The Jewish Study Bible

SECOND EDITION

JEWISH PUBLICATION SOCIETY

TANAKH TRANSLATION

EDITORS AND CONTRIBUTORS

Yairah Amit: *Judges*
Shimon Bar-Efrat: *First and Second Samuel* [revised by Marc Zvi Brettler]
Amitai Baruchi-Unna: *Geography of Biblical Land of Israel*
Ehud Ben Zvi: *Introduction to The Twelve and The Twelve Minor Prophets*
Adele Berlin: Editor; *Introduction: What Is the Jewish Study Bible?* [with Marc Zvi Brettler], *Psalms* [with Marc Zvi Brettler], *Introduction to The Five Megillot* [with Marc Zvi Brettler], *Lamentations, Esther, Introduction to the Essays* [with Marc Zvi Brettler], *Reading Biblical Poetry*
Oded Borowski: *Daily Life in Biblical Times*
Marc Zvi Brettler: Editor; *Introduction: What is the Jewish Study Bible?* [with Adele Berlin], *Introduction to Torah, Introduction to Nevi'im, Introduction to Kethuvim, Psalms* [with Adele Berlin], *Introduction to The Five Megillot* [with Adele Berlin], *Introduction to the Essays* [with Adele Berlin], *Modern Jewish Interpretation, The Canonization of the Bible, Gender in the Bible*
Edward Breuer: *Jewish Biblical Scholarship from the 17th to the 19th Centuries*
Yaakov Elman: *Classical Rabbinic Interpretation*
Esther Eshel: *The Bible in the Dead Sea Scrolls* Steven E. Fassberg: *Languages of the Bible*
Michael Fishbane: *The Bible in the Jewish Mystical Tradition*
Michael V. Fox: *Proverbs* Nili S. Fox: *Numbers* Tova Ganzel: *Ezekiel*
Stephen A. Geller: *The Religion of the Bible* Leonard J. Greenspoon: *Jewish Translations of the Bible*
Edward L. Greenstein: *Job* Shalom E. Holtz: *Reading Biblical Law*
Victor Avigdor Hurowitz: *The Temple* [edited by Adele Berlin and Marc Zvi Brettler]
Jonathan Klawans: *Concepts of Purity in the Bible* Ruth Langer: *The Bible in the Liturgy*
Jacob Lassner: *The Hebrew Bible and Biblical Exegesis in the Qur'an and Muslim Tradition*
Jon D. Levenson: *Genesis* Amy-Jill Levine: *Use of the Hebrew Bible in the New Testament*
Baruch A. Levine: *Biblical Festivals and Fast Days* Bernard M. Levinson: *Deuteronomy*
Oded Lipschits: *The History of Israel in the Biblical Period* Peter Machinist: *Ecclesiastes*
Aren M. Maeir: *Archeology and the Hebrew Bible*
Hindy Najman: *Ezra, Nehemiah, Early Nonrabbinic Interpretation*
Jordan S. Penkower: *The Development of the Masoretic Bible*
Adele Reinhartz: *Ruth, Jewish Women's Scholarly Writings on the Bible*
Dalit Rom-Shiloni: *Jeremiah* David Rothstein: *First and Second Chronicles*
Jonathan D. Sarna: *The Jewish Bible in America*
Jack M. Sasson: *On the Bible and the Ancient Near East* Baruch J. Schwartz: *Leviticus*
Avigdor Shinan: *The Bible in the Synagogue* Uriel Simon: *The Bible in Israeli Life*
Benjamin D. Sommer: *Isaiah, Inner-biblical Interpretation* Daniel Sperber: *Jewish Customs*
David Stern: *Midrash and Jewish Exegesis* Elsie Stern: *The Song of Songs*
Sacha Stern: *Biblical Calendars*
Marvin A. Sweeney: *Historical and Ideal Davidic Kingship, The Modern Study of the Bible*
Jeffrey H. Tigay: *Exodus* Hava Tirosh-Samuelson: *The Bible in the Jewish Philosophical Tradition*
Emanuel Tov: *Textual Criticism* Barry D. Walfish: *Medieval Jewish Interpretation*
Nili Wazana: *Joshua* Lawrence M. Wills: *Daniel* Jacob L. Wright: *War and Peace in the Bible*
Yair Zakovitch: *Reading Biblical Narrative* Ziony Zevit: *First and Second Kings*

The Jewish Study Bible

Second Edition

Adele Berlin and Marc Zvi Brettler

EDITORS

Jewish Publication Society

TANAKH *Translation*

OXFORD
UNIVERSITY PRESS

OXFORD
UNIVERSITY PRESS

Oxford New York
Auckland Cape Town Dar es Salaam Hong Kong Karachi
Kuala Lumpur Madrid Melbourne Mexico City Nairobi
New Delhi Shanghai Taipei Toronto
With offices in
Argentina Austria Brazil Chile Czech Republic France Greece
Guatemala Hungary Italy Japan Poland Portugal Singapore
South Korea Switzerland Thailand Turkey Ukraine Vietnam

Published by Oxford University Press USA
198 Madison Avenue, New York, New York 10016

www.oup.com

Cloth 10 9 8 7 6 5 4
Leather 10 9 8 7 6 5 4 3 2 1

Contents

Maps, Charts and Diagrams

Color Maps follow the last page of the Index

Introduction: What is *The Jewish Study Bible*?

MORE THAN TWENTY-FIVE CENTURIES have passed since an anonymous Jewish poet wrote an elaborate and lengthy prayer that included this exclamation:

O how I love Your teaching!
It is my study all day long (Ps. 119.97).

These two themes—the love for Torah (teaching) and dedication to the study of it—have characterized Jewish reading and interpretation of the Bible ever since. The love is the impetus for the study; the study is the expression of the love. Indeed the intensity with which Jews have examined this text through the centuries testifies both to their love of it—a love combined with awe and deep reverence—and to their intellectual curiosity about it. That tradition of impassioned intellectual engagement continues to the present day.

The tradition of biblical interpretation has been a constant conversation, at times an argument, among its participants; at no period has the text been interpreted in a monolithic fashion. If anything marks Jewish biblical interpretation, it is the diversity of approaches employed and the multiplicity of meanings produced. This is expressed in the famous rabbinic saying; "There are seventy faces to the Torah" (*Num. Rab.* 13.15 and parallels), meaning that biblical texts are open to seventy different interpretations, seventy symbolizing a large and complete number. Thus, there is no official Jewish interpretation of the Bible. In keeping with this attitude, the interpreters who contributed to this volume have followed a variety of methods of interpretation, and the editors have not attempted to harmonize the contributions, so an array of perspectives is manifest. In addition, we do not claim any privileged status for this volume; we can only hope that it will find its place among the myriad Jewish interpretations that preceded and that will follow. We hope that Jewish readers will use this book as a resource to better understand the multiple traditions that have informed, and continue to inform, their tradition. We also hope that the *The Jewish Study Bible* will serve as a compelling introduction for students of the Bible from other backgrounds and traditions, who are curious about contemporary academic Jewish biblical interpretation.

Jews have been engaged in reading and interpreting the Hebrew Bible, or Tanakh, since its inception. Even before the biblical canon was complete, some of its early writings were becoming authoritative, and were cited, alluded to, and reworked in later writings, which themselves would become part of the Bible. Jewish biblical interpretation continued in various forms in early translations into Greek and Aramaic, in the Dead Sea scrolls, in rabbinic literature, and in medieval and modern commentaries; it continues in the present. We therefore have kept in mind two overarching goals in the commissioning and editing of the study materials in this volume. The first goal is to convey the best of modern academic scholarship on the Bible, that is, scholarship that reflects the way the Bible is approached in the university. This desire comes from a strong conviction that this approach does not undermine Judaism, as leading figures of previous generations had argued, but can add significant depth to Jewish belief and values. The second goal is to reflect, in as broad a fashion as possible, the range of Jewish engagement with the Bible over the past two and a half millennia. The breadth of this engagement, as well as its depth, should not be underestimated. In fact, as a group, the contributors reflect divergent Jewish commitments and beliefs, which infuse their commmentaries. They employ state-of-the-art scholarship and a wide range of modern approaches; at the same time, they are sensitive to Jewish readings of the Bible, to classical Jewish interpretation, and to the place of the Bible in Jewish life. In this respect they are actually quite "traditional," in that Jewish interpreters have a long history of drawing on ideas and methods from the non-Jewish world in which they lived and incorporating them into Jewish writings.

Although there is no single notion of Jewish biblical interpretation, our contributors share some commonalities:

- They view the Tanakh as complete in itself, not as a part of a larger Bible or a prelude to the New Testament. For all of them, the Tanakh is "the Bible," and for this reason *The Jewish Study Bible* uses the terms "Tanakh" and "the Bible" interchangeably.
- We minimize use of the term "Hebrew Bible," a redundancy in the Jewish view. Jews have no Bible but the "Hebrew Bible." (Some Christians use "Hebrew Bible," a sensitive substitute for "Old Testament," to distinguish it from the Greek Bible, or New Testament.)
- They take seriously the traditional Hebrew (Masoretic) text of the Bible.
- They take cognizance of and draw upon traditional Jewish interpretation, thereby placing themselves in the larger context of Jewish exegesis.
- They point out where biblical passages have influenced Jewish practice.
- They call attention to biblical passages that are especially meaningful in the life of the Jewish community.

Just as there is no one Jewish interpretation, there is no authorized Jewish translation of the Bible into English. In fact, translation has always been less important in Jewish communal life than in Christian communities, because public liturgical readings from the Bible have always been in Hebrew, a language understood until recent centuries by many within the community. For Jews, the official Bible is the Hebrew Masoretic Text; it has never been replaced by an official translation (like the Vulgate, for instance, which is the official Bible of the Roman Catholic Church). Nevertheless, because many Jews since postbiblical times did not understand biblical Hebrew, translations into vernacular languages were made. For contemporary English-speaking Jews, the best and most widely read Jewish translation is the most recent one commissioned and published by the Jewish Publication Society, begun in 1955 and completed in 1982, with revisions to the earlier books incorporated in the 1985 edition, and with a revised and corrected second edition in 1999. That second edition of the translation (NJPS *Tanakh*) serves as the basis for this volume.

There is no single way to read through the Bible—this is reflected in the variety of orders found for the biblical books in manuscripts and rabbinic texts. In fact, some may prefer first to read background material about the Bible, and only then to read the text. For this reason, we have taken an expansive approach in offering numerous essays that explore many aspects of the Bible and its interpretation. Some of these are of the type found in other study Bibles, exploring issues such as canon, the history of the biblical period, and modern methods of studying the Bible. Others reflect the specific interests of *The Jewish Study Bible*, including essays on the history of the Jewish interpretation of the Bible, Jewish Bible translation, midrash, and the Bible in the Jewish philosophical, mystical, and liturgical traditions. Each essay is self-standing, and there is often overlap between them. As a whole, however, they convey the important place of the Bible within Judaism, and many of the varieties of uses that this text has found throughout the ages. We hope that, along with the annotations, these essays will introduce a wide audience to the world of Jewish tradition as it relates to the Bible. (A brief introduction to the essays, pp. 1833–34, sets out their arrangement and aims in greater detail.)

For each book of the Bible, our contributors have provided an introduction that sets it in its context—its original setting, so far as that can be determined; the wider corpus of which it is a part; its genre; and its place within Judaism—and provides an overview of the issues involved in reading it. Like many traditional rabbinic texts, the main text, here the NJPS translation, is surrounded by commentary, or more precisely annotations, often quite extensive, that comment on specific points in the text but also bring the reader back to the larger issues raised in the introduction and elsewhere. These annotations frequently refer to other portions of the biblical text, and further insight can be gained by checking these references and reading those texts and their associated annotations.

Besides the essays, described above, the volume has further information. A timeline lists rulers in the land of Israel and the surrounding empires during the biblical period. A chart of weights and measures gives modern approximations to the quantities specified at various points in the text (these are usually explained in the annotations as well). A table of chapter/verse numbering differences between the Hebrew text and standard, non-Jewish English translations, will be of help to those who come to this volume from a different translation tradition. A list of biblical readings provides the citations of texts for use in the synagogue. A glossary, explaining technical terms in biblical studies, various literary terms, and numerous words specific to the Jewish interpretive tradition, provides further information for the technical vocabulary that was sometimes unavoidable. An index to the entirety of the study materials—book introductions, annotations, and essays—keyed by page number, facilitates pursuing particular topics through the full range of the study materials. Finally, a set of full-color maps and a map index present geographical background for the events detailed in the text, the annotations, and the historical essays.

From *Acknowledgments for the First Edition*

In order to produce a work of this length and complexity, many people must play a role. We especially wish to thank Dr. Ellen Frankel, chief executive and editor-in-chief of the Jewish Publication Society (now retired), who first suggested this publishing project to Oxford University Press, and Prof. Michael Fishbane, the academic advisor to the Jewish Publication Society, who participated in the initial planning and whose scholarly dedication both to the biblical text and to the tradition of Jewish interpretation served as a model for our endeavors. We are grateful to JPS, and particularly to the Board of Trustees of the Society, for agreeing to make their translation available for this study edition.

We are also mindful of all the scholarship that has gone before us, and on which we have relied throughout the volume. In particular, we have followed the model of the *New Oxford Annotated Bible*, and have, with the permission of Oxford University Press, adapted some of the excellent auxiliary materials in that work for use in this one. The introductory essays to the three canonical groups, *Torah, Nevi'im*, and *Kethuvim* are expanded versions of the essays written for the *Annotated*: "The Pentateuch" (Marc Z. Brettler), "The Historical Books" (Marc Z. Brettler), "The Poetical and Wisdom Books" (Marc Z. Brettler), and "The Prophetic Books" (Carol A. Newsom). The essay on "The Canonization of the Bible" is adapted from the essay "The Canons of the Bible" (Marc Z. Brettler and Pheme Perkins).

In addition, the editors would especially like to thank:
The contributors, from whom we have learned so much, and hope that they will be pleased with the whole, to which each contributed an invaluable part. Both editors, coming from different perspectives, have read every word of every annotation and essay, often more than once. Our editing sessions became wonderful opportunities for serious discussion between ourselves and with our contributors on a wide range of fundamental issues in biblical and Jewish studies. We invite our readers to partake of the fruits of this productive collaboration, the seventy faces of the Torah that await them in this volume.

We are completing our work on this volume as we approach the holiday of Shavuʿot, the time when, according to postbiblical Jewish tradition, the Torah was given to Moses. The volume is being published close to the holiday of Simḥat Torah, the Rejoicing of the Torah, when the annual liturgical reading cycle of the Torah is completed and immediately begun again. As we have worked on the Bible for the last three years, we have gained even greater respect and appreciation for the "gift" of the Bible and for the never-ending, ever-renewing Jewish interpretive traditions. We share with even more profound conviction the sentiment of the psalmist with whose words we opened this introduction:

O how I love Your teaching!
It is my study all day long.

ADELE BERLIN

MARC ZVI BRETTLER

June 2003

Sivan 5762

Preface to the Second Edition

THE RECEPTION OF THE FIRST EDITION of *The Jewish Study Bible,* completed a decade ago, has been extremely gratifying. The book has found a place in many homes and synagogues, in college and seminary courses, and in adult study groups. Jews and non-Jews alike, in both religious and secular settings, have read it. It has fulfilled our goal of increasing biblical literacy and showing that traditional Jewish learning and modern academic biblical scholarship can be integrated successfully. One measure of its success is the National Jewish Book Award bestowed on the volume in 2004.

The first edition of any book is an experiment. In addition to the biblical books and their annotations, we decided that the volume should contain essays about the Bible and its study. We saw those essays as an essential part of the work; they provided a broader context for the study of the Bible. Many readers found the essays to be an extremely valuable resource for learning about the world of the Bible, the history of Jewish Bible study, and the methods of modern scholarship. We received so many positive reactions to the essay section that we thought it would be useful to augment it substantially, offering even more background on a wider variety of topics.

The addition of new essays is the most significant enhancement in this edition. We commissioned six new essays in the area of "Biblical Ideas and Institutions," on topics including daily life in biblical times, the Temple, calendars, festivals, David, and war and peace. In the section on "The Bible in Jewish Life," we added an essay on Jewish customs, and an essay on the Bible in America, to complement the essay "The Bible in Israeli Life." In the previous edition, we revised several essays from *The New Oxford Annotated Bible* for the section on "Backgrounds for Reading the Bible"; for this edition, we commissioned entirely new essays on history, geography, archeology, the Bible and the ancient Near East, textual criticism, and modern study of the Bible. In addition, we have augmented this section through new essays on gender, and on reading biblical narrative and biblical law, complementing the essay from the first edition on reading biblical poetry. Finally, we have added a new section of essays, "The Hebrew Bible in Other Scriptures," showing how the New Testament and the Qur'an engage the Hebrew Bible.

But the essays are not the only new feature of this edition. Biblical scholarship is dynamic and ever-changing. We have therefore encouraged all the original contributors of both annotations and essays to revise their work; and in some cases, we sought new annotators to reflect more recent scholarship and to include more women and Israeli scholars. Thus, this volume is over one-third new.

Sadly, the annotations on the book of Samuel, by Shimon Bar-Efrat, could not be revised by the author, who died in 2010; Marc Zvi Brettler revised these annotations. Our friend and colleague Victor Avigdor Hurowitz completed his essay "The Temple" shortly before his untimely death a year ago, and was unable to see our revisions. In both of these cases, we revised with an acute awareness of our responsibility toward the departed scholar, and approached our task as a *ḥesed shel ʾemet,* an act of lovingkindness toward the deceased. We hope that they would have looked with favor on our revisions.

It continues to be a great personal and intellectual pleasure to work together with each other and with our many contributors. We have a great team. This volume could not possibly have been written by one or two individuals, and we were fortunate to be able to draw on the finest expertise in biblical studies. We are grateful to our contributors for sharing their vast knowledge with our readers, and for making this volume as successful as we know it will be.

We also express our gratitude to the Jewish Publication Society, for once again permitting the use of their Tanakh translation in this publication. In addition, the Jewish Publication Society graciously agreed to allow us to modify the translation of *ḥat'at,* "sin offering," to "purification offering," in agreement with current scholarship.

We thank all those who labored to bring this project to publication: the staff at Oxford University Press, particularly Susan Lee and Claudia Dukeshire, who oversaw the complex process of typesetting; Jan Gibbs of Peachtree Editorial and Proofreading Service, who copy-edited the entire text; Peachtree Editorial and Proofreading Service, who proofread the entire book and checked numerous elements within it; Kate Mertes, who prepared the index to the study materials; and Mr. Lenin Prado, who updated the list of "Translations of Primary Sources."

And *aḥaron aḥaron ḥaviv*—the best is saved for last. With great pleasure we again express our special thanks to Donald Kraus, executive editor in the Bible department at Oxford University Press, U.S.A. Don is the dean of annotated Bibles, and has shepherded this new edition of *The Jewish Study Bible* as he did with the first edition, through every stage with grace and acuity. He is smart, knowledgeable, politic, and a wonderful stylist, who has contributed so much to biblical literacy through the many annotated Bibles and other works he has supervised. Though, like Saul, he shuns the limelight, preferring to hide backstage (1 Sam. 10.22), we would like to publicly acknowledge his invaluable work and thank him for his patience and his good judgment at every step along the way, from the initial planning through the publication of this volume. His faith in this project never flagged and his determination to bring it to fruition never diminished. Don deserves much of the credit for the success of the first edition of *The Jewish Study Bible,* and no less for what we hope will be the success of the second edition.

ADELE BERLIN

MARC ZVI BRETTLER

February 2014

Adar Aleph / Adar Rishon

Preface to the 1985 JPS Edition

THIS TRANSLATION OF TANAKH, THE HOLY SCRIPTURES, produced by the Jewish Publication Society, was made directly from the traditional Hebrew text into the idiom of modern English. It represents the collaboration of academic scholars with rabbis from the three largest branches of organized Jewish religious life in America. Begun in 1955, the ongoing translation was published in three main stages: *The Torah* in 1962, *The Prophets (Nevi'im)* in 1978, and *The Writings (Kethuvim)* in 1982. These three volumes, with revisions, are now brought together in a complete English *Tanakh (Torah-Nevi'im-Kethuvim),* the latest link in the chain of Jewish Bible translations.

On the History of Bible Translation

Bible translation began about 2200 years ago, in the 3rd century BCE, as the large Jewish population of Alexandria, Egypt, came under the influence of Hellenism. When the Greek language replaced Hebrew and Aramaic as their vernacular, and the Torah in its Hebrew original was no longer commonly understood, a translation into Greek was made for the Jewish community of Alexandria. This translation came to be known as the Septuagint, Latin for "seventy," because of the legend that the committee of translators numbered seventy-two, six elders from each of the twelve tribes of Israel.

In the last few centuries BCE, the Jews who lived to the north and east of Judea also found the Hebrew Bible difficult to understand, for their spoken language had become largely Aramaic. Translations into Aramaic, first of the Torah and then of the rest of the Bible, became known as the Targums.

The Septuagint and the Targums are not only the oldest translations of the Bible but also the most influential. Down to our own day, virtually every Christian translation has followed the methods of the Jewish translators who created the Septuagint, and generally followed their renderings of the Hebrew as well. The Christian translators also were influenced by the interpretation of the Hebrew text set forth in the Targums (much of it in oral form at the time) and by the writings of the Jewish philosopher-interpreter Philo of Alexandria (died about 45 CE).

The forerunners and leaders of the Renaissance and the Reformation (14th–15th centuries), and especially Martin Luther and William Tyndale (16th century), made use of Latin translations of the classic Jewish commentators Rashi, Ibn Ezra, and Kimḥi (11th–13th centuries), whose works were imbued with the direct knowledge of the Targums. Luther was greatly indebted to Nicholas of Lyre (1270–1349), who had adopted Rashi's exegesis for his Latin Bible commentary. Rashi's influence on all authorized and most unofficial English translations of the Hebrew Bible becomes evident when Tyndale's dependence on Luther is considered. Tyndale is central to many subsequent English translations: the King James Version of 1611, the (British) Revised Version of 1881–1885, the American Standard Version of 1901, and especially the Revised Standard Version of 1952.

Alongside the close, literal method of Bible translation, the earliest Jewish translators were also influenced by the widely held view that, along with the Written Law *(torah she-bikhtav),* God had given Moses on Mount Sinai an Oral Law *(torah she-be'al peh)* as well; so that to comprehend God's Torah fully and correctly, it was essential to make use of both. Thus, when a translation of the Hebrew Bible into the Judeo-Arabic vernacular was deemed necessary for Jewry in Moslem countries toward the end of the first millennium, the noted philologian, philosopher, and community leader Saadia Gaon (882–942) produced a version that incorporated traditional Jewish interpretation but was not based on word-for-word translation; at the same time, it was a model of clarity and stylistic elegance. The present version is in the spirit of Saadia.

With the growth of Christianity in the 1st century, the Church adopted the Septuagint as its Bible, and the Septuagint was translated into the languages of the various Christian communities. As Greek began to give way to Latin in the Roman empire, it was only a matter of time before a Latin translation of Scripture became the recognized Bible of the Church. The Church father Jerome (ca. 340–420) produced the official Latin version. Drawing on Jewish tradition and consulting Jewish teachers, he achieved what came to be known as the Vulgate, the Bible in the language of the common people. The Vulgate, the Bible of European Christianity until the Reformation, is clearly the most significant Bible translation after the Septuagint.

With the rise of Protestantism in Europe, scholars within this movement set themselves the task of making the Bible available in the various vernaculars of the time. By 1526 the first parts of two notable translations began to appear: Martin Luther's in German and William Tyndale's in English. The latter, by way of several subsequent revisions, became the King James Version of 1611. The more modern English versions—such as *The Holy Scriptures* by the American rabbi Isaac Leeser (1855), the (British) Revised Version (1881–1885), the American Standard Version (1901), the Jewish Publication Society's *The Holy Scriptures* (1917), and the (American) Revised Standard Version (1952)—made extensive use of the King James.

On the Making of the New Translation

After World War II, when the Jewish Publication Society began to consider a new edition of the Bible, the idea of a modest revision of the 1917 translation met with resistance, and the concept of a completely new translation gradually took hold. The proposed translation would reproduce the Hebrew idiomatically and reflect contemporary scholarship, thus laying emphasis upon intelligibility and correctness. It would make critical use of the early rabbinic and medieval Jewish commentators, grammarians, and philologians and would rely on the traditional Hebrew text, avoiding emendations. The need for this new translation was the focus of the Jewish Publication Society's annual meeting in 1953. Later that year the Society announced its intention to proceed with the project, and in 1955 the committee of translators began their task.

Harry M. Orlinsky, Professor of Bible at Hebrew Union College–Jewish Institute of Religion (New York), was asked to serve as editor-in-chief for the new translation, along with H. L. Ginsberg, Professor of Bible at the Jewish Theological Seminary, and Ephraim A. Speiser, Professor of Semitic and Oriental Languages at the University of Pennsylvania, as fellow editors. Associated with them were three rabbis: Max Arzt, Bernard J. Bamberger, and Harry Freedman, representing the Conservative, Reform, and Orthodox branches of organized Jewish religious life. Solomon Grayzel, editor of the Jewish Publication Society, served as secretary of the committee.

The committee profited much from the work of previous translators; the present rendering, however, is essentially a new translation. A few of its characteristics may be noted. The committee undertook to follow faithfully the traditional Hebrew text, but there were certain points at which footnotes appeared necessary: (1) where the committee had to admit that it did not understand a word or passage; (2) where an alternative rendering was possible; (3) where an old rendering, no longer retained, was so well known that it would very likely be missed, in which case the traditional translation was given in the name of "Others" (usually referring to the Society's version of 1917); (4) where the understanding of a passage could be facilitated by reference to another passage elsewhere in the Bible; and (5) where important textual variants are to be found in some of the ancient manuscripts or versions of the Bible.

The translators avoided obsolete words and phrases and, whenever possible, rendered Hebrew idioms by means of their normal English equivalents. For the second person singular, the modern "you" was used instead of the archaic "thou," even when referring to the Deity ("You"). A further obvious difference between this translation and most of the older ones is in the rendering of the Hebrew particle *waw,* which is usually translated "and." Biblical Hebrew demanded the frequent use of the *waw,* but in that style it had the force not only of "and" but also of "however," "but," "yet," "when," and any number of other such words and particles, or none at all that can be translated into English. Always to render it as "and" is to misrepresent the Hebrew rather than be faithful to it. Consequently, the committee translated the particle as the sense required, or left it untranslated.

The chapter and verse divisions found in the printed Bible are indispensable as a system of precise reference, but they do not always coincide with the organic divisions of the text. The chapter divisions, whose origin is neither ancient nor Jewish but medieval Christian, sometimes join or separate the wrong paragraphs, sentences, or even parts of sentences. The verse divisions, though considerably older and of Jewish origin, sometimes join together parts of different sentences or separate from each other parts of the same sentence. The translation of Saadia Gaon often does not correspond to our chapter divisions, which did not exist in his day. More noteworthy is the readiness with which he joined separate verses of the Hebrew text (whose authority he did not question) into single sentences when the sense required it. Thus, in joining Genesis 7.24 and 8.1 into a single sentence, or combining the last part of 1 Kings 6.38 with 7.1, the present translation is following the example of Saadia. The attentive reader will discover other instances in which the translators have followed what they considered to be the logical units of meaning even when they did not coincide with the conventional chapters and verses. The latter, however, are marked and numbered throughout.

The preface to the first edition of *The Torah* was dated September 25, 1962, Erev Rosh Ha-Shanah 5723. A second edition, incorporating some changes by the translators, came out five years later. The committee also produced translations of *The Five Megilloth and Jonah* (1969), *Isaiah* (1973), and *Jeremiah* (1974). The latter two books and Jonah were incorporated, with some corrections and revisions, into the complete translation of *The Prophets (Nevi'im).* For this volume, which was published in 1978, Professor Ginsberg served as editor, in association with Professor Orlinsky. Whereas Professor Orlinsky had initially prepared a draft translation of the entire Torah, individual members of the committee undertook to prepare a draft of an entire prophetic book or part of a book; but, as in translating the Torah, everyone had an opportunity to criticize the draft and to offer detailed suggestions at periodic committee sessions, which were presided over by Rabbi Bamberger. Differences of opinion were settled by majority vote.

In preparing the translation of *The Prophets,* the translators faced a recurring problem that deserves special mention. The prophetic books contain many passages whose meaning is uncertain. Thus, in order to provide an intelligible rendering, modern scholars have resorted to emending the Hebrew text. Some of these emendations derive from the ancient translators, especially of the Septuagint and the Targums, who had before them a Hebrew text that sometimes differed from today's traditional text. Where these ancient versions provide no help, some scholars have made conjectural emendations of their own. Many modern English versions contain translations of emended texts, sometimes without citing any departure from the traditional Hebrew text.

Like the translation of *The Torah,* the present translation of the prophetic books adheres strictly to the traditional Hebrew text; but where the text remains obscure and an alteration provides marked clarification, a footnote is offered with a rendering of the suggested emendation.

If the emendation is based on one or two ancient versions, they are mentioned by name; if more than two versions agree, they are summed up as "ancient versions." Conjectural emendations are introduced by "Emendation yields." Sometimes, however, it was deemed sufficient to offer only a change of vowels, and such modifications are indicated by "Change of vocalization yields." In all cases, the emendation is given in a footnote, which may be readily disregarded by those who reject it on either scholarly or religious grounds. The only exceptions involve such changes in grammatical form as those, say, from second person to third or from singular to plural. In such rare instances, the change is incorporated in the text, and the traditional Hebrew is translated in a footnote.

The committee of translators for *The Writings (Kethuvim),* the third part of the Hebrew Bible, was set up by the Jewish Publication Society in 1966. It consisted of Moshe Greenberg, now Professor of Bible at the Hebrew University, Jonas C. Greenfield, then Professor of Semitic Languages at the Hebrew University, and Nahum M. Sarna, then Professor of Biblical Studies at Brandeis University, in association with Rabbis Saul Leeman, Martin S. Rozenberg, and David Shapiro of the Conservative, Reform, and Orthodox movements. Chaim Potok, then editor of the Society, served as secretary of the committee.

The present English rendering of *Kethuvim,* like *Torah* and *Nevi'im,* is based on the traditional Hebrew text—its consonants, vowels, and syntactical divisions—although the traditional accentuation occasionally has been replaced by an alternative construction. Following the approach of the original committee, the entire gamut of biblical interpretation, ancient and modern, Jewish and non-Jewish, has been consulted, and, whenever possible, the results of modern study of the languages and cultures of the ancient Near East have been brought to bear on the biblical text. In choosing between alternatives, however, just as antiquity was not in itself a disqualification, so modernity was not in itself a recommendation. Divergences of the present translation from recent renderings reflect the committee's judgment that certain innovations, though interesting, are too speculative for adoption in the present state of knowledge. The as-yet-imperfect understanding of the language of the Bible, or what appears to be some disorder in the Hebrew text, makes sure translation of many passages impossible. This uncertainty in *Kethuvim* is indicated in a note, and, where the Hebrew text permits, alternative renderings have been offered. However, emendations of the text of *Kethuvim*—except for the five *Megilloth*—were not proposed, and notes were kept to a minimum.

Some passages in Kethuvim are identical or very similar to passages in *Torah* and *Nevi'im.* The rendering of these passages in *Kethuvim* generally follows the wording in the earlier books; on occasion, however, owing to various considerations, divergences in style and translation will be found. For example, in the presentation of the poetry of the Psalms, it was deemed fitting, because of their liturgical use, to indicate the thought units through appropriate indentation. The text of *Kethuvim* frequently presented the translators with extraordinary difficulties, for it is hardly possible to convey in English the fullness of the Hebrew, with its ambiguities, its overtones, and the richness that it carries from centuries of use. Still, it was their goal to transmit something of the directness, the simplicity, and the uniquely Israelite expressions of piety that are so essential to the sublimity of the Hebrew Bible.

The committee's translation of *The Psalms* appeared in 1973; of *The Book of Job,* in 1980. The two were incorporated, with revisions, into the complete translations of *The Writings (Kethuvim),* which appeared in 1982.

For this one-volume English edition of *Tanakh,* the translation of *The Torah,* first published twenty years earlier, underwent more revision than the more recent publications of *The Prophets* and *The Writings.* A number of the changes had already been projected in *Notes on the New Translation of the Torah,* edited by Harry M. Orlinsky and published by the Society in 1969.

Subsequent research on the text has led to further revisions in the translation of *Torah* and some revisions in *Nevi'im* as well.

Ephraim Speiser, of the original committee, died in June 1965. Max Arzt, also an active member of the original committee, died in 1975, when the work of translating the prophetic books was almost complete. Since the appearance of *The Prophets* and *The Writings*, Bernard J. Bamberger, Solomon Grayzel, and Harry Freedman have also passed on.* Their memory, and their scholarship, will be for a blessing.

The Jewish Publication Society joins the members of the committees of translators in the hope that the results of their labors will find favor with God and man.

THE JEWISH PUBLICATION SOCIETY
SEPTEMBER 15, 1985
ערב ראש השנה תשמ״ו

*Deceased and lamented since 1985: H. L. Ginsberg, Harry Orlinsky, and Jonas Greenfield.

Alphabetical Listing of the Books of the Bible

Hebrew Transliteration

Although we have tried to be consistent and simple in transliteration, we have kept certain standard or traditional spellings to avoid confusion.

CHARACTER	TRANSLITERATION	CHARACTER	TRANSLITERATION
א	ʾ	מ	m
בּ ב	b, v	נ	n
ג	g	ס	s
ד	d	ע	ʿ
ה	h	פּ פ	p, f
ו	v, w	צ	ts, tz
ז	z	ק	k, q
ח	π	ר	r
ט	t	שׂ	s
י	y	שׁ	š, sh
כּ כ	k, kh	ת	t
ל	l		

Guide to Abbreviations and Terms

Abbreviations Used for the Books of the Bible

Amos	Amos	Hos.	Hosea	Mic.	Micah
1 Chron.	Chronicles, First	Isa.	Isaiah	Nah.	Nahum
2 Chron.	Chronicles, Second	Jer.	Jeremiah	Neh.	Nehemiah
Dan.	Daniel	Job	Job	Num.	Numbers
Deut.	Deuteronomy	Joel	Joel	Obad.	Obadiah
Eccl.	Ecclesiastes	Jonah	Jonah	Prov.	Proverbs
Esth.	Esther	Josh.	Joshua	Ps(s).	Psalms
Exod.	Exodus	Judg.	Judges	Ruth	Ruth
Ezek.	Ezekiel	1 Kings	Kings, First	1 Sam.	Samuel, First
Ezra	Ezra	2 Kings	Kings, Second	2 Sam.	Samuel, Second
Gen.	Genesis	Lam.	Lamentations	Song	The Song of Songs
Hab.	Habakkuk	Lev.	Leviticus	Zech.	Zechariah
Hag.	Haggai	Mal.	Malachi	Zeph.	Zephaniah

Abbreviations and Terms Used in the Footnotes to the Translation

Akkadian	An ancient Semitic language spoken in Mesopotamia; its chief dialects were Babylonian and Assyrian.
Aquila	A 2nd-century convert to Judaism who made a literal translation of the Bible into Greek.
Berakhot	One of the treatises of the Mishnah and the Talmud.
Cf.	A reference to another version, or to a cognate language, that justified the translation adopted.
Heb.	The Hebrew word or phrase in transliteration, especially when necessary to point out a pun, homonym, or the like. *Heb.* is also used to indicate the literal wording for which a superior rendering was employed; see Genesis 46.23, note *a*, or 49.9, note *a-a*. An example of a somewhat different type may be seen at Exodus 21.22, note *a*.
Ibn Ezra	Rabbi Abraham Ibn Ezra, a Bible commentator and grammarian who lived in Spain in the 12th century.
I.e.	An explanation, to avoid adding words to the text, in order to clarify the translation; see Exodus 22.29, note *b*.
Kethib	The way a word, usually unvocalized, is written in the Bible; see *qere*.
Kimhi	Rabbi David Kimḥi (Radak), a Bible commentator and grammarian who lived in southern France in the late 12th and early 13th centuries.
Lit.	For the literal translation of a word or phrase that was given an idiomatic or somewhat free translation in the text; see Genesis 30.27, note *a*, and 30.38, note *b*; or 43.21, note *a*, and 43.34, note *b*; or Deuteronomy 18.1, note *b* (where the Hebrew and English cannot agree in number).
Masorah	The text of the Bible as transmitted, with vowel signs and accents.
Meaning of Heb. uncertain.	Where the translation represents the best that the committee could achieve with an elusive or difficult text. In some cases the text may be unintelligible because of uncertain corruption.
Mishnah	The code of Jewish law prepared by Rabbi Judah ha-Nasi about 200 CE. The word is usually followed by the name of the relevant treatise.
Moved up	Where clarity required the shifting of a word or phrase within a verse or from one verse to another; see Genesis 10.14, note *a*.
Or	Indicates an alternative reading that the committee found almost as acceptable as the one adopted for the text.
Others	Indicates a well-known traditional translation, especially if it was used in the older (1917) JPS version, that the committee does not find acceptable even as an alternate reading.
Peshitta	A translation of the Bible into Syriac, parts of which are said to have been made in the 1st century CE.

Qere	The way the Masorah requires a word to be read, especially when it diverges from the *kethib.*
Qumran	The site of the caves where Bible manuscripts were found in 1949–1950. The manuscripts are identified by such symbols as 4QSam^{a} (for manuscript *a* of Samuel, found in the fourth cave of Qumran); 1QIs^{a} (for manuscript *a* of Isaiah found in the first cave of Qumran).
Rashbam	Rabbi Shmuel ben Meir, a grandson of Rashi, who commented on the Torah.
Rashi	Rabbi Shlomo Yitzḥaki, the best-known Jewish commentator on the Bible. He lived in France at the end of the 11th century.
Saadia	A *gaon,* i.e., a head of a Babylonian talmudic academy, in the early part of the 10th century. His works include the famous translation of the Bible into Arabic.
See	Frequently used in place of *cf.,* but usually intended to begin a note attached to another passage in the Bible.
Septuagint	The oldest Jewish translation of the Bible, into Greek. The Torah translation dates from the 3rd century BCE; other books of the Bible were translated somewhat later.
Syriac	See *Peshitta.*
Targum	A Jewish translation of the Bible into Aramaic, a language once widely spoken in western Asia, of which Syriac was a later development.
Ugaritic	A language of inscriptions found at Ras Shamra, on the Syrian coast, in the second millennium BCE. Both the language and its literature have shed much light on the Hebrew Bible.
Vulgate	The Latin translation of the Bible made by the Church father Jerome about the year 400 CE. It became the official Bible of the Roman Catholic Church.

Abbreviations Used in the Annotations, Introductions, and Essays

1Q13	Phylactery
1QapGen ar	*Genesis Apocryphon* (1Q20)
1QIsa^{a}	Isaiah^{a}
1QIsa^{b}	Isaiah^{b} (1Q8)
1QM	*Milḥamah* or *War Scroll* (1Q33)
1QpHab	*Pesher Habakkuk*
1QS	*Serek Hayaḥad* or *Rule of the Community*
4Q12	paleo-Hebrew Genesis (paleoGen^{m})
4Q30	Deut^{c}
4Q158	Biblical paraphrases (BibPar) (=4QRP^{a})
4Q161–65	*Pesher Isaiah* $^{a-e}$
4Q166	*Pesher Hosea* (pHos^{a})
4Q167	*Pesher Hosea* (pHos^{b})
4Q169	*Pesher Nahum* (pNah)
4Q171	*Pesher Psalms* (4QpPs^{a})
4Q248	Historical Text A
4Q252	*Commentary on Genesis A*, formerly *Patriarchal Blessings* or *Pesher Genesis* (4QCommGen A)
4Q266	*Damascus Document*^{a} (4QD^{a})
4Q319	Otot
4Q320–30	Calendar Doc. Mishmarot A-I
4Q331	Papyrus Historical Text C
4Q332	Historical Text D
4Q354	Accounts of Cereal (Account B ar or heb)
4Q364	*Reworked Pentateuch*^{b} (4QRP^{b})
4Q365	*Reworked Pentateuch*^{c} (4QRP^{c})
4Q366	*Reworked Pentateuch*^{d} (4QRP^{d})
4Q367	*Reworked Pentateuch*^{e} (4QRP^{e})
4Q380–81	Non-Canonical Psalms A, B
4Q452	Prayer D?
4Q491	*War Scroll* (M^{a})
4Q511	*Shir* (*Songs of the Sage*)
4Q530	*Enoch, Giants* (EnGiants^{b} ar)
4Q540	apocrLevi^{a} ar
4Q541	apocrLevi^{b} ar
4Q542	*Aramaic Testament of Qahat* (TQahat ar)
4Q550–550e	*Prayers of Esther* (PrEsther^{a-f} ar)
4QDeut^{c}	Deuteronomy (4Q30)
4QDeut^{n}	Deuteronomy (4Q41)
4QDeut^{q}	Deuteronomy (4Q44)
4QDibHam^{a}	*Dibre Hame'orot*^{a} or *Words of the Luminaries*^{a} (4Q504)
4QExod^{d}	Exodus (4Q15)
4QExod-Lev^{f}	4Q17
4QGen^{b}	Genesis (4Q2)
4QJer^{a}	Jeremiah (4Q70)
4QJer^{b}	Jeremiah (4Q71)
4QJer^{c}	Jeremiah (4Q72)
4QJer^{d}	Jeremiah (4Q72a)
4QJosh^{a}	Joshua (4Q47)
4QJudg^{a}	Judges (4Q49)
4QMMT^{a}	*Miqsat Ma'ase ha-Torah* ("matter of the Torah") (4Q394)
4QMMT^{d}	*Miqsat Ma'ase ha-Torah*^{d} (4Q397)
4QpaleoExod^{m}	4Q22
4QPrNab ar	*Prayer of Nabonidus* (4Q242)
4QNum^{b}	4Q27
4QSam^{a}	Samuel (4Q51)
4QSam^{b}	Samuel (4Q52)
4QShirShabb^{a}	*Songs of the Sabbath Sacrifice*^{a} (4Q400)
4QTest	*Testimonia* (4Q175)
4QtgLev	*Targum of Leviticus* (4Q156)

4QtgJob	*Targum of Job* (4Q157)
4QX11	4Q76–81 (=XII^{a-f}), oldest mss of The Twelve
8ḤevXII gr	Greek copy of the Minor Prophets (8Ḥev 1)
11Q19	*Temple Scroll*^{a} (11QT^{a})
11QMelch	*Melchizedek Scroll* (11Q13)
11QPs	*Psalms Scroll* (11QS)
11QPs^{a}	*Psalms Scroll*^{a}
11QSTemple	*Temple Scroll*^{a} (11Q19); *Temple Scroll*^{b} (11Q20)
11QT	*Temple Scroll*
11QtgJob	*Targum of Job* (11Q10)

Note: The abbreviation "Q" refers to Qumran, and manuscripts from Qumran are identified by the cave number, which precedes the Q, and the official manuscript number, which follows it; thus 1Q13= Manuscript 13 from Cave 1 at Qumran; 4Q166 from Cave 4; etc.

Abr.	Philo, *On the Life of Abraham*
ad loc.	*ad locum*, to or at that place
AEL	*Ancient Egyptian Literature*. M. Lichtheim. 3 vols. Berkeley, 1971–1980
Ag. Ap.	Josephus, *Against Apion*
ANEP	*The Ancient Near East in Pictures Relating to the Old Testament*. J. B. Pritchard, ed. Princeton, 1954
ANET	*Ancient Near Eastern Texts Relating to the Old Testament*. J. B. Pritchard, ed. Princeton, 1969
Ant.	Josephus, *Antiquities of the Jews*
ʿArak.	*ʿArakhin* (Talmudic Tractate)
Aram.	Aramaic (language)
ʾAvot R. Nat.	*ʾAvot of Rabbi Nathan*
A. Z.	*ʿAvodah Zarah* (Talmudic Tractate)
b.	Babylonian Talmud
b.	born
B. Bat.	*Bava Batra* (Talmudic Tractate)
B. K.	*Bava Kamma* (Talmudic Tractate)
B. M.	*Bava Metziʿa* (Talmudic Tractate)
BCE	before the Common Era (= BC)
Bek.	*Bekhorot* (Talmudic Tractate)
Ber.	*Berakhot* (Talmudic Tractate)
Bik.	*Bikkurim* (Talmudic Tractate)
c.	century
ca.	circa
CD	Cairo Genizah copy of the *Damascus Document*
CE	Common Era (= AD)
cf.	compare
ch, chs	chapter, chapters
col(s)	column(s)
Contempl.	Philo, *On the Contemplative Life*
cm	centimeter(s)
cu	cubit(s)
D	Deuteronomic or Deuteronomistic source (of the Torah)
d.	died
Det.	Philo, *Quod deterius potiori insidari soleat, That the Worse Attacks the Better*
Dtr^{1}	the first Deuteronomistic writer
Dtr^{2}	the second (later) Deuteronomistic writer
E	Elohist or Elohistic source (of the Torah)
e.g.	*exempli gratia*, for example
ed.	editor, edited by, or edition
ʿEd.	*ʿEduyyot*
ʿEruv.	*ʿEruvin* (Talmudic Tractate)
Esd.	Esdras
esp.	especially
et al.	*et alii*, and others
etc.	*et cetera*, and the rest
ff.	following
fol.	folio
Frg. Tg.	*Fragmentary Targum*
ft	feet
g	gram(s)
gal	gallon(s)
Gal.	New Testament book of Galatians
Git.	*Gittin* (Talmudic Tractate)
Gk	Greek (language)
Guide	Maimonides, *The Guide for the Perplexed*
H	Holiness Collection (or Code or Legislation)
Ḥag.	*Ḥagigah* (Talmudic Tractate)
Ḥal.	*Ḥallah* (Talmudic Tractate)
HB	Hebrew Bible
Heb	Hebrew (language)
Ḥev	Ḥever, Naḥal
Hor.	*Horayot* (Talmudic Tractate)
HUBP	Hebrew University Bible Project
HUC	Hebrew Union College
Ḥul.	*Ḥullin* (Talmudic Tractate)
i.e.	*id est*, that is
ibid.	*ibidem*, in the same place
in	inch(es)
intro.	introduction, introductory
J	Jahwist or Yahwist source (of the Torah)
Jdt.	Judith
JPS	Jewish Publication Society
JTS	Jewish Theological Seminary
Jub.	*Jubilees*
J. W.	Josephus, *Jewish War*
Ker.	*Keritot* (Talmudic Tractate)
Ketub.	*Ketubbot* (Talmudic Tractate)
kg	kilogram(s)
Kid.	*Kiddushin* (Talmudic Tractate)
Kil.	*Kilʾayim* (Talmudic Tractate)

KJV	King James Version
km	kilometer(s)
Kod.	*Kodoshim* (Talmudic Order)
Let. Aris.	*Letter of Aristeas*
lit.	literally
L.A.B.	*Liber antiquitatum biblicarum* (Pseudo-Philo)
LXX	Septuagint
m	meter(s)
m.	Mishnah
Maʿas.	*Maʿaserot* (Talmudic Tractate)
Maʿas. S.	*Maʿaser Sheni* (Talmudic Tractate)
Macc.	Maccabees
Mak.	*Makkot* (Talmudic Tractate)
Maks.	*Makhshirin* (Talmudic Tractate)
MAL	Middle Assyrian Laws
Mas	Masada
Matt.	Matthew (gospel)
Meg.	*Megillah* (Talmudic Tractate)
Meʿil.	*Meʿilah*
Mek.	*Mekhilta* (midrashic text on Exodus)
Menaḥ.	*Menaḥot* (Talmudic Tractate)
mi	mile(s)
Mid.	*Middot* (Talmudic Tractate)
Midr. + book	*Midrash* + biblical book (e.g., *Midr. Prov. = Midrash Proverbs*)
Mikv.	*Mikvaʾot* (Talmudic Tractate)
MMT	*Miqṣat Maʿase ha-Torah* (a Dead Sea Scroll)
Moʿed Kat.	*Moʿed Katan* (Talmudic Tractate)
Mos.	Philo, *On the Life of Moses*
ms, mss	manuscript, manuscripts
Mt.	Mount
MT	Masoretic Text
n., nn.	annotation(s)
Nash.	*Nashim* (Talmudic Order)
Naz.	*Nazir* (Talmudic Tractate)
Ned.	*Nedarim* (Talmudic Tractate)
Neg.	*Negaʿim* (Talmudic Tractate)
Nez.	*Nezikin* (Talmudic Order)
Nid.	*Niddah* (Talmudic Tractate)
NJPS	*Tanakh: The Holy Scriptures: The New JPS Translation according to the Traditional Hebrew Text*
NRSV	New Revised Standard Version
ʾOhal.	*ʾOhalot* (Talmudic Tractate)
op. cit.	*opere citato,* in the work cited
Opif.	Philo, *De opificio mundi, On the Creation of the World*
ʿOr.	*ʿOrlah* (Talmudic Tractate)
oz	ounce(s)
P	Priestly source (of the Torah)
p., pp.	page, pages
par.	paragraph
Pes.	*Pesaḥim* (Talmudic Tractate)
Pesik. Rab.	*Pesikta Rabbati*
Pesik. Rav Kah.	*Pesikta de Rav Kahana*
Pirqe R. El.	*Pirqe Rabbi Eliezer*
pl.	plural
Post.	Philo, *On the Posterity of Cain*
Q	manuscripts found at Qumran (Dead Sea Scrolls)
QE	Philo, *Questions and Answers on Exodus*
QG	Philo, *Questions and Answers on Genesis*
q.v.	*quod vide,* which see
R	redactor(s)
R.	Rabbi
RB	Rabbinic Bible *(Miqraʾot Gedolot)*
Rab.	*Rabbah* (book + *Rabbah,* e.g., *Gen. Rab. = Genesis Rabbah*)
Rom.	New Testament book of Romans
Rosh Hash.	*Rosh Ha-Shanah* (Talmudic Tractate)
RSV	Revised Standard Version
Sacr.	Philo, *On the Sacrifices of Cain and Abel*
Sanh.	*Sanhedrin* (Talmudic Tractate)
Seder ʿOlam Rab.	"Order of the world" teaching
Sem.	*Semahot* (minor tractate)
sg.	singular
Shab.	*Shabbat*
Shek.	*Shekalim* (Talmudic Tractate)
Shev.	*Sheviʿit* (Talmudic Tractate)
Shevu.	*Shevuʿot* (Talmudic Tractate)
Shir haShir. Rab.	*Shir ha-Shirim Rabbah* (Song of Songs commentary)
Sir.	The Wisdom of Jesus ben Sirach (Ecclesiasticus)
Sot.	*Sotah* (Talmudic Tractate)
SP	Samaritan Pentateuch
Spec. Laws	Philo, *On the Special Laws*
Sukk.	*Sukkah* (Talmudic Tractate)
s.v.	*sub verbum,* under the heading
t.	*Tosefta*
T. Job	*Testament of Job*
Taʿan.	*Taʿanit* (Talmudic Tractate)
Tanḥ.	*Tanḥuma* (midrashic text on the Torah)
Tehar.	*Teharot* (Talmudic Order)
Tem.	*Temurah* (Talmudic Tractate)
Ter.	*Terumot* (Talmudic Tractate)
Tg.	Targum
Tg. Chron.	*Targum Chronicles*
Tg. Esth. II	*Second Targum of Esther* (*Targum Sheni*)
Tg. Jon.	*Targum Jonathan*
Tg. Neof.	*Targum Neofiti*
Tg. Onk.	*Targum Onkelos*
Tg. Ps.-J.	*Targum Pseudo-Jonathan*
Tg. Rishon	*Targum Rishon* (*First Targum of Esther*)
Tg. Yerushalmi	*Targum Jerusalem* (*Targum Pseudo-Jonathan*)
tr.	translated

T. Yom	*Tevul Yom* (Talmudic Tractate)	*Yad.*	*Yadayim* (Talmudic Tractate)
ʿUk.	*ʿUktzin* (Talmudic Tractate)	*Yebam.*	*Yebamot* (Talmudic Tractate)
v., vv.	verse, verses	Wisd.	The Wisdom of Solomon
Vg	Vulgate	*Zera.*	*Zeraʿim* (Talmudic Order)
Virt.	Philo, *On the Virtues*	*Zevaḥ.*	*Zevaḥim* (Talmudic Tractate)
viz.	*videlicet,* namely	=	equals
vs.	versus	||	parallel
VTE	Vassal Treaty of Esarhaddon	§(§)	section(s)
y.	Jerusalem Talmud		

Note: In chapter/verse references, or following a verse number, the letter "a" means the first section of the verse, "b" means the second section, and so on.

For a complete listing of the divisions and tractates of the Mishnah, Talmud, and Tosefta see p. 1878.

The Jewish Study Bible

SECOND EDITION

JEWISH PUBLICATION SOCIETY

TANAKH TRANSLATION

תּוֹרָה

TORAH

Terminology, Contents, and Traditional Views of Authorship

THE TERM TORAH, "TEACHINGS, INSTRUCTION," derives from the homonymic Hebrew root "y-r-h." This root means "to teach," one possible etymology of Torah is "teaching," or "to shoot (an arrow)," and thus refers to that which "hits the mark." Jewish tradition, from the late biblical period on, uses "Torah" to refer to the first section of the Bible, the books Genesis, Exodus, Leviticus, Numbers, and Deuteronomy. These books are also called "The Five Books of Moses" or the "Pentateuch," which derives (via Latin) from the Greek *penta* (five) *teuchoi* (books). In the early first millennium of the common era, as the technology for creating thin parchment developed, these five books were sometimes written on one long scroll, signaling unambiguously that they are one unit. Unlike other canonical divisions, where there is significant debate within and between different religious traditions (see the essay on "Canonization," pp. 2153–58), both Jewish and Christian traditions view the books Genesis through Deuteronomy in this order as a single unit, standing first in the Bible. The unanimity of tradition and the initial placement of these five books reflect their significant place within religious life. In Judaism, the Torah is accorded the highest level of sanctity, above that of the other books of the Bible. One symbol of its significance is that the Torah scrolls are kept in an ark or cabinet at the very front of the synagogue, and when the ark is opened, the congregation stands; in addition, only the Torah text is read in its entirety; this is not true for the reading in the synagogue of any other canonical section (though individual books are read as a whole).

Despite their traditional perception as a unity, it is not so obvious how these five books cohere. They do not form a single book in the modern sense, with a single author; modern scholarship has persuasively argued that each of these books is a composite, reflecting many traditions and sources (see below). While the plot progresses chronologically, from the creation of the world to the end of the wandering in the wilderness, a large part of this story is retold in Deuteronomy. Moreover, the story does not end here, but continues into the book of Joshua and beyond. While Moses is the central human character in much of the Torah, he is introduced only in ch 2 of Exodus, and is absent from all of Genesis. There are several major themes, including the early development of Israel as a people, the covenant between God and Israel, and the promise of the land; but none of these is present throughout the Torah and all continue beyond it. Theme alone does not define what the Torah is. In fact, if this final theme of promise of the land and its fulfillment is determinative, we should speak of the Hexateuch, the six books of Genesis through Joshua, rather than the Pentateuch or Torah.

The Hebrew terms *torah* and *torat moshe* ("the Torah of Moses"), already in use in late biblical literature to describe what is later called the Torah, offer a better clue to the nature and unity of these books. *Torah* is often understood as "law," and indeed this is one of its frequent meanings in the Bible, as in Exod. 12.49: "There shall be one law [Heb *torah*] for the citizen and for the stranger who dwells among you." Law is a predominant genre of the Torah, which contains not only the Decalogue in Exod. ch 20 and Deut. ch 5, but extensive legal collections in Exod. chs 21–23, Lev. chs 17–26, and Deut. chs 12–26, as well as selected laws within various narratives, such as the law of circumcision in the narrative about Abraham in Gen. ch 17 and the law concerning inheritance of the land by women in Num. ch 36, embedded within a section about the possession of the land. Many narrative sections also contain material that is of legal significance. For example, the first creation story in Genesis culminates with the "creation" of the Sabbath (Gen. 2.2–3), though this would only be legislated in Exod. ch 16, and then as part of the Decalogue, in Exod. 20.8–11 and in the legal collection in Exod. 23.10–12. Similarly, the story of the construction of the Tabernacle (Exod. chs 25–40), a temporary temple for God in the wilderness, is not narrated for its own sake, but as an introduction to the various laws of sacrifice, narrated at the beginning of Leviticus, the book that immediately follows these chapters. Given that so much of the Torah is comprised of laws, it is not surprising that in the pre-Christian Jewish community of Alexandria, Egypt, Torah was often translated into Greek as *nomos*, "law." This tradition continued in Christianity, where the Torah is often called "the Law."

Yet "law" is not the only possible translation of *torah*, and the Torah should not be typified as a book of law. The Heb term *torah* also means "instruction" or "teaching," as in Prov. 1.8, "My son, heed the discipline of your father, / And do not forsake the instruction [Heb *torah*] of your mother." Teaching is not confined to law; indeed narratives or stories are as effective a medium of instruction. Given the predominance of narrative in significant portions of the Torah, especially in Genesis, the beginning of Exodus, and Numbers, it is best to understand the biblical term *torat moshe*, an early term for these five books, as "the instruction of Moses." This instruction was realized through narratives and laws, which together elucidate the proper norms of living and the relationship between God and the world. That the Torah is more than a set of laws is made explicit in the comments of Rashi, the great Jewish medieval interpreter, who, quoting earlier sources, defends the fact that Torah begins with the stories of Genesis rather than with the laws of Exodus.

The terms *torat moshe, and torat (ha)elohim/Yhvh*, "God's/the Lord's torah," are found predominantly in various late biblical sections and books, such as Ezra, Nehemiah, and Chronicles. These phrases suggest that the Torah was then understood to be a divine revelation mediated by Moses, as explicitly stated in Ezra 7.6 (cf. Neh. 8.1), "The Torah of Moses which the Lord God of Israel had given." The Torah in the time of Ezra is more or less identical to the Torah as it now exists. It is significant, however, that these terms for it never appear in the Torah itself, suggesting that in the Torah, the word *torah* never refers to the Torah. In fact, the Torah does not explicitly suggest that it was compiled by Moses himself. (The phrase "the Torah" in passages such as Deut. 4.44, "This is the *torah* that Moses set before the Israelites," never refers to the complete Torah—there the reference is to [most of] the book of Deuteronomy.)

After the books came to be viewed as authoritative, it was natural that they should be considered a coherent body of writing given by God through one special "author," Moses. In several places, the Bible suggests that Moses stayed on Mount Sinai for forty days and forty nights (Exod. 24.18; 34.28; Deut. 9.9; 10.10). Clearly, this was too long a time for short legal collections such as Exod. chs 21–23 to have been conveyed to him, and thus traditions developed that Moses received the entire written Torah from God at that point; according to the classical rabbis, Moses simultaneously received the oral law, which served as the authoritative interpretation of the written law. In other words, the concept of the divinely inspired Torah expanded to include the Written Torah and all that would derive from it. The Written Torah, according to all rabbinic sources (which are followed by the early church), included events before the time of Moses—the book of Genesis, which thus represents God's authoritative narration to Moses of the early history of the world and of Abraham and his family—and the death of Moses. Some rabbinic sources suggest that the final chapter of the Torah, Deut. ch 34, which narrates the death of Moses, was dictated by God to Moses, who wrote it with his tears. The view that the Torah is the divine word mediated by Moses was the standard view through the Renaissance.

This view is explicitly contradicted by the Torah's narrative, as was sometimes (though rarely) recognized in the Middle Ages. Thus, Abraham Ibn (son of) Ezra, a 12th-century CE exegete, noted that Gen. 12.6 states that "The Canaanites were *then* in the land." The word "then" suggests that when the author of this passage wrote it, the Canaanites were no longer in the land, and thus the text must have been written after the time of Moses, because during Moses' time the Canaanites were still in the land. A small number of other places that suggest authorship later than Moses were pointed out by a few medieval scholars, but these were not systematized into a thesis which could challenge the dominant view concerning Moses' authorship of the Torah.

Modern Source Theories

SLOWLY, WITH THE RISE OF RATIONALISM, particularly as associated with figures such as Thomas Hobbes (1588–1679) and especially Benedict (Baruch) Spinoza (1632–1677), the view that the Torah was a unified whole, written by Moses, began to be questioned. (For additional information on this development, see "Modern Jewish Interpretation," pp. 1971–77, and "Modern Study of the Bible," pp. 2166–77). This culminated in the development of the model of the Documentary Hypothesis in the 19th century, according to which the Torah (or Hexateuch) is comprised of four main sources or documents which were edited or redacted together: J, E, P, and D. Each of these sources or documents is embedded in a (relatively) complete form in the current Torah, and is typified by vocabulary, literary style, and theological perspective.

J and E are so called after the names for God that each of them uses in Genesis: J uses the name "Yahveh" (German "Jahwe," hence "J"), translated in NJPS as "LORD," though it is really a personal name whose exact meaning is unknown; E prefers to call the deity "Elohim" (translated "God"), an epithet which also serves as the generic term for God or gods in the Bible. P, which also uses "Elohim" (and other names, such as "Shaddai"), is an abbreviation for the Priestly material, and D refers to the Deuteronomist, primarily in Deuteronomy.

The difference in divine names, however, is not the main criterion used by scholars for suggesting that the Torah is not a unified composition. Much more significant are doublets and contradictions, in both narrative and legal material. For example, it has long been noted that Gen. chs 1–3 twice narrate the creation of the world. People are created first in 1.27—"And God created man in His image, in the image of God He created him; male and female He created them"—and then again in 2.7—"The LORD God formed man from the dust of the earth. He blew into his nostrils the breath of life, and man became a living being." Furthermore, the second creation account does not simply mirror or repeat the first, but differs from the first in both outline and detail. Gen. 1.1–2.3, the first account, narrates the creation of a highly symmetrical world by a very powerful deity who creates through the word. In this story, for example, man and woman are created together (1.27) after the creation of the land animals (1.25). In contrast, the second story, in 2.4–3.24, suggests that man was created (2.7), then the animals (2.19), and then woman (2.21–22). Its focus is on the creation of humanity, not of the entire physical world, and God anthropomorphically "forms" various beings, rather than creating them through the spoken word. Thus, these are two separate stories, written by two authors, representing different worldviews about the nature of creation, humanity, and God.

The two creation stories appear as two totally separate blocks of material in 1.1–2.3 and 2.4–3.24. In several cases, however, the sources do not appear in distinct, long blocks but are intertwined. This is the case in the flood story, a combination of J and P. According to P, two of each type of animal shall come into the ark (Gen. 6.19–20), but J says that of the clean animals, seven pairs shall come in, and of the unclean, one pair (Gen. 7.2). Similarly, the story of the plague of blood (Exod. 7.14–24) contains two accounts which are intertwined; in one (J), Moses is the protagonist, and the blood only affects the Nile (e.g., vv. 17–18), while in the other (P), Aaron appears as well, and the flood affects all Egyptian water sources (e.g., vv. 19, 24). In such cases, the narratives are combined with great skill, though careful attention to plot and vocabulary help to discern the original building blocks or sources of the story in its final form.

In addition to narrative, the legal material in the Torah is also the product of several sources. For example, slave laws concerning the Hebrew or Israelite slave are found in the Torah in Exod. 21.1–6, Lev. 25.39–46, and Deut. 15.12–18. These laws cannot be reconciled in a straightforward fashion since they represent three different notions of slavery. Most significant is the way in which Exodus differentiates between the treatment of a male and female slave, whereas Deuteronomy insists that they should both be treated similarly. While Exodus and Deuteronomy agree that a slave who loves his master may opt to remain a slave "for life" (Exod. 21.6) or "in perpetuity" (Deut. 15.17), Lev. ch 25 insists that slavery of Israelites does not really exist, since slaves must be treated "as a hired or bound laborer," and they may only serve "until the jubilee year" (v. 40). Such legal differences are not surprising once we are open to the hypotheses that the Bible is composite, and the different legal collections reflect norms or ideals of different groups living in different time periods. Traditional Jewish interpretation, on the other hand, reconciles these various traditions through a process of harmonization, by assuming, for example, that "for life" or "in perpetuity" should in these cases be interpreted as "until the jubilee year."

It is possible to trace distinctive styles and theological notions that typify individual Torah sources. For example, the J source is well known for its highly anthropomorphic God, who has a close relationship with humans, as seen in Gen. 2.4–3.24, which includes, for example, a description of God "moving about [or walking] in the garden" (3.8) and says that God "made garments of skins for Adam and his wife, and clothed them" (3.21). On the other hand, in E, the Elohist source, God is more distant from people, typically communicating with them by dreams or via intermediaries, such as heavenly messengers (NJPS "angels") and prophets. The P or Priestly source is characterized by a strong interest in order and boundaries (see Gen. ch 1), as well as an overriding concern with the priestly family of Aaron and the Temple-based religious system. D, or Deuteronomy, is characterized by a unique hortatory or preaching style, and insists strongly that God cannot be seen, as in this source's description of revelation: "The LORD spoke to you out of the fire; you heard the sound of words but perceived no shape—nothing but a voice" (Deut. 4.12). This explains why this source insists that God does not physically dwell in the Temple or Tabernacle; rather, the Temple is "the site where the LORD your God will choose to establish His name" (Deut. 12.11 and elsewhere). D also emphasizes that this one God must be worshipped in one place only (see esp. Deut. ch 12); this place is understood to be Jerusalem.

The narrative sources J, E, P, and D also have legal collections associated with them. The Covenant Collection (see Exod. 24.7) in Exod. 20.19–23.33 is associated with J or E. The Holiness Collection of Lev. chs 17–26 is so named because of its central injunction (Lev. 19.2), "You shall be holy, for I the LORD your God am holy." Though not composed by the Priestly author (P), it represents Priestly theology. The Deuteronomic law collection appears in Deut. chs 12–26. These blocks of material were called "codes" by earlier scholars; since the blocks are neither complete nor organized for the law court, however, as a "code" might be, the term "collection" is more suitable.

The identification of these narrative sources with associated legal material is not based solely on contradictions within the Torah. Using modern source theory, it is possible to divide the Torah into separate , consistent, more or less complete documents; it is difficult to imagine that this is a result of an accident or modern imagination.

Critical biblical scholarship, through the latter part of the 20th century, was quite confident in dating each of these Torah sources along with the legal collections that they incorporated. Thus, J was seen as the earliest collection, often dated to the period of David and Solomon in the 10th century BCE, followed by E, which was often associated with the Northern Kingdom. D was connected to the reforms of King Josiah in the late 7th century, and P was seen as deriving from the community in exile in Babylonia in the 6th century BCE. The arguments for these specific dates were in some cases tinged with anti-Semitism. Many of these scholars deprecated rabbinic Judaism and the Priestly source that was most proximate to it chronologically as legalistic, seeing it as a degeneration of the more ideal, early Hebrew religion. There was also an element of Christian supersessionism among some source critics: Biblical Israel is held in high esteem; early Judaism (in the late biblical and postbiblical periods) is not, for it was to be superseded by Christianity. For this reason, many academic Jewish scholars have until recently shied away from source-critical models.

Scholars now agree that many of the reasons usually given for assigning these dates to the individual sources are problematic, and a lively debate has developed concerning such fundamental issues as the relative order of these sources and the extent to which any of them are as early as previous scholars had suggested. The scholarly consensus, however, remains that the text is composite, unlike the assumptions of pre-modern scholarship, which continue to be influential among some religious groups. The existence of E as a complete source has been questioned as well, especially since E first appears well after the beginning of the Torah and is very difficult to disentangle from J after the beginning of Exodus. Thus, many scholars now talk of JE together as an early narrative source, incorporating diverse traditions. Some scholars, especially in Europe, do not see each source as independent, but view the Torah as coming together from an original core that has been supplemented by various authors. Additionally, most scholars no longer see each source as representative of a single author writing at one particular time but recognize that each may reflect a long historical period within a single group or "school." Thus, it is best to speak of streams or strands of tradition and to contrast their basic underpinnings, rather than to speak of sources reflecting a single author, period, and locale. For example, despite the unraveling of a consensus on the exact date of the sources, it is still valid to contrast the Deuteronomic view of Israel's fundamental, intrinsic holiness—as seen, for example, in Deut. 7.6, "For you are a people consecrated [holy] to the LORD your God"—with the Priestly view, articulated most clearly in the Holiness Collection (H), which suggests that Israel must aspire to holiness—as in Lev. 19.2, "You shall be holy." These fundamental differences cannot easily be reconciled, suggesting that despite certain problems with the classical source-critical method, certain elements of source criticism remain useful alongside other methods of analyzing biblical texts.

Compilation and Redaction of the Torah

WE DO NOT KNOW HOW THESE VARIOUS SOURCES and legal collections, which now comprise the Torah, came together to form a single book. Scholars have posited an editor or series of editors or redactors, conveniently called R, who combined the various sources, perhaps in several stages, over a long time. Certainly not all ancient Israelite traditions were preserved in the Torah. Much was probably lost. Without knowing what was lost, we cannot suggest how and why the redactor(s), R, made their selection and by what principles they ordered their materials. It must suffice to note that in contrast to modern editing, which works toward articulating a single viewpoint, the redaction of the Torah, like the editing of other ancient works, did not create a purely consistent, singular perspective but incorporated a variety of voices and perspectives. Others suggest that the final Torah reflects little editing in our sense of the word, since the sources were hardly revised in the process and the editorial hand was slight; these scholars thus prefer to use the term "compiler" rather than "redactor."

The ultimate result of this process, most likely completed during the Babylonian exile (586–538 BCE) or soon thereafter in the early Persian period, was the creation of a very long book, narrating what must have been felt to be the formative period of Israel, from the period of the creation of the world through the death of Moses. The events narrated in Gen. chs 1–11 describing the creation of the world and its population by many nations serve as an introduction to the singling out of one nation, Israel. The stories of Abraham, Isaac, and Jacob, the ancestors of Israel, form the national prehistory. Israel comes into existence as a nation in Exodus, and the foremost events of its national history are the exodus from Egypt, the revelation at Sinai, and the coming to the promised land. These events are central to Exodus-Deuteronomy.

The ancient Near Eastern world produced no other work of comparable length in the span of time its narrative covers or in the inclusiveness of the literary genres and sources incorporated into it. This extensive and inclusive nature of the Torah creates a fundamental problem for biblical interpreters. Should we concentrate on interpreting the individual sources, on hearing the voices of the component parts of the text before they were redacted together? Or should we follow the traditional way in which the Bible was read for many centuries before the rise of modern source criticism, and focus on the final product? This latter approach has been called holistic reading, and it is often advocated by modern literary scholars who are most focused on the final version of the text. In the annotations of the biblical books that follow we will aim for a balance, maintaining our critical stance toward the sources but never forgetting that it is their combination into a whole that has preserved them and given them meaning. We will show how meaning may be uncovered by looking both at the early building blocks of the text, and at the text in its final, redacted form.

[MARC ZVI BRETTLER]

בראשית

Genesis

THE BOOK OF GENESIS RECEIVED its English name from the Greek translation of the Heb word *toledot,* which is used thirteen times in Genesis and is translated as "story" (2.4), "record" (5.1), or "line" (10.1). In Heb, it is known, like many books in the Tanakh, by its first word, *bereshit,* which means, "In the beginning." Genesis is indeed a book about beginnings—the beginning of the natural world, the beginning of human culture, and the beginning of the people Israel, whose story occupies most of this book and will dominate the rest of the Torah. In the ancient Near Eastern world in which Israel emerged, beginnings were deemed to be crucial, for the origins of things were thought to disclose their character and purpose. In Genesis, the origins of Israel—the people known later as the "Jews"—lie in God's mysterious promise to a Mesopotamian whose name is Abram (changed in ch 17 to "Abraham"). The essence of the promise is that God will make of him a great nation, bless him abundantly, and grant him the land of Canaan. Ostensibly absurd when it first comes, the promise faces one obstacle after another throughout the course of Genesis—principally, the barrenness of Abraham's primary wife (and of other matriarchs in the next two generations) and the murderous fraternal rivalry among his descendants. And yet, by the end of Genesis, all the obstacles notwithstanding, the twelve tribes that make up the people Israel have indeed come into existence, an Israelite effectively rules a superpower (Egypt), and the promise of the land, though far from fulfillment (which comes about only in the book of Joshua), is anything but forgotten.

The book of Genesis is thus, in more senses than one, a primary source for Jewish theology. It presents its ideas on the relationship of God to nature, to humanity in general, and to the people Israel in particular in ways that are, however, foreign to the expectations of most modern readers. It is therefore all too easy to miss the seriousness and profundity of its messages. For the vehicle through which Genesis conveys its worldview is neither the theological tract nor the rigorous philosophical proof nor the confession of faith. That vehicle is, rather, narrative. The theology must be inferred from stories, and the lived relationship with God takes precedence over abstract theology. Those who think of stories (including mythology) as fit only for children not only misunderstand the thought-world and the literary conventions of the ancient Near East; they also condemn themselves to miss the complexity and sophistication of the stories of Genesis. For these are narratives that have evoked interpretation upon interpretation from biblical times into our own day and have occupied the attention of some of the keenest thinkers in human history.

One aspect of narrative in Genesis that requires special attention is its high tolerance for different versions of the same event, a well-known feature of ancient Near Eastern literature, from earliest times through rabbinic midrash. The book presents, for example, two accounts of Abram/Abraham's attempting to pass his wife off as his sister (12.10–20; 20.1–18; cf. 26.1–11, where Isaac does the same), two accounts of God's making a covenant with him (ch 15 and 17), and two accounts of how Jacob's name was changed to Israel (32.23–33; 35.9–15). In these instances, most modern biblical scholars see different antecedent documents that editors (known as redactors or compilers) have combined to give us the text now in our hands. This could not have happened, however, if the existence of variation was seen as a serious defect or if rigid consistency was deemed essential to effective storytelling. Rather, the redactors have chosen a different approach, retaining variant versions and treating them as sequential events in the same longer story. The result is a certain measure of repetition, to be sure, but the repetition is in the service of a sophisticated presentation of themes with variations in a book rich in narrative analogy, revealing echoes, and suggestive contrasts. For the Rabbis of Talmudic times and their successors through the centuries, the exploration of those subtle literary features provided an indispensable insight not only into the first book of the Torah (the most sacred part of the Tanakh) but also into the mind of God.

The book is composed of four major sections: 1.1–11.25, the primeval story; 11.26–25.18, the story of Abraham; 25.19–36.43, the Jacob cycle; and 37.1–50.26, the story of Joseph. (There is little independent narrative about Isaac, the second patriarch.)

The first section, the primeval story, takes us from the creation of the world through the birth of Abram's father nineteen generations later. Its stories are short, loosely strung together, and connected only by genealogies that identify the generation in which the action takes place. There is, however, an overriding theme: the spread of human wickedness, the refusal of humankind to accept their creaturely status, as they seek to blur the all-important boundary between the human and the divine and, as a result, bring catastrophe upon themselves. The center of attention is God, who is portrayed rather anthropomorphically and speaks directly and frequently to human beings, condemning or sparing, announcing His judgment or His merciful forbearance.

Largely because of its focus on creation, the primeval story exhibits a number of contacts with Mesopotamian mythology. The account of creation with which Genesis opens (1.1–2.3), for example, has affinities with *Enuma elish,* a Babylonian epic, which tells how one god, Marduk, attained supremacy over the others and created the world by splitting his aquatic enemy Tiamat (cf. Heb *tehom*, "the deep") in half. The story of Adam and Eve's sin in the garden of Eden (2.25–3.24) displays similarities with *Gilgamesh,* an epic poem that tells how its hero lost the opportunity for immortality and came to terms with his humanity. And the story of Noah (6.5–9.17) has close connections with *Atrahasis,* a Mesopotamian story in which the gods send a flood to wipe out the human race, with the exception of one man and his children from whom humankind begins afresh (the story was eventually incorporated into *Gilgamesh* as well). In each case, the biblical narrator has made use of the Mesopotamian forerunner but also adapted it to Israelite theology. The primeval story thus evidences both the deep continuities and the striking points of discontinuity between biblical Israel and its Mesopotamian antecedents and contemporaries.

In the story of Abraham (11.26–25.11), the narrative becomes more continuous. Abra(ha)m dominates almost every episode. Seeing him in a wide variety of situations, we have a sense of his personality and of the human dimension of the events that God has mysteriously set into motion. Whereas God's relationship to human beings in the primeval story is marked mostly (but not exclusively) by judgment, expulsion, and exile, in the story of Abraham the dominant notes are the contrasting ones of blessing and promise, especially the promise of the land and of progeny. But the narrative does not spare us the knowledge that while the blessings and promises are as yet unrealized, Abraham's family have their moments of anguish and even ugliness. God, who is generally portrayed less anthropomorphically than in the primeval story, overcomes the obstacles to His promises and blessings, so that Abraham finally acquires both the son from whom the promised nation shall descend and a foothold in the promised land.

The LORD accomplishes this partly through palpable miracles and partly through His silent guidance of the course of human events. As the story of Abraham unfolds, its human protagonist, despite some arguably serious lapses, gradually assumes the role of the ideal religious person—obedient to God's commands (even at the cost of the most painful sacrifice); faithful even when the promise seems impossible; gracious, generous, and hospitable, yet committed to justice and compassion even to the point of firmly (if deferentially) questioning God's counsel.

The stories in the Jacob cycle (25.19–36.43) are even more connected and less self-contained than those in the story of Abraham. Here, we are entitled to speak not simply of a general theme, like the theme of blessing and promise in the Abraham story (which continues in this section), but of a plot as well. In its broadest outlines, the plot has to do with how the second son acquires his older brother's superior status and the attendant rights to the Abrahamic promise, yet eventually reconciles with the brother he has wronged and emerges legitimately as the patriarch from whom the people Israel takes its name. Various types of trickery play a major role as this plot develops. The human dimension is more central here than in the Abraham narrative, and the resourcefulness of the protagonists, especially Jacob himself and his mother Rebekah, proportionately more important. Accordingly, God speaks less frequently and intervenes less dramatically. Indeed, His presence is less available and assumes an eerie cast ("Surely the LORD is present in this place, and I did not know it!" [28.16]).

The closing section of the book of Genesis, the story of Joseph (37.1–50.26), represents a narrative so coherent and so continuous that it has justly been termed a novella. Indeed, it offers the deepest psychological portraits and the most subtle and complex plot in Genesis and constitutes one of the gems of biblical prose narrative. Whereas in the first section of Genesis, the primeval story, God booms forth His pronouncements, in this last section He does not speak at all, with the exception of one apparition to Jacob while he is still in Canaan (46.1–4). Rather, He communicates through dreams (in which, significantly, He does not appear) and, more importantly, through people, especially through Joseph's God-given wisdom to interpret dreams and to administer effectively. Here, even more than in the Jacob cycle, God works through the ambivalent and devious designs of flawed human beings, providentially bringing good out of human evil and arranging "the survival of many people" (50.20)—including the brothers who, seething with resentment, once plotted Joseph's death and enslavement but now graciously accept subordination to the younger brother who has saved their lives.

How much history lies behind the story of Genesis? Because the action of the primeval story is not represented as taking place on the plane of ordinary human history and has so many affinities with ancient mythology, it is very far-fetched to speak of its narratives as historical at all. In the cases of the succeeding three large sections of the book, the matter is more complicated, for scholars continue to sift the evidence and to debate the question. Although enormous amounts of data about ancient Mesopotamia, Canaan, and Egypt have been uncovered over the last two centuries, no evidence has turned up that establishes that Abraham, (his son) Isaac, Jacob, or Joseph existed. At best, we can speak of accurate local color, although this may mean only that the Israelites knew something about the lands in which they placed their legendary forebears (see "History of Israel," pp. 2107–19). Negative evidence, however, is not necessarily evidence of a negative, and historians are likely to continue examining the reports of Israel's Mesopotamian origins and Egyptian sojourn for the foreseeable future. More to the point, these stories are less important for the history they convey than for the theology they develop.

The authorship of Genesis is a similarly controversial issue, although here the consensus among critical scholars is somewhat more secure (see "Modern Study of the Bible," pp. 2166–77). The book itself names no one as its author, and makes no claim to be divinely revealed or inspired (though it does contain many reports of divine speech). When other biblical books refer to a Torah of Moses, they cite legal texts, and there is no reason to think that Genesis formed part of the corpus so designated. Indeed, there are several indications that the Genesis narrative assumes a post-Mosaic narrator without embarrassment (see the comments on 12.6, 14.14, and 36.31). In Second Temple and rabbinic Judaism, however, Genesis is treated as part of the Torah of Moses. Despite a number of demurrals on a few particular passages by major rabbis in the Middle Ages, this became the consensus of the tradition. Historical-critical scholarship, however, has identified three main sources, which it denotes with the symbols J, E, and P, that have been woven together to produce Genesis (see "Torah," pp. 1–6). The relationship of compositional history to religious faith is not a simple one. If Moses is the human author of Genesis, nothing ensures that God is its ultimate Author. If J, E, P, and various equally anonymous sources and redactors are its human authors, nothing ensures that God is not its ultimate Author.

[JON D. LEVENSON]

BERE'SHIT בראשית

1 When God began to create[a] heaven and earth—[2] the earth
being unformed and void, with darkness over the surface
of the deep and a wind from[b] God sweeping over the water—[3] God said, "Let there be light"; and there was light. [4] God
saw that the light was good, and God separated the light from
the darkness. [5] God called the light Day, and the darkness He

a Others "In the beginning God created." *b Others "the spirit of."*

1.1–2.3: Creation in seven days. The book of Genesis—and thus the Bible itself—opens with an account of creation that is extraordinary for its austerity. Other ancient Near Eastern evocations of God's (or the gods') world-ordering activity, including many in the Bible itself (e.g., Ps. 104), provide high drama and graphic description of the events and their protagonists (even the LORD). Gen. 1.1–2.3, however, is utterly devoid of sensory detail. This eerie abstractness, combined with the highly schematic and formulaic structure of the narrative, conveys a sense of the awe-inspiring majesty and inviolable sovereignty of the God on whom the narrative is unswervingly focused. This narrative is structured by a pattern of seven days, six in which God accomplishes all His creative labors, and one in which He rests in regal repose, blessing and hallowing that climactic day. The correlations between things created on the various days exhibit a high degree of symmetry (see diagram, next page). The first three days describe the creation of generalities or domains; the next three chronicle the creation of the specifics or the inhabitants of the domains in the same order. Creation comes to its culmination, however, only in the one day that has no counterpart, the Sabbath ("Shabbát" in modern Heb, or "Shábbes" in the Eastern European pronunciation), here observed by God above and not yet enjoined upon His people Israel (who first hear of it in Exod. ch 16). The organization of time into seven-day units has become so familiar and so widespread that it is easy to forget that unlike the month (which in the Bible is lunar) and the year (which in the Bible never moves too far from its solar base), the biblical week corresponds to no astronomical event. The notion that seven signifies completeness and that things come to their fit conclusion on the seventh day did, however, have wide resonance in the ancient Near Eastern world in which Israel emerged, and that idea doubtless stands in the background of our passage. The role of the number seven in 1.1–2.3 extends, in fact, beyond the obvious division of the acts of creation into a seven-day sequence. For example, the expression, *And God saw that* [something He made] *was good* or *very good* occurs seven times, but not on every day of the primordial week. Missing on the second and seventh, it appears twice on the adjacent third and sixth days (1.10, 12, 25, 31). Similarly, the word "God" occurs exactly thirty-five times (i.e., five times seven) in our passage, and the section devoted to the seventh day (2.1–3) has exactly thirty-five words in the Heb. The organization of the process of creation into a sequence of seven days is familiar to most readers not only from the opening of the Tanakh but also from the Sabbath commandment of the Decalogue in Exod. 20.8–11. But we must not forget that this connection is far from universal in the Tanakh. In fact, most biblical descriptions of creation know nothing of a seven-day sequence (e.g., Ps. 104; Prov. 8.22–31), and most texts about the Sabbath (including the version of the Decalogue in Deut. 5.12–15) make no reference to creation. The suspicion arises that 1.1–2.3 derives from a distinct school of thought, one that dates to a relatively late period in the history of Israelite religion. On the

called Night. And there was evening and there was morning, a
first day.[a]
6 God said, "Let there be an expanse in the midst of the water, that it may separate water from water." 7 God made the
expanse, and it separated the water which was below the expanse from the water which was above the expanse. And it was
so. 8 God called the expanse Sky. And there was evening and
there was morning, a second day.
9 God said, "Let the water below the sky be gathered into
one area, that the dry land may appear." And it was so. 10 God
called the dry land Earth, and the gathering of waters He called
Seas. And God saw that this was good. 11 And God said, "Let
the earth sprout vegetation: seed-bearing plants, fruit trees
of every kind on earth that bear fruit with the seed in it." And
it was so. 12 The earth brought forth vegetation: seed-bearing
plants of every kind, and trees of every kind bearing fruit with
the seed in it. And God saw that this was good. 13 And there was
evening and there was morning, a third day.

a *Others "one day."*

basis of these considerations, and a multitude of others, critical scholars attribute the passage to the P (for "Priestly") source. And God does function here in ways reminiscent of a "kohen" (priest), giving blessings, for example (1.22, 28; 2.3; cf. Lev. 9.22–23; Num. 6.22–27), and consecrating the Sabbath (2.3; cf. Ezek. 44.24). The concern shown in this story for order and clear boundaries typifies the Priestly corpus. More importantly, the creation of the world in 1.1–2.3 bears several striking resemblances to the Priestly construction of the Tabernacle mandated in Exod. chs 25–31 and executed in Exod. chs 35–40 (e.g., see Gen. 2.1–3; Exod. 39.32, 42–43)—the prototype of the Jerusalem Temple and the focus of the priestly service of the LORD. Other ancient Near Eastern creation stories also conclude with the construction of a temple for the creation god. In the Tanakh, the world is sometimes seen as the LORD's temple, and the Temple as a microcosm (e.g., Isa. 66.1–2). **1:** A tradition over two millennia old sees 1.1 as a complete sentence: "In the beginning God created the heavens and the earth." In the 11th century, the great Jewish commentator Rashi made a case that the verse functions as a temporal clause. This is, in fact, how some ancient Near Eastern creation stories begin—including the one that starts at 2.4b. Hence the translation, *When God began to create heaven and earth.* **2:** This clause describes things just before the process of creation began. To modern people, the opposite of the created order is "nothing," that is, a vacuum. To the ancients, the opposite of the created order was something much worse than "nothing." It was an active, malevolent force we can best term "chaos." In this verse, chaos is envisioned as a dark, undifferentiated mass of water. In 1.9, God creates the dry land (and the seas, which can exist only when water is bounded by dry land). But in 1.1–2.3, water itself and darkness, too, are primordial (contrast Isa. 45.7). In the midrash, Bar Kappara upholds the troubling notion that the Torah shows that God created the world out of preexistent material. But other rabbis worry that acknowledging this would cause people to liken God to a king who had built his palace on a garbage dump, thus arrogantly impugning His majesty (*Gen. Rab.* 1.5). In the ancient Near East, however, to say that a deity had subdued chaos is to give him the highest praise. **3–5:** Since the sun is not created until the fourth day (1.14–19), the light of the first three days is of a different order from what we know. A midrash teaches that when God saw the corruption of the generations of the flood and of the tower of Babel, He hid that primordial light away for the benefit of the righteous in the world-to-come (*b. Ḥag.* 12a). Other ancient Near Eastern myths similarly assume the existence of light before the creation of the luminaries. **6–8:** The word translated *expanse* refers to a piece of metal that has been hammered flat. Here, the function of the sky is to separate the waters above (which fall as rain) from the subterranean waters (which rise as springs; see 7.11).

SABBATH DAY 7 (2.1–3)	
LAND AND PLANTS DAY 3 (1.9–13)	LAND ANIMALS AND HUMANS DAY 6 (1.24–31)
SKY *(separating waters above from waters below)* DAY 2 (1.6–8)	FISH/BIRDS DAY 5 (1.20–23)
LIGHT DAY 1 (1.1–5)	LIGHTS *(i.e., sun, moon, and stars)* DAY 4 (1.14–19)

14 God said, "Let there be lights in the expanse of the sky to
separate day from night; they shall serve as signs for the set
times—the days and the years; 15 and they serve as lights in
the expanse of the sky to shine upon the earth." And it was so.
16 God made the two great lights, the greater light to dominate
the day and the lesser light to dominate the night, and the
stars. 17 And God set them in the expanse of the sky to shine
upon the earth, 18 to dominate the day and the night, and to
separate light from darkness. And God saw that this was good.
19 And there was evening and there was morning, a fourth day.
20 God said, "Let the waters bring forth swarms of living
creatures, and birds that fly above the earth across the expanse of the sky." 21 God created the great sea monsters, and
all the living creatures of every kind that creep, which the waters brought forth in swarms, and all the winged birds of every
kind. And God saw that this was good. 22 God blessed them,
saying, "Be fertile and increase, fill the waters in the seas, and
let the birds increase on the earth." 23 And there was evening
and there was morning, a fifth day.
24 God said, "Let the earth bring forth every kind of living
creature: cattle, creeping things, and wild beasts of every kind."
And it was so. 25 God made wild beasts of every kind and cattle
of every kind, and all kinds of creeping things of the earth. And
God saw that this was good. 26 And God said, "Let us make man
in our image, after our likeness. They shall rule the fish of the
sea, the birds of the sky, the cattle, the whole earth, and all the
creeping things that creep on earth." 27 And God created man
in His image, in the image of God He created him; male and
female He created them. 28 God blessed them and God said to
them, "Be fertile and increase, fill the earth and master it; and
rule the fish of the sea, the birds of the sky, and all the living
things that creep on earth."
29 God said, "See, I give you every seed-bearing plant that is
upon all the earth, and every tree that has seed-bearing fruit;
they shall be yours for food. 30 And to all the animals on land, to
all the birds of the sky, and to everything that creeps on earth,
in which there is the breath of life, [I give] all the green plants

16: The sun and moon are created only on the fourth day and are not named, but referred to only as *the greater light* and *the lesser light*. This may be an implicit polemic against the worship of astral bodies (see 2 Kings 23.5). **21:** A similar point can be made about the creation of *the great sea monsters* on the fifth day. In some ancient myths—and biblical texts as well (see Ps. 74.12–17; Job 26.5–14)—creation results from the slaying of a sea monster. Isa. 27.1 uses the same word to describe the frightening sea monster that the LORD will kill at the end of time. **26–28:** The plural construction *(Let us ...)* most likely reflects a setting in the divine council (cf. 1 Kings 22.19–22; Isa. ch 6; Job chs 1–2): God the King announces the proposed course of action to His cabinet of subordinate deities, though He alone retains the power of decision. The midrash manifests considerable uneasiness with God's proposal to create something so capable of evil as human beings are. Playing on Ps. 1.6, one midrash reports that God told his ministering angels only of "the way of the righteous" and hid from them "the way of the wicked" (*Gen. Rab.* 8.4). Another midrash reports that while the angels were debating the proposal among themselves, God took the matter in hand. "Why are you debating?" He asked them. "Man has already been created!" (*Gen. Rab.* 8.5). Whereas the earth and the waters (at God's command) bring forth the plants, fish, birds, and other animals (1.12, 20, 24), humankind has a different origin and a different character. In the ancient Near East, the king was often said to be the "image" of the god and thus to act with divine authority. So here, the creation of humanity in God's *image* and *likeness* carries with it a commission to rule over the animal kingdom (1.26b, 28b; cf. Ps. 8.4–9). Some have seen in that commission a license for ecological irresponsibility. Elsewhere, however, the Tanakh presents humanity not as the owner of nature but as its steward, strictly accountable to the true Owner (see Lev. 25.23–24). This theology is one source of the important institutions of the sabbatical and jubilee years (see Exod. 23.10–11; Lev. ch 25). Whereas the next account of human origins (Gen. 2.4b–24) speaks of God's creation of one male from whom one female subsequently emerges, Gen. ch 1 seems to speak of groups of men and women created simultaneously. The division of humankind into two sexes is closely associated with the divine mandate to *Be fertile and increase.* In Jewish law, this is a positive commandment, although it is obligatory only on Jewish men, not women (*b. Yebam.* 65b). **29–30:** Humankind, animals, and birds all seem originally meant to be neither vegetarians nor carnivores, but frugivores, eating the seeds of plants and trees. **2.1–3:** In the Jewish liturgy, this

for food." And it was so. 31 And God saw all that He had made,
and found it very good. And there was evening and there was
morning, the sixth day.

2 The heaven and the earth were finished, and all their array.
2 On the seventh day God finished the work that He had
been doing, and He ceased[a] on the seventh day from all the
work that He had done. 3 And God blessed the seventh day and
declared it holy, because on it God ceased from all the work
of creation that He had done. 4 Such is the story of heaven and
earth when they were created.

When the LORD God made earth and heaven— 5 when no
shrub of the field was yet on earth and no grasses of the field
had yet sprouted, because the LORD God had not sent rain
upon the earth and there was no man to till the soil, 6 but a flow
would well up from the ground and water the whole surface of
the earth— 7 the LORD God formed man[b] from the dust of the
earth.[c] He blew into his nostrils the breath of life, and man became a living being.
8 The LORD God planted a garden in Eden, in the east, and
placed there the man whom He had formed. 9 And from the
ground the LORD God caused to grow every tree that was
pleasing to the sight and good for food, with the tree of life in
the middle of the garden, and the tree of knowledge of good
and bad.
10 A river issues from Eden to water the garden, and it then
divides and becomes four branches. 11 The name of the first is
Pishon, the one that winds through the whole land of Havilah,

a *Or "rested."* b *Heb.* ʾadam. c *Heb.* ʾadamah.

passage serves as an introduction to the Kiddush, the prayer over wine to sanctify the Sabbath that is recited just before the first meal of the holy day, on Friday night (see Exod. 20.8–11). It also appears in the traditional Friday evening service. The passage is characterized by the type of repetition that suggests it might have served as a liturgy already in antiquity.

2.4–25: The creation of Adam and Eve. Whereas 1.1–2.3 presented a majestic God-centered scenario of creation, 2.4–25 presents a very different but equally profound story of origins. This second account of creation is centered more on human beings and familiar human experiences, and its deity is conceived in more anthropomorphic terms. Source critics attribute the two accounts to different documents (P and J, respectively) later combined into the Torah we now have. The classical Jewish tradition tends to harmonize the discrepancies by intertwining the stories, using the details of one to fill in the details of the other. Even on the source-critical reading, however, the contrasts and interactions of the two creation accounts offer a richer understanding of the relationship of God to humankind than we would have if the accounts were read in isolation from each other. **4:** The Jewish textual tradition places a major break between 2.3 and 2.4, rather than in the middle of v. 4, where many modern interpreters put it, and for good reason. If the latter verse, or even its first half (2.4a), is read with 1.1–2.3, then several of the multiples of seven in 1.1–2.3, of which we gave a sample above (see intro. to 1.1–2.3), disappear. Most likely, 2.4a is an editorial linkage between the two accounts of creation. **4b–6:** For the first time, we see the Tetragrammaton (YHVH), or the four-letter proper name of the God of Israel, the pronunciation of which rabbinic law forbids categorically. The name is conventionally rendered in English as "LORD" and in Heb as "Adonai" (in prayer and in liturgical reading of Scripture) or "ha-Shem" (in other contexts). The use of this name is one of several features that cause source critics to attribute this second creation account to the J source. Note that the expression "heaven and earth" (1.1; 2.4a) now appears in the reverse order ("earth and heaven"), as befits the more earth-centered character of this story. Whereas in the first account of creation the primordial problem was too much water, requiring God to split the waters and create dry land (1.6–7, 9–10), here the problem is too little water. The variation may reflect the difference between the situation in Babylonia, in which the saline waters of the sea threatened human life, and a setting in the land of Israel, where a deficiency of water was (and is) a constant threat. **7:** Here, man has a lowlier origin than in the parallel in 1.26–28. He is created not in the image of God but from the dust of the earth. But he also has a closer and more intimate relationship with his Creator, who blows the breath of life into him, transforming that lowly, earth-bound creature into a living being. In this understanding, the human being is not an amalgam of perishable body and immortal soul, but a psychophysical unity who depends on God for life itself. **8–11:** The root of *Eden* denotes fertility. Where the wondrously fertile garden was thought to have

where the gold is. (12 The gold of that land is good; bdellium is
there, and lapis lazuli.[a]) 13 The name of the second river is Gihon, the one that winds through the whole land of Cush. 14 The
name of the third river is Tigris, the one that flows east of Asshur. And the fourth river is the Euphrates.
15 The LORD God took the man and placed him in the garden
of Eden, to till it and tend it. 16 And the LORD God commanded
the man, saying, "Of every tree of the garden you are free to eat;
17 but as for the tree of knowledge of good and bad, you must
not eat of it; for as soon as you eat of it, you shall die."
18 The LORD God said, "It is not good for man to be alone; I
will make a fitting helper for him." 19 And the LORD God formed
out of the earth all the wild beasts and all the birds of the sky,
and brought them to the man to see what he would call them;
and whatever the man called each living creature, that would
be its name. 20 And the man gave names to all the cattle and to
the birds of the sky and to all the wild beasts; but for Adam no
fitting helper was found. 21 So the LORD God cast a deep sleep
upon the man; and, while he slept, He took one of his ribs and
closed up the flesh at that spot. 22 And the LORD God fashioned
the rib that He had taken from the man into a woman; and He
brought her to the man. 23 Then the man said,

"This one at last
Is bone of my bones
And flesh of my flesh.
This one shall be called Woman,[b]
For from man[c] was she taken."

24 Hence a man leaves his father and mother and clings to
his wife, so that they become one flesh.

25 The two of them were naked,[d] the man and his wife, yet
3 they felt no shame. 1 Now the serpent was the shrewdest of
all the wild beasts that the LORD God had made. He said to
the woman, "Did God really say: You shall not eat of any tree of
the garden?" 2 The woman replied to the serpent, "We may eat
of the fruit of the other trees of the garden. 3 It is only about fruit
of the tree in the middle of the garden that God said: 'You shall

a Others "onyx"; meaning of Heb. shoham *uncertain.* *b Heb.* 'ishshah.
c Heb. 'ish. *d Heb.* 'arummim, *play on* 'arum *"shrewd" in 3.1.*

been located (if a realistic location was ever conceived) is unclear. The Tigris and Euphrates are the two great rivers of Mesopotamia (now found in modern Iraq). But the Pishon is unidentified, and the only Gihon in the Bible is a spring in Jerusalem (1 Kings 1.33, 38). Adam is conceived as a farmer, and work—albeit in an exceedingly easy form, given the miraculous fertility of Eden—is part of the divine plan. **16–17:** *Knowledge of good and bad* may be a merism, a figure of speech in which polar opposites denote a totality (like *heaven and earth* in 1.1). But *knowledge* can have an experiential, not only an intellectual, sense in biblical Heb, and *good and bad* can mean either "weal and woe" or "moral good and moral evil." The forbidden tree offers an experience that is both pleasant and painful; it awakens those who partake of it to the higher knowledge and to the pain that both come with moral choice. **18–24:** Man's fulfillment requires companionship. As a talmudic rabbi observes about v. 18, "Even though a man has several sons, it is forbidden to him to be without a wife" (*b. Yebam.* 61b). The LORD's creation of woman from man emphasizes the close connection between them and lays the groundwork for the understanding of marriage (and its association with procreation) in v. 24. The creation of the woman after the man and from a part of his body need not imply the subordination of women to men. According to Ramban (Naḥmanides, a great 13th-century Spanish rabbi), the point of v. 24 is that men are to be different from the males of the animal world, who mate and move on to the next partner: A man "wishes [his wife] to be with him always." Promiscuity is thus a degradation of God's intentions in creating human beings male and female. It is interesting that although polygamy is amply attested in the Tanakh, v. 24 may suggest that the ideal, Edenic condition is monogamy (see also Mal. 2.14–16; Prov. 5.15–23).

2.25–3.24: Disobedience, knowledge, exile. 2.25–3.1a: That the primal couple were nude (Heb "'arummim") but not ashamed attests to their innocence but also to their ignorance. It contrasts with the shrewd ("'arum") nature of the snake who will tempt them into losing both of these. Unlike some later Jewish and Christian literature, Genesis does not identify the talking snake with Satan or any other demonic being. **3.1b–3:** His question is tricky and does not admit of a yes-or-no answer. The woman, who has never heard the commandment directly (2.16–17), paraphrases it closely. Why she

not eat of it or touch it, lest you die.'" 4 And the serpent said to the woman, "You are not going to die, 5 but God knows that as soon as you eat of it your eyes will be opened and you will be like [a-]divine beings who know[-a] good and bad." 6 When the woman saw that the tree was good for eating and a delight to the eyes, and that the tree was desirable as a source of wisdom, she took of its fruit and ate. She also gave some to her husband, and he ate. 7 Then the eyes of both of them were opened and they perceived that they were naked; and they sewed together fig leaves and made themselves loincloths.

8 They heard the sound of the LORD God moving about in the garden at the breezy time of day; and the man and his wife hid from the LORD God among the trees of the garden. 9 The LORD God called out to the man and said to him, "Where are you?" 10 He replied, "I heard the sound of You in the garden, and I was afraid because I was naked, so I hid." 11 Then He asked, "Who told you that you were naked? Did you eat of the tree from which I had forbidden you to eat?" 12 The man said, "The woman You put at my side—she gave me of the tree, and I ate." 13 And the LORD God said to the woman, "What is this you have done!" The woman replied, "The serpent duped me, and I ate." 14 Then the LORD God said to the serpent,

"Because you did this,
More cursed shall you be
Than all cattle
And all the wild beasts:
On your belly shall you crawl
And dirt shall you eat
All the days of your life.
15 I will put enmity
Between you and the woman,
And between your offspring and hers;
They shall strike at your head,
And you shall strike at their heel."

16 And to the woman He said,

"I will make most severe
Your pangs in childbearing;
In pain shall you bear children.
Yet your urge shall be for your husband,
And he shall rule over you."

a-a Others "God, who knows."

adds the prohibition on touching the fruit is unclear. A talmudic rabbi sees here an illustration of the dictum that "he who adds [to God's words] subtracts [from them]" (*b. Sanh.* 29a). Another rabbinic source presents a more complicated explanation. In relaying the prohibition to his wife, Adam has obeyed the rabbinic principle that one should "make a [protective] hedge for the Torah" (*m. 'Avot* 1.1). Tragically, according to this rabbinic interpretation, this praiseworthy act gave the snake his opening. He "touched the tree with his hands and his feet, and shook it until its fruits dropped to the ground," thus undermining the credibility of God's entire commandment in the woman's mind (*'Avot. R. Nat.* A,1). **4–5:** The serpent impugns God's motives, attributing the command to jealousy. Whereas in the first creation account human beings are God-like creatures exercising dominion (1.26–28), here their ambition to be like God or like divine beings is the root of their expulsion from Eden. **6:** The fatal progression in the woman's mind begins with the physical *(eating)*, moves to the aesthetic *(a delight to the eyes)*, and culminates in the intellectual *(a source of wisdom)*. The progression may reflect the process of rationalization to which she succumbed just before she engaged in humanity's first act of disobedience. **7:** As the serpent had predicted (v. 5), their eyes are opened, and they have enhanced knowledge (v. 7). **8–17:** But with the new knowledge comes the shame of nudity that they had lacked in their childlike innocence (vv. 10–11; cf. 2.25), a symbol of a much more encompassing sense of guilt and an ominous estrangement between God and the primal couple. The man lamely attempts to pass the buck to his wife, and thus, also to the God who put her at his side (v. 12). She, with more credibility, blames the serpent (v. 13). **14–19:** The LORD God then reverses this order and punishes the malefactors in the order of their misdeeds instead. The serpent is to lose his legs, slither in the dirt, and suffer from the hostility of human beings (vv. 14–15). The woman will suffer pain in childbirth and experience sexual desire for her husband, yet be subordinate to him (v. 16). The man, for having obeyed her rather than God, will toil over unproductive soil all the days of his life, until the ground from which he was taken reabsorbs him (vv. 17–19; cf. 2.7). The primal couple have left

17 To Adam He said, "Because you did as your wife said and
ate of the tree about which I commanded you, 'You shall not
eat of it,'

Cursed be the ground because of you;
By toil shall you eat of it
All the days of your life:
18 Thorns and thistles shall it sprout for you.
But your food shall be the grasses of the field;
19 By the sweat of your brow
Shall you get bread to eat,
Until you return to the ground—
For from it you were taken.
For dust you are,
And to dust you shall return."

20 The man named his wife Eve,[a] because she was the mother
of all the living.[b] 21 And the LORD God made garments of skins
for Adam and his wife, and clothed them.
22 And the LORD God said, "Now that the man has become
like one of us, knowing good and bad, what if he should stretch
out his hand and take also from the tree of life and eat, and live
forever!" 23 So the LORD God banished him from the garden of
Eden, to till the soil from which he was taken. 24 He drove the
man out, and stationed east of the garden of Eden the cherubim and the fiery ever-turning sword, to guard the way to the
tree of life.

4 Now the man knew[c] his wife Eve, and she conceived and
bore Cain, saying, "I have gained[d] a male child with the
help of the LORD." 2 She then bore his brother Abel. Abel became a keeper of sheep, and Cain became a tiller of the soil.
3 In the course of time, Cain brought an offering to the LORD
from the fruit of the soil; 4 and Abel, for his part, brought the

a Heb. ḥawwah. *b Heb.* ḥay. *c Heb.* yadaʿ, *often in a sexual sense.*
d Heb. qanithi, *connected with "Cain."*

the magical garden of childhood innocence and entered into the harsh, real world of adulthood and its painful realities. **20–21:** God's clothing the naked indicates that His anger was not the last word in the divine-human relationship. The Jewish ethical tradition finds in this unmerited kindness a paradigm for human behavior as well. "Great are acts of kindness," a talmudic rabbi remarks, "for the Torah begins with an act of kindness and ends with an act of kindness"—it begins with God's clothing the naked and ends with His burying the dead (Moses) (Deut. 34.6) (*b. Sot.* 14a). **22–24:** Neither the first nor the second account of creation portrays humankind as created immortal. Nor does the punishment of v. 19, which speaks of Adam's returning to the ground from which he was taken, mean that he would have lived forever, had it not been for his disobedience. In this passage, the LORD, alarmed at the very real, God-like status that the man has suddenly attained, resolves to deny him the opportunity to make himself immortal and banishes him from the garden in which the tree of life was found. The cherubim are supernatural beings who sometimes act as protectors of sacred items or places (e.g., Exod. 25.17–22; 1 Kings 8.6–7). The stance of jealousy about His status and anxiety about human beings' acquiring immortality is not the only one taken by the God of Israel. Prov. 3.18 asserts that the tree of life, in the form of Wisdom (therein personified as a woman), remains available to "those who grasp her." The Rabbis identified wisdom with Torah and could therefore cite Prov. 3.18 in support of their characteristic affirmation that Torah "gives life to those who practice it, in this world and in the world-to-come" (*m. 'Avot* 6.7). In Judaism, the estrangement caused by the innate human appetite for evil does not require an act of messianic redemption to be healed. Rather, the practice and study of Torah renew intimacy with the God of Israel and lead to eternal life. "The Holy One (blessed be He) created the Evil Inclination; He created Torah as its antidote" (*b. B. Bat.* 16a).

4.1–16: The first murder. This story of the LORD's preference for the younger brother and the older brother's resentment and exile looks both back to the episode in the garden of Eden and forward to other stories of mysterious divine preference, sibling rivalry, and exile later in the book of Genesis (chs 21, 27, 37). **1:** The verb translated *knew* may have the sense of "had known" in this context. Rashi thinks the conception of Cain occurred in the garden of Eden before his parents had sinned. **3–5:** The Torah does not say why the LORD accepted Abel's offering, but not Cain's. Perhaps we are to infer that Abel offered his with greater devotion (*the choicest of the firstlings* as opposed to *the fruit of the soil*). Alternately, the episode may evidence the high

choicest of the firstlings of his flock. The LORD paid heed to
Abel and his offering, 5 but to Cain and his offering He paid
no heed. Cain was much distressed and his face fell. 6 And the
LORD said to Cain,

"Why are you distressed,
And why is your face fallen?
7[a] Surely, if you do right,
There is uplift.
But if you do not do right
Sin couches at the door;
Its urge is toward you,
Yet you can be its master."

8 Cain said to his brother Abel[b]... and when they were in the
field, Cain set upon his brother Abel and killed him. 9 The LORD
said to Cain, "Where is your brother Abel?" And he said, "I do not
know. Am I my brother's keeper?" 10 Then He said, "What have
you done? Hark, your brother's blood cries out to Me from the
ground! 11 Therefore, you shall be more cursed than the ground,[c]
which opened its mouth to receive your brother's blood from
your hand. 12 If you till the soil, it shall no longer yield its strength
to you. You shall become a ceaseless wanderer on earth."
13 Cain said to the LORD, "My punishment is too great to
bear! 14 Since You have banished me this day from the soil, and
I must avoid Your presence and become a restless wanderer on
earth—anyone who meets me may kill me!" 15 The LORD said
to him, "I promise, if anyone kills Cain, sevenfold vengeance
shall be taken on him." And the LORD put a mark on Cain, lest
anyone who met him should kill him. 16 Cain left the presence
of the LORD and settled in the land of Nod, east of Eden.

17 Cain knew his wife, and she conceived and bore Enoch.
And he then founded a city, and named the city after his son
Enoch. 18 To Enoch was born Irad, and Irad begot Mehujael,
and Mehujael[d] begot Methusael, and Methusael begot Lamech. 19 Lamech took to himself two wives: the name of the
one was Adah, and the name of the other was Zillah. 20 Adah
bore Jabal; he was the ancestor of those who dwell in tents and
amidst herds. 21 And the name of his brother was Jubal; he was
the ancestor of all who play the lyre and the pipe. 22 As for Zillah, she bore Tubal-cain, who forged all implements of copper
and iron. And the sister of Tubal-cain was Naamah.
23 And Lamech said to his wives,

"Adah and Zillah, hear my voice;
O wives of Lamech, give ear to my speech.

a *Meaning of verse uncertain.*
b *Ancient versions, including the Targum, read "Come, let us go out into the field."*
c *See 3.17.* d *Heb.* Meḥijael.

regard for shepherds and the pastoral life manifest, for example, in the early life of national heroes such as Joseph, Moses, and David. Like Abel, however, all the latter—and many others chosen by God in the Tanakh (e.g., Isaac, Jacob, and Solomon)—were younger brothers. The story of Cain and Abel thus demonstrates a theme widespread in the Tanakh: the difference between God's will and human conventions, such as primogeniture. In this text, the emphasis falls, however, not on the reasons for God's preference, but on Cain's fatal and culpable refusal to reconcile himself to it. **7:** The end of the verse is strikingly reminiscent of the words of God to Eve in 3.16, just as Cain's punishment in 4.11–12 recalls Adam's in 3.17–19. It is possible that the story of Cain and Abel itself once served as an account of the primal sin and expulsion from paradise. **9:** The LORD's question to Cain recalls His question to Adam in 3.9. In both cases, He asks about more than location. Cain's flippant answer offends against the Torah's ethic of responsibility for one's kinsman and neighbor (e.g., Lev. 19.16; Deut. 21.1–9). **13–15:** Although murder is a capital offense in biblical law (e.g., Exod. 21.12), the LORD yields to Cain's plea and protects him from the fate He inflicted on Abel. The irony is pungent: The man who could not tolerate God's inscrutable grace now benefits from it. A midrash sees Cain as the first penitent and attributes his pardon to his repentance (*Gen. Rab.* 22.13).

4.17–26: The growth of culture. This highly compressed passage may be an epitome of well-known legends that have not survived. The emergence of occupations and technologies that it records is reminiscent of the Mesopotamian tradition about the pre-flood sages who founded the basic institutions of civilization. The culminating v. 26 speaks of what is, in the Jewish view, the most important of these:

the proper worship of the true God. This comes not from the line of Cain, but from Adam and Eve's third son, Seth. The poem of Lamech in vv. 23–24 continues the dark theme of violence associated with his ancestor Cain and attests to the increasing evil of the human race.

5.1–32: The ten generations from Adam to Noah. This genealogy can be seen, in part, as the parallel to the list in 4.17–26, though they are not always identical: Cain/*Kenan*, Enoch/*Enoch*, Irad/*Jared*, Mehujael/*Mehalalel*, Methusael/*Methuselah*, Lamech/*Lamech*. Even if these figures were originally thought to be descendants of Cain, ch 5 treats them all as descendants of Seth. Cain's line will not survive the flood, and the people Israel will emerge from the lineage of the younger son's replacement (4.25), not from that of the murderous first-born son of Adam. **1–3:** The ostensibly natural process of procreation has high theological import: It continues the creation of human beings in God's likeness (1.26–28). **5:** The enormous life spans of Adam and his antediluvian descendants find a parallel in the Sumerian King List, an ancient Mesopotamian text, in which the pre-flood kings rule much longer than those who came afterward (the longest reign was 65,000 years). The underlying conception is that things proceeded on a grander scale in those days. These life spans are thus akin to the biblical allusions to primordial giants or heroes (e.g., 6.4; Deut. 2.20–21). **21–23:** Significantly, Enoch occupies the seventh position and lives only 365 years (suggesting a connection with the solar cycle). Like Noah (6.9), he *walked with God,* though the meaning of the statement that *God took him* is unclear. Rashi thinks it means that God caused his death prematurely to spare him from sinning. It is possible that Enoch's earthly life, like Elijah's (2 Kings 2.11–12), ended without death, and there is much speculation about this in postbiblical Jewish literature.

I have slain a man for wounding me,
And a lad for bruising me.
24 If Cain is avenged sevenfold,
Then Lamech seventy-sevenfold."
25 Adam knew his wife again, and she bore a son and named
him Seth, meaning, "God has [a]provided me with[a] another offspring in place of Abel," for Cain had killed him. 26 And to Seth,
in turn, a son was born, and he named him Enosh. It was then
that men began to invoke the LORD by name.

5 This is the record of Adam's line.—When God created man,
He made him in the likeness of God; 2 male and female He
created them. And when they were created, He blessed them
and called them Man.—3 When Adam had lived 130 years, he
begot a son in his likeness after his image, and he named him
Seth. 4 After the birth of Seth, Adam lived 800 years and begot
sons and daughters. 5 All the days that Adam lived came to 930
years; then he died.
6 When Seth had lived 105 years, he begot Enosh. 7 After the
birth of Enosh, Seth lived 807 years and begot sons and daughters. 8 All the days of Seth came to 912 years; then he died.
9 When Enosh had lived 90 years, he begot Kenan. 10 After
the birth of Kenan, Enosh lived 815 years and begot sons and
daughters. 11 All the days of Enosh came to 905 years; then he
died.
12 When Kenan had lived 70 years, he begot Mahalalel. 13 After the birth of Mahalalel, Kenan lived 840 years and begot
sons and daughters. 14 All the days of Kenan came to 910 years;
then he died.
15 When Mahalalel had lived 65 years, he begot Jared. 16 After the birth of Jared, Mahalalel lived 830 years and begot sons
and daughters. 17 All the days of Mahalalel came to 895 years;
then he died.
18 When Jared had lived 162 years, he begot Enoch. 19 After
the birth of Enoch, Jared lived 800 years and begot sons and
daughters. 20 All the days of Jared came to 962 years; then he
died.
21 When Enoch had lived 65 years, he begot Methuselah.
22 After the birth of Methuselah, Enoch walked with God 300
years; and he begot sons and daughters. 23 All the days of
Enoch came to 365 years. 24 Enoch walked with God; then he
was no more, for God took him.
25 When Methuselah had lived 187 years, he begot Lamech.
26 After the birth of Lamech, Methuselah lived 782 years and
begot sons and daughters. 27 All the days of Methuselah came
to 969 years; then he died.

a-a Or "established for me"; Heb. shath, *connected with "Seth."*

28 When Lamech had lived 182 years, he begot a son. 29 And he named him Noah, saying, "This one will provide us relief[a] from our work and from the toil of our hands, out of the very soil which the LORD placed under a curse." 30 After the birth of Noah, Lamech lived 595 years and begot sons and daughters. 31 All the days of Lamech came to 777 years; then he died.

32 When Noah had lived 500 years, Noah begot Shem, Ham, and Japheth.

6 When men began to increase on earth and daughters were born to them, 2 the divine beings[b] saw how beautiful the daughters of men were and took wives from among those that pleased them.—3 The LORD said, "My breath shall not abide[c] in man forever, since he too is flesh; let the days allowed him be one hundred and twenty years."—4 It was then, and later too, that the Nephilim appeared on earth—when the divine beings cohabited with the daughters of men, who bore them offspring. They were the heroes of old, the men of renown.

5 The LORD saw how great was man's wickedness on earth, and how every plan devised by his mind was nothing but evil all the time. 6 And the LORD regretted that He had made man on earth, and His heart was saddened. 7 The LORD said, "I will blot out from the earth the men whom I created—men together with beasts, creeping things, and birds of the sky; for I regret that I made them." 8 But Noah found favor with the LORD.

NOAH נח

9 This is the line of Noah.—Noah was a righteous man; he was blameless in his age; Noah walked with God.—10 Noah begot three sons: Shem, Ham, and Japheth.

11 The earth became corrupt before God; the earth was filled with lawlessness. 12 When God saw how corrupt the earth was, for all flesh had corrupted its ways on earth, 13 God said to Noah, "I have decided to put an end to all flesh, for the earth is filled with lawlessness because of them: I am about to destroy them with the earth. 14 Make yourself an ark of gopher wood; make it an ark with compartments, and cover it inside and out with pitch. 15 This is how you shall make it: the length of the ark shall be three hundred cubits, its width fifty cubits, and its

a *Connecting Noah with Heb.* niḥam *"to comfort"; cf. 9.20 ff.*
b *Others "the sons of God."* c *Meaning of Heb. uncertain.*

29: The allusion to 3.17 is one of several indications that Noah is the new Adam—a righteous antidote to the wickedness of the father of universal mankind. Remarked an early rabbi, "When a righteous person comes into the world, goodness comes into the world" (*b. Sanh.* 113b). **31:** The suspicious figure of 777 is undoubtedly related to (the Cainite) Lamech's mention of "sevenfold" and "seventy-sevenfold" in 4.24.

6.1–8: The prelude to the flood. 1–4: This brief narrative reads like a condensation of a much longer, well-known myth. It records yet another breach of the all-important boundary between the divine and the human (vv. 1–2) and explains why human beings no longer attain to the great ages of their primordial forebears (v. 3). It also explains the origin of the Nephilim (v. 4), the preternatural giants that Israelites thought once dwelt in the land (Num. 13.31–33). These verses as well served as the basis for much post-biblical speculation. **5–8:** Whereas in ch 1 God seven times "saw" what He had made and pronounced it "good," this passage reports that He *saw how great was man's wickedness* and *regretted that He had made man.* The flood narrative that ensues, a characteristically Israelite adaptation of a well-known and widespread Mesopotamian story, emphasizes human immorality as the provocation for the cataclysm. Most strikingly, the narrator depicts God's heart as *saddened.* The sudden mention of Noah (v. 8)—whose Heb name ("n-ḥ") is "favor" ("ḥ-n") spelled backwards—indicates that human perversion and divine grief will not be the last word.

6.9–9.17: The flood: corruption, destruction, re-creation, covenant. 6.9–10: The mention of Noah's righteousness and blamelessness serves as a counterpoint to the reports of human wickedness and lawlessness that both precede and follow it (vv. 1–7, 11–13). **8:** The *favor* that *Noah found … with the LORD* derives, in part or in whole, from his lonely role as the one moral man in an immoral society. As such, he also serves as the one who provides relief from the LORD's curse, as his father predicted when he named him (5.29). **11–16:** The word translated *ark* occurs only in the flood story of Genesis and in the account of Moses' mother's effort to save her baby by putting him in the Nile in Exod. 2.3, 5 (where the term is rendered

height thirty cubits. [16] Make an opening for daylight in the ark, and [a]terminate it within a cubit of the top.[-a] Put the entrance to the ark in its side; make it with bottom, second, and third decks.

[17] "For My part, I am about to bring the Flood—waters upon the earth—to destroy all flesh under the sky in which there is breath of life; everything on earth shall perish. [18] But I will establish My covenant with you, and you shall enter the ark, with your sons, your wife, and your sons' wives. [19] And of all that lives, of all flesh, you shall take two of each into the ark to keep alive with you; they shall be male and female. [20] From birds of every kind, cattle of every kind, every kind of creeping thing on earth, two of each shall come to you to stay alive. [21] For your part, take of everything that is eaten and store it away, to serve as food for you and for them." [22] Noah did so; just as God commanded him, so he did.

7 Then the LORD said to Noah, "Go into the ark, with all your household, for you alone have I found righteous before Me in this generation. [2] Of every clean animal you shall take seven pairs, males and their mates, and of every animal that is not clean, two, a male and its mate; [3] of the birds of the sky also, seven pairs, male and female, to keep seed alive upon all the earth. [4] For in seven days' time I will make it rain upon the earth, forty days and forty nights, and I will blot out from the earth all existence that I created." [5] And Noah did just as the LORD commanded him.

[6] Noah was six hundred years old when the Flood came, waters upon the earth. [7] Noah, with his sons, his wife, and his sons' wives, went into the ark because of the waters of the Flood. [8] Of the clean animals, of the animals that are not clean, of the birds, and of everything that creeps on the ground, [9] two of each, male and female, came to Noah into the ark, as God had commanded Noah. [10] And on the seventh day the waters of the Flood came upon the earth.

[11] In the six hundredth year of Noah's life, in the second month, on the seventeenth day of the month, on that day

All the fountains of the great deep burst apart,
And the floodgates of the sky broke open.

a-a Meaning of Heb. uncertain.

"basket"). Noah foreshadows Moses, even as Moses, removed from the water, foreshadows the people Israel, whom he leads to safety through the death-dealing sea that drowns their oppressors (Exod. chs 14–15). The great biblical tale of redemption occurs first in a shorter, universal form, then in a longer, particularistic one. **14–16:** The cubit being roughly one and a half feet, the ark measures about 137.2 m × 22.9 m × 13.7 m (450 ft × 75 ft × 45 ft). Unlike other ancient boats, it is entirely enclosed, with the exception of the *opening for daylight* (v. 16). Covered *inside and out with pitch* (v. 14) to protect its passengers from the cataclysm, the ark symbolizes the tender mercies and protective grace with which God envelopes the righteous even in the harshest circumstances.

6.17–22: Further introduction and a pledge. 18: This v. records the first mention of *covenant* ("berit") in the Tanakh. In the ancient Near East, a covenant was an agreement that the parties swore before the gods, and expected the gods to enforce. In this case, God is Himself a party to the covenant, which is more like a pledge than an agreement or contract (this was sometimes the case in the ancient Near East as well). The covenant with Noah will receive longer treatment in 9.1–17. **19–20:** This contradicts 7.2, in which the LORD instructs Noah to take seven pairs of the clean animals and two unclean animals ("clean" and "unclean" refer to ritual categories and not to hygiene; the terminology of "pure" and "impure" would be less misleading). Critical scholars explain the contradiction by attributing 6.19–20 to the Priestly source (P) but 7.2 to the J source. Only the latter reports Noah's sacrifice when he emerges from the ark (8.20–21). If there were only one pair of each animal, this sacrifice would actually lead to the extinction of the species offered. The source-critical explanation receives corroboration from the use of *God* in 6.9–22 but "LORD" in 7.1–5, which suggests (as do other features of the flood story) that two slightly differing stories have been interwoven. Traditional commentators have other explanations: for example, that *two* in 6.19 means "at least two" (Rashi) or that a pair of each species would come of their own accord, but Noah would later have to capture seven pairs of the "clean" species to use for the sacrifice (Ramban).

7.1–23: The flood comes. 4: The *forty days and forty nights* of rainfall here and in v. 12 conflict with the one hundred fifty days of swelling waters in v. 24. Once again, critical scholars detect a difference between J and P, respectively.

(12 The rain fell on the earth forty days and forty nights.)
13 That same day Noah and Noah's sons, Shem, Ham, and
Japheth, went into the ark, with Noah's wife and the three
wives of his sons—14 they and all beasts of every kind, all cattle of every kind, all creatures of every kind that creep on the
earth, and all birds of every kind, every bird, every winged
thing. 15 They came to Noah into the ark, two each of all flesh in
which there was breath of life. 16 Thus they that entered comprised male and female of all flesh, as God had commanded
him. And the LORD shut him in.
17 The Flood continued forty days on the earth, and the
waters increased and raised the ark so that it rose above the
earth. 18 The waters swelled and increased greatly upon the
earth, and the ark drifted upon the waters. 19 When the waters
had swelled much more upon the earth, all the highest mountains everywhere under the sky were covered. 20 Fifteen cubits
higher did the waters swell, as the mountains were covered.
21 And all flesh that stirred on earth perished—birds, cattle,
beasts, and all the things that swarmed upon the earth, and
all mankind. 22 All in whose nostrils was the merest breath of
life, all that was on dry land, died. 23 All existence on earth was
blotted out—man, cattle, creeping things, and birds of the sky;
they were blotted out from the earth. Only Noah was left, and
those with him in the ark.

24 And when the waters had swelled on the earth one
8 hundred and fifty days, 1 God remembered Noah and all
the beasts and all the cattle that were with him in the ark,
and God caused a wind to blow across the earth, and the waters subsided. 2 The fountains of the deep and the floodgates
of the sky were stopped up, and the rain from the sky was held
back; 3 the waters then receded steadily from the earth. At
the end of one hundred and fifty days the waters diminished,
4 so that in the seventh month, on the seventeenth day of the
month, the ark came to rest on the mountains of Ararat. 5 The
waters went on diminishing until the tenth month; in the tenth
month, on the first of the month, the tops of the mountains
became visible.
6 At the end of forty days, Noah opened the window of the
ark that he had made 7 and sent out the raven; it went to and
fro until the waters had dried up from the earth. 8 Then he sent
out the dove to see whether the waters had decreased from the
surface of the ground. 9 But the dove could not find a resting
place for its foot, and returned to him to the ark, for there was
water over all the earth. So putting out his hand, he took it into
the ark with him. 10 He waited another seven days, and again
sent out the dove from the ark. 11 The dove came back to him
toward evening, and there in its bill was a plucked-off olive

7.24–8.22: The flood ends. 8.1: The statement that *God remembered Noah* is the turning point of the whole flood narrative, marking the triumph of mercy over judgment. It recalls other incidents in the Torah in which God remembers and rescues: remembering Abraham and thus saving his nephew Lot from death in Sodom (19.29); remembering Rachel and thus rescuing her from the humiliation of infertility (30.22); and, most importantly, remembering "His covenant with Abraham and Isaac and Jacob" and finally saving Israel from enslavement to Pharaoh (Exod. 2.23–25). Here, too, the remembrance at issue is associated with God's reliable faithfulness to His covenant (6.18). **4:** *The mountains of Ararat* refers to the mountainous country of ancient Urartu, a country in eastern Asia Minor occupying parts of what is now Turkey, Iraq, Armenia, and Iran (cf. 2 Kings 19.37; Jer. 51.27). Contrary to a common misimpression, the Tanakh knows of no individual mountain named "Ararat."

leaf! Then Noah knew that the waters had decreased on the
earth. 12 He waited still another seven days and sent the dove
forth; and it did not return to him any more.
13 In the six hundred and first year, in the first month, on the
first of the month, the waters began to dry from the earth; and
when Noah removed the covering of the ark, he saw that the
surface of the ground was drying. 14 And in the second month,
on the twenty-seventh day of the month, the earth was dry.
15 God spoke to Noah, saying, 16 "Come out of the ark, together with your wife, your sons, and your sons' wives. 17 Bring
out with you every living thing of all flesh that is with you:
birds, animals, and everything that creeps on earth; and let
them swarm on the earth and be fertile and increase on earth."
18 So Noah came out, together with his sons, his wife, and his
sons' wives. 19 Every animal, every creeping thing, and every
bird, everything that stirs on earth came out of the ark by families.
20 Then Noah built an altar to the LORD and, taking of every
clean animal and of every clean bird, he offered burnt offerings on the altar. 21 The LORD smelled the pleasing odor, and
the LORD said to Himself: "Never again will I doom the earth
because of man, since the devisings of man's mind are evil
from his youth; nor will I ever again destroy every living being,
as I have done.

22 So long as the earth endures,
Seedtime and harvest,
Cold and heat,
Summer and winter,
Day and night
Shall not cease."

9 God blessed Noah and his sons, and said to them, "Be fertile and increase, and fill the earth. 2 The fear and the dread
of you shall be upon all the beasts of the earth and upon all
the birds of the sky—everything with which the earth is astir—
and upon all the fish of the sea; they are given into your hand.
3 Every creature that lives shall be yours to eat; as with the
green grasses, I give you all these. 4 You must not, however, eat
flesh with its life-blood in it. 5 But for your own life-blood I will
require a reckoning: I will require it of every beast; of man, too,
will I require a reckoning for human life, of every man for that
of his fellow man!

6 Whoever sheds the blood of man,
By man shall his blood be shed;
For in His image
Did God make man.

7 Be fertile, then, and increase; abound on the earth and increase on it."

13: At some point in Israelite tradition, the first day of the first month (which occurs in the spring, two weeks before Passover) must have served as New Year's Day. In rabbinic law, it is listed as one of four New Year's Days, the most familiar being the autumnal holiday known today as Rosh Ha-Shanah (*m. Rosh Hash.* 1.1). It is significant that in the Tanakh, the first day of the first month is the day that the Tabernacle—the portable temple of the wilderness period—goes up (Exod. 40.2, 17). For the Mesopotamian epic known as *Enuma elish,* which was associated with a New Year's festival, the date celebrates both the creation of the world from the severed body of the creator god's aquatic enemy and the raising of a palace to the victorious creator. In Gen. ch 8, too, the world is, as it were, being created anew from the watery chaos that had undone God's original work of creation. A new beginning is at hand, with Noah as the new Adam. **20–22:** Nothing would seem more natural to a biblical Israelite who had survived a life-threatening crisis than to offer a sacrifice to the God of his salvation (v. 20). In this case, the sacrifice appeases the LORD (cf. Num. 17.8–15), who thus moves from anger at human beings to acceptance of them in their weakness. The correspondence of v. 21, at the end of the flood narrative, with 6.5, at its beginning, is striking: Human beings have not improved. "Harsh indeed is the Evil Inclination," goes a saying in the Talmud that quotes v. 21, "for even its own Creator called it *evil.*" (*b. Kid.* 30b). Yet God will spare them nonetheless, and the rhythm of human life goes on (v. 22).

9.1–17: The covenant with Noah. Having rescued the righteous remnant from the lethal waters, God now makes a covenant with them, just as He will with the people Israel at Sinai after enabling them to escape across the Sea of Reeds (Exod. chs 14–15, 19). The closest parallel to our passage, however, is Gen. ch 17 (the covenant with Abraham), also ascribed to P. In each case, God

[8] And God said to Noah and to his sons with him, [9] "I now establish My covenant with you and your offspring to come, [10] and with every living thing that is with you—birds, cattle, and every wild beast as well—all that have come out of the ark, every living thing on earth. [11] I will maintain My covenant with you: never again shall all flesh be cut off by the waters of a flood, and never again shall there be a flood to destroy the earth."

[12] God further said, "This is the sign that I set for the covenant between Me and you, and every living creature with you, for all ages to come. [13] I have set My bow in the clouds, and it shall serve as a sign of the covenant between Me and the earth. [14] When I bring clouds over the earth, and the bow appears in the clouds, [15] I will remember My covenant between Me and you and every living creature among all flesh, so that the waters shall never again become a flood to destroy all flesh. [16] When the bow is in the clouds, I will see it and remember the everlasting covenant between God and all living creatures, all flesh that is on earth. [17] That," God said to Noah, "shall be the sign of the covenant that I have established between Me and all flesh that is on earth."

[18] The sons of Noah who came out of the ark were Shem, Ham, and Japheth—Ham being the father of Canaan. [19] These three were the sons of Noah, and from these the whole world branched out.

[20] Noah, the tiller of the soil, was the first to plant a vineyard. [21] He drank of the wine and became drunk, and he uncovered himself within his tent. [22] Ham, the father of Canaan, saw his father's nakedness and told his two brothers outside. [23] But Shem and Japheth took a cloth, placed it against both their backs and, walking backward, they covered their father's nakedness; their faces were turned the other way, so that they did

makes an *everlasting covenant* or "pact" (9.16; 17.13, 19) memorialized by a distinctive *sign,* the rainbow in the case of Noah (9.12, 13, 17) and circumcision in the case of Abraham and the Jewish people who, he is promised, shall descend from him (17.11). **1–4:** V. 1 repeats the charge to primordial humanity (1.28) verbatim (if only in part), but then enhances mankind's status relative to the animals: The animals shall be afraid of them, and God licenses humans to use animals for food (vv. 2–3). The only qualification is that the *blood,* which the Tanakh identifies with the life-force (Lev. 17.11, 14; Deut. 12.23), must be drained out first. This is the origin of the Jewish practice of "kashering" meat, by salting it before cooking to remove its blood. **5–6:** *By man* in v. 6 may be more accurately rendered as "for man," or "in compensation for a human being." Human life is sharply distinguished from animal life; the idea that human beings are created in the image of God (1.26–27) requires a higher degree of respect for human life. In the Talmud, v. 5 is interpreted as a prohibition of killing oneself (*b. B. K.* 91b), and v. 6 is cited in support of the prohibition of abortion (*b. Sanh.* 57b). Jewish law strictly forbids suicide and allows abortion only in rare circumstances, and never for the purpose of birth control. **8–17:** In the Talmud, it is taught that "descendants of Noah"—that is, universal humanity—are obligated by seven commandments: (1) to establish courts of justice, (2) to refrain from blaspheming the God of Israel, as well as from (3) idolatry, (4) sexual perversion, (5) bloodshed, (6) robbery, and (7) not to eat meat cut from a living animal (*b. Sanh.* 56a). Whereas Jews have hundreds of commandments in addition to these seven (traditionally, 613 altogether), Gentiles who observe the "seven commandments of the descendants of Noah" meet with God's full approval.

9.18–28: The sin of Ham and the cursing of Canaan. 20–21: The ancient Rabbis saw in Noah an object lesson about the dangers of intoxication (*Gen. Rab.* 36.4), but whether the first person to grow grapes should have foreseen the degrading consequences of excessive alcohol consumption is unclear. In any event, mentioning the failures of its human heroes is characteristic of the Tanakh; only God is perfect, and even He is at times the target of protest (e.g., see 18.22–33). **22–24:** This perplexing passage serves as an explanation of the sexual perverseness that Israelite culture sometimes thought to be typical of the Canaanites (cf. Lev. 18.3–4, 24–30). Note that it is Canaan who is cursed (Gen. 9.25), although Ham perpetuated the atrocity. The author (or perhaps a redactor) softens the contradiction by twice pointing out that Ham is *the father of Canaan* (vv. 18, 22). The identity of the act in question is murky. "To uncover the nakedness" of a man means to have sexual relations with his wife (e.g., Lev. 20.11). This makes Ham guilty of incest. In Lev. 20.17, the less common expression "to see the nakedness" means to have sex. This would make Ham guilty of homosexual rape. In an effort to explain why Canaan is cursed for Ham's sin, on the

not see their father's nakedness. 24 When Noah woke up from
his wine and learned what his youngest son had done to him,
25 he said,

"Cursed be Canaan;
The lowest of slaves
Shall he be to his brothers."

26 And he said,

"Blessed be the LORD,
The God of Shem;
Let Canaan be a slave to them.
27 May God enlarge[a] Japheth,
And let him dwell in the tents of Shem;
And let Canaan be a slave to them."

28 Noah lived after the Flood 350 years. 29 And all the days of
Noah came to 950 years; then he died.

10 These are the lines of Shem, Ham, and Japheth, the sons
of Noah: sons were born to them after the Flood.
2 The descendants of Japheth: Gomer, Magog, Madai, Javan, Tubal, Meshech, and Tiras. 3 The descendants of Gomer:
Ashkenaz, Riphath, and Togarmah. 4 The descendants of Javan: Elishah and Tarshish, the Kittim and the Dodanim.[b]
5 From these the maritime nations branched out. [These are
the descendants of Japheth][c] by their lands—each with its language—their clans and their nations.
6 The descendants of Ham: Cush, Mizraim, Put, and Canaan.
7 The descendants of Cush: Seba, Havilah, Sabtah, Raamah,
and Sabteca. The descendants of Raamah: Sheba and Dedan.
8 Cush also begot Nimrod, who was the first man of might
on earth. 9 He was a mighty hunter by the grace of the LORD;
hence the saying, "Like Nimrod a mighty hunter by the grace
of the LORD." 10 The mainstays of his kingdom were Babylon,
Erech, Accad, and Calneh[d] in the land of Shinar. 11 From that
land Asshur went forth and built Nineveh, Rehoboth-ir, Calah,
12 and Resen between Nineveh and Calah, that is the great city.

a Heb. yapht, *play on Heb.* yepheth *"Japheth."*
b Septuagint and 1 Chron. 1.7 "Rodanim." *c Cf. vv. 20 and 31.*
d Heb. we-khalneh, *better vocalized* we-khullanah *"all of them being."*

other hand, the midrash sees Ham as castrating his father. Just as Ham prevented Noah from ever having a fourth son, so will his own fourth son, Canaan (10.6), be cursed (*Gen. Rab.* 36.7). V. 23, however, suggests that the words *saw his father's nakedness* are better taken literally. If so, Ham violated two norms highly stressed in both the Tanakh and rabbinic Judaism, the ethic of bodily modesty and the norm to honor and respect one's parents. **25–27:** The cursing of Canaan may be intended, in part, to explain why non-Israelite slaves do not have to be emancipated (e.g., Lev. 25.39–46). Understanding Japheth to be Greece, an early rabbi cited v. 27 in defense of his ruling that scriptural scrolls may be written (other than in Heb) only in Gk: "May the beauty ('yefifut') of Japheth ('yefet') be in the tents of Shem" (*b. Meg.* 9b).

10.1–32: The seventy nations of the world. As if in fulfillment of God's command to Noah and his sons to "Be fertile and increase, and fill the earth" (9.1), the three sons of Noah rapidly engender nations that *branched out over the earth* (v. 32). The fluidity of identity, which allows a name to refer both to an individual and to a nation, is characteristic of the Tanakh and is especially prominent in Genesis. This table of nations, strikingly universal in scope, represents an early exercise in ethnography. But, as in biblical genealogies generally, political relationships are at least as important as ethnicity and linguistic affinity in establishing lines of descent. Thus, the Canaanites are classed with Egypt (*Mizraim*) as *Ham*ites (v. 6), though the geographic and linguistic relations of the Canaanites ought to put them in the same class as Israel (who have not yet emerged), the class of Shemites. The genealogy probably reflects the political reality that for a long time prior to the emergence of Israel, Egypt had dominated Canaan. Race in our contemporary sense of the term is not a basis for human division in Gen. ch 10, and no mention of physical characteristics is made. **3:** *Ashkenaz* refers to the Scythians, who occupied the area to the north of the Black Sea (cf. Jer. 51.27). In the Middle Ages, Jews reused the term to refer to Germany and, later, to the Jewish communities of central and northeastern Europe. **8–12:** Nimrod joins the growing company of inventors of culture (cf. 4.17–22; 9.20). He is the first emperor (the term *mighty hunter* has royal connotations), uniting different parts of Mesopotamia under his rule. It is likely that these verses allude to a lost epic about the figure of Nimrod. Interpreting his name as a form of the Heb verb that means "to rebel," a midrash sees him as the archetypal rebel against the will of God (*Tg. Ps.-J.*)—to which Rabbi Abraham Ibn Ezra, the 12th-century commentator, replies, "Don't look for a reason for every name!"

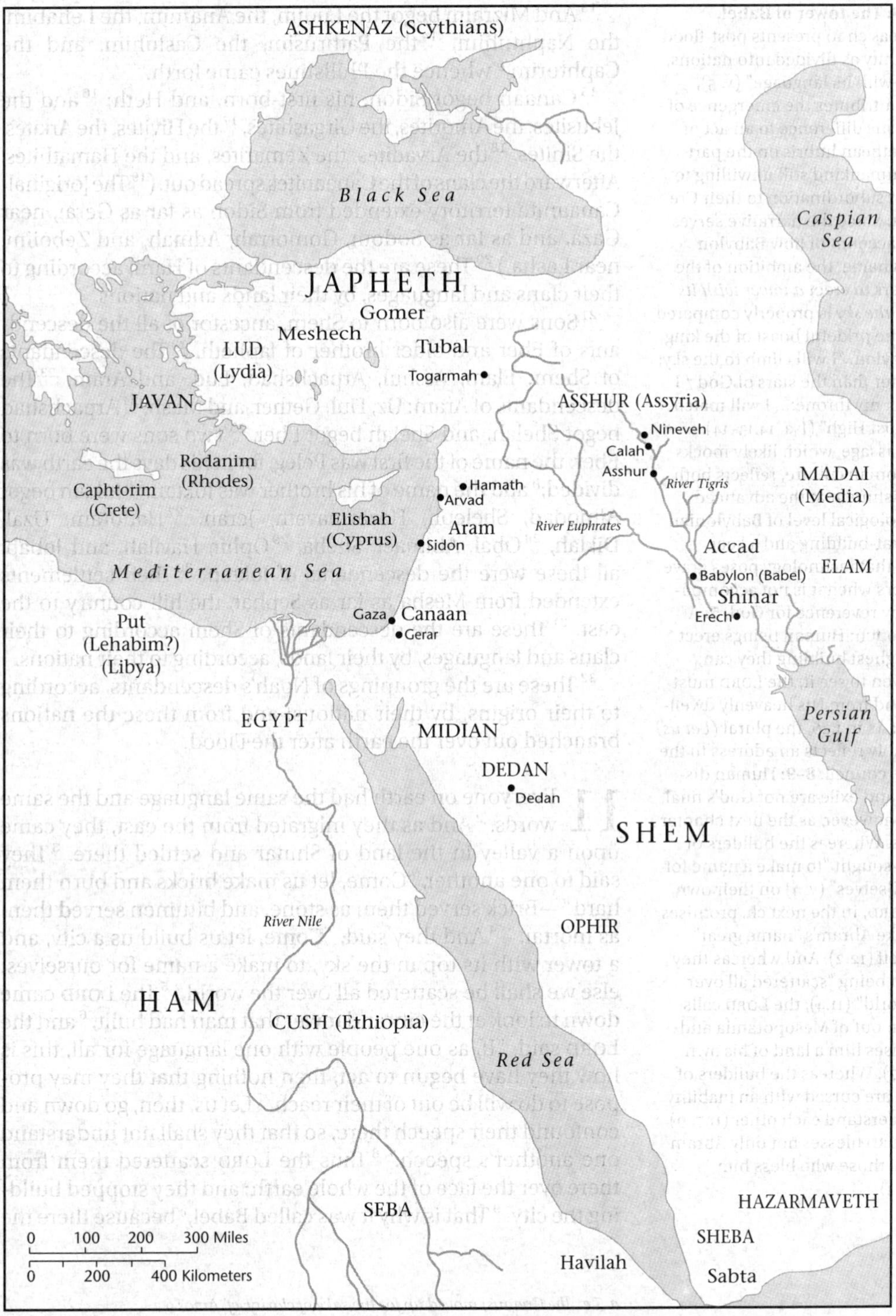

The table of nations. Only places that can be identified with probability are shown.

[13] And Mizraim begot the Ludim, the Anamim, the Lehabim, the Naphtuhim, [14] the Pathrusim, the Casluhim, and the Caphtorim,[a] whence the Philistines came forth.

[15] Canaan begot Sidon, his first-born, and Heth; [16] and the Jebusites, the Amorites, the Girgashites, [17] the Hivites, the Arkites, the Sinites, [18] the Arvadites, the Zemarites, and the Hamathites. Afterward the clans of the Canaanites spread out. ([19] The [original] Canaanite territory extended from Sidon as far as Gerar, near Gaza, and as far as Sodom, Gomorrah, Admah, and Zeboiim, near Lasha.) [20] These are the descendants of Ham, according to their clans and languages, by their lands and nations.

[21] Sons were also born to Shem, ancestor of all the descendants of Eber and older brother of Japheth. [22] The descendants of Shem: Elam, Asshur, Arpachshad, Lud, and Aram. [23] The descendants of Aram: Uz, Hul, Gether, and Mash. [24] Arpachshad begot Shelah, and Shelah begot Eber. [25] Two sons were born to Eber: the name of the first was Peleg, for in his days the earth was divided;[b] and the name of his brother was Joktan. [26] Joktan begot Almodad, Sheleph, Hazarmaveth, Jerah, [27] Hadoram, Uzal, Diklah, [28] Obal, Abimael, Sheba, [29] Ophir, Havilah, and Jobab; all these were the descendants of Joktan. [30] Their settlements extended from Mesha as far as Sephar, the hill country to the east. [31] These are the descendants of Shem according to their clans and languages, by their lands, according to their nations.

[32] These are the groupings of Noah's descendants, according to their origins, by their nations; and from these the nations branched out over the earth after the Flood.

11 Everyone on earth had the same language and the same words. [2] And as they migrated from the east, they came upon a valley in the land of Shinar and settled there. [3] They said to one another, "Come, let us make bricks and burn them hard."—Brick served them as stone, and bitumen served them as mortar.—[4] And they said, "Come, let us build us a city, and a tower with its top in the sky, to make a name for ourselves; else we shall be scattered all over the world." [5] The LORD came down to look at the city and tower that man had built, [6] and the LORD said, "If, as one people with one language for all, this is how they have begun to act, then nothing that they may propose to do will be out of their reach. [7] Let us, then, go down and confound their speech there, so that they shall not understand one another's speech." [8] Thus the LORD scattered them from there over the face of the whole earth; and they stopped building the city. [9] That is why it was called Babel,[c] because there the

a I.e., the Cretans; moved up for the sake of clarity; cf. Amos 9.7.
b Heb. niphlegah, *play on "Peleg."* *c I.e., "Babylon."*

11.1–9: The tower of Babel. Whereas ch 10 presents post-flood humanity as divided into nations, "each with its language" (v. 5), 11.1–9 attributes the emergence of linguistic difference to an act of Promethean hubris on the part of a humankind still unwilling to accept subordination to their Creator. **4:** Since the narrative serves as an account of how Babylon got its name, the ambition of the builders to erect *a tower with its top in the sky* is properly compared with the prideful boast of the king of Babylon, "I will climb to the sky; / Higher than the stars of God / I will set my throne.... I will match the Most High" (Isa. 14.13–14). Our passage, which likely mocks Babylonian culture, reflects both astonishment at the advanced technological level of Babylonian ziggurat-building and a keen sense that technology poses grave dangers when it is not accompanied by reverence for God. **5:** A nice touch: Human beings erect the highest building they can, but even to see it, the LORD must descend from His heavenly dwelling. **7:** As in 1.26, the plural *(Let us)* probably reflects an address to the divine council. **8–9:** Human disunity and exile are not God's final wish, however, as the next chapter shows. Whereas the builders of Babel sought "to make a name for [them]selves" (v. 4) on their own, the LORD, in the next ch, promises to make Abram's "name great" Himself (12.2). And whereas they feared being "scattered all over the world" (11.4), the LORD calls Abram out of Mesopotamia and promises him a land of his own (12.1, 7). Whereas the builders of Babel are cursed with an inability to understand each other (11.7, 9), the LORD blesses not only Abram but all those who bless him (12.2–3).

LORD confounded[a] the speech of the whole earth; and from
there the LORD scattered them over the face of the whole earth.

10 This is the line of Shem. Shem was 100 years old when he
begot Arpachshad, two years after the Flood. 11 After the birth of[b]
Arpachshad, Shem lived 500 years and begot sons and daughters.
12 When Arpachshad had lived 35 years, he begot Shelah.
13 After the birth of Shelah, Arpachshad lived 403 years and begot sons and daughters.
14 When Shelah had lived 30 years, he begot Eber. 15 After
the birth of Eber, Shelah lived 403 years and begot sons and
daughters.
16 When Eber had lived 34 years, he begot Peleg. 17 After the
birth of Peleg, Eber lived 430 years and begot sons and daughters.
18 When Peleg had lived 30 years, he begot Reu. 19 After the
birth of Reu, Peleg lived 209 years and begot sons and daughters.
20 When Reu had lived 32 years, he begot Serug. 21 After the
birth of Serug, Reu lived 207 years and begot sons and daughters.
22 When Serug had lived 30 years, he begot Nahor. 23 After
the birth of Nahor, Serug lived 200 years and begot sons and
daughters.
24 When Nahor had lived 29 years, he begot Terah. 25 After
the birth of Terah, Nahor lived 119 years and begot sons and
daughters.
26 When Terah had lived 70 years, he begot Abram, Nahor,
and Haran. 27 Now this is the line of Terah: Terah begot Abram,
Nahor, and Haran; and Haran begot Lot. 28 Haran died in the
lifetime of his father Terah, in his native land, Ur of the Chaldeans. 29 Abram and Nahor took to themselves wives, the name
of Abram's wife being Sarai and that of Nahor's wife Milcah,
the daughter of Haran, the father of Milcah and Iscah. 30 Now
Sarai was barren, she had no child.
31 Terah took his son Abram, his grandson Lot the son of
Haran, and his daughter-in-law Sarai, the wife of his son
Abram, and they set out together from Ur of the Chaldeans for
the land of Canaan; but when they had come as far as Haran,
they settled there. 32 The days of Terah came to 205 years; and
Terah died in Haran.

LEKH LEKHA לך לך

12 The LORD said to Abram, "Go forth from your native
land and from your father's house to the land that I will
show you.
2 I will make of you a great nation,
And I will bless you;

a *Heb.* balal *"confound," play on "Babel."*
b *Lit. "After he begot," and so throughout.*

11.10–32: Ten generations from Shem to Abram. The text rapidly works its way from Noahide humankind to the particular subject that will dominate the rest of the Torah: God's dealing with the people Israel, descended from Abram and thus from *Shem*. Compared to the previous genealogical list in ch 5, which recorded the pre-flood figures, this one displays lifespans that are markedly shorter. In fact, they tend to decrease over the generations, and the ages at which these men beget their first-born sons are generally realistic. At least two of the personal names listed here, *Serug* and *Nahor*, are known from Mesopotamian literature as place names. **31–32:** The idea that Abram began his trek to Canaan together with his father contradicts the implication of 12.1, wherein Abram leaves his "father's house" to go to an unnamed land that turns out, of course, to be Canaan (cf. 15.7). Source critics solve the problem by assigning vv. 31–32 to P, but the account of Abram's leaving his "father's house" for Canaan to J. A more traditional approach speaks of two stages to Abram's trek, the first from Ur to Haran with Terah, the second from Haran to Canaan without him. If one computes the life span of 205 years given for Terah in v. 32 with other numbers in the life of Abram—born when his father is seventy (v. 26), seventy-five when he left Haran (12.4)—then Terah lived for sixty years after Abram's departure. The difference between the narrative order and the chronological order provides Rashi with the basis for a pungent observation: "The wicked are called 'dead' even in their lifetime" (according to Josh. 24.2, Terah was an idolater).

12.1–9: The command and the promise to Abram. 1–3: The universalism that marked Gen. chs 1–11 having now failed, the LORD begins anew, singling out one Mesopotamian—in no way distinguished from his peers as yet—and promising to make of him *a great nation,* not numbered in the

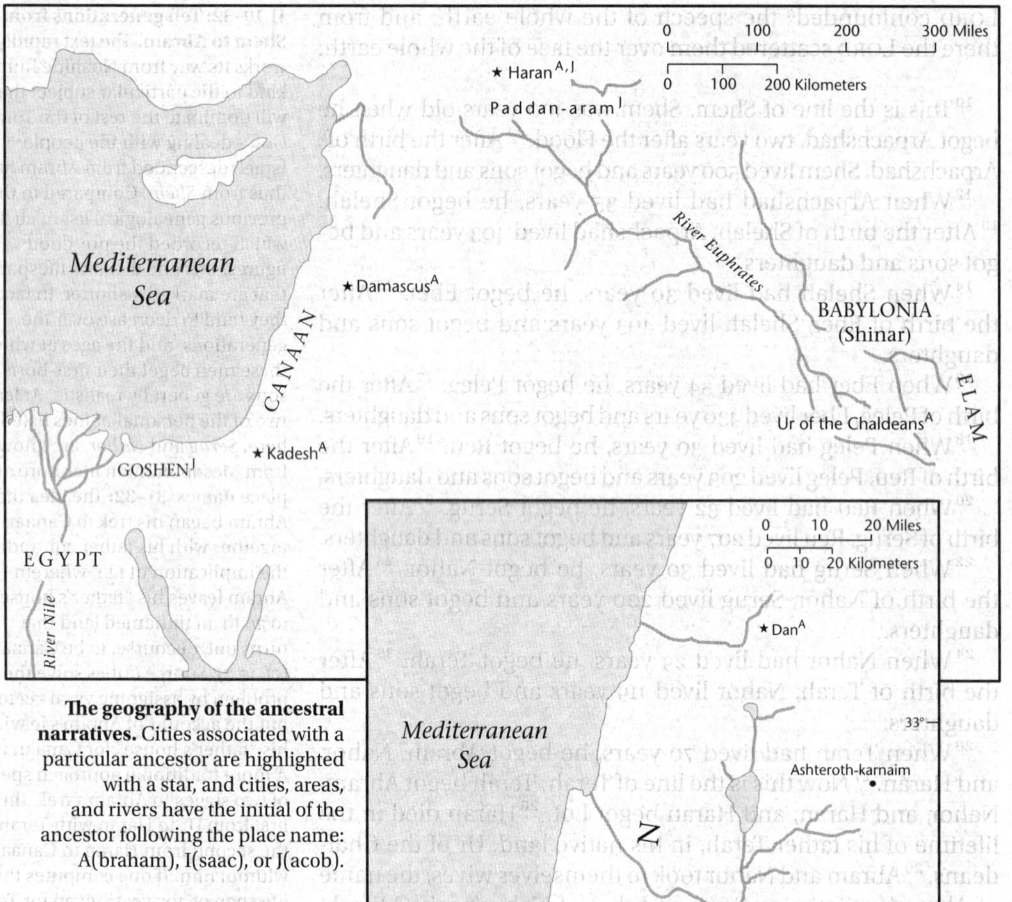

The geography of the ancestral narratives. Cities associated with a particular ancestor are highlighted with a star, and cities, areas, and rivers have the initial of the ancestor following the place name: A(braham), I(saac), or J(acob).

I will make your name great,
And you shall be a blessing.[a]
3 I will bless those who bless you
And curse him that curses you;
And all the families of the earth
Shall bless themselves by you."
4 Abram went forth as the LORD had commanded him, and
Lot went with him. Abram was seventy-five years old when
he left Haran. 5 Abram took his wife Sarai and his brother's
son Lot, and all the wealth that they had amassed, and the
persons that they had acquired in Haran; and they set out for
the land of Canaan. When they arrived in the land of Canaan,
6 Abram passed through the land as far as the site of Shechem,
at the terebinth of Moreh. The Canaanites were then in the
land.

7 The LORD appeared to Abram and said, "I will assign this
land to your offspring." And he built an altar there to the LORD
who had appeared to him. 8 From there he moved on to the hill
country east of Bethel and pitched his tent, with Bethel on the
west and Ai on the east; and he built there an altar to the LORD
and invoked the LORD by name. 9 Then Abram journeyed by
stages toward the Negeb.

10 There was a famine in the land, and Abram went down to
Egypt to sojourn there, for the famine was severe in the land.
11 As he was about to enter Egypt, he said to his wife Sarai, "I
know[b] what a beautiful woman you are. 12 If the Egyptians see
you, and think, 'She is his wife,' they will kill me and let you
live. 13 Please say that you are my sister, that it may go well with
me because of you, and that I may remain alive thanks to you."
14 When Abram entered Egypt, the Egyptians saw how
very beautiful the woman was. 15 Pharaoh's courtiers saw her
and praised her to Pharaoh, and the woman was taken into
Pharaoh's palace. 16 And because of her, it went well with
Abram; he acquired sheep, oxen, asses, male and female
slaves, she-asses, and camels.

a *I.e., a standard by which blessing is invoked; cf. v. 3 end.*

b *Or "You"; cf. the second person feminine form* -ti *in Judg. 5.7; Jer. 2.20; Mic. 4.13, etc.*

seventy nations of ch 10. What the LORD promises Abram (his name is changed to "Abraham" only in ch 17)—land, numerous offspring, and blessing—constitutes to a large extent a reversal of some of the curses on Adam and Eve—exile, pain in childbirth, and uncooperative soil (3.16–24). The twin themes of land and progeny inform the rest of the Torah. In Gen. ch 12, these extraordinary promises come like a bolt from the blue, an act of God's grace alone; no indication has been given as to why or even whether Abram merits them. In 22.15–18, the promises will be reinterpreted as the LORD's condign response to Abraham's great act of obedience when he proved willing to sacrifice his beloved son, Isaac. In Second Temple and rabbinic sources, various details of Abraham's early life are filled in, and he sometimes appears as the first monotheist, discovering the one true God even before God calls him. **6:** The statement that *The Canaanites were then in the land* poses an obstacle to the doctrine of Mosaic authorship, since the Canaanites were still firmly in control of the land when Moses died. Ibn Ezra suggests that the Canaanites may have taken the land from some prior occupants, and "if not, [this verse] has a great secret." The "great secret," according to Joseph Bonfils, a commentator on Ibn Ezra, was that "Joshua or another of the other prophets wrote it.... And since we are to have trust in the words of tradition and the prophets," Bonfils concludes, "what should I care whether it was Moses or another prophet who wrote it, since the words of all of them are true and inspired?" *(Tzafenat Pa'aneaḥ).*

12.10–20: Exile and danger. No sooner has Abram been promised the land and taken his tour of it than the promise is thrown into great danger. In the extreme and life-threatening circumstance of famine, Abram leaves Canaan for Egypt, a land that had a reputation in the Israelite mind for sexual impropriety (e.g., Gen. ch 39; Lev. ch 18; Ezek. 23.1–3, 8, 19, 21, 27). Although Abram is sometimes chastised for passing his beautiful wife off as his sister, it is hard to see how Sarai (whose name becomes "Sarah" in ch 17) would have fared better if he died at the hands of the lecherous and adulterous Egyptians. Ramban, however, makes a powerful theological criticism of Abram, observing that the patriarch "committed a great sin inadvertently" by not trusting in God's protection, leaving the promised land, and subjecting his righteous wife to the possibility of sexual victimization. This, Ramban remarks, will be the cause of his descendants' painful exile in Egypt (Ramban on 12.10).

17 But the LORD afflicted Pharaoh and his household with mighty plagues on account of Sarai, the wife of Abram. 18 Pharaoh sent for Abram and said, "What is this you have done to me! Why did you not tell me that she was your wife? 19 Why did you say, 'She is my sister,' so that I took her as my wife? Now, here is your wife; take her and begone!" 20 And Pharaoh put men in charge of him, and they sent him off with his wife and all that he possessed.

13

From Egypt, Abram went up into the Negeb, with his wife and all that he possessed, together with Lot. 2 Now Abram was very rich in cattle, silver, and gold. 3 And he proceeded by stages from the Negeb as far as Bethel, to the place where his tent had been formerly, between Bethel and Ai, 4 the site of the altar that he had built there at first; and there Abram invoked the LORD by name.

5 Lot, who went with Abram, also had flocks and herds and tents, 6 so that the land could not support them staying together; for their possessions were so great that they could not remain together. 7 And there was quarreling between the herdsmen of Abram's cattle and those of Lot's cattle.—The Canaanites and Perizzites were then dwelling in the land.— 8 Abram said to Lot, "Let there be no strife between you and me, between my herdsmen and yours, for we are kinsmen. 9 Is not the whole land before you? Let us separate:[a] if you go north, I will go south; and if you go south, I will go north." 10 Lot looked about him and saw how well watered was the whole plain of the Jordan, all of it—this was before the LORD had destroyed Sodom and Gomorrah—all the way to Zoar, like the garden of the LORD, like the land of Egypt. 11 So Lot chose for himself the whole plain of the Jordan, and Lot journeyed eastward. Thus they parted from each other; 12 Abram remained in the land of Canaan, while Lot settled in the cities of the Plain, pitching his tents near Sodom. 13 Now the inhabitants of Sodom were very wicked sinners against the LORD.

14 And the LORD said to Abram, after Lot had parted from him, "Raise your eyes and look out from where you are, to the north and south, to the east and west, 15 for I give all the land that you see to you and your offspring forever. 16 I will make your offspring as the dust of the earth, so that if one can count the dust of the earth, then your offspring too can be counted.

a *Lit. "Please separate from me."*

17: The LORD's infliction of *plagues* on Pharaoh foreshadows the story of the exodus. Indeed, Abram's experience in 12.10–20 pre-enacts major themes of his descendants' experience at the end of Genesis and in Exodus: descent into Egypt because of famine, the death (feared or realized) of the male and survival of the female (cf. Exod. 1.15–22), discussions with Pharaoh, plagues, release, and the acquisition of great wealth (cf. Exod. 12.35). "None of the events that happened to the father failed to happen to the descendants" (Ramban on 12.10, based on *Gen. Rab.* ad loc.). The wife-sister motif, in this instance ascribed to J, recurs with King Abimelech of Gerar in Pharaoh's place in ch 20 (ascribed to E) and with Isaac and Rebekah, instead of Abraham and Sarah, confronting Abimelech in 26.6–11 (again attributed to J). Thus, no one source repeats the story with the same couple and the same king.

13.1–18: Lot and Abram separate. Abram's childlessness (11.30) has raised the possibility that the "great nation" that God promises to make of him will descend, biologically, from his nephew Lot, whom he may have adopted (11.31; 12.5). Now, the blessing on Abram having worked too well, so to speak, the land cannot support the huge flocks that the two kinsmen have acquired, and they must separate. **8–13:** Abram is characteristically generous and conciliatory, offering Lot the first choice of land (vv. 8–9). Lot, by contrast, is self-interested and immediately selects what he mistakenly takes to be the best. The narrator's comparison of his portion to *the garden of the LORD,* a place of disobedience and curse, and to Egypt, a place of exile and oppression, suggests the short-sightedness of Lot's choice (v. 10). His settling near the archetypal sinners of Sodom contrasts with Abram, who faithfully *remained in the land of Canaan* (vv. 12–13). **14–18:** Whereas Lot "raised his eyes" (v. 10, translated here as "looked about him"), Abram does not do likewise until the LORD so instructs him (v. 14). Whereas Lot "chose for himself" land that the LORD would, in his own lifetime, destroy utterly (v. 11; 19.23–25), the LORD *gives* Abram and his progeny the land of Canaan *forever* (v. 15). And whereas Lot pitches his tent near the archsinners of Sodom (vv. 12–13), Abram dwells in Hebron and builds an altar to the God he serves. This contrast of

[17] Up, walk about the land, through its length and its breadth, for I give it to you." [18] And Abram moved his tent, and came to dwell at the terebinths of Mamre, which are in Hebron; and he built an altar there to the LORD.

14 Now, when King Amraphel of Shinar, King Arioch of Ellasar, King Chedorlaomer of Elam, and King Tidal of Goiim [2] made war on King Bera of Sodom, King Birsha of Gomorrah, King Shinab of Admah, King Shemeber of Zeboiim, and the king of Bela, which is Zoar, [3] all the latter joined forces at the Valley of Siddim, now the Dead Sea.[a] [4] Twelve years they served Chedorlaomer, and in the thirteenth year they rebelled. [5] In the fourteenth year Chedorlaomer and the kings who were with him came and defeated the Rephaim at Ashteroth-karnaim, the Zuzim at Ham, the Emim at Shaveh-kiriathaim, [6] and the Horites in their hill country of Seir as far as El-paran, which is by the wilderness. [7] On their way back they came to En-mishpat, which is Kadesh, and subdued all the territory of the Amalekites, and also the Amorites who dwelt in Hazazon-tamar. [8] Then the king of Sodom, the king of Gomorrah, the king of Admah, the king of Zeboiim, and the king of Bela, which is Zoar, went forth and engaged them in battle in the Valley of Siddim: [9] King Chedorlaomer of Elam, King Tidal of Goiim, King Amraphel of Shinar, and King Arioch of Ellasar—four kings against those five.

[10] Now the Valley of Siddim was dotted with bitumen pits; and the kings of Sodom and Gomorrah, in their flight, threw themselves into them, while the rest escaped to the hill country. [11] [The invaders] seized all the wealth of Sodom and Gomorrah and all their provisions, and went their way. [12] They also took Lot, the son of Abram's brother, and his possessions, and departed; for he had settled in Sodom.

[13] A fugitive brought the news to Abram the Hebrew, who was dwelling at the terebinths of Mamre the Amorite, kinsman of Eshkol and Aner, these being Abram's allies. [14] When Abram heard that his kinsman had been taken captive, he mustered his retainers,[b] born into his household, numbering three hundred and eighteen, and went in pursuit as far as Dan. [15] At night, he and his servants deployed against them and defeated them; and he pursued them as far as Hobah, which is north of Damascus. [16] He brought back all the possessions; he also brought back his kinsman Lot and his possessions, and the women and the rest of the people.

a Heb. "Salt Sea." *b Meaning of Heb.* ḥanikh *uncertain.*

the two kinsmen, with Lot serving as a foil for his uncle, will appear again in chs 18–19.

14.1–24: Abram's heroic campaign. 1–9: Both in content and in style, ch 14 is very different from the rest of the story of Abram/Abraham. Its depiction of him as a warrior is unusual. Vv. 1–9 read like an excerpt from a battle report in an ancient Near Eastern royal inscription. Whether or not this indicates a historical basis for the campaigns reported here has been a matter of debate. Although most of the nations mentioned can be identified, confirmation of the individuals involved has not been forthcoming. The names of the four Canaanite kings are arranged in two sets of alliterating pairs, *Bera-Birsha*, *Shinab-Shemeber* (v. 2), and at least the names of the kings of Sodom and Gomorrah are likely symbolic (Bera = "in evil," Birsha = "in wickedness"). **12–13:** The narrowing of the vast international perspective down to Lot and Sodom and the mention of Abram's *dwelling at the terebinths of Mamre* connect this anomalous narrative to the previous chapter (cf. 13.10–13, 18). Why Abram is called *the Hebrew* (if this is the correct translation) is unclear. In the Tanakh, the term seems to refer to an ethnic group (e.g., 39.14; Exod. 1.19; Jonah 1.9). Here, the ethnic group not having as yet appeared, it may be anachronistic. **14:** It is surprising that Abram has 318 retainers. Although the previous stories have mentioned his rapid acquisition of wealth (12.16; 13.2), he remains a humbler and more vulnerable figure throughout the other narratives and is never again portrayed with his own army. Sensing the anomaly, an ancient rabbi identifies the 318 retainers with Abram's steward Eliezer (15.2) alone, the letters of whose name, if assigned numerical equivalents, total 318 (*Gen. Rab.* 43.2). Since the town of Dan did not acquire that name until long after Abram's time (Josh. 19.47; Judg. 18.27–29), *Dan* here is also anachronistic, reflecting the situation of a much later author. **16:** Separated from Abram, Lot is weak and despoiled (v. 12). Rejoined with Abram (through the latter's heroism), he is restored and recovers his property (cf. 12.3; 19.29).

17 When he returned from defeating Chedorlaomer and the
kings with him, the king of Sodom came out to meet him in the
Valley of Shaveh, which is the Valley of the King. 18 And King
Melchizedek of Salem brought out bread and wine; he was a
priest of God Most High.[a] 19 He blessed him, saying,
"Blessed be Abram of God Most High,
Creator of heaven and earth.
20 And blessed be God Most High,
Who has delivered your foes into your hand."
And [Abram] gave him a tenth of everything.
21 Then the king of Sodom said to Abram, "Give me the persons, and take the possessions for yourself." 22 But Abram said
to the king of Sodom, "I swear[b] to the LORD, God Most High,
Creator of heaven and earth: 23 I will not take so much as a
thread or a sandal strap of what is yours; you shall not say, 'It is
I who made Abram rich.' 24 For me, nothing but what my servants have used up; as for the share of the men who went with
me—Aner, Eshkol, and Mamre—let them take their share."

15 Some time later, the word of the LORD came to Abram in
a vision. He said,
"Fear not, Abram,
I am a shield to you;
Your reward shall be very great."
2 But Abram said, "O Lord GOD, what can You give me, seeing
that I shall die childless, [c]and the one in charge of my household is Dammesek Eliezer!"[c] 3 Abram said further, "Since You
have granted me no offspring, my steward will be my heir."
4 The word of the LORD came to him in reply, "That one shall
not be your heir; none but your very own issue shall be your
heir." 5 He took him outside and said, "Look toward heaven and
count the stars, if you are able to count them." And He added,
"So shall your offspring be." 6 And because he put his trust in
the LORD, He reckoned it to his merit.

a Heb. El 'Elyon. *b Lit. "lift up my hand." c-c Meaning of Heb. uncertain.*

18–20: The blessing on Abram that *Melchizedek*, king of Salem (probably Jerusalem, cf. Ps. 76.3), delivers abruptly interrupts the approach of the king of Sodom, which resumes in v. 21. Nothing is known about Melchizedek, who is also mentioned in Ps. 110.4 (see translators' note), and is a central figure in some postbiblical texts, such as 11QMelch from the Dead Sea Scrolls and the New Testament Letter to the Hebrews chs 5–7. The term *Most High* is a common epithet of deities in the area of ancient Israel, applied, for example, to the god El at Ugarit (a Canaanite city along the coast of what is now Syria), with whom the LORD is sometimes equated in the Tanakh (e.g., 33.20; Num. 23.8). *Most High* is itself a not uncommon epithet of the LORD (e.g., Ps. 47.3). That a foreigner should recognize and revere the God of Israel is not unusual in Genesis, though it is so in much of the rest of the Tanakh. The account of Abram's interaction with the priest-king of Salem may have served to establish the antiquity of Israel's holiest site and the priestly and royal dynasties associated with it. (Strikingly, Jerusalem/Salem is never again mentioned by name in the Torah.) **21–24:** Refusing the Sodomite king's offer to split the booty, Abram again displays his generosity and his graciousness. In v. 22, he employs the liturgical language Melchizedek introduced in v. 19, only this time explicitly equating *God Most High* with *the LORD*, as Melchizedek did not. Vv. 22–24 underscore Abram's exemplary faith in God: In Abram's view, the true hero of the victorious campaign is not himself, but the LORD.

15.1–21: The LORD promises Abram an heir and a land. This ch falls into two sections, the first (vv. 1–6) focuses on God's promise to provide Abram with an heir who will be his own son, and the second (vv. 7–20) on God's covenantal pledge to redeem Abram's descendants from enslavement abroad and to give them a land. Note that in each section, Abram raises a question that expresses some doubt about the promise (vv. 2–3, 8), and in each case the LORD responds with a renewed promise of staggering proportions (vv. 5, 13, 18–20). **2–3:** These difficult verses (v. 3 reads like a gloss on v. 2) may imply that Abram had adopted *Eliezer*, on the presumption, of course, that he would have no children of his own. In any event, the mention of Abram's *childless*ness draws our attention again to Sarai's infertility (11.30) and to the pointlessness of all Abram's recent financial and military success in the absence of a son from whom the promised "great nation" (12.2) can descend. **6:** With nothing more than an extravagant reiteration of the promise of offspring, Abram drops his question and trusts in the LORD. "And thus you find," observes an ancient midrash about this verse, "that our father Abraham inherited this world and the world-to-come only as a reward for the faith that he had" (*Mek. of Rabbi Ishmael, beshallaḥ* 7). In the Tanakh, faith (from the Heb root "ʾ-m-n") does not mean believing in spite of the evidence. It means trusting profoundly in a person, in this case the

[7] Then He said to him, "I am the LORD who brought you out from Ur of the Chaldeans to assign this land to you as a possession." [8] And he said, "O Lord GOD, how shall I know that I am to possess it?" [9] He answered, "Bring Me a three-year-old heifer, a three-year-old she-goat, a three-year-old ram, a turtledove, and a young bird." [10] He brought Him all these and cut them in two, placing each half opposite the other; but he did not cut up the bird. [11] Birds of prey came down upon the carcasses, and Abram drove them away. [12] As the sun was about to set, a deep sleep fell upon Abram, and a great dark dread descended upon him. [13] And He said to Abram, "Know well that your offspring shall be strangers in a land not theirs, and they shall be enslaved and oppressed four hundred years; [14] but I will execute judgment on the nation they shall serve, and in the end they shall go free with great wealth. [15] As for you,

You shall go to your fathers in peace;
You shall be buried at a ripe old age.

[16] And they shall return here in the fourth generation, for the iniquity of the Amorites is not yet complete."

[17] When the sun set and it was very dark, there appeared a smoking oven, and a flaming torch which passed between those pieces. [18] On that day the LORD made a covenant with Abram, saying, "To your offspring I assign this land, from the river of Egypt to the great river, the river Euphrates: [19] the Kenites, the Kenizzites, the Kadmonites, [20] the Hittites, the Perizzites, the Rephaim, [21] the Amorites, the Canaanites, the Girgashites, and the Jebusites."

16 Sarai, Abram's wife, had borne him no children. She had an Egyptian maidservant whose name was Hagar. [2] And Sarai said to Abram, "Look, the LORD has kept me from bearing. Consort with my maid; perhaps I shall have a son[a] through her." And Abram heeded Sarai's request. [3] So Sarai, Abram's wife, took her maid, Hagar the Egyptian—after Abram had dwelt in the land of Canaan ten years—and gave her to her husband Abram as concubine. [4] He cohabited with Hagar and she conceived; and when she saw that she had conceived, her

a Lit. "be built up," play on ben *"son" and* banah *"build up."*

personal God who has reiterated His promise. **7:** The resemblance to the beginning of the Decalogue (Exod. 20.2) further reinforces the sense that Abraham's life foreshadows that of his descendants, the people of Israel, whose enslavement in Egypt and subsequent exodus is about to be predicted (15.13–14). **9–11:** The ritual of cutting animals in half and passing between them is found both in the Bible and in Mesopotamia. The parallel in Jer. 34.17–22 makes it likely that the essence of the ritual is a self-curse: Those walking between the pieces will be like the dead animals if they violate the covenant. In the case at hand, remarkably, it is the LORD, symbolized by the "smoking oven" and "flaming torch" (15.17) who invokes the self-curse, and nothing is said about any covenantal obligations that Abram is to fulfill. This type of covenant is called a covenant of grant, which is a reward for past loyalty, and does not involve any obligations upon the grantee. The same pattern is prominent in texts about the covenant with David (2 Sam. 7.8–16; Ps. 89.20–37). **12–16:** The good news that has marked Abram's previous interactions with God here gives way to a dark prophecy of his offspring's separation from the promised land and enslavement in Egypt. Like the birds of prey swooping toward the carcasses of the severed animals (v. 11), horrors will befall the people Israel, but Israel will go free and return to the land. *Amorites* in v. 16 is used as a general term for all the Canaanite nations. They lose the land not only because of the LORD's promise to Abram, but also because of their own sin (cf. Lev. 18.24–30). **18–21:** These are the most extensive borders of the promised land given in the Tanakh. They encompass, for example, much more territory than the borders specified in Num. 34.1–12, and reflect an ideal that was never realized.

16.1–16: A tale of two women. **1–3:** God's uncompromising reiterations of the promise of offspring in the previous chapter (15.4–5, 13–16, 18) render Sarai's infertility all the more problematic: *ten years* in Canaan but still no child! Nothing in the promises given to Abram to date having specified the matriarch of the great nation to come, so Sarai takes matters into her own hands and, in accordance with documented ancient Near Eastern practice, offers her slave woman as a surrogate mother. Abram (who might have solved his problem by divorcing Sarai but stayed with her nonetheless) accepts. **4:** Given the high estimation of motherhood in biblical culture, the status of Sarai and Hagar now reverses. Among the four things at which "the earth shudders," according to the book of Proverbs, is "a slave-girl who supplants her mistress" (Prov. 30.23).

mistress was lowered in her esteem. 5 And Sarai said to Abram,
"The wrong done me is your fault! I myself put my maid in your
bosom; now that she sees that she is pregnant, I am lowered in
her esteem. The LORD decide between you and me!" 6 Abram
said to Sarai, "Your maid is in your hands. Deal with her as you
think right." Then Sarai treated her harshly, and she ran away
from her.

7 An angel of the LORD found her by a spring of water in the
wilderness, the spring on the road to Shur, 8 and said, "Hagar,
slave of Sarai, where have you come from, and where are you
going?" And she said, "I am running away from my mistress
Sarai."

9 And the angel of the LORD said to her, "Go back to your mistress, and submit to her harsh treatment." 10 And the angel of
the LORD said to her,

"I will greatly increase your offspring,
And they shall be too many to count."

11 The angel of the LORD said to her further,

"Behold, you are with child
And shall bear a son;
You shall call him Ishmael,[a]
For the LORD has paid heed to your suffering.
12 He shall be a wild ass of a man;
His hand against everyone,
And everyone's hand against him;
He shall dwell alongside of all his kinsmen."

13 And she called the LORD who spoke to her, "You Are El-roi,"[b]
by which she meant, [c-]"Have I not gone on seeing after He saw
me!"[-c] 14 Therefore the well was called Beer-lahai-roi;[d] it is between Kadesh and Bered.—15 Hagar bore a son to Abram, and
Abram gave the son that Hagar bore him the name Ishmael.
16 Abram was eighty-six years old when Hagar bore Ishmael to
Abram.

17 When Abram was ninety-nine years old, the LORD appeared to Abram and said to him, "I am El Shaddai.[e] Walk
in My ways and be blameless. 2 I will establish My covenant between Me and you, and I will make you exceedingly numerous."

a I.e., "God heeds." *b Apparently "God of Seeing."*
c-c Meaning of Heb. uncertain.
d Apparently "the Well of the Living One Who sees me."
e Traditionally rendered "God Almighty."

5–6: Sarai demands justice from Abram, and he gives her carte blanche. A midrash sees in Sarai's behavior an object lesson in the dangers of litigiousness: Had she not been so single-mindedly and insensitively preoccupied in demanding justice for herself, her life span would have equaled Abram's. Instead, whereas he lived to 175, she died at 127 (25.7; 23.1) (*Gen. Rab.* 45.5). **7–9:** The flight of the oppressed slave into the wilderness, only to meet a divine being there, foreshadows again the experience of the exodus, prophesied in the previous chapter (15.13–14; cf. Exod. 3.1–2). But this time the oppressor is Israelite, the slave is Egyptian, and the angel of the LORD commands the escapee to return to her cruel mistress and *submit to her harsh treatment.* God's sympathy with the oppressed is potent in the Tanakh, but so is His election of Israel, and it is the latter that trumps in this instance. **10–12:** But God does take note of Hagar's suffering and rewards her with the Abrahamic blessing of *offspring … too many to count* (cf. 13.16; 15.5). Indeed, her high-spirited and militarily formidable son will bear the name *Ishmael* ("God heeds/heeded") as testimony to the LORD's concern about her affliction. **13–14:** The basis for Hagar's exclamation at the end of v. 13 is the idea that one who sees a divine being must die (cf. Exod. 33.20; Judg. 13.22).

17.1–27: An everlasting covenant with Abraham and a promise about Sarah. Source critics identify ch 17 as the P(riestly) version of the covenant with Abraham (of which the J version appears in ch 15). Nothing in ch 17 indicates any awareness that a covenant has, in fact, already been established two chapters earlier. In our chapter, the two chief innovations are that the covenant acquires a sign (circumcision, v. 10) and that it is Sarah who, despite her advanced age, shall bear the promised son (vv. 15–16, 19). The closest parallel to ch 17 in style and diction is 9.1–17, the account of the covenant with Noah. **1:** *El Shaddai* is believed to have originally meant "God, the One of the Mountain" and thus to have expressed the association of a deity with his mountain abode well known in Canaanite literature (cf. the "LORD, Him of Sinai" in Judg. 5.5). In the Priestly conception, the four-letter name translated as LORD was disclosed only in the time of Moses (Exod. 6.2–3), and El Shaddai was the name by which God revealed Himself to the patriarchs.

3 Abram threw himself on his face; and God spoke to him further, 4 "As for Me, this is My covenant with you: You shall be the father of a multitude of nations. 5 And you shall no longer be called Abram, but your name shall be Abraham,[a] for I make you the father of a multitude of nations. 6 I will make you exceedingly fertile, and make nations of you; and kings shall come forth from you. 7 I will maintain My covenant between Me and you, and your offspring to come, as an everlasting covenant throughout the ages, to be God to you and to your offspring to come. 8 I assign the land you sojourn in to you and your offspring to come, all the land of Canaan, as an everlasting holding. I will be their God."

9 God further said to Abraham, "As for you, you and your offspring to come throughout the ages shall keep My covenant. 10 Such shall be the covenant between Me and you and your offspring to follow which you shall keep: every male among you shall be circumcised. 11 You shall circumcise the flesh of your foreskin, and that shall be the sign of the covenant between Me and you. 12 And throughout the generations, every male among you shall be circumcised at the age of eight days. As for the homeborn slave and the one bought from an outsider who is not of your offspring, 13 they must be circumcised, homeborn, and purchased alike. Thus shall My covenant be marked in your flesh as an everlasting pact. 14 And if any male who is uncircumcised fails to circumcise the flesh of his foreskin, that person shall be cut off from his kin; he has broken My covenant."

15 And God said to Abraham, "As for your wife Sarai, you shall not call her Sarai, but her name shall be Sarah.[b] 16 I will bless her; indeed, I will give you a son by her. I will bless her so that she shall give rise to nations; rulers of peoples shall issue from her." 17 Abraham threw himself on his face and laughed, as he said to himself, "Can a child be born to a man a hundred years old, or can Sarah bear a child at ninety?" 18 And Abraham said to God, "O that Ishmael might live by Your favor!" 19 God said, "Nevertheless, Sarah your wife shall bear you a son, and you shall name him Isaac;[c] and I will maintain My covenant with him as an everlasting covenant for his offspring to come. 20 As for Ishmael, I have heeded you.[d] I hereby bless him. I will make him fertile and exceedingly numerous. He shall be the father of twelve chieftains, and I will make of him a great nation. 21 But My covenant I will maintain with Isaac, whom Sarah shall bear to you at this season next year." 22 And when He was done speaking with him, God was gone from Abraham.

a Understood as "father of a multitude." *b I.e., "princess."*
c Heb. Yiṣḥaq, *from* ṣaḥaq, *"laugh."* *d Heb.* shemaʿtikha, *play on "Ishmael."*

5: The change of *name* here and in v. 15 signifies a change in destiny: The childless couple will become the ancestors of many *nations*, including royal dynasties (v. 6). **9–14:** Just as the rainbow is the sign of the Noahide covenant (9.12–17), so circumcision is the sign of the Abrahamic. It thus becomes a matter of the highest importance in Judaism. A Second Temple source reports that when the Seleucid King Antiochus IV prohibited circumcision (a favorite target of anti-Semites), Jewish mothers chose martyrdom over neglect of the commandment (1 Macc. 1.60–61). Rabbinic law requires that a (healthy) Jewish boy be circumcised on the eighth day of his life (v. 12), even if it is the Sabbath. Although arguments for the hygienic value of circumcision have been made since the mid-19th century, the Torah knows nothing of these and sees circumcision ("berit milah," the "covenant of circumcision," or in shorthand, "berit" or "beris," "covenant") as a religious duty incumbent only on Jews. The procedure of medical circumcision is not identical to that performed by a "mohel" (ritual circumciser) in a "berit milah." **15–22:** Unlike its parallel in ch 15 (J), the P account of the Abrahamic covenant specifies *Sarah* as the mother of the promised son, and thus makes her indispensable to the fulfillment of the promise to her husband. The natural impossibility of her giving birth at 90 (not to mention her lifelong infertility) only highlights the supernatural origin of *Isaac* and the nation descended from him (v. 17). *Ishmael*, however, is not dispossessed. Whereas only Isaac inherits the covenant (and its attendant promise of land), Ishmael inherits a large measure of the Abrahamic promise (vv. 20–21; 12.2). Like his nephew Jacob (35.22b–26), he will become the patriarch of a twelve-tribe confederation and thus the father of *a great nation* (v. 20; cf. 25.12–18; 12.2).

[23] Then Abraham took his son Ishmael, and all his homeborn slaves and all those he had bought, every male in Abraham's household, and he circumcised the flesh of their foreskins on that very day, as God had spoken to him. [24] Abraham was ninety-nine years old when he circumcised the flesh of his foreskin, [25] and his son Ishmael was thirteen years old when he was circumcised in the flesh of his foreskin. [26] Thus Abraham and his son Ishmael were circumcised on that very day; [27] and all his household, his homeborn slaves and those that had been bought from outsiders, were circumcised with him.

VA-YERA' וירא

18 The Lord appeared to him by the terebinths of Mamre; he was sitting at the entrance of the tent as the day grew hot. [2] Looking up, he saw three men standing near him. As soon as he saw them, he ran from the entrance of the tent to greet them and, bowing to the ground, [3] he said, "My lords,[a] if it please you, do not go on past your servant. [4] Let a little water be brought; bathe your feet and recline under the tree. [5] And let me fetch a morsel of bread that you may refresh yourselves; then go on—seeing that you have come your servant's way." They replied, "Do as you have said."

[6] Abraham hastened into the tent to Sarah, and said, "Quick, three seahs of choice flour! Knead and make cakes!" [7] Then Abraham ran to the herd, took a calf, tender and choice, and gave it to a servant-boy, who hastened to prepare it. [8] He took curds and milk and the calf that had been prepared and set these before them; and he waited on them under the tree as they ate.

[9] They said to him, "Where is your wife Sarah?" And he replied, "There, in the tent." [10] Then one said, "I will return to you next year,[b] and your wife Sarah shall have a son!" Sarah was listening at the entrance of the tent, which was behind him. [11] Now Abraham and Sarah were old, advanced in years; Sarah had stopped having the periods of women. [12] And Sarah laughed to herself, saying, "Now that I am withered, am I to have enjoyment—with my husband so old?" [13] Then the Lord said to Abraham, "Why did Sarah laugh, saying, 'Shall I in truth bear a child, old as I am?' [14] Is anything too wondrous for the Lord? I will return to you at the same season next year, and Sarah shall have a son." [15] Sarah lied, saying, "I did not laugh," for she was frightened. But He replied, "You did laugh."

a Or "My Lord."
b Cf. Gen. 17.21; 2 Kings 4.16–17.

18.1–19.38: The conception of Isaac and the destruction of Sodom. Chs 18 and 19 display a chiastic structure (ABB'A'): 18.1–15 is the annunciation of Isaac's conception (A); 18.16–33 is the announcement of Sodom's destruction (B); 19.1–29 reports the destruction of Sodom (B'); and 19.30–38 reports Moab's and Ammon's conception (A'). In the process, Abraham emerges again as a heroic figure, one who deeply reveres God yet politely demands justice from Him. Lot is once again (as in ch 13) a foil for Abraham—self-interested, passive, and, finally, victimized. **18.1–2:** The relationship of the Lord to the men is unclear. Perhaps, as in some Canaanite literature, we are to imagine a deity accompanied by his two attendants (cf. 22.3). **3–8:** Note the contrast between Abraham's self-deprecating language *(a little water, a morsel)* and the enormous efforts to which he goes to serve his guests. **9–18:** Source analysis identifies this as the J parallel to the annunciation of Isaac's birth in ch 17 (P). Note that in 17.17 it is Abraham, whereas in 18.12 it is Sarah, who laughs (and thus gives Isaac his name). **13:** The Lord's citation to Abraham of Sarah's monologue in the preceding verse is not quite accurate (*old as I am* as opposed to *with my husband so old*). "Great is peace," remarks a rabbi in the Talmud about this point, "for even the Holy One (blessed be He) made a change on account of it," sparing the couple the discord that might have come had Abraham known Sarah's true thought (*b. B. M.* 87a).

16 The men set out from there and looked down toward Sodom, Abraham walking with them to see them off. 17 Now the
LORD had said, "Shall I hide from Abraham what I am about to
do, 18 since Abraham is to become a great and populous nation
and all the nations of the earth are to bless themselves by him?
19 For I have singled him out, that he may instruct his children
and his posterity to keep the way of the LORD by doing what is just
and right, in order that the LORD may bring about for Abraham
what He has promised him." 20 Then the LORD said, "The outrage
of Sodom and Gomorrah is so great, and their sin so grave! 21 I
will go down to see whether they have acted altogether according
to the outcry that has reached Me; if not, I will take note."
22 The men went on from there to Sodom, while Abraham remained standing before the LORD. 23 Abraham came forward and
said, "Will You sweep away the innocent along with the guilty?
24 What if there should be fifty innocent within the city; will You
then wipe out the place and not forgive it for the sake of the innocent fifty who are in it? 25 Far be it from You to do such a thing,
to bring death upon the innocent as well as the guilty, so that
innocent and guilty fare alike. Far be it from You! Shall not the
Judge of all the earth deal justly?" 26 And the LORD answered, "If I
find within the city of Sodom fifty innocent ones, I will forgive the
whole place for their sake." 27 Abraham spoke up, saying, "Here
I venture to speak to my Lord, I who am but dust and ashes:
28 What if the fifty innocent should lack five? Will You destroy the
whole city for want of the five?" And He answered, "I will not destroy if I find forty-five there." 29 But he spoke to Him again, and
said, "What if forty should be found there?" And He answered, "I
will not do it, for the sake of the forty." 30 And he said, "Let not my
Lord be angry if I go on: What if thirty should be found there?"
And He answered, "I will not do it if I find thirty there." 31 And he
said, "I venture again to speak to my Lord: What if twenty should
be found there?" And He answered, "I will not destroy, for the
sake of the twenty." 32 And he said, "Let not my Lord be angry if I
speak but this last time: What if ten should be found there?" And
He answered, "I will not destroy, for the sake of the ten."
33 When the LORD had finished speaking to Abraham, He departed; and Abraham returned to his place.

19 The two angels arrived in Sodom in the evening, as Lot
was sitting in the gate of Sodom. When Lot saw them, he
rose to greet them and, bowing low with his face to the ground,
2 he said, "Please, my lords, turn aside to your servant's house
to spend the night, and bathe your feet; then you may be on
your way early." But they said, "No, we will spend the night in
the square." 3 But he urged them strongly, so they turned his
way and entered his house. He prepared a feast for them and
baked unleavened bread, and they ate.

16–33: In this section, God treats Abraham as a prophet (cf. 20.7, where he is the first person so designated in Tanakh), disclosing His plans to him (vv. 17–21; cf. Amos 3.7), and Abraham, like one of the prophets of Israel, eloquently demands justice from God (vv. 23–25; cf. Jer. 12.1–4) and pleads for mercy (Gen. 18.26–32; cf. Amos 7.1–6). **24:** Notice that Abraham's demand is not that the guilty be punished and the innocent spared, but rather that the Lord *forgive* [the entire city] *for the sake of the innocent ... who are in it.* The point is made more explicit in v. 26. The underlying theology maintains that the righteous effect deliverance for the entire community. This idea, found elsewhere in the Tanakh (e.g., Jer. 5.1), is prominent in rabbinic literature, where it underlies the notion of the thirty-six righteous individuals for whose sake the world endures. **27:** Recognizing the sovereignty of God and his own subordinate status, Abraham speaks with great deference and scrupulously avoids chutzpah (also in vv. 30–32). The Talmud remarks about this verse, "The Holy One (blessed be He) said to Israel, I deeply love you, for even when I give you abundant greatness, you make yourselves small before Me. I gave greatness to Abraham, and he said *I who am but dust and ashes*" (*b. Ḥul.* 89a). **19.1–3:** The contrast between Abraham and Lot (discussed above, on ch 13) continues. Whereas Abraham sees the LORD (18.1), Lot sees only His two angelic attendants (19.1). Whereas Abraham runs to greet his visitors (18.2), Lot only rises (19.1). Whereas Abraham offers a sumptuous feast (18.6–8), Lot offers *unleavened bread* (19.3).

4–5: The story in Judg. 19.10–30 is quite possibly patterned after this episode. The wrong that the men of Sodom attempt involves not only the sin of homosexual conduct (defined as an "abhorrence" in Lev. 18.22), but also a gross violation of the conventions of hospitality. According to one opinion in the Mishnah, a lack of generosity is characteristic of Sodom, as epitomized in the saying, "What is mine is mine; what is yours is yours" (*m. 'Avot* 5.10; cf. Ezek. 16.46–50). **7–8:** Lot's offer of his two daughters prefigures the tragicomic scene at the end of the chapter when they get him drunk and engage in incestuous relations with him (19.30–38). **10:** Lot's passivity is patent and contrasts with Abraham's daring challenge to God's justice in the previous chapter (18.22–33). Gen. 19.29 will make it explicit that Lot's escape is owing not to his own deeply irresolute character, but to God's reliable commitment to Abraham. **14:** Whereas Abraham, taking the impending destruction with the utmost seriousness, functions prophetically in hopes of averting the catastrophe, Lot is taken for a buffoon even by his own sons-in-law and cannot save them. Since Lot's two daughters mentioned in v. 8 are unmarried, these sons-in-law are either engaged to them (so the Vg and Rashi) or married to two other daughters, who die in the conflagration along with their husbands. **15–22:** Lot's weakness and inconstancy would have done him in, had it not been for *the LORD's mercy on him* (v. 16). His weakness and self-interest, however, result in the sparing of one town (vv. 18–22), whereas Abraham's audacious and principled intervention (18.22–33) proved unable to save anyone.

4 They had not yet lain down, when the townspeople, the men of Sodom, young and old—all the people to the last man—gathered about the house. 5 And they shouted to Lot and said to him, "Where are the men who came to you tonight? Bring them out to us, that we may be intimate with them." 6 So Lot went out to them to the entrance, shut the door behind him, 7 and said, "I beg you, my friends, do not commit such a wrong. 8 Look, I have two daughters who have not known a man. Let me bring them out to you, and you may do to them as you please; but do not do anything to these men, since they have come under the shelter of my roof." 9 But they said, "Stand back! The fellow," they said, "came here as an alien, and already he acts the ruler! Now we will deal worse with you than with them." And they pressed hard against the person of Lot, and moved forward to break the door. 10 But the men stretched out their hands and pulled Lot into the house with them, and shut the door. 11 And the people who were at the entrance of the house, young and old, they struck with blinding light, so that they were helpless to find the entrance.

12 Then the men said to Lot, "Whom else have you here? Sons-in-law, your sons and daughters, or anyone else that you have in the city—bring them out of the place. 13 For we are about to destroy this place; because the outcry against them before the LORD has become so great that the LORD has sent us to destroy it." 14 So Lot went out and spoke to his sons-in-law, who had married his daughters, and said, "Up, get out of this place, for the LORD is about to destroy the city." But he seemed to his sons-in-law as one who jests.

15 As dawn broke, the angels urged Lot on, saying, "Up, take your wife and your two remaining daughters, lest you be swept away because of the iniquity of the city." 16 Still he delayed. So the men seized his hand, and the hands of his wife and his two daughters—in the LORD's mercy on him—and brought him out and left him outside the city. 17 When they had brought them outside, one said, "Flee for your life! Do not look behind you, nor stop anywhere in the Plain; flee to the hills, lest you be swept away." 18 But Lot said to them, "Oh no, my lord! 19 You have been so gracious to your servant, and have already shown me so much kindness in order to save my life; but I cannot flee to the hills, lest the disaster overtake me and I die. 20 Look, that town there is near enough to flee to; it is such a little place! Let me flee there—it is such a little place—and let my life be saved." 21 He replied, "Very well, I will grant you this favor too, and I will not annihilate the town of which you have spoken. 22 Hurry, flee there, for I cannot do anything until you arrive there." Hence the town came to be called Zoar.[a]

a Connected with miṣʿar *"a little place," v. 20.*

23 As the sun rose upon the earth and Lot entered Zoar, 24 the LORD rained upon Sodom and Gomorrah sulfurous fire from the LORD out of heaven. 25 He annihilated those cities and the entire Plain, and all the inhabitants of the cities and the vegetation of the ground. 26 Lot's[a] wife looked back,[b] and she thereupon turned into a pillar of salt.

27 Next morning, Abraham hurried to the place where he had stood before the LORD, 28 and, looking down toward Sodom and Gomorrah and all the land of the Plain, he saw the smoke of the land rising like the smoke of a kiln.

29 Thus it was that, when God destroyed the cities of the Plain and annihilated the cities where Lot dwelt, God was mindful of Abraham and removed Lot from the midst of the upheaval.

30 Lot went up from Zoar and settled in the hill country with his two daughters, for he was afraid to dwell in Zoar; and he and his two daughters lived in a cave. 31 And the older one said to the younger, "Our father is old, and there is not a man on earth to consort with us in the way of all the world. 32 Come, let us make our father drink wine, and let us lie with him, that we may maintain life through our father." 33 That night they made their father drink wine, and the older one went in and lay with her father; he did not know when she lay down or when she rose. 34 The next day the older one said to the younger, "See, I lay with Father last night; let us make him drink wine tonight also, and you go and lie with him, that we may maintain life through our father." 35 That night also they made their father drink wine, and the younger one went and lay with him; he did not know when she lay down or when she rose.

36 Thus the two daughters of Lot came to be with child by their father. 37 The older one bore a son and named him Moab;[c] he is the father of the Moabites of today. 38 And the younger also bore a son, and she called him Ben-ammi;[d] he is the father of the Ammonites of today.

20 Abraham journeyed from there to the region of the Negeb and settled between Kadesh and Shur. While he was sojourning in Gerar, 2 Abraham said of Sarah his wife, "She is my sister." So King Abimelech of Gerar had Sarah brought to him. 3 But God came to Abimelech in a dream by night and said to him, "You are to die because of the woman that you have taken, for she is a married woman." 4 Now Abimelech had not approached her. He said, "O Lord, will You slay people even though innocent? 5 He himself said to me, 'She is my sister!' And she also said, 'He is my brother.' When I did this, my heart was blameless and my hands were clean." 6 And God said

a Lit. "His." *b Lit. "behind him."* *c As though* me-'ab *"from (my) father."*
d As though "son of my (paternal) kindred."

26: The report of the fate of *Lot's wife* serves as an explanation for salt formations still evident in the vicinity of the Dead Sea. **30–38:** This passage has strong affinities with the story of Ham's sin in 9.20–27. Here, however, it is possible to construct a defense of Lot's daughters on the grounds that they genuinely and plausibly believed that the human race would die out unless they bore children from the one surviving male, their hapless father (vv. 31–32). The passage is partly a comic inversion of the opening of this two-chapter section, which centers on the unlikely birth of a son to Sarah (18.1–15). Note the similarity of Sarah's remark "with my husband so old" (18.12) and the older daughter's words, *our father is old* (19.31). Gen. 19.30–38 provides an unflattering account of the origins of two of Israel's traditional enemies, the *Moabites* and the *Ammonites* (cf. Deut. 23.4–7). Nonetheless, a midrash sees in these acts the origins of two of the great mothers of Israel, the Moabite Ruth, ancestor of King David (Ruth 4.13–22), and the Ammonite Naamah, wife of King Solomon and mother of his successor King Rehoboam (1 Kings 14.21). "I found David" (Ps. 89.21), a rabbi observed. "Where did He find him?—in Sodom!" A seed of messianic redemption thus lies in the squalid events of Gen. 19.30–38 (*Gen. Rab.* 41.4).

20.1–18: Abraham and Sarah in Abimelech's court. Attributed by source criticism to the Elohist (E), this episode parallels the accounts of Abram and Sarai in Pharaoh's court in 12.10–20 and of Isaac and Rebekah in Abimelech's court in 26.1–11 (both ascribed to J). In this version, the emphasis lies on points of law and ethics and on the motivation of the protagonists, and the moral and psychological situation is much more complex than in either of the parallel narratives. **3–7:** Even though Abimelech has not consummated his relationship with Sarah (v. 6), he is still culpable for abducting another man's wife (v. 3). V. 7 implies that he may still harbor erotic

to him in the dream, "I knew that you did this with a blameless heart, and so I kept you from sinning against Me. That was
why I did not let you touch her. 7 Therefore, restore the man's
wife—since he is a prophet, he will intercede for you—to save
your life. If you fail to restore her, know that you shall die, you
and all that are yours."

8 Early next morning, Abimelech called his servants and
told them all that had happened; and the men were greatly
frightened. 9 Then Abimelech summoned Abraham and said
to him, "What have you done to us? What wrong have I done
that you should bring so great a guilt upon me and my kingdom? You have done to me things that ought not to be done.
10 What, then," Abimelech demanded of Abraham, "was your
purpose in doing this thing?" 11 "I thought," said Abraham,
"surely there is no fear of God in this place, and they will kill
me because of my wife. 12 And besides, she is in truth my sister, my father's daughter though not my mother's; and she
became my wife. 13 So when God made me wander from my
father's house, I said to her, 'Let this be the kindness that you
shall do me: whatever place we come to, say there of me: He
is my brother.'"

14 Abimelech took sheep and oxen, and male and female
slaves, and gave them to Abraham; and he restored his wife
Sarah to him. 15 And Abimelech said, "Here, my land is before
you; settle wherever you please." 16 And to Sarah he said, "I
herewith give your brother a thousand pieces of silver; this will
serve you as vindication[a] before all who are with you, and you
are cleared before everyone." 17 Abraham then prayed to God,
and God healed Abimelech and his wife and his slave girls, so
that they bore children; 18 for the LORD had closed fast every
womb of the household of Abimelech because of Sarah, the
wife of Abraham.

21 The LORD took note of Sarah as He had promised, and
the LORD did for Sarah as He had spoken. 2 Sarah conceived and bore a son to Abraham in his old age, at the set time
of which God had spoken. 3 Abraham gave his newborn son,
whom Sarah had borne him, the name of Isaac. 4 And when
his son Isaac was eight days old, Abraham circumcised him,

a Lit. "a covering of the eyes"; meaning of latter half of verse uncertain.

aspirations toward Sarah and may lack a full understanding of just who Abraham is. **8:** The servants' fear gives the lie to Abraham's attempt at self-exoneration on the grounds that "there is no fear of God in this place" (v. 11). **9–10:** The image of a Gentile king righteously upbraiding an Israelite prophet (v. 7) for the latter's moral failures is a fine comic inversion of our expectations. **12:** Abraham tries a new line of defense based on a semantic ambiguity: Since *sister* can mean "half-sister" (e.g., Lev. 18.9), he really was not lying. But was Sarah even his half-sister? On the plain sense of the biblical text, there is no evidence that she was. Ibn Ezra thinks that with this claim, Abraham simply "put Abimelech off according to the need of the moment." A midrash, however, identifies Iscah, Abraham's niece (11.29), with Sarah and thus makes Abraham's father Sarah's grandfather (*b. Meg.* 14a). Since "father" in ancient Heb could also mean grandfather (e.g., 28.13), this midrash serves to validate Abraham's defense. Ramban notes that even if Sarah really was Abraham's half-sister, Abraham was still in the wrong for not mentioning the vastly more important point that she was his wife. **17:** "Pray" in biblical Heb very often denotes intercession. Abraham is the first person called a prophet in the Bible, and here functions as a prophetic intercessor, as God predicted he would in v. 7. **18:** This conclusion is less surprising than it first seems. It is consistent with 12.17, which speaks of the LORD's afflicting "Pharaoh and his household with mighty plagues" in the analogous situation. It also correlates with the harsh tone that God takes when He first confronts Abimelech in 20.3. Though God recognizes the king's innocence, He also takes special measures to ensure that no untoward act occurs (v. 6).

21.1–8: The promise to Sarah fulfilled at last. With its heavy emphasis on God's fulfillment of His promise of a son to Sarah and Abraham (vv. 1–2) and its note that the father circumcised his son on the eighth day in accordance with God's command (v. 3), this passage marks a major turning point in the story. Despite seemingly insurmountable obstacles (including Abimelech's abduction of Sarah in the previous ch), things have gone according to plan. A midrash reports that it was on Rosh Ha-Shanah that *The LORD took note of Sarah* (*b. Rosh Hash.* 11a); Gen. ch 21 is thus the Torah reading for the first day of Rosh Ha-Shanah.

as God had commanded him. 5 Now Abraham was a hundred years old when his son Isaac was born to him. 6 Sarah said, "God has brought me laughter; everyone who hears will laugh with[a] me." 7 And she added,

"Who would have said to Abraham
That Sarah would suckle children!
Yet I have borne a son in his old age."

8 The child grew up and was weaned, and Abraham held a great feast on the day that Isaac was weaned.

9 Sarah saw the son whom Hagar the Egyptian had borne to Abraham playing. 10 She said to Abraham, "Cast out that slave-woman and her son, for the son of that slave shall not share in the inheritance with my son Isaac." 11 The matter distressed Abraham greatly, for it concerned a son of his. 12 But God said to Abraham, "Do not be distressed over the boy or your slave; whatever Sarah tells you, do as she says, for it is through Isaac that offspring shall be continued[b] for you. 13 As for the son of the slave-woman, I will make a nation of him, too, for he is your seed."

14 Early next morning Abraham took some bread and a skin of water, and gave them to Hagar. He placed them over her shoulder, together with the child, and sent her away. And she wandered about in the wilderness of Beer-sheba. 15 When the water was gone from the skin, she left the child under one of the bushes, 16 and went and sat down at a distance, a bowshot away; for she thought, "Let me not look on as the child dies." And sitting thus afar, she burst into tears.

17 God heard the cry of the boy, and an angel of God called to Hagar from heaven and said to her, "What troubles you, Hagar? Fear not, for God has heeded the cry of the boy where he is. 18 Come, lift up the boy and hold him by the hand, for I will make a great nation of him." 19 Then God opened her eyes and she saw a well of water. She went and filled the skin with water, and let the boy drink. 20 God was with the boy and he grew up; he dwelt in the wilderness and became a bowman. 21 He lived in the wilderness of Paran; and his mother got a wife for him from the land of Egypt.

22 At that time Abimelech and Phicol, chief of his troops, said to Abraham, "God is with you in everything that you do.

a *Lit. "for."* *b* *Lit. "called."*

5: Abraham's life divides into seven periods of 25 years each: three of them in Mesopotamia (12.4), one in Canaan without the promised son (21.5), and three in Canaan after Isaac's birth (25.7). The period of his life in which Abraham lived with the promise unfulfilled, though the shortest, is the pivotal and central one and occupies the most space in the narrative.

21.9–21: The expulsion of Ishmael and Hagar. This passage closely parallels ch 16. Source criticism accounts for this by attributing ch 16 to J, but 21.9–21 to E. Note that the J-name ("LORD") never appears here; the E-name ("God") is used throughout. **9:** *Playing* is another pun on Isaac's name (cf. 17.17; 18.12; 19.14; 26.8). Ishmael was "Isaacing," or "taking Isaac's place." **10:** Sarah's omission of the names of the two individuals who have aroused her jealousy indicates the depth of her contempt. **12:** Yet it is Sarah's protection of Isaac's rights, rather than Abraham's solicitude for Ishmael, that mediates God's will in this tragic situation (cf. ch 27). In the Talmud, this is cited as evidence that Sarah was a prophet (*b. Meg.* 14a). God's command to Abraham to *do as she says* uses the same term with which He rebuked Adam for obeying Eve in 3.17—only with the opposite intent. **13:** Like 17.20 (and 21.18), this verse stresses that Isaac does not altogether displace Ishmael (whatever Sarah's designs). Ishmael inherits a substantial portion of the promise to his father Abraham. **14:** There is room to wonder just how far Abraham expected Hagar and Ishmael to travel before the bread and skin of water gave out. Did he not realize that by provisioning them so slimly, he was putting them in mortal danger? Ibn Ezra, surmising that Sarah must have determined the provisions, concludes that had Abraham done otherwise, he would have violated God's command. **15–16:** The narrator presupposes a child small enough to be carried by his mother. But since Ishmael was 13 before Isaac was even conceived (17.25), and Isaac's weaning, which likely occurred at 3, has already taken place (21.8), Ishmael is at least 16. In an analysis informed by source criticism, the problem is easily explained, since the present narrative stems from E, but the chronology from P. Calculating Ishmael's age as 27, a midrash takes a different tack: Sarah had cast the evil eye on him and made him ill, thus incapable of walking (*Gen. Rab.* 53.12).

21.22–34: Abimelech and Abraham make a pact. The focus shifts from the promise of offspring, on whose fulfillment the chapter has so far

23 Therefore swear to me here by God that you will not deal
falsely with me or with my kith and kin, but will deal with me
and with the land in which you have sojourned as loyally as I
have dealt with you." 24 And Abraham said, "I swear it."
25 Then Abraham reproached Abimelech for the well of water which the servants of Abimelech had seized. 26 But Abimelech said, "I do not know who did this; you did not tell me, nor
have I heard of it until today." 27 Abraham took sheep and oxen
and gave them to Abimelech, and the two of them made a pact.
28 Abraham then set seven ewes of the flock by themselves,
29 and Abimelech said to Abraham, "What mean these seven
ewes which you have set apart?" 30 He replied, "You are to accept these seven ewes from me as proof that I dug this well."
31 Hence that place was called Beer-sheba,[a] for there the two
of them swore an oath. 32 When they had concluded the pact
at Beer-sheba, Abimelech and Phicol, chief of his troops, departed and returned to the land of the Philistines. 33 [Abraham]
planted a tamarisk at Beer-sheba, and invoked there the name
of the LORD, the Everlasting God. 34 And Abraham resided in
the land of the Philistines a long time.

22 Some time afterward, God put Abraham to the test. He
said to him, "Abraham," and he answered, "Here I am."
2 And He said, "Take your son, your favored one, Isaac, whom
you love, and go to the land of Moriah, and offer him there as
a burnt offering on one of the heights that I will point out to
you." 3 So early next morning, Abraham saddled his ass and
took with him two of his servants and his son Isaac. He split
the wood for the burnt offering, and he set out for the place of
which God had told him. 4 On the third day Abraham looked
up and saw the place from afar. 5 Then Abraham said to his
servants, "You stay here with the ass. The boy and I will go up
there; we will worship and we will return to you."

a *I.e., "well of seven" or "well of oath."*

focused, to the promise of land, as Abraham acquires rights to wells he has dug. Abimelech appears here as another important figure who recognizes Abraham's special status and prospers as a result (cf. 14.18–20; 23.6–16). The passage has close affinities with 26.26–31.

22.1–19: Abraham's last and greatest test. This magnificently told story, known in Judaism as the "ʿAkedah" ("binding"), is one of the gems of biblical narrative. It also comes to occupy a central role in rabbinic theology and eventually to be incorporated into the daily liturgy. Jewish tradition regards the ʿAkedah as the tenth and climactic test of Abraham, the first Jew. **1:** There is no good English equivalent for the Heb "hineni," translated in this verse as *Here I am.* The term indicates readiness, alertness, attentiveness, receptivity, and responsiveness to instructions. It serves as a kind of refrain throughout the ʿAkedah. Abraham employs it in answer to God here, to Isaac in v. 7 (where it is rendered as "Yes"), and to the angel of the LORD in v. 11. **2:** The order of the Heb is "your son, your favored one, the one whom you love, Isaac" and indicates increasing tension. Not only is Isaac the son upon whom Abraham's life has centered; he also loves him. If Abraham did not love Isaac, the commandment to sacrifice him would not have constituted much of a test. The expression *go to* ("lekh-lekha"), which otherwise occurs only in 12.1, the initial command to Abraham, ties this narrative to the beginning of Abraham's dealings with God. *On one of the heights that I will point out to you* also parallels "to the land that I will show you" (12.1). The location of Moriah (here the name of a land, not a mountain) is unknown. The late biblical book of Chronicles calls the Temple Mount in Jerusalem "Moriah" (2 Chron. 3.1), probably on the understanding that the ʿAkedah is the foundation legend for the service of God that took place there. **3:** The verse resembles 21.14. The expulsion of Ishmael in the preceding chapter and the ʿAkedah have much in common, but the latter is the more wrenching, since Abraham is directly commanded to sacrifice his son, and the angelic intervention (vv. 11–12) is thus more surprising. Some have wondered why Abraham, who protested God's apparent decision to destroy the innocent with the guilty in Sodom (18.22–32), here obeys without objection. The essence of the answer is that the context in ch 18 is forensic, whereas the context of the ʿAkedah is sacrificial. A sacrifice is not an execution, and in a sacrificial context the unblemished condition of the one offered does not detract from, but rather commends, the act. **5:** Abraham may be concealing the truth from his servants (lest they prevent him from carrying out God's will), from Isaac (lest he flee), and from himself (lest the frank acknowledgement of his real intention cause his resolve to break). Alternately, he may be expressing his profound trust in God's promise, casting his faith and hope as a prediction.

6 Abraham took the wood for the burnt offering and put it
on his son Isaac. He himself took the firestone[a] and the knife;
and the two walked off together. 7 Then Isaac said to his father
Abraham, "Father!" And he answered, "Yes, my son." And he
said, "Here are the firestone and the wood; but where is the
sheep for the burnt offering?" 8 And Abraham said, "God will
see to the sheep for His burnt offering, my son." And the two of
them walked on together.

9 They arrived at the place of which God had told him. Abraham built an altar there; he laid out the wood; he bound his
son Isaac; he laid him on the altar, on top of the wood. 10 And
Abraham picked up the knife to slay his son. 11 Then an angel
of the LORD called to him from heaven: "Abraham! Abraham!"
And he answered, "Here I am." 12 And he said, "Do not raise
your hand against the boy, or do anything to him. For now
I know that you fear God, since you have not withheld your
son, your favored one, from Me." 13 When Abraham looked up,
his eye fell upon a[b] ram, caught in the thicket by its horns. So
Abraham went and took the ram and offered it up as a burnt
offering in place of his son. 14 And Abraham named that site
Adonai-yireh,[c] whence the present saying, "On the mount of
the LORD there is vision."[d]

15 The angel of the LORD called to Abraham a second time
from heaven, 16 and said, "By Myself I swear, the LORD declares: Because you have done this and have not withheld
your son, your favored one, 17 I will bestow My blessing upon
you and make your descendants as numerous as the stars of
heaven and the sands on the seashore; and your descendants
shall seize the gates of their foes. 18 All the nations of the earth
shall bless themselves by your descendants, because you have
obeyed My command." 19 Abraham then returned to his servants, and they departed together for Beer-sheba; and Abraham
stayed in Beer-sheba.

20 Some time later, Abraham was told, "Milcah too has borne
children to your brother Nahor: 21 Uz the first-born, and Buz
his brother, and Kemuel the father of Aram; 22 and Chesed,

a *Lit. "fire."*

b *Reading* 'eḥad *with many Heb. mss. and ancient versions; text* 'aḥar *"after."*

c *I.e., "the* LORD *will see"; cf. v. 8.*

d *Heb.* Behar Adonai yera'eh.

6: The image of Isaac's carrying the wood on which he is to be burned adds enormous power to the story. A midrash relates this to a Roman (not Jewish) method of execution that was sometimes used on Jewish martyrs: "It is like a person who carries his cross on his own shoulder" (*Gen. Rab.* 56.3). **7:** Our ignorance of Isaac's age makes it difficult to interpret his poignant question. Most rabbinic commentators see him as an adult and thus a willing participant in his own sacrifice—the prototype, that is, of the Jewish martyr. **8:** The same possibilities that we outlined for v. 5 apply here as well. The verse ends with the same Heb words with which v. 6 ends. Even after their exchange, father and son still have a single resolve: "the one to bind, and the other to be bound; the one to sacrifice, and the other to be sacrificed" (*Gen. Rab.* 56.3). **12:** In the Tanakh, the "fear of God" denotes an active obedience to the divine will. God is now able to call the last trial of Abraham off because Abraham has demonstrated that this obedience is uppermost for him, surpassing even his paternal love for Isaac. **13:** The substitution of a male sheep for the first-born son has parallels in the ancient Near East and foreshadows the story of the paschal lamb (Exod. 12.1–42). Contrary to a widespread misperception, however, the story is not about the superiority of animal to human sacrifice, nor is it a polemic against human sacrifice: God commands the sacrifice of Isaac at the beginning of the story (v. 2) and commends and rewards Abraham for being willing to carry it through at the end (vv. 12, 15–18). A midrash has Abraham praying that God "see the blood of this ram as if it were the blood of my son Isaac, the entrails of this ram as if they were the entrails of my son Isaac" (*Gen. Rab.* 56.9). **14:** The name of the otherwise unattested site plays on Abraham's words in v. 8. This enigmatic verse may connect the site of the 'Akedah to the Temple mount (see v. 2 n.). **15–18:** The second angelic address conveys the LORD's final blessing on Abraham, picking up the language of several earlier addresses (cf. 12.3; 13.16; 15.5). Only this time, the earlier promises are reinterpreted as a consequence of the 'Akedah. Much Jewish prayer calls upon God to remember the 'Akedah for the benefit of Abraham's descendants. **19:** Too much should not be made of the omission of Isaac. The story closes where it opened (v. 1): with the focus on Abraham alone.

22.20–24: The children of Nahor. Like Abraham's as yet unborn grandson, Jacob/Israel (35.22b–26), his *brother Nahor* becomes the

Hazo, Pildash, Jidlaph, and Bethuel"—23 Bethuel being the father of Rebekah. These eight Milcah bore to Nahor, Abraham's
brother. 24 And his concubine, whose name was Reumah, also
bore children: Tebah, Gaham, Tahash, and Maacah.

ḤAYYEI SARAH חיי שרה

23 Sarah's lifetime—the span of Sarah's life—came to
one hundred and twenty-seven years. 2 Sarah died in
Kiriath-arba—now Hebron—in the land of Canaan; and Abraham proceeded to mourn for Sarah and to bewail her. 3 Then
Abraham rose from beside his dead, and spoke to the Hittites,
saying, 4 "I am a resident alien among you; sell me a burial
site among you, that I may remove my dead for burial." 5 And
the Hittites replied to Abraham, saying to him, 6 "Hear us, my
lord: you are the elect of God among us. Bury your dead in the
choicest of our burial places; none of us will withhold his burial place from you for burying your dead." 7 Thereupon Abraham bowed low to the people of the land, the Hittites, 8 and
he said to them, "If it is your wish that I remove my dead for
burial, you must agree to intercede for me with Ephron son of
Zohar. 9 Let him sell me the cave of Machpelah that he owns,
which is at the edge of his land. Let him sell it to me, at the full
price, for a burial site in your midst."

10 Ephron was present among the Hittites; so Ephron the
Hittite answered Abraham in the hearing of the Hittites, all
who entered the gate of his town,[a] saying, 11 "No, my lord,
hear me: I give you the field and I give you the cave that is
in it; I give it to you in the presence of my people. Bury your
dead." 12 Then Abraham bowed low before the people of the
land, 13 and spoke to Ephron in the hearing of the people of
the land, saying, "If only you would hear me out! Let me pay
the price of the land; accept it from me, that I may bury my
dead there." 14 And Ephron replied to Abraham, saying to him,
15 "My lord, do hear me! A piece of land worth four hundred
shekels of silver—what is that between you and me? Go and
bury your dead." 16 Abraham accepted Ephron's terms. Abraham paid out to Ephron the money that he had named in the
hearing of the Hittites—four hundred shekels of silver at the
going merchants' rate.

a I.e., all his fellow townsmen.

patriarch of eight children by his primary wife and four by his secondary wife. Rebekah, who will marry Isaac and thus become the second matriarch of Israel, is the only person of her generation mentioned here (v. 23), suggesting that the promise of descendants reiterated and reinterpreted in v. 17 is already on its way to fulfillment. Note the near-identity of v. 17b with the blessing on Rebekah in 24.60.

23.1–20: Abraham acquires a burial ground. After the climactic episode of the ʿAkedah, all Abraham's actions are in the nature of putting his affairs in order. In ch 23, he acquires a burial plot for Sarah. In the next chapter, he arranges for a wife for Isaac, and in ch 25, he decrees the distribution of his assets and passes away. **2:** *Hebron,* in the hill country of Judah, 20 miles south-southwest of Jerusalem, was also the first seat of David's kingship (2 Sam. 2.1–4; 5.1–5). Its principal claim upon the Jewish imagination over the centuries is owing to the biblical reports that not only Sarah but also Abraham, Isaac and Rebekah, and Jacob and Leah are buried there (Gen. 23.19; 35.27; 49.29–32; 50.13). **3:** The *Hittites* mentioned here have no connection to the Indo-European peoples with that name who ruled a mighty empire based in what is now eastern Turkey in the second millennium BCE. Rather, they are one of the Canaanite nations (cf. 10.15; 15.20). **4–6:** The tension in the story lies in Abraham's contradictory status. On the one hand, he is but a *resident alien* without hereditary land-rights or a secure place in the social and legal order. On the other, he is *the elect of God* (v. 6), to whom the whole land has been promised. A text in Leviticus describes the entire people Israel as resident aliens, living on land owned by God (Lev. 25.23), and the same terms are used to describe the transience of human life and the unworthiness of human beings in the face of God's bounty (1 Chron. 29.15). **7–8:** As a "resident alien," Abraham probably needed the approval of *the people of the land* (a local council) before he could approach a landowner. **10–16:** It would not behoove Abraham, as "the elect of God" (v. 5) and a man of exemplary generosity and hospitality (13.8–9; 18.1–8), to accept a gift (cf. 14.23–24). It is hard to know what the field and its cave were worth on the market. Compared to the 17 shekels that Jeremiah pays to redeem ancestral land (Jer. 32.9), the price of 400 shekels that Abraham paid (v. 16) is probably exorbitant, and thus Ephron's statement in v. 15 seems disingenuous.

17 So Ephron's land in Machpelah, near Mamre—the field with its cave and all the trees anywhere within the confines of that field—passed 18 to Abraham as his possession, in the presence of the Hittites, of all who entered the gate of his town.[a] 19 And then Abraham buried his wife Sarah in the cave of the field of Machpelah, facing Mamre—now Hebron—in the land of Canaan. 20 Thus the field with its cave passed from the Hittites to Abraham, as a burial site.

24 Abraham was now old, advanced in years, and the LORD had blessed Abraham in all things. 2 And Abraham said to the senior servant of his household, who had charge of all that he owned, "Put your hand under my thigh 3 and I will make you swear by the LORD, the God of heaven and the God of the earth, that you will not take a wife for my son from the daughters of the Canaanites among whom I dwell, 4 but will go to the land of my birth and get a wife for my son Isaac." 5 And the servant said to him, "What if the woman does not consent to follow me to this land, shall I then take your son back to the land from which you came?" 6 Abraham answered him, "On no account must you take my son back there! 7 The LORD, the God of heaven, who took me from my father's house and from my native land, who promised me on oath, saying, 'I will assign this land to your offspring'—He will send His angel before you, and you will get a wife for my son from there. 8 And if the woman does not consent to follow you, you shall then be clear of this oath to me; but do not take my son back there." 9 So the servant put his hand under the thigh of his master Abraham and swore to him as bidden.[b]

10 Then the servant took ten of his master's camels and set out, taking with him all the bounty of his master; and he made his way to Aram-naharaim, to the city of Nahor. 11 He made the camels kneel down by the well outside the city, at evening time, the time when women come out to draw water. 12 And he said, "O LORD, God of my master Abraham, grant me good fortune this day, and deal graciously with my master Abraham: 13 Here I stand by the spring as the daughters of the townsmen come out to draw water; 14 let the maiden to whom I say, 'Please, lower your jar that I may drink,' and who replies, 'Drink, and I will also water your camels'—let her be the one whom You have decreed for Your servant Isaac. Thereby shall I know that You have dealt graciously with my master."

15 He had scarcely finished speaking, when Rebekah, who was born to Bethuel, the son of Milcah the wife of Abraham's brother Nahor, came out with her jar on her shoulder. 16 The maiden was very beautiful, a virgin whom no man had known.

24.1–67: Abraham procures a proper wife for Isaac. This sophisticated and beautifully wrought narrative constitutes the longest chapter in Genesis. In certain important ways, it functions as Abraham's deathbed scene, recapitulating the promise that impelled him on his course and foreshadowing events in the life of his grandson Jacob/Israel, eponymous ancestor of the Jewish people. **2:** The rabbinic tradition assumes that Abraham's *senior servant* is Eliezer, but the latter is never termed a "servant" (15.2–4), and precise identification of the man, unnamed throughout the story, is unnecessary. *Thigh* seems to be a euphemism for the male organ (cf. 46.26; Exod. 1.5). Perhaps by touching it, the person swearing the oath calls sterility or loss of children upon himself, should he violate it. The parallel in Gen. 47.29 suggests that ch 24 once functioned as Abraham's last request. **3:** Intermarriage with the Canaanites, a lethal threat to Abraham's identity and destiny, is strictly forbidden in Deut. 7.1–4. The prohibition is extended to intermarriage with other groups in Ezra chs 9–10. **4:** The phrasing rather precisely recalls God's original commandment to Abraham in 12.1 (cf. 24.7, 38, 40). Similarly, Rebekah's consent ("I will [go]," v. 58) recalls God's first word to Abraham in that same verse, "Go." Rebekah thus becomes a kind of Abraham figure in her own right. Abraham's dispatch of his senior servant back to his native land and his kinfolk brings his story full circle and ensures his legacy will continue in the next generation. **14:** Rashi points out the aptness of the sign that the servant requests: The woman appropriate to marry into Abraham's household must practice the extraordinary kindness and generosity characteristic of her future father-in-law.

a *I.e., all his fellow townsmen.* b *Lit. "about this matter."*

20: Rebekah's running to serve the visitor (who has not yet introduced himself) recalls Abraham's response to the visit of the unidentified men in 18.6–7. **30:** Laban's instantaneous notice of the jewelry suggests the materialism and stinginess that he will display in dealing with his own son-in-law, Jacob (29.27; 31.14–16, 33–43), and contrasts with his sister's innate generosity.

She went down to the spring, filled her jar, and came up. [17] The
servant ran toward her and said, "Please, let me sip a little water from your jar." [18] "Drink, my lord," she said, and she quickly
lowered her jar upon her hand and let him drink. [19] When she
had let him drink his fill, she said, "I will also draw for your
camels, until they finish drinking." [20] Quickly emptying her jar
into the trough, she ran back to the well to draw, and she drew
for all his camels.

[21] The man, meanwhile, stood gazing at her, silently wondering whether the LORD had made his errand successful
or not. [22] When the camels had finished drinking, the man
took a gold nose-ring weighing a half-shekel,[a] and two gold
bands for her arms, ten shekels in weight. [23] "Pray tell me," he
said, "whose daughter are you? Is there room in your father's
house for us to spend the night?" [24] She replied, "I am the
daughter of Bethuel the son of Milcah, whom she bore to Nahor." [25] And she went on, "There is plenty of straw[b] and feed at
home, and also room to spend the night." [26] The man bowed
low in homage to the LORD [27] and said, "Blessed be the LORD,
the God of my master Abraham, who has not withheld His
steadfast faithfulness from my master. For I have been guided on my errand by the LORD, to the house of my master's
kinsmen."

[28] The maiden ran and told all this to her mother's household. [29] Now Rebekah had a brother whose name was Laban.
Laban ran out to the man at the spring—[30] when he saw the
nose-ring and the bands on his sister's arms, and when he
heard his sister Rebekah say, "Thus the man spoke to me." He
went up to the man, who was still standing beside the camels at the spring. [31] "Come in, O blessed of the LORD," he said,
"why do you remain outside, when I have made ready the
house and a place for the camels?" [32] So the man entered the
house, and the camels were unloaded. The camels were given
straw and feed, and water was brought to bathe his feet and
the feet of the men with him. [33] But when food was set before
him, he said, "I will not eat until I have told my tale." He said,
"Speak, then."

[34] "I am Abraham's servant," he began. [35] "The LORD has
greatly blessed my master, and he has become rich: He has
given him sheep and cattle, silver and gold, male and female
slaves, camels and asses. [36] And Sarah, my master's wife, bore
my master a son in her old age, and he has assigned to him
everything he owns. [37] Now my master made me swear, saying, 'You shall not get a wife for my son from the daughters
of the Canaanites in whose land I dwell; [38] but you shall go to

a Heb. beqa'.

b Heb. teben, *shredded straw, which in the East is mixed with feed; cf. v. 32.*

my father's house, to my kindred, and get a wife for my son.' [39] And I said to my master, 'What if the woman does not follow me?' [40] He replied to me, 'The LORD, whose ways I have followed, will send His angel with you and make your errand successful; and you will get a wife for my son from my kindred, from my father's house. [41] Thus only shall you be freed from my adjuration: if, when you come to my kindred, they refuse you—only then shall you be freed from my adjuration.'

[42] "I came today to the spring, and I said: O LORD, God of my master Abraham, if You would indeed grant success to the errand on which I am engaged! [43] As I stand by the spring of water, let the young woman who comes out to draw and to whom I say, 'Please, let me drink a little water from your jar,' [44] and who answers, 'You may drink, and I will also draw for your camels'—let her be the wife whom the LORD has decreed for my master's son.' [45] I had scarcely finished praying in my heart, when Rebekah came out with her jar on her shoulder, and went down to the spring and drew. And I said to her, 'Please give me a drink.' [46] She quickly lowered her jar and said, 'Drink, and I will also water your camels.' So I drank, and she also watered the camels. [47] I inquired of her, 'Whose daughter are you?' And she said, 'The daughter of Bethuel, son of Nahor, whom Milcah bore to him.' And I put the ring on her nose and the bands on her arms. [48] Then I bowed low in homage to the LORD and blessed the LORD, the God of my master Abraham, who led me on the right way to get the daughter of my master's brother for his son. [49] And now, if you mean to treat my master with true kindness, tell me; and if not, tell me also, that I may turn right or left."

[50] Then Laban and Bethuel answered, "The matter was decreed by the LORD; we cannot speak to you bad or good. [51] Here is Rebekah before you; take her and go, and let her be a wife to your master's son, as the LORD has spoken." [52] When Abraham's servant heard their words, he bowed low to the ground before the LORD. [53] The servant brought out objects of silver and gold, and garments, and gave them to Rebekah; and he gave presents to her brother and her mother. [54] Then he and the men with him ate and drank, and they spent the night. When they arose next morning, he said, "Give me leave to go to my master." [55] But her brother and her mother said, "Let the maiden remain with us [a-]some ten days;[-a] then you may go." [56] He said to them, "Do not delay me, now that the LORD has made my errand successful. Give me leave that I may go to my master." [57] And they said, "Let us call the girl and ask for her reply." [58] They called Rebekah and said to her, "Will you go with this man?" And she said, "I will." [59] So they sent off their sister

47: The servant reverses the order of events given in vv. 22–23 to give Rebekah's family the impression that it was her pedigree rather than her character that most commended her. **50:** The appearance of *Bethuel* here is very strange, since everywhere else in the chapter it is his son, *Laban*, sometimes together with the girl's mother, who conducts the negotiations (vv. 28–29, 53, 55, 59). Rabbi David Kimḥi (Radak), the great 13th-century Provençal scholar, suggests that Bethuel was aged and the management of the household had fallen upon Laban.

a-a Lit. "days or ten."

Rebekah and her nurse along with Abraham's servant and his
men. [60] And they blessed Rebekah and said to her,

"O sister!
May you grow
Into thousands of myriads;
May your offspring seize
The gates of their foes."

[61] Then Rebekah and her maids arose, mounted the camels,
and followed the man. So the servant took Rebekah and went
his way.

[62] Isaac had just come back from the vicinity of Beer-lahai-
roi, for he was settled in the region of the Negeb. [63] And Isaac
went out walking[a] in the field toward evening and, looking up,
he saw camels approaching. [64] Raising her eyes, Rebekah saw
Isaac. She alighted from the camel [65] and said to the servant,
"Who is that man walking in the field toward us?" And the
servant said, "That is my master." So she took her veil and covered herself. [66] The servant told Isaac all the things that he had
done. [67] Isaac then brought her into the tent of his mother Sarah, and he took Rebekah as his wife. Isaac loved her, and thus
found comfort after his mother's death.

25 Abraham took another wife, whose name was Keturah.
[2] She bore him Zimran, Jokshan, Medan, Midian,
Ishbak, and Shuah. [3] Jokshan begot Sheba and Dedan. The
descendants of Dedan were the Asshurim, the Letushim,
and the Leummim. [4] The descendants of Midian were Ephah,
Epher, Enoch,[b] Abida, and Eldaah. All these were descendants
of Keturah. [5] Abraham willed all that he owned to Isaac; [6] but
to Abraham's sons by concubines Abraham gave gifts while
he was still living, and he sent them away from his son Isaac
eastward, to the land of the East.

[7] This was the total span of Abraham's life: one hundred and
seventy-five years. [8] And Abraham breathed his last, dying at
a good ripe age, old and contented; and he was gathered to
his kin. [9] His sons Isaac and Ishmael buried him in the cave
of Machpelah, in the field of Ephron son of Zohar the Hittite,
facing Mamre, [10] the field that Abraham had bought from the
Hittites; there Abraham was buried, and Sarah his wife. [11] After
the death of Abraham, God blessed his son Isaac. And Isaac
settled near Beer-lahai-roi.

[12] This is the line of Ishmael, Abraham's son, whom Hagar the
Egyptian, Sarah's slave, bore to Abraham. [13] These are the names
of the sons of Ishmael, by their names, in the order of their birth:
Nebaioth, the first-born of Ishmael, Kedar, Adbeel, Mibsam,
[14] Mishma, Dumah, Massa, [15] Hadad, Tema, Jetur, Naphish,

a Others "to meditate"; meaning of Heb. uncertain. *b Or "Hanoch."*

60: The near-identity of the last two lines with the latter words of the angel after the ʿAkedah (end of 22.17) reinforces the appropriateness of Rebekah for Abraham's son and the providential nature of the match. **65:** Everywhere else in the chapter, *my master* refers to Abraham, and Isaac has been called "his/my master's son." Perhaps Abraham has died while his steward was on his sacred mission. If so, the events narrated in 25.1–18 had happened beforehand.

25.1–18: Abraham's death and descendants. Abraham's descendants are here mentioned in the reverse order of their ancestors' births: first the many descendants of Keturah, then Isaac, and, lastly, the line of Ishmael, Abraham's first-born son. This puts Isaac in the central position, and it is he alone who inherits his father's estate, Abraham having honorably discharged his obligations to his other sons through gifts (vv. 5–6). **1:** Nothing more is known about the mysterious Keturah, whose name is related to the word for incense ("ketoret"), and whose children reflect names related to the Arabian peninsula, a main source of aromatics in antiquity. A midrash identifies her with Hagar and explains the name on the grounds that Hagar was "perfumed ('mekuteret') with commandments and good deeds" (*Gen. Rab.* 61.4). **6:** It is possible that *by concubines* is better translated "by concubinage" and thus refers only to the sons of Keturah listed in v. 2. Rabbi Samuel ben Meir (Rashbam, northern France, 12th century) thinks the *concubines* are Hagar and Keturah. **7:** If Abraham was 100 when Isaac was born (21.5), Isaac 60 when Esau and Jacob were born (25.26), and Abraham died at 175 (25.7), then Abraham passed away only when his twin grandsons were 15. This suggests that the notice of Abraham's death is premature here. Source critics resolve the problem by attributing the chronology to P, but the bulk of the ancestral narrative to J. See 11.31–32 n.

and Kedmah. 16 These are the sons of Ishmael and these are
their names by their villages and by their encampments: twelve
chieftains of as many tribes.—17 These were the years of the
life of Ishmael: one hundred and thirty-seven years; then he
breathed his last and died, and was gathered to his kin.—18 They
dwelt from Havilah, by Shur, which is close to Egypt, all the way
to Asshur; they camped alongside all their kinsmen.

TOLEDOT תולדות

19 This is the story of Isaac, son of Abraham. Abraham begot
Isaac. 20 Isaac was forty years old when he took to wife Rebekah,
daughter of Bethuel the Aramean of Paddan-aram, sister of Laban the Aramean. 21 Isaac pleaded with the LORD on behalf of
his wife, because she was barren; and the LORD responded to
his plea, and his wife Rebekah conceived. 22 But the children
struggled in her womb, and she said, "If so, why do I exist?"[a]
She went to inquire of the LORD, 23 and the LORD answered her,

"Two nations are in your womb,
Two separate peoples shall issue from your body;
One people shall be mightier than the other,
And the older shall serve the younger."

24 When her time to give birth was at hand, there were twins in
her womb. 25 The first one emerged red, like a hairy mantle all
over; so they named him Esau.[b] 26 Then his brother emerged,
holding on to the heel of Esau; so they named him Jacob.[c] Isaac
was sixty years old when they were born.

27 When the boys grew up, Esau became a skillful hunter, a
man of the outdoors; but Jacob was a mild man who stayed in
camp. 28 Isaac favored Esau because [d-]he had a taste for game;[-d]
but Rebekah favored Jacob. 29 Once when Jacob was cooking a
stew, Esau came in from the open, famished. 30 And Esau said
to Jacob, "Give me some of that red stuff to gulp down, for I am
famished"—which is why he was named Edom.[e] 31 Jacob said,
"First sell me your birthright." 32 And Esau said, "I am at the
point of death, so of what use is my birthright to me?" 33 But
Jacob said, "Swear to me first." So he swore to him, and sold
his birthright to Jacob. 34 Jacob then gave Esau bread and lentil
stew; he ate and drank, and he rose and went away. Thus did
Esau spurn the birthright.

26 There was a famine in the land—aside from the previous famine that had occurred in the days of Abraham—
and Isaac went to Abimelech, king of the Philistines, in Gerar.
2 The LORD had appeared to him and said, "Do not go down to

a *Meaning of Heb. uncertain.* b *Synonym of "Seir," play on Heb.* seʿar *"hair."* c *Play on Heb.* ʿaqeb *"heel."* d-d *Lit. "game was in his mouth."* e *Play on Heb.* ʾadom *"red."*

25.19–34: Birth and birthright. This passage tells of the birth of Esau and Jacob, and of the former's ominous sale of his status as first-born to the latter. **21:** Rebekah's barrenness puts her again in line of succession to her late mother-in-law, Sarah (cf. 24.67), though the narrative about Rebekah is much more compressed and much less complex than the corresponding story of Sarai/Sarah (cf. ch 16). The "barren mother" is a common motif in special birth stories. Compare also Rachel (Gen. ch 30) and Hannah (1 Sam. ch 1). A midrash sees in God's response to Isaac's plea an object lesson in the power of prayer to move God from anger to mercy (*b. Yebam.* 64a). **25:** In addition to the pun on "Seir" and "seʿar" ("hair"), there is also a play on *red* ("ʾadmoni") and "Edom," another name for Esau and the kingdom descended from him. (See translators' note *b* and 36.9.) **26:** *Jacob*'s naming (as usual in the Tanakh) is based on a folk etymology. "Jacob" probably derives from "y-ʿ-k-b-ʾ-l," "may God protect." **27:** To the ancient Israelite, Esau's hunting, like his hairiness, suggested uncouthness and even a certain degree of danger. The uncouthness is also apparent in his blunt speech and impulsive behavior in the ensuing tale (vv. 30–34). **28:** Once again, the mother mediates God's preference (cf. 21.9–13; Mal. 1.2–5). The father seems blind to the higher purpose (cf. Gen. 27.1–45). God's favoring the younger son is already familiar from the story of Cain and Abel (4.4–5) and, in a different way, Ishmael and Isaac (21.12), and will be a prominent feature of the story of Joseph (37.3).

26.1–33: Episodes in the life of Isaac. In comparison with the two larger-than-life figures who are his father (Abraham) and his son (Jacob), there is remarkably little narrative about Isaac. Indeed, he generally appears passive and, in places, even comic (e.g., 26.8–9; 27.18–23). Gen. 26.1–33 is the only collection of biblical narrative centrally devoted to the middle patriarch. **1–5:** Here,

Egypt; stay in the land which I point out to you. [3] Reside in this land, and I will be with you and bless you; I will assign all these lands to you and to your heirs, fulfilling the oath that I swore to your father Abraham. [4] I will make your heirs as numerous as the stars of heaven, and assign to your heirs all these lands, so that all the nations of the earth shall bless themselves by your heirs—[5] inasmuch as Abraham obeyed Me and kept My charge: My commandments, My laws, and My teachings."

[6] So Isaac stayed in Gerar. [7] When the men of the place asked him about his wife, he said, "She is my sister," for he was afraid to say "my wife," thinking, "The men of the place might kill me on account of Rebekah, for she is beautiful." [8] When some time had passed, Abimelech king of the Philistines, looking out of the window, saw Isaac fondling his wife Rebekah. [9] Abimelech sent for Isaac and said, "So she is your wife! Why then did you say: 'She is my sister?' " Isaac said to him, "Because I thought I might lose my life on account of her." [10] Abimelech said, "What have you done to us! One of the people might have lain with your wife, and you would have brought guilt upon us." [11] Abimelech then charged all the people, saying, "Anyone who molests this man or his wife shall be put to death."

[12] Isaac sowed in that land and reaped a hundredfold the same year. The LORD blessed him, [13] and the man grew richer and richer until he was very wealthy: [14] he acquired flocks and herds, and a large household, so that the Philistines envied him. [15] And the Philistines stopped up all the wells which his father's servants had dug in the days of his father Abraham, filling them with earth. [16] And Abimelech said to Isaac, "Go away from us, for you have become far too big for us."

[17] So Isaac departed from there and encamped in the wadi of Gerar, where he settled. [18] Isaac dug anew the wells which had been dug in the days of his father Abraham and which the Philistines had stopped up after Abraham's death; and he gave them the same names that his father had given them. [19] But when Isaac's servants, digging in the wadi, found there a well of spring water, [20] the herdsmen of Gerar quarreled with Isaac's herdsmen, saying, "The water is ours." He named that well Esek,[a] because they contended with him. [21] And when they dug another well, they disputed over that one also; so he named it Sitnah.[b] [22] He moved from there and dug yet another well, and they did not quarrel over it; so he called it Rehoboth, saying, "Now at last the LORD has granted us ample space[c] to increase in the land."

[23] From there he went up to Beer-sheba. [24] That night the LORD appeared to him and said, "I am the God of your father

a *I.e., "contention."* b *I.e., "harassment."*
c Heb. hirḥib, *connected with "Rehoboth."*

the LORD affirms the continuity of Isaac with his father, whose experience he in part relives (vv. 1–2; cf. 12.10; 20.1–18). Isaac will fall heir to the Abrahamic promise of offspring, blessing, and land (vv. 3–5; cf. 12.1–3, 7; 15.5). V. 5 may be a reference to the ʿAkedah (cf. 22.15–18), the only explicit one in the Tanakh outside of ch 22. In Judaism, Abraham is generally thought to have exemplified not only faith in God and love for Him but also meticulous obedience to His commands. Traditional commentators differ, however, on the extent of the *charge, commandments, laws,* and *teachings* that Abraham had observed, to his son's benefit (v. 5). Rashi, following strong rabbinic precedents (e.g., *b. Yoma* 28b), thinks that Abraham observed all categories of Jewish law, even the Oral Torah. His grandson, Rashbam, more dedicated to the plain sense, thinks that Abraham observed only those commandments that had been communicated to him in Genesis or that human reason can intuit without revelation. **6–11:** This is the last of the three stories of a patriarch's attempting unsuccessfully to pass his wife off as his sister (cf. 12.10–20; 20.1–18), and the only one in which the matriarch is never brought into the foreign king's quarters. A note of comedy relieves its blandness in comparison with the other two when Abimelech sees *Isaac* ("yitzḥaq") *"fondling"* ("met-zaḥeq") *Rebekah* and draws the all too obvious conclusion (vv. 8–9). Is Isaac here over-confident, careless, or foolish? **12–33:** The image of Isaac as a landholder and farmer (v. 12) is in tension with the picture of him as a seminomad (cf. v. 17). His acquisition of vast wealth (vv. 13–14) underscores the continuity with his father (cf. 12.5, 16; 13.2), just as the ensuing conflict with the Philistines (vv. 15–22) recalls the prologue to the separation of Abraham and Lot (13.5–7). Most historians consider the reference to Philistines here (and in v. 1) anachronistic, since the Philistines did not arrive in Canaan until about 1200 BCE. The dispute about the wells and the covenant-making ceremony

Abraham. Fear not, for I am with you, and I will bless you and
increase your offspring for the sake of My servant Abraham."
25 So he built an altar there and invoked the LORD by name.
Isaac pitched his tent there and his servants started digging a
well. 26 And Abimelech came to him from Gerar, with Ahuz-
zath his councilor and Phicol chief of his troops. 27 Isaac said to
them, "Why have you come to me, seeing that you have been
hostile to me and have driven me away from you?" 28 And they
said, "We now see plainly that the LORD has been with you,
and we thought: Let there be a sworn treaty between our two
parties, between you and us. Let us make a pact with you 29 that
you will not do us harm, just as we have not molested you but
have always dealt kindly with you and sent you away in peace.
From now on, be you blessed of the LORD!" 30 Then he made for
them a feast, and they ate and drank.

31 Early in the morning, they exchanged oaths. Isaac then
bade them farewell, and they departed from him in peace.
32 That same day Isaac's servants came and told him about the
well they had dug, and said to him, "We have found water!"
33 He named it Shibah;[a] therefore the name of the city is Beer-
sheba to this day.

34 When Esau was forty years old, he took to wife Judith
daughter of Beeri the Hittite, and Basemath daughter of Elon
the Hittite; 35 and they were a source of bitterness to Isaac and
Rebekah.

27 When Isaac was old and his eyes were too dim to see,
he called his older son Esau and said to him, "My son."
He answered, "Here I am." 2 And he said, "I am old now, and I
do not know how soon I may die. 3 Take your gear, your quiver
and bow, and go out into the open and hunt me some game.
4 Then prepare a dish for me such as I like, and bring it to me to
eat, so that I may give you my innermost blessing before I die."

5 Rebekah had been listening as Isaac spoke to his son Esau.
When Esau had gone out into the open to hunt game to bring
home, 6 Rebekah said to her son Jacob, "I overheard your father speaking to your brother Esau, saying, 7 'Bring me some
game and prepare a dish for me to eat, that I may bless you,
with the LORD's approval, before I die.' 8 Now, my son, listen

a As though "oath."

that resolves it (vv. 17–33) are highly reminiscent of King Abimelech's previous dealing with Isaac's father in 21.22–32. Incidentally, nothing in this episode, or in the rest of the chapter, gives any indication that the couple's twins have already been born (25.21–26), and one can imagine that the episode once stood elsewhere.

26.34–35: Esau intermarries. Source critics attribute these verses to P and see them as the prologue to 27.46–28.9, the Priestly explanation for Jacob's flight to his uncle's homestead. In the genealogical notice in 36.2–4, Elon's daughter is not Basemath but Adah; Basemath is the daughter of Ishmael, not Elon; and Judith is absent altogether. Esau's intermarriages to specifically Canaanite women are a jarring contrast to Abraham's strenuous effort to find a wife for Isaac from within the clan (ch 24) and demonstrate Esau's unworthiness to serve as the next figure in the patriarchal line.

27.1–45: Jacob acquires Esau's blessing. This story, one of the masterpieces of biblical narrative artistry, exhibits both charming comedy and intense pathos. Jacob, having purchased his brother's status of first-born in a questionable fashion (25.29–34), acquires his paternal blessing as well. He does so in a way that advances the divine plan but also utilizes deceit and thus brings hardship on all involved. **1–4:** Gen. 25.28 has already established Isaac's preference for Esau, who, as the first-born son (27.19), should receive his father's prime blessing anyway. Isaac's instruction to *hunt* him *some game* recalls the rather shallow reason for his favoring the uncouth Esau. There may also be a notion here that eating will fortify his innermost self, that is, his life-force ("nefesh," v. 4) so that he may impart a more powerful blessing to his son. Since Isaac is blind, this chapter emphasizes his other senses. He identifies "Esau" by touching his hands, tasting him through a kiss, and smelling his clothing. His sense of hearing tells him that something may be amiss. Esau's response to his aged father's summons, *Here I am* (v. 1), recalls the refrain of the ʿAkedah (22.1, 7, 11), another but very different story of a loving father and the near-loss of his beloved son. **5–13:** Once again, it is the mother who arranges the fulfillment of the divine plan, to the benefit of the second-born son, and in a manner that is morally offensive

carefully as I instruct you. 9 Go to the flock and fetch me two choice kids, and I will make of them a dish for your father, such as he likes. 10 Then take it to your father to eat, in order that he may bless you before he dies." 11 Jacob answered his mother Rebekah, "But my brother Esau is a hairy man and I am smooth-skinned. 12 If my father touches me, I shall appear to him as a trickster and bring upon myself a curse, not a blessing." 13 But his mother said to him, "Your curse, my son, be upon me! Just do as I say and go fetch them for me."

14 He got them and brought them to his mother, and his mother prepared a dish such as his father liked. 15 Rebekah then took the best clothes of her older son Esau, which were there in the house, and had her younger son Jacob put them on; 16 and she covered his hands and the hairless part of his neck with the skins of the kids. 17 Then she put in the hands of her son Jacob the dish and the bread that she had prepared.

18 He went to his father and said, "Father." And he said, "Yes, which of my sons are you?" 19 Jacob said to his father, "I am Esau, your first-born; I have done as you told me. Pray sit up and eat of my game, that you may give me your innermost blessing." 20 Isaac said to his son, "How did you succeed so quickly, my son?" And he said, "Because the LORD your God granted me good fortune." 21 Isaac said to Jacob, "Come closer that I may feel you, my son—whether you are really my son Esau or not." 22 So Jacob drew close to his father Isaac, who felt him and wondered. "The voice is the voice of Jacob, yet the hands are the hands of Esau." 23 He did not recognize him, because his hands were hairy like those of his brother Esau; and so he blessed him.

24 He asked, "Are you really my son Esau?" And when he said, "I am," 25 he said, "Serve me and let me eat of my son's game that I may give you my innermost blessing." So he served him and he ate, and he brought him wine and he drank. 26 Then his father Isaac said to him, "Come close and kiss me, my son"; 27 and he went up and kissed him. And he smelled his clothes and he blessed him, saying, "Ah, the smell of my son is like the smell of the fields that the LORD has blessed.

28 "May God give you
Of the dew of heaven and the fat of the earth,
Abundance of new grain and wine.
29 Let peoples serve you,
And nations bow to you;
Be master over your brothers,
And let your mother's sons bow to you.
Cursed be they who curse you,
Blessed they who bless you."

30 No sooner had Jacob left the presence of his father Isaac—after Isaac had finished blessing Jacob—than his brother Esau came back from his hunt. 31 He too prepared a dish and brought

to a high degree (cf. 21.9–13). It is curious, however, that in seeking to allay her favored son's worry (vv. 11–13), Rebekah never mentions the prenatal oracle that announced the LORD's preference for the younger twin (25.23). Rashbam thinks it was trust in that oracle that enabled her to discount the curse Jacob fears. But note that the Tanakh gives no indication that Jacob ever saw his mother alive again after this disquieting episode. **18–27:** The passage is full of suspense and high drama, as Isaac uses his senses of touch, hearing, taste, and smell to ascertain that it is Esau rather than an impersonator who is serving him the tasty game. There is probably also a note of broad humor in vv. 22–23. Should not a blind man have put more trust in his hearing than in his touch, and just how hairy was Esau that the skin of a goat could be mistaken for his hands? Jacob's answer in v. 20 beautifully encapsulates the dual causation that drives this narrative. On the one hand, he is lying to his father. On the other, he is expressing, perhaps unwittingly, the fact that it is God's preference, not his father's, that has arranged his unlikely success. **29:** Jacob's mastery over his brothers (the plural need not be taken literally) may be connected to the subjection of the Edomites (On Esau = Edom see 25.25 n.) beginning, according to the Bible, with King David (2 Sam. 8.13–14). Note also the Abrahamic resonance of the end of the verse (cf. Gen. 12.3).

it to his father. And he said to his father, "Let my father sit up
and eat of his son's game, so that you may give me your innermost blessing." 32 His father Isaac said to him, "Who are you?"
And he said, "I am your son, Esau, your first-born!" 33 Isaac was
seized with very violent trembling. "Who was it then," he demanded, "that hunted game and brought it to me? Moreover,
I ate of it before you came, and I blessed him; now he must remain blessed!" 34 When Esau heard his father's words, he burst
into wild and bitter sobbing, and said to his father, "Bless me
too, Father!" 35 But he answered, "Your brother came with guile
and took away your blessing." 36 [Esau] said, "Was he, then,
named Jacob that he might supplant me[a] these two times?
First he took away my birthright and now he has taken away
my blessing!" And he added, "Have you not reserved a blessing
for me?" 37 Isaac answered, saying to Esau, "But I have made
him master over you: I have given him all his brothers for servants, and sustained him with grain and wine. What, then, can
I still do for you, my son?" 38 And Esau said to his father, "Have
you but one blessing, Father? Bless me too, Father!" And Esau
wept aloud. 39 And his father Isaac answered, saying to him,

"See, your abode shall [b-]enjoy the fat of the earth
And[-b] the dew of heaven above.
40 Yet by your sword you shall live,
And you shall serve your brother;
But when you grow restive,
You shall break his yoke from your neck."

41 Now Esau harbored a grudge against Jacob because of the
blessing which his father had given him, and Esau said to himself, "Let but the mourning period of my father come, and I will
kill my brother Jacob." 42 When the words of her older son Esau
were reported to Rebekah, she sent for her younger son Jacob
and said to him, "Your brother Esau is consoling himself by
planning to kill you. 43 Now, my son, listen to me. Flee at once
to Haran, to my brother Laban. 44 Stay with him a while, until your brother's fury subsides—45 until your brother's anger
against you subsides—and he forgets what you have done to
him. Then I will fetch you from there. Let me not lose you both
in one day!"

46 Rebekah said to Isaac, "I am disgusted with my life because of the Hittite women. If Jacob marries a Hittite woman
28 like these, from among the native women, what good
will life be to me?" 1 So Isaac sent for Jacob and blessed
him. He instructed him, saying, "You shall not take a wife from
among the Canaanite women. 2 Up, go to Paddan-aram, to the
house of Bethuel, your mother's father, and take a wife there

a *Heb.* ʿaqab, *connected with "Jacob."*
b-b *Others "be away from the fat of the earth and from."*

34–35: The pathos is palpable, and the sympathy for Esau is in marked contrast to exilic and postexilic literature in which Esau/Edom epitomizes evil and betrayal (e.g., Ps. 137.7; Jer. 49.7–22; Obadiah; Isa. 34.5; 63.1–6). In rabbinic and medieval Jewish literature, Esau becomes a cipher for the Roman empire and then Christendom, and the highly pejorative portrayal of him there reflects the painful experience of the Jews at the hands of those powers. **36:** *Birthright* ("bekhora") and *blessing* ("berakha") have the same three consonants. Though continuing to believe passionately in the chosenness of Jacob/Israel, the prophet Jeremiah sees in Jacob's deceit a paradigm of the chosen people at their worst, and just cause for God's impending punishment (Jer. 9.3–8). **37:** The reversal of the order of fertility and domination of vv. 28–29 reflects the reversal of Esau's expectations. **39–40:** Like Ishmael (17.20; 21.13, 18), Esau receives a blessing that is formidable but inferior to his younger brother's. The prophecy of Esau's breaking free from subjugation to Jacob may be connected to Edom's successful rebellions in the 9th or 8th centuries (2 Kings 8.20–22; 2 Chron. 28.17). **41–45:** Esau's murderous grudge (v. 41) recalls the incident of Cain and Abel (4.3–8); less directly, Rebekah's intervention foreshadows tragic events in the life of David (2 Sam. 14.1–24, esp. vv. 4–7).

27.46–28.9: Isaac blesses Jacob (again) and Jacob departs. Most source-critical analysts view this passage as the continuation of 26.34–35 and thus see in it the P version of Isaac's blessing of Jacob and the latter's flight to his uncle Laban (27.1–45 is attributed to J). In this version, Jacob does not flee for his life from a brother he has swindled; rather, he dutifully follows the family tradition of finding a wife from within the clan, rather than intermarrying, as Esau had done. Appended to 27.1–45, however, our passage takes on a new and more complex meaning. The distaste for Hittite women (26.34–35) that Isaac and Rebekah

from among the daughters of Laban, your mother's brother,
3 May El Shaddai[a] bless you, make you fertile and numerous,
so that you become an assembly of peoples. 4 May He grant
the blessing of Abraham to you and your offspring, that you
may possess the land where you are sojourning, which God assigned to Abraham."
5 Then Isaac sent Jacob off, and he went to Paddan-aram,
to Laban the son of Bethuel the Aramean, the brother of Rebekah, mother of Jacob and Esau.

6 When Esau saw that Isaac had blessed Jacob and sent him
off to Paddan-aram to take a wife from there, charging him,
as he blessed him, "You shall not take a wife from among the
Canaanite women," 7 and that Jacob had obeyed his father and
mother and gone to Paddan-aram, 8 Esau realized that the Canaanite women displeased his father Isaac. 9 So Esau went to
Ishmael and took to wife, in addition to the wives he had, Mahalath the daughter of Ishmael son of Abraham, sister of Nebaioth.

VA-YETSE' ויצא

10 Jacob left Beer-sheba, and set out for Haran. 11 He came upon
a certain place and stopped there for the night, for the sun had
set. Taking one of the stones of that place, he put it under his
head and lay down in that place. 12 He had a dream; a stairway[b] was set on the ground and its top reached to the sky, and
angels of God were going up and down on it. 13 And the LORD
was standing beside him and He said, "I am the LORD, the God
of your father Abraham and the God of Isaac: the ground on
which you are lying I will assign to you and to your offspring.
14 Your descendants shall be as the dust of the earth; you shall
spread out to the west and to the east, to the north and to the
south. All the families of the earth shall bless themselves by
you and your descendants. 15 Remember, I am with you: I will
protect you wherever you go and will bring you back to this
land. I will not leave you until I have done what I have promised you."
16 Jacob awoke from his sleep and said, "Surely the LORD is
present in this place, and I did not know it!" 17 Shaken, he said,
"How awesome is this place! This is none other than the abode
of God, and that is the gateway to heaven." 18 Early in the morning, Jacob took the stone that he had put under his head and
set it up as a pillar and poured oil on the top of it. 19 He named

a See note at 17.1. *b Or "ramp"; others "ladder."*

both truly share becomes the pretext for Rebekah's saving her favorite son from his vindictive brother's rage. **28.3:** On *El Shaddai*, see 17.1 n. **8–9:** It seems fitting that the one nonfavored older brother (a hunter, 25.27) marries into the immediate family of the other (a bowman, 21.20). A midrash points out that Esau's attempt at rectification missed the point: "If he had put out the first wives, [he would have been all right]. But *in addition to the wives he had*—one source of pain upon another!" (*Gen. Rab.* 67.13). *Mahalath* is missing from the list of Esau's wives in 36.2–3, where Basemath is Ishmael's daughter (cf. 26.34).

28.10–22: Jacob's dream at Bethel. This passage, which according to most source critics is a combination of J and E, is the continuation of 27.45, and records Jacob's first direct encounter with God. In a dream, he sees a *stairway* (not a "ladder") or ramp of the sort with which Mesopotamian temple towers (ziggurats) were equipped and atop which the deity was thought to appear to communicate to his worshippers (28.12). The LORD assures Jacob that he will inherit the patriarchal promise, thus demonstrating that, however deceitfully it was gotten, Isaac's blessing on him conforms to God's will and that Jacob's exile will be temporary (vv. 13–15). Waking, Jacob realizes the awesomeness of the place and consecrates it as a sanctuary (vv. 16–19), vowing to give God a tithe if He protects him as He has promised (vv. 20–22). **18:** The Tanakh frequently associates sacred pillars, an important element of ancient worship, especially in Canaan, with idolatry (e.g., Deut. 12.3; 16.22; Hos. 10.1–2; Mic. 5.12). Nonetheless, Moses sets up twelve of them at the foot of Mount Sinai (Exod. 24.4), and Joshua erects one in the temple at Shechem (Josh. 24.26). Ibn Ezra (here and on Deut. 16.22) thinks that sacred pillars were prohibited only if they were erected to the honor of other gods. More likely is a midrash that sees in the practice a vestige of an early form of worship that was later proscribed (*Sifre Deut.* 146; see also Rashi on Deut. 16.22). **19:** Given the importance of *Bethel* in Israelite worship and the positive evaluation of it in several biblical texts (e.g., Judg. 20.18, 26–28; 21.2–4; 1 Sam. 7.16), it is appropriate that its foundation should be attributed to

that site Bethel;[a] but previously the name of the city had been
Luz.
[20] Jacob then made a vow, saying, "If God remains with me, if
He protects me on this journey that I am making, and gives me
bread to eat and clothing to wear, [21] and if I return safe to my
father's house—the LORD shall be my God. [22] And this stone,
which I have set up as a pillar, shall be God's abode; and of all
that You give me, I will set aside a tithe for You."

29 Jacob [b]resumed his journey[b] and came to the land of
the Easterners. [2] There before his eyes was a well in the
open. Three flocks of sheep were lying there beside it, for the
flocks were watered from that well. The stone on the mouth of
the well was large. [3] When all the flocks were gathered there,
the stone would be rolled from the mouth of the well and the
sheep watered; then the stone would be put back in its place
on the mouth of the well.
[4] Jacob said to them, "My friends, where are you from?" And
they said, "We are from Haran." [5] He said to them, "Do you
know Laban the son of Nahor?" And they said, "Yes, we do."
[6] He continued, "Is he well?" They answered, "Yes, he is; and
there is his daughter Rachel, coming with the flock." [7] He said,
"It is still broad daylight, too early to round up the animals;
water the flock and take them to pasture." [8] But they said, "We
cannot, until all the flocks are rounded up; then the stone is
rolled off the mouth of the well and we water the sheep."
[9] While he was still speaking with them, Rachel came with
her father's flock; for she was a shepherdess. [10] And when Jacob saw Rachel, the daughter of his uncle[c] Laban, and the flock
of his uncle Laban, Jacob went up and rolled the stone off the
mouth of the well, and watered the flock of his uncle Laban.
[11] Then Jacob kissed Rachel, and broke into tears. [12] Jacob told
Rachel that he was her father's kinsman, that he was Rebekah's
son; and she ran and told her father. [13] On hearing the news
of his sister's son Jacob, Laban ran to greet him; he embraced
him and kissed him, and took him into his house. He told Laban all that had happened, [14] and Laban said to him, "You are
truly my bone and flesh."

When he had stayed with him a month's time, [15] Laban said
to Jacob, "Just because you are a kinsman, should you serve
me for nothing? Tell me, what shall your wages be?" [16] Now Laban had two daughters; the name of the older one was Leah,
and the name of the younger was Rachel. [17] Leah had weak
eyes; Rachel was shapely and beautiful. [18] Jacob loved Rachel;
so he answered, "I will serve you seven years for your younger
daughter Rachel." [19] Laban said, "Better that I give her to you

a *I.e., "house of God."* *b-b* *Lit. "lifted up his feet."* *c* *Lit. "his mother's brother."*

the patriarch Jacob. Nonetheless, after King Jeroboam I established a temple there to rival the one in Jerusalem, some texts loyal to the latter saw in Bethel a hotbed of idolatry and condemned it roundly (e.g., 1 Kings 12.25–13.34). Our passage presumes that it was the site of a legitimate temple. **22:** Jacob's pledge of *a tithe* at Bethel may thus have functioned as a counterpoint to Abraham's gift of a tithe at Salem (Jerusalem) in 14.20.

29.1–30: Jacob marries twice. In a scene remarkably similar to the one in ch 24, when Abraham's servant finds a wife for Isaac, Jacob no sooner arrives in Haran than he encounters Laban's daughter, *Rachel,* and begins the negotiations to marry her. But this time things do not go smoothly, and Jacob the trickster must drink a hefty dose of his own bitter medicine. **3:** The implication is that it would take the collective strength of all the shepherds to roll the rock off the well. Jacob, energized by the sight of his cousin, will soon do so alone (v. 10). **6:** The immediate appearance of *Rachel* recalls that of Rebekah in 24.15 and again suggests a hidden hand behind the events. **10:** The future bridegroom's heroism at the well foreshadows Moses' scene of the victimized daughters of Reuel in Exod. 2.16–22. **12:** Rachel's running to Laban recalls Rebekah's (24.28) and adds to our mounting suspicion that she is to be the next matriarch of the chosen family. But, as we shall soon see, things are not so simple. **18:** This is one of the very few explicit references to romantic love in the Tanakh. Interestingly, the subject of one of the others is Jacob's father, Isaac, who loved Rebekah (24.67).

than that I should give her to an outsider. Stay with me." 20 So Jacob served seven years for Rachel and they seemed to him but a few days because of his love for her.

21 Then Jacob said to Laban, "Give me my wife, for my time is fulfilled, that I may cohabit with her." 22 And Laban gathered all the people of the place and made a feast. 23 When evening came, he took his daughter Leah and brought her to him; and he cohabited with her.—24 Laban had given his maidservant Zilpah to his daughter Leah as her maid.—25 When morning came, there was Leah! So he said to Laban, "What is this you have done to me? I was in your service for Rachel! Why did you deceive me?" 26 Laban said, "It is not the practice in our place to marry off the younger before the older. 27 Wait until the bridal week of this one is over and we will give you that one too, provided you serve me another seven years." 28 Jacob did so; he waited out the bridal week of the one, and then he gave him his daughter Rachel as wife.—29 Laban had given his maidservant Bilhah to his daughter Rachel as her maid.—30 And Jacob cohabited with Rachel also; indeed, he loved Rachel more than Leah. And he served him another seven years.

31 The LORD saw that Leah was unloved and he opened her womb; but Rachel was barren. 32 Leah conceived and bore a son, and named him Reuben;[a] for she declared, "It means: 'The LORD has seen[b] my affliction'; it also means: 'Now my husband will love me.'"[c] 33 She conceived again and bore a son, and declared, "This is because the LORD heard[d] that I was unloved and has given me this one also"; so she named him Simeon. 34 Again she conceived and bore a son and declared, "This time my husband will become attached[e] to me, for I have borne him three sons." Therefore he was named Levi. 35 She conceived again and bore a son, and declared, "This time I will praise[f] the LORD." Therefore she named him Judah. Then she stopped bearing.

30 When Rachel saw that she had borne Jacob no children, she became envious of her sister; and Rachel said to Jacob, "Give me children, or I shall die." 2 Jacob was incensed at Rachel, and said, "Can I take the place of God, who has denied

a *Understood as "See a son."*
b *Heb.* ra'ah, *connected with the first part of "Reuben."*
c *Heb.* ye'ehabani, *connected with the last part of "Reuben."*
d *Heb.* shama', *connected with "Simeon."* e *Heb.* yillaweh, *connected with "Levi."*
f *Heb.* 'odeh, *connected with "Judah."*

25–26: *What is this you have done to me?* echoes Pharaoh's and Abimelech's indignation after Abraham and Isaac tried to pass their wives off as their sisters (12.18; 20.9; 26.10). Jacob's accusation of deceit is richly ironic in light of his own deceit in passing himself off as his older brother (27.35). Similarly, Laban's answer in v. 26 is an exquisitely ironic reaffirmation of the principle that Jacob has violated in buying Esau's birthright (25.29–34) and defrauding him of his father's highest blessing (27.1–45). Having acquired his older brother's birthright for a bowl of lentils, he now proves unable to acquire the woman he loves even with seven years of harsh labor (31.38–41). A remarkable midrash in the Talmud speaks of Rachel's selflessness and her concern to spare her unloved older sister humiliation. Jacob, the midrash reports, had given Rachel certain tokens by which he could identify her, lest her deceitful father succeed in substituting Leah. Worried that her sister would then be put to shame in her wedding bed, she handed the tokens over to Leah. In reward for Rachel's self-effacement, the midrash concludes, King Saul was numbered among her descendants (*b. Meg.* 13b).

29.31–30.24: The origins of the tribes of Israel. This passage accounts for the birth of twelve of Jacob's thirteen children and eleven of his twelve sons. Only Benjamin, who will be born after the return to Canaan (35.16–20), is missing from the roster of the eponymous ancestors of the twelve tribes of Israel (in some lists, Levi is missing, and Joseph appears as two tribes, Ephraim and Manasseh. See 48.5–7 n.). **29.31:** As in the case of Hagar (16.10–12; 21.17–18), God shows compassion to the unfavored mate, thus partly equalizing the disparity between her and her co-wife. Barrenness, in some instances a punishment (e.g., 2 Sam. 6.20–23), serves in Rachel's case to place her in succession to Sarah and Rebekah (11.30; 25.21). **32–35:** The names Leah gives her first three sons communicate her deep distress at not being the preferred wife. In Heb, *The LORD has seen my affliction* (v. 32) is close to the message of the angel to Hagar, "For the LORD has paid heed to your suffering" (16.11). **30.1:** The theme of bad relations between a fertile co-wife and a barren one, with the latter as their husband's favorite, appears in more developed form in the story of Hannah in 1 Sam. ch 1. **2:** The question *Can I take the place*

you fruit of the womb?" 3 She said, "Here is my maid Bilhah. Consort with her, that she may bear on my knees and that through her I too may have children." 4 So she gave him her maid Bilhah as concubine, and Jacob cohabited with her. 5 Bilhah conceived and bore Jacob a son. 6 And Rachel said, "God has vindicated me;[a] indeed, He has heeded my plea and given me a son." Therefore she named him Dan. 7 Rachel's maid Bilhah conceived again and bore Jacob a second son. 8 And Rachel said, [b-]"A fateful contest I waged[-b] with my sister; yes, and I have prevailed." So she named him Naphtali.

9 When Leah saw that she had stopped bearing, she took her maid Zilpah and gave her to Jacob as concubine. 10 And when Leah's maid Zilpah bore Jacob a son, 11 Leah said, "What luck!"[c] So she named him Gad. 12 When Leah's maid Zilpah bore Jacob a second son, 13 Leah declared, "What fortune!"[d] meaning, "Women will deem me fortunate." So she named him Asher.

14 Once, at the time of the wheat harvest, Reuben came upon some mandrakes in the field and brought them to his mother Leah. Rachel said to Leah, "Please give me some of your son's mandrakes." 15 But she said to her, "Was it not enough for you to take away my husband, that you would also take my son's mandrakes?" Rachel replied, "I promise, he shall lie with you tonight, in return for your son's mandrakes." 16 When Jacob came home from the field in the evening, Leah went out to meet him and said, "You are to sleep with me, for I have hired you with my son's mandrakes." And he lay with her that night. 17 God heeded Leah, and she conceived and bore him a fifth son. 18 And Leah said, "God has given me my reward[e] for having given my maid to my husband." So she named him Issachar. 19 When Leah conceived again and bore Jacob a sixth son, 20 Leah said, "God has given me a choice gift;[f] this time my husband will exalt me,[g] for I have borne him six sons." So she named him Zebulun. 21 Last, she bore him a daughter, and named her Dinah.

22 Now God remembered Rachel; God heeded her and opened her womb. 23 She conceived and bore a son, and said, "God has taken away[h] my disgrace." 24 So she named him Joseph, which is to say, "May the LORD add[i] another son for me."

25 After Rachel had borne Joseph, Jacob said to Laban, "Give me leave to go back to my own homeland. 26 Give me my wives and my children, for whom I have served you, that I may go;

a Heb. danánni, *connected with "Dan."*
b-b Heb. naphtule ... naphtalti, *connected with "Naphtali." Lit. "A contest of God ..."*
c Kethib begad; *the* qere *reads* ba gad *"luck has come"; connected with "Gad."*
d Heb. be'oshri, *connected with "Asher."* *e Heb.* sekhari, *connected with "Issachar."*
f Heb. zebadani ... zebed. *g Heb.* yizbeleni; *others "will dwell with me."*
h Heb. 'asaph. *i Heb.* yoseph.

of God? reappears in 50.19 (where it is translated, "Am I a substitute for God?"). There, probably not coincidentally, it is Rachel's first-born who asks it, and in a context of reconciliation of siblings once riven by jealousy. **3:** The words *that through her I too may have children* is another connection to the story of Hagar (16.2). Ancient Near Eastern evidence suggests that placing a child on one's knees represents acknowledgment of that child as one's own. **14–18:** The *mandrake*, a plant with purplish flowers and branching roots, was thought to have aphrodisiac properties (cf. Song 7.14). The bitterness of Leah's tragic position as the wife Jacob never wanted and never loved is especially poignant in vv. 15–16. She has to bargain with her sister to hire her husband just to sleep with her. **22:** What Rachel does with the mandrakes she buys is strangely unreported. One expects them to play a role in her overcoming her infertility, but it is God alone who is given credit for that. His *remembering Rachel* underscores her favored status (cf. 8.1). On the basis of a word for "remembering" in Lev. 23.24 (translated "commemorated"), the Talmud dates Rachel's conceiving (as well as Sarah's [see 21.1–8 n.] and Hannah's) to Rosh Ha-Shanah (*b. Rosh Hash.* 11a). The matriarchs thus play a prominent role in the traditional Rosh Ha-Shanah liturgy, in which God's remembering the ancestors and His faithfulness to them are major themes.

30.25–43: Jacob grows wealthy. After strained negotiations about payment for Jacob's services, Laban agrees to his son-in-law's terms, but then tries to cheat him anyway. Jacob outsmarts Laban, cleverly arranging for the rapid proliferation of his own share of the flocks. **25–26:** The underlying assumption seems to be that Jacob had accepted the status of an indentured servant. Thus, he could not leave without his master's permission, and his wives and children would belong

for well you know what services I have rendered you." 27 But Laban said to him, "If you will indulge me,[a] I have learned by divination that the LORD has blessed me on your account." 28 And he continued, "Name the wages due from me, and I will pay you." 29 But he said, "You know well how I have served you and how your livestock has fared with me. 30 For the little you had before I came has grown to much, since the LORD has blessed you wherever I turned. And now, when shall I make provision for my own household?" 31 He said, "What shall I pay you?" And Jacob said, "Pay me nothing! If you will do this thing for me, I will again pasture and keep your flocks: 32 let me pass through your whole flock today, removing from there every speckled and spotted animal—every dark-colored sheep and every spotted and speckled goat. Such shall be my wages. 33 In the future when you go over my wages, let my honesty toward you testify for me: if there are among my goats any that are not speckled or spotted or any sheep that are not dark-colored, they got there by theft." 34 And Laban said, "Very well, let it be as you say."

35 But that same day he removed the streaked and spotted he-goats and all the speckled and spotted she-goats—every one that had white on it—and all the dark-colored sheep, and left them in the charge of his sons. 36 And he put a distance of three days' journey between himself and Jacob, while Jacob was pasturing the rest of Laban's flock.

37 Jacob then got fresh shoots of poplar, and of almond and plane, and peeled white stripes in them, laying bare the white of the shoots. 38 The rods that he had peeled he set up in front of the goats[b] in the troughs, the water receptacles, that the goats came to drink from. Their mating occurred when they came to drink, 39 and since the goats mated by the rods, the goats brought forth streaked, speckled, and spotted young. 40 But Jacob dealt separately with the sheep; he made these animals face the streaked or wholly dark-colored animals in Laban's flock. And so he produced special flocks for himself, which he did not put with Laban's flocks. 41 Moreover, when the sturdier[c] animals were mating, Jacob would place the rods in the troughs, in full view of the animals, so that they mated by the rods; 42 but with the feebler[d] animals he would not place them there. Thus the feeble ones[d] went to Laban and the sturdy to Jacob. 43 So the man grew exceedingly prosperous, and came to own large flocks, maidservants and menservants, camels and asses.

a *Lit. "If I have found favor in your eyes."*
b *Lit. "flocks."*
c *Or "early-breeding."*
d *Or "late-breeding."*

to the master (Exod. 21.2–4; cf. Gen. 31.43). The verb translated *Give me leave* serves as the standard term for manumission in the story of the exodus (e.g., Exod. 4.23). **27:** Even Laban, ascertaining the divine will by a method that is later prohibited (Lev. 19.26; Deut. 18.10), can see that Jacob is a graced person who brings good luck to those around him (cf. 2 Sam. 6.12). **28:** According to Deut. 15.12–15, the master is obligated to endow his newly manumitted indentured servant liberally. **35–42:** Laban proves his offer to have been in bad faith, but Jacob overcomes the trickery with a clever technique of his own. The basis for Jacob's actions in vv. 37–42 is the folkloristic belief that what animals see while mating determines the appearance of their young. Thus, when the goats (which are ordinarily dark in the Near East) see *the white of the shoots* (v. 37; the word for *white* is the same as Laban's name), they conceive kids with patches of white. Similarly, Jacob positioned the sheep (which are normally white) in view of the *streaked or wholly dark-colored animals* (v. 40), so that they would bear lambs with dark patches. Thus was the master trickster Laban finally and justly tricked, and thus did Jacob, by the blessing of God and by his own ingenuity, achieve the wealth that had been characteristic of his grandfather and father as well (13.2; 26.13–14). The refugee is becoming a patriarch.

31 Now he heard the things that Laban's sons were saying: "Jacob has taken all that was our father's, and from that which was our father's he has built up all this wealth." 2 Jacob also saw that Laban's manner toward him was not as it had been in the past. 3 Then the LORD said to Jacob, "Return to the land of your fathers where you were born, and I will be with you." 4 Jacob had Rachel and Leah called to the field, where his flock was, 5 and said to them, "I see that your father's manner toward me is not as it has been in the past. But the God of my father has been with me. 6 As you know, I have served your father with all my might; 7 but your father has cheated me, changing my wages time and again.[a] God, however, would not let him do me harm. 8 If he said thus, 'The speckled shall be your wages,' then all the flocks would drop speckled young; and if he said thus, 'The streaked shall be your wages,' then all the flocks would drop streaked young. 9 God has taken away your father's livestock and given it to me.

10 "Once, at the mating time of the flocks, [b-]I had a dream in which I saw[-b] that the he-goats mating with the flock were streaked, speckled, and mottled. 11 And in the dream an angel of God said to me, 'Jacob!' 'Here,' I answered. 12 And he said, 'Note well that all the he-goats which are mating with the flock are streaked, speckled, and mottled; for I have noted all that Laban has been doing to you. 13 I am the God of Beth-el, where you anointed a pillar and where you made a vow to Me. Now, arise and leave this land and return to your native land.' "

14 Then Rachel and Leah answered him, saying, "Have we still a share in the inheritance of our father's house? 15 Surely, he regards us as outsiders, now that he has sold us and has used up our purchase price. 16 Truly, all the wealth that God has taken away from our father belongs to us and to our children. Now then, do just as God has told you."

17 Thereupon Jacob put his children and wives on camels; 18 and he drove off all his livestock and all the wealth that he had amassed, the livestock in his possession that he had acquired in Paddan-aram, to go to his father Isaac in the land of Canaan.

19 Meanwhile Laban had gone to shear his sheep, and Rachel stole her father's household idols. 20 Jacob [c-]kept Laban the Aramean in the dark,[-c] not telling him that he was fleeing,

a Lit. "ten times." *b-b Lit. "I raised my eyes and saw in a dream, behold."*
c-c Lit. "stole the mind of Laban the Aramean"; similarly in v. 26.

31.1–54: Jacob breaks free of Laban. This chapter marks the final resolution of the ever more difficult relationship between the emerging patriarch and his selfish and duplicitous father-in-law. Jacob first persuades his wives to leave their father (vv. 1–16) and then contends with Laban's accusations, making a few of his own along the way (vv. 22–42). Finally, at Laban's suggestion, the two make a nonaggression pact, solemnly delimiting the terms of their separation and the boundary between their territories (vv. 43–54). **1:** The complaint of Laban's sons (who are mentioned only here) echoes Esau's charge in 27.36. In this case, however, Jacob will not only receive divine validation of his behavior, but also vigorously defend its legality (vv. 36–42). **3:** The verse recalls the LORD's words to Jacob in 28.15, when he first set out for Haran, and thus suggests that He has indeed been protecting the chosen son of Isaac during his long and painful sojourn outside the promised land all along. Functioning as bookends around the story of Jacob in Haran, these two verses illustrate the principle that, in the psalmist's words, "The LORD will guard your going and your coming/now and forever" (Ps. 121.8). **4–13:** Jacob here presents a different account of the increase in his flocks from the one that appears in 30.25–43. Source criticism can explain the divergence through the attribution of this text to E, whereas 30.25–43 is J. Note that 31.4–13 always uses the E-name *(God)* and that v. 13 seems to be a variant of v. 3. Reading the two texts as part of one now unified document presents us with two options: Is Jacob here dissembling to his wives in order to make himself look innocent, or is he giving a profound theological interpretation of the events that happened in the previous chapter on a human plane? **14–16:** Rachel and Leah refer to the institution of the bride-price, a gift that the groom paid his fiancee's father; this text suggests that in some cases it was used to benefit the bride herself. Laban, they complain (in agreement for once), has consumed the bride-price (probably in the form of Jacob's labor) without concern for them, in effect disowning them. **19–21:** Concerning these household idols, see 1 Sam. 19.13. "Stealing" (the Heb has a wider range of meaning than the English), in any event, is a recurrent theme in this chapter and points to one of its major ironies. Whereas

21 and fled with all that he had. Soon he was across the Euphrates and heading toward the hill country of Gilead.
22 On the third day, Laban was told that Jacob had fled. 23 So
he took his kinsmen with him and pursued him a distance of
seven days, catching up with him in the hill country of Gilead.
24 But God appeared to Laban the Aramean in a dream by night
and said to him, "Beware of attempting anything with Jacob,
good or bad."
25 Laban overtook Jacob. Jacob had pitched his tent on the
Height, and Laban with his kinsmen encamped in the hill country of Gilead. 26 And Laban said to Jacob, "What did you mean by
keeping me in the dark and carrying off my daughters like captives of the sword? 27 Why did you flee in secrecy and mislead
me and not tell me? I would have sent you off with festive music,
with timbrel and lyre. 28 You did not even let me kiss my sons and
daughters good-by! It was a foolish thing for you to do. 29 I have
it in my power to do you harm; but the God of your father said to
me last night, 'Beware of attempting anything with Jacob, good
or bad.' 30 Very well, you had to leave because you were longing
for your father's house; but why did you steal my gods?"
31 Jacob answered Laban, saying, "I was afraid because I
thought you would take your daughters from me by force.
32 But anyone with whom you find your gods shall not remain
alive! In the presence of our kinsmen, point out what I have of
yours and take it." Jacob, of course, did not know that Rachel
had stolen them.
33 So Laban went into Jacob's tent and Leah's tent and the
tents of the two maidservants; but he did not find them. Leaving Leah's tent, he entered Rachel's tent. 34 Rachel, meanwhile,
had taken the idols and placed them in the camel cushion and
sat on them; and Laban rummaged through the tent without
finding them. 35 For she said to her father, "Let not my lord take
it amiss that I cannot rise before you, for the period of women
is upon me." Thus he searched, but could not find the household idols.
36 Now Jacob became incensed and took up his grievance
with Laban. Jacob spoke up and said to Laban, "What is my
crime, what is my guilt that you should pursue me? 37 You rummaged through all my things; what have you found of all your
household objects? Set it here, before my kinsmen and yours,
and let them decide between us two.
38 "These twenty years I have spent in your service, your
ewes and she-goats never miscarried, nor did I feast on rams
from your flock. 39 That which was torn by beasts I never
brought to you; I myself made good the loss; you exacted it of
me, whether snatched by day or snatched by night. 40 Often,[a]

Jacob vigorously defends himself against the charge that he defrauded Laban (vv. 8–12, 39), he, in fact, had "to steal the mind of Laban the Aramean" (see translators' note *c-c* on previous p.) in order to effect his getaway. Unbeknownst to him, his wife had indeed stolen her father's household idols. Given Laban's own deceit (29.21–28), the phrase "stole the mind of Laban the Aramean" constitutes a delicious wordplay. In Heb, "mind" ("lev") sounds like "Laban" ("lavan"), and "Aramean" ("'arami") sounds like "deceive" ("rima"). **32:** According to a midrash, it was Jacob's well-intentioned curse that brought about his beloved Rachel's premature death (*Gen. Rab.* 74.4; see 35.16–20). **33–35:** Note the two-fold satire, against the miserly Laban, vainly rummaging through his own family's tents, and against the household idols themselves, escaping detection only because of Rachel's menstrual period. In the purity system of the Torah, anything on which a menstruant has sat communicates impurity (Lev. 15.22). Whereas Laban refers to his *gods* (v. 30), the narrator is careful to call them *household idols* (Heb "terafim") (v.35). And whereas Laban is fiercely devoted to his *gods,* it is God who has stripped him of his wealth and given it to his daughters (v. 16). Note also the connection of Laban's "rummaging" ("mishesh") and Isaac's "feeling" ("mash") Jacob in 27.21–22. In each case, Jacob escapes detection, but in each case he also pays a steep price. **39:** By the standards of the law in Exod. 22.12, and known in other ancient Near Eastern law collections as well, Jacob went beyond his obligations when he made good *that which was torn by beasts.*

a Lit. *"I was."*

scorching heat ravaged me by day and frost by night; and sleep fled from my eyes. 41 Of the twenty years that I spent in your household, I served you fourteen years for your two daughters, and six years for your flocks; and you changed my wages time and again.[a] 42 Had not the God of my father, the God of Abraham and the Fear[b] of Isaac, been with me, you would have sent me away empty-handed. But God took notice of my plight and the toil of my hands, and He gave judgment last night."

43 Then Laban spoke up and said to Jacob, "The daughters are my daughters, the children are my children, and the flocks are my flocks; all that you see is mine. Yet what can I do now about my daughters or the children they have borne? 44 Come, then, let us make a pact, you and I, that there may be a witness between you and me." 45 Thereupon Jacob took a stone and set it up as a pillar. 46 And Jacob said to his kinsmen, "Gather stones." So they took stones and made a mound; and they partook of a meal there by the mound. 47 Laban named it Yegar-sahadutha,[c] but Jacob named it Gal-ed.[d] 48 And Laban declared, "This mound is a witness between you and me this day." That is why it was named Gal-ed; 49 and [it was called] Mizpah, because he said, "May the LORD watch[e] between you and me, when we are out of sight of each other. 50 If you ill-treat my daughters or take other wives besides my daughters—though no one else be about, remember, God Himself will be witness between you and me."

51 And Laban said to Jacob, "Here is this mound and here the pillar which I have set up between you and me: 52 this mound shall be witness and this pillar shall be witness that I am not to cross to you past this mound, and that you are not to cross to me past this mound and this pillar, with hostile intent. 53 May the God of Abraham and the god of Nahor"—their ancestral deities—"judge between us." And Jacob swore by the Fear[b] of his father Isaac. 54 Jacob then offered up a sacrifice on the Height, and invited his kinsmen to partake of the meal. After the meal, they spent the night on the Height.

32 Early in the morning, Laban kissed his sons and daughters and bade them good-by; then Laban left on his journey homeward. 2 Jacob went on his way, and angels of God encountered him. 3 When he saw them, Jacob said, "This is God's camp." So he named that place Mahanaim.[f]

a Lit. "ten times." *b Meaning of Heb.* paḥad *uncertain.*
c Aramaic for "the mound (or, stone-heap) of witness."
d Heb. for "the mound (or, stone-heap) of witness," reflecting the name Gilead, v. 23.
e Heb. yiṣeph, *associated with* Mizpah.
f Connected with Heb. maḥaneh, *"camp."*

44: *Witness* ("ʿed") may involve a pun on a similar Semitic word ("ʿad") that means a "pact" or "covenant"; here, it may even be a variant of it. If the word does mean *witness,* the reference is unclear. Most likely, it is God Himself who is to play that role, as in v. 50. **47:** The narrative gives a folk etymology for Gilead (v. 23), a mountainous area in Transjordan, southeast of the Sea of Galilee (Kinneret). 1 Kings 22.1–38 and 2 Kings 9.14–15 report wars between Israelites and Arameans over one of its major cities in the 9th century BCE. Gen. 31.44–54 may reflect a pact between these two peoples. Laban's giving *Gal-ed* an Aram. name is a wonderful little touch. According to the Talmud, one should not esteem the Aram. language lightly, for, as these two words show, it appears in the Torah itself (*y. Sot.* 7.7).

32.1–3: A good-bye and a revelation. 1: Laban omits kissing Jacob, in pointed contrast to their initial encounter (29.13). **3:** Retrospectively, this verse recalls Jacob's experience at Bethel on his way to Laban (28.10–22). Cf. especially 28.17, "This is none other than the abode of God." Prospectively, the name *Mahanaim,* understood as "two camps," anticipates Jacob's precautionary division of his entourage in 32.8–9.

VA-YISHLAḤ וישלח

4 Jacob sent messengers ahead to his brother Esau in the land of Seir, the country of Edom, 5 and instructed them as follows, *a-*"Thus shall you say, 'To my lord Esau, thus says your servant Jacob:*-a* I stayed with Laban and remained until now; 6 I have acquired cattle, asses, sheep, and male and female slaves; and I send this message to my lord in the hope of gaining your favor.'" 7 The messengers returned to Jacob, saying, "We came to your brother Esau; he himself is coming to meet you, and there are four hundred men with him." 8 Jacob was greatly frightened; in his anxiety, he divided the people with him, and the flocks and herds and camels, into two camps, 9 thinking, "If Esau comes to the one camp and attacks it, the other camp may yet escape."

10 Then Jacob said, "O God of my father Abraham and God of my father Isaac, O LORD, who said to me, 'Return to your native land and I will deal bountifully with you'! 11 I am unworthy of all the kindness that You have so steadfastly shown Your servant: with my staff alone I crossed this Jordan, and now I have become two camps. 12 Deliver me, I pray, from the hand of my brother, from the hand of Esau; else, I fear, he may come and strike me down, mothers and children alike. 13 Yet You have said, 'I will deal bountifully with you and make your offspring as the sands of the sea, which are too numerous to count.'"

14 After spending the night there, he selected from what was at hand these presents for his brother Esau: 15 200 she-goats and 20 he-goats; 200 ewes and 20 rams; 16 30 milch camels with their colts; 40 cows and 10 bulls; 20 she-asses and 10 he-asses. 17 These he put in the charge of his servants, drove by drove, and he told his servants, "Go on ahead, and keep a distance between droves." 18 He instructed the one in front as follows, "When my brother Esau meets you and asks you, 'Whose man are you? Where are you going? And whose [animals] are these ahead of you?' 19 you shall answer, 'Your servant Jacob's; they are a gift sent to my lord Esau; and [Jacob] himself is right behind us.'" 20 He gave similar instructions to the second one, and the third, and all the others who followed the droves, namely, "Thus and so shall you say to Esau when you reach him. 21 And you shall add, 'And your servant Jacob himself is right behind us.'" For he reasoned, "If I propitiate him with presents in advance, and then face him, perhaps he will show me favor." 22 And so the gift went on ahead, while he remained in camp that night.

23 That same night he arose, and taking his two wives, his two maidservants, and his eleven children, he crossed the ford of the Jabbok. 24 After taking them across the stream, he sent across all his possessions. 25 Jacob was left alone. And a man

a-a Or "Thus you shall say to my lord Esau, 'Thus says your servant Jacob: . . .'"

32.4–22: Jacob prepares to meet Esau. 4: *Messengers* is the same Heb word as "angels" in v. 2. The term communicates a premonition that, however fearful the encounter with Esau may seem, God's protective grace will not depart from Jacob. **7:** The mention of Esau's 400 men underscores Jacob's vulnerability. For all his wives, offspring, slaves, and animals, he lacks the military might of the brother he has wronged. Things are looking grim. **10–13:** Jacob's prayer opens and closes with quotations of those promises of God that the looming confrontation with Esau threatens (vv. 10, 13). V. 11 expresses his humility and his gratitude for previous favors, and v. 12 asks for deliverance, appealing to God's mercy. A talmudic rabbi, however, is critical of Jacob on the grounds that one should never put himself in a dangerous place and then ask that a miracle be performed (*b. Shab.* 32a). The danger should be avoided, if at all possible. **17–22:** The Heb word for *face* ("panim") occurs seven times in this passage (in some instances, it is translated as *ahead, in advance*). This suggests a connection with Peniel, "face of God" (vv. 31–32) and underscores the association of Esau with the mysterious figure with whom Jacob is about to wrestle (cf. 33.10).

32.23–33: Jacob wrestles with a divine being. The fateful encounter at the Jabbok is one of the best-known episodes in the life of Jacob, but also surely the most enigmatic. **23–25:** Peniel is on the north bank of the *Jabbok* (the wadi Zerka). Why Jacob returned there after fording his wives and children is unclear. In the Talmud, it is suggested that he had returned to retrieve some little jars he had forgotten there (*b. Ḥul.* 91a). In any case, his solitude and lack of property recall his status when he first fled his brother's wrath, before God had showered His bounty upon him (28.11). **25:** The identity of the *man* is as unclear as his reason for attacking Jacob (cf. Exod. 4.24–26). In the Tanakh, God and angels can appear in human form, as in 18.2 (cf. 19.1); Josh. 5.13–15; Judg. 13.6, 10.

wrestled with him until the break of dawn. [26]When he saw that he had not prevailed against him, he wrenched Jacob's hip at its socket, so that the socket of his hip was strained as he wrestled with him. [27]Then he said, "Let me go, for dawn is breaking." But he answered, "I will not let you go, unless you bless me." [28]Said the other, "What is your name?" He replied, "Jacob." [29]Said he, "Your name shall no longer be Jacob, but Israel, for you have striven[a] with [b]beings divine and human,[-b] and have prevailed." [30]Jacob asked, "Pray tell me your name." But he said, "You must not ask my name!" And he took leave of him there. [31]So Jacob named the place Peniel,[c] meaning, "I have seen a divine being face to face, yet my life has been preserved." [32]The sun rose upon him as he passed Penuel, limping on his hip. [33]That is why the children of Israel to this day do not eat the thigh muscle that is on the socket of the hip, since Jacob's hip socket was wrenched at the thigh muscle.

33 Looking up, Jacob saw Esau coming, accompanied by four hundred men. He divided the children among Leah, Rachel, and the two maids, [2]putting the maids and their children first, Leah and her children next, and Rachel and Joseph last. [3]He himself went on ahead and bowed low to the ground seven times until he was near his brother. [4]Esau ran to greet him. He embraced him and, falling on his neck, he kissed him; and they wept. [5]Looking about, he saw the women and the children. "Who," he asked, "are these with you?" He answered, "The children with whom God has favored your servant." [6]Then the maids, with their children, came forward and bowed low; [7]next Leah, with her children, came forward and bowed low; and last, Joseph and Rachel came forward and bowed low; [8]And he asked, "What do you mean by all this company which I have met?" He answered, "To gain my lord's favor." [9]Esau said, "I have enough, my brother; let what you have remain yours." [10]But

a Heb. saritha, *connected with first part of "Israel."*

*b-b Or "God (*Elohim, *connected with second part of 'Israel') and men."*

c Understood as "face of God."

Jacob's mysterious adversary is surely supernatural, and most traditional Jewish commentators have taken him to be angelic. A well-known midrash sees him as the "patron angel of Esau" and thus interprets this episode as a warning to all future enemies of the Jewish people: "Your patron angel could not withstand him [i.e., Jacob/Israel] and you seek to attack his descendants?" (*Gen. Rab.* 77.3). **29:** The scientific etymology of *Israel* is unclear, a good guess being "[The God] El rules." The folk etymology in this verse appears again in Hos. 12.4. **30:** Cf. Exod. 3.13–14; Judg. 13.18. *He took leave of him* could also be rendered "he blessed him." If so, Jacob wins his blessing after all. **33:** The Rabbis saw this norm, unparalleled in the Tanakh, as a commandment ("mitzvah") and thus an indispensable element of the Jewish dietary system ("kashrut"). A majority position in the Mishnah maintains that this "mitzvah" was first announced when the Torah was given on Mount Sinai and only written down in its current location to draw attention to its underlying rationale (*m. Ḥul.* 7.6). In other words, the prohibition did not come into force until the revelation on Sinai.

33.1–20: The reconciliation of Jacob and Esau. The keynotes of this ch are Jacob's obsequiousness and Esau's gracious forbearance. The murderous revenge that the former had feared (32.12) and the latter had vowed (27.41) thus averted, Jacob succeeds in effecting a definitive separation from his brother and maintaining his own distinctive identity. **1–2:** Jacob graphically reaffirms his preference for Rachel (now extended to her son Joseph), which once caused so much ill will between his wives (29.31–30.21). His preference for Joseph will be the cause of the next tear in the fabric of familial relations. It will nearly result in his beloved son's death (ch 37). **3:** Sevenfold prostration appears in the Amarna Letters (14th c. BCE) as a gesture of homage to one's suzerain. The scene reverses the dominance of Jacob over Esau prophesied in 25.23 and 27.29, 37. **4:** *He kissed him* is missing in the LXX, an ancient Gk translation of the Torah produced by Jewish scholars in Egypt. In the Masoretic Text (the traditional rabbinic version codified in the late first millennium CE), dots appear over the phrase, probably to indicate its doubtful status in the manuscript tradition. One midrash interprets the dots to mean that, uncharacteristically, Esau felt compassion for Jacob and kissed him wholeheartedly. Another midrash, however, thinks that Esau intended to "bite" ("nashakh") rather than to "kiss" ("nashak") his brother, but God hardened Jacob's neck, foiling his brother's deceitful attack (*Gen. Rab.* 78.9). **9:** *Enough* ("rav") may echo the prophecy that "the older ('rav') shall serve the younger" (25.23). Esau, confronted with his brother's conspicuous obeisance, renounces any claim to his younger brother's property.

Jacob said, "No, I pray you; if you would do me this favor, accept from me this gift; for to see your face is like seeing the face of God, and you have received me favorably. 11 Please accept my present which has been brought to you, for God has favored me and I have plenty." And when he urged him, he accepted.

12 And [Esau] said, "Let us start on our journey, and I will proceed at your pace." 13 But he said to him, "My lord knows that the children are frail and that the flocks and herds, which are nursing, are a care to me; if they are driven hard a single day, all the flocks will die. 14 Let my lord go on ahead of his servant, while I travel slowly, at the pace of the cattle before me and at the pace of the children, until I come to my lord in Seir."

15 Then Esau said, "Let me assign to you some of the men who are with me." But he said, "Oh no, my lord is too kind to me!" 16 So Esau started back that day on his way to Seir. 17 But Jacob journeyed on to Succoth, and built a house for himself and made stalls for his cattle; that is why the place was called Succoth.[a]

18 Jacob arrived safe in the city of Shechem which is in the land of Canaan—having come thus from Paddan-aram—and he encamped before the city. 19 The parcel of land where he pitched his tent he purchased from the children of Hamor, Shechem's father, for a hundred *kesitahs*.[b] 20 He set up an altar there, and called it El-elohe-yisrael.[c]

34 Now Dinah, the daughter whom Leah had borne to Jacob, went out to visit the daughters of the land. 2 Shechem son of Hamor the Hivite, chief of the country, saw her, and took her and lay with her by force. 3 Being strongly drawn to Dinah daughter of Jacob, and in love with the maiden, he spoke to the maiden tenderly. 4 So Shechem said to his father Hamor, "Get me this girl as a wife."

5 Jacob heard that he had defiled his daughter Dinah; but since his sons were in the field with his cattle, Jacob kept silent until they came home. 6 Then Shechem's father Hamor came out to Jacob to speak to him. 7 Meanwhile Jacob's sons, having heard the news, came in from the field. The men were distressed and very angry, because he had committed an outrage in Israel by lying with Jacob's daughter—a thing not to be done.

8 And Hamor spoke with them, saying, "My son Shechem longs for your daughter. Please give her to him in marriage. 9 Intermarry with us: give your daughters to us, and take our

a *Meaning "stalls," "huts," "booths."* b *Heb.* qesitah, *a unit of unknown value.* c *"El, God of Israel."*

11: *Accept my present* can also be translated as "take my blessing," with Jacob acknowledging the truth in Esau's charge that "he has taken away my blessing" (27.35–36) and offering amends. It is precisely God's generosity toward the chosen son that enables him to be generous, in turn, to his unchosen brother. **14:** Jacob never comes to his brother in Seir, but instead journeys to Succoth. He once again succeeds in securing his independence from the larger family, thus maintaining the distinctive identity of his lineage against the threat of assimilation into the surrounding nations. **20:** Through this confession El, the supreme Canaanite deity, is identified as the God of Israel.

34.1–31: Dinah. No sooner does Jacob succeed in separating from Esau (33.12–17) than a new threat to the distinctive identity of his family emerges when a Canaanite prince seeks to marry the daughter of Jacob whom he has seduced or raped (the Heb is somewhat ambiguous). And no sooner is an old rent in the family healed through the reconciliation of Jacob and Esau (33.1–11) than a new one opens when Simeon and Levi defy their father and avenge the crime against their sister. **1–2:** Given the extraordinary lengths to which the chosen family has gone to preserve its identity, Dinah's departure from her family's quarters is ominous. In the event, though she goes out "to see" (here rendered *to visit*), she is the one seen, with tragic consequences. *Shechem* is the name not only of a person but also of an important Canaanite city. The book of Joshua concludes with Joshua's making a covenant with Israel at Shechem (Josh. ch 24). It is striking that there is no account of Israel's having taken the city by force of arms during the conquest of the land recounted in Joshua and Judges. It is possible that complex ethnic and political history lies behind the powerful tale in Gen. ch 34. **2:** Some scholars suggest that the final verb refers to improper sexual relations, in this case nonmarital sex, and not specifically rape. **3:** Without justifying his crime, the narrative builds up considerable sympathy for Shechem. **8–12:** According to biblical law (and strong

daughters for yourselves: 10 You will dwell among us, and the land will be open before you; settle, move about, and acquire holdings in it." 11 Then Shechem said to her father and brothers, "Do me this favor, and I will pay whatever you tell me. 12 Ask of me a bride-price ever so high, as well as gifts, and I will pay what you tell me; only give me the maiden for a wife."

13 Jacob's sons answered Shechem and his father Hamor—speaking with guile because he had defiled their sister Dinah—14 and said to them, "We cannot do this thing, to give our sister to a man who is uncircumcised, for that is a disgrace among us. 15 Only on this condition will we agree with you; that you will become like us in that every male among you is circumcised. 16 Then we will give our daughters to you and take your daughters to ourselves; and we will dwell among you and become as one kindred. 17 But if you will not listen to us and become circumcised, we will take our daughter and go."

18 Their words pleased Hamor and Hamor's son Shechem. 19 And the youth lost no time in doing the thing, for he wanted Jacob's daughter. Now he was the most respected in his father's house. 20 So Hamor and his son Shechem went to the *a-*public place*-a* of their town and spoke to their fellow townsmen, saying, 21 "These people are our friends; let them settle in the land and move about in it, for the land is large enough for them; we will take their daughters to ourselves as wives and give our daughters to them. 22 But only on this condition will the men agree with us to dwell among us and be as one kindred: that all our males become circumcised as they are circumcised. 23 Their cattle and substance and all their beasts will be ours, if we only agree to their terms, so that they will settle among us." 24 All *b-*who went out of the gate of his town*-b* heeded Hamor and his son Shechem, and all males, *b-*all those who went out of the gate of his town,*-b* were circumcised.

25 On the third day, when they were in pain, Simeon and Levi, two of Jacob's sons, brothers of Dinah, took each his sword, came upon the city unmolested, and slew all the males. 26 They put Hamor and his son Shechem to the sword, took Dinah out of Shechem's house, and went away. 27 The other sons of Jacob came upon the slain and plundered the town, because their sister had been defiled. 28 They seized their flocks and herds and asses, all that was inside the town and outside; 29 all

a-a Lit. "gate." *b-b I.e., all his fellow townsmen.*

Assyrian precedents), a man who rapes an unattached woman must pay a fine to her father, marry her, and forfeit the right to divorce her (Deut. 22.28–29). On the other hand, biblical law elsewhere strictly forbids the marriage of an Israelite to a Hivite (one of the indigenous nations of the land of Canaan; Deut. 7.1–5), and the patriarchs have gone to great lengths to avoid intermarriage with Canaanite nations (Gen. ch 24; 27.46–28.9). From the perspective of these (later) laws, a happy resolution to the love-struck Shechem's dilemma is impossible. **13–17:** In this ch, the sons of Jacob have already become adults, and the perspective is that of a later period in the national history (e.g., "he had committed an outrage in Israel," v. 7). The brothers' devious proposal seems to be that the Israelites and the Hivites enter into a covenant, an act that is prohibited in the Torah as inevitably an inducement to break faith with the LORD (Exod. 23.27–33). **23:** *Hamor* and *Shechem* change the terms of the offer so as to appeal to their kinsmen. Now the projected deal is said to enrich the *townsmen* at the expense of Jacob and his family. **26:** Were the Hivites holding Dinah as a hostage throughout the elaborate negotiations? Some scholars suggest that this was an abduction marriage, whereby abducting and holding the woman constituted a legal marriage. Or had she stayed in Shechem's house voluntarily, recognizing that he had done what the law required (see vv. 8–12 n.) and that the marriage prospects for a raped woman were not good (cf. 2 Sam. 13.12–16)? **27–29:** *Other* does not appear in the Heb of v. 27, and it is unclear whether Simeon and Levi were involved in the plundering; conversely, it is also possible those two brothers alone were responsible for it. The Bible commends those who abstain from plunder in situations of righteous war (e.g., Deut. 13.13–19; 1 Sam. 15.13–26; Esth. 9.10, 15, 16). Given the emphasis Hamor and Shechem had placed on material benefits (vv. 34.10–12, 23), however, and the fact that the whole episode began with an act of violence (v. 2), the plundering of their town exemplifies the widespread biblical principle that the punishment fit the crime (e.g., Deut. 19.16–21). That Simeon and Levi *slew all the males* when the latter *were in pain* from an operation on their

their wealth, all their children, and their wives, all that was in
the houses, they took as captives and booty.
30 Jacob said to Simeon and Levi, "You have brought trouble
on me, making me odious among the inhabitants of the land,
the Canaanites and the Perizzites; my men are few in number,
so that if they unite against me and attack me, I and my house
will be destroyed." 31 But they answered, "Should our sister be
treated like a whore?"

35 God said to Jacob, "Arise, go up to Bethel and remain
there; and build an altar there to the God who appeared
to you when you were fleeing from your brother Esau." 2 So Jacob said to his household and to all who were with him, "Rid
yourselves of the alien gods in your midst, purify yourselves,
and change your clothes. 3 Come, let us go up to Bethel, and
I will build an altar there to the God who answered me when
I was in distress and who has been with me wherever I have
gone." 4 They gave to Jacob all the alien gods that they had, and
the rings that were in their ears, and Jacob buried them under
the terebinth that was near Shechem. 5 As they set out, a terror
from God fell on the cities round about, so that they did not
pursue the sons of Jacob.
6 Thus Jacob came to Luz—that is, Bethel—in the land of
Canaan, he and all the people who were with him. 7 There he
built an altar and named the site El-bethel,[a] for it was there
that God had revealed Himself to him when he was fleeing
from his brother.
8 Deborah, Rebekah's nurse, died, and was buried under the
oak below Bethel; so it was named Allon-bacuth.[b]
9 God appeared again to Jacob on his arrival from Paddan-
aram, and He blessed him. 10 God said to him,

"You whose name is Jacob,
You shall be called Jacob no more,
But Israel shall be your name."

Thus He named him Israel.
11 And God said to him,

"I am El Shaddai.[c]
Be fertile and increase;
A nation, yea an assembly of nations,
Shall descend from you.
Kings shall issue from your loins.

a *"The God of Bethel."* *b* *Understood as "the oak of the weeping."* *c* *Cf. 17.1.*

male organs (v. 25) manifests the same principle. **31:** Appropriately, this tragic and ambiguous tale ends with a question, not an assertion. There is room to question the two brothers' zeal here. The same men who kill for the sake of the family's honor (against their father's wishes) in ch 34 consent to have their own little brother slain or sold into slavery in ch 37. Gen. 49.5–7, in which Jacob curses the anger of Simeon and Levi, explicitly condemns these brothers for their excessive zeal, and explains the curious fates of the tribes of Simeon (which was absorbed into Judah) and Levi (which became the clerical tribe, without land).

35.1–29: Jacob and his household return to Bethel and travel in the promised land. Marked by three deaths (Deborah, Rachel, and Isaac) and one birth (Jacob's last child, Benjamin), this disjointed chapter provides closure to one phase of Jacob's life and prepares the way for his next set of trials, the apparent loss of Joseph and all that it involves (chs 37–50). **1–7:** This passage functions as a kind of fulfillment to Jacob's vow in 28.20–22. God's protection has indeed been with him, and he is about to return safely to his father's house. **2:** The actions Jacob commands to his entourage are associated with preparations for ritual service (e.g., Num. 19.7–8) and with a deepened and renewed consecration to the one God (cf. Josh. 24.14). **5:** This verse may be the conclusion to the tale told in ch 34. **8:** Nothing else is known about this *Deborah*. The story of her death serves as an etymology for the name of what must have been a well-known landmark. A different story suggests that a tree in the same region is named after the more famous Deborah, a heroine of the book of Judges (Judg. 4.4–5). A midrash, ingeniously connecting *oak* (Heb "'alon") with a form of the Gk word for "other" ("alon"), reports that while still mourning Rebekah's nurse, Jacob received the news of another death, that of Rebekah herself (*Gen. Rab.* 81.5)—an event strangely unreported in the Torah. Another midrash gives a reason: Her funeral was held at night so that "everybody would not say, Cursed be the breasts that suckled a person like this [i.e., her wicked son Esau]" (*Tanḥ., ki-tetze* 4). **9–13:** These verses are characterized by the vocabulary of P, and vv. 9–10 are the Priestly

12 The land that I assigned to Abraham and Isaac
I assign to you;
And to your offspring to come
Will I assign the land."
13 God parted from him at the spot where He had spoken to
him; 14 and Jacob set up a pillar at the site where He had spoken to him, a pillar of stone, and he offered a libation on it and
poured oil upon it. 15 Jacob gave the site, where God had spoken to him, the name of Bethel.

16 They set out from Bethel; but when they were still some
distance short of Ephrath, Rachel was in childbirth, and she
had hard labor. 17 When her labor was at its hardest, the midwife said to her, "Have no fear, for it is another boy for you."
18 But as she breathed her last—for she was dying—she named
him Ben-oni;[a] but his father called him Benjamin.[b] 19 Thus Rachel died. She was buried on the road to Ephrath—now Bethlehem. 20 Over her grave Jacob set up a pillar; it is the pillar at
Rachel's grave to this day. 21 Israel journeyed on, and pitched
his tent beyond Migdal-eder.
22 While Israel stayed in that land, Reuben went and lay with
Bilhah, his father's concubine; and Israel found out.

Now the sons of Jacob were twelve in number. 23 The sons
of Leah: Reuben—Jacob's first-born—Simeon, Levi, Judah, Issachar, and Zebulun. 24 The sons of Rachel: Joseph and Benjamin. 25 The sons of Bilhah, Rachel's maid: Dan and Naphtali.
26 And the sons of Zilpah, Leah's maid: Gad and Asher. These
are the sons of Jacob who were born to him in Paddan-aram.

27 And Jacob came to his father Isaac at Mamre, at Kiriath-
arba—now Hebron—where Abraham and Isaac had sojourned. 28 Isaac was a hundred and eighty years old 29 when
he breathed his last and died. He[c] was gathered to his kin in
ripe old age; and he was buried by his sons Esau and Jacob.

36 This is the line of Esau—that is, Edom.
2 Esau took his wives from among the Canaanite
women—Adah daughter of Elon the Hittite, and Oholibamah
daughter of Anah daughter of Zibeon the Hivite[d]— 3 and also
Basemath daughter of Ishmael and sister of Nebaioth. 4 Adah
bore to Esau Eliphaz; Basemath bore Reuel; 5 and Oholibamah

a *Understood as "son of my suffering (or, strength)."*
b *I.e., "son of the right hand," or "son of the south."*
c *Lit. "Isaac."* d *Cf. v. 20, "Horite."*

version of the change of Jacob's name that J reports in 32.28–29. **14–15:** This is the third time Jacob names Bethel. The passage seems to be a variant of 28.18–19, which it more closely resembles than 35.7. The source analysis of v. 7 and vv. 14–15 is more uncertain than usual.

18-19: According to 1 Sam. 10.2, the tomb of Rachel was in the territory of Benjamin, as befits this account of her death, and not near Bethlehem, which is in Judah. Similarly, in Jer. 31.15, Rachel is depicted as weeping for her children in Ramah, a Benjaminite city (Josh. 18.21–28). Ephrathah/Bethlehem and Judah, however, attained high status because of their later association with David (e.g., Ruth 4.11–12, 18–22), and this may have contributed to the identification of Rachel's tomb with the site mentioned in v. 19. **22a:** The details are missing, and the text breaks off abruptly mid-verse; even the written Hebrew text contains a paragraph break in the middle (49.4 seems to allude to the same episode), suggesting that some material has been lost, or that there is more to say about this episode. A son's having intercourse with his father's concubine was a declaration of rebellion (2 Sam. 16.20–22; 1 Kings 2.13–25). Eager to protect the good names of all involved, a midrash denies that the report of Reuben's sin is to be taken literally (e.g., *b. Shab.* 55b). **28:** Abraham's life span of 175 years (25.7) and Isaac's of 180 suggest a pattern: $175 = 7 \times 5^2$, and $180 = 5 \times 6^2$. Following that progression, Jacob should live 147 years ($= 3 \times 7^2$), and so he does (47.28)!

36.1–43: The descendants of Esau. This chapter consists of several overlapping but not altogether consistent genealogies, most likely compiled from a variety of sources. Its placement here is perhaps owing to the list of Jacob's twelve sons in 35.22b–26; it also serves to divide the Jacob cycle from the Joseph story. The generation of Rebekah and Isaac's twins is now passing, and the focus for the rest of Genesis will lie on Jacob's troubled descendants alone. The attention given to Esau's family here suggests considerable fraternal feeling for him (cf. Deut. 23.8), which clashes with later biblical and postbiblical attitudes toward him. See 27.34–35 n. **2–3:** See 26.34–35 n.; 28.8–9 n.

6–8: The passage is reminiscent of the separation of Abraham and Lot in 13.5–13 and serves a similar purpose. **9–14:** This list provides the names of Esau's sons and their sons in turn. Amalek's conception by a concubine may be a disparagement related to his identity as the ruthless enemy of the people Israel and their God (Exod. 17.8–16; Deut. 25.17–19). **15–19:** The individuals in vv. 9–14 are here listed as the eponymous heads of the Edomite clans. **20–30:** This is a list of the individuals and the clans of *Seir the Horite.* According to Deut. 2.12, a group called *Horites* inhabited the land of Seir before the descendants of Esau wiped them out. The exact identity of these Horites—whether, for example, they are the same as the "Hurrians" known from cuneiform sources—is still a matter of debate. Note that Zibeon (vv. 20, 24) appears in v. 2 as the name of a Hivite. **24:** Nothing more is known about *Anah*'s enigmatic discovery. The report reads like an allusion to a story well known to the original listeners.

bore Jeush, Jalam, and Korah. Those were the sons of Esau, who were born to him in the land of Canaan.

6 Esau took his wives, his sons and daughters, and all the members of his household, his cattle and all his livestock, and all the property that he had acquired in the land of Canaan, and went to another land because of his brother Jacob.
7 For their possessions were too many for them to dwell together, and the land where they sojourned could not support them because of their livestock.
8 So Esau settled in the hill country of Seir—Esau being Edom.

9 This, then, is the line of Esau, the ancestor of the Edomites, in the hill country of Seir.

10 These are the names of Esau's sons: Eliphaz, the son of Esau's wife Adah; Reuel, the son of Esau's wife Basemath.
11 The sons of Eliphaz were Teman, Omar, Zepho, Gatam, and Kenaz.
12 Timna was a concubine of Esau's son Eliphaz; she bore Amalek to Eliphaz. Those were the descendants of Esau's wife Adah.
13 And these were the sons of Reuel: Nahath, Zerah, Shammah, and Mizzah. Those were the descendants of Esau's wife Basemath.
14 And these were the sons of Esau's wife Oholibamah, daughter of Anah daughter of Zibeon: she bore to Esau Jeush, Jalam, and Korah.

15 These are the clans of the children of Esau. The descendants of Esau's first-born Eliphaz: the clans Teman, Omar, Zepho, Kenaz,
16 Korah, Gatam, and Amalek; these are the clans of Eliphaz in the land of Edom. Those are the descendants of Adah.
17 And these are the descendants of Esau's son Reuel: the clans Nahath, Zerah, Shammah, and Mizzah; these are the clans of Reuel in the land of Edom. Those are the descendants of Esau's wife Basemath.
18 And these are the descendants of Esau's wife Oholibamah: the clans Jeush, Jalam, and Korah; these are the clans of Esau's wife Oholibamah, the daughter of Anah.
19 Those were the sons of Esau—that is, Edom—and those are their clans.

20 These were the sons of Seir the Horite, who were settled in the land: Lotan, Shobal, Zibeon, Anah,
21 Dishon, Ezer, and Dishan. Those are the clans of the Horites, the descendants of Seir, in the land of Edom.

22 The sons of Lotan were Hori and Hemam; and Lotan's sister was Timna.
23 The sons of Shobal were these: Alvan, Manahath, Ebal, Shepho, and Onam.
24 The sons of Zibeon were these: Aiah[a] and Anah—that was the Anah who discovered the hot springs[b] in the wilderness while pasturing the asses of his father Zibeon.
25 The children of Anah were these: Dishon and Anah's daughter Oholibamah.
26 The sons of Dishon[c] were these: Hemdan, Eshban, Ithran, and Cheran.
27 The sons of

a Heb. *"and Aiah."* *b* *Meaning of Heb.* yemim *uncertain.*
c Heb. Dishan; *but cf. vv. 21, 25, 28, and 30, and 1 Chron. 1.41.*

Ezer were these: Bilhan, Zaavan, and Akan.
28 And the sons of Dishan were these: Uz and Aran.

29 These are the clans of the Horites: the clans Lotan, Shobal, Zibeon, Anah,
30 Dishon, Ezer, and Dishan. Those are the clans of the Horites, clan by clan, in the land of Seir.

31 These are the kings who reigned in the land of Edom before any king reigned over the Israelites.
32 Bela son of Beor reigned in Edom, and the name of his city was Dinhabah.
33 When Bela died, Jobab son of Zerah, from Bozrah, succeeded him as king.
34 When Jobab died, Husham of the land of the Temanites succeeded him as king.
35 When Husham died, Hadad son of Bedad, who defeated the Midianites in the country of Moab, succeeded him as king; the name of his city was Avith.
36 When Hadad died, Samlah of Masrekah succeeded him as king.
37 When Samlah died, Saul[a] of Rehoboth-on-the-river succeeded him as king.
38 When Saul died, Baal-hanan son of Achbor succeeded him as king.
39 And when Baal-hanan son of Achbor died, Hadar succeeded him as king; the name of his city was Pau, and his wife's name was Mehetabel daughter of Matred daughter of Me-zahab.

40 These are the names of the clans of Esau, each with its families and locality, name by name: the clans Timna, Alvah, Jetheth,
41 Oholibamah, Elah, Pinon,
42 Kenaz, Teman, Mibzar,
43 Magdiel, and Iram. Those are the clans of Edom—that is, of Esau, father of the Edomites—by their settlements in the land which they hold.

VA-YESHEV וישב

37 Now Jacob was settled in the land where his father had sojourned, the land of Canaan.
2 This, then, is the line of Jacob:

At seventeen years of age, Joseph tended the flocks with his brothers, as a helper to the sons of his father's wives Bilhah and Zilpah. And Joseph brought bad reports of them to their father.
3 Now Israel loved Joseph best of all his sons, for he was the child of his old age; and he had made him an ornamented tunic.[b]
4 And when his brothers saw that their father loved him more than any of his brothers, they hated him so that they could not speak a friendly word to him.

a *Or "Shaul."* b *Or "a coat of many colors"; meaning of Heb. uncertain.*

31–39: None of the kings listed here succeeded his father, and different capitals are given for different rulers. It is likely that the *kings* listed here were more like the nondynastic leaders known as "judges" in the biblical book of that name. **31:** The reference to kings reigning in Israel is difficult to reconcile with the traditional attribution of Genesis to Moses, who died long before the monarchy. Ibn Ezra, who is elsewhere open to the idea of post-Mosaic passages (see 12.6 n.), defends the traditional doctrine by identifying Moses himself as the first Israelite king (also in Deut. 33.5)—a title he never holds in the Tanakh, however. **40–43:** The ch closes with another list of Edomite clans, overlapping with vv. 15–19, but not identical with it.

37.1–36: Joseph's brothers sell him into slavery. Ch 37 begins the story of Joseph, a figure who dominates most of the remaining narrative in Genesis. In structure, the Joseph story is quite different from the preceding material centering on Abraham, Isaac, and Jacob. Whereas the latter takes the form, predominantly, of small, self-contained passages, the story of Joseph resembles a coherent novella, with a subtle and well-crafted plot. Its theology, too, is different. Whereas the patriarchal narrative is replete with appearances of God or His messengers, and oracles from them, Joseph never sees or hears God or His messengers (the only direct revelation in these chs comes to Jacob, in 46.1–4). Rather, God works here in a hidden way, secretly guiding the course of human events, even bringing good out of human evil (50.20). Lastly, whereas the stories of Abraham, Isaac, and Jacob take place in Canaan and Mesopotamia, the novella of Joseph and his brothers takes place mostly in Egypt. The events that result in the return to the promised land will begin only after Joseph's death. Many of these special characteristics of the Joseph story are found in wisdom literature. **1–3:** The order of presentation is revealing—Jacob, Joseph, his brothers. Joseph is caught between his doting father and his envious siblings. Although he is the first-born son of Jacob's preferred wife, Rachel (30.22–24), his older brothers seem to have stationed him with the sons of the slave women (30.3–13), the lowest ranking siblings. Like his dreams (vv. 5–11), this contradiction may foreshadow the radical reversal of Joseph's status. **4:** The end of the verse can be translated more literally as, "they could not (even) say 'Shalom' to him."

5 Once Joseph had a dream which he told to his brothers; and they hated him even more. 6 He said to them, "Hear this dream which I have dreamed: 7 There we were binding sheaves in the field, when suddenly my sheaf stood up and remained upright; then your sheaves gathered around and bowed low to my sheaf." 8 His brothers answered, "Do you mean to reign over us? Do you mean to rule over us?" And they hated him even more for his talk about his dreams.

9 He dreamed another dream and told it to his brothers, saying, "Look, I have had another dream: And this time, the sun, the moon, and eleven stars were bowing down to me." 10 And when he told it to his father and brothers, his father berated him. "What," he said to him, "is this dream you have dreamed? Are we to come, I and your mother and your brothers, and bow low to you to the ground?" 11 So his brothers were wrought up at him, and his father kept the matter in mind.

12 One time, when his brothers had gone to pasture their father's flock at Shechem, 13 Israel said to Joseph, "Your brothers are pasturing at Shechem. Come, I will send you to them." He answered, "I am ready." 14 And he said to him, "Go and see how your brothers are and how the flocks are faring, and bring me back word." So he sent him from the valley of Hebron.

When he reached Shechem, 15 a man came upon him wandering in the fields. The man asked him, "What are you looking for?" 16 He answered, "I am looking for my brothers. Could you tell me where they are pasturing?" 17 The man said, "They have gone from here, for I heard them say: Let us go to Dothan." So Joseph followed his brothers and found them at Dothan.

18 They saw him from afar, and before he came close to them they conspired to kill him. 19 They said to one another, "Here comes that dreamer! 20 Come now, let us kill him and throw him into one of the pits; and we can say, 'A savage beast devoured him.' We shall see what comes of his dreams!" 21 But when Reuben heard it, he tried to save him from them. He said, "Let us not take his life." 22 And Reuben went on, "Shed no blood! Cast him into that pit out in the wilderness, but do not touch him yourselves"—intending to save him from them and restore him to his father. 23 When Joseph came up to his brothers, they stripped Joseph of his tunic, the ornamented tunic that he was wearing, 24 and took him and cast him into the pit. The pit was empty; there was no water in it.

25 Then they sat down to a meal. Looking up, they saw a caravan of Ishmaelites coming from Gilead, their camels bearing

5: Like the "bad reports [that] he brought to his father" (v. 2), his telling his brothers the dream evidences Joseph's immaturity and lack of foresight—both of which will be dramatically remedied as his tale unfolds. **7–8:** In each of the three pairs of dreams in the Joseph story, one dream focuses on grain or grain products (40.16–19; 41.5–7). The brothers see only dominance in Joseph's own first dream, missing altogether the symbolism of the grain imagery. When they do bow down to him, it will be in supplication that he—who has grain when they do not—will feed them (42.6–7). **9–11:** Joseph tells his first dream to the brothers alone, the second to his brothers and his father. Similarly, his brothers come to Egypt alone and bow down to him (42.6); only afterwards does Jacob come (46.6) and bow to his son (47.31). Jacob is doubly incredulous of the dream, perhaps because it appears to mention Rachel, who has already died giving birth to Benjamin (35.16–20). In the Talmud, a rabbi observes that this illustrates the rule that only part of any given dream comes true, not the whole (*b. Ber.* 55a). Rashi, on the other hand, cites a midrash that identifies Joseph's mother with Bilhah, Rachel's slave and surrogate (*Gen. Rab.* 44.11). Some modern scholars have speculated that the second dream presupposes a different form of the ancestral stories, in which Rachel had not yet passed away. **12–13:** Joseph's response, *I am ready* ("hineni"), recalls instances in which the same Heb word appears in contexts in which earlier fathers were about to lose, or seemed about to lose, their favored sons (22.1, 7, 11; 27.1). **14:** *How your brothers are,* lit. "the shalom of your brothers," is telling, given the absence of "shalom" in the family (see v. 4 n.). Shechem being quite a distance from Hebron, there is room to wonder why Jacob did not foresee danger, even before his beloved son reached his angry brothers. Eventually, Joseph does reach Shechem in peace—after his death (Josh. 24.32)! **23:** The clothing and unclothing of Joseph mark pivotal moments in the course of the narrative (cf. 37.3; 39.15–18; 41.14, 42). **25:** The brothers' meal displays their extraordinary callousness and insensitivity to human life (cf. Esth. 3.15). Later, the tables turn, and Joseph arranges a meal in which he is the master, and they, his nervous

gum, balm, and ladanum to be taken to Egypt. [26] Then Judah said to his brothers, "What do we gain by killing our brother and covering up his blood? [27] Come, let us sell him to the Ishmaelites, but let us not do away with him ourselves. After all, he is our brother, our own flesh." His brothers agreed. [28] When Midianite traders passed by, they pulled Joseph up out of the pit. They sold Joseph for twenty pieces of silver to the Ishmaelites, who brought Joseph to Egypt.

[29] When Reuben returned to the pit and saw that Joseph was not in the pit, he rent his clothes. [30] Returning to his brothers, he said, "The boy is gone! Now, what am I to do?" [31] Then they took Joseph's tunic, slaughtered a kid, and dipped the tunic in the blood. [32] They had the ornamented tunic taken to their father, and they said, "We found this. Please examine it; is it your son's tunic or not?" [33] He recognized it, and said, "My son's tunic! A savage beast devoured him! Joseph was torn by a beast!" [34] Jacob rent his clothes, put sackcloth on his loins, and observed mourning for his son many days. [35] All his sons and daughters sought to comfort him; but he refused to be comforted, saying, "No, I will go down mourning to my son in Sheol." Thus his father bewailed him.

[36] The Midianites,[a] meanwhile, sold him in Egypt to Potiphar, a courtier of Pharaoh and his chief steward.

38 About that time Judah left his brothers and camped near a certain Adullamite whose name was Hirah. [2] There Judah saw the daughter of a certain Canaanite whose name was Shua, and he married her and cohabited with her. [3] She conceived and bore a son, and he named him Er. [4] She conceived again and bore a son, and named him Onan. [5] Once again she bore a son, and named him Shelah; he was at Chezib when she bore him.

[6] Judah got a wife for Er his first-born; her name was Tamar. [7] But Er, Judah's first-born, was displeasing to the LORD, and the LORD took his life. [8] Then Judah said to Onan, "Join with your brother's wife and do your duty by her as a brother-in-law,[b] and provide offspring for your brother." [9] But Onan, knowing that

a Heb. "Medanites." *b Cf. Deut. 25.5.*

dependents (43.29–34). **26–27:** It is Judah's advice that is ultimately heeded, reflecting the importance of this brother elsewhere in the Joseph story. **28:** In its current form, the text mentions both Ishmaelite caravaneers (v. 25) and *Midianite traders,* just as it mentions two different attempts to save Joseph's life, one by Reuben (vv. 21–22, 29–30) and one by Judah (vv. 26–28). Although arguments have been made that Midianites and Ishmaelites are the same group (cf. Judg. 8.24), many modern scholars think the explanation lies in source analysis: Reuben and the Midianites derive from the E version of the story, and Judah and the Ishmaelites from the J version, though it is difficult to find complete J and E versions throughout the narrative. In the story in its current form, it is unclear who is the subject of *pulled* in v. 28—the brothers or the *Midianite traders.* If it is the latter, Joseph's brothers truly do not know what became of him. But the idea that it was the Midianites rather than the brothers who sold him to the Ishmaelites cannot explain the reports that it is the Midianites who bring him to Egypt (v. 36; cf. 39.1). **30:** Reuben's cry is strikingly similar to the wording of the oracle about Rachel's lament in Jer. 31.15. **31:** There is a certain poetic justice to the brothers' cruel deception of their father, since Jacob had used kids to deceive his own father (27.5–23). **35:** That Jacob *refused to be comforted* recalls what is said of Rachel in Jer. 31.15, in a lament for the lost members of the nation. See 37.30 n.

38.1–30: Judah and Tamar. This chapter, which treats the origins of the Judahite clans (cf. Num. 26.19–22), is, on the one hand, independent of the novella of Joseph in which it now appears; Judah lives apart from his brothers and already has grown children when the tale begins. On the other hand, a number of verbal and thematic connections to the Joseph story bespeak the exquisite fitness of its placement therein. **8:** The duty in question, known in English as "levirate marriage" (from Latin "levir," "husband's brother"), is spelled out in Deut. 25.5–10. If a man dies childless, his brother is obligated to marry his widow, and her first son is reckoned as the offspring of the deceased. In Deuteronomy, the surviving brother can decline and undergo a procedure that the Rabbis named "ḥalitzah," but Gen. ch 38 presupposes a practice in which "ḥalitzah" is unknown (cf. Ruth 4.5–6). Today, levirate marriage is discouraged and "ḥalitzah" is substituted among traditionally observant Ashkenazic Jews. Some Sephardic groups still practice levirate marriage. **9:** *Onan* would have to expend his own resources to support a child that is legally

the seed would not count as his, let it go to waste[a] whenever
he joined with his brother's wife, so as not to provide offspring
for his brother. 10 What he did was displeasing to the LORD, and
He took his life also. 11 Then Judah said to his daughter-in-law
Tamar, "Stay as a widow in your father's house until my son
Shelah grows up"—for he thought, "He too might die like his
brothers." So Tamar went to live in her father's house.
12 A long time afterward, Shua's daughter, the wife of Judah,
died. When [b]his period of mourning was over,[b] Judah went up
to Timnah to his sheepshearers, together with his friend Hirah
the Adullamite. 13 And Tamar was told, "Your father-in-law is
coming up to Timnah for the sheepshearing." 14 So she took
off her widow's garb, covered her face with a veil, and, wrap-
ping herself up, sat down at the entrance to Enaim,[c] which is
on the road to Timnah; for she saw that Shelah was grown up,
yet she had not been given to him as wife. 15 When Judah saw
her, he took her for a harlot; for she had covered her face. 16 So
he turned aside to her by the road and said, "Here, let me sleep
with you"—for he did not know that she was his daughter-in-
law. "What," she asked, "will you pay for sleeping with me?"
17 He replied, "I will send a kid from my flock." But she said,
"You must leave a pledge until you have sent it." 18 And he said,
"What pledge shall I give you?" She replied, "Your seal and
cord, and the staff which you carry." So he gave them to her
and slept with her, and she conceived by him. 19 Then she went
on her way. She took off her veil and again put on her widow's
garb.
20 Judah sent the kid by his friend the Adullamite, to redeem
the pledge from the woman; but he could not find her. 21 He
inquired of the people of that town, "Where is the cult prostitute, the one at Enaim, by the road?" But they said, "There has
been no prostitute here." 22 So he returned to Judah and said, "I
could not find her; moreover, the townspeople said: There has
been no prostitute here." 23 Judah said, "Let her keep them, lest
we become a laughingstock. I did send her this kid, but you did
not find her."
24 About three months later, Judah was told, "Your daughter-
in-law Tamar has played the harlot; in fact, she is with child by
harlotry." "Bring her out," said Judah, "and let her be burned."
25 As she was being brought out, she sent this message to her
father-in-law, "I am with child by the man to whom these belong." And she added, "Examine these: whose seal and cord
and staff are these?" 26 Judah recognized them, and said, "She
is more in the right than I, inasmuch as I did not give her to my
son Shelah." And he was not intimate with her again.

someone else's, and the child, as the heir to a first-born son, would displace Onan in the line of inheritance to boot. **11:** Judah's loss of two sons and reluctance to surrender the third foreshadows the tragic situation of Jacob, who will soon lose Joseph and Simeon (or so it will appear to him) and refuse to surrender Benjamin, though he must surrender him if the family is to survive (42.36–38). **14–15:** The use of a disguise in pursuit of a purpose that conforms to the will of God (and, in this case, religious law) recalls Jacob's deceit in ch 27. **17:** Note the echo of the preceding ch, where a kid also played a key role in deceiving a parent (37.31–35). **21:** *Cult prostitute* and *prostitute* are the same word in Heb; many scholars doubt that cultic prostitution as it is usually understood existed in ancient Israel. A different term underlies "harlot" in vv. 15, 24. **24:** Tamar's ostensible capital offense is not prostitution, but adultery (see Deut. 22.23–24), since she is still in a state akin to betrothal to Judah's family. Adultery is the false charge in the next ch as well (39.7–18). **25:** *Examine these* is identical in the Heb to "Please examine it" in the previous chapter (37.32). These are, in fact, the only two instances of this expression in the Tanakh. Recognition (the same word in Heb) is a major theme in the Joseph story (see also 42.7–8). **26:** Tamar's actions are justified in Judah's eyes, and in the eyes of the author. She ensured that the family line of Judah was preserved. A midrash in the Talmud sees Judah's Heb name (which includes every letter of the four-letter name of the LORD) as a reward for his public confession of wrongdoing in this episode (*b. Sot.* 10b). According to 1 Chron. 4.21, Shelah named his first son Er, suggesting that Judah did finally release him to the first Er's widow, Tamar.

a Lit. "spoil on the ground." *b-b Lit. "he was comforted."*
c Cf. Enam, Josh. 15.34. Others "in an open place" or "at the crossroad."

[27] When the time came for her to give birth, there were twins in her womb! [28] While she was in labor, one of them put out his hand, and the midwife tied a crimson thread on that hand, to signify: This one came out first. [29] But just then he drew back his hand, and out came his brother; and she said, "What a breach[a] you have made for yourself!" So he was named Perez. [30] Afterward his brother came out, on whose hand was the crimson thread; he was named Zerah.[b]

39 When Joseph was taken down to Egypt, a certain Egyptian, Potiphar, a courtier of Pharaoh and his chief steward, bought him from the Ishmaelites who had brought him there. [2] The LORD was with Joseph, and he was a successful man; and he stayed in the house of his Egyptian master. [3] And when his master saw that the LORD was with him and that the LORD lent success to everything he undertook, [4] he took a liking to Joseph. He made him his personal attendant and put him in charge of his household, placing in his hands all that he owned. [5] And from the time that the Egyptian put him in charge of his household and of all that he owned, the LORD blessed his house for Joseph's sake, so that the blessing of the LORD was upon everything that he owned, in the house and outside. [6] He left all that he had in Joseph's hands and, with him there, he paid attention to nothing save the food that he ate. Now Joseph was well built and handsome.

[7] After a time, his master's wife cast her eyes upon Joseph and said, "Lie with me." [8] But he refused. He said to his master's wife, "Look, with me here, my master gives no thought to anything in this house, and all that he owns he has placed in my hands. [9] He wields no more authority in this house than I, and he has withheld nothing from me except yourself, since you are his wife. How then could I do this most wicked thing, and sin before God?" [10] And much as she coaxed Joseph day after day, he did not yield to her request to lie beside her, to be with her.

[11] One such day, he came into the house to do his work. None of the household being there inside, [12] she caught hold of him by his garment and said, "Lie with me!" But he left his garment in her hand and got away and fled outside. [13] When she saw

a Heb. pereṣ
b I.e., "brightness," perhaps alluding to the crimson thread.

27–30: The birth story of *Perez* and *Zerah* is highly reminiscent of that of Jacob and Esau in 25.21–26. It is from Perez that King David was descended, as reported, for example, in Ruth (Ruth 4.18–22), a book with striking similarities to Gen. ch 38 (see also Ruth 4.11–12).

39.1–23: Joseph in Potiphar's house. Genesis rejoins the story of Joseph after the digression of ch 38. The bulk of ch 39 centers on the hero's resistance to seduction and the ensuing false accusation of the spurned matron. It shows remarkable similarities to an Egyptian tale, "The Story of Two Brothers." Although some dependence is likely, the biblical narrative adapts its prototype to characteristic Israelite theological and ethical convictions. **39.1–6a:** As in ch 37, which speaks of Jacob's preference for Joseph (vv. 3–4), so here the latter is the beneficiary of a mysterious favor, this time from the LORD. Unbeknownst to all at the time, Jacob's favoritism for the son of his old age had been the medium for a higher purpose. Like Laban (30.27–30), Potiphar benefits mightily from association with this descendant of Abraham. **6–7:** Good looks are often a sign of divine favor in the Tanakh (e.g., 1 Sam. 9.2; 16.12), but here they set up the one who bears them for a potentially catastrophic temptation. A midrash, finding it difficult to believe that Joseph was altogether innocent, likens him to one "who would stand in the market place, put make-up around his eyes, straighten up his hair, and swing his heels." Mrs. Potiphar's proposition was thus a punishment for his narcissism and machismo (*Gen. Rab.* 87.3). **8–9:** Joseph's pointed deference to his *master* stands in striking contrast with his dreams of dominance in 37.5–11. The brash and unreflective teenager of ch 37 has matured into a more responsible man, with the appropriate humility. Joseph's mention of *God* is his first. No one mentioned the deity in the previous two chs. **12:** The garment left *in her hand* (also in v. 13) contrasts with Potiphar's placing "in his hands all that he owned" (v. 4). The use of a garment as fraudulent evidence recalls Joseph's brothers' displaying the bloodstained tunic to their father (37.31–33) and contrasts with Tamar's truthful presentation to Judah of his "seal and cord and staff" (38.25–26). Note the telling contrast between the woman who attempts to dishonor her marriage without success (Mrs. Potiphar) and the woman who, also acting boldly and seductively, succeeds in implementing the law and thus ensures the survival of her family (Tamar).

that he had left it in her hand and had fled outside, 14 she called out to her servants and said to them, "Look, he had to bring us a Hebrew to dally with us! This one came to lie with me; but I screamed loud. 15 And when he heard me screaming at the top of my voice, he left his garment with me and got away and fled outside." 16 She kept his garment beside her, until his master came home. 17 Then she told him the same story, saying, "The Hebrew slave whom you brought into our house came to me to dally with me; 18 but when I screamed at the top of my voice, he left his garment with me and fled outside."

19 When his master heard the story that his wife told him, namely, "Thus and so your slave did to me," he was furious. 20 So Joseph's master had him put in prison, where the king's prisoners were confined. But even while he was there in prison, 21 the LORD was with Joseph: He extended kindness to him and disposed the chief jailer favorably toward him. 22 The chief jailer put in Joseph's charge all the prisoners who were in that prison, and he was the one to carry out everything that was done there. 23 The chief jailer did not supervise anything that was in Joseph's[a] charge, because the LORD was with him, and whatever he did the LORD made successful.

40 Some time later, the cupbearer and the baker of the king of Egypt gave offense to their lord the king of Egypt. 2 Pharaoh was angry with his two courtiers, the chief cupbearer and the chief baker, 3 and put them in custody, in the house of the chief steward, in the same prison house where Joseph was confined. 4 The chief steward assigned Joseph to them, and he attended them.

When they had been in custody for some time, 5 both of them—the cupbearer and the baker of the king of Egypt, who were confined in the prison—dreamed in the same night, each his own dream and each dream with its own meaning. 6 When Joseph came to them in the morning, he saw that they were distraught. 7 He asked Pharaoh's courtiers, who were with him in custody in his master's house, saying, "Why do you appear downcast today?" 8 And they said to him, "We had dreams, and there is no one to interpret them." So Joseph said to them, "Surely God can interpret! Tell me [your dreams]."

9 Then the chief cupbearer told his dream to Joseph. He said to him, "In my dream, there was a vine in front of me. 10 On the vine were three branches. It had barely budded, when out came its blossoms and its clusters ripened into grapes. 11 Pharaoh's

a Lit. "his."

14: Her clever phrasing suggests a hope to profit from her staff's resentment of a foreigner and perhaps of their boss as well *(he had to bring us a Hebrew).* Here she sides with her servants *(bring us),* whereas in v. 17 she sides with her husband ("whom you brought into our house"), although in both cases she blames him for introducing Joseph into the household. **17–18:** Now she blames Joseph primarily, and her husband only indirectly. Note that here (as in v. 15) she describes the garment that was left "in her hand" (v. 12) as *with me,* instead, subtly disguising her true involvement. **19–23:** The tale ends where it began (v. 2), with an affirmation of God's presence in Joseph's affairs and the success it brings. Even in prison, the young man who had been second in rank in his family (37.3) and second in rank in the chief steward's household (vv. 4–6) achieves the same status, when the warden puts him in charge of the other prisoners.

40.1–23: Joseph the dream interpreter. In this chapter, we hear of the second of the three pairs of dreams that mark pivotal moments in Joseph's life. The first pair (37.5–11) were Joseph's own, and their interpretation came not from him, but from his outraged brothers and incredulous father. Taken for dreams of kingship, they nearly result in the dreamer's death and leave him in slavery (37.18–28). Joseph decodes the second set of dreams himself, through a hitherto unmentioned God-given talent. They treat of the same polarity, favor from the king (v. 13), reminiscent of the nearly lethal favor Joseph received from his father (37.3), on the one hand, and death, on the other (v. 19). **8:** *Surely God can interpret!* may imply a critique of divination practices prominent in the ancient world. The contrast between Joseph, with his God-given talent for dream interpretation, and the bankruptcy of the Egyptian magicians is more pronounced in the next chapter, which deals with Pharaoh's dreams (41.8). The theme foreshadows Moses and Aaron's decisive confrontation with Pharaoh's magicians in Exod. chs 7–11 (see esp. Exod. 8.15) and serves as the basis of the depiction of Daniel as a great dream interpreter (see, for example, Dan. ch 2).

cup was in my hand, and I took the grapes, pressed them into Pharaoh's cup, and placed the cup in Pharaoh's hand." [12] Joseph said to him, "This is its interpretation: The three branches are three days. [13] In three days Pharaoh will pardon you[a] and restore you to your post; you will place Pharaoh's cup in his hand, as was your custom formerly when you were his cupbearer. [14] But think of me when all is well with you again, and do me the kindness of mentioning me to Pharaoh, so as to free me from this place. [15] For in truth, I was kidnapped from the land of the Hebrews; nor have I done anything here that they should have put me in the dungeon."

[16] When the chief baker saw how favorably he had interpreted, he said to Joseph, "In my dream, similarly, there were three openwork baskets[b] on my head. [17] In the uppermost basket were all kinds of food for Pharaoh that a baker prepares; and the birds were eating it out of the basket above my head." [18] Joseph answered, "This is its interpretation: The three baskets are three days. [19] In three days Pharaoh will lift off your head and impale you upon a pole; and the birds will pick off your flesh."

[20] On the third day—his birthday—Pharaoh made a banquet for all his officials, and he singled out[c] his chief cupbearer and his chief baker from among his officials. [21] He restored the chief cupbearer to his cupbearing, and he placed the cup in Pharaoh's hand; [22] but the chief baker he impaled—just as Joseph had interpreted to them.

[23] Yet the chief cupbearer did not think of Joseph; he forgot him.

MIKKETS מקץ

41 After two years' time, Pharaoh dreamed that he was standing by the Nile, [2] when out of the Nile there came up seven cows, handsome and sturdy, and they grazed in the reed grass. [3] But presently, seven other cows came up from the Nile close behind them, ugly and gaunt, and stood beside the cows on the bank of the Nile; [4] and the ugly gaunt cows ate up the seven handsome sturdy cows. And Pharaoh awoke.

[5] He fell asleep and dreamed a second time: Seven ears of grain, solid and healthy, grew on a single stalk. [6] But close behind them sprouted seven ears, thin and scorched by the east wind. [7] And the thin ears swallowed up the seven solid and full ears. Then Pharaoh awoke: it was a dream!

[8] Next morning, his spirit was agitated, and he sent for all the magicians of Egypt, and all its wise men; and Pharaoh told them his dreams, but none could interpret them for Pharaoh.

a Lit. "lift up your head."
b Others "baskets with white bread" or "white baskets"; meaning of Heb. ḥori *uncertain.*
c Lit. "lifted the head of."

16–19: The chief baker altogether misses the key point that Joseph's gift for interpretation depends on the grace of God. Instead, he imagines that it is all a matter of technique: Similar dreams must lead to similar interpretations (not an unreasonable expectation in light of the other pairs in 37.5–11 and 41.1–32). But Joseph notices a crucial detail that the chief baker has missed: Not Pharaoh but birds eat from the basket on his head. Having missed God's grace, the chief baker will be denied Pharaoh's as well.

41.1–57: Joseph interprets Pharaoh's dreams and becomes vizier. Vv. 1–32 deal with the last of the three pairs of dreams in the Joseph story, the dreams of Pharaoh. Vv. 33–57 detail Joseph's unsolicited recommendation of a course to enable Egypt to survive the crisis, and then report the king's enthusiastic appointment of the young Hebrew man to implement his own policy. **1–7:** Pharaoh's dreams revert to the pattern of the first pair, Joseph's own (37.5–11), in that they both mean the same thing (v. 32) and deal with the triumph of the weak over the strong. And like the intervening pair, those of the chief cupbearer and chief baker (40.9–22), each of the two dreams deals with themes of good fortune and ill, in that order. **8:** See 40.8 n. The inability of the pagan magicians to interpret dreams and accurately predict the future is developed at greater length in Dan. ch 2, a narrative influenced by the Joseph story. Cf. Isa. 41.21–24.

14: The Heb word for *dungeon* (also in 40.15) is the same as that for the "pit" into which Joseph's brothers threw him in 37.20, 22, 24, 28. The chief cupbearer's belated act of remembrance has suddenly reversed Joseph's repeated descents—into the pit, into Egypt, into prison. The pattern is familiar from prayers of thanksgiving (e.g., Ps. 30, esp. vv. 4, 10). For the fourth time, Joseph's clothes are changed (the previous instances are in 37.3, 23; 39.12), this time (like the first) as a sign of elevation. **16:** See 39.8–9 n.

9 The chief cupbearer then spoke up and said to Pharaoh, "I must make mention today of my offenses. 10 Once Pharaoh was angry with his servants, and placed me in custody in the house of the chief steward, together with the chief baker. 11 We had dreams the same night, he and I, each of us a dream with a meaning of its own. 12 A Hebrew youth was there with us, a servant of the chief steward; and when we told him our dreams, he interpreted them for us, telling each of the meaning of his dream. 13 And as he interpreted for us, so it came to pass: I was restored to my post, and the other was impaled."

14 Thereupon Pharaoh sent for Joseph, and he was rushed from the dungeon. He had his hair cut and changed his clothes, and he appeared before Pharaoh. 15 And Pharaoh said to Joseph, "I have had a dream, but no one can interpret it. Now I have heard it said of you that for you to hear a dream is to tell its meaning." 16 Joseph answered Pharaoh, saying, "Not I! God will see to Pharaoh's welfare."

17 Then Pharaoh said to Joseph, "In my dream, I was standing on the bank of the Nile, 18 when out of the Nile came up seven sturdy and well-formed cows and grazed in the reed grass. 19 Presently there followed them seven other cows, scrawny, ill-formed, and emaciated—never had I seen their likes for ugliness in all the land of Egypt! 20 And the seven lean and ugly cows ate up the first seven cows, the sturdy ones; 21 but when they had consumed them, one could not tell that they had consumed them, for they looked just as bad as before. And I awoke. 22 In my other dream, I saw seven ears of grain, full and healthy, growing on a single stalk; 23 but right behind them sprouted seven ears, shriveled, thin, and scorched by the east wind. 24 And the thin ears swallowed the seven healthy ears. I have told my magicians, but none has an explanation for me."

25 And Joseph said to Pharaoh, "Pharaoh's dreams are one and the same: God has told Pharaoh what He is about to do. 26 The seven healthy cows are seven years, and the seven healthy ears are seven years; it is the same dream. 27 The seven lean and ugly cows that followed are seven years, as are also the seven empty ears scorched by the east wind; they are seven years of famine. 28 It is just as I have told Pharaoh: God has revealed to Pharaoh what He is about to do. 29 Immediately ahead are seven years of great abundance in all the land of Egypt. 30 After them will come seven years of famine, and all the abundance in the land of Egypt will be forgotten. As the land is ravaged by famine, 31 no trace of the abundance will be left in the land because of the famine thereafter, for it will be very severe. 32 As for Pharaoh having had the same dream twice, it means that the matter has been determined by God, and that God will soon carry it out.

33 "Accordingly, let Pharaoh find a man of discernment and wisdom, and set him over the land of Egypt. 34 And let Pharaoh take steps to appoint overseers over the land, and organize[a] the land of Egypt in the seven years of plenty. 35 Let all the food of these good years that are coming be gathered, and let the grain be collected under Pharaoh's authority as food to be stored in the cities. 36 Let that food be a reserve for the land for the seven years of famine which will come upon the land of Egypt, so that the land may not perish in the famine."

37 The plan pleased Pharaoh and all his courtiers. 38 And Pharaoh said to his courtiers, "Could we find another like him, a man in whom is the spirit of God?" 39 So Pharaoh said to Joseph, "Since God has made all this known to you, there is none so discerning and wise as you. 40 You shall be in charge of my court, and by your command shall all my people be directed;[b] only with respect to the throne shall I be superior to you." 41 Pharaoh further said to Joseph, "See, I put you in charge of all the land of Egypt." 42 And removing his signet ring from his hand, Pharaoh put it on Joseph's hand; and he had him dressed in robes of fine linen, and put a gold chain about his neck. 43 He had him ride in the chariot of his second-in-command, and they cried before him, "Abrek!"[c] Thus he placed him over all the land of Egypt.

44 Pharaoh said to Joseph, "I am Pharaoh; yet without you, no one shall lift up hand or foot in all the land of Egypt." 45 Pharaoh then gave Joseph the name Zaphenath-paneah;[d] and he gave him for a wife Asenath daughter of Poti-phera, priest of On. Thus Joseph emerged in charge of the land of Egypt.— 46 Joseph was thirty years old when he entered the service of Pharaoh king of Egypt.—Leaving Pharaoh's presence, Joseph traveled through all the land of Egypt.

47 During the seven years of plenty, the land produced in abundance. 48 And he gathered all the grain of [e]the seven years that the land of Egypt was enjoying,[e] and stored the grain in the cities; he put in each city the grain of the fields around it. 49 So Joseph collected produce in very large quantity, like the sands of the sea, until he ceased to measure it, for it could not be measured.

50 Before the years of famine came, Joseph became the father of two sons, whom Asenath daughter of Poti-phera, priest of On, bore to him. 51 Joseph named the first-born Manasseh, meaning, "God has made me forget[f] completely my hardship

a Others "take a fifth part of"; meaning of Heb. uncertain.

b Others "order themselves" or "pay homage"; meaning of Heb. yishshaq *uncertain.*

c Others "Bow the knee," as though from Heb. barakh *"to kneel"; perhaps from an Egyptian word of unknown meaning.*

d Egyptian for "God speaks; he lives," or "creator of life."

e-e Lit. "the seven years that were in the land of Egypt."

f Heb. nashshani, *connected with "Manasseh"* (Menashsheh).

33–36: Unlike the implication of Joseph's own two dreams (37.5–11), the domination of the weak over the strong is not the last word. Foresight and prudence, Joseph tells Pharaoh, can enable the land to survive catastrophe. As things turn out, the survival of Egypt will have a more particular meaning as well: It foreshadows and enables the healing of the rift between Joseph and his brothers. **40:** Joseph is once again second in rank. See 39.19–23 n. Joseph will indeed rule, just as his brothers feared (37.8, 10–11), but with this crucial qualification: His rule will be rooted not in sheer power, but in the benefit he provides to the less fortunate. This corresponds to an ideal of kingship widespread in the ancient Near East, in which the king is the rescuer and servant of the people (cf. Judg. 11.4–11). **42:** This is Joseph's fifth and final change of clothes. See v. 14 n. **45:** In Egyptian, *Asenath* means "the one who belongs to (the goddess) Neith." Since Jewish law does not recognize any marriage between a Jew and a Gentile (see 26.34–35 n.), Jewish tradition came to interpret Asenath as the prototypical convert to Judaism. Her powerful story is told at length in an important Hellenistic novella, "Joseph and Asenath." Rabbinic tradition identifies her father, Poti-phera, with the Potiphar of ch 39 (*b. Sot.* 13b), but this is unlikely. This verse, as others in Gen., suggests that biblical lineage was patrilineal, and that the foreign wife adopted the religious practices of her husband (though rites of formal conversion were not yet in existence). **51:** Saved by the cupbearer's act of remembrance (vv. 9–13), Joseph nonetheless gives his first-born son a name that celebrates forgetfulness. The family history that he has repressed will, however, return to confront him with great force in the next chapter (42.8–9).

and my parental home." 52 And the second he named Ephraim, meaning, "God has made me fertile[a] in the land of my affliction."

53 The seven years of abundance that the land of Egypt enjoyed came to an end, 54 and the seven years of famine set in, just as Joseph had foretold. There was famine in all lands, but throughout the land of Egypt there was bread. 55 And when all the land of Egypt felt the hunger, the people cried out to Pharaoh for bread; and Pharaoh said to all the Egyptians, "Go to Joseph; whatever he tells you, you shall do."— 56 Accordingly, when the famine became severe in the land of Egypt, Joseph laid open all that was within, and rationed out grain to the Egyptians. The famine, however, spread over the whole world. 57 So all the world came to Joseph in Egypt to procure rations, for the famine had become severe throughout the world.

42 When Jacob saw that there were food rations to be had in Egypt, he[b] said to his sons, "Why do you keep looking at one another? 2 Now I hear," he went on, "that there are rations to be had in Egypt. Go down and procure rations for us there, that we may live and not die." 3 So ten of Joseph's brothers went down to get grain rations in Egypt; 4 for Jacob did not send Joseph's brother Benjamin with his brothers, since he feared that he might meet with disaster. 5 Thus the sons of Israel were among those who came to procure rations, for the famine extended to the land of Canaan.

6 Now Joseph was the vizier of the land; it was he who dispensed rations to all the people of the land. And Joseph's brothers came and bowed low to him, with their faces to the ground. 7 When Joseph saw his brothers, he recognized them; but he acted like a stranger toward them and spoke harshly to them. He asked them, "Where do you come from?" And they said, "From the land of Canaan, to procure food." 8 For though Joseph recognized his brothers, they did not recognize him. 9 Recalling the dreams that he had dreamed about them, Joseph said to them, "You are spies, you have come to see the land in its nakedness." 10 But they said to him, "No, my lord! Truly, your servants have come to procure food. 11 We are all of us sons of the same man; we are honest men; your servants have never been spies!" 12 And he said to them, "No, you have come to see the land in its nakedness!" 13 And they replied, "We your servants were twelve brothers, sons of a certain man in the land of Canaan; the youngest, however, is now with our father, and one is no more." 14 But Joseph said to them, "It is just as I have told you: You are spies! 15 By this you shall be put to the test: unless your youngest brother comes here, by Pharaoh,

a Heb. hiphrani, *connected with "Ephraim."* *b Lit. "Jacob."*

52: Fertility in the land of affliction will eventually prove a mixed blessing. When "the Israelites were fertile and prolific;.... A new king arose over Egypt who did not know Joseph" (Exod. 1.7–8) and sought to inflict upon them the fate decided for Joseph in Gen. ch 37: enslavement and death (Exod. 1.9–12, 15–22).

42.1–38: The first reunion of Joseph and his brothers. In this chapter, Joseph and his brothers meet again, though in radically different and, in fact, reversed roles from the ones in which we last saw them (ch 37). Now, just as he has dreamt, it is they who are the subordinates, and, moreover, he is the only one who recognizes the situation. Joseph reenacts his brothers' mistreatment of him, only with them now as the victims—and with a dose of mercy altogether missing in ch 37 (with the exception of Reuben's botched attempt to rescue him). **3–4:** Once again, Jacob shows preference for a son of Rachel (cf. 37.3). As the events unfold, Benjamin, Joseph's only full brother and the youngest of the brood, serves as Joseph's alter ego. **6:** Their prostration fulfills the dreams of 37.5–11. Little did anyone suspect at the time, however, that their prostration would be in supplication for their very lives or that Joseph would keep them from death. **9:** *To see the land in its nakedness* recalls the episode in ch 39, in which Joseph is unfairly accused (and convicted) of a sexual crime (see 9.22–24 n.). **11:** The first clause is truer than the brothers recognize; the second remains to be established; only the third is straightforward fact. **13–14:** Having lied to their father about Joseph's fate (37.31–33), the brothers now find themselves unable to convince Pharaoh's vizier of the truth. The Heb of the clause *and one is no more* echoes Reuben's cry of desperation in 37.30 (cf. 42.36). **15–17:** By reaffirming the specialness of the favored son, Joseph's test requires the brothers

you shall not depart from this place! 16 Let one of you go and bring your brother, while the rest of you remain confined, that your words may be put to the test whether there is truth in you. Else, by Pharaoh, you are nothing but spies!" 17 And he confined them in the guardhouse for three days.

18 On the third day Joseph said to them, "Do this and you shall live, for I am a God-fearing man. 19 If you are honest men, let one of you brothers be held in your place of detention, while the rest of you go and take home rations for your starving households; 20 but you must bring me your youngest brother, that your words may be verified and that you may not die." And they did accordingly. 21 They said to one another, "Alas, we are being punished on account of our brother, because we looked on at his anguish, yet paid no heed as he pleaded with us. That is why this distress has come upon us." 22 Then Reuben spoke up and said to them, "Did I not tell you, 'Do no wrong to the boy'? But you paid no heed. Now comes the reckoning for his blood." 23 They did not know that Joseph understood, for there was an interpreter between him and them. 24 He turned away from them and wept. But he came back to them and spoke to them; and he took Simeon from among them and had him bound before their eyes. 25 Then Joseph gave orders to fill their bags with grain, return each one's money to his sack, and give them provisions for the journey; and this was done for them. 26 So they loaded their asses with the rations and departed from there.

27 As one of them was opening his sack to give feed to his ass at the night encampment, he saw his money right there at the mouth of his bag. 28 And he said to his brothers, "My money has been returned! It is here in my bag!" Their hearts sank; and, trembling, they turned to one another, saying, "What is this that God has done to us?"

29 When they came to their father Jacob in the land of Canaan, they told him all that had befallen them, saying, 30 "The man who is lord of the land spoke harshly to us and accused us of spying on the land. 31 We said to him, 'We are honest men; we have never been spies! 32 There were twelve of us brothers, sons by the same father; but one is no more, and the youngest is now with our father in the land of Canaan.' 33 But the man who is lord of the land said to us, 'By this I shall know that you are honest men: leave one of your brothers with me, and take something for your starving households and be off. 34 And bring your youngest brother to me, that I may know that you are not spies but honest men. I will then restore your brother to you, and you shall be free to move about in the land.' "

35 As they were emptying their sacks, there, in each one's sack, was his money-bag! When they and their father saw their money-bags, they were dismayed. 36 Their father Jacob said to them, "It is always me that you bereave: Joseph is no more and

to confront anew the factor that led them to commit their infamous crime. Having taken one "child of [Jacob's] old age" (37.3) away from his father on the basest motivation, they must now persuade the old man to give up his stand-in (cf. 44.20) in the interest of life itself. Similarly, their imprisonment reenacts Joseph's own fate after they sold or abandoned him (39.1, 20). **21–22:** Just as his brothers saw only domination (and not deliverance) in his dreams (37.5–11), so here they see only punishment, never suspecting the larger design that will lead to survival and reconciliation (45.5; 50.20). **24:** As Leah's second son (29.31–33), Simeon is the appropriate hostage for Benjamin, Rachel's second son (35.18). His name echoes the Heb of "paid no heed" in 42.21, 22. **25:** Joseph's returning their silver (which was weighed out and used as money for much of the biblical period) deftly symbolizes the movement of the whole chapter: The brothers are getting what they gave! **34:** *I will then restore your brother to you* (not reported in vv. 18–20) refers most immediately to Simeon, but unbeknownst to the brothers (and perhaps even to Joseph himself at this point), the release of Benjamin will result in the restoration of Joseph as well. **35:** Practitioners of source criticism tend to see this verse as a variant of vv. 27–28, with the latter as the secondary passage (note that the brothers say nothing about any returned money in vv. 29–34). The supplementation (if such it be) was aided by the difference between the two variants: vv. 27–28 speak literally of only one brother, whereas v. 35 speaks of all of them. **36–38:** Reuben once again proves ineffectual (cf. 37.18–30; 42.22). A midrash paraphrases Jacob's decline of Reuben's offer this way: "This is a foolish first-born son! Are your sons not my sons?" (*Gen. Rab.* 91.9). The theme of the loss of two sons—Jacob's and Reuben's—recalls ch 38, in which Judah loses two sons and withholds the third. Reuben's foolish offer thus sets the

Simeon is no more, and now you would take away Benjamin.
These things always happen to me!" 37 Then Reuben said to his
father, "You may kill my two sons if I do not bring him back to
you. Put him in my care, and I will return him to you." 38 But
he said, "My son must not go down with you, for his brother
is dead and he alone is left. If he meets with disaster on the
journey you are taking, you will send my white head down to
Sheol in grief."

43 But the famine in the land was severe. 2 And when they
had eaten up the rations which they had brought from
Egypt, their father said to them, "Go again and procure some
food for us." 3 But Judah said to him, "The man warned us, [a-]'Do
not let me see your faces[-a] unless your brother is with you.' 4 If
you will let our brother go with us, we will go down and procure food for you; 5 but if you will not let him go, we will not go
down, for the man said to us, [a-]'Do not let me see your faces[-a]
unless your brother is with you.'" 6 And Israel said, "Why did
you serve me so ill as to tell the man that you had another
brother?" 7 They replied, "But the man kept asking about us
and our family, saying, 'Is your father still living? Have you another brother?' And we answered him accordingly. How were
we to know that he would say, 'Bring your brother here'?"
8 Then Judah said to his father Israel, "Send the boy in my
care, and let us be on our way, that we may live and not die—
you and we and our children. 9 I myself will be surety for him;
you may hold me responsible: if I do not bring him back to you
and set him before you, I shall stand guilty before you forever.
10 For we could have been there and back twice if we had not
dawdled."
11 Then their father Israel said to them, "If it must be so, do
this: take some of the choice products of the land in your baggage, and carry them down as a gift for the man—some balm
and some honey, gum, ladanum, pistachio nuts, and almonds.
12 And take with you double the money, carrying back with you
the money that was replaced in the mouths of your bags; perhaps it was a mistake. 13 Take your brother too; and go back
at once to the man. 14 And may El Shaddai dispose the man
to mercy toward you, that he may release to you your other
brother, as well as Benjamin. As for me, if I am to be bereaved,
I shall be bereaved."
15 So the men took that gift, and they took with them double
the money, as well as Benjamin. They made their way down
to Egypt, where they presented themselves to Joseph. 16 When
Joseph saw Benjamin with them, he said to his house steward, "Take the men into the house; slaughter and prepare an

a-a *Lit. "Do not see my face."*

stage for Judah's successful interventions in 43.8–14 and 44.18–34.

43.1–34: The brothers' second trip to Egypt. Chs 43–45 repeat the pattern of ch 42, only with variations, greater detail, and much greater emotional tension. Once again, the brothers depart for Egypt, approach Joseph fearfully, find themselves subjected to a frightening test of their honesty as well as accusations of deceit, and once again they return to their father. Ch 43 records, first, Judah's persuasion of a reluctant Jacob to release his beloved Benjamin and, second, the ensuing encounter of Joseph and his brothers—this time all eleven of them. **6–8:** Jacob, to whom the brothers once lied about Joseph (37.31–35), now accuses them of telling too much of the truth. The brothers are, in fact, still lying, though with a more benign intention. For, according to 42.9–13, they volunteered the information about their youngest brother. **9:** *Surety* (Heb "'arav") recalls the "pledge" ("'eravon") that Judah offered Tamar in 38.17. In this speech, Judah persuades his father, who believes he has lost two sons, to surrender the third—exactly the act that he had dangerously sought to avoid in ch 38. The commercial terminology is especially apt on the lips of the son that suggested his brother be sold (37.26–27). **11:** As in 37.21–30, Judah's plan succeeds where Reuben's had failed (42.37–38). This is another indication that one function of the Joseph story is to explain why Joseph (the dominant tribe of the North) and Judah (the royal tribe of the South) became more important than Reuben (the first-born). See 1 Chron. 5.1–2. The *balm* and *ladanum* (a fragrant resin) recall the commodities conveyed by the Ishmaelite caravan in 37.25. Once again, Jacob's beloved son is being brought to Egypt—only this time with his father's knowledge and consent and as a sign (unknown to all but Joseph) of healing rather than estrangement.

animal, for the men will dine with me at noon." 17 The man did as Joseph said, and he brought the men into Joseph's house. 18 But the men were frightened at being brought into Joseph's house. "It must be," they thought, "because of the money replaced in our bags the first time that we have been brought inside, as a pretext to attack us and seize us as slaves, with our pack animals." 19 So they went up to Joseph's house steward and spoke to him at the entrance of the house. 20 "If you please, my lord," they said, "we came down once before to procure food. 21 But when we arrived at the night encampment and opened our bags, there was each one's money in the mouth of his bag, our money in full.[a] So we have brought it back with us. 22 And we have brought down with us other money to procure food. We do not know who put the money in our bags." 23 He replied, "All is well with you; do not be afraid. Your God, the God of your father, must have put treasure in your bags for you. I got your payment." And he brought out Simeon to them.

24 Then the man brought the men into Joseph's house; he gave them water to bathe their feet, and he provided feed for their asses. 25 They laid out their gifts to await Joseph's arrival at noon, for they had heard that they were to dine there.

26 When Joseph came home, they presented to him the gifts that they had brought with them into the house, bowing low before him to the ground. 27 He greeted them, and he said, "How is your aged father of whom you spoke? Is he still in good health?" 28 They replied, "It is well with your servant our father; he is still in good health." And they bowed and made obeisance.

29 Looking about, he saw his brother Benjamin, his mother's son, and asked, "Is this your youngest brother of whom you spoke to me?" And he went on, "May God be gracious to you, my boy." 30 With that, Joseph hurried out, for he was overcome with feeling toward his brother and was on the verge of tears; he went into a room and wept there. 31 Then he washed his face, reappeared, and—now in control of himself—gave the order, "Serve the meal." 32 They served him by himself, and them by themselves, and the Egyptians who ate with him by themselves; for the Egyptians could not dine with the Hebrews, since that would be abhorrent to the Egyptians. 33 As they were seated by his direction, from the oldest in the order of his seniority to the youngest in the order of his youth, the men looked at one another in astonishment. 34 Portions were served them from his table; but Benjamin's portion was several[b] times that of anyone else. And they drank their fill with him.

a Lit. "by its weight."
b Lit. "five."

23: Joseph's steward senses the hand of a beneficent providence in these strange events. Much to their surprise, the brothers' honesty works to their advantage. It even restores one lost brother, the hostage Simeon. **30–31:** Joseph's emotion is described as more intense here than in 42.24. The harsh self-presentation of Pharaoh's vizier is rapidly yielding to the Hebrew man's love of father and brothers. **32:** It is unclear why Egyptians would find it abhorrent to dine with Hebrews. The phenomenon is probably connected to the reports that Egyptians found shepherds to be "abhorrent" (46.34; cf. Exod. 8.22), a tradition lacking historical corroboration. **33–34:** Joseph no sooner reaffirms the principle of seniority—the brothers are amazed that the Egyptian vizier knows their order of birth—than he reenacts the favoritism for the youngest that once proved so problematic to the family. This time, however, the brothers show no resentment. This meal contrasts poignantly with the meal to which the brothers sat down after throwing Joseph into the pit (37.25; see also 42.21).

44 Then he instructed his house steward as follows, "Fill the men's bags with food, as much as they can carry, and put each one's money in the mouth of his bag. [2] Put my silver goblet in the mouth of the bag of the youngest one, together with his money for the rations." And he did as Joseph told him.

[3] With the first light of morning, the men were sent off with their pack animals. [4] They had just left the city and had not gone far, when Joseph said to his steward, "Up, go after the men! And when you overtake them, say to them, 'Why did you repay good with evil? [5] It is the very one from which my master drinks and which he uses for divination. It was a wicked thing for you to do!'"

[6] He overtook them and spoke those words to them. [7] And they said to him, "Why does my lord say such things? Far be it from your servants to do anything of the kind! [8] Here we brought back to you from the land of Canaan the money that we found in the mouths of our bags. How then could we have stolen any silver or gold from your master's house! [9] Whichever of your servants it is found with shall die; the rest of us, moreover, shall become slaves to my lord." [10] He replied, "Although what you are proposing is right, only the one with whom it is found shall be my slave; but the rest of you shall go free."

[11] So each one hastened to lower his bag to the ground, and each one opened his bag. [12] He searched, beginning with the oldest and ending with the youngest; and the goblet turned up in Benjamin's bag. [13] At this they rent their clothes. Each reloaded his pack animal, and they returned to the city.

[14] When Judah and his brothers reentered the house of Joseph, who was still there, they threw themselves on the ground before him. [15] Joseph said to them, "What is this deed that you have done? Do you not know that a man like me practices divination?" [16] Judah replied, "What can we say to my lord? How can we plead, how can we prove our innocence? God has uncovered the crime of your servants. Here we are, then, slaves of my lord, the rest of us as much as he in whose possession the goblet was found." [17] But he replied, "Far be it from me to act thus! Only he in whose possession the goblet was found shall be my slave; the rest of you go back in peace to your father."

VA-YIGGASH ויגש

[18] Then Judah went up to him and said, "Please, my lord, let your servant appeal to my lord, and do not be impatient with your

44.1–17: The incident of the silver goblet. This passage recalls Joseph's clandestine return of his brothers' money to their sacks (42.25–38), except this time Joseph specifically targets Jacob's favored son (and Joseph's stand-in), Benjamin (absent in the prior episode). This seems to be a test: Will the older ten brothers jettison Benjamin when his presence becomes inconvenient, as they once did Joseph, or have they finally learned the painful lesson about family solidarity and filial obedience? **5:** *It is the very one from which my master drinks* seems abrupt. An ancient Jewish translation into Gk (the LXX) gives evidence that a second question, "Why have you stolen my silver goblet?" once followed the one at the end of v. 4. In contrast to other passages in the Torah (Lev. 19.26; Num. 23.23; Deut. 18.10–11), divination (fortune-telling) is not here condemned (cf. 30.27). The practice suggests Joseph's ominous dreams, the immediate cause of his brothers' selling him into slavery, and the silver of the goblet recalls the "twenty pieces of silver" they received for selling him (37.18–28). **7–9:** The accusation strikingly recalls Laban's charge that Jacob had stolen his household icons (31.25–37). The latter's defense, "anyone with whom you find your gods shall not remain alive!" (31.32) is probably connected to Rachel's premature death giving birth to Benjamin (35.16–20). Here, too, the curse involves death for the malefactor, but it also entails slavery for the rest of the brothers (44.9). Not coincidentally, death and slavery were the two punishments that the brothers plotted to inflict on Joseph in 37.18–28. **14–17:** Judah again assumes the leading position (see 43.11 n.). Having devised the plan to sell Joseph into slavery (37.26–27), he now offers to accept slavery upon himself and his brothers rather than abandon Benjamin, as he (and they, with the exception of the ineffectual Reuben) had once callously and criminally abandoned Joseph. **17:** Joseph forces his older brothers to face and, moreover, to accept the special place that Benjamin (Joseph's alter ego) has in his father's heart.

44.18–45.28: The turning point. With all apparently lost and Benjamin about to enter into slavery (and Jacob about to die as a result), Judah again assumes the lead role, with results that amaze all concerned.

18: "Va-Yiggash," translated here as *went up*, appears also in the introduction to Abraham's bold intercession for Sodom in 18.23 (where it is rendered "came forward"). Both Judah's speech and Abraham's

servant, you who are the equal of Pharaoh. [19] My lord asked his servants, 'Have you a father or another brother?' [20] We told my lord, 'We have an old father, and there is a child of his old age, the youngest; his full brother is dead, so that he alone is left of his mother, and his father dotes on him.' [21] Then you said to your servants, 'Bring him down to me, that I may set eyes on him.' [22] We said to my lord, 'The boy cannot leave his father; if he were to leave him, his father would die.' [23] But you said to your servants, 'Unless your youngest brother comes down with you, do not let me see your faces.' [24] When we came back to your servant my father, we reported my lord's words to him.

[25] "Later our father said, 'Go back and procure some food for us.' [26] We answered, 'We cannot go down; only if our youngest brother is with us can we go down, for we may not [a-]show our faces to the man[-a] unless our youngest brother is with us.' [27] Your servant my father said to us, 'As you know, my wife bore me two sons. [28] But one is gone from me, and I said: Alas, he was torn by a beast! And I have not seen him since. [29] If you take this one from me, too, and he meets with disaster, you will send my white head down to Sheol in sorrow.'

[30] "Now, if I come to your servant my father and the boy is not with us—since his own life is so bound up with his—[31] when he sees that the boy is not with us, he will die, and your servants will send the white head of your servant our father down to Sheol in grief. [32] Now your servant has pledged himself for the boy to my father, saying, 'If I do not bring him back to you, I shall stand guilty before my father forever.' [33] Therefore, please let your servant remain as a slave to my lord instead of the boy, and let the boy go back with his brothers. [34] For how can I go back to my father unless the boy is with me? Let me not be witness to the woe that would overtake my father!"

45 Joseph could no longer control himself before all his attendants, and he cried out, "Have everyone withdraw from me!" So there was no one else about when Joseph made himself known to his brothers. [2] His sobs were so loud that the Egyptians could hear, and so the news reached Pharaoh's palace.

[3] Joseph said to his brothers, "I am Joseph. Is my father still well?" But his brothers could not answer him, so dumfounded were they on account of him.

[4] Then Joseph said to his brothers, "Come forward to me." And when they came forward, he said, "I am your brother Joseph, he whom you sold into Egypt. [5] Now, do not be distressed or reproach yourselves because you sold me hither; it was to save life that God sent me ahead of you. [6] It is now two

exhibit a delicate balance of deference and assertion, and both succeed in moving the addressee from judgment to mercy. Abraham's argument, however, rests on the possibility that there is an innocent minority in the evil city (18.23–32), whereas Judah makes no argument for Benjamin's innocence (even if he believed in it, he could hardly make the case without incriminating Joseph or his staff). Instead, he appeals to the vizier's compassion for the foreigners' father and courageously offers himself in Benjamin's stead. **30–31:** Judah is unwittingly accusing Pharaoh's vizier of killing his own father, catching Joseph in his own stratagem. **32–33:** See 43.9 n., where the same verb ("'arav," "pledged himself") appears. **33:** Judah offers to take the place of Benjamin, who takes the place of Joseph (vv. 27–28). The brother responsible for selling Joseph into slavery (37.26–27) now freely offers himself as a slave to Joseph in order to save Jacob's life. Things have come full circle, and the long-standing and nearly fatal rift in the family is about to be healed. **45.4–8:** Joseph no sooner reminds his brothers of their great sin (v. 4) than he renounces retribution, interpreting the events that have overtaken the House of Israel as he had interpreted Pharaoh's dreams (41.25–36): God has arranged things so that the disaster (though very real and very painful) is not the last word. The last word is a word of life, not death (vv. 5–8; cf. 50.19–21). *Father to Pharaoh* (v. 8) has some parallels in the Egyptian language, and seems to denote Joseph's office of vizier and head counselor. *Ruler over the whole land of Egypt* echoes the brothers' angry and incredulous question in 37.8 ("Do you mean to rule over us?").

a-a Lit. "see the man's face."

years that there has been famine in the land, and there are still five years to come in which there shall be no yield from tilling. [7] God has sent me ahead of you to ensure your survival on earth, and to save your lives in an extraordinary deliverance. [8] So, it was not you who sent me here, but God; and He has made me a father to Pharaoh, lord of all his household, and ruler over the whole land of Egypt.

[9] "Now, hurry back to my father and say to him: Thus says your son Joseph, 'God has made me lord of all Egypt; come down to me without delay. [10] You will dwell in the region of Goshen, where you will be near me—you and your children and your grandchildren, your flocks and herds, and all that is yours. [11] There I will provide for you—for there are yet five years of famine to come—that you and your household and all that is yours may not suffer want.' [12] You can see for yourselves, and my brother Benjamin for himself, that it is indeed I who am speaking to you. [13] And you must tell my father everything about my high station in Egypt and all that you have seen; and bring my father here with all speed."

[14] With that he embraced[a] his brother Benjamin around the neck and wept, and Benjamin wept on his neck. [15] He kissed all his brothers and wept upon them; only then were his brothers able to talk to him.

[16] The news reached Pharaoh's palace: "Joseph's brothers have come." Pharaoh and his courtiers were pleased. [17] And Pharaoh said to Joseph, "Say to your brothers, 'Do as follows: load up your beasts and go at once to the land of Canaan. [18] Take your father and your households and come to me; I will give you the best of the land of Egypt and you shall live off the fat of the land.' [19] And you are bidden [to add], 'Do as follows: take from the land of Egypt wagons for your children and your wives, and bring your father here. [20] And never mind your belongings, for the best of all the land of Egypt shall be yours.' "

[21] The sons of Israel did so; Joseph gave them wagons as Pharaoh had commanded, and he supplied them with provisions for the journey. [22] To each of them, moreover, he gave a change of clothing; but to Benjamin he gave three hundred pieces of silver and several[b] changes of clothing. [23] And to his father he sent the following: ten he-asses laden with the best things of Egypt, and ten she-asses laden with grain, bread, and provisions for his father on the journey. [24] As he sent his brothers off on their way, he told them, "Do not be quarrelsome on the way."

[25] They went up from Egypt and came to their father Jacob in the land of Canaan. [26] And they told him, "Joseph is still alive; yes, he is ruler over the whole land of Egypt." His heart

a Lit. "fell on." *b Lit. "five"; cf. 43.34.*

9: *Come down to me* recalls Jacob's plaintive words in 37.35, "I will go down mourning to my son in Sheol." Now he goes down to Joseph not in Sheol, but in Egypt, over which the once rejected son now rules by the grace of God. **14:** The scene is highly reminiscent of the reconciliation of Esau and Jacob in 33.4. **22:** Joseph's giving extra clothing to Benjamin recalls Jacob's giving him an "ornamental tunic" in 37.3. The fraternal reconciliation does not mean that the old favoritism has come to an end and all the brothers are equal. It means, rather, that all concerned are now at last able to live with and accept the favoritism with grace and good will. **24:** Rashi thinks the plain sense is that the brothers should refrain from blaming each other for the sale of Joseph and for defaming him so as to make him hateful to them—not bad advice in light of past experience (42.22).

went numb, for he did not believe them. [27] But when they recounted all that Joseph had said to them, and when he saw the wagons that Joseph had sent to transport him, the spirit of their father Jacob revived. [28] "Enough!" said Israel. "My son Joseph is still alive! I must go and see him before I die."

46 So Israel set out with all that was his, and he came to Beer-sheba, where he offered sacrifices to the God of his father Isaac. [2] God called to Israel in a vision by night: "Jacob! Jacob!" He answered, "Here." [3] And He said, "I am God, the God of your father. Fear not to go down to Egypt, for I will make you there into a great nation. [4] I Myself will go down with you to Egypt, and I Myself will also bring you back; and Joseph's hand shall close your eyes."

[5] So Jacob set out from Beer-sheba. The sons of Israel put their father Jacob and their children and their wives in the wagons that Pharaoh had sent to transport him; [6] and they took along their livestock and the wealth that they had amassed in the land of Canaan. Thus Jacob and all his offspring with him came to Egypt: [7] he brought with him to Egypt his sons and grandsons, his daughters and granddaughters—all his offspring.

[8] These are the names of the Israelites, Jacob and his descendants, who came to Egypt.

Jacob's first-born Reuben; [9] Reuben's sons: Enoch,[a] Pallu, Hezron, and Carmi. [10] Simeon's sons: Jemuel, Jamin, Ohad, Jachin, Zohar, and Saul[b] the son of a Canaanite woman. [11] Levi's sons: Gershon, Kohath, and Merari. [12] Judah's sons: Er, Onan, Shelah, Perez, and Zerah—but Er and Onan had died in the land of Canaan; and Perez's sons were Hezron and Hamul. [13] Issachar's sons: Tola, Puvah, Iob, and Shimron. [14] Zebulun's sons: Sered, Elon, and Jahleel. [15] Those were the sons whom Leah bore to Jacob in Paddan-aram, in addition to his daughter Dinah. Persons in all, male and female: 33.[c]

[16] Gad's sons: Ziphion, Haggi, Shuni, Ezbon, Eri, Arodi, and Areli. [17] Asher's sons: Imnah, Ishvah, Ishvi, and Beriah, and their sister Serah. Beriah's sons: Heber and Malchiel. [18] These were the descendants of Zilpah, whom Laban had given to his daughter Leah. These she bore to Jacob—16 persons.

[19] The sons of Jacob's wife Rachel were Joseph and Benjamin. [20] To Joseph were born in the land of Egypt Manasseh and Ephraim, whom Asenath daughter of Poti-phera priest of On bore to him. [21] Benjamin's sons: Bela, Becher, Ashbel, Gera, Naaman, Ehi, Rosh, Muppim, Huppim, and Ard. [22] These were the descendants of Rachel who were born to Jacob—14 persons in all.

a Or "Hanoch." *b Or "Shaul."* *c Including Jacob.*

46.1–7: Jacob sets out for Egypt. With Jacob's departure for Egypt, the tale of Joseph rejoins the ancestral story from which it separated when Joseph was sold into slavery in ch 37. At the same time, these verses look forward to the next seemingly insurmountable challenge to the House of Israel, the affliction in Egypt. **2–4:** God's only speech in chs 37–50 reiterates the promise to Abraham and Isaac (cf. 12.2–3; 26.2–5), assuring Jacob that his departure from the promised land will not void God's commitment to his forebears. *I Myself will also bring you back* (v. 4) looks forward to the exodus and underscores the fact that, as the Passover *Haggadah* puts it, "Our father Jacob did not come down to strike roots in Egypt but only to sojourn there." *Joseph's hand shall close your eyes* (v. 4) means that Joseph will lovingly attend to his father's needs at the moment of the latter's death.

46.8–27: Joseph's household. A list of Jacob's children and grandchildren interrupts the account of his journey to Egypt. **12:** The mention of *Er and Onan* who *died in the land of Canaan* indicates that the list was once independent of its current role as a census of the Israelites *who came to Egypt* (v. 8). **15:** The figure 33 requires that Er and Onan be counted but Dinah be excluded, despite the unambiguous expression *male and female.* If we replace Judah's two deceased sons with Dinah, we arrive at a figure of 32 descendants of Leah—exactly twice the number of her handmaiden Zilpah (v. 18). The symmetry with Rachel, who has twice as many descendants as her handmaiden Bilhah (vv. 22, 25), commends this interpretation. In order to reach 33, we must then count Jacob himself in the census. A midrash solves the problem by postulating that Moses' mother, Jochebed (Exod. 6.20), was born between the city walls as her parents entered Egypt (i.e., she was counted before she was named)—hence the plural "daughters" in v. 7 (*b. B. Bat.* 123b).

27: *Seventy persons,* seventy was considered a perfect number. The quest for progeny—the fulfillment of the promise to Abraham—is now complete. The opening vv. of Exodus will recapitulate the numbering of Jacob's family and continue the narrative with the quest for the land promised to Abraham.

46.28–30: The reunion of father and son. The narrative of Jacob's journey to Egypt resumes after the census of vv. 8–27. Having seen for himself that his beloved son lives and that his own life has been fulfilled beyond his wildest dreams, the elderly Jacob is at last prepared to accept his death (contrast 37.35; 42.38).

46.31–47.12: Audience with Pharaoh. Joseph carefully prepares his family for an audience in the royal court. He presents his brothers and then his father to the king of Egypt (the family members make their appearances in the same order as in his dreams in 37.5–11). **46.34:** *Goshen* is a fertile region in the eastern delta of the Nile. It is unclear why *all shepherds are abhorrent to Egyptians.* Pharaoh has herds of his own (47.6). Some scholars connect this with a late folk etymology of "Hyksos" associated with the Egyptian word for "shepherd." The Hyksos were a Syro-Palestinian group who ruled Lower Egypt about 1680–1540 BCE; they were likely despised by later native Egyptians.

23 Dan's son:[a] Hushim. 24 Naphtali's sons: Jahzeel, Guni, Jezer, and Shillem. 25 These were the descendants of Bilhah, whom Laban had given to his daughter Rachel. These she bore to Jacob—7 persons in all.

26 All the persons belonging to Jacob who came to Egypt[b]—his own issue, aside from the wives of Jacob's sons—all these persons numbered 66. 27 And Joseph's sons who were born to him in Egypt were two in number. Thus the total of Jacob's household who came to Egypt was seventy persons.[c]

28 He had sent Judah ahead of him to Joseph, to point the way before him to Goshen. So when they came to the region of Goshen, 29 Joseph ordered[d] his chariot and went to Goshen to meet his father Israel; he presented himself to him and, embracing him around the neck, he wept on his neck a good while. 30 Then Israel said to Joseph, "Now I can die, having seen for myself that you are still alive."

31 Then Joseph said to his brothers and to his father's household, "I will go up and tell the news to Pharaoh, and say to him, 'My brothers and my father's household, who were in the land of Canaan, have come to me. 32 The men are shepherds; they have always been breeders of livestock, and they have brought with them their flocks and herds and all that is theirs.' 33 So when Pharaoh summons you and asks, 'What is your occupation?' 34 you shall answer, 'Your servants have been breeders of livestock from the start until now, both we and our fathers'—so that you may stay in the region of Goshen. For all shepherds are abhorrent to Egyptians."

47 Then Joseph came and reported to Pharaoh, saying, "My father and my brothers, with their flocks and herds and all that is theirs, have come from the land of Canaan and are now in the region of Goshen." 2 And selecting a few[e] of his brothers, he presented them to Pharaoh. 3 Pharaoh said to his brothers, "What is your occupation?" They answered Pharaoh, "We your servants are shepherds, as were also our fathers. 4 We have come," they told Pharaoh, "to sojourn in this land, for there is no pasture for your servants' flocks, the famine being severe in the land of Canaan. Pray, then, let your servants stay in the region of Goshen." 5 Then Pharaoh said to Joseph, "As regards your father and your brothers who have come to you, 6 the land of Egypt is open before you: settle your father and your brothers in the best part of the land; let them stay in the region of Goshen. And if you know any capable men among them, put them in charge of my livestock."

a *Heb. "sons."* b *Not including Joseph and Joseph's two sons.*
c *Including Jacob and Joseph.* d *Lit. "hitched."* e *Lit. "five."*

[7] Joseph then brought his father Jacob and presented him to Pharaoh; and Jacob greeted Pharaoh. [8] Pharaoh asked Jacob, "How many are the years of your life?" [9] And Jacob answered Pharaoh, "The years of my sojourn [on earth] are one hundred and thirty. Few and hard have been the years of my life, nor do they come up to the life spans of my fathers during their sojourns." [10] Then Jacob bade Pharaoh farewell, and left Pharaoh's presence.

[11] So Joseph settled his father and his brothers, giving them holdings in the choicest part of the land of Egypt, in the region of Rameses, as Pharaoh had commanded. [12] Joseph sustained his father, and his brothers, and all his father's household with bread, down to the little ones.

[13] Now there was no bread in all the world, for the famine was very severe; both the land of Egypt and the land of Canaan languished because of the famine. [14] Joseph gathered in all the money that was to be found in the land of Egypt and in the land of Canaan, as payment for the rations that were being procured, and Joseph brought the money into Pharaoh's palace. [15] And when the money gave out in the land of Egypt and in the land of Canaan, all the Egyptians came to Joseph and said, "Give us bread, lest we die before your very eyes; for the money is gone!" [16] And Joseph said, "Bring your livestock, and I will sell to you against your livestock, if the money is gone." [17] So they brought their livestock to Joseph, and Joseph gave them bread in exchange for the horses, for the stocks of sheep and cattle, and the asses; thus he provided them with bread that year in exchange for all their livestock. [18] And when that year was ended, they came to him the next year and said to him, "We cannot hide from my lord that, with all the money and animal stocks consigned to my lord, nothing is left at my lord's disposal save our persons and our farmland. [19] Let us not perish before your eyes, both we and our land. Take us and our land in exchange for bread, and we with our land will be serfs to Pharaoh; provide the seed, that we may live and not die, and that the land may not become a waste."

[20] So Joseph gained possession of all the farm land of Egypt for Pharaoh, every Egyptian having sold his field because the famine was too much for them; thus the land passed over to Pharaoh. [21] And he removed the population town by town,[a] from one end of Egypt's border to the other. [22] Only the land of the priests he did not take over, for the priests had an allotment from Pharaoh, and they lived off the allotment which Pharaoh had made to them; therefore they did not sell their land.

a Meaning of Heb. uncertain.

47.9: Since Jacob dies at 147 (47.28), he has two periods of seventeen years with Joseph, the first seventeen of the latter's life (37.2) and the last seventeen of his own. See 25.7 n.; 35.28 n. **10:** *Bade ... farewell* can also be translated "blessed." The theme that contact with the family of Abraham results in blessing for Gentiles (or at least for those Gentiles who treat them well) is widespread in Genesis (12.3; 22.18; 26.4; 28.14; 30.27–30; 39.5, 23).

47.13–27: Joseph saves and enslaves the Egyptians. This passage describes the progressive impoverishment of the Egyptian population, Joseph's rescue of them through skillful administration, and, finally and most troublingly, his enslavement of them to Pharaoh. The tables have indeed turned: The man who was brought to Egypt as a slave now reduces the Egyptians to slavery, all the while, however, saving their lives just as he saved the lives of his own family. The cruelty of Joseph's enslavement of Egypt does not seem to bother the narrator. When Joseph died, however, and "a new king arose over Egypt who did not know Joseph" (Exod. 1.8), the House of Israel found themselves once again on the wrong end of the enslavement process. **21:** The Heb MT seems to refer to a forced transfer of the rural population as part of the program of nationalization of the farmland. Other versions evidence a slightly variant wording with a very different meaning: "He made the population into slaves."

23 Then Joseph said to the people, "Whereas I have this day acquired you and your land for Pharaoh, here is seed for you to sow the land. 24 And when harvest comes, you shall give one-fifth to Pharaoh, and four-fifths shall be yours as seed for the fields and as food for you and those in your households, and as nourishment for your children." 25 And they said, "You have saved our lives! We are grateful to my lord, and we shall be serfs to Pharaoh." 26 And Joseph made it into a land law in Egypt, which is still valid, that a fifth should be Pharaoh's; only the land of the priests did not become Pharaoh's.

27 Thus Israel settled in the country of Egypt, in the region of Goshen; they acquired holdings in it, and were fertile and increased greatly.

VA-YEḤI ויחי

28 Jacob lived seventeen years in the land of Egypt, so that the span of Jacob's life came to one hundred and forty-seven years. 29 And when the time approached for Israel to die, he summoned his son Joseph and said to him, "Do me this favor, place your hand under my thigh as a pledge of your steadfast loyalty: please do not bury me in Egypt. 30 When I lie down with my fathers, take me up from Egypt and bury me in their burial-place." He replied, "I will do as you have spoken." 31 And he said, "Swear to me." And he swore to him. Then Israel bowed at the head of the bed.

48 Some time afterward, Joseph was told, "Your father is ill." So he took with him his two sons, Manasseh and Ephraim. 2 When Jacob was told, "Your son Joseph has come to see you," Israel summoned his strength and sat up in bed.

3 And Jacob said to Joseph, "El Shaddai appeared to me at Luz in the land of Canaan, and He blessed me, 4 and said to me, 'I will make you fertile and numerous, making of you a community of peoples; and I will assign this land to your offspring to come for an everlasting possession.' 5 Now, your two sons, who were born to you in the land of Egypt before I came to you in Egypt, shall be mine; Ephraim and Manasseh shall be mine no less than Reuben and Simeon. 6 But progeny born to you after them shall be yours; they shall be recorded instead[a] of their brothers in their inheritance. 7 I [do this because], when I was returning from Paddan, Rachel died, to my sorrow, while

a Lit. "under the name."

27: Whereas the Egyptians lose their land to Pharaoh because of Joseph's administrative policy, the Israelites acquire holdings through the generosity of Pharaoh, grateful for Joseph's managerial skills. Similarly, the fertility and increase of Israel contrasts with the devastation and impoverishment of the Egyptians, once again underscoring the special role of the former in God's designs.

47.28–48.22: Jacob's deathbed adoption of Joseph's sons. As befits a deathbed scene, this passage looks both to the past and to the future. Jacob gives a retrospective of his experience of the patriarchal promise and his loss of his favored wife, Rachel (48.3–7), but he also makes Joseph promise to bury him in the promised land (47.29–30), thus reiterating and deepening familial devotion to the patrimony of which they have yet to take possession. Similarly, Jacob's blessing of Joseph's two sons, in the reverse of the birth order (48.8–20), looks back to his own supplanting of his older brother early in life (25.22–33; 27.1–45), but it also authorizes the establishment of Ephraim and Manasseh among the twelve tribes that comprise Israel. **47.28:** See 35.28 n. **29–30:** The scene recalls that of 24.2–9. Once again the patriarchal promise is at risk, and once again an ailing and aged patriarch solemnly undertakes to reconnect with the family tradition. **31:** The meaning of Jacob/Israel's bowing is unclear (cf. 1 Kings 1.47). If he bows to Joseph, he fulfills the second of the latter's two predictive dreams (37.9–10). **48.3:** On *El Shaddai,* see 17.1 n. **5–7:** Jacob adopts his two grandsons born in Egypt, explaining this by reference to his affection for their departed grandmother, Rachel. This promotes them to the status of tribal founders and makes his favored wife their mother in place of the Egyptian priest's daughter Asenath (41.50–52). Moreover, the end of v. 5 seems to mean that Ephraim and Manasseh will become the senior tribes, replacing Reuben and Simeon, both of whom earn their father's censure (34.30; 35.22; 49.3–7; cf. 1 Chron. 5.1). V. 6 stipulates that any other children that Joseph has or will have (the Tanakh lists no others) shall be classified under Ephraim and Manasseh and not hold the status of the sons of Jacob. Note that whereas some

I was journeying in the land of Canaan, when still some distance short of Ephrath; and I buried her there on the road to
Ephrath"—now Bethlehem.
8 Noticing Joseph's sons, Israel asked, "Who are these?"
9 And Joseph said to his father, "They are my sons, whom God
has given me here." "Bring them up to me," he said, "that I may
bless them." 10 Now Israel's eyes were dim with age; he could
not see. So [Joseph] brought them close to him, and he kissed
them and embraced them. 11 And Israel said to Joseph, "I never
expected to see you again, and here God has let me see your
children as well."
12 Joseph then removed them from his knees, and bowed
low with his face to the ground. 13 Joseph took the two of
them, Ephraim with his right hand—to Israel's left—and
Manasseh with his left hand—to Israel's right—and brought
them close to him. 14 But Israel stretched out his right hand
and laid it on Ephraim's head, though he was the younger,
and his left hand on Manasseh's head—thus crossing his
hands—although Manasseh was the first-born. 15 And he
blessed Joseph, saying,

"The God in whose ways my fathers Abraham and Isaac
walked,
The God who has been my shepherd from my
birth to this day—
16 The Angel who has redeemed me from all harm—
Bless the lads.
In them may my name be recalled,
And the names of my fathers Abraham and Isaac,
And may they be teeming multitudes upon the earth."

17 When Joseph saw that his father was placing his right hand
on Ephraim's head, he thought it wrong; so he took hold of his
father's hand to move it from Ephraim's head to Manasseh's.
18 "Not so, Father," Joseph said to his father, "for the other is
the first-born; place your right hand on his head." 19 But his father objected, saying, "I know, my son, I know. He too shall
become a people, and he too shall be great. Yet his younger
brother shall be greater than he, and his offspring shall be
plentiful enough for nations." 20 So he blessed them that day,
saying, "By you shall Israel invoke blessings, saying: God make
you like Ephraim and Manasseh." Thus he put Ephraim before
Manasseh.
21 Then Israel said to Joseph, "I am about to die; but God
will be with you and bring you back to the land of your fathers.
22 And now, I assign to you one portion[a] more than to your
brothers, which I wrested from the Amorites with my sword
and bow."

lists of the twelve include Joseph and the clerical tribe Levi (e.g., Deut. 27.12–13), others omit Levi and divide Joseph into Ephraim and Manasseh (e.g., Num. 1.5–15). **8:** Israel's question is odd, since he has just spoken about Ephraim and Manasseh in considerable detail and with no deficit of clarity. The problem disappears if v. 8 is seen as the continuation of v. 2, and vv. 3–7 (which employ classic P language) are understood as an interpretation. In the text as it comes to us, however, the effect of v. 8 is to suggest that the aged Israel is confused and forgetful, somewhat like his own father in ch 27. If so, this time the suggestion proves wrong (vv. 17–20)! **10:** Cf. 27.1. **17–20:** Both tribes became important, though it is from Ephraim that Moses' successor Joshua, the prophet Samuel, and Jeroboam I, the founder of the Northern Kingdom (Israel) all hailed (Num. 13.8; 1 Sam. 1.1; 1 Kings 11.26). In fact, "Ephraim" eventually became another name for the Northern Kingdom itself (e.g., Hos. 5.3; Isa. 7.1–17). **20:** Jacob's words are used in the blessing that a Jewish father traditionally bestows upon his sons just before the first Sabbath meal (Friday night). In the case of daughters, the tradition devised a functional equivalent that does not actually appear in the Tanakh: "God make you like Sarah, Rebekah, Rachel, and Leah." In both cases, the Aaronic blessing follows (Num. 6.24–26). **22:** *One portion more than to your brothers* probably refers to the "double portion" that the first-born son inherits (Deut. 21.17). The word for *portion* ("shekhem") in this difficult verse puns on the name of (the city) Shechem. Note that Shechem appears as a Manassite clan in Josh. 17.2 but as an Ephraimite city in Josh. 20.7.

a *Meaning of Heb.* shekhem *uncertain; others "mountain slope."*

49 And Jacob called his sons and said, "Come together that I may tell you what is to befall you in days to come.
2 Assemble and hearken, O sons of Jacob;
Hearken to Israel your father:

3 Reuben, you are my first-born,
My might and first fruit of my vigor,
Exceeding in rank
And exceeding in honor.
4 Unstable as water, you shall excel no longer;
For when you mounted your father's bed,
You brought disgrace—my couch he mounted!

5 Simeon and Levi are a pair;
Their weapons are tools of lawlessness.
6 Let not my person be included in their council,
Let not my being be counted in their assembly.
For when angry they slay men,
And when pleased they maim oxen.
7 Cursed be their anger so fierce,
And their wrath so relentless.
I will divide them in Jacob,
Scatter them in Israel.

8 You, O Judah, your brothers shall praise;
Your hand shall be on the nape of your foes;
Your father's sons shall bow low to you.
9 Judah is a lion's whelp;
On prey, my son, have you grown.

49.1–28: Jacob's tribal sayings. Although the prose superscription has Jacob speaking to his sons (v. 1), the content of the poetry that follows applies to the tribes descended from these twelve men. The closest parallel to this collection of tribal sayings is thus Deut. ch 33, in which Moses blesses most of the tribes just before he dies. A more distant parallel is Judg. 5.14–18, in which the judge, Deborah, and her general, Barak, sing of the courage of some of the tribes and the failure of others in a time of military crisis. Like Judg. 5.14–18, and unlike the Blessing of Moses, however, 49.1–28 interlaces commendation and condemnation. Rich in wordplays impossible to capture in English as well as cryptic phrasings and rare expressions (including unusual, and probably very ancient, divine names), Jacob's tribal sayings have long provoked disagreements among interpreters. There are also considerable variations in wording among the ancient versions. The collection of sayings is organized according to the tribal mothers, in the order of Leah, Zilpah (her handmaiden), Bilhah (Rachel's handmaiden), and Rachel (29.31–30.24; 35.16–19). The first four Leah tribes—Reuben, Simeon, Levi, and Judah—appear in the order of their births, as do those descended from Rachel—Joseph and Benjamin. But whereas in the narrative the sons of the handmaidens appear in the order of Dan, Naphtali, Gad, Asher, and are followed by Leah's last two sons, Issachar and Zebulun, in the tribal sayings of ch 49 the order is Zebulun, Issachar, Dan, Gad, Asher, Naphtali. Many scholars consider this chapter to be among the oldest portions of the Torah. **4:** The allusion is probably to the event cryptically reported in 35.22. Although the tribe of Reuben, the first-born, may once have been important, it has left little mark in biblical history. The Blessing of Moses regards it as small and in danger of extinction (Deut. 33.6), and the Song of Deborah chastises it for its indecision (Judg. 5.15b–16; see Gen. 42.36–38 n.). **5–7:** *Simeon and Levi are a pair* only in Gen. ch 34, where they also suffer their father's rebuke (v. 30). The dividing and scattering predicted here probably refers to Simeon's absorption into Judah and Levi's redefinition as a priestly tribe, without land of its own (Deut. 18.1–2). **8–10:** The preeminence of Judah (v. 8; cf. 27.29) is doubtless associated with King David's derivation from that tribe (see 38.27–30 n.). *Scepter* and *ruler's staff* may thus be royal symbols, although they can also designate the stick or club of any military commander or tribal leader (cf. Num. 21.18, where the word rendered here as *ruler's staff* is translated as the "maces" of "the nobles of the people"). V. 10 has traditionally been viewed as a messianic prophecy in both the Jewish and Christian traditions, though this is not its likely original meaning. Some commentators, beginning as early as the Aram. translation known as *Tg. Onk.*, read the word rendered here as *tribute ... to him* as "his due" (Heb "shelo"): God shall uphold His promise to Judah even till the royal figure comes to claim the dominion that is his due. Ibn Ezra, on the other hand, considers it possible to retain the traditional wording, "Shiloh," in place of "shai loh" *(tribute ... to him).* Reading *shall come* in the sense of "shall come down," like the setting sun (in Lev. 22.7, the verb is translated "sets"), he connects this verse to Ps. 78, which reports that God "forsook the

He crouches, lies down like a lion,
Like [a]the king of beasts[a]—who dare rouse him?
10 The scepter shall not depart from Judah,
Nor the ruler's staff from between his feet;
So that tribute shall come to him[b]
And the homage of peoples be his.

11 He tethers his ass to a vine,
His ass's foal to a choice vine;
He washes his garment in wine,
His robe in blood of grapes.
12 [c]His eyes are darker than wine;
His teeth are whiter than milk.[c]

13 Zebulun shall dwell by the seashore;
He shall be a haven for ships,
And his flank shall rest on Sidon.

14 Issachar is a strong-boned ass,
Crouching among the sheepfolds.
15 When he saw how good was security,
And how pleasant was the country,
He bent his shoulder to the burden,
And became a toiling serf.

16 Dan shall govern his people,
As one of the tribes of Israel.
17 Dan shall be a serpent by the road,
A viper by the path,
That bites the horse's heels
So that his rider is thrown backward.
18 I wait for Your deliverance, O LORD!

19 Gad shall be raided by raiders,
But he shall raid at their heels.

20 Asher's bread shall be rich,
And he shall yield royal dainties.

21 Naphtali is a hind let loose,
Which yields lovely fawns.

a-a Heb. labi, *another word for "lion."*
b Shiloh, understood as shai loh *"tribute to him," following Midrash; cf. Isa. 18.7. Meaning of Heb. uncertain; lit. "Until he comes to Shiloh."*
c-c Or "His eyes are dark from wine,
And his teeth are white from milk."

tabernacle of Shiloh," "did choose the tribe of Judah" and "David, His servant" (vv. 60, 68, 70; see 1 Sam. 3.19–4.22; Jer. 7.12–15). **11–12:** The images suggest preternatural fertility, prosperity, and vigor. According to Rabbi Ovadiah Sforno, an Italian commentator of the 16th century, the messianic king rides an *ass* rather than a horse because it is God who wages the wars by which he comes to rule, "and he will become king in peace" (cf. Zech. 4.6b; 9.9). **13:** The boundaries of Zebulun in Josh. 19.10–15 suggest that it was an inland tribe, but perhaps this was not always the case. **15:** The pronouncement on Issachar seems to be a criticism. It is a strong, but lazy, tribe that became *a toiling serf,* presumably for Canaanites in the northern regions that were its home (cf. Judg. 1.33). There is probably a play here on the tribe's name (as if it were "'ish sakhar," "hired man"). Influenced by 1 Chron. 12.33, the midrash reconceives Issachar's service as the teaching of Torah and the rendering of halakhic (i.e., legal) rulings (*Gen. Rab.* 99.10). **16:** *Govern* ("yadin") puns on the tribe's name ("dan"). **18:** This verse seems to be a devout interpolation unrelated to the context (cf. Ps. 119.166). It contains the only mention of the four-letter name of God (*LORD*) in ch 49, indeed in all of chs 40–50. **19:** The Heb plays repeatedly on Gad's name. **20:** The *royal dainties* may have been served to Canaanite kings (cf. Judg. 1.32, on Naphtali; and v. 15 n., above).

22 [a-]Joseph is a wild ass,
A wild ass by a spring
—Wild colts on a hillside.[-a]

23 Archers bitterly assailed him;
They shot at him and harried him.
24 Yet his bow stayed taut,
And his arms[b] were made firm
By the hands of the Mighty One of Jacob—
There, the Shepherd, the Rock of Israel—
25 The God of your father who helps you,
And Shaddai who blesses you
With blessings of heaven above,
Blessings of the deep that couches below,
Blessings of the breast and womb.
26 [c-]The blessings of your father
Surpass the blessings of my ancestors,
To the utmost bounds of the eternal hills.[-c]
May they rest on the head of Joseph,
On the brow of the elect of his brothers.

27 Benjamin is a ravenous wolf;
In the morning he consumes the foe,[d]
And in the evening he divides the spoil."

28 All these were the tribes of Israel, twelve in number, and this
is what their father said to them as he bade them farewell, addressing to each a parting word appropriate to him.
29 Then he instructed them, saying to them, "I am about to be
gathered to my kin. Bury me with my fathers in the cave which is
in the field of Ephron the Hittite, 30 the cave which is in the field
of Machpelah, facing Mamre, in the land of Canaan, the field that
Abraham bought from Ephron the Hittite for a burial site— 31 there

a-a *Others "Joseph is a fruitful bough,*
A fruitful bough by a spring,
Its branches run over a wall."
b *Heb. "the arms of his hands."*
c-c *Meaning of Heb. uncertain.*
d *Meaning of Heb. uncertain; others "booty."*

22: Like Judah (v. 9), Issachar (v. 14), Naphtali (v. 21), and Benjamin (v. 27), Joseph is described as an animal. (Even if the alternative suggested in the translation note is accepted, the image is still one of fertility and vigor.) **23–24:** Like the rest of the tribal sayings, the image of Joseph under assault relates to the subsequent history of the tribe. It also recalls, however, Joseph's brothers' early hostility in the preceding narrative (ch 37). **24:** The unusual titles of the deity, *the Mighty One of Jacob* (or "Bull of Jacob"), *the Shepherd,* and *the Rock of Israel,* may attest to an early date and Canaanite affinities. **25:** *Shaddai* is presumably a shortened form of El Shaddai (see 17.1 n.). **26:** The term *my ancestors* ("horay") is otherwise unattested. The LXX and the parallels in Deut. 33.15 and Hab. 3.6 suggest that the word is actually "mountains" ("harerei") and that the word after it ("ʿad") means not "to," but "ancient." *Utmost bounds* ("taʾavat"), another unique term, is then more plausibly derived from a root associated with "desire" ("ʾvh"). If this reconstruction were to be accepted, the first sentence would read: "The blessings of your father / Surpass the blessings of the ancient mountains / That which is most desired in the eternal hills." **28:** And so, just before he leaves this world, Jacob has bidden farewell to the twelve tribes of Israel—the people promised to his grandfather long ago (12.2), the people that against all odds and in the face of multiple and formidable challenges, external and internal, has now, by the grace of God, come into existence, the people that at long last stands united as it faces the new challenges that lie ahead.

49.29–50.26: The deaths of Jacob and Joseph. The book of Genesis draws to a rapid close with accounts of the deaths of Jacob and Joseph. The overall mood is marked by reverence for these larger-than-life figures and awareness that the promise that started their ancestor Abraham on his fateful journey (12.1–3) has now, amazingly, been largely fulfilled. Only two discordant notes are sounded: the anxiety of Joseph's brothers that their erstwhile victim will seek revenge now that he is no longer accountable to his father (50.15–21), and Joseph's last words, which draw attention to the fact that the Israelites in Egypt, for all their material comfort, do not yet possess the land of Israel, and the solemn promise of God to grant Abraham, Isaac, and Jacob the land thus remains unfulfilled (50.24–25). Joseph allays his brothers' anxiety by affirming God's mysterious providential design, which can bring good out of human evil (50.20–21). Similarly, by affirming the reliability of God's sworn promise to the patriarchs, he expresses his firm faith that their exile will end (50.24–25).

Abraham and his wife Sarah were buried; there Isaac and his wife
Rebekah were buried; and there I buried Leah—[32] the field and
the cave in it, bought from the Hittites." [33] When Jacob finished
his instructions to his sons, he drew his feet into the bed and,
breathing his last, he was gathered to his people.

50 Joseph flung himself upon his father's face and wept
over him and kissed him. [2] Then Joseph ordered the
physicians in his service to embalm his father, and the physicians embalmed Israel. [3] It required forty days, for such is the
full period of embalming. The Egyptians bewailed him seventy
days; [4] and when the wailing period was over, Joseph spoke to
Pharaoh's court, saying, "Do me this favor, and lay this appeal
before Pharaoh: [5] 'My father made me swear, saying, "I am
about to die. Be sure to bury me in the grave which I made ready
for myself in the land of Canaan." Now, therefore, let me go up
and bury my father; then I shall return.'" [6] And Pharaoh said,
"Go up and bury your father, as he made you promise on oath."
[7] So Joseph went up to bury his father; and with him went
up all the officials of Pharaoh, the senior members of his court,
and all of Egypt's dignitaries, [8] together with all of Joseph's
household, his brothers, and his father's household; only their
children, their flocks, and their herds were left in the region
of Goshen. [9] Chariots, too, and horsemen went up with him; it
was a very large troop.
[10] When they came to Goren[a] ha-Atad, which is beyond the
Jordan, they held there a very great and solemn lamentation;
and he observed a mourning period of seven days for his father. [11] And when the Canaanite inhabitants of the land saw
the mourning at Goren ha-Atad, they said, "This is a solemn
mourning on the part of the Egyptians." That is why it was
named Abel-mizraim,[b] which is beyond the Jordan. [12] Thus his
sons did for him as he had instructed them. [13] His sons carried
him to the land of Canaan, and buried him in the cave of the
field of Machpelah, the field near Mamre, which Abraham had
bought for a burial site from Ephron the Hittite. [14] After burying
his father, Joseph returned to Egypt, he and his brothers and all
who had gone up with him to bury his father.

[15] When Joseph's brothers saw that their father was dead,
they said, "What if Joseph still bears a grudge against us and
pays us back for all the wrong that we did him!" [16] So they
sent this message to Joseph, "Before his death your father left
this instruction: [17] So shall you say to Joseph, 'Forgive, I urge
you, the offense and guilt of your brothers who treated you so
harshly.' Therefore, please forgive the offense of the servants of

a *Or "the threshing floor of."* *b* *Interpreted as "the mourning of the Egyptians."*

49.33: *He drew his feet into the bed* closes the action begun at 48.2, when he "sat up in bed." The intervening material is thus presented as Jacob's last will and testament. **50.2–3:** The embalming and the periods of mourning follow Egyptian rather than Israelite custom. Jewish law forbids embalming (and cremating). The body must, instead, be interred in such a way that it will "return to the ground from which [it was] taken" (Gen. 3.19). **5:** *The grave which I made ready for myself*: Jacob had designated the burial place (49.29-30) but had not actually readied the grave. When speaking to Pharaoh, Joseph models his father's preparations for death on Egyptian kings who erected elaborate monuments for their burial. **10:** It is unclear why the state procession approached Hebron by way of Transjordan. Perhaps vv. 10–11 derive from a lost tradition that did not locate Jacob's grave in the cave of Machpelah, as vv. 12–13 do, but spoke of an interment at the otherwise unattested site of Goren ha-Atad. Whether this is the case or not, the itinerary foreshadows the route Israel takes after their miraculous escape from Egypt, when they entered Canaan from Transjordan (Num. 33.1–49; Josh. ch 3). As God had promised (46.4), Jacob, in short, is given his own personal exodus. The Talmud derives from this verse the institution of "shiv'ah," the seven days of most intense mourning incumbent upon Jews who have lost close kin (*y. Mo'ed Kat.* 3.5). Unlike the situation here, however, "shiv'ah" begins after burial. **15:** Cf. 27.41. **16–17:** No such words appear on the lips of Jacob himself. On the basis of this, a rabbi in the Talmud ruled that "it is permissible for a person to modify a statement in the interest of peace," and another rabbi maintained that one was required to do so (*b. Yebam.* 65b). The brothers' lie is defensible because of the good relations it ensured—a result that Jacob, on a plain-sense reading, surely desired.

the God of your father." And Joseph was in tears as they spoke
to him.
18 His brothers went to him themselves, flung themselves before him, and said, "We are prepared to be your slaves." 19 But
Joseph said to them, "Have no fear! Am I a substitute for God?
20 Besides, although you intended me harm, God intended it
for good, so as to bring about the present result—the survival
of many people. 21 And so, fear not. I will sustain you and your
children." Thus he reassured them, speaking kindly to them.

22 So Joseph and his father's household remained in Egypt.
Joseph lived one hundred and ten years. 23 Joseph lived to see
children of the third generation of Ephraim; the children of
Machir son of Manasseh were likewise born upon Joseph's
knees. 24 At length, Joseph said to his brothers, "I am about to
die. God will surely take notice of you and bring you up from
this land to the land that He promised on oath to Abraham, to
Isaac, and to Jacob." 25 So Joseph made the sons of Israel swear,
saying, "When God has taken notice of you, you shall carry up
my bones from here."
26 Joseph died at the age of one hundred and ten years; and
he was embalmed and placed in a coffin in Egypt.

18–21: Joseph's dreams in 37.5–11 suggest that the enslavement of Joseph's brothers to him would indeed occur and be, in fact, the last word in this complex and suspenseful novella. As they sold him into slavery (37.25–28), so would he (who had already enslaved the Egyptians, 47.13–26) enslave them. In fact, Joseph adheres to the ethic that forbids an Israelite to "take vengeance or bear a grudge" (Lev. 19.18). His rationale rests on the idea that the malignant intentions of human beings can realize the benign intentions of God. The people Israel, ironically, survives the worldwide famine because Joseph's brothers sold him into slavery (50.19–20; cf. 30.2 n.). **22:** *One hundred and ten years* appears in Egyptian sources as the ideal life span (cf. 6.3; Ps. 90.10). **23:** *Born upon Joseph's knees* implies adoption (cf. 30.3; 48.12). Not surprisingly, therefore, in Judg. 5.14 Machir appears as a tribe of Israel. **24–25:** *Will surely take notice.... has taken notice* (both are "pakod yifkod" in Heb) came to fulfillment in Exod. 3.16, when the LORD instructs Moses to declare to the "elders of Israel" that "I have taken note" ("pakod pakadti") of "you and what is being done to you in Egypt." In fact, it is none other than Moses himself who carries out Joseph's charge. The Mishnah finds in this an illustration of the important rabbinic principle, "By the measure by which a person metes out, it shall be meted out to him." Because "Joseph went up to bury his father" (50.7), Moses, generations later (as reported in Exod. 13.19) "took with him the bones of Joseph" (*m. Sot.* 1.7, 9). Ultimately, those bones were buried in Shechem (Josh. 24.32), the very city to which Jacob had sent Joseph, then a brash teenager, at the beginning of this astonishing tale of discord and reconciliation in the family that bears God's promise (37.13).

שמות

Exodus

THE ENGLISH NAME OF EXODUS derives from the Greek title *Exodos,* short for *Exodos Aigyptou,* "Departure from Egypt," used in the Septuagint (LXX). The Hebrew title, *Sefer ve'eleh shemot,* "the book of 'And these are the names' " (usually abbreviated to *Shemot,* "Names"), is based on the opening words of the book.

Exodus, in its present form, is not an independent book, but an intrinsic part of the Torah which narrates the story of Israel from the creation of the world through the death of Moses. The Torah in its final form is divided into five separate books because ancient scrolls could not contain a work of that length. Nevertheless, the books were not divided arbitrarily but at natural transition points. Exodus begins where the Hebrews grow from a family into the people of Israel (1.1–7; cf. v. 9), and it ends on the first day of the new year following the exodus from Egypt as the sanctuary is erected and the divine Presence takes up Its abode in the Israelites' midst. The opening section (1.1–6, which recapitulates Gen. 46.8–27) and the closing section (40.36–38, which anticipates Num. 9.15–23) look as if they were composed to serve as prologue and epilogue, marking the book as a distinct subunit within the Torah. Thematically, the book marks the transition from God's promises of progeny, land, and a permanent relationship with Israel (e.g., Gen. chs 12–15; 17.1–8) to the fulfillment of these promises, beginning with the Israelites' phenomenal growth, the exodus, and the covenant at Sinai (Exod. 1.1–7; 12.1–36; chs 19–24).

Exodus presents the seminal events in Israel's history and the definitive institutions of its religion, themes that have reverberated through all subsequent Jewish and Western history. These include Pharaoh's enslavement of the Israelites, the leadership of Moses, the beginnings of prophecy, the revelation of God's name YHVH to Moses, the ten plagues, the Pesaḥ ("Passover") festival, the splitting and crossing of the sea, the manna, the revelation of the Decalogue at Mount Sinai, the covenant formally constituting Israel as God's people, the first of the Torah's law collections and rules about the Sabbath and sacrificial worship, the sin of the golden calf, and the construction of the sanctuary.

Structure and Focus

THE BOOK FALLS ROUGHLY INTO FOUR MAIN SECTIONS: (1) enslavement and liberation (1.1–15.21), during which Israel and Egypt come to "know" the LORD and His name; (2) the journey to Sinai (15.22–17.16), marked by a series of dangers, Israelite complaints, and deliverance by God; (3) covenant and lawgiving at Sinai (18.1–24.18), featuring the public revelation of God; and (4) the sanctuary and the golden calf (chs 25–40), dealing with the authorized and unauthorized ways of securing God's Presence and worshipping Him. The division between sections 1 and 2 is not certain.

The narrative in Exodus focuses on the paradigmatic significance of the events and on celebrating them rather than on historical details. The names of the pharaohs (the generic name for Egyptian kings, meaning "great house" [i.e., palace])—so important for historians—are nowhere mentioned, although those of the midwives who demonstrated "fear of God" are (1.15). Emphasized instead is the contest of wills between Pharaoh, who does not know YHVH (5.2), and YHVH Himself, who is determined to show Egypt, Israel, and the world that He is YHVH and what that means (7.5; 9.16; 14.4; etc.): that He is incomparable (8.6); that He is present in the world (8.18); that the earth is His (9.29). The book points out the lessons of the events, to be repeated to subsequent generations, and ordains commemorative rites to celebrate them (10.2; chs 12–13). The narrative is full of the miraculous, such as the plagues against Egypt and the atmospherics at Sinai. Based on these accounts, Deuteronomy would later declare that the exodus and the revelation at Sinai "clearly demonstrate ... that the LORD alone is God in heaven above and on earth below; there is no other" (Deut. 4.32–39).

Historicity

THE BOOK'S LACK OF ATTENTION to historical details has left historians grasping at bits of incidental information, and at indirect evidence from ancient Egypt, that might permit dating of the exodus or assessment of its historicity. None of its narratives in their current form is likely to be contemporary with the events they describe, though at least some have roots in earlier oral tradition. Nor is there reference to an exodus in contemporary Egyptian sources. Such a reference is not really to be expected, however: Egyptian royal inscriptions avoided mentioning setbacks and defeats unless they were followed by victories, and administrative records from the time and place of the exodus have mostly perished. Still, some data suggest that there is a plausible historical kernel to the story. Northwestern Semites of the same ethno-linguistic stock as the Hebrews, from Canaan, Transjordan, and Syria, had for centuries migrated to Egypt, especially the eastern Nile delta, for food and water during times of famine, as the Bible reports of Abraham and later of Jacob and his family, who settled in the eastern delta (1.8 n.; 8.18 n.). Others were brought there as slaves captured by the Egyptian army during raids. Egyptian documents refer to all of them as "Asiatics," rather than the specific ethnic groups to which they belong (e.g., Hebrew/Israelite, Moabite, Phoenician; some mention people called Ḥapiru, but they are probably not Hebrews; see 1.15 n.). Some Asiatics served as domestic or state slaves, the latter in royal building projects, like the Hebrews of Exodus. According to the biblical account, the Hebrew slaves worked on the construction of the city of Rameses (1.11). If there is a historical kernel to the story, the Pharaoh who enslaved them was Rameses II (1279–1213 BCE), the greatest builder in ancient Egypt, who built the city named after himself as his new capital, in the eastern delta. Rameses also built a series of forts in the delta to secure Egypt's borders; this is perhaps reflected in the biblical Pharaoh's concern about foreign invasion (1.10).

While we have no extrabiblical record of the ten plagues or of a mass escape of slaves from Egypt, natural disasters did take place periodically (though so many in rapid succession is implausible), and mass escapes of slaves are known from elsewhere in the ancient world, such as the later revolt of 100,000 slaves in Italy led by Spartacus. The Egyptian origin of the name "Moses" (a common element in such Egyptian names as Thutmosis and Rameses) is consistent with the Israelites having spent time in Egypt. If the Pharaoh of the enslavement was Rameses II, the Pharaoh under whom the Israelites left Egypt may have been his son, Merneptah (1213–1203 BCE), one of whose inscriptions claims a victory over "Israel," described as a nonsedentary people somewhere in the vicinity of Canaan, an encounter that would have taken place after the exodus. This fits the archeological evidence that suggests that the Israelites appeared in Canaan around the beginning of the Iron Age (ca. 1200 BCE). None of this proves that the exodus happened, but it does indicate that the outline of the story, of Hebrews migrating to Egypt during a famine and being enslaved there under Rameses II, and later leaving under Moses, during or by the time of Merneptah, is not inherently implausible. Moreover, if the Israelites had invented their history, it seems more likely that they would have portrayed themselves as the original inhabitants of their land rather than as interlopers with a humiliating background as slaves.

Composition and Date

MODERN CRITICAL SCHOLARSHIP has shown that Exodus, like the Torah as a whole and some other ancient literature as well, was composed by one or more compilers, or redactors, who wove together several earlier written versions of the same events (see "Torah," pp. 1–6). These versions often disagreed with each other about ideology or the course of events. Their preservation side by side has led modern scholars to conclude that the redactor(s) was/were fundamentally conservative. Perhaps they believed all the traditions valid, perhaps even inspired, and therefore preserved them with minimal revision even if that left inconsistencies, non sequiturs, and redundancies.

For example, in Exodus 6.3 God tells Moses that He did not make Himself known to the patriarchs by the name YHVH, but according to Genesis 15.7 He did. Within Exodus itself, Moses' father-in-law has different names in 2.18; 3.1; 4.18, and the description of the Tent of Meeting in 33.7–11 is inconsistent with, and oblivious to, both the immediately surrounding narrative and the description of the differently described Tent in chs 25–31 and 35–40. Inconsistencies such as these have alerted scholars to the presence of different written sources that were woven together to form the version we now have, and characteristic variations in vocabulary and ideas have guided them in identifying the sources from which various components stem. Most easily identified is the Priestly document (P), the source of sections of chs 1–24 and most of chs 25–31 and 35–40, although recently scholars have found signs of the Holiness Document (H), a later compilation of the Priestly school, there as well. P is also found in some of the narratives of the book, but there it shares space with material from the Yahwist (J) and Elohist (E) sources. J and E can sometimes, but not always, be distinguished; thus scholars often speak simply of the JE (or early narrative) source. Some also believe that there are some sections that are Deuteronomic, that is, related to ideas found in Deuteronomy. In numerous cases, although it is clear that we are dealing with an amalgam of two or three sources, we cannot fully disentangle them (see introductory comments to chs 19–24 and 31.18–34.35).

Once the components of the text have been assigned as best they can be to their original sources, the differing views of those sources emerge. For example, J represents the oppression of the Israelites as corvée (forced) labor (1.11), P as full enslavement (1.13–14); arranging them in sequence, the redactor portrays them as two successive stages of oppression. According to J the Israelites lived in Goshen, apart from the Egyptians (9.26); according to E they lived side by side with them (3.22). P (6.2) and E (3.13–15) hold that the name YHVH was first revealed to Moses, while J believes that it was known earlier (Gen. 15.7). The patterned sequence of ten plagues noted at 7.14–10.29 was shaped by the redactor, who wove together material from J, P, and possibly E, which each had fewer, partly overlapping, partly different, plagues.

The sources all represent the events at Mount Sinai very differently. For example, P reports neither a public revelation, the conclusion of a covenant, nor a golden calf episode. All that happened on the mountain was that God's Presence or Glory (Heb "kavod") rested there in a cloud and Moses entered the cloud and privately received the tablets of the "Pact" and the instructions for the sanctuary (19.1–2a; 24.15–31.18a); all other lawgiving took place later in the Tabernacle, starting in Leviticus ch 1. It was J and E that reported the covenant, the visual (J) and auditory (E) manifestations of God, the proclamation of the Decalogue and the other covenant laws, and the breach of the covenant in the golden calf episode (chs 19–24; 32–34). It was the redactor(s) who wove these varying and conflicting details together in their present order, making them represent different stages of the events. The care and literary skill of the redactor(s) is illustrated by the patterning of the plagues (7.14–10.29) and the location of the golden calf episode between the instructions for the sanctuary and their execution (31.18–32.35 n.). Whether or not the redactors believed that the inconsistencies could be harmonized is unclear. The contradictions and redundancies, however, had an important effect on later Judaism because they encouraged—in fact, forced—readers to create fine distinctions and nonliteral interpretations to enable them to coexist (*Thirteen Hermeneutic Rules of Rabbi Ishmael,* no. 13; *Thirty-two Hermeneutic Rules of Rabbi Eliezer ben Rabbi Jose the Galilean,* no. 15; Saadia, *Book of Beliefs and Opinions,* ch 7), thus paving the way in Judaism for innovations in theology and law.

Exodus and the Jewish Tradition

MANY OF THE FUNDAMENTAL BELIEFS and practices of Judaism are rooted in Exodus. The first of the book's two central events, the exodus itself, is recounted daily in Jewish prayers. It and the other central event, the proclamation of the Decalogue at Mount Sinai, are celebrated and retold at Jewish festivals every year, the exodus on the festival of Pesaḥ, whose rituals, including the Seder, are based on the rules prescribed in chs 12–13, and the proclamation of the Decalogue (ch 20) on the festival of Shavuʿot. The two festivals are known in later liturgical texts, respectively, as *zeman ḥerutenu,* "the time of our freedom," and *zeman matan toratenu,* "the time when our Torah was given." The inextricable link between them, expressed in the fact that Pesaḥ begins a fifty-day countdown to Shavuʿot (see Lev. 23.15–21), proclaims that the freedom attained on the former only reaches fulfillment with the laws received on the latter. These two festivals plus Sukkot, the Feast of Booths, constitute the three "Pilgrimage Festivals" *(shalosh regalim)* of the Jewish religious calendar. Two other rituals that began as commemorations of the exodus are daily wearing of tefillin (13.9–10 n.) and the redemption of first-born sons (*pidyon haben,* 13.13 n.).

The exodus also served to orient Jewish festivals increasingly toward God's actions in history, in contrast to polytheistic festivals which focused on the gods' actions in nature. The role of Pesaḥ and the Feast of Unleavened Bread as commemorations of the exodus completely eclipsed their presumed earlier significance as spring agricultural and livestock festivals (12.6–14 n., 14–20 n.). Sukkot, although essentially an agricultural festival, ultimately comes to commemorate the Israelites' dwelling in booths following the exodus (Lev. 23.43). At least since Second Temple times Shavuʿot—in the Torah an entirely agricultural festival—has been recognized as commemorating the giving of the Torah at Mount Sinai. Theologically, God's manifestation as Israel's redeemer at the exodus has fortified Jewish belief in redemption even in the throes of oppression.

Fundamental principles of Judaism based on Exodus are the belief that the relationship between God and the Jewish people is defined by the covenant *(berit)* established between them at Mount Sinai (chs 19; 24) and the belief that God gave the Torah there, ordaining the Jewish way of life (chs 19–24). (This latter idea, however, of the revelation of the entire Torah on Sinai, is never explicit in the Torah.) The momentous encounter with God at Sinai is, for Judaism, the defining moment in Jewish history, the moment when God came down on earth and spoke to all Jews, present and future, giving them His rules for life, which they accepted enthusiastically (20.16; 24.3, 7 n.). These laws (according to rabbinic belief both the Written Torah and its oral interpretation were communicated simultaneously) became the basis of all of Judaism: "Moses received Torah—written and oral—at Sinai and passed it on" down through the generations (*Pirkei ʾAvot* 1.1). Because these laws were presented to the entire people (21.1 n.), it became the duty of every Jew, not just an intellectual or clerical elite, to study them. Finally, the Thirteen Attributes of God, recited on various occasions in Jewish liturgy, are based on the attributes that God reveals to Moses in 34.6–7.

The laws that God proclaimed to the Israelites in the Decalogue (20.2–14), include laws both "between humankind and God" and "between one human being and another." Three of the laws in the first group became defining characteristics of Judaism which Jews have defended, often with their lives: the requirement to worship only the LORD (YHVH) and have no other gods, the requirement to have no idols, and the requirement to observe the Sabbath. Of the latter, the Zionist philosopher Aḥad Ha-ʿAm (Asher Ginzberg, 1856–1927) observed: "Even more than the Jews kept the Sabbath, the Sabbath preserved the Jews." The exodus has reverberated down through world history. Many early American settlers understood their flight from Europe and settlement in America as a new exodus, and later, Benjamin Franklin and Thomas Jefferson recommended that the great seal of the United States depict Moses leading the Israelites across the parted sea as a symbol of the American experience. African-Americans in the United States, hoping for freedom in the 19th century and fighting for civil rights in the 20th century, likewise saw themselves as reliving the Israelite experience. In the 1970s and 1980s, the mass departure of hundreds of thousands of Jews from the Soviet Union was known as "Operation Exodus." The exodus has clearly resonated strongly in Western history.

[JEFFREY H. TIGAY]

SHEMOT שמות

1 These are the names of the sons of Israel who came to
Egypt with Jacob, each coming with his household: 2 Reuben, Simeon, Levi, and Judah; 3 Issachar, Zebulun, and Benjamin; 4 Dan and Naphtali, Gad and Asher. 5 The total number
of persons that were of Jacob's issue came to seventy, Joseph
being already in Egypt. 6 Joseph died, and all his brothers, and
all that generation. 7 But the Israelites were fertile and prolific;
they multiplied and increased very greatly, so that the land
was filled with them.

8 A new king arose over Egypt who did not know Joseph.
9 And he said to his people, "Look, the Israelite people are
much too numerous for us. 10 Let us deal shrewdly with them,
so that they may not increase; otherwise in the event of war
they may join our enemies in fighting against us and [a]rise
from the ground."[a] 11 So they set taskmasters over them to oppress them with forced labor; and they built garrison cities[b] for

a-a Meaning perhaps from their wretched condition, cf. Hos. 2.2; or "gain ascendancy over the country." Others "get them up out of the land."
b Others "store cities."

1.1–2.22: Prologue. This section sets the stage for the exodus by telling how the family of Jacob grew into a people in Egypt and fell into bondage (as God foretold in Gen. 15.13), and how Moses, the human agent of their deliverance, arose. It is composed of a combination of early narrative sources (JE) and P material.

1.1–7: Transition from Genesis. A recapitulation of Gen. 46.8–27 (cf. Gen. 35.23–26) leads to the account of how Jacob's family grew in Egypt from seventy individuals (a number signifying perfect completion) to a huge population—indeed, from a family to a people. **7:** Many terms in this v. (and in vv. 12 and 20) are also used in God's blessings and promises in Genesis, to humanity and then the patriarchs (Gen. 1.20, 28; 9.1, 7; 17.2; 18.18; 28.14; 48.4), implying that these ancestral promises were now being fulfilled by God, who was causing the Israelites' proliferation and thwarting Pharaoh's attempts to check it.

1.8–22: The oppression. 8: This may refer to the rise of the 19th Dynasty, particularly Rameses II (ca. 1279–1213 BCE). This dynasty, founded by military officers, sought to protect Egypt's vulnerable coast and northeastern and northwestern borders from the Sea Peoples, the Libyans, and infiltrators from the Sinai, and to protect access to Egypt's empire in western Asia. Given the Israelites' background in Canaan and current residence in Goshen (8.18 n.), adjacent to the Sinai, Pharaoh may have feared that they would ally with invaders from that direction. **11–22:** Pharaoh's attempts to check the Israelites' proliferation unfold in

Pharaoh: Pithom and Rameses. 12 But the more they were oppressed, the more they increased and spread out, so that the [Egyptians] came to dread the Israelites.

13 The Egyptians ruthlessly imposed upon the Israelites 14 [a-]the various labors that they made them perform. Ruthlessly[-a] they made life bitter for them with harsh labor at mortar and bricks and with all sorts of tasks in the field.

15 The king of Egypt spoke to the Hebrew midwives, one of whom was named Shiphrah and the other Puah, 16 saying, "When you deliver the Hebrew women, look at the birthstool:[b] if it is a boy, kill him; if it is a girl, let her live." 17 The midwives, fearing God, did not do as the king of Egypt had told them; they let the boys live. 18 So the king of Egypt summoned the midwives and said to them, "Why have you done this thing, letting the boys live?" 19 The midwives said to Pharaoh, "Because the Hebrew women are not like the Egyptian women: they are vigorous. Before the midwife can come to them, they have given birth." 20 And God dealt well with the midwives; and the people multiplied and increased greatly. 21 And because the midwives feared God, He established households[c] for them. 22 Then Pharaoh charged all his people, saying, "Every boy that is born you shall throw into the Nile, but let every girl live."

2 A certain man of the house of Levi went and married a Levite woman. 2 The woman conceived and bore a son; and when she saw how beautiful he was, she hid him for three months. 3 When she could hide him no longer, she got a wicker

a-a Brought up from the end of the verse for clarity.
b More exactly, the brick or stone supports used by Egyptian women during childbirth.
c Meaning of Heb. batim *uncertain.*

four stages, increasingly more oppressive: subjection to corvée (forced or draft) labor (vv. 11–12), slavery (vv. 13–14), a secret attempt to murder newborn boys (vv. 15–21), and a public attempt to do the same (v. 22). The presentation of these as four successive, intensifying stages is the work of the redactor who drew them from the earlier sources J (corvée), P (slavery), and perhaps E (one or both attempts at infanticide). **11:** Pharaoh hopes to check the Israelites' proliferation by exhausting them. *Taskmasters,* foremen of corvée contingents (1 Kings 5.27–28). *Garrison cities,* rather "store cities" of a type that usually served military purposes (1 Kings 9.19; 2 Chron. 8.4–6; 17.12–13; 32.27–28). These were not the pyramids; nothing in the biblical text or elsewhere suggests that the Israelites built pyramids. *Pithom and Rameses* stood at strategic points guarding the entry to Egypt from the north and northeast. *Pithom,* Egyptian Pir-Atum, "House of (the god) Atum," was probably Tel e-Retabeh or Tel el-Maskhutah in the Wadi Tumilat, the entrance to Egypt from the Sinai Peninsula; both sites have archeological remains from the time of Rameses II. The city of Rameses was Pir-Rameses-Meri-Amon, "House of Rameses, beloved of [the god] Amon," capital of the delta region under the 19th and part of the 20th dynasties (1292–1137 BCE). It occupied a very large area that extended over Kantir and Khataana and other nearby sites. Seti I (1294–1279 BCE) built a summer palace there, and it was considerably expanded by Rameses II. **13–14:** *Ruthlessly imposed … labors,* reduced them to full slavery (Lev. 25.39–46). **15:** *Hebrew,* an old term for Israelites, usually used when contrasting Israelites with other peoples (Gen. 14.13; 39.14, 17; 40.15; Exod. 21.2; Deut. 15.12); it is not normally used after the time of David (an exception is Jonah 1.9). A relationship with the groups known as ʿApiru (sometimes spelled Ḥapiru) in ancient Near Eastern sources has been suggested, but the connection is problematic since the latter refers to a social class of outcasts, whereas "Hebrew" refers to an ethnic group. *Hebrew midwives,* the phrase could mean "midwives to the Hebrews" or "midwives who were Hebrew." The former interpretation, found in LXX, Josephus, Abravanel, and Judah he-Ḥasid, understands them as righteous Gentiles; hence their motive is said to be fear of God (v. 17) rather than loyalty to their people. **16:** Killing the males and leaving only females would eliminate potential Israelite military power. Pharaoh's efforts are of no avail, as women thwart him (v. 17) and rescue Israel's future deliverer (2.1–10). *Birthstool,* parturient women sat or crouched on a seat of stone or bricks. **17:** *Fearing God,* restrained by an awareness that murder would bring divine retribution; here as elsewhere in the Bible, "fearing God" reflects an action which derives from fear, or awe, and not the emotion itself. **22:** *Throw into the Nile,* rather "expose in the Nile," that is, to be floated in baskets down the Nile where the babies would sink and drown. This attempt also fails. Ironically, the Nile will become the means by which Moses is saved and raised by Pharaoh's own daughter (2.1–10), and drowning will become the means of Pharaoh's ultimate defeat (Exod. 14.28).

2.1–22: The origins of Moses.

2.1–10: Moses' infancy. The story of Moses' birth and Pharaoh's attempted infanticide may

basket for him and caulked it with bitumen and pitch. She put
the child into it and placed it among the reeds by the bank of
the Nile. 4 And his sister stationed herself at a distance, to learn
what would befall him.
5 The daughter of Pharaoh came down to bathe in the Nile,
while her maidens walked along the Nile. She spied the basket
among the reeds and sent her slave girl to fetch it. 6 When she
opened it, she saw that it was a child, a boy crying. She took pity
on it and said, "This must be a Hebrew child." 7 Then his sister
said to Pharaoh's daughter, "Shall I go and get you a Hebrew
nurse to suckle the child for you?" 8 And Pharaoh's daughter
answered, "Yes." So the girl went and called the child's mother. 9 And Pharaoh's daughter said to her, "Take this child and
nurse it for me, and I will pay your wages." So the woman took
the child and nursed it. 10 When the child grew up, she brought
him to Pharaoh's daughter, who made him her son. She named
him Moses,[a] explaining, "I drew him out of the water."

11 Some time after that, when Moses had grown up, he went
out to his kinsfolk and witnessed their labors. He saw an Egyptian beating a Hebrew, one of his kinsmen. 12 He turned this
way and that and, seeing no one about, he struck down the
Egyptian and hid him in the sand. 13 When he went out the
next day, he found two Hebrews fighting; so he said to the offender, "Why do you strike your fellow?" 14 He retorted, "Who
made you chief and ruler over us? Do you mean to kill me as
you killed the Egyptian?" Moses was frightened, and thought:
Then the matter is known! 15 When Pharaoh learned of the
matter, he sought to kill Moses; but Moses fled from Pharaoh.
He arrived[b] in the land of Midian, and sat down beside a well.

16 Now the priest of Midian had seven daughters. They came
to draw water, and filled the troughs to water their father's
flock; 17 but shepherds came and drove them off. Moses rose
to their defense, and he watered their flock. 18 When they returned to their father Reuel, he said, "How is it that you have
come back so soon today?" 19 They answered, "An Egyptian
rescued us from the shepherds; he even drew water for us
and watered the flock." 20 He said to his daughters, "Where

a Heb. Mosheh *from Egyptian for "born of"; here associated with* mashah *"draw out."*
b Lit. "sat" or "settled."

be a relatively late addition to the tradition; the following narratives about the exodus show no awareness of them (e.g., 2.23 and 6.6 are aware only of bondage), and they are never mentioned elsewhere in the Bible. This story has parallels in birth legends of other heroes, some of which pre-date the Bible, such as Sargon of Akkad who in infancy was born in secret and exposed in a river in a reed basket sealed with pitch, but was found and later became king. In an Egyptian story, the god Horus was endangered as an infant by the god Seth and was hidden (but not abandoned) in a papyrus thicket of the Nile delta by his mother Isis to save him. **1:** Moses' parents, nameless here, are identified in a different source (6.16–20; P) as Amram and Amram's aunt Jochebed. **2–4:** *The woman conceived and bore a son:* As the subsequent narrative indicates, this was not the couple's first child. This episode knows of an older sister, (v. 4ff.), and other passages recognize an older brother, Aaron (e.g., 4.14; 6.20; 7.7). All the actions to thwart Pharaoh's decree are taken by women—Moses' mother and sister, the midwives (1.17), and Pharaoh's daughter (2.5–10); the Hebrew men have been reduced to inactivity. **4:** *His sister,* elsewhere identified as Miriam (15.20; Num. 26.59). **7–9:** This sister contrives to return Moses temporarily to his mother's care by means of a wetnursing agreement (such agreements are well-attested in ancient Near Eastern documents). **10:** *Moses* is an Egyptian name meaning "gave birth"; it is a shortened form of names compounded with names of deities, such as Thut-mose and Rameses, meaning "Thut/Ra gave birth (to this child)." Here, in a popular etymology typical of biblical and other ancient Near Eastern literature, it is interpreted as if it were derived from Heb "m-sh-h," "draw out" (cf. Isa. 63.11).

2.11–22: Moses' young adulthood. In the first two episodes (vv. 11–12, 13–14) Moses plays the royal role of defending his people and adjudicating among them (cf. 1 Sam. 8.5, 20)—actions that prefigure his later activities—and in the third he defends foreigners and strangers (vv. 16–17), showing that his passion for justice makes no distinctions between nations. **11:** *An Egyptian,* presumably one of the taskmasters (1.11). **15:** *Midian,* a region in northwest Arabia. **18:** *Their father Reuel,* Moses' father-in-law is called Jethro in 3.1 (Jether in 4.18) and elsewhere, and Hobab son of Reuel in Num. 10.29

is he then? Why did you leave the man? Ask him in to break bread." 21 Moses consented to stay with the man, and he gave Moses his daughter Zipporah as wife. 22 She bore a son whom he named Gershom,[a] for he said, "I have been a stranger in a foreign land."

23 A long time after that, the king of Egypt died. The Israelites were groaning under the bondage and cried out; and their cry for help from the bondage rose up to God. 24 God heard their moaning, and God remembered His covenant with Abraham and Isaac and Jacob. 25 God looked upon the Israelites, and God took notice of them.

3 Now Moses, tending the flock of his father-in-law Jethro, the priest of Midian, drove the flock into the wilderness, and came to Horeb, the mountain of God. 2 An angel of the LORD appeared to him in a blazing fire out of a bush. He gazed, and there was a bush all aflame, yet the bush was not consumed. 3 Moses said, "I must turn aside to look at this marvelous sight; why doesn't the bush burn up?" 4 When the LORD saw that he had turned aside to look, God called to him out of the bush: "Moses! Moses!" He answered, "Here I am." 5 And He said, "Do not come closer. Remove your sandals from your feet, for the place on which you stand is holy ground. 6 I am," He said, "the God of your father, the God of Abraham, the God

a Associated with ger sham, *"a stranger there."*

and Judg. 4.11. These different names reflect different ancient traditions. **19:** *An Egyptian,* so Moses must have seemed because of his clothing and speech. **22:** Since Moses was raised as an Egyptian, it is only in Midian that he begins to feel the sense of alienness that his kinsfolk have experienced in Egypt.

2.23–25: Prelude to redemption. Pharaoh's death clears the way for Moses' return to Egypt (4.19). The Israelites' outcry rises up to God, who takes note of it and remembers His commitments to their ancestors. *His covenant* refers both to God's promise of nationhood and territory in Canaan and the promise to free Israel after a long period of servitude (12.1–3; 15.13–20; 17.1–14; Gen. 26.2–5; 46.3–4). God's resolve to carry out these commitments is put into effect immediately, starting with His appearance to Moses in the burning bush (3.7–10).

3.1–22: Moses' call and departure for Egypt. The current narrative is the result of an artful combination of the two early sources, J and E. This is intimated by the different names used for God in 3.4a and b, but the clearest indication is that 3.9–15 seem intrusive: vv. 9, 10, and 15a are redundant with, respectively, vv. 7, 18b, and 16a; the people never ask for God's name as Moses expects in v. 13; and vv. 10 and 18 describe the goal of Moses' mission to Pharaoh differently and use different terms for the Egyptian king. Vv. 16–18 read like, and probably once were, a direct continuation of v. 8. The consistent use of the name "God" (ʾelohim) in 3.9–15 identifies its source as E; the remainder of this section is mostly from J with a few other passages from E (such as vv. 1, 4b, 6b, and 20b). By incorporating material from both sources the redactor preserved multiple themes, such as the explanation of God's name in v. 14 (E) and the fact that God both "appeared" to Moses (3.2, 16; 4.1, 5, from J) and "sent" him (vv. 10, 12–15, from E).

3.1–10: God appears to Moses and gives him his charge. The burning bush is both a means of attracting Moses' attention and a manifestation of God's Presence. **1:** *Horeb,* alternate name for Mount Sinai (in E and in Deuteronomy). It is generally thought to be located in the Sinai Peninsula, though some believe it is in northwest Arabia, near Midian. Its designation *mountain of God* may indicate that it was already considered a sacred place, or it may be anticipatory. The first possibility may gain support from Egyptian inscriptions of the 14th century BCE that refer to an area, apparently in this region, as "land of the nomads, Yahve"; this might also be understood as "land of the nomads who worship Yahve." **2:** *An angel of the LORD,* a manifestation of God. Angels (lit. "messengers") usually take human form, but this one takes the form of *fire,* a substance evocative of the divine because it is insubstantial yet powerful, dangerous, illuminating, and purifying. (For God's manifestation in, and comparison to, fire, see also Gen. 15.17; Exod. 19.18; Deut. 4.24; Ezek. 1.27; Ps. 104.4.) **6:** *The God of Abraham, the God of Isaac, and the God of Jacob:* This phrase later became the way that God is addressed in the ʿAmidah prayer. The repetition of "God" before each patriarch is explained in *ʿEtz Yosef,* a commentary on the Jewish prayerbook, as meaning that, like the patriarchs, each person should believe in God on the basis of personal investigation, not merely tradition. *He was afraid to look at God:* Although the Bible assumes that God has a physical (usually humanlike) form, many passages suggest that seeing Him would be too awesome for humans to survive (Gen. 32.31; Exod. 19.21; 33.20–23; Judg. 13.22; Isa. 6.5; exceptions include Exod. 24.10–11; Num. 12.8; Deut. 34.10; Ezek. 1.26–28). Later

of Isaac, and the God of Jacob." And Moses hid his face, for he
was afraid to look at God.
7 And the LORD continued, "I have marked well the plight
of My people in Egypt and have heeded their outcry because
of their taskmasters; yes, I am mindful of their sufferings. 8 I
have come down to rescue them from the Egyptians and to
bring them out of that land to a good and spacious land, a land
flowing with milk and honey, the region of the Canaanites, the
Hittites, the Amorites, the Perizzites, the Hivites, and the Jebusites. 9 Now the cry of the Israelites has reached Me; moreover,
I have seen how the Egyptians oppress them. 10 Come, therefore, I will send you to Pharaoh, and you shall free My people,
the Israelites, from Egypt."
11 But Moses said to God, "Who am I that I should go to Pharaoh and free the Israelites from Egypt?" 12 And He said, "I will
be with you; that shall be your sign that it was I who sent you.
And when you have freed the people from Egypt, you shall
worship God at this mountain."
13 Moses said to God, "When I come to the Israelites and
say to them, 'The God of your fathers has sent me to you,' and
they ask me, 'What is His name?' what shall I say to them?"
14 And God said to Moses, "Ehyeh-Asher-Ehyeh."[a] He continued, "Thus shall you say to the Israelites, 'Ehyeh[b] sent me to
you.' " 15 And God said further to Moses, "Thus shall you speak
to the Israelites: The LORD,[c] the God of your fathers, the God

a *Meaning of Heb. uncertain; variously translated: "I Am That I Am"; "I Am Who I Am"; "I Will Be What I Will Be"; etc.*

b *Others "I Am" or "I Will Be."*

c *The name* YHWH *(traditionally read* Adonai *"the LORD") is here associated with the root* hayah *"to be."*

Jewish philosophers, most notably Maimonides, held that God does not in fact have a physical form and that the biblical passages in question are meant as metaphors. **8:** *A land flowing with milk and honey,* a proverbial expression of the fertility of the land of Israel, representing the products of animals and the earth, of herders and farmers ("honey" refers primarily to the nectar of fruit, esp. of dates, figs, and grapes). *The Canaanites . . . :* The Bible offers several different lists of peoples who lived in the promised land prior to the Israelites. (Cf., e.g., Gen. 10.15–20; Num. 13.29; Deut. 7.1.) **10:** *I will send you:* As a prophet, Moses' primary role is to serve as God's emissary. Phrases with "send" ("sh-l-ḥ") typify the selection of prophets elsewhere as well (e.g., Isa. 6.8; Jer. 1.7).

3.11–4.17: Moses raises five objections to his assignment (3.11, 13; 4.1, 10, 13), **but God overcomes each.** Prophets are often reluctant to accept their commission; cf. Jer. ch. 1. **12:** *I will be with you:* The verb *be* ("'ehyeh") anticipates the etymology of the divine name YHVH in v. 14. *That shall be your sign,* or, "this shall be your sign." It is unclear whether the sign is God's Presence with Moses, the fact that He sent him, or the future return to Horeb and worship there. **13:** Not having been raised among his own people, Moses (like Pharaoh in 5.2) is ignorant of their God's name and fears he will therefore lack credibility with them. He is told God's name, which the people evidently knew already, though 6.3 implies otherwise. (Source critics assign 6.3 to the Priestly source, while 3.9–15 are said to be from E.) **14–15:** God discloses His proper name, preceded by its explanation. In Hebrew the name is spelled with the consonants "yod-he-vav-he" (more precisely "yod-he-waw-he," since the vav was originally pronounced "w"). The exact pronunciation is uncertain since the vowels were forgotten in ancient times; hence scholars often refer to the name only by its consonants YHVH or, more precisely, YHWH. It was probably pronounced Yahweh. God's answer in v. 14, *Ehyeh-Asher-Ehyeh,* is actually an explanation of its meaning, probably best translated as "I Will Be What I Will Be," meaning "My nature will become evident from My actions." (Compare God's frequent declarations below, that from His future acts Israel and Egypt "shall know that I am the LORD [YHVH]," as in 7.5; 10.2; etc.). Then He answers Moses' question about what to say to the people: "Tell them: 'Ehyeh' ("I Will Be," a shorter form of the explanation) sent me." This explanation derives God's name from the verb "h-wh," a variant form of "h-yh," "to be." Because God is the speaker, He uses the first-person form of the verb. This explanation is probably either a folk etymology or a learned etymology, not necessarily precise. Grammatically YHWH means "He who is," or "He who will be" or, perhaps most likely, "He who causes things to be." This translation renders YHWH as *the LORD* , which is actually a translation of "'adonai" (lit. "my Lord"), the word that Jews say instead of pronouncing YHWH. The practice of saying this and other surrogate words in place of YHWH developed in Second Temple times when, as an expression of reverence, Jews began to avoid uttering YHWH. This is why the exact pronunciation was forgotten and the vocalization is uncertain. (As a reminder to say "'adonai", in printed Hebrew Bibles the consonants YHVH are accompanied by the vowels of the surrogate words, leading to such hybrid English forms as Jehovah [i.e., "Yehovah"] which combines the consonants Y-H-V-H with the vowels from "'adonai"].) **18:** The Egyptians are known to have granted to their workers time off for worship. The request may be simply to test Pharaoh's disposition, or to deceive the tyrant (cf. the deception commanded by God in 1 Sam. 16.1–3). **22:** *Borrow*, better, "request." The text need not imply deception, but a favor God will cause the Egyptians to bestow upon the departing Israelites (see v. 21). Cf. God's promise in Gen. 15.14. Already in antiquity some commentators saw this as Egyptian compensation for the Israelites' slave labor, or treatment in accord with Deut. 15.13–14 (*Jub.* 48.18; Philo, *Mos.* 141; *b. Sanh.* 91a; Baḥya). **4.1–9:** Three supernatural signs will confirm that Moses was indeed sent by God. All are ominous, portending harm for Egypt if it resists. **6:** The snowy encrustation looks like the skin disease that renders a person ritually impure. (On "leprosy," see Lev. 13.1–14.57 n.) **9:** *Blood* here is a sign for the Israelites, in contrast to the plague in ch 7.

of Abraham, the God of Isaac, and the God of Jacob, has sent me to you:

This shall be My name forever,
This My appellation for all eternity.

16 "Go and assemble the elders of Israel and say to them: the LORD, the God of your fathers, the God of Abraham, Isaac, and Jacob, has appeared to me and said, 'I have taken note of you and of what is being done to you in Egypt, 17 and I have declared: I will take you out of the misery of Egypt to the land of the Canaanites, the Hittites, the Amorites, the Perizzites, the Hivites, and the Jebusites, to a land flowing with milk and honey.' 18 They will listen to you; then you shall go with the elders of Israel to the king of Egypt and you shall say to him, 'The LORD, the God of the Hebrews, manifested Himself to us. Now therefore, let us go a distance of three days into the wilderness to sacrifice to the LORD our God.' 19 Yet I know that the king of Egypt will let you go only because of a greater might. 20 So I will stretch out My hand and smite Egypt with various wonders which I will work upon them; after that he shall let you go. 21 And I will dispose the Egyptians favorably toward this people, so that when you go, you will not go away empty-handed. 22 Each woman shall borrow from her neighbor and the lodger in her house objects of silver and gold, and clothing, and you shall put these on your sons and daughters, thus stripping the Egyptians."

4 But Moses spoke up and said, "What if they do not believe me and do not listen to me, but say: The LORD did not appear to you?" 2 The LORD said to him, "What is that in your hand?" And he replied, "A rod." 3 He said, "Cast it on the ground." He cast it on the ground and it became a snake; and Moses recoiled from it. 4 Then the LORD said to Moses, "Put out your hand and grasp it by the tail"—he put out his hand and seized it, and it became a rod in his hand—5 "that they may believe that the LORD, the God of their fathers, the God of Abraham, the God of Isaac, and the God of Jacob, did appear to you."

6 The LORD said to him further, "Put your hand into your bosom." He put his hand into his bosom; and when he took it out, his hand was encrusted with snowy scales![a] 7 And He said, "Put your hand back into your bosom."—He put his hand back into his bosom; and when he took it out of his bosom, there it was again like the rest of his body.—8 "And if they do not believe you or pay heed to the first sign, they will believe the second. 9 And if they are not convinced by both these signs and still do not heed you, take some water from the Nile and pour it on the dry ground, and it—the water that you take from the Nile—will turn to blood on the dry ground."

a Cf. Lev. 13.2–3.

10 But Moses said to the LORD, "Please, O Lord, I have never been a man of words, either in times past or now that You have spoken to Your servant; I am slow of speech and slow of tongue." 11 And the LORD said to him, "Who gives man speech? Who makes him dumb or deaf, seeing or blind? Is it not I, the LORD? 12 Now go, and I will be with you as you speak and will instruct you what to say." 13 But he said, "Please, O Lord, make someone else Your agent."[a] 14 The LORD became angry with Moses, and He said, "There is your brother Aaron the Levite. He, I know, speaks readily. Even now he is setting out to meet you, and he will be happy to see you. 15 You shall speak to him and put the words in his mouth—I will be with you and with him as you speak, and tell both of you what to do— 16 and he shall speak for you to the people. Thus he shall serve as your spokesman, with you playing the role of God[b] to him, 17 and take with you this rod, with which you shall perform the signs."

18 Moses went back to his father-in-law Jether[c] and said to him, "Let me go back to my kinsmen in Egypt and see how they are faring."[d] And Jethro said to Moses, "Go in peace."

19 The LORD said to Moses in Midian, "Go back to Egypt, for all the men who sought to kill you are dead." 20 So Moses took his wife and sons, mounted them on an ass, and went back to the land of Egypt; and Moses took the rod of God with him.

21 And the LORD said to Moses, "When you return to Egypt, see that you perform before Pharaoh all the marvels that I have put within your power. I, however, will stiffen his heart so that he will not let the people go. 22 Then you shall say to Pharaoh, 'Thus says the LORD: Israel is My first-born son. 23 I have said to you, "Let My son go, that he may worship Me," yet you refuse to let him go. Now I will slay your first-born son.' "

a *Lit. "send through whomever You will send."* *b* *Cf. 7.1.*
c *I.e., Jethro.* *d* *Lit. "whether they are still alive."*

10: *Slow of speech and ... tongue,* encumbered with a speech impediment. **13–17:** Moses' continued resistance, after God has answered all his concerns, causes God to lose patience, but even then He further modifies His plan to accommodate Moses: Aaron will go as Moses' spokesman. No matter what, success will depend on God "being with" the spokesman (v. 15). **16:** Aaron shall speak Moses' words, just as the prophet speaks God's words (cf. 7.1).

4.18–31: Moses returns to Egypt. **20:** *The rod of God* with which Moses will perform some of the signs and plagues (v. 17; cf. vv. 2–4; 7.20; 9.23; 10.13; 17.5, 9). This designation suggests that it was given him by God. *Sons,* Gershom and Eliezer (2.22; 18.3–5). **21:** *I ... will stiffen his heart,* make him unyielding, impermeable to reason. The narrative makes different statements as to whether Pharaoh's obduracy is self-motivated or caused by God. Here and in 7.3; 9.12; 10.1, 20, 27; 11.10; 14.4, 8, 17, God stiffens Pharaoh's heart, but in 7.13, 14, 22; 8.11, 15, 28; 9.7, 34, 35 Pharaoh stiffens his own heart. These different ideas about Pharaoh's motivation are consistent with a tendency in the Bible to see dual causality operating in history: the protagonists act according to their own character and motives, yet at the same time they are acting according to God's plan (Gen. 45.4–8; 50.20; 1 Sam. 2.25; 1 Kings 2.15; 12.15; the different explanations of the seventh and eighth plagues in 9.35 and 10.1). But commentators have also noted that the different depictions of Pharaoh's motives fall basically into two stages: he stiffens his own heart for the first five plagues, and God stiffens it in plagues six, eight and nine. Assuming that 4.21 and 7.3 refer to the final stage of the confrontation (for 4.21 cf. v. 23), and setting aside the difference between 9.35 and 10.1, it seems that the narrative has arranged the plagues to indicate that God did not stiffen Pharaoh's heart initially, but only after Pharaoh had done so himself many times. In essence, God punished Pharaoh in kind, depriving him of the freedom to change his mind and escape further punishment (thus the process is perceived by *Exod. Rab.* 13.3; Maimonides, *Introduction to Abot,* ch 8 and *Hilkhot Teshuva,* ch 6). The process is drawn out so that God's power can be made abundantly clear (7.3–5; 10.1–2). **22:** *Thus says the LORD:* This is the formula with which a messenger introduces the words of the one who sent him (Gen. 32.5; 45.9; Exod. 5.10; etc.). It is commonly used by prophets, reflecting their role as God's messengers and further marks Moses as a prophet. The designation of Israel as YHVH's *first-born son* reflects God's special attachment to Israel (cf. Gen. 49.3; Deut. 21.17; Jer. 31.9, 20; Ps. 89.28). **23:** *I will slay your first-born son:* In the Bible God may punish or reward offspring for their parents' actions. This is part of the ancient view of families as organic units. (See 20.5 n.)

[24] At a night encampment on the way, the LORD encountered him and sought to kill him. [25a] So Zipporah took a flint and cut off her son's foreskin, and touched his legs with it, saying, "You are truly a bridegroom of blood to me!" [26] And when He let him alone, she added, "A bridegroom of blood because of the circumcision."

[27] The LORD said to Aaron, "Go to meet Moses in the wilderness." He went and met him at the mountain of God, and he kissed him. [28] Moses told Aaron about all the things that the LORD had committed to him and all the signs about which He had instructed him. [29] Then Moses and Aaron went and assembled all the elders of the Israelites. [30] Aaron repeated all the words that the LORD had spoken to Moses, and he performed the signs in the sight of the people, [31] and the people were convinced. When they heard that the LORD had taken note of the Israelites and that He had seen their plight, they bowed low in homage.

5 Afterward Moses and Aaron went and said to Pharaoh, "Thus says the LORD, the God of Israel: Let My people go that they may celebrate a festival for Me in the wilderness." [2] But Pharaoh said, "Who is the LORD that I should heed Him and let Israel go? I do not know the LORD, nor will I let Israel go." [3] They answered, "The God of the Hebrews has manifested Himself to us. Let us go, we pray, a distance of three days into the wilderness to sacrifice to the LORD our God, lest He strike us with pestilence or sword." [4] But the king of Egypt said to them, "Moses and Aaron, why do you distract the people from their tasks? Get to your labors!" [5] And Pharaoh continued, [b-]"The people of the land are already so numerous,[-b] and you would have them cease from their labors!"[c]

[6] That same day Pharaoh charged the taskmasters and foremen of the people, saying, [7] "You shall no longer provide the people with straw for making bricks as heretofore; let them go and gather straw for themselves. [8] But impose upon them the same quota of bricks as they have been making heretofore; do not reduce it, for they are shirkers; that is why they cry, 'Let us go and sacrifice to our God!' [9] Let heavier work be laid upon the men; let them keep at it and not pay attention to deceitful promises."

a Meaning of vv. 25–26 uncertain.
b-b Samaritan "Even now they are more numerous than the people of the land," i.e., than the native population (cf. Gen. 23.7).
c See 1.5–11.

24–26: This episode, possibly abridged from a fuller, clearer version, is extraordinarily puzzling because the motive for God's attack is unclear, the pronouns are equivocal, and Zipporah's remarks are enigmatic. Cf. the similarly enigmatic episode in Gen 32.25–33 in which Jacob is attacked by a divine being while journeying, at God's command (Gen. 31.3), from one land to another. **25:** Here circumcision seems to have apotropaic (magically protective) power, and by touching her son's foreskin to Moses' "legs," possibly a euphemism for genitals, Zipporah saved him. The saving power of the bloody foreskin may foreshadow the protective role of the blood on the Israelites' doorposts on the eve of the exodus (12.7, 13, 22–23). *Bridegroom of blood,* cognates of Heb "ḥatan," *bridegroom,* mean "protect" in Akkadian and Arabic, and "circumcise" in Arabic. **31:** The theme that God has taken note of Israel's plight ends the episode, just as it opened it in 2.23–25 and 3.7.

5.1–6.1: The first encounter with Pharaoh. The ensuing narrative of the plagues and the defeat of the Egyptians in chs 6–15 may be viewed as God's answer to Pharaoh's contemptuous question, *Who is the LORD?* (v. 2). **5.1:** Here and in v. 3 Moses and Aaron request only a leave for worship, as instructed by God in 3.18. **3:** *Lest He strike us,* a reason Pharaoh should understand; failure to worship the deity would lead to punishment. **5:** This v. is best understood on the assumption that the Samaritan reading ("m'm" instead of MT "'m" [see translators' note *b-b*]) is correct: Pharaoh claims that the Israelites already outnumber the Egyptians, and if they cease their labors they will increase even more—the very thing he sought to prevent by enslaving them (1.9–14). **7–8:** Bricks were made of Nile mud mixed with sand and straw gathered from harvested fields and chopped. Egyptian documents refer to daily brickmaking quotas and, in one case, to a lack of straw. Pharaoh's new requirement was a severe additional hardship. **9:** *Deceitful promises,* of liberation, by Moses and Aaron.

[10] So the taskmasters and foremen of the people went out and said to the people, "Thus says Pharaoh: I will not give you any straw. [11] You must go and get the straw yourselves wherever you can find it; but there shall be no decrease whatever in your work." [12] Then the people scattered throughout the land of Egypt to gather stubble for straw. [13] And the taskmasters pressed them, saying, "You must complete the same work assignment each day as when you had straw." [14] And the foremen of the Israelites, whom Pharaoh's taskmasters had set over them, were beaten. "Why," they were asked, "did you not complete the prescribed amount of bricks, either yesterday or today, as you did before?"

[15] Then the foremen of the Israelites came to Pharaoh and cried: "Why do you deal thus with your servants? [16] No straw is issued to your servants, yet they demand of us: Make bricks! Thus your servants are being beaten, when the fault is with your own people." [17] He replied, "You are shirkers, shirkers! That is why you say, 'Let us go and sacrifice to the LORD.' [18] Be off now to your work! No straw shall be issued to you, but you must produce your quota of bricks!"

[19] Now the foremen of the Israelites found themselves in trouble because of the order, "You must not reduce your daily quantity of bricks." [20] As they left Pharaoh's presence, they came upon Moses and Aaron standing in their path, [21] and they said to them, "May the LORD look upon you and punish you for making us loathsome to Pharaoh and his courtiers—putting a sword in their hands to slay us." [22] Then Moses returned to the LORD and said, "O Lord, why did You bring harm upon this people? Why did You send me? [23] Ever since I came to Pharaoh to speak in Your name, he has dealt worse with this people; and still You have not delivered Your people."

6 Then the LORD said to Moses, "You shall soon see what I will do to Pharaoh: he shall let them go because of a greater might; indeed, because of a greater might he shall drive them from his land."

VA-'ERA' וארא

[2] God spoke to Moses and said to him, "I am the LORD. [3] I appeared to Abraham, Isaac, and Jacob as El Shaddai, but I did not make Myself known to them by My name יהוה.[a] [4] I also established My covenant with them, to give them the land of Canaan, the land in which they lived as sojourners. [5] I have now heard the moaning of the Israelites because the Egyptians are holding them in bondage, and I have remembered

a This divine name is traditionally not pronounced; instead, Adonai, *"(the) LORD," is regularly substituted for it.*

10: The *foremen of the people,* Israelites whom the Egyptian taskmasters placed in charge of the Israelite laborers. **6.1:** *Drive them:* Ultimately Pharaoh will be forced to expel the Israelites as quickly as possible (12.31–33).

6.2–7.13: God's promises and Moses' mission reaffirmed. The vindication and glorification of God's name is the main theme of the plagues. This section, from the P source, is a variant of 3.1–6.1 (from JE), partly inconsistent and redundant with it. For example, the introduction of God's name and the promise of liberation (6.2–8) duplicate 3.7–15; Moses is to demand unconditional release (6.11, 13; 7.2), not merely three days' religious leave (3.18; 5.1); and Moses uses a different idiom to describe his speech impediment (6.12, 30; contrast 4.10). In its present context, however, this section reads as a response to the challenges of ch 5. **6.2:** God begins His reply to Moses (and to the people in v. 6) and concludes it in v. 8, by identifying Himself with the name that conveys His full power ("to know that He is YHVH" [6.7; 7.5] means to experience or witness His power [1 Kings 20.13, 28; Isa. 52.6; Jer. 9.2]). The people are thus reassured of the power and authority that guarantee His promises. **3:** YHVH is the same God who, under the name of El Shaddai, made a covenant with Israel's ancestors (see v. 4 and cf. Gen. 17.1–8; 28.3–4; 35.11–12; 48.3–4), and He now intends to fulfill that covenant. *But I did not make Myself known to them by My name YHVH:* They did not experience the full power that is expressed by the name YHVH, as Israel now will. From a critical point of view, this statement is inconsistent with such vv. as Gen. 15.7; 28.13; it is another indication that multiple, earlier sources underlie the present narrative. One source (J) holds that the name YHVH was first known in the days of Enosh (Gen. 4.26), while others (E and P) hold that it was first revealed in the days of Moses. These variations reflect different theologies: Was God fully known before Israel existed as a people, or only once Israel was formed?

My covenant. 6 Say, therefore, to the Israelite people: I am the LORD. I will free you from the labors of the Egyptians and deliver you from their bondage. I will redeem you with an outstretched arm and through extraordinary chastisements. 7 And I will take you to be My people, and I will be your God. And you shall know that I, the LORD, am your God who freed you from the labors of the Egyptians. 8 I will bring you into the land which I swore[a] to give to Abraham, Isaac, and Jacob, and I will give it to you for a possession, I the LORD." 9 But when Moses told this to the Israelites, they would not listen to Moses, their spirits crushed by cruel bondage.

10 The LORD spoke to Moses, saying, 11 "Go and tell Pharaoh king of Egypt to let the Israelites depart from his land." 12 But Moses appealed to the LORD, saying, "The Israelites would not listen to me; how then should Pharaoh heed me, a man of impeded speech!" 13 So the LORD spoke to both Moses and Aaron in regard to the Israelites and Pharaoh king of Egypt, instructing them to deliver the Israelites from the land of Egypt.

14 The following are the heads of their respective clans.

The sons of Reuben, Israel's first-born: Enoch[b] and Pallu, Hezron and Carmi; those are the families of Reuben. 15 The sons of Simeon: Jemuel, Jamin, Ohad, Jachin, Zohar, and Saul[c] the son of a Canaanite woman; those are the families of Simeon. 16 These are the names of Levi's sons by their lineage: Gershon, Kohath, and Merari; and the span of Levi's life was 137 years. 17 The sons of Gershon: Libni and Shimei, by their families. 18 The sons of Kohath: Amram, Izhar, Hebron, and Uzziel; and the span of Kohath's life was 133 years. 19 The sons of Merari: Mahli and Mushi. These are the families of the Levites by their lineage.

20 Amram took to wife his father's sister Jochebed, and she bore him Aaron and Moses; and the span of Amram's life was 137 years. 21 The sons of Izhar: Korah, Nepheg, and Zichri. 22 The sons of Uzziel: Mishael, Elzaphan, and Sithri. 23 Aaron took to wife Elisheba, daughter of Amminadab and sister of Nahshon, and she bore him Nadab and Abihu, Eleazar and Ithamar. 24 The sons of Korah: Assir, Elkanah, and Abiasaph. Those are the families of the Korahites. 25 And Aaron's son Eleazar took to wife one of Putiel's daughters, and she bore him Phinehas. Those are the heads of the fathers' houses of the Levites by their families.

26 It is the same Aaron and Moses to whom the LORD said, "Bring forth the Israelites from the land of Egypt, troop by troop."

a Lit. "raised My hand." *b Or "Hanoch"; cf. on Gen. 46.9.*
c Or "Shaul"; cf. on Gen. 46.10.

7: *I will take you to be My people, and I will be your God:* This bilateral relationship refers to the covenant that will be established at Mount Sinai (cf. El Shaddai's covenant promise in Gen. 17.7, 8 and those in Lev. 26.12; Jer. 31.33; Hos. 2.25). The expression of this relationship ("take" and "be someone's x") is modeled on idioms for marrying and adopting (Gen. 4.19; Exod. 2.10; Deut. 24.1–2; 2 Sam. 7.14), implying the intimate nature of the intended relationship between God and Israel. (Marriage and the parent-child relationship are used as metaphors for the relationship between God and Israel in many biblical passages, e.g., Exod. 4.22; Deut. 14.2; Isa. 54.5–7; 62.5; Jer. 2.2; 3.19, 22; Hos. ch 2.) *And you shall know that I, the LORD, am your God:* See v. 2 n.

6.14–27: The pedigree of Moses and Aaron. This is apparently an extract from a larger genealogy (cf. Gen. 46.8–11; Num. 3.17–39; 26.5–14, 57–60), beginning with the descendants of Jacob's first two sons (see Exod 1.2; Gen. 29.32–34), but only for the sake of showing the place of his third son, Levi, the ancestor of Moses and Aaron. Levi's descendants are listed in detail, particularly Aaron and his immediate successors as high priest (v. 25). The rest of the tribes are omitted here as they are not pertinent to identifying Moses and Aaron. **20:** *His father's sister:* Marriage with an aunt, is forbidden in Lev. 18.12–13; this text may reflect an earlier or different norm (cf. the marriage of Jacob to Rachel and Leah, two sisters, to Lev. 18.18). Jochebed must have been a much younger sister of Kohath. *Aaron and Moses:* Miriam (Num. 26.59) is omitted as the list names only men, apart from the mothers of the most prominent individuals. **21:** *Korah,* see Num. ch 16. **22:** *Mishael, Elzaphan,* see Lev. 10.4. **23:** *Nadab and Abihu,* see Lev. 10.1–5. **25:** *Eleazar,* Aaron's successor, Num. 20.26–28. *Phinehas,* Eleazar's successor and ancestor of the subsequent high priests; see Num. 25.1–13. **26:** *Troop by troop:* The Israelites would not leave Egypt as fleeing slaves but as an army marching to the promised land in military formation (7.4; 12.17; 18.21b; Num. 1.52; etc.). In order to pick up the narrative following the genealogical digression, 6.28–30 and 7.1–2 recapitulate 6.9–13.

27 It was they who spoke to Pharaoh king of Egypt to free the
Israelites from the Egyptians; these are the same Moses and
Aaron. 28 For when the LORD spoke to Moses in the land of
Egypt 29 and the LORD said to Moses, "I am the LORD; speak to
Pharaoh king of Egypt all that I will tell you," 30 Moses appealed
to the LORD, saying, "See, I am of impeded speech; how then
should Pharaoh heed me!"

7 The LORD replied to Moses, "See, I place you in the role of
God to Pharaoh, with your brother Aaron as your prophet.[a]
2 You shall repeat all that I command you, and your brother
Aaron shall speak to Pharaoh to let the Israelites depart from
his land. 3 But I will harden Pharaoh's heart, that I may multiply My signs and marvels in the land of Egypt. 4 When Pharaoh
does not heed you, I will lay My hand upon Egypt and deliver
My ranks, My people the Israelites, from the land of Egypt with
extraordinary chastisements. 5 And the Egyptians shall know
that I am the LORD, when I stretch out My hand over Egypt
and bring out the Israelites from their midst." 6 This Moses and
Aaron did; as the LORD commanded them, so they did. 7 Moses
was eighty years old and Aaron eighty-three, when they made
their demand on Pharaoh.

8 The LORD said to Moses and Aaron, 9 "When Pharaoh
speaks to you and says, 'Produce your marvel,' you shall say
to Aaron, 'Take your rod and cast it down before Pharaoh.' It
shall turn into a serpent." 10 So Moses and Aaron came before
Pharaoh and did just as the LORD had commanded: Aaron
cast down his rod in the presence of Pharaoh and his courtiers, and it turned into a serpent. 11 Then Pharaoh, for his part,
summoned the wise men and the sorcerers; and the Egyptian
magicians, in turn, did the same with their spells; 12 each cast
down his rod, and they turned into serpents. But Aaron's rod
swallowed their rods. 13 Yet Pharaoh's heart stiffened and he
did not heed them, as the LORD had said.

14 And the LORD said to Moses, "Pharaoh is stubborn; he refuses to let the people go. 15 Go to Pharaoh in the morning, as

a *Cf. 4.16.*

7.3–5: See 4.21. This common biblical device is called a resumptive repetition. *The Egyptians shall know that I am the LORD:* God's "signs and marvels" will answer Pharaoh's contemptuous declaration that he does "not know the LORD" (5.2). **9:** *Produce your marvel,* produce evidence corroborating that you were sent by a god. The marvel is one of those Moses used to convince the people of his divine mission (4.1–5). **11–13:** Since Pharaoh's magicians are able to duplicate this marvel (vv. 7–12a), he is unimpressed. Nonetheless, this early confrontation foreshadows the eventual outcome of the contest between Moses and Aaron and the Egyptian magicians. The magicians use "their spells" (v. 11; 7.22), conventional magic; while Aaron works silently, relying not on his own power or on magical technique, but on an unknown power that he identifies as the LORD, whose superiority is shown when Aaron's serpent overcomes those of the magicians.

7.14–10.29: The first nine plagues. There are ten plagues in all. Source analysis indicates that the narrative is drawn from the J, E, and P sources, which differed in the number of plagues and their details; none of these delineate all ten plagues, which is why the number ten is never stated—the redactor or compiler tended not to add information to the preexisting material. Indications of multiple sources include inconsistencies regarding whether Aaron or Moses is to bring about the first plague and the nature of the gesture that will initiate it (7.17, 19), whether the first two plagues will involve the Nile only or all the waters of Egypt (7.17, 19, 21, 28; 8.1), and the different terms used for Pharaoh's obstinacy, "stiffening his heart" (7.22; 8.15; 9.12, 35; 10.20, 27; 11.10) and "stubbornness [lit. heaviness] of heart" (8.11, 28; 9.7, 34; rendered "harden" in 10.1). The passages from P see the plagues as demonstrations of God's power; those from J and E conceive of them as punishment. By fusing the sources, the redactor adds to the narrative a sense of the multivalence of events. In addition, he has skillfully woven the sources into three triads, each with a consistent pattern, followed by a capstone tenth plague. In introducing the first plague of each triad, God tells Moses the main lesson that triad will teach (7.17; 8.18; 9.14). The first two plagues of each triad are preceded by warnings to Pharaoh, while the third is not. Before the first plague in each group God sends Moses to Pharaoh in the morning, saying "station yourself before [Pharaoh]," and before the second he says "Go to Pharaoh" without specifying the time of day. All the plagues in the first triad are brought on by an action of Aaron; in the second triad, the first two are brought about directly by God and the third by

Moses; in the third triad, all are brought on by an action of Moses. These nine plagues resemble calamities that occur in nature (many are attested in ancient Near Eastern literature), but their patterns, their timing and rapid succession, and their announcement and removal by Moses show that they are not a random succession of natural events but the purposeful workings of divine power. The tenth plague stands by itself: Moses, still in Pharaoh's presence following the ninth plague, receives word from God and warns Pharaoh immediately of the final plague, one that will be manifestly supernatural, unlike anything known in human experience.

7.14–8.15: The first three plagues. In this triad, the Egyptians will begin to experience the LORD's power. **7.14–24: The first plague: blood. 17:** Like Israel in 6.7 and Moses in 7.5, Pharaoh is now told what the coming events will show, though he will grasp the lesson by fits and starts and more slowly than his courtiers will. **17–18:** This plague is far more ominous than the sign in 4.9 because here the river itself—the deified source of Egypt's life—is affected. **22:** The magicians' ability to duplicate the plague can only make matters worse for the Egyptians, but it again (see 7.11–13) convinces Pharaoh that nothing but magic is involved, so he remains unmoved. **7.25–8.11: The second plague: frogs. 8.4:** Despite the magicians' duplication of the plague (which, again, makes matters worse), this time Pharaoh apparently realizes that his magicians cannot end the plague, and therefore that the LORD is behind it. This is the first of several partial or temporary concessions by Pharaoh, each of which is soon withdrawn (see also vv. 21, 24; 9.27–28; 10.8–11, 16–17, 24–28).

he is coming out to the water, and station yourself before him
at the edge of the Nile, taking with you the rod that turned into
a snake. 16 And say to him, 'The LORD, the God of the Hebrews,
sent me to you to say, "Let My people go that they may worship
Me in the wilderness." But you have paid no heed until now.
17 Thus says the LORD, "By this you shall know that I am the
LORD." See, I shall strike the water in the Nile with the rod that
is in my hand, and it will be turned into blood; 18 and the fish
in the Nile will die. The Nile will stink so that the Egyptians will
find it impossible to drink the water of the Nile." '
19 And the LORD said to Moses, "Say to Aaron: Take your rod
and hold out your arm over the waters of Egypt—its rivers, its
canals, its ponds, all its bodies of water—that they may turn
to blood; there shall be blood throughout the land of Egypt,
even in vessels of wood and stone." 20 Moses and Aaron did
just as the LORD commanded: he lifted up the rod and struck
the water in the Nile in the sight of Pharaoh and his courtiers,
and all the water in the Nile was turned into blood 21 and the
fish in the Nile died. The Nile stank so that the Egyptians could
not drink water from the Nile; and there was blood throughout
the land of Egypt. 22 But when the Egyptian magicians did the
same with their spells, Pharaoh's heart stiffened and he did not
heed them—as the LORD had spoken. 23 Pharaoh turned and
went into his palace, paying no regard even to this. 24 And all
the Egyptians had to dig round about the Nile for drinking water, because they could not drink the water of the Nile.
25 When seven days had passed after the LORD struck the
Nile, 26 the LORD said to Moses, "Go to Pharaoh and say to him,
'Thus says the LORD: Let My people go that they may worship
Me. 27 If you refuse to let them go, then I will plague your whole
country with frogs. 28 The Nile shall swarm with frogs, and they
shall come up and enter your palace, your bedchamber and
your bed, the houses of your courtiers and your people, and
your ovens and your kneading bowls. 29 The frogs shall come
up on you and on your people and on all your courtiers.' "

8 And the LORD said to Moses, "Say to Aaron: Hold out your
arm with the rod over the rivers, the canals, and the ponds,
and bring up the frogs on the land of Egypt." 2 Aaron held out
his arm over the waters of Egypt, and the frogs came up and
covered the land of Egypt. 3 But the magicians did the same
with their spells, and brought frogs upon the land of Egypt.
4 Then Pharaoh summoned Moses and Aaron and said,
"Plead with the LORD to remove the frogs from me and my people, and I will let the people go to sacrifice to the LORD." 5 And
Moses said to Pharaoh, "You may have this triumph over me:
for what time shall I plead in behalf of you and your courtiers
and your people, that the frogs be cut off from you and your

houses, to remain only in the Nile?" [6]"For tomorrow," he replied. And [Moses] said, "As you say—that you may know that there is none like the LORD our God; [7]the frogs shall retreat from you and your courtiers and your people; they shall remain only in the Nile." [8]Then Moses and Aaron left Pharaoh's presence, and Moses cried out to the LORD in the matter of the frogs which He had inflicted upon Pharaoh. [9]And the LORD did as Moses asked; the frogs died out in the houses, the courtyards, and the fields. [10]And they piled them up in heaps, till the land stank. [11]But when Pharaoh saw that there was relief, he became stubborn and would not heed them, as the LORD had spoken.

[12]Then the LORD said to Moses, "Say to Aaron: Hold out your rod and strike the dust of the earth, and it shall turn to lice throughout the land of Egypt." [13]And they did so. Aaron held out his arm with the rod and struck the dust of the earth, and vermin came upon man and beast; all the dust of the earth turned to lice throughout the land of Egypt. [14]The magicians did the like with their spells to produce lice, but they could not. The vermin remained upon man and beast; [15]and the magicians said to Pharaoh, "This is the finger of God!" But Pharaoh's heart stiffened and he would not heed them, as the LORD had spoken.

[16]And the LORD said to Moses, "Early in the morning present yourself to Pharaoh, as he is coming out to the water, and say to him, 'Thus says the LORD: Let My people go that they may worship Me. [17]For if you do not let My people go, I will let loose [a]swarms of insects[a] against you and your courtiers and your people and your houses; the houses of the Egyptians, and the very ground they stand on, shall be filled with swarms of insects. [18]But on that day I will set apart the region of Goshen, where My people dwell, so that no swarms of insects shall be there, that you may know that I the LORD am in the midst of the land. [19]And I will make a distinction[b] between My people and your people. Tomorrow this sign shall come to pass.'" [20]And the LORD did so. Heavy swarms of insects invaded Pharaoh's palace and the houses of his courtiers; throughout the country of Egypt the land was ruined because of the swarms of insects.

[21]Then Pharaoh summoned Moses and Aaron and said, "Go and sacrifice to your God within the land." [22]But Moses replied, "It would not be right to do this, for what we sacrifice to the LORD our God is untouchable to the Egyptians. If we sacrifice that which is untouchable to the Egyptians before their very eyes, will they not stone us! [23]So we must go a distance of three days into the wilderness and sacrifice to the LORD our God as He may command us." [24]Pharaoh said, "I will let you go to sacrifice to the LORD your God in the wilderness; but do not go very far. Plead, then, for me." [25]And Moses said, "When I

a-a Others "wild beasts." *b Meaning of* peduth *uncertain.*

6: Allowing Pharaoh to specify the time for removing the frogs should reinforce the lesson of the LORD's unique power: He can end a plague at the very moment specified. **8.12–15: The third plague: vermin.** The Heb term refers to some small insect, such as mosquitoes or lice. **14–15:** The magicians' inability to duplicate this plague with their spells leads them to explicitly recognize that this is not magic but divine power.

8.16–9.12: The second three plagues. In this triad God applies the punishments only to the Egyptians and not to the Israelites (8.18–19; 9.4, 6–7; cf. 9.11), showing that He is "in the midst of the land," on the scene directing events closely and discriminatingly. **8.16–28: The fourth plague. 17:** *Swarms of insects,* as the translators' note indicates, the meaning of Heb "ʿarov" is uncertain. **18:** *The region of Goshen,* the area in the eastern part of the Nile delta (near the Sinai peninsula), where Joseph had settled his family (Gen. 46.29, 34; 47.6; 50.8; see Map, p. 122). **21–24:** Pharaoh weakens further and begins to recognize God, saying *Plead, then, for me.* He makes partial concessions but will not grant all that is asked. **22:** *Untouchable to the Egyptians:* This is consistent with the Egyptian aversion mentioned in Gen. 43.32, but whether Moses means what he says or is being evasive is unclear. **24:** *Do not go very far,* less than *a distance of three days* (v. 23).

9.1–7: The fifth plague: pestilence. Some type of deadly epidemic affecting livestock. **9.8–12: The sixth plague: boils.** A severe skin inflammation (cf. Deut. 28.27).

9.13–10.29: The third triad of plagues. The unprecedented character of the plagues in this triad shows the incomparability of the LORD who causes them (9.14, 18; 10.6, 14). **9.13–35: The seventh plague: hail. 16:** One of God's aims in prolonging the confrontation is to show the Egyptians the consequences of resisting His authority and to make Himself known to the world. See also 10.1–2.

leave your presence, I will plead with the LORD that the swarms of insects depart tomorrow from Pharaoh and his courtiers and his people; but let not Pharaoh again act deceitfully, not letting the people go to sacrifice to the LORD."

26 So Moses left Pharaoh's presence and pleaded with the LORD. 27 And the LORD did as Moses asked: He removed the swarms of insects from Pharaoh, from his courtiers, and from his people; not one remained. 28 But Pharaoh became stubborn this time also, and would not let the people go.

9 The LORD said to Moses, "Go to Pharaoh and say to him, 'Thus says the LORD, the God of the Hebrews: Let My people go to worship Me. 2 For if you refuse to let them go, and continue to hold them, 3 then the hand of the LORD will strike your livestock in the fields—the horses, the asses, the camels, the cattle, and the sheep—with a very severe pestilence. 4 But the LORD will make a distinction between the livestock of Israel and the livestock of the Egyptians, so that nothing shall die of all that belongs to the Israelites. 5 The LORD has fixed the time: tomorrow the LORD will do this thing in the land.' " 6 And the LORD did so the next day: all the livestock of the Egyptians died, but of the livestock of the Israelites not a beast died. 7 When Pharaoh inquired, he found that not a head of the livestock of Israel had died; yet Pharaoh remained stubborn, and he would not let the people go.

8 Then the LORD said to Moses and Aaron, "Each of you take handfuls of soot from the kiln, and let Moses throw it toward the sky in the sight of Pharaoh. 9 It shall become a fine dust all over the land of Egypt, and cause an inflammation breaking out in boils on man and beast throughout the land of Egypt." 10 So they took soot of the kiln and appeared before Pharaoh; Moses threw it toward the sky, and it caused an inflammation breaking out in boils on man and beast. 11 The magicians were unable to confront Moses because of the inflammation, for the inflammation afflicted the magicians as well as all the other Egyptians. 12 But the LORD stiffened the heart of Pharaoh, and he would not heed them, just as the LORD had told Moses.

13 The LORD said to Moses, "Early in the morning present yourself to Pharaoh and say to him, 'Thus says the LORD, the God of the Hebrews: Let My people go to worship Me. 14 For this time I will send all My plagues upon your person, and your courtiers, and your people, in order that you may know that there is none like Me in all the world. 15 I could have stretched forth My hand and stricken you and your people with pestilence, and you would have been effaced from the earth. 16 Nevertheless I have spared you for this purpose: in order to show you My power, and in order that My fame may

resound throughout the world. [17] Yet you continue to thwart[a] My people, and do not let them go! [18] This time tomorrow I will rain down a very heavy hail, such as has not been in Egypt from the day it was founded until now. [19] Therefore, order your livestock and everything you have in the open brought under shelter; every man and beast that is found outside, not having been brought indoors, shall perish when the hail comes down upon them!' " [20] Those among Pharaoh's courtiers who feared the LORD's word brought their slaves and livestock indoors to safety; [21] but those who paid no regard to the word of the LORD left their slaves and livestock in the open.

[22] The LORD said to Moses, "Hold out your arm toward the sky that hail may fall on all the land of Egypt, upon man and beast and all the grasses of the field in the land of Egypt." [23] So Moses held out his rod toward the sky, and the LORD sent thunder and hail, and fire streamed down to the ground, as the LORD rained down hail upon the land of Egypt. [24] The hail was very heavy—fire flashing in the midst of the hail—such as had not fallen on the land of Egypt since it had become a nation. [25] Throughout the land of Egypt the hail struck down all that were in the open, both man and beast; the hail also struck down all the grasses of the field and shattered all the trees of the field. [26] Only in the region of Goshen, where the Israelites were, there was no hail.

[27] Thereupon Pharaoh sent for Moses and Aaron and said to them, "I stand guilty this time. The LORD is in the right, and I and my people are in the wrong. [28] Plead with the LORD that there may be an end of God's thunder and of hail. I will let you go; you need stay no longer." [29] Moses said to him, "As I go out of the city, I shall spread out my hands to the LORD; the thunder will cease and the hail will fall no more, so that you may know that the earth is the LORD's. [30] But I know that you and your courtiers do not yet fear the LORD God."—[31] Now the flax and barley were ruined, for the barley was in the ear and the flax was in bud; [32] but the wheat and the emmer[b] were not hurt, for they ripen late.—[33] Leaving Pharaoh, Moses went outside the city and spread out his hands to the LORD: the thunder and the hail ceased, and no rain came pouring down upon the earth. [34] But when Pharaoh saw that the rain and the hail and the thunder had ceased, he became stubborn and reverted to his guilty ways, as did his courtiers. [35] So Pharaoh's heart stiffened and he would not let the Israelites go, just as the LORD had foretold through Moses.

a Others "exalt yourself over."
b A kind of wheat.

20: Some Egyptians have come to understand God's power, but others still resist, along with Pharaoh (vv. 21, 30, 34; 10.1). **25:** The first plague that takes human life (cf. vv. 19–21); it represents an escalation of the plagues. **27–28:** Now Pharaoh capitulates completely, albeit temporarily. **29:** *The earth is the LORD's:* He controls nature.

10.1–20: The eighth plague: locusts, one of the most devastating natural disasters (see Joel chs 1–2). **1–2:** An extension of the idea of 9.16, but noting explicitly that the real point of the plagues is so that the Israelites, not only the Egyptians, will appreciate the LORD's power. **5:** *The surviving remnant,* particularly the wheat and emmer of 9.32. **7–11:** Now all of Pharaoh's courtiers are convinced and urge him to submit. When he hears Moses' terms, he offers only a partial concession.

BO' בא

10 Then the LORD said to Moses, "Go to Pharaoh. For I
have hardened his heart and the hearts of his courtiers,
in order that I may display these My signs among them, 2 and
that you may recount in the hearing of your sons and of your
sons' sons how I made a mockery of the Egyptians and how I
displayed My signs among them—in order that you may know
that I am the LORD." 3 So Moses and Aaron went to Pharaoh
and said to him, "Thus says the LORD, the God of the Hebrews,
'How long will you refuse to humble yourself before Me? Let
My people go that they may worship Me. 4 For if you refuse to
let My people go, tomorrow I will bring locusts on your territory. 5 They shall cover the surface of the land, so that no one will
be able to see the land. They shall devour the surviving remnant that was left to you after the hail; and they shall eat away
all your trees that grow in the field. 6 Moreover, they shall fill
your palaces and the houses of all your courtiers and of all the
Egyptians—something that neither your fathers nor fathers'
fathers have seen from the day they appeared on earth to this
day.'" With that he turned and left Pharaoh's presence.
7 Pharaoh's courtiers said to him, "How long shall this one be
a snare to us? Let the men go to worship the LORD their God!
Are you not yet aware that Egypt is lost?" 8 So Moses and Aaron
were brought back to Pharaoh and he said to them, "Go, worship the LORD your God! Who are the ones to go?" 9 Moses replied, "We will all go, young and old: we will go with our sons
and daughters, our flocks and herds; for we must observe the
LORD's festival." 10 But he said to them, "The LORD be with you
the same as I mean to let your children go with you! Clearly,
you are bent on mischief. 11 No! You menfolk go and worship
the LORD, since that is what you want." And they were expelled
from Pharaoh's presence.
12 Then the LORD said to Moses, "Hold out your arm over the
land of Egypt for the locusts, that they may come upon the land
of Egypt and eat up all the grasses in the land, whatever the hail
has left." 13 So Moses held out his rod over the land of Egypt,
and the LORD drove an east wind over the land all that day and
all night; and when morning came, the east wind had brought
the locusts. 14 Locusts invaded all the land of Egypt and settled
within all the territory of Egypt in a thick mass; never before
had there been so many, nor will there ever be so many again.
15 They hid all the land from view, and the land was darkened;
and they ate up all the grasses of the field and all the fruit of the
trees which the hail had left, so that nothing green was left, of
tree or grass of the field, in all the land of Egypt.

16 Pharaoh hurriedly summoned Moses and Aaron and
said, "I stand guilty before the LORD your God and before you.
17 Forgive my offense just this once, and plead with the LORD

your God that He but remove this death from me.” 18 So he left Pharaoh’s presence and pleaded with the LORD. 19 The LORD caused a shift to a very strong west wind, which lifted the locusts and hurled them into the Sea of Reeds;[a] not a single locust remained in all the territory of Egypt. 20 But the LORD stiffened Pharaoh’s heart, and he would not let the Israelites go.

21 Then the LORD said to Moses, “Hold out your arm toward the sky that there may be darkness upon the land of Egypt, a darkness that can be touched.” 22 Moses held out his arm toward the sky and thick darkness descended upon all the land of Egypt for three days. 23 People could not see one another, and for three days no one could get up from where he was; but all the Israelites enjoyed light in their dwellings.

24 Pharaoh then summoned Moses and said, “Go, worship the LORD! Only your flocks and your herds shall be left behind; even your children may go with you.” 25 But Moses said, “You yourself must provide us with sacrifices and burnt offerings to offer up to the LORD our God; 26 our own livestock, too, shall go along with us—not a hoof shall remain behind: for we must select from it for the worship of the LORD our God; and we shall not know with what we are to worship the LORD until we arrive there.” 27 But the LORD stiffened Pharaoh’s heart and he would not agree to let them go. 28 Pharaoh said to him, “Be gone from me! Take care not to see me again, for the moment you look upon my face you shall die.” 29 And Moses replied, “You have spoken rightly. I shall not see your face again!”

11 And the LORD said to Moses, “I will bring but one more plague upon Pharaoh and upon Egypt; after that he shall let you go from here; indeed, when he lets you go, he will drive

a *Traditionally, but incorrectly, “Red Sea.”*

10.21–29: The ninth plague: darkness. Since the darkness “can be touched” (v. 21), it may reflect a “hamsin,” the hot southerly wind from the Sahara desert, carrying unusually dense concentrations of sand and dust that block out sunlight. **24–26:** Pharoah will permit the people to go but not their flocks, as if to undermine the purpose for which the Israelites are leaving—to sacrifice, which requires animals from the flocks. Moses counters by demanding that Pharaoh also provide the sacrificial animals from his own livestock, and also insists that the Israelite livestock go with them. Moses seeks Pharaoh’s total capitulation to God. **28:** Pharaoh, who has not absorbed the lessons of the plagues, clings to his own sovereignty, refusing to the end to accept God’s. **29:** Moses only partially quotes Pharaoh, acknowledging that they will never again meet, but undermining Pharaoh’s claim that it is Moses who will die.

11.1–13.16: The tenth plague, the exodus, and commemorative festivals. The composite nature of this section is indicated by differences in the ritual instructions (e.g., 13.3–10 n.), discontinuities in the narrative, and verbal and other links to the various sources in the Torah. Source critics agree that one component of this section is from the Priestly source (11.9–12.20; 12.28, 40–41; 12.43–13.2); they disagree over which parts of the remainder belong to J, E, and (in some views) D. The most puzzling issue is the premature location of 12.14–20: God refers to the exodus in the past tense (v. 17a), though the event does not occur until vv. 37–41, and He commands that the day be commemorated by eating unleavened bread for a week, though the reason for doing so does not occur until vv. 34 and 39. Vv. 21–27 (J) are unaware of this command: When Moses conveys God’s instructions about the pesaḥ sacrifice, he tells the people instead to commemorate the event in the future by reenacting the sacrifice. He informs them of the seven-day festival of unleavened bread only later in 13.3–10, after the text explains why the people ate unleavened bread on the day of the exodus. The redactor’s reason for placing 12.14–20 right after vv. 1–13 (both units are from P), despite the resultant disturbance of the continuity, was evidently his desire to fuse the festival of unleavened bread and the pesaḥ offering—originally separate rites (see 12.14–20 n.)—into a single holiday with the same date (vv. 6, 18). He may have believed that the fact that the meal accompanying the pesaḥ offering included unleavened bread implied that they are part of the same festival, as if the Feast of Unleavened Bread commemorated the fact that the people ate matzah with the pesaḥ offering (v. 8).

11.1–10: The announcement of the tenth plague. The final and decisive plague would be a virulent epidemic (Ps. 78.49–51) of preternatural specificity, causing the sudden death of all first-born Egyptians. This plague corresponds to the Egyptians’ murder of the Hebrew baby boys (1.22; the Egyptian people’s cooperation with Pharaoh’s decree is implied by 2.2–3). Exod. 4.22–23 explains it as measure-for-measure punishment for Pharaoh’s refusal to free Israel, God’s “first-born.” **11.1:** *He will drive you out,* see 6.1. **2–3:** See 3.22. *Much*

you out of here one and all. 2 Tell the people to borrow, each man from his neighbor and each woman from hers, objects of silver and gold." 3 The LORD disposed the Egyptians favorably toward the people. Moreover, Moses himself was much esteemed in the land of Egypt, among Pharaoh's courtiers and among the people.

4 Moses said, "Thus says the LORD: Toward midnight I will go forth among the Egyptians, 5 and every first-born in the land of Egypt shall die, from the first-born of Pharaoh who sits on his throne to the first-born of the slave girl who is behind the millstones; and all the first-born of the cattle. 6 And there shall be a loud cry in all the land of Egypt, such as has never been or will ever be again; 7 but not a dog shall snarl[a] at any of the Israelites, at man or beast—in order that you may know that the LORD makes a distinction between Egypt and Israel.

8 "Then all these courtiers of yours shall come down to me and bow low to me, saying, 'Depart, you and all the people who follow you!' After that I will depart." And he left Pharaoh's presence in hot anger.

9 Now the LORD had said to Moses, "Pharaoh will not heed you, in order that My marvels may be multiplied in the land of Egypt." 10 Moses and Aaron had performed all these marvels before Pharaoh, but the LORD had stiffened the heart of Pharaoh so that he would not let the Israelites go from his land.

12 The LORD said to Moses and Aaron in the land of Egypt: 2 This month shall mark for you the beginning of the months; it shall be the first of the months of the year for you.

a Others "move (or whet) his tongue."

esteemed, held in awe because of the power he has displayed. **4–8:** Although God does not tell Moses the nature of the final plague in vv. 1–3, according to the present form of the narrative Moses already knew it from God's words in 4.22–23. To make the narrative read more clearly, the Samaritan Pentateuch has Moses quote those words to Pharaoh here, and it also copies vv. 4–7 into God's words in vv. 1–3. According to that reading, then, in vv. 4–7 Moses is telling Pharaoh what God previously told him. Such additions to smooth out the narrative are typical of the Samaritan Pentateuch, and are also found in some Dead Sea Scrolls. **6–7:** This plague manifests the probative qualities of the second and third triads of plagues: It will be unprecedented (9.18; 10.6, 14), and God will make *a distinction between Egypt and Israel* (see 8.18–19; 9.4, 6–7)—signs of the unique divine power beyond the event. **6:** *Loud cry,* measure-for-measure punishment for causing the outcry of the Israelites (2.23). **7:** *Not a dog shall snarl at any of the Israelites:* In contrast to the loud cry among the Egyptians, peace and quiet will prevail among the Israelites; even the Egyptians' dogs won't snarl at them; alternatively, even the Israelites' dogs will be calm and will not snarl (understanding the Heb as "Not a dog of the Israelites shall snarl"). **10:** *The LORD had stiffened the heart of Pharaoh:* See 4.21 n.

12.1–28: Preparations for the exodus. Israel is to prepare for the coming deliverance with a sacrificial banquet while the final plague is occurring and is to commemorate the event in the future on its anniversary by eating unleavened bread for a week and reenacting the banquet. This feast became the prototype of the postbiblical Seder, the festive meal at which the exodus story is retold and expounded each year to this day on the holiday of Pesaḥ (Passover), as explained below. **2:** Since the exodus will be commemorated on its anniversary every year (vv. 6, 17–18), the preparatory instructions begin with the calendar (see the essay "Biblical Calendars," pp. 2021–25). Henceforth the year will commence with the month of the exodus, and months will be referred to by ordinal numbers rather than names (see v. 18; 16.1; 19.1; Lev. 23.24; etc.). Since the numbers will mean essentially "in the Xth month since the day on which we gained freedom," every reference to a month will commemorate the redemption. The first month (later called Nisan [Esth. 3.7; Neh. 2.1]— corresponds to March or April (the later month names were borrowed from the Babylonian calendar during the Exile [see p. 2230]). In Jewish practice, this is the beginning of the liturgical year (see e.g., the calendars in Exod. 23.14–16, Lev. ch 23 and elsewhere); it was also the beginning of the Babylonian year. The calendar year, starting with what came to be called Rosh Ha-Shanah (the New Year holiday, in the seventh month!), begins in Tishri (September or October). (The older, nature-based, names of a few months are mentioned in 13.4; Deut. 16.1; 1 Kings 6.1, 37, 38; 8.2.) Because vv. 1–20 deal with the month in which Pesaḥ falls and with preparations for the holiday, they are read as an additional Torah portion (maftir) on the Sabbath preceding the month of Nisan, or on the first of Nisan if it is a Sabbath, and that Sabbath is called Shabbat ha-Ḥodesh, "the Sabbath of the passage (beginning) 'This month.'" The rest of the ch, which includes the observance of the first Pesaḥ and the exodus, is read on the first day of Pesaḥ.

3 Speak to the whole community of Israel and say that on the
tenth of this month each of them shall take a lamb[a] to a family,
a lamb to a household. 4 But if the household is too small for a
lamb, let him share one with a neighbor who dwells nearby,
in proportion to the number of persons: you shall contribute
for the lamb according to what each household will eat. 5 Your
lamb shall be without blemish, a yearling male; you may take
it from the sheep or from the goats. 6 You shall keep watch over
it until the fourteenth day of this month; and all the assembled congregation of the Israelites shall slaughter it at twilight.
7 They shall take some of the blood and put it on the two doorposts and the lintel of the houses in which they are to eat it.
8 They shall eat the flesh that same night; they shall eat it roasted over the fire, with unleavened bread and with bitter herbs.
9 Do not eat any of it raw, or cooked in any way with water, but
roasted—head, legs, and entrails—over the fire. 10 You shall
not leave any of it over until morning; if any of it is left until
morning, you shall burn it.

11 This is how you shall eat it: your loins girded, your sandals
on your feet, and your staff in your hand; and you shall eat it

a Or "kid." Heb. seh *means either "sheep" or "goat"; cf. v. 5.*

5: *Without blemish,* a standard requirement of sacrificial animals (Lev. 22.17–25; Deut. 15.21; 17.1; cf. Mal. 1.6–8). **6–14:** Some of the vv. about the sacrifice reflect a different view of the tenth plague from that in the rest of the narrative. In the rest of the narrative, God Himself slays the Egyptian firstborn; no special measures are necessary to protect the Israelites (11.4–7; 12.29; 13.15). But in some of the vv. about the sacrifice God is accompanied by "the Destroyer," an angel of death who presumably kills the Egyptians on God's command (v. 23; cf. Gen. 19.13–14; 2 Sam. 24.16; 2 Kings 19.35; 1 Chron. 21.15); the Israelites must apply the blood of the sacrifice to their doorways to prevent the plague from harming them (vv. 7, 13, 22 and 23), although no such measures were needed to protect them from the earlier plagues (8.18; 9.4, 6, 26—all from J; 10.23, E); in v. 22 God warns all Israelites (not just the firstborn) to remain indoors; in v. 23 He "protects" their houses from the Destroyer; and again in v. 27 He "protects" and "saves" them, presumably from the Destroyer. From these and other details (such as the slaughter of a lamb or goat and cooking by roasting) scholars have conjectured that the sacrifice was not an original part of the narrative about the plagues but was based on an older shepherds' rite observed on a spring night (perhaps the night before they set out for summer pasture) when shepherds believed they were endangered by demons who could be warded off by remaining inside and applying blood to their entrances. This view of the sacrifice and its blood as apotropaic (magically protective) is consistent with its Heb name, "pesaḥ," "protection"; see v. 11. According to this theory, the Israelites inherited this rite from their pastoral ancestors (see Gen. 46.32) but, because of its proximity in the calendar to the time of the exodus, they reinterpreted it as a memorial of the exodus and introduced it into the narrative of the tenth plague. Gradually they abandoned its demonological-apotropaic aspects in favor of its meaning as a commemoration of the exodus. Traces of this process are visible here: Of the vv. attributed to the earlier sources that precede P, only v. 23 implies that the Destroyer does the killing; vv. 27 and 29 say that God did the killing, but v. 27, in stating that God "protected" and "saved" the Israelites' houses, preserves a trace of the older tradition that it was the Destroyer. In vv. attributed to P (12–13), only God does the killing; the Destroyer becomes merely a destructive plague, and the blood is merely a sign to identify Israelite houses (like the red cord in Josh. 2.12, 18, 19), not an apotropaic substance (see v. 23 n.). **6:** *Keep watch,* to prevent it from becoming blemished or escaping during the interval. **8:** *Bitter herbs* are pungent condiments (popular among pastoral nomads) and *unleavened bread* (Heb "matzah," bread that has not risen) frequently accompanied sacrifices (29.2; Lev. 2.4–5; 6.9; 7.12; Judg. 6.19–21; etc.; leavened bread was forbidden with most sacrifices: Exod. 23.18; 34.25; Lev. 2.11; 6.10). Following the prescription of vv. 24–27, this banquet is reenacted annually at the Seder, the ritual banquet which includes the eating of unleavened bread, bitter herbs ("maror," interpreted as recalling the bitterness of slavery; romaine lettuce or horseradish are commonly used), and other symbolic foods. A roasted shankbone is displayed as a token of the roasted meat, and the story of the exodus, accompanied by rabbinic interpretations, is expounded, based on vv. 26–27 and 13.8. **10:** The sacrifice must be used only for its sacred purpose; hence no leftovers may be saved for eating later. **11:** The Israelites are to eat while prepared to leave on a moment's notice. *Passover offering,* Heb "pesaḥ," which originally referred only to the sacrifice. Later it became the name of the entire festival, including the seven days of the Festival of Unleavened Bread ("Ḥag ha-Matzot"), originally a separate holiday. In most European languages it is also the name of Easter (as in French "Pâques"). The

hurriedly: it is a passover offering[a] to the LORD. 12 For that night
I will go through the land of Egypt and strike down every first-
born in the land of Egypt, both man and beast; and I will mete
out punishments to all the gods of Egypt, I the LORD. 13 And
the blood on the houses where you are staying shall be a sign
for you: when I see the blood I will pass over[b] you, so that no
plague will destroy you when I strike the land of Egypt.
14 This day shall be to you one of remembrance: you shall
celebrate it as a festival to the LORD throughout the ages; you
shall celebrate it as an institution for all time. 15 Seven days
you shall eat unleavened bread; on the very first day you shall
remove leaven from your houses, for whoever eats leavened
bread from the first day to the seventh day, that person shall be
cut off from Israel.
16 You shall celebrate a sacred occasion on the first day, and
a sacred occasion on the seventh day; no work at all shall be

a *Or "protective offering"; Heb.* pesaḥ.
b *Or "protect"* (*Heb.* pasaḥ); *cf. v. 11, note a.*

translation "passover" (and hence the English name of the holiday) is probably incorrect. The alternative translation "protective offering" is more likely; see v. 13. **12:** *Mete out punishments to all the gods of Egypt:* This probably means that the Egyptians' idols would be destroyed in the course of the plague *(Tg. Ps.-J.; Mek.),* just as the Philistine idol Dagon is smashed, and other plagues are inflicted on the Philistines, in 1 Sam. ch 5 (Ibn Ezra), and just as Assyrian armies sometimes smashed the idols of conquered cities (2 Kings 19.18). **13:** *Pass over* (Heb "pasaḥ"): The use of this verb in Isa. 31.5, "Like the birds that fly, even so will the LORD of Hosts shield Jerusalem, shielding and saving, protecting ("p-sḥ") and rescuing," favors the translation "protect." So does the context in v. 23 of the present ch. **14–20:** The Feast of Unleavened Bread. The haste of the Israelites' departure from Egypt would leave them no time to bake leavened bread (see vv. 34, 39). In the future, their annual week-long abstention from leavened bread will serve as a reminder that God so overwhelmed the Egyptians that the latter ultimately hastened the departure of the slaves they had earlier refused to free. As it does here, the Torah usually speaks of this festival as something distinct and separate from the pesaḥ sacrifice rather than part of the same holiday (see vv. 24–27, 43–49; 13.3–9; 23.15; 34.18; Lev. 23.5–6; Num. 9.1–14; 28.16–17; see also Ezra 6.19–22; 2 Chron. 35.17; only Deut. 16.1–8, 16; Ezek. 45.21; and 2 Chron. 30.2, 5, 13, 15 describe them as a single festival). This has led to the theory that the pesaḥ sacrifice and the Feast of Unleavened Bread have separate origins, the former pastoral (see vv. 6–14 n.) and the latter agrarian. The avoidance of leaven in favor of unleavened bread, called "bread of distress" in Deut. 16.3, suggests that the Feast of Unleavened Bread may have begun as a rite of abstinence, perhaps expressing anxiety over the success of the coming grain harvest. The two rites were eventually brought together because of their proximity in the calendar and because unleavened bread was also eaten with the pesaḥ sacrifice (v. 8). In this view, then, the Festival of Unleavened Bread became a commemoration of the exodus because, like the pesaḥ sacrifice, it was observed at the time of year when the exodus took place. In the Bible, any agrarian significance the festival once had has been set aside in favor of its meaning as a commemoration of the exodus. See further, "Exodus and the Jewish Tradition" in the intro. to Exodus. **15:** *Unleavened bread:* The "matzah" was probably similar to the flat unleavened bread like pita that Bedouin still bake on embers. In earlier times it was disk-shaped and thicker than now. *Leaven* refers to leavening agents, such as sourdough or yeast, while *leavened bread* is any food prepared from dough to which a leavening agent was added to make it rise faster. (In antiquity, starter dough that was already fermented and contained yeast was used to make most bread.) According to rabbinic exegesis the prohibition covers any leavened product of wheat, barley, spelt, rye, or oats; in traditional Ashkenazic practice, rice, millet, corn, and legumes are also forbidden. *Remove leaven from your houses:* In traditional Jewish practice, the home is cleansed of leavened products in preparation for Pesaḥ and, on the night before the Seder, a few pieces of bread or other leavened products are hidden and "found" in a ceremonial search; the next morning the pieces are burned. Halakhic exegesis construes Deut. 16.4 to mean "no leaven *of yours* shall be seen," meaning that only leaven belonging to Jews must be eliminated. Leavened goods sold to non-Jews for the duration of the festival may be kept and stored out of sight in one's home. This avoids the economic hardship that would result from the destruction of large quantities of leavened goods. *Cut off:* The probable meaning is that God will cut him off (see Lev. 17.10; 20.1–6; 23.29–30), that is, cause him to die early and childless. This is also the punishment for noncircumcision and cultic and sexual sins (v. 19; 30.33, 38; 31.14; Gen. 17.14; Lev. 7.20, 21, 25, 27; 17.4, 9, 14; 18.29; 19.8; 20.1–6, 17, 18; 22.3, 29; Num. 9.13; 19.13, 20) that are committed "defiantly" (Num. 15.30–31). **16:** The sacredness of these days is to be expressed by

done on them; only what every person is to eat, that alone may be prepared for you. [17] You shall observe the [Feast of] Unleavened Bread, for on this very day I brought your ranks out of the land of Egypt; you shall observe this day throughout the ages as an institution for all time. [18] In the first month, from the fourteenth day of the month at evening, you shall eat unleavened bread until the twenty-first day of the month at evening. [19] No leaven shall be found in your houses for seven days. For whoever eats what is leavened, that person shall be cut off from the community of Israel, whether he is a stranger or a citizen of the country. [20] You shall eat nothing leavened; in all your settlements you shall eat unleavened bread.

[21] Moses then summoned all the elders of Israel and said to them, "Go, pick out lambs for your families, and slaughter the passover offering. [22] Take a bunch of hyssop, dip it in the blood that is in the basin, and apply some of the blood that is in the basin to the lintel and to the two doorposts. None of you shall go outside the door of his house until morning. [23] For when the LORD goes through to smite the Egyptians, He will see the blood on the lintel and the two doorposts, and the LORD will pass over[a] the door and not let the Destroyer enter and smite your home.

[24] "You shall observe this as an institution for all time, for you and for your descendants. [25] And when you enter the land that the LORD will give you, as He has promised, you shall observe this rite. [26] And when your children ask you, 'What do you mean by this rite?' [27] you shall say, 'It is the passover sacrifice[b] to the LORD, because He passed over[a] the houses of the Israelites in Egypt when He smote the Egyptians, but saved our houses.'"

a See v. 13, note b. *b See v. 11, note a.*

ceasing from work, as on the Sabbath (20.8–11; cf. Gen. 2.2–3), except that, on the festival, food may be cooked (contrast 16.23). **17:** A literal reading of the text as "You shall guard (from the Heb root "sh-m-r") the unleavened bread," led to an especially stringent custom of carefully guarding the grain from the time it is harvested to ensure that there is no fermentation. Matzah made in this way is called "matzah shemurah," "guarded matzah." **18:** Since holy days begin and end in the evening (Lev. 23.32), the festival lasts from the evening at the end of the fourteenth day through the evening at the end of the twenty-first day. **19:** *Stranger,* a foreigner residing among the Israelites. Although strangers are not obligated to offer a pesaḥ sacrifice (v. 48), they may not eat leavened food during the festival. This is perhaps to prevent them from accidentally contaminating Israelites' food with leaven, since bread was sometimes baked in shared or communal ovens (Lev. 26.26; Jer. 37.21; Neh. 3.11; 12.38). **23:** *Pass over,* rather, "protect" (see above, v. 13 n.). *Destroyer,* see introductory comment to vv. 6–14. The tradition that an angelic figure served as God's agent in the exodus and subsequent events is also reflected in 14.19; 23.20–23 (see also the plan announced by God in 32.34 and 33.2 but withdrawn in 33.14; Num. 20.16; Josh. 5.13–15; Judg. 2.1–5; and Ps. 78.49). This tradition is rejected in other passages which hold that God was the only actor, using no intermediary (Exod. 33.14–15; Deut. 4.37; 7.1 [based on but modifying Exod. 23.20]; 32.12; see also the probably original text of Isa. 63.9 reflected in the readings of the ancient versions). This disagreement was still alive in talmudic times and led to the well-known midrashic passage quoted in the Haggadah which declares that Israel was taken out of Egypt by God personally, "not by means of an angel." This declaration indicates that the Rabbis, like the authors of the biblical vv. denying a role to angels, considered the tradition of angelic involvement incompatible with absolute monotheism. **24:** *Observe this:* According to talmudic tradition (*m. Pes.* 9.5) only the sacrifice itself is to be repeated annually, not the rites accompanying it in vv. 3, 7, 10–11, 23. Ibn Ezra accepts this tradition on authority but observes that one would not infer this from the text itself. **26–27:** Here and in 13.8, 14–15 and Deut. 6.20–25, the Torah anticipates that children will ask what the various commemorative rites and other laws mean (see also Josh. 4.21–24). The Israelites are to use these questions as opportunities to teach loyalty to God by explaining what He did for them. The religious value of such lessons about the past accounts for why much of the Bible is devoted to past events and for the theological viewpoint of biblical historiography. A midrashic elaboration of these passages about children figures prominently in the Haggadah as part of the answer to the children's Four Questions about the unique procedures at the Seder banquet. It explains that the wording of the question in each passage reflects a different type of personality. The Seder itself is postbiblical, postdating the destruction of the Second Temple in 70 CE, but it has roots in the biblical period.

The people then bowed low in homage. 28 And the Israelites
went and did so; just as the LORD had commanded Moses and
Aaron, so they did.

29 In the middle of the night the LORD struck down all the
first-born in the land of Egypt, from the first-born of Pharaoh
who sat on the throne to the first-born of the captive who was in
the dungeon, and all the first-born of the cattle. 30 And Pharaoh
arose in the night, with all his courtiers and all the Egyptians—
because there was a loud cry in Egypt; for there was no house
where there was not someone dead. 31 He summoned Moses
and Aaron in the night and said, "Up, depart from among my
people, you and the Israelites with you! Go, worship the LORD
as you said! 32 Take also your flocks and your herds, as you said,
and begone! And may you bring a blessing upon me also!"
33 The Egyptians urged the people on, impatient to have
them leave the country, for they said, "We shall all be dead."
34 So the people took their dough before it was leavened, their
kneading bowls wrapped in their cloaks upon their shoulders. 35 The Israelites had done Moses' bidding and borrowed
from the Egyptians objects of silver and gold, and clothing.
36 And the LORD had disposed the Egyptians favorably toward
the people, and they let them have their request; thus they
stripped the Egyptians.
37 The Israelites journeyed from Rameses to Succoth, about
six hundred thousand men on foot, aside from children.
38 Moreover, a mixed multitude went up with them, and very
much livestock, both flocks and herds. 39 And they baked unleavened cakes of the dough that they had taken out of Egypt,
for it was not leavened, since they had been driven out of Egypt
and could not delay; nor had they prepared any provisions for
themselves.
40 The length of time that the Israelites lived in Egypt was
four hundred and thirty years; 41 at the end of the four hundred

12.29–42: The tenth plague and the exodus. 31–33: Pharoah and his people press the Israelites to leave (see also v. 39). Cf. 6.1; 11.1. **31:** *As you said,* 3.18; 5.3; 7.16. Pharaoh is granting no more than Moses asked, three days' leave for worship (only in 14.5 does he realize they mean to leave for good, though he suspected that earlier [8.24; 10.10]). **32:** *May you bring a blessing upon me also,* i.e., leave with your cattle to worship the LORD (v. 31) with sacrifice, as you said (3.18; 5.3, 8, 17; 8.4, 21–25; 10.25–26), and when you sacrifice and ask for His blessing (see 20.21 end; Lev. 9.22), ask Him to bless me as well. Pharoah may have a specific blessing—cessation of the tenth plague—in mind (cf. 8.4, 24; 9.28; 10.17), but in any case his plea indicates that his capitulation to the LORD is complete. **35–36:** See 3.22. **37:** *From Rameses to Succoth:* On *Rameses,* the capital, see 1.11. *Succoth* was the name of both a place and a region in the eastern Nile delta, in or near the land of Goshen where the Israelites lived (see 8.18 and Map, p. 122). An Egyptian letter from the period of Pharaoh Seti II (1204–1198 BCE) indicates that the place Succoth was one day's journey from the palace, which was presumably in Rameses. On the reasons for the Israelites following this route, see 13.17 n. *Six hundred thousand men,* a round number; see also Num. 11.21; Num. 1.46 and 2.32 give the number more precisely as 603,550 (Num. 3.39 adds 22,000 Levites). According to Exod. 38.26 and Num. 1.46–47, these figures refer to men of military age, twenty and older. Adding women and children yields a population of at least two and a half million. Some scholars believe that in census contexts the word translated *thousand* ("'elef") does not have numerical significance but means "clan" or "squad" (as in Num. 1.16; Judg. 6.15; 1 Sam. 10.19; and elsewhere), in which case the number of people need not be that high, but this is unlikely since 38.24–26 and other passages indicate that individuals, not groups, are being counted. This exaggerated number certainly accords with Exodus' assertions that the Israelites in Egypt were extraordinarily prolific (1.7–12), though it conflicts with the reality that the land of Goshen and later the Sinai peninsula could not have sustained such a population. The number probably originated in hyperbole, perhaps as an expansion of the common 600-man military unit (14.7; Judg. 18.11; 1 Sam. 13.15; 23.13; etc.). Comparably, the Haggadah inflates the number of plagues from ten to fifty, and Arabian Bedouin often magnify numbers by factors of ten; Assyrian inscriptions and annals also sometimes contain inflated numbers. Note also the thousand-fold population growth wished for by Moses (Deut. 1.11) and the 3-million-person army attributed to Kirta, the king of the city-state of Ugarit. **38:** *Mixed multitude,* non-Israelites, most likely members of other enslaved groups in Egypt. Egyptian texts and art show the presence of such groups, including Semites and Nubians. **39:** In their haste, the Israelites made unleavened bread because it can be made quickly (for that reason, it is made for unexpected guests [Gen. 19.3; Judg.

and thirtieth year, to the very day, all the ranks of the LORD departed from the land of Egypt. 42 That was for the LORD a night
of vigil to bring them out of the land of Egypt; that same night
is the LORD's, one of vigil for all the children of Israel throughout the ages.

43 The LORD said to Moses and Aaron: This is the law of the
passover offering: No foreigner shall eat of it. 44 But any slave a
man has bought may eat of it once he has been circumcised.
45 No bound or hired laborer shall eat of it. 46 It shall be eaten
in one house: you shall not take any of the flesh outside the
house; nor shall you break a bone of it. 47 The whole community of Israel shall offer it. 48 If a stranger who dwells with you

6.19; 1 Sam. 28.24], as Arab peasants still do). **40–41:** The figure of 430 years of Israelite residence in Egypt (P) is compatible with the 400 years of slavery and oppression predicted in Gen. 15.13 (JE or E), assuming that the oppression began thirty years after Israel arrived in Egypt. Gen. 15.16 (also JE or E), however, states that the Israelites would return in the fourth generation (of living there), a statement compatible with the fact that Moses is the great-grandson of Levi, who went down to Egypt (Exod. 6.16–20). If a generation is the period between a man's birth and the birth of his first child, these two traditions cannot be reconclied: Even assuming a generation of forty years (although twenty to twenty-five is more likely), four generations would be no more than 160 years. The LXX, the Samaritan Pentateuch, and midrashic traditions (*Seder Olam* 1 and 3; *Mek. R. Shimon bar Yohai,* p. 34 at 12.40; *Mek. Pisḥa* 14 [Horovitz p. 50]; *Pirqe R. El.* 48, p. 114a) minimize the problem by including in the 400 or 430 years the time the patriarchs lived in Canaan, starting with the covenant of Gen. ch 15 or the birth of Isaac, though that is not what our v. or Gen. ch 15 says. **41:** *The ranks of the LORD:* The Israelites are organized as an army, their goal being the conquest of Canaan; cf. v. 51 and 13.18 and their designation as "men on foot," that is, infantry, in v. 37. **42:** *Vigil,* Heb "shimurim." Although derivatives of the root "sh-mr," "watch, guard, observe" are common (they occur five other times in this ch: vv. 6, 17 twice [see n. there], 24, 25), this exact form is unparalleled in the Bible. In rabbinic Heb it means "guarding, care." If that is the meaning here, this v. may represent an interpretation of the term "pesaḥ" (see vv. 11, 13 n.). The sense would be that God guarded the Israelites from the Destroyer on the night of the exodus and will guard them against malevolent forces on the anniversaries of this night (thus *Tg. Ps.-J.* and *b. Pes.* 109b; in that case the v. is a vestige of a magical notion that this date is particularly dangerous, as in the presumed shepherds' belief mentioned in vv. 6–14 n.). Possibly, the term has different nuances and different subjects in each clause; e.g., it was a night of God's protection of Israel at the exodus, so in the future it will be a night of Israel's observance of the pesaḥ sacrifice. The translation "vigil" implies that it was a night of God's vigilance, protecting Israel (or of Israel's vigilance waiting for God to deliver them [taking "for the LORD a night of vigil" as "a night of waiting for the LORD"]), and in the future it will be a night of wakefulness for Israel to offer the pesaḥ sacrifice ("a night of vigil in honor of the LORD").

12.43–51: Seven supplementary rules about the pesaḥ offering (vv. 43b, 44, 45, 46a, 46b, 47, 48–49). V. 50, which recapitulates v. 28, implies that these instructions were given before the Israelites departed. They define who is eligible to take part in the pesaḥ offering and other details concerning it. Those instructions pertaining to foreigners, "strangers" (resident aliens—see v. 19 n.), and slaves and employees of Israelites seem, like those in vv. 24–27, to apply primarily to the future, after Israel settles in the promised land, rather than to their circumstances in Egypt; note particularly that once circumcised the stranger becomes "as a citizen of the country" (of Israel). **43:** *Foreigner,* Heb "ben nekhar," a non-Israelite; normally used of foreigners living or visiting in the land of Israel temporarily, usually for business. It is contrasted with "stranger" ("ger"), which refers to a long-term foreign resident. Here it could also refer to Egyptians or other foreigners in Egypt on friendly terms with the Israelites (cf. Isa. 56.3). Because the pesaḥ sacrifice is integrally connected with the exodus, which was a national experience, those who do not identify with Israelites as a nation are ineligible to partake of it. Likewise, according to Lev. 23.42, only native Israelites are obligated to dwell in booths, another rite that commemorates Israel's national experience. **44–45:** The implications of the pesaḥ sacrifice being a family-household ceremony (vv. 3, 4, 7, 27, 46). **44:** Privately owned foreign slaves, as members of the household, may partake if they are circumcised in accordance with Gen. 17.12–13. **45:** *Bound or hired laborer:* This phrase (lit. "resident and hireling") is better taken as a hendiadys meaning "resident hireling" (as in Lev. 22.10; 25.6, 40), a long-term hired hand who lives on his employer's property. He is not integrated into his employer's household. If a foreigner, he is ineligible for the pesaḥ; if an Israelite, the v. seems to imply that he should partake of his own family's pesaḥ sacrifice, not that of his employer. **46:** All those sharing the same lamb were to eat it together and to remain indoors. See vv. 4, 7, 22–23. *Break a bone of it,* to eat the marrow. **47:** Offering the pesaḥ sacrifice is incumbent on all Israelites, like the obligation to eat nothing leavened

would offer the passover to the LORD, all his males must be circumcised; then he shall be admitted to offer it; he shall then be as a citizen of the country. But no uncircumcised person may eat of it.
49 There shall be one law for the citizen and for the stranger who dwells among you.

50 And all the Israelites did so; as the LORD had commanded Moses and Aaron, so they did.

51 That very day the LORD freed the Israelites from the land of Egypt, troop by troop.

13 The LORD spoke further to Moses, saying,
2 "Consecrate to Me every first-born; man and beast, the first issue of every womb among the Israelites is Mine."

during the festival (vv. 15, 19; cf. Num. 9.11). **48–49:** Resident aliens, though they must abstain from leaven (v. 19), are not obligated to offer a pesaḥ sacrifice but may do so voluntarily. They must first undergo circumcision. Then they may make the offering and become "as a citizen of the country," at least for purposes of this offering. This is not necessarily a full religious conversion—the stranger's motivation is to make a pesaḥ offering, not to become an Israelite—but since circumcision is a sign of the covenant, and the

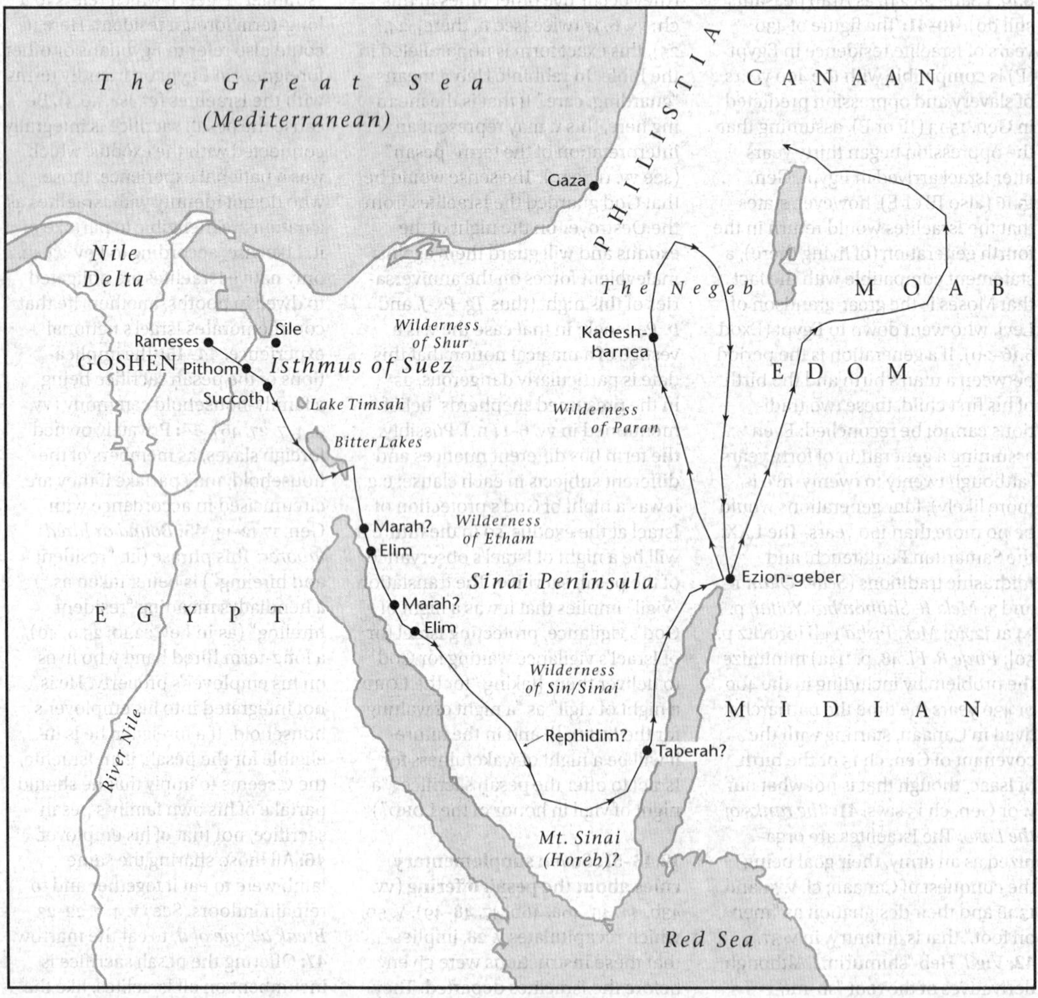

Probable exodus route according to the Bible

3 And Moses said to the people,
"Remember this day, on which you went free from Egypt,
the house of bondage, how the LORD freed you from it with a
mighty hand: no leavened bread shall be eaten. 4 You go free
on this day, in the month[a] of Abib. 5 So, when the LORD has
brought you into the land of the Canaanites, the Hittites, the
Amorites, the Hivites, and the Jebusites, which He swore to
your fathers to give you, a land flowing with milk and honey,
you shall observe in this month the following practice:
6 "Seven days you shall eat unleavened bread, and on the
seventh day there shall be a festival of the LORD. 7 Throughout
the seven days unleavened bread shall be eaten; no leavened
bread shall be found with you, and no leaven shall be found in
all your territory. 8 And you shall explain to your son on that
day, 'It is because of what the LORD did for me when I went
free from Egypt.'
9 "And this shall serve you as a sign on your hand and as a
reminder on your forehead[b]—in order that the Teaching of

a Or "on the new moon." *b Lit. "between your eyes."*

sacrifice celebrates the exodus, he must first become a quasi-Israelite in order to identify with Israel's defining national experience. If so, this ceremony is unique in the Bible; there is no other reference to a formal procedure for converting foreigners to Israelites, even quasi-Israelites. Foreigners normally became Israelites only by marriage or the informal, generations-long process of ethnic assimilation that resulted from living in the land. By the rabbinic period, a procedure for religious conversion, including circumcision of males, was created and the Heb word for stranger, "ger," acquired the meaning "proselyte." Since the idea of strangers joining Israel is explicitly mentioned in exilic or postexilic passages (Isa. 14.1; 56.3–8; Ezek. 47.22–23), it is possible that the present passage is also from that period. **49:** *One law for the citizen and for the stranger,* see also Lev. 24.22; Num. 9.14; 15.14–16, 29. In each of these instances strangers and Israelites follow the same specific procedure (cf. Lev. 7.7); the requirement that there be *one law* is not a generality covering all laws. In later halakhic exegesis, when "ger" ("stranger") is understood as "proselyte," this v. is understood as prescribing equality between proselytes and born Jews with respect to all the laws of the Torah (*Mek. Pisḥa* 14, end). **51:** This v. recapitulates v. 40, indicating that the digression in vv. 43–49 is concluded and the narrative resumes.

13.1–16: Further commemorative rituals. 2: The first issue of humans and domestic animals is holy and reserved for the LORD; they must be given to Him or redeemed. According to Gen. 4.4, the sacrifice of firstling cattle goes back to the beginning of the human race when Abel brought "the choicest of the firstlings of his flock" as a gift to the LORD. In vv. 12–15 this practice is given a new raison d'etre as a commemoration of God's slaying the first-born of Egypt and sparing those of Israel at the time of the exodus. *The first issue of every womb* defines *first-born* as the first-born of the mother, not the father. **3–10:** The Festival of Unleavened Bread, repeating 12.14–20. Because of this duplication and some conflicting details (such as the use here of a name instead of a number for the first month, and the emphasis only on the seventh day and not on the first as well), scholars assign this paragraph to the J source and 12.14–20 to the P source. **4:** *The month of Abib:* The old name of the first month (12.2), now called Nisan. "'Aviv" means "new ears of grain"; this month begins when immature ears of grain have begun to grow on the stalks. The alternative translation "on the new moon of Abib" is based on the preceding phrase "on this day," which seems to refer to a specific date (see also Deut. 16.1). If that is the meaning, this may be a variant tradition that the exodus occurred, and was celebrated, on the first day of the month rather than the fourteenth and fifteenth. **5:** See 3.8. **8:** See 12.26–27. *Explain,* Heb "vehigadta," lit. "tell, relate." The Rabbis derived the injunction to relate the story of the exodus at the Seder from this v., and the name of the text recited at the Seder, "Haggadah shel Pesaḥ" ("The Pesaḥ narrative"; Haggadah for short) from this verb. *What the LORD did for me:* Because every future Israelite is to speak thus, the Rabbis inferred that "In every generation one should look upon himself as if he personally had gone out of Egypt.... It was not only our ancestors whom the Holy One, Blessed is He, redeemed, but also us along with them" (Haggadah). The effect is that every individual Jew will identify personally with the exodus experience. **9–10:** *This shall serve you as a sign:* It is not clear what shall serve as a sign: either something mentioned in the preceding vv. (such as the Festival of Unleavened Bread) or in the second half of v. 9 (the fact that the LORD brought the Israelites out of Egypt). One or more of these things must be remembered well so that the LORD's teaching will be remembered well. The same interpretation applies to v. 16: The sacrifice or redemption of the first-born (vv. 12–15), or the fact "that with a mighty hand the LORD freed us from Egypt" (the second half of v. 16), is to be "as a sign ... and as a frontlet" (see translators' note). As noted by Rashbam, "sign," "memorial," and "frontlet" are here used metaphorically to indicate that these things are to be remembered well (cf. the metaphoric use of other

the LORD may be in your mouth—that with a mighty hand the LORD freed you from Egypt. 10 You shall keep this institution at its set time from year to year.

11 "And when the LORD has brought you into the land of the Canaanites, as He swore to you and to your fathers, and has given it to you, 12 you shall set apart for the LORD every first issue of the womb: every male firstling that your cattle drop shall be the LORD's. 13 But every firstling ass you shall redeem with a sheep; if you do not redeem it, you must break its neck. And you must redeem every first-born male among your children. 14 And when, in time to come, your son asks you, saying, 'What does this mean?' you shall say to him, 'It was with a mighty hand that the LORD brought us out from Egypt, the house of bondage. 15 When Pharaoh stubbornly refused to let us go, the LORD slew every first-born in the land of Egypt, the first-born of both man and beast. Therefore I sacrifice to the LORD every first male issue of the womb, but redeem every first-born among my sons.'

16 "And so it shall be as a sign upon your hand and as a symbol[a] on your forehead that with a mighty hand the LORD freed us from Egypt."

BE-SHALLAH בשלח

17 Now when Pharaoh let the people go, God did not lead them by way of the land of the Philistines, although it was nearer; for God said, "The people may have a change of heart

a *Others "frontlet."*

ornaments and items of apparel in Isa. 62.3; Jer. 13.11; Prov. 6.21; 7.3; and elsewhere). In neither case does "it shall be a sign," represent an additional observance beyond those mentioned in vv. 2–8 and 12–15. In Deut. 6.8 and 11.18, however, the same phrases are used literally to indicate that God's words are to be "bound" as a sign on the arm and as a frontlet on the forehead, and this is accompanied by the injunction to write those words on the doorposts and city gates. In that context, the command is meant literally. Jewish tradition reinterpreted Exod. 13.9 and 16 in line with Deuteronomy, and took all four passages as referring to tefillin, or phylacteries, small leather capsules fastened to the forehead and the upper arm by leather straps, and containing the paragraphs in which these vv. appear (Exod. 13.1–10, 11–16; Deut. 6. 5–9; 11.13–21). Evidence for this interpretation is already found in the community that produced the Dead Sea Scrolls, whose archaeological remains include numerous tefillin. In talmudic times they were worn throughout the day on weekdays (that is, not on the Sabbath or festivals); today they are usually worn only during weekday morning prayers. **10:** *This institution,* the eating of unleavened bread. *At its set time:* According to Naḥmanides, this v. is the basis of the practice of creating leap years by periodically adding an extra month at the end of a lunar year to adjust it to the longer solar year so that the festival falls "at its set time," that is, in the spring. This is done in order to delay the festival in years when it would otherwise occur before spring arrives (Hayim Dov Chavel, "Sefer ha-mitsvot leha-Rambam ... 'im hasagot ha-Ramban" [Jerusalem: Mosad Harav Kook, 1981], pp. 26–27). **11–16:** The sacrifice and redemption of first-borns. **12–13:** See also 22.28–29; 34.19–20; Lev. 27.27; Num. 18.15–18; Deut. 15.19–23 for further, and in some cases conflicting, details. **12:** *Set apart,* for sacrifice (v. 15). *Shall be the LORD's,* that is, sacrificed. **13:** *Every firstling ass:* Asses are domestic animals, but are ritually impure and thus may not be sacrificed (cf. Lev. 27.26; Num. 18.15); hence the owner must redeem an ass by sacrificing a sheep in its place or breaking its neck (a nonsacrificial method of slaughter). *Among your children:* Since humans are not sacrificed, they must be redeemed from the priests (see also 34.20; Num. 18.15; for a possible, but unlikely, exception see 22.28 n.). Based on Num. 18.16, the ceremony, called "Pidyon ha-ben" ("Redemption of the Son"), takes place on the thirty-first day after birth (or the next day if that is a Sabbath or major holiday). The son is "redeemed" by giving a "kohen" (a descendant of the priestly family) five units of the local currency (e.g., five dollars). The money is generally returned to the father or donated to charity. Sons whose parents are the offspring of a kohen or a Levite are not redeemed, since they have been "set apart for the LORD" by virtue of their divine service, and sons born by Caesarian section or after the birth of a daughter or a miscarriage are not redeemed because they are not the first issue of the womb. **16:** *Symbol,* the translation "frontlet"(see translators' note) i.e., headband, is preferable. The headband was the characteristic headdress in Canaan and nearby lands in biblical times, as illustrated in Egyptian and Assyrian art.

13.17–15.21: The crossing of the sea. The final episode of God's defeat of the Egyptians. God lures Egypt to a crushing blow so as to "gain glory through Pharaoh and all his host" and show them that "I am the LORD" (14.4, 18). The Sabbath on which this pericope is read in the annual Torah reading cycle is known as Shabbat Shirah, the "Sabbath of the Song,"

when they see war, and return to Egypt." 18 So God led the people roundabout, by way of the wilderness at the Sea of Reeds.
Now the Israelites went up armed[a] out of the land of Egypt.
19 And Moses took with him the bones of Joseph, who had exacted an oath from the children of Israel, saying, "God will be
sure to take notice of you: then you shall carry up my bones
from here with you."
20 They set out from Succoth, and encamped at Etham, at the
edge of the wilderness. 21 The LORD went before them in a pillar of cloud by day, to guide them along the way, and in a pillar
of fire by night, to give them light, that they might travel day
and night. 22 The pillar of cloud by day and the pillar of fire by
night did not depart from before the people.

14 The LORD said to Moses: 2 Tell the Israelites to turn back
and encamp before Pi-hahiroth, between Migdol and
the sea, before Baal-zephon; you shall encamp facing it, by the

a *Meaning of Heb.* ḥamushim *uncertain.*

referring to the poem of 15.1–18. It is also read on the seventh day of Pesaḥ, when, according to tradition, the crossing of the sea took place. See also v. 18 n. **13.17:** *By way of the land of the Philistines,* or "by The Way to the Land of the Philistines" (the name of the road)—in either case, the route leading from Egypt to Philistia in southern Canaan (see Map, no. 2). This is presumably the route, called "The Ways of Horus" by the Egyptians, that ran parallel to the Mediterranean coast, from Zilu (Sile) to Gaza, and was the shortest route to Canaan (along it an army could reach Gaza in nine or ten days). If the exodus took place in the 13th century BCE, the reference to the Philistines is anachronistic, since the Philistines were among the "Sea Peoples" who migrated to the Levant from the Aegean region and did not settle in southern Canaan until the early 12th century. *Have a change of heart,* as they do in 14.11–12. *When they see war,* either with the Canaanites in the promised land or the Egyptian forces stationed in Zilu (Sile) and the other fortresses Egypt maintained all along the Ways of Horus in the 13th century BCE to protect its access to Canaan. To avoid demoralization, God leads the Israelites via the arduous but less guarded southerly route through the marshy lake-land of the eastern delta to Sukkot and thence to the wilderness. **18:** *By way of the wilderness,* or, "by The Way to the Wilderness," possibly the name of an ancient road leading to the Sinai wilderness. *At the Sea of Reeds,* Heb "yam suf" [often incorrectly translated as the Red Sea], an unidentified body of water, probably in the Isthmus of Suez, the strip of land, lakes, and marshes between the Gulf of Suez and the Mediterranean (the strip traversed by the Suez Canal today). See Map, p. 122. The same name is used for the Gulf of Eilat [23.31; Deut. 1.40; etc.]. **19:** See Gen. 50.24–25. According to Josh. 24.32, Joshua buried Joseph in Shechem (modern Nablus; see Map no. 1). **20:** *Etham,* an unidentified place, perhaps at the eastern end of the Wadi Tumilat, where the wadi meets the wilderness, near Lake Timsah (see Map, p. 122). (Cf. Num. 33.8, "the wilderness of Etham.") **21:** *The LORD went before them in a pillar of cloud … and in a pillar of fire:* The two pillars were probably one, a columnar cloud enveloping a fire that was visible through it only in the dark. Hence 14.24 refers to a single "pillar of fire and cloud" at daybreak, when the fire was still partly visible as the cloud gradually became opaque. Their role here may reflect the ancient practice of carrying a burning, smoking brazier at the head of an army or caravan to indicate the line of march by day and night. See further 14.19 n. **22:** For an exception to this statement, see 14.19. According to P, once the Tabernacle was erected, the pillar or cloud and fire remained above it even when directing the Israelites' march (Exod. 40.33–38; Num. 9.15–23; 10.11–12, 34). (For a reflection of this image in United States history, see the intro. to Exodus.)

14.1–31: The crossing of the Sea of Reeds. The composite nature of this narrative is indicated by inconsistencies and redundancies. For example, God's stiffening Pharaoh's heart to chase the Israelites (vv. 8–9) is redundant after Pharaoh has already decided to give chase (vv. 5–7). V. 19a says that the angel leading the Israelites moves to their rear, while 19b says that it was the cloud. V. 21b (through "dry ground") presents a relatively naturalistic picture of God causing a strong wind to blow back the waters of the sea, while the remainder of the v. and v. 22 present a more miraculous picture of the sea splitting, with the waters forming walls on either side of the Israelites. Source critics assign the components of the narrative to J, E, and P. By skillfully combining the sources, the redactor has harmonized the differences so as to show, for example, that Pharaoh's independent decision to pursue the Israelites is, in a mysterious way, carrying out God's plan (cf. v. 4), that the cloud is indeed the angel, and that God used the natural means of the wind to carry out His miraculous splitting of the sea. **2:** *Pi-hahiroth* cannot be clearly identified with any known Egyptian toponym. *Migdol* ("watchtower") figures in several toponyms in and near the eastern delta. An Egyptian letter (see 12.37 n.) mentions one apparently in or near the Sinai desert not far from Wadi Tumilat. *Baal-zephon* must refer to a site at which the Canaanite deity of that name was worshipped

sea. 3 Pharaoh will say of the Israelites, "They are astray in the land; the wilderness has closed in on them." 4 Then I will stiffen Pharaoh's heart and he will pursue them, that I may gain glory through Pharaoh and all his host; and the Egyptians shall know that I am the LORD.

And they did so.

5 When the king of Egypt was told that the people had fled, Pharaoh and his courtiers had a change of heart about the people and said, "What is this we have done, releasing Israel from our service?" 6 He ordered[a] his chariot and took his men with him; 7 he took six hundred of his picked chariots, and the rest of the chariots of Egypt, with officers[b] in all of them. 8 The LORD stiffened the heart of Pharaoh king of Egypt, and he gave chase to the Israelites. As the Israelites were departing defiantly,[c] 9 the Egyptians gave chase to them, and all the chariot horses of Pharaoh, his horsemen, and his warriors overtook them encamped by the sea, near Pi-hahiroth, before Baal-zephon.

10 As Pharaoh drew near, the Israelites caught sight of the Egyptians advancing upon them. Greatly frightened, the Israelites cried out to the LORD. 11 And they said to Moses, "Was it for want of graves in Egypt that you brought us to die in the wilderness? What have you done to us, taking us out of Egypt? 12 Is this not the very thing we told you in Egypt, saying, 'Let us be, and we will serve the Egyptians, for it is better for us to serve the Egyptians than to die in the wilderness'?" 13 But Moses said to the people, "Have no fear! Stand by, and witness the deliverance which the LORD will work for you today; for the Egyptians whom you see today you will never see again. 14 The LORD will battle for you; you hold your peace!"

15 Then the LORD said to Moses, "Why do you cry out to Me? Tell the Israelites to go forward. 16 And you lift up your rod and hold out your arm over the sea and split it, so that the Israelites may march into the sea on dry ground. 17 And I will stiffen the hearts of the Egyptians so that they go in after them; and I will gain glory through Pharaoh and all his warriors, his chariots and his horsemen. 18 Let the Egyptians know that I am LORD, when I gain glory through Pharaoh, his chariots, and his horsemen."

19 The angel of God, who had been going ahead of the Israelite army, now moved and followed behind them; and the pillar of cloud shifted from in front of them and took up a place behind them, 20 and it came between the army of the Egyptians and the army of Israel. Thus there was the cloud with the

a *See on Gen. 46.29.*

b *Heb.* shalish; *originally "third man on royal chariot"; hence "adjutant," "officer."*

c *Lit. "with upraised hand."*

in Egypt. Several in the eastern delta region are known. **4:** *Gain glory* (etymologically "weightiness," honor, authority), by punishing those who disobey Him. *The Egyptians shall know that I am the LORD,* see 6.2 n. **5:** Only now do the Egyptians realize that the Israelites have left for good (see 12.31). **11–12:** The Israelites' continual complaining in the wilderness, a dominant theme of the Torah, is introduced here. (See 15.24; 16.2–3; 17.2–3; Num. 11.4–6; 14.2–3; 16.13–14; 20.2–5, 13; 21.4–5; Deut. 1.27–28.) **12:** *We told you in Egypt:* No such comment is recorded earlier, but the Samaritan Pentateuch adds it after 6.9. (See 11.4–8 n.) **15–31:** Some believe that the action of the sea reflects the rising and falling tides or shallow waters being blown back by wind in the southern part of the isthmus, or a combination of both. A document from Mari, in Syria, reports that an army escaped across a river one night at low tide and the pursuing army was prevented from overtaking them when the tide later rose again. In the present case the heavy Egyptian chariots became mired in the mud and were engulfed by the returning waters. The text, however, claims that miraculously the waters were split and stood up like walls (vv. 16, 22, 29). **19:** The first clause of the v. (from the E source) says that the angel of God was at the head of the Israelites; the next clause (from J) indicates that the pillar of cloud led them, while 13.21 (also J) says that it was the LORD in the cloud. These three statements picture the divine manifestation in different ways (cf. 3.2 n.). **20:** *Cast a spell,* turned it totally dark so that the Egyptians could not approach the Israelites (cf. 10.22–23a; Josh. 24.7). *The one could not come near the other all through the night:* According to a midrashic interpretation, this refers to the angels, who sought to sing a hymn praising God as the Egyptians were drowning; God rebuked them, saying: "While my creatures are drowning in the sea you would sing a hymn?!" showing that He does not rejoice in the death of the wicked (*b. Sanh.* 39b, prompted either by the similar phraseology in Isa. 6.3 or by an interpretation of "k-rv"

darkness, and it cast a spell[a] upon the night, so that the one
could not come near the other all through the night.
21 Then Moses held out his arm over the sea and the LORD
drove back the sea with a strong east wind all that night, and
turned the sea into dry ground. The waters were split, 22 and
the Israelites went into the sea on dry ground, the waters forming a wall for them on their right and on their left. 23 The Egyptians came in pursuit after them into the sea, all of Pharaoh's
horses, chariots, and horsemen. 24 At the morning watch, the
LORD looked down upon the Egyptian army from a pillar of
fire and cloud, and threw the Egyptian army into panic. 25 He
locked[b] the wheels of their chariots so that they moved forward
with difficulty. And the Egyptians said, "Let us flee from the
Israelites, for the LORD is fighting for them against Egypt."
26 Then the LORD said to Moses, "Hold out your arm over the
sea, that the waters may come back upon the Egyptians and
upon their chariots and upon their horsemen." 27 Moses held out
his arm over the sea, and at daybreak the sea returned to its normal state, and the Egyptians fled at its approach. But the LORD
hurled the Egyptians into the sea. 28 The waters turned back
and covered the chariots and the horsemen—Pharaoh's entire
army that followed them into the sea; not one of them remained.
29 But the Israelites had marched through the sea on dry ground,
the waters forming a wall for them on their right and on their left.
30 Thus the LORD delivered Israel that day from the Egyptians. Israel saw the Egyptians dead on the shore of the sea.
31 And when Israel saw the wondrous power which the LORD
had wielded against the Egyptians, the people feared the LORD;
they had faith in the LORD and His servant Moses.

15 Then Moses and the Israelites sang this song to the LORD. They said:

I will sing to the LORD, for He has triumphed
gloriously;
Horse and driver He has hurled into the sea.
2 The LORD[c] is my strength and might;[d]
He is become my deliverance.

a *From root* ʿrr, *"cast a spell" or "curse." Others "and it lit up."*
b *From root* ʾsr, *with several ancient versions. Others "took off."*
c *Heb.* Yah. d *Others "song."*

["come near"] as a term for prayer). **25:** *Locked:* They became stuck in the mud. **31:** *Feared:* No longer frightened of the Egyptians (v. 10), they were awe-struck at God's power. *Had faith,* i.e., trusted, now that their fears were proven groundless. "Faith" in the Bible means trust, rather than an abstract belief in the existence of God or assent to a doctrine. *His servant Moses:* The people now realize that Moses is truly God's servant and representative. Cf. Num. 12.7–8; Deut. 34.10.

15.1–21: The Song at the Sea, a lyric poem, sung as a hymn, celebrating God's defeat of Egypt at the sea. Rich in imagery, hyperbole, and poetic license, it expresses the unrestrained enthusiasm of the Israelites over their miraculous rescue from disaster. Formally it is divided into three sections, each ending with a simile followed by a bicolon addressed to God in which the opening phrase is repeated in the second colon (vv. 5b–6, 10b–11, 16a–b), and a conclusion (vv. 17–18). In terms of content, however, the sections are an introduction (vv. 1–3), the defeat of Pharaoh's forces (vv. 4–12), God's guidance of Israel to the promised land and the Temple Mount and the terrified reaction of its inhabitants and neighbors (vv. 13–17), and a coda acclaiming His eternal rule (v. 18). The general plot of the poem—God's control of the sea followed by the building of His sanctuary and the acclamation of His kingship—and some of its vocabulary allude to motifs found in other biblical poems that tell of His primordial defeat of the sea and assumption of kingship (e.g., Pss. 74.12–16; 89.10–14; 93), which themselves hark back to ancient Near Eastern myths about the storm god's defeat of the sea god followed by the building of his palace/temple. The language and style of the poem are archaic and share many features with Ugaritic poetry of the Late Bronze Age, suggesting that it is one of the oldest poems in the Bible. On the other hand, the mention of Philistia (v. 14; see 13.22 n.) and the building of the Temple as the culmination of the exodus imply a date in the monarchic period, later than the putative date of the exodus. In Jewish prayer, the entire poem is recited every morning in the preliminary prayers, and vv. 11 and 18 are recited following the Shema prayer morning and evening, as part of the daily acceptance of God's kingship, the Jewish declaration of allegiance to God. **2:** The first half of this v. also appears in Isa. 12.2 and Ps. 118.14, suggesting that it became a liturgical saying. *I will enshrine Him,* another interpretation of the enigmatic Heb verb is

This is my God and I will enshrine[a] Him;
The God of my father, and I will exalt Him.
3 The LORD, the Warrior—
LORD is His name!
4 Pharaoh's chariots and his army
He has cast into the sea;
And the pick of his officers
Are drowned in the Sea of Reeds.
5 The deeps covered them;
They went down into the depths like a stone.
6 Your right hand, O LORD, glorious in power,
Your right hand, O LORD, shatters the foe!
7 In Your great triumph You break Your opponents;
You send forth Your fury, it consumes them like straw.
8 At the blast of Your nostrils the waters piled up,
The floods stood straight like a wall;
The deeps froze in the heart of the sea.
9 The foe said,
"I will pursue, I will overtake,
I will divide the spoil;
My desire shall have its fill of them.
I will bare my sword—
My hand shall subdue them."
10 You made Your wind blow, the sea covered them;
They sank like lead in the majestic waters.
11 Who is like You, O LORD, among the celestials;[b]
Who is like You, majestic in holiness,
Awesome in splendor, working wonders!
12 You put out Your right hand,
The earth swallowed them.
13 In Your love You lead the people You redeemed;
In Your strength You guide them to Your holy abode.
14 The peoples hear, they tremble;
Agony grips the dwellers in Philistia.

a Others "glorify." *b Others "mighty."*

"glorify" or "beautify Him," from which a midrash derived the duty of beautifying religious objects used in His worship, such as the sukkah, tallit, shofar, and Torah scroll; another midrash takes the verb as meaning "show His beauty" by imitating His compassion (*Mek. Shirta,* 3; *b. Shab.* 133b; *Torah Temimah*). *The God of my father,* see 3.6. **3:** *The LORD, the Warrior,* see 14.14, 25. One of the various metaphors applied to God. The warrior metaphor was frequently applied to deities in the ancient world, reflecting the conviction that victory is in reality an achievement of God, not of human warriors. Cf. Deut. 20.4; 1 Sam. 17.47; Zech. 4.6. *LORD is His name:* That is, YHVH ("'adonai") is His name (see 3.15). This declaration reflects the further fulfillment of God's promises that all would come to know that "I am the LORD" (see 5.1–6.1 n., 6.2 n.). **6:** *Your right hand:* In this poem Moses' arm, so prominent in the prose narrative of ch 14 (vv. 16, 21, 26, 27), is not mentioned. Only God's role—the ultimate reality behind the event—is celebrated. In this respect the poem is a forerunner of the Haggadah, which mentions only God, not Moses. **7:** *It consumes them like straw:* The poem mixes metaphors. Although the Egyptians drowned, the image here is of fire burning them. In vv. 6b and 7a God "shatters" and "breaks" the enemy. **8:** *The blast of Your nostrils,* a metaphor for the wind of 14.21. **9:** *Desire,* i.e., appetite. **10:** After all the enemy's boasts, God sinks them in an instant. **11:** *Celestials,* lit. "gods." Exclamations of God's uniqueness among the "gods" (2 Sam. 7.22; 1 Kings 8.23; Ps. 86.8) proclaim Him the greatest power in the universe. They go back to ancient Near Eastern polytheistic prototypes (cf. Jethro in 18.11), and understand YHVH as the supreme, incomparable deity. Later texts and interpretations retain the term "gods" vestigially to refer to the celestial or supernatural beings that surround God in the manner of a royal court—that is, the "host of heaven," including the sun, moon, stars, spirits, winds, flames, seraphs, and angels (Deut. 4.35–39; Pss. 86.10; 96.4–5; 135.5, 15–17). The translation "celestials" invokes the latter concept so that the v. conforms more closely to the modern sense of monotheism, but whether this ancient poem is referring to angelic beings or actual gods is debated. **13:** *Love,* Heb "ḥesed," better rendered "faithfulness." It refers to acts of kindness that are expected between parties in a relationship—husband and wife, parents and children, relatives, and allies—and to reciprocation of kindness (Gen. 40.14; Deut. 7.9; 1 Sam. 20.8; 2 Sam. 9.1; 10.2). Here, as frequently, it refers to God's covenantal faithfulness to Israel (2.24; 6.4–8; cf. 20.6; 34.6, 7). *To Your holy abode,* to the destination mentioned in v. 17, the land of Israel (cf. the sequence of events in Ps. 78.53–55) and/or the Temple Mount in Jerusalem (2 Sam. 15.25; Isa. 33.20); cf. Jer. 25.30; 31.23. **14–16:** Terrified by the power God exercised against Egypt on

15 Now are the clans of Edom dismayed;
The tribes of Moab—trembling grips them;
All the dwellers in Canaan are aghast.
16 Terror and dread descend upon them;
Through the might of Your arm they are still as stone—
Till Your people cross over, O LORD,
Till Your people cross whom You have ransomed.

17 You will bring them and plant them in Your own mountain,
The place You made to dwell in, O LORD,
The sanctuary, O LORD, which Your hands established.
18 The LORD will reign for ever and ever!

19 For the horses of Pharaoh, with his chariots and horsemen,
went into the sea; and the LORD turned back on them the waters of the sea; but the Israelites marched on dry ground in the
midst of the sea.

20 Then Miriam the prophetess, Aaron's sister, took a timbrel
in her hand, and all the women went out after her in dance
with timbrels. 21 And Miriam chanted for them:

Sing to the LORD, for He has triumphed gloriously;
Horse and driver He has hurled into the sea.

22 Then Moses caused Israel to set out from the Sea of Reeds.
They went on into the wilderness of Shur; they traveled three

Israel's behalf, the Canaanites and neighboring nations are petrified at Israel's approach (cf. Josh. 2.9–11). **16:** *Still as stone,* like the Egyptians, who sank "like a stone" (v. 5). *Cross over:* This refers either to Israel's passing these nations (excepting the Canaanites) on its way to Canaan (Deut. 2.8, 18) or crossing the Jordan into the land (Josh. 1.11; 4.1). *Ransomed,* i.e., redeemed. **17:** *Plant them,* permanently settle them (Amos 9.15; Pss. 44.3; 80.9). *In Your own mountain:* "Mountain" refers to the promised land, which is mountainous (Deut. 3.25; Isa. 11.9; 57.13; Ps. 78.54), or to the Temple Mount, called "God's mountain" (Isa. 2.3; Ezek. 20.40; Zech. 8.3; Ps. 24.3), which the following phrases *the place You made to dwell in* and *the sanctuary ...* clearly refer to. The v. blends the concepts of the promised land and the Temple Mount: The Israelites, settled throughout the land with the Temple in the center, are pictured as dwelling around the Temple in which God dwells in their midst (cf. Exod. 25.8; 29.45–46; 1 Kings 6.13; Ezek. 37.25–28). This climactic v. indicates that the conquest of the promised land will not be an end in itself. The redemption will culminate when the Temple is built and Israel dwells there in the Presence of God. *You made ... Your hands established:* As in the victory over Egypt and the conquest of the promised land (vv. 6, 16b–17a), human agency in building the Temple (1 Kings chs 6–8, esp. 8.13) is ignored. In a theological sense it is God who will build the Temple (cf. Ps. 78.69). **18:** God's kingship is acclaimed here because the Temple, as His palace ("heikhal," 1 Kings 6.3, 5, and elsewhere), symbolizes His kingship. This is the first explicit mention of the biblical metaphor "God is king," which is rarely explicit in the Torah, though common elsewhere. **20–21:** In keeping with the custom of women celebrating the victor after a battle (Judg. 11.34; 1 Sam. 18.6), the women dance and play music, led by Miriam who summons them, or all the Israelites, to sing God's praises (either the hymn of vv. 1–18 or a refrain). *Miriam the prophetess:* This title could refer to Miriam's recitation of the hymn, or part of it (cf. 1 Chron. 25.1–3) or to her prophetic status mentioned in Num. 12.2. The activities of Deborah the prophetess also include singing a hymn praising God for a victory (Judg. 4.4; ch 5), while Huldah delivers a prophetic oracle (2 Kings 22.14; cf. Ezek. 13.17; Joel 3.1; Neh. 6.14).

15.22–17.16: Challenges in the wilderness. Four episodes in which the Israelites face typical dangers of the wilderness: shortages of food and water and attack by marauders. In the face of the shortages the people grumble against Moses and Aaron. God here responds to their complaints without anger or punishment, perhaps because they have not previously seen His ability to meet their material needs, or because these incidents occur before the covenant at Sinai at which God promised to meet such needs (23.25). Having seen God's ability to defeat armies (14.30–31), they do not complain (as in 14.10–12) when the Amalekites attack.

15.22–27: Complaints (14.11–12 n.) about food and water recur throughout the wilderness wanderings. See 16.2–3; 17.2–3; Num. 11.4–6; 16.13–14; 20.2–5; 21.4–5. **22:** *The wilderness of Shur,* east of the Isthmus of Suez, apparently named for the defensive wall ("shur") that the Egyptians erected to prevent incursions from the east. *Three days ... no water:* The midrash, which interprets "water" as Torah (since Torah is as essential

days in the wilderness and found no water. 23 They came to Marah, but they could not drink the water of Marah because it was bitter; that is why it was named Marah.[a] 24 And the people grumbled against Moses, saying, "What shall we drink?" 25 So he cried out to the LORD, and the LORD showed him a piece of wood; he threw it into the water and the water became sweet.

There He made for them a fixed rule, and there He put them to the test. 26 He said, "If you will heed the LORD your God diligently, doing what is upright in His sight, giving ear to His commandments and keeping all His laws, then I will not bring upon you any of the diseases that I brought upon the Egyptians, for I the LORD am your healer."

27 And they came to Elim, where there were twelve springs of water and seventy palm trees; and they encamped there beside the water.

16 Setting out from Elim, the whole Israelite community came to the wilderness of Sin, which is between Elim and Sinai, on the fifteenth day of the second month after their departure from the land of Egypt. 2 In the wilderness, the whole Israelite community grumbled against Moses and Aaron. 3 The Israelites said to them, "If only we had died by the hand of the LORD in the land of Egypt, when we sat by the fleshpots, when we ate our fill of bread! For you have brought us out into this wilderness to starve this whole congregation to death."

4 And the LORD said to Moses, "I will rain down bread for you from the sky, and the people shall go out and gather each day that day's portion—that I may thus test them, to see whether they will follow My instructions or not. 5 But on the sixth day, when they apportion what they have brought in, it

a I.e., "bitter."

for well-being as water), infers that it was three days without Torah that made the people rebellious, and holds that the practice of reading the Torah in the synagogue every Sabbath, Monday, and Thursday was instituted so that three days would not pass without Torah (*Mek. Beshallah, Vayassa'*, 1; *b. B. K.* 82a). **23:** *Marah,* lit. "bitter." Brackish pools and wells are common in deserts (cf. the "Bitter Lakes" in the Isthmus of Suez). Assuming that the Israelites are now heading south, the site could be Bir el-Murrah, Arabic for "Bitter Well," nine miles east of Suez, or the oasis Ein Hawarah, 75 km (47 mi) southeast of Suez, near Wadi Amarah which has a similar sounding name. **25:** *A piece of wood,* or a branch with its foliage. Even today, Bedouin sweeten brackish water with shrubs that pull the salt to the bottom. *There He made for them a fixed rule, and there He put them to the test:* The context suggests that this enigmatic sentence refers to the next v. and means that God told Israel the conditions of their future relationship, against which they will be tested (see 16.4; Deut. 8.2, 16). Some see this as an alternative to the Sinai traditions, suggesting that Israel received laws immediately upon leaving Egypt. The promise in v. 26, which also implies a warning, is prompted by Israel's grumbling against Moses, God's servant (14.31), which contained the seeds of rebellion against God Himself (cf. 16.8). **26:** *The diseases that I brought upon the Egyptians,* such as the sixth plague, skin inflammation (9.8–11). *Healer:* This quality of God, with its implicit warning of punishment by disease, is prompted by His purifying the water of its bitterness, which was regarded as "healing" the water (the same verb is translated "make wholesome" in 2 Kings 2.22; Ezek. 47.8, 9, 11). **27:** *Elim,* possibly Wadi Gharandel, the best-watered site in western Sinai, about 15 km (9 mi) south of Ein Hawarah, or Uyun Musa, 12 km (7.5 mi) southwest of Bir el-Murrah, which has a palm grove and twelve springs even today.

16.1–36: Provision of food in the wilderness. Most of this narrative is assigned to the Priestly source, but redundancies (such as God's two responses to the people's complaint [vv. 4–5 and 11–12]) and difficulties in the order (vv. 6–8 presuppose vv. 9–12) suggest the presence of a second source (JE) as well. Another episode in which God provides quail, which also refers to the manna, appears in Num. ch 11. These episodes are in part doublets of each other. **1–3:** A month after the exodus (Num. 33.3), having left the oasis of Elim and run low on food, the Israelites turn on Moses and Aaron and begin to idealize life in Egypt (cf. 14.11–12; Num. 11.5). **4:** The people's need for food is real, but their accusatory complaint portends rebellion, so God determines to provide food subject to rules that test their obedience and trust (vv. 19–20, 25–29). **5:** When it is apportioned, the manna collected on the sixth day will miraculously double and suffice for the next day as well. Cf. Lev. 25.20–22. *Apportion:* Halakhic exegesis construes the Heb verb in its better-known sense of "prepare," and infers a general rule that cooked food for the Sabbath must be prepared before the Sabbath (*b. Shab.* 117b; *b. Pes.* 47b; *b. Betzah* 2b; see also v. 23).

shall prove to be double the amount they gather each day."
[6] So Moses and Aaron said to all the Israelites, "By evening you shall know it was the LORD who brought you out from the land of Egypt; [7] and in the morning you shall behold the Presence[a] of the LORD, because He has heard your grumblings against the LORD. For who are we that you should grumble against us?
[8] Since it is the LORD," Moses continued, "who will give you flesh to eat in the evening and bread in the morning to the full, because the LORD has heard the grumblings you utter against Him, what is our part? Your grumbling is not against us, but against the LORD!"

[9] Then Moses said to Aaron, "Say to the whole Israelite community: Advance toward the LORD, for He has heard your grumbling." [10] And as Aaron spoke to the whole Israelite community, they turned toward the wilderness, and there, in a cloud, appeared the Presence of the LORD.

[11] The LORD spoke to Moses: [12] "I have heard the grumbling of the Israelites. Speak to them and say: By evening you shall eat flesh, and in the morning you shall have your fill of bread; and you shall know that I the LORD am your God."

[13] In the evening quail appeared and covered the camp; in the morning there was a fall of dew about the camp. [14] When the fall of dew lifted, there, over the surface of the wilderness, lay a fine and flaky substance, as fine as frost on the ground.
[15] When the Israelites saw it, they said to one another, "What is it?"[b]—for they did not know what it was. And Moses said to them, "That is the bread which the LORD has given you to eat.
[16] This is what the LORD has commanded: Gather as much of it as each of you requires to eat, an *omer* to a person for as many of you as there are; each of you shall fetch for those in his tent."

[17] The Israelites did so, some gathering much, some little.
[18] But when they measured it by the *omer,* he who had gathered much had no excess, and he who had gathered little had no deficiency: they had gathered as much as they needed to eat. [19] And Moses said to them, "Let no one leave any of it over until morning." [20] But they paid no attention to Moses; some of them left of it until morning, and it became infested with maggots and stank. And Moses was angry with them.

a Others "glory." *b Heb.* man hu; *others "It is manna."*

6–7: Divinely provided food and the appearance of God's Presence will remind the people that, contrary to their charge in v. 3, it was God, not Moses and Aaron, who took them from Egypt (cf. 15.6 n., 17.11 n.) and that their complaints are really against Him. *The Presence of the LORD*: God's kavod, the visual form in which He appears to humans, usually described as fiery or as enveloped in cloud or fire (v. 10; 24.17; 40.34–38), though sometimes as a human form (33.18, 22; Ezek. 1.26–28). But since this is to happen *in the morning,* Rashi holds that this v. does not refer to the theophany of vv. 9–10 but to the manna, which appeared in the morning (vv. 8, 12–13). In that case *the Presence of the LORD* refers to an act of providence or miracle that manifests His power, as in Num. 14.22; Ps. 96.3. **8:** *Flesh ... bread,* in the form of quail and manna (v. 13). **9–10:** *Advance toward the LORD,* perhaps toward the pillar of cloud/fire (13.21–22). If so, *there, in a* [or "the"] *cloud, appeared the Presence of the LORD* would seem to mean that His fiery Presence became more visible within the cloud. **12:** *You shall know that I the LORD am your God:* See 7.3–5 n. **13:** *Quail:* Quail migrating, often in great numbers, between Africa and Europe in the spring and fall often drop exhausted in the Sinai and are caught by hunters. This experience was repeated in Num. 11.31–32 but did not become a regular occurrence as did the manna. The quail were not a supernatural phenomenon, but their timely appearance at God's promise was an act of divine providence. **14:** *A fine and flaky substance,* named manna in v. 31. The tradition about the manna may have its origin in the sweet, edible honeydew (still called "manna" in Arabic) found in parts of the Sinai in June and July. Scale insects and plant lice ingest the sap of tamarisk trees and excrete it onto the branches, from which it crystallizes and falls to the ground as sticky solids. Bedouin use it as a sweetener. If this was the manna, the miracle was that it arrived just when the Israelites needed it, that enough was produced to feed the entire people but never more than an omer (about 2.3 liters, 2.1 quarts [dry measure]) per person daily, that it doubled on the sixth day and did not appear on the Sabbath, and that contrary to its natural pattern it appeared year-round. **16:** *Omer:* See v. 36. **19:** Using up the manna before morning shows trust that God will provide more the next day (hence Moses' anger in v. 20).

21 So they gathered it every morning, each as much as he
needed to eat; for when the sun grew hot, it would melt. 22 On
the sixth day they gathered double the amount of food, two
omers for each; and when all the chieftains of the community
came and told Moses, 23 he said to them, "This is what the LORD
meant: Tomorrow is a day of rest, a holy sabbath of the LORD.
Bake what you would bake and boil what you would boil; and
all that is left put aside to be kept until morning." 24 So they put
it aside until morning, as Moses had ordered; and it did not
turn foul, and there were no maggots in it. 25 Then Moses said,
"Eat it today, for today is a sabbath of the LORD; you will not
find it today on the plain. 26 Six days you shall gather it; on the
seventh day, the sabbath, there will be none."
27 Yet some of the people went out on the seventh day to
gather, but they found nothing. 28 And the LORD said to Moses,
"How long will you men refuse to obey My commandments
and My teachings? 29 Mark that the LORD has given you the
sabbath; therefore He gives you two days' food on the sixth
day. Let everyone remain where he is: let no one leave his
place on the seventh day." 30 So the people remained inactive
on the seventh day.
31 The house of Israel named it manna;[a] it was like coriander seed, white, and it tasted like wafers[b] in honey. 32 Moses
said, "This is what the LORD has commanded: Let one *omer* of
it be kept throughout the ages, in order that they may see the
bread that I fed you in the wilderness when I brought you out
from the land of Egypt." 33 And Moses said to Aaron, "Take a jar,
put one *omer* of manna in it, and place it before the LORD, to
be kept throughout the ages." 34 As the LORD had commanded
Moses, Aaron placed it before the Pact,[c] to be kept. 35 And the
Israelites ate manna forty years, until they came to a settled
land; they ate the manna until they came to the border of the
land of Canaan. 36 The *omer* is a tenth of an *ephah*.

a Heb. man. *b Meaning of Heb.* ṣappiḥith *uncertain.* *c Others "Testimony."*

21–30: The Sabbath. Since God observes the Sabbath, He will not provide manna on the seventh day but will provide a double portion on the sixth day and Israel will observe the Sabbath as well. The Sabbath, having been "created" in Gen. ch 2, is first revealed to Israel here. **22:** See v. 5 n. *Told Moses,* of the mysterious fact that the day's yield turned out to be *double the amount of food* (Heb "leḥem mishneh," "double the bread/food"). This v. is the source of the Jewish custom of placing two loaves of bread (called "leḥem mishneh") on the table at the main Sabbath and festival meals. **23:** *Day of rest ... sabbath,* Heb "shabbaton ... shabbat." Both Heb terms literally refer to "cessation" of particular activities; the doubling of terms suggests a superlative, complete cessation. The seventh day is a day of cessation from normal labor (20.10), such as gathering and cooking food, because it is a holy day of cessation to God: He does not provide manna on it because He ceased creative activity on it, blessed it and declared it holy (Gen. 2.1–3). *Bake ... and boil ... :* cf. Num. 11.8. *And all that is left put aside ... :* This means either "cook today for two days, and save what you don't eat today for tomorrow" (Rashi) or "cook what you will eat today and eat the rest raw tomorrow" (Ibn Ezra). **28:** *Refuse to obey My commandments ... :* Unless this means simply that they refused to believe that there would be no manna on the Sabbath, it must mean that they violated the implicit command not to go out for manna on the Sabbath (vv. 25b–26) or the explicit command to eat the manna that was kept overnight (v. 25a). **29:** *Given you the sabbath:* God has given the Sabbath, previously holy only to Him (Gen. 2.1–3), as a gift to Israel. *Let no one leave his place,* to gather manna. Rabbinic exegesis saw here a broader prohibition on all Sabbath travel and inferred that one may not walk more than 2,000 cubits (roughly 914.4 m, 3,000 ft) beyond the city limits on the Sabbath. This distance (based on Num. 35.5) is called the "Sabbath boundary" ("teḥum shabbat"). **31:** *Named it manna* (Heb "man"), playfully reinterpreting their original question, "what (Heb 'man') is it?" (v. 15), as a declaration, "it is 'man.' " In essence, then, the term means "whatchamacallit" and expresses the manna's unprecedented character in Israelite experience. *Tasted:* Num. 11.8, a different tradition, says "it tasted like rich cream" and notes various ways to prepare it. This gave rise to the rabbinic tradition that the manna had many different tastes, suiting the palate of each person. **32–34:** One day's portion of manna is to be preserved as a future reminder of God's care for the Israelites in the wilderness. Cf. Lev. 23.42–43. **34:** *Before the Pact,* before the Ark of the Pact (25.10–22), P's term for the Ark of the Covenant (Num. 10.33; Josh. 3.6); the suggestion is that the jar of manna stored in front of the Ark could be taken out to show to future generations. **35:** *Until they came to the border of the land of Canaan,* see Josh. 5.10–12. **36:** *Ephah,* about 23 liters (21 quarts).

17 From the wilderness of Sin the whole Israelite community continued by stages as the LORD would command. They encamped at Rephidim, and there was no water for the people to drink. 2 The people quarreled with Moses. "Give us water to drink," they said; and Moses replied to them, "Why do you quarrel with me? Why do you try the LORD?" 3 But the people thirsted there for water; and the people grumbled against Moses and said, "Why did you bring us up from Egypt, to kill us and our children and livestock with thirst?" 4 Moses cried out to the LORD, saying, "What shall I do with this people? Before long they will be stoning me!" 5 Then the LORD said to Moses, "Pass before the people; take with you some of the elders of Israel, and take along the rod with which you struck the Nile, and set out. 6 I will be standing there before you on the rock at Horeb. Strike the rock and water will issue from it, and the people will drink." And Moses did so in the sight of the elders of Israel. 7 The place was named Massah[a] and Meribah,[b] because the Israelites quarreled and because they tried the LORD, saying, "Is the LORD present among us or not?"

8 Amalek came and fought with Israel at Rephidim. 9 Moses said to Joshua, "Pick some men for us, and go out and do battle with Amalek. Tomorrow I will station myself on the top of the hill, with the rod of God in my hand." 10 Joshua did as Moses told him and fought with Amalek, while Moses, Aaron, and Hur went up to the top of the hill. 11 Then, whenever Moses held up his hand, Israel prevailed; but whenever he let down his hand, Amalek prevailed. 12 But Moses' hands grew heavy; so they took a stone and put it under him and he sat on it, while Aaron and Hur, one on each side, supported his hands; thus

a I.e., "Trial." *b I.e., "Quarrel."*

17.1–7: The incident at Massah and Meribah. 1: *Rephidim,* the last station before Sinai (19.2; Num. 33.14–15) and, to judge from v. 6, near Sinai/Horeb. **2:** *Why do you quarrel with me? Why do you try the LORD?* Cf. 16.8. *Try,* i.e., test, demanding proof that God was present among them and controlling the events (see v. 7; cf. 8.18; Deut. 7.21; 31.17; Josh. 3.10). **3:** Cf. 16.3b. **5–6:** Moses is to take some of the elders, perhaps as witnesses, and set out for *Horeb* (Sinai), "the mountain of God" (3.1), to obtain water. *Strike the rock:* The Sinai contains limestone rocks from which small amounts of water drip, and a blow to their soft surface can expose a porous inner layer containing water. Apparently the water thus obtained by Moses would flow from Horeb back to Rephidim via a wadi (cf. 32.20; Deut. 9.21). A similar but enigmatic episode, an oral variant of this one, appears in Num. 20.2–13 (mostly from P in its present form). According to talmudic legend, the water came from the "Well of Miriam" which henceforth accompanied the Israelites on their journeys through the wilderness; it was given to them because of Miriam's merits and named after her (*Seder Olam* 5; *t. Sot.* 11.1, 8; *b. Ta'an.* 9a; see Num. 20.1 n.). **7:** *The place,* Rephidim (v. 1), not Horeb. *Massah and Meribah,* meaning "The Place of Testing and Quarreling." These names, playing on the verbs "quarrel" and "try" used in v. 2, became bywords for Israel's lack of trust in God (Deut. 6.16; 9.22; Ps. 95.8).

17.8–16: The attack of the Amalekites. The Amalekites are depicted as marauding nomads living in the Negev and Sinai. In later times they periodically raided and pillaged Israel and joined other enemies in threatening to wipe Israel out (Judg. 3.13; 6.3–5; 30.1; 1 Sam. 30.1–2; Ps. 83.4–9). They are not mentioned in extrabiblical records. This passage is read in the synagogue on Purim because Haman, the arch anti-Semite who sought to exterminate all the Jews in the Persian empire, was an Agagite, a descendant of the Amalekite king Agag (cf. Esth. 3.1; 1 Sam. 15.32). In later Jewish tradition Amalek came to symbolize anti-Semites in general. **8:** *Fought with Israel:* According to Deut. 25.18 this was a sneak attack on the defenseless weak lagging at the rear, which showed that Amalekites had no fear of God, or conscience (see 1.17 n.). **9:** *Joshua,* Moses' attendant and eventual successor who led the Israelites in conquering the promised land. See 24.13; 33.11; Num. 11.28; 27.15–23; Deut. 1.38; ch 31. **10:** *Hur,* a public figure, associated again with Aaron in 24.14; possibly the Hur who was Bezalel's grandfather (31.2). **11:** *Whenever Moses held up his hand* [or "hands," v. 12], a gesture of uncertain meaning, perhaps a gesture of prayer (Pss. 28.2; 63.5; Lam. 2.19), a sign of triumph (see 14.8, translators' note; Deut. 32.27; Mic. 5.8), or in order to raise his staff and focus God's power against the enemy (7.20; 14.16; cf. Josh. 8.18–26). In any case, the victory is not won by military efforts alone. Rabbinic sources, sensitive to the impression that Moses magically controls the battle (he acts without divine command), state that his uplifted hands merely directed the Israelites' thoughts to God in heaven who thereupon gave them victory (*m. Rosh Hash.* 3.5; *Mek. Amalek* 1).

his hands remained steady until the sun set. [13] And Joshua
overwhelmed the people of Amalek[a] with the sword.
[14] Then the LORD said to Moses, "Inscribe this in a document
as a reminder, and read it aloud to Joshua: I will utterly blot
out the memory of Amalek from under heaven!" [15] And Moses
built an altar and named it Adonai-nissi.[b] [16] He said, "It means,
'Hand upon the throne[c] of the LORD!' The LORD will be at war
with Amalek throughout the ages."

YITRO יתרו

18 Jethro priest of Midian, Moses' father-in-law, heard all
that God had done for Moses and for Israel His people,
how the LORD had brought Israel out from Egypt. [2] So Jethro,
Moses' father-in-law, took Zipporah, Moses' wife, after she
had been sent home, [3] and her two sons—of whom one was
named Gershom, that is to say, "I have been a stranger[d] in a
foreign land"; [4] and the other was named Eliezer,[e] meaning,
"The God of my father was my help, and He delivered me from
the sword of Pharaoh." [5] Jethro, Moses' father-in-law, brought
Moses' sons and wife to him in the wilderness, where he was
encamped at the mountain of God. [6] He sent word to Moses,
"I, your father-in-law Jethro, am coming to you, with your wife
and her two sons." [7] Moses went out to meet his father-in-law;
he bowed low and kissed him; each asked after the other's welfare, and they went into the tent.
[8] Moses then recounted to his father-in-law everything that
the LORD had done to Pharaoh and to the Egyptians for Israel's
sake, all the hardships that had befallen them on the way,
and how the LORD had delivered them. [9] And Jethro rejoiced
over all the kindness that the LORD had shown Israel when He
delivered them from the Egyptians. [10] "Blessed be the LORD,"
Jethro said, "who delivered you from the Egyptians and from
Pharaoh, and who delivered the people from under the hand
of the Egyptians. [11] Now I know that the LORD is greater than

a Lit. "Amalek and his people." *b I.e., "The LORD is my banner."*
c Meaning of Heb. kes *uncertain.* *d Heb.* ger. *e Lit. "(My) God is help."*

14: This event, too, is to be memorialized (cf. 12.14, 26–27; 13.3, 8–9, 14–16; 16.32–34), both in writing and orally (cf. Deut. 25.17). This is the first time writing is mentioned among the Israelites. *Document,* a scroll or an inscription. Heb "sefer," commonly translated as "book" (as in Num. 21.14; Deut. 31.26), means any kind of written text—even one as brief as a letter, a legal document, or an inscription—whether written on a scroll or a hard surface such as stone or plaster. The same word is rendered *record* in 24.7 and 32.32ff. *I will utterly blot out,* cf. Num. 24.20. In Deut. 25.19 Israel is commanded to wipe out the Amalekites, apparently acting as God's agents. **15:** The event is also commemorated with a monument, in the shape of an altar. Named memorial altars are also mentioned in Gen. 33.20; 35.7; Josh. 22.26–27; Judg. 6.24. **16:** *Hand upon the throne of the LORD:* The anomalous Heb word rendered "throne" ("kes") may be a scribal error for the graphically similar "nes," "banner," that is, battle standard, which would make the connection to v. 15 clearer. This difficult phrase is possibly an oath formula meaning "I swear by the LORD's throne/banner."

18.1–27: The visit of Jethro. The fact that v. 3 seems unaware of 2.22, and that Moses' father-in-law was called Reuel in that episode (2.16–22, from J), suggests that this episode is drawn from a different source; the predominance of the name "God" ("'elohim") here and other details indicate that it is E.

18.1–12: Jethro's arrival. 1: *Jethro,* see 2.18 n. **2:** This source assumes that Zipporah and the children (2.21–22; 4.20) had been sent back from Egypt to Midian. **3–4:** Moses' two sons, and the name of one (Gershom), were mentioned in 2.21 and 4.20; this is the first we hear of Eliezer's name. *Delivered me from the sword of Pharaoh,* see 2.15. **5:** *At the mountain of God,* Sinai/Horeb (3.1). Since Israel does not reach Sinai until 19.2, this episode evidently took place afterwards. This is also implied by the context in Deut. 1.6–17 and by the presumption in Exod. 24.14b that the pre-Jethro judicial system is still in place, with Aaron and Hur substituting for Moses. Thus, this passage is not where it belongs chronologically. Talmudic sages recognized that the Torah sometimes narrates events out of their chronological sequence for literary or rhetorical purposes ("there is no earlier or later in the Torah;" see introductory comment to 25.1–31.17). Radak suggested that the Torah's aim was to juxtapose Jethro's visit with the attack of the Amalekites (17.8–16) so as to contrast the Midianites' friendliness with the Amalekites' enmity as a guide for future dealings with these two nations (Radak at Judg. 1.16; see 1 Sam. 15.5–7). **11:** *Now I know:* In a further fulfillment of the LORD's aim that all come to know His name and acknowledge Him (see 5.1–6.1 n.; 6.2 n.; 14.4; 15.3), Jethro recognizes His superiority, though

all gods, [a]yes, by the result of their very schemes against [the
people].”[-a] 12 And Jethro, Moses' father-in-law, brought a burnt
offering and sacrifices for God; and Aaron came with all the
elders of Israel to partake of the meal before God with Moses'
father-in-law.

13 Next day, Moses sat as magistrate among the people, while
the people stood about Moses from morning until evening.
14 But when Moses' father-in-law saw how much he had to do
for the people, he said, “What is this thing that you are doing to
the people? Why do you act[b] alone, while all the people stand
about you from morning until evening?” 15 Moses replied to his
father-in-law, “It is because the people come to me to inquire
of God. 16 When they have a dispute, it comes before me, and
I decide between one person and another, and I make known
the laws and teachings of God.”
17 But Moses' father-in-law said to him, “The thing you are
doing is not right; 18 you will surely wear yourself out, and these
people as well. For the task is too heavy for you; you cannot do
it alone. 19 Now listen to me. I will give you counsel, and God be
with you! You represent the people before God: you bring the
disputes before God, 20 and enjoin upon them the laws and the
teachings, and make known to them the way they are to go and
the practices they are to follow. 21 You shall also seek out from
among all the people capable men who fear God, trustworthy
men who spurn ill-gotten gain. Set these over them as chiefs
of thousands, hundreds, fifties, and tens, and 22 let them judge
the people at all times. Have them bring every major dispute
to you, but let them decide every minor dispute themselves.
Make it easier for yourself by letting them share the burden
with you. 23 If you do this—and God so commands you—you
will be able to bear up; and all these people too will go home
unwearied.”

a-a Meaning of Heb. uncertain. *b Lit. “sit” as magistrate; cf. v. 13.*

he does not renounce other gods (contrast Naaman in 2 Kings 5.15, 17). The Torah does not expect Gentiles to become monotheists (see Deut. 4.19), only to recognize the LORD's superiority and authority when He asserts it, as in the case of Egypt. The ideal of universal monotheism first appears in the later classical prophets (Jer. 16.19–20; Zech. 14.9). Neither the prophets nor Jewish tradition call for Gentiles, even monotheistic ones, to convert to Judaism, though later Jewish tradition—characteristically reading the Bible through the prism of the prophets—believed that Jethro did abandon idolatry (*Exod. Rab.* 1.32) and, going even further, became a Jew (*Tg. Ps.-J. Exod.* 18.6, 27; *Tanḥ.* Buber *Yitro,* 5). *Yes, by the result of ...,* i.e., “Yes, they perished as the result of ...” **12:** *A burnt offering and sacrifices:* A burnt offering was entirely burnt as a tribute to God on the altar (Lev. ch 1). The *sacrifice* (short for “sacrifice of well-being,” Lev. 3.1), in contrast, was partly burnt, but most of it was eaten by the donor and guests at a sacrificial meal (cf. 24.5, 9–11; 32.6; Deut. 12.27; 27.7).

18.13–27: The organization of a judiciary, also related (with variations) in Deut. 1.9–18. Remarkably, the judicial institution is ascribed to a priest of the Midianites, a nation with whom the Israelites later had hostile relations. **13:** *As magistrate,* better, “to judge” the people's disputes. **15:** *To inquire of God:* To ask Moses either to consult God for a verdict (cf. 22.8) or to render a verdict himself based on prior rulings by God (cf. the laws generated by Moses' continued consultation with God in Lev. 24.10–23; Num. 9.1–14; 15.32–36; chs 27, 36). The judicial role of the prophets Deborah and Samuel (Judg. 4.4–5; 1 Sam. 7.15–17) may also have involved oracular consultation of God. **19:** *And God be with you:* Jethro may be either praying or promising that if Moses follows his advice, God will grant him success (= “you will be able to bear up,” v. 23), or he may mean “and if God agrees” (= “and God so commands you,” v. 23). **19–22:** Jethro advises Moses to continue consulting God in cases without legal precedent, but to make the resulting *laws and ... teachings* (v. 20) public, to reduce the need for adjudication and enable him to delegate authority to officials who could judge most remaining cases, leaving only the difficult ones for him (cf. Deut. 17.8–13). **21:** Jethro defines the ideal qualities of character required of judges. *Fear God,* men of conscience (1.17 n.). *Trustworthy men,* or “men of truth.” *Spurn ill-gotten gain,* unsusceptible to bribes (23.8). In recounting this event in Deut. 1.13, 15, Moses lists intellectual qualifications. Maimonides, in defining the qualifications for judges, holds that the qualities of both lists, character as well as intellect, are required (*Hilkhot Sanh.* 2.7). *Chiefs of thousands, hundreds, fifties, and tens:* These are military ranks, consistent with the fact that the Israelites are organized as an army (12.41 n.) and have just fought a battle (17.8–16). Military officers sometimes held judicial responsibilities in the ancient Near East. **22:** *Major* (lit. “large”), explained in v. 26 as “difficult.” **23:** *And God so commands you,* i.e., authorizes you to follow this suggestion.

24 Moses heeded his father-in-law and did just as he had said.
25 Moses chose capable men out of all Israel, and appointed
them heads over the people—chiefs of thousands, hundreds,
fifties, and tens; 26 and they judged the people at all times: the
difficult matters they would bring to Moses, and all the minor
matters they would decide themselves. 27 Then Moses bade his
father-in-law farewell, and he went his way to his own land.

19 On the third new moon after the Israelites had gone
forth from the land of Egypt, on that very day, they entered the wilderness of Sinai. 2 Having journeyed from Rephidim, they entered the wilderness of Sinai and encamped in the
wilderness. Israel encamped there in front of the mountain,
3 and Moses went up to God. The LORD called to him from the
mountain, saying, "Thus shall you say to the house of Jacob
and declare to the children of Israel: 4 'You have seen what I did
to the Egyptians, how I bore you on eagles' wings and brought

27: According to Num. 10.29–32, from a different source, Moses sought to persuade Jethro to remain with the Israelites and share God's bounty with them in the promised land, but he declined.

Chs 19–24: The theophany, covenant, and laws at Sinai. The momentous encounter with God at Sinai is, for the Torah, the defining and seminal moment in Israel's relationship with God. Nevertheless, it is extraordinarily difficult to follow. It was transmitted in multiple versions that differed about the nature of the event and what God communicated to the people. The text clearly combines material from J, E, and P, but the relative paucity of identifying characteristics in several vv. has made it difficult to reach a consensus about which source they belong to. The combination of these sources, based on the redactor's perception that they are all true, resulted in significant tensions within the narrative. For example, according to 19.9, the theophany was to be auditory: The people would hear God speaking to Moses, although it is not clear what they would hear. According to v. 19 it was a dialogue (possibly consisting of vv. 20–25), but 20.1 says that it was the Decalogue. In contrast, in 19.11 God speaks of a visual rather than auditory theophany, although in v. 21 He warns against the people trying "to gaze." The account of Moses' writing and communicating the laws during the covenant ceremony in 24.3 and 7 apparently refers to the laws of 20.19–23.33 and seems unaware of the Decalogue; only in 24.12 does God summon him to receive the stone tablets, which played no role in the covenant just concluded (24.3–8). Moses' reports in 19.8b and 9b are redundant, as are God's two descents to the mountain (19.18a, 20a), while "Come up to the LORD" (24.1) is a non sequitur since Moses has already done so (20.18). Despite, or perhaps because of, these tensions, the narrative has great power, expressing the multifaceted, ambiguous nature of revelation. Remarkably, the theophany and giving of the law on Sinai does not play a significant role outside of the Torah except for (the very late) Neh. 9.13; by rabbinic times, it was regarded as one of the most—if not *the* most—central event in Jewish history.

19.1–25: The theophany. 1–2: The anomalous order (contrast 16.1) seems designed to foreground the date because of the historic significance of what will happen at Sinai. *The third new moon,* the new moon of Sivan, counting the new moon of Nisan as the first (12.2 n.). The Israelites will remain at Sinai for just short of a year (Num. 10.11). *The wilderness of Sinai,* the wilderness surrounding Mount Sinai, where Moses' mission had begun (see 3.1 and n.). The arrival there heralds the fulfillment of God's promise to Moses (3.12). **3–6:** God announces the purpose, first revealed in 6.6–7, toward which everything has led: Having redeemed Israel, as promised, He proposes a covenant relationship, as promised in 6.7. This relationship is modeled on ancient royal covenants, in which a citizenry accepted a king, and on suzerainty treaties, in which a weaker king accepted a more powerful one as his suzerain. The covenant proposed here goes beyond the one established with Israel's ancestors (Gen. chs 15, 17). Here, God imposes specific, detailed obligations and, in return, promises Israel an especially close relationship with Him. This covenant, along with the earlier one, became the basis on which Judaism defined its relationship with God. As befits the solemnity of the proposal, much of God's statement is in a quasi-poetic style, marked by parallelism and metaphors. According to the final form of the narrative, the terms of the covenant—which is formally established in 24.7–8—are the Decalogue (20.2–14) and the "Book of the Covenant" (20.19–23.33; see 24.7 n.). **3:** *House of Jacob,* the Israelites, Jacob's descendants (1.1–5). According to *Mek. Baḥodesh* 2, this phrase refers specifically to the women, while *the children of Israel* refers to the men; rabbinic interpretation finds different meanings in the parallel lines. **4:** God reminds Israel of what He has already done, since in the ancient Near East a suzerain's prior benefactions to a vassal, such as delivering him from enemies, are the vassal's motivation to accept a treaty with him (cf. 20.2–3). *You have seen:* The premise of the covenant is Israel's national experience. From biblical times on, Jewish belief has

you to Me. 5 Now then, if you will obey Me faithfully and keep
My covenant, you shall be My treasured possession among all
the peoples. Indeed, all the earth is Mine, 6 but you shall be
to Me a kingdom of priests and a holy nation.' These are the
words that you shall speak to the children of Israel."
7 Moses came and summoned the elders of the people and
put before them all that the LORD had commanded him. 8 All
the people answered as one, saying, "All that the LORD has spoken we will do!" And Moses brought back the people's words to
the LORD. 9 And the LORD said to Moses, "I will come to you in
a thick cloud, in order that the people may hear when I speak
with you and so trust you ever after." Then Moses reported the
people's words to the LORD, 10 and the LORD said to Moses, "Go
to the people and warn them to stay pure[a] today and tomorrow. Let them wash their clothes. 11 Let them be ready for the
third day; for on the third day the LORD will come down, in the
sight of all the people, on Mount Sinai. 12 You shall set bounds
for the people round about, saying, 'Beware of going up the
mountain or touching the border of it. Whoever touches the
mountain shall be put to death: 13 no hand shall touch him, but

a Cf. v. 15.

been based primarily on Jewish historical experience rather than on speculative thought. *On eagles' wings:* God led Israel swiftly and safely through the wilderness, like an eagle training its young to fly, catching them on its back when they tire or fall. Cf. Deut. 32.11–12. *To Me,* to Mount Sinai/Horeb, "the mountain of God." **5:** *Treasured possession,* Heb "segulah" is personal property: the private property of a king, as distinct from that used for public purposes (1 Chron. 29.3; Eccl. 2.8), or of economic dependents, such as a wife's nest egg or the "peculium" of a son or slave. One's personal stake in his private property gives it the connotation of something "treasured." Although God owns all things, if Israel accepts His covenant He will cherish Israel because of His personal relationship with them. A Hittite king described one of his vassals by this term, and an ancient Syrian royal seal describes the king as the servant, beloved, and treasure of the gods. **5b–6a:** Although all the (peoples of the) world are mine, if you obey My covenant it is you who shall be My *kingdom of priests and a holy nation:* enjoying the status of priests, close to God and sacrosanct (Deut. 26.19; 28.9; and esp. Isa. 61.6; 62.12; for "holy meaning sacrosanct and inviolable," see Jer. 2.3). Deuteronomy (Deut. 7.1–6; 14.2, 21) and later Jewish tradition converted this from a promise to a responsibility (noblesse oblige) requiring the entire Jewish people, not just the priests, to live by a code of holiness—God's commandments—and to serve as priests, bringing knowledge of Him to the world. **7:** *All that the LORD had commanded him,* in vv. 3–6. **8:** Although they have not yet heard the terms of the covenant, the people willingly and unanimously accept God's proposal and promise to obey Him, as they reconfirm twice in 24.3, 7. **8b–13:** Vv. 8b–9a and 9b–13 seem to be alternative versions of Moses' report to God and God's reply. According to 8b–9a, God replied by telling Moses, privately, that He would come and speak to Moses in the people's hearing in order to confirm Moses' credibility. According to vv. 9b–13 He told Moses to prepare the people for His coming appearance, but did not divulge its purpose (cf. 20.17). **9a:** *In order that the people may hear when I speak with you and so trust you ever after:* Once the people personally overhear God and Moses conversing (v. 19b), they will be convinced once and for all that Moses really is God's prophet. This conviction, first instilled in 4.1–9 and 14.31, is essential for their acceptance of all the rest of the Torah, which God communicates through Moses after the people decline to hear Him directly following the Decalogue (20.16). In classical Jewish thought, the fact that the entire nation witnessed God speaking to Moses is the definitive evidence that the Torah is from God (Judah Halevi, *Kuzari* 1:87–88; Maimonides, *Hilkhot Yesodei Hatorah* 8:1), though according to Saadia Gaon, this demonstration of the truth of Judaism was only a stopgap until the Jewish people could derive the same lesson by the slower process of reasoning (*Beliefs and Opinions,* Introductory Treatise, sec. 6). **9b–13:** God's descent to the mountain will turn it into a holy place and it will accordingly have to be safeguarded from impurity and encroachment by zones of increasingly restricted access, as the Tabernacle (a portable Mt. Sinai, as it were) would be. **10:** *Warn them to stay pure,* lit. "purify them," possibly meaning "have them purify themselves"—by laundering (cf. Lev. 11.25, 28, 40, etc.), abstaining from sexual relations (v. 15), and possibly by bathing as well (2 Sam. 11.2, 4). **11:** Purification the day before witnessing a manifestation of God's power is also prescribed in Num. 11.18; Josh. 3.5; cf. Josh. 7.13. Here an extra day is prescribed because of the momentousness of the event. *Come down,* from His dwelling-place in heaven. **12:** *Set bounds,* temporarily (see v. 13b). Cf. 3.5; Josh. 5.15. *Whoever touches the mountain shall be put to death,* like unauthorized persons who encroach upon the sanctuary (Num. 3.10, 38). **13:** Since violators become subject to death for touching the holy mountain (cf.

he shall be either stoned or shot; beast or man, he shall not
live.' When the ram's horn [a]sounds a long blast,[a] they may go
up on the mountain."

14 Moses came down from the mountain to the people and
warned the people to stay pure, and they washed their clothes.
15 And he said to the people, "Be ready for the third day: do not
go near a woman."

16 On the third day, as morning dawned, there was thunder,
and lightning, and a dense cloud upon the mountain, and a
very loud blast of the horn; and all the people who were in the
camp trembled. 17 Moses led the people out of the camp toward God, and they took their places at the foot of the mountain.
18 Now Mount Sinai was all in smoke, for the LORD had come
down upon it in fire; the smoke rose like the smoke of a kiln,
and the whole mountain[b] trembled violently. 19 The blare of the
horn grew louder and louder. As Moses spoke, God answered
him in thunder. 20 The LORD came down upon Mount Sinai,
on the top of the mountain, and the LORD called Moses to the
top of the mountain and Moses went up. 21 The LORD said to
Moses, "Go down, warn the people not to break through to
the LORD to gaze, lest many of them perish. 22 The priests also,
who come near the LORD, must stay pure, lest the LORD break
out against them." 23 But Moses said to the LORD, "The people
cannot come up to Mount Sinai, for You warned us saying, 'Set
bounds about the mountain and sanctify it.'" 24 So the LORD
said to him, "Go down, and come back together with Aaron;
but let not the priests or the people break through to come
up to the LORD, lest He break out against them." 25 And Moses
went down to the people and spoke to them.

a-a Meaning of Heb. uncertain.
b Some Hebrew manuscripts and the Greek read "all the people"; cf. v. 16.

Num. 4.15; 1 Chron. 13.10), they must be executed by methods that do not require touching them, lest they infect their executioners with its fatal holiness. *Shot,* by arrow. *When the ram's horn sounds a long blast, they may go up on the mountain:* It is never reported that this happened. The meaning is obscure. The v. could mean that a final, long blast of the trumpet will later indicate when God has left the mountain and it is safe for people to go up; alternately, it reflects a different tradition that allowed contact with the mountain. **15:** *Do not go near a woman:* Sexual relations produce ritual impurity, which disqualifies one from entering the sanctuary (Lev. 15.18; 1 Sam. 21.5–6). Some modern Jewish feminist exegesis, noting that this clause is clearly addressed to the men only and that it was not part of God's instructions in vv. 10–13, infers that not regarding women as part of the active community reflects Moses' own, male-centered, viewpoint, not God's. For a more inclusive view of women, see Deut. 29.10; 31.12; Neh. 8.2–3. **16:** *Thunder ... lightning ... dense cloud ...:* The arrival of God (v. 18) is heralded by these awesome forces of nature serving like a king's outrunners (2 Sam. 15.1; 1 Kings 1.5) and by a *loud blast of the horn.* See also 1 Kings 19.11–13; Hab. 3.3–5; Pss. 18.8–16; 68.9–10. Outside the Bible these phenomena also appear in theophanies, particularly of storm gods. In Israelite tradition, although the LORD is not merely a storm god, these motifs were taken over to describe the overwhelming power and majesty of the direct experience of the divine. **18:** *The LORD had come down upon it in fire,* see 3.2 n. *Like the smoke of a kiln,* cf. Gen. 19.28. **19:** *As Moses spoke, God answered him:* The Heb verbs are iterative, indicating that Moses kept speaking and God kept answering him; what the people overheard was a dialogue. Its contents are not specified (it cannot be the dialogue of vv. 20–24 since Moses conveyed its contents to the people [v. 25], and it cannot be the Decalogue since that is a monologue; in the present context, however, the redactor may have believed it was one of those). *In thunder,* in a thunderous voice; cf. Pss. 18.14; 29.3–9; Job 40.9. **21–24:** Further instructions to prevent the people from encroaching and dying. **21:** *Lest many of them perish,* see 3.6 n.; 33.20; cf. Num. 4.20; 1 Sam. 6.19. **22:** Even the priests *who come near the LORD* when performing their sacrificial duties (28.43; Ezek. 44.13) *must stay pure,* or "purify themselves," like the rest of the people. Although priests will later have access to the sanctuary, at the theophany they are restricted like the rest of the people. *Break out,* strike them down; cf. 2 Sam. 6.8. **23:** *Sanctify it,* treat it like a sanctuary, by the restrictions specified above. **24:** *Come back together with Aaron:* The summit of the mountain, like the Holy of Holies, is here accessible only to Moses (25.22; 26.33; Lev. 16.3). **25:** *Spoke to them:* He told them what God had said in vv. 21–24.

20 God spoke all these words,[a] saying:
2 I the LORD am your God who brought you out of the
land of Egypt, the house of bondage: 3 You shall have no other
gods besides Me.
4 You shall not make for yourself a sculptured image, or any
likeness of what is in the heavens above, or on the earth below,

a Tradition varies as to the division of the Commandments in vv. 2–14, and as to the numbering of the verses from 13 on.

20.1–14: The Decalogue. The Decalogue, Heb "'aseret hadevarim," lit. "the ten words," i.e., "dictums," "commandments" (see 34.28; Deut. 4.13; 10.4), is the initial stipulation of the covenant. The commandments are addressed directly to the people. No punishments are stated; obedience is motivated not by fear of punishment but by God's absolute authority and the people's desire to live in accordance with His will. The belief that God is the author of the laws is a distinctive feature of biblical law. Elsewhere in the ancient Near East the laws were believed to be the product of human minds, particularly the king. While Mesopotamian kings claimed to have learned the principles of truth and justice from the gods, they themselves turned those principles into specific laws. Implicit in this biblical view is that God is Israel's king, hence its legislator. This elevated the status of law beyond matters of practicality and endowed it with sanctity. Obedience to law—civil no less than moral and ritual law—became a religious duty; obedience made one holy and crimes were sins, a flouting of God's authority.

The items in the Decalogue are arranged in two groups. Duties to God come first. Each commandment in this group contains the phrase, "the LORD your God." The second group contains duties toward fellow humans, which are depicted as being of equal concern to God. The first five are accompanied by explanatory comments or exhortations. The remaining five, as widely recognized ethical requirements, need no such support. Exod. 34.28 and Deut. 4.13 and 10.4 all indicate that there are ten commandments, but do not clarify how they should be divided to reach that number; several approaches developed in antiquity and they continue in use today (the most prominent are listed in the chart on p. 141). The translation follows the view of Philo, Josephus, and some talmudic sources.

The Decalogue is repeated in Deut. 5.6–17 with a few variations, especially in the Sabbath commandment. Many believe that the variants between the Decalogue here and in Deut. ch 5 suggest that they both derived from an earlier, shorter version, though the exact form of that version, and its original use, are debated. It seems to have been well known, to judge from apparent allusions to it by prophets and psalmists (see Jer. 7.9 n.; Hos. 4.2 n.; Pss. 50.7 n., 50.18 n.; 81.10–11 n.). This may be due to the fact that it contains the initial stipulations of the covenant and concisely represents most of the categories of biblical law. Nevertheless, the Bible does not endow it with the iconic status that is sometimes accorded to it in modern times. **1:** The addressee is not specified. The present sequence of the narrative suggests that it was the people, as stated in Deut. 5.4 and 19, but according to Deut. 5.5 and, possibly, Exod. 20.15–18, God spoke only to Moses, who later communicated His words to the people. Talmudic exegesis resolves the inconsistency by explaining that the people heard the first two commandments (v. 2 and vv. 3–6 in this view), in which God speaks in the first person, directly from Him, while in the remainder, in which God is spoken of in the third person, the nation heard via Moses (*b. Mak.* 24a). **2–3:** The first commandment. **2:** *I the LORD am your God:* This v. lacks an imperative verb and is not itself a commandment but an introduction to the entire Decalogue. The LORD identifies Himself by name to solemnly indicate that His authority stands behind the following stipulations. His authority derives from His freeing Israel from bondage (cf. 19.4 n.). This v. also serves as the motive clause for the first commandment (v. 3), explaining that since the LORD alone freed Israel from Egypt, He alone is Israel's God, and the worship of other gods is prohibited (cf. Judg. 6.8–10; Ps. 81.9–11). This is a central doctrine of biblical religion, which is based on the historical experience of the Israelites (see 19.4 n.). The logic is that of covenants, which establish an exclusive relationship: A subject or vassal may have only one sovereign or suzerain, and ancient oaths of allegiance and treaties explicitly prohibit subjects and vassals from accepting another. As noted (19.4 n.), subjects entered into such relationships because of the past benefactions of the king or suzerain, such as delivering them from enemies. The covenant was thus an apt metaphor for Israel's exclusive relationship with YHVH because of the exodus. Although this v. lacks an imperative verb, and thus cannot be called a commandment, later Jewish tradition interpreted it as a command in itself requiring belief in God (Maimonides, *Hilkhot Yesodei Hatorah* 1:6; *Sefer Hamitsvot*, positive no. 1; Ramban) or belief that the LORD alone is God (Ibn Ezra). **3:** *You shall have no other gods:* This is not a theological statement denying the existence of other gods (such as Deut. 4.35–39) but a behavioral injunction ruling out worship of the other beings and objects known as gods (see 15.11 n.). This prohibition, banning the worship of all but one deity, was unique in the ancient Near Eastern world. Polytheism was inherently tolerant of the worship of many gods since no single god was believed to control all the phenomena of nature that are vital to human life. *Besides Me,* in addition to Me.

or in the waters under the earth. 5 You shall not bow down to
them or serve them. For I the LORD your God am an impassioned God, visiting the guilt of the parents upon the children,
upon the third and upon the fourth generations of those who
reject Me, 6 but showing kindness to the thousandth generation of those who love Me and keep My commandments.
7 You shall not [a]-swear falsely by-[a] the name of the LORD your
God; for the LORD will not clear one who swears falsely by His
name.
8 Remember the sabbath day and keep it holy. 9 Six days
you shall labor and do all your work, 10 but the seventh day is

a-a *Others "take in vain."*

Israelites tempted to worship other gods would not abandon the LORD but would worship others in addition to Him. **4–6:** The second commandment. **4:** *A sculptured image:* Only images made for worship (v. 5) are prohibited. Nonidolatrous statues of certain creatures were permitted, such as the cherubs (Exod. 25.18–20) and the oxen supporting the water tank in Solomon's Temple (1 Kings 7.25); see also Num. 21.8–9. *What is in the heavens above,* such as birds (Deut. 4.17), the sun, moon, and stars, or other members of God's heavenly retinue (see 15.11 n.). Not even an idol of the LORD is permitted. *On the earth below,* such as animals (Deut. 4.17–18a) or sacred trees (Exod. 34.13). *In the waters under the earth,* i.e., in oceans, lakes, and rivers. The surface of the earth is conceived as standing or floating on a huge body of water which surrounds it in the form of oceans and breaks through to the earth's surface in the form of lakes, springs, and rivers. For the reasons for this commandment, see vv. 19–20; Deut. 4.9–18. **5:** *An impassioned God:* This is a warning against provoking God's jealous indignation—the rage felt by one whose prerogatives are given to another (cf. Isa. 42.8; 48.11). God's reaction reflects His emotional tie with Israel, described metaphorically by the prophets as a marital bond (see 6.7 n.). Hence, worship of other gods is as repugnant as adultery (34.15–16; Ezek. ch 16) and God's response, like that of an aggrieved husband, is jealousy (see the use of this term ["k-n'"] in Prov. 6.34). In the biblical view, this is an aspect of His passionate involvement with human beings and no more a character flaw than is human jealousy over marital infidelity. But postbiblical commentators found the implications of divine jealousy troubling, and Maimonides interpreted the term as merely an anthropomorphism based on the necessity of borrowing terms from human experience to describe God based on His actions: "[In reality, His punitive actions] are in accordance with the guilt of those who are to be punished, and not the result of any emotion; for He is above all defect!" (*Guide of the Perplexed,* 1.54). *Visiting the guilt of the parents upon the children:* God does not punish the idolater alone, but his descendants as well, just as He rewards descendants for their ancestors' loyalty and obedience. This view of divine retribution as extending to descendants corresponds to the concept of family solidarity in ancient societies, especially those with a tribal background, like Israel. It is stated most starkly in 34.7 and Num. 14.18. Here, the phrases *of those who reject Me* and *of those who love Me* (v. 6) modify it to indicate that God punishes or rewards descendants for ancestral sins and virtues only if they act as their ancestors did (but contrast 34.7, where this phrase is absent). For outright rejection of transgenerational retribution, see Deut. 24.16 (forbidding human authorities to impose it) and Jer. 31.29–30; Ezek. 18.1–20 (declaring that God does not, or in the future will not, impose it). *Upon the third and ... fourth generations:* That is, upon grandchildren and great-grandchildren—the descendants the guilty may live long enough to see. This may indicate that the punishment of descendants is intended as a deterrent to, and punishment of, their ancestors, not a transfer of guilt to the descendants in their own right. *Those who reject Me:* A polytheistic Israelite would not literally reject the LORD but would worship Him together with other gods or, at worst, ignore Him, but since He demands total fidelity, worshipping another god alongside Him is tantamount to rejection. **6:** *Showing kindness,* better, "keeping faith" or "dealing faithfully." On Heb "ḥesed" see 15.13 n. This v. assures Israel, which is covenanted to God, that He will faithfully reciprocate its devotion and obedience. *To the thousandth generation,* forever. God's favor far exceeds His wrath, which extends only to the third and fourth generation. *Those who love Me,* those who are loyal to Me. In biblical Heb, "love" includes the loyalty of allies and of a vassal toward his suzerain (1 Sam. 18.1, 3; 20.17; 1 Kings 5.15). **7:** The third commandment. *Swear falsely by the name of the LORD:* Assertions in court, in public affairs, and even in ordinary conversation were often backed up with conditional self-curses that would take effect if the swearer's assertion were false or his promise unfulfilled. Typical formulations were: "By the life of the LORD, I will (or will not) ...," or, "May the LORD do such and such to me if I did (or if I didn't) ..." The swearer proved his sincerity by invoking punishment from God, who cannot be deceived or evaded. A false oath would show contempt for God by implying that the swearer does not fear His punishment. Cf. Lev. 19.12. *Will not clear,* will not leave unpunished. **8–11:** The fourth commandment. The first three prohibit acts of disrespect for

a sabbath of the Lord your God: you shall not do any work—
you, your son or daughter, your male or female slave, or your
cattle, or the stranger who is within your settlements. 11 For
in six days the Lord made heaven and earth and sea, and all
that is in them, and He rested on the seventh day; therefore the
Lord blessed the sabbath day and hallowed it.

God; this requires a positive act of honoring Him. This is the longest commandment in the Decalogue, indicating the sabbath's importance as one of the quintessential expressions of loyalty to God. **8:** *Sabbath,* See 16.23 n. *Keep it holy,* withdraw it from common use (by desisting from labor [v. 10]) and reserve it for a special purpose associated with God. Dedication to God was expressed by visits to sanctuaries and prophets (2 Kings 4.23; Isa. 1.13; 66.23), by special sacrifices and other activities in the Temple (Num. 28.9–10; Lev. 24.8), by the recitation of a special psalm for the day (Ps. 92), and by a joyous atmosphere (Hos. 2.13; Isa. 58.13; Lam. 2.6). **10:** *A sabbath of the Lord your God:* Since He observes the Sabbath (Gen. 2.2; Exod. 16.21–30) it must be used for His purposes, not one's own (cf. Isa. 58.13). *You shall not do any work,* defined by various biblical passages to include gathering food and fuel, kindling fire, agriculture, and business activities (16.23–30; 34.21; 35.3; Num. 15.32–36; Amos 8.5; Jer. 17.21–22; Neh. 13.15–21). The Rabbis defined more precisely what kinds of work fell under this prohibition, identifying thirty-nine categories (e.g., weaving, hammering, writing) based on the inference that the activities performed in constructing the Tabernacle—forbidden on the Sabbath—exemplified the definition of "work" (Exod. 31.13–17; 35.2; *m. Shab.* 7.2; *b. Shab.* 49b). *Your male or female slave:* This one day a week the servant is treated as the master's equal. *The stranger,* the resident alien (12.19 n., 43 n.). Cf. 23.12. The text reads lit. "your stranger," which implies that the resident alien was, at least in some cases, dependent on a specific individual. **11:** Keeping the Sabbath holy honors God by emulating His actions at the time of creation (Gen. 2.1–3; cf. Exod. 31.16–17). In place of the explanation found here of the origin of the Sabbath, agreeing with Priestly texts, the Decalogue in Deuteronomy states its purpose of providing rest to servants and cites the exodus as the reason for observing it (Deut. 5.14–15).

CHART OF THE DECALOGUE IN EXODUS

NUMBERING OF THE TEN COMMANDMENTS IN EXODUS 20.2–14

NJPS	MOST JEWISH TRADITION	ALTERNATIVE JEWISH TRADITION AND THIS TRANSLATION	VERSE NUMBERING IN OTHER BIBLES	EASTERN ORTHODOX, ANGLICAN, MOST PROTESTANT CHURCHES (= ALTERNATIVE JEWISH TRADITION)	ROMAN CATHOLIC AND LUTHERAN CHURCHES
Exod. 20.2	1	1	Exod. 20.2	1	1
20.3	2	1	20.3	1	1
20.4–6	2	2	20.4–6	2	1
20.7	3	3	20.7	3	2
20.8–11	4	4	20.8–11	4	3
20.12	5	5	20.12	5	4
20.13a	6	6	20.13	6	5
20.13b	7	7	20.14	7	6
20.13c	8	8	20.15	8	7
20.13d	9	9	20.16	9	8
20.14	10	10	20.17a	10	9
20.14	10	10	20.17b	10	10

12 Honor your father and your mother, that you may long endure on the land that the LORD your God is assigning to you.
13 You shall not murder.
You shall not commit adultery.
You shall not steal.
You shall not bear false witness against your neighbor.
14 You shall not covet your neighbor's house: you shall not
covet your neighbor's wife, or his male or female slave, or his
ox or his ass, or anything that is your neighbor's.

15 All the people witnessed the thunder and lightning, the
blare of the horn and the mountain smoking; and when the
people saw it, they fell back and stood at a distance. 16 "You
speak to us," they said to Moses, "and we will obey; but let not
God speak to us, lest we die." 17 Moses answered the people,
"Be not afraid; for God has come only in order to test you, and
in order that the fear of Him may be ever with you, so that you
do not go astray." 18 So the people remained at a distance, while
Moses approached the thick cloud where God was.

12: The fifth commandment. Honoring one's parents is a counterpart to the honor due God; it forms a bridge between duties toward God and toward humans. *Honor:* One aspect of this duty is respect, which includes obedience and forbids hitting, insulting and behaving disrespectfully toward them, and misappropriating their property (21.15, 17; Lev. 20.9; Deut. 27.16; Prov. 30.17). Another is caring for them when they are infirm, as recognized in the Talmud: "What is honoring? Providing them food and drink, clothing and covers, and taking them in and out" (*b. Kid.* 31b). *That you may long endure on the land:* This does not refer to personal longevity. Ancient Near Eastern legal documents make children's right to inherit their parents' property contingent on honoring them by providing and caring for them. Here God applies this condition on a national scale: The right of future generations of Israelites to inherit the land of Israel from their parents is contingent upon honoring them. **13:** The sixth through ninth commandments. *You shall not murder:* This refers to illicit killing. The King James Version's "thou shalt not kill" is too broad; it implies that even capital punishment and war are prohibited, whereas the Torah sometimes mandates these. *You shall not commit adultery:* In the Bible, adultery means voluntary sexual relations between a married or engaged woman and a man other than her husband or fiancé. It did not refer to the extramarital relations of a married man (in polygynous societies a wife might share her husband with other wives and did not have an exclusive right to him). The Torah views adultery as a sin against God (Gen. 20.6; 39.9; cf. Ps. 51.6; Prov. 2.7) and a capital crime (Lev. 20.10; Deut. 22.22–27). *You shall not steal:* Although *b. Sanh.* 86a, followed by some modern scholars, holds that this refers to stealing of persons, i.e., kidnapping (21.16), the plain sense is, as Ibn Ezra recognized, theft. *You shall not bear false witness:* This covers both false accusation and false testimony in court. False accusation is a means of depriving one's fellow of what belongs to him, as when the accuser falsely claims ownership of something in another's possession and the accused cannot disprove it (cf. 22.8). The penalty for false testimony is described in Deut. 19.16–21. **14:** *You shall not covet:* Some view this as an ethical exhortation to master the kinds of impulses that would lead to violation of the preceding commandments, but the Heb verb sometimes refers to having designs on a desired object, perhaps even to scheming or maneuvering to acquire it (see esp. 34.24). Hence, the sense could be "do not scheme to acquire ..." *Your neighbor's house,* that is, "household," which the second clause explicates as consisting of wife, servants, and livestock. In Deut. 5.18, which places the wife in the first clause and house, field, servants, and cattle in the second, "house" means dwelling. The wording in Exodus reflects conditions when the Israelites lived as nomadic herders without real estate (Gen. 12.5, 16; 26.14; Num. 16.30, 32; Deut. 11.6); Deut. refers to the kinds of property people will own after settlement in Canaan.

20.15–18: The people's response to the theophany. 15: Since the people do not refer to God's words but only to *the thunder and lightning,* etc. (cf. 19.16–19), Ramban infers that this scene took place before God spoke the Decalogue. **16:** Moses' office and authority as prophet are now made permanent at the people's request (cf. Deut. 5.19–28; 18.15–19). The circumstances explain why God continued to communicate to Israel through prophets rather than directly. *You speak to us,* anything further that God says. If this scene preceded the Decalogue, the people (who already know that God will proclaim laws [19.5]) mean that Moses should hear the Decalogue by himself and convey it to them. *Lest we die:* They fear that auditory contact with God may be as lethal as visual contact (3.6 n.; 19.21 n.). **17:** *In order to test you:* It is not clear what is tested. Another possible translation is "to give you an experience (of Him)," meaning that the theophany would give the people a vivid, sensory experience of God. This interpretation fits the rest of the v., *That the fear of Him may be ever with you, so that you do not go astray,* namely the experience would instill "fear of God," a deterrent to sin (1.17 n.; cf. Deut. 5.26). **18:** *Moses approached the thick cloud where God was:* to hear either the Decalogue or further instructions (20.19–23.33), depending on when this scene took place.

19 The LORD said to Moses:
Thus shall you say to the Israelites: You yourselves saw that
I spoke to you from the very heavens: 20 With Me, therefore,
you shall not make any gods of silver, nor shall you make for
yourselves any gods of gold. 21 Make for Me an altar of earth
and sacrifice on it your burnt offerings and your sacrifices of
well-being,[a] your sheep and your oxen; in every place where I
cause My name to be mentioned I will come to you and bless
you. 22 And if you make for Me an altar of stones, do not build it
of hewn stones; for by wielding your tool upon them you have

a Others "peace-offering." Meaning of shelamin *uncertain.*

20.19–23.33: The Book of the Covenant (or Covenant Code or Collection) lays out the terms of the covenant in detail, beginning with a law about idolatry and proper worship (20.19–23), followed by a series of civil and criminal laws (21.1–22.16) and then a collection of ethical and religious exhortations concluding with further laws about worship (22.17–23.19), and an epilogue containing promises of reward for fidelity and warnings about idolatry (23.20–33). These laws may reflect a settled society of farmers and herders in premonarchic times (since the highest official of whom they are aware is the chieftain, not the king; 22.27 n.). Like the laws of the Torah as a whole, they are not a complete, systematic code. Practical details of how to apply the law are rarely spelled out, and areas such as commerce, real estate, marriage, inheritance, and government are mentioned barely or not at all. Apparently only part of the existing laws have been selected, perhaps to illustrate certain ideal principles of justice and religion. Other areas and details of enforcement must have been governed by custom, courts, and administrative agencies. These details became the subject of the Oral Torah in rabbinic times, embodied in the Mishnah, Talmud, and halakhic midrashim. The Book of the Covenant (for this term, see Exod. 24.7, where it is translated as "the record of the covenant") constitutes the first of four major collections of law in the Torah. The others (in addition to the brief variant of the Book of the Covenant in 34.11–26) are the Priestly laws (primarily Exod. chs 25–40, most of Leviticus, and the laws in Numbers), the Holiness Collection (Lev. chs 17–26), and the Deuteronomic laws (Deut. 11.31–28.69). Unlike most narratives, these law collections were not blended by a redactor into a single, integrated whole but were left separate. The resolution of their discrepancies is a fundamental feature of rabbinic exegesis.

20.19–23: The altar. All of the Torah's law collections begin with laws contrasting forbidden, pagan means of worship with permitted ones at a proper place of worship (see also chs 25–31 in contrast to Exod. ch 32 [see introductory n. to 31.18–32.35]; Lev. ch 17; Deut. ch 12). **19–21:** Since Israel has seen that God communicates with them directly from heaven without the use of idols (which idolaters use to draw the gods close), they should not make idols to secure His Presence and blessing but instead build Him an altar, offer sacrifices, and invoke His name. Cf. the similar argument in Deut. 4.9–18. **19:** *I spoke to you from the very heavens:* This v. (probably from E, which distances God from human beings and avoids anthropomorphism) contradicts ch 19, according to which God came down onto Mount Sinai (19.3, 9, 11, 18, 20, 21, from J). The midrash reconciled the contradiction by inferring from Deut. 4.36 that God spoke from heaven and only the fire and His power were on earth; another view is that He lowered the heavens to the top of Mount Sinai (*Mek. Baḥodesh* 9; Rashi). **20:** *With Me, therefore, you shall not make any gods of silver, nor shall you make for yourselves any gods of gold,* to draw God close and secure His blessings (v. 21b). Idolatry assumes that the deity is somehow present in (though not limited to) its image where it is especially available to bless its worshippers. Israel is to eschew such means and instead follow the instructions in the next v. **21:** *In every place:* This law permits numerous places of sacrifice (Maimonides, *Sefer Hamitzvot,* positive commandment no. 20); contrast the later restriction of sacrifice to a single site in Deut. ch 12. *Where I cause My name to be mentioned:* The Heb is problematic; the original reading may have been "In every place where you invoke My name," as implied by the Peshitta, *Tg. Neofiti, Frg. Tg.,* and *Pirkei ʾAvot* 3.6. Invoking God's name refers to calling upon Him in worship. *I will come to you and bless you:* Altars, instead of idols, will serve as the locus and symbol of God's Presence, as does the altar in 24.4–8. **22:** *And if you make for Me an altar of stones:* An exception to the requirement that the altar be made of earth (v. 21); perhaps the clause has in mind locations where the soil is sandy and cannot be packed firmly, but where stones are available. *Do not build it of hewn stones; for by wielding your tool upon them you have profaned them:* The stones must be in their natural state, uncut. Cf. Deut. 27.5–6. The reason for the prohibition is uncertain. Rashbam suggests that it is to preclude the temptation to carve images on them, an explanation consistent with the idea that the altar symbolizes God's Presence. The Mishnah explains that "iron was created to shorten man's days [through its use in weapons], while the altar was created to lengthen man's days [by means of sacrifice]: what shortens may not rightly be lifted up against what lengthens" (*m. Mid.* 3:4). This v. served as the basis for the midrashic legend that Solomon's Temple was built with the assistance of the Shamir, a magical worm or

profaned them. 23 Do not ascend My altar by steps, that your
nakedness may not be exposed upon it.

MISHPATIM משפטים

21 These are the rules that you shall set before them:
2 When you acquire a Hebrew slave, he shall serve six
years; in the seventh year he shall go free, without payment.
3 If he came single, he shall leave single; if he had a wife, his
wife shall leave with him. 4 If his master gave him a wife, and
she has borne him children, the wife and her children shall
belong to the master, and he shall leave alone. 5 But if the slave
declares, "I love my master, and my wife and children: I do not
wish to go free," 6 his master shall take him before God.[a] He
shall be brought to the door or the doorpost, and his master
shall pierce his ear with an awl; and he shall then remain his
slave for life.

7 When a man sells his daughter as a slave, she shall not be
freed as male slaves are. 8 If she proves to be displeasing to
her master, who designated her for himself, he must let her be

a Others "to the judges."

mineral used to cut rocks (see e.g., *b. Sot.* 48b). **23:** *Do not ascend My altar by steps, that your nakedness may not be exposed upon it:* The altar must either be low or, if built on a platform, have a ramp rather than stairs to climb onto it, lest one's private parts be exposed beneath the skirtlike garments that were worn. According to the Priestly legislation, in the Tabernacle the priests were required to wear undergarments for this reason (28.42).

21.1–22.16: Civil and criminal laws to establish a just society, the purpose for which, according to Gen. 18.19, God chose Abraham and his descendants. The Torah's strong emphasis on law led to the important place that law and its study have in Judaism. The casuistic formulation of most of these laws ("if /when x happens, [then] y shall happen") is typical of all the ancient Near Eastern legal collections, and several laws are notably similar to their counterparts in those collections and later Arabic law, though they also display uniquely Israelite values, as in the treatment of murder and crimes against property and the concern for slaves and strangers. **21.1:** Teaching the laws to the entire people is practically unparalleled in the ancient world. See further, "Exodus and the Jewish Tradition" in the intro. to Exodus. **21.2–11:** These laws begin with limitations on servitude, a subject that connects with Israel's recent liberation from slavery. **2–6:** Manumission of indentured servants. Biblical law deals with two types of bondsmen: Israelite ("Hebrew"; see 1.15 n.) slaves, who are really indentured servants, and full, permanent slaves, who were foreigners. Hebrew slaves (v. 2) must be freed after six years unless they choose to remain with their masters (vv. 5–6; Deut. 15.12–18); lifelong slavery is in principle limited to foreigners (Lev. 25.39–55). Both types were domestic slaves living in their owners' homes (see 12.44 n.), not members of slave gangs working on plantations. Biblical law and ethical teachings require humane treatment of slaves, based on the shared humanity of master and servant (Job 31.13–15) and the Israelites' own experience as slaves (Deut. 5.15; 15.15; 16.12; 24.18, 22). *When you acquire a Hebrew slave:* An indigent Israelite might indenture himself or a member of his household to obtain financial support (see Lev. 25.39, 47), and a convicted thief who could not make restitution would be sold to raise the money to pay it (Exod. 22.2). Debtors and members of their households might also be seized to work off defaulted loans (2 Kings 4.1; Neh. 5.1–6); it is questionable whether the Torah permits this, but in any case the present law would have the effect of limiting debt servitude. *In the seventh year he shall go free,* so, too, Deut. 15.12. According to the Babylonian laws of Hammurabi (par. 117; in M. Roth, *Law Collections from Mesopotamia and Asia Minor,* p. 103 = *Context of Scripture* 2, p. 343), debt servants went free after three years. Lev. 25.10, 40–41 prescribe an entirely different system: All Hebrew slaves go free simultaneously in the jubilee year no matter how long they have served. **5:** The servant might become attached to his master or the family he has established in the master's household, or consider security in subservience preferable to the financial risks of independence. **6:** *Before God.... to the door or the doorpost,* either at a sanctuary near the master's home or before some symbol of God kept at the master's door. *Pierce his ear:* This may symbolize the servant's obligation to have his ear permanently open to hear his master's orders or (see Deut. 15.17) permanent attachment to the master's house. The midrash saw the ceremony as symbolic: The ear, which heard God say that Israelites are His servants and may not be sold into permanent servitude (Lev. 25.42), is punished for electing to remain a servant to a human master (*b. Kid.* 22b). *For life:* According to later rabbinic interpretation, for the rest of the master's life, unless a jubilee year (Lev. ch 25) comes first; even if the servant chooses to remain with the master, he does not remain beyond the jubilee (*Mek. Nezikin* 2). This reconciles Exod. ch 21 with Lev. ch 25. **7–11:** According to the parallel law in Deut. 15.12–18, females sold into slavery go free, like males, after

redeemed; he shall not have the right to sell her to outsiders, since he broke faith with her. 9 And if he designated her for his son, he shall deal with her as is the practice with free maidens. 10 If he marries another, he must not withhold from this one her food, her clothing, or her conjugal rights.[a] 11 If he fails her in these three ways, she shall go free, without payment.

12 He who fatally strikes a man shall be put to death. 13 If he did not do it by design, but it came about by an act of God, I will assign you a place to which he can flee.

14 When a man schemes against another and kills him treacherously, you shall take him from My very altar to be put to death.

15 He who strikes his father or his mother shall be put to death.

16 He who kidnaps a man—whether he has sold him or is still holding him—shall be put to death.

17 He who insults[b] his father or his mother shall be put to death.

18 When men quarrel and one strikes the other with stone or fist, and he does not die but has to take to his bed—19 if he then gets up and walks outdoors upon his staff, the assailant shall go unpunished, except that he must pay for his idleness and his cure.

20 When a man strikes his slave, male or female, with a rod, and he dies there and then,[c] he must be avenged. 21 But if he

a Or "ointments." *b Or "reviles."* *c Lit. "under his hand."*

six years. The present law may deal with a special case, that of a father selling his minor daughter for the purpose of marriage or concubinage in the purchaser's family. (Similar arrangements are known from the ancient Near East, where a poor father might arrange for his daughter's adoption by a well-to-do family in order to ensure a marriage for her.) Since the sale is for marriage, it is not terminated after six years, but the purchaser must meet certain conditions. If he reneges on these conditions (either those of v. 10 or those of vv. 8–10), she goes free. *Conjugal rights,* alternatively "ointments," or "lodging." **12–32:** Crimes against persons. **12–14:** Capital punishment for murder. Unlike ancient Near Eastern and Arabic law, the Bible does not permit compensation of the victim's family for economic loss instead of capital punishment (Num. 35.31). Human life is sacred and beyond economic value because human beings were created in the divine image (Gen. 1.26; 9.6). **13–14:** In tribal societies lacking strong central authority the kinship group is the primary defender of its members. When a person is killed a kinsman is obliged to "redeem" the blood by slaying the killer (2 Sam. 3.27–30). Such "blood-vengeance" was originally exacted even if the killing was accidental. This v. limits it to deliberate murder and allows the accidental killer to seek refuge from the victim's kin at an altar or perhaps other places of sanctuary until a court can determine whether he acted intentionally (see the development of this idea in Num. 35.9–34; Deut. 19.1–13; Josh. ch 20). Originally in the ancient world the innocent and guilty alike could claim sanctuary; this v. subjects the institution to a moral criterion. **15:** Obedience toward parents is considered the cornerstone of all order and authority, especially in a tribal, patriarchal society like ancient Israel. In the Laws of Hammurabi (par. 195; in Roth, *Law Collections,* p. 120 = *Context,* p. 348) a son who strikes his father is punished by cutting off his hand. The biblical law applies to both parents. The death penalty suggests that the Bible regards this crime as posing a severe danger to society. **16:** The primary purpose of kidnapping was to enslave the victim. See also Deut. 24.7, where some details differ. **17:** See 20.12 n. *Insults:* The Heb verb (lit. "treat lightly") has a wide range of meanings from "disrespect" to "revile, treat contemptuously, curse." The death penalty may be meant only rhetorically as a deterrent, like *in terrorem* provisions in some contracts, or modern laws that are enacted simply "to make a statement" (some believe the same applies to Deut. 21.18–21, see n.), though if the verb means "curse" it may be meant literally because of the potentially serious consequences that cursing was thought to entail. **18–19:** This law and the next provide a rule of thumb for assessing the killer's motive: immediate death from a fight or disciplinary beating is presumptive evidence of murderous intent and calls for capital punishment, but death following temporary recovery, and a lingering death, are not. *Idleness,* income lost during convalescence. *Cure:* From this clause the Rabbis determined that the Bible permits medical care and people should not refuse it on the grounds that their injury or illness is the will of God and that the cure must come from Him alone (*b. B. K.* 85a, and Rashi and Tosafot ad loc.). **20–21:** This law and vv. 26–27 protect slaves from extreme corporal punishment. They do not distinguish between Hebrew slaves and others. **21:** *Since he is the other's property:* That is, the slave is the master's property. This means either that the master was within his rights to

survives a day or two, he is not to be avenged, since he is the
other's property.
22 When men fight, and one of them pushes a pregnant
woman and a miscarriage results, but no other damage ensues,
the one responsible[a] shall be fined according as the woman's
husband may exact from him, the payment to be based on
reckoning.[b] 23 But if other damage ensues, the penalty shall be
life for life, 24 eye for eye, tooth for tooth, hand for hand, foot
for foot, 25 burn for burn, wound for wound, bruise for bruise.
26 When a man strikes the eye of his slave, male or female,
and destroys it, he shall let him go free on account of his eye.
27 If he knocks out the tooth of his slave, male or female, he
shall let him go free on account of his tooth.
28 When an ox gores a man or a woman to death, the ox shall
be stoned and its flesh shall not be eaten, but the owner of the
ox is not to be punished. 29 If, however, that ox has been in the
habit of goring, and its owner, though warned, has failed to
guard it, and it kills a man or a woman—the ox shall be stoned
and its owner, too, shall be put to death. 30 If ransom is laid
upon him, he must pay whatever is laid upon him to redeem
his life. 31 So, too, if it gores a minor, male or female, [the own-
er] shall be dealt with according to the same rule. 32 But if the
ox gores a slave, male or female, he shall pay thirty shekels of
silver to the master, and the ox shall be stoned.
33 When a man opens a pit, or digs a pit and does not cover
it, and an ox or an ass falls into it, 34 the one responsible for the

a Heb. "he." *b Others "as the judges determine."*

punish the slave corporally, or that (in addition to the slave's lingering death) his investment in the slave makes it unlikely that he would have intentionally killed him. **22:** *Other damage* to the woman. *Based on reckoning:* perhaps reckoning the age of the fetus, but both this translation and the alternative "as the judges determine" are questionable. Halakhic exegesis infers that, since the punishment is monetary rather than execution, the unborn fetus is not considered a living person and feticide is not murder (cf. 12–14 n.); hence, abortion is permitted when necessary to save the mother (Rashi and Yad Ramah to *b. Sanh.* 72b; see also Gen. 9.5–6 n.). **23–25:** *Life for life, eye for eye:* This is the "lex talionis," measure-for-measure punishment by which the law strives to make punishment for death or injury fit the crime perfectly. See Deut. 19.21 and esp. Lev. 24.17–21. It may not be an obligatory requirement (Num. 35.31 implies that for injuries other than death an indemnity could be accepted instead; Josephus, *Ant.* 4.280) but a limitation of vengeance: The punishment may not exceed the original injury (contrast Gen. 4.23). The Talmud considered the equitable application of talion impossible and, construing the law loosely, inferred that it requires the assailant to pay damages corresponding to the severity of the injury (*m. B. K.* 8.1; *b. B. K.* 83b–84a). In Mesopotamia, perpetrators were originally required to pay monetary indemnities; later, talion was imposed when the victim was a member of the upper class. Biblical law is the same for all classes. **28–32:** These laws have especially close parallels in Babylonian law (Laws of Eshnunna, pars. 53–55; Laws of Hammurabi pars. 250–252; in Roth, *Law Collections*, pp. 67, 128 = *Context of Scripture* 2, pp. 335, 350), suggesting that the Bible might have borrowed and revised them. **28:** *The ox shall be stoned:* Stoning, otherwise used only for humans, treats the ox as a criminal because it has killed a human (see Gen. 9.5). This and the avoidance of the ox's flesh express abhorrence at its taking of a human life. The owner is not punished because the accident was unpredictable. **29:** If the owner ignored warnings that the ox had previously gored, he may be executed for criminal negligence. The penalties in these vv. are not paralleled in Babylonian law, where nothing is done to the ox and the owner is only required to pay damages. V. 30 permits this, if the victim's family agrees, because the owner's responsibility was only indirect and unintentional (contrast Num. 35.31). **31:** *According to the same rule* apparently means that if the ox kills somebody's child, it is still the owner who is executed and not his child (cf. Deut. 24.16), as would apparently have been done as a form of talion under Babylonian law (cf. Laws of Hammurabi pars. 209–210, 229–230; in Roth, *Law Collections*, pp. 122, 125 = *Context* 2, pp. 348, 349). **32:** The anomalous prescription of monetary compensation for killing a human being is puzzling since v. 20 prescribes capital punishment for killing a slave and the stoning of the ox treats the slave's death like that of freemen (v. 28). Perhaps in this case the slave is a foreigner, and the master, acting in lieu of the slave's absent family, has agreed to accept a ransom as in v. 30. This case differs from v. 30 by setting a fixed amount for the ransom, perhaps because a slave has a market value (thirty silver shekels is the price of a slave in several documents from Nuzi).

21.33–22.16: Offenses against property. 21.34: *He ... shall keep the dead animal,* which has some

pit must make restitution; he shall pay the price to the owner,
but shall keep the dead animal.
35 When a man's ox injures his neighbor's ox and it dies, they
shall sell the live ox and divide its price; they shall also divide
the dead animal. 36 If, however, it is known that the ox was in
the habit of goring, and its owner has failed to guard it, he must
restore ox for ox, but shall keep the dead animal.
37[a] When a man steals an ox or a sheep, and slaughters it or
sells it, he shall pay five oxen for the ox, and four sheep for the
22 sheep.—1 If the thief is seized while tunneling,[b] and he
is beaten to death, there is no bloodguilt in his case. 2 If
the sun has risen on him, there is bloodguilt in that case.—
He[c] must make restitution; if he lacks the means, he shall be
sold for his theft. 3 But if what he stole—whether ox or ass or
sheep—is found alive in his possession, he shall pay double.
4 When a man lets his livestock loose to graze in another's
land, and so allows a field or a vineyard to be grazed bare, he
must make restitution for the impairment[d] of that field or vineyard.
5 When a fire is started and spreads to thorns, so that stacked,
standing, or growing[e] grain is consumed, he who started the
fire must make restitution.
6 When a man gives money or goods to another for safekeeping, and they are stolen from the man's house—if the thief
is caught, he shall pay double; 7 if the thief is not caught, the
owner of the house shall depose before God[f] that he has not
laid hands on the other's property. 8 In all charges of misappropriation—pertaining to an ox, an ass, a sheep, a garment, or
any other loss, whereof one party alleges, "This is it"—the case
of both parties shall come before God: he whom God declares
guilty shall pay double to the other.

a This constitutes chap. 22.1 in some editions.
b I.e., under a wall for housebreaking. *c I.e., the thief of 21.37.*
d Lit. "excellence." *e Lit. "field."* *f See note on 21.6.*

value. Thus the owner of the dead animal receives full restitution, but no more, and the person who dug the pit can recover some of his costs. **35–36:** If the goring was an unpredictable accident, both parties share in the loss, but if the owner of the goring ox was negligent, he must make full restitution. **37:** This law continues in 22.2b–3. It establishes the principle that a thief (whose action was direct, intentional, and intended for profit) owes the victim more than restitution. **22.1–2a:** These vv., set between hyphens, are a separate law about theft. It is not clear why it is interposed here rather than placed after v. 3. *There is no bloodguilt in his case,* i.e., if the circumstances are such that the homeowner has reason to fear for his or his family's life, such as where the thief is not visible to witnesses. But if he catches the thief in broad daylight, when the thief would presumably fear detection and not risk killing anybody, the homeowner is guilty of homicide. In the absence of danger to life, there is no right to kill a thief. Jer. 2.34 alludes to this law. The law would presumably apply in all such circumstances, but in its present location it seems to have in mind a burglar tunneling into a house to steal an animal. In multi-story homes, especially in villages, the ground floor often served as a stable (Deut. 22.2; 1 Sam. 28.24; *'Avot R. Nat.* 8, end; cf. the case of a tunneling goat thief reported in *b. Sanh.* 72a). **2b–3:** These vv. continue 21.37. *He shall be sold for his theft,* to raise funds to pay restitution and the fine. According to the Laws of Hammurabi, a thief who is unable to make restitution is executed (par. 8; in Roth, *Law Collections,* p. 82 = *Context* 2, p. 337). Mesopotamian law often prescribes death for property offenses (Laws of Hammurabi, pars. 6–13, 21–22; in Roth, *Law Collections,* pp. 82–85 = *Context* 2, pp. 337–38). Biblical law, which considers human life beyond economic value (vv. 12–14 n.), does not. **4–5:** Damaging another's field or crops. V. 4 continues the theme of theft. The owner of the livestock must make restitution, either by replacing the crop or by giving the owner another field. *For the impairment* [rather: "from the best part"] *of that field or vineyard:* Whatever the quality of the damaged field or crops, the damages are assessed as if they were of the highest quality. **5:** If a fire spreads accidentally, the one who started it must repay only the actual value of the loss. **6–14:** When property is lost or damaged while in another's care, liability depends on the degree of responsibility implicitly assumed by the bailee. The comments below list the four main cases, followed by comments on other matters. **6–7:** (a) In the case of small movables deposited for safekeeping, since the bailee is expected simply to keep them in his house without taking precautions beyond those he takes with his own property, if they are stolen he may clear himself with an oath (20.7 n.) that he did not misappropriate them.

[9] When a man gives to another an ass, an ox, a sheep or any
other animal to guard, and it dies or is injured or is carried off,
with no witness about, [10] an oath before the LORD shall decide
between the two of them that the one has not laid hands on
the property of the other; the owner must acquiesce, and no
restitution shall be made. [11] But if [the animal] was stolen from
him, he shall make restitution to its owner. [12] If it was torn by
beasts, he shall bring it as evidence; he need not replace what
has been torn by beasts.

[13] When a man borrows [an animal] from another and it dies
or is injured, its owner not being with it, he must make restitution. [14] If its owner was with it, no restitution need be made;
but if it was hired, he is entitled to the hire.

[15] If a man seduces a virgin for whom the bride-price has
not been paid,[a] and lies with her, he must make her his wife
by payment of a bride-price. [16] If her father refuses to give her
to him, he must still weigh out silver in accordance with the
bride-price for virgins.

[17] You shall not tolerate[b] a sorceress.

[18] Whoever lies with a beast shall be put to death.

[19] Whoever sacrifices to a god other than the LORD alone
shall be proscribed.[c]

[20] You shall not wrong a stranger or oppress him, for you
were strangers in the land of Egypt.

[21] You shall not ill-treat any widow or orphan. [22] If you do
mistreat them, I will heed their outcry as soon as they cry out

a So that she is unmarried; cf. Deut. 20.7; 22.23 ff.
b Lit. "let live." *c See Lev. 27.29.*

9–12: (b) But if he was asked to keep cattle, which roam in the field, extra precautions are expected and if they are stolen (v. 11) he is held negligent and must pay for the loss. If, however, the loss was unpreventable, he may establish this by oath (v. 10) or by producing the carcass (v. 12; cf. Gen. 31.39; Amos 3.12). **13–14a:** (c) If the bailee borrowed an animal for his own use, since all the benefit is his, he assumes liability for whatever causes its death or injury unless its owner was with it (presumably because the owner would then be expected to protect it). **14b:** This may introduce a fourth case: (d) where the bailee has hired the animal and any damage to it is covered by the fee. The Talmud identifies these four types of bailee as the unpaid and paid guardians, the borrower and the hirer, and holds that their different degrees of liability depend on the benefit each receives or expects from the arrangement (*m. B. M.* 7.8 and Gemara). **8:** This covers the case when, in these or other circumstances, a man claims to have identified his possessions among another's (such as the bailee's); the matter is to be decided by an oracle (*he whom God declares guilty*), such as the Urim and Thummim (28.29–30; cf. Josh. 7.14–18; 1 Sam. 14.37–42). **9:** *Carried off,* captured in war or a raid, as distinct from being stolen. **10:** *An oath before the LORD:* The use of the Tetragrammaton suggests that this law was drawn from a different source than vv. 7–8, which use "God." **13:** *And it dies or is injured,* rather, "and it is injured and dies" or "and it is injured or dies." **15:** *For whom the bride-price has not been paid:* Betrothal normally consisted of paying a bride-price to a girl's father (Gen. 34.12; Deut. 20.7). Seduction of an unbetrothed virgin diminishes her chances of marriage and her father may never receive the full bride-price (hence this law's inclusion with economic damages; if the girl is already betrothed the seduction counts as adultery, Deut. 22.23–27). Her seducer must make good on both losses. Contrast the case of rape, Deut. 22.28–29. **16:** *If her father refuses to give her to him:* According to later halakhah, the girl also has the right to refuse the marriage (*Mek. Nez.* 17).

22.17–23.19: Ethical and religious exhortations. 17: *Sorceress,* a practitioner of malevolent magic (usually a woman, as here, but male sorcerers are mentioned, and banned, in Deut. 18.10), who is punished severely because they were dangerous and antisocial. The Bible does not deny the efficacy of magic, but bans it as rebellion against God (Deut. 18.9–15). **18:** See Lev. 18.23; 20.15–16; Deut. 27.21. **19:** *Proscribed,* executed. This law applies only to Israelites; only they are subject to the first commandment (Exod. 20.3) and punished for violating it. Cf. 18.11 n.; Deut. 4.19–20; 32.8–9. (The Canaanites are to be punished for abominable rituals, such as child sacrifice [Lev. 18.24–29; Deut. 12.31; 20.18], not for idolatry per se.) **20–26:** Resident aliens (12.19 n., 43 n.), the poor, widows, and orphans are often mentioned together because, lacking social or family protection, they are vulnerable to exploitation. The duty of treating these groups fairly and compassionately is reiterated frequently (e.g., 20.10; 23.6, 9, 12; Lev. 19.33–34; 23.22; Deut. 1.16; 10.18–19; 24.17–22; 27.19). Concern for foreigners, not found in other ancient Near Eastern law collections, is here and often grounded in Israel's recalling its own experience as foreigners in

to Me, 23 and My anger shall blaze forth and I will put you to
the sword, and your own wives shall become widows and your
children orphans.
24 If you lend money to My people, to the poor among you,
do not act toward them as a creditor; exact no interest from
them. 25 If you take your neighbor's garment in pledge, you
must return it to him before the sun sets; 26 it is his only clothing, the sole covering for his skin. In what else shall he sleep?
Therefore, if he cries out to Me, I will pay heed, for I am compassionate.
27 You shall not revile God, nor put a curse upon a chieftain
among your people.
28 You shall not [a]put off the skimming of the first yield of
your vats.[-a] You shall give Me the first-born among your sons.
29 You shall do the same with your cattle and your flocks: seven
days it[b] shall remain with its mother; on the eighth day you
shall give it to Me.
30 You shall be holy people to Me: you must not eat flesh torn
by beasts in the field; you shall cast it to the dogs.

a-a Meaning of Heb. uncertain. *b I.e., the male first-born.*

Egypt. **22:** *I will heed their outcry,* cf. v. 25. God is the ultimate patron of the powerless and He will punish those who mistreat them. This warning may imply that human government was not well equipped to protect their rights and that God was their only recourse. Cf. Deut. 24.13, 15. **23:** Measure-for-measure punishment, a very common principle in the Bible. **24:** Charitable loans to countrymen who have fallen on hard times. Lending to them is a moral obligation and must be done without further increasing the borrower's poverty by requiring interest, which could be ruinous (rates of 20 to 50 percent were common in the short-term loans that typified the ancient Near East). Loans to non-resident foreigners were not subject to this rule; these people were normally businessmen. If they borrowed, it was for business and not to survive poverty. **25–26:** *Take ... in pledge,* rather, as noted by Rashi, "seize ... as collateral." Creditors might legally seize property from defaulting debtors to induce them to repay. The poorest debtors might have nothing left but the cloaks they slept in (Amos 2.8; Job 22.6). In such circumstances, the present law subordinates the creditor's right to repayment to the welfare of the debtor. See also Deut. 24.6, 10–13, 17. *You must return it to him before the sun sets* each day, to sleep in, and he must return it to you in the morning. **27:** *Revile,* cf. Lev. 24.10–16; Job 2.9. *Chieftain,* of a clan or tribe, the highest human civil authority prior to the monarchy. The two offenses covered by this v. are mentioned together in 1 Kings 21.10, 13, where "chieftain" is reasonably construed as applying to the king and the law is (falsely) enforced. **28–29:** The first fruits of the soil and first-born animals (13.2) must be given to God, thereby acknowledging Him as the source of the land's fertility and the true owner of its produce. **28:** The uncertain nouns refer to the first wine and oil, and possibly to the first grain as well (see also Num. 18.27; Deut. 22.9). *Give Me the first-born among your sons,* see 13.2, 12–13. Since no provision for redemption is mentioned here, some have taken this as a command to sacrifice all first-born sons, like first-born cattle (cf. the next v., *You shall do the same with your cattle ...*). It is true that some Israelites and neighbors in the region *voluntarily* sacrificed children in extreme situations (Judg. 11.29–40 n.; 2 Kings 3.26–27; Jer. 7.31; Ezek. 20.25 n.; Mic. 6.7 n.), a practice that the Bible condemns (e.g., Lev. 20.1–5; Deut. 12.31; Jer. 7.31). But a general requirement to sacrifice all first-born sons would have wiped them out, and it is inconceivable that a society in which firstborns were highly valued (4.22 n.) and were their fathers' chief heirs (Gen. 25.31–34; 27.18–29; Deut. 21.15–17; 2 Kings 3.27), would have had such a requirement. "Give me" here must be meant in a general way, with the specific meaning depending on the different types of firstborns, like "consecrate" and "is Mine" in 13.2 and "set apart" in 13.12 (for both vv., see v. 13; see also Num. 8.17). In the case of humans it may mean set aside for redemption, or perhaps for sacral duties (as in Num. 8.16–19; 1 Sam. 1.11; see Num. 3.11–13 n.). **29:** On first-born animals, see 13.2, 12–13. This is a humane law, respecting the mother-child relationship among animals. See also 23.19; Lev. 22.27–28; Deut. 22.6–7. **30:** *You shall be holy people to Me:* The prohibition of eating torn flesh, and the related one in Deut. 14.21, are addressed to priests in Lev. 22.8 and Ezek. 44.31. The present v. requires all Israelites to maintain a quasi-priestly level of holiness (cf. Lev. 19.2). *You must not eat flesh torn by beasts:* Only properly slaughtered animals may be eaten by Israelites. The word for "torn" (Heb "terefah") is the source of the postbiblical Heb term "taref" (in English [from Yiddish] "treif"), referring to any animal or food that does not conform to the Jewish dietary laws. Food that does conform is termed in postbiblical Heb "kasher" ("kosher" in Yiddish and English), which in the Bible meant more generally "fit," "proper," "right" (Esth. 8.5). The system of dietary laws as a whole is called "kashrut."

23 You must not carry false rumors; you shall not join hands with the guilty to act as a malicious witness: 2 You shall neither side with the mighty[a] to do wrong—you shall not give perverse testimony in a dispute so as to pervert it in favor of the mighty[a]— 3 nor shall you show deference to a poor man in his dispute.

4 When you encounter your enemy's ox or ass wandering, you must take it back to him.

5 When you see the ass of your enemy lying under its burden and would refrain from raising[b] it, you must nevertheless raise it with him.

6 You shall not subvert the rights of your needy in their disputes. 7 Keep far from a false charge; do not bring death on those who are innocent and in the right, for I will not acquit the wrongdoer. 8 Do not take bribes, for bribes blind the clear-sighted and upset the pleas of those who are in the right.

9 You shall not oppress a stranger, for you know the feelings of the stranger, having yourselves been strangers in the land of Egypt.

10 Six years you shall sow your land and gather in its yield; 11 but in the seventh you shall let it rest and lie fallow. Let the needy among your people eat of it, and what they leave let the wild beasts eat. You shall do the same with your vineyards and your olive groves.

12 Six days you shall do your work, but on the seventh day you shall cease from labor, in order that your ox and your ass may rest, and that your bondman and the stranger may be refreshed.

a Others "multitude."
b For this use of the verb ʿzb, cf. Neh. 3.8, 34. For the whole verse see Deut. 22.4.

23.1–3: These vv. and vv. 6–8, perhaps originally contiguous, concern judicial procedures. **1:** Cf. 20.13; Lev. 19.11, 16; Deut. 19.15–21. **2:** *So as to pervert it in favor of the mighty:* The ambiguity of the Heb permitted this to be construed by the rabbis as a separate, positive command meaning "follow the majority" in determining the law. As a jurisprudential principle this meant that, in general, judicial rulings and legal questions are to be decided not simply by invoking the literal interpretation of the Torah nor by invoking new revelations, but by flexible interpretation (loose construction) of the Torah, based on the circumstances, as determined by a majority of competent sages (*b. Ḥul.* 11a; *y. Sanh.* 4:2, p. 22a). **3:** This v. and Lev. 19.15 presume that the Bible's concern for the poor will be internalized, and warn against taking it to an unjust extreme: It is wrong to favor the powerful in a trial, and also wrong to favor the poor. **4–5:** One must assist others facing difficulty or possible economic loss (Deut. 22.1–4), even a personal enemy. **4:** *Ox or ass,* the usual beasts of burden; according to the halakhah the obligation applies to any animal (*m. B. K.* 5.7; *b. B. K.* 54b). *Wandering:* Since much of the population was engaged in herding and animals were used for transport, it was common to come upon strays (cf. 1 Sam. 9.3, 20). **5:** A pack animal might collapse or lose its balance under its load. The fastest way to raise it was for two people to lift the load simultaneously, one on each side of the animal. Talmudic sages hold that this commandment is meant to benefit the animal as well as its owner, citing it as the basis of the obligation to prevent animals from suffering (called "tzaʿar baʿalei ḥayim") (*b. B. M.* 32a-b). **6–8:** Another group of rules about judicial procedures. **6:** You must not rule unfairly against the poor in a trial. **7:** *The wrongdoer,* the judge or witness who causes the death of the innocent. **8:** *Bribes,* lit. "gifts" (Prov. 21.14; perhaps 17.8). This could refer to a payoff to influence judges (see Deut. 27.25; Isa. 5.23; Prov. 17.23) or to a fee charged by judges merely for hearing cases (Isa. 1.23; Mic. 3.11; cf. 7.3). *For bribes blind the clear-sighted,* see also Deut. 16.19. The explanation is in a poetic parallelistic style resembling that of wisdom literature; cf. Eccl. 7.7. *Upset the pleas of those who are in the right,* i.e., influence the judge against the claims of the innocent party. **9:** See 22.20. This v. may be repeated here because strangers, who lack kin to protect their rights, are at a disadvantage in courts composed of local or tribal leaders (cf. Ps. 127.5). **10–19:** The religious calendar and related requirements. Vv. 10–12 and 14–17 deal with requirements that occur at fixed intervals. **10–13:** The sabbatical fallow year (cf. Lev. 25.1–7, 20–22) and the Sabbath day. In line with the theme of vv. 1–9, only their social and humanitarian goals are stated here; Exod. 16.23; 20.10; Lev. 25.2, 4 describe both as "a sabbath of the LORD," indicating their religious significance. According to Deut. 15.1–3, debts were also canceled in the seventh year, possibly because debts commonly came due at harvest time, when farmers realized their income, and there would be no harvest in the seventh year. Neh. 10.32 mentions both fallowing and debt cancellation in the seventh year.

13 Be on guard concerning all that I have told you. Make no
mention of the names of other gods; they shall not be heard
on your lips.
14 Three times a year you shall hold a festival for Me: 15 You
shall observe the Feast of Unleavened Bread—eating unleavened bread for seven days as I have commanded you—at the
set time in the month[a] of Abib, for in it you went forth from
Egypt; and none shall appear before Me empty-handed; 16 and
the Feast of the Harvest, of the first fruits of your work, of what
you sow in the field; and the Feast of Ingathering at the end of
the year, when you gather in the results of your work from the
field. 17 Three times a year all your males shall appear before
the Sovereign, the LORD.

a *See note at 13.4.*

13: *Be on guard ... :* This may be intended as a conclusion to all the preceding laws and exhortations (21.1–23.12) or to the mostly negative commandments in 22.17–23.12 (or just 23.1–12) before turning to the laws of worship in vv. 14–19. Or, in view of its position between v. 12 and the next clause ("Make no mention ... "), it may mean: Remember not only the Sabbath, but all of the first four commandments (20.2–11) and have nothing to do with any other god. Note the similar sequence of commands in Lev. 19.3–4 followed by laws about worship in vv. 5–8 (cf. Exod. 34.17 followed by vv. 18–23). *Make no mention ... :* That is, do not invoke other gods in worship (cf. 20.21); instead, worship the LORD, as prescribed in vv. 14–19. This warning is especially pertinent to the agricultural festivals mentioned in those vv., since several non-Israelite deities mentioned in the Bible were closely associated with fertility. The Bible teaches that the LORD alone controls nature. **14–17:** A brief festival calendar. The festivals fall in the two agricultural seasons. The Feast of Unleavened Bread and the Feast of the Harvest, respectively, precede and follow the spring grain harvest, while the Feast of Ingathering occurs in the fall when the new grain and wine are stored away for the winter (see the essay, "Biblical Festivals and Fast Days," pp. 2025–34; see also 34.18–26; Lev. ch 23; Num. 9.1–14; chs 28–29; Deut. 16.1–17). This calendar contains no mention of the pesaḥ sacrifice (see 12.14–20 n.). **15:** In Jewish tradition *the Feast of Unleavened Bread* (see 12.14–20 n.), which commemorates the exodus, is called "zeman ḥerutenu," "the time of our freedom." The Bible does not connect it to the harvest, which follows the festival, but (as noted above, 12.14–20 n.) in the popular mind eating primitive, unleavened bread was possibly perceived as a type of abstinence expressing anxiety about the success of the coming harvest. *The month of Abib,* see 13.4 n. Lev. 23.6 gives a specific date, the fifteenth of the month. *As I have commanded you,* see 12.14–20, 34, 39. *None shall appear before Me empty-handed:* All must bring offerings. In Deut. 16.16–17 this obligation is explicitly applied to all three festivals. Here it is emphasized in connection with the Feast of Unleavened Bread since it falls when no new agricultural produce is ready. **16:** *The Feast of the Harvest,* also called "the day of the first fruits" (of the grain harvest, Num. 28.26) and "the Feast of Weeks" ("Shavu'ot," 34.22), because it is observed, according to Lev. 23.15–21 and Deut. 16.10, exactly seven weeks after the harvest begins. Because of the later tradition that this festival falls on the anniversary of the giving of the Torah, it is also known as "zeman matan toratenu," "the time when our Torah was given." Here it is an agricultural festival only, and is not connected to the previous Feast of Unleavened Bread by the counting of seven weeks, as it is in Lev. and Deut. *The Feast of Ingathering,* at the end of the summer, celebrates the gathering of the processed grain and new wine into storage for the coming year, the goal of all the preceding agricultural activities. It is known elsewhere as "the Feast of Booths" ("Sukkot," Lev. 23.34; Deut. 16.13), after the practice of dwelling in booths during the festival (Lev. 23.42; Neh. 8.14, 17), or simply "the Feast," meaning "the festival par excellence" (1 Kings 8.2, 65; Ezek. 45.25; Neh. 8.14). In Jewish tradition it is also called "zeman simḥatenu," "the time of our rejoicing," because it was the most joyous festival, coming at a time when the bounty of the harvest was manifest, and work in the fields was complete. *At the end of the year,* at the close of the agricultural year. Cf. 34.22. According to Lev. 23.34, 39 the festival begins on the fifteenth day of the seventh month (September-October). **17:** *All your males:* The obligation is limited to males, probably because pregnant and nursing women could not travel to distant sanctuaries. *Appear before ... the LORD,* visit a sanctuary in any of the country's temple cities (34.24; Deut. 31.11; 1 Sam. 1.22; Isa. 1.12). Deut. later limited this to a single sanctuary (Deut. 12.4–14; 16.2–7; cf. 2 Kings 23.21–23; 2 Chron. ch 30). This clause may originally have read "see the face of the LORD," meaning to visit Him and pay Him homage at His sanctuary. The reading was probably changed to "Appear before" to prevent the impression that God could literally be seen there. God's designation as *the Sovereign* ('adon, related to the divine name 'adonai; see also 34.23; cf. Zech. 14.16) emphasizes that He is Israel's king, and therefore His subjects must appear before Him regularly to acknowledge His sovereignty, just as subjects of a human suzerain were required to do.

18 You shall not offer the blood of My sacrifice with anything leavened; and the fat of My festal offering shall not be left lying until morning.

19 The choice first fruits of your soil you shall bring to the house of the LORD your God.

You shall not boil a kid in its mother's milk.

20 I am sending an angel before you to guard you on the way and to bring you to the place that I have made ready. 21 Pay heed to him and obey him. Do not defy him, for he will not pardon your offenses, since My Name is in him; 22 but if you obey him and do all that I say, I will be an enemy to your enemies and a foe to your foes.

23 When My angel goes before you and brings you to the Amorites, the Hittites, the Perizzites, the Canaanites, the Hivites, and the Jebusites, and I annihilate them, 24 you shall not bow down to their gods in worship or follow their practices, but shall tear them down and smash their pillars to bits. 25 You shall serve the LORD your God, and He will bless your bread

18–19: These rules about offerings and food seem to apply both year-round and also specifically to the festivals just mentioned. **18:** Leavened bread was forbidden with most sacrifices (12.8 n.), and several types of sacrifice must be consumed before morning (29.34; Lev. 7.15; 22.30), but 12.8, 10 apply both rules to the "pesaḥ" sacrifice in particular, as does 34.25b to the second rule. *The fat of* [the] *festal offering* refers to the fat on the entrails of sacrificial animals; it is burnt as part of the sacrifice, and eating it is forbidden (Lev. 3.17; 7.23, 25; 17.6). **19:** *First fruits,* see 22.28–29 n. Farmers probably brought first-fruit offerings at various times of the year, when each species was harvested, but in v. 16 the practice is mentioned particularly in connection with the Feast of the Harvest. See also Lev. 23.16–20; Num. 28.26; Deut. 26.1–11. *You shall not boil a kid in its mother's milk:* Meat boiled in sour milk ("leben") was probably considered a delicacy, as it is by Arabs, since it is tastier and more tender than meat boiled in water. As noted by Philo (*Virt.* 143–144), Ibn Ezra, and Rashbam, this law is similar to the rules that forbid acts of insensitivity against animals such as slaughtering cattle on the same day as their young, sacrificing cattle in their first week, and taking a mother bird along with her fledglings or her eggs (22.29; Lev. 22.27–28; Deut. 22.6–7). It is therefore likely that it also applied to lambs and calves, kids being mentioned only because goats were the most common type of cattle or because their meat is most in need of tenderizing and flavoring. Jewish law construes this rule broadly, forbidding cooking or eating any domestic cattle with the milk or milk products of any domestic cattle. Supplementary regulations also prohibited eating fowl or game with milk and required the use of separate utensils for milk and meat, including their products (Maimonides, *Hilkhot Ma'akhalot 'Asurot,* ch 9). The association of this rule with the festivals is probably due to the fact that meat was eaten infrequently but was part of festival meals. Since in Israel goats typically begin to give birth in the fall, the Feast of Ingathering was probably the one at which kids were typically eaten.

23.20–33: Conclusion. The Book of the Covenant (see 24.7) concludes with an epilogue containing promises of the reward for fidelity to the preceding laws. This is comparable to ancient Near Eastern treaties, which conclude with promises and warnings about the consequences of fidelity to or betrayal of the treaty, though here (contrast Lev. ch 26 and Deut. ch 28) only rewards are described. The final exhortations against idolatry (vv. 24, 32–33) hark back to the book's first law (20.19–20) and the begininning of the Decalogue (20.2–6). **20:** *Angel,* lit. "messenger," "emissary" (from God); see 3.2 n. and 12.23 n. and cf. Num. 20.16 (see translators' note). *To guard you,* cf. 14.19; 33.2; Gen. 24.7; 48.16. *The place that I have made ready,* the promised land. **21:** The angel will instruct and chastise the people on God's behalf since God's *Name is in him,* that is, God's Presence and authority are manifest in him (3.2 n.). Cf. Judg. 2.1–4. **22:** A classic expression of a treaty relationship in which the parties agree that the enemy of one is the enemy of the other. Cf. Gen. 12.3; Ps. 139.21–22. **24–26:** Cf. 34.11–17; Num. 33.52; Deut. 7.5, 25–26. Victors sometimes worshipped the gods of the nations they defeated, believing that they had abandoned their people to enable the victor to triumph (2 Chron. 25.14; cf. 1 Sam. 5.2). **24:** *Follow their practices,* i.e., (according to Deut. 12.2–4, 29–31), adapt Canaanite rituals for worshipping the LORD. Israel may not even take Canaanite idols as booty (2 Sam. 5.21) but must *tear them down:* At Hazor archeologists found a statue with its head deliberately chopped off in the stratum likely destroyed by the incoming Israelites. *Pillars,* stones erected for a cultic purpose, whether plain or engraved with images of a deity or its symbols. Apparently they were thought to embody the presence of a deity, either by representing it or serving as its residence (cf. Gen. 28.16–22; 2 Kings 3.2; 10.27). Sacrifices were offered to them and they were treated like idols. Although they were sometimes used in the worship of the LORD (Gen. 21.13; 28.16–22; 35.14; cf. Isa. 19.19; Hos. 3.4), Deut. 16.22 bans even such use because of their associations with idolatry. **25–26:** These are rewards typically promised in ancient treaties; see also Lev. 26.3–10; Deut. 11.13–15, 21; 28.1–13. **27:** *My terror,* a divinely induced panic, here reified as in Gen. 35.5; 1 Sam. 14.15; Isa. 24.17; Jer. 48.44. Alternatively, in view of the following verb, "My terror" might refer to God's fearsome aura, comparable to

and your water. And I will remove sickness from your midst. 26 No woman in your land shall miscarry or be barren. I will let you enjoy the full count of your days.

27 I will send forth My terror before you, and I will throw into panic all the people among whom you come, and I will make all your enemies turn tail[a] before you. 28 I will send a plague[b] ahead of you, and it shall drive out before you the Hivites, the Canaanites, and the Hittites. 29 I will not drive them out before you in a single year, lest the land become desolate and the wild beasts multiply to your hurt. 30 I will drive them out before you little by little, until you have increased and possess the land. 31 I will set your borders from the Sea of Reeds to the Sea of Philistia, and from the wilderness to the Euphrates; for I will deliver the inhabitants of the land into your hands, and you will drive them out before you. 32 You shall make no covenant with them and their gods. 33 They shall not remain in your land, lest they cause you to sin against Me; for you will serve their gods—and it will prove a snare to you.

24 Then He said to Moses, "Come up to the LORD, with Aaron, Nadab and Abihu, and seventy elders of Israel, and bow low from afar. 2 Moses alone shall come near the

a *Lit. "back."* *b* *Others "hornet"; meaning of Heb. uncertain.*

the fearsome aura of Mesopotamian gods and kings which overwhelms their enemies; cf. Isa. 2.10, 19, 21. *Throw into panic,* rather, "rout" (14.24; Deut. 7.23; Josh. 10.10; Judg. 4.15; 1 Sam. 7.10; Esth. 9.24). **28:** *Plague,* better, "hornets" or "wasps," meaning either that ferocious swarms of wasps will chase the Canaanites or that God will induce a panic or frenzy like that caused by wasps and cause the Canaanites to flee. **31:** Starting at a line running *from the Sea of Reeds* (here the Gulf of Eilat, 13.18 n.) *to the Sea of Philistia* (the Mediterranean off the coast of Philistia—roughly the Gaza Strip today), Israel's territory will extend *from the* (Sinai-Negev) *wilderness* in the south *to the Euphrates* in the northeast (see also Gen. 15.18; Deut. 1.7; 11.24; Josh. 1.4); other passages in the Torah place the northern boundary in Lebanon's Bekaa Valley in Lebanon (Num. 13.21; 34.8). *You will drive them out,* see also 33.2; 34.11 (cf. Lev. 18.25b, 28; Num. 33.52–55; Josh. 24.12, 18; Judg. 6.9). According to Deut. 7.2, 16; 20.15–18, however, the Canaanites are to be killed. Jewish exegesis resolves the inconsistency by holding that the Canaanites were given the option of fighting, emigrating, or remaining in the land as forced laborers, provided they accept the seven Noahide laws (Gen. 9.8–17 n.) (Maimonides, *Hilkhot Melakhim* 6.5). Historically speaking, there was probably no policy of either expulsion or extermination. Archeological evidence and passages such as Josh. 15.63; 16.10; 17.12–13; Judg. 1.19, 27–36; 1 Kings 9.20–21 indicate that Canaanites remained in the land. Driving out or killing the Canaanites are both probably late, theoretical reconstructions. **32:** *Covenant,* a treaty allowing the Canaanites or their idolatry to remain. **33:** *Lest they cause you to sin ...,* cf. 34.15–16; Deut. 7.3–4. According to Deut. 20.18 the danger is that the Canaanites would influence Israelites to adopt their abhorrent rites, such as child sacrifice and various occult practices (Deut. 12.31; 18.9–12). According to Genesis and Leviticus, God will expel the Canaanites because of immorality, occult practices, and child sacrifice (see Gen. 9.22–27; 15.16; 19.4–5; Lev. chs 18, 20).

24.1–18: The covenant ceremony. The covenant proposed in 19.4–6 is formally established when Moses reads its terms to the people in the course of a blood rite in which they ratify its terms, followed by a sacrificial meal for the leaders in the presence of God. The sequence of events is hard to follow because of the interweaving of conflicting versions of the narrative (see chs 19–24, introductory comment), though the ch as a whole is organized to suggest that different groups, according to their status, ascended the mountain to different levels. Vv. 1–2 (*Come up ...*) interrupt the preceding narrative, since 20.18 shows that Moses was already on the mountain when he received the laws of 20.19–23.33. The immediate sequel to that narrative is 24.3–8, followed by vv. 12–15a and 18b (from E). Vv. 1–2 and 9–11, in which Moses is called up to God, are the sequel to 19.25; they are from J, while 15b–18a—the sequel of 19.1–2—are from P. There are differences in detail between these groups of vv. In J, Moses is to be accompanied part way by the priests and elders (vv. 1–2, 9); in E he is apparently accompanied part way by Joshua (vv. 13–14; cf. 32.17) but leaves the elders, Aaron and Hur, behind; while in P (vv. 15b–18a) he seems not to be accompanied at any time. J does not tell of any lawgiving; to it the event at Sinai was a visual encounter with God, experienced in differing degrees by the people, the leaders, and Moses, and the covenant was established by a meal (24.1–2, 9–11; cf. 19.11, 18, 21). E, preserved more fully, tells of a primarily auditory experience, the establishment of the covenant by a blood rite and ratification of the "Book of the Covenant," and Moses' ascent to receive the tablets of the Decalogue (19.9, 16, 19; chs 20–23; 24.3–8, 12–15a). To P the event consisted primarily of Moses going up on the mountain to receive the instructions for constructing the Tabernacle (chs 25–31) in which God will dwell among the Israelites and give Moses laws, and where they will worship Him; He also gave Moses the "Pact" to put in the Ark (25.8, 22; 29.38–46; 31.18). **1–2:** The summons is answered, and this source is

LORD; but the others shall not come near, nor shall the people
come up with him."
3 Moses went and repeated to the people all the commands
of the LORD and all the rules; and all the people answered with
one voice, saying, "All the things that the LORD has commanded we will do!" 4 Moses then wrote down all the commands of
the LORD.

Early in the morning, he set up an altar at the foot of the
mountain, with twelve pillars for the twelve tribes of Israel.
5 He designated some young men among the Israelites, and
they offered burnt offerings and sacrificed bulls as offerings
of well-being to the LORD. 6 Moses took one part of the blood
and put it in basins, and the other part of the blood he dashed
against the altar. 7 Then he took the record of the covenant and
read it aloud to the people. And they said, "All that the LORD
has spoken [a]we will faithfully do!"[-a] 8 Moses took the blood
and dashed it on the people and said, "This is the blood of the
covenant that the LORD now makes with you concerning all
these commands."
9 Then Moses and Aaron, Nadab and Abihu, and seventy elders of Israel ascended; 10 and they saw the God of Israel: under
His feet there was the likeness of a pavement of sapphire, like
the very sky for purity. 11 Yet He did not raise His hand against
the leaders[b] of the Israelites; they beheld God, and they ate
and drank.
12 The LORD said to Moses, "Come up to Me on the mountain
and wait there, and I will give you the stone tablets with the

a-a Lit. "we will do and obey." *b Meaning of Heb.* ʾaṣilim *uncertain.*

continued in vv. 9–11. *Nadab and Abihu,* 6.23 n. For the various zones of permitted access, cf. 19.12, 24. **3:** *Repeated to the people,* as they had requested in 20.16 and as God had commanded in 21.1. After hearing the specific terms of the covenant, the people repeat the assent they first expressed in 19.8. *All the commands of the LORD,* 20.19–23.33. *All the people answered with one voice,* the redundant language emphasizes the unanimity of their assent, as in 19.8. *We will do,* as they promised in 20.16. **4:** Once the people assent to the terms of the covenant, Moses prepares for a ceremony formally establishing it. In the ceremony the *altar* (cf. 20.21) and *twelve pillars* will represent, respectively, God and Israel. These pillars are not cultic as in 23.24. **5:** *Young men,* perhaps the first-borns (Targum; Rashi) assisting Moses. Apparently E, like P (28.1), assumes that the Aaronide priestly order has not yet been established (J, in vv. 1, 9 and 19.22, assumes otherwise). Priests' assistants are called "young men" in 1 Sam. 2.13–18; 3.1. *Burnt offerings ... offerings of well-being,* 18.12 n. **6–8:** Dashing the blood on the altar and on the people (v. 8) joins God and Israel in the covenant. Here the altar represents God, as in 20.21; cf. Ps. 42.3 with 43.4; 1 Kings 8.22, 31, 54; 2 Kings 18.22; Isa. 19.19 (cf. Gen. 15.17, where a torch and smoking oven represent God in a covenant ceremony). Establishing a covenant by the parties sharing blood, each other's or that of an animal, is attested in many places; Aeschylus, for example, describes a covenant in which the parties dip their hands in the blood of a slaughtered animal (Aeschylus, *Seven Against Thebes,* 43–48). **7:** *Record,* i.e., a scroll or a stone inscription (cf. Deut. 27.2–3, 8), containing, apparently, 20.19–23.33. On the basis of this phrase, modern scholars call the legal collection of 20.19–23.33 "the Book of the Covenant" (cf. 17.14 n.). *We will faithfully do,* a hendiadys. The literal translation is "we will do and listen," and the midrash inferred from this that the people trusted God so thoroughly that they committed themselves to obeying all of His commands before they even heard their contents (*b. Shab.* 88a). **8:** *On the people,* perhaps, on the pillars representing the people. **9:** See v. 1. **10:** For this unique occasion the people's leaders and representatives are granted a visual experience of God. Later Jewish writers, who believed that God is not visible, held that the experience was not literally visual but was either an intellectual perception (Maimonides, *Guide,* 1.4) or a prophetic vision such as those in Isa. 6.1 and Ezek. ch 1 (Ibn Ezra). The Bible does not deny that God is visible, but the text is reticent about describing Him. By focusing on what was *under His feet,* it seems to suggest that the leaders did not see God directly but from below, through a transparent sapphire (or rather, lapis-lazuli) colored pavement. Cf. Ezek. 1.26–28; 10.1–2. This lapis-lazuli pavement is the floor of God's heavenly palace; it explains why the sky is blue. **11:** *He did not raise His hand:* Despite their seeing God, no harm befell them; see 3.6 n. *They ate and drank:* A well-attested way of celebrating the establishment of a covenant; see Gen. 26.28–30; 31.54; and the ceremony reaffirming the covenant in Deut. 27.1–8; cf. the parallelism in Obad. 1.7 and Ps. 41.10. In covenants between humans both parties share the meal. Here, one of the parties, God, does not eat, and Moses and the leaders merely eat in His Presence. **12:** In addition to the Book of the Covenant (v. 7), the Israelites would receive two tablets containing the Decalogue inscribed by God Himself (31.18; 32.16) as a

teachings and commandments which I have inscribed to instruct them." 13 So Moses and his attendant Joshua arose, and Moses ascended the mountain of God. 14 To the elders he had said, "Wait here for us until we return to you. You have Aaron and Hur with you; let anyone who has a legal matter approach them."

15 When Moses had ascended the mountain, the cloud covered the mountain. 16 The Presence of the LORD abode on Mount Sinai, and the cloud hid it for six days. On the seventh day He called to Moses from the midst of the cloud. 17 Now the Presence of the LORD appeared in the sight of the Israelites as a consuming fire on the top of the mountain. 18 Moses went inside the cloud and ascended the mountain; and Moses remained on the mountain forty days and forty nights.

TERUMAH תרומה

25 The LORD spoke to Moses, saying: 2 Tell the Israelite people to bring Me gifts; you shall accept gifts for Me from every person whose heart so moves him. 3 And these are

monument to their revelation at Sinai. Stone was normally used only for permanent inscriptions, such as royal and ceremonial inscriptions, boundary inscriptions, and treaties. The tablets may have resembled a square stone tablet containing a 7th-century BCE Aramaic decree. Two such tablets, 15 or 16 inches square and inscribed on both sides (like the Decalogue, 32.16), could have contained the entire Decalogue. This shape is consistent with Jewish tradition and early Christian art, which conceived of the tablets as rectangular. The tablets with curved tops, familiar today, reflect later Roman practice, and were first introduced in Christian art around the 11th century. *With the teachings and commandments,* according to 34.28, the Decalogue. The Heb can also be construed as *"and* the teachings and commandments," which midrashic exegesis took to mean the rest of the written Torah (or of the entire Bible) plus the Oral Torah; in other words, all were given to Moses at Mount Sinai *(b. Ber.* 5a; *Lekaḥ Tov; Midrash HaGadol).* **13:** *Joshua* (17.9 n.) apparently accompanied Moses part way (see v. 14; cf. 32.17). **14:** *Aaron and Hur,* 17.10 n. They are to perform Moses' duties in his absence (18.16a). **15:** *The cloud,* in which God's Presence is manifest; see 13.21 n., 22 n. **16:** *The Presence of the LORD,* 16.6–7 n. This *Presence* is the main manifestation of the divine in Priestly thought. *Abode on Mount Sinai:* The main thrust of the instructions in chs 25–32 is the construction of the Tabernacle (Heb "mishkan," lit. "abode") to which God will transfer His abode (40.34–38) and which will accompany Israel; see 25.8, where "dwell" should be rendered "abide" to indicate that it is the same Heb verb (sh-kn) as here. The Tabernacle, in other words, is essentially a portable Mount Sinai, the locus of God's presence. **17:** On the appearance of God's Presence, see 16.6–7 n. **18:** Cf. 34.28. The tradition that Moses was on Mt. Sinai for forty days and nights probably helped to facilitate the idea that the entire Torah was revealed to him there; forty days is much too long for the revelation of the Decalogue or even the entire Book of the Covenant.

25.1–31.17: Instructions for building the Tabernacle (see diagram, p. 156) **and inaugurating the priesthood.** The sanctuary will enable God to abide among the Israelites, and will be the place from which He issues commands for Israel (25.22 n.). It will also be the place of sacrificial worship (v. 30; 29.38–42; Lev. chs 1–7), where the priests officiate daily (29.9–12, 21, 29). Its main purpose, however, is for the benefit of Israel, that they may experience God's guiding presence, and not for the benefit of God, who has no need for sacrifice (see also 29.42b–46 n.). In contrast, an important purpose of sanctuaries in polytheistic religions was to serve as places where worshippers feed the gods. Like Mount Sinai (19.9b–13 n.), the sanctuary will have three carefully delimited zones of holiness and restricted access. They are, in descending order of holiness: (a) the "Holy of Holies," where the Ark and Tablets of the Covenant are kept, (b) its antechamber, "the Holy Place"—both of these inside the Tent of Meeting, the Tabernacle proper—and (c) the surrounding courtyard. Nonpriests will be admitted only to the courtyard (c); the Holy Place (b) will be accessible only to priests and Moses; and the Holy of Holies (a) only to the High Priest on the Day of Atonement (Lev. 16.2; whether Moses may enter the Holy of Holies is unclear; see below, 25.22 n.). In all cases, access will be limited to those who are ritually pure (cf. Lev. 12.4; Num. 5.3; 2 Chron. 23.19). These restrictions will protect the Ark, above which God's Presence is situated (25.22 n.), from impurity so that the Tabernacle will remain fit for His Presence (Lev. 15.31; 20.3).

The materials used in constructing the Tabernacle, its paraphernalia, and the priestly vestments reflect its varying levels of holiness: the closer to the Ark and the Holy of Holies, the more precious the materials. For example, all the furniture in the Tent of Meeting is made of gold or wood overlaid with gold, while the altar and laver outside in the courtyard are overlaid or made with bronze; the fabric directly covering the Tent of Meeting is made of fine twisted linen and blue, purple, and crimson yarns, while the layers of fabric above that one are made of less precious fabrics. The outer vestments of Aaron, who ministers inside the

the gifts that you shall accept from them: gold, silver, and copper; 4 blue, purple, and crimson yarns, fine linen, goats' hair;
5 tanned ram skins,[a] dolphin[b] skins, and acacia wood; 6 oil for
lighting, spices for the anointing oil and for the aromatic incense; 7 lapis lazuli[c] and other stones for setting, for the ephod

a Others "rams' skins dyed red."
b Or "dugong"; meaning of Hebrew taḥash *uncertain.*
c Cf. Gen. 2.12 and note.

Tent, are made of gold thread, blue, purple, and crimson yarns and fine twisted linen, while the garments of the other priests, who officiate only in the courtyard, are made mostly of linen.

The instructions for the Tabernacle fall into two main sections: The Tabernacle structure and its contents (25.10–27.19) and its activities (27.20–30.38). These are preceded by an introduction (25.1–9) and followed by two paragraphs dealing with the builders of the Tabernacle (31.1–11) and suspending its construction on Sabbaths (31.12–17). These instructions, and the narrative of their implementation in chs 35–40, are drawn from the Priestly source (P), with some additions from the Holiness Collection (H; see comments on Lev. chs 17–26). In many respects they echo the Priestly account of creation in Gen. 1.1–2.4a: The instructions are divided into seven separate divine commands, culminating in the Sabbath (see 25.1; 30.11, 17, 22, 34; 31.1, 12), the lampstand holds seven candles (25.37), Aaron wears seven sacral vestments (28.1–39), the account of the building of the Tabernacle culminates in several allusions to the creation account (compare 39.32 to Gen. 2.1, 3; 39.43 to Gen. 1.31; and 40.33 to Gen. 2.2), and the Tabernacle is completed on New Year's day (40.17). See nn. on 39.32, 43; 40.16, 33.

The Priestly Tabernacle instructions are an unexpected sequel to 24.12–18, according to which Moses was summoned to receive the stone tablets (24.12, E), which the present order of the text delays for seven chs until 31.18. In the present sequence it seems that God's first order of business was to arrange for the housing of the tablets (the role of the Tabernacle according to 25.10–16 n.; 38.21). Rashi, invoking the talmudic dictum that " there is no earlier or later in the Torah" (18.5 n.), holds that the Tabernacle instructions were actually not given until after the entire golden calf episode was concluded (Rashi at 31.18, following *Tanḥ. Ki Tissa* 31). For a likely reason for the present sequence, see the introductory comments to 31.18–34.35. To modern readers, the quantity of detail in this section and

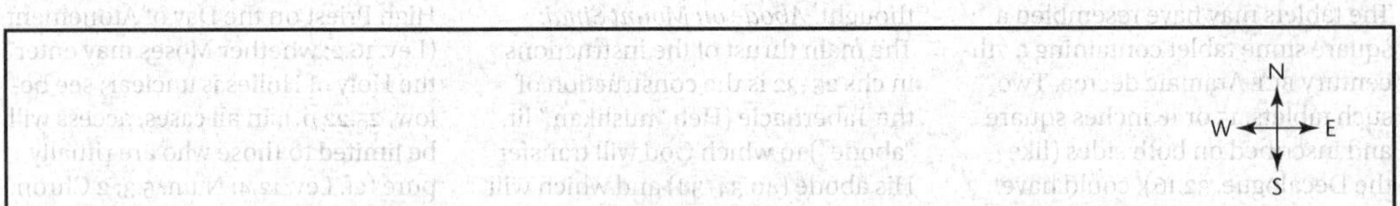

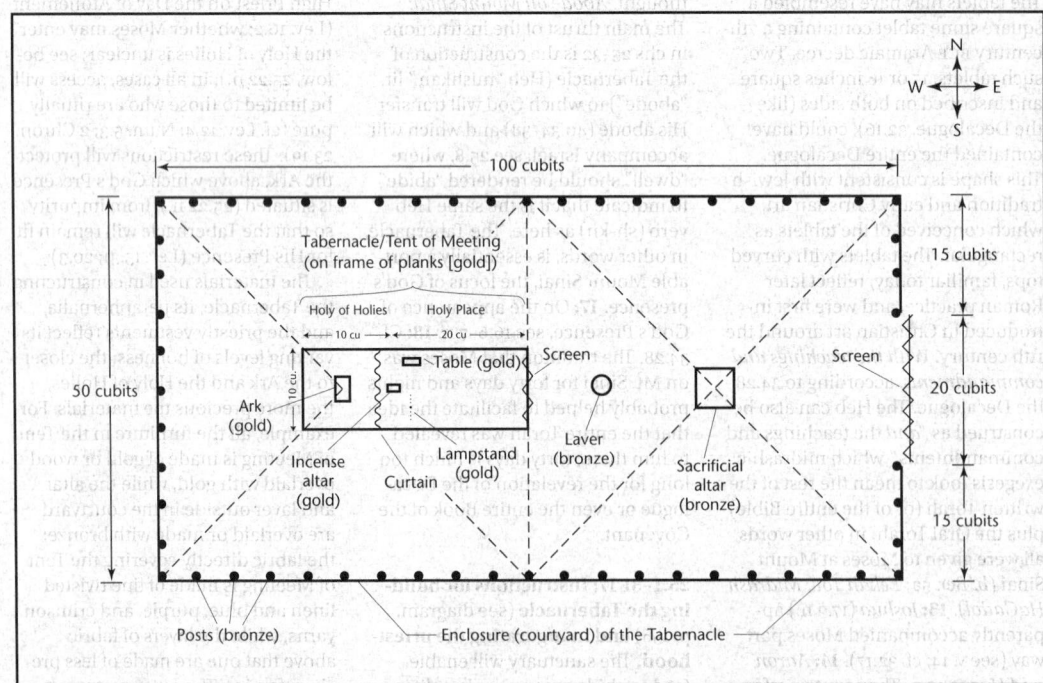

The structure of the Tabernacle

and for the breastpiece. 8 And let them make Me a sanctuary
that I may dwell among them. 9 Exactly as I show you—the pattern of the Tabernacle and the pattern of all its furnishings—so
shall you make it.
10 They shall make an ark of acacia wood, two and a half
cubits long, a cubit and a half wide, and a cubit and a half

much of the end of Exodus, which repeats these commands with minor variations in describing their execution, seems excessive. The explanation is found in 25.8, "And let them make Me a sanctuary that I may dwell among them." The indwelling of God, along with the blessing and protection that this offers, is crucial for the well-being of the community; thus it is crucial to construct a "house" to exact divine specifications. Scholars debate the existence of the Tabernacle. Some believe that some form of the First Temple is being described, and that it was historically retrojected into the period of the wanderings to give it legitimacy. Others note that aspects of the Tabernacle's architecture are paralleled in second millennium Egypt and Syria (Mari) and that portable shrines are attested among Arab tribes, and suggest that at least in broad strokes, the Tabernacle here reflects a recollection of a premonarchic sanctuary, perhaps one that antedates the settlement of the Israelites in Canaan.

25.1–9: Introduction. 1: *The Lord spoke to Moses,* while he was on Mount Sinai (24.18). For the Priestly author, the instructions for the Tabernacle, rather than laws, are given on Sinai. **2:** *Gifts ... from every person whose heart so moves him:* The Tabernacle is to be built entirely of voluntary gifts from the entire community. **3:** *Gold, silver, and copper,* for the Tabernacle paraphernalia and the priestly vestments. The metal of which each object is made will depend on its proximity to the Holy of Holies. *Copper,* more likely bronze. **4–5:** *Blue, purple, and crimson yarns, fine linen, goats' hair, tanned ram skins, dolphin skins,* the finest fabrics, for the Tabernacle curtains, hangings, and covers, and the priests' vestments. As with the metals, these are listed in descending order of quality, and the material of which an item is made depends on its proximity to the Holy of Holies. *Blue, purple,* bluish and reddish-purple colors manufactured from fluid obtained from the murex snails found in abundance along the Mediterranean coast north of Acco, also called Acre (the ancient name of the region, "Phoenicia," is related to Gk "phoinix," "purple," "crimson"). *Dolphin skins,* more likely, dyed sheep or goat leather. *Acacia wood,* for the frame of the Tabernacle, its furniture and carrying-poles. **8:** *Sanctuary:* The sanctuary is referred to by three main terms, each expressing different aspects of it: "mikdash" ("sanctuary"), lit. "holy place," "sanctum," referring to its sacred dimension; "mishkan" ("Tabernacle"), lit. "abode," referring to it as God's dwelling (v. 9 and frequently); and "ʾohel moʿed" ("Tent of Meeting"), referring to it as an oracle site, the place where God would communicate with Moses (29.42–43; 30.6, 36; cf. 33.7–11; 25.22 n.; cf. 29.45–46 n.). "Sanctuary" refers to the entire compound described below—the covered structure and the courtyard surrounding it. "Tabernacle" and "Tent of Meeting" sometimes refer to the entire compound and at other times only the covered structure (see also 26.1; 27.19). *That I may dwell among them,* rather, "that I may abide among them," the same verb as that used in 24.16, "the Presence of the Lord abode on Mount Sinai." This verb and the Heb word for Tabernacle ("mishkan"; see above) are from the same root, as is "Shekhinah," a term for the divine Presence in later Jewish tradition. **9:** God showed Moses either "blueprints," pictures, or a model of the Tabernacle. This information is repeated in connection with the table and the lampstand, the Tabernacle structure, and the sacrificial altar and its utensils (v. 40; 26.30; 27.8; Num. 8.4; cf. 1 Chron. 28.11–19; Ezek. chs 40–42). The Tabernacle is not to be a product of human creativity but must conform exactly to divine specifications ("One cannot approach God except by [the ways that] He commands" [Judah Halevi, *Kuzari* 3.23; cf. 1.79, 98, 99]).

25.10–27.19: The Tabernacle structure and its contents. 25.10–49: The furnishings of the building. The furnishings of both chambers of the Tabernacle building—the Holy of Holies and the Holy Place—are to be of solid gold or overlaid with gold. **10–16: The Ark.** The instructions begin with the Ark (Heb "ʾaron," lit. "chest"). The Ark will hold the "Pact," the two tablets containing the Decalogue (31.18). For that reason it will be placed in the innermost chamber of the Tabernacle, the "Holy of Holies" (meaning "the holiest" chamber; 26.31–44). As the container of the Pact, the Ark is the heart of the Tabernacle, which is called "the Tabernacle [lit. the Abode] of the Pact" in 38.21, as if the main purpose of the Tabernacle is to serve as the housing for the Pact (Rashbam at v. 10). It is significant that the heart of the sanctuary is a symbol of God's law, rather than an image as was the case in non-Israelite sanctuaries. In postbiblical Judaism the Torah scroll, housed in the Holy Ark (see below) and taken out to be carried in procession around the synagogue, came to symbolize God's Presence, and the study of the Torah's laws and teachings became one of the primary means of access to Him. (Nowadays the term "Ark," more fully "Holy Ark" ["ʾaron kodesh"], is used of the wall cabinet that houses the Torah scrolls in the synagogue.) **10:** *Cubits:* A cubit is the distance from the elbow to the tip of the middle finger, approximately 18 inches. The Ark's dimensions were 1.1 m by

high. 11 Overlay it with pure gold—overlay it inside and out—and make upon it a gold molding round about. 12 Cast four gold rings for it, to be attached to its four feet, two rings on one of its side walls and two on the other. 13 Make poles of acacia wood and overlay them with gold; 14 then insert the poles into the rings on the side walls of the ark, for carrying the ark. 15 The poles shall remain in the rings of the ark: they shall not be removed from it. 16 And deposit in the Ark [the tablets of] the Pact which I will give you.

17 You shall make a cover of pure gold, two and a half cubits long and a cubit and a half wide. 18 Make two cherubim of gold—make them of hammered work—at the two ends of the cover. 19 Make one cherub at one end and the other cherub at the other end; of one piece with the cover shall you make the cherubim at its two ends. 20 The cherubim shall have their wings spread out above, shielding the cover with their wings. They shall confront each other, the faces of the cherubim being turned toward the cover. 21 Place the cover on top of the Ark, after depositing inside the Ark the Pact that I will give you. 22 There I will meet with you, and I will impart to you—from above the cover, from between the two cherubim that are on top of the Ark of the Pact—all that I will command you concerning the Israelite people.

23 You shall make a table of acacia wood, two cubits long, one cubit wide, and a cubit and a half high. 24 Overlay it with pure gold, and make a gold molding around it. 25 Make a rim of a hand's breadth around it, and make a gold molding for its rim round about. 26 Make four gold rings for it, and attach the rings to the four corners at its four legs. 27 The rings shall be next to the rim, as holders for poles to carry the table. 28 Make the poles of acacia wood, and overlay them with gold; by these the table shall be carried. 29 Make its bowls, ladles, jars and jugs with which to offer libations; make them of pure gold.

.7 m by .7 m (3.75 ft long, 2.25 ft wide, 2.25 ft high). **16:** Cf. 1 Kings 8.9.

25.17–22: The Ark cover. The Ark is to be covered with a lid of gold hammered into the shape of two cherubs standing on a base. Cherubs are not the chubby, naked, winged boys known from medieval art, but winged composite creatures (cf. Ezek. 1.6–11; 10.14–22). Various types of such creatures are known from ancient Near Eastern art, such as winged sphinxes, with lions' bodies, eagles' wings, and human faces (sometimes with a second, animal face), and winged anthropoids with eagles' wings and birds' heads. Such creatures, frequently in pairs, often serve as protective spirits for kings, their palaces and thrones. Images of royal thrones with cherubs sculpted on their sides, several of which were found in Canaan and ancient Israel, are consistent with v. 22, which indicates that God would be present between the cherubs. They suggest that the Ark cover represented God's throne (cf. 1 Sam. 4.4; 2 Sam. 6.2; 2 Kings 19.15; Pss. 80.2; 99.1) and the Ark His footstool. The symbolism thus represents God as King and the Holy of Holies as the seat of divine government. This symbolism is consistent with the fact that architecturally the Tabernacle resembles a royal residence, particularly the royal tent in Egyptian military camps. It also is similar in structure to temples of surrounding nations. **20:** Unlike the cherubs flanking royal thrones, and the free-standing cherubs in Solomon's Temple (1 Kings 6.23–27), the Tabernacle cherubs face each other. **21:** Ancient Near Eastern treaties were often stored in sanctuaries in the presence of the deities who were expected to enforce their observance. In some cases treaties and other documents are explicitly said to be placed beneath the deity's feet; this is consistent with the conception of the Ark as God's footstool. **22:** See 29.42–43; 30.36; Num. 7.89; 17.19; and cf. Lev. 16.2, 13. Appropriately, the place where the first revelation is stored will serve as the site of future revelations. The text expresses this by paronomasia (punning), since the Heb words for "Pact" ("ʿedut") and "meet" ("noʿad") sound alike (though they are from different roots), as if to say that the site of the Pact ("ʿedut") is the site of meeting ("noʿad"). Whether Moses enters the Holy of Holies or listens to God from the Holy Place (Sforno at Lev. 1.1) is debated.

25.23–40: The table and lampstand. The furnishings of the antechamber, the Holy Place. **23–30:** The *table* was to hold the "bread of display," that is, "the Bread of the (Divine) Presence" (also called "showbread"), explained as bread placed "before (that is, in the presence of) God." Twelve loaves of bread were placed on the table every Sabbath and replaced a week later and then eaten by the priests (see Lev. 24.5–9; cf. Num. 4.7; 1 Sam. 21.4–7; 1 Chron. 9.32). Ancient Near Eastern art often shows tables holding gifts of food before enthroned royalty and deities. In Mesopotamian ritual, curtains were drawn around the image of the deity and the table when sacrificial food was brought in for the deity to eat. It is significant that here the table is in the antechamber, separated from the Holy of Holies by the curtain (26.31–35).

30 And on the table you shall set the bread of display, to be before Me always.

31 You shall make a lampstand of pure gold; the lampstand shall be made of hammered work; its base and its shaft, its cups, calyxes, and petals shall be of one piece. 32 Six branches shall issue from its sides; three branches from one side of the lampstand and three branches from the other side of the lampstand. 33 On one branch there shall be three cups shaped like almond-blossoms, each with calyx and petals, and on the next branch there shall be three cups shaped like almond-blossoms, each with calyx and petals; so for all six branches issuing from the lampstand. 34 And on the lampstand itself there shall be four cups shaped like almond-blossoms, each with calyx and petals: 35 a calyx, of one piece with it, under a pair of branches; and a calyx, of one piece with it, under the second pair of branches, and a calyx, of one piece with it, under the last pair of branches; so for all six branches issuing from the lampstand. 36 Their calyxes and their stems shall be of one piece with it, the whole of it a single hammered piece of pure gold. 37 Make its seven lamps—the lamps shall be so mounted as to give the light on its front side—38 and its tongs and fire pans of pure gold. 39 It shall be made, with all these furnishings, out of a talent of pure gold. 40 Note well, and follow the patterns for them that are being shown you on the mountain.

26 As for the Tabernacle,[a] make it of ten strips of cloth; make these of fine twisted linen, of blue, purple, and crimson yarns, with a design of cherubim worked into them. 2 The length of each cloth shall be twenty-eight cubits, and the width of each cloth shall be four cubits, all the cloths to have the same measurements. 3 Five of the cloths shall be joined to one another, and the other five cloths shall be joined to one another. 4 Make loops of blue wool on the edge of the outermost cloth of the one set; and do likewise on the edge of the outermost cloth of the other set: 5 make fifty loops on the one cloth, and fifty loops on the edge of the end cloth of the other set, the loops to be opposite one another. 6 And make fifty gold clasps, and couple the cloths to one another with the clasps, so that the Tabernacle becomes one whole.

7 You shall then make cloths of goats' hair for a tent over the Tabernacle; make the cloths eleven in number. 8 The length of each cloth shall be thirty cubits, and the width of each cloth shall be four cubits, the eleven cloths to have the same measurements. 9 Join five of the cloths by themselves, and the other six cloths by themselves; and fold over the sixth cloth at the front of the tent. 10 Make fifty loops on the edge of the outermost

a Here the lowest of the covers of the Tabernacle.

This partition between God and the Table makes it clear that the bread of display is not actually consumed by God but is only a symbolic gift—this is also underlined by the fact that it was eaten by priests. That its purpose was display, not consumption, is also indicated by the fact that it is replaced weekly, not daily as elsewhere in the ancient Near East. See also vv. 31–40 n. and 30.9 n. **31–40:** The *lampstand* ("menorah") for illuminating the interior of the Holy Place each night (27.20–21). Its location in the antechamber indicates that the light is for the benefit of the officiating priests, not God. With its central shaft and three branches emerging from each side it resembled a stylized tree, possibly symbolizing fertility or the sustenance of life. It held seven *lamps* (v. 37), i.e., cups to hold the oil and wicks (it is debated whether six of these were on the branches or all seven were on the central shaft). The seven-branched lampstand later became a popular Jewish symbol in synagogues, tombs, and amulets, and today it is a symbol of the State of Israel. According to the Talmud it is forbidden to make exact replicas of the menorah except for use in the Tabernacle or the Temple (*b. Rosh Hash.* 24a–b); hence many synagogue menorahs have six or eight branches instead of seven. **40:** Cf. v. 9 n.

26.1–37: The Tabernacle structure. The Holy of Holies and the Holy Place will be housed in a structure of gold-overlaid wood roofed with four layers of material. **1–6:** *The Tabernacle* (lit. "abode"): Here, apparently, this term means the lowest, innermost layer of the covers (cf. v. 6); it is so called because as the layer closest to the Ark it is the "abode" proper (Rashbam). It is to be made of the finest materials: *fine twisted linen, of blue, purple, and crimson yarns, with a design of cherubim worked into them,* corresponding to the cherubs on the Ark cover. Because it is contiguous with the Holy of Holies and the Holy Place, the clasps holding its sections together are to be made of gold. **7–13:** The *tent over the Tabernacle,* the second layer, is to be made of less precious material, goats' hair, and its clasps are to be made of *copper* (rather, bronze; v. 11). **14:** The upper layer is to be made of the least expensive of the Tabernacle materials, tanned ram skins and "dolphin skins" (see 25.4–5 n.). These constitute two separate layers (39.34), making four in all. **15–30:** The wooden structure, made of vertical planks of gold-overlaid acacia wood stabilized by silver sockets, or bases, and gold-overlaid wooden bars held in place by gold rings. The structure, with its opening facing east, was 30 cubits (13.7 m, 45 ft) long and 10 cubits (4.6 m, 15 ft) high and wide (see 25.10 n.). Silver is probably chosen for the sockets despite the fact that the planks are inside the Tabernacle because gold is not strong enough to support the planks. **30:** See 25.9 n. **31–35:** The curtain ("parokhet") for the Holy of Holies, again made of the finest materials and decorated with cherubs because of its contiguity with the Holy of Holies (cf. vv. 1–6 n.). The same Heb term is now used for the curtain that covers the Holy Ark in synagogues. The *blue, purple, and crimson yarns* must have been woollen since only wool could be dyed successfully in ancient times. Hence the curtain, which also contained *linen,* consisted of a combination of fabrics that the laity are forbidden to wear (Lev. 19.19; Deut. 22.11) precisely because the combination is reserved for sacred use. See also 28.6, 15. **33:** *Under the clasps,* the clasps holding together the two halves of the innermost cover (v. 6). Since this cover is 40 cubits (approx. 18.3 m, 60 ft) from front to back (including the part that hangs over the back of the structure), the clasps, and hence the curtain, are placed 20 cubits (approx 9.1 m, 30 ft) from the entrance. Since the entire structure is 30 cubits (approx. 13.7 m, 45 ft) from front to back, the Holy Place occupies its eastern two-thirds and the Holy of Holies the westernmost third. The latter, then, is a perfect cube, 10 cubits (approx 4.6 m, 15 ft) wide, long, and tall.

cloth of the one set, and fifty loops on the edge of the cloth of
the other set. 11 Make fifty copper clasps, and fit the clasps into
the loops, and couple the tent together so that it becomes one
whole. 12 As for the overlapping excess of the cloths of the tent,
the extra half-cloth shall overlap the back of the Tabernacle,
13 while the extra cubit at either end of each length of tent cloth
shall hang down to the bottom of the two sides of the Tabernacle and cover it. 14 And make for the tent a covering of tanned
ram skins, and a covering of dolphin skins above.

15 You shall make the planks for the Tabernacle of acacia
wood, upright. 16 The length of each plank shall be ten cubits
and the width of each plank a cubit and a half. 17 Each plank
shall have two tenons, parallel[a] to each other; do the same
with all the planks of the Tabernacle. 18 Of the planks of the
Tabernacle, make twenty planks on the south[b] side: 19 making
forty silver sockets under the twenty planks, two sockets under
the one plank for its two tenons and two sockets under each
following plank for its two tenons; 20 and for the other side wall
of the Tabernacle, on the north side, twenty planks, 21 with
their forty silver sockets, two sockets under the one plank and
two sockets under each following plank. 22 And for the rear of
the Tabernacle, to the west, make six planks; 23 and make two
planks for the corners of the Tabernacle at the rear. 24 [c]They
shall match at the bottom, and terminate alike at the top inside
one ring;[-c] thus shall it be with both of them: they shall form
the two corners. 25 Thus there shall be eight planks with their
sockets of silver: sixteen sockets, two sockets under the first
plank, and two sockets under each of the other planks.

26 You shall make bars of acacia wood: five for the planks of
the one side wall of the Tabernacle, 27 five bars for the planks
of the other side wall of the Tabernacle, and five bars for the
planks of the wall of the Tabernacle at the rear to the west.
28 The center bar halfway up the planks shall run from end to
end. 29 Overlay the planks with gold, and make their rings of
gold, as holders for the bars; and overlay the bars with gold.
30 Then set up the Tabernacle according to the manner of it that
you were shown on the mountain.

31 You shall make a curtain of blue, purple, and crimson
yarns, and fine twisted linen; it shall have a design of cherubim
worked into it. 32 Hang it upon four posts of acacia wood overlaid with gold and having hooks of gold, [set] in four sockets of
silver. 33 Hang the curtain under the clasps, and carry the Ark of
the Pact there, behind the curtain, so that the curtain shall serve
you as a partition between the Holy and the Holy of Holies.

a Meaning of Heb. meshullaboth *uncertain.* *b Heb. uses two terms for "south."*
c-c Meaning of Heb. uncertain.

[34] Place the cover upon the Ark of the Pact in the Holy of Holies.
[35] Place the table outside the curtain, and the lampstand by the
south wall of the Tabernacle opposite the table, which is to be
placed by the north wall.

[36] You shall make a screen for the entrance of the Tent, of
blue, purple, and crimson yarns, and fine twisted linen, done
in embroidery. [37] Make five posts of acacia wood for the screen
and overlay them with gold—their hooks being of gold—and
cast for them five sockets of copper.

27 You shall make the altar of acacia wood, five cubits
long and five cubits wide—the altar is to be square—
and three cubits high. [2] Make its horns on the four corners,
the horns to be of one piece with it; and overlay it with copper. [3] Make the pails for removing its ashes, as well as its scrapers, basins, flesh hooks, and fire pans—make all its utensils of
copper. [4] Make for it a grating of meshwork in copper; and on
the mesh make four copper rings at its four corners. [5] Set the
mesh below, under the ledge of the altar, so that it extends to
the middle of the altar. [6] And make poles for the altar, poles of
acacia wood, and overlay them with copper. [7] The poles shall
be inserted into the rings, so that the poles remain on the two
sides of the altar when it is carried. [8] Make it hollow, of boards.
As you were shown on the mountain, so shall they be made.

[9] You shall make the enclosure of the Tabernacle:
On the south side,[a] a hundred cubits of hangings of fine twisted linen for the length of the enclosure on that side—[10] with its

a *Cf.* note at 26.18.

35: On the location of the table and the lampstand *outside the curtain,* see 25.23–30 n.; 25.31–40 n. **36–37:** The *screen for the entrance of the Tent* (here *Tent* means the Tabernacle structure). It is made of the same fine materials as the "parokhet" but, since it is not contiguous with the Holy of Holies, it is not adorned with cherubs, its sockets are of a less valuable metal (copper [bronze] rather than silver), and it is *done in embroidery*—apparently a less sophisticated weave than that used for the "parokhet."

27.1–19: The altar and the courtyard. Just as chs 25–26 first described the main contents of the Tabernacle and then the Tabernacle structure, the text now describes the most important object placed in the courtyard—the altar—and then the courtyard itself. Since all of this is outside the Tabernacle structure, it is mostly made of less precious materials: The altar, its utensils, and the posts and sockets supporting the courtyard wall are made of bronze and bronzed wood, and the hangings are made of *fine twisted linen* but without blue, purple, or crimson. **1–8:** *The altar:* This is the main altar on which animal and grain offerings were burnt and wine offerings (libations) were poured. It is called "the altar of burnt offering" (30.28), after the type of offering made on it twice daily (29.38–43)—though in fact it is used for all types of offering (Lev. chs 1–7). It is also called "the copper [rather, bronze] altar" (38.30). Sacrifice is regarded as an expression of honor and gratitude and a means of purification and expiation, not a way of feeding God; God derives from it only the "pleasing odor" (29.18, 25, 41; Lev. 1.9 n.), an expression possibly meant literally or perhaps to indicate God's pleasure at the worshipper's devotion. That the sacrificial altar is located outside the Tabernacle building, and that none of the sacrifices are ever taken inside, where God's presence abides, clearly expresses the idea that the sacrifices are not His food (cf. 25.23–30 n., 31–40 n.; 30.9 n.). **2:** *Horns,* horn-like projections pointing vertically at the upper corners of the altar (see also 30.2–3). Horned altars have been found by archeologists at several sites in Israel and elsewhere; they usually have four horns, though a recent altar from Tell es-Safi (ancient Gath in Philistia) contains two. The horns are an essential part of the altar: The blood of the "purification offering"(Heb "ḥata't"; see Lev. 4.4–12 n.) is daubed on them (29.12; Lev. 4.29–30), and those seeking asylum at the altar (21.13–14 n.) would grasp them (1 Kings 1.50; 2.28). Their significance is not known, though Ps. 118.27 mentions tying sacrifices to them. **8:** *Hollow:* Unlike the case of the incense altar (30.3), no top is mentioned here, indicating that there was an open space inside the four walls of this altar. It may, then, have resembled in a general way the pit altars used by the Samaritans. It would have been very difficult, however, for the priests to reach down over the sides (which were 3 cubits = 1.4 m, 4.5 ft high [v. 1]) to handle the sacrifice at the bottom of such an open space, and the heat of the sacrificial fire would probably have damaged the bronzed wooden structure. It is traditionally assumed that, in keeping with the requirement of 20.21, the empty space was filled with earth each time the Israelites encamped, producing an earthen altar on which the sacrifices would be burnt (*Tg. Jon.;* Rashi; Rashbam). **9–19:** *The enclosure* of the Tabernacle (that is, its courtyard) will be 100 by

twenty posts and their twenty sockets of copper, the hooks and
bands of the posts to be of silver.
11 Again a hundred cubits of hangings for its length along the
north side—with its twenty posts and their twenty sockets of
copper, the hooks and bands of the posts to be of silver.
12 For the width of the enclosure, on the west side, fifty cubits
of hangings, with their ten posts and their ten sockets.
13 For the width of the enclosure on the front, or east side,
fifty cubits: 14 fifteen cubits of hangings on the one flank, with
their three posts and their three sockets; 15 fifteen cubits of
hangings on the other flank, with their three posts and their
three sockets; 16 and for the gate of the enclosure, a screen of
twenty cubits, of blue, purple, and crimson yarns, and fine
twisted linen, done in embroidery, with their four posts and
their four sockets.
17 All the posts round the enclosure shall be banded with silver
and their hooks shall be of silver; their sockets shall be of copper.
18 The length of the enclosure shall be a hundred cubits, and
the width fifty throughout; and the height five cubits—[with
hangings] of fine twisted linen. The sockets shall be of copper:
19 all the utensils of the Tabernacle,[a] for all its service, as well
as all its pegs and all the pegs of the court, shall be of copper.

TETSAVVEH תצוה

20 You shall further instruct the Israelites to bring you clear
oil of beaten olives for lighting, for kindling lamps regularly.
21 Aaron and his sons shall set them up in the Tent of Meeting, outside the curtain which is over [the Ark of] the Pact, [to
burn] from evening to morning before the LORD. It shall be a
due from the Israelites for all time, throughout the ages.

28 You shall bring forward your brother Aaron, with his
sons, from among the Israelites, to serve Me as priests:
Aaron, Nadab and Abihu, Eleazar and Ithamar, the sons of

a *I.e., of the Tabernacle enclosure; the furnishings inside were of gold.*

50 cubits (45.7 by 22.9 m, 150 by 75 ft) and five cubits (2.3 m, 7.5 ft) high—half as high as the Tabernacle itself (26.16). **13–16:** The eastern wall will have a 20-cubit-wide opening (9.1 m, 30 ft), shielded by a screen of the same width, to serve as its entrance. The screen will be made of the same quality materials as the screen for the entrance of the Tent (v. 36) which it faces, except for its bronze rather than gold overlay. **19:** *The Tabernacle:* Here this means the courtyard.

27.20–30.38: The Tabernacle activities. After describing most of the fixed, permanent items of the sanctuary structure made of the materials listed in 25.3–5, the text turns to items made from the materials listed in 25.6–7. These items are described along with the activities (particularly the regular ["tamid"], daily priestly activities) performed with them: oil for the lamps (of 25.31–40) that are kindled regularly, the vestments worn by the priests when officiating (and hence also their ordination), culminating in the regular daily sacrifices (chs 28–29), the incense altar and the incense burned on it regularly (30.1–10, 34–38), the census (30.11–16), the laver where the priests would wash before officiating (30.17–21), and the sacred anointing oil (30.22–33). The shift in subject matter (from sacred objects to activities) is reflected in the fact that in Jewish liturgical practice a new weekly Torah portion ("Tetsavveh," "You shall ... instruct") begins here.

27.20–21: Oil for the lamps. 20: *Further instruct the Israelites to bring you clear oil:* In addition to the original request (25.6), oil will have to be requested regularly since, unlike the materials used to construct the sanctuary (25.3–5), the oil supply is depletable. *For kindling lamps* (those of 25.31–40; see Lev. 24.4) *regularly,* every evening, to burn until morning (v. 21; Lev. 24.3–4; cf. 1 Sam. 3.3). In current Jewish practice this command is emulated by suspending a lamp from the ceiling in the synagogue above and in front of the Torah Ark. The lamp is kept lit perpetually and called the "ner tamid," "eternal light," based on an alternative understanding of the Heb words for *lamps regularly.* This lamp identifies the synagogue as a "miniature sanctuary" (Ezek. 11.16) and serves as a symbol that the divine Presence accompanies the Jewish people (*b. Shab.* 22b). **21:** *Aaron and his sons,* the priests (28.1). According to 30.8; Lev. 24.3; Num. 8.2–3, only Aaron was to kindle the lamps; his sons—if their mention is not a scribal error—may have assisted him with the preparations. *Tent of Meeting,* see 25.8 n.

Chs 28–29: The priests. Having mentioned the priests in 27.21, the text turns to their identity, their vestments, and their ordination.

28.1–43: The priestly vestments. *Bring forward:* This is to take place after the sanctuary is constructed (29.4; Lev. 8.6). *Aaron, with his sons,* 6.23; 24.1. The priesthood will be hereditary (29.8). The Bible never explains why Aaron was granted the priesthood. Later Jewish tradition praises him as a lover of peace who

Aaron. [2]Make sacral vestments for your brother Aaron, for dignity and adornment. [3]Next you shall instruct all who are *a*-skillful, whom I have endowed with the gift of skill,-*a* to make Aaron's vestments, for consecrating him to serve Me as priest. [4]These are the vestments they are to make: a breastpiece, an ephod, a robe, a fringed*b* tunic, a headdress, and a sash. They shall make those sacral vestments for your brother Aaron and his sons, for priestly service to Me; [5]they, therefore, shall receive the gold, the blue, purple, and crimson yarns, and the fine linen.

[6]They shall make the ephod of gold, of blue, purple, and crimson yarns, and of fine twisted linen, worked into designs. [7]It shall have two shoulder-pieces attached; they shall be attached at its two ends. [8]And the decorated band that is upon it shall be made like it, of one piece with it: of gold, of blue, purple, and crimson yarns, and of fine twisted linen. [9]Then take two lazuli stones and engrave on them the names of the sons of Israel: [10]six of their names on the one stone, and the names of the remaining six on the other stone, in the order of their birth. [11]On the two stones you shall make seal engravings—the work of a lapidary—of the names of the sons of Israel. Having bordered them with frames of gold, [12]attach the two stones to the shoulder-pieces of the ephod, as stones for remembrance

a-a Lit. "wise of heart, whom I have filled with a spirit of wisdom."
b Others "checkered."

encouraged reconciliation and who brought people near to Torah (*Pirkei 'Avot* 1.12). One midrash holds that he was granted the privilege of wearing the Urim and Thummim over his heart (v. 29) because instead of being jealous of Moses' greater stature he "rejoiced in his heart" (4.14, literal translation; *Tanḥ., Shemot* 27). Another credits his receipt of the high priesthood to his employing delaying tactics when the Israelites decided to make the golden calf (*Exod. Rab.* 37.2). **2:** Aaron's *sacral vestments ... for dignity and adornment* number seven in all, the six listed here plus a frontlet (vv. 36–38). An eighth item, *breeches* (vv. 42–43), is listed separately because they are neither visible nor sacral (contrast Lev. 16.4). These garments will be worn by the priests when officiating (Lev. 6.3; Ezek. 42.14; 44.17–19). No foot-wear is mentioned; 30.19 implies that they officiated barefoot (Naḥmanides; cf. 3.5; Josh. 5.14; *Exod. Rab.* 2, end), as their descendants still do nowadays when reciting the priestly benediction (Num. 6.24–26) in the synagogue. The four main vestments mentioned first are listed in order from the outermost to the innermost: the breastpiece, which was attached to the front of the ephod, the ephod itself, the robe, and the tunic (see 29.5; cf., with a slight difference, Lev. 8.7–8). **3:** *Skillful ... skill:* See translators' note *a-a*. Artistic skills, no less than intellectual ones, are recognized as forms of wisdom. *Gift,* lit. "spirit." Extraordinary skills are gifts from God. *For consecrating him to serve Me:* Placing these vestments on Aaron (and his sons) will be a constitutive part of their ordination ceremony (v. 41; 29.1–9; Lev. 8.7–9, 13; Num. 29.26, 28). **5:** *They, therefore, shall receive,* those with artistic skill (v. 3). The finest materials called for in 25.3–4 shall be given to the artisans to make the priestly vestments. These will be made of the same materials as the most sacred parts of the sanctuary itself. **6–38:** Aaron's sacral vestments. **6–30:** The ephod (vv. 6–12) and the breastpiece (vv. 15–30). The order of these two items is the reverse of v. 4; in essence the two constitute a unit both physically, since the breastpiece is attached to the ephod (vv. 22–28), and functionally, since both are involved in ascertaining the divine will. Elsewhere the term ephod (and cognates in other Semitic languages) refers to a garment of uncertain appearance (1 Sam. 2.18; 2 Sam. 6.14) and also to a device carried by priests and used to determine God's will (1 Sam. 2.28; 14.3; 23.6, 9–12; 30.7–8). Here it is clearly a garment (sometimes translated as "apron"), and the divinatory device—the breastpiece containing the Urim and Thummim (vv. 15–30)—is attached to it. Using the Urim and Thummim to determine God's will is one of the most important functions of the priest. Because of the importance of this function and Aaron's access to the interior of the sanctuary, the ephod and the breastpiece are, like it, made of the most precious materials (vv. 6, 15) including the sacred mixture of wool and linen (26.31–35 n.); cf. 39.29. **9–12:** The inscriptions on the epaulets of the ephod. **9:** *Lazuli,* translation not certain. **10:** *In the order of their birth,* see Gen. 29.32–30.24; 35.16–18. **11:** *Seal engravings—the work of a lapidary,* cf. v. 21. The stones are to be inscribed by the technique used by lapidaries to engrave people's names on gems and other stones used as seals. **12:** *For remembrance ... before the* L*ORD:* This phrase evokes the formula of ancient graffiti and votive inscriptions that pray that "so-and-so may be remembered (for good) before the deity" (an expanded form of the formula appears in the Hebrew prayer ya'aleh veyavo'). The ancients sought by various means to make the gods mindful of them: by placing votive statues of themselves

of the Israelite people, whose names Aaron shall carry upon his two shoulder-pieces for remembrance before the LORD. 13 Then make frames of gold 14 and two chains of pure gold; braid these like corded work, and fasten the corded chains to the frames.

15 You shall make a breastpiece of decision,[a] worked into a design; make it in the style of the ephod: make it of gold, of blue, purple, and crimson yarns, and of fine twisted linen. 16 It shall be square and doubled, a span in length and a span in width. 17 Set in it mounted stones, in four rows of stones. The first row shall be a row of [b]carnelian, chrysolite, and emerald; 18 the second row: a turquoise, a sapphire, and an amethyst; 19 the third row: a jacinth, an agate, and a crystal; 20 and the fourth row: a beryl, a lapis lazuli, and a jasper. They shall be framed with gold in their mountings. 21 The stones shall correspond [in number] to the names of the sons of Israel: twelve, corresponding to their names. They shall be engraved like seals, each with its name, for the twelve tribes.

22 On the breastpiece make braided chains of corded work in pure gold. 23 Make two rings of gold on the breastpiece, and fasten the two rings at the two ends of the breastpiece, 24 attaching the two golden cords to the two rings at the ends of the breastpiece. 25 Then fasten the two ends of the cords to the two frames, which you shall attach to the shoulder-pieces of the ephod, at the front. 26 Make two rings of gold and attach them to the two ends of the breastpiece, at its inner edge, which faces the ephod. 27 And make two other rings of gold and fasten them on the front of the ephod, low on the two shoulder-pieces, close to its seam above the decorated band. 28 The breastpiece shall be held in place by a cord of blue from its rings to the rings of the ephod, so that the breastpiece rests on the decorated band and does not come loose from the ephod. 29 Aaron shall carry the names of the sons of Israel on the breastpiece of decision over his heart, when he enters the sanctuary, for remembrance before the LORD at all times. 30 Inside the breastpiece of decision you shall place the Urim and Thummim,[c] so that they are over Aaron's heart when he comes before the LORD. Thus Aaron shall carry the instrument of decision for the Israelites over his heart before the LORD at all times.

31 You shall make the robe of the ephod of pure blue.[d] 32 The opening for the head shall be in the middle of it; the opening

a See v. 30 below; others "judgment."
b The identity of several of these twelve stones is uncertain.
c Meaning of these two words uncertain. They designate a kind of oracle; cf. Num. 27.21.
d Others "all of blue."

in an attitude of prayer in sanctuaries—a method forbidden in the Bible—by donating ritual objects inscribed with their names to sanctuaries, and by writing graffiti praying for remembrance by the deity. Most reminiscent of the present v. are seals inscribed with both the owner's name and a prayer for divine blessing. Some of these are written in positive rather than mirror-writing and hence were not intended as functional seals; they were likely placed in sanctuaries to secure divine remembrance. Thus, each time Aaron entered the sanctuary wearing these inscriptions he not only represented the Israelites but carried before God an implicit prayer on their behalf. **15–30:** The *breastpiece of decision,* a pouch, approx. 24 cm (9.5 in) square and attached to the ephod, containing *the instrument of decision* (v. 30). **17–20:** The inscribed stones on the breastpiece function like the inscribed epaulets (vv. 9–12). The translation of the names of the twelve stones is not certain. **21:** *Engraved like seals,* see v. 11 n. **29:** See v. 12 n. **30:** *Urim and Thummim ... the instrument of decision:* The Urim and Thummim was a device for obtaining God's *decision* on important questions on which human judgment was found inadequate, such as military actions, allocation of land, legal verdicts in the absence of evidence, and choice of leaders (Num. 27.21; 1 Sam. 14.37–42 [see v. 41 translators' note *d-d*]; Ezra 2.63; cf. Exod. 22.8 n.; Josh. 7.14–18; Judg. 1.1–2; 20.18; 1 Sam. 10.20–22; 2 Sam. 2.1; 5.23–24). It apparently consisted of two or more lots (Prov. 16.33) which the priest drew out of the breastpiece and which signified a positive, negative, or noncommittal answer to a question or indicated a particular message (see esp. 1 Sam. 14.41 with translators' note *d-d*). *Urim and Thummim* may have been the names of the lots. Derivation of these terms from Heb "'or," "light," and "tom," "completeness, perfection, integrity," is suggestive but far from certain. *Thus Aaron shall carry the instrument of decision for the Israelites ... before the LORD at all times:* This may indicate that the Urim and Thummim were consulted (at least in the view of the Priestly source) only in the sanctuary.

shall have a binding of woven work round about—it shall be
like the opening of a coat of mail—so that it does not tear.
33 On its hem make pomegranates of blue, purple, and crimson yarns, all around the hem, with bells of gold between them
all around: 34 a golden bell and a pomegranate, a golden bell
and a pomegranate, all around the hem of the robe. 35 Aaron
shall wear it while officiating, so that the sound of it is heard
when he comes into the sanctuary before the LORD and when
he goes out—that he may not die.

36 You shall make a frontlet of pure gold and engrave on it
the seal inscription: "Holy to the LORD." 37 Suspend it on a cord
of blue, so that it may remain on the headdress; it shall remain
on the front of the headdress. 38 It shall be on Aaron's forehead,
that Aaron may take away any sin arising from the holy things
that the Israelites consecrate, from any of their sacred donations; it shall be on his forehead at all times, to win acceptance
for them before the LORD.

39 You shall make the fringed tunic of fine linen.

You shall make the headdress of fine linen.

You shall make the sash of embroidered work.

40 And for Aaron's sons also you shall make tunics, and make
sashes for them, and make turbans for them, for dignity and

31–35: *The robe of the ephod* indicates that it is part of the same unit as the ephod and the breastpiece of decision; they would all be worn together. Its shape seems to resemble an ankle-length sleeveless shirt, and its single color, with no gold or linen admixture, indicates its lesser importance than the other two items. **33:** The robe's most distinctive feature is its hemline with dyed wool pomegranate-shaped tassels and golden bells. The pomegranate—a well-known symbol of fertility—was a popular artistic motif in ancient Israel and adorned Solomon's Temple in several places (1 Kings 7.42; 2 Kings 25.17; Jer. 52.23; 2 Chron. 3.16; 4.13). A miniature ivory pomegranate with a dove atop it was discovered recently in the City of David excavations in Jerusalem. **35:** The purpose of the bells is not clear. The ominous explanation *that he may not die* may indicate that the bells were apotropaic devices to protect the priest from demons that were widely believed to haunt thresholds (cf. Gen. 4.7; the rites mentioned in 1 Sam. 5.5 and Zeph. 1.9 may have originated in a similar belief); that is why the sound must be heard when the priest leaves the sanctuary as well as when he enters. If that was the original purpose it seems to have been abandoned by the Bible, which gives similar warnings with the requirements that the priests wear underpants and wash their hands and feet before ministering (v. 43; 30.20–21); this suggests that these items and actions are expressions of respect for God: One does not approach Him unannounced, unwashed, or immodestly dressed. Most significantly, all such warnings reflect the potential lethality of the sanctuary and its contents (19.21 n., 22 n.; see also 30.33, 37; Lev. 10.6, 9; 16.2, 13; Num. 4.15, 19–20; 17.28; 18.3, 22). **36–38:** The *frontlet* (lit. "blossom, flower," perhaps indicating its shape; it is called a "diadem" in 29.6 and both terms are used in 39.30 and Lev. 8.9) was attached to the front of Aaron's *headdress* (v. 39). The frontlet functions in relation to sin that might occur in the sanctuary because of imperfections or impurities in the Israelites' sacrifices. Aaron, by wearing the inscription "Holy to the LORD"—presumably meaning that he is sacrosanct and hence protected by God from harm (19.5b–6a n.)—will be able to expiate any such sin and eliminate it. Coming as it does after the bells (and pomegranates) on Aaron's hem that may have originated as apotropaic devices, it is noteworthy that the frontlet is called "blossom, flower" and is worn on Aaron's forehead, since in Mesopotamian iconography the most common apotropaic head-ornament (worn even by gods for their own protection) is the rosette, a blossom-shaped decoration worn on the forehead, and that it is held in place by a blue cord, since blue is frequently used in apotropaic devices. Here, however, the text says that *Aaron*—not the frontlet—[shall] *take away ... sin* and that his wearing it is *to win acceptance for* Israel *before the LORD*—indicating that Aaron will take away sin because wearing the frontlet pleases God, not because it has any inherent apotropaic power. **39:** In addition to the preceding vestments, Aaron was to wear a *fringed tunic of fine linen* ("of woven work" according to 39.27) under them, a *headdress* of unknown appearance, and an ornate *sash* which, like the ephod and the breastpiece, was made of the sacred mixture of wool and linen (39.29). Since the sash was an emblem of office (Isa. 22.21) and ornate in appearance, it was naturally to be worn over Aaron's other vestments (29.5–9). **40:** The other priests have three vestments, similar to the last three of Aaron's vestments but simpler, reflecting their lower status: *tunics* ("of fine linen, of woven work," 39.27), like Aaron's, but not fringed; *sashes,* whether identical to Aaron's or simpler depends on whether 39.29 refers only to Aaron's sash or to those of all the priests; and *turbans* (translation uncertain, but presumably different in appearance from Aaron's *headdress*), also made

adornment. 41 Put these on your brother Aaron and on his sons as well; anoint them, and ordain them[a] and consecrate them to serve Me as priests.

42 You shall also make for them linen breeches to cover their nakedness; they shall extend from the hips to the thighs. 43 They shall be worn by Aaron and his sons when they enter the Tent of Meeting or when they approach the altar to officiate in the sanctuary, so that they do not incur punishment and die. It shall be a law for all time for him and for his offspring to come.

29 This is what you shall do to them in consecrating them to serve Me as priests: Take a young bull of the herd and two rams without blemish; 2 also unleavened bread, unleavened cakes with oil mixed in, and unleavened wafers spread with oil—make these of choice wheat flour. 3 Place these in one basket and present them in the basket, along with the bull and the two rams. 4 Lead Aaron and his sons up to the entrance of the Tent of Meeting, and wash them with water. 5 Then take the vestments, and clothe Aaron with the tunic, the robe of the ephod, the ephod, and the breastpiece, and gird him with the decorated band of the ephod. 6 Put the headdress on his head, and place the holy diadem upon the headdress. 7 Take the anointing oil and pour it on his head and anoint him. 8 Then bring his sons forward; clothe them with tunics 9 and wind turbans upon them. And gird both Aaron and his sons with sashes. And so they shall have priesthood as their right for all time.

You shall then ordain Aaron and his sons. 10 Lead the bull up to the front of the Tent of Meeting, and let Aaron and his sons lay their hands upon the head of the bull. 11 Slaughter the bull before the LORD, at the entrance of the Tent of Meeting, 12 and take some of the bull's blood and put it on the horns of the altar

a *Lit. "and fill their hands."*

of fine linen (39.28) but lacking a frontlet. In contrast to Aaron's vestments, which are made of materials used in the interior of the sanctuary, those of the other priests, possibly excluding their sashes, match the material of the courtyard hangings (linen, 27.9), as befits their lesser sanctity. **41:** That is: Robe the priests in their vestments and then anoint them and ordain them, thereby consecrating them as priests; see 29.1–37, introductory n. *Anoint:* Sacred anointing oil is to be poured on Aaron's head and sprinkled on his sons (29.7, 21) to sanctify them for their duties (29.21; 30.22–33). Anointing with oil actuated a change of status for kings as well (see e.g., 1 Sam. 16.13). *Ordain:* lit. "fill their hand," an expression that probably originated in an induction ceremony in which a symbol of office was placed in the inductee's hand. Conceivably it refers to the temporary placement of parts of the "ordination offering" in the priests' hands (29.24; see Lev. 8.22–29 n.), but it may be no more than an idiom here. **42–43:** The priests' *breeches,* that is, underpants, are separated from the list of sacral vestments by v. 41 because they are not sacral and hence not part of the ordination ceremony (cf. 29.5–6 n.); they are purely functional, to prevent exposure of the genitals. Evidently breeches were not regularly worn by men, hence the need to require them for priests. See 20.23 n. **43:** *To officiate,* to offer sacrifices (Ezek. 44.15; 2 Chron. 29.11). *And die,* v. 35 n.

29.1–37: The consecration of the priests. This ceremony consists of six parts: washing, robing, and anointing the priests and three sacrifices. The three elements unique to priests (robing with the vestments, anointing with holy oil, and the ordination sacrifice [28.41]) constitute their consecration; washing and the first two sacrifices are preparatory. The performance of the ceremony is narrated in Lev. chs 8–9, which are the natural continuation of this unit; cf. Exod. 40.12–16. **3:** *Present them,* "before the LORD" (v. 23), probably before the altar (Deut. 26.4, 10). **4:** *Entrance of the Tent of Meeting,* the courtyard in front of the Tent. *Wash them with water,* as part of the process of purification (Lev. chs 14–17). **5–6:** For the vestments, see ch 28. Only those that have ceremonial significance are mentioned here; that the priests would put on their breeches (28.42–43) goes without saying. **7:** *Anointing oil,* 30.22–33; *anoint,* 28.41 n. **9b–14:** The *purification offering* (Heb "ḥata't"; preferred rather than sin offering, see Lev. 4.3 n.) follows the procedure prescribed in Lev. ch 4; cf. Num. 15.22–31. On the purpose of this type of offering, see introductory nn. to Lev. 4.1–5.26; 4.1–35; chs 12–25; 16.1–34; 15.31 n. Here the altar is purified (v. 12), either from impurities stemming from its builders and the donors of its materials or (since purification offerings normally purge impurities stemming from the individuals who bring them) from the priests. **10:** *Lay their hands upon the head of the bull:* The meaning of the act is uncertain; it likely identifies Aaron and his sons as the ones on whose behalf the sacrifice is being made. For another view, see Lev. 1.4 n. **12:** *Take some of the bull's blood and put it on* with your finger; then pour out the rest of the blood at the base of the altar. [13]Take all the fat that covers the entrails, the protuberance on the liver, and the two kidneys with the fat on them, and turn them into smoke upon the altar. [14]The rest of the flesh of the bull, its hide, and its dung shall be put to the fire outside the camp; it is a purification offering.

[15]Next take the one ram, and let Aaron and his sons lay their hands upon the ram's head. [16]Slaughter the ram, and take its blood and dash it against all sides of the altar. [17]Cut up the ram into sections, wash its entrails and legs, and put them with its quarters and its head. [18]Turn all of the ram into smoke upon the altar. It is a burnt offering to the LORD, a pleasing odor, an offering by fire to the LORD.

[19]Then take the other ram, and let Aaron and his sons lay their hands upon the ram's head. [20]Slaughter the ram, and take some of its blood and put it on the ridge[a] of Aaron's right ear and on the ridges of his sons' right ears, and on the thumbs of their right hands, and on the big toes of their right feet; and dash the rest of the blood against every side of the altar round about. [21]Take some of the blood that is on the altar and some of the anointing oil and sprinkle upon Aaron and his vestments, and also upon his sons and his sons' vestments. Thus shall he and his vestments be holy, as well as his sons and his sons' vestments.

[22]You shall take from the ram the fat parts—the broad tail, the fat that covers the entrails, the protuberance on the liver, the two kidneys with the fat on them—and the right thigh; for this is a ram of ordination. [23]Add one flat loaf of bread, one cake of oil bread, and one wafer, from the basket of unleavened bread that is before the LORD. [24]Place all these on the palms of Aaron and his sons, and offer them as an elevation offering before the LORD. [25]Take them from their hands and turn them into smoke upon the altar with the burnt offering, as a pleasing odor before the LORD; it is an offering by fire to the LORD.

[26]Then take the breast of Aaron's ram of ordination and offer it as an elevation offering before the LORD; it shall be your

a *Or "lobe."*

the horns of the altar: The animal's blood serves as the purifying agent, the "ritual detergent" in purification offerings. Applying the blood to the horns of the altar (27.2)—its vulnerable extremities representing all of the altar—purifies the altar (cf. Ezek. 43.20). *Pour out the rest of the blood at the base of the altar,* Lev. 4.4–12 n. **13:** Lev. 3.3–4 n. **14:** Lev. 4.11; 6.23 (see n.). **15–18:** The burnt offering, following the procedure prescribed in Lev. ch 1. See the comments there. **19–34:** The ordination offering. This is the most elaborate offering, completing the priests' consecration by further anointment and then ordaining them. It follows the procedure for offering sheep as "sacrifices of well-being" (18.12 n.) prescribed in Lev. 3.6–11 and 7.11–34 with modifications specific to this occasion. **20:** As in the case of applying blood to the horns of the altar (v. 12), vulnerable extremities of the priests, representing their entire bodies, are daubed with blood, apparently to purge them of impurity (cf. v. 33 and the similar rite in Lev. 14.14–20, 25–31). *Dash the rest of the blood against every side of the altar,* a standard procedure in sacrifices (see Lev. 1.5 n.). **21:** The mixture of blood from the altar and anointing oil makes the priests and their garments holy; the anointing oil because that is its function (30.25–30) and the blood because being on the altar has made it holy (v. 37b) and capable of transmitting holiness to anything it touches (Hizkuni; see Lev. 6.11 n.). **22:** The fat parts of the sacrifice of well-being are burnt on the altar, as Lev. 3.9–11 prescribes. *And the right thigh; for this is a ram of ordination:* The right thigh of a sacrifice of well-being is normally given to the officiating priest (Lev. 7.32–33), but not in an ordination offering. **23:** Sacrifices of well-being commonly include grain offerings (Lev. 7.11–13; cf. Lev. ch 2; Exod. 12.8). These, too, are normally eaten by the officiating priest (Lev. ch 2; 6.7–11; 7.14), but when, as on the present occasion, the offering is on his own behalf, it is burnt on the altar (Lev. 6.12–16). *Unleavened bread:* As v. 2 indicates, all the items mentioned in this v. must be unleavened, like most grain offerings (12.8 n.; Lev. 2.11–12; 6.9–10). **24:** Moses is to place these items in the priests' hands, to indicate that they are from them (Lev. 7.30; Num. 6.19–20) and then cause them to *offer* (lit. "elevate") *them as an elevation offering,* a gesture indicating that the offering is donated to God (Lev. 7.30 n.). **25:** *With the burnt offering,* of vv. 15–18. The combination of burnt offerings and sacrifices of well-being is common (10.25; 18.12; 20.21; 24.5; 32.6; Lev. 17.8; etc.). The former is given entirely to God, while parts of the latter are eaten by the donor, guests, and the priests. **26:** *Your portion:* Since the priests' consecration is not yet complete and Moses is officiating in their stead, he is to receive the portion that will

portion. 27 You shall consecrate the breast that was offered as an elevation offering and the thigh that was offered as a gift offering from the ram of ordination—from that which was Aaron's and from that which was his sons'— 28 and those parts shall be a due for all time from the Israelites to Aaron and his descendants. For they are a gift; and so shall they be a gift from the Israelites, their gift to the LORD out of their sacrifices of well-being.

29 The sacral vestments of Aaron shall pass on to his sons after him, for them to be anointed and ordained in. 30 He among his sons who becomes priest in his stead, who enters the Tent of Meeting to officiate within the sanctuary, shall wear them seven days.

31 You shall take the ram of ordination and boil its flesh in the sacred precinct; 32 and Aaron and his sons shall eat the flesh of the ram, and the bread that is in the basket, at the entrance of the Tent of Meeting. 33 These things shall be eaten only by those for whom expiation was made with them when they were ordained and consecrated; they may not be eaten by a layman, for they are holy. 34 And if any of the flesh of ordination, or any of the bread, is left until morning, you shall put what is left to the fire; it shall not be eaten, for it is holy.

35 Thus you shall do to Aaron and his sons, just as I have commanded you. You shall ordain them through seven days, 36 and each day you shall prepare a bull as a purification offering for expiation; you shall purge the altar by performing purification upon it, and you shall anoint it to consecrate it. 37 Seven days you shall perform purification for the altar to consecrate it, and the altar shall become most holy; whatever touches the altar shall become consecrated.

38 Now this is what you shall offer upon the altar: two yearling lambs each day, regularly. 39 You shall offer the one lamb in the morning, and you shall offer the other lamb at twilight. 40 There

in the future go to them (vv. 27–28). **27–28:** A parenthetic note indicating that the disposition of the ram is to be the precedent for all future sacrifices of well-being, with one exception: both the *breast ... and* (unlike on the present occasion, v. 22) the right *thigh* shall be given to the priests (Lev. 7.34–35; 10.15). **28:** In addition to the fat parts, which are burnt (vv. 22, 25), the breast and right thigh of sacrifices of well-being are also donated by the people to God, who assigns them to the priests for their maintenance. **29–30:** A second parenthetic note: The robing of the high priest and the seven-day duration of the ceremony (v. 35) shall be the precedent for the ordination of future high priests. **31–33:** The consecration continues: The remainder of the ram is cooked and eaten, along with the remainder of the unleavened bread, by the priests in the courtyard. **31:** *The sacred precinct,* lit. "in a holy place," either anywhere in the courtyard or in a specific part of it, perhaps the area between the altar and the Tent of Meeting (cf. Lev. 6.9, 19; 8.31). **33:** *They may not be eaten by a layman, for they are holy,* a blanket rule concerning the sacrificial portions assigned to the priests (Lev. 22.10–16). Cf. 30.31–33. **34:** This rule also applies to other sacrifices of well-being, namely the pesaḥ and other festival offerings and the thanksgiving offering (12.10; 23.28; 34.25; Lev. 7.15; 22.30; contrast 7.16–17; 19.6). **35–37:** The consecration of the priests and the altar is to go on for a week. Cf. Ezek. 43.25–26; 2 Chron. 7.9. *Shall become consecrated:* Once the altar is sanctified, its holiness will become contagious. As with other sanctuary furniture and parts of certain sacrifices, anything that touches it will likewise become holy and unfit for ordinary activity and will become the property of the sanctuary. See 30.29; Lev. 6.11 n., 20; Num. 17.1–4 (Ezek. 44.19; 46.20 holds that even people can become consecrated in this way).

29.38–42: The obligatory daily offering. After the procedure for sanctifying the altar and the priests, the text again (as in vv. 28–30) turns to the future, first describing the regular daily offering which the priests will henceforth be fit to make (cf. Ezek. 43.18–27). This offering, made twice daily and known as the "tamid" ("regular" [sacrifice], Dan. 8.11), became the core of the sacrificial system (Num. 28.3–8). With this the text resumes the theme of regular ("tamid") rites begun in 27.20–21. The "tamid" offering consists of the simple staples of the Israelites' diet: the meat of lambs (the least expensive meat), wheat, oil, and wine. No attempt is made to provide delicacies or sumptuous quantities as would befit God's greatness (contrast the royal diet in 1 Kings 5.2–3). This reflects the token nature of biblical sacrifice, expressive of the worshippers' attitude, as distinct from actually feeding God (27.1–8 n.). **39:** *In the morning ... at twilight:* With reference to sacrifices the day is reckoned as beginning in the morning (cf. Lev. 6.13; 2 Kings 16.15; likewise the singing of psalms in the Temple, Ps. 92.2–4; 1 Chron. 23.30; contrast Lev. 23.32 with reference to

shall be a tenth of a measure of choice flour with a quarter of a *hin* of beaten oil mixed in, and a libation of a quarter *hin* of wine for one lamb; [41] and you shall offer the other lamb at twilight, repeating with it the meal offering of the morning with its libation—an offering by fire for a pleasing odor to the LORD, [42] a regular burnt offering throughout the generations, at the entrance of the Tent of Meeting before the LORD.

For there I will meet with you, and there I will speak with you, [43] and there I will meet with the Israelites, and it shall be sanctified by My Presence. [44] I will sanctify the Tent of Meeting and the altar, and I will consecrate Aaron and his sons to serve Me as priests. [45] I will abide among the Israelites, and I will be their God. [46] And they shall know that I the LORD am their God, who brought them out from the land of Egypt that I might abide among them, I the LORD their God.

self-denial on the Day of Atonement). **40:** Cf. Lev. 6.12–16. *A tenth of a measure,* a tenth of an "ʾefah" measure, about 2.3 liters (2.1 dry quarts); see 16.36 n. *Hin,* a liquid measure of uncertain size (possibly about a gallon, in which case a quarter of a "hin" would be a liter or a quart). *Libation:* Libations of wine often accompany burnt and well-being offerings (Lev. 23.13, 18, 27; Num. 15.1–12; Num. chs 28–29; 2 Kings 6.13, 15), though no standalone libation is prescribed. **41:** *An offering by fire for a pleasing odor to the LORD,* see Lev. 1.9 n. **42:** *At the entrance of the Tent of Meeting,* i.e., at the altar in the courtyard.

29.42b–46: The divine Presence in the sanctuary. The sanctuary will be ready to serve its various functions as the site of divine-human communication, as a sanctuary, and as the locus of God's Presence among the Israelites. In this climactic passage, all these functions are alluded to by the verbs (each occurring at least twice) from which the three main terms for the sanctuary (25.8) are derived—thereby explaining these terms. God will *meet* ("ʾivaʿed," "noʿad") there with Moses and Israel, echoing "Tent of Meeting" ("ʾohel moʿed"), it will be *sanctified* ("nikdash," "kadesh," echoing "mikdash," "sanctuary"), and God will *abide* ("shakhan") there, echoing "abode" ("mishkan"). That these goals are mentioned after the regular daily sacrifice may reflect the idea that sacrificial worship is the means by which God is drawn to the sanctuary (20.21 n.). Sacrifice is presented as a means, not as a goal in itself: The sanctuary is for the benefit of Israel, not God (see introductory n. to 25.1–31.17). **42b–43:** *For there I will meet with you ...*, see 25.22. The threefold repetition of "there" emphasizes that it is the sanctuary that will become the regular place of communication between God and Israel, replacing Mt. Sinai. **43:** The ordination ceremony will culminate in a theophany in which God's Presence will appear at the Tent of Meeting in the sight of the entire people (Lev. 9.4, 6, 23–24), thus sanctifying it by His Presence. *I will meet* [Heb "noʿadti"] *with the Israelites:* This statement is unexpected since elsewhere God meets only with Moses (25.22; 30.6, 36) (seeming exceptions are the first "you" in v. 42 and the one in Num. 17.19, which are in the plural, but the LXX and Samaritan Pentateuch read the singular in both cases). Perhaps the text originally read "I shall make Myself known ("nodaʿti") to the Israelites"; cf. Ezek. 20.5, 9; 36.23. (This assumes that an ancient scribe accidentally reversed the order of two letters.) **44:** Perhaps this refers to God's sending fire to consume the offerings on the altar (Lev. 9.24), meaning that the fire sanctified the altar and the sanctuary, and hence the priests who made the offerings. But this v. and v. 43 seem redundant with each other and inconsistent with vv. 21, 36–37 and 30.29–30 which state that it is Moses who will sanctify the sanctuary, the altar, and the priests by sacrifice and anointment. This has led to the suggestion that vv. 42b–46 are not from the Priestly source but stem from the "Holiness Collection" ("H") in which God regularly concludes His statements with "I, the LORD your/their God," and which holds that it is God who sanctifies the priests and the sanctuary (Lev. 21.15, 23; 2.16). If so, the aim of the interpolation is apparently to override the message of vv. 21, 36–37; 30.29–30 by indicating that sacrifice and anointment are not efficacious by themselves; the real source of sanctification is God. **45–46:** These concluding vv. echo the promises of 25.8 and 6.7, tying the exodus narrative and the Tabernacle instructions into one overarching structure of meaning: With the Tabernacle finished God will abide among the Israelites, as promised in 25.8, and fulfill His covenant with them by being their God, as promised in 6.7, and the Israelites will understand that these, rather than freedom from servitude, were the ultimate purpose of the exodus: *that I might abide among them* and that they might live in God's presence. In this respect the goal of the exodus will be achieved even before reaching the promised land. This might explain why the Torah is complete without the narrative of the conquest in the book of Joshua—it is the indwelling of the divine Presence, rather than the conquest of the land that culminates the exodus. (According to 15.17 [see also 6.8] the same goal will be achieved in the promised land when the Temple is built [15.17 n.]).

30 You shall make an altar for burning incense; make it of acacia wood. [2] It shall be a cubit long and a cubit wide—it shall be square—and two cubits high, its horns of one piece with it. [3] Overlay it with pure gold: its top, its sides round about, and its horns; and make a gold molding for it round about. [4] And make two gold rings for it under its molding; make them on its two side walls, on opposite[a] sides. They shall serve as holders for poles with which to carry it. [5] Make the poles of acacia wood, and overlay them with gold.

[6] Place it in front of the curtain that is over the Ark of the Pact—in front of the cover that is over the Pact—where I will meet with you. [7] On it Aaron shall burn aromatic incense: he shall burn it every morning when he tends the lamps, [8] and Aaron shall burn it at twilight when he lights the lamps—a regular incense offering before the LORD throughout the ages. [9] You shall not offer alien incense on it, or a burnt offering or a meal offering; neither shall you pour a libation on it. [10] Once a year Aaron shall perform purification upon its horns with blood of the purification offering; purification shall be performed upon it once a year throughout the ages. It is most holy to the LORD.

KI TISSA כי תשא

[11] The LORD spoke to Moses, saying: [12] When you take a census of the Israelite people according to their enrollment, each shall pay the LORD a ransom for himself on being enrolled, that

a *Lit. "its two."*

30.1–31.17: Supplementary instructions concerning the sanctuary. This section begins with instructions for constructing the incense altar, taking a census, constructing the laver, and for compounding the anointing oil and sacred incense (ch 30). These five supplementary instructions are followed by the designation of the chief artisans for the entire construction project and a final injunction to suspend all construction and manufacture on the Sabbath (31.1–17). There are phraseological similarities among the five subsections of ch 30, and their order may reflect the fact that the first three deal with items made, respectively, of gold, silver, and bronze (see 25.1–31.17 n.) and that items two through five employ materials acquired from special contributions, not those donated by the public at large or in response to the initial appeal (25.2–7; 35.4–9): silver from the census levy (v. 13), the bronze for the laver "from the mirrors of the women who performed tasks at the entrance of the Tent" (38.8), and the spices and oil from the chieftains (35.27–28). It is unclear, however, why all these items appear after 29.42b–46, which seems to conclude the manufacturing instructions. Why were the incense altar and the laver not mentioned earlier along with the other items in, respectively, the Holy Place (25.23–40; 26.35) and the courtyard (27.1–19) where they will stand, and why do the census, the anointing oil, and the incense appear here? In subsequent lists of the contents of the Tabernacle, the incense altar, the laver, the anointing oil, and the incense are listed in their proper physical or functional location (30.26–28; 31.7–11; 35.11–19; 39.33–40; 40.1–15, 18–33). Their location here indicates that their organizing principles elude us and, perhaps, that they were added to this text (though not necessarily composed) at a later date.

30.1–10: The incense altar. This altar would stand in the Holy Place and was, accordingly, overlaid with gold. Its location directly in front of the curtain of the Holy of Holies, flanked by the table and the lampstand (40.5, 22–26) indicates its importance. The burning of incense on it was, like the activities performed on the table and lampstand, one of the regular ("tamid"), daily activities of the Tabernacle (27.20–30.38 n.; 27.20 n.). It was .5 m (1.5 ft) square and .9 m (3 ft) high. Burning incense was common in ancient religions and numerous incense altars, some with horns as prescribed here, have been found among archeological remains from ancient Israel and elsewhere. The altar found at Tell es-Safi (27.2 n.) has dimensions nearly identical to those prescribed here. Since burning incense is part of the complex of daily activities inside the Holy Place that includes kindling lamps (v. 7), it is perhaps regarded as a natural activity in a courtly residence, creating a pleasing aroma inside; as Maimonides noted, it may have counteracted the stench of the animals being slaughtered and sacrificed (*Guide of the Perplexed* 3.45). **9:** *Alien,* unauthorized, compounded with a formula different from that prescribed in vv. 34–36 (cf. Lev. 10.1). *Or a burnt offering or a meal offering; neither shall you pour a libation on it:* No food or drink offerings may be made inside the Tent. Only the "bread of display," which is eaten by the priests, is presented there. This shows again that the offerings are tokens, not consumed by God. See 25.23–30 n.; 29.38–42 n. **10:** *Once a year,* on the Day of Atonement (Lev. 16.16; cf. 4.18; *m. Yoma* 5.5).

30.11–16: Census. This regulation is apparently placed here because the census involves collecting silver

no plague may come upon them through their being enrolled. 13 This is what everyone who is entered in the records shall pay: a half-shekel by the sanctuary weight—twenty *gerah*s to the shekel—a half-shekel as an offering to the LORD. 14 Everyone who is entered in the records, from the age of twenty years up, shall give the LORD's offering: 15 the rich shall not pay more and the poor shall not pay less than half a shekel when giving the LORD's offering as expiation for your persons. 16 You shall take the expiation money from the Israelites and assign it to the service of the Tent of Meeting; it shall serve the Israelites as a reminder before the LORD, as expiation for your persons.

17 The LORD spoke to Moses, saying: 18 Make a laver of copper and a stand of copper for it, for washing; and place it between the Tent of Meeting and the altar. Put water in it, 19 and let Aaron and his sons wash their hands and feet [in water drawn] from it. 20 When they enter the Tent of Meeting they shall wash with water, that they may not die; or when they approach the

that will be used for the construction of the Tabernacle (v. 16) and because the donations serve as "expiation" (vv. 15–16), thus creating a link with v. 10 where "purification" is expressed by the same Heb word ("Kipper"/"kipurim"; see Lev. 4.3 n.). The juxtaposition of this law with the incense altar may also have been prompted by the apotropaic function (i.e., one that averts ill consequences) of the census donation in preventing a plague (v. 12), since incense sometimes has an apotropaic function (Num. 17.11–13). Censuses were normally taken for purposes of military (v. 14 n.; Num. 1.2–3; 2 Sam. 24.9) or other forms of public service (Num. 4.2–3, 22–23, 29–30; 1 Chron. 23.24–32), land distribution (Num. 26.52) and redistribution, and taxation (some of these uses are also known from ancient Mari where the Akkadian term for census literally means "purification"). The link with expiation is evidently due to popular fear that counting people or listing their names might expose them to supernatural danger (Rashi; cf. 2 Sam. 24.1–15; 2 Chron. 21.1–14). Hence when a census was necessary, a payment would be made to "ransom" the lives of those counted and protect them from danger (cf. Num. 31.48–50). The same fear is known from many places in the world and evidently underlies the talmudic dictum not to count Israelites directly; where counting is necessary, objects representing each person, such as ostraca, are counted (*b. Yoma* 22b; Maimonides, *Hilkhot Temidin* 4.4). This practice survives in a Jewish custom for determining whether a prayer quorum ("minyan") of ten is present: ten words of a biblical v., rather than numbers, are applied to those being counted. Similarly, in the present case Rashi says that the half-shekels, not the people, are to be counted. That would explain why all must pay the same amount (v. 15); that is the only way to determine the number of people from the total collected. Although this regulation is limited here to when a census is taken, in Second Temple times it became the basis of an annual impost for maintaining the Temple (possibly reflected in 2 Chron. 24.4–10 [cf. 2 Kings 12.12–25]). The details are spelled out in the talmudic tractate *Shekalim.* Since the payment was due in the month of Adar (early spring), in order to announce it the present law, called "the Section concerning Shekels" *(Parashat Shekalim),* was added as the *maftir* to the weekly Torah reading on the Sabbath of, or preceding, the New Moon of Adar (*m. Meg.* 3.4), and the Sabbath is called "the Sabbath of Shekels" *(Shabbat Shekalim).* Nowadays half of the local currency (e.g., a half-dollar) is collected on Purim, which falls in Adar, and the proceeds are used for the support of synagogues and the poor. **12:** *Ransom,* a payment made to escape death or physical punishment (21.30; Prov. 6.35). **13:** *Half-shekel,* of silver (38.25–26). The shekel was the standard weight. Coinage was not widely used until the Persian period; before that silver was weighed out to serve as currency. *By the sanctuary weight:* Shekels varied in weight: the standard shekel, weighing ca. 11.4 grams (or .4 oz) and possibly the same as the "shekel at the going merchant's weight" (Gen. 23.16), the "sanctuary shekels" (as here), and the "shekel by the royal weight" (2 Sam. 14.26). Examples have been found at excavations. **14:** *From the age of twenty years up,* i.e., of military age (Num. 1.3; etc.). The envisioned censuses would be for military purposes, since the Israelites were organized as an army (12.41 n.). **16:** *Assign it to the service of the Tent of Meeting,* rather, "for the (construction) work on the Tent of Meeting." See 35.21 n. and, for the use to which the silver would be put, 38.25–28. The items made with the silver will stand in the sanctuary *as a reminder before the LORD, as expiation,* that is, for favorable remembrance (28.12 n.) which, by expiating, will prevent a plague. Cf. Num. 31.50, 54.

30.17–21: The laver, a basin containing water for washing, is to be placed between the sacrificial altar and the Tent. Before entering the Tent or offering sacrifices (activities just mentioned in 29.38–42; 30.7–8) the priests must wash their hands and feet (28.2 n.), with which they touch the sacrifices, the sanctuary, and its ground. Talmudic sources describe this as "sanctifying" the hands and feet (*m. Yoma* 3.2). Ramban explains it as an act of respect for God. **18:** *Copper,* rather, bronze, like the other items in the courtyard. For the source of this bronze, see 38.8. **20:** *That they may not die,* 28.35 n.

30.22–33: The sacred anointing oil. The formula of the sacred anointing oil is now given, along with the instruction that it be used to sanctify the sanctuary and all its other furniture as well. It is a fragrant compound of olive oil and the finest spices, and because it is sacred to the LORD it may be used only for the stated purpose, not for everyday hygienic and cosmetic anointing; nor may it be duplicated or used by the laity. **29:** *Whatever touches them shall be consecrated,* 29.35–37 n. **33:** *Cut off from his kin,* 12.15 n.; 28.35 n.

30.34–38: The sacred incense, to be burned on the incense altar (vv. 1–10). Like the anointing oil, it is sacred to the LORD and may not be duplicated and used for any other purpose. **36:** *Put some before the Pact:* See v. 6.

31.1–11: The master builders. Having completed all the instructions for the sanctuary, God designates two master builders to be in charge of executing His plans, Bezalel and his associate Oholiab from the tribes of Judah and Dan, respectively. The construction is supervised and executed by skilled people from all the tribes (v. 6b), not just priests and Levites. **2:** *Bezalel,* possibly meaning "in the shade (i.e., shelter) of God." *Hur,* possibly, but not necessarily, the Hur mentioned in 17.11 and 24.14. **3:** *Divine spirit,* 28.3 n. **6:** *Oholiab,* apparently meaning "the Father (God) is a tent (i.e., shelter)," an apt name for one of the builders of the Tent of Meeting. **7:** *Ark for the Pact,* 25.10–16 n.

altar to serve, to turn into smoke an offering by fire to the LORD,
[21] they shall wash their hands and feet, that they may not die. It shall be a law for all time for them—for him and his offspring—throughout the ages.

[22] The LORD spoke to Moses, saying: [23] Next take choice spices: five hundred weight of solidified[a] myrrh, half as much—two hundred and fifty—of fragrant cinnamon, two hundred and fifty of aromatic cane, [24] five hundred—by the sanctuary weight—of cassia, and a *hin* of olive oil. [25] Make of this a sacred anointing oil, a compound of ingredients expertly blended, to serve as sacred anointing oil. [26] With it anoint the Tent of Meeting, the Ark of the Pact, [27] the table and all its utensils, the lampstand and all its fittings, the altar of incense, [28] the altar of burnt offering and all its utensils, and the laver and its stand. [29] Thus you shall consecrate them so that they may be most holy; whatever touches them shall be consecrated. [30] You shall also anoint Aaron and his sons, consecrating them to serve Me as priests.

[31] And speak to the Israelite people, as follows: This shall be an anointing oil sacred to Me throughout the ages. [32] It must not be rubbed on any person's body, and you must not make anything like it in the same proportions; it is sacred, to be held sacred by you. [33] Whoever compounds its like, or puts any of it on a layman, shall be cut off from his kin.

[34] And the LORD said to Moses: Take the herbs stacte, onycha, and galbanum—these herbs together with pure frankincense; let there be an equal part of each. [35] Make them into incense, a compound expertly blended, refined, pure, sacred. [36] Beat some of it into powder, and put some before the Pact in the Tent of Meeting, where I will meet with you; it shall be most holy to you. [37] But when you make this incense, you must not make any in the same proportions for yourselves; it shall be held by you sacred to the LORD. [38] Whoever makes any like it, to smell of it, shall be cut off from his kin.

31 The LORD spoke to Moses: [2] See, I have singled out by name Bezalel son of Uri son of Hur, of the tribe of Judah. [3] I have endowed him with a divine spirit of skill, ability, and knowledge in every kind of craft; [4] to make designs for work in gold, silver, and copper, [5] to cut stones for setting and to carve wood—to work in every kind of craft. [6] Moreover, I have assigned to him Oholiab son of Ahisamach, of the tribe of Dan; and I have also granted skill to all who are skillful, that they may make everything that I have commanded you: [7] the Tent of Meeting, the Ark for the Pact and the cover upon it, and all the furnishings of the Tent; [8] the table and its utensils, the pure

a Others "flowing."

lampstand[a] and all its fittings, and the altar of incense; 9 the
altar of burnt offering and all its utensils, and the laver and its
stand; 10 the service[b] vestments, the sacral vestments of Aaron
the priest and the vestments of his sons, for their service as
priests; 11 as well as the anointing oil and the aromatic incense
for the sanctuary. Just as I have commanded you, they shall do.
12 And the LORD said to Moses: 13 Speak to the Israelite people and say: Nevertheless, you must keep My sabbaths, for this
is a sign between Me and you throughout the ages, that you
may know that I the LORD have consecrated you. 14 You shall
keep the sabbath, for it is holy for you. He who profanes it shall
be put to death: whoever does work on it, that person shall be
cut off from among his kin. 15 Six days may work be done, but
on the seventh day there shall be a sabbath of complete rest,
holy to the LORD; whoever does work on the sabbath day shall
be put to death. 16 The Israelite people shall keep the sabbath,
observing the sabbath throughout the ages as a covenant for
all time: 17 it shall be a sign for all time between Me and the
people of Israel. For in six days the LORD made heaven and
earth, and on the seventh day He ceased from work and was
refreshed.

18 When He finished speaking with him on Mount Sinai, He
gave Moses the two tablets of the Pact, stone tablets inscribed
with the finger of God.

a *Or "lampstand of pure gold."* *b* *Others "plaited."*

11: *Just as I have commanded you, they shall do:* The design is entirely God's (25.9 n.); the artisans merely follow God's blueprint. That is why they are designated only after the construction plans are given.

31.12–17: The Sabbath. The last of the seven divine commands about building the sanctuary concerns the seventh day of the week, the Sabbath (20.8–11; cf. 25.1–31.17 n.). Thus far, the instructions concerned a holy place; now the instructions emphasize a holy time. As God created a holy time after constructing the world, Israel must observe that holy time even while constructing the sanctuary, indicating that holy time is more important than holy space. **13:** *Nevertheless,* notwithstanding the instructions to construct the sanctuary; thus the building of the sanctuary is to be suspended on the Sabbath (Rashi). *My sabbaths:* Since the Sabbath belongs to God (20.10 n.), observing it serves as *a sign between Me and you* indicating to Israel that God has consecrated them, making them His people, dedicated to His service and sacrosanct to Him (19.5b–6a n.). The notion of *a sign* is key to Priestly thinking about the Sabbath—it is not merely a day of rest. **14:** Because the Sabbath is God's and holy to Him (vv. 13, 15), it must also be holy to Israel (20.8 n.) like the sanctuary and its parts (30.29). Hence, profaning it—treating it as unholy, common—is no less a capital crime than encroaching on the sanctuary (28.35 n.) or Mount Sinai (19.12). *Put to death,* Num. 15.32–36. *Work,* 20.10 n. *Cut off,* 12.15 n.; 28.35 n. **15:** *Rest,* rather, "cessation (of labor)"; see 16.23 n. **16–17:** The Sabbath serves as a sign of Israel's relationship with God because it commemorates God's own actions and, in observing it, Israel follows His example (Gen. 2.1–3; for emulating God, cf. Lev. 19.2); as such, in Priestly thinking, it is also *a covenant for all time. Covenant* may be used here in the sense of a binding obligation or commitment, particularly a covenant obligation (Gen. 17.10; see also Lev. 2.13 n.; Lev. 24.8). These two vv. are part of the Sabbath afternoon Kiddush, the blessing over wine that consecrates the Sabbath.

31.18–34.35: The violation and restoration of the covenant. See also Deut. 9.8–10.11 (with differences), Ps. 106.19–23. Like chs 19–24, this section shows evidence of being based on multiple sources that differ about the course of the events. It clearly combines material from J, E, P, and perhaps other hands as well, but, as in the case of chs 19–24, there is wide disagreement about which passages belong to which source. In 32.7, e.g., God renounces punishment, but in v. 35 He punishes the people, though Aaron is excepted despite his acknowledged complicity (vv. 21–24). Moses' request in 33.15 that God accompany Israel personally is redundant, since God already promised that in v. 14. God's promise to do wonders in 34.10 is not a direct answer to Moses' plea that He go in Israel's midst (v. 9). The description in 33.7–11 about what Moses regularly did with "the tent" interrupts his dialogue with God, and the surrounding narrative (32.30; 34.2, 4, 28–29) is oblivious to it. What is more, although the tent is here regularly in use, and is called the Tent of Meeting (v. 7), it is very different from the tent of the same name in chs 25–31, which is not erected until ch 40 (see 33.7–11 n.). It represents a non-Priestly variant tradition about the Tent and was placed here because its location outside the camp seemed compatible with God's alienation from the people in ch 32. It seems unlikely that its author, who writes that God and Moses spoke "face to face" (33.11), was the same one who wrote that Moses may not see God's face

32 When the people saw that Moses was so long in coming down from the mountain, the people gathered against Aaron and said to him, "Come, make us a god who shall go before us, for that man Moses, who brought us from the land of Egypt—we do not know what has happened to him." 2 Aaron said to them, "Take off the gold rings that are on the ears of your wives, your sons, and your daughters, and bring them to me." 3 And all the people took off the gold rings that were in their ears and brought them to Aaron. 4 This he took from them

(v. 20). God's words about making a covenant in 34.10, 27 give no indication that they refer to the restoration of a prior covenant, and 34.27–28 give confusing information about which document is the basis of the covenant—the document in vv. 11–26 (a doublet, with contextually inexplicable variations, of 23.12–33) or the Decalogue. Possibly ch 34 contains a parallel account of the original Sinai covenant, and the redactor, confronted with both accounts, reinterpreted this account as describing the covenant's renewal.

31.18–32.35: The golden calf episode. The location of the Tabernacle instructions prior to the golden calf episode is puzzling (see introductory comments to 25.1–31.17). The present order, by giving precedence to the Tabernacle as the divinely authorized means of securing God's Presence among the people, shows that the calf is a perverted, humanly devised means of doing the same thing (see 32.4 n.), already forbidden in 20.4–5, 20. The connection between the two pericopes is highlighted by the sequence of events in the calf episode that parallels God's instructions for the Tabernacle and the people's response: The people command Aaron to make them a god, Aaron responds with a public appeal for gold, all the people bring him the gold, he makes the calf with it, builds an altar and offers sacrifices, and the people celebrate (cf. chs 25–31; 35.4–9, 20–29; 36.8–38.20; Lev. chs 8–9). The people's celebration of the calf also bears an ironic resemblance to the covenant ceremony in ch 24: An altar is built, burnt offerings and sacrifices of well-being are made, and the people eat and drink (cf. 24.4–5, 10–11). Their declaration that the calf is the God who brought them out of Egypt contrasts ironically with God's declaration that it is through the Tabernacle that He will abide among the Israelites and they will know that He is their God who brought them out of Egypt (29.45–46). In fact, making the calf leads to the annulment of the covenant (v. 19 n.) and to God's refusal to abide among the people (33.3, 5), and threatens their very existence (32.10). The present arrangement conveys these messages and shows that the people's generous and obedient response to the Tabernacle instructions (chs 35–39, esp. 36.3–7; 39.42–43) is a sign of their repentance, while God's Presence entering the Tabernacle (40.34–38) is a sign of His forgiveness. The narrative has similarities to the account of the golden calves that Jeroboam (the first king of the Northern Kingdom) erected in Bethel and Dan (1 Kings 12.25–33), and some scholars believe that the present Exodus narrative goes back to a putative northern legend that portrayed Aaron's making of the calf in positive terms and served to legitimize Jeroboam's calves by giving them an ancient and prestigious precedent, since Aaron was the archetypical priest. In this view, the original northern legend portrayed the calf not as an idol but as a pedestal or mount for God (see 32.4 n.; see also v. 24 n.). A Judahite writer who viewed Jeroboam's golden calves as idolatrous revised the story about Aaron's calf to characterize the phenomenon as sinful from the outset and, implicitly, to condemn the Bethel and Dan sanctuaries. In this view, that is the version that we find here. **31.18:** The Jewish Masoretic paragraph system starts this episode here (unlike the medieval Christian ch divisions, which start it at 32.1), highlighting the outrage of the people's behavior: At the very moment that God was giving Moses the Tablets of the Pact, which forbids idolatry (20.4–5), the people were demanding just that (see also Deut. 9.8–13). In modern terms, "the ink was not yet dry" on the covenant when the people violated it. **32.1:** With Moses now gone for forty days (24.18), the people fear that he has disappeared, and since he had been their sole conduit to God they ask Aaron to make them a "god" to replace him (Radak at 1 Kings 12.28) and lead them. Although most commentators believe that they mean "god" literally, they more likely mean it as a metonymy for an object that would serve as a conduit for securing God's Presence. See v. 4 n. *That man Moses:* In the people's view, Moses disappeared because he was a mortal; that is why they want a "god" to replace him. **3:** *Gold rings,* 3.22; 11.2–3; 12.35–36. **4:** *Cast in a mold,* rather, as Rashi notes, "tied them in a garment (or bag)" (2 Kings 5.23). *And made it into a molten calf,* from the melted earrings. *And they exclaimed, "This is your God, O Israel, who brought you out of the land of Egypt!":* As Rashbam notes, the people cannot be so foolish as to believe that the resultant image is the God who had brought them out of Egypt. They must view it either as an image that represents Him and will attract His Presence (20.20 n.) or as a pedestal on which He will stand invisibly (cf. the cherub throne, 25.17–22 n.). Images of calves and bulls in these roles have been found in archeological excavations in Israel and neighboring lands. The Heb reads lit. "These are your gods," and "brought" is also plural, as is the verb for "go" and "lead" in vv. 1 and

and [a-]cast in a mold,[-a] and made it into a molten calf. And they
exclaimed, [b-]"This is your god,[-b] O Israel, who brought you out
of the land of Egypt!" [5]When Aaron saw this, he built an altar
before it; and Aaron announced: "Tomorrow shall be a festival
of the LORD!" [6]Early next day, the people offered up burnt offerings and brought sacrifices of well-being; they sat down to
eat and drink, and then rose to dance.
[7]The LORD spoke to Moses, "Hurry down, for your people,
whom you brought out of the land of Egypt, have acted basely.
[8]They have been quick to turn aside from the way that I enjoined upon them. They have made themselves a molten calf
and bowed low to it and sacrificed to it, saying: 'This is your
god, O Israel, who brought you out of the land of Egypt!' "
[9]The LORD further said to Moses, "I see that this is a stiffnecked people. [10]Now, let Me be, that My anger may blaze
forth against them and that I may destroy them, and make of
you a great nation." [11]But Moses implored the LORD his God,
saying, "Let not Your anger, O LORD, blaze forth against Your
people, whom You delivered from the land of Egypt with great
power and with a mighty hand. [12]Let not the Egyptians say, 'It
was with evil intent that He delivered them, only to kill them
off in the mountains and annihilate them from the face of the
earth.' Turn from Your blazing anger, and renounce the plan
to punish Your people. [13]Remember Your servants, Abraham,

a-a Cf. Zech. 11.13 (beth hayyoṣer, *"foundry"); others "fashioned it with a graving tool."*
b-b Others "These are your gods."

23. The translation construes this as a meaningless grammatical technicality, much like the English use of "data" as a singular even though it is technically plural; since Heb "'elohim," "god/God," is grammatically plural in form even when its meaning is singular, it is occasionally accompanied by a plural verb as here (Josh. 24.19; 2 Sam. 7.23). But since the plural verb is also found in Jeroboam's nearly identical words about the *two* calves he made (1 Kings 12.28), it seems possible that, in the putative northern legend underlying our account, the people's words were originally singular and that the plural is part of the pejorative recasting of the legend, highlighting their similarity to Jeroboam's and characterizing the people's request as idolatrous and polytheistic from the outset. **5:** *A festival of the LORD:* Since the image does not represent a different god, the people are not in violation of the Decalogue's prohibition against worshipping other gods but rather, as v. 8 indicates, the prohibition of making and worshipping idols (20.4–5). **6:** *Dance,* cf. vv. 18–19, where singing and dancing are both mentioned. The people are honoring the calf as they had honored God in 15.20–21. **7:** *Your people, whom you brought out of the land of Egypt:* God normally refers to Israel as "My people" "whom I brought out of Egypt" (3.7; 29.46). Here He feels alienated from them and speaks of them as Moses' people, much as an exasperated parent may refer to a misbehaving child as the other spouse's child. Contrast Moses' language in vv. 11 and 33.13. **9:** *Stiffnecked,* obstinate. The Heb idiom is close in meaning to English "headstrong." **10:** *Let Me be:* God implies that Moses can restrain Him from destroying Israel. Midrashic commentaries understand this as a hint for Moses to do just that by praying on Israel's behalf and making the case for sparing them. Prophets frequently play this intercessory role (1 Sam. 12.23; Jer. 18.20; Ezek. 22.30–31; Ps. 106.23; cf. Gen. 18.17–32). *Make of you a great nation:* God would fulfill His promise to the patriarchs, to make their descendants a great nation, through Moses and his descendants alone. **11–14:** Moses mounts a multifaceted plea: Israel is God's own people on whose behalf He has invested much effort; destroying His own people will injure His reputation among other nations; and He has a sworn obligation to the Israelites' ancestors, who were His loyal servants. In Jewish practice this passage and 34.1–10 are read in the synagogue on the public fast days that commemorate national disasters or near-disasters. **11:** *Your people, whom You delivered from the land of Egypt:* Here Moses counters God's disassociation of Himself from Israel in v. 7. All the effort that God has invested in Israel would be for naught if He were to destroy them. **12:** Moses argues that annihilating Israel would damage God's reputation in the world; He would appear diabolical and lose the stature that He had gained from the exodus. This suggests that God cares about His reputation. **13:** By destroying the Israelites God would, furthermore, violate His oath to the patriarchs to give them countless descendants and eternal possession of the promised land (Gen. 12.7; 13.15–16; 15.5; 17.7–8). Even Israel's violation of the conditional covenant made at Sinai (19.5–6) would not justify destroying Israel, since the earlier covenant with the patriarchs was unconditional and irrevocable (Gen. 17.7; Deut. 4.31). Moses' invocation of the patriarchs became the precedent for the postbiblical idea of the "merit of the ancestors" ("zekhut 'avot") in Jewish prayers. Going beyond the idea that God rewards later generations for their ancestors' merits (20.6), and the

Isaac, and Israel, how You swore to them by Your Self and said to them: I will make your offspring as numerous as the stars of heaven, and I will give to your offspring this whole land of which I spoke, to possess forever." 14 And the LORD renounced the punishment He had planned to bring upon His people.

15 Thereupon Moses turned and went down from the mountain bearing the two tablets of the Pact, tablets inscribed on both their surfaces: they were inscribed on the one side and on the other. 16 The tablets were God's work, and the writing was God's writing, incised upon the tablets. 17 When Joshua heard the sound of the people in its boisterousness, he said to Moses, "There is a cry of war in the camp." 18 But he answered,

"It is not the sound of the tune of triumph,
Or the sound of the tune of defeat;
It is the sound of song that I hear!"

19 As soon as Moses came near the camp and saw the calf and the dancing, he became enraged; and he hurled the tablets from his hands and shattered them at the foot of the mountain. 20 He took the calf that they had made and burned it; he ground it to powder and strewed it upon the water and so made the Israelites drink it.

21 Moses said to Aaron, "What did this people do to you that you have brought such great sin upon them?" 22 Aaron said, "Let not my lord be enraged. You know that this people is bent on evil. 23 They said to me, 'Make us a god to lead us; for that man Moses, who brought us from the land of Egypt—we do not know what has happened to him.' 24 So I said to them, 'Whoever has gold, take it off!' They gave it to me and I hurled it into the fire and out came this calf!"

25 Moses saw that the people were out of control—since Aaron had let them get out of control—so that they were a menace[a] to any who might oppose them. 26 Moses stood up in the gate of the camp and said, "Whoever is for the LORD, come here!" And all the Levites rallied to him. 27 He said to them, "Thus says the LORD, the God of Israel: Each of you put sword

a Others "an object of derision."

notion that the ancestral promise may never be broken, this concept holds that even when Israel lacks merit—as in the present case—its ancestors' merits can sustain it and God may grant mercy for their sake. **14:** God's agreement not to destroy the people responds to Moses' plea in v. 12, but not to the request to bring Israel to the promised land in v. 13 (see v. 34). In fact, full reconciliation will require several further pleas by Moses. See v. 34; 33.12–17; 34.9. **15:** *Bearing the two tablets of the Pact,* which he has just received (31.18). **16:** *Incised* (Heb "ḥarut") *upon the tablets:* In a verbal play, a midrash interprets the text as if it read "(there was) freedom ("ḥerut") upon the tablets," explaining that no one is free except one who studies the Torah (*Pirkei 'Avot* 6.2). Ironically, subjugation to law is viewed as bringing true freedom. **17–18:** Joshua, waiting for Moses part-way up the mountain (24.13 n.), hears the people's noise but misjudges its nature, but Moses discerns that it is singing. The Heb word for singing ("'anot") is the same one used for Miriam's singing of God's praises in 15.21, again suggesting that the people are honoring the calf as they had honored God (v. 6 n.). **19:** Breaking the tablets expresses not only Moses' rage but (as in Mesopotamian law) the annulment of the covenant, since its most fundamental condition has been violated. His action is the equivalent of tearing up a contract. **20:** Rabbinic exegesis, followed by some modern scholars, takes the forced drinking as a kind of ordeal designed to identify the guilty, comparable to the "waters of bitterness" ritual for testing the suspected adulteress (Num. 5.11–31; *b. A. Z.* 44a). Ramban suggests that when the people drink the water with the powdered ashes of the calf, the idol would be degraded further by being turned into human waste. **21:** Moses demands an accounting of Aaron because he had left him in charge (24.14). **24:** *Out came this calf!:* Aaron denies responsibility for making the calf: it made itself! Some see here evidence for a version of the story in which the calf was created supernaturally (which supports the view that the story was originally an approving one), like midrashim that describe how the Tabernacle and Solomon's Temple, respectively, erected and built themselves (e.g., *Exod. Rab.* 52.4) and a Ugaritic myth that tells how Baal's palace was built by simply firing silver and gold for six days (D. Pardee in W. W. Hallo and K. L. Younger, eds., *The Context of Scripture* 1.261). **26:** *Whoever is for the LORD:* As far as Moses is concerned, whatever the intention of its worshippers, worshipping an image is tantamount to worshipping another god and must be opposed by those loyal to the LORD. The Levites, Moses' fellow tribesmen, step forward. This story thus justifies the Levites' later important cultic role (see v. 29 n.). **27:** With Israel's

on thigh, go back and forth from gate to gate throughout the camp, and slay brother, neighbor, and kin." [28] The Levites did as Moses had bidden; and some three thousand of the people fell that day. [29] And Moses said, "Dedicate yourselves[a] to the LORD this day—for each of you has been against son and brother—that He may bestow a blessing upon you today."

[30] The next day Moses said to the people, "You have been guilty of a great sin. Yet I will now go up to the LORD; perhaps I may win forgiveness for your sin." [31] Moses went back to the LORD and said, "Alas, this people is guilty of a great sin in making for themselves a god of gold. [32] Now, if You will forgive their sin [well and good]; but if not, erase me from the record which You have written!" [33] But the LORD said to Moses, "He who has sinned against Me, him only will I erase from My record. [34] Go now, lead the people where I told you. See, My angel shall go before you. But when I make an accounting, I will bring them to account for their sins."

[35] Then the LORD sent a plague upon the people, [b]for what they did with the calf that Aaron made.[-b]

33 Then the LORD said to Moses, "Set out from here, you and the people that you have brought up from the land of Egypt, to the land of which I swore to Abraham, Isaac, and Jacob, saying, 'To your offspring will I give it'—[2] I will send an angel before you, and I will drive out the Canaanites, the

a Lit. "fill your hands." *b-b Meaning of Heb. uncertain.*

fate in the balance (v. 30), Moses orders the Levites, in God's name, to summarily execute the guilty, not sparing even their own kin. **29:** The Heb is difficult. Taking the verbs as past tense (thus LXX), the v. may mean that by their action the Levites have dedicated themselves to God's service. In view of the idiom "fill the hand" (28.41 n.) the v. may mean, "Today you have ordained yourselves/been ordained for the service of the LORD ... and so have brought a blessing upon yourselves (or: He has granted you a blessing) today." This has been seen as referring to the Levites' future role as sanctuary attendants (Num. 1.48–54; chs 3–4), but in P texts in the Torah only priests are ordained, and according to Deut. 10.8 it was at this time that God chose the Levites for their future priestly role. Deut. holds, contrary to P (Exod. 28.1), that all Levites, not only descendants of Aaron, may be priests (Deut. 18.1–8); the present non-P narrative may share that view. Having battled illegitimate worship, the Levites are made the ministers of legitimate worship. See also Deut. 33.8–10. **30:** *Perhaps I may win forgiveness for your sin:* From God's incomplete response in v. 14 Moses realizes that He has not yet forgiven the people. Moses wants more than simply their survival. But he is not certain that God will grant forgiveness. The idea that divine forgiveness is not automatic is found elsewhere (see e.g., Joel 2.14; Jonah 3.9). **32:** *Erase me from the record which You have written,* i.e., "the book of life" (or, "the book of the living," Ps. 69.29; cf. Isa. 4.3; for the translation *record* see 17.14 n.), a notion (based on Mesopotamian tablets of life and destiny written by the gods) developed in much detail in the postbiblical liturgy for Rosh Ha-Shanah and Yom Kippur. Moses demands that his own life be taken if God will not forgive Israel. According to Ramban, he means that if God will not forgive Israel, He should take Moses' life in Israel's place. In either case, Moses here goes beyond his earlier refusal to supplant Israel (v. 10 n.). **33–34:** God declines both of Moses' requests: He will not take Moses' life or waive further punishment of the people, but says that only the guilty will be punished (cf. Ezek. ch 18). He does agree that the people may proceed to the promised land, but led only by an angel (23.20 n.), not Himself personally. **35:** Here, in contrast to v. 33, punishment was not limited to those directly involved in worshipping the calf but, in keeping with the concept of collective responsibility, strikes "the people," i.e., others as well (Num. 25.8–9; Josh. 7.1–5, 24–26).

33.1–6: The LORD's further displeasure. 1–3: Explaining what He meant in 32.34, God's reference to *the people that you* (Moses) *have brought up from the land of Egypt* indicates that He is still alienated from Israel. Despite the similarity of His words in v. 2 to His promise in 23.20–23, vv. 3b–5 make clear that here the promise of angelic guidance is punitive: God Himself will not accompany a rebellious people. The people's misguided attempt to secure God's Presence and guidance (32.1) has backfired, and God's plan to abide among the people in the Tabernacle (25.8; 29.45–46) is implicitly withdrawn. All of Moses' efforts in chs 33–34 are directed toward ending this alienation and restoring God's direct Presence among the people, and he succeeds step by step; see vv. 14, 17; 34.1, 10. In the present, redacted form of Exodus, with this narrative (from J and E) followed by chs 35–40 (P), Moses' crowning success is the resumption of plans to build God's abode among the people in chs 35–40. **2–3a:** *The Canaanites ... milk and honey,* 3.8 n.

Amorites, the Hittites, the Perizzites, the Hivites, and the Jebusites—3 a land flowing with milk and honey. But I will not go
in your midst, since you are a stiffnecked people, lest I destroy
you on the way."
4 When the people heard this harsh word, they went into
mourning, and none put on his finery.
5 The LORD said to Moses, "Say to the Israelite people, 'You
are a stiffnecked people. If I were to go in your midst for one
moment, I would destroy you. Now, then, leave off your finery,
and I will consider what to do to you.'" 6 So the Israelites remained stripped of the finery from Mount Horeb on.

7 Now Moses would take the Tent and pitch it outside the
camp, at some distance from the camp. It was called the Tent
of Meeting, and whoever sought the LORD would go out to the
Tent of Meeting that was outside the camp. 8 Whenever Moses
went out to the Tent, all the people would rise and stand, each
at the entrance of his tent, and gaze after Moses until he had
entered the Tent. 9 And when Moses entered the Tent, the pillar
of cloud would descend and stand at the entrance of the Tent,
while He spoke with Moses. 10 When all the people saw the pillar of cloud poised at the entrance of the Tent, all the people
would rise and bow low, each at the entrance of his tent. 11 The
LORD would speak to Moses face to face, as one man speaks to
another. And he would then return to the camp; but his attendant, Joshua son of Nun, a youth, would not stir out of the Tent.

12 Moses said to the LORD, "See, You say to me, 'Lead this
people forward,' but You have not made known to me whom
You will send with me. Further, You have said, 'I have singled
you out by name, and you have, indeed, gained My favor.'
13 Now, if I have truly gained Your favor, pray let me know Your
ways, that I may know You and continue in Your favor. Consider, too, that this nation is Your people." 14 And He said, [a-]"I
will go in the lead and will[-a] lighten your burden." 15 And he
said to Him, "Unless You go in the lead, do not make us leave
this place. 16 For how shall it be known that Your people have

a-a Lit. "My face will go and I will."

33.7–11: The Tent of Meeting moved outside the camp. As a consequence of God's refusal to abide among the people, Moses moves the site for communicating with Him outside the camp and (v. 12) resumes his dialogue with Him. Since this tent is also called "the Tent of Meeting," scholars consider it part of a variant tradition (found also in Num. 11.16–30; 12.4–13; Deut. 31.14–15) which sees the "Tent of Meeting" not as a sanctuary or a place of sacrifice, as does P (chs 25–31, 35–40), but purely as an oracle-site. Kept outside the camp, it is tended by Joshua rather than priests, and anybody who wants to consult God may come to it. God does not abide in it but descends to it in a pillar of cloud to converse with Moses *face to face, as one man speaks to another* (v. 11), rather than by voice only from between the cherubs (25.27; Num. 7.89). The statement that Moses *would … pitch* [the Tent] *outside the camp* supports the theory that this passage was not originally part of the present context; it indicates that Moses would regularly pitch the Tent outside the camp, not inside the camp as P requires (Num. 2.2, 17); cf. Num. 11.26, 30; 12.4. **7:** *Tent of Meeting:* The explanation that *whoever sought the LORD* would resort to the Tent is consistent with the etymology of the name (25.8 n.). **11:** *Face to face,* cf. Num. 12.8; Deut. 34.10. Even if meant figuratively, this is incompatible with vv. 20–22, which is from a different source. *Would not stir out of the Tent,* cf. 1 Sam. 3.3, 15.

33.12–23: Moses pleads with God. 12: *You have not made known to me whom You will send with me,* namely the angel of God mentioned in v. 2. **13:** *Let me know Your ways,* Your ways in dealing with humankind, meaning—as indicated by God's response in 34.6–7 and Ps. 103.7–13—the principles by which you deal with human sin. God had said that the angel would be unforgiving (23.21). What is God's own way? *Consider, too, that this nation is Your people:* Perhaps: What is Your way, considering that Israel is Your own people? (32.7 n., 11 n.; cf. v. 16 n. below). **14:** *I will go in the lead and will lighten your burden:* Rather: "I personally will go and will deliver you to safety." "Deliver to a safe haven" is a common meaning of the second verb (Deut. 3.20; 25.19). This is essentially the role God had promised the angel would play in v. 2 and 23.20–23, and is therefore a further concession to Moses, though he has not yet agreed to go in Israel's midst (34.9). **15:** *Unless You go in the lead:* Rather, "unless you personally go," as in v. 14. **16:** A preferable translation would be: "For how shall it be known that I have gained Your favor—I and Your people—unless You go with us, so that we may be distinguished—I and Your

gained Your favor unless You go with us, so that we may be distinguished, Your people and I, from every people on the face of the earth?"

[17] And the LORD said to Moses, "I will also do this thing that you have asked; for you have truly gained My favor and I have singled you out by name." [18] He said, "Oh, let me behold Your Presence!" [19] And He answered, "I will make all My goodness pass before you, and I will proclaim before you the name LORD, [a-]and the grace that I grant and the compassion that I show.[-a] [20] But," He said, "you cannot see My face, for man may not see Me and live." [21] And the LORD said, "See, there is a place near Me. Station yourself on the rock [22] and, as My Presence passes by, I will put you in a cleft of the rock and shield you with My hand until I have passed by. [23] Then I will take My hand away and you will see My back; but My face must not be seen."

34 The LORD said to Moses: "Carve two tablets of stone like the first, and I will inscribe upon the tablets the words that were on the first tablets, which you shattered. [2] Be ready by morning, and in the morning come up to Mount Sinai and present yourself there to Me, on the top of the mountain. [3] No one else shall come up with you, and no one else shall be seen anywhere on the mountain; neither shall the flocks and the herds graze at the foot of this mountain."

[4] So Moses carved two tablets of stone, like the first, and early in the morning he went up on Mount Sinai, as the LORD had commanded him, taking the two stone tablets with him. [5] The LORD came down in a cloud; He stood with him there, and proclaimed the name LORD. [6] The LORD passed before him [b-]and proclaimed: "The LORD! the LORD![-b] a God compassionate and

a-a Lit. "and I will grant the grace that I will grant and show the compassion that I will show."

b-b Or "and the Lord proclaimed: The LORD! a God compassionate," etc.; cf. Num. 14.17–18.

people—from every people on the face of the earth?" Moses insists that Israel enjoy the same favor that he does and reiterates that it is God's people. The proof of divine favor is being led by God Himself, not by an intermediary. **18:** Emboldened by God's favorable reply, Moses supplements his request to know God's ways (v. 13) with a request to behold God's Presence (16.6–7 n.), that is, to know Him visually as well (see vv. 20–23). He seeks total familiarity with God. **19–23:** God replies to both of Moses' requests: He will let him know His ways (v. 19) and grant him a partial visual experience, but a full visual experience would be fatal (vv. 20–23). **19:** *Proclaim ... the name LORD:* God will disclose all the qualities embodied in His name, YHVH (3.14–15 n.; 6.2 n.); this is fulfilled in 34.6–7. According to rabbinic exegesis, the name YHVH ("LORD") expresses God's attribute of mercy while "God" ("'elohim") expresses His attribute of strict justice, but as 34.6–7 shows, the name YHVH expresses both attributes (cf. 34.13). *And the grace that I grant and the compassion that I show:* Better, "but I shall grant grace to whom I will and shall be merciful to whom I will." Notwithstanding His gracious qualities, God remains sovereign and decides whom or whether to forgive. Justice may not be viewed as automatic (see v. 3). **20:** See 3.6 n.; cf. 24.10 n. According to Num. 12.8, Moses sees God's "likeness" (Heb "temunah," which appears in poetic parallelism with "face" in Ps. 17.15). This may represent a different tradition than the present v., or it may represent a later stage in Moses' relationship with God. **21:** *On the rock,* better "mountain," namely on the top of Mount Sinai. **22–23:** *My hand ... My back ... My face:* As noted in the comment to 3.6, the Bible assumes that God has a human form; but that seeing Him would be too awesome for humans to survive.

34.1–35: Restoration of the covenant. Exod. 34.1–10, containing the list of God's attributes and the phrase "Pardon our iniquity and our sin, and take us for Your own!" (v. 9), is part of the Torah reading on public fast days (see 32.11–14 n.). **1:** God now prepares to formally restore the covenant by replacing the broken tablets (32.19 n.). But whereas the first tablets were made by God (32.16), these would be man-made, though inscribed by God. Sforno infers from the difference that God did not forgive Israel completely. **3:** As when the terms of the covenant were first proclaimed, access to the mountain is restricted (cf. 19.12, 21–24) in preparation for God's descending to it (v. 5). **5–7:** God grants both of Moses' requests, passing His Presence before him (33.22) and proclaiming His ways (33.13). *The name LORD [YHVH],* that is, the attributes it represents. These attributes include both magnanimity (vv. 6–7a) and justice (v. 7b; cf. v. 14). *Kindness and faithfulness,* rather as a hendiadys, "steadfast faithfulness" (Heb "ḥesed" [15.13 n.; 20.6 n.] and "'emet"), extending Himself to those in covenant with Him; cf. Ps. 25.10 (rendered "steadfast love").

gracious, slow to anger, abounding in kindness and faithfulness, 7 extending kindness to the thousandth generation, forgiving iniquity, transgression, and sin; yet He does not remit
all punishment, but visits the iniquity of parents upon children
and children's children, upon the third and fourth generations."
8 Moses hastened to bow low to the ground in homage, 9 and
said, "If I have gained Your favor, O Lord, pray, let the Lord go
in our midst, even though this is a stiffnecked people. Pardon
our iniquity and our sin, and take us for Your own!"
10 He said: I hereby make a covenant. Before all your people
I will work such wonders as have not been wrought on all the
earth or in any nation; and all the people [a]who are with you[a]
shall see how awesome are the LORD's deeds which I will perform for you. 11 Mark well what I command you this day. I will
drive out before you the Amorites, the Canaanites, the Hittites,
the Perizzites, the Hivites, and the Jebusites. 12 Beware of making a covenant with the inhabitants of the land against which
you are advancing, lest they be a snare in your midst. 13 No, you
must tear down their altars, smash their pillars, and cut down
their sacred posts; 14 for you must not worship any other god,
because the LORD, whose name is Impassioned, is an impassioned God. 15 You must not make a covenant with the inhabitants of the land, for they will lust after their gods and sacrifice
to their gods and invite you, and you will eat of their sacrifices.
16 And when you take wives from among their daughters for

a-a Lit. "in whose midst you are."

7: *Extending kindness ... visits the iniquity ...*, 20.5, 6 nn. This v. closely parallels the latter but it reverses the order, giving precedence to God's magnanimous attributes in response to Moses' plea for pardon. At the same time, its characterization of transgenerational reward and punishment is unconditional, unlike that in 20.5–6 which limits it to descendants who follow their ancestors' ways. God's sovereign right to dispense reward and punishment is not bound by the limits He imposes on human justice (Deut. 24.16). *Yet He does not remit all punishment,* Num. 14.19. God never entirely waives punishment, although it may be deferred, even to a later generation (see esp. 1 Kings 21.29). **8–9:** Ignoring God's punitive attributes, Moses invokes His magnanimous attributes and pleads that He cancel His refusal to go in Israel's midst (vv. 3, 5) and forgive its sin. *Take us for Your own,* reestablish Israel as His own people. The Heb means "take us (back) as your inalienable hereditary property," a metaphor frequently applied to Israel to express God's attachment to them (Deut. 4.20; 9.29), "since a person's personal property and his portion are dear to him" (Saadia Gaon, *Book of Beliefs and Opinions,* 2:11). Moses' ignoring of God's punitive qualities became a precedent in the Bible and in later Jewish practice; both frequently recite only God's magnanimous attributes (e.g., Jonah 4.2; Joel 2.23; Ps. 86.15; and esp. Neh. 9.17–18, which refers to the golden calf episode; Ps. 25.4–11 is virtually a commentary on the magnanimous attributes), reflecting a firm belief that God is more magnanimous than punitive (Ezek. 18.23, 32). Jewish tradition calls the list of God's magnanimous qualities His "Thirteen Attributes." It is recited as a prayer for forgiveness on various holidays, fast days, and other penitential occasions, especially the Days of Awe (the High Holidays). **10:** God will (re) establish the covenant. He will lead Israel to the promised land with unprecedented miracles (cf. 9.13–10.29 n.). In return, Israel is to obey the following terms. **11–26:** In view of the people's recent religious sin, these terms restate their religious duties; they are a variant—in some details stricter—of the pertinent section of the Book of the Covenant (23.12–33; see comments there). In light of the people's sin of idolatry, the order in the parallel section in ch 23 is reversed, presenting the laws against idolatry first and in greater detail (vv. 11–17 || 23.20–33) and then the religious calendar (vv. 18–26 || 23.12–19). **11:** Cf. 23.23, 31b. **12–13:** An expanded list (based on 23.32–33) of Canaanite cult objects that must be destroyed. *Sacred posts,* Heb "'asherah," a wooden object standing at a place of worship. It was a natural or artificial tree, an image, a tree trunk, or a pole (Deut. 16.21; Judg. 6.25–32; 1 Kings 21.3, 7). It may have been regarded as a symbol of the Canaanite goddess Asherah or of the protection, fertility, or nourishment worshippers hoped to receive from a deity. **14:** Exod. 23.24 is restated in the more comprehensive terms of 20.3, 5, including the prohibition of worshipping *any* other god and the warning against provoking God's indignation (20.5 n.). This passage goes beyond 20.5 in stating that the LORD's very *name is Impassioned,* meaning that jealous indignation (20.5 n.) is another of the qualities embodied in His name or essence (33.19). This is possibly a play on the name YHVH, equating its root "h-vh" with "h-wy" used in Arabic with the meaning "passion." **15–16:** This explains v. 12, warning that Canaanites remaining in the land would, especially through intermarriage, seduce the Israelites

your sons, their daughters will lust after their gods and will
cause your sons to lust after their gods.
17 You shall not make molten gods for yourselves.
18 You shall observe the Feast of Unleavened Bread—eating
unleavened bread for seven days, as I have commanded you—
at the set time of the month[a] of Abib, for in the month of Abib
you went forth from Egypt.
19 Every first issue of the womb is Mine, from all your livestock that drop a male[b] as firstling, whether cattle or sheep.
20 But the firstling of an ass you shall redeem with a sheep; if
you do not redeem it, you must break its neck. And you must
redeem every first-born among your sons.
None shall appear before Me empty-handed.
21 Six days you shall work, but on the seventh day you shall
cease from labor; you shall cease from labor even at plowing
time and harvest time.
22 You shall observe the Feast of Weeks, of the first fruits of
the wheat harvest; and the Feast of Ingathering at the turn of
the year. 23 Three times a year all your males shall appear before the Sovereign LORD, the God of Israel. 24 I will drive out
nations from your path and enlarge your territory; no one will
covet your land when you go up to appear before the LORD
your God three times a year.
25 You shall not offer the blood of My sacrifice with anything
leavened; and the sacrifice of the Feast of Passover shall not be
left lying until morning.
26 The choice first fruits of your soil you shall bring to the
house of the LORD your God.
You shall not boil a kid in its mother's milk.
27 And the LORD said to Moses: Write down these commandments, for in accordance with these commandments I make a
covenant with you and with Israel.
28 And he was there with the LORD forty days and forty nights;
he ate no bread and drank no water; and he wrote down on the
tablets the terms of the covenant, the Ten Commandments.

a See note at 13.4. *b Heb.* tizzakhar, *form uncertain.*

into participating in their idolatry (cf. Num. 25.1–3). This law is, however, less stringent than Deut. 20.17, which commands the complete destruction of the Canaanites. **17:** *You shall not make molten gods for yourselves,* a command not stated in 23.20–23 but essentially a restatement of 20.4 in terms relevant to the present circumstances (32.4, 8). **18–26:** Since in worshipping the calf the Israelites created an illicit religious festival (32.5), the calendar of legitimate festivals and related obligations is restated. **18:** Cf. 23.14–15. **19–20a:** A digression prompted by the connection of dedicating the first-born with the exodus; cf. 13.2, 11–15 and cf. 22.28–29. **20b:** *None shall appear before Me empty-handed,* continuing v. 18; cf. 23.15b. **21:** A further digression, prompted by the mention of the harvest in the next v. *Even at plowing time and harvest time:* The Sabbath (cf. 23.12) takes precedence even at the busiest time of the agricultural year, as it does when building the Tabernacle (31.12–17; 35.2–3). **22:** Cf. 23.16. *The Feast of Weeks* is another name for the Feast of the Harvest. According to Lev. 23.15–16 and Deut. 16.9–10 it is observed seven weeks ("the weeks appointed for reaping," Jer. 5.24) after the Feast of Unleavened Bread. **23:** *Three times a year,* on the three pilgrimage festivals (23.14–17 n.; Deut. 16.16). See 23.17. **24:** The men need have no fear of an attack on their homes when they leave for the festivals (23.17 n.). *Covet,* rather, have designs on, scheme against (20.14). **25–26:** See 12.6–11, 21–26; 23.18–19. **27:** The commandments just received are to form the basis of the restored covenant. **28:** *Forty days and forty nights,* as when he received the first tablets (24.18). *Ate no bread and drank no water:* During his private, intimate encounter with God Moses was beyond human needs and concerns (contrast 24.9–11). *He wrote down on the tablets the terms of the covenant, the Ten Commandments:* In view of v. 1 and Deut. 10.4 this seems to mean that God wrote down the Decalogue, so that two covenant documents—vv. 11–26 and the Decalogue—resulted from this encounter, just as the terms of the earlier covenant included both the Decalogue and the Book of the Covenant (24.4, 7–8, 12; 31.18). But in the immediate context *he wrote* is most naturally construed as referring to Moses and *the terms of the covenant* as referring to the terms mentioned in vv. 11–26. This is why some scholars call vv. 11–26 the Ritual Decalogue or Cultic Decalogue. But dividing the commandments of those vv. into ten is difficult and why the text designates them as the Decalogue—which according to v. 1 God was going to write on the tablets—is puzzling. The present text appears to combine two different traditions about what the terms of the covenant were.

29 So Moses came down from Mount Sinai. And as Moses
came down from the mountain bearing the two tablets of the
Pact, Moses was not aware that the skin of his face was radiant,
since he had spoken with Him. 30 Aaron and all the Israelites
saw that the skin of Moses' face was radiant; and they shrank
from coming near him. 31 But Moses called to them, and Aaron
and all the chieftains in the assembly returned to him, and
Moses spoke to them. 32 Afterward all the Israelites came near,
and he instructed them concerning all that the LORD had imparted to him on Mount Sinai. 33 And when Moses had finished
speaking with them, he put a veil over his face.
34 Whenever Moses went in before the LORD to speak with
Him, he would leave the veil off until he came out; and when
he came out and told the Israelites what he had been commanded, 35 the Israelites would see how radiant the skin of
Moses' face was. Moses would then put the veil back over his
face until he went in to speak with Him.

VA-YAKHEL ויקהל

35 Moses then convoked the whole Israelite community
and said to them:
These are the things that the LORD has commanded you to
do: 2 On six days work may be done, but on the seventh day
you shall have a sabbath of complete rest, holy to the LORD;
whoever does any work on it shall be put to death. 3 You shall
kindle no fire throughout your settlements on the sabbath day.
4 Moses said further to the whole community of Israelites:
This is what the LORD has commanded: 5 Take from among
you gifts to the LORD; everyone whose heart so moves him shall
bring them—gifts for the LORD: gold, silver, and copper; 6 [a]blue,
purple, and crimson yarns, fine linen, and goats' hair; 7 tanned
ram skins, dolphin skins, and acacia wood; 8 oil for lighting, spices for the anointing oil and for the aromatic incense; 9 lapis lazuli
and other stones for setting, for the ephod and the breastpiece.
10 And let all among you who are skilled come and make all that
the LORD has commanded: 11 the Tabernacle, its tent and its covering, its clasps and its planks, its bars, its posts, and its sockets;
12 the ark and its poles, the cover, and the curtain for the screen;

a *See 25.4 ff. and the notes there.*

29–35: Not only was Moses beyond human needs while with God (v. 28 n.), but his face came to radiate an awe-inspiring light. According to passages such as Ezek. 1.27–28; Hab. 3.4; Ps. 104.2, the divine Presence is surrounded by a radiant luminosity (a concept also found in Mesopotamian literature, called "fearsome radiance"). Thus, from his lengthy and intense encounter with God, Moses' face came to reflect the divine radiance and his status was even greater than before. In this way, the golden calf episode ends with the theme with which it began: Moses' role as Israel's conduit to God, which the people feared they had lost (32.1 n.), is reaffirmed and he is shown to be more than a common "man" (32.1). **29:** *Radiant,* Heb "karan," from "keren," "horn," in the sense of projection, emanation, as in Hab. 3.4 ("rays"). In the Vg, Jerome, in an over-etymological translation, rendered "was horned," although he knew from the LXX that the meaning was figurative. Nevertheless, his translation led to the image of Moses with horns in medieval and Renaissance art (see esp. Michelangelo's Moses), and eventually, coupled with the notion of Satan's horns, to the anti-Semitic belief that Jews have horns.

Chs 35–40: The construction of the Tabernacle and God's entrance into it. The people's change of heart following their rebellion is shown by their punctilious obedience to God's commands, highlighted by near verbatim correspondence between the instructions in chs 25–31 and their execution in 35–40, and by the recurring phrase "as the LORD had commanded Moses" in 38.32, 42, 43 and ch 39, and by the people's enthusiasm, indicated by recurrent references in ch 35 to their hearts and spirits moving them to give, to their freewill offerings (35.29; 36.3), and by their giving so much that they had to be stopped (36.3–7).

35.1–3: The Sabbath reiterated. Moses begins with the Sabbath, the same subject with which God's instructions concluded in 31.12–17. It is an appropriate introduction to a section in which the word "work" (Heb "mela'khah") appears twenty-one more times, further emphasizing that no work is to be done on the Sabbath. **3:** *You shall kindle no fire throughout your settlements on the sabbath day:* Rabbinic exegesis holds that this prohibition allows for letting a previously kindled fire burn, so long as it is not refueled on the Sabbath. Karaite (non-Rabbanite) Jews, however, took the law to prohibit the use even of a previously kindled fire; they spent the Sabbath in darkness.

35.4–29: The call for donations and craftspeople and the people's response. 10–19: The contents of the

13 the table, and its poles and all its utensils; and the bread of display; 14 the lampstand for lighting, its furnishings and its lamps,
and the oil for lighting; 15 the altar of incense and its poles; the
anointing oil and the aromatic incense; and the entrance screen
for the entrance of the Tabernacle; 16 the altar of burnt offering, its
copper grating, its poles, and all its furnishings; the laver and its
stand; 17 the hangings of the enclosure, its posts and its sockets,
and the screen for the gate of the court; 18 the pegs for the Tabernacle, the pegs for the enclosure, and their cords; 19 the service
vestments for officiating in the sanctuary, the sacral vestments of
Aaron the priest and the vestments of his sons for priestly service.
20 So the whole community of the Israelites left Moses' presence. 21 And everyone who excelled in ability and everyone
whose spirit moved him came, bringing to the LORD his offering for the work of the Tent of Meeting and for all its service
and for the sacral vestments. 22 Men and women, all whose
hearts moved them, all who would make an elevation offering
of gold to the LORD, came bringing brooches, earrings, rings,
and pendants[a]—gold objects of all kinds. 23 And everyone who
had in his possession blue, purple, and crimson yarns, fine lin-
en, goats' hair, tanned ram skins, and dolphin skins, brought
them; 24 everyone who would make gifts of silver or copper
brought them as gifts for the LORD; and everyone who had in
his possession acacia wood for any work of the service brought
that. 25 And all the skilled women spun with their own hands,
and brought what they had spun, in blue, purple, and crimson
yarns, and in fine linen. 26 And all the women who excelled in
that skill spun the goats' hair. 27 And the chieftains brought lapis lazuli and other stones for setting, for the ephod and for the
breastpiece; 28 and spices and oil for lighting, for the anointing
oil, and for the aromatic incense. 29 Thus the Israelites, all the
men and women whose hearts moved them to bring anything
for the work that the LORD, through Moses, had commanded
to be done, brought it as a freewill offering to the LORD.
30 And Moses said to the Israelites: See, the LORD has singled
out by name Bezalel, son of Uri son of Hur, of the tribe of Judah. 31 He has endowed him with a divine spirit of skill, ability,
and knowledge in every kind of craft 32 and [b-]has inspired him[-b]
to make designs for work in gold, silver, and copper, 33 to cut
stones for setting and to carve wood—to work in every kind
of designer's craft—34 and to give directions. He and Oholiab
son of Ahisamach of the tribe of Dan 35 have been endowed
with the skill to do any work—of the carver, the designer, the
embroiderer in blue, purple, crimson yarns, and in fine linen,
36 and of the weaver—as workers in all crafts and as makers of designs. 1 Let, then, Bezalel and Oholiab and all

Tabernacle are listed in more systematic order than in chs 25–31 (see introductory n. to 30.1–31.17). **21:** *For the work of the Tent of Meeting and for all its service,* rather, "for the work on the Tent of Meeting, all the labor on it." The materials contributed were for the construction of the Tabernacle, not for the worship that would be conducted there afterwards. Heb "'avodah," translated "service" here and in 27.19; 30.16; 35.24; 36.1, 3, 5; 39.40, is better rendered "labor" (referring to construction). See esp. 36.1 where the "'avodah," performed by nonpriests, cannot refer to the worship service, which was conducted by the priests. **22:** *Elevation offering,* 29.24 n. *Gold objects of all kinds:* The jewelry given by the Egyptians is now used to obey rather than violate God's commands (contrast 32.2–3). **25–26:** *And all the skilled women spun:* Women had a role in the building of the Tabernacle (cf. 38.8). Spinning was women's work (Prov. 31.19).

35.30–36.1: The appointment of the master builders. The translation correctly ignores the ch break (a medieval innovation; there is none here in the Heb MT) since Moses' announcement continues through 36.1. **35.30:** *See, the LORD has singled out.* Moses informs the public of Bezalel and Oholiab's appointment. The Talmud, interpreting "see" as meaning "do you agree?" inferred that one must not appoint a public leader without first consulting the public (*b. Ber.* 54a with Rashi). **34:** *And to give directions,* to instruct others in these skills.

a *Meaning of Heb.* kumaz *uncertain.* b-b *Moved up from v. 34 for clarity.*

36.2–7: The overabundance of donations. 3: *Continued,* even after the work began; see v. 4. The commencement of the work is related in v. 8.

36.8–38.20: The construction of the Tabernacle. As in 35.10–19, the contents are listed in a more systematic order than earlier.

36.8–37: The Tabernacle structure. See 26.1–37. **35:** *The curtain* for the entrance to the Holy of Holies (26.31–33).

the skilled persons whom the LORD has endowed with skill and ability to perform expertly all the tasks connected with the service of the sanctuary carry out all that the LORD has commanded.
[2] Moses then called Bezalel and Oholiab, and every skilled person whom the LORD had endowed with skill, everyone who excelled in ability, to undertake the task and carry it out.
[3] They took over from Moses all the gifts that the Israelites had brought, to carry out the tasks connected with the service of the sanctuary. But when these continued to bring freewill offerings to him morning after morning, [4] all the artisans who were engaged in the tasks of the sanctuary came, each from the task upon which he was engaged, [5] and said to Moses, "The people are bringing more than is needed for the tasks entailed in the work that the LORD has commanded to be done." [6] Moses thereupon had this proclamation made throughout the camp: "Let no man or woman make further effort toward gifts for the sanctuary!" So the people stopped bringing: [7] their efforts had been more than enough for all the tasks to be done.

[8] Then all the skilled among those engaged in the work made the Tabernacle of ten strips of cloth, which they made of fine twisted linen, blue, purple, and crimson yarns; into these they worked a design of cherubim. [9] The length of each cloth was twenty-eight cubits, and the width of each cloth was four cubits, all cloths having the same measurements. [10] They joined five of the cloths to one another, and they joined the other five cloths to one another. [11] They made loops of blue wool on the edge of the outermost cloth of the one set, and did the same on the edge of the outermost cloth of the other set: [12] they made fifty loops on the one cloth, and they made fifty loops on the edge of the end cloth of the other set, the loops being opposite one another. [13] And they made fifty gold clasps and coupled the units[a] to one another with the clasps, so that the Tabernacle became one whole.

[14] They made cloths of goats' hair for a tent over the Tabernacle; they made the cloths eleven in number. [15] The length of each cloth was thirty cubits, and the width of each cloth was four cubits, the eleven cloths having the same measurements.
[16] They joined five of the cloths by themselves, and the other six cloths by themselves. [17] They made fifty loops on the edge of the outermost cloth of the one set, and they made fifty loops on the edge of the end cloth of the other set. [18] They made fifty copper clasps to couple the Tent together so that it might become one whole. [19] And they made a covering of tanned ram skins for the tent, and a covering of dolphin skins above.

a Lit. "strip of cloth," here used collectively.

[20] They made the planks for the Tabernacle of acacia wood, upright. [21] The length of each plank was ten cubits, the width of each plank a cubit and a half. [22] Each plank had two tenons, parallel[a] to each other; they did the same with all the planks of the Tabernacle. [23] Of the planks of the Tabernacle, they made twenty planks for the south side,[b] [24] making forty silver sockets under the twenty planks, two sockets under one plank for its two tenons and two sockets under each following plank for its two tenons; [25] and for the other side wall of the Tabernacle, the north side, twenty planks, [26] with their forty silver sockets, two sockets under one plank and two sockets under each following plank. [27] And for the rear of the Tabernacle, to the west, they made six planks; [28] and they made two planks for the corners of the Tabernacle at the rear. [29] [c-]They matched at the bottom, but terminated as one at the top into one ring;[-c] they did so with both of them at the two corners. [30] Thus there were eight planks with their sockets of silver: sixteen sockets, two under each plank.

[31] They made bars of acacia wood, five for the planks of the one side wall of the Tabernacle, [32] five bars for the planks of the other side wall of the Tabernacle, and five bars for the planks of the wall of the Tabernacle at the rear, to the west; [33] they made the center bar to run, halfway up the planks, from end to end. [34] They overlaid the planks with gold, and made their rings of gold, as holders for the bars; and they overlaid the bars with gold.

[35] They made the curtain of blue, purple, and crimson yarns, and fine twisted linen, working into it a design of cherubim. [36] They made for it four posts of acacia wood and overlaid them with gold, with their hooks of gold; and they cast for them four silver sockets.

[37] They made the screen for the entrance of the Tent, of blue, purple, and crimson yarns, and fine twisted linen, done in embroidery; [38] and five posts for it with their hooks. They overlaid their tops and their bands with gold; but the five sockets were of copper.

37 Bezalel made the ark of acacia wood, two and a half cubits long, a cubit and a half wide, and a cubit and a half high. [2] He overlaid it with pure gold, inside and out; and he made a gold molding for it round about. [3] He cast four gold rings for it, for its four feet: two rings on one of its side walls and two rings on the other. [4] He made poles of acacia wood, overlaid them with gold, [5] and inserted the poles into the rings on the side walls of the ark for carrying the ark.

[6] He made a cover of pure gold, two and a half cubits long and a cubit and a half wide. [7] He made two cherubim of

37.1–9: The Ark and its cherub-cover. See 25.10–22. These would stand in the Holy of Holies.

a *See note at 26.17.* *b* *See note at 26.18.* *c-c* *See note at 26.24.*

37.10–28: The table, the lampstand, and the incense altar. See 25.23–40; 31.1–10. These would stand in the Holy Place. Here the incense altar is not separated from the other items that it would stand with as it is in 31.1–10.

37.29: The anointing oil and the incense. See 30.22–37. The incense is mentioned here because it would be burnt on the incense altar. The anointing oil is mentioned with it by association, since it too is a compound.

gold; he made them of hammered work, at the two ends of
the cover: 8 one cherub at one end and the other cherub at
the other end; he made the cherubim of one piece with the
cover, at its two ends. 9 The cherubim had their wings spread
out above, shielding the cover with their wings. They faced
each other; the faces of the cherubim were turned toward
the cover.

10 He made the table of acacia wood, two cubits long, one
cubit wide, and a cubit and a half high; 11 he overlaid it with
pure gold and made a gold molding around it. 12 He made a
rim of a hand's breadth around it and made a gold molding
for its rim round about. 13 He cast four gold rings for it and attached the rings to the four corners at its four legs. 14 The rings
were next to the rim, as holders for the poles to carry the table.
15 He made the poles of acacia wood for carrying the table, and
overlaid them with gold. 16 The utensils that were to be upon
the table—its bowls, ladles, jugs, and jars with which to offer
libations—he made of pure gold.

17 He made the lampstand of pure gold. He made the
lampstand—its base and its shaft—of hammered work; its
cups, calyxes, and petals were of one piece with it. 18 Six
branches issued from its sides: three branches from one side
of the lampstand, and three branches from the other side of
the lampstand. 19 There were three cups shaped like almond-
blossoms, each with calyx and petals, on one branch; and
there were three cups shaped like almond-blossoms, each
with calyx and petals, on the next branch; so for all six
branches issuing from the lampstand. 20 On the lampstand
itself there were four cups shaped like almond-blossoms,
each with calyx and petals: 21 a calyx, of one piece with it,
under a pair of branches; and a calyx, of one piece with it,
under the second pair of branches; and a calyx, of one piece
with it, under the last pair of branches; so for all six branches
issuing from it. 22 Their calyxes and their stems were of one
piece with it, the whole of it a single hammered piece of pure
gold. 23 He made its seven lamps, its tongs, and its fire pans of
pure gold. 24 He made it and all its furnishings out of a talent
of pure gold.

25 He made the incense altar of acacia wood, a cubit long
and a cubit wide—square—and two cubits high; its horns
were of one piece with it. 26 He overlaid it with pure gold: its
top, its sides round about, and its horns; and he made a gold
molding for it round about. 27 He made two gold rings for it
under its molding, on its two walls—on opposite sides—as
holders for the poles with which to carry it. 28 He made the
poles of acacia wood, and overlaid them with gold. 29 He prepared the sacred anointing oil and the pure aromatic incense,
expertly blended.

38 He made the altar for burnt offering of acacia wood, five cubits long and five cubits wide—square—and three cubits high. 2 He made horns for it on its four corners, the horns being of one piece with it; and he overlaid it with copper. 3 He made all the utensils of the altar—the pails, the scrapers, the basins, the flesh hooks, and the fire pans; he made all these utensils of copper. 4 He made for the altar a grating of meshwork in copper, extending below, under its ledge, to its middle. 5 He cast four rings, at the four corners of the copper grating, as holders for the poles. 6 He made the poles of acacia wood and overlaid them with copper; 7 and he inserted the poles into the rings on the side walls of the altar, to carry it by them. He made it hollow, of boards.

8 He made the laver of copper and its stand of copper, from the mirrors of the women who performed tasks[a] at the entrance of the Tent of Meeting.

9 He made the enclosure:

On the south[b] side, a hundred cubits of hangings of fine twisted linen for the enclosure—10 with their twenty posts and their twenty sockets of copper, the hooks and bands of the posts being silver.

11 On the north side, a hundred cubits—with their twenty posts and their twenty sockets of copper, the hooks and bands of the posts being silver.

12 On the west side, fifty cubits of hangings—with their ten posts and their ten sockets, the hooks and bands of the posts being silver.

13 And on the front side, to the east, fifty cubits: 14 fifteen cubits of hangings on the one flank, with their three posts and their three sockets, 15 and fifteen cubits of hangings on the other flank—on each side of the gate of the enclosure[c]—with their three posts and their three sockets.

16 All the hangings around the enclosure were of fine twisted linen. 17 The sockets for the posts were of copper, the hooks and bands of the posts were of silver, the overlay of their tops was of silver; all the posts of the enclosure were banded with silver.—18 The screen of the gate of the enclosure, done in embroidery, was of blue, purple, and crimson yarns, and fine twisted linen. It was twenty cubits long. [d-]Its height—or width—was five cubits, like that of[-d] the hangings of the enclosure. 19 The posts were four; their four sockets were of copper, their hooks of silver; and the overlay of their tops was of silver, as were also their bands.—20 All the pegs of the Tabernacle and of the enclosure round about were of copper.

a Meaning of Heb. uncertain. *b Cf. note at 26.18.*
c Which accounts for the remaining 20 cubits; cf. v. 18.
d-d Meaning of Heb. uncertain.

38.1–8: The altar of burnt offering and the laver. See 27.1–8; 30.17–21. These would stand in the courtyard; they are not separated from each other as they were when first mentioned. **8:** The laver is not made from the copper (bronze) donated by the general public (vv. 29–31) but from a separate gift from *the women who performed tasks at the entrance of the Tent of Meeting:* The same class of women is mentioned in 1 Sam. 2.22 but there is no indication of what they did. In Num. 4.23; 8.24 the Heb phrase translated *performed tasks* refers to the Levites performing physical labor. This notice here is doubly enigmatic since the Tent has not yet been erected. Nevertheless, it clearly indicates some role for women not only in building the Tabernacle (35.25–26) but also in its functioning.

38.9–20: The enclosure. See 27.9–19.

PEKUDEI פקודי

21 These are the records of the Tabernacle, the Tabernacle of the Pact, which were drawn up at Moses' bidding—the work of the Levites under the direction of Ithamar son of Aaron the priest. 22 Now Bezalel, son of Uri son of Hur, of the tribe of Judah, had made all that the LORD had commanded Moses; 23 at his side was Oholiab son of Ahisamach, of the tribe of Dan, carver and designer, and embroiderer in blue, purple, and crimson yarns and in fine linen.

24 All the gold that was used for the work, in all the work of the sanctuary—the elevation offering of gold—came to 29 talents[a] and 730 shekels by the sanctuary weight. 25 The silver of those of the community who were recorded came to 100 talents and 1,775 shekels by the sanctuary weight: 26 a half-shekel[b] a head, half a shekel by the sanctuary weight, for each one who was entered in the records, from the age of twenty years up, 603,550 men. 27 The 100 talents of silver were for casting the sockets of the sanctuary and the sockets for the curtain, 100 sockets to the 100 talents, a talent a socket. 28 And of the 1,775 shekels he made hooks for the posts, overlay for their tops, and bands around them.

29 The copper from the elevation offering came to 70 talents and 2,400 shekels. 30 Of it he made the sockets for the entrance of the Tent of Meeting; the copper altar and its copper grating and all the utensils of the altar; 31 the sockets of the enclosure round about and the sockets of the gate of the enclosure; and all the pegs of the Tabernacle and all the pegs of the enclosure round about.

39 Of the blue, purple, and crimson yarns they also[c] made the service vestments for officiating in the sanctuary; they made Aaron's sacral vestments—as the LORD had commanded Moses.

2 The ephod was made[d] of gold, blue, purple, and crimson yarns, and fine twisted linen. 3 They hammered out sheets of gold and cut threads to be worked into designs among the blue, the purple, and the crimson yarns, and the fine linen. 4 They made for it attaching shoulder-pieces; they were attached at its two ends. 5 The decorated band that was upon it was made like it, of one piece with it; of gold, blue, purple, and crimson yarns, and fine twisted linen—as the LORD had commanded Moses.

6 They bordered the lazuli stones with frames of gold, engraved with seal engravings of the names of the sons of Israel.

a A talent here equals 3,000 shekels. *b Heb.* beqaʿ. *c See 36.8.*
d Here and elsewhere in this chapter the singular active verb (lit. "he made") is used impersonally.

38.21–31: The tally of materials. A tally of donations was being made as they were given (cf. 36.3–7). (Egyptian art shows metal being weighed and recorded before being used by artisans [*ANEP* no. 133].) The items are listed in descending order of value. The list is not balanced. It includes the total of all the gold donated by the general public and used throughout the sanctuary, but does not identify the specific items made with it. On the other hand, it tallies, and specifies the items made with the silver acquired from the census (30.11–16), but not that given in the general donation (35.24; it is not known what was done with the latter, since the former was used for everything that is supposed to be made of silver [26.19–32; 27.10–11, 17]). In contrast to the silver, it tallies, and specifies articles made with the copper/bronze given in the general donation (35.25), but not that obtained from the women's mirrors (38.8). For the fabrics in 39.1 (if they are part of this list), no quantities are given at all. **21:** *These are the records,* better, "this is the tally." *The Tabernacle of the Pact,* 25.10–16 n. *The work of the Levites:* They conducted the tally. *Under the direction of Ithamar son of Aaron the priest:* The later censuses were also under priestly supervision (Num. 1.2–3, 17–18; 26.1–3, 63). *Ithamar* (6.23; 28.1) would later supervise some of the Levites in their porterage duties (Num. 4.28, 33; 7.8). **22–23:** The cooperation of Bezalel and Oholiab was necessary for the Levites to supervise how the metals were used. **25–26:** It is unclear when this census was carried out since none is ordered until a month after the sanctuary was completed (Num. 1.1, 18; see Exod. 40.2, 17). **26:** *Half-shekel:* Stone weights inscribed with this term in Heb script ("bekaʿ," a different term than that used in 30.13, 15) have been found in excavations. *603,550 men,* men of military age, excluding the Levites. See Num. 1.46; 2.32 and the estimated tally in Exod. 12.37. **30:** *The copper altar,* the main sacrificial altar, overlaid with copper (27.1–8).

39.1–31: The making of the priestly vestments. See ch 28. **1:** The first half of this v. may belong with the tally of materials in 29.21–31.

7 They were set on the shoulder-pieces of the ephod, as stones
of remembrance for the Israelites—as the LORD had commanded Moses.
8 The breastpiece was made in the style of the ephod: of
gold, blue, purple, and crimson yarns, and fine twisted linen.
9 It was square; they made the breastpiece doubled—a span
in length and a span in width, doubled. 10 They set in it four
rows of stones. The first row was a row of[a] carnelian, chrysolite,
and emerald; 11 the second row: a turquoise, a sapphire, and
an amethyst; 12 the third row: a jacinth, an agate, and a crystal;
13 and the fourth row: a beryl, a lapis lazuli, and a jasper. They
were encircled in their mountings with frames of gold. 14 The
stones corresponded [in number] to the names of the sons of
Israel: twelve, corresponding to their names; engraved like
seals, each with its name, for the twelve tribes.
15 On the breastpiece they made braided chains of corded
work in pure gold. 16 They made two frames of gold and two
rings of gold, and fastened the two rings at the two ends of
the breastpiece, 17 attaching the two golden cords to the two
rings at the ends of the breastpiece. 18 They then fastened the
two ends of the cords to the two frames, attaching them to the
shoulder-pieces of the ephod, at the front. 19 They made two
rings of gold and attached them to the two ends of the breastpiece, at its inner edge, which faced the ephod. 20 They made
two other rings of gold and fastened them on the front of the
ephod, low on the two shoulder-pieces, close to its seam above
the decorated band. 21 The breastpiece was held in place by a
cord of blue from its rings to the rings of the ephod, so that the
breastpiece rested on the decorated band and did not come
loose from the ephod—as the LORD had commanded Moses.
22 The robe for the ephod was made of woven work, of pure
blue.[b] 23 The opening of the robe, in the middle of it, was like
the opening of a coat of mail, with a binding around the opening, so that it would not tear. 24 On the hem of the robe they
made pomegranates of blue, purple, and crimson yarns, twisted. 25 They also made bells of pure gold, and attached the bells
between the pomegranates, all around the hem of the robe,
between the pomegranates: 26 a bell and a pomegranate, a bell
and a pomegranate, all around the hem of the robe for officiating in—as the LORD had commanded Moses.
27 They made the tunics of fine linen, of woven work, for
Aaron and his sons; 28 and the headdress of fine linen, and the
decorated turbans of fine linen, and the linen breeches of fine
twisted linen; 29 and sashes of fine twisted linen, blue, purple,
and crimson yarns, done in embroidery—as the LORD had
commanded Moses.

a See note at 28.17. *b See note at 28.31.*

30 They made the frontlet for the holy diadem of pure gold, and incised upon it the seal inscription: "Holy to the LORD." 31 They attached to it a cord of blue to fix it upon the headdress above—as the LORD had commanded Moses.

32 Thus was completed all the work of the Tabernacle of the Tent of Meeting. The Israelites did so; just as the LORD had commanded Moses, so they did.

33 Then they brought the Tabernacle to Moses, with the Tent and all its furnishings: its clasps, its planks, its bars, its posts, and its sockets; 34 the covering of tanned ram skins, the covering of dolphin skins, and the curtain for the screen; 35 the Ark of the Pact and its poles, and the cover; 36 the table and all its utensils, and the bread of display; 37 the pure lampstand,[a] its lamps—lamps in due order—and all its fittings, and the oil for lighting; 38 the altar of gold, the oil for anointing, the aromatic incense, and the screen for the entrance of the Tent; 39 the copper altar with its copper grating, its poles and all its utensils, and the laver and its stand; 40 the hangings of the enclosure, its posts and its sockets, the screen for the gate of the enclosure, its cords and its pegs—all the furnishings for the service of the Tabernacle, the Tent of Meeting; 41 the service vestments for officiating in the sanctuary, the sacral vestments of Aaron the priest, and the vestments of his sons for priestly service. 42 Just as the LORD had commanded Moses, so the Israelites had done all the work. 43 And when Moses saw that they had performed all the tasks—as the LORD had commanded, so they had done—Moses blessed them.

40 And the LORD spoke to Moses, saying: 2 On the first day of the first month you shall set up the Tabernacle of the Tent of Meeting. 3 Place there the Ark of the Pact, and screen off the ark with the curtain. 4 Bring in the table and lay out its due setting; bring in the lampstand and light its

a See note at 31.8.

39.32–43: The completion and inspection of the Tabernacle's components. This section begins and ends by indicating that everything was made exactly as God had commanded. See chs 35–40 n. As in 35.10–19; 36.8–38.20, the contents of the Tabernacle are listed in a more systematic order than earlier. **32:** *Thus was completed all the work of the Tabernacle of the Tent of Meeting:* The phraseology, "completed" and "all" (see also 40.33 n.), alludes to the completion of the creation of the world in Gen. 2.1, 3, one of several echoes of the Priestly source's account of creation here in its account of the creation of the Tabernacle (see 25.1–31.17 n.). The leitmotif of this section, mentioned seven times, that each item was made exactly "as the LORD had commanded Moses" (supplemented in vv. 32, 42, 43 with "so they did/had done") echoes the sevenfold repetition of the formula "and there was/it was so" in Gen. ch 1, indicating that all happened as God commanded (see also. 40.17–33 with reference to setting up the Tabernacle). Paralleling Genesis, the section ends with Moses inspecting ("seeing") everything that was made and blessing the people (cf. Gen. 1.31; 2.3; see v. 43 n. regarding phraseology), and the Tabernacle is completed on New Year's day (40.17). See also 40.9 n. All of these allusions reflect the view that the sanctuary and the world mirror each other and that actions of the priests officiating in the sanctuary mirror God's actions in creating the world (note esp. the role of dividing/discriminating ["havdel"] in creation and in the priests' duties, Gen. 1.4, 6, 14; Lev. 10.10). *The Tabernacle of the Tent of Meeting:* This designation (see also v. 40) combines the two main terms for the sanctuary, expressing its two main functions. See 25.8 n. **34:** *And the curtain for the screen,* the screen at the entrance to the Holy of Holies (26.31–33). *The curtain,* for the entrance to the Holy of Holies (26.31–33). **38:** *The altar of gold,* the incense altar, overlaid with gold (31.1–9). **39:** *The copper altar,* the main sacrificial altar (27.1–8). **43:** *And when Moses saw that they had performed all the tasks,* lit. "And Moses saw all the work, and behold ..." echoing Gen. 1.31, lit. "And God saw all that He had made, and behold ..." "Work" (Heb "mela'khah") is the term used for God's work of creation in Gen. 2.2–3 (see also introductory n. to 35.2–3). *Moses blessed them,* another echo of the Priestly creation account, though here it is Moses who blesses; cf. Gen. 1.22, 28; 2.3.

40.1–16: Instructions for setting up and consecrating the Tabernacle and the priests. Only Moses can set up the components of the Tabernacle because only he has been shown how it should look (25.9 n.). He must also perform certain priestly tasks because the priests are not yet consecrated and eligible to perform them (vv. 4, 23, 25, 27).

40.1–8: The Tabernacle. 2: *On the first day of the first month,* an appropriate date for beginning the

lamps; [5] and place the gold altar of incense before the Ark of the Pact. Then put up the screen for the entrance of the Tabernacle.

[6] You shall place the altar of burnt offering before the entrance of the Tabernacle of the Tent of Meeting. [7] Place the laver between the Tent of Meeting and the altar, and put water in it. [8] Set up the enclosure round about, and put in place the screen for the gate of the enclosure.

[9] You shall take the anointing oil and anoint the Tabernacle and all that is in it to consecrate it and all its furnishings, so that it shall be holy. [10] Then anoint the altar of burnt offering and all its utensils to consecrate the altar, so that the altar shall be most holy. [11] And anoint the laver and its stand to consecrate it.

[12] You shall bring Aaron and his sons forward to the entrance of the Tent of Meeting and wash them with the water. [13] Put the sacral vestments on Aaron, and anoint him and consecrate him, that he may serve Me as priest. [14] Then bring his sons forward, put tunics on them, [15] and anoint them as you have anointed their father, that they may serve Me as priests. This their anointing shall serve them for everlasting priesthood throughout the ages.

[16] This Moses did; just as the LORD had commanded him, so he did.

[17] In the first month of the second year, on the first of the month, the Tabernacle was set up. [18] Moses set up the Tabernacle, placing its sockets, setting up its planks, inserting its bars, and erecting its posts. [19] He spread the tent over the Tabernacle, placing the covering of the tent on top of it—just as the LORD had commanded Moses.

[20] He took the Pact and placed it in the ark; he fixed the poles to the ark, placed the cover on top of the ark, [21] and brought the ark inside the Tabernacle. Then he put up the curtain for screening, and screened off the Ark of the Pact—just as the LORD had commanded Moses.

[22] He placed the table in the Tent of Meeting, outside the curtain, on the north side of the Tabernacle. [23] Upon it he laid out the setting of bread before the LORD—as the LORD had commanded Moses. [24] He placed the lampstand in the Tent of Meeting opposite the table, on the south side of the Tabernacle. [25] And he lit the lamps before the LORD—as the LORD had commanded Moses. [26] He placed the altar of gold in the Tent of Meeting, before the curtain. [27] On it he burned aromatic incense—as the LORD had commanded Moses.

[28] Then he put up the screen for the entrance of the Tabernacle. [29] At the entrance of the Tabernacle of the Tent of Meeting he placed the altar of burnt offering. On it he offered up the burnt offering and the meal offering—as the LORD had commanded Moses. [30] He placed the laver between the Tent of

sanctuary service. **4:** *Its due setting,* i.e., the bread of display (25.23–30 n.).

40.9–16: Consecrating the Tabernacle and the priests. See 30.26–30; 29.4–9. **9:** *Consecrate it ... so that it shall be holy,* lit. "make it holy ... so that it shall be holy." This phrase in this context, with its allusions to the creation story (39.32 n.), is reminiscent of God's consecrating the seventh day in Gen. 2.3 where "declared it holy" is the same Heb word. **16:** *This Moses did,* referring to the instructions in vv. 1–15, which Moses carries out in two stages: He sets up the Tabernacle in vv. 17–33, and consecrates it and the priests in Lev. 8.1–13. *Just as the LORD had commanded him, so he did:* A slightly different form of this statement appears seven times in vv. 17–33.

40.17–33a: Setting up the Tabernacle. 27: There is no explicit command for Moses to burn the incense or offer the sacrifices (v. 29), but his doing so is consistent with God's commands that he perform the other priestly duties of laying out the bread and lighting the lamps (vv. 4, 23, 25) prior to the priests' consecration. The reference to Moses approaching the altar in vv. 31–32 must refer to the same pre-consecration period.

Meeting and the altar, and put water in it for washing. [31] From it Moses and Aaron and his sons would wash their hands and feet; [32] they washed when they entered the Tent of Meeting and when they approached the altar—as the LORD had commanded Moses. [33] And he set up the enclosure around the Tabernacle and the altar, and put up the screen for the gate of the enclosure.

When Moses had finished the work, [34] the cloud covered the Tent of Meeting, and the Presence of the LORD filled the Tabernacle. [35] Moses could not enter the Tent of Meeting, because the cloud had settled upon it and the Presence of the LORD filled the Tabernacle. [36] When the cloud lifted from the Tabernacle, the Israelites would set out, on their various journeys; [37] but if the cloud did not lift, they would not set out until such time as it did lift. [38] For over the Tabernacle a cloud of the LORD rested by day, and fire would appear in it[a] by night, in the view of all the house of Israel throughout their journeys.

a I.e., in the cloud.

40.33b–38: The divine Presence enters the Tabernacle. With the Tabernacle complete, God's Presence (16.6–7 n.) leaves Mount Sinai (this is implicit) and takes up Its abode amidst the Israelites, fulfilling the promise of 29.43, 45 and signifying the complete repair of the rupture between God and Israel occasioned by the golden calf. From there God will communicate with Moses from now on (Lev. 1.1) and will accompany the Israelites on their journeys (24.16 n.; 25.1–31.17 n.). **33:** *When Moses had finished the work,* another echo of creation; see Gen. 2.2. **34:** *The cloud,* in which God's Presence is manifest; see 13.21 n., 22 n.; 24.15. As it covered Mount Sinai, it now covers the Tabernacle, where it will remain to guide Israel. For the appearance of fire within it at night, see 13.21 n. **36–38:** These vv. look ahead to Israel's future journeys accompanied by God (Num. 9.15–23; 10.11–28). The narrative will resume in Leviticus with God's call to Moses from the Tent (Lev. 1.1) and the consecration of the priests in Lev. chs 8–9. But at this point Exodus ends, allowing the reader to contemplate the phenomenon of God dwelling on earth with a symbol of His Presence in full view of the Israelites (cf. 1 Kings 8.27).

ויקרא

Leviticus

LEVITICUS, THE THIRD BOOK OF THE TORAH, is traditionally called *vayikra'* ("and He [the LORD] called," but see 1.1 n.), after the first word in the book. It was also called *torat kohanim,* "instruction of (or 'for') the priests" in rabbinic times, hence its Greek name *Levitikon,* "things pertaining to the Levites" (i.e., the priests, who are of the tribe of Levi), referring to the book's main concern with commandments connected with the worship of God, for which the priests were responsible.

Context

LEVITICUS IS PART OF A LONG NARRATIVE, extending from Exodus ch 25 to Numbers ch 10, that may be called "When the Tabernacle Stood at Sinai." It begins with God's instructions to Moses to provide a portable residence (called a *mishkan,* "tabernacle," lit. "dwelling," or *mikdash,* "holy place") for the divine Presence (the LORD's *kavod*) and to consecrate his brother Aaron and the latter's sons as priests. The Tabernacle was also the place for God to meet regularly with Moses to impart His laws (Exod. 25.22); thus it is also called the *'ohel mo'ed,* "Tent of Meeting." The Tabernacle and all its appurtenances were manufactured at the foot of Mount Sinai; the divine Presence took up residence; the priests were consecrated and sacrificial worship commenced; the laws were conveyed; the priests, Levites, and remaining tribes were mustered and arranged and instructions for the journey to Canaan were given; and finally the Israelites departed from Sinai on their journey to Canaan.

The Tabernacle narrative stands at the center of the Torah, and although it takes up almost a third of the Torah, it covers a timespan of less than one year. This indicates its crucial importance. All the institutions that ultimately shaped Israel's national and religious existence—the law, the priesthood, the forms of Temple worship and the tribal foundation of its society—are said to have been ordained and established during this brief period in Israel's history.

According to the story that emerges from the Torah as a whole, the Tabernacle narrative is a stage in Israel's sojourn at Sinai, interwoven with the theophany and proclamation of the Decalogue (Exod. chs 19–20), the giving of the laws and the covenant ceremony (Exod. chs 21–24), the giving of the two sets of tablets, and the incident of the golden calf (Exod. chs 32–34). However, according to the critical theory that separates the Torah into sources that were originally distinct and independent (see "Modern Study of the Bible," pp. 2166–77), the literary source that contained the Tabernacle narrative, called the Priestly document, or P, contained none of these other events. In P's view, only the events recounted by the Tabernacle narrative took place. The centrality of the Tabernacle narrative is therefore far more pronounced in P than in the redacted Torah, since in P, only in connection with the arrival of the divine Presence to dwell among the Israelites, was a code of law given and the social structure established; no other theophany or covenant preceded it and no sin of collective apostasy followed.

Content and Structure

LEVITICUS IS THE DIRECT CONTINUATION of what precedes it at the end of Exodus, and the narrative at the end of Leviticus continues directly into Numbers. Ch 1 takes up the story from the time the divine Presence enters the Tabernacle, on the first day of Nisan (the first month, in the spring) in the year following the exodus (Exod. ch 40). From within, God calls to Moses and imparts to him, in a series of encounters (Lev. chs 1–27), His laws and commandments. Since Numbers begins on the first day of ʾIyar (the second month) in the same year (Num. 1.1), it emerges that the entire book of Leviticus covers but one month.

The first group of laws, on sacrifice (chs 1–7), are given on the first day of the month, the day the Presence entered the Tabernacle (see 7.37–38). Then, interrupting the law-giving, is the consecration of the priesthood (ch 8), the dedication of the Tabernacle (ch 9), and the crime and immediate death of Aaron's sons (10.1–7, 12–20). The law-giving resumes as Moses is given the commandments concerning permitted and forbidden foods (ch 11), the purification and atonement following physical defilement (chs 12–15), the annual "Day of Atonement" (ch 16), prohibitions of profane slaughter and blood (ch 17), sexual crimes (chs 18, 20), miscellaneous regulations assuring Israel's holiness (ch 19), the sanctity of the priests (ch 21), the qualifications for sacrificial animals (ch 22), the weekly Sabbath and annual festivals (ch 23), the oil for the Tabernacle lamp (24.1–4), and the showbread (24.5–9). Again the law-giving is briefly interrupted, this time to recount the crime of the blasphemer and his execution (24.10–16, 23). It concludes with the laws of the sabbatical and jubilee years, including laws of slavery and property rights (25.1–26.2), a lengthy speech promising reward for compliance and punishment for failure to obey (26.3–45), and a summarizing caption (26.46). Then the laws of vows and tithes (ch 27) are appended and the caption is repeated (27.34).

The two narratives that interrupt the laws lead to brief legal sections. Thus following the crime of Nadab and Abihu, Moses clarifies for Aaron and his surviving sons the law regulating the proper disposal of sacrificial offerings (10.12–19); and while pronouncing sentence upon the blasphemer, God also imparts the laws of damages, governed by the eye-for-an-eye principle (24.17–22).

The complex interaction of narrative and law displayed in Leviticus is the defining literary feature of the Torah and of the Priestly document in particular. Both are narrative works, but the purpose of the narrative is to provide the literary framework, and thus the historical rationale and theological explanation, for the laws and commandments which are embedded within the narrative.

Composition

MODERN BIBLE SCHOLARS AGREE that all of Leviticus belongs to the Priestly source (P). If, however, the Torah is treated as a unified whole, the laws and narratives belonging to the Priestly source must be reconciled and harmonized with the non-Priestly material, so that they all interact and complement each other. This is done by traditional Jewish interpretation, and also by modern scholars who hold that the Priestly source was composed as a supplement to the non-Priestly sources. This commentary, however, believes that the Priestly work does not interact on any primary level with the non-Priestly material, so its main aim is to demonstrate the uniqueness of the Priestly tradition by pointing out the contrast between P and the other sources. The harmonistic approach will be illustrated only for the purpose of comparison and to explain the basis of traditional Jewish interpretations.

Date

THE BOOK OF LEVITICUS, like the other books of the Torah, came into existence as a defined literary entity no earlier than the time of the Babylonian exile in the 6th century BCE. On the date of P there is much disagreement. This commentary will espouse the view that the Priestly source was the product of learned scribes of the Jerusalemite priesthood of the last centuries of the Judean kingdom and that it took shape in two phases, the Holiness Legislation (H) (chs 17–26) being added to the Priestly work in the final years before the exile.

Leviticus and Judaism

THE STUDY OF THE LAWS in Leviticus stood at the center of rabbinic learning, and the halakhic midrash on Leviticus was called simply *Sifra*, or "the Book." It was customary for small children to begin their study of the Bible with Leviticus. The traditional explanation for this is that "the pure" (i.e., children) should be engaged in the study of purity (i.e., the laws of purification and atonement). A more likely reason is that Leviticus contains most of the laws that the Jew is commanded to observe on a regular basis, and it was only natural that the child's program of study should begin with the practical knowledge required for the life of *mitzvot* (commandments).

Even after the destruction of the Temple and the cessation of sacrificial worship and Temple ritual, Leviticus remains at the foundation of Jewish life. Among the institutions still central to Judaism which have their biblical origins in Leviticus are most of the dietary laws (the permitted and forbidden animals, and the blood prohibition); many of the festival rituals; most of the laws regulating sex, marriage, and family purity; and the commandments governing the seventh year, still applicable in the land of Israel. Moreover, the religious life of the congregation, centered upon the synagogue and the daily prayers offered at fixed times and in precisely ordained ritual forms, is a direct outgrowth of, and according to rabbinic tradition a substitute for, the Temple ritual as envisioned in Leviticus.

Another aspect of the heritage of Leviticus that has become normative in Judaism is its unique theology of the performance of *mitzvot.* Leviticus teaches that the ritual commandments and the ethical or social ones (in rabbinic terms: *mitzvot* between a human being and God and *mitzvot* between fellow human beings) are equally important and equally valid. To be precise, there is really no such thing as a *mitzvah* pertaining solely to interpersonal relations; the love of one's neighbor is a divine command (see 19.18), and every offense against one's fellow human being desecrates the name of God. This idea, which has taken shape and developed over the centuries and has ultimately become a central pillar of Jewish religious thought, derives directly from the book of Leviticus, where it is summed up in a single verse: "You shall each revere his mother and his father, and keep My sabbaths: I the LORD am your God" (19.3).

Finally, nowhere outside of Leviticus is there a clearer articulation of the reason for the Jewish people's existence. God has entered into a relationship with the people of Israel so that they might perpetually sanctify His name. Their role in the world, and in history, is to attest to His existence, to publicize His oneness, and to advertise His greatness. This they are commanded to do by worshipping Him and keeping His laws. When they fail to do so, His name is profaned, that is, His fame is diminished and His reputation tarnished; when they live up to this charge and duty, He and His name are sanctified. This statement, explicit in 22.31–33 and implicit throughout the book, has remained fundamental to Jewish belief and consciousness throughout all generations.

[BARUCH J. SCHWARTZ]

VA-YIKRA' ויקרא

1 The Lord called to Moses and spoke to him from the Tent
of Meeting, saying: 2 Speak to the Israelite people, and say
to them:
When any of you presents an offering of cattle to the Lord,
[a-]he shall choose his[-a] offering from the herd or from the flock.
3 If his offering is a burnt offering from the herd, he shall
make his offering a male without blemish. He shall bring it to
the entrance of the Tent of Meeting, for acceptance in his behalf
before the Lord. 4 He shall lay his hand upon the head of the
burnt offering, that it may be acceptable in his behalf, in expiation for him. 5 The bull shall be slaughtered before the Lord;
and Aaron's sons, the priests, shall offer the blood, dashing the
blood against all sides of the altar which is at the entrance of
the Tent of Meeting. 6 The burnt offering shall be flayed and cut
up into sections. 7 The sons of Aaron the priest shall put fire on
the altar and lay out wood upon the fire; 8 and Aaron's sons, the
priests, shall lay out the sections, with the head and the suet,
on the wood that is on the fire upon the altar. 9 Its entrails and
legs shall be washed with water, and the priest shall turn the
whole into smoke on the altar as a burnt offering, an offering
by fire of pleasing odor to the Lord.

a-a Lit. "you shall offer your."

1.1–7.38: The Types of Offerings. Chs 1–7 consist of a series of divine speeches to Moses in which the major types of sacrificial offerings, their purpose, the circumstances requiring them, the details of their performance and their distribution after the sacrifice is performed are delineated. These laws were all given on a single day; see the summary at 7.37–38 and nn.

1.1–3.17: Gift offerings. Chs 1–3 are a single, uninterrupted divine speech. The theme is "gift offerings," expressed in the word "ʾisheh," "food gift," used in each ch to characterize the offering prescribed (see 1.9 n.). Gift offerings, as distinct from expiatory sacrifices (treated in chs 4–5), express the worshipper's desire to present something to the Lord as a token of love and reverence. The Rabbis referred to them as "nedavah," "voluntary offerings," since they could be made at will—in fulfillment of vows, at private visits to the sanctuary, in supplication in times of distress, in gratitude for deliverance from danger or harm, or simply in a spontaneous urge to pay homage to God. Each of the subsections corresponds to one of the three types of gift offering: the burnt offering (ch 1), the cereal offering (ch 2), and the sacrifice of well-being (ch 3). While the burnt offering and cereal offering also figure prominently in the ordained public rituals performed by the priests on specified occasions, the sacrifice of well-being belongs almost entirely to the realm of individual piety.
1.1–17: Burnt offerings from the herd and flock. As with the other offerings in chs 1–3, only some of the procedures are detailed here. Some have already been given with the instructions for the consecration ceremonies (Exod. 29.15–18), and others are implicit in the instructions for other sacrifices. The text economizes, preferring not to repeat material found in other contexts. The defining feature of the burnt offering is that none of the meat is eaten; it is burned on the altar in its entirety. This makes it the gift-offering par excellence. The text does not specify the circumstances that might occasion a burnt offering, but Noah's sacrifices of thanksgiving or propitiation after the flood (Gen. 8.20), Abraham's near-sacrifice of Isaac (Gen. ch 22), Balaam's sacrifices entreating divine vision (Num. 23.15; etc.), Saul's sacrifices before battle (1 Sam. 13.12), and Job's sacrifices of atonement for his sons' hypothetical sins (Job 1.5), among many others, were burnt offerings. Since it also comprised the central component of the statutory public offerings, the altar in the Tabernacle court is called "the altar of burnt offering" (e.g., Exod. 30.28). **1:** This is connected to the P narrative at the end of Exodus, so it should be translated "and it [the Presence of the Lord (Exod. 40.35)] called out to Moses." After it filled the Tabernacle, the Presence called to Moses from within. A distinction is made between the Presence, which called, and the Lord Himself, who spoke; this is similar to the first encounter with God experienced by the prophet Ezekiel (Ezek. 1.28–2.1ff.). *Tent of Meeting,* one of the names for the Tabernacle; see the intro. **2: The heading for chs 1–3.** According to the Masoretic accents, the v. should be translated as two separate provisions. The first, "When any of you presents an offering, [it must be] to the Lord," is the basic postulate of all Israelite worship: Sacrifices are to be made to the Lord alone. The second goes on to stipulate: "He shall make his offering of livestock, that is, from the herd or from the flock." This preserves the original intent of the second half of the v.: Offerings must be of livestock. Later, when the laws allowing burnt offerings from fowl (vv. 14–17) and cereal offerings (2.1–16) were added, the v. was understood to mean that when one wished to sacrifice livestock, the choice was limited to domestic animals. *Any of you:* Heb "ʾadam," "human being," refers to male and female alike (see Gen. 1.27; 5.2, also P). In P opportunities for individual worship are identical

10 If his offering for a burnt offering is from the flock, of sheep
or of goats, he shall make his offering a male without blemish. 11 It shall be slaughtered before the LORD on the north side
of the altar, and Aaron's sons, the priests, shall dash its blood
against all sides of the altar. 12 When it has been cut up into sections, the priest shall lay them out, with the head and the suet,
on the wood that is on the fire upon the altar. 13 The entrails
and the legs shall be washed with water; the priest shall offer
up and turn the whole into smoke on the altar. It is a burnt offering, an offering by fire, of pleasing odor to the LORD.
14 If his offering to the LORD is a burnt offering of birds, he
shall choose his offering from turtledoves or pigeons. 15 The
priest shall bring it to the altar, pinch off its head, and turn
it into smoke on the altar; and its blood shall be drained out
against the side of the altar. 16 He shall remove its crop with its
contents,[a] and cast it into the place of the ashes, at the east side
of the altar. 17 The priest shall tear it open by its wings, without
severing it, and turn it into smoke on the altar, upon the wood
that is on the fire. It is a burnt offering, an offering by fire, of
pleasing odor to the LORD.

a Others "feathers."

for male and female; only the public ritual was confined to males, namely, the Aaronic priesthood. **3–13:** The burnt offering. See also 6.1–6; 7.8. **3–9:** Making a burnt offering from the herd. Instructions follow for a third type of burnt offering, made from fowl (vv. 14–17). The fowl offering, which does not fit the explicit provision "you shall choose your offering from the herd or from the flock" (v. 2), was apparently not part of the original text. The offerer is responsible for acquiring the proper animal (see 22.17–20), bringing it to the Tabernacle entrance, placing his hand upon its head as an act of presentation, slaughtering it, removing the hide and flaying the animal. The priest performs the remaining actions: presenting the blood, dashing some of it around the altar in the Tabernacle courtyard, placing the quarters, head, and suet on the altar fire, washing the entrails and legs and placing them too on the altar, and seeing that all the flesh is "turned into smoke," that is, consumed completely until nothing but ashes remain. **3:** An *offering,* Heb "korban," a term expressing the notion of something presented (from Heb "k-r-b," "near") in homage. It does not mean "sacrifice" in the sense of "giving something up." *Burnt offering,* Heb "ʿolah," from the verb "ʿ-l-h," "go up, ascend"; the distinguishing visible feature of all altar sacrifices was the smoke ascending heavenward. *For acceptance in his behalf:* Central to all gift-offerings is the worshipper's need to know that the deity has accepted his gift; this is consistently referred to as "ratzon," "acceptance" (see 22.17–20). **4:** *Lay his hand,* to signify the transfer of ownership of the animal to the deity. *Acceptable,* correctly: "accepted"; see 7.18; 19.5–8; 22.17–30. In expiation for him, Heb "kipper," often translated "atone," has two meanings in P: "decontaminate [the sacred precincts] of sin or defilement" (see 4.1–5.26 n.) and "serve as ransom or payment [for one's life]" (see 17.11 n.). The latter seems to be intended here; that is why it is mentioned along with the hand-laying ritual: The moment ownership of the animal is transferred to the deity, it is accepted as payment, i.e., as a substitute for the worshipper himself. The lay person's private burnt offering would then be one way of symbolically offering oneself to God. The Rabbis ruled that the burnt offering be given in expiation for the failure to carry out performative commandments. **5:** *The bull shall be slaughtered,* better, [the offerer] shall slaughter the bull. This is not strictly a part of the ritual in that no sacral significance was attached to the animal's death. Heb "sh-ḥ-t" implies that the slaughter is performed by slitting the throat, but since the Bible provides no details, rabbinic tradition held that the specifics were communicated orally by God to Moses. *Offer the blood ... against all sides of the altar:* This is a symbolic method of offering the blood to the LORD. **6:** *Shall be flayed* by the offerer. The division of labor is clear: The offerer is responsible for the mundane tasks of transferring ownership of the animal and transforming it from a living animal into food fit for consumption; the priests are responsible for the sacred tasks of dashing the blood and offering the flesh as a gift to the LORD. **7:** *Fire* here, as in many passages, probably means burning coals. The priests were required to maintain a constant altar fire on the altar (see 6.6). **9:** *An offering by fire:* Heb "ʾisheh" is not derived from "ʾesh," "fire," but from a root meaning "gift." Thus a better translation is "food gift," since the word denotes burnt offerings, cereal offerings, and sacrifices of well-being. It is not used for the purification and reparation offerings, as the latter are not gifts but rituals of expiation. *Of pleasing odor to the LORD:* P's unique anthropomorphism attributes to God the sensual, carnal pleasure derived from inhaling the fragrant odor of roasting meat while at the same time denying that He actually consumes it as food. Similarly, P portrays God's Presence as abiding within the Tabernacle, but offerings presented to Him are turned into smoke and ascend heavenward. The LORD's contrasting human and supernatural traits, as well as His opposite attributes of immanence and transcendence, exist in P side by side. **10–13:** A burnt

2 When a person presents an offering of meal to the LORD,
his offering shall be of choice flour; he shall pour oil upon
it, lay frankincense on it, 2 and present it to Aaron's sons, the
priests. The priest shall scoop out of it a handful of its choice
flour and oil, as well as all of its frankincense; and this token
portion he shall turn into smoke on the altar, as an offering by
fire, of pleasing odor to the LORD. 3 And the remainder of the
meal offering shall be for Aaron and his sons, a most holy portion from the LORD's offerings by fire.
4 When you present an offering of meal baked in the oven, [it
shall be of] choice flour: unleavened cakes with oil mixed in,
or unleavened wafers spread with oil.
5 If your offering is a meal offering on a griddle, it shall be of
choice flour with oil mixed in, unleavened. 6 Break it into bits
and pour oil on it; it is a meal offering.
7 If your offering is a meal offering in a pan, it shall be made
of choice flour in oil.
8 When you present to the LORD a meal offering that is made
in any of these ways, it shall be brought to the priest who shall
take it up to the altar. 9 The priest shall remove the token portion from the meal offering and turn it into smoke on the altar
as an offering by fire, of pleasing odor to the LORD. 10 And the
remainder of the meal offering shall be for Aaron and his sons,
a most holy portion from the LORD's offerings by fire.

offering from the flock (sheep and goats) is like offerings from the herd (cattle). **14–17:** Making a burnt offering from fowl, presumably for those who could not afford a sacrifice of livestock. The birds that qualify as offerings, turtledoves and pigeons, are the two types of domesticated fowl used for human consumption. The particulars of the procedure stem from the nature of fowl and its small size. The wingspread is left intact so that the carcass placed upon the altar will not appear ridiculously small. **16:** The first part of the v. should be translated "He shall remove its feathers and its excrement." These are to be cast into the ash-heap alongside the altar.

2.1–16: The offering of grain. Instructions for the "minḥa" (see also 6.7–16). The word means tribute paid to a superior (e.g., Gen. 32.14, 22; etc.) or a ruler (e.g., Judg. 3.15ff.; 1 Sam. 10.27), and is used in non-Priestly texts to refer to sacrifices in general, e.g., Cain and Abel's offerings (Gen. 4.3–5) and the offerings at the Shiloh sanctuary (1 Sam. 2.17). This expresses the basic notion underlying the sacrificial system: that the Israelites, as a people and as individuals, are expected to offer to God regular tokens of His lordship over them. P uses the term in a specific sense of "offering made of grain." This ch interrupts the original sequence of burnt offering and well-being offering; it was introduced here to provide an opportunity for even the poorest Israelite to make a freewill offering, from grain. The "minḥa" also figures prominently among the statutory public offerings, accompanying the burnt offerings made each morning and evening. The public "minḥa" (see Exod. 29.40; 40.29; Num. 28.5; etc.), especially that which was a part of the daily evening sacrifice, eventually gave its name to the afternoon prayer, known since rabbinic times as the "minḥa" prayer. **1–8:** Types of grain offering. The two essential ingredients are semolina of wheat and [olive] oil; these give it its character of a food gift (the oil was also necessary to facilitate the burning). Several variations exist. The uncooked mixture (v. 1) requires the addition of frankincense, so it is the most costly. The remaining types, requiring no frankincense, involve some preparation of unleavened cakes: oven-baked (as loaves or wafers, v. 4), griddle-toasted (and crumbled, vv. 5–6), and pan-fried (v. 7); see also 7.9–10. The grain offering is prepared by the worshipper and presented in its entirety to the priest. Unlike the burnt offering, however, only an "'azkara," a "reminder" or token portion, is placed on the altar; the remainder is eaten by the priest (see 6.11; 7.9); God thus gives the priests the "leftover" portions of his own food gift (see 6.10). The "'azkara" of the uncooked "minḥa" includes the frankincense, all of which belongs to the deity. **2:** *Offering by fire,* see 1.9 n. *Of pleasing odor,* see 1.9 n.; as v. 9 confirms, this is not simply the result of the frankincense. In P, the "minḥa" itself, like the flesh of animals, is by definition a *pleasing odor,* whereas in non-Priestly texts it is assumed that the addition of fragrant spice renders the offering pleasing (see Isa. 1.13; 43.23; Jer. 6.20; 17.26; 41.5; Ps. 141.2). **3:** *A most holy portion,* Heb "kodesh kodashim" (see also v. 10), a term applied to the purification offering and the reparation offering as well, although not to the burnt offering, perhaps simply because no flesh remains of it that needs to be treated as most holy. Gradation of sanctity or holiness (see 6.11), thought of as an effusion of the divine Presence varying in degree, is an essential aspect of the Tabernacle and its worship. The most holy among the food gifts are those of which a portion is eaten by the priests but not by the worshippers. **8–10:** The procedure for the prepared "minḥa." The three types in vv. 4–7 are offered in the same manner as the uncooked type. **8–9:** *Take it up to the altar:* Before the token portion is removed, the entire offering is symbolically presented to the deity. This gives ritual expression to the fact that the cakes, loaves, or wafers were prepared for God and

11 No meal offering that you offer to the LORD shall be made
with leaven, for no leaven or honey may be turned into smoke
as an offering by fire to the LORD. 12 You may bring them to the
LORD as an offering of choice products;[a] but they shall not be
offered up on the altar for a pleasing odor. 13 You shall season
your every offering of meal with salt; you shall not omit from
your meal offering the salt of your covenant with God; with all
your offerings you must offer salt.
14 If you bring a meal offering of first fruits to the LORD, you
shall bring new ears parched with fire, grits of the fresh grain, as
your meal offering of first fruits. 15 You shall add oil to it and lay
frankincense on it; it is a meal offering. 16 And the priest shall
turn a token portion of it into smoke: some of the grits and oil,
with all of the frankincense, as an offering by fire to the LORD.

3 If his offering is a sacrifice of well-being[b]—
If he offers of the herd, whether a male or a female, he shall
bring before the LORD one without blemish. 2 He shall lay his
hand upon the head of his offering and slaughter it at the entrance of the Tent of Meeting; and Aaron's sons, the priests, shall
dash the blood against all sides of the altar. 3 He shall then present from the sacrifice of well-being, as an offering by fire to the
LORD, the fat that covers the entrails and all the fat that is about
the entrails; 4 the two kidneys and the fat that is on them, that is
at the loins; and the protuberance on the liver, which he shall remove with the kidneys. 5 Aaron's sons shall turn these into smoke
on the altar, with the burnt offering which is upon the wood that
is on the fire, as an offering by fire, of pleasing odor to the LORD.
6 And if his offering for a sacrifice of well-being to the LORD
is from the flock, whether a male or a female, he shall offer
one without blemish. 7 If he presents a sheep as his offering,
he shall bring it before the LORD 8 and lay his hand upon the
head of his offering. It shall be slaughtered before the Tent of
Meeting, and Aaron's sons shall dash its blood against all sides
of the altar. 9 He shall then present, as an offering by fire to the
LORD, the fat from the sacrifice of well-being: the whole broad
tail, which shall be removed close to the backbone; the fat that
covers the entrails and all the fat that is about the entrails; 10 the
two kidneys and the fat that is on them, that is at the loins; and

a *Exact meaning of Heb. uncertain.*
b *Others "peace offering." Exact meaning of* shelamim *uncertain.*

not simply brought from the supply of foods kept at home for common consumption. **11–12:** The prohibition of leaven. In the Heb v. 11a is a general prohibition of "ḥametz," leavened cakes or loaves, while v. 11b gives the details: In order to prevent fermentation, neither "se᾿or," the leavening agent (sourdough) nor "devash," *honey,* may be used in any of the LORD's food gifts (see 1.9 n.) Though both date-honey and the honey of bees are leavening agents, in the Bible "devash" is almost always the honey of fruits (see Gen. 43.11; Deut. 8.8; 2 Chron. 31.5; etc.). There is nothing intrinsically unacceptable about leaven and honey; they may be offered (v. 12) but not placed on the altar. Rather it is the fermentation of the grain offering specifically that is prohibited, most likely for practical reasons, so that the preparation, offering, and eating of food gifts would all take place within a short period of time and in proximity to the altar. The preparation of leavened cakes would take much longer. The presentation to God of ready-made loaves of bread is known outside of P (1 Sam. 10.3; 21.5; 22.13). **13:** The requirement to salt the grain offering is a corollary of the prohibition of leaven: Salt is an anti-fermentation agent and would impede natural leavening. *The salt of your covenant:* Heb "berit," *covenant,* is used here in the sense of imposed obligation, and simply means that the salting of offerings is to be observed perpetually. *With all your offerings ... offer salt:* Characteristically, the Rabbis took this summary to mean that animal offerings as well, and not only the "minḥa," required salting; this eventually became normative. In commemoration of this, Jewish custom requires salt on the table. **14–16:** A final type of "minḥa" is described, *a meal offering of first fruits.* This gift offering of grain, before it has fully matured and before flour can be produced from it, is prepared and offered in the same way as the uncooked offering, and provides a means for approaching God the moment one's grain begins to ripen, when the natural impulse to make an offering is strongest.

3.1–17: The sacrifice of well-being. V. 1a introduces the possibility of offering a third type of gift offering, namely, the sacrifice of well-being; vv. 1b–5 lay out the procedure for making such an offering if the animal is taken from the herd; vv. 6–16 lay out the procedure if the animal is from the flock (v. 6a)—either a sheep (vv. 7–11) or a goat (vv. 12–16).

the protuberance on the liver, which he shall remove with the kidneys. 11 The priest shall turn these into smoke on the altar as food, an offering by fire to the LORD.

12 And if his offering is a goat, he shall bring it before the LORD 13 and lay his hand upon its head. It shall be slaughtered before the Tent of Meeting, and Aaron's sons shall dash its blood against all sides of the altar. 14 He shall then present as his offering from it, as an offering by fire to the LORD, the fat that covers the entrails and all the fat that is about the entrails; 15 the two kidneys and the fat that is on them, that is at the loins; and the protuberance on the liver, which he shall remove with the kidneys. 16 The priest shall turn these into smoke on the altar as food, an offering by fire, of pleasing odor.

All fat is the LORD's. 17 It is a law for all time throughout the ages, in all your settlements: you must not eat any fat or any blood.

4 The LORD spoke to Moses, saying: 2 Speak to the Israelite people thus:

When a person unwittingly incurs guilt in regard to any of the LORD's commandments about things not to be done, and does one of them—

3 If it is the anointed priest who has incurred guilt, so that blame falls upon the people, he shall offer for the sin of which

This follows the basic outline of ch 1. The prohibition of suet and blood (v. 17) ends the ch. **1:** *A sacrifice of well-being:* Heb consists of two components: "zevaḥ" denotes a sacrifice of a slaughtered animal of which the offerer partakes in a festive meal; in P this is the only way in which the eating of meat is permitted (see 17.3–7). Several interpretations have been suggested for the word "shelamim." The translation "sacrifice of well-being" reflects the fact that in P a "zevaḥ" offered by the individual is an expression of joy, gladness, gratitude, or relief; see 7.11–21 n. Additional regulations concerning the "shelamim" sacrifice are given in 7.11–38; 19.5–8; 22.21–30. The distinctive feature is that only the blood and token fatty portions of the animal are placed on the altar, and only certain prescribed portions of the meat are eaten by the priests; most of the animal is eaten by the offerer and invited guests as a festive meal "in the LORD's presence." Well-being offerings are thus the natural expression of gladness, the worshipper celebrating by feasting in the presence of God in acknowledgment of His loving-kindness. The feast is a sacrifice because ownership of the animal is first transferred to God, after which the portions eaten by the priest and the worshipper are considered to have been given to them by God—much as a king is sustained by the tribute provided by his subjects, yet the subjects are nevertheless honored to be invited to dine at the royal table. **1b–5:** The procedure for a "shelamim" sacrifice from the herd. The animal may be male or female. The tasks of the worshipper are similar to those for a burnt offering (1.3–9). No mention is made of the distribution of the remainder of the animal (see 7.11ff.) since the sole interest of this ch is the manner in which the food-gift is presented to the deity. **2:** *Shall dash the blood against ... the altar,* as an offering; see 1.5 n. **3–4:** The LORD's portion of the sacrifice. Fatty portions of slaughtered animals were considered to be the richest, tastiest morsels. Best of all are the layers of suet (Heb "ḥelev," translated as "fat"), the hard, subcutaneous fatty tissue surrounding the internal organs; therefore these portions would be assigned to God. That which is "too good" for mortals might logically be assumed to be a proper repast for a deity. Burning suet also provides a dense smoke of sweet, meaty fragrance, suggesting that pleasure is derived from it by a transcendent divine being. Biblical tradition is thus unanimous that the suet of sacrificial flesh is offered to the deity (below, v. 16; see also 1 Sam. 2.15–16; Deut. 32.38; Isa. 1.11; 34.6; 43.24; Ezek. 44.7, 15). In addition to the suet, two organs—the *kidneys* and *the protuberance on the liver* (the caudate lobe)—are offered to God; these are surrounded by so much fatty tissue that they are considered as suet. **3:** Entrails, i.e., intestines. **4:** *Loins* (Heb "kesalim"), better, "sinews." **5:** *With the burnt offering ... on the fire:* The public burnt offering is made each morning and evening; the assumption is that it is either being burned, or at least its remains are smoldering, on the altar fire at all times. For *the wood,* see 6.1ff. *Pleasing odor,* see 1.9 n. **6–16:** The procedure for a "shelamim" sacrifice from the flock. Sheep and goats are treated separately because only sheep possess the heavy fat-tail which, like suet, needs to be removed and added to the portions placed upon the altar. **16:** *All fat,* better, "all suet," as explained above. However, the words *all fat [is]* are evidently a scribal error, copied unintentionally from the next v. (where they are translated "any fat"); v. 16 should conclude "of pleasing odor to the LORD" just like vv. 5 and 11. **17:** What belongs to the LORD is not to be eaten by humans, thus, all blood and suet are prohibited. The details of the blood prohibition are given in 17.10–16; for elaboration on the prohibition of suet, see 7.22–27. This prohibition is appropriately placed here, since, according to P, the "shelamim" offering is the one occasion on which lay people would have eaten the flesh of domestic livestock.

he is guilty a bull of the herd without blemish as a purification offering[a] to the LORD. 4 He shall bring the bull to the entrance of the Tent of Meeting, before the LORD, and lay his hand upon the head of the bull. The bull shall be slaughtered before the LORD, 5 and the anointed priest shall take some of the bull's blood and bring it into the Tent of Meeting. 6 The priest shall dip his finger in the blood, and sprinkle of the blood seven times before the LORD, in front of the curtain of the Shrine. 7 The priest shall put some of the blood on the horns of the altar of aromatic incense, which is in the Tent of Meeting, before the LORD; and all the rest of the bull's blood he shall pour out at the base of the altar of burnt offering, which is at the entrance of the Tent of Meeting. 8 He shall remove all the fat from the bull of purification offering: the fat that covers the entrails and all the fat that is about the entrails; 9 the two kidneys and the fat that is on them, that is at the loins; and the protuberance on the liver, which he shall remove with the kidneys—10 just as it is removed from the ox of the sacrifice of well-being. The priest shall turn them into smoke on the altar of burnt offering. 11 But the hide of the bull, and all its flesh, as well as its head and legs, its entrails and its dung—12 all the rest of the bull—he shall carry to a clean place outside the camp, to the ash heap, and burn it up in a wood fire; it shall be burned on the ash heap.

13 If it is the whole community of Israel that has erred and the matter escapes the notice of the congregation, so that they do any of the things which by the LORD's commandments ought not to be done, and they realize their guilt—14 when the sin through which they incurred guilt becomes known, the

a Traditionally "sin offering."

4.1–5.26: The purification and reparation offerings. Chs 4–5 present three speeches of God to Moses (4.1–5.13; 5.14–19; 5.20–26). The first contains the laws concerning the "ḥata't" or purification offering; the second and third give regulations governing the "'asham" or reparation offering. This completes instructions for the five types of occasional sacrifice. The sacrifices in these two chs do not reflect the individual's voluntary resolve to serve God, but are occasioned by specific violations or wrongdoing. The Rabbis therefore called these sacrifices "ḥova": debts, penalties incurred. Such sacrificial rituals are said to "atone" (Heb "kipper"), traditionally understood as amends for wrongdoing. Atonement, in this view, is a sort of payment made to propitiate an angry deity and be reconciled with him. However, Heb "kipper" literally means "wipe clean," and the atoning act consists of the application of the blood of the animal to the sanctuary as a whole and to the objects within it. This is strikingly reminiscent of Mesopotamian ritual texts where the root "k-p-r" is used to refer to the ritual cleansing of temples. It follows that "atonement" in P is actually a type of expiation, i.e., cleansing, by which the divine abode is ritually purged of contamination that has accumulated there (see 1.4 n.). According to P, this contamination comes from the Israelites' bodily impurities (see chs 12–15) and from certain acts of wrongdoing they commit. It defiles the sanctuary and, if allowed to collect there, threatens the community's collective existence. "Atonement," which is really Temple purification, is thus of critical importance (see 15.31 n.). Chs 4–5 provide basic instructions for sacrificial atonement initiated by, and performed on behalf of, individual offending parties as the need arises; these are the basis for regulations regarding public rituals of atonement and atonement for bodily impurities in later chs. The order of chs 1–5 is also significant. In Israel's cultic system, the natural impulse to petition and to worship (chs 1–3) is primary, while the obligation to expiate (chs 4–5), i.e., to purge the sacred of impurities, is the result of circumstance.

4.1–35: The purification offering. If an Israelite has inadvertently transgressed a prohibition (v. 2), a "ḥata't" or purification offering (see below, v. 3) must be made (vv. 3–35). The details differ according to the identity of the guilty party, the main distinction pertaining to the objects to which the blood is applied. Since the more severe the contamination, the more deeply it penetrates the sacred sphere, the instructions regarding where the blood is to be applied are an exact indication of the severity of the impurity or sin for which atonement is being made. This determines the division of the ch into two main sections. The first section (vv. 3–21) speaks of offenses that have brought guilt upon the community. The transgression may be committed by the high priest (vv. 3–12) or by "the whole community of Israel" (vv. 13–21); in both cases the purgation of the interior of the Tabernacle is required and a bull, the largest sacrificial animal, is slaughtered. The second section (vv. 22–35) pertains to offenses that have not resulted in communal guilt; these require only the purgation of the outer sphere, by applying blood to the altar in the Tabernacle court. The type of animal used varies according to the social status of the individual. Ch 16 completes this picture: Deliberate sins penetrate to the inner sanctum; see 16.11–17.

congregation shall offer a bull of the herd as a purification offering, and bring it before the Tent of Meeting. [15] The elders of the community shall lay their hands upon the head of the bull before the LORD, and the bull shall be slaughtered before the LORD. [16] The anointed priest shall bring some of the blood of the bull into the Tent of Meeting, [17] and the priest shall dip his finger in the blood and sprinkle of it seven times before the LORD, in front of the curtain. [18] Some of the blood he shall put on the horns of the altar which is before the LORD in the Tent of Meeting, and all the rest of the blood he shall pour out at the base of the altar of burnt offering, which is at the entrance of the Tent of Meeting. [19] He shall remove all its fat from it and turn it into smoke on the altar. [20] He shall do with this bull just as is done with the [priest's] bull of purification offering; he shall do the same with it. Thus the priest shall make expiation for them, and they shall be forgiven. [21] He shall carry the bull outside the camp and burn it as he burned the first bull; it is the purification offering of the congregation.

[22] In case it is a chieftain who incurs guilt by doing unwittingly any of the things which by the commandment of the LORD his God ought not to be done, and he realizes his guilt—[23] or the sin of which he is guilty is brought to his knowledge—he shall bring as his offering a male goat without blemish. [24] He shall lay his hand upon the goat's head, and it shall be slaughtered

Additional regulations concerning the "ḥata't" are given in 6.17–23; see also 10.16–20. A variant tradition is found in Num. 15.22–31. **2:** *A person,* Heb "nefesh," "a living being" (see 17.10 n.), male or female. *Unwittingly incurs guilt,* better, "sins inadvertently." "Sin" (Heb "ḥata'") basically means to err, to miss the mark, and the qualifier "bishgagah," "in error," makes it clear that the offender did not know the act was prohibited. A basic postulate of Israelite thought is that inadvertent acts are just as harmful as deliberate ones, the need to atone for them just as real, and the desire to do so, once they are realized, greater. *Any of the LORD's commandments:* Since in P the overwhelming majority of commandments belong to the category of prohibited acts, "commandment" in P is essentially defined as a prohibition, and "sin" is primarily an act of commission, not of omission. **3–12:** The purification offering of the high priest. In P the high priest is not a public official, a teacher or a leader (contrast the role of Joshua in Zech. 3.3–7), but rather a divinely designated, sacred representative of the Israelite people. His entire function is ceremonial. In his person, dressed in the priestly vestments, he represents the body politic (see esp. Exod. 28.9–12), serving within God's earthly abode, paying uninterrupted homage to the enshrined deity on behalf of the Israelite tribes, and calling attention to their needs in the twice-daily regimen of worship. He is also the sole officiant in the annual Day of Atonement ceremonies (ch 16), which means he is the only person ever to enter the inner sanctum. **3:** *The anointed priest:* He alone has the sacred anointing oil poured on his head at his investiture (Exod. 29.7; Lev. 8.12; 21.10). He is also called "the high priest" (Heb "ha-kohen ha-gadol" [Num. 35.25, 28; Josh. 20.6]), short for "the highest priest among his brothers" (Lev. 21.10), which parallels the Ugaritic "rb khnm," and "[ha-]kohen ha-rosh," "the head priest" (e.g., 2 Kings 25.18). *Incurred guilt,* better, "sinned"; see above, v. 2. *So that blame falls upon the people:* Corporate guilt for the crimes of leaders is assumed elsewhere in the Bible. In this case, because the high priest is the representative of the people, his sins of commission are accounted to the people as a whole, and since he serves on their behalf in the innermost sphere of sanctity, his misdeeds contaminate the Tabernacle interior by his very presence there. *For the sin of which he is guilty,* better, "for the sin which he committed." *A purification offering:* The traditional translation of "ḥata't," associating it with "ḥet'," "sin, misdeed" and "ḥata'," "to sin, err" (see above), was "sin offering." The noun is actually derived, however, from the verb "ḥite'," "purge, decontaminate" (8.15; 9.15; 14.49, 52; Num. 8.21; 19.12, 13, 20; 31.19–20, 23; Ezek. 43.22–23; 45.18; Ps. 51.9) which is virtually synonymous with "kipper," "atone" (see also Exod. 29.36; Ezek. 43.20), and so the preferred translation is "purification offering"; note also the "ḥata't"-water (Num. 8.7), which means "water of purification." **4–12:** The procedure. The high priest is both the offerer and the officiant. The requirement *to lay his hand upon the head of the bull* here too symbolically transfers ownership of the animal to the deity. Having slaughtered the bull *before the LORD,* i.e., "in the LORD's presence," at *the entrance of the Tent of Meeting,* the priest begins the sprinkling of blood in order to cleanse the areas that have become contaminated. Here and in the next subsection (see vv. 17–18a), the priest is to bring some of the blood into the Tabernacle's outer sanctum. The sevenfold sprinkling of blood toward the curtain (see Exod. 26.31–33) and the application of blood on the horns (rounded protuberances) of the incense altar (see Exod. 30.1–10) serve to purify the entire outer sanctum. The remaining blood is poured out at the base of the sacrificial altar in the court, that is, drained onto the ground as it is not a

at the spot where the burnt offering is slaughtered[a] before the
LORD; it is a purification offering. 25 The priest shall take with
his finger some of the blood of the purification offering and
put it on the horns of the altar of burnt offering; and the rest
of its blood he shall pour out at the base of the altar of burnt
offering. 26 All its fat he shall turn into smoke on the altar, like
the fat of the sacrifice of well-being. Thus the priest shall make
expiation on his behalf for his sin, and he shall be forgiven.

27 If any person from among the populace[b] unwittingly incurs guilt by doing any of the things which by the LORD's
commandments ought not to be done, and he realizes his
guilt—28 or the sin of which he is guilty is brought to his knowledge—he shall bring a female goat without blemish as his offering for the sin of which he is guilty. 29 He shall lay his hand
upon the head of the purification offering, and the purification
offering shall be slaughtered at the place of the burnt offering.
30 The priest shall take with his finger some of its blood and put
it on the horns of the altar of burnt offering; and all the rest of
its blood he shall pour out at the base of the altar. 31 He shall
remove all its fat, just as the fat is removed from the sacrifice of
well-being; and the priest shall turn it into smoke on the altar,
for a pleasing odor to the LORD. Thus the priest shall make expiation for him, and he shall be forgiven.

a Cf. 1.11. *b Lit. "people of the country."*

sacrifice, but kept within the sacred precincts since it has been consecrated. After this, the fatty portions of the bull are turned into smoke upon the altar just as is done with sacrifices of well-being (see 3.3–4). Significantly, though the LORD's portion of the sacrificial animal is presented to Him in the customary way, it is not called a "gift" nor is it said to be of pleasing odor (but see v. 31). Further, the remaining meat of the animal is not eaten by anyone; it is rather incinerated along with the refuse, outside the camp upon the ash-heap. On this total disposal of the animal's flesh, see 6.23 and 10.16–20. **13–21:** The community's purification offering. The ritual is the same as the one preceding, except for the fact that since the offense has been committed by the community as a whole, the offerer is *the congregation,* represented by *the elders of the community* who perform the hand-laying gesture on behalf of the people. Rabbinic tradition found the notion that the *whole community* might sin spontaneously to be farfetched, and also rejected the idea that if only some, even a majority, of the population sinned the entire community was obligated to atone. They therefore interpreted the case as one in which the High Court errs in instructing the community how to behave and the latter commits the resulting offense. **13:** *The whole community of Israel that has erred and the matter escapes the notice of the congregation:* The entire community has somehow performed an act thought at the time to be innocuous but subsequently determined to have been in violation of a prohibition, for instance, laboring on a day which they were unaware had been proclaimed sacred. And they realize their guilt: This may result from the reinvestigation of past actions spurred by pangs of conscience, or even from some form of suffering suspected to be a divine punishment or warning (see also vv. 22 and 27; the phrase is implicit in the previous section). **14:** *When the sin ... becomes known,* better, "or the sin they committed becomes known" (similarly the opening clauses of vv. 23 and 28). Alternatively, the offense may come to one's attention as a result of information learned from others. Atonement in P is possible only when the realization of wrongdoing and the feeling of guilt move the offender to remorse and to an active desire to rid the sanctuary of the resulting contamination. **20:** *Thus the priest shall make expiation for them, and they shall be forgiven:* Though this summary result clause (cf. vv. 26, 31, 35) is absent from the first section, it must be understood there too. In P, forgiveness is not a grace to be hoped for; it is rather the promised result of the completed atonement process. When, following the realization and remorse, the sacred sphere has been rid of the contamination one's act has caused, one is assured that no further consequences will result. **21:** *As he burned the first bull,* i.e., the bull described in the previous subsection; the two rituals would not necessarily be performed on the same occasion. **22–35:** The remaining purification offerings. The misdeeds of individual commoners and even of tribal chieftains are their own. Their severity is less than that of the sins of the high priest or of the community, their contaminating force penetrates less deeply, and so the blood of the animal is applied to the horns of the sacrificial altar that stood in the Tabernacle court. The instructions regarding the disposal of the meat in these three subsections is spelled out in 6.19, 22–23, and its rationale is provided in 10.17. **22–23:** *And he realizes his guilt—or the sin ... is brought to his knowledge:* The translation here and in vv. 27–28 reflects more accurately the two possible ways in which the offending party is eventually moved to atone; see vv. 13–14. **31:** *For a pleasing odor to the LORD:* This phrase appears nowhere else in reference to the atoning sacrifices and is indeed out

32 If the offering he brings as a purification offering is a sheep, he shall bring a female without blemish. 33 He shall lay his hand upon the head of the purification offering, and it shall be slaughtered as a purification offering at the spot where the burnt offering is slaughtered. 34 The priest shall take with his finger some of the blood of the purification offering and put it on the horns of the altar of burnt offering, and all the rest of its blood he shall pour out at the base of the altar. 35 And all its fat he shall remove just as the fat of the sheep of the sacrifice of well-being is removed; and this the priest shall turn into smoke on the altar, over the LORD's offering by fire. Thus the priest shall make expiation on his behalf for the sin of which he is guilty, and he shall be forgiven.

5 If a person incurs guilt—
When he has heard a public imprecation[a] and—although able to testify as one who has either seen or learned of the matter—he does not give information, so that he is subject to punishment;

2 Or when a person touches any unclean thing—be it the carcass of an unclean beast or the carcass of unclean cattle or the carcass of an unclean creeping thing—and the fact has escaped him, and then, being unclean, he realizes his guilt;

3 Or when he touches human uncleanness—any such uncleanness whereby one becomes unclean—and, though he has known it, the fact has escaped him, but later he realizes his guilt;

4 Or when a person utters[b] an oath to bad or good purpose—whatever a man may utter in an oath—and, though he has known it, the fact has escaped him, but later he realizes his guilt in any of these matters—

5 when he realizes his guilt in any of these matters, he shall confess that wherein he has sinned. 6 And he shall bring as his penalty to the LORD, for the sin of which he is guilty, a female from the flock, sheep or goat, as a purification offering; and the priest shall make expiation on his behalf for his sin.

a Namely, against one who withholds testimony. *b Lit. "utters with his lips."*

of place; many scholars believe it to be a scribal error. **35:** *Over the LORD's offering by fire,* better, "on top of (or along with) the LORD's food gifts" (see 1.9); i.e., together with the other offerings smoldering on the altar. This proves that the purification offering itself is not a food gift; see 4.1–5.26 n.

5.1–13: Further instructions on the purification offering. Next comes a specific list of wrongs that require atonement by means of the "ḥata't" sacrifice. No instructions for performing the sacrifice are given; the listener is to rely on the previous ch. The rest of the section provides for the sacrifice of two fowl by a person who cannot afford an animal from the flock (vv. 7–10) and for a "ḥata't" of a grain offering by the person of even more limited means. These adjustments gave the sacrifice its rabbinic name of "korban ʿole veyored," "graduated offering"—but see below (vv. 7–13 n.). **1–4:** The cases. The situations requiring sacrifice are: (1) A person has refrained from coming forward with testimony about some matter to which he was an eyewitness or about which he has indirect knowledge, even though a public imprecation, solemnly adjuring all that have knowledge about the matter to speak up, has been heard (v. 1); (2) a person has neglected to cleanse himself of a secondary impurity within the prescribed time period (see 11.4–8, 24–40), or (3) of corpse-contamination (see Num. 19.10a–22) of which he was originally aware but subsequently forgot, only later realizing his negligence (vv. 2–3); (4) a person has sworn verbally to perform some action but subsequently forgot to do so, only to realize his negligence at some later date. This list differs greatly from the general stipulation in ch 4. The cases aim to counter the notion that duties weaken with time and eventually cease to exist ("forget it and it will simply go away"). In P's view, the opposite is the case: Severity of negligence, whether of physical impurity or of moral or legal obligation, intensifies the longer it lasts. **1:** *Incurs guilt,* rather, "sins"; see 4.2. *So that he is subject to punishment,* actually, "and he bears his sin." Protracted negligence is an objective guilt that continues to weigh upon the sinner until the appropriate measures are taken to be rid of it; see 7.18. **2:** *The carcass of an unclean beast or ... cattle,* correctly "of an unclean animal"; see 7.21; 11.40. *And then, being unclean, he realizes his guilt,* correctly: "though he had been unclean, and then he realizes his guilt." An emendation yields the more logical: "the fact escaped him, though he had known it, and then he realizes his guilt." **5–6:** The procedure. Unique to these four cases is the requirement that the guilty party supplement his realization and remorse with verbal confession. P's idea is thus that

7 But if his means do not suffice for a sheep, he shall bring to the LORD, as his penalty for that of which he is guilty, two turtledoves or two pigeons, one for a purification offering and the other for a burnt offering. 8 He shall bring them to the priest, who shall offer first the one for the purification offering, pinching its head at the nape without severing it. 9 He shall sprinkle some of the blood of the purification offering on the side of the altar, and what remains of the blood shall be drained out at the base of the altar; it is a purification offering. 10 And the second he shall prepare as a burnt offering, according to regulation. Thus the priest shall make expiation on his behalf for the sin of which he is guilty, and he shall be forgiven.

11 And if his means do not suffice for two turtledoves or two pigeons, he shall bring as his offering for that of which he is guilty a tenth of an *ephah* of choice flour for a purification offering; he shall not add oil to it or lay frankincense on it, for it is a purification offering. 12 He shall bring it to the priest, and the priest shall scoop out of it a handful as a token portion of it and turn it into smoke on the altar, with the LORD's offerings by fire; it is a purification offering. 13 Thus the priest shall make expiation on his behalf for whichever of these sins he is guilty, and he shall be forgiven. It shall belong to the priest, like the meal offering.

14 And the LORD spoke to Moses, saying:

15 When a person commits a trespass, being unwittingly remiss about any of the LORD's sacred things, he shall bring as his penalty to the LORD a ram without blemish from the flock, convertible into payment in silver by the sanctuary weight, as a guilt offering. 16 He shall make restitution for that wherein he was remiss about the sacred things, and he shall add a fifth part to it and give it to the priest. The priest shall make expiation on his behalf with the ram of the guilt offering, and he shall be forgiven.

17 And when a person, without knowing it, sins in regard to any of the LORD's commandments about things not to be done, and then realizes his guilt, he shall be subject to punishment.

verbalizing what one ought to have done but failed to do is part of expiation. In later Jewish tradition, verbal confession of all sin, whether communal or individual, became an essential requirement for atonement. **7–13:** Unlike the allowances made in 1.14–17 and 2.1–16, which serve to alleviate the poor person's sense of being excluded, the reason for the concessions here is that the sacred precincts must be decontaminated and sin must be eradicated from Israel's midst. It is not clear why the necessity to provide a means for the poor Israelite to atone for sin should be restricted to the four cases enumerated here. Perhaps these vv. are a subscript to the entire "ḥata᾽t" section, applying equally to 4.27–35. **7–10:** If the offender cannot afford a sheep or goat, he is to bring two birds. One serves as the "ḥata᾽t" itself, supplying the blood to cleanse the altar; the other is presented as a burnt offering. The burnt offering does not atone; rather it provides for the altar a respectable amount of flesh (in place of the fatty portions of the "ḥata᾽t") which would otherwise be negligible. See also 12.8; 14.22–31. **10:** *According to regulation,* according to the procedure outlined in 1.14–17. **11–13:** The possibility of substituting a cereal offering for an animal is remarkable here, since the essential step in the "ḥata᾽t" procedure is the application of blood to the altar. Perhaps the use of flour in some Mesopotamian purification ceremonies has cleared the way for its admission to Israel's cult, at least in this one case.

5.14–26: The reparation offering. Two concluding sections (vv. 14–19 and 20–26) convey the regulations concerning the other atonement offering, the "᾽asham," required when trespass against the sacred sphere, deliberate or unintentional, has taken place. The first section prescribes the sacrifice in cases of trespass against sacred objects and the sacred domain (vv. 14–16) and in cases of undiscovered violations (vv. 17–19). In the second section the obligation is extended to instances of false oath in property offenses. Since the verb "᾽-sh-m" often means "to be guilty" or "realize one's guilt" (see 4.13 n.; 5.17, 20–26 n.), the "᾽asham" sacrifice is generally translated "guilt offering." Its literal meaning, however, is "to incur liability," and "᾽asham" as a noun denotes the payment of damages (Num. 5.7–8; 1 Sam. 6.3–4, 8; see also Lev. 5.6). This fact, along with the importance attached by P, as well as in the Mesopotamian cultic texts, to the need to guard against misuse of the sacred and to make reparations when this has occurred, make it preferable to translate "reparation offering." Further cases requiring the reparation offering are found in 14.10–14; 19.21–22; Num. 6.12. Additional regulations appear in 7.1–7. **15:** *Trespass,* or "sacrilege"; Heb "ma῾al." The Tabernacle and its furnishings and appurtenances, as well as offerings and gifts that have been presented to it, are sacrosanct; their misuse or misappropriation is a crime against the deity Himself.

[18]He shall bring to the priest a ram without blemish from the flock, or the equivalent,[a] as a guilt offering. The priest shall make expiation on his behalf for the error that he committed unwittingly, and he shall be forgiven. [19]It is a guilt offering; he has incurred guilt before the LORD.

[20]The LORD spoke to Moses, saying: [21]When a person sins and commits a trespass against the LORD by dealing deceitfully with his fellow in the matter of a deposit or a pledge,[b] or through robbery, or by defrauding his fellow, [22]or by finding something lost and lying about it; if he swears falsely regarding any one of the various things that one may do and sin thereby—[23]when one has thus sinned and, realizing his guilt, would restore that which he got through robbery or fraud, or the deposit that was entrusted to him, or the lost thing that he found, [24]or anything else about which he swore falsely, he shall repay the principal amount and add a fifth part to it. He shall pay it to its owner when he realizes his guilt. [25]Then he shall bring to the priest, as his penalty to the LORD, a ram without blemish from the flock, or the equivalent,[a] as a guilt offering. [26]The priest shall make expiation on his behalf before the LORD, and he shall be forgiven for whatever he may have done to draw blame thereby.

TSAV צו

6 The LORD spoke to Moses, saying: [2]Command Aaron and his sons thus:

This is the ritual of the burnt offering: The burnt offering itself shall remain where it is burned upon the altar all night until morning, while the fire on the altar is kept going on it.

a I.e., in currency; cf. v. 15. *b Meaning of Heb. uncertain.*

See also 22.14. *Convertible ... by the sanctuary weight:* According to this translation, the animal need not be sacrificed; it may be converted into its monetary equivalent. Another possibility is that the ram, which is to be offered in every case, must be one whose value is symbolically commensurate with that of the misappropriated sacred property. This would also account for the name of the offering. *The sanctuary weight:* better, "the sacred shekel," i.e., the official shekel in use in the sanctuary treasury (about 11.5 g, less than half an oz). **16:** *Restitution ... add a fifth part:* The payment of damages in addition to restitution is common to biblical and Near Eastern law. *The priest shall make expiation on his behalf:* It may be presumed that this is accomplished through the blood application as performed with the "ḥata't," but this is not certain. **17–19:** The case is unclear. The circumstances are almost identical to those requiring the "ḥata't" in ch 4, the only difference being the words "without knowing it" in v. 17, repeated in v. 18 ("unwittingly"). Perhaps the offender, though he feels guilty of something, never becomes fully aware of what he has done; the "unknown sin" is a common motif in ancient religion. The Rabbis suggest that if the offender eventually becomes aware of his offense, he will be obligated to bring a "ḥata't" as well. But why make a reparation offering if no sacrilege has taken place? There is no persuasive solution to the text in its given form. **17:** *He shall be subject to punishment,* correct to "and bears his sin"; see 5.1; 7.18. **18:** *Or the equivalent,* see v. 15. **20–26:** The "'asham" for fraud. Defrauding one's fellow over property disputes is an act of sacrilege when a false oath using God's name has been sworn. The misuse of the divine name is probably the most common form of desecration of the sacred, since every Israelite has immediate access to it at all times (see 24.10–13). The restitution and fine are paid to the injured party, while the sacrificial expiation is made as above. This law is supplemented by Num. 5.5–8. **25:** *Or the equivalent,* see v. 15.

Chs 6–7: These chs complete the sacrificial instructions conveyed to Moses on the first of Nisan. They are transmitted in five speeches (6.1–11; 6.12–16; 6.17–7.21; 7.22–27; 7.28–36) and followed by a typical P caption summing up the whole of chs 1–7 (7.37–38). Each of the five types of sacrifice prescribed in chs 1–5 is taken up again, with added regulations. Each new topic is introduced by the phrase "this is the 'torah' of ...," i.e., "these are the instructions regarding ..." (6.2; 6.7; 6.18; 7.1; 7.11). Some suggest that while chs 1–5 are addressed to the lay Israelite, chs 6–7 are addressed to the priests. More accurately, in contrast to chs 1–5, which outline who offers what sort of sacrifice and how this is done, the primary purpose of chs 6–7 is to spell out precisely how the sacrifice is to be apportioned and disposed of following the altar ritual (see 7.35–36 n.). The three passages addressed specifically to the priesthood (6.1, 12, 17) are a logical subcategory.

6.1–6: The burnt offering. This refers to the burnt offering of the individual, discussed in 1.3–13, and not the "tamid" or daily burnt offering (Exod. 29.38 and elsewhere). Two regulations are added here: the stipulation that the flesh may burn throughout the night but by morning the ash should be removed (v. 2) and the instructions for the ash removal by the priest (vv. 3–4). A corollary follows: The fire on the altar must be kept burning at all

3 The priest shall dress in linen raiment, with linen breeches
next to his body; and he shall take up the ashes to which the
fire has reduced the burnt offering on the altar and place them
beside the altar. 4 He shall then take off his vestments and put
on other vestments, and carry the ashes outside the camp to a
clean place. 5 The fire on the altar shall be kept burning, not to
go out: every morning the priest shall feed wood to it, lay out
the burnt offering on it, and turn into smoke the fat parts of the
offerings of well-being. 6 A perpetual fire shall be kept burning
on the altar, not to go out.

7 And this is the ritual of the meal offering: Aaron's sons shall
present it before the LORD, in front of the altar. 8 A handful of
the choice flour and oil of the meal offering shall be taken from
it, with all the frankincense that is on the meal offering, and
this token portion shall be turned into smoke on the altar as
a pleasing odor to the LORD. 9 What is left of it shall be eaten
by Aaron and his sons; it shall be eaten as unleavened cakes,
in the sacred precinct; they shall eat it in the enclosure of the
Tent of Meeting. 10 It shall not be baked with leaven; I have giv-
en it as their portion from My offerings by fire; it is most holy,
like the purification offering and the guilt offering. 11 Only the
males among Aaron's descendants may eat of it, as their due
for all time throughout the ages from the LORD's offerings by
fire. Anything that touches these shall become holy.

12 The LORD spoke to Moses, saying: 13 This is the offering
that Aaron and his sons shall offer to the LORD on the occasion of his[a] anointment: a tenth of an *ephah* of choice flour
as a regular meal offering, half of it in the morning and half
of it in the evening, 14 shall be prepared with oil on a griddle.
You shall bring it well soaked, and offer it as a meal offering of
baked slices,[b] of pleasing odor to the LORD. 15 And so shall the

a Or "their." *b Meaning of Heb.* tuphine *uncertain.*

times (vv. 5–6). Since none of the flesh is eaten, these two regulations are the counterpart of the corresponding instructions for distribution and consumption given below for the remaining types of sacrifice. **2:** *Command Aaron and his sons* because handling the flesh of the burnt offering is their task; see above, ch 1. *This is the ritual of,* better, "these are the instructions concerning"; Heb "torah" means "body of instruction pertaining to." **3:** *The priest,* not necessarily the high priest. *In linen raiment,* with linen breeches next to his body, see Exod. 28.39–43. Since collecting the ashes involves contact with the high degree of sanctity attached to the altar, linen vestments are required. In order to exit the sphere of the sacred, however, nonsacred vestments must be worn. **4:** A clean place: Since the ashes derive from a sacred offering, they must be disposed of in a ritually pure spot. **5–6:** The altar fire, once ignited (see 9.24), must never be allowed to die out; it serves as a perpetual sign that the enshrined deity is being worshipped constantly. Later tradition derived from this v. the obligation to supply a regular "wood offering" to keep the altar aflame; see Neh. 10.35; 13.31.

6.7–11: The grain offering. Further instructions concerning the "minḥah" of the individual, prescribed in 2.1–13. They include (vv. 7–9a) a restatement of 2.2–3 and 2.9–10, along with the precise regulations regarding the priests' preparation and consumption of the "minḥah" and the consequences of the sacred portions of the offering coming into contact with the laity. **7:** *Ritual,* see v. 2 n., above. **9b–10a:** The prohibition of leaven (see 2.11) is here extended specifically to the priests' portion of the "minḥah." *In the sacred precinct ... of the Tent of Meeting,* within the Tabernacle courtyard. Offerings of the highest degree of sanctity could not leave the sacred precincts. **10–11:** The priests' portion of the sacrifice is not a gift from the person who presents the offering. Rather, the entire sacrifice is a gift to the LORD, who graciously "shares" it with the priests for their service (see 2.1–10; 7.34). *Offerings by fire,* see 1.9. *It is most holy,* see 2.3. **11:** *Only the males,* more precisely, "any male." The priests' portions of most holy offerings may be eaten only by priests qualified to offer them; namely, males. Female members of the priestly families are permitted to eat the meat of the well-being sacrifices. *Anything that touches these shall become holy:* Direct contact with any of the most holy food-gifts of the LORD communicates holiness, conceived of as a contagious, dynamic effervescence of the deity's Presence that renders whatever comes into contact with it holy. See also v. 20; Exod. 29.37; 30.29; Num. 17.1–4.

6.12–16: The grain offering of the priest. The "minḥah" of the high priest, half to be offered each morning and the other half each evening (v. 13), is incumbent upon the high priest's successors for all time (v. 15). These regulations are appended here as an exception to the preceding lay grain offering, since the priestly offering is turned into smoke in its entirety. The priest does not receive a share of his own gift. **13:** *Aaron and his sons,* i.e., the first high priest and his successors; see v. 15. *On the*

priest, anointed from among his sons to succeed him, prepare it; it is the LORD's—a law for all time—to be turned entirely into smoke. [16] So, too, every meal offering of a priest shall be a whole offering: it shall not be eaten.

[17] The LORD spoke to Moses, saying: [18] Speak to Aaron and his sons thus: This is the ritual of the purification offering: the purification offering shall be slaughtered before the LORD, at the spot[a] where the burnt offering is slaughtered: it is most holy. [19] The priest who offers it as a purification offering shall eat of it; it shall be eaten in the sacred precinct, in the enclosure of the Tent of Meeting. [20] Anything that touches its flesh shall become holy; and if any of its blood is spattered upon a garment, you shall wash the bespattered part in the sacred precinct. [21] An earthen vessel in which it was boiled shall be broken; if it was boiled in a copper vessel, [the vessel] shall be scoured and rinsed with water. [22] Only the males in the priestly line may eat of it: it is most holy. [23] But no purification offering may be eaten from which any blood is brought into the Tent of Meeting for expiation in the sanctuary; any such shall be consumed in fire.

7 This is the ritual of the guilt offering: it is most holy. [2] The guilt offering shall be slaughtered at the spot where the burnt offering is slaughtered, and the blood shall be dashed on all sides of the altar. [3] All its fat shall be offered: the broad tail; the fat that covers the entrails; [4] the two kidneys and the fat that is on them at the loins; and the protuberance on the liver, which shall be removed with the kidneys. [5] The priest shall turn them into smoke on the altar as an offering by fire to the LORD; it is a guilt offering. [6] Only the males in the priestly line may eat of it; it shall be eaten in the sacred precinct: it is most holy.

[7] The guilt offering is like the purification offering. The same rule applies to both: it shall belong to the priest who makes

a *Cf.* 1.11.

occasion of his anointment, most likely "from the time of his anointment [onward]." *A regular meal offering,* better: "as a grain offering, perpetually." **16:** Like the high priest, lesser priests too receive no share of a "minḥah" they offer on their own behalf. *Shall be a whole offering,* more precisely: "shall be turned completely into smoke."

6.17–23: Further instructions concerning the purification offering ("ḥata't"). For the types and procedure see 4.1–5.13. The paragraph stipulates where the "ḥata't" is to be slaughtered, defines its degree of sanctity, prescribes who may eat of its flesh and where (vv. 18–19, 22), and sets forth the ramifications of contact with the sacrificial flesh (vv. 20–21). It concludes by spelling out the crucial distinction between the eaten "ḥata't" and the burned one (v. 23); see 10.16–20 n. **18:** *Ritual,* see v. 2 n. *At the spot,* see 1.11. *Purification offering,* see 4.3 n. **19, 22:** These vv. refer to the eaten "ḥata't" (see v. 23 n.), and seem to contradict each other. The simplest resolution is that the flesh must be eaten and the officiating priest is entitled to it (see also 7.7, 14); he may, however, share it with other male members of the priesthood (see v. 11 n.). A single priest could hardly eat all of it, likely consumed within the space of a single day (see 10.19; cf. 7.15). **20:** *Shall become holy,* see v. 11 n. **20b–21:** These vv. confirm that the purification offering removes impurity by absorbing it. As a result, whatever flesh and blood have not been disposed of by consumption or burning communicate impurity to objects with which they come in contact, requiring them to be cleansed. **23:** As explained in ch 4.1–35 n., there are two types of purification offering: those whose blood purges the interior of the Tabernacle and those whose blood decontaminates the courtyard. Here the implications are spelled out. The flesh of the "ḥata't" for severe offenses may not be eaten; it must be burned. That of the "ḥata't" for less severe offenses and impurities must be eaten; thus the impurity is disposed of and the purification process made complete (see 10.16–20).

7.1–10: Further instructions concerning the reparation offering ("'asham") **and priestly share.** See 5.14–26. **1:** *Ritual,* see 6.2 n. *Guilt offering,* see 5.14–26 n. It is most holy, see 2.3. **2:** See 1.11. **2b–5a:** These details are not mentioned in connection with the "'asham" in 5.14–26, though they are included in the ritual prescribed for other sacrifices in chs 1–5 (e.g., 3.2b–5; 4.7–10; etc.). **3:** *The broad tail,* included since the animal prescribed for the "'asham" offering is a ram (5.15, 18, 25); see 3.6–16 n. **5:** *Offering by fire,* see 1.9 n. This is the only time this term is used of expiatory sacrifices; probably it refers to the portions given to the LORD and not to the sacrifice as a whole. **6–7:** As is the case with the "ḥata't" (6.19ff.), only male priests are eligible to eat the meat of the "'asham." The officiating priest receives the meat and may share it

expiation thereby. [8] So, too, the priest who offers a man's burnt offering shall keep the skin of the burnt offering that he offered. [9] Further, any meal offering that is baked in an oven, and any that is prepared in a pan or on a griddle, shall belong to the priest who offers it. [10] But every other meal offering, with oil mixed in or dry, shall go to the sons of Aaron all alike.

[11] This is the ritual of the sacrifice of well-being that one may offer to the LORD:

[12] If he offers it for thanksgiving, he shall offer together with the sacrifice of thanksgiving unleavened cakes with oil mixed in, unleavened wafers spread with oil, and cakes of choice flour with oil mixed in, well soaked. [13] This offering, with cakes of leavened bread added, he shall offer along with his thanksgiving sacrifice of well-being. [14] Out of this he shall offer one of each kind[a] as a gift to the LORD; it shall go to the priest who dashes the blood of the offering of well-being. [15] And the flesh of his thanksgiving sacrifice of well-being shall be eaten on the day that it is offered; none of it shall be set aside until morning. [16] If, however, the sacrifice he offers is a votive or a freewill offering, it shall be eaten on the day that he offers his sacrifice, and what is left of it shall be eaten on the morrow. [17] What is then left of the flesh of the sacrifice shall be consumed in fire on the third day. [18] If any of the flesh of his sacrifice of well-being is eaten on the third day, it shall not be acceptable; it shall not count for him who offered it. It is an offensive thing, and the person who eats of it shall bear his guilt.

[19] Flesh that touches anything unclean shall not be eaten; it shall be consumed in fire. As for other flesh, only he who is clean may eat such flesh. [20] But the person who, in a state of uncleanness, eats flesh from the LORD's sacrifices of well-being, that person shall be cut off from his kin. [21] When a person touches anything unclean, be it human uncleanness or an unclean animal or any unclean creature,[b] and eats flesh from the LORD's sacrifices of well-being, that person shall be cut off from his kin.

a Lit. "offering."

b Heb. sheqeṣ, *lit. "abomination"; several mss. and ancient versions read* shereṣ *"swarming things."*

with other male priests. **8–10:** The discussion of most holy sacrifices is concluded, with remaining details regarding the distribution of the priestly portions; v. 8 supplements 1.3–13 and 6.1–6, and vv. 9–10 supplement 2.1–13 and 6.7–11. **10:** *Dry,* the cereal "ḥata't" of 5.11 and the "minḥah" of the suspected adulteress (Num. 5.15).

7.11–34: Instructions for the sacrifice of well-being. See ch 3. **11–21:** As explained in 3.1 n., the meat of the well-being offering is eaten primarily by the offerer and his guests in a sacred meal. There are three types of well-being offerings; the distinctions are reflected also in 19.5–8 and 22.29–30. **11:** *Ritual,* see 6.2 n. **12–15:** The first type, the "todah" or sacrifice of thanksgiving, is offered according to Ps. 107 (and rabbinic law) by one who has recovered from illness, been rescued from danger, or returned safely from a journey. It is accompanied by prayers of thanksgiving, proclaiming to all present the beneficence of God enjoyed by the offerer. Mandated by happy circumstance, it is more of an obligation than a voluntary offering. It is accompanied by leavened cakes and wafers; one of each type is presented to the officiating priest. The meat is to be consumed by the following morning. **16–18:** The second and third types, here lumped together but distinguished in 22.21–23, are the "neder" or votive offering, obligatory in that it is made in fulfillment of a vow, though the vow itself was undertaken freely, and the "nedavah" or freewill offering, entirely an act of spontaneous devotion. No loaves are required and two days are allowed for the consumption of the meat. The burning of uneaten meat prescribed in v. 17 applies to the thanksgiving offering as well but would take place on the second day. **18:** Violating the time restriction invalidates the sacrifice retroactively. *It shall not be acceptable,* more precisely: "it shall not be accepted." See 1.3, 4; 19.5–8; 22.17–30. An *offensive thing,* Heb "pigul," meaning uncertain; perhaps "foul" or "desecrated." *Shall bear his guilt,* lit. "shall bear his sin"; see 5.1. P uses this phrase to mean that the act of wrongdoing remains with the individual until he has cleansed himself of it or, if this is impossible (as with particularly heinous misdeeds) or he fails to do so, until he has suffered its consequences. **19–21:** Sacred meat that comes into contact with a source of impurity may not be eaten. Further, if an impure individual, or one who has contracted impurity by means of direct contact, eats of the sacrificial meat, he is subject to the penalty of extirpation. **20, 21:** *Shall be cut off from his kin:* This threat recurs throughout the Priestly writings and is applied to many crimes committed against the sacred. Traditional commentators correctly understood

22 And the LORD spoke to Moses, saying: 23 Speak to the Israelite people thus: You shall eat no fat[a] of ox or sheep or goat. 24 Fat from animals that died or were torn by beasts may be put to any use, but you must not eat it. 25 If anyone eats the fat of animals from which offerings by fire may be made to the LORD, the person who eats it shall be cut off from his kin. 26 And you must not consume any blood, either of bird or of animal, in any of your settlements. 27 Anyone who eats blood shall be cut off from his kin.

28 And the LORD spoke to Moses, saying: 29 Speak to the Israelite people thus: The offering to the LORD from a sacrifice of well-being must be presented by him who offers his sacrifice of well-being to the LORD: 30 his own hands shall present the LORD's offerings by fire. He shall present the fat with the breast, the breast to be elevated as an elevation offering before the LORD; 31 the priest shall turn the fat into smoke on the altar, and the breast shall go to Aaron and his sons. 32 And the right thigh from your sacrifices of well-being you shall present to the priest as a gift; 33 he from among Aaron's sons who offers the blood and the fat of the offering of well-being shall get the right thigh as his portion. 34 For I have taken the breast of elevation offering and the thigh of gift offering from the Israelites, from their sacrifices of well-being, and given them to Aaron the priest and to his sons as their due from the Israelites for all time.

35 Those shall be the perquisites[b] of Aaron and the perquisites of his sons from the LORD's offerings by fire, once they have been inducted[c] to serve the LORD as priests; 36 these the LORD commanded to be given them, once they had been anointed, as a due from the Israelites for all time throughout the ages.

a I.e., hard, coarse fat (suet); cf. 3.3–5.
b Lit. "anointment," i.e., accruing from anointment. *c Lit. "brought forward."*

that it implies a penalty inflicted by God and not a form of ostracism or excommunication. They often saw it as death by divine agency or the denial of eternal bliss in the next world, but it is more probable that "cutting off" is extirpation, i.e., the eventual total extinction of one's line, by whatever means God sees fit. **21:** *Any unclean creature,* referring only to the carcasses of impure animals; for the question this poses, see 5.2; 11.40. **22–27:** Elaborating on the brief stipulation of 3.17; the fat mentioned here is suet (see 3.3–4 n. and translators' note *a* at 7.23). Eating the suet of permitted animals, whether sacrificed or not, just as ingesting their blood (v. 26; see also 17.10–16), is prohibited. The Israelite is commanded to abstain from the "food" of the LORD even when no sacrifice is made. **24:** *Animals,* i.e., domestic animals, named in the previous v., that have not been slaughtered as sacrifice but rather have been killed by beasts or died of themselves. Their meat, according to P, may be eaten (see 11.39–40 n.; 17.15–16 n.), but since no sacrificial ritual has taken place, no sanctity attaches to the meat, so household use of the suet is permissible. Torn by beasts, Heb "terefah," which in postbiblical phraseology became a term for all prohibited foods. **25:** *Offerings by fire,* see 1.9 n. **26–27:** The blood prohibition of 3.17 is also repeated in this context; see 17.10–16. **28–34:** The distribution of the well-being sacrifice. The altar portions are presented by the worshipper to be turned by the priest into smoke (see 3.3–5a). The priests' share of the well-being sacrifice is treated last. As elsewhere, the priests' portion is perceived as a gift from God (see v. 34), not from the offerer, as remuneration for their service and in compensation for their having been given no land (see also Num. 18.8–24). **30:** *Elevation offering,* Heb "tenufah." The ritualized transfer of ownership from the offerer to the deity. The Rabbis understood the presentation ritual as waving the offering back and forth, but the translation "elevation," also known from ancient times as well as from the depiction of the rite in an ancient Egyptian relief, is more accurate. *Offerings by fire,* see 1.9 n. **34:** *Breast of elevation offering and the thigh of gift offering:* Deut. 18.3, which assigns to the priests "the shoulder, cheeks and the stomach," has a different view of the priests' portions. Rabbinic law reconciled the two passages by interpreting Deut. ch 18 as referring to nonsacrificial meat slaughtered for food.

7.35–36: Summary. A summary of chs 6–7 in their entirety: The two chs refer primarily to the apportionment of the sacrificial offerings in general, and in particular to the priests' share. **35:** *Perquisites,* Heb "mishḥah," a rare word (see also Num. 18.8, there vocalized as "moshḥah"), meaning the priests' due, their assigned portion. *Offerings by fire,* see 1.9 n.; here alone it refers to all the sacrifices.

7.37–38: Overall summary. A summary of chs 1–7, closing the account of what was communicated to Moses on the first day of Nisan. **37:** *Offering of ordination:* These rituals were included in the instructions

37 Such are the rituals of the burnt offering, the meal offering, the purification offering, the guilt offering, the offering of ordination, and the sacrifice of well-being, 38 with which the LORD charged Moses on Mount Sinai, when He commanded that the Israelites present their offerings to the LORD, in the wilderness of Sinai.

8 The LORD spoke to Moses, saying: 2 Take Aaron along with his sons, and the vestments, the anointing oil, the bull of purification offering, the two rams, and the basket of unleavened bread; 3 and assemble the whole community at the entrance of the Tent of Meeting. 4 Moses did as the LORD commanded him. And when the community was assembled at the entrance of the Tent of Meeting, 5 Moses said to the community, "This is what the LORD has commanded to be done."

6 Then Moses brought Aaron and his sons forward and washed them with water. 7 He put the tunic on him, girded him with the sash, clothed him with the robe, and put the ephod on him, girding him with the decorated band with which he tied it to him. 8 He put the breastpiece on him, and put into the breastpiece the Urim and Thummim.[a] 9 And he set the headdress on his head; and on the headdress, in front, he put the gold frontlet, the holy diadem—as the LORD had commanded Moses.

10 Moses took the anointing oil and anointed the Tabernacle and all that was in it, thus consecrating them. 11 He sprinkled some of it on the altar seven times, anointing the altar, all its utensils, and the laver with its stand, to consecrate them. 12 He poured some of the anointing oil upon Aaron's head and anointed him, to consecrate him. 13 Moses then brought

a See note on Exod. 28.30.

given to Moses before the building of the Tabernacle (Exod. ch 29) and will be re-introduced in ch 8 (see 8.22–29). Their inclusion in the caption is puzzling. **38:** *When,* on 1 Nisan. *On Mount Sinai:* As is clear from *in the wilderness of Sinai* at the end of the v., this phrase means "[in the Tabernacle which stood] at [the foot of] Mount Sinai"; see also 25.1; 26.46; 27.34.

8.1–10.20: This is the major narrative section of Lev., describing the events connected with the inauguration of the Tabernacle and its rituals. These events occurred during the first eight days of Nisan.

8.1–36: The consecration of Aaron and his sons. Aaron and his sons are consecrated to the priesthood. According to P, God, many months earlier, had informed Moses that Aaron and his sons were to become His priests (Exod. ch 28), and outlined the details of this ceremony (Exod. ch 29). Now the consecration is to take place. Most of the ch (vv. 6–30) thus consists of a past-tense repetition of Exod. ch 29 with minor differences and the added refrain "as the LORD had commanded Moses." The ceremony of induction into the priesthood consists of five elements. (1) Investiture: The priests are clothed for the first time in the garments required to perform their service (vv. 7–9, 13). (2) Invocation: The priests present a burnt offering (vv. 18–21). (3) Consecration: The blood of a ram of offering is applied to the priests' bodies (vv. 22–24a). (4) "Filling the hands": The priests receive for the first time their allotted share of the sacrifices; they offer a portion to the LORD (vv. 26–29) and eat the remaining meat and loaves (v. 31). (5) Anointment: The priests are anointed with the sacred oil, infusing them with holiness (vv. 12, 30). Afterwards the priests remain within the Tabernacle for seven full days, completing their consecration (vv. 31–36). Three preparatory rituals are also performed, each at the appropriate moment. Before their investiture the priests must be bathed (v. 6); before the first sacrifices to be offered in the divine abode are made, the Tabernacle and its furnishings must be anointed (vv. 10–11); before being used, the altar must be purified (vv. 15–17). The latter two rituals sanctify the Tabernacle itself; its consecration thus takes place simultaneously with that of the priests. **2:** *The vestments,* see Exod. chs 28, 39. *The anointing oil,* see Exod. 30.22–33; 37.29. *The bull of purification offering* (see 4.3), *the two rams, and the basket of unleavened bread,* as already prescribed in Exod. 29.1–2. **7–9:** The outer "garments" of the high priest are marks of "dignity and adornment" (Exod. 28.2) and appurtenances of the daily regimen of perpetual worship, each one having a specific ritual function as enumerated in Exod. 28.12, 30, 35, 38. **8:** *Urim and Thummim,* see Exod. 28.30 n. **10–13:** In P, the anointing of persons and objects infuses them with holiness (see 6.11). Anointing Aaron and his sons (v. 30) transforms them into God's personal servants; they belong permanently to the sphere of the divine. All contact with the nonsacred is restricted and any contact with the impure is potentially fatal and must be avoided (see 21.1–15). **12:** *Upon Aaron's head,* see 4.3. **13:** The *tunics, sashes,* and *turbans* of Aaron's sons are for "dignity and adornment" (Exod. 28.40); they (and probably Aaron as well) also wore breeches for modesty (Exod. 28.42). **14–17:** The purification offering of the high priest, a bull, is offered and its parts are disposed of (see 4.3–12). This decontaminates the sacred sphere, in particular the altar, of the impurities that have collected there prior to the induction of the priests and the inauguration of worship. *Purification offering,* see 4.3. **15:** *Thus ... to make expiation upon it,* better, "and made expiation upon it." **18–21:** The first "food gift" to be presented is a burnt offering (see 1.3–9); it invokes the deity and summons His presence. Prior to the consummation of the induction ceremony, Aaron is the individual offerer, while Moses assumes the role of priest. **19:** *And it was slaughtered,* by Aaron; see 1.5. **22–29:** The central feature of the induction ceremony, translated here as ordination, is in Heb "milu'im," "filling," an ellipsis for "filling the hand" (see v. 33; 16.32; 21.10; also Exod. 28.41; 29.3ff.; 32.29; Judg. 17.5, 12; etc.). This phrase, also attested in Akkadian, expresses the priests' entitlement to their allotted portions of the sacrifices. Along with the "filling" comes the added consecration ritual of daubing some of the ram's blood upon Aaron and his sons and on the altar. **23:** *Ear ... thumb ... big toe,* probably the extremities of the body represent the whole. **25–29:** One of each of the loaves and cakes, along with the *right thigh,* is symbolically placed in the hands of the ordinands. They in turn present them to the LORD by elevating them (see 7.30) and then have them turned into smoke on the altar; priests do not receive a portion of their own offerings (see 6.12–15; 6.16). However, one of the priestly portions, the breast, is treated differently. As Moses serves on this occasion in the role of priest, he performs the elevation and receives the breast as his "priest's share" of the sacrificial meat.

Aaron's sons forward, clothed them in tunics, girded them with sashes, and wound turbans upon them, as the LORD had commanded Moses.

[14] He led forward the bull of purification offering. Aaron and his sons laid their hands upon the head of the bull of purification offering, [15] and it was slaughtered. Moses took the blood and with his finger put some on each of the horns of the altar, cleansing the altar; then he poured out the blood at the base of the altar. Thus he consecrated it in order to make expiation upon it.

[16] Moses then took all the fat that was about the entrails, and the protuberance of the liver, and the two kidneys and their fat, and turned them into smoke on the altar. [17] The rest of the bull, its hide, its flesh, and its dung, he put to the fire outside the camp—as the LORD had commanded Moses.

[18] Then he brought forward the ram of burnt offering. Aaron and his sons laid their hands upon the ram's head, [19] and it was slaughtered. Moses dashed the blood against all sides of the altar. [20] The ram was cut up into sections and Moses turned the head, the sections, and the suet into smoke on the altar; [21] Moses washed the entrails and the legs with water and turned all of the ram into smoke. That was a burnt offering for a pleasing odor, an offering by fire to the LORD—as the LORD had commanded Moses.

[22] He brought forward the second ram, the ram of ordination. Aaron and his sons laid their hands upon the ram's head, [23] and it was slaughtered. Moses took some of its blood and put it on the ridge[a] of Aaron's right ear, and on the thumb of his right hand, and on the big toe of his right foot. [24] Moses then brought forward the sons of Aaron, and put some of the blood on the ridges of their right ears, and on the thumbs of their right hands, and on the big toes of their right feet; and the rest of the blood Moses dashed against every side of the altar. [25] He took the fat—the broad tail, all the fat about the entrails, the protuberance of the liver, and the two kidneys and their fat—and the right thigh. [26] From the basket of unleavened bread that was before the LORD, he took one cake of unleavened bread, one cake of oil bread, and one wafer, and placed them on the fat parts and on the right thigh. [27] He placed all these on the palms of Aaron and on the palms of his sons, and elevated them as an elevation offering before the LORD. [28] Then Moses took them from their hands and turned them into smoke on the altar with the burnt offering. This was an ordination offering for a pleasing odor; it was an offering by fire to the LORD. [29] Moses took the breast and elevated it as an elevation offering before the LORD; it was Moses' portion of the ram of ordination—as the LORD had commanded Moses.

a *Or "lobe."*

[30] And Moses took some of the anointing oil and some of the
blood that was on the altar and sprinkled it upon Aaron and
upon his vestments, and also upon his sons and upon their
vestments. Thus he consecrated Aaron and his vestments, and
also his sons and their vestments.
[31] Moses said to Aaron and his sons: Boil the flesh at the entrance of the Tent of Meeting and eat it there with the bread
that is in the basket of ordination—as I commanded:[a] Aaron
and his sons shall eat it; [32] and what is left over of the flesh
and the bread you shall consume in fire. [33] You shall not go
outside the entrance of the Tent of Meeting for seven days,
until the day that your period of ordination is completed. For
your ordination will require seven days. [34] Everything done
today, the LORD has commanded to be done [seven days], to
make expiation for you. [35] You shall remain at the entrance
of the Tent of Meeting day and night for seven days, keeping
the LORD's charge—that you may not die—for so I have been
commanded.
[36] And Aaron and his sons did all the things that the LORD
had commanded through Moses.

SHEMINI שמיני

9 On the eighth day Moses called Aaron and his sons, and
the elders of Israel. [2] He said to Aaron: "Take a calf of the
herd for a purification offering and a ram for a burnt offering,
without blemish, and bring them before the LORD. [3] And speak
to the Israelites, saying: Take a he-goat for a purification offering; a calf and a lamb, yearlings without blemish, for a burnt
offering; [4] and an ox and a ram for an offering of well-being to
sacrifice before the LORD; and a meal offering with oil mixed
in. For today the LORD will appear to you."

a Or, vocalizing ṣuwwethi, *"I have been commanded"; cf. below, vv. 35 and 10.13.*

30: The sanctifying oil, previously poured on Aaron's head (v. 12), is now applied to the person of Aaron and his sons. It is mixed with blood from the altar and is sprinkled, rather than smeared, on them, completing his consecration and accomplishing theirs. **31–36:** The newly ordained priests may now eat of the sacred meat and bread, making sure to consume it all and to observe the time restriction (see Exod. 29.34). They then remain within the Tabernacle for seven days of "milu'im." Exod. 29.30 also ordains that the "milu'im" ritual be repeated when a new high priest is installed. **33:** *Your ordination will require seven days,* lit. "he [Moses] will fill your hands for seven days"; i.e., the ceremony of vv. 22–29 will be repeated on each of the next six days (see Exod. 29.35–37). **34:** *Everything done today,* all of the purification and ordination rituals. *Make expiation for you,* specifically, purge the altar of impurities that accrue there during the seven-day period that you are in such close proximity to it. **35:** If the priests fail to keep *the LORD's charge* and exit the Tabernacle during the critical first seven days of their priesthood, the contact between their heightened state of sanctity and the realm of the nonsacred will be fatal.

9.1–10.20: The Day of Revelation and the transgression of Aaron's sons. Chs 9 and 10 comprise one unit recounting the events of the eighth day. In the Heb text no new division occurs at 10.1. After Aaron and his sons have been ordained, Moses orders them to perform their first sacrificial service in preparation for the appearance of the divine Presence (9.1–6). This consists of a number of offerings, including a well-being offering made on behalf of the entire people in celebration of the great event (9.7–23a). When the deity's Presence manifests itself in the sight of the people, signaling that He is pleased with their worship and has agreed to abide in the shrine they have built for Him, the people burst into rejoicing (9.23b–24). At the very moment that the inauguration of Israel's cult seems to have reached its auspicious climax, however, two of Aaron's sons commit a blatant act of sacrilege, overstepping the strictly prescribed bounds of acceptable worship (10.1). The LORD sanctifies His name by striking them down on the spot (10.2–3), and the surviving members of the priestly family are forbidden to mourn their demise (10.4–7). They are reminded of their sacred charge—to keep the sacred separate from the nonsacred (10.8–11)—and told to continue the day's ceremonies (10.12–15). When Moses discovers that they have deviated from the normal manner of disposing of the "ḥata't" meat, he is incensed (10.16–18); it takes some convincing before he agrees that their act was justified (10.19–20). **9.1–6:** After their seven-day seclusion, Aaron and his sons are told to emerge from the Tabernacle and to begin preparations for the Revelation Day ritual. Moses has them prepare the offerings they will make and tells Aaron to order the people, represented by the elders (see 4.15), to prepare the sacrifices that will be offered on their behalf. Thus the high priest takes up, for the first time, his crucial role of informing the Israelite people of their cultic duties. **1:** *The eighth day,* beginning with the first day of the seven-day

5 They brought to the front of the Tent of Meeting the things that Moses had commanded, and the whole community came forward and stood before the LORD. 6 Moses said: "This is what the LORD has commanded that you do, that the Presence of the LORD may appear to you." 7 Then Moses said to Aaron: "Come forward to the altar and sacrifice your purification offering and your burnt offering, making expiation for yourself and for the people; and sacrifice the people's offering and make expiation for them, as the LORD has commanded."

8 Aaron came forward to the altar and slaughtered his calf of purification offering. 9 Aaron's sons brought the blood to him; he dipped his finger in the blood and put it on the horns of the altar; and he poured out the rest of the blood at the base of the altar. 10 The fat, the kidneys, and the protuberance of the liver from the purification offering he turned into smoke on the altar—as the LORD had commanded Moses; 11 and the flesh and the skin were consumed in fire outside the camp. 12 Then he slaughtered the burnt offering. Aaron's sons passed the blood to him, and he dashed it against all sides of the altar. 13 They passed the burnt offering to him in sections, as well as the head, and he turned it into smoke on the altar. 14 He washed the entrails and the legs, and turned them into smoke on the altar with the burnt offering.

15 Next he brought forward the people's offering. He took the goat for the people's purification offering, and slaughtered it, and presented it as a purification offering like the previous one. 16 He brought forward the burnt offering and sacrificed it according to regulation. 17 He then brought forward the meal offering and, taking a handful of it, he turned it into smoke on the altar—in addition to the burnt offering of the morning.[a] 18 He slaughtered the ox and the ram, the people's sacrifice of well-being. Aaron's sons passed the blood to him—which he

a See Exod. 29.38–46.

ordination. **2:** *Purification offering,* see 4.3. Here too the purification of the Tabernacle is necessary before acts of worship can begin. *Burnt offering:* The first gift the priests offer the LORD is a sublime act of devotion and serves also as an act of attraction, invoking the deity's presence. **3:** The people too are to offer a purification offering, confirming that in P all are responsible for eradicating impurities from the divine abode; see ch 4. **4:** One of the few occasions on which a well-being offering ("shelamim"; see ch 3) is made by the public (see also 23.19). Since all will be present for the manifestation of the divine Presence shortly to occur, all will celebrate the joyous event in the appropriate manner, partaking of a sacred repast in God's presence. *Meal offering,* "minḥah" or grain offering; see ch. 2. One of each of the three types of gift offerings (see 1.1–3.17 n.) is to be made by the people, inaugurating the perpetual regimen of worship. *For today the LORD will appear to you:* This is echoed in v. 6 by "[in order] that the Presence of the LORD may appear to you," confirming Rashi's view that the purpose of these rituals is to bring about the theophany, i.e., to induce the divine Presence to make its appearance. **5:** *And the whole community came forward,* i.e., after having collected the prescribed materials, presumably so instructed by the elders. **6:** *Moses said: "This is what the LORD has commanded,"* see also v. 7, "as the LORD has commanded." But nowhere is it recounted that God issued these commands, so most commentators assume that the text economizes for the sake of brevity. Rabbinic tradition acknowledges that Moses often commanded in the name of the LORD actions about which he had received no prior orders (e.g., Exod. 19.15; 32.27; elsewhere in P this occurs in Num. 30.2), implying that Moses' prophetic intuition was tantamount to explicit divine authority. Note that v. 21 says that the offerings were made "as Moses had commanded." **7:** *And for the people:* This apparently refers to the second purification offering, subsequently to be made on behalf of the people (see vv. 3, 15–16). The LXX here reads "and for your house" (i.e., Aaron's family). **8–14:** The priests' purification and burnt offerings are made in accordance with their prescribed rituals. **15–21:** The people's sacrifices are offered, again following the logical sequence: purification, then the burnt offering and grain offering (since it too is in the "most-holy" category; see 6.10), and finally the well-being offering which is to constitute the sacred feast of celebration. **15:** *Like the previous one:* The text does not state specifically (as it did above regarding the priests' "ḥata't") what was done with the meat; this omission prepares us for what is to follow (10.16–20). **17:** Unlike the "minḥah" of the individual (2.3, etc.; 6.9–11), this public one is offered in its entirety (as is the priest's; 6.16). *The burnt offering of the morning,* apparently the daily burnt offering prescribed in Exod. 29.38–39 (= Num. 28.3–4), indicating that its regular practice has already commenced (see Exod. 40.29). **18–21:** Though the ritual of the "shelamim" is performed

dashed against every side of the altar—19 and the fat parts of
the ox and the ram: the broad tail, the covering [fat], the kidneys, and the protuberances of the livers. 20 They laid these
fat parts over the breasts; and Aaron[a] turned the fat parts into
smoke on the altar, 21 and elevated the breasts and the right
thighs as an elevation offering before the LORD—as Moses had
commanded.
22 Aaron lifted his hands toward the people and blessed
them; and he stepped down after offering the purification offering, the burnt offering, and the offering of well-being. 23 Moses and Aaron then went inside the Tent of Meeting. When
they came out, they blessed the people; and the Presence of
the LORD appeared to all the people. 24 Fire came forth from
before the LORD and consumed the burnt offering and the fat
parts on the altar. And all the people saw, and shouted, and fell
on their faces.

10 Now Aaron's sons Nadab and Abihu each took his fire
pan, put fire in it, and laid incense on it; and they offered
before the LORD alien fire, which He had not enjoined upon
them. 2 And fire came forth from the LORD and consumed
them; thus they died [b]at the instance of[b] the LORD. 3 Then Moses said to Aaron, "This is what the LORD meant when He said:

Through those near to Me I show Myself holy,
And gain glory before all the people."

And Aaron was silent.

a This word moved up from v. 21 for clarity. *b-b Others "before."*

meticulously, the celebration to follow will be aborted. **22–24:** Some rabbinic commentators suggest that Aaron's initial blessing was a plea for God to appear, consisting of the priestly blessing prescribed in Num. 6.22–27 (which includes the words "May the LORD shine His face upon you" and "May the LORD lift up His face toward you"). When this was not answered, Aaron realized he had been found wanting, either in his priestly abilities, in which case he needed to enter the Tabernacle for instruction, or in his personal merits, in which case he needed Moses to pray on his behalf. After Moses accompanied him into the Tabernacle and the situation was rectified, the subsequent blessing pronounced by two of them (consisting of the words of Ps. 90.17) was answered and the LORD appeared. This interpretation is fanciful. Taken in context, the vv. indicate two separate acts. In Aaron's first blessing he asks the LORD to deal favorably with the people; he and Moses then enter the Tabernacle and invite the deity to emerge, after which they bless the people again—this time praying on their behalf that God favor them all with His manifest Presence—to which the LORD then responds by making His long-awaited appearance. Similarly, in the account of the dedication of Solomon's Temple in 1 Kings ch 8, Solomon blesses the people, prays, then—when the festivities are concluded—blesses the people again, after which God makes an appearance. **22:** *Lifted his hands toward the people,* to convey to them the blessings he has solicited on their behalf from God. *Stepped down:* The author anachronistically assumes the later Temple with which he is familiar, in which the altar would have been raised high above the ground; the Tabernacle altar was a portable one and was but three cubits (1.5 m, about 4.5 ft) high (Exod. 27.1). **23–24:** The Presence appears in the entrance of the Tabernacle and divine fire emerges from within, igniting the altar fire and consuming the sacrificial portions arrayed there. At this the people cry out, an expression of joy, and fall prostrate, a mark of obeisance. The non-Priestly narratives too tell of a theophany at Sinai/Horeb (Exod. chs 19–20; 24.1–15a). The Priestly counterpart of these accounts relates nothing of a thunderous voice booming out from heaven and proclaiming the Decalogue or of a fiery descent of the LORD in the sight of all the people on the mountain. For P the theophany began with the arrival of the divine Presence at Sinai (Exod. 24.15–18a) where it lingered until the Israelites finished building the Tabernacle. It continued with the entrance of the divine Presence to dwell in its abode (Exod. 40.34–35), and reaches its culmination here.

10.1–3: The sin and death of Nadab and Abihu follow directly (see 9.1–10.20 n.). **1:** *Fire pan,* a metal utensil with a handle used for offering smoking incense. *Fire,* Heb "'esh" here means kindling material; see also Num. 17.2, 11. The brothers placed unlit coals (or wood for kindling) in the pans, in order to attract the divine fire to light them (see 1 Kings 18.38). *Offered,* i.e., presented, "brought near"; alien fire, unauthorized coals. They thus prepared an incense offering upon kindling of their own. *Which He had not enjoined upon them:* No offering of incense had been ordered; the only legitimate incense offerings are those made daily, by the high priest, upon the sacred altar (see Exod. 30.7–8). In public worship, only what is prescribed is legitimate; what is not is sacrilege. The Rabbis and medieval commentators thought otherwise, incredulous at the idea that God had struck down

4 Moses called Mishael and Elzaphan, sons of Uzziel the uncle of Aaron, and said to them, "Come forward and carry your
kinsmen away from the front of the sanctuary to a place outside the camp." 5 They came forward and carried them out of
the camp by their tunics, as Moses had ordered. 6 And Moses
said to Aaron and to his sons Eleazar and Ithamar, "Do not
[a-]bare your heads[-a] and do not rend your clothes, lest you die
and anger strike the whole community. But your kinsmen, all
the house of Israel, shall bewail the burning that the LORD has
wrought. 7 And so do not go outside the entrance of the Tent of
Meeting, lest you die, for the LORD's anointing oil is upon you."
And they did as Moses had bidden.

8 And the LORD spoke to Aaron, saying: 9 Drink no wine or
other intoxicant, you or your sons, when you enter the Tent
of Meeting, that you may not die. This is a law for all time
throughout the ages, 10 for you must distinguish between the
sacred and the profane, and between the unclean and the
clean; 11 and you must teach the Israelites all the laws which
the LORD has imparted to them through Moses.

12 Moses spoke to Aaron and to his remaining sons, Eleazar
and Ithamar: Take the meal offering that is left over from the
LORD's offerings by fire and eat it unleavened beside the altar, for it is most holy. 13 You shall eat it in the sacred precinct,
inasmuch as it is your due, and that of your children, from
the LORD's offerings by fire; for so I have been commanded.
14 But the breast of elevation offering and the thigh of gift offering you, and your sons and daughters with you, may eat in
any clean place, for they have been assigned as a due to you
and your children from the Israelites' sacrifices of well-being.

a-a Or "dishevel your hair."

two young priests for a "mere" ritual offense, especially since it seemed to stem from a sincere, though perhaps overenthusiastic, desire to serve the LORD. They therefore suggested other reasons for the severe fate suffered by the two (such as drunkenness, celibacy, arrogant impatience for Moses and Aaron to die, or neglect of their sacred obligations). In biblical thought, however, ritual crimes are dire. Further, the sin of the two brothers was not simply that they went too far in their misguided super-piety. Rather, they acted in utter disregard for the deity. God intended that the manifestation of His Presence would ignite the altar fire, marking His acceptance of His people's devotion. Their intent was for the divine fire to ignite their own pans; that is, they were attempting to arrogate control of the deity to themselves. **2:** *Fire came forth from the LORD,* from the Holy of Holies; similarly 9.24. The sacrilege of Nadab and Abihu evokes a spontaneous response: Crimes of trespass upon the sacred are automatically fatal. **3:** *This is what the LORD meant:* The reference may be to Exod. 29.43; otherwise one must assume that the statement was made at an earlier point but recorded only here. Those near to Me, perhaps more simply, "those who come too near to Me." *Show Myself holy ... gain glory:* Frequently in biblical thought, God's holiness is displayed, and His glory made manifest, in the swift and unrelenting punishment of those who offend His majesty. **4–5:** The corpses must be removed immediately; to allow such a potent source of contamination to remain in contact with the most sacred sphere would be particularly dangerous. **5:** *By their tunics:* Direct physical contact with the bodies is also avoided. **6–7:** Mourning rituals, as well as contact with the dead, are forbidden to priests (21.1–6, 10–12). The surviving priests are warned that if they compound the offense of Nadab and Abihu with further ritual infraction their fate will be no less severe, and the community too will be placed in jeopardy; see 4.3. Their first concern must be to prevent the holy from being defiled and the service of the deity from being disrupted. *Bare your heads,* correctly "dishevel your heads [i.e., your hair]"; a bared head was not a sign of mourning. *Shall bewail the burning that the LORD has wrought:* The death of Aaron's sons is all the more tragic for the fact that it was deserved. Although the officiating priests are forbidden to display any outward manifestations of grief, the people at large are under no such restriction (but see 19.27–28). **8–10:** Priests need to maintain sobriety in order to discharge their sacred tasks, not only their ritual duties but also priestly instruction, which require the ability to make precise distinctions and rulings. This parenthetical passage, which seems out of place here, could well serve as the introduction to the remainder of Lev., in which the priestly tasks of distinguishing *between the sacred and the profane, and between the unclean and the clean* are described. **12–16:** Internal feelings notwithstanding, Aaron, Eleazar, and Ithamar are to continue as though nothing has occurred. The priests' portions of the well-being offerings are given to them; they, and their families, may eat the meat later in the day and perhaps the next day as well (see 7.15–16). The festive

[15] Together with the fat of fire offering, they must present the thigh of gift offering and the breast of elevation offering, which are to be elevated as an elevation offering before the LORD, and which are to be your due and that of your children with you for all time—as the LORD has commanded.

[16] Then Moses inquired about the goat of purification offering, and it had already been burned! He was angry with Eleazar and Ithamar, Aaron's remaining sons, and said, [17] "Why did you not eat the purification offering in the sacred area? For it is most holy, and He has given it to you to remove the guilt of the community and to make expiation for them before the LORD. [18] Since its blood was not brought inside the sanctuary,[a] you should certainly have eaten it in the sanctuary, as I commanded." [19] And Aaron spoke to Moses, "See, this day they brought their purification offering and their burnt offering before the LORD, and such things have befallen me! Had I eaten purification offering today, would the LORD have approved?" [20] And when Moses heard this, he approved.

11 The LORD spoke to Moses and Aaron, saying to them: [2] Speak to the Israelite people thus:

These are the creatures that you may eat from among all the land animals: [3] any animal that has true hoofs, with clefts through the hoofs, and that chews[b] the cud—such you may eat.

a As is done in the case of the most solemn offerings; see 4.3–21; 16.11–17.
b Lit. "brings up."

repast to be held by the people (see 9.18–21) following the day's ceremonies was probably canceled. **16–20:** Diligently keeping track that each of the day's offerings has been handled properly, Moses finally arrives at the people's "ḥata't" (9.15). Since this, though public, was performed for preventive purification, its blood, unlike that for a communal offense (4.13–21), was not brought into the Tabernacle interior. Yet, Moses discovers, Aaron and his surviving sons, instead of eating the meat, have had it burned, in apparent violation of 6.23. Aaron's response means that what has occurred is a one-time exception in light of the tragic circumstances; no ritual reform has been attempted nor is there any dispute as to the proper procedure. Thus is Moses' apprehension put to rest.

11.1–47: Laws regulating the consumption of flesh. Communication of laws to Moses now resumes. The Priestly doctrine of prohibited and permitted foodstuffs derives from the belief that human beings, having dominion over the world and all it contains, are permitted, since the flood, to eat all vegetation and all (nonhuman) meat. There is but one stipulation: Humans must not consume an animal's blood along with its flesh. All this, P believes, has been known since the time of Noah (Gen. 9.1–4). Now, however, Moses is informed that the Israelite people are to be subject to a host of additional restrictions. These extend to all five categories of the animal kingdom: (1) large land animals (vv. 2–8), (2) beings that dwell in the water (vv. 9–12), (3) fowl (vv. 13–19), (4) flying insects (vv. 20–23), and (5) small land animals (vv. 41–42). Each category is subdivided into those animals that Israelites may eat and those that they may not. The criteria of division are present in nature itself: The distinction between forbidden and permitted meat, while incumbent upon Israelites alone, is a part of creation as reflected in Gen. 1.1–2.4a. This is similar to the Sabbath: Though it was sanctified at creation, its observance was obligatory only for the Israelites. By maintaining a set of dietary restrictions corresponding to the distinctions held to be present in the natural world, the Israelites, in Priestly thought, are kept holy, that is, separate from the remainder of humanity (vv. 44–45; see also 20.25–26) and within the inner circle of proximity to the divine. In both categories of land animals (1 and 5), an additional dimension exists: Contact with the carcasses of the prohibited animals also communicates impurity. Though this is mentioned briefly in (1) (vv. 4, 7, 8), its ramifications are detailed in the vv. preceding (5) (vv. 24–40). This ch anticipates the next four (chs 12–15), in which the issue of impurity and the need to eradicate it will be taken up in full. The laws of permitted and forbidden meat (also in briefer form in Deut. 14.3–20) constitute only a portion of the biblical dietary laws. Elsewhere in P are prohibitions of blood and suet (3.16–17; 7.22–27; 17.10–14; see also 19.26); also outside of P blood is prohibited (Deut. 12.16, 23–24). The non-Priestly laws also forbid Israelites to eat carrion (Exod. 22.30; Deut. 14.21), a prohibition that P does not accept (see vv. 39–40 n.), and prohibit cooking a kid in its mother's milk (Exod. 23.19; 34.26; Deut. 14.21), which P does not mention. Together with the law of slaughter, traditionally believed to have been communicated to Moses orally (see 1.5 n.), these laws provide the biblical basis for the laws of "kashrut" practiced to this day. **1:** These laws are communicated to Aaron along with Moses, in view of the priests' responsibility for scrupulously maintaining the

4 The following, however, of those that either chew the cud or
have true hoofs, you shall not eat: the camel—although it chews
the cud, it has no true hoofs: it is unclean for you; 5 the daman—
although it chews the cud, it has no true hoofs: it is unclean for
you; 6 the hare—although it chews the cud, it has no true hoofs:
it is unclean for you; 7 and the swine—although it has true hoofs,
with the hoofs cleft through, it does not chew the cud: it is unclean for you. 8 You shall not eat of their flesh or touch their carcasses; they are unclean for you.
9 These you may eat of all that live in water: anything in water,
whether in the seas or in the streams, that has fins and scales—
these you may eat. 10 But anything in the seas or in the streams
that has no fins and scales, among all the swarming things of
the water and among all the other living creatures that are in
the water—they are an abomination for you 11 and an abomination for you they shall remain: you shall not eat of their flesh
and you shall abominate their carcasses. 12 Everything in water
that has no fins and scales shall be an abomination for you.
13 The following[a] you shall abominate among the birds—
they shall not be eaten, they are an abomination: the eagle, the
vulture, and the black vulture; 14 the kite, falcons of every variety; 15 all varieties of raven; 16 the ostrich, the nighthawk, the sea
gull; hawks of every variety; 17 the little owl, the cormorant, and
the great owl; 18 the white owl, the pelican, and the bustard;
19 the stork; herons of every variety; the hoopoe, and the bat.
20 All winged swarming things that walk on fours shall be
an abomination for you. 21 But these you may eat among all
the winged swarming things that walk on fours: all that have,
above their feet, jointed legs to leap with on the ground—22 of
these you may eat the following:[a] locusts of every variety; all

a A number of these cannot be identified with certainty.

prescribed distinctions; see 10.10–11. **2–8:** Category (1): large land animals. It is assumed that domestic livestock (cattle, sheep, and goats) may be eaten; since these animals are fit for sacrifice, they are obviously permitted. In Priestly law, however, domestic livestock may only be eaten as sacrificial meat (see 17.3–8). Therefore the text here must be dealing with nondomestic animals, as is the case throughout the ch. These vv. establish that Israelites may eat the meat of other large land animals only if they resemble domestic livestock, i.e., if they possess the latter's characteristics. They are listed in Deut. 14.5: the deer, the gazelle, the roebuck, the wild goat, the ibex, the antelope, the mountain sheep. There, however, they are equated with the domestic ones, since Deuteronomic law disagrees with P, permitting the nonsacrificial slaughter of cattle, sheep, and goats as well. **3:** *Has true hoofs ... chews the cud:* These characteristics have no intrinsic or symbolic significance; they are simply the distinguishing features of cattle, sheep, and goats and therefore serve as a simple means for identifying other permitted animals. **4–7:** The four illustrations—the *camel,* the *daman,* the *hare,* and the *swine*—show that one characteristic is not enough; only animals that both ruminate and have cloven hooves are permitted. Swine are not singled out here. *Unclean:* In addition to being forbidden as food, the meat of these animals communicates impurity. This is elaborated upon below (see vv. 24–28). **8:** *You shall not eat of their flesh or touch their carcasses,* probably equivalent to the parallel v. 11 "you shall not eat of their flesh [and you shall avoid] (see vv. 10–12 n.) their carcasses." Throughout P contact with sources of impurity is not forbidden; it is to be avoided when possible, and when it has occurred purification is mandatory but no misdeed has been committed (see chs 12–15). As is clear from vv. 24ff., this applies here as well. **9–12:** Category (2): water creatures. The Israelites may eat the flesh of beings that populate the waters only if they have the characteristics peculiar to fish. **9–10:** *Fins and scales:* The water creatures divide into two groups: fish, thought of as the "proper" or normal form of maritime life, and all others, *all the swarming things of the water.* Those in the former group are easily identified by the two features characteristic of fish; those in the latter are forbidden. **10–12:** *Abomination* (Heb "sheketz"), *abominate* (Heb "sh-k-tz"), in this ch refer specifically to forbidden animals. Perhaps *you shall abominate* and an abomination for you mean that although there is nothing intrinsically loathsome about these animals, the Israelite is to abhor them simply because they are prohibited. But abominate may be too strong and in P may mean "avoid." Unlike forbidden land creatures, forbidden water creatures and flying creatures do not communicate impurity. **13–19:** Category (3): fowl. This section does not provide a set of distinguishing markings to identify the permitted species; it simply enumerates the prohibited ones, implying that all others are allowed. Rabbinic tradition attempted to supply the missing key, suggesting that the prohibited fowl are all birds of prey; the permitted fowl are nonpredators. This category

varieties of bald locust; crickets of every variety; and all varieties of grasshopper. [23] But all other winged swarming things that have four legs shall be an abomination for you.

[24] And the following shall make you unclean—whoever touches their carcasses shall be unclean until evening, [25] and whoever carries the carcasses of any of them shall wash his clothes and be unclean until evening—[26] every animal that has true hoofs but without clefts through the hoofs, or that does not chew the cud. They are unclean for you; whoever touches them shall be unclean. [27] Also all animals that walk on paws, among those that walk on fours, are unclean for you; whoever touches their carcasses shall be unclean until evening. [28] And anyone who carries their carcasses shall wash his clothes and remain unclean until evening. They are unclean for you.

[29] The following[a] shall be unclean for you from among the things that swarm on the earth: the mole, the mouse, and great lizards of every variety; [30] the gecko, the land crocodile, the lizard, the sand lizard, and the chameleon. [31] Those are for you the unclean among all the swarming things; whoever touches them when they are dead shall be unclean until evening. [32] And anything on which one of them falls when dead shall be unclean: be it any article of wood, or a cloth, or a skin, or a sack—any such article that can be put to use shall be dipped in water, and it shall remain unclean until evening; then it shall be clean. [33] And if any of those falls into an earthen vessel, everything inside it shall be unclean and [the vessel] itself you shall break. [34] As to any food that may be eaten, it shall become unclean if it came in contact with water;[b] as to any liquid that may be drunk, it shall become unclean if it was inside any vessel.[c] [35] Everything on which the carcass of any of them falls shall be unclean: an oven or stove shall be smashed. They are unclean and unclean they shall remain for you. [36] However, a spring or cistern in which water is collected shall be clean, but whoever touches such a carcass in it shall be unclean. [37] If such a carcass falls upon seed grain that is to be sown, it is clean;

a A number of these cannot be identified with certainty.
b I.e., if the food then came in contact with the carcass of any animal named in vv. 29–30. *c I.e., a vessel that had become contaminated by such contact.*

may be analogous to (1): It is taken for granted that the turtledove and the pigeon are permitted since they are fit for the altar; the list of forbidden fowl would then be an enumeration of all known fowl that are dissimilar in their appearance and habits to the fowl used in sacrifice. *The eagle, the vulture, ... :* Some of the translations are uncertain. **20–23:** Category (4): flying insects, *winged swarming things.* Those with jointed legs above their feet for leaping on the ground are permissible. These are named; all others, as stressed by the repetition in v. 23, are forbidden. Unlike the previous categories, here the basic category itself is forbidden; only insects that diverge from the characteristics of the category and may have been thought to resemble birds more than insects may be eaten. **24–40:** These parenthetical vv. interrupt the flow, introducing a series of laws pertaining to impurities generated or communicated by the flesh of creatures mentioned in (1) and (5). This is anticipated by, and elaborates on, what has preceded, but since v. 41 is the direct continuation of v. 23, it seems most likely that these vv. are secondary. Perhaps they were inserted here, instead of after (5) which would have been more natural, in order for v. 43 to follow vv. 41–42 directly. **24–25:** The superscription and its explanation: The carcasses of the following creatures communicate impurity by direct contact and carrying. The impurity is minor; only a brief time, until sunset, followed by laundering (and, presumably, bathing), is needed for it to dissipate. **26–28:** Elaborating on (1). The first to be mentioned (v. 26) are those whose impurity was noted above (vv. 3–8); to these, such animals as bears, dogs and cats, which would not be eaten in any case and are therefore omitted above, are added (v. 27). The opening statement is then repeated (v. 28). **29–38:** Anticipating (5) (vv. 41–42). The realities of life are such that the carcasses of small land animals are not only likely to come into direct contact with humans, thus communicating impurity directly; they are especially likely to come into contact with foodstuffs, vessels and utensils, seeds, and water supplies. **31–35:** Like humans who have contracted this impurity and are governed by the rule in vv. 24–25 (see v. 31), articles of wood and leather require washing and the lapse of one day in order for the impurity to dissipate (v. 32). Earthen vessels that have absorbed impurity cannot be cleansed (v. 33). Liquid in vessels becomes impure if the unclean animal has fallen in (v. 34b), but sources of fresh water, while not cleansing the unclean animal, remain pure and do not communicate impurity, since they are constantly washing it away (v. 36).

38 but if water is put on the seed and any part of a carcass falls
upon it, it shall be unclean for you.
39 If an animal that you may eat has died, anyone who touches its carcass shall be unclean until evening; 40 anyone who
eats of its carcass shall wash his clothes and remain unclean
until evening; and anyone who carries its carcass shall wash
his clothes and remain unclean until evening.
41 All the things that swarm upon the earth are an abomination; they shall not be eaten. 42 You shall not eat, among all
things that swarm upon the earth, anything that crawls on its
belly, or anything that walks on fours, or anything that has
many legs; for they are an abomination. 43 You shall not draw
abomination upon yourselves through anything that swarms;
you shall not make yourselves unclean therewith and thus become unclean. 44 For I the LORD am your God: you shall sanctify
yourselves and be holy, for I am holy. You shall not make yourselves unclean through any swarming thing that moves upon
the earth. 45 For I the LORD am He who brought you up from the
land of Egypt to be your God: you shall be holy, for I am holy.
46 These are the instructions concerning animals, birds,
all living creatures that move in water, and all creatures that
swarm on earth, 47 for distinguishing between the unclean and
the clean, between the living things that may be eaten and the
living things that may not be eaten.

TAZRIA' תזריע

12 The LORD spoke to Moses, saying: 2 Speak to the Israelite
people thus: When a woman at childbirth[a] bears a male,
she shall be unclean seven days; she shall be unclean as at the
time of her menstrual infirmity.—3 On the eighth day the flesh of
his foreskin shall be circumcised.—4 She shall remain in a state
of blood purification[b] for thirty-three days: she shall not touch
any consecrated thing, nor enter the sanctuary until her period

a Heb. tazria', *lit. "brings forth seed."* *b Meaning of Heb. uncertain.*

Dry foodstuffs are not susceptible to impurity, but are if they have been moistened by water (v. 34a). **34:** *If it came in contact with water:* This translation is misleading; the water does not render it unclean. Rather, it becomes capable of contracting impurity if, prior to coming in contact with the unclean object, it is moistened at any time by water; see v. 38. **35:** *An oven or stove shall be smashed:* These too are of earthenware; earthenware, being porous, thoroughly absorbs impurity and cannot be cleansed. **37–38:** Seed and grain, like foodstuffs, are not susceptible to impurity until they come into contact with water; thenceforth contact with an unclean animal renders them unclean. **39–40:** These vv. confirm that according to P "nevelah," the meat of an animal that has died by itself rather than being slaughtered, is permitted as long as the animal is one that may be eaten. Impurity results and must be remedied, but no sin has been committed. Elsewhere in P this is extended to "terefah," the meat of an animal that has been "torn," i.e., killed by another beast; see 17.15–16. In P, only priests are commanded to abstain from "nevelah" and "terefah"; see 17.15–16 and 22.8. **39:** *An animal that you may eat:* Above, and in 5.2 and 7.21, it is only the meat of unclean animals that communicates impurity. Here, and in 17.15–16 (see also 7.23) the meat of permitted animals does so as well. It may be possible to reconcile this conflict; perhaps the carcass and flesh of an unclean animal (which may not be eaten) communicates impurity no matter how the animal has died, whereas that of permitted animals does so only if the animal has died on its own or been killed by a beast (though it may be eaten, see above); if it has been slaughtered, no impurity results. **41–42:** Category (5): small land animals. Like (4), the category per se is prohibited, but here there are no exceptions. The only permitted land animals are thus domestic livestock and fowl and those which resemble them, and a few exceptions to the general rule prohibiting all others, namely the explicitly named types of flying insects. **43–45:** The conclusion of the instructions stresses the aim of the food restrictions. By restricting consumption of meat to clean animals, the Israelites sanctify themselves and become holy; for the idea expressed by these terms see 11.1–47 n. **43:** *Draw abomination upon yourselves:* Heb actually means "make your throats loathsome," a straightforward way of saying "eat that which is loathsome." **45:** *Who brought you up from the land of Egypt to be your God,* see 26.13 n. *You shall be holy, for I am holy,* see 19.2. **46–47:** This typically Priestly caption, like 7.37–38, summarizes what precedes it.

Chs 12–15: Disposal of impurity. The next four chs prescribe how to dispose of the types of impurity identified by the Priestly tradition. "Impurity" (Heb "tum'ah") is often translated as contamination, defilement, pollution, or uncleanness. In P "tum'ah" is like an atmospheric layer or coating, enveloping the

of purification is completed. 5 If she bears a female, she shall be unclean two weeks as during her menstruation, and she shall remain in a state of blood purification[a] for sixty-six days.

6 On the completion of her period of purification, for either son or daughter, she shall bring to the priest, at the entrance of the Tent of Meeting, a lamb in its first year for a burnt offering, and a pigeon or a turtledove for a purification offering.[b] 7 He shall offer it before the LORD and make expiation on her behalf; she shall then be clean from her flow of blood. Such are the rituals concerning her who bears a child, male or female.

a Meaning of Heb. uncertain. *b See note at 4.3.*

impure person or object. Though invisible, it is believed to be quite real; though amorphous it is substantive. Its causes are four: human corpses, carcasses of animals, fluxes of life fluids, and a specific condition known as "tzaraʿat" (see chs 13–14). The common denominator is that all these are manifestations of death, or more precisely, of the escape of the forces of life. Thus the corpse and the carcass, out of which life may be thought to "leak," defile; similarly semen, menstrual fluid, the blood lost in childbirth, and other genital discharge (though not human waste, which has nothing to do with the escape of life, and not blood, apparently because it is the purifying agent) defile as well. The disease or condition known as "tzaraʿat" too is thought of as a form of gradually escaping life (see Num. 12.12). Impurity is distinct from its causes: Corpses, carcasses, fluids, and "tzaraʿat" are not the defilement itself; rather, they produce the defilement, by process of spontaneous generation. We may compare "tumʾah" to a miasma, an aura of invisible vapors, expanding to fill available space and polluting all that it touches, contagiously contaminating persons and objects with which they come into contact and communicating to them various degrees of indirect (secondary or tertiary) impurity, which in turn needs to be disposed of. Unlike similar notions found outside the Bible, "tumʾah" in P is not demonic, not created by or connected with evil spirits or malicious deities. Neither is it the same as modern notions of dirt or filth, or of infection. Rather, it is a simple fact of life, a part of nature; certain phenomena in the created world are empirically sources of impurity. These phenomena are not necessarily bad; there is nothing morally repugnant about a human corpse or the carcass of an animal, there is nothing sinful about menstruation or sexual intercourse, and there is no evil in a genital flux or a disease of the skin. For this reason, nowhere in the Priestly law is there a prohibition of the lay Israelite's becoming "tameʾ" per se; people and objects routinely and unavoidably contract impurity at all times. The grievous and dangerous sin connected with impurity is rather that of remaining impure, of failing to dispose of impurity once one has contracted it, thereby allowing it to spread and to come into contact with the sacred, i.e., the sanctuary and its furnishings. For "tumʾah," as pictured by Priestly thought, is drawn irresistibly to the sacred sphere, which is particularly vulnerable to its penetration, and there it accumulates. If this goes unchecked, i.e., if too much of this odious matter collects in the divine abode, the divine Presence will depart and then Israel is doomed (see 15.31 n.). Only priests, who are in constant contact with the sacred sphere, are explicitly cautioned to shun all but the most unavoidable impurity; lay Israelites are under no such obligation; they are simply required to attend conscientiously to its disposal. Three elements effect the disposal of impurity: the passage of time, cleansing (usually in water), and the purification offering. The first two purify the individual, the third purges the sanctuary. The minor types of impurity require only the bathing of the impure individual and the laundering of clothing, after which the impurity dissipates on its own by nightfall. Contamination of the Tabernacle by such minor impurities is negligible and is presumably cleansed by routine public offerings. Major impurities, on the other hand, directly contaminate the Tabernacle. When they occur, in addition to the passage of time and cleansing, a "ḥataʾt" sacrifice must be made on behalf of the impure individual, in order to eradicate the impurity that he has caused to accumulate in the Tabernacle. Later tradition tended to adopt a less literal, more practical view of biblical "tumʾah," and often reinterpreted it symbolically. Further, by rejecting the idea that impurity is drawn to the sanctuary from afar, the Rabbis made it less of a concern—only those who planned actually to visit the Temple need worry about purifying themselves. Ultimately "tumʾah" became simply an arbitrarily decreed ritual "state." In biblical teaching, in contrast to its later interpretation, impurity is not simply a condition; it is real.

12.1–8: Impurity after childbirth. Neither procreation nor childbirth is sinful. Like other bodily impurities, the defilement attached to childbirth has no moral significance whatsoever; it is a fact of nature. As the text explicitly says, the woman who has given birth needs to be purified *from her flow of blood* (v. 7). The observable discharge of heavy, dark fluid ("lochia rubra"), which lasts for a number of days, followed by a lighter flow ("lochia alba") which may last for a number of weeks, provides the empirical explanation of the two phases of her purification. In order to prescribe unified legislation, these two approximate periods are standardized into the "round" numbers seven and forty used throughout the Bible, which are then doubled (see v. 5). The ch outlines the stages of the

8 If, however, her means do not suffice for a sheep, she shall
take two turtledoves or two pigeons, one for a burnt offering
and the other for a purification offering. The priest shall make
expiation on her behalf, and she shall be clean.

13 The LORD spoke to Moses and Aaron, saying:
2 When a person has on the skin of his body a swelling,
a rash, or a discoloration, and it develops into a scaly affection
on the skin of his body, it shall be reported[a] to Aaron the priest
or to one of his sons, the priests. 3 The priest shall examine the
affection on the skin of his body: if hair in the affected patch
has turned white and the affection appears to be deeper than
the skin of his body, it is a leprous affection;[b] when the priest
sees it, he shall pronounce him unclean. 4 But if it is a white
discoloration on the skin of his body which does not appear to
be deeper than the skin and the hair in it has not turned white,
the priest shall isolate the affected person for seven days. 5 On
the seventh day the priest shall examine him, and if the affection has remained unchanged in color and the disease has

a Or "he shall be brought."

b Heb. ṣaraʿath *is used for a variety of diseases. Where a human being is declared unclean by reason of* ṣaraʿath, *the traditional translation "leprosy" has been retained without regard to modern medical terminology.*

mother's purification if a male child has been born (vv. 2–4), explains how they differ if a female child is born (v. 5), and prescribes how the mother is obligated to see to the purification of the sanctuary, whether she is a person of means (vv. 6–7) or not (v. 8). **2:** *She shall be unclean seven days:* During the first phase the mother is severely unclean; her impurity penetrates to the sphere of the sacred, requiring her to offer a "ḥata't." This, however, she cannot do until she is completely purified, several weeks later (vv. 6–7a). *Unclean as at the time of her menstrual infirmity:* In addition to the fact that her impurity contaminates the sanctuary from afar, the regulations pertaining to the parturient are identical to those pertaining to the menstruant, as given in 15.19–24. She communicates minor impurity to whatever and whomever she touches by direct or almost direct contact. **3:** Circumcision is not a stage in the purification process. It is noted here by association; mention of the seventh day of a male child's life quite naturally calls to mind the event of the eighth day. Halakhic exegesis also notes that since the command of circumcision was given not to Moses but to Abraham (Gen. 17.9–14), it needed to be repeated here, in the context of the giving of the law to Israel in the wilderness, in order to be valid. **4:** *In a state of blood purification,* lit. "in the blood of becoming pure," that is, she will continue to observe some discharge, and thus remain impure to a lesser degree, before becoming fully purified. *Thirty-three days:* The number thirty-three, which has no significance, when combined with the first seven days yields forty, a "round" number of purification days. *Not touch any consecrated thing,* better, "anything holy." During the second phase, she continues to contaminate sacred objects and the sanctuary, but only by direct contact, no longer from afar; she no longer communicates impurity to the nonsacred (to other humans or objects) at all. Thus she is permitted to resume relations with her husband in this second phase. Rabbinic law is more stringent, requiring a longer period of time; see also 15.19. **5:** The reason the length of each phase is doubled when a female child is born is difficult to determine. Modern medicine recognizes no difference between the postpartum genital flow of the mother of a boy and that of the mother of a girl. The ancients, however, may have believed there was a difference, or they may have noted that there is occasionally vaginal flow from the infant girl herself and viewed this as necessitating a longer purification by the mother. **6–7a:** The expiation, that is, decontamination of the sanctuary, is accomplished elsewhere by means of the "ḥata't" sacrifice (see ch 4). Uniquely, the mother is also required to offer a burnt offering (see ch 1), though generally this is not needed for expiation. It may be an expression of thanks or a required gesture of obeisance. **6:** *Purification offering* (see 4.3 n.), no sin has been committed. **7b:** The summary caption. **8:** An appended provision made for the woman who cannot afford the costly sacrifice (see 5.7–10 n.). Here the concern is to ensure that every parturient, even the poorest, performs her expiation, so that the divine abode is cleansed.

13.1–14.57: Impurity caused by "tzaraʿat." These two chs are a unit (see summary at 14.54–57), prescribing the elimination of the impurity caused by "tzaraʿat." This has sometimes been translated as "leprosy" (or "leprous affection"), but the disease today called leprosy (Hansen's disease) was not known in biblical times and the description given in the Bible is not consistent with it. Further, since "tzaraʿat" afflicts not only humans but also fabrics (13.47–59) and building materials (14.33–47), it cannot be identified with a single pathology. The distinctive symptom of "tzaraʿat" in humans is scale-like eruptions of the skin. Lacking modern microbiology, the Bible referred to conditions with similar outward manifestations by a single name. "Tzaraʿat" in fabrics and building materials are types of mildew. The Bible does not

not spread on the skin, the priest shall isolate him for another
seven days. 6 On the seventh day the priest shall examine him
again: if the affection has faded and has not spread on the
skin, the priest shall pronounce him clean. It is a rash; he shall
wash his clothes, and he shall be clean. 7 But if the rash should
spread on the skin after he has presented himself to the priest
and been pronounced clean, he shall present himself again to
the priest. 8 And if the priest sees that the rash has spread on
the skin, the priest shall pronounce him unclean; it is leprosy.

9 When a person has a scaly affection, it shall be reported[a]
to the priest. 10 If the priest finds on the skin a white swelling
which has turned some hair white, with [b-]a patch of undiscolored flesh[-b] in the swelling, 11 it is chronic leprosy on the skin of
his body, and the priest shall pronounce him unclean; he need
not isolate him, for he is unclean. 12 If the eruption spreads out
over the skin so that it covers all the skin of the affected person
from head to foot, wherever the priest can see—13 if the priest
sees that the eruption has covered the whole body—he shall
pronounce the affected person clean; he is clean, for he has
turned all white. 14 But as soon as undiscolored flesh appears in
it, he shall be unclean; 15 when the priest sees the undiscolored
flesh, he shall pronounce him unclean. The undiscolored flesh
is unclean; it is leprosy. 16 But if the undiscolored flesh again
turns white, he shall come to the priest, 17 and the priest shall
examine him: if the affection has turned white, the priest shall
pronounce the affected person clean; he is clean.

18 When an inflammation appears on the skin of one's body
and it heals, 19 and a white swelling or a white discoloration
streaked with red develops where the inflammation was, he

a *See note a at 13.2.* *b-b* *Others "quick raw flesh."*

view disease per se as defiling. Only those having "tzaraʿat" or abnormal genital fluxes (see 15.1–33 n., 15.1–15, 25–30) are considered to be impure. "Tzaraʿat," seen as a gradual erosion of the skin, was thought to culminate, unless the patient recovered, in the ultimate disintegration of the flesh, which was taken as a manifestation of the gradual escape of life. The person afflicted with it was looked upon as potentially dead (see Num. 12.12), death itself having begun to consume his body (Job 18.13). This "leakage" of life, according to P, creates impurity (see chs 12–15 n.). For the steps necessary to dispose of the impurity lest it spread to the sanctuary, the priest, in his sacred role of distinguishing the pure from the impure (see 10.10; cf. 11.47) is given the task of "diagnosing" "tzaraʿat" in humans, fabrics, and buildings. But the priest is not a physician, and has no role in the healing process; the commands detail only the procedure to be followed, and the information necessary, for him to determine if the lesion is "tzaraʿat" or not. If it is, purification and expiation are prescribed; if not, the priest pronounces it clean. In the Bible, the onset and progress of disease, its persistence or eventual disappearance, are essentially outside of human control. In other biblical books "tzaraʿat" is seen as a divine penalty (e.g., Num. 12.10; 2 Kings 15.5). Rabbinic thought agreed, suggesting that the person afflicted with "tzaraʿat" (the "metzoraʿ") was being punished thereby for the sin of slander (the same consonants in Heb: "motzi raʿ"). But none of this is expressed here. P seems to view "tzaraʿat" quite matter-of-factly as a feature of the natural world created by God, like unclean animals, gonorrhea, and menstruation. No moral judgment is passed on the afflicted individuals, who are accountable only if they fail to attend to the prompt eradication of impurity once the disease has disappeared. **13.1:** As in 11.1, the laws are communicated to Aaron as well as Moses, reflecting the central role of the priest in what follows. **1–46:** Each set of symptoms is taken up separately, and directions are provided in order to determine whether "tzaraʿat" is present or not. If it is not, the priest declares the person pure. If it is, the person is declared impure until such time as the affliction is healed and the purification rituals have been completed (ch 14). If a conclusive diagnosis cannot be made, seven-day waiting periods ensue, after which the condition is examined again. **2–8:** *A swelling, a rash, or a discoloration* (better: "shiny mark"): These are immediately deemed to be "tzaraʿat" if the two symptoms in v. 3 are present. Otherwise a seven-day quarantine commences, after which, if the condition has spread or if the two symptoms appear, it is pronounced to be "tzaraʿat." If not, a second seven-day period is observed; during it, if the condition spreads the afflicted person must immediately report back to the priest and be pronounced unclean. At the end of the second week, a final check is made: If the affection has faded it is deemed to be merely a rash and the person is pronounced clean; if at that time, or subsequently, it has spread or the two symptoms have appeared, it is deemed "tzaraʿat." **3:** *A leprous affection,* Heb "tzaraʿat"; better, "scale disease" (see above) or "surface affection." **4:** *Shall isolate the affected person:* This quarantine is not aimed at arresting the spread of the disease, but is an attempt to contain the spread of an intolerable

shall present himself to the priest. 20 If the priest finds that it appears lower than the rest of the skin and that the hair in it has turned white, the priest shall pronounce him unclean; it is a leprous affection that has broken out in the inflammation. 21 But if the priest finds that there is no white hair in it and it is not lower than the rest of the skin, and it is faded, the priest shall isolate him for seven days. 22 If it should spread in the skin, the priest shall pronounce him unclean; it is an affection. 23 But if the discoloration remains stationary, not having spread, it is the scar of the inflammation; the priest shall pronounce him clean.

24 When the skin of one's body sustains a burn by fire, and the patch from the burn is a discoloration, either white streaked with red, or white, 25 the priest shall examine it. If some hair has turned white in the discoloration, which itself appears to go deeper than the skin, it is leprosy that has broken out in the burn. The priest shall pronounce him unclean; it is a leprous affection. 26 But if the priest finds that there is no white hair in the discoloration, and that it is not lower than the rest of the skin, and it is faded, the priest shall isolate him for seven days. 27 On the seventh day the priest shall examine him: if it has spread in the skin, the priest shall pronounce him unclean; it is a leprous affection. 28 But if the discoloration has remained stationary, not having spread on the skin, and it is faded, it is the swelling from the burn. The priest shall pronounce him clean, for it is the scar of the burn.

29 If a man or a woman has an affection on the head or in the beard, 30 the priest shall examine the affection. If it appears to go deeper than the skin and there is thin yellow hair in it, the priest shall pronounce him unclean; it is a scall, a scaly eruption in the hair or beard. 31 But if the priest finds that the scall affection does not appear to go deeper than the skin, yet there is no black hair in it, the priest shall isolate the person with the scall affection for seven days. 32 On the seventh day the priest shall examine the affection. If the scall has not spread and no yellow hair has appeared in it, and the scall does not appear to go deeper than the skin, 33 the person with the scall shall shave himself, but without shaving the scall; the priest shall isolate him for another seven days. 34 On the seventh day the priest shall examine the scall. If the scall has not spread on the skin, and does not appear to go deeper than the skin, the priest shall pronounce him clean; he shall wash his clothes, and he shall be clean. 35 If, however, the scall should spread on the skin after he has been pronounced clean, 36 the priest shall examine him. If the scall has spread on the skin, the priest need not look for yellow hair: he is unclean. 37 But if the scall has remained unchanged in color, and black hair has grown in it, the scall is healed; he is clean. The priest shall pronounce him clean.

amount of severe impurity in case "tzaraʿat" is present. **9–11:** *A scaly affection:* This is immediately deemed to be "tzaraʿat" if it shows the three symptoms given in v. 10; no period of waiting is needed. **10:** *Undiscolored flesh,* lit. "raw" or "living" flesh. It appears where scales have rubbed off, indicating that the disease is still active. **11–13:** The spreading of the scales to the entire body rather than deepening and causing erosion in specific spots indicates that healing is under way and the person is pronounced pure. **14–17:** *Undiscolored flesh,* see v. 10. Its reappearance indicates the disease has not yet healed; that is established only when the "raw" flesh again turns white and remains so. **18–23:** A boil that heals and is followed by a white swelling or a whitish-reddish mark is deemed on sight to be "tzaraʿat" if the two symptoms outlined in v. 20 are present. If they are not, a seven-day waiting period is observed, after which, if the condition has spread, it is pronounced "tzaraʿat"; otherwise the person is pronounced pure. **24–28:** A *burn* displaying the symptoms is subjected to the same scrutiny and diagnostic procedure as boils (vv. 19–23). **29–37:** *On the head or in the beard,* i.e., on the scalp or on the skin beneath the beard. A mark appearing here is immediately deemed "tzaraʿat" if it is a scall (Heb "netek," detachment), that is, hairs have become detached from their follicles, and both of the symptoms described in v. 30 are present. If they are not, the person is reexamined after a seven-day quarantine, after which, if both symptoms fail to appear and the condition has not spread, the procedures given in vv. 33–37 are carried out. The presence of yellow hair is not necessary to prove the presence of "tzaraʿat" if the condition has spread, but the presence of dark hair in the scall is a sure sign of healing.

38 If a man or a woman has the skin of the body streaked with white discolorations, 39 and the priest sees that the discolorations on the skin of the body are of a dull white, it is a tetter broken out on the skin; he is clean.

40 If a man loses the hair of his head and becomes bald, he is clean. 41 If he loses the hair on the front part of his head and becomes bald at the forehead, he is clean. 42 But if a white affection streaked with red appears on the bald part in the front or at the back of the head, it is a scaly eruption that is spreading over the bald part in the front or at the back of the head. 43 The priest shall examine him: if the swollen affection on the bald part in the front or at the back of his head is white streaked with red, like the leprosy of body skin in appearance, 44 the man is leprous; he is unclean. The priest shall pronounce him unclean; he has the affection on his head.

45 As for the person with a leprous affection, his clothes shall be rent, his head shall be left bare,[a] and he shall cover over his upper lip; and he shall call out, "Unclean! Unclean!" 46 He shall be unclean as long as the disease is on him. Being unclean, he shall dwell apart; his dwelling shall be outside the camp.

47 When an eruptive affection occurs in a cloth of wool or linen fabric, 48 in the warp or in the woof of the linen or the wool, or in a skin or in anything made of skin; 49 if the affection in the cloth or the skin, in the warp or the woof, or in any article of skin, is streaky green[b] or red, it is an eruptive affection. It shall be shown to the priest; 50 and the priest, after examining the affection, shall isolate the affected article for seven days. 51 On the seventh day he shall examine the affection: if the affection has spread in the cloth—whether in the warp or the woof, or in the skin, for whatever purpose the skin may be used—the affection is a malignant eruption; it is unclean. 52 The cloth—whether warp or woof in wool or linen, or any article of skin—in which the affection is found, shall be burned, for it is a malignant eruption; it shall be consumed in fire. 53 But if the priest sees that the affection in the cloth—whether in warp or in woof, or in any article of skin—has not spread, 54 the priest shall order the affected article washed, and he shall isolate it for another seven days. 55 And if, after the affected article has been washed, the priest sees that the affection has not changed color and that it has not spread, it is unclean. It shall be consumed in fire; it

a *See note at 10.6.* *b* *Or "yellow."*

38–39: *Streaked with white discolorations,* better, "shiny white marks." This supplements vv. 2–8, providing a method for determining if the mark is merely a tetter or white patch. **40–44:** Normal baldness is not a sign of "tzaraʿat." If, however, it is accompanied by the symptoms given in v. 43, it is immediately deemed to be "tzaraʿat" and no waiting period is required. **45–46:** These vv. detail the behavior required of the person found to have "tzaraʿat" of any type from the moment the diagnosis is certain until he or she is cured, after which the instructions given in ch 14 are followed. **45:** *His head shall be left bare,* better, "[the hair of] his head shall be disheveled"; this, together with the rending of garments, is a sign of mourning (see 10.6), appropriate for a person diagnosed with a disease equivalent to death itself. Covering of the upper lip was also a sign of mourning (see Ezek. 24.17, 22). *He shall call out, "Unclean! Unclean!"* to warn others that the impurity (not the disease) is contagious. **46:** *He shall dwell apart:* Since he remains removed from society, no details regarding how his impurity is transmitted to other persons and objects are given. Most likely the person with "tzaraʿat" also contaminates whatever is under the same roof; therefore he must dwell apart. His impurity also defiles the sacred, from afar, which is why he will need to perform expiation when he is able (see 14.19). *Outside the camp:* This refers to the wilderness period; in later periods, outside the city (see 2 Kings 7.3). **47–58:** Types of mildew or mold in fabrics that cause erosion and destruction were yet another manifestation of the same leakage of life-force that is the source of all impurity in P and are therefore also "tzaraʿat." As with humans, the fabric suspected of impurity is isolated for seven days; if the condition has spread the suspicion is confirmed. If not, the fabric is cleaned and isolated for seven more days. If the affection has not spread and has begun to clear up the fabric is pronounced pure; otherwise it is deemed to have "tzaraʿat." Fabrics with confirmed cases cannot be "cured," and must be destroyed promptly; they cannot be purified through a ritual. This explains why these vv., which would perhaps read more naturally after 14.32, are placed here, before the laws prescribing the purification of persons and objects that have been cured. **55:** *Whether on its inner side or on its outer side,* Heb is identical to v. 42

is a fret,[a] whether on its inner side or on its outer side. 56 But if the priest sees that the affected part, after it has been washed, is faded, he shall tear it out from the cloth or skin, whether in the warp or in the woof; 57 and if it occurs again in the cloth—whether in warp or in woof—or in any article of skin, it is a wild growth; the affected article shall be consumed in fire. 58 If, however, the affection disappears from the cloth—warp or woof—or from any article of skin that has been washed, it shall be washed again, and it shall be clean.

59 Such is the procedure for eruptive affections of cloth, woolen or linen, in warp or in woof, or of any article of skin, for pronouncing it clean or unclean.

METSORAʿ מצרע

14 The LORD spoke to Moses, saying: 2 This shall be the ritual for a leper at the time that he is to be cleansed.

When it has been reported[b] to the priest, 3 the priest shall go outside the camp. If the priest sees that the leper has been healed of his scaly affection, 4 the priest shall order two live clean birds, cedar wood, crimson stuff, and hyssop to be brought for him who is to be cleansed. 5 The priest shall order one of the birds slaughtered over fresh water in an earthen vessel; 6 and he shall take the live bird, along with the cedar wood, the crimson stuff, and the hyssop, and dip them together with the live bird in the blood of the bird that was slaughtered over the fresh water. 7 He shall then sprinkle it seven times on him who is to be cleansed of the eruption and cleanse him; and he shall set the live bird free in the open country. 8 The one to be cleansed shall wash his clothes, shave off all his hair, and bathe in water; then he shall be clean. After that he may enter the camp, but he must remain outside his tent seven days. 9 On the seventh day he shall shave off all his hair—of head, beard, and eyebrows. When he

a Meaning of Heb. pehetheth *uncertain.* *b Cf. note a at 13.2.*

"the bald part in the front or at the back of the head" and is translated appropriately to the context. Most likely these words are a scribal error and should be deleted. **59:** *Procedure,* better, "instructions" (Heb "torat"; see 6.2 n.). This summary caption refers only to vv. 47–58; the entire "tzaraʿat" section is summed up at 14.54–57. **14.1–32:** Resuming 13.46, these vv. prescribe the steps required of the person cured to dispose of the impurity he has created. Anthropologically and sociologically these rituals have been seen as rites of passage, marking the return of the outcast to normal life in human society and in God's presence. Rabbinic interpretation, which tended to view the person afflicted as under divine sanction for wrongdoing, generally explained these rituals as acts of contrition, penance, and thanksgiving. In fact, however, they are for ridding the person and the environment of the impurity that has been generated, and the afflicted person is under no disapprobation unless he or she fails to carry them out. **2–3:** The process begins when the priest has examined the afflicted person and declared him cured. The cure itself is God's affair; the priest's task begins where God's ends. **2:** *This shall be the ritual for,* better, "these are the instructions concerning"; see 6.2. A *leper* (Heb "metzoraʿ," i.e., a person afflicted with "tzaraʿat"); see 13.3 and 13.1–14.57 n. **3–20:** The purification of the "metzoraʿ" and the expiation, in three stages. **3–7:** Stage one takes place outside the camp as soon as the priest pronounces the afflicted person cured. Its purpose is to rid the person of the impurity that has enveloped the physical body during the ailment. The purging agent is the blood of the first of two birds. This is the only instance in which purifying blood is applied to a human. The sprinkling of the reconstituted blood of the red heifer on the person contaminated by contact with a corpse (Num. ch 19) is the closest parallel and further indicates the close connection between "tzaraʿat" and death. The second bird is kept alive and set free to carry off the impurity, like the scapegoat on the annual Day of "Atonement" (or Purification); see ch 16. **4:** *Live,* i.e., wild birds, that live in the open country. *Clean birds,* see 11.13–19. *Cedar wood, crimson stuff,* agents of purification throughout biblical and ancient Near Eastern tradition. *Hyssop,* used for dipping and sprinkling, and therefore associated with purification (Ps. 51.9). **5:** *Over fresh water in an earthen vessel,* to dilute the substance, so that there is a sufficient quantity that may easily be sprinkled. **7:** The two birds are considered one entity. Thus the impurity, after being removed by the blood of the slaughtered bird, is believed to be transferred to the second, live bird which is then dispatched, thereby permanently disposing of it. **8–9:** Stage two, on the seventh day, consists of the cleansing of the individual. That cleansing is not sufficient in itself, but must be preceded by the removal and disposal rituals and the lapse of a seven-day period, indicates the severity of

has shaved off all his hair, he shall wash his clothes and bathe his body in water; then he shall be clean. 10 On the eighth day he shall take two male lambs without blemish, one ewe lamb in its first year without blemish, three-tenths of a measure of choice flour with oil mixed in for a meal offering, and one *log* of oil. 11 These shall be presented before the LORD, with the man to be cleansed, at the entrance of the Tent of Meeting, by the priest who performs the cleansing.

12 The priest shall take one of the male lambs and offer it with the *log* of oil as a guilt offering, and he shall elevate them as an elevation offering before the LORD. 13 The lamb shall be slaughtered at the spot in the sacred area where the purification offering and the burnt offering are slaughtered.[a] For the guilt offering, like the purification offering, goes to the priest; it is most holy. 14 The priest shall take some of the blood of the guilt offering, and the priest shall put it on the ridge of the right ear of him who is being cleansed, and on the thumb of his right hand, and on the big toe of his right foot. 15 The priest shall then take some of the *log* of oil and pour it into the palm of his own left hand. 16 And the priest shall dip his right finger in the oil that is in the palm of his left hand and sprinkle some of the oil with his finger seven times before the LORD. 17 Some of the oil left in his palm shall be put by the priest on the ridge of the right ear of the one being cleansed, on the thumb of his right hand, and on the big toe of his right foot—over the blood of the guilt offering. 18 The rest of the oil in his palm the priest shall put on the head of the one being cleansed. Thus the priest shall make expiation for him before the LORD. 19 The priest shall then offer the purification offering and make expiation for the one being cleansed of his uncleanness. Last, the burnt offering shall be slaughtered, 20 and the priest shall offer the burnt offering and the meal offering on the altar, and the priest shall make expiation for him. Then he shall be clean.

21 If, however, he is poor and his means are insufficient, he shall take one male lamb for a guilt offering, to be elevated in expiation for him, one-tenth of a measure of choice flour with oil mixed in for a meal offering, and a *log* of oil; 22 and two turtledoves or two pigeons, depending on his means, the one to be the purification offering and the other the burnt offering. 23 On the eighth day of his cleansing he shall bring them to the priest at the entrance of the Tent of Meeting, before the LORD. 24 The priest shall take the lamb of guilt offering and the *log* of oil, and elevate them as an elevation offering before the LORD. 25 When the lamb of guilt offering has been slaughtered, the priest shall take some of the blood of the guilt offering and put it on the ridge of the right ear of the one being cleansed, on the

a See 1.11; 4.24.

this impurity. **10–20:** In stage three, on the eighth day, the “metzoraʿ” makes his offerings. **12:** *Guilt offering:* The presence of an “ʾasham” sacrifice (see 5.14–26), its prominence evidenced among other things by the elevation ritual, is a mystery, since being afflicted with “tzaraʿat” is not an obvious trespass against the sacred. One theory is that the “metzoraʿ” is under the strong presumption of having committed sacrilege; otherwise why would he have been stricken (see 2 Chron. 26.16–19)? Another possibility is that the inherent sanctity of the Israelite individual (see 19.2) has been compromised, though this would be unexpected in this portion of the book (see 19.1–37 n.). Perhaps the “ʾasham” is brought simply to provide blood for the final removal of residual impurity a week after the initial decontamination. **14–18:** The application of consecrated oil in addition to the blood of the “ʾasham” sacrifice apparently adds a measure of sanctification to the purification process. **19:** *Purification offering,* (see ch 4), by means of which the “metzoraʿ” rids the sacred sphere of the impurity that has accumulated there during the course of his illness. **20:** *The burnt offering and the meal offering:* These complete the full set of offerings by the “metzoraʿ.” These acts of homage express rejoining the society of living Israelites engaged in the worship of the LORD. *Then he shall be clean:* This sums up the entire process; it does not mean that the offerings purify the person. **21–32:** The provisions for the healed “metzoraʿ” of modest means; see 5.7–13 n.; 12.8 n. Note that the “ʾasham” lamb (v. 12) is not reducible even in this case (see v. 24).

33–53: Mildew or rot in the walls of a house. Since the condition resembled "tzara'at" in humans, it was believed to be a manifestation of the same deadly leakage of life. *Greenish or reddish streaks ... deep into the wall* (v. 37) are deemed on sight to be "tzara'at," but the measures taken depend on the reexamination of the house after a seven-day quarantine. If the condition has spread, the affected stones and plaster are removed and replaced. (If it has not spread, perhaps another week of quarantine follows; the text is silent.) If it returns, the house must be demolished and the materials disposed of, since the condition has pervaded the entire dwelling. Otherwise the "tzara'at" is determined to have run its course and the priest pronounces the house to be clean. To eradicate the impurity that has accumulated, a ritual similar to the first stage in the purification of the affected human (vv. 3–7) is performed (vv. 49–53). **36:** Once the priest determines that "tzara'at" is present, everything in the house susceptible to contamination will be declared impure. To prevent this, the house is cleared in advance and the foods and objects that have been removed remain under the presumption of purity. Rabbinic interpretation correctly recognized that this is designed to prevent undue economic hardship.

thumb of his right hand, and on the big toe of his right foot.
26 The priest shall then pour some of the oil into the palm of his
own left hand, 27 and with the finger of his right hand the priest
shall sprinkle some of the oil that is in the palm of his left hand
seven times before the LORD. 28 Some of the oil in his palm
shall be put by the priest on the ridge of the right ear of the one
being cleansed, on the thumb of his right hand, and on the big
toe of his right foot, over the same places as the blood of the
guilt offering; 29 and what is left of the oil in his palm the priest
shall put on the head of the one being cleansed, to make expiation for him before the LORD. 30 He shall then offer one of the
turtledoves or pigeons, depending on his means—31 whichever he can afford—the one as a purification offering and the
other as a burnt offering, together with the meal offering. Thus
the priest shall make expiation before the LORD for the one being cleansed. 32 Such is the ritual for him who has a scaly affection and whose means for his cleansing are limited.

33 The LORD spoke to Moses and Aaron, saying:

34 When you enter the land of Canaan that I give you as a
possession, and I inflict an eruptive plague upon a house in
the land you possess, 35 the owner of the house shall come and
tell the priest, saying, "Something like a plague has appeared
upon my house." 36 The priest shall order the house cleared before the priest enters to examine the plague, so that nothing in
the house may become unclean; after that the priest shall enter
to examine the house. 37 If, when he examines the plague, the
plague in the walls of the house is found to consist of greenish[a]
or reddish streaks[b] that appear to go deep into the wall, 38 the
priest shall come out of the house to the entrance of the house,
and close up the house for seven days. 39 On the seventh day
the priest shall return. If he sees that the plague has spread on
the walls of the house, 40 the priest shall order the stones with
the plague in them to be pulled out and cast outside the city
into an unclean place. 41 The house shall be scraped inside all
around, and the coating[c] that is scraped off shall be dumped
outside the city in an unclean place. 42 They shall take other
stones and replace those stones with them, and take other
coating and plaster the house.

43 If the plague again breaks out in the house, after the stones
have been pulled out and after the house has been scraped and
replastered, 44 the priest shall come to examine: if the plague
has spread in the house, it is a malignant eruption in the house;
it is unclean. 45 The house shall be torn down—its stones and
timber and all the coating on the house—and taken to an unclean place outside the city.

a *Or "yellowish."* b *Meaning of Heb.* sheqa'aruroth *uncertain.*
c *Lit. "dust," "mud."*

46 Whoever enters the house while it is closed up shall be unclean until evening. 47 Whoever sleeps in the house must wash his clothes, and whoever eats in the house must wash his clothes.

48 If, however, the priest comes and sees that the plague has not spread in the house after the house was replastered, the priest shall pronounce the house clean, for the plague has healed. 49 To purge the house, he shall take two birds, cedar wood, crimson stuff, and hyssop. 50 He shall slaughter the one bird over fresh water in an earthen vessel. 51 He shall take the cedar wood, the hyssop, the crimson stuff, and the live bird, and dip them in the blood of the slaughtered bird and the fresh water, and sprinkle on the house seven times. 52 Having purged the house with the blood of the bird, the fresh water, the live bird, the cedar wood, the hyssop, and the crimson stuff, 53 he shall set the live bird free outside the city in the open country. Thus he shall make expiation for the house, and it shall be clean.

54 Such is the ritual for every eruptive affection—for scalls, 55 for an eruption on a cloth or a house, 56 for swellings, for rashes, or for discolorations—57 to determine when they are unclean and when they are clean.

Such is the ritual concerning eruptions.

15 The LORD spoke to Moses and Aaron, saying: 2 Speak to the Israelite people and say to them:

When any man has a discharge issuing from his member,[a] he is unclean. 3 The uncleanness from his discharge shall mean the following—whether his member runs with the discharge or is stopped up so that there is no discharge, his uncleanness means this: 4 Any bedding on which the one with the discharge lies shall be unclean, and every object on which he sits shall be unclean. 5 Anyone who touches his bedding shall wash his clothes, bathe in water, and remain unclean until evening. 6 Whoever sits on an object on which the one with the discharge has sat shall wash his clothes, bathe in water, and remain unclean until evening. 7 Whoever touches the body of the one with the discharge shall wash his clothes, bathe in water, and remain unclean until evening. 8 If one with a discharge spits on one who is clean, the latter shall wash his clothes, bathe in water, and remain unclean until evening. 9 Any means for riding that one with a discharge has mounted shall be unclean; 10 whoever touches anything that was under him shall be unclean until evening; and whoever carries such things shall wash his clothes, bathe in water, and remain unclean until evening. 11 If one with a discharge, without having rinsed his

a *Lit. "flesh."*

46–47: The impurity is contagious during the week of quarantine. **53:** *Make expiation for,* Heb "kipper" is used anomalously here (see 16.1–34 n.) to refer to the decontamination of a person. No purification of the sacred sphere is prescribed, since if the "tzaraʿat" is deemed severe the house is destroyed before the impurity spreads to the sanctuary. **54–57:** Concluding subscription to chs 13–14. *Ritual,* better, "instructions"; see 6.2 n.

15.1–33: Impurity from bodily discharges. Concluding the laws of purification from bodily impurities, this ch deals with defilement caused by the flow of life fluids from the genital organs: semen, menstrual fluid, and the discharge accompanying various urethral infections or gonorrhea. They are treated as facts of nature: some normal, some abnormal. The only sin connected with them is failure to purify oneself from them. The ch is arranged chiastically. Section (A) speaks of abnormal discharge from a male (vv. 2b–15) and parallels section (A'), which speaks of abnormal discharge from a female (vv. 25–30). These are severe impurities; since they reach the sacred sphere, their bearers must make purification offerings to decontaminate the sanctuary after they have been cleansed. Section (B) speaks of normal discharge from a male, i.e., the emission of semen (vv. 16–17); this parallels section (B'), which speaks of normal discharge from a female; i.e., menstruation (vv. 19–24). These are lesser impurities; they require only the cleansing of the individual which, if performed promptly, arrests any possible contamination of the sacred. At the center is section (C) (v. 18), which deals with the impurity contracted during sexual intercourse by both males and females. **1:** *Moses and Aaron,* see 11.1; 13.1. **2b–15:** Abnormal discharge in a male; the symptoms are consistent with urethral infections of various types and not only gonorrhea. In biblical times it was not known that these ailments are transmitted by sexual contact. **2:** *His member,* lit. "his flesh" (see

hands in water, touches another person, that person shall wash
his clothes, bathe in water, and remain unclean until evening.
12 An earthen vessel that one with a discharge touches shall be
broken; and any wooden implement shall be rinsed with water.
13 When one with a discharge becomes clean of his discharge, he shall count off seven days for his cleansing, wash
his clothes, and bathe his body in fresh water; then he shall
be clean. 14 On the eighth day he shall take two turtledoves or
two pigeons and come before the LORD at the entrance of the
Tent of Meeting and give them to the priest. 15 The priest shall
offer them, the one as a purification offering and the other as
a burnt offering. Thus the priest shall make expiation on his
behalf, for his discharge, before the LORD.
16 When a man has an emission of semen, he shall bathe his
whole body in water and remain unclean until evening. 17 All
cloth or leather on which semen falls shall be washed in water
and remain unclean until evening. 18 And if a man has carnal
relations with a woman, they shall bathe in water and remain
unclean until evening.
19 When a woman has a discharge, her discharge being blood
from her body, she shall remain in her impurity seven days;
whoever touches her shall be unclean until evening. 20 Anything that she lies on during her impurity shall be unclean;
and anything that she sits on shall be unclean. 21 Anyone who
touches her bedding shall wash his clothes, bathe in water, and
remain unclean until evening; 22 and anyone who touches any
object on which she has sat shall wash his clothes, bathe in water, and remain unclean until evening. 23 Be it the bedding or be
it the object on which she has sat, on touching it he shall be unclean until evening. 24 And if a man lies with her, her impurity is
communicated to him; he shall be unclean seven days, and any
bedding on which he lies shall become unclean.
25 When a woman has had a discharge of blood for many
days, not at the time of her impurity, or when she has a discharge beyond her period of impurity, she shall be unclean,

translators' note *a*), a euphemism; see v. 19. **4–12:** The communication of impurity by direct or indirect contact. The details provided here and in vv. 19–27 are given in this ch only, to be applied by appropriate analogy in other cases of bodily impurity of similar degree; see, e.g., 12.2 n. and 13.46 n. Secondary impurity is less severe than that borne by the affected person himself; after washing (traditionally understood to mean immersion) and laundering it dissipates by nightfall and does not spread to the sacred sphere. It is taken for granted that contact with impure persons will occur in the normal course of everyday life. Impure individuals are not "off limits," but since contact with them communicates minor impurity, the necessary measures must be taken to rid oneself of it. **11:** *Touches another person,* i.e., with his hands (which have probably come into contact with his genitals). *Without having rinsed his hands in water:* In rabbinic law this too was taken to mean immersion, thus equating it with the washing required in the preceding cases. **12:** See 11.31–35 n. **13–15:** The impurity is severe; thus it lasts for seven days after the condition has passed, after which the final cleansing of the man takes place. Then, when he is finally rid of his impurity and may approach the divine abode, the "ḥata't" is offered and the sacred area decontaminated. **14:** *Two turtledoves or two pigeons,* see 5.7–10 n.; 12.8 n. Here, however, the two birds are prescribed for all, not just for those too poor to offer livestock; for the reason, see v. 29 n. **16–17:** See also Deut. 23.10–12; 1 Sam. 20.26; here, however, the law is not restricted to involuntary nocturnal emission. The emission of semen per se, deliberate or accidental, during intercourse or not, creates a minor impurity which, after cleansing, is gone by nightfall. **17:** Being minor, this impurity is not communicated to others by contact, but it is communicated to objects (and perhaps persons too) if the semen itself touches them. **18:** This stipulation is a function of the previous section and serves also as a transition to the next. Sexual intercourse defiles both participants; their impurity, after cleansing, lasts until nightfall. **19–24:** The menstruant. According to this ch, everyday nonsexual contact with the menstruating woman merely confers a minor impurity which, after cleansing, dissipates by nightfall. Even sexual intercourse with the menstruant is not forbidden; although it communicates a more severe impurity lasting seven days (v. 24), if the necessary purification takes place no sin has been committed. Thus the law in 18.19, forbidding sexual relations with a menstruant on pain of "karet" (see 7.20), directly contradicts this ch. Jewish tradition not only accepted the stricter view, forbidding intercourse with the menstruant, but interpreted the latter law in such a way as to prohibit other forms of physical contact with her as well. The need to comply with 18.19 led to the survival of the laws restricting marital relations to the days between menstrual cycles, forbidding physical contact with menstruating women and requiring

as though at the time of her impurity, as long as her discharge lasts. [26] Any bedding on which she lies while her discharge lasts shall be for her like bedding during her impurity; and any object on which she sits shall become unclean, as it does during her impurity: [27] whoever touches them shall be unclean; he shall wash his clothes, bathe in water, and remain unclean until evening.

[28] When she becomes clean of her discharge, she shall count off seven days, and after that she shall be clean. [29] On the eighth day she shall take two turtledoves or two pigeons, and bring them to the priest at the entrance of the Tent of Meeting. [30] The priest shall offer the one as a purification offering and the other as a burnt offering; and the priest shall make expiation on her behalf, for her unclean discharge, before the LORD.

[31] You shall put the Israelites on guard against their uncleanness, lest they die through their uncleanness by defiling My Tabernacle which is among them.

[32] Such is the ritual concerning him who has a discharge: concerning him who has an emission of semen and becomes unclean thereby, [33] and concerning her who is in menstrual infirmity, and concerning anyone, male or female, who has a discharge, and concerning a man who lies with an unclean woman.

ʾAḤAREI MOT אחרי מות

16 The LORD spoke to Moses after the death of the two sons of Aaron who died when they drew too close to the presence of the LORD. [2] The LORD said to Moses:

Tell your brother Aaron that he is not to come at will[a] into the Shrine behind the curtain, in front of the cover that is upon the ark, lest he die; for I appear in the cloud over the cover. [3] Thus only shall Aaron enter the Shrine: with a bull of the herd for a purification offering and a ram for a burnt offering.—[4] He shall be dressed in a sacral linen tunic, with linen breeches next to his flesh, and be girt with a linen sash, and he shall wear a linen turban. They are sacral vestments; he shall bathe his body in water and then put them on.—[5] And from the Israelite

a *Lit. "at any time."*

the monthly immersion of the wife ("tohorat hamishpaḥah," lit. "family purity") in Jewish law. The case is unique among the purification laws in the Bible, virtually all of which fell into disuse after the destruction of the Temple. **19:** *Blood,* menstrual fluid was thought to be blood. *Body,* a euphemism; see v. 2. *Seven days,* approximating the maximum number of days each month during which most women menstruate. Rabbinic law, however, on the analogy of v. 28, eventually prescribed that the seven "clean" days commence after the actual flow has ceased. **25–30:** Paralleling 2b–15, above, but taking into account a second possibility as well: menstrual flow that lasts beyond its normal duration. **29:** Inexpensive animals are prescribed since prolonged menstrual flow or irregular discharges are relatively frequent, so requiring livestock would impose economic hardship and the purification of the sanctuary would be neglected. By simple analogy birds are prescribed for males as well in v. 14. **31:** The rationale for all of the purification laws in P; see chs 12–15 n. *Lest they die through their uncleanness:* The "death" is the collective destruction of Israel *by defiling My Tabernacle which is among them.* Failing to eradicate defilement causes it to collect in the divine abode, leading to its abandonment by the deity. See also 16.16; Num. 5.3; 19.13, 20. Rabbinic tradition reinterpreted this and similar passages to mean that the divine abode would be defiled only if the unclean person entered it; thus it severed the laws of purification from their biblical moorings.

16.1–34: Purging the Tabernacle annually. The preceding chs have established that sins and bodily impurities contaminate the Tabernacle. Regular atonement for unintentional sin and the routine eradication of impurity eliminate as much of both types of defilement as possible. Yet, since not all unintentional wrongs are discovered and not everyone is diligent about atonement, a certain amount of defilement remains. In particular, deliberate crimes, which contaminate the inner sanctum where the divine Presence itself is said to dwell, are not expurgated by the regular atonement rituals. This ch thus provides the instructions for purging the inner sanctum along with the rest of the Tabernacle once a year, so that defilement does not accumulate. It logically follows the laws of purification (chs 12–15), as they conclude with the statement that only by preventing the spread of impurity can the Israelites ensure God's continual presence among them (15.31). The annual purification ritual, briefly alluded to in Exod. 30.10, is to be performed on the tenth day of the seventh month (v. 29). Elsewhere (23.27, 28; 25.9) this day is referred to as "yom hakippurim"—often translated as "Day of Atonement,"

community he shall take two he-goats for a purification offering and a ram for a burnt offering.

[6] Aaron is to offer his own bull of purification offering, to make expiation for himself and for his household. [7] Aaron[a] shall take the two he-goats and let them stand before the LORD at the entrance of the Tent of Meeting; [8] and he shall place lots upon the two goats, one marked for the LORD and the other marked for Azazel. [9] Aaron shall bring forward the goat designated by lot for the LORD, which he is to offer as a purification offering; [10] while the goat designated by lot for Azazel shall be left standing alive before the LORD, to make expiation with it and to send it off to the wilderness for Azazel.

[11] Aaron shall then offer his bull of purification offering, to make expiation for himself and his household. He shall slaughter his bull of purification offering, [12] and he shall take a panful of glowing coals scooped from the altar before the LORD, and two handfuls of finely ground aromatic incense, and bring this behind the curtain. [13] He shall put the incense on the fire

a Moved up from v. 8 for clarity.

with the verb "kipper," "atone," being used in the sense of "decontaminate [the sacred precincts] of sin or defilement" (see 1.4; 4.1–5.26 n.). This day is found only in the Priestly calendar of sacred times (23.26–32; see also Num. 29.7–11). Sanctuary purification rites are known in the ancient Near East outside of Israel. The biblical Day of Atonement, while unique in its conceptual and ritual complexity and in its nondemonic view of defilement, shares with them the specific ritual aim of decontaminating the sanctuary. It also, however, brings about a sort of purification of the Israelite people, since the thorough eradication and disposal of their sins and impurities serves as a personal and communal catharsis. Further, the people have a role in the process: vv. 29–34a prescribe that they must observe a fast and a cessation of labor. The Israelites emerge from this day secure in the knowledge that the equilibrium in their relationship with God has been restored and "all is forgiven." This too is expressed by the text: "For on this day atonement shall be made for you to cleanse you of all your sins; you shall be clean before the LORD" (v. 30). Long after the original notion that God threatened to abandon His people if His abode became impure had receded, the Day of Atonement, as an annual occasion for repentance and forgiveness, continued to have crucial importance. Even since the destruction of the Second Temple, when fasting, prayer, and penitence are all that survive of the day's ritual, it has remained a central feature of the liturgical year in Jewish tradition. **1:** *After the death of the two sons of Aaron,* related in 10.1–2. Some have assumed a connection between the offense of Aaron's sons and the annual purgation, suggesting either that the priest is cautioned not to repeat their actions or that the purgation was necessitated by their deaths or their dire sins. But the narrator probably means that this ch was actually imparted to Moses immediately after Revelation Day, while chs 11–15, conveyed to Moses later in the month, have been placed here so that the reader may correctly grasp what is meant by "the uncleanness ... of the Israelites" in v. 16 and understand why the Tabernacle needs to be purged (see 16.1–34 n.). **2:** *At will,* lit. "at any time." Only once a year may Aaron or his successor enter the inner sanctum. *The Shrine behind the curtain, in front of the cover that is upon the ark,* the inner sanctum, known as the "holy of holies" and here called "haqodesh," "the holy place." *Lest he die; for I appear in the cloud over the cover:* How Aaron is to avoid death when purging the inner sanctum is explained in vv. 12–13. **3–22:** The thorough purification of the Tabernacle, focusing on the inner sanctum. **4:** Since the tasks to be performed on Purification Day are for purgation, not for worship, the priest is to remove the vestments worn for the daily service and to don simple linen garments, which, when soiled by the sprinkling of blood, are easily laundered. **5–22:** The ritual includes the following components: (1) a slaughtered bull, to serve as a purification offering on behalf of the high priest and his household (cf. 4.3–12); (2) a slaughtered goat to serve as a purification offering on behalf of the Israelite people; (3) a live goat, to carry away the transgressions of the Israelites to the wilderness; (4) two burnt offerings, one on Aaron's own behalf and the other on behalf of the people. **7–10:** The use of the two goats is similar to that of the two birds in 14.4–7, 49–53. The lottery determines at random how each goat is to be used. **8:** *Azazel:* The Rabbis cleverly divided this name into two words "'ez 'azel," "the goat that goes away," from which the traditional "scapegoat" is derived. It literally means "fierce god" and as intimated by the medieval exegete Abraham Ibn Ezra is evidently the name of a demon or deity believed to inhabit the wilderness. Thus the sins of the people are symbolically cast into the realm beyond civilization, to become the property of a being who is the antithesis of the God of Israel. Though Azazel accepts the goat bearing Israel's sins as a sacrifice to him, this is no disloyalty to God since He Himself commands it, as Naḥmanides (Ramban) says: It is as though a king ordered "Give a portion [of this feast] to my servant so-and-so." **11–14:** Aaron's first entry into the inner sanctum, to expiate for

before the LORD, so that the cloud from the incense screens
the cover that is over [the Ark of] the Pact, lest he die. 14 He
shall take some of the blood of the bull and sprinkle it with his
finger over the cover on the east side; and in front of the cover
he shall sprinkle some of the blood with his finger seven times.
15 He shall then slaughter the people's goat of purification offering, bring its blood behind the curtain, and do with its blood
as he has done with the blood of the bull: he shall sprinkle it
over the cover and in front of the cover.

16 Thus he shall purge the Shrine of the uncleanness and
transgression of the Israelites, whatever their sins; and he shall
do the same for the Tent of Meeting, which abides with them in
the midst of their uncleanness. 17 When he goes in to make expiation in the Shrine, nobody else shall be in the Tent of Meeting until he comes out.

When he has made expiation for himself and his household,
and for the whole congregation of Israel, 18 he shall go out to
the altar that is before the LORD and purge it: he shall take
some of the blood of the bull and of the goat and apply it to
each of the horns of the altar; 19 and the rest of the blood he
shall sprinkle on it with his finger seven times. Thus he shall
cleanse it of the uncleanness of the Israelites and consecrate it.

20 When he has finished purging the Shrine, the Tent of Meeting, and the altar, the live goat shall be brought forward. 21 Aaron
shall lay both his hands upon the head of the live goat and confess over it all the iniquities and transgressions of the Israelites,
whatever their sins, putting them on the head of the goat; and
it shall be sent off to the wilderness through a designated[a] man.
22 Thus the goat shall carry on it all their iniquities to an inaccessible region; and the goat shall be set free in the wilderness.

23 And Aaron shall go into the Tent of Meeting, take off the
linen vestments that he put on when he entered the Shrine,

a Meaning of Heb. ʿitti *uncertain.*

his own transgressions and impurities. **13:** *The cover that is over [the Ark of] the Pact,* the platform upon which the two winged cherubs stand, serving to shield the divine Presence which is situated there (Exod. 25.10–22). The incense is placed on the coals to create a cloud of smoke, preventing Aaron from viewing the deity. The blood is sprinkled in front of the Ark and behind it, purging the area most vulnerable to contamination. **15–16a:** Aaron's second entry into the inner sanctum, to expiate for the transgressions and impurities of the people. The blood of the goat is sprinkled in the same way as that of the bull. **16:** *Of the uncleanness:* A better translation is "of the impurities of the Israelites and, among all their sins, of their deliberate transgressions"; see v. 22 n. **16b:** The cleansing of the inner sanctum is followed by the purification of the outer sanctum. Probably the procedure in 4.6–7a and 4.17–18a is intended, performed first with the blood of the bull and then with that of the goat. *The Tent ... abides,* better, "the Tent of Meeting of the One who abides." **17:** The first half of the v. confirms that in the outer sanctum too Aaron is to be alone (translate "the holy place" instead of the Shrine); the second half sums up the cleansing of the Tabernacle. **18–19a:** The next step: purging the altar. *The altar that is before the LORD:* Rabbinic interpretation took this to mean the incense altar located in the inner sanctum. The words *he shall go out* would thus refer to Aaron's exiting the inner sanctum. But the v. would then be out of place, and the summary vv. 20 and 33 distinguish between the inner sanctum, the outer sanctum, and the altar. It is preferable to explain he shall go out as meaning "he shall exit the Tent of Meeting." The altar is the sacrificial altar that stood in the courtyard, the purgation of the incense altar having been accomplished already (see v. 16b). **19:** *And consecrate it:* The translation reflects the rabbinic midrash, according to which the altar was not only purged but reconsecrated for the coming year, but the word "vekidesho" stands before *of the uncleanness of the Israelites* and means "and purge it." **20–22:** Having removed the impurities from the inner and outer sanctums, Aaron now transfers them to the live goat for dispatch to the wilderness. The transfer is accomplished by placing both hands on the goat's head and making verbal declaration of the people's sins. Rabbinic law, reinterpreting the term "vekipper," "he shall make expiation" in vv. 6 and 11, added two more confessions to the Day of Atonement ritual. **21:** *Lay both his hands:* Elsewhere single-hand leaning (e.g., 1.4) reflects designation of an animal; the gesture here is one of transfer to the animal. **22:** *All their iniquities,* rather, "all the intentional sins and deliberate transgressions of the Israelites among all their sins." The impurities (see v. 16 n.) have disappeared, eradicated by the blood of the "ḥataʾt" offerings. Deliberate sins, however, are indestructible; they can only be sent away, in the hope that they may never return. The idea is that intentional acts of wrongdoing, once committed, can never really be undone.

and leave them there. [24] He shall bathe his body in water in the holy precinct and put on his vestments; then he shall come out and offer his burnt offering and the burnt offering of the people, making expiation for himself and for the people. [25] The fat of the purification offering he shall turn into smoke on the altar.

[26] He who set the Azazel-goat free shall wash his clothes and bathe his body in water; after that he may reenter the camp.

[27] The bull of purification offering and the goat of purification offering whose blood was brought in to purge the Shrine shall be taken outside the camp; and their hides, flesh, and dung shall be consumed in fire. [28] He who burned them shall wash his clothes and bathe his body in water; after that he may re-enter the camp.

[29] And this shall be to you a law for all time: In the seventh month, on the tenth day of the month, you shall practice self-denial; and you shall do no manner of work, neither the citizen nor the alien who resides among you. [30] For on this day atonement shall be made for you to cleanse you of all your sins; you shall be clean before the LORD. [31] It shall be a sabbath of complete rest for you, and you shall practice self-denial; it is a law for all time. [32] The priest who has been anointed and ordained to serve as priest in place of his father shall make expiation. He shall put on the linen vestments, the sacral vestments. [33] He shall purge the innermost Shrine; he shall purge the Tent of Meeting and the altar; and he shall make expiation for the priests and for all the people of the congregation.

[34] This shall be to you a law for all time: to make atonement for the Israelites for all their sins once a year.

And Moses did as the LORD had commanded him.

17 The LORD spoke to Moses, saying:
[2] Speak to Aaron and his sons and to all the Israelite people and say to them:

This is what the LORD has commanded: [3] if anyone of the house of Israel slaughters an ox or sheep or goat in the camp, or does so outside the camp, [4] and does not bring it to the entrance of the Tent of Meeting to present it as an offering to the LORD, before the LORD's Tabernacle, bloodguilt shall be

23–28: The remaining offerings, the cleansing of Aaron, the removal of the contaminated garments, the disposal of the flesh, and the purification of those who have become secondarily defiled as a result of their roles in the ritual. **29–34a:** The rituals are to be performed on a specific date, annually, in perpetuity, by Aaron's successors in the high priesthood, accompanied by a community-wide fast and cessation of labor, observed by citizen and resident alien alike (see 23.26–32). **29:** *Practice self-denial,* lit. "deprive your throats," i.e., fast (see Isa. 58.3, 5). The translation reflects the halakhic midrash, according to which "nefesh" is used in the sense of "self"; based on this the Rabbis decreed additional forms of self-affliction besides the abstinence from food and drink indicated explicitly by the text, including abstaining from washing, anointing, wearing leather shoes, and engaging in sexual intercourse (*m. Yoma* 8:1). *Citizen,* Heb "'ezraḥ," "native," referring to the Israelite born in the land of Israel of bona fide Israelite ancestry. *The alien who resides among you:* The "ger," or resident alien, is a person of non-Israelite ancestry residing more or less permanently in the land of Israel. He is not considered a descendant of the Canaanite peoples, since they are believed to have been evacuated (see 18.24–30). Rabbinic tradition understands the "ger" as a proselyte or convert, but this is anachronistic; neither religious conversion nor gradual assimilation is contemplated anywhere in P. Laws pertaining to the "ger" appear throughout the remaining chs of Lev. and elsewhere in the Priestly law; see, e.g., 17.8, 10, 12, 15; 18.26; 19.33–36; 24.16 n.; 25.47–54 n. The "ger" is not required to worship Israel's God but may do so voluntarily; thus the "ger" is not obligated to observe the performative commands, but must comply with all prohibitions, and must observe the laws of fairness and justice (see 24.17–22). The Israelite must refrain from oppressing or exploiting the "ger." **31:** *A sabbath of complete rest for you,* see 23.32 n.

Chs 17–26: Scholars agree that chs 17–26, along with some other passages in Lev. and elsewhere in P, belong to a literary stratum distinct from the remainder of the Priestly work. Although this section is not structurally differentiated from the rest, and does echo and supplement the ritual and sacral regulations in P in many ways, on substantive and stylistic grounds it appears to have been composed by Priestly authors other than those responsible for the remainder of P. Its most characteristic feature is a concern for holiness. Throughout Priestly thought, holiness is conceived of as an effervescence of the Presence of the LORD.

imputed to that man: he has shed blood; that man shall be cut off from among his people. 5 This is in order that the Israelites may bring the sacrifices which they have been making in the open—that they may bring them before the LORD, to the priest, at the entrance of the Tent of Meeting, and offer them as sacrifices of well-being to the LORD; 6 that the priest may dash the blood against the altar of the LORD at the entrance of the Tent of Meeting, and turn the fat into smoke as a pleasing odor to the LORD; 7 and that they may offer their sacrifices no more to the goat-demons after whom they stray. This shall be to them a law for all time, throughout the ages.

8 Say to them further: If anyone of the house of Israel or of the strangers who reside among them offers a burnt offering or a sacrifice, 9 and does not bring it to the entrance of the Tent of Meeting to offer it to the LORD, that person shall be cut off from his people.

10 And if anyone of the house of Israel or of the strangers who reside among them partakes of any blood, I will set My face against the person who partakes of the blood, and I will cut him off from among his kin. 11 For the life of the flesh is in the blood, and I have assigned it to you for making expiation for your lives upon the altar; it is the blood, as life, that effects expiation. 12 Therefore I say to the Israelite people: No person among you shall partake of blood, nor shall the stranger who resides among you partake of blood.

13 And if any Israelite or any stranger who resides among them hunts down an animal or a bird that may be eaten, he shall pour out its blood and cover it with earth. 14 For the life of all flesh—its blood is its life. Therefore I say to the Israelite people: You shall not partake of the blood of any flesh, for the life of all flesh is its blood. Anyone who partakes of it shall be cut off.

15 Any person, whether citizen or stranger, who eats what has died or has been torn by beasts shall wash his clothes, bathe in water, and remain unclean until evening; then he shall be clean. 16 But if he does not wash [his clothes] and bathe his body, he shall bear his guilt.

It infuses everything with which it comes into contact (see 6.11; 8.10–13), transforming it into the designated "personal" property of the deity. In these chs we hear for the first time that holiness is not confined to the realm of the Tabernacle and priesthood; rather, the Israelite people as a whole can and must attain holiness (chs 19–20). This section also contains legislation concerning the holiness of the priests and of sacred offerings (chs 21–22), the annual festivals, here called holy times (ch 23), the holiness of the name of God (ch 24), and the holiness of the fiftieth year (ch 25). Implied also is the holiness of the land of Israel (chs 18 and 26). Holiness as the all-encompassing theme of these chs has given them their name, the Holiness Legislation (or Holiness Code or Collection), or H. While earlier critics believed H to be more ancient than P, many scholars now think that H was added to, and is therefore probably later than, the kernel of the Priestly document. If so, the addition of the Holiness Collection to the preexisting Priestly document marks an important development in Priestly tradition and thought. The earlier Priestly work reflects the idea that the commandments given by God to the Israelites at Sinai were concerned solely with worship and the maintenance of the purity of the divine abode; all else was a matter of universal morality but not the stuff of divine legislation for Israel. The H chs constitute a transformation; they claim that the laws given to Israel at Sinai included civil and criminal legislation and pertained to every sphere of interpersonal relationships and social behavior as well as ritual activity. H thereby makes explicit through specific commands what was only implicit in the earlier stratum of P, namely, that Israel's compliance with God's expectations in these areas impinges on the sacred no less than the maintenance of the institutions of worship. Among the unique characteristics of H are its distinct rationale for the blood prohibition (see 17.10–12), its peculiar understanding of sacrificial atonement (17.11), its strict prohibition of sexual relations with the menstruating woman (18.19), the new meaning it instills into the concept of impurity (18.24–30), its incorporation of popular ritual into the observance of the holy days (23.1–44), its detailed exploration of the full ramifications of God's lordship over His people and land (25.1–55), and its explicit historicization of the Priestly promise of divine indwelling and threat of divine abandonment (26.3–45).

17.1–16: Slaughter and blood. Three laws are communicated to Moses: the prohibition of common, or "profane," slaughter of domestic livestock (vv. 3–7), the prohibition of sacrifice outside of the Tabernacle (vv. 8–9), and the prohibition of "eating" any blood (vv. 10–12). The third law draws in its wake two corollaries: the requirement to drain the blood of wild

18 The LORD spoke to Moses, saying: [2] Speak to the Israelite
people and say to them:
I the LORD am your God. [3] You shall not copy the practices
of the land of Egypt where you dwelt, or of the land of Canaan
to which I am taking you; nor shall you follow their laws. [4] My
rules alone shall you observe, and faithfully follow My laws: I
the LORD am your God.
[5] You shall keep My laws and My rules, by the pursuit of which
man shall live: I am the LORD.
[6] None of you shall come near anyone of his own flesh to uncover nakedness: I am the LORD.

animals killed for food (vv. 13–14), and the need to dispose of the impurity one contracts from eating carrion (vv. 15–16). All five sections are thus concerned with proper disposal of the blood of slain animals. They derive from P's view of the commands given to Noah and his descendants in Gen. 9.1–7 (see 11.1–47 n.), and they supplement the laws of sacrifice in chs 1–7, the dietary laws given in ch 11, and the laws of purification given in chs 12–15. **2:** *To Aaron and his sons and to all the Israelite people:* As the laws commanded here require specific activity on the part of the priests, Aaron and his sons are singled out, but the laws in the ch apply to the people as a whole. **3–4:** *Ox or sheep or goat:* Since animals from the herd and flock are fit for the altar, they are considered as belonging to God. Thus, according to this law, the Israelites may not simply slaughter domestic livestock for food; they are required to offer them as a sacrifice of well-being ("shelamim"; see 3.1–17 and 7.11–34), after which they may partake of the offerers' share of the flesh. **4:** *Bloodguilt ... he has shed blood:* In P's view, until the time of the flood it was a capital crime to shed the blood of any animal; thereafter it was permissible as long as the blood was not ingested (Gen. 9.3–4). Now that the Tabernacle has been erected, Israelites may slay sheep and cattle for food only as well-being offerings; if they fail to present the animal as an offering, it is as if they had slain the animal in the antediluvian period when such an act was considered murder. *Shall be cut off,* see 7.20, 21. **5–7:** These three vv. are spoken only for Moses' ears, and they provide the actual rationale for the prohibition. **5:** *The sacrifices ... in the open:* This rests on the Priestly belief that the worship of the LORD began with the establishment of the Israelite cult at Sinai and until then the LORD was never worshipped. (The stories of sacrifices in Gen. and the first part of Exod.—such as those offered by Cain and Abel, by Noah after the flood and by the patriarchs—all belong to the non-Priestly material.) Heretofore, any slaughter of domestic livestock has been meaningless, "in the open"—in the Rabbis' phrase, "profane" or common slaughter. **7:** *That they may offer their sacrifices no more to the goat-demons:* Conceptually, however, the nonsacrificial slaughter of domestic livestock actually is a sacrifice—not to God but to the demons thought to inhabit the open fields and desolate regions. Now that the Tabernacle cult is established, any further activity of this sort is an unpardonable sin. *A law for all time, throughout the ages:* The law is thus irreconcilable with that in Deut. 12.15, 20–27, according to which, after the Temple is built, it will become permissible to slaughter and eat livestock anywhere without making an offering. Though the law in H seems oppressive, it may not be entirely utopian. It imposes no restriction on the consumption of permitted nondomestic livestock (see 11.1–8), fowl, fish, or flying creatures (11.9–23). It is also conceivable that blemished sheep and cattle, not fit for the altar (22.21–24), might be slaughtered for food. The law in Deut. ultimately became normative in Judaism. **8–9:** Having established that all domestic livestock may be consumed only after having been presented as "shelamim" offerings, the law commands that all offerings must be made at the Tabernacle; anyone presenting a sacrifice elsewhere is threatened with the "karet" penalty (see 7.20, 21 n.). The Priestly legislator clearly has in mind a single legitimate sanctuary, agreeing with Deut. ch 12 in its demand that all sacrificial worship be centralized in one location, but disagreeing on whether nonsacrificial slaughter may be practiced after the centralization has been accomplished. **8:** *The strangers who reside among them,* Heb "ger" ("resident alien"); see 16.29 n. **10–12:** The blood prohibition. See Gen. 9.4; Lev. 3.17; 7.26–27. Deut. also records this prohibition (Deut. 12.16, 23–24; 15.23). H offers its peculiar rationale for this law (see vv. 11–12 n.). **10:** *Partakes of any blood,* lit. "eats" any blood. The act referred to is that of eating meat without first draining the blood. *I will set My face,* I will give it My personal, undivided and immediate attention (26.17). For this phrase, along with the active form of the threat of "karet" (see 7.20, 21 n.), both characteristic of H, see 20.3, 5, 6; cf. 23.30. **11–12:** H's unique rationale for the blood prohibition (intended like vv. 5–7 for Moses' ears alone) differs from that implied in 3.17 and 7.26–27, where blood, like suet, is God's food. It differs too from that given in Deut. 12.16, 23–24, where ingesting the animal's meat along with its "life" is inherently improper. Here, since the blood of sacrificial offerings has been assigned to the altar as ransom (see below), the blood of all flesh is strictly forbidden. **11:** *The life of the flesh is in the blood:* Since loss of blood brings about swift death, it would be natural to assume that the life-force (Heb "nefesh," lit. "gullet" but often figuratively "life-force") is contained in the blood. *For making expiation for your lives,* better, "to serve as ransom for your lives"; see 1.4 n. This too is unique to H; sacrificial atonement is not

[7] [a]Your father's nakedness, that is, the nakedness of your mother, you shall not uncover; she is your mother—you shall not uncover her nakedness.

[8] Do not uncover the nakedness of your father's wife;[-a] it is the nakedness of your father.

[9] The nakedness of your sister—your father's daughter or your mother's, whether born into the household or outside—do not uncover their nakedness.

a-a A man and his wife are one flesh (Gen. 2.24), even if he should die or divorce her.

the decontamination of the sacred precincts but rather a symbolic payment in exchange for one's life which would otherwise be forfeit. **13–14:** In order to prevent the ingestion of the blood of nondomestic quadrupeds (which may be eaten if they conform to the stipulations of 11.3) and fowl (those not listed in 11.13–19), which would presumably be hunted, the Israelite is commanded to drain out the blood on the ground. *Cover it with earth:* Jewish tradition viewed this as a command in its own right; some interpreters saw it as a symbolic way of returning the "life" of the animal, i.e., its blood, to God. But the explicit reason for the draining and covering of the blood is to prevent its being eaten. **15–16:** As mentioned in 7.24, permitted animals that have not been slaughtered as sacrifice but rather have died of themselves ("nevelah") or were killed by beasts ("terefah") may be eaten, although, as stated in 11.40, impurity results. This law is repeated here because it is an exception to the blood prohibition. When the blood of a permitted animal has cooled and coagulated within it, it no longer contains the animal's "nefesh" or life-force (see v. 11) and may be eaten. In opposition, the non-Priestly law collections prohibit the eating of "nevelah" (Deut. 14.21) and "terefah" (Exod. 22.30). The opposing views share the idea that refraining from "nevelah" and "terefah" is a mark of sanctity. Since according to the non-Priestly sources all Israelites are on an equal plane of sanctity, all must avoid "nevelah" and "terefah." In P, only priests are so commanded (22.8), while lay Israelites are not. This opinion is held by Ezekiel as well (Ezek. 44.31). In the Priestly view, there are different grades of holiness and only the priests, who belong to the innermost sphere of sanctity, must observe the restriction. Rabbinic law accepts the stricter view, and even uses the term "terefah" as a general designation for all prohibited ("nonkosher") food (see 7.24 n.). **15:** *Citizen or stranger,* see 16.29 n.

18.1–30: The Abominations of the Canaanites. A list of prohibited sexual unions (vv. 6–23), including incestuous relationships (vv. 6–18), and the prohibition of sacrificing children to Molech (v. 21). These laws, rather than merely being proclaimed, are presented as part of a speech warning the Israelites not to practice the "abominations" characteristic of the peoples of Egypt and Canaan lest they suffer their dire fate. H thus conveys the idea that refraining from forbidden sexual practices and child sacrifice, no less than the scrupulous maintenance of the purity of the divine abode as emphasized by the earlier part of P, is the key to Israel's national survival in its land. This ch is read in the synagogue at the afternoon service on the Day of Atonement, a practice for which various interpretations have been suggested. **2–5:** The introductory vv. lay the groundwork for what will follow. To survive, Israel must shun the practices of Egypt and Canaan and adhere only to God's commands. **2:** *I the LORD am your God,* better, "I am the LORD your God" (or "I am YHVH your God"). This formula (with variations) is one of the hallmarks of H's style; here it sets up the contrast between "My rules/laws" and those of Egypt and Canaan. **3:** *The practices of the land of Egypt ... or of the land of Canaan:* The Egyptians and Canaanites are characterized in biblical tradition, particularly P, by rampant sexual licentiousness and perversion. This, however, does not emerge from Canaanite and Egyptian literature, at least not to the extent that the biblical authors seem to have imagined, and it is now thought that the biblical writers used this accusation as a means of stigmatizing Israel's cultural rivals (in the guise of long-extinct enemies) by attributing to them the most heinous crimes. Thus they provided moral justification for the displacement of the Canaanites, while at the same time polemicizing against such practices in Israelite society itself. *Nor shall you follow their laws:* The midrash took these words as an indication that the Egyptians and the Canaanites actually had laws requiring these sexual practices (*Sifre Aḥare Mot Perek,* 18 parashah 8 [8]). **5:** *By the pursuit of which man shall live,* better, "which, if a person follows, he/she will live," most simply understood as the converse of vv. 24–30, which detail how violation of these laws leads to collective death and to "karet" for the individual. Here too rabbinic law introduced a legislative import into an originally nonlegislative phrase, interpreting that one must "live by them [but do not die by them]," and ruling that all the laws of the Torah (except idolatry, unlawful sexual intercourse, and bloodshed) are set aside if their observance will endanger the preservation of human life (*b. Sanh.* 74a). **6–23:** *My laws and My rules* mentioned in v. 5 are now spelled out. **6:** *Anyone of his own flesh,* the extended family; see 25.49; cf. 21.2. *Uncover nakedness,* "uncover the sexual organ." This term is used throughout vv. 6–19 (see also 20.11, etc.) to denote sexual intercourse. It focuses on the shamelessness of engaging in sexual relations with a member of one's family in flagrant disregard for the repulsion that

[10] The nakedness of your son's daughter, or of your daughter's daughter—do not uncover their nakedness; for their nakedness is yours.[a]

[11] The nakedness of your father's wife's daughter, who was born into your father's household—she is your sister; do not uncover her nakedness.

[12] Do not uncover the nakedness of your father's sister; she is your father's flesh.

[13] Do not uncover the nakedness of your mother's sister; for she is your mother's flesh.

[14] Do not uncover the nakedness of your father's brother: do not approach his wife; she is your aunt.

[15] Do not uncover the nakedness of your daughter-in-law: she is your son's wife; you shall not uncover her nakedness.

[16] [b-]Do not uncover the nakedness of your brother's wife; it is the nakedness of your brother.[-b]

[17] Do not uncover the nakedness of a woman and her daughter; nor shall you marry her son's daughter or her daughter's daughter and uncover her nakedness: they are kindred; it is depravity.

[18] Do not marry a woman as a rival to her sister and uncover her nakedness in the other's lifetime.

a *Meaning uncertain.*
b-b *A man and his wife are one flesh (Gen. 2.24), even if he should die or divorce her.*

viewing the nakedness of a close relative was thought to arouse. In postbiblical terminology, the phrase "uncover nakedness," ("gilui ʿarayot") losing its literal meaning, became the standard Talmudic term for unlawful sexual intercourse, and the word "nakedness" became a euphemism for a forbidden sexual partner or act. **7–18:** The list of prohibited sexual unions extends over four generations, with the male addressed in the text placed in the second. All female members of his immediate family who might be the object of his sexual desire during his adulthood are named. (1) Directly related women: in the generation preceding, his mother (v. 7) and step-mother (v. 8); in his own generation, his sister (v. 9); in the vertical line, his granddaughter (v. 10). (There is no satisfactory explanation for the omission of the daughter.) Supplementing the immediate relatives is the step-sister, pronounced here to be of the same degree as a true sister (v. 11). (2) Indirectly related women: in the generation preceding, his true aunt (vv. 12–13) and his aunt by marriage, pronounced here to be of the same degree (v. 14); in the next generation, his daughter-in-law (v. 15); in his own generation, his brother's wife. (3) Women related to each other: mother and daughter, grandmother and granddaughter (v. 17); sisters (v. 18). It cannot be determined whether analogous prohibitions, such as one's mother's brother's wife and one's niece, are implied or not. **7:** *Your father's nakedness, that is, the nakedness of your mother:* A woman's sexual organs are permitted only to her husband; by engaging in intercourse with the wife of one's close relation one commits a crime against the male relation as well. **9:** *Your father's daughter or your mother's,* referring specifically to the half-sister. The full sister may be supplied by inference since she is in both categories; see v. 14. *Whether born into the household or outside,* better: whether belonging (now) to the household of the parent to which you (now) belong or to another household.

10: *For their nakedness is yours,* obscure. **11:** *She is your sister:* Similarly "she is your aunt" (v. 14), meant figuratively; the step-sister and uncle's wife are declared to be on the same level as blood-relations. **14:** *Your aunt:* The legislator would thus view Amram's marriage to his aunt (Exod. 6.20) as an improper act. Similarly Abraham's marriage to his half-sister (Gen. 20.12), which violates v. 9, and Jacob's marriage to Rachel and Leah (Gen. 29.16–28), which violates v. 18, but these marriages are recounted only in the non-Priestly sources. **16:** *Your brother's wife,* in direct opposition to the levirate law in Deut. 25.5–9. Rabbinic law resolved the conflict by viewing the latter as an exception: Intercourse with one's sister-in-law is prohibited in every case except that described in Deut. The midrash even suggests that the two laws were spoken in the same utterance, so that the general rule and the exception would become known at one and the same time (*Mek. de R. Yishmael, Yitro, ba-Ḥodesh* 7 [Horowitz-Rabin, p. 229]; *Sifre* Ki Tetze 223 [Finkelstein, p. 266]). **17:** *Nor shall you marry,* Heb "tikkaḥ," "take" (so v. 18) does not always refer to marriage (see 20.17, 21), and may refer to sexual contact in general. Since the rhetorical aim of the ch is to enumerate the abhorrent sexual practices of the Canaanites, perhaps illicit unions too are contemplated. The halakhic tradition understood the entire series as a table of prohibited marriages, and legal systems throughout the Jewish and Christian worlds have based the impediments to lawful marriage on it. **18:** *A woman as a rival to her sister,* see 1 Sam. 1.6. See v. 14 n. above. *In the other's lifetime:* After the death of one sister, however, it might be considered meritorious to marry the other. **19–23:** Additional sexual prohibitions, arranged as follows: (1) intercourse with women, first, one's own wife, when menstruating (v. 19),

19 Do not come near a woman during her period of uncleanness to uncover her nakedness.
20 Do not have carnal relations with your neighbor's wife and
defile yourself with her.
21 Do not allow any of your offspring to be offered up to Molech,
and do not profane the name of your God: I am the LORD.
22 Do not lie with a male as one lies with a woman; it is an
abhorrence.
23 Do not have carnal relations with any beast and defile
yourself thereby; and let no woman lend herself to a beast to
mate with it; it is perversion.
24 Do not defile yourselves in any of those ways, for it is by
such that the nations that I am casting out before you defiled
themselves. 25 Thus the land became defiled; and I called it to
account for its iniquity, and the land spewed out its inhabitants. 26 But you must keep My laws and My rules, and you must
not do any of those abhorrent things, neither the citizen nor
the stranger who resides among you; 27 for all those abhorrent
things were done by the people who were in the land before
you, and the land became defiled. 28 So let not the land spew
you out for defiling it, as it spewed out the nation that came
before you. 29 All who do any of those abhorrent things—such
persons shall be cut off from their people. 30 You shall keep

second, another's wife (v. 20); (2) nonprocreative intercourse, first, with a male (v. 22), second, with an animal (v. 23a); (3) intercourse in which no human seed is emitted, i.e., between a woman and an animal (v. 23b). **19:** See 15.19–24 n. This stricter law is probably an indication of H's espousal of popular tradition, viewing the menstruating woman as taboo, overriding P's concern with purely formal, technical definitions according to which menstruation is no different from any other bodily impurity. **20:** The adultery prohibition is included here since it too was thought to be characteristic of the Canaanites. *Defile yourself:* Note the wider sense of "defile" in H; in the strict, Priestly sense all sexual intercourse is defiling (see 15.18). **21:** The inclusion in this ch of the prohibition of Molech sacrifice (see 20.2–5 n.) is unexpected. Apparently H shares the view of Deut. 12.31; 18.9–12 that child sacrifice was among the abominable practices for which the Canaanites were expelled from their land, so he adds it to the list of sexual offenses, which he believes are equally responsible. Other biblical texts confirm that it was in fact practiced in Israel at certain times during the monarchy (see 2 Kings 16.3; 17.17; 21.6; 23.10; Isa. 30.33 [see translators' note g]; Jer. 7.31; 19.5; 32.35; Ezek. 16.21; 23.37; Ps. 106.37–38), and this accounts for the Torah sources having attributed it to the Canaanites: to serve as a warning for Israel. **22:** Biblical and ancient Near Eastern culture was not familiar with homosexuality in the sense of a defined sexual orientation or lifestyle (the Bible gives no indication that David and Jonathan had a sexual relationship). It acknowledges only the occasional act of male anal intercourse, usually as an act of force associated with humiliation, revenge, or subjection (for the biblical examples see Gen. 19.4–5; Judg. 19.22). Of the biblical legal collections only H mentions it (here and in 20.13), declaring it to be an abominable act and a capital offense. One possible explanation might be that H views certain sexual acts that are not potentially procreative as aberrant. **24–30:** The concluding exhortation, extrapolating from abhorrence in v. 22 and from the defilement mentioned in vv. 19 and 20, speaks of defilement as a destructive force emanating from all of the acts mentioned. These acts *defile* those who commit them, and this in turn defiles the land of Canaan which then spits out its inhabitants. This is the automatic reaction of the land of Canaan to abominations, no matter who commits them, Canaanites or Israelites. The intent of the exhortation is to say that what was, will be, unless the listeners themselves prevent it. *The nations that I am casting out before you:* The Egyptians, mentioned in v. 3, have disappeared from view; the focus is entirely on the Canaanites. See also 20.23. **25:** *Spewed out,* lit. "vomited"; not actions performed upon the land by attackers from outside but rather performed by the land upon its population. As recognized by the midrash, "the land of Israel is not like the rest of the earth in that it does not sustain those who commit [sexual] offenses" (*Sifre* to v. 28 [Kod. 11:14], mistakenly placed in the *Sifra* at 20.22 because of similarity to the v. there). The land is so sensitive to the criminal behavior of its inhabitants that when abominable acts are performed, "defiling" the land, it ceases to yield its bounty and its population is forced to emigrate. Of course, as the previous v. confirms, God has imbued the land of Israel with its delicate constitution. This is unique to H; elsewhere in the Torah it is presumed that the pre-Israelite inhabitants of Canaan were either destroyed or expelled by the conquering Israelites. **26:** *Neither the citizen nor the stranger who resides among you,* see 16.29. **28:** *Spewed out the nation that came before you:* Unique also is the idea that the evacuation of Canaan has already occurred. **29:** Not only is the national fate sealed by failing to avoid the abominations, each perpetrator is punished with "karet" (see 7.20, 21 n.).

My charge not to engage in any of the abhorrent practices that
were carried on before you, and you shall not defile yourselves
through them: I the LORD am your God.

KEDOSHIM קדשים

19 The LORD spoke to Moses, saying: 2 Speak to the whole
Israelite community and say to them:
You shall be holy, for I, the LORD your God, am holy.
3 You shall each revere his mother and his father, and keep
My sabbaths: I the LORD am your God.
4 Do not turn to idols or make molten gods for yourselves: I
the LORD am your God.
5 When you sacrifice an offering of well-being to the LORD,
sacrifice it so that it may be accepted on your behalf. 6 It shall
be eaten on the day you sacrifice it, or on the day following;
but what is left by the third day must be consumed in fire. 7 If it
should be eaten on the third day, it is an offensive thing, it will
not be acceptable. 8 And he who eats of it shall bear his guilt,

19.1–37: Holiness of individuals. Commands pertaining to virtually every area of Israelite life; there is no such thing as a command pertaining merely to relations between human beings ("ben ʾadam laḥavero"); every commanded or prohibited action affects the sacred realm and is in the category of laws between God and human beings ("ben ʾadam lamakom"). The ch expresses this by presenting an admixture of laws from every sphere—from worship to fairness in commerce, from legal proceedings to reverence for the Temple, from idolatry and the avoidance of pagan practices to family relations, from the use of the name of God in oaths to support for the needy, from the sanctity of first fruits to theft and fraud—all on equal footing; punctuating the separate paragraphs with the repeated refrain *I am the LORD* or *I the LORD am your God,* which is approximately equivalent to "because I, the LORD, say so." The opening and closing vv. (2 and 37) provide the key to meaning: *You shall be holy, for I, the LORD your God, am holy* (v. 2). *You shall faithfully observe all My laws and all My rules: I am the LORD* (v. 37). These vv. resemble two that occur alongside each other in the next ch, 20.7–8. Only through faithful observance of God's commands can the Israelite fulfill the sacred charge of being holy. This is repeated in Num. 15.39–40, recited every morning and evening as part of the Shema prayer, where the function of the fringe on the tallit is that one may "look at it and recall all the commandments of the LORD and observe them.... Thus you shall be reminded to observe all My commandments and be holy to your God." Through this miscellany of laws H expresses the idea that through the performance of all commanded deeds and the avoidance of all prohibited actions, all Israelites are able to absorb the effusion of the divine Presence in their midst (see 6.11) and be holy. A number of rabbinic and modern interpreters, noting that the prohibitions of idolatry (v. 4), theft and falsehood (v. 11), and false witness (v. 12), along with the command to keep the Sabbath and to revere one's mother and father (v. 3), are included in this collection, have suggested that this ch is the Priestly version of the Decalogue (see Exod. ch 20; Deut. ch 5). This is unlikely. The Priestly literature is completely unfamiliar with the Decalogue tradition; there is no logical explanation for the missing commands; and the six scattered parallels are outweighed by the remainder of ch 19, which does not resemble the Decalogue at all. **2:** *You shall be holy, for I, the LORD your God, am holy:* This is the caption; what follows is its elaboration. Later interpreters often took it as a general command to emulate divine attributes such as compassion and forgiveness ("imitatio dei"). But "holy" in the Bible does not refer to superior moral qualities. God's holiness is His essential "otherness," His being separate from all that is not divine; humans are not called upon to be holy in this sense (the text does not say "as I am holy"). Holiness in humans, as in time, space, objects, and speech, is the state of belonging to the deity, being designated God's "personal" property. In the non-Priestly tradition Israel is holy simply by virtue of having been chosen (see Exod. 19.5–6; Deut. 7.6; 14.2, 21). In Priestly thought, holiness is the desired result of an effusion of God's immanent Presence (see Exod. 29.43), which, according to H, Israel must actively absorb by performing the commandments. **3:** The legislative part of the ch leads with a command pertaining to the ethical realm, reverence for parents, alongside one obviously belonging—in priestly tradition at least—to the sacred sphere, the Sabbath, together with the formulaic *I the LORD am your God. Revere:* The Rabbis correctly sensed that this differs from "honor" in Exod. 20.12 and Deut. 5.16; the Decalogue refers to the do's; this v. refers to the don'ts. *And keep My sabbaths,* see 23.3. **5–8:** See 7.11–21. This refers to the well-being offerings of the votive and freewill types (see 7.16–18; 22.21–23). The third type of well-being offering, the thanksgiving offering (see 7.12–15) is mentioned in 22.29–30, marking the close of this section of H (chs 19–22). **7:** *It is an offensive thing,* see 7.18. *It will not be acceptable,* correctly, "it will not be accepted." See 1.3; 7.18 n.; 22.17–30. **8:** *He has profaned what is sacred to the LORD:* This theme connects the passage with the holiness motif. *Cut off from his kin,* see 7.20, 21 n. **9–10:** Four prohibitions, two in the

for he has profaned what is sacred to the LORD; that person
shall be cut off from his kin.
9 When you reap the harvest of your land, you shall not reap
all the way to the edges of your field, or gather the gleanings of
your harvest. 10 You shall not pick your vineyard bare, or gather
the fallen fruit of your vineyard; you shall leave them for the
poor and the stranger: I the LORD am your God.
11 You shall not steal; you shall not deal deceitfully or falsely
with one another. 12 You shall not swear falsely by My name,
profaning the name of your God: I am the LORD.
13 You shall not defraud your fellow. You shall not commit
robbery. The wages of a laborer shall not remain with you until
morning.
14 You shall not insult the deaf, or place a stumbling block
before the blind. You shall fear your God: I am the LORD.
15 You shall not render an unfair decision: do not favor the
poor or show deference to the rich; judge your kinsman fairly.
16 Do not [a-]deal basely with[-a] your countrymen. Do not [b-]profit
by[-b] the blood of your fellow: I am the LORD.
17 You shall not hate your kinsfolk in your heart. Reprove
your kinsman but[c] incur no guilt because of him. 18 You shall
not take vengeance or bear a grudge against your countrymen.
Love your fellow as yourself: I am the LORD.

a-a Others "go about as a talebearer among"; meaning of Heb. uncertain.
b-b Lit. "stand upon"; precise meaning of Heb. phrase uncertain.
c Exact force of we- *uncertain.*

field and two in the vineyard. The first in each pair is observed while reaping, the second during ingathering. All lead up to you shall leave them for the poor and the stranger. The command to care for the needy is fulfilled by inaction. *I the LORD am your God* transforms social legislation into a sacred act. Cf. Deut. 24.19–21. *The stranger,* see 16.29. **11–18:** Four two-v. paragraphs, each ending with *I am the LORD,* indicating that decency and honesty, ostensibly pertaining to interpersonal affairs, are in fact divine concerns. All four deal with matters of conscience: Since all of the crimes are to some degree committed in secret, their perpetrators imagine that they will go undetected. The progression is from the crimes most difficult to conceal to those which can never be proven and whose victims have no remedy whatsoever, leaving detection and punishment in the hands of God alone. **11–12:** Falsehood in commerce and its ramifications; see 5.20–26. Theft naturally leads to deceit, denial, and cover-up; these are likely to be aggravated by false oath, thus profaning the sacred name of God, so God becomes a party to what began as a purely civil matter. **13–14:** Taking unfair advantage. The first v. prohibits fraud, extortion, and withholding wages from the defenseless laborer; the second, speaking metaphorically and not of those literally deaf or blind, extends the principle to include exploitation of others by capitalizing on their ignorance or vulnerability. Rabbinic tradition extended the metaphoric reading even further, to include the prohibition of tempting someone to commit a sinful act. **14:** *You shall fear your God:* The victims of such exploitation may never know how they have been used; fear of God is the only real sanction (see also v. 32 as well as 25.17, 36, 43). As noted by the Rabbis, this phrase occurs when compliance is a matter of conscience rather than legal enforcement. **15–16:** Perversion of justice. The first v. speaks directly of the corruption of judicial proceedings on the part of judges. A better rendering of v. 16 is: "Do not spread [false] rumors among your countrymen [to have unjust charges brought against a person]; do not stand by the blood of your fellow [i.e., ignore bloodshed, thus preventing charges from being brought against the perpetrator]." **15:** *Render an unfair decision,* lit. "commit distortion in judgment"; see v. 35. **17–18:** Pent-up hatred and its consequences. The two vv. are a unit, better rendered: "Do not hate your kinsfolk in your heart, rather, reprove your kinsman so as to incur no guilt because of him. In other words: Do not take vengeance or bear a grudge against your countrymen, rather, love your fellow as yourself." The first v. prohibits one whose fellow has wronged him from keeping his resentment inside instead of informing the wrongdoer of his action, lest the bottled-up hatred result in incurring guilt. The second v. explains: Such bearing of grudges results ultimately in vengeance, while by refraining from this course one treats his fellow with the same "love," i.e., understanding and forgiveness, one normally extends toward one's own shortcomings. Traditional interpretation tended to treat each phrase as a general command in its own right. For instance the words reprove your kinsman were seen as obligating competent persons to chastise their fellow Israelites for failings in their religious and ethical duties and returning them to the path of righteousness (*b. 'Arak.* 16 b and many other places). Most notably, love your fellow as yourself was generalized in Jewish and Christian tradition to serve as a brief encapsulation of the Torah's ethics (e.g., *b. Shab.* 31a; Matt. 22.34–40) and as a blanket command covering all ethical duties not specifically mentioned (e.g., Maimonides *Yad*

19 You shall observe My laws.
You shall not let your cattle mate with a different kind; you
shall not sow your field with two kinds of seed; you shall not
put on cloth from a mixture of two kinds of material.
20 If a man has carnal relations with a woman who is a slave
and has been designated for another man, but has not been
redeemed or given her freedom, there shall be an indemnity;
they shall not, however, be put to death, since she has not been
freed. 21 But he must bring to the entrance of the Tent of Meeting, as his guilt offering to the LORD, a ram of guilt offering.
22 With the ram of guilt offering the priest shall make expiation
for him before the LORD for the sin that he committed; and the
sin that he committed will be forgiven him.
23 When you enter the land and plant any tree for food, you
shall regard its fruit as forbidden.[a] Three years it shall be forbidden[a] for you, not to be eaten. 24 In the fourth year all its fruit
shall be set aside for jubilation before the LORD; 25 and only in
the fifth year may you use its fruit—that its yield to you may be
increased: I the LORD am your God.
26 You shall not eat anything with its blood. You shall not
practice divination or soothsaying. 27 You shall not round off
the side-growth on your head, or destroy the side-growth of
your beard. 28 You shall not make gashes in your flesh for the
dead, or incise any marks on yourselves: I am the LORD.
29 Do not degrade your daughter and make her a harlot, lest
the land fall into harlotry and the land be filled with depravity.
30 You shall keep My sabbaths and venerate My sanctuary: I am
the LORD.
31 Do not turn to ghosts and do not inquire of familiar spirits,
to be defiled by them: I the LORD am your God.

a Heb. root ʿrl, *commonly "to be uncircumcised."*

ʾAvelut 14:1; Matt. 19.16–19). **18:** *I am the LORD:* In the Priestly worldview, ethical behavior is a religious act only when performed as an act of obedience to God. **19:** *My laws,* "ḥukkotay" should be understood here more literally as "the boundaries I have fixed in the natural world"; cf. Isa. 5.14; Jer. 5.22; 33.25; Job 38.33. As explained in ch 11, according to P's view Israel is to maintain the distinctions present in the created order. *Different kind, two kinds,* Heb "kilʾayim," used in the parallel law in Deut. 22.9 as well. *Mixture,* Heb "shaʿatnez." However, wool and linen are woven together in the priestly vestments (Exod. 28.6; 39.29) and in the fringes (tzitzit) Israelites are obligated to place on their clothing (Num. 15.37–40). The "unnatural" mixture is therefore taboo for mundane use but not for sacred garments. **20–22:** If one's female slave is designated for marriage to another man, sexual relations with her are illicit. Only by legal technicality (since the woman is not yet free, she is not strictly "betrothed" in the legally binding sense) are the two exempt from the death penalty mandated for adultery (see 20.10 n.) but the offense against God must be expiated. The "ʾasham" sacrifice is prescribed (see 5.14–26) even though no desecration of the sacred has taken place, because the "ḥataʾt" sacrifice (see 4.1–35 n.) does not atone for deliberate acts.
20: *There shall be an indemnity:* This translation is uncertain. A simpler one is: "a distinction shall be made." **23–25:** The fruit of a tree is off-limits for the first three years, and offered to the LORD in the fourth; only then may it be eaten. **23:** You shall regard its fruit as forbidden, lit. "treat it as uncircumcised." Figuratively speaking, the fruit tree is to be regarded as though sealed off from use. **24:** Set aside, Heb "kodesh," a sacred or "holy" object, thus connecting this law with the theme of the ch as a whole. The text does not state how the fruit is to be set aside and what is to be done with it. *For jubilation before the LORD,* see Judg. 9.27. **25:** *That its yield to you may be increased:* Abstaining from the first three years' fruit will result not in material loss but rather in divine blessing. **26–28:** From context it appears that *You shall not eat anything with its blood,* which refers to eating meat without having drained the blood (see 17.10–14; 1 Sam. 14.32–35), must, like the two prohibitions that follow, be associated with pagan forms of divination and magic. The acts prohibited in the next two vv. are extreme expressions of grief and mourning (see Deut. 14.1–2; 1 Kings 18.28); as they are associated with conjuring up dead spirits and the gods of the netherworld, they are not to be copied from the pagan peoples. Similar restrictions are placed on priests (see 21.5). **29:** *Degrade,* lit. "profane." This is the opposite of holiness. **30–32:** These three vv. mark the close of the main section of the unit, returning to the themes with which it opened and adding to them. **30:** *Keep My sabbaths,* corresponding to v. 3a. *Venerate My sanctuary,* i.e., do not trespass the bounds of the sacred. The verb corresponds to that used in the second law in 3a. This v. occurs again in 26.2. **31:** *Do not turn to,* corresponding to v. 4. *Ghosts ... familiar spirits,* Heb "ʾov" and "yideʿoni," mentioned throughout the Bible as spirits conjured up by

32 You shall rise before the aged and show deference to the
old; you shall fear your God: I am the LORD.
33 When a stranger resides with you in your land, you shall not
wrong him. 34 The stranger who resides with you shall be to you
as one of your citizens; you shall love him as yourself, for you
were strangers in the land of Egypt: I the LORD am your God.
35 You shall not falsify measures of length, weight, or capacity.
36 You shall have an honest balance, honest weights, an honest
ephah, and an honest *hin.*
I the LORD am your God who freed you from the land of Egypt.
37 You shall faithfully observe all My laws and all My rules: I am
the LORD.

20 And the LORD spoke to Moses: 2 Say further to the Israelite people:
Anyone among the Israelites, or among the strangers residing in Israel, who gives any of his offspring to Molech, shall be
put to death; the people of the land shall pelt him with stones.

necromancers. Biblical tradition admits that this method of gaining knowledge of the occult is effective (see 1 Sam. 28.3–25) but places it strictly off-limits for Israelites; see 20.6, 27; cf. Deut. 18.9ff.
32: *Rise ... show deference to the old,* corresponding to v. 3a. *You shall fear your God,* see v. 14 n. **33–36:** These vv. make up the appendix, extending two of the laws mentioned in the main body of the ch to the "ger" or resident alien (see 16.29 n.). Elsewhere in P, when the law is extended to include resident aliens, it is to enable them to perform positive commands if they desire or to obligate them to observe prohibitions. Here, the purpose is to obligate the Israelite to treat the "ger" with the same decency he is required to show his fellow Israelite.
33–34: Reinterpreting and extending the law in v. 18 to the resident alien. *Love* of the "ger" is manifest in treating him as a citizen, though he is not one, in financial dealings. **33:** *Wrong him,* the sense is "cheat him in commerce." **34:** *For you were strangers in the land of Egypt:* The prohibition of exploiting the "ger" is logically grounded in Israel's own experience; see Exod. 22.20; 23.9; Deut. 10.19. **35–36:** Extending the law in v. 15, "do not commit distortion in judgment," by employing "mishpat," "judgment," in its additional meaning of "correct portion." These two vv. likely also refer to the "ger," warning the Israelite not to take advantage of the alien's lack of familiarity with local weights and measures. A similar law, not connected with "gerim" specifically, appears in Deut. 25.13–16.
36: *Ephah,* a dry measure, about 23 liters (21 quarts); *hin,* a liquid measure, a little less than 4 liters, 1 gal). *I the LORD am your God who freed you from the land of Egypt:* The elongated self-assertion formula (cf. for instance 26.13) signals the end of the ch; it also indicates that this paragraph is connected with the one preceding. **37:** Concluding summation; see 19.1–37 n.

20.1–27: Molech worship and sexual crimes. A single speech, introduced in v. 1 and divided into four parts: (1) penalties for Molech worship (vv. 2–5); (2) exhortation (vv. 7–8); (3) a series of prescribed penalties for sexual and other crimes (vv. 9–21); (4) exhortation (vv. 22–26). Two appendices, dealing with conjuring up the spirits of the dead, have been placed at the conclusions of sections (1) and (4), respectively (vv. 6 and 27). Sacrifice to Molech and sexual crimes were treated at length in ch 18 as direct commands ("Do not uncover the nakedness of ..."), while here they are phrased conditionally ("If a man [commits such-and-such], he shall [suffer such-and-such punishment]"). Many commentators have therefore assumed that this ch provides the punishments for the crimes given in ch 18. But this is unlikely for many reasons. Several of the acts prohibited in ch 18 are missing (intercourse with one's mother, granddaughter, half-sister, step-granddaughter, and wife's sister). Conversely, this ch mentions crimes not included in ch 18 (cursing one's parents and consulting spirits). Even some of the parallels are not exact: 20.14, 17, 18 do not quite correspond to the commands in 18.9, 17, 19. Further, according to 18.29 all the crimes enumerated are punished by "karet," whereas this ch mentions "karet" in a few cases only, and prescribes capital punishment in the others. Finally, the very existence of two separate chs devoted to one theme, with an entire ch standing between them, indicates that the two chs were composed separately. The compilers of H, in their endeavor to include as much legislation as possible, preserved and included overlapping and contradictory compositions without harmonization. This illustrates the reverence ancient authors had for texts that they inherited from earlier bearers of tradition.
2–5: *Molech* is the Heb for an ancient Near Eastern deity associated with the netherworld. Biblical tradition is unanimous that the worship of Molech consisted of the sacrifice of children, and there is evidence that this cult of death was occasionally practiced in Israel, and that at times Israelites engaged in child sacrifice (see Micah 6.7 n.). In 18.21 this monstrous crime is included among the "abominations" which caused (and will again cause) the land of Canaan to spew out its inhabitants.
2–3: Sacrificing to Molech is a capital offense. The *people of the land* (which may refer to a designated body of citizens) are required to see

3 And I will set My face against that man and will cut him off
from among his people, because he gave of his offspring to
Molech and so defiled My sanctuary and profaned My holy
name. 4 And if the people of the land should shut their eyes to
that man when he gives of his offspring to Molech, and should
not put him to death, 5 I Myself will set My face against that
man and his kin, and will cut off from among their people
both him and all who follow him in going astray after Molech.
6 And if any person turns to ghosts and familiar spirits and goes
astray after them, I will set My face against that person and cut
him off from among his people.

7 You shall sanctify yourselves and be holy, for I the LORD
am your God. 8 You shall faithfully observe My laws: I the LORD
make you holy.

9 If anyone insults his father or his mother, he shall be put to
death; he has insulted his father and his mother—his bloodguilt is upon him.

10 If a man commits adultery with a married woman, committing adultery with another man's wife, the adulterer and the
adulteress shall be put to death. 11 If a man lies with his father's
wife, it is the nakedness of his father that he has uncovered; the
two shall be put to death—their bloodguilt is upon them. 12 If a
man lies with his daughter-in-law, both of them shall be put to
death; they have committed incest—their bloodguilt is upon
them. 13 If a man lies with a male as one lies with a woman, the
two of them have done an abhorrent thing; they shall be put
to death—their bloodguilt is upon them. 14 If a man marries a
woman and her mother, it is depravity; both he and they shall
be put to the fire, that there be no depravity among you. 15 If a
man has carnal relations with a beast, he shall be put to death;
and you shall kill the beast. 16 If a woman approaches any beast
to mate with it, you shall kill the woman and the beast; they
shall be put to death—their bloodguilt is upon them.

17 If a man marries his sister, the daughter of either his father
or his mother, so that he sees her nakedness and she sees his
nakedness, it is a disgrace; they shall be excommunicated[a] in
the sight of their kinsfolk. He has uncovered the nakedness of

a Lit. "cut off."

the death by stoning of the perpetrators. In addition, God will personally attend to the eventual extinction of their line ("karet," see 7.20, 21 n.). *Defiled My sanctuary:* Sacrifices to Molech were not made in the LORD's sanctuary; rather, the contamination of God's abode results from this crime wherever it is committed. *Profaned My holy name,* by attributing salvific power to another deity, or by imagining that the God of Israel desires the sacrifice of children. **4–5:** If those charged with prosecuting the criminal neglect their duty, God will extend the "karet" threat to the perpetrator's larger family and all those *who follow him in going astray after Molech.* **6:** *Ghosts and familiar spirits,* see 19.31 n. In v. 27 the death penalty is prescribed for those who "have" ghosts and familiar spirits. Thus the "providers" are punished by death, and the "consumers" are punished by "karet." **7–8:** See ch 19. These two vv. provide the transition to the second set of laws in the ch. **9–21:** The series of penalties for severe crimes. For those in vv. 9–16 the death penalty is prescribed, with burning mentioned as the method in one case (v. 14). For the remainder, "karet" (see 7.20, 21 n.) is either pronounced (vv. 17–18) or implied (vv. 19–21). It is unclear why particular punishments are legislated for particular offenses. Many of the terms used to characterize the crimes are unclear (e.g., "depravity," "disgrace"), and it is uncertain why only some vv. contain such characterizations and others do not. These and other features of the text indicate that this ch, like the remainder of H, was not composed to be studied as a precise legal document but rather as an exhortation, with all the rhetorical technique and emotional expression that this entails. **9:** *Insults,* Heb "curses." *His bloodguilt is upon him:* This phrase, here and in the following vv., emphasizes that although the crime was not one of bloodshed, the guilty parties have indeed incurred the death penalty and the executioners are not accountable. **10:** *Adultery* is defined as sexual relations between any man, married or single, and a woman betrothed or married to someone else. Both parties to the crime are guilty; see Deut. 22.22. **11:** See 18.8. **12:** See 18.15. *They have committed incest,* Heb "tevel," taken to mean "improper mixing." **13:** See 18.22 n. **14:** See 18.17, where the formulation is "a woman and her daughter." **15–16:** See 18.23. **17:** See 18.9 n. *Marries,* see 18.17 n.; here too the Heb "yikaḥ," "takes," may suggest a sexual relationship. *They shall be excommunicated,* Heb (see translators' note *a*) simply says "shall be cut off," precisely as in the "karet" threat in the next v. and throughout the Priestly law (see 7.20, 21 n.). *He shall bear his guilt,* for this phrase, used also in vv. 19 and 20, see 5.1;

his sister, he shall bear his guilt. 18 If a man lies with a woman in her infirmity and uncovers her nakedness, he has laid bare her flow and she has exposed her blood flow; both of them shall be cut off from among their people. 19 You shall not uncover the nakedness of your mother's sister or of your father's sister, for that is laying bare one's own flesh; they shall bear their guilt. 20 If a man lies with his uncle's wife, it is his uncle's nakedness that he has uncovered. They shall bear their guilt: they shall die childless. 21 If a man marries the wife of his brother, it is indecency. It is the nakedness of his brother that he has uncovered; they shall remain childless.

22 You shall faithfully observe all My laws and all My regulations, lest the land to which I bring you to settle in spew you out. 23 You shall not follow the practices of the nation that I am driving out before you. For it is because they did all these things that I abhorred them 24 and said to you: You shall possess their land, for I will give it to you to possess, a land flowing with milk and honey. I the LORD am your God who has set you apart from other peoples. 25 So you shall set apart the clean beast from the unclean, the unclean bird from the clean. You shall not draw abomination upon yourselves through beast or bird or anything with which the ground is alive, which I have set apart for you to treat as unclean. 26 You shall be holy to Me, for I the LORD am holy, and I have set you apart from other peoples to be Mine.

27 A man or a woman who has a ghost or a familiar spirit shall be put to death; they shall be pelted with stones—their bloodguilt shall be upon them.

ʾEMOR אמר

21

The LORD said to Moses: Speak to the priests, the sons of Aaron, and say to them:

None shall defile himself for any [dead] person among his kin, 2 except for the relatives that are closest to him: his mother, his father, his son, his daughter, and his brother; 3 also for a virgin sister, close to him because she has not married, for her he may defile himself. 4 But he shall not defile himself [a]as a kinsman by marriage,[a] and so profane himself.

5 They shall not shave smooth any part of their heads, or cut the side-growth of their beards, or make gashes in their flesh.

a-a Lit. "as a husband among his kin"; meaning uncertain.

7.18. **18:** See 15.19–24 n. and 18.19 n. *In her infirmity,* during her menstrual period; see 12.2; 15.33. **19:** *You shall not uncover the nakedness,* see 18.12, 13. This v. abandons the conditional formulation found throughout this ch and reverts to the "you shall not" formulation of ch 18. **20:** *Uncle's wife:* This may include the wife of the mother's brother as well as the wife of the father's brother mentioned specifically in 18.14. *They shall die childless:* This penalty, found here and in the next v., is probably a specific form of "karet" (see 7.20, 21 n.), since the childless person's line is thereby made extinct. **21:** See 18.16 n. **22–26:** The concluding exhortation returns briefly (vv. 22–24) to the themes of 18.24–30, adding the description of the land of Canaan as *a land flowing with milk and honey.* It then (vv. 25–26) introduces the motif of "setting apart": As God has separated Israel from the nations, they must separate pure (clean) from impure (unclean) foods, and thus be *holy.* Since *holy* means set apart, the text is saying that in order to be holy (*to be Mine,* v. 26) they are required to act accordingly (*So you shall set apart,* v. 25). Vv. 25–26 resemble 11.43–45 and would read well as an alternate conclusion to ch 11. **27:** The appendix, evidently a secondary addition to the ch; see v. 6.

21.1–22.33: Worship and holiness. Whereas earlier chs were concerned with the proper procedure for sacrifice (chs 1–7, 17) and with the prompt disposal of impurity (chs 11–16), this section revolves primarily around holiness, that of the priests (ch 21) and that of sacrificial offerings (22.1–16). The sacred, which belongs to the divine sphere and has been "saturated" with holiness (see 6.11 n.), is vulnerable to attack; it is subject to desecration if it is not kept apart from impurity, disqualifying imperfections, and unauthorized contact or use. Desecration of the holy redounds to God, profaning His abode and His holy name, and brings disastrous consequences in its wake. The second topic, arising from the mention of disqualifying blemishes, is the acceptance of offerings, first mentioned in 1.3–4 (see also 7.18; 19.5–8). The chs consist of five speeches to Moses, the first four of which he is to convey to Aaron and his sons: (1) avoiding the desecration of the priests (21.1–15); (2) avoiding the desecration of the sanctuary and the offerings by contact with defective priests (21.16–24); (3) avoiding the desecration of the sanctuary and the sacred offerings by contact with impure priests and consumption by ineligible persons

6 They shall be holy to their God and not profane the name of
their God; for they offer the LORD's offerings by fire, the food of
their God, and so must be holy.
7 They shall not marry a woman defiled by harlotry, nor shall
they marry one divorced from her husband. For they are holy
to their God 8 and you must treat them as holy, since they offer
the food of your God; they shall be holy to you, for I the LORD
who sanctify you am holy.
9 When the daughter of a priest defiles herself through harlotry, it is her father whom she defiles; she shall be put to the fire.
10 The priest who is exalted above his fellows, on whose head
the anointing oil has been poured and who has been ordained
to wear the vestments, shall not bare his head[a] or rend his vestments. 11 He shall not go in where there is any dead body; he
shall not defile himself even for his father or mother. 12 He shall
not go outside the sanctuary and profane the sanctuary of his
God, for upon him is the distinction of the anointing oil of his
God, Mine the LORD's. 13 He may marry only a woman who is
a virgin. 14 A widow, or a divorced woman, or one who is degraded by harlotry—such he may not marry. Only a virgin of
his own kin may he take to wife— 15 that he may not profane
his offspring among his kin, for I the LORD have sanctified him.
16 The LORD spoke further to Moses: 17 Speak to Aaron and say:
No man of your offspring throughout the ages who has a defect

a See note at 10.6.

(22.1–16); (4) offerings deemed unacceptable due to physical defect or pagan origin (22.17–25); (5) offerings deemed unacceptable because of time factors, and concluding vv. of a general nature (22.26–33).

21.1–15: The holiness of the priesthood. 1–4: The priests, in contrast to the lay Israelite, must stay clear of avoidable impurity and must refrain from nearing the sacred when they become unavoidably impure since they are holy in the highest degree. Thus, while lay Israelites may come into contact with a corpse as long as they dispose of their impurity afterwards (see Num. ch 19), priests may not do so, unless it be in order to mourn the death of a first-degree blood relative—in which case they must, of course, avoid contact with the sacred until they have been cleansed. **2–3:** *The relatives that are closest to him,* a narrower group than those denoted by the phrase "anyone of his own flesh" in 18.6; 25.49. *His mother, his father,* etc.: In Jewish tradition, this (along with the wife, who is not mentioned but was supplied exegetically) is the basis for the list of relatives for whom one is required to observe the statutory mourning periods. **4:** *Defile himself as a kinsman by marriage:* Others translate this difficult phrase literally: "a 'master' [i.e., a priest] must not defile himself for his kinsmen," a recapitulation of v. 1b. **5:** Desecration of the priest results also from observing the widespread rituals of mourning detailed here; see 10.6–7. According to 19.27–28 these expressions of grief are also forbidden to lay Israelites. **6:** The rationale for the preceding. The priests must maintain the sanctity with which they, like the Tabernacle and its furnishings, have been imbued (see 8.10–13). Since they offer the deity food gifts, any desecration of their persons would profane the name of God. *Offerings by fire,* see 1.9. **7:** The holiness of the priests is held to be genetically transmitted; they may marry only women about whom there can be no suspicion of the presence of another man's seed. See v. 14 n. *A woman defiled by harlotry,* lit. "a harlotrous woman and one defiled," taken by most exegetes as two distinct categories. Traditionally, the former is defined as a woman who has had prohibited intercourse (see 18.6–23) and the latter as a woman born of such a relationship, or of a union between a priest and a woman prohibited to him. Halakhah derives the prohibition of marriage between a priest and a proselyte from this phrase. **8:** The repeated rationale, including a reference to God's own holiness. **9:** The lay Israelite too is forbidden to allow his daughter to engage in harlotry (19.29). The priest's daughter, however, is a more serious case; her father's sanctity would thereby be desecrated, and the offense is therefore a capital one. **10–14:** The high priest is subject to even stricter safeguards against possible desecration, since he is required to enter the Tabernacle daily. He must refrain even from benign expressions of grief, and may not contract corpse contamination even in order to mourn for a close relative (similarly the Nazirite; see Num. 6.6). Further, he must marry a virgin; even a widow (whom a lesser priest may marry, presumably because her husband has been dead long enough to nullify any suspicion of paternity) is off-limits; since another man's seed has entered her at some time in her life, the high priest's union with her is thought to desecrate his own seed. Ezekiel forecasts that in the rebuilt Temple all priests will be subject to the same restrictions (Ezek. 44.22–26); halakhah maintained the Torah's leniency. **10:** *On whose head,* see 4.3 n. Bare his head, better: dishevel his head [i.e., his hair]; see 10.6. *Or rend his vestments,* see 10.6. **14:** *Of his own kin,* i.e., of priestly descent. In contrast Ezekiel permits the priest to marry any virgin of the seed

shall be qualified to offer the food of his God. [18] No one at all who has a defect shall be qualified: no man who is blind, or lame, or [a]-has a limb too short or too long;-[a] [19] no man who has a broken leg or a broken arm; [20] or who is a hunchback, or a dwarf, or who has a growth in his eye, or who has a boil-scar, or scurvy, or crushed testes. [21] No man among the offspring of Aaron the priest who has a defect shall be qualified to offer the LORD's offering by fire; having a defect, he shall not be qualified to offer the food of his God. [22] He may eat of the food of his God, of the most holy as well as of the holy; [23] but he shall not enter behind the curtain or come near the altar, for he has a defect. He shall not profane these places sacred to Me, for I the LORD have sanctified them.

[24] Thus Moses spoke to Aaron and his sons and to all the Israelites.

22 The LORD spoke to Moses, saying: [2] Instruct Aaron and his sons to be scrupulous about the sacred donations that the Israelite people consecrate to Me, lest they profane My holy name, Mine the LORD's. [3] Say to them:

Throughout the ages, if any man among your offspring, while in a state of uncleanness, partakes of any sacred donation that the Israelite people may consecrate to the LORD, that person shall be cut off from before Me: I am the LORD. [4] No man of Aaron's offspring who has an eruption or a discharge[b] shall eat of the sacred donations until he is clean. If one touches anything made unclean by a corpse, or if a man has an emission of semen, [5] or if a man touches any swarming thing by which he is made unclean or any human being by whom he is made unclean—whatever his uncleanness—[6] the person who touches such shall be unclean until evening and shall not eat of the sacred donations unless he has washed his body in water. [7] As soon as the sun sets, he shall be clean; and afterward he may eat of the sacred donations, for they are his food. [8] He shall not eat anything that died or was torn by beasts, thereby becoming unclean: I am the LORD. [9] They shall keep My charge, lest they incur guilt thereby and die for it, having committed profanation: I the LORD consecrate them.

a-a Or "mutilated or has a limb too long." *b See chapters 13 and 15.*

of Israel (44.22). Here the halakhah follows Ezekiel, once again adopting the more lenient view—perhaps understanding Ezekiel's view as an interpretation of our v. **15:** *Have sanctified,* better, "sanctify him," reflecting Priestly thought, where God sanctifies constantly by His very Presence (Exod. 29.43–44; see also v. 8 above; Exod. 31.13; Lev. 20.8; 22.9, 16, 32; cf. Ezek. 37.28).

21.16–24: Priests' desecration of the sacred. Physical defects, broadly defined as the absence or permanent malformation of external parts of the human body in its "completed," adult, male form, disqualify the priest from offering the sacred food gifts to God. Though he may not officiate, the defective priest remains a priest, as this is a fact of birth, and is entitled to eat the priestly portions of the sacrificial flesh. **21:** See 1.9 n. **23:** The specific ineligibility of the defective priest, i.e., the prohibition of approaching the altar and beyond, may indicate the precise rationale for the law. According to Priestly teaching, the human being is made in the image of the deity (Gen. 1.26–27; 5.1). The priest, as God's palace servant, profanes the abode of the deity if he cannot adequately reflect the divine form; only the fully formed specimens of the image of God can serve in His earthly habitation. Alternatively, the rationale for the law may be a matter of dignity as judged by human standards; see Mal. 1.6–13. *These places sacred to Me,* "mikdashay," lit. "My sanctuaries." This does not, however, indicate that P or H accepted a decentralized cult with multiple sanctuaries (see also 26.31 n.) *Have sanctified,* as in v. 15, "sanctify them."

22.1–16: Desecration of the offerings. Even minor impurities desecrate the sacred (vv. 2–9); moreover, the consumption of sacred flesh by nonpriests desecrates it (vv. 10–16). **2:** Be scrupulous about, lit. "keep away from [whenever they are impure]." This v. thus provides the caption for vv. 2–9. *Lest they profane My holy name:* Allowing impurity to come into contact with the sacred profanes the divine name, since the divine abode and the food gifts of the deity are thereby treated as though they were common. *Mine the LORD's,* better, "I am the LORD [who commands this]." **3–7:** Contact impurities (see ch 11) and bodily impurities (see chs 13–15). **3:** *Shall be cut off,* see 7.20, 21. **4:** Until he is clean, as stipulated by the laws that apply in each case. **7:** *Sun sets:* The rule applies to vv. 4b–6 (see 11.24, etc.; 15.17). **8:** See 11.39–40 n.; 17.15–16 n. **9:** *And die for it:* Death is depicted as the automatic and inevitable consequence of desecrating the sacred; see 10.2 n.

[10] No lay person shall eat of the sacred donations. No bound
or hired laborer of a priest shall eat of the sacred donations;
[11] but a person who is a priest's property by purchase may eat
of them; and those that are born into his household may eat of
his food. [12] If a priest's daughter marries a layman, she may not
eat of the sacred gifts; [13] but if the priest's daughter is widowed
or divorced and without offspring, and is back in her father's
house as in her youth, she may eat of her father's food. No lay
person may eat of it: [14] but if a man eats of a sacred donation
unwittingly, he shall pay the priest for the sacred donation,
adding one-fifth of its value. [15] But [the priests] must not allow the Israelites to profane the sacred donations that they set
aside for the LORD, [16] or to incur guilt requiring a penalty payment, by eating such sacred donations: for it is I the LORD who
make them sacred.

[17] The LORD spoke to Moses, saying: [18] Speak to Aaron and
his sons, and to all the Israelite people, and say to them:

When any man of the house of Israel or of the strangers in
Israel presents a burnt offering as his offering for any of the votive or any of the freewill offerings that they offer to the LORD,
[19] it must, to be acceptable in your favor, be a male without
blemish, from cattle or sheep or goats. [20] You shall not offer any
that has a defect, for it will not be accepted in your favor.

[21] And when a man offers, from the herd or the flock, a sacrifice of well-being to the LORD for an explicit[a] vow or as a freewill offering, it must, to be acceptable, be without blemish;
there must be no defect in it. [22] Anything blind, or injured, or
maimed, or with a wen, boil-scar, or scurvy—such you shall
not offer to the LORD; you shall not put any of them on the altar
as offerings by fire to the LORD. [23] You may, however, present
as a freewill offering an ox or a sheep with a limb extended or
contracted; but it will not be accepted for a vow. [24] You shall not
offer to the LORD anything [with its testes] bruised or crushed
or torn or cut. You shall have no such practices[b] in your own
land, [25] nor shall you accept such [animals] from a foreigner for
offering as food for your God, for they are mutilated, they have
a defect; they shall not be accepted in your favor.

[26] The LORD spoke to Moses, saying: [27] When an ox or a sheep
or a goat is born, it shall stay seven days with its mother, and

a Or "unspecified" or "extraordinary"; meaning of Heb. lephalle *uncertain.*
b I.e., mutilations.

10–16: The portions of the sacrificial offerings whose consumption is restricted to the priests are considered among the most sacred; contact between them and the lay person leads to their desecration. Nonpriests in the priest's employ, and the daughters of priests, may eat of them only as long as they are formally a part of the priest's household. **14:** On unwitting desecration of the sacred, see also 5.14–16. **15–16:** These vv. make it clear that actively preserving the boundaries between the sacred and the profane is the responsibility of the priests; see also 10.10.

22.17–25: Animals unfit for sacrifice. The disqualifying defects of a priest, just enumerated, and of a potential offering are analogous, but their ramifications are not. Whereas defective priests must not approach the altar lest they desecrate the sacred, they are not thereby excluded from the priesthood per se and may eat sacred flesh. Deformed animals do not cause desecration, but are simply not accepted and the person's sacrifice is deemed not to have been offered. For the underlying idea that what is placed on God's table must be without defect, see Mal. 1.6–14. **17–20:** The disqualifying blemishes in the burnt offering; see 1.3 n. **19:** *Acceptable,* see 1.3–4; 7.18 n. **21–23:** The disqualifying blemishes in the well-being sacrifice. From this passage it becomes evident that the votive offering is of a greater sanctity since all of the blemishes enumerated disqualify it, whereas the freewill offering, in which the deformities mentioned in v. 23 are acceptable, is of a lesser sanctity. Taken along with 7.12–18, these vv. confirm that the hierarchy of the three classes is "todah" (thanksgiving offering), "neder" (votive offering),"nedavah" (freewill offering), in descending order. **24:** Animals with defective or mutilated genitalia; this v. appears to pertain to all sacrificial animals. *No such practices in your own land:* The Rabbis took this as a general prohibition of castrating animals, even outside of the sacrificial context (*b. Ḥag.* 14b; *b. Shab.* 110b).

22.26–33: Rules of acceptability. The fifth and final speech of the section, containing three laws pertaining to the acceptability of sacrificial animals as a function of the time factor and concluding with a general exhortation. **26–27:** From the context (see also Exod. 22.29), an animal is not considered fit for sacrifice until it is viable, i.e., has safely gotten beyond the stage of a newborn and is a creature in its own right. **27:** *Offering*

from the eighth day on it shall be acceptable as an offering by fire to the LORD. 28 However, no animal from the herd or from the flock shall be slaughtered on the same day with its young.
29 When you sacrifice a thanksgiving offering to the LORD, sacrifice it so that it may be acceptable in your favor. 30 It shall be eaten on the same day; you shall not leave any of it until morning: I am the LORD.
31 You shall faithfully observe My commandments: I am the LORD. 32 You shall not profane My holy name, that I may be sanctified in the midst of the Israelite people—I the LORD who sanctify you, 33 I who brought you out of the land of Egypt to be your God, I the LORD.

23 The LORD spoke to Moses, saying: 2 Speak to the Israelite people and say to them:
These are My fixed times, the fixed times of the LORD, which you shall proclaim as sacred occasions.
3 On six days work may be done, but on the seventh day there shall be a sabbath of complete rest, a sacred occasion. You shall do no work; it shall be a sabbath of the LORD throughout your settlements.
4 These are the set times of the LORD, the sacred occasions, which you shall celebrate each at its appointed time: 5 In the

by fire, see 1.9 n. **28:** In contrast to the preceding, the humane concern seems to be the only plausible explanation for this restriction; see Exod. 23.19 (= 34.26; Deut. 14.21) and Deut. 22.6–7. All of the Torah law collections thus exhibit the same motif. It is not clear whether it expresses the sense that animals have emotional attachment to their young and experience distress at their fate or whether the aim is to sensitize humans to avoid unnecessary cruelty. **29–30:** See 7.12–15. Together with 19.5–8, these vv. are a repetition of 7.12–18. **31–33:** Elsewhere in the Holiness Legislation we have been told that compliance with the commandments enables the Israelites to absorb the holiness of God (19.2, 37; 20.7–8). This hortatory conclusion expresses the converse: that the failure to obey the commandments desecrates the name of God. This is only logical: The purpose of Israel's existence is to sanctify God's name, that is, to attest to His existence, to publicize His oneness, and to advertise His greatness, by worshipping Him and by keeping His laws. Their failure to do so has the opposite effect: His name is profaned, that is, His fame is diminished and His reputation tarnished.

23.1–44: Sacred times. God conveys to Moses, in five speeches, the laws of the weekly Sabbath and the annual holy days. Each of the Torah law collections contains a calendar of annual festivities, and most include a Sabbath law (some mention the Sabbath more than once). The command to abstain from labor on the Sabbath is found in all the collections, as is the tradition of festivals coinciding with the major events in the agricultural year: the early grain ripening, the reaping of the first produce, and the final ingathering. Some of the names of the festivals are shared by more than one law collection, as is the intrinsic connection between the springtime "matzot" festival ("Unleavened Bread") and the commemorative "pesaḥ" ("Passover") offering. The collections also agree that a central feature of at least some of the festivals is the "ḥag," which means "pilgrimage" (later called "ʿaliyah" or "ascent"), namely, the obligation to appear before the LORD. Despite these similarities, the Sabbath laws and festival calendars in the separate law collections differ in many ways. Tradition managed to combine all of the legislation into a coherent whole, creatively reconciling the contradictions and interpreting each repeated passage as providing some further detail. Critical scholarship generally views each version of the festival calendar as reflecting a stage in the historical development of the festivals. The laws in this ch provide a glimpse of the unique Priestly vision of the Sabbath and festivals. They are "sacred times," i.e., dates set apart from the remainder of the calendar and designated as "belonging to" the deity. Like sacred objects, persons, areas, and utterances, they may not be treated as common. Thus, only in P are the festivals, like the Sabbath, days of cessation from work, since engaging in daily activity (that is, labor) would amount to the desecration of the holy, which Priestly law, especially H, is at such pains to prevent. Further, in the Priestly view, though the festivals are determined by the agricultural year, they are primarily God's special occasions. Thus they are days on which He is worshipped—by His priests, in His abode—in a manner exceeding the daily routine. The literary structure of the ch reflects these two features. It is organized as a calendar of precise dates on which a cessation from labor is to be observed and a special "food-gift" offered to the LORD. Another Priestly festival calendar appears in Num. chs 28–29; that calendar is primarily concerned with the required offerings. **1–2:** The caption. The terms *fixed times of the LORD* and *sacred occasions* express the underlying idea for the festival legislation. *Which you shall proclaim:* The translation reflects the rabbinic tradition (*b. Rosh Hash.* 24a) that the dates of the festivals are determined by the Israelites, i.e., the proclamation of the New Moon and the

first month, on the fourteenth day of the month, at twilight,
there shall be a passover offering to the LORD, [6]and on the
fifteenth day of that month the LORD's Feast of Unleavened
Bread. You shall eat unleavened bread for seven days. [7]On the
first day you shall celebrate a sacred occasion: you shall not
work at your occupations. [8]Seven days you shall make offerings by fire to the LORD. The seventh day shall be a sacred occasion: you shall not work at your occupations.

[9]The LORD spoke to Moses, saying: [10]Speak to the Israelite
people and say to them:

When you enter the land that I am giving to you and you
reap its harvest, you shall bring the first sheaf of your harvest
to the priest. [11]He shall elevate the sheaf before the LORD for
acceptance in your behalf; the priest shall elevate it on the
day after the sabbath. [12]On the day that you elevate the sheaf,

introduction of the intercalated month, upon which the entire calendar depends, are the responsibility of the Sages. **3:** The weekly Sabbath. In the Priestly version of history, the weekly "shabbat" (lit. "cessation") was consecrated at creation (see Gen. 2.1–3) but was not implemented until the Israelites had become a people, the Tabernacle was ready to be erected, and the worship of the LORD was about to be inaugurated there (Exod. 31.12–17; 35.1–3). The Sabbath law is repeated several times in H (Lev. 19.3, 30; 26.2; see also Num. 15.32–36). In the non-Priestly literature the Sabbath and festivals are two distinct topics; only Priestly law, with its notion of sacred times, calls the Sabbath holy and mentions it alongside the festivals (see also Exod. 34.21, the location of which may have been influenced by this text). **4:** The repetition of the caption (see v. 2) may indicate that the inclusion of the weekly Sabbath among the "sacred times" was not part of an earlier version of the ch. See vv. 37–38 n. **5–8:** The annual "pesaḥ" sacrifice, which is not a sacred occasion but which immediately precedes the first of these, the "matzot" pilgrimage. The historical explanation for each, the connection between the two, and the details of their observance, including the abstention from leaven, are given by P in Exod. ch 12; here only those aspects relevant to the calendar of "sacred occasions" are mentioned. **5:** *The first month,* see Exod. 12.2 n. *On the fourteenth day of the month, at twilight:* The date of the evening is that of the preceding day (see v. 32; Exod. 12.18); only in postbiblical tradition was the method reversed and evenings given the date of the following day. *A passover offering,* "pesaḥ" (see Exod. 12.11–13) is the name of the sacrifice made in commemoration of the exodus; in postbiblical Judaism it became the name of the ensuing festival, the Feast of Unleavened Bread. **6:** *Feast,* Heb "ḥag," "pilgrimage." In the non-Priestly calendars there are three annual pilgrimages: the pilgrimage of Unleavened Bread ("ḥag ha-matzot"), the pilgrimage of Harvest ("katzir"), also called Weeks ("shavu'ot") and the pilgrimage of Ingathering ("ḥag ha'asif") or Booths ("sukkot"). Here and in Num. 28.26–31 there are only two, and "shavu'ot" is observed as a sacred occasion but not as a pilgrimage. In addition, in the non-Priestly tradition, the three pilgrimages are an absolute requirement, incumbent upon all males (Exod. 23.14, 17; 34.23–24; Deut. 16.16); in P, no such unqualified obligation is present. Those who do not make the pilgrimages must, however, observe the cessation from labor on the days designated as holy. *You shall eat unleavened bread:* Nowhere does P provide the rationale for this; the non-Priestly traditions explain it as a commemoration of the haste in which the Israelites left Egypt (see Exod. 12.39; Deut. 16.3). The Priestly tradition thus preserves the agricultural origin of the eating of "matzot" in the early spring, marking the very beginning of the barley harvest. *For seven days:* The eating of unleavened bread lasts seven days; the pilgrimage, unlike "sukkot" (see vv. 34, 39–40) does not. According to Exod. 13.6 only the seventh day was observed as a pilgrimage; in our text it appears that the pilgrimage was observed on the first day, the day after the "pesaḥ" offering, followed by six more days of eating unleavened bread; this is stated explicitly in Deut. 16.7–8. **7:** *You shall not work at your occupations:* This phrase recurs in vv. 8, 21, 25, 35, 36, prohibiting labor on the fully sacred festival days. It differs from the phrase "You shall do no work" used with regard to the weekly Sabbath and the Day of Atonement in vv. 3, 28, 31. Relying on Exod. 12.16, Ramban interpreted the difference to mean that labors required for the preparation of food are permissible on festival days but not on the Sabbath and Day of Atonement. **8:** *Offerings by fire,* see 1.9 n. *The seventh day:* The observance of the first and last days of the festival as full holy days, which became normative Jewish practice, is peculiar to the Priestly tradition (see vv. 36, 39; Exod. 12.16; Num. 28.24–25; 29.35). **9–22:** The second speech contains a lengthy set of instructions for the rituals commencing after the "matzot" festival and culminating seven weeks later with the second of the sacred occasions. **9–14:** The presentation (lit. "elevation"; see 7.30 n.) of the "'omer," or first sheaf of the new barley harvest, with its accompanying offerings, performed each year to secure the deity's blessing for the new crops. **11:** *For acceptance in your behalf,* see 1.3–4; 7.18 n.; 19.5; 22.19. *On the day after the sabbath:* This phrase (appearing also in v. 15) became a major source of

you shall offer as a burnt offering to the LORD a lamb of the first year without blemish. 13 The meal offering with it shall be two-tenths of a measure of choice flour with oil mixed in, an offering by fire of pleasing odor to the LORD; and the libation with it shall be of wine, a quarter of a *hin*. 14 Until that very day, until you have brought the offering of your God, you shall eat no bread or parched grain or fresh ears;[a] it is a law for all time throughout the ages in all your settlements.

15 And from the day on which you bring the sheaf of elevation offering—the day after the sabbath—you shall count off seven weeks. They must be complete: 16 you must count until the day after the seventh week—fifty days; then you shall bring an offering of new grain to the LORD. 17 You shall bring from your settlements two loaves of bread as an elevation offering; each shall be made of two-tenths of a measure of choice flour, baked after leavening, as first fruits to the LORD. 18 With the bread you shall present, as burnt offerings to the LORD, seven yearling lambs without blemish, one bull of the herd, and two rams, with their meal offerings and libations, an offering by fire of pleasing odor to the LORD. 19 You shall also offer one he-goat as a purification offering and two yearling lambs as a sacrifice of well-being. 20 The priest shall elevate these—the two lambs[b]—together with the bread of first fruits as an elevation offering before the LORD; they shall be holy to the LORD, for the priest. 21 On that same day you shall hold a celebration; it shall be a sacred occasion for you; you shall not work at your occupations. This is a law for all time in all your settlements, throughout the ages.

22 And when you reap the harvest of your land, you shall not reap all the way to the edges of your field, or gather the gleanings

a I.e., of the new crop. *b Meaning of Heb. uncertain.*

controversy in talmudic times (*Sifra ʾEmor* 12:4; *b. Menaḥ.* 66a). The Pharisaic sages, claiming that the word "sabbath" is used here in its nonspecific, literal sense ("cessation") and does not indicate the weekly Sabbath day, vehemently asserted that the "ʿomer" is presented on the day after the day of rest at the beginning of the "matzot" pilgrimage, namely, the sixteenth of Nisan; otherwise the definite article in the phrase "*the* sabbath" would have no referent. Though this view has been accepted by Jewish tradition, the more natural sense of the phrase is that the ceremony was to take place on the first day of the week (Sunday) following the pilgrimage. This was the view of the Boethusians as well as the Qumran sect, while the Samaritans and the Karaites held that the Sunday during the "matzot" pilgrimage was intended. **14:** As the presentation of the "ʿomer" marks the beginning of the new harvest, partaking of the new grain is prohibited until the ceremony has taken place. **15–22:** The new-grain ("first fruits"; see v. 20) offering, performed seven weeks later. **15–16:** The precise counting of seven weeks is required in order for the cessation from labor observed by the population at large, wherever they are, to coincide with the Temple observances prescribed, since in P this festival is not marked by a pilgrimage (see v. 6). Only with the acceptance of the rabbinic interpretation of "the day after the sabbath" (see v. 11) and the establishment of the calendar did it become possible to specify a fixed date (6 Sivan) for this holy day; prior to this the fiftieth day would have fallen on a different date each year. The counting later became a ceremony in its own right, called, in commemoration of the sheaf of barley presented at its start, the "Counting of [i.e., from] the ʿomer." The counting of seven weeks is also prescribed in Deut. 16.9, and even gives its name ("shavuʿot," "Weeks") to the festival observed at its conclusion (vv. 10 and 16; see also Exod. 34.22), but there it is to enable each landowner to determine the appropriate day for his own family's visit to the Temple. Here it has no name, but Num. 28.26 calls it "yom ha-bikkurim," "the Day of First Fruits" (see v. 20) and describes it further as "your Weeks." The connection of "shavuʿot" with the giving of the Torah at Sinai is not found in biblical tradition; it was implied in Jub. 6.17-31 and derived by the Rabbis, who held that the dates coincide. **17–20:** The offerings presented on the fiftieth day (in addition to those enumerated in Num. 28.26–31). They consist of a unique offering of two leavened loaves called the "bread of first fruits" (see v. 20), in thanks for the new grain harvest and accompanied by appropriate additional offerings. Among the latter are two yearling lambs offered as a well-being offering ("shelamim"). This is the only such offering made on behalf of the public, functioning here as a communal offering of thanksgiving. **20:** *First fruits:* The word "fruit" is misleading; the reference here is to the new crop of wheat (see Exod. 23.16; 34.22) from which these loaves are produced; see also 2.14–17. **21:** *On that same day,* see vv. 15–16 n. **22:** A partial quotation from 19.9–10, added here by association to the context of harvest time. **23–25:** The

of your harvest; you shall leave them for the poor and the stranger: I the LORD am your God.
23 The LORD spoke to Moses, saying: 24 Speak to the Israelite people thus: In the seventh month, on the first day of the
month, you shall observe complete rest, a sacred occasion
commemorated with loud blasts. 25 You shall not work at your
occupations; and you shall bring an offering by fire to the LORD.
26 The LORD spoke to Moses, saying: 27 Mark, the tenth day of
this seventh month is the Day of Atonement. It shall be a sacred occasion for you: you shall practice self-denial, and you
shall bring an offering by fire to the LORD; 28 you shall do no
work throughout that day. For it is a Day of Atonement, on
which expiation is made on your behalf before the LORD your
God. 29 Indeed, any person who does not practice self-denial
throughout that day shall be cut off from his kin; 30 and whoever
does any work throughout that day, I will cause that person to
perish from among his people. 31 Do no work whatever; it is a
law for all time, throughout the ages in all your settlements. 32 It
shall be a sabbath of complete rest for you, and you shall practice self-denial; on the ninth day of the month at evening, from
evening to evening, you shall observe this your sabbath.

33 The LORD spoke to Moses, saying: 34 Say to the Israelite
people:
On the fifteenth day of this seventh month there shall be
the Feast of Booths[a] to the LORD, [to last] seven days. 35 The
first day shall be a sacred occasion: you shall not work at your
occupations; 36 seven days you shall bring offerings by fire to

a. Others "Tabernacles."

third speech ordains the sacred occasion observed on the first day of the seventh month. The beginning of the seventh month marks the beginning of the agricultural year and opens the season of holy days culminating two weeks later in the Ingathering pilgrimage. The non-Priestly calendars are unfamiliar with this observance. **24:** *Commemorated with loud blasts,* correctly, "remembrance by shouting"; compare "a day of shouting" [NJPS: "a day when the horn is sounded"] in the parallel law in Num. 29.1. The Priestly literature contains a number of observances to remind God of the Israelite people (Exod. 28.12, 29; 30.16; Num. 31.54). These may be compared to the rainbow, designated by God as a reminder (to Himself!) of His promise to preserve humanity (Gen. 9.14–16). Num. 10.9–10 states that this is the function of the trumpet blasts sounded when Israel is in distress, to call their plight to God's attention and secure His assistance, or when celebrating festivals, New Moons, and appointed seasons. The annual "Day of Shouting" would thus be envisaged by the Priestly tradition as a day of Israel's crying out to God, to remind Him that they are His people and to secure His aid. In later tradition this observance developed in several directions. Though "teruʿah" literally means "raise a cry, shout," it is used in Num. 10.5–10 in conjunction with the sounding of trumpets, and in Lev. 25.9 in reference to the ram's horn. This led to the conclusion that here too the sound is to be made by the ram's horn or shofar. With the eventual adoption of the autumnal New Year as the primary one, the first day of the seventh month in the vernal calendar became New Year's Day ("Rosh Ha-Shanah"). Since, in ancient Near Eastern cultural milieu the heralding of the New Year was particularly associated with celebrations of kingship, Rosh Ha-Shanah became, among other things, a day to mark God's sovereignty as king. This development was certainly influenced by the numerous biblical references both to "teruʿah" "shouting" and to the sounding of ram's horns in contexts associated with kingship, both earthly and divine (e.g., 1 Kings 1.39; Pss. 47.2, 6; 98.6). Finally, since it opens a period leading up to the annual Day of Atonement (see ch 16; 23.26–32), Rosh Ha-Shanah became invested with the significance of the latter, and now marks the beginning of Judaism's annual ten-day penitential period. **26–32:** The Day of Atonement, also unknown outside of Priestly literature. On this day the Tabernacle is purged of the accumulated impurities and transgressions of the Israelite people (ch 16). The cessation of labor, which serves (along with the fast) to effect the purification and atonement rituals performed, marks this day too as holy time, a "sacred occasion," thus incorporating it into the annual cycle of such dates. **27:** *Practice self-denial,* fast; see 16.29 n. **28:** *For it is a Day of Atonement,* see 16.30. **29–30:** See 7.20, 21 n.; 17.10. **32:** *A sabbath of complete rest,* a phrase used only of the Sabbath (v. 3; Exod. 31.15; 35.2) and the Day of Atonement (see also 16.31), highlighting the strict and total abstention from labor required in order for the atonement rituals to be effective. *On the ninth day of the month at evening, from evening to evening,* see v. 5. *Sabbath,* cessation from labor. **33–42:** The final speech, containing the laws for the Sukkot festival and the concluding captions. **34:** *Feast,* "pilgrimage"; see v. 6. *Booths,* Heb "sukkot," "huts" serving as makeshift, temporary

the LORD. On the eighth day you shall observe a sacred occasion and bring an offering by fire to the LORD; it is a solemn
gathering:[a] you shall not work at your occupations.

37 Those are the set times of the LORD that you shall celebrate
as sacred occasions, bringing offerings by fire to the LORD—
burnt offerings, meal offerings, sacrifices, and libations, on each
day what is proper to it— 38 apart from the sabbaths of the LORD,
and apart from your gifts and from all your votive offerings and
from all your freewill offerings that you give to the LORD.

39 Mark, on the fifteenth day of the seventh month, when you
have gathered in the yield of your land, you shall observe the festival of the LORD [to last] seven days: a complete rest on the first
day, and a complete rest on the eighth day. 40 On the first day you
shall take the product of *hadar*[b] trees, branches of palm trees,
boughs of leafy[c] trees, and willows of the brook, and you shall rejoice before the LORD your God seven days. 41 You shall observe
it as a festival of the LORD for seven days in the year; you shall observe it in the seventh month as a law for all time, throughout the
ages. 42 You shall live in booths seven days; all citizens in Israel
shall live in booths, 43 in order that future generations may know
that I made the Israelite people live in booths when I brought
them out of the land of Egypt, I the LORD your God.
44 So Moses declared to the Israelites the set times of the LORD.

a Precise meaning of Heb. ʿaṣereth *uncertain.*
b Others "goodly"; exact meaning of Heb. hadar *uncertain. Traditionally the product is understood as "citron."* *c Meaning of Heb.* aboth *uncertain.*

shelters while working in the field or vineyard for several days at a time (see Isa. 1.8). The autumn pilgrimage is so named because its long duration—seven full days—necessitates the erection of such shelters to accommodate the many pilgrims during their stay in the Temple city (see vv. 43–44 n.). Notably, the texts that do not specify the fall pilgrimage lasts for seven days (Exod. 23.16; 34.22) do not call it Sukkot, whereas vv. 39 and 42, as well as Num. 29.12, refer to it as "the pilgrimage of the LORD"—the pilgrimage par excellence. Rabbinic tradition too called it simply "ḥag," (the) pilgrimage. **36:** *On the eighth day:* As distinct from the "matzot" observance, the concluding holy day is added to the first seven. Apparently, the pilgrimage is to last seven days, while on the eighth day, not called a "ḥag" but simply a "sacred occasion," a cessation from labor is to be observed by all—those who do not make the pilgrimage, those who do so but return home for the eighth day, and those who remain an additional day. The eighth day is unknown in the Torah outside of the Priestly tradition. *A solemn gathering,* Heb "ʿatzeret" (see Isa. 1.13; Joel 2.15; Amos 5.21; etc); this day is therefore later called "shemini ʿatzeret," "the solemn gathering of the eighth [day]." In Deut. 16.8 "ʿatzeret" refers to the solemnities on the final day of the "matzot" festival. Both apparently signify local festive gatherings, as distinct from the pilgrimage to the Temple city denoted by the word "ḥag." **37–38:** A summary caption. *Apart from the sabbaths of the LORD:* The Sabbath law in v. 3 may not have originally been part of the ch; see v. 4 n. **39–43:** The closing section repeats the date and length of the autumn pilgrimage, and the cessation of labor on the first and eighth days. Here, however, in place of the refrain "you shall offer food gifts to the LORD" are the additional observances of the festival. Since these are not sacrificial rites performed by the priests but are rather observed by the public at large, during their week-long visit to the Temple city, they are not included in what comes before the caption in vv. 37–38. **39:** *Observe the festival,* lit. "make a pilgrimage"; see v. 6 n. **40:** The "taking" of the four species of branches and boughs is evidently a ritual of joyous acknowledgment of the current year's agricultural abundance. It may also have been a form of supplication for the next year's rainfall, expected to begin at this period of the year; in later times it was so interpreted. In Neh. 8.14–15 (see nn. there) the branches (the list of trees is slightly different) were used for the construction of the booths, while according to rabbinic practice, they were gathered together in a bouquet and waved. Product, Heb "peri," "fruit"; possibly also boughs or branches. *Of hadar trees,* lit. "majestic" or beautiful trees (see translators' note *b*). Though no specific identification can be determined, ancient tradition (*b. Sukk.* 31a) ruled that the fruit of the citron (the "ʾetrog") is to be used. *Boughs of leafy trees,* traditionally, the myrtle. *You shall rejoice,* mentioned only here, a stark contrast to Deut., where rejoicing on the pilgrimages is mentioned several times (Deut. 16.11, 14, 15). **41:** *As a festival,* "as a pilgrimage"; see v. 6 n. **43–44:** Dwelling in booths for the seven days of the pilgrimage is here prescribed as a requirement, incumbent upon the entire population. The rationale differs from the one suggested above (see v. 34 n.) and is obscure. It is an attempt to historicize the central observance of the pilgrimage, suggesting that it commemorates the period of dwelling in the presence of the LORD's abode, the Tabernacle, in

24 The LORD spoke to Moses, saying:
2 Command the Israelite people to bring you clear oil of
beaten olives for lighting, for kindling lamps regularly. 3 Aaron
shall set them up in the Tent of Meeting outside the curtain of
the Pact [to burn] from evening to morning before the LORD
regularly; it is a law for all time throughout the ages. 4 He shall
set up the lamps on the pure[a] lampstand before the LORD [to
burn] regularly.

5 You shall take choice flour and bake of it twelve loaves, two-
tenths of a measure for each loaf. 6 Place them on the pure[a] table before the LORD in two rows, six to a row. 7 With each row
you shall place pure frankincense, which is to be a token offering[b] for the bread, as an offering by fire to the LORD. 8 He shall
arrange them before the LORD regularly every sabbath day—it
is a commitment for all time on the part of the Israelites. 9 They
shall belong to Aaron and his sons, who shall eat them in the
sacred precinct; for they are his as most holy things from the
LORD's offerings by fire, a due for all time.

10 There came out among the Israelites one whose mother was
Israelite and whose father was Egyptian. And a fight broke out
in the camp between that half-Israelite[c] and a certain Israelite.

a See note at Exod. 31.8. b See Lev. 2.2.
c Lit. "the son of an Israelite woman."

the wilderness. The notion that God housed the Israelites in booths in the wilderness is not attested elsewhere.

24.1–9: Oil and loaves. A divine speech containing two laws. The first law (vv. 2–4), instructions for the oil for the Tabernacle lampstand, is almost a repetition of Exod. 27.20–21; the second (vv. 5–9), the procedure for the loaves to be displayed on the table in the Tabernacle, completes the legislation of Exod. 25.23–30. Both laws pertain to the ritual acts performed by the high priest regularly, inside the Tabernacle, and constituting a perpetual (Heb "tamid") display of worship. The daily lighting and tending of the lampstand is also mentioned in Exod. 30.7–8, in the context of the high priest's incense offering, the third component of the ritual complex. The laws relating to daily Tabernacle routine may supplement the preceding ch, which details the calendar of perpetually recurring special occasions. **2–3:** See Exod. 27.20–21. **4:** The instructions for fashioning the Tabernacle lampstand ("menorah") in Exod. 25.31–40 do not explain how the lampstand is to be used. The legislation here clarifies the command to have light burn from evening to morning in the Tabernacle (Exod. 27.20–21). *The pure lampstand,* an ellipsis meaning "the lampstand made of pure gold"; see Exod. 25.31, 39; 31.8 (see translators' note *a*); 37.17; 39.37 (see translators' note *a*); Num. 8.4. **5–9:** The twelve loaves, known as the "showbread" or "Bread of Presence," are a symbolic offering, displayed but not sacrificed. They represent the twelve tribes of Israel and suggest dramatically their constant devotion to the deity who abides in their midst. In the Priestly Tabernacle, the deity is enshrined in the inner sanctum, but the furnishings and the acts of devotion performed upon them all belong to the outer sanctum, and the partition dividing the two realms is never breached. Thus God, even as His Presence dwells among the Israelites, is perceived as separate from them and noncorporeal. The pure table, i.e., "the table overlaid with pure gold"; see Exod. 25.23–24; 37.10–11. **7, 9:** *Offering(s) by fire,* better, "food gifts" (see 1.9 n.) **8:** *Every sabbath day:* The weekday morning entry of the high priest into the Tabernacle consisted of offering incense and tending the lampstand; on the Sabbath, the removal and replacement of the twelve display loaves is added. **9:** The loaves, having absorbed permanent, contagious sanctity from their close contact with the deity's Presence, can neither be discarded nor eaten by the laity. Conceptually, the loaves are a gift made by the Israelite people to the LORD, who gives it to the priests in recognition of their service (see 6.10–11).

24.10–23: The blasphemer. The report of an extraneous event interrupts the giving of the laws. A similar interruption is found in ch 10. In both cases, the resolution of the unforeseen situation requires direct divine intervention, and both times this leads to a brief legal discussion arising from the events (10.12–19; 24.17–22). Most significantly, both passages tell of flagrant crimes committed by individual Israelites in violation of the divinely imposed order established in the preceding chs: the crime of Nadab and Abihu against the indwelling deity, and the crime of the blasphemer against the sacred Name. Thus, both strata of the Priestly work, P and H (see ch 17), tell of a primal sin occurring shortly after the revelation of God, upsetting what should have been an untroubled relationship between God and His people and necessitating immediate action. The motif is also found in the non-Priestly tradition (Exod. chs 32–34; Deut. chs 9–10). **10:** *Half-Israelite:* The case was initially puzzling because of the blasphemer's mixed ancestry, but v. 16 renders the decision that both Israelites (citizens) and resident aliens were equally liable for blasphemy.

11 The son of the Israelite woman pronounced the Name in blasphemy, and he was brought to Moses—now his mother's name was Shelomith daughter of Dibri of the tribe of Dan— 12 and he was placed in custody, until the decision of the LORD should be made clear to them.

13 And the LORD spoke to Moses, saying: 14 Take the blasphemer outside the camp; and let all who were within hearing lay their hands upon his head, and let the whole community stone him.

15 And to the Israelite people speak thus: Anyone who blasphemes his God shall bear his guilt; 16 if he also pronounces the name LORD, he shall be put to death. The whole community shall stone him; stranger or citizen, if he has thus pronounced the Name, he shall be put to death.

17 If anyone kills any human being, he shall be put to death. 18 One who kills a beast shall make restitution for it: life for life. 19 If anyone maims his fellow, as he has done so shall it be done to him: 20 fracture for fracture, eye for eye, tooth for tooth. The injury he inflicted on another shall be inflicted on him. 21 One who kills a beast shall make restitution for it; but one who kills a human being shall be put to death. 22 You shall have one standard for stranger and citizen alike: for I the LORD am your God.

23 Moses spoke thus to the Israelites. And they took the blasphemer outside the camp and pelted him with stones. The Israelites did as the LORD had commanded Moses.

11: *Pronounced the Name in blasphemy:* Merely uttering "YHVH" is not a crime in P; throughout the Bible this is a normal and even commendable action. Nor is uttering God's name in falsehood or "in vain," though prohibited in the Decalogue (Exod. 20.7 || Deut. 5.11), a case of blasphemy. Blasphemy consists of cursing God (see Exod. 22.27 and n.; 1 Kings 21.10–13), that is, uttering an imprecation against Him in which His name is included ("May such-and-such befall YHVH"). As the divine Name is the one sacred "object" that can be used, or misused, by anyone at any time (see 5.20–26 n.), it is only logical that in the Holiness Legislation this is a sacrilege par excellence. **12–13:** The blasphemer is apprehended and held in custody until Moses seeks and receives oracular instruction from God (probably by means of the "'urim" on Aaron's breastplate; see Exod. 28.15, 30). Moses' inability to render a decision before consulting God occurs three more times in P, in the accounts of the second Passover, the Sabbath wood-gatherer, and the daughters of Zelophehad (Num. 9.1–14; 15.32–36; 27.1–11), and in all four cases the remedy for a specific circumstance becomes a permanent law applicable for future generations as well. **14:** The laying-on of hands (see 16.21) transfers to the blasphemer the guilt that the listeners have incurred by hearing the desecration of the sacred Name. This guilt will be eradicated along with the offender, who is stoned as an expression of the community's collective horror and its urgent need to be rid of the instrument of desecration. **15–16:** The legal decision is now generalized for future use. *Blasphemes his God ... also pronounces the name LORD,* lit. "curses his God and pronounces the name of YHVH"; thus, one who maligned God or invoked evil upon Him without actually pronouncing the Tetragrammaton would be exempt from the death penalty, since no actual desecration of the sacred Name would have taken place. **16:** *Stranger or citizen,* see 16.29 n. The logical counterpart to the "ger" or resident alien, familiar in the author's own period, would have been a non-Israelite accompanying the Israelites in the wilderness. In the author's mind such persons would have been the offspring of Israelite women and Egyptian men, conceived and born while still in Egypt (the non-Priestly tradition probably agrees; see Exod. 12.38). Such a person is cast in the central role of the narrative in order to establish the legal principle that the desecration of YHVH's name is a capital offense by definition, whether performed by an Israelite or a "ger." The Bible's principle of patrilineal descent would consider such a person Egyptian rather than Israelite. **17–22:** This short collection of laws is parenthetical and the narrative flow of vv. 10–16 continues, and concludes, in v. 23. It has been inserted here in accord with H's principle that laws pertaining to wrongs committed against one's fellow are the stuff of divine commands only if they impinge on the realm of the sacred. This brief law collection has a simple theme: With regard to the talionic or measure-for-measure ("eye-for-eye") rule in crimes and damages, the resident alien has precisely the same obligation as the citizen (v. 22). God's laws of fairness and justice are to be observed throughout the land where His Presence, with the holiness it effuses, resides. Unlike the obligation to worship Him, which rests upon Israel alone, the obligation to make fair restitution applies wherever God's Presence dwells. The similar statement in the law of the blasphemer (v. 16) accounts for the addition of this section here. **17:** See Gen. 9.6; Num. 35.31–34; outside of P: Exod. 21.12. The laws of asylum for unintentional homicide are designed to circumvent the death penalty when it is patently

BE-HAR בהר

25 The LORD spoke to Moses on Mount Sinai: [2] Speak to the Israelite people and say to them:

When you enter the land that I assign to you, the land shall observe a sabbath of the LORD. [3] Six years you may sow your field and six years you may prune your vineyard and gather in the yield. [4] But in the seventh year the land shall have a sabbath of complete rest, a sabbath of the LORD: you shall not sow your field or prune your vineyard. [5] You shall not reap the aftergrowth of your harvest or gather the grapes of your untrimmed vines; it shall be a year of complete rest for the land. [6] But you may eat whatever the land during its sabbath will produce—you, your male and female slaves, the hired and bound laborers who live with you, [7] and your cattle and the beasts in your land may eat all its yield.

[8] You shall count off seven weeks of years—seven times seven years—so that the period of seven weeks of years gives you a total of forty-nine years. [9] Then you shall sound the horn loud; in the seventh month, on the tenth day of the month—the Day

unethical; see in P Num. 35.9–33. **18:** Restitution can always be made for destruction of livestock; see Exod. 21.33–37. **19–20:** On the law of talion, or "eye-for-eye" principle, for bodily harm, see Exod. 21.23–25, where monetary compensation equivalent to the damages is probably meant (see v. 22). Rabbinic law interprets our text and Deut. 19.21 in the same fashion, but from the formulation of v. 20 it would seem that in Lev. the literal sense is intended. **21:** The recapitulation indicates the end of the interpolated section and reemphasizes the legal distinction between human life and the life of animals. **23:** The narrative resumes and concludes: The people carry out the instructions given to Moses in v. 14.

25.1–26.46: As the end of the first month of the second year after the exodus approaches (see Num. 1.1), the law-giving at Sinai draws to a close. During the first three weeks of the second month, some additional laws will be communicated (see Num. chs 5, 6; 8.23–26; 9.1–14; 10.1–10), but most of what is presented as divine communication to Moses during that period will consist of instructions for the journey to commence on the twentieth of the month. Thus, chs 25 and 26 mark the final stage of the law-giving. This is evident from the content of 26.3–45 and is stated explicitly in the concluding v. (26.46). (Ch 27 is chronologically displaced.) Chs 25 and 26 contain two integrally connected sections, the laws of the sabbatical and jubilee (25.1–26.2) and the speech of promise and threat (26.3–45). The theme of the first section is God's ownership of the land of Israel and the Israelites' status as hired tenants on His estate; the second details the wages promised to the tenants if they acquiesce in all the Landowner's demands and the measures He will take if they do not, culminating, if necessary, in their being evicted from His property. By combining two speeches into one, the longest in Lev., with the legal section flowing directly into the concluding exhortation, the author establishes this connection.

25.1–26.2: Sabbatical and jubilee laws. 25.1: *On Mount Sinai:* Midrashic interpretation took this to mean that the divine speech recorded here was communicated to Moses during one of his visits to the top of the mountain. In P, however, Moses ascended Sinai only once, for the sole purpose of receiving the instructions for the Tabernacle and the priesthood. Thus here the words "behar sinay" mean "at (not on) Mount Sinai," i.e., [in the Tabernacle which stood] at [the foot of] Mount Sinai; see 7.38 n. **2–7:** The sabbatical year. The command to release and abandon the produce of the seventh year appears in Exod. 23.11, where its purpose is to allow the poor to gather and eat what the owner leaves behind. The year of release in Deut. also highlights social concerns, but it pertains to the cancellation of debts rather than the produce of the land (Deut. 15.1–6). Here, uniquely, it is forbidden to work the land in the seventh year, while its produce may be gathered and eaten—by the landholder. In Priestly law the poor are provided for by other measures (19.9–10; 23.22). **2:** *Assign to you,* correctly, "give you" as in 14.34. *A sabbath of the LORD:* Only here is the seventh year called "shabbat of the LORD," thus making it equivalent to the other appointed times and sacred occasions of the LORD (see ch 23). **4:** *Sabbath of complete rest,* a sabbath of the LORD, similarly with regard to the weekly Sabbath and the Day of Atonement; see 23.32 n. **5:** *Aftergrowth,* plants that spring up on their own, without deliberate sowing. **6:** Normal, wholesale reaping and harvesting is not permitted; rather, the landholder may gather as needed in order to feed his own household, and his livestock may graze. **8–22:** The jubilee year. It is not known whether the jubilee was ever observed in actual practice. There is no mention of the jubilee in biblical books dating from First Temple times, and according to the Rabbis it was not observed in Second Temple times at all (*b. 'Arak.* 32b). There are, however, indications that a fifty-year cycle was employed in the calendar in ancient times; traditions of calculating the jubilees survived beyond the biblical period. The primary law of the jubilee (vv. 8–13) introduces its frequency and onset, its inauguration, its

of Atonement—you shall have the horn sounded throughout
your land 10 and you shall hallow the fiftieth year. You shall
proclaim release[a] throughout the land for all its inhabitants.
It shall be a jubilee[b] for you: each of you shall return to his
holding and each of you shall return to his family. 11 That fiftieth year shall be a jubilee for you: you shall not sow, neither
shall you reap the aftergrowth or harvest the untrimmed vines,
12 for it is a jubilee. It shall be holy to you: you may only eat the
growth direct from the field.

13 In this year of jubilee, each of you shall return to his holding. 14 When you sell property to your neighbor,[c] or buy any
from your neighbor, you shall not wrong one another. 15 In
buying from your neighbor, you shall deduct only for the number of years since the jubilee; and in selling to you, he shall
charge you only for the remaining crop years: 16 the more such
years, the higher the price you pay; the fewer such years, the
lower the price; for what he is selling you is a number of harvests. 17 Do not wrong one another, but fear your God; for I the
LORD am your God.

a Others "liberty." *b Heb.* yobel, *"ram" or "ram's horn."*
c I.e., fellow Israelite; see v. 46.

sanctity, and its two central features: the land release and the release of indentured persons. This is followed by a brief section detailing the implications for the sale of real estate between jubilees (vv. 14–17). The law then promises prosperity and security as reward for faithful observance (vv. 18–19) and concludes by reassuring the uneasy that God will provide (vv. 20–22). **8:** *Weeks of years,* lit. "sabbaths of years"; "shabbat" in the sense of "week" is common in later Heb. **9:** The fiftieth year follows the seventh sabbatical year (though rabbinic tradition records other views as well). Unlike the seventh year, which is called a "shabbat" but not referred to as holy, it is sacred. The jubilee year is inaugurated in the seventh month because the autumnal New Year, which later became dominant in the Jewish calendar but has biblical roots, is the start of the agricultural cycle (see Exod. 23.16 n.; 34.22 n.). *On the tenth day of the month—the Day of Atonement:* Perhaps the tenth of the month was thought of, as it was in later times, as the conclusion of the New Year's celebrations. **10:** *Release,* Heb "deror"; see Isa. 61.1; Jer. 34.8; Ezek. 46.17. A related term, "andurāru," is known from Mesopotamia, where it indicates the general release proclaimed occasionally by kings in order to create or restore economic stability. This second aspect of the jubilee, the release of indentured persons, is detailed in vv. 39–46. *Jubilee:* Ancient translators drew an artificial connection between Heb "yovel" and the similar sounding Latin "jubilare," "shout for joy"; thus the English "jubilee" suggests the idea of jubilation not present in the Heb. Outside of the Priestly literature "yovel" indicates a ram (Josh. 6.4–6) or a ram's horn (Exod. 19.13), and since the fiftieth year is inaugurated by the sounding of the ram's horn (v. 9), some feel that this has given its name to the institution. But the word "shofar" rather than "yovel" is mentioned in v. 9, and throughout the ch (and in 27.17–24; Num. 36.4) it is used to denote what takes place during the fiftieth year and not the manner in which the year is heralded. "Yovel" here seems to be derived from "y-b-l," "bring" and to mean "sending forth, homebringing" or simply liberation, as reflected in LXX and realized in the 12th c. by Abraham Ibn Ezra. *Each of you shall return to his holding:* The basic postulate of the jubilee, from which the legislation in this ch (and that in 27.17–24; Num. 36.4) derives, is that once the Israelites have entered Canaan, the land is divided up (by lot, see Num. 33.54) in perpetuity. The land of Canaan is not the Israelites' property, it is rather a "holding" ("'aḥuzah"; see 14.34; Gen. 17.8; 48.4; Deut. 32.49); so are the plots of land held by each tribe, clan, and family. Collectively and individually, these holdings are not theirs to buy, sell, and reapportion. The Israelites are mere leaseholders, tenants on the divine estate, and the holdings God has parceled out to them are inalienable. Though the ultimate effect of this far-reaching legislation may be social, the pervasive concern is religious, indeed theocentric. The jubilee, like the Sabbath and festivals, is an assertion of God's exclusive proprietorship and dominion, designed to keep the Israelites constantly aware that they are His indentured servants (vv. 42, 55). Once again the law-giver expresses the idea that social legislation is included among God's commands only insofar as it impinges on the sacred; see nn. to chs 17–26, 18, 19; 24.17–22. **11:** See vv. 5–6. Since the fiftieth year always follows a sabbatical year, a two-year cessation of agricultural activity is entailed. **14–17:** *Buying* and *selling* of land in Canaan is actually a matter of leasing until the jubilee. **17:** *Wrong:* i.e., cheat, by deceitfully inflating the price. But fear your God, see 19.14 n.; 25.36.

18 You shall observe My laws and faithfully keep My rules, that you may live upon the land in security; 19 the land shall yield its fruit and you shall eat your fill, and you shall live upon it in security. 20 And should you ask, "What are we to eat in the seventh year, if we may neither sow nor gather in our crops?" 21 I will ordain My blessing for you in the sixth year, so that it shall yield a crop sufficient for three years. 22 When you sow in the eighth year, you will still be eating old grain of that crop; you will be eating the old until the ninth year, until its crops come in.

23 But the land must not be sold beyond reclaim, for the land is Mine; you are but strangers resident with Me. 24 Throughout the land that you hold, you must provide for the redemption of the land.

25 If your kinsman is in straits and has to sell part of his holding, his nearest redeemer[a] shall come and redeem what his kinsman has sold. 26 If a man has no one to redeem for him, but prospers and acquires enough to redeem with, 27 he shall compute the years since its sale, refund the difference to the man to whom he sold it, and return to his holding. 28 If he lacks sufficient means to recover it, what he sold shall remain with the purchaser until the jubilee; in the jubilee year it shall be released, and he shall return to his holding.

29 If a man sells a dwelling house in a walled city, it may be redeemed until a year has elapsed since its sale; the redemption period shall be a year. 30 If it is not redeemed before a full year has elapsed, the house in the walled city shall pass to the purchaser beyond reclaim throughout the ages; it shall not be released in the jubilee. 31 But houses in villages that have no encircling walls shall be classed as open country: they may be redeemed, and they shall be released through the jubilee. 32 As for the cities of the Levites, the houses in the cities they hold—the Levites shall forever have the right of redemption. 33[b] Such property as may be redeemed from the Levites—houses sold in a city they hold—shall be released through the jubilee; for the houses in the cities of the Levites are their holding among the Israelites. 34 But the unenclosed land about their cities cannot be sold, for that is their holding for all time.

a *I.e., the closest relative able to redeem the land.*
b *Meaning of first half of verse uncertain.*

20: *And should you ask:* Though the issue should properly have arisen after v. 7, it applies even more urgently here; see below. **21–22:** The people are told to trust in God and do as commanded. The promise given is most easily understood elliptically. Crops sown in the fall of the sixth year and reaped in the spring will suffice for (1) the remainder of that year and (2) the entire seventh year. In the fall of the eighth year new crops may be sown, so the grain from the sixth year will suffice until the spring of the eighth, two years altogether. And if the eighth year is a jubilee, the produce of the sixth year will last until (3) the spring of the ninth year, when the crops sown in the fall following the jubilee come in, a total of three years. **23–55:** While the jubilee effects a general, universal release, throughout the years leading up to it society must provide for the restoration of property and liberty whenever possible; the jubilee is the last resort. The basic law stating this (vv. 23–24) is followed by a series of specific cases spelling out its specific ramifications. **23:** *But,* better, "Furthermore"; that is, in addition to all of the above and prior to it. *Strangers resident,* see 16.29 n. **24:** *Redemption:* In the Bible this term retains its literal, commercial sense, as in reclaiming a pawned item or mortgaged property. A person who has lost his property or liberty must be enabled to regain it. This obligation is twofold: It devolves upon the buyer, who is required to allow the person in question to repurchase property or liberty, and upon the kinsmen of the person in question, who must assist if the means to do so do not suffice. Otherwise the jubilee, when it eventually arrives, effects the redemption by default. Speaking of God as Israel's "Redeemer" is thus a metaphor. Since Israel is God's near kinsman, when Israel is in distress it is God's veritable obligation to come to its aid and make whatever efforts are necessary to extricate it from its predicament. **25–28:** An Israelite is forced to sell (i.e., lease) a portion of an ancestral heritage. Prior to the jubilee, the buyer must enable the seller, or a kinsman acting on the seller's behalf, to reclaim at a price calculated in view of the number of years remaining until the jubilee. But even if neither the seller nor the kinsmen can come up with the necessary funds, the sale remains in effect only until the jubilee. **29–34:** The only exception to the above is the sale (i.e., lease) of strictly urban property. The seller and the kinsmen have but one year to come up with the redemption price; if they default, the sale is final. But even here, several exceptions are enumerated. **35–37:** According to the simplest interpretation, the

35 If your kinsman, being in straits, comes under your authority, and you hold him as though a resident alien, let him live by your side: 36 do not exact from him advance or accrued interest,[a] but fear your God. Let him live by your side as your kinsman. 37 Do not lend him your money at advance interest, or give him your food at accrued interest. 38 I the LORD am your God, who brought you out of the land of Egypt, to give you the land of Canaan, to be your God.

39 If your kinsman under you continues in straits and must give himself over to you, do not subject him to the treatment of a slave. 40 He shall remain with you as a hired or bound laborer; he shall serve with you only until the jubilee year. 41 Then he and his children with him shall be free of your authority; he shall go back to his family and return to his ancestral holding.—42 For they are My servants, whom I freed from the land of Egypt; they may not give themselves over into servitude.—43 You shall not rule over him ruthlessly; you shall fear your God. 44 Such male and female slaves as you may have—it is from the nations round about you that you may acquire male and female slaves. 45 You may also buy them from among the children of aliens resident among you, or from their families that are among you, whom they begot in your land. These shall become your property: 46 you may keep them as a possession for your children after you, for them to inherit as property for all time. Such you may treat as slaves. But as for your Israelite kinsmen, no one shall rule ruthlessly over the other.

47 If a resident alien among you has prospered, and your kinsman being in straits, comes under his authority and gives himself over to the resident alien among you, or to an offshoot of an alien's family, 48 he shall have the right of redemption even after he has given himself over. One of his kinsmen shall

a I.e., interest deducted in advance, or interest added at the time of repayment.

impoverished Israelite may have no recourse but to enter the kinsman's household and become a dependent. The kinsman, however, is commanded to refrain from exacting interest on the sustenance provided, so that the poor relative may save enough to regain economic independence. The prohibition of interest, which outside of the Priestly law is universal (Exod. 22.24; Deut. 23.20–21) and stems from explicitly humanitarian concerns, is restricted here to the live-in relative attempting to redeem property or liberty. Here, the land of Canaan is God's estate, and the command for the tenants to behave charitably toward one another derives from this. **38:** A transitional v. concluding the laws of land release; the remainder of the ch deals with the release of indentured persons. **39–46:** In contrast to the picture emerging from the non-Priestly law collections (see Exod. 21.2–11 n.; Deut. 15.12–18 n.), the Priestly legal tradition recognizes no Israelite slavery as such. What appears to be servitude is not; an Israelite forced to become indentured to another Israelite has the status of a hired laborer. Moreover, this servitude is temporary, and the option of remaining in slavery forever, available in the non-Priestly collections (Exod. 21.5–6; Deut. 15.16–18), is not provided. **39:** *Continues,* not reflected in the Heb. The dependent relative, in a dire situation, may become a kinsman's indentured laborer even without the prior, dependent stage. **40:** *Only until the jubilee year:* Logical, but not explicit, is the possibility that the indentured servant may save enough to redeem himself before the jubilee arrives or that his kinsmen may help him to do so. **41:** This v. indicates that the servitude envisaged was subsequent to the sale of property. When the jubilee arrives, the servants are released from their servitude and their ancestral property is released from its buyers, so persons and lands are reunited. *And his children with him:* Here, in contrast to Exod. 21.3–4, even children born during the long years of servitude do not become the property of the employer. **42–43:** Israelites, like landholdings in Canaan, are divine property; thus they are released in the jubilee. Israelites are servants of God alone: He took them out of Egypt not in order to make them free but to make them slaves—of His own. This idea has practical as well as theological implications: Indentured Israelites may not be exploited or treated with the harshness with which a master may legitimately treat actual slaves. **44–46:** These vv. make clear that the Priestly law has no principled objection to slavery per se. Non-Israelites may be enslaved, and they and their progeny become the permanent property of their master. **44:** *The nations round about you:* According to the picture of history envisaged by H, the land of Canaan itself will have been evacuated of its former inhabitants (see 18.24–30), so non-Israelite slaves can only be purchased from foreign nations. **47–54:** The Israelite forced to sell (i.e., indenture) himself to a non-Israelite is entitled to redeem himself; moreover, the members of his immediate and even extended family are obligated to make every effort to redeem him if he cannot redeem himself. As with landholdings (see vv. 14–17), the redemption price depends on the number of years

redeem him, 49 or his uncle or his uncle's son shall redeem
him, or anyone of his family who is of his own flesh shall redeem him; or, if he prospers, he may redeem himself. 50 He
shall compute with his purchaser the total from the year he
gave himself over to him until the jubilee year; the price of
his sale shall be applied to the number of years, as though it
were for a term as a hired laborer under the other's authority.
51 If many years remain, he shall pay back for his redemption
in proportion to his purchase price; 52 and if few years remain
until the jubilee year, he shall so compute: he shall make payment for his redemption according to the years involved. 53 He
shall be under his authority as a laborer hired by the year; he
shall not rule ruthlessly over him in your sight. 54 If he has not
been redeemed in any of those ways, he and his children with
him shall go free in the jubilee year. 55 For it is to Me that the Israelites are servants: they are My servants, whom I freed from
the land of Egypt, I the LORD your God.

26 You shall not make idols for yourselves, or set up for
yourselves carved images or pillars, or place figured[a]
stones in your land to worship upon, for I the LORD am your
God. 2 You shall keep My sabbaths and venerate My sanctuary,
Mine, the LORD's.

BE-ḤUKKOTAI בחקתי

3 If you follow My laws and faithfully observe My commandments, 4 I will grant your rains in their season, so that the earth
shall yield its produce and the trees of the field their fruit.
5 Your threshing shall overtake the vintage, and your vintage
shall overtake the sowing; you shall eat your fill of bread and
dwell securely in your land.

6 I will grant peace in the land, and you shall lie down untroubled by anyone; I will give the land respite from vicious
beasts, and no sword shall cross your land. 7 You shall give
chase to your enemies, and they shall fall before you by the
sword. 8 Five of you shall give chase to a hundred, and a hundred of you shall give chase to ten thousand; your enemies
shall fall before you by the sword.

a *Meaning of Heb.* maskith *uncertain.*

remaining until the jubilee, since at that time the Israelite will be released in any case. **47:** *Resident alien,* see. 16.29 n. It is assumed that the "ger" must, and can be compelled to, comply with the law requiring Israelite self-redemption or the release of the Israelite when the jubilee arrives. *An offshoot of an alien's family,* mentioned only here, but clearly indicating that in the Priestly view the "ger" does not eventually become an Israelite by assimilation, much less by conversion (unknown in biblical times). Rather, though he and his descendants may dwell and prosper in the land of Israel, they retain their non-Israelite status. For P, the only Israelites are the biological descendants of Jacob. **54:** *He and his children with him,* see v. 41. **55:** Repeating the rationale of v. 42, pertinent here and serving to conclude the corpus of jubilee legislation.

26.1–2: The ch division misconstrues these two vv. as the introduction to what follows, but they are in fact the conclusion to what precedes. They echo commands in ch 19; v. 1 elaborates on 19.4, and v. 2 repeats 19.30. They act as concluding refrains, expressing three of the basic concerns of the Holiness legislation and signaling the end of its body of laws.

26.3–45: Promise and threat. The promise of reward and the threat of divine chastisement. By analogy to Deut. ch 28 and the treaty curses found in Mesopotamian texts, scholars generally refer to this section as the "blessings and curses" of the Holiness Legislation. But neither "bless" nor "curse" appears in the text, nor does the idea that these terms imply. **3–13:** The reward for compliance: God will give the Israelites peace and prosperity, safety from wild beasts, population increase, and victory over their enemies. Further, He will give them the security that comes from the certain knowledge that all this is assured them. The aim of the exodus will be accomplished: Israel will become God's people, that is, His loyal servants; He will take up residence in their midst, enshrined in the earthly abode which they will fashion for Him, and reign over them as their liege Lord. **3:** *If you follow My laws,* all the laws that have been conveyed, from the beginning of Lev. **5:** *Threshing shall overtake the vintage, and your vintage shall overtake the sowing:* There will be so much grain that threshing will continue into late summer, when the vines are picked; this will continue until fall when sowing begins. See Amos 9.13. **9:** *Maintain My covenant:* In P this means "uphold My promise." In Priestly tradition the covenant is the commitment made by God to Abraham (Gen. 17.4–8) and

9 I will look with favor upon you, and make you fertile and
multiply you; and I will maintain My covenant with you. 10 You
shall eat old grain long stored, and you shall have to clear out
the old to make room for the new.
11 I will establish My abode in your midst, and I will not
spurn you. 12 I will be ever present in your midst: I will be your
God, and you shall be My people. 13 I the LORD am your God
who brought you out from the land of the Egyptians to be their
slaves no more, who broke the bars of your yoke and made you
walk erect.

14 But if you do not obey Me and do not observe all these
commandments, 15 if you reject My laws and spurn My rules,
so that you do not observe all My commandments and you
break My covenant, 16 I in turn will do this to you: I will wreak
misery upon you—[a]consumption and fever, which cause the
eyes to pine and the body to languish; you shall sow your seed
to no purpose, for your enemies shall eat it. 17 I will set My face
against you: you shall be routed by your enemies, and your
foes shall dominate you. You shall flee though none pursues.
18 And if, for all that, you do not obey Me, I will go on to discipline you sevenfold for your sins, 19 and I will break your
proud glory. I will make your skies like iron and your earth like

a Precise nature of these ills is uncertain.

repeated to Moses (Exod. 6.2–8): to make Israel numerous and to give them the land of Canaan as a hereditary holding (see 25.10 n.). **11:** *Spurn,* see v. 15 n. **13:** *To be their slaves no more,* for the implication, see 25.42, 55. *Broke the bars:* Though God's purpose in bringing Israel out of Egyptian slavery was to make them His own slaves, in the course of doing so He did indeed break their yoke and enable them to walk erect. The point is to remind Israel what He is capable of doing for them if they comply with His wishes. **14–45:** The results of noncompliance. As in Deut. ch 28, considerably more space is given to the threats than the promises; but in direct contrast to Deut. 11.13–17 (recited daily as part of the Shema) and 28.15–68, the disasters threatened here are not punishments. Rather they are warnings arranged as a series of successive attempts to discipline the Israelites, that is, to force them into obedience. Each stage demonstrates an example of the sort of deadly disaster God may let loose upon them if they persist in their refusal to obey. Even the final stage, though it includes the element of vengeance and seems at first to be aimed at bringing Israel's national existence to an end (as in Deut.), is finally revealed to be yet another attempt at making Israel walk the straight and narrow. This stage, entailing destruction and exile, will culminate in Israel's remorse; when this occurs God will remember His covenant and try once again to implement His plan of abiding in their midst and ruling over them. The effect of this diatribe is complex. On the one hand, it rains down upon the listener an unending barrage of fire and brimstone. The very contemplation of the horrors described forces the individual to consider the consequences of acting against the will of a God so uncompromising and so powerful. On the other hand, it casts God not in the role of the petty tyrant exacting retaliation for each infringement but rather as the undeterred ruler, patient but far from passive, who realizes that He may not achieve His end immediately and that severe measures may be necessary. God is pictured here as compelled to give repeated second chances, since He is bound and determined to have His way and cannot simply give up. In Priestly thought, the covenant cannot ever become null and void. **15:** *Reject, spurn,* lit. graphic expressions of distaste: "you will find disgusting and your throat will vomit up"; see vv. 11, 30, 43, 44. *So that you do not observe all My commandments:* This is not a gradual abandonment of God's laws after a period during which they were obeyed (as in Deut.), but rather an initial, wholesale rejection of the commandments and successive attempts by God to "try again" to beat Israel into submission. Thus it is incorrect to speak of repentance here, since repentance consists of the return to former righteousness. *And you break My covenant:* This seems inconsistent with the Priestly view that the covenant is God's to keep (or break), not Israel's; only in the non-Priestly tradition is the covenant thought to be mutual. Probably, as in Gen. 17.14, the idea is that by refusing to obey God's commands the Israelites move God to abrogate His promise. **16–17:** The first attempt. An onslaught of diseases, followed by enemy incursions upon Israel's territory and despoilation of her crops. The fear instilled by the occupier's force will become so all-pervasive that the Israelites will flee though none pursues (v. 17). **16:** *Misery,* better: "shock." **18–20:** The second attempt. If the measures described do not succeed, they will be followed by the withholding of rain and the resultant crop failure. **18:** *Sevenfold for your sins,* an expression signifying the maximum punishment; see Gen. 4.15, 24. **21–22:** The third attempt; the reverse of v. 6. *Wild beasts* are one of God's four weapons of destruction in Ezek. 14.12–23. **23–26:** Sword, pestilence, and

copper, 20 so that your strength shall be spent to no purpose. Your land shall not yield its produce, nor shall the trees of the land yield their fruit.

21 And if you remain hostile toward Me and refuse to obey Me, I will go on smiting you sevenfold for your sins. 22 I will loose wild beasts against you, and they shall bereave you of your children and wipe out your cattle. They shall decimate you, and your roads shall be deserted.

23 And if these things fail to discipline you for Me, and you remain hostile to Me, 24 I too will remain hostile to you: I in turn will smite you sevenfold for your sins. 25 I will bring a sword against you to wreak vengeance for the covenant; and if you withdraw into your cities, I will send pestilence among you, and you shall be delivered into enemy hands. 26 When I break your staff of bread, ten women shall bake your bread in a single oven; they shall dole out your bread by weight, and though you eat, you shall not be satisfied.

27 But if, despite this, you disobey Me and remain hostile to Me, 28 I will act against you in wrathful hostility; I, for My part, will discipline you sevenfold for your sins. 29 You shall eat the flesh of your sons and the flesh of your daughters. 30 I will destroy your cult places and cut down your incense stands, and I will heap your carcasses upon your lifeless fetishes.

I will spurn you. 31 I will lay your cities in ruin and make your sanctuaries desolate, and I will not savor your pleasing odors. 32 I will make the land desolate, so that your enemies who settle in it shall be appalled by it. 33 And you I will scatter among the nations, and I will unsheath the sword against you. Your land shall become a desolation and your cities a ruin.

34 Then shall the land make up for its sabbath years throughout the time that it is desolate and you are in the land of your enemies; then shall the land rest and make up for its sabbath years. 35 Throughout the time that it is desolate, it shall observe the rest that it did not observe in your sabbath years while you

famine, the three other divine judgments mentioned in Ezek. ch 14. Typically all three occur together, the latter two being the horrible results of the siege brought about by the former. Yet they are three separate phenomena, bringing the total number of measures employed by God to pressure His people into compliance to seven, a number commonly used in biblical literature to express completeness. **23:** *Hostile,* uncertain; it probably means something like "uncaring, indifferent"; see v. 24. **24:** *I too will remain hostile to you:* He will treat them as they have treated Him. The mutuality is telling: God requires Israel's obedience the same way that they require His providence and kindness; if they withhold what He demands, He will do likewise. **26:** *Staff of bread,* what one leans upon in order to remain erect; see Isa. 3.1. **27–33:** The final blow. The enemy's siege of Israel's towns will culminate in the worst of its horrors, cannibalism resulting from dire famine (a common ancient Near Eastern trope in accounts of siege). It will end with the utter destruction of the towns, followed by desolation of the land and the dispersion of the population. **28:** *Wrathful hostility,* see v. 21. **30:** The invading enemy will destroy all the local shrines and cultic objects in its path, the very existence of which is a symptom of Israel's widespread, ongoing insubordination. The image of heaping the carcasses of slaughtered Israelites upon the lifeless idols of the false deities they worshipped is a particularly ironic instance of poetic justice. *I will spurn you:* The translation makes this the beginning of a new thought, but this is not warranted. For the meaning of the phrase see v. 15 n. **31:** *Sanctuaries:* The existence of multiple local sanctuaries is another manifestation of Israel's chronic disobedience. See 17.8–9 n. **33:** *And I will unsheath the sword against you,* "after you," as you go into exile. *Your land shall become a desolation and your cities a ruin:* The enemies who will have by then settled in their land (v. 32) are not pictured as rebuilding it. **34–35:** Israel's sustained failure to obey God's commands will necessarily have included the repeated nonobservance of the sabbatical year (25.2–7). But when Israel goes into exile and its land is deserted with none to work it, it will have a permanent "sabbath" and be repaid the rest it was denied. Rabbinic tradition interpreted these vv. more literally, viewing restitution for the land's missed sabbaths as the actual purpose of the exile and taking the sin of ignoring the sabbatical year as its specific cause. The plain sense of the text does not imply this, however. In contrast to the Deuteronomic doctrine that Israel's demise will have a particular cause, the worship of foreign deities, this ch insists that it is the nonobservance of the totality of the commandments that will bring about the horrible fate described. **36–38:** After focusing momentarily on the land, the speaker now returns to the fate of the dispersed former inhabitants, not all of whom will survive the enemy assault. They will

were dwelling upon it. 36 As for those of you who survive, I will cast a faintness into their hearts in the land of their enemies. The sound of a driven leaf shall put them to flight. Fleeing as though from the sword, they shall fall though none pursues. 37 With no one pursuing, they shall stumble over one another as before the sword. You shall not be able to stand your ground before your enemies, 38 but shall perish among the nations; and the land of your enemies shall consume you.

39 Those of you who survive shall be heartsick over their iniquity in the land of your enemies; more, they shall be heartsick over the iniquities of their fathers; 40 and they shall confess their iniquity and the iniquity of their fathers, in that they trespassed against Me, yea, were hostile to Me. 41 When I, in turn, have been hostile to them and have removed them into the land of their enemies, then at last shall their obdurate[a] heart humble itself, and they shall atone for their iniquity. 42 Then will I remember My covenant with Jacob; I will remember also My covenant with Isaac, and also My covenant with Abraham; and I will remember the land.

43 For the land shall be forsaken of them, making up for its sabbath years by being desolate of them, while they atone for their iniquity; for the abundant reason that they rejected My rules and spurned My laws. 44 Yet, even then, when they are in the land of their enemies, I will not reject them or spurn them so as to destroy them, annulling My covenant with them: for I the LORD am their God. 45 I will remember in their favor the covenant with the ancients, whom I freed from the land of Egypt in the sight of the nations to be their God: I, the LORD.

46 These are the laws, rules, and instructions that the LORD established, through Moses on Mount Sinai, between Himself and the Israelite people.

a Others "uncircumcised"; lit. "blocked."

be persecuted by their captors and consumed by fear of dangers real and imagined; finally they will simply cease to exist. **39:** *Those of you who survive:* The repetition of the phrase (see v. 36) indicates that only a fraction of those who survive to go into exile will also survive the tribulations of the exile itself. After a few generations, hardly any will be left even of these. *Be heartsick over,* correctly, "will rot away because of," become fewer and fewer with the passage of time. The repeated refusal of earlier generations to obey God's commands will be the cause of the misery of later ones. **40–42:** At last, the remaining survivors will consider the cause of what has happened, will realize it was their own (and their ancestors' own) obduracy that caused their plight, and God will respond appropriately. *Confess:* It is not the ceremonial, ritual confession that accompanies sacrificial atonement (as in 16.21; Num. 5.7) that is predicted; in their exilic condition the remnant of the Israelite people will simply acknowledge their guilt and that of their ancestors, and this contrition will suffice. **41:** *Obdurate heart,* lit. "uncircumcised heart." *Atone for,* better, "make full restitution for." When they finally take upon themselves the commitment to comply with God's demands, the slate will be wiped clean of the accumulated guilt. **42:** *Then will I remember My covenant:* This event, to take place at some future time, is a fitting conclusion to the Priestly history of the nation of Israel, which begins when God hears Israel's cry in bondage and is moved to remember His covenant (Exod. 6.5). In the predicted future, He will hear not their cry of misery but their confession of guilt; recalling His promise to the patriarchs, He will try again to implement His plan. *Jacob ... Isaac ... Abraham:* The inverted order may express the gradual motion of God's recollection backwards in history. In P, God gives His promise to Abraham in Gen. 17.4–8 and reiterates it to Jacob in Gen. 35.11–12. No surviving P text tells of His repeating it to Isaac, though Isaac passes it on to Jacob (Gen. 28.1–4). **43:** Eloquently elaborating on the end of v. 42, the v. describes God thinking of His abandoned estate. **45:** *The covenant with the ancients, whom I freed from the land of Egypt:* Nowhere in P is God explicitly said to have made a covenant with the generation of the exodus. The reference is not to the Sinai events, as these are not called a covenant in P. The promise made to Abraham, Isaac, and Jacob was, however, communicated to the generation of the exodus as well, by Moses; see Exod. 6.6–9. *I, the LORD,* better, "I am the LORD"; cf. 18.2 n.; ch 19. **46:** The caption to the Priestly account of the law-giving in the Tabernacle; cf. 7.37–38; see 25.1. *On Mount Sinai,* see 25.1 n.

27 The LORD spoke to Moses, saying:
[2] Speak to the Israelite people and say to them: When
anyone explicitly[a] vows to the LORD the equivalent for a human
being, [3] the following scale shall apply: If it is a male from twenty
to sixty years of age, the equivalent is fifty shekels of silver by the
sanctuary weight; [4] if it is a female, the equivalent is thirty shekels. [5] If the age is from five years to twenty years, the equivalent
is twenty shekels for a male and ten shekels for a female. [6] If the
age is from one month to five years, the equivalent for a male
is five shekels of silver, and the equivalent for a female is three
shekels of silver. [7] If the age is sixty years or over, the equivalent is fifteen shekels in the case of a male and ten shekels for
a female. [8] But if one cannot afford the equivalent, he shall be
presented before the priest, and the priest shall assess him; the
priest shall assess him according to what the vower can afford.
[9] If [the vow concerns] any animal that may be brought as an
offering to the LORD, any such that may be given to the LORD
shall be holy. [10] One may not exchange or substitute another
for it, either good for bad, or bad for good; if one does substitute one animal for another, the thing vowed and its substitute
shall both be holy. [11] If [the vow concerns] any unclean animal
that may not be brought as an offering to the LORD, the animal
shall be presented before the priest, [12] and the priest shall assess it. Whether [b-]high or low,[-b] whatever assessment is set by
the priest shall stand; [13] and if he wishes to redeem it, he must
add one-fifth to its assessment.

a Cf. note at Lev. 22.21. *b-b Lit. "good or bad."*

27.1–34: Monetary and other dedications. The laws in this ch prescribe how monetary and other dedications are made to the sanctuary, the values or method for determining them, and whether or not such dedications may be redeemed. If the dedication is of land or property, the effect of the jubilee release on its value is prescribed. Objects that belong intrinsically to God and those that have been irrevocably consecrated cannot be dedicated; in the case of tithes, however, redemption is possible. Voluntary contributions might be made by anyone, at any time, as spontaneous acts of devotion. Besides constituting the most important source of revenue for the Temple, they allowed individual Israelites to achieve a sense that the regimen of public worship performed by the priests was being conducted on their behalf. The placement of this ch after the concluding caption in 26.46 can be explained on literary grounds. Since a section of the ch (vv. 16–24) is dependent upon the laws of land tenure, it would have been unclear if it had been placed before ch 25. On the other hand, placing this ch between chs 25 and 26 would have interrupted their thematic continuity. Wishing to keep distinct topics of legislation separate and at the same time to make the laws as intelligible as possible, the author occasionally saw the need to stray somewhat from the order in which he imagined the laws were conveyed to Moses, taking care not to hide this from the reader (see also 16.1 n.). **2–8:** A vow to dedicate the value of a human being. The person wishes to make a significant monetary contribution to the upkeep of the sanctuary. Through the procedure described, a purely fiscal transaction takes on the character of the ultimate act of devotion, that of consecrating oneself or a member of one's household to the LORD. Thus biblical religion preserves vicariously the notion of self-consecration without requiring one actually to sacrifice oneself. **3–7:** The scale is evidently based on size and strength, and thus on potential productivity in terms of physical labor. It does not indicate a social hierarchy. **8:** If a poor person wishes to "dedicate" himself or a member of his family, the scale is flexible, in contrast to the previous section. **9–13:** Vows to donate animals. Animals are of two types: those fit for the altar (vv. 9–10) and those that may not be sacrificed (vv. 11–13). In the former category, once dedicated to the sanctuary, the pledged animal must be brought in fulfillment of the vow and may not be substituted, and the consequence of substitution is that both animals are dedicated. Animals in the latter category, since they cannot be sacrificed, can be dedicated only in order to be sold by the sanctuary for their monetary value. Unlike persons, animals must have their values fixed ad hoc by the priest. The consecration of an animal not fit for sacrifice may sound strange, but the aim of this system is to enable anyone to devote a portion of his wealth to the upkeep of the divine abode. A person whose wealth consists, say, of asses rather than of herds of sheep is thus not disenfranchised. **12–13:** *Whether high or low:* The priest's assessment is final, i.e., it is valid for the outside buyer or for the donor *if he wishes to redeem it;* i.e., if, instead of donating the animal, he would prefer to make his contribution and also keep the animal, he may pay a twenty percent surcharge (compare 5.16, 24). This would apply also to persons wishing to extricate themselves from vows they regret having made. It is not clear whether this option exists for animals in both categories or only

14 If anyone consecrates his house to the LORD, the priest
shall assess it. Whether [a]high or low,[a] as the priest assesses
it, so it shall stand; 15 and if he who has consecrated his house
wishes to redeem it, he must add one-fifth to the sum at which
it was assessed, and it shall be his.
16 If anyone consecrates to the LORD any land that he holds,
its assessment shall be in accordance with its seed requirement: fifty shekels of silver to a *ḥomer* of barley seed. 17 If
he consecrates his land as of the jubilee year, its assessment
stands. 18 But if he consecrates his land after the jubilee, the
priest shall compute the price according to the years that are
left until the jubilee year, and its assessment shall be so reduced; 19 and if he who consecrated the land wishes to redeem
it, he must add one-fifth to the sum at which it was assessed,
and it shall pass to him. 20 But if he does not redeem the land,
and the land is sold to another, it shall no longer be redeemable: 21 when it is released in the jubilee, the land shall be holy
to the LORD, as land proscribed; it becomes the priest's holding.
22 If he consecrates to the LORD land that he purchased,
which is not land of his holding, 23 the priest shall compute for
him the proportionate assessment up to the jubilee year, and
he shall pay the assessment as of that day, a sacred donation
to the LORD. 24 In the jubilee year the land shall revert to him
from whom it was bought, whose holding the land is. 25 All assessments shall be by the sanctuary weight, the shekel being
twenty *gerahs*.
26 A firstling of animals, however, which—as a firstling—is
the LORD's, cannot be consecrated by anybody; whether ox or
sheep, it is the LORD's. 27 But if it is of unclean animals, it may
be ransomed as its assessment, with one-fifth added; if it is not
redeemed, it shall be sold at its assessment.

a-a Lit. "good or bad."

for nonsacrificial ones. **14–15:** Similarly, one may choose to dedicate his house, that is, to donate it to the sanctuary for sale, or, if his primary intention is actually to make a monetary contribution in the amount of his home, he may effect this by dedicating the house and redeeming it for silver, adding twenty percent to the price that has been fixed. **16–24:** Dedication of fields. These too may be donated for sale, the proceeds going to the sanctuary treasury, or the donor may redeem them at a twenty percent surcharge, with proper adjustment for the number of years remaining until the jubilee. **16:** *Any land that he holds,* any portion of the land belonging to his ancestral holding. *In accordance with its seed requirement:* The sale price is thus a function of size, which is constant, whereas fixing it in accordance with how much it has produced in past years would be a function of divine blessing, which may change from one year, or from one owner, to the next. *Fifty shekels of silver:* Probably one shekel (see 5.15 n.) per year; maximally fifty, if the jubilee is fifty years away. *A ḥomer of barley seed,* a measure of seed equal to the normal load carried by an ass; see Ezek. 45.11. It was about 230 liters (a little more than 6.5 bushels). **17:** *Its assessment stands,* see v. 12. **20–21:** The original holder's right to reclaim his land expires when the Temple treasury has sold it to another or when the jubilee arrives, whichever comes first. *When it is released in the jubilee,* in the former case. If not sold to another person, it remains the property of the Temple. *The land shall be holy to the LORD:* Since the whole point of the jubilee is that the land is the LORD's property, land that has been dedicated to the LORD obviously remains His when the next jubilee comes, the proprietorship passing to the priests. *As land proscribed,* see vv. 28–29. **22–24:** Dedication of purchased fields, i.e., lands that will revert to their original owners at the jubilee. The donor is not donating something of his own, and he does not have the option of transferring ownership to the sanctuary for sale to a third party. *Purchased* fields thus, like humans (vv. 3–8), may be consecrated only by donating their monetary value, as assessed by the priest, and in the jubilee they revert to their original owner. **25:** *All assessments:* This applies to all of the preceding legislation. *The sanctuary weight,* see 5.15 n. *Twenty gerahs,* see Exod. 30.13; Num. 3.47; 18.16. **26–33:** A set of restrictions on the above: objects that cannot be consecrated to the LORD since they belong to Him already. **26–27:** A *firstling* of livestock may not be dedicated, as it belongs to the LORD by definition (see Exod. 13.2; 22.28–29; 34.19; Num. 3.40ff.; Deut. 15.19–20). Firstlings of the flock and herd must be sacrificed and cannot be redeemed; firstlings of nonsacrificial animals may be redeemed or sold. The law here differs from the non-Priestly regulation in Exod. 13.13; 34.20, according to which impure animals must be exchanged for a lamb or destroyed. **27:** *Ransomed,* Heb "padah," usually synonymous with "ga'al," "redeem." Since they are the property of God, the person is not regaining ownership of them but gaining it for the first time.

28 But of all that anyone owns, be it man or beast or land of
his holding, nothing that he has proscribed for the LORD may
be sold or redeemed; every proscribed thing is totally consecrated to the LORD. 29 No human being who has been proscribed can be ransomed: he shall be put to death.

30 All tithes from the land, whether seed from the ground or
fruit from the tree, are the LORD's; they are holy to the LORD. 31 If
anyone wishes to redeem any of his tithes, he must add one-
fifth to them. 32 All tithes of the herd or flock—of all that passes
under the shepherd's staff, every tenth one—shall be holy to
the LORD. 33 He must not look out for good as against bad, or
make substitution for it. If he does make substitution for it, then
it and its substitute shall both be holy: it cannot be redeemed.

34 These are the commandments that the LORD gave Moses
for the Israelite people on Mount Sinai.

28–29: The second restriction: *proscribed* things (Heb "ḥerem"). This term is used outside of the Priestly writings for those condemned to destruction, such as defeated military enemies, those guilty of idolatry, and persons who fail to comply with the terms of a communal oath (the so-called "ban") requiring all to "do or die." It refers also to the spoils confiscated from those so condemned, consisting of animals, which were also destroyed, and inanimate objects, which were probably reserved for the sanctuary (see also the contrast between Deut. 20.13–14 and 1 Sam. 15.2–3). Such items are "off-limits" and their taboo nature is contagious. Further, this destruction or confiscation of spoils is said to be *for the LORD.* This indicates that the obligation to condemn, destroy, and despoil is a divinely sanctioned one, and implies that the destroyed persons and animals are, like the silver and gold confiscated for the sanctuary, a form of offering to God. This passage seems to mean another type of "ḥerem": the "proscribing" by an individual (rather than by the community or God) of an object by pledging that no use would ever be made of it and that it would become the permanent property of the LORD, with no option to sell, redeem, or exchange. **28:** *Be it man or beast,* see next v. *Totally consecrated,* Heb "kodesh kodashim," "most holy" (see also 2.3, etc.). Consistent with Priestly thought and law, such objects are here deemed to be sacred; since they have been made immutably so, they are called "most holy." The use of the term is not entirely consistent with its use elsewhere. **29:** The text shockingly says that one may sentence oneself, one's slave, or a household member under one's authority to death as a consecration to the LORD, and once this is done there is no reprieve or remedy. Commentators have interpreted the text differently, but there is little basis for this. **30–33:** *Tithes* constitute the third and final restriction: They belong to God already and cannot be dedicated. **30–31:** It is not clear whether this tithe, which belongs to the LORD, is in addition to the crop tithe assigned to the Levites in Num. 18.21ff. for their upkeep, or whether our ch views all crop tithes as a tax given to the central sanctuary. **32–33:** A tithe of herds and flocks is not mentioned elsewhere in the Torah. According to 1 Sam. 8.15–17, kings are notorious for imposing such tithes as a form of taxation. **33:** *He must not look out for good as against bad:* He must offer the tenth sheep to pass under the staff, without regard to its size or quality. *Make substitution,* see vv. 9–13 n. **34:** The caption of 26.46 is repeated in abbreviated form; see 27.1–34 n. *On Mount Sinai,* see 7.38 n.; 25.1 n.

במדבר

Numbers

THE FOURTH BOOK OF THE TORAH, Numbers, recounts memorable events of the Israelite wanderings from Sinai, God's mountain, to the plains of Moab, just opposite the promised land. Thus, Numbers continues the story begun in Exodus and continued in Leviticus of the escape from Egyptian servitude, the desert journey to Mount Sinai, the revelation at Sinai and giving of the law, and the building of the Tabernacle with instruction on its operation. The current Hebrew name of this book, *Bemidbar,* "in the wilderness [of Sinai]," taken from the fifth Hebrew word in ch 1, reflects this theme. In contrast, the English name, Numbers, derives from the Greek translation, the LXX, which titled the book after the censuses mentioned in the first four chs. This name reflects an earlier Hebrew name for the book, ḥapikudim, "the fifth concerning the census," well-attested in classical rabbinic sources, from a period when books of the Torah were named thematically rather than after one of their initial words.

Composition

NUMBERS IS A COMPLEX COLLECTION of texts containing an assortment of interwoven literary genres: historical narratives, legal texts, ritual prescriptions, and poetic folk traditions. Its final form reflects a long and complex literary history. Modern critical scholarship—based on stylistic, linguistic, and contextual criteria—identifies separate sources underlying the final version of the book. (See essay "Modern Study of the Bible," pp. 2166–77.) Primarily, the texts derive from various layers of the Priestly school (P), with additional texts from the two older narrative sources, the Yahwist (J) and Elohist (E). The predominant Priestly material often functions to expand, supplement, or recast ideologically the earlier (JE) texts to fit the agenda of Priestly circles. The lengthy Balaam pericope (chs 22–24) in its entirety stands untouched by the Priestly writer and may represent the hand of yet another author(s), neither J, E, or P; quite remarkably, one rabbinic tradition considered it to be a self-standing book (*b. B. Bat.* 14b). As is the case for the entire Torah, Jewish tradition views the seemingly disparate texts in Numbers as a unified work, part of the Torah written by Moses. Although modern biblical scholarship does not recognize Mosaic authorship, it has begun to emphasize the merits of a holistic approach, one that studies the parts in the context of the whole.

Some scholars who favor a synchronic approach identify a recurring chiastic literary structure in the book of Numbers. Chiasm is a device used by a writer to emphasize ideas and/or for aesthetic purposes. The technique is evident in small or large units of text where pairs of items (ideas, subjects, etc.) are inverted like an X (ABB'A' etc.) to create symmetry. An example is God's description of Moses' unique status as a prophet (12.6–8):

A. When a prophet of the LORD arises among you,
B. I make Myself known to him in a vision,
C. I speak with him in a dream
D. Not so with My servant Moses;
D'. He is trusted throughout My household.
C'. With him I speak mouth to mouth,
B'. Plainly and not in riddles,
A'. And he beholds the likeness of the LORD.

The technique is common in biblical poetry but less so in prose. Positing large units of chiasm, sometimes encompassing chs or even larger units, suggests a more uniform textual whole composed in a literary style that clearly communicates its ideas within a framework.

Recent literary interpretations of the structure of the book of Numbers focus on how the parts are woven together to shape the entire narrative and what that reveals about underlying goals of its authors. The collection of stories recounting the forty years of wandering, for example, provide an understanding of Israel's past that serves to create a worldview for its future, perhaps in a postexilic context, after the return of some Judahites from the Babylonian exile, beginning in 538 BCE. Key to that worldview is the apparent priestly agenda highlighting laws and rituals, which the author(s) present as sanctioned with divine endorsement. Questions of historicity are ancillary to such approaches; whether the traditions are real, invented, or a combination of both matters little in the creation of a people's collective memory.

Matters relating to the historicity of the wilderness accounts, however, continue to be debated among scholars. But literary criticism need not discount the presence of historical facts in the texts. On one hand, an argument can be advanced that usage of Egyptian terms, geography of the Sinai, and political realities of periods corresponding to Israel's prehistory bespeak some knowledge of a residency in Egypt and wilderness sojourn. On the other hand, studies of genre show that ancient historiography, even if peppered with authentic data, is not necessarily synonymous with history writing in the modern sense. For example, in Numbers the content of historiographic texts often deals with the ritual calendar, thus demonstrating a disconnection between form and function. It is important, therefore, to distinguish between the author's ideological motive for writing an account and the literary style of that account. A genre may have been chosen to give the text a certain appearance.

Content

THE BOOK OF NUMBERS can easily be divided by subject and other criteria into several primary units; these can be further subdivided into smaller sections and subsections. It is, however, often difficult to determine the relationship between contiguous segments. Based on geographical criteria and ideological motifs, three major units can be distinguished, reflecting a literary sandwich of sorts: (1) the final encampment at Sinai and preparation to resume the wilderness trek (1.1–10.10); (2) the generation-long march in the desert from Sinai to Moab (10.11–22.1); (3) the encampment on the plains of Moab and preparation to enter Canaan (22.2–36.13). Unit one marks the period when Israel, having received God's teaching, readies itself for the desert march to its final destination. This is the first time that the people enter the wilderness while they are bonded by covenant to the LORD. The wanderings in the second unit form a bridge between the first and last units. The generation of the Egyptian bondage dies in the desert and a new generation matures. In unit three this new generation prepares to embark on a journey once more, this time to enter the promised land as a national entity.

The Final Encampment at Sinai

THE THEME OF THIS UNIT (1.1–10.10), comprised entirely of Priestly material, centers on the organization of the Israelite camp around the Tabernacle and the maintenance of cult purity within the camp, assuring God's Presence in the Tabernacle. This material is mainly prescriptive. The first section of the unit opens with a census of eligible military-age males and an election of tribal chieftains (1.1–46). A description of duties for the military-exempt Levites follows (1.47–54). Next is a description of the traveling tribal camp (2.1–34). Much space is devoted to the roles of the Levites, who are stationed closest to the Tabernacle, performing guard duty there, making sure that no non-priests approach the Tabernacle. Topics include the consecration of the Levites in place of first-born Israelites, two Levite censuses, and a detailed outline of the familial relationships of the Levitical clans and their duties (chs 3–4).

The next sections shift focus from camp organization to the maintenance of camp purity. Conditions for removal and readmission of persons who have become ritually impure are delineated (parts of ch 5). Laws regarding Nazirite vows and the formula for the priestly blessing follow (ch 6). The next few sections focus again on the Tabernacle and its functionaries: the initiatory gifts brought by the tribal chieftains to the sanctuary (ch 7); the procedure for lighting the lampstand (menorah); and the purification of the Levites (ch 8). The last section of unit one (9.1–10.10) discusses the final preparations for departure from Sinai. Israel celebrates the first Passover in the wilderness, and Moses makes provisions for ritually impure persons to celebrate a second Passover one month later. Directives concerning the fire-cloud, to guide Israel's travels, and the silver trumpets, to herald movement of the camp divisions, conclude the unit.

The Generation-long March in the Desert from Sinai to Moab

THIS MIDDLE UNIT (10.11–22.1) is composed of narratives from various sources woven into a story line interspersed by sacrificial law, injunctions against certain transgressions, and expiation processes. A recurring cycle of murmuring and rebellion against the authority of God and Moses, by individuals or by the community as a whole, characterizes this unit. Even Miriam, Aaron, and Moses have moments of disloyalty to God. In certain cases, where rebellion by a few persons spreads to the group or where it is enacted by the leadership, punishment is severe.

The unit opens with a description of the camp's departure (10.11–36) followed by a litany of grievances and their resolutions (11.1–35). After the first complaint God responds with deadly fire; Moses then successfully intercedes on Israel's behalf. This cycle repeats in one form or another. Eventually Moses appoints seventy elders to relieve his burden, but displays of disloyalty continue, even among the community leaders. Miriam and Aaron criticize Moses on account of his Cushite wife while ultimately protesting against his unique status as prophet (ch 12). The mood of rebellion intensifies in the spy episode (chs 13–14). Israel sides with the ten spies who declare Canaan unconquerable and ponder returning to Egypt, and God reacts by condemning the entire exodus generation to death in the wilderness. Soon thereafter a Levite named Korah and his followers stage a rebellion against Moses and Aaron (chs 16–17). Finally, in frustration, Moses and Aaron defy God (20.1–13). For their lack of trust God, in an unexpected decree, bars Moses and Aaron from entering the promised land.

Interspersed between these accounts of human infidelity and divine retribution are prescriptive, Priestly passages detailing ordinances regarding sacrifices and purification (chs 15, 19), and the duties and privileges of priests and Levites (ch 18), including the commandment for Israelites to attach tzitzit (fringes) to their garments (15.37–41). At the end of unit two Israel emerges from the wilderness to face the peoples inhabiting Transjordan. Not surprisingly, the rulers of those small kingdoms deny Israel passage through their territory. Nevertheless, Israel moves ever closer to its final destination and prevails in encounters with its enemies (20.14–21.35).

Encampment on the Plains of Moab and Preparation to Enter Canaan

UNIT THREE (22.2–36.13) finds the Israelites encamped on the eastern side of the Jordan opposite Jericho, their destination within visible reach. This unit, like the previous two, is composed of narrative and legal material; it also contains lengthy poetic folk traditions. The theme centers on the new Israelite community's final preparations to inherit the land of Canaan, and as such, much of the legal material here focuses on inheritance.

The first section, composed of narrative and poetry, is the story of the Moabite king Balak and the prophet Balaam whom he hires to curse the Israelites (chs 22–24). God thwarts Balaam's mission, turning the intended curse into a blessing. Israel's apostasy at Baal-peor follows (25.1–18); the plague that God inflicts upon the sinners eliminates the last members of the exodus generation.

The opening of ch 26 is an alternate juncture for the end of unit two and the beginning of unit three. With the demise of the older generation and the crossing into Canaan imminent, Moses conducts a second census and apportions the land to the tribes (ch 26). As in the first census, the Levitical clans, who are not allotted landholdings, are counted separately. Arising from the process of apportioning land is the special case of Zelophehad's daughters, who petition for the right of women to inherit when there are no male heirs (27.1–11). That case is followed by the succession of Joshua (27.12–23). Next is an insertion of ritual prescriptions establishing the cultic calendar and governing the daily, new moon, Sabbath, and festival offerings (28.1–30.1). The section ends with a discussion on the annulment of vows and oaths. Following a statement that men are bound by their vows and oaths comes a list of conditions under which women's vows can be annulled (30.2–17). The narrative resumes with a war against the Midianites, allegedly in retaliation for their seduction of the Israelites at Baal-peor (ch 31).

Having routed its enemies in Transjordan, Israel begins the settlement process. The tribes of Reuben and Gad ask to receive a portion of land on the eastern side of the Jordan (ch 32). Part of the tribe of Manasseh settles there as well. A summary of the wilderness itinerary that highlights key events follows (33.1–49). The next narrative section continues where the previous one left off (32.42); having appropriated land to two and a half tribes in Transjordan, Moses reformulates the division of Canaan among the remaining nine and a half tribes (33.50–35.8). As part of the process, he defines the boundaries of Canaan and assigns Levitical towns in place of tribal land for Levites.

Unit three ends with several final prescriptions (35.9–36.13). Moses designates six cities of refuge, three of which are across (west of) the Jordan River, in the land about to be conquered; furthermore he distinguishes between involuntary and deliberate homicide. The last section outlines marriage regulations for female heirs, using the case of Zelophehad's daughters as a model. The issue of land inheritance projects into the future since it is significant only after the land of Israel is settled. The book of Numbers ends by stating that the precepts in this unit were enjoined upon the Israelites "on the steppes of Moab, at the Jordan near Jericho." This phrase forms an inclusio with the last phrase of the second unit (22.1), a transition between units two and three.

[NILI S. FOX]

BE-MIDBAR במדבר

1 On the first day of the second month, in the second year
following the exodus from the land of Egypt, the LORD
spoke to Moses in the wilderness of Sinai, in the Tent of Meeting, saying:
2 Take a census of the whole Israelite community by the clans
of [a]its ancestral houses,[a] listing the names, every male, head
by head. 3 You and Aaron shall record them by their groups,
from the age of twenty years up, all those in Israel who are able
to bear arms. 4 Associated with you shall be a man from each
tribe, each one the head of his ancestral house.
5 These are the names of the men who shall assist you:
From Reuben, Elizur son of Shedeur.
6 From Simeon, Shelumiel son of Zurishaddai.
7 From Judah, Nahshon son of Amminadab.
8 From Issachar, Nethanel son of Zuar.
9 From Zebulun, Eliab son of Helon.
10 From the sons of Joseph:
from Ephraim, Elishama son of Ammihud;
from Manasseh, Gamaliel son of Pedahzur.
11 From Benjamin, Abidan son of Gideoni.
12 From Dan, Ahiezer son of Ammishaddai.
13 From Asher, Pagiel son of Ochran.
14 From Gad, Eliasaph son of Deuel.
15 From Naphtali, Ahira son of Enan.
16 Those are the elected of the assembly, the chieftains of their
ancestral tribes: they are the heads of the contingents of Israel.
17 So Moses and Aaron took those men, who were designated
by name, 18 and on the first day of the second month they convoked the whole community, who were registered by the clans
of their ancestral houses—the names of those aged twenty years
and over being listed head by head. 19 As the LORD had commanded Moses, so he recorded them in the wilderness of Sinai.
20 They totaled as follows:
The descendants of Reuben, Israel's first-born, the registration of the clans of their ancestral house, as listed by name,
head by head, all males aged twenty years and over, all who
were able to bear arms—21 those enrolled from the tribe of
Reuben: 46,500.
22 Of the descendants of Simeon, the registration of the clans
of their ancestral house, their enrollment as listed by name,
head by head, all males aged twenty years and over, all who
were able to bear arms—23 those enrolled from the tribe of
Simeon: 59,300.
24 Of the descendants of Gad, the registration of the clans of
their ancestral house, as listed by name, aged twenty years and

a-a I.e., of its tribes.

1.1–46: First Israelite census and appointment of tribal chieftains. Numbers opens with the Israelites still encamped at the base of Mt. Sinai (1.1–10.10). They already have received the laws, have constructed the portable Tabernacle, and have been instructed on formal worship procedures and regulated observances both for priests and lay persons (Exod. chs 20–31; 34–40; Lev. chs 1–27). Now they must be organized into a mobile war camp to resume their travels in the wilderness and in readiness to meet any foes along the way. Ch 1 begins with a census. **2:** The purpose of a census is to determine military strength or potential taxation revenues (cf. 2 Sam. ch 24), though later Jewish interpretation suggests that God counts Israel because they are dear to Him (see Rashi). All males twenty years and older are eligible for military duty, and tribal chieftains who function as census supervisors are appointed, one from each tribe. A separate census is taken of the Levites who are exempt from military service (ch 3; 26.57–62). **5–15:** Heading the list of chieftains is the representative of Reuben, Jacob's first-born son, though elsewhere in Num., Judah is typically listed first. The other sons follow Reuben in chronological order of birth with Leah's sons first, Rachel's second, and the concubines' last. None of the names on the list contains a theophoric element, that is, an element with the name of God as prefix ("yeho-" or "yo-") or suffix ("-yahu" or "-yah"). In the latter period of the monarchy such names are commonplace (e.g., Jehoiada, Zechariah). **20–46:** The census figures for each tribe, with a grand total of 603,550, are vastly inflated by any realistic standards. The final tally, however, is generally consistent in the biblical literature (cf. Exod. 12.37; 38.26; Num. 11.21; 26.51). Earlier biblical scholars posited that this number reflected a census at a later period, perhaps under David, but this is incorrect.

27: *Judah* has the largest number, reflecting its later importance.

over, all who were able to bear arms—[25] those enrolled from
the tribe of Gad: 45,650.
[26] Of the descendants of Judah, the registration of the clans
of their ancestral house, as listed by name, aged twenty years
and over, all who were able to bear arms—[27] those enrolled
from the tribe of Judah: 74,600.
[28] Of the descendants of Issachar, the registration of the
clans of their ancestral house, as listed by name, aged twenty
years and over, all who were able to bear arms—[29] those enrolled from the tribe of Issachar: 54,400.
[30] Of the descendants of Zebulun, the registration of the
clans of their ancestral house, as listed by name, aged twenty
years and over, all who were able to bear arms—[31] those enrolled from the tribe of Zebulun: 57,400.
[32] Of the descendants of Joseph:
Of the descendants of Ephraim, the registration of the clans
of their ancestral house, as listed by name, aged twenty years
and over, all who were able to bear arms—[33] those enrolled
from the tribe of Ephraim: 40,500.
[34] Of the descendants of Manasseh, the registration of the
clans of their ancestral house, as listed by name, aged twenty
years and over, all who were able to bear arms—[35] those enrolled from the tribe of Manasseh: 32,200.
[36] Of the descendants of Benjamin, the registration of the
clans of their ancestral house, as listed by name, aged twenty
years and over, all who were able to bear arms—[37] those enrolled from the tribe of Benjamin: 35,400.
[38] Of the descendants of Dan, the registration of the clans of
their ancestral house, as listed by name, aged twenty years and
over, all who were able to bear arms—[39] those enrolled from
the tribe of Dan: 62,700.
[40] Of the descendants of Asher, the registration of the clans
of their ancestral house, as listed by name, aged twenty years
and over, all who were able to bear arms—[41] those enrolled
from the tribe of Asher: 41,500.
[42] [Of] the descendants of Naphtali, the registration of the
clans of their ancestral house as listed by name, aged twenty
years and over, all who were able to bear arms—[43] those enrolled from the tribe of Naphtali: 53,400.
[44] Those are the enrollments recorded by Moses and Aaron
and by the chieftains of Israel, who were twelve in number, one
man to each ancestral house. [45] All the Israelites, aged twenty
years and over, enrolled by ancestral houses, all those in Israel
who were able to bear arms—[46] all who were enrolled came to
603,550.
[47] The Levites, however, were not recorded among them by
their ancestral tribe. [48] For the LORD had spoken to Moses, saying: [49] Do not on any account enroll the tribe of Levi or take a

census of them with the Israelites. 50 You shall put the Levites
in charge of the Tabernacle of the Pact, all its furnishings, and
everything that pertains to it: they shall carry the Tabernacle
and all its furnishings, and they shall tend it; and they shall
camp around the Tabernacle. 51 When the Tabernacle is to set
out, the Levites shall take it down, and when the Tabernacle is
to be pitched, the Levites shall set it up; any outsider who encroaches shall be put to death. 52 The Israelites shall encamp
troop by troop, each man with his division and each under his
standard. 53 The Levites, however, shall camp around the Tabernacle of the Pact, that wrath may not strike the Israelite community; the Levites shall stand guard around the Tabernacle
of the Pact.

54 The Israelites did accordingly; just as the LORD had commanded Moses, so they did.

2 The LORD spoke to Moses and Aaron, saying: 2 The Israelites shall camp each with his standard, under the banners
of their ancestral house; they shall camp around the Tent of
Meeting at a distance.

3 Camped on the front, or east side: the standard of the division of Judah, troop by troop.

Chieftain of the Judites: Nahshon son of Amminadab. 4 His troop, as enrolled: 74,600.

5 Camping next to it:

The tribe of Issachar.

Chieftain of the Issacharites: Nethanel son of Zuar. 6 His troop, as enrolled: 54,400.

7 The tribe of Zebulun.

Chieftain of the Zebulunites: Eliab son of Helon. 8 His troop, as enrolled: 57,400.

9 The total enrolled in the division of Judah: 186,400, for all troops.
These shall march first.

10 On the south: the standard of the division of Reuben, troop
by troop.

Chieftain of the Reubenites: Elizur son of Shedeur. 11 His troop, as enrolled: 46,500.

12 Camping next to it:

The tribe of Simeon.

Chieftain of the Simeonites: Shelumiel son of Zurishaddai. 13 His troop, as enrolled: 59,300.

14 And the tribe of Gad.

Chieftain of the Gadites: Eliasaph son of Reuel. 15 His troop, as enrolled: 45,650.

16 The total enrolled in the division of Reuben: 151,450, for all
troops. These shall march second.

1.47–54: Levites are charged with the Tabernacle. This is part one of a lengthy, detailed outline of Levitical duties (continued in chs 3–4). Being exempt from military service, the Levites are charged with guarding the Tabernacle as well as dismantling it for travel and erecting it when encamped. As such, their position in the layout of the camp is closest to the Tabernacle. Rabbinic midrash (*Num. Rab.* 1.12) attributes their prestigious responsibilities to a reward they receive for remaining loyal to God by not having participated in the golden calf worship (Exod. 32.25–29).

2.1–34: The plan of the camp. The camp description, according to God's instruction, situates the Tabernacle in the center surrounded by the twelve tribes. Each tribe is assigned a location in this military-style camp. **2:** Each tribal group marches and camps with its *standard, under the banners* of its ancestral house. The meaning of the Heb term "degel," rendered in NJPS as "standard," is uncertain. It may refer to an attached banner or flag bearing the insignia of the tribe or may refer to a military unit, a subdivision of the tribe. Medieval commentators suggest that the tribal animal totem is depicted on the banner (Ibn Ezra) or that a colored cloth corresponding to the color of the tribe's stone on the priest's breastplate hangs from the banner (Rashi). Levites and priests are not assigned a position in this account (see ch 3), and the Joseph tribe is broken into his two sons, Ephraim and Manasseh (see Gen. 48.1–20) to reach the number twelve. **3–31:** The twelve tribes are arranged to form a square camp of four divisions with three tribes in each. The Leah tribes are situated to the east and south of the Tabernacle; Gad, a son of Leah's maidservant Zilpah, replaces Levi. Benjamin and Joseph's sons Ephraim and Manasseh, the Rachel tribes, take their position west of the Tabernacle. The remaining concubine tribes are located to the north. Judah's eastern position facing the Tabernacle entrance is a mark of the tribe's distinction as the progenitor of the Davidic royal house (see Gen. 49.10). Each of the four camp divisions has a designated leading tribe; the choice is based on traditions regarding attributes of Jacob's sons (Gen. ch 49). **32–34:** These summary vv. repeat the census grand total of ch 1, adding the information about the military organization, which is the main purpose of the census. The concluding v. confirms that subsequently the Israelites camped and marched according to this plan (Num. 10.14–28). Such summary vv. at the end of a unit typify Priestly literature, which also emphasizes that God's command was fulfilled exactly (v. 34).

3.1–51: The first Levite census, their ranking, and special roles. This is the first of three Levite censuses (ch 4; 26.57–62). The tribe of Levi is divided into clans; each bears the name of a son of Gershon, Kohath, or Merari, Levi's three sons. Preserving the genealogy of the Levites and especially that of the Aaronite priests is of great importance to the Priestly writer(s). P considers the Aaronites as the sole legitimate priestly line. Non-Aaronite Levites function in subordinate roles to the priests. Any challenge to Aaron's divinely ordained authority is summarily crushed (see Korah rebellion, chs 16–17). **1–3:** *This is the line of Aaron and Moses:* It is most unusual for Aaron's name to precede Moses', and this is an indication of the priorities of the P source in emphasizing Aaron's importance; elsewhere this occurs only in other genealogical texts of the P source (Exod. 6.20; Num. 26.59; 1 Chron. 5.29; 23.13). Rashi notes that Aaron's sons are named but not Moses', and he concludes that Moses is, figuratively, the father of Aaron's sons as well because he (Moses) taught them Torah on the day God spoke to him on Mt. Sinai. **4:** A reference to the obscure incident described in Lev. ch 10.

17 Then, midway between the divisions, the Tent of Meeting, the division of the Levites, shall move. As they camp, so they shall march, each in position, by their standards.

18 On the west: the standard of the division of Ephraim, troop by troop.
Chieftain of the Ephraimites: Elishama son of Ammihud.
19 His troop, as enrolled: 40,500.
20 Next to it:
The tribe of Manasseh.
Chieftain of the Manassites: Gamaliel son of Pedahzur.
21 His troop, as enrolled: 32,200.
22 And the tribe of Benjamin.
Chieftain of the Benjaminites: Abidan son of Gideoni.
23 His troop, as enrolled: 35,400.
24 The total enrolled in the division of Ephraim: 108,100 for all troops. These shall march third.

25 On the north: the standard of the division of Dan, troop by troop.
Chieftain of the Danites: Ahiezer son of Ammishaddai.
26 His troop, as enrolled: 62,700.
27 Camping next to it:
The tribe of Asher.
Chieftain of the Asherites: Pagiel son of Ochran. 28 His troop, as enrolled: 41,500.
29 And the tribe of Naphtali.
Chieftain of the Naphtalites: Ahira son of Enan. 30 His troop, as enrolled: 53,400.
31 The total enrolled in the division of Dan: 157,600. These shall march last, by their standards.

32 Those are the enrollments of the Israelites by ancestral houses. The total enrolled in the divisions, for all troops: 603,550. 33 The Levites, however, were not recorded among the Israelites, as the LORD had commanded Moses.

34 The Israelites did accordingly; just as the LORD had commanded Moses, so they camped by their standards, and so they marched, each with his clan according to his ancestral house.

3

This is the line of Aaron and Moses at the time that the LORD
spoke with Moses on Mount Sinai. 2 These were the names
of Aaron's sons: Nadab, the first-born, and Abihu, Eleazar and
Ithamar; 3 those were the names of Aaron's sons, the anointed
priests who were ordained for priesthood. 4 But Nadab and
Abihu died [a]by the will of[a] the LORD, when they offered alien

a-a *Others "before."*

fire before the LORD in the wilderness of Sinai; and they left no
sons. So it was Eleazar and Ithamar who served as priests in
the lifetime of their father Aaron.
5 The LORD spoke to Moses, saying: 6 Advance the tribe of
Levi and place them in attendance upon Aaron the priest
to serve him. 7 They shall perform duties for him and for the
whole community before the Tent of Meeting, doing the work
of the Tabernacle. 8 They shall take charge of all the furnishings
of the Tent of Meeting—a duty on behalf of the Israelites—doing the work of the Tabernacle. 9 You shall assign the Levites to
Aaron and to his sons: they are formally assigned to him from
among the Israelites. 10 You shall make Aaron and his sons responsible for observing their priestly duties; and any outsider
who encroaches shall be put to death.
11 The LORD spoke to Moses, saying: 12 I hereby take the Levites
from among the Israelites in place of all the first-born, the first
issue of the womb among the Israelites: the Levites shall be
Mine. 13 For every first-born is Mine: at the time that I smote
every first-born in the land of Egypt, I consecrated every first-
born in Israel, man and beast, to Myself, to be Mine, the LORD's.
14 The LORD spoke to Moses in the wilderness of Sinai, saying: 15 Record the Levites by ancestral house and by clan; record every male among them from the age of one month up.
16 So Moses recorded them at the command of the LORD, as he
was bidden. 17 These were the sons of Levi by name: Gershon,
Kohath, and Merari. 18 These were the names of the sons of
Gershon by clan: Libni and Shimei. 19 The sons of Kohath by
clan: Amram and Izhar, Hebron and Uzziel. 20 The sons of Merari by clan: Mahli and Mushi.

These were the clans of the Levites within their ancestral
houses:
21 To Gershon belonged the clan of the Libnites and the clan
of the Shimeites; those were the clans of the Gershonites. 22 The
recorded entries of all their males from the age of one month
up, as recorded, came to 7,500. 23 The clans of the Gershonites
were to camp behind the Tabernacle, to the west. 24 The chieftain of the ancestral house of the Gershonites was Eliasaph son
of Lael. 25 The duties of the Gershonites in the Tent of Meeting comprised: the Tabernacle,[a] the tent, its covering, and the
screen for the entrance of the Tent of Meeting; 26 the hangings
of the enclosure, the screen for the entrance of the enclosure
which surrounds the Tabernacle, the cords thereof, and the altar—all the service connected with these.
27 To Kohath belonged the clan of the Amramites, the clan
of the Izharites, the clan of the Hebronites, and the clan of the
Uzzielites; those were the clans of the Kohathites. 28 All the

a *See note on Exod. 26.1.*

5–10: The main role of the Levites is guarding the Tabernacle from non-priestly encroachers while it is stationary and guarding its furnishings during travel. The purview of the priests is the interior of the Tabernacle, its sacred objects, and performing the rites associated with them. *Any outsider* (v. 10), that is, a non-priest, is forbidden contact with the holy place or holy articles, on penalty of death. Only the sanctified priests may enter the sacred space of the Tabernacle. Naḥmanides (Ramban) compares the boundaries of the Tabernacle with the bounds set for Mt. Sinai when Moses ascends the mountain to receive the law (Exod. 19.12). **11–13:** Another role of the Levites is to replace first-born Israelites who are consecrated to God. Levites serve the priests *in place* of Israelite first-born males, who by birth are destined to minister to God. The dedication of Samuel to Eli at Shiloh reflects this practice (1 Sam. 1.10–11, 24–28). Rabbinic interpretation understands the substitution by Levites as an indication that originally first-born children were sacrificed to the deity, comparable to the offering of first-born animals (Exod. 13.2; Lev. 27.26–27; Num. 8.17; 18.15–16), but no proof exists for that assumption. **14–39:** The first census of Levites states that they are counted from the age of one month up, probably P's conception of the age of a viable infant; contrast the Israelite census from age 20 up in 1.3, the age of military conscription. The various clans of Gershonites, Kohathites, and Merarites are numbered and assigned a position from which to guard the Tabernacle: the west side, south side, and north side, respectively; the priests are stationed at the eastern entrance. The specific duties of each clan are also delineated.

40–51: Although Levites function as substitutes for first-born Israelites, apparently the Levite population is short by 273 of the number of Israelite first-borns. The excess children are redeemed with a payment to the priests of five shekels per head. The numbers here are problematic as well; it is difficult to understand how the number of first-born children from all the tribes was nearly equivalent to the number of Levites; this would assume that each mother had over twenty children. **47:** *By the sanctuary weight, twenty gerahs to the shekel:* Two standards of weights coexisted in ancient Israel, the sanctuary weight (Exod. 30.13, 24; Lev. 5.15; Num. 7.13) and the royal weight (2 Sam. 14.26). The gloss "twenty gerahs" specifies the number of small units of weight in the lighter sanctuary shekel. The royal shekel (24 gerahs), also known as the shekel of the king, is widely attested in the archeological record. A gerah was about .5 g; the royal shekel was about 11.5 g, the sanctuary shekel about 9.5 g (less than .5 oz).

listed males from the age of one month up came to 8,600, attending to the duties of the sanctuary. [29] The clans of the Kohathites were to camp along the south side of the Tabernacle.
[30] The chieftain of the ancestral house of the Kohathite clans
was Elizaphan son of Uzziel. [31] Their duties comprised: the
ark, the table, the lampstand, the altars, and the sacred utensils that were used with them, and the screen[a]—all the service
connected with these. [32] The head chieftain of the Levites was
Eleazar son of Aaron the priest, in charge of those attending to
the duties of the sanctuary.

[33] To Merari belonged the clan of the Mahlites and the clan
of the Mushites; those were the clans of Merari. [34] The recorded entries of all their males from the age of one month up came
to 6,200. [35] The chieftain of the ancestral house of the clans of
Merari was Zuriel son of Abihail. They were to camp along the
north side of the Tabernacle. [36] The assigned duties of the Merarites comprised: the planks of the Tabernacle, its bars, posts,
and sockets, and all its furnishings—all the service connected
with these; [37] also the posts around the enclosure and their
sockets, pegs, and cords.

[38] Those who were to camp before the Tabernacle, in front—
before the Tent of Meeting, on the east—were Moses and Aaron
and his sons, attending to the duties of the sanctuary, as a duty
on behalf of the Israelites; and any outsider who encroached
was to be put to death. [39] All the Levites who were recorded,
whom at the LORD's command Moses and Aaron recorded by
their clans, all the males from the age of one month up, came
to 22,000.

[40] The LORD said to Moses: Record every first-born male of
the Israelite people from the age of one month up, and make
a list of their names; [41] and take the Levites for Me, the LORD,
in place of every first-born among the Israelite people, and
the cattle of the Levites in place of every first-born among the
cattle of the Israelites. [42] So Moses recorded all the first-born
among the Israelites, as the LORD had commanded him. [43] All
the first-born males as listed by name, recorded from the age
of one month up, came to 22,273.

[44] The LORD spoke to Moses, saying: [45] Take the Levites in place
of all the first-born among the Israelite people, and the cattle of
the Levites in place of their cattle; and the Levites shall be Mine,
the LORD's. [46] And as the redemption price of the 273 Israelite
first-born over and above the number of the Levites, [47] take five
shekels per head—take this by the sanctuary weight, twenty
gerahs to the shekel—[48] and give the money to Aaron and his
sons as the redemption price for those who are in excess. [49] So
Moses took the redemption money from those over and above

a I.e., the screening curtain; cf. 4–5.

the ones redeemed by the Levites; [50] he took the money from the first-born of the Israelites, 1,365 sanctuary shekels. [51] And Moses gave the redemption money to Aaron and his sons at the LORD's bidding, as the LORD had commanded Moses.

4 The LORD spoke to Moses and Aaron, saying:
[2] Take a [separate] census of the Kohathites among the Levites, by the clans of their ancestral house, [3] from the age of thirty years up to the age of fifty, all who are subject to service, to perform tasks for the Tent of Meeting. [4] This is the responsibility of the Kohathites in the Tent of Meeting: the most sacred objects.

[5] At the breaking of camp, Aaron and his sons shall go in and take down the screening curtain and cover the Ark of the Pact with it. [6] They shall lay a covering of dolphin[a] skin over it and spread a cloth of pure blue on top; and they shall put its poles in place.

[7] Over the table of display they shall spread a blue cloth; they shall place upon it the bowls, the ladles, the jars, and the libation jugs; and the regular bread shall rest upon it. [8] They shall spread over these a crimson cloth which they shall cover with a covering of dolphin skin; and they shall put the poles in place.

[9] Then they shall take a blue cloth and cover the lampstand for lighting, with its lamps, its tongs, and its fire pans, as well as all the oil vessels that are used in its service. [10] They shall put it and all its furnishings into a covering of dolphin skin, which they shall then place on a carrying frame.

[11] Next they shall spread a blue cloth over the altar of gold and cover it with a covering of dolphin skin; and they shall put its poles in place. [12] They shall take all the service vessels with which the service in the sanctuary is performed, put them into a blue cloth and cover them with a covering of dolphin skin, which they shall then place on a carrying frame. [13] They shall remove the ashes from the [copper] altar and spread a purple cloth over it. [14] Upon it they shall place all the vessels that are used in its service: the fire pans, the flesh hooks, the scrapers, and the basins—all the vessels of the altar—and over it they shall spread a covering of dolphin skin; and they shall put its poles in place.

[15] When Aaron and his sons have finished covering the sacred objects and all the furnishings of the sacred objects at the breaking of camp, only then shall the Kohathites come and lift them, so that they do not come in contact with the sacred objects and die. These things in the Tent of Meeting shall be the porterage of the Kohathites.

a See note at Exod. 25.5.

4.1–49: The second Levite census and delineation of Levite duties. The second census of Levites is restricted to the work force between the ages of 30 and 50, who transport the Tabernacle's structural parts, its curtains, and its sacred objects during travel in the wilderness. Responsibilities for specific components of the Tabernacle are divided among the Levitical clan groups. **4–20:** The most important components of the Tabernacle are dealt with first. Since the Levites are not empowered to handle these sacred objects or even view them, on pain of death, those objects, including the Ark, are first wrapped by priests. Coverings of different material and color distinguish the sacred objects transported by the Kohathite clans. The Ark of the Covenant, the most sacred article, is covered with three cloths. The Ark is considered the divine throne of God (1 Sam. 4.4; 2 Sam. 6.2), who in Priestly literature is envisioned as dwelling in the Tabernacle itself (contrast Deut. ch 12, where God's name dwells in the Temple). For that reason the Ark is sometimes brought into battle (1 Sam. ch 4). According to a rabbinic midrash, the earthly Ark is a counterpart of the heavenly throne (*Num. Rab.* 4:13).

21–28: The Gershonite clans are responsible for transporting the four layers of tent curtains. They are supervised by Aaron's son Ithamar. **29–33:** The Merarites, the third group of clans, are charged with carrying the structural parts of the Tabernacle. Ithamar oversees their duties as well. **34:** *The chieftains of the community:* The tribal leaders assist Moses and Aaron in recording the Levite census; this also connects ch 4 to ch 1.

16 Responsibility shall rest with Eleazar son of Aaron the
priest for the lighting oil, the aromatic incense, the regular
meal offering, and the anointing oil—responsibility for the
whole Tabernacle and for everything consecrated that is in it
or in its vessels.
17 The LORD spoke to Moses and Aaron, saying: 18 Do not let
the group of Kohathite clans be cut off from the Levites. 19 Do
this with them, that they may live and not die when they approach the most sacred objects: let Aaron and his sons go in
and assign each of them to his duties and to his porterage.
20 But let not [the Kohathites] go inside and [a-]witness the dismantling of the sanctuary,[-a] lest they die.

NASO' נשא

21 The LORD spoke to Moses: 22 Take a census of the Gershonites
also, by their ancestral house and by their clans. 23 Record them
from the age of thirty years up to the age of fifty, all who are subject to service in the performance of tasks for the Tent of Meeting. 24 These are the duties of the Gershonite clans as to labor
and porterage: 25 they shall carry the cloths of the Tabernacle,
the Tent of Meeting with its covering, the covering of dolphin
skin that is on top of it, and the screen for the entrance of the
Tent of Meeting; 26 the hangings of the enclosure, the screen
at the entrance of the gate of the enclosure that surrounds the
Tabernacle, the cords thereof, and the altar, and all their service
equipment and all their accessories; and they shall perform the
service. 27 All the duties of the Gershonites, all their porterage
and all their service, shall be performed on orders from Aaron
and his sons; you shall make them responsible for attending
to all their porterage. 28 Those are the duties of the Gershonite
clans for the Tent of Meeting; they shall attend to them under
the direction of Ithamar son of Aaron the priest.
29 As for the Merarites, you shall record them by the clans of
their ancestral house; 30 you shall record them from the age of
thirty years up to the age of fifty, all who are subject to service in
the performance of the duties for the Tent of Meeting. 31 These
are their porterage tasks in connection with their various duties for the Tent of Meeting: the planks, the bars, the posts, and
the sockets of the Tabernacle; 32 the posts around the enclosure and their sockets, pegs, and cords—all these furnishings
and their service: you shall list by name the objects that are
their porterage tasks. 33 Those are the duties of the Merarite
clans, pertaining to their various duties in the Tent of Meeting
under the direction of Ithamar son of Aaron the priest.
34 So Moses, Aaron, and the chieftains of the community
recorded the Kohathites by the clans of their ancestral house,

a-a Others "look at the sacred objects even for a moment."

35 from the age of thirty years up to the age of fifty, all who were
subject to service for work relating to the Tent of Meeting.
36 Those recorded by their clans came to 2,750. 37 That was the
enrollment of the Kohathite clans, all those who performed
duties relating to the Tent of Meeting, whom Moses and Aaron
recorded at the command of the LORD through Moses.
38 The Gershonites who were recorded by the clans of their
ancestral house, 39 from the age of thirty years up to the age
of fifty, all who were subject to service for work relating to the
Tent of Meeting—40 those recorded by the clans of their ancestral house came to 2,630. 41 That was the enrollment of the Gershonite clans, all those performing duties relating to the Tent
of Meeting whom Moses and Aaron recorded at the command
of the LORD.
42 The enrollment of the Merarite clans by the clans of their
ancestral house, 43 from the age of thirty years up to the age
of fifty, all who were subject to service for work relating to
the Tent of Meeting—44 those recorded by their clans came to
3,200. 45 That was the enrollment of the Merarite clans which
Moses and Aaron recorded at the command of the LORD
through Moses.
46 All the Levites whom Moses, Aaron, and the chieftains of
Israel recorded by the clans of their ancestral houses, 47 from
the age of thirty years up to the age of fifty, all who were subject
to duties of service and porterage relating to the Tent of Meeting—48 those recorded came to 8,580. 49 Each one was given
responsibility for his service and porterage at the command of
the LORD through Moses, and each was recorded as the LORD
had commanded Moses.

5 The LORD spoke to Moses, saying: 2 Instruct the Israelites
to remove from camp anyone with an [a]eruption or a discharge[a] and anyone defiled by a corpse. 3 Remove male and
female alike; put them outside the camp so that they do not
defile the camp of those in whose midst I dwell.
4 The Israelites did so, putting them outside the camp; as the
LORD had spoken to Moses, so the Israelites did.

5 The LORD spoke to Moses, saying: 6 Speak to the Israelites:
When a man or woman commits any wrong toward a fellow
man, thus breaking faith with the LORD, and that person realizes his guilt, 7 he shall confess the wrong that he has done.
He shall make restitution in the principal amount and add
one-fifth to it, giving it to him whom he has wronged. 8 If the
man has no kinsman[b] to whom restitution can be made, the
amount repaid shall go to the LORD for the priest—in addition

a-a See Lev. 13, 15. *b Lit. "redeemer."*

5.1–31: Laws of purity and the role of the priests. Priestly tasks include responsibilities over worldly as well as sacred matters; in the ancient world the two were inseparable. Laws concerned with the maintenance of religious purity inside the Israelite camp reflect this ideology, and the purity of the camp was essential if the Israelites wanted God to continue dwelling in their midst (see essay "Concepts of Purity," pp. 1998–2005). This explains why these regulations immediately follow the instructions for the proper organization and transport of the wilderness camp (chs 1–4). **1–4:** The sacred status of the Tabernacle, which sits in the center of the camp, necessitates that the entire area within the bounds of the camp preserve a state of cultic (religious) purity. According to the Priestly writer(s), contact with impurity is contagious to both persons and objects. Therefore, that which is in a state of impurity must be removed from the camp, lest it pollute the holiness of the sanctuary and endanger the Presence of God. The most dangerous conditions, those marked by severe impurity, require a seven-day purification process (Lev. chs 13–16; Num. ch 19). They include persons with certain skin diseases, abnormal sexual discharges, menstruating women, or those who are defiled by a corpse. **5–10:** Lev. ch 5 details the "'asham," or guilt offering, and the expiation processes for transgressions that require this category of sacrifices. Here in Num. two provisions supplement the guilt offering for sins involving robberies and accompanying false oaths: (1) A confession must precede the act of restitution. (2) If the injured party has no living relative the reparation payment goes to the officiating priest (as does the meat from the expiatory sacrifice).

11–31: The ordeal, or more correctly, the trial of the suspected adulteress, is a means of allaying or confirming the fears of a husband that his wife was unfaithful. Marital infidelity by the woman is a grave offense because it threatens the purity of the lineage. Adultery is defined as involving sexual contact between a married woman and a man other than her husband, and is a capital crime (Lev. 20.10). (Sexual contact between a married man and an unmarried woman was not considered adultery, although it was not encouraged.) When conclusive evidence is lacking, judgment and subsequent punishment is left in the hands of the divine. Water ordeals of varying types are attested from the ancient Near East. In the Babylonian Laws of Hammurabi, §132, (18th c. BCE), one method of determining the guilt or innocence of a suspected adulteress is the river ordeal, in which the woman is thrown into the water and her fate is left to the river god. According to the Mishnah, the biblical ordeal for a suspected adulteress was suspended after the destruction of the Second Temple, in part due to the uncontrollable number of cases of adultery (*m. Sot.* 9.9). The episode of the suspected adulteress is narrated here for two reasons: The ritual utilizes earth from the floor of the Tabernacle (v. 17), the focus of the previous ch, and the ritual, like the guilt offering, is connected to broken faith (see vv. 6, 12). **12:** If a man's wife *has gone astray:* The initial sin of the woman may be a violation of the marriage oath. Rashi, following *m. Tanḥ.*, understands it as the woman having gone mad. **14:** The reason for the husband's jealousy is not stated but may be that his wife is pregnant and he questions the paternity of the child. But apparently, no concrete reason is required for a husband to bring his wife to trial. **15–26:** The husband brings a menial meal offering, and the priest prepares a mixture of sacral water, dust from the sanctuary floor, and ink rubbed off the inscription of the curse for the woman to drink. Most importantly, the priest administers the woman's

to the ram of expiation with which expiation is made on his
behalf.[a] 9 So, too, any gift among the sacred donations that the
Israelites offer shall be the priest's. 10 And each shall retain his
sacred donations: each priest shall keep what is given to him.

11 The LORD spoke to Moses, saying: 12 Speak to the Israelite
people and say to them:
If any man's wife has gone astray and broken faith with him
13 in that a man has had carnal relations with her unbeknown
to her husband, and she keeps secret the fact that she has
defiled herself without being forced, and there is no witness
against her—14 but a fit of jealousy comes over him and he is
wrought up about the wife who has defiled herself; or if a fit of
jealousy comes over one and he is wrought up about his wife
although she has not defiled herself—15 the man shall bring his
wife to the priest. And he shall bring as an offering for her one-tenth of an *ephah* of barley flour. No oil shall be poured upon
it and no frankincense shall be laid on it, for it is a meal offering of jealousy, a meal offering of remembrance which recalls
wrongdoing.

16 The priest shall bring her forward and have her stand before the LORD. 17 The priest shall take sacral water in an earthen vessel and, taking some of the earth that is on the floor of
the Tabernacle, the priest shall put it into the water. 18 After he
has made the woman stand before the LORD, the priest shall
bare the woman's head[b] and place upon her hands the meal
offering of remembrance, which is a meal offering of jealousy.
And in the priest's hands shall be the water of bitterness [c]that
induces the spell.[c] 19 The priest shall adjure the woman, saying to her, "If no man has lain with you, if you have not gone
astray in defilement while married to your husband, be immune to harm from this water of bitterness that induces the
spell. 20 But if you have gone astray while married to your
husband and have defiled yourself, if a man other than your
husband has had carnal relations with you"—21 here the priest
shall administer the curse of adjuration to the woman, as the
priest goes on to say to the woman—"may the LORD make you
a curse and an imprecation among your people, as the LORD
causes your thigh to sag and your belly to distend; 22 may this
water that induces the spell enter your body, causing the belly to distend and the thigh to sag." And the woman shall say,
"Amen, amen!"
23 The priest shall put these curses down in writing and rub
it off into the water of bitterness. 24 He is to make the woman
drink the water of bitterness that induces the spell, so that the

a Cf. Lev. 5.15 f. *b See note at Lev. 10.6.* *c-c Meaning of Heb. uncertain.*

spell-inducing water may enter into her to bring on bitterness.
25 Then the priest shall take from the woman's hand the meal
offering of jealousy, elevate the meal offering before the LORD,
and present it on the altar. 26 The priest shall scoop out of the
meal offering a token part of it and turn it into smoke on the
altar. Last, he shall make the woman drink the water.

27 Once he has made her drink the water—if she has defiled
herself by breaking faith with her husband, the spell-inducing
water shall enter into her to bring on bitterness, so that her belly shall distend and her thigh shall sag; and the woman shall
become a curse among her people. 28 But if the woman has not
defiled herself and is pure, she shall be unharmed and able to
retain seed.

29 This is the ritual in cases of jealousy, when a woman goes
astray while married to her husband and defiles herself, 30 or
when a fit of jealousy comes over a man and he is wrought up
over his wife: the woman shall be made to stand before the
LORD and the priest shall carry out all this ritual with her. 31 The
man shall be clear of guilt; but that woman shall suffer for her
guilt.

6 The LORD spoke to Moses, saying: 2 Speak to the Israelites
and say to them: If anyone, man or woman, explicitly[a]
utters a nazirite's vow, to set himself apart for the LORD, 3 he
shall abstain from wine and any other intoxicant; he shall not
drink vinegar of wine or of any other intoxicant, neither shall
he drink anything in which grapes have been steeped, nor eat
grapes fresh or dried. 4 Throughout his term as nazirite, he may
not eat anything that is obtained from the grapevine, even
seeds or skin.[b]

5 Throughout the term of his vow as nazirite, no razor shall
touch his head; it shall remain consecrated until the completion of his term as nazirite of the LORD, the hair of his head being left to grow untrimmed. 6 Throughout the term that he has
set apart for the LORD, he shall not go in where there is a dead
person. 7 Even if his father or mother, or his brother or sister
should die, he must not defile himself for them, since [c-]hair set
apart for his God[-c] is upon his head: 8 throughout his term as
nazirite he is consecrated to the LORD.

a See note at Lev. 22.21. *b Meaning of Heb.* ḥarṣannim *and* zag *uncertain.*
c-c Others "his consecration unto God."

oath and utters the curse that takes effect if she is guilty. **18:** *Water of bitterness* seems to refer to the bitter taste of the water, which contains ink and dust, probably mixed with ashes fallen to the sanctuary floor from the altar. Alternatively, the "bitterness" can refer to the punishment, apparently a distended uterus, a possible miscarriage, and ultimate infertility (so medieval commentators). A third interpretation translates the Heb term "hamarim" as "instructing," derived from a different verbal root ("y-r-h"). Thereby, the waters reveal the woman's innocence or guilt. **21:** This v. repeats the curse; it can be explained as an interpolation that adds God to the formula. **22:** *The woman shall say, "Amen, amen!"*: Amen or twice amen is an affirmation of truth often attached to oaths (Deut. 27.15–26; Neh. 5.13). An archeological discovery of a letter from the 7th century BCE that records the petition of an Israelite worker to his officer, uses "Amen" to affirm the truth of the worker's statement. Oaths and curses similar in formula to those uttered in this biblical case are known from ancient Near Eastern treaties. In the case of the biblical adulteress, as well as in some nonbiblical examples, the function of the water mixture is to effectuate the oath. **27–28:** These vv. repeat the two possible results of the trial. **29–31:** *This is the ritual,* or instruction, "torah." Priestly legislation often introduces units or concludes them with these types of summary statements (see concluding vv. in Lev. chs 7, 11, 15). The husband of an innocent woman is free of guilt, that is, he is not charged and punished for bringing a false accusation (cf. Deut. 19.16–19—a false witness).

6.1–21: Vow of the Nazirite. By taking the vow of a Nazirite an Israelite becomes consecrated to God for a limited time period, becoming a type of lay priest, with restrictions similar to those of priests. The vow entails a number of restrictions: abstaining from fermented drinks and grape products, abstaining from cutting the hair, and abstaining from coming in contact with the dead. (This explains why Samson, who was a Nazirite, was not supposed to cut his hair.) The Rabbis explain that the passage on Nazirite vows follows the section on the suspected adulteress to teach that abstinence from drink is commendable, since drinking intoxicants can lead to adultery (*b. Sot.* 2a). Modern critical approaches connect the sections by their emphasis on the key roles of the priests.

9 If a person dies suddenly near him,[a] defiling his consecrated hair, he shall shave his head on the day he becomes clean;
he shall shave it on the seventh day. 10 On the eighth day he
shall bring two turtledoves or two pigeons to the priest, at the
entrance of the Tent of Meeting. 11 The priest shall offer one as a
purification offering and the other as a burnt offering, and make
expiation on his behalf for the guilt that he incurred through
the corpse. That same day he shall reconsecrate his head 12 and
rededicate to the LORD his term as nazirite; and he shall bring a
lamb in its first year as a penalty offering. The previous period
shall be void, since his consecrated hair was defiled.

13 This is the ritual for the nazirite: On the day that his term
as nazirite is completed, he[b] shall be brought to the entrance
of the Tent of Meeting. 14 As his offering to the LORD he shall
present: one male lamb in its first year, without blemish, for a
burnt offering; one ewe lamb in its first year, without blemish,
for a purification offering; one ram without blemish for an offering of well-being; 15 a basket of unleavened cakes of choice
flour with oil mixed in, and unleavened wafers spread with oil;
and the proper meal offerings and libations.

16 The priest shall present them before the LORD and offer
the purification offering and the burnt offering. 17 He shall offer the ram as a sacrifice of well-being to the LORD, together
with the basket of unleavened cakes; the priest shall also offer
the meal offerings and the libations. 18 The nazirite shall then
shave his consecrated hair, at the entrance of the Tent of Meeting, and take the locks of his consecrated hair and put them on
the fire that is under the sacrifice of well-being.

19 The priest shall take the shoulder of the ram when it has
been boiled, one unleavened cake from the basket, and one
unleavened wafer, and place them on the hands of the nazirite
after he has shaved his consecrated hair. 20 The priest shall elevate them as an elevation offering before the LORD; and this
shall be a sacred donation for the priest, in addition to the
breast of the elevation offering and the thigh of gift offering.
After that the nazirite may drink wine.

21 Such is the obligation of a nazirite; except that he who
vows an offering to the LORD of what he can afford, beyond his
nazirite requirements, must do exactly according to the vow
that he has made beyond his obligation as a nazirite.

22 The LORD spoke to Moses: 23 Speak to Aaron and his sons:
Thus shall you bless the people of Israel. Say to them:

24 The LORD bless you and protect you!

25 The LORD [c]deal kindly and graciously with you![c]

a Cf. Num. 19.14–16. *b Or "it," i.e., the consecrated hair; cf. v. 19.*
c-c Others "make His face to shine upon thee and be gracious to thee."

9–12: Contamination by a corpse requires shaving the hair and following the purification process outlined in ch 19. After purification, the Nazirite restarts his or her original vow timetable. Defilement of a Nazirite affects the consecrated hair rather than the person. **13–20:** The rites that the Nazirite undergoes at the completion of the vow not only commemorate the fulfillment of the vow but function as a transitional ritual that allows the person to return to his or her former status. In this Priestly passage, the role of the priest in the ceremony is central to the discussion of the Nazirite. These vv. concern a Nazirite for a prescribed period of time; Judg. ch 13 depicts Samson as a lifetime Nazirite, with similar restrictions. However, Samson's warrior ventures are inconsistent with Nazirite vows as outlined in Num. **18:** The significance of the hair is also apparent at the completion ceremony, at which time it is burnt in the fire underneath (the pot of) the Nazirite's sacrifice of well-being. Hair offerings are known from ancient practices in the Aegean.

6.22–27: The priestly blessing. Another duty of priests is to bless the community of Israel (Lev. 9.22–23; Deut. 10.8; 21.5) or individual Israelites (1 Sam. 2.20) in the name of the LORD. The three-part blessing here invokes God's mercy and favor toward the children of Israel for the sake of their general well-being, "shalom." Each of the three parts is longer than the preceding one, emphasizing the overflowing of blessing that is hoped for. Ibn Ezra connects Aaron's blessing of Israel at the dedication of the Tabernacle (Lev. 9.22–23) to the priestly blessing in Num. An interpretive version of the priestly blessing, contained in the sectarian literature of the Dead Sea Scrolls, expands the biblical text to more clearly define the particulars of God's blessing (1QS 2.2–4). **25–26:** *Deal kindly* is more literally "shine His face," a sign of favor. Similarly in v. 26, *bestow his favor* is "raise His head." The Bible often

26 The LORD [a]bestow His favor[a] upon you and grant you
peace![b]
27 Thus they shall link My name with the people of Israel,
and I will bless them.

7 On the day that Moses finished setting up the Tabernacle,
he anointed and consecrated it and all its furnishings, as
well as the altar and its utensils. When he had anointed and
consecrated them, 2 the chieftains of Israel, the heads of ancestral houses, namely, the chieftains of the tribes, those who
were in charge of enrollment, drew near[c] 3 and brought their
offering before the LORD: six draught carts and twelve oxen, a
cart for every two chieftains and an ox for each one.
When they had brought them before the Tabernacle, 4 the
LORD said to Moses: 5 Accept these from them for use in the
service of the Tent of Meeting, and give them to the Levites according to their respective services.
6 Moses took the carts and the oxen and gave them to the
Levites. 7 Two carts and four oxen he gave to the Gershonites,
as required for their service, 8 and four carts and eight oxen
he gave to the Merarites, as required for their service—under
the direction of Ithamar son of Aaron the priest. 9 But to the
Kohathites he did not give any; since theirs was the service of
the [most] sacred objects, their porterage was by shoulder.
10 The chieftains also brought the dedication offering for the
altar upon its being anointed. As the chieftains were presenting their offerings before the altar, 11 the LORD said to Moses:
Let them present their offerings for the dedication of the altar,
one chieftain each day.
12 The one who presented his offering on the first day was
Nahshon son of Amminadab of the tribe of Judah. 13 His offering: one silver bowl weighing 130 shekels and one silver
basin of 70 shekels by the sanctuary weight, both filled with
choice flour with oil mixed in, for a meal offering; 14 one gold

a-a *Others "lift up His countenance."* *b* *Or "friendship."* *c* *Cf. Exod. 14.10.*

refers to God in such anthropomorphic terms. **27:** The prescription to place God's name upon Israel may refer to amulets inscribed with the name of the LORD worn around the neck. This interpretation is supported by the discovery in a Jerusalem tomb of two silver amulets incised with slightly shorter versions of the priestly benediction in Num. These First Temple-period amulets testify to the antiquity of the blessing. The priestly blessing has been preserved to modernity in Jewish liturgy as part of the "Amidah" and in the blessing recited by parents for their children on Friday night. *And I will bless them:* The Heb reads, "and I will bless you (plural)." Ibn Ezra correctly explains that "you" refers to the priests; the priests bless Israel and God in turn blesses the priests.

7.1–89: Final preparation for the operation of the Tabernacle cult. After the organization of the camp and the relegation of duties to the Levites and priests, Moses consecrates the Tabernacle and its implements and outfits it with supplies necessary for its operation. The consecration of the altar repeats the account in Lev. chs 8–9, expanding the narrative in Lev. by adding the chieftains' gifts. The tribal chieftains bring joint gifts, representing all Israel equally (cf. Exod. 30.15), as well as gifts from their separate tribes. Joint initiatory gifts for the sanctuary consist of six carts and twelve oxen. The carts and oxen are given to the Gershonite and Merarite Levitic clans for transporting the portable Tabernacle. The Kohathites do not receive carts because they must carry the sacred objects on their shoulders. Individual chieftains bring their tribe's gifts and dedication offerings for twelve consecutive days, one chieftain per day. The insertion of this information at this point fits with the previous assignment of Levitic tasks and the appointment of tribal heads. **1:** Anointing the Tabernacle and its implements with oil as an act of consecration is an ancient Near Eastern practice. In the Bible, a comparable act is performed by Jacob at Bethel when he anoints the pillar that he erects to mark the holiness of the site, designating it as a future shrine (Gen. 28.18–22). **2:** According to Rashi, the chieftains of Israel are the same officers who were in charge of the slaves in Egypt and beaten on their (the Israelites') account (see Exod. 5.14, where they are called "foremen"); they are now rewarded. **10:** *Dedication offering for the altar:* In Heb "ḥanukah" is the term for the opening dedication of a house, temple, or altar (cf. Deut. 20.5; 1 Kings 8.63; 2 Chron. 7.9). Similarly, the holiday of Hanukkah celebrates the purification and rededication of the Jerusalem Temple by the Maccabees (1 Macc. 4.36–61). The Torah reading for Hanukkah is taken from this ch in Num. **12–83:** The group of gifts brought by each tribal chieftain is substantial by any standard: a heavy silver bowl and a silver basin, a solid gold ladle, 21 herd animals of various kinds, incense, flour and oil. Despite the fact that each chieftain brings the identical items, these are listed separately following the chief's name. Such lists are reminiscent of accounting practices for temples in Syria, Mesopotamia, and Egypt. Like modern accounting records, at times the ancient ones are laid out in columns, using numeral characters to specify amounts, and even ditto marks (Egypt) for repeated items. Several inscriptions (receipts on pottery sherds) from ancient Arad (7th–6th c. BCE), a military fort in the northern Negev, are Israelite examples of similar accounting methods. **12:** *Judah,* as most important, is mentioned first.

ladle of 10 shekels, filled with incense; 15 one bull of the herd,
one ram, and one lamb in its first year, for a burnt offering;
16 one goat for a purification offering; 17 and for his sacrifice
of well-being: two oxen, five rams, five he-goats, and five
yearling lambs. That was the offering of Nahshon son of Amminadab.

18 On the second day, Nethanel son of Zuar, chieftain of Issachar, made his offering. 19 He presented as his offering: one
silver bowl weighing 130 shekels and one silver basin of 70
shekels by the sanctuary weight, both filled with choice flour
with oil mixed in, for a meal offering; 20 one gold ladle of 10
shekels, filled with incense; 21 one bull of the herd, one ram,
and one lamb in its first year, for a burnt offering; 22 one goat
for a purification offering; 23 and for his sacrifice of well-being:
two oxen, five rams, five he-goats, and five yearling lambs. That
was the offering of Nethanel son of Zuar.

24 On the third day, it was the chieftain of the Zebulunites,
Eliab son of Helon. 25 His offering: one silver bowl weighing
130 shekels and one silver basin of 70 shekels by the sanctuary weight, both filled with choice flour with oil mixed in, for
a meal offering; 26 one gold ladle of 10 shekels, filled with incense; 27 one bull of the herd, one ram, and one lamb in its first
year, for a burnt offering; 28 one goat for a purification offering;
29 and for his sacrifice of well-being: two oxen, five rams, five
he-goats, and five yearling lambs. That was the offering of Eliab
son of Helon.

30 On the fourth day, it was the chieftain of the Reubenites,
Elizur son of Shedeur. 31 His offering: one silver bowl weighing
130 shekels and one silver basin of 70 shekels by the sanctuary weight, both filled with choice flour with oil mixed in, for
a meal offering; 32 one gold ladle of 10 shekels, filled with incense; 33 one bull of the herd, one ram, and one lamb in its first
year, for a burnt offering; 34 one goat for a purification offering;
35 and for his sacrifice of well-being: two oxen, five rams, five
he-goats, and five yearling lambs. That was the offering of Elizur son of Shedeur.

36 On the fifth day, it was the chieftain of the Simeonites,
Shelumiel son of Zurishaddai. 37 His offering: one silver bowl
weighing 130 shekels and one silver basin of 70 shekels by the
sanctuary weight, both filled with choice flour with oil mixed
in, for a meal offering; 38 one gold ladle of 10 shekels, filled with
incense; 39 one bull of the herd, one ram, and one lamb in its
first year, for a burnt offering; 40 one goat for a purification offering; 41 and for his sacrifice of well-being: two oxen, five rams,
five he-goats, and five yearling lambs. That was the offering of
Shelumiel son of Zurishaddai.

42 On the sixth day, it was the chieftain of the Gadites, Eliasaph son of Deuel. 43 His offering: one silver bowl weighing

130 shekels and one silver basin of 70 shekels by the sanctuary weight, both filled with choice flour with oil mixed in, for
a meal offering; 44 one gold ladle of 10 shekels, filled with incense; 45 one bull of the herd, one ram, and one lamb in its first
year, for a burnt offering; 46 one goat for a purification offering;
47 and for his sacrifice of well-being: two oxen, five rams, five
he-goats, and five yearling lambs. That was the offering of Eliasaph son of Deuel.

48 On the seventh day, it was the chieftain of the Ephraimites, Elishama son of Ammihud. 49 His offering: one silver bowl
weighing 130 shekels and one silver basin of 70 shekels by the
sanctuary weight, both filled with choice flour with oil mixed
in, for a meal offering; 50 one gold ladle of 10 shekels, filled with
incense; 51 one bull of the herd, one ram, and one lamb in its
first year, for a burnt offering; 52 one goat for a purification offering; 53 and for his sacrifice of well-being: two oxen, five rams,
five he-goats, and five yearling lambs. That was the offering of
Elishama son of Ammihud.

54 On the eighth day, it was the chieftain of the Manassites,
Gamaliel son of Pedahzur. 55 His offering: one silver bowl
weighing 130 shekels and one silver basin of 70 shekels by the
sanctuary weight, both filled with choice flour with oil mixed
in, for a meal offering; 56 one gold ladle of 10 shekels, filled with
incense; 57 one bull of the herd, one ram, and one lamb in its
first year, for a burnt offering; 58 one goat for a purification offering; 59 and for his sacrifice of well-being: two oxen, five rams,
five he-goats, and five yearling lambs. That was the offering of
Gamaliel son of Pedahzur.

60 On the ninth day, it was the chieftain of the Benjaminites,
Abidan son of Gideoni. 61 His offering: one silver bowl weighing 130 shekels and one silver basin of 70 shekels by the sanctuary weight, both filled with choice flour with oil mixed in, for
a meal offering; 62 one gold ladle of 10 shekels, filled with incense; 63 one bull of the herd, one ram, and one lamb in its first
year, for a burnt offering; 64 one goat for a purification offering; 65 and for his sacrifice of well-being: two oxen, five rams,
five he-goats, and five yearling lambs. That was the offering of
Abidan son of Gideoni.

66 On the tenth day, it was the chieftain of the Danites,
Ahiezer son of Ammishaddai. 67 His offering: one silver bowl
weighing 130 shekels and one silver basin of 70 shekels by the
sanctuary weight, both filled with choice flour with oil mixed
in, for a meal offering; 68 one gold ladle of 10 shekels, filled with
incense; 69 one bull of the herd, one ram, and one lamb in its
first year, for a burnt offering; 70 one goat for a purification offering; 71 and for his sacrifice of well-being: two oxen, five rams,
five he-goats, and five yearling lambs. That was the offering of
Ahiezer son of Ammishaddai.

[72]On the eleventh day, it was the chieftain of the Asherites, Pagiel son of Ochran. [73]His offering: one silver bowl weighing 130 shekels and one silver basin of 70 shekels by the sanctuary weight, both filled with choice flour with oil mixed in, for a meal offering; [74]one gold ladle of 10 shekels, filled with incense; [75]one bull of the herd, one ram, and one lamb in its first year, for a burnt offering; [76]one goat for a purification offering; [77]and for his sacrifice of well-being: two oxen, five rams, five he-goats, and five yearling lambs. That was the offering of Pagiel son of Ochran.

[78]On the twelfth day, it was the chieftain of the Naphtalites, Ahira son of Enan. [79]His offering: one silver bowl weighing 130 shekels and one silver basin of 70 shekels by the sanctuary weight, both filled with choice flour with oil mixed in, for a meal offering; [80]one gold ladle of 10 shekels, filled with incense; [81]one bull of the herd, one ram, and one lamb in its first year, for a burnt offering; [82]one goat for a purification offering; [83]and for his sacrifice of well-being: two oxen, five rams, five he-goats, and five yearling lambs. That was the offering of Ahira son of Enan.

[84]This was the dedication offering for the altar from the chieftains of Israel upon its being anointed: silver bowls, 12; silver basins, 12; gold ladles, 12. [85]Silver per bowl, 130; per basin, 70. Total silver of vessels, 2,400 sanctuary shekels. [86]The 12 gold ladles filled with incense—10 sanctuary shekels per ladle—total gold of the ladles, 120.

[87]Total of herd animals for burnt offerings, 12 bulls; of rams, 12; of yearling lambs, 12—with their proper meal offerings; of goats for purification offerings, 12. [88]Total of herd animals for sacrifices of well-being, 24 bulls; of rams, 60; of he-goats, 60; of yearling lambs, 60. That was the dedication offering for the altar after its anointing.

[89]When Moses went into the Tent of Meeting to speak with Him, he would hear the Voice addressing him from above the cover that was on top of the Ark of the Pact between the two cherubim; thus He spoke to him.

BE-HAʿALOTEKHA בהעלתך

8 The LORD spoke to Moses, saying: [2]Speak to Aaron and say to him, "When you mount[a] the lamps, let the seven lamps give light at the front of the lampstand." [3]Aaron did so; he mounted the lamps at the front of the lampstand, as the LORD had commanded Moses.—[4]Now this is how the lampstand was made: it was hammered work of gold, hammered from base to petal. According to the pattern that the LORD had shown Moses, so was the lampstand made.

a *Cf. Exod.* 25.37.

84–88: A typically Priestly summary of the account. **89:** This appended v. reiterates how Moses communicates with God in the Tent of Meeting, the portable site for revelation where God dwells (Exod. 25.17–22; Lev. 9.23). God's name is not mentioned but is substituted by *the Voice,* a term that is the precursor of the rabbinic "bat kol," "daughter of the voice," or "echo," signifying a divine voice from the heavens.

8.1–4: Lighting the lampstand. Several passages in Exod. (25.31–40; 27.20–21; 30.7–8; 37.17–24; 40.4) and one in Lev. (24.1–4) deal with the construction and lighting instructions for the lampstand (menorah). Here the instructions are fulfilled. Lighting the lampstand inside the Tabernacle is a logical conclusion to 7.89, where Moses enters the Tent of Meeting and communicates with God. Ibn Ezra explains the textual placement as a lesson that God's word also comes at night, necessitating the light to burn day and night. **2:** *Let the seven lamps give light at the front of the lampstand:* The lamps are positioned on the stand facing forward, northward, to cast light on the altar and the table with showbread situated in front of the menorah. Seven-spouted ceramic lamps excavated from the shrine at Dan, dating to the First Temple period, are shaped differently; they are circular with spouts for wicks projecting in all directions. **4:** The unit concludes in typically Priestly fashion, that God's command was executed exactly.

[5] The LORD spoke to Moses, saying: [6] Take the Levites from among the Israelites and cleanse them. [7] This is what you shall do to them to cleanse them: sprinkle on them water of purification, and let them go over their whole body with a razor, and wash their clothes; thus they shall be cleansed. [8] Let them take a bull of the herd, and with it a meal offering of choice flour with oil mixed in, and you take a second bull of the herd for a purification offering. [9] You shall bring the Levites forward before the Tent of Meeting. Assemble the whole Israelite community, [10] and bring the Levites forward before the LORD. Let the Israelites lay their hands upon the Levites, [11] and let Aaron designate[a] the Levites before the LORD as an elevation offering from the Israelites, that they may perform the service of the LORD. [12] The Levites shall now lay their hands upon the heads of the bulls; one shall be offered to the LORD as a purification offering and the other as a burnt offering, to make expiation for the Levites.

[13] You shall place the Levites in attendance upon Aaron and his sons, and designate them as an elevation offering to the LORD. [14] Thus you shall set the Levites apart from the Israelites, and the Levites shall be Mine. [15] Thereafter the Levites shall be qualified for the service of the Tent of Meeting, once you have cleansed them and designated them as an elevation offering. [16] For they are formally assigned to Me from among the Israelites: I have taken them for Myself in place of all the first issue of the womb, of all the first-born of the Israelites. [17] For every first-born among the Israelites, man as well as beast, is Mine; I consecrated them to Myself at the time that I smote every first-born in the land of Egypt. [18] Now I take the Levites instead of every first-born of the Israelites; [19] and from among the Israelites I formally assign the Levites to Aaron and his sons, to perform the service for the Israelites in the Tent of Meeting and to make expiation for the Israelites, so that no plague may afflict the Israelites [b-]for coming[-b] too near the sanctuary.

[20] Moses, Aaron, and the whole Israelite community did with the Levites accordingly; just as the LORD had commanded Moses in regard to the Levites, so the Israelites did with them. [21] The Levites purified themselves and washed their clothes; and Aaron designated them as an elevation offering before the LORD, and Aaron made expiation for them to cleanse them. [22] Thereafter the Levites were qualified to perform their service in the Tent of Meeting, under Aaron and his sons. As the LORD had commanded Moses in regard to the Levites, so they did to them.

[23] The LORD spoke to Moses, saying: [24] This is the rule for the Levites. From twenty-five years of age up they shall participate

a *Lit. "elevate."* *b-b* *Lit. "when the Israelites come."*

8.5–26: Ritual purification of the Levites. The duties of the Levites are explicated in the previous chs. Here they undergo rites of ritual purification so that they can handle the Tabernacle and its contents. **7:** Cleansing entails being sprinkled with water of purification (fresh water mixed with the ashes of the red cow; see ch 19), shaving the entire body, and washing one's clothing. **9–16:** These preparatory rituals are followed by sacrifices and a laying-on-of-hands ceremony in front of the Tent of Meeting. In a gesture reminiscent of laying hands upon the heads of sacrificial animals (8.12), a group of Israelite representatives lay their hands on the Levites as Aaron designates them (the Levites) as an elevation offering from Israel. These rituals officially separate the Levites from other Israelites and dedicate them to God's service. **23–26:** The last vv. of this section specify the age limits for Levitic duties. The starting age for joining the Levite work force, age 25, conflicts with the starting age for being counted in the census, age 30 (ch 4). This suggests that the Priestly material in Num. has a complex history, though rabbinic interpretation harmonizes the conflicting numbers by surmising that between the ages of 25 and 30 Levites function as assistants and only at age 30 are they counted as full-fledged members of the work force.

in the work force in the service of the Tent of Meeting; 25 but at the age of fifty they shall retire from the work force and shall serve no more. 26 They may assist their brother Levites at the Tent of Meeting by standing guard, but they shall perform no labor. Thus you shall deal with the Levites in regard to their duties.

9 The LORD spoke to Moses in the wilderness of Sinai, on the first new moon of the second year following the exodus from the land of Egypt, saying: 2 Let the Israelite people offer the passover sacrifice at its set time: 3 you shall offer it on the fourteenth day of this month, at twilight, at its set time; you shall offer it in accordance with all its rules and rites.

4 Moses instructed the Israelites to offer the passover sacrifice; 5 and they offered the passover sacrifice in the first month, on the fourteenth day of the month, at twilight, in the wilderness of Sinai. Just as the LORD had commanded Moses, so the Israelites did.

6 But there were some men who were unclean by reason of a corpse and could not offer the passover sacrifice on that day. Appearing that same day before Moses and Aaron, 7 those men said to them,[a] "Unclean though we are by reason of a corpse, why must we be debarred from presenting the LORD's offering at its set time with the rest of the Israelites?" 8 Moses said to them, "Stand by, and let me hear what instructions the LORD gives about you."

9 And the LORD spoke to Moses, saying: 10 Speak to the Israelite people, saying: When any of you or of your posterity who are defiled by a corpse or are on a long journey would offer a passover sacrifice to the LORD, 11 they shall offer it in the second month, on the fourteenth day of the month, at twilight. They shall eat it with unleavened bread and bitter herbs, 12 and they shall not leave any of it over until morning. They shall not break a bone of it. They shall offer it in strict accord with the law of the passover sacrifice. 13 But if a man who is clean and not on a journey refrains from offering the passover sacrifice, that person shall be cut off from his kin, for he did not present the LORD's offering at its set time; that man shall bear his guilt.

14 And when a stranger who resides with you would offer a passover sacrifice to the LORD, he must offer it in accordance with the rules and rites of the passover sacrifice. There shall be one law for you, whether stranger or citizen of the country.

15 On the day that the Tabernacle was set up, the cloud covered the Tabernacle, the Tent of the Pact; and in the evening it

a *Lit. "him."*

9.1–14: First Passover in the wilderness. Israel observed the first Passover in Egypt just prior to the exodus (Exod. ch 12). Now, one year later, as Israel prepares to depart from Sinai, it celebrates the first Passover in the wilderness. Here the Passover is connected to the Sinaitic covenant, including the laws of ritual purity that must be observed inside the camp in the presence of the Tabernacle. The time-bound obligation to partake of the Passover sacrifice presents a legal problem for Israelites who are ritually impure from contact with a corpse. The issue is resolved with the designation of an alternate Passover, one month later, for persons in a state of impurity or on a distant journey. According to the Chronicler, King Hezekiah (late 8th c. BCE) also postponed one Passover to the second month since not enough priests were in a state of purity and those Israelites residing in the north needed time to assemble in Jerusalem (2 Chron. ch 30). Passover is the only festival or ritual for which a "make-up" is scheduled; this is because of the importance of the festival as an acknowledgment of God's role as redeemer from Egypt. **10:** *Defiled by a corpse or are on a long journey:* Both of these exemptions require further definition. According to the Rabbis, corpse defilement is inclusive of all other impurities; the distance that qualifies as a long journey from the Temple is debated. Even though the setting of this legislation is in the wilderness, it is imagining the reality of life after the wilderness wanderings. **14:** Observance of the Passover is mandatory both for Israelites and resident aliens, though according to Exod. 12.48, only circumcised resident aliens may partake.

9.15–23: The divine fire-cloud. This passage is strategically placed just prior to Israel's resumption of the desert march which was interrupted by their encampment at Sinai (Exod. 19.1–Num. 10.1). The fire-cloud, God's manifestation to Israel, guides the movement of the traveling camp as a cloud by day and a fire at night.

rested over the Tabernacle in the likeness of fire until morning. [16] It was always so: the cloud covered it, appearing as fire by night. [17] And whenever the cloud lifted from the Tent, the Israelites would set out accordingly; and at the spot where the cloud settled, there the Israelites would make camp. [18] At a command of the LORD the Israelites broke camp, and at a command of the LORD they made camp: they remained encamped as long as the cloud stayed over the Tabernacle. [19] When the cloud lingered over the Tabernacle many days, the Israelites observed the LORD's mandate and did not journey on. [20] At such times as the cloud rested over the Tabernacle for but a few days, they remained encamped at a command of the LORD, and broke camp at a command of the LORD. [21] And at such times as the cloud stayed from evening until morning, they broke camp as soon as the cloud lifted in the morning. Day or night, whenever the cloud lifted, they would break camp. [22] Whether it was two days or a month or a year—however long the cloud lingered over the Tabernacle—the Israelites remained encamped and did not set out; only when it lifted did they break camp. [23] On a sign from the LORD they made camp and on a sign from the LORD they broke camp; they observed the LORD's mandate at the LORD's bidding through Moses.

10 The LORD spoke to Moses, saying: [2] Have two silver trumpets made; make them of hammered work. They shall serve you to summon the community and to set the divisions in motion. [3] When both are blown in long blasts,[a] the whole community shall assemble before you at the entrance of the Tent of Meeting; [4] and if only one is blown, the chieftains, heads of Israel's contingents, shall assemble before you. [5] But when you sound short blasts,[a] the divisions encamped on the east shall move forward; [6] and when you sound short blasts a second time, those encamped on the south shall move forward. Thus short blasts shall be blown for setting them in motion, [7] while to convoke the congregation you shall blow long blasts, not short ones. [8] The trumpets shall be blown by Aaron's sons, the priests; they shall be for you an institution for all time throughout the ages.

[9] [b]When you are at war[-b] in your land against an aggressor who attacks you, you shall sound short blasts on the trumpets, that you may be remembered before the LORD your God and be delivered from your enemies. [10] And on your joyous occasions—your fixed festivals and new moon days—you shall sound the trumpets over your burnt offerings and your sacrifices of well-being. They shall be a reminder of you before your God: I, the LORD, am your God.

a Meaning of Heb. uncertain. *b-b Meaning of Heb. uncertain.*

When the fire-cloud descends over the Tabernacle, Israel camps; when it rises, Israel marches (also Exod. 40.36–38). The cloudy fiery aura of the LORD is a divine feature also found in non-Israelite societies; it arrives over the Tabernacle once that structure is completed (v. 15) and serves as a sign of divine favor. In other Priestly writings this divine fire is called "kavod," God's Presence or glory (Exod. 24.16–17; 2 Chron. 7.3). In the account of the burning bush (Exod. ch 3) and Ezekiel's vision of the divine chariot (Ezek. ch 1), God also manifests Himself as, or from within, fire.

10.1–10: The silver trumpets. The trumpets, like the fire-cloud, summon the Israelite divisions to march. Together, the fire-cloud and trumpets appeal to the senses of hearing and sight just as both senses are invoked in the revelation at Sinai by thunder, lightning, and dense cloud cover (Exod. 19.16). Usually an animal horn, a shofar, is used to signal the people to assemble for religious or military purposes (i.e., Lev. 25.9; Judg. 3.27). Trumpets, presumably of metal, are attested in a number of biblical texts, primarily of Priestly authorship. Only trumpets explicitly manufactured of silver are mentioned in this text. Trumpets play a significant role in the postbiblical "War Scroll," a description of the eschatological war found among the Dead Sea Scrolls. **9–10:** In wartime, the sound of the trumpets, like a siren, alerts God that Israel is in trouble; at festivals, the sound of the trumpets is a reminder that Israel stands before God, no doubt as a blessing. The Rabbis used the final v. in this section as the foundation on which they constructed the three-part "Musaf" (additional prayer) of Rosh Ha-Shanah. *I, the LORD, am your God* stands for God's kingship ("malkhuyot"—kingship); *you shall sound the trumpets* stands for trumpets or horns ("shofarot"—related to the shofar or ram's horn); *they shall be a reminder of you before your God* stands for memorials ("zikhronot"—remembrance).

11 In the second year, on the twentieth day of the second
month, the cloud lifted from the Tabernacle of the Pact 12 and
the Israelites set out on their journeys from the wilderness of
Sinai. The cloud came to rest in the wilderness of Paran.
13 When the march was to begin, at the LORD's command
through Moses, 14 the first standard to set out, troop by troop,
was the division of Judah. In command of its troops was Nahshon son of Amminadab; 15 in command of the tribal troop of
Issachar, Nethanel son of Zuar; 16 and in command of the tribal
troop of Zebulun, Eliab son of Helon.
17 Then the Tabernacle would be taken apart; and the Gershonites and the Merarites, who carried the Tabernacle, would
set out.
18 The next standard to set out, troop by troop, was the division of Reuben. In command of its troop was Elizur son of Shedeur; 19 in command of the tribal troop of Simeon, Shelumiel son
of Zurishaddai; 20 and in command of the tribal troop of Gad,
Eliasaph son of Deuel.
21 Then the Kohathites, who carried the sacred objects,
would set out; and by the time they arrived, the Tabernacle
would be set up again.
22 The next standard to set out, troop by troop, was the division of Ephraim. In command of its troop was Elishama son of
Ammihud; 23 in command of the tribal troop of Manasseh, Gamaliel son of Pedahzur; 24 and in command of the tribal troop
of Benjamin, Abidan son of Gideoni.
25 Then, as the rear guard of all the divisions, the standard
of the division of Dan would set out, troop by troop. In command of its troop was Ahiezer son of Ammishaddai; 26 in command of the tribal troop of Asher, Pagiel son of Ochran; 27 and
in command of the tribal troop of Naphtali, Ahira son of Enan.
28 Such was the order of march of the Israelites, as they
marched troop by troop.

29 Moses said to Hobab son of Reuel the Midianite, Moses'
father-in-law, "We are setting out for the place of which the
LORD has said, 'I will give it to you.' Come with us and we will
be generous with you; for the LORD has promised to be generous to Israel."

10.11–12.16: The march from Sinai to the desert of Paran. 10.11–28: Order of march. The second major literary unit in Numbers begins here. (The ch numbers in our Bibles date from the 13th c. CE, so it is not surprising that a major unit may begin in the middle of a ch.) It starts with the Israelite departure from Sinai to resume their journey through the wilderness. The four camp divisions travel in a single column while maintaining the same order as in camp. The division of Judah leads, reflecting yet again the importance of this tribe; they are followed by the Gershonites and Merarites who carry the structural parts of the Tabernacle. The division of Reuben is next, followed by the Kohathites with the sacred objects. In that way the structure of the Tabernacle can be reassembled by the time the sanctuary objects reach an encampment stop. The last two divisions, those led by Ephraim and then Dan, bring up the rear. **29–32:** From this point until the end of ch 12 the narrative style and contents reflect the writing of the JE source(s). The focus switches to the story of the journey, without the features that characterize the Priestly source: genealogical lists, lengthy discussions of priestly laws, and ritual regulations. At the outset of the march, Moses persuades his father-in-law to help guide Israel through the wilderness. **29:** *Hobab son of Reuel the Midianite:* In Exod., the name of Moses' father-in-law appears as Reuel (2.18) or Jethro (18.1ff.). One of those names, Reuel, may be his Midianite clan name (Gen. 36.17). Some scholars think that Hobab (Jethro), who was a priest of Midian, was a worshipper of the LORD and that Moses actually adopted this deity as Israel's God after learning of Him from his father-in-law. These scholars refer to the theophoric place-name YHW' in the Sinai which is mentioned in an Egyptian text (14th c. BCE), as well as biblical references that the LORD came from that region (Deut. 33.2; Judg. 5.4; Hab. 3.3). As a biblical prooftext they cite Jethro's exclamation to Moses that "the LORD is greater than all gods" (Exod. 18.11). This is highly hypothetical; in the latter statement, however, Jethro may simply be reacting in awe to Israel's redemption from Egypt. In any case, Hobab (Jethro) is welcome in the Israelite camp, reflecting a non-particularistic view. **33–36:** According to this JE tradition, the Ark travels in front of the Israelite camp rather than in its midst (cf. vv. 11–28). It is striking that the two different traditions about the place of the Ark are juxtaposed so closely to each other, but this typifies the Torah (compare, e.g., the two conflicting creation accounts that open Gen.). Ibn Ezra and Ramban reconcile this contradiction by suggesting that initially, to alleviate Israel's fears, the Ark led the group. **35–36:** The song

30 "I will not go," he replied to him, "but will return to my
native land." 31 He said, "Please do not leave us, inasmuch as
you know where we should camp in the wilderness and can be
our guide.[a] 32 So if you come with us, we will extend to you the
same bounty that the LORD grants us."

33 They marched from the mountain of the LORD a distance
of three days. The Ark of the Covenant of the LORD traveled in
front of them on that three days' journey to seek out a resting
place for them; 34 and the LORD's cloud kept above them by
day, as they moved on from camp.
35 When the Ark was to set out, Moses would say:

Advance, O LORD!
May Your enemies be scattered,
And may Your foes flee before You!

36 And when it halted, he would say:

[b-]Return, O LORD,
You who are Israel's myriads of thousands![-b]

11 The people took to complaining bitterly before the LORD.
The LORD heard and was incensed: a fire of the LORD
broke out against them, ravaging the outskirts of the camp.
2 The people cried out to Moses. Moses prayed to the LORD, and
the fire died down. 3 That place was named Taberah,[c] because a
fire of the LORD had broken out against them.
4 The riffraff in their midst felt a gluttonous craving; and
then the Israelites wept and said, "If only we had meat to eat!
5 We remember the fish that we used to eat free in Egypt, the
cucumbers, the melons, the leeks, the onions, and the garlic.
6 Now our gullets are shriveled. There is nothing at all! Nothing
but this manna to look to!"
7 Now the manna was like coriander seed, and in color it was
like bdellium. 8 The people would go about and gather it, grind
it between millstones or pound it in a mortar, boil it in a pot,
and make it into cakes. It tasted like rich cream.[d] 9 When the
dew fell on the camp at night, the manna would fall upon it.

10 Moses heard the people weeping, every clan apart, each
person at the entrance of his tent. The LORD was very angry,
and Moses was distressed. 11 And Moses said to the LORD,
"Why have You dealt ill with Your servant, and why have I not
enjoyed Your favor, that You have laid the burden of all this
people upon me? 12 Did I conceive all this people, did I bear
them, that You should say to me, 'Carry them in your bosom as

a *Lit. "eyes."*

b-b *Others "Return, O LORD, unto the ten thousands of the families of Israel!"*

c *From root* b'r, *"to burn."* d *Lit. "cream of oil (or, fat)."*

of the Ark, evidently part of a Mosaic tradition, is a type of victory song praising God as a divine warrior, the defender of Israel. Its insertion here may be related to the first word of the song, "binsoa'," which picks up on the key word of this subsection, "travel" (of the Ark). Here the Ark can be understood as God's chariot. This poem is used in Jewish tradition in the liturgy as part of the Torah service. **36:** *Myriads of thousands* is an epithet of the LORD as a warrior similar to the more common biblical epithet LORD of Hosts (1 Sam. 17.45; Isa. 1.24; 21.10; Zeph. 2.9).

11.1–35: Murmuring in the wilderness. As the Israelites resume their long trek in the wilderness, they fall into a pattern of complaining. After each incident God reacts by punishing the people, essentially because the grievances reflect disloyalty to the Sinaitic covenant. Moses responds to God's action by interceding on Israel's behalf—this is a typical role of biblical prophets (see, e.g., Jer. 7.16; 11.14; 14.11). The biblical writer preserves the incident in the collective memory of Israel by naming the location after the event that occurred there. This cycle repeats in one form or another throughout the wanderings. Two complaint stories are found in this ch. **1–3:** The grievance in the first case is not specified, but God's punishment, deadly fire, is mentioned. The place name, *Taberah,* recalls the punishment by fire, and might be connected to the manifestation of God as fire in ch 9. Clearly, there is an intended lesson for Israel, but it is not heeded and the murmuring continues. **4–35:** The second incident is far more detailed and complex. It originates from the camp's non-Israelite contingent which joined the Israelites in the exodus (Exod. 12.38). The people crave a more varied diet than just manna, like the one they claim was available in Egypt. As commonly happens, the complaints of a few are echoed by the entire group. This larger section seems to combine two originally independent stories concerning the quail and the seventy elders. **4–5:** *If*

a nurse carries an infant,' to the land that You have promised on oath to their fathers? 13 Where am I to get meat to give to all this people, when they whine before me and say, 'Give us meat to eat!' 14 I cannot carry all this people by myself, for it is too much for me. 15 If You would deal thus with me, kill me rather, I beg You, and let me see no more of my wretchedness!"

16 Then the LORD said to Moses, "Gather for Me seventy of Israel's elders of whom you have experience as elders and officers of the people, and bring them to the Tent of Meeting and let them take their place there with you. 17 I will come down and speak with you there, and I will draw upon the spirit that is on you and put it upon them; they shall share the burden of the people with you, and you shall not bear it alone. 18 And say to the people: [a-]Purify yourselves[-a] for tomorrow and you shall eat meat, for you have kept whining before the LORD and saying, 'If only we had meat to eat! Indeed, we were better off in Egypt!' The LORD will give you meat and you shall eat. 19 You shall eat not one day, not two, not even five days or ten or twenty, 20 but a whole month, until it comes out of your nostrils and becomes loathsome to you. For you have rejected the LORD who is among you, by whining before Him and saying, 'Oh, why did we ever leave Egypt!'"

21 But Moses said, "The people [b-]who are with me[-b] number six hundred thousand men; yet You say, 'I will give them enough meat to eat for a whole month.' 22 Could enough flocks and herds be slaughtered to suffice them? Or could all the fish of the sea be gathered for them to suffice them?" 23 And the LORD answered Moses, [c-]"Is there a limit to the LORD's power?[-c] You shall soon see whether what I have said happens to you or not!"

24 Moses went out and reported the words of the LORD to the people. He gathered seventy of the people's elders and stationed them around the Tent. 25 Then the LORD came down in a cloud and spoke to him; He drew upon the spirit that was on him and put it upon the seventy elders. And when the spirit rested upon them, they [d-]spoke in ecstasy,[-d] but did not continue.

26 Two men, one named Eldad and the other Medad, had remained in camp; yet the spirit rested upon them—they were among those recorded, but they had not gone out to the Tent—and they [d-]spoke in ecstasy[-d] in the camp. 27 A youth ran out and told Moses, saying, "Eldad and Medad are acting the prophet in the camp!" 28 And Joshua son of Nun, Moses' attendant from his youth, spoke up and said, "My lord Moses, restrain them!" 29 But Moses said to him, "Are you wrought up on my account?

a-a *I.e., as for a sacrificial meal.* b-b *Lit. "in whose midst I am."*
c-c *Lit. "Is the LORD's hand too short?"* d-d *Others "prophesied."*

only we had meat.... We remember the fish: Meat may actually refer to fish, a cheap and ample food from the Nile. Why the Israelites do not slaughter animals from their herds (Exod. 12.38; Num. 32.1) is not explained in the text. **7–9:** *Manna* is described here as a rich and tasty food suitable for various modes of preparation. This positive depiction of manna underscores the unjustified complaints of the people. Some scholars identify the manna with the edible sap of the tamarisk tree that forms flaky sweet pellets in conjunction with the activity of plant lice. Its description here differs from Exod. 16.31; this is reconciled in classical Jewish thought by suggesting that the manna could take on various flavors (see, e.g., *m. Yoma* 75a). **10–35:** Utterly frustrated, Moses questions his heavy burden of leadership and his ability to succeed at it. He is ready to die if no relief comes. The point of this episode, including Moses' desire to satisfy the people, is to elicit divine solutions for the problems. Most important is the appointment of seventy elders to assist Moses. The judicial roles of Israel's elders are legitimated for all time because of their endowment with Moses' spirit. Simultaneously, this scene affirms Moses' human traits and limitations. God's solution to the meat crisis differs from an earlier rendition of the story. In Exod. ch 16, quail and manna are God's gift to Israel; here in Num. the wording of their grievance bespeaks their desire to return to Egypt, clearly a rejection of God that warrants punishment. Therefore, when the quail finally arrive, many people become fatally ill from gorging themselves with meat. Appropriately, the place name for this event becomes *Kibroth-hattaavah* (v. 34), "burials of the craving." **26–29:** This account is connected to the broader story since both involve the transmission of some of Moses' "spirit" to other individuals (vv. 17, 26; cf. v. 31 which uses the same Heb word "ruaḥ" in its other sense of "wind"). This story may reflect an ancient debate concerning whether there is only one legitimate prophet at a

Would that all the LORD's people were prophets, that the LORD
put His spirit upon them!" 30 Moses then reentered the camp
together with the elders of Israel.

31 A wind from the LORD started up, swept quail from the
sea and strewed them over the camp, about a day's journey
on this side and about a day's journey on that side, all around
the camp, and some two cubits deep on the ground. 32 The
people set to gathering quail all that day and night and all the
next day—even he who gathered least had ten *ḥomers*—and
they spread them out all around the camp. 33 The meat was
still between their teeth, nor yet chewed,[a] when the anger of
the LORD blazed forth against the people and the LORD struck
the people with a very severe plague. 34 That place was named
Kibroth-hattaavah,[b] because the people who had the craving
were buried there.

35 Then the people set out from Kibroth-hattaavah for Hazeroth.

12 When they were in Hazeroth, 1 Miriam and Aaron spoke
against Moses because of the Cushite woman he had
married: "He married a Cushite woman!"

2 They said, "Has the LORD spoken only through Moses?
Has He not spoken through us as well?" The LORD heard it.
3 Now Moses was a very humble man, more so than any other
man on earth. 4 Suddenly the LORD called to Moses, Aaron,
and Miriam, "Come out, you three, to the Tent of Meeting."
So the three of them went out. 5 The LORD came down in a pillar of cloud, stopped at the entrance of the Tent, and called
out, "Aaron and Miriam!" The two of them came forward;
6 and He said, "Hear these My words: [c-]When a prophet of the
LORD arises among you, I[-c] make Myself known to him in a
vision, I speak with him in a dream. 7 Not so with My servant
Moses; he is trusted throughout My household. 8 With him I
speak mouth to mouth, plainly and not in riddles, and he beholds the likeness of the LORD. How then did you not shrink
from speaking against My servant Moses!" 9 Still incensed with
them, the LORD departed.

10 As the cloud withdrew from the Tent, there was Miriam
stricken with snow-white scales![d] When Aaron turned toward
Miriam, he saw that she was stricken with scales. 11 And Aaron said to Moses, "O my lord, account not to us the sin which
we committed in our folly. 12 Let her not be as one dead, who

a *Meaning of Heb.* yikkareth *uncertain.* b *I.e., "the graves of craving."*
c-c *Meaning of Heb. uncertain. Others "If there be a prophet among you, I the LORD."*
d *Cf. Lev.* 13.2–3.

time, as assumed perhaps by Deut. 18.15–18, or if there may be many prophets in a single era.

12.1–16: Miriam and Aaron speak against Moses. Miriam and Aaron, like other Israelites, are subject to complaining. Their grievance against Moses is founded on two issues: his wife, and more seriously, his authority. This narrative continues the themes from the previous ch, namely, prophecy and the questioning of Moses' leadership capabilities and his limitations. The first objection that Miriam and Aaron raise is to Moses' marriage to a Cushite woman; the second questions his special role as a prophet. Moses remains silent in the face of these accusations so that God takes up his defense. The message of the narrative is clear: God chose Moses to be His unique prophet and no one, not even other key Israelite leaders, may challenge that decision. Miriam's severe punishment underscores the point and makes clear that any other person who arises to challenge Moses is doomed from the start. **1:** *He married a Cushite woman:* Moses' wife Zipporah is Midianite (Exod. 2.21). Two explanations are possible: (1) This reference is to Zipporah, "Cushan" being part of Midian (Hab. 3.7). (2) Moses married a second woman in Egypt, a Nubian (= Cush). The latter is more plausible since Nubia was part of the Egyptian empire and dark-skinned women were considered beautiful, as reflected in the Tg.'s rendition of Cushite as "beautiful." **3:** Moses' attribute of humility is underscored as praiseworthy. It stands in stark contrast to Miriam's and Aaron's arrogance. **6–8:** These vv. are poetic, showing an introverted, triangular-shaped, literary structure (chiasmus) with v. 7 as the climax. God distinguishes Moses' prophetic privileges from those accorded any other prophet. Moses can speak to God directly, in live dialogue rather than in dreams or visions. God is at His most anthropomorphic in these vv. **10:** *Snow-white scales:* This disease is mentioned in Lev. ch 13 as

emerges from his mother's womb with half his flesh eaten
away." 13 So Moses cried out to the LORD, saying, "O God, pray
heal her!"

14 But the LORD said to Moses, "If her father spat in her face,
would she not bear her shame for seven days? Let her be shut
out of camp for seven days, and then let her be readmitted."
15 So Miriam was shut out of camp seven days; and the people
did not march on until Miriam was readmitted. 16 After that the
people set out from Hazeroth and encamped in the wilderness
of Paran.

SHELAH-LEKHA שלח לך

13 The LORD spoke to Moses, saying, 2 "Send men to scout
the land of Canaan, which I am giving to the Israelite
people; send one man from each of their ancestral tribes, each
one a chieftain among them." 3 So Moses, by the LORD's command, sent them out from the wilderness of Paran, all the men
being leaders of the Israelites. 4 And these were their names:
From the tribe of Reuben, Shammua son of Zaccur.
5 From the tribe of Simeon, Shaphat son of Hori.
6 From the tribe of Judah, Caleb son of Jephunneh.
7 From the tribe of Issachar, Igal son of Joseph.
8 From the tribe of Ephraim, Hosea[a] son of Nun.
9 From the tribe of Benjamin, Palti son of Rafu.
10 From the tribe of Zebulun, Gaddiel son of Sodi.
11 From the tribe of Joseph, namely, the tribe of Manasseh,
Gaddi son of Susi.
12 From the tribe of Dan, Ammiel son of Gemalli.
13 From the tribe of Asher, Sethur son of Michael.
14 From the tribe of Naphtali, Nahbi son of Vophsi.
15 From the tribe of Gad, Geuel son of Machi.
16 Those were the names of the men whom Moses sent to scout
the land; but Moses changed the name of Hosea[a] son of Nun
to Joshua.

a Or "Hoshea."

one causing severe impurity that requires a 14-day purification process. It was previously identified as leprosy, but recent thinking rejects this in favor of curable skin diseases, since persons afflicted with this condition in the Bible are often cured after being quarantined. Furthermore, the symptoms of the disease do not correlate with leprosy (Hansen's disease). Disease, in general, was believed to be divine retribution for sin (2 Sam. 3.29). The Rabbis understood the name of the skin condition, "metzora'," as indicative of its cause, the sin of slander, "motzi' shem ra'" ("uttering an evil name") (*Lev. Rab.* 16.1–6). They conclude that Miriam and not Aaron was punished because she instigated the gossip and vocalized it, as indicated by the feminine gender of the verb *spoke* in 12.1, and the placement of Miriam before Aaron. Ibn Ezra speculates that Aaron was silent or simply agreed. **13:** *"O God, pray heal her!":* Moses' brief plea for Miriam is an example of biblical prose prayer. The terseness of Moses' prayer may reflect his disappointment with his siblings or, conversely, may point to the immediacy of Moses' response. Prayer expressed in poetic style, used for more public or ceremonial occasions, is far more common in the Bible; for example, Hannah's lengthy prayer of thanksgiving after Samuel's birth (1 Sam. ch 2) in contrast to her previous brief prose prayer (1 Sam. 1.11). **14:** *If her father spat in her face:* Apparently, this is an act of rebuke that entails shame plus seven days of banishment. Usually the purpose of spitting is to shame someone, but the custom of banishment is unknown (cf. Deut. 25.9). Seclusion outside the camp is undoubtedly related to a notion of impurity from the skin disease.

13.1–33: The scouts' expedition and report. The goal of this expedition is two-fold: to assess the strength of the indigenous population and the strongholds in which they reside, and to investigate the productivity of the land. This narrative is a conflation of at least two traditions that reflect different sources (JE and P). Discrepancies in the story revolve around two issues: What area of Canaan is scouted and how many scouts bring a positive report. In the earlier JE version the scouts reconnoiter the southern portion of Canaan (13.17); Caleb alone recommends that Israel proceed with the conquest (13.30). The Priestly account expands the scouting expedition over the entire land of Canaan (13.21) and it adds Joshua as a spokesman for undertaking the conquest (14.6–9). **1–15:** Moses chooses tribal leaders, presumably those capable of such a mission. Some rabbis, who take note of the fact that Moses chooses the scouts rather than asking God to do it (by lot), attribute the ill-fated scouting expedition to Moses, assuming that God could foresee the scouts' sin (*Num. Rab.* 16.4). **16:** Moses expands *Joshua*'s name, *Hosea* (13.8), by adding the prefix "ye," possibly a

[17] When Moses sent them to scout the land of Canaan, he said to them, "Go up there into the Negeb and on into the hill country, [18] and see what kind of country it is. Are the people who dwell in it strong or weak, few or many? [19] Is the country in which they dwell good or bad? Are the towns they live in open or fortified? [20] Is the soil rich or poor? Is it wooded or not? And take pains to bring back some of the fruit of the land."—Now it happened to be the season of the first ripe grapes.

[21] They went up and scouted the land, from the wilderness of Zin to Rehob, at Lebo-hamath.[a] [22] They went up into the Negeb and came to Hebron, where lived Ahiman, Sheshai, and Talmai, the Anakites.—Now Hebron was founded seven years before Zoan of Egypt.—[23] They reached the wadi Eshcol, and there they cut down a branch with a single cluster of grapes—it had to be borne on a carrying frame by two of them—and some pomegranates and figs. [24] That place was named the wadi Eshcol[b] because of the cluster that the Israelites cut down there.

[25] At the end of forty days they returned from scouting the land. [26] They went straight to Moses and Aaron and the whole Israelite community at Kadesh in the wilderness of Paran, and they made their report to them and to the whole community, as they showed them the fruit of the land. [27] This is what they told him: "We came to the land you sent us to; it does indeed flow with milk and honey, and this is its fruit. [28] However, the people who inhabit the country are powerful, and the cities are fortified and very large; moreover, we saw the Anakites there. [29] Amalekites dwell in the Negeb region; Hittites, Jebusites, and Amorites inhabit the hill country; and Canaanites dwell by the Sea and along the Jordan."

[30] Caleb hushed the people before Moses and said, "Let us by all means go up, and we shall gain possession of it, for we shall surely overcome it."

[31] But the men who had gone up with him said, "We cannot attack that people, for it is stronger than we." [32] Thus they spread calumnies among the Israelites about the land they had scouted, saying, "The country that we traversed and scouted is one that devours its settlers. All the people that we saw in it are men of great size; [33] we saw the Nephilim[c] there—the Anakites are part of the Nephilim—and we looked like grasshoppers to ourselves, and so we must have looked to them."

a Others "the entrance to Hamath." *b I.e., "cluster."* *c See Gen. 6.4.*

theophoric element associated with the Israelite God. In the sources of the names of the tribal leaders, only Joshua's name bears such an element. **22:** The gloss added to the mention of *Hebron* stresses the antiquity of that city which was David's capital for the first seven years of his reign (1 Kings 2.11). *Zoan,* the Egyptian capital city of Tanis, was (re)built at the same time as Jerusalem. **22, 28, 33:** *Anakites,* or giants, are mentioned in several texts (Deut. 2.11; Josh. 11.21–22). An etiological account for the Nephilim is found in Gen. 6.1–4. The reference to Anakites in Joshua notes that even after the conquest some survived in Philistine cities (11.22). David's adversary Goliath, a Philistine from Gath, is depicted as a giant (1 Sam. 17.4) descended from a group of giants from Raphah (1 Chron. 20.5–6). The tall headdresses of the Philistines may have contributed to their gigantic image. More importantly, the report of giants in the land makes the Canaanites more intimidating and their eventual defeat by the Israelites more spectacular. This literary device is also found in Egyptian literature where Shasu nomads, enemies of Egypt, are depicted as giants 7–8 ft tall. **23:** *Grapes, pomegranates,* and *figs* are late summer fruits. **24:** This is an etiological account (origin story) for the name of the wadi, *Eshcol*—in Heb, a cluster of grapes. **27:** *Flow with milk and honey:* This biblical phrase describing the promised land (also Exod. 3.8, 17) has been preserved in Jewish tradition to modernity. Honey could refer to bee or date honey, both attested in antiquity, although a recent archaeological discovery in the Beit She'an Valley of a large beehive complex dated to the 10th–9th c. BCE attests to a honey production industry in ancient Israel. **29:** For the indigenous population of Canaan, see the table of nations in Gen. 10.15–20; there is tremendous variability in the lists of these nations found in various texts. **30:** The place of Judah is again emphasized, as *Caleb* the Judaean (see v. 6) is represented as the faithful scout. **32:** Canaan as a country that devours its settlers may refer to the land's infertility. More likely, however, the metaphor alludes to the results of frequent warfare (cf. Ezek. 36.13–14).

14 The whole community broke into loud cries, and the
people wept that night. [2] All the Israelites railed against
Moses and Aaron. "If only we had died in the land of Egypt,"
the whole community shouted at them, "or if only we might
die in this wilderness! [3] Why is the LORD taking us to that land
to fall by the sword? Our wives and children will be carried
off! It would be better for us to go back to Egypt!" [4] And they
said to one another, "Let us [a-]head back for[-a] Egypt."
[5] Then Moses and Aaron fell on their faces before all the
assembled congregation of the Israelites. [6] And Joshua son of
Nun and Caleb son of Jephunneh, of those who had scouted
the land, rent their clothes [7] and exhorted the whole Israelite
community: "The land that we traversed and scouted is an
exceedingly good land. [8] If the LORD is pleased with us, He
will bring us into that land, a land that flows with milk and
honey, and give it to us; [9] only you must not rebel against the
LORD. Have no fear then of the people of the country, for they
are our prey:[b] their protection has departed from them, but
the LORD is with us. Have no fear of them!" [10] As the whole
community threatened to pelt them with stones, the Presence of the LORD appeared in the Tent of Meeting to all the
Israelites.
[11] And the LORD said to Moses, "How long will this people
spurn Me, and how long will they have no faith in Me despite
all the signs that I have performed in their midst? [12] I will
strike them with pestilence and disown them, and I will make
of you a nation far more numerous than they!" [13] But Moses
said to the LORD, "When the Egyptians, from whose midst You
brought up this people in Your might, hear the news, [14] they
will tell it to the inhabitants of that land. Now they have heard
that You, O LORD, are in the midst of this people; that You, O
LORD, appear in plain sight when Your cloud rests over them
and when You go before them in a pillar of cloud by day and
in a pillar of fire by night. [15] If then You slay this people to a
man, the nations who have heard Your fame will say, [16] 'It must
be because the LORD was powerless to bring that people into
the land He had promised them on oath that He slaughtered
them in the wilderness.' [17] Therefore, I pray, let my Lord's forbearance be great, as You have declared, saying,[c] [18] 'The LORD!
slow to anger and abounding in kindness; forgiving iniquity
and transgression; yet not remitting all punishment, but visiting the iniquity of fathers upon children, upon the third and
fourth generations.' [19] Pardon, I pray, the iniquity of this people according to Your great kindness, as You have forgiven this
people ever since Egypt."

a-a Lit. "set the head and return to"; cf. Neh. 9.17. Others "Let us make a captain and return to." *b Lit. "food (or, bread)."* *c Cf. Exod. 34.6–7.*

14.1–45: Aftermath of the scouting expedition. In the continuous cycle of rebellions, this one constitutes the most serious. The ten scouts who incite the populace advocate abandoning Israel's ultimate goal, to settle the promised land. The fear they instill in the Israelites supersedes the memory of Egyptian oppression. This extreme display of faithlessness before God exacts the ultimate punishment, forty years of wandering in the desert and the death of the exodus generation. **4:** *Let us head back:* This phrase can also be translated, "Let us appoint a leader," indicating that the Israelites were ready to replace Moses and return to Egypt under new leadership. **6–10:** Rending the garment is a sign of mourning that has survived in modern times, albeit a ribbon sometimes substitutes for an article of clothing. Joshua and Caleb are not only frustrated by the negative report of the other scouts but they fear God's harsh punishment, as evidenced by their plea to the people not to rebel against God. The imminence of Israel's rebellion is apparent by the people's intent to stone Moses and Aaron, and probably also Joshua and Caleb (cf. Exod. 17.4). *The Presence of the LORD* (v. 10) is God's typical manner of manifestation in Priestly material. **11–19:** Here God is prepared to eradicate all Israel save Moses (cf. Exod. 32.10), offering to create a new people from the descendants of Moses. This is followed by one of the longest prose prayers in the Torah. Moses' initial argument centers on preserving God's reputation among the nations (cf. Ezek. 36.16–36; 39.21–29); his second argument appeals to God's attribute of mercy (see Exod. 34.6–7 in the context of the second set of Decalogue tablets). The long prayer of Moses after the entire nation sins grievously stands in marked contrast to his short prayer on behalf of his sister in 12.13. **18:** *Visiting the iniquity of fathers upon children,* a quotation of the divine attributes found in the Decalogue (Exod. 20.5–6; Deut. 5.9–10) and in Exod. 34.6–7.

[20] And the LORD said, "I pardon, as you have asked. [21] Nevertheless, as I live and as the LORD's Presence fills the whole
world, [22] none of the men who have seen My Presence and the
signs that I have performed in Egypt and in the wilderness,
and who have tried Me these many[a] times and have disobeyed
Me, [23] shall see the land that I promised on oath to their fathers; none of those who spurn Me shall see it. [24] But My servant Caleb, because he was imbued with a different spirit and
remained loyal to Me—him will I bring into the land that he
entered, and his offspring shall hold it as a possession. [25] Now
the Amalekites and the Canaanites occupy the valleys. Start
out, then, tomorrow and march into the wilderness by way of
the Sea of Reeds."[b]

[26] The LORD spoke further to Moses and Aaron, [27] "How
much longer shall that wicked community keep muttering
against Me? Very well, I have heeded the incessant muttering
of the Israelites against Me. [28] Say to them: 'As I live,' says the
LORD, 'I will do to you just as you have urged Me. [29] In this
very wilderness shall your carcasses drop. Of all of you who
were recorded in your various lists from the age of twenty
years up, you who have muttered against Me, [30] not one shall
enter the land in which I swore[c] to settle you—save Caleb son
of Jephunneh and Joshua son of Nun. [31] Your children who,
you said, would be carried off—these will I allow to enter;
they shall know the land that you have rejected. [32] But your
carcasses shall drop in this wilderness, [33] while your children roam the wilderness for forty years, suffering for your
faithlessness, until the last of your carcasses is down in the
wilderness. [34] You shall bear your punishment for forty years,
corresponding to the number of days—forty days—that you
scouted the land: a year for each day. Thus you shall know
what it means to thwart Me. [35] I the LORD have spoken: Thus
will I do to all that wicked band that has banded together
against Me: in this very wilderness they shall die to the last
man.'"

[36] As for the men whom Moses sent to scout the land, those
who came back and caused the whole community to mutter
against him by spreading calumnies about the land—[37] those
who spread such calumnies about the land died of plague, by
the will of the LORD. [38] Of those men who had gone to scout
the land, only Joshua son of Nun and Caleb son of Jephunneh
survived.

[39] When Moses repeated these words to all the Israelites,
the people were overcome by grief. [40] Early next morning they
set out toward the crest of the hill country, saying, "We are

a Lit. "ten"; cf. note at Gen. 31.41. *b See note at Exod. 10.19.*
c Lit. "raised My hand."

20–38: God reduces the people's punishment: The entire nation will not be wiped out immediately, but the current generation will not inherit Canaan. The rebellious adult generation will perish in the desert according to their wish (14.2). **21, 28:** *As I live* is an oath formula. **36–37:** The ten scouts who incited the rebellion with their negative report die in a plague on the spot. **39–45:** The people attempt to invade Canaan either because they regret their previous behavior and lack of trust in God, or because they hope to reverse God's decree. In any case, the invasion fails and they are defeated. The writer's message here is clear: Without God's blessing and Presence (accompanying the Ark) conquest is impossible. The function of the Ark in the military camp is also emphasized in the passage (see 10.35–36 n.).

prepared to go up to the place that the LORD has spoken of,
for we were wrong.” 41 But Moses said, “Why do you transgress
the LORD’s command? This will not succeed. 42 Do not go up,
lest you be routed by your enemies, for the LORD is not in your
midst. 43 For the Amalekites and the Canaanites will be there
to face you, and you will fall by the sword, inasmuch as you
have turned from following the LORD and the LORD will not be
with you.”
44 Yet defiantly[a] they marched toward the crest of the hill
country, though neither the LORD’s Ark of the Covenant nor
Moses stirred from the camp. 45 And the Amalekites and the
Canaanites who dwelt in that hill country came down and
dealt them a shattering blow at Hormah.

15 The LORD spoke to Moses, saying: 2 Speak to the Israelite
people and say to them:
When you enter the land that I am giving you to settle in,
3 and would present an offering by fire to the LORD from the
herd or from the flock, be it burnt offering or sacrifice, in fulfillment of a vow explicitly uttered,[b] or as a freewill offering,
or at your fixed occasions, producing an odor pleasing to the
LORD:
4 The person who presents the offering to the LORD shall
bring as a meal offering: a tenth of a measure of choice flour
with a quarter of a *hin* of oil mixed in. 5 You shall also offer, with
the burnt offering or the sacrifice, a quarter of a *hin* of wine as
a libation for each sheep.
6 In the case of a ram, you shall present as a meal offering:
two-tenths of a measure of choice flour with a third of a *hin* of
oil mixed in; 7 and a third of a *hin* of wine as a libation—as an
offering of pleasing odor to the LORD.
8 And if it is an animal from the herd that you offer to the
LORD as a burnt offering or as a sacrifice, in fulfillment of a vow
explicitly uttered or as an offering of well-being, 9 there shall be
offered a meal offering along with the animal: three-tenths of
a measure of choice flour with half a *hin* of oil mixed in; 10 and
as libation you shall offer half a *hin* of wine—these being offerings by fire of pleasing odor to the LORD.
11 Thus shall be done with each ox, with each ram, and with
any sheep or goat, 12 as many as you offer; you shall do thus
with each one, as many as there are. 13 Every citizen, when presenting an offering by fire of pleasing odor to the LORD, shall
do so with them.
14 And when, throughout the ages, a stranger who has taken
up residence with you, or one who lives among you, would
present an offering by fire of pleasing odor to the LORD—as

45: *Hormah* means destruction; thus the site name.

15.1–41: A variety of laws. The narrative of the forty years in the wilderness is interrupted here by the insertion of legal material. Medieval commentators suggest that the placement of the laws, immediately following the condemnation of the adult generation to death in the desert, reiterates God’s promise that the children will indeed inherit Canaan, thus the introduction to the first two sets of laws—*When you enter the land* (vv. 2, 18). The first set of laws deals with accompaniments to the sacrifices: meal, oil, and wine (vv. 1–16). These are followed by the bread dough offering, “ḥalah” (vv. 17–21), and then by those sacrifices required for individual or communal inadvertent violations of any law (vv. 22–31). The delineation of laws is interrupted by a case study that contrasts the preceding type of violations. That case entails extreme, willful breaking of the law through the desecration of the Sabbath (vv. 32–36). The prescriptive passages resume with the commandment to wear fringes, tzitzit, on one’s garment (vv. 37–41). The purpose of the fringes, to remind the wearer of God’s laws, clearly ties into the previous case of the Sabbath violator. **3–16:** Animal burnt offerings and offerings of well-being are accompanied by a grain and oil mixture and wine (Lev. chs 1–3) reminiscent of a complete meal. In the case of sacrifices, the meal is for the deity. Although the Bible describes these offerings as *producing an odor pleasing to the LORD*, it never states that God actually eats them. **4:** *Hin* is an Egyptian measure equal to approximately 4 liters (1 gal). **14–16:** In most matters, including sacrificial matters (except for the paschal lamb, see Exod. 12.48), the resident alien must be treated as the native Israelite (e.g., Deut. 1.16; 5.14).

a Meaning of Heb. uncertain. *b See note at Lev. 22.21.*

you do, so [a]shall it be done by 15 the rest of the congregation.[-a]
There shall be one law for you and for the resident stranger;
it shall be a law for all time throughout the ages. You and the
stranger shall be alike before the LORD; 16 the same ritual and
the same rule shall apply to you and to the stranger who resides among you.

17 The LORD spoke to Moses, saying: 18 Speak to the Israelite
people and say to them:
When you enter the land to which I am taking you 19 and you
eat of the bread of the land, you shall set some aside as a gift to
the LORD: 20 as the first yield of your baking,[b] you shall set aside
a loaf as a gift; you shall set it aside as a gift like the gift from the
threshing floor. 21 You shall make a gift to the LORD from the
first yield of your baking, throughout the ages.
22 If you unwittingly fail to observe any one of the commandments that the LORD has declared to Moses—23 anything that
the LORD has enjoined upon you through Moses—from the day
that the LORD gave the commandment and on through the ages:
24 If this was done unwittingly, through the inadvertence of
the community, the whole community shall present one bull
of the herd as a burnt offering of pleasing odor to the LORD,
with its proper meal offering and libation, and one he-goat as
a purification offering. 25 The priest shall make expiation for
the whole Israelite community and they shall be forgiven; for
it was an error, and for their error they have brought their offering, an offering by fire to the LORD and their purification offering before the LORD. 26 The whole Israelite community and
the stranger residing among them shall be forgiven, for it happened to the entire people through error.
27 In case it is an individual who has sinned unwittingly, he
shall offer a she-goat in its first year as a purification offering.
28 The priest shall make expiation before the LORD on behalf of
the person who erred, for he sinned unwittingly, making such
expiation for him that he may be forgiven. 29 For the citizen
among the Israelites and for the stranger who resides among
them—you shall have one ritual for anyone who acts in error.
30 But the person, be he citizen or stranger, who acts defiantly[c] reviles the LORD; that person shall be cut off from among
his people. 31 Because he has spurned the word of the LORD
and violated His commandment, that person shall be cut off—
he bears his guilt.

32 Once, when the Israelites were in the wilderness, they
came upon a man gathering wood on the sabbath day. 33 Those

a-a *Meaning of Heb. uncertain.* b *Meaning of Heb.* ʿarisah *uncertain.*
c *Lit. "with upraised hand."*

17–21: The dough offering is the first part of the dough prepared in the kneading basin, somewhat analogous to the first-fruits offering, though the latter is a once-a-year event (Lev. 19.24–25; 23.10–11). The dough is given to the priest; in turn, the homes of the Israelites are blessed (cf. Ezek. 44.30). According to the Rabbis in the Talmud, this "ḥalah" offering brings blessings to the nonfarmer as well because it constitutes his labor (*b. Shab.* 32b), and in postbiblical times, a portion of the dough was burned rather than given to the priests. The sweet Sabbath bread is called "ḥalah" after this custom. **22–31:** This section continues the previous one. Sacrifices for inadvertent violations are applicable to all laws (for more details, see Lev. ch 4). **29:** *One ritual,* more correctly, "one law" ("torah") applies to both Israelites and alien residents. Breaking a law has a negative effect on the "terra sancta," therefore an expiation is required of all inhabitants. **30–31:** Defiant, willful violation of ritual law cannot be expiated in the manner of an inadvertent sin. "Karet," literally the cutting off, is a punishment enacted by the divine. Its exact nature is not defined here but can be gleaned from other biblical passages which indicate punishments affecting both the sinner and his progeny (e.g., Mal. 2.12; Ps. 109.13). Traditional Jewish interpretation includes childlessness, early death, and the death of the soul together with the body. **32–36:** The case of the wood gatherer is distinct from the above. It illustrates a most severe violation of ritual law, the desecration of the Sabbath which is a capital offense, here punished by stoning (cf. Exod. 31.14). It is possible that Moses here asks God what to do because earlier legislative texts note that the punishment is death, but are unclear about whether it should be carried out by people or God (Exod. 31.14–15). The case of the wood gatherer, which combines law and narrative (story), is one of four such legislative accounts in the Torah (also Lev. 24.10–16; Num. 9.6–13; 27.1–11; 36.1–12).

who found him as he was gathering wood brought him before Moses, Aaron, and the whole community. 34 He was placed in custody, for it had not been specified what should be done to him. 35 Then the LORD said to Moses, "The man shall be put to death: the whole community shall pelt him with stones outside the camp." 36 So the whole community took him outside the camp and stoned him to death—as the LORD had commanded Moses.

37 The LORD said to Moses as follows: 38 Speak to the Israelite people and instruct them to make for themselves fringes on the corners of their garments throughout the ages; let them attach a cord of blue to the fringe at each corner. 39 That shall be your fringe; look at it and recall all the commandments of the LORD and observe them, so that you do not follow your heart and eyes in your lustful urge. 40 Thus you shall be reminded to observe all My commandments and to be holy to your God. 41 I the LORD am your God, who brought you out of the land of Egypt to be your God: I, the LORD your God.

KORAH קרח

16 Now Korah, son of Izhar son of Kohath son of Levi, [a]betook himself,[a] along with Dathan and Abiram sons of Eliab, [b]and On son of Peleth—descendants of Reuben[b]— 2 to rise up against Moses, together with two hundred and fifty Israelites, chieftains of the community, chosen in the assembly, men of repute. 3 They combined against Moses and Aaron and said to them, "You have gone too far! For all the community are holy, all of them, and the LORD is in their midst. Why then do you raise yourselves above the LORD's congregation?"

a-a Lit. "took"; meaning of Heb. uncertain.
b-b According to Num. 26.5, 8–9, Eliab was son of Pallu, son of Reuben.

35–36: God Himself sentences the violator. Stoning signifies the serious nature of the infraction, which is an affront to the entire community. **37–41:** The fringes or tassels on the corners of the outer garments call the Israelites to action regarding the fulfillment of the commandments. Remembering, Heb "zakhar," is often a verb of action rather than simply thought (e.g., Gen. 8.1; 30.22; Exod. 12.14). In antiquity, fringes were common on Canaanite and Mesopotamian dress. Prophets from the Babylonian city of Mari legitimated their oracles before the king by sending a fringe from their garment, which is a symbolic way of sending part of themselves, like a signature. The imprinting of fringes on clay tablets, like the touching of the fringe of the prayer shawl to the Torah today when one is called to the Torah during its reading, is a way of verifying or endorsing the written document. Like garments and hair, fringes are considered part of the individual's identity, and by giving them to the ruler, a person is pledging his loyalty. It is no accident that the violet-blue wool cord that must be attached to the fringes (according to P) is identical to the cord that hangs from the priest's headdress (Exod. 28.37). The tzitzit on the garments of Israelites identifies them as being holy to God and symbolically connects them to the priests. Thereby, Israelites pledge their loyalty to God as well as to the priests who oversee the laws (cf. the nonspecific garment fringes called "gedilim" [lit. "twisted threads"] in Deut. 22.12). The commandment to wear fringed garments is an example of biblical sanctification of dress—imbuing aspects of traditional dress with cultic meaning. Modern prayer shawls, tallit (sing.), and the small tallit, worn daily under the shirt by observant Jews, no longer require a violet-blue cord for their tzitzit. That aspect of the commandment was suspended in talmudic times because of the scarcity and expense of the blue dye derived from the murex snail. Most likely because of the reference "to observe all My commandments," this paragraph came to be recited daily as part of the Shema prayer (see Deut. 6.4). **41:** The redemption from Egyptian slavery is often employed as grounds for Israelite allegiance to God (Exod. 6.7; 20.2–3; Lev. 11.45; Deut. 26.17–19).

16.1–35: The rebellions of Korah and Dathan and Abiram. These rebellions against the divinely appointed leadership of Moses and Aaron constitute public defiance that requires swift and harsh retribution. Like other rebellions in the wilderness, these begin with a few individuals and spread to the community at large. Two insurrection stories are interwoven by the redactor. One involves Korah, a Kohathite Levite who demands a share in the Aaronite priesthood; the second has three Reubenites, two brothers, Dathan and Abiram, and a third individual, On, who question the authority of Moses. The rebel leaders assemble followers. Defiance of Moses is clearly tied to miseries of the wilderness experience and doubts surrounding the eventual settlement of Canaan. On the other hand, the challenge of Aaron deals with the legitimacy of the priests' exclusive position vis-à-vis the Levites, who had a secondary role in the cult that

4 When Moses heard this, he fell on his face.[a] 5 Then he spoke
to Korah and all his company, saying, "Come morning, the
LORD will make known who is His and who is holy, and will
grant him access to Himself; He will grant access to the one
He has chosen. 6 Do this: You, Korah and all your[b] band, take
fire pans, 7 and tomorrow put fire in them and lay incense on
them before the LORD. Then the man whom the LORD chooses,
he shall be the holy one. You have gone too far, sons of Levi!"

8 Moses said further to Korah, "Hear me, sons of Levi. 9 Is it
not enough for you that the God of Israel has set you apart from
the community of Israel and given you access to Him, to perform the duties of the LORD's Tabernacle and to minister to the
community and serve them? 10 Now that He has advanced you
and all your fellow Levites with you, do you seek the priesthood too? 11 Truly, it is against the LORD that you and all your
company have banded together. For who is Aaron that you
should rail against him?"

12 Moses sent for Dathan and Abiram, sons of Eliab; but they
said, "We will not come! 13 Is it not enough that you brought us
from a land flowing with milk and honey to have us die in the
wilderness, that you would also lord it over us? 14 [c-]Even if you
had[-c] brought us to a land flowing with milk and honey, and
given us possession of fields and vineyards, should you gouge
out those men's eyes?[d] We will not come!" 15 Moses was much
aggrieved and he said to the LORD, "Pay no regard to their oblation. I have not taken the ass of any one of them, nor have I
wronged any one of them."

16 And Moses said to Korah, "Tomorrow, you and all your
company appear before the LORD, you and they and Aaron.
17 Each of you take his fire pan and lay incense on it, and each
of you bring his fire pan before the LORD, two hundred and fifty
fire pans; you and Aaron also [bring] your fire pans." 18 Each of
them took his fire pan, put fire in it, laid incense on it, and took
his place at the entrance of the Tent of Meeting, as did Moses
and Aaron. 19 Korah gathered the whole community against
them at the entrance of the Tent of Meeting.

a Perhaps in the sense of "his face fell."
b Lit. "his." *c-c Lit. "You have not even."*
d "Those men's" is a euphemism for "our"; cf. 1 Sam. 29.4. Gouging out the eyes was punishment for runaway slaves and rebellious vassals; cf. 2 Kings 25.4–7; Jer. 39.4–7, 52.7–11.

was much less prestigious than the priestly role. Both situations are resolved by divine wrath. In the case of Dathan and Abiram, they, their families, and all their possessions are literally swallowed up by the earth. In a twist of fate, they who had refused to *come* (up) to Moses (v. 12), *went down* into the earth (v. 33). Korah's contingent is first offered a test to settle the matter of the priesthood for all time. For their punishment, they who had sought the right to make fire for God's offerings are consumed themselves by divine fire. Such cases of measure-for-measure punishment are frequent in the Bible (see e.g., Eccl. 10.8a). **1:** *Descendants of Reuben:* This story may help to explain why the tribe of Reuben, the first-born, was supplanted by Judah. In fact, Ibn Ezra maintains that Reubenites challenged Moses because he did not give them their just due as descendants of Jacob's first-born. Instead he chose Joshua, an Ephraimite of the House of Joseph, as his assistant. **2:** Two hundred fifty Israelite chieftains join the uprising against Moses (v. 2), though later these chieftains are connected to the Levites who challenge Aaron (v. 35). This is a clear example of a redactor tightly weaving two separate accounts. **3:** *All the community are holy:* Korah's group argues against the notion that only the priests are sanctified to perform religious rituals. The fact that Korah and his followers are proven wrong demonstrates that popular holiness attached to the tzitzit (15.40) still renders wearers subordinate to priests. The people's holiness is not intrinsic and of the same level as that of the priests, and it derives from their obligation to follow the commandments (Lev. 19.2). **8–11:** Moses rebukes Korah and the Levites for not being satisfied with their God-appointed positions as guardians of the Tabernacle. Their sin is challenging God's authority rather than that of Aaron. **13–14:** The rebels call Egypt a land flowing with milk and honey, thus attributing the bounty of the promised land to Egypt, the land of enslavement. **15:** Moses defends his conduct as an honorable leader. The prophet Samuel responds similarly when the Israelites demand that a king replace him (1 Sam. 12.3). The prayer for their punishment sharply contrasts with Moses' other prayers for the nation's forgiveness. **16–18:** It is not specified that the fire which burnt the incense in the Levites' fire pans was taken from the altar. Thus, their sin may be compounded by the use of unauthorized *fire* (cf. Nadab and Abihu, Lev. 10.1–2).

Then the Presence of the LORD appeared to the whole community, 20 and the LORD spoke to Moses and Aaron, saying,
21 "Stand back from this community that I may annihilate them
in an instant!" 22 But they fell on their faces and said, "O God,
Source[a] of the breath of all flesh! When one man sins, will You
be wrathful with the whole community?"

23 The LORD spoke to Moses, saying, 24 "Speak to the community and say: Withdraw from about the abodes of Korah,
Dathan, and Abiram."

25 Moses rose and went to Dathan and Abiram, the elders
of Israel following him. 26 He addressed the community, saying, "Move away from the tents of these wicked men and touch
nothing that belongs to them, lest you be wiped out for all their
sins." 27 So they withdrew from about the abodes of Korah, Dathan, and Abiram.

Now Dathan and Abiram had come out and they stood at
the entrance of their tents, with their wives, their children,
and their little ones. 28 And Moses said, "By this you shall
know that it was the LORD who sent me to do all these things;
that they are not of my own devising: 29 if these men die as
all men do, if their lot be the common fate of all mankind, it
was not the LORD who sent me. 30 But if the LORD brings about
something unheard-of, so that the ground opens its mouth
and swallows them up with all that belongs to them, and they
go down alive into Sheol, you shall know that these men have
spurned the LORD." 31 Scarcely had he finished speaking all
these words when the ground under them burst asunder,
32 and the earth opened its mouth and swallowed them up
with their households, all Korah's people and all their possessions. 33 They went down alive into Sheol, with all that belonged to them; the earth closed over them and they vanished
from the midst of the congregation. 34 All Israel around them
fled at their shrieks, for they said, "The earth might swallow
us!"

35 And a fire went forth from the LORD and consumed the
two hundred and fifty men offering the incense.

17 The LORD spoke to Moses, saying: 2 Order Eleazar son of
Aaron the priest to remove the fire pans—for they have
become sacred—from among the charred remains; and scatter the coals abroad. 3 [b][Remove] the fire pans of those who
have sinned at the cost of their lives, and let them be made
into hammered sheets as plating for the altar—for once they
have been used for offering to the LORD, they have become sacred—and let them serve as a warning to the people of Israel.
4 Eleazar the priest took the copper fire pans which had been

a Lit. "God." *b Meaning of parts of verse uncertain.*

20–22: Apparently God is ready to annihilate Israel. Moses and Aaron appeal to God as Creator of humanity (v. 22a) and appeal to His sense of justice: Sin must be punished individually rather than communally (v. 22b; see Ezek. ch 18). **33:** *Sheol* is the underworld, the place where the dead, both the righteous and the sinners, dwell (1 Kings 2.6; Isa. 14.9–20). **35:** Korah is not mentioned as having died in the LORD's fire, although it is implied that he did (cf. 26.10, Korah perishes with Dathan and Abiram). The phrase *a fire went forth from the LORD and consumed* is used in Lev. 10.2 as well, in reference to Nadab and Abihu, thereby connecting these two units that focus on improper worship of God.

17.1–18.7: The aftermath of Korah's insurrection. This ch continues the previous narratives, tying up some loose ends. First, the copper fire pans of the Levites, which were exposed to divine fire, must be preserved since they are sacred. Second, the Israelites who question the fate of their rebel leaders are punished by plague. Third, the absolute divinely ordained authority of the Aaronide Levites is confirmed in the test of the staffs. Fourth, the Aaronide priests and their Levite subordinates take all sanctuary responsibilities and consequences of misconduct upon themselves. **17.3–5:** The fire pans rescued from the conflagration become copper plating for the altar, thereby serving as a *warning* sign, a visible *reminder,* aimed at stopping future would-be encroachers on the Tabernacle. The same Heb terms are used to describe the function of the tefillin (phylacteries) in Exod. 13.9, and the rainbow at the end of the flood story, though in that account God is the one being reminded (Gen. 9.12–17). These words refer to an action or object that is of symbolic rather than intrinsic significance. **6–15:** The Israelite community blames Moses and Aaron for the death of their leaders, here called *the LORD's people,* so Moses and Aaron must act to show

used for offering by those who died in the fire; and they were hammered into plating for the altar, 5 as the LORD had ordered him through Moses. It was to be a reminder to the Israelites, so that no outsider—one not of Aaron's offspring—should presume to offer incense before the LORD and suffer the fate of Korah and his band.

6 Next day the whole Israelite community railed against Moses and Aaron, saying, "You two have brought death upon the LORD's people!" 7 But as the community gathered against them, Moses and Aaron turned toward the Tent of Meeting; the cloud had covered it and the Presence of the LORD appeared.

8 When Moses and Aaron reached the Tent of Meeting, 9 the LORD spoke to Moses, saying, 10 "Remove yourselves from this community, that I may annihilate them in an instant." They fell on their faces. 11 Then Moses said to Aaron, "Take the fire pan, and put on it fire from the altar. Add incense and take it quickly to the community and make expiation for them. For wrath has gone forth from the LORD: the plague has begun!" 12 Aaron took it, as Moses had ordered, and ran to the midst of the congregation, where the plague had begun among the people. He put on the incense and made expiation for the people; 13 he stood between the dead and the living until the plague was checked. 14 Those who died of the plague came to fourteen thousand and seven hundred, aside from those who died on account of Korah. 15 Aaron then returned to Moses at the entrance of the Tent of Meeting, since the plague was checked.

16 The LORD spoke to Moses, saying: 17 Speak to the Israelite people and take from them—from the chieftains of their ancestral houses[a]—one staff for each chieftain of an ancestral house: twelve staffs in all. Inscribe each man's name on his staff, 18 there being one staff for each head of an ancestral house; also inscribe Aaron's name on the staff of Levi. 19 Deposit them in the Tent of Meeting before the Pact, where I meet with you. 20 The staff of the man whom I choose shall sprout, and I will rid[b] Myself of the incessant mutterings of the Israelites against you.

21 Moses spoke thus to the Israelites. Their chieftains gave him a staff for each chieftain of an ancestral house, twelve staffs in all; among these staffs was that of Aaron. 22 Moses deposited the staffs before the LORD, in the Tent of the Pact. 23 The next day Moses entered the Tent of the Pact, and there the staff of Aaron of the house of Levi had sprouted: it had brought forth sprouts, produced blossoms, and borne almonds. 24 Moses then brought out all the staffs from before the LORD to all the Israelites; each identified and recovered his staff.

a I.e., of their tribes. *b Meaning of Heb.* wahashikkothi *uncertain.*

that God is responsible. It is thus Aaron's expiation ritual that halts the plague. Similarly, David stops a plague by building an altar and offering a sacrifice on it (2 Sam. 24.18–25). The efficacy of ritual is apparent in both accounts. **16–26:** By collecting a staff from each tribal chieftain, the election of the tribe of Levi for sanctuary duties and the Aaronides as priests is reconfirmed. Aaron's name is inscribed on the staff of Levi, thus affirming his clan's status among the Levites. The contest, however, is not to determine who among the Levites can function as priests, as that issue was already settled with the death of Korah's group. **19:** *In the Tent of Meeting before the Pact:* The staffs are placed in front of the deity, or more correctly at His throne, the Ark. **23:** Aaron's *staff* not only sprouts but it produces *blossoms* which in turn develop into *almonds* overnight. The sprouting of a staff or pillar for the purpose of identifying a hero or priest is also known from Herodotus (IV.67–68). Almonds are considered among the choicest products of Canaan (Gen. 43.11). **25:** *Aaron's staff* is placed in the sanctuary as a warning sign, like the copper plating of fire pans on the altar. Alternatively, Aaron's staff was kept as a memorial attesting God's choice of Aaron (Rashi). **27–28:** The people fear that even approaching the Tabernacle could constitute encroachment and result in death; this concern is allied in the following unit, which is incorrectly separated by a new ch number.

18.1: God speaks to Aaron directly rather than through Moses (only in this ch and in Lev. 10.8). The priests are responsible to keep other priests who are in a state of cultic impurity out of the sanctuary (Exod. 28.43; 30.20; Lev. 10.9; 16.2; 21.23). **2–5:** Levite guard duties concerning the Tabernacle and its contents protect the Israelites from the consequences of encroachment. These vv. also contain a popular or folk etymology of Levites: They are the cultic functionaries who are *attached* to (vv. 2 and 4, from the root "l-v-h") the priests.

18.8–32: Compensation for the priests and Levites. This section, which by and large repeats Priestly legislation found in other books of the Torah, continues the subject of the previous section by delineating a system of compensation for priestly and Levitic services. In their responsibilities vis-à-vis the Tabernacle, religious functionaries work on behalf of the people, who, in turn, support them and their families. Regular tax revenues designated for the sanctuary satisfy those needs. Naturally, those holding the highest status and charged with the most sacred duties, the priests, are allocated the most desirable gifts, those marked "holy to the LORD, for the priests" (Lev. 23.20). Priestly portions are divided into two categories *most sacred* and *sacred,* and accordingly, are designated for consumption by only ritually pure males in the sacred precinct, and by their female relatives living at home, respectively. A statement regarding these priestly emoluments is found in the writings of the prophet Ezekiel, himself a priest (44.29–30). The Levites, on the other hand, receive the tithes. **9–10:** *Most sacred* includes that part of purification and guilt offerings which is not burnt (see Lev. 6.1–7.10).

25 The LORD said to Moses, "Put Aaron's staff back before the
Pact, to be kept as a lesson to rebels, so that their mutterings
against Me may cease, lest they die." 26 This Moses did; just as
the LORD had commanded him, so he did.
27 But the Israelites said to Moses, "Lo, we perish! We are lost,
all of us lost! 28 Everyone who so much as ventures near the
LORD's Tabernacle must die. Alas, we are doomed to perish!"

18 The LORD said to Aaron: You and your sons and the
ancestral house under your charge shall bear any guilt
connected with the sanctuary; you and your sons alone shall
bear any guilt connected with your priesthood. 2 You shall also
associate with yourself your kinsmen the tribe of Levi, your ancestral tribe, to be attached to you and to minister to you, while
you and your sons under your charge are before the Tent of the
Pact.[a] 3 They shall discharge their duties to you and to the Tent
as a whole, but they must not have any contact with the furnishings of the Shrine or with the altar, lest both they and you
die. 4 They shall be attached to you and discharge the duties of
the Tent of Meeting, all the service of the Tent; but no outsider
shall intrude upon you 5 as you discharge the duties connected
with the Shrine and the altar, that wrath may not again strike
the Israelites.
6 I hereby take your fellow Levites from among the Israelites;
they are assigned to you in dedication to the LORD, to do the
work of the Tent of Meeting; 7 while you and your sons shall
be careful to perform your priestly duties in everything pertaining to the altar and to what is behind the curtain. I make
your priesthood a service of dedication; any outsider who encroaches shall be put to death.
8 The LORD spoke further to Aaron: I hereby give you charge
of My gifts, all the sacred donations of the Israelites; I grant
them to you and to your sons as a perquisite,[b] a due for all
time. 9 This shall be yours from the most holy sacrifices, [c]the
offerings by fire:[-c] every such offering that they render to Me
as most holy sacrifices, namely, every meal offering, purification offering, and guilt offering of theirs, shall belong to you
and your sons. 10 You shall partake of them as most sacred
donations: only males may eat them; you shall treat them as
consecrated.[d]
11 This, too, shall be yours: the gift offerings[e] of their contributions, all the elevation offerings of the Israelites, I give to you, to
your sons, and to the daughters that are with you, as a due for
all time; everyone of your household who is clean may eat it.

a *Meaning of latter part of verse uncertain.* b *See note at Lev. 7.35.*
c-c *Meaning of Heb. uncertain; lit. "from the fire."*
d *Or "they are consecrated for your use."* e *Cf. Lev. 7.29 ff.*

12 All the best of the new oil, wine, and grain—the choice parts that they present to the LORD—I give to you. 13 The first fruits of everything in their land, that they bring to the LORD, shall be yours; everyone of your household who is clean may eat them. 14 Everything that has been proscribed in Israel[a] shall be yours. 15 The first issue of the womb of every being, man or beast, that is offered to the LORD, shall be yours; but you shall have the first-born of man redeemed, and you shall also have the firstling of unclean animals redeemed. 16 Take as their redemption price,[b] from the age of one month up, the money equivalent of five shekels by the sanctuary weight, which is twenty *gerah*s. 17 But the firstlings of cattle, sheep, or goats may not be redeemed; they are consecrated. You shall dash their blood against the altar, and turn their fat into smoke as an offering by fire for a pleasing odor to the LORD. 18 But their meat shall be yours: it shall be yours like the breast of elevation offering and like the right thigh.

19 All the sacred gifts that the Israelites set aside for the LORD I give to you, to your sons, and to the daughters that are with you, as a due for all time. It shall be an everlasting covenant of salt[c] before the LORD for you and for your offspring as well. 20 And the LORD said to Aaron: You shall, however, have no territorial share among them or own any portion in their midst; I am your portion and your share among the Israelites.

21 And to the Levites I hereby give all the tithes in Israel as their share in return for the services that they perform, the services of the Tent of Meeting. 22 Henceforth, Israelites shall not trespass on the Tent of Meeting, and thus incur guilt and die: 23 only Levites shall perform the services of the Tent of Meeting; others[d] would incur guilt. It is the law for all time throughout the ages. But they shall have no territorial share among the Israelites; 24 for it is the tithes set aside by the Israelites as a gift to the LORD that I give to the Levites as their share. Therefore I have said concerning them: They shall have no territorial share among the Israelites.

25 The LORD spoke to Moses, saying: 26 Speak to the Levites and say to them: When you receive from the Israelites their tithes, which I have assigned to you as your share, you shall set aside from them one-tenth of the tithe as a gift to the LORD. 27 This shall be accounted to you as your gift. As with the new grain from the threshing floor or the flow from the vat, 28 so shall you on your part set aside a gift for the LORD from all the tithes that you receive from the Israelites; and from them you shall bring the gift for the LORD to Aaron the priest. 29 You shall

a *See Lev. 27.28.*
b *I.e., for human first-born; cf. Num. 3.44 ff. For animals see Exod. 34.19 f.*
c *See Lev. 2.13.* d *Lit. "they."*

11–18: "Sacred" is a much larger category which includes the following: portions of nonsacrificial gifts and elevation offerings (see Lev. 7.11–38); offerings of first fruits, grain, wine, and oil (see Exod. 23.16–19; Lev. 2.14; 23.17–18; Deut. 18.4; 26.1–11); anything proscribed or dedicated that becomes the property of the LORD under the law of "ḥerem" (the ban; see Lev. 27.21, 28–29; Deut. 7.26; Josh. chs 6–7); all human and animal first-born males, both those to be redeemed—man and animals unfit for sacrifice—and those animals sacrificed (see Exod. 13.2, 11–13; 22.28; 34.19–20; Lev. 27.1–13; Deut. 12.17; 14.23; 15.19–23). **16:** For the values of the sanctuary weight, the shekel, and *gerah* see 3.47 n. **19:** *An everlasting covenant of salt:* Salt, a valuable food preservative, is symbolic of the permanence of the covenant agreement. It is used with sacrifices (Lev. 2.13; 2 Chron. 13.5). Based on this v., the Rabbis maintain that the covenant between the priests and God is eternal, even following the destruction of the Temple and the end of the sacrificial system (*Lev. Rab.* 24.2). This explains why in some contemporary groups of Judaism, the priests retain certain privileges, especially blessing the congregation (see 6.22–27) or being called first to the Torah. **20:** *I am your portion:* The personal name Hilkiah, "Yah (the LORD) is my portion," which is the name of several priests (2 Kings 22.10; Ezra 7.1; 1 Chron. 5.39; and on the personal seal of a priest), reflects the sense of this phrase. **21–24:** Laws concerning tithes are outlined in Lev. 27.30–32 and Deut. 12.17–19; 14.22–29. **25–32:** Levites are compensated for their service by the tithes. They are required to donate to the priests one-tenth of the tithes that they collect, however. Thus, Levites are obligated to pay tithes like other Israelites; only priests are exempt since they cannot pay themselves tithes. This final section of the ch is an addition or amendment to the law in Lev.

set aside all gifts due to the LORD from everything that is donated to you, from each thing its best portion, the part thereof
that is to be consecrated.
30 Say to them further: When you have removed the best part
from it, you Levites may consider it the same as the yield of
threshing floor or vat. 31 You and your households may eat it
anywhere, for it is your recompense for your services in the
Tent of Meeting. 32 You will incur no guilt through it, once you
have removed the best part from it; but you must not profane
the sacred donations of the Israelites, lest you die.

ḤUKKAT חקת

19 The LORD spoke to Moses and Aaron, saying: 2 This is the
ritual law that the LORD has commanded:
Instruct the Israelite people to bring you a red cow without
blemish, in which there is no defect and on which no yoke
has been laid. 3 You shall give it to Eleazar the priest. It shall
be taken outside the camp and slaughtered in his presence.
4 Eleazar the priest shall take some of its blood with his finger and sprinkle it seven times toward the front of the Tent of
Meeting. 5 The cow shall be burned in his sight—its hide, flesh,
and blood shall be burned, its dung included—6 and the priest
shall take cedar wood, hyssop, and crimson stuff, and throw
them into the fire consuming the cow. 7 The priest shall wash
his garments and bathe his body in water; after that the priest
may reenter the camp, but he shall be unclean until evening.
8 He who performed the burning shall also wash his garments
in water, bathe his body in water, and be unclean until evening.
9 A man who is clean shall gather up the ashes of the cow and
deposit them outside the camp in a clean place, to be kept for
water of lustration[a] for the Israelite community. It is for purification. 10 He who gathers up the ashes of the cow shall also
wash his clothes and be unclean until evening.
This shall be a permanent law for the Israelites and for the
strangers who reside among you.
11 He who touches the corpse of any human being shall be
unclean for seven days. 12 He shall cleanse himself with it[b] on
the third day and on the seventh day, and then be clean; if

a Lit. "water for impurity." *b I.e., the ashes, as in v. 9.*

19.1–22: Ritual of purification with the ashes of a red cow. Contamination through contact with a corpse, or any part thereof, whether by actual touch or through proximity in an enclosed space, is considered a severe impurity (cf. 5.1–4) requiring a complex purification process. While impurities in general are discussed elsewhere (Lev. chs 11–15), the process of erasing corpse pollution is delineated only here (and briefly in 31.19–24 in connection with combat). Contaminated persons or objects must be cleansed lest they communicate their contagious state to other humans or objects within the camp and ultimately defile the sanctuary. Classical Judaism understands the term "ḥukah" (NJPS *ritual law,* v. 2), as a law that defies rational explanation. However, the types of procedures described here have parallels in ancient Near Eastern literature, and may be understood using anthropological understandings of how rituals function. The seven-day purification process involves a type of "ḥata't," a purification offering. The affected person or object is sprinkled on the third and seventh day with a prepared mixture of fresh water and the ashes of a red cow, cedar wood, hyssop plant, and red dye. Essentially on the principle of sympathetic magic, the red-colored ash mixture absorbs the corpse pollution. (Note also how blood functions as a type of "ritual detergent" in Lev. ch 16.) This ritual is unique in biblical practices, one reason being that those officiating at the cleansing contract a measure of impurity in the process of performing it. Ch 19 consists of two subsections. The first, vv. 1–13, contains instructions on the preparation of the ashes and the mixture. It also details the purification procedure for persons preparing the concoction. The second part, vv. 14–22, details conditions that qualify persons or objects to undergo this rite and the actual sprinkling ritual. Failure to undergo this process is subject to "karet," divine retribution (vv. 13, 20). **2:** *Ritual law:* The Rabbis derive justification for this seemingly peculiar rite, over which the nations of the world taunt Israel, by this reference to law, "Torah." *A red cow:* Red, symbolic of blood, ensures the efficacy of the rite. The ashes of a cow rather than a bull are used for individuals (cf. Deut. 21.1–9); the bull "ḥata't" is used for the high priest and the community (Lev. 4.1–21; 16.11). Generations have puzzled over the color of this cow. The best explanation is that it is a brown, or reddish-brown cow with no spots of other color on it. **6–10:** The priest who oversees the incineration of the cow, and the persons who conduct the various tasks associated with it, become ritually unclean. **9:** *It is for purification:* The translation of "ḥata't" reflects the fact

he fails to cleanse himself on the third and seventh days, he shall not be clean. 13 Whoever touches a corpse, the body of a person who has died, and does not cleanse himself, defiles the LORD's Tabernacle; that person shall be cut off from Israel. Since the water of lustration was not dashed on him, he remains unclean; his uncleanness is still upon him.

14 This is the ritual: When a person dies in a tent, whoever enters the tent and whoever is in the tent shall be unclean seven days; 15 and every open vessel, with no lid fastened down, shall be unclean. 16 And in the open, anyone who touches a person who was killed[a] or who died naturally, or human bone, or a grave, shall be unclean seven days. 17 Some of the ashes[b] from the fire of purification shall be taken for the unclean person, and fresh water shall be added to them in a vessel. 18 A person who is clean shall take hyssop, dip it in the water, and sprinkle on the tent and on all the vessels and people who were there, or on him who touched the bones or the person who was killed or died naturally or the grave. 19 The clean person shall sprinkle it upon the unclean person on the third day and on the seventh day, thus cleansing him by the seventh day. He[c] shall then wash his clothes and bathe in water, and at nightfall he shall be clean. 20 If anyone who has become unclean fails to cleanse himself, that person shall be cut off from the congregation, for he has defiled the LORD's sanctuary. The water of lustration was not dashed on him: he is unclean.

21 That shall be for them a law for all time. Further, he who sprinkled the water of lustration shall wash his clothes; and whoever touches the water of lustration shall be unclean until evening. 22 Whatever that unclean person touches shall be unclean; and the person who touches him shall be unclean until evening.

20 The Israelites arrived in a body at the wilderness of Zin on the first new moon,[d] and the people stayed at Kadesh. Miriam died there and was buried there.

2 The community was without water, and they joined against Moses and Aaron. 3 The people quarreled with Moses, saying, "If only we had perished when our brothers perished at

a Lit. "slain by the sword." *b Lit. "earth" or "dust."*
c I.e., the person being cleansed. *d Of the fortieth year; cf. Num. 33.36–38.*

that this is not a sacrifice in the true sense of a sin offering which is made on the altar inside the camp. **14:** Pollution from a corpse seems to be airborne. **16:** Any portion of a corpse is defiling. Contact with sacred objects defiles them permanently, and so King Josiah used human ashes to desecrate illegitimate altars and other cult objects and to invalidate sacred space in perpetuity (2 Kings chs 22–23). **17:** *Fresh water,* lit. "living water," is water running from its source rather than taken from a storage unit (cf. Lev. 14.5, 50). In postbiblical Jewish law such running water must be used in the mikveh or ritual bath. **20:** The sin of defiling the sanctuary only applies if a contaminated Israelite or foreign resident does not undergo this cleansing process. Priests, on the other hand, are restricted to contact with a corpse of immediate family members (Lev. 21.1–4). The consequences of defiling the sanctuary are severe: God will abandon it when it becomes sufficiently defiled (see Ezek. chs 1–11). The biblical Day of Atonement ritual (Lev. ch 16) is a purification ritual, which cleanses the sanctuary from accumulated impurities or pollution.

20.1–13: The sin of Moses and Aaron. Chs 20–21 continue the wilderness narrative. This section opens with the Israelites at Kadesh. According to the Priestly writer(s) this marks the end of the 40-year period in the desert, which was spent primarily in northern Sinai. In contrast, the JE tradition (see Exod. ch 16) places this stop early in the forty-year march, claiming that Israel traveled only one to two years in the Sinai, with the balance of the forty years being spent in the wilderness of Edom and Moab en route to the crossing at the Jordan River. (32.8 states that the spies were distracted from Kadesh; 13.26 records the spies' return to the Israelite camp at Kadesh. The punishment of forty years of wandering follows their report. Num. 14.25 instructs the Israelites to head for the Red Sea immediately, then cross into the wilderness of Edom.) Vv. 1–13 comprise the first of three subsections of ch 20. This part recounts Miriam's death, Israel's murmuring to Moses and Aaron over a water shortage, Moses' and Aaron's handling of the crisis, and their tragic banning from entering Canaan. The incident involving water is the second of its kind, and is likely P's version of the JE account of a water shortage at Massah and Meribah (Exod. 17.1–7). In the Exod. narrative God instructs Moses to hit the rock with his rod to bring forth water. In the Priestly version here in Num., Moses and Aaron are to speak to the rock in front of the Israelites (v. 8). When Moses strikes the rock

the instance of the LORD! 4 Why have you brought the LORD's congregation into this wilderness for us and our beasts to die there? 5 Why did you make us leave Egypt to bring us to this wretched place, a place with no grain or figs or vines or pomegranates? There is not even water to drink!"

6 Moses and Aaron came away from the congregation to the entrance of the Tent of Meeting, and fell on their faces. The Presence of the LORD appeared to them, 7 and the LORD spoke to Moses, saying, 8 "You and your brother Aaron take the rod and assemble the community, and before their very eyes order the rock to yield its water. Thus you shall produce water for them from the rock and provide drink for the congregation and their beasts."

9 Moses took the rod from before the LORD, as He had commanded him. 10 Moses and Aaron assembled the congregation in front of the rock; and he said to them, "Listen, you rebels, shall we get water for you out of this rock?" 11 And Moses raised his hand and struck the rock twice with his rod. Out came copious water, and the community and their beasts drank.

12 But the LORD said to Moses and Aaron, "Because you did not trust Me enough to affirm My sanctity in the sight of the Israelite people, therefore you shall not lead this congregation into the land that I have given them." 13 Those are the Waters of Meribah[a]—meaning that the Israelites quarrelled with the LORD—through which He affirmed His sanctity.

14 From Kadesh, Moses sent messengers to the king of Edom: "Thus says your brother Israel: You know all the hardships that have befallen us; 15 that our ancestors went down to Egypt, that we dwelt in Egypt a long time, and that the Egyptians dealt harshly with us and our ancestors. 16 We cried to the LORD and He heard our plea, and He sent a messenger[b] who freed us from Egypt. Now we are in Kadesh, the town on the border of your territory. 17 Allow us, then, to cross your country. We will not

a *I.e., "Quarrel"; cf. Exod. 17.7 and note b there.* *b* *Or "angel."*

instead of speaking to it, God, in an unexpected move, hands down the ultimate punishment to His appointed leaders. Puzzled by the apparent harshness of God's verdict, biblical readers past and present have tried to reconcile Moses' and Aaron's punishment with their sin (see v. 10). The deaths of Aaron and, especially, of Moses in Transjordan overlooking the promised land have become a symbol epitomizing the human condition. **1:** *On the first new moon:* This is the first month of the fortieth year according to 33.38, which places Kadesh before Aaron's death in the fifth month of that year. Some rabbinic traditions connect Miriam to water, and find significance in the juxtaposition of Miriam's death (v. 1) to the absence of water (*Song Rab.* 4.12). **10:** *"Shall we get water for you out of this rock?":* Striking the rock, as in the Exod. version, does not seem to account for the gravity of Moses' sin, even though according to some interpretations, it constitutes public disobedience of God's instructions, which in itself is punishable. A plausible, interpretation is found among medieval commentators who focus on the pronoun "we" in "shall we get water." By attributing the act of drawing water from a rock to himself and Aaron, Moses, standing before Israel, fails to credit the miracle to God; this is particularly significant because in vv. 4–5 the nation seems to attribute the exodus to Moses and Aaron rather than to God. The distinction carries theological implications in light of the Bible's need to show the superiority of Israel's God over Pharaoh and the gods of Egypt (Exod. ch 5–12). Of significance is an Egyptian inscription on a roadside rock temple in the eastern desert dedicated by Pharaoh Seti I (late 14th c.) to his gods: "He (god) has made water come forth for me from the mountain."

20.14–21: Confrontation with Edom. Since the Israelites fail to enter Canaan from the south (14.40–45) they now plan to cut through the territory of Edom, follow the main road north to Moab, and then cross the Jordan from the east. Moses twice petitions the ruler of Edom for permission to cross his country, emphasizing Israel's misfortunes as he appeals for sympathy. But the Edomites deny Israel access to their territory and confront them with a large military force. Israel must circumvent the entire region of Edom by detouring south to the Red Sea and marching around the eastern border of Edom. It is this detour that according to the JE tradition took thirty-eight years to complete. A variant version in Deut. recalls that Israel did indeed march through Edom (2.1–8). **14:** *Your brother Israel* may refer to Edom's relationship to Jacob (Gen. 25.24–26), a legacy reflected in certain laws (Deut. 23.8). On the other hand, in the ancient Near East "brother" signifies someone of equal status. Here Moses may be indicating that the two groups, the Edomites and Israelites, are essentially of equal status and should therefore practice a "brother" relationship when dealing with each other. **17:** *The king's highway* is an

pass through fields or vineyards, and we will not drink water from wells. We will follow the king's highway, turning off neither to the right nor to the left until we have crossed your territory."

18 But Edom answered him, "You shall not pass through us, else we will go out against you with the sword." 19 "We will keep to the beaten track," the Israelites said to them, "and if we or our cattle drink your water, we will pay for it. We ask only for passage on foot—it is but a small matter." 20 But they replied, "You shall not pass through!" And Edom went out against them in heavy force, strongly armed. 21 So Edom would not let Israel cross their territory, and Israel turned away from them.

22 Setting out from Kadesh, the Israelites arrived in a body at Mount Hor. 23 At Mount Hor, on the boundary of the land of Edom, the LORD said to Moses and Aaron, 24 "Let Aaron be gathered to his kin: he is not to enter the land that I have assigned to the Israelite people, because you disobeyed my command about the waters of Meribah. 25 Take Aaron and his son Eleazar and bring them up on Mount Hor. 26 Strip Aaron of his vestments and put them on his son Eleazar. There Aaron shall be gathered[a] unto the dead."[a]

27 Moses did as the LORD had commanded. They ascended Mount Hor in the sight of the whole community. 28 Moses stripped Aaron of his vestments and put them on his son Eleazar, and Aaron died there on the summit of the mountain. When Moses and Eleazar came down from the mountain, 29 the whole community knew that Aaron had breathed his last. All the house of Israel bewailed Aaron thirty days.

21

When the Canaanite, king of Arad, who dwelt in the Negeb, learned that Israel was coming by the way of Atharim,[b] he engaged Israel in battle and took some of them captive. 2 Then Israel made a vow to the LORD and said, "If You deliver this people into our hand, we will proscribe[c] their towns." 3 The LORD heeded Israel's plea and delivered up the Canaanites; and they and their cities were proscribed. So that place was named Hormah.[d]

a-a *Lit. "and die."*

b *Meaning of Heb.* ha-'atharim *uncertain. Targum and other ancient versions render "the way [taken by] the scouts."*

c *I.e., utterly destroy, reserving no booty except what is deposited in the Sanctuary; see Josh. 6.24.* d *Connected with* heḥerim *"to proscribe."*

important ancient trade route leading from Damascus to the delta in Egypt via Elath.

20.22–29: Aaron's death. The Priestly narrative continues with the transference of the office of high priest to Eleazar and the death of Aaron on Mount Hor. Mount Hor is the site of Aaron's death according to 33.38 and Deut. 32.50; but in Deut. 10.6 he dies at Moserah. For P it is important to record in detail Eleazar's inheritance of his father's priestly garments along with his office. The fact that all Israel mourned Aaron for thirty days, instead of the customary seven (Gen. 50.10; 1 Sam. 31.13), reflects his stature in the community. Moses is also mourned for thirty days (Deut. 34.8). In later Jewish law, these different durations of periods of mourning are reconciled by having a more stringent period of seven days of mourning followed by a period of moderate mourning that lasts for an additional twenty-three days. According to a midrashic tradition, Aaron was loved, and thus mourned extensively by the people because he was a harbinger of peace, especially between husband and wife (*'Avot R. Nat.* 12).

21.1–22.1: The final events of the wilderness experience. This ch consists of four subsections. The first and last focus on Israel's encounters with different ethnic groups that inhabit the eastern Negev and Transjordan; the middle two recount events on this part of the journey. These travels end the wilderness period bringing the Israelites from Kadesh-barnea to the eastern bank of the Jordan River in Moab just opposite Canaan. The Deuteronomistic History calculates that period as thirty-eight years (Deut. 2.13–15). Previously, Israel had met an armed group of indigenous people when attempting to invade Canaan from the south, but without success (14.43–45); a fruitless encounter with Edomites is also mentioned (20.14–21). In this ch, the confrontations with the inhabitants on the borders of Canaan proper mark a turning point in Israel's fortunes. With God at their side, their victories preview coming events during the conquest of Canaan. Two ancient poems are preserved in this section. **1–3:** This encounter with Canaanites in the northern Negev in the region of Arad is an alternate tradition concerning the naming of Hormah (14.43–45). In this version, God ends up by championing Israel's cause after the people vow to proscribe the enemy as "ḥerem," utter

4 They set out from Mount Hor by way of the Sea of Reeds[a] to
skirt the land of Edom. But the people grew restive on the journey, 5 and the people spoke against God and against Moses,
"Why did you make us leave Egypt to die in the wilderness?
There is no bread and no water, and we have come to loathe
this miserable food." 6 The LORD sent *seraph*[b] serpents against
the people. They bit the people and many of the Israelites died.
7 The people came to Moses and said, "We sinned by speaking against the LORD and against you. Intercede with the LORD
to take away the serpents from us!" And Moses interceded for
the people. 8 Then the LORD said to Moses, "Make a *seraph*[b] figure and mount it on a standard. And if anyone who is bitten
looks at it, he shall recover." 9 Moses made a copper serpent
and mounted it on a standard; and when anyone was bitten
by a serpent, he would look at the copper serpent and recover.

10 The Israelites marched on and encamped at Oboth.
11 They set out from Oboth and encamped at Iye-abarim, in the
wilderness bordering on Moab to the east. 12 From there they
set out and encamped at the wadi Zered. 13 From there they set
out and encamped beyond the Arnon, that is, in the wilderness
that extends from the territory of the Amorites. For the Arnon
is the boundary of Moab, between Moab and the Amorites.
14 Therefore the Book of the Wars of the LORD speaks of[c] "... Wa-
heb in Suphah, and the wadis: the Arnon 15 with its tributary
wadis, stretched along the settled country of Ar, hugging the
territory of Moab..."

16 And from there to Beer,[d] which is the well where the LORD
said to Moses, "Assemble the people that I may give them water." 17 Then Israel sang this song:

Spring up, O well—sing to it—
18 The well which the chieftains dug,
Which the nobles of the people started
With maces, with their own staffs.

And from Midbar[e] to Mattanah, 19 and from Mattanah to
Nahaliel, and from Nahaliel to Bamoth, 20 and from Bamoth to
the valley that is in the country of Moab, at the peak of Pisgah,
overlooking the wasteland.[f]

a See Exod. 10.19 note.
b Cf. Isa. 14.29; 30.6. Others "fiery"; exact meaning of Heb. saraph *uncertain.*
c The quotation that follows is a fragment; text and meaning are uncertain.
d Lit. "well." *e Septuagint "the well"* (= Beer)*; cf. v. 16.* *f Or "Jeshimon."*

destruction with the booty dedicated to the sanctuary. **1:** *King of Arad:* Archeological excavations show no evidence of a settlement at Arad in the second millennium. Probably, a writer living at a later time, when Israelite Arad was inhabited, assumed that during the exodus period a Canaanite king resided there. On Hormah, see 14.45. **4–9:** This incident is the final recurrence of wilderness murmuring. Complaints again center around a lack of water and poor food. The bronze serpent as an apotropaic (evil-averting, from Gk "turn from") symbol seems to be the etiological account for the bronze serpent, Neḥushtan, which was worshipped in Jerusalem until the late 8th century when King Hezekiah destroyed it (2 Kings 18.4). Winged serpents associated with the divine are attested in Isaiah (6.6–7; 14.20–30) and elsewhere in the ancient Near East. In Egypt, the uraeus, an amulet of an upreared cobra, symbolized kingship and divinity. It was worn on the pharaoh's forehead and was believed to protect him with its fiery saliva. A serpent attached to a staff is the source of the caduceus symbol of the modern medical profession. **4:** This v. continues 20.21; *from Mount Hor* is a Priestly interpolation. *The Sea of Reeds* here must refer to the Red Sea (see Map, p. 122). **5:** Once again, the people revolt against God and Moses. *This miserable food* refers to the manna. **6:** *Seraph serpents,* based on the verb, means "burning serpents," because of their poisonous bite. **9:** *A copper serpent* more likely refers to one made of bronze, a copper-tin alloy. Heb "neḥoshet" (copper) resembles the word for snake, "naḥash." Rabbinic interpreters were disturbed by the magical nature of this cure, and suggested that it was the glance of the afflicted to their Father in heaven (which is why the *seraph* was placed on a standard), rather than the snake itself, which effected the cure (*b. Rosh Hash.* 29a, cited in Rashi). **10–20:** This subsection summarizes Israel's trek through Transjordan (cf. 33.41–49); another similar list is found in 33.1–49. **14:** *Book of the Wars of the LORD* is a reference to an ancient collection, not extant, probably epic poems describing Israel's battles (cf. Book of Jashar in Josh. 10.13; 2 Sam. 1.18). **17–18:** The song of the well celebrates God providing Israel with water (cf. Song at the Sea, Exod. 15.1–18; Song of Deborah, Judg. ch 5). It is an etiology for the toponym Beer, "well" (v. 16).

21 Israel now sent messengers to Sihon king of the Amorites,
saying, 22 "Let me pass through your country. We will not turn
off into fields or vineyards, and we will not drink water from
wells. We will follow the king's highway until we have crossed
your territory." 23 But Sihon would not let Israel pass through
his territory. Sihon gathered all his people and went out against
Israel in the wilderness. He came to Jahaz and engaged Israel
in battle. 24 But Israel put them to the sword, and took possession of their land, from the Arnon to the Jabbok, as far as [Az] of
the Ammonites, for Az[a] marked the boundary of the Ammonites. 25 Israel took all those towns. And Israel settled in all the
towns of the Amorites, in Heshbon and all its dependencies.
26 Now Heshbon was the city of Sihon king of the Amorites,
who had fought against a former king of Moab and taken all
his land from him as far as the Arnon. 27 Therefore the bards
would recite:

[b]"Come to Heshbon; firmly built
And well founded is Sihon's city.
28 For fire went forth from Heshbon,
Flame from Sihon's city,
Consuming Ar of Moab,
The lords of Bamoth[c] by the Arnon.
29 Woe to you, O Moab!
You are undone, O people of Chemosh!
His sons are rendered fugitive
And his daughters captive
By an Amorite king, Sihon."
30[d] Yet we have cast them down utterly,
Heshbon along with Dibon;
We have wrought desolation at Nophah,
Which is hard by Medeba.

31 So Israel occupied the land of the Amorites. 32 Then Moses
sent to spy out Jazer, and they captured its dependencies and
dispossessed the Amorites who were there.

33 They marched on and went up the road to Bashan, and
King Og of Bashan, with all his people, came out to Edrei to
engage them in battle. 34 But the LORD said to Moses, "Do not
fear him, for I give him and all his people and his land into
your hand. You shall do to him as you did to Sihon king of the
Amorites who dwelt in Heshbon." 35 They defeated him and
his sons and all his people, until no remnant was left him; and

a Septuagint "Jazer," cf. v. 32. Others "for the boundary of the Ammonites was strong."

b The meaning of several parts of this ancient poem is no longer certain.

c Cf. vv. 19 and 20 and Num. 22.21.

d Meaning of verse uncertain. Alternatively: "Their dominion is at an end / From Heshbon to Dibon / And from Nashim to Nophah, / Which is hard by Medeba."

21.21–22.1: The conquest narrative begins here with Israel's triumph over two Amorite kinglets in Transjordan. Accounts of victories in Transjordan provide the backdrop for settlement in that region by the tribes of Reuben, Gad, and half of Manasseh. **21.21–32:** Israel must conquer the Amorite king Sihon in order to advance. The territory ruled by Sihon is in Moab; apparently it has changed hands. **27–30:** The ballad of Heshbon celebrates Sihon's conquest of Moabite territory. Various theories have been proposed as to why it is preserved in the Bible. According to the Rabbis, it justifies Israel's defeat of Sihon (*Num. Rab.* 19.30). Israel was prohibited from provoking the Moabites to battle (Deut. 2.9). **29:** *Chemosh* is the national god of the Moabites. **33–35:** The record of the victory over Og king of the Bashan region (see Map, p. 482) parallels Deut. 3.1–2. In this encounter God directs the military action.

22 they took possession of his country. 1 The Israelites then
marched on and encamped in the steppes of Moab,
across the Jordan from Jericho.

BALAK בלק

2 Balak son of Zippor saw all that Israel had done to the Amorites.
3 Moab was alarmed because that people was so numerous.
Moab dreaded the Israelites, 4 and Moab said to the elders of
Midian, "Now this horde will lick clean all that is about us as
an ox licks up the grass of the field."
Balak son of Zippor, who was king of Moab at that time,
5 sent messengers to Balaam son of Beor in Pethor, which is by
the Euphrates,[a] in the land of his kinsfolk, to invite him, saying,
"There is a people that came out of Egypt; it hides the earth
from view, and it is settled next to me. 6 Come then, put a curse
upon this people for me, since they are too numerous for me;
perhaps I can thus defeat them and drive them out of the land.
For I know that he whom you bless is blessed indeed, and he
whom you curse is cursed."
7 The elders of Moab and the elders of Midian, [b-]versed in
divination,[-b] set out. They came to Balaam and gave him Balak's
message. 8 He said to them, "Spend the night here, and I shall
reply to you as the LORD may instruct me." So the Moabite dignitaries stayed with Balaam.

a *Lit. "the River."* *b-b* *Lit. "with divination in their power (hand)."*

22.1: This v., which also contextualizes the subsequent Balaam pericope, is a postscript to ch 21.

22.2–24.25: The story of the seer Balaam. Inserted into the narrative of Israel's final preparation to enter Canaan is the story of the Moabite king Balak and the non-Israelite prophet Balaam whom he hires to curse Israel into oblivion. A visionary named Balaam is attested outside the Bible, on a fragmentary inscription on a wall plaster (late 9th to 8th c.) from a temple at Deir ʿAlla in Transjordan, which records the night vision of a certain Balaam. The seer Balaam may have been a legendary character of antiquity or a real person well known in the region. This independent composition, possibly originating from a different scribal circle than those associated with the rest of the Torah, is composed of narrative and poetry. It is inserted at this juncture, the beginning of Israel's period of encampment in Moab, because the outcome of Balak's scheme determines if Israel will inherit the promised land. The account is a contest in the divine realm between the God of Israel and those supernatural elements available to Balak. At times amusing, and somewhat mocking of the non-Israelite prophet, the message of this pericope is serious: The intent of the LORD reigns supreme and cannot be superseded. Even the powers of a well-known non-Israelite prophet are ultimately controlled by God. In the end nothing in Balaam's four oracles exacts a curse upon Israel; in fact, his prophecies function in reverse, blessing Israel and cursing her enemies. The biblical traditions are not consistent in their assessment of Balaam's intentions. In Deut. (23.4–7) and Josh. (24.9–10) it is God who reverses Balaam's actual intent. Num. 31.16 blames Balaam for Israel's apostasy at Baal-peor (ch 25), implying that he previously sought to curse them. The memory preserved in the writings of the 8th-c. BCE prophet Micah (6.5) is more compatible with most of the favorable Num. chs 22–24 accounts. Postbiblical literature is divided as well in evaluations of Balaam (cf. *Tg. Num.* chs 22–24; *Num. Rab.* 14.20).

The complete biblical story of Balaam is composed of several subsections: (1) Balak hires Balaam to curse Israel (22.2–40). Within this narrative is inserted the tale of Balaam and his talking she-ass (22.21–35). (2) Balaam's first oracle (22.41–23.10); (3) Balak's response and Balaam's second oracle (23.11–24); (4) Balak's response and Balaam's third oracle (23.25–24.9); (5) Balak's response and Balaam's fourth oracle; their departure (24.10–25). Each subsection containing an oracle is composed of narrative followed by a poetic oracle. If read detached from the narrative, the four poems connect to tell the story in poetic form, suggesting that the entire poem derives from an older independent source. Like much biblical poetry, this poem contains many words and phrases that are obscure or possibly have become corrupted over time.

22.2–40: Balak hires Balaam to curse Israel. 4: *The elders of Midian* refers to the leaders of Midianite groups who lived in Moab (cf. Gen. 36.35). **5:** *Balaam son of Beor in Pethor:* The seer of the Deir ʿAlla inscription bears the same name and patronymic. The place name Pethor, Balaam's home, is identified as a site on the Sajur River in Aram (Syria) some 644 km (400 mi) from Moab. **6–7:** Balaam apparently has a reputation not only as a seer, but also as a diviner who can effectuate curses. The elders of Moab and Midian, sent to fetch him, are versed in divinatory techniques. Execration texts (written curses) on pottery cursing rulers of Canaanite cities are known from Egypt (early 2nd millennium). Prophets from the same period are mentioned in letters from the Mesopotamian city-state of Mari.

9 God came to Balaam and said, "What do these people want
of you?" 10 Balaam said to God, "Balak son of Zippor, king of
Moab, sent me this message: 11 Here is a people that came out
from Egypt and hides the earth from view. Come now and
curse them for me; perhaps I can engage them in battle and
drive them off." 12 But God said to Balaam, "Do not go with
them. You must not curse that people, for they are blessed."

13 Balaam arose in the morning and said to Balak's dignitaries, "Go back to your own country, for the LORD will not let me
go with you." 14 The Moabite dignitaries left, and they came to
Balak and said, "Balaam refused to come with us."

15 Then Balak sent other dignitaries, more numerous and
distinguished than the first. 16 They came to Balaam and said
to him, "Thus says Balak son of Zippor: Please do not refuse to
come to me. 17 I will reward you richly and I will do anything
you ask of me. Only come and damn this people for me." 18 Balaam replied to Balak's officials, "Though Balak were to give me
his house full of silver and gold, I could not do anything, big or
little, contrary to the command of the LORD my God. 19 So you,
too, stay here overnight, and let me find out what else the LORD
may say to me." 20 That night God came to Balaam and said to
him, "If these men have come to invite you, you may go with
them. But whatever I command you, that you shall do."

21 When he arose in the morning, Balaam saddled his ass
and departed with the Moabite dignitaries. 22 But God was incensed at his going; so an angel of the LORD placed himself in
his way as an adversary.

He was riding on his she-ass, with his two servants alongside, 23 when the ass caught sight of the angel of the LORD
standing in the way, with his drawn sword in his hand. The ass
swerved from the road and went into the fields; and Balaam
beat the ass to turn her back onto the road. 24 The angel of the
LORD then stationed himself in a lane between the vineyards,
with a fence on either side. 25 The ass, seeing the angel of the
LORD, pressed herself against the wall and squeezed Balaam's
foot against the wall; so he beat her again. 26 Once more the
angel of the LORD moved forward and stationed himself on a
spot so narrow that there was no room to swerve right or left.
27 When the ass now saw the angel of the LORD, she lay down
under Balaam; and Balaam was furious and beat the ass with
his stick.

28 Then the LORD opened the ass's mouth, and she said to
Balaam, "What have I done to you that you have beaten me
these three times?" 29 Balaam said to the ass, "You have made a
mockery of me! If I had a sword with me, I'd kill you." 30 The ass
said to Balaam, "Look, I am the ass that you have been riding
all along until this day! Have I been in the habit of doing thus
to you?" And he answered, "No."

8–21: The biblical writer makes it clear that the Israelites are a blessed people. In this account, which views Balaam postively, his words and actions are bound to God's will and no reward of riches can enable him to counter it. **22–35:** This episode of Balaam and the she-ass derives from a different tradition that contradicts the favorable view of Balaam expressed by the main story (contrast esp. v. 20). In this version God is angry with the prophet (v. 22) and in turn depicts the donkey as the actual visionary. Balaam becomes the object of mockery: He is portrayed as being blind to divine will; it is the ass that sees what the seer cannot. **22:** *As an adversary:* In the Bible the term "satan" is used attributively (1 Sam. 29.4), or when personified it refers to a divine being who answers to God (Job 1.6–12; 1 Chron. 21.1), rather than to an independent entity who is God's adversary ("Satan"). The concept only later developed into the "Devil."

36–40: Balak offers a sacrifice of well-being, which is eaten by Balaam and his entourage.

22.41–23.10: Balaam's first oracle. **23.1:** Seven is a significant number in the Bible, often signaling complete perfection (cf. Josh. 6.4; 1 Kings 18.43; 2 Kings 5.10, 14), and is frequent in Northwest Semitic literature. The sacrifice of seven animals, as in Job 42.8, would signify the completeness of an offering to the deity. Balaam's offerings seem to invoke the deity's message. Ibn Ezra notes the frequency of the number seven in the cultic calendar.

31 Then the LORD uncovered Balaam's eyes, and he saw the
angel of the LORD standing in the way, his drawn sword in his
hand; thereupon he bowed [a]right down to the ground.[-a] 32 The
angel of the LORD said to him, "Why have you beaten your ass
these three times? It is I who came out as an adversary, for
the errand is obnoxious[b] to me. 33 And when the ass saw me,
she shied away because of me those three times. If she had
not shied away from me, you are the one I should have killed,
while sparing her." 34 Balaam said to the angel of the LORD, "I
erred because I did not know that you were standing in my
way. If you still disapprove, I will turn back." 35 But the angel of
the LORD said to Balaam, "Go with the men. But you must say
nothing except what I tell you." So Balaam went on with Balak's
dignitaries.
36 When Balak heard that Balaam was coming, he went out
to meet him at Ir-moab, which is on the Arnon border, at its
farthest point. 37 Balak said to Balaam, "When I first sent to
invite you, why didn't you come to me? Am I really unable to
reward you?" 38 But Balaam said to Balak, "And now that I have
come to you, have I the power to speak freely? I can utter only
the word that God puts into my mouth."
39 Balaam went with Balak and they came to Kiriath-huzoth.
40 Balak sacrificed oxen and sheep, and had them served to
Balaam and the dignitaries with him. 41 In the morning Balak
took Balaam up to Bamoth-baal. From there he could see a
portion of the people.

23 Balaam said to Balak, "Build me seven altars here and
have seven bulls and seven rams ready here for me."
2 Balak did as Balaam directed; and Balak and Balaam offered
up a bull and a ram on each altar. 3 Then Balaam said to Balak,
"Stay here beside your offerings while I am gone. Perhaps the
LORD will grant me a manifestation, and whatever He reveals
to me I will tell you." And he went off alone.[c]
4 God manifested Himself to Balaam, who said to Him, "I
have set up the seven altars and offered up a bull and a ram on
each altar." 5 And the LORD put a word in Balaam's mouth and
said, "Return to Balak and speak thus."
6 So he returned to him and found him standing beside his
offerings, and all the Moabite dignitaries with him. 7 He took
up his theme, and said:

From Aram has Balak brought me,
Moab's king from the hills of the East:

a-a Lit. "and prostrated himself to his nostrils."
b Precise meaning of Heb. uncertain.
c Others "to a bare height"; exact meaning of Heb. shephi *uncertain.*

Come, curse me Jacob,
Come, tell Israel's doom!
8 How can I damn whom God[a] has not damned,
How doom when the LORD has not doomed?
9 As I see them from the mountain tops,
Gaze on them from the heights,
There is a people that dwells apart,
Not reckoned among the nations,
10 Who can count the dust[b] of Jacob,
Number[c] the dust-cloud of Israel?
May I die the death of the upright,[d]
May my fate be like theirs!

[11] Then Balak said to Balaam, "What have you done to me? Here I brought you to damn my enemies, and instead you have blessed them!" [12] He replied, "I can only repeat faithfully what the LORD puts in my mouth." [13] Then Balak said to him, "Come with me to another place from which you can see them—you will see only a portion of them; you will not see all of them—and damn them for me from there." [14] With that, he took him to Sedehzophim,[e] on the summit of Pisgah. He built seven altars and offered a bull and a ram on each altar. [15] And [Balaam] said to Balak, "Stay here beside your offerings, while I seek a manifestation yonder."

[16] The LORD manifested Himself to Balaam and put a word in his mouth, saying, "Return to Balak and speak thus." [17] He went to him and found him standing beside his offerings, and the Moabite dignitaries with him. Balak asked him, "What did the LORD say?" [18] And he took up his theme, and said:

Up, Balak, attend,
Give ear unto me, son of Zippor!
19 God is not man to be capricious,
Or mortal to change His mind.
Would He speak and not act,
Promise and not fulfill?
20 My message was to bless:
When He blesses, I cannot reverse it.
21 No harm is in sight for Jacob,
No woe in view for Israel.
The LORD their God is with them,
And their King's acclaim in their midst.
22 God who freed them from Egypt
Is for them like the horns[f] of the wild ox.

a Heb. El, *as often in these poems.* *b Cf. Gen. 13.16.*
c Lit. "and the number of."
d Heb. yesharim, *a play on* yeshurun *(Jeshurun in Deut. 32.15), a name for Israel.*
e Or "Lookout Point." *f Lit. "eminences," used figuratively.*

8: The deity name "El" (see translators' note *a)* probably short for "Elohim," God, appears in parallel construction to the Tetragrammaton (YHVH). Some scholars believe that the designations refer to two separate deities, El being the Canaanite high God also worshipped by Israel. This v. is a poetic variant of the idea expressed in prose in 22.18. More extensive prose and poetic variants of the same story are found in Exod. chs 14–15 and Judg. chs 4–5. **10:** Balak's fear that the Israelite multitude will be triumphant (22.3) is confirmed already in Balaam's first oracle. *Who can count the dust of Jacob* reverberates the patriarchal blessing (Gen. 13.16). This English translation assumes a textual error, that the single Heb word "umispar" ("and the number of") should be read as two words: "umiy safar" ("[who can] number"). The parallelism of the v. supports this emendation; ancient texts from Israel used dots or later, small spaces as word dividers, and these could easily become lost.

23.11–24: The second oracle. **11–17:** Sandwiched between the poems of the first and second oracles is a narrative section containing reactions to the initial poem. In a dialogue between Balak and Balaam, Balak expresses shock at Balaam's blessing of Israel; Balaam responds with a disclaimer to his own words. Balak then attempts to elicit a curse from Balaam by having the prophet view the Israelite camp from a less threatening angle. Fresh sacrifices need to be offered to attain another vision. The narrator is mocking Balak, who fails to understand that God's desire may not be contravened in this manner. **18–24:** The poem of the second oracle underscores the message of the first. Emphasis is placed on God's constancy in general and specifically in connection with His devotion to Israel's welfare. Other gods may be capricious, subject to human manipulation through magic, but the LORD is not. **22:** The redemption from Egypt is cited as evidence of God's power and allegiance to Israel.

23 Lo, there is no augury in Jacob,
No divining in Israel:[a]
Jacob is told at once,
Yea Israel, what God has planned.[b]
24 Lo, a people that rises like a lion,
Leaps up like the [c]king of beasts,[-c]
Rests not till it has feasted on prey
And drunk the blood of the slain.

25 Thereupon Balak said to Balaam, "Don't curse them and don't bless them!" 26 In reply, Balaam said to Balak, "But I told you: Whatever the LORD says, that I must do." 27 Then Balak said to Balaam, "Come now, I will take you to another place. Perhaps God will deem it right that you damn them for me there." 28 Balak took Balaam to the peak of Peor, which overlooks the wasteland.[d] 29 Balaam said to Balak, "Build me here seven altars, and have seven bulls and seven rams ready for me here." 30 Balak did as Balaam said: he offered up a bull and a ram on each altar.

24 Now Balaam, seeing that it pleased the LORD to bless Israel, did not, as on previous occasions, go in search of omens, but turned his face toward the wilderness. 2 As Balaam looked up and saw Israel encamped tribe by tribe, the spirit of God came upon him. 3 Taking up his theme, he said:

[e]Word of Balaam son of Beor,
Word of the man whose eye is true,[f]
4 Word of him who hears God's speech,
Who beholds visions from the Almighty,
Prostrate, but with eyes unveiled:
5 How fair are your tents, O Jacob,
Your dwellings, O Israel!
6 Like palm-groves that stretch out,
Like gardens beside a river,
Like aloes planted by the LORD,
Like cedars beside the water;
7 Their boughs drip with moisture,
Their roots[g] have abundant water.
Their king shall rise above Agag,
Their kingdom shall be exalted.

a Cf. Deut. 18.10–15.
b Or, "Else would it be told to Jacob, / Yea to Israel, what God has planned."
c-c Heb. 'ari, another term for "lion." *d Cf. note on 21.20.*
e Some of the poetic portions of this chapter are unclear.
f Others "whose eye is (or, eyes are) open"; meaning of Heb. uncertain.
g Lit. "and its seed."

24: The simile of a lion previews Israel's military victories and kingdom in Canaan (cf. Gen. 49.9–10).

23.25–24.9: The third oracle. **23.25–24.2:** In this second narrative segment between oracles, Balak, in distress, wants to abandon cursing Israel if that will nullify the blessing. The foolish Moabite king, in contrast to the seer, is not resigned to God's will as a fait accompli. Sacrifices are offered for the third time from yet another location. This time Balaam does not search for omens in the process of seeking divine spirit, implying that he did so previously. **2:** For the first time Balaam views the entire Israelite camp (cf. 22.41; 23.13). **3–4:** Balaam opens this oracle with self-praise. He considers himself a true prophet of God. **4:** *The Almighty* (also v. 16): Heb "shadai" is an epithet of God common in the Priestly patriarchal stories (e.g., Gen. 17.1; 28.3; 35.11). Its likely meaning, "high," is related to the Akkadian term for mountain. **5:** This idyllic portrayal of the Israelites in their homes is noted in the midrash. In Jewish liturgy this line begins the daily morning service, since *tents* and *dwellings* are understood to refer to the synagogue. **6–7:** The depiction of lush vegetation contrasts with the wilderness background of Balaam's view of Israel's encampment (24.1). **7:** *Agag* is the king of Amalek at the time of Saul's reign (1 Sam. 15.8). Saul's victory is foretold here, suggesting to many scholars a date for the text in the monarchic period.

8 God who freed them from Egypt
Is for them like the horns[a] of the wild ox.
They shall devour enemy nations,
Crush their bones,
And smash their arrows.
9 They crouch, they lie down like a lion,
Like the king of beasts;[b] who dare rouse them?
Blessed are they who bless you,
Accursed they who curse you!

10 Enraged at Balaam, Balak struck his hands together. "I
called you," Balak said to Balaam, "to damn my enemies,
and instead you have blessed them these three times! 11 Back
with you at once to your own place! I was going to reward you
richly, but the LORD has denied you the reward." 12 Balaam replied to Balak, "But I even told the messengers you sent to me,
13 'Though Balak were to give me his house full of silver and
gold, I could not of my own accord do anything good or bad
contrary to the LORD's command. What the LORD says, that I
must say.' 14 And now, as I go back to my people, let me inform
you of what this people will do to your people in days to come."
15 He took up his theme, and said:

Word of Balaam son of Beor,
Word of the man whose eye is true,
16 Word of him who hears God's speech,
Who obtains knowledge from the Most High,
And beholds visions from the Almighty,
Prostrate, but with eyes unveiled:
17 What I see for them is not yet,
What I behold will not be soon:
A star rises from Jacob,
A scepter comes forth from Israel;
It smashes the brow of Moab,
The foundation of[c] all children of Seth.
18 Edom becomes a possession,
Yea, Seir a possession of its enemies;
But Israel is triumphant.
19 A victor issues from Jacob
To wipe out what is left of Ir.

20 He saw Amalek and, taking up his theme, he said:
A leading nation is Amalek;
But its fate is to perish forever.

a See note at 23.22. *b Heb.* labi, *another word for "lion"; cf. note at 23.24.*
c Samaritan "the pate of," cf. Jer. 48.45; others "breaks down."

8–9: The oracle ends by returning to the lion imagery at the end of the previous oracle (23.24), and reiterating the promise to the patriarchs that anyone who blesses Israel will be blessed in turn, but anyone who curses her is himself cursed (Gen. 12.3; 27.29).

24.10–25: The fourth oracle. **10–14:** Balak's reaction to Balaam's third oracle is one of outrage, no doubt exacerbated by the pronouncement that he who curses Israel will be cursed in turn; Balak thus sends Balaam home. **10:** *Balak struck his hands together:* This is a gesture of anguish and anger (cf. Ezek. 6.11; 21.19, 22; 22.13; Lam. 2.15). **15–25:** Before returning to his home, Balaam utters one more oracle, this one containing a prophecy about Moab's future and that of Israel's other enemies. A very common pattern in biblical literature, followed here, is the 3–4 pattern, where the fourth element is climactic. **17:** This v. predicts the destruction of Moab by an Israelite king. Either David or Omri qualifies (2 Sam. 8.2; the Mesha Stele[or Moabite Stone]). This v. played a significant role in the 2nd c. CE, when the star (Heb "kokhav") was connected by some to Bar Kosiba, a Jewish leader who headed an unsuccessful revolt against Rome in 132–35. Based on this v., some sages renamed this leader as Bar Kokhba, "the son of the star," and viewed him as a messianic figure (see esp. *y. Ta'an.* 68d). The revolt was a miserable failure. **18–24:** Balaam predicts the conquest of several national or ethnic groups, including Edomites, Amalekites, and Midianites. Kittim, people from Cyprus, are mentioned as invaders into the region of Syria and Mesopotamia; the historical setting for this is unclear. In the Dead Sea Scrolls, "Kittim" represents the Romans.

21 He saw the Kenites and, taking up his theme, he said:
Though your abode be secure,
And your nest be set among cliffs,
22 Yet shall Kain[a] be consumed,
When Asshur takes you captive.

23 He took up his theme and said:
Alas, who can survive except God has willed it!
24 Ships come from the quarter of Kittim;
They subject Asshur, subject Eber.
They, too, shall perish forever.

25 Then Balaam set out on his journey back home; and Balak
also went his way.

25 While Israel was staying at Shittim, the people [b-]pro-
faned themselves by whoring[-b] with the Moabite wom-
en, 2 who invited the people to the sacrifices for their god. The
people partook of them and worshiped that god. 3 Thus Israel
attached itself to Baal-peor, and the LORD was incensed with
Israel. 4 The LORD said to Moses, "Take all the ringleaders[c]
and have them publicly[d] impaled before the LORD, so that the
LORD's wrath may turn away from Israel." 5 So Moses said to
Israel's officials, "Each of you slay those of his men who attached themselves to Baal-peor."
6 Just then one of the Israelites came and brought a Midianite
woman over to his companions, in the sight of Moses and of the
whole Israelite community who were weeping at the entrance of
the Tent of Meeting. 7 When Phinehas, son of Eleazar son of Aaron the priest, saw this, he left the assembly and, taking a spear
in his hand, 8 he followed the Israelite into the chamber and
stabbed both of them, the Israelite and the woman, through the
belly. Then the plague against the Israelites was checked. 9 Those
who died of the plague numbered twenty-four thousand.

a I.e., the Kenites. *b-b Others "began to commit harlotry."*
c Lit. "heads of the people." *d Others "in face of the sun."*

25: The narrative ends with Balaam and Balak returning home, the latter's mission having failed.

25.1–19: Worship of Baal-peor and its aftermath. Ch 25 continues the narrative begun in 22.1, which was interrupted by the insertion of the story of Balak and Balaam. While encamped on the plains of Moab awaiting crossing into Canaan, Israelite men mingle with local, non-Israelite women. As predicted in warnings to Israel (Exod. 34.16; cf. 1 Kings 11.1–6), marriage with idolaters leads to idolatry, in this case worship of the local god Baal-peor. This ch can be divided into three smaller segments: vv. 1–5, 6–9, and 10–19. Scholars often attribute the latter two segments to a Priestly expansion of the first five vv., a JE account. In P's rendition, the role of Phinehas, Aaron's grandson, is central in the expiation process of the sin (vv. 7–18), even superseding that of Moses. Furthermore, it offers historical support for the divine appointment of the Aaronide priesthood. Memory of Israel's apostasy of Baal-peor and subsequent punishment is preserved in several biblical accounts outside the book of Numbers (cf. Deut. 4.3; Josh. 22.17; Hos. 9.10; Ps. 106.28). **1:** Ramban suggests that it was Balaam's evil advice that provoked the incident. Otherwise, he reasons, why would the Israelites have killed Balaam (31.8)? **2–3:** Ps. 106 identifies the sacrificial feast as a ritual associated with a funerary cult. Baal-peor is the local manifestation of the fertility storm-god Baal, the high god of Canaanite religion; Peor is a geographic name previously mentioned in the Balaam saga (23.28; also Deut. 3.29). The calf image that Israel fashioned of gold and then worshipped at Sinai (Exod. ch 32) is a common representation of the deity Baal, apparently, as well as the LORD in the sanctuaries of Dan and Bethel (see 1 Kings 12.28–29). **4:** *Take all the ringleaders and have them publicly impaled. Ringleaders* is an interpretive translation of the Heb. A literal understanding, "all the heads of the people," implies that the leadership, both guilty individuals and innocent ones, are liable for the people's action. Their execution and subsequent public impalement is to serve as expiation for Israel's violation of the Sinaitic covenant, which prohibits foreign worship. Similarly, Saul's sons are executed and publicly impaled for their father's violation of a treaty with the Gibeonites (2 Sam. 21.1–14). In that case, a drought, attributed to the violation of the oath, ends when the princes' deaths appease the deity. In both cases, extreme measures need to be taken to control the divine wrath. **5:** Moses intercedes here (cf. 11.2; 14.13–19; 16.22), instructing Israel's officials to slay only the guilty (cf. the role of the Levites in Exod. 32.25–29). **6–9:** The Israelite man is later identified as Zimri son of Salu, a chieftain of Simeon (v. 14); the woman is Cozbi daughter of Zur, a Midianite chief (v. 15). Thus, both are influential members of

PINḤAS פינחס
10 The LORD spoke to Moses, saying, 11 "Phinehas, son of Eleazar son of Aaron the priest, has turned back My wrath from
the Israelites by displaying among them his passion for Me,
so that I did not wipe out the Israelite people in My passion.
12 Say, therefore, 'I grant him My pact of friendship. 13 It shall be
for him and his descendants after him a pact of priesthood for
all time, because he took impassioned action for his God, thus
making expiation for the Israelites.'"
14 The name of the Israelite who was killed, the one who was
killed with the Midianite woman, was Zimri son of Salu, chieftain of a Simeonite ancestral house. 15 The name of the Midianite woman who was killed was Cozbi daughter of Zur; he was
the tribal head of an ancestral house in Midian.
16 The LORD spoke to Moses, saying, 17 "Assail the Midianites
and defeat them—18 for they assailed you by the trickery they
practiced against you—because of the affair of Peor and because of the affair of their kinswoman Cozbi, daughter of the
Midianite chieftain, who was killed at the time of the plague
on account of Peor."

26 19 When the plague was over, 1 the LORD said to Moses
and to Eleazar son of Aaron the priest, 2 "Take a census of
the whole Israelite community from the age of twenty years up,
by their ancestral houses, all Israelites able to bear arms." 3 [a]So
Moses and Eleazar the priest, on the steppes of Moab, at the Jordan near Jericho, gave instructions about them, namely, 4 those
from twenty years up, as the LORD had commanded Moses.
The descendants of the Israelites who came out of the land
of Egypt were:
5 Reuben, Israel's first-born. Descendants of Reuben: [Of]
Enoch,[b] the clan of the Enochites; of Pallu, the clan of the Pal-
luites; 6 of Hezron, the clan of the Hezronites; of Carmi, the
clan of the Carmites. 7 Those are the clans of the Reubenites.
The persons enrolled came to 43,730.
8 [c]Born to[c] Pallu: Eliab. 9 The sons of Eliab were Nemuel, and
Dathan and Abiram. These are the same Dathan and Abiram,
chosen in the assembly, who agitated against Moses and Aaron
as part of Korah's band when they agitated against the LORD.

a Meaning of parts of vv. 3 and 4 uncertain. *b Or "Hanoch."*
c-c Or "descendants of."

their respective communities. **6:** For the association of Midianites and Moabites (v. 1), see 22.4 n. **8:** *The chamber,* Heb "ha-kubah," probably refers to a tent (also in Arabic) that is part of the cultic area, rendering the transgression as pagan worship. No evidence exists, however, for any act of cultic prostitution. **9:** Those who died in the plague would have included any remnant of the exodus generation (26.64–65). **10–13:** God rewards Phinehas's zealous act, which appeases His wrath and makes expiation for Israel (cf. Aaron's act, 17.11–12), with a *pact of friendship* guaranteeing divine protection (cf. Isa. 54.10; Ezek. 34.25; 37.26). *A pact of priesthood for all time* reiterates the eternal and exclusive election of the Aaronides to the priesthood (chs 16–17). **16–19:** God's command that Israel take vengeance on the Midianites for their part in the apostasy of Baal-peor is realized in the continuation of this account in ch 31, where v. 1 completes the v. fragment of 25.19 (for the association of Midianites and Moabites, see 22.4 n.). Thus, chs 26–30 have been placed here secondarily.

26.1–65: The second census. Initially, the Israelites were counted at Sinai prior to their forty-year wilderness trek (ch 1). That population consisted of the exodus generation. This second census takes place after the death of that entire population (26.64–65). Levites are again numbered separately (cf. 3.14–39). The statistics of the second census are necessary for determining the allotment of the land of Canaan (see Josh. chs 14–19), the subject of the end of this ch (vv. 52–56). This ch also precedes a major battle, the war against the Midianites (ch 31), since a count of military-age males is required in preparation for this battle and for others planned in the conquest of Canaan. **1–4:** The instructions for the second census, like the first, come directly from God who addresses both Moses and the current high priest (cf. 1.1–3). **5–51:** The Israelites are numbered by tribes, excluding Levi. Each tribe's total is derived from the sum of its clans. Whereas clan chieftains are named in connection with the first census (1.5–15), the names of the clans appear in the account of the second census. Some scholars attempt to understand these vast, unrealistic numbers symbolically. **9–11:** These vv. recall the fate of the Reubenites Dathan and Abiram who were part of the Korah rebellion (chs 16–17). Similar short notices are sometimes placed in the genealogies that open Chron. **29–34:** The tribe of Manasseh increases in size more than any other tribe (five tribes decrease in number), almost doubling its population (cf. 1.34–35). Five Manassite clan names (Iezer [= Abiezer], Helek, Asriel, Shechem, and Shemida) and two names of Zelophehad's daughters (Noah and Hoglah) appear as place names on the Samaria Ostraca pottery sherds from the 8th century BCE inscribed as receipts for wine and oil, which were excavated in the remains of the palace complex at Samaria. Thus, it is possible that the names mentioned in this ch do not refer to actual individuals, but to geographical regions whose connection is expressed through genealogical language. **33:** The legal implications of the inheritance of Zelophehad's daughters are discussed in 27.1–11; 36.1–12.

10 Whereupon the earth opened its mouth and swallowed them
up with Korah—when that band died, when the fire consumed
the two hundred and fifty men—and they became an example.
11 The sons of Korah, however, did not die.
12 Descendants of Simeon by their clans: Of Nemuel, the
clan of the Nemuelites; of Jamin, the clan of the Jaminites; of
Jachin, the clan of the Jachinites; 13 of Zerah, the clan of the
Zerahites; of Saul,[a] the clan of the Saulites. 14 Those are the
clans of the Simeonites; [persons enrolled:] 22,200.
15 Descendants of Gad by their clans: Of Zephon, the clan
of the Zephonites; of Haggi, the clan of the Haggites; of Shuni,
the clan of the Shunites; 16 of Ozni, the clan of the Oznites; of
Eri, the clan of the Erites; 17 of Arod, the clan of the Arodites;
of Areli, the clan of the Arelites. 18 Those are the clans of Gad's
descendants; persons enrolled: 40,500.
19 b-Born to-b Judah: Er and Onan. Er and Onan died in the
land of Canaan.
20 Descendants of Judah by their clans: Of Shelah, the clan of
the Shelanites; of Perez, the clan of the Perezites; of Zerah, the
clan of the Zerahites. 21 Descendants of Perez: of Hezron, the
clan of the Hezronites; of Hamul, the clan of the Hamulites.
22 Those are the clans of Judah; persons enrolled: 76,500.
23 Descendants of Issachar by their clans: [Of] Tola, the clan
of the Tolaites; of Puvah, the clan of the Punites; 24 of Jashub,
the clan of the Jashubites; of Shimron, the clan of the Shim-
ronites. 25 Those are the clans of Issachar; persons enrolled:
64,300.
26 Descendants of Zebulun by their clans: Of Sered, the clan
of the Seredites; of Elon, the clan of the Elonites; of Jahleel, the
clan of the Jahleelites. 27 Those are the clans of the Zebulunites;
persons enrolled: 60,500.
28 The sons of Joseph were Manasseh and Ephraim—by their
clans.
29 Descendants of Manasseh: Of Machir, the clan of the
Machirites.—Machir begot Gilead.—Of Gilead, the clan of the
Gileadites. 30 These were the descendants of Gilead: [Of] Iezer,
the clan of the Iezerites; of Helek, the clan of the Helekites; 31 [of]
Asriel, the clan of the Asrielites; [of] Shechem, the clan of the
Shechemites; 32 [of] Shemida, the clan of the Shemidaites; [of]
Hepher, the clan of the Hepherites.—33 Now Zelophehad son
of Hepher had no sons, only daughters. The names of Zelophehad's daughters were Mahlah, Noah, Hoglah, Milcah, and Tirzah.—34 Those are the clans of Manasseh; persons enrolled:
52,700.
35 These are the descendants of Ephraim by their clans: Of
Shuthelah, the clan of the Shuthelahites; of Becher, the clan of

a *Or "Shaul."* *b-b* *Or "descendants of."*

the Becherites; of Tahan, the clan of the Tahanites. 36 These are
the descendants of Shuthelah: Of Eran, the clan of the Eran-
ites. 37 Those are the clans of Ephraim's descendants; persons
enrolled: 32,500.
Those are the descendants of Joseph by their clans.
38 The descendants of Benjamin by their clans: Of Bela, the
clan of the Belaites; of Ashbel, the clan of the Ashbelites; of
Ahiram, the clan of the Ahiramites; 39 of Shephupham, the clan
of the Shuphamites; of Hupham, the clan of the Huphamites.
40 The sons of Bela were Ard and Naaman: [Of Ard,] the clan of
the Ardites; of Naaman, the clan of the Naamanites. 41 Those
are the descendants of Benjamin by their clans; persons enrolled: 45,600.
42 These are the descendants of Dan by their clans: Of Shu-
ham, the clan of the Shuhamites. Those are the clans of Dan,[a]
by their clans. 43 All the clans of the Shuhamites; persons enrolled: 64,400.
44 Descendants of Asher by their clans: Of Imnah, the clan
of the Imnites; of Ishvi, the clan of the Ishvites; of Beriah, the
clan of the Beriites. 45 Of the descendants of Beriah: Of Heber,
the clan of the Heberites; of Malchiel, the clan of the Malchiel-
ites.—46 The name of Asher's daughter was Serah.—47 These
are the clans of Asher's descendants; persons enrolled: 53,400.
48 Descendants of Naphtali by their clans: Of Jahzeel, the clan
of the Jahzeelites; of Guni, the clan of the Gunites; 49 of Jezer,
the clan of the Jezerites; of Shillem, the clan of the Shillemites.
50 Those are the clans of the Naphtalites, clan by clan; persons
enrolled: 45,400.
51 This is the enrollment of the Israelites: 601,730.
52 The LORD spoke to Moses, saying, 53 "Among these shall the
land be apportioned as shares, according to the listed names:
54 with larger groups increase the share, with smaller groups
reduce the share. Each is to be assigned its share according to
its enrollment. 55 The land, moreover, is to be apportioned by
lot; and the allotment shall be made according to the listings of
their ancestral tribes. 56 Each portion shall be assigned by lot,
whether for larger or smaller groups."
57 This is the enrollment of the Levites by their clans: Of Gershon, the clan of the Gershonites; of Kohath, the clan of the
Kohathites; of Merari, the clan of the Merarites. 58 These are
the clans of Levi: The clan of the Libnites, the clan of the Hebronites, the clan of the Mahlites, the clan of the Mushites, the
clan of the Korahites.—Kohath begot Amram. 59 The name of
Amram's wife was Jochebed daughter of Levi, who was born
to Levi in Egypt; she bore to Amram Aaron and Moses and
their sister Miriam. 60 To Aaron were born Nadab and Abihu,

a Meaning of parts of vv. 42 and 43 uncertain.

51: The total of 601,730 indicates a net loss of 1,820 males aged 20 and up (cf. 603,550 in 1.46). **52–56:** Here are the directions for apportioning the land of Canaan. The size of each tribal territory is determined by the population of the tribe; the geographical area, however, is assigned to the tribes by lot. Casting lots is a common ancient Near Eastern divination practice; according to several biblical passages, God controls the results (Josh. 18.8; 19.51; 1 Sam. 10.20–24; 14.41).

26.57–62: The Levites are numbered for the third time (cf. chs 3–4). They are listed separately because they do not serve in the military, nor do they receive a portion of land. They are, however, assigned Levitical towns (see 35.1–8), the number of which is determined by the size of the group. **58–59:** These vv. trace the genealogy of Moses and Aaron, Israel's leaders.

Eleazar and Ithamar. 61 Nadab and Abihu died when they offered alien fire before the LORD.—62 Their enrollment of 23,000
comprised all males from a month up. They were not part of
the regular enrollment of the Israelites, since no share was assigned to them among the Israelites.

63 These are the persons enrolled by Moses and Eleazar the
priest who registered the Israelites on the steppes of Moab, at the
Jordan near Jericho. 64 Among these there was not one of those
enrolled by Moses and Aaron the priest when they recorded the
Israelites in the wilderness of Sinai. 65 For the LORD had said of
them, "They shall die in the wilderness." Not one of them survived, except Caleb son of Jephunneh and Joshua son of Nun.

27 The daughters of Zelophehad, of Manassite family—son
of Hepher son of Gilead son of Machir son of Manasseh
son of Joseph—came forward. The names of the daughters
were Mahlah, Noah, Hoglah, Milcah, and Tirzah. 2 They stood
before Moses, Eleazar the priest, the chieftains, and the whole
assembly, at the entrance of the Tent of Meeting, and they said,
3 "Our father died in the wilderness. He was not one of the faction, Korah's faction, which banded together against the LORD,
but died for his own sin; and he has left no sons. 4 Let not our
father's name be lost to his clan just because he had no son!
Give us a holding among our father's kinsmen!"
5 Moses brought their case before the LORD.
6 And the LORD said to Moses, 7 "The plea of Zelophehad's
daughters is just: you should give them a hereditary holding
among their father's kinsmen; transfer their father's share to
them.
8 "Further, speak to the Israelite people as follows: 'If a man
dies without leaving a son, you shall transfer his property to
his daughter. 9 If he has no daughter, you shall assign his property to his brothers. 10 If he has no brothers, you shall assign his
property to his father's brothers. 11 If his father had no brothers, you shall assign his property to his nearest relative in his
own clan, and he shall inherit it.' This shall be the law of procedure for the Israelites, in accordance with the LORD's command to Moses."

61: For the episode surrounding the death of Nadab and Abihu, see Lev. 10.1–3. **63–65:** The ch ends by stating that God's punishment of the wilderness generation was fulfilled, preparing the way for the death of Moses and the conquest of the land.

27.1–11: The case of Zelophehad's daughters. A specific case is used here seemingly to introduce a revision to existing laws of inheritance. The special case of Zelophehad, who died leaving daughters but no sons, is foreshadowed in 26.33 in the census record of his clan. The detailed account that follows in ch 27 and continues in ch 36 addresses questions surrounding this case and uses it to explore more generally female inheritance of property in Israel, a patriarchal society. In contrast, ancient texts from Mesopotamia, Syria, and Egypt attest to inheritance rights of women even in the presence of male heirs. In light of ancient Near East practices, it is doubtful that Israelite women were barred from inheriting property. Rather, the case of Zelophehad's daughters presented in ch 27 likely creates a backdrop for the legal revision of female inheritance as outlined in ch 36. Underlying the discussion in Num. is the biblical precept that ancestral lands are divinely granted in perpetuity and may not be alienated from their original tribes or families (see Lev. 25.25–34; 1 Kings 21.1–19). **1–4:** Zelophehad's daughters present the arguments for their case. **2:** *At the entrance of the Tent of Meeting,* a location in the camp analogous to the city gate of permanent settlements where courts convened (cf. Jer. 26.10; Ruth 4.1). **3:** *Korah's faction,* see ch 16. *But* [Zelophehad] *died for his own sin,* difficult to interpret. It may refer to the condemnation of Zelophehad as part of the entire sinful exodus generation (14.29) or imply an assumed transgression explaining his lack of male heirs (cf. 1 Kings 1.17–18). Traditional Jewish commentary makes the latter connection. **4:** *Let not our father's name be lost:* Preserving a person's name is of tantamount importance and clearly connected to his estate (Deut. 25.5–6). **5:** Moses brings this difficult case before God (Deut. 1.17), as he did earlier with the person gathering stubble on the Sabbath (15.32–36). **8–11:** Granting the women's request is a divine decision, and this presents an opportunity to expand on the particular case by offering a hierarchical list of potential heirs, thereby establishing a legal principle. Num. 36.1–13 will further clarify that since the women actually *transfer* the patrimony to future male heirs, they are bound by certain marriage requirements.

12 The LORD said to Moses, "Ascend these heights of Abarim and view the land that I have given to the Israelite people. 13 When you have seen it, you too shall be gathered to your
kin, just as your brother Aaron was. 14 For, in the wilderness
of Zin, when the community was contentious, you disobeyed
My command to uphold My sanctity in their sight by means of
the water." Those are the Waters of Meribath-kadesh,[a] in the
wilderness of Zin.
15 Moses spoke to the LORD, saying, 16 "Let the LORD, Source
of the breath of all flesh, appoint someone over the community
17 [b-]who shall go out before them and come in before them, and
who shall take them out and bring them in,[-b] so that the LORD's
community may not be like sheep that have no shepherd."
18 And the LORD answered Moses, "Single out Joshua son of
Nun, an inspired man, and lay your hand upon him. 19 Have
him stand before Eleazar the priest and before the whole community, and commission him in their sight. 20 Invest him with
some of your authority, so that the whole Israelite community
may obey. 21 But he shall present himself to Eleazar the priest,
who shall on his behalf seek the decision of the Urim before
the LORD. By such instruction they shall go out and by such instruction they shall come in, he and all the Israelites, the whole
community."
22 Moses did as the LORD commanded him. He took Joshua
and had him stand before Eleazar the priest and before the
whole community. 23 He laid his hands upon him and commissioned him—as the LORD had spoken through Moses.

28 The LORD spoke to Moses, saying: 2 Command the Israelite people and say to them: Be punctilious in presenting to Me at stated times [c-]the offerings of food due Me,[-c] as
offerings by fire of pleasing odor to Me.
3 Say to them: These are the offerings by fire that you are to
present to the LORD:
As a regular burnt offering every day, two yearling lambs
without blemish. 4 You shall offer one lamb in the morning,
and the other lamb you shall offer at twilight. 5 And as a meal
offering, there shall be a tenth of an *ephah* of choice flour with

a See note at 20.13.
b-b I.e., who shall lead them in all matters and whom they shall follow in all matters.
c-c Lit. "My offering, My food."

27.12–23: The transfer of leadership to Joshua. Key to the success of Israel's inheritance of Canaan is the succession of Moses by a competent and worthy leader. The role is filled by Joshua, one of two spies who gave a positive report claiming that Canaan can be conquered (chs 13–14). Certain other texts as well (e.g., Exod. 17.9–14; 24.13; Num. 11.28) also prepare the reader for the role that Joshua would play as Moses' successor. **12–14:** The beginning of the narrative suggests that Moses is about to die in fulfillment of God's punishment (20.12; cf. Aaron's death and Eleazar's assumption of leadership of the priesthood, 20.22–29). His death, however, is postponed to Deut. ch 34. **12:** Mount Nebo, the site of Moses' death (Deut. ch 34) is part of the heights of Abarim (33.47; Deut. 32.49). **15–17:** Moses requests that God appoint his successor. In this period, national leadership, unlike the priesthood, is not hereditary. Moses' own descendants were not suitable for leadership (see Judg. 18.30 n.). **18–23:** Joshua's investiture is witnessed by Eleazar the priest and the entire community, probably to avoid challenges to the legitimacy of his authority. **18:** *An inspired man,* lit. "a man in whom there is spirit," anticipates the transfer of Mosaic attributes to Joshua. *Lay your hand* [*hands,* v. 23] *upon him,* for the purpose of transferring *authority* (v. 20). The spirit may refer to prophetic ability (see 1 Kings 22.21–23), and the ritual may express Moses' transferring his prophetic abilities to Joshua. The rite of laying hands is employed for animals as well as persons (Lev. 16.21; Num. 8.10). Contrast the transfer of power from Elijah to Elisha (2 Kings 2.9–15). Jewish tradition refers to the ceremony of rabbinic ordination as "semikhah," the laying of hands. **21:** *Seek the decision of the Urim:* The Urim and Thummim (here abbreviated) are consulted as an oracle (1 Sam. 14.41 [LXX]; 28.6). According to the Priestly tradition, they fit into a pouch of the breastplate worn by the high priest (Exod. 28.30; Lev. 8.8), many scholars believe that they were cast like dice to answer yes-or-no questions. Clearly, Joshua cannot commune directly with God as does Moses.

28.1–30.1: Calendar of sacrifices in the public cult. Chs 28–29 are an insertion into the narrative consisting of ritual prescriptions that delineate the daily, Sabbath, new moon, and festival schedule of offerings. The variety and number of sacrificial animals vary, but all are males: bulls, rams, lambs, and goats. Meal offerings and wine libations

a quarter of a *hin* of beaten oil mixed in—6 the regular burnt offering instituted at Mount Sinai[a]—an offering by fire of pleasing odor to the LORD.
7 The libation with it shall be a quarter of a *hin* for each lamb,
to be poured in the sacred precinct as an offering of fermented
drink[b] to the LORD. 8 The other lamb you shall offer at twilight,
preparing the same meal offering and libation as in the morning—an offering by fire of pleasing odor to the LORD.
9 On the sabbath day: two yearling lambs without blemish,
together with two-tenths of a measure[c] of choice flour with oil
mixed in as a meal offering, and with the proper libation—10 a
burnt offering for every sabbath, in addition to the regular
burnt offering and its libation.
11 On your new moons you shall present a burnt offering
to the LORD: two bulls of the herd, one ram, and seven yearling lambs, without blemish. 12 As meal offering for each bull:
three-tenths of a measure of choice flour with oil mixed in. As
meal offering for each ram: two-tenths of a measure of choice
flour with oil mixed in. 13 As meal offering for each lamb: a
tenth of a measure of fine flour with oil mixed in. Such shall
be the burnt offering of pleasing odor, an offering by fire to the
LORD. 14 Their libations shall be: half a *hin* of wine for a bull, a
third of a *hin* for a ram, and a quarter of a *hin* for a lamb. That
shall be the monthly burnt offering for each new moon of the
year. 15 And there shall be one goat as a purification offering to
the LORD, to be offered in addition to the regular burnt offering
and its libation.
16 In the first month, on the fourteenth day of the month,
there shall be a passover sacrifice to the LORD, 17 and on the fifteenth day of that month a festival. Unleavened bread shall be
eaten for seven days. 18 The first day shall be a sacred occasion:
you shall not work at your occupations. 19 You shall present an
offering by fire, a burnt offering, to the LORD: two bulls of the
herd, one ram, and seven yearling lambs—[d]see that they are[d]
without blemish. 20 The meal offering with them shall be of
choice flour with oil mixed in: prepare three-tenths of a measure for a bull, two-tenths for a ram; 21 and for each of the seven
lambs prepare one-tenth of a measure. 22 And there shall be one

a Exod. 29.38–41. *b I.e., wine.* *c I.e., of an* ephah.
d-d Lit. "they shall be to you."

are also part of the formulas. Num. 28.1–15 deals with daily, weekly, and monthly sacrifices. Num. 28.16–29.38 is an outline of the annual cycle of festivals, beginning with Passover in the first month and ending with Sukkot in the seventh month. The Num. calendar expands on the calendar in Lev. ch 23, also a product of the Priestly tradition, by adding the daily and new moon rituals. A third, non-Priestly calendar, Deut. 16.1–17, describes the three pilgrimage festivals (Passover, Feast of Weeks, Feast of Booths) in conjunction with the requirement of a central sanctuary. The Num. complete cultic calendar is a guide for ritual observances required of a settled community, especially those rites pertaining to harvest festivals. Therefore, it is included in the text at a point prior to the Israelite crossing into Canaan. **28.2:** *Offerings of food due Me,* lit. "My food," designates sacrifices as divine food. This notion pervades the ancient Near East, where food was placed daily at mealtime before statues of deities. Vestiges of such beliefs appear in the Bible (Gen. 8.20–21). In Priestly writings, however, anthropomorphic concepts of God are generally absent, although the pleasing odor of offerings to the LORD is commonly mentioned (Lev. 21.6; Num. 15.3–13); it is unclear if this should be understood literally, or is vestigial, and should be understood metaphorically. **3–8:** The daily offering, "tamid," is the standard to which the special holy day sacrifices are added. **9–10:** The Sabbath offering doubles the daily one. Cf. the larger Sabbath offering described by the prophet Ezekiel (46.4–5). The Sabbath labor prohibition is mentioned in Lev. (23.3) but not in Num. **11–15:** The sacrificial animals offered on the new moon parallel those offered on other festivals, though their number varies (cf. Ezek. 46.6–7). They include a goat purification offering, which the Rabbis connect to the purification of the sanctuary (*m. Shevu.* 1.4–5). **16–25:** Passover is the first festival of the cultic calendar (Exod. 12.2) and marks the beginning of the barley harvest. The holy day on which the Passover sacrifice ("pesaḥ") is offered is distinct from the seven-day Festival of Unleavened Bread ("matzot"); in other words, we have a festival complex of an evening festival (Pesaḥ) followed immediately by a seven-day Matzot festival. Neither here nor in Lev. (23.5–8) is the commemoration of the exodus from Egypt mentioned, though it is noted elsewhere (Exod. 23.15; Deut. 16.1–3). Biblical records of Passover celebrations in the preexilic period are associated with the reigns of two Judean kings, Hezekiah (2 Chron. 30.1–27) and Josiah (2 Kings 23.21–23;

goat for a purification offering, to make expiation in your behalf. [23] You shall present these in addition to the morning portion of the regular burnt offering. [24] You shall offer the like daily
for seven days as food, an offering by fire of pleasing odor to the
LORD; they shall be offered, with their libations, in addition to
the regular burnt offering. [25] And the seventh day shall be a sacred occasion for you: you shall not work at your occupations.

[26] On the day of the first fruits, your Feast of Weeks, when
you bring an offering of new grain to the LORD, you shall observe a sacred occasion: you shall not work at your occupations. [27] You shall present a burnt offering of pleasing odor to
the LORD: two bulls of the herd, one ram, seven yearling lambs.
[28] The meal offering with them shall be of choice flour with oil
mixed in, three-tenths of a measure for a bull, two-tenths for a
ram, [29] and one-tenth for each of the seven lambs. [30] And there
shall be one goat for expiation in your behalf. [31] You shall present them—[a]see that they are[a] without blemish—with their
libations, in addition to the regular burnt offering and its meal
offering.

29 In the seventh month, on the first day of the month,
you shall observe a sacred occasion: you shall not work
at your occupations. You shall observe it as [b]a day when the
horn is sounded.[b] [2] You shall present a burnt offering of pleasing odor to the LORD: one bull of the herd, one ram, and sev-
en yearling lambs, without blemish. [3] The meal offering with
them—choice flour with oil mixed in—shall be: three-tenths
of a measure for a bull, two-tenths for a ram, [4] and one-tenth
for each of the seven lambs. [5] And there shall be one goat for
a purification offering, to make expiation in your behalf—[6] in
addition to the burnt offering of the new moon with its meal
offering and the regular burnt offering with its meal offering,
each with its libation as prescribed, offerings by fire of pleasing
odor to the LORD.

[7] On the tenth day of the same seventh month you shall observe a sacred occasion when you shall practice self-denial.
You shall do no work. [8] You shall present to the LORD a burnt
offering of pleasing odor: one bull of the herd, one ram, seven
yearling lambs; see that they are[c] without blemish. [9] The meal
offering with them—of choice flour with oil mixed in—shall
be: three-tenths of a measure for a bull, two-tenths for the
one ram, [10] one-tenth for each of the seven lambs. [11] And there
shall be one goat for a purification offering, in addition to the
purification offering of expiation and the regular burnt offering with its meal offering, each with its libation.

a-a Lit. "they shall be to you." *b-b Or "a day of festivity."*
c See note at 28.19.

2 Chron. 35.1–19); Ezra the scribe notes that the returning exiles in the Persian period celebrated Passover (Ezra 6.19–22). **26–31:** The Feast of Weeks, celebrated seven weeks from Passover, marks the wheat harvest. No calendrical date is given here (contrast Lev. 23.15–21), perhaps because the new grain might ripen at different times in different years. In Priestly writings, including Ezekiel, it is not considered a pilgrimage festival; indeed, the population would have been very busy with the harvest then. The Deuteronomist, following Exod. 23.14–17, however, does count the Feast of Weeks as one of three pilgrimage festivals (Deut. 16.16). **26:** *First fruits* refers to the new crop of wheat and perhaps the grapes and olives used in preparation of the offering (Lev. 23.17). **29.1–6:** The new moon of the seventh month is like a sabbath of new moon celebrations. According to the earlier covenant collection in Exod., the seventh month marks the transition between the end and the beginning of the agricultural year (Exod. 23.16). Jewish tradition adopted the new moon of the seventh month as the start of the new year, Rosh Ha-Shanah. The oddity of having the new year begin in the seventh month comes from the fact that two calendrical systems are reflected in the Bible: one in which the year begins in the fall (Tishri), and one beginning in the spring (Nisan), as the Babylonian year did. We have here a hybrid: the year beginning in the fall but the month named according to the spring beginning. The sounding of the horn (v. 1), the shofar, is still practiced on Rosh Ha-Shanah. The shofar, from an animal, differs from the metal trumpets sounded by the priests (10.2–10). **7–11:** In Lev. (23.27) the tenth day of the seventh month is called "yom ha-kippurim," the Day of Atonement. It is designated as a Sabbath of complete rest (Lev. 16.31; 23.32). For the priestly expiation rites associated with it, see Lev. 16.29–34. **7:** *Self-denial* elsewhere refers to fasting (Isa. 58.3–5; Ps. 35.13), as observed by Ibn Ezra; in rabbinic practice, fasting is one of the

fundamental requirements on Yom Kippur (see essay on "Biblical Festivals and Fast Days," pp. 2025–34). **12–34:** This festival, lasting from the fifteenth to the twenty-first day of the seventh month is also known by more descriptive names: Feast of Booths, "sukkot" (Lev. 23.34; Deut. 16.13) and Feast of Ingathering (Exod. 23.16; 34.22). A far larger amount of livestock is offered on this festival than on any other, perhaps reflecting its importance. For the nonsacrificial rituals, like that of the "lulav," palm bough, see Lev. 23.33–36, 39–43. King Solomon celebrated Sukkot, called "the Feast," at the time he dedicated the Temple (1 Kings 8.65; 2 Chron. 7.8–10). Judahites in the Persian period observed Sukkot at the bidding of Ezra (Neh. 8.14–18). In more modern times, the Pilgrims modeled their thanksgiving celebration in the New World after this biblical harvest festival. **35–38:** An eighth day of Sukkot, characterized as a concluding solemn gathering, may have been originally a distinct holy day, as indicated by the contradiction between v. 12, *seven days,* and v. 35, *on the eighth day.* This gives rise to significant confusion in Jewish legal texts concerning the nature and status of the eighth day. **39:** A Priestly summary v. Public cult observances are required in addition to private votive or freewill offerings. Examples of the latter include Elkanah's family sacrifice at the Shiloh shrine (1 Sam. 1.3–6) and Absalom's fulfillment of a vow in Hebron (2 Sam. 15.7–8).

[12] On the fifteenth day of the seventh month, you shall observe a sacred occasion: you shall not work at your occupations.—Seven days you shall observe a festival of the LORD.—[13] You shall present a burnt offering, an offering by fire of pleasing odor to the LORD: Thirteen bulls of the herd, two rams, fourteen yearling lambs; they shall be without blemish. [14] The meal offerings with them—of choice flour with oil mixed in—shall be: three-tenths of a measure for each of the thirteen bulls, two-tenths for each of the two rams, [15] and one-tenth for each of the fourteen lambs. [16] And there shall be one goat for a purification offering—in addition to the regular burnt offering, its meal offering and libation.

[17] Second day: Twelve bulls of the herd, two rams, fourteen yearling lambs, without blemish; [18] the meal offerings and libations for the bulls, rams, and lambs, in the quantities prescribed; [19] and one goat for a purification offering—in addition to the regular burnt offering, its meal offering and libations.

[20] Third day: Eleven bulls, two rams, fourteen yearling lambs, without blemish; [21] the meal offerings and libations for the bulls, rams, and lambs, in the quantities prescribed; [22] and one goat for a purification offering—in addition to the regular burnt offering, its meal offering and libation.

[23] Fourth day: Ten bulls, two rams, fourteen yearling lambs, without blemish; [24] the meal offerings and libations for the bulls, rams, and lambs, in the quantities prescribed; [25] and one goat for a purification offering—in addition to the regular burnt offering, its meal offering and libation.

[26] Fifth day: Nine bulls, two rams, fourteen yearling lambs, without blemish; [27] the meal offerings and libations for the bulls, rams, and lambs, in the quantities prescribed; [28] and one goat for a purification offering—in addition to the regular burnt offering, its meal offering and libation.

[29] Sixth day: Eight bulls, two rams, fourteen yearling lambs, without blemish; [30] the meal offerings and libations for the bulls, rams, and lambs, in the quantities prescribed; [31] and one goat for a purification offering—in addition to the regular burnt offering, its meal offering and libations.

[32] Seventh day: Seven bulls, two rams, fourteen yearling lambs, without blemish; [33] the meal offerings and libations for the bulls, rams, and lambs, in the quantities prescribed; [34] and one goat for a purification offering—in addition to the regular burnt offering, its meal offering and libation.

[35] On the eighth day you shall hold a solemn gathering;[a] you shall not work at your occupations. [36] You shall present a burnt offering, an offering by fire of pleasing odor to the LORD; one bull, one ram, seven yearling lambs, without blemish; [37] the

a See note at Lev. 23.36.

meal offerings and libations for the bull, the ram, and the
lambs, in the quantities prescribed; 38 and one goat for a purification offering—in addition to the regular burnt offering, its
meal offering and libation.
39 All these you shall offer to the LORD at the stated times,
in addition to your votive and freewill offerings, be they burnt
30 offerings, meal offerings, libations, or offerings of well-
being. 1 So Moses spoke to the Israelites just as the LORD
had commanded Moses.

MATTOT מטות

2 Moses spoke to the heads of the Israelite tribes, saying: This is
what the LORD has commanded:
3 If a man makes a vow to the LORD or takes an oath imposing an obligation[a] on himself, he shall not break his pledge; he
must carry out all that has [b-]crossed his lips.[-b]
4 If a woman makes a vow to the LORD or assumes an obligation while still in her father's household by reason of her
youth, 5 and her father learns of her vow or her self-imposed
obligation and offers no objection, all her vows shall stand and
every self-imposed obligation shall stand. 6 But if her father
restrains her on the day he finds out, none of her vows or self-
imposed obligations shall stand; and the LORD will forgive her,
since her father restrained her.
7 If she should marry while her vow or the commitment[c] to
which she bound herself is still in force, 8 and her husband
learns of it and offers no objection on the day he finds out, her
vows shall stand and her self-imposed obligations shall stand.
9 But if her husband restrains her on the day that he learns of it,
he thereby annuls her vow which was in force or the commitment[c] to which she bound herself; and the LORD will forgive
her.—10 The vow of a widow or of a divorced woman, however, whatever she has imposed on herself, shall be binding
upon her.—11 So, too, if, while in her husband's household,
she makes a vow or imposes an obligation on herself by oath,
12 and her husband learns of it, yet offers no objection—thus
failing to restrain her—all her vows shall stand and all her self-
imposed obligations shall stand. 13 But if her husband does annul them on the day he finds out, then nothing that has crossed
her lips shall stand, whether vows or self-imposed obligations.
Her husband has annulled them, and the LORD will forgive her.
14 Every vow and every sworn obligation of self-denial may be
upheld by her husband or annulled by her husband. 15 If her
husband offers no objection from that day to the next, he has
upheld all the vows or obligations she has assumed: he has

a Or "a prohibition." *b-b Lit. "come out of his mouth."*
c Lit. "utterance of her lips."

30.1: This type of subscript statement, which belongs to what precedes (the beginning of a new unit in 30.1 is a mistake), is common in Priestly literature, and attests to the fact that the LORD's instructions were carried out (cf. 5.4).

30.2–17: Annulling vows and oaths. The section of cult regulations begun in ch 28 ends with the subject of the annulment of vows and oaths. This topic connects to the aforementioned votive and freewill offerings (29.39), which most often constitute the pledge. A sworn statement in the name of God defines the seriousness of the pledge (Exod. 20.7; Deut. 5.11). Vow and oath obligations differ from each other in that a vow is conditional. It binds the devotee only after God fulfills the requested blessing. For example, Jacob vows to erect a shrine at Bethel if God delivers him safely from the wrath of his brother (Gen. 28.20, 22); Jephthah vows to sacrifice whatever comes out first from his house if he returns having defeated the Ammonites (Judg. 11.30–31); and Hannah vows to dedicate her son to sanctuary service if she conceives (1 Sam. 1.11). **3:** This initial statement affirms the obligation of men to any vows and oaths they take (Deut. 23.22–24). This case is simple: Since all men are independent, they are thus responsible for their vows. However, one might expect some delineation pertaining to age status. Clearly the focus is on women. The rest of the ch deals with women's vows; the status of these depends on the status of the woman, particularly if she is dependent on a man, that is, under his legal authority, specifically her father or husband. **4–13:** The discussion turns to the responsibility of women regarding such promises. Four cases are presented: (1) the vow or oath of a young woman (but presumably not a minor) living in her father's house and under his authority (vv. 4–6), (2) the vow or oath of a married woman made while still in her father's house but now under the authority of her husband (vv. 7–9), (3) the vow of a widow or divorced woman (v. 10),

upheld them by offering no objection on the day he found out.
[16] But if he annuls them after [the day] he finds out, he shall
bear her guilt.

[17] Those are the laws that the LORD enjoined upon Moses
between a man and his wife, and as between a father and his
daughter while in her father's household by reason of her youth.

31 The LORD spoke to Moses, saying, [2] "Avenge the Israelite
people on the Midianites; then you shall be gathered to
your kin."

[3] Moses spoke to the people, saying, "Let men be picked out
from among you for a campaign, and let them fall upon Midian
to wreak the LORD's vengeance on Midian. [4] You shall dispatch
on the campaign a thousand from every one of the tribes of
Israel."

[5] So a thousand from each tribe were furnished from the
divisions of Israel, twelve thousand picked for the campaign.
[6] Moses dispatched them on the campaign, a thousand from
each tribe, with Phinehas son of Eleazar serving as a priest
on the campaign, equipped with the sacred utensils[a] and the
trumpets for sounding the blasts. [7] They took the field against
Midian, as the LORD had commanded Moses, and slew every
male. [8] Along with their other victims, they slew the kings of
Midian: Evi, Rekem, Zur, Hur, and Reba, the five kings of Midian. They also put Balaam son of Beor to the sword.

[9] The Israelites took the women and children of the Midianites captive, and seized as booty all their beasts, all their
herds, and all their wealth. [10] And they destroyed by fire all
the towns in which they were settled, and their encampments. [11] They gathered all the spoil and all the booty, man
and beast, [12] and they brought the captives, the booty, and
the spoil to Moses, Eleazar the priest, and the whole Israelite
community, at the camp in the steppes of Moab, at the Jordan near Jericho.

[13] Moses, Eleazar the priest, and all the chieftains of the
community came out to meet them outside the camp. [14] Moses became angry with the commanders of the army, the officers of thousands and the officers of hundreds, who had come
back from the military campaign. [15] Moses said to them, "You
have spared every female! [16] Yet they are the very ones who,
at the bidding of Balaam, induced[b] the Israelites to trespass
against the LORD in the matter of Peor, so that the LORD's community was struck by the plague. [17] Now, therefore, slay every
male among the children, and slay also every woman who has
known a man carnally; [18] but spare every young woman who
has not had carnal relations with a man.

a Perhaps the Urim; cf. 27.21. *b Meaning of Heb.* hayu ... limsor *uncertain.*

(4) the vow or oath of a widowed or divorced woman made prior to her husband's death or before their divorce (vv. 11–13). Nullification of a woman's vows and oaths is only possible if the woman is in a state of dependency, either on her father or husband. Independent women, such as widows or divorcees, who take on these obligations are bound to them in the same way as men. These laws suggest that a woman's vows and oaths required validation by a male if she was legally dependent on him. The Dead Sea Scrolls, however, placed almost equal weight on the oaths of adult females and limited a husband's or father's right of annulment to oaths and vows which transgress the laws of the Torah (CD 16.10–12). **14–16:** A husband (or father) who annuls a woman's vow or oath outside the prescribed parameters bears the woman's guilt and is liable for punishment. Problems arising from vows made in error or haste prompted the Rabbis to assert that four kinds of vows were not binding: vows of incitement, vows of exaggeration, vows made in error, and vows of constraint (*m. Ned.* 3.1). **17:** This v. formally concludes these legal prescriptions.

31.1–54: War of vengeance against the Midianites. Ch 31 consists of a Priestly narrative that picks up from the end of ch 25 (see 25.16–19 n.). The divine command to defeat the Midianites in retaliation for their seduction of the Israelites at Baal-peor (25.17–18) is realized in this ch, which opens with a call to battle (for the association of Midianites and Moabites, see 22.4 n.). The brevity and somewhat legendary nature of the war account point to several issues of real concern underlying the lengthy ch, which integrates several laws mentioned in the book, and adduces some new ones. Clearly evident is the Priestly writer's agenda: the key military role of the priesthood; the fate of male and female captives in a holy war, ritual purification of soldiers and booty, and the taxation of spoils for the sanctuary. Thus, the main

19 "You shall then stay outside the camp seven days; every one among you or among your captives who has slain a person or touched a corpse shall cleanse himself on the third and seventh days. 20 You shall also cleanse every cloth, every article of skin, everything made of goats' hair, and every object of wood."

21 Eleazar the priest said to the troops who had taken part in the fighting, "This is the ritual law that the LORD has enjoined upon Moses: 22 Gold and silver, copper, iron, tin, and lead— 23 any article that can withstand fire—these you shall pass through fire and they shall be clean, except that they must be cleansed with water of lustration; and anything that cannot withstand fire you must pass through water. 24 On the seventh day you shall wash your clothes and be clean, and after that you may enter the camp."

25 The LORD said to Moses: 26 "You and Eleazar the priest and the family heads of the community take an inventory of the booty that was captured, man and beast, 27 and divide the booty equally between the combatants who engaged in the campaign and the rest of the community. 28 You shall exact a levy for the LORD: in the case of the warriors who engaged in the campaign, one item in five hundred, of persons, oxen, asses, and sheep, 29 shall be taken from their half-share and given to Eleazar the priest as a contribution to the LORD; 30 and from the half-share of the other Israelites you shall withhold one in every fifty human beings as well as cattle, asses, and sheep—all the animals—and give them to the Levites, who attend to the duties of the LORD's Tabernacle."

31 Moses and Eleazar the priest did as the LORD commanded Moses. 32 The amount of booty, other than the spoil that the troops had plundered, came to 675,000 sheep, 33 72,000 head of cattle, 34 61,000 asses, 35 and a total of 32,000 human beings, namely, the women who had not had carnal relations.

36 Thus, the half-share of those who had engaged in the campaign [was as follows]: The number of sheep was 337,500, 37 and the LORD's levy from the sheep was 675; 38 the cattle came to 36,000, from which the LORD's levy was 72; 39 the asses came to 30,500, from which the LORD's levy was 61. 40 And the number of human beings was 16,000, from which the LORD's levy was 32. 41 Moses gave the contributions levied for the LORD to Eleazar the priest, as the LORD had commanded Moses.

42 As for the half-share of the other Israelites, which Moses withdrew from the men who had taken the field, 43 that half-share of the community consisted of 337,500 sheep, 44 36,000 head of cattle, 45 30,500 asses, 46 and 16,000 human beings. 47 From this half-share of the Israelites, Moses withheld one in every fifty humans and animals; and he gave them to the Levites, who attended to the duties of the LORD's Tabernacle, as the LORD had commanded Moses.

focus is not the battle, but the legal precedents that it sets. **4:** *A thousand from every one of the tribes:* The term "'elef" can also refer to "division" (a military unit), hence twelve divisions. **6:** *Phinehas son of Eleazar* the high priest serves as the military priest (cf. 25.7–8; Deut. 20.2–4). According to the midrash (*Num. Rab.* 22.4), Phinehas was assigned this role so that he could finish the sacred task he began when he smote the Midianite woman in the affair of Baal-peor (25.1–9). *The sacred utensils* are not specified but probably include the Ark (1 Sam. 4.3–11) and the Urim and Thummim (1 Sam. 14.41; 28.6). The *trumpets* are mentioned earlier in 10.1–10. **7:** *Slew every male:* Total annihilation is an expression of victory not to be taken literally. It is a common propagandistic statement in ancient Near Eastern battle accounts. **8:** *Put Balaam son of Beor to the sword:* According to this tradition (also v. 16) he is killed for his association with the Midianites, through whom he incited the Israelites to the apostasy of Baal-peor (see 22.2–24.25 n.). **15–18:** Only young girls who are virgins are left alive and presumably taken captive (Deut. 20.14; 21.10–14). Since lineage was determined patriarchally, they do not pose the danger of producing Midianite sons who can avenge their fathers. **19–24:** Soldiers returning from battle as well as captives must be purified from corpse defilement; this recalls ch 19. In addition, their metal implements must be cleansed by fire, a new law. **22–23:** This process of cleansing vessels and other objects is perpetuated, with adaptations, in the Jewish tradition of preparing kitchen utensils for Passover. **25–30:** A similar practice concerning distribution of booty is noted in 1 Sam. 30.22–31; both cases, by different authors, are in-tended as illustrative precedents. **28–30:** A form of the laws concerning tithing, detailed in ch 18, is carried out. **31–47:** The amount of booty recorded here, including the share designated for the sanctuary, is fantastic by any standards.

48 The commanders of the troop divisions, the officers of thousands and the officers of hundreds, approached Moses. 49 They said to Moses, "Your servants have made a check of the warriors in our charge, and not one of us is missing. 50 So we have brought as an offering to the LORD such articles of gold as each of us came upon: armlets, bracelets, signet rings, earrings, and pendants,[a] that expiation may be made for our persons before the LORD." 51 Moses and Eleazar the priest accepted the gold from them, all kinds of wrought articles. 52 All the gold that was offered by the officers of thousands and the officers of hundreds as a contribution to the LORD came to 16,750 shekels.—53 But in the ranks, everyone kept his booty for himself.—54 So Moses and Eleazar the priest accepted the gold from the officers of thousands and the officers of hundreds and brought it to the Tent of Meeting, as a reminder in behalf of the Israelites before the LORD.

32 The Reubenites and the Gadites owned cattle in very great numbers. Noting that the lands of Jazer and Gilead were a region suitable for cattle, 2 the Gadites and the Reubenites came to Moses, Eleazar the priest, and the chieftains of the community, and said, 3 "Ataroth, Dibon, Jazer, Nimrah, Heshbon, Elealeh, Sebam, Nebo, and Beon—4 the land that the LORD has conquered for the community of Israel is cattle country, and your servants have cattle. 5 It would be a favor to us," they continued, "if this land were given to your servants as a holding; do not move us across the Jordan."

6 Moses replied to the Gadites and the Reubenites, "Are your brothers to go to war while you stay here? 7 Why will you turn the minds of the Israelites from crossing into the land that the LORD has given them? 8 That is what your fathers did when I sent them from Kadesh-barnea to survey the land. 9 After going up to the wadi Eshcol and surveying the land, they turned the minds of the Israelites from invading the land that the LORD had given them. 10 Thereupon the LORD was incensed and He swore, 11 'None of the men from twenty years up who came out of Egypt shall see the land that I promised on oath to Abraham, Isaac, and Jacob, for they did not remain loyal to Me—12 none except Caleb son of Jephunneh the Kenizzite and Joshua son of Nun, for they remained loyal to the LORD.' 13 The LORD was incensed at Israel, and for forty years He made them wander in the wilderness, until the whole generation that had provoked the LORD's displeasure was gone. 14 And now you, a breed of sinful men, have replaced your fathers, to add still further to the LORD's wrath against Israel. 15 If you turn away from Him and He abandons them once more in the wilderness, you will bring calamity upon all this people."

a See note at Exod. 35.22.

48–54: Conducting a census not initiated by God was believed to provoke divine anger (see 2 Sam. ch 24 where God in anger incites David to take a census that results in a plague). To avert that possibility, the army commanders donate precious articles of gold to God as a ransom for the Israelites (cf. Exod. 30.12). **54:** *As a reminder:* The gold ransom is used in the Tent of Meeting as a continual ritual reminder (Exod. 30.16). This recalls the earlier fire pans, which serve the same purpose (17.5).

32.1–42: Settlement of Transjordan. The settlement process begins. Since the Israelites had already routed a number of their enemies in Transjordan (21.21–35; 31.1–12), the tribes of Reuben and Gad consider it prudent to settle that land with their families and livestock. Subsequently, half the tribe of Manasseh also settles east of the Jordan River. The narrative in this ch primarily serves to legitimate Israelite occupation of land outside Canaan proper (see also Josh. ch 22). A nonbiblical text, the Mesha Stele (Moabite Stone) (9th c. BCE), confirms Gadite occupation of Ataroth—a town assigned to that tribe in 32.34—since antiquity. **1–5:** These introductory vv. provide a backdrop for the narrative. **3:** The cities of Gad and Reuben are more fully discussed in vv. 34–38; variant traditions about each tribe's holdings are found elsewhere (cf. Josh. 13.17–23). **6–15:** Moses interprets Gad's and Reuben's request as a sign that they are unwilling to fight in the conquest of Canaan, comparing them with the ten scouts who disheartened Israel in the wilderness (chs 13–14). **15:** Moses fears for the fate of Israel on account of the actions of Gad and Reuben (cf. Josh. 22.16–19; Judg. 5.16–17); this v. assumes corporate responsibility, where a serious infraction by part of the nation endangers the nation as a whole.

16 Then they stepped up to him and said, "We will build here
sheepfolds for our flocks and towns for our children. 17 And we
will hasten[a] as shock-troops in the van of the Israelites until we
have established them in their home, while our children stay
in the fortified towns because of the inhabitants of the land.
18 We will not return to our homes until every one of the Israelites is in possession of his portion. 19 But we will not have a
share with them in the territory beyond the Jordan, for we have
received our share on the east side of the Jordan."
20 Moses said to them, "If you do this, if you go to battle as
shock-troops, at the instance of the LORD, 21 and every shock-
fighter among you crosses the Jordan, at the instance of the
LORD, until He has dispossessed His enemies before Him,
22 and the land has been subdued, at the instance of the LORD,
and then you return—you shall be clear before the LORD and
before Israel; and this land shall be your holding under the
LORD. 23 But if you do not do so, you will have sinned against
the LORD; and know that your sin will overtake you. 24 Build
towns for your children and sheepfolds for your flocks, but do
what you have promised."
25 The Gadites and the Reubenites answered Moses, "Your
servants will do as my lord commands. 26 Our children, our
wives, our flocks, and all our other livestock will stay behind[b]
in the towns of Gilead; 27 while your servants, all those recruit-
ed for war, cross over, at the instance of the LORD, to engage in
battle—as my lord orders."
28 Then Moses gave instructions concerning them to Eleazar
the priest, Joshua son of Nun, and the family heads of the Israelite tribes. 29 Moses said to them, "If every shock-fighter among
the Gadites and the Reubenites crosses the Jordan with you to
do battle, at the instance of the LORD, and the land is subdued
before you, you shall give them the land of Gilead as a holding.
30 But if they do not cross over with you as shock-troops, they
shall receive holdings among you in the land of Canaan."
31 The Gadites and the Reubenites said in reply, "Whatever
the LORD has spoken concerning your servants, that we will
do. 32 We ourselves will cross over as shock-troops, at the instance of the LORD, into the land of Canaan; and we shall keep
our hereditary holding across the Jordan."[c]
33 So Moses assigned to them—to the Gadites, the Reubenites, and the half-tribe of Manasseh son of Joseph—the kingdom of Sihon king of the Amorites and the kingdom of King Og
of Bashan, the land with its various cities and the territories of
their surrounding towns. 34 The Gadites rebuilt Dibon, Ataroth,
Aroer, 35 Atroth-shophan, Jazer, Jogbehah, 36 Beth-nimrah, and

17: *Shock-troops:* Gad and Reuben commit to frontline action as vanguard troops. The modern Heb "ḥalutz," a pioneer who settled the land of Israel in the early 20th century, is derived from this word, specifically from the idea that they are the vanguard of settling the land. **20–22:** *At the instance of the LORD,* lit. "before the LORD": Moses repeats this phrase emphasizing Gad's and Reuben's commitment to march in front of the Ark. In the wilderness the Ark leads (cf. 10.33). **22:** *You shall be clear before the LORD:* Freedom from obligation in legal terms indicates that the Gadites and Reubenites took an oath (Gen. 24.8). **28:** Moses instructs Joshua about the obligation of the Transjordanian tribes because the conquest will take place under Joshua's leadership. **31–32:** The Gadites and Reubenites repeat their acceptance of the terms. **33:** Moses assigns Gad, Reuben, and half the tribe of Manasseh the lands of conquered kings (21.21–35) as their inheritance (see Map, p. 482). Settlement of Manasseh in Transjordan first appears here, perhaps indicating a secondary addition, although one attested elsewhere (Deut. 3.12–16; Josh. 13.29–31).

a *Meaning of Heb.* hushim *uncertain.* b *Lit. "there."*
c *I.e., in Transjordan.*

Beth-haran as fortified towns or as enclosures for flocks. [37] The Reubenites rebuilt Heshbon, Elealeh, Kiriathaim, [38] Nebo, Baal-meon—some names being changed—and Sibmah; they gave [their own] names to towns that they rebuilt.[a] [39] The descendants of Machir son of Manasseh went to Gilead and captured it, dispossessing the Amorites who were there; [40] so Moses gave Gilead to Machir son of Manasseh, and he settled there. [41] Jair son of Manasseh went and captured [b]their villages,[-b] which he renamed Havvoth-jair.[c] [42] And Nobah went and captured Kenath and its dependencies, renaming it Nobah after himself.

MASEʿEI מסעי

33 These were the marches of the Israelites who started out from the land of Egypt, troop by troop, in the charge of Moses and Aaron. [2] Moses recorded the starting points of their various marches as directed by the LORD. Their marches, by starting points, were as follows:

[3] They set out from Rameses in the first month, on the fifteenth day of the first month. It was on the morrow of the passover offering that the Israelites started out defiantly,[d] in plain view of all the Egyptians. [4] The Egyptians meanwhile were burying those among them whom the LORD had struck down, every first-born—whereby the LORD executed judgment on their gods.

[5] The Israelites set out from Rameses and encamped at Succoth. [6] They set out from Succoth and encamped at Etham, which is on the edge of the wilderness. [7] They set out from Etham and turned about toward Pi-hahiroth, which faces Baal-zephon, and they encamped before Migdol. [8] They set out from Pene[e]-hahiroth and passed through the sea into the wilderness; and they made a three-days' journey in the wilderness of Etham and encamped at Marah. [9] They set out from Marah and came to Elim. There were twelve springs in Elim and seventy palm trees, so they encamped there. [10] They set out from Elim and encamped by the Sea of Reeds.[f] [11] They set out from the Sea of Reeds and encamped in the wilderness of Sin. [12] They set out from the wilderness of Sin and encamped at Dophkah. [13] They set out from Dophkah and encamped at Alush. [14] They set out from Alush and encamped at Rephidim; it was there that the people had no water to drink. [15] They set out from Rephidim and encamped in the wilderness of Sinai. [16] They set out from the wilderness of Sinai and encamped at Kibroth-hattaavah. [17] They set out from Kibroth-hattaavah and encamped at Hazeroth.

a Cf. vv. 41, 42. *b-b Or "the villages of Ham"; cf. Gen. 14.5.*
c I.e., "the villages of Jair." *d See note at Exod. 14.8.*
e Many Hebrew manuscripts and ancient versions read "Pi."
f See note at Exod. 10.19.

39–42: In contrast to other tribes, Manassites conquer a portion of their inheritance on their own. A tradition in Judg. 10.4 ascribes the origin of *Havvoth-jair* to a later period.

33.1–49: A comprehensive wilderness itinerary. This record encompasses the itinerary of Israel's travels from their point of departure in Egypt to their final encampment in Transjordan (42 stations; see Map, p. 122). The writer seems to correct geographical problems, such as alternate routes, in the previous wilderness accounts (Exod. and Num.) in order to create a coherent itinerary. Notably, some toponyms appear here for the first time, being absent from accounts of the exodus in other biblical texts (see Deut. chs 1–3 for another summary). The literary style of the itinerary, the repetition of campsite names, and the highlighting of events in those places closely resemble extant military records from the ancient Near East, especially from Assyria. Accordingly, the notation in this Priestly source that Moses *recorded the starting points of their various marches* (v. 2) fits the genre. Some scholars, however, consider ch 33 a composite text extracted from other portions of Num., Exod., and Deut. As in the census in ch 26, at some points small expansions appear here (e.g., vv. 38–39). **3–5:** On *Rameses,* see Exod. 12.37. **6–7:** For *Succoth* and *Etham* (= Shur in Exod. 15.22), see Exod. 13.20. **8:** For the incident at *Marah,* see Exod. 15.23–25.
9–10: For *Elim,* see Exod. 15.27.
11–12: For the story of the manna in the *wilderness of Sin,* see Exod. ch 16.
14: At *Rephidim* Moses brought forth water by striking the rock; Israel was attacked there by Amalek (Exod. ch 17). **15:** Sinai still cannot be identified with any degree of certainty. Accounts of events associated with Mount Sinai begin in Exod. ch 19.
16–17: For *Kibroth-hattaavah* and *Hazeroth,* see 11.34–35.

18 They set out from Hazeroth and encamped at Rithmah. 19 They
set out from Rithmah and encamped at Rimmon-perez. 20 They
set out from Rimmon-perez and encamped at Libnah. 21 They set
out from Libnah and encamped at Rissah. 22 They set out from
Rissah and encamped at Kehelath. 23 They set out from Kehelath
and encamped at Mount Shepher. 24 They set out from Mount
Shepher and encamped at Haradah. 25 They set out from Haradah and encamped at Makheloth. 26 They set out from Makheloth and encamped at Tahath. 27 They set out from Tahath and
encamped at Terah. 28 They set out from Terah and encamped
at Mithkah. 29 They set out from Mithkah and encamped at
Hashmonah. 30 They set out from Hashmonah and encamped
at Moseroth. 31 They set out from Moseroth and encamped at
Bene-jaakan. 32 They set out from Bene-jaakan and encamped
at Hor-haggidgad. 33 They set out from Hor-haggidgad and encamped at Jotbath. 34 They set out from Jotbath and encamped at
Abronah. 35 They set out from Abronah and encamped at Ezion-
geber. 36 They set out from Ezion-geber and encamped in the
wilderness of Zin, that is, Kadesh. 37 They set out from Kadesh
and encamped at Mount Hor, on the edge of the land of Edom.

38 Aaron the priest ascended Mount Hor at the command of
the LORD and died there, in the fortieth year after the Israelites
had left the land of Egypt, on the first day of the fifth month.
39 Aaron was a hundred and twenty-three years old when he
died on Mount Hor. 40 And the Canaanite, king of Arad, who
dwelt in the Negeb, in the land of Canaan, learned of the coming of the Israelites.[a]

41 They set out from Mount Hor and encamped at Zalmonah. 42 They set out from Zalmonah and encamped at Punon.
43 They set out from Punon and encamped at Oboth. 44 They
set out from Oboth and encamped at Iye-abarim, in the territory of Moab. 45 They set out from Iyim and encamped at
Dibon-gad. 46 They set out from Dibon-gad and encamped at
Almon-diblathaim. 47 They set out from Almon-diblathaim
and encamped in the hills of Abarim, before Nebo. 48 They set
out from the hills of Abarim and encamped in the steppes of
Moab, at the Jordan near Jericho; 49 they encamped by the Jordan from Beth-jeshimoth as far as Abel-shittim, in the steppes
of Moab.

50 In the steppes of Moab, at the Jordan near Jericho, the
LORD spoke to Moses, saying: 51 Speak to the Israelite people
and say to them: When you cross the Jordan into the land of
Canaan, 52 you shall dispossess all the inhabitants of the land;
you shall destroy all their figured[b] objects; you shall destroy
all their molten images, and you shall demolish all their cult

a *See 21.1–3.* *b* *See note at Lev. 26.1.*

18–29: The toponyms listed in these vv. are unattested elsewhere. **30–34:** For these sites, see Deut. 10.6–7. **36:** In non-Priestly sources *Kadesh* was an early stop on the wilderness trek (cf. 13.26; Deut. 2.14). **37–39:** Aaron's death, a memorable event for the Priestly writer, is described here in detail with the addition of the date and his age (cf. 20.22–29). **38:** *At the command of the LORD*, lit. "at the mouth of the LORD." Rashi (following *b. B. Bat.* 17a) comments that Aaron dies by the divine kiss, as does Moses (Deut. 34.5). **40:** Cf. 21.1–3. **41–42:** These are two unknown toponyms. **41–49:** The location of these sites, although not all are known, suggest a route through Edomite and Moabite territory, in keeping with Deut. (chs 2–13) but contra Num. 20.19–21. **49:** *Abel-shittim* is the site from which Israel crosses the Jordan River into Canaan in Josh. 3.1.

33.50–35.8: Instructions on the conquest and division of Canaan. The final task before crossing into Canaan is to delineate the boundaries of the land so that it can be divided among the nine-and-a-half tribes that will inhabit it. The Levites, who are not allotted tribal territory, are provided with towns and pastureland within the holdings of the other tribes. A repetition of the method by which the land will be apportioned (26.52–56) and, more importantly, the command to utterly destroy the indigenous Canaanite population together with its religious objects and shrines (33.50–56) precede instructions relating to the division of Canaan. **33.50–56:** The eradication of the Canaanites and their cult is a divine command. Failure to do so will result in the demise of Israel (cf. Deut. 7.16; Josh. 23.13). **52:** *Figured objects* may refer to stone images in relief (cf. Lev. 26.1). Such objects have been uncovered in archeological excavations from Syria to Israel. *Their cult places*, Heb "bamah," high place, is difficult to define but probably refers to a shrine smaller than a full-scale temple with an elevated

places. 53 And you shall take possession of the land and settle in it, for I have assigned the land to you to possess. 54 You shall apportion the land among yourselves by lot, clan by clan: with larger groups increase the share, with smaller groups reduce the share. Wherever the lot falls for anyone, that shall be his. You shall have your portions according to your ancestral tribes. 55 But if you do not dispossess the inhabitants of the land, those whom you allow to remain shall be stings in your eyes and thorns in your sides, and they shall harass you in the land in which you live; 56 so that I will do to you what I planned to do to them.

34 The LORD spoke to Moses, saying: 2 Instruct the Israelite people and say to them: When you enter the land of Canaan, this is the land that shall fall to you as your portion, the land of Canaan with its various boundaries:

3 Your southern sector shall extend from the wilderness of Zin alongside Edom. Your southern boundary shall start on the east from the tip of the Dead Sea. 4 Your boundary shall then turn to pass south of the ascent of Akrabbim and continue to Zin, and its limits shall be south of Kadesh-barnea, reaching Hazar-addar and continuing to Azmon. 5 From Azmon the boundary shall turn toward the Wadi of Egypt and terminate at the Sea.[a]

6 For the western boundary you shall have the coast of the Great Sea;[a] that shall serve as your western boundary.

7 This shall be your northern boundary: Draw a line from the Great Sea to Mount Hor; 8 from Mount Hor draw a line to Lebo-hamath,[b] and let the boundary reach Zedad. 9 The boundary shall then run to Ziphron and terminate at Hazar-enan. That shall be your northern boundary.

10 For your eastern boundary you shall draw a line from Hazar-enan to Shepham. 11 From Shepham the boundary shall descend to Riblah on the east side of Ain; from there the boundary shall continue downward and abut on the eastern slopes of the Sea of Chinnereth.[c] 12 The boundary shall then descend along the Jordan and terminate at the Dead Sea.

That shall be your land as defined by its boundaries on all sides.

13 Moses instructed the Israelites, saying: This is the land you are to receive by lot as your hereditary portion, which the LORD has commanded to be given to the nine and a half tribes. 14 For the Reubenite tribe by its ancestral houses, the Gadite tribe by its ancestral houses, and the half-tribe of Manasseh have

a I.e., the Mediterranean Sea. *b See note at 13.21.*
c I.e., the Sea (or Lake) of Galilee.

cult platform, like those uncovered in archeological excavations at Megiddo and Tel Dan. **34.1–15:** The exact boundaries of the promised land are delineated from south to north, the direction corresponding to the scouting account (13.21). Scholars have observed a correlation between the Levantine territory under Egyptian control at the end of the 13th century and the borders as defined in vv. 3–12 (cf. Josh. 15.1–12; Ezek. 47.13–20). The large size of Israel's domain is clearly idealized. **3–5:** Israel's territory begins at the southern tip of the Dead Sea, extending in a southern arc through Kadesh-barnea and west to the Mediterranean Sea at the Brook of Egypt, Wadi El-ʿArish (see Maps no. 2 and no. 6). **6–9:** From the west it extends northward. The northernmost border, at Hazar-enan, is tentatively identified with the oasis of Qayatein 113 km (70 mi) northeast of Damascus. **7–8:** *Mount Hor* is not the site in the region of Edom where Aaron died (20.22; 33.38). **10–12:** The border then extends south around the eastern banks of the Sea of Galilee and further southward along the Jordan River to the Dead Sea. **14–15:** These vv. serve as a reminder that Reuben, Gad, and half of Manasseh received land in Transjordan.

already received their portions: 15 those two and a half tribes
have received their portions across the Jordan, opposite Jericho, on the east, the orient side.

16 The LORD spoke to Moses, saying: 17 These are the names
of the men through whom the land shall be apportioned for
you: Eleazar the priest and Joshua son of Nun. 18 And you
shall also take a chieftain from each tribe through whom the
land shall be apportioned. 19 These are the names of the men:
from the tribe of Judah: Caleb son of Jephunneh. 20 From the
Simeonite tribe: Samuel[a] son of Ammihud. 21 From the tribe
of Benjamin: Elidad son of Chislon. 22 From the Danite tribe: a
chieftain, Bukki son of Jogli. 23 For the descendants of Joseph:
from the Manassite tribe: a chieftain, Hanniel son of Ephod;
24 and from the Ephraimite tribe: a chieftain, Kemuel son of
Shiphtan. 25 From the Zebulunite tribe: a chieftain, Elizaphan
son of Parnach. 26 From the Issacharite tribe: a chieftain, Paltiel
son of Azzan. 27 From the Asherite tribe: a chieftain, Ahihud
son of Shelomi. 28 From the Naphtalite tribe: a chieftain, Peda-
hel son of Ammihud.

29 It was these whom the LORD designated to allot portions
to the Israelites in the land of Canaan.

35 The LORD spoke to Moses in the steppes of Moab at the
Jordan near Jericho, saying: 2 Instruct the Israelite people to assign, out of the holdings apportioned to them, towns
for the Levites to dwell in; you shall also assign to the Levites
pasture land around their towns. 3 The towns shall be theirs to
dwell in, and the pasture shall be for the cattle they own and
all their other beasts. 4 The town pasture that you are to assign
to the Levites shall extend a thousand cubits outside the town
wall all around. 5 You shall measure off two thousand cubits
outside the town on the east side, two thousand on the south
side, two thousand on the west side, and two thousand on the
north side, with the town in the center. That shall be the pasture for their towns.

6 The towns that you assign to the Levites shall comprise the
six cities of refuge that you are to designate for a manslayer to
flee to, to which you shall add forty-two towns. 7 Thus the total
of the towns that you assign to the Levites shall be forty-eight
towns, with their pasture. 8 In assigning towns from the holdings of the Israelites, take more from the larger groups and less
from the smaller, so that each assigns towns to the Levites in
proportion to the share it receives.

9 The LORD spoke further to Moses: 10 Speak to the Israelite
people and say to them: When you cross the Jordan into the

a Or "Shemuel."

16–29: New tribal chieftains, with the exception of Caleb (13.6), are appointed to assist Eleazar the priest and Joshua in allotting portions of land to the nine-and-a-half remaining tribes. The tribal chieftains are listed here more or less in an order corresponding to the geographical tribal distribution in Canaan, from south to north. For the delineation of each tribe's territory, see Josh. chs 15–19. **35.1–8:** Each tribe must allocate land from its holdings for the Levites. The towns and pastureland apportioned to the Levites by each tribe is proportional to the size of its tribal territory. These instructions diverge from the division of the forty-eight Levitical towns among the tribes in Joshua (21.1–40), where nine of the tribes allocate four towns each, Judah gives eight, Simeon one, and Naphtali three. **4–5:** Pastureland extends from the town 1000 cubits (1 cubit = approximately .5 meter [18 in]) in all directions, thereby forming a square of at least 2000 × 2000 cubits, depending on the town size. **6:** The mention of *cities of refuge* serves as a bridge to the following unit.

35.9–34: Cities of refuge and laws governing intentional and unintentional homicide. Different traditions concerning accidental homicide and the cities of refuge are found in Exod. 21.12–14; Deut. 4.41–43; 19.1–13; Josh. ch 20. **9–15:** Levitical towns also serve another purpose. Six (of the forty-eight) designated towns, three in Transjordan and three in Canaan, function as places of asylum for perpetrators of involuntary manslaughter.

12: *The avenger,* lit. "redeemer," is a kinsman of the victim who is obligated (vv. 19–27) to avenge (or restore) the lost blood of the slain family member with the blood of the murderer. **15:** Aliens are offered asylum like Israelites. These laws, while protecting persons from unjustified vengeance, clearly reflect the Priestly concern over bloodshed as a source of defilement of the land (vv. 33–34). **16–23:** Listed are concrete examples that distinguish intentional from unintentional homicide; as is typical of the Bible and ancient Near Eastern law, specific cases rather than general principles are adduced. **24:** *The assembly* probably refers to the court of elders (cf. 11.16–25). **25:** Apparently, court is not held in cities of refuge. The death of the high priest seems to atone accidental homicide. Cf. other purgings of impurity and sin by the high priest in his lifetime (Lev. 16.16–22). For the ritual of anointing the high priest, see Lev. 21.10. **26–28:** The perpetrator of involuntary manslaughter is only protected from the blood avenger inside the city of refuge.

land of Canaan, 11 you shall provide yourselves with places to serve you as cities of refuge to which a manslayer who has killed a person unintentionally may flee. 12 The cities shall serve you as a refuge from the avenger,[a] so that the manslayer may not die unless he has stood trial before the assembly.

13 The towns that you thus assign shall be six cities of refuge in all. 14 Three cities shall be designated beyond the Jordan, and the other three shall be designated in the land of Canaan: they shall serve as cities of refuge. 15 These six cities shall serve the Israelites and the resident aliens among them for refuge, so that anyone who kills a person unintentionally may flee there.

16 Anyone, however, who strikes another with an iron object so that death results is a murderer; the murderer must be put to death. 17 If he struck him with a stone tool[b] that could cause death, and death resulted, he is a murderer; the murderer must be put to death. 18 Similarly, if the object with which he struck him was a wooden tool[b] that could cause death, and death resulted, he is a murderer; the murderer must be put to death. 19 The blood-avenger himself shall put the murderer to death; it is he who shall put him to death upon encounter. 20 So, too, if he pushed him in hate or hurled something at him on purpose and death resulted, 21 or if he struck him with his hand in enmity and death resulted, the assailant shall be put to death; he is a murderer. The blood-avenger shall put the murderer to death upon encounter.

22 But if he pushed him without malice aforethought or hurled any object at him unintentionally, 23 or inadvertently[c] dropped upon him any deadly object of stone, and death resulted—though he was not an enemy of his and did not seek his harm—24 in such cases the assembly shall decide between the slayer and the blood-avenger. 25 The assembly shall protect the manslayer from the blood-avenger, and the assembly shall restore him to the city of refuge to which he fled, and there he shall remain until the death of the high priest who was anointed with the sacred oil. 26 But if the manslayer ever goes outside the limits of the city of refuge to which he has fled, 27 and the blood-avenger comes upon him outside the limits of his city of refuge, and the blood-avenger kills the manslayer, there is no bloodguilt on his account. 28 For he must remain inside his city of refuge until the death of the high priest; after the death of the high priest, the manslayer may return to his land holding.

29 Such shall be your law of procedure throughout the ages in all your settlements.

a Lit. "redeemer," i.e., next of kin; cf. note at Lev. 25.25. *b Lit. "of the hand."*
c Lit. "without seeing."

[30] If anyone kills a person, the manslayer may be executed
only on the evidence of witnesses; the testimony of a single
witness against a person shall not suffice for a sentence of
death. [31] You may not accept a ransom for the life of a murderer
who is guilty of a capital crime; he must be put to death. [32] Nor
may you accept ransom in lieu of flight to a city of refuge, enabling one to return to live on his land before the death of the
priest. [33] You shall not pollute the land in which you live; for
blood pollutes the land, and the land can have no expiation for
blood that is shed on it, except by the blood of him who shed
it. [34] You shall not defile the land in which you live, in which I
Myself abide, for I the LORD abide among the Israelite people.

36 The family heads in the clan of the descendants of Gilead son of Machir son of Manasseh, one of the Josephite
clans, came forward and appealed to Moses and the chieftains,
family heads[a] of the Israelites. [2] They said, "The LORD commanded my lord to assign the land to the Israelites as shares
by lot, and my lord was further commanded by the LORD to
assign the share of our kinsman Zelophehad to his daughters.
[3] Now, if they marry persons from another Israelite tribe, their
share will be cut off from our ancestral portion and be added to
the portion of the tribe into which they marry; thus our allotted
portion will be diminished. [4] And even when the Israelites observe the jubilee, their share will be added to that of the tribe
into which they marry, and their share will be cut off from the
ancestral portion of our tribe."
[5] So Moses, at the LORD's bidding, instructed the Israelites,
saying: "The plea of the Josephite tribe is just. [6] This is what the
LORD has commanded concerning the daughters of Zelophehad: They may marry anyone they wish, provided they marry
into a clan of their father's tribe. [7] No inheritance of the Israelites may pass over from one tribe to another, but the Israelites
must remain bound each to the ancestral portion of his tribe.

a I.e., tribal heads.

30–34: These vv., only loosely connected to the preceding, outline the procedure for convicting and punishing persons guilty of intentional homicide. **30:** At least two witnesses are required in capital cases (cf. Deut. 17.6). **31:** In cases of intentional homicide monetary compensation is explicitly prohibited. It does not compensate for the victim's lost blood as does the death of the killer (cf. Deut. 21.1–9). Biblical law differs in this respect from practices among other ancient Near Eastern societies, especially the Hittites, where monetary restitution to the family of the victim was an option. Thus, murder in the Bible was seen as a crime beyond an offense against the family of the deceased. **33–34:** The notion that bloodshed and other transgressions pollute the land, thereby endangering its inhabitants with divine wrath, is common in the Bible (see Gen. 4.10–12; Lev. 18.28; 2 Sam. 21.1–14; Ezek. 36.17–19; Hos. 4.2–3. See also essay on "Concepts of Purity," pp. 1998–2005).

36.1–13: Marriage of Zelophehad's daughters. Previously, the case of Zelophehad's daughters elicited divine permission for females to inherit in the absence of male heirs (27.1–11). This ch, which completes the third unit of Num. as well as of the entire book, addresses practical issues arising from female inheritance of land. It balances two important, but potentially conflicting principles: the right of women to inherit land in certain special circumstances and the idea of not alienating land from its original tribe or clan. The narrative provides legal instruction for heiresses so that their marriage will not result in the transfer of ancestral tribal lands from one tribe to another. Some scholars, citing the marriage of Zelophehad's daughters to their first cousins, maintain that originally the real concern centered on the preservation of smaller clan holdings, rather than those of the larger tribal unit. The discussion of the distribution of permanent tribal holdings in chs 32 and 34 may account for the placement of this explanatory text to 27.1–11 following ch 34. **1–4:** These vv. outline the potential problem surrounding female inheritance of property. **1:** The opening of the narrative parallels that of 27.1–11. **3–4:** The property still passes through the male line, the daughter's possession being interim. As a result of Israel's patrilineal and patrilocal system, a consequence of the daughter's marriage is that the property permanently passes to the husband's tribe via the inheritance of her sons. **4:** *Jubilee:* According to the Priestly system, every fiftieth year all sold land reverts to its original owner (see Lev. 25.8–16; 27.16–24). The jubilee law does not apply in this case since the land is inherited, not sold. **5–9:** These vv. contain broader stipulations for marriages of female heirs in order to preserve tribal holdings. The redundancy in vv. 7 and 9 pertaining to the inviolability of tribal estates prompted Ramban to view v. 9 as a separate commandment that in cases where a woman is already married to a man from a different tribe, any property she stands

8 Every daughter among the Israelite tribes who inherits a
share must marry someone from a clan of her father's tribe, in
order that every Israelite may keep his ancestral share. 9 Thus
no inheritance shall pass over from one tribe to another, but
the Israelite tribes shall remain bound each to its portion."

10 The daughters of Zelophehad did as the LORD had commanded Moses: 11 Mahlah, Tirzah, Hoglah, Milcah, and Noah,
Zelophehad's daughters, were married to sons of their uncles,
12 marrying into clans of descendants of Manasseh son of Joseph; and so their share remained in the tribe of their father's
clan.

13 These are the commandments and regulations that the
LORD enjoined upon the Israelites, through Moses, on the
steppes of Moab, at the Jordan near Jericho.

to inherit from her father subsequently must go to another relative. **5:** The validity of the clan elders' case evokes divine justice, as did the case of Zelophehad's daughters (27.6). **10–12:** The narrative concludes with the marriage of Zelophehad's daughters according to the conditions of the law. **13:** This v. is a postscript to the preceding laws, those commanded by God while Israel was encamped in Moab (22.1), and is not a concluding formula encompassing the book as a whole. Its form is typical of Priestly literature (e.g., Lev. 26.46; 27.34).

דברים

Deuteronomy

DEUTERONOMY MAY WELL BE the first book to pose the problem of modernity. Its authors struggled with issues conventionally viewed as exclusively modern ones, such as the historical distance between past and present, the tension between tradition and the needs of the contemporary generation, and the distinction between divine revelation and human interpretation. Seen from this perspective, ancient Israel's Deuteronomy becomes a remarkably contemporary text, one that challenges its readers to rethink their assumptions about time, about Scripture, and about religion. Of course, Deuteronomy is also a deeply traditional text that, more than any other book of the Bible, provides the foundation of Judaism. The religious conviction that God made a covenant with Israel at Sinai, and that the Torah embodies the terms of that covenant, is fundamental to Deuteronomy. Many familiar Jewish ritual objects, like the mezuzah, the tefillin, and the tzitzit (fringed garment), are, in part, based on Deuteronomy, as is Judaism's most important prayer, the Shema (6.4–9). But the Shema is more than a prayer. Judaism understands its recitation to be a binding legal act in which individuals pledge their commitment to God. By reciting the Shema, the congregation in the synagogue brings the plot of Deuteronomy to life in the present, as it enacts and renews that oath of allegiance to God that, it believes, Israel first vowed on the plains of Moab.

The story begins just as the Israelites, encamped on the plains of Moab, stand poised finally to enter the promised land. The entry into Canaan would provide the long-awaited climax of the story that had begun with the promises to the ancestors in Genesis, and whose fulfillment had been delayed by the enslavement in Egypt and the wandering in the wilderness. Now, on the eve both of his death and of the nation's entry into the land without him, Moses, portrayed as Deuteronomy's speaker, arrests the narrative action in order to deliver a series of three speeches, grouped together as a long valedictory address. He reviews the nation's history, expounds upon their laws, and instructs them about the importance of loyalty to God. He also adjures the nation, from the plains of Moab, to uphold this combination of law and theological instruction as a covenant, one that supplements the covenant previously sworn at Horeb (the name for the mountain of revelation, called Sinai elsewhere; 28.69). Only after the conclusion of these discourses and a following appendix (chs 31–34) does the overall narrative line resume with the account of the nation's entry into Canaan in Joshua and Judges.

The Historical Context and Literary Background

THE SECOND WORD OF THE BOOK, Devarim, "[the] words," gives the book its most common Hebrew title, following an ancient Near Eastern convention of naming books after their opening phrase or incipit. In contrast, the standard English name of the book, "Deuteronomy," goes back to the Greek Septuagint (LXX) (to deuteronomion, yielding Latin Deuteronomium), meaning "Second Law." That approach to naming the book represents the Greek translation of the Hebrew phrase "Mishneh Torah" found in Deuteronomy's Law of the King, where it refers to "a copy of the law" (17.18 n.). That phrase was understood in ancient rabbinic sources as a reference to the book of Deuteronomy itself (*Sifre* §160), understood as a "second law" or "repetition of the law," because of the extent to which Moses, throughout the book, revisits the earlier laws and narratives of the Tetrateuch (the first four books of the Bible) and teaches Israel about them (see Naḥmanides on Deut. 1.1 and Ibn Ezra on Deut. 1.5).

Despite the literary attribution of the text to Moses as its speaker, from the vantage point of modern biblical scholarship, Deuteronomy more likely arose in its present form at a later period of Israelite history. The main sections of the book fit best in the 7th c. BCE as the composition of educated scribes associated with Jerusalem's royal court. It has been long recognized that there are very striking similarities between the distinctive religious and legal requirements of Deuteronomy and the account of the major religious reform carried out by King Josiah in 622 BCE. That reform had been inspired by the discovery in the Temple of a "scroll of the Teaching" (Heb "torah") (2 Kings 22.8). Josiah's reform restricted all sacrificial worship of God to Jerusalem and removed foreign elements from the system of worship (technically, the "cult"); it culminated in the celebration of the first nationally centralized Passover at the Temple in Jerusalem (2 Kings chs 22–23). So strongly do these royal initiatives correspond to the distinctive requirements of Deuteronomy that scholars have long identified the "scroll of the Teaching" discovered in Josiah's Temple as Deuteronomy, and thus have assigned the book a 7th-century date.

Josiah's reform, with some form of Deuteronomy as its catalyst, was much more a revolution than a simple return to older forms of worship, as the book of Kings suggests. Previously, it was entirely legitimate to sacrifice to God throughout the land, as did Abraham at Shechem and Bethel (Gen. 12.7–8); Jacob at Bethel (Gen. 35.1–7); Samuel at Mizpah, Ramah, Gilgal, and Bethlehem (1 Sam. 7.9, 17; 9.11–14; 10.8; 16.1–5); and Elijah upon Mount Carmel (1 Kings 18.20–46). Indeed, even earlier biblical law, associated with the revelation at Sinai, stipulated that God would grant blessing "in every place where I [God] cause My name to be mentioned" (Exod. 20.21). Deuteronomy challenged that older norm, prohibiting sacrifice "at any [or, every] place" and restricting it to a single site, understood to be Jerusalem (Deut. 12.13–14). It is therefore striking that Deuteronomy presents itself as both an explication of the prior covenant (1.1–5) and as a supplement to it (28.69). Deuteronomy justifies itself in two ways, yet neither description acknowledges the extent to which Deuteronomy actually challenges and revises earlier law.

The historical background of Josiah's reforms was the increasing threat of imperial domination. The Northern Kingdom of Israel had fallen under the Neo-Assyrian invasion a scant century before (722 BCE; 2 Kings ch 17). Continuing Assyrian incursions down the coastal littoral had all but reduced Judah to a rump-state (2 Kings 18.13). In a desperate bid to preserve the nation's autonomy, Hezekiah had already made a pact with Assyria (2 Kings 18.13–18). Subsequently, Judah's political and religious independence seemed to hover uncertainly between the threats presented by Assyria and resurgent Babylon (2 Kings 20.12–15). The resulting military allegiances led to religious syncretism, as Judean officials introduced various foreign forms of worship into the Temple (2 Kings 16.10–20; 21.1–6).

In this context, Josiah's religious reforms represented an important bid for Judean cultural, political, and religious autonomy. The monarch extended his reforms into the area of the former Northern Kingdom of Israel and thus implicitly into territory under Assyrian control (2 Kings 23.15–20). Deuteronomy, apparently written sometime during this historical crisis, likewise reflects the desire to preserve Judean cultural and religious integrity. Its authors had the conviction that older conventions of worship and social organization were no longer viable. If the religion of YHVH was to survive the crisis, renewal and adaptation were necessary.

Deuteronomy's legal corpus (chs 12–26) provides a comprehensive program for cultural renewal. It addresses worship; the festival calendar; the major institutions of public life (justice, kingship, priesthood, prophecy); criminal, family, and civil law; and ethics. The law is presented as a covenant between God and nation, which the people take an oath to uphold, upon penalty of sanctions, while maintaining unconditional loyalty to their God. That covenant structure closely corresponds to the Neo-Assyrian state treaties that have been recovered from this period, the most famous of which is the Vassal Treaty of Esarhaddon (VTE) (672 BCE). At a number of points, the authors of Deuteronomy seem consciously to have patterned their covenant after this treaty tradition, which they could have known either directly or in Aramaic translation. From this perspective, Deuteronomy represents a counter-treaty: Its authors turned the weapon of Assyrian imperialism into a bid for Judean independence, shifting its oath of loyalty from the Assyrian overlord to their divine sovereign.

Thus tutored in international treaty conventions, the authors of Deuteronomy elsewhere reveal their knowledge of two additional important literary genres from the ancient Near East: the legal collection (15.1–18 n.; 17.8–13 n., 14–20 n.; 22.13–23.1 n.) and wisdom literature (1.13 n.; 4.2 n.). Moreover, they also employed a convention of authorship familiar in their time. They did not directly attach their name to their composition or write in their own voice. Instead, they attributed their composition to a prestigious figure from the past. By employing "Moses" as their spokesperson, they established a link with tradition at precisely the time when tradition, for the sake of survival, had to be transformed. This convention of ascribing a text to an ancient personage, called "pseudepigraphy," is well known in the literature of the Second Temple period; examples include *Jubilees*, *4 Ezra*, the *Testament of Abraham*, and (among the Dead Sea Scrolls) the *Temple Scroll*.

The Layers of Tradition

DEUTERONOMY PRESERVES SEVERAL LAYERS of tradition: The structure of three different discourses with an appendix already suggests a process of literary growth. That growth is closely connected to the gradual formation of the Hebrew Bible. To appreciate what is involved, it helps to imagine the time before there was an assembled, complete Bible as we now know it.

(1) When Deuteronomy was first promulgated, it would not have been part of any larger whole. Instead, it would have stood by itself as a "scroll of the torah" (i.e., the "scroll of the Teaching" in 2 Kings 22.8). It would have consisted primarily of some form of most of the laws of chs 12–26, framed by a relatively simple introduction and conclusion. This form of Deuteronomy presented itself as a treaty concluded between the nation and its God in a formal ceremony whereby each citizen took an oath of loyalty under penalty of strict sanctions (28.1–46). This was very likely the preexilic form of Deuteronomy.

(2) At a later stage, presumably sometime during the exile (586–538 BCE), Deuteronomy would have been incorporated into the Deuteronomistic History (Joshua through 2 Kings) to serve as its introduction. At this point, the Deuteronomistic (D) editors would have given the book its present literary frame (1.1–4.40, chs 31–34), while also adding to the legal corpus, selectively tying its promises or expectations to the later historical material (see 12.8 n.). Expansions in Deuteronomy that reflect the Babylonian exile may derive from this stage (i.e., 4.25–31; 28.47–56; 30.1–10).

(3) At a still later point, in the postexilic period, Priestly (P) editors appended Deuteronomy to the nascent Torah, to serve as its conclusion. Ironically, the decision to conclude the Pentateuch with Deuteronomy interrupted and delayed the overall narrative plot of Genesis through Numbers, which reaches its climax in an account of the conquest of the land. This narrative climax was delayed until Joshua.

The placement of Deuteronomy between the larger literary units of the other Pentateuchal material and the Deuteronomistic History makes an important theological statement. The Pentateuchal story of the promise of the land to the patriarchs, the enslavement in Egypt, the exodus, and the wilderness wandering now ends with Moses' death in Deuteronomy's last chapter (ch 34), which brings to a close both the book and the Torah. But that formal conclusion now separates not only Moses but also the reader from access to the land whose covenantal promise was the point of departure for the entire narrative (Gen. 12.1). Early on, from the vantage point of the Judean hills, Abram viewed the panorama of that promised land, as it extended in every direction of the compass (Gen. 13.14–17). But at the end of his life he was constrained to bargain for a small plot of land where he might bury his wife, Sarah (Gen. 23.1–20), poignant testimony that Abraham never gained full possession of the land promised him. So too, now, closing the circle, does the Torah conclude with a panorama that symbolizes dislocation and loss, as Moses looks out over Canaan from the heights of Mount Pisgah. Prohibited from entering the very promised land to which he successfully led his people, he finds his only access in that forlorn prospect. Like Abraham, Moses saw the promised land stretched out before him, but he would never possess it. Looking into the land from the outside without possession of it thus forms a literary and theological inclusio for the Pentateuchal narrative.

As with Abraham and Moses, so, too, the reader. Ancient editors have deliberately defined the Torah as a literary unit so as, first, to accommodate the addition of Deuteronomy and, second, to sever it from its logically expected fulfillment. The possession of the land is diverted instead into the next literary unit, which is to say, into the future. So profound a reconfiguration both of the patriarchal promise and of the overall plot is conceivable only in light of the historical experience of exile, which profoundly called the possession of the land into question. Had possession of the land remained central to the covenant during the exile, Israelite religion would have collapsed. By concluding the Torah with Deuteronomy and not Joshua, the fulfillment of the Torah is defined as obedience to the requirements of covenantal law rather than the acquisition of a finite possession.

The Transformation of Deuteronomy in the Second Temple Period

IN BIBLICAL NARRATIVE, "THIS BOOK OF TEACHING" (TORAH) crosses the symbolic geographic divide of the Jordan, carried, in the Ark of the Covenant, upon the shoulders of the Levitical priests (Deut. 31.25–26; Josh. 3.14–17). So did the text of Deuteronomy cross the historical divide of the Babylonian exile, borne on the shoulders of the multiple Jewish communities that survived the exile and that developed their distinct identities thereafter. This crucial transition from the First Temple to the Second Temple periods, from preexilic Israelite religion to postexilic Jewish religion, represents a major pivot in the history of Israelite literature, thought, and belief. The wrenching force of that transition, as institutions and assumptions underwent profound transformations, created "stress fractures" in the text of Deuteronomy. In many cases, preexilic religious and legal norms became unintelligible to these postexilic communities. Therefore in the process of teaching and translating Deuteronomy, they were forced to translate not only the language of the text but also its ideas: from one language into another, from one historical period into another, from one set of assumptions into another. Sometimes this overlay of postexilic ideas may interfere with understanding the original meaning of the text, even though that overlay now represents the conventional way that Deuteronomy has come to be read and understood. Such cases require attention in the annotations.

As a broader model for understanding such issues, it is helpful to view the religion of Israel reflected by Deuteronomy in the preexilic period as in many ways a "Near Eastern" religion.

This applies preeminently to the original theology of the text, which, like all religions of its time and place, viewed its god as presiding over a "divine council" of lesser deities (5.7 n.; 6.4 n.). From this perspective, texts like the Shema called for exclusive loyalty to God, without thereby denying the existence of other deities, just as Near Eastern treaties required that a vassal swear allegiance to a single political monarch (6.4–9 n.). But once radical monotheism became the Jewish norm in the Second Temple period, under the influence of exilic prophecy, the original "Israelite" view gradually became "foreign" and unintelligible. The Shema could only be understood as affirming the later "truth" of Jewish monotheism. This authentically Israelite religious language seems to have become so alien that the Hebrew text was "corrected" in several cases to bring it into conformity with later Jewish theology (32.8 n; 32.43 n.).

The same issue applies to law. In certain cases, the preexilic authors of Deuteronomy clearly followed Near Eastern procedures. For example, they required the immediate, summary execution of those disloyal to God, as if under the emergency conditions of martial law (13.10 n.). In the Second Temple period, however, this breach of Deuteronomy's own requirement for due process (17.2–7 n.) was understandably seen as contradicting the norms of Jewish law! The text was therefore read and taught as if the requirement for execution were to take place only after the due process that, in fact, it originally bypassed. As a next step, this originally oral legal interpretation of the law was introduced into the text of the law, when Deuteronomy was translated into Greek for the Jewish community of Alexandria (in the LXX, ca. 225 BCE; see 13.10 n.). The conscientious translator could do no less, since that revision of the law was what the law "had" to mean, lest the Torah here contradict Jewish law!

Just as the LXX later updates the Hebrew in light of the Jewish law of its time, elsewhere the reverse may hold true. On occasion, the Greek version retains classical views of preexilic Israelite religion that have been updated or corrected in the standardized Masoretic Text (MT) of the Bible (see nn. at 28.69; 32.8; 32.43). In such cases, the LXX or the Dead Sea Scrolls may open a window into the original meaning of a passage that has been lost in the MT. The commentary will therefore take these ancient textual "witnesses" to the text into account, in the hope of recovering what Deuteronomy's earlier authors sought to say. Since the NJPS translation follows the Masoretic Hebrew version, which is familiar from synagogue worship, it should simply be pointed out that these additional versions are themselves part of Jewish history. Because the LXX was later accepted as the Bible of the Church, it is often no longer recognized that it was a Jewish translation, prepared for the thriving Jewish community of Alexandria. In translating the Bible into their living language of Greek, that community saw the Torah as also telling their story. Thus, where Deuteronomy's Hebrew refers to the "horror" of foreign invasion as punishment for national wrongdoing, the LXX reinterprets that punishment as the contemporary experience of "diaspora" (28.25 n.). The multiple Judaisms of the Second Temple period each had their own way of reading Deuteronomy, and thereby understanding themselves as being addressed by Moses in his oration.

Deuteronomy and Interpretation

DEUTERONOMY REWARDS THE ATTENTION of contemporary readers and thinkers, whether religiously committed or secular, whether Jewish or non-Jewish. The modernity of Deuteronomy is that it does not permit itself to be read literally or passively. It challenges its readers actively to confront the problem of the relation between divine revelation and human interpretation, even as it breaks down the conventional boundaries between Scripture and tradition. It makes paradox central to its structure. As the book narrates the story of its formation, it also anticipates its prior existence as a complete literary work (31.1–34.12 n.). Interpretation is directly and indirectly a theme of Deuteronomy (1.5 n.). At many points, the authors of

Deuteronomy reinterpret earlier laws and narratives (6.1–3 n.). Moreover, the process of the book's editing intentionally preserves conflicting perspectives on a full range of key issues central to Israelite religion: on whether the revelation of the Decalogue at Sinai/Horeb was direct or required the mediation of Moses (5.5 n.); on the stature of Moses relative to other prophets (34.10 n.); on the nature of divine punishment for sin (5.9–10 nn.; 7.10 n.); on whether God rules as head of a pantheon or is the only God who exists (see nn. at 4.15–31, 35; and 32.8); and even on Deuteronomy's own setting in time and place (see nn. at 1.1; 2.12; and 3.11). As with many other biblical texts, there is no facile "air-brushing" away of this interplay of perspectives, which reflects an ongoing ancient debate about fundamental religious assumptions. There is finally, for Deuteronomy, no access to God in the covenant without joining this debate. The reader of Deuteronomy must become, like the authors of Deuteronomy, an interpreter.

Outline and Structure of Deuteronomy

I. The first discourse of Moses (1.1–4.43)
  A. Editorial headnote (1.1–5)
  B. Historical review (1.6–3.29)
  C. Exhortation to obey the Torah (4.1–40)
  D. Appendix: cities of refuge in Transjordan (4.41–43)

II. The second discourse of Moses (4.44–28.68)
  A. Introduction (4.44–49)
  B. The revelation of the Decalogue at Sinai/Horeb (5.1–30)
  C. Preamble to the laws: the requirement of loyalty to God (6.1–11.32)
    1. Validation of Mosaic instruction as revealed upon Horeb (6.1–3)
    2. A sermon on the first commandment of the Decalogue (6.4–25)
    3. The war of conquest (7.1–26)
    4. The temptation to pride and self-sufficiency in the land (8.1–20)
    5. The already broken and renewed covenant (9.1–10.11)
    6. Obedience as the condition for prosperity in the land (10.12–11.32)
  D. The legal corpus (12.1–26.15)
    1. Centralization and purification of sacrificial worship (12.1–13.1)
    2. The requirement for unconditional loyalty (13.2–19)
    3. The obligations of holiness (14.1–29)
    4. Remission of debts and manumission of slaves (15.1–18)
    5. Sacrifice of firstlings (15.19–23)
    6. The festival calendar (16.1–17)
    7. Laws of public officials (16.18–18.22)
      a. The organization of justice (16.18–17.13)
      b. The law of the king (17.14–20)
      c. The Levitical priesthood (18.1–8)
      d. The Mosaic prophet (18.9–22)
    8. Cities of refuge (19.1–13)
    9. Boundary markers (19.14)
    10. The integrity of the judicial system (19.15–21)
    11. Rules for waging holy war (20.1–20)
    12. Atonement for an unsolved murder (21.1–9)
    13. Miscellaneous criminal, civil, and family laws (21.10–25.19)
    14. Concluding liturgies (26.1–15)

- E. Formal conclusion: the reciprocity of the covenant (26.16–19)
- F. Ceremonies at Shechem upon entry to the land (27.1–26; cf. 11.29–32)
- G. The consequences of obedience or disobedience: blessing or curse (28.1–68)

III. The third discourse of Moses: the ratification ceremony for the covenant on the plains of Moab (28.69–30.20)

- A. Editorial heading: the relation between Moab and Horeb (28.69)
- B. Didactic review of Israel's history (29.1–8)
- C. Imprecation to ensure loyalty to the covenant (29.9–28)
- D. Reassurance of restoration (30.1–10)
- E. The accessibility of Torah (30.11–14)
- F. The necessity of choice (30.15–20)

IV. The death of Moses and the formation of the Torah (31.1–34.12)

- A. Moses makes arrangements for his death (31.1–29)
- B. The Song of Moses (31.30–32.44)
- C. Double conclusion to the Song (32.45–47)
- D. Moses commanded to die (32.48–52)
- E. The Blessing of Moses (33.1–29)
- F. The death of Moses (34.1–12)

[BERNARD M. LEVINSON]

DEVARIM דברים

1 These are the words that Moses addressed to all Israel on the
other side of the Jordan.—[a]Through the wilderness, in the Arabah near Suph, between Paran and Tophel, Laban, Hazeroth, and
Di-zahab, 2 it is eleven days from Horeb to Kadesh-barnea by the
Mount Seir route.—3 It was in the fortieth year, on the first day of
the eleventh month, that Moses addressed the Israelites in accordance with the instructions that the LORD had given him for them,
4 after he had defeated Sihon king of the Amorites, who dwelt in
Heshbon, and King Og of Bashan, who dwelt at Ashtaroth [and[b]]

a *The rest of this verse and v. 2 are unclear; cf. v. 19 and Num. 33.16–36.*
b *Cf. Josh. 12.4; 13.12, 31.*

1.1–4.43: The first discourse of Moses. This first of Deut.'s three discourses has two subsections: an historical retrospective (1.6–3.29) and a sermon on the importance of obeying Torah (4.1–40). An editorial headnote (1.1–5) and appendix (4.41–43) frame the discourse. **1.1–5: Editorial headnote.** Refers to Moses in the third person, attributes the book to him, and locates the book historically and geographically. **1:** *On the other side of the Jordan,* designating the land east of the Jordan River (Transjordan), where the Israelites have stopped, awaiting entry to the land. That geographical frame of reference places the speaker west of the Jordan and thus already in Canaan. According to the narrative line, however, the Israelites have not yet reached the promised land and Moses never does. From this and similar anachronisms, a small number of medieval Jewish commentators already recognized that not all of the Torah could be attributed to Moses (see also 2.12 n.; 3.11 n.); this is the modern consensus as well. *The Arabah,* the rift valley that includes the Jordan River and stretches south from the Dead Sea through Eilat (biblical Elath, see Map no. 6) and the Red Sea into Africa. The places mentioned cannot be identified with certainty. **2:** *Eleven days* implies a scathing indictment of the nation. As a result of their rebellion in the desert (Num. chs 13–14), it actually took them thirty-eight years, eight months, and twenty days to reach this point after they first broke camp (Num. 10.11). *Horeb* (Exod. 3.1; 17.6; 33.6) is Deut.'s term for the mount of revelation. "(Mount) Sinai," in contrast, is the more standard term used by the J and P writers elsewhere in the Torah (see Exod. 19.11; 34.29); it occurs in Deut. only in the poetry of 33.2. **4:** Num. 21.21–35. **5:** *Expound* the Heb seems intentionally ambiguous about whether Moses here proclaims new religious teachings, not previously heard, or

Edrei. 5 On the other side of the Jordan, in the land of Moab,
Moses undertook to expound this Teaching. He said:
6 The LORD our God spoke to us at Horeb, saying: You have
stayed long enough at this mountain. 7 Start out and make your
way to the hill country of the Amorites and to all their neighbors in the Arabah, the hill country, the Shephelah,[a] the Negeb,
the seacoast, the land of the Canaanites,[b] and the Lebanon, as
far as the Great River, the river Euphrates. 8 See, I place the land
at your disposal. Go, take possession of the land that the LORD
swore to your fathers, Abraham, Isaac, and Jacob, to assign to
them and to their heirs after them.
9 Thereupon I said to you, "I cannot bear the burden of you by
myself. 10 The LORD your God has multiplied you until you are
today as numerous as the stars in the sky.—11 May the LORD,
the God of your fathers, increase your numbers a thousandfold,
and bless you as He promised you.—12 How can I bear unaided
the trouble of you, and the burden, and the bickering! 13 Pick
from each of your tribes men who are wise, discerning, and experienced, and I will appoint them as your heads." 14 You answered me and said, "What you propose to do is good." 15 So
I took your tribal leaders, wise and experienced men, and appointed them heads over you: chiefs of thousands, chiefs of
hundreds, chiefs of fifties, and chiefs of tens, and officials for
your tribes. 16 I charged your magistrates at that time as follows,
"Hear out your fellow men, and decide justly between any man
and a fellow Israelite or a stranger. 17 You shall not be partial in
judgment: hear out low and high alike. Fear no man, for judgment is God's. And any matter that is too difficult for you, you
shall bring to me and I will hear it." 18 Thus I instructed you, at
that time, about the various things that you should do.
19 We set out from Horeb and traveled the great and terrible
wilderness that you saw, along the road to the hill country of
the Amorites, as the LORD our God had commanded us. When

a Others "Lowland." *b I.e., Phoenicia.*

simply explicates material already proclaimed. *This Teaching,* Heb "this torah" (4.8, 44; 27.3, 8, 26; 28.58, 61; 29.20, 28; 30.10; 31.9, 11, 12; 32.46). The word designates not only the combination of ritual, civil, family, and ethical law found in chs 12–26, but also the religious instructions of chs 5–11. Here, as elsewhere in Deut., the reference is not to the entire Torah, but specifically to Deut. itself (cf. 2 Kings 14.5–6 n.).

1.6–3.29: Historical review. Moses rehearses the exodus, revelation at Horeb, and rebellion in the desert for the generation who arose after these events and did not directly witness them, so that they may understand what brought them to the present moment. At a number of points, this narrative diverges from that of Exod.–Num. **6:** The original of the divine command quoted has not been preserved (cf. Num. ch 10). **7:** *Amorites,* as at Gen. 15.16, is used generically for the family of nations who are the original inhabitants of Canaan, rather than for one specific nation (contrast Gen. 15.19–21; Exod. 3.8, 17). *The Shephelah* is the region of foothills between the hill country on the east and the *seacoast* on the west. *The Negeb* is the semi-arid region south of the hill country. *Great River:* The ideal borders of the Israelite empire extended to the *Euphrates* (Gen. 15.18), the northern limit of David's conquests according to 2 Sam. 8.3. **8:** *See ... at your disposal:* With this binding oral proclamation, God symbolically displays the land and transfers its legal title to Israel (similarly, Gen. 13.14–15).

1.9–18: Leadership institutionalized. This account combines and reinterprets two previous accounts of the creation of a military-judicial system to share the burden of leadership (compare vv. 9–12 with Num. 11.14–17 and vv. 13–17 with Exod. 18.13–27). This new version places the institutionalization of leadership after the departure from Sinai rather than before it and omits the important advisory role of Jethro, Moses' non-Israelite father-in-law (contrast Exod. ch 18). **10:** *Stars in the sky,* thus fulfilling the promises to the ancestors (Gen. 15.5; 22.17; 26.4; Exod. 32.13). **11:** *God of your fathers:* Deut.'s normal phrase is "the LORD your/our God" (i.e., vv. 6, 10, 19–21; 6.1, 4, 10). This departure from that formula ties this new generation to its past by recalling God's earlier promises (Gen. 26.24; 32.10; Exod. 3.6). **13:** *Wise* (contrast Exod. 18.21), an attribute regularly stressed by Deut. (4.6; 32.29), suggesting the influence of wisdom literature upon its authors. *Experienced,* lit. "knowing," continuing the emphasis upon wisdom as a criterion for leadership. **16:** *Stranger,* better, "resident alien," referring to a non-Israelite who lives in the community without title to land and who is therefore economically vulnerable. Deut. insists upon a single law in civil and religious matters that applies to Israelite and non-Israelite alike (5.14; 10.18–19; 14.29; 16.11; 24.14, 17, 19–21). **17:** Similarly, 16.18–20.

1.19–46: From Horeb to Kadesh: A retelling, with significant variations,

we reached Kadesh-barnea, [20] I said to you, "You have come to the hill country of the Amorites which the LORD our God is giving to us. [21] See, the LORD your God has placed the land at your disposal. Go up, take possession, as the LORD, the God of your fathers, promised you. Fear not and be not dismayed."

[22] Then all of you came to me and said, "Let us send men ahead to reconnoiter the land for us and bring back word on the route we shall follow and the cities we shall come to." [23] I approved of the plan, and so I selected twelve of your men, one from each tribe. [24] They made for the hill country, came to the wadi Eshcol, and spied it out. [25] They took some of the fruit of the land with them and brought it down to us. And they gave us this report: "It is a good land that the LORD our God is giving to us."

[26] Yet you refused to go up, and flouted the command of the LORD your God. [27] You sulked[a] in your tents and said, "It is because the LORD hates us that He brought us out of the land of Egypt, to hand us over to the Amorites to wipe us out. [28] [b]What kind of place[b] are we going to? Our kinsmen have taken the heart out of us, saying, 'We saw there a people stronger and taller than we, large cities with walls sky-high, and even Anakites.'"

[29] I said to you, "Have no dread or fear of them. [30] None other than the LORD your God, who goes before you, will fight for you, just as He did for you in Egypt before your very eyes, [31] and in the wilderness, where you saw how the LORD your God carried you, as a man carries his son, all the way that you traveled until you came to this place. [32] Yet for all that, you have no faith in the LORD your God, [33] who goes before you on your journeys—to scout the place where you are to encamp—in fire by night and in cloud by day, in order to guide you on the route you are to follow."

[34] When the LORD heard your loud complaint, He was angry. He vowed: [35] Not one of these men, this evil generation, shall see the good land that I swore to give to your fathers—[36] none except Caleb son of Jephunneh; he shall see it, and to him and his descendants will I give the land on which he set foot, because he remained loyal to the LORD.

[37] Because of you the LORD was incensed with me too, and He said: You shall not enter it either. [38] Joshua son of Nun, who attends you, he shall enter it. Imbue him with strength, for he shall allot it to Israel. [39] Moreover, your little ones who you said would be carried off, your children who do not yet know good from bad, they shall enter it; to them will I give it and they shall possess it. [40] As for you, turn about and march into the wilderness by the way of the Sea of Reeds.

[41] You replied to me, saying, "We stand guilty before the LORD. We will go up now and fight, just as the LORD our God

of the spies' reconnaissance of the land (Num. ch 13), the people's complaining of God's inability to fulfill the promises made to Israel's ancestors (Num. 14.1–38), and the abortive attempt to penetrate Canaan from the south despite the divine command not to do so (Num. 14.39–45; cf. 21.1–3). **28:** *Anakites,* see Num. 13.22, 28, 33 n. **30:** Exod. 14.14. **33:** *Fire ... cloud,* see Exod. 13.21–22 nn. **34–36:** See Num. 14.28–30. **37:** Here Moses is not punished for his own sin (contrast Num. 20.10–13; 27.12–23), but instead vicariously bears the punishment due Israel for its sin (see 3.24–28).

a Precise meaning of Heb. uncertain. *b-b Lit. "Where."*

2.1–25: The circuit via Transjordan. 1–8a: Num. 20.14–21. From Kadesh Israel turned south through the Arabah to the Gulf of Aqaba in order to go around Edom (Num. 21.4; cf. 33.47–49). **4:** *Descendants of Esau,* see Gen. 36.1. **8a:** *Elath,* see 1 Kings 9.26. *Ezion-geber,* see Num. 33.35. **8b–25:** Num. 21.4–20, significantly revised. Turning along the brook Zered (modern Wadi el-Hasa), which formed Edom's southern boundary, Israel detoured through the wilderness of Moab toward the Amorite kingdom of Sihon. **9:** Moab and Ammon (v. 19) were traditionally related through Lot (Gen. 19.36–38). **10–12:** These vv. are slightly indented in the translation, setting them off from the rest of the passage so as to mitigate the anachronistic post-conquest perspective (see v. 12 n.). **10–11:** *Emim, Rephaim* (cf. v. 20; 3.11–13), names reflecting the legendary view that the aboriginal inhabitants of the land were fearsome giants. **12:** *Horites,* see Gen. 36.20–30 n. *As Israel did ... to possess:* Here the Israelite conquest of the land is represented as already having been completed, conflicting with the attribution to Moses and the narrative setting in Transjordan, prior to the conquest. The anachronism reflects the date of composition of this section (see 1.1 n.; 3.11 n.). **13:** *Wadi,* a winter stream that dries up in the summer.

commanded us." And you all girded yourselves with war gear
and recklessly[a] started for the hill country. 42 But the LORD said
to me, "Warn them: Do not go up and do not fight, since I am
not in your midst; else you will be routed by your enemies." 43 I
spoke to you, but you would not listen; you flouted the LORD's
command and willfully marched into the hill country. 44 Then
the Amorites who lived in those hills came out against you like
so many bees and chased you, and they crushed you at Hormah in Seir. 45 Again you wept before the LORD; but the LORD
would not heed your cry or give ear to you.

2 46 Thus, after you had remained at Kadesh [b]all that long
time,[b] 1 we marched back into the wilderness by the way
of the Sea of Reeds, as the LORD had spoken to me, and skirted
the hill country of Seir a long time.
2 Then the LORD said to me: 3 You have been skirting this hill
country long enough; now turn north. 4 And charge the people as follows: You will be passing through the territory of your
kinsmen, the descendants of Esau, who live in Seir. Though
they will be afraid of you, be very careful 5 not to provoke
them. For I will not give you of their land so much as a foot can
tread on; I have given the hill country of Seir as a possession
to Esau. 6 [c]What food you eat you shall obtain from them for
money; even the water you drink you shall procure from them
for money.[c] 7 Indeed, the LORD your God has blessed you in
all your undertakings. He has watched over your wanderings
through this great wilderness; the LORD your God has been
with you these past forty years: you have lacked nothing.
8 We then moved on, away from our kinsmen, the descendants of Esau, who live in Seir, away from the road of the Arabah,
away from Elath and Ezion-geber; and we marched on in the
direction of the wilderness of Moab. 9 And the LORD said to me:
Do not harass the Moabites or provoke them to war. For I will
not give you any of their land as a possession; I have assigned
Ar as a possession to the descendants of Lot.—
10 It was formerly inhabited by the Emim, a people great
and numerous, and as tall as the Anakites. 11 Like the
Anakites, they are counted as Rephaim; but the Moabites
call them Emim. 12 Similarly, Seir was formerly inhabited
by the Horites; but the descendants of Esau dispossessed
them, wiping them out and settling in their place, just
as Israel did in the land they were to possess, which the
LORD had given to them.—
13 Up now! Cross the wadi Zered!

a Meaning of Heb. uncertain. *b-b Lit. "many days, like the days that you remained."*
c-c Or "You may obtain food from them to eat for money; and you may also procure water from them to drink for money."

So we crossed the wadi Zered. [14] The time that we spent in travel from Kadesh-barnea until we crossed the wadi Zered was thirty-eight years, until that whole generation of warriors had perished from the camp, as the LORD had sworn concerning them. [15] Indeed, the hand of the LORD struck them, to root them out from the camp to the last man.

[16] When all the warriors among the people had died off, [17] the LORD spoke to me, saying: [18] You are now passing through the territory of Moab, through Ar. [19] You will then be close to the Ammonites; do not harass them or start a fight with them. For I will not give any part of the land of the Ammonites to you as a possession; I have assigned it as a possession to the descendants of Lot.—

> [20] It, too, is counted as Rephaim country. It was formerly inhabited by Rephaim, whom the Ammonites call Zamzummim, [21] a people great and numerous and as tall as the Anakites. The LORD wiped them out, so that [the Ammonites] dispossessed them and settled in their place, [22] as He did for the descendants of Esau who live in Seir, when He wiped out the Horites before them, so that they dispossessed them and settled in their place, as is still the case.[a] [23] So, too, with the Avvim who dwelt in villages in the vicinity of Gaza: the Caphtorim, who came from Crete,[b] wiped them out and settled in their place.—

[24] Up! Set out across the wadi Arnon! See, I give into your power Sihon the Amorite, king of Heshbon, and his land. Begin the occupation: engage him in battle. [25] This day I begin to put the dread and fear of you upon the peoples everywhere under heaven, so that they shall tremble and quake because of you whenever they hear you mentioned.

[26] Then I sent messengers from the wilderness of Kedemoth to King Sihon of Heshbon with an offer of peace, as follows, [27] "Let me pass through your country. I will keep strictly to the highway, turning off neither to the right nor to the left. [28] What food I eat you will supply for money, and what water I drink you will furnish for money; just let me pass through[c]— [29] as the descendants of Esau who dwell in Seir did for me, and the Moabites who dwell in Ar—that I may cross the Jordan into the land that the LORD our God is giving us."

[30] But King Sihon of Heshbon refused to let us pass through, because the LORD had stiffened his will and hardened his heart in order to deliver him into your power—as is now the case. [31] And the LORD said to me: See, I begin by placing Sihon and his land at your disposal. Begin the occupation; take possession of his land.

14: Fulfilling God's angry oath (1.34–35; Num. 14.28–30). Without the death of the generation of the exodus, here marked as accomplished, there can be no entry into the promised land. **15:** *Hand of the LORD,* thus indicating that they did not die merely of old age or natural causes. The imagery inverts the standard idea of holy war: God had turned against Israel rather than fighting on its behalf (32.30 n.; see 3.22; 7.1–5; 12.29–31; 20.1–20). **20:** Cf. vv. 10–11 n.; Gen. 14.5. **23:** *Caphtorim ... Crete* refers to the conquest of the coastal plain by Sea Peoples such as Philistines shortly after 1200 BCE (see Gen. 10.14; Amos 9.7). See essay "History of Israel," pp. 2107–19. **24:** *Arnon,* see Num. 21.13–14. **26–37:** The victory over *Sihon,* whose capital was at Heshbon. The earlier source in Num. 21.21–32 is here supplemented and revised. **30:** See Exod. 4.21 n.

a *Lit. "until this day."* *b* *Heb. "Caphtor."* *c* *Lit. "with my feet."*

34: *Doomed,* see 7.2 n. **37:** The river *Jabbok* makes a wide bend south and thus forms the western border of Ammon (3.16) (see Map no. 1).

3.1–11: The victory over Bashan (Num. 21.33–35). **1:** *Edrei,* on the extreme southern border of *Bashan;* see Num. 21.33. **11:** The oversized bed of *Og,* one of the legendary *Rephaim* (2.10–11), was a "museum piece" in *Rabbah,* a city on the Ammonite border. The claim that this bed *is now* there places the historical perspective of the narrator, and thus of Deut.'s composition, long after the events here recounted (1.1 n.; 2.12 n.). A *cubit* was about approximately 45 cm (18 in), so the bed was 1.8 m (6 ft) wide and 4 m (13 ft) long. **12–22:** The allotment of tribal territories in Transjordan (Num. ch 32; Josh. ch 13).

32 Sihon with all his men took the field against us at Jahaz,
33 and the LORD our God delivered him to us and we defeated
him and his sons and all his men. 34 At that time we captured
all his towns, and we doomed[a] every town—men, women, and
children—leaving no survivor. 35 We retained as booty only
the cattle and the spoil of the cities that we captured. 36 From
Aroer on the edge of the Arnon valley, including the town[b] in
the valley itself, to Gilead, not a city was too mighty for us; the
LORD our God delivered everything to us. 37 But you did not
encroach upon the land of the Ammonites, all along the wadi
Jabbok and the towns of the hill country, just as the LORD our
God had commanded.

3 We made our way up the road toward Bashan, and King
Og of Bashan with all his men took the field against us at
Edrei. 2 But the LORD said to me: Do not fear him, for I am delivering him and all his men and his country into your power,
and you will do to him as you did to Sihon king of the Amorites,
who lived in Heshbon.
3 So the LORD our God also delivered into our power King
Og of Bashan, with all his men, and we dealt them such a blow
that no survivor was left. 4 At that time we captured all his
towns; there was not a town that we did not take from them:
sixty towns, the whole district of Argob, the kingdom of Og in
Bashan— 5 all those towns were fortified with high walls, gates,[c]
and bars—apart from a great number of unwalled towns. 6 We
doomed them as we had done in the case of King Sihon of
Heshbon; we doomed every town—men, women, and children— 7 and retained as booty all the cattle and the spoil of the
towns.
8 Thus we seized, at that time, from the two Amorite kings,
the country beyond the Jordan, from the wadi Arnon to Mount
Hermon— 9 Sidonians called Hermon Sirion, and the Amorites
call it Senir— 10 all the towns of the Tableland and the whole
of Gilead and Bashan as far as Salcah[d] and Edrei, the towns of
Og's kingdom in Bashan. 11 Only King Og of Bashan was left
of the remaining Rephaim. His bedstead, an iron bedstead, is
now in Rabbah of the Ammonites; it is nine cubits long and
four cubits wide, by [e-]the standard cubit![-e]
12 [f]And this is the land which we apportioned at that time:
The part from Aroer along the wadi Arnon, with part of the hill
country of Gilead and its towns, I assigned to the Reubenites
and the Gadites. 13 The rest of Gilead, and all of Bashan under

a *I.e., placed under* ḥerem, *which meant the annihilation of the population. Cf. note c at Num. 21.2; Josh. 6.24.*
b *Meaning of Heb. uncertain.*
c *I.e., two-leaf doors.*
d *Others "Salecah" or "Salchah."*
e-e *Lit. "by a man's forearm."*
f *Vv. 12–13 proceed from south to north; vv. 14–16 from north to south.*

Og's rule—the whole Argob district, all that part of Bashan
which is called Rephaim country—I assigned to the half-tribe
of Manasseh. 14 Jair son of Manasseh received the whole Argob
district (that is, Bashan) as far as the boundary of the Geshurites
and the Maacathites, and named it after himself: Havvoth-
jair[a]—as is still the case. 15 To Machir I assigned Gilead. 16 And
to the Reubenites and the Gadites I assigned the part from
Gilead down to the wadi Arnon, the middle of the wadi being
the boundary, and up to the wadi Jabbok, the boundary of the
Ammonites.

17[b] [We also seized] the Arabah, from the foot of the slopes of
Pisgah on the east, to the edge of the Jordan, and from Chinnereth down to the sea of the Arabah, the Dead Sea.

18 At that time I charged you,[c] saying, "The LORD your God
has given you this country to possess. You must go as shock-
troops, warriors all, at the head of your Israelite kinsmen.
19 Only your wives, children, and livestock—I know that you
have much livestock—shall be left in the towns I have assigned
to you, 20 until the LORD has granted your kinsmen a haven
such as you have, and they too have taken possession of the
land that the LORD your God is assigning them, beyond the Jordan. Then you may return each to the homestead that I have
assigned to him."

21 I also charged Joshua at that time, saying, "You have seen
with your own eyes all that the LORD your God has done to
these two kings; so shall the LORD do to all the kingdoms into
which you shall cross over. 22 Do not fear them, for it is the
LORD your God who will battle for you."

VA-'ETHANNAN ואתחנן

23 I pleaded with the LORD at that time, saying, 24 "O Lord GOD,
You who let Your servant see the first works of Your greatness
and Your mighty hand, You whose powerful deeds no god in
heaven or on earth can equal! 25 Let me, I pray, cross over and
see the good land on the other side of the Jordan, that good hill
country, and the Lebanon." 26 But the LORD was wrathful with
me on your account and would not listen to me. The LORD said
to me, "Enough! Never speak to Me of this matter again! 27 Go
up to the summit of Pisgah and gaze about, to the west, the
north, the south, and the east. Look at it well, for you shall not
go across yonder Jordan. 28 Give Joshua his instructions, and
imbue him with strength and courage, for he shall go across at
the head of this people, and he shall allot to them the land that
you may only see."

29 Meanwhile we stayed on in the valley near Beth-peor.

a I.e., "villages of Jair." *b Continuing vv. 8–10; cf. 4.47–49.*
c I.e., the two and a half tribes.

14: Num. 32.41. **17:** The territory included the eastern part of the Jordan Valley or Arabah. **22:** The whole story of the exodus, wilderness journey, and invasion of Canaan is governed by the conventions of holy war, whereby God is a divine warrior who engages in battle on behalf of Israel. **23–29:** Num. 27.12–23. **24:** *No god ... can equal:* The assertion of God's superior power, relative to other gods *in heaven,* assumes the existence of other gods (5.7 n; 6.4 n.; 32.8 n.; Exod. 15.11; Ps. 89.5–8). For the later perspective of monotheism, see 4.35 n. **26:** On the vicarious suffering of Moses, see 1.37 n. **27:** Mount *Pisgah,* see 34.1 n.

4 And now, O Israel, give heed to the laws and rules that I
am instructing you to observe, so that you may live to enter
and occupy the land that the LORD, the God of your fathers, is
giving you. 2 You shall not add anything to what I command
you or take anything away from it, but keep the commandments of the LORD your God that I enjoin upon you. 3 You saw
with your own eyes what the LORD did in the matter of Baal-
peor, that the LORD your God wiped out from among you every
person who followed Baal-peor; 4 while you, who held fast to
the LORD your God, are all alive today.
5 See, I have imparted to you laws and rules, as the LORD my
God has commanded me, for you to abide by in the land that
you are about to enter and occupy. 6 Observe them faithfully,
for that will be proof of your wisdom and discernment to other
peoples, who on hearing of all these laws will say, "Surely, that
great nation is a wise and discerning people." 7 For what great
nation is there that has a god so close at hand as is the LORD
our God whenever we call upon Him? 8 Or what great nation
has laws and rules as perfect as all this Teaching that I set before you this day?
9 But take utmost care and watch yourselves scrupulously,
so that you do not forget the things that you saw with your own
eyes and so that they do not fade from your mind as long as
you live. And make them known to your children and to your
children's children: 10 The day you stood before the LORD your
God at Horeb, when the LORD said to me, "Gather the people
to Me that I may let them hear My words, in order that they

4.1–40: Exhortation to obey the Torah. While preceding the Decalogue in narrative terms (5.6–18), this unit provides a historically later theological reflection upon it, focusing on the second commandment of the Decalogue (5.8–10) and broadening its significance. Admonitions to obedience (vv. 1, 40) frame the unit, which systematically contrasts: obedience (vv. 5–24)/disobedience (vv. 25–31); remembering/forgetting (vv. 9, 23); the LORD/other gods (vv. 7, 34); Israel's revealed Torah/the laws of other nations (vv. 8, 28); and God/idols (vv. 12–20). The central lesson is that the correct worship of God is aniconic: Images (whether of God or of objects in nature) should play no role in Israelite religion. This becomes so strong a theme that idolatry, in and of itself, is asserted to be the cause of the nation's exile from its land (vv. 25–31). The explicit reference to exile suggests that the unit is a late theological explanation for the Babylonian exile (586–538 BCE). The focus on idolatry as the basis for the divine punishment diverges significantly from the perspective elsewhere that views failure to heed "all his [God's] commandments and decrees" as the cause of exile (28.15; cf. 28.1, 45, 58–59).

4.1–4: The incident at Baal-peor (Num. 25.1–9) **is recalled** to emphasize the importance of fidelity to God and the dire consequences of worshipping other gods. **2:** This admonition not to alter the Torah, whether by addition or subtraction (cf. 13.1), parallels similar admonitions in wisdom literature (Prov. 30.6; Eccl. 3.14; 12.12–13; Sir. 42.21; cf. Revelation 22.18–19). It seems to originate in ancient Near Eastern literature (Egyptian wisdom literature; Babylonian law codes; Neo-Assyrian state treaties; cf. 1 Macc. 8.30). **3:** *Followed,* see 6.14 n. **5–8:** The Torah as Israel's "wisdom." The author here challenges the prevailing Near Eastern idea that wisdom was a royal prerogative. Whereas, for example, the ancient Babylonian Laws of Hammurabi (ca. 1755 BCE) praised the "just decisions" of its "wise" king (cols 47.1; 4.7), here it is rather the nation Israel who will be internationally renowned as "wise" for its "just" laws (vv. 6, 8). See also 29.28 n. and 30.11–14 n. **7–8:** Israel is distinguished both by its God and by its law: The two ideas are interlocked. **7:** God is *close at hand,* both in having entered history on behalf of Israel and in revealing His will as Torah (30.14). **8:** The laws are *perfect* (better "righteous"), not only in their morality but also as embodying the will of God. This Israelite idea of law as divine revelation diverges from Near Eastern views of law as royal wisdom (see 5.1–30 n.).

4.9–14: The revelation at Horeb (Exod. chs 19–20 [in which the location of revelation is referred to as Sinai]; Deut. ch 5) is recalled in order to instruct the present generation, who did not experience it. **9:** The paired injunctions not to *forget* the powerful experience of God's actions and to educate *your children,* so that the past becomes "present" also to them, represent a prominent aim of Deut.: to overcome the historical distance of the past and to maintain it as a source of identity (vv. 23, 25; 6.2, 7, 20–25; 8.11; 9.7; 31.13; 32.18). *You saw,* and the following *you stood* (v. 10) are highly paradoxical assertions. Neither is literally true: The actual generation of the exodus had died off and been replaced by this new one, who had experienced none of the events here being recounted (2.14–15 nn.). This paradoxical structure of thought, whereby Moses addresses those who had not witnessed the events as if they had, while insisting that they inculcate the events to posterity, is central to Deut.'s theology of history (5.3–4, 20; 11.7; 29.13–14). This

may learn to revere Me as long as they live on earth, and may so teach their children." 11 You came forward and stood at the foot of the mountain. The mountain was ablaze with flames to the very skies, dark with densest clouds. 12 The LORD spoke to you out of the fire; you heard the sound of words but perceived no shape—nothing but a voice. 13 He declared to you the covenant that He commanded you to observe, the Ten Commandments; and He inscribed them on two tablets of stone. 14 At the same time the LORD commanded me to impart to you laws and rules for you to observe in the land that you are about to cross into and occupy.

15 For your own sake, therefore, be most careful—since you saw no shape when the LORD your God spoke to you at Horeb out of the fire—16 not to act wickedly and make for yourselves a sculptured image in any likeness whatever: the form of a man or a woman, 17 the form of any beast on earth, the form of any winged bird that flies in the sky, 18 the form of anything that creeps on the ground, the form of any fish that is in the waters below the earth. 19 And when you look up to the sky and behold the sun and the moon and the stars, the whole heavenly host, you must not be lured into bowing down to them or serving them. These the LORD your God allotted to other peoples everywhere under heaven; 20 but you the LORD took and brought out of Egypt, that iron blast furnace, to be His very own people, as is now the case.

21 Now the LORD was angry with me on your account and swore that I should not cross the Jordan and enter the good land that the LORD your God is assigning you as a heritage.

develops further in postbiblical Judaism to the idea that all Jews, past, present, and future, were at Sinai (see *b. Shevu.* 39a, which defines the group adjured at Sinai/Horeb as including "the coming generations, and proselytes who were later to be proselytised"). Because of their sharp divergence from the narrative setting, these vv. may well represent a different source or literary layer in Deut. **10:** *My words,* here, the Decalogue ("Ten Commandments"; v. 13; 10.4). Elsewhere, however, the reference to God's "words" designates the legal corpus of chs 12–26 (12.28). *Revere* (lit. "fear"): This important Deuteronomic characterization for the proper relation between the nation and God seems to originate with wisdom literature (Prov. 1.7; Job 28.28) and refers to obedience. **11:** The manifestation of a god ("theophany") was often associated with disturbances of nature in Ugaritic (Canaanite) literature (see 5.1–30 n.). This motif was taken over by Israelite writers and applied to God (Exod. 19.16–19; 20.15; Pss. 18.7–15; 29.3–9). **12:** *Shape* (also vv. 15; "likeness" vv. 16, 23, 25), directly alluding to the second commandment of the Decalogue (5.8 = Exod. 20.4). **13:** A subtle reinterpretation of Sinai: The specification of that event as one where God proclaimed the *Ten Commandments* occurs only here, at 10.4, and at Exod. 34.28. There is no special number of or name for the commandments (lit. "words") in Exod. chs 19–20 or Deut. ch 5. The rationale for *two tablets of stone* (as at 5.19) derives from ancient Near Eastern state treaties, whereby both sovereign and vassal would retain a separate copy of the treaty. The popular image of two arched tablets, each containing only part of the Decalogue, misunderstands that historical context.

4.15–31: Reinterpretation of the second commandment. The Decalogue concedes the existence of other gods, while prohibiting Israel from worshipping them (5.7; cf. 32.8; Exod. 15.11; Ps. 82.1). It then separately prohibits the making of images (5.8). The distinction between those two commandments is dissolved here. The existence of other gods is no longer conceivable; the sole focus is the prohibition against idols. Here and elsewhere (see v. 19 n.), key ideas in Deut. are reinterpreted from a later theological perspective; such passages therefore represent a later textual layer within Deut. that dates to the exilic period. **16b–19a:** This catalogue follows the order of creation in Gen. ch 1 in reverse order, consistent with an ancient scribal practice when quoting an earlier text. **18:** *Waters below the earth,* seas, rivers, and lakes. Ancient cosmology conceived the earth to be a disk floating on such waters (cf. Gen. 1.9). **19:** *Sun ... heavenly host:* This polemic against astral cults may reflect images derived from the Neo-Assyrian pantheon that were brought into the Jerusalem Temple by Manasseh but removed by Josiah (2 Kings 21.5; 23.4–5; Jer. 8.2). The idea of idols or of celestial phenomena literally being worshipped sharply distorts ancient Near Eastern religion, which regarded such phenomena as visible manifestations or emblems of a deity, not as themselves alive or divine. This polemic, with the idea that God *allotted* the celestial phenomena to other nations while reserving Israel as "his very own people" (v. 20; cf. 7.6 n.), reinterprets the earlier biblical idea that God, as head of the pantheon, assigned other nations to the supervision of lesser gods but retained Israel as "His allotment" (lit. "His very own possession"; 32.8–9 nn.). The author de-animates those gods, reducing them to lifeless celestial objects. **21:** See 1.37 n.

26: *Heaven ... witness,* similarly, 30.19; 31.28; 32.1; Isa. 1.2; 44.23; Pss. 69.35; 96.11. **27–28:** These vv. allude to the exile of conquered populations, a policy used effectively by the Assyrians and the Babylonians.

4.32–40: Continuation of the double focus on the uniqueness of God's revelation to Israel and of the covenant He made with the nation. This passage fits best in the historical context of the Babylonian exile (see v. 35 n.). **33:** This alludes to the normal expectation that no human can look directly upon God and survive (Gen. 16.13; 32.30; Exod. 3.6; 19.21; 33.20). **34:** *Prodigious acts ... portents* refers to the signs performed by Moses and Aaron in Egypt, including the plagues, to persuade Pharaoh to release Israel (Exod. 7.3; 8.19; 10.1, 2; 11.9, 10). **35:** *There is none beside Him:* This affirmation of full or radical monotheism (contrast v. 7; 5.7) corresponds to the thought of the contemporaneous Second Isaiah (Isa. 43.10–13; 44.6–8; 45.6–7, 22).

22 For I must die in this land; I shall not cross the Jordan. But
you will cross and take possession of that good land. 23 Take
care, then, not to forget the covenant that the LORD your God
concluded with you, and not to make for yourselves a sculptured image in any likeness, against which the LORD your God
has enjoined you. 24 For the LORD your God is a consuming
fire, an impassioned God.

25 When you have begotten children and children's children
and are long established in the land, should you act wickedly
and make for yourselves a sculptured image in any likeness,
causing the LORD your God displeasure and vexation, 26 I call
heaven and earth this day to witness against you that you shall
soon perish from the land that you are crossing the Jordan to
possess; you shall not long endure in it, but shall be utterly
wiped out. 27 The LORD will scatter you among the peoples, and
only a scant few of you shall be left among the nations to which
the LORD will drive you. 28 There you will serve man-made gods
of wood and stone, that cannot see or hear or eat or smell.

29 But if you search there for the LORD your God, you will
find Him, if only you seek Him with all your heart and soul—
30 when you are in distress because all these things have befallen you and, in the end, return to the LORD your God and
obey Him. 31 For the LORD your God is a compassionate God:
He will not fail you nor will He let you perish; He will not forget
the covenant which He made on oath with your fathers.

32 You have but to inquire about bygone ages that came
before you, ever since God created man on earth, from one
end of heaven to the other: has anything as grand as this ever
happened, or has its like ever been known? 33 Has any people
heard the voice of a god speaking out of a fire, as you have, and
survived? 34 Or has any god ventured to go and take for himself
one nation from the midst of another by prodigious acts, by
signs and portents, by war, by a mighty and an outstretched
arm and awesome power, as the LORD your God did for you
in Egypt before your very eyes? 35 [a]It has been clearly demonstrated to you[a] that the LORD alone is God; there is none
beside Him. 36 From the heavens He let you hear His voice to
discipline you; on earth He let you see His great fire; and from
amidst that fire you heard His words. 37 And because He loved
your fathers, He chose their heirs after them; He Himself,[b] in
His great might, led you out of Egypt, 38 to drive from your path
nations greater and more populous than you, to take you into
their land and assign it to you as a heritage, as is still the case.
39 Know therefore this day and keep in mind that the LORD

a-a Lit. "You have been shown to know."
b Lit. "With His face (or Presence)"; cf. note at Exod. 33.14.

alone is God in heaven above and on earth below; there is no other. 40 Observe His laws and commandments, which I enjoin upon you this day, that it may go well with you and your children after you, and that you may long remain in the land that the LORD your God is assigning to you for all time.

41 Then Moses set aside three cities on the east side of the Jordan 42 to which a manslayer could escape, one who unwittingly slew a fellow man without having been hostile to him in the past; he could flee to one of these cities and live: 43 Bezer, in the wilderness in the Tableland, belonging to the Reubenites; Ramoth, in Gilead, belonging to the Gadites; and Golan, in Bashan, belonging to the Manassites.

44 This is the Teaching that Moses set before the Israelites: 45 these are the decrees, laws, and rules that Moses addressed to the people of Israel, after they had left Egypt, 46 beyond the Jordan, in the valley at Beth-peor, in the land of King Sihon of the Amorites, who dwelt in Heshbon, whom Moses and the Israelites defeated after they had left Egypt. 47 They had taken possession of his country and that of King Og of Bashan—the two kings of the Amorites—which were on the east side of the Jordan 48 from Aroer on the banks of the wadi Arnon, as far as Mount Sion,[a] that is, Hermon; 49 also the whole Arabah on the east side of the Jordan, as far as the Sea of the Arabah, at the foot of the slopes of Pisgah.

5 Moses summoned all the Israelites and said to them: Hear, O Israel, the laws and rules that I proclaim to you this day! Study them and observe them faithfully!

a *Cf. "Sirion," 3.9.*

4.41–43: An appendix: the cities of refuge to be established in Transjordan (cf. Num. 35.9–15; Josh. 20.8). Since Deut.'s law concerned with these cities (ch 19) does not refer to this passage, these vv. are most likely an editorial appendix composed after the completion of ch 19. Similar disconnected appendices often appear in the Bible at the conclusion of longer literary units (e.g., Lev. ch 27), suggesting that Deut. 1.1–4.43 as a whole was added to 4.44ff.

4.44–28.68: The second discourse of Moses. 4.44–49: Introduction. Cf. 1.1–5. **44:** This v. is recited in synagogue during the Torah service; the original referent of "Torah" is Deut. (see 1.5 n.), though later Jewish tradition understands it as the entire Torah. **49:** *Sea of the Arabah,* the Dead Sea.

5.1–30: The revelation of the Ten Commandments at Sinai/Horeb. The Decalogue is distinctive in the context of ancient Near Eastern literature and religion, transforming the literary conventions of both theophany and law. In Ugaritic myth, for example, the manifestation of a god was accompanied by disturbances of nature like thunder, lightning, and earthquake. But the same phenomena here (Exod. 19.16–19; 20.15) simply provide the dramatic background for Israel's distinctive infusion of law into the older theophany tradition. Similarly, several ancient Mesopotamian legal collections (most famously, the Laws of Hammurabi, 1755 BCE) were attributed to a human monarch. King Hammurabi sought in his legal corpus to embody the cosmic principles of justice and equity. In the Decalogue, by contrast, law derives from God and represents divine will. As a result, law and ethics provide the foundation for the nation's covenantal relationship to God. This revision of Near Eastern literary convention is underscored by the markedly public nature of the divine revelation at Sinai/Horeb. Previously, neither theophany nor law was public and universally accessible. In this account, however, God reveals Himself to the whole nation, cutting across boundaries of gender, race, and class.

The literary form of the Decalogue is also significant. It differs from the casuistic "if [infraction]—then [punishment]" form standard to both biblical law (Exod. chs 21–23) and Near Eastern law. That form, which seeks to mete out appropriate punishment, nonetheless presupposes a status quo in which infraction of the law is inevitable. The Decalogue's prohibitions, in contrast, are "apodictic" (universal and absolute). The "thou shalt not" form in effect stipulates, "You must never!" The intent is to transform society by creating a moral community in which murder, theft, etc. cease to exist. Equally meaningful is the literary structure of the Decalogue, with one pentad of laws directed toward God and one toward the neighbor. Obedience to God's will (vv. 6–16) here demands active respect for the integrity of the neighbor (vv. 17–18). The Decalogue thus ties love of God inextricably together with love of neighbor: There is no separation of religious duties to God from moral commitments as a member of the divinely created community. Further, the direct address to the entire nation is grammatically unusual. It employs a singular form of "you," rather than the expected plural form, to stress that God directly addresses each former slave as an individual human being.

2 The LORD our God made a covenant with us at Horeb. 3 It
was not with our fathers that the LORD made this covenant, but
with us, the living, every one of us who is here today. 4 Face to
face the LORD spoke to you on the mountain out of the fire—5 I
stood between the LORD and you at that time to convey the
LORD's words to you, for you were afraid of the fire and did not
go up the mountain—saying:

The ch emphasizes that there is no access to God or revelation without mediation and interpretation (vv. 5, 25–29). The editing drives that point home. It preserves two mutually independent viewpoints about whether God spoke directly to the people, with them standing on the mountain (v. 4), or only through the mediation of Moses, while the people remained at the foot of the mountain (v. 5 n.). Similarly, there seems to be a disagreement about the terror involved in hearing the divine voice directly (vv. 21–22). That the editing of the ch preserves this play of perspectives requires the attentive reader to join that ancient debate about the nature of revelation.

5.1–5: Making the past present. **3:** *Not with our fathers ... but with us* contrasts literally with the earlier emphasis that the generation who experienced these events has now died off (2.14–15). The aim is to overcome the limits of historical time and place through participation in the covenant, which makes revelation "present" (see 4.9 n.; 29.13–14 n.). *Our fathers* may refer either to the exodus generation (2.14–15 nn.) or to the patriarchs Abraham, Isaac, and Jacob (1.11 n.). **5:** NJPS sets off the entire sentence (except for the final word) within dashes to suggest that it serves to clarify the preceding v. More likely, the statement presents an alternative perspective inconsistent with v. 4. *I stood between the LORD and you,* contrast "Face to face" (v. 4). *To convey the LORD's words to you,* contrast "Face to face the LORD spoke" (v. 4). *You ... did not go up the mountain* (lit. "up on the mountain") contradicts v. 4, "the LORD spoke to you on the mountain." *Saying* provides the original transition from the end of v. 4 directly to the Decalogue.

5.6–18: The Decalogue. The narrative of the Decalogue affirms that God wrote "Ten Words" or statements on two stone tablets and gave them to Moses following the revelation at Horeb (4.13; 10.4). The actual enumeration, however, of the text of the Decalogue into 'ten commandments' is complicated because there are more than ten verbs expressing commands. This is further complicated by v. 6, which is a divine self-introduction without any imperative verb and thus not an explicit command. Because of these ambiguities, three different divisions of the text emerged in ancient Judaism as shown in the chart on p. 357.

The text's punctuation for synagogue worship preserves each of the three different systems simultaneously: (1) The cantillation marks that accompany the text for oral chanting (from Yiddish, the "trope") include an "upper" set (above the consonants), organizing the text according to the conventional rabbinic division; and (2) the "lower" set of cantillation marks (below the consonants), which reflects the sequence of Hellenistic Judaism. (3) The system of open and closed paragraphs, which divides the final prohibition (v. 18) into two separate laws, is reflected in the later Roman Catholic and Protestant enumeration. None of these enumerations is definitively correct or original. (The layout in the translation, with vv. 6–7 presented as the first commandment, follows Philo, Josephus, and some Talmudic sources.)

Within the narrative frame, Deut.'s authors present the Decalogue as a precise reprise of that found in Exod. 20.2–14. This presentation is complicated by the fact that the text diverges in several places from the Exod. version. The most substantial inconsistency lies in the motivation to observe the Sabbath (see vv. 12–15 nn.). Deut. also expands the command to honor the mother and father (v. 16) and presents a slightly different version of the prohibition on coveting (see v. 18 n.). Other factors also challenge any simple reading of the narrative's claim. Whereas what follows the Decalogue in Exod. is the Book of the Covenant (Exod. chs 21–23), here, what follows is a legal collection that, while patterned after the Book of the Covenant, at key points sharply contradicts it (e.g., 12.13–14 n.; 15.12–18 n.). These and other inconsistencies suggest that the reuse of the Decalogue serves to anchor Deut.'s religious and legal innovations (chs 12–26) to the tradition of divine revelation at Sinai/Horeb. But by borrowing the authority of tradition for their new legal compilation, Deut.'s authors displace the earlier, competing collection of law: the Book of the Covenant (see further 6.1–3 n.).

It is almost certain that Exod. and Deut. existed independently of one another in the preexilic period. However, once Second Temple period editors integrated both into a single literary work, the Torah, subsequent generations of readers had to struggle to make sense of how it contained two mutually inconsistent Decalogues! The Rabbis developed elaborate interpretive strategies in order to resolve the inevitable difficulties that resulted. Their exegetical model presupposed that the Torah had a single author and that it was free of contradiction. On that basis, for example, the two different formulations of the Sabbath commandment were resolved by arguing that God had spoken both simultaneously (see v. 12 n.). Similarly, the inconsistency in the narrative frame about whether God spoke directly to the people or only through the mediation of Moses

[6][a]I the LORD am your God who brought you out of the land
of Egypt, the house of bondage: [7]You shall have no other gods
beside Me.
[8]You shall not make for yourself a sculptured image, any likeness of what is in the heavens above, or on the earth below, or
in the waters below the earth. [9]You shall not bow down to them
or serve them. For I the LORD your God am an impassioned

a Tradition varies as to the divisions of the Commandments in vv. 6–18 and the numbering of the verses. Cf. Exod. 20.1, note a.

(see v. 5 n.), coupled with the abrupt change from first-person to third-person reference to God in the Decalogue (see v. 11 n.), was resolved by suggesting that God Himself spoke only the first two commandments while Moses spoke the rest on behalf of God, because the people complained of their fear of God (5.20–24). In contrast to this model of interpretation that "harmonizes" inconsistencies, modern biblical scholarship shows that the Torah was compiled by multiple authors and editors who lived at different times and places (see essay "Modern Study of the Bible," pp. 2166–77). Consequently, the editorial "seams" implicitly recognized by the ancient Rabbis as contradictions in need of harmonization are explained in different ways by modern scholars. For example, the inconsistency in the Decalogue's narrative frame about whether revelation was direct or indirect probably points to the intentional splicing together of originally different traditions, each of which is here preserved. The two different versions of the Decalogue most likely derive from two different historical contexts and communities, and may represent different revisions of a shorter, earlier Decalogue. **7:** This first commandment takes for granted the existence of other gods; its concern is only to ensure Israel's exclusive loyalty to YHVH. This perspective, called "monolatry," is found frequently within Deut. (see 6.4; 32.8–9, 43; 33.2–3, 27). The idea of monolatry is often expressed by representing YHVH as the ruler of the divine council (see 32.8 n.; Pss. 82; 89.6–8; cf. Exod. 15.11). That perspective almost certainly represents a predominant preexilic form of Israelite religion. Ancient Near Eastern sources similarly envision a chief god ruling over a council of other gods. During the Babylonian exile, as reflected dramatically in Second Isaiah, a very different understanding developed. Radical "monotheism" affirms God's greatness, not by portraying Him as more powerful than other gods but, instead, by denying the existence of other deities altogether (see 4.15–31 n.; Isa. 43.10–12; 44.6–8; 45.5–6, 14, 18–19, 22). Once that perspective became normative in the period following the exile, the earlier view was no longer intelligible. As a result, in the process of reading, teaching, and translating the biblical text, Second Temple Jewish communities sometimes read the later perspective of monotheism into earlier texts that actually had in mind the idea of God as ruling a divine council (see v. 9 n.; 6.4 n.; 32.8 n.). That original theology has also become unavailable to most contemporary readers, since many of the translations found in synagogue prayer books employ euphemisms to explain away the

CHART OF THE DECALOGUE IN DEUTERONOMY

Numbering of the Ten Commandments in Deuteronomy 5.6–18

NJPS	MOST JEWISH TRADITION	ALTERNATIVE JEWISH TRADITION AND THIS TRANSLATION	VERSE NUMBERING IN OTHER BIBLES	EASTERN ORTHODOX, ANGLICAN, MOST PROTESTANT CHURCHES (= ALTERNATIVE JEWISH TRADITION)	ROMAN CATHOLIC AND LUTHERAN CHURCHES
Deut. 5.6	1	1	Deut. 5.6	1	1
5.7	2	1	5.7	1	1
5.8–10	2	2	5.8–10	2	1
5.11	3	3	5.11	3	2
5.12–15	4	4	5.12–15	4	3
5.16	5	5	5.16	5	4
5.17a	6	6	5.17	6	5
5.17b	7	7	5.18	7	6
5.17c	8	8	5.19	8	7
5.17d	9	9	5.20	9	8
5.18	10	10	5.21	10	9
5.18	10	10	5.21	10	10

God, visiting the guilt of the parents upon the children, upon
the third and upon the fourth generations of those who reject
Me, 10 but showing kindness to the thousandth generation of
those who love Me and keep My commandments.
11 You shall not swear falsely by the name of the LORD your
God; for the LORD will not clear one who swears falsely by His
name.
12 Observe the sabbath day and keep it holy, as the LORD
your God has commanded you. 13 Six days you shall labor and
do all your work, 14 but the seventh day is a sabbath of the LORD
your God; you shall not do any work—you, your son or your
daughter, your male or female slave, your ox or your ass, or any
of your cattle, or the stranger in your settlements, so that your
male and female slave may rest as you do. 15 Remember that
you were a slave in the land of Egypt and the LORD your God

Bible's clear references to the existence of other gods. **9:** *You shall not bow down to them or serve them:* As it stands, the grammar of the text is illogical. The two references to "them" require a plural antecedent. The intended reference cannot be to the immediately previous v. 8, which refers only to "a sculptured image," in the singular. The grammatical difficulty suggests that, at an earlier stage of the text, v. 9 directly continued v. 7, which prohibits the Israelites from expressing their allegiance to "other gods," in the plural. The sequence of thought in the original form of the Decalogue would thus have prohibited allegiance to other gods (v. 7) by bowing down to them in worship (v. 9). Under the impact of later prophetic thought, the standard preexilic idea of monolatry became inconceivable and the existence of deities other than YHVH was denied (see previous n.). The "other gods" of older texts were reinterpreted as mere lifeless "idols" (see Isa. 40.18–20; 44.9–20). On the basis of such an association, the original direct connection between vv. 6–7 and v. 9 (prohibiting first allegiance to and then worship of other gods) was severed by the later theological perspective represented by v. 8, with its prohibition merely of a "sculptured image." *Serve:* The same verb is translated "worship" at 13.3. This variation reflects the word's two different basic meanings: "to perform a service or labor" (Exod. 21.2; Num. 3.7–8) and "to make sacrificial offerings to a deity," whether to God (Exod. 3.12; 4.23; 13.5) or to other gods (Deut. 7.16; 12.2, 30). Here the latter meaning is clearly intended. A postbiblical sermonic interpretation of this commandment is preserved by the word's grammatically impossible vocalization (see also 13.3; Exod. 20.5; 23.24; the vocalization of the Bible dates from the second half of the first millennium CE). The MT implies that the prohibition warns: "You shall not be enslaved by them." This theological vocalization unites the word's two meanings: False worship leads to slavery (4.28); only in the worship of YHVH is there freedom (5.6; Lev. 25.55; 26.13). The daily recitation of the Decalogue in the developing liturgy of the Second Temple period provides the context for such ongoing interpretive activity, here witnessed by the formal vocalization of the text. The same understanding is reflected in the spelling of a phylactery from Qumran (1Q13). *Visiting the guilt of the parents upon the children:* Punishment for sins against God extends across three generations. This principle of divine vicarious punishment contrasts sharply with the Israelite norm for civil and criminal law, which restricts punishment to the agent alone (24.16). Later layers of tradition challenged this theological principle of divine justice (see 7.10 n.; Jer. 31.29–30; Ezek. ch 18). **10:** *Kindness* or "grace," loyalty of action as an expectation of the covenant (2 Sam. 7.15: "favor"; Hos. 6.6: "goodness"). *Who love Me* employs the technical language of Near Eastern treaties, where "love" refers to the loyalty the vassal owes to the sovereign. See also 6.14 n. **11:** The intent is to prohibit careless use of the divine name in the context of swearing an oath ("May God do X to me unless I do Y"); such oaths were viewed as dangerous and legally binding (see Judg. 11.29–40). *The LORD your God:* The grammatical perspective here shifts from direct reference to God by God Himself (i.e., "those who love Me and keep My commandments"; v. 10) to a reference to God in relation to Israel by a third party ("your God"). Both ancient rabbinic interpreters and modern scholars have sought to explain this shift. The rabbis resolved the inconsistency by claiming that it was only the first two commandments that God revealed directly to the people (in the first person). In response to the people's fear (v. 5), Moses then mediated the remaining commandments to the people, now logically referring to God in the third person (*b. Mak.* 24a; *b. Hor.* 8a). From a modern perspective, the more likely explanation for the shift lies in the nature of the text as divine decree: Many Near Eastern royal inscriptions reflect the same alternation in the monarch's reference to himself. The shift may also point to different layers of composition. **12:** *Observe,* contrast Exod. 20.8, "Remember." Faced with two different versions of the Decalogue, rabbinic interpretation held that God uttered both versions simultaneously: " 'Observe' and 'Remember' in a single utterance" (*b. Shevu.* 20b). This interpretation recurs in the hymn for Sabbath eve, "Lekha Dodi." *As the LORD ... commanded you:* A phrase characteristic of Deut., here a reference to the Decalogue of Exod. The ostensibly precise repetition

freed you from there with a mighty hand and an outstretched arm; therefore the LORD your God has commanded you to observe the sabbath day.

16 Honor your father and your mother, as the LORD your God has commanded you, that you may long endure, and that you may fare well, in the land that the LORD your God is assigning to you.

17 You shall not murder.
You shall not commit adultery.
You shall not steal.
You shall not bear false witness against your neighbor.

18 You shall not covet your neighbor's wife. You shall not crave your neighbor's house, or his field, or his male or female slave, or his ox, or his ass, or anything that is your neighbor's.

19 The LORD spoke those words—those and no more—to your whole congregation at the mountain, with a mighty voice out of the fire and the dense clouds. He inscribed them on two tablets of stone, which He gave to me.
20 When you heard the voice out of the darkness, while the mountain was ablaze with fire, you came up to me, all your tribal heads and elders,
21 and said, "The LORD our God has just shown us His majestic Presence, and we have heard His voice out of the fire; we have seen this day that man may live though God has spoken to him.
22 Let us not die, then, for this fearsome fire will consume us; if we hear the voice of the LORD our God any longer, we shall

nonetheless here diverges from the original (Exod. 20.8). The Decalogue embeds the perspective of Moses as speaker, whose reference to God's prior proclamation now itself becomes part of the revelation. **14:** The law equally benefits slaves and non-Israelites (1.16 n.; 15.15; 16.11; 24.17). **15:** Contrast the rationale provided for the Sabbath at Exod. 20.11, where it is associated with the creation of the world. Here it is associated with the origin of Israel as a people. Here also, as elsewhere, Deut. emphasizes the exodus as a central motivation for religious and social practices, though how and why the Sabbath might be connected to the exodus are open to interpretation. **16:** See v. 12 n. *And that you may fare well* is absent from the Exod. version (Exod. 20.12). This motivational phrase is typical of Deut.'s exhortations to obedience (4.40; 5.26; 6.3, 18; 12.25, 28; 22.7). **17:** The prohibition against adultery in the Decalogue is absolute. The Decalogue has transformed the ancient Near Eastern breach of the contractual rights of the woman's husband (see Laws of Hammurabi §129) into an offense against both God and the larger community. Biblical law here removes the wife from the disposal of the husband and grants her the status of legal person (see 22.22 n.). **18:** *Wife ... house,* contrast the order "house ... wife" in the Exod. Decalogue (Exod. 20.14). There the sequence suggests that "house" is the inclusive term, with the following list (wife, slave, ox, or ass) serving to itemize its contents. Consistent with their view elsewhere, the authors of Deut. here completely separate family law from property law. They invert the earlier sequence, placing the wife first. By removing her altogether from the list of other chattels, they establish that the law does not regard the woman as merely one commodity among others comprising a "house" (see also 22.22–23.1 n.). This is consistent with Deut.'s general view of women.

5.19–30: Moses as mediator. While the Decalogue was given directly to the people (v. 4; 4.10–13), the rest of the laws were mediated to the people by Moses, at their plea (vv. 22–24; 4.14). **19–23:** See 4.33; cf. Exod. 20.15–18. **19:** *The LORD spoke ... at the mountain ... out of the fire,* lit. "The LORD spoke ... on the mountain out of the fire." The more precise translation of the Heb shows its exact correspondence to v. 4: "Face to face the LORD spoke to you on the mountain out of the fire ..." The Decalogue is thus set in a precise literary frame, with both vv. affirming the direct nature of the divine revelation. In this view, God spoke the Decalogue directly to Israel without the mediation of Moses. *Those and no more,* lit. "He did not add [anything more]." There is no source for this comment in Exod. ch 20. The authors of Deut. here seem to be arguing that the Book of the Covenant, which immediately follows the Decalogue in Exod., was not included in the revelation at Sinai/Horeb. The phrase thus makes way for the presentation of the laws of Deut. alone as the further words of God to Moses at Sinai/Horeb. **20–24:** This section expands Exod. 20.15–18, while also revising that narrative in several key aspects. The editor here recognizes the existence of the two mutually inconsistent traditions about the Decalogue: that it was spoken directly by God to the people (vv. 4, 19); that it was mediated by Moses (v. 5). In this section, he establishes a compromise between the two views: While the Decalogue was proclaimed by God directly, thereafter all law was mediated by Moses. The editor's careful reuse and expansion of Exod. 20.15–18 facilitates this attempt to reconcile the conflicting perspectives. **22:** *Let us not die:* The people's anxiety explains their request that Moses serve as mediator. The emphasis upon the mortal threat of the divine voice conflicts, however, with the affirmation of safety in v. 21.

die. [23] For what mortal ever heard the voice of the living God
speak out of the fire, as we did, and lived? [24] You go closer and
hear all that the LORD our God says, and then you tell us everything that the LORD our God tells you, and we will willingly
do it."
[25] The LORD heard the plea that you made to me, and the
LORD said to me, "I have heard the plea that this people made
to you; they did well to speak thus. [26] May they always be of
such mind, to revere Me and follow all My commandments,
that it may go well with them and with their children forever!
[27] Go, say to them, 'Return to your tents.' [28] But you remain
here with Me, and I will give you the whole Instruction—the
laws and the rules—that you shall impart to them, for them to
observe in the land that I am giving them to possess."
[29] Be careful, then, to do as the LORD your God has commanded you. Do not turn aside to the right or to the left: [30] follow only the path that the LORD your God has enjoined upon
you, so that you may thrive and that it may go well with you,
and that you may long endure in the land you are to possess.

6 And this is the Instruction—the laws and the rules—that
the LORD your God has commanded [me] to impart to you,
to be observed in the land that you are about to cross into and
occupy, [2] so that you, your children, and your children's children may revere the LORD your God and follow, as long as you
live, all His laws and commandments that I enjoin upon you,
to the end that you may long endure. [3] Obey, O Israel, willingly

Therefore this v. is less a continuation of the previous one than an alternative to it, consistent with the idea of divine revelation in v. 5. *If we hear ... any longer:* This formulation presupposes that God has already spoken to them directly. The Exod. source, however, does not presuppose God's prior speech. Its formulation is unconditional and absolute: "Let God not speak to us, lest we die" (Exod. 20.16). Deut.'s editor has added *any longer* in order to adapt the v. to the new context. It now supports the editorial compromise: God spoke (only) the Decalogue directly; Moses mediated (only) the following legal material. **25–30:** The idea that Moses mediates between God and the people will be used in two ways: (1) to justify the laws that Moses subsequently propounds as revelation (chs 12–26); (2) to justify the institution of "Mosaic" prophecy (18.15–22). **28:** *Instruction,* lit. "commandment." Note the deliberate allusion to this v. in 6.1 (see 6.1–3 n.).

6.1–11.32: The requirement of loyalty to God. A sermonic preamble to the laws of chs 12–26. **6.1–3:** An introduction to this separate literary unit, validating Mosaic instruction as revealed at Horeb. NJPS correctly follows the standard ch division and recognizes that this paragraph begins a new literary unit. Whereas Moses speaks about the past in ch 5, as he recalls the revelation at Horeb, he now shifts into the present, to explain the significance of that revelation for the new generation whom he addresses in Moab. The Masoretic division of the text follows a different logic from that of the NJPS, regarding 5.19–6.3 as a single paragraph. That organization attempts to show that there is no "break" whatsoever between Horeb and Moab. It maintains that "the laws and rules" that God originally proclaimed to Moses subsequent to the revelation on Sinai/Horeb (5.28) are identical to "the laws and the rules" (6.1; 12.1) of the following sermon (chs 6–11) and legal code (chs 12–26). That claim, however, runs counter to the tradition found in Exod., whereby the Book of the Covenant (Exod. chs 21–23)—not Deut.'s laws—records the "rules" that God spoke to Moses on the mountain (Exod. 21.1; 24.3). The attribution of the following speech and law corpus to Sinaitic revelation by Deut.'s authors thus reuses the earlier tradition in order to lend authority to Deut.'s new vision of law and religion. The entire Mosaic reprise of ostensibly earlier law is therefore more sophisticated than at first evident, since repetition here entails competition, as Deut. seeks to displace the Book of the Covenant. Accordingly, while the present ch division is formally correct, the Masoretic division preserves an important insight into the original aims of the text's authors. The sophistication of their literary strategy should not be underestimated. The *Temple Scroll* from Qumran and the laws in the pseudepigraphic book of *Jub.* similarly present sectarian law as deriving from Sinaitic revelation. The development during the early rabbinic movement (ca. 70–300 CE) of the doctrine of Oral Torah as a tradition that originates in revelation at Mount Sinai also corresponds to this model. **1:** *And,* marking the transition from past retrospective about Horeb (chs 4–5) to the speaker's addressing the Israelites in the present, in Moab, about the requirements of the covenant. *The Instruction ... occupy:* The Heb is nearly identical to 5.28. The precise repetition of terminology is important. It legitimates the entire second discourse—both *the Instruction* (chs 6–11) and *the laws and the rules* (the legal corpus of chs 12–26; see 12.1)—as originating in direct divine revelation from God on Horeb (5.28). **2:** *Revere,* see 4.10 n.

and faithfully, that it may go well with you and that you may
increase greatly [in] [a-]a land flowing with milk and honey,[-a] as
the LORD, the God of your fathers, spoke to you.
4 Hear, O Israel! The LORD is our God, the LORD alone.[b] 5 You
shall love the LORD your God with all your heart and with all
your soul and with all your might. 6 Take to heart these instructions with which I charge you this day. 7 Impress them upon
your children. Recite them when you stay at home and when

a-a According to Ibn Ezra this phrase connects with the end of v. 1.
b Cf. Rashbam and Ibn Ezra; see Zech. 14.9. Others "The LORD our God, the LORD is one."

6.4–25: A sermon on the first commandment of the Decalogue, incorporating direct allusions to it: vv. 4 and 14 refer to 5.7; vv. 12, 21, 23 refer to 5.6; v. 15 ("impassioned God") refers to 5.9; vv. 5 and 17 refer to 5.10. **4–9: The Shema.** These vv. form the first paragraph of the important Jewish prayer called the Shema, after its first word, Heb for "Hear!" During the late Second Temple period, this prayer rose to special prominence both in the synagogue liturgy and in individual piety, a position that it still maintains. Strikingly, Deut. itself gives no indication that this passage is theologically central or liturgically important. Nor do any of the biblical passages that incorporate liturgical prayer refer to it (see Ezra 3.10–11; Neh. ch 9; 1 Chron. 16.7–36; 2 Chron. 5.11–14; 7.3); its formal recitation is not attested until late in the Second Temple period. The centrality of this text is likely the result of early rabbinic interpretation of the requirement to "recite [these words] ... when you lie down and when you get up" (vv. 6–7). This interpretation led to recitation of the Shema twice daily, in the morning and at night. A similar injunction to "recite ... these My words" is found at 11.18–19. Because of the double reference to "these words," the prayer was formally defined as including both paragraphs (6.4–9; 11.13–21). A third paragraph was also added (Num. 15.37–41): the requirement to wear a garment whose fringes (tzitzit) provide a further context for reflection upon Torah and fulfilling its precepts.

Many modern readers regard the Shema as an assertion of monotheism, a view that is anachronistic. In the context of ancient Israelite religion, it served as a public proclamation of exclusive loyalty to YHVH as the sole LORD of Israel. Subsequently, as the Shema became incorporated into the synagogue liturgy, its recitation was also given legal significance. The prayer was regarded as a legally binding oath to carry out the requirements of the Torah. Through the liturgical recitation of the Shema the worshipper thus reaffirms, twice daily, the original covenant ratification ceremony that, in the narrative of Deut., took place on the plains of Moab. **4–5:** The Shema, with its call for complete personal devotion to God, became normative for the various Judaisms of the Second Temple period; in fact, vv. 4–5 were cited by Jesus as the "first" of all commandments (Mark 12.29–30). **4:** *The LORD ... alone:* NJPS correctly departs from the more familiar translation, "The LORD [YHVH] our God, the LORD is one" (see translators' note *b,* end). Each of the two interpretations is theoretically possible because, in Heb, it is possible to form a sentence by simply joining a subject and a predicate, without specifying the verb "to be." The Heb here thus allows either "YHVH, our God, YHVH *is* one" or "YHVH *is* our God, YHVH alone." The first, older translation, which makes a statement about the unity and the indivisibility of God, does not do full justice to this text (though it makes sense in a later Jewish context as a polemic against Christianity). The v. makes not a quantitative argument (about the number of deities) but a qualitative one, about the nature of the relationship between God and Israel. Almost certainly, the original force of the v., as the medieval Jewish exegetes in translators' note *b* recognized, was to demand that Israel show exclusive loyalty to *our God,* YHVH—but not thereby to deny the existence of other gods. In this way, it assumes the same perspective as the first commandment of the Decalogue, which, by prohibiting the worship of other gods, presupposes their existence (see 5.7 n.). Once true monotheism became more normative in the Second Temple period, this earlier perspective became unintelligible. Second Temple readers and translators of the Shema were thus forced to read this and similar passages in a way that made them consistent with monotheism (see 32.8 n.; cf. 4.15–31 n.; 5.9 n.). That process of reinterpretation is already evident in the LXX's translation (3rd c. BCE): "the LORD is one." As the basis for most subsequent translations, that reading is the source for the common understanding of the v. *Alone:* The traditional translation (see translators' note *b)* preserves the usual meaning of Heb "'eḥad," "one," which may have contributed to interpreting the Shema as a declaration of monotheism. But what it might mean to say that God is "one" is unclear, since that is not the same as affirming that there is only one God (Isa. 44.6; 45.5–7, 14, 18, 21; 46.9). Nor is it likely that the v. intends to clarify that there is only one YHVH, as opposed to many YHVHS, since it was recognized that different manifestations of a divinity could derive from a single god (Exod. 6.3). NJPS thus is probably correct to understand "'eḥad" to mean "alone," i.e., "exclusively." This understanding receives support in the prophet Zechariah's interpretation of this v.: "In that day there shall be one LORD with one name" (Zech. 14.9 and translators' note *e*). **5:** *Love,* see 5.10 n. The paradox of commanding a feeling (as in Lev. 19.17–18) is resolved with the recognition that covenantal "love" does not refer to internal sentiment or to private emotion, but rather to loyalty of action toward both deity

you are away, when you lie down and when you get up. [8] Bind them as a sign on your hand and let them serve as a symbol[a] on your forehead;[b] [9] inscribe them on the doorposts of your house and on your gates.

a Others "frontlet"; cf. Exod. 13.16. b Lit. "between your eyes"; cf. Exod. 13.9.

and neighbor (see 5.1–30 n.). *With all your soul:* This phrase, in rabbinic interpretation, meant that one should be willing to give one's life for God. This interpretation led to the practice of reciting the Shema on one's deathbed (Zohar, *Terumah* 141) or during acts of martyrdom, a custom that seems to have arisen among the Jews of the Rhineland in response to the massacres conducted against them during the call to the first Crusade in spring 1096 CE (see Ivan G. Marcus, *The Jewish Life Cycle,* p. 200). There is also a narrative of Rabbi Akiva (2nd c.) reciting the evening Shema while being martyred by the Romans (*Ber.* 61a). *Might:* Heb "me'od" is elsewhere an adverb meaning "very" or "exceedingly." It is used as a noun only here and in the Deuteronomistic description of King Josiah, which cites this v. (2 Kings 23.25). While the word's basic meaning is "might" or "strength," it was understood as "wealth" or "property" both at Qumran (CD 9.11; 12.10) and in early rabbinic literature (*Tg. Jon.; Sifre*). The two interpretations each call for full commitment to God, whether psychological or practical; both are preserved in the Mishnah (*m. Ber.* 9.5). **6:** *These instructions,* lit. "these words," as at 11.19, a likely reference to the Decalogue. **7:** *Impress them,* a difficult word, used only here, likely in the sense of "teach them incisively." *Recite them:* This translation reflects the formal liturgical recitation of the prayer, a ritual that is postbiblical. The Heb is better rendered "speak about them" (see also Ps. 119.13, 46): to be mindful of and discuss the laws of the Torah. *When you lie down and when you get up,* possibly a merism signifying that one should reflect upon these Deuteronomic teachings at all times. Rabbinic interpretation, however, understands the phrase to refer literally to two distinct times: "in the evening" and "in the morning." On that basis, the Shema is formally recited twice daily. So important is this obligation that the Mishnah begins with a debate about how to fulfill it properly: "From what time in the evening should one recite the Shema?" (*m. Ber.* 1.1). **8:** *Bind them:* Taken literally, this law provides the basis for the Jewish practice of binding tefillin (phylacteries) upon the arm and forehead. Tefillin have been found at Qumran, and it is clear that their use dates from at least the 2nd c. BCE. However, some mss of the LXX, as well as the customs reflected in Samaritan practice, understood the law metaphorically. There was thus a debate within Second Temple Judaism about the correct interpretation of this prescription: whether literally to bind an object or symbolically to take instruction to heart (Exod. 13.9, 16; Prov. 3.3; 6.21; 7.3). Both perspectives have merit, but since the instructions to write upon the doorposts are intended literally (see v. 9 n.), it is possible, even likely, that the authors of Deut. expected their audience to wear portions of the text upon the body. There is archeological evidence for similar practices. Inscribed silver amulets (with the text on, not in, them) that date to the 7th and 6th centuries BCE have been found at Jerusalem. Similar amulets are depicted in Egyptian and Mesopotamian art and literature. Such amulets, however, were likely worn as magic charms in order to ward off evil. In Deut., the text is worn to express the wearer's dedication and obedience to Torah. In refocusing the purpose of wearing texts upon the body, Deut. takes over an established practice but transforms its meaning. The same subordination of older custom to Deuteronomic Torah occurs elsewhere; see 6.9 n.; 12.13–19 n.; 17.14–20 n.; 18.15–22 n. Ironically, the Gk translation "phylakterion" (the source of "phylactery") means "amulet," thereby semantically connecting it with magic, which was rejected by the authors of Deut. *Sign:* Based on the archeological evidence, it seems that the passages would originally have been inscribed on metal and displayed in full view. Only later, in the Second Temple period, did the practice develop of enclosing the text in small leather cases. According to rabbinic sources, the texts placed in the tefillin always included the four biblical passages that refer to the practice (Exod. 13.3–10, 11–16; Deut. 6.4–9; 11.13–21), though the tefillin found at Qumran sometimes contain different passages, including the Decalogue and other selections from the Torah. **9:** *Doorposts:* The doorways of houses and temples were regarded in Israel and the ancient Near East as important transitional spaces in which religious-legal ceremonies were performed and where divine images might be stored (see Exod. 12.7, 21–23; 21.6; Isa. 57.8). The practice of inscribing these liminal spaces with cultic or religious invocations is also well known throughout the ancient Near East. Deut. adopts that custom but subordinates the doorway, as a religiously significant space, to the authority of Deuteronomic law. Originally, the words were to be directly displayed on the doorposts, as can be seen from the stone plaques inscribed with the words of the Decalogue found outside Samaritan dwellings. By the late Second Temple period, as evidenced at Qumran, in some Jewish communities the texts were written on parchment, placed in small boxes (mezuzot), and affixed to the doorpost. The texts placed in the mezuzot varied: Most contained this passage (vv. 4–9) and Deut. 11.13–21, and at Qumran, the Decalogue and Deut. 10.12–11.12 were sometimes added. However, Samaritan mezuzot contain only the Decalogue.

10 When the LORD your God brings you into the land that He swore to your fathers, Abraham, Isaac, and Jacob, to assign to you—great and flourishing cities that you did not build, 11 houses full of all good things that you did not fill, hewn cisterns that you did not hew, vineyards and olive groves that you did not plant—and you eat your fill, 12 take heed that you do not forget the LORD who freed you from the land of Egypt, the house of bondage. 13 Revere only the LORD your God and worship Him alone, and swear only by His name. 14 Do not follow other gods, any gods of the peoples about you—15 for the LORD your God in your midst is an impassioned God—lest the anger of the LORD your God blaze forth against you and He wipe you off the face of the earth.

16 Do not try the LORD your God, as you did at Massah.[a] 17 Be sure to keep the commandments, decrees, and laws that the LORD your God has enjoined upon you. 18 Do what is right and good in the sight of the LORD, that it may go well with you and that you may be able to possess the good land that the LORD your God promised on oath to your fathers, 19 and that all your enemies may be driven out before you, as the LORD has spoken.

20 When, in time to come, your children ask you, "What mean the decrees, laws, and rules that the LORD our God has enjoined upon you?"[b] 21 you shall say to your children, "We were slaves to Pharaoh in Egypt and the LORD freed us from Egypt with a mighty hand. 22 The LORD wrought before our eyes marvelous and destructive signs and portents in Egypt, against Pharaoh and all his household; 23 and us He freed from there, that He might take us and give us the land that He had promised on oath to our fathers. 24 Then the LORD commanded us to observe all these laws, to revere the LORD our God, for our lasting good and for our survival, as is now the case. 25 It will be therefore to our merit before the LORD our God to observe faithfully this whole Instruction, as He has commanded us."

7 When the LORD your God brings you to the land that you are about to enter and possess, and He dislodges many nations before you—the Hittites, Girgashites, Amorites, Canaanites, Perizzites, Hivites, and Jebusites, seven nations much larger than you—2 and the LORD your God delivers them to you and you defeat them, you must doom them to destruction: grant them no terms and give them no quarter. 3 You shall not intermarry with them: do not give your daughters to their sons or take their daughters for your sons. 4 For they will turn your children away from Me to worship other gods, and the LORD's anger will blaze forth against you and He will promptly wipe

a Cf. Exod. 17.1–7.

b Septuagint and rabbinic quotations read "us."

10–11: The list *land ... houses ... cisterns ... olive groves* (cf. Josh. 24.13; Neh. 9.24–25) defines the elements of a society established in its land. Israel is about to both inherit its land and become an established society. **12:** The threat of forgetting and the risk of apostasy are repeatedly stressed (4.9–14 n.; 8.11–20; 32.18; cf. 5.26; Hos. 2.5–13). **14:** *Do not follow,* lit. "do not go after," employs the technical language of Neo-Assyrian state treaties, which were concerned to ensure that the vassal show obedience and commitment to the suzerain alone. Deut. redeploys that language of international diplomacy in a new context: the covenant with Israel in which YHVH functions as divine suzerain. **16:** *Try ... Massah:* For the incident and the Heb pun, see Exod. 17.2–7; see also Matthew 4.7. **20:** The Passover Haggadah includes this and similar didactic questions (Exod. 12.21–27; 13.1–10, 11–16) in the section about the Four Sons. **22:** See 4.34 n.

7.1–10.11: Risks to covenantal fidelity upon entering the land. The first risk is that Israel enters an already inhabited land, whose greater population and different religious practices it must confront (ch 7). Thereafter, successful habitation carries its own risks of complacency and loss of historical memory (ch 8).

7.1–26: The war of conquest. Two topics are treated: (1) the command to destroy the original occupants of Canaan (vv. 1–3, 6, 17–24); and (2) the command not to worship their gods (vv. 4–5, 7–15, 25–26). The two themes are joined at v. 16. **1:** We may infer from a number of factors that this list is primarily an after-the-fact literary compilation rather than an historical portrayal. The identity, sequence, and number of the peoples included in the "table of nations" vary considerably (Gen. 15.19–21; Exod. 3.8, 17; 13.5; 23.23; 33.2; 34.11; Deut. 20.17; Josh. 3.10; 9.1; 11.3; 12.8; 24.11; Judg. 3.5; 1 Kings 9.20; Ezra 9.1; Neh. 9.8; 2 Chron. 8.7). *Hittites* (e.g., Gen. 23.10; 25.9; 49.29–30; 50.13; Num. 13.29) are presented as one of

you out. 5 Instead, this is what you shall do to them: you shall
tear down their altars, smash their pillars, cut down their sacred posts, and consign their images to the fire.
6 For you are a people consecrated to the LORD your God:
of all the peoples on earth the LORD your God chose you to
be His treasured people. 7 It is not because you are the most
numerous of peoples that the LORD set His heart on you and
chose you—indeed, you are the smallest of peoples; 8 but it
was because the LORD favored you and kept the oath He made
to your fathers that the LORD freed you with a mighty hand and
rescued you from the house of bondage, from the power of
Pharaoh king of Egypt.
9 Know, therefore, that only the LORD your God is God, the
steadfast God who keeps His covenant faithfully to the thousandth generation of those who love Him and keep His commandments, 10 but who instantly requites with destruction
those who reject Him—never slow with those who reject Him,
but requiting them instantly. 11 Therefore, observe faithfully
the Instruction—the laws and the rules—with which I charge
you today.

the original inhabitants of Canaan, in contrast to the historically important Hittite empire which flourished in Anatolia, in central Turkey, ca. 1700–1200 BCE. The *Jebusites,* according to the Bible the pre-Israelite inhabitants of Jerusalem, retained control of the city until it was conquered by David several centuries after the period in which the conquest is set (2 Sam. 5.6–7). The latter narrative implies that this law was never implemented. The ideal number *seven,* which signifies completion or totality (Gen. ch 1; the plague list of Pss. 78.44–51 and 105.28–36 in contrast to Exod. chs 7–12), suggests that the enumeration may be artificial. The number of peoples included in the "table" elsewhere in the Bible varies considerably: twelve, seven, six, or fewer. **2:** This requirement for destruction is anomalous in several ways. Earlier sources contemplate only the expulsion of these groups (Exod. 23.27–33; cf. 34.11). The definition and requirements of the "ban" (Heb "ḥerem") vary considerably throughout the Bible: total destruction of people and property (here; 13.15–17; 20.16–17; 1 Sam. 15.3); sparing of property (2.34–35; 3.6–7); sparing of women, children, and property (20.10–14). Finally, other narratives, which seem far more realistic, speak of the failure to carry out the conquest except in very limited areas and the use of conquered populations for labor (Josh. chs 15–17; Judg. ch 1; 3.1–6). These factors suggest that the law of the ban is an anachronistic literary formulation. It first arose centuries after the settlement; it was never implemented because there was no population extant against whom it could be implemented. Its polemic in favor of religious purity is directed at internal issues in 6th c. Judah. Often the authors of Deut. use the term "Canaanite" rhetorically to stigmatize older forms of Israelite religion that they no longer accept (see v. 5 n.; 18.9–14 n.). *Doom them to destruction,* or "place under the ban," or "devote." That which is "devoted" is set aside for divine use and denied to humans. The war of conquest, as a holy war, should not be one where the individual profits through plunder (see 12.29–31 n.; 13.14 n.; 20.1–20 n.; Josh. ch 7). The law addresses apostasy as opposed to ethnicity; it is directed against apostate Israelites in 8.20; 13.15–17. **3:** This prohibition against intermarriage does not fit easily after v. 2, suggesting several layers of editing. It is also inconsistent with 21.10–14, which seems to reflect a more original policy. **5:** See Exod. 34.12–13 n. *Pillars:* stone monuments that marked places where God appeared and were thus originally legitimate in worship (Gen. 35.14; Exod. 24.4; Hos. 3.4). Only subsequently were they prohibited as alien (Exod. 23.24; 34.13; Lev. 26.1; Deut. 12.3; 16.22; 2 Kings 18.4). *Sacred posts,* Heb "'Asherim." The singular, "'Asherah," preserves the name of an important Canaanite goddess known from Ugarit (1 Kings 18.19). Archeological evidence suggests this goddess may also have been popular in Israel. Here the word designates merely a tree or wooden pole (16.21; Judg. 6.25, 26, 28).

7.6–16: The meaning of Israel's covenantal relationship to God. **6:** *For* suggests that the v. originally continued v. 3, since it provides the rationale for total separation from the Canaanites, not for the destruction of their cult sites. This v., repeated at 14.2, summarizes Deut.'s view of Israel's relation to God. *Consecrated,* lit., "set aside as separate," as is clear here. *Chose,* the precondition of Israel's elected status. *His treasured people* (14.2 n.; 26.18; Exod. 19.5; Mal. 3.17; Ps. 135.4), designating Israel as the exclusive property of God; similarly, 4.20, using a different Heb word. The term originates in Near Eastern treaty language for the special relationship of vassal to overlord. **9–11:** A sermon on the second commandment that radically revises its meaning. The reuse of key phrases and inversion of the order of punishment and blessing in 5.9–10 mark the citation (see 4.16b–19a n.). **9:** *Keeps His covenant faithfully:* NJPS translates the same phrase as "showing kindness" at 5.10 (see n.). **10:** *Instantly requites ... requiting them instantly:* Note the ABB'A' frame, at whose center is the key idea that God is *never slow.* The idea is that the sinner is punished directly, as already recognized by Rashi (cf. NRSV "in their own person"). At issue is the rejection of the norm

'EKEV עקב
[12] And if you do obey these rules and observe them carefully, the LORD your God will maintain faithfully for you the covenant that He made on oath with your fathers: [13] He will favor you and bless you and multiply you; He will bless the issue of your womb and the produce of your soil, your new grain and wine and oil, the calving of your herd and the lambing of your flock, in the land that He swore to your fathers to assign to you. [14] You shall be blessed above all other peoples: there shall be no sterile male or female among you or among your livestock. [15] The LORD will ward off from you all sickness; He will not bring upon you any of the dreadful diseases of Egypt, about which you know, but will inflict them upon all your enemies.

[16] You shall destroy all the peoples that the LORD your God delivers to you, showing them no pity. And you shall not worship their gods, for that would be a snare to you. [17] Should you say to yourselves, "These nations are more numerous than we; how can we dispossess them?" [18] You need have no fear of them. You have but to bear in mind what the LORD your God did to Pharaoh and all the Egyptians: [19] the wondrous acts that you saw with your own eyes, the signs and the portents, the mighty hand, and the outstretched arm by which the LORD your God liberated you. Thus will the LORD your God do to all the peoples you now fear. [20] The LORD your God will also send a plague[a] against them, until those who are left in hiding perish before you. [21] Do not stand in dread of them, for the LORD your God is in your midst, a great and awesome God.

[22] The LORD your God will dislodge those peoples before you little by little; you will not be able to put an end to them at once, else the wild beasts would multiply to your hurt. [23] The LORD your God will deliver them up to you, throwing them into utter panic until they are wiped out. [24] He will deliver their kings into your hand, and you shall obliterate their name from under the heavens; no man shall stand up to you, until you have wiped them out.

[25] You shall consign the images of their gods to the fire; you shall not covet the silver and gold on them and keep it for yourselves, lest you be ensnared thereby; for that is abhorrent to the LORD your God. [26] You must not bring an abhorrent thing into your house, or you will be proscribed like it; you must reject it as abominable and abhorrent, for it is proscribed.

8 You shall faithfully observe all the Instruction that I enjoin upon you today, that you may thrive and increase and be able to possess the land that the LORD promised on oath to your fathers.

a Others "hornet"; meaning of Heb. uncertain. Cf. note at Exod. 23.28.

of vicarious or transgenerational punishment previously propounded in the Decalogue (5.9 = Exod. 20.5; cf. Exod. 34.7; Num. 14.18). Instead, the sermon argues for individual retribution, as in criminal law (24.16), while deleting any reference to the transmission of punishment across generations. There is a similar rejection of transgenerational punishment in Ezek. 18.1–4 (cf. Jer. 31.27–30, where the elimination of transgenerational punishment is anticipated in the future); it is nevertheless quite remarkable that Deut. here directly polemicizes against the Decalogue. **12–14:** The blessings of fertility do not come from the nature gods of Canaan but from Israel's God (see Hos. ch 2). Natural fertility is here made contingent upon obedience to the covenant. **13:** *Calving ... lambing* (28.4, 18, 51), originally two Ugaritic fertility deities; the second, "Astarte," is named at 1 Kings 11.5. **15:** Cf. Exod. 15.26. **17–26:** Israel need not fear more powerful nations since, according to the idea of the holy war, God "is in your midst" in battle (v. 21; 6.15; cf. 20.1–4). These vv. echo ideas in Exod. 23.20–33. **20:** *Plague,* see Exod. 23.28 n.; Josh. 24.12. **22:** Abbreviating Exod. 23.29–30; contrast Deut. 9.3.

8.1–20: The temptation to pride and self-sufficiency in the land. Moses warns the people that success in Canaan will tempt them to forget the wilderness lesson of complete dependence upon God.

1–10: An appeal to Israel's memory: In the wilderness God sustained the people daily (Exod. 12.37–17.16; Num. chs 11–14). **3:** *Manna,* see Exod. ch 16; Num. 11.7–8. **5:** Suffering is here interpreted as discipline, as in a parent's correction of a child (Hos. ch 11); like many others in Deut., this idea reflects the influence of wisdom literature (see Prov. 3.11–12; cf. Deut. 1.13 n.; 4.2 n.; 4.5–8 n.; 4.10 n.; 11.2). **10:** *When you have eaten your fill, give thanks to the* Lord *your God* serves as the rabbinic justification for reciting the grace after meals (*b. Ber.* 21a).

8.11–20: The peril of prosperity. **11:** Disobedience to Deut.'s laws becomes tantamount to forgetting God and transgressing the first commandment (see v. 19 n.). **15:** *Water ... from the flinty rock,* Exod. 17.1–7; Num. 20.2–13; Ps. 114.8. **19:** *Follow,* see 6.14 n. *Other gods ... serve ... bow down to,* citing the first and second commandments of the Decalogue (5.7, 9). **20:** *Like the nations:* Here Israel is itself placed under the ban if it commits apostasy (see 7.1–26 n.). *Cause to perish ... perish:* The repeated word underscores the precise "measure-for-measure" nature of the punishment. Israel's election (7.6 n.) grants no exemption from upholding the law. Rightful habitation in the promised land, like its fertility (7.12–14 n.), depends upon covenantal obedience, not ethnic identity (7.2 n.).

2 Remember the long way that the Lord your God has made
you travel in the wilderness these past forty years, that He might
test you by hardships to learn what was in your hearts: whether you would keep His commandments or not. 3 He subjected
you to the hardship of hunger and then gave you manna to eat,
which neither you nor your fathers had ever known, in order to
teach you that man does not live on bread alone, but that man
may live on anything that the Lord decrees. 4 The clothes upon
you did not wear out, nor did your feet swell these forty years.
5 Bear in mind that the Lord your God disciplines you just as a
man disciplines his son. 6 Therefore keep the commandments
of the Lord your God: walk in His ways and revere Him.

7 For the Lord your God is bringing you into a good land,
a land with streams and springs and fountains issuing from
plain and hill; 8 a land of wheat and barley, of vines, figs, and
pomegranates, a land of olive trees and honey; 9 a land where
you may eat food without stint, where you will lack nothing; a
land whose rocks are iron and from whose hills you can mine
copper. 10 When you have eaten your fill, give thanks to the
Lord your God for the good land which He has given you.

11 Take care lest you forget the Lord your God and fail to
keep His commandments, His rules, and His laws, which I
enjoin upon you today. 12 When you have eaten your fill, and
have built fine houses to live in, 13 and your herds and flocks
have multiplied, and your silver and gold have increased, and
everything you own has prospered, 14 beware lest[a] your heart
grow haughty and you forget the Lord your God—who freed
you from the land of Egypt, the house of bondage; 15 who led
you through the great and terrible wilderness with its seraph[b]
serpents and scorpions, a parched land with no water in it,
who brought forth water for you from the flinty rock; 16 who
fed you in the wilderness with manna, which your fathers had
never known, in order to test you by hardships only to benefit
you in the end—17 and you say to yourselves, "My own power
and the might of my own hand have won this wealth for me."
18 Remember that it is the Lord your God who gives you the
power to get wealth, in fulfillment of the covenant that He
made on oath with your fathers, as is still the case.

19 If you do forget the Lord your God and follow other gods
to serve them or bow down to them, I warn you this day that
you shall certainly perish; 20 like the nations that the Lord will
cause to perish before you, so shall you perish—because you
did not heed the Lord your God.

9 Hear, O Israel! You are about to cross the Jordan to go in
and dispossess nations greater and more populous than

a Heb. pen *moved down from v. 12 for clarity.* b *See note at Num. 21.6.*

you: great cities with walls sky-high; 2 a people great and tall, the Anakites, of whom you have knowledge; for you have heard it said, "Who can stand up to the children of Anak?" 3 Know then this day that none other than the LORD your God is crossing at your head, a devouring fire; it is He who will wipe them out. He will subdue them before you, that you may quickly dispossess and destroy them, as the LORD promised you. 4 And when the LORD your God has thrust them from your path, say not to yourselves, "The LORD has enabled us to possess this land because of our virtues"; it is rather because of the wickedness of those nations that the LORD is dispossessing them before you. 5 It is not because of your virtues and your rectitude that you will be able to possess their country; but it is because of their wickedness that the LORD your God is dispossessing those nations before you, and in order to fulfill the oath that the LORD made to your fathers, Abraham, Isaac, and Jacob.

6 Know, then, that it is not for any virtue of yours that the LORD your God is giving you this good land to possess; for you are a stiffnecked people. 7 Remember, never forget, how you provoked the LORD your God to anger in the wilderness: from the day that you left the land of Egypt until you reached this place, you have continued defiant toward the LORD.

8 At Horeb you so provoked the LORD that the LORD was angry enough with you to have destroyed you. 9 I had ascended the mountain to receive the tablets of stone, the Tablets of the Covenant that the LORD had made with you, and I stayed on the mountain forty days and forty nights, eating no bread and drinking no water. 10 And the LORD gave me the two tablets of stone inscribed by the finger of God, with the exact words that the LORD had addressed to you on the mountain out of the fire on the day of the Assembly.

11 At the end of those forty days and forty nights, the LORD gave me the two tablets of stone, the Tablets of the Covenant. 12 And the LORD said to me, "Hurry, go down from here at once, for the people whom you brought out of Egypt have acted wickedly; they have been quick to stray from the path that I enjoined upon them; they have made themselves a molten image." 13 The LORD further said to me, "I see that this is a stiffnecked people. 14 Let Me alone and I will destroy them and blot out their name from under heaven, and I will make you a nation far more numerous than they."

15 I started down the mountain, a mountain ablaze with fire, the two Tablets of the Covenant in my two hands. 16 I saw how you had sinned against the LORD your God: you had made yourselves a molten calf; you had been quick to stray from the path that the LORD had enjoined upon you. 17 Thereupon I gripped the two tablets and flung them away with both my hands, smashing them before your eyes. 18 I threw myself down

9.1–10.11: The already broken and renewed covenant. God does not give the land to the people as a reward for righteousness, for in the wilderness they acted rebelliously. **9.2:** See Num. 13.22, 33. **4–5:** Victory will be given in the holy war because (negatively) Canaan has been irrevocably corrupted by the actions of its present occupants and because (positively) of God's enduring commitment to the promises made to Israel's ancestors. **6–24:** The historical record shows that Israel has been rebellious since the exodus (Ezek. 20.5–8; contrast Jer. 2.2–3; Hos. 2.14–20). **8–10:** Exod. 24.12–18; 31.18. **11–21:** Exod. ch 32, revised. **17:** *Smashing them,* not simple anger but a legal ceremony to confirm breach of treaty (Exod. 32.19 n.).

22: Num. 11.1–3; Exod. 17.1–7; and Num. 11.31–34. **23:** Num. chs 13–14. **25–29:** A paraphrase of Exod. 32.11–14. Deut. portrays Moses as the ideal prophet (34.10–12); he intercedes for the people and suffers because of them (1.37 n.; cf. Isa. ch 53).

10.1–11: The second ascent of the mountain (this narrative is abstracted at Exod. 34.1–4, 27–28). **1–3:** These vv. rest on a tradition that Moses made the Ark and put the stone tablets in it (1 Kings 8.9); it is fundamentally different from the P tradition and its gold-covered ark (Exod. 25.10–12). **6–9:** An editorial insertion concerning Levites, the Ark and other Levitical matters; vv. 6–7 seem to quote a wilderness itinerary from P (cf. Num. 33.30–38). **6:** Num. 20.22–29. **8:** Exod. 32.25–29. The Levites' role is to bear the Ark (Num. 4.4–15), to *stand in attendance,* i.e., conduct the sacrificial services (Num. ch 18), and to *bless* the people (Num. 6.22–27). **9:** See 12.12 n.; 18.2 n.

before the LORD—eating no bread and drinking no water forty
days and forty nights, as before—because of the great wrong
you had committed, doing what displeased the LORD and vexing Him. 19 For I was in dread of the LORD's fierce anger against
you, which moved Him to wipe you out. And that time, too,
the LORD gave heed to me.—20 Moreover, the LORD was angry
enough with Aaron to have destroyed him; so I also interceded for Aaron at that time.—21 As for that sinful thing you had
made, the calf, I took it and put it to the fire; I broke it to bits
and ground it thoroughly until it was fine as dust, and I threw
its dust into the brook that comes down from the mountain.

22 Again you provoked the LORD at Taberah, and at Massah,
and at Kibroth-hattaavah.

23 And when the LORD sent you on from Kadesh-barnea, saying, "Go up and take possession of the land that I am giving
you," you flouted the command of the LORD your God; you did
not put your trust in Him and did not obey Him.

24 As long as I have known you, you have been defiant toward the LORD.

25 When I lay prostrate before the LORD [a]those forty days
and forty nights,[a] because the LORD was determined to destroy you, 26 I prayed to the LORD and said, "O Lord GOD, do
not annihilate Your very own people, whom You redeemed in
Your majesty and whom You freed from Egypt with a mighty
hand. 27 Give thought to Your servants, Abraham, Isaac, and
Jacob, and pay no heed to the stubbornness of this people, its
wickedness, and its sinfulness. 28 Else the country from which
You freed us will say, 'It was because the LORD was powerless to bring them into the land that He had promised them,
and because He rejected them, that He brought them out to
have them die in the wilderness.' 29 Yet they are Your very own
people, whom You freed with Your great might and Your outstretched arm."

10 Thereupon the LORD said to me, "Carve out two tablets
of stone like the first, and come up to Me on the mountain; and make an ark of wood. 2 I will inscribe on the tablets
the commandments that were on the first tablets that you
smashed, and you shall deposit them in the ark."

3 I made an ark of acacia wood and carved out two tablets of
stone like the first; I took the two tablets with me and went up
the mountain. 4 The LORD inscribed on the tablets the same
text as on the first, the Ten Commandments that He addressed
to you on the mountain out of the fire on the day of the Assembly; and the LORD gave them to me. 5 Then I left and went
down from the mountain, and I deposited the tablets in the

a-a *Lit. "the forty days and forty nights that I lay prostrate."*

ark that I had made, where they still are, as the LORD had commanded me.
[6]From Beeroth-bene-jaakan[a] the Israelites marched to Moserah. Aaron died there and was buried there; and his son Eleazar became priest in his stead. [7]From there they marched
to Gudgod,[b] and from Gudgod to Jotbath, a region of running
brooks.
[8]At that time the LORD set apart the tribe of Levi to carry the
Ark of the LORD's Covenant, to stand in attendance upon the
LORD, and to bless in His name, as is still the case. [9]That is why
the Levites have received no hereditary portion along with
their kinsmen: the LORD is their portion, as the LORD your God
spoke concerning them.

[10]I had stayed on the mountain, as I did the first time, forty
days and forty nights; and the LORD heeded me once again:
the LORD agreed not to destroy you. [11]And the LORD said to
me, "Up, resume the march at the head of the people, that they
may go in and possess the land that I swore to their fathers to
give them."

[12]And now, O Israel, what does the LORD your God demand
of you? Only this: to revere the LORD your God, to walk only
in His paths, to love Him, and to serve the LORD your God
with all your heart and soul, [13]keeping the LORD's commandments and laws, which I enjoin upon you today, for your good.
[14]Mark, the heavens [c]to their uttermost reaches[c] belong to the
LORD your God, the earth and all that is on it! [15]Yet it was to
your fathers that the LORD was drawn in His love for them, so
that He chose you, their lineal descendants, from among all
peoples—as is now the case. [16]Cut away, therefore, the thickening about your hearts and stiffen your necks no more. [17]For
the LORD your God is [d]God supreme and Lord supreme,[d] the
great, the mighty, and the awesome God, who shows no favor
and takes no bribe, [18]but upholds the cause of the fatherless
and the widow, and befriends the stranger, providing him with
food and clothing.—[19]You too must befriend the stranger, for
you were strangers in the land of Egypt.

a Lit. "wells of Bene-jaakan"; cf. Num. 33.31–32.
b "Hor-haggidgad" in Num. 33.32–33.
c-c Lit. "and the heaven of heavens."
d-d Lit. "the God of gods and the Lord of lords."

10.12–11.32: Obedience as the condition for prosperity in the land. This section provides the climax and conclusion of the historical review in 8.1–10.11. **10.12–13:** Earlier, breach of the first and second Decalogue commandments, with their focus specifically on God, had been redefined and equated with failing to "keep His commandments ... rules ... and ... laws" (8.11 n.). Now obedience to God is similarly redefined as compliance with the fixed *commandments and laws* (v. 13) of Deut., i.e., the laws of chs 12–26 (see 28.15, 45). **13:** *Keeping,* the precise antithesis of 8.11. The sequence *love ... keeping ... commandments* (vv. 12–13) cites 5.10. **16:** *Cut away ... the thickening about your hearts* (lit. "circumcise ... the foreskin of your heart") means to open oneself to God (Lev. 26.41); no distinction is intended between mind, will, and emotion. The metaphorical formulation, which challenges any attempt to reduce Deut. to narrow "legalism," corresponds to prophetic ideals (cf. Jer. 4.4; 31.33). **17–18:** Integrity in the administration of court justice (v. 17; cf. 1.17; 16.19) and protection of the marginalized (v. 18) are together given a theological foundation, making the remarkable argument that human social ethics amounts to "imitatio dei." Ensuring justice in court and defending the marginalized were conventional royal prerogatives (Laws of Hammurabi prologue; Ps. 72.4). Deut. contemplates no such role for the monarch (17.14–20 n.). Instead, it is God who protects the rights of the marginalized, entering history to do so (cf. Exod. 3.7–10; similarly Philippians 2.5–8). Love of neighbor thus originates in divine action as ethics receive a theological foundation. In its use of the consecutive adjectives *the great, the mighty, and the awesome* to describe God, this section echoes the style of Mesopotamian royal inscriptions, but projects these royal attributes onto God. This phrase becomes significant in later Judaism when it is quoted as part of the first blessing of the daily statutory prayer (*'Amidah*). **18–19:** *Stranger ... strangers,* better, "resident alien" in both cases; see 1.16 n. The Israelite is not urged simply to protect a fellow Israelite, but to "love" the non-Israelite, who resides in the community. Just as justice must be rendered to Israelite and alien alike (see 1.16 n.), so must "love" reach across national or ethnic lines (cf. Lev. 19.33–34). **18:** *Befriends* (lit., "loves"): Note the concrete expression of love in action and service (see 5.10 n.; 6.5 n.). **19:** *For you were,* see Exod. 23.9.

22: *Seventy persons* (Gen. 46.27; Exod. 1.5), here a stereotypical number expressing completeness, comes first in the Heb, emphasizing Israel's miraculous transformation into a nation. *Stars of heaven,* see 1.10 n.

11.1–32: Loyalty to the covenant provides the condition for life in Canaan. The punishments and rewards in this section are predominantly addressed to a plural "you," stressing communal rather than individual responsibility. **2:** The frequent phrase *this day* in Deut. emphasizes the contemporaneity of the covenant (see 5.3 n.). *Lesson,* see 8.5 n. **4:** See Exod. ch 14. **6:** The address is based upon the early tradition of the revolt of Dathan and Abiram (Num. ch 16). There is no mention of Korah's rebellion (Num. 16.3–11), which was very likely added to the narrative in Num. by the Priestly school after this abstract was made. **10–12:** Though the Nile provided sufficient water, the Nile valley had to be irrigated through human effort, since rainfall was minimal; Canaan's crops are irrigated by seasonal rainfall. The difference is mentioned to stress Israel's dependence upon God, who gives and withholds rain (Amos 4.7–8), as well as the fundamental sanctity of the land of Israel. **14:** *I,* God (see translators' note *d*). Moses as speaker here shifts from referring to God in the third person to speaking directly on God's behalf, in the first person (see 28.20 n.). The *early rain* ends the summer dry season (October–November); the *late* comes in the spring (March–April).

20 You must revere the LORD your God: only Him shall you
worship, to Him shall you hold fast, and by His name shall you
swear. 21 He is your glory and He is your God, who wrought for
you those marvelous, awesome deeds that you saw with your
own eyes. 22 Your ancestors went down to Egypt seventy persons in all; and now the LORD your God has made you as numerous as the stars of heaven.

11 Love, therefore, the LORD your God, and always keep
His charge, His laws, His rules, and His commandments.
2 [a]Take thought this day that it was not your children, who
neither experienced nor witnessed the lesson of the LORD your
God—

His majesty, His mighty hand, His outstretched arm; 3 the
signs and the deeds that He performed in Egypt against
Pharaoh king of Egypt and all his land; 4 what He did to
Egypt's army, its horses and chariots; how the LORD rolled
back upon them the waters of the Sea of Reeds when they
were pursuing you, thus destroying them [b-]once and for
all;[-b] 5 what He did for you in the wilderness before you
arrived in this place; 6 and what He did to Dathan and Abiram, sons of Eliab son of Reuben, when the earth opened
her mouth and swallowed them, along with their households, their tents, and every living thing in their train,
from amidst all Israel—

7 but that it was you who saw with your own eyes all the marvelous deeds that the LORD performed.

8 Keep, therefore, all the Instruction that I enjoin upon you
today, so that you may have the strength to enter and take possession of the land that you are about to cross into and possess,
9 and that you may long endure upon the soil that the LORD
swore to your fathers to assign to them and to their heirs, a
land flowing with milk and honey.

10 For the land that you are about to enter and possess is not
like the land of Egypt from which you have come. There the
grain you sowed had to be watered by your own labors,[c] like
a vegetable garden; 11 but the land you are about to cross into
and possess, a land of hills and valleys, soaks up its water from
the rains of heaven. 12 It is a land which the LORD your God
looks after, on which the LORD your God always keeps His eye,
from year's beginning to year's end.

13 If, then, you obey the commandments that I enjoin upon
you this day, loving the LORD your God and serving Him with
all your heart and soul, 14 I[d] will grant the rain for your land in
season, the early rain and the late. You shall gather in your new

a Syntax of Heb. uncertain. b-b Lit. "to this day." c Lit. "by your foot."
d I.e., the LORD; Samaritan reads "He."

grain and wine and oil—[15] I[a] will also provide grass in the fields for your cattle—and thus you shall eat your fill. [16] Take care not to be lured away to serve other gods and bow to them. [17] For the LORD's anger will flare up against you, and He will shut up the skies so that there will be no rain and the ground will not yield its produce; and you will soon perish from the good land that the LORD is assigning to you.

[18] Therefore impress these My words upon your [b]very heart:[b] bind them as a sign on your hand and let them serve as a [c]symbol on your forehead,[c] [19] and teach them to your children—reciting them when you stay at home and when you are away, when you lie down and when you get up; [20] and inscribe them on the doorposts of your house and on your gates—[21] to the end that you and your children may endure, in the land that the LORD swore to your fathers to assign to them, as long as there is a heaven over the earth.

[22] If, then, you faithfully keep all this Instruction that I command you, loving the LORD your God, walking in all His ways, and holding fast to Him, [23] the LORD will dislodge before you all these nations: you will dispossess nations greater and more numerous than you. [24] Every spot on which your foot treads shall be yours; your territory shall extend from the wilderness to the Lebanon and from the River—the Euphrates—to the Western[d] Sea. [25] No man shall stand up to you: the LORD your God will put the dread and the fear of you over the whole land in which you set foot, as He promised you.

RE'EH ראה

[26] See, this day I set before you blessing and curse: [27] blessing, if you obey the commandments of the LORD your God that I enjoin upon you this day; [28] and curse, if you do not obey the commandments of the LORD your God, but turn away from the path that I enjoin upon you this day and follow other gods, [e]whom you have not experienced.[e] [29] When the LORD your God brings you into the land that you are about to enter and possess, you shall pronounce the blessing at Mount Gerizim and the curse at Mount Ebal.—[30] Both are on the other side of the Jordan, beyond the west road that is in the land of the Canaanites who dwell in the Arabah—near Gilgal, by the terebinths of Moreh.

[31] For you are about to cross the Jordan to enter and possess the land that the LORD your God is assigning to you. When you have occupied it and are settled in it, [32] take care to observe all the laws and rules that I have set before you this day.

a I.e., the LORD; Samaritan reads "He." *b-b Lit. "heart and self."*
c-c See notes on 6.8. *d I.e., Mediterranean.*
e-e I.e., who have not proved themselves to you; cf. Hos. 13.4.

16–17: See 7.12–14 n. **18–21:** See 6.6–9 nn. **24:** *Every spot ... yours,* a legal ritual that effected transfer of title by pacing out the perimeter of the territory (Gen. 13.17). The territory is described in terms of the ideal limits noted of biblical King David's empire (see 1.7 n.). **26–32:** The two ways (see ch 28; 30.15–20). **26:** *Curse,* the sanctions for violating a treaty, which a vassal assumes in a sworn oath (see 28.15–68). **28:** *Follow,* see 6.14 n. **29–30:** These vv. represent an editorial intrusion, hinting ahead to ch 27. Previously, *blessing ... and the curse* identify the benefits of covenantal obedience and the sanctions for breach of covenant (vv. 26–28; 28.2, 15). That theme is the expected climax of this ch. Here, "blessing" and "curse" are restricted to a series of positive and negative sayings shouted from mounts *Gerizim and ... Ebal,* in anticipation of ch 27. *Gerizim,* on the south, and *Ebal,* on the north, flank the pass guarded by the city of Shechem in the central hill country. This geographic restriction fits poorly in a ch otherwise directed to the entire land (vv. 22–25, 31–32). **30:** *The terebinths of Moreh,* at Shechem (see Gen. 12.6). **31–32:** Transition to the legal corpus. **32:** *Take care to observe ... laws and rules,* cited chiastically at 12.1 ("laws ... rules ... carefully observe") to effect the transition from the literary frame of Deut. (chs 1–11) into the laws (chs 12–26).

12 These are the laws and rules that you must carefully observe in the land that the LORD, God of your fathers, is
giving you to possess, as long as you live on earth.
[2] You must destroy all the sites at which the nations you are
to dispossess worshiped their gods, whether on lofty mountains and on hills or under any luxuriant tree. [3] Tear down their
altars, smash their pillars, put their sacred posts to the fire,
and cut down the images of their gods, obliterating their name
from that site.
[4] Do not worship the LORD your God in like manner, [5] but
look only to the site that the LORD your God will choose amidst
all your tribes as His habitation, to establish His name there.
There you are to go, [6] and there you are to bring your burnt
offerings and other sacrifices, your tithes and contributions,[a]
your votive and freewill offerings, and the firstlings of your
herds and flocks. [7] Together with your households, you shall
feast there before the LORD your God, happy in all the undertakings in which the LORD your God has blessed you.
[8] You shall not act at all as we now act here, every man as he
pleases, [9] because you have not yet come to the allotted haven
that the LORD your God is giving you. [10] When you cross the
Jordan and settle in the land that the LORD your God is allotting

a Lit. "the contribution(s) of your hands."

12.1–26.15: The legal corpus, the core of Deuteronomy's transformation of Israelite religion. For the topical organization, see the intro.

12.1–13.1: Centralization and purification of the sacrificial worship, two of the most distinctive features of Deut.'s idea of religion and law. These two requirements radically transformed Israelite religion, which in its formative stages, like all religions of antiquity, viewed sacrifice as indispensable to honor and to communicate with the deity. Historically, they are associated with the reform movements of King Hezekiah (2 Kings 18.3–6, 22; 727/715–698/687 BCE) and, especially, of King Josiah (2 Kings chs 22–23; 640–609 BCE). The ch requires the removal of foreign elements from the cult (the system of sacrificial worship of God). It also centralizes the cult by restricting sacrifice to a single, exclusively legitimate sanctuary. Four paragraphs (vv. 2–7, 8–12, 13–19, 20–28) each contain the centralization command; a fifth paragraph (vv. 29–31), concerned with cultic purification, vividly warns of the consequences of introducing alien worship into the Israelite system. An editorial superscription (v. 1) and conclusion (13.1) frame the unit, as each urges obedience. **1:** *Earth,* more accurately, "land." **2–7:** Israel must violently reject the Canaanite precedent of worshipping God at multiple sanctuaries distributed throughout the land; instead, no matter where the members of the covenant live, they must travel to the single, legitimate sanctuary. **2:** *You:* The ch alternates between primarily plural (vv. 1–12) and primarily singular (vv. 13–31). This unexplained grammatical shift, combined with six repetitions of the command for cultic centralization (vv. 5, 11, 14, 18, 21, 26), suggests a complex compositional history. *Destroy:* Similar commands to destroy all implements associated with the worship of foreign gods are found at Exod. 23.23–24; 34.11–14; Deut. 7.5. *Lofty mountains ... luxuriant tree,* formulaic language of the school of Deut. for Canaanite sanctuaries, also known as "high places" (1 Kings 3.2; 2 Kings 16.4). Such sanctuaries were not only used to worship alien deities, however. During the monarchy, God could also be worshipped at such locations (1 Kings 3.4). **5:** *The site that the LORD ... will choose:* This frequent formula consistently refers to Jerusalem, where Solomon built the Temple. Since Jerusalem played no role in Israel's history until David conquered it, made it his capital, and brought the Ark of the Covenant there (2 Sam. 5.6–6.19), the city cannot be named explicitly without undermining the literary form of Deut. as a Mosaic address. *To establish His name there:* Deut. rejects the common older idea that a nation's God would inhabit the Temple (contrast 1 Kings 8.12–13). Thus, *as His habitation* would better be translated "to establish it" (the divine name), indicating possession and special relationship. **6:** A list of different types of sacrificial offerings. *Burnt offerings* is a technical term for a type of sacrifice where all of the animal's flesh was burnt on the altar (v. 27; cf. the Priestly sacrificial laws in Lev. 1.3–17). *Other sacrifices* refers to offerings where portions of the animal were assigned to the priests or shared by the worshippers (v. 27; 18.1–3; cf. Priestly law in Lev. ch 3; 7.29–36). **8–12:** This paragraph understands centralization of worship as part of a divine plan that awaits future fulfillment. The idea here that sacrificial worship at multiple sanctuaries was intended from the beginning to have limited temporal validity differs from the viewpoint of Exod. 20.21, where it is chronologically unconditional. **8:** *Every man as he pleases,* lit. "each person doing what is right in his own eyes" in the absence of a central authority; a negative judgment, as in Judg. 17.6; 21.25. **9–10:** *Allotted haven* is a typical Deuteronomic term for the land as a whole. These vv. designate territorial security as the

to you, and He grants you safety from all your enemies around you and you live in security, [11] then you must bring everything that I command you to the site where the LORD your God will choose to establish His name: your burnt offerings and other sacrifices, your tithes and contributions,[a] and all the choice votive offerings that you vow to the LORD. [12] And you shall rejoice before the LORD your God with your sons and daughters and with your male and female slaves, along with the Levite in your settlements, for he has no territorial allotment among you.

[13] Take care not to sacrifice your burnt offerings in any place you like, [14] but only in the place that the LORD will choose in one of your tribal territories. There you shall sacrifice your burnt offerings and there you shall observe all that I enjoin upon you. [15] But whenever you desire, you may slaughter and eat meat in any of your settlements, according to the blessing that the LORD your God has granted you. The unclean and the clean alike may partake of it, as of the gazelle and the deer.[b] [16] But you must not partake of the blood; you shall pour it out on the ground like water.

[17] You may not partake in your settlements of the tithes of your new grain or wine or oil, or of the firstlings of your herds and flocks, or of any of the votive offerings that you vow, or of your freewill offerings, or of your contributions.[a] [18] These you must consume before the LORD your God in the place that the LORD your God will choose—you and your sons and your daughters, your male and female slaves, and the Levite in your settlements—happy before the LORD your God in all your undertakings. [19] Be sure not to neglect the Levite as long as you live in your land.

a Lit. "the contribution(s) of your hands."
b I.e., animals that may be eaten (cf. 14.5; Lev. 11.1 ff.), but not sacrificed (Lev. 1.1 ff.).

precondition for the inauguration of centralization. This condition was fulfilled, according to the Deuteronomistic historian, only with David's conquest of Jerusalem, which then allowed the construction of the Temple (2 Sam. 7.1, 11; 1 Kings 8.56; cf. Josh. 21.43–45). **12:** Since *the Levites* were not assigned land (see Josh. 13.14; cf. Ezek. 44.28), they had to depend upon voluntary offerings (see 10.9; 18.2 n.). **13–19:** This section, the earliest in the ch, is concentrically arranged in a chiasm, a literary device frequently used by the authors and editors of antiquity to structure diverse material in an ABC:C'B'A' pattern (see diagram below). **13–16:** The paragraph introduces two important distinctions in Israelite religion, each of which was revolutionary. **13–14:** The first distinction is between sacrificial worship *any place* (i.e., at sites scattered throughout the land), which is here rejected as illegitimate, and legitimate sacrifice performed at a single sanctuary, *the place that the LORD will choose* (v. 14). The prohibition of sacrifice at multiple sites marks a dramatic contrast with the nation's previous norms. It was formerly common to erect altars and sacrifice to God throughout the land (Gen. 12.7; 35.1–7; 1 Sam. 7.17; 1 Kings 18.20–46); indeed, earlier biblical law assures God's blessing at multiple sacrificial altars: "in every place" (Exod. 20.21). **14–16:** The second distinction is between the ritual sacrifice of animals at an altar and the secular slaughter of domestic animals for food. Prior to Deut., that distinction almost certainly did not exist; all sacrifice was ritual. The existence of multiple altars throughout the land made it easy to comply with the requirement that the slaughter of a domestic animal should take place upon an altar, on the base of which its blood would be spilled in devotion to God (Lev. 17.1–9). This requirement lies behind the condemnation of Saul's troops for slaughtering domestic animals "on the ground," without an altar (1 Sam. 14.31–35). The prohibition of

CHIASTIC STRUCTURE OF 12.13–19

v. 13	*Take care not* (Heb "hishamer lekha pen")	A
v. 14	*but only* ("ki 'im") + central location	B
v. 15	*But* ("rak") + secular slaughter elsewhere	C
v. 16	*But* ("rak") + secular slaughter elsewhere	C'
v. 18	But rather ("ki 'im"; not translated) + central location	B'
v. 19	*Be sure not* ("hishamer lekha pen")	A'

[20] When the LORD enlarges your territory, as He has promised
you, and you say, "I shall eat some meat," for you have the urge
to eat meat, you may eat meat whenever you wish. [21] If the place
where the LORD has chosen to establish His name is too far from
you, you may slaughter any of the cattle or sheep that the LORD
gives you, as I have instructed you; and you may eat to your
heart's content in your settlements. [22] Eat it, however, as the
gazelle and the deer are eaten: the unclean may eat it together
with the clean. [23] But make sure that you do not partake of the
blood; for the blood is the life, and you must not consume the
life with the flesh. [24] You must not partake of it; you must pour
it out on the ground like water: [25] you must not partake of it, in
order that it may go well with you and with your descendants to
come, for you will be doing what is right in the sight of the LORD.

[26] But such sacred and votive donations as you may have
[a]-shall be taken by you-[a] to the site that the LORD will choose.
[27] You shall offer your burnt offerings, both the flesh and the
blood, on the altar of the LORD your God; and of your other
sacrifices, the blood shall be poured out on the altar of the
LORD your God, and you shall eat the flesh.

[28] Be careful to heed all these commandments that I enjoin
upon you; thus it will go well with you and with your descendants after you forever, for you will be doing what is good and
right in the sight of the LORD your God.

[29] When the LORD your God has cut down before you the nations that you are about to enter and dispossess, and you have
dispossessed them and settled in their land, [30] beware of being lured into their ways after they have been wiped out before
you! Do not inquire about their gods, saying, "How did those
nations worship their gods? I too will follow those practices."

a-a Lit. "you shall pick up and come."

all local altars, however, created a real difficulty for those living *in any of your settlements* (v. 15), without easy access to the central sanctuary. In order that those far from the Temple could continue to eat meat, the legislator sought a legal precedent for the innovation of permitting the slaughter of domestic animals without performing that slaughter at an altar. The precedent employed was, paradoxically, the convention that applied to wild game such as the *gazelle and ... deer* (v. 15). Although permissible for consumption, these animals could not be sacrificed (see translators' note *b*). Accordingly, Priestly law allowed the slaughter of wild game in the open field: i.e., away from an altar (Lev. 17.13–14). (Later rabbinic law also provides specific rules concerning how any animal should be slaughtered, seeking to prevent suffering.) The one condition imposed was not to consume the animal's blood but to "pour out its blood and cover it with earth" (Lev. 17.13). Deut.'s legislator applies that model to domestic animals, which may now—paradoxically in contravention of Priestly norms (Lev. 17.3–7)—similarly be slaughtered throughout the land, on condition that their blood is not consumed but poured *out on the ground like water* (v. 16). Blood was accorded special status because it symbolized the vitality and "life" of animals and humans (v. 23; 15.23; Gen. 9.4–5; Lev. 17.14; 19.26); later Jewish ritual law clarified how the blood was to be removed (e.g., by soaking and salting the meat). Ritually pure and impure alike *(the unclean and the clean)* may now eat meat slaughtered under the new regulations (v. 15; contrast Lev. 7.19–21) since this meat no longer must be consumed at a temple. **17:** *Tithes,* see 14.22–29 n. **20–28:** This section repeats the permission for secular slaughter. It presents it in a new light, however, now explaining it as a necessary consequence of the expansion of Israel's boundaries and resulting distance from the cultic shrine. The assumption of a 7th c. date for the composition of Deut. would imply that the paragraph's future formulation reflects an after-the-fact explanation. **23–27:** Although secular slaughter does not require an altar, common to it and the rules for sacrifice are special procedures for handling the animal's blood (see vv. 13–16 n.). In neither case may the blood ever be consumed by humans. Slaughter requires the blood to be poured on the ground (vv. 23–25). Similarly, the rules for each of the two main types of animal sacrifice direct the blood away from human consumption (v. 27). With *burnt offerings, both the flesh and the blood* are offered to God on the altar (see v. 6 n.). With *your other sacrifices,* the blood is directed *on the altar,* at or upon its base. **28:** *Commandments,* lit. "words." **29–31:** Here the focus shifts to purification of worship. **30:** The new covenant requires that Israelites not imitate the more established sacrificial practices of the Canaanites, by whose antiquity the newcomers might be *lured.* Elsewhere, the corruption of Israelite religion is presented as resulting from the attractions of marital contract (7.1–5, 25) or political treaty (Exod. 23.33; 34.12).

[31] You shall not act thus toward the LORD your God, for they
perform for their gods every abhorrent act that the LORD detests; they even offer up their sons and daughters in fire to
13 their gods. [1] Be careful to observe only that which I enjoin upon you: neither add to it nor take away from it.
[2] If there appears among you a prophet or a dream-diviner
and he gives you a sign or a portent, [3] saying, "Let us follow
and worship another god"—whom you have not experienced[a]
—even if the sign or portent that he named to you comes
true, [4] do not heed the words of that prophet or that dream-
diviner. For the LORD your God is testing you to see whether
you really love the LORD your God with all your heart and soul.
[5] Follow none but the LORD your God, and revere none but
Him; observe His commandments alone, and heed only His
orders; worship none but Him, and hold fast to Him. [6] As for
that prophet or dream-diviner, he shall be put to death; for he

a See note on 11.28.

31: *Offer up their sons and their daughters in fire:* The Canaanites are accused of child sacrifice (see 2 Kings 3.27; 23.10; Jer. 19.5–6), elsewhere associated with the deity Molech (Lev. 18.2; 20.2–5). This practice may have entrenched itself during the monarchy, with a cult center in the Hinnom Valley, just southwest of Jerusalem (2 Kings 23.10; Jer. 7.31; 19.5–6). The historical evidence for such practices, however, remains disputed. **13.1:** NJPS, following the Masoretic paragraph divisions, correctly regards this v. as the conclusion to ch 12; contrast the standard ch and v. numbers, which were first added to the Heb text in the 13th c. CE. The demarcation of the unit is here important. In form, ch 12 is thus framed by an inclusio (see next n.) that urges fidelity to law and tradition, even though, in its content, the unit has just profoundly transformed both. *Be careful to observe,* the same idiom found at 12.1 (also 11.32), frames the unit with an inclusio. Moreover, *Neither add to it nor take away from it* reflects an ancient Near Eastern scribal formula that was often included in the epilogue of treaties, inscriptions, or law collections to protect them from being defaced, altered, or written over. Although in 4.2 the admonition begins a section, more frequently, as here, it serves as an ending marker or "colophon" to conclude the literary unit (Prov. 30.6; Eccl. 3.14; cf. Revelation 22.18–19).

13.2–19: The requirement for unconditional loyalty to God. Three hypothetical test cases introduced by "if," each of which requires a difficult choice between competing social or personal commitments and allegiance to Israel's God. In the first case (vv. 2–6), a prophet or interpreter of dreams, symbolizing powerful religious authority, invites the citizen to worship other gods and thereby betray God by committing apostasy. The second test case (vv. 7–12) presents the incitement to apostasy as coming from an intimate family member, spouse, or close friend. The third case (vv. 13–19) concerns the successful conversion to apostasy of an entire city. In each instance, the crime is capital, and the citizen must act decisively by executing the prophet or dream interpreter (v. 6), killing the family member, spouse, or friend (v. 10), or conducting a war of attrition against a town of fellow citizens (v. 16). The literary model for these requirements is found in ancient Near Eastern treaties, which stipulated that vassals subject to a suzerain owed absolute loyalty to that suzerain and his designated successor. Political conspiracy had to be reported and was punishable by death. (See, e.g., the Neo-Assyrian VTE [672 BCE]). The author of this ch has transformed that treaty requirement into a demand for absolute covenantal loyalty to Israel's divine suzerain. **2–6:** While Deut. presents Moses as the founder of Israelite prophecy, establishing both its standard (18.15–22) and its pinnacle (34.10–12), the book is nonetheless concerned to regulate prophecy. No other Torah law collection legislates concerning the prophet. Deut. does so twice, in each case requiring the execution of the prophet who contravenes Deut.'s Torah (vv. 1–5; 18.19–22) and thus subordinating prophecy to covenantal law. At the same time, Deut. sharply reworks the role of the prophet. Older forms of charismatic revelation *(dream ... sign or a portent),* once the touchstone of the legitimate prophet and employed by Moses himself, now become suspect. No longer is the power to perform signs the test of a prophet's legitimacy (contrast v. 2 with 34.11–12; Exod. 4.1–9, 21; 1 Kings 18.20–40). The true prophet will now proclaim Torah (18.18). **2:** As a mediator of divine communications, *a prophet or a dream-diviner* (lit. "a prophet or dreamer of dreams") would by definition command public credibility and authority, making it the more difficult to resist his incitement to apostasy. *Dream-diviner:* Predicting the future by dream interpretation was one of the most common techniques of divination (Gen. 37.5–10; Num. 12.6; Jer. 23.25; Joel 3.1). The two sources of religious authority identified here correspond closely to the nearly contemporary Neo-Assyrian VTE (672 BCE), which requires loyalty even in the face of conspiracy from "your brothers, your sons, your daughters, or from the mouth of a prophet, an ecstatic, or an inquirer of oracles" (§10).

urged disloyalty to the LORD your God—who freed you from
the land of Egypt and who redeemed you from the house of
bondage—to make you stray from the path that the LORD your
God commanded you to follow. Thus you will sweep out evil
from your midst.
7 If your brother, [a]your own mother's son,[-a] or your son or
daughter, or the wife of your bosom, or your [b-]closest friend[-b] entices you in secret, saying, "Come let us worship other gods"—
whom neither you nor your fathers have experienced[c]— 8 from
among the gods of the peoples around you, either near to you
or distant, anywhere from one end of the earth to the other:
9 do not assent or give heed to him. Show him no pity or compassion, and do not shield him; 10 but take his life. Let your
hand be the first against him to put him to death, and the hand
of the rest of the people thereafter. 11 Stone him to death, for
he sought to make you stray from the LORD your God, who
brought you out of the land of Egypt, out of the house of bondage. 12 Thus all Israel will hear and be afraid, and such evil
things will not be done again in your midst.
13 If you hear it said, of one of the towns that the LORD your
God is giving you to dwell in, 14 that some scoundrels from
among you have gone and subverted the inhabitants of their
town, saying, "Come let us worship other gods"—whom you

a-a Samaritan reads, "the son of your father or the son of your mother."
b-b Lit. "your friend who is as yourself." *c See note on 11.28.*

Signs or *portents* were also used by legitimate prophets to authenticate their proclamations (34.11; Exod. 4.1–9, 21; 7.9; Judg. 6.17). **3:** *Follow ... another god:* The incitement to apostasy is formulated in the language of Neo-Assyrian treaties; see 6.14 n. *Worship,* specifically, with sacrifice; see 5.9 n. **6:** *Disloyalty,* as betrayal of the divine suzerain to whom covenant loyalty is owed. *Sweep out evil from your midst:* a formula that emphasizes the community's obligation to eliminate particularly offensive religious transgressions (e.g., 17.7, 12; 19.19; 21.21). **7–12:** The possible conflict between love of family, spouse, or friend—exclusive loyalty to God (cf. Luke 14.26). **7:** *In secret,* i.e., in private, without witnesses. *Your own mother's son* (lit. "the son of your mother"), that is, "your full brother." In the context of Second Temple Judaism, the law was read as incomplete because of its asymmetrical formulation. Seeking to fill the perceived gap in the law, the Samaritan Pentateuch, the LXX, and a fragment of Deut. found at Qumran (4Q30) add: "the son of your father" (in translators' note *a-a*), so that it would include both the full and the half-brother. The addition no longer understands the original intent of this law, which demands that the addressee choose between loyalty to God and loyalty to the closest possible member of the immediate family. Thus, the Masoretic version preserves the better reading by restricting the focus to the full brother. **10:** *But take his life,* lit. "But you shall surely kill him." This verb is almost never used for a standard judicial execution. Here it demands that the inciter should be killed on the spot. Only the religious emergency of a grave threat to the covenant, requiring urgent action, explains this type of summary execution (see also Exod. 32.27; Num. 25.5; Ezek. 9.6; cf. Lev. 20.15–16). Similar requirements for summarily executing traitors may be found in the Neo-Assyrian loyalty treaties that serve as a partial literary source for this ch. Historically, the requirement for unconditional loyalty to YHVH, at all costs, modeled after the political treaty's similar demand for loyalty to the suzerain, accounts for the law's stringency. Nonetheless, compliance with the law conflicts with Deut.'s requirement elsewhere for due process (17.2–7 n.; 19.15; similarly, Num. 35.30). Later editors therefore added another layer to bring the law into conformity with the normal protocol for a public, judicial execution (v. 11 n.). In the Second Temple period, the law could only be taught and understood in that light: as consistent with the standard requirement that any execution require a prior legal conviction based upon the testimony of two witnesses. The LXX embeds that later reinterpretation of the law into its translation of the initial command: "You shall report." **11:** *Stone:* Stoning was reserved for a particular class of offenses regarded as violating the community's fundamental values or sources of authority: apostasy or treason (here; 17.2–7; Lev. 20.2; Josh. 7.10–26; 1 Kings 21.8–14), blasphemy (Lev. 24.13–23), defying parental authority (21.18–21; 22.20–21), betraying marriage (22.23–24). Each of these offenses is prohibited by the Decalogue (5.6–7, 11, 16, 17). This form of punishment compelled the entire community to act collectively to repudiate the offense. **14:** *Scoundrels,* lit., "sons of worthlessness," or "children of Belial" (KJV), a very strong derogatory term. **16–18:** In the sphere of clan life, little could be more horrifying and socially divisive than to have to "join battle with our kinsmen" (Judg. 20.23). Nonetheless, the infidelity of the entire town represents so significant a betrayal of the covenant that its entire population must be placed under the same ban as that otherwise reserved for the Canaanite population (7.1–6, 25–26; 12.29–30; 20.16–18). **17:** Normally in antiquity, new occupants

have not experienced—15 you shall investigate and inquire and
interrogate thoroughly. If it is true, the fact is established—that
abhorrent thing was perpetrated in your midst—16 put the
inhabitants of that town to the sword and put its cattle to the
sword. Doom it and all that is in it to destruction: 17 gather all
its spoil into the open square, and burn the town and all its
spoil as a holocaust to the LORD your God. And it shall remain
an everlasting ruin, never to be rebuilt. 18 Let nothing that has
been doomed stick to your hand, in order that the LORD may
turn from His blazing anger and show you compassion, and in
His compassion increase you as He promised your fathers on
oath—19 for you will be heeding the LORD your God, obeying
all His commandments that I enjoin upon you this day, doing
what is right in the sight of the LORD your God.

14 You are children of the LORD your God. You shall not
gash yourselves or shave the front of your heads because
of the dead. 2 For you are a people consecrated to the LORD
your God: the LORD your God chose you from among all other
peoples on earth to be His treasured people.
3 You shall not eat anything abhorrent. 4 These are the animals that you may eat: the ox, the sheep, and the goat; 5a the
deer, the gazelle, the roebuck, the wild goat, the ibex, the antelope, the mountain sheep, 6 and any other animal that has true
hoofs which are cleft in two and brings up the cud—such you
may eat. 7 But the following, which do bring up the cud or have
true hoofs which are cleft through, you may not eat: the camel, the hare, and the daman—for although they bring up the
cud, they have no true hoofs—they are unclean for you; 8 also
the swine—for although it has true hoofs, it does not bring up
the cud—is unclean for you. You shall not eat of their flesh or
touch their carcasses.

a A number of these creatures cannot be identified with certainty.

would rebuild cities after their military destruction, right on top of the *ruin* (Heb "tel"). The word yields the term for the city-mounds that remain visible throughout the Near East, where archeological digs are conducted. In cases of particular cataclysm, the mounds sometimes were not rebuilt, and served as visible reminders of the destruction (Josh. 8.28; Jer. 26.18; 49.2; Mic. 3.12).

14.1–29: The obligations of holiness. 1–21: The special status that the covenant grants Israel as *a people consecrated to the LORD* (v. 2) entails special obligations upon them, one focus of which is dietary. The affirmation of holiness (vv. 2, 21) therefore frames the list of permitted and prohibited foods (vv. 3–21). That the nation's holiness requires special selectivity regarding food is also evident in earlier biblical law (Exod. 22.30). **1:** *Children of the LORD,* the first of three metaphors used in vv. 1–2 to emphasize the special relation between God and Israel. The divine parent has special custody for the child (Exod. 2.22–23; Hos. 1.10) but, equally, special indignation at wrongdoing (32.5–6, 19–20; Isa. 1.2). *Gash ... shave ... dead:* Gashing and head shaving were customary mourning rituals within Israel and the larger Near East (1 Kings 18.28; Jer. 16.6–7; 41.4–5; 47.5; Amos 8.10). Many see the rationale for their prohibition (see also Lev. 19.27–28; 21.1–6) as their association with foreign religion. More likely, such rituals were associated with ancestor worship or cults of the dead, an aspect of Israelite family religion rejected by Deut. (see 18.10–11). **2:** *For you are a people consecrated to the LORD:* Just as priests observe more stringent purity rules than other Israelites, so must Israel distinguish itself from other nations by observing the special requirements of the Torah. This second metaphor of election departs from the idea of Israel's status found in the other biblical legal collections. Both the Book of the Covenant and the Holiness Collection understand the nation's holiness as a goal to be achieved in the future ("you shall be": Exod. 22.30; Lev. 19.2). In contrast, Deut. affirms Israel's present, intrinsic status as already holy. *His treasured people:* The third metaphor is political. Just as the monarch is entitled to a "private hoard" of treasure not in the public domain (1 Chron. 29.3), so does God single Israel out for a special relationship. Both the second and third metaphors *(consecrated; treasured people)* derive from God's affirmation just prior to Sinai (Exod. 19.5–6). **3–21:** The word "kosher" is never used in the Bible in reference to food. Nor is there in the Torah a comprehensive set of rules, similar to the later rabbinic system of kashrut, which covers permitted and nonpermitted foods, combinations of foods, means of preparation, rules for slaughter, etc. Deut. nevertheless begins to build toward such a system. In contrast to Priestly law (Lev. ch 11), it brings together a list of creatures that may or may not be eaten (vv. 3–20), which it combines with laws implicitly concerned with slaughter and food preparation (v. 21). Deut.'s dietary restrictions abridge and revise the

9 These you may eat of all that live in water: you may eat anything that has fins and scales. 10 But you may not eat anything that has no fins and scales: it is unclean for you.

11 You may eat any clean bird. 12 The following you may not eat: [a]the eagle, the vulture, and the black vulture; 13 the kite, the falcon, and the buzzard of any variety; 14 every variety of raven; 15 the ostrich, the nighthawk, the sea gull, and the hawk of any variety; 16 the little owl, the great owl, and the white owl; 17 the pelican, the bustard, and the cormorant; 18 the stork, any variety of heron, the hoopoe, and the bat.

19 All winged swarming things are unclean for you: they may not be eaten. 20 You may eat only clean winged creatures.

21 You shall not eat anything that has died a natural death; give it to the stranger in your community to eat, or you may sell it to a foreigner. For you are a people consecrated to the LORD your God.

You shall not boil a kid in its mother's milk.

22 You shall set aside every year a tenth part of all the yield of your sowing that is brought from the field. 23 You shall consume the tithes of your new grain and wine and oil, and the firstlings of your herds and flocks, in the presence of the LORD your God, in the place where He will choose to establish His name, so that you may learn to revere the LORD your God forever. 24 Should the distance be too great for you, should you be unable to transport them, because the place where the LORD your God has chosen to establish His name is far from you and because the LORD your God has blessed you,[b] 25 you may convert them into money. Wrap up the money and take it with you to the place that the LORD your God has chosen, 26 and spend the money on anything you want—cattle, sheep, wine, or other intoxicant, or anything you may desire. And you shall feast there, in the presence of the LORD your God, and rejoice with your household.

a A number of these creatures cannot be identified with certainty.
b I.e., with abundant crops.

more detailed list of permitted and prohibited foods provided by P (Lev. 11.2–23). For example, the list of land animals prohibited by vv. 7–9 is more limited than the fuller list, including individual explanations, of Lev. 11.4–8. Similarly, vv. 9–10 offer a précis of Lev. 11.9–12; and v. 19 issues a blanket prohibition against insects in contrast to the lengthy distinctions between permitted and prohibited insects of Lev. 11.20–23. This textual relationship, where Deut. uses and revises P material, is highly unusual; by and large, it seems unaware of these texts. The classification of creatures as permitted or nonpermitted employs unexplained criteria to establish three basic divisions of species: creatures of the land (Deut. 14.1–8), water (vv. 9–10), or air (vv. 11–20). The same tripartite division occurs in the P creation account (Gen. 1.20–25). Species that fail to satisfy the defining characteristics established for each category are not permitted: the pig (v. 8) and shellfish (v. 10). It is important to recognize that the classification system reflects the desire to imprint a human system of categorization upon nature and is based on a concern for systematic order rather than on hygiene or health. Thus, the term *unclean* (v. 8) does not imply that an animal is dirty. Ritually "impure" conveys the idea more clearly (see essay "Concepts of Purity," pp. 1998–2005). **21:** *Anything that has died a natural death:* Israelites may not eat carrion (Exod. 22.30) or any other animal that is not slaughtered according to Deut.'s stringent requirement that the blood be drained (12.16, 23–25). Again, the motivation is not hygiene but the enforcement of rules for slaughter. Carrion may therefore be donated to resident aliens or sold to foreigners, since the laws of slaughter apply only to Israelites. *Boil a kid:* This law is repeated three times in the Torah (here; Exod. 23.19; 34.26). The rabbinic assumption that no law in the Bible is redundant led to the postbiblical generalization that prohibited the consumption of meat and milk products together and even prohibited enjoying any benefit from such a combination. On its own terms, the law seems to have had a more restricted application, and originally applied specifically to the pilgrimage festival offerings (Exod. 23.19; 34.26). Deut. now reinterprets it as a general law of food preparation. Philo viewed it as directing the mind away from the body; Maimonides (Rambam) viewed it as directed against idolatry. Some moderns have viewed the prohibition as directed against Canaanite religious rituals; others view it as concerned to prevent the abuse of animals. **22–29:** The requirement to *set aside every year a tenth* of crops and livestock as a tax or honorarium paid to a monarch is common (Gen. 14.20; 28.22; 1 Sam. 8.15, 17). Here the rule signifies that Israel is God's steward, working but not owning God's land. **23:** The standard rules of the tithe (Lev. 27.30–33; Num. 18.21–32; cf. Exod.

27 But do not neglect the Levite in your community, for he
has no hereditary portion as you have. 28 [a]Every third year[a]
you shall bring out the full tithe of your yield of that year, but
leave it within your settlements. 29 Then the Levite, who has no
hereditary portion as you have, and the stranger, the fatherless, and the widow in your settlements shall come and eat
their fill, so that the LORD your God may bless you in all the
enterprises you undertake.

15 [b]Every seventh year[b] you shall practice remission of
debts. 2 This shall be the nature of the remission: every
creditor shall remit the due that he claims from his fellow; he
shall not dun his fellow or kinsman, for the remission proclaimed is of the LORD. 3 You may dun the foreigner; but you
must remit whatever is due you from your kinsmen.
4 There shall be no needy among you—since the LORD your
God will bless you in the land that the LORD your God is giving you as a hereditary portion—5 if only you heed the LORD
your God and take care to keep all this Instruction that I enjoin
upon you this day. 6 For the LORD your God will bless you as He
has promised you: you will extend loans to many nations, but
require none yourself; you will dominate many nations, but
they will not dominate you.
7 If, however, there is a needy person among you, one of your
kinsmen in any of your settlements in the land that the LORD

a-a *Lit. "After a period of three years"; cf. Deut. 26.12.* *b-b* *Cf. 14.28.*

22.29) are revised to direct offerings to the single sanctuary. Later rabbinic norms for tithing do not recognize this, and attempt to harmonize these various laws by insisting that they all be observed. *You shall consume:* Whereas Deut. assigns the tithe to the landholder, Lev. 27.30 directs it to the sanctuary and Num. 18.21 to the Levites. **24–25:** In light of centralization, sanctified crops (designated for the sanctuary) may be converted *into money* (better "silver," v. 25) to facilitate the journey. That *firstlings* (v. 23) may also be sold for silver is at variance with Lev. 27.32. *Distance be too great,* as in 12.21 ("too far"). **28–29:** *Every third year* the tithe is shifted away from the central sanctuary to focus on the needs of the disadvantaged and the marginalized in the local community, to ensure that they too may *eat their fill.*

15.1–18: Remission of debts (vv. 1–11) **and manumission of slaves** (vv. 12–18). On accession to the throne, ancient Near Eastern rulers would sometimes grant one-time cancellation of debts, return land confiscated by the crown, and free indentured slaves. That custom, Akkadian "duraru," is reflected in the Heb "deror," "jubilee" or "release," of Lev. 25.10; Isa. 61.1; Jer. 34.15, 17. Deut.'s conception of the covenant between Israel and God entails a similar fresh start in which prior economic obligations are canceled at the initiative of the divine monarch. Now, however, it is not financial obligations to a privileged monarch that are canceled. Instead, the covenant requires the wealthy to forgive the debts of the poor. Moreover, this remission of debts and still unpaid labor contracts is no longer to be a voluntary, one-time act but a covenantal obligation that recurs every seven years. This blueprint for social justice is highly idealistic. By providing specific mechanisms to eliminate poverty and financial inequality every seven years, Deut. seeks to prevent economic injustice from becoming entrenched in society.

There is evidence that the authors are aware of the gap between this aspiration and worldly convention: Perspectives that are idealistic (v. 4) and pragmatic (v. 11) alternate in the ch. For reflections of the injustices at issue, see Amos 2.6–8; Jer. 34.8–22; Ezek. 18.16–18; Job 24.9; Neh. 5.1–13. In the concern for social justice, the ch reworks earlier laws found in the Book of the Covenant (Exod. chs 21–23), adjusting their requirements to the innovation of centralization of worship. The sequence of the paragraphs reflects increasingly severe stages of financial distress: from debt to indentured servitude, an ancient form of bankruptcy (see Lev. 25.13–55 for a similar sequence). Slavery and manumission serve as rich theological metaphors for both Jews and Christians (see Lev. 25.42, 55; Romans 6.20–23; Philippians 2.5–8). **1–6:** Cancellation of debts. **1:** *Seventh year:* This law presupposes the requirement of the Book of the Covenant that agricultural land should be permitted to lie fallow each "seventh year" (Exod. 23.10–11). **2:** *Remission,* using the same verb found in Exod. 23.11 for "lie fallow," but now reapplying that agricultural requirement to command the cancellation of all existing debts. **3:** The utopian requirement is restricted to fellow citizens (cf. Exod. 22.24). In not canceling the debts of foreigners, the legislator makes a concession to the pragmatic concerns of the creditor. **4:** *There shall be no needy,* or, "no poor." This contrasts with the unconditional utopian affirmation and the pragmatism of v. 7. **7–11:** An appeal to conscience, anticipating the problem of implementing and enforcing such a law.

your God is giving you, do not harden your heart and shut
your hand against your needy kinsman. 8 Rather, you must
open your hand and lend him sufficient for whatever he needs.
9 Beware lest you harbor the base thought, "The seventh year,
the year of remission, is approaching," so that you are mean to
your needy kinsman and give him nothing. He will cry out to
the LORD against you, and you will incur guilt. 10 Give to him
readily and have no regrets when you do so, for in return the
LORD your God will bless you in all your efforts and in all your
undertakings. 11 For there will never cease to be needy ones in
your land, which is why I command you: open your hand to
the poor and needy kinsman in your land.

12 If a fellow Hebrew, man or woman, is sold to you, he
shall serve you six years, and in the seventh year you shall set
him free. 13 When you set him free, do not let him go empty-
handed: 14 Furnish him out of the flock, threshing floor, and
vat, with which the LORD your God has blessed you. 15 Bear in
mind that you were slaves in the land of Egypt and the LORD
your God redeemed you; therefore I enjoin this commandment upon you today.

16 But should he say to you, "I do not want to leave you"—
for he loves you and your household and is happy with you—
17 you shall take an awl and put it through his ear into the door,
and he shall become your slave in perpetuity. Do the same
with your female slave. 18 When you do set him free, do not feel
aggrieved; for in the six years he has given you double the service of a hired man. Moreover, the LORD your God will bless you
in all you do.

19 You shall consecrate to the LORD your God all male firstlings that are born in your herd and in your flock: you must not
work your firstling ox or shear your firstling sheep. 20 You and
your household shall eat it annually before the LORD your God

9: *Cry ... guilt.* The law has no judicial penalty or sanction. The neighbor's appeal is to the divine judge for enforcement (similarly, 24.15; Exod. 22.22–23). **12–18:** Manumission: This law adjusts the older laws regulating male (Exod. 21.2–6) and female slaves (Exod. 21.7–11) in four significant ways. (1) It rejects separate procedures for the female bondservant and creates a single law that applies to both sexes, strikingly abrogating the older law (contrast v. 17b with Exod. 21.7b)! (2) It secularizes the procedure for a slave who voluntarily relinquishes the right to freedom (vv. 16–17) by eliminating the former requirement that the ceremony take place "before God," i.e., at one of the now prohibited local sanctuaries or before the household deities (Exod. 21.6). (3) The master must now grant the slave a gift (vv. 13–14) rather than simply releasing him or her empty-handed (contrast Exod. 21.2). (4) In the Book of the Covenant, there is no connection between the manumission law (Exod. 21.2–6) and the land sabbatical law (Exod. 23.10–11). Nor should one be expected, since the year of manumission would not be uniform throughout the land but would vary with each household, depending upon when a slave began to labor. By conjoining the two originally separate laws, Deut. creates a single year of release that now applies to both remission of debts (vv. 1–6) and manumission (vv. 12–18). Deut. thus transforms manumission, which used to be based in the individual household, into a year of universal liberty (see Lev. ch 25). That perspective lies behind Zedekiah's last-ditch attempt to curry divine favor by implementing this law on the eve of the Babylonian invasion of Jerusalem in 587 BCE, with a universal emancipation of slaves (Jer. 34.6–22). And whereas the legislator of Deut. can only appeal to individual moral conscience to urge obedience (v. 18), Jeremiah explains the Babylonian destruction as divine punishment for Jerusalem's citizens reneging on the law by immediately reenslaving those whom they freed (Jer. 34.11–22). With national exile thus made the penalty for infringement, setting slaves free every seven years becomes, in this view, a central requirement of the covenant. The delay of manumission from every seventh to every fiftieth year in the Holiness Collection may reflect the difficulty of implementing this idealistic law (Lev. 25.39–44). **12:** *Is sold,* alternately, "sells himself," expressing the two alternative ways of understanding the contractual and economic nature of this slavery, which is not based on race, nationality, or religion. The court might require that a thief, unable to repay a theft, "be sold," i.e., indenture his labor to compensate the victim (Exod. 21.37–22.3). Alternatively, if overcome by debt, a serf might "sell himself," i.e., assign his labor to repay a loan (Lev. 25.39–44). **14–15:** The gift provided the manumitted slave recalls and reenacts the nation's own manumission by God from slavery in Egypt. **18:** As in vv. 8–10, an appeal to conscience that anticipates the difficulty of enforcing a law that lacks judicial sanction.

15.19–23: Sacrifice of firstlings. Older religious convention required that each first-born male domestic

in the place that the LORD will choose. 21 But if it has a defect, lameness or blindness, any serious defect, you shall not sacrifice it to the LORD your God. 22 Eat it in your settlements, the unclean among you no less than the clean, just like the gazelle and the deer. 23 Only you must not partake of its blood; you shall pour it out on the ground like water.

16 Observe the month[a] of Abib and offer a passover sacrifice to the LORD your God, for it was in the month[a] of Abib, at night, that the LORD your God freed you from Egypt. 2 You shall slaughter the passover sacrifice for the LORD your God, from the flock and the herd, in the place where the LORD will choose to establish His name. 3 You shall not eat anything leavened with it; for seven days thereafter[b] you shall eat unleavened bread, bread of distress—for you departed from the land of Egypt hurriedly—so that you may remember the day of your departure from the land of Egypt as long as you live. 4 For seven days no leaven shall be found with you in all your territory, and none of the flesh of what you slaughter on the evening of the first day shall be left until morning.

5 You are not permitted to slaughter the passover sacrifice in any of the settlements that the LORD your God is giving you; 6 but at the place where the LORD your God will choose to establish His name, there alone shall you slaughter the passover sacrifice, in the evening, at sundown, the time of day when you departed from Egypt. 7 You shall cook and eat it at the place that the LORD your God will choose; and in the morning you may start back on your journey home. 8 After eating unleavened bread six days, you shall hold a solemn gathering[c] for the LORD your God on the seventh day: you shall do no work.

a Cf. Exod. 13.4; 23.15; 34.18. *b Lit. "upon it."* *c See note at Lev. 23.36.*

animal be offered as a sacrifice to God at one of the local sanctuaries (Exod. 13.1–2, 11–16; 22.28–29; 34.19–20). The author now adjusts that law to the new one stipulating a single sanctuary. **19:** *Not work,* so as to reserve the animal for God. **20:** *Before the LORD* refers to sacrifice at an altar, which now requires a pilgrimage to the central sanctuary of Jerusalem, *the place that the LORD will choose.* **21–23:** Blemished first-born livestock need not be taken to the central sanctuary. They may be slaughtered locally, *in your settlements,* following the requirements for secular slaughter (12.15–16, 21–25).

16.1–17: The festival calendar. Deut. strikingly transforms older religious celebrations in order to accommodate them to its requirement for centralization of worship. Previously, each male Israelite was commanded to undertake three pilgrimages to "appear before the LORD," i.e., to make an offering at one of the multiple local sanctuaries (v. 16; Exod. 23.14–18). The Heb term for these important events in ancient Israel's religious calendar is "Ḥag" (as in the still common greeting, "Ḥag Sameaḥ," "[may you enjoy] a joyous festival"). Often translated as "feasts" (v. 16; Exod. 23.14), the original idea is "pilgrimage festival"; indeed the word "ḥag" is related to the Arabic hajj, the pilgrimage to Mecca. As a consequence of restricting sacrifice to a single, central sanctuary, Deut. redirects the required pilgrimage from the prohibited local sanctuaries (v. 5) to the central one, *the place where the LORD will choose* (vv. 2, 6, 7, 11, 15, 16; 12.17–18). These three festivals were Unleavened Bread (Heb "Matzot"), Harvest, and Ingathering (Exod. 23.14–17; 34.18, 23). Deut. renames the latter two "Weeks" (v. 10; Heb "Shavu'ot") and "Booths" (v. 13; Heb "Sukkot"), which remain their current names.

16.1–8: The blend of Passover and the Festival of Unleavened Bread is the most remarkable section of this calendar. Passover was originally a separate observance, celebrated within the family or clan. Since it did not require a sacrifice at the sanctuary, it was not included among the three pilgrimage festivals (Exod. 23.14–17; 34.18, 21–23). Instead, it was distinguished by a nighttime slaughter of a sheep or goat in the doorway of the house, where the blood was smeared to demarcate the house as Israelite (Exod. 12.7, 21–22). First performed to protect the Israelites in Egypt from the plague against the first-born, the ritual thereafter annually commemorated Israel's deliverance from that plague (Exod. 12.1–13, 21–28). But Deut.'s restriction of sacrifice to the single sanctuary prohibited Passover from being observed locally (v. 5) and required that the observance be redirected to the central sanctuary (vv. 2, 6–7). Now made into a pilgrimage festival, the older blood ritual in the doorway of the private home—the defining act of the original Passover observance—is no longer mentioned. The new observance then merges with the Festival of Unleavened Bread, which was also celebrated in early spring. Traces of the separate identity of Passover and Unleavened Bread remain evident in their distinct dates and naming in Lev. 23.5, 6; Num. 28.16, 17–25. **1:** *Abib* (lit. "new ear of grain"), in early spring, when ears of barley, the first crop, began to

9 You shall count off seven weeks; start to count the seven
weeks when the sickle is first put to the standing grain. 10 Then
you shall observe the Feast of Weeks for the LORD your God,
offering your freewill contribution according as the LORD your
God has blessed you. 11 You shall rejoice before the LORD your
God with your son and daughter, your male and female slave,
the Levite in your communities, and the stranger, the fatherless, and the widow in your midst, at the place where the LORD
your God will choose to establish His name. 12 Bear in mind
that you were slaves in Egypt, and take care to obey these laws.
13 After the ingathering from your threshing floor and your
vat, you shall hold the Feast of Booths for seven days. 14 You
shall rejoice in your festival, with your son and daughter, your
male and female slave, the Levite, the stranger, the fatherless,
and the widow in your communities. 15 You shall hold a festival
for the LORD your God seven days, in the place that the LORD

ripen (Exod. 13.4; 23.15; 34.18). It was originally the first month of the Hebrew calendar (Exod. 12.2); later this month was called by the Babylonian month name "Nisan." **2:** *From the flock and the herd* expands the earlier restriction of the paschal offering to "a lamb ... from the sheep or from the goats" (Exod. 12.4–5, 21). **3:** *For seven days:* This section, through v. 4a, splices the seven-day observance of the Festival of Unleavened Bread (Exod. 12.14–20; 23.15) into the one-day observance of Passover (vv. 1–3a, 4b–7). **7:** *Cook:* more accurately, "boil," like other standard sacrifices (Exod. 29.1; Lev. 6.21; 8.31; Num. 6.19; 1 Sam. 2.13, 15; Zech. 14.21). This prescription is at odds with the earlier stipulation that the paschal offering be "roasted by fire," not "boiled in water" (Exod. 12.8–9; Heb). The Passover is now being treated as a standard sacrifice. These two mutually inconsistent laws are harmonized at 2 Chron. 35.13, where the Heb paradoxically reads: "They boiled the Passover offering by fire, according to the law." (NJPS translates as "They roasted the passover sacrifice in fire, as prescribed ....") **8:** *After eating unleavened bread six days:* The Heb reads simply, "For six days you shall eat unleavened bread." The NJPS rendering, *"after ... six days,"* models the festivals of Passover and Unleavened Bread after the P version of the calendar: 1 evening (Passover) + 6 days (Unleavened Bread) + 1 day (the solemn gathering); see Lev. 23.5–8. In contrast, Deut. intended to fuse the two holidays into a single seven-day observance.

16.9–12: The Festival of Weeks (Exod. 34.22; Lev. 23.15–16; Num. 28.26), originally, as the earliest name signifies, the "Festival of Harvest" (Exod. 23.16), celebrated in May–June. In postbiblical Judaism, the festival came to be associated with the revelation at Mount Sinai (Exod. chs 19–20). The idea underlies the New Testament narrative of the Holy Spirit's activity at "Pentecost" (Acts 2.1; cf. 20.16; 1 Corinthians 16.8), the Gk term for which reflects the calculation of "fifty days" (Lev. 23.16). **9:** *Start to count the seven weeks when the sickle is first put to the standing grain:* The date of this festival is not a fixed date set by the calendar but is based upon the cycle of the agricultural year. The seven-week period delays the celebration until the safe conclusion of the harvest, a precarious period when the important crop might be damaged by natural forces, especially early rains. This kind of calculation implies that different parts of the land might celebrate the festival on different dates. This ambiguity gave rise to a chain of successive interpretations in Second Temple literature that attempted to clarify the precise date of the festival. The first of these attempts may well be that of the Holiness Collection, which dates the seven weeks "from the day on which you bring the sheaf of elevation offering—the day after the sabbath" (Lev. 23.15). But that calculation remains ambiguous, since the "sabbath" to which the text refers is not identified. Contextually, "the day after the sabbath" refers to the first Sunday after the first ripe sheaf of grain is harvested, but precisely that absence of a specific date for Weeks led to sectarian disagreement in Second Temple times over when to observe it. Pharisees understood the sabbath in question simply as a reference to the Passover, no matter on which day of the week it fell; Sadducees regarded it as the Sabbath during the week of Passover/Unleavened Bread; and the Qumran community viewed it as the Sabbath of the following week. The proliferation of sects in the Second Temple period may well reflect, in part, the mutually exclusive interpretations of different groups who struggled to resolve the Bible's calendrical ambiguities. **11:** *With your son and daughter:* The command to rejoice before God at the central sanctuary specifies the inclusion of women (as v. 14; 12.12, 18). That the wife is not named separately in the list implies that the law regards the male and female adult citizen as equals. Contrast the more formulaic vv. 16–17, which is slavishly adopted from its source in Exod. *Slave ... widow:* The marginalized and the disadvantaged are also included in this comprehensive list. *Stranger,* better, "resident alien," see 10.18–19 n.

16.13–15: The Feast of Booths. Curiously, the law provides no explanation for the name of the festival, which is elsewhere called "Ingathering" (Exod. 23.16; 34.22), reflecting its origins as the fall harvest festival. The Holiness Collection fills in this gap with the explanation that the name recalls how God "made the Israelite people live in booths when I brought them out of the

will choose; for the LORD your God will bless all[a] your crops and all your undertakings, and you shall have nothing but joy.
[16] Three times a year—on the Feast of Unleavened Bread, on the Feast of Weeks, and on the Feast of Booths—all your males shall appear before the LORD your God in the place that He will choose. They shall not appear before the LORD empty-handed, [17] but each with his own gift, according to the blessing that the LORD your God has bestowed upon you.

SHOFETIM שפטים

[18] You shall appoint magistrates and officials for your tribes, in all the settlements that the LORD your God is giving you, and they shall govern the people with due justice. [19] You shall not judge unfairly: you shall show no partiality; you shall not take bribes, for bribes blind the eyes of the discerning and upset the plea of the just. [20] Justice, justice shall you pursue, that you may thrive and occupy the land that the LORD your God is giving you.

a Lit. "you in all."

land of Egypt" (Lev. 23.43). But that explanation is inconsistent with the narrative tradition that the Israelites lived in tents during the wilderness sojourn (Num. 11.10; 16.27; 25.8). More likely, the name reflects the agricultural custom of farmers erecting temporary shelters, *booths,* in the fields during the summer while the grapes, olives, and other crops are tended and then harvested (see Isa. 1.8). **15:** *Seven days:* Deut.'s observance differs from that of the Holiness Collection, which requires a total of eight days (Lev. 23.36, 40). Moreover, Deut. does not require that the first and the final days of the festival involve a "holy convocation" or "solemn assembly," when work was prohibited (Lev. 23.35–36).

16.16–17: The formulaic summary (colophon) reuses the conclusion of the older festival calendar in the Book of the Covenant (Exod. 23.17), which it now updates to specify that the three annual pilgrimages must be to the central sanctuary, *the place that He will choose.* Two elements, however, reflect older assumptions inconsistent with the rest of this ch: Passover (vv. 1–8) is not mentioned, and the pilgrimage requirement is directed to *all your males* (as Exod. 23.17), despite the gender inclusivity of vv. 11, 14.

16.18–18.22: Laws of public officials. Although western political theory is normally traced back to ancient Athens, this section is remarkable for providing what seems to be the first blueprint for a constitutional system of government. The carefully thought-out plan is designed to ensure that no single branch of government and no single religious institution should have sole power. Each is brought into relationship to the others and, more importantly, each is made subordinate to the one true authority: the Torah of Deut. Even institutions that might justifiably claim absolute authority—whether political, as in the case of the king (see Ps. 2.6–7), or religious, as in the case of the prophet (see Exod. 3.10–12)—are integrated into Deut.'s comprehensive vision. It is unlikely that the ambitious program envisioned by this draft constitution was ever fully implemented. Upon the return from exile, when Judah regained some measure of political autonomy under Persian rule, different religious and political priorities preempted this blueprint. There is a great deal of scholarly disagreement about the precise dating of this section: how much to ascribe to the original legislation of Deut., associated with the Josianic period shortly before the exile, and how much may derive from the Babylonian exile itself, as Judahite thinkers reflected on their national history and mapped out a new model of society, structured by Torah. Most likely, an original Josianic layer underwent elaboration during the exile.

In its organization, this section addresses the full range of public officials in the judicial, executive, and religious branches: the local and the central courts (16.18–17.13), kingship (17.14–20), the Levitical priesthood (18.1–8), and prophecy (18.9–22). Although the focus on public officials ostensibly marks a significant change from the previous section's focus on the sacrificial system (12.1–16.17), the concern of the legislator in both sections is consistent: the impact of centralization of worship upon all spheres of life. The desire to bridge from the first section to the new one explains the puzzling way in which ritual laws (16.21–17.1) seem to intrude between two paragraphs concerned with justice (16.18–20; 17.2–7). By means of the repetition, the editor provides a transition into the new section, while establishing the underlying unity of both areas of community life:

A Cult (12.1–16.17)
B Justice (16.18–20)
A' Cult (16.21–17.1)
B' Justice (17.2–7, 8–13)

16.18–17.13: The organization of justice. 16.18–20: Deut. here establishes a professionalized local judiciary. **18:** *Settlements,* lit., "gates," Deut.'s metaphor for the local sphere (12.15, 17, 21; 16.5), as distinguished from the central sanctuary. Here the metaphor takes on an additional meaning, because the city gate served as the location where justice was traditionally dispensed by the village elders (Job 29.7; Ruth 4.1, 11; Lam. 5.14). By appointing

21 You shall not set up a sacred post—any kind of pole beside
the altar of the LORD your God that you may make—22 or erect
a stone pillar; for such the LORD your God detests.

17 You shall not sacrifice to the LORD your God an ox or a
sheep that has any defect of a serious kind, for that is
abhorrent to the LORD your God.

2 If there is found among you, in one of the settlements
that the LORD your God is giving you, a man or woman who
has affronted the LORD your God and transgressed His covenant—3 turning to the worship of other gods and bowing
down to them, to the sun or the moon or any of the heavenly
host, something I never commanded—4 and you have been informed or have learned of it, then you shall make a thorough
inquiry. If it is true, the fact is established, that abhorrent thing
was perpetrated in Israel, 5 you shall take the man or the woman who did that wicked thing out to the public place, and you
shall stone them, man or woman, to death.—6 A person shall
be put to death only on the testimony of two or more[a] witnesses; he must not be put to death on the testimony of a single
witness.—7 Let the hands of the witnesses be the first against
him to put him to death, and the hands of the rest of the people
thereafter. Thus you will sweep out evil from your midst.

a Lit. "three."

professional *magistrates and officials* to just that location, while leaving the elders unmentioned, Deut. significantly contracts the elders' sphere of authority, if not altogether eliminating it. The professionalization of the judicial system thus entails a disruption of traditional patterns of clan authority. The elders are mentioned elsewhere in the legal corpus as involved with judicial matters (21.1–9, 19; 22.15; 25.7). These references may preserve an older perspective; otherwise, they show how the elders' role in justice has now been restricted to family and marital law. **19:** *You shall not judge unfairly:* This admonition to the judges, sometimes called a "Mirror for Magistrates," quotes Exod. 23.6a (where the same verb is translated "subvert"). *For bribes blind the eyes of the discerning* (lit. "of the wise"): The older law of Exod. 23.8, which refers to "the clear-sighted" as being blinded by bribery, is revised in light of Deut.'s stress upon wisdom. The failure of Samuel's sons to meet this standard of judicial probity (1 Sam. 8.3) is viewed by the Deuteronomistic historian as the justification for the establishment of the monarchy (1 Sam. 8.5).

16.21–17.1: Prohibitions against Canaanite cultic objects (7.5; 12.3; Exod. 34.13). **16.21–22:** See 7.5 n. **17.1:** This v. broadens the prohibition against sacrificing blemished firstlings (15.21) into a general law of sacrifice.

17.2–7: Local justice. Because of the extent to which this law so closely overlaps with 13.7–12, both in its wording and in the topic of apostasy by an individual, many scholars have incorrectly viewed it as out of place and as belonging to ch 13. Whereas the theme of ch 13 is incitement, at issue here are the procedures and the jurisdiction of the local courts. Under the professionalized judiciary (16.18), the law grants the local courts maximal autonomy, enabling them to try even capital cases and to address religious matters (the accusation of apostasy). Just one essential condition is imposed: that a trial be conducted according to strictly rational standards that assure empirical proof for the verdict. Thus v. 4 provides the procedures to put a vague rumor *(you have been informed)* to the formal test of *a thorough inquiry* in order to verify its truth. The law stipulates the criteria necessary to establish judicial "proof": *the testimony of two or more witnesses* (v. 6). This law may be the first place in the Bible, historically speaking, where norms of justice regarding witness law were established. (Scholars normally date P, and thus the parallel requirement of more than one witness in Num. 35.30, later than Deut.) The power of this law is that it rejects the summary execution in the case of incitement required by Deut. 13.7–12. By stipulating that *he must not be put to death on the testimony of a single witness* (v. 6b), the law seeks to impose rigorous requirements for evidence even in cases of apostasy. The older law is then subordinated to the new standard of justice: No longer is the execution carried out by the single witness ("your hand," 13.10); rather the agents carrying out the execution are now plural: *the hands of the witnesses* (v. 7). **2:** *A man or woman:* The law views the woman as a legally responsible individual. The viewpoint in marriage and family law differs, however (see 22.13–29). **3:** Contravening the Decalogue (5.8–9); see 4.19; 2 Kings 23.5; Jer. 8.2. **6:** A travesty of the condition for *two or more witnesses* occurs in the kangaroo court set up by Jezebel to execute Naboth (1 Kings 21.10, 13). The prohibition against execution on the basis of testimony by a *single witness* is also found at 19.15–16; Num. 35.30.

17.8–13: Justice at the central sanctuary. In the pre-Deuteronomic period, the local sanctuaries served a judicial function in addition to

[8] If a case is too baffling for you to decide, be it a controversy over homicide, civil law, or assault—matters of dispute in your courts—you shall promptly repair to the place that the LORD your God will have chosen, [9] and appear before the levitical priests, or the magistrate in charge at the time, and present your problem. When they have announced to you the verdict in the case, [10] you shall carry out the verdict that is announced to you from that place that the LORD chose, observing scrupulously all their instructions to you. [11] You shall act in accordance with the instructions given you and the ruling handed down to you; you must not deviate from the verdict that they announce to you either to the right or to the left. [12] Should a man act presumptuously and disregard the priest charged with serving there the LORD your God, or the magistrate, that man shall die. Thus you will sweep out evil from Israel: [13] all the people will hear and be afraid and will not act presumptuously again.

[14] If, after you have entered the land that the LORD your God has assigned to you, and taken possession of it and settled in it, you decide, "I will set a king over me, as do all the nations about me," [15] you shall be free to set a king over yourself, one chosen by the LORD your God. Be sure to set as king over yourself one of your own people; you must not set a foreigner over you, one who is not your kinsman. [16] Moreover, he shall not keep many horses or send people back to Egypt to add to his

providing a place for the sacrificial worship of God. In legal cases where there was an absence either of physical evidence or of witnesses, no court could make a ruling. Such cases were remanded to divine jurisdiction at the local sanctuary on the assumption that God could determine guilt or innocence without being bound by empirical criteria. The parties to the dispute would swear a judicial oath at the altar, symbolically "before God" (19.17; 1 Kings 8.31–32; see also Exod. 21.6). In special circumstances, a priest might conduct a judicial ordeal (Num. 5.11–31). In both cases, Israelite judicial procedures conform closely to those evident in ancient Babylonian legal collections like The Laws of Hammurabi (§§9, 23, 266, 281) or the Laws of Eshnunna. Deut.'s prohibition of the local sanctuaries (ch 12) therefore created an important local judicial void. The intent of these two laws (17.2–7, 8–13) is to fill the void. Deut. grants the local courts absolute judicial autonomy, extending even to capital cases and to religious matters, on condition that all such cases meet the standard of sufficient evidence (17.2–7). Cases that do not meet that empirical standard, and that once would have been remanded to the local sanctuary for divine resolution, must now be remanded instead to the central sanctuary (17.8–13). Deut. is thus completely consistent in its transformation of sacrifice and in its revolution of the judicial system. The local sphere is completely secularized (12.15–16, 20–25; 17.2–7); the central sanctuary provides the sole legitimate context for either sacrifice (12.13–14, 26–27; 16.2, 5–7a) or divine resolution of ambiguous legal cases (17.8–13). **8:** *Too baffling for you to decide,* going beyond what is possible for human knowledge to resolve. *A controversy over homicide,* when it is unclear whether the defendant is guilty of murder or manslaughter (Exod. 21.12–14; Num. 35.16–23). In each of these pairs, the distinction is between premeditated and unintentional offenses. **9:** The tribunal at the sanctuary includes both priestly and lay members, assuming that *the magistrate* refers to a secular official (as in 19.17). The account of Jehoshaphat's setting up tribunals throughout Judah composed of lay and clerical judges reflects this law (2 Chron. 19.5–11).

17.14–20: The law of the king. Deut.'s conception of the kingship entails an extraordinary restriction of royal authority. Whereas generally Near Eastern monarchs like Hammurabi themselves promulgated law, here the monarch is subject to the law and required to read the Torah daily (v. 19). Conventionally the monarch was assigned a crucial role in the administration of justice, serving as a court of last appeal to defend the rights of the oppressed (Ps. 72.1–4). Deut. remarkably denies the king any role whatsoever in justice, granting the local courts and the central sanctuary complete jurisdiction. The king is also denied his customary Near Eastern role in supervising the public cult. This law far more emphasizes what the king may not do than what he may do. The remarkable subordination of the king to *this Teaching* (v. 18)—Deuteronomic Torah—thus envisions something like a constitutional monarchy. This notion exists in some tension to the views of the Deuteronomistic historian, who returns the king to his public religious function as Josiah leads the national Passover celebration (2 Kings 23.21–23), and to the royalist concerns of the Chronicler. **14:** *As do all the nations,* see 1 Sam. 8.5. **16–18:** The offenses specified here allude to the warnings against royal autocracy outlined at the very founding of the monarchy (1 Sam. 8.10–18). They almost certainly presuppose Solomon's trade in horses (1 Kings 10.26–29) and his multiple marital alliances with foreign wives (1 Kings 11.1–8). The Deuteronomistic historian understood those marriages to lead to religious syncretism and the corruption of Israelite religion (1 Kings 11.1–8), with the breakup of the united monarchy the

horses, since the LORD has warned you, "You must not go back
that way again." 17 And he shall not have many wives, lest his
heart go astray; nor shall he amass silver and gold to excess.
18 When he is seated on his royal throne, he shall have a copy
of this Teaching written for him on a scroll by[a] the levitical
priests. 19 Let it remain with him and let him read in it all his
life, so that he may learn to revere the LORD his God, to observe
faithfully every word of this Teaching as well as these laws.
20 Thus he will not act haughtily toward his fellows or deviate
from the Instruction to the right or to the left, to the end that
he and his descendants may reign long in the midst of Israel.

18 The levitical priests, the whole tribe of Levi, shall have
no territorial portion with Israel. They shall live only off
the LORD's offerings by fire as their[b] portion, 2 and shall have
no portion among their brother tribes: the LORD is their portion, as He promised them.
3 This then shall be the priests' due from the people: Everyone who offers a sacrifice, whether an ox or a sheep, must give
the shoulder, the cheeks, and the stomach to the priest. 4 You
shall also give him the first fruits of your new grain and wine
and oil, and the first shearing of your sheep. 5 For the LORD
your God has chosen him and his descendants, out of all your
tribes, to be in attendance for service in the name of the LORD
for all time.

6 If a Levite would go, from any of the settlements throughout Israel where he has been residing, to the place that the
LORD has chosen, he may do so whenever he pleases. 7 He may
serve in the name of the LORD his God like all his fellow Levites who are there in attendance before the LORD. 8 They shall
receive equal shares of the dues, [c]without regard to personal
gifts or patrimonies.[c]

a Nuance of Heb. milliphne *uncertain.* *b Lit. "its," i.e., the tribe's.*
c-c Meaning of Heb. uncertain.

divine punishment for these transgressions (1 Kings 11.9–13). **16:** *People,* lit. "the people," i.e., the Israelites. *Back to Egypt to add to his horses:* The reference is difficult. Elsewhere, the idea of Israel's returning to Egypt implies divine punishment and the reimposition of slavery (28.68; Hos. 8.13; 9.3). But here that idea is combined with a veiled critical reference to Judah's attempt to forge a military alliance with Egypt against Assyria in 701 BCE, when Isaiah challenged "those who go down to Egypt for help/And rely upon horses!" (Isa. 31.1). *Since the LORD has warned you,* see 28.68 n. **18:** The law requires the king to be subject to the law, not above it. The common status of the monarch throughout the ancient Near East as promulgator of the law (as in the Laws of Hammurabi) and as enjoying a special relationship with the divinity (so also Ps. 2) might suggest that the king would be exempt from the law's requirements. To emphasize its rejection of that norm, Deut. requires the king to have *a copy of this Teaching written for him:* The king must daily read the law that limits his powers. The literal Heb phrase, "a copy of this Teaching (torah)," provides the basis for one of the two ancient Jewish designations of the book: "Mishneh Torah" (*Sifre* §160; see the intro. to Deut. for a more detailed discussion of its name). "Mishneh Torah" was translated into Gk by Philo and the LXX as "Deuteronomion" and is the source of the book's familiar English title, "Deuteronomy." That title, however, is based on a misunderstanding of this phrase in 17.18 as referring to Deut. as a whole, rather than to just the law of the king.

18.1–8: The Levitical priesthood. Centralization of worship also had an impact upon the Israelite priesthood, to which the legislator now turns. Deut. provides a concise "job description" of the priesthood (vv. 1–5) and then addresses the impact of centralization upon its livelihood (vv. 6–8). **1:** The phrase *levitical priests* marks a distinctively D conception of the priesthood, one that significantly differs from that found in the P literature, where "the priests" and "the Levites" are separate from one another. P establishes a hierarchy within the tribe of Levi between the direct descendants of Aaron and the rest of the tribe (Num. ch 18). Only the Aaronides are called "priests" and thereby permitted to officiate at the altar before God (Num. 18.5, 7). For their support they are assigned the priestly share of the sacrificial offerings brought by Israelites to the sanctuary (Num. 18.8–20). In contrast, the remainder of the tribe, the "Levites," serve the priests and are prohibited from officiating at the altar (Num. 18.3–4, 6). For their support, they receive the tithes of produce and cattle. In turn, they pay a tithe of what they have received to the priests (Num. 18.21–31). Deut.'s approach is very different. There is no genealogical hierarchy within the tribe; all are deemed equally Levitical priests and are eligible to serve at the altar and to receive sacrifices.

9 When you enter the land that the LORD your God is giving you, you shall not learn to imitate the abhorrent practices of those nations. 10 Let no one be found among you who
consigns his son or daughter to the fire, or who is an augur, a
soothsayer, a diviner, a sorcerer, 11 one who casts spells, or one
who consults ghosts or familiar spirits, or one who inquires of
the dead. 12 For anyone who does such things is abhorrent to
the LORD, and it is because of these abhorrent things that the
LORD your God is dispossessing them before you. 13 You must
be wholehearted with the LORD your God. 14 Those nations
that you are about to dispossess do indeed resort to soothsayers and augurs; to you, however, the LORD your God has not
assigned the like.

The emphatic appositional phrase, *the whole tribe of Levi,* seems to rule out precisely the hierarchy presupposed by Num. ch 18. Continuing scholarly debate about the dating of P makes it very difficult to establish the relative dating and sequence of these two diverging approaches to the priesthood. **2:** They *shall have no portion:* Levi does not participate in the tribal land distribution at the time of the settlement (see Gen. 49.7; Josh. 13.14; Ezek. 44.28). Without their own land allocation, the tribe has no independent means of agricultural support or income. As an alternative, *the LORD is their portion:* God grants them a share of the sacrificial offerings brought to the sanctuary. This system in effect made the Levitical priests completely dependent upon other Israelites for their support. The system must have run into difficulty because the priest-prophet Ezekiel allocates land both to the priests and the Levites in his vision of the future restoration of Judah after the exile (Ezek. 48.10–14). **3:** These specific portions of the sacrificial offerings are reserved for the priests. The abuse of this privilege by the greedy sons of Eli led to divine punishment (1 Sam. 2.12–17, 22–36). **5:** *To be in attendance for service* refers technically to officiating at the altar. **6–8:** While rejecting any genealogical hierarchy within the tribe, the law anticipates a geographical one and seeks to prevent it. **6:** With Deut.'s prohibition of local altars (12.8–12; chs 13–15), the Levites serving at those altars would face sudden unemployment. With no independent landholding as a means of support, the local Levite would thus become completely destitute. Accordingly, *if a Levite would go, from any of the settlements* to the central sanctuary in Jerusalem, seeking to serve there as a priest, he must be provided for. **7:** The concern is to guarantee the Levite who had not lived in Jerusalem equal access to the altar. This admonition correctly anticipates that the Levites who had long been stationed at the Jerusalem Temple would hardly welcome such newcomers, fearing that their own income and power would be threatened. The emphasis that each displaced Levite *may serve in the name of the LORD his God* implies that the countryside altars prohibited by Deut. were not entirely devoted to Canaanite cults, as 12.2–4 asserts. They clearly included sanctuaries officiated over by a priesthood loyal to the God of Israel. **8:** *Equal shares,* the choice meats, grains, and oil assigned the tribe in vv. 3–4. The Deuteronomistic historian, while narrating the accomplishments of Josiah's reform, concedes that the priests at the Temple failed to implement this requirement. The displaced countryside Levites thus became second-class citizens, able to eat only "unleavened bread" (2 Kings 23.9).

18.9–22: The Mosaic prophet. This section divides into two main paragraphs. The first condemns various types of divination as illegitimate and associates them with the Canaanites (vv. 9–14). The second establishes a uniquely Israelite model of prophecy, patterned after Moses, which understands the prophet to mediate God's word to the people (vv. 15–22). **9–14:** Just as the legal corpus prohibits forms of sacrificial worship that it condemns as Canaanite (12.1–4, 29–31; also 7.1–6, 25–26; Exod. 23.24; 34.11–16), so here does it prohibit certain forms of divination, which are repeatedly branded as Canaanite, almost as a refrain (vv. 9, 12, 14). In each case, Deut. consistently requires its own alternative: here, prophecy rather than divination; previously, centralization of worship rather than multiple altar sites (12.5–7). At the same time, the condemnation of the rejected practices as Canaanite warrants further consideration. Strikingly, when divination or necromancy are elsewhere mentioned and even challenged (in sources that do not depend upon this list), there is no accusation or hint that they are foreign or not efficacious. They seem completely Israelite (1 Sam. 28.3–25; Isa. 8.19–22; 29.4). The same applies to the rejected forms of sacrificial worship (see 12.14–16 n.; 16.21–22 n.). Indeed, in the 7th c., the generally accepted date of Deut.'s composition (see the intro.), the Canaanites would no longer have been a live issue. Most likely the authors of the legal corpus represented prior norms as "Canaanite" in order to gain acceptance for their trenchant critique of Israelite popular religion (see 14.1 n.). **10:** *Consigns ... to the fire:* It is unclear if this refers to child sacrifice, and if so, why this law is included in this context. *Who is an augur, a soothsayer ... :* The AB sequence of these two initial terms is reversed at the end of the list, in the B'A' of "soothsayers and augurs" (v. 14), thereby providing the long list of vv. 10–14 with a frame. The list provides the most comprehensive compilation of such activities in the Bible (Exod. 22.17; Lev. 19.30–31; 20.6, 27; Isa. 8.19). It is no longer

15 The LORD your God will raise up for you a prophet from
among your own people, like myself; him you shall heed.
16 This is just what you asked of the LORD your God at Horeb,
on the day of the Assembly, saying, "Let me not hear the voice
of the LORD my God any longer or see this wondrous fire any
more, lest I die." 17 Whereupon the LORD said to me, "They have
done well in speaking thus. 18 I will raise up a prophet for them
from among their own people, like yourself: I will put My words
in his mouth and he will speak to them all that I command him;
19 and if anybody fails to heed the words he speaks in My name,
I Myself will call him to account. 20 But any prophet who presumes to speak in My name an oracle that I did not command
him to utter, or who speaks in the name of other gods—that
prophet shall die." 21 And should you ask yourselves, "How can
we know that the oracle was not spoken by the LORD?"— 22 if the
prophet speaks in the name of the LORD and the oracle does not
come true, that oracle was not spoken by the LORD; the prophet
has uttered it presumptuously: do not stand in dread of him.

possible to identify precisely each of the prohibited forms of divination. Indeed, because the list is so comprehensive, it is unclear whether each term represented a distinct activity still known to the author or whether the list represents more of a scholastic compilation. *Sorcerer* reflects the standard Akkadian term for magic ("kishpu"). **11:** *Who consults ghosts or familiar spirits ... dead,* necromancy, or conjuring the dead (1 Sam. 28.7–15; Isa. 29.4). As in some contemporary religions, family religion in antiquity devoted extensive attention to communicating with the dead, especially with ancestors. **12:** *Abhorrent:* This condemnation of necromancy as obnoxious to God is remarkable for what is not said. There is no claim that it is ineffective. The Deuteronomistic historian narrates the ability of the witch of En-dor to raise Samuel's ghost on demand (1 Sam. 28.7–25). **15–22:** Deut. transforms prophecy, viewing the prophet as the spokesperson of Torah (see 13.2–6 n.) and defining Moses as the paradigmatic prophet. **15:** *The LORD ... will raise up:* The continuity of prophecy is assured by means of divine election. Other offices achieve their continuity by means of professional training and appointment (as with the judges of 16.18–20; 17.2–13), or dynastically (the king of 17.14–20), or by tribal membership (the Levitical priesthood of vv. 1–8). That God alone appoints the prophet makes the prophet independent of all institutions and able to challenge them. Yet the laws in vv. 20–22, which emphasize various cases in which the prophets are to be executed, also curb the power of prophets, especially their ability to undo the contents of Deut.'s laws. *A prophet,* while grammatically singular, is likely distributive in its meaning: "I will repeatedly raise up for you a prophet." More than one prophet is clearly intended. A much later Jewish reinterpretation that was accepted by the Christian church (John 1.21, 45; 6.14; 7.40; Acts 3.22; 7.37) understands the v. to promise a single, messianic prophet at the end of time. *Like myself:* At Horeb (5.20–30), Moses established the distinctively Israelite model of prophecy as mediating God's word to the people. This model contrasts with the prophet as diviner (vv. 9–14), where the prophet does not represent the God of Israel and where the supernatural communication about the future bears no relation to covenantal law. Thus the prophet, like the king (17.15), should be *from among your own people.* **16–17:** See 5.20–28; Exod. 20.16–18. **18:** The prophet's oracles do not originate from other deities, from dead spirits, from skilled manipulation of objects, or from the prophet's own reflections. God instead affirms, *I will put My words in his mouth.* The prophet reiterates the word of Israel's God. That metaphorical promise is reused in the call narrative of Jeremiah (Jer. 1.9) and then dramatically enacted in Ezekiel's call, where the metaphor is taken literally (Ezek. 2.9–3.3). **20:** Having established an Israelite model of prophecy, the law provides two criteria to distinguish true from false prophecy. The first is that the prophet should speak exclusively on behalf of God, and report only God's words. Breach of that rule is a capital offense (Jer. 28.12–17). **21–23:** The second criterion makes the fulfillment of a prophet's oracle the measure of its truth. That approach attempts to solve a critical problem: If two prophets each claim to speak on behalf of God yet make mutually exclusive claims—(1 Kings 22.6 vs. 22.17; Jer. 27.8 vs. 28.2)—how may one decide which prophet speaks the truth? The solution offered is not free of difficulty. If a false prophet is distinguished by the failure of his oracle to come true, then making a decision in the present about which prophet to obey becomes impossible. Nor can this criterion easily be reconciled with 13.3, which concedes that the oracles of false prophets might come true. Finally, the prophets frequently threatened judgment, hoping to bring about repentance (Jer. ch 7; 26.1–6). If the prophet succeeds, and the people repent and thereby avert doom (Jonah chs 3–4), one would assume the prophet to be authentic, since he has accomplished God's goal of repentance. Yet according to the criteria here (but contrast Jer. 28.9), the prophet who fostered repentance is nonetheless a false prophet, since the judgment oracle that was proclaimed remains unfulfilled. These texts, with their questions and differences of opinion on such issues, reflect the vigorous debate that took place in Israel about prophecy.

19 When the LORD your God has cut down the nations whose
land the LORD your God is assigning to you, and you
have dispossessed them and settled in their towns and homes,
2 you shall set aside three cities in the land that the LORD your
God is giving you to possess. 3 You shall survey the distances,
and divide into three parts the territory of the country that the
LORD your God has allotted to you, so that any manslayer may
have a place to flee to.—4 Now this is the case of the manslayer
who may flee there and live: one who has killed another unwittingly, without having been his enemy in the past. 5 For instance, a man goes with his neighbor into a grove to cut wood;
as his hand swings the ax to cut down a tree, the ax-head flies
off the handle and strikes the other so that he dies. That man
shall flee to one of these cities and live.—6 Otherwise, when the
distance is great, the blood-avenger, pursuing the manslayer in
hot anger, may overtake him and kill him; yet he did not incur
the death penalty, since he had never been the other's enemy.
7 That is why I command you: set aside three cities.

8 And when the LORD your God enlarges your territory, as
He swore to your fathers, and gives you all the land that He
promised to give your fathers—9 if you faithfully observe all

19.1–13: Cities of refuge. Under the old system of clan justice, the kin of a homicide victim assumed the burden of killing the slayer to avenge the death. Deut. limits but cannot eradicate that older system. In cases of murder, the capital punishment is not carried out by the state but by the kinsman ("the blood-avenger," v. 12; cf. Num. 35.19, 21, which also refers to the older system). Similarly, while the law can insist that unintentional homicide is not a capital crime, it cannot simply declare the person innocent. It must also provide a city to serve as sanctuary where the avenging kinsman may not enter. The law concedes that it can provide no protection should the avenger overtake the unintentional slayer before he reaches sanctuary (v. 6; cf. Num. 35.26–28).

The literary model for the law, like many of Deut.'s laws, may be found in the Book of the Covenant, which stipulated that criminal homicide was a capital crime but exempted unintentional homicide: "He who fatally strikes a man shall be put to death. If he did not do it by design, but it came about by an act of God, I will assign you a place to which he can flee" (Exod. 21.12–13). But should that person have committed murder rather than manslaughter, "you shall take him from My very altar to be put to death" (Exod. 21.14). The coordination of these two laws establishes that the "place" of refuge refers specifically to the "altar" of the sanctuary (so also 1 Kings 1.49–53; 2.28–35). The same Heb word ("place" or "site") also designates the altar in 12.5, 11, 13, 18, 21, 26; Exod. 20.21.

Once centralization declared those local altars illegitimate, Deut. had to update the law of sanctuary. Simply shifting the location of sanctuary from the local to the central sanctuary was clearly not feasible, since the distance for the trip would jeopardize the person needing protection (v. 6). Instead, Deut. retains the local setting of the law but secularizes the site of refuge. No longer the altar but three neutral "cities" are designated to fill the void, with provision made for an additional three when necessary (vv. 8–9). Even the language of the older law is updated. According to the older law in the Book of the Covenant, the accidental homicide takes place when "the god deflected his [the slayer's] hand" (Exod. 21.13, lit.). But that attribution of the accident to the agency of a generic god, following an archaic formula inherited from Near Eastern law, is no longer acceptable even as a cliché of speech. The scrupulous authors of Deut. eliminate the superstitious element and redefine the accident neutrally: "the ax-head flies off the handle" (v. 5).

The later Deuteronomistic introduction to the book (4.44) provides a concise summary of the law but understands the six cities to refer to three in Transjordan and three in Israel (4.41–44), rather than to all six within the land, three in the present and three in the future (vv. 2, 8–9). P correctly recognizes the original cultic basis of the law, which had been rooted in the local altars. It accepts Deut.'s designation of the city as the new sanctuary site but defines those cities as belonging to the Levites (Num. 35.6). It extends the law to non-Israelites and follows 4.41–44 in concluding that three of the six cities are located in Transjordan (Num. 35.13–15). Josh. 20.7–8 reconciles these different reflections of the law of asylum while narrating its enactment at the time of the settlement, following the enumeration of 4.41–44 while conforming to Num. 35.9–34 in selecting cities assigned to the Levites. **1:** For the formulaic introduction, see 12.29. **4:** *Who may flee there,* more literally, "where he might flee (there)," an exact citation of the older law that requires revision (Exod. 21.13b; translated "to which he can flee" in NJPS). Whereas the law in Exod. refers specifically to the altar at the local sanctuary as the site of refuge, Deut. redefines the word so that, in the new context, it now refers to one of the three "cities" of vv. 2–3. (The same cited phrase also occurs in the Heb of v. 3.) **5:** *Shall flee to one of these cities:* The same key phrase is now explicitly amended to include the city reference. **6:** *When the distance is great:* The formula marks Deut.'s updating of older law; see 14.24. *In hot anger,* lit. "for his heart

this Instruction that I enjoin upon you this day, to love the LORD your God and to walk in His ways at all times—then you shall add three more towns to those three. [10]Thus blood of the innocent will not be shed, bringing bloodguilt upon you in the land that the LORD your God is allotting to you.

[11]If, however, a person who is the enemy of another lies in wait for him and sets upon him and strikes him a fatal blow and then flees to one of these towns, [12]the elders of his town shall have him brought back from there and shall hand him over to the blood-avenger to be put to death; [13]you must show him no pity. Thus you will purge Israel of the blood of the innocent,[a] and it will go well with you.

[14]You shall not move your countryman's landmarks, set up by previous generations, in the property that will be allotted to you in the land that the LORD your God is giving you to possess.

[15]A single witness may not validate against a person any guilt or blame for any offense that may be committed; a case can be valid only on the testimony of two witnesses or more.[b] [16]If a man appears against another to testify maliciously and gives false testimony against him, [17]the two parties to the dispute shall appear before the LORD, before the priests or magistrates in authority at the time, [18]and the magistrates shall make a thorough investigation. If the man who testified is a false witness, if he has testified falsely against his fellow, [19]you shall do to him as he schemed to do to his fellow. Thus you will sweep out evil from your midst; [20]others will hear and be afraid, and such evil things will not again be done in your midst. [21]Nor must you show pity: life for life, eye for eye, tooth for tooth, hand for hand, foot for foot.

a *Cf. Num. 35.33–34.* *b* *See note at 17.6.*

is incensed." If the kinsman kills the slayer while in hot pursuit, the law is powerless. **8:** *Enlarges your territory:* This formula provides a means for updating older law to address present realities (see 12.20; Exod. 34.24) by casting the provision for change as intended from the beginning, rather than something that takes place after the fact. **10:** *Blood of the innocent,* a bold conception of innocence. The law insists that wrongfully killing someone who has unintentionally committed homicide—yet who is innocent of murder—would itself constitute murder. *Bloodguilt:* The spilling of innocent blood defiles the land (see Num. 35.33–34; Deut. 21.1–9). **12:** *Brought back from there,* secularizing the original law of Exod. 21.14, "You shall take him from My very altar." *Hand him over to the blood-avenger to be put to death.* The law here regulates but does not replace the clan-based system of justice, surrendering the murderer to the kinsman to serve as executioner.

19.14: Boundary marker. The sacrosanct status of a *landmark* (lit. "boundary marker") was a legal tradition in the ancient Near East (see 27.17; Isa. 5.8; Hos. 5.10; Job 24.2; Prov. 22.28). The v. also marks a topical boundary within the legal corpus and provides a transition marker. In the next law, the legislator will conclude the section devoted to the impact of centralization upon justice.

19.15–21: The integrity of the judicial system. This section, whose theme is the public order (16.18–19.21), began with a law that required probity on the part of the newly established judges (16.18–20). The section therefore appropriately concludes with a law that demands corresponding integrity from witnesses. The two laws thus frame the unit with an inclusio that emphasizes the honesty required of all participants in the judicial system. The same emphasis, symbolizing the legal collection's commitment to justice, is also evident in Near Eastern law (Laws of Hammurabi §§1–5). **15:** *Validate against a person any guilt or blame for any offense:* Heb is even more insistent on the universal application of this law, repeating the "any" before each of the three nouns. *A case can be valid ... two witnesses or more,* broadening the specific focus of 17.6 on capital crimes: "A person shall be put to death only on the testimony of two or more witnesses." That principle is here made a universal requirement for justice. It prohibits hearsay or spurious accusation (one person's word against another's) from having any legal force whatsoever. **17:** *Before the LORD,* testimony before the altar at the central sanctuary (12.7; 14.23; 17.8–13). **19:** *You shall do to him* [the false witness] *as he schemed to do to his fellow:* This reciprocal formulation of justice is called "talion," the technical term from Latin for "measure-for-measure" or "an eye for an eye." That principle is elsewhere employed in the context of bodily injury or homicide (Exod. 21.23–25; Lev. 24.17–21). It distinguishes crimes against the person (which require talion) from property crimes (where alone financial compensation is permitted). By applying the principle of talion to the category of crimes against the judicial system, the legislators here seek to ensure the integrity of the law by using the highest sanction available to them (see also Laws of Hammurabi §§1–5).

20 When you take the field against your enemies, and see
horses and chariots—forces larger than yours—have
no fear of them, for the LORD your God, who brought you from
the land of Egypt, is with you. 2 Before you join battle, the priest
shall come forward and address the troops. 3 He shall say to
them, "Hear, O Israel! You are about to join battle with your enemy. Let not your courage falter. Do not be in fear, or in panic,
or in dread of them. 4 For it is the LORD your God who marches
with you to do battle for you against your enemy, to bring you
victory."
5 Then the officials shall address the troops, as follows: "Is
there anyone who has built a new house but has not dedicated
it? Let him go back to his home, lest he die in battle and another dedicate it. 6 Is there anyone who has planted a vineyard but
has never harvested it? Let him go back to his home, lest he die
in battle and another harvest it. 7 Is there anyone who has paid
the bride-price for a wife,[a] but who has not yet married her?
Let him go back to his home, lest he die in battle and another
marry her." 8 The officials shall go on addressing the troops

a Thereby making her his wife legally, even though the marriage has not yet taken place.

20.1–20: Rules for waging holy war. In contrast to the other biblical legal collections, which include only brief sections concerning military engagement (Exod. 23.23–33; 34.11–16; Num. 34.50–56), Deut., reflecting a literary setting of Israel about to enter the land, concerns itself extensively with the laws of holy war. Underlying this theology of holy war is the idea that Israel's God joins the fray as a divine warrior and directly confronts the adversary on behalf of the nation. God's Presence in the military camp imposes additional purity requirements upon the people (23.11–15). Although wars of conquest would normally be waged for the sake of empire building and profit, Israel's holy war is fought for religious reasons: to extirpate iniquity and to create a covenantal community organized by divine law (Lev. 18.24–29; 20.22–24). Accordingly, the usual seizing of plunder—property, animals, and humans—is prohibited (7.25b; 13.15–17). Throughout the Near East, the kinds of spoils taken in war would include men, for their labor, and women, for sex, labor and child-rearing (v. 11). For that reason, the rules for holy war must stipulate that no prisoners be taken (vv. 16–18; 7.1–5). All the normal spoils of war had to be devoted exclusively to God, like the sacrificial "holocaust" offering (13.17) from which neither priest nor lay Israelite could take any portion (see 12.23–27 n.). A contemporary inscription, the Moabite Stone (or Mesha Stele, ca. 850 BCE), establishes that similar theologies of holy war were shared by a number of nations. In the case of Deut., it is important to recognize that the conception of the conquest as a holy war represents, paradoxically, a highly schematized idealization, formulated half a millennium after the settlement, at a time when ethnic Canaanites would already long have assimilated into the Israelite population. (See 18.9–14 n.) **1:** *When you take the field against your enemies:* This introductory formula enables the editor to group a series of various laws loosely together (21.10–14; cf. 23.9–14; 24.5). *Horses and chariots:* The adversary is superior both in numbers and in military equipment (see Exod. 14.9; 15.4; Josh. 11.4). *Forces* (lit. "people"): Deut. imagines both Israel and the adversary less as a professionally organized army than as an entire nation arrayed for a common purpose. This conception, also reflected in the conquest account in Josh., is an idealization about the past that is inconsistent with earlier accounts, which represent the settlement as a series of initiatives by individual tribes who achieved very restricted penetration into the land, and who did not act in concert as a unified nation (Judg. 1.18–20, 27–36). The ideal national perspective outlined by Deut. lies behind the account in Josh., which is part of the work of the Deuteronomistic historian. *Have no fear of them, for the LORD your God ... is with you:* The narrator, in this introductory formula, summarizes the priest's oracle of military reassurance in vv. 3–4. **3–4:** See 9.1–3; 31.3–6; cf. Exod. 14.14, 25; 15.1–4. **5–9:** The primary intent is to help ensure the future of the community by allowing young conscripts to finish establishing their own households, symbolized by taking possession of house, vineyard, and wife (cf. Jer. 29.5–6), before sending them to a war in which they may die. The same items are included in the curses for disobedience (28.30), where they signify dispossession by the enemy. The sequence of the three together symbolizes the home as an entirety. **5:** *Dedicated* (or "inaugurated"): Although Solomon's dedication of the Temple is narrated (1 Kings ch 8), there are no specific rituals of home dedication recorded in the Bible. The parallel curse employs "live" (28.30). **6:** *Harvested it,* lit. "profaned it"; Priestly law stipulated that newly planted fruit trees were only available for common use in the fifth year (Lev. 19.23–25). **7:** *Paid the bride-price ... married:* Marriage was a two-step process; see NJPS translators' note *a;* 22.23–27 n. *Wife:* For the order in which "wife" follows "house," see Exod. 20.14. The wife comes first at 5.18; 28.30. **8:** *Comrades:* The Heb employs "brother," to which Deut. frequently, and distinctively, gives the meaning "fellow citizen." The same word is elsewhere

and say, "Is there anyone afraid and disheartened? Let him go
back to his home, lest the courage of his comrades flag like his."
9 When the officials have finished addressing the troops, army
commanders shall assume command of the troops.
10 When you approach a town to attack it, you shall [a]offer it
terms of peace.[a] 11 If it responds peaceably and lets you in, all
the people present there shall serve you at forced labor. 12 If it
does not surrender to you, but would join battle with you, you
shall lay siege to it; 13 and when the LORD your God delivers it
into your hand, you shall put all its males to the sword. 14 You
may, however, take as your booty the women, the children, the
livestock, and everything in the town—all its spoil—and enjoy
the use of the spoil of your enemy, which the LORD your God
gives you.
15 Thus you shall deal with all towns that lie very far from you,
towns that do not belong to nations hereabout. 16 In the towns
of the latter peoples, however, which the LORD your God is giving you as a heritage, you shall not let a soul remain alive. 17 No,
you must proscribe[b] them—the Hittites and the Amorites, the
Canaanites and the Perizzites, the Hivites and the Jebusites—
as the LORD your God has commanded you, 18 lest they lead
you into doing all the abhorrent things that they have done for
their gods and you stand guilty before the LORD your God.
19 When in your war against a city you have to besiege it a
long time in order to capture it, you must not destroy its trees,
wielding the ax against them. You may eat of them, but you
must not cut them down. Are trees of the field human to withdraw before you into the besieged city? 20 Only trees that you
know do not yield food may be destroyed; you may cut them
down for constructing siegeworks against the city that is waging war on you, until it has been reduced.

21 If, in the land that the LORD your God is assigning you
to possess, someone slain is found lying in the open,
the identity of the slayer not being known, 2 your elders and
magistrates shall go out and measure the distances from the

a-a Or "call on it to surrender." *b See Lev. 27.29.*

translated "a fellow Hebrew" (15.12). **11:** The use of a defeated people for *forced labor* was widespread. Some narratives in the Deuteronomistic History establish that the Israelites employed the indigenous population of Canaan as such a resource (Judg. 1.27–36). So important was it to the monarchy that David's cabinet, according to 2 Sam. 20.24, included an official responsible for "forced labor." **15–18:** *Thus you shall deal with all towns that lie very far from you:* The law now retroactively restricts the preceding rules of engagement (vv. 10–14), which tolerate the taking of captives as "forced labor," so that they apply only to foreign wars. That restriction comes unexpectedly and contradicts the unconditional formulation of v. 10, which imposed no geographical restriction. Moreover, the stipulation that the indigenous population of Canaan should uniformly be exterminated is inconsistent both with the earliest narratives of the settlement and with the administrative list of the monarchy (see v. 11 n.). Most likely, therefore, the law sanctioning the negotiation of peace treaties and the taking of captives (vv. 10–14) originally applied to warfare within Canaan. The editor preserves the earliest rules of engagement, but redefines them using the geographical restriction in vv. 15–16. Deut.'s formulaic prohibition against taking Canaanite prisoners (see 7.1–6; 12.29–31) thus represents a later addition reflecting the 7th c. theology of Deut. The rationale for the literary fiction may be an ex post facto desire to construct an ideal of cultural independence and religious purity at the very historical moment that Judah was in fact a vassal state paying tribute to Assyria (2 Kings 18.7–19.35). **15:** The *nations hereabout* refers to the Canaanites. With that turn of language, the narrator places himself in the land of Canaan (as at 1.1). According to the narrative, however, the nation has not yet entered the land and Moses died before entering Canaan (34.5). Similar anachronisms (2.12b; 3.11; 34.5; Gen. 12.6b) led a few medieval Jewish biblical commentators, like Abraham Ibn Ezra (1089–1164 CE), to recognize that both Deut. and the Torah include post-Mosaic material. **16:** *In the towns of the latter peoples* refers to the Canaanites. **17:** *You must proscribe them:* The Heb phrase is elsewhere translated as "doom … to destruction" (7.2; 13.16; see also translators' note *b*). **19–20:** Wars often involved the kind of "scorched earth policy" prohibited here (2 Kings 3.19, 25). **20:** *Siegeworks* were regularly built against walled cities (1 Sam. 20.15; 2 Kings 25.1). Remnants of Roman siegeworks (70–74 CE) remain visible at Masada.

21.1–9: Atonement for an unsolved murder. This archaic law is concerned to maintain the moral and ritual purity of the land of Israel. Since contact with a murder victim's

corpse to the nearby towns. [3]The elders of the town nearest to the corpse shall then take a heifer which has never been worked, which has never pulled in a yoke; [4]and the elders of that town shall bring the heifer down to an everflowing wadi, which is not tilled or sown. There, in the wadi, they shall break the heifer's neck. [5]The priests, sons of Levi, shall come forward; for the LORD your God has chosen them to minister to Him and to pronounce blessing in the name of the LORD, and every lawsuit and case of assault[a] is subject to their ruling. [6]Then all the elders of the town nearest to the corpse shall wash their hands over the heifer whose neck was broken in the wadi. [7]And they shall make this declaration: "Our hands did not shed this blood, nor did our eyes see it done. [8]Absolve, O LORD, Your people Israel whom You redeemed, and do not let guilt for the blood of the innocent remain among Your people Israel." And they will be absolved of bloodguilt. [9]Thus you will remove from your midst guilt for the blood of the innocent, for you will be doing what is right in the sight of the LORD.

KI TETSE' כי תצא

[10]When you take the field against your enemies, and the LORD your God delivers them into your power and you take some of them captive, [11]and you see among the captives a beautiful woman and you desire her and would take her to wife, [12]you shall bring her into your house, and she shall trim her hair, pare her nails, [13]and discard her captive's garb. She shall spend a month's time in your house lamenting her father and mother; after that you may come to her and possess her, and

a Cf. 17.8. Or "skin affection"; cf. 24.8.

blood rendered the land impure (Gen. 4.10; Num. 35.33–34), it was imperative to "purge Israel of the blood of the innocent" (19.13). The established method for doing so was to restore justice by putting the murderer to death (Gen. 9.5–6). However, this law addresses circumstances when doing so is impossible because the perpetrator of the murder cannot be identified. There are similar cases involving corpses found between two cities in older Near Eastern law (Laws of Hammurabi §§23–24; Hittite Laws §6), where the primary focus is to clarify whether financial liability exists. Here, in contrast, the primary concern is ethical and religious: how to atone for the spilled blood of the victim. The law shows evidence of several stages of literary reworking, making it difficult to recover the exact meaning of its rituals. **1:** *In the open,* a technical term, meaning beyond the legal jurisdiction of any particular town (see 22.23, 25). The reference implies the absence of witnesses to identify the culprit. **2:** For the judicial role of the *elders* in cases of homicide, see 19.12; 21.18–21; for the *magistrates,* see 16.18 n. *Measure the distances* in order to establish legal jurisdiction, as in the Hittite Laws §6. **3:** *Never been worked ... never pulled in a yoke:* The heifer's immaturity and physically intact state symbolize the human victim's innocence (similarly, Num. 19.2). **4:** *Everflowing wadi,* lit. "with reliable water" (Amos 5.24), in contrast to unreliable seasonal streams (Jer. 15.18). *Break the heifer's neck,* nonsacrificial slaughter; sacrifice requires ritual slitting of the throat (see Exod. 13.13; 34.20). **5:** *The priests, sons of Levi* were not mentioned among the officials of v. 2 and play no subsequent role in the law. Their inclusion therefore seems like a later addition, perhaps prompted by the prayer. *Every lawsuit and case of assault* contrasts with 17.9, where the Levitical priests, officiating at the central sanctuary, had jurisdiction only in cases that could not be resolved locally. The NJPS translation is correct as it stands. The alternative translation mentioned in translators' note *a* is valid only when the word here properly translated "assault" is combined with another word specifying "skin" (as at 24.8). **6:** *Wash their hands over the heifer,* with no laying on of hands, thus entailing no ritual transfer of culpability from the elders to the animal (contrast Lev. 16.21–22). Instead, the ritual seems symbolically to contrast this slaughter with that of the human victim. **7:** *Our hands ... nor did our eyes see it done:* The formula extends the notion of responsibility from direct *(our hands)* to indirect: mere failure to avert or report a witnessed crime (cf. Lev. 5.1). **8:** *Absolve, O LORD:* The extended ritual of vv. 3–6 has no intrinsic efficacy; prayer in combination with the ritual is the means of absolution. *Your people Israel:* The v.'s double reference to the nation drives home that the frame of reference is no longer the "elders of the town nearest to the corpse" (v. 6) but the people's collective responsibility (19.10, 13). The prayer has a chiastic structure: "Absolve ... Your people Israel ... Your people Israel ... will be absolved" (AB:B'A'). *And they will be absolved,* better, "so that they may be absolved." The v.'s literary symmetry and grammar together establish that absolution ultimately depends upon divine action, not human ritual.

21.10–25.19: Miscellaneous criminal, civil, and family laws. The following laws are concerned with individual family, civil, and ethical issues; in comparison, the preceding section was more broadly

she shall be your wife. [14]Then, should you no longer want her,
you must release her outright. You must not sell her for money:
since you had your will of her, you must not enslave her.

[15]If a man has two wives, one loved and the other unloved,
and both the loved and the unloved have borne him sons, but
the first-born is the son of the unloved one—[16]when he wills
his property to his sons, he may not treat as first-born the son of
the loved one in disregard of the son of the unloved one who is
older. [17]Instead, he must accept the first-born, the son of the unloved one, and allot to him a double portion[a] of all he possesses;
since he is the first fruit of his vigor, the birthright is his due.

[18]If a man has a wayward and defiant son, who does not
heed his father or mother and does not obey them even after
they discipline him, [19]his father and mother shall take hold of
him and bring him out to the elders of his town at the public
place of his community. [20]They shall say to the elders of his
town, "This son of ours is disloyal and defiant; he does not
heed us. He is a glutton and a drunkard." [21]Thereupon the men
of his town shall stone him to death. Thus you will sweep out
evil from your midst: all Israel will hear and be afraid.
[22]If a man is guilty of a capital offense and is put to death,
and you impale him on a stake, [23]you must not let his corpse
remain on the stake overnight, but must bury him the same

a Lit. two-thirds.

concerned with the system of worship, the judicial procedures, and the public administration of the nation as a whole. Laws extending legal protection to women in contexts where they would otherwise be disenfranchised concern female captives (21.10–14), the property rights of the less-favored wife (21.15–17), and false charges of infidelity (22.13–19).

21.10–14: Legal obligations toward female captives. In light of 20.10–18, the law would apply only to female captives taken in wars outside of the land; most likely, however, it also applied to the Canaanite population (20.15–18 n.). Female war captives routinely became concubines of their captors. This law regulates that convention and accords such women some dignity and protection against enslavement. **12–13:** The rituals provide both captive and captor means to effect a transition from one status to another. **13:** *A month's time,* the full mourning period, as for Aaron and Moses (Num. 20.29; Deut. 34.8). *Lamenting:* Contextually it is unclear whether the captive's parents actually died in the war or are mourned as lost to her because of her captivity. The prescribed time to grieve implies legal respect for the female captive as a person. **13:** *Come to her* sexually; consummation provides the legal means for her to become *your wife.* **14:** Manumission to protect female concubines from being sold as slaves is also prescribed at Exod. 21.7–8. *Had your will of her,* more specifically, "violated her" sexually (22.24, 29; Gen. 34.2; Judg. 19.24; 2 Sam. 13.12).

21.15–17: Legal protection of the less-favored wife. The law uses the norm of primogeniture (Gen. 25.29–34; Laws of Hammurabi §§165–70) to protect the son of the less-favored wife from disinheritance. **17:** *Double portion,* two-thirds (see Zech. 13.8), leaving one third for the other son. *The birthright,* the technical legal term for the preferential share of the inheritance. The foundation narratives concerning Isaac, Jacob, and Joseph do not recognize the legal norm here affirmed (Gen. 17.15–22; 21.8–14; 27.1–40; 48.8–22).

21.18–21: The rebellious son. The Decalogue requirement to honor the parents (5.16; Exod. 20.12) carries no explicit sanction; here flagrant and sustained disobedience is a capital offense. Nevertheless, the Rabbis (*m. Sanh.* 8) attenuated the force of this law by making the son's violation much more stringent than the text suggests, essentially eliminating cases in which the penalty would apply. The law becomes, then, an ideal law teaching respect for parents. Other Near Eastern law collections included similar laws but did not require capital punishment (Law of Hammurabi §195). This law concerning sons should be read in tandem with the law concerning daughters in 22.13–21. **18:** *Not heed his father or mother:* The Heb more emphatically ascribes equal authority to each parent: "obey either his father or his mother." *Discipline:* The term extends to physical measures such as flogging (1 Kings 12.11). **19:** *The elders* functioned as judges of family law and held court at the city gate, which served as a public forum (22.15; 25.7; Job. 29.7; Ruth 4.1–2, 11; Lam. 5.14). This system contrasts with the professionalized judiciary established at the same site (16.18), which may specifically have had jurisdiction over religious and criminal law (17.2–7). **21:** In contrast to 13.14 and 17.4, no investigation is required; only parental testimony. *Stone him,* see 13.10 n.

21.22–23: Treatment of the executed. Public exposure of the corpse of an executed criminal, which was not the norm, was a form of reproach directed against enemies of the state (Josh. 8.29; 10.26; 1 Sam. 31.10; Esth.

day. For an impaled body is an affront to God: you shall not
defile the land that the LORD your God is giving you to possess.

22 If you see your fellow's ox or sheep gone astray, do not
ignore it; you must take it back to your fellow. 2 If your
fellow does not live near you or you do not know who he is, you
shall bring it home and it shall remain with you until your fellow claims it; then you shall give it back to him. 3 You shall do
the same with his ass; you shall do the same with his garment;
and so too shall you do with anything that your fellow loses
and you find: you must not remain indifferent.
4 If you see your fellow's ass or ox fallen on the road, do not
ignore it; you must help him raise it.
5 A woman must not put on man's apparel, nor shall a man
wear woman's clothing; for whoever does these things is abhorrent to the LORD your God.
6 If, along the road, you chance upon a bird's nest, in any tree
or on the ground, with fledglings or eggs and the mother sitting over the fledglings or on the eggs, do not take the mother
together with her young. 7 Let the mother go, and take only the
young, in order that you may fare well and have a long life.
8 When you build a new house, you shall make a parapet for
your roof, so that you do not bring bloodguilt on your house if
anyone should fall from it.
9 You shall not sow your vineyard with a second kind of seed,
else the crop—from the seed you have sown—and the yield of
the vineyard may not be used. 10 You shall not plow with an
ox and an ass together. 11 You shall not wear cloth combining
wool and linen.
12 You shall make tassels on the four corners of the garment
with which you cover yourself.

9.6–14). Out of respect for the body, to prevent it from serving as carrion (2 Sam. 21.10), this law sets stringent limits to that procedure. The law applies to Israelites and non-Israelites alike (Josh. 8.29; 10.27), since the ritual purity of the land is involved. **22:** *Impale him on a stake:* The Heb phrase may also mean death caused by hanging from a tree or gallows, or suspending someone who has already been executed from a pole or gallows (Josh. 10.26; Esth. 9.11–14).

22.1–12: Various moral and religious responsibilities of citizenship. The rationale for the sequence and selection of these laws is often unclear.

22.1–4: Moral duties toward the neighbor. Two laws (vv. 1–3, 4) that develop, in sequence, two corresponding laws from the earlier Book of the Covenant. **1–3:** The earlier law governing the return of wandering animals (Exod. 21.1–3) is here revised and extended. **1:** *Your fellow's ox,* in contrast to "your enemy's ox" (Exod. 23.4). **3:** *Anything:* The earlier law has now been universalized to apply to any lost property, even that which cannot independently have "gone astray" (v. 1). *You must not remain indifferent:* The law makes a moral appeal to conscience but possesses no legal sanction. **4:** Reworking Exod. 23.5 to emphasize the neighbor, as in v. 1.

22.5–12: Miscellaneous laws. 5: The prohibition against cross-dressing likely seeks to maintain gender boundaries; a similar concern for boundaries is evident in vv. 10–12. **6–7:** The respect for the life of other creatures here parallels that shown for the integrity of the natural environment even in the context of war (20.19–20). Desire to avoid the simultaneous consumption of two generations of the same creature is also evident in other laws (14.21; Exod. 23.19; 34.26; Lev. 22.28). **7:** To elicit compliance, the legislator makes an appeal to enlightened self-interest; as in v. 3, there is no legal sanction for noncompliance. **8:** The *roof* was used as living space (Josh. 2.6; Judg. 3.20–25; 2 Sam. 11.2), and according to most reconstructions was where people slept in the typical Israelite four-room house. (See essay "Daily Life," pp. 2005–11.) *Bloodguilt* defines the negligence in criminal rather than civil terms, with the implication that the offense is capital (see 19.10 n.). For other examples of criminal negligence, see Exod. 21.29 and, also involving liability for faulty construction, Laws of Hammurabi §229. **9–10:** These laws attempt to maintain specific boundaries between categories seen as incompatible (as in v. 5; 14.3–20); see the corresponding laws in Lev. 19.19. The rationale for the specific examples selected, however, is hard to establish. **9:** *May not be used,* lit. becomes "set apart" or "holy"; that is, not permitted for human consumption. **12:** *Tassels:* No reason is given for this requirement, although the law receives a theological rationale at Num. 15.37–40. Since Neo-Assyrian palace reliefs distinguish royalty by their fringed garments, it may symbolize the application of a royal dress code to the nation as a whole. The command's original intention was that the tassels were to be worn in full view. Only during the persecution of the Middle Ages did the practice develop of wearing tassels (the "tallit katan") underneath the clothing. Based on this law and its parallel in Num., rabbinic law requires that a tasseled shawl (tallit)

13 A man marries a woman and cohabits with her. Then he
takes an aversion to her 14 and makes up charges against her
and defames her, saying, "I married this woman; but when I approached her, I found that she was not a virgin." 15 In such a case,
the girl's father and mother shall produce the evidence of the
girl's virginity before the elders of the town at the gate. 16 And the
girl's father shall say to the elders, "I gave this man my daughter
to wife, but he has taken an aversion to her; 17 so he has made up
charges, saying, 'I did not find your daughter a virgin.' But here is
the evidence of my daughter's virginity!" And they shall spread
out the cloth before the elders of the town. 18 The elders of that
town shall then take the man and flog him, 19 and they shall fine
him a hundred [shekels of] silver and give it to the girl's father;
for the man has defamed a virgin in Israel. Moreover, she shall
remain his wife; he shall never have the right to divorce her.

20 But if the charge proves true, the girl was found not to
have been a virgin, 21 then the girl shall be brought out to the
entrance of her father's house, and the men of her town shall
stone her to death; for she did a shameful thing in Israel, committing fornication while under her father's authority. Thus
you will sweep away evil from your midst.

22 If a man is found lying with another man's wife, both of
them—the man and the woman with whom he lay—shall die.
Thus you will sweep away evil from Israel.

be worn during certain prayers. *Yourself:* Here, the requirement is not explicitly restricted to males. Some rabbis argued that women, too, are to wear tassels, although the majority view exempted women from this requirement (see *Sifre Num.* §115; *b. Menaḥ.* 43a).

22.13–23.1: Violations of marriage law. In the ancient Near East, marriage was a contractual arrangement between the woman's father and the husband. She remained in her father's household until a suitor paid a bride-price (vv. 28–29; Exod. 22.15–16) to compensate the father for the reduction of the household. At that point she became formally engaged, legally contracted for, although still living "under her father's authority" (v. 21; lit. "in her father's house"). Later, at the marriage feast, the union was consummated (Gen. 29.22–25) and the woman took up residence in the household of her husband. The following laws presuppose these contractual norms and terminology.

22.13–21: False accusation of breach of marital contract. 13: *Cohabits with her* to consummate the marriage (as 21.13). *Takes an aversion to her,* cf. 21.15. **14:** *Makes up charges against her:* His reason for using this option to end the relation may well be mercenary. Displeasure with a wife provided grounds for divorce (24.1), but divorce would almost certainly have required the man to provide financial support, as presupposed by the requirement for a "bill of divorce" (24.3; Isa. 50.1; Jer. 3.8; cf. Exod. 21.10) and stipulated by Near Eastern law (e.g., Laws of Hammurabi §§137–40). In contrast, the slander, *I found that she was not a virgin,* would entail the refund of the bride-price and payment of a penalty for breach of contract (see Hittite Laws §§28–29). **15:** The *evidence* sought is the blood-stained cloth of v. 17. *Elders of the town at the gate,* see 16.18 n.; 21.19 n. **17:** *The cloth* upon which husband and wife slept upon consummation of the relationship. There is scant medical support for the underlying assumptions: that intercourse would cause the first perforation of the hymen and that such perforation would cause bleeding upon the bedding, which is here held up in public display as legal evidence. No other biblical text refers to this *cloth.* Nor is it likely that such a cloth was kept by the parents, but it would have been easy for them to manufacture one. This entire case is set up to deter false accusations against the bride and her family. **18:** *Flog him,* the same Heb word as "discipline him" (21.18); it may refer to flogging or simply to the following fine. **19:** *They shall fine him:* The penalty for his slanderous accusation is financial, although the penalty for her lack of virginity, if proven true, is capital (vv. 20–21). This disproportion is an exception to Deut.'s requirement that "you shall do to the false witness just as the false witness had meant to do to the other" (19.19). *A hundred [shekels of] silver,* about 1.1 kg (2.5 pounds), is twice the fine for rape (v. 29). **21:** *Entrance of her father's house,* the very site of the offense. *Stone her to death,* see 13.11 n. *Shameful thing in Israel,* a violation of basic community sexual and religious norms (Gen. 34.7; Josh. 7.15; Judg. 19.23–34; 20.6, 10). *Sweep away evil,* see 13.6 n. These are strong terms of condemnation.

22.22–23.1: Adultery and rape. The editors' placement of these laws suggests their concern to establish sex and family law as a moral category, rather than as a financial one, as in the Book of the Covenant. There, the law of the seduced virgin (Exod. 22.15–16) came at the end of a sequence of property law (Exod. 21.35–22.14), implying that the daughter was seen as an extension of her father's estate. In contrast, the corresponding law found here (22.28–29) concludes a series of similar laws (22.13–23.1); there is no longer any connection to property law (see also 5.18 n.). **22:** Adultery, when defined as a man having sex with a woman betrothed or married

23 In the case of a virgin who is [a]-engaged to a man-[a]—if a
man comes upon her in town and lies with her, 24 you shall take
the two of them out to the gate of that town and stone them to
death: the girl because she did not cry for help in the town, and
the man because he violated another man's wife. Thus you will
sweep away evil from your midst. 25 But if the man comes upon
the engaged girl in the open country, and the man lies with
her by force, only the man who lay with her shall die, 26 but
you shall do nothing to the girl. The girl did not incur the death
penalty, for this case is like that of a man attacking another and
murdering him. 27 He came upon her in the open; though the
engaged girl cried for help, there was no one to save her.
28 If a man comes upon a virgin who is not engaged and he
seizes her and lies with her, and they are discovered, 29 the
man who lay with her shall pay the girl's father fifty [shekels of]
silver, and she shall be his wife. Because he has violated her, he
can never have the right to divorce her.

23 No man shall marry his father's former wife, so as [b]-to
remove his father's garment.-[b]
2 No one whose testes are crushed or whose member is cut
off shall be admitted into the congregation of the LORD.

a-a *I.e., for whom a bride-price has been paid; see 20.7.*
b-b *I.e., lay claim to what his father had possessed. Cf. Lev. 18.8; 20.11; Ezek. 16.8; Ruth 3.9.*

to another man, is a violation of the Decalogue's seventh commandment (5.17) and a capital offense (Lev. 18.20; 20.10). *Both of them ... shall die:* This stipulation makes a sharp contrast with ancient Near Eastern legal norms, which required the adulterer's death but left the fate of the adulterous wife to the disposition of her husband (but cf. Prov. 6.34). That the wife is here removed from the authority of the husband defines her as a legal person who is accountable for her own actions. **23–27:** Two laws determining the woman's culpability (vv. 23–24) or nonculpability (vv. 25–27) in cases of rape or seduction. The distinction hangs upon the expectation of protest to express refusal (v. 24). **23:** *Engaged to a man* (cf. v. 25): This distinction in legal status between the betrothed and married woman permits another distinction between adultery and rape: Although the woman still resides with her father, she is contractually bound to her future husband (see translators' note *a-a*). Therefore consensual sex with the betrothed woman would constitute adultery. *In town,* where there are potential witnesses. The contrast with "in the open country" (v. 25) symbolically determines the availability or unavailability of witnesses who could testify or come to the rescue. Similarly, Middle Assyrian Laws §A 12 (ca. 1076 BCE). **24:** *Cry for help:* A sign that she tried to resist. The fabrication of such a cry in the false accusation against Joseph therefore has legal significance (Gen. 39.14–15). **25:** The assault *in the open country,* where rescuers or witnesses are unlikely, suggests planned malice. **26:** *For this case is like:* A distinctive cross-reference to another legal case (19.11–13), used to make an argument from analogy. *A man attacking another and murdering him,* criminal assault. The importance of the analogy is not in the definition of the crime, however. Rather, it is in the determination of the legal status of the participants in the crime; the analogy absolves the woman of legal culpability for adultery. **28–29:** The seizure and rape of a virgin who is not engaged, the enforced marriage, and the prohibition of divorce correspond to Middle Assyrian Laws §A 55. The law also follows the model of Exod. 22.16–17, which specifies sexual intercourse with, but not forced rape of, a "virgin who is not engaged." The conflation of the two different models blurs the distinction between consensual and nonconsensual intercourse on the woman's part. **28:** *Seizes her:* The Heb word differs from that in v. 25, where force is clearly intended; here the degree of physical force is more ambiguous. *And lies with her,* as in Exod. 22.15. **29:** *Fifty ... silver:* As in Exod. 22.15, the intercourse does not constitute adultery, because the woman is neither married nor betrothed. In contrast to Exod. 22.16, however, the payment to the father does not directly represent compensation for the loss of the bride-price, which is normally a negotiated amount (Gen. 34.12). As a fixed amount externally imposed by the law, the payment here seems closer to a fine (v. 19). Both Deut. and Exod. require the man now also legally and contractually to marry the woman by paying the bride-price to the father. In contrast to Exod. 22.16, the father's consent is not sought, and therefore he must negotiate the bride-price with the man who had intercourse with his daughter and no other. Thus the fine paid by the man seems intended to compensate the father for diminished potential earnings had he been able to negotiate a higher bride-price with another man. Postbiblical Jewish law granted both the father and the daughter the right to refuse such marriages (Maimonides, *Mishneh Torah, Nash.,* Hilkhot Na'arah Betulah 1:3). **23.1:** A transition from marriage law to the next section, which resembles the previous one in form (prohibition) and content (prohibited sexual relations). The Heb ch division that

3 No one misbegotten[a] shall be admitted into the congregation of the LORD; none of his descendants, even in the tenth
generation, shall be admitted into the congregation of the
LORD.
4 No Ammonite or Moabite shall be admitted into the
congregation of the LORD; none of their descendants, even
in the tenth generation, shall ever be admitted into the congregation of the LORD, 5 because they did not meet you with
food and water on your journey after you left Egypt, and because they hired Balaam son of Beor, from Pethor of Aram-
naharaim, to curse you.— 6 But the LORD your God refused to
heed Balaam; instead, the LORD your God turned the curse
into a blessing for you, for the LORD your God loves you.—
7 You shall never concern yourself with their welfare or benefit as long as you live.
8 You shall not abhor an Edomite, for he is your kinsman.
You shall not abhor an Egyptian, for you were a stranger in his
land. 9 Children born to them may be admitted into the congregation of the LORD in the third generation.[b]

10 When you go out as a troop against your enemies, be on
your guard against anything untoward. 11 If anyone among you
has been rendered unclean by a nocturnal emission, he must
leave the camp, and he must not reenter the camp. 12 Toward
evening he shall bathe in water, and at sundown he may reenter the camp. 13 Further, there shall be an area for you outside the camp, where you may relieve yourself. 14 With your
gear you shall have a spike, and when you have squatted you

a *Meaning of Heb.* mamzer *uncertain; in Jewish law, the offspring of adultery or incest between Jews.* b *I.e., of residence in Israel's territory.*

assigns this law to ch 23 instead of ch 22, with the other family laws, reflects the law's closer connection to what follows. *Father's former wife* presupposes the death of the father and almost certainly refers to the widowed stepmother, not the birth mother (see Lev. 18.7–8). *Remove his father's garment:* The intent is to respect the sexual privacy of the father and to avoid even indirect sexual contact with him (Gen. 9.23–24; 49.4; Lev. 18.8; 20.11).

23.2–9: Restrictions on access to Israel's assembly. *The congregation of the LORD* (v. 2) served as the national governing body, akin to a popular legislature, that was charged with a broad range of judicial, political, and policy matters (Judg. 20.2). **2:** *Testes ... member,* any physical damage to the male genitalia. Deut. here seems to impose the same physiological qualification for membership in the assembly that the Holiness Collection requires of the priesthood (Lev. 21.17–23; see also Deut. 14.2 n.). Alternatively, eunuchs may be here excluded for reasons of their cultural association, since they served as officials in Near Eastern bureaucracies. **3:** *Misbegotten,* the offspring of a marriage viewed as incestuous (see vv. 1, 4; Lev. 18.6–18; translators' note *a*). *Tenth generation,* see v. 4 n. **4–9:** The restriction on access to Israel's national assembly does not entail denial of residence rights. Those named retain the protection afforded by the legal status of "resident alien" (see 1.16; 5.14; Lev. 19.10, 33–34; 23.22). It is likely, however, that those excluded could not marry within the community, and could not enter the Temple precincts. **4–7:** These laws were reused and extended in the postexilic context to prohibit intermarriage (Ezra chs 9–10; Neh. 13.1–3). **4:** *Ammonite or Moabite,* perhaps introduced after v. 3 because of an older tradition concerning their incestuous origins (Gen. 19.30–38). *Tenth generation,* "forever," as explicitly stated in the Heb. **5:** The rationale, which could be a late addition, substantially varies from the earlier report that Israel detoured around Ammon without requesting assistance and received food and water from Moab (2.19, 29, 37). *Balaam,* see Num. chs 22–24. **8:** *Not abhor an Edomite:* The retention of this exhortation is extraordinary, since the Edomites participated in the destruction of Jerusalem (Ps. 137.7; Obad.; cf. Amos 1.11). *Kinsman,* through Esau (Gen. 25.24–26; 36.1). *Egyptian:* This equally remarkable injunction must reflect stories about Egypt as a site of sanctuary (Gen. chs 12; 37–50), while managing to overlook the enslavement (26.6; 28.60, 68; Exod. chs 1–15).

23.10–15: Special rules for the military camp. These laws move forward from the rules determining the composition of the assembly to the special rules that apply to the military camp. The focus is no longer on the rules of engagement (20.1–20; 21.10–14) but rather matters of personal hygiene that effect ritual purity. The theology of holy war assumes God's direct participation in the campaign (7.17–24; 20.4), creating a demand for heightened purity such as was demanded of the entire people at Sinai (Exod. 19.10, 14). Sexual abstinence seems also to have been required (1 Sam. 21.4–5; 2 Sam. 11.8–11; cf. Exod. 19.15). **10–11:** Cf. Lev. 15.16–18. **13:** *Area for you outside the camp,* a latrine. These laws are reused in the Dead Sea Scrolls (1QM; 11QSTemple), each of which also specifies the exact distance of the latrine from the camp.

shall dig a hole with it and cover up your excrement. 15 Since
the LORD your God moves about in your camp to protect you
and to deliver your enemies to you, let your camp be holy; let
Him not find anything unseemly among you and turn away
from you.
16 You shall not turn over to his master a slave who seeks refuge with you from his master. 17 He shall live with you in any
place he may choose among the settlements in your midst,
wherever he pleases; you must not ill-treat him.
18 No Israelite woman shall be a cult prostitute, nor shall any
Israelite man be a cult prostitute. 19 You shall not bring the fee
of a whore or the pay of a dog[a] into the house of the LORD your
God in fulfillment of any vow, for both are abhorrent to the
LORD your God.
20 You shall not deduct interest from loans to your countrymen, whether in money or food or anything else that can be deducted as interest; 21 but you may deduct interest from loans to
foreigners. Do not deduct interest from loans to your countrymen, so that the LORD your God may bless you in all your undertakings in the land that you are about to enter and possess.
22 When you make a vow to the LORD your God, do not put
off fulfilling it, for the LORD your God will require it of you, and
you will have incurred guilt; 23 whereas you incur no guilt if you
refrain from vowing. 24 You must fulfill what has crossed your
lips and perform what you have voluntarily vowed to the LORD
your God, having made the promise with your own mouth.

a *I.e., a male prostitute.*

15: *Moves about,* see 20.4; 31.6. *Anything unseemly,* as in 24.1.

23.16–25.19: The heightened moral responsibilities of the covenant community. The text moves from membership (vv. 2–9) and military camp rules (vv. 10–15) to broader ethical and religious norms imposed upon Israel.

23.16–17: Prohibition against the return of escaped slaves. The law rejects the almost universal stipulation within ancient Near Eastern law that escaped slaves must be returned to their owner, usually under penalty of death, and that rewards bounty hunters for their return (Laws of Hammurabi §§16–20; Hittite Laws §§22–24). **17:** The extraordinary fivefold repetition of phrases designating the location of residence emphasizes that the entire community must be open to them.

23.18–19: Restrictions on prostitution. Prostitution is presupposed, and not illegal, but is regulated in such a way as to preserve the Temple's sanctity. **18:** *Cult prostitute:* The translation reflects the widely held belief in the existence of sacred prostitution in Israel and the ancient Near East, for which there is scant evidence. Heb "kedesha" here more likely serves as a standard euphemism for the coarser term for a regular prostitute that appears in v. 19. The same alternation between the two terms appears in the narrative of Tamar, whom Judah privately regards as a "whore" but who is publicly referred to as a "kedesha" (Gen. 38.15, 21). The word might better be translated as "one set aside." **19:** *Dog,* in context, a euphemism for the male counterpart to a common female prostitute. To maintain holiness, the law proscribes the donation of income gained from prostitution to the Temple (cf. Hos. 4.14; Mic. 1.7).

23.20–26: Laws of financial ethics, vows, gathering by the needy. 20–21: As Israelites must not sexually exploit one another (vv. 18–19), so must they avoid exploiting each other economically. This law builds on Exod. 22.25, which clarifies that, in this economy, lending served primarily as a means of social support for "the poor among you" (similarly Lev. 25.36–37). Charging interest would amount to profiteering from the misfortunes of others. **21:** *Foreigners,* as distinct from the "resident alien" or "stranger," who fully participated in Israel's social welfare system (5.14; 14.29; 16.11; 24.14, 17, 19, 20, 21; for similar distinctions, see 15.3; Lev. 25.44–45). **22–24:** A *vow* (v. 22) promises payment to God (usually a sacrifice at a temple) for granting a petitioner's request (see 1 Sam. 1.11). The cautious reserve expressed here closely corresponds to wisdom teachings (Eccl. 5.4–6). The precedent of stories like Jephthah's vow (Judg. 11.29–40) trenchantly explains such reserve. For a more positive view, see Ps. 50.14. **25–26:** These rules prohibit exploitation of Deut.'s extensive support system for the needy (14.28–29; 24.19–22; 25.4). **26:** *Pluck ... hand,* to address immediate hunger (illustrated in a later period in Luke 6.1; cf. Matt. 12.1; Mark 2.23).

24.1–22: Restriction on marriage and care for those in need. The ch, like the previous one, begins with a restriction on marriage and concludes by stipulating care for those in need. **1–4:** This complex law, theologically applied by two prophets (Isa. 50.1; Jer. 3.1, 8), addresses only the specific case of remarriage after divorce to a wife who subsequently married another; it does not prohibit remarriage in general. No general laws of either marriage or divorce

25 When you enter another man's vineyard, you may eat as
many grapes as you want, until you are full, but you must not
put any in your vessel. 26 When you enter another man's field
of standing grain, you may pluck ears with your hand; but you
must not put a sickle to your neighbor's grain.

24 A man takes a wife and possesses her. She fails to please
him because he finds something obnoxious about her,
and he writes her a bill of divorcement, hands it to her, and
sends her away from his house; 2 she leaves his household and
becomes the wife of another man; 3 then this latter man rejects
her, writes her a bill of divorcement, hands it to her, and sends
her away from his house; or the man who married her last dies.
4 Then the first husband who divorced her shall not take her to
wife again, since she has been defiled[a]—for that would be abhorrent to the LORD. You must not bring sin upon the land that
the LORD your God is giving you as a heritage.

5 When a man has taken a bride, he shall not go out with the
army or be assigned to it for any purpose; he shall be exempt
one year for the sake of his household, to give happiness to the
woman he has married.

6 A handmill or an upper millstone shall not be taken in
pawn, for that would be taking someone's life in pawn.

7 If a man is found to have kidnapped a fellow Israelite, enslaving him or selling him, that kidnapper shall die; thus you
will sweep out evil from your midst.

8 In cases of a skin affection[b] be most careful to do exactly
as the levitical priests instruct you. Take care to do as I have
commanded them. 9 Remember what the LORD your God did
to Miriam on the journey after you left Egypt.[c]

10 When you make a loan of any sort to your countryman,
you must not enter his house to seize his pledge. 11 You must
remain outside, while the man to whom you made the loan
brings the pledge out to you. 12 If he is a needy man, you shall
not go to sleep in his pledge; 13 you must return the pledge to
him at sundown, that he may sleep in his cloth and bless you;
and it will be to your merit before the LORD your God.

14 You shall not abuse a needy and destitute laborer, whether
a fellow countryman or a stranger in one of the communities
of your land. 15 You must pay him his wages on the same day,
before the sun sets, for he is needy and urgently depends on it;
else he will cry to the LORD against you and you will incur guilt.

a I.e., disqualified for him. *b Cf. Lev. 13.1 ff.* *c See Num. 12.10 ff.*

survive from ancient Israel; biblical law includes only special cases that raise particular ethical or religious issues. **1:** Male-initiated divorce was the norm, though there is some evidence in the Near East and in the Jewish Elephantine Papyri (5th c. BCE) of marriage contracts permitting either party to initiate divorce proceedings (cf. Exod. 21.10–11). *He finds ... about her,* a legal formula used to charge someone with disloyal action or betrayal of trust (1 Sam. 29.3, 6, 8; 2 Kings 17.4; cf. 1 Sam. 12.5). *Obnoxious,* "unseemly" (23.15). It is unclear from the Heb, whose exact meaning is debated in early Jewish texts, what valid criteria for divorce were. *Bill of divorcement,* legally freeing her to remarry (22.14 n.). **4:** *Since she has been defiled,* not in general, since she is permitted to remarry, but specifically as regards relations with her first husband. **5:** Another of the rules for holy war (20.1–20; 21.10–14; 23.10–15). Newly *married,* see 20.7 n. *To give happiness to,* including conjugal joy, for the purpose of having children. **6:** The law prohibits economic oppression (like vv. 10–15). *Taken ... in pawn,* held as collateral for a loan. *Handmill ... upper millstone:* Like the garment taken as "pledge" in vv. 10–12, they lack significant intrinsic value but are essential to the owner's survival; thus, only as incentive for repayment would they be taken in pawn. The law prohibits extortion. **7:** Restricts the application of Exod. 21.16 to kidnappers of fellow Israelites; perhaps also an interpretation of Deut. 5.17 (cf. Laws of Hammurabi §14; Hittite Laws §§19–21). **8–9:** *Remember ... Miriam,* see Num. 12.1–15. *Skin affection,* not leprosy but an unidentified inflammation; see Lev. chs 13–14 and 13.1–14.57 n. **10–13:** Expands upon Exod. 22.25–26 (cf. Amos. 2.8; Prov. 20.16; 22.27; 27.13; Job 22.6). As in Exod., the *pledge* refers to a garment. The Yavneh Yam inscription, a legal petition written on a pottery sherd from the late 7th c. BCE, documents a similar case. **14–15:** See Exod. 22.21–24; Lev. 19.13. Israel's ethics are based upon the conviction that God identifies with and vindicates the oppressed. **14:** The prohibition against economic exploitation applies equally to the non-Israelite; it is not contingent upon ethnicity or nationality (see 1.16 n.). **16:** This law, restricting punishment to the responsible individual, applies specifically to civil and criminal law; it is

16 Parents shall not be put to death for children, nor children
be put to death for parents: a person shall be put to death only
for his own crime.
17 You shall not subvert the rights of the stranger or the fatherless; you shall not take a widow's garment in pawn. 18 Remember that you were a slave in Egypt and that the LORD your
God redeemed you from there; therefore do I enjoin you to observe this commandment.
19 When you reap the harvest in your field and overlook a
sheaf in the field, do not turn back to get it; it shall go to the
stranger, the fatherless, and the widow—in order that the LORD
your God may bless you in all your undertakings.
20 When you beat down the fruit of your olive trees, do not
go over them again; that shall go to the stranger, the fatherless,
and the widow. 21 When you gather the grapes of your vineyard, do not pick it over again; that shall go to the stranger, the
fatherless, and the widow. 22 Always remember that you were a
slave in the land of Egypt; therefore do I enjoin you to observe
this commandment.

25 When there is a dispute between men and they go to
law, and a decision is rendered declaring the one in
the right and the other in the wrong—2 if the guilty one is to be
flogged, the magistrate shall have him lie down and be given
lashes in his presence, by count, as his guilt warrants. 3 He may
be given up to forty lashes, but not more, lest being flogged
further, to excess, your brother be degraded before your eyes.
4 You shall not muzzle an ox while it is threshing.
5 When brothers dwell together and one of them dies and
leaves no son, the wife of the deceased shall not be married
to a stranger, outside the family. Her husband's brother shall
unite with her: he shall take her as his wife and perform the

cited in 2 Kings 14.6. In contrast, collective responsibility for wrongdoing operates in the realm of offenses against God (5.9–10; Exod. 34.7; Num. 16.31–33; Josh. 7.24–25; 2 Sam. 21.1–9). That theological principle was subsequently brought into conformity with the law of individual liability (7.10; Ezek. ch 18). **17:** *You shall not subvert the rights,* identical to the comprehensive "You shall not judge unfairly" (16.19). This law, therefore, ensures full judicial protection of the most vulnerable members of the community, the *stranger* (or "resident alien") and the *fatherless. Take ... in pawn,* better, "seize" or "distrain" to force payment (see Job 24.3). This law accords the *widow* special protection; for day laborers, the garment could be taken but must be returned daily (vv. 10–13). **18:** See 15.15. **19–22:** Lev. 19.9–10; 23.22. The story of Ruth, both widow and alien, presupposes such laws, which assign harvest gleanings to the needy, allowing them to eat without begging for food. **20:** *Beat,* with poles, so as to harvest the olives (Isa. 17.6).

25.1–3: This law imposes a double restriction upon the Near Eastern convention of judicial flogging (22.18 n.), which was also employed for discipline in nonjudicial contexts (21.18 n.; Exod. 21.20; Prov. 10.13; 26.3; 1 Kings 12.14). **2:** First, the sentence must be carried out under the judge's direct supervision: *in his presence,* with the lashes delivered *by* [his] *count.* **3:** Second, the number is restricted to *forty lashes* (reduced by the rabbis to thirty-nine; see *Mak.* 22a). No parallel restriction exists in Near Eastern law; the Middle Assyrian Laws stipulate floggings of five to one hundred lashes (MAL B §§7–10). The rationale for the restriction is an extrajudicial notion of human dignity: The criminal, despite his judicial status, remains *your brother.* **4:** For similar humane treatment of animals, see 22.6–7; Prov. 12.10.

25.5–10: Levirate marriage. Biblical, Near Eastern, and Roman inheritance law assigned special responsibilities to the "husband's brother" (vv. 5–7), Heb "yavam" (cf. Latin "levir"). Should a man die, leaving his widow childless, his brother was expected to marry the widow, thereby continuing the deceased's line (see variant versions of this law in Gen. 38.8; Ruth 4.5–6). **5:** *When brothers dwell together,* in joint tenancy on patrimonial land not yet subdivided among them as heirs. The law addresses the contingency of a father who dies leaving sons who are not yet ready to set up their own independent households. In such circumstances, the patrimony would be managed jointly until the land could be properly divided. However, should one of the heirs die childless prior to this division of property, he and his line would never inherit his share; it would be subsumed into the others' shares. Thus, the purpose of the levirate law was to "build up the house" of the deceased son (v. 6), to ensure he had an heir to inherit his fair share of the jointly held property. *Stranger,* not a brother of the deceased. *Her husband's brother shall unite with her:* This requirement conflicts with the prohibition against incest with the sister-in-law in the later Holiness Collection (Lev. 18.16 n.; 20.21). Possibly, as in the Hittite Laws (§193), levirate marriage provided an exception to the normal prohibition

levir's duty. 6 The first son that she bears shall be accounted to
the dead brother, that his name may not be blotted out in Israel. 7 But if the man does not want to marry his brother's widow, his brother's widow shall appear before the elders in the
gate and declare, "My husband's brother refuses to establish a
name in Israel for his brother; he will not perform the duty of a
levir." 8 The elders of his town shall then summon him and talk
to him. If he insists, saying, "I do not want to marry her," 9 his
brother's widow shall go up to him in the presence of the elders, pull the sandal off his foot, spit in his face, and make this
declaration: Thus shall be done to the man who will not build
up his brother's house! 10 And he shall go in Israel by the name
of "the family of the unsandaled one."

11 If two men get into a fight with each other, and the wife
of one comes up to save her husband from his antagonist and
puts out her hand and seizes him by his genitals, 12 you shall
cut off her hand; show no pity.

13 You shall not have in your pouch alternate weights, larger and smaller. 14 You shall not have in your house alternate
measures, a larger and a smaller. 15 You must have completely
honest weights and completely honest measures, if you are to
endure long on the soil that the LORD your God is giving you.
16 For everyone who does those things, everyone who deals
dishonestly, is abhorrent to the LORD your God.

17 Remember what Amalek did to you on your journey, after
you left Egypt— 18 how, undeterred by fear of God, he surprised
you on the march, when you were famished and weary, and
cut down all the stragglers in your rear. 19 Therefore, when the
LORD your God grants you safety from all your enemies around
you, in the land that the LORD your God is giving you as a hereditary portion, you shall blot out the memory of Amalek from
under heaven. Do not forget!

KI TAVO' כי תבוא

26 When you enter the land that the LORD your God is giving you as a heritage, and you possess it and settle in it,
2 you shall take some of every first fruit of the soil, which you
harvest from the land that the LORD your God is giving you,

of such relations. **6:** *The first son* alone here counts to the brother in terms of inheritance rights; cf. Gen. 38.8; Ruth 4.5–6. This mitigates the potential loss to the brother who complied with its requirements, who would effectively disinherit himself if all future children counted as the deceased's. **9:** The intent of the ceremony, with the man passive and spat upon, is public shaming, for his dereliction of duty. **10:** *Shall go ... by the name of,* thus explicitly applying a form of talionic justice (19.19 n.). For refusing to build up the deceased's "name" (vv. 6, 7) and "house" (v. 9), the brother's own *family* (lit. "house") is stigmatized by its new *name.* **11–12:** This law, like the preceding one, deals with threats to reproduction; it provides a corollary to Exod. 21.22–25, where a case involving a pregnant woman is used to develop the law of talion. The rationale for the punishment is difficult. While physical mutilation is characteristic in the Middle Assyrian Laws, it is nowhere else prescribed in the Bible, except in the general formula for talion (19.21; Exod. 21.23–24; Lev. 24.19–20). That formula does not apply here, however, since there can be no symmetry between injury and punishment. Since no physical injury to the male is actually specified, the issue may rather be the perceived insult to dignity or to decency (cf. Laws of Hammurabi §195). **13–16:** Compare Laws of Hammurabi §108; Lev. 19.35–36; Amos 8.5. **14:** By fraudulently using two different sets of counterweights—small ones to sell grain but large ones to purchase it—a merchant could turn a tidy profit. **17–19:** The tradition builds upon Exod. 17.8–17, in which the Amalekites, a fierce desert tribe, attacked Israel (cf. Ps. 83.4–8). Within later Jewish tradition, these vv. are read liturgically on the Sabbath before Purim, since according to Jewish tradition, Haman, is an Amalekite (see 1 Sam. 15.8 and Esth. 3.1; 8.3); Amalek later became a symbol for any enemy of Israel. **18:** These details are not reflected in Exod. 17.8–17; the Deuteronomic author may have supplied them in order to justify the extirpation of Amalek (v. 19; cf. Exod. 17.14; 1 Sam. 15.2–3). **19:** *Grants you safety,* see 3.20; 12.9–10 n.

26.1–15: Concluding liturgies. Two already prescribed laws (14.22–29) are given a historical and theological foundation (similarly, 16.12, for the Festival of Weeks). **1–11:** The context is the Festival of Weeks (16.9–12), when the Israelite was to make an annual pilgrimage to the central sanctuary, bringing the first fruits of the harvest, to thank God for the land's bounty. **4:** *The priest shall take the basket ... and set it down in front*

put it in a basket and go to the place where the LORD your God
will choose to establish His name. 3 You shall go to the priest
in charge at that time and say to him, "I acknowledge this day
before the LORD your God that I have entered the land that the
LORD swore to our fathers to assign us."
4 The priest shall take the basket from your hand and set it
down in front of the altar of the LORD your God.
5 You shall then recite as follows before the LORD your God:
"My father was a fugitive Aramean. He went down to Egypt
with meager numbers and sojourned there; but there he became a great and very populous nation. 6 The Egyptians dealt
harshly with us and oppressed us; they imposed heavy labor
upon us. 7 We cried to the LORD, the God of our fathers, and the
LORD heard our plea and saw our plight, our misery, and our
oppression. 8 The LORD freed us from Egypt by a mighty hand,
by an outstretched arm and awesome power, and by signs and
portents. 9 He brought us to this place and gave us this land,
a land flowing with milk and honey. 10 Wherefore I now bring
the first fruits of the soil which You, O LORD, have given me."
You shall leave it[a] before the LORD your God and bow low
before the LORD your God. 11 And you shall enjoy, together with
the Levite and the stranger in your midst, all the bounty that the
LORD your God has bestowed upon you and your household.
12 When you have set aside in full the tenth part of your
yield—in the third year, the year of the tithe[b]—and have given
it to the Levite, the stranger, the fatherless, and the widow, that
they may eat their fill in your settlements, 13 you shall declare
before the LORD your God: "I have cleared out the consecrated

a I.e., the basket of v. 4. *b See Deut. 14.28–29.*

of the altar, in contrast to the stipulation, "You shall leave it before the LORD" (v. 10). On that basis, vv. 3–4 may represent a later addition, emphasizing the role of the priests in the ceremony. That would account for the absence of references to the priests elsewhere in the unit; the double tradition about what is recited at the sanctuary (v. 3, vv. 5–10); and the two versions of who is to set the basket before the altar. Thus, v. 5 would originally have continued v. 2. **5:** *My father was a fugitive Aramean:* This v. (through v. 8) is deployed in the Passover Haggadah (just following the section on the Four Sons) in a famous passage that emphasizes God's miraculous sparing of Israel from a long line of persecutors, beginning with Laban's attack on Jacob (Gen. ch 31). The Rabbis interpret this v. to mean "an Aramean sought to destroy my ancestor." That midrashic reworking departs from the actual grammar of the v. and almost certainly reflects the politics of the Second Temple period, when the Seleucid empire, which ruled Israel from Syria (198–168 BCE), was referred to obliquely as Laban, the Aramean. The hyperbolic claim in the Haggadah that Laban's oppression of Israel/Jacob was more invidious than the Egyptian enslavement points to a polemic against the Seleucids, whose policies triggered the Hasmonean revolt in 167 BCE. **8–9:** The thanksgiving prayer recited by the pilgrim provides a précis of the main narrative line of the Pentateuch and Joshua (the Hexateuch). For that reason, the vv. have been seen by some scholars as an ancient confession of faith, or creed, that is older than its present context. Strikingly, this summary of the main events of Israel's religious history makes no mention of the revelation of law at Sinai/Horeb. The same is true for many similar "confessions" in the Bible (see 6.20–24; Josh. 24.2–13; 1 Sam. 12.8; Pss. 78; 105; 136). The existence of such a strong tradition that makes no mention of Sinai has suggested to a number of scholars the possibility that the inclusion of the Sinai/Horeb experience in the overall Torah narrative represents a relatively late, secondary addition. Sinai seems to have been incorporated into the larger narrative only in exilic or later texts (Ps. 106; Neh. ch 9). Some scholars have explained this by reasoning that only a minority of the tribes or groups eventually comprising Israel experienced Sinai/Horeb; thus, only at a late stage of the tradition was their experience extended to all Israel and incorporated into the narrative of the Torah. Alternately, this act of thanksgiving commemorates Israel's wondrous transformation from a single, landless, persecuted individual into a populous nation, secure and at home in its land. In this thanksgiving for the double miracle—the individual has now become a nation and those who were homeless now harvest crops from their land—mention of the journey to Sinai to receive the law would have been disruptive and irrelevant. **6:** *Oppressed ... heavy labor,* see Exod. 1.11–14. **11:** *Enjoy,* or "rejoice" (16.11, 14–15), specifically in a festive meal consumed at the central sanctuary (12.7, 18), which must include *the Levite and the stranger,* for whose benefit (along with other disadvantaged groups) the following law is directed. **12–15:** Produce was tithed annually and consumed by the farmer and his household at the central sanctuary (14.22–27); every third year that tithe was used locally to support the poor (14.28–29). **12:** *The stranger, the fatherless, and the widow,* see 1.16 n.; 14.28–29 n.; 23.25–26 n., 23.20–21 n.

portion from the house; and I have given it to the Levite, the
stranger, the fatherless, and the widow, just as You commanded me; I have neither transgressed nor neglected any of Your
commandments: 14 [a] I have not eaten of it while in mourning, I have not cleared out any of it while I was unclean, and I
have not deposited any of it with the dead.[b] I have obeyed the
LORD my God; I have done just as You commanded me. 15 Look
down from Your holy abode, from heaven, and bless Your people Israel and the soil You have given us, a land flowing with
milk and honey, as You swore to our fathers."

16 The LORD your God commands you this day to observe
these laws and rules; observe them faithfully with all your heart
and soul. 17 You have affirmed[c] this day that the LORD is your
God, that you will walk in His ways, that you will observe His
laws and commandments and rules, and that you will obey Him.
18 And the LORD has affirmed[c] this day that you are, as He promised you, His treasured people who shall observe all His commandments, 19 and that He will set you, in fame and renown and
glory, high above all the nations that He has made; and that you
shall be, as He promised, a holy people to the LORD your God.

27 Moses and the elders of Israel charged the people, saying:
Observe all the Instruction that I enjoin upon you this
day. 2 [d] As soon as you have crossed the Jordan into the land that
the LORD your God is giving you, you shall set up large stones.
Coat them with plaster 3 and inscribe upon them all the words

a Meaning of first part of verse uncertain.
b No part of the tithe may be left as food for the dead.
c Exact nuance of Heb. uncertain. *d Construction of vv. 2–4 uncertain.*

14: The triple confession of the donor's ritual purity implies that the formula was originally used for donations of produce to God at a sanctuary, where purity would be expected. That formula has now been reused for the donation of food to the poor in a noncultic setting: "in your settlements" (v. 12). *Deposited any of it with the dead:* The duty of the living to care for dead ancestors through food offerings at their place of burial was widely assumed in the ancient Near East (see the Ugaritic *Aqhat Epic*), is confirmed archeologically, and continued to be held in Second Temple times (Tobit 4.17). Here the practice is not condemned; it is viewed as improper specifically when coming into contact with cultic donations, because the impurity associated with death would render food unfit for donation to the Temple (Lev. 22.2–4). **15:** *From Your holy abode, from heaven* (as in 1 Kings 8.30): The double preposition may point to the correction of an older theology in light of a newer one, following Deut.'s older view that only God's name resides in the Temple (12.11; 16.11; 26.2). For the earlier idea, that God Himself inhabits the Temple, see 1 Kings 8.13; cf. Deut. 12.5. *Bless Your people Israel and the soil:* The farmer prays for the blessing of the community and of the land, not directly for fertility or the abundance of his own crops.

26.16–19: Formal conclusion, which presents the legal corpus as a mutually binding relationship between God and Israel. Having just read the law to the people, Moses presents it to them in a formal ratification ceremony (vv. 17–18; cf. 2 Kings 23.1–3). **16:** *Laws and rules ... observe ... faithfully* forms an inclusio with 12.1, providing the laws of chs 12–26 with an elegant frame to mark their conclusion. **17–18:** *You have affirmed:* The past tense points to a prior action or speech in which each party has proclaimed what is here described. No record of such an event or ceremony survives. Deut. emphasizes that both God and Israel have explicitly assented to the covenant and have affirmed the mutuality of the obligations that each undertakes. God's proclamation (v. 17) specifies His responsibility (to be God) and then identifies His three expectations of Israel. Symmetrically, Israel proclaims (v. 18) one responsibility (to obey the commandments) while then outlining the three responsibilities of God toward Israel (to grant treasured status, election, holiness). This reciprocal model contrasts with the Sinai covenant in Exod., which was unilaterally offered by God (Exod. 19.3–6) and unilaterally agreed to by Israel (Exod. 19.8; 24.3, 7). Deut. invokes the language of the Sinai covenant as a model, while revising that model significantly in the process. **18:** *His treasured people,* see 7.6 n.; 14.2 n. *As He promised you,* Exod. 19.5–6. **19:** *High above all the nations,* see 28.13–14 nn. *That He has made,* see Exod. 19.5b. *A holy people to the LORD your God* continues the reference to Exod. 19.5–6, while substituting *people* for "nation," which Deut. uses for non-Israelites (12.29). *In fame and renown and glory:* NJPS implies that the accolades will be given to Israel; the Heb also allows for the possibility that the honors will go to God because of His action on Israel's behalf (see Jer. 13.11; 33.9).

27.1–26: The ceremonies at Shechem. The injunctions of 11.29–32 are here reiterated and detailed. The laws of chs 12–26 are thus framed with ceremonies that connect entry into the land with

of this Teaching. When you cross over to enter the land that the
LORD your God is giving you, a land flowing with milk and honey, as the LORD, the God of your fathers, promised you—[4] upon
crossing the Jordan, you shall set up these stones, about which I
charge you this day, on Mount Ebal, and coat them with plaster.
[5] There, too, you shall build an altar to the LORD your God, an
altar of stones. Do not wield an iron tool over them; [6] you must
build the altar of the LORD your God of unhewn[a] stones. You
shall offer on it burnt offerings to the LORD your God, [7] and you
shall sacrifice there offerings of well-being and eat them, rejoicing before the LORD your God. [8] And on those stones you shall
inscribe every word of this Teaching most distinctly.
[9] Moses and the levitical priests spoke to all Israel, saying:
Silence! Hear, O Israel! Today you have become the people of
the LORD your God: [10] Heed the LORD your God and observe
His commandments and His laws, which I enjoin upon you
this day.
[11] Thereupon Moses charged the people, saying: [12] [b]After you
have crossed the Jordan, the following shall stand on Mount
Gerizim when the blessing for the people is spoken: Simeon,
Levi, Judah, Issachar, Joseph, and Benjamin. [13] And for the
curse, the following shall stand on Mount Ebal: Reuben, Gad,

a *Lit. "whole."* *b* *Construction of vv. 12–13 uncertain.*

obedience to Torah. The ch joins four separate sections that are only loosely connected to one another and to the rest of Deut. An editor has aligned the sections with one another, while breaking up the continuity of the Mosaic speech of chs 26 and 28. The resulting digression preserves several competing traditions about how and where the covenant between God and Israel was concluded: at Sinai; or on the plains of Moab; or at Gilgal immediately upon entering the land; or at the important northern shrine of Shechem (see 11.29–30 n.). **1–8:** This section combines two separate requirements: the raising of plastered-over stones inscribed with the Torah (vv. 1–4, 8), and the construction of a stone altar for sacrifice (vv. 5–7). **1:** Moses is referred to in the third person, interrupting his first-person address (chs 5–26, 28). *And the elders:* Nowhere else in Deut. do they join Moses in addressing the people; this plural subject does not easily fit the following singular *I.* **2:** *As soon as you have crossed the Jordan ... you shall set up large stones:* The Deuteronomistic historian understands this command to have been fulfilled at Gilgal, just across the Jordan and less than a mile from Jericho (see Josh. ch 4). *Coat them with plaster,* to serve as a surface for an inscription. Archeology attests the use of plaster-covered inscriptions. **4:** *Mount Ebal,* at over 1,000 m (3,280 ft) high, the tallest mountain in the region, lies in central Canaan, adjacent to the city of Shechem. But that site, more than 50 km (30 mi) from the Jordan, is inconsistent with v. 2 and the beginning of this v., which each anticipate that the ceremony will take place immediately upon crossing the river. It would be impossible to reach Shechem in a day. The most logical explanation is that Josh. ch 4 points to the original form of these vv., with Gilgal, which later became an important sanctuary (1 Sam. 11.15; Hos. 4.15; 9.15; 12.12; Amos 4.4; 5.5) as the site where Israel complied with this command. That older tradition was replaced here by the reference to the mountains around Shechem, the chief town of the northern tribes (Josh. 24.1, 32). **5–7:** These vv. are an insertion that reinterprets the plastered stones on which the Torah is to be inscribed as an altar of *unhewn stones,* following Exod. 20.22. Such an altar, outside of Jerusalem, conflicts with the centralization requirement of ch 12, further suggesting this tradition's antiquity and its independence from the rest of Deut. The Deuteronomistic historian understood this law to be fulfilled at Mount Ebal some time after the Israelite entry into the land, following the defeats of Jericho and Ai (Josh. 8.30–35). **8:** *On those stones you shall inscribe every word of this Teaching,* repeats and resumes the key terms of vv. 3–4, thus bracketing the insertion of vv. 5–7. Since the term "Teaching" (Heb "torah") is elastic, there is significant debate in traditional and critical scholarship about what was meant to be written on these stones. **9–10:** This paragraph, which has its own beginning, is independent of what precedes it. **9:** *And the levitical priests,* see v. 1 n.; here too the plural subject is continued by "I" (v. 10). *Today:* The assertion here that Israel becomes God's people just now, in Moab, contrasts with statements that define the bond as previously formed, either at the time of the exodus (Exod. 6.6–7) or at Sinai (4.20; Exod. 19.5–6). **11–13:** A fragment that refers to an ancient covenant ceremony at Shechem, instituted at the command of Moses (Josh. 8.30–35). The antiquity of the tribal list is seen in the facts that Levi is listed as a tribe (Gen. 49.5–7) and that the division of the House of Joseph into Manasseh and Ephraim has not yet occurred (Gen. 49.22–26; contrast Deut. 33.17). The division of the tribes into two groups of six is attested only here. **11:** *Thereupon,* lit., "on that day," without further specification. **12–13:** *Mount Gerizim ... Mount Ebal,* see 11.29–30 n. One group of tribes, on Gerizim, proclaims a set of blessings (see 28.1–14); the other, on Ebal, a set of curses (see 28.15–68).

Asher, Zebulun, Dan, and Naphtali. 14 The Levites shall then
proclaim in a loud voice to all the people of Israel:
15 Cursed be anyone who makes a sculptured or molten image, abhorred by the LORD, a craftsman's handiwork, and sets
it up in secret.—And all the people shall respond, Amen.
16 Cursed be he who insults his father or mother.—And all
the people shall say, Amen.
17 Cursed be he who moves his fellow countryman's landmark.—And all the people shall say, Amen.
18 Cursed be he who misdirects a blind person on his way.—
And all the people shall say, Amen.
19 Cursed be he who subverts the rights of the stranger, the
fatherless, and the widow.—And all the people shall say, Amen.
20 Cursed be he who lies with his father's wife, for he has
removed his father's garment.[a]—And all the people shall say,
Amen.
21 Cursed be he who lies with any beast.—And all the people
shall say, Amen.
22 Cursed be he who lies with his sister, whether daughter of
his father or of his mother.—And all the people shall say, Amen.
23 Cursed be he who lies with his mother-in-law.—And all
the people shall say, Amen.
24 Cursed be he who strikes down his fellow countryman in
secret.—And all the people shall say, Amen.
25 Cursed be he who accepts a bribe [b]in the case of the murder of[b] an innocent person.—And all the people shall say,
Amen.
26 Cursed be he who will not uphold the terms of this Teaching and observe them.—And all the people shall say, Amen.

28 Now, if you obey the LORD your God, to observe faithfully all His commandments which I enjoin upon you
this day, the LORD your God will set you high above all the nations of the earth. 2 All these blessings shall come upon you
and take effect, if you will but heed the word of the LORD your
God:

a See note at 23.1. *b-b I.e., to acquit the murderer; others "to slay."*

14–26: Despite the paragraphing in NJPS, v. 14 more likely begins a new section with a very different conception of the ceremony. Here the tribe of Levi alone proclaims a set of prohibited actions and *all the people*—acting in unison and not divided into tribes—respond, *Amen* (see Jer. 11.3–5). There is no list of blessings (cf. v. 12). Nor is "the curse" intended by v. 13—a description of divine punishment for wrongful action, as in 28.15–68—provided. In contrast, the "cursed be" proclamations here employ an unrelated Heb word and stigmatize a summary list of rejected actions, making no references to the consequences of the transgressions. **14:** *The Levites:* Contrast Deut.'s normal term "levitical priests" (v. 9; 18.1). **15–26:** In context, the twelve curses correspond to the twelve tribes, although this section makes no reference to the tribal division, and the people function as a single entity (v. 14). The resulting incongruence points to the many editorial revisions that this ch has undergone.

28.1–68: The consequences of obedience or disobedience: blessing or curse. The Mosaic covenant specifies a series of blessings and curses that follow upon national obedience or disobedience to the law. These are modeled after ancient Near Eastern state treaties, which spell out, at their conclusion, the consequences of breaching the treaty. This ch has several close parallels to the VTE, a Neo-Assyrian treaty dating to 672 BCE. The present strong disproportion between the sections devoted to blessing (vv. 1–14) and to curse (vv. 15–68) most likely reflects the actual historical experience of the Babylonian conquest, deportation, and exile of Judah (597 and 586 BCE), here recast as a prophetic warning. The two appendices (vv. 47–57, 58–68) each seek to make theological sense of that catastrophe. The two other legal collections of the Torah (the Book of the Covenant in Exod. chs 21–23; the Holiness Collection of Lev. chs 17–26) similarly end with exhortations to obedience, accompanied by blessings and curses (Exod. 23.20–33; Lev. ch 26), as do the Laws of Hammurabi. Here an inclusio frames and defines the blessings section: *if you obey ... observe faithfully* (vv. 1, 13). **1–2:** The proem emphasizes the conditionality of the elected status of Israel. The repetition of the conditional nature of the fulfillment, *If you obey the LORD your God* (vv. 1 and 2), places a frame around the central idea of divine election of Israel. *Set you high above all the nations of the earth* (see also v. 13): The metaphor, which is also used to denote the elected status of the Davidic dynasty (Ps. 89.28), here denotes the divine election of the nation. The same affirmation of Israel's election appears at 26.19, where it is not conditional; instead, it fulfills God's past promises. Here,

3 Blessed shall you be in the city and blessed shall you be in
the country.
4 Blessed shall be the issue of your womb, the produce of
your soil, and the offspring of your cattle, the calving of your
herd and the lambing of your flock.
5 Blessed shall be your basket and your kneading bowl.
6 Blessed shall you be in your comings and blessed shall you
be in your goings.
7 The LORD will put to rout before you the enemies who attack you; they will march out against you by a single road, but
flee from you by many[a] roads. 8 The LORD will ordain blessings
for you upon your barns and upon all your undertakings: He
will bless you in the land that the LORD your God is giving you.
9 The LORD will establish you as His holy people, as He swore to
you, if you keep the commandments of the LORD your God and
walk in His ways. 10 And all the peoples of the earth shall see
that the LORD's name is proclaimed over you,[b] and they shall
stand in fear of you. 11 The LORD will give you abounding prosperity in the issue of your womb, the offspring of your cattle,
and the produce of your soil in the land that the LORD swore to
your fathers to assign to you. 12 The LORD will open for you His
bounteous store, the heavens, to provide rain for your land in
season and to bless all your undertakings. You will be creditor
to many nations, but debtor to none.
13 The LORD will make you the head, not the tail; you will always be at the top and never at the bottom—if only you obey
and faithfully observe the commandments of the LORD your
God that I enjoin upon you this day, 14 and do not deviate to
the right or to the left from any of the commandments that I
enjoin upon you this day and turn to the worship of other gods.

15 But if you do not obey the LORD your God to observe faithfully all His commandments and laws which I enjoin upon you
this day, all these curses shall come upon you and take effect:

a Lit. "seven." *b I.e., the LORD recognizes you as His own; cf. Isa. 4.1.*

in contrast, the nation's elected status is presented as a future promise that is conditional upon obedience. The marked change may well reflect the revision of earlier expectations in light of the catastrophe of exile. **3–6:** The six benedictions have their malediction counterpart at vv. 16–19. The two antonym pairs (vv. 3, 6) provide a frame to the unit. The opposites form a merism to stress totality (like "night and day"); see 6.7 n. **3:** *City* and *country,* "everywhere," urban and rural. **4:** *Issue ... lambing:* Fecundity for humans, crops, and livestock is contingent upon obedience to the covenant—and thus not upon either natural fertility or competing fertility gods (see 7.12–14 n.). **6:** *Comings ... goings,* whenever and wherever you go. **7:** Military success is conditional upon covenantal obedience rather than strength of arms (9.1–3; Josh. 1.6–8). **9:** *The LORD will establish you ... if you keep:* The assertion here that the nation's holiness or election is conditional upon obedience represents a remarkable shift from other contexts in Deut. where Israel's holiness is not future but present, and not conditional but unconditional (7.6; 14.2; cf. 26.18). **10:** *The LORD's name is proclaimed over you* signifies a special relationship with God, which includes particular accountability to God and corresponding divine oversight. The formula can apply to either the nation (here; Isa. 63.19; Jer. 14.9; 2 Chron. 7.14) or an individual (Exod. 33.12; Jer. 15.16). **12:** *Store:* In Israelite and Near Eastern cosmology, primordial waters remained above the dome of the sky and were released as rain (Gen. 1.7; 7.11). *Creditor ... debtor:* For the same image as a metaphor for national sovereignty, see 15.6. **13:** Further metaphors for autonomy, as at 15.6. **14:** *And turn ... gods,* lit. "to go after other gods to worship them." See 6.14 n.

28.15–68: Consequences of disobedience. This long section has two subsections. The focus of the first (vv. 15–46) is a broad range of misfortunes, extending from infertility of crops, livestock, or the human population through to military defeat. The second unit (vv. 47–68) places its focus specifically on foreign invasion, siege, national defeat, and exile, reversing key components of the covenantal promises and of the nation's history of salvation. By disobeying the covenant, the nation undoes its own history. **15–46:** The first section is framed by an ancient literary device, a chiastic inclusio, whereby the initial sequence AB is repeated in reverse at the end of the unit as B'A'. Thus, the sequence in v. 15, *not obey ... to observe* (A) and *these curses shall come upon you and take effect* (B) is reversed in v. 45 as *these curses shall befall you ... overtake you* (B', identical in the Heb) and *not heed ... keep the commandments* (A'). **15:** A precise negation of v. 1: Disobedience negates blessing and occasions punishment. *Come upon you and take effect:* The verbs are animate and active; the curses are personified, as if they had agency or acted by themselves to punish those who infringe the covenant (cf.

16 Cursed shall you be in the city and cursed shall you be in
the country.
17 Cursed shall be your basket and your kneading bowl.
18 Cursed shall be the issue of your womb and the produce of
your soil, the calving of your herd and the lambing of your flock.
19 Cursed shall you be in your comings and cursed shall you
be in your goings.
20 The LORD will let loose against you calamity, panic, and
frustration in all the enterprises you undertake, so that you
shall soon be utterly wiped out because of your evildoing in
forsaking Me. 21 The LORD will make pestilence cling to you,
until He has put an end to you in the land that you are entering
to possess. 22 The LORD will strike you with [a]consumption, fever, and inflammation, with scorching heat and drought, with
blight and mildew; they shall hound you until you perish. 23 The
skies above your head shall be copper and the earth under you
iron. 24 The LORD will make the rain of your land dust, and sand
shall drop on you from the sky, until you are wiped out.
25 The LORD will put you to rout before your enemies; you
shall march out against them by a single road, but flee from
them by many[b] roads; and you shall become a horror to all the
kingdoms of the earth. 26 Your carcasses shall become food for
all the birds of the sky and all the beasts of the earth, with none
to frighten them off.
27 The LORD will strike you with the Egyptian inflammation,[c]
with hemorrhoids, boil-scars, and itch, from which you shall
never recover.
28 The LORD will strike you with madness, blindness, and
dismay.[d] 29 You shall grope at noon as a blind man gropes in
the dark; you shall not prosper in your ventures, but shall be
constantly abused and robbed, with none to give help.
30 If you pay the bride-price for a wife, another man shall enjoy her. If you build a house, you shall not live in it. If you plant
a vineyard, you shall not harvest it.[e] 31 Your ox shall be slaughtered before your eyes, but you shall not eat of it; your ass shall

a Exact nature of these afflictions uncertain. *b Lit. "seven."* *c See Exod. 9.9–10.* *d Lit. "numbness of heart."* *e Cf. 20.6.*

Exod. 12.23). **16–19:** Negating vv. 3–6. **20:** Corresponding to the promise of tripartite blessing for obedience (v. 8: agriculture, activity, and land) stands the triple threat of *calamity, panic, and frustration.* The first term would more accurately be translated "curse," as the precise negation of blessing. The threats summarized by this v. are spelled out in the rest of the section (vv. 21–44). *Me:* Moses speaks on behalf of God directly: Note the shift to the first person from third person reference to God (as at 7.4; 17.3). The shift takes place in the opposite direction in the Decalogue (cf. 5.6, 11). **21–44:** This section echoes the state treaties imposed by the Neo-Assyrian empire upon its vassal states in order to ensure loyalty and tribute (826–625 BCE). The degree of similarity suggests that the curse section of these state treaties, either directly or by way of Aram. translation, provided a model for the authors of this ch to use in describing Israel's relationship to God. According to biblical narratives, Judah was a vassal to the Assyrian empire (2 Kings 18.13–18) and both Neo-Assyrian and Judean officials freely employed Aram., the international language of diplomacy (2 Kings 18.26–27). **23:** *Copper ... iron:* See VTE §§63–64: "May [the gods] make your ground like iron ... Just as rain does not fall from a bronze sky ... " (D. J. Wiseman, in *ANET*, p. 539). **25:** The routers of v. 7 become the routed. *You shall become a horror:* The LXX reads "you shall become a 'diaspora,' " reinterpreting the Heb to reflect the historical circumstances of its 3rd-c. BCE Alexandrian authors. **26:** Deuteronomic law requires even executed criminals to be buried by sundown, lest their corpses become carrion (21.22–23); the abrogation of that religious norm here underscores the punishment's horror (Jer. 7.33). **27–35:** The sequence of punishments specified in this section initially seems arbitrary: skin inflammation (v. 27); blindness (vv. 28–29); and loss of wife, house, and property (vv. 30a, 30b, 33). The sequence finds its explanation, however, in VTE §§39–43, where each curse is associated with a particular god within the Neo-Assyrian pantheon. The moon god Sin is responsible for leprosy; the sun god Shamash for blindness; and Dilipat (the planet Venus) for rape, dispossession, and pillage by a foreign army. The arrangement of the curses follows the rank of the deities within that pantheon's hierarchy. **27:** *Egyptian inflammation,* inversion of 7.15; see Exod. 9.9–11. **28–29:** *Blindness:* The Mesopotamian sun god Shamash punishes disobedience by withholding light and vision. Shamash is also the god of justice. Thus, his punishment entails the breakdown of civil order and legal standards: You *shall be constantly abused and robbed.* **30:** *Wife ... house ... vineyard:* Contrast 20.7, which provides the same conditions for exemption

be seized in front of you, and it shall not be returned to you;
your flock shall be delivered to your enemies, with none to help
you. 32 Your sons and daughters shall be delivered to another
people, while you look on; and your eyes shall strain for them
constantly, but you shall be helpless. 33 A people you do not
know shall eat up the produce of your soil and all your gains;
you shall be abused and downtrodden continually, 34 until you
are driven mad by what your eyes behold. 35 The LORD will afflict you at the knees and thighs with a severe inflammation,
from which you shall never recover—from the sole of your foot
to the crown of your head.

36 The LORD will drive you, and the king you have set over
you, to a nation unknown to you or your fathers, where you
shall serve other gods, of wood and stone. 37 You shall be a consternation, a proverb, and a byword among all the peoples to
which the LORD will drive you.

38 Though you take much seed out to the field, you shall
gather in little, for the locust shall consume it. 39 Though you
plant vineyards and till them, you shall have no wine to drink
or store, for the worm shall devour them. 40 Though you have
olive trees throughout your territory, you shall have no oil for
anointment, for your olives shall drop off. 41 Though you beget
sons and daughters, they shall not remain with you, for they
shall go into captivity. 42 The cricket shall take over all the trees
and produce of your land.

43 The stranger in your midst shall rise above you higher
and higher, while you sink lower and lower: 44 he shall be your
creditor, but you shall not be his; he shall be the head and you
the tail.

45 All these curses shall befall you; they shall pursue you
and overtake you, until you are wiped out, because you did
not heed the LORD your God and keep the commandments
and laws that He enjoined upon you. 46 They shall serve as
signs and proofs against you and your offspring for all time.
47 Because you would not serve the LORD your God in joy and
gladness over the abundance of everything, 48 you shall have to
serve—in hunger and thirst, naked and lacking everything—
the enemies whom the LORD will let loose against you. He will
put an iron yoke upon your neck until He has wiped you out.

from conscription, in different order. Here, all hope of establishing households is dashed. Society will lack its essential structures for building family, community, and economy. **32:** The children will be enslaved to foreigners; that is, taken captive by foreign conquerers. **36:** Both the Neo-Assyrian army (2 Kings ch 17) and the Neo-Babylonian invaders (2 Kings chs 24–25) practiced deportation. **37:** *Byword:* The nation's fate will become a negative standard that all other peoples will hope to avoid. The opposite idea was central to God's covenant with Abraham, whose people were to become the paradigm of divine providence (Gen. 12.3). **38–42:** Futility curses. The frustration of human labor through infertility of the harvest (caused by insects or other natural enemies) is here presented as punishment for infringement of the covenant, reversing the blessings of vv. 7–14. From this perspective, crop failure is interpreted as divine judgment (Lev. 26.20; Amos 4.7–12). **43–44:** Reversing vv. 12b–13. **45–46:** Summary statement that, in conjunction with vv. 38–44, shows systematically how disobedience undoes blessing: (A) the blessings of agricultural and reproductive fertility (vv. 11–12a) and (B) economic independence and political sovereignty (vv. 12b–13), which result from (C) obedience (vv. 13b–14), are reversed with (A') failure of crops and loss of progeny (vv. 38–42) and (B') political and economic domination by foreigners (vv. 43–44), all of which result from (C') disobedience to the covenant (v. 45). **46:** *Signs and proofs,* more commonly translated "sign(s) and marvel(s)," as at 29.2. These terms normally specify the miracles performed by God on behalf of Israel at the time of the exodus (4.34; 6.22; 7.19; 34.11; Exod. 7.3; 8.19; 10.1–2; 11.9–10). They now threaten instead to immortalize the divine punishment of Israel, as even language is now inverted against the nation.

28.47–57: Scenario of foreign invasion. This unit, outside the frame provided by vv. 15, 45–46, seems like a later appendix. **47:** *Because you would not serve:* Here the detailed depiction of the future curse is based upon wrongdoing already committed in the past, in contrast to the conditional formulation of v. 15, which presents the disobedience as a future possibility. *Abundance:* The threat that prosperity in the land will cause Israel to forget the source of that comfort is here realized (see 6.11–12; 8.11–20; 33.15, 18). **48:** The punishment corresponds precisely to the offense: *Because you would not serve* ... (v. 47) *you shall have to serve:* Israel is judged by talionic justice ("an eye for an eye"). The formulation works on the double meaning of the key Heb word: "to serve" can refer to sacrificial worship of God (13.5) as

49 The LORD will bring a nation against you from afar, from
the end of the earth, which will swoop down like the eagle—a
nation whose language you do not understand, 50 a ruthless nation, that will show the old no regard and the young no mercy.
51 It shall devour the offspring of your cattle and the produce
of your soil, until you have been wiped out, leaving you nothing of new grain, wine, or oil, of the calving of your herds and
the lambing of your flocks, until it has brought you to ruin. 52 It
shall shut you up in all your towns throughout your land until
every mighty, towering wall in which you trust has come down.
And when you are shut up in all your towns throughout your
land that the LORD your God has assigned to you, 53 you shall
eat your own issue, the flesh of your sons and daughters that
the LORD your God has assigned to you, because of the desperate straits to which your enemy shall reduce you. 54 He who is
most tender and fastidious among you shall be too mean to
his brother and the wife of his bosom and the children he has
spared 55 to share with any of them the flesh of the children
that he eats, because he has nothing else left as a result of the
desperate straits to which your enemy shall reduce you in all
your towns. 56 And she who is most tender and dainty among
you, so tender and dainty that she would never venture to set
a foot on the ground, shall begrudge the husband of her bosom, and her son and her daughter, 57 the afterbirth that issues
from between her legs and the babies she bears; she shall eat
them secretly, because of utter want, in the desperate straits to
which your enemy shall reduce you in your towns.

58 If you fail to observe faithfully all the terms of this Teaching that are written in this book, to reverence this honored and
awesome Name, the LORD your God, 59 the LORD will inflict
extraordinary plagues upon you and your offspring, strange
and lasting plagues, malignant and chronic diseases. 60 He will
bring back upon you all the sicknesses of Egypt that you dreaded so, and they shall cling to you. 61 Moreover, the LORD will
bring upon you all the other diseases and plagues that are not

well as to labor as a servant or slave (see 5.14 n.). God thus redeemed Israel from servitude in Egypt so that, in freedom, they serve Him in the covenant (Lev. 25.42, 55). *Iron yoke,* symbolizing vassal status, as in Jer. chs 27–28. **49–57:** Systematic presentation of foreign conquest, proceeding from invasion (vv. 48–50), to the invaders' plunder and despoiling of the land (v. 51), to crippling siege (v. 52), and culminating in the horrors of starvation that arise from the siege (vv. 53–57). These descriptions of the invader and of the consequences of the siege are based upon the literary model of the VTE. **49–52:** Closely parallels Jer. 5.15–19. **49:** *Like the eagle,* cf. Ezek. 17.3–7; Hab. 1.8. **51:** Contrast the idealistic war laws of 20.19–20, which prohibit occupiers from despoiling the land. **52:** *It shall shut you up ... until every ... wall ... has come down:* The Neo-Assyrian (2 Kings 17.5) and Neo-Babylonian armies (2 Kings 24.3; 25.1–7) employed advanced engineering to mount a siege campaign involving ramparts, battering rams, and catapults. **53–57:** The starvation resulting from the siege causes a complete breakdown of the normal social order, as parents become predators of their children and family members compete for food. Cannibalism under siege conditions is a common literary trope, see Lev. 26.29; 2 Kings 6.28–32; Jer. 19.9; Ezek. 5.10; Lam. 2.20; 4.10; and VTE §§47, 69, 71, 75.

28.58–68: Undoing the exodus. The orientation here, with a new introduction, differs considerably from what precedes; the unit seems to represent a third layer to the ch. **58:** The Mosaic speaker has thus far urged Israel to obey God's "commandments which I enjoin upon you this day" (v. 1; similarly, vv. 13–14). Here, in contrast, Israel must obey *the terms of this Teaching that are written in this book.* How the commandments have already become transformed from oral proclamation into a written text, i.e., Torah in its later sense, is unexplained, since it is not until 31.9, 24 that Moses commands that the Torah be put into writing as a book. Moreover, previously the required obedience was to the plural "commandments" (vv. 1, 9, 13, 15, 45). Here, for the first time in the ch, Israel must obey a codified, single *Teaching. This ... Name:* distinctively, *Name* stands directly for God (elsewhere in the Torah only Lev. 24.11; in later Judaism "the Name," "ha-Shem," becomes an important circumlocution for God's name). The word's special reference is explained by the following *the LORD,* which denotes the Tetragrammaton (YHVH), God's personal name. **59–68:** Consistent with the "book" perspective, the consequences for breach of the written Torah have a different focus than the preceding horrors of foreign invasion. Contravention of the Torah triggers a systematic reversal of the national history, covenantal promises, and theology included in that Torah. The punishment amounts to an anti-Torah that will dissolve the national identity. **59–61:** *Bring back ... sicknesses:* After the miracle

mentioned in this book of Teaching, until you are wiped out.
62 You shall be left a scant few, after having been as numerous
as the stars in the skies, because you did not heed the command of the LORD your God. 63 And as the LORD once delighted
in making you prosperous and many, so will the LORD now delight in causing you to perish and in wiping you out; you shall
be torn from the land that you are about to enter and possess.
64 The LORD will scatter you among all the peoples from one
end of the earth to the other, and there you shall serve other
gods, wood and stone, whom neither you nor your ancestors
have experienced.[a] 65 Yet even among those nations you shall
find no peace, nor shall your foot find a place to rest. The LORD
will give you there an anguished heart and eyes that pine and a
despondent spirit. 66 The life you face shall be precarious; you
shall be in terror, night and day, with no assurance of survival.
67 In the morning you shall say, "If only it were evening!" and in
the evening you shall say, "If only it were morning!"—because
of what your heart shall dread and your eyes shall see. 68 The
LORD will send you back to Egypt in galleys, by a route which I
told you you should not see again. There you shall offer yourselves for sale to your enemies as male and female slaves, but
none will buy.

69 These are the terms of the covenant which the LORD commanded Moses to conclude with the Israelites in the land of
Moab, in addition to the covenant which He had made with
them at Horeb.

a See note at 11.28.

of the exodus, God had promised, if the people obeyed, "I will not bring upon you any of the diseases that I brought upon the Egyptians" (Exod. 15.26). Now the threat implicit in that conditional promise becomes realized (also vv. 21–22, 35; 7.15). **62:** *Stars ... skies:* God will cancel the promise made to Abraham that his people shall be as numerous as the stars of heaven (Gen. 15.5–6; cf. Deut. 1.10; 10.22). The covenantal promise of peoplehood (Gen. 12.2) will thus be rescinded. **63:** Dispossession and exile (as in 4.26; Lev. 26.33–39) rescinds the covenantal promise of the land, contravening even the unconditional divine promises of Gen. 12.7 and 13.17. **64:** The double loss of Israel's identity: Dispersion of the population dissolves its political identity, and idol worship dissolves its religious identity. **65–67:** In the absence of the national destiny provided by the covenant, historical existence has no meaning. **68:** Forced return to Egypt, where the former taskmasters now spurn Israel's desperate bid to sell itself back into slavery and thus to undo its own history. For selling oneself into slavery under financial hardship to pay off debts or gain support ("indenture"), see Lev. 25.39. *Route which I told you you should not see again* (cf. 17.16): Although the reference to the "route" or "direction" is unclear, the threat reverses the unconditional promise by Moses at the time of the exodus: "the Egyptians whom you see today you will never see again" (Exod. 14.13). The covenant violations by Israel are so serious that Moses threatens to abrogate that promise.

28.69–30.20: The third discourse of Moses: The ratification ceremony for the covenant on the plains of Moab. Israel is formally adjured to enter the covenant: to swear to obey the laws of chs 12–26 under penalty of the sanctions of ch 28. **28.69–29.28:** A didactic review of Israel's history (29.1–8) precedes an imprecation to ensure loyal adherence to the covenant (vv. 9–28). The people are formally assembled and instructed in the serious consequences of what they are about to undertake.

28.69: Editorial Heading. NJPS follows the Masoretic textual division, understanding the v. as a colophon that concludes the second discourse of Moses (4.44–28.69). In contrast, most English translations follow the more logical LXX division, which regards the v. (as 29.1) as a superscription to the third discourse (29.1–30.20). Similar formulae *(these are the ...)* are used to introduce the first and second discourses (1.1; 4.45). *The covenant ... Moab:* This editorial heading provides two new perspectives on the legal corpus. (1) The earlier "laws and rules" (12.1) are now seen as a unified, single *covenant* between God and Israel. This perspective is absent from the legal corpus itself, where the word "covenant" appears only at 17.2. In this third discourse, however, that understanding becomes the norm (see 28.69; 29.8, 11, 13, 20, 24; 31.16, 20). (2) The second new perspective regards the laws of Moab as a covenant *in addition to* the one made at Horeb; the phrase suggests an editor's attempt to work in a later version of a law or narrative alongside an earlier one (Gen. 26.1; Lev. 23.38). This view stylizes Deut.—originally intended as an independent body of law—as now working in tandem with prior law. It is striking that, in other contexts, Deut. does not take the covenant at Horeb into account but presents itself as an independent and autonomous covenant. There is no reference to Horeb in the redundant introductory formulae of 4.44–45 or, more importantly, in the superscription to the legal corpus at 12.1.

29 Moses summoned all Israel and said to them:
You have seen all that the LORD did before your very
eyes in the land of Egypt, to Pharaoh and to all his courtiers
and to his whole country: 2 the wondrous feats that you saw
with your own eyes, those prodigious signs and marvels. 3 Yet
to this day the LORD has not given you a mind to understand or
eyes to see or ears to hear.
4 I led you through the wilderness forty years; the clothes on
your back did not wear out, nor did the sandals on your feet;
5 you had no bread to eat and no wine or other intoxicant to
drink—that you might know that I the LORD am your God.
6 When you reached this place, King Sihon of Heshbon and
King Og of Bashan came out to engage us in battle, but we defeated them. 7 We took their land and gave it to the Reubenites,
the Gadites, and the half-tribe of Manasseh as their heritage.
8 Therefore observe faithfully all the terms of this covenant,
that you may succeed in all that you undertake.

NITSAVIM נצבים

9 You stand this day, all of you, before the LORD your God—
your tribal heads, your elders and your officials, all the men
of Israel, 10 your children, your wives, even the stranger within
your camp, from woodchopper to water drawer— 11 to enter
into the covenant of the LORD your God, which the LORD your
God is concluding with you this day, with its sanctions;[a] 12 to
the end that He may establish you this day as His people and
be your God, as He promised you and as He swore to your fathers, Abraham, Isaac, and Jacob. 13 I make this covenant, with
its sanctions, not with you alone, 14 but both with those who
are standing here with us this day before the LORD our God
and with those who are not with us here this day.
15 Well you know that we dwelt in the land of Egypt and that
we passed through the midst of various other nations; 16 and

a I.e., the curses that violations of the covenant will entail.

29.1–8: Didactic review of Israel's history. 29.1: *You have seen:* As at 5.2–4, Moses addresses the present generation, who are actually one generation removed from the miraculous events, as if they had themselves lived through the exodus and the wilderness wandering. **2:** *Signs ... marvels,* see 28.46 n. **3:** *Yet to this day ... given you,* more accurately, "the LORD has not given you until today." The thrust is to stress informed consent. The admonition creates a tension with the preceding two vv.: the addressees who "have seen" the miraculous events (v. 1), which their own "eyes" saw (v. 2), are accused of having lacked *eyes to see.* The castigation reflects the episodes of rebellion (9.7–24). **4–5:** The Mosaic homily reinterprets the wilderness wandering, full of trials and tribulations according to Num., and presents it positively, as a miraculous experience that led Israel to know God. **4:** *I:* For the intrusion of divine speech into Mosaic speech, see 7.4; 17.3; 28.20, 68. *Clothes ... feet,* see 8.4. **5:** *You had no bread to eat ... no wine ... to drink:* You had no normal food. The manna, quail, and water that Israel consumed were instead miraculous food supplied by divine providence (8.2–5; Exod. ch 16; Num. 11.4–9, 31–33). *Know:* The miraculous sustenance of Israel in the desert was intended didactically to bring the people to know God (8.3). This knowledge is not abstract speculation but the recognition of God's historical actions on behalf of the nation. *I the LORD am your God,* better, "I, YHVH, am your God" (6.4; Exod. 20.2). **6–7:** See 1.4; 2.26–3.22; Num. 21.21–35.

29.9–28: Imprecation to ensure loyalty to the covenant. 9: *Stand ... all of you,* in formal array for a public legal ceremony (see Ps. 82.1). *This day,* making the transition from historical review (28.69–29.7) to present adjuration (similarly, VTE §33). **10:** In Deut., all, including women, are included in the covenantal community. **11:** *Covenant ... with its sanctions:* This legal formula recurs at v. 13, thus framing the central idea of the covenant: the binding relationship between God and Israel. *Sanctions,* more accurately, "its imprecation" or "its curse" (see translators' note *a*). Treaty infraction is punished with "all the curses of the covenant" (v. 20, more accurately translating the same Heb terms), which are named and sworn to in advance. As in the colloquial expression that joins a promise ("Cross my heart") to a pronouncement dooming oneself for noncompliance ("and hope to die"), so in the ancient Near East were covenants validated by means of a concluding imprecation (VTE §§37–56, 58–106). On that model, the preceding laws of chs 12–26 represent the treaty stipulations; ch 28, its sanctions; and ch 29, the formal ceremony of the imprecation. **13–14:** The covenant binds even future generations (as in VTE §§25, 33, 34, 57); consequently, the punishment for infraction of its terms extends to the third and fourth generation (5.9; Exod. 20.5; 34.7). **16–26:** A stark, two-part warning, showing how the attempt even of a single individual secretly to withdraw from

you have seen the detestable things and the fetishes of wood
and stone, silver and gold, that they keep. [17] Perchance there is
among you some man or woman, or some clan or tribe, whose
heart is even now turning away from the LORD our God to go
and worship the gods of those nations—perchance there is
among you a stock sprouting poison weed and wormwood.
[18] When such a one hears the words of these sanctions, he may
fancy himself immune, thinking, "I shall be safe, though I follow my own willful heart"—to the utter ruin of moist and dry
alike.[a] [19] The LORD will never forgive him; rather will the LORD's
anger and passion rage against that man, till every sanction recorded in this book comes down upon him, and the LORD blots
out his name from under heaven.

[20] The LORD will single them[b] out from all the tribes of Israel
for misfortune, in accordance with all the sanctions of the covenant recorded in this book of Teaching. [21] And later generations will ask—the children who succeed you, and foreigners
who come from distant lands and see the plagues and diseases
that the LORD has inflicted upon that land, [22] all its soil devastated by sulfur and salt, beyond sowing and producing, no
grass growing in it, just like the upheaval of Sodom and Gomorrah, Admah and Zeboiim, which the LORD overthrew in
His fierce anger—[23] all nations will ask, "Why did the LORD do
thus to this land? Wherefore that awful wrath?" [24] They will be
told, "Because they forsook the covenant that the LORD, God
of their fathers, made with them when He freed them from the
land of Egypt; [25] they turned to the service of other gods and
worshiped them, gods whom they had not experienced[c] and
whom He had not allotted[d] to them. [26] So the LORD was incensed at that land and brought upon it all the curses recorded
in this book. [27] The LORD uprooted them from their soil in anger, fury, and great wrath, and cast them into another land, as
is still the case."

[28] Concealed acts concern the LORD our God; but with overt
acts, it is for us and our children ever to apply all the provisions
of this Teaching.

a I.e., everything. *b I.e., clan or tribe, v. 17.* *c See note at 11.28.*
d See 4.19–20.

the covenant (vv. 16–18) jeopardizes the entire nation (vv. 19–27). **17:** *Turning away,* transferring loyalty from God to other gods (13.6–11; 17.2–7). *Poison weed and wormwood,* both toxic and bitter; see Hos. 10.4; Amos 5.7; 6.12. **18:** *Fancy himself immune,* rather than proclaim the imprecation, hoping to escape the sanctions of the covenant. *Moist and dry:* Most likely the paired antonyms are a merism designating totality (see 28.3–6 n.), but the exact meaning is lost. **19:** *Passion:* God is described as an "impassioned God" (5.9; Exod. 34.14; with the adjectival form of the same word), referring to His zeal to defend the mutual exclusivity of the covenant relation. *Comes down upon him,* more literally, "will crouch down upon them" (cf. Gen. 4.7), with the imprecation here almost animate. *Blots out his name:* Like the erasure of a tablet or scroll (Num. 5.23), given a theological cast based on the Mesopotamian idea that the divine decree of human fate is inscribed in a heavenly book. Erasure from this book, then, symbolizes punishment (9.14; Gen. 6.7; Exod. 17.14; 32.32; 2 Kings 14.27; Ps. 9.6). This ancient Mesopotamian idea figures prominently in the later Jewish liturgy for Rosh Ha-Shanah (the Jewish New Year) and Yom Kippur (the Day of Atonement). **21–27:** The negative instruction. As the wilderness wandering provided an instructional lesson for the nation (vv. 4–5), so will Israel, now transformed into a devastation, provide an object lesson for future generations and other nations. Normally this question-and-answer model, which anticipates the child's question, seeks to provide the rationale for ritual observance with reference to God's redemptive acts (4.32–38; Exod. 12.25–27; 13.8–10). Reversing that scenario, the lesson here involves divine punishment for breach of covenant (see 1 Kings 9.9). **22:** *Sulfur and salt* were used in antiquity as chemical defoliants by invading armies. *Sodom ... Zeboiim:* The land's resulting sterility will recall the divine devastation of the proverbial wicked cities located in the arid area around the Dead Sea (Gen. 19.24–25; Isa. 1.9–10). **24:** *The covenant,* conflating the covenants of Horeb and Moab (28.69). **25:** *Gods ... not allotted to them:* As at 32.8–9, the idea is that each nation is allocated its own god, and that YHVH is the God of Israel. As at 5.7–9, the existence of other deities is here conceded. Contrast 4.19, where it is rather only inanimate "stars ... [that] God allotted," which reinterprets the polytheistic image from the later perspective of monotheism. **27:** *Cast them into another land, as is still the case:* The reference to the present implies that the ch was composed subsequent to the Babylonian exile of 586 BCE. **28:** *Concealed acts* may, as here, refer to acts that God will punish (vv. 17–18); or to future events.

30 When all these things befall you—the blessing and the
curse that I have set before you—and you take them to
heart amidst the various nations to which the LORD your God
has banished you, 2 and you return to the LORD your God, and
you and your children heed His command with all your heart
and soul, just as I enjoin upon you this day, 3 then the LORD
your God will restore your fortunes[a] and take you back in love.
He will bring you together again from all the peoples where the
LORD your God has scattered you. 4 Even if your outcasts are
at the ends of the world,[b] from there the LORD your God will
gather you, from there He will fetch you. 5 And the LORD your
God will bring you to the land that your fathers possessed, and
you shall possess it; and He will make you more prosperous
and more numerous than your fathers.
6 Then the LORD your God will open up[c] your heart and the
hearts of your offspring to love the LORD your God with all your
heart and soul, in order that you may live. 7 The LORD your God
will inflict all those curses upon the enemies and foes who
persecuted you. 8 You, however, will again heed the LORD and
obey all His commandments that I enjoin upon you this day.
9 And the LORD your God will grant you abounding prosperity
in all your undertakings, in the issue of your womb, the offspring of your cattle, and the produce of your soil. For the LORD
will again delight in your well-being, as He did in that of your
fathers, 10 since you will be heeding the LORD your God and
keeping His commandments and laws that are recorded in this
book of the Teaching—once you return to the LORD your God
with all your heart and soul.

a Others "captivity." *b Lit. "sky."* *c Others "circumcise."*

More likely, the antithesis rejects religions that define truth in terms of esoteric speculation and restrict access to such truth to a learned few. Instead, the Torah, based upon a public revelation (ch 5) and Mosaic instruction (chs 12–26), is accessible to all. Similarly, Israel's God is "near" and obedience to the revealed Torah constitutes "wisdom" (4.6–7). *For us and our children ever,* tripartite emphasis on lasting open access. *To apply* continues the antithesis: The Torah requires not esoteric speculation but moral and religious action.

30.1–10: Reassurance of restoration. The promise of restoration here contradicts the unconditional denial of divine pardon and the blotting out of Israel's name in 29.19. Indeed, this section, with its emphasis on restoration, does not logically follow ch 29, which urges obedience to the covenant by stressing the seriousness of its sanctions. The unit makes most sense as a later insertion that serves the religious needs of a community different from that of the book's original audience (see v. 5 n.). Its literary and theological elegance is difficult to represent in English. The author uses the Heb word "shuv" (which can mean "return," "repent," or "restore") seven times, in seven different ways to establish the close bond between human repentance and divine forgiveness: (v. 1) If you *take them to heart* ..., (v. 2) and *return* ..., (v. 3) then the LORD will *restore your fortunes and take you back* ..., (v. 8) Then you shall *again* obey ..., (v. 9) For the LORD will *again* take delight ..., (v. 10) because you *return.* This notion of returning (using "shuv") is central to Deut. ch 4 as well, and to prophetic literature, and is further developed into the rabbinic doctrine of "teshuvah" or repentance, which replaces the Priestly idea of "kapparah" or atonement (see Lev. 16.1–34 n.). **4:** Contrast Amos 9.2–3. **5:** *Bring you to the land that your fathers possessed:* The "you" no longer refers to the desert generation whom Moses, according to the narrative, addresses on the plains of Transjordan, as they are about to enter the land (ca. 1220 BCE). Instead, the perspective has shifted to that of the Judahite exiles in Babylonia (586–539 BCE), who look forward to returning to the land they once inhabited, and from which they have since been displaced. *More numerous,* using the language of the covenantal promise (Gen. 17.2; 22.17). For similar claims that the future will repeat the past while also surpassing it, see Isa. 42.9; 43.6–20; 51.9–11. **6:** *The LORD ... will open up* [lit. "circumcise"] *your heart:* God is the agent, in contrast with the previous call for Israel itself to "cut away ... the thickening about your hearts" (see 10.16 n.). The change in perspective suggests skepticism about the people's ability to effect such a change of heart independently. Still more skepticism is evident in the prophetic vision of a divine "reprogramming" of the human heart by inscribing the Torah upon it (Jer. 31.31–34; Ezek. 11.19–20; 36.26–27). **7:** The curses remain in effect, but are deflected from Israel to the adversary; contrast 28.47, 49, where the foreign nation functions as God's agent to punish Israel for its disobedience. **9:** *Issue ... offspring ... produce:* The blessings upon return from exile conform to those promised upon initial entry into the land (28.4). **10:** *Heeding the LORD ... and keeping His ... laws that are recorded in this book of the Teaching:* The reference is to the text of Deut. itself, which replaces the live speech of Moses (12.28; 13.1) or prophetic speech (18.18–9) as authoritative revealer of God's word.

11 Surely, this Instruction which I enjoin upon you this day is not too baffling for you, nor is it beyond reach. 12 It is not in the heavens, that you should say, "Who among us can go up to the heavens and get it for us and impart it to us, that we may observe it?" 13 Neither is it beyond the sea, that you should say, "Who among us can cross to the other side of the sea and get it for us and impart it to us, that we may observe it?" 14 No, the thing is very close to you, in your mouth and in your heart, to observe it.

15 See, I set before you this day life and prosperity, death and adversity. 16 For[a] I command you this day, to love the LORD your God, to walk in His ways, and to keep His commandments, His laws, and His rules, that you may thrive and increase, and that the LORD your God may bless you in the land that you are about to enter and possess. 17 But if your heart turns away and you give no heed, and are lured into the worship and service of other gods, 18 I declare to you this day that you shall certainly perish; you shall not long endure on the soil that you are crossing the Jordan to enter and possess. 19 I call heaven and earth to witness against you this day: I have put before you life and death, blessing and curse. Choose life—if you and your offspring would live—20 by loving the LORD your God, heeding His commands, and holding fast to Him. For thereby you shall have life and shall long endure upon the soil that the LORD swore to your ancestors, Abraham, Isaac, and Jacob, to give to them.

VA-YELEKH וילך

31 [b]Moses went and spoke[b] these things to all Israel. 2 He said to them:

I am now one hundred and twenty years old, I can no longer [c]be active.[c] Moreover, the LORD has said to me, "You shall not go across yonder Jordan." 3 The LORD your God Himself will cross over before you; and He Himself will wipe out those nations from your path and you shall dispossess them.—Joshua is the one who shall cross before you, as the LORD has spoken.—4 The LORD will do to them as He did to Sihon and Og, kings of the Amorites, and to their countries, when He wiped them out. 5 The LORD will deliver them up to you, and you shall deal with them in full accordance with the Instruction that I have enjoined upon you. 6 Be strong and resolute, be not in fear

a Septuagint reads "If you obey the commandments of the LORD your God, which."
b-b An ancient Heb. ms. and the Septuagint read: "When Moses had finished speaking…"; cf. 29.1. *c-c Lit. "come and go."*

30.11–20: The original continuation of ch 29, with two sections: vv. 11–14, 15–20. **11–14: The accessibility of Torah.** Turning their own characteristic imagery against them, the passage challenges the assumptions of Near Eastern wisdom schools about the inaccessibility of divine wisdom and the limits of human knowledge (cf. Job ch 28). **11:** *Surely,* better, "because," logically continuing 29.28 and emphasizing the ready accessibility of the Torah. The NJPS translation is an accommodation to the insertion of vv. 1–10. *This Instruction,* in the singular refers to Deut. as a whole (as at 6.1); the contrasting plural use designates the individual stipulations (v. 10; 4.2, 40; 5.10; 6.17). **12:** See Prov. 30.4. *That we may observe it,* lit. "so that He may proclaim it to us." **14:** *In your mouth:* In antiquity, written texts were normally read, taught, and recited aloud rather than silently (6.7; 31.19, 21; Josh. 1.8). **15–20:** The necessity of choice. As the nation is about to enter the land, Moses presents Israel with a stark choice: its future well-being lies entirely in its own hands, depending upon whether each Israelite commits himself or herself to covenantal obedience. By providing a clear statement of the consequences that follow upon the responsibility of each individual to decide, this v. becomes a major source for the later Jewish doctrine of free will, as expressed in the idea that humans are free to choose between good and evil (see Maimonides, *Hilkhot Teshuvah* 5:3). **16:** *Love … walk in His ways:* In the technical language of Near Eastern treaties, "love" means to act loyally and to honor the commitments of the treaty (see 6.5 n.). **19:** *Heaven and earth to witness,* see 4.26; 32.1. *Choose life:* Joshua reiterates the necessity of choice (Josh. 24.15). The didactic use of life and death suggests the influence of wisdom teachings upon the authors (Prov. 11.19; 14.27; 18.21; cf. Jer. 8.3; 21.8).

31.1–34.12: The death of Moses and the formation of the Torah. With the imprecation of ch 30 marking the conclusion of the treaty between God and Israel, Deut. now returns to Moses, the mediator of the treaty, as his life draws to a close. The inevitable question of succession is here given a twofold answer, as befits the role of Moses as both political and religious leader of Israel. Moses invests Joshua with leadership in

or in dread of them; for the LORD your God Himself marches
with you: He will not fail you or forsake you.
7 Then Moses called Joshua and said to him in the sight of
all Israel: "Be strong and resolute, for it is you who shall go
with this people into the land that the LORD swore to their
fathers to give them, and it is you who shall apportion it to
them. 8 And the LORD Himself will go before you. He will be
with you; He will not fail you or forsake you. Fear not and be
not dismayed!"

political and military matters (31.1–8, 14–15, 23; 32.44, 48–52; 34.9), while also "putting down in writing the words of this Teaching" (31.24) to instruct the nation in matters of religion. Deut. thus ends in paradox: Moses, ostensibly the book's narrator, narrates his own death (ch 34); and the book of the Torah, which is already presupposed (29.26), nevertheless provides an account of its own formation (31.9–13, 24–29). The conclusion of Deut. also marks, however, the conclusion of the Pentateuch. As they set Deut. as the conclusion of that larger work, later editors with the background of the exile contributed their perspectives on the function of the Torah in the people's life. Finally, the Pentateuch's literary precedent of a patriarch's deathbed bequest and blessing (Gen. chs 27; 48–49) led to the incorporation of "The Song of Moses" (32.1–43) and of "The Blessing of Moses" (ch 33), each of which may originally have circulated independently. What results is a heavily "written over" text that blends several viewpoints. Themes like the Mosaic appointment of Joshua begin, then begin again from a different perspective, and then are continued only after a digression, which marks the insertion of new material. The editors incorporated later layers by patterning them after earlier ones, often repeating their key terms, while arranging the whole in an overarching chiastic pattern (AB:B'A'A''). See diagram on page 417.

31.1–29: Moses makes arrangements for his death. Publicly announcing his imminent death, Moses invests Joshua with leadership and initiates the writing down of the Torah, which is to be taught regularly to the entire people. These two legacies seem independent of each other and suggest that an earlier narrative, concerned with the leadership issue, has been expanded to provide an account of the formation of the book of Deut. But, perhaps because of the importance of each of these two traditions, and the pivotal role occupied by Deut. in the Pentateuch, each tradition is itself doubled. The ch is thus quite complex and contains many layers of tradition. (1) There is a double announcement of the imminent mortality of Moses: v. 1 (at the initiative of Moses, citing previous divine commandment) and vv. 14–15 (with no reference to a previous announcement). (2) There is a corresponding double tradition concerning the transfer of leadership. Although Moses begins a public ceremony in order himself to appoint the new leader (vv. 7–8), a variant tradition has God commissioning Joshua directly (vv. 14–15, 23). (3) There is a double tradition concerning what Moses writes: one of "the words ... of this Teaching" (v. 24) and one of "this poem" (v. 19). These traditions are harmonized, as each is to serve as a "witness" (vv. 21, 26). The first, which refers to Deut., was supplemented by the second in order to integrate the following "Song of Moses" (32.1–43). (4) In the "Song" tradition, Israel's future apostasy is already a foregone conclusion (vv. 16–22; 28–29); in the covenant-making tradition, there is yet hope that, by taking the law to heart, Israel might avoid catastrophe (vv. 9–13, 24–27). **1:** *Moses went and spoke:* The LXX and a Qumran text attest an alternate version, "Moses finished speaking" (see translators' note *b-b;* in Heb, the difference between the two involves only the transposition of two consonants, "vylk" vs. "vykl"). The latter reading may make more sense since it creates an exact parallel between this v. and 32.45, each of which marks a transition between two sections of text and is continued by "and he said to them ..." (v. 2; 32.46). **2:** *I am now one hundred and twenty years old:* The Heb places the age first, thereby forefronting the key issue. Moses has reached the maximum age allocated by God to humans (Gen. 6.3); the imminence of death makes it urgent to assure continuity of leadership. *I can no longer be active,* lit. "go out and come in," referring specifically to military leadership (Num. 27.17; 1 Kings 3.7; cf. 2 Sam. 11.1). **2–3:** Refers back to 1.37–38; 3.27–28. The death of a major leader and the transfer of his authority mark important turning points within the larger context of the Deuteronomistic History and partially follow a common model (cf. Josh. 23.2; 1 Sam. 12.2; 1 Kings 2.1–2). **4:** The successful military campaigns in Transjordan provide assurance in the conquest of Canaan; Moses aims to counter Israel's intimidation (1.27–28; Num. chs 13–14). **5:** *The Instruction that I have enjoined upon you* refers to the ban (7.1–7; 12.29–31; 20.16–18). **7–8:** The speech commissioning Joshua into office includes three formal elements: encouragement *(Be strong and resolute),* description of the task *(for it is you who ...),* and assurance of support *(the LORD ... will be with you).* **9–13:** The institution of a covenant ceremony to be held every seven years, in the sabbatical year (15.1–11), during the *Feast of Booths* (16.13–15). **12:** The requirement that the law must be read publicly and taught to the assembled nation

9 Moses wrote down this Teaching and gave it to the priests,
sons of Levi, who carried the Ark of the LORD's Covenant, and
to all the elders of Israel.
10 And Moses instructed them as follows: Every seventh
year,[a] the year set for remission, at the Feast of Booths, 11 when
all Israel comes to appear before the LORD your God in the
place that He will choose, you shall read this Teaching aloud in
the presence of all Israel. 12 Gather the people—men, women,
children, and the strangers in your communities—that they
may hear and so learn to revere the LORD your God and to observe faithfully every word of this Teaching. 13 Their children,
too, who have not had the experience, shall hear and learn to
revere the LORD your God as long as they live in the land that
you are about to cross the Jordan to possess.

14 The LORD said to Moses: The time is drawing near for
you to die. Call Joshua and present yourselves in the Tent of
Meeting, that I may instruct him. Moses and Joshua went and
presented themselves in the Tent of Meeting. 15 The LORD appeared in the Tent, in a pillar of cloud, the pillar of cloud having come to rest at the entrance of the tent.

a See note at 15.1.

specifies the inclusion of women, minors, and non-Israelite resident aliens. The law does not restrict the responsibility to observe the covenant to males (cf. Neh. 8.2; contrast Exod. 19.15 [see n.]). **14:** *Tent of Meeting,* in the J source, the site outside of the camp where God speaks to Moses, with Joshua in attendance (see Exod. 33.7–11 n.). This tent should be distinguished from the Tabernacle of the P literature, located in the center of the Israelite encampment and housing the Ark of the Covenant and the altar (Exod. chs 26–27; Num. 7.1–3; 18.1–7). *That I may instruct him:* The more standard tradition involves direct commission by Moses at God's command (3.27–28; 34.9; Num. 27.18–23). **15:** The double reference to the *pillar of cloud,* located both *in the Tent* (cf. Exod. 30.36; 40.34–35; Lev. 16.2) and *at the entrance of the tent* (cf. Exod. 33.9–10; Num. 12.5) blends the separate traditions associated with each of the two tents (see v. 14 n.)

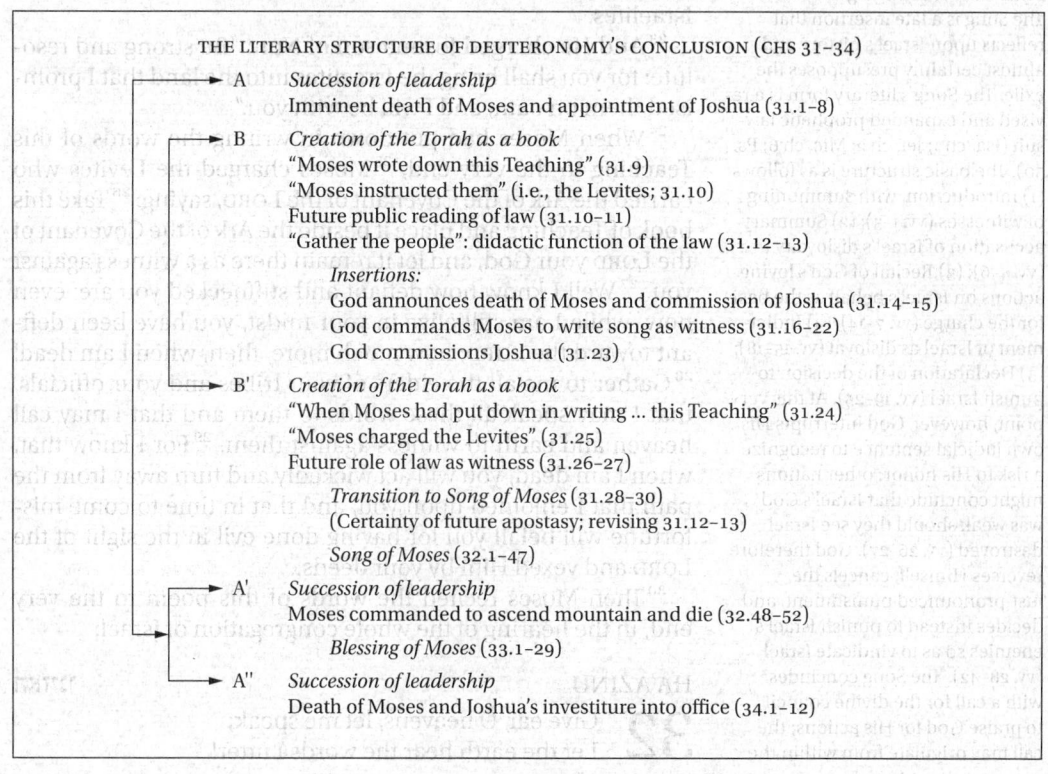

THE LITERARY STRUCTURE OF DEUTERONOMY'S CONCLUSION (CHS 31–34)

A *Succession of leadership*
Imminent death of Moses and appointment of Joshua (31.1–8)

B *Creation of the Torah as a book*
"Moses wrote down this Teaching" (31.9)
"Moses instructed them" (i.e., the Levites; 31.10)
Future public reading of law (31.10–11)
"Gather the people": didactic function of the law (31.12–13)
Insertions:
God announces death of Moses and commission of Joshua (31.14–15)
God commands Moses to write song as witness (31.16–22)
God commissions Joshua (31.23)

B' *Creation of the Torah as a book*
"When Moses had put down in writing ... this Teaching" (31.24)
"Moses charged the Levites" (31.25)
Future role of law as witness (31.26–27)
Transition to Song of Moses (31.28–30)
(Certainty of future apostasy; revising 31.12–13)
Song of Moses (32.1–47)

A' *Succession of leadership*
Moses commanded to ascend mountain and die (32.48–52)
Blessing of Moses (33.1–29)

A'' *Succession of leadership*
Death of Moses and Joshua's investiture into office (34.1–12)

regarding the site of divine communication. **16:** *Forsake:* The punishment is measure-for-measure (v. 17). **17:** *Our God:* Although the word generally has this meaning, the Heb could also mean "our gods," suggesting that the people will have strayed so far from the covenant that they attribute the resulting divine punishment to other gods. This interpretation explains God's angry response (v. 18). **22–23:** The sequence of *Moses wrote down* (v. 22) and … *charged* (v. 23) uses the same key terms as "When Moses had put down in writing … Moses charged" (vv. 24–25). The repetition of the paired terms provided a means for editors to insert the section on the song (vv. 16–22). **23:** *And He charged,* lit. "He commanded," with no subject identified. NJPS, by capitalizing the pronoun, indicates that the reference is God, not Moses, since the v. does not continue from v. 22, but directly resumes vv. 14–15.

31.30–32.44: The Song of Moses. The Song is a late insertion that reflects upon Israel's history and almost certainly presupposes the exile. The Song's literary form is a revised and expanded prophetic lawsuit (Isa. ch 1; Jer. ch 2; Mic. ch 6; Ps. 50). The basic structure is as follows: (1) Introduction, with summoning of witnesses (vv. 1–3); (2) Summary accusation of Israel's disloyalty (vv. 4–6); (3) Recital of God's loving actions on Israel's behalf as the basis for the charge (vv. 7–14); (4) Indictment of Israel as disloyal (vv. 15–18); (5) Declaration of the decision to punish Israel (vv. 19–25). At this very point, however, God interrupts His own judicial sentence to recognize a risk to His honor: other nations might conclude that Israel's God was weak should they see Israel destroyed (vv. 26–27). God therefore reverses Himself, cancels the just-pronounced punishment, and decides instead to punish Israel's enemies so as to vindicate Israel (vv. 28–42). The Song concludes with a call for the divine council to praise God for His actions; the call may originate from within the

16 The LORD said to Moses: You are soon to lie with your fathers. This people will thereupon go astray after the alien gods
in their midst, in the land that they are about to enter; they
will forsake Me and break My covenant that I made with them.
17 Then My anger will flare up against them, and I will abandon them and hide My countenance from them. They shall be
ready prey; and many evils and troubles shall befall them. And
they shall say on that day, "Surely it is because our God is not in
our midst that these evils have befallen us." 18 Yet I will keep My
countenance hidden on that day, because of all the evil they
have done in turning to other gods. 19 Therefore, write down
this poem and teach it to the people of Israel; put it in their
mouths, in order that this poem may be My witness against
the people of Israel. 20 When I bring them into the land flowing
with milk and honey that I promised on oath to their fathers,
and they eat their fill and grow fat and turn to other gods and
serve them, spurning Me and breaking My covenant, 21 and
the many evils and troubles befall them—then this poem shall
confront them as a witness, since it will never be lost from the
mouth of their offspring. For I know what plans they are devising even now, before I bring them into the land that I promised
on oath.

22 That day, Moses wrote down this poem and taught it to the
Israelites.

23 And He charged Joshua son of Nun: "Be strong and resolute: for you shall bring the Israelites into the land that I promised them on oath, and I will be with you."

24 When Moses had put down in writing the words of this
Teaching to the very end, 25 Moses charged the Levites who
carried the Ark of the Covenant of the LORD, saying: 26 Take this
book of Teaching and place it beside the Ark of the Covenant of
the LORD your God, and let it remain there as a witness against
you. 27 Well I know how defiant and stiffnecked you are: even
now, while I am still alive in your midst, you have been defiant toward the LORD; how much more, then, when I am dead!
28 Gather to me all the elders of your tribes and your officials,
that I may speak all these words to them and that I may call
heaven and earth to witness against them. 29 For I know that,
when I am dead, you will act wickedly and turn away from the
path that I enjoined upon you, and that in time to come misfortune will befall you for having done evil in the sight of the
LORD and vexed Him by your deeds.

30 Then Moses recited the words of this poem to the very
end, in the hearing of the whole congregation of Israel:

HA'AZINU האזינו

32 Give ear, O heavens, let me speak;
Let the earth hear the words I utter!

2 May my discourse come down as the rain,
My speech distill as the dew,
Like showers on young growth,
Like droplets on the grass.[a]
3 For the name of the LORD I proclaim;
Give glory to our God!

4 The Rock!—His deeds are perfect,
Yea, all His ways are just;
A faithful God, never false,
True and upright is He.
5[b] Children unworthy of Him—
That crooked, perverse generation—
Their baseness has played Him false.
6 Do you thus requite the LORD,
O dull and witless people?
Is not He the Father who created you,
Fashioned you and made you endure!

7 Remember the days of old,
Consider the years of ages past;
Ask your father, he will inform you,
Your elders, they will tell you:
8 When the Most High gave nations their homes
And set the divisions of man,
He fixed the boundaries of peoples
In relation to Israel's numbers.
9 For the LORD's portion is His people,
Jacob His own allotment.

10 He found him in a desert region,
In an empty howling waste.
He engirded him, watched over him,
Guarded him as the pupil of His eye.
11 Like an eagle who rouses his nestlings,

a I.e., may my words be received eagerly; cf. Job 29.22–23.
b Meaning of Heb. uncertain.

divine council itself (v. 43; similarly, Ps. 29.1). A prose frame links the Song to Deut. by identifying Moses, otherwise unmentioned in the poem, as its speaker (31.30; 32.44). **2:** The reference to *discourse,* and the criticism of Israel as "dull and witless" (v. 6) show how the original prophetic lawsuit has been combined with ideas taken from wisdom literature (Prov. 1.5; 4.2; 7.21). **4:** *Rock,* better, "Mountain," a title applied to the high god of ancient Canaanite literature (see v. 8 n.) and to the biblical God (vv. 15, 18, 30, 31, 37; Isa. 44.8; Ps. 78.35). **6:** *Created you,* when God redeemed Israel from Egypt (Exod. 15.16). **8:** *Most High,* or "Elyon," is a formal title of El, the senior god who presided over the divine council in the Ugaritic literature of ancient Canaan. The reference thus invokes, as do other biblical texts, the Near Eastern convention of a pantheon of gods ruled by the chief deity (Pss. 82.1; 89.6–8). Israelite authors regularly applied El's title to Israel's God (Gen. 14.18–22; Num. 24.16; Pss. 46.5; 47.3). *In relation to Israel's numbers* is unintelligible as it stands. The variant attested by the LXX and at Qumran, "according to the sons of El" (cf. NRSV), which preserves the mythological reference to *Most High* ("ʿElyon") earlier in the v., makes much more sense. Here, the idea is that the chief god allocates the nations to lesser deities in the pantheon. (A postbiblical notion that seventy angels are in charge of the world's seventy nations echoes this idea.) Almost certainly, the unintelligible reading of the MT represents a "correction" of the original text (whereby God presides over other gods) to make it conform to the later standard of pure monotheism: There are no other gods! The polytheistic imagery of the divine council is also deleted in the Heb at 32.43; 33.2–3, 7. **9:** *Portion:* This and the following term reflect ancient estate law: Israel is God's special inheritance (4.20; cf. 7.6; 14.2; 26.18). *Own allotment:* NJPS has added *own* in order to avoid the impression that ʿElyon, as head of the pantheon, has assigned Israel to YHVH, as merely a member of the pantheon. The translation suggests that Israel's God, here identified with ʿElyon, reserves Israel for Himself until the end. The Heb permits either reading. **10:** *Found* (Hos. 9.10): Overlooking the traditions about the slavery in Egypt, the Song here traces the beginnings of Israel to the wilderness period, romanticizing its ideal purity (similarly, Hos. 2.14–15; Jer. 2.2–3; contrast Deut. 9.6–7, 22–27; Ezek. ch 20). **11:** God, as an eagle, tenderly bears Israel as a fledgling (see Exod. 19.4).

Gliding down to his young,
So did He spread His wings and take him,
Bear him along on His pinions;
12 The LORD alone did guide him,
No alien god at His side.

13 He set him atop the highlands,
To feast on the yield of the earth;
He fed him honey from the crag,
And oil from the flinty rock,
14 Curd of kine and milk of flocks;
With the best[a] of lambs,
And rams of Bashan, and he-goats;
With the [b]very finest[b] wheat—
And foaming grape-blood was your drink.

15 So Jeshurun grew fat and kicked—
You grew fat and gross and coarse[c]—
He forsook the God who made him
And spurned the Rock of his support.
16 They incensed Him with alien things,
Vexed Him with abominations.
17 They sacrificed to demons, no-gods,
Gods they had never known,
New ones, who came but lately,
[d]Who stirred not your fathers' fears.[d]
18 You neglected the Rock that begot you,
Forgot the God who brought you forth.

19 The LORD saw and was vexed
And spurned His sons and His daughters.
20 He said:
I will hide My countenance from them,
And see how they fare in the end.
For they are a treacherous breed,
Children with no loyalty in them.
21 They incensed Me with no-gods,
Vexed Me with their futilities;[e]
I'll incense them with a no-folk,
Vex them with a nation of fools.
22 For a fire has flared in My wrath
And burned to the bottom of Sheol,
Has consumed the earth and its increase,
Eaten down to the base of the hills.

a Lit. "fat." *b-b Lit. "kidney fat of."* *c Meaning of Heb. uncertain.*
d-d Meaning of Heb. uncertain; Arabic sha'ara *suggests the rendering "Whom your fathers did not know."* *e I.e., idols.*

13: *Highlands,* see Exod. 15.17. **14:** *Curd,* symbolic of extravagant hospitality offered to special guests (Gen. 18.8; Judg. 5.25). **15:** *Jeshurun,* probably meaning "upright," a poetic term for Israel (33.5, 26; Isa. 44.2). **17:** *Demons,* better, "protective spirits," using a word borrowed from Akkadian (also Ps. 106.37). *No-gods:* The language is intentionally sarcastic (see also v. 21). **18:** *The Rock that begot you ... brought you forth:* The Heb much more vividly presents God as going through childbirth: "The Rock (better: mountain) who gave birth to you ... who writhed in labor (to bear) you." The same verb is elsewhere applied to Sarah, who "writhed in labor" to bring Israel forth (so Isa. 51.2, lit.). That God had to suffer labor pains to bear Israel only increases the injustice of Israel's forgetting its divine parent. For the metaphor of God panting as a woman in labor, see Isa. 42.14. Such cases provide an important alternative to the normal masculine imagery associated with God. **21:** *Incensed* refers to the covenant's demand for exclusive loyalty to God (5.8; 6.15; Num. 25.11). Accordingly, the punishment for breach of the covenant metes out precise talionic justice (see 19.19 n.). Heb emphasizes the sarcasm: thus, *with no-gods* and *no-folk. Their futilities,* lit. "their vapors" or "their vanities," even "their vapidities" (Jer. 8.19, "futilities"; 10.15, "delusion"; 16.19, "delusions"; Eccl. 1.2, "futility"). **22:** *Sheol,* the underworld (Gen. 37.25; 1 Sam. 2.6; Ps. 139.8), the abode of all the dead, not a place of damnation like the later idea of hell.

23 I will sweep[a] misfortunes on them,
Use up My arrows on them:
24 Wasting famine, ravaging plague,
Deadly pestilence, and fanged beasts
Will I let loose against them,
With venomous creepers in dust.
25 The sword shall deal death without,
As shall the terror within,
To youth and maiden alike,
The suckling as well as the aged.
26 [b-]I might have reduced them to naught,[-b]
Made their memory cease among men,
27 But for fear of the taunts of the foe,
Their enemies who might misjudge
And say, "Our own hand has prevailed;
None of this was wrought by the LORD!"
28[c] For they are a folk void of sense,
Lacking in all discernment.
29 Were they wise, they would think upon this,
Gain insight into their future:
30 "How could one have routed a thousand,
Or two put ten thousand to flight,
Unless their Rock had sold them,
The LORD had given them up?"
31 For their rock is not like our Rock,
[d-]In our enemies' own[e] estimation.[-d]

32 Ah! The vine for them is from Sodom,
From the vineyards of Gomorrah;
The grapes for them are poison,
A bitter growth their clusters.
33 Their wine is the venom of asps,
The pitiless poison of vipers.
34 Lo, I have it all put away,
Sealed up in My storehouses,
35 To be My vengeance and recompense,
At the time that their foot falters.
Yea, their day of disaster is near,
And destiny rushes upon them.

36 For the LORD will vindicate His people
[f-]And take revenge for[-f] His servants,

a *Meaning of Heb. uncertain.*
b-b *Lit. "I said, I will reduce..."; meaning of Heb.* 'aph'ehem *uncertain.*
c *Here, apparently, Moses is the speaker; God resumes in v. 32.*
d-d *I.e., as everyone must admit.*
e *For Heb.* pelilim *see Exod. 21.22; cf. Gen. 48.11.*
f-f *Cf. Isa. 1.24. Others "and repent Himself concerning."*

23: *My arrows,* divine punishments (v. 42; Ezek. 5.16; Pss. 7.14; 18.15; 38.3). **24:** *Ravaging plague* reflects the name of the Ugaritic god of pestilence, thus better, "devoured by Plague." **25:** *Youth ... maiden,* better, "young man ... young woman," to emphasize along with *suckling ... aged* the double merism (28.3–6 n.), which symbolizes the totality of the slaughter. **26–27:** The Song here pivots from judgment of Israel to its vindication at the expense of the foreign invaders. **27:** *For fear:* God has feelings and vulnerabilities (as at Gen. 6.6). *Our own hand has prevailed,* lit., "our hand is held high" in victory (Num. 33.3, "defiantly"; Ps. 89.14). **28–31:** God's soliloquy is interrupted by another voice that refers to God in the third person and speaks on behalf of Israel (vv. 30–31). The voice is contextually that of Moses (see translators' note *c*), but it is one that assumes the perspective of scribal wisdom. The section therefore seems to be an addition to the text, separating God's abrupt change of heart (vv. 25–27) from the explicit announcement of judgment upon the foreign nation (vv. 34–38). **28–29:** The insertion here directs against the foreign nation the same critique already made of Israel: God's judgment is justified by the nation's lack of wisdom (vv. 6, 20). **30:** A citation within a citation: The v., attributed to Israel's enemy, in effect reproaches the foreign nation for failing to understand that it owes its triumph over Israel to God rather than force of arms. The imagery ironically inverts the holy war idea (3.22; 20.1), now turning it against Israel. **32:** *Sodom ... Gomorrah,* here symbolizing moral corruption more than ruinous devastation (cf. 29.22 n.). **34:** *It,* the punishment of the foreign nation, which is about to be announced (vv. 35–42). *Put away, Sealed up* refers to the formal legal procedures for rolling and then sealing a witnessed deed or contract with a wax seal, so that the unaltered document can subsequently be introduced into court as evidence (Isa. 8.16; Jer. 32.9–15). **35:** *Vengeance,* better, "vindication," since the idea is not revenge but justice.

When He sees that their might is gone,
And neither bond nor free is left.
37 He will say: Where are their gods,
The rock in whom they sought refuge,
38 Who ate the fat of their offerings
And drank their libation wine?
Let them rise up to your help,
And let them be a shield unto you!
39 See, then, that I, I am He;
There is no god beside Me.
I deal death and give life;
I wounded and I will heal:
None can deliver from My hand.
40 Lo, I raise My hand to heaven
And say: As I live forever,
41 When I whet My flashing blade
And My hand lays hold on judgment,
Vengeance will I wreak on My foes,
Will I deal to those who reject Me.
42 I will make My arrows drunk with blood—
As My sword devours flesh—
Blood of the slain and the captive
From the long-haired enemy chiefs.

43 O nations, acclaim His people!
For He'll avenge the blood of His servants,
Wreak vengeance on His foes,
And cleanse the land of His people.[a]

44 Moses came, together with Hosea son of Nun, and recited all the words of this poem in the hearing of the people.

a Cf. Num. 35.33. Meaning of Heb. uncertain; Ugaritic 'udm't *"tears" suggests the rendering "And wipe away His people's tears." Cf. Isa. 25.8.*

ORIGINAL FORM OF 32.43

RECONSTRUCTED TEXT	NJPS (MASORETIC TEXT)
Rejoice, *O heavens,* with Him!	*O nations,* acclaim His people!
Worship Him, O every god!	
For He'll avenge the blood of His *children,*	For He'll avenge the blood of His *servants,*
Wreak vengeance on His foes;	Wreak vengeance on His foes,
He will repay those who hate him,	
And cleanse the land of His people.	And cleanse the land of His people.

36: *Their might is gone, And neither bond nor free is left:* God will act when no one survives who can take charge or provide assistance (2 Kings 14.26; cf. 1 Kings 14.10; 21.21; 2 Kings 9.8). **37–38:** Further sarcasm. **39:** Similar to exilic Second Isaiah (Isa. 41.4; 43.10, 13; 44.6; 45.6–7, 22; 48.12). **40:** *I raise My hand,* elsewhere translated "I swear," which clarifies the meaning here. God is represented anthropomorphically, as performing the physical gesture that marks a formal legal oath (see Exod. 6.7 n.; Num. 14.30; Ezek. 20.5–6, 15, 23, 28, 42; 36.7; 44.12; 47.14; Neh. 9.15). **41:** *Wreak,* lit. "return," in talionic justice. Thus, because of the judicial connotation, *vengeance* gives the wrong idea (v. 35 n.). *Reject Me,* treaty language that refers to disloyal action that violates the covenant. **43:** As it stands, the Heb presents numerous difficulties. The opening vocative *O nations* is illogical in this context. The v. demands that the very nations judged guilty of spilling Israel's blood suddenly join in the chorus of those praising Israel—in the moment before their destruction! The expected poetic parallelism (AA'BB', as in v. 2) is absent. Here the second line presents a completely different idea than the first line, rather than repeating it with a variation. The absence of parallelism is not simply a formal stylistic issue: It renders the climax of the poem unintelligible. The incoherence of v. 43 in its present form suggests that the original text has been disrupted. Alternative reflections of the text, as preserved by the LXX and a Dead Sea Scrolls ms, restore the poem's lost coherence. A reconstruction of the original form of the v. is shown in the diagram on this page. The restoration opens up an entire world of meaning and provides the expected poetic parallelism for the first, second, and third pairs of lines, which is absent in the MT. In the ancient versions, it is logically the "heavens" who are addressed (as in v. 1 and Isa. 1.2) and who rejoice with God. That makes more sense than illogically requiring the *nations*

[45] And when Moses finished reciting all these words to all Israel, [46] he said to them: Take to heart all the words with which I have warned you this day. Enjoin them upon your children, that they may observe faithfully all the terms of this Teaching. [47] For this is not a trifling thing for you: it is your very life; through it you shall long endure on the land that you are to possess upon crossing the Jordan.

[48] That very day the LORD spoke to Moses: [49] Ascend these heights of Abarim to Mount Nebo, which is in the land of Moab facing Jericho, and view the land of Canaan, which I am giving the Israelites as their holding. [50] You shall die on the mountain that you are about to ascend, and shall be gathered to your kin, as your brother Aaron died on Mount Hor and was gathered to his kin; [51] for you both broke faith with Me among the Israelite people, at the waters of Meribath-kadesh in the wilderness of Zin, by failing to uphold My sanctity among the Israelite people. [52] You may view the land from a distance, but you shall not enter it—the land that I am giving to the Israelite people.

VE-ZO'T HA-BERAKHAH וזאת הברכה

33 This is the blessing with which Moses, the man of God, bade the Israelites farewell before he died. [2] He said:

The LORD came from Sinai;
He shone upon them from Seir;

to praise Israel. The restoration also provides a frame at the poem's conclusion; "heavens ... *land*" (v. 43) forms an inclusio with its beginning, "heavens ... earth" (v. 1). It also continues the mythological imagery of God presiding over the divine council and acting as Divine Warrior (see vv. 8–9 nn.; vv. 41–42). Almost certainly, the challenge to monotheism in the original form of the v. is what triggered the attempts to purge the text of polytheistic elements, i.e., the shift from "heavens" to "nations" and the elision of the parallelism, with its reference to plural deities. Note the similar "correction" of the text at v. 8. *Avenge the blood:* These lines present God as divine blood-avenger (cf. 19.6), who removes the stain of Israel's blood from the land by requiting the aggressor for having spilled it (19.11–13). *Cleanse:* The line makes sense as it stands; the textual emendation suggested by NJPS in translators' note *a* is neither necessary nor linguistically valid. The moral stain on the land can only be "wiped clean" (the word's literal meaning) with the blood of the murderer (Num. 35.33–34; cf. Deut. 21.8): here, the foreign nation. God's position is nonetheless morally ambiguous, since it was God who had sanctioned the foreign invasion as just punishment for Israel's wrongdoing (vv. 19–26).

32.44–47: Double conclusion to the Song. Two originally separate conclusions joined by Deut.'s editors. **44:** *All the words* ... frames the Song of Moses in a perfect inclusio (see 31.30), thus concluding that unit. **45–47:** A separate section, the original continuation of 31.29 prior to the insertion of the Song. **46:** *All the words,* specifically, the laws of Deut. (31.24); now, following the insertion of the Song, and thus referring to both. **47:** *Not a trifling thing,* using the same word as the Laws of Hammurabi: "My laws ... are trifling only to the fool" (Epilogue).

32.48–52: Moses commanded to die. This section repeats the announcement of Moses' death (Num. 27.12–14) and thus joins it to its logical continuation, the narrative of that death (Deut. ch 34). The original connection between these two P sections was interrupted by Deut.'s insertion into the Torah. **49:** *These heights of Abarim to Mount Nebo,* as in the P narrative (Num. 27.12; 33.47); but, according to D, Pisgah (3.27). The two traditions are joined at 34.1. **50:** *You shall die,* a command, "Die ... !" This unusual imperative establishes that Moses both lives and dies at God's command (34.5 n.). *Gathered to your kin:* buried in a family tomb, where the bones of the generations would be gathered together (2 Kings 8.24; 22.20; cf. 1 Kings 13.31). Here the phrase is used metaphorically, since Moses' burial place is unknown (34.6). *Mount Hor,* consistent with P (Num. 20.22–29; 33.37–39); but, in D, "Moserah" (10.6). **51:** *You both broke faith,* see Num. 20.1–13.

33.1–29: The Blessing of Moses. Based upon the literary genre of a father's blessing of his progeny when death is imminent (Gen. 27.27–29; 48.15–16; 49.1–28; cf. 1 Kings 2.1–4), Moses addresses the tribes, arrayed before him (29.1, 9; 31.7, 30) as if all Israel were his own progeny, gathered before the deathbed (Gen. 48.2; 49.33). Conforming to the literary model of the blessing, the tribes are primarily addressed in the singular, as if they were individual sons (cf. v. 19). Surprisingly, Deut. makes no reference to the two sons of Moses (Exod. 2.22; 18.3–4; see also 34.6 n.). This poem is an insertion into Deut., intruding between God's command to Moses to ascend Nebo to prepare for his death (32.49–50) and Moses' compliance (34.1–5).

In its present form the poem was created by editors who have consciously combined several older literary models, in three stages, to create something new. (1) The literary convention of the patriarchal blessing addressed individually to each of the twelve tribes (vv. 6–25)

He appeared from Mount Paran,
And approached from Ribeboth-kodesh,[a]
Lightning flashing at them from His right.[b]
3c Lover, indeed, of the people,
Their hallowed are all in Your hand.
They followed in Your steps,
Accepting Your pronouncements,
4 When Moses charged us with the Teaching
As the heritage of the congregation of Jacob.
5 Then He became King in Jeshurun,
When the heads of the people assembled,
The tribes of Israel together.

a Cf. Meribath-kadesh, 32.51.
b Meaning of Heb. mimino 'eshdath *uncertain, perhaps a place name.*
c The meaning of vv. 3–5 is uncertain. An alternative rendering, with v. 3 apostrophizing Moses, is: [3]Then were, O lover of the people, / All His worshippers in your care; / They followed your lead, / Accepted your precepts. / [4]Moses charged us with the Teaching / As the heritage of the congregation of Jacob. / [5]Thus was he king in Jeshurun …

has been (2) embedded in a framing poem, which is rather addressed to a united Israel (vv. 1–5, 26–29). The focus of the framing poem is not on tribal destiny but on YHVH as the Divine Warrior who departs from the distant mountains that are His home. Accompanied by His divine pantheon, God comes to the rescue of His people in a powerful theophany that disturbs nature, defeats foreign adversaries, and results in His proclamation as Divine King, while ensuring His nation's rule. This model goes back to the classical victory hymns to the Divine Warrior (Judg. ch 5, Hab. ch 3; Ps. 18.8–16; cf. Exod. ch 15). That older model has been (3) significantly transformed, however. In vv. 1–4, the expected climax of the divine theophany in the military defeat of the enemy has been totally eclipsed (cf. vv. 26–29), although it is the logical precondition for the proclamation of God as King (v. 5). The editors have instead introduced a new climax: Moses' proclamation of Torah (v. 4 n.). The reference here to Sinai instead of Deut.'s usual Horeb (see 1.2 n.) is an attempt by the later editors of the Blessing to integrate Deut. with the other literary sources of the Torah (Exod. chs 19–20; Lev. 25.1; Num. 10.12). The editors have used an inclusio pattern to embed the Blessing (with its focus upon the individual tribes) into the framing hymn to the Divine Warrior (where united Israel is the focus). Thus the chiasm LORD: Jacob:Jeshurun::Jeshurun':Jacob': LORD' (A:B:C::C':B':A'; vv. 2, 4, 5, 26, 28, 29) brackets the inserted Blessing. Older hymns to the Divine Warrior sometimes list the tribes' contributions to the battle (Judg. 5.14–18), facilitating the combination of the two models. Although it draws upon older textual traditions, the poem in its present form is almost certainly exilic or postexilic. The combination of two separate literary models and the emphasis on Torah rather than on the Divine Warrior's manifestation in battle suggests the later literary setting. **1:** *Man of God,* a type of prophet, concerning whom "everything that he says comes true" (1 Sam. 9.6; see also Josh. 14.6; 1 Kings 13.1–32; 17.18, 24; 2 Kings 4.7–41). This term is not used of Moses elsewhere in Deut. **2:** *The LORD came from Sinai; He shone:* God's departure from His distant mountain stronghold, dramatically coming to the rescue of His people, closely follows the model of Judg. 5.4; Hab. 3.3. *Sinai … Seir:* The geography intended by the parallelism is anomalous. Normally Sinai is located in the Sinai Peninsula, south of Israel, while Seir, associated with Edom (Judg. 5.4), lies in the east, in southern Transjordan. *And approached from Ribeboth-kodesh:* The place name is otherwise unknown; and the alternative in translators' note *a,* "-kadesh," has no connection to God's theophany. The Heb can also be understood (with LXX, Samaritan Pentateuch; cf. NRSV) as "with Him were thousands of holy ones," i.e., the divine council who accompany God into battle (32.8 n.; Pss. 68.18; 89.8). This alternative translation, which only changes the vowels of one word in the MT, (from *approached* to "with Him,") is to be preferred since it preserves the poem's representation of God as Divine Warrior (see 33.1–29 n.). God similarly ventures forth from Sinai, at the head of a divine host of "thousands upon thousands," to appear in theophany in Ps. 68.18. **3:** *Their hallowed,* originally, the divine council. The poem's editors seem to have shifted it to refer to Israel (7.6; 14.2, 21; 26.19; 28.9; Lev. 19.2; Num. 16.3) to permit a transition to v. 4. **4:** *Moses charged us:* Since Moses is himself the speaker (v. 1), the change of perspective is disruptive and suggests that the v. was inserted so as to present the promulgation of the Mosaic Torah as the climax of the Divine Warrior's theophany! (See 33.1–29 n.) **5:** *Then He became King:* Although the subject is not specified, it almost certainly refers to God as Divine King of Israel (Exod. 15.18; Num. 23.21; Judg. 8.22–23; 1 Sam. 8.7; Isa. 33.22; Ps. 29.10), as reflected in NJPS's capitalized pronoun. The idea of God's kingship is central to the Bible, but is rarely explicit in the Torah (see Exod. 15.18 n.). *Jeshurun,* see 32.15 n.

6 May Reuben live and not die,
Though few be his numbers.

7 And this he said of Judah:
Hear, O LORD the voice of Judah
And restore him to his people.
[a-]Though his own hands strive for him,[-a]
Help him against his foes.

8 And of Levi he said:
Let Your Thummim and Urim
Be with Your faithful one,
Whom You tested at Massah,
Challenged at the waters of Meribah;
9 Who said of his father and mother,
"I consider them not."
His brothers he disregarded,
Ignored his own children.
Your precepts alone they observed,
And kept Your covenant.
10 They shall teach Your laws to Jacob
And Your instructions to Israel.
[b-]They shall offer You incense to savor[-b]
And whole-offerings on Your altar.
11 Bless, O LORD, his substance,
And favor his undertakings.
Smite the loins of his foes;
Let his enemies rise no more.

12 Of Benjamin he said:
Beloved of the LORD,
He rests securely beside Him;
Ever does He protect him,
[c-]As he rests between His shoulders.[-c]

13 And of Joseph he said:
Blessed of the LORD be his land
With the bounty of dew[d] from heaven,
And of the deep that couches below;
14 With the bounteous yield of the sun,
And the bounteous crop of the moons;
15 With the best from the ancient mountains,

6: *Reuben,* who once had the leadership of the first-born (see Gen. 49.3–4), is apparently threatened with extinction, owing to military pressures in Transjordan. (Simeon, Jacob's second-born, is missing from the list entirely.) **7:** *Judah,* in sore trouble because of an unnamed adversary (perhaps the Philistines), should be helped by other tribes. This depiction contrasts sharply with Gen. 49.8–12. **8–11:** *Levi,* once a warlike tribe (Gen. 49.5–7), is to receive the prerogatives of the priesthood: to teach *law,* or Torah (v. 10), and to officiate at the altar. **8:** *Thummim and Urim,* the priestly divination devices (see Exod. 28.30 and n.; Ezra 2.63). *Massah* and *Meribah,* see Exod. 17.1–7; Num. 20.2–13. **9:** On Levi's zealous loyalty to the covenant, at the expense of *father and mother ... brothers ... his own children,* thus complying with 13.7, see Exod. 32.25–29. **13–17:** See Gen. 49.25–26.

a-a Better (vocalizing rab *with* pathaḥ) *"Make his hands strong for him."* *Cf.* rabbeh, *Judg.* 9.29.

b-b Lit. "They shall place incense in Your nostril."

c-c Or "He dwells amid his slopes."

d Targum Onkelos and two Hebrew manuscripts read: "With the bounty of heaven above" (meʿal *for* miṭṭal, *cf. Gen.* 49.25).

16–17: By ascribing primacy of rule and the status of *firstling* to Joseph, this blessing conflicts with the law affirming the norm of primogeniture (21.15–17). **16:** *Presence in the Bush* refers to Exod. 3.1–6. *Elect* goes back to a time when Joseph (the Northern Kingdom, destroyed in 722 BCE) enjoyed greater prestige than Judah (v. 7). **17:** *Ephraim* and *Manasseh,* the two tribes making up "the house of Joseph" (Gen. 48.13–14). **18–19:** *Zebulun* and *Issachar* will enjoy great influence owing to the resources of the Mediterranean and Sea of Chinnereth, later known as the Sea of Galilee (Gen. 49.13). **20–21:** *Gad* occupied the *best* tableland in Transjordan but aided the other tribes in the occupation of Canaan (Num. ch 32). **22:** *Dan,* vigorous as a *lion's whelp,* must here already have migrated from its original tribal allotment on the coastal plain, adjacent to the Philistine pentapolis, to the far north, at the base of Mount Hermon (Judg. ch 18). *Bashan,* in northern Transjordan. **23:** *Naphtali,* located in the region of the Sea of Galilee and the Ginnesar (Chinnereth) plain, *west* and *south* of Dan. **24–25:** *Asher,* located below Phoenicia, is to be strong and prosperous.

And the bounty of hills immemorial;
16 With the bounty of earth and its fullness,
And the favor of the Presence[a] in the Bush.
May these rest on the head of Joseph,
On the crown of the elect of his brothers.
17 Like a firstling bull in his majesty,
He has horns like the horns of the wild-ox;
With them he gores the peoples,
The ends of the earth one and all.
These[b] are the myriads of Ephraim,
Those[c] are the thousands of Manasseh.

18 And of Zebulun he said:
Rejoice, O Zebulun, on your journeys,
And Issachar, in your tents.
19 They invite their kin to the mountain,
Where they offer sacrifices of success.
For they draw from the riches of the sea
And the hidden hoards of the sand.

20 And of Gad he said:
Blessed be He who enlarges Gad!
Poised is he like a lion
To tear off arm and scalp.
21 [d-]He chose for himself the best,
For there is the portion of the revered chieftain,
Where the heads of the people come.
He executed the LORD's judgments
And His decisions for Israel.[-d]

22 And of Dan he said:
Dan is a lion's whelp
That leaps forth from Bashan.

23 And of Naphtali he said:
O Naphtali, sated with favor
And full of the LORD's blessing,
Take possession on the west and south.

24 And of Asher he said:
Most blessed of sons be Asher;
May he be the favorite of his brothers,
May he dip his foot in oil.

a Lit. "Dweller"; cf. Exod. 3.1 ff.
b I.e., the one horn. *c I.e., the other horn.*
d-d Meaning of Heb. uncertain; cf. vv. 3–5 (with note c) above, and saphun *"esteemed" in post-biblical Heb.*

25[a] May your doorbolts be iron and copper,
And your security last all your days.

26 O Jeshurun, there is none like God,
Riding through the heavens to help you,
Through the skies in His majesty.
27[a] The ancient God is a refuge,
A support are the arms everlasting.
He drove out the enemy before you
By His command: Destroy!
28 Thus Israel dwells in safety,
Untroubled is Jacob's abode,[b]
In a land of grain and wine,
Under heavens dripping dew.
29 O happy Israel! Who is like you,
A people delivered by the LORD,
Your protecting Shield, your Sword triumphant!
Your enemies shall come cringing before you,
And you shall tread on their backs.

34 Moses went up from the steppes of Moab to Mount
Nebo, to the summit of Pisgah, opposite Jericho, and
the LORD showed him the whole land: Gilead as far as Dan;
2 all Naphtali; the land of Ephraim and Manasseh; the whole
land of Judah as far as the Western[c] Sea; 3 the Negeb; and the
Plain—the Valley of Jericho, the city of palm trees—as far as
Zoar. 4 And the LORD said to him, "This is the land of which
I swore to Abraham, Isaac, and Jacob, 'I will assign it to your
offspring.' I have let you see it with your own eyes, but you shall
not cross there."
5 So Moses the servant of the LORD died there, in the land
of Moab, at the command of the LORD. 6 He buried him in the

a *Meaning of Heb. uncertain.* b *Others "fountain."*
c *I.e., Mediterranean; cf. note at 11.24.*

26–29: The resumption of the hymn to the Divine Warrior (vv. 2–5) and a return to the focus upon *Jeshurun* (v. 26), meaning all *Israel* (v. 28). **26:** Much like the Canaanite storm god Ba'al (see, e.g., the battle with Sea in the Baal cycle [Hallo and Younger, *Context of Scripture,* vol. 1, p. 248]), Israel's Divine Warrior is represented as riding upon the clouds (Isa. 19.1; Pss. 18.10; 68.33). **27:** As translators' note *a* indicates, the Heb is difficult. NJPS's translation, although plausible, seems inconsistent with the emphasis of v. 26 upon God as Divine Warrior. On that basis, the alternate reconstruction of the Heb by the NRSV seems more appropriate: "He subdues the ancient gods, / shatters the forces of old; / he drove out the enemy before you, / and said, 'Destroy!' " **28:** As in the Ugaritic epic, the theophany of the Divine Warrior and His proclamation as King results in the fertility of the land. **29:** *Tread on their backs,* the standard biblical and Near Eastern symbol of military triumph (Josh. 10.24; Ps. 110.1; also illustrated in Neo-Assyrian reliefs).

34.1–12: The death of Moses. After the insertion of the Song of Moses (ch 32) and the Blessing of Moses (ch 33), the ch directly continues the narrative concerning the death of Moses and the transfer of leadership to Joshua, his successor (ch 31). At another level, however, the ch also directly continues the narrative thread of Num. ch 27, where God had commanded Moses to "ascend these heights" to survey the promised land before his death, and to "lay your hand" upon Joshua, to transfer the mantle of authority to him (vv. 12, 18). The belated resumption of that narrative, with its two themes of Mosaic death and succession, forms a literary bracket around the book of Deut., suggesting that editors interrupted an earlier form of the narrative in order to work Deut. into the Torah. **1:** *Went up,* responding to the command of 32.49; Num. 27.12. The v. joins two different traditions about the site of Moses' death: *Mount Nebo,* in Transjordan, east of Jericho; and *the summit of Pisgah,* which is slightly to its west, and unmentioned in 32.49. To preserve both traditions, the editor presents them as if they were the same. **2–3:** The lofty vantage point allows Moses to look northward to the Sea of Galilee (area of the tribal allotment of Dan and *Naphtali*), to the *Western Sea* (the Mediterranean), south to the *Negeb* desert and along the Jordan rift valley as far south as *Zoar* (once located at the southern end of the Dead Sea as one of the "cities of the Plain" and thus likely destroyed according to biblical tradition; Gen. 14.2, 8; 19.29). **5:** *At the command of the LORD,* see 32.50 n. The unusual formulation greatly honors Moses, who, despite advanced age, does not die of old age nor succumb to physical or intellectual infirmity. **6:** *He buried him:* The clear indication is that God Himself buried Moses, as He Himself sealed Noah into the ark (Gen. 7.16). Instead of Moses' progeny assuming the important legal responsibility of caring for the dead, God undertook it personally. This divine care fits the image of Moses in Deut.

valley in the land of Moab, near Beth-peor; and no one knows
his burial place to this day.
7 Moses was a hundred and twenty
years old when he died; his eyes were undimmed and his vigor
unabated.
8 And the Israelites bewailed Moses in the steppes of
Moab for thirty days.

The period of wailing and mourning for Moses came to an
end.
9 Now Joshua son of Nun was filled with the spirit of wisdom because Moses had laid his hands upon him; and the
Israelites heeded him, doing as the LORD had commanded
Moses.

10 Never again did there arise in Israel a prophet like Moses—whom the LORD singled out, face to face,
11 for the vari-
ous signs and portents that the LORD sent him to display in
the land of Egypt, against Pharaoh and all his courtiers and
his whole country,
12 and for all the great might and awesome
power that Moses displayed before all Israel.

Beth-peor, see 3.29; 4.46; Josh. 13.20. *No one knows his burial place,* thus precluding pilgrimages to the site as a shrine. **7:** *A hundred and twenty,* see 31.2 n. **8:** *Thirty days,* so also for Aaron (Num. 20.29). Israel mourns the loss of Moses for the full mourning period stipulated for a parent (21.13). **9:** *Joshua ... was filled with the spirit of wisdom:* As at 1.13 and 16.18–20, Deut. revises earlier traditions to stress wisdom as the essential qualification of office, and thus what Joshua receives from Moses. Num. 27.18 depicts Joshua as already "an inspired man" (often associated with prophecy or possession), while Moses was to transfer his "authority" to him. Here "the spirit of wisdom" is what Joshua receives from Moses. *Because Moses had laid his hands upon him,* as at Num. 27.22–23, a means of transfer of attributes (Lev. 16.21; Num. 8.10–13), here used for investiture into office. **10–12:** An editor eulogizes Moses as marking the pinnacle of prophecy, both because of his direct access to divine revelation and his power to work miracles. This double elevation of Moses to an ideal standard differs from his more human representation elsewhere in the book. The contrast between the two suggests that an editor's later, idealizing retrospective operates here, as Deut. is now worked into the Torah. **10:** *Never again:* Note the tension between the perspective of this v. and the divine promise to Moses that the line of prophetic succession will continue in the future: "I will raise up a prophet for them ... like yourself" (18.18). *Face to face,* rather than through dreams or visions (13.2); similarly, Exod. 33.11; Num. 12.8–10. Other traditions reject that Moses had such direct access to God (Exod. 33.20–23).

נביאים

NEVI'IM

Terminology and Content

ACCORDING TO JEWISH TRADITION, the second canonical division, Nevi'im or Prophets, is comprised of the eight books Joshua, Judges, Samuel, Kings, Isaiah, Jeremiah, Ezekiel, and the Twelve Minor (in the sense of short) Prophets. (In the Christian tradition, the Historical Books and the Prophetic Books are two separate groupings, with Joshua, Judges, Samuel, and Kings in the first and the other prophetic books, including Daniel, in the second. Jewish tradition locates Daniel in Writings. Samuel and Kings, which are now each divided into two books, are each considered as a single book in Jewish tradition, though the NJPS translation follows the practice, first found in the Septuagint (LXX), of dividing these long books in two. In the classical rabbinic period, the eight books in Nevi'im were seen as a single unit; in the medieval period, these books were divided in half thematically, with Joshua through Kings called the former prophets *(nevi'im rishonim),* and Isaiah through the Twelve called the latter prophets *(nevi'im 'aḥaronim).* The terms "former" and "latter" refer to the placement of these collections within Nevi'im rather than to the chronological order of the events they recount, since, for example, some of the events narrated in Kings, the fourth book of Nevi'im, transpire later than the period of some of the Twelve Minor Prophets.

It is likely that these eight books came to be seen as authoritative after the Torah had taken shape, and that at some point an early canon (or established collection) was comprised of Torah plus Nevi'im (see "Canonization," pp. 2153–58). It is not clear why the first four books were called "prophets" and how they became part of a larger collection called Nevi'im. Perhaps, the name Nevi'im reflects an awareness that prophets and prophetic activity play important roles in each of the first four books as well. In the book of Joshua, Joshua is depicted as the prophetic successor to Moses (see esp. ch 1); in Judges oracles are often consulted (e.g., 1.1; 20.18) and a prophet is mentioned in 6.8; Samuel the prophet is a central figure of the book that bears his name; and Elijah, Elisha, and several other named and unnamed prophets figure prominently in Kings; in fact, no king or dynasty arises without the approval of a prophet. Stated differently, Joshua through Kings might be categorized as historical books according to their genre, and are so placed in non-Jewish Bibles, which follow the order of the LXX (see the chart "Canons of the Bible" on p. 2155). The inclusion of these four books in Nevi'im reflects an ancient tradition that reflects the history of canonization rather than a thematic or generic arrangement of the books. It is thus appropriate to treat each section of Nevi'im separately in this introduction.

The Former Prophets and Historiography

THE BOOKS OF JOSHUA THROUGH KINGS are in narrative prose, in contrast to the other prophetic books (except Jonah), which consist largely of poetic speeches. The prose narratives are often categorized as historical texts. Yet the idea that historical writing should capture the events "as they really were," that historians should attempt to write an objective account of the events of the past, is a relatively recent notion which developed in European universities in the 19th c. Before that, history was typically didactic in nature, teaching the readers how to be good citizens or how to lead proper religious lives. Sometimes histories were produced in the royal court, in which case they were apologetic, showing how the king fulfilled his royal duties. Surviving historical documents from the ancient Near East show similar religious and ideological goals. Biblical writers, like their ancient Near Eastern contemporaries, were not primarily interested in the accurate recording of real events; rather, they used narratives set in the past to illustrate various issues of significance to their earliest audience, the ancient Israelite community.

It is easiest to understand the biblical notion of history by first focusing on an earlier work, Exod. ch 13. Verse 3 begins: "And Moses said to the people, 'Remember this day, on which you went free from Egypt, the house of bondage.' " This would seem to suggest the importance of history for its own sake. This unit continues, however, with a set of commandments that directly result from this event: "No leavened bread shall be eaten" (v. 3); "seven days you shall eat unleavened bread, and on the seventh day there shall be a festival of the LORD" (v. 6); "no leavened bread shall be found with you, and no leaven shall be found in all your territory" (v. 7); "And you shall explain to your son on that day ..." (v. 8); "and this shall serve you as a sign on your hand and as a reminder on your forehead" (v. 9); "you shall set apart for the LORD every first issue of the womb: every male firstling that your cattle drop shall be the LORD's" (v. 12). Taken as a whole, this passage indicates that the exodus is not significant as a disembodied historical event, as the beginning of v. 3 might suggest; rather, the exodus is a key occurrence because it serves as the basis for the observance of a central set of laws or norms.

The use of historical material in Psalms is even more instructive, since there these traditions about the past are typically surrounded by a framework which explicitly highlights their theological significance or purpose. For example, in Ps. 78, a particular set of traditions is chosen and shaped so:

> that a future generation might know
> —children yet to be born—
> and in turn tell their children
> that they might put their confidence in God,
> and not forget God's great deeds,
> but observe His commandments,
> and not be like their fathers,
> a wayward and defiant generation,
> a generation whose heart was inconstant,
> whose spirit was not true to God. (vv. 6–8)

Ps. 106 tells how God saved Israel time after time, despite their covenant violations. This is used as an argument to God that they should be rescued again:

> Deliver us, O LORD our God,
> and gather us from among the nations,
> to acclaim Your holy name,
> to glory in Your praise. (v. 47)

Unfortunately, the material collected in Joshua through Kings is not as explicit about its purposes as these psalms or Exodus; for this reason, these books require internal analysis, in order to see what motivations and interests best explain their shape.

The Former Prophets and the Deuteronomistic History

NOT ONLY ARE JOSHUA THROUGH KINGS separated from the other prophetic books that follow on the basis of content, but Joshua, Judges, Samuel, and Kings, along with the preceding book of Deuteronomy, fit so well together that it is likely that at some point these five books were edited together as a single work. Scholars call this hypothetical work the Deuteronomistic History, meaning the history written or edited under the influence of ideas found in the book of Deuteronomy. This theory has much to commend it: These five books do read as a unified whole from a chronological perspective, narrating a continuous history from the end of the life of Moses to beyond the Babylonian exile (586 BCE), and they share many phrases and ideas, such as an insistence on exclusive worship of God and the catastrophic consequences of idolatry, a concern with the centrality of Jerusalem, and a belief in the permanence of the Davidic dynasty. If this theory is correct, the size of the Deuteronomistic History, and the long period that it depicts, is quite remarkable, especially for an ancient historical work.

Many details of this theory remain debated; some scholars suggest that these books are not quite unified enough to represent the product of a single individual, intellectual school, or movement. For example, the book of Samuel has remarkably few echoes of the language of Deuteronomy, and the book of Kings contains narratives in which the great prophets Elijah and Elisha are legitimately active outside of the Jerusalem Temple (see esp. Elijah on Mt. Carmel, 1 Kings ch 18). There is some tension about whether the promise of an eternal dynasty to David is unconditional or conditional. Scholars have thus suggested various theories concerning successive editions of the Deuteronomistic History, which many believe was begun in the 7th c. under the Judean King Josiah (640–609 BCE), but was completed only in the Babylonian exile (586–538 BCE) or later. Some suggest that the lack of unity is due to non-Deuteronomistic material that has been added at a late stage to an earlier Deuteronomistic History. There have also been attempts to isolate narratives which might have preceded the Deuteronomistic History and other sources used by the Deuteronomist(s), and to discern their original purposes before these narratives and sources became integrated into the larger literary work. In sum, this collection has a long and complicated history, so it is impossible to speak of a totally unified purpose or interest in the compilation of the books of Joshua, Judges, Samuel, and Kings. These four books were not written by a single author, and reflect many different interests and stages of development: pre-Deuteronomic, Deuteronomistic, and later, postexilic concerns. The interests of the individual books are thus discussed in the introduction at the beginning of each book.

The Former Prophets and the History of Israel

THE PROBLEMATIC NATURE OF THESE BOOKS as historical documents does not mean that they are entirely useless as historical sources. Each unit needs to be weighed individually in terms of its date of composition and its likely goals. Using these criteria, there are reasons to accept the veracity of, for example, the dry notice in 1 Kings 14.25–26 ("In the fifth year of King Rehoboam, King Shishak of Egypt marched against Jerusalem and carried off the treasures of the House of the LORD and the treasures of the royal palace. He carried off everything; he even carried off all the golden shields that Solomon had made"), which might even come from an archival source, and has some confirmation from Egyptian sources. In contrast, we should be suspicious of the historicity of the long, detailed, and embellished story of David slaying Goliath in 1 Sam. ch 17; this story uses late biblical Hebrew language, comes from a different source than the surrounding material in Samuel, and is structured like a fairy-tale, in that the poor, short, unlikely hero gets to marry the tall king's daughter by killing the giant who had vilified God. Additionally, 2 Sam. 21.19 reads: "Again there was fighting with the Philistines at Gob; and Elhanan son of Jaare-oregim the Bethlehemite killed Goliath the Gittite, whose spear had a shaft like a weaver's bar." It is much more likely that a short tradition in which Goliath is killed by a relatively unknown figure (Elhanan) would be the source for the long, elaborate tale attributing the same event to the well-known David, rather than vice versa. Thus, the modern historian must subject each text in the Former Prophets to the type of analysis used on ancient nonbiblical historical texts when external information bearing on the text is lacking.

There are a number of cases where we do have external, ancient Near Eastern written evidence that deals with events depicted in the Former Prophets. For example, the events surrounding the siege of Jerusalem by the Assyrian King Sennacherib in 701 BCE are narrated in several Assyrian sources, and are also depicted in the palace reliefs of that king, now found in the British Museum. These sources suggest that part of the terse account in 2 Kings 18.13–16 is quite accurate, while the highly developed continuation of the story in chs 19 and 20, especially the note in 19.35, that the angel of the LORD killed 185,000 Assyrian soldiers in a single night, is imaginative. Similarly, from various Mesopotamian sources, we know of a "house of Omri"; Omri's name is also mentioned on the Moabite Mesha Stele. This confirms the existence of the Northern (Israelite) king mentioned in 1 Kings 16.23–28. Kings, however, tells little of his achievements during his twelve years as monarch, other than his building of Samaria and the notice that: "Omri did what was displeasing to the LORD; he was worse than all who preceded him. He followed all the ways of Jeroboam son of Nebat and the sins which he committed and caused Israel to commit, vexing the LORD, the God of Israel, with their futilities" (vv. 25–26). The external sources, however, suggest that Omri was a powerful king who established a significant name for himself through his military activities. This highlights the extreme selectivity of the biblical sources.

Archeological evidence confirms the picture suggested above: There may be some truth (or a kernel of truth) to some of the biblical stories, but in their current form, they often lack historical veracity, because that is not their prime concern. Recent decades, for example, have seen a remarkable reevaluation of the evidence concerning the conquest of the land of Canaan by Joshua. As more sites have been excavated, there has been a growing consensus that the main story of Joshua, that of a speedy and complete conquest (e.g., Josh. 11.23: "Thus Joshua conquered the whole country, just as the LORD had promised Moses") is contradicted by the archeological record, though there are indications of *some* destruction and conquest at the appropriate time. Various events and traditions have been reworked very substantially over time and ultimately included in the Bible in order to substantiate a particular picture of God.

In sum, though Joshua through Kings are often viewed as early historical texts, they should not be viewed as historical in the contemporary sense as accurately depicting the real past. Many of these texts do contain the raw materials for the reconstruction of the history of ancient Israel from the time of the conquest through the 6th c. BCE or later, but this material can only be teased out using sophisticated and complex tools. Not only did these accounts have their own agendas that were not necessarily invested in historical accuracy, but these accounts did not remain stagnant; they were changed by later tradents, authors and editors, who revised them in accordance with their own beliefs and purposes. It is these religious and religio-political perspectives that we must try to appreciate as we study these books; if we read them as we read modern historical accounts, we will misunderstand these texts in the most fundamental way. Thus, given that prophets frequently are depicted as the vehicles of religious and religio-political perspectives, "the former prophets" is a suitable name for the first part of this collection.

The Latter Prophets and Their Order

THE BOOKS OF ISAIAH, JEREMIAH, EZEKIEL, AND THE TWELVE are fundamentally different from the previous four books: With the exception of Jonah in the Twelve, they all contain collections of oracles (prophetic speeches, generally in poetic form) attributed to various prophets. In contrast with the prophets described in the Former Prophets, whose mission was largely directed to individuals in private audiences, mostly to kings, and whose prestige was often established through performing unusual ("magical") actions (see esp. Elijah and Elisha, 1 Kings chs 17–19, 21; 2 Kings chs 1–9), these books suggest that prophets such as Isaiah or Amos spoke the divine word in elevated rhetorical speeches at public settings, where the people, as well as their leaders, would hear them.

There is some variation in the ordering of these four latter prophetic books. The typical manuscript order of the first three, Isaiah, Jeremiah, Ezekiel, reflects chronological ordering. (First) Isaiah was active mostly in the later 8th c., Jeremiah prophesied in the late 7th through the early 6th c., while Ezekiel spoke in the Babylonian exile in the 6th c. The Twelve is then placed last as reflecting prophets working in diverse time periods; the latest prophets (Haggai, Zechariah, Malachi) are later than Ezekiel, reflecting the return from exile. A different order is noted in the Babylonian Talmud (*b. B. Bat.* 14b): Jeremiah, Ezekiel, Isaiah, the Twelve. This is explained in terms of thematic continuity: The pessimistic Jeremiah follows the destruction noted at the end of Kings, and this is followed by Ezekiel, which opens with destruction and finishes with consolation.

The Nature and Composition of the Prophetic Books

THE PROPHETIC BOOKS ARE UNUSUAL and complex compositions. While the books in places preserve authentic words of the prophets in question, we should not think of them simply as transcriptions of the words of prophets. Although much remains unknown about the composition of these books, it is possible to reconstruct a general picture. Scholars generally agree that some of the poetic materials of most of the prophetic books originated as oral pronouncements by the prophet to a public audience. These oral sayings were subsequently written down, perhaps by the prophet or a disciple. Various circumstances led to the compilation of these original written collections. A reference in Isaiah suggests that oracles might be written down as a form of authentication (Isa. 30.8). The book of Jeremiah describes a situation in which Jeremiah, having been banned from speaking publicly in the Temple, had his assistant Baruch write down a selection of his prophetic words so that they could be taken into the Temple and read to the people (Jer. 36.5–6). When King Jehoiakim destroyed the scroll, Jeremiah had Baruch write out another copy, to which they added additional material (Jer. 36.27–32). This collection may have formed the nucleus of the book of Jeremiah. (Unlike most of the other prophetic books, Ezekiel may have been composed as a written document from the beginning.) It is unclear if what was written was identical to what the prophet recited, or if the prophet or his disciples even at this earliest stage introduced changes, reflecting the difference between the oral form of a publicly recited oracle versus the written form of a scroll.

Once small collections of prophetic oracles and pronouncements were made, they were subject to further editing, rearranging, annotating, and expansion. Like other biblical texts, these prophetic works did not fossilize. In some cases narratives about the prophet were added; these are presented both as autobiographical (e.g., Isa. chs 6, 8; Jer. 1.4–19; 13.1–11; Hos. chs 1–2; Amos 7.1–7) and biographical (e.g., Isa. chs 7, 36–39; Jer. chs 26, 36–44; Hos. ch 3; Amos 7.10–17). The occasions for such editorial activity will have differed, but national crises may have prompted some of this process. Most likely, written collections of the oracles of Amos and Hosea, which were originally addressed to the Northern Kingdom (Israel) were brought to Judah after the fall of the Northern Kingdom in 722 BCE, and edited and circulated, and eventually expanded there (see Amos 1.1, 2 nn.). Isaiah of Jerusalem seems to have knowledge of Amos's oracles, and Jeremiah is unquestionably influenced by Hosea. Many of the prophetic books originating before the fall of Judah to the Babylonians in 586 BCE show evidence of editorial additions and reorganizations that reflect the circumstances of exilic and postexilic times. The book of Amos, for example, now includes material that presupposes the fall of Judah (9.11–15). The most extensive example of the expansion and reworking of prophetic materials is the book of Isaiah. Although it contains extensive material from the 8th-century prophet, chs 40–66 clearly reflect the situation of the Babylonian exile and the subsequent period of the restoration of the Judean community after the exile. Yet even though the book contains materials dating from several centuries, it is unified by a number of motifs, themes, and topics that recur throughout the work.

The complex activity of preserving and developing the prophetic oracle collections reflects a conviction that a prophet's words were not only significant for the circumstance in which they were originally pronounced but potentially relevant for later ones as well. (This notion, which became more significant in the exilic and postexilic period, is very well established in the Dead Sea Scrolls and in later early Christian and rabbinic literature.) At the same time, the freedom with which later generations could rework the prophetic oracles indicates that the prophets' words did not at first possess the kind of fixed authority that is later associated with canonical Scripture. Although the processes by which the prophetic books came to assume a relatively final form and canonical status are difficult to trace, this probably occurred during the Persian and early Hellenistic periods (the 5th through the 3rd centuries BCE). Most likely, during this time scribal editors added the superscriptions that introduce most of the books, indicating the identity of the prophet (name, father's name, and occasionally other information) and often the kings of Israel or Judah during whose reigns the prophets were active (e.g., Isa. 1.1; Jer. 1.1–3; Hos. 1.1). In addition to editorial additions to the individual prophetic books, the smaller prophetic books (Hosea through Malachi) were arranged and edited to form a group known as "the book of the Twelve," which was copied on a single scroll. By the beginning of the 2nd c. BCE Ben Sirach refers to these prophets as "the twelve" (Sir. 49.10). The number twelve is symbolic of the twelve sons of Jacob and the twelve tribes of Israel, and considerable editorial work was required to organize these prophetic materials into a grouping of twelve; for example, the book of Zechariah consists of three separate collections (chs 1–8, 9–11, 12–14) grouped together editorially. Only the first of these comes from the prophet Zechariah, whereas the other two are anonymous. The final book in the collection, Malachi, is also an anonymous piece, since "Malachi" is not a personal name but a phrase meaning "my messenger," picked up from 3.1 to serve as the name of the prophet in the superscription.

The Phenomenon of Prophecy

THE PHENOMENON OF PROPHECY was known in the ancient Near East, and many important themes and genres familiar from biblical prophecy have parallels there. It should be viewed as part of a larger belief in that area that the deity's will is accessible in the world, either through omen interpretation, as was typical in Mesopotamia, or through prophecy, the preferred method in Israel.

Contrary to popular perception, the prophets were not predominantly forecasters of the future, ancient fortune-tellers. Rather, they were intermediaries between God and the people, spokesmen, and had a crucial role in critiquing and trying to change society to bring it in line with God's commandments. Predictions of doom and destruction were intended to get Israel to repent and change its behavior. But when it seemed that Israel had gone too far, and must be punished (see esp. Jer. ch 25), the main role of the prophet was to assure the nation that their punishment, which derived from God, was deserved.

Since in the canon the prophets follow the Torah, Jewish tradition typically reads the prophets as interpreters of the Torah, whose role was to make sure that the people adhered to the Torah. Protestant tradition, on the other hand, often emphasized the apparently antinomian tendencies in such prophecies as Isa. 1.10–20 or Amos 5.21–25. Neither of these views is correct from a scholarly perspective. Critical biblical scholarship has ascertained that the Torah and Prophets developed simultaneously from a chronological perspective; thus, not all prophets knew all the Torah since the Torah had not yet been completed by the time that most of the prophets were active. The Protestant view is problematic because it ignores the fact that certain prophetic oracles are very interested in punctilious performance of particular ritual laws (see esp. Jer. 17.19–27). Furthermore, a close reading of prophets such as Isaiah or Amos suggests that they are not anti-law or anti-Temple, but are rhetorically emphasizing that ritual behavior alone, without proper moral behavior, is insufficient to assure divine blessing.

Many more prophets were active in ancient Israel and Judah than those whose work is represented in the prophetic books of the Bible, and their activities were more varied than these writings suggest. The books of Samuel and Kings provide important additional information. Since our sources are limited, it is difficult to reconstruct the history of prophecy. Some of the features are clear, however. The prophet was essentially an intermediary between God and the people, and one of the major functions was that of messenger (Heb *mal'akh*). Often prophets introduced their communications with a version of the formula typically used by messengers, "thus says the LORD." But prophets might also carry inquiries from the people to God or make intercession on behalf of the people. In contrast to the priesthood, which was exclusively male, both women and men could be prophets. Women prophets included Deborah (Judg. 4.4) and Huldah (2 Kings 22.14); see also Joel 3.1. Additional aspects of the prophetic role are suggested by the various terms used to identify them. In addition to "prophet" (Heb *navi'*, perhaps meaning "one who is called"), the prophets are identified as seers (Heb *ro'eh*), visionaries (Heb *ḥozeh*), and holy men (Heb *'ish 'elohim,* lit. "man of God"). It is uncertain if these different titles reflect different types of prophets.

The religious phenomenon of Israelite prophecy can be traced for more than a thousand years, from the premonarchical period to the turn of the era. Over such a long period of time the nature and function of prophecy altered in response to changing historical, social, and religious circumstances. One may divide the development of prophecy loosely into four periods, although this division is not absolute : the early monarchical period (11th through 9th centuries), the Assyrian crisis (8th c.), the Babylonian crisis (late 7th through early 6th centuries), and the postexilic restoration (mid-6th through mid-5th centuries).

In the earliest period prophets may have been local or itinerant men and women who were revered for their special religious powers and who might be consulted on a variety of private matters, from locating lost property (1 Sam. 9.1–10) to learning whether a sick child would live or die (1 Kings 14.1–18). Some lived in prophetic communities which cultivated ecstatic forms of religious experience (1 Sam. 19.18–24; 2 Kings 6.1–7); these are called "sons of (the) prophets" in the sense of members of prophetic guilds. Prophets also had the public function of declaring God's will concerning whether the people should go to war (Judg. 4.4–10). The emergence of the monarchy in ancient Israel may have changed aspects of the prophets' role. Prophets appear as king-makers and king-breakers, as they announce that God has designated an individual to become king or has rejected a reigning king (1 Sam. 10.1; 15.23; 1 Kings 11.29–39; 14.1–18). Though prophets continued their role in advising about matters of war (1 Kings ch 22), they also served as critics of the king in religious and social affairs. The consolidation of royal power and the foreign religious practices introduced through royal marriages often threatened older tribal institutions and values. The conflict between Elijah, the prophet, and Ahab and Jezebel, the king and queen, illustrates these tensions between prophet and king (1 Kings chs 18–21).

Prophecy appears to have undergone a dramatic change during the 8th c., although this impression may be affected by the change in the nature of the sources of information. From the 8th c. onward collections of prophetic oracles are preserved, yet, with the exception of Jeremiah, few extended narratives about prophets exist. It does appear, however, that in this period prophets began to function less as private counselors and critics of kings and more as public figures who influenced opinion through their pronouncements in the Temple courts and in other public places. Prophets of the 8th c. (Amos, Hosea, Isaiah, Micah) interpreted international affairs, critiqued complacent religious practices, and condemned the abuses of social justice that accompanied the increasing urbanization and centralization of state power characteristic of the 8th c. The prophetic careers of Hosea, Micah, and Isaiah took place in the shadow of the expansionist Assyrian empire, which eventually put an end to the Northern Kingdom of Israel and subjected Judah to the condition of vassalage. The prophets interpreted these events, however, in terms of the judgment of the LORD, not simply as the success of a powerful Assyrian empire. This perspective allowed Isaiah, for example, to anticipate the ultimate downfall of Assyria because of its overweening arrogance.

The third major period of prophecy occurred during the Babylonian crisis. The prophet Nahum celebrated the defeat of Assyria (612–609 BCE), but the excitement he expressed was soon turned to confusion as Babylonia succeeded Assyria as the dominant empire (see the intro. and nn. to Habakkuk and the essay "History of Israel," pp. 2107–19). Jeremiah's prophetic career (ca. 627–586 BCE) spanned the time from the decline of Assyria through the Babylonian overlordship of Judah, to the revolt and destruction of Judah and the exile of a portion of its population. Although it is difficult to correlate many of his poetic oracles with specific events in this period, the narratives about Jeremiah give a vivid picture of a nation and its leadership deeply conflicted about what political course to follow and the religious significance of the political choices that were forced upon it. Even the prophetic community was bitterly divided and gave contradictory advice to the king concerning the will of the LORD (Jer. chs 26–29, 36–44). Overlapping the career of Jeremiah, the prophet Ezekiel (active 593–ca. 571 BCE) was among the Judeans exiled to Babylonia after the revolt of 597 BCE, a decade before the final revolt and the destruction of Jerusalem. Ezekiel's prophetic work was, first, to persuade the exiled Judeans of the inevitability of Jerusalem's destruction, and to justify this event. Following the fall of the city, he began to articulate the theological grounds for conceiving a possible future, including a return of the exiles and a rebuilding of the destroyed Temple. In contrast to most of the prophets who preceded him, Ezekiel drew strongly on Priestly traditions for his categories of thought, forms of speech, and evocative symbols.

The defeat of the Babylonian empire by the Persian king Cyrus in 539 BCE altered political conditions dramatically. Although Judah did not regain its independence but became a part of the Persian empire, Cyrus and his successors authorized the rebuilding of the Temple and of Jerusalem, allowing members of the exiled community in Babylonia who so desired to return to Yehud, the name of the small Persian province that was formerly Judah. Thus the prophetic task during this period largely concerned the restoration of the community and its institutions in a context significantly different from that which prevailed during the Israelite and Judean monarchy. The anonymous prophet whose work is found in Isa. chs 40–55 (often called "Second Isaiah") addressed the Babylonian exiles just at the time that Cyrus was engaged in the conquest of Babylonia. Second Isaiah had to persuade the exilic community that unfolding events represented God's action in history, to interpret the significance of Cyrus (God's "anointed" who would rebuild Jerusalem [44.28–45.1]), and to encourage the exiles to return to Jerusalem. The process of rebuilding the Temple (520–515 BCE) provides the context for the prophets Haggai and Zechariah. Zechariah's work in particular suggests this was a time of expectation that perhaps the Davidic monarchy might be restored, an event that did not occur. Issues concerning reorganization of the Judean community and tensions regarding economic justice, institutional corruption, and the boundaries of the community are variously reflected in Zechariah, Isa. chs 56–66 (sometimes called Trito-Isaiah), and Malachi, prophets who were active in roughly the period 525–475 BCE.

Although prophets in all periods might speak of the dramatic intervention of God in historical events and the consequent transformation of the conditions of life, this type of language seems to have become more common and more vivid in the postexilic prophets (e.g., Isa. chs 56–66, Zechariah, Malachi, Joel, and postexilic additions to earlier prophetic books, such as Isa. chs 24–27). Some of the passages anticipate a war or other cataclysmic event of cosmic proportions that will precede a time of deliverance, peace, and virtual re-creation of the world, themes associated with apocalypticism. Such imagery and the expectations it expresses suggest to some scholars that apocalypticism emerges out of postexilic prophecy. Though it is true that apocalyptic literature is influenced by these prophetic writings and their imagery, apocalyptic cannot simply be understood as an outgrowth of the phenomenon of prophecy.

The book of Daniel, a prophetic book which is found in the Kethuvim (in Christian Bibles it is included among the prophets), is the only book in the Hebrew Bible that could be called an apocalypse. In the latter part of the book, Daniel is the recipient of visions which disclose the future. These vision reports do bear significant similarities to those found in Ezekiel and especially in Zechariah, though their almost allegorical style is quite different. Similarly, although general claims about God's foreknowledge of historical events can be found in Second Isaiah, Daniel's representation of history as predetermined both with respect to its epochal structure and its specific events is strikingly different from the representation of history by the prophets. A clue to the relationship of apocalyptic to prophecy may be found in Dan. ch 9, where Daniel is presented as studying the book of Jeremiah and receiving an angelic interpretation of its significance. As suggested by the representation of Daniel as a technically trained sage, the authors of apocalyptic books, many of which were produced in the Hellenistic period, were perhaps themselves learned scribes who studied and appropriated aspects of the prophetic tradition and combined them with other influences in their attempts to understand the nature of the cosmos and the course of history. The movement from receiving the prophetic word directly, as in the first three periods, to receiving it via an intermediary angel in the fourth period, and of understanding what God wants by studying earlier prophetic texts, would ultimately become responsible for the perception in the Second Temple period that prophecy as a living, core institution had died. With the canonization of God's revelation in the form of the written books of the Bible, new revelations through prophets became superfluous. Prophecy was gradually replaced by scriptural study and interpretation, and prophets by scribes, sages, and rabbis.

[MARC ZVI BRETTLER]

יהושע

Joshua

Introduction

THE BOOK OF JOSHUA, named for its main character, begins after the death of Moses and continues until the death and burial of Joshua. It recounts how the people of Israel entered the Land of Israel and settled it. Chapters 1–12 depict Israel's national beginnings as a story of newcomers clashing with a densely settled and fortified land, disinheriting the native Canaanites, and taking possession of their land through violent military attacks. Under the leadership of Joshua, a second Moses, Israel marched united, crossed the Jordan River in a ceremonial procession (chs 1–5), and set up camp in Gilgal. From there they embarked on a series of four strategic and representative military campaigns. The first two were mounted against fortified towns, Jericho in the east and Ai in the central area (chs 6–8); the two following campaigns were sweeping and "sudden" (10.9; 11.7) attacks against broad coalitions of kings of the southwest cities and of the northern area. The four victorious battles resulted in the complete conquest of the entire land and its population (11.17–19). Only when the land was emptied of its former inhabitants did the Israelites settle it (11.23). This settlement process, and the apportionment of the land among the tribes, is described in great detail (chs 13–21). The book closes with an epilogue—matters relating to the Transjordanian tribes (ch 22) and a set of speeches and ceremonies centered around Joshua (chs 23–24).

The story of the conquest in Joshua does not accord, either in its general outlook or its specific details, with the archeological data (see "Archeology," pp. 2124–36). These data suggest that instead of a violent entry into a populated land, the first Israelites settled a mostly empty part of the region, the central hill country. Archeology also contradicts the detailed stories of the conquest of the two cities, Jericho and Ai, which were apparently not inhabited during the Late Bronze Age. Some of the Late Bronze Canaanite centers, such as Hazor, did experience a violent destruction, though it is not certain who destroyed them. Some archeologists attribute the destruction to the Israelites; others point to the significant time gap separating the destruction from the subsequent Iron I settlement and conclude that there is no relation between the destroyers of Late Bronze Hazor and the settlers of the next phase. The current excavator of Hazor evaluates the destruction of Hazor at the first half of the 13th century BCE as the final phase of a long process of decline. The story of the conquest and settlement as it now appears in the book of Joshua is a literary, ideological construct, the result of many editions, revisions, and additions, reflecting changing concepts of the fulfillment of the divine promise of the land over a long period of time. See the introduction to Nevi'im, particularly the sections on "The Former Prophets and Historiography," (pp. 429–30) and "The Former Prophets and the History of Israel," (pp. 431–33). The book is best read as an ideological manifesto rather than as an attempt at accurate historiography.

Like much of the Former Prophets, concern for national and religious issues takes precedence over historicity. The book shows an overall concern with following God's teaching.

Institutions like circumcision and the Passover mark the entry to the land. The Ark of the Covenant, along with the priests, altars, and sacrifices, play a significant role, underlining the integral relationship between the sacral and the political in Israelite life. Frequent allusions to the language and themes of Deuteronomy reinforce the book's didactic intent, rather than its interest in the accurate recording of historical events. The book portrays the conquest of the promised land as a complete and outright victory directed by God, led by a Moses-like figure, and accomplished by a people who have sworn allegiance to God. The book of Joshua, indeed, carries forward the story and themes of the Torah.

Now part of the Deuteronomistic History (Deut.–2 Kings), the book, like many other biblical books, has a long and complicated literary history; it came into being over hundreds of years, in several subsequent editions. Its diverse materials are, in some cases, used for purposes other than those for which they were originally intended. The book depicts the fulfillment of the promise of inheriting the land in two distinct stages: conquest and settlement. First, in chs 1–12, the land was conquered in its entirety by the nation as a whole; scholars call this section "The Book of Conquest." Then, in chs 13–21, the land was divided and settled by the tribes, in what scholars label "The Book of Settlement." These were two distinct literary compositions that have been combined.

The detailed conquest stories revolve around sites in the territory of Benjamin (Gilgal, Jericho, Ai, Gibeon), and reflect a pro-northern Israelite viewpoint. These have been supplemented by summaries (10.40–42; 11.16–17) with a pro-Judahite tendency. The first written version of the story of the conquest (chs 6–11) was produced at the end of the 8th or early 7th century BCE in Judah. At that time, the country was under the control of the Assyrian empire. Through this story of Israel's epic entrance into the promised land, depicting Israel as a great victorious people with God on their side, the authors reversed roles with their Assyrian overlords: Israel was the mighty force, not Assyria. At the same time, the story reinforced their right to the land, based on divine grant and assistance.

The Book of Settlement (chs 13–21) includes a story of conquest (chs 14–17). Unlike in the Book of Conquest (chs 1–12), however, Joshua is not a military commander, but the national leader, in charge of the division of the land and its settlement. Shiloh, in the territory of Ephraim, Joshua's tribe, is central, and the role of the priest Eleazar, who is not mentioned in the Book of Conquest, is prominent. The importance of Shiloh, which has ties to the book of Jeremiah (Jer. 7.12–14; 26.9; cf. 41.5), points to Judah in the early 6th century BCE. The Book of Settlement made use of various preexistent administrative documents from the end of the 7th century (e.g., relating to taxation) that had nothing to do with the settlement and allocation of the land. The editor of this section added unifying opening and closing formulae for each tribal allotment. Josh. chs 13–21 and Judg. ch 1 agree that foreign enclaves were present in the midst of Israel; they both likely relied on a third source that depicted local clashes; remnants of such a source may be found in 1 Chron. 4.39–43; 5.7–17; 7.20–29.

A Priestly summary (19.51) concludes the entire settlement process; this is, supplemented by several episodes, mostly derived from Priestly circles, concerning the inheritance of the land (chs 20–21). Another, mostly Deuteronomistic summary in 21.41–43 concludes the settlement process, bringing to a close both parts of the process— conquest and settlement—presented as the fulfillment of the divine promise to the ancestors; here the people are called, uniquely, "the House of Israel," who have settled in the land and have "rest on all sides ... of all their enemies" (21.42), similar to Deut. 12.10. The final Deuteronomistic summary, all of ch 23, explains why worship was then not centralized, as demanded by Deut. 12.11–18, by acknowledging the threat to religious observance by the "remaining nations" in the land.

The initial chs and the final ch of Joshua reflect late stages of development. The book now opens with incidents relating to the entrance into the land (chs 1–5). The events reflect almost perfectly the acts of Moses in reverse order, and this organizing pattern superseded considerations of chronology and continuity. Chapters 3–4 and 5 display an amalgam of different traditions, some very late. The current structure of chs 1–5 belongs to the Persian period, when diverse materials from the Priestly and Deuteronomistic schools were woven together. Joshua ch 24, the final ch of the book, like the book's beginning, portrays Joshua as a second Moses, concluding a covenant, giving the people "law and rule," and writing it all in a book of divine instruction. The editing at the beginning and end of Joshua manifests a postexilic viewpoint (note the mention of exile in 23.15–16), using materials found in the Torah, and is thus probably to be dated to the 5th century BCE. All of these literary stages rest on earlier materials—oral and written—some of which may go back to the beginning of the first millennium. The LXX version differs from the Masoretic Text in various ways throughout the book, and is altogether about five percent shorter. This shows the fluidity of the text even in very late times, or suggests that the book was known in more than one edition.

[NILI WAZANA]

1 After the death of Moses the servant of the LORD, the LORD
said to Joshua son of Nun, Moses' attendant:
2 "My servant Moses is dead. Prepare to cross the Jordan,
together with all this people, into the land that I am giving to
the Israelites. 3 Every spot on which your foot treads I give to
you, as I promised Moses. 4 Your territory shall extend from
the wilderness and the Lebanon to the Great River, the River
Euphrates [on the east]—the whole Hittite country—and up to
the Mediterranean[a] Sea on the west. 5 No one shall be able to
resist you as long as you live. As I was with Moses, so I will be
with you; I will not fail you or forsake you.

a *Heb. "Great."*

1.1–5.15: The entrance into the land. Chs 1–5 relate Israel's entrance into the land preceding the conquest. This period is presented as a transition stage from Moses, who led the people through the wilderness, to Joshua his successor, the designated commander of the conquest of the land (see Num. 27.18–23; Deut. 1.38; 3.21, 28; 31.3, 23; 33.9). The events reflect in reverse order almost perfectly the acts of Moses: Joshua's address to the two-and-a-half Transjordanian tribes to fulfill their obligation and lead the conquest of the promised land (1.12–15) matches Moses' conditional agreement to the settlement of the two-and-a-half tribes east of the Jordan (Num. ch 32); Joshua sending spies in advance to Jericho (ch 2) parallels Moses' spies (Num. ch 13); the miraculous crossing of the Jordan River (chs 3–4) explicitly relates to the wondrous crossing of the Reed Sea (Exod. ch 14); the circumcision of all the men, the celebration of Passover and the cessation of the manna (5.2–12) recall the circumcision of Moses' son (Exod. 4.24–26), the first Passover (Exod. ch 12) and the initial manna account (Exod. ch 16). Joshua's meeting with the captain of the LORD's host, before the first attack, when he is told to remove his sandals from his feet (5.13–15), recalls Moses' similar experience during his call at the burning bush (Exod. ch 3). Such reversals of order often point to connections between two narratives; their presence here suggests that the following material is not arranged in complete chronological order.

1.1–18. Introduction. The many connections of this ch with the end of Deut. make it appropriate as the haftarah of the last section of the Torah, Ve-zo't Ha-berakhah (Deut. 33.1–34.12), read on Simḥat-Torah, when the annual reading cycle of the Torah is completed.

1.1–9: Joshua's call and commissioning. The book opens with divine words of encouragement to Joshua to fulfill his role. This divine speech makes the transition to a new phase in national history, while, at the same time echoing familiar phrases from Deut., stressing continuity. Moses, the leader of the initial stage of the formation of the nation and the mediator of the law, is dead and Joshua is depicted as a second, somewhat lesser, Moses: "the face of Moses like the sun, the face of Joshua like the moon" (*b. B. Bat.* 75a). **1:** *After the death of Moses,* both a literary link to Deut. 34.5–6 and indicating a change of era (cf. similarly Judg. 1.1; 2 Sam. 1.1). *The servant* ["'ebed"]

6 "Be strong and resolute, for you shall apportion to this people the land that I swore to their fathers to assign to them. 7 But
you must be very strong and resolute to observe faithfully all the
Teaching that My servant Moses enjoined upon you. Do not deviate from it to the right or to the left, that you may be successful
wherever you go. 8 Let not this Book of the Teaching cease from
your lips, but recite it day and night, so that you may observe
faithfully all that is written in it. Only then will you prosper in
your undertakings and only then will you be successful.
9 "I charge you: Be strong and resolute; do not be terrified or
dismayed, for the LORD your God is with you wherever you go."

10 Joshua thereupon gave orders to the officials of the people: 11 "Go through the camp and charge the people thus: Get
provisions ready, for in three days' time you are to cross the
Jordan, in order to enter and possess the land that the LORD
your God is giving you as a possession."
12 Then Joshua said to the Reubenites, the Gadites, and the
half-tribe of Manasseh, 13 "Remember what Moses the servant of
the LORD enjoined upon you, when he said: 'The LORD your God
is granting you a haven; He has assigned this territory to you.'

of the LORD ... Joshua son of Nun, Moses' attendant ["mesharet"]: While derived from the meaning "to serve" like "'ebed," "mesharet" indicates primarily service to a person (cf. Elisha to Elijah, 1 Kings 19.21; 2 Kings 4.43). Its mention here alone in the book refers to Exod. 24.13; 33.11; Num. 11.28. Joshua would only be named "the servant ("'ebed") of the LORD" posthumously (Josh. 24.29; Judg. 2.8), echoing Moses. **2:** "Now," in the Heb, indicating transition to the major issue in an address. *Prepare to cross the Jordan ... into the land:* The Jordan is the border of the promised land; Transjordan is not part of it. Accordingly, the crossing will occupy chs 3–4, epitomizing a transition from "promise" to "fulfillment." **3–4:** *Every spot on which your foot treads I give to you, as I promised Moses. Your territory shall extend from ... to the Great River, the River Euphrates ... and up to the Mediterranean Sea on the west,* quoting Deut. 11.24–25, this is a promise of great power and unlimited dominion. Despite mentioning the Euphrates River, this is not a clearly demarcated territorial unit different than the land west of the Jordan. It reflects imperialistic, utopian language that was prevalent in the ancient Near East when Israel was under the rule of the Neo-Assyrian empire. **6:** *Be strong and resolute,* direct divine encouragement echoing and reestablishing Moses' words (Deut. 3.28; 31.7, 23; cf. Josh. 10.25). The imperatives ("ḥazak ve-'ematz," a blessing in Heb even today) are here thrice repeated for emphasis and clarity (vv. 6, 7, 9), cited again at the conclusion of the ch, tying its two parts together (v. 18). *Apportion,* in the second half of the book this root refers to the distribution of the land (11.23; 13.6, 7, 32; 16.4; 17.6; 19.9, 49, 51). At this stage however, it reflects Deut. 1.38; 3.28; 31.7, meaning to give the land to the people in fulfillment of the divine oath to the patriarchs. **7–9:** A later reinterpretation of the meaning of the divine encouragement. The key to success is to follow the teaching, Torah—which Moses *enjoined* (v. 7; again in 23.6; cf. 8.34), and furthermore, to recite constantly the Book of the Teaching—Torah (v. 8). Joshua is thus requested to behave similarly to the ideal future king (Deut. 17.18–19) and the ideal man of Ps. 1.2. This book is the Deuteronomic corpus of law (Deut. chs 12–26). *Be strong ... your God is with you:* The words of God end with an inverse repetition of the assurance with the same military sense as in v. 6, God mentioned in the third person (cf. v. 5).

1.10–11: Joshua prepares the people for the crossing. 10: *Officials,* Heb "shotri[m]," related to the Akkadian verb "shatāru" - to write. These are the mediators of the instructions to the people. **11:** *Provisions,* for the camp will move in three days to cross the River Jordan (see 3.2). *To enter and possess the land ...,* typical Deuteronomistic language (cf. Deut. 4.22, 26; 6.1; etc.). *Three days,* reminiscent of the preparation at the foot of Mount Sinai (Exod. 19.10–11).

1.12–18: Obligation of the tribes of Transjordan. Joshua reminds the men of the Transjordanian tribes of their obligation to join the other tribes in the conquest of the land, repeating the words of Moses (Deut. 3.18–20; cf. Num. 32.16–32). The "real promised land" lies west of the River Jordan, and participation in its conquest is a prerequisite to being a part of the people. 4.12–13 will relate the crossing of the Jordan by the two-and-a-half east Jordanian tribes, and 22.1–8 will continue the story of their settlement, using repeated terminology (22.4), forming an inclusio for the body of the book concerning conquest and settlement. Josh. 13.8–33, on the other hand, details their tribal boundaries without mentioning their obligatory participation in the western campaigns. That ch "upgrades" the Transjordanian inheritances, placing their status parallel to the ones on the west. **13:** *Granting ... haven,* lit. "gives you rest," this is found again in v. 15 and in the conclusion of the book (21.42; 22.4; 23.1), and is often a precondition for transitioning to the next historical phase (1 Sam. 7.1, 11; 1 Kings 5.18). *This territory* ("ha-'aretz ha-zot"), usually designating the promised land, here Transjordan, as in Deut. 3.18.

14 Let your wives, children, and livestock remain in the land that Moses assigned to you [a]-on this side of-[a] the Jordan; but every one of your fighting men shall go across armed[b] in the van of your kinsmen. And you shall assist them 15 until the LORD has given your kinsmen a haven, such as you have, and they too have gained possession of the land that the LORD your God has assigned to them. Then you may return to the land on the east side of the Jordan, which Moses the servant of the LORD assigned to you as your possession, and you may possess it."

16 They answered Joshua, "We will do everything you have commanded us and we will go wherever you send us. 17 We will obey you just as we obeyed Moses; let but the LORD your God be with you as He was with Moses! 18 Any man who flouts your commands and does not obey every order you give him shall be put to death. Only be strong and resolute!"

2 Joshua son of Nun secretly sent two spies from Shittim, saying, "Go, reconnoiter the region of Jericho." So they set out, and they came to the house of a harlot named Rahab and lodged there. 2 The king of Jericho was told, "Some men have come here tonight, Israelites, to spy out the country." 3 The king of Jericho thereupon sent orders to Rahab: "Produce the men who came to you and entered your house, for they have

a-a *Lit. "across."* b *Meaning of Heb. uncertain.*

14–15: Cf. Deut. 3.19–20. *On this side of* (lit. "across") *the Jordan,* east of the Jordan (see v. 15), reflecting an anachronistic viewpoint from west of the Jordan (contrast Deut. 3.20). *Armed* ("ḥamushim"), armed or lined up for war perhaps in five ("ḥamesh") corps, or in a special unit of fifty ("ḥamishim"). **16–18:** The reaction of all the people to Joshua's words. *Any man who flouts your commands ... shall be put to death:* This presupposes the incident of Achan, the only sinner in the period of the conquest. Indeed God there claims He can no longer "be with you (pl.)" (7.12) while they have transgressed. The particle *only* is twice repeated in the Heb (1.17, 18), first in relation to God's assistance (*let but,* v. 17), then at the culmination of the introductory ch with the repetition of the reassuring divine words of v. 7: *Only be strong and resolute!*

2.1–24: The spies' debacle in Jericho. Joshua sends a pair of spies to Jericho, the first city targeted. Jericho is identified as tel e-Sultan, ca. 8 km (5 mi) west of the Jordan. Ch 2 is disconnected from its natural conclusion, the conquest of Jericho (ch 6). The spies stay the night at Rahab's house, then flee to the mountains, waiting three days before safely returning to the camp (2.22). Placed here, the story presents Joshua as a second Moses, his actions matching those of his master in reverse order (see 1.1–5.15 n. above). Yet, coming immediately after the divine assurances of victory (ch 1), this mission seems absurd. The story focuses on a woman of low status, the prostitute Rahab, the only character besides Joshua and Achan given a name in chs 1–9. Rahab is the central and active character, even pronouncing a glorious declaration of faith in God (2.9–11), repeated by the spies in their report to Joshua, who should have known this in advance (2.24). It is therefore not surprising that a midrashic tradition marries her to Joshua, making her the ancestor of eight prophets and priests, and one prophetess (*b. Meg.* 14:2), and in the New Testament she is the mother of Boaz, thus an ancestress of David and Jesus (Matt. 1.5). This ch is the haftarah reading for the weekly portion Shelaḥ-Lekha (Num. 13.1–15.41), dealing with the spies Moses sent. **1:** *Shittim,* the first geographical site mentioned is the place where Israel sinned by cohabiting with Moabite women (Num. ch 25). Mentioned in Num. 33.49 ("Abel-shittim"), and again in Josh. 3.1, *Shittim* was viewed as a place of divine national wonders, listed among other "gracious acts of the LORD" by the prophet Micah (Mic. 6.5). Joshua learns a theological lesson of faith from a local prostitute at this location. *Secretly:* The adverb *secretly* ("ḥeresh") is derived from the root indicating silence (Judg. 16.2), deafness and dumbness (Mic. 7.16). Traditional exegesis read this unusual word as "clay" ("ḥeres"), depicting them as pretending to be merchants selling clay. *Go, reconnoiter the region of Jericho,* lit. "the land, and Jericho." Jericho seems to represent the land, and the report indeed relates to "the whole land" (v. 24; cf. 24.11). The Rabbis appropriately referred to Jericho as "the key of the land." *Lodged there,* lit. "lay there," the only act initiated by the anonymous spies. While this is a suitable place for gathering information undetected, coming to and lying down in a prostitute's house carries implicit sexual undertones (cf. Judg. 16.1–3). *Rahab* could be an actual name (compare Rehoboam), but probably indicates her profession, the house of Rahab meaning most likely "brothel." The Aram. Tg. and most medieval exegetes interpreted "zonah" as innkeeper, from the root "z-w-n," yet the Rabbis also acknowledge the ordinary meaning, prostitute (*b. Zevah.* 116.2). **2:** *The king of Jericho was told:* The passive verb does not indicate who told, but considering who stood to gain the most, Rahab is the immediate suspect, yet the spies remain deaf and dumb to this as to everything

come to spy out the whole country." 4 The woman, however, had taken the two men and hidden them. "It is true," she said, "the men did come to me, but I didn't know where they were from. 5 And at dark, when the gate was about to be closed, the men left; and I don't know where the men went. Quick, go after them, for you can overtake them."—6 Now she had taken them up to the roof and hidden them under some stalks of flax which she had lying on the roof.—7 So the men pursued them in the direction of the Jordan down to the fords; and no sooner had the pursuers gone out than the gate was shut behind them.

8 [a-]The spies[-a] had not yet gone to sleep when she came up to them on the roof. 9 She said to the men, "I know that the LORD has given the country to you, because dread of you has fallen upon us, and all the inhabitants of the land are quaking before you. 10 For we have heard how the LORD dried up the waters of the Sea of Reeds for you when you left Egypt, and what you did to Sihon and Og, the two Amorite kings across the Jordan, whom you doomed.[b] 11 When we heard about it, we lost heart, and no man had any more spirit left because of you; for the LORD your God is the only God in heaven above and on earth below. 12 Now, since I have shown loyalty to you, swear to me by the LORD that you in turn will show loyalty to my family. Provide me with a reliable sign 13 that you will spare the lives of my father and mother, my brothers and sisters, and all who belong to them, and save us from death." 14 The men answered her, "Our persons are pledged for yours, even to death! If you do not disclose this mission of ours, we will show you true loyalty when the LORD gives us the land."

15 She let them down by a rope through the window—for her dwelling was at the outer side of the city wall and she lived in the actual wall. 16 She said to them, "Make for the hills, so that the pursuers may not come upon you. Stay there in hiding three days, until the pursuers return; then go your way."

a-a Heb. "They."

b I.e., placed under herem, *which meant the annihilation of the inhabitants. Cf. Deut. 2.34 ff.*

else. *To spy out,* from an unexpected root "to dig," found again only in Deut.'s version of the story of the spies (Deut. 1.22). **3:** *The men who came to you and entered your house,* retaining the sexual innuendo. **4–5:** *I didn't/don't know,* twice repeated: Rahab refers conspicuously to the information "told" to the king— the origin of the men and their whereabouts. *When the gate was about to be closed, the men left:* The Heb suggests that they either left as the gate was closing, or immediately before. **6:** *Now,* better "but." *Stalks of flax,* lying on the flat roof to dry. For a similar scene see 2 Sam. 17.18–20, where the woman hides the two men down the well. **7:** *In the direction of the Jordan,* eastwards; the actions in the v. are happening at the same time as the previous v., and the hapless spies are trapped. **8:** Back in the house the men *had not yet gone to sleep,* though they had already lain down before (v. 1; indicated also in v. 6). The same phrase appears in another dangerous nocturnal visit of foreign men on a mission—the story of Sodom (Gen. 19.4). This echo heightens the tension, and further ridicules the passive spies. **9–11:** Unlike her claims of ignorance to the king's messengers, Rahab's declaration of faith is full of *I know that ... and ...* A foreign prostitute, the most dangerous trap according to wisdom literature, is here presented as being well acquainted with the typical acts of salvation God had bestowed upon His people. As she says twice (vv. 10, 11), the locals have *heard* of the acts of God. The result is great fear, emphasized four times (twice in vv. 9, 11). Rahab ends with a Deuteronomistic declaration of faith in God (see Deut. 4.39; 1 Kings 8.23). Rahab and the Gibeonites, who say similar words (9.9–10, 24), are the only local people exempt from the proscription of all the native Canaanites ("ḥerem"). **12–13:** Rahab asks for an oath of *loyalty* to her family. Her request for "a token ("ʾot") of truthfulness" (NJPS, *a reliable sign)* is missing in the LXX, and is perhaps a later addition related to the crimson thread (v. 18). **15:** *She ... through the window,* a typical rescue-by-a-woman scene (see Michal and David, 1 Sam. 19.12). *She lived in the actual wall:* Archeology testifies to this typical feature of Israelite cities, where casemate walls composed of two parallel walls were sometimes filled in with rubble and sometimes divided into rooms. This is anachronistic in a description of Canaanite Jericho, which like many other Late Bronze cities, did not have walls at all. The notice that Rahab's house was in the wall is missing from the LXX, perhaps because it was understood as problematic, for when the city's walls tumble down, Rahab's house stays intact (6.22). **16–21:** The sequence of vv. presents this part of the conversation as taking place when the spies are hanging by the rope, like puppets on a string. *Make for the hills,* westward, in the opposite direction from their destination. Many natural caves are found in the mountains above Jericho.

[17] But the men warned her, “We will be released from this
oath which you have made us take [18] [unless,] when we invade
the country, you tie this length of crimson cord to the window
through which you let us down. Bring your father, your mother, your brothers, and all your family together in your house;
[19] and if anyone ventures outside the doors of your house, his
blood will be on his head, and we shall be clear. But if a hand is
laid on anyone who remains in the house with you, his blood
shall be on our heads. [20] And if you disclose this mission of
ours, we shall likewise be released from the oath which you
made us take.” [21] She replied, “Let it be as you say.”

She sent them on their way, and they left; and she tied the
crimson cord to the window.

[22] They went straight to the hills and stayed there three days,
until the pursuers turned back. And so the pursuers, searching
all along the road, did not find them.

[23] Then the two men came down again from the hills and
crossed over. They came to Joshua son of Nun and reported to
him all that had happened to them. [24] They said to Joshua, “The
Lord has delivered the whole land into our power; in fact, all
the inhabitants of the land are quaking before us.”

3 Early next morning, Joshua and all the Israelites set out
from Shittim and marched to the Jordan. They did not cross
immediately, but spent the night there. [2] Three days later, the
officials went through the camp [3] and charged the people as follows: “When you see the Ark of the Covenant of the Lord your
God being borne by the levitical priests, you shall move forward.
Follow it—[4] but keep a distance of some two thousand cubits
from it, never coming any closer to it—so that you may know
by what route to march, since it is a road you have not traveled
before.” [5] And Joshua said to the people, “Purify yourselves,[a] for
tomorrow the Lord will perform wonders in your midst.”

[6] Then Joshua ordered the priests, “Take up the Ark of the Covenant and advance to the head of the people.” And they took up
the Ark of the Covenant and marched at the head of the people.

[7] The Lord said to Joshua, “This day, for the first time, I will
exalt you in the sight of all Israel, so that they shall know that
I will be with you as I was with Moses. [8] For your part, command the priests who carry the Ark of the Covenant as follows:

a See Exod. 19.10, 15.

18: *Crimson cord,* another motif missing from ch 6, indicating perhaps that the act of favor requested by Rahab was in return for her insider’s help in a military attack, by means of a crimson thread signal (cf. similar motifs in the story of the conquest of Bethel, Judg. 1.23–26). An actual battle is further hinted at in Josh. 24.11. The superimposed miraculous story rendered all these motifs superfluous. **22–24:** The two men return to Joshua, their report concluding the story with the message of divine deliverance of *the whole land,* adding the element of the fear-struck locals stressed by Rahab.

3.1–4.24: The crossing of Jordan. The dramatic crossing of Jordan is the first feat that draws detailed parallels between Joshua and Moses (3.7; 4.14). The miraculous crossing of the Reed Sea is echoed in the story through the stopping of the waters of Jordan and the passage of Israel on dry ground (4.23). In one part of the story, likely an addition, the priests, bearers of the Ark, play an important role; in another part, at Gilgal, twelve representatives of the people take stones from the Jordan and erect them in memory of the act. **3.1:** *Early next morning,* designating Joshua’s eagerness to fulfill his role (again in 6.12; 7.16; 8.10). **2:** *Three days later, the officials ...,* continuing 1.10–11. *The Ark of the Covenant of the Lord your God,* containing the document of the covenant (Deut. 10.1–5), is carried by *the levitical priests:* priests who were Levites (cf. Deut. 18.1; 21.5). **4:** *Two thousand cubits,* almost 1 km (0.57 mi), a very long distance from an object that is leading the way across a rather narrow river; it seems this is a later addition, emphasizing the Ark’s dangerousness (cf. 2 Sam. 6.7). **5:** *Purify yourselves,* recalling the covenant ceremony (Exod. 19.10, 14, 15), which also mentions the motifs of three days’ preparations, and keeping the people at a distance (Exod. 19.12). *Perform wonders* (“niflaʾot”), only here in Josh., this word denotes the miraculous acts of God in Israel’s formative period (cf. Exod. 3.20; 34.10; Judg. 6.13 and often in Ps.). **7–8:** Divine address to Joshua. *I will be with you ... Moses,* echoes for the last time the reassurances of the introduction (1.5, 9, 17), and the end of Deut. (Deut. 31.8, 23). This will be realized in 4.14. *Make a halt in the Jordan:* The double mention of the Jordan anticipates the two descriptions of where the priests carrying the Ark stood: at the edge of the water (v. 15) or in the middle of the Jordan (v. 17; 4.10).

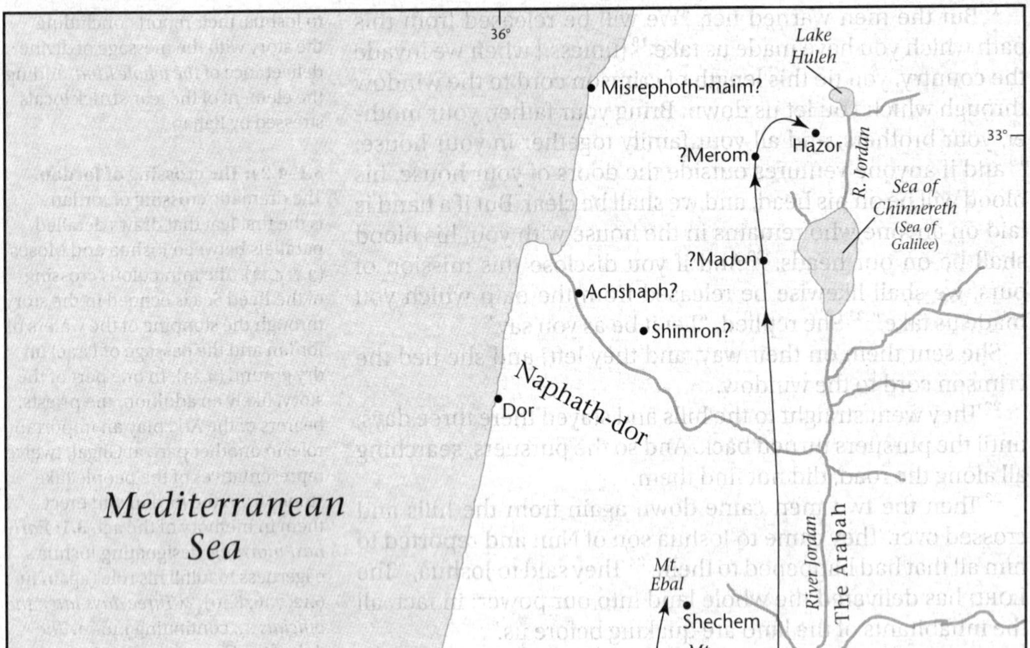

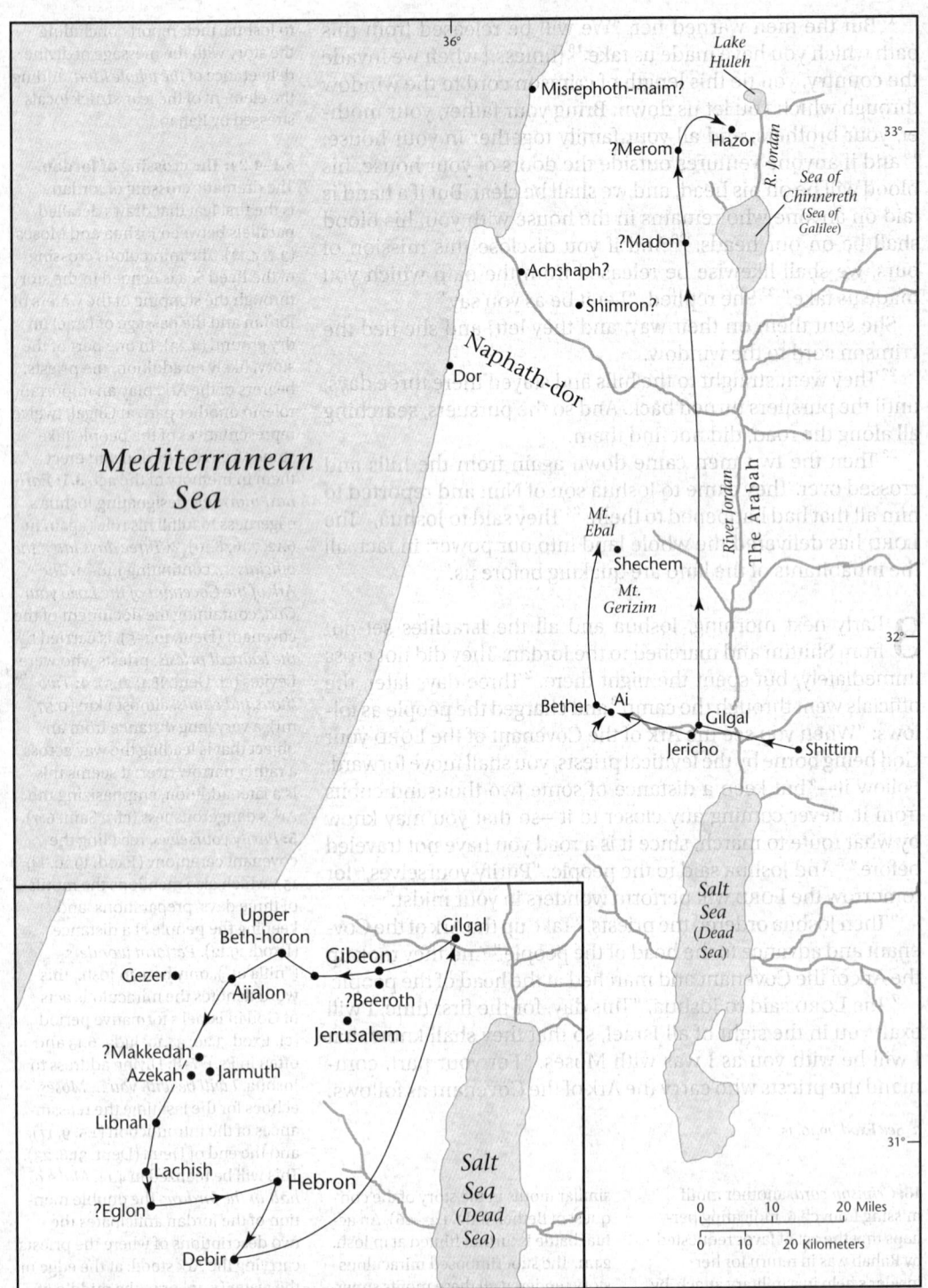

The conquest of Canaan according to the book of Joshua

When you reach the edge of the waters of the Jordan, make a halt in the Jordan."

9 And Joshua said to the Israelites, "Come closer and listen to the words of the LORD your God. 10 By this," Joshua continued, "you shall know that a living God is among you, and that He will dispossess for you the Canaanites, Hittites, Hivites, Perizzites, Girgashites, Amorites, and Jebusites: 11 the Ark of the Covenant of the Sovereign of all the earth is advancing before you into the Jordan. 12 Now select twelve men from the tribes of Israel, one man from each tribe. 13 When the feet of the priests bearing the Ark of the LORD, the Sovereign of all the earth, come to rest in the waters of the Jordan, the waters of the Jordan—the water coming from upstream—will be cut off and will stand in a single heap."

14 When the people set out from their encampment to cross the Jordan, the priests bearing the Ark of the Covenant were at the head of the people. 15 Now the Jordan keeps flowing over its entire bed throughout the harvest season. But as soon as the bearers of the Ark reached the Jordan, and the feet of the priests bearing the Ark dipped into the water at its edge, 16 the waters coming down from upstream piled up in a single heap a great way off, at[a] Adam, the town next to Zarethan; and those flowing away downstream to the Sea of the Arabah (the Dead Sea) ran out completely. So the people crossed near Jericho. 17 The priests who bore the Ark of the LORD's Covenant stood on dry land exactly in the middle of the Jordan, while all Israel crossed over on dry land, until the entire nation had finished crossing the Jordan.

4 When the entire nation had finished crossing the Jordan, the LORD said to Joshua, 2 "Select twelve men from among the people, one from each tribe, 3 and instruct them as follows: Pick up twelve stones from the spot exactly in the middle of the Jordan, where the priests' feet are standing; take them along with you and deposit them in the place where you will spend the night."

4 Joshua summoned the twelve men whom he had designated among the Israelites, one from each tribe; 5 and Joshua said to them, "Walk up to the Ark of the LORD your God, in the middle of the Jordan, and each of you lift a stone onto his

a So kethib; qere *"from."*

9–13: Joshua speaks to the people. **10:** *By this,* the imminent miraculous crossing; cf. similar phrasing by Moses (Num. 27.28). *Living God,* potent (Hos. 2.1; Pss. 42.3; 84.3). *Dispossess,* the Heb root indicates either expulsion or eradication. The typical list of seven nations (Deut. 7.1) denoting ethnic diversity of the pre-Israelite population appears here for the first time. It will reappear, often with six members, at key points of the book (9.1; 11.3; 12.8; 24.11). **11:** *Sovereign of all the earth,* appearing only here and in v. 13 in Josh. This is a rare, late, universalistic title (Zech. 4.14; 6.5; Ps. 97.5), suggesting the complex layering of this ch. **12:** Interrupts the predicted crossing of the Ark (v. 11) and the stopping of the water (v. 13). It is a secondary, fragmentary comment anticipating the erection of the stones (ch 4). **13:** *A single heap,* repeated in v. 16, alluding to the Song of the Sea (Exod. 15.8; cf. Ps. 78.3). **14–17:** The crossing. **14:** *The people set out from their encampment:* The mention of the tents is repeated at the end of the book (22.4, 6, 7–8). **15:** *Jordan ... over its entire bed,* at harvest time in the early summer, when the river was typically high, magnifying the miracle. **16:** *A great way off, at Adam,* Tel ed-Damyieh, 27 km (17 mi) north of Jericho. **17:** *Until the entire nation* ("goy"), usually denoted "'am" (4.11). This phrase, repeated in 4.1a, is from one of the late layers of the book (cf. 5.8), and connects the crossing (ch 3) with the theme of the twelve stones (ch 4). **4.2–3:** A divine command to erect memorial stones, followed by Joshua's expanded command to the people (vv. 4–7). The stones parallel the twelve standing stones erected after the revelation on Mt. Sinai (Exod. 24.4). **2:** *Select* [pl.] *twelve men ... one from each tribe,* this was already ordered by Joshua (3.12), where the pl. makes more sense. **3:** *From the spot exactly in the middle of the Jordan, where the priests' feet are standing:* The twelve memorial stones are to be taken from the riverbed. The second clause adds the motif of the Ark to that of the memorial stones. The position of the priests' feet is mentioned again in v. 9, in an alternative tradition concerning the stones. *In the place where you will spend the night,* later identified as Gilgal (v. 20). **5:** *Walk up to the Ark ... and ... lift a stone,* another combination of the motif of the memorial stones and the Ark. It is unclear whether the men were to take the stones from the eastern bank of the river, where the priests' feet touched the edge of the water, or to return to where the

shoulder—corresponding to the number of the tribes of Israel.
6 This shall serve as a symbol among you: in time to come,
when your children ask, 'What is the meaning of these stones
for you?' 7 you shall tell them, 'The waters of the Jordan were
cut off because of the Ark of the LORD's Covenant; when it
passed through the Jordan, the waters of the Jordan were cut
off.' And so these stones shall serve the people of Israel as a
memorial for all time."
8 The Israelites did as Joshua ordered. They picked up twelve
stones, corresponding to the number of the tribes of Israel,
from the middle of the Jordan—as the LORD had charged
Joshua—and they took them along with them to their night
encampment and deposited them there.
9 Joshua also set up twelve stones in the middle of the Jordan, at the spot where the feet of the priests bearing the Ark
of the Covenant had stood; and they have remained there to
this day.
10 The priests who bore the Ark remained standing in the
middle of the Jordan until all the instructions that the LORD
had ordered Joshua to convey to the people had been carried
out. And so the people speedily crossed over, [a-]just as Moses
had assured Joshua in his charge to him.[-a] 11 And when all the
people finished crossing, the Ark of the LORD and the priests
advanced to the head of the people.
12 The Reubenites, the Gadites, and the half-tribe of Manasseh
went across armed[b] in the van of the Israelites, as Moses had
charged them.[c] 13 About forty thousand shock troops went across,
at the instance of the LORD, to the steppes of Jericho for battle.
14 On that day the LORD exalted Joshua in the sight of all Israel, so that they revered him all his days as they had revered
Moses.
15 The LORD said to Joshua, 16 "Command the priests who
bear the Ark of the Pact to come up out of the Jordan." 17 So
Joshua commanded the priests, "Come up out of the Jordan."
18 As soon as the priests who bore the Ark of the LORD's Covenant came up out of the Jordan, and the feet of the priests
stepped onto the dry ground, the waters of the Jordan resumed
their course, flowing over its entire bed as before.

a-a Connection of clause uncertain; cf. Deut. 31.7–8.
b Meaning of Heb. uncertain. *c See Num. 32.20–22.*

priests were standing after crossing. **6:** *Symbol* ("ot"), this refers to the pedagogical function of various cultic acts, which are meant to evoke questions from future generations (Exod. 12.26–27; 13.14–16; cf. the symbol in Exod. 13.8–9). *In time to come, when your children ask,* similarly Deut. 6.20–25. **7:** *These stones ... as a memorial,* used only in this passage for standing stones. Joshua's words are repeated in vv. 21–24, after the erection of the stones at Gilgal, without mention of the Ark. **9:** *The feet of the priests,* these play an important, almost magical role in the crossing. Once they touch the water, at the edge of the Jordan, the water flow is cut off (3.13, 15), and returns only when the feet reach dry ground (v. 18). Joshua erects twelve stones in the Jordan, presumably the very stones that the priests stood on. Vv. 10–11 repeat 3.17. **10:** *Just as Moses had assured Joshua,* missing in the LXX, as there is no passage in which Moses had said this to Joshua. The hierarchy God-Moses-Joshua is later underscored in the summation of the entire conquest (11.15). **11:** *To the head of the people:* After all the people have passed while the priests bearing the Ark stand still, the priests pass the people, resuming their place before them (3.6). **12–13:** In describing the order of those crossing, the warriors of the two-and-a-half Transjordanian tribes are mentioned. **13:** *Forty thousand shock troops ... for battle:* The word *thousand* ("elef") can mean the number 1,000, but can also mean a tribal-based military unit (1 Sam. 10.19) of indeterminate but probably smaller size. The number here likely refers to the entire Israelite army. *The steppes of Jericho,* mentioned again in 5.10, appears elsewhere only in the account of the destruction of the kingdom of Judah (2 Kings 25.5), perhaps framing the story of the people in the land, from entry to exile. **14:** The fulfillment of the divine promise to make Joshua as great as Moses (3.7); this is the original culmination of the crossing. *They revered him ... Moses:* Fear of Moses is mentioned only in Exod. 34.30, when his face was radiant.

15–18: God commands Joshua who in turn orders the priests, who come out of the water. This concludes the tradition of the feet of the priests stopping the flow of the water (3.11, 13–17). **16:** *Ark of the Pact,* ("aron ha-ʿedut"), the Priestly term, is only used here; cf. Exod. 25.16. **19:** *On the tenth day of the first month,* Nissan, in preparation for the celebration of Passover (5.10). *Gilgal,* an important Benjaminite cultic center located here to the east of Jericho. Its exact site is unknown. The name indicates a circle of standing stones, and this name was common for

19 The people came up from the Jordan on the tenth day of
the first month, and encamped at Gilgal on the eastern border of Jericho. 20 And Joshua set up in Gilgal the twelve stones
they had taken from the Jordan. 21 He charged the Israelites
as follows: "In time to come, when your children ask their
fathers, 'What is the meaning of those stones?' 22 tell your
children: 'Here the Israelites crossed the Jordan on dry land.'
23 For the LORD your God dried up the waters of the Jordan
before you until you crossed, just as the LORD your God did
to the Sea of Reeds, which He dried up before us until we
crossed. 24 Thus all the peoples of the earth shall know how
mighty is the hand of the LORD, and you shall fear the LORD
your God always."

5 When all the kings of the Amorites on the western side
of the Jordan, and all the kings of the Canaanites near
the Sea, heard how the LORD had dried up the waters of the
Jordan for the sake of the Israelites until they crossed over,
they lost heart, and no spirit was left in them because of the
Israelites.

2 At that time the LORD said to Joshua, "Make flint knives
and proceed with a second circumcision of the Israelites." 3 So
Joshua had flint knives made, and the Israelites were circumcised at Gibeath-haaraloth.[a]

4 This is the reason why Joshua had the circumcision performed: All the people who had come out of Egypt, all the males
of military age, had died during the desert wanderings after
leaving Egypt. 5 Now, whereas all the people who came out of
Egypt had been circumcised, none of the people born after the
exodus, during the desert wanderings, had been circumcised.

a I.e., "the Hill of Foreskins."

many sites, yet a secondary etiology later connects it to the root "to roll away" ("galloti," 5.9). **20–24:** The act of erecting the stones is again described, this time explicitly at Gilgal, and is connected to the children's question (vv. 6–7). **23:** *Sea of Reeds, which He dried up before us,* Reed Sea, identical to Rahab's words (2.10). **24:** The account of the crossing ends with the recognition on the part of *all the peoples of the earth* (!) of *how mighty is the hand of the LORD:* Its only appearance in Josh., *mighty is the hand* usually refers to the exodus (Exod. 13.9; Deut. 6.21; etc.). The ch ends with Israel's fear of God, on top of their fear of Joshua (4.14). The entire account of the crossing combines various traditions. One version highlights Gilgal and its twelve standing stones. These huge stones (each 40 "se'ah" [approximately 300 liters in volume] according to *b. Sot.* 34:1) were said to have been pulled out from the middle of the Jordan by twelve representatives of the tribes (4.1–8, 10–14, 19–24). Another tradition emphasizes the semi-magical role of the priests' feet, whose mere touch in the eastern edge of the Jordan stopped the water (3.9–11, 13–17; 4.15–18). Perhaps there were two separate memorial sites, one at the very edge of the Jordan and one at Gilgal, of twelve standing stones. (Alternatively, the tradition of the standing stones may reflect an effort to supplant the Gilgal tradition, marginalizing the site, relating the crossing to Jericho (3.16), and calling Gilgal "the overnight stay.") In the text the two versions are blended. According to another version, perhaps connected to the Gilgal tradition, the Ark does not stop in the middle of Jordan but rather leads the people, who must leave a large distance between themselves and the Ark carried by the Levitical priests (3.1–4).

5.1–15: The conquest nears. **1:** *When ... heard,* indicating a new phase in the conquest (see 9.1; 10.1; 11.1). The kings of the land are divided into *Amorites* and *Canaanites,* though either of these terms usually designates the entire pre-Israelite population (cf. 7.7, 9 and Deut. 1.7; see Num. 13.29 for the Canaanites dwelling by the sea). *They lost heart,* repeating Rahab's words (2.11) in preparation of the miraculous conquest of Jericho (ch 6). **2–9:** The story of circumcision is one of three units (vv. 10–12, 13–15) before the conquest. Reversing the order of the events of the exodus, circumcision is renewed followed by the first celebration of Passover in the land (vv. 10–12). **2:** *At that time,* usually indicates the introduction of a separate source. *Flint knives,* these were put in Joshua's tomb, according to a tradition preserved in LXX (24.31). Such knives would have been outdated in this period, and reflect a desire to perform the custom in an ancient, traditional manner. *A second circumcision,* Joshua is to reinstate the custom. **3:** *Gibeath-haaraloth* ("foreskins hill"), mentioned only here, referring perhaps to a practice of burying the foreskins after circumcision. A secondary note (see v. 9) will transform this story into an etiology of the name Gilgal. **4–7:** *This is the reason,* beginning a series of justifications for the need to re-establish circumcision.

6 For the Israelites had traveled in the wilderness forty years,
until the entire nation—the men of military age who had left
Egypt—had perished; because they had not obeyed the LORD,
and the LORD had sworn never to let them see the land that the
LORD had sworn to their fathers to assign to us, a land flowing
with milk and honey. 7 But He had raised up their sons in their
stead; and it was these that Joshua circumcised, for they were
uncircumcised, not having been circumcised on the way. 8 After the circumcising of the whole nation was completed, they
remained where they were, in the camp, until they recovered.
9 And the LORD said to Joshua, "Today I have rolled away
from you the disgrace of Egypt."[a] So that place was called
Gilgal,[b] as it still is.
10 Encamped at Gilgal, in the steppes of Jericho, the Israelites offered the passover sacrifice on the fourteenth day of the
month, toward evening.
11 On the day after the passover offering, on that very day,
they ate of the produce of the country, unleavened bread
and parched grain. 12 On that same day,[c] when they ate of
the produce of the land, the manna ceased. The Israelites got
no more manna; that year they ate of the yield of the land of
Canaan.

13 Once, when Joshua was near Jericho, he looked up and
saw a man standing before him, drawn sword in hand. Joshua
went up to him and asked him, "Are you one of us or of our
enemies?" 14 He replied, "No, I am captain of the LORD's host.
Now I have come!" Joshua threw himself face down to the
ground and, prostrating himself, said to him, "What does my
lord command his servant?" 15 The captain of the LORD's host
answered Joshua, "Remove your sandals from your feet, for
the place where you stand is holy." And Joshua did so.

a I.e., of the Egyptian bondage. *b Interpreted as "rolling."*
c Lit. "on the day after."

6: *A land flowing with milk and honey,* a stock phrase appearing only here in Josh., though common in promise-terminology (Exod. 3.8, 17; Lev. 20.24; Num. 16.13; Deut. 6.3; and many other places). **8:** *After ... completed,* a redactional note, similar to 4.1. *In the camp,* identified in the next v. as Gilgal. **9:** *Gilgal* is connected to the verb "roll" ("g-l-l"), perhaps to undermine the original connotation of a circle of standing stones, seen as forbidden divine images ("pesilim," Judg. 3.19). *Disgrace of Egypt:* The disgrace is that of being uncircumcised (Gen. 34.14); the author of this v. is unaware of the tradition that the Israelites were circumcised in Egypt (5.5–7), or the *disgrace* refers to their status as slaves. **10–12:** The first Passover in the land follows circumcision (Exod. 12.48). **10:** *Encamped at Gilgal,* after v. 9, this is redundant, and is missing in the LXX; it associates initiation of religious rites in the land with the shrine of Gilgal. **11:** *The produce of the country* ("me-'avur ha-'aretz"), found only here and in the following v., a wordplay with the former v. "toward evening" ("ba-'erev"), "in the steppes of Jericho" ("be-'arvot yeriḥo"). *On the day after the passover,* (cf. Num. 33.3) is missing in the LXX. This seems problematic alongside the following *on that very day,* but matches the Priestly descriptions of Passover (Lev. 23.5–7), and may be a Priestly gloss. *Unleavened bread and parched grain,* "fast food" for special conditions, here also matching the celebration of the feast. **12:** *The manna ceased,* as predicted in Exod. 16.35, this is another indication that the borders of the promised land do not include Transjordan. *On that same day ...,* lit. "on the day after when they ate," "after eating" according to the LXX—another link to Priestly traditions. **13–15:** Circumcision, Passover and cessation of manna were connected to Gilgal, perhaps secondarily (5.9, 10). Joshua's meeting with the commander of the army of the LORD is a very late tradition, paralleling Joshua with Moses (Exod. 3.5), thus placed at the conclusion of preparations for the conquest. **13:** *Once, when Joshua was near Jericho:* This episode speaks of the sanctity ("kodesh") of "the place" ("ha-maqom"; v. 15), yet the location is obscure. *He looked up ... drawn sword in hand,* similarly in Balaam's story (Num. 23.31) and David's encounter in Jerusalem (1 Chron. 21.16). This is usually a threatening motif, but Joshua boldly approaches the man asking him *"Are you one of us or of our enemies?"* **14:** Identifying himself as *captain of the LORD's host,* he plays no role in the forthcoming stories of conquest. *Now I have come,* as said the angel Gabriel (Dan. 9.22–23), his words indicate his heavenly character as well as the late origin of the episode; yet, unlike angels from the late Second Temple period, he is unnamed. **15:** *Remove your sandals from your feet ... holy,* in preparation for a divine message, yet none follows. Perhaps this passage is truncated, or the message is the act itself, placed here in order to elevate Joshua as a second Moses, just before the first battle of conquest of the land.

6 Now Jericho was shut up tight because of the Israelites; no
one could leave or enter.
2 The LORD said to Joshua, "See, I will deliver Jericho and her
king [and her] warriors into your hands. 3 Let all your troops
march around the city and complete one circuit of the city. Do
this six days, 4 with seven priests carrying seven ram's horns
preceding the Ark. On the seventh day, march around the city
seven times, with the priests blowing the horns. 5 And when a
long blast is sounded on the horn—as soon as you hear that
sound of the horn—all the people shall give a mighty shout.
Thereupon the city wall will collapse, and the people shall advance, every man straight ahead."
6 Joshua son of Nun summoned the priests and said to them,
"Take up the Ark of the Covenant, and let seven priests carrying
seven ram's horns precede the Ark of the LORD." 7 And he instructed the people, "Go forward, march around the city, with
the vanguard marching in front of the Ark of the LORD." 8 When
Joshua had instructed the people, the seven priests carrying
seven ram's horns advanced before the LORD, blowing their
horns; and the Ark of the LORD's Covenant followed them. 9 The
vanguard marched in front of the priests who were blowing the
horns, and the rear guard marched behind the Ark, with the
horns sounding all the time. 10 But Joshua's orders to the rest of
the people were, "Do not shout, do not let your voices be heard,
and do not let a sound issue from your lips until the moment
that I command you, 'Shout!' Then you shall shout."
11 So he had the Ark of the LORD go around the city and complete one circuit; then they returned to camp and spent the
night in camp. 12 Joshua rose early the next day; and the priests
took up the Ark of the LORD, 13 while the seven priests bearing
the seven ram's horns marched in front of the Ark of the LORD,
blowing the horns as they marched. The vanguard marched in
front of them, and the rear guard marched behind the Ark of
the LORD, with the horns sounding all the time. 14 And so they

6.1–11.23: The conquest of the land. Following the entrance into the land, its conquest (chs 6–11) is presented through four schematic battles, two against walled cities, in the east and in the center of the land, and two battles against coalitions of kings, in the southwest and in the north.

6.1–27: The Israelites first conquer Jericho. Otherwise a relatively insignificant city in the Hebrew Bible, Jericho plays the role of a key site in the capture of the land (*Midr. Tanḥ.* Be-haʿalotekha 10). The story of its conquest is unique. Jericho falls by a miraculous feat, not human action, and then is treated very harshly. Not only is the population proscribed according to the Deuteronomic law of "ḥerem" (the "ban": Deut. 7.2, 26; 20.17), but its property as well is consecrated to God, with its valuable metals going into the treasury of the LORD. In other battles, the Israelites could enjoy the spoils of war. This denotes Jericho as the "first fruit offering" of the promised land (*Ant.* 5.26; *J.W.* 4.459), and equates Jericho with the fate decreed for a town whose inhabitants were found to have worshipped other gods (Deut. 13.13–18). Jericho is burned and Joshua further pronounces a curse upon any person who will rebuild it, an additional feature reminiscent of the conquered town which shall "remain an everlasting ruin, never to be rebuilt" (Deut. 13.17). In the light of extrabiblical practices, Joshua's curse of Jericho is another indication of the consecration to God of the first site. **1:** *Now Jericho was shut up tight,* originally continuing 5.1. *No one could leave or enter,* this is meant lit. indicating a siege, but the phrase is also reminiscent of military language, meaning "leave or enter to fight" (cf. 14.11; 1 Sam. 18.13). **2:** *I will deliver ... into your hands:* Divine assurance is repeated in each phase of the conquest (8.1, 18; 10.8; 11.6), already mentioned by Rahab and the spies (2.9, 24) and recalled at the final ch (24.11). [Valiant] *warriors* ("gibborey he-ḥayil"): While the people of Gibeon (later incorporated in Israel) are described as "warriors" ("gibborim"), it seems that "gibborey ḥayil" is reserved for the Israelite forces everywhere else in Josh. (1.14; 8.3; 10.7), thus a misplaced gloss to the words "all the warriors" ("kol ʾanshey ha-milḥama," v. 3; cf. 10.7). **3:** *March around ... circuit:* The roots "s-b-b" and "n-q-f" here and in v. 11 can denote siege (1 Kings 6.14–15) but are also used in religious ceremonies (Ps. 48.13). **4:** The emphasis on the number *seven* indicates ritual rather than military activity. *Ram's horns,* (sg. "qeren ha-yovel"; v. 5). "Yovel," usually indicating jubilee, originally meant ram. **5:** *A long blast,* lit. "pulling" ("m-sh-k"), reminiscent of the revelation at Mt. Sinai (Exod. 19.13). *A mighty shout,* again, used in both military and cultic contexts. **6:** *Ark of the Covenant* plays an important role in the miraculous conquest. **7:** *The vanguard* ("he-ḥalutz"), a military term (see 4.13). **8–9:** The order of the procession: The vanguard followed by seven priests blowing the ram's horn, then the Ark, and last, the rear guard, *the horns sounding all the time.* **11:** *They ... spent the night in camp:* The explicit mention of Gilgal is likely

marched around the city once on the second day and returned
to the camp. They did this six days.
15 On the seventh day, they rose at daybreak and marched
around the city, in the same manner, seven times; that was the
only day that they marched around the city seven times. 16 On
the seventh round, as the priests blew the horns, Joshua commanded the people, "Shout! For the LORD has given you the
city. 17 The city and everything in it are to be proscribed for the
LORD; only Rahab the harlot is to be spared, and all who are
with her in the house, because she hid the messengers we sent.
18 But you must beware of that which is proscribed, or else you
will be proscribed:[a] if you take anything from that which is
proscribed, you will cause the camp of Israel to be proscribed;
you will bring calamity upon it. 19 All the silver and gold and
objects of copper and iron are consecrated to the LORD; they
must go into the treasury of the LORD."
20 So the people shouted when the horns were sounded. When
the people heard the sound of the horns, the people raised a
mighty shout and the wall collapsed. The people rushed into
the city, every man straight in front of him, and they captured
the city. 21 They exterminated everything in the city with the
sword: man and woman, young and old, ox and sheep and ass.
22 But Joshua bade the two men who had spied out the land,
"Go into the harlot's house and bring out the woman and all
that belong to her, as you swore to her." 23 So the young spies
went in and brought out Rahab, her father and her mother, her
brothers and all that belonged to her—they brought out her
whole family and left them outside the camp of Israel.
24 They burned down the city and everything in it. But the
silver and gold and the objects of copper and iron were deposited in the treasury of the House of the LORD. 25 Only Rahab
the harlot and her father's family were spared by Joshua, along
with all that belonged to her, and she dwelt among the Israelites—as is still the case. For she had hidden the messengers
that Joshua sent to spy out Jericho.
26 At that time Joshua pronounced this oath: "Cursed of the
LORD be the man who shall undertake to fortify this city of Jericho: he shall lay its foundations at the cost of his first-born, and
set up its gates at the cost of his youngest."

a I.e., be put to death; cf. Lev. 27.28–29.

suppressed. **15:** *In the same manner,* missing in the LXX, emphasizing in the Heb that the order of the procession remained as described before (vv. 8–9). *The only day ... seven times,* also missing from the LXX, furthering the uniqueness of the pivotal day. **17–19:** Between Joshua's command to the people to shout (v. 16) and their shouting (v. 20) these vv. refer to past events, Rahab's favor and promised reward, and hint ahead, foreshadowing Achan's violation (note the verb in v. 18, *bring calamity* "vehe'ekhartem"; cf. 7.25). **17–18:** *Proscribed* ("ḥerem"), set aside and forbidden for use, whether due to consecration to the LORD (Lev. 27.28) or because it is an abomination (Deut. 7.26). The root is repeated five times in vv. 17–18. *The messengers* ("ha-mal'akhim"), another allusion to the story of Sodom and Gomorrah (Gen. ch 19). Jericho is to be completely destroyed by fire, but Rahab, like Lot, will be taken out of the city together with her family and their lives will be saved. **19:** *Silver and gold and objects of copper and iron:* Deut. forbids only the taking of the images of the gods, warning not to covet the silver and gold on them (7.25). **20:** *Every man straight in front of him,* repeating v. 5, depicting a complete shattering of the wall, rather than a breach in it. **21:** *Everything ... man and woman ... ox and sheep and ass,* a series of merisms, depicting the totality of the "ḥerem" (cf. 1 Sam. 15.3; 22.19). **22–23:** This ending of Rahab's story does not recognize that Rahab's house was built in the wall which collapsed (2.15) nor does it recall the crimson thread she was to hang in the window in the wall from which she let the spies down (2.18). In this story of divine conquest, there is no room for human initiative. **24:** *In the treasury of the House of the LORD,* an anachronism, missing in the LXX. This treasury (sg.) is mentioned only in 1 Chron. 29.8. **25:** *As is still the case,* lit. "to this day." This etiology adds credibility to the story. **26:** *At that time,* indicating a different issue, or source. The whole v. is missing in the Lucianic version of the LXX. The curse of the rebuilder of Jericho is a double merism: the *foundations* and the *gates* stand for its entire fortification system, *his first-born ... his youngest* refer to the cutting off of all his offspring. This merism was misunderstood and taken literally by the author of 1 Kings 16.34 who identified the builder as Hiel from Bethel, whose first-born Abiram, and youngest Segub, were used to fulfill Joshua's curse in the days of the wicked king Ahab. Similar curses against conquered cities are known

27 The LORD was with Joshua, and his fame spread throughout the land.

7 The Israelites, however, violated the proscription: Achan
son of Carmi son of Zabdi son of Zerah, of the tribe of Judah, took of that which was proscribed, and the LORD was incensed with the Israelites.
2 Joshua sent men from Jericho to Ai, which lies close to
Beth-aven—east of Bethel—with orders to go up and spy out
the country. So the men went up and spied out Ai. 3 They returned to Joshua and reported to him, "Not all the troops need
go up. Let two or three thousand men go and attack Ai; do
not trouble all the troops to go up there, for [the people] there
are few." 4 So about three thousand of the troops marched up
there; but they were routed by the men of Ai. 5 The men of Ai
killed about thirty-six of them, pursuing them outside the gate
as far as Shebarim, and cutting them down along the descent.
And the heart of the troops [a]-sank in utter dismay.-[a]
6 Joshua thereupon rent his clothes. He and the elders of Israel lay until evening with their faces to the ground in front of
the Ark of the LORD; and they strewed earth on their heads.
7 "Ah, Lord GOD!" cried Joshua. "Why did You lead this people across the Jordan only to deliver us into the hands of the

a-a Lit. "melted and turned to water."

from other ancient cultures, such as Hatti, Assyria and Carthage. **27:** *The LORD was with Joshua,* as foreseen in 1.5, 9, 17, and as realized by Israel at the miraculous crossing of Jordan (3.7). After Jericho *his fame spread throughout the land* (cf. 9.9, referring to God's fame).

7.1–8.35: The sin of Achan and the conquest of Ai. The story of Achan is connected to the preceding conquest of Jericho, where Achan violated the "ḥerem," and to the subsequent conquest of Ai, which can succeed only once the perpetrator is caught and punished. Achan is the only Israelite character besides Joshua to appear with a name (and even with developed lineage), in the first part of the book. A Judahite, he is the only sinner in this golden age of promise fulfillment, and his sin is disobedience, not idolatry. **7.1:** *Violated the proscription:* "Maʿal" means to betray trust, here violating sacred items (see Lev. 5.15). The sin of the individual is contagious, and visited upon all Israel. *Achan:* 1 Chron. 2.7 calls him "'Achar, the troubler ['"okher"] of Israel," and Achar is his name according to one of the LXX's versions, the Peshitta, and Josephus (*Ant.* 5.1.10, 14). This version of the name fits the words of Joshua (7.25) and the etiology concluding the story, connecting it to the Valley of Achor, "calamity" (see 7.26). **2:** *Ai ... close to Beth-aven—east of Bethel:* Ai, the second fortified town in the conquest of the land, is the first Israelite foothold in the hill country. Like Jericho it plays a marginal role in national memory. Abraham wandered between Bethel and Ai, where he built an altar (Gen. 12.8; 13.3). Unlike Bethel which was one of Israel's major religious sites (Gen. ch 28), a "king's sanctuary and a royal palace" (Amos 7.13), Ai remained desolate, in accordance with its name, meaning "the ruin" (8.28). Indeed, this entire story is an etiology of how the city gained that name. *Beth-aven,* house of sin, an intentional misspelling of Beth-On, house of power ("On" is a divine name)—a site close to Bethel (8.12–13), elsewhere also a pejorative designation for Bethel (Hos. 4.15; 10.5, 8; Amos 5.5). Bethel itself, while mentioned in the list of conquered cities in 12.16, appears as the destination of Israelite conquest only in Judg. 1.22–26, suggesting that several different traditions about the city's conquest circulated in antiquity. A combination of human resourcefulness and divine assistance (see Judg. 1.22, "and the LORD was with them"), the conquest of Bethel shares many motifs with the conquest stories of Jericho and Ai, including the spies and the help of a local person who is consequently allowed to live with his family, albeit in a distant place. **5:** *About thirty-six,* better "thirty-six exactly." *Pursuing them ... as far as Shebarim,* a place otherwise never mentioned; the name is a wordplay on the root "sh-b-r" ("to break"), referring to the geological characteristic of the rock-strewn, "broken" landscape, as well as to the catastrophic "breaking" of the Israelite troops (cf. 1 Kings 13.26; Jer. 17.18), as reflected in the Tg. and the Peshitta, "until they were broken." *And the heart of the troops sank in utter dismay,* lit. "melted and turned into water," a complete reversal of the description of the previous fear of the people of the land (2.11; 5.1). **6:** *Rent his clothes.... strewed earth on their heads,* because of the calamity (cf. 2 Sam. 1.2; 13.19). *In front of the Ark of the LORD,* elsewhere usually "in front of the LORD" (cf. v. 23); the word *Ark* is missing from the LXX. *The elders of Israel,* mentioned here for the first time in the book, are recalled only once more in the conquest of Ai (8.10). The elders were tribal leaders involved in political and military decisions, and led Israel after Joshua's death (24.31; Judg. 2.7). **7–9:** Achan's sin creates an opportunity for Joshua to act as an interceding prophet, like Moses. **7:** *Ah,* a cry of sorrow, mostly by prophets (cf. Jer. 32.17; Ezek. 11.13).

Amorites, to be destroyed by them? If only we had been content to remain on the other side of the Jordan! 8 O Lord, what can I say after Israel has turned tail before its enemies? 9 When the Canaanites and all the inhabitants of the land hear of this, they will turn upon us and wipe out our very name from the earth. And what will You do about Your great name?"

10 But the LORD answered Joshua: "Arise! Why do you lie prostrate? 11 Israel has sinned! They have broken the covenant by which I bound them. They have taken of the proscribed and put it in their vessels; they have stolen; they have broken faith! 12 Therefore, the Israelites will not be able to hold their ground against their enemies; they will have to turn tail before their enemies, for they have become proscribed. I will not be with you any more unless you root out from among you what is proscribed. 13 Go and purify the people. Order them: Purify yourselves for tomorrow. For thus says the LORD, the God of Israel: Something proscribed is in your midst, O Israel, and you will not be able to stand up to your enemies until you have purged the proscribed from among you. 14 Tomorrow morning you shall present yourselves by tribes. Whichever tribe the LORD indicates[a] shall come forward by clans; the clan that the LORD indicates shall come forward by ancestral houses, and the ancestral house that the LORD indicates shall come forward man by man. 15 Then he who is [b]indicated for proscription,[b] and all that is his, shall be put to the fire, because he broke the Covenant of the LORD and because he committed an outrage in Israel."

16 Early next morning, Joshua had Israel come forward by tribes; and the tribe of Judah was indicated. 17 He then had the clans of Judah come forward, and the clan of Zerah was indicated. Then he had the clan of Zerah come forward by [c]ancestral houses,[c] and Zabdi was indicated. 18 Finally he had his ancestral house come forward man by man, and Achan son of Carmi, son of Zabdi, son of Zerah, of the tribe of Judah, was indicated.

19 Then Joshua said to Achan, "My son, pay honor to the LORD, the God of Israel, and make confession to Him. Tell me what you have done; do not hold anything back from me." 20 Achan answered Joshua, "It is true, I have sinned against the

a *Lit. "catches."* *b-b* *Or "caught in the net."*
c-c *So some Heb. mss. and some ancient versions; most mss. and editions have "men."*

Why ... to be destroyed by them? If only ... on the other side of the Jordan, this echoes the people's complaint after the sin of the spies (Num. 14.2–3). Joshua is aware that Israel's advantage after the miraculous crossing is now lost. **9:** *What will You do about Your great name?,* repeating Moses' pleas on behalf of the people after the sin of the spies (Num. 14.13–16) and other sins (Deut. 9.7–29). **10:** *Arise!:* This imperative begins the explanation of the failure, then is repeated in the Heb at the beginning of the orders to purify the people (v. 13). It also appears twice in the description of Israel's defeated state. As long as they possess devoted things they will not be able to stand up to their enemies (vv. 12, 13). **11:** *Broken the covenant,* lit. "crossed," recalling their miraculous crossing of the Jordan (v. 7). *They have ... they have ...,* by five times repeating in the Heb "and also" ("vegam"), the sin is detailed and multiplied. **12:** *I will not be with you any more:* As stressed from the start of the book, divine Presence is the one condition for success, for Joshua (1.5, 9, 17; 3.7), and now for the entire people. **13:** *Purify,* as before the crossing of the Jordan (3.5), this prepares the people for the divine Presence required for the identification of the sinner by lot. **14:** *Come forward ... the LORD indicates:* The process of divine elimination is known from the election of Saul to kingship (1 Sam. 10.19–21), and from the story of finding his son Jonathan's guilt (1 Sam. 14.37–44), where the casting of lots involved the "urim vetumim" (1 Sam. 14.41). The detailed genealogy of Achan (7.1) parallels the introduction to the story of Saul's rise to kingship (1 Sam. 9.1–2). That the villain comes from the tribe of Judah and is caught by the same process by which Saul was elected to kingship indicates the Benjaminite influence on the conquest stories; in addition the majority of the stories relate to Benjaminite sites— Gilgal, Jericho, Ai and Gibeon. (Sections of Samuel may have been written before sections of Joshua.)

15: *Because he committed an outrage in Israel,* this phrase typically refers to sexual crimes (Gen. 34.7; Deut. 22.21; Judg. 19.23, 24; 20.6; 2 Sam. 13.12–13; Jer. 29.23), though here it refers to fulfilling one's desires regardless of consequences (cf. Job 42.8).

19: Although no confession is necessary, Joshua is requesting one, to validate the outcome of the casting of the lots (*b. Sanh.* 43:2). Joshua asks Achan to please *pay honor* and to *make confession,* all late terms. His request, *do not hold anything back,* is answered in full.

LORD, the God of Israel. This is what I did: 21 I saw among the
spoil a fine Shinar mantle, two hundred shekels of silver, and
a wedge of gold weighing fifty shekels, and I coveted them and
took them. They are buried in the ground in my tent, with the
silver under it."[a]
22 Joshua sent messengers, who hurried to the tent; and there
it[a] was, buried in his tent, with the silver underneath. 23 They
took them from the tent and brought them to Joshua and all
the Israelites, and displayed[b] them before the LORD. 24 Then
Joshua, and all Israel with him, took Achan son of Zerah—and
the silver, the mantle, and the wedge of gold—his sons and
daughters, and his ox, his ass, and his flock, and his tent, and
all his belongings, and brought them up to the Valley of Achor.
25 And Joshua said, "What calamity you have brought upon us!
The LORD will bring calamity upon you this day." And all Israel
pelted him with stones. They put them to the fire and stoned
them. 26 They raised a huge mound of stones over him, which
is still there. Then the anger of the LORD subsided. That is why
that place was named the Valley of Achor[c]—as is still the case.

8 The LORD said to Joshua, "Do not be frightened or dismayed. Take all the fighting troops with you, go and march
against Ai. See, I will deliver the king of Ai, his people, his city,
and his land into your hands. 2 You shall treat Ai and her king
as you treated Jericho and her king; however, you may take the
spoil and the cattle as booty for yourselves. Now set an ambush against the city behind it."
3 So Joshua and all the fighting troops prepared for the
march on Ai. Joshua chose thirty thousand men, valiant warriors, and sent them ahead by night. 4 He instructed them as
follows: "Mind, you are to lie in ambush behind the city; don't
stay too far from the city, and all of you be on the alert. 5 I and
all the troops with me will approach the city; and when they
come out against us, as they did the first time, we will flee from
them. 6 They will come rushing after us until we have drawn
them away from the city. They will think, 'They are fleeing from
us the same as last time'; but while we are fleeing before them,

a I.e., the mantle. *b Meaning of Heb. uncertain.*
c Connected with 'akhar *"to bring calamity upon"; cf. v. 25.*

21: *A fine Shinar mantle:* Shinar is Sumer in southern Mesopotamia (Gen. 10.10; 11.2), yet in light of the common construct "'aderet she'ar" ("wool garment"; Gen. 25.25; Zech. 13.4), perhaps the nun is a scribal error, and a "wool garment" was meant. *Two hundred shekels of silver,* a shekel is around 11 grams (about a sixth of an ounce). *In the ground,* for this meaning of "'aretz" see the late text, 2 Chron. 32.4. **22:** The messengers Joshua sent *hurried,* eager to restore God's goodwill. **23:** *Displayed,* lit. "poured out," perhaps in relation to the metals (but cf. 2 Sam. 15.24), *before the LORD,* as they belong to Him. **24:** The punishment involves Achan and all that is his, like Korah and his followers (Num. 16.32–33), emphasized by a long list, followed by a summation *all his belongings.* Some Rabbis suggested his children were not killed, but just taken to view the punishment (*b. Sanh.* 44:1), while some found them guilty of not reporting the crime (*Pirqe R. El.* 38). In much of the biblical view, however, the fate of the children was an integral part of the life of the father (see, e.g., Exod. 34.7; contrast Ezek. ch 18). *The Valley of Achor,* mentioned in the Benjaminite-Judahite border (Josh. 15.7), identified with el-Buqei'a. The meaning of the name, "valley of calamity," here connected to the fate of Achan by a pun (v. 25), probably reflects the dryness of the area. **25:** *Pelted him ... put them to the fire and stoned them:* The two verbs for stoning ("r-g-m" and "s-q-l") are parallel. The orders were to burn (v. 15) in accordance with the special "ḥerem" of Jericho (6.24), yet the etiology for the pile of stones in the Valley of Achor (v. 26), perhaps a border-marker, required stoning too. **26:** *The anger of the LORD subsided,* bringing the story to its close (cf. 7.1). *As is still the case,* lit. "to this day"; the etiological formula appears twice, referring to the pile of stones and to the name of the valley.

8.1–29: The destruction of Ai. **1:** *Do not be frightened or dismayed:* After the first military defeat at Ai (7.4–5), the divine encouragement formula (cf. 1.9) is repeated (see also 10.8; 11.6, in pl.). *Take all the fighting troops,* in contrast to the first attempt. *The king of Ai,* mentioned for his role in the etiology of another pile of stones (8.29). **2:** *You may take ... booty,* unlike Jericho. *Ambush:* The noun refers to both the people and the place (v. 7). *Behind it,* west of Ai. **3:** *By night,* undetected by the enemy. The conquest of fortified towns had to be accomplished by unconventional or miraculous means, or by a surprise ploy. **4:** *Be on the alert,* better "ready."

[7]you will dash out from your ambush and seize the city, and the LORD your God will deliver it into your hands. [8]And when you take the city, set it on fire. Do as the LORD has commanded. Mind, I have given you your orders."

[9]Joshua then sent them off, and they proceeded to the ambush; they took up a position between Ai and Bethel—west of Ai—while Joshua spent the night with the rest of the troops.

[10]Early in the morning, Joshua mustered the troops; then he and the elders of Israel marched upon Ai at the head of the troops. [11]All the fighting force that was with him advanced near the city and encamped to the north of Ai, with a hollow between them and Ai.—[12]He selected about five thousand men and stationed them as an ambush between Bethel and Ai, west of the city. [13]Thus the main body of the army was disposed on the north of the city, but the far end of it was on the west. (This was after Joshua had [a-]spent the night[-a] in the valley.[b])—[14]When the king of Ai saw them, he and all his people, the inhabitants of the city, rushed out in the early morning to the [c-]meeting place,[-c] facing the Arabah, to engage the Israelites in battle; for he was unaware that a force was lying in ambush behind the city. [15]Joshua and all Israel fled in the direction of the wilderness, as though routed by them. [16]All the troops in the city gathered to pursue them; pursuing Joshua, they were drawn out of the city. [17]Not a man was left in Ai or in Bethel who did not go out after Israel; they left the city open while they pursued Israel.

[18]The LORD then said to Joshua, "Hold out the javelin in your hand toward Ai, for I will deliver it into your hands." So Joshua held out the javelin in his hand toward the city. [19]As soon as he held out his hand, the ambush came rushing out of their station. They entered the city and captured it; and they swiftly set fire to the city. [20]The men of Ai looked back and saw the smoke of the city rising to the sky; they had no room for flight in any direction.

The people who had been fleeing to the wilderness now became the pursuers. [21]For when Joshua and all Israel saw that the ambush had captured the city, and that smoke was rising from the city, they turned around and attacked the men of Ai. [22]Now the other [Israelites] were coming out of the city against them,

a-a So with some mss. (cf. v. 9); most mss. and editions read "marched."
b Syriac reads "with the troops"; cf. v. 9.
c-c Emendation yields "descent"; cf. 7.5.

7: *You will dash out,* better "But you will ..."; while Joshua and the troops will flee as before, the forces of the ambush will attack from the rear. **9:** *Sent them,* already mentioned in v. 3, their sending is repeated after Joshua's instructions. *Between Ai and Bethel,* identified as e-Tel, Ai is but 3 km (1.86 mi) to the southeast of Bethel (Beitin), yet they are separated by a mountain range. Vv. 10–13 present an alternative version of the ambush. A similar sentence appears at the end of v. 13 (cf. 10.9 for the nocturnal march motif), and this repetition (a resumptive repetition) resumes the story after the insertion. **10:** *Elders of Israel:* Two rare mentions of the elders put them beside Joshua in his two major roles—imploring God after military failure (7.6), and leading the army, in preparation for their leadership after his death. **11:** *To the north of Ai, with a hollow between them and Ai,* the topographical specifics are stressed, perfectly matching the site of et-Tell. Since Ai was left a perpetual ruin, the identification of the site required details. **12:** *Five thousand men ... as an ambush,* thirty thousand people were sent at night according to v. 3. **13:** The v. probably refers to the ambush, hiding west of Ai. **14:** *Meeting place,* of the former encounter (7.5), *facing the Arabah,* in the direction of the Jordan valley. **16:** *Pursuing Joshua,* this juxtaposes the two military leaders, Joshua and the king of Ai. **17:** *Or in Bethel,* missing in the LXX, perhaps inserted because of 7.2. The participation of Bethel warriors is impossible, as they would have stumbled upon the ambush, situated between Bethel and Ai (8.9, 12). **18:** *Hold out the javelin in your hand toward Ai,* a new motif, requiring divine direction. **19:** *As soon as he held out his hand,* recalling Moses' hands in the battle against Amalek (Exod. 17.8–13). God's staff is mentioned there (Exod. 17.9), and is paralleled here by the javelin, a sort of sword, which reflects a military sign here, undermining the magical tone of the action. Realistically, the warriors lying in ambush could not have seen Joshua, and Joshua's hand is held toward the city (v. 18). **20:** *They had no room for flight:* Conquest by means of an ambush and tactical flight is common in ancient descriptions. A particularly close parallel is found in the (secondary account of the) capture of Gibeah of Benjamin by Israel after the rape of the concubine (Judg. ch 20). **22:** *No one escaped or got away:* This will be repeated in a shorter form in the following battles (10.28, 30, 33,

so that they were between two bodies of Israelites, one on each side of them. They were slaughtered, so that no one escaped or got away. 23 The king of Ai was taken alive and brought to Joshua.

24 When Israel had killed all the inhabitants of Ai who had pursued them into the open wilderness, and all of them, to the last man, had fallen by the sword, all the Israelites turned back to Ai and put it to the sword.

25 The total of those who fell that day, men and women, the entire population of Ai, came to twelve thousand.

26 Joshua did not draw back the hand with which he held out his javelin until all the inhabitants of Ai had been exterminated. 27 However, the Israelites took the cattle and the spoil of the city as their booty, in accordance with the instructions that the LORD had given to Joshua.

28 Then Joshua burned down Ai, and turned it into a mound of ruins for all time, a desolation to this day. 29 And the king of Ai was impaled on a stake until the evening. At sunset, Joshua had the corpse taken down from the stake and it was left lying at the entrance to the city gate. They raised a great heap of stones over it, which is there to this day.

30 At that time Joshua built an altar to the LORD, the God of Israel, on Mount Ebal, 31 as Moses, the servant of the LORD, had commanded the Israelites—as is written in the Book of the Teaching of Moses[a]—an altar of unhewn stone upon which no iron had been wielded. They offered on it burnt offerings to the LORD, and brought sacrifices of well-being. 32 And there, on the stones, he inscribed a copy of the Teaching that Moses had written for the Israelites. 33 All Israel—stranger and citizen alike—with their elders, officials, and magistrates, stood

a See Deut. 27.3–8.

37, 39; 11.8) and in the summaries (10.40; similarly 11.11, 14). **27:** *In accordance with the instructions ... Joshua,* ending the story by referring to the divine orders of v. 2. **28:** Like Jericho, Ai is to remain *a desolation to this day.* **29:** The fate of the king of Ai continues the account of his capture in v. 23. The five kings of the south will be dealt with in a similar way (10.26–27). *Impaled on a stake until the evening.... at the entrance to the city:* The public hanging and removal of the king's corpse before sunset accord with Deut. 21.22–23, yet the initiative here is ascribed to Joshua, with no mention of Deut. (see also 10.27). The law refers to criminal execution, this account to military norms of behavior. It is as a polemic against the Assyrian norm of pressing the enemy to surrender by impaling live and dead dignitaries near the city gate, without burial, as reflected in the Assyrian palace reliefs of Sennacherib's conquest of Lachish. **30–35:** This short passage, which interrupts the conquest sequence, describes a religious ceremony in which the entire assembly of Israel participated at the site of Mount Ebal and Mount Gerizim (near Shechem); it parallels the ones described after the crossing of the Jordan River (chs 3–4; 5) and is a fulfillment of Deut. 11.29; 27.2–13. It was placed here since Ai is near Shechem. The late character of the passage is reflected by its various placements in different textual and exegetical sources: after the crossing of the Jordan, preceding the circumcision account (Josh. 5.2) according to a Dead Sea Scrolls text (4QJosh^{a}); after the gathering of the kings of the land according to the LXX (9.2); after the complete conquest (ch 12) according to Josephus (*Ant.* 5.69); and after the division of the land according to the opinion of R. Ishmael (placing it at the end of the book, *y. Sot.* 7:3). **30:** *At that time,* indicating the beginning of a new subject, and likely reliance on a source (cf. 10.12). **31:** *As Moses ... had commanded the Israelites— as is written in the Book of the Teaching of Moses:* Joshua piously executes the orders of God as communicated to Moses (cf. 11.12, 15), here explicitly a written document: *"sefer Torat Moshe"* (cf. 1.7–8; 23.6), referring to Deut. Joshua built *an altar of unhewn stone ...* on which Israel *offered on it burnt offerings ... and ... sacrifices of well-being,* in accordance with Deut. 27.5–7. These sacrifices are identical with those at the Sinai covenant ceremony (Exod. 24.5). The building of the altar further ties the conquest with the arrival of Abraham in the promised land and the altars he built in it, first at Shechem and then between Bethel and Ai (Gen. 12.6–8). **32:** *On the stones, he inscribed a copy of the Teaching that Moses had written for the Israelites:* Joshua wrote a copy of the Teaching of Moses, as in Deut.'s law of the king (Deut. 17.18), though uniquely, Joshua wrote it on the altar stones. This unifies two separate instructions juxtaposed in the book of Deut.: setting up stones, coating them with plaster (absent here) and writing the Teaching on them (Deut. 27.2–4, 8), and building a stone altar and offering on it (Deut. 27.5–7). The juxtaposition of the laws in Deut. may have encouraged our author to see them as a single ritual. **33:** *All Israel ... stood on either side of the Ark:* absent in Deut. ch 27. The Ark and the *levitical priests who carried the Ark of the LORD's Covenant*

on either side of the Ark, facing the levitical priests who carried the Ark of the LORD's Covenant. Half of them faced Mount Gerizim and half of them faced Mount Ebal, as Moses the servant of the LORD had commanded them of old, in order to bless the people of Israel. 34 After that, he read all the words of the Teaching, the blessing and the curse, just as is written in the Book of the Teaching.[a] 35 There was not a word of all that Moses had commanded that Joshua failed to read in the presence of the entire assembly of Israel, including the women and children and the strangers who accompanied them.

9 When all the kings [b]west of[b] the Jordan—in the hill country, in the Shephelah, and along the entire coast of the Mediterranean Sea up to the vicinity of Lebanon, the [land of the] Hittites, Amorites, Canaanites, Perizzites, Hivites, and Jebusites—learned of this, 2 they gathered with one accord to fight against Joshua and Israel.

3 But when the inhabitants of Gibeon learned how Joshua had treated Jericho and Ai, 4 they for their part resorted to cunning. They set out [c]in disguise:[c] they took worn-out sacks for their asses, and worn-out waterskins that were cracked and patched; 5 they had worn-out, patched sandals on their feet, and threadbare clothes on their bodies; and all the bread they took as provision was dry and crumbly. 6 And so they went to Joshua in the camp at Gilgal and said to him and to the men of Israel, "We come from a distant land; we propose that you make a pact with us." 7 The men of Israel replied to the Hivites, "But perhaps you live among us; how then can we make a pact with you?"[d]

a See Deut. 27.11–28.68. *b-b Lit. "across."* *c-c Meaning of Heb. uncertain.* *d Cf. Deut. 7.2.*

tie the ceremony to the description of the crossing of the Jordan (3.3). *All Israel* includes resident aliens and citizens alike, this Priestly terminology (cf. Lev. 24.16, 22) is added here to designate that the two groups facing each other are not arranged by their tribal affinity (Deut. 27.12–13), but in relation to their origins. **34:** The reading of *all the words of the Teaching* recalls Exod. 24.7, yet here *the blessing and the curse* is read. **35:** The concluding v. repeats the main message of the passage, that Joshua excelled in his religious tasks just as he would in his military tasks (11.15). He read the Teaching *in the presence of the entire assembly of Israel* (cf. Deut. 21.12; 1 Kings 8.22). The text is laden with references to the Sinai covenant, to the crossing of the Jordan and to the inauguration of the Temple, and places the adherence to the Book of the Teaching of Moses above all.

9.1–27: The covenant with the Gibeonites. This is an etiological story, explaining at minimum why some Gibeonites, natives of Canaan, functioned as lowly Temple servants. More broadly it justifies the survival of other Canaanites who were supposed to be killed according to the law of the ban ("ḥerem"). Like Rahab in ch 2, these Canaanites recognize God's power and are spared from destruction. **1:** *When ... learned,* lit. "heard," introducing a new stage of the conquest; see 5.1 (cf. 10.1, 11.1). *All the kings,* a general introduction to the second phase of the conquest, against coalitions and initiated by the locals. This phase consists of two battles, against the south (ch 10), and the north (ch 11). **2:** *Gathered with one accord:* The locals not only take the initiative, they unite and act as one, lit. "with one mouth." **3–4:** *But when ... learned,* in opposition to the nations uniting their forces against the Israelites, the Gibeonites had also heard—but reacted differently. *The inhabitants of Gibeon,* no king is mentioned. *Resorted to cunning,* Heb uses "also" ("gam"), perhaps referring to the cunning of Rahab (ch 2). *In disguise,* the Heb is homonymic, meaning either "pretended to be messengers," or "disguised themselves"; or "they took provisions" (cf. vv. 12, 14). *Worn-out ... cracked and patched,* the holes of the water sacks were tied up with string. **5:** *Patched sandals ... threadbare clothes,* recalling in reverse order the miraculously intact clothes and sandals of the Israelites during the desert wanderings, emphasizing the folly of the covenant with the locals (see Deut. 29.4, 10, where hewers of wood and drawers of water are also mentioned). **6:** *And to the men of Israel,* a body consisting of every adult male citizen that acted as the military (10.24) and legal body of Israel (cf. Judg. 8.22). This is the only account in Joshua where this body acts independently; Joshua is added secondarily. *A distant land ... a pact,* in accordance with the addition to the Deuteronomic law of war (Deut. 20.15–18), which distinguishes between the fate of Canaanite cities and "very distant cities," which need not be totally proscribed. **7:** *The Hivites,* the only time the Gibeonites are so called in this account (see 11.19), emphasizing their connection to the list of local nations that must be proscribed (v. 1). *Live among us:* This well-founded suspicion (see 9.16) hints that the men of Israel could easily know the truth, since they wondered *how then can we make a pact with you.* **8:** *We will be your subjects,* a request for a vassal treaty, Joshua fulfilling the role of the

8 They said to Joshua, "We will be your subjects." But Joshua
asked them, "Who are you and where do you come from?"
9 They replied, "Your servants have come from a very distant
country, because of the fame of the LORD your God. For we
heard the report of Him: of all that He did in Egypt, 10 and of
all that He did to the two Amorite kings on the other side of the
Jordan, King Sihon of Heshbon and King Og of Bashan who
lived in Ashtaroth. 11 So our elders and all the inhabitants of
our country instructed us as follows, 'Take along provisions for
a trip, and go to them and say: We will be your subjects; come
make a pact with us.' 12 This bread of ours, which we took from
our houses as provision, was still hot when we set out to come
to you; and see how dry and crumbly it has become. 13 These
wineskins were new when we filled them, and see how they
have cracked. These clothes and sandals of ours are worn out
from the very long journey." 14 The men [a]took [their word] because of[a] their provisions, and did not inquire of the LORD.
15 Joshua established friendship with them; he made a pact
with them to spare their lives, and the chieftains of the community gave them their oath.

16 But when three days had passed after they made this
pact with them, they learned that they were neighbors, living
among them. 17 So the Israelites set out, and on the third day
they came to their towns; these towns were Gibeon, Chephirah, Beeroth, and Kiriath-jearim. 18 But the Israelites did not
attack them, since the chieftains of the community had sworn
to them by the LORD, the God of Israel. The whole community muttered against the chieftains, 19 but all the chieftains
answered the whole community, "We swore to them by the
LORD, the God of Israel; therefore we cannot touch them.
20 This is what we will do to them: We will spare their lives, so
that there may be no wrath against us because of the oath that
we swore to them." 21 And the chieftains declared concerning
them, "They shall live!" And they became hewers of wood and
drawers of water for the whole community, as the chieftains
had decreed concerning them.

a-a Meaning of Heb. uncertain.

head of an empire (cf. 2 Kings 16.7). The story plays on their words, punishing the Gibeonites by granting them their wish literally—they are to become sanctuary slaves. **9–10:** Like Rahab (2.11), the Gibeonites know of God's saving acts, but their praise of God is no excuse for their survival. Strikingly, the conquest story never mentions the idolatry of the local population, nor explains the divine directive for their extermination because of their theological threat (contrast Deut. 20.17). Even Achan steals metals (7.21), not idols (cf. Deut. 7.25). Nevertheless, Joshua assumes that the "ḥerem" simply needed to be carried out. The only way to avoid complete "ḥerem" that was mandated by God (10.40; 11.14–15) is by cunning and deceit. **14:** *The men took ... their provisions:* Eating together is part of the treaty-making ceremony. *And did not inquire of the LORD,* by the "'urim ve-tumim" (Num. 27.21). This inaction hints at Joshua's earlier sending the spies without divine order (ch 2), both having similar results. **15:** *Joshua ... made a pact with them,* lit. a friendship pact, sparing their lives. *The chieftains of the community:* Mentioned here for the first time, this is the Priestly designation of the tribal leaders, elsewhere called elders. *The community* ("ha-ʿeda") is also a Priestly term for the men of Israel. The three components of the treaty ceremony are divided among three different parties: the men of Israel eat with them (v. 14); Joshua concludes the covenant; and the chieftains *gave them their oath.* **16:** *Living among them,* like Rahab (6.25). **17–21:** Distinct Priestly language suggests that these vv. are added to the story, together with the end of v. 15. **17:** *Set out,* referring to a moving camp rather than the permanent one situated at Gilgal for the duration of the conquest. *On the third day:* According to this v., missing in the LXX, the three day period followed the discovery of the truth, not the conclusion of the covenant (v. 16). *These towns,* four towns forming a ten km (6.2 mi) long strip of land within the territory of Benjamin. Together with Jericho in the east and Ai in the eastern slopes of the mountainous spine running north to south (see Map no. 3), the Israelites now control a narrow corridor, dividing the land in its middle. **18:** *Muttered:* This motif appears only here outside the Priestly traditions of the desert wanderings; here, unlike the cases in the Torah, the muttering is justified, targeting the chieftains. **20:** *Wrath* elsewhere leads to national catastrophes—military defeat (22.20; 2 Kings 3.27), plague (1 Chron. 27.24), or exile (Deut. 29.27). 2 Sam. 21.1–2 tells how in the days of Saul a solemn oath was violated, resulting in three years of famine. **21:** *Hewers ... water,* wood and water are the basic and cheapest (normally free) provisions for subsistence (see Lam. 5.4); a merism designating low social status (Deut. 29.10).

22 Joshua summoned them and spoke to them thus: "Why
did you deceive us and tell us you lived very far from us, when
in fact you live among us? 23 Therefore, be accursed! Never
shall your descendants cease to be slaves, hewers of wood and
drawers of water for the House of my God." 24 But they replied
to Joshua, "You see, your servants had heard that the LORD
your God had promised His servant Moses to give you the
whole land and to wipe out all the inhabitants of the country
on your account; so we were in great fear for our lives on your
account. That is why we did this thing. 25 And now we are at
your mercy; do with us what you consider right and proper."
26 And he did so; he saved them from being killed by the Israelites. 27 That day Joshua made them hewers of wood and drawers of water—as they still are—for the community and for the
altar of the LORD, in the place that He would choose.

10 When King Adoni-zedek of Jerusalem learned that Joshua had captured Ai and proscribed it, treating Ai and its
king as he had treated Jericho and its king, and that, moreover,
the people of Gibeon had come to terms with Israel and remained among them, 2 [a]he was[a] very frightened. For Gibeon
was a large city, like one of the royal cities—in fact, larger than
Ai—and all its men were warriors. 3 So King Adoni-zedek of
Jerusalem sent this message to King Hoham of Hebron, King
Piram of Jarmuth, King Japhia of Lachish, and King Debir of
Eglon: 4 "Come up and help me defeat Gibeon; for it has come
to terms with Joshua and the Israelites."
5 The five Amorite kings—the king of Jerusalem, the king of
Hebron, the king of Jarmuth, the king of Lachish, and the king
of Eglon, with all their armies—joined forces and marched on
Gibeon, and encamped against it and attacked it. 6 The people
of Gibeon thereupon sent this message to Joshua in the camp
at Gilgal: "Do not fail your servants; come up quickly and aid
us and deliver us, for all the Amorite kings of the hill country
have gathered against us." 7 So Joshua marched up from Gilgal
with his whole fighting force, all the trained warriors.

a-a Heb. "they were."

22: A continuation of v. 16. *Joshua summoned them,* to Gilgal (v. 6). **23:** *Be accursed!* Their status is viewed here not as punishment, but as a curse. *Never ... cease* [cf. 2 Sam. 3.29] ... *for the House of my God,* and not to the whole community (v. 21). This concretizes their status: from political vassals to actual service in a specific, albeit unnamed, temple. (Given the time of this section's composition, the Jerusalem Temple was probably meant, but since it had not yet been built in Joshua's time, it could not be mentioned.) **24–25:** The Gibeonites' actions are justified using heavily Deuteronomistic language. **26:** *Saved them:* At the end of the narrative, Joshua's actions are validated; the men of Israel, it is noted, suspected deception but did not ask the LORD (v. 14); and the Gibeonites deceived and were cursed (vv. 22–23). **27:** *That day,* indicating a later addition. *For the community and for the altar of the LORD:* The two earlier traditions (vv. 21, 23) are merged. *In the place that He would choose,* using the language of Deut. (e.g., 12.5, 11) an additional reference to Jerusalem added after the etiological final formula *as they still are,* lit. "to this day," bringing the account up to the present and to an end.

10.1–43: The battle against the southern coalition. The pact with the Gibeonites leads to the collective battle against the southern kings at Gibeon (vv. 1–15), the execution of the five kings (vv. 16–27), and the conquest of the southwest area (vv. 28–39); the ch concludes with a summary (vv. 40–43). **1:** *Adoni-zedek of Jerusalem,* the ringleader, the first king identified by name. His name recalls Melchizedek who greeted Abraham (Gen. 14.18); the divine element "zedek" ("righteous, just") is rooted in Jerusalem (see also Zadok the high priest, 1 Kings 1.39). The LXX calls him Adoni-bezek, as in the story of the conquest of Bezek, probably originally Jerusalem in the book of Judg. (Judg. 1.4–7). This is the first explicit mention of Jerusalem in the Bible, yet the story does not refer to the capture of the city, which is accomplished later by David. **2:** *He was* [better "they were"] *very frightened,* cf. 2.9, 11, 24; 5.1; 9.24. His fear however creates a union of forces against the invading army. **3:** Except for Hebron, all the other cities are located in the Lowland. *King Debir of Eglon,* here the name of the king, Debir, is also one of the cities conquered (vv. 38–39). The LXX reads Adulam, another Lowland city, instead of Eglon. **4:** *Help me,* a technical term indicating military cooperation (10.6, 33; 2 Sam. 8.5). **6:** *Do not fail your servants:* Referring to their vassal status, the Gibeonites ask for military help from their overlord against their aggressive neighbors, since their pact with the Israelites is the very reason for the attack (cf. 2 Kings 16.7).

8 The LORD said to Joshua, "Do not be afraid of them, for I
will deliver them into your hands; not one of them shall withstand you." 9 Joshua took them by surprise, marching all night
from Gilgal. 10 The LORD threw them into a panic before Israel:
[Joshua] inflicted a crushing defeat on them at Gibeon, pursued them in the direction of the Beth-horon ascent, and harried them all the way to Azekah and Makkedah. 11 While they
were fleeing before Israel down the descent from Beth-horon,
the LORD hurled huge stones on them from the sky, all the way
to Azekah, and they perished; more perished from the hailstones than were killed by the Israelite weapons.
12 On that occasion, when the LORD routed the Amorites before the Israelites, Joshua addressed the LORD; he said in the
presence of the Israelites:

"Stand still, O sun, at Gibeon,
O moon, in the Valley of Aijalon!"
13 And the sun stood still
And the moon halted,
While a nation wreaked judgment on its foes

—as is written in the Book of Jashar.[a] Thus the sun halted in
midheaven, and did not press on to set, for a whole day; 14 for
the LORD fought for Israel. Neither before nor since has there
ever been such a day, when the LORD acted on words spoken
by a man. 15 Then Joshua together with all Israel returned to
the camp at Gilgal.
16 Meanwhile, those five kings fled and hid in a cave at
Makkedah. 17 When it was reported to Joshua that the five
kings had been found hiding in a cave at Makkedah, 18 Joshua
ordered, "Roll large stones up against the mouth of the cave,
and post men over it to keep guard over them. 19 But as for the
rest of you, don't stop, but press on the heels of your enemies
and harass them from the rear. Don't let them reach their
towns, for the LORD your God has delivered them into your
hands." 20 When Joshua and the Israelites had finished dealing
them a deadly blow, they were wiped out, except for some fugitives who escaped into the fortified towns. 21 The whole army

a *Presumably a collection of war songs.*

8: *Do not be afraid ... not one of them shall withstand you,* similar phrases occur at key points in Josh. (1.3, 5, 9; 6.2; 8.1; 11.6). **9:** *By surprise,* only here and in the next battle (11.7), the motif of swift victory expresses the notion of a divinely-assisted attack. *Marching all night ... Gilgal:* The nocturnal march recalls the battle against Ai (8.3, 9, 13). The repetition of the march first mentioned in v. 7 returns to the main storyline, after God's encouragement. **10:** *Threw them into a panic,* also typical of divine intervention (cf. Exod. 14.24; Judg. 4.15). The direction of the pursuit after enemy forces is westwards via the Beth-horon ascent, then southwards, to Azekah in the Elah valley and Makkedah, in the southern Shephelah (Lowlands). **11:** *Huge stones ... from the sky,* explicit miraculous intervention. **12:** *On that occasion:* This marks a different source. *Joshua addressed the LORD,* qualifying his control of the elements reflected in his direct order to them. *Sun, at Gibeon, O moon, in the Valley of Aijalon,* this "freezes" the morning conditions, as the sun remains at the back of the Israelites heading west from Gibeon, to the valley of Aijalon. **13:** *As is written in the Book of Jashar* ("ha-yashar"), a collection of war songs mentioned again as the source of David's eulogy for Jonathan (2 Sam. 1.18), equated with "the book of song" ("ha-shir") mentioned in the LXX version of 1 Kings 8.13(53), named perhaps after its opening word "he will sing" ("ya-sher"). This is one of more than twenty non-extant books mentioned in the Bible, suggesting that the biblical authors sometimes drew on earlier works. **14:** *The LORD fought for Israel:* The arrest of the sun and moon for a whole day is attributed to God, not to Joshua (cf. Judg. 5.20). *Neither before nor since:* Joshua's achievement is nonetheless unparalleled, comparing Joshua to Moses (Deut. 34.10–12). **15:** *Returned ... Gilgal,* repeated in v. 43, while v. 21 locates the camp at Makkedah, which perhaps is a mistake, since the v. is missing in the LXX. The v. indicates the end of the battle, and the following unit (vv. 16–27) focuses on the fate of the kings, in an etiological story relating to a cave near Makkedah (Kh. El-Qom). **16–18:** *Five kings ... a cave .... large stones up against the mouth of the cave:* All the elements of the etiology are here from the start, motivating the story. **20:** A *deadly blow,* lit. "a very great blow" is an escalation from v. 10, "a crushing defeat," lit. "a great blow." *Except for some fugitives who escaped into the fortified towns,* a qualification in anticipation of the third part of the story (vv. 28–39). *Fortified towns:* Although this concept underlies the entire narrative, this is the only time the local towns in the conquest narrative are thus described (cf. Num. 13.19, 28; Deut. 1.28). **21:** *Snarled at the Israelites,* i.e., threatened them.

returned in safety to Joshua in the camp at Makkedah; no one
so much as snarled[a] at the Israelites. 22 And now Joshua ordered, "Open the mouth of the cave, and bring those five kings
out of the cave to me." 23 This was done. Those five kings—the
king of Jerusalem, the king of Hebron, the king of Jarmuth, the
king of Lachish, and the king of Eglon—were brought out to
him from the cave. 24 And when the kings were brought out to
Joshua, Joshua summoned all the men of Israel and ordered
the army officers who had accompanied him, "Come forward
and place your feet on the necks of these kings." They came
forward and placed their feet on their necks. 25 Joshua said to
them, "Do not be frightened or dismayed; be firm and resolute. For this is what the LORD is going to do to all the enemies
with whom you are at war." 26 After that, Joshua had them put to
death and impaled on five stakes, and they remained impaled
on the stakes until evening. 27 At sunset Joshua ordered them
taken down from the poles and thrown into the cave in which
they had hidden. Large stones were placed over the mouth of
the cave, [and there they are] to this very day.

28 At that time Joshua captured Makkedah and put it and its
king to the sword, proscribing it[b] and every person in it and
leaving none that escaped. And he treated the king of Makkedah as he had treated the king of Jericho.

29 From Makkedah, Joshua proceeded with all Israel to Libnah, and he attacked it. 30 The LORD delivered it and its king
into the hands of Israel; they put it and all the people in it to the
sword, letting none escape. And he treated its king as he had
treated the king of Jericho.

31 From Libnah, Joshua proceeded with all Israel to Lachish;
he encamped against it and attacked it. 32 The LORD delivered
Lachish into the hands of Israel. They captured it on the second day and put it and all the people in it to the sword, just as
they had done to Libnah.

33 At that time King Horam of Gezer marched to the help of
Lachish; but Joshua defeated him and his army, letting none
of them escape.

a Cf. Exod. 11.7. *b So several mss.; most mss. and the editions read "them."*

23: The enumeration of the five kings connects this section to the former story (v. 3). **24:** *Placed their feet on their necks,* a symbol of complete subjugation, familiar in ancient Near Eastern art and literature (e.g., 1 Kings 5.17). **25:** Joshua repeats the divine exhortation (1.9; 8.1; 10.8; 11.6). **26:** *After that,* a temporal reference indicating the secondary nature of vv. 26–27. *Put to death and impaled,* similar to the treatment of the king of Ai (8.29), though here specifying that the execution was prior to impalement. **27:** *At sunset,* recalling the miracle of the former story (v. 13). *Joshua ordered:* Here and in the case of the king of Ai (8.29) the emphasis is on Joshua as a leader, rather than on his obedience to the Deuteronomic law, which is not mentioned. This passage is a polemic against Assyrian war norms.

10.28–39: The conquest and conscription of six cities. The third narrative in this ch gives brief accounts of the conquest of six cities, which are only partially identical with the five in the battle of the first stage. The cities of Lachish, Eglon and Hebron were members of the coalition (vv. 31-32, 34–37), but three more cities are mentioned alongside them: Makkedah, a link to the former story, Libnah and Debir (vv. 28–30, 38–39); Debir was perhaps hinted at in the name of the king of Eglon. **31:** *Encamped against it,* a siege is mentioned only against Lachish and Eglon (v. 34). **33:** *At that time King Horam of Gezer marched to the help of Lachish,* an unusual notice. The second and third traditions (vv. 16–27, 28–39) take place in the same geographical area of Sennacherib's 701 BCE campaign. The cities Jerusalem, Lachish and Libnah are mentioned together only here in Josh. ch 10 and in the story of Sennacherib's campaign (2 Kings 18.17; 19.8). Horam king of Gezer, who came to help Lachish (v. 33) is reflex of the much later Egyptian involvement in 701 (2 Kings 19.9); in both cases the battle is fought in the open field. The battle at Gibeon (10.1–15) is also best explained as a mirror of the battle of Sennacherib against Hezekiah. In 701, the king of Jerusalem and his allies imprisoned Padi, king of Ekron, who was reluctant to join the anti-Assyrian initiative. Josh. ch 10 is an exercise in role-reversal: the king of Jerusalem who initiates the southern coalition is not the Judean Hezekiah, ringleader of the rebellion against Sennacherib, but the enemy. Similarly, the devastating army that comes to aid its loyal vassals, captures Lachish after a siege, and carries out a rapid attack—seizing the cities of the Lowland—is not the Assyrian force, but Joshua and the Israelites. The treatment of the bodies is thus another polemic against the standard Assyrian punishment, reflecting the viewpoint of the victims of this practice.

34 From Lachish, Joshua proceeded with all Israel to Eglon;
they encamped against it and attacked it. 35 They captured it on
the same day and put it to the sword, proscribing all the people
that were in it, as they had done to Lachish.
36 From Eglon, Joshua marched with all Israel to Hebron and
attacked it. 37 They captured it and put it, its king, and all its
towns, and all the people that were in it, to the sword. He let
none escape, proscribing it and all the people in it, just as he
had done in the case of Eglon.
38 Joshua and all Israel with him then turned back to Debir
and attacked it. 39 He captured it and its king and all its towns.
They put them to the sword and proscribed all the people in it.
They let none escape; just as they had done to Hebron, and as
they had done to Libnah and its king, so they did to Debir and
its king.
40 Thus Joshua conquered the whole country:[a] the hill country, the Negeb, the Shephelah, and the slopes, with all their
kings; he let none escape, but proscribed everything that
breathed—as the LORD, the God of Israel, had commanded.
41 Joshua conquered them from Kadesh-barnea to Gaza, all
the land of Goshen, and up to Gibeon. 42 All those kings and
their lands were conquered by Joshua at a single stroke, for the
LORD, the God of Israel, fought for Israel. 43 Then Joshua, with
all Israel, returned to the camp at Gilgal.

11 When the news reached King Jabin of Hazor, he sent messages to King Jobab of Madon, to the king of Shimron, to
the king of Achshaph, 2 and to the other kings in the north—in
the hill country, in the Arabah south of Chinnereth, in the lowlands, and in the district[b] of Dor on the west; 3 to the Canaanites
in the east and in the west; to the Amorites, Hittites, Perizzites,
and Jebusites in the hill country; and to the Hivites at the foot
of Hermon, in the land of Mizpah. 4 They took the field with all
their armies—an enormous host, as numerous as the sands on

a *I.e., the whole southern part of Canaan.* b *Meaning of Heb. uncertain.*

10.40–42: A summary of the conquest. This is the first of three summaries that divides the book into sections. Another will follow the battle against the northern coalition (11.16–20); the third will introduce the list of the conquered kings (12.7–8). **40:** *The whole country,* an anticipatory note, since at this point the people have not yet taken full possession of the land. The area delineated is congruent with the territory of the kingdom of Judah. **41:** *From Kadesh-barnea to Gaza, all the land of Goshen, and up to Gibeon,* four sites represent the cities Joshua has conquered thus far. The first three do not appear in the conquest tradition, while Gibeon was never conquered (ch 9). The summary hints at the existence of additional conquest stories that were not incorporated here (for Gaza cf. 15.47; Judg. 1.18). **42:** *At a single stroke,* depicting the miraculous character of the conquest, *for the LORD ... fought for Israel,* cf. v. 14. The first summary is by a Judean author who sought to narrate the conquest of Judah separately from that detailing the possession of the land in its entirety.

11.1–23: The battle against the northern coalition at the Waters of Merom. The final battle leads to the conquest of the north, and completes the conquest of the land. Unlike earlier events which all took place in Benjaminite or Judahite territory, the description of the war in upper Galilee is poor in details and leans heavily upon the pattern of the earlier battles. This disparity may suggest that the author was from the later kingdom of Judah, and was intimately familiar only with that region. **1:** *When the news reached,* indicating the last phase of the conquest (see 5.1; 9.1; 10.1). *King Jabin of Hazor:* As with the earlier king of Jerusalem (10.1), the ringleader of the northern coalition's name is known. "King Jabin of Canaan, who reigned in Hazor" is also, somewhat problematically, mentioned in the later period of the judges (Judg. 4.2); his title reflects Hazor's prominence among Canaanite city-states (see Josh. 11.10). The relation between Josh. ch 11 and Judg. ch 4 is disputed, though Jabin was an ancient royal name in Hazor, known from external sources as well. *He sent messages to ...,* patterned after the description of the battle with the southern coalition. Aside from Jabin, only one other king is named, followed by three place names. The participants are *the other kings in the north* (v. 2), dwelling in all regions, including *the Arabah* (v. 2), which geographically belongs to the land of Judah in the south. **2–3:** *North ... south ... Canaanites in the east and in the west ... Amorites ...,* listing the usual six local peoples as well as all four compass points. **4:** *They took the field ... a vast multitude of horses and chariots:* Borrowing the opening formula from 10.5, the author depicts a new element, a field battle against an advanced army with chariots. Chariots play a central role also in the tradition of the clash with Sisera, Jabin's army commander (Judg. 4.3, 13, 15–17).

the seashore—and a vast multitude of horses and chariots. [5] All these kings joined forces; they came and encamped together at the Waters of Merom to give battle to Israel.

[6] But the LORD said to Joshua, "Do not be afraid of them; tomorrow at this time I will have them all lying slain before Israel. You shall hamstring their horses and burn their chariots." [7] So Joshua, with all his fighting men, came upon them suddenly at the Waters of Merom, and pounced upon them. [8] The LORD delivered them into the hands of Israel, and they defeated them and pursued them all the way to Great Sidon [a-]and Misrephothmaim,[-a] and all the way to the Valley of Mizpeh[b] on the east; they crushed them, letting none escape. [9] And Joshua dealt with them as the LORD had ordered him; he hamstrung their horses and burned their chariots.

[10] Joshua then turned back and captured Hazor and put her king to the sword.—Hazor was formerly the head of all those kingdoms.—[11] They proscribed and put to the sword every person in it. Not a soul survived, and Hazor itself was burned down. [12] Joshua captured all those royal cities and their kings. He put them to the sword; he proscribed them in accordance with the charge of Moses, the servant of the LORD. [13] However, all those towns that are still standing on their mounds were not burned down by Israel; it was Hazor alone that Joshua burned down. [14] The Israelites kept all the spoil and cattle of the rest of those cities as booty. But they cut down their populations with the sword until they exterminated them; they did not spare a soul. [15] Just as the LORD had commanded His servant Moses, so Moses had charged Joshua, and so Joshua did; he left nothing undone of all that the LORD had commanded Moses.

[16] Joshua conquered the whole of this region: the hill country [of Judah], the Negeb, the whole land of Goshen, the Shephelah, the Arabah, and the hill country and coastal plain of Israel—[17] [everything] from Mount Halak, which ascends to Seir, all the way to Baal-gad in [c-]the Valley of the Lebanon[-c] at the foot of Mount Hermon; and he captured all the kings there and executed them.

a-a Change of vocalization yields "and Misrephoth on the west."
b Apparently identical with Mizpah in v. 3.
c-c I.e., the valley between the Lebanon and Anti-Lebanon ranges.

5: *Encamped together at the Waters of Merom:* Aside from the place name—somewhere in the Upper Galilee—details are scant, since the southern author is unfamiliar with this area. **6:** *Tomorrow at this time ... lying slain:* While somewhat formulaic (cf. 1.9; 8.1; 10.8), this divine encouragement includes three unparalleled elements: (1) a notice concerning the brevity of the forecasted battle, underscoring divine assistance; (2) the word *slain* "ḥalalim" to describe enemy's defeat, rare in Joshua (cf. 13.22); and (3) a unique divine order: *hamstring their horses and burn their chariots,* put them out of action, with no explicit reason. Chariot forces were identified as the weapons of the ultimate "other," the Philistines (cf. 2 Sam. 8.4). **7:** *Came upon them suddenly:* This is patterned after the previous battle (10.9), though Gilgal is not mentioned here since it is too distant. **8:** *Great Sidon ... Misrephothmaim, ... to the Valley of Mizpeh on the east:* Coming from the south the Israelites pursue their enemies to the north, west and east. **10:** *Then,* lit. "at that time," a marker of a change in subject or source. *Hazor was formerly the head of all those kingdoms:* Tel Hazor is the largest Canaanite tel in Israel. **13:** *All those towns that are still standing on their mounds ... it was Hazor alone that Joshua burned down,* distinguishing between Canaanite towns which were inhabited by Israelites, lit. "standing on their mounds" (cf. Jer. 30.18), and the towns which were burnt. In the south Jericho and Ai were set on fire, never to be inhabited again, while in the north, Hazor alone was burned. Israelite Hazor was a thriving town inhabiting only the upper part of the tel. **15:** *He left nothing undone of all that the LORD had commanded Moses:* Concluding the conquest, the key to a full success is once more repeated—complete obedience to divine orders according to the commandments of Moses. **16–17:** The second of three summaries of the inheritance (cf. 10.40–42; 12.7–8) comprises three parallel members: a general statement ("the whole of this region"); an enumeration of the geographical locations contained within it ("the Negeb," "the hill country," etc.); and a spatial merism ("from Mount Halak ... to Baal-gad ..."). **16:** *The hill country and coastal plain of Israel,* an anachronism, reflecting the author's awareness that this account includes the conquest of what would later be both Judah and Israel. **17:** *From Mount Halak ... to Baal-gad:* The spatial merism mentions two unusual mountains that delimit the scope of the territory of the land of Canaan (cf. Num. 34.1–14) that Joshua fully conquered.

18 Joshua waged war with all those kings over a long period.
19 Apart from the Hivites who dwelt in Gibeon, not a single city
made terms with the Israelites; all were taken in battle. 20 For
it was the LORD's doing to stiffen their hearts to give battle to
Israel, in order that they might be proscribed without quarter
and wiped out, as the LORD had commanded Moses.
21 At that time, Joshua went and wiped out the Anakites from
the hill country, from Hebron, Debir, and Anab, from the entire hill country of Judah, and from the entire hill country of
Israel; Joshua proscribed them and their towns. 22 No Anakites
remained in the land of the Israelites; but some remained in
Gaza, Gath, and Ashdod.
23 Thus Joshua conquered the whole country, just as the
LORD had promised Moses; and Joshua assigned it to Israel to
share according to their tribal divisions. And the land had rest
from war.

12 The following are the local kings whom the Israelites
defeated and whose territories they took possession of:
East of the Jordan, from the Wadi Arnon to Mount Hermon,
including the eastern half of the Arabah: 2 [a]King Sihon of the
Amorites, who resided in Heshbon and ruled over part of
Gilead—from Aroer on the bank of the Wadi Arnon and the
wadi proper up to the Wadi Jabbok [and] the border of the
Ammonites—3 and over the eastern Arabah up to the Sea of
Chinnereth and, southward by way of Beth-jeshimoth at the
foot of the slopes of Pisgah on the east, down to the Sea of
the Arabah, that is, the Dead Sea. 4 Also the territory of King
Og of Bashan—one of the last of the Rephaim—who resided

a *Meaning of vv. 2 and 3 uncertain.*

18: *Over a long period,* a tradition inconsistent with the detail that the battle against the northern coalition lasted one day (v. 6), and with the former summary note that the conquest of Judah was accomplished "at a single stroke" (10.42). This v. thus distinguishes between the conquest of the "kingdom of Judah"—which proceeded quickly and smoothly and was accompanied by signs and wonders—and the conquest of the future "kingdom of Israel," which required "a long period," and lacked earth-shattering divine assistance. **19–20:** As opposed to the command that all the nations of Canaan must be proscribed (Deut. 20.16–18), this passage suggests that the residents of the land could have escaped slaughter had they made peace with the Israelites. But God stiffened their hearts, as He had done to Pharaoh (Exod. 4.21) and Sihon king of Heshbon (Deut. 2.30), so that Israel could enter an empty land. Based on this paragraph, the Rabbis suggested that Joshua sent letters to the residents of Canaanites, offering three choices: evacuate the land (the Girgashites chose to leave—that explains why they are absent from most of the lists), make peace (as did the Gibeonites), or do battle (thus the thirty-one kings enumerated in ch 12; *y. Shev.* 6.1; [= 36:3]). **19:** *Apart from the Hivites who dwelt in Gibeon:* Lacking in the LXX, this clause, likely a later addition, relieves the inconsistency between the complete conquest (cf. 10.40–42) and the story of the Gibeonites. **20:** *Proscribed without quarter,* Heb "ṭhina," mercy (cf. Ezra 9.8). **21–22:** *At that time,* a secondary addition built upon the promise/command to destroy all the Anakites (Deut. 9.1–3). *Joshua ... the Anakites from ... Hebron ...:* Joshua mixes two traditions regarding who captured Hebron, Joshua or Caleb (14.12–15). **22:** *Some remained in Gaza ...,* the first note in the book regarding incomplete conquest. **23:** *Joshua assigned it to Israel ... according to their tribal divisions:* Anticipating the following theme of tribal settlements, the conquest narrative ends here. *The land had rest from war* (also 14.15): This usage indicates peace as a lasting rather than provisional state. Joshua the commander conquered the promised land in totality—the territory of which corresponds to the "land of Canaan" (Num. 34.1–14)—defeated all its kings, and realized God's promise to His people in full. An explicit description of this status appears at the end of Josh. ch 21, "everything was fulfilled" (21.43).

12.1–24: List of conquered kings. This ch presents a summary of the conquest of the land, beginning with the land east of the Jordan, and continuing with that on the west, the book's focus. The concept of the promised land is thus broadened to include Transjordan, albeit it is of a somewhat lower status. The book of Joshua commences with the command to cross the Jordan (1.2), and its crossing symbolizes a transition from "promise" to "fulfillment." Yet there too Joshua's statements to the Transjordanian tribes (1.12–18) present the conquest of Cisjordan as the second phase of a process that Moses had begun. **1:** *From the Wadi Arnon to Mount Hermon ... Arabah,* spatial merism indicating Transjordan. Wadi Arnon marked the northern Moabite border (Num. 21.13), and Israel was allowed to inherit the land north of it, inhabited by the two legendary kings (Num. ch 21; Deut. 1.4)—Sihon, king of Heshbon (vv. 2–3) and Og, king of Bashan (vv. 4–5).

in Ashtaroth and in Edrei 5 and ruled over Mount Hermon,
Salcah, and all of Bashan up to the border of the Geshurites
and the Maacathites, as also over part of Gilead [down to] the
border of King Sihon of Heshbon. 6 These were vanquished by
Moses, the servant of the LORD, and the Israelites; and Moses,
the servant of the LORD, assigned [a]that territory[a] as a possession to the Reubenites, the Gadites, and the half-tribe of
Manasseh.

7 And the following are the local kings whom Joshua and the
Israelites defeated on the west side of the Jordan—from Baal-
gad in the Valley of the Lebanon to Mount Halak, which ascends to Seir—which Joshua assigned as a possession to the
tribal divisions of Israel: 8 in the hill country, in the lowlands,
in the Arabah, in the slopes,[b] in the wilderness, and in the
Negeb—[in the land of] the Hittites, the Amorites, the Canaanites, the Perizzites, the Hivites, and the Jebusites. 9 They were:

the king of Jericho 1
the king of Ai, near Bethel, 1
10 the king of Jerusalem 1
the king of Hebron 1
11 the king of Jarmuth 1
the king of Lachish 1
12 the king of Eglon 1
the king of Gezer 1
13 the king of Debir 1
the king of Geder 1
14 the king of Hormah 1
the king of Arad 1
15 the king of Libnah 1
the king of Adullam 1
16 the king of Makkedah 1
the king of Bethel 1
17 the king of Tappuah 1
the king of Hepher 1
18 the king of Aphek 1
the king of Sharon 1
19 the king of Madon 1
the king of Hazor 1

a-a Lit. "it." *b I.e., the slopes of Pisgah; cf. 13.20.*

6: *Moses ... assigned that territory as a possession to the Reubenites ... :* Vv. 1 and 6 combined are parallel to v. 7, suggesting that the Transjordanian territories are equal in status to Cisjordan. **7:** *From Baal-gad ... to Mount Halak:* This quotes the same two elements of 11.17, but in reverse order, a sign that an earlier source is quoted. *Joshua assigned as a possession,* similar to 11.23, presupposing the tribal divisions which will be defined in the second half of the book. **8:** A list of six geographical areas followed by the typical six nations of the land complement the spatial merism (v. 7), defining the territory west of the Jordan. Together, they depict a totality (cf. 9.1; 10.40; 11.2–3), this time heading the list of the thirty-one kings "whom Joshua and the Israelites defeated" (v. 7), another enumeration depicting totality. **9–24:** *The king of Jericho 1 ... Total number of kings 31:* The list does not correlate fully with the conquest stories, failing to mention some conquered cities, such as Azekah (10.10–11) or Aijalon (10.12), while encompassing sites which appear in conquest traditions outside the book of Joshua such as *Hormah* and *Arad* (v. 14; Num. 21.1–3; Judg. 1.17), and *Bethel* (v. 16; missing in LXX; cf. Judg. 1.22–26). *Aphek,* mentioned in the list (v. 18) is elsewhere an Aramean city conquered when its wall tumbled down after seven days (1 Kings 20.29–30). The list also mentions sites for which we have no conquest traditions at all such as *Adullam* (v. 15; however, LXX reads Adullam instead of Eglon in 10.3, 23), or *Hepher* (v. 17). Yet, the list does follow loosely the order of conquests in Josh. chs 6–11, beginning with *Jericho* and *Ai* (v. 9), and reflecting the majority of sites mentioned in chs 10 (vv. 10–13, 15–16a) and 11 (vv. 19–20). Some of the additional sites are mentioned only in the second half of Josh., such as *Tappuah* (v. 17; cf. 16.8; 17.7–8) or *Jokneam* (v. 22; cf. 21.34). *Tirzah,* ending the list (v. 24) was the Israelite capital prior to Samaria (see, e.g., 1 Kings 15.33; 16.6, 8). The list serves both as a summary of the conquest—the enumeration of conquered sites together with a numerical summation was a common feature in ancient Near eastern conquest narratives—as well as a linchpin connecting the two sections of the book, and perhaps even incorporating traditions relating to the Northern Kingdom. **24:** *Number of kings 31:* LXX mentions twenty-nine kings in total, and lacks also the repetitive "one" following each name. While the exact number is secondary, it appears that approximately thirty kings was an appropriate number signifying a great force (cf. the thirty-two kings fighting alongside Ben-hadad in 1 Kings 20.1, 16; 22.31).

20 the king of Shimron-meron 1
the king of Achshaph 1
21 the king of Taanach 1
the king of Megiddo 1
22 the king of Kedesh 1
the king of Jokneam in the Carmel 1
23 the king of Dor in the district[a] of Dor 1
the king of Goiim in Gilgal 1
24 the king of Tirzah 1
Total number of kings 31.

13 Joshua was now old, advanced in years. The LORD said
to him, "You have grown old, you are advanced in years;
and very much of the land still remains to be taken possession of. 2 This is the territory that remains: all the districts of the
Philistines and all [those of] the Geshurites, 3 from the Shihor,
which is close to Egypt, to the territory of Ekron on the north,
are accounted Canaanite, namely, those of the five lords of the
Philistines—the Gazites, the Ashdodites, the Ashkelonites, the
Gittites, and the Ekronites—and those of the Avvim 4 on the
south; further, all the Canaanite country from Mearah of the Sidonians to Aphek at the Amorite border 5 and the land of the Ge-
balites, with the whole [Valley of the] Lebanon, from Baal-gad at
the foot of Mount Hermon to Lebo-hamath on the east, 6 with all
the inhabitants of the hill country from the [Valley of the] Lebanon to [b-]Misrephoth-maim,[-b] namely, all the Sidonians. I Myself
will dispossess [c-]those nations[-c] for the Israelites; you have only
to apportion [d-]their lands[-d] by lot among Israel, as I have commanded you. 7 Therefore, divide this territory into hereditary
portions for the nine tribes and the half-tribe of Manasseh."

a Meaning of Heb. uncertain. *b-b See note on 11.8.* *c-c Lit. "them."* *d-d Lit. "it."*

13.1–6: The land that yet remains. After the accounts of complete victory followed by summaries of total conquest (10.40–42; 11.16–17), a surprising paragraph refers to territory in the promised land that Joshua and the Israelites failed to conquer. **1:** *Joshua was now old, advanced in years,* mentioned again in 23.1, before Joshua's farewell speech. His advanced years and the failure to completely subjugate the land are causally related, as old age often indicates sexual and military impotence (Abraham, Gen. 18.1; Moses, Deut. 31.2; David, 1 Kings 1.1). *The LORD said to him:* This is the only biblical passage referring to the partial conquest in which God directly addresses the leader. **2–3:** *This is the territory that remains:* Although remaining peoples are mentioned elsewhere (23.4, 7, 12; Judg. 2.21, 23; 3.1), only here is the subject of the remaining territory fully delineated. *All ... the Geshurites ... the five lords of the Philistines,* two general statements, followed by a spatial merism (v. 3), an ethnic comment, and a list of nations describe the southern sector of the land that yet remains. *From the Shihor, which is close to Egypt:* Although the term "Shihor" may elsewhere mean "wadi" (see 19.26), here it reflects its original signification—the Nile. The area demarcated covers the Sinai Desert, in distinction from the more limited southern border of the "land of Canaan" (Num. 34.2–5; cf. Josh. 15.2–4) that follows the course of the "Wadi of Egypt" (identified with Wadi el-Arish). **4–6:** The northern sector of the land that yet remains is described by four general statements and three merisms. **5:** *From Baal-gad at the foot of Mount Hermon to Lebo-hamath:* Baal-gad is linked to the battle against the northern coalition (11.3) and the conquest summaries (11.17; 12.7). *Lebo-hamath,* a prominent border post on the northern boundary (Num. 13.21; 34.8). **6:** *From the ... Lebanon to Misrephoth-maim, ... all the Sidonians,* also appearing in the depiction of the enemy's rout following the battle at the Waters of Merom (11.8). Oddly, the region whose residents Joshua "crushed ..., letting none escape" (11.8) is now part of the "territory that remains." *You have only to apportion their lands by lot,* lit. "bequeath it to Israel," referring not to the division of the land into portions, but to the actual taking possession of it. Vv. 1–6 thus present a picture of an incomplete conquest, referring to wide expanses of unconquered territory. Philistia in the south and the hill country of the Lebanon in the north were depicted as areas that remained outside the spheres of conquest. In the south, the land's borders extended up to "Shihor ... close to Egypt" (v. 3), leaving a vast strip of unconquered land. Chs 1–12 describe how the promise had been fulfilled in full in the past. According to this passage, however, possession of the land had been only partially accomplished, and the full promise would only be fulfilled in the future. This will be accomplished by God Himself: *I Myself will dispossess those nations for the Israelites.*

13.7–19.51: The tribal territories. This section describes the various tribal territories, the second phase of the inheritance of the land: the

8 Now the Reubenites and the Gadites, along with [a]the other
half-tribe,[a] had already received the shares which Moses assigned to them on the east side of the Jordan—as assigned to
them by Moses the servant of the LORD: 9 from Aroer on the
edge of the Wadi Arnon and the town in the middle of the
wadi, the entire Tableland [from] Medeba to Dibon, 10 embracing all the towns of King Sihon of the Amorites, who had
reigned in Heshbon, up to the border of the Ammonites; 11 further, Gilead, the territories of the Geshurites and the Maacathites, and all of Mount Hermon, and the whole of Bashan up
to Salcah— 12 the entire kingdom of Og, who had reigned over
Bashan at Ashtaroth and at Edrei. (He was the last of the remaining Rephaim.) These were defeated and dispossessed by
Moses; 13 but the Israelites failed to dispossess the Geshurites
and the Maacathites, and Geshur and Maacath remain among
Israel to this day. 14 No hereditary portion, however, was assigned to the tribe of Levi, their portion being the fire offerings
of the LORD, the God of Israel, as He spoke concerning them.[b]
15 And so Moses assigned [the following] to the tribe of the
Reubenites, for their various clans, 16 and it became theirs:

a-a Lit. "it." *b See Deut. 18.1.*

settlement that follows the conquest. Yet an examination of its contents reveals that it too contains conquest stories, intertwined with descriptions of the tribal allotments. The chs suggest that the settlement occurs in three stages: (1) While the people were encamped on the steppes of Moab (13.32), Moses assigned the Reubenites, Gadites, and the half-tribe of Manasseh territory conquered on the east of the Jordan (13.8–32). (2) The two largest tribes, the Judahites and the Josephites (Ephraimites and western Manassites) received their allotments (chs 15–17). These portions were assigned by the priest Eleazar, Joshua son of Nun, and the heads of the ancestral houses (14.1). The settlement process included personal conquest initiatives, conflicting with the perspective that Joshua had already completely vanquished the former residents. The territories of these tribes likewise contained foreign enclaves (15.63; 16.10; 17.11–12). (3) Finally, the seven remaining smaller tribes received their inheritance: Benjamin, Simeon, Zebulun, Issachar, Asher, Naphtali, and Dan. These tribes required goading and direction from Joshua (18.1–10). Having surveyed the land and depicting it "in a document, town by town, in seven parts" (18.9), they returned to Joshua at Shiloh, where he cast lots for them and assigned them their territories. No individual conquest initiatives are describe for these tribes, for "the land was now under their control" (18.1), nor does the passage recognize any unconquered enclaves within their allotments. This version of the conquest was overshadowed by the dominant narrative set before it in the first part of the book, chs 6–11. **13.7–33:** This whole section is a flashback to the days of Moses, using earlier traditions from Num. and Deut. Like 12.1–6 which sets the conquest of the land west of the Jordan as the second phase of the conquest started by Moses in Transjordan, 13.8–32 sets the settlement of Israel west of the River Jordan as the second stage of a settlement process which Moses had begun. **13.7:** *Therefore:* Heb "ve-'ata" indicates a transition in the divine address (cf. 1.2; 14.12). *Divide this territory:* As opposed to the former six vv. which dealt with taking possession of the land as a whole, this directive relates to the forthcoming tribal division of *this territory,* which was conquered in totality (cf. 11.16). According to the LXX the v. concluded with a description of the land west of the Jordan "from the Jordan to the Great Sea on the west," parallel to 23.4, and providing a merism that envelopes the second section of the book. **8–12:** The eastern territories in general. **8:** *Which Moses assigned to them:* Although the settlement process in Transjordan is linked to that on the west side, the eastern heritages are not an integral part of the promised land which was assigned by God (1.2; cf. 1.15). *Moses the servant of the LORD,* cf. 1.1, 13, 15; 14.7. **9–10:** *From Aroer ... the entire Tableland ... to Dibon,* a merism depicting the territory of the legendary Sihon king of Heshbon. **11–12:** Enumerations of the regions in the kingdom of Og, king of the Bashan; cf. 12.1–5. The description of Transjordan (in vv. 9–12) as total is expressed by the fivefold repetition of the Heb "kol," meaning "whole" or "all." **13:** *But the Israelites failed ... Geshurites and the Maacathites,* foreign enclaves located within the Transjordanian territories. Unlike similar lists, which combine nations and cities (15.63; 16.10; 17.12; Judg. 1.21, 27–35), this v. mentions peoples, probably referring to small kingdoms (2 Sam. 3.3; 10.6). **14:** *... To the tribe of Levi,* similar to v. 33 that ends the ch. The second half of the book repeatedly refers to the Levites' status (13.33; 14.3–4; 18.7; ch 21). The content and the language of this v. reflect Deut. 18.1–2. **15–23:** The territory of Reuben. **15:** *Moses assigned ... clans:* The same title appears in the following headings of Gad (v. 24) and the half-tribe of Manasseh (v. 29). The word for tribe here is "matteh" rather than "shebet," which was the predominant word for tribe in the first part of the book. "Matteh" creates a link to the following titles of the territories of the western tribes (15.1; 17.1; 18.11; etc.).

The territory from Aroer, on the edge of the Wadi Arnon and the town in the middle of the wadi, up to Medeba—the entire Tableland—17 Heshbon and all its towns in the Tableland: Dibon, Bamoth-baal, Beth-baal-meon, 18 Jahaz, Kedemoth, Mephaath, 19 Kiriathaim, Sibmah, and Zereth-shahar [a-]in the hill of the valley,[-a] 20 Beth-peor, the slopes of Pisgah, and Beth-jeshimoth—21 all the towns of the Tableland and the entire kingdom of Sihon, the king of the Amorites, who had reigned in Heshbon. (For Moses defeated him and the Midianite chiefs Evi, Rekem, Zur, Hur, and Reba, who had dwelt in the land as princes of Sihon. 22 Together with the others that they slew, the Israelites put Balaam son of Beor, the augur, to the sword.) 23 The boundary of the Reubenites was the edge of the Jordan. That was the portion of the Reubenites for their various clans—those towns with their villages.

24 To the tribe of Gad, for the various Gadite clans, Moses assigned [the following], 25 and it became their territory: Jazer, all the towns of Gilead, part of the country of the Ammonites up to Aroer, which is close to Rabbah, 26 and from Heshbon to Ramath-mizpeh and Betonim, and from Mahanaim to the border of Lidbir;[b] 27 and in the Valley, Beth-haram, Beth-nimrah, Succoth, and Zaphon—the rest of the kingdom of Sihon, the king of Heshbon—down to the edge of the Jordan and up to the tip of the Sea of Chinnereth on the east side of the Jordan. 28 That was the portion of the Gadites, for their various clans—those towns with their villages.

29 And to the half-tribe of Manasseh Moses assigned [the following], so that it went to the half-tribe of Manasseh, for its various clans, 30 and became their territory: Mahanaim,[c] all of Bashan, the entire kingdom of Og, king of Bashan, and all of Havvoth-jair[d] in Bashan, sixty towns; 31 and part of Gilead, and Ashtaroth and Edrei, the royal cities of Og in Bashan, were assigned to the descendants of Machir son of Manasseh—to a part of the descendants of Machir—for their various clans.

32 Those, then, were the portions that Moses assigned in the steppes of Moab, on the east side of the Jordan. 33 But no portion was assigned by Moses to the tribe of Levi; the LORD, the God of Israel, is their portion, as He spoke concerning them.[e]

a-a Emendation yields "in the hill country; and in the Valley..."
b Change of vocalization yields "Lo-debar"; cf. 2 Sam. 9.4, 5; 17.27.
c Lit. "from Mahanaim." *d See note on Num. 32.41.* *e See Deut. 18.1.*

21–22: *Midianite chiefs,* a reminder of the battle of Israel against the Midianites (Num. 31.8). *Princes of Sihon:* Under the premise that the two legendary kingdoms of Sihon and Og contained all the territories inherited by the two-and-a-half Transjordanian tribes, the Midianite chiefs are depicted as vassals of Sihon, ignoring their connection to Moab (Num. 22.4, 7), which was not a legitimate target for conquest (Deut. 2.9). **22:** *Balaam,* likewise disassociated from the Moabites (Num. 22.2). *The augur,* ("ha-qosem"), a pejorative term; an added insult to his already negative association with the Midianites in Num. 31.8, based on the use of the word "divination," "qesamim" in the story of Balaam (Num. 22.7). **24–28:** Gad's allotment. **25:** *Jazer, all ... Gilead,* a general depiction relying on Num. 32.1. The conquest of Amorite Jazer was depicted sketchily in Num. 21.32. *Part of the country of the Ammonites:* In the light of Deut.'s (2.19) prohibition to inherit the land of Ammon, the settlement of Israelites there was justified as settlement in territory taken from the kingdom of Sihon (v. 27; cf. the apologetic message of Jephthah to the king of Ammon, Judg. 11.12–27). **27:** *The rest of the kingdom of Sihon,* which was divided between Reuben (v. 21) and Gad. **29–31:** The allotment of the half-tribe of Manasseh. The combination of ancestry within a tribe, spatial merism, and selective listing characterize the account of the allotments east of the Jordan. This description does not include a list of cities as in Reuben and Gad, and the territory is depicted by enumerating geographical areas only. **30:** *The entire kingdom of Og, king of Bashan,* following Deut. 3.13–14. *All of Havvoth-jair:* Here as in Deut. 3.13–14, these villages are situated in the Bashan, while in Num. 32.39–41 and Judg. 10.3–4, they are in the Gilead. **31:** *Part of Gilead ... part of ... Machir,* lit. "half," paralleling half of Manasseh. *Gilead* is most frequently a geographical name, in Transjordan, inhabited also by Gadites (v. 25). *Machir* is a tribal designation, connected to the land west of the Jordan as well (Judg. 5.14). **32:** *The steppes of Moab ...,* quoted from Num. 22.1 (cf. Num. 36.13). **33:** See v. 14 n.

14 And these are the allotments of the Israelites in the land
of Canaan, that were apportioned to them by the priest
Eleazar, by Joshua son of Nun, and by the heads of the ancestral houses of the Israelite tribes, 2 the portions that fell to them
by lot, as the LORD had commanded through Moses for the
nine and a half tribes. 3 For the portion of the other two and a
half tribes had been assigned to them by Moses on the other
side of the Jordan. He had not assigned any portion among
them to the Levites; 4 for whereas the descendants of Joseph
constituted two tribes, Manasseh and Ephraim, the Levites
were assigned no share in the land, but only some towns to
live in, with the pastures for their livestock and cattle. 5 Just as
the LORD had commanded Moses, so the Israelites did when
they apportioned the land.
6 The Judites approached Joshua at Gilgal, and Caleb son of
Jephunneh the Kenizzite said to him: "You know what instructions the LORD gave at Kadesh-barnea to Moses, the man of
God, concerning you and me. 7 I was forty years old when Moses the servant of the LORD sent me from Kadesh-barnea to
spy out the land, and I gave him a forthright report. 8 While my
companions who went up with me took the heart out of the
people, I was loyal to the LORD my God. 9 On that day, Moses
promised on oath, 'The land on which your foot trod shall be
a portion for you and your descendants forever, because you
were loyal to the LORD my God.' 10 Now the LORD has preserved
me, as He promised. It is forty-five years since the LORD made
this promise to Moses, when Israel was journeying through
the wilderness; and here I am today, eighty-five years old.

14.1–5: Another introduction to the inheritance of the land west of the Jordan, again presenting it as parallel to the inheritance of the two-and-a-half eastern tribes (vv. 1–2), and again referring to the non-inheritance of the Levites (3–4; see 13.14 n.). **1:** ... *The priest Eleazar, by Joshua son of Nun, and by the heads of the ancestral houses,* fulfilling Num. 34.13–14, 17–18, 29, following the description of the boundaries of the land of Canaan. The v. is repeated in 19.51, framing the story of the distribution of the land. The mention of Eleazar the priest, Aaron's son and successor (Num. 20.25–28), before Joshua, points to the Priestly origins of this tradition and to Eleazar's role in casting the lots (Num. 27.21). **3–4:** *For .... for ... :* These vv. explain why the Josephites received two inheritances, repeating that the Levites did not get an inheritance (cf. 13.33; 18.7). These are connected, since adding one inheritance while omitting another keeps the number of tribes at twelve. *Towns to live in,* referring to the directive in Num. 35.2, and anticipating its fulfilment in ch 21. **5:** *Apportioned the land:* For the first time in the book the verb "ḥalak," divide, apportion is used (cf. 18.2; Num. 26.53–57), rather than "naḥal," inherit. This accords with the preceding mention of two nouns indicating a "portion," "naḥala" (v. 3), and "share," "ḥelek" (v. 4), from the same root as the verb "ḥalak."

14.6–15.63: The inheritance of Judah is constructed from three genres: (1) personal initiatives of conquest and settlement (14.7–15; 15.13–19); (2) description of the border and a list of Judah's cities (15.1–12, 20, 21–62); and (3) one tribal failure to dispossess, leading to the existence of a foreign enclave within its territory (15.63). The story of Caleb's conquests is split, appearing before and after the border description (15.1–12), suggesting that conquest and settlement are intertwined processes. As in Judg. ch 1, this version of the conquest begins with Judah, not with sites in Benjamin: Jericho, Ai and Gibeon.

14.6–15: The conquest initiative of Caleb. *The Judites,* placing the story of Caleb within its tribal context. A similar story appears in Judg. ch 1, likely based on this one; there the conquest of Hebron is attributed to the tribe of Judah first (Judg. 1.10) then to Caleb (Judg. 1.20). **6:** *Joshua at Gilgal,* parallel to chs 6–11, this places the Israelites in Gilgal and Joshua as their leader, yet Joshua is no military hero here, but more of a Moses figure. *At Kadesh-barnea,* referring to Deut.'s rather than Num.'s version of the story (Deut. 1.19–46). *Moses, the man of God:* This epithet of Moses appears in the titles of two hymns (Deut. 33.1; Ps. 90.1), and in late books (Ezra 3.2; 1 Chron. 23.14; 2 Chron. 30.16). *Concerning you and me:* Caleb and Joshua were the sole survivors of the entire wilderness generation (Num. chs 13–14). **8:** *Took the heart out of the people,* following Deut. 1.28. *I was loyal ... God:* This phrase is repeated here three times (vv. 8, 9, 14), and appears elsewhere only in 1 Kings 11.6; it refers back to the story in Num. 14.24; 32.11–12; Deut. 1.36. **9:** *The land on which your foot trod,* as in Deut. 1.36 (cf. the promise terminology in Deut. 11.24; Josh. 1.3). The spying mission referred to the entire land, though it concentrates on the area of Hebron in the mountains (Deut. 1.24) where the Anakites dwell (Deut. 1.28). **10:** *Eighty-five years old:* According to Deut., after leaving Kadesh-barnea thirty-eight years passed until the entire generation was wiped out (Deut. 2.14). In Kadesh-barnea Caleb was forty years old (v. 7). Now he is eighty-five years old; based on this the Rabbis calculated the

11 I am still as strong today as on the day that Moses sent me;
my strength is the same now as it was then, for battle and for
activity.[a] 12 So assign to me this hill country as the LORD promised on that day. Though you too heard on that day that Anakites are there and great fortified cities, if only the LORD is with
me, I will dispossess them, as the LORD promised."
13 So Joshua blessed Caleb son of Jephunneh and assigned
Hebron to him as his portion. 14 Thus Hebron became the portion of Caleb son of Jephunneh the Kenizzite, as it still is, because he was loyal to the LORD, the God of Israel.—15 The name
of Hebron was formerly Kiriath-arba: [Arba] was the great man
among the Anakites.
And the land had rest from war.

15 The portion that fell by lot to the various clans of the
tribe of Judah lay farthest south, down to the border of
Edom, which is the Wilderness of Zin. 2 Their southern boundary began from the tip of the Dead Sea, from the tongue that
projects southward. 3 It proceeded to the south of the Ascent of
Akrabbim, passed on to Zin, ascended to the south of Kadesh-
barnea, passed on to Hezron, ascended to Addar, and made
a turn to Karka. 4 From there it passed on to Azmon and proceeded to the Wadi of Egypt; and the boundary ran on to the
Sea. That shall be your southern boundary.
5 The boundary on the east was the Dead Sea up to the mouth
of the Jordan. On the northern side, the boundary began at the
tongue of the Sea at the mouth of the Jordan. 6 The boundary
ascended to Beth-hoglah and passed north of Beth-arabah;

a *Lit. "and to go out and come in."*

conquest lasted seven years (*b. Zevaḥ.* 118:b). Yet Caleb's words show no awareness of the complete conquest narrative. Perhaps these implicit seven years assume other traditions of conquest (cf. Judg. 1.1–9). **11:** *I am still as strong today:* This declaration of potency is important for his request *for battle and for activity,* lit. "to go out and come back," an expression referring to military activity, similar to Joshua's role according to Num. 27.17, 21. **12:** *So,* lit. "now" ("ve-'ata"), indicating a transition. *Anakites ... great fortified cities:* Caleb's story shows no awareness of the entire conquest narrative, particularly of the conquest of Hebron (10.37), or the tradition relating Hebron's capture to Joshua himself (11.21), suggesting that nothing has changed in Hebron since Caleb's spying escapade forty-five years earlier. *I will dispossess them:* The verb used is typical of the Deuteronomistic conquest language (cf. 15.63). **14:** *Of Caleb son of Jephunneh the Kenizzite,* ending the story, as it began, with Caleb's full name and affiliation (v. 6). *As it still is,* lit. "to this day." This etiological formula marks the conclusion of foundational stories. **15:** *The name of Hebron ...,* an added note relating to the earlier name of Hebron (see 15.13, 15). *And the land had rest from war:* The final note is a repetition of 11.23, also following the annihilation of the Anakites from Hebron. Yet the wars are not over; Debir, for example, remains to be conquered (15.17).

15.1–19.51: Further distributions. The geographical system reflected in the descriptions that follow is not related to any particular historical period or specific administrative source. It expresses the author's ideological conviction about the land's parameters and tribal allocations, which was drawn from various diverse archival materials augmented by artificial delineations. In their secondary literary life, the tribal-allotment descriptions represent a religious notion linking the triad God–people–land. This section illustrates how God now grants His people tribal land within the broader land whose parameters He noted in the wilderness (Num. 34.1–12). **15.1:** *The portion that fell by lot ... Zin,* a general definition of the territory of Judah in relation to the areas bordering it as in the Benjaminite (18.11); Simeonite (19.1); and Manassite (17.1) allotments. The opening formulation of the tribes belonging to the first Cisjordanian group, Judah and the Josephites (15.1; 16.1; 17.1) indicates that their inheritance was bestowed through the casting of lots (cf. 19.51); this is likely a reworking of an earlier tradition, now found in the LXX, which does not suggest allotment by lots. **2–4:** *Their southern boundary ... :* The description of the southern border of Judah was the source of the almost identical depiction of the southern sector of the land of Canaan (Num. 34.3–5). The border is described as an east-west line via verbs and place names, forming a kind of verbal map in the shape of a virtual tour, from the southern tip of the Dead Sea, via Kadesh-barnea to the Mediterranean. **5–11:** After noting that the Dead Sea demarcated the eastern border, the northern border runs east to west, from the northern tip of the Dead Sea to the Mediterranean. This description parallels the southern boundary of Benjamin (18.15–19). The appearance of the same sites in both descriptions makes it impossible to determine to which tribal territory they belonged, except where the depiction explicitly defines the side

then the boundary ascended to the Stone of Bohan son of Reuben. 7 The boundary ascended [a]from the Valley of Achor
to Debir and turned north[a] to Gilgal,[b] facing the Ascent of
Adummim which is south of the wadi; from there the boundary continued to the waters of En-shemesh and ran on to
En-rogel. 8 Then the boundary ascended into the Valley of
Ben-hinnom, along the southern flank of the Jebusites—
that is, Jerusalem. The boundary then ran up to the top of
the hill which flanks the Valley of Hinnom on the west, at the
northern end of the Valley of Rephaim. 9 From that hilltop the
boundary curved to the fountain of the Waters of Nephtoah
and ran on to the towns of Mount Ephron; then the boundary curved to Baalah—that is, Kiriath-jearim. 10 From Baalah
the boundary turned westward to Mount Seir,[c] passed north
of the slope of Mount Jearim—that is, Chesalon—descended
to Beth-shemesh, and passed on to Timnah. 11 The boundary
then proceeded to the northern flank of Ekron; the boundary curved to Shikkeron, passed on to Mount Baalah, and
proceeded to Jabneel; and the boundary ran on to the Sea.
12 And the western boundary was the edge of the Mediterranean Sea. Those were the boundaries of the various clans of
the Judites on all sides.

13 In accordance with the LORD's command to Joshua, Caleb
son of Jephunneh was given a portion among the Judites,
namely, Kiriath-arba—that is, Hebron. ([Arba] was the father
of Anak.) 14 Caleb dislodged from there the three Anakites:
Sheshai, Ahiman, and Talmai, descendants of Anak. 15 From
there he marched against the inhabitants of Debir—the
name of Debir was formerly Kiriath-sepher—16 and Caleb announced, "I will give my daughter Achsah in marriage to the
man who attacks and captures Kiriath-sepher." 17 His kinsman
Othniel the Kenizzite[d] captured it; and Caleb gave him his
daughter Achsah in marriage.

18 [e]When she came [to him], she induced him[e] to ask her father for some property. She dismounted from her donkey, and
Caleb asked her, "What is the matter?" 19 She replied, "Give
me a present; for you have given me away as Negeb-land;[f] so
give me springs of water." And he gave her Upper and Lower
Gulloth.[g]

a-a Meaning of Heb. uncertain. *b Apparently identical with Geliloth, 18.17.*
c Not the Seir of Edom. *d Cf. 14.6, 14.*
e-e Meaning of Heb. uncertain. Some Greek mss. read "he induced her"; cf. Judg. 1.14.
f I.e., as a dry land, that is, without a dowry. *g I.e., "springs."*

on which the border passed, such as v. 8, *along the southern flank of the Jebusites—that is, Jerusalem* (similarly 18.16), indicating that Jerusalem clearly lay within the territory of the Benjaminites. **12:** *And the western boundary ... Mediterranean Sea:* The western sector of Judah also demonstrates literary affinities with the description of the borders of the land of Canaan (Num. 34.6). The term for the Mediterranean Sea "ha-yam(ah) ha-gadol," typical of the Deuteronomistic layer of Joshua (1.4; 23.4; cf. 13.7–8 [LXX]), indicates that this may have been added.

15.13–19: Conquests and settlements of the house of Caleb (Caleb, Othniel, and his daughter Achsah). This tradition is likely copied from here to Judg. 1.10–15, another depiction of the conquest of the land. The story here parallels and continues 14.6–15. **13–14:** *In accordance with the LORD's command to Joshua:* This command was not previously narrated, and this formulation reflects another case of Joshua echoing Moses (cf. 14.6, 10, 12). *Caleb dislodged from there the three Anakites,* another reference to the foundational tradition of the Calebites in Hebron (cf. 14.6–15). The intentional separation of Calebite traditions by the border description (15.1–12) indicates that according to this part of the book conquest and settlement are inseparable processes. **16:** *I will give my daughter Achsah ... Kiriath-sepher:* This motif resembles David bravely winning the hand of Saul's daughters (1 Sam. 17.25; 18.17, 27). **17:** *His kinsman Othniel,* lit. "his brother," his younger brother according to Judg. 1.13, just as David was the youngest brother in his family. **18:** *She induced him,* yet nothing is reported about his actions; Achsah is the sole initiator of the following scene. *She dismounted from her donkey:* The verb "va-titznah" is rare (found again only in Judg. 4.21); the context determines she did something to display her anxiety that attracted her father's attention, perhaps like Rebekah dismounting from her camel when meeting with Isaac (Gen. 24.64). **19:** *Give me a present,* lit. "a blessing." *And he gave her Upper and Lower Gulloth,* explaining why these springs were part of the territory of the southern Calebite tribal element. **20:** Closing phrase for the border description (cf. 16.8; 18.20, 28).

20 This was the portion of the tribe of the Judites by their clans:
21 The towns at the far end of the tribe of Judah, near the border of Edom, in the Negeb, were: Kabzeel, Eder, Jagur, 22 Kinah,
Dimonah, Adadah, 23 Kedesh, Hazor, Ithnan, 24 Ziph, Telem,
Bealoth, 25 Hazor-hadattah, Kerioth-hezron—that is, Hazor—26 Amam, Shema, Moladah, 27 Hazar-gaddah, Heshmon,
Beth-pelet, 28 Hazar-shual, Beer-sheba, Biziothiah, 29 Baalah,
Iim, Ezem, 30 Eltolad, Chesil, Hormah, 31 Ziklag, Madmannah,
Sansannah, 32 [a]Lebaoth, Shilhim,[a] Ain and Rimmon.[b] Total:
29[c] towns, with their villages.
33 In the Lowland: Eshtaol, Zorah, Ashnah, 34 Zanoah,
En-gannim, Tappuah, Enam, 35 Jarmuth, Adullam, Socoh, Azekah, 36 Shaaraim, Adithaim, Gederah, and Gederothaim—14[d]
towns, with their villages.
37 Zenan, Hadashah, Migdal-gad, 38 Dilan, Mizpeh, Joktheel,
39 Lachish, Bozkath, Eglon, 40 Cabbon, Lahmas, Chithlish,
41 Gederoth, Beth-dagon, Naamah, and Makkedah: 16 towns,
with their villages.
42 Libnah, Ether, Ashan, 43 Iphtah, Ashnah, Nezib, 44 Keilah,
Achzib, and Mareshah: 9 towns, with their villages.
45 Ekron, with its dependencies and villages. 46 From Ekron
westward, all the towns in the vicinity of Ashdod, with their villages—47 Ashdod, its dependencies and its villages—Gaza, its
dependencies and its villages, all the way to the Wadi of Egypt
and the edge of the Mediterranean Sea.
48 And in the hill country: Shamir, Jattir, Socoh, 49 Dannah,
Kiriath-sannah[e]—that is, Debir—50 Anab, Eshtemoh, Anim,
51 Goshen, Holon, and Giloh: 11 towns, with their villages.
52 Arab, Dumah, Eshan, 53 Janum, Beth-tappuah, Aphekah,
54 Humtah, Kiriath-arba—that is, Hebron—and Zior: 9 towns,
with their villages.
55 Maon, Carmel, Ziph, Juttah, 56 Jezreel, Jokdeam, Zanoah,
57 Kain, Gibeah, and Timnah: 10 towns, with their villages.
58 Halhul, Beth-zur, Gedor, 59 Maarath, Beth-anoth, and Eltekon: 6 towns, with their villages.[f]
60 Kiriath-baal—that is, Kiriath-jearim—and Rabbah: 2 towns,
with their villages.
61 In the wilderness: Beth-arabah, Middin, Secacah, 62 Nibshan, Ir-melah,[g] and En-gedi: 6 towns, with their villages.

a-a Cf. below 19.6.
b Cf. Ain, Rimmon, 19.7 below, and 1 Chron. 4.32; En-rimmon, Neh. 11.29.
c The number is uncertain. Some of the same towns are listed under Simeon, cf. 19.1–9; so Rashi.
d The number is uncertain. Tappuah and Enam may have been one place; so Rashi on basis of 17.7.
e Emendation yields "Kiriath-sepher"; cf. Septuagint.
f Septuagint adds: Tekoa, Ephrathah—that is, Bethlehem—Peor, Etam, Kulon, Tatam, Sores, Karem, Gallim, Bether, and Manach—11 towns, with their villages.
g Or "the City of Salt."

15.21–63: The list of the cities of Judah, arranged according to four geographical zones – the Negev (vv. 21–32), the Lowlands (vv. 33–47), the hill country (vv. 48–60), and the wilderness (vv. 61–62). These are divided into districts, probably a dozen originally, each summarized by the total sum of cities included in them (vv. 32, 36, 41, 44, 51, 54, 57, 59, 60, 62). The summaries do not always agree with the cities enumerated in the text before us, indicating that the lists changed over time. **45–47:** The district of the Philistine cities contains diverse material, including the phrase *Ekron ... Ashdod ... Gaza, its dependencies and its villages,* fragments of border descriptions such as *all the way to the Wadi of Egypt* (v. 47), and it lacks a numerical summary. It is an addition to the postulated original administrative document. **59:** One district in the hill country is missing in the Heb, although it appears in the LXX at the end of this v. It includes the cities in the area of Bethlehem and a summary of eleven cities. **63:** *The Judites could not,* this very failure is attributed to the Benjaminites in Judg. 1.21. Indeed the border description of Judah indicates Jerusalem lay in Benjaminite territory (v. 8; cf. 18.16, 28). Whereas the Benjaminites "did not" dispossess the Jebusites (Judg. 1.21), the Judites *could not* dispossess them, though no explanation is offered why (cf. Judg. 1.19). The various traditions regarding the history of Jerusalem indicate its centrality. *To this day:* This conclusion to an etiological formula also characterizes the wording of the Ephraimite failure in Gezer (16.10; cf. Judg. 1.29). In the light of the tradition of the conquest of Jerusalem by David, it cannot be taken as historical, but is a concluding expression of a foundational text.

63 But the Judites could not dispossess the Jebusites, the inhabitants of Jerusalem; so the Judites dwell with the Jebusites in Jerusalem to this day.

16 The portion that fell by lot to the Josephites ran from the Jordan at Jericho—from the waters of Jericho east of the wilderness. From Jericho it ascended through the hill country to Bethel. 2 From Bethel it ran to Luz and passed on to the territory of the Archites at Ataroth, 3 descended westward to the territory of the Japhletites as far as the border of Lower Beth-horon and Gezer, and ran on to the Sea. 4 Thus the Josephites—that is, Manasseh and Ephraim—received their portion.

5 The territory of the Ephraimites, by their clans, was as follows: The boundary of their portion ran from Atroth-addar on the east to Upper Beth-horon, 6 and the boundary ran on to the Sea. And on the north, the boundary proceeded from Michmethath to the east of Taanath-shiloh and passed beyond it up to the east of Janoah; 7 from Janoah it descended to Ataroth and Naarath, touched on Jericho, and ran on to the Jordan. 8 Westward, the boundary proceeded from Tappuah to the Wadi Kanah and ran on to the Sea. This was the portion of the tribe of the Ephraimites, by their clans, 9 together with the towns marked off[a] for the Ephraimites within the territory of the Manassites—all those towns with their villages. 10 However, they failed to dispossess the Canaanites who dwelt in Gezer; so the Canaanites remained in the midst of Ephraim, as is still the case. But they had to perform forced labor.

17 And this is the portion that fell by lot to the tribe of Manasseh—for he was Joseph's first-born. Since Machir, the first-born of Manasseh and the father of Gilead, was a valiant warrior, Gilead and Bashan were assigned to him. 2 And now assignments were made to the remaining Manassites, by their clans: the descendants of Abiezer, Helek, Asriel, Shechem,

a Meaning of Heb. uncertain.

16.1–17.18: The inheritance of the Josephites too is constructed of three genres: (1) personal and tribal initiative of settlement (17.1–6, 14–18); (2) descriptions of the borders of the Josephites in general (16.1–3); of the Ephraimites followed by a note regarding cities (16.5–9); of the Manassites (17.7–10); and (3) tribal failures to dispossess leading to the existence of foreign enclaves within its territory, even within territories of other tribes, namely Issachar and Asher, though this failure is attributed to Manasseh (16.10; 17.11–13). The depiction of the Josephites in general is followed by its components, Ephraim and Manasseh, and is associated with terms found in the wilderness census (Num. 26.28–37). **16.1–4:** For the Josephite territory, only the southern border line is described from the Jordan in the east to the Mediterranean in the west, parallel to the Benjaminite northern line (18.12–13). This was the historical border between the northern kingdom of Israel and the kingdom of Judah. **5–8:** The description of the Ephraimite border depicts the southern and northern lines from a central point, eastwards then westwards. **9:** *The towns marked off for the Ephraimites within the territory of the Manassites,* mentioned again in 17.9, these tribal enclaves, which were not detailed here, were probably significant for taxation reasons. **10:** *Failed to dispossess the Canaanites ... Gezer ... as is still the case:* Ephraim's territory, like Judah's, encompasses a foreign enclave. This note parallels Judg. 1.29, which lacks an etiological end-formula. In the light of the tradition of the complete conquest of Gezer by Pharaoh who gave it to Solomon as a wedding present (1 Kings 9.16) this note too does not indicate historical fact, but functions as a concluding expression of a foundational text. *But they had to perform forced labor:* This addition, missing in the LXX, undermines the previous etiological final note, and equates the fate of the Canaanites in Gezer to that of those in other Josephite enclaves (17.13).

17.1–6: Manassite settlement initiatives. 1: *The portion that fell by lot,* according to LXX "the borders" (similarly in 15.1 and 16.1; the words "boundary" ["gevul"] and portion ["goral"] are similar in Heb). Casting of lots is not mentioned for the large tribes. *For he was Joseph's first-born:* Manasseh is the only tribe to have settled both east and west of the Jordan, justified here by his status as the first-born (of Joseph) who receives a double portion (Deut. 21.17). *Since Machir ... was a valiant warrior:* Gilead and Bashan in Transjordan (Josh. 13.29–31) are attributed to the personal initiative of Machir or his son, Gilead, and not to Moses as in 13.9–12 (cf. Num. 32.39–42). This is in line with the rest of the personal/tribal achievements highlighted in the inheritances of Judah and the

Hepher, and Shemida. Those were the male descendants of
Manasseh son of Joseph, by their clans.
3 [a]Now Zelophehad son of Hepher son of Gilead son of
Machir son of Manasseh had no sons, but only daughters. The
names of his daughters were Mahlah, Noah, Hoglah, Milcah,
and Tirzah. 4 They appeared before the priest Eleazer, Joshua
son of Nun, and the chieftains, saying: "The LORD commanded
Moses to grant us a portion among our male kinsmen." So, in
accordance with the LORD's instructions, they were granted a
portion among their father's kinsmen. 5 Ten districts fell to Manasseh, apart from the lands of Gilead and Bashan, which are
across the Jordan. 6 Manasseh's daughters inherited a portion
in these together with his sons, while the land of Gilead was
assigned to the rest of Manasseh's descendants.
7 The boundary of Manasseh ran from Asher to Michmethath,
which lies near Shechem. The boundary continued to the right,
toward the inhabitants of En-tappuah.—8 The region of Tappuah belonged to Manasseh; but Tappuah, on the border of
Manasseh, belonged to the Ephraimites.—9 Then the boundary descended to the Wadi Kanah. Those towns to the south of
the wadi belonged to Ephraim as an enclave among the towns
of Manasseh. The boundary of Manasseh lay north of the wadi
and ran on to the Sea. 10 What lay to the south belonged to
Ephraim, and what lay to the north belonged to Manasseh,
with the Sea as its boundary. [This territory] was contiguous
with Asher on the north and with Issachar on the east. 11 Within Issachar and Asher, Manasseh possessed Beth-shean and its
dependencies, Ibleam and its dependencies, the inhabitants
of Dor and its dependencies, the inhabitants of En-dor and its
dependencies, the inhabitants of Taanach and its dependencies, and the inhabitants of Megiddo and its dependencies:
[b-]these constituted three regions.[-b]

12 The Manassites could not dispossess [the inhabitants of]
these towns, and the Canaanites stubbornly remained in this
region. 13 When the Israelites became stronger, they imposed
tribute on the Canaanites; but they did not dispossess them.

a *Cf. Num. 27.1–11.* b-b *Meaning of Heb. uncertain.*

Josephites. **2–3:** *Remaining Manassites,* "ha-notarim," here refers to the western Manassites, but in the unit's conclusion in v. 6, to the eastern. *By their clans:* Manasseh is the only tribe whose clans are mentioned; this detail is required to explain the initiative of Zelophehad's daughters. The six clan names are taken from the census list in Num. 26.30–32. *The names of his daughters,* the "sons" of Manasseh were areas in his tribal territory; the "daughters" were cities. Most of them—Abiezer, Helek, Asriel, Shechem, Shemida, Noah and Hoglah—were mentioned in the Samaria Ostraca as sites in Israel ca. 800–750 BCE. Elsewhere in the Bible, personal names may also refer to geographical locations. Hepher and Tirzah appear in the list of Canaanite cities that Joshua conquered (12.17, 24), and Gen. contains traditions referring to former conquests of Shechem (Gen. ch 34; 48.22). Yet the Book of Settlement (13.7–19.51) says nothing about how the Manassites inherited their share. **4:** *They appeared before ... :* The tradition rests upon Num. 26.33; 27.1–11, when they came forward and stood before "Moses, Eleazar the priest, the chieftains, and the whole assembly, at the entrance of the Tent of Meeting" (Num. 27.2). Now they come forward before the priest Eleazar, Joshua and the chieftains, demanding fulfillment of that promise (cf. Caleb's demand from Joshua, 14.6, 13). As in the case of Achsah (15.18–19), female initiative is not connected to conquests, but to inner-Israelite tribal divisions. **5–6:** *Ten districts,* the five "daughters" take the place of their "father's" one district, together with five more Manassite clans. *The land of Gilead was assigned to the rest,* the conclusion returns to the beginning (see vv. 1–2).

17.7–13: The allotment of Manasseh. Only the southern boundary is delineated in detail, parallel to the northern boundary of Ephraim (16.6–9). **8:** *The region of Tappuah belonged to Manasseh; but Tappuah ... belonged to the Ephraimites:* This elucidation of the specific side to which the border sites belonged reflects the conjectured administrative source defining territorial allocations for tax-collection purposes. (See the similar note in v. 9.) **10:** *With the Sea as its boundary. [This territory] was contiguous with Asher on the north, and with Issachar on the east,* all sides but the southern are referred to loosely, in an effort to present an all-encompassing account. **11–13:** This is a lengthy roster of Canaanite cities that belong to the Manassites, while located in the allotments of Issachar and Asher. The list of Canaanite enclaves parallels the register that appears (alongside an additional catalog) in Judg. 1.27–28 as foreign enclaves in Manasseh.

14 The Josephites complained to Joshua, saying, "Why have
you assigned as our portion a single allotment and a single district, seeing that we are a numerous people whom the LORD has
blessed so greatly?" 15 "If you are a numerous people," Joshua
answered them, "go up to the forest country and clear an area
for yourselves there, in the territory of the Perizzites and the
Rephaim, seeing that you are cramped in the hill country of
Ephraim." 16 "The hill country is not enough for us," the Josephites replied, "and all the Canaanites who live in the valley area
have iron chariots, both those in Beth-shean and its dependencies and those in the Valley of Jezreel." 17 But Joshua declared to the House of Joseph, to Ephraim and Manasseh, "You
are indeed a numerous people, possessed of great strength;
you shall not have one allotment only. 18 The hill country shall
be yours as well; true, it is forest land, but you will clear it and
possess it to its farthest limits. And you shall also dispossess
the Canaanites, even though they have iron chariots and even
though they are strong."

18 The whole community of the Israelite people assembled at Shiloh, and set up the Tent of Meeting there.
The land was now under their control; 2 but there remained
seven tribes of the Israelites which had not yet received their

17.14–18: The Josephites' complaint, and Joshua's solution. 14: *The Josephites complained to Joshua:* The conquest-settlement process of the two-and-a-half big western tribes begins and ends with a tribe approaching Joshua (cf. 14.6). *A numerous people:* This refers back to the divine order in Num. (26.54; 33.54a) to increase the share assigned to larger groups. **16:** *Canaanites who live in the valley area have iron chariots:* According to archeology the valleys of *Beth-shean* and *Jezreel* were inhabited by Canaanites during the transition between the Bronze (Canaanite) and Iron (Israelite) ages. Mentioning their control of advanced military technology reflects the more realistic attitude of the Book of Settlement (see intro.) towards the conquest-settlement process, which does not cite the decree of total destruction of all Canaanites, nor refer to miraculous divine intervention. **17:** *Possessed of great strength:* Joshua affirms the Josephites' claim of being numerous, yet stresses that this signifies their strength. **18:** *The hill country shall be yours as well:* The final explanatory v. repeats the Heb word "ki," meaning "for" or "if" five times. *And you shall also dispossess the Canaanites, even though they have iron chariots and even though they are strong,* alternately, according to the LXX, "because you are stronger than them."

This tribal initiative completes the conquest and settlement of the two-and-a-half largest tribes in Cisjordan: Judah and the Josephites. The tribes approach Joshua, who assigned them their territories, and went ahead to settle them, dealing with military and environmental issues, such as Anakites, dry land or forests. Inheritance precedes tribal conquest. The combination of personal or tribal initiatives with border descriptions and notes regarding foreign enclaves is intentional. The process of settlement is local, protracted and realistic, though not necessarily precisely historical. The tribes inherit portions according to their size, failures mix with successes, and there is no separation between conquest and settlement. In contrast to the beginning of the book, Joshua is not a military leader; his role is confined to dividing the land, together with the priest Eleazar and the chieftains, apportioning it to the various tribes and families and encouraging them to actualize their inheritance.

18.1–19.51: The allotments of the seven smaller tribes. After the settlement of the large tribes, the clans assembled at Shiloh in the territory of Ephraim (16.6), where they set up the Tent of Meeting. The seven remaining smaller tribes received their inheritance: Benjamin, Simeon, Zebulun, Issachar, Asher, Naphtali, and Dan. The description begins with Benjamin and ends with Dan (19.40–48), the tribes whose territories lay between the large tribes, Judah and the Josephites. The small tribes are described as requiring goading and direction from Joshua. The tribes do not engage in battle, nor need they worry about remaining in foreign enclaves, for "the land was now under their control" (18.1).

18.1–10: Introduction: Survey and division of territories by lots. 1: *The whole community ... assembled:* The words *community* ("eda"), and *assembled* ("va-yiqahalu"), as well as the mention of the *Tent of Meeting* point to the Priestly orientation of this v. *At Shiloh,* the important pre-monarchic religious center about 30 km (18.64 mi) north of Jerusalem (1 Sam. chs 1–4), recalled also in later times (Jer. 26.6). *Set up the Tent of Meeting there:* This desert institution (Exod. 29.42) is found in the book of Joshua in Priestly additions only here and at the end of this unit (19.51), in connection to the division by casting of lots. *The land was now under their control:* The same verb ("k-b-sh") in passive form is found in the Priestly story of the Transjordanian tribes (Num. 32.22, 29; cf. the late description of David's days, 1 Chron. 22.18), and resonates with the Priestly account of the creation (Gen. 1.28). No details are given in this part of the book as to how the completion of the conquest of the promised land

portions. 3 So Joshua said to the Israelites, "How long will
you be slack about going and taking possession of the land
which the LORD, the God of your fathers, has assigned to
you? 4 Appoint three men of each tribe; I will send them out
to go through the country and write down a description of it
for purposes of apportionment, and then come back to me.
5 They shall divide it into seven parts—Judah shall remain by
its territory in the south, and the house of Joseph shall remain
by its territory in the north.—6 When you have written down
the description of the land in seven parts, bring it here to me.
Then I will cast lots for you here before the LORD our God.
7 For the Levites have no share among you, since the priesthood of the LORD is their portion; and Gad and Reuben and
the half-tribe of Manasseh have received the portions which
were assigned to them by Moses the servant of the LORD, on
the eastern side of the Jordan."

8 The men set out on their journeys. Joshua ordered the men
who were leaving to write down a description of the land—
"Go, traverse the country and write down a description of it.
Then return to me, and I will cast lots for you here at Shiloh
before the LORD."

9 So the men went and traversed the land; they described
it in a document, town by town, in seven parts, and they returned to Joshua in the camp at Shiloh. 10 Joshua cast lots for
them at Shiloh before the LORD, and there Joshua apportioned
the land among the Israelites according to their divisions.

11 The lot of the tribe of the Benjaminites, by their clans,
came out first. The territory which fell to their lot lay between
the Judites and the Josephites. 12 The boundary on their northern rim began at the Jordan; the boundary ascended to the
northern flank of Jericho, ascended westward into the hill
country and ran on to the Wilderness of Beth-aven. 13 From
there the boundary passed on southward to Luz, to the flank

was achieved. **3:** *How long will you be slack:* Joshua's role is still that of goading and directing, though here he initiates the process, rather than reacting to tribal or personal initiatives. **4:** *Go through the country and write down a description of it,* reflecting a ground survey preceding the determination of borders. This inspired the prevalent method of describing land boundaries in Josh., in which they are delineated as a consecutive line, reflecting a virtual tour. "Walking" through the length and breadth of the land also symbolizes taking possession of it (cf. Gen. 13.7 and R. Eliezer's statement in *b. B. Bat.* 100a). **6:** *When you have written down ... in seven parts ... I will cast lots for you:* Biblical traditions describe two conflicting methods of assigning land portions: casting lots of shares of presumably similar size, reflecting practices of inheritance of private lots, and assigning lots according to the size of the groups (Num. 26.54; 33.54a). The Book of Settlement (see intro.) distinguishes between the larger tribes who inherited according to size (cf. Josh. 17.14, 17; 19.9) and between the remaining seven tribes, which divided the land into seven equal shares and cast lots. The Rabbis reconciled these two different ways by suggesting that the entire division was of unequal shares according to the group's size, and then this division was divinely sanctioned through lot (*b. B. Bat.* 122a). **8:** *Joshua ordered ... "Go, traverse the country .... return to me ... at Shiloh ...,"* a repetition of v. 6, adding the name of Shiloh. **9:** *Described it in a document,* "sepher" refers to any written document and reflects real customs of surveys of land and people (cf. David's census, 2 Sam. 24.5–9). **10:** *Joshua apportioned the land ... their divisions,* missing in the LXX. The Heb text highlights that the account ends as it started, before the LORD at Shiloh (see v. 1).

18.11–28: The first lot: the boundary of Benjamin and its town list. The description of Benjamin's allotment is the largest of the small tribes, comprising eighteen vv. compared to the common seven or eight. It also shares many characteristics with that of Judah's: both present full delineations of the border; include continuous and detailed border delineations that use verbs to highlight places, followed by a list of towns; and their lists include summaries at the end of each district (as does the Simeonite list of cities in 19.6, 7). These similarities may reflect a time when Benjamin was, along with Judah, part of the Southern Kingdom of Judah. Both also reflect conspicuous inconsistencies between the border demarcations and inventory of towns. The case of Bethel is illustrative—while the Benjaminite boundary runs south of Bethel (v. 13), Bethel itself is listed as a Benjaminite city (v. 22). No such discrepancies appear in the accounts of the northern tribes. **11:** *The territory ... lay between the Judites and the Josephites:* A prefatory comment identifies the Benjaminite allotment's relation to the areas bordering it, like the Judahite boundary description (15.1; cf. the opening to the Simeonite allotment, 19.1). **12–13:** The northern boundary parallels part of the southern boundary of the Josephites (16.1–3; cf. 16.5). **12:** *Began at the Jordan,* the boundary also ends at the Jordan, presenting a full

of Luz—that is, Bethel; then the boundary descended to
Atroth-addar [and] to the hill south of Lower Beth-horon.
14 The boundary now turned and curved onto the western
rim; and the boundary ran southward from the hill on the
south side of Beth-horon till it ended at Kiriath-baal—that is,
Kiriath-jearim—a town of the Judites. That was the western
rim. 15 The southern rim: From the outskirts of Kiriath-jearim,
the boundary passed westward[a] and ran on to the fountain of
the Waters of Nephtoah. 16 Then the boundary descended to
the foot of the hill by the Valley of Ben-hinnom at the northern
end of the Valley of Rephaim; then it ran down the Valley of
Hinnom along the southern flank of the Jebusites to En-rogel.
17 Curving northward, it ran on to En-shemesh and ran on to
Geliloth, facing the Ascent of Adummim, and descended to
the Stone of Bohan son of Reuben. 18 It continued northward
to the edge of the Arabah and descended into the Arabah.
19 The boundary passed on to the northern flank of Beth-
hoglah, and the boundary ended at the northern tongue of
the Dead Sea, at the southern end of the Jordan. That was the
southern boundary. 20 On their eastern rim, finally, the Jordan
was their boundary. That was the portion of the Benjaminites,
by their clans, according to its boundaries on all sides.

21 And the towns of the tribe of the Benjaminites, by its
clans, were: Jericho, Beth-hoglah, Emek-keziz, 22 Beth-arabah,
Zemaraim, Bethel, 23 Avvim, Parah, Ophrah, 24 Chephar-
ammonah, Ophni, and Geba—12 towns, with their villages.
25 Also Gibeon, Ramah, Beeroth, 26 Mizpeh, Chephirah, Mo-
zah, 27 Rekem, Irpeel, Taralah, 28 Zela, Eleph, and Jebus[b]—that
is, Jerusalem—Gibeath [and] Kiriath:[c] 14 towns, with their villages. That was the portion of the Benjaminites, by their clans.

19 The second lot fell to Simeon. The portion of the tribe of
the Simeonites, by their clans, lay inside the portion of
the Judites. 2 Their portion comprised: Beer-sheba—or Sheba—
Moladah, 3 Hazar-shual, Balah, Ezem, 4 Eltolad, Bethul,[d] Hormah, 5 Ziklag, Beth-marcaboth, Hazar-susah, 6 [e-]Beth-lebaoth,
and Sharuhen[-e]—13 towns, with their villages. 7 Ain, Rimmon,
Ether, and Ashan: 4 towns, with their villages—8 together with
all the villages in the vicinity of those towns, down to Baalath-
beer [and] Ramath-negeb. That was the portion of the tribe of
the Simeonites, by their clans. 9 The portion of the Simeonites
was part of the territory of the Judites; since the share of the
Judites was larger than they needed, the Simeonites received a
portion inside their portion.

a *Emendation yields "eastward."* *b* *Heb. "the Jebusite."*
c *Emendation yields "and Kiriath-jearim."* *d* *15.30 reads "Chesil."*
e-e *15.32 reads "Shilhim."*

circle (vv. 19–20). The description of the southern border (vv. 15–19) parallels most of the Judahite northern boundary (15.5–9), yet is drawn from west to east. This suggests the incorporation of segments from originally independent sources. **21–28:** The list of Benjaminite towns is arranged in two districts, with numerical summaries (vv. 24, 28). **25–28:** *Gibeon ... Beeroth ... Chephirah ... Kiriath* [-jearim]: The list does not distinguish between these Gibeonite towns, which according to ch 9 remained Hivite (9.17), and other Benjaminite cities. **28:** *Jebus—that is, Jerusalem:* Although the v. mentions "the Jebusite" (see translators' note *b*), elsewhere a foreign nation, there is no indication here that Jerusalem is a foreign enclave, contra 15.63 and Judg. 1.21.

19.1–9: The second lot: the town list of Simeon. 1: *Lay inside the portion of the Judites,* mentioned again in v. 9, cf. Judg. 1.3. The Simeonite heritage is defined solely by a list of towns. The majority of the list parallels Judah's Negev district (15.26–32) and a few cities from the district of the Shephelah (15.42). The list also appears in 1 Chron. 4.28–33. The identification of the allotment's location parallels that of the Judahites (15.1) and the Benjaminites (18.11), which share the same format of the town list divided into districts, with numerical summaries at the end of each district. These three tribes, Judah, Simeon, and Benjamin, comprised the territory of the kingdom of Judah. While discrepancies within the lists and border descriptions suggest they were taken from various sources, these were official lists, constructed in a similar format. **9:** *Since the share of the Judites was larger than they needed:* Following the pattern of division according to size underlying the inheritances of the larger tribes, this claim is the opposite of the Josephites' complaint (17.14–18). It contradicts the order of Joshua not to include the territories of Judah and Joseph in the survey of the seven remaining tribes (18.5).

[10] The third lot emerged for the Zebulunites, by their clans.
The boundary of their portion: Starting at Sarid, [11] their boundary[a] ascended westward to Maralah, touching Dabbesheth and
touching the wadi alongside Jokneam. [12] And it also ran from
Sarid along the eastern side, where the sun rises, past the territory of Chisloth-tabor and on to Daberath and ascended to
Japhia. [13] From there it ran [back] to the east, toward the sunrise, to Gath-hepher, to Eth-kazin, and on to Rimmon, where
it curved to Neah. [14] Then it turned—that is, the boundary on
the north—to Hannathon. Its extreme limits[b] were the Valley
of Iphtah-el, [15] Kattath, Nahalal, Shimron, Idalah, and Bethlehem: 12 towns, with their villages. [16] That was the portion of the
Zebulunites by their clans—those towns, with their villages.
[17] The fourth lot fell to Issachar, the Issacharites by their clans.
[18] Their territory comprised: Jezreel, Chesulloth, Shunem,
[19] Hapharaim, Shion, Anaharath, [20] Rabbith, Kishion, Ebez,
[21] Remeth, En-gannim, En-haddah, and Beth-pazzez. [22] The
boundary touched Tabor, Shahazimah, and Beth-shemesh;
and their boundary ran to the Jordan: 16 towns, with their villages. [23] That was the portion of the tribe of the Issacharites, by
their clans—the towns with their villages.
[24] The fifth lot fell to the tribe of the Asherites, by their clans.
[25] Their boundary[a] ran along Helkath, Hali, Beten, Achshaph,
[26] Allammelech, Amad, and Mishal; and it touched Carmel on
the west, and Shihor-libnath. [27] It also ran[c] along the east side
to Beth-dagon, and touched Zebulun and the Valley of Iphtah-
el to the north, [as also] Beth-emek and Neiel; [d-]then it ran to
Cabul on the north,[-d] [28] Ebron,[e] Rehob, Hammon, and Kanah,
up to Great Sidon. [29] The boundary turned to Ramah and on
to the fortified city of Tyre; then the boundary turned to Hosah [d-]and it ran on westward to Mehebel,[-d] Achzib, [30] Ummah,
Aphek, and Rehob: 22 towns, with their villages. [31] That was
the portion of the tribe of the Asherites, by their clans—those
towns, with their villages.

a *I.e., the southern one.*
b *I.e., the northwest corner, opposite the starting point, Sarid.*
c *I.e., from Helkath, v. 25.* *d-d* *Meaning of Heb. uncertain.*
e *Some Heb. mss., as well as Josh. 21.30 and 1 Chron. 6.59, read "Abdon."*

19.10–39: The inheritance of the northern tribes. The boundary depictions of the northern tribes—Zebulun, Issachar, Asher, and Naphtali—are intertwined with city rosters and are fragmentary and incomplete. The descriptions of the first and last Galilean tribes, Zebulun and Naphtali, follow closely the pattern of Judah and Benjamin, yet they are much briefer and incomplete. The southern author, while trying to depict a complete system, seems to have had only limited information regarding their territories.

19.10–16: The third lot: the inheritance of Zebulun. Zebulun's inheritance is the first of the Galilean tribes, situated in the lower Galilee between the mountains of Carmel in the west (near modern-day Haifa) and Tabor in the east. While the inheritance of Zebulun includes a border description followed by a town list like that of Judah and Benjamin, the account is not homogenous and some of the syntax is problematic (see v. 13). The inventories of the cities refer to a limited number of towns (v. 15), not arranged by districts. The author of this account may have employed a list of stations located on the caravan route that crossed the Jordan south of the Kinneret (Sea of Galilee) and proceeded westward. **15:** *Nahalal,* mentioned in Judg. 1.30 as an unsubdued Canaanite city in the territory of Zebulun, together with Kitron (perhaps *Kattath* here). In Josh. these are regular Zebulunite towns. **16:** *Towns, with their villages:* Identical summary formulations appear also in the Issacharite, Asherite, and Naphtalite heritages (vv. 22, 30, 38), yet the summaries refer to all the cities mentioned, not just in the lists. The LXX, which omits the summary formulas in the northern tribes, is more original; the summaries were probably added to enhance the uniformity among the descriptions of the tribal allotments.

19.17–23: The fourth lot: the inheritance of Issachar. Issachar's lot is east of Manasseh (17.10) and Zebulun's, extending from Mount Tabor in the west to the River Jordan in the east. Primarily a roster of cities, it also includes a border-like note (v. 22). Judg. ch 1 does not refer to foreign enclaves in Issachar's lot, but Jacob's blessing supports Joshua's depiction, when it mentions Issachar's willingness to live in his pleasant country even as a serf, using the familiar term for performing forced labor (Gen. 49.15).

19.24–31: The fifth lot: the inheritance of Asher. Asher's inheritance lay west of Zebulun's (v. 27), north of Manasseh (17.10), and included the coastline from Carmel to Sidon. Like Issachar's lot, the delineation of the Asherite portion is principally a city roster with some border terminology. Judg. ch 1 mentions a lengthy

32 The sixth lot fell to the Naphtalites, the Naphtalites by their
clans. 33 *a* Their boundary ran from Heleph, Elon-bezaanannim,
Adami-nekeb, and Jabneel to Lakkum, and it ended at the Jordan. 34 The boundary then turned westward to Aznoth-tabor
and ran from there to Hukok. It touched Zebulun on the south,
and it touched Asher on the west, and Judah at the Jordan on
the east. 35 Its fortified towns were Ziddim, Zer, Hammath, Rak-
kath, Chinnereth, 36 Adamah, Ramah, Hazor, 37 Kedesh, Edrei,
En-hazor, 38 Iron, Migdal-el, Horem, Beth-anath, and Beth-
shemesh: 19 towns, with their villages. 39 That was the portion
of the tribe of the Naphtalites, by their clans—the towns, with
their villages.

40 The seventh lot fell to the tribe of the Danites, by their
clans. 41 Their allotted territory comprised: Zorah, Eshtaol,
Ir-shemesh, 42 Shaalabbin, Aijalon, Ithlah, 43 Elon, Timnah, Ekron, 44 Eltekeh, Gibbethon, Baalath, 45 Jehud, Bene-berak, Gath-
rimmon, 46 Me-jarkon, and Rakkon, at the border near Joppa.
47 But the territory of the Danites slipped from their grasp. So
the Danites migrated and made war on Leshem.[b] They captured
it and put it to the sword; they took possession of it and settled
in it. And they changed the name of Leshem to Dan, after their
ancestor Dan. 48 That was the portion of the tribe of the Danites,
by their clans—those towns, with their villages.

49 When they had finished allotting the land by its boundaries,
the Israelites gave a portion in their midst to Joshua son of Nun.

a The geography of vv. 33–35 is unclear in part. *b Called Laish in Judg. 18.7 ff.*

roster of unsubdued cities in Asher's territory defining the Asherites as dwelling among the Canaanites (Judg. 1.31–32), but the same sites are listed here among Asherite cities. The list of foreign enclaves in the territories of Issachar and Asher which belonged to the Manassites (see 17.11–13) is not mentioned here. The description of the Asherite allotment lacks a northern border.

19.32–39: The sixth lot: the inheritance of the Naphtalites. The Naphtalite inheritance lay north of Zebulun, east of Asher, from the area of the Tabor to Jordan (v. 34). Like the descriptions of Judah, Benjamin, and Zebulun it includes continuous border delineations followed by a list of towns, yet Naphtali's description is confined to a denotation of the southern border (vv. 32–34). *And Judah at the Jordan on the east* (v. 34): The mention of Judah here is a mistake. As in the description of the Asherites, Judg. ch 1 depicts the Naphtalites as Israelites dwelling among the Canaanite populace (Judg. 1.33). Those Canaanite unsubdued cities are listed here as belonging to the Naphtalites with no reservation. The northern Naphtalite border is missing, too (as is Asher's). Maps of the tribal inheritances accordingly often lack a northern border altogether. The author's vagueness is due to a lack of sources, clarity, or information concerning the northern region.

19.40–48: The seventh lot: the inheritance of the Danites. Of the seven tribes whose heritages were assigned by lot at Shiloh, only the Danites engaged in conflict (v. 47). These operations were nevertheless conducted outside the original territory assigned to the tribe in the Shephelah. The Danite description is composed primarily of a roster of towns (vv. 41–45), followed by a border notation (v. 46). The list looks as though it is aligned to the Judah-Benjamin-Simeon group, with some of the names appearing in the roster of towns belonging to the Judahites (15.33) and forming part of the account of the northern Judahite border (15.10–11). This roster is not divided into provinces, however, and the numerical summary is also absent (19.48). Some of the cities listed appear in Judg. ch 1 as Amorite settlements on which the Ephraimites imposed forced labor (Judg. 1.35). Although the Danite inheritance is here in the south, they eventually lived in the far north (see Judg. 1.34; 5.17; 18.1–31), and thus they are included here with other northern tribes. **47:** *But the territory of the Danites slipped from their grasp,* avoiding any hint that human forces are responsible for the non-conquest (contrast Judg. 1.34–35; 18.1), neglecting to clarify what happened or why. The verb *slipped,* "va-yetzeʾ," "went out" with "gevul," "border" as its subject is reminiscent of border descriptions. The Danites were the only tribe whose territory remained theoretical. It is uncertain what became of their cities in the south, yet a list of their actual cities in the north is not provided.

19.49–51: Conclusion. 49: *When they had finished:* The concluding remarks begin and end with the same verb, mentioned only here in the book: they had finished "va-yekhalu," first allotting the land (v. 49), then to divide it (v. 51), corresponding to the beginning of this part of the book (13.7; 14.1). The language is reminiscent of the Priestly story of the creation of the world (Gen. 2.1–2), hinting that the real creation has only now been completed. *The land by its boundaries,* alluding to the conception of the "land of Canaan" (Num. 34.2). *The Israelites gave a portion ... to Joshua,* a unique reversal of roles.

50 At the command of the LORD they gave him the town that
he asked for, Timnath-serah in the hill country of Ephraim; he
fortified the town and settled in it.
51 These are the portions assigned by lot to the tribes of Israel
by the priest Eleazar, Joshua son of Nun, and the heads of the
ancestral houses, before the LORD at Shiloh, at the entrance of
the Tent of Meeting.

20

When they had finished dividing the land, 1 the LORD
said to Joshua: 2 "Speak to the Israelites: Designate the
cities of refuge—about which I commanded you through Moses—3 to which a manslayer who kills a person by mistake, unintentionally, may flee. They shall serve you as a refuge from
the blood avenger. 4 He shall flee to one of those cities, present
himself at the entrance to the city gate, and plead his case before the elders of that city; and they shall admit him into the city
and give him a place in which to live among them. 5 Should the
blood avenger pursue him, they shall not hand the manslayer
over to him, since he killed the other person without intent
and had not been his enemy in the past. 6 He shall live in that
city until he can stand trial before the assembly, [and remain
there] until the death of the high priest who is in office at that
time. Thereafter, the manslayer may go back to his home in his
own town, to the town from which he fled."

50: *At the command of the LORD,* not mentioned explicitly, yet hinted at in Caleb's request recalling the divine instructions "concerning you and me" (14.6). Thus the Book of Settlement is framed by the personal portions that the two survivors of the desert generation, Caleb and Joshua, had asked for in Judah and in Ephraim (14.12; 19.50). *He fortified the town,* in the manner of founding kings (1 Kings 12.25; 16.24). *Timnath-serah,* this will also be his place of burial (24.30, Judg. 12.9). **51:** *These are the portions assigned by lot ... at Shiloh:* The final statement joins two separate elements. Its first half relates to the heading of the section dealing with the Judahites and Josephites, whose lots "were apportioned to them by the priest Eleazar, by Joshua son of Nun, and by the heads of the ancestral houses" (14.1). The second half refers to the seven tribes whose heritages were assigned by lot at Shiloh (18.1–10). The amalgamation blurs the divergence between the two groups by denoting that all received their share from Eleazar, Joshua, and the ancestral heads, by lot, at Shiloh (similarly in Num. 34.13, 16–18).

20.1–22.8: Addenda to the "Book of Settlement." After concluding the division of the land and its settlement, three additional chs deal with other geographical issues related to settlement. The cities of refuge (ch 20) and Levitical cities (ch 21) are connected in reverse order to Num. ch 35. There they follow a detailed border description of the perimeters of the land of Canaan (Num. 34.1–12) and a reference to the leaders— the priest Eleazar, Joshua, and the chieftains—who will apportion the land (Num. 34.16–29), themes developed in the preceding chs of Josh. The content of 22.1–8 concludes the settlement east of the Jordan, corresponding to its appearance at the beginning of the book (1.12–18).

20.1–9: The cities of refuge. The LXX version of this ch is significantly shorter, lacking vv. 4–6a and the note regarding the death of the high priest in v. 6b. The shorter version corresponds more closely to the Priestly account of the divine command to appoint cities of refuge (Num. 35.9–15), while the longer Heb version integrates more passages about the cities of refuge, especially from Deut. 19.1–13. The account in Josh. lists the names of the six designated cities, three in Cisjordan and three in Transjordan; the latter are found in Deut. 4.43. The MT additions relate mostly to the Deuteronomic law of refuge cities (Deut. 19.1–7); the MT story thus includes both Priestly and Deuteronomistic elements, a sign of its late composition. **1–2:** *The LORD said to Joshua: "Speak to the Israelites ...":* Everywhere else in the book direct divine speech to Joshua is marked by Heb "va-yo'mer" (1.1; 4.1, 16; 6.2; etc.). This unique use of "va-yedaber" reflects a common Priestly formula (cf. Num. 6.22–23; 9.9–10), perhaps a direct borrowing from the opening of the Priestly city of refuge laws in Num. 35.9–10. *Designate,* follows the Priestly use of the root "n-t-n," as in Num. 35.13–14, vs. Deuteronomic "b-d-l" (Deut. 4.41; 19.2, 7). **3:** *By mistake,* Priestly terminology (cf. Num. 35.15); *unintentionally,* Deuteronomistic terminology (cf. Deut. 4.42; 19.4), missing in the LXX, suggesting that at a later stage of the story, it was brought more in line with the laws of Deut. (See 20.1–9 n.) **4:** *At the entrance to the city gate:* A trial by the elders of the refuge city determining the killer's right to enter the city is unique, refining the Deuteronomic law that any manslayer who flees to the cities of refuge may be retrieved from there by the elders of his home town and handed to the blood avenger (see Deut. 19.3, 12). *Give him a place,* citing the law in Exod. 21.13: "I will assign you a place to which he can flee" (cf. 1 Sam. 27.5). **5:** *Had not been his enemy in the past,* see Deut. 4.42; 19.4, 6. **6:** *Until he can stand trial before the assembly,* based on the Priestly version (Num. 35.24–25), resulting in a process of

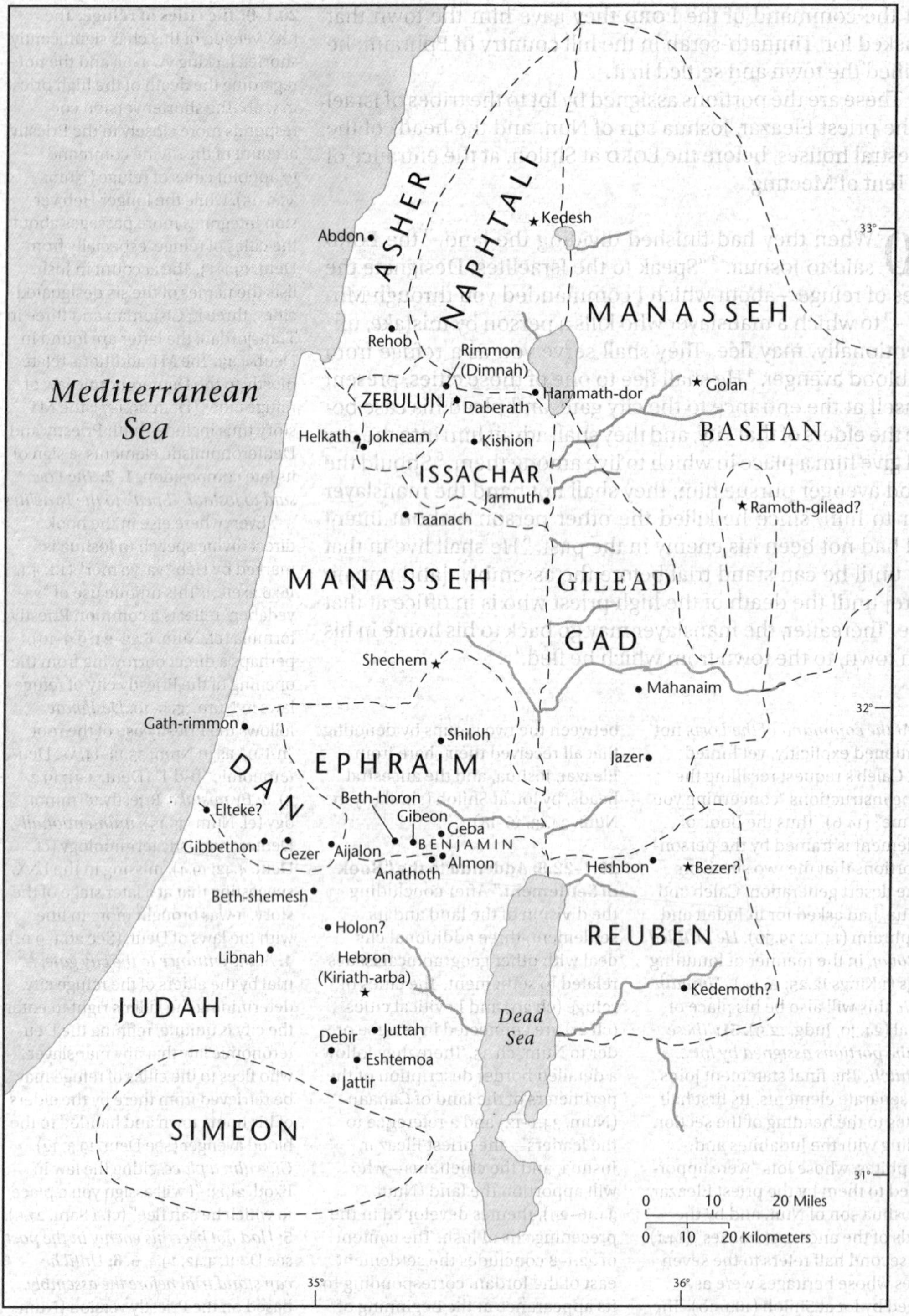

The Levitical cities. Cities of refuge are highlighted with a star. The tribal boundaries are shown by a dashed line.

[7]So they set aside Kedesh in the hill country of Naphtali in
Galilee, Shechem in the hill country of Ephraim, and Kiriath-
arba—that is, Hebron—in the hill country of Judah. [8]And
across the Jordan, east of Jericho, they assigned Bezer in the
wilderness, in the Tableland, from the tribe of Reuben; Ramoth in Gilead from the tribe of Gad; and Golan in Bashan
from the tribe of Manasseh. [9]Those were the towns designated[a]
for all the Israelites and for aliens residing among them, to
which anyone who killed a person unintentionally might flee,
and not die by the hand of the blood avenger before standing
trial by the assembly.

21 The heads of the ancestral houses of the Levites approached the priest Eleazar, Joshua son of Nun, and the
heads of the ancestral houses of the Israelite tribes, [2]and spoke
to them at Shiloh in the land of Canaan, as follows: "The LORD
commanded through Moses that we be given towns to live in,
along with their pastures for our livestock." [3]So the Israelites,
in accordance with the LORD's command, assigned to the Levites, out of their own portions, the following towns with their
pastures:
[4]The [first] lot among the Levites fell to the Kohathite clans.
To the descendants of the priest Aaron, there fell by lot 13 towns
from the tribe of Judah, the tribe of Simeon, and the tribe of
Benjamin; [5]and to the remaining Kohathites [there fell] by lot
10 towns from the clans of the tribe of Ephraim, the tribe of
Dan, and the half-tribe of Manasseh.
[6]To the Gershonites [there fell] by lot 13 towns from the clans
of the tribe of Issachar, the tribe of Asher, the tribe of Naphtali,
and the half-tribe of Manasseh in Bashan.
[7][And] to the Merarites, by their clans—12 towns from the
tribe of Reuben, the tribe of Gad, and the tribe of Zebulun.
[8]The Israelites assigned those towns with their pastures by lot
to the Levites—as the LORD had commanded through Moses.

a Meaning of Heb. uncertain.

a double trial. *Until the death of the high priest.... from which he fled,* an addition based on Num. 35.24, 28, missing in the LXX. **7–8:** The three cities west of the Jordan appear only here, matching the three designated Transjordanian cities of Deut. 4.43. While in Deut. 4.41–43 Moses had already designated the Transjordanian cities, Josh. ch 20 agrees with Num. 35.10 that this will happen only after the crossing of the Jordan. Hence Moses is mentioned as the recipient of the original instruction (20.2), but not as the designator of cities (v. 8). **9:** A summation, based on Num. 35.12, 15, in reverse order—such reversals may indicate that an earlier source is being quoted.

21.1–43: The Levitical cities. The non-inheritance of the Levites was mentioned in key points of the framework of the Book of Settlement, both in sections using Priestly (14.3–4; 18.7; cf. Num. 35.2–3) and Deuteronomistic terminology (13.14, 33; cf. Deut. 18.1–2). This ch refers to the fulfillment of the divine injunction to designate cities to the Levites in the Priestly source (Num. 35.1–8). The framework of forty-eight cities altogether, including six refuge cities and forty-two other cities, is described there (Num. 35.6). The plan is schematic, with each tribe contributing approximately four cities, and the Levites divided into four groups. The list appears again in 1 Chron. 6.39–66.

21.1–3: Introduction. 1: *The heads of the ancestral houses,* cf. Num. 36.1. *Approached the priest Eleazar, Joshua ... and the heads ... :* The tribal initiative is reminiscent of that of the Judahites (14.6) and Josephites (17.14). The large tribes approached Joshua alone, whereas the Levites approach the triadic leadership as in the story of Zelophehad's daughters (17.4; cf. Num. 27.1–2; 36.1). Eleazar, Joshua and the heads of the ancestral houses were considered responsible for the entire division of Cisjordan according to the frame in 14.1 and 19.51.

21.4–8: General lists of Levitical groups and their cities in the tribal territories. 4: *Descendants of the priest Aaron:* The priests received the cities in the territories of the tribes Judah, Simeon, and Benjamin, that is, the kingdom of Judah. **5:** *The remaining,* appearing five times in the Heb in this ch (vv. 5, 20, 26, 34, 40; cf. 17.2, 6). **8:** *The Israelites assigned ... by lot to the Levites,* repetition of v. 3, closure of the general introduction.

21.9–19: The Priestly cities. 9: *Which will be listed by name,* lit. "give names," "va-yiqra'," a mark of ownership (cf. Num. 32.38, 41). **11–12:** *Kiriath-arba— that is, Hebron:* These vv. try to reconcile two different traditions regarding Hebron by distinguishing between the city and its pastures around it (assigned to the Levites) and its fields and villages (assigned to Caleb; see 14.13–15; 15.13). **13:** *The city of refuge for manslayers,* the term is unique to our ch, appearing four more times (vv. 21, 27, 32, 36). The list repeats the assignment of Hebron to the Aaronites while establishing its status as a refuge city according to the rule that all refuge cities were also Levitical (Num. 35.6). The Rabbis inferred that the opposite was also true: the other forty-two Levitical cities were also cities of refuge (*b. Mak.* 10:1; 13:1). **19:** *Descendants of the priest Aaron:* The concluding v. repeats the term found in v. 10, here explicitly calling them priests.

21.20–38: The cities of the remaining three groups of Levites. Two vv. including four more names of cities in Reuben dropped out of the list after v. 35; they are found in some Bibles (see translators' note at v. 35). They can be restored according to 1 Chron. 6.63–64, matching the sum stated in v. 38.

9 From the tribe of the Judites and the tribe of the Simeonites
were assigned the following towns, which will be listed by
name; 10 they went to the descendants of Aaron among the Kohathite clans of the Levites, for the first lot had fallen to them.
11 To them were assigned in the hill country of Judah Kiriath-
arba—that is, Hebron—together with the pastures around it.
[Arba was] the father of the Anokites.[a] 12 They gave the fields
and the villages of the town to Caleb son of Jephunneh as his
holding. 13 But to the descendants of Aaron the priest they assigned Hebron—the city of refuge for manslayers—together
with its pastures, Libnah with its pastures, 14 Jattir with its pastures, Eshtemoa with its pastures, 15 Holon with its pastures,
Debir with its pastures, 16 Ain with its pastures, Juttah with its
pastures, and Beth-shemesh with its pastures—9 towns from
those two tribes. 17 And from the tribe of Benjamin: Gibeon
with its pastures, Geba with its pastures, 18 Anathoth with its
pastures, and Almon with its pastures—4 towns. 19 All the
towns of the descendants of the priest Aaron, 13 towns with
their pastures.

20 [b]As for the other clans of the Kohathites, the remaining
Levites descended from Kohath, the towns in their lot were:
From the tribe of Ephraim 21 they were given, in the hill country of Ephraim, Shechem—the city of refuge for manslayers—
with its pastures, Gezer with its pastures, 22 Kibzaim with its
pastures, and Beth-horon with its pastures—4 towns. 23 From
the tribe of Dan, Elteke with its pastures, Gibbethon with its
pastures, 24 Aijalon with its pastures, and Gath-rimmon with
its pastures—4 towns. 25 And from the half-tribe of Manasseh,
Taanach with its pastures, and Gath-rimmon with its pastures—2 towns. 26 All the towns for the remaining clans of the
Kohathites came to 10, with their pastures.

27 To the Gershonites of the levitical clans: From the half-
tribe of Manasseh, Golan in Bashan—the city of refuge for
manslayers—with its pastures, and Beeshterah with its pastures—2 towns. 28 From the tribe of Issachar: Kishion with its
pastures, Dobrath with its pastures, 29 Jarmuth with its pastures, and En-gannim with its pastures—4 towns. 30 From
the tribe of Asher: Mishal with its pastures, Abdon with its
pastures, 31 Helkath with its pastures, and Rehob with its
pastures—4 towns. 32 From the tribe of Naphtali, Kedesh in
Galilee—the city of refuge for manslayers—with its pastures,
Hammoth-dor with its pastures, and Kartan with its pastures—3 towns. 33 All the towns of the Gershonites, by their
clans, came to 13 towns, with their pastures.

34 To the remaining Levites, the clans of the Merarites: From
the tribe of Zebulun, Jokneam with its pastures, Kartah with its

a Elsewhere Anakites; cf. Num. 13.22; Deut. 9.2. *b Explicating v. 5.*

pastures, 35 Dimnah with its pastures, and Nahalal with its pastures—4 towns.[a] 36 From the tribe of Gad, Ramoth in Gilead—the city of refuge for manslayers—with its pastures, Mahanaim with its pastures, 37 Heshbon with its pastures, and Jazer with its pastures—4 towns in all. 38 All the towns which went by lot to the Merarites, by their clans—the rest of the levitical clans—came to 12 towns. 39 All the towns of the Levites within the holdings of the Israelites came to 48 towns, with their pastures. 40 [b]Thus those towns were assigned, every town with its surrounding pasture; and so it was with all those towns.

41 The LORD gave to Israel the whole country which He had sworn to their fathers that He would assign to them; they took possession of it and settled in it. 42 The LORD gave them rest on all sides, just as He had promised to their fathers on oath. Not one man of all their enemies withstood them; the LORD delivered all their enemies into their hands. 43 Not one of the good things which the LORD had promised to the House of Israel was lacking. Everything was fulfilled.

22 Then Joshua summoned the Reubenites, the Gadites, and the half-tribe of Manasseh, 2 and said to them, "You have observed all that Moses the servant of the LORD commanded you, and have obeyed me in everything that I commanded you. 3 You have not forsaken your kinsmen through the long years down to this day, but have faithfully observed the Instruction of the LORD your God. 4 Now the LORD your God has given your kinsmen rest, as He promised them. Therefore turn and go to your homes, to the land of your holdings beyond the Jordan that Moses the servant of the LORD assigned to you. 5 But be very careful to fulfill the Instruction and the Teaching that Moses the servant of the LORD enjoined upon you, to love the LORD your God and to walk in all His ways, and to keep His commandments and hold fast to Him, and to serve Him with all your heart and soul."

a *Some mss. and editions add the following (cf. 1 Chron. 6.63–64): "And from the tribe of Reuben: Bezer with its pastures, Jahaz with its pastures, Kedemoth with its pastures, and Mephaath with its pastures—4 towns."*
b *Meaning of verse uncertain.*

21.39–40: Summary. 40: *Thus those towns were assigned,* Heb "tihiyena," "they shall be," used only here in Josh., is reiterated four times in the Priestly Num. 35.11–15 to assign refuge cities. *And so it was with all those towns:* The concluding v. is almost lyrical, beginning and ending with the phrase *those towns,* with the word "town" doubled in the middle, meaning "every town."

21.41–43: A conclusion of the book. This glorious Deuteronomistic ending of the entire conquest-settlement process testifies to one of the stages of the formation of the book, which once may have ended here (cf. 11.23). Heb "kol," "all," "everything," or "whole," is a key word, appearing six times: God gave Israel the *whole* country; His oath to the forefathers was "completely" fulfilled; *not one man of all their enemies withstood them; the LORD delivered all their enemies;* not one of "all" the good things was lacking; *Everything was fulfilled.* This repetition emphasizes the completeness of the conquest, the predominant idea of the book. The motifs correspond to the introduction to the book: God giving them the land (1.2) that He had sworn to their fathers (1.6); God giving them rest (1.15); not one man of their enemies will withstand them (1.5, in the address to Joshua; LXX, Vg and Syriac versions there render the verb in pl., as in 21.42).

22.1–34: Transjordanian matters. After the inheritance and settlement of the land, Joshua is sending the two-and-a-half eastern tribes back to their land (vv. 1–8) in conclusion to their exchange at the beginning of the book (1.12–18). Following, the story of the building of an altar by the Jordan leads to the establishment of the religious relationship between the two-and-a-half eastern tribes and the people settled in the land of Canaan.

22.1–8: The Transjordanian tribes go home. 1: *Then,* Heb "'az," indicating the change of subject and/or source (cf. 8.30 n.; 10.12 n.). *Joshua summoned,* his role as leader and initiator of events resumed, as in the first half of the book (cf. 4.4; 6.6). **2:** *You have observed ...,* echoing 1.13, 16–17. **3:** *The long years,* mentioned in the summary of the conquest (11.18). *To this day,* a common Deuteronomistic formula (cf. e.g., 4.3; 7.26). *Faithfully observed,* a Deuteronomistic term (Deut. 11.1; 1 Kings 2.3). **4:** *To the land of your holdings,* Priestly terminology, as opposed to Deuteronomistic "the land ... your possession" (1.15). Its appearance here may reflect the influence of the following Priestly story, which uses the term (cf. 22.9, 19). **5:** *But ... :* The particle (Heb "raq") introduces a typical Deuteronomistic directive to adhere to the Instruction and the Teaching of Moses (cf. Deut. 11.13, 22; 30.16, 20). This v. parallels and completes 1.7, also beginning with "raq."

6 Then Joshua blessed them and dismissed them, and they
went to their homes.
7 To the one half-tribe of Manasseh Moses had assigned territory in Bashan, and to the other Joshua assigned [territory]
on the west side of the Jordan, with their kinsmen.[a]
Furthermore, when Joshua sent them[b] off to their homes, he
blessed them 8 and said to them, "Return to your homes with
great wealth—with very much livestock, with silver and gold,
with copper and iron, and with a great quantity of clothing. Share
the spoil of your enemies with your kinsmen." 9 So the Reubenites, the Gadites, and the half-tribe of Manasseh left the Israelites at Shiloh, in the land of Canaan, and made their way back to
the land of Gilead, the land of their own holding, which they had
acquired by the command of the LORD through Moses. 10 When
they came to the region of the Jordan in the land of Canaan, the
Reubenites and the Gadites and the half-tribe of Manasseh built
an altar there by the Jordan, a great conspicuous altar.
11 A report reached the Israelites: "The Reubenites, the Gadites, and the half-tribe of Manasseh have built an altar opposite the land of Canaan, in the region of the Jordan, across
from the Israelites." 12 When the Israelites heard this, the whole
community of the Israelites assembled at Shiloh to make war
on them. 13 But [first] the Israelites sent the priest Phinehas
son of Eleazar to the Reubenites, the Gadites, and the half-
tribe of Manasseh in the land of Gilead, 14 accompanied by ten
chieftains, one chieftain from each ancestral house of each of
the tribes of Israel; they were every one of them heads of ancestral houses of the contingents of Israel. 15 When they came
to the Reubenites, the Gadites, and the half-tribe of Manasseh
in the land of Gilead, they spoke to them as follows:

a I.e., the other nine tribes. *b I.e., the two and a half tribes.*

6: *Joshua blessed them ... and they went to their homes,* a typical ending of a story, as in 24.28 (cf. 1 Kings 8.66). **7:** The emphasis on the split tribe of Manasseh suggests that perhaps vv. 1–6 originally dealt only with the tribes of Reuben and Gad (cf. 22.32–34; Num. 32.1–38). **8:** *With great wealth,* Heb "nekhasim" appears in very late texts (Eccl. 5.18; 6.2; 2 Chron. 1.11, 12; cf. Ezek. 6.8; 7.26). The blessing turns out to be an instruction: *Share the spoil of your enemies with your kinsmen,* probably with the western tribes (cf. 1.14–15; 22.3–4). The story of the conquest rarely mentioned spoils, whether consecrated to God (6.19, 24), or approved for taking (8.27). This addition was made in a later period to define the Transjordanian tribes as equals to their western brethren.

22.9–34: The "altar" by the Jordan. **22.9–12:** The opening of the story. In this unique story of religious confrontation between the Israelites settled to the west and those to the east of the Jordan River, Israel is led by the priest Phinehas son of Eleazar, while Joshua is not mentioned. Phinehas is known to have saved the people from the wrath of God at Peor (Num. ch 25), a sin which is recalled here expressly (v. 17). The story follows the pattern of a foundation tale of a site, but the location remains vague, and the "altar"—in shape but not in function—is not given a name. The story focuses on the altar's newly-found religious status agreed upon by both sides. The historical background of this dispute could be the 5th c. BCE debate over whether or not the Transjordanians, headed by Tobiah, were a part of the community centered in Jerusalem (Neh. 2.10, 19, 20; 13.1–9). Alternately, the Transjordan community may represent all those who live outside of Israel, and the story aims to teach that in order for them to retain their identity and ties with Israel they must not conduct sacrificial practices elsewhere, because only one altar is legitimate, that which stands before His Tabernacle (22.29). **9:** *At Shiloh,* connecting the story to the Book of Settlement (18.1, 8–10; 19.51; cf. 21.1). *In the land of Canaan,* four of the eight times this name appears in the book are in our story, in its beginning (vv. 9, 10, 11), and end (v. 32). Jordan is the border of the land of Canaan (v. 25; see Num. 34.1–12), and by using this term the story distinguishes between the status of Canaan and that of Transjordan, designated *the land of Gilead* (vv. 9, 13, 15, 32). Similarly, the story distinguishes between *the Reubenites* ("benei Reuben"), *the Gadites* ("benei Gad"), *and the half-tribe of Manasseh,* vs. *the Israelites* ("benei Israel"). **10:** *The region of the Jordan in the land of Canaan:* According to this v., the spectacular altar was built next to the Jordan, on its western side. **11:** *Opposite the land of Canaan ... across from the Israelites:* According to this translation the altar was built east of the Jordan, yet the Heb might refer to its western side, as in the previous v. In either case, the altar is not at the centralized place of worship. **12:** *The whole community ... assembled at Shiloh,* same as 18.1. *To make war on them:* The phrase used is found only in our story, and possibly indicates late language.

16 “Thus said the whole community of the LORD: What is this
treachery that you have committed this day against the God
of Israel, turning away from the LORD, building yourselves
an altar and rebelling this day against the LORD! 17 Is the sin
of Peor, which brought a plague upon the community of the
LORD, such a small thing to us? We have not cleansed ourselves from it to this very day; 18 and now you would turn away
from the LORD! If you rebel against the LORD today, tomorrow
He will be angry with the whole community of Israel. 19 If it is
because the land of your holding is unclean, cross over into
the land of the LORD's own holding, where the Tabernacle of
the LORD abides, and acquire holdings among us. But do not
rebel against the LORD, and do not rebel against us by building for yourselves an altar other than the altar of the LORD our
God. 20 When Achan son of Zerah violated the proscription,
anger struck the whole community of Israel; he was not the
only one who perished for that sin.”

21 The Reubenites, the Gadites, and the half-tribe of Manasseh replied to the heads of the contingents of Israel: They
said, 22 “God, the LORD God! God, the LORD God! He knows,
and Israel too shall know! If we acted in rebellion or in treachery against the LORD, do not vindicate us this day! 23 If we built
an altar to turn away from the LORD, if it was to offer burnt
offerings or meal offerings upon it, or to present sacrifices of
well-being upon it, may the LORD Himself demand [a reckon-
ing]. 24 We did this thing only out of our concern that, in time
to come, your children might say to our children, ‘What have
you to do with the LORD, the God of Israel? 25 The LORD has
made the Jordan a boundary between you and us, O Reubenites and Gadites; you have no share in the LORD!’ Thus your
children might prevent our children from worshiping the
LORD. 26 So we decided to provide [a witness] for ourselves by
building an altar—not for burnt offerings or [other] sacrifices,

22.13–32: The inquiry conducted by the delegation headed by the priest Phinehas and ten chieftains, acting as a judicial tribunal. **15:** *In the land of Gilead:* The main story locates the scene in the heart of the land of Gilead.

22.16–29: The charge of the western delegation (vv. 16–20) is answered by self-justification of the eastern tribes (vv. 22–29). **16:** *Treachery … against the God of Israel:* The religious charge refers to building an altar outside of the centralized sanctuary. The story nowhere suggests that the altar was dedicated to another god, yet the tribes are accused of *treachery,* “ma‘al,” the same strong term used of Achan (22.20; cf. 7.1); the root is used seven times in this story (vv. 16, 20, 22, 31); of *turning away from the LORD*—mentioned four times in this story (22.16, 18, 23, 29); and of *rebelling … against* Him, “m-r-d” is repeated six times (vv. 16, 18, 19, 22, 29), borrowed from the realm of international relations (2 Kings 18.7; 24.1; cf. Num. 14.9). **17:** *The sin of Peor:* See Num. 31.16 where the noun treachery (“ma‘al”) appears. *Such a small thing to us?* See Num. 16.9, 13; the syntax resembles Neh. 9.32. **18:** *He will be angry with the whole community,* recalling the plague due to the sin of Peor (v. 17) and the divine anger (“qetzef”) following Achan's violation of the ban (v. 20). After the rising of Korah and his company Moses and Aaron oppose this paradigm of divine anger at the entire community for one group's sin (Num. 16.22). **19:** *If it is because the land of your holding is unclean,* (cf. Amos 7.17), namely ritually impure. This conception is suggested, but not here presented as a fact, as a possible motive for building the altar. It is eventually implicitly rejected, together with the entire “case.” *The land of the LORD's own holding,* a unique phrase, formulated to distinguish between *the land of your holding* (cf. also vv. 4, 9), a Priestly term designating the land of Canaan (Lev. 14.34; 25.24) as well as Transjordan (cf. Num. 32.22, 29) as here, and between the land proper, west of the Jordan. *An altar other than the altar of the LORD our God,* reflecting the concept that sacrifices may be carried out in one place only, since the days of the desert wanderings (cf. Lev. 17.1–7). **22:** *God, the LORD God! …* : Stating three divine names twice, this cry is both an oath formula to refute the legal charges and a statement of faith (cf. 1 Kings 18.39). **22–24:** *If we acted … do not vindicate us,* a typical oath formula, formed as a conditional phrase, introduced by the word *if* (“'im”) repeated five times (vv. 22–24), four times referring to the allegations, and finally defining the real purpose of the altar, by a negative emphatic expression “if not” (“'im lo'”), translated *only.* **24:** *Your children might say to our children:* The children's question is a common motif in etiological stories (see Exod. 13.14; Josh. 4.6, 21), but is here used rhetorically as a statement (see 2 Sam. 16.10). **25:** *You have no share in the LORD:* Like the rebellious cries of political separatism (2 Sam. 20.1; 1 Kings 12.16), here the core tribes, signify exclusivity and ban groups living outside the land from belonging to the same religious community. This is the major concern of the story, twice repeated (again in v. 27).

27 but as a witness between you and us, and between the generations to come—that we may perform the service of the
LORD before Him[a] with our burnt offerings, our sacrifices, and
our offerings of well-being; and that your children should not
say to our children in time to come, 'You have no share in the
LORD.' 28 We reasoned: should they speak thus to us and to our
children in time to come, we would reply, 'See the replica of
the LORD's altar,[a] which our fathers made—not for burnt offerings or sacrifices, but as a witness between you and us.' 29 Far
be it from us to rebel against the LORD, or to turn away this day
from the LORD and build an altar for burnt offerings, meal offerings, and sacrifices other than the altar of the LORD our God
which stands before His Tabernacle."
30 When the priest Phinehas and the chieftains of the community—the heads of the contingents of Israel—who were with
him heard the explanation given by the Reubenites, the Gadites,
and the Manassites, they approved. 31 The priest Phinehas son
of Eleazar said to the Reubenites, the Gadites, and the Manassites, "Now we know that the LORD is in our midst, since you
have not committed such treachery against the LORD. You have
indeed saved the Israelites from punishment by the LORD."
32 Then the priest Phinehas son of Eleazar and the chieftains
returned from the Reubenites and the Gadites in the land of Gilead to the Israelites in the land of Canaan, and gave them their
report. 33 The Israelites were pleased, and the Israelites praised
God; and they spoke no more of going to war against them, to
ravage the land in which the Reubenites and Gadites dwelt.
34 The Reubenites and the Gadites named the altar ["Witness"], meaning, "It is a witness between us and them that the
LORD is [our] God."

23 Much later, after the LORD had given Israel rest from
all the enemies around them, and when Joshua was
old and well advanced in years, 2 Joshua summoned all Israel,
their elders and commanders, their magistrates and officials,
and said to them: "I have grown old and am advanced in years.

a *I.e., at Shiloh.*

27–28: *As a witness between you and us,* recalling the pillar set by Laban and Jacob at Gilead as a witness to their covenant, followed by a sacrifice and a meal (Gen. 31.44–54). *Your children should not say to our children .... should they speak thus to us ... :* This repetition is typical of legal terminology—a direct prohibition followed by a case describing what will happen if the prohibition is violated. **29:** *Far be it from us:* As it begins, the rebuttal of the charges of treachery also ends with an oath (cf. 1 Sam. 26.10–11; 1 Kings 21.3).

22.30–34: The resolution of the difficulty. 30: *They approved:* The approval is later confirmed again by the entire community (v. 33). **31:** *The LORD is in our midst:* God has not left His abode, and will not spurn His people (Lev. 26.11). *You have indeed saved the Israelites,* a complete reversal of affairs: The outsiders did the right thing all along and saved the people. This contrasts with Phinehas (Num. ch 25), who single-handedly saved the community. **34:** *Named the altar:* The name is missing, and Rashi suggested filling it in as "Witness," in the light of the following explanation *meaning, "It is a witness between us and them ..."* The story of the confrontation takes place in the heart of Transjordan (v. 15). "Witness" (Heb "ʿed") referred originally to the name of the region Gilead, and to the tradition that etymologizes its meaning as "gal ʿed," "the mound of witness" (see Gen. 31.44–54). The etiology of the missing name of this altar indicates this eastern site was original, and it was secondarily "moved" in the story's introduction to the western side of the Jordan (22.10–11). *The LORD is [our] God:* This story establishes the concept that people living outside the land can worship God and belong to His community, as long as they remain loyal to the cultic center in Israel and refrain from creating competing sacrificial sites.

23.1–16: Joshua's farewell speech. The Deuteronomistic authors divided the history of ancient Israel into different periods by inserting speeches at key moments. These speeches, saturated with Deuteronomistic phraseology and ideas, serve both to unite the various epochs, leading to eventual destruction and exile, but also to distinguish between the various periods. Joshua's speech ends the period of conquest and settlement, highlighting past victories and cautioning the people to keep the covenant. The site of the farewell speech is not mentioned (contrast Deut. 1.1). **1:** *Much later, after the LORD had given Israel rest ... around them,* a time formula, indicating a change of subject or a different source. This resumes 21.42. *Joshua was old ... :* Repeated in his own words (v. 2), this was also the opening to the description of "the land [that] still remains" (13.1). Joshua's senescence is the grounds for his farewell speech, as in

[3]You have seen all that the LORD your God has done to all
those nations on your account, for it was the LORD your God
who fought for you. [4]See, I have allotted to you, by your tribes,
[the territory of] these nations that still remain, and that of all
the nations that I have destroyed, from the Jordan to the Mediterranean Sea in the west. [5]The LORD your God Himself will
thrust them out on your account and drive them out to make
way for you, and you shall possess their land as the LORD your
God promised you.
[6]"But be most resolute to observe faithfully all that is written
in the Book of the Teaching of Moses, without ever deviating
from it to the right or to the left, [7]and without intermingling
with these nations that are left among you. Do not utter the
names of their gods or swear by them; do not serve them or
bow down to them. [8]But hold fast to the LORD your God as you
have done to this day.
[9]"The LORD has driven out great, powerful nations on your
account, and not a man has withstood you to this day. [10]A single man of you would put a thousand to flight, for the LORD
your God Himself has been fighting for you, as He promised
you. [11]For your own sakes, therefore, be most mindful to love
the LORD your God. [12]For should you turn away and attach
yourselves to the remnant of those nations—to those that are
left among you—and intermarry with them, you joining them
and they joining you, [13]know for certain that the LORD your
God will not continue to drive these nations out before you;
they shall become a snare and a trap for you, a scourge to your
sides and thorns in your eyes, until you perish from this good
land that the LORD your God has given you.
[14]"I am now going the way of all the earth. Acknowledge with
all your heart and soul that not one of the good things that the
LORD your God promised you has failed to happen; they have
all come true for you, not a single one has failed. [15]But just as
every good thing that the LORD your God promised you has
been fulfilled for you, so the LORD can bring upon you every
evil thing until He has wiped you off this good land that the

the cases of other significant figures (Abraham in Gen. 24.1, Samuel in 1 Sam. 12.2, and David in 1 Chron. 23.1; 29.28). **2–3:** *Summoned all Israel, ... "you have seen ...,"* as did Moses (Deut. 29.1). *Their elders ... and officials,* again in 24.1, recalling Deut. 29.9 (cf. Josh. 8.33). **3:** *All those nations:* This Heb term seven times in this ch designates the inhabitants of the land (vv. 3, 4, 7, 9, 12, 13), emphasizing that those who remained (vv. 4, 7, 12, 13) are dangerous since they might lead Israel astray (cf. Deut. 7.17, 22; 12.2, 29, 30). *It was the LORD your God who fought for you,* again in v. 10, recalling Deut. 3.22 (cf. Josh. 10.14). **4:** *These nations that still remain:* The issue here is not unconquered land (13.1–6), but the foreign people dwelling within the conquered territory. *From the Jordan to the Mediterranean Sea:* The same merism is found also in the LXX version of Josh. 13.7–8a, serving as a framework to the Book of Settlement. **5:** *Will thrust them out,* Deuteronomistic language, as in Deut. 6.19; 9.4. This v. recognizes that the conquest was partial and postpones the completion of the conquest to the future. **6:** Repeats 1.7, here as a warning rather than divine encouragement. **7:** *Without intermingling with these nations:* The principal concern is the danger of religious contamination by the remaining nations through assimilation and idolatry (see vv. 12, 16; see also Exod. 23.32–33; Deut. 7.22–26; Judg. 2.22; 3.4–6). **8:** *Hold fast,* see Deut. 13.5. *As you have done to this day,* a prerequisite for the successes Israel had experienced so far (see 24.31). **9:** *Driven out great, powerful nations,* enumerating past divine favors again (see v. 3) in Deuteronomistic language (Deut. 4.38; 7.1; 9.1). *Not a man has withstood you,* see 21.42 (cf. 1.5). *To this day,* repeating the same phrase as the previous v. **10:** *A single man ... would put a thousand to flight:* Cf. Deut. 32.30, emphasizing that it was God who fought for Israel (v. 3). **11–13:** Parallel to vv. 6–8. **13:** *Will not continue to drive these nations out:* As in Num. 33.55, their continued presence is explained as a warning to Israel about the threat of apostasy and exile, and is thus meant to control and restrain Israel's future behavior. Other texts view the presence of these nations differently, e.g., as a test (Judg. 2.22; cf. Judg. 3.4) or for military training (Judg. 3.2; cf. Exod. 23.29–33). *Until you perish from this good land:* The historical horizon of this Deuteronomistic speech is the eventual loss of land (cf. Deut. 11.17).

14–16: The final part of the speech. **14:** *Going the way of all the earth,* returning to the motif of his old age (v. 2; cf. 1 Kings 2.2). *They have all come ... not a single one has failed,* repeating 21.43 in reverse order. Although recognizing the remaining nations, the glorious depiction of the period is not dampened, twice negating the possibility that something failed. **15:** *Just as ... so ... every evil thing ...,* covenant curse language (Deut. 28.63). *Wiped you off this good land ...,* repeating v. 13; foreshadowing the exile.

LORD your God has given you. 16 If you break the covenant that the LORD your God enjoined upon you, and go and serve other gods and bow down to them, then the LORD's anger will burn against you, and you shall quickly perish from the good land that He has given you."

24 Joshua assembled all the tribes of Israel at Shechem. He summoned Israel's elders and commanders, magistrates and officers; and they presented themselves before God. 2 Then Joshua said to all the people, "Thus said the LORD, the God of Israel: In olden times, your forefathers—Terah, father of Abraham and father of Nahor—lived beyond the Euphrates and worshiped other gods. 3 But I took your father Abraham from beyond the Euphrates and led him through the whole land of Canaan and multiplied his offspring. I gave him Isaac, 4 and to Isaac I gave Jacob and Esau. I gave Esau the hill country of Seir as his possession, while Jacob and his children went down to Egypt.

5 "Then I sent Moses and Aaron, and I plagued Egypt with [the wonders] that I wrought in their midst, after which I freed you—6 I freed your fathers—from Egypt, and you came to the Sea. But the Egyptians pursued your fathers to the Sea of Reeds with chariots and horsemen. 7 They cried out to the LORD, and He put darkness between you and the Egyptians; then He brought the Sea upon them, and it covered them. Your own eyes saw what I did to the Egyptians.

16: *If you break the covenant ... and go and serve other gods,* noting a causal relationship between idolatry and possession of the land. The days of Joshua were depicted as free of idolatry and apostasy, hence the total success of the conquest, while the opposite will lead to God's anger and loss of the good land (see Deut. 11.16–17). The Deuteronomistic introduction to the book (ch 1), parallel in many respects to ch 23, did not mention the possibility of apostasy, suggesting that Joshua's farewell speech is the end of this ideal era, which will be followed by a period that will eventually lead to loss and ruin.

24.1–28: The covenant at Shechem. This ch describes a ceremony initiated by Joshua that describes the Israelite covenantal relationship with God along with inauguration of its terms, the divine laws (v. 25). Uniquely, this is set in Shechem, after the conquest. It partakes in the basic form of ancient Near Eastern treaty ceremonies: summoning the people in front of the suzerain (here YHVH instead of a human overlord), at the altar of Shechem (v. 1); reading aloud the treaty starting with a historical introduction (vv. 2–13); and demanding exclusive loyalty (vv. 14–15). A discourse leading to covenantal commitment is repeated three times (vv. 16–24), concluding with a ceremony of recording the covenant and setting a pillar as a witness (vv. 25–27). Joshua then sends the people to their settlements (v. 28). **1:** *Shechem:* This tradition most likely originated at Shechem. This northern site is associated with other major religious traditions in the Deuteronomistic (see 8.30–35; Deut. 11.29; 27.2–13) and other traditions (Gen. 12.6–7; 33.18–20; 35.4). *He summoned ... and they presented ... :* This redundant Deuteronomistic sentence (see Deut. 29.1, 9) links to the previous ch (23.2) and to 8.33. *Before God,* formerly in Shiloh (18.8, 10; 19.51); here Shechem. **2–13:** One of many places in the Bible where a review of past events is presented. These reviews differ; the events recalled and the way they are phrased depends upon the purpose of the review. Here the emphasis is on the land: the promise of the land to the patriarchs, the sojourn in and the exodus from Egypt, the incident of Balak and Balaam, and the (un-miraculous but divinely achieved) taking of Jericho. V. 13 concludes with the idea that Israel acquired the land by God's will, not by their own strength, and is enjoying a land for which they did not labor. **2:** *Beyond the Euphrates,* usually designating the western side, including Canaan, but here, the eastern side (cf. 1 Kings 14.15). *And worshiped other gods,* a tradition lacking in Gen. although perhaps hinted at in Gen. 35.2, 4. *Jub.* 11–12 and rabbinic traditions (e.g., *Ber. Rab.* 38:13) supply details of the life of Abraham and his religious practices in his pagan homeland. **3:** *Led him through the whole land of Canaan,* a symbolic act representing the transfer of ownership of the land (Gen. 13.17). *And multiplied his offspring,* thus fulfilling to Abraham himself the divine promises of land and progeny (Gen. 15.5, 7; 17.6, 8). **4:** *I gave Esau ... as his possession,* connecting to the Deuteronomic tradition forbidding Israel to invade Edomite (as well as Moabite and Ammonite) territory (Deut. 2.5). The message here may be subversive: the Edomites who had spread from Mount Seir to southern Judah in the 7th–6th centuries were trespassing and violating divine borders. **5:** *Then I sent Moses and Aaron,* see 1 Sam. 12.8. This phrase, missing in the LXX, is the only reference to Moses in this story; it may thus be a later expansion. **5–6:** *I freed you—I freed your fathers,* the same redundancy appears in v. 17 (though there the words "and our fathers" are missing in the Peshitta). **7:** *They cried out to the LORD,* see Exod. 14.10. Except for

"After you had lived a long time in the wilderness, 8 I brought
you to the land of the Amorites who lived beyond the Jordan.
They gave battle to you, but I delivered them into your hands;
I annihilated them for you, and you took possession of their
land. 9 Thereupon Balak son of Zippor, the king of Moab, made
ready to attack Israel. He sent for Balaam son of Beor to curse
you, 10 but I refused to listen to Balaam; he had to bless you,
and thus I saved you from him.

11 "Then you crossed the Jordan and you came to Jericho.
The citizens of Jericho and the Amorites, Perizzites, Canaanites, Hittites, Girgashites, Hivites, and Jebusites fought you,
but I delivered them into your hands. 12 I sent a plague[a] ahead
of you, and it drove them out before you—[just like] the two
Amorite kings—not by your sword or by your bow. 13 I have
given you a land for which you did not labor and towns which
you did not build, and you have settled in them; you are enjoying vineyards and olive groves which you did not plant.

14 "Now, therefore, revere the LORD and serve Him with undivided loyalty; put away the gods that your forefathers served
beyond the Euphrates and in Egypt, and serve the LORD. 15 Or,
if you are loath to serve the LORD, choose this day which ones
you are going to serve—the gods that your forefathers served
beyond the Euphrates, or those of the Amorites in whose land
you are settled; but I and my household will serve the LORD."

16 In reply, the people declared, "Far be it from us to forsake
the LORD and serve other gods! 17 For it was the LORD our God
who brought us and our fathers up from the land of Egypt, the
house of bondage, and who wrought those wondrous signs before our very eyes, and guarded us all along the way that we
traveled and among all the peoples through whose midst we
passed. 18 And then the LORD drove out before us all the peoples—the Amorites—that inhabited the country. We too will
serve the LORD, for He is our God."

a *See note at Exod. 23.28.*

vv. 6b–7a, where God is mentioned in third person, the historical preamble is God's direct speech to the audience, emphasizing: *your own eyes saw what I did to the Egyptians* (again in v. 17; cf. Exod. 14.30–31). *A long time in the wilderness,* cf. Deut. 1.46, with Kadesh instead of *the wilderness.* **8:** *The land of the Amorites who lived beyond the Jordan,* see 2.10; 9.10. **9–10:** *Balak son of Zippor ... made ready to attack Israel:* Before noting the curse of Balaam (Num. chs 22–24 and elsewhere), the text alludes to a confrontation between Moab and Israel, which is not attested elsewhere (Judg. 11.25 appears to deny this confrontation). *To curse you, but I refused to listen,* Deuteronomistic language (see Deut. 23.5–6; cf. Num. 22.6, 11). The recollection of the past in Mic. 6.4–5 has a similar sequence of divine favors (the exodus followed by Balak-Balaam). *I saved you from him,* a common designation of God's past favors, see 1 Sam. 10.18; 12.11. **11:** *The citizens of Jericho ... fought you:* Jericho is the only place mentioned, representing the whole land, yet the tradition here seems oblivious to the miraculous conquest of that city as reported in ch 6. **12:** *I sent a plague,* lit. "hornet," as in Exod. 23.28 and Deut. 7.20. *Drove them out before you,* as foretold in Exod. 23.28 (cf. Judg. 6.9), in opposition to the total annihilation of the inhabitants of the land depicted in Josh. chs 1–12. *The two Amorite kings,* are out of place here; perhaps a misplaced gloss to v. 8. *Not by your sword or by your bow,* reflecting a polemic with Gen. 48.22, which attributes the taking of Shechem from the Amorite by the sword and the bow (cf. Ps. 44.4, 7). **14:** *Now,* indicating transition in an address (see 1.2 n.). *Revere the* LORD *and serve Him,* the language resembles Deut. 6.13. *With undivided loyalty,* "be-tamim uve-'emet," "in wholeness and truth [or reliability]": this hendiadys (a figure of speech in which two terms are linked by a conjunction rather than one modifying the other, obscured here in the translation) appears in reverse order in Judg. 9.16, 19, another Shechemite tradition. *Put away ... that your forefathers served beyond the Euphrates and in Egypt,* referring to v. 2, but adding that Israel was idolatrous in Egypt as well (cf. Ezek. 20.7–8). **15:** *Choose ... which ones you are going to serve,* the motif of choice is found in international treaties, the vassal depicted as choosing his overlord just as cattle choose their stable (e.g., the treaty between Hatti and Kizzuwatna, ca. 1400 BCE). *But I ... will serve the* LORD*:* possibly alluding to the traditions that God would start a new nation with Moses (Num. 14.12; Deut. 9.14), implying that if all Israel is not obedient, God could start anew with the pious Joshua and his family. **16–18:** The people affirm their allegiance to God by first asserting that they will not serve other gods, then reiterating God's past favors during the exodus, the wilderness, and the early conquest (vv. 17–18a summarize vv. 5–12). They conclude with a pledge, *We too*—in addition to Joshua and his household (v. 15)—*will serve the* LORD*, for He is our God.*

19 Joshua, however, said to the people, "You will not be able
to serve the LORD, for He is a holy God. He is a jealous God;
He will not forgive your transgressions and your sins. 20 If you
forsake the LORD and serve alien gods, He will turn and deal
harshly with you and make an end of you, after having been
gracious to you." 21 But the people replied to Joshua, "No, we
will serve the LORD!" 22 Thereupon Joshua said to the people,
"You are witnesses against yourselves that you have by your
own act chosen to serve the LORD." "Yes, we are!" they responded. 23 "Then put away the alien gods that you have among you
and direct your hearts to the LORD, the God of Israel." 24 And
the people declared to Joshua, "We will serve none but the
LORD our God, and we will obey none but Him."

25 On that day at Shechem, Joshua made a covenant for the
people and he made a fixed rule for them. 26 Joshua recorded
all this in a book of divine instruction. He took a great stone
and set it up at the foot of the oak in the sacred precinct of the
LORD; 27 and Joshua said to all the people, "See, this very stone
shall be a witness against us, for it heard all the words that the
LORD spoke to us; it shall be a witness against you, lest you
break faith with your God." 28 Joshua then dismissed the people to their allotted portions.

19–24: The dialogue between Joshua and the people is unique in leading to two confirmations of the people's commitment, three times in total (vv. 18, 21, 24). **19:** *You will not be able to serve the LORD:* This statement sounds prophetic, in which case it would be undermining free choice. *For He is a holy God:* "Elohim qedoshim," a hapax legomenon (a unique occurrence). The word "Elohim," "God," is grammatically pl., but when used of the one LORD, takes sg. adjectives. This is one of the few exceptions, since "qedoshim," "holy," is grammatically pl., though the pronoun, "hwʾ," *He (is),* is in the sg. This v. emphasizes divine exclusivity, and foretells the people's inability to refrain from serving other gods, igniting God's jealousy and fury. It thus anticipates the exile. **20:** *Serve alien gods:* The situation anticipates the Deuteronomistic portrayal of the days of the judges (Judg. 2.11–15; 10.10–16) and hints ahead to the events surrounding the Ark of the Covenant when the "holy God" inflicted a great slaughter upon the people of Beth-shemesh (1 Sam. 6.20), eventually leading to the removal of alien gods, directing the heart to God and serving Him alone (1 Sam. 7.3). **22:** *You are witnesses … :* The people witness their own commitment (cf. 1 Sam. 12.5). *Chosen,* repeating the motif from v. 15. **23:** *Then,* lit. "and now," a transition to the next demand. *Put away the alien gods,* repeating v. 14. A similar ceremony is reflected in Gen. 35.2, 4; Judg. 10.16; 1 Sam. 7.3–4. **24:** *We will serve none but the LORD our God … obey:* The third and last statement of commitment, offered by the people entering covenantal relationship (see Deut. 13.5). The verb "to serve," "ʿ-b-d," used in reference to serving God or other gods, is repeated fifteen times in vv. 1–28, underlining the theme of this unit. **25:** *Joshua made a covenant … and he made a fixed rule,* cf. Exod. 15.25. This refers to the laws that comprise the terms of the covenant (cf. Exod. 21.1). **26:** *Joshua recorded all this in a book of divine instruction:* While other people are said to have set new rules (David – 1 Sam. 31.25; Ezek. 44.5) and even to have written them in a book that is placed before the LORD (Samuel – 1 Sam. 10.25), only Moses and Joshua are said to have made a covenant and written it in a book (cf. Exod. 24.7). *Book of divine instruction,* "sefer Torat Elohim," lit. "book of God's teaching"—this designation appears again only in Neh. 8.18 (cf. Neh. 8.8), where it refers to the book of the teaching of Moses—"sefer Torat Moshe" (Neh. 8.1; cf. Josh. 8.31; 23.6). Various connections between Josh. ch 24 and Deut., and even the Torah more broadly, have suggested to some that at an earlier point in its history the ch was a conclusion to the hexateuch, a six-book composition of the Torah plus Josh. The Rabbis interpreted this v. quite differently, as referring to Joshua adding to the "book of Moses" (the Torah), writing the last eight vv. of Deut. describing Moses' death, or the cities of refuge (Josh. ch 20; *b. Mak.* 12:1). Yet ch 24 ignores Moses almost completely (see v. 5 n.), depicting Joshua as the sole leader, the deliverer of laws and the author of the "book of divine instruction." *He took a great stone and set it up,* like Moses who set twelve pillars for the twelve tribes of Israel (Exod. 24.4), *at the foot of the oak in the sacred precinct,* the same Heb words describe the site where Jacob buried the alien gods when back in Canaan (Gen. 35.4). A tree and an altar in Shechem are also mentioned as the first sacred site in Canaan (Gen. 12.6). Abimelech was proclaimed king at "the terebinth of the pillar at Shechem" (Judg. 9.6), and Rehoboam came to Shechem to be proclaimed king over all Israel there (1 Kings 12.1). **27:** *This very stone … a witness:* For stones as witnesses for covenants see Gen. 31.52 (cf. Josh. 22.28, 34). Earlier, a different tradition depicts Joshua appointing the people themselves as witnesses (v. 22). **28:** *Joshua then dismissed the people,* ending the story (see 22.6 n.), *to their allotted portions,* at some point in its history, the book ended here, forming a frame with 1.6.

29 After these events, Joshua son of Nun, the servant of the
LORD, died at the age of one hundred and ten years. 30 They
buried him on his own property, at Timnath-serah in the hill
country of Ephraim, north of Mount Gaash. 31 Israel served the
LORD during the lifetime of Joshua and the lifetime of the elders who lived on after Joshua, and who had experienced all the
deeds that the LORD had wrought for Israel.
32 The bones of Joseph, which the Israelites had brought up
from Egypt, were buried at Shechem, in the piece of ground
which Jacob had bought for a hundred *kesitahs*[a] from the children of Hamor, Shechem's father, and which had become a
heritage of the Josephites.
33 Eleazar son of Aaron also died, and they buried him on the
hill of his son Phinehas, which had been assigned to him in the
hill country of Ephraim.

a See note at Gen. 33.19.

24.29–33: Death and burial of the leaders. The concluding vv. of the book tell the death and burial of the leaders Joshua (vv. 29–30) and Eleazar (v. 33), the burial of the bones of Joseph (v. 32), and the end of an era (v. 31). These vv. are repeated in a slightly different order together with the conclusion of the former unit (v. 28) in Judg. 2.6–9. LXX presents a different, expanded text, containing notes regarding the deposition of the flint knives (see 5.2–3) in Joshua's grave, a note regarding the Ark of God, and the death of the priest Phinehas, the son of Eleazar. The LXX ends the book with a direct link to Judg. 3.12, indicating the existence of an early version of Judg. that lacked Judg. 1.1–3.11. **29:** *After these events,* a transition formula (cf. Gen. 22.20; 48.1). *The servant of the LORD:* Moses' title (1.1), granted to Joshua only here. *One hundred and ten years,* like Joseph, his forefather (Gen. 50.22, 26), whose burial is mentioned in v. 32. In Egyptian sources, this lifespan is ideal, yet the Rabbis noted that Joshua lived ten years less than Moses, because he prolonged the conquest unnecessarily ("over a long period" 11.18; *Num. Rab.* 22:6). **30:** *They buried him ... at Timnath-serah,* unlike Moses, whose burial site remains unknown (Deut. 34.6). Joshua's tomb became the site of buried relics according to the LXX: "they put with him, in the grave where they buried him, the flint knives with which he had circumcised Israel at Gilgal (see 5.2–3), when he had taken them out of Egypt as God had ordered them, where they remain to this day." **31:** *Israel served the LORD ... experienced all the deeds:* Serving ("ʿ-b-d") the LORD is the major theme of ch 24 (see v. 24 n.; ch 23, from a different source, uses the verbs "d-b-q" and "ʾ-h-b" [23.8, 11]). In Judg. 2.10 the death of the generation that "experienced" was the dawn of a new era of a generation that did not, and was prone to apostasy. **32:** *The bones of Joseph ... were buried at Shechem ...,* concluding the story of Joseph according to his instructions (Gen. 50.25; Exod. 13.19). *Which Jacob had bought ... from the children of Hamor,* recalling Gen. 33.19. Through these concluding motifs the end of Josh. refers back to Gen., framing the hexateuch. **33:** This ch, which is largely Deuteronomistic in nature, ends with a note regarding Eleazar's death and burial, indicating Priestly interests. It shows that in its current form, the book of Joshua is a blend of Deuteronomistic and Priestly materials, composed at a late period.

שופטים

Judges*

THE BOOK OF JUDGES is the second of Former Prophets. Its place was determined chronologically—it covers the period after Joshua's death at the end of the book of Joshua and before the anointing of Saul as king in 1 Samuel chs 8–12. The book is named after its central characters, "judges" (typically translated in NJPS as "chieftains"). Although the book of Judges ends before the birth of Samuel the prophet (1 Sam. ch 1), the book of Samuel, suggests that Eli and Samuel and his sons should be considered judges as well (see 1 Sam. 4.18; 7.15–17; 8.1).

The judges are mostly portrayed as tribal leaders who became regional leaders and delivered their people from oppression. Some are depicted as military leaders (Othniel, Ehud, Barak, Gideon, and Jephthah), some as lone warriors (Shamgar and Samson), and one as both leader and commander (Jephthah). Some judges are shown as prophets (Deborah and Samuel), one as a Nazirite (Samson), some as also being priests (Eli and Samuel), or as one who sat in judgment (Deborah, Samuel, and his sons), while the acts of others are not specified (Tola, Jair, Ibzan, Elon, and Abdon). The term "judge," Hebrew *shofet* (see esp. 2 Sam. 7.11; 2 Kings 23.22; Ruth 1.1; 1 Chron. 17.6, 10), thus covers the range of diverse leaders who flourished, according to the book, in the period prior to the monarchy, and it should not be understood in a narrow juridical sense.

The book of Judges does not describe the entire period between Joshua and Samuel, nor is it organized chronologically. It opens in the time of the elders who survived Joshua (Judg. 1.1–2.10) and concludes the sequence of the judges with Samson (13–16), so the last judges, Eli, Samuel, and his sons, now appear in the book of Samuel. The ending of the book of Judges, however, deals with events that took place at the start of the period: the conquest of Dan (17–18) and the war against Gibeah (19–21), both of which are placed in the third generation after the exodus from Egypt (18.30; 20.28). Its nonchronological order shows that the editors' purpose was not only to describe and record the period, but to draw lessons from the stories he uses.

The book's main theme is the inefficacy of the judges. They could influence and deliver their people for only a limited time; then the people would relapse, would be punished, and would cry to the LORD to save them again. This recurrent theme of sin, punishment, crying out, rescue, and peace gives the book a cyclical structure.

The book offers two principal lessons: about God's role in history and about the preferred type of leader. The book describes the course of history as an interaction between God and His people, with God punishing and afterwards heeding His people's cries, and saving them through various judges. As for human leadership, the judges are not depicted, by and large, as successful leaders, and thus they pave the way for the establishment of a more successful political institution, the monarchy. The ideal king could confront the people's enemies and prevent anarchy, though the book warns that the king may also be a villain, as in the case of Abimelech, symbolized by the bramble (ch 9).

* This is a traditional rendering of *shofetim*, which, however, in the text is rendered "chieftains." The corresponding verb *shafat* is usually translated not "judged" but "ruled" or "led."

The book can be divided into three parts. The first, an exposition, provides the background for the rise of the judges (1.1–3.6). The second, main part of the book is devoted largely to the acts of the judges (3.7–16.31). The third, final part describes two episodes: that of Micah's graven image and the shrine built at Dan, and the story of the rape in Gibeah and the subsequent civil war (chs 17–21). These final episodes create the impression that monarchy alone could end the chaotic period of the judges, because when "there was no king in Israel; every man did as he pleased" (17.6; 21.25).

The rabbinic Sages (*b. B. Bat.* 14b) assumed that the book of Judges was written by the prophet Samuel, who lived not long after the events described. Biblical scholars, however, maintain that the book was written later and should not be viewed as a unified work by a single author. Scholars suggest that it could only have been produced in an established social culture possessing self-consciousness, appropriate institutions, and a receptive public. Scholars distinguish between the judges' stories, which are based on local-tribal traditions of deliverance and which do not interpret events with theological causality, and their frameworks, which depict the deliverer in a broad national context, characterized by a cycle that begins with sin and ends with peace. There is widespread agreement that these frameworks reflect a Deuteronomistic redaction which took the tribal stories, gave them a national-religious character, and fitted the whole into the great Deuteronomistic work that describes the history from the years in the wilderness (the book of Deuteronomy) to the Babylonian exile (the end of the book of Kings). At a later stage, they suggest, post-Deuteronomistic redactors added certain passages, such as the ones about the Canaanite nations that were or were not driven out, in the exposition (1.1–2.5) and the concluding chs (17–21).

But the assumption that the book of Judges reflects the ideological world of Deuteronomy is not certain. Deuteronomy's ideology and style are only partly evident in the book of Judges. Deuteronomistic literature criticizes monarchy (Deut. 17.14–20), places prophets above it (Deut. 18.15–19; 1 Kings 12.22–24, etc.), demands centralization of cult (Deut. 12.5–28; 1 Kings 8.16ff., etc.), and depicts the deity as a remote being whose name alone dwells in the Temple (Deut. 12.5; 1 Kings 8.27, etc.). By contrast, the book of Judges has positive expectations from the monarchy, scarcely refers to prophecy and its function of predicting historical events, does not call for the centralization of the cult, and shows God intervening in the events, directly or by means of angels. (Some of these features are true of the following book of Samuel as well.) Moreover, the phrases that are typical of Deuteronomistic literature are concentrated only in the opening part of the book (2.6–3.4). It would seem, therefore, that the main redaction of the book of Judges was completed in the pre-Deuteronomistic stage—namely, in the late 8th or in the 7th century BCE—and that it reflected the shocked mood in Judah after the downfall of the Northern Kingdom of Israel in 722 (see the allusion to exile in 18.30). This would explain the negative portrayal of the northern tribes throughout the book, from the exposition that accuses them of the sin of failing to drive out the local inhabitants (1.21–36), to the final chs that speak of Mount Ephraim and the shrine at Dan as sinful places. By contrast, the tribe of Judah is depicted in the book's opening as a tribe that succeeded completely in driving out the local inhabitants and was faithful to the covenant with God (1.1–20). The redaction sought to justify the punishment that befell the Northern Kingdom by showing it as a group of sinful tribes; this theme is evident in each of the sections of the book.

The book later was slightly adapted when it became part of the great Deuteronomistic work of Deuteronomy-Kings. Additions from this period or later may include: Deuteronomistic phrases noticeable in the exposition (2.11–19), the text criticizing Gideon for making the ephod (8.27b), and the episode of the concubine in Gibeah (chs 19–21), which is mainly a veiled polemical attack on the house of Saul. In general, the history of the composition of the book, and its relation to the surrounding books, deserves serious reconsideration as scholars debate the validity of the idea of a single Deuteronomistic History, from Deuteronomy-Kings.

The book of Judges presents itself as covering a period of more than 400 years—111 years of subjugation, and 299 of judgeship and peace (or possibly 319 years, given the uncertainty about the length of Samson's period [see 15.20; 16.31 n.]). These data do not agree either with the chronology of 1 Kings 6.1, according to which 480 years passed from the exodus to the building of the Jerusalem Temple, or with the historical and archeological findings, which suggest that less than 200 years passed from the end of the 13th century, when the hill country was settled, to the latter half of the 11th century BCE and the beginning of the monarchy according to the book of Samuel.

Modern research has abandoned the view that the bulk of the book of Judges is historically authentic, although it acknowledges that ancient traditions sometimes preserve echoes of historical reality. Thus, while some scholars chose not to speak of a "period of the judges" at all, other scholars regard this period—namely, the time of settlement leading up to the monarchy—as a decisive one in the history of the people of Israel, in the course of which groups of settling nomads grew into an established society, developed a sense of national identity with a cultural-religious heritage, and came to form the people of Israel. Comparative study suggests that local chieftains typically develop during this pre-monarchic stage, so in most general terms (only), the picture in Judges reflects some reality. At the same time, modern scholarship has emphasized certain ideological themes such as an anti-Northern Kingdom bias, an anti-Saul, pro-David predisposition, and the role of God in history. The poetics of the book as a whole and the artistry of its individual narratives has become a subject of investigation, and the prominent role of women who appear through the book and the place of gender—a subject of examination. Recent studies have also shown how methods applied to folklore may explain the form and development of the book's individual stories. Moreover, as a book that describes a transitional period in the history of the relations between God and His people, Judges offers a rich background for social, political and theological insights.

[YAIRAH AMIT]

1 After the death of Joshua, the Israelites inquired of the
LORD, "Which of us shall be the first to go up against the
Canaanites and attack them?" 2 The LORD replied, "Let [the
tribe of] Judah go up. I now deliver the land into their hands."
3 Judah then said to their brother-tribe Simeon, "Come up with
us to our allotted territory and let us attack the Canaanites, and
then we will go with you to your allotted territory." So Simeon
joined them.
4 When Judah advanced, the LORD delivered the Canaanites and the Perizzites into their hands, and they defeated
ten thousand of them at Bezek. 5 At Bezek, they encountered

1.1–3.6: Introduction to the book of Judges. 1.1–2.10: The days of the elders. The period from the death of Joshua to the beginning of the age of the judges is called here the days of the elders (cf. 2.7). This period is created to explain how the people, who during the days of Joshua were noted for their loyalty to the LORD, became transformed into one that repeatedly did evil in His eyes. During this period the tribes needed to fight against the nations who remained in the land after Joshua's death. According to the editor, the tribe of Judah did so with his brother Simeon, but most of the tribes preferred to subjugate the remaining nations and allowed them to remain in their territories, thereby laying the groundwork for assimilation and sin.

1.1–20: The conquests of Judah. The tribe of *Judah* and the tribe of *Simeon* that *joined them* destroyed the *Canaanites,* with the exception of the inhabitants of the valley, who had iron chariots and therefore could not be destroyed (cf. v. 19). This presentation shows the preference of Judah, which characterizes the whole passage. Joshua's death is recorded again in 2.8. **2:** The claim that *Judah* should *go up* first, God will *deliver the land into their* (Judah's) *hands* is the theme of this unit. **3:** The connection between *Judah* and *Simeon* reflects the geographical-historical reality of the absorption of the tribe of Simeon into Judah's holdings (Josh. 19.1–9; 15.26–32). **5:** Bezek is the site where

Adoni-bezek, engaged him in battle, and defeated the Canaanites and the Perizzites. 6 Adoni-bezek fled, but they pursued
him and captured him; and they cut off his thumbs and his big
toes. 7 And Adoni-bezek said, "Seventy kings, with thumbs and
big toes cut off, used to pick up scraps under my table; as I have
done, so God has requited me." They brought him to Jerusalem
and he died there.

8 The Judites attacked Jerusalem and captured it; they put it
to the sword and set the city on fire. 9 After that the Judites went
down to attack the Canaanites who inhabited the hill country,
the Negeb, and the Shephelah.

10 The Judites marched against the Canaanites who dwelt in
Hebron, and they defeated Sheshai, Ahiman, and Talmai. (The
name of Hebron was formerly Kiriath-arba.) 11 From there they
marched against the inhabitants of Debir (the name of Debir
was formerly Kiriath-sepher). 12 And Caleb announced, "I will
give my daughter Achsah in marriage to the man who attacks
and captures Kiriath-sepher." 13 His younger kinsman, Othniel
the Kenizzite,[a] captured it; and Caleb gave him his daughter
Achsah in marriage. 14 [b-]When she came [to him], she induced
him to ask her father for some property. She dismounted from
her donkey, and Caleb asked her, "What is the matter?" 15 She
replied, "Give me a present, for you have given me away as
Negeb-land; give me springs of water." And Caleb gave her Upper and Lower Gulloth.[-b]

16 The descendants of the Kenite, the father-in-law of Moses,
went up with the Judites from the City of Palms to the wilderness of Judah; and they went and settled among the people[c] in
the Negeb of Arad. 17 And Judah with its brother-tribe Simeon
went on and defeated the Canaanites who dwelt in Zephath.
They proscribed it, and so the town was named Hormah.[d]
18 And Judah captured[e] Gaza and its territory, Ashkelon and its
territory, and Ekron and its territory.

19 The LORD was with Judah, so that they took possession
of the hill country; but they were not able to dispossess the

a *Cf. Josh. 14.6, 14.* *b-b* *Cf. Josh. 15.18–19 and notes.*
c *Meaning of Heb. uncertain. Emendation yields "Amalekites"; cf. 1 Sam. 15.6.*
d *I.e., "Proscribed." Cf. notes at Num. 21.2–3.*
e *Septuagint reads "But Judah did not capture Gaza..." Gaza is in the coastal plain referred to in v. 19.*

Saul mustered his army in his first war (1 Sam. 11.8). It is generally identified with Khirbet Ibzik, about 24 km (15 miles) northeast of Shechem. *Adoni-bezek:* The name of this king is likely a corruption of Adoni-zedek, who was king of Jerusalem according to Josh. 10.1. The fact that the king was buried in Jerusalem (v. 7) supports this conjecture. **7:** The king's servants took him to die in Jerusalem. **8:** In the description of the conquest of Jerusalem by the Judites, there is no hint that any inhabitants were left. Further on (v. 21), the blame for not dispossessing the Jebusites from Jerusalem is placed on Benjamin, while in Josh. 15.63 it is placed on Judah, thus various conflicting traditions have been collected in Joshua and Judges. According to many modern historians, Jerusalem remained a non-Israelite enclave until it was conquered by David (2 Sam. 5.9–16). **9:** A general summary of Judah's conquests south of Jerusalem. **10:** The biblical *Hebron* is identified with Tel Romeda, 29 km (18 miles) southwest of Jerusalem. The conquest of Hebron and its giants ("Anakites," v. 20) is here attributed to Judah. Other traditions appear in Josh. 10.36–37; 14.6–14, as well as in v. 20 below. Hebron is an important city in the ancestral narratives in Genesis (see esp. Gen. ch 23), and in the early part of David's reign (2 Sam. chs 2–5). **11:** *Debir* is identified with Khirbet Rabud, 15 km (9 miles) southwest of Hebron. **12–13:** The families of *Caleb* and Kenaz are presented here as part of the tribe of Judah. **13:** The representation of *Othniel* as *younger* than Caleb indicates that Caleb's clan was a more important one. **14:** According to this v., Achsah persuaded Othniel, but further on the negotiation occurs between Achsah and Caleb; hence, many scholars prefer the reading of the LXX, according to which Othniel persuaded Achsah. Dismounting from the donkey is a gesture of politeness. **15:** In addition to the dry *Negeb-land,* she asks for land with *springs.* **16:** The Kenites were another group integrated into the tribe of Judah. The origins of the connection with them is told through the story of Moses' marriage to Zipporah, daughter of Jethro (Exod. 2.16–22). *The City of Palms:* As the name is applicable to any settlement in which there are date palms, it is difficult to identify. The Kenites settled in the *Negeb of Arad,* east of Beer-sheba. **18:** *Gaza ... Ashkelon ... Ekron:* The conquest of three of the five Philistine royal city-states, which elsewhere were only conquered in the days of David, is here attributed to *Judah.* **19:** Only in the case of Judah

inhabitants of the plain, for they had iron chariots. 20 They gave Hebron to Caleb, as Moses had promised; and he drove the three Anakites out of there. 21 The Benjaminites did not dispossess the Jebusite inhabitants of Jerusalem; so the Jebusites have dwelt with the Benjaminites in Jerusalem to this day.

22 The House of Joseph, for their part, advanced against Bethel, and the LORD was with them. 23 While the House of Joseph were scouting at Bethel (the name of the town was formerly Luz), 24 their patrols[a] saw a man leaving the town. They said to him, "Just show us how to get into the town, and we will treat you kindly." 25 He showed them how to get into the town; they put the town to the sword, but they let the man and all his relatives go free. 26 The man went to the Hittite country. He founded a city and named it Luz, and that has been its name to this day.

27 Manasseh did not dispossess [the inhabitants of] Beth-shean and its dependencies, or [of] Taanach and its dependencies, or the inhabitants of Dor and its dependencies, or the inhabitants of Ibleam and its dependencies, or the inhabitants of Megiddo and its dependencies. The Canaanites persisted in dwelling in this region. 28 And when Israel gained the upper hand, they subjected the Canaanites to forced labor; but they did not dispossess them. 29 Nor did Ephraim dispossess the Canaanites who inhabited Gezer; so the Canaanites dwelt in their midst at Gezer.

30 Zebulun did not dispossess the inhabitants of Kitron or the inhabitants of Nahalol; so the Canaanites dwelt in their midst, but they were subjected to forced labor. 31 Asher did not dispossess the inhabitants of Acco or the inhabitants of Sidon, Ahlab, Achzib, Helbah, Aphik, and Rehob. 32 So the Asherites dwelt in the midst of the Canaanites, the inhabitants of the land, for they did not dispossess them. 33 Naphtali did not dispossess the inhabitants of Beth-shemesh or the inhabitants of Beth-anath. But they settled in the midst of the Canaanite inhabitants of the land, and the inhabitants of Beth-shemesh and Beth-anath had to perform forced labor for them.

34 The Amorites pressed the Danites into the hill country; they would not let them come down to the plain. 35 The Amorites also persisted in dwelling in Har-heres, in Aijalon, and in Shaalbim. But the hand of the House of Joseph bore heavily on them and they had to perform forced labor. 36 The territory of the Amorites[b] extended from the Ascent of Akrabbim—from Sela—onward.

2 An angel of the LORD came up from Gilgal to Bochim and said, "I brought you up from Egypt and I took you into the land which I had promised on oath to your fathers. And

a Lit. "watchmen." *b Some Septuagint mss. read "Edomites."*

is there a justification for non-dispossessing. **20:** Judah gave the city to Caleb and he dispossessed the giants (Anakites), whose names are mentioned in v. 10 above. The story of a struggle with giants appears in the narratives of the conquest (see, e.g., Num. 13.28, 32–33).

1.21–36: The conquests of the northern tribes. The northern tribes, who here number only seven, are mentioned in order from south to north, from Benjamin to Dan, who was forced to leave his inheritance and later settled in the north. This order is similar to that of the whole book, which begins with Ehud the Benjaminite (3.12–30) and concludes with Samson from Dan (chs 13–16) and the northward wandering of his tribe (chs 17–18). The northern tribes are represented as responsible for most of the failures to take possession of the land, reflecting the pro-Judean attitude of the book's editor. **22–29:** Similar to Judah who conquered Jerusalem (v. 8), the first conquest of the *House of Joseph* is their central cultic city, *Bethel.* Bethel is identified with the Arab village Beitin, about 19 km (12 mi) north of Jerusalem. **30–33:** The tribes dwelling north of the valley of Jezreel are described as a minority that ruled the Canaanite population. **34–35:** The tribe of Dan did not succeed in taking hold of its allotted land in the western south throughout the sea shore, and was forced by the Amorites to move eastward into the hill country, the area of Har-heres near Beth-shemesh; this is told in details in ch 18. The House of Joseph, unlike Judah who cooperated with Simeon his brother, did not help the tribe of Dan, but preferred to subjugate the Amorites as forced labor.

2.1–5: The assembly in Bochim and the punishment for non-dispossessing. This episode is obscure. **1:** The *angel* is evidently a prophet sent by the LORD to the city of *Bochim,* which the LXX renders as Bethel, and is elsewhere connected to "weeping" (vv. 4–5; see 20.26, 17–23; 21.2). It was only natural that

I said, 'I will never break My covenant with you. [2] And you,
for your part, must make no covenant with the inhabitants of
this land; you must tear down their altars.' But you have not
obeyed Me—look what you have done! [3] Therefore, I have resolved not to drive them out before you; they shall become
your oppressors,[a] and their gods shall be a snare to you." [4] As
the angel of the LORD spoke these words to all the Israelites,
the people broke into weeping. [5] So they named that place
Bochim,[b] and they offered sacrifices there to the LORD.

[6] When Joshua dismissed the people, the Israelites went to
their allotted territories and took possession of the land. [7] The
people served the LORD during the lifetime of Joshua and the
lifetime of the older people who lived on after Joshua and
who had witnessed all the marvelous deeds that the LORD
had wrought for Israel. [8] Joshua son of Nun, the servant of the
LORD, died at the age of one hundred and ten years, [9] and was
buried on his own property, at Timnath-heres[c] in the hill country of Ephraim, north of Mount Gaash. [10] And all that generation were likewise gathered to their fathers.
Another generation arose after them, which had not experienced [the deliverance of] the LORD or the deeds that He had
wrought for Israel. [11] And the Israelites did what was offensive
to the LORD. They worshiped the Baalim [12] and forsook the
LORD, the God of their fathers, who had brought them out of the
land of Egypt. They followed other gods, from among the gods
of the peoples around them, and bowed down to them; they
provoked the LORD. [13] They forsook the LORD and worshiped
Baal and the Ashtaroth.[d] [14] Then the LORD was incensed at Israel, and He handed them over to foes[e] who plundered them.
He surrendered them to their enemies on all sides, and they
could no longer hold their own against their enemies. [15] In
all their campaigns, the hand of the LORD was against them
to their undoing, as the LORD had declared and as the LORD
had sworn to them; and they were in great distress. [16] Then
the LORD raised up chieftains who delivered them from those
who plundered them. [17] But they did not heed their chieftains
either; they went astray after other gods and bowed down to
them. They were quick to turn aside from the way their fathers
had followed in obedience to the commandments of the LORD;
they did not do right. [18] When the LORD raised up chieftains for
them, the LORD would be with the chieftain and would save
them from their enemies during the chieftain's lifetime; for the
LORD would be moved to pity by their moanings because of

a So Targum and other ancient versions. Meaning of Heb. uncertain.
b I.e., "weepers." *c Some mss. read "Timnath-serah"; cf. Josh. 24.30.*
d Canaanite female deities. *e Lit. "plunderers."*

Bethel, which is identified with the golden calf (1 Kings 12.25–30), was chosen to serve as the place of rebuke to the northern tribes, who violated the covenant and sinned in non-dispossessing.

2.6–3.6: Characterization of the age of the judges. 2.6–8: This retells Josh. 24.29–31. **6–10:** The first generation of the age of the judges, just after the days of the elders, did not know the deliverance of the LORD. **11–19:** The period of the judges is characterized by repeating cycles comprised here of four stages: the sin of doing evil in the eyes of the LORD (vv. 11–13); punishment by subjugation to the surrounding nations (vv. 14–15), deliverance by judges (v. 16), and the days during which the judges ruled, which were periods of calm following the deliverance (vv. 17–19). Sometimes the people returned to sin during the judge's lifetime (v. 17), and at others only after his death (vv. 18–19); in any event the period of sin always returns. Later in the book, the stage of deliverance (see 3.9, etc.) is also preceded by a stage of crying out or turning to the LORD, though full-scale repentance is mentioned only once (10.10–16). The absence of this stage here emphasizes the nation's apostasy. This description is rich in repetitions and in Deuteronomistic expressions, suggesting that it is a late framework, created to incorporate stories about individual judges. **11:** *Baalim:* Baal, whose name means "master," was one of the heads of the Canaanite pantheon. The use of the plural may indicate the existence of a multiplicity of cults of which Baal is the center, or various other kinds of idolatry. **13:** *Ashtaroth:* The name Ashtoreth also appears here in the plural. This goddess, one of the consorts of Baal, was responsible for love and fertility.

those who oppressed and crushed them. 19 But when the chieftain died, they would again act basely, even more than [a]the
preceding generation[a]—following other gods, worshiping
them, and bowing down to them; they omitted none of their
practices and stubborn ways.
20 Then the LORD became incensed against Israel, and He
said, "Since that nation has transgressed the covenant that I
enjoined upon their fathers and has not obeyed Me, 21 I for My
part will no longer drive out before them any of the nations that
Joshua left when he died." 22 For it was in order to test Israel by
them—[to see] whether or not they would faithfully walk in the
ways of the LORD, as their fathers had done—23 that the LORD
had left those nations, instead of driving them out at once, and
had not delivered them into the hands of Joshua.

3 [b]These are the nations that the LORD left so that He might
might test by them all the Israelites who had not known
any of the wars of Canaan, 2 so that succeeding generations of
Israelites might be made to experience war—but only those
who had not known the [c]former wars:[c] 3 the five principali-
ties[d] of the Philistines and all the Canaanites, Sidonians, and
Hivites who inhabited the hill country of the Lebanon from
Mount Baal-hermon to Lebo-hamath.[e] 4 These served as a
means of testing Israel, to learn whether they would obey the
commandments which the LORD had enjoined upon their fathers through Moses.
5 The Israelites settled among the Canaanites, Hittites,
Amorites, Perizzites, Hivites, and Jebusites; 6 they took their
daughters to wife and gave their own daughters to their sons,
and they worshiped their gods. 7 The Israelites did what was
offensive to the LORD; they ignored the LORD their God and
worshiped the Baalim and the Asheroth. 8 The LORD became
incensed at Israel and surrendered them to King Cushan-
rishathaim of Aram-naharaim; and the Israelites were subject
to Cushan-rishathaim for eight years. 9 The Israelites cried out
to the LORD, and the LORD raised a champion for the Israelites
to deliver them: Othniel the Kenizzite, a younger kinsman of
Caleb. 10 The spirit of the LORD descended upon him and he
became Israel's chieftain. He went out to war, and the LORD

a-a Lit. "their fathers." *b The sentence structure of vv. 1–2 is uncertain.*
c-c Lit. "them formerly." *d Lit. "lords."* *e See note at Num. 13.21.*

2.20–3.6: Three answers to why the nations remained. This is clearly a composite text, reflecting various answers to the central question: Why was the conquest of the indigenous population not complete? **2.20–21:** The sins of the period of the judges caused the LORD to decide not to continue to dispossess the nations. **22–23; 3.4:** According to a second view, God intended from the outset to leave the nations in order to test Israel's loyalty to Him. **3.1–3:** According to a third view, incorporated into the previous one, God planned from the outset to leave the other nations in order to give the Israelites practice in the art of war. **3:** The Bible depicts the Philistines as organized in a Pentapolis comprised of Ashdod, Ashkelon, Ekron, Gath and Gaza. **5–6:** The result was that the lack of complete annihilation of the local population led to assimilation (see Deut. 7.1–6; 20.16–18), and thus explains the faithlessness of the Israelites in the rest of the book.

3.7–11: Othniel the Kenizzite. The first judge was from Judah (since according to v. 9 he is Caleb's kinsman; see also 1.13), and he waged war against an enemy from the far north, thus lending a national character to the event. The description of the deliverance gives no details about the war itself, but is rich in terms found elsewhere in the cyclical formulae. This description serves as a transitional stage from the introduction of the book to its specific narratives. Othniel's success is complete, suggesting the preeminence of Judah. **7:** *Asheroth:* The plural indicates multiple cults. In the Ugaritic pantheon Asherah is the consort of El, the old chief god. The Bible uses the word both as the name of the goddess and as the term for a cultic object made of wood, which was evidently her symbol (see, e.g., Deut. 16.21–22). **8:** *Cushan-rishathaim:* The name, meaning "Dark double-wickedness," is strange, and is likely symbolic. The dual ending ("ayim") seems to suggest a particularly wicked enemy. *Aram-naharaim:* The land beween and near the two rivers (Tigris and Euphrates), in northeast Syria. Some think that the name Aram is a corruption of Edom, which borders Judah, but it is more likely that the whole war is symbolic and that its intention is to attribute to Othniel from Judah a national war against a powerful distant nation in the far north and thus to indicate the superiority of Judah. **10:** *The spirit of the LORD:* This refers to a temporary endowment

delivered King Cushan-rishathaim of Aram into his hands. He
prevailed over Cushan-rishathaim, 11 and the land had peace
for forty years.
When Othniel the Kenizzite died, 12 the Israelites again did
what was offensive to the LORD. And because they did what
was offensive to the LORD, the LORD let King Eglon of Moab
prevail over Israel. 13 [Eglon] brought the Ammonites and the
Amalekites together under his command, and went and defeated Israel and occupied the City of Palms. 14 The Israelites
were subject to King Eglon of Moab for eighteen years.
15 Then the Israelites cried out to the LORD, and the LORD
raised up a champion for them: the Benjaminite Ehud son
of Gera, a left-handed man. It happened that the Israelites
sent tribute to King Eglon of Moab through him. 16 So Ehud
made for himself a two-edged dagger, a *gomed* in length,
which he girded on his right side under his cloak. 17 He presented the tribute to King Eglon of Moab. Now Eglon was a
very stout man. 18 When [Ehud] had finished presenting the
tribute, he dismissed the people who had conveyed the tribute. 19 But he himself returned from Pesilim, near Gilgal, and
said, "Your Majesty, I have a secret message for you." [Eglon]
thereupon commanded, "Silence!" So all those in attendance left his presence; 20 and when Ehud approached him,
he was sitting alone in his cool upper chamber. Ehud said,
"I have a message for you from God"; whereupon he rose
from his seat. 21 Reaching with his left hand, Ehud drew the
dagger from his right side and drove it into [Eglon's][a] belly.
22 The fat closed over the blade and the hilt went in after the
blade—for he did not pull the dagger out of his belly—and
the filth[b] came out.
23 Stepping out into the vestibule,[b] Ehud shut the doors of
the upper chamber on him and locked them. 24 After he left,
the courtiers returned. When they saw that the doors of the
upper chamber were locked, they thought, "He must be relieving himself in the cool chamber." 25 They waited a long
time; and when he did not open the doors of the chamber,
they took the key and opened them—and there their master was lying dead on the floor! 26 But Ehud had made good
his escape while they delayed; he had passed Pesilim and

a Heb. "his." *b Meaning of Heb. uncertain.*

of power or charisma that allows him to be a successful warrior and leader.

3.12–30: Ehud son of Gera. In this story, the deliverance by Ehud the Benjaminite is accomplished with military tactics, some planned and others improvised. The victory suggests that divine providence stands behind the success of human tactics. **13:** *The City of Palms:* Here, unlike 1.16, most commentators, following Josephus, identify this place with Jericho. **15:** *A left-handed man:* One who could use his left hand as if it was his right hand (cf. 1 Chron. 12.2). **16:** *Two-edged dagger:* Ordinary daggers were curved and sharp only on the inner edge. Ehud's dagger, intended for stabbing, was short, perhaps a foot long, and sharpened on both edges, probably so that he could wield it in his left hand, contrary to the usual practice. **17:** The king's stoutness is emphasized because it complicated the planned assassination, as Ehud had a short sword. The picture of the dagger buried in the fleshy king's abdomen (vv. 21–22) adds to the humorous put-down of Eglon. **18:** *Had finished ... he dismissed the people:* These expressions create the impression of an elaborate gift-offering ceremony. The time consumed by the ceremony enabled Ehud to become familiar with the place and to create the impression of a submissive subject. Ehud alone remained, thereby obviating the need to reenter the well-guarded palace. **19:** Ehud arrived at Eglon's residence after having previously visited the *Pesilim* ("idols"), evidently a cultic site with statues of the gods near Gilgal, next to Jericho. **20:** *From God:* Ehud anticipated that, upon hearing God's name, the fat king would stand up and stretch himself, thereby making it easier to kill him. Eglon expects a divine oracle, but receives a divinely sanctioned stabbing. Some sages emphasized the positive aspect in Eglon's behavior, namely, that he stood up out of respect for the LORD, and therefore they considered Ruth the Moabite to be Eglon's daughter, making David one of his descendants (*Ruth Rab.* 2.9). **23:** The architectural details are unclear. It seems that the doors were locked by the act of shutting them. **24:** Eglon is indeed relieving himself in that his guts are spilling out; the entire story partakes of a vulgar humorousness, debasing the enemy. **25:** *Lying dead:* The servants did not sense the murder, as the fat covering the dagger prevented bleeding. They therefore did not suspect Ehud, who had enough time to escape. **26:** *Seirah,* unidentified site in the hill country of Ephraim.

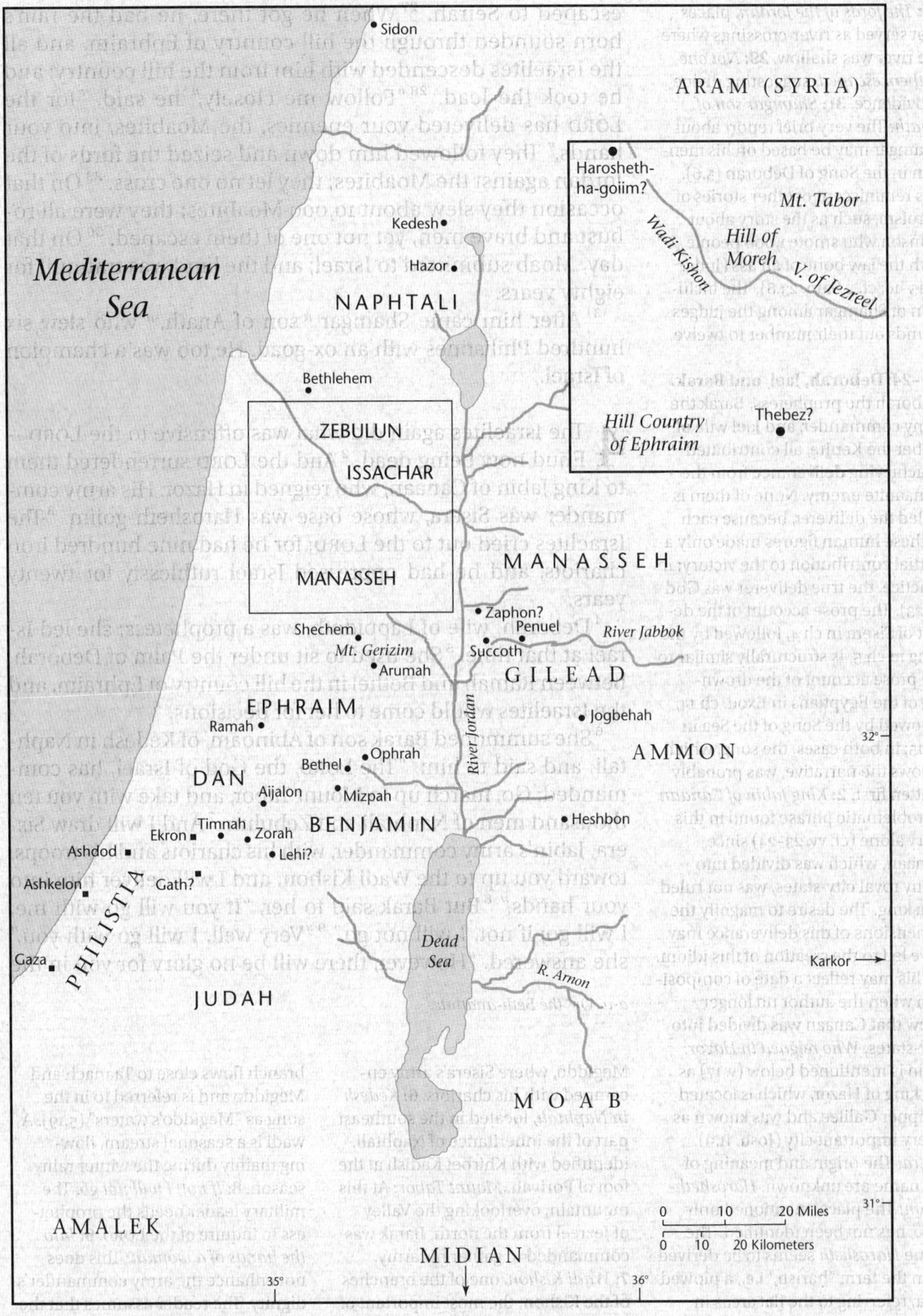

Important cities mentioned in the book of Judges. Square boxes indicate Philistine cities.

escaped to Seirah. [27] When he got there, he had the ram's horn sounded through the hill country of Ephraim, and all the Israelites descended with him from the hill country; and he took the lead. [28] "Follow me closely," he said, "for the LORD has delivered your enemies, the Moabites, into your hands." They followed him down and seized the fords of the Jordan against the Moabites; they let no one cross. [29] On that occasion they slew about 10,000 Moabites; they were all robust and brave men, yet not one of them escaped. [30] On that day, Moab submitted to Israel; and the land was tranquil for eighty years.

[31] After him came Shamgar [a]son of Anath,[-a] who slew six hundred Philistines with an ox-goad. He too was a champion of Israel.

4 The Israelites again did what was offensive to the LORD—Ehud now being dead. [2] And the LORD surrendered them to King Jabin of Canaan, who reigned in Hazor. His army commander was Sisera, whose base was Harosheth-goiim. [3] The Israelites cried out to the LORD; for he had nine hundred iron chariots, and he had oppressed Israel ruthlessly for twenty years.

[4] Deborah, wife of Lappidoth, was a prophetess; she led Israel at that time. [5] She used to sit under the Palm of Deborah, between Ramah and Bethel in the hill country of Ephraim, and the Israelites would come to her for decisions.

[6] She summoned Barak son of Abinoam, of Kedesh in Naphtali, and said to him, "The LORD, the God of Israel, has commanded: Go, march up to Mount Tabor, and take with you ten thousand men of Naphtali and Zebulun. [7] And I will draw Sisera, Jabin's army commander, with his chariots and his troops, toward you up to the Wadi Kishon; and I will deliver him into your hands." [8] But Barak said to her, "If you will go with me, I will go; if not, I will not go." [9] "Very well, I will go with you," she answered. "However, there will be no glory for you in the

a-a *Or "the Beth-anathite."*

28: *The fords of the Jordan,* places that served as river-crossings where the river was shallow. **29:** *Not one of them escaped,* suggesting divine providence. **31:** *Shamgar son of Anath:* The very brief report about Shamgar may be based on his mention in the Song of Deborah (5.6). It is reminiscent of other stories of heroism, such as the story about Samson who smote 1,000 people with the jaw bone of an ass (Judg. 15.15–16; cf. 2 Sam. 23.8). The inclusion of Shamgar among the judges rounds out their number to twelve.

4.1–24: Deborah, Jael, and Barak. Deborah the prophetess, Barak the army commander, and Jael wife of Heber the Kenite, all contributed to achieving deliverance from the Canaanite enemy. None of them is called the deliverer, because each of these human figures made only a partial contribution to the victory; in practice, the true deliverer was God (v. 23). The prose account of the defeat of Sisera in ch 4, followed by the song in ch 5, is structurally similar to the prose account of the drowning of the Egyptians in Exod. ch 14, followed by the Song of the Sea in ch 15; in both cases, the song, which follows the narrative, was probably written first. **2:** *King Jabin of Canaan,* a problematic phrase found in this story alone (cf. vv. 23–24) since Canaan, which was divided into many royal city-states, was not ruled by a king. The desire to magnify the dimensions of this deliverance may have led to the creation of this idiom, or this may reflect a date of composition when the author no longer knew that Canaan was divided into city-states. *Who reigned in Hazor:* Jabin is mentioned below (v. 17) as the king of Hazor, which is located in upper Galilee and was known as a very important city (Josh. 11.9). *Sisera:* The origin and meaning of the name are unknown. *Harosheth-goiim:* The place, mentioned only here, has not been identified. The name *Harosheth* seems to be derived from the term "ḥarish," i.e., a plowed area, referring to the flat areas in the Jezreel Valley near Taanach and Megiddo, where Sisera's army encamped with his chariots. **6:** *Kedesh in Naphtali,* located in the southeast part of the inheritance of Naphtali, identified with Khirbet Kadish at the foot of Poriyah. *Mount Tabor:* At this mountain, overlooking the Valley of Jezreel from the north, Barak was commanded to gather his army. **7:** *Wadi Kishon,* one of the branches of the Kishon, the most important of the brooks of the Jezreel Valley. This branch flows close to Taanach and Megiddo and is referred to in the song as "Megiddo's waters" (5.19). A wadi is a seasonal stream, flowing mainly during the winter rainy season. **8:** *If not, I will not go:* The military leader needs the prophetess to inquire of the LORD. **9:** *Into the hands of a woman:* This does not enhance the army commander's dignity. The reader assumes that the woman is Deborah, but by the end

course you are taking, for then the LORD will deliver Sisera into
the hands of a woman." So Deborah went with Barak to Kedesh.
[10] Barak then mustered Zebulun and Naphtali at Kedesh; ten
thousand men marched up [a]after him;[-a] and Deborah also
went up with him.

[11] Now Heber the Kenite had separated [b]from the other
Kenites,[-b] descendants of Hobab, father-in-law of Moses, and
had pitched his tent at Elon-bezaanannim, which is near
Kedesh.

[12] Sisera was informed that Barak son of Abinoam had
gone up to Mount Tabor. [13] So Sisera ordered all his chariots—nine hundred iron chariots—and all the troops he had
to move from Harosheth-goiim to the Wadi Kishon. [14] Then
Deborah said to Barak, "Up! This is the day on which the
LORD will deliver Sisera into your hands: the LORD is marching before you." Barak charged down Mount Tabor, followed
by the ten thousand men, [15] and the LORD threw Sisera and
all his chariots and army into a panic [c]before the onslaught
of Barak.[-c] Sisera leaped from his chariot and fled on foot
[16] as Barak pursued the chariots and the soldiers as far as
Harosheth-goiim. All of Sisera's soldiers fell by the sword;
not a man was left.

[17] Sisera, meanwhile, had fled on foot to the tent of Jael, wife
of Heber the Kenite; for there was friendship between King Jabin of Hazor and the family of Heber the Kenite. [18] Jael came
out to greet Sisera and said to him, "Come in, my lord, come
in here, do not be afraid." So he entered her tent, and she covered him with a blanket. [19] He said to her, "Please let me have
some water; I am thirsty." She opened a skin of milk and gave
him some to drink; and she covered him again. [20] He said to
her, "Stand at the entrance of the tent. If anybody comes and
asks you if there is anybody here, say 'No.' " [21] Then Jael wife of
Heber took a tent pin and grasped the mallet. When he was
fast asleep from exhaustion, she approached him stealthily
and drove the pin through his temple till it went down to the
ground. Thus he died.

[22] Now Barak appeared in pursuit of Sisera. Jael went out to
greet him and said, "Come, I will show you the man you are
looking for." He went inside with her, and there Sisera was lying
dead, with the pin in his temple.

[23] On that day God subdued King Jabin of Canaan before the
Israelites. [24] The hand of the Israelites bore harder and harder
on King Jabin of Canaan, until they destroyed King Jabin of
Canaan.

a-a *Lit. "at his feet."*
b-b *Lit. "from Cain"; cf. 1.16.*
c-c *Lit. "at the edge of the sword before Barak."*

realizes that she is Jael. Thus, Deborah's "prophecy" in this v. is fulfilled. **11:** *Heber the Kenite,* a tribal unit that became separated from the Kenites who were annexed to Judah (1.16). **14:** *The LORD is marching before you:* These words of Deborah indicate the LORD's direct participation in the battle, as the leader going at the head of the army. **15:** *"At the edge of the sword"* (see translators' note *c-c*). Nowhere else in the entire Bible does the LORD throw the enemy into a panic by the sword, and this first mention may be a dittography from the following v. **16:** *Not a man was left:* This unrealistic detail alludes to divine intervention (cf. 3.29). **17:** *To the tent of Jael ... for there was friendship:* Sisera preferred the tent of the Kenites to Harosheth-goiim, because he was convinced that this direction of flight would not occur to his pursuers, due to the friendship between the Kenites and the Israelites. **18:** The final maternal image of Jael covering *him with a blanket* becomes ironic, when the reader discovers that she kills him. **19:** Even though he asked for water, she gave him milk, because of its soothing qualities; Jael wanted to assure that Sisera would sleep deeply. **21:** Here it is revealed that Jael is the woman into whose hands the LORD delivered Sisera (see v. 9). **23:** *God subdued:* The conclusion emphasizes the LORD's central role in accomplishing the general victory and the partial contribution of the human figures.

5 On that day Deborah and Barak son of Abinoam sang:

2[a] When [b]locks go untrimmed[b] in Israel,
When people dedicate themselves—
Bless the LORD!

3 Hear, O kings! Give ear, O potentates!
I will sing, will sing to the LORD,
Will hymn the LORD, the God of Israel.

4 O LORD, when You came forth from Seir,
Advanced from the country of Edom,
The earth trembled;
The heavens dripped,
Yea, the clouds dripped water,
5 The mountains quaked[c]—
Before the LORD, Him of Sinai,
Before the LORD, God of Israel.

6 In the days of Shamgar [d]son of Anath,[d]
In the days of Jael, caravans[e] ceased,
And wayfarers went
By roundabout paths.
7 Deliverance ceased,
Ceased in Israel,
Till you[f] arose, O Deborah,
Arose, O mother, in Israel!

a *In many parts of this poem the meaning is uncertain.*
b-b *Apparently an expression of dedication; cf. Num. 6.5.*
c *Taking* nazelu *as a by-form of* nazollu; *cf. Targum.*
d-d *Or "the Beth-anathite."* e *Or "roads."*
f *Heb.* qamti, *archaic second-person singular feminine.*

5.1–31: The Song of Deborah. This is a hymn of praise thanking and extolling God for overcoming the enemies that threatened His people. It incorporates calls and addresses expressing the joy of victory and the need to offer thanksgiving. The poem is written in the first person, presented from the viewpoint of the speaker; readers in effect sing the song and identify with the speaker. Besides the opening (vv. 2–3) and closing (v. 31a) it consists of three sections. The first (vv. 4–11c) depicts God's appearance or theophany, the difficult situation of His people and its hope for salvation; the second (vv. 11d–23) portrays the Israelite warriors in contrast with the Canaanite kings; the third (vv. 24–30) focuses upon the non-Israelite Jael, who represents victory, contrasted with Sisera's mother, who represents defeat. Although there are similarities between the song in ch 5 and the story in ch 4, there are also numerous differences: e.g., the story only mentions two tribes who participate in battle, the song mentions at least six; according to the song Sisera headed the Canaanite alliance and Jabin is not mentioned. Some scholars believe that the story was composed as an interpretation of the song. Stylistically, the song is in archaic Heb, and is extremely difficult, and in some places, corrupt. It makes use of extensive contrasts and extreme transitions: from the LORD's might to Israel's unfortunate situation; from the Israelite tribes to their enemies; from Jael to Sisera's mother. It also conveys an atmosphere of spontaneous enthusiasm. The poem does not mention Judah, Simeon, and Levi, suggesting that it was composed in the north. **1:** According to the editor, Deborah and Barak uttered the song in immediate reaction to the joy of victory. This song is recited as the haftarah for parashat Beshalaḥ, which contains the Song of the Sea (Exod. ch 15); it is preceded by most of ch 4 in the Ashkenazic rite.

5.2–3: Opening explaining the circumstances of reciting the song. 2: *When locks go untrimmed,* the Heb is difficult. The translation alludes to Nazirites who dedicated themselves to warfare wearing long hair (see Num. ch 6). Rashi's interpretation, that the phrase refers to disturbances or even disasters that confronted Israel, is preferable. *Dedicate,* volunteer of one's own will. *Bless,* addressed to the people of Israel. **3:** *I will sing . . . :* The repetition emphasizes the function of the speaker and strengthens the involvement of the person later reciting the song.

5.4–5: God's theophany and His influence on the mighty forces of nature. 4: *Seir . . . Edom,* synonyms referring to God's revelation in the land of Edom, southeast of Judah. On the tradition of God's theophany there, see Deut. 32.2 and Hab. 3.3. **5:** *Quaked,* some interpret the Heb in the sense of flowing, liquid matter. On the connection between earthquakes and liquid imagery, see Amos 9.5. *Sinai* is here connected to a theophany, as in Exod. ch 19, but not to the giving of the Torah.

5.6–11c: Description of the difficult situation in Israel. 6: *Shamgar,* see 3.31 n. **7:** *Deliverance ceased:* In the Aram. Targum and in traditional exegesis the Heb word "perazon" is taken as referring to "open" cities. People were afraid to live in towns without a wall, and fled to fortified

8 When they chose new gods,
[a]Was there a fighter then in the gates?[a]
No shield or spear was seen
Among forty thousand in Israel!

9 My heart is with Israel's leaders,
With the dedicated of the people—
Bless the LORD!
10 You riders on tawny she-asses,
You who sit on saddle rugs,
And you wayfarers, declare it!
11 Louder than the [b]sound of archers,[b]
There among the watering places
Let them chant the gracious acts of the LORD,
His gracious deliverance of Israel.
Then did the people of the LORD
March down to the gates!
12 Awake, awake, O Deborah!
Awake, awake, strike up the chant!
Arise, O Barak;
Take your captives, O son of Abinoam!

13 Then was the remnant made victor over the mighty,
The LORD's people[c] won my victory over the warriors.

14 From Ephraim came they whose roots are in Amalek;
After you, your kin Benjamin;
From Machir came down leaders,
From Zebulun such as hold the marshal's staff.
15 And Issachar's chiefs were with Deborah;
As Barak, so was Issachar—
Rushing after him into the valley.

a-a *Meaning of Heb. uncertain; others "then was war in the gates."*
b-b *Or "thunder peals"; meaning of Heb. uncertain.*
c *Reading* ʿam (*with* pathaḥ) Adonai; *so many Heb. mss.*

cities. *You arose:* Here the speaker addresses Deborah; see v. 12. **8:** *New gods:* The cause of the difficult situation is the people's abandonment of the LORD for the gods of Canaan. See Deut. 32.15–19. *Then:* This word is repeated five times (vv. 8, 11, 13, 19, 22), indicating various stages in the course of the war: danger, gathering together, arrival at the battlefield, war, retreat. *Forty thousand,* an exaggerated typological number, suggesting a war of national dimensions. **9:** *Leaders:* The Heb carries the connotation of legislators. **10:** *You riders ... :* Riding on a donkey was a symbol of wealth; see 10.4 n. **11:** *Sound of archers:* Alternately, the Heb may refer to the noise made by shepherds while dividing their flocks to water them. The sound of those who tell God's victories will be louder than this sound. *His gracious deliverance:* The LORD's deliverance restored confidence.

5.11d–13: General description of preparation for war. 11: *Gates:* The city gate served as a public gathering place. Those who had left the unwalled cities gathered at the gates of the fortified cities in order to set out to battle. **12:** Deborah is given here the primary position. *Strike up the chant:* Deborah is expected to prophesy on the eve of the war. *Take your captives:* On the connection between victory and booty, see v. 30. **13:** *Then was the remnant ... :* The use of the Heb verb is difficult, as is calling Israel a "remnant" (Heb "sarid"). A preferable reading is "Then they went down to Sarid [a city in the Jezreel Valley] against the mighty ones [i.e., the Canaanite kings; see v. 25], the LORD's people with their warriors."

5.14–18: Description of the Israelite side. Most commentators say that six tribes went to war (Ephraim, Benjamin, Machir [i.e., Manasseh], Zebulun, Issachar and Naphtali), while four other tribes (Reuben, Gilead [i.e., Gad and the other half of Manasseh], Dan and Asher) refused to join. According to the interpretation suggested here, all ten northern tribes participated. **14:** *They whose roots are in Amalek:* This phrase is unclear; hence one should adopt the emendation based on the similarity of the Heb letters: "From Ephraim chieftains (instead of roots) [went down] to the valley (Heb ʿmk instead of ʿmlk)." *Your kin:* The collective noun here follows the plural in the Heb, which may be interpreted as: "After you, Benjamin, among your kinfolk." This usage strengthens the sense of Benjamin's large army. Benjamin is a fighting tribe in ch 20, in the blessing of Jacob (Gen. 49.27), and in the description of the establishment of the kingdom (2 Sam. ch 11). *Machir:* The first-born son of Manasseh; cf. Josh. 17.1. *Marshal's staff:* The Heb word suggests commanders, who recorded the number of those going to war (see 2 Kings 25.19). **15:** *So was Issachar:* It is strange that Issachar is repeated twice in this v., while Naphtali is absent. It therefore seems likely that it originally read "Naphtali." This conjecture is strengthened by the fact that Barak

Among the clans of Reuben
Were great decisions of heart.
16 Why then did you stay among the sheepfolds
And listen as they pipe for the flocks?
Among the clans of Reuben
Were great searchings of heart!
17 Gilead tarried beyond the Jordan;
And Dan—why did he linger [a-]by the ships?[-a]
Asher remained at the seacoast
And tarried at his landings.
18 Zebulun is a people [b-]that mocked at death,[-b]
Naphtali—on the open heights.

19 Then the kings came, they fought:
The kings of Canaan fought
At Taanach, by Megiddo's waters—
They got no spoil of silver.
20 The stars fought from heaven,
From their courses they fought against Sisera.
21 The torrent Kishon swept them[c] away,
The raging torrent, the torrent Kishon.

March on, my soul, with courage!

22 Then the horses' hoofs pounded
[d-]As headlong galloped the steeds.[-d]
23 "Curse Meroz!" said the angel of the LORD.
"Bitterly curse its inhabitants,
Because they came not to the aid of the LORD,
To the aid of the LORD among[e] the warriors."

24 Most blessed of women be Jael,
Wife of Heber the Kenite,
Most blessed of women in tents.
25 He asked for water, she offered milk;
In a princely bowl she brought him curds.

a-a Or "at Onioth," a presumed designation of Dan's region.
b-b Lit. "belittled its life to die." *c I.e., the kings of Canaan (v. 19).*
d-d Lit. "From the gallopings, the gallopings of his steeds." *e Or "against."*

was from Kedesh-Naphtali, and by the affinity of this v. to the description of Naphtali in the blessing of Jacob (Gen. 49.21). *Heart:* The ancients thought of the heart as the center of thinking and wisdom (see, e.g., 1 Kings 3.12). **16:** *Why then:* Heb "lamah" (why) does not necessarily imply a query. Here and in v. 17 it seems preferable to read it as a term of negation with an emphatic mem. Thus, it is not a denunciation of Reuben, and later Dan, for not taking part in the battle, and should be translated: "You [certainly] did not stay among the sheepfolds ... !" **17:** *Tarried,* alternately, "dwelled" or "lived," suggesting that even though the inhabitants of Gilead (Gad and the half tribe of Manasseh) lived far away from the location of the events, they took part in them. *And Dan ... ships,* alternately, "Dan [certainly] did not linger by the ships." The mention of ships is difficult, because the territory of Dan, both in the south and in the north, has no connection to the sea. *Asher:* The tribe Asher, who dwelt on the northern coastal plain, also joined the war. **18:** *Zebulun ... Naphtali:* These two tribes alone are mentioned as bold warriors, and they alone are mentioned in the prose story (ch 4). *Open heights:* The war was in the valley; the expression alludes to Naphtali's inheritance.

5.19–23: The battle. 19: *Kings of Canaan:* Jabin, who is mentioned in the prose story, does not appear here; v. 20 notes Sisera as heading the alliance. *At Taanach, by Megiddo's waters:* The battlefield was between Taanach and one of the tributaries of the Kishon next to Megiddo, in Jezreel Valley, near the ancient international road connecting Egypt and Mesopotamia (see 4.7). **20:** *The stars,* representing minor deities and part of the heavenly host, are imagined to be participating along with God in helping Israel. **21:** *The raging torrent:* The Heb is obscure, and an emendation suggests "the brook Kishon came in front of them." *March on:* The joy of victory finds expression as the speaker addresses himself. **22:** A description of the noise of the enemy's horses' feet fleeing from the battle's confusion. **23:** *Meroz,* which has not been identified and whose inhabitants did not join the battle, is cursed. *The warriors:* Here and in v. 13 it speaks of the warriors of Israel who joined the LORD's battle.

5.24–27: Description of the killing of Sisera in Jael's tent. Death at the hands of a woman was considered shameful; cf. 9.54. The appearance of Jael in the poem is not explained; furthermore, the song does not suggest that Sisera slept, implying instead that Jael struggled with Sisera. The poem describes Sisera's

26 Her [left] hand reached for the tent pin,
Her right for the workmen's hammer.
She struck Sisera, crushed his head,
Smashed and pierced his temple.
27 At her feet he sank, lay outstretched,
At her feet he sank, lay still;
Where he sank, there he lay—destroyed.

28 Through the window peered Sisera's mother,
Behind the lattice she whined:[a]
"Why is his chariot so long in coming?
Why so late the clatter of his wheels?"
29 The wisest of her ladies give answer;
She, too, replies to herself:
30 "They must be dividing the spoil they have found:
A damsel or two for each man,
Spoil of dyed cloths for Sisera,
Spoil of embroidered cloths,
A couple of embroidered cloths
Round every neck as spoil."

31 So may all Your enemies perish, O LORD!
But may His friends be as the sun rising in might!

And the land was tranquil forty years.

6 Then the Israelites did what was offensive to the LORD, and the LORD delivered them into the hands of the Midianites for seven years. 2 The hand of the Midianites prevailed over Israel; and because of Midian, the Israelites [b-]provided themselves with refuges in the caves and strongholds of the mountains.[-b] 3 After the Israelites had done their sowing, Midian, Amalek, and the Kedemites would come up and raid them; 4 they would attack them, destroy[c] the produce of the land all the way to Gaza, and leave no means of sustenance in Israel,

a *Or "gazed"; meaning of Heb. uncertain.* b-b *Meaning of Heb. uncertain.*
c *I.e., by grazing their livestock.*

death in slow motion, and the term *at her feet,* Heb "between her legs," may depict Jael as a temptress.

5.28–30: Transition to Sisera's house. The mother's apprehension contrasts with the ladies' expectations of booty. This scene, which is not found in the narrative in ch 4, portrays Sisera's demise from a different perspective. **28:** The picture of a woman looking through the window is repeated in the Bible (2 Sam. 6.16; 2 Kings 9.30) and in other ancient Near Eastern texts and artistic depictions. **29:** Irony pervades, as *the wisest of her ladies* are completely mistaken. **30:** *Dyed cloths ... embroidered:* The making of dye was expensive; hence colored clothing was expensive, as were garments embroidered with colored threads. Cf. Exod. 26.36. *Every neck:* Presumably the necks of those who took the spoils.

5.31a: Closing. *His friends:* The people of the LORD are compared to the sun, rising with great intensity.

5.31b: Editorial conclusion. These words are not part of the song, but are the closing frame of the Deborah-Barak cycle. In its present location it emphasizes the transition to a new cycle of stories.

6.1–8.28: The cycle of Gideon stories. The description of Gideon's deliverance of the Israelites is divided into two sections, distinctive in subject matter, events, and characterization. The former (6.1–7.23) depicts the period from the people's sin and consequent subjugation to the Midianites until Gideon's victory. This section is rich with miracles, while Gideon is portrayed as a coward requiring divine support. By contrast, the second section (7.24–8.28) is concerned with problems of leadership, there are no miracles, and Gideon is displayed as a charismatic leader. The two sections illustrate the central problem of Judges: What is the preferred type of leadership? Divine leadership rich in miraculous signs, as in the first section, or human rule, as in the second? Gideon's victory is also mentioned in Isa. 10.26 and Ps. 83.10–13. Given the length of the section about Gideon, and the likelihood that it was composed from smaller units, it is best characterized as a "cycle," as are the Samson stories.

6.1–10: Exposition. 1–2: The period of oppression lasted for only seven years, but since it involved subjugation by nomadic tribes with grazing flocks, they succeeded in causing great damage by destroying all the crops. The Israelites were forced to go into hiding and to conceal their grain in the hills. **2:** *The caves* were also used to hide grain from the marauding tribes. **3:** *Amalek ... Kedemites,* wandering tribes from southern and eastern deserts who joined the Midianites. **4:** *Gaza,* located in the southwest of

not a sheep or an ox or an ass. 5 For they would come up with
their livestock and their tents, swarming as thick as locusts;
they and their camels were innumerable. Thus they would invade the land and ravage it. 6 Israel was reduced to utter misery
by the Midianites, and the Israelites cried out to the LORD.
7 When the Israelites cried to the LORD on account of Midian, 8 the LORD sent a prophet to the Israelites who said to them,
"Thus said the LORD, the God of Israel: I brought you up out of
Egypt and freed you from the house of bondage. 9 I rescued you
from the Egyptians and from all your oppressors; I drove them
out before you, and gave you their land. 10 And I said to you, 'I
the LORD am your God. You must not worship the gods of the
Amorites in whose land you dwell.' But you did not obey Me."

11 An angel of the LORD came and sat under the terebinth at
Ophrah, which belonged to Joash the Abiezrite. His son Gideon
was then beating out wheat inside a winepress in order to keep
it safe from the Midianites. 12 The angel of the LORD appeared
to him and said to him, "The LORD is with you, valiant warrior!"
13 Gideon said to him, "Please, my lord, if the LORD is with
us, why has all this befallen us? Where are all His wondrous
deeds about which our fathers told us, saying, 'Truly the LORD
brought us up from Egypt'? Now the LORD has abandoned us
and delivered us into the hands of Midian!" 14 The LORD turned
to him and said, "Go in this strength of yours and deliver Israel
from the Midianites. I herewith make you My messenger." 15 He
said to Him, "Please, my lord, how can I deliver Israel? Why,
my clan is the humblest in Manasseh, and I am the youngest
in my father's household." 16 The LORD replied, "I will be with
you, and you shall defeat Midian to a man." 17 And he said to
Him, "If I have gained Your favor, give me a sign that it is You
who are speaking to me: 18 do not leave this place until I come
back to You and bring out my offering and place it before You."
And He answered, "I will stay until you return."
19 So Gideon went in and prepared a kid, and [baked] unleavened bread from an ephah of flour. He put the meat in a
basket and poured the broth into a pot, and he brought them

Israel, later marking the boundary of the land (1 Kings 5.4). Its mention here suggests that the entire land was devastated. **5:** *As locusts,* an image emphasizing a large number and severe damage. Cf. Joel 1.6–7. **7–10:** Israel *cried to the LORD,* but this time He delayed the deliverer and sent a prophet to rebuke the people for being ungrateful and violating the covenant. Vv. 7–10 are absent in the variant from a Dead Sea Scroll version of Judges, 4QJudg[a], and may be a later element in the text.

6.11–24: Gideon's appointment as savior. A stereotypic scene composed of seven stages: meeting (vv. 11–13), presentation of the mission (v. 14), refusal (v. 15), encouragement (v. 16), request for and giving of a sign (vv. 17–22), acknowledgment and fear (v. 23), and further encouragement (v. 24). The appointment of Moses in Exod. 3.1–4.17 has a similar structure, but in a different sequence. **11:** *Ophrah:* Several other places bear this name. Ophrah of the Abiezrites (v. 24) is located within the territory of the Abiezer clan, one of the important families in Manasseh, who is mentioned in the Samaria Ostraca from the mid-8th century BCE. *Gideon:* This story offers a folk etymology of his name from the root "g-d-ʿ," "to hack," mentioned in connection with destroying sacred posts (Deut. 7.5). *Winepress:* The winepress, in contrast to a threshing floor, is sunk in the ground, and thus is a better hiding place for the grain. **12:** *Angel:* Angels, or messengers from God, appear as adult human beings; therefore Gideon does not know that he is confronted by an angel. *The LORD is with you:* A conventional formula of blessing and encouragement (Ruth 2.4). *Valiant warrior:* An anticipatory allusion to the military role that Gideon is expected to play. **13:** The angel uses the same language in the prophet's rebuke in vv. 7–10, or the prophet's words may be based on this passage. **14:** *The LORD,* as the angel of the LORD. *This strength,* Rashi: "By virtue of the fact that you spoke in defense of my sons." *I herewith make you My messenger* is more literally "I now send you." The root "sh-l-ḥ" is generally used for commissioning messengers and prophets (e.g., Exod. 2.10; 3.13; Isa. 6.8; Jer. 1.7). **15:** *Humblest ... youngest,* a polite refusal characteristic of appointment stories, since Gideon's family is depicted as prosperous (vv. 19, 25, 27; cf. 1 Sam. 9.21). The choice of the youngest is also a repeated motif (e.g., 1 Sam. 16.11) that emphasizes divine intervention through the unexpected. **17:** *A sign that it is You:* Gideon is skeptical that the messenger is God's angel and asks for proof. **18:** The proof is based upon the belief that angels do not usually participate in human meals (cf. 13.15; Tobit 12.19). **19:** Prepared from dough that has not risen, *unleavened bread* bakes quickly. *Ephah,* about 23 liters (21 dry quarts), a huge quantity, signifying

out to Him under the terebinth. As he presented them, [20] the
angel of God said to him, "Take the meat and the unleavened
bread, put them on yonder rock, and spill out the broth." He
did so. [21] The angel of the LORD held out the staff that he carried, and touched the meat and the unleavened bread with its
tip. A fire sprang up from the rock and consumed the meat and
the unleavened bread. And the angel of the LORD vanished
from his sight. [22] Then Gideon realized that it was an angel of
the LORD; and Gideon said, "Alas, O Lord GOD! For I have seen
an angel of the LORD face to face."
[23] But the LORD said to him, "All is well; have no fear, you
shall not die." [24] So Gideon built there an altar to the LORD and
called it [a-]Adonai-shalom.[-a] To this day it stands in Ophrah of
the Abiezrites.
[25] That night the LORD said to him: "Take the [b-]young bull[-b]
belonging to your father and another bull seven years old; pull
down the altar of Baal which belongs to your father, and cut
down the sacred post which is beside it. [26] Then build an altar to the LORD your God, on [b-]the level ground[-b] on top of this
stronghold. Take the other bull and offer it as a burnt offering,
using the wood of the sacred post that you have cut down."
[27] So Gideon took ten of his servants and did as the LORD had
told him; but as he was afraid to do it by day, on account of
his father's household and the townspeople, he did it by night.
[28] Early the next morning, the townspeople found that the altar of Baal had been torn down and the sacred post beside it
had been cut down, and that the second bull had been offered
on the newly built altar. [29] They said to one another, "Who did
this thing?" Upon inquiry and investigation, they were told,
"Gideon son of Joash did this thing!" [30] The townspeople said
to Joash, "Bring out your son, for he must die: he has torn
down the altar of Baal and cut down the sacred post beside it!"
[31] But Joash said to all who had risen against him, "Do you have
to contend for Baal? Do you have to vindicate him? Whoever
fights his battles shall be dead by morning! If he is a god, let
him fight his own battles, since it is his altar that has been torn
down!" [32] That day they named him[c] Jerubbaal, meaning "Let
Baal contend with him, since he tore down his altar."

a-a I.e., "The LORD, 'All-is-well.'"
b-b Meaning of Heb. uncertain.
c I.e., Gideon.

an honorable portion. **20:** The first sign that this mysterious stranger is an angel is his abstaining from eating; instead he uses the materials from the meal for a cultic ceremony. The meat is a sacrificial offering, the cakes are a meal offering, and the gravy is a substitute for the libation. **21:** The second sign is the appearance of fire from the rock (cf. 13.20; 1 Kings 18.38; etc.) consuming the materials of the meal; the third sign is the miraculous disappearance of the angel. This piling up of signs is later mirrored in the signs that Gideon requests at the end of the ch. **22:** Once Gideon realized that he had seen God's angel, he was afraid that this contact with the divine might prove fatal, since encounter with the divine is typically fraught with danger (see Exod. 20.15; Judg. 13.22). **24:** The name of the altar is related to God's comforting words in v. 23: "All is well."

6.25–32: Gideon wages war against the Baal cult. On the night after his appointment, the LORD commands Gideon to destroy his father's altar of Baal, to cut down the sacred post next to it, and to build an altar to the LORD. Gideon fears the townspeople and works with ten of his servants under cover of darkness. In the morning, after a short investigation, the townspeople want to kill Gideon, but his father prevents them from doing so by saying that, if Baal is god, he can fight his own battles. This story mocks Baal worship, and explains the additional name given to Gideon: Jerubbaal (see v. 32), emphasizing that Gideon did battle with the cult of Baal. **25:** *Another bull seven years old:* The reference to two bulls here, and to the second bull in vv. 26 and 28, is problematic, and may reflect a textual error; a better reading is: "the bull that had been fattened for seven years." *Sacred post,* symbol of the goddess Asherah (see 3.7 n.). **26:** The building of the LORD's altar in place of Baal's symbolizes the LORD's victory over Baal, who is unable to wage his own battles. **27:** Gideon is shown as a coward, a feature repeated in the first section (until 7.23). **31:** Joash puts Baal to the test in the eyes of his believers. This motif is reminiscent of Elijah's test at Mount Carmel (1 Kings 18.20–40). *By morning,* i.e., of the next day. Joash left time for Baal to act. **32:** *Jerubbaal,* originally a theophoric name, praising Baal as founder. The component "Jeru," also found in the name "Jerusalem," means "to establish." The derivation of the name here as *Let Baal contend ...* is a folk etymology.

33 All Midian, Amalek, and the Kedemites joined forces; they
crossed over and encamped in the Valley of Jezreel. 34 The spirit of the LORD enveloped Gideon; he sounded the horn, and
the Abiezrites rallied behind him. 35 And he sent messengers
throughout Manasseh, and they too rallied behind him. He
then sent messengers through Asher, Zebulun, and Naphtali,
and they came up to meet the Manassites.[a]
36 And Gideon said to God, "If You really intend to deliver Israel through me as You have said—37 here I place a fleece of
wool on the threshing floor. If dew falls only on the fleece and
all the ground remains dry, I shall know that You will deliver Israel through me, as You have said." 38 And that is what happened.
Early the next day, he squeezed the fleece and wrung out the dew
from the fleece, a bowlful of water. 39 Then Gideon said to God,
"Do not be angry with me if I speak just once more. Let me make
just one more test with the fleece: let the fleece alone be dry,
while there is dew all over the ground." 40 God did so that night:
only the fleece was dry, while there was dew all over the ground.

7 Early next day, Jerubbaal—that is, Gideon—and all the
troops with him encamped above En-harod,[b] while the
camp of Midian was in the plain to the north of him, at Gibeath-
moreh.[c] 2 The LORD said to Gideon, "You have too many troops
with you for Me to deliver Midian into their hands; Israel might
claim for themselves the glory due to Me, thinking, 'Our own
hand has brought us victory.' 3 Therefore, announce to the men,
'Let anybody who is timid and fearful turn back, [d-]as a bird flies
from Mount Gilead.'"[-d] Thereupon, 22,000 of the troops turned
back and 10,000 remained.
4 "There are still too many troops," the LORD said to Gideon. "Take them down to the water and I will sift[e] them for
you there. Anyone of whom I tell you, 'This one is to go with
you,' that one shall go with you; and anyone of whom I tell
you, 'This one is not to go with you,' that one shall not go."
5 So he took the troops down to the water. Then the LORD said
to Gideon, "Set apart all those who [f-]lap up the water with
their tongues like dogs[-f] from all those who get down on their
knees to drink." 6 Now those who "lapped" the water into their
mouths by hand numbered three hundred; all the rest of the
troops got down on their knees to drink. 7 Then the LORD said
to Gideon, "I will deliver you and I will put Midian into your
hands through the three hundred 'lappers'; let the rest of the
troops go home." 8 [d-]So [the lappers] took the provisions and
horns that the other men had with them,[-d] and he sent the

a Heb. "them." *b Or "the Spring of Harod."* *c Or "the Hill of Moreh."*
d-d Meaning of Heb. uncertain. *e Lit. "smelt."*
f-f Actually, using their hands as a dog uses its tongue; see v. 6.

6.33–35: The military mustering. The Midianite army had spread out across the Jezreel Valley; troops from Gideon's father's house were not sufficient, so he called to his assistance his own house and the neighboring tribes who were harmed by the Midianites. **34:** On *the spirit of the LORD*, see 3.10 n.

6.36–40: The signs of the fleece. Gideon requires additional signs and tests God with two opposite tests, in order to be certain that it was not by chance, but by the LORD's will, that Gideon will deliver Israel. This is the culmination of a ch that has as its theme Gideon's fear.

7.1–8: The three hundred lappers. Gideon's army was reduced from a force of 32,000 warriors to a band of 300 lappers of water, in order to convince the people that the deliverance comes from God. According to rabbinic tradition the lappers were chosen because, unlike those who bent on their knees, they did not bow down to an idol (*Tanḥuma,* ed. Buber, *Toledot* 19; *Yalqut Shim'oni,* Judges 62; 1 Kings 29). According to Josephus the lappers were the cowards. This is more likely, and thus Gideon highlights the miracle of the victory by choosing cowards (Josephus, *Ant.,* 5.6.3 [216–17]). **1:** *Plain:* The Midianites encamped on the plain at the feet of *Gibeath-moreh,* south of Afula. **2:** The concern was that Israel would be haughty and attribute the victory to themselves and not to God (see Deut. 8.17–18). **3:** A call to those fearful of war to return to their homes appears in the laws of war in Deut. 20.8. **6:** The v. seems to be corrupt, the phrase "into their mouths by hand" belongs at its end, as a dog does not lap water by bringing its hand to its mouth.

rest of the men of Israel back to their homes, retaining only
the three hundred men.
The Midianite camp was below him, in the plain. [9] That night
the LORD said to him, "Come, attack[a] the camp, for I have delivered it into your hands. [10] And if you are afraid to attack, first
go down to the camp with your attendant Purah [11] and listen
to what they say; after that you will have the courage to attack
the camp." So he went down with his attendant Purah to the
outposts of the warriors who were in the camp.—[12] Now Midian, Amalek, and all the Kedemites were spread over the plain,
as thick as locusts; and their camels were countless, as numerous as the sands on the seashore.—[13] Gideon came there just
as one man was narrating a dream to another. "Listen," he was
saying, "I had this dream: There was a commotion[b]—a loaf
of barley bread was whirling through the Midianite camp. It
came to a tent and struck it, and it fell; it turned it upside down,
and the tent collapsed." [14] To this the other responded, "That
can only mean the sword of the Israelite Gideon son of Joash.
God is delivering Midian and the entire camp into his hands."[c]

[15] When Gideon heard the dream told and interpreted,
he bowed low. Returning to the camp of Israel, he shouted,
"Come on! The LORD has delivered the Midianite camp into
your hands!" [16] He divided the three hundred men into three
columns and equipped every man with a ram's horn and an
empty jar, with a torch in each jar. [17] "Watch me," he said, "and
do the same. When I get to the outposts of the camp, do exactly
as I do. [18] When I and all those with me blow our horns, you
too, all around the camp, will blow your horns and shout, 'For
the LORD and for Gideon!'"

[19] Gideon and the hundred men with him arrived at the outposts of the camp, at the beginning of the middle watch, just
after the sentries were posted. [d-]They sounded the horns and
smashed the jars that they had with them,[-d] [20] and the three
columns blew their horns and broke their jars. Holding the
torches in their left hands and the horns for blowing in their
right hands, they shouted, "A sword for the LORD and for Gideon!" [21] They remained standing where they were, surrounding
the camp; but the entire camp ran about yelling, and took to
flight. [22] For when the three hundred horns were sounded, the
LORD turned every man's sword against his fellow, throughout
the camp, and the entire host fled as far as Beth-shittah and
on to Zererah—as far as the outskirts of Abel-meholah near
Tabbath.

a Lit. "descend upon"; so in vv. 10 and 11. *b Meaning of Heb. uncertain.*
c The loaf of bread symbolizes the agricultural Israelites; the tent, the nomadic Midianites.
d-d Emendation yields "He sounded the horn and smashed the jar that he had with him."

7.9–15a: The dream of the Midianite soldier and its meaning. Gideon, who remains fearful of battle, is given another encouraging sign. God commands him to go close to the Midianite camp; there he hears a Midianite telling his friend a dream, whose interpretation signifies their defeat. Gideon thanks God. **12:** See 6.5. **13:** A dream was understood by the ancients as revealing God's will. (See esp. Gen. chs 37; 40; 41; Dan. ch 2.) *A commotion—a loaf…*: The Midianite dreamer heard a commotion in which a loaf of barley bread whirled through the camp until it knocked over a tent. **14:** The falling of the tent is interpreted as the defeat of Midian, while the barley bread, the peasants' product, symbolizes Gideon's sword. **15a:** Gideon *bowed low* in thanks and recognition to God.

7.15b–23: The battle. The battle description consists of three stages: the preparations (vv. 15b–18), the battle itself (vv. 19–22), and the pursuit (v. 23). The description emphasizes the passivity of the (cowardly) fighters, whose only task is to blow the ram's horns, cry out "For the LORD and for Gideon," and watch God's deliverance. **16:** The army is divided into three parts in order to surround the camp. **19:** *Middle watch:* The night is divided into three watches. During the middle watch sleep is deepest; hence, at the time of changing guards, the soldiers are likely to be groggy and to panic at every sound. **20:** To emphasize that the sword is the LORD's, Gideon's soldiers are shown as having both their hands occupied: in the right hand the horns to blow, and in the left, the torches, so that all they can do is to shout. **21:** Unlike "real" soldiers, Gideon's soldiers stood at their places while the Midianites called for help and began to flee. **22:** The blowing of 300 horns, coupled with the LORD's intervention, caused the Midianites to kill one another. Those who escaped fled southeast, to the fords of the Jordan. The places mentioned have not been identified.

23 And now the men of Israel from Naphtali and Asher and
from all of Manasseh rallied for the pursuit of the Midianites.
24 Gideon also sent messengers all through the hill country of
Ephraim with this order: [a]"Go down ahead of the Midianites
and seize their access to the water all along the Jordan down to
Beth-barah." So all the men of Ephraim rallied and seized the
waterside down to Beth-barah by the Jordan. 25 They pursued
the Midianites and captured Midian's two generals, Oreb and
Zeeb. They killed Oreb at the Rock of Oreb and they killed Zeeb
at the Winepress of Zeeb; and they brought the heads of Oreb
and Zeeb from the other side of the Jordan to Gideon.

8 And the men of Ephraim said to him, "Why did you do that
to us—not calling us when you went to fight the Midianites?" And they rebuked him severely. 2 But he answered them,
"After all, what have I accomplished compared to you? Why,
Ephraim's gleanings are better than Abiezer's vintage! 3 God
has delivered the Midianite generals Oreb and Zeeb into your
hands, and what was I able to do compared to you?" And when
he spoke in this fashion, their anger against him abated.
4 Gideon came to the Jordan and crossed it. The three hundred men with him were famished, but still in pursuit. 5 He
said to the people of Succoth, "Please give some loaves of
bread to the men who are following me, for they are famished,
and I am pursuing Zebah and Zalmunna, the kings of Midian." 6 But the officials of Succoth replied, [b-]"Are Zebah and
Zalmunna already in your hands,[-b] that we should give bread
to your troops?" 7 "I swear," declared Gideon, "when the LORD
delivers Zebah and Zalmunna into my hands, I'll thresh[c] your
bodies upon desert thorns and briers!" 8 From there he went
up to Penuel and made the same request of them; but the
people of Penuel gave him the same reply as the people of

a Meaning of rest of verse uncertain.

b-b Lit. "Is the palm of Zebah and Zalmunna in your hand."

c I.e., throw them naked in a bed of thorns and trample them; but exact meaning uncertain.

23: *The men of Israel ... rallied:* The fighting units of Naphtali, Asher, and all of Manasseh joined in the chase.

7.24–8.3: The confrontation with Ephraim. Ephraim's warriors were insulted because they were invited to the chase but not to the battle itself, and were concerned for their status among the tribes. Gideon calmed them, preventing a civil war while displaying responsible leadership and diplomatic talent. This story opens the second section, in which there are no divine interventions or miracles, and Gideon is not fearful. This episode anticipates 12.1–7 and the comparison emphasizes the responsible leadership of Gideon. **7.24:** Upon setting out in pursuit, Gideon called the men of Ephraim, imposing upon them responsibility for the pursuit adjacent to their territory. *Beth-barah* has not been identified. Gideon's instruction was to seize all the water sources flowing into the Jordan. **25:** The names *Oreb* and *Zeeb* mean "wolf" and "raven"; we have no Midianite literature, so we do not know if animal names were typical in that culture. *Rock of ... :* The places where the Midianite generals were killed, north of Jericho and to the west of the Jordan, are named for them. *The other side of the Jordan,* east of the Jordan. **8.1:** *When you went to fight:* Ephraim's warriors were angry that Gideon did not involve them earlier when he called Manasseh, Asher, and Naphtali (6.35). **2:** *Gleanings,* the grapes that remain after the main part of the harvest has been completed. Gideon explained to the warriors in a diplomatic way that the killing of the two generals was even more important than the battle itself, in which he and his family, the house of Abiezer, had taken part.

8.4–21: The confrontation with Succoth and Penuel. Gideon, leading 300 men, crosses the Jordan to smite the camp of Midian in the east and to capture Zebah and Zalmunna, the kings of Midian. The inhabitants of the Israelite cities Succoth and Penuel question the ability of Gideon's troops to defeat the Midianites and refuse to give them bread. After smiting the Midianites, Gideon comes back to severely punish these two towns. In this second confrontation, Gideon is again shown as an authoritative and decisive leader. **5:** *Succoth* is located east of the Jordan, in Gad's territory. It is first mentioned in the tradition of Jacob (Gen. 33.17), and is usually identified with Tel Deir ʿAlla. *Kings of Midian:* Earlier Oreb and Zeeb were described as generals. Both titles refer to heads of tribes. **6:** The response of the Succoth officials indicates that they had not yet heard about Gideon's mighty deeds in the west. This situation also reflects the fragmented nature of Israel before the establishment of the monarchy. **8:** *Penuel* is located east of Succoth, close to it and to the Jabbok. It is mentioned in the tradition of Jacob (Gen. 32.23–31) and served as the temporary capital of Jeroboam I

Succoth. 9 So he also threatened the people of Penuel: "When
I come back safe, I'll tear down this tower!"
10 Now Zebah and Zalmunna were at Karkor with their army
of about 15,000; these were all that remained of the entire host
of the Kedemites, for the slain numbered 120,000 fighting
men.[a] 11 Gideon marched up the road of the tent dwellers, up to
east of Nobah and Jogbehah, and routed the camp, which was
off guard. 12 Zebah and Zalmunna took to flight, with Gideon[b]
in pursuit. He captured Zebah and Zalmunna, the two kings of
Midian, and threw the whole army into panic.
13 On his way back from the battle at the Ascent of Heres,
Gideon son of Joash 14 captured a boy from among the people
of Succoth and interrogated him. The latter drew up for him
a list of the officials and elders of Succoth, seventy-seven in
number. 15 Then he came to the people of Succoth and said,
"Here are Zebah and Zalmunna, about whom you mocked me,
saying, [c-]'Are Zebah and Zalmunna already in your hands,[-c] that
we should give your famished men bread?' " 16 And he took the
elders of the city and, [bringing] desert thorns and briers, he
punished[d] the people of Succoth with them. 17 As for Penuel,
he tore down its tower and killed the townspeople.
18 Then he asked Zebah and Zalmunna, "Those men you killed
at Tabor, [e-]what were they like?"[-e] "They looked just like you,"
they replied, "like sons of a king." 19 "They were my brothers," he
declared, "the sons of my mother. As the LORD lives, if you had
spared them, I would not kill you." 20 And he commanded his
oldest son Jether, "Go kill them!" But the boy did not draw his
sword, for he was timid, being still a boy. 21 Then Zebah and Zalmunna said, "Come, you slay us; for strength comes with manhood." So Gideon went over and killed Zebah and Zalmunna,
and he took the crescents that were on the necks of their camels.
22 Then the men of Israel said to Gideon, "Rule over us—
you, your son, and your grandson as well; for you have saved
us from the Midianites." 23 But Gideon replied, "I will not rule
over you myself, nor shall my son rule over you; the LORD
alone shall rule over you." 24 And Gideon said to them, "I have

a Lit. "men who drew the sword." *b Heb. "him."*
c-c Lit. "Is the palm of Zebah and Zalmunna in your hand."
d Meaning of Heb. uncertain; emendation yields "threshed"; cf. v. 7.
e-e Others "Where are they?"

(1 Kings 12.25). Its identification has not been fixed definitively. **9:** *Tower,* a fortified building that served for defense and observation. **10:** *Karkor,* a desert oasis on the caravan route of pilgrims to Mecca, about 161 km (100 miles) southeast of Amman. The numbers are exaggerated, as is the notion that Gideon had a battle so far away. **11:** A nomadic route east of Amman. *Off guard:* The Midianites did not suspect that Gideon and his army would get so far. **17:** Gideon did not threaten to kill the people of the city, but to destroy the tower. Therefore Radak concludes: "Perhaps they were warring with him when he came to destroy the tower." **18:** *Tabor:* Mount Tabor is in the northeastern corner of Jezreel Valley. *Zebah and Zalmunna* relate to Gideon as to a king; their behavior is the opposite of that of Succoth and Penuel. **20:** The description of Jether as fearful is reminiscent of Gideon's behavior in the first section, and highlights the changed attitude of Gideon in the second section. **21:** The kings of Midian preferred that Gideon, and not the youth, should kill them, both as a matter of honor and because they wanted to die quickly at the hand of an experienced warrior.

8.22–23: The offer of kingship to Gideon. Gideon's refusal to rule as king is interpreted in different ways. Some see it as an early text reflecting the ideology that God alone may be king; others claim that it is a later interpolation critical of the monarchy; still others suggest that it has nothing to do with this political issue, and Gideon is simply offering a polite refusal, although the text depicts him later as a king with many wives and a son who inherited a ruling position (vv. 29–31). In the larger context of the Deuteronomistic History, Gideon's refusal may reflect the awareness that Israelite society was not yet ripe for a monarch. If the army of a few tribes should offer kingship to someone, there would likely be civil war, as may be seen from the case of Abimelech in the following ch. **22:** *The men of Israel,* the army of some tribes, which in this case is composed of five: Manasseh, Asher, Zebulun, Naphtali, and Ephraim (6.35; 7.24). *You, your son,* a rule that passes from father to son, that is, a royal dynasty. *You have saved us:* The army sees Gideon and not the LORD as their deliverer. **23:** Gideon emphasizes that the LORD raises up the redeemer and therefore He is the ruler. Throughout these vv., the verb used is "to rule" (Heb "m-sh-l"), not "to reign" (Heb "m-l-k").

8.24–28: The golden ephod. 24: The substitution of *Ishmaelites,* who were

a request to make of you: Each of you give me the earring he
received as booty." (They[a] had golden earrings, for they were
Ishmaelites.) 25 "Certainly!" they replied. And they spread out
a cloth, and everyone threw onto it the earring he had received
as booty. 26 The weight of the golden earrings that he had requested came to 1,700 shekels of gold; this was in addition to
the crescents and the pendants and the purple robes worn by
the kings of Midian and in addition to the collars on the necks
of their camels. 27 Gideon made an ephod of [b-]this gold[-b] and
set it up in his own town of Ophrah. There all Israel went astray
after it, and it became a snare to Gideon and his household.

28 Thus Midian submitted to the Israelites and did not raise
its head again; and the land was tranquil for forty years in
Gideon's time.

29 So Jerubbaal son of Joash retired to his own house. 30 Gideon had seventy sons of his own issue, for he had many wives.
31 A son was also born to him by his concubine in Shechem,
and he named him Abimelech. 32 Gideon son of Joash died at a
ripe old age, and was buried in the tomb of his father Joash at
Ophrah of the Abiezrites.

33 After Gideon died, the Israelites again went astray after the
Baalim, and they adopted Baal-berith as a god. 34 The Israelites
gave no thought to the LORD their God, who saved them from
all the enemies around them. 35 Nor did they show loyalty to
the house of Jerubbaal-Gideon in return for all the good that
he had done for Israel.

9 Abimelech son of Jerubbaal went to his mother's brothers
in Shechem and spoke to them and to the whole clan of
his mother's family. He said, 2 "Put this question to all the citizens of Shechem: Which is better for you, to be ruled by seventy men—by all the sons of Jerubbaal—or to be ruled by one

a I.e., the Midianites. The author explains that the Midianites wore earrings like the Ishmaelites, who were better known to his contemporaries. *b-b Heb. "it."*

descendants of Hagar, for Midianites, who were descendants of Keturah, also appears in the Joseph story (Gen. 37.25–36), and the author may thereby indicate a relationship between them. Alternatively, the term "Ishmaelites" may be a generic designation for nomadic traders rather than a mark of ethnic identity. **25:** Willingness to forgo the booty indicates Gideon's status and influence. **27:** *Ephod:* The ephod is mentioned in various contexts: a means of inquiring of God (1 Sam. 23.6–12), or a part of the priestly garment (Exod. 28.6–8; 1 Sam. 2.18). The reference here seems to be to a statue intended to commemorate the deliverance, which over the course of time became an object of pagan adulation. The making of the statue is reminiscent of the golden calf story (Exod. 32.2–4). *In his own town of Ophrah:* Ophrah is depicted as Gideon's capital city for those tribes who recognized his leadership. *There all ... a snare ...:* The description of Gideon as one who sinned and caused Israel to sin is inappropriate to the whole cycle and to the view that he did good for Israel (8.35; 9.16ff.). Thus, this phrase seems to be an addition by a late editor, who criticized the making of the ephod and wished to justify the murder of Gideon's sons. **28:** *Tranquil for forty years,* a formulaic conclusion, likely an earlier ending of the story (see 5.31b).

8.29–9.57: The rule of Abimelech. Abimelech was the son of Gideon by his concubine from Shechem, and thus of lower status than his brothers. Unlike his father, he was willing to pay any price to become king. He murdered his brothers, conducted a civil war, and was ultimately killed in battle. His brief and bloody reign marks the failure of the first attempt at monarchy. **8.30:** *Seventy,* a large typological number (cf. 2 Kings 10.1, 7). Having many wives and sons is a sign of a significant social position; see 10.4 n.; 12.9, 14. **31:** At that time marriage also had political significance; therefore Abimelech is closely tied to his mother's city of Shechem. *Abimelech,* a theophoric name: "My/The (divine) father is king." It is ironic that the person with a name highlighting divine kingship attempts to become the first king of Israel. **33:** *Baal-berith,* also called El-berith (9.46), had a temple in Shechem (9.3–4). He is not known from other sources. **35:** From here on Gideon is mentioned only by his name *Jerubbaal;* the switching between names is one indication that these stories should be understood as an edited cycle rather than a composition of a single author.

9.1–6: Abimelech's enthronement. Abimelech is depicted as a powerful figure, who became king through his own bloody deception and not by the will of God. He is negatively characterized through the contrast between his actions and those of Gideon. **1:** He first convinces his mother's brothers, then the family of his maternal grandfather, and only afterwards addresses the other city citizens. **2:** His suggestion that being *ruled by seventy men* is an actual

man? And remember, I am your own [a]flesh and blood."[-a] 3 His mother's brothers said all this in his behalf to all the citizens of Shechem, and they were won over to Abimelech; for they thought, "He is our kinsman." 4 They gave him seventy shekels from the temple of Baal-berith; and with this Abimelech hired some worthless and reckless fellows, and they followed him. 5 Then he went to his father's house in Ophrah and killed his brothers, the sons of Jerubbaal, seventy men on one stone. Only Jotham, the youngest son of Jerubbaal, survived, because he went into hiding.

6 All the citizens of Shechem and all Beth-millo convened, and they proclaimed Abimelech king at the terebinth of the pillar[b] at Shechem. 7 When Jotham was informed, he went and stood on top of Mount Gerizim and called out to them in a loud voice. "Citizens of Shechem!" he cried, "listen to me, that God may listen to you.

8 "Once the trees went to anoint a king over themselves. They said to the olive tree, 'Reign over us.' 9 But the olive tree replied, 'Have I, through whom God and men are honored, stopped yielding my rich oil, that I should go and wave above the trees?' 10 So the trees said to the fig tree, 'You come and reign over us.' 11 But the fig tree replied, 'Have I stopped yielding my sweetness, my delicious fruit, that I should go and wave above the trees?' 12 So the trees said to the vine, 'You come and reign over us.' 13 But the vine replied, 'Have I stopped yielding my new wine, which gladdens God and men, that I should go and wave above the trees?' 14 Then all the trees said to the thornbush, 'You come and reign over us.' 15 And the thornbush said to the trees, 'If you are acting honorably in anointing me king over you, come and take shelter in my shade; but if not, may fire issue from the thornbush and consume the cedars of Lebanon!'

16 "Now then, if you acted honorably and loyally in making Abimelech king, if you have done right by Jerubbaal and his house and have requited him according to his deserts—17 considering that my father fought for you and saved you from the

a-a *Lit. "bone and flesh."* *b* *Meaning of Heb. uncertain.*

possibility is absurd and rhetorical. **4:** *From the temple ... :* Ancient Near Eastern temples often have large treasuries (cf. 1 Kings 7.51). *Worthless ... :* Jephthah (11.3) and David (1 Sam. 22.2) also utilized such people at the beginning of their path. **5:** *One stone:* One stone was used for all seventy people, a particularly horrific image. *Jotham,* a theophoric name meaning "God acts with integrity." **6:** *Beth-millo* seems to refer to a quarter of the city that was built upon a filling of earth near Shechem (see v. 20). *The terebinth:* There may be a relationship between this tree and the oak mentioned in the stories of Jacob (Gen. 35.4) and Joshua (Josh. 24.23–27). Many of these stories concerning Shechem are connected to the fact that this city was significant in the Northern Kingdom (see esp. 1 Kings 12.1).

9.7–21: Jotham's parable. Jotham, who was saved from being slaughtered, stood at the top of Mount Gerizim and told the Shechemites a parable (vv. 7–15) and its interpretation (vv. 16–20). The connection between the parable and what it represents is not exact, but this is true of other biblical parables as well (see esp. Jonah 4.6–11). Abimelech, for example, unlike the trees in the parable, was not offered the monarchy, and he and his supporters, unlike the explanation, were not burned by the citizens of Shechem. It seems, therefore, that the parable was an independent anti-monarchic work, used here to criticize Abimelech and to inform the reader that when all the trees are interested in having a king, they must beware of the thornbush and look carefully for a suitable tree. The parable is based upon a pattern of three and four, where the fourth element is different and climactic: three refusals by the useful trees—olive, fig, and grapevine—opposed to the agreement of the fourth, the thornbush. This structure emphasizes that the refusal of the useful trees cleared the way for an aggressive figure, and that Abimelech is totally useless. **7:** It would have been impossible for the Shechemites to hear things uttered at the top of Mount Gerizim; this follows a literary model of uttering from a high place (cf. e.g., Num. 23.14; 1 Sam. 26.13–14). **9:** *God and men are honored:* The oil and the wine (v. 13) were used in the cult and in everyday life. *Wave above,* to supervise, to rule. **14:** *Thornbush,* a barren shrub whose fruit is inedible. **15:** *Shade,* an ironic description, because the thornbush hardly provides shade. *Cedars,* archetypal tall and strong trees. The thornbush warns those interested in his protection that, if they attempt to rebel, his fire will be so powerful that it will consume even the highest and strongest trees. **16:** *Now,* a transitional formula to a new subject, used here to introduce the parable's explanation. **16b–19b:** Many scholars consider this passage to be an addition, intended to strengthen the connection

Midianites at the risk of his life, 18 and now you have turned
on my father's household, killed his sons, seventy men on
one stone, and set up Abimelech, the son of his handmaid,
as king over the citizens of Shechem just because he is your
kinsman—19 if, I say, you have this day acted honorably and
loyally toward Jerubbaal and his house, have joy in Abimelech
and may he likewise have joy in you. 20 But if not, may fire issue
from Abimelech and consume the citizens of Shechem and
Beth-millo, and may fire issue from the citizens of Shechem
and Beth-millo and consume Abimelech!"
21 With that, Jotham fled. He ran to Beer and stayed there,
because of his brother Abimelech.
22 Abimelech held sway over Israel for three years. 23 Then
God sent a spirit of discord between Abimelech and the citizens of Shechem, and the citizens of Shechem broke faith with
Abimelech—24 to the end that the crime committed against the
seventy sons of Jerubbaal might be avenged, and their blood
recoil upon their brother Abimelech, who had slain them, and
upon the citizens of Shechem, who had abetted him in the slaying of his brothers. 25 The citizens of Shechem planted ambus-
cades against him on the hilltops; and they robbed whoever
passed by them on the road. Word of this reached Abimelech.
26 Then Gaal son of Ebed and his companions came passing through Shechem, and the citizens of Shechem gave him
their confidence. 27 They went out into the fields, gathered
and trod out the vintage of their vineyards, and made a festival. They entered the temple of their god, and as they ate and
drank they reviled Abimelech. 28 Gaal son of Ebed said, "Who
is Abimelech and who are [we] Shechemites, that we should
serve him? [a]This same son of Jerubbaal and his lieutenant Zebul once served the men of Hamor, the father of Shechem;[a] so
why should we serve him? 29 Oh, if only this people were under
my command, I would get rid of Abimelech! One[b] would challenge Abimelech, 'Fill up your ranks and come out here!'"
30 When Zebul, the governor of the city, heard the words of
Gaal son of Ebed, he was furious. 31 He sent messages to Abimelech at Tormah[c] to say, "Gaal son of Ebed and his companions
have come to Shechem and they are inciting[d] the city against

a-a Meaning of Heb. uncertain. *b Septuagint reads "I."*
c Called "Arumah" in v. 41. *d Meaning of Heb. uncertain.*

between the Abimelech and Gideon cycles. **18:** Jotham belittles Abimelech further by calling him *the son of his handmaid* (see 8.31). **21:** *Beer,* an unidentified locale.

9.22: The kingship of Abimelech. *Held sway,* Heb "sarar" may be interpreted as arbitrary rule (translated "lord it over" in Num. 16.13). The more typical verb "malak," "reigned," is not used. *Over Israel:* This does not refer to all Israel, but to Shechem and its environs, and perhaps to additional areas in the hill country of Ephraim that were interested in kingship. *Three years:* The number indicates a brief reign, and prepares for the description of Abimelech's downfall.

9.23–41: First stage: the first battle in Shechem. The editor explains that Abimelech's fall is a measure-for-measure divine punishment (see also vv. 56–57). **23:** The power of the evil spirit also affects King Saul (1 Sam. 16.14; 18.10). Here the God of justice intervened directly. **24:** The punishment will also fall upon the citizens of Shechem who supported Abimelech. **26:** It is difficult to determine whether the name of his father was *Ebed* (Heb for "slave") or whether *Gaal* was the son of a slave. Gaal was apparently the head of a brigade, similar to Jephthah (11.3) and David (1 Sam. 22.2). Gaal and his men did not intend to settle in Shechem; rather, they were mere mercenaries hired by the citizens of the city for purposes of the battle, just as Achish hired the services of David (1 Sam. 28.1–2). **27:** *They entered the temple* in order to thank their god for the grape harvest. **28:** *Who is ... and who are ... :* Gaal incites the citizens by means of his rhetorical questions: Who is Abimelech that he should rule over Shechem, and why should we Shechemites maintain loyalty to him? He represents himself as one of the Shechemites. *Son of Jerubbaal:* Gaal represents Abimelech as a foreigner, mentioning the name of his Israelite father but not of his Shechemite mother. *Lieutenant:* Further on Zebul, whose name means "exalted," appears as the ruler of the city (v. 30). *The men of Hamor:* The family of Hamor represents the old Canaanite element in the city (Gen. 34.2), who should not accept this upstart ruler. **29:** *This people,* the people of Shechem. Gaal proposes the Shechemites accept his rule and unite to free the city of the rule of Abimelech and his men. **30–31:** Abimelech is mentioned as being at *Tormah,* a corruption of Arumah (see v. 41). *Zebul,* who remained loyal to Abimelech,

you. [32] Therefore, set out at night with the forces you have with you and conceal yourself in the fields. [33] Early next morning, as the sun rises, advance on the city. He and his men will thereupon come out against you, and you will do to him whatever you find possible."

[34] Abimelech and all the men with him set out at night and disposed themselves against Shechem in four hiding places. [35] When Gaal son of Ebed came out and stood at the entrance to the city gate, Abimelech and the army with him emerged from concealment. [36] Gaal saw the army and said to Zebul, "That's an army marching down from the hilltops!" But Zebul said to him, "The shadows of the hills look to you like men." [37] Gaal spoke up again, "Look, an army is marching down from Tabbur-erez, and another column is coming from the direction of Elon-meonenim." [38] "Well," replied Zebul, "where is your boast, 'Who is Abimelech that we should serve him'? There is the army you sneered at; now go out and fight it!"

[39] So Gaal went out at the head of the citizens of Shechem and gave battle to Abimelech. [40] But he had to flee before him, and Abimelech pursued him, and many fell slain, all the way to the entrance of the gate. [41] Then Abimelech stayed in Arumah,[a] while Zebul expelled Gaal and his companions and kept them out of Shechem.

[42] The next day, when people went out into the fields, Abimelech was informed. [43] Taking the army, he divided it into three columns and lay in ambush in the fields; and when he saw the people coming out of the city, he pounced upon them and struck them down. [44] While Abimelech and the column[b] that followed him dashed ahead and took up a position at the entrance of the city gate, the other two columns rushed upon all that were in the open and struck them down. [45] Abimelech fought against the city all that day. He captured the city and massacred the people in it; he razed the town and sowed it with salt.

[46] When all the citizens of the Tower of Shechem[c] learned of this, they went into the tunnel[d] of the temple of El-berith.[e] [47] When Abimelech was informed that all the citizens of the Tower of Shechem had gathered [there], [48] Abimelech and all the troops he had with him went up on Mount Zalmon. Taking an ax[f] in his hand, Abimelech lopped off a tree limb and lifted it onto his shoulder. Then he said to the troops that accompanied him, "What you saw me do—quick, do the same!" [49] So each

a Cf. "Tormah" in v. 31. *b Heb. "columns."*
c Perhaps identical with Beth-millo of vv. 6 and 20.
d Cf. 1 Sam. 13.6; others "citadel." *e Called "Baal-berith" in v. 4.*
f Heb. plural.

secretly sent messengers, informing him that he needed to go to war against Shechem. **34:** *Four hiding places,* in order to surround the city. **36:** *The shadows ... :* It is difficult to determine whether visibility was poor, whether Zebul wanted to distract Gaal, or whether he was mocking and alluding to the fears of Gaal, who began to understand the severity of the situation. **37:** *From Tabbur-erez:* The expression is also found in Ezek. 38.12. The LXX and most commentators interpret it as "the navel of the earth." *Elon-meonenim:* A road named for a sacred terebinth that was adjacent to it, where necromancers (Heb "meʿonenim") were evidently active. **39:** Many men from Gaal's army fell in the area between the battle location and the city gate. **41:** After his victory Abimelech returned to dwell in *Arumah.*

9.42–45: Second stage: the second battle in Shechem. The harsh means taken by Abimelech against the Shechemites is directly connected to the depiction of Abimelech in the parable and its explanation: He is a fire that consumes all its environs. **45:** *Sowed it with salt,* a symbolic action to signify that the destruction is final and the city would be barren and could not be rebuilt. Assyrian kings behaved in a similar manner. Already in the days of Jeroboam I, however, Shechem is mentioned as a central place (1 Kings 12.1).

9.46–49: Third stage: the battle at the Tower of Shechem. Once again the narrative gives no reason for the war. Here the fire imagery is strengthened, because Abimelech himself made use of fire. On the other hand, he is described as a charismatic, though excessively cruel leader. It would appear that the Tower of Shechem (Heb "migdal shekhem") was not part of Shechem, which had already been destroyed, but was a nearby settlement whose name was Migdal-shechem. **46:** *Of this,* the destruction of Shechem. **48:** *Zalmon,* a mountain near Shechem, whose identification is uncertain. *Do the same:* These words are reminiscent of Gideon (7.17). **49:** The mention of non-combatant

of the troops also lopped off a bough; then they marched behind Abimelech and laid them against the tunnel, and set fire
to the tunnel over their heads. Thus all the people of the Tower
of Shechem also perished, about a thousand men and women.
50 Abimelech proceeded to Thebez; he encamped at Thebez and occupied it. 51 Within the town was a fortified tower;
and all the citizens of the town, men and women, took refuge
there. They shut themselves in, and went up on the roof of the
tower. 52 Abimelech pressed forward to the tower and attacked
it. He approached the door of the tower to set it on fire. 53 But a
woman dropped an upper millstone on Abimelech's head and
cracked his skull. 54 He immediately cried out to his attendant,
his arms-bearer, "Draw your dagger and finish me off, that
they may not say of me, 'A woman killed him!'" So his attendant stabbed him, and he died. 55 When the men of Israel saw
that Abimelech was dead, everyone went home.
56 Thus God repaid Abimelech for the evil he had done to his
father by slaying his seventy brothers; 57 and God likewise repaid the men of Shechem for all their wickedness. And so the
curse of Jotham son of Jerubbaal was fulfilled upon them.

10 After Abimelech, Tola son of Puah son of Dodo, a man of
Issachar, arose to deliver Israel. He lived at Shamir in the
hill country of Ephraim. 2 He led Israel for twenty-three years;
then he died and was buried at Shamir.
3 After him arose Jair the Gileadite, and he led Israel for twenty-
two years. (4 He had thirty sons, who rode on thirty burros and

women heightens his cruelty, and points ahead to the next episode.

9.50–54: Fourth stage: the battle of Thebez and Abimelech's death. In this fourth, climactic stage, Abimelech meets his ignominious death (see 2 Sam. 11.20–21). **50:** *Thebez:* Contemporary scholars think that this name is a corruption of Tirzah, located 11 km (7 miles) northeast of Shechem. **51:** *Went up:* They went up on the roof in order to fight by throwing rocks, arrows, and the like. **53:** The Sages (*Tanḥuma,* Buber ed., *Vayera* 51b [102]) emphasize the principle of measure for measure, connecting Abimelech's death from a stone to the stone upon which he slew his brothers. **54:** Abimelech's request to his armor-bearer is similar to that of Saul in the battle of Gilboa (1 Sam. 31.4), and emphasizes how even in his death he was concerned for his honor. Yet Abimelech is remembered as the one killed by a woman (2 Sam. 11.20–21).

9.55–57: Denoument: the dispersion of the army and the end of the cycle. 55: Upon Abimelech's death, the army that supported him was dispersed, thereby ending the first attempt to establish monarchical rule over Israel. The fall of his kingship showed that a charismatic king who is supported by the army is insufficient to assure quiet and stability. **56–57:** The story concludes by alluding to the various units that opened it: the murder and the parable.

10.1–5: Consecutive judges: The book includes two lists: 10.1–5 and 12.8–15. First list. The judges mentioned after Abimelech appear one after another, without intervening periods of sin and punishment; they may therefore be described as consecutive judges. (Other scholars call them "minor judges," because the accounts of their actions are "minor" or short [compare "Minor Prophets"].) Although Tola is mentioned as a deliverer (v. 1), the account referring to him and to the other judges in the lists does not describe any acts of deliverance, but merely lists the place where they lived, their burial place, the period they were judges, and sometime their descendants and property. Scholars debate whether they are to be seen as a distinct type of judge, or if they were similar to the other judges, but for whatever reasons, less information has been recorded about them. Their appearance one after the other helps create the impression that leadership continuity may prevent a return to a period of sin, and thus on the one hand, softens the negative impression created by the kingdom of Abimelech, and on the other, confirms the final conclusion of the book concerning the advantages of monarchy. A second list appears in 12.8–15. Some scholars believe that these two lists were originally joined, and that Jephthah was in the middle of this list, and the expanded Jephthah story now interrupts the list. However, the separation into two lists creates repetition and thus emphasizes the advantage of leadership continuity and balances the impression of Abimelech's kingship. **1:** *To deliver:* Although it is not told from whom or how he delivered Israel, the sequence creates the impression that he delivered them from the rule of Abimelech. *Tola:* This name is connected with the families of the tribe of Issachar (Gen. 46.13; Num. 26.23–25; 1 Chron. 7.1–5). *Shamir ... Ephraim:* Not identified, but the existence of families from Issachar in the central mountain suggests that they began taking possession there, before they went down to the Jezreel Valley. **3:** Sources outside the book of Judges (Num. 32.41; Deut. 3.14; 1 Chron. 2.22–23) relate this tradition to an earlier Jair, who conquered territory in Gilead. **4:** The large number of

owned thirty boroughs[a] in the region of Gilead; these are called
Havvoth-jair[b] to this day.) 5 Then Jair died and was buried at Kamon.

6 The Israelites again did what was offensive to the LORD.
They served the Baalim and the Ashtaroth, and the gods of
Aram, the gods of Sidon, the gods of Moab, the gods of the Ammonites, and the gods of the Philistines; they forsook the LORD
and did not serve Him. 7 And the LORD, incensed with Israel,
surrendered them to the Philistines and to the Ammonites.
8 That year they battered and shattered the Israelites—for[c]
eighteen years—all the Israelites beyond the Jordan, in [what
had been] the land of the Amorites in Gilead. 9 The Ammonites
also crossed the Jordan to make war on Judah, Benjamin, and
the House of Ephraim. Israel was in great distress.

10 Then the Israelites cried out to the LORD, "We stand guilty
before You, for we have forsaken our God and served the Baalim." 11 But the LORD said to the Israelites, "[I have rescued you]
from the Egyptians, from the Amorites, from the Ammonites,
and from the Philistines. 12 The Sidonians, Amalek, and Maon[d]
also oppressed you; and when you cried out to Me, I saved you
from them. 13 Yet you have forsaken Me and have served other
gods. No, I will not deliver you again. 14 Go cry to the gods you
have chosen; let them deliver you in your time of distress!"
15 But the Israelites implored the LORD: "We stand guilty. Do
to us as You see fit; only save us this day!" 16 They removed the
alien gods from among them and served the LORD; and He
could not bear the miseries of Israel.

17 The Ammonites mustered and they encamped in Gilead; and the Israelites massed and they encamped at Mizpah.

a *Imitating the pun in the Heb., which employs* ʿayarim *first in the sense of "donkeys" and then in the sense of "towns."*

b *I.e., "the villages of Jair"; cf. Num. 32.41.*

c *Meaning of Heb. uncertain; perhaps "enough for" or "continuing for."*

d *Septuagint reads "Midian."*

offspring and *burros* indicates his established position. **5:** *Kamon,* located in northern Gilead.

10.6–16: Introduction to the Jephthah cycle. Following Jair the Gileadite no other judge appears, and as a result the people return to sin. The stages of sin, punishment, and crying out that precede Jephthah are particularly detailed and represented as graver than those that preceded it and thus point to a process of escalation in the sins and the punishment. **6:** The text enumerates seven types of idolatry, and notes in a doubled fashion *they forsook … and did not serve Him,* emphasizing that Israel had completely abandoned the LORD. **7:** The subjugation is also presented as more severe. This time the LORD gave His people to the Philistines in the west and the Ammonites in the east. The reference to the Philistines may also foreshadow the stories of Samson. The sequel of this description focuses on the Ammonites. **8:** *The land of the Amorites:* It follows from the sequel (11.22) that this refers to southern Gilead, the territory lying between the Rivers Arnon and Jabbok. **10–16:** This time God rebuked His people directly and not by a prophet (2.1–5; 6.7–10), and they acknowledged their sin and removed the foreign gods. **10:** *We stand guilty before You:* This v. and v. 15 are the only explicit references to repentance in the entire book, and may be a later addition; elsewhere, the Israelites simply "cry out." **12:** *Maon:* The Maonites were a nomadic tribe in the southwest of Judah (1 Chron. 4.41; 2 Chron. 26.7); therefore their mention here is surprising. Some mss of the LXX read Midian as do most scholars. **16:** It is possible that some ritual action stands behind the activity depicted here and in Gen. 35.1; Josh. 24.23 and 1 Sam. 7.3. All these show that the cyclical system can bring back the people to the LORD, but cannot stop them from returning to sin.

10.17–11.11: Jephthah's appointment. Jephthah, whose brothers expelled him and prevented him from inheriting their father's property, established himself as the head of a band of ruffians in the eastern border area. It seems that his expulsion was with the approval of the elders of Gilead. Thanks to his military experience, and the absence of any other candidate, the elders were forced to ask him to lead the army. But he made his appointment conditional: If he won the war, he would be leader of all the inhabitants of Gilead. The elders agreed and appointed Jephthah before the LORD in Mizpah, not only as commander, but also as chieftain. This story depicts Jephthah similarly to Abimelech, hinting at his problematic rule. The story of Jephthah's appointment and his victory over the Ammonites (11.1–12.7, omitting the story of Jephthah's daughter) is read as the haftarah for the parashah of Ḥukkat (Num. chs 19–21), which describes Israel's war against Sihon king of the Amorites, a subject that arises in the negotiation between Jephthah and the king of the Ammonites. **10.17:** *Mizpah:* which is located in east Jordan and its name means "outlook" has not been identified but appears here as a cultic center and the town of Jephthah (11.11, 34).

18 The troops—the officers of Gilead—said to one another, "Let
the man who is the first to fight the Ammonites be chieftain
over all the inhabitants of Gilead."

11 Jephthah the Gileadite was an able warrior, who was the
son of a prostitute. Jephthah's father was Gilead; 2 but
Gilead also had sons by his wife, and when the wife's sons
grew up, they drove Jephthah out. They said to him, "You shall
have no share in our father's property, for you are the son of an
outsider."[a] 3 So Jephthah fled from his brothers and settled in
the Tob country. Men of low character gathered about Jephthah and went out raiding with him.

4 Some time later, the Ammonites went to war against Israel. 5 And when the Ammonites attacked Israel, the elders
of Gilead went to bring Jephthah back from the Tob country. 6 They said to Jephthah, "Come be our chief, so that we
can fight the Ammonites." 7 Jephthah replied to the elders of
Gilead, "You are the very people who rejected me and drove
me out of my father's house. How can you come to me now
when you are in trouble?" 8 The elders of Gilead said to Jephthah, "Honestly, we have now turned back to you. If you come
with us and fight the Ammonites, you shall be our commander over all the inhabitants of Gilead." 9 Jephthah said to the
elders of Gilead, "[Very well,] if you bring me back to fight
the Ammonites and the LORD delivers them to me, I am to
be your commander." 10 And the elders of Gilead answered
Jepthah, "The LORD Himself shall be witness between us: we
will do just as you have said."

11 Jephthah went with the elders of Gilead, and the people
made him their commander and chief. And Jephthah repeated
all these terms before the LORD at Mizpah.

12 Jephthah then sent messengers to the king of the Ammonites, saying, "What have you against me that you have come to

a *Lit. "another woman."*

18: *The first ... :* The phrasing emphasizes their despair. The leadership is promised to whoever will dare to fight, and not necessarily to the one who achieves victory. *Chieftain:* not "shofet," but "ro'sh," lit. "head," a leader whose authority is not only military, but also judicial and administrative. The people are prepared to convey this authority to the one who dares to fight the Ammonites even during the period following the war. **11.1:** Being the son of a prostitute may have lowered his status but did not make him illegitimate. According to the Sumerian law of Lipit-Ishtar, when a man has no sons by his wife but does have sons by a harlot, those sons are allowed to inherit his estate. Perhaps a similar law applied in Israel. His status, however, places him one rung below Abimelech, the son of a concubine (8.31). **2:** Gilead's wife apparently bore him sons after Jephthah's birth. *Outsider,* in this context, a euphemism for a prostitute. **3:** *Tob country,* located in the northeast of Gilead; presumably a border district to which law-breakers and banished people came. *Men of low character,* see 9.4. **4:** This v. belongs before 10.17. **5:** *The elders of Gilead:* They are so desperate, they come themselves rather than sending messengers. **6:** *Chief,* in this context, a man of war ("katzin"), whose authority is less than that of the "head" ("ro'sh"); neither approaches the king ("melech") in power or importance. Jephthah understands this adverse proposal, and therefore begins negotiations. **7–9:** From Jephthah's viewpoint the elders are responsible for his expulsion because they did not stop his brothers. The elders do not deny it and thus offer him all the authority he asks for. Jephthah magnanimously states that he will accept the position only if he is victorious. **10:** Invoking God as a witness was usual in Israel (Gen. 31.50; etc.) and divine witnesses are well known from treaties in the ancient Near East. **11:** *Before the LORD,* in a place sanctified to the LORD, such as a temple or an altar.

11.12–28: The negotiation with the king of the Ammonites. Jephthah attempted to prevent war by negotiation, where he questions the Ammonites' motivation for war. Against the argument of the Ammonite king that the territory "from the Arnon to the Jabbok as far as the Jordan" belongs to the Ammonites (v. 13), Jephthah justifies the Israelite conquest by the following arguments: (1) the area under dispute never belonged to Ammon, but to Sihon king of the Amorites (vv. 14–19); (2) Israel was forced to wage war against Sihon because he did not allow them to pass through his land (v. 20); (3) the conquest of Sihon's land was the LORD's will (vv. 21–24); (4) for the past 300 years the Ammonites have not questioned Israelite settlement in these areas (vv. 25–26). Once the king of the Ammonites rejected these arguments, war was inevitable. For a variety of reasons, including the fact that Chemosh (v. 24) is the national god of Moab,

make war on my country?" 13 The king of the Ammonites replied to Jephthah's messengers, "When Israel came from Egypt,
they seized the land which is mine, from the Arnon to the Jabbok as far as the Jordan. Now, then, restore it peaceably."
14 Jephthah again sent messengers to the king of the Ammonites. 15 He said to him, "Thus said Jephthah: Israel did not
seize the land of Moab or the land of the Ammonites. 16 When
they left Egypt, Israel traveled through the wilderness to the
Sea of Reeds and went on to Kadesh. 17 Israel then sent messengers to the king of Edom, saying, 'Allow us to cross your
country.' But the king of Edom would not consent. They also
sent a mission to the king of Moab, and he refused. So Israel,
after staying at Kadesh, 18 traveled on through the wilderness,
skirting the land of Edom and the land of Moab. They kept to
the east of the land of Moab until they encamped on the other
side of the Arnon; and, since Moab ends at the Arnon, they
never entered Moabite territory.
19 "Then Israel sent messengers to Sihon king of the Amorites, the king of Heshbon. Israel said to him, 'Allow us to cross
through your country to our homeland.' 20 But Sihon would not
trust Israel to pass through his territory. Sihon mustered all his
troops, and they encamped at Jahaz; he engaged Israel in battle. 21 But the LORD, the God of Israel, delivered Sihon and all
his troops into Israel's hands, and they defeated them; and Israel took possession of all the land of the Amorites, the inhabitants of that land. 22 Thus they possessed all the territory of the
Amorites from the Arnon to the Jabbok and from the wilderness to the Jordan.
23 "Now, then, the LORD, the God of Israel, dispossessed the
Amorites before His people Israel; and should you possess
their land? 24 Do you not hold what Chemosh your god gives
you to possess? So we will hold on to everything that the LORD
our God has given us to possess.
25 "Besides, are you any better than Balak son of Zippor, king
of Moab? Did he start a quarrel with Israel or go to war with
them?
26 "While Israel has been inhabiting Heshbon and its dependencies, and Aroer and its dependencies, and all the
towns along the Arnon for three hundred years, why have you
not tried to recover them all this time? 27 I have done you no
wrong; yet you are doing me harm and making war on me. May
the LORD, who judges, decide today between the Israelites and
the Ammonites!"
28 But the king of the Ammonites paid no heed to the message that Jephthah sent him.

not of Ammon, and that the story mentions the Moabite King Balak (v. 25), many scholars believe that much of this ch was a separate document concerning the relations between Israel and Moab; once this became integrated here, Moab was changed to Ammon—at the beginning and at the end (vv. 12–14, 27–28), although other details of the story were left as they were. The subject is discussed in the Torah in Num. 20.14–21; 21.21–35 and Deut. chs 2–3. **13:** *Arnon ... Jabbok ... Jordan:* The brook Arnon, which spills into the Dead Sea, marks the southern border of Gilead and the land of Sihon, and the northern boundary of Moab. The Jabbok spills into the Jordan north of the city Adam and divides Gilead into two parts. The western border is the Jordan and the eastern is the desert. Reuben and Gad settled in the land of Sihon. **16:** The narrator describes events from the beginning of the period of wandering briefly, focusing upon those that preceded the conquest of the disputed region. *Kadesh,* Kadesh-barnea, a desert oasis in northern Sinai. **17:** See Num. 20.14–21; this episode is lacking in Deut. ch 2. **19:** *Heshbon,* located about 10 km (6 miles) north of Medeba, and described as a royal city from which Sihon ruled his country. **20:** *Jahaz,* identification uncertain; it is also mentioned in the Moabite Mesha inscription (lines 18–20). **24:** *Chemosh,* the national god of Moab, mentioned in the Mesha inscription (e.g., lines 5–6). As noted, the reference to Chemosh, rather than Milcom, the high god of Ammon, indicates the source of this document. This v. reflects ancient Near Eastern theology, where each national god gives its people the land they merit. **25:** On *Balak,* who wished to curse Israel and ended up blessing them, see Num. 22.2–24.25. **26:** *Aroer:* Located on the northern shore of the Arnon, it marks the southern border of Sihon's kingdom. It is mentioned in the Moabite Mesha inscription as a city he built (line 26). *Three hundred:* A round and inexact number that has no relation to the length of the period of the judges. The author thought that 300 years had passed from the conquest until Jephthah.

29 Then the spirit of the LORD came upon Jephthah. He
marched through Gilead and Manasseh, passing Mizpeh of
Gilead; and from Mizpeh of Gilead he crossed over [to] the
Ammonites. 30 And Jephthah made the following vow to the
LORD: "If You deliver the Ammonites into my hands, 31 then
whatever comes out of the door of my house to meet me on my
safe return from the Ammonites shall be the LORD's and shall
be offered by me as a burnt offering."
32 Jephthah crossed over to the Ammonites and attacked
them, and the LORD delivered them into his hands. 33 He utterly routed them—from Aroer as far as Minnith, twenty towns—
all the way to Abel-cheramim. So the Ammonites submitted to
the Israelites.

34 When Jephthah arrived at his home in Mizpah, there was
his daughter coming out to meet him, with timbrel and dance!
She was an only child; he had no other son or daughter. 35 On
seeing her, he rent his clothes and said, "Alas, daughter! You
have brought me low; you have become my troubler! For I have
[a]uttered a vow[a] to the LORD and I cannot retract." 36 "Father,"
she said, "you have uttered a vow to the LORD; do to me as you
have vowed, seeing that the LORD has vindicated you against
your enemies, the Ammonites." 37 She further said to her father,
"Let this be done for me: let me be for two months, and I will
go with my companions and lament[b] upon the hills and there
bewail my maidenhood." 38 "Go," he replied. He let her go for
two months, and she and her companions went and bewailed
her maidenhood upon the hills. 39 After two months' time, she
returned to her father, and he did to her as he had vowed. She
had never known a man. So it became a custom in Israel 40 for
the maidens of Israel to go every year, for four days in the year,
and chant dirges for the daughter of Jephthah the Gileadite.

12 The men of Ephraim mustered and crossed [the Jordan]
to Zaphon. They said to Jephthah, "Why did you march
to fight the Ammonites without calling us to go with you?

a-a *Lit. "opened my mouth."* b *Lit. "descend," i.e., with weeping; cf. Isa. 15.3.*

11.29–40: The war and the oath. Before going out to battle Jephthah makes a vow, stating that if the LORD will give him victory, he will make Him an offering of the first thing that comes out of his house. The vow's purpose was to secure divine favor by promising something valuable to God. After defeating the Ammonites he returns home, where he is met by his only daughter, who had come out to greet him, and he is forced to carry out his vow. In practice, the brief account of the war is incorporated within the account of the vow, depicted in detail and in a way that emphasizes the tragedy of this fateful, irreversible error. Biblical literature struggles with the norm of offering human sacrifices, which was apparently practiced during the First Temple period (2 Kings 16.3; 17.31; 21.6; 23.10; Jer. 7.31; etc.). Hence, this incident shows Jephthah in a negative light. Jephthah is, genealogically speaking, a marginal person both in his ancestry and in his progeny. **29:** Jephthah advanced in a northeasterly direction. The places mentioned here and in v. 33 have not been identified. **31:** The formulation of the oath, referring to one coming out of the door of his house, suggests a human rather than animal sacrifice. **34:** The v. describes women celebrating a military victory, and the safe return home of the men (see Exod. 15.21; 1 Sam. 18.7). *Mizpah:* This is not Mizpeh of Gilead mentioned in v. 29, but is apparently Mizpah which is mentioned in 11.11. **35:** You have brought me low: in effect, Jephthah is saying "I am emotionally devastated." *I cannot retract:* Jephthah and his daughter understand the oath as an obligation that cannot be nullified, since vows were taken very seriously in the biblical period (see Deut. 23.22–23; Prov. 20.25; Eccl. 5.3–4). **36:** It is noteworthy that Jephthah's daughter does not attempt to flee. **37:** *My maidenhood:* I will weep because I will die as a childless virgin. **39:** The text shies away from explicitly depicting her sacrifice, which leads some ancient and modern interpreters (e.g., Radak) to suggest that she was not actually killed. **40:** The story has an etiological conclusion, and perhaps originated as an independent etiology of a custom, unattested elsewhere in the Bible, that had presumably existed since hoary antiquity: to sing dirges four days a year in memory of Jephthah's daughter. In its present location, it signals the end of Jephthah's family line.

12.1–7: Jephthah's battle with Ephraim and the conclusion. This story likewise shows Jephthah in a negative light. The men of Ephraim had threatened to burn Jephthah's house because he had not called them to participate in the war against the Ammonites. Jephthah replies that he had attempted to call them in the past, but they refused. He went to war against

We'll burn your house down over you!" [2] Jephthah answered them, "I and my people were in a bitter conflict with the Ammonites; and I summoned you, but you did not save me from them. [3] When I saw that you were no saviors, I risked my life and advanced against the Ammonites; and the LORD delivered them into my hands. Why have you come here now to fight against me?" [4] And Jephthah gathered all the men of Gilead and fought the Ephraimites. The men of Gilead defeated the Ephraimites; for [a-]they had said, "You Gileadites are nothing but fugitives from Ephraim—being in Manasseh is like being in Ephraim."[-a] [5] The Gileadites held the fords of the Jordan against the Ephraimites. And when any fugitive from Ephraim said, "Let me cross," the men of Gilead would ask him, "Are you an Ephraimite?"; if he said "No," [6] they would say to him, "Then say *shibboleth*"; but he would say *"sibboleth,"* not being able to pronounce it correctly. Thereupon they would seize him and slay him by the fords of the Jordan. Forty-two thousand Ephraimites fell at that time.

[7] Jephthah led Israel six years. Then Jephthah the Gileadite died and he was buried in one of the towns of Gilead.

[8] After him, Ibzan of Bethlehem[b] led Israel. [9] He had thirty sons, and he married off thirty daughters outside the clan and brought in thirty girls from outside the clan for his sons. He led Israel seven years. [10] Then Ibzan died and was buried in Bethlehem.

[11] After him, Elon the Zebulunite led Israel; he led Israel for ten years. [12] Then Elon the Zebulunite died and was buried in Aijalon, in the territory of Zebulun.

[13] After him, Abdon son of Hillel the Pirathonite led Israel. [14] He had forty sons and thirty grandsons, who rode on seventy jackasses. He led Israel for eight years. [15] Then Abdon son of Hillel the Pirathonite died. He was buried in Pirathon, in the territory of Ephraim, on the hill of the Amalekites.

a-a Meaning of Heb. uncertain. *b I.e., Bethlehem in Zebulun; cf. Josh. 19.15.*

Ephraim, and this concluded with the death of 42,000 Ephraimites. This conflict mirrors Gideon's conflict with Ephraim (8.1–3) and presents Ephraim negatively in a struggle for inter-tribal hegemony, but unlike ch 8, many Ephraimites are killed here as a result of their behavior—the stakes have escalated. Within the broader book, this fits the pro-Judean, anti-northern ideology of the editor. (Ephraim is used elsewhere in the Bible to refer to the Northern Kingdom.) While Gideon succeeded in preventing a civil war, Jephthah conducted a bloody conflict. The blocking of the Jordan crossings was a tactic used by Ehud (3.28), but while Ehud made war against the Moabites, Jephthah did so against his own people. These comparisons stress that Jephthah is not fit to lead. **1:** *Zaphon:* This may refer to the settlement Zaphon, located in the territory of Gad near the city of Succoth (Josh. 13.27). **4:** The men of Gilead were insulted by the Ephraimites. According to one interpretation, even the lowest of Ephraim, naming the fugitives, despised the people of Gilead, telling them that they had no importance in Ephraim and Manasseh. Others suggest that the phrase "fugitives of Ephraim" relates to the inhabitants of Gilead as refugees who left the region of Ephraim and Manasseh. **5:** The Gileadites seized the Jordan fords even before the men of Ephraim arrived. **6:** The difference in pronunciation, *"sibboleth"* instead of *"shibboleth"* (s/sh) reflected dialectical variation in the different areas of settlement; dialectical differences are rarely present in the Bible, written mostly in Judean Heb. It is uncertain whether the word "shibboleth" refers to the current of the river (Ps. 69.3) or to sheaves of grain (Gen. 41.5–7). This episode is the origin of the English word "shibboleth." **7:** While Jephthah the commander did indeed save his people from the Ammonites, he did not prove himself as a leader, and his term only lasted six years. The final burial notice is odd: it would be expected that he would be buried in his city, Mizpah. The LXX version is preferable: "and was buried in his city in Gilead" (cf. Josephus, *Ant.* 5.7.12).

12.8–15: Consecutive judges: Second list. Three consecutive judges appear after Jephthah, suggesting an additional period without sin, punishment, or deliverance. On these judges, see 10.1–5 n. **8:** Except Othniel, who was from Judah, all the judges throughout the book are from northern Israel. Hence, the *Bethlehem* mentioned here is a city in the territory of Zebulun (Josh. 19.15). **9:** Such extensive connections through marriage were one of the means of creating foreign alliances. **13:** Pirathon is elsewhere the city of Benaiah of Ephraim, one of David's warriors (2 Sam. 23.30; 1 Chron. 27.14). **15:** *The hill of the Amalekites* implies that there was an ancient settlement of Amalekites, and may be an implicit criticism of Ephraim for not eradicating them (see Deut. 25.19; 1 Sam. 15.3).

13 The Israelites again did what was offensive to the LORD,
and the LORD delivered them into the hands of the Philistines for forty years.
2 There was a certain man from Zorah, of the stock of Dan,
whose name was Manoah. His wife was barren and had borne
no children. 3 An angel of the LORD appeared to the woman
and said to her, "You are barren and have borne no children;
but you shall conceive and bear a son. 4 Now be careful not to
drink wine or other intoxicant, or to eat anything unclean. 5 For
you are going to conceive and bear a son; let no razor touch his
head, for the boy is to be a nazirite to God from the womb on.
He shall be the first to deliver Israel from the Philistines."
6 The woman went and told her husband, "A man of God
came to me; he looked like an angel of God, very frightening.
I did not ask him where he was from, nor did he tell me his
name. 7 He said to me, 'You are going to conceive and bear a
son. Drink no wine or other intoxicant, and eat nothing unclean, for the boy is to be a nazirite to God from the womb to
the day of his death!'"
8 Manoah pleaded with the LORD. "Oh, my Lord!" he said,
"please let the man of God that You sent come to us again, and
let him instruct us how to act with the child that is to be born."
9 God heeded Manoah's plea, and the angel of God came to
the woman again. She was sitting in the field and her husband
Manoah was not with her. 10 The woman ran in haste to tell
her husband. She said to him, "The man who came to me before[a] has just appeared to me." 11 Manoah promptly followed

a *Lit. "in the day."*

Chs 13–16: The Samson cycle. Samson was different from the other judges. His actions are of a miraculous nature, he fights as an individual rather than as a commander, and his heroic acts are the result of personal involvement with Philistine women. The stories about him are filled with remnants of myth, legends, and folk traditions. He is not, however, portrayed as a giant or other superhuman being, but he does have a direct connection with God, both through his being a Nazirite and through his prayers. Concluding the stories of the judges with a hero who does not deliver his people but only himself, and who dies in enemy captivity, contributes to the feeling of disappointment with the type of leadership that the judges represent. This bolsters the book's ultimate conclusion, that permanent kingship over all of Israel must be established. This cycle, like the others in the book, comprises originally distinct stories; for example, his status as a Nazirite is only operative in the first and last stories. In their final form here, they have been structured to focus on three subjects: his birth (ch 13), women in his life (chs 14–15), and his death (ch 16).

13.1–25: Samson's birth. The story resembles other annunciation stories where God or His messengers appear (Gen. 18.1–15; Judg. 6.11–24; 1 Sam. ch 1; 2 Kings 4.8–37). This story serves as the haftarah for the Torah portion of Naso' (Num. 4.21–7.89), which includes the Nazirite laws (6.1–21), since Samson is designated as a Nazirite from before his birth. **1:** Subjugation of 40 years is the longest in the book. The absence of the stage of crying out strengthens the impression of distance from the LORD. **2:** *Zorah,* located in the territory of Dan, near the modern kibbutz of that name. Nearby is an altar carved into rock, commonly known as "the altar of Manoah." *Stock:* The Heb word used here is "family," referring to the entire tribe, as this small tribe consisted of only one family (Num. 26.42). *His wife was barren and had borne no children* raises the expectation of divine intervention, like the special birth stories of the matriarchs in Genesis. **5:** Samson's Nazirite-hood is exceptional, referred to by the Sages as "the Nazirite-hood of Samson"—namely, even when his hair grew heavy he did not thin it (*m. Naz.* 1.2). Here the prohibition of drinking wine applies only to his mother. The word for *razor* differs from the one used in Num. 6.5, suggesting that that text is not this story's source; in addition, in Numbers the nazirite vow is only for a prescribed time-period. *The first,* the Heb and KJV: "he shall begin," meaning that he will not deliver them fully, but only in a partial manner (Rashi ad loc). **6:** From the woman's report to her husband, she seems to suspect that the man of God (her term) was an angel (the narrator's term), and therefore she was frightened and did not ask him usual questions, such as his name or where he was from; Manoah, her husband, does not catch on. **7:** *To the day of his death:* The woman does not repeat the angel's words exactly. She focuses upon the prohibitions that relate to her, and interprets the partial deliverance as predicting the premature death of the child. The gaps she creates lead Manoah to ask for another appearance of the visitor. According to some scholars the language in this v. and elsewhere allows for the possibility that the angel impregnated the woman (see Gen. 6.1–4). **8:** *Us:* Manoah wants to be a full partner in the additional visit; he seems to mistrust his wife's report. **9:** Due to the woman's preferred status in birth stories (cf. 2 Kings 4.8–17), the angel, notwithstanding Manoah's request, reappears to the woman, not to Manoah. **11:** That Manoah *promptly followed his wife* is unusual and underlines the

his wife. He came to the man and asked him: "Are you the man who spoke to my wife?" "Yes," he answered. 12 Then Manoah said, "May your words soon come true! What rules shall be observed for the boy?" 13 The angel of the LORD said to Manoah, "The woman must abstain from all the things against which I warned her. 14 She must not eat anything that comes from the grapevine, or drink wine or other intoxicant, or eat anything unclean. She must observe all that I commanded her."

15 Manoah said to the angel of the LORD, "Let us detain you and prepare a kid for you." 16 But the angel of the LORD said to Manoah, "If you detain me, I shall not eat your food; and if you present a burnt offering, offer it to LORD."—For Manoah did not know that he was an angel of the LORD. 17 So Manoah said to the angel of the LORD, "What is your name? We should like to honor you when your words come true." 18 The angel said to him, "You must not ask for my name; it is unknowable!"

19 Manoah took the kid and the meal offering and offered them up on the rock to the LORD; [a]and a marvelous thing happened[a] while Manoah and his wife looked on. 20 As the flames leaped up from the altar toward the sky, the angel of the LORD ascended in the flames of the altar, while Manoah and his wife looked on; and they flung themselves on their faces to the ground.—21 The angel of the LORD never appeared again to Manoah and his wife.—Manoah then realized that it had been an angel of the LORD. 22 And Manoah said to his wife, "We shall surely die, for we have seen a divine being." 23 But his wife said to him, "Had the LORD meant to take our lives, He would not have accepted a burnt offering and meal offering from us, nor let us see all these things; and He would not have made such an announcement to us."

24 The woman bore a son, and she named him Samson. The boy grew up, and the LORD blessed him. 25 The spirit of the LORD first moved him in the encampment of Dan, between Zorah and Eshtaol.

14 Once Samson went down to Timnah; and while in Timnah, he noticed a girl among the Philistine women. 2 On his return, he told his father and mother, "I noticed one of the

a-a Meaning of Heb. uncertain.

role reversal of man and woman in this ch. Manoah then presumably saw the angel but this is not made explicit. **12:** *Your words,* i.e., of prophecy. *For the boy:* Manoah asks how to behave regarding the child who is to be born. **13–14:** The angel's answer ignores Manoah's question and only relates to the woman. **15:** Manoah invites the angel to a meal—behavior reminiscent of Gideon's in 6.18. Perhaps the function of the meal is to determine whether he is in fact an angel; alternatively, the text suggests that Manoah has no clue that this man is actually an angel. **16:** The angel, as angels do, refuses to eat and suggests that the goat be offered to the LORD. The second half of this v. *(For Manoah ...)* may belong at the end of v. 15. **17:** Manoah continues to examine the angel and asks for his name. He justifies this question by stating that he wishes to honor the messenger once his tidings are realized. Since angels do not have names, at least until the late biblical period (see Gen. 32.30), this may be Manoah's way of testing whether the man is an angel, or it may be the narrator's way of showing that Manoah is not very clever, and in contrast to his wife, still does not realize that an angel is before him. **18:** The angel refuses to disclose his name. The Heb is phrased as a question: "Why do you ask my name?" **19–20:** Miraculously, the angel disappears when the sacrifice is offered, while Manoah and his wife watch. **20:** *Altar,* the rock. **21:** Only after the angel disappears does Manoah realize what his wife already felt at the first encounter, that God's messenger had visited them. **22:** The idea that seeing the LORD brings death (cf. 6.22 and elsewhere) causes Manoah to express his fear. **23:** Manoah's wife is logical. She calms him by stating that if God had wished to kill them He would not have sent His angel twice. The narrator's depiction of Manoah in this ch supports the Rabbis' observation that "Manoah was a boorish, ignorant person" (*b. Ber.* 61a). **24a:** The woman names the infant. Many commentators connect the name with the sun (Heb "Shimshon" [Samson]/"shemesh" [sun]), seeing in this a mythological allusion. **24b–25:** These vv. summarize Samson's unique growth and development under divine blessing and protection. *Eshtaol,* near Zorah.

14.1–15.20: Samson's marriage to the Timnite and its consequences. Samson's marriage to a Philistine woman is part of a deliberate divine strategy that might be described as a policy of "pretext"(14.4), by which Samson's connection with Philistine women was intended to provide him justification for harming the Philistines by a series of annoyances and not by wars of deliverance. God acts here in mysterious ways that are not known to human observers (see esp. 14.4). **14.1:** *Timnah,* located between Beth Shemesh and Ekron. **2:** Marriage was typically an economic

Philistine women in Timnah; please get her for me as a wife."
3 His father and mother said to him, "Is there no one among
the daughters of your own kinsmen and among all our[a] people, that you must go and take a wife from the uncircumcised
Philistines?" But Samson answered his father, "Get me that
one, for she is the one that pleases me." 4 His father and mother
did not realize that this was the LORD's doing: He was seeking
a pretext against the Philistines, for the Philistines were ruling
over Israel at that time. 5 So Samson and his father and mother
went down to Timnah.

When he[b] came to the vineyards of Timnah [for the first
time], a full-grown lion came roaring at him. 6 The spirit of
the LORD gripped him, and he tore him asunder with his bare
hands as one might tear a kid asunder; but he did not tell his
father and mother what he had done. 7 Then he went down and
spoke to the woman, and she pleased Samson.

8 Returning the following year to marry her, he turned aside
to look at the remains of the lion; and in the lion's skeleton he
found a swarm of bees, and honey. 9 He scooped it into his
palms and ate it as he went along. When he rejoined his father
and mother, he gave them some and they ate it; but he did not
tell them that he had scooped the honey out of a lion's skeleton.

10 So his father came down to the woman, and Samson made
a feast there, as young men used to do. 11 When they[c] saw him,
they designated thirty companions to be with him. 12 Then
Samson said to them, "Let me propound a riddle to you. If you
can give me the right answer during the seven days of the feast,
I shall give you thirty linen tunics and thirty sets of clothing;
13 but if you are not able to tell it to me, you must give me thirty
linen tunics and thirty sets of clothing." And they said to him,
"Ask your riddle and we will listen." 14 So he said to them:

"Out of the eater came something to eat,
Out of the strong came something sweet."

For three days they could not answer the riddle.

15 On the seventh[d] day, they said to Samson's wife, "Coax
your husband to provide us with the answer to the riddle;
else we shall put you and your father's household to the fire;
have you invited us here[e] in order to impoverish us?" 16 Then
Samson's wife harassed him with tears, and she said, "You
really hate me, you don't love me. You asked my countrymen a riddle, and you didn't tell me the answer." He replied,

a Heb. "my." *b Heb. "they."*
c I.e., the people of Timnah.
d Septuagint and Syriac read "fourth."
e Reading halom, *with some Heb. mss. and Targum.*

transaction arranged between the parents. **3:** The Bible does not recognize conversion. Other texts assume that the woman simply followed her husband's religious practices (Joseph and Moses marry non-Israelite women), but intermarriage with Philistines seems to have been distasteful. **5:** Although Samson went with his parents, during the journey he left the main road, so that they did not know of his struggle with the lion (v. 6; see also v. 9). Gilgamesh, the hero of the Babylonian myth, and Hercules, the Greek mythic hero, also overcame lions. **6:** Killing the lion would have rendered Samson ritually impure, and would have invalidated his status as a Nazirite, but these episodes do not recognize that status. **8:** The removal of honey—it would have been wild honey—from the skeleton of a lion has parallels in the literature of the ancient world. These two acts provide the material for the riddle. **9:** Samson gave his parents some of the honey, but did not tell them its source. **10:** The father alone is mentioned here; the mention of Samson's mother at the beginning of the ch may help connect this story, an originally separate narrative (note that Samson is never depicted as a Nazirite in chs 14–15), with the previous ch, in which the mother plays a central role. *A feast there:* Usually the feast is in the groom's house. **11:** *To be with him,* to provide him with companionship, as he was a stranger. **12:** *A riddle:* The proposal of a riddle accompanied by betting was part of the feast entertainment. The postponement of the riddle's solution until the seventh day indicates that Samson was convinced that it could be impossible to solve. **13:** Samson takes upon himself an obligation 30 times greater than that of any other. **14:** Samson's riddle is personal, and could not be solved without knowledge of his earlier acts. **15:** *On the seventh day:* Some versions of the LXX suggest the fourth day, which is more likely in context. *Have you invited us here:* The Philistines accuse the bride and her family of collaboration with Samson, with the intent of impoverishing them. **16:** *My countrymen:* This formulation emphasizes the national confrontation: she and her countrymen against Samson.

"I haven't even told my father and mother; shall I tell you?"
[17] During the rest of the seven days of the feast she continued
to harass him with her tears, and on the seventh day he told
her, because she nagged him so. And she explained the riddle
to her countrymen. [18] On the seventh day, before the sunset,
the townsmen said to him:

"What is sweeter than honey,
And what is stronger than a lion?"

He responded:

"Had you not plowed with my heifer,
You would not have guessed my riddle!"

[19] The spirit of the LORD gripped him. He went down to
Ashkelon and killed thirty of its men. He stripped them and
gave the sets of clothing to those who had answered the riddle.
And he left in a rage for his father's house.
[20] Samson's wife then married one of those who had been
his wedding companions.

15 Some time later, in the season of the wheat harvest,
Samson came to visit his wife, bringing a kid as a gift. He
said, "Let me go into the chamber to my wife." But her father
would not let him go in. [2] "I was sure," said her father, "that you
had taken a dislike to her, so I gave her to your wedding companion. But her younger sister is more beautiful than she; let
her become your wife instead." [3] Thereupon Samson declared,
"Now the Philistines can have no claim against me for the
harm I shall do them."
[4] Samson went and caught three hundred foxes. He took
torches and, turning [the foxes] tail to tail, he placed a torch
between each pair of tails. [5] He lit the torches and turned [the
foxes] loose among the standing grain of the Philistines, setting fire to stacked grain, standing grain, vineyards, [and][a] olive trees.
[6] The Philistines asked, "Who did this?" And they were
told, "It was Samson, the son-in-law of the Timnite, who took
Samson's[b] wife and gave her to his wedding companion."
Thereupon the Philistines came up and put her and her father[c]
to the fire. [7] Samson said to them, "If that is how you act, I will
not rest until I have taken revenge on you." [8] [d-]He gave them
a sound and thorough thrashing.[-d] Then he went down and
stayed in the cave of the rock of Etam.
[9] The Philistines came up, pitched camp in Judah and spread
out over Lehi. [10] The men of Judah asked, "Why have you come
up against us?" They answered, "We have come to take Samson

a So Targum. *b Heb. "his."*
c Many mss. read "her father's household"; cf. 14.15.
d-d Lit. "He smote them leg as well as thigh, a great smiting."

18: Samson responds with a riddle. He compares the woman to a heifer and the way of discovering to plowing. Thus he suggests that he knows how they arrived at the solution. His parable is phrased in a poetic formulation identical to the solution that they proposed, thereby concealing his anger and allowing the festive atmosphere to continue. **19:** Samson responds measure for measure, without deviating from the number 30. **20:** After his vengeance, Samson returns to his father's house, perhaps before the marriage was consummated. In any case, Samson abandoned his wife and she married another man. Compare Michal, David's wife, who was married off to Paltiel while apparently still married to David. David later reclaimed her, as Samson apparently tried to reclaim his wife in 15.1–3 (cf. 1 Sam. 25.44; 2 Sam. 3.14–16). **15.1:** Perhaps to consummate their wedding. **2:** *Taken a dislike* may be a technical term for divorce (see Deut. 24.1). **3:** In accordance with the policy of pretexts, Samson takes revenge not only against his wife's family, but against the Philistines in general. **4:** The motif of using foxes to damage fields is also known from other ancient literature (cf. Song 2.15). The *three hundred* builds on and escalates the thirty of the previous ch. **6:** The Philistines justify Samson's anger by taking revenge against his wife and her father. **7:** The violence escalates. **8:** *A sound and thorough thrashing:* The exact meaning of the Heb expression, lit. "calf as well as thigh," is unknown, but it is clear that the sense is a severe beating. *Etam:* Samson goes to live in the cleft of a rock in Judah, near Zorah; see 1 Chron. 4.3, 32; 2 Chron. 11.6. **9:** Samson's presence in the territory of Judah led the Philistines to apply further pressure on the tribe of Judah. *Lehi,* not identified. The folk etymology of the name, which means "jaw," appears in v. 17. **10–13:** Samson is not afraid of the Philistines, but of an attack by Judah. He therefore makes them take an oath. **10:** The measure-for-measure language is emphasized.

prisoner, and to do to him as he did to us.” 11 Thereupon three thousand men of Judah went down to the cave of the rock of Etam, and they said to Samson, “You knew that the Philistines rule over us; why have you done this to us?” He replied, “As they did to me, so I did to them.” 12 “We have come down,” they told him, “to take you prisoner and to hand you over to the Philistines.” “But swear to me,” said Samson to them, “that you yourselves will not attack me.” 13 “We won't,” they replied. “We will only take you prisoner and hand you over to them; we will not slay you.” So they bound him with two new ropes and brought him up from the rock.

14 When he reached Lehi, the Philistines came shouting to meet him. Thereupon the spirit of the LORD gripped him, and the ropes on his arms became like flax that catches fire; the bonds melted off his hands. 15 He came upon a fresh jawbone of an ass and he picked it up; and with it he killed a thousand men. 16 Then Samson said:

“With the jaw of an ass,
Mass upon mass!
With the jaw of an ass
I have slain a thousand men.”

17 As he finished speaking, he threw the jawbone away; hence that place was called Ramath-lehi.[a]

18 He was very thirsty and he called to the LORD, “You Yourself have granted this great victory through Your servant; and must I now die of thirst and fall into the hands of the uncircumcised?” 19 So God split open the hollow which is at Lehi, and the water gushed out of it; he drank, regained his strength, and revived. That is why it is called to this day “En-hakkore[b] of Lehi.”

20 He led Israel in the days of the Philistines for twenty years.

16 Once Samson went to Gaza; there he met a whore and slept with her. 2[c] The Gazites [learned][d] that Samson had come there, so they gathered and lay in ambush for him in the town gate the whole night; and all night long they kept whispering to each other, “When daylight comes, we'll kill him.” 3 But Samson lay in bed only till midnight. At midnight he got up, grasped the doors of the town gate together with the two

a I.e., “Jawbone Heights.” *b Understood as “The Spring of the Caller.”*
c Meaning of parts of verse uncertain. *d Septuagint reads “were told.”*

11: The numbers escalate further, moving from three hundred (v. 4) to *three thousand.* **12:** This foreshadows the binding of Samson in the following ch by Delilah. **15:** The *jawbone of an ass* was the first chance object that came to hand. This act of bravery is reminiscent of the heroic acts of Shamgar son of Anath (3.31); cf. 2 Sam. 23.8–23. **16:** Samson does not mention God in his song of victory. The word-play in the English (*ass ... mass ... mass*) mimics the Heb. **18:** Samson's thirst is interpreted as a result of the battle, but it also has educational meaning. He realizes that his might and life are dependent upon God's will. *Your servant:* This time, in contrast to the song of victory, Samson represents himself as a servant before his master and admits that the victory came from God. Especially in Samuel, *the uncircumcised* is used as a derogatory term for the Philistines (see 1 Sam. 14.6 n.). **19:** The folk etymology connects the name of the spring with Samson's calling upon God (v. 18). **20:** The appearance here of the closing formula, citing the number of years that he judged Israel, may suggest that the cycle originally ended here (cf. 16.31). Alternately, it indicates that the period when he was a judge occurred between his marriage and the events in ch 16 that led to his death. *In the days of the Philistines:* The emphasis that Samson judged Israel during the period of Philistine rule indicates that his mighty acts did not bring about deliverance or quiet.

16.1–21: Samson's betrayal and capture. Samson's final acts, all of which are associated with the city of Gaza, end with his death in Philistine captivity. As in all the Samson stories, a woman plays a prominent role. **1–3:** *Gaza:* Samson easily carried off the city gates, leaving the Philistines ashamed and exposed. This explains the Philistines' readiness to pay Delilah any price in order to catch Samson. **2:** The town gate was an extremely heavy, fortified structure with numerous rooms. **3:** Against the preparations of the townspeople “the whole night” (repeated twice), the author repeats that already “at midnight” Samson had left. Thus, while they were still waiting to catch him, he was no longer in the place. *To the top of the hill ... :* The geographical details emphasize the miracle. Samson walked a distance of some 56 km (35 miles), from the lowlands to the mountains, carrying the doors, the gateposts, and the bar on his shoulders. This story may be an etiology for part of an old

gateposts, and pulled them out along with the bar. He placed
them on his shoulders and carried them off to the top of the
hill that is near Hebron.

[4] After that, he fell in love with a woman in the Wadi Sorek,
named Delilah. [5] The lords of the Philistines went up to her and
said, "Coax him and find out what makes him so strong, and
how we can overpower him, tie him up, and make him helpless; and we'll each give you eleven hundred shekels of silver."
[6] So Delilah said to Samson, "Tell me, what makes you so
strong? And how could you be tied up and made helpless?"
[7] Samson replied, "If I were to be tied with seven fresh tendons
that had not been dried,[a] I should become as weak as an ordinary man." [8] So the lords of the Philistines brought up to her
seven fresh tendons that had not been dried. She bound him
with them, [9] while an ambush was waiting in her room. Then
she called out to him, "Samson, the Philistines are upon you!"
Whereat he pulled the tendons apart, as a strand of tow comes
apart at the touch of fire. So the secret of his strength remained
unknown.
[10] Then Delilah said to Samson, "Oh, you deceived me; you
lied to me! Do tell me now how you could be tied up." [11] He
said, "If I were to be bound with new ropes that had never
been used, I would become as weak as an ordinary man." [12] So
Delilah took new ropes and bound him with them, while an
ambush was waiting in a room. And she cried, "Samson, the
Philistines are upon you!" But he tore them off his arms like
a thread. [13] Then Delilah said to Samson, "You have been deceiving me all along; you have been lying to me! Tell me, how
could you be tied up?" He answered her, "If you weave seven
locks of my head into the web."[b] [14] And she pinned it with a
peg[c] and cried to him, "Samson, the Philistines are upon you!"
Awaking from his sleep, he pulled out the peg, the loom,[d] and
the web.
[15] Then she said to him, "How can you say you love me, when
you don't confide in me? This makes three times that you've
deceived me and haven't told me what makes you so strong."

a For use as bowstrings.
b Septuagint adds "and pin it with a peg to the wall, I shall become as weak as an ordinary man. So Delilah put him to sleep and wove the seven locks of his head into the web."
c Septuagint adds "to the wall."
d Meaning of Heb. uncertain.

gate structure found near Hebron. **4–21:** *Delilah:* Delilah exploits Samson's love and, in exchange for a handsome sum, discovers the secret of his strength and betrays him to the Philistines. Samson is taken, blind and humiliated, to a prison in Gaza. The story of Delilah's attempts to uncover the source of his strength are structured on the model of ascending numbers, three and four (see Jotham's parable: 9.8–15). Three times she fails (vv. 6–9, 10–12, 13–14), but in the climactic fourth time (vv. 15–21) he reveals his secret to her. In so doing he betrays his destiny and is punished. **4:** *He fell in love:* For the first time we are told that Samson was in love, and the woman is named. This indicates that this time Samson was emotionally involved and was bound to behave differently. *A woman:* We are not told that Delilah was a Philistine. *Wadi Sorek,* adjacent to Zorah and Eshtaol, rather than to the Philistine cities. *Delilah:* The etymology of Delilah may relate to woven braids of hair (Song 7.6), and thus may foreshadow Samson's undoing. **5:** *Each ... eleven hundred shekels:* Hence Delilah was offered the enormous sum of 5,500 shekels, as there were five Philistine lords, heading the five cities: Gaza, Ashkelon, Gath, Ekron, and Ashdod. **7:** Evidently, *tendons* taken from the intestines or sinews of animals. Their being fresh assures their flexibility and makes it more difficult to tear them. **9:** *A strand of tow* is a very weak cord. **10:** By the second attempt Delilah is angry that Samson misled her. This attempt is reminiscent of the incident at Lehi (15.13–14). **12:** *Thread* was slightly stronger than "a strand of tow" (v. 9). **13:** In the third attempt Delilah's tone is more imperious, and Samson reveals the object of his undoing, his hair, but not how it might undo him. Samson's answer is incomplete: It begins with a conditional sentence, but lacks the second half in the Heb (though it is complete in the LXX). This time the ambush is not mentioned. *Locks:* In this connection and from the continuation (v. 19), we may understand that his hair was divided into seven plaits, which were tied into a braid. *Into the web,* into the threads of the warp of the loom. **14:** *The loom, and the web,* the weave and the threads of the warp, which are part of the loom. **15:** On the fourth attempt, Delilah marshals her femininity and claims that Samson's declarations of love are false. He can convince her that his love is true only by revealing his secret.

16 Finally, after she had nagged him and pressed him constantly, he was wearied to death 17 and he confided everything to
her. He said to her, "No razor has ever touched my head, for I
have been a nazirite to God since I was in my mother's womb.
If my hair were cut, my strength would leave me and I should
become as weak as an ordinary man."
18 Sensing that he had confided everything to her, Delilah
sent for the lords of the Philistines, with this message: "Come
up once more, for he has confided everything to me." And the
lords of the Philistines came up and brought the money with
them. 19 She lulled him to sleep on her lap. Then she called in
a man, and she had him cut off the seven locks of his head;
thus she weakened him[a] and made him helpless: his strength
slipped away from him. 20 She cried, "Samson, the Philistines
are upon you!" And he awoke from his sleep, thinking he would
break loose[b] and shake himself free as he had the other times.
For he did not know that the LORD had departed from him.
21 The Philistines seized him and gouged out his eyes. They
brought him down to Gaza and shackled him in bronze fetters,
and he became a mill slave in the prison. 22 After his hair was
cut off, it began to grow back.
23 Now the lords of the Philistines gathered to offer a great
sacrifice to their god Dagon and to make merry. They chanted,

"Our god has delivered into our hands
Our enemy Samson."

24 [c]When the people saw him, they sang praises to their god,
chanting,

"Our god has delivered into our hands
The enemy who devastated our land,
And who slew so many of us."

25 As their spirits rose, they said, "Call Samson here and let
him dance for us." Samson was fetched from the prison, and he
danced for them. Then they put him between the pillars. 26 And
Samson said to the boy who was leading him by the hand, "Let
go of me and let me feel the pillars that the temple rests upon,
that I may lean on them." 27 Now the temple was full of men
and women; all the lords of the Philistines were there, and
there were some three thousand men and women on the roof
watching Samson dance. 28 Then Samson called to the LORD,
"O Lord GOD! Please remember me, and give me strength just
this once, O God, to take revenge of the Philistines, if only for
one of my two eyes." 29 He embraced the two middle pillars
that the temple rested upon, one with his right arm and one
with his left, and leaned against them; 30 Samson cried, "Let
me die with the Philistines!" and he pulled with all his might.

a Taking wattaḥel *as equivalent to* wattaḥal; *cf. vv. 7, 11, and 17.*
b Meaning of Heb. uncertain. *c This verse would read well after v. 25.*

16: This attempt continued during a long period of nagging until Samson felt his life wasn't worth living. This is reminiscent of the woman in 14.16. **19:** As he fell asleep on her knees, she called a man to assist her in cutting his hair because she was afraid that he might waken.

16.22–31: Samson's death and burial. The Philistines gathered at Dagon's temple (see 1 Sam. 5.2 n.) to offer sacrifices and to thank their god for catching Samson. The taunting of the defeated enemy is a form of entertainment; cf. Ps. 137.3. Samson turned to the LORD to assist him in taking a final vengeance upon the Philistines, by enabling him to pull down the pillars supporting the temple, destroying all that was within it. Thus, even Samson's death became a pretext for a strike against the Philistines. Members of his tribe took his body and buried him in his father's grave. **22:** The regrowth of his hair signals the renewal of his strength and may connect to ch 13 and the Nazirite vow; only in this ch is his strength connected to his "magical" locks. **24:** In Heb. this poem is exuberant and joyful, containing a very unusual example of end-rhyme. **25:** The Philistines wished to enjoy the sight of Samson humiliated (the Heb text does not explicitly mention dancing). **28:** As in the earlier story, Samson prays (15.18), but this time the prayer is a supplication for vengeance. In En-hakkore (15.19) one could hear in his prayer an element of questioning and even complaint. **29:** The pillars were likely placed closely together. **30:** Samson, upon feeling his strength returning to him, utters a cry of encouragement to himself.

The temple came crashing down on the lords and on all the
people in it. Those who were slain by him as he died outnumbered those who had been slain by him when he lived.
31 His brothers and all his father's household came down
and carried him up and buried him in the tomb of his father
Manoah, between Zorah and Eshtaol. He had led Israel for
twenty years.

17 There was a man in the hill country of Ephraim whose
name was Micah.[a] 2 He said to his mother, "The eleven
hundred shekels of silver that were taken from you, so that you
uttered an imprecation[b] which you repeated in my hearing—I
have that silver; I took it." "Blessed of the LORD be my son," said
his mother.[c] 3 He returned the eleven hundred shekels of silver
to his mother; but his mother said, "I herewith consecrate the
silver to the LORD, transferring it to my son to make a sculptured image and a molten image. I now return it to you." 4 So
when he gave the silver back to his mother, his mother took
two hundred shekels of silver and gave it to a smith. He made
of it a sculptured image and a molten image, which were kept
in the house of Micah.
5 Now the man Micah had a house of God; he had made an
ephod and teraphim and he had inducted one of his sons to be
his priest. 6 In those days there was no king in Israel; every man
did as he pleased.
7 There was a young man from Bethlehem of Judah, from the
clan seat of Judah; he was a Levite and had resided there as a
sojourner. 8 This man had left the town of Bethlehem of Judah
to take up residence wherever he could find a place. On his way,
he came to the house of Micah in the hill country of Ephraim.
9 "Where do you come from?" Micah asked him. He replied,
"I am a Levite from Bethlehem of Judah, and I am traveling to

a *"Micaihu" here and in v. 4.*
b *Cursing anyone who knew the whereabouts of the silver and did not disclose it; cf. Lev. 5.1; 1 Kings 8.31.* c *In order to nullify the imprecation.*

31: *His brothers,* his compatriots. *He had led . . . :* This refers to the period preceding what is related in ch 16. This phrase returns the reader to 15.20.

17.1–18.31: Micah's house of God and the temple of Dan. This story, focused upon cultic sites, criticizes the period of the judges by representing it as an age of anarchy: "In those days there was no king in Israel; every man did as he pleased." In terms of chronology, the story is set at the beginning of the age of the judges (see 18.30 and the introduction), but is placed at the end of the book to emphasize that the end of the period was similar to its beginning and that the judges were unable to correct the situation; hence, the solution is monarchy. In several details, including its setting (cf. 16.31 to 18.2, 8, 11) and the sum of money—1,100 silver shekels (16.5 and 17.3), this story is connected to the Samson cycle. Its emphasis on the illegitimacy of northern cultic site accords with the criticism of 1 Kings 12.25–13.34; 2 Kings 17.16–18 and other passages. **17.1–13:** Micah's *house of God:* The account of establishing Micah's house of God (vv. 1-5) is a negative portrayal of the manner in which God was worshipped during the period of the judges: A statue made by means of stolen silver was the center of the cult, and the priest was Micah's son, whom he himself appointed. During this period Levites sought a livelihood; hence Micah hired a Levite and appointed him as priest rather than his son (vv. 7–13). Some scholars think that Micah's temple in the hill country of Ephraim is an allusion to Bethel, which was connected with Dan, and that the criticism here is of the two central temples of the Northern Kingdom. **1:** *Hill country of Ephraim:* The name of Micah's town is not specified, but rather the broad region of the central hill country. Cf. v. 8; 18. 2, 13. **4:** *Two hundred shekels:* His mother said that she had consecrated the money to the LORD, but in practice she only set aside 200 out of 1,100 shekels—this too reflects poorly on the cult center that is ultimately established. *Sculptured image and a molten image:* This may refer to a single article, namely a molten (cast) sculpture. In any event, these are expressions related to pagan worship or worship of the LORD in a pagan manner (see Deut. 27.15; Exod. 20.3; 34.17; etc.). Micah and his mother are described as serving the LORD, but not in the proper way. **5:** *Ephod and teraphim,* means of inquiring of God. *One of his sons,* an illegitimate appointment, as he was not a Levite. **6:** This statement, which serves as a refrain in the last five chs of the book (18.1; 21.25), criticizes what precedes it, and serves as a critical introduction to what follows. It also suggests that Micah's specific act is representative of the whole. **7:** A Levite could not be a resident in Judah, but only a temporary sojourner (Deut. 18.2 n.). **8:** *A place,* where he would be able to earn a livelihood. The Levite came to Micah's house to rest from his travels and did not imagine that he would find his livelihood there.

take up residence wherever I can find a place." [10] "Stay with me," Micah said to him, "and be a father and a priest to me, and I will pay you ten shekels of silver a year, an allowance of clothing, and your food." [a-]The Levite went.[-a] [11] The Levite agreed to stay with the man, and the youth became like one of his own sons. [12] Micah inducted the Levite, and the young man became his priest and remained in Micah's shrine. [13] "Now I know," Micah told himself, "that the LORD will prosper me, since the Levite has become my priest."

18 In those days there was no king in Israel, and in those days the tribe of Dan was seeking a territory in which to settle; for to that day no territory had fallen to their lot among the tribes of Israel. [2] The Danites sent out five of their number, from their clan seat at Zorah and Eshtaol—valiant men—to spy out the land and explore it. "Go," they told them, "and explore the land." When they had advanced into the hill country of Ephraim as far as the house of Micah, they stopped there for the night. [3] While in the vicinity of Micah's house, they recognized the speech[b] of the young Levite, so they went over and asked him, "Who brought you to these parts? What are you doing in this place? What is your business here?" [4] He replied, "Thus and thus Micah did for me—he hired me and I became his priest." [5] They said to him, "Please, inquire of God; we would like to know if the mission on which we are going will be successful." [6] "Go in peace," the priest said to them, "the LORD views with favor the mission you are going on." [7] The five men went on and came to Laish. They observed the people in it dwelling carefree, after the manner of the Sidonians, a tranquil and unsuspecting people, with no one in the land to molest them and [c-]with no hereditary ruler.[-c] Moreover, they were distant from the Sidonians and had no dealings with anybody.

[8] When [the men] came back to their kinsmen at Zorah and Eshtaol, their kinsmen asked them, "How did you fare?" [9] They replied, "Let us go at once and attack them! For we found that the land was very good, and you are sitting idle! Don't delay; go and invade the land and take possession of it, [10] for God has delivered it into your hand. When you come, you will come to an unsuspecting people; and the land is spacious and nothing on earth is lacking there."

a-a Force of Heb. uncertain.
b Lit. "voice." The men could tell by his dialect that he came from Judah and was therefore a former neighbor of the Danites; cf. vv. 11–12.
c-c Meaning of Heb. uncertain.

10: *A father:* Micah promises the Levite a respected position (cf. Gen. 45.8). *Ten shekels ... a year:* The gap between the annual wage of the Levite and the amount of money stolen by Micah indicates his great wealth and maybe his stinginess too. *The Levite went:* This expression seems superfluous and may be an erroneous duplication (dittography) of the nearly identical Heb words that follow ("the Levite agreed").

18.1–31: The conquest of Dan and the setting up of its temple. The Danites' wandering may reflect the intertribal relations during the period of the judges, the difficult situation of the individual, and the status of the cultic sites. **1:** *In those days ... :* A truncated version of 17.6, suggesting its critical sequel: "every man did as he pleased." Here too this statement is integrated within the transition from one scene to another, bearing on both what precedes and what follows. The tribe of Dan was forced to leave its territory in the coastal lowlands, near Zorah and Eshtaol (where the Samson stories are set—it might have been that these towns are mentioned to strengthen the connection between the stories), and to seek a new territory, while none of the other tribes came to their help (see 1.34–35; Josh. 19.47). **4:** *Thus and thus ... :* The narrator abbreviates the information already known from ch 17. **5:** *Inquire of God:* Before carrying out any task it was customary to inquire of God; see 1 Sam. 23.1–13 and the opening v. of Judges (1.1). **6:** The Levite's answer is ambiguous, because a failure could have been the LORD's will too. **7:** *Laish,* the former name of Dan (see v. 29), referred to in Josh. 19.47 as Leshem. The description of the city is from the viewpoint of the spies, who emphasized that it was peaceful and isolated, and therefore could easily be conquered. *Distant from ... :* The Galilee separates Laish and the area of the Sidonians in Phoenicia. *With anybody:* The LXX reads: "with Aram," to the north of Laish; *anybody* ('adam) and "Aram" ('aram) are nearly identical in the Heb. **9:** *Sitting idle:* The spies criticize the apathy of their tribe and enumerate the virtues of the place and the ease with which it might be conquered. Their enthusiasm is reminiscent of Joshua and Caleb (Num. 14.7ff.).

[11] They departed from there, from the clan seat of the Danites, from Zorah and Eshtaol, six hundred strong, girt with weapons of war. [12] They went up and encamped at Kiriath-jearim in Judah. That is why that place is called "the Camp of Dan" to this day; it lies west of Kiriath-jearim. [13] From there they passed on to the hill country of Ephraim and arrived at the house of Micah. [14] Here the five men who had gone to spy out the Laish region remarked to their kinsmen, "Do you know, there is an ephod in these houses, and teraphim, and a sculptured image and a molten image? Now you know what you have to do." [15] So they turned off there and entered the home of the young Levite at Micah's house and greeted him. [16] The six hundred Danite men, girt with their weapons of war, stood at the entrance of the gate, [17] while the five men who had gone to spy out the land went inside and took the sculptured image, the ephod, the teraphim, and the molten image. The priest was standing at the entrance of the gate, and the six hundred men girt with their weapons of war, [18] while those men entered Micah's house and took [a]the sculptured image, the molten image, the ephod, and the household gods.[a] The priest said to them, "What are you doing?" [19] But they said to him, "Be quiet; put your hand on your mouth! Come with us and be our father and priest. Would you rather be priest to one man's household or be priest to a tribe and clan in Israel?" [20] The priest was delighted. He took the ephod, the household gods, and the sculptured image, and he joined the people.

[21] They set out again, placing the children, the cattle, and their household goods in front. [22] They had already gone some distance from Micah's house, when the men in the houses near Micah's mustered and caught up with the Danites. [23] They called out to the Danites, who turned around and said to Micah, "What's the matter? Why have you mustered?" [24] He said, "You have taken my priest and the gods that I made, and walked off! What do I have left? How can you ask, 'What's the matter'?" [25] But the Danites replied, "Don't do any shouting at us, or some desperate men might attack you, and you and your family would lose your lives." [26] So Micah, realizing that they were stronger than he, turned back and went home; and the Danites went on their way, [27] taking the things Micah had made and the priest he had acquired. They proceeded to Laish, a people tranquil and unsuspecting, and they put them to the sword and burned down the town. [28] There was none to come to the rescue, for it was distant from Sidon and they had no dealings with anyone; it lay in the valley of Beth-rehob.

They rebuilt the town and settled there, [29] and they named the town Dan, after their ancestor Dan who was Israel's son.

a-a Lit. "the sculptured image of the ephod, and the household gods, and the molten image."

11: Six hundred indicates a military unit. See 1 Sam. 30.9. **12:** *Kiriath-jearim,* located on the border of Judah and Benjamin, west of Jerusalem, and identified with modern Abu-Ghosh. *The Camp of Dan:* The site has not been identified. *To this day,* the days of the author (see v. 30). **14:** *In these houses:* Micah's house was not an isolated house in the hill country of Ephraim, but was located within a settlement whose name is not given. It seems to refer to Bethel (cf. Jer. 4.15). *You know what you have to do,* an agreed signal among conspirators. **15:** *The home of the young Levite,* i.e., the temple in which he serves. **20:** *The priest was delighted:* The narrator criticizes the Levite's thoughts, representing him as one who prefers his own interest—to be a priest for an entire tribe—over ethics and loyalty. **21:** *In front:* As they wished to protect their property and the weak among them, they placed them in the front, so that the fighting men would serve as a buffer against marauders from the rear. In the case of Jacob, Esau was approaching him, so he behaved in the opposite manner, placing the women and children in the rear. **22:** See v. 14 above. **23:** The Danites' questions were sarcastic, as they knew the real reason. **24:** Micah's answer indicates the depth of divine worship in an improper manner, which fits the Danites too. **27:** Here too there is implicit criticism of the northerners, who massacre *a people tranquil and unsuspecting.* **28:** See v. 7. *Beth-rehob,* an Aramean kingdom (2 Sam. 10.6) whose locale is unidentified.

Originally, however, the name of the town was Laish. [30] The
Danites set up the sculptured image for themselves; and Jonathan son of Gershom son of Manasseh,[a] and his descendants,
served as priests to the Danite tribe until the land went into
exile. [31] They maintained[b] the sculptured image that Micah
had made throughout the time that the House of God stood
at Shiloh.

19 In those days, when there was no king in Israel, a Levite
residing at the other end of the hill country of Ephraim
took to himself a concubine from Bethlehem in Judah. [2] Once
his concubine deserted[c] him, leaving him for her father's house
in Bethlehem in Judah; and she stayed there a full four months.
[3] Then her husband set out, with an attendant and a pair of donkeys, and went after her to woo her and to win her back. She
admitted him into her father's house; and when the girl's father
saw him, he received him warmly. [4] His father-in-law, the girl's
father, pressed him, and he stayed with him three days; they
ate and drank and lodged there. [5] Early in the morning of the
fourth day, he started to leave; but the girl's father said to his
son-in-law, "Eat something to give you strength, then you can
leave." [6] So the two of them sat down and they feasted together.
Then the girl's father said to the man, "Won't you stay overnight
and enjoy yourself?" [7] The man started to leave, but his father-
in-law kept urging him until he turned back and spent the night
there. [8] Early in the morning of the fifth day, he was about to

a Heb. מנשה *with* נ *suspended, indicating an earlier reading "Moses"; cf. Exod. 2.22.*
b Meaning of Heb. uncertain. *c Lit. "played the harlot."*

30: *Jonathan ... :* Here the Levite's identity is revealed, being a grandson of Moses, the third generation from the exodus. The name Moses is obscured and turned into Manasseh (an evil Judean king; some scholars think that this name points to a Samaritan high priest too) by means of a hanging letter "nun" to clear Moses from his grandson's misdeeds. (According to Exod. 2.22, *Gershom* is Moses' son.) *Exile:* This seems to refer to 732 BCE, when the Galilee was exiled by Assyria (2 Kings 15.29), or the exile of the Northen Kingdom in 722. **31:** This v. does not fit the one that precedes it. Shiloh was destroyed in the days of Samuel (1 Sam. chs 4–5), more than 300 years before the Assyrian invasion. It seems that this v. is an editorial addition, introduced to connect the story with the book of Samuel, which begins with the temple of Shiloh (1 Sam. ch 1). The mention of Kiriath-jearim in v. 12 also connects Judges to Samuel (see 1 Sam. 7.1–2).

Chs 19–21: The happenings with Gibeah and Benjamin. This account concerns a brutal rape in the town of Gibeah, following which all the tribes of Israel set out to punish those responsible. The tribe of Benjamin covered for the townspeople, and as a result a war broke out and Benjamin was nearly decimated. After the war, the other tribes arranged for the surviving Benjaminites to marry women from Jabesh-gilead and Shiloh. A distinctive feature of this episode is the anonymity of the figures involved and the focus upon place names. Gibeah, which fails to provide hospitality, is contrasted with the exemplary hospitality of Bethlehem in Judah. Through the named places and what occurred there the author strongly hints his preference for David from Bethlehem over the Benjaminite Saul from Gibeah. Even though the story is framed by the motto "in those days there was no king in Israel" (19.1; 21.25), it seems doubtful that this was intended to endorse anarchy. The story depicts a unified society, sensitive to problems of ethics and serving the LORD. It therefore appears that by using the motto the episode was appended by an editor to chs 17–18 as their continuation on the one hand, and on the other hand to the ending of the book of Judges as an anticipatory hint to the book of Samuel, preparing specifically for the disappointment from Saul of Gibeah and the hope from Bethlehem. The story includes numerous allusions to stories from the Torah and from the early prophets. It likewise raises many strange questions that have no solution (see the commentary)—suggesting that its composition was not completed. Finally, it contains several echoes to the beginning of Judges (see 20.18 and 1.1–2; 21.24 and 2.6), using the literary device of an inclusio to frame the book and bring it to a close.

19.1–30: Between two cities. A concubine from the hill country of Ephraim left her husband and returned to her father's home in Bethlehem in Judah. Her husband came to take her back and enjoyed outstanding hospitality. On the way home they stopped to sleep in Gibeah, where the woman was raped by the townspeople until she died. The husband conveyed this terrible news to all the tribes of Israel. There are many points of similarity between this incident and the story of Sodom (Gen. ch 19), which it knows; Gibeah, Saul's city, is thus portrayed as a wicked Sodom. **1:** *Concubine,* a woman in a lower legal status than a wife. **3–9:** The repeated entreaties of the father-in-law, the focus upon the feasts and staying overnight, and the emphasis that the hospitality

leave, when the girl's father said, "Come, have a bite." The two
of them ate, dawdling until past noon. 9 Then the man, his concubine, and his attendant started to leave. His father-in-law,
the girl's father, said to him, "Look, the day is waning toward
evening; do stop for the night. See, the day is declining; spend
the night here and enjoy yourself. You can start early tomorrow
on your journey and head for home."
10 But the man refused to stay for the night. He set out and
traveled as far as the vicinity of Jebus—that is, Jerusalem; he had
with him a pair of laden donkeys, and his concubine [a-]was with
him.[-a] 11 Since they were close to Jebus, and the day was very far
spent, the attendant said to his master, "Let us turn aside to this
town of the Jebusites and spend the night in it." 12 But his master
said to him, "We will not turn aside to a town of aliens who are
not of Israel, but will continue to Gibeah. 13 Come," he said to his
attendant, "let us approach one of those places and spend the
night either in Gibeah or in Ramah." 14 So they traveled on, and
the sun set when they were near Gibeah of Benjamin.
15 They turned off there and went in to spend the night in
Gibeah. He went and sat down in the town square, but nobody took them indoors to spend the night. 16 In the evening,
an old man came along from his property [b-]outside the town.[-b]
(This man hailed from the hill country of Ephraim and resided
at Gibeah, where the townspeople were Benjaminites.) 17 He
happened to see the wayfarer in the town square. "Where," the
old man inquired, "are you going to, and where do you come
from?" 18 He replied, "We are traveling from Bethlehem in
Judah to the other end of the hill country of Ephraim. That is
where I live. I made a journey to Bethlehem of Judah, and now
I am on my way [c-]to the House of the LORD,[-c] and nobody has
taken me indoors. 19 We have both bruised straw and feed for
our donkeys, and bread and wine for me and your handmaid,[d]
and for the attendant [e-]with your servants.[-e] We lack nothing."
20 "Rest easy," said the old man. "Let me take care of all your
needs. Do not on any account spend the night in the square."
21 And he took him into his house. He mixed fodder for the
donkeys; then they bathed their feet and ate and drank.
22 While they were enjoying themselves, the men of the
town, a depraved lot, had gathered about the house and were

a-a Emendation yields "and his attendant." *b-b Lit. "in the field."*
c-c Meaning of Heb. uncertain; emendation yields "to my home"; cf. v. 29.
d I.e., the concubine. *e-e I.e., "with us."*

continued for five days—all these emphasize the generous hospitality offered in Bethlehem in Judah. **10:** There is no external corroboration that Jebus was the previous name of Jerusalem; the Jebusites are not recorded in any extrabiblical source. The name Jerusalem is known from the beginning of the second millenium BCE. The repetition that *His concubine was with him* (cf. v. 9) makes her seem like an afterthought, anticipating what follows. **12:** According to 2 Sam. ch 5, Jerusalem was conquered only in the days of David, so that during the period of the judges it was a foreign city (contrast Judg. 1.8). It is mentioned here to emphasize the lack of expectations from an alien city as opposed to the Israelite city of Gibeah. **13:** The mention of Ramah, located 10 km (6 miles) north of Jerusalem, alludes to Samuel, who anointed Saul and David. The mention of these specific cities suggests that the travelers avoid the good cities, associated with David and Samuel, and choose the evil city associated with Saul. **14–21:** The man who hosted the Levite and his company in his house was not from Gibeah—all of its residents were inhospitable—but a stranger from the hill country of Ephraim. The mention of this location helps to tie this story to the previous one (18.2, 12, 13). Similarly, in the episode of Sodom it was the stranger Lot who provided hospitality to the strangers (Gen. 19.2–3). **22–26:** The violence of the people of Gibeah is reminiscent of the Sodomites: Both try to break into the host's house and want to sodomize the guests. But while in Sodom the guests were angels, here they were ordinary human beings; hence the different result. The host protected the Levite, offering his own virgin daughter and the concubine. At the end the Levite gave them his concubine, whom they abused all night long, until in the morning she was found at the threshold of the house. This description entails many strange features, indicating its relation to the story of Sodom, yet incompletely. It is strange that the host offers them the concubine, who was a guest. It is strange that the people of Gibeah were satisfied with the concubine and did not insist upon receiving the Levite and his attendant or the virgin daughter. It is also strange that once the woman fell at the entrance to the house and her hands were on the threshold no one heard her; were they asleep? Was she dead? **22:** The characterization of

pounding on the door. They called to the aged owner of the
house, "Bring out the man who has come into your house, so
that we can be intimate with him." 23 The owner of the house
went out and said to them, "Please, my friends, do not commit such a wrong. Since this man has entered my house, do
not perpetrate this outrage. 24 Look, here is my virgin daughter,
and his concubine. Let me bring them out to you. Have your
pleasure of them, do what you like with them; but don't do that
outrageous thing to this man." 25 But the men would not listen
to him, so the man seized his concubine and pushed her out
to them. They raped her and abused her all night long until
morning; and they let her go when dawn broke.
26 Toward morning the woman came back; and as it was
growing light, she collapsed at the entrance of the man's house
where her husband was. 27 When her husband arose in the
morning, he opened the doors of the house and went out to
continue his journey; and there was the woman, his concubine, lying at the entrance of the house, with her hands on the
threshold. 28 "Get up," he said to her, "let us go." But there was
no reply. So the man placed her on the donkey and set out for
home. 29 When he came home, he picked up a knife, and took
hold of his concubine and cut her up limb by limb into twelve
parts. He sent them throughout the territory of Israel. 30 And
everyone who saw it cried out, "Never has such a thing happened or been seen from the day the Israelites came out of the
land of Egypt to this day! Put your mind to this; take counsel
and decide."

20 Thereupon all the Israelites—from Dan to Beer-sheba
and [from] the land of Gilead—marched forth, and the
community assembled to a man before the LORD at Mizpah.
2 All the leaders of the people [and] all the tribes of Israel presented themselves in the assembly of God's people, 400,000
fighting men on foot.—3 The Benjaminites heard that the Israelites had come up to Mizpah.[a]—The Israelites said, "Tell us,
how did this evil thing happen?" 4 And the Levite, the husband
of the murdered woman, replied, "My concubine and I came
to Gibeah of Benjamin to spend the night. 5 The citizens of
Gibeah set out to harm me. They gathered against me around
the house in the night; they meant to kill me, and they ravished
my concubine until she died. 6 So I took hold of my concubine

a *This sentence is continued at v. 14 below.*

the city's inhabitants as *depraved,* a very strong word, hints at the trouble ahead. **23:** *Outrage,* a strong term, used in the context of sexual transgressions (see Gen. 34.7; Deut. 22.21; etc.). **24:** Although v. 22 consists of the threat of intercourse between the male attackers and the male outsider, the point of the threat is to express dominance. The concubine and the host's daughter, who are female, would also serve to demonstrate the dominant status of the attackers, over both the outsider and the host (who is responsible for the well-being of the guests). **25:** The numerous descriptions of time ("all night," "long until morning," "when dawn broke") emphasize the brutality. **27–28:** The Levite's behavior was strange as well. He prepares to leave as though nothing had happened, and upon seeing the concubine's body, he calls her to get up and go and then treats her like a sack of grain, and it is not mentioned explicitly that she is dead. **29:** The dismemberment of the body and the sending of its pieces are also strange. It is meant to recall the incident in which Saul divided a pair of cattle (1 Sam. 11.7), but there the purpose is clear: to dramatize what Saul would do to the cattle of those who refused to join him. All these strange details suggest that the story is a kind of polemic against Saul and his town, Gibeah.

20.1–48: The war against Benjamin. Benjamin's refusal to turn over those who were guilty in Gibeah led to a bloody war. On the first two days Israel was defeated, for reasons that are not clear. On the third day they overpowered Benjamin, leaving only 600 people. This description relies upon the well-known story of Israel's war against Ai (Josh. chs 7–8). **1:** There is no other unification of this type throughout the book of Judges; the phrase from Dan to Beer-sheba appears five times in the following book of Samuel, where it is used four times in the monarchic period (e.g., 2 Sam. 3.10; 24.2, 15). **2:** The number *400,000* is very exaggerated. **3:** It is strange that the examination of the Levite is only performed once the army had been mustered. **4:** There is no proportion between the sin and its punishment. Moreover, there are other problems related to the process of the war that we shall see in what follows. **4–11:** The Levite's account is brief and not entirely truthful; nevertheless, the Israelite side does not feel a need to investigate, but adopts

and I cut her in pieces and sent them through every part of
Israel's territory. For an outrageous act of depravity had been
committed in Israel. 7 Now you are all Israelites; produce a
plan of action here and now!"
8 Then all the people rose, as one man, and declared, "We
will not go back to our homes, we will not enter our houses!
9 But this is what we will do to Gibeah: [we will wage war]
against it according to lot. 10 We will take from all the tribes of
Israel ten men to the hundred, a hundred to the thousand, and
a thousand to the ten thousand to supply provisions for the
troops—[a]to prepare for their going to Geba in Benjamin[a] for
all the outrage it has committed in Israel." 11 So all the men of
Israel, united as one man, massed against the town. 12 And the
tribes of Israel sent men through the whole tribe[b] of Benjamin,
saying, "What is this evil thing that has happened among you?
13 Come, hand over those scoundrels in Gibeah so that we may
put them to death and stamp out the evil from Israel." But the
Benjaminites would not yield to the demand of their fellow Israelites.
14 So the Benjaminites gathered from their towns to Gibeah
in order to take the field against the Israelites. 15 [c]On that day
the Benjaminites mustered from the towns 26,000 fighting
men, mustered apart from the inhabitants of Gibeah; 700
picked men 16 of all this force—700 picked men—were left-
handed. Every one of them could sling a stone at a hair and
not miss. 17 The men of Israel other than Benjamin mustered
400,000 fighting men, warriors to a man. 18 They proceeded to
Bethel and inquired of God; the Israelites asked, "Who of us
shall advance first to fight the Benjaminites?" And the LORD
replied, "Judah first." 19 So the Israelites arose in the morning
and encamped against Gibeah.
20 The men of Israel took the field against the Benjaminites;
the men of Israel drew up in battle order against them at Gibeah. 21 But the Benjaminites issued from Gibeah, and that day
they struck down 22,000 men of Israel.
22 Now the army—the men of Israel—rallied and again drew
up in battle order at the same place as they had on the first
day. 23 For the Israelites had gone up and wept before the LORD
until evening. They had inquired of the LORD, "Shall we again
join battle with our kinsmen the Benjaminites?" And the LORD
had replied, "March against them." 24 The Israelites advanced
against the Benjaminites on the second day. 25 But the Benjaminites came out from Gibeah against them on the second
day and struck down 18,000 more of the Israelites, all of them
fighting men.

a-a Emendation yields "for those who go to requite Gibeah."

b Heb. plural. *c Meaning of parts of vv. 15 and 16 uncertain.*

a decision to go to war. **8:** *Go back to our homes ... enter our houses* recalls the opening section of the book (2.6). **9:** *According to lot:* The casting of lots determines when to go to war and which of the tribes will go first (v. 18); this also returns us to the beginning of the book (1.3). **10:** Ten percent were responsible for the supplies to the combatants. **11–13:** The men of Israel were interested in punishing only the scoundrels from Gibeah, but the tribe of Benjamin did not agree to turn them over, preferring to fight. **13:** *And stamp out the evil from Israel* is otherwise only found in Deut. (e.g., 17.7). **15–17:** The number of combatants from Benjamin is problematic. The number mentioned here (26,700 fighters) conflicts with the number in v. 35 (25,100, with 600 surviving), as well as with vv. 44–47 (25,000, with 600 left). **16:** *Left-handed,* otherwise only in 3.15. On a group of chosen people from Benjamin who used both hands, see 1 Chron. 12.2. **17:** The number 400,000 seems to include the tenth appointed over the supplies. **18:** *And the LORD replied, "Judah first":* As Judah is not mentioned later, this seems to have been an addition introduced under the influence of the beginning of the book (1.1–2), and intended to round the book out through an inclusio. **19–25:** It would seem that v. 22 ought to appear after v. 23. In the first two battles Israel acted after asking the LORD, nevertheless the Benjaminite warriors killed 40,000 of them; the text does not explain this theological difficulty.

26 Then all the Israelites, all the army, went up and came to
Bethel and they sat there, weeping before the LORD. They fasted that day until evening, and presented burnt offerings and
offerings of well-being to the LORD. 27 The Israelites inquired
of the LORD (for the Ark of God's Covenant was there in those
days, 28 and Phinehas son of Eleazar son of Aaron the priest
ministered before Him in those days), "Shall we again take the
field against our kinsmen the Benjaminites, or shall we not?"
The LORD answered, "Go up, for tomorrow I will deliver them
into your hands."

29 Israel put men in ambush against Gibeah on all sides.
30 And on the third day, the Israelites went up against the Benjaminites, as before, and engaged them in battle at Gibeah.
31 The Benjaminites dashed out to meet the army and were
drawn away from the town onto the roads, of which one runs
to Bethel and the other to Gibeah. As before, they started out
by striking some of the men dead in the open field, about 30
men of Israel.

32 The Benjaminites thought, "They are being routed before us as previously." But the Israelites had planned: "We
will take to flight and draw them away from the town to
the roads." 33 And while the main body of the Israelites had
moved away from their positions and had drawn up in battle order at Baal-tamar, the Israelite ambush was rushing out
from its position at Maareh-geba.[a] 34 Thus 10,000 picked men
of all Israel came to a point south of[b] Gibeah, and the battle
was furious. Before they realized that disaster was approaching, 35 the LORD routed the Benjaminites before Israel. That
day the Israelites slew 25,100 men of Benjamin, all of them
fighting men. 36 Then the Benjaminites realized that they
were routed.[c] Now the Israelites had yielded ground to the
Benjaminites, for they relied on the ambush which they had
laid against Gibeah. 37 One ambush quickly deployed against
Gibeah, and the other ambush advanced and put the whole
town to the sword.

a Emendation yields "west of Gibeah."

b So many Heb. mss. and Targum; most mss. and the editions read "opposite."

c This sentence is continued by v. 45.

26–28: The army of Israel went up a third time to Bethel, where the Ark of God was at that time and where Phinehas son of Eleazar son of Aaron, third generation from the exodus, served as priest. This connects the end of Judges to the end of Joshua (Josh. 24.33), while much of the rest of the story connects it to the following book of Samuel. The army fasted, offered burnt offerings, and inquired of the LORD. God promised that this time He would give Benjamin into their hands. **29–47:** According to most scholars this story has been expanded and reworked here. Abravanel already wrote: "The verses in this narrative seem to be repeated and inconsistent, and the interpreters did not solve them properly." Most likely two versions have been imperfectly reworked into a single story. Underlying both versions is a combined strategy trick of ambush and decoy, known from Joshua's battle with Ai (Josh. chs 7–8). The function of the ambush was to besiege the city and set fire to it after tempting its inhabitants to chase an Israelite decoy force that would stage a retreat. Once the pursuers saw their city going up in flames, they would lose their fighting spirit, and the pursued would become pursuers. Thus the Benjaminites would find themselves caught between the ambush and the new pursuers, while the city and its protectors were destroyed. While the first version (vv. 29–36a) refers to the task of the main Israelite force that encamped at Baal-tamar and was counted neither with the decoy force nor with the ambush, the second version (vv. 36b–44) relates to the agreed signal between the decoy force and the ambush. **29:** According to vv. 33–34 the main force was east of Gibeah, the ambush west of the city, while the decoy force was opposite the city. **30:** This refers to the decoy force alone; see v. 34. **31:** *To Gibeah:* It is preferable to read "to Geba," located east of Gibeah. The choice of two directions of flight divides the pursuing force. *About 30 men:* The small number of the fallen, in comparison to the first two wars, is evidently influenced by the story of Ai (Josh. 7.5). **33:** The main Israelite force had been mustered before in Baal-tamar, whose location has not been identified. **34:** *Before they realized,* i.e., before the Benjaminites realized. **35:** See the interpretation of vv. 15–17. **36b:** The beginning of the second version emphasizes that the Israelite army, who had relied upon the ambush, placed to the west of Gibeah, waited for a sign to enter into battle, giving the decoy time to lead the inhabitants of Gibeah away from their city. **37:** The English translation divides the ambush into two parts, which is unnecessary. It should read: "The ambush quickly deployed against Gibeah and advanced ..."

[38]A time had been agreed upon by the Israelite men with
those in ambush: When a huge column of smoke was sent up
from the town, [39]the Israelite men were to turn about in battle.
Benjamin had begun by striking dead about 30 Israelite men,
and they thought, "They are being routed before us as in the previous fighting." [40]But when the column, the pillar of smoke, began to rise from the city, the Benjaminites looked behind them,
and there was the whole town going up in smoke to the sky!
[41]And now the Israelites turned about, and the men of Benjamin
were thrown into panic, for they realized that disaster had overtaken them. [42]They retreated before the men of Israel along the
road to the wilderness, where the fighting caught up with them;
meanwhile those [a]-from the towns-[a] were massacring them in
it. [43][b]They encircled the Benjaminites, pursued them, and trod
them down [from] Menuhah to a point opposite Gibeah on the
east. [44]That day 18,000 men of Benjamin fell, all of them brave
men. [45]They turned and fled to the wilderness, to the Rock of
Rimmon; but [the Israelites] picked off another 5,000 on the
roads and, continuing in hot pursuit of them up to Gidom, they
slew 2,000 more. [46]Thus the total number of Benjaminites who
fell that day came to 25,000 fighting men, all of them brave. [47]But

a-a Meaning of Heb. uncertain; emendation yields "in the town" (i.e., Gibeah).
b Meaning of verse uncertain.

38–39a: The Israelite decoy force and the ambush agreed upon a sign—a great cloud of smoke rising from the city—to determine when the pursued would turn into pursuers. **39b:** See vv. 31–32. **41:** *The Israelites turned about,* the decoy force. **42:** The Benjaminites attempted to escape from the pincer motion of the ambush and the decoy force by fleeing in the direction of the desert, but the war overtook them there as well. *From the towns:* Those who fled from the town of Gibeah were killed in the middle. **43:** The v. is in the form of a (difficult) poem, which may be a remnant of a poem in whose center is the victory over Benjamin. Israel surrounded Benjamin and pursued them from a settlement called Nohah (see 1 Chron. 8.2) until close to Gibeah. **45–47:** Here, the total number of the fallen Benjaminites was 25,000. Six hundred men found shelter in the *Rock of Rimmon* on the edge of the desert east of Bethel, where they remained for four months. **47:** *Four months,* connecting the story to

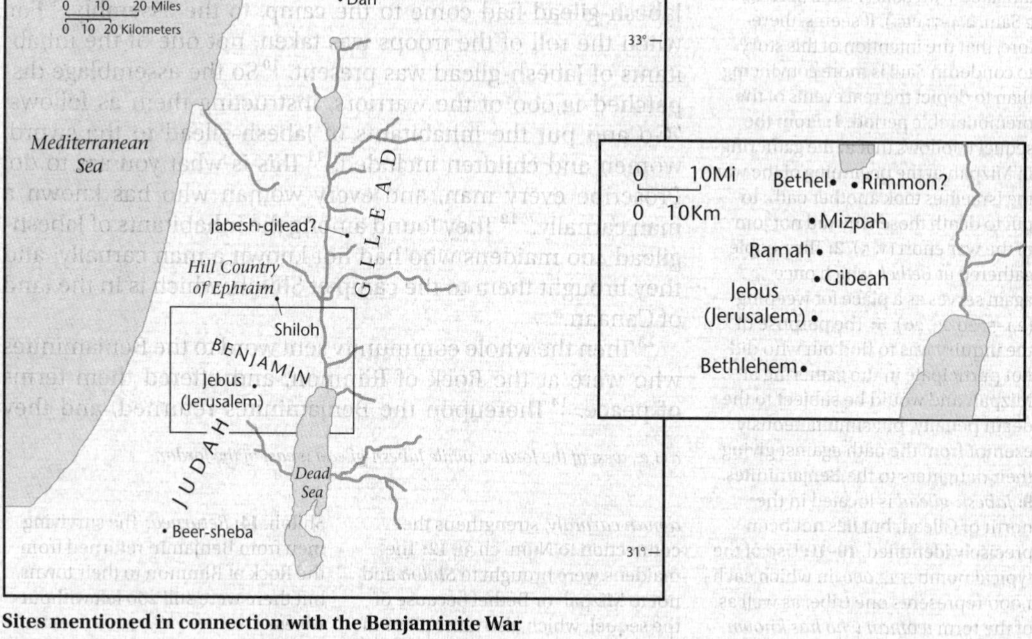

Sites mentioned in connection with the Benjaminite War

600 men turned and fled to the wilderness, to the Rock of Rimmon; they remained at the Rock of Rimmon four months. 48 The
men of Israel, meanwhile, turned back to the rest of the Benjaminites and put them to the sword—towns, people, cattle—
everything that remained. Finally, they set fire to all the towns
that were left.

21 Now the men of Israel had taken an oath at Mizpah:
"None of us will give his daughter in marriage to a Benjaminite."
2 The people came to Bethel and sat there before God until evening. They wailed and wept bitterly, 3 and they said, "O
LORD God of Israel, why has this happened in Israel, that one
tribe must now be missing from Israel?" 4 Early the next day,
the people built an altar there, and they brought burnt offerings and offerings of well-being.
5 The Israelites asked, "Is there anyone from all the tribes of
Israel who failed to come up to the assembly before the LORD?"
For a solemn oath had been taken concerning anyone who did
not go up to the LORD at Mizpah: "He shall be put to death."
6 The Israelites now relented toward their kinsmen the Benjaminites, and they said, "This day one tribe has been cut off
from Israel! 7 What can we do to provide wives for those who
are left, seeing that we have sworn by the LORD not to give any
of our daughters to them in marriage?"

8 They inquired, "Is there anyone from the tribes of Israel
who did not go up to the LORD at Mizpah?" Now no one from
Jabesh-gilead had come to the camp, to the assembly. 9 For,
when the roll of the troops was taken, not one of the inhabitants of Jabesh-gilead was present. 10 So the assemblage dispatched 12,000 of the warriors, instructing them as follows:
"Go and put the inhabitants of Jabesh-gilead to the sword,
women and children included. 11 This is what you are to do:
Proscribe every man, and every woman who has known a
man carnally." 12 They found among the inhabitants of Jabesh-
gilead 400 maidens who had not known a man carnally; and
they brought them to the camp at Shiloh, which is in the land
of Canaan.[a]

13 Then the whole community sent word to the Benjaminites
who were at the Rock of Rimmon, and offered them terms
of peace. 14 Thereupon the Benjaminites returned, and they

a I.e., west of the Jordan, while Jabesh-gilead is east of the Jordan.

the previous episode (19.2). **48:** The army of Israel treated Benjamin worse than a proscribed Canaanite city (see Deut. 20.16–18), not only destroying its population, but its property and cities too (cf. Deut. 13.13–19).

21.1–14: The war against Jabesh-gilead. The Israelite army had taken an oath at Mizpah (20.1, 3) not to marry their daughters to the Benjaminites and to put to death those who did not join the battle. In order to allow the tribe of Benjamin to continue, it was necessary to find them wives. Investigation revealed that Jabesh-gilead had not joined the war; therefore it was decided to kill its inhabitants except for the virgins, who would then be given as wives to the surviving Benjaminites. This story, which condemns Jabesh-gilead, relates to the story of Israel's war against the Midianites at the time of the wanderings in the desert (Num. ch 31), which combines putting to death the males of Midian and taking their women captive. The story thus reflects negatively on Jabesh-gilead which, according to the traditions preserved in Samuel, was closely affiliated with Saul (1 Sam. 31.11–13; 2 Sam. 2.4–7; etc.). It seems, therefore, that the intention of this story to condemn Saul is more convincing than to depict the real events of the premonarchic period. **1:** From the sequel it follows that at the gathering in Mizpah at the beginning of the war the Israelites took another oath: to put to death those who did not join in the war effort (v. 5). **2:** The people gathered at *Bethel,* which once again serves as a place for weeping (2.1–5; 20.23, 26). **5:** The purpose of the inquiry was to find out who did not participate in the gathering at Mizpah and would be subject to the death penalty, but simultaneously exempt from the oath against giving their daughters to the Benjaminites. **9:** *Jabesh-gilead* is located in the north of Gilead, but has not been precisely identified. **10–11:** Use of the typical number *12,000,* in which each 1,000 represents one tribe, as well as of the term *woman who has known a man carnally,* strengthens the connection to Num. ch 31. **12:** The maidens were brought to *Shiloh* and not to Mizpah or Bethel because of the sequel, which also takes place in Shiloh. **14:** *Returned:* The surviving men from Benjamin returned from the Rock of Rimmon to their towns, but there were still 200 left without wives.

gave them the girls who had been spared from the women of
Jabesh-gilead. [a]But there were not enough of them.[a]
15 Now the people had relented toward Benjamin, for the
LORD had made a breach in the tribes of Israel. 16 So the elders of the community asked, "What can we do about wives for
those who are left, since the women of Benjamin have been
killed off?" 17 For they said, "There must be a saving remnant
for Benjamin, that a tribe may not be blotted out of Israel; 18 yet
we cannot give them any of our daughters as wives," since the
Israelites had taken an oath: "Cursed be anyone who gives a
wife to Benjamin!"
19 They said, "The annual feast of the LORD is now being held
at Shiloh." (It lies north of Bethel, east of the highway that runs
from Bethel to Shechem, and south of Lebonah.)
20 So they instructed the Benjaminites as follows: "Go and
lie in wait in the vineyards. 21 As soon as you see the girls of
Shiloh coming out to join in the dances, come out from the
vineyards; let each of you seize a wife from among the girls of
Shiloh, and be off for the land of Benjamin. 22 And if their fathers or brothers come to us to complain, we shall say to them,
[a]'Be generous to them for our sake! We could not provide any
of them with a wife on account of the war, and you would have
incurred guilt if you yourselves had given them [wives].' "[a]
23 The Benjaminites did so. They took to wife, from the dancers whom they carried off, as many as they themselves numbered. Then they went back to their own territory, and rebuilt
their towns and settled in them. 24 Thereupon the Israelites
dispersed, each to his own tribe and clan; everyone departed
for his own territory.
25 In those days there was no king in Israel; everyone did as
he pleased.

a-a Meaning of Heb. uncertain.

21.15–25: The abduction at Shiloh. In order to resolve the problem of the 200 additional Benjaminites who were left without wives, the elders of the community suggested that the others circumvent the oath by lying in wait in the vineyards of Shiloh to abduct from there the young women dancing at the feast of the LORD. The motif of stealing women on a festival day is known from Greek (Herodotus) and Roman (Livy) literature. The story connecting Benjamin with Shiloh prepares the ground for the decline of the town's status in the days of Eli and his sons in the following book of Samuel. **15:** The blow struck to the Benjaminites harmed the overall structure of the Israelite tribes. **19:** *The annual feast:* It is not clear what feast this refers to. According to Josephus this was one of the three pilgrimage festivals, while a rabbinic tradition knows of a similar festival commemorated on the 15th of Av (the fifth month, in the mid-summer) or the Day of Atonement (*m. Ta'an.* 4.8). It may simply refer to a local grape-harvest festival similar to the vintage festival in Shechem (9.27). The detailed geographical description of Shiloh's location is unusual in the Bible, suggesting that it may be an addition from the period when Shiloh, which is identified with Khirbet Sailun, north of Bethel, was destroyed. **20:** The Heb for *lie in wait* is the same as "ambush" in the previous episode (e.g., 20.29), tying the two together and implying the warlike character of the situation. **22:** *Fathers or brothers* were generally responsible for their daughters' or sisters' marriage. The continuation of this v. is unclear in Heb. **24:** Once a solution had been found, the Israelites left Bethel and returned to their own territories. The end of the final section of Judges returns to the end of the first sections (2.6). **25:** The book concludes with the motto that expresses disappointment in the judges and hope in the monarchy. Given the negative associations in the story with Saul, it is the Davidic monarchy, established in the following book of Samuel, to which Judges looks forward.

שמואל א

1 Samuel

Name and Contents

THE BOOKS OF SAMUEL were originally one book. In the Septuagint (LXX) it was divided into two, owing to its length, and the Christian tradition followed this division. In Hebrew Bibles used by the Jewish community, this division was not accepted until the 15th century, under the influence of the Vulgate. Following a pattern found in some other biblical books, which end with the death of a main character, the division in the book of Samuel was made at the point of Saul's death. Thus, 1 Samuel recounts the periods of Eli (chs 1–4), Samuel (chs 5–12), and Saul (chs 13–31); 2 Samuel tells of the reign of David, although David, before he became king, is a central character for much of the end of 1 Samuel. In the Hebrew tradition, the work was named after the prophet Samuel (*b. B. Bat.* 14b), because the story of his birth opens the book and he is the principal figure in the first part. According to the book that bears his name, he greatly influenced events during his life and even after his death, since he anointed the first two kings, whose actions and fate occupy the major part of the book of Samuel. In the Greek tradition, the books are called 1 and 2 Kingdoms, and are followed by 3 and 4 Kingdoms, our 1–2 Kings, thereby tying together more tightly the books that deal with the rise and fall of the monarchy in ancient Israel.

The book of Samuel consists chiefly of narratives, which are supplemented with a few songs, lists, and brief notices. Its central concern is with the personal lives of the leaders. Their aspirations, feelings, and passions are depicted realistically, displaying negative qualities as well as positive ones. Through the events of their lives the main ideas of the book are expressed. As a rule, human beings, not God, occupy the central stage, their lot being determined by their conduct. God acts behind the scenes, usually refraining from direct, supernatural intervention, shaping individual destinies through the natural course of events. The ancient Near East offers no other example of such a long, extended and detailed narrative focused on such a brief time period.

Samuel, whose biography begins before his birth and extends after his death, acted as both judge and prophet. Saul, the first king, who led Israel after Samuel, is depicted in most of the book as an unstable character. When he tries to free himself from Samuel's stern tutelage, a break ensues between the two men, and Saul is rejected in favor of David—the focal figure in both books. David, as opposed to Saul, is generally portrayed in a favorable light. His personality is many-faceted and richer than any other figure in the Bible. He is a strong leader, successful in war and peace, a gifted musician and poet, deeply religious, endowed with a strong sense of justice, respectful and loyal towards Saul. Only in his dealings with his children does he appear weak. He sins, abusing his power, but repents wholeheartedly. At the peak of his reign he receives God's promise that his dynasty will reign forever.

Background

THE BOOK OF SAMUEL describes the transition from the rule of the judges to the monarchic system of government. It tells of the foundation of the monarchy and its early struggles, paying special attention to questions concerning the rights, duties, and restrictions of the kings. It depicts how, through clashes between King Saul and the prophet Samuel, and between King David and the prophet Nathan, a type of kingship emerged that radically differed from the absolute kingship prevalent in the ancient Near East. According to the Bible, kings in Israel were not allowed to do whatever they fancied. They were subject to a higher power and to the rule of law and morality (see esp. Deut. 17.14–20), upheld by the prophets.

The book also deals with the transfer of government from the old leaders to the new. Though hereditary succession was not unknown (see esp. Judg. chs 6–9), the three leaders Eli, Samuel, and Saul were not succeeded by their sons, but by others—each of whom had initially been under the patronage of his predecessor. The transfer was effected smoothly in the case of Eli and Samuel, with difficulty in the case of Samuel and Saul, and with bitter conflict in the case of Saul and David, culminating in Saul's recurring attempts to kill David.

Literary Form

THE BOOK OF SAMUEL is a work of literary art and is best read as such. Though only partly visible in translation, the literary and stylistic features are unmistakable, bearing witness to the book's artistry. The narratives excel in dramatic force and human appeal. Almost all contain a large amount of direct speech, which gives them their vivid character. Some are made up almost exclusively of direct speech, as in the narrative of Saul, who went to look for his father's asses and was anointed king of Israel (9.1–10.16). Though numerous, conversations are usually brief, including only what is essential for the development of the plot. The same holds true for descriptions. Unlike conversations, however, descriptions of people, places, and objects are relatively rare and in many narratives wholly absent. This is typical of most biblical literature, and plays an important role in expressing or highlighting the narratives' ideas and values and impressing them on the readers. The book's literary character has no bearing on the question of its historical veracity, since both fact and fiction may be cast in an aesthetic mold. The book, however, should not be understood as a straightforward history of the early monarchic period. The goals of the book are theological and political, rather than a straightforward telling of the history of the early monarchy.

Text

A CONSIDERABLE NUMBER OF CORRUPTIONS are found in the traditional Hebrew text of Samuel, generally resulting from scribal errors. For instance, 13.1 reads literally "Saul was a year old when he became king and he reigned over Israel two years." It is clear that a number was accidentally omitted before the word "year" ("a" is not expressed in Heb). The number "two" at the end of the sentence is also implausible because it seems quite impossible to accommodate all the events of Saul's kingship within a span of two years (see, e.g., 27.7). (See also 1 Sam. 11.1–13 n.) In some cases it is possible to correct the Masoretic Text of Samuel with the help of alternative texts. Parallel passages to Samuel, containing partly divergent readings, are found in the book of Psalms and the book of Chronicles. Among the Dead Sea Scrolls fragments of four different manuscripts of Samuel have been discovered, which contain pre-Masoretic texts. The LXX and other ancient translations also testify to different readings. In some cases even *Antiquities of the Jews* by Josephus, whose readings are often similar to those of the LXX and one of the Dead Sea manuscripts, may be helpful. The following annotations will be based on the Hebrew Masoretic Text and the NJPS translation, but whenever the text seems corrupt, attention will be paid to alternative readings.

Composition

SEVERAL STORIES IN THE BOOK OF SAMUEL occur twice, though in different versions. Cases in point include the stories about the election of Saul (9.15–10.9; 10.20–24), his rejection by Samuel (13.8–14; 15.9–33), David's first meeting with Saul (16.14–23; 17.31–37, 55–58), the killing of Goliath (in one case by David, in the other by Elhanan, 17.40–51; 2 Sam. 21.19), Saul's attempt to kill David by throwing his spear at him (18.10–11; 19.9–10), David's escape from Saul (19.11–12; 20.1–21.1), his taking refuge with Achish (21.11–16; 27.1–28.2; 29.1–11), and his refusal to kill Saul when he had the opportunity to do so (24.1–22; 26.1–25). The origin of the saying, "Is Saul too among the prophets?" is explained twice and in different ways (10.10–12; 19.18–24), and there are two divergent accounts of Saul's death (31.1–7; 2 Sam. 1.3–10).

Different versions of the same story, which are often met with in folk tales, arose, in all likelihood, when these stories were transmitted orally, before they were written down. Consistency was not considered essential by the editor(s) who compiled these earlier tales into a single book, especially since multiple stories, even if contradictory, could shed light on the protagonists.

Jewish sources ascribe the composition of the book of Samuel to Samuel himself (*b. B. Bat.* 14b). But since his death is already recorded in 1 Sam. ch 25, the prophets Gad and Nathan, who are mentioned together with Samuel as the authors of a history of David (1 Chron. 29.29), are said to have finished the work (*b. B. Bat.* 15a). In the book of Samuel itself one source is mentioned: the Book of Jashar, from which David's elegy for Saul and Jonathan was taken (2 Sam. 1.18).

Biblical scholarship has posited a plurality of sources. In this respect three main theories have been put forward. First, like the Torah, the book of Samuel is composed of two or three parallel and continuous narrative strands, which run through the whole length of the book. This view was current in the 19th and the beginning of the 20th centuries, and has largely, and correctly, been abandoned. Second, the book of Samuel consists of many single, independent narratives. Third, the book of Samuel is a compilation of large thematic units—such as the Ark narrative, the Saul cycle, the history of David's rise, the so-called succession narrative (which continues into the first chs of Kings)—which are not parallel, but arranged one after the other. Most scholars hold that the book of Samuel should be read as part of the Deuteronomistic History (Deuteronomy-Kings), and was also subjected to a Deuteronomistic redaction (that is, based on the tenets of the book of Deuteronomy), but it is generally agreed that this redaction was much slighter than in the book of Judges or the book of Kings. Some scholars assume a prophetic stratum between the older narrative material and the Deuteronomistic redaction. There is likely truth in the second and third models, and thus many hands have contributed to the formation of the book of Samuel, as is also borne out by the differences in plot, style and narrative method. Thus various sources have been unified into one whole.

In its final form the book of Samuel, and particularly the figures of David and Saul, have had a great impact on Jewish and Western thought and art. Many compositions—religious, moral, and political—as well as innumerable works of poetry, drama, narrative prose, painting, sculpture, and music have been influenced by them, and they continue to be a source of inspiration even today.

[SHIMON BAR-EFRAT, Z"L, REVISED BY MARC ZVI BRETTLER]

1 There was a man from [a-]Ramathaim of the Zuphites,[-a] in the
hill country of Ephraim, whose name was Elkanah son of
Jeroham son of Elihu son of Tohu son of Zuph, an Ephraimite.
2 He had two wives, one named Hannah and the other Peninnah; Peninnah had children, but Hannah was childless. 3 This
man used to go up from his town every year to worship and
to offer sacrifice to the LORD of Hosts at Shiloh.—Hophni and
Phinehas, the two sons of Eli, were priests of the LORD there.
4 One such day, Elkanah offered a sacrifice. He used to give
portions to his wife Peninnah and to all her sons and daughters;
5 but to Hannah he would give one portion [b-]only—though[-b]
Hannah was his favorite—for the LORD had closed her womb.
6 Moreover, her rival, to make her miserable, would taunt her
that the LORD had closed her womb. 7 [c-]This happened[-c] year
after year: Every time she went up to the House of the LORD,
the other would taunt her, so that she wept and would not eat.
8 Her husband Elkanah said to her, "Hannah, why are you crying and why aren't you eating? Why are you so sad? Am I not
more devoted to you than ten sons?"
9 After they had eaten and drunk at Shiloh, Hannah rose.[d]—
The priest Eli was sitting on the seat near the doorpost of the
temple of the LORD.— 10 In her wretchedness, she prayed to
the LORD, weeping all the while. 11 And she made this vow:
"O LORD of Hosts, if You will look upon the suffering of Your
maidservant and will remember me and not forget Your maidservant, and if You will grant Your maidservant a male child, I
will dedicate him to the LORD for all the days of his life; and no
razor shall ever touch his head."
12 As she kept on praying before the LORD, Eli watched her
mouth. 13 Now Hannah was praying in her heart; only her lips

a-a Heb. "Ramathaim-zophim." In 1.19, 2.11, 7.17, 15.34, 19.18, etc., the town is called Ramah; and 9.5 ff. shows that it was in the district of Zuph.
b-b Meaning of Heb. uncertain. *c-c Lit. "Thus he did."*
d Septuagint adds "and stood before the LORD."

1.1–2.11a: The vow. The book of Samuel begins with the story of the remarkable birth of Samuel. The focus is on Samuel's mother, who was barren and so desperate for a child that she vowed to part from him and dedicate him to God, if her prayer for a son were answered. The motif of formerly barren women who give birth to national leaders or ancestors is well attested in the Bible (Sarah, Rebekah, Rachel, Samson's mother; see Gen. 21.1–8; 25.19–26; 30.1–2, 22–24; Judg. 13.2–3, 24), the exceptional birth hinting at divine concern and purpose for the child. The narrative gives details about the persons, the background, and relevant customs in three parts. The first part takes place at Shiloh, the second at Ramah, and the third at Shiloh again. Sections of the the episode in 2.18–21 round off the story. **1:** The list of Elkanah's ancestors shows that he was of distinguished lineage. The exact location of *Ramathaim,* lit. "double heights," is uncertain, though see the map on p. 551. **2:** Polygyny was allowed and probably widely practiced in well-to-do families. **3:** The Ark of the LORD was housed in the sanctuary *at Shiloh.* The information concerning the worship every year at Shiloh links the beginning of the book of Samuel with the end of the book of Judges, where an annual feast of God at Shiloh is mentioned (Judg. 21.19). The two sons of Eli, who have Egyptian names, are mentioned because the stories about Samuel anticipate their role in the following ch. **5:** *One portion only—though:* The Heb may also be interpreted, "one twofold portion—for" (cf. the fivefold portion Joseph gave to Benjamin, Gen. 43.34); this interpretation better explains Peninnah's reaction. **6:** Fertility is understood throughout the Bible as a divine gift. Barrenness, here understood as *the LORD* closing a woman's *womb,* was considered humiliating, causing great distress to the woman who suffered from it (e.g., Gen. 30.1, 22–23). **7:** Peninnah is the opposite of Hannah. Not only does Peninnah have many children, whereas Hannah has none, but Peninnah deliberately hurts her rival, while Hannah refrains from paying back, weeping in silence. The *House of the LORD* may refer to local temples (e.g., Judg. 19.18), and would later refer to the Temple in Jerusalem (e.g., 1 Kings 9.10). **8:** *Am I not more devoted to you than ten sons,* cf. Ruth 4.15, which uses the number seven instead of ten. **9:** Though Hannah does not eat, she waits until all have finished their meal. **11:** The structure of Hannah's vow is typical of vows in the Bible: First a condition is stated, and this is followed by a commitment if the condition is fulfilled (cf. Gen. 28.20–22; Judg. 11.30–31). Here the vow is preceded by an invocation of God. Long hair was characteristic of Nazirites, who devoted themselves to God (Num. 6.5). The word "Nazirite" is used by the LXX in the present v. and by the Dead Sea manuscript 4QSam[a] in v. 22, and Samuel is also called a Nazirite in the postbiblical book of Sirach (46.13). Later Judaism recognized Hannah's prayer as the basis for statutory prayer (*b. Ber.* 31a-b). **13:** Silent prayer was uncommon;

moved, but her voice could not be heard. So Eli thought she was drunk. 14 Eli said to her, "How long will you make a drunken spectacle of yourself? [a-]Sober up!"[-a] 15 And Hannah replied, "Oh no, my lord! I am a very unhappy woman. I have drunk no wine or other strong drink, but I have been pouring out my heart to the LORD. 16 Do not take your maidservant for a worthless woman; I have only been speaking all this time out of my great anguish and distress." 17 "Then go in peace," said Eli, "and may the God of Israel grant you what you have asked of Him." 18 She answered, "You are most kind to your handmaid." So the woman left, and she ate, and was no longer downcast. 19 Early next morning they bowed low before the LORD, and they went back home to Ramah.

Elkanah knew[b] his wife Hannah and the LORD remembered her. 20 Hannah conceived, and at the turn of the year bore a son. She named him Samuel,[c] meaning, "I asked the LORD for him." 21 And when the man Elkanah and all his household were going up to offer to the LORD the annual sacrifice and his votive sacrifice, 22 Hannah did not go up. She said to her husband, "When the child is weaned, I will bring him. For when he has appeared before the LORD, he must remain there for good." 23 Her husband Elkanah said to her, "Do as you think best. Stay home until you have weaned him. May the LORD fulfill [d-]His word."[-d] So the woman stayed home and nursed her son until she weaned him.

24 When she had weaned him, she took him up with her, along with [e-]three bulls,[-e] one *ephah* of flour, and a jar of wine. And [f-]though the boy was still very young,[-f] she brought him to the House of the LORD at Shiloh. 25 After slaughtering the bull, they brought the boy to Eli. 26 She said, "Please, my lord! As you live, my lord, I am the woman who stood here beside you and prayed to the LORD. 27 It was this boy I prayed for; and the LORD has granted me what I asked of Him. 28 I, in turn, hereby lend[g] him to the LORD. For as long as he lives he is lent to the LORD." And they[h] bowed low there before the LORD.

a-a Lit. "Remove your wine from you."
b Cf. note at Gen. 4.1.
c Connected with sha'ul me'el *"asked of God"; cf. vv. 17, 27–28.*
d-d Septuagint and 4QSam[a] (a Samuel fragment from Qumran) read "the utterance of your mouth." The translators express their thanks to Professor Frank M. Cross, Jr., for graciously making available to them copies of his unpublished Samuel fragments.
e-e Septuagint and 4QSam[a] read "a three-year-old [cf. Gen. 15.9] bull and bread"; cf. v. 25.
f-f Meaning of Heb. uncertain.
g From the same root as that of the verb rendered "asked for" in v. 20.
h Heb. "he"; cf. 2.11. A reading in the Talmud (Berakhot 61a) implies that Elkanah was there.

the text suggests that there was nothing unusual about a woman praying. **19:** *They went back home:* This phrase often serves to mark the end of a story or an episode (e.g., 2.11). *The LORD remembered her:* This is shown when Hannah's womb is opened (see v. 11), enabling her to conceive. **20:** The verb "sha'al" (= ask) recurs in the narrative several times, more than is expressed in the translation (see also 2.20); oddly, it is more associated with Saul's name (Heb sha'ul) rather than Samuel's (Heb shemu'el), suggesting to some that this story originally told of Saul's, not Samuel's birth. **22:** Weaning used to take place after several years; according to 2 Macc. 7.27 after three years. **24:** *One ephah,* about 23 liters (21 quarts). **27:** Hannah uses the same words as Eli did before (v. 17), to indicate to the priest that his blessing has materialized. **28:** *Lend* in the sense of dedicate him for temple service as a type of priest; in contrast to the priestly material in the Torah, this story assumes that those not descended from Levi or Aaron may officiate in temples.

2 And Hannah prayed:

My heart exults in the LORD;
[a-]I have triumphed[-a] through the LORD.
[b-]I gloat[-b] over my enemies;
I rejoice in Your deliverance.

2 There is no holy one like the LORD,
Truly, there is none beside You;
There is no rock like our God.

3 Talk no more with lofty pride,
Let no arrogance cross your lips!
For the LORD is an all-knowing God;
By Him actions are measured.

4 The bows of the mighty are broken,
And the faltering are girded with strength.
5 Men once sated must hire out for bread;
Men once hungry hunger no more.
While the barren woman bears seven,
The mother of many is forlorn.
6 The LORD deals death and gives life,
Casts down into Sheol and raises up.
7 The LORD makes poor and makes rich;
He casts down, He also lifts high.
8 He raises the poor from the dust,
Lifts up the needy from the dunghill,
Setting them with nobles,
Granting them seats of honor.
For the pillars of the earth are the LORD's;
He has set the world upon them.
9 He guards the steps of His faithful,
But the wicked perish in darkness—
For not by strength shall man prevail.

10 The foes of the LORD shall be shattered;
He will thunder against them in the heavens.
The LORD will judge the ends of the earth.
He will give power to His king,
[c-]And triumph to[-c] His anointed one.

a-a Lit. *"My horn is high."* *b-b* Lit. *"My mouth is wide."*
c-c Lit. *"And will raise the horn of."*

2.1–10: Hannah's song, which is similar in style and content to certain psalms (cf. v. 8 with Ps. 113.7–8), expresses thanks and praise to God for a victory over an enemy. It fits neither Hannah's situation nor her personality. Moreover, a king is mentioned in v. 10, whereas at Hannah's time the monarchy had not yet been established in Israel. The song was probably a self-standing composition put in Hannah's mouth. V. 5, *while the barren woman bears seven,* suggests Hannah's situation, as does the psalm's general idea, that God often completely reverses the fortunes of human beings. This idea of reversal is underscored by the contrasts between or within the lines of the parallelisms in the central part of the song. **1:** The horn (see translators' note *a-a*), a symbol of strength (Deut. 33.17), is mentioned in the Heb text both at the beginning and the end of the song, thus stressing the idea of triumph. **2:** The middle of the v. prevents understanding the rest as if other gods existed. *Rock* may also be translated as "mountain," the image is of height and/or strength and stability. **3:** Here the enemies are addressed. The thought that God is all-knowing does not pervade the Bible (see e.g., Gen. 22.12, "For now I know"), though the idea and vocabulary used here is also found in Prov. 24.12, and other wisdom motifs pervade the poem. **5:** The number *seven* denotes multiplicity, and perfection. **6–8a:** The LORD is the cause of all changes in life. **6:** *Sheol,* the place beneath the earth, where, according to biblical belief, all people go after death. Sheol differs from the "'olam haba'" (the next world), the belief in which developed in Judaism in the Second Temple period, because in Sheol there is no retribution and all its inhabitants are equal, without regard to their former status or behavior in life. Raising up from Sheol, a common biblical motif, does not refer to resurrection from death—a later belief as well—but to deliverance from near death (see Ps. 30.4 n.). **8:** *Dust* and *dunghill* are metaphorical for utter degradation. The earth was believed to be flat and resting upon pillars. **9:** *Not by strength,* but by the LORD's providence (see similarly 8.18). **10:** *The ends of the earth,* all peoples, even the most remote ones. *His anointed one* (Heb "mashiah," from which comes the English word "messiah") denotes the king, since kings were

[11] Then Elkanah[a] [and Hannah] went home to Ramah; and the
boy entered the service of the LORD under the priest Eli.
[12] Now Eli's sons were scoundrels; they paid no heed to
the LORD. [13] This is how the priests used to deal with the people: When anyone brought a sacrifice, the priest's boy would
come along with a three-pronged fork while the meat was boiling, [14] and he would thrust it into [b]the cauldron, or the kettle,
or the great pot, or the small cooking-pot;[b] and whatever the
fork brought up, the priest would take away [c]on it.[c] This was
the practice at Shiloh with all the Israelites who came there.

a See note h at 1.28. *b-b These vessels have not been distinguished precisely.*
c-c Targum and Septuagint add "for himself."

anointed with oil; the use of "messiah" for the future ideal Davidic king is postbiblical. **11a:** See 1.19 n.

2.11b–36: Ascent versus descent. Samuel's ascent is contrasted with the descent of the house of Eli, both processes taking place simultaneously at the sanctuary of Shiloh. Most of the space is allotted to the house of Eli, highlighting that leaders who abuse their office and exploit their people will not escape punishment. In the first part (vv. 12–17) the recurring sins of Eli's

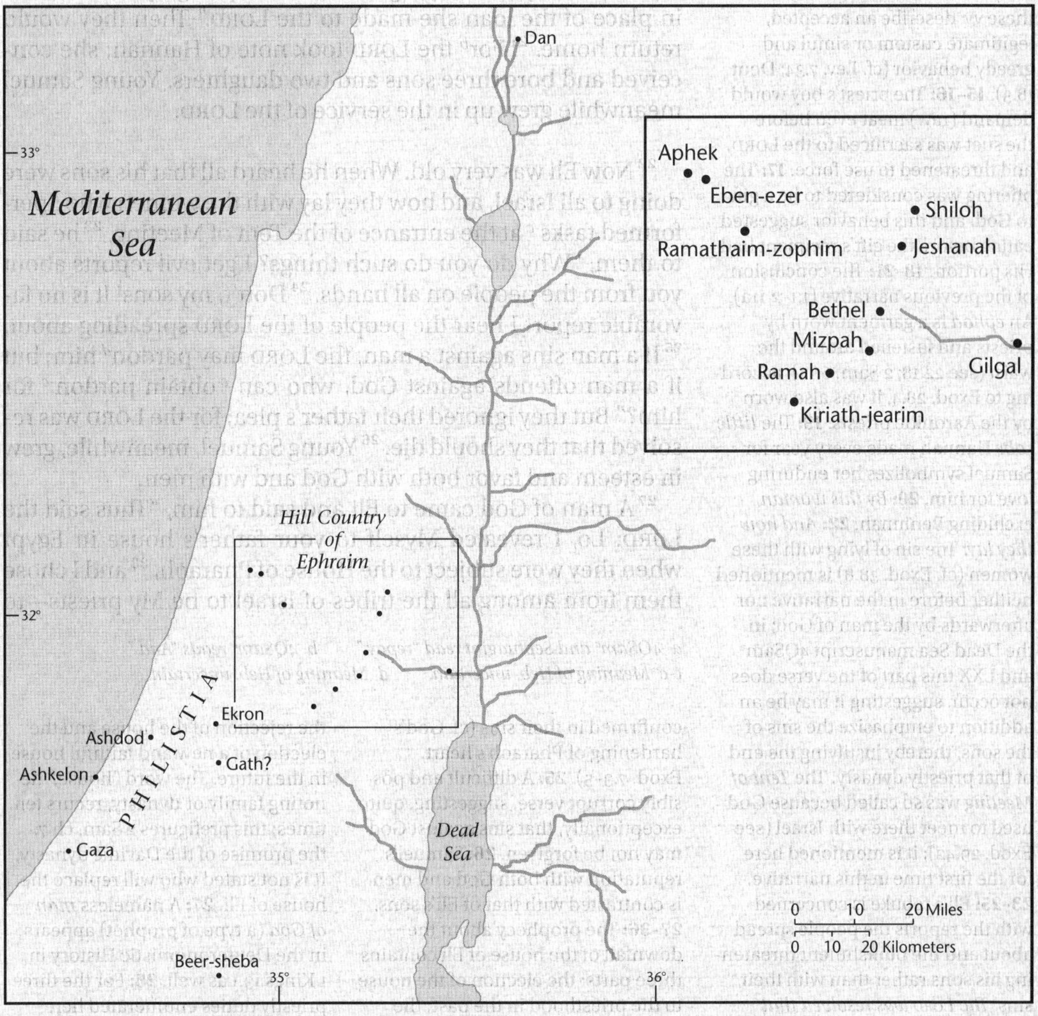

The activity of Samuel according to First Samuel

15 [But now] even before the suet was turned into smoke, the
priest's boy would come and say to the man who was sacrificing,
"Hand over some meat to roast for the priest; for he won't accept
boiled meat from you, only raw." 16 And if the man said to him,
"Let them first turn the suet into smoke, and then take as much
as you want," he would reply, "No, hand it over at once or I'll take
it by force." 17 The sin of the young men against the LORD was
very great, for the men treated the LORD's offerings impiously.
18 Samuel was engaged in the service of the LORD as an attendant, girded with a linen ephod. 19 His mother would also
make a little robe for him and bring it up to him every year,
when she made the pilgrimage with her husband to offer
the annual sacrifice. 20 Eli would bless Elkanah and his wife,
and say, "May the LORD grant[a] you offspring by this woman
in place of the loan she made to the LORD." Then they would
return home. 21 For[b] the LORD took note of Hannah; she conceived and bore three sons and two daughters. Young Samuel
meanwhile grew up in the service of the LORD.

22 Now Eli was very old. When he heard all that his sons were
doing to all Israel, and how they lay with the women who [c-]per-
formed tasks[-c] at the entrance of the Tent of Meeting, 23 he said
to them, "Why do you do such things? I get evil reports about
you from the people on all hands. 24 Don't, my sons! It is no favorable report I hear the people of the LORD spreading about.
25 If a man sins against a man, the LORD may pardon[d] him; but
if a man offends against God, who can [c-]obtain pardon[-c] for
him?" But they ignored their father's plea; for the LORD was resolved that they should die. 26 Young Samuel, meanwhile, grew
in esteem and favor both with God and with men.
27 A man of God came to Eli and said to him, "Thus said the
LORD: Lo, I revealed Myself to your father's house in Egypt
when they were subject to the House of Pharaoh, 28 and I chose
them from among all the tribes of Israel to be My priests—to

a 4QSam[a] and Septuagint read "repay." *b 4QSam[a] reads "And."*
c-c Meaning of Heb. uncertain. *d Meaning of Heb. uncertain.*

sons are described; the second part (vv. 22–25) tells how Eli reprimanded them, which they ignore; and the third part (vv. 27–36) specifies the future punishment to the House of Eli. These parts alternate with short pieces of information about Samuel. **11b:** Both context and the syntax of the Heb suggest that this opens a new episode, contrary to the v. divisions. **12:** It is unusual for a biblical narrator to judge the characters explicitly; here he does so because of the graveness of their sins (see also v. 17). *They paid no heed,* lit. "they did not know" (similarly e.g., Judg. 2.10). **13–14:** It is uncertain whether these vv. describe an accepted, legitimate custom or sinful and greedy behavior (cf. Lev. 7.34; Deut. 18.3). **15–16:** The priest's boy would demand (raw) meat even before the suet was sacrificed to the LORD, and threatened to use force. **17:** The offering was considered to be a gift to God, and this behavior suggested eating before the gift's recipient had His portion. **18–21:** The conclusion of the previous narrative (1.1–2.11a). An *ephod* is a garment worn by priests and fastened around the waist (see 22.18; 2 Sam. 6.14); according to Exod. 28.4, it was also worn by the Aaronide priests. **19:** The *little robe* Hannah made every year for Samuel symbolizes her enduring love for him. **20:** *By this woman,* excluding Peninnah. **22:** *And how they lay:* The sin of lying with these women (cf. Exod. 38.8) is mentioned neither before in the narrative nor afterwards by the man of God; in the Dead Sea manuscript 4QSam[a] and LXX this part of the verse does not occur, suggesting it may be an addition to emphasize the sins of the sons, thereby justifying the end of that priestly dynasty. The *Tent of Meeting* was so called because God used to meet there with Israel (see Exod. 29.42); it is mentioned here for the first time in this narrative. **23–25:** Eli's rebuke is concerned with the reports the people spread about and the punishment threatening his sons rather than with their sins. *The LORD was resolved that they should die,* because they were confirmed in their sins (cf. God's hardening of Pharaoh's heart, Exod. 7.3–5). **25:** A difficult and possibly corrupt verse, suggesting, quite exceptionally, that sins against God may not be forgiven. **26:** Samuel's reputation with both God and men is contrasted with that of Eli's sons. **27–36:** The prophecy about the downfall of the house of Eli contains three parts: the election of the house to the priesthood in the past; the abuse of its office in the present; the rejection of the house and the election of a new and faithful house in the future. The word "house," denoting family or dynasty, recurs ten times; this prefigures 2 Sam. ch 7, the promise of the Davidic dynasty. It is not stated who will replace the house of Eli. **27:** A nameless *man of God* (a type of prophet) appears in the Deuteronomistic History in 1 Kings 13.1 as well. **28:** For the three priestly duties enumerated here see Deut. 33.8–10. **30:** This promise

ascend My altar, to burn incense, [and] to carry an ephod[a] before Me—and I assigned to your father's house all offerings by fire of the Israelites. 29 Why, then, do you [b]maliciously trample upon the sacrifices and offerings that I have commanded?[-b] You have honored your sons more than Me, feeding on the first portions of every offering of My people Israel.[c] 30 Assuredly—declares the LORD, the God of Israel—I intended for you and your father's house to remain in My service forever. But now—declares the LORD—far be it from Me! For I honor those who honor Me, but those who spurn Me shall be dishonored. 31 A time is coming when I will break your power and that of your father's house, and there shall be no elder in your house. 32 You will gaze grudgingly[d] at all the bounty that will be bestowed on Israel, but there shall never be an elder in your house. 33[e]I shall not cut off all your offspring from My altar; [but,] to make your eyes pine and your spirit languish, all the increase in your house shall die as [ordinary] men.[-e] 34 And this shall be a sign for you: The fate of your two sons Hophni and Phinehas—they shall both die on the same day. 35 And I will raise up for Myself a faithful priest, who will act in accordance with My wishes and My purposes. I will build for him an enduring house, and he shall walk before My anointed evermore. 36 And all the survivors of your house shall come and bow low to him for the sake of a money fee and a loaf of bread, and shall say, 'Please, assign me to one of the priestly duties, that I may have a morsel of bread to eat.'"

3 Young Samuel was in the service of the LORD under Eli. In those days the word of the LORD was rare; prophecy was not widespread. 2 One day, Eli was asleep in his usual place; his eyes had begun to fail and he could barely see. 3 The lamp of God had not yet gone out, and Samuel was sleeping in the temple of the LORD where the Ark of God was. 4 The LORD called out to Samuel, and he answered, "I'm coming." 5 He ran to Eli and said, "Here I am; you called me." But he replied, "I didn't call you; go back to sleep." So he went back and lay down. 6 Again the LORD called, "Samuel!" Samuel rose and went to Eli and said, "Here I am; you called me." But he replied, "I didn't

a *Here a device for obtaining oracles (cf. 14.3; 23.6, 9–12), not a garment as in v. 18 above.*

b-b *Meaning of Heb. uncertain. Emendation yields "gaze [cf. Septuagint] grudgingly upon the sacrifices and offerings which I have commanded" (connecting* maʿon *with* ʿoyen, *"keeping a jealous eye"; see 1 Sam. 18.9); cf. v. 32 and note d below.*

c *See vv. 15–16.* *d* *Cf. note b-b above.* *e-e* *Meaning of Heb. uncertain.*

is not elsewhere preserved; quite remarkably, an eternal promise (note *forever*) is revoked by God. **31:** *And there shall be no elder in your house* is repeated in the next v.; in the Dead Sea manuscript 4QSam[a] and LXX these words do not occur in the present v. **33:** *Shall die as ... men:* The Dead Sea manuscript 4QSam[a] and LXX read "shall fall by the sword of men." This may refer to the massacre of the priests of Nob (ch 22). **34:** For identical language, see 2 Kings 19.29 (and Isa. 38.7). **35:** *Faithful* and *enduring:* The Heb uses the same word, indicating that because the priest will be faithful, his house shall be enduring. Possibly the priest meant is Zadok, who replaced Abiathar, a descendant of Eli (1 Kings 2.26–27). *My anointed,* see v. 10 n.

3.1–4.1a: Revelation. God's revelation to Samuel, which elevates him to the rank of prophet, contains a second message of calamity to the house of Eli. The narrative consists of five parts: an introduction, dialogues between Eli and Samuel, the revelation (in the center), again dialogue between Eli and Samuel, and a conclusion. The humor at the beginning of the unit tempers its more serious message. **1–3:** The exposition supplies the background information. Because *the word of the LORD was rare* and *prophecy* (i.e., revelations) *was not widespread,* neither Samuel nor Eli recognizes at first who is calling. In this way an ironic situation is created (dramatic irony). Samuel, who waits upon the almost blind Eli, sleeps near the Ark of God (from where God's voice is heard, see Exod. 25.22; Num. 7.89). *The lamp of God,* which used to burn from evening to morning (cf. Exod. 27.20–21), *had not yet gone out*—so it is still night, a frequent time for revelations in the Bible and the ancient Near Eastern world. *The Ark of God,* see 4.4 n. **4–9:** Because Samuel is humble and inexperienced, and because visions were not frequent, it does not enter Samuel's mind that it is God who is calling to him. Though aware that Samuel was mistaken before, he again and again gets up and goes to Eli. By repeating the situation with slight changes, the narrative builds dramatic tension. **6:** To reassure Samuel, Eli fondly adds *my son.*

call, my son; go back to sleep."—7 Now Samuel had not yet experienced the LORD; the word of the LORD had not yet been revealed to him.—8 The LORD called Samuel again, a third time, and he rose and went to Eli and said, "Here I am; you called me." Then Eli understood that the LORD was calling the boy. 9 And Eli said to Samuel, "Go lie down. If you are called again, say, 'Speak, LORD, for Your servant is listening.'" And Samuel went to his place and lay down.

10 The LORD came, and stood there, and He called as before: "Samuel! Samuel!" And Samuel answered, "Speak, for Your servant is listening." 11 The LORD said to Samuel: "I am going to do in Israel such a thing that both ears of anyone who hears about it will tingle. 12 In that day I will fulfill against Eli all that I spoke concerning his house, from beginning to end. 13 And I declare to him that I sentence his house to endless punishment for the iniquity he knew about—how his sons committed sacrilege [a]at will[-a]—and he did not rebuke them. 14 Assuredly, I swear concerning the house of Eli that the iniquity of the house of Eli will never be expiated by sacrifice or offering."

15 Samuel lay there until morning; and then he opened the doors of the House of the LORD. Samuel was afraid to report the vision to Eli, 16 but Eli summoned Samuel and said, "Samuel, my son"; and he answered, "Here." 17 And [Eli] asked, "What did He say to you? Keep nothing from me. [b]Thus and more may God do to you[-b] if you keep from me a single word of all that He said to you!" 18 Samuel then told him everything, withholding nothing from him. And [Eli] said, "He is the LORD; He will do what He deems right."

a-a Meaning of Heb. uncertain. Septuagint reads "against God."
b-b A formula of adjuration.

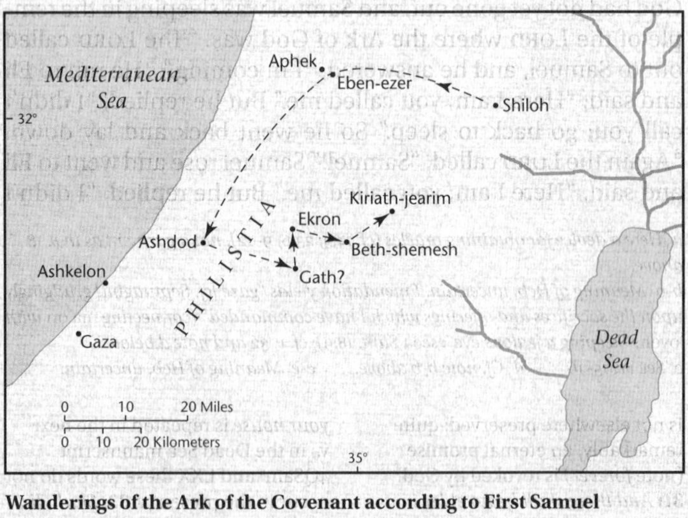

Wanderings of the Ark of the Covenant according to First Samuel

7: The v. explains why at the third call the inexperienced Samuel still does not understand who is calling, whereas Eli now realizes that it is the LORD. **10:** Samuel's state of awe causes him not to add "LORD" in his response, as Eli has instructed him to do. Other instances of God standing before a human are Gen. 28.13 (of Jacob/Israel) and Exod. 34.5 (Moses). **11–14:** In the first half of the revelation God announces His intention to inflict dreadful calamities upon Israel and the house of Eli; in the second half He states the reason why He will do so and will not forgive them. Though repentance is a major theme in the Bible, not all sins may be forgiven. **11:** *Both ears ... will tingle:* The figure refers to the shock felt at learning of a terrible disaster (see 2 Kings 21.12; Jer. 19.3). **12:** *All that I spoke,* through the man of God (2.27–36). **13:** According to Jewish tradition *at will* is a "scribes' emendation." Initially the Heb text read, "against God" (like LXX), but this was changed by the ancient scribes to avoid affronting His dignity. *Not rebuke,* better, "not restrain." Eli did rebuke his sons (see 2.23–25), though insufficiently. **14:** *Sacrifice or offering* will not atone, as they were trampled upon (2.29). *Will never be* harks back to the promise in 2.30, that they would "remain in My service forever." **15:** *He opened the doors:* In spite of his numinous experience Samuel continues to carry out his daily duties as usual. He does not report the vision to Eli so as not to distress him. **16:** *My son ... here,* a reprise of the dialogue of the previous night (v. 6). **17:** *Thus and more,* disproportionately found in Samuel (e.g., 2 Sam. 3.9, 35), in a formula of adjuration refers to harmful occurrences, which the adjurer shrinks from mentioning explicitly.

19 Samuel grew up and the LORD was with him: He did not
leave any of Samuel's[a] predictions unfulfilled. 20 All Israel,
from Dan to Beer-sheba, knew that Samuel was trustworthy as
a prophet of the LORD. 21 And the LORD continued to appear
at Shiloh: the LORD revealed Himself to Samuel at Shiloh with
4 the word of the LORD; 1 and Samuel's word went forth to
all Israel.
[b]Israel marched out to engage the Philistines in battle; they
encamped near Eben-ezer, while the Philistines encamped at
Aphek. 2 The Philistines arrayed themselves against Israel; and
when the battle was fought,[c] Israel was routed by the Philistines, who slew about four thousand men on the field of battle.
3 When the [Israelite] troops returned to the camp, the elders of
Israel asked, "Why did the LORD put us to rout today before the
Philistines? Let us fetch the Ark of the Covenant of the LORD
from Shiloh; thus He will be present among us and will deliver
us from the hands of our enemies." 4 So the troops sent men
to Shiloh; there Eli's two sons, Hophni and Phinehas, were in
charge of the Ark of the Covenant of God, and they brought
down from there the Ark of the Covenant of the LORD of Hosts
Enthroned on the Cherubim.
5 When the Ark of the Covenant of the LORD entered the
camp, all Israel burst into a great shout, so that the earth re-
sounded. 6 The Philistines heard the noise of the shouting and
they wondered, "Why is there such a loud shouting in the camp
of the Hebrews?" And when they learned that the Ark of the
LORD had come to the camp, 7 the Philistines were frightened;
for they said, "God has come to the camp." And they cried,

a Heb. "his."
b Preceding this, Septuagint has "In those days, the Philistines gathered for war against Israel."
c Meaning of Heb. uncertain.

3.19–4.1a: These vv. (again, the division into vv. and chs is later and often problematic) conclude the story. After the first revelation Samuel had many more, and since all his predictions came true, he was recognized as a *trustworthy* prophet (the Heb uses the same adjective rendered as "faithful" at 2.35), in accordance with the criterion of a true prophet in Deut. 18.22. **20:** The expression *from Dan to Beer-sheba* means from the northern to the southern limit of Israel (see Judg. 20.1). **21a:** The situation at the end of the story is opposed to that at the beginning (v. 1). This unit thus outlines the transition of prophecy from a rare to a commonplace phenomenon.

4.1b–22: Disaster. In chs 4–6 the Ark of the Covenant is the main subject, and Samuel is not mentioned at all. Some scholars believe that these chs were once continued in 2 Sam. ch 6, about David bringing the Ark to Jerusalem, and they were split up and redistributed in chronologically appropriate places throughout Samuel. 1 Sam. ch 4 relates the capture of the Ark by the Philistines, the death of Eli's sons on one day (as predicted in 2.34), and the death of Eli himself. It consists of two parts: the first, located at Eben-ezer, tells of the battles between Israel and the Philistines; the second, at Shiloh, describes the events in the wake of the defeat. It introduces a main theme of the book: the conflict between Israel and the Philistines. **1b:** The *Philistines*—from which the name Palestine was derived in the Hellenistic-Roman period—came from the area of the Aegean Sea and settled on the eastern Mediterranean coast about 1200 BCE. According to the Bible their origin was from Caphtor (Jer. 47.4; Amos 9.7), which is identified with Crete. Archeological excavations in the coastal cities have brought their material culture to light, but little is known of their religious culture. Having better fighting equipment, including chariots and perhaps having introduced iron-working technology (see 1 Sam. 13.19–22), they were militarily superior to Israel. **3:** It was not unusual to bring the Ark of the Covenant to the battlefield, as a physical sign of the Presence of the LORD (see 2 Sam. 11.11), in the same way that ancient Near Eastern nations would bring images of their gods to battle and modern armies may bring flags or national symbols. **4:** The *Ark of the Covenant* was a chest containing the Tablets of the Covenant between the LORD and Israel (Exod. 25.16; Deut. 9.11; 10.5). It was the holiest object in the First Temple, but was absent from the Second Temple, despoiled some time before the Second Temple's destruction. The Ark served as a throne for the *LORD of Hosts* (= armies). On its cover were two *Cherubim,* composite creatures, possibly with the body of a lion or bull, the head of a human, and the wings of an eagle (see Ezek. 1.5–11). In the ancient Near East such creatures flanked royal thrones, or were placed as protection in liminal spaces. **6:** *Hebrews* as the designation of the Israelites is employed primarily by foreigners and by Israelites when talking to foreigners (e.g., Exod. 1.15–16, 19). **7–9:** Several voices are cited, mainly expressing fear and despair, but, finally, also encouragement.

"Woe to us! Nothing like this has ever happened before. 8 Woe to us! Who will save us from the power of this mighty God? He is the same God who struck the Egyptians with every kind of plague in the wilderness! 9 Brace yourselves and be men, O Philistines! Or you will become slaves to the Hebrews as they were slaves to you. Be men and fight!" 10 The Philistines fought; Israel was routed, and they all fled to their homes. The defeat was very great, thirty thousand foot soldiers of Israel fell there. 11 The Ark of God was captured, and Eli's two sons, Hophni and Phinehas, were slain.

12 A Benjaminite ran from the battlefield and reached Shiloh the same day; his clothes were rent and there was earth on his head.[a] 13 When he arrived, he found Eli sitting on a seat, waiting beside the road—his heart trembling for the Ark of God. The man entered the city to spread the news, and the whole city broke out in a cry. 14 And when Eli heard the sound of the outcry and asked, "What is the meaning of this uproar?" the man rushed over to tell Eli. 15 Now Eli was ninety-eight years old; his eyes were fixed in a blind stare. 16 The man said to Eli, "I am the one who came from the battlefield; I have just fled from the battlefield." [Eli] asked, "What happened, my son?" 17 The bearer of the news replied, "Israel fled before the Philistines and the troops also suffered a great slaughter. Your two sons, Hophni and Phinehas, are dead, and the Ark of God has been captured." 18 When he mentioned the Ark of God, [Eli] fell backward off the seat beside[b] the gate, broke his neck and died; for he was an old man and heavy. He had been a chieftain of Israel for forty years.

19 His daughter-in-law, the wife of Phinehas, was with child, about to give birth. When she heard the report that the Ark of God was captured and that her father-in-law and her husband were dead, she was seized with labor pains, and she crouched down and gave birth. 20 As she lay dying, the women attending her said, "Do not be afraid, for you have borne a son." But she did not respond or pay heed. 21 She named the boy Ichabod, meaning, "The glory has departed from Israel"—referring to the capture of the Ark of God and to [the death of] her father-in-law and her husband. 22 "The glory is gone from Israel," she said, "for the Ark of God has been captured."

5 When the Philistines captured the Ark of God, they brought it from Eben-ezer to Ashdod. 2 The Philistines took the Ark of God and brought it into the temple of Dagon and they set it

a I.e., as a sign of mourning. *b Meaning of Heb. uncertain.*

8: *God,* better, "gods" in the plural, as in the Heb, which suggests that the Philistines believe that the Hebrews, like themselves, worship many gods. They are also confused as to the location of the plagues of Egypt. This depiction creates humor and irony—the Philistines don't understand theology or history, but nevertheless will defeat the Israelites. **9:** *Be men,* brave (see 1 Kings 2.2), following standard ancient gender roles. **10:** *Thirty thousand* likely exaggerated like many of the numbers in similar literature, but brings home the magnitude of the defeat. **11:** *The Ark of God was captured,* in keeping with the ancient custom of taking the statue of the god of the defeated people as booty. **12:** Rent clothes and earth on the head were signs of mourning (see 2 Sam. 1.2). **13:** *Trembling for the Ark of God,* more than for his sons. **15:** Physical or personal information about a character is given only when it is crucial for the understanding of the narrative. **17:** The bad news is conveyed in increasing order, seen from Eli's perspective; the Heb suggests the breathlessness of the messenger. **18:** *The Ark of God,* see v. 13 n. *Forty years,* a round number (Judg. 3.11; 5.31; 8.28). The concluding observation *He had been a chieftain* suggests to many that this story was originally part of an earlier book of Judges, that focuses on chieftains. **19–22:** The story of Eli's daughter-in-law shows another outcome of the disaster. The report of the calamities is again arranged in increasing order, but now from her perspective. **19:** *She crouched down,* the customary position for childbirth in antiquity. **21–22:** Names were often given by the mothers. *Ichabod* means "no-glory," or "where is glory." Glory (Heb "kavod") is elsewhere associated with divine Presence and especially with the Ark (e.g., Exod. 24.16–17; Pss. 24.7–10; 79.9), thus the name explains the capture of the Ark. The name's pattern is rare, reflecting names that express misfortune at the time of birth, such as the Aram. name "Ayezer," "where is the divine helper?" or "Jezebel," "where is the (divine) prince?". Instead of *departed* and *gone* the Heb reads "exiled."

5.1–12: The hand of the LORD. The point of this episode is that God has the power to help any nation He chooses; the Philistine victory was

up beside Dagon. [3] Early the next day, the Ashdodites found
Dagon lying face down on the ground in front of the Ark of the
LORD. They picked Dagon up and put him back in his place;
[4] but early the next morning, Dagon was again lying prone
on the ground in front of the Ark of the LORD. The head and
both hands of Dagon were cut off, lying on the threshold; only
[a-]Dagon's trunk was left intact.[-a] [5] That is why, to this day, the
priests of Dagon and all who enter the temple of Dagon do not
tread on the threshold of Dagon in Ashdod.

[6] The hand of the LORD lay heavy upon the Ashdodites, and
He wrought havoc among them: He struck [b-]Ashdod and its
territory[-b] with hemorrhoids. [7] When the men of Ashdod saw
how matters stood, they said, "The Ark of the God of Israel must
not remain with us, for His hand has dealt harshly with us and
with our god Dagon." [8] They sent messengers and assembled all
the lords of the Philistines and asked, "What shall we do with
the Ark of the God of Israel?" They answered, "Let the Ark of
the God of Israel be removed to Gath." So they moved the Ark
of the God of Israel [to Gath]. [9] And after they had moved it, the
hand of the LORD came against the city, causing great panic;
He struck the people of the city, young and old, so that hemorrhoids [a-]broke out[-a] among them. [10] Then they sent the Ark of
God to Ekron. But when the Ark of God came to Ekron, the Ekronites cried out, "They have moved the Ark of the God of Israel
to us to slay us and our kindred." [11] They too sent messengers
and assembled all the lords of the Philistines and said, "Send
the Ark of the God of Israel away, and let it return to its own
place, that it may not slay us and our kindred." For the panic of
death pervaded the whole city, so heavily had the hand of God
fallen there; [12] and the men who did not die were stricken with
hemorrhoids. The outcry of the city went up to heaven.

6 The Ark of the LORD remained in the territory of the Philistines seven months.[c] [2] Then the Philistines summoned
the priests and the diviners and asked, "What shall we do

a-a Meaning of Heb. uncertain.

b-b Meaning of Heb. uncertain. Septuagint reads differently from our Heb. text; it also mentions mice swarming in the Philistine ships and invading their fields. Cf. the mention of "mice" in 6.4, 18; and the note at 6.1.

c Septuagint continues "and mice invaded their fields"; cf. vv. 4, 5, 18, and note at 5.6.

not proof of the superiority of the Philistine god Dagon over YHVH, as the Philistines might have thought. The narrator takes no interest in the political and military consequences of their victory, likely including their penetration into the heart of the country and the destruction of Shiloh and its sanctuary (see Jer. 7.12–14; Ps. 78.60). He is concerned only with their affliction by the *hand of the LORD* (which is mentioned four times in this ch and three times in the next). "Hand" here and elsewhere means "power." The recurrence of the situations in the temple of Dagon and in the Philistine towns shows that the described misfortunes did not happen accidentally. As in the previous ch, the narrative mocks the Philistines. **1:** *Ashdod,* one of the five cities of the Philistines. The others are Gaza, Gath, Ekron, and Ashkelon. **2:** *Dagon,* a Near Eastern deity (Dagan) eventually associated with grain, who was adopted by the Philistines. Placing war trophies in the sanctuary was not uncommon (see 21.10; 31.10). **3–5:** The description of Dagon lying face down on the ground before the Ark makes a mockery of the Philistine god; this is even more pronounced when the fallen god has also lost his head and hands. The mockery extends to the custom not to tread on the threshold because parts of the god have lain on it (cf. Zeph. 1.9). **3:** *Lying face down* may also be understood as bowing down (see e.g., Gen. 44.14). **5:** *To this day:* A temple of Dagon stood at Ashdod as late as the Maccabean period (1 Macc. 10.83–84; 11.4).
6: *Hemorrhoids:* Cf. Ps. 78.66, where "He beat back his foes" is explained in the ancient Aram. translation of Jonathan: "He beat his foes with hemorrhoids at their back." Some scholars, however, identify the disease as bubonic plague, since instead of *hemorrhoids,* the Heb "ketiv" ("what is written") reads "tumors," which are characteristic of bubonic plague, and the LXX mentions mice, which are known to have spread it. In addition, hemorrhoids are neither fatal nor epidemic, whereas according to vv. 11–12 the disease in question was. A new suggestion based on the discovery of phalluses in the excavation of Philistine Gath, suggests that the Philistines were afflicted with a venereal disease or genital disfunction, and the offerings described in 6.4 were phalluses. **8:** *The lords,* Heb "seren" (perhaps cognate to Gk "tyrannos" = tyrant), the title of the five Philistine rulers. **12:** *To heaven,* where God dwells according to many biblical texts (Gen. 11.4; Ps. 2.4).

6.1–7.1: The Ark's return. The first part of the narrative, located at Ekron, tells about the Philistines'

about the Ark of the LORD? Tell us with what we shall send
it off to its own place.” [3] They answered, “If you are going to
send the Ark of the God of Israel away, do not send it away
without anything; you must also pay an indemnity to Him.
Then you will be healed, and [a-]He will make Himself known to
you; otherwise His hand will not turn away from you.”[-a] [4] They
asked, “What is the indemnity that we should pay to Him?”
They answered, “Five golden hemorrhoids and five golden
mice, corresponding to the number of lords of the Philistines;
for the same plague struck all of you[b] and your lords. [5] You
shall make figures of your hemorrhoids and of the mice that
are ravaging your land; thus you shall honor the God of Israel, and perhaps He will lighten the weight of His hand upon
you and your gods and your land. [6] Don't harden your hearts
as the Egyptians and Pharaoh hardened their hearts. As you
know, when He made a mockery of them, they had to let Israel[b] go, and they departed. [7] Therefore, get a new cart ready
and two milch cows that have not borne a yoke; harness the
cows to the cart, but take back indoors the calves that follow
them. [8] Take the Ark of the LORD and place it on the cart; and
put next to it in a chest the gold objects you are paying Him as
indemnity. Send it off, and let it go its own way. [9] Then watch:
If it goes up the road to Beth-shemesh, to His own territory, it
was He who has inflicted this great harm on us. But if not, we
shall know that it was not His hand that struck us; it just happened to us by chance.”
[10] The men did so. They took two milch cows and harnessed
them to the cart, and shut up their calves indoors. [11] They
placed the Ark of the LORD on the cart together with the chest,
the golden mice, and the figures of their hemorrhoids. [12] The
cows went straight ahead along the road to Beth-shemesh.
They went along a single highroad, lowing as they went, and
turning off neither to the right nor to the left; and the lords
of the Philistines walked behind them as far as the border of
Beth-shemesh.

[13] The people of Beth-shemesh were reaping their wheat
harvest in the valley. They looked up and saw the Ark, and they
rejoiced [c-]when they saw [it].[-c] [14] The cart came into the field of
Joshua of Beth-shemesh and it stopped there. They split up the
wood of the cart and presented the cows as a burnt offering to
the LORD. A large stone was there; [15] and the Levites took down
the Ark of the LORD and the chest beside it containing the gold
objects and placed them on the large stone. Then the men of
Beth-shemesh presented burnt offerings and other sacrifices

a-a Or “and you will know why His hand would not turn away from you.” Meaning of Heb. uncertain. *b Heb. “them.”*
c-c Septuagint reads “As they met it.”

decision to return the Ark to its place; the second part, located at Beth-shemesh, describes the reaction of the people there to the Ark's arrival. **2:** As experts on matters of ritual and predicting the future, *the priests and the diviners* will know how to deal with the Ark. Soothsaying was characteristic of the Philistines according to Isa. 2.6. For the Israelites, divining is prohibited (e.g., Deut. 18.10, but the text suggests that it may be effective). See 28.12–14 n. **3:** Instead of *He will make Himself known to you,* the Dead Sea manuscript 4QSam[a] and LXX read “there will be atonement for you.” *His hand,* see 5.1–12 n. **4–5:** The golden hemorrhoids and golden mice correspond to the nature of the plagues; they are a gift to *honor the God of Israel* and to appease Him. *The mice that are ravaging* the land by destroying the grain crops are a blow to Dagon, the god of grain (but see also 5.6 n.). *Upon you,* who are afflicted by disease, *and your gods,* who are deeply humiliated, *and your land,* which is ravaged by mice. **6:** The precedent of Egypt (see also 4.8) serves to convince those Philistines who, believing that their misfortunes happened by chance (see v. 9), are still unwilling to part with their precious trophy. **7:** As a mark of reverence for the Ark, the cart and the cows transporting it should not have been defiled by previous use (see similarly Num. 19.2). Cows were kept for work rather than for milk or meat; milch cows would have young calves and naturally be drawn to them. **9:** The Philistine's theology is remarkable—an event may either reflect divine activity, or *chance.* **12:** *The cows went straight ahead,* as if they knew the way. *Lowing as they went,* better, “lowing continuously,” expressing their distress at being unable to follow their instinctive urge and return to their calves. **13:** Here the viewpoint of the narrative switches to Beth-shemesh, which was the nearest Israelite town. **14:** Stones could mark the place of temples or temporary altars (Gen. 28.22; 1 Sam. 14.33–35). **15:** According to the beginning of

to the LORD that day. 16 The five lords of the Philistines saw this
and returned the same day to Ekron.
17 The following were the golden hemorrhoids that the Philistines paid as an indemnity to the LORD: For Ashdod, one; for
Gaza, one; for Ashkelon, one; for Gath, one; for Ekron, one.
18[a] As for the golden mice, their number accorded with all the
Philistine towns that belonged to the five lords—both fortified towns and unwalled [b-]villages, as far as[-b] the great stone[c]
on which the Ark of the LORD was set down, to this day, in the
field of Joshua of Beth-shemesh.
19 [The LORD] struck at the men of Beth-shemesh because
[d-]they looked into the Ark of the LORD; He struck down seventy men among the people [and] fifty thousand men.[-d] The
people mourned, for He had inflicted a great slaughter upon
the population. 20 And the men of Beth-shemesh asked, "Who
can stand in attendance on the LORD, this holy God? And to
whom shall He go up from us?" 21 They sent messengers to the
inhabitants of Kiriath-jearim to say, "The Philistines have sent
back the Ark of the LORD. Come down and take it into your
7 keeping." 1 The men of Kiriath-jearim came and took up
the Ark of the LORD and brought it into the house of Abinadab on the hill; and they consecrated his son Eleazar to have
charge of the Ark of the LORD.
2 A long time elapsed from the day that the Ark was housed
in Kiriath-jearim, twenty years in all; and all the House of Israel
[e-]yearned after[-e] the LORD. 3 And Samuel said to all the House
of Israel, "If you mean to return to the LORD with all your heart,
you must remove the alien gods and the Ashtaroth from your
midst and direct your heart to the LORD and serve Him alone.
Then He will deliver you from the hands of the Philistines."
4 And the Israelites removed the Baalim and Ashtaroth and
they served the LORD alone.
5 Samuel said, "Assemble all Israel at Mizpah, and I will
pray to the LORD for you." 6 They assembled at Mizpah, and
they drew water and poured it out before the LORD; they fasted that day, and there they confessed that they had sinned

a *Meaning of vv. 18 and 19 uncertain in part.*
b-b *Emendation yields "villages, as witness there is."*
c *Reading* 'eben *with some Heb. mss., Septuagint, and Targum, most mss. and editions* 'abel, *"meadow [?]."* d-d *Force of Heb. uncertain.*
e-e *Meaning of Heb. uncertain.*

this v., possibly a late addition to accommodate Priestly norms, only Levites, who had been consecrated to serve the LORD, were allowed to handle the Ark; Josephus does not mention Levites in his recounting of this episode. **18:** Instead of *as far as the great stone,* read as a new sentence: "There still is the great stone" (requiring a small change in the Heb vocalization, and as reflected in some ancient versions). **19:** The number *fifty thousand* is far too big for a little town like Beth-shemesh. Read only *seventy,* as in *Antiquities of the Jews* by Josephus. **20:** God's holiness is awesome—approaching the Ark, without being consecrated, involves peril of death (Num. 4.19–20). The Ark cannot return to Shiloh because the town has been destroyed (see 5.1–12 n.). **7.1:** The text does not suggest that this was a priestly or Levitical family (contrast 6.15 n.).

7.2–17: The spiritual leader. After the Ark narrative, in which Samuel was not mentioned at all, the present narrative again focuses on him. Samuel is depicted as the last of the judges or chieftains, but unlike most of his predecessors, he does not deliver Israel from its enemies by military means. His leadership is religious and judicial (see Judg. 4.5). The narrative demonstrates that if Israel gets rid of its idols and serves the LORD alone, it will overcome its enemies and live in peace. **2:** *Twenty years,* half a generation. This number fits the chronology of the book of Judges, which is based on periods of forty years, but also twenty and eighty years. **3–4:** *Ashtaroth* (plural), images of Ashtoreth, the main Canaanite goddess (of fertility and love). *Baalim* (plural), images of Baal, the god of heaven and earth, who was the head of the Canaanite pantheon. The use of *Baalim and Ashtaroth* as generic for male and female foreign deities is likely late. The removal of foreign deities is also mentioned in the related Gen. 35.2–4; Josh. 24.23; Judg. 10.16. **5:** There was probably a religious center at *Mizpah,* where the community used to assemble before the LORD (see Judg. 20.1; 1 Sam. 10.17). Samuel, who later became renowned for his success in praying (Jer. 15.1; Ps. 99.6), will beseech the LORD to forgive Israel its sins and deliver them from the Philistines; prophets had important roles as intercessors (see already Gen. 20.7, of Abraham). **6:** The ritual of pouring out water is mentioned nowhere else in the Bible. In the Second Temple period water was poured out on the festival of Sukkot, probably as a request for

against the LORD. And Samuel acted as chieftain of the Israelites at Mizpah.
[7] When the Philistines heard that the Israelites had assembled at Mizpah, the lords of the Philistines marched out
against Israel. Hearing of this, the Israelites were terrified of
the Philistines [8] and they implored Samuel, "Do not neglect us
and do not refrain from crying out to the LORD our God to save
us from the hands of the Philistines." [9] Thereupon Samuel took
a suckling lamb and sacrificed it as a whole burnt offering to
the LORD; and Samuel cried out to the LORD in behalf of Israel,
and the LORD responded to him. [10] For as Samuel was presenting the burnt offering and the Philistines advanced to attack
Israel, the LORD thundered mightily against the Philistines that
day. He threw them into confusion, and they were routed by
Israel. [11] The men of Israel sallied out of Mizpah and pursued
the Philistines, striking them down to a point below Beth-car.
[12] Samuel took a stone and set it up between Mizpah and
Shen,[a] and named it Eben-ezer:[b] "For up to now," he said, "the
LORD has helped us." [13] The Philistines were humbled and did
not invade the territory of Israel again; and the hand of the
LORD was set against the Philistines as long as Samuel lived.
[14] The towns which the Philistines had taken from Israel, from
Ekron to Gath, were restored to Israel; Israel recovered all her
territory from the Philistines. There was also peace between
Israel and the Amorites.
[15] Samuel judged Israel as long as he lived. [16] Each year he
made the rounds of Bethel, Gilgal, and Mizpah, and acted as
judge over Israel at all those places. [17] Then he would return to
Ramah, for his home was there, and there too he would judge
Israel. He built an altar there to the LORD.

8 When Samuel grew old, he appointed his sons judges over
Israel. [2] The name of his first-born son was Joel, and his second son's name was Abijah; they sat as judges in Beer-sheba.

a Otherwise unknown; perhaps identical with "Jeshanah"; cf. Septuagint; also 2 Chron. 13.19. *b I.e., "Stone of Help."*

rain. But here it is done as a request for remission of sins, just as are the prayer, fasting, and confession. The Heb suggests that the text of the confession was we "sinned against the LORD"; a similarly short confession is recited by David in 2 Sam. 12.23, where it is properly rendered as a quotation. **9:** According to Jewish traditional interpretation, sacrifice was permitted everywhere before there was a central sanctuary. Modern scholarship, however, holds that sacrifice outside the central sanctuary became prohibited only when the law of Deuteronomy, demanding centralization of the cult, was introduced during the reign of King Josiah (640–609 BCE). See nn. to Deut. ch 12. **10:** *Thundered:* The LORD uses the forces of nature to help Israel (cf. Judg. 5.20–21). **12:** The recurrence of the name *Eben-ezer* (see 4.1) points to the reversal in the situation: then defeat by the Philistines, now victory over them (after Israel's return to the LORD). **13:** *The hand of the LORD,* see 5.1–12 n. Contrary to the statement here, which aims at glorifying Samuel, in the ensuing narratives Israel is still in the hands of the Philistines, even in Samuel's lifetime (e.g., 9.16). This suggests that the book is a compilation of various sources; see the intro. **14:** *Amorites,* like "Canaanites," is a general designation of the inhabitants of Canaan before the Israelite conquest. Many Amorites remained in the country after the conquest. **15–17:** In order to facilitate the administration of justice Samuel makes yearly rounds of the towns in the central region of the country, going out to the people instead of requiring them to come to him (contrast Judg. 4.5).

Chs 8–12: The foundation of the monarchy. No less than five chs are devoted to the foundation of the monarchy, highlighting its importance. Their attitude towards kingship is not uniform—in chs 8, 10.17–27, and 12 it is negative, in the other chs positive. This reflects ancient controversy concerning the merits of kingship. Many biblical scholars explain the difference by assuming different sources: The pro-monarchic chs 9.1–10.16 and 11 are believed to belong to an older source, the anti-monarchic chs 8, 10.17–27 and 12 to a later one. The materials are arranged artistically, in a broad chiasm: The first and last chs, 8 and 12, contain speeches by Samuel, the second and penultimate ones (9.1–10.16 and 11.1–13) embody narratives having Saul as protagonist, and the middle section (10.17–27) recounts the election of Saul as king.

8.1–22: The request for a king. This narrative is concerned with the advantages and disadvantages of the monarchy. The people desire a strong, centralized government, where the king will lead them in battle, whereas Samuel warns against the likely burden of taxation and oppression that will be a consequence of choosing a king. God, though disapproving, yields to the wish of the people. The first part of the narrative recounts the people's request,

3 But his sons did not follow in his ways; they were bent on
gain, they accepted bribes, and they subverted justice.
4 All the elders of Israel assembled and came to Samuel at
Ramah, 5 and they said to him, "You have grown old, and your
sons have not followed your ways. Therefore appoint a king for
us, to govern us like all other nations." 6 Samuel was displeased
that they said "Give us a king to govern us." Samuel prayed to
the LORD, 7 and the LORD replied to Samuel, "Heed the demand of the people in everything they say to you. For it is not
you that they have rejected; it is Me they have rejected as their
king. 8 Like everything else they have done ever since I brought
them out of Egypt to this day—forsaking Me and worshiping
other gods—so they are doing to you. 9 Heed their demand; but
warn them solemnly, and tell them about the practices of any
king who will rule over them."
10 Samuel reported all the words of the LORD to the people,
who were asking him for a king. 11 He said, "This will be the
practice of the king who will rule over you: He will take your
sons and appoint them as his charioteers and horsemen, and
they will serve as outrunners for his chariots. 12 He will appoint
them as his chiefs of thousands and of fifties; or they will have
to plow his fields, reap his harvest, and make his weapons and
the equipment for his chariots. 13 He will take your daughters
as perfumers, cooks, and bakers. 14 He will seize your choice
fields, vineyards, and olive groves, and give them to his courtiers. 15 He will take a tenth part of your grain and vintage and
give it to his eunuchs and courtiers. 16 He will take your male
and female slaves, your choice *a*young men,*-a* and your asses,
and put them to work for him. 17 He will take a tenth part of
your flocks, and you shall become his slaves. 18 The day will
come when you cry out because of the king whom you yourselves have chosen; and the LORD will not answer you on that
day."
19 But the people would not listen to Samuel's warning. "No,"
they said. "We must have a king over us, 20 that we may be like
all the other nations: Let our king rule over us and go out at our
head and fight our battles." 21 When Samuel heard all that the
people said, he reported it to the LORD. 22 And the LORD said to
Samuel, "Heed their demands and appoint a king for them."
Samuel then said to the men of Israel, "All of you go home."

a-a Septuagint reads "cattle."

Samuel's appeal to God, and God's reply; the central part contains the "king's practice"; and the last part again tells of the people's request, Samuel's appeal to God and God's reply. **1–3:** Background information regarding the people's request. Like Eli, Samuel is old and his sons are corrupt and unworthy to succeed him; these vv. justify the end of judges or chieftains as an institution, and the necessity of the monarchy.

3: Cf. Deut. 16.19. **5:** Cf. Deut. 17.14. In both places it is the example of the *nations* that appeals to the people. **6:** Samuel *prays* to receive divine guidance. **7:** God's kingship is presumed to be conflicting with human kingship. For God's kingship, see Exod. 15.18; Judg. 8.23. **8:** In a very sharp critique the desire for a king is equated with abandoning YHVH. **11–17:** The "king's practice" is based on the reality of the ancient Near East, in accordance with the people's request to have a king "like all other nations" (v. 5). It is not meant to enumerate the rights of the king in Israel, but to deter the people from desiring one. The king will load a heavy burden upon all individuals—unlike the existing regime, which rarely interfered with personal life. He will *take*—Samuel repeats this verb many times—their sons to the army, impose corvée (forced labor) upon their sons and daughters, confiscate their lands, levy taxes, and use their property. **11:** *Outrunners* served as bodyguards to the king (see 22.17). **12:** *Chiefs of thousands and of fifties,* cf. Exod. 18.21, 25, where also hundreds and tens are mentioned. **15:** *Eunuchs,* better "high officials." **17:** *Slaves:* As a result of the foregoing the citizens will be further burdened; instead of being servants to YHVH, whose demands are reasonable (Lev. 25.42), they will be exploited by human kings. **18:** Instead of crying out because of their enemies (Judg. 3.9, 15; 6.6–7; 10.10) they will cry out because of their king, and God who answered their cry in the past will then refrain from answering them. **20:** The people want a king to rule the country in times of peace and lead the army in times of war. *Go out at our head* is a military term (see 18.13). Their request reflects the Philistine incursion, which demanded a standing army with strong leadership. **22:** Because of Samuel's objection the LORD reiterates His command (v. 7), adding explicitly that Samuel appoint a king. Samuel, however, not eager to execute the order, does not transmit this to the people, but tells them to go home.

9 There was a man of Benjamin whose name was Kish son of Abiel son of Zeror son of Becorath son of Aphiah, a Benjaminite, a man of substance. 2 He had a son whose name was Saul, an excellent young man; no one among the Israelites was handsomer than he; [a-]he was a head taller[-a] than any of the people.

3 Once the asses of Saul's father Kish went astray, and Kish said to his son Saul, "Take along one of the servants and go out and look for the asses." 4 He passed into the hill country of Ephraim. He crossed the district of Shalishah, but they did not find them. They passed through the district of Shaalim, but they were not there. They traversed the [entire] territory of Benjamin, and still they did not find them. 5 When they reached the district of Zuph, Saul said to the servant who was with him, "Let us turn back, or my father will stop worrying about the asses and begin to worry about us." 6 But he replied, "There is a man of God in that town, and the man is highly esteemed; everything that he says comes true. Let us go there; perhaps he will tell us about the errand on which we set out." 7 "But if we go," Saul said to his servant, "what can we bring the man? For the food in our bags is all gone, and there is nothing we can bring to the man of God as a present. What have we got?" 8 The servant answered Saul again, "I happen to have a quarter-shekel of silver. I can give that to the man of God and he will tell us about our errand."—9 [b]Formerly in Israel, when a man went to inquire of God, he would say, "Come, let us go to the seer," for the prophet of today was formerly called a seer.—10 Saul said to his servant, "A good idea; let us go." And they went to the town where the man of God lived.

11 As they were climbing the ascent to the town, they met some girls coming out to draw water, and they asked them, "Is the seer in town?" 12 "Yes," they replied. "He is up there ahead of you. [c-]Hurry, for he has just come to the town[-c] because the people have a sacrifice at the shrine today. 13 As soon as you enter the town, you will find him before he goes up to the shrine to eat; the people will not eat until he comes; for he must first bless the sacrifice and only then will the guests eat. Go up at once, for you will find him right away." 14 So they went up to the town; and as they were entering the town,[d] Samuel came out toward them, on his way up to the shrine.

a-a Lit. "taller from his shoulders up." *b This verse explains the term "seer" in v. 11.* *c-c Emendation yields "Hurry, for he has just reached* ('attah kayyom ba, *so Septuagint) the gate"; cf. v. 18.* *d Emendation yields "gate"; cf. v. 18.*

9.1–10.16: The anointing. The story of the young man who went to search for lost asses and found a kingdom is told vividly. Everything happens in a natural way, yet, as elsewhere in the Bible (see esp. the Joseph story in Gen.), God's directing the course of events is manifested in the "accidental" occurrences. Only thanks to his persevering servant—and against his own intention—does Saul happen to get to Samuel's town, and only thanks to the chance encounter with some girls does he enter the town at the precise moment when Samuel comes out, thus meeting the prophet who will anoint him. The first part of the narrative describes Saul's journey up to his arrival at Samuel's town, the second part tells of the encounter between the two men and of Saul's anointing, and the third part recounts Saul's way back home. The narrative expresses Saul's stellar character before he becomes king. **1–2:** The exposition provides details about the hero. Regarding the list of ancestors, cf. 1.1. *Benjamin,* the land of the tribe of Benjamin. Being *handsome* was considered a royal quality in ancient Israel; in the broader context of Samuel, Saul's height will become important when David, rather than Saul confronts the giant, Goliath (1 Sam. ch 17). **5:** *Zuph,* Samuel's home district (1.1). The depiction of Saul's caring is touching, but may suggest that he is too sensitive to rule as king. **6:** *That town,* Ramah. **7:** It was customary to bring some food or presents when making inquiries of a prophet concerning the future or other hidden matters (see 1 Kings 14.3; 2 Kings 8.8–9; Ezek. 13.19. **8:** Were it not for the *quarter-shekel* (a measure of weight, approximately 2.5 gram or a little less than 0.1 oz.) *of silver* the servant happened to possess, Saul and Samuel would not have met. **9:** This late explanatory note, which separates Saul's reply from the servant's proposal, is inserted here in order to explain the term "seer" in v. 11 and to provide the background for the expression "come, let us go" (so in the Heb), used by Saul in v. 10. Ruth 4.7 contains a similarly parenthetic note.

11: The source of water was downhill outside the town. **12–13:** Several voices of the girls can be distinguished, all eager to supply more information than asked for. Samuel has come to the town from one of his circuits (7.16–17). Regarding the sacrifice, see 7.9 n.

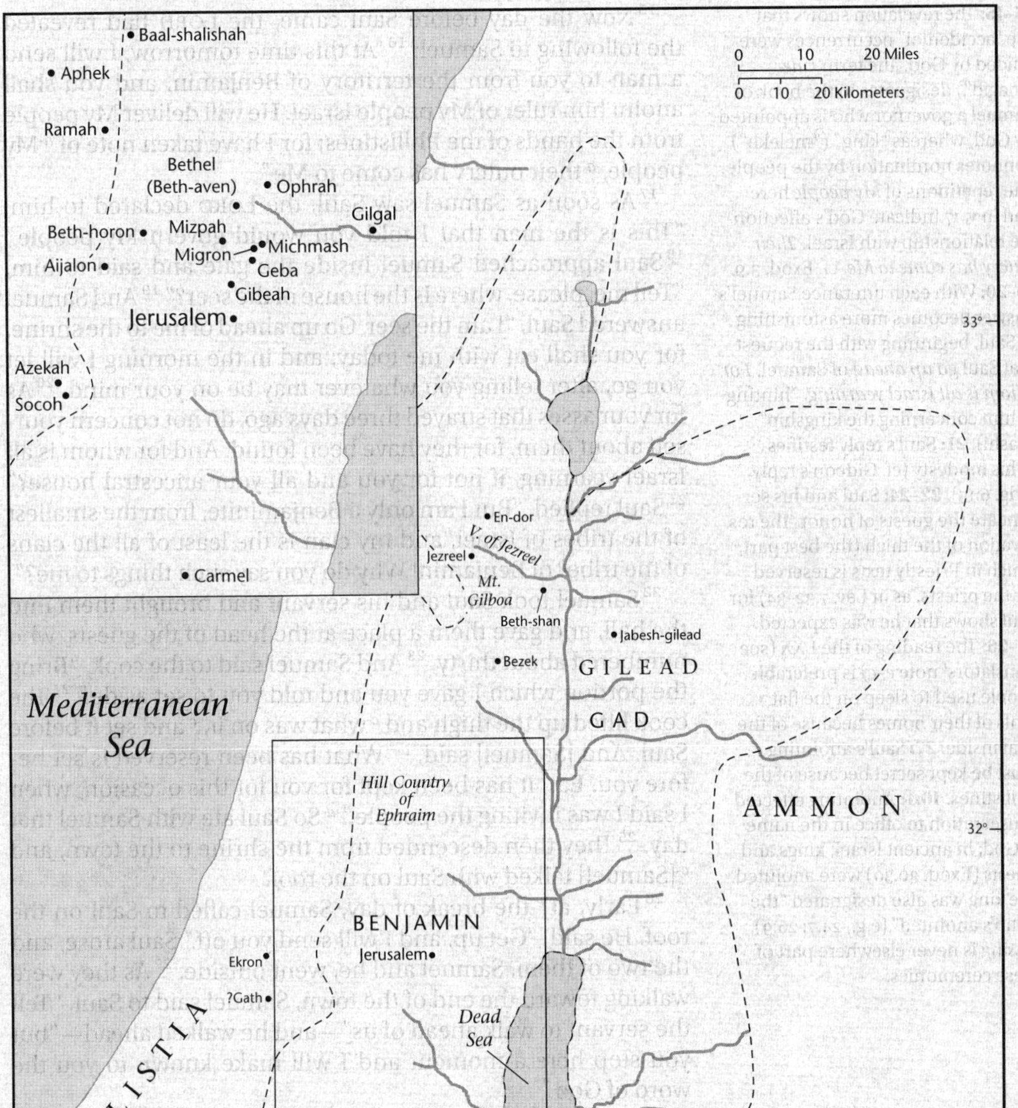

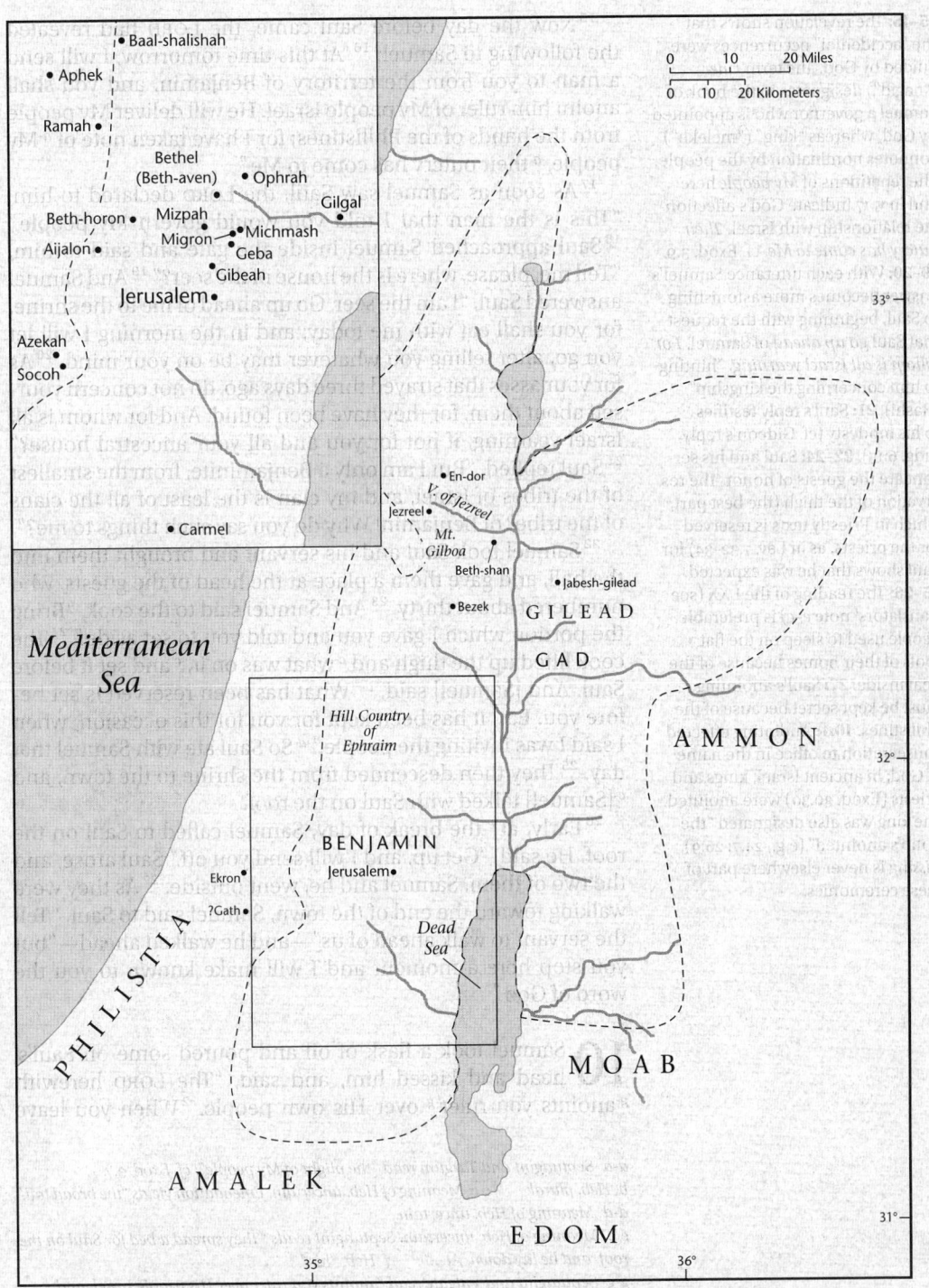

The kingdom of Saul according to First Samuel. The dashed line shows the approximate outer boundary of his kingdom.

15 Now the day before Saul came, the LORD had revealed
the following to Samuel: 16 "At this time tomorrow, I will send
a man to you from the territory of Benjamin, and you shall
anoint him ruler of My people Israel. He will deliver My people
from the hands of the Philistines; for I have taken note of [a-]My
people,[-a] their outcry has come to Me."
17 As soon as Samuel saw Saul, the LORD declared to him,
"This is the man that I told you would govern My people."
18 Saul approached Samuel inside the gate and said to him,
"Tell me, please, where is the house of the seer?" 19 And Samuel
answered Saul, "I am the seer. Go up ahead of me to the shrine,
for you shall eat with me today; and in the morning I will let
you go, after telling you whatever may be on your mind. 20 As
for your asses that strayed three days ago, do not concern yourself about them, for they have been found. And for whom is all
Israel yearning, if not for you and all your ancestral house?"
21 Saul replied, "But I am only a Benjaminite, from the smallest
of the tribes of Israel, and my clan is the least of all the clans
of the tribe[b] of Benjamin! Why do you say such things to me?"
22 Samuel took Saul and his servant and brought them into
the hall, and gave them a place at the head of the guests, who
numbered about thirty. 23 And Samuel said to the cook, "Bring
the portion which I gave you and told you to set aside." 24 The
cook lifted up the thigh and [c-]what was on it,[-c] and set it before
Saul. And [Samuel] said, [d-]"What has been reserved is set before you. Eat; it has been kept for you for this occasion, when
I said I was inviting the people."[-d] So Saul ate with Samuel that
day. 25 They then descended from the shrine to the town, and
[e-][Samuel] talked with Saul on the roof.
26 Early, at[-e] the break of day, Samuel called to Saul on the
roof. He said, "Get up, and I will send you off." Saul arose, and
the two of them, Samuel and he, went outside. 27 As they were
walking toward the end of the town, Samuel said to Saul, "Tell
the servant to walk ahead of us"—and he walked ahead—"but
you stop here a moment and I will make known to you the
word of God."

10 Samuel took a flask of oil and poured some on Saul's[f]
head and kissed him, and said, "The LORD herewith
[g-]anoints you ruler[-g] over His own people. 2 When you leave

a-a Septuagint and Targum read "the plight of My people"; cf. Exod. 3.7.
b Heb. plural. *c-c Meaning of Heb. uncertain. Emendation yields "the broad tail."*
d-d Meaning of Heb. uncertain.
e-e Meaning of Heb. uncertain. Septuagint reads "They spread a bed for Saul on the roof, and he lay down. At . . ." *f Heb. "his."*
g-g Septuagint and Vulgate read "anoints you ruler over His people Israel, and you will govern the people of the LORD and deliver them from the hands of their foes roundabout. And this is the sign for you that the LORD anoints you."

15–16: The revelation shows that the "accidental" occurrences were guided by God. The term *ruler* ("nagid") designates in the book of Samuel a governor who is appointed by God, whereas "king" ("melekh") connotes nomination by the people. The repetitions of *My people* here and in v. 17 indicate God's affectionate relationship with Israel. *Their outcry has come to Me,* cf. Exod. 3.9. **19–20:** With each utterance Samuel's answer becomes more astonishing to Saul, beginning with the request that Saul *go up ahead* of Samuel. *For whom is all Israel yearning,* "hinting to him concerning the kingship" (Rashi). **21:** Saul's reply testifies to his modesty (cf. Gideon's reply, Judg. 6.15). **22–24:** Saul and his servant are the guests of honor. The reservation of the thigh (the best part, which in Priestly texts is reserved for the priests, as in Lev. 7.32–34) for Saul shows that he was expected. **25–26:** The reading of the LXX (see translators' note *e–e)* is preferable. People used to sleep on the flat roofs of their homes because of the heat inside. **27:** Saul's anointing must be kept secret because of the Philistines. **10.1:** Anointing effected consecration to office in the name of God; in ancient Israel, kings and priests (Exod. 30.30) were anointed. The king was also designated "the LORD's anointed" (e.g., 24.7; 26.9). *Kissing* is never elsewhere part of these ceremonies.

me today, you will meet two men near the tomb of Rachel in
the territory of Benjamin, [a-]at Zelzah,[-a] and they will tell you
that the asses you set out to look for have been found, and that
your father has stopped being concerned about the asses and
is worrying about you, saying: 'What shall I do about my son?'
3 You shall pass on from there until you come to the terebinth of
Tabor. There you will be met by three men making a pilgrimage
to God at Bethel. One will be carrying three kids, another will
be carrying three loaves of bread, and the third will be carrying
a jar of wine. 4 They will greet you and offer you two loaves of
bread, which you shall accept. 5 After that, you are to go on to
[b-]the Hill[-b] of God, where the Philistine prefects reside. There, as
you enter the town, you will encounter a band of prophets coming down from the shrine, preceded by lyres, timbrels, flutes,
and harps, and they will be [c-]speaking in ecstasy.[-c] 6 The spirit of
the LORD will grip you, and you will speak in ecstasy along with
them; you will become another man. 7 And once these signs
have happened to you, [d-]act when the occasion arises,[-d] for God
is with you. 8 After that, you are to go down to Gilgal ahead of
me, and I will come down to you to present burnt offerings and
offer sacrifices of well-being. Wait seven days until I come to
you and instruct you what you are to do next."
9 As [Saul] turned around to leave Samuel, God gave him another heart; and all those signs were fulfilled that same day.
10 And when they came there, to [b-]the Hill,[-b] he saw a band of
prophets coming toward him. Thereupon the spirit of God
gripped him, and he spoke in ecstasy among them. 11 When all
who knew him previously saw him speaking in ecstasy together with the prophets, the people said to one another, "What's
happened to [e-]the son of Kish?[-e] Is Saul too among the prophets?" 12 But another person there spoke up and said, "And who
are their fathers?" Thus the proverb arose: "Is Saul too among
the prophets?" 13 And when he stopped speaking in ecstasy, he
entered the shrine.
14 Saul's uncle asked him and his servant, "Where did you
go?" "To look for the asses," he replied. "And when we saw
that they were not to be found, we went to Samuel." 15 "Tell
me," said Saul's uncle, "what did Samuel say to you?" 16 Saul
answered his uncle, "He just told us that the asses had been

a-a Meaning of Heb. uncertain. *b-b Or "Gibeah."*
c-c Others "prophesying"; cf. Num. 11.25 and note. *d-d See 11.5–13.*
e-e To refer to a person merely as "the son (ben) *of…" is slighting; cf. 20.27, 30, 31; Isa. 7.4.*

2–6: The three signs are to convince Saul of the truth of Samuel's words and to persuade him that he will indeed be king. **2:** The tradition that the tomb of Rachel, the ancestress of Saul's tribe Benjamin, was located near Ramah in Benjaminite territory contradicts the tradition that it was near Bethlehem (Gen. 35.19), but is corroborated by Jer. 31.15; different traditions about her burial place existed already in antiquity. **3–4:** From the items intended for the sanctuary of Bethel two loaves of bread will be given to Saul, whose food has run out (9.7). **5:** *The Hill of God* (Gibeah of God) is also called Gibeah of Saul, Gibeah of Benjamin, or just Gibeah. Music served to induce a state of ecstasy (see 2 Kings 3.15). The ecstatic, communal prophets were essentially different from the later, lone, literary prophets. **6:** *The spirit of the LORD* manifests itself in some exceptional ability, like prophesying or leadership. The *gripping* of *the spirit* connects Saul, the first king, to Samson, the last judge (Judg. 14.6, 19; 15.14). **8:** Samuel informs Saul of their relationship right from the beginning: The king is subordinate to the prophet and must follow his instructions. **9:** *Another heart,* another personality. From a simple, diffident peasant Saul is transformed into a charismatic leader. The text summarizes the first two *signs,* saying merely that they were *fulfilled,* and will focus on the third, around which a popular story developed. **10–12:** The episode demonstrates that Saul has become *another man* (v. 6). **10:** *He spoke in ecstasy* reflects a form of the verb "n-b-ʾ," related to the noun "nabi," prophet, but is generally used pejoratively, and is never used in this form for the classical prophets. **11:** Here *son of Kish* is not necessarily slighting (contrast translators' note *e–e*). Kish is a well-known and prosperous citizen, and his son's conduct arouses astonishment. **12:** *And who are their fathers,* a disdainful rhetorical question. The other prophets do not come from distinguished families like Saul, which makes his affiliation with them even more astonishing. *"Is Saul too among the prophets?"* The proverb, whose origin is explained differently at 19.24, expresses surprise at a person who engages in something foreign to him or associates with people unlike himself. **16:** The last sentence may also be translated: "But he did not tell him anything about the kingship, as Samuel had said." In compliance with Samuel's instructions (v. 8; see

found." But he did not tell him anything of what Samuel had
said about the kingship.

17 Samuel summoned the people to the LORD at Mizpah
18 and said to them, "Thus said the LORD, the God of Israel: 'I
brought Israel out of Egypt, and I delivered you from the hands
of the Egyptians and of all the kingdoms that oppressed you.'
19 But today you have rejected your God who delivered you
from all your troubles and calamities. For you said, 'No,[a] set
up a king over us!' Now station yourselves before the LORD, by
your tribes and clans."
20 Samuel brought forward each of the tribes of Israel, and
the lot indicated the tribe of Benjamin. 21 Then Samuel brought
forward the tribe of Benjamin by its clans, and the clan of the
Matrites was indicated; and then[b] Saul son of Kish was indicated. But when they looked for him, he was not to be found.
22 They inquired of the LORD again, [c-]"Has anyone else come
here?"[-c] And the LORD replied, "Yes; he is hiding among the
baggage." 23 So they ran over and brought him from there; and
when he took his place among the people, he stood a head taller than all the people. 24 And Samuel said to the people, "Do
you see the one whom the LORD has chosen? There is none like
him among all the people." And all the people acclaimed him,
shouting, "Long live the king!"
25 Samuel expounded to the people the rules of the monarchy, and recorded them in a document which he deposited before the LORD. Samuel then sent the people back to their homes.
26 Saul also went home to Gibeah, accompanied by [d-]upstanding
men[-d] whose hearts God had touched. 27 But some scoundrels
said, "How can this fellow save us?" So they scorned him and
brought him no gift. [e-]But he pretended not to mind.[-e]

11 Nahash the Ammonite marched up and besieged Jabesh-
gilead. All the men of Jabesh-gilead said to Nahash,
"Make a pact with us, and we will serve you." 2 But Nahash the

a So many Heb. mss. and ancient versions. Other mss. and editions read "to Him."
b Septuagint reads "then he brought up the family of the Matrites by their men and..."
c-c Septuagint reads "Has the man come here?"
d-d In contrast to "scoundrels" (v. 27); understanding Heb. *ḥayil* as the equivalent of *bene ḥayil*, as read by Septuagint and 4QSam[a].
e-e Lit. "But he was as one who holds his peace." Septuagint and 4QSam[a] read "About a month later," connecting with what follows.

also 9.27 n.), Saul keeps the kingship a secret, even from his close relatives.

10.17–27: The election. The people, convened by Samuel, acclaim—now openly—the king chosen by the LORD. Samuel again expresses his objection to the monarchy, but he does not object to Saul as a person, deeming him most suitable for the office. **17:** On *Mizpah,* see 7.5 n. **18–19:** The people are ungrateful. In demanding a king they are rejecting their God (cf. 8.7), who has always saved them. **20–21:** Finding someone by lot proceeded by narrowing down: First the person's tribe was indicated, then the clan, then the family, and finally the person himself (cf. Josh. 7.14). **22:** According to Radak, Saul is *hiding among the baggage,* because "he shunned authority." **23:** *A head taller than all the people,* cf. 9.2. **24:** The cry *"Long live the king!"* marks the acclamation of the king by the people and was part of the coronation ceremony (cf. 2 Samuel 16.16; 1 Kings 1.25, 39; 2 Kings 11.12). **25:** The expression *rules of the monarchy* is in the Heb almost identical to "practice of the king" (8.11). This probably indicates that Samuel repeats and records his previous account of the practice of the king (8.11–17) as a warning and witness for the future (cf. Deut. 31.19–21). But it is also possible that the slightly different phrase indicates the rights and duties of the monarch. *Before the LORD,* in the sanctuary (see Exod. 16.33; Num. 17.22). **26–27:** Two extreme reactions to Saul's election are recounted: on the one hand warm support from *upstanding men,* on the other, scorn from *scoundrels,* who do not believe in his ability to help. *This fellow* (lit. "this one"), a contemptuous phrase.

11.1–13: Deliverance. This story demonstrates Saul's ability to assume leadership and help his countrymen; a specific Ammonite threat, rather than a more generalized Philistine one, provides the opportunity. Saul is depicted here after the model of the judges: The spirit of God grips him (see 10.6 n.), he gathers the people, leads them to victory, and delivers them from the neighboring people that oppressed them. The first part of the narrative is located east of the Jordan at Jabesh-gilead, the second part west of the Jordan, mainly at Gibeah, and the third part again east of the Jordan at Jabesh-gilead (see map, p. 563). At the beginning of the narrative the Dead Sea manuscript 4QSam[a] and Josephus have an additional passage, which supplies the background to

Ammonite answered them, "I will make a pact with you on this condition, that everyone's right eye be gouged out; I will make this a humiliation for all Israel." 3 The elders of Jabesh said to him, "Give us seven days' respite, so that we may send messengers throughout the territory of Israel; if no one comes to our aid, we will surrender to you." 4 When the messengers came to Gibeah of Saul and gave this report in the hearing of the people, all the people broke into weeping.

5 Saul was just coming from the field driving the cattle; and Saul asked, "Why are the people crying?" And they told him about the situation of the men of Jabesh. 6 When he heard these things, the spirit of God gripped Saul and his anger blazed up. 7 He took a yoke of oxen and cut them into pieces, which he sent by messengers throughout the territory of Israel, with the warning, "Thus shall be done to the cattle of anyone who does not follow Saul and Samuel into battle!" Terror from the LORD fell upon the people, and they came out as one man. 8 [Saul] mustered them in Bezek, and the Israelites numbered 300,000, the men of Judah 30,000. 9 The messengers who had come were told, "Thus shall you speak to the men of Jabesh-gilead: Tomorrow, when the sun grows hot, you shall be saved." When the messengers came and told this to the men of Jabesh-gilead, they rejoiced. 10 The men of Jabesh then told [the Ammonites], "Tomorrow we will surrender to you, and you can do to us whatever you please."

11 The next day, Saul divided the troops into three columns; at the morning watch they entered the camp and struck down the Ammonites until the day grew hot. The survivors scattered; no two were left together.

12 The people then said to Samuel, "Who was it said, 'Shall Saul be king over us?' Hand the men over and we will put them to death!" 13 But Saul replied, "No man shall be put to death this day! For this day the LORD has brought victory to Israel."

14 Samuel said to the people, "Come, let us go to Gilgal and there inaugurate the monarchy." 15 So all the people went to Gilgal, and there at Gilgal they declared Saul king before the LORD. They offered sacrifices of well-being there before the LORD; and Saul and all the men of Israel held a great celebration there.

the story. The passage relates that Nahash, king of the Ammonites, oppressed the Gadites and the Reubenites, gouging out the right eye of each of them, but 7,000 men escaped and came to Jabesh-gilead. Scholars debate if this passage was original, and fell out of the main (proto-Masoretic) Heb text, or was added later to provide the background of the story. **1:** The Ammonites, who lived east of the Jordan, clashed with the Israelite tribes settled there (Judg. 10.6–11.33). **2:** Gouging out eyes was considered deeply humiliating (Judg. 16.21; 2 Kings 25.7); the Ammonites did not deem the initial offer of vassaldom sufficient. **4:** Gibeah belonged to Benjamin, and members of that tribe were related to the people of Jabesh (Judg. 21.14). **5:** Saul, not yet publicly inaugurated king, still works in the field. **6:** *The spirit of God,* see 10.6 n. **7:** Military service was not compulsory, but Saul, with violent threats, manages to recruit the people. For a similar act, also performed at Gibeah, likely a parody of this text, see Judg. 19.29 n. **8:** Israel and Judah are thought of as different entities. This may be an anachronism, or possibly, David united them, but after Solomon they divided into two separate states. **10:** *We will surrender to you,* lit. "we will come out to you." This is understood by the Ammonites as "we will surrender," but given the ambiguity of the Heb, meant by the people of Jabesh as "we will fight." **11:** During *the morning watch,* the last of the three watches into which the night was divided, sleep is deepest. Saul attacks from three directions (cf. Gideon's tactic, Judg. 7.16). **12–13:** *Who was it said* refers to 10.27. After Saul's imposing victory opposition is tolerated no more, but Saul himself is prepared to forgive.

11.14–12.25: The prophet's address. At the inception of the monarchy Samuel addresses the people, denouncing their request for a king and urging them to obey the LORD, but also trying to maintain the position of prophet as a religious leader alongside that of the new political leadership of the king. The address begins with the vindication of Samuel's past leadership and ends with his continuing task as mediator between God and the people. In its ideas and language it evinces Deuteronomistic influence, unlike much of the book of Samuel. **14–15:** After Saul's great achievement the time is fit to inaugurate him as king. Offering sacrifices and holding a *great celebration,* lit. "great rejoicing," were part of the royal inauguration ceremony (1 Kings 1.25, 40; 2 Kings 11.14). No other text describes kingship being renewed (that is a better translation of *inaugurate*); this is likely redactional, as a way of combining what follows with the tradition that Saul had already been inaugurated in 10.1.

12 Then Samuel said to all Israel, "I have yielded to you in
all you have asked of me and have set a king over you.
2 Henceforth the king will be your leader.

"As for me, I have grown old and gray—but my sons are still
with you—and I have been your leader from my youth to this day.
3 Here I am! Testify against me, in the presence of the LORD and
in the presence of His anointed one: Whose ox have I taken, or
whose ass have I taken? Whom have I defrauded or whom have I
robbed? From whom have I taken a bribe [a-]to look the other way?[-a]
I will return it to you." 4 They responded, "You have not defrauded
us, and you have not robbed us, and you have taken nothing from
anyone." 5 He said to them, "The LORD then is witness, and His
anointed is witness, [b-]to your admission[-b] this day that you have
found nothing in my possession." They[c] responded, "He is!"

6 Samuel said to the people, [d-]"The LORD [is witness], He who
appointed[-d] Moses and Aaron and who brought your fathers
out of the land of Egypt. 7 Come, stand before the LORD while
I cite against you all the kindnesses that the LORD has done to
you and your fathers.

8 "When Jacob came to Egypt,[e] ... your fathers cried out to the
LORD, and the LORD sent Moses and Aaron, who brought your
fathers out of Egypt and settled them in this place. 9 But they forgot the LORD their God; so He delivered them into the hands of
Sisera the military commander of Hazor, into the hands of the
Philistines, and into the hands of the king of Moab; and these
made war upon them. 10 They cried to the LORD, 'We are guilty,
for we have forsaken the LORD and worshiped the Baalim and
Ashtaroth. Oh, deliver us from our enemies and we will serve
You.' 11 And the LORD sent Jerubbaal and Bedan[f] and Jephthah
and Samuel, and delivered you from the enemies around you;
and you dwelt in security. 12 But when you saw that Nahash
king of the Ammonites was advancing against you, you said
to me, 'No, we must have a king reigning over us'—though the
LORD your God is your King.

13 "Well, the LORD has set a king over you! Here is the king
that you have chosen, that you have asked for.

14 "If you will revere the LORD, worship Him, and obey Him,
and will not flout the LORD's command, if both you and the
king who reigns over you will follow the LORD your God, [well
and good]. 15 But if you do not obey the LORD and you flout the
LORD's command, the hand of the LORD will strike you [d-]as it
did your fathers.[-d]

a-a Septuagint reads "or a pair of sandals? [cf. Amos 2.6] Testify against me."
b-b Lit. "against you." *c Heb. "he."* *d-d Meaning of Heb. uncertain.*
e Septuagint adds "the Egyptians oppressed them." *f Septuagint "Barak."*

12.2–5: Samuel asserts—and his assertion is confirmed by the people—that he never abused his office for his own profit (whereas corruption among leaders is widespread), implying that his rejection is unjustified and an act of ingratitude (cf. Num. 16.15), especially since he has not engaged in any of the typical abuses of the king (8.11–17). **3:** *His anointed one,* see 2.10 n. **7–12:** The LORD directly delivered Israel from its enemies, even when their plight was caused by their own guilt, so there was no need to ask for a king in order to be delivered. **8:** *Cried out to the LORD,* see Exod. 2.23; this v. telescopes the events. **9:** The interpretation of the historical events largely conforms to the book of Judges: Deliverance into the hands of the enemies is seen as punishment for forsaking the LORD and worshipping other gods, deliverance from the enemies as the result of returning to Him. *Sisera,* see Judg. 4.2. *Philistines,* see Judg. 13.1. *Moab,* see Judg. 3.12. **10:** *They cried to the LORD ...,* see Judg. 10.10. *The Baalim and Ashtaroth,* see 7.3–4 n. **11:** *Jerubbaal,* also called Gideon (see Judg. 7.1). *Bedan,* no judge by that name is known. The Rabbis stated, "Bedan is Samson" (*b. Rosh Hash.* 25a), since Bedan means "in Dan," and Samson belonged to the tribe of Dan. But perhaps Barak should be read (see Judg. 4.6). Alternately, this refers to a judge not mentioned in the extant book of Judges. The ancient versions show significant variation in this list of judges, probably because they are attempting to harmonize it with the book of Judges. **12:** The advance of Nahash is not mentioned in ch 8 among the reasons for requesting a king. Moreover, according to the order of the narratives, the request for a king (ch 8) preceded the war against Nahash (ch 11). But according to a passage in the Dead Sea manuscript 4QSam[a] and in Josephus (see 11.1–13 n.), Nahash troubled Israel already before the war at Jabesh-gilead. According to that narrative, these earlier attacks (together with the Philistine occupation; see 9.16) probably inspired the wish for a strong military leader. **15:** This is the same *hand of the LORD* which earlier afflicted the Philistines (see 5.1–12 n.).

[16] "Now stand by and see the marvelous thing that the LORD will do before your eyes. [17] It is the season of the wheat harvest.[a] I will pray to the LORD and He will send thunder and rain; then you will take thought and realize what a wicked thing you did in the sight of the LORD when you asked for a king."

[18] Samuel prayed to the LORD, and the LORD sent thunder and rain that day, and the people stood in awe of the LORD and of Samuel. [19] The people all said to Samuel, "Intercede for your servants with the LORD your God that we may not die, for we have added to all our sins the wickedness of asking for a king." [20] But Samuel said to the people, "Have no fear. You have, indeed, done all those wicked things. Do not, however, turn away from the LORD, but serve the LORD with all your heart. [21] Do not turn away to follow worthless things, which can neither profit nor save but are worthless. [22] For the sake of His great name, the LORD will never abandon His people, seeing that the LORD undertook to make you His people.

[23] "As for me, far be it from me to sin against the LORD and refrain from praying for you; and I will continue to instruct you in the practice of what is good and right. [24] Above all, you must revere the LORD and serve Him faithfully with all your heart; and consider how grandly He has dealt with you. [25] For if you persist in your wrongdoing, both you and your king shall be swept away."

13 Saul was...[b] years old when he became king, and he reigned over Israel two years. [2] Saul picked 3,000 Israelites, of whom 2,000 were with Saul in Michmas[c] and in the hill country of Bethel, and 1,000 with Jonathan in Gibeah of Benjamin; the rest of the troops he sent back to their homes. [3] Jonathan struck down the Philistine prefect in Geba;[d] and the Philistines heard about it. [e-]Saul had the ram's horn sounded throughout the land, saying, "Let the Hebrews hear."[-e]

[4] When all Israel heard that Saul had struck down the Philistine prefect, and that Israel had [f-]incurred the wrath of[-f] the Philistines, all the people rallied to Saul at Gilgal. [5] The

a *When thunderstorms do not occur in the land of Israel.*
b *The number is lacking in the Heb. text; also, the precise context of the "two years" is uncertain. The verse is lacking in the Septuagint.*
c *So in oldest mss.; other mss. and editions read "Michmash" throughout the chapter.*
d *Apparently identical with Gibeah in v. 2.* e-e *Meaning of Heb. uncertain.*
f-f *Lit. "became malodorous to."*

18: The miracle demonstrates both the anger of the LORD and the power of Samuel's prayer. In the land of Israel rain only falls from the late fall to the early spring. Rain during the harvest in the summer would cause the crop to rot. **21:** *Worthless things* refer to idolatry; see 2 Kings 17.15, using a different word to express the same idea, concerning why the Northern Kingdom was exiled: "They went after delusion and were deluded." **22:** Abandonment of Israel would damage the LORD's *great name* among the nations, who would attribute it to His impotence (cf. Num. 14.15–16; Josh. 7.9), thus the covenant between God and Israel must be eternal. **23:** Samuel, whose authority is reconfirmed by the miracle, will continue in his prophetic role, to represent the people before God by means of prayer and to represent God before the people by means of instruction. **24:** The beginning of the v. is a clichéd combination of Deuteronomistic language: *revere* (lit. "fear") *the LORD and serve Him faithfully with all your heart.* The referent of God dealing *grandly* is uncertain; it may refer to general divine beneficence or to His show through an unseasonal thunder storm (v. 18—so Radak), or perhaps God's willingness to overlook the people's request for a king, and stating instead that they will be judged on their continued ability to serve God. **25:** The fate of the people and the king are often intertwined.

13.1–14.52: The king's failure and the prince's success. Saul, in his first war against the Philistines, dreads their superior force, whereas Jonathan his son, convinced that God can grant victory "by many or by few" (14.6), takes action and achieves an impressive victory. The Heb text of this unit is unusually difficult, and has suffered significant corruption; the LXX, is often superior here, reflecting a better-preserved Heb text (see e.g., 14.40–42 n.). **1:** This formula—here incomplete—often introduces the reign of kings, e.g., 2 Sam. 2.10; 1 Kings 14.21; 22.42. **2:** Saul sets up a standing army. *Gibeah of Benjamin,* see 10.5 n. **3:** By killing the Philistine prefect Jonathan initiates the revolt. Sounding *the ram's horn* serves to mobilize the *Hebrews.* To incite the Israelites to arms Saul uses the Philistine designation, "Hebrews" (see 4.6 n.). **4:** Saul, as king, is credited with Jonathan's deed. **5:** The Philistine army exceeds the Israelite force by far. Unlike the Israelites, it has chariots, though the numbers mentioned

Philistines, in turn, gathered to attack Israel: 30,000[a] chariots
and 6,000 horsemen, and troops as numerous as the sands of
the seashore. They marched up and encamped at Michmas,
east of Beth-aven.
6 [b]-When the men of Israel saw that they were in trouble—for
the troops were hard pressed—the people hid in caves, among
thorns, among rocks, in tunnels, and in cisterns. 7 Some Hebrews
crossed the Jordan, [to] the territory of Gad and Gilead. Saul was
still at Gilgal, and the rest of the people rallied to him in alarm.-[b]
8 He waited seven days, the time that Samuel [had set].[c] But
when Samuel failed to come to Gilgal, and the people began to
scatter, 9 Saul said, "Bring me the burnt offering and the sacrifice of well-being"; and he presented the burnt offering. 10 He
had just finished presenting the burnt offering when Samuel
arrived; and Saul went out to meet him and welcome him.
11 But Samuel said, "What have you done?" Saul replied, "I saw
the people leaving me and scattering; you had not come at the
appointed time, and the Philistines had gathered at Michmas.
12 I thought the Philistines would march down against me at
Gilgal before I had entreated the LORD, so I [b]-forced myself-[b]
to present the burnt offering." 13 Samuel answered Saul, [d]-"You
acted foolishly in not keeping the commandments that the
LORD your God laid upon you! Otherwise-[d] the LORD would
have established your dynasty over Israel forever. 14 But now
your dynasty will not endure. The LORD will seek out a man
after His own heart, and the LORD will appoint him ruler over
His people, because you did not abide by what the LORD had
commanded you."
15 [e]-Samuel arose and went up from Gilgal-[e] to Gibeah[f] of
Benjamin. Saul numbered the troops who remained with
him—about 600 strong. 16 Saul and his son Jonathan, and the
troops who remained with them, stayed in Geba of Benjamin,
while the Philistines were encamped at Michmas. 17 The raiders came out of the Philistine camp in three columns: One column headed for the Ophrah road that leads to the district of
Shual, 18 another column headed for the Beth-horon road, and
the third column headed for the border[g] road that overlooks
the valley of Zeboim toward the desert.
19 No smith was to be found in all the land of Israel, for the
Philistines were afraid that the Hebrews would make swords

a Septuagint and other versions read "three thousand."
b-b Meaning of Heb. uncertain.
c So some Heb. mss.; other mss., Septuagint, and Targum read "said." Cf. 10.8.
d-d Change of vocalization yields, "You acted foolishly. If you had kept the commandment the LORD your God laid upon you..."
e-e Septuagint reads here, "Samuel rose and left Gilgal and went his way. The rest of the people followed Saul to meet the soldiers, and they went from Gilgal."
f Sometimes called Geba; cf. vv. 3, 16; 14.5. *g Septuagint reads "Geba."*

seem greatly exaggerated. The Heb word translated *horsemen* can also mean "horses"; these were used for pulling the chariots, not for riding. *As the sands of the seashore* is a common figure (e.g., Gen. 22.17; Josh. 11.4). **8–15a:** The episode of Samuel's clash with Saul connects with 10.8, where Samuel explicitly told Saul to wait for him. **9:** It was customary to offer a sacrifice before battle (see 7.10). There are several instances of kings sacrificing, e.g., David (2 Sam. 6.17), Solomon (1 Kings 8.62–64), Jeroboam (1 Kings 13.1). **11–12:** To Samuel's short question, Saul, to justify himself, gives a lengthy answer. **13–14:** Samuel is angry that Saul did not obey him and offered the sacrifice, a task that Samuel, as religious leader, wished to retain for himself. Samuel acknowledges Saul as the political leader of the people, not as the religious one. The words *commandments* and *commanded* are in Heb of the same root as *appoint* ("tz-v-h"), thus connecting the punishment with the sin according to the principle of measure-for-measure. *Ruler,* see 9.15–16 n. **15:** Unlike the LXX, the Masoretic version fails to record that Saul goes from Gilgal to Gibeah (see v. 16). The omission is probably due to haplography (the copyist's eye skipping from the first *Gilgal* to the second). Samuel refrains from accompanying Saul. **16:** *Geba* and *Michmas* were across from each other, separated by a ravine with precipitous sides. **17–18:** The raiders disperse in different directions in order to devastate the area (cf. 2 Sam. 11.1). **19–22:** The Israelites are inferior to the Philistines not only in number, but also in the quality of their weapons. Not being allowed by the Philistines to manufacture or repair iron tools (the period described coincides with the beginning of the Iron Age), they do not have iron weapons, and are also dependent on the Philistines for the (expensive) maintenance of their agricultural implements. The story may reflect the idea that iron-working technology was introduced by the Philistines from the Aegean. **21:** The word *pim* occurs only here.

or spears. 20 So all the Israelites had to go down to the Philistines to have their plowshares, their mattocks, axes, and colters[a] sharpened. 21 [b]The charge for sharpening was a *pim*[c] for plowshares, mattocks, three-pronged forks, and axes, and for setting the goads. 22 Thus on the day of the battle, no sword or spear was to be found in the possession of any of the troops with Saul and Jonathan; only Saul and Jonathan had them.

23 Now the Philistine garrison had marched out to the pass of Michmas.

14 One day, Jonathan son of Saul said to the attendant who carried his arms, "Come, let us cross over to the Philistine garrison on the other side"; but he did not tell his father. 2 Now Saul was staying on the outskirts of Gibeah,[d] under the pomegranate tree at Migron, and the troops with him numbered about 600. 3 Ahijah son of Ahitub brother of Ichabod son of Phinehas son of Eli, the priest of the LORD at Shiloh, was there bearing an ephod.—The troops did not know that Jonathan had gone. 4 [e]At the crossing[e] by which Jonathan sought to reach the Philistine garrison, there was a rocky crag on one side, and another rocky crag on the other, the one called Bozez and the other Seneh. 5 One crag was located on the north, near Michmas, and the other on the south, near Geba.

6 Jonathan said to the attendant who carried his arms, "Come, let us cross over to the outpost of those uncircumcised fellows. Perhaps the LORD will act in our behalf, for nothing prevents the LORD from winning a victory by many or by few." 7 His arms-bearer answered him, "Do whatever [f]you like. You go first,[f] I am [g]with you, whatever you decide."[g] 8 Jonathan said, "We'll cross over to those men and let them see us. 9 If they say to us, 'Wait until we get to you,' then we'll stay where we are, and not go up to them. 10 But if they say, 'Come up to us,' then we will go up, for the LORD is delivering them into our hands. That shall be our sign." 11 They both showed themselves to the Philistine outpost and the Philistines said, "Look, some Hebrews are coming out of the holes where they have been hiding." 12 The men of the outpost shouted to Jonathan and his arms-bearer, "Come up to us, and we'll teach you a lesson." Then Jonathan said to his arms-bearer, "Follow me, for the LORD will deliver them into the hands of Israel." 13 And Jonathan clambered up on his hands and feet, his arms-bearer behind him; [the Philistines] fell before Jonathan, and his arms-bearer finished them

Its meaning became clear when stone weights inscribed with this word were unearthed (see translators' note *c*). **22:** *No sword or spear,* made of iron. **14.1:** *One day* often introduces a sub-episode or a shift in scene (as in 1 Sam. 1.4; Job 1.6, 13); it does not represent a new major episode, as the ch divisions suggest; indeed, the end of ch 13 is essential background to the episode that follows. **3:** *Ichabod,* see 4.21. The ephod was a device used by priests for consulting the LORD, and its mention here heightens the irony that Saul did not know that Jonathan had left the camp. The mention of *Ahijah* anticipates his role in v. 18. **4–5:** These vv. offer unusually detailed geographical and geological detail, giving great verisimilitude to this unit. **6:** The repetition (see 14.1) serves to resume the thread of the story after the interruption depicting the background (vv. 2–5). *Uncircumcised fellows,* a contemptuous way to refer to the Philistines, who, unlike the Israelites and many peoples in the area, were not circumcised. This was considered a disgrace (cf. Gen. 34.14). Jonathan's belief, that victory is determined by God, is frequent in the Bible (see e.g., Ps. 20.8–10). **11–12:** The presumptuous Philistines belittle the two Israelites. *Hebrews,* see 4.6 n. *The holes,* see 13.6. **13:** Jonathan climbs the precipice at a difficult, unexpected site, thus surprising the Philistine outpost.

a *Meaning of Heb. uncertain. Septuagint reads "sickle."*
b *Meaning of several terms in this verse uncertain.* *c* *I.e., two-thirds of a shekel.*
d *See note f at 13.15.* *e-e* *Meaning of Heb. uncertain.*
f-f *Lit. "is in your heart. Incline yourself." Septuagint reads "your heart inclines to."*
g-g *Lit. "with you, according to your heart." Septuagint reads "with you; my heart is like your heart."*

15: *The very earth quaked,* lit. "the land trembled," metonymical for "the people trembled." *Terror from God,* immense terror (cf. 11.7; Gen. 35.5); Heb uses the divine name to express enormity. **18:** The *Ark* has a divinatory role in Judg. 20.27–28, though the reading of "ephod" in some LXX manuscripts may make more sense in context (see v. 3). **19:** *Withdraw your hand:* Do not continue consulting the LORD, because, in view of the confusion, there is neither need nor time for it. **21–22:** Israelites who were in the service of the Philistines as well as those who were hiding (13.6) now join Saul's army. **24:** Saul does not want the people to pause in the pursuit of the Philistines, but the result of his curse is that they become faint from hunger (cf. the rash vow of Jephthah, which also afflicted his own child, Judg. 11.30–31). The curse was an attempt to show that God, and not human strength or endurance, will ultimately determine victory (see v. 6), but it has backfired. **25–27:** *Beehives,* rather "honeycombs." The same Heb word is also translated "forest" (in vv. 25–26). Honey was produced in the Iron Age mostly by wild bees (see Judg. 14.8–9) and was considered a delicacy. This ch assumes that even though Jonathan did not hear the adjuration, he is still responsible. **29–30:** Jonathan openly criticizes his father: If the troops had eaten, they would have had more strength to pursue the Philistines.

off behind him. 14 The initial attack that Jonathan and his arms-bearer made accounted for some twenty men, [a]within a space about half a furrow long [in] an acre of land.[a] 15 Terror broke out among all the troops both in the camp [and] in the field; the outposts and the raiders were also terrified. The very earth quaked, and a terror from God ensued.

16 Saul's scouts in Gibeah of Benjamin saw that the multitude was [b]scattering in all directions.[b] 17 And Saul said to the troops with him, "Take a count and see who has left us." They took a count and found that Jonathan and his arms-bearer were missing. 18 Thereupon Saul said to Ahijah, "Bring the Ark[c] of God here"; for the Ark[c] of God was at the time among[d] the Israelites. 19 But while Saul was speaking to the priest, the confusion in the Philistine camp kept increasing; and Saul said to the priest, "Withdraw your hand." 20 Saul and the troops with him assembled and rushed into battle; they found [the Philistines] in very great confusion, every man's sword turned against his fellow. 21 [a]And the Hebrews who had previously sided with the Philistines, who had come up with them in the army [from] round about—they too joined the Israelites[a] who were with Saul and Jonathan. 22 When all the men of Israel who were hiding in the hill country of Ephraim heard that the Philistines were fleeing, they too pursued them in battle. 23 Thus the LORD brought victory to Israel that day.

The fighting passed beyond Beth-aven. 24 [e]The men of Israel were distressed[e] that day. For Saul had laid an oath upon the troops: "Cursed be the man who eats any food before night falls and I take revenge on my enemies." So none of the troops ate anything. 25 Everybody came to a [f]stack of beehives[f] where some honey had spilled on the ground. 26 When the troops came to the beehives[g] and found the flow of honey there, no one put[h] his hand to his mouth, for the troops feared the oath. 27 Jonathan, however, had not heard his father adjure the troops. So he put out the stick he had with him, dipped it into the beehive of honey, and brought his hand back to his mouth; and his eyes lit up. 28 At this one of the soldiers spoke up, "Your father adjured the troops: 'Cursed be the man who eats anything this day.' And so the troops are faint." 29 Jonathan answered, "My father has brought trouble on the people. See for yourselves how my eyes lit up when I tasted that bit of honey. 30 If only the troops had eaten today of spoil captured

a-a Meaning of Heb. uncertain.
b-b Lit. "shaken and going thither." Meaning of Heb. uncertain.
c Septuagint reads "ephod," and cf. vv. 3, 23.9, 30.7. *d Heb. "and."*
e-e Meaning of Heb. uncertain. Septuagint reads "And all the troops, about 10,000 men, were with Saul; and the battle spread into the hill country of Ephraim. Now Saul committed a rash act." *f-f Meaning of Heb. uncertain; cf. Song of Songs 5.1.*
g Meaning of Heb. uncertain; cf. Song of Songs 5.1. *h Meaning of Heb. uncertain.*

from the enemy, the defeat of the Philistines would have been
greater still!"
[31] They struck down the Philistines that day from Michmas to
Aijalon, and the troops were famished. [32] The troops pounced
on the spoil; they took the sheep and cows and calves and
slaughtered them on the ground, and the troops ate with the
blood.[a] [33] When it was reported to Saul that the troops were sinning against the LORD, eating with the blood, he said, "You have
acted faithlessly. Roll a large stone over to me today."[b] [34] And
Saul ordered, "Spread out among the troops and tell them that
everyone must bring me his ox or his sheep and slaughter it
here, and then eat. You must not sin against the LORD and eat
with the blood." Every one of the troops brought [c-]his own ox
with him[-c] that night and slaughtered it there. [35] Thus Saul set up
an altar to the LORD; it was the first altar he erected to the LORD.
[36] Saul said, "Let us go down after the Philistines by night and
plunder among them until the light of morning; and let us not
leave a single survivor among them." "Do whatever you please,"
they replied. But the priest said, "Let us approach God here."
[37] So Saul inquired of God, "Shall I go down after the Philistines? Will You deliver them into the hands of Israel?" But this
time He did not respond to him. [38] Then Saul said, "Come forward, all chief officers of the troops, and find out how this guilt
was incurred today. [39] For as the LORD lives who brings victory
to Israel, even if it was through my son Jonathan, he shall be
put to death!" Not one soldier answered him. [40] And he said to
all the Israelites, "You stand on one side, and my son Jonathan
and I shall stand on the other." The troops said to Saul, "Do
as you please." [41] Saul then said to the LORD, the God of Israel,
[d-]"Show Thammim."[-d] Jonathan and Saul were indicated by lot,
and the troops were cleared. [42] And Saul said, "Cast the lots between my son and me"; and Jonathan was indicated.
[43] Saul said to Jonathan, "Tell me, what have you done?" And
Jonathan told him, "I only tasted a bit of honey with the tip of
the stick in my hand. I am ready to die." [44] Saul said, "Thus and
more may God do:[e] You shall be put to death, Jonathan!" [45] But
the troops said to Saul, "Shall Jonathan die, after bringing this
great victory to Israel? Never! As the LORD lives, not a hair of
his head shall fall to the ground! For he brought this day to pass
with the help of God." Thus the troops saved Jonathan and he
did not die. [46] Saul broke off his pursuit of the Philistines, and
the Philistines returned to their homes.

a *I.e., without the proper rites.* *b* *Septuagint reads "here."*
c-c *Septuagint reads "whatever he had in his possession."*
d-d *Meaning of Heb. uncertain. Septuagint reads "Why have You not responded to Your servant today? If this iniquity was due to my son Jonathan or to me, O LORD, God of Israel, show Urim; and if You say it was due to Your people Israel, show Thummim."*
e *Many mss. and Septuagint add "to me."*

32–34: It was forbidden to eat meat with the blood, which was considered to be the life (Lev. 19.26; Deut. 12.23). Accordingly, for meat to be kosher, rabbinic law requires that all traces of blood be meticulously removed. By slaughtering on the ground the blood will not drain out properly and will mix with the meat, whereas by slaughtering on a stone the blood can drain out and flow down, leaving the meat fit for consumption. **36–39:** It was customary to inquire of God before going to battle (Num. 27.21). The lack of response is an indication of divine distance as a result of the people's guilt. **39:** The text offers no reason that Saul should suspect Jonathan. **40–42:** The guilty person was found by means of the Urim and Thummim (see Exod. 28.30 n.). These were lots allowing only yes-or-no answers (cf. Saul's questions in v. 37), so the people had to be divided into two groups, one group being indicated at each stage. The Heb text of v. 41 has been shortened accidentally, and the longer LXX text more clearly explains the method used: The appearance of Urim meant yes; of Thummim, no (the omission in the MT is probably due to haplography, the copyist's eye skipping from the first *Israel* to the last—see translators' note *d-d*). **43:** The lack of proportion between the "crime" (Jonathan only *tasted* and just *a bit)* and the punishment is manifest. Jonathan has broken a vow, however, and vows had to be observed unconditionally (Deut. 23.22–24). **44:** *Thus and more,* see 3.17. **45:** *Not a hair of his head shall fall to the ground:* The same hyperbolic expression occurs in 2 Sam. 14.11; 1 Kings 1.52. *Saved,* lit. "redeemed." Jonathan did not hear his father's oath; although he is considered formally guilty; in such cases he may redeemed (cf. *Mid. Sam.:* "Israel gave his weight in gold and redeemed him"). Biblical law allows redemption of the offender in exceptional cases (see Exod. 21.30). **46:** The statement that people returned home, here, as elsewhere, marks the end of a narrative (e.g., 15.34; 26.25).

47 After Saul had secured his kingship over Israel, he waged
war on every side against all his enemies: against the Moabites, Ammonites, Edomites, the Philistines, and the kings[a] of
Zobah; and wherever he turned he worsted [them]. 48 He was
triumphant, defeating the Amalekites and saving Israel from
those who plundered it.
49 Saul's sons were: Jonathan, Ishvi,[b] and Malchishua; and
the names of his two daughters were Merab, the older, and
Michal, the younger. 50 The name of Saul's wife was Ahinoam
daughter of Ahimaaz; and the name of his army commander
was Abiner[c] son of Saul's uncle Ner. 51 Kish, Saul's father, and
Ner, Abner's father, were sons of Abiel.
52 There was bitter war against the Philistines all the days of
Saul; and whenever Saul noticed any stalwart man or warrior,
he would take him into his service.

15 Samuel said to Saul, "I am the one the LORD sent to
anoint you king over His people Israel. Therefore, listen
to the LORD's command!
2 "Thus said the LORD of Hosts: I am exacting the penalty
for what Amalek did to Israel, for the assault he made upon
them on the road, on their way up from Egypt. 3 Now go, attack
Amalek, and proscribe[d] all that belongs to him. Spare no one,
but kill alike men and women, infants and sucklings, oxen and
sheep, camels and asses!"
4 Saul mustered the troops and enrolled them at Telaim:
200,000 men on foot, and 10,000 men of Judah. 5 Then Saul
advanced as far as the city of Amalek and [e]lay in wait[e] in the
wadi. 6 Saul said to the Kenites, "Come, withdraw at once from
among the Amalekites, that I may not destroy you along with
them; for you showed kindness to all the Israelites when they
left Egypt." So the Kenites withdrew from among the Amalekites.
7 Saul destroyed Amalek from Havilah all the way to Shur,
which is close to Egypt, 8 and he captured King Agag of Amalek
alive. He proscribed all the people, putting them to the sword;
9 but Saul and the troops spared Agag and the best of the sheep,
the oxen, the second-born,[f] the lambs, and all else that was of

a Septuagint and 4QSam[a] read "king."
b The same as Ishbosheth (2 Sam. 2.8) and Eshbaal (1 Chron. 8.33).
c Usually "Abner." *d See note at Josh. 6.18.* *e-e Meaning of Heb. uncertain.*
f Targum and Syriac read "fatlings."

47–52: A summary of Saul's kingship, with regard to his wars and family; this summary may separate units in which Saul is viewed positively from what follows, where he is vilified. The *Amalekites* are mentioned separately in v. 48 to anticipate the subject of the next story, and v. 52, which refers to *all the days of Saul,* may very well be the introduction to the chs that follow, until the death of Saul.

15.1–35: Rejection. As in 13.8–14 Saul and Samuel clash over the king's insubordination to the prophet, and Samuel tells Saul that his kingship will not abide. But whereas in the earlier narrative the rejection referred to his dynasty, here it applies to Saul himself. There the clash occurred in connection with the war against the Philistines, here against Amalek, a nomadic people to the south of Israel. The Amalekites are regarded in the Bible as vicious adversaries of Israel; in later times the name Amalek came to signify "archenemy of the Jews" (see Exod. 17.8–16 n.). Although the entire book of Samuel was incorporated into the Deuteronomstic History, the hand of the Deuteronomist is very light throughout the book. This ch is an exception; his hand is heavier as he introduces the main justification for the dynasty of David, his hero. **1:** At the beginning of the narrative—without an introduction—Samuel stresses Saul's obligation to obey, and thus the subservience of the king to God and His prophet. **2:** The Amalekites' vile attack upon Israel is described in Exod. 17.8–16; Deut. 25.17–19; the phrase *on the road* reflects Deut. 25.17, 18. **3:** Proscription, practiced by Israel and other peoples in the ancient Near East, was a way of consecrating the fruits of victory to the deity; it meant exterminating all the people and all their belongings, as emphasized in the present v. **4:** The numbers are exaggerated; however, the Heb word for "thousand" may refer to a much smaller military unit. **5:** *The city of Amalek,* their main settlement; no information about Amalek or its cities is known from extrabiblical sources. **6:** The *Kenites* were a nomadic tribe in the south of the country. It is unknown wherein their kindness to the Israelites consisted. According to Judg. 1.16; 4.11, Moses' father-in-law was a Kenite, and he extended help to the Israelites (Exod. 18.1–27; Num. 10.29). **8–9:** These vv. highlight the sin—only *the people* are *proscribed,* and *Agag* and the best animal are spared. The vv. emphasize Saul's

value. They would not proscribe them; they proscribed only
[a-]what was cheap and worthless.[-a]
10 The word of the LORD then came to Samuel: 11 "I regret
that I made Saul king, for he has turned away from Me and has
not carried out My commands." Samuel was distressed and
he entreated the LORD all night long. 12 Early in the morning
Samuel went to meet Saul. Samuel was told, "Saul went to Carmel, where he erected a monument for himself; then he left
and went on down to Gilgal."
13 When Samuel came to Saul, Saul said to him, "Blessed are
you of the LORD! I have fulfilled the LORD's command." 14 "Then
what," demanded Samuel, "is this bleating of sheep in my ears,
and the lowing of oxen that I hear?" 15 Saul answered, "They
were brought from the Amalekites, for the troops spared the
choicest of the sheep and oxen for sacrificing to the LORD your
God. And we proscribed the rest." 16 Samuel said to Saul, "Stop!
Let me tell you what the LORD said to me last night!" "Speak,"
he replied. 17 And Samuel said, "You may look small to yourself,
but you are the head of the tribes of Israel. The LORD anointed
you king over Israel, 18 and the LORD sent you on a mission,
saying, 'Go and proscribe the sinful Amalekites; make war on
them until you have exterminated them.' 19 Why did you disobey the LORD and swoop down on the spoil [b-]in defiance of
the LORD's will?"[-b] 20 Saul said to Samuel, "But I did obey the
LORD! I performed the mission on which the LORD sent me:
I captured King Agag of Amalek, and I proscribed Amalek,
21 and the troops took from the spoil some sheep and oxen—
the best of what had been proscribed—to sacrifice to the LORD
your God at Gilgal." 22 But Samuel said:

"Does the LORD delight in burnt offerings and
sacrifices
As much as in obedience to the LORD's command?
Surely, obedience is better than sacrifice,
Compliance than the fat of rams.
23 For rebellion is like the sin of divination,
Defiance, like the iniquity of teraphim.[c]
Because you rejected the LORD's command,
He has rejected you as king."

24 Saul said to Samuel, "I did wrong to transgress the LORD's
command and your instructions; but I was afraid of the troops
and I yielded to them. 25 Please, forgive my offense and come

a-a Meaning of Heb. uncertain. *b-b Lit. "and do what was evil in the sight of the LORD."* *c Idols consulted for oracles; see Ezek. 21.26; Zech. 10.2.*

involvement in this. *Agag:* In Esth. 3.1 Haman is called the Agagite. **11:** Samuel is likely *entreat*ing God to relent, but as v. 29 makes clear, God does not relent in such circumstances. **12:** *Carmel,* a town in the south of Judah. **13:** Did Saul believe he had fulfilled God's command by killing most of the Amalekites, or was he lying? **15:** Saul shifts the blame for the violation of the proscription to the troops, but in the proscription's execution he includes himself (*we*). He also contends that though the choicest animals were spared, this was done for a most worthy purpose. He possibly believes that he has in fact performed the LORD's command. **17:** *You may look small to yourself* (cf. 9.21), but as head of Israel you bear responsibility. **18:** *Sinful,* absent in the command in v. 2, refers to all Amalekites, those at the time of the exodus as well as those living at the time of Saul; atypically in the Bible, the entire nation is condemned forever for its ancestors' actions. **19:** Doing what is evil in the sight of the LORD (see translators' note *b-b)* is a common Deuteronomistic formula of condemnation (see e.g., Deut. 4.25; Judg. 3.12; 1 Kings 15.26). **20–21:** To Samuel's accusation Saul replies by repeating his previous arguments more emphatically and in greater detail, indicating that he has missed Samuel's point. **22–23:** The poetic form of these vv. serves to highlight their significance. They convey the message that right is more important than rite. Samuel is the first in the line of prophets such as Amos, Isaiah, and Micah, who do not attribute paramount importance to sacrifices. Most of the literary prophets demand moral behavior along with ritual; Jeremiah 7.21–23, likely a Deuteronomistic addition to Jeremiah, resembles Samuel in demanding obedience to the LORD. *The fat of rams,* the best part. *Rebellion* against the LORD is like *the sin of divination* (which is a form of idolatry; see Deut. 18.9–14), both involving turning away from Him. The repetition of *rejected* hints at the common biblical principle of measure-for-measure, the punishment corresponding to the sin (see Deut. 19.19 n.). By enthroning Saul the people rejected the LORD as king (8.7); now the LORD rejects Saul as king. **24:** Though now admitting his guilt, Saul justifies himself by shifting the blame to the troops. **25:** In asking for forgiveness Saul hopes that his

back with me, and I will bow low to the LORD." 26 But Samuel
said to Saul, "I will not go back with you; for you have rejected
the LORD's command, and the LORD has rejected you as king
over Israel."
27 As Samuel turned to leave, Saul seized the corner of his
robe, and it tore. 28 And Samuel said to him, "The LORD has
this day torn the kingship over Israel away from you and has
given it to another who is worthier than you. 29 Moreover, the
Glory[a] of Israel does not deceive or change His mind, for He
is not human that He should change His mind." 30 But [Saul]
pleaded, "I did wrong. Please, honor me in the presence of
the elders of my people and in the presence of Israel, and
come back with me until I have bowed low to the LORD your
God." 31 So Samuel followed Saul back, and Saul bowed low
to the LORD.
32 Samuel said, "Bring forward to me King Agag of Amalek."
Agag approached him [b-]with faltering steps;[-b] and Agag said,
"Ah, bitter death is at hand!"[a]
33 Samuel said:

"As your sword has bereaved women,
So shall your mother be bereaved among women."

And Samuel [c-]cut Agag down[-c] before the LORD at Gilgal.
34 Samuel then departed for Ramah, and Saul went up to his
home at Gibeah of Saul.
35 Samuel never saw Saul again to the day of his death. But
Samuel grieved over Saul, because the LORD regretted that He

16

had made Saul king over Israel. 1 And the LORD said to
Samuel, "How long will you grieve over Saul, since I
have rejected him as king over Israel? Fill your horn with oil
and set out; I am sending you to Jesse the Bethlehemite, for I
have decided on one of his sons to be king." 2 Samuel replied,
"How can I go? If Saul hears of it, he will kill me." The LORD
answered, "Take a heifer with you, and say, 'I have come to
sacrifice to the LORD.' 3 Invite Jesse to the sacrificial feast, and
then I will make known to you what you shall do; you shall
anoint for Me the one I point out to you." 4 Samuel did what the

a Meaning of Heb. uncertain. *b-b From root* ma'ad, *"to falter"; cf. Septuagint.*
c-c Meaning of Heb. uncertain.

rejection will be revoked. *Forgiving* and *coming back* are connected; in the next v., Samuel refuses to *go back* with him indicating that Saul has not been forgiven. **28:** Samuel gives a symbolic interpretation to the tearing of the robe (for a similar interpretation, see 1 Kings 11.30–31) an action that David would later repeat, reinforcing the message of this ch that Saul is unsuitable to rule (1 Sam. 24.5). **29:** This v. seems to contradict vv. 11 and 35. The LORD does occasionally regret His previous decisions, for instance when a person's behavior displeases Him (see Gen. 6.6). Perhaps the sense is that He is not fickle like human beings. **30:** This time Saul does not shift the blame to others, but he still accompanies his confession with a personal request to prevent his public humiliation. **31:** Samuel's compliance with Saul's request does not mean that he has forgiven him. **32:** Instead of *with faltering steps,* the Heb may be translated "with delight"; and instead of *is at hand,* "has gone away." According to this interpretation Agag expects that the prophet will save his life. Ironically, however, the opposite happens. **33:** Samuel's second set of poetic lines justify Agag's punishment by stressing its correspondence with his sins, a second case of measure-for-measure in the ch. **34:** See 14.46 n. **35:** The final v. of the unit looks ahead (as in 14.52), but also backwards, highlighting God's *regret* at anointing Saul (v. 11).

16.1–13: Anointing renewed. In this first story about David he still plays a passive role. Even his name is not mentioned until the last v. His being chosen, though the youngest and least esteemed of eight brothers, agrees with the biblical motif of the younger being preferred to the elder: Abel to Cain (Gen. 4.2–5), Isaac to Ishmael (Gen. 21.9–13), Jacob to Esau (Gen. 27.28–40), Joseph to Reuben (Gen. 37.3–11; 49.3–4, 22–26). This indicates that not seniority, but suitability, is the decisive factor. The motif of the younger, or youngest son being chosen (as in the patriarchal stories) may reflect Israel's feeling that it was a latecomer on the world scene, much younger than the great surrounding civilizations of Egypt and Mesopotamia. **1:** Samuel's grieving over Saul links the beginning of this narrative to the end of the previous one. The verb *rejected* evokes not only 15.23, but also 8.7; 10.19; 15.26. The hollow ram's *horn* was used as a vessel. **2:** *He will kill me,* for subversive action. The sacrifice serves to disguise Samuel's mission. Although Deuteronomic principle (see esp. Deut. ch 12) is that sacrifice may only be performed at the central sanctuary. **4:** *In alarm,* in fear that a visit by a prophet like Samuel portends evil. **5:** It is not clear how this ritual purification was carried out. **6–7:** Eliab's *stature* reminds

LORD commanded. When he came to Bethlehem, the elders
of the city went out in alarm to meet him and said, "Do you
come on a peaceful errand?" 5 "Yes," he replied, "I have come
to sacrifice to the LORD. Purify yourselves and join me in the
sacrificial feast." He also instructed Jesse and his sons to purify
themselves and invited them to the sacrificial feast.
6 When they arrived and he saw Eliab, he thought: "Surely
the LORD's anointed stands before Him." 7 But the LORD said to
Samuel, "Pay no attention to his appearance or his stature, for
I have rejected him. For not as man sees [does the LORD see];[a]
man sees only what is visible, but the LORD sees into the heart."
8 Then Jesse called Abinadab and had him pass before Samuel;
but he said, "The LORD has not chosen this one either." 9 Next
Jesse presented Shammah; and again he said, "The LORD has
not chosen this one either." 10 Thus Jesse presented seven of his
sons before Samuel, and Samuel said to Jesse, "The LORD has
not chosen any of these."
11 Then Samuel asked Jesse, "Are these all the boys you
have?" He replied, "There is still the youngest; he is tending
the flock." And Samuel said to Jesse, "Send someone to bring
him, for we will not [b-]sit down to eat[-b] until he gets here." 12 So
they sent and brought him. He was [b-]ruddy-cheeked, bright-
eyed,[-b] and handsome. And the LORD said, "Rise and anoint
him, for this is the one." 13 Samuel took the horn of oil and
anointed him in the presence of his brothers; and the spirit
of the LORD gripped David from that day on. Samuel then set
out for Ramah.
14 Now the spirit of the LORD had departed from Saul, and an
evil spirit from the LORD began to terrify him. 15 Saul's courtiers said to him, "An evil spirit of God is terrifying you. 16 Let our

a These words are preserved in the Septuagint. *b-b Meaning of Heb. uncertain.*

Samuel of Saul, who was also tall (9.2; 10.23). But height and outward appearance are unimportant: God, who knows each person from within, has *rejected* Eliab, just as He rejected Saul. **10:** For the names of Jesse's sons, see 1 Chron. 2.13–15; 27.18. *Seven* is often a number of completion; here it highlights the surprise at the existence of an eighth son. **11:** The shepherd who tends the flock is the one suited to tend the people (cf. Ps. 78.70–71). Moses is depicted as a shepherd (Exod. 3.1) and "shepherd" was a common epithet of the king in the ancient Near East. **12:** David, like Saul, is handsome, and thus suitable for kingship (see 9.1–2 n.). **13:** On anointing, see 10.1 n. *In the presence of his brothers,* without strangers, to keep the anointing secret. *The spirit of the LORD,* see 10.6 n.

16.14–23: The king's musician. David, on arriving at the court, immediately wins Saul's affection, and the initial relations between the king and the young musician are most promising. Saul's problem, the subject of the first part of the narrative, is solved by David in the second part. **14:** The *spirit of the LORD* departed from Saul when it gripped David (v. 13), and in its place came *an evil spirit,* manifested in attacks of mental disorder.
16: Music therapy may be beneficial in relieving mental distress.

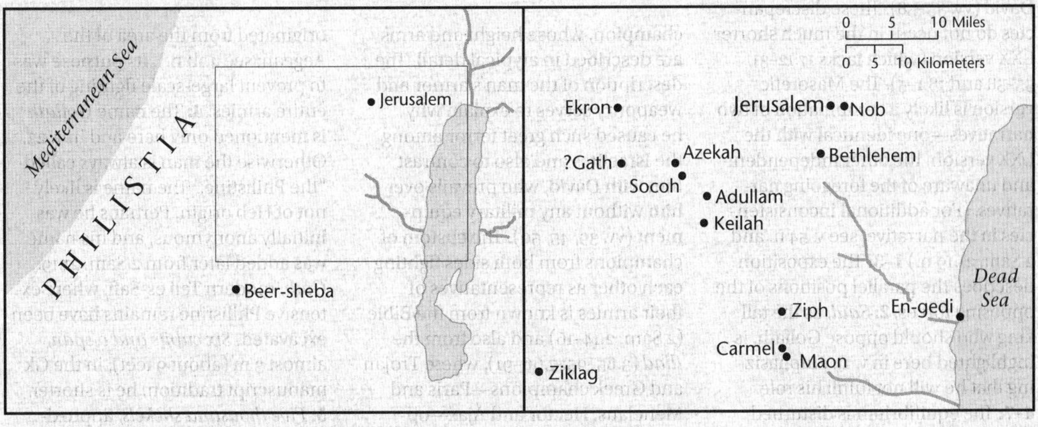

David's early career and his flight from Saul according to First Samuel

lord give the order [and] the courtiers in attendance on you
will look for someone who is skilled at playing the lyre; whenever the evil spirit of God comes over you, he will play it[a] and
you will feel better." 17 So Saul said to his courtiers, "Find me
someone who can play well and bring him to me." 18 One of the
attendants spoke up, "I have observed a son of Jesse the Bethlehemite who is skilled in music; he is a stalwart fellow and a
warrior, sensible in speech, and handsome in appearance, and
the LORD is with him." 19 Whereupon Saul sent messengers to
Jesse to say, "Send me your son David, who is with the flock."
20 Jesse took [b]an ass [laden with][-b] bread, a skin of wine, and a
kid, and sent them to Saul by his son David. 21 So David came
to Saul and entered his service; [Saul] took a strong liking to
him and made him one of his arms-bearers. 22 Saul sent word
to Jesse, "Let David remain in my service, for I am pleased with
him." 23 Whenever the [evil] spirit of God came upon Saul, David would take the lyre and play it;[a] Saul would find relief and
feel better, and the evil spirit would leave him.

17 The Philistines assembled their forces for battle; they
massed at Socoh of Judah, and encamped at Ephes-
dammim, between Socoh and Azekah. 2 Saul and the men of
Israel massed and encamped in the valley of Elah. They drew
up their line of battle against the Philistines, 3 with the Philistines stationed on one hill and Israel stationed on the opposite
hill; the ravine was between them. 4 A champion[c] of the Philistine forces stepped forward; his name was Goliath of Gath,
and he was six cubits and a span tall. 5 He had a bronze helmet
on his head, and wore a breastplate of scale armor, a bronze
breastplate weighing five thousand shekels. 6 He had bronze

a Meaning of Heb. uncertain. *b-b Meaning of Heb. uncertain.*
c Lit. "the man of the space between," i.e., between the armies.

18: The person recommended is not only a skilled musician (cf. Amos 6.5), but excels in many other fields as well. The characterization summarizes David's traits that make him suitable for kingship; these will emerge in the following narratives. Saul, however, is oblivious to the fact that these traits qualify David as a competitor for the throne. David's depiction as a musician contributed to the tradition that he composed the psalms. **20:** The presents serve to express Jesse's loyalty and to secure a favorable treatment for his son.

17.1–18.5: The shepherd boy and the giant. The story of David and Goliath demonstrates the triumph of faith over physical strength. The detailed description of Goliath's weapons and the rejection of Saul's armor by David serve, together with David's speech before the battle (vv. 45–47), to underscore this idea. Fairy-tale motifs have been incorporated in the narrative: A giant terrifies the community; riches and the king's daughter are promised to him who slays the giant; three elder brothers are unable to do so; and only the youngest and least esteemed brother achieves success by the use of clever, unconventional means. Several details in the narrative are inconsistent with the preceding ch: David and his family are introduced as new characters (vv. 12–14); David is with his family in Bethlehem and not with Saul (vv. 17–20); and Saul does not know David (vv. 55–58). These discrepancies do not occur in the much shorter LXX version (which lacks 17.12–31, 55–58 and 18.1–5). The Masoretic version is likely a combination of two narratives—one identical with the LXX version, the other independent and unaware of the foregoing narratives. (For additional inconsistencies in the narrative, see v. 54 n. and 2 Sam. 21.19 n.) **1–3:** The exposition describes the parallel positions of the opposing forces. **2:** *Saul,* as the tall king who should oppose Goliath, is highlighted here in v. 11, emphasizing that he will not fulfill his role. **4–7:** The equilibrium is disturbed by the appearance of the Philistine champion, whose height and arms are described in atypical detail. The description of the man's armor and weaponry serves to explain why he caused such great terror among the Israelites and also to contrast him with David, who prevails over him without any military equipment (vv. 39, 45, 50). The custom of champions from both sides fighting each other as representatives of their armies is known from the Bible (2 Sam. 2.14–16) and also from the *Iliad* (3.85–95; 7.66–91), where Trojan and Greek champions—Paris and Menelaus, Hector and Ajax—oppose each other (the Philistines originated from the area of the Aegean; see 4.1b n.). Its purpose was to prevent large-scale fighting of the entire armies. **4:** The name *Goliath* is mentioned only here and in v. 23. Otherwise the man is always called "the Philistine." The name is likely not of Heb origin. Perhaps he was initially anonymous, and his name was added later from 2 Sam. 21.19. *Gath,* modern Tell es-Safi, where extensive Philistine remains have been excavated. *Six cubits and a span,* almost 3 m (about 9 feet); in the Gk manuscript tradition, he is shorter. **5:** *Five thousand shekels,* approximately 60 kg (about 130 pounds).

greaves on his legs, and a bronze javelin [slung] from his shoulders. [7] The shaft of his spear was like a weaver's bar, and the
iron head of his spear weighed six hundred shekels; and the
shield-bearer marched in front of him.
[8] He stopped and called out to the ranks of Israel and he said
to them, "Why should you come out to engage in battle? I am
the Philistine [champion], and you are Saul's servants. Choose[a]
one of your men and let him come down against me. [9] If he
bests me in combat and kills me, we will become your slaves;
but if I best him and kill him, you shall be our slaves and serve
us." [10] And the Philistine ended, "I herewith defy the ranks of
Israel. Get me a man and let's fight it out!" [11] When Saul and all
Israel heard these words of the Philistine, they were dismayed
and terror-stricken.
[12] David was the son of a certain Ephrathite of Bethlehem
in Judah whose name was Jesse. He had eight sons, and in
the days of Saul the man was already old, advanced in years.[a]
[13] The three oldest sons of Jesse had left and gone with Saul
to the war. The names of his three sons who had gone to the
war were Eliab the first-born, the next Abinadab, and the third
Shammah; [14] and David was the youngest. The three oldest
had followed Saul, [15] and David would go back and forth from
attending on Saul to shepherd his father's flock at Bethlehem.
[16] The Philistine stepped forward morning and evening and
took his stand for forty days.
[17] Jesse said to his son David, "Take an ephah of this parched
corn and these ten loaves of bread for your brothers, and carry
them quickly to your brothers in camp. [18] Take these ten chees-
es[a] to the captain of their thousand. Find out how your brothers are and bring some token[a] from them." [19] Saul and [b-]the
brothers[-b] and all the men of Israel were in the valley of Elah,
in the war against the Philistines.
[20] Early next morning, David left someone in charge of the
flock, took [the provisions], and set out, as his father Jesse had
instructed him. He reached the barricade[a] as the army was
going out to the battle lines shouting the war cry. [21] Israel and
the Philistines drew up their battle lines opposite each other.
[22] David left his baggage with the man in charge of the baggage
and ran toward the battle line and went to greet his brothers.
[23] While he was talking to them, the champion, whose name
was Goliath, the Philistine of Gath, stepped forward from the
Philistine ranks and spoke the same words as before; and David heard him.
[24] When the men of Israel saw the man, they fled in terror.
[25] And the men of Israel were saying [among themselves], "Do
you see that man coming out? He comes out to defy Israel!

a *Meaning of Heb. uncertain.* *b-b* *Heb. "they."*

7: *Like a weaver's bar:* The comparison refers either to the size of the shaft or to a loop attached to it to facilitate hurling. In the first case, the weaver's bar is the beam to which the warp is fastened in a loom; in the second, it denotes the shaft carrying the eyed strings for separating the threads of the warp. *Six hundred shekels,* about 7 kg (15 pounds). **10:** *Defy* is a major key word in this story (vv. 25, 26, 36, 45)—of course, the giant's defiance will be unsuccessful. **12:** Instead of *certain* the Heb has "this," which serves to connect the present narrative to the preceding ones, where Jesse was already mentioned. **14:** The beginning of the v. may also be rendered "and David was the shortest," in contrast to Goliath (and Saul). **15:** This v. alone serves to reconcile this narrative, in which David is at home, with the preceding one, in which he is with Saul. **16:** *Forty days* is a stereotypical biblical number for a long time (see e.g., Gen. 7.4; Exod. 24.18). **17:** The protraction of the war necessitates sending food to the warriors. *Ephah,* 23 liters (about 21 quarts). **18:** *Captain of … thousand,* officer in charge of a large military unit. **19:** These are probably still the words of Jesse, instructing David where to go (instead of *were,* the Heb may be translated "are"). **20:** *Barricade,* lit. "circle," round the army camp (cf. 26.5, where the same word is used). **25:** The text here offers information that was not reported previously; coming from the men of Israel and conveying their perspective it makes Saul recede even further into the background. The exemption refers to "practice of the king" in 8.11–17.

26: *Uncircumcised,* see 14.6 n. In the Heb, *disgrace* and *defy* are from the same root, tying these ideas together. **28:** The eldest brother had great authority in the family, and the younger ones had to obey him. Eliab accuses David of irresponsible behavior, vicious intent, and malice (rather than impudence and impertinence), but David, on the contrary, has acted responsibly (v. 20) and carried out his father's mission faithfully. **31:** As noted in the introduction to the ch, Saul does not know David, in contrast to the previous ch. **33:** The contrast in the Heb is sharper: "you are a boy, and he has been a warrior since his boyhood." **34–35:** *If,* the Heb expresses "each time that." Having fought wild animals more than once, David is not inexperienced in fighting strong opponents. This and the following v. suggest that David does not need the elaborate weapons that Goliath has to kill wild animals or a Philistine foe. **38–39:** David has no military experience and is *not used* to wearing armor; the vv. are comical. **40:** David prefers the simple implements of the shepherd. *Wadi,* a dry streambed. *Sling,* a strip of cloth or leather folded double, in the center of which a stone is placed. The sling is held at the ends and rotated, and then one end is suddenly released, which causes the stone to fly with great force to its target. Exactly hitting the mark requires considerable dexterity (cf. Judg. 20.16). The sling was used by shepherds, hunters, and soldiers, and is illustrated in the Assyrian reliefs showing the conquest of Lachish by Sennacherib in 701 BCE. **42:** Cf. 16.12. **43–47:** Delivering speeches before the battle, which is also attested in the *Iliad* (see vv. 4–7 n.), served to strengthen the spirit of one side and demoralize the other. Whereas the Philistine trusts in his arms, David trusts in the *LORD of Hosts, the God of the ranks of Israel,* who determines *the battle. Dogs* were frequently used as a deprecatory image in the ancient world. In his speech, David turns the battle into one of warring deities. **44:** See the similar curse in

The man who kills him will be rewarded by the king with great
riches; he will also give him his daughter in marriage and grant
exemption[a] to his father's house in Israel." 26 David asked the
men standing near him, "What will be done for the man who
kills that Philistine and removes the disgrace from Israel? Who
is that uncircumcised Philistine that he dares defy the ranks of
the living God?" 27 The troops told him in the same words what
would be done for the man who killed him.

28 When Eliab, his oldest brother, heard him speaking to
the men, Eliab became angry with David and said, "Why did
you come down here, and with whom did you leave those few
sheep in the wilderness? I know your impudence and your
impertinence:[b] you came down to watch the fighting!" 29 But
David replied, "What have I done now? I was only asking!"
30 And he turned away from him toward someone else; he
asked the same question, and the troops gave him the same
answer as before.

31 The things David said were overheard and were reported to
Saul, who had him brought over. 32 David said to Saul, "Let [c]no
man's[c] courage fail him. Your servant will go and fight that Philistine!" 33 But Saul said to David, "You cannot go to that Philistine and fight him; you are only a boy, and he has been a warrior
from his youth!" 34 David replied to Saul, "Your servant has been
tending his father's sheep, and if a lion or[d] a bear came and carried off an animal from the flock, 35 I would go after it and fight
it and rescue it from its mouth. And if it attacked me, I would
seize it by the beard and strike it down and kill it. 36 Your servant
has killed both lion and bear; and that uncircumcised Philistine
shall end up like one of them, for he has defied the ranks of the
living God. 37 The LORD," David went on, "who saved me from
lion and bear will also save me from that Philistine." "Then go,"
Saul said to David, "and may the LORD be with you!"

38 Saul clothed David in his own garment; he placed a bronze
helmet on his head and fastened [e]a breastplate on him.[e] 39 David girded his sword over his garment. Then he [f]tried to walk;
but[f] he was not used to it. And David said to Saul, "I cannot
walk in these, for I am not used to them." So David took them
off. 40 He took his stick, picked a few[g] smooth stones from the
wadi, put them in the pocket[d] of his shepherd's bag and, sling
in hand, he went toward the Philistine.

41 The Philistine, meanwhile, was coming closer to David,
preceded by his shield-bearer. 42 When the Philistine caught
sight of David, he scorned him, for he was but a boy, ruddy

a I.e., freedom from royal levies. *b Lit. "badness of heart."*
c-c Septuagint reads "not my lord's." *d Meaning of Heb. uncertain.*
e-e Heb. "clothed him in a breastplate" (cf. v. 5), because a breastplate was combined with a leather jerkin. *f-f Septuagint reads "was unable to walk, for..."*
g Lit. "five."

and handsome. 43 And the Philistine called out to David, "Am I a dog that you come against me with sticks?" The Philistine cursed David by his gods; 44 and the Philistine said to David, "Come here, and I will give your flesh to the birds of the sky and the beasts of the field."

45 David replied to the Philistine, "You come against me with sword and spear and javelin; but I come against you in the name of the LORD of Hosts, the God of the ranks of Israel, whom you have defied. 46 This very day the LORD will deliver you into my hands. I will kill you and cut off your head; and I will give [a]the carcasses[a] of the Philistine camp to the birds of the sky and the beasts of the earth. All the earth shall know that there is a God in[b] Israel. 47 And this whole assembly shall know that the LORD can give victory without sword or spear. For the battle is the LORD's, and He will deliver you into our hands."

48 When the Philistine began to advance toward him again, David quickly ran up to the battle line to face the Philistine. 49 David put his hand into the bag; he took out a stone and slung it. It struck the Philistine in the forehead; the stone sank into his forehead, and he fell face down on the ground. 50 Thus David bested the Philistine with sling and stone; he struck him down and killed him. David had no sword; 51 so David ran up and stood over the Philistine, grasped his sword and pulled it from its sheath; and with it he dispatched him and cut off his head.

When the Philistines saw that their warrior was dead, they ran. 52 The men of Israel and Judah rose up with a war cry and they pursued the Philistines all the way to Gai[c] and up to the gates of Ekron; the Philistines fell mortally wounded along the road to Shaarim up to Gath and Ekron. 53 Then the Israelites returned from chasing the Philistines and looted their camp.

54 David took the head of the Philistine and brought it to Jerusalem;[d] and he put his weapons in his own tent.

55 When Saul saw David going out to assault the Philistine, he asked his army commander Abner, "Whose son is that boy, Abner?" And Abner replied, "By your life, Your Majesty, I do not know." 56 "Then find out whose son that young fellow is," the king ordered. 57 So when David returned after killing the Philistine, Abner took him and brought him to Saul, with the head of the Philistine still in his hand. 58 Saul said to him, "Whose son are you, my boy?" And David answered, "The son of your servant Jesse the Bethlehemite."

Deut. 28.26. **48:** The heavily armed Philistine moves slowly; David runs quickly. **49:** While still at a distance, David hurls the stone at the unsuspecting Philistine, striking him with the very first shot. **50–51:** Though killed by the stone, Goliath is finished off with his own sword (though vv. 50 and 51 may be from different sources; see intro above). **54:** Since *Jerusalem* was not yet in Israelite hands and David did not yet have his own tent, the v. must be anticipatory (cf. v. 57). David takes Goliath's *weapons* as booty; Goliath's sword will reappear in 21.10 and 22.10. **55–58:** Saul inquires about David's father, though in the preceding narrative he is said to have sent a message to Jesse (see 17.1–18.5 n.). In the past a person's identity was mainly determined by his or her ancestry (see Gen. 24.23–24; 1 Sam. 1.1; 9.1; for David's ancestors, see Ruth 4.18–22). *Abner* was introduced in 14.50, and will play a major role in the later Saul stories.

a-a Septuagint reads "your carcass and the carcasses."
b So many Heb. mss. and ancient versions; other mss. and the editions read "to."
c Septuagint reads "Gath"; cf. end of verse.
d I.e., after David's capture of Jerusalem (2 Sam. 5).

18 When [David] finished speaking with Saul, Jonathan's soul became bound up with the soul of David; Jonathan loved David as himself. 2 Saul took him [into his service] that day and would not let him return to his father's house.—3 Jonathan and David made a pact, because [Jonathan] loved him as himself. 4 Jonathan took off the cloak and tunic he was wearing and gave them to David, together with his sword, bow, and belt. 5 David went out [with the troops], and he was successful in every mission on which Saul sent him, and Saul put him in command of all the soldiers; this pleased all the troops and Saul's courtiers as well. 6 When the [troops] came home [and] David returned from killing the Philistine, [a]the women of all the towns of Israel came out singing and dancing to greet King Saul[a] with timbrels, shouting, and sistrums.[b] 7 The women sang as they danced, and they chanted:

> Saul has slain his thousands;
> David, his tens of thousands!

8 Saul was much distressed and greatly vexed about the matter. For he said, "To David they have given tens of thousands, and to me they have given thousands. All that he lacks is the kingship!" 9 From that day on Saul kept a jealous eye on David. 10 The next day an evil spirit of God gripped Saul and he began to rave in the house, while David was playing [the lyre], as he did daily. Saul had a spear in his hand, 11 and Saul threw[c] the spear, thinking to pin David to the wall. But David eluded him twice. 12 Saul was afraid of David, for the LORD was with him and had turned away from Saul. 13 So Saul removed him from his presence and appointed him chief of a thousand, [d]to march at the head of the troops.[d] 14 David was successful in all his undertakings, for the LORD was with him; 15 and when Saul saw that he was successful, he dreaded him. 16 All Israel and Judah loved David, for he marched at their head.

17 Saul said to David, "Here is my older daughter, Merab; I will give her to you in marriage; in return, you be my warrior and fight the battles of the LORD." Saul thought: "Let not my hand strike him; let the hand of the Philistines strike him." 18 David replied to Saul, "Who am I and [e]what is my life[e]—my

a-a Meaning of Heb. uncertain. Septuagint reads "the dancing women came out to meet David from all the towns of Israel."

b Meaning of Heb. uncertain. *c Change of vocalization yields "raised."*

d-d Lit. "and he went out and came in before the troops."

e-e Meaning of Heb. uncertain. Change of vocalization yields "who are my kin."

18.1–5: Jonathan's love for David is expressed practically in the pact between them, and symbolically in the bestowal of the garments and arms—which, however, were also of considerable real value. These vv. do not necessarily express a homoerotic relationship between David and Jonathan, as often suggested. **5:** This v. hints at trouble ahead, suggesting that David was already perceived as having ideal royal abilities. *Soldiers,* lit. "men of war," i.e., professional soldiers or perhaps raiders.

18.6–30: Jealousy. David, who after his victory over Goliath is successful in all his undertakings and loved by everyone, including the king's son and daughter, arouses the jealousy and enmity of Saul, who schemes to get rid of his perceived rival, but his attempts all fail. Three times the narrative states that David is successful (vv. 5, 14, 30), and three times that Saul fears David because the LORD is with him (vv. 12, 14–15, 28–29). The narrative makes Saul completely transparent by repeatedly and explicitly disclosing his feelings and motives. **6:** For the custom of women greeting the victors with dance and song, see Exod. 15.20–21; Judg. 11.34; 2 Sam. 1.20. **7–8:** *Thousands* and *tens of thousands* are regularly paired in the parallelisms of biblical poetry (e.g., Deut. 32.30; Ps. 91.7), the greater number always appearing in the second line. Thus, although a stereotypical phrase is being used, and this does not imply David's superiority, Saul infers from the order of the numbers that the women praise David more than him. **10:** *The next day:* The indication of time hints at a causal relation between Saul's vexation and his fit of mental disorder. *Rave,* lit. "speak in ecstasy" (see 10.5–6, 10). David *was playing,* see 16.23. **11:** *David eludes* Saul, but foreshadowing later chs, does not try to harm him. **13:** *Chief of a thousand,* 17.18 n. The text hints that Saul attempted to get David killed in battle. **14–15:** The contrast between these two vv. is striking; Saul does not realize that David's success is because *the LORD was with him.* **17:** Saul is prepared to give his daughter to David as promised (17.25), but he imposes additional conditions in a further attempt to have him killed. *Warrior,* lit. "man of strength," i.e., of courage. Saul wants David to undertake daring and dangerous exploits. *The battles of the LORD* are in fact the battles of Israel; as is typical in the ancient Near East, the army fights on behalf of the deity. **18:** David's reply shows his humility. **20:** Michal is the only named woman in all biblical

father's family in Israel—that I should become Your Majesty's son-in-law?" 19 But at the time that Merab, daughter of Saul, should have been given to David, she was given in marriage to Adriel the Meholathite. 20 Now Michal daughter of Saul had fallen in love with David; and when this was reported to Saul, he was pleased. 21 Saul thought: "I will give her to him, and she can serve as a snare for him, so that the Philistines may kill him." So Saul said to David, [a]-"You can become my son-in-law even now through the second one."-[a] 22 And Saul instructed his courtiers to say to David privately, "The king is fond of you and all his courtiers like you. So why not become the king's son-in-law?" 23 When the king's courtiers repeated these words to David, David replied, "Do you think that becoming the son-in-law of a king is a small matter, when I am but a poor man of no consequence?" 24 Saul's courtiers reported to him, "This is what David answered." 25 And Saul said, "Say this to David: 'The king desires no other bride-price than the foreskins of a hundred Philistines, as vengeance on the king's enemies.'"—Saul intended to bring about David's death at the hands of the Philistines.—26 When his courtiers told this to David, David was pleased with the idea of becoming the king's son-in-law. [a]-Before the time had expired,-[a] 27 David went out with his men and killed two hundred[b] Philistines; David brought their foreskins and [a]-they were counted out-[a] for the king, that he might become the king's son-in-law. Saul then gave him his daughter Michal in marriage. 28 When Saul realized that the LORD was with David [c]-and that Michal daughter of Saul loved him,-[c] 29 Saul grew still more afraid of David; and Saul was David's enemy ever after.

30 The Philistine chiefs marched out [to battle]; and every time they marched out, David was more successful than all the other officers of Saul. His reputation soared.

19 Saul urged his son Jonathan and all his courtiers to kill David. But Saul's son Jonathan was very fond of David, 2 and Jonathan told David, "My father Saul is bent on killing you. Be on your guard tomorrow morning; get to a secret place and remain in hiding. 3 I will go out and stand next to my father in the field where you will be, and I will speak to my father about you. If I learn anything, I will tell you." 4 So Jonathan spoke well of David to his father Saul. He said to him, "Let not Your Majesty wrong his servant David, for he has not wronged you; indeed, all his actions have been very much to your advantage. 5 He took his life in his hands and killed the Philistine,

a-a Meaning of Heb. uncertain.

b Septuagint reads "one hundred" and cf. 2 Sam. 3.14.

c-c Septuagint reads "and that all Israel loved him."

narrative of whom it is said that she loves a man (see also v. 28). **25:** Since David is poor (v. 23) he cannot pay the expected bride-price (see Exod. 22.15 n.). *Foreskins:* This would prove that David has killed Philistines, who were not circumcised (see 14.6 n.), and not men of another group. **27:** According to the MT (but not the LXX) David doubles the bride-price, which shows his prowess in battle. He becomes the king's son-in-law at Saul's, not his own, initiative. This position gives him right of succession, though Saul's own sons have precedence. **28:** It took a long time for Saul to understand that *the LORD was with David.*

19.1–24: Escape. All three stories in this ch deal with Saul's unconcealed efforts to kill David. Saul's own children, Jonathan and Michal, prove their love for David by acting in his behalf, opposing their father. **1:** See 18.1-4. **2:** *Tomorrow morning,* the time fixed for killing David. **4:** *Wrong,* lit. "sin against." *Wronged,* lit. "sinned against." **5:** *Incur the guilt of,* lit. "sin by." The repetitions of "sin" emphasize that by killing a man without sin Saul will gravely sin himself. This contrasts with David's behavior throughout the book, when he refuses to kill the guilty Saul.

and the LORD wrought a great victory for all Israel. You saw it
and rejoiced. Why then should you incur the guilt of shedding
the blood of an innocent man, killing David without cause?"
6 Saul heeded Jonathan's plea, and Saul swore, "As the LORD
lives, he shall not be put to death!" 7 Jonathan called David,
and Jonathan told him all this. Then Jonathan brought David
to Saul, and he served him as before.

8 Fighting broke out again. David went out and fought the
Philistines. He inflicted a great defeat upon them and they fled
before him. 9 Then an evil spirit of the LORD came upon Saul
while he was sitting in his house with his spear in his hand,
and David was playing [the lyre]. 10 Saul tried to pin David to
the wall with the spear, but he eluded Saul, so that he drove the
spear into the wall. David fled and got away.

That night 11 Saul sent messengers to David's home to keep
watch on him and to kill him in the morning. But David's wife
Michal told him, "Unless you run for your life tonight, you will
be killed tomorrow." 12 Michal let David down from the window and he escaped and fled. 13 Michal then took the household idol, laid it on the bed, and covered it with a cloth; and
at its head she put a net of goat's hair. 14 Saul sent messengers
to seize David; but she said, "He is sick." 15 Saul, however, sent
back the messengers to see David for themselves. "Bring him
up to me in the bed," he ordered, "that he may be put to death."
16 When the messengers came, they found the household idol
in the bed, with the net of goat's hair at its head. 17 Saul said to
Michal, "Why did you play that trick on me and let my enemy
get away safely?" "Because," Michal answered Saul, "he said to
me: 'Help me get away or I'll kill you.' "

18 David made good his escape, and he came to Samuel at
Ramah and told him all that Saul had done to him. He and
Samuel went and stayed at Naioth. 19 Saul was told that David
was at Naioth in Ramah, 20 and Saul sent messengers to seize
David. They[a] saw a band of prophets [b-]speaking in ecstasy,[-b]
with Samuel standing by [c-]as their leader;[-c] and the spirit of God
came upon Saul's messengers and they too began to speak in
ecstasy. 21 When Saul was told about this, he sent other messengers; but they too spoke in ecstasy. Saul sent a third group
of messengers; and they also spoke in ecstasy. 22 So he himself
went to Ramah. When he came to [d-]the great cistern at Secu,[-d]
he asked, "Where are Samuel and David?" and was told that
they were at Naioth in Ramah. 23 He was on his way there, to
Naioth in Ramah, when the spirit of God came upon him too;
and he walked on, speaking in ecstasy, until he reached Naioth
in Ramah. 24 Then he too stripped off his clothes and he too

a *Heb. "He."* *b-b* *Cf. note at 10.5.* *c-c* *Meaning of Heb. uncertain.*
d-d *Septuagint reads "the cistern of the threshing floor on the bare height."*

6: Saul will almost immediately break this vow, becoming guilty not only of attempted murder, but of violating a vow. **8–10:** David's success again arouses Saul's jealousy, and Saul attempts to kill David. This may be a doublet of 18.10–11, though in this case, David flees from Saul, unlike the earlier instance. **11:** *To keep watch,* so that David cannot escape. Saul imagined it unseemly to kill David while sleeping at night, or perhaps he just wanted to wait until he woke up and left the house (see Judg. 16.2). **13:** Michal risks her life in order to gain time for David and enable him to get farther away; she thus joins Jonathan in favoring David over her own father. *Household idol,* see Gen. 31.19, 35. **15:** The image is fantastic, and further denigrates Saul, who would consider carrying an ailing man in his bed—just to be murdered! **17:** Michal lies to her father, telling him that self-preservation prompted her to help her husband to escape, while in fact she acted out of love for David. Her explanation does not account for the deception of her father with the household idol (v. 16). **18:** David flees north to Samuel, who has anointed him, and not south to his family in Bethlehem, where Saul would probably look for him. **20–24:** Just like Balaam and Balak (Num. chs 22–24), Saul and his officers do not learn from repeated experience that the divine will cannot be contravened. **20:** *The spirit of God* plays a disproportionate role in the Saul stories (see 10.10; 11.6; 16.15, 23; 18.10), uniting them. **24:** *"Is Saul too among the prophets?"* The origin of this saying was explained differently at 10.10–12. There, following Saul's election, it referred to him in a positive sense; here, after his rejection, it alludes to his disgraceful, degrading behavior; using different words, the v. twice emphasizes Saul's nakedness.

spoke in ecstasy before Samuel; and he lay naked all that day and all night. That is why people say, "Is Saul too among the prophets?"

20 David fled from Naioth in Ramah; he came to Jonathan and said, "What have I done, what is my crime and my guilt against your father, that he seeks my life?" 2 He replied, "Heaven forbid! You shall not die. My father does not do anything, great or small, without disclosing it to me; why should my father conceal this matter from me? It cannot be!" 3 David [a]swore further,[a] "Your father knows well that you are fond of me and has decided: Jonathan must not learn of this or he will be grieved. But, as the LORD lives and as you live, there is only a step between me and death." 4 Jonathan said to David, "Whatever you want, I will do it for you."

5 David said to Jonathan, "Tomorrow is the new moon, and I [b]am to sit with the king at the meal. Instead, let[b] me go and I will hide in the countryside until the third[c] evening. 6 If your father notes my absence, you say, 'David asked my permission to run down to his home town, Bethlehem, for the whole family has its annual sacrifice there.' 7 If he says 'Good,' your servant is safe; but if his anger flares up, know that he is resolved to do [me] harm. 8 Deal faithfully with your servant, since you have taken your servant into a covenant of the LORD with you. And if I am guilty, kill me yourself, but don't make me go back to your father." 9 Jonathan replied, "Don't talk like that! If I learn that my father has resolved to kill you, I will surely tell you about it." 10 David said to Jonathan, "Who will tell me if[d] your father answers you harshly?" 11 Jonathan said to David, "Let us go into the open"; and they both went out into the open.

12 [e]Then Jonathan said to David, "By the LORD, the God of Israel! I will sound out my father at this time tomorrow, [or] on the third day; and if [his response] is favorable for David, I will send a message to you at once and disclose it to you. 13 But if my father intends to do you harm, may the LORD do thus to Jonathan and more if I do [not] disclose it to you and send you off to escape unharmed. May the LORD be with you, as He used to be with my father. 14 Nor shall you fail to show me the [f]LORD's faithfulness,[f] while I am alive; nor, when I am dead, 15 shall you ever discontinue your faithfulness to my house—not even after the LORD has wiped out every one of David's

a-a Septuagint reads "replied to him."
b-b Septuagint reads "will not sit ... meal. Let ..."
c Septuagint lacks "third."
d Meaning of Heb. uncertain.
e The meaning of several parts of vv. 12–16 is uncertain.
f-f I.e., the faithfulness pledged in the covenant before the LORD.

20.1–21.1: Friendship. The story demonstrates Jonathan's profound friendship for David, in spite of his knowledge that David's success will be at his expense. The narrative consists of four parts. The first part, in Jonathan's house, and the second part, in the open, deal with planning; the third part, in Saul's house, and the fourth, in the open again, tell of the execution of the plans. Like the previous narrative, it shows Saul being deceived by a member of his own family. **1:** The repetitions in David's question express his distress (the Heb contains three questions). **2:** Jonathan is unaware of Saul's attempts to kill David (see 19.6). **5:** The *new moon* was celebrated as a festival (see Num. 28.11; 2 Kings 4.23; Isa. 1.13; Amos 8.5), which included a festive meal. In postbiblical times the day lost its importance as a festival, but great significance was attached to the Rabbis' official proclamation of the new moon since that determined when festivals would be commemorated. The moon's renewal is still marked in Jewish liturgy by special prayers and by the ceremony of Blessing the Moon, which is performed at night, when the new moon can clearly be seen. *Third,* counting from and including the present day. **6:** We know little about the annual sacrifice (see 1.21), though this context seems to suggest that different families observed this festival at different times—it functions as an annual family reunion. **8:** *Faithfully,* in accordance with the covenant (see 18.3). *Don't make me go back,* as you did last time (19.7). **11:** *The open,* where one can talk in private (cf. Gen. 31.4). **12:** *Third,* see v. 5 n. **13:** *Thus ... and more,* see 3.17 n. If Saul's response is favorable, Jonathan will inform David through a messenger; if harmful, Jonathan will come and disclose it himself, because a messenger could reveal David's whereabouts to Saul. *As He used to be with my father,* a hint that David will be king. **14–16:** Jonathan, who deals faithfully with David now, wants David to deal faithfully with him and his offspring in the future. **15:** *My house:* To secure his throne the king of a

enemies from the face of the earth. 16 Thus has Jonathan covenanted with the house of David; and may the LORD requite the enemies of David!"

17 Jonathan, out of his love for David, adjured[a] him again, for he loved him as himself. 18 Jonathan said to him, "Tomorrow will be the new moon; and you will be missed when your seat remains vacant.[b] 19 So the day after tomorrow, go down [c-]all the way[-c] to the place where you hid [d-]the other time,[-d] and stay close to the Ezel stone. 20 Now I will shoot three arrows to one side of it, as though I were shooting at a mark, 21 and I will order the boy to go and find the arrows. If I call to the boy, 'Hey! the arrows are on this side of you,' be reassured[e] and come, for you are safe and there is no danger—as the LORD lives! 22 But if, instead, I call to the lad, 'Hey! the arrows are beyond you,' then leave, for the LORD has sent you away. 23 As for the promise we made to each other,[f] may the LORD be [witness] between you and me forever."

24 David hid in the field. The new moon came, and the king sat down to partake of the meal. 25 When the king took his usual place on the seat by the wall, Jonathan rose[g] and Abner sat down at Saul's side; but David's place remained vacant. 26 That day, however, Saul said nothing. "It's accidental," he thought. [h-]"He must be unclean and not yet cleansed."[-h] 27 But on the day after the new moon, the second day, David's place was vacant again. So Saul said to his son Jonathan, "Why didn't the son of Jesse[i] come to the meal yesterday or today?" 28 Jonathan answered Saul, "David begged leave of me to go to Bethlehem. 29 He said, 'Please let me go, for we are going to have a family feast in our town and my brother has summoned me to it. Do me a favor, let me slip away to see my kinsmen.' That is why he has not come to the king's table."

30 Saul flew into a rage against Jonathan. "You son of a perverse, rebellious woman!" he shouted. "I know that you side with the son of Jesse—to your shame, and to the shame of your mother's nakedness! 31 For as long as the son of Jesse lives on earth, neither you nor your kingship will be secure. Now then, have him brought to me, for he is marked for death." 32 But Jonathan spoke up and said to his father, "Why should he be put to death? What has he done?" 33 At that, Saul threw[j] his spear at him to strike him down; and Jonathan realized that his father was determined to do away with David. 34 Jonathan rose from the table in a rage. He ate no food on the second day of the new moon, because he was grieved about David, and because his father had humiliated him.

a Septuagint reads "swore to." *b At the festal meal.* *c-c Lit. "very much."*
d-d Lit. "on the day of the incident"; see 19.2 ff. *e Lit. "accept it."*
f See above, vv. 12–17. *g Force of Heb. uncertain; Septuagint "faced him."*
h-h Heb. construction unclear. *i See note at 10.11.* *j See 18.11 and note.*

new dynasty often killed the former king's relatives (1 Kings 15.29; 16.11; 2 Kings 10.11). Jonathan recognizes that David will succeed his father. References to *house* and *ever* (better rendered "forever") foreshadow the promise of an eternal dynasty to David in 2 Sam. ch 7. **17:** Jonathan's motive to help David is his deep love for him, not his desire to secure his and his offspring's future destiny. **20–22:** The sign with the *arrows* is both practical and symbolic. If the arrows fly far, that means David must leave, and this gives him time to flee, and vice versa. **23:** *May the LORD be [witness] between you and me:* May the LORD watch over each of us that we keep the covenant (cf. Gen. 31.49). **26:** Ritual impurity prevented one from participating in ritual meals. A frequent cause of impurity was the emission of semen, but in that event one could become pure again in the evening according to the legislation in Lev. 15.16–18; see similarly 1 Sam. 16.5. **29:** *My brother has summoned me,* probably the eldest brother (see 17.28 n.). *Slip away,* elsewhere the Heb conveys "escape," hinting that this is precisely what David is doing. **30:** It is clear from Jonathan's answer that he sides with David. This infuriates Saul and causes him to use obscene language. Both *shame* (besides its usual meaning) and *nakedness* denote the genitals. The insult is directed at the son, not the mother. **31:** *Marked for death,* better "legally deserving to die" (see 1 Sam. 26.16; 2 Sam. 12.5); Saul is baselessly accusing David of treason. **33:** Saul has no answer to Jonathan's questions, because David has committed no capital crime, so Saul throws his spear at him. This action mirrors 18.11 and 19.10, where Saul tried to kill David with his spear; the situation has escalated and Saul wants to kill his own son. **34:** *Grieved,* see v. 3.

[35] In the morning, Jonathan went out into the open for the
meeting with David, accompanied by a young boy. [36] He said
to the boy, "Run ahead and find the arrows that I shoot." And as
the boy ran, he shot the arrows past him. [37] When the boy came
to the place where the arrows shot by Jonathan had fallen, Jonathan called out to the boy, "Hey, the arrows are beyond you!"
[38] And Jonathan called after the boy, "Quick, hurry up. Don't
stop!" So Jonathan's boy gathered the arrows and came back to
his master.—[39] The boy suspected nothing; only Jonathan and
David knew the arrangement.—[40] Jonathan handed the gear to
his boy and told him, "Take these back to the town." [41] When
the boy got there, David [a-]emerged from his concealment at[-a]
the Negeb.[b] He flung himself face down on the ground and
bowed low three times. They kissed each other and wept together; David wept the longer.
[42] Jonathan said to David, "Go in peace! For we two have
sworn to each other in the name of the LORD: 'May the LORD be
21 [witness] between you and me, and between your offspring and mine, forever!' " [1] David then went his way,
and Jonathan returned to the town.
[2] David went to the priest Ahimelech at Nob. Ahimelech
came out in alarm to meet David, and he said to him, "Why are
you alone, and no one with you?" [3] David answered the priest
Ahimelech, "The king has ordered me on a mission, and he
said to me, 'No one must know anything about the mission on
which I am sending you and for which I have given you orders.'
So I have [c-]directed [my] young men to[-c] such and such a place.
[4] Now then, what have you got on hand? Any[d] loaves of bread?
Let me have them—or whatever is available." [5] The priest answered David, "I have no ordinary bread on hand; there is only
consecrated bread—provided the young men have kept away
from women." [6] In reply to the priest, David said, "I assure you
that women have been kept from us, as always. Whenever
I went on a mission, even if the journey was a common one,
the vessels of the young men were consecrated; all the more
then [e-]may consecrated food be put into their vessels today."[-e]
[7] So the priest gave him consecrated bread, because there was
none there except the bread of display, which had been removed from the presence of the LORD, to be replaced by warm
bread as soon as it was taken away.—[8] Now one of Saul's officials was there that day, [f-]detained before the LORD;[-f] his name
was Doeg the Edomite, Saul's [g-]chief herdsman.[-g]

38: Jonathan's words are directed at the boy and David at the same time. **41:** This is a modification of the original plan, according to v. 22, David was supposed to flee immediately. **42:** An expansion of the oath in v. 23. **21.1:** This v. serves to mark the end of the story (cf. 26.25); 21.2 starts the next episode, which focuses on David (without Jonathan).

21.2–10: The helpful priest. David, finding himself, after his hasty flight, without food or weapon, gets consecrated bread and Goliath's sword. **2:** *Ahimelech* was the great-grandson of Eli and brother of Ahijah (see 14.3). *In alarm,* because David, a high army commander, came unaccompanied; this also creates a parallel to the arrival of Samuel in 16.4. **3:** In order to obtain food David lies to Ahimelech. His lie has dire consequences. **5:** *Consecrated bread,* see Lev. 24.5–9. The bread in the Tabernacle was renewed once a week, and the old bread was eaten by the priests in the sacred precinct; perhaps the same practice took place here at the shrine in Nob. *Provided the young men have kept away from women:* According to Lev. 15.18 sexual intercourse entails ritual impurity. Ahimelech respectfully refrains from mentioning David himself, but he is of course included in the provision. **6:** Deut. 23.10–12 implies that soldiers were prohibited from having sexual relations. Not only the persons but the eating *vessels* as well are ritually pure, and thus may come in contact with the consecrated showbread. **8:** Doeg's presence at the sanctuary is noted because of its importance for the story in the next ch. According to 1 Chron. 27.30–31, foreigners were also employed in David's young kingdom. There is no value judgment in being singled out as a foreigner; this information is given to explain why, unlike all Israel (18.16), he is not aligned with David.

a-a Lit. "rose up from beside." *b Identical with the "Ezel Stone," v. 19.*
c-c Meaning of Heb. uncertain. 4QSam[b] (cf. Septuagint) reads "made an appointment with [my] young men at..."
d Lit. "five." *e-e Meaning of Heb. uncertain in part.*
f-f I.e., excluded from the shrine, perhaps because of ritual impurity.
g-g Meaning of Heb. uncertain.

9 David said to Ahimelech, "Haven't you got a spear or sword on hand? I didn't take my sword or any of my weapons with me, because the king's mission was urgent." 10 The priest said, "There is the sword of Goliath the Philistine whom you slew in the valley of Elah; it is over there, wrapped in a cloth, behind the ephod. If you want to take that one, take it, for there is none here but that one." David replied, "There is none like it; give it to me."

11 That day David continued on his flight from Saul and he came to King Achish of Gath. 12 The courtiers of Achish said to him, "Why, that's David, king of the land! That's the one of whom they sing as they dance:

Saul has slain his thousands;
David, his tens of thousands."

13 These words worried David and he became very much afraid of King Achish of Gath. 14 So he concealed his good sense from them; he feigned madness [a-]for their benefit.[-a] He scratched marks on the doors of the gate and let his saliva run down his beard. 15 And Achish said to his courtiers, "You see the man is raving; why bring him to me? 16 Do I lack madmen that you have brought this fellow to rave for me? Should this fellow enter my house?"

22 David departed from there and escaped to the cave[b] of Adullam; and when his brothers and all his father's house heard, they joined him down there. 2 Everyone who was in straits and everyone who was in debt and everyone who was desperate joined him, and he became their leader; there were about four hundred men with him. 3 David went from there to Mizpeh of Moab, and he said to the king of Moab, "Let my father and mother come [and stay] with you, until I know what God will do for me." 4 So he [c-]led them to[-c] the king of Moab, and they stayed with him as long as David remained in the stronghold.[b] 5 But the prophet Gad said to David, "Do not stay in the stronghold; go at once to the territory of Judah." So David left and went to the forest of Hereth.

6 When Saul heard that David and the men with him had been located—Saul was then in Gibeah, sitting under the tamarisk

a-a Lit. "in their hand"; meaning of Heb. uncertain.
b The "cave" in v. 1 is referred to as "stronghold" in vv. 4–5; cf. the same variation in 2 Sam. 23.13–14; 1 Chron. 11.15–16. *c-c Targum and Syriac read "left them with."*

10: The sword of Goliath was kept at the sanctuary as a trophy (cf. 5.1–2; 31.10). Its exact place is described because it will play a role in the next ch. *Ephod,* see 14.3 n.

21.11–16: In Philistia. David flees to the Philistine city of Gath, believing that there he will be out of danger, but he barely succeeds in saving his life. It is ironic that he flees there, having just secured the sword of Goliath the Gittite. **12:** The song of the women (18.7) has spread to the Philistines (see 29.5), and the courtiers infer from it that David, who features in the song together with Saul, is master of the land—a conclusion not far from that of Saul himself (18.8). **13:** David, understanding that he has been recognized, fears for his life, because the cited song celebrates his victory over the Philistines and particularly over Goliath, whose origin was from Gath. **14:** *For their benefit,* the Heb can also be interpreted, "[when] in their control." The Lachish reliefs showing Sennacherib's deportation of the city depict the Judeans as bearded. **15:** David's clever ruse succeeds. It is clear that Achish wants David to be expelled (the expulsion is mentioned explicitly at the heading of Ps. 34, which likely knows this ch).

22.1–5: Head of a band. David, as leader of a group of people who fled from the established order, now has a force of his own at his disposal. **1:** The members of David's family, who are in danger from Saul, join David at *Adullam,* situated in the border region between Judah and Philistia. **3:** David takes care of his parents, for whom a fugitive's life would be too strenuous. He probably has family relations in Moab, since, according to Ruth, his great-grandmother was a Moabite, who married into a family from Bethlehem (Ruth 1.1, 4; 4.17). This story is a remarkable exception to the normally hostile relations between Israel and Moab found throughout the Bible. **4:** *Stronghold,* probably at Adullam. But perhaps all the "strongholds of the wilderness" (23.14) are meant, and the space of time mentioned refers to all the wanderings of David in the wilderness. **5:** *Gad,* mentioned only here and in 2 Sam. ch 24, where in v. 11 he is called "David's seer." Passages such as 2 Sam. 2.1 may suggest that David had a personal seer to advise him on military matters.

22.6–23: The massacre. This narrative continues the story of 21.2–10: All priests and inhabitants of Nob are killed because of Ahimelech's help to David. Saul, fearing David, whom he considers a rebel, wants to set a deterring example, and does not even shrink from sacrilege. In his

tree on the height, spear in hand, with all his courtiers in attendance upon him—7 Saul said to the courtiers standing about him, "Listen, men of Benjamin! Will the son of Jesse[a] give fields and vineyards to every one of you? And will he make all of you captains of thousands or captains of hundreds? 8 Is that why all of you have conspired against me? For no one informs me when my own son makes a pact with the son of Jesse; no one is concerned[b] for me and no one informs me when my own son has set my servant [c]in ambush[c] against me, as is now the case."

9 Doeg the Edomite, who was standing among the courtiers of Saul, spoke up: "I saw the son of Jesse come to Ahimelech son of Ahitub at Nob. 10 He inquired of the LORD on his behalf and gave him provisions; he also gave him the sword of Goliath the Philistine." 11 Thereupon the king sent for the priest Ahimelech son of Ahitub and for all the priests belonging to his father's house at Nob. They all came to the king, 12 and Saul said, "Listen to me, son[a] of Ahitub." "Yes, my lord," he replied. 13 And Saul said to him, "Why have you and the son of Jesse conspired against me? You gave him food and a sword, and inquired of God for him—that he may rise [c]in ambush[c] against me, as is now the case."

14 Ahimelech replied to the king, "But who is there among all your courtiers as trusted as David, son-in-law of Your Majesty and [d]obedient to your bidding,[d] and esteemed in your household? 15 This is the first time that I inquired of God for him; [e]I have done no wrong.[e] Let not Your Majesty find fault with his servant [or] with any of my father's house; for your servant knew nothing whatever about all this." 16 But the king said, "You shall die, Ahimelech, you and all your father's house." 17 And the king commanded the guards standing by, "Turn about and kill the priests of the LORD, for they are in league with David; they knew he was running away and they did not inform me." But the king's servants would not raise a hand to strike down the priests of the LORD. 18 Thereupon the king said to Doeg, "You, Doeg, go and strike down the priests." And Doeg the Edomite went and struck down the priests himself; that day, he killed eighty-five men [f]who wore the linen ephod.[f] 19 He put Nob, the town of the priests, to the sword: men and women, children and infants, oxen, asses, and sheep—[all] to the sword.

20 But one son of Ahimelech son of Ahitub escaped—his name was Abiathar—and he fled to David. 21 When Abiathar

a See note at 10.11. *b For this meaning of* ḥoleh, *cf. Amos 6.6.*
c-c Septuagint reads "as an enemy."
d-d Cf. Isa. 11.14; but meaning of Heb. uncertain. *e-e Lit. "Far be it from me!"*
f-f Septuagint reads "bearers of the ephod"; cf. note at 2.28.

insanity he suspects everyone of conspiring against him. This ch is part of the main pattern of the second half of 1 Sam.: David spares Saul, who is guilty, while Saul kills and attempts to kill those who are innocent (David, Jonathan, and here, the priests of Nob). **6:** *Sitting under the tamarisk tree,* cf. 14.2; Judg. 4.5. *Spear in hand,* as symbol of his rule (see 26.11 n.), but also hinting that he is about to use it improperly, as he did against David and Jonathan. **7:** Saul's courtiers belong to his tribe, Benjamin. Kings used to distribute *fields and vineyards* and appoint army officers as signs of personal favor to those closest to them (see 8.12, 14), and Saul is saying that David, from the tribe of Judah, will not benefit the men of Benjamin. **8:** *My servant:* Saul makes it clear that David is his subordinate. **9:** *Doeg the Edomite,* see 21.8. **10:** The giving of provisions and the sword of Goliath to David was reported in 21.7, 10, but no mention was made there of inquiring of the LORD. Either Doeg lied or when Ahimelech went behind the ephod to take the sword and unwrap it from its cloth, Doeg imagined that the priest went to inquire of the LORD (see 21.10 n.). **11–13:** Saul summons Ahimelech and all the priests, accusing them of conspiracy. **14–15:** Ahimelech justifies himself, arguing that he aided David because he knew of the latter's esteemed and trusted position at the court and he was not aware that this had changed. **15:** The Heb can also be translated: "Did I begin now to inquire of God for him? Far be it from me!" According to this rendering Ahimelech denies that he inquired of God for David, perhaps the most serious charge leveled by Saul. **18:** Only Doeg, not being Israelite, is prepared to execute the king's order and kill the priests of the LORD. *Linen ephod,* see 2.18–21 n. **19:** Compare the enumeration here with 15.3. The similarity of the two lists (there camels are also mentioned, because those animals were kept by the Amalekites, who were desert nomads) suggests that what Saul failed to do to Amalek, though commanded by the LORD, he did to his own town of priests of the LORD, strongly condemning Saul. **20:** The massacre of the priests may be the fulfillment of the prophecy of 2.33, and the "offspring" mentioned there may refer to Abiathar. This prophecy-fulfillment pattern is a

told David that Saul had killed the priests of the LORD, 22 David said to Abiathar, "I knew that day, when Doeg the Edomite
was there, that he would tell Saul. I [a]am to blame for all the
deaths[a] in your father's house. 23 Stay with me; do not be
afraid; for [a]whoever seeks your life must seek my life also.[a] It
will be my care to guard you."

23 David was told: "The Philistines are raiding Keilah and
plundering the threshing floors." 2 David consulted the
LORD, "Shall I go and attack those Philistines?" And the LORD
said to David, "Go; attack the Philistines and you will save
Keilah." 3 But David's men said to him, "Look, we are afraid
here in Judah, how much more if we go to Keilah against the
forces of the Philistines!" 4 So David consulted the LORD again,
and the LORD answered him, "March down at once to Keilah,
for I am going to deliver the Philistines into your hands." 5 David and his men went to Keilah and fought against the Philistines; he drove off their cattle and inflicted a severe defeat on
them. Thus David saved the inhabitants of Keilah.

6 When Abiathar son of Ahimelech fled to David at Keilah,
[a]he brought down an ephod with him.[a]

7 Saul was told that David had come to Keilah, and Saul
thought, "God has delivered[b] him into my hands, for he has
shut himself in by entering a town with gates and bars." 8 Saul
summoned all the troops for war, to go down to Keilah and besiege David and his men. 9 When David learned that Saul was
planning[b] to harm him, he told the priest Abiathar to bring
the ephod forward. 10 And David said, "O LORD, God of Israel,
Your servant has heard that Saul intends to come to Keilah and
destroy the town because of me. 11 Will the citizens of Keilah
deliver me into his hands? Will Saul come down, as Your servant has heard? O LORD, God of Israel, tell Your servant!" And
the LORD said, "He will." 12 David continued, "Will the citizens
of Keilah deliver me and my men into Saul's hands?" And the
LORD answered, "They will." 13 So David and his men, about
six hundred in number, left Keilah at once and moved about
wherever they could. And when Saul was told that David had
got away from Keilah, he did not set out.

14 David was staying [a]in the strongholds of the wilderness
[of Judah];[a] he stayed in the hill country, in the wilderness of
Ziph. Saul searched for him constantly, but God did not deliver him into his hands. 15 David was once at Horesh in the
wilderness of Ziph, when David learned that Saul had come

a-a *Meaning of Heb. uncertain.* b *Meaning of Heb. uncertain.*

central characteristic of the Deuteronomistic History. **22–23:** David feels responsible for the disaster, and he promises to protect Abiathar's life like his own.

23.1–13: Consulting the LORD. In the preceding narrative Ahimelech was (falsely) accused of having consulted God for David; in the present one Ahimelech's son Abiathar actually and repeatedly consults God for David. Consulting God is a recurring theme through ch 30. When successful, it is a sign that God is with David; when unsuccessful, that He is not with Saul. The first part of this narrative tells of David's deliverance of Keilah, the second part of his escape from Keilah. **1:** The Philistines came at the end of the harvest to plunder the crops (cf. Judg. 6.3). **2–3:** David wants to use his force to help Keilah, but his motley band (see 22.1–5) lacks the courage. **4:** The LORD's second reply, explicitly promising to deliver the Philistines into David's hands, aids in instilling confidence in the men. **5:** *He drove off their cattle:* The Philistines had come with their livestock, taking over the town (cf. Judg. 6.5). **6:** Abiathar's flight to David was already reported in 22.20, before David's rescue of Keilah. *Keilah* here may be the result of dittography. An *ephod* probably contained Urim and Thummim, the means for consulting the LORD; it likely offered yes-no answers only. Regarding the technique of consulting the LORD, see 14.40–42 n. **7:** The only way to leave the walled town was through the gates, and there David could easily be captured. **11:** David asks two questions, but because it was possible to ask only one at a time, he has to repeat his first question. **12:** Notwithstanding their rescue by David the citizens of Keilah will deliver him into Saul's hands. They greatly fear Saul after he massacred the whole town of Nob because of the help extended to David. **13:** *Six hundred:* According to 22.2 there were about 400 men with David, so meanwhile the number has increased.

23.14–18: Encouragement. Jonathan comes to David's hiding place to encourage him, assuring his friend that eventually he will become king. **14:** *Strongholds,* table mountains with steep sides, providing natural

out to seek his life. [16] And Saul's son Jonathan came to David at Horesh and encouraged him in [the name of] God. [17] He said to him, "Do not be afraid: the hand of my father Saul will never touch you. You are going to be king over Israel and I shall be second to you; and even my father Saul knows this is so." [18] And the two of them entered into a pact before the LORD. David remained in Horesh, and Jonathan went home.

[19][a]Some Ziphites went up to Saul in Gibeah and said, "David is hiding among us in the strongholds of Horesh, at the hill of Hachilah south of Jeshimon. [20] So if Your Majesty has the desire to come down, come down, and it will be our task to deliver him into Your Majesty's hands." [21] And Saul replied, "May you be blessed of the LORD for the compassion you have shown me! [22] Go now and prepare further. Look around and learn what places he sets foot on [and] who has seen him there, for I have been told he is a very cunning fellow. [23] Look around and learn in which of all his hiding places he has been hiding, and return to me when you are certain. I will then go with you, and if he is in the region, I will search him out among all the clans of Judah."

[24] They left at once for Ziph, ahead of Saul; David and his men were then in the wilderness of Maon, in the Arabah, to the south of Jeshimon. [25] When Saul and his men came to search, David was told about it; and he went down to [b-]the rocky region[-b] and stayed in the wilderness of Maon. On hearing this, Saul pursued David in the wilderness of Maon. [26] Saul was making his way along one side of a hill, and David and his men were on the other side of the hill. [b-]David was trying hard to elude Saul, and Saul and his men were trying to encircle David and his men and capture them,[-b] [27] when a messenger came and told Saul, "Come quickly, for the Philistines have invaded the land." [28] Saul gave up his pursuit of David and went to meet the Philistines. That is why that place came to be called the Rock of Separation.[c]

24 David went from there and stayed in the wildernesses of En-gedi.

[2] When Saul returned from pursuing the Philistines, he was told that David was in the wilderness of En-gedi. [3] So Saul took three thousand picked men from all Israel and went in search of David and his men [b-]in the direction of the rocks of the wild goats;[-b] [4] and he came to the sheepfolds along the way. There

a The meaning of many parts of 23.19 ff. is uncertain. The events described in 23.19–24.22 are partly paralleled in chapter 26, with variations.
b-b Meaning of Heb. uncertain. *c Meaning of Heb. uncertain.*

protection. **17:** Saul knows that David will be king, and yet he continues pursuing him, driven by jealousy and enmity. **18:** *A pact* ("berit"), stipulating that when David will be king, Jonathan shall rank next to him. The *pact* here strengthens, and extends the *pact* they made in 18.3.

23.19–28: Narrow escape. At the last moment, when his capture by Saul seems unavoidable, David is saved. The first part of the narrative contains the dialogue between Saul and the Ziphites concerning David's capture; the second part relates Saul's pursuit and its unexpected outcome. **19–20:** The Ziphites, in proving their loyalty to Saul, are probably under the influence of the massacre of Nob, whose priests were accused of failing to inform Saul (22.17). **21:** *May you be blessed of the LORD,* a customary blessing (see 15.13; 2 Sam. 2.5; Ps. 115.15). The king, uttering satisfaction at being pitied, makes a sorry figure. **26:** Instead of *trying to encircle,* read "encircling" (*trying* is not expressed in the Heb). David is already encircled by Saul's men and on the verge of being captured, when suddenly the messenger appears. This may be seen as directed by God to save David. **28:** *Rock of Separation,* "because there Saul separated and departed from David" (Abravanel); such etiologies (stories of origin) typically contain folk etymologies of well-known places rather than historical facts.

24.1–23: Magnanimity. David has the opportunity to kill Saul, but refrains from doing so. When the king falls into his hands, David does not take revenge, but shows himself magnanimous and loyal towards him. In the first part of the narrative the event itself is described; the second part contains a speech by David, stating that he never wronged the king; the third part consists of a speech by Saul, who is impressed by David's generosity. The word "hand(s)" recurs frequently (in the Heb even more than in the translation): Though he has Saul in his hands, David will not raise his hand against him. A variant of this story appears in ch 26. **4:** *Sheepfolds* were often attached to caves, which provided shelter to the animals from heat and cold. The depiction of Saul relieving himself

was a cave there, and Saul went in [a-]to relieve himself.[-a] Now
David and his men were sitting in the back of the cave.
[5] David's men said to him, "This is the day of which the LORD
said to you, 'I will deliver your enemy into your hands; you can
do with him as you please.'" [b]David went and stealthily cut off
the corner of Saul's cloak. [6] But afterward [c-]David reproached
himself[-c] for cutting off [d-]the corner of Saul's cloak.[-d] [7] He said
to his men, "The LORD forbid that I should do such a thing to
my lord—the LORD's anointed—that I should raise my hand
against him; for he is the LORD's anointed." [8] David rebuked[e]
his men and did not permit them to attack Saul.

Saul left the cave and started on his way. [9] Then David also
went out of the cave and called after Saul, "My lord king!" Saul
looked around and David bowed low in homage, with his face
to the ground. [10] And David said to Saul, "Why do you listen
to the people who say, 'David is out to do you harm?' [11] You
can see for yourself now that the LORD delivered you into my
hands in the cave today. And though [f-]I was urged[-f] to kill you,
I showed you pity;[g] for I said, 'I will not raise a hand against
my lord, since he is the LORD's anointed.' [12] Please, sir,[h] take a
close look at the corner of your cloak in my hand; for when I
cut off the corner of your cloak, I did not kill you. You must see
plainly that I have done nothing evil or rebellious, and I have
never wronged you. Yet you are bent on taking my life. [13] May
the LORD judge between you and me! And may He take vengeance upon you for me, but my hand will never touch you. [14] As
the ancient proverb has it: 'Wicked deeds come from wicked
men!' My hand will never touch you. [15] Against whom has the
king of Israel come out? Whom are you pursuing? A dead dog?
A single flea? [16] May the LORD be arbiter and may He judge between you and me! May He take note and uphold my cause,
and vindicate me against you."

[17] When David finished saying these things to Saul, Saul
said, "Is that your voice, my son David?" And Saul broke down
and wept. [18] He said to David, "You are right, not I; for you have
treated me generously, but I have treated you badly. [19] Yes,
you have just revealed how generously you treated me, for
the LORD delivered me into your hands and you did not kill
me. [20] If a man meets his enemy, does he let him go his way
unharmed? Surely, the LORD will reward you generously for
[i-]what you have done for me this day.[-i] [21] I know now that you

a-a Lit. "to cover his feet." *b Vv. 5b–6 read well after 8a.*
c-c Lit. "David's heart struck him."
d-d So several mss. and ancient versions; cf. v. 5. Most mss. and editions read "Saul's corner."
e Meaning of Heb. uncertain. *f-f Meaning of Heb. uncertain.*
g Understanding the Heb. as an ellipsis of wattaḥos ʿeni *(cf., e.g., Deut. 7.16).*
h Lit. "[my] father," cf. 2 Kings 5.13.
i-i Meaning of Heb. uncertain. Emendation yields "the generosity you have shown me."

is most unbecoming to the king. **5:** The LORD's promise cited by David's men has not been mentioned before; perhaps the men interpret Saul's entering the cave as directed by the LORD, in order to enable David to strike his pursuer down. David, however, only cuts off the corner of Saul's cloak as proof that he could have killed him. He is not aware that the cutting of the cloak also has symbolic significance, namely, cutting off the kingdom (cf. 15.27–28; 1 Kings 11.29–32). **6–7:** According to biblical scholars, vv. 5b–6 should be placed after vv. 7–8a. According to Rashi, since the narrator began to talk about the cutting of the cloak, he finishes the subject, remarking that—some time later—David reproached himself even for having cut the cloak; the narrator then returns to the first subject and reports David's reply to his men. *The LORD's anointed:* Because the king was anointed by a prophet in the name of the LORD, he is inviolable (see 2 Sam. 1.16 and 1 Sam. 2.10 n.). **9:** Though persecuted by Saul, David honors the king. **12:** As the translators' note indicates, the Heb is literally "my father," which may serve as an honorific, like *sir.* David may be using it in the more literal sense, suggesting that he in some sense is Saul's son (he is his son-in-law), and thus a legitimate successor to the throne. **14:** *Wicked deeds come from wicked men,* i.e., not from me. **15:** David designates Saul here *king of Israel* to contrast him with himself, who is as insignificant and harmless as *a dead dog* or (even) *a single flea.* Such expressions of submissiveness were customary in the ancient Near East. **16:** David puts his case in the hands of the LORD. **17:** Saul's question expresses his astonishment. *My son,* in response to "my father" (v. 12), indicates close relationship, and perhaps a recognition by Saul that David should be his successor. **21:** Saul acknowledges that David will be king and that his kingship will endure—as opposed to Saul's kingship. This follows Jonathan's similar acknowledgment in 23.17.

will become king, and that the kingship over Israel will remain in your hands. [22] So swear to me by the LORD that you will not destroy my descendants or wipe out my name from my father's house." [23] David swore to Saul, Saul went home, and David and his men went up to the strongholds.

25 Samuel died, and all Israel gathered and made lament for him; and they buried him in Ramah, his home.

David went down to the wilderness of Paran.[a]

[2] There was a man in Maon whose possessions were in Carmel. The man was very wealthy; he owned three thousand sheep and a thousand goats. At the time, he was shearing his sheep in Carmel. [3] The man's name was Nabal, and his wife's name was Abigail. The woman was intelligent and beautiful, but the man, a Calebite, was a hard man and an evildoer. [4] David was in the wilderness when he heard that Nabal was shearing his sheep. [5] David dispatched ten young men, and David instructed the young men, "Go up to Carmel. When you come to Nabal, greet him in my name. [6] Say [b]as follows: 'To life![b] Greetings to you and to your household and to all that is yours! [7] I hear that you are now doing your shearing. As you know, your shepherds have been with us; we did not harm them, and nothing of theirs was missing all the time they were in Carmel. [8] Ask your young men and they will tell you. So receive these young men graciously, for we have come on a festive occasion. Please give your servants and your son David whatever you can.' "

[9] David's young men went and delivered this message to Nabal in the name of David. When they stopped speaking, [10] Nabal answered David's servants, "Who is David? Who is the son of Jesse? There are many slaves nowadays who run away from their masters. [11] Should I then take my bread and my water,[c] and the meat that I slaughtered for my own shearers, and give them to men who come from I don't know where?" [12] Thereupon David's young men retraced their steps; and when they got back, they told him all this. [13] And David said to his men, "Gird on your swords." Each girded on his sword; David too girded on his sword. About four hundred men went up after David, while two hundred remained with the baggage.

[14] One of [Nabal's] young men told Abigail, Nabal's wife, that David had sent messengers from the wilderness to greet their master, and that he had spurned[d] them. [15] "But the men had been very friendly to us; we were not harmed, nor did we miss anything all the time that we went about with them while we were in the open. [16] They were a wall about us both by night and by day all the time that we were with them tending the

a Septuagint reads "Maon," cf. v. 2 and 23.24, 25. *b-b Meaning of Heb. uncertain.*
c Septuagint reads "wine," and cf. v. 18. *d Meaning of Heb. uncertain.*

22: See 20.15 n. **23:** See 14.46 n. Saul abandons the pursuit, yet David and his men go up to the *stronghold* (in the Heb the word is in the singular), because they do not trust Saul.

25.1–44: The evil husband and the clever wife. The violent clash between David and the boorish, evil, foolish Nabal is prevented by Nabal's clever wife Abigail, who succeeds in persuading David to refrain from spilling blood. She also alludes to David's future kingship, as did Saul in the preceding narrative. The placement of this story here separates the two parallel stories in chs 24 and 26. This story may have a polemical overtone, combatting the idea that Abigail became David's wife under less proper circumstances. **1:** The note concerning Samuel's death, which has no connection with the following narrative, is unexpected (cf. 28.3). **2–3:** The exposition specifies Nabal's wealth even before stating his name and qualities and those of his wife. *Carmel,* see 15.12 n. *Calebite:* The clan of Caleb was part of Judah, but Kenizzite in origin (Gen. 15.19; Num. 32.12; Josh. 14.14). **4:** Sheepshearing was an occasion for celebration (see 2 Sam. 13.23). **5:** *Ten young men,* to carry the generous gift David expects to receive as reward for his services. **6:** Before the request itself good wishes are uttered. The Heb may also be translated: "Say: 'So be it (also) next year: May you be well and may your household be well and all that is yours be well!' " **7:** *Your shepherds have been with us,* under our protection. **10:** *"Who is David?":* Nabal's rude reply expresses contempt (cf. Exod. 5.2). By implying that they are runaway slaves he insults both David, who escaped from Saul, and his men, who fled from society. **11:** *My bread and my water,* food and drink in general (Hos. 2.7). **13:** David is determined to use force; girding the swords is mentioned three times. **14:** The narrative's point of view switches to Abigail. **15–16:** The young man (or rather, servant), confirming David's statement (v. 7), specifies

flocks. 17 So consider carefully what you should do, for harm
threatens our master and all his household; he is such a nasty
fellow that no one can speak to him."
18 Abigail quickly got together two hundred loaves of bread,
two jars of wine, five dressed sheep, five *seahs* of parched
corn, one hundred cakes of raisin, and two hundred cakes
of pressed figs. She loaded them on asses, 19 and she told her
young men, "Go on ahead of me, and I'll follow you"; but she
did not tell her husband Nabal. 20 She was riding on the ass and
going down a trail[a] on the hill, when David and his men appeared, coming down toward her; and she met them.—21 Now
David had been saying, "It was all for nothing that I protected
that fellow's possessions in the wilderness, and that nothing he owned is missing. He has paid me back evil for good.
22 May God do thus and more to [b]the enemies of[b] David if, by
the light of morning, I leave [c]a single male[c] of his."—23 When
Abigail saw David, she quickly dismounted from the ass and
threw herself face down before[a] David, bowing to the ground.
24 Prostrate at his feet, she pleaded, "Let the blame be mine,
my lord, but let your handmaid speak to you; hear your maid's
plea. 25 Please, my lord, pay no attention to that wretched fellow Nabal. For he is just what his name says: His name means
'boor' and he is a boor.

"Your handmaid did not see the young men whom my lord
sent. 26 I swear, my lord, as the LORD lives and as you live—
the LORD who has kept you from seeking redress by blood
with your own hands—let your enemies and all who would
harm my lord fare like Nabal! 27 Here is the present which
your maidservant has brought to my lord; let it be given to the
young men who are the followers of my lord. 28 Please pardon your maid's boldness. For the LORD will grant my lord
an enduring house, because my lord is fighting the battles of
the LORD, and no wrong is ever to be found in you. 29 And if
anyone sets out to pursue you and seek your life, the life of

a *Meaning of Heb. uncertain.*
b-b *The phrase is intended to avoid the imprecation of David against himself; it is lacking in the Septuagint.*
c-c *Lit. "one who pees against a wall."*

the protection Nabal's shepherds received. *They were a wall:* The metaphor denotes defense against marauders. **17:** *Nasty,* better, "evil" (lit. "good-for-nothing"). Because speaking to Nabal is impossible, the servant appeals to Abigail. **18:** The wise Abigail understands that she has to act quickly in order to anticipate David and that first of all his request must be generously satisfied. Other wise women are depicted in 2 Sam. 14.2 and 20.16. *Seahs:* A *seah* was probably about 7 liters (more than 6 quarts). **19:** *Go on ahead of me:* Abigail wants to placate David before she meets him; as a wise woman who knows her husband's true personality, *she did not tell her husband Nabal.* **22:** *Thus and more,* see 3.17 n. **23:** Though a wealthy and distinguished woman, Abigail hastens to display profuse gestures of respect to the runaway chieftain. She begins by taking the blame—either for Nabal's behavior or for addressing David. **24–31:** Abigail's speech shows her intelligence and eloquence. She refers throughout to David as *my* lord and to herself as his *handmaid.* In the first part she expresses agreement with David as regards Nabal; in the second part she cautions David that by spilling blood now he will do harm to himself in the future. **24:** *At his feet,* a gesture of pleading (see 2 Kings 4.27; Esth. 8.3). **25:** *Wretched,* better, "evil." Nabal's wife uses the same strong term as Nabal's servant (see v. 17 n.), which indicates that she shares his opinion—evidently the common sentiment. *For he is just what his name says:* In the Bible people are aware of the meaning of names. Some names occur that, like Nabal, have unpleasant meanings, e.g., Mahlon and Chilion in Ruth 1.2, whose names mean "sickness" and "destruction," and that reflect the person's character or destiny (e.g., Gen. 27.36). *Boor:* According to Isa. 32.6 the Heb word "naval" denotes a villain, who "leaves the hungry unsatisfied and deprives the thirsty of drink," just as Nabal did to David (see also Prov. 17.7, 21). **26:** *Fare like Nabal,* a hint that Nabal is surely going to die (cf. 2 Sam. 18.32)—therefore David need take no action himself. **27:** *Let it be given to the young men,* a polite expression, implying that the present is too humble for David himself. **28:** *Enduring house:* Abigail knows that David will be king and that his dynasty will endure (see 2 Sam. 7.16, which uses a nearly identical phrase), because he is fighting *the battles of the LORD* (see 18.17 n.). **29:** *Anyone,* an allusion to Saul, who set out to *pursue* David (23.25, 28; 24.15) and *seek* his *life* (20.1; 22.23; 23.15). *The life ... will be bound up in the bundle of life,* a metaphor denoting long life. The LORD's bundle of life was believed to contain the names of the living, similar to His

my lord will be bound up in the bundle of life in the care of the LORD; but He will fling away the lives of your enemies as from the hollow of a sling. 30 And when the LORD has accomplished for my lord all the good He has promised you, and has appointed you ruler of Israel, 31 do not let this be a cause of stumbling and of faltering courage to my lord that you have shed blood needlessly and that my lord sought redress with his own hands. And when the LORD has prospered my lord, remember your maid."

32 David said to Abigail, "Praised be the LORD, the God of Israel, who sent you this day to meet me! 33 And blessed be your prudence, and blessed be you yourself for restraining me from seeking redress in blood by my own hands. 34 For as sure as the LORD, the God of Israel, lives—who has kept me from harming you—had you not come quickly to meet me, not [a]a single male[a] of Nabal's line would have been left by daybreak." 35 David then accepted from her what she had brought him, and he said to her, "Go up to your home safely. See, I have heeded your plea and respected your wish."

36 When Abigail came home to Nabal, he was having a feast in his house, a feast fit for a king; Nabal was in a merry mood and very drunk, so she did not tell him anything at all until daybreak. 37 The next morning, when Nabal had slept off the wine, his wife told him everything that had happened; and his courage died within him, and he became like a stone. 38 About ten days later the LORD struck Nabal and he died. 39 When David heard that Nabal was dead, he said, "Praised be the LORD who championed my cause against the insults of Nabal and held back His servant from wrongdoing; the LORD has brought Nabal's wrongdoing down on his own head."

David sent messengers [b]to propose marriage to[b] Abigail, to take her as his wife. 40 When David's servants came to Abigail at Carmel and told her that David had sent them to her to make her his wife, 41 she immediately bowed low with her face to the ground and said, "Your handmaid is ready to be your maidservant, to wash the feet of my lord's servants." 42 Then Abigail rose quickly and mounted an ass, and with five of her maids in attendance she followed David's messengers; and she became his wife.

43 Now David had taken Ahinoam of Jezreel; so both of them became his wives. 44 Saul had given his daughter Michal, David's wife, to Palti son of Laish from Gallim.

a-a *Lit. "one who pees against a wall."*
b-b *Lit. "and spoke for"; cf. Song of Songs 8.8.*

"book of life" (Ps. 69.29). In postbiblical times the bundle of life came to signify eternal life in the next world, and therefore the expression is found regularly on Jewish tombstones and in "Yizkor," the memorial service for the dead. *Fling away the lives,* a metaphor denoting the opposite of the preceding one. *The hollow of a sling,* the middle of the sling, where the stone would be placed (see 17.40 n.). **30:** *The good* refers to the enduring house (v. 28). On *ruler,* see 9.15–16 n. **31:** Refraining from bloodshed is in David's own interest. *Faltering courage,* lit. "faltering of heart," i.e., weakness. *Remember your maid,* rewarding her. **34:** David's present oath annuls his previous one (v. 22). *From harming you:* David refers to Abigail as representative of Nabal's household. **36:** Nabal's feasting shows him to be quite oblivious of any danger. It is strikingly called *a feast* (that is, a drinking party, as in Esth.) *fit for a king,* making Abigail the queen and setting Nabal in contrast to David, who will become king. **37:** *His courage,* lit. "his heart." The simile *like a stone* points to paralysis, which was presumably understood as death of the heart, in accordance with the tendency of the Bible to attribute to the heart not only feelings, but also thoughts, traits, and some physical functions. It seems that when Nabal hears what happened and to what terrible danger he was exposed, he suffers a stroke and becomes paralyzed and ten days later he dies. David then marries the widow because of her intelligence, beauty, and wealth. He thereby gains the wealth and influence that Nabal had possessed. **41:** *To wash the feet of my lord's servants,* an expression of extreme politeness and humility. **42:** The five maids are mentioned to show Abigail's economic and social status. **43:** *Jezreel,* near Carmel in southern Judah. **44:** Since Michal was David's wife, Saul had no right to give her to someone else. By doing so he intentionally hurt both David and his daughter, who had deceived him in order to help her husband (19.11–17).

26 [a]The Ziphites came to Saul at Gibeah and said, "David
is hiding in the hill of Hachilah facing Jeshimon." 2 Saul
went down at once to the wilderness of Ziph, together with
three thousand picked men of Israel, to search for David in the
wilderness of Ziph, 3 and Saul encamped on the hill of Hachilah
which faces Jeshimon, by the road. When David, who was then
living in the wilderness, learned that Saul had come after him
into the wilderness, 4 David sent out scouts and made sure that
Saul had come. 5 David went at once to the place where Saul
had encamped, and David saw the spot where Saul and his
army commander, Abner son of Ner, lay asleep. Saul lay asleep
inside the barricade[a] and the troops were posted around him.
6 David spoke up and asked Ahimelech the Hittite and
Abishai son of Zeruiah, Joab's brother, "Who will go down with
me into the camp to Saul?" And Abishai answered, "I will go
down with you." 7 So David and Abishai approached the troops
by night, and found Saul fast asleep inside the barricade,[b] his
spear stuck in the ground at his head, and Abner and the troops
sleeping around him. 8 And Abishai said to David, "God has
delivered your enemy into your hands today. Let me pin him
to the ground with a single thrust of the spear. I will not have
to strike him twice." 9 But David said to Abishai, "Don't do him
violence! No one can lay hands on the LORD's anointed with
impunity." 10 And David went on, "As the LORD lives, the LORD
Himself will strike him down, or his time will come and he will
die, or he will go down to battle and perish. 11 But the LORD forbid that I should lay a hand on the LORD's anointed! Just take
the spear and the water jar at his head and let's be off." 12 So
David took away the spear and the water jar at Saul's head, and
they left. No one saw or knew or woke up; all remained asleep;
a deep sleep from the LORD had fallen upon them.
13 David crossed over to the other side and stood afar on top
of a hill; there was considerable distance between them. 14 And
David shouted to the troops and to Abner son of Ner, "Abner,
aren't you going to answer?" And Abner shouted back, "Who
are you to shout at the king?" 15 And David answered Abner,
"You are a man, aren't you? And there is no one like you in
Israel! So why didn't you keep watch over your lord the king?
For one of [our] troops came to do violence to your lord the
king. 16 You have not given a good account of yourself! As the
LORD lives, [all of] you deserve to die, because you did not keep
watch over your lord, the LORD's anointed. Look around, where
are the king's spear and the water jar that were at his head?"

a Cf. 23.19 and note. *b Meaning of Heb. uncertain; cf. 17.20.*

26.1–25: Magnanimity repeated. The present story is similar to the one in ch 24. In both, David has the opportunity to kill Saul, but though urged by his men to do so, he refuses to harm the LORD's anointed. Instead, he takes one object from him to prove that he could have killed him, and when Saul sees this, he expresses regret at having persecuted David. In addition, there are verbal similarities (e.g., the simile in 24.15 and 26.20, and the question in 24.17 and 26.17). It seems that two variants of the same story have been included in the book—probably because of the differences between them (e.g., in one Saul comes to David in a cave by day and David takes a corner of Saul's coat, in the other David comes to Saul in an army camp by night and takes Saul's spear and water jar), and because they both serve to show that David did not usurp the kingship from Saul. The repetition also causes David's magnanimity to emerge as a constant character trait. **1:** The presence of *Ziphites* suggests that this episode was originally connected to the end of ch 23. **5:** *Barricade,* see 17.20 n. Saul is surrounded by his troops. **6:** *Ahimelech the Hittite* is not mentioned elsewhere. The Hittite empire had its center in present-day Turkey, but Hittites (perhaps a different group of people) are also mentioned as residing in the land of Canaan (Gen. 23.3; 26.34; 27.46; 2 Sam. 11.3). *Abishai,* who is willing to accompany David on his dangerous exploit, and his more famous brother *Joab,* David's future army commander, are always designated sons of *Zeruiah,* who was David's sister. **7:** *His spear:* The same spear that Saul used against David can now be used by David against Saul. **9:** See 24.6–7 n. **10:** *Strike him down,* by means of an illness (see 25.38). **11:** The spear, besides being a useful weapon, was a symbol of Saul's kingship (see 13.22; 18.10; 19.9; 20.33; 22.6; 2 Sam. 1.6). A water jar was vitally important in the desert. **12:** In coming close to Saul's head David exposes himself to extreme danger. *No one saw or knew or woke up; all remained asleep:* The repetitiveness serves to ridicule the defective watch. This v. introduces a supernatural element that is missing in ch 24. **15:** *A man,* a hero. **17–18:** Saul's question aims at achieving certainty, since in the dark

[17] Saul recognized David's voice, and he asked, "Is that your voice, my son David?" And David replied, "It is, my lord king." [18] And he went on, "But why does my lord continue to pursue his servant? What have I done, and what wrong am I guilty of? [19] Now let my lord the king hear his servant out. If the LORD has incited you against me, let Him be appeased[a] by an offering; but if it is men, may they be accursed of the LORD! For they have driven me out today, so that I cannot have a share in the LORD's possession, but am told, 'Go and worship other gods.' [20] Oh, let my blood not fall to the ground, away from the presence of the LORD! For the king of Israel has come out to seek a single flea—as if he were hunting a partridge in the hills."

[21] And Saul answered, "I am in the wrong. Come back, my son David, for I will never harm you again, seeing how you have held my life precious this day. Yes, I have been a fool, and I have erred so very much." [22] David replied, "Here is Your Majesty's spear. Let one of the young men come over and get it. [23] And the LORD will requite every man for his right conduct and loyalty—for this day the LORD delivered you into my[b] hands and I would not raise a hand against the LORD's anointed. [24] And just as I valued your life highly this day, so may the LORD value my life and may He rescue me from all trouble." [25] Saul answered David, "May you be blessed, my son David. You shall achieve, and you shall prevail."

David then went his way, and Saul returned home.

27 David said to himself, "Some day I shall certainly perish at the hands of Saul. The best thing for me is to flee to the land of the Philistines; Saul will then give up hunting me throughout the territory of Israel, and I will escape him." [2] So David and the six hundred men with him went and crossed over to King Achish son of Maoch of Gath. [3] David and his men stayed with Achish in Gath, each man with his family, and David with his two wives, Ahinoam the Jezreelite and Abigail wife of Nabal the Carmelite. [4] And when Saul was told that David had fled to Gath, he did not pursue him any more.

[5] David said to Achish, "If you please, let a place be granted me in one of the country towns where I can live; why should your servant remain with you in the royal city?" [6] At that time Achish granted him Ziklag; that is how Ziklag came to belong to the kings of Judah, as is still the case. [7] The length of time that David lived in Philistine territory was a year and four months.

[8] David and his men went up and raided the Geshurites, the Gizrites, and the Amalekites—who were the inhabitants

a Cf. Amos 5.21.
b So many mss.; other mss. and editions omit.

he is unable to see David. David, who politely addresses Saul as *my* lord and calls himself *his servant,* tries to dissuade Saul from pursuing him. Saul again calls David *my son* (see 24.17). **19:** *They have driven me out:* They have compelled me to flee from *the LORD's possession*—i.e., the land of Israel—to a foreign country, where I will be obliged to *worship other gods.* This probably alludes to David's intention to flee to the Philistines (see ch 27) and to the popular belief that each nation has its own god, who rules over that nation's territory (cf. 2 Kings 5.17; 17.24–28). In the land of Israel the LORD must be worshipped, in other countries the local gods. **20:** David begs not to have to die in a foreign country. *King of Israel, a single flea,* see 24.15 n. **21:** Saul, trying to reassure David, again calls him *my son* (see vv. 17 and 25). This time, Saul keeps his promise (see 27.4). **22:** David, who does not trust Saul anymore, ignores his invitation and promise. **25:** Saul's final words ever to David are a blessing, assuring him of success. The verbs *achieve* and *prevail* are emphasized in the Heb. The concluding sentence, which marks the end of the story (cf. 21.1), makes it clear that David rejects Saul's call to return to him.

27.1–28.2: In Philistia again. For the second time David flees to Achish and deceives the Philistine king. But whereas the first time (21.11–16) he came alone and was expelled, now he comes at the head of a useful unit of 600 men and is received favorably. **1:** Because David's decision to enter the enemy's service is rather questionable, his considerations are recounted at some length and in his own words. **3:** *Stayed with Achish,* as his vassal. **5:** It was customary for a suzerain to give an estate to his vassal in return for his services. David's aim is to get away from Achish's watchful eyes. **6:** *Ziklag* was evidently crown property at the time of the narrator, during the reign of the kings of Judah—i.e., after Solomon and before the Babylonian exile. **8–11:** Achish expects David

of the region of Olam,[a] all the way to Shur and to the land of
Egypt.—9 When David attacked a region, he would leave no
man or woman alive; he would take flocks, herds, asses, camels, and clothing. When he returned and came[b] to Achish,
10 Achish would ask, "Where[c] did you raid today?" and David
would reply, "The Negeb[d] of Judah," or "the Negeb of the Jerahmeelites," or "the Negeb of the Kenites." 11 David would leave
no man or woman alive to be brought to Gath; for he thought,
"They might tell about us: David did this." Such was his practice
as long as he stayed in the territory of the Philistines. 12 Achish
trusted David. He thought: [e-]"He has aroused the wrath of[-e] his
own people Israel, and so he will be my vassal forever."

28 At that time the Philistines mustered their forces for
war, to take the field against Israel. Achish said to David, "You know, of course, that you and your men must march
out with my forces." 2 David answered Achish, "You surely
know what your servant will do." "In that case," Achish replied
to David, "I will appoint you my bodyguard for life."
3 [f]Now Samuel had died and all Israel made lament for him;
and he was buried in his own town of Ramah. And Saul had
forbidden [recourse to] ghosts and familiar spirits in the land.
4 The Philistines mustered and they marched to Shunem and
encamped; and Saul gathered all Israel, and they encamped at
Gilboa. 5 When Saul saw the Philistine force, his heart trembled
with fear. 6 And Saul inquired of the LORD, but the LORD did
not answer him, either by dreams or by Urim[g] or by prophets.
7 Then Saul said to his courtiers, "Find me a woman who consults ghosts, so that I can go to her and inquire through her."
And his courtiers told him that there was a woman in En-dor
who consulted ghosts.
8 Saul disguised himself; he put on different clothes and set
out with two men. They came to the woman by night, and he
said, "Please divine for me by a ghost. Bring up for me the one I

a *Septuagint reads "Telam" (cf. "Telaim" in 15.4; and "Telem" in Josh. 15.24).*
b *Change of vocalization yields "brought it"; cf. v. 11.*
c *So some mss. and Targum; Septuagint and 4QSam[a] read "Whom."*
d *I.e., the part of the Negeb occupied by these clans.* *e-e* *Cf. note at 13.4.*
f *The rest of this chapter would read well after chapters 29 and 30.*
g *A kind of oracle; see note at Exod. 28.30 and 1 Sam. 14.41.*

to make raids on Judah. But David refuses to fight his own people, so he raids non-Israelite tribes and clans. After killing their population so as not to leave witnesses, he lies to Achish about the object of his raids. *The Negeb,* the desert region in the south. The clans of *Jerahmeelites* and *Kenites* were attached to Judah. David is not condemned for taking Amalekite property as Saul was (ch 15). He kills all the Amalekites as part of his strategy, but not to proscribe them. **28.1–2:** This time lying cannot solve David's problem: how to reconcile his obligations to his suzerain with his unwillingness to fight against Israel. Meanwhile David gives an ambiguous answer to Achish, who, however, interprets it as expressing loyalty. As a sign of his trust, he appoints David to the sensitive office of bodyguard. Here the narrative breaks off, leaving open the question of what course David will take in the impending war.

28.3–25: Prophecy of doom. This narrative, which explains the reason for Saul's imminent defeat and death in the battle against the Philistines, seems misplaced. It would fit better immediately before ch 31, where that battle is described. Moreover, placed there the break between 28.1–2 and ch 29, which clearly belong together, would be avoided. That position would also solve the difficulty that according to 28.4 the Philistines are already at Shunem in the valley of Jezreel, whereas according to 29.1 they are only at Aphek, close to their territory, and from there they march to Jezreel (29.11). Such misplacements are common in Samuel. The narrative consists of five parts, arranged concentrically around Samuel's prophecy: narrator's report, dialogue between Saul and the necromancer, dialogue between Samuel and Saul, dialogue between Saul and the necromancer, narrator's report. **3:** The exposition mentions two events, which happened previously, but provide important background for the present story: Samuel's death and Saul's removal of necromancers. **4:** *Shunem* and Mount *Gilboa* lie on opposite sides of the valley of Jezreel. Saul's fear is an indication of his decline. **6:** Saul's inability to receive a divine oracle contrasts with David's easy access to the divine word in ch 23. **7:** Since discovering the future by legitimate means failed—a bad sign in itself—Saul has recourse to an illegitimate one. It is ironic that he who banned necromancers now consults one himself. **8:** *Saul disguised himself* so the necromancer would not recognize him as the king who banned her profession. Sheol, the abode of the dead, was believed to be beneath the

shall name to you.” 9 But the woman answered him, “You know what Saul has done, how he has banned [the use of] ghosts and familiar spirits in the land. So why are you laying a trap for me, to get me killed?” 10 Saul swore to her by the LORD: “As the LORD lives, you won’t get into trouble over this.” 11 At that, the woman asked, “Whom shall I bring up for you?” He answered, “Bring up Samuel for me.” 12 Then the woman recognized Samuel,[a] and she shrieked loudly, and said to Saul, “Why have you deceived me? You are Saul!” 13 The king answered her, “Don’t be afraid. What do you see?” And the woman said to Saul, “I see a divine being coming up from the earth.” 14 “What does he look like?” he asked her. “It is an old man coming up,” she said, “and he is wrapped in a robe.” Then Saul knew that it was Samuel; and he bowed low in homage with his face to the ground.

15 Samuel said to Saul, “Why have you disturbed me and brought me up?” And Saul answered, “I am in great trouble. The Philistines are attacking me and God has turned away from me; He no longer answers me, either by prophets or in dreams. So I have called you to tell me what I am to do.” 16 Samuel said, “Why do you ask me, seeing that the LORD has turned away from you and has become your adversary?[b] 17 The LORD has done [c]for Himself[c] as He foretold through me: The LORD has torn the kingship out of your hands and has given it to your fellow, to David, 18 because you did not obey the LORD and did not execute His wrath upon the Amalekites. That is why the LORD has done this to you today. 19 Further, the LORD will deliver the Israelites who are with you into the hands of the Philistines. Tomorrow your sons and you will be with me; and the LORD will also deliver the Israelite forces into the hands of the Philistines.”

20 At once Saul flung himself prone on the ground, terrified by Samuel’s words. Besides, there was no strength in him, for he had not eaten anything all day and all night. 21 The woman went up to Saul and, seeing how greatly disturbed he was, she said to him, “Your handmaid listened to you; I took my life in my hands and heeded the request you made of me. 22 So now you listen to me: Let me set before you a bit of food. Eat, and then you will have the strength to go on your way.” 23 He refused, saying, “I will not eat.” But when his courtiers as well as the woman urged him, he listened to them; he got up from the ground and sat on the bed. 24 The woman had a stall-fed calf in the house; she hastily slaughtered it, and took flour and kneaded it, and baked some unleavened cakes. 25 She set this before Saul and his courtiers, and they ate. Then they rose and left the same night.

a Some Septuagint mss. read “Saul.” *b Meaning of Heb. uncertain.*
c-c Some mss. and Septuagint read “to you.”

earth. **11:** Though dead, Samuel the prophet is still expected to be able to foretell the future. **12–14:** Apparently only the woman could see the ghost, whereas Saul could only hear him. The appearance of Samuel’s ghost is considered to be real—not trickery by the woman or imagination of Saul. The Bible believes in the possibility of sorcery, soothsaying and necromancy, but prohibits them as heathen practices (Deut. 18.9–14). See 6.2 n. *A divine being,* Heb “᾿elohim,” is the same word often used for God. *Wrapped in a robe:* Samuel’s robe was distinctive, and played a role before; see 2.19; 15.27. **17–18:** See 15.18–19, 28. **19:** *With me,* namely with Samuel in Sheol, the underworld (see 2.6 n.). **20:** *He had not eaten,* owing to his depression. **21–24:** In contrast to the stern Samuel, the woman is depicted as concerned for Saul’s well-being. She has compassion for him and urges him to eat (she mentions only *a bit of food,* but slaughters *a stall-fed calf,* a luxury fit for a king, and bakes *cakes*). She uses the argument that because she listened to Saul, he should listen to her in return. Much urging, by the woman as well as by the courtiers, is needed to persuade Saul to eat. **23:** It was customary to sit *on the bed* (or couch) while eating (Ezek. 23.41; Amos 6.4). **25:** Saul and his courtiers leave as soon as they finish eating, before anyone can recognize them.

29
The Philistines mustered all their forces at Aphek, while
Israel was encamping at the spring in Jezreel. 2 The Philistine lords came marching, each with his units of hundreds
and of thousands; and David and his men came marching last,
with Achish. 3 The Philistine officers asked, "Who are those Hebrews?" "Why, that's David, the servant of King Saul of Israel,"
Achish answered the Philistine officers. "He has been with me
[a-]for a year or more,[-a] and I have found no fault in him from the
day he defected until now." 4 But the Philistine officers were
angry with him; and the Philistine officers said to him, "Send
the man back; let him go back to the place you assigned him.
He shall not march down with us to the battle, or else he may
become our adversary in battle. For with what could that fellow
appease his master if not with [b-]the heads of these men?[-b] 5 Remember, he is the David of whom they sang as they danced:

> Saul has slain his thousands;
> David, his tens of thousands."

6 Achish summoned David and said to him, "As the LORD
lives, you are an honest man, and I would like to have you
serve[c] in my forces; for I have found no fault with you from the
day you joined me until now. But you are not acceptable to the
other lords. 7 So go back in peace, and do nothing to displease
the Philistine lords."
8 David, however, said to Achish, "But what have I done, what
fault have you found in your servant from the day I appeared
before you to this day, that I should not go and fight against the
enemies of my lord the king?" 9 Achish replied to David, "I know;
you are as acceptable to me as an angel of God. But the Philistine officers have decided that you must not march out with us
to the battle. 10 So rise early in the morning, you and your lord's
servants who came with you—[d-]rise early in the morning,[-d] and
leave as soon as it is light." 11 Accordingly, David and his men
rose early in the morning to leave, to return to the land of the
Philistines, while the Philistines marched up to Jezreel.

30
By the time David and his men arrived in Ziklag, on
the third day, the Amalekites had made a raid into
the Negeb and against Ziklag; they had stormed Ziklag and

a-a Meaning of phrase uncertain. *b-b A euphemism for "our heads."*
c Lit. "go out and come in." *d-d Meaning of parts of verse uncertain. Septuagint reads "and go to the place that I have assigned you; and harbor no evil thought in your heart, for you are acceptable to me."*

29.1–11: The problem solved. This narrative continues 28.1–2. It shows again that God is with David: It cleverly resolves the problem of how to refrain from fighting against his own people without violating his suzerain's order, solved by the Philistine lords, who mistrust David. The narrative is composed of two rounds of dialogues—the first between the Philistine officers and Achish, the second between Achish and David. **2:** *The Philistine lords,* see 5.8 n. **3:** *Hebrews,* see 4.6 n. **4:** *Angry,* because in the officers' opinion, David endangers them. *The place you assigned him,* Ziklag. *That fellow,* a disdainful phrase. *These men,* the Philistines in front of them. **5:** Like Achish's courtiers earlier in 21.12, the Philistine officers base their argument on the song of the Israelite women (18.7), which celebrated David for his glorious victory over the Philistines. **6–7:** Before ordering David back, Achish praises him and stresses his faith in him. It is ironic that Achish has complete confidence in David, who repeatedly deceived him. *As the LORD lives:* Achish even swears by the God of David. Polytheistic peoples believed in the power of other peoples' gods (see 4.8). *The other lords,* the Philistine lords adopted the officers' opinion. **8:** David, who is happy not to have to participate in the war, pretends to be offended so as to underscore his (feigned) loyalty to Achish. **9:** *Acceptable to me,* lit. "good in my eyes." Achish intensifies his praise of David, even comparing him to an *angel of God.* The same rather extreme comparison is applied to David—and to no one else—three more times (2 Sam. 14.17, 20; 19.28). **10:** *Your lord's servants:* David's men became Achish's servants together with David himself. **11:** *To Jezreel,* where the Israelite army was encamping (v. 1).

30.1–30: Defeat turned into victory. In David's absence the Amalekites raided Ziklag, taking captives and spoil. Thanks to the Philistine lords' distrust, and particularly to Achish's order to leave early in the morning, David arrives home soon enough to be able to overtake the Amalekites and rescue the captives and spoil. The first part of the narrative is devoted to the encounter with the Amalekites, the second part to the distribution of the spoils taken from them. The narrative presents some important contrasts between David and Saul: David successfully consults God, Saul does not; David is victorious in battle, Saul suffers defeat; David rescues all women and children,

burned it down. 2 They had taken the women in it captive,
low-born and high-born alike; they did not kill any, but
carried them off and went their way. 3 When David and his
men came to the town and found it burned down, and their
wives and sons and daughters taken captive, 4 David and the
troops with him broke into tears, until they had no strength
left for weeping. 5 David's two wives had been taken captive,
Ahinoam of Jezreel and Abigail wife of Nabal from Carmel.
6 David was in great danger, for the troops threatened to stone
him; for all the troops were embittered on account of their
sons and daughters.

But David sought strength in the LORD his God. 7 David said
to the priest Abiathar son of Ahimelech, "Bring the ephod up
to me." When Abiathar brought up the ephod[a] to David, 8 David inquired of the LORD, "Shall I pursue those raiders? Will I
overtake them?" And He answered him, "Pursue, for you shall
overtake and you shall rescue."

9 So David and the six hundred men with him set out, and
they came to the Wadi Besor, where a halt was made by those
who were to be left behind. 10 David continued the pursuit
with four hundred men; two hundred men had halted, too
faint to cross the Wadi Besor. 11 They came upon an Egyptian
in the open country and brought him to David. They gave him
food to eat and water to drink; 12 he was also given a piece of
pressed fig cake and two cakes of raisins. He ate and regained
his strength, for he had eaten no food and drunk no water
for three days and three nights. 13 Then David asked him,
"To whom do you belong and where are you from?" "I am an
Egyptian boy," he answered, "the slave of an Amalekite. My
master abandoned me when I fell ill three days ago. 14 We had
raided the Negeb of the Cherethites, and [the Negeb] of Judah,
and the Negeb of Caleb; we also burned down Ziklag." 15 And
David said to him, "Can you lead me down to that band?" He
replied, "Swear to me by God that you will not kill me or deliver me into my master's hands, and I will lead you down to that
band." 16 So he led him down, and there they were, scattered
all over the ground, eating and drinking and making merry
because of all the vast spoil they had taken from the land of
the Philistines and from the land of Judah. 17 David attacked
them from [b]before dawn until the evening of the next day;[-b]
none of them escaped, except four hundred young men who
mounted camels and got away. 18 David rescued everything
the Amalekites had taken; David also rescued his two wives.
19 Nothing of theirs was missing—young or old, sons or daughters, spoil or anything else that had been carried off—David
recovered everything. 20 David took all the flocks and herds,

a See note at 2.28. *b-b Meaning of Heb. uncertain.*

Saul and his children die, together with many of his troops. The contrasts are highlighted by the fact that David's battle against the Amalekites and Saul's battle against the Philistines took place at approximately the same time (see 2 Sam. 1.1–2). Furthermore, this battle should not have taken place since Saul should have killed all the Amalekites (ch 15); David thus corrects Saul's lapse. **1:** The Amalekites attacked *Ziklag* (see 27.6), when there were only women and children in the town. **2:** The Amelikites took the Israelites as slaves, which is why they *did not kill any.* **4:** Compare their legitimate lack of strength to Saul's in 28.20. **5:** See 25.42–43. **6:** David, as leader, is held responsible for the disaster; as an ideal leader, he trusts God, not humans (see Ps. 118.8–9). **7:** See 23.6 n. **8:** In contrast to Saul (28.6), the LORD answers David, telling him that he will surely *overtake* and *rescue* (these verbs are emphasized in the Heb). **10:** *Too faint:* After marching home from Aphek, the men immediately had to set out again and hurry into the desert in pursuit of the Amalekites. **11–15:** Thanks to the Egyptian boy, David soon discovers the Amalekites and is able to rescue captives and spoil. Because the boy, being ill, was cruelly abandoned by his master, without food or drink, he is prepared to help David—only concerned that he not be killed or delivered to his Amalekite master. And since he is Egyptian, not Amalekite, David need not kill him. **14:** *Cherethites,* Philistines (cf. v. 16; Ezek. 25.16). The name probably points to their origin from the island of Crete (see 4.1b n.). *Caleb,* see 25.2–3 n. *Burned down Ziklag,* in revenge for David's raid (27.8). **15:** The law in the ancient Near East required returning slaves to their masters—Israelite law only being an exception (Deut. 23.16–17). **16:** The feasting Amalekites are completely oblivious of a possible attack. **17:** *The next day* after coming there David attacks from before dawn until evening. As wilderness-dwelling nomads, the Amalekites had camels (see Judg. 6.3, 5; 7.12). **20:** *This is David's spoil,*

[a-]which [the troops] drove ahead of the other livestock;[-a]
and they declared, "This is David's spoil."
[21] When David reached the two hundred men who were too
faint to follow David and who had been left at the Wadi Besor,
they came out to welcome David and the troops with him; David came forward with the troops and greeted them. [22] But all
the mean and churlish fellows among the men who had accompanied David spoke up, "Since they did not accompany us,[b] we
will not give them any of the spoil that we seized—except that
each may take his wife and children and go." [23] David, however,
spoke up, "You must not do that, [c-]my brothers, in view of[-c] what
the LORD has granted us, guarding us and delivering into our
hands the band that attacked us. [24] How could anyone agree
with you in this matter? The share of those who remain with the
baggage shall be the same as the share of those who go down to
battle; they shall share alike." [25] So from that day on it was made
a fixed rule for Israel, continuing to the present day.
[26] When David reached Ziklag, he sent some of the spoil to
the elders of Judah [a-][and] to his friends,[-a] saying, "This is a
present for you from our spoil of the enemies of the LORD."
[27] [He sent the spoil to the elders] in Bethel,[d] Ramoth-negeb,
and Jattir; [28] in Aroer, Siphmoth, and Eshtemoa; [29] in Racal, in
the towns of the Jerahmeelites, and in the towns of the Kenites; [30] in Hormah, Bor-ashan, and Athach; [31] and to those in
Hebron—all the places where David and his men had roamed.

31

[e] The Philistines attacked Israel, and the men of Israel
fled before the Philistines and [many] fell on Mount Gilboa. [2] The Philistines pursued Saul and his sons, and the Philistines struck down Jonathan, Abinadab, and Malchishua, sons
of Saul. [3] The battle raged around Saul, and [f-]some of the archers[-f] hit him, and he [g-]was severely wounded[-g] by the archers.
[4] Saul said to his arms-bearer, "Draw your sword and run me
through, so that the uncircumcised may not run me through
and make sport of me." But his arms-bearer, in his great awe,
refused; whereupon Saul grasped the sword and fell upon it.
[5] When his arms-bearer saw that Saul was dead, he too fell on
his sword and died with him. [6] Thus Saul and his three sons

a-a Meaning of Heb. uncertain.
b So some mss. and versions; most mss. and editions read "me."
c-c Meaning of Heb. uncertain. Septuagint reads "after."
d Called Bethul in Josh. 19.4.
e 1 Chron. 10 reproduces this chapter, with minor variations.
f-f Meaning of Heb. uncertain. Lit. "the archers, men with the bow."
g-g Construed as hophal *form; cf. 1 Kings 2.34.*

a sign of the men's gratitude, and a radical reversal of their attitude at the beginning of the narrative (v. 6). **24:** The men who guard the supplies, thereby allowing the others to move swiftly, have contributed to the victory (cf. 25.13). **25:** The incident is used as an etiology, explaining that a rule existing in his time originated from David's prescription. In the ancient Near Eastern world, kings typically offered legislation; this passage thus supports David's right to be king. **26–31:** David sends parts of the spoil to the elders of Judah, to express his gratitude for their help when he roamed through their territory, and to gain their support in the future. All places mentioned were situated in the area of Hebron and Beer-sheba. The style of the list is odd, found only again in Josh. 17.16; its climactic conclusion with Hebron is connected to the importance of that city, especially as David's first capital (2 Sam. 2.11).

31.1–13: Tragic end. Saul, who was anointed king in order to liberate Israel from the Philistines (9.16), dies while being defeated by the Philistines. Not only did he fail in liberating Israel, but at his death the Philistines gained domination over most of the country. Saul's career began with the rescue of Jabesh-gilead (ch 11), and it ended with the men of Jabesh-gilead rescuing his dead body. The first part of the narrative tells of Israel's defeat and Saul's death, the second part of the treatment of his and his sons' corpses. **1:** This narrative takes no interest in the details of the battle, only in its outcome. **2:** Only in 2 Sam. 2.8 do we realize that Saul had a son who survived. **4:** A few cases of suicide, mostly committed to escape being killed by the enemy, are recorded in the Bible (Judg. 9.54; 16.30; 2 Sam. 17.23; 1 Kings 16.18). The Bible does not view these suicides negatively, in the way later Judaism would. *The uncircumcised,* a deprecatory designation (see 14.6). Instead of *make sport of,* the Heb may be translated "abuse." The abuse of enemy corpses springs from feelings of rage and hatred towards them. **5:** The death of Saul's *arms-bearer* leaves Saul's body unprotected, allowing it to be mutilated. **6:** *All his men,* those close to him; the others fled (Radak). **7:** The people living near the battlefield fled in fear of the Philistines.

and his arms-bearer, [a]as well as all his men,[a] died together on
that day. 7 And when the men of Israel [b]on the other side of the
valley and on the other side of the Jordan[b] saw that the men
of Israel had fled and that Saul and his sons were dead, they
abandoned the towns and fled; the Philistines then came and
occupied them.

8 The next day the Philistines came to strip the slain, and they
found Saul and his three sons lying on Mount Gilboa. 9 They
cut off his head and stripped him of his armor, and they sent
them throughout the land of the Philistines, to spread the news
[c]in the temples of their idols[c] and among the people. 10 They
placed his armor in the temple of Ashtaroth, and they impaled
his body on the wall of Beth-shan. 11 When [d]the inhabitants
of Jabesh-gilead heard about it—what[d] the Philistines had
done to Saul—12 all their stalwart men set out and marched all
night; they removed the bodies of Saul and his sons from the
wall of Beth-shan and came[e] to Jabesh and burned them there.
13 Then they took the bones and buried them under the tamarisk tree in Jabesh, and they fasted for seven days.

a-a Lacking in the Septuagint; 1 Chron. 10.6 reads "all his house."
b-b Meaning of Heb. uncertain. 1 Chron. 10.7 reads "in the valley."
c-c Septuagint and 1 Chron. 10.9 read "among their idols."
d-d 1 Chron. 10.11 reads "all [the inhabitants of] Jabesh-gilead heard all that."
e 1 Chron. 10.12 reads "brought them."

9: *The temples of their idols,* a strong derogatory term, is only used here. **10:** *They placed his armor in the temple,* cf. 21.10. *Ashtaroth,* see 7.3. Impalement of corpses was designed to shame and demoralize the enemy; the Lachish reliefs, depicting the Assyrian victory over Judah in 701 BCE, show three impaled Judeans. **12:** By their courageous deed, intended to prevent further desecration of the corpses, the men of Jabesh-gilead pay their debt to Saul for the rescue of their city (ch 11). Cremation was not practiced in Israel. In this particular case the flesh was probably burned because it was in a state of decay, and only the bones were buried. **13:** *They fasted,* as an act of mourning. According to the Bible mourning rites were observed *for seven days* (see Gen. 50.10; Job 2.13), and that is still the case in Judaism today (the mourning period is called "shivʿah," from the Heb word for seven). This story continues directly in 2 Sam. ch 1, which was originally not a separate book (see intro. to 1 Sam.).

שמואל ב

2 Samuel

AS STATED IN THE INTRODUCTION to 1 Samuel, the two books of Samuel were originally, and should still be read as one work. For information about the background, literary form, text, and composition of 2 Samuel, see the introduction to 1 Samuel.

The reign of King David is the subject of 2 Samuel, which is composed of two main parts. The first part (1.1–8.18) tells of David's rise to power, and the second (9.1–20.26) of his sin and the ensuing troubles in his family. The book concludes with an appendix (chs 21–24) consisting of miscellaneous prose and poetic materials that offer many new details concerning David. A list of David's chief officials (8.16–18; 20.23–26) is found between the major sections of the book.

The book depicts David as highly successful in his career: He conquers Jerusalem, makes it his administrative and religious center, liberates Israel definitively from Philistine domination, and even creates an empire. In 2 Sam. ch 7, which many see as the key theological chapter in the book, David is promised an eternal dynasty. In the second half of the book, David makes grave mistakes, and he consequently undergoes great suffering, though he ultimately retains kingship. The book's final four chapters break the implied chronological order of the rest of the book, and may be seen as an appendix comprised of miscellaneous prose and poetic materials.

[SHIMON BAR-EFRAT, Z"L, REVISED BY MARC ZVI BRETTLER]

1 After the death of Saul—David had already returned from
defeating the Amalekites—David stayed two days in Ziklag.
2 On the third day, a man came from Saul's camp, with his clothes
rent and earth on his head; and as he approached David, he flung
himself to the ground and bowed low. 3 David said to him, "Where
are you coming from?" He answered, "I have just escaped from
the camp of Israel." 4 "What happened?" asked David. "Tell me!"

1.1–16: Message of death. This narrative, a direct continuation of the end of 1 Sam., reports David's reaction to the message of Saul's death. The account of Saul's death here disagrees with the account in 1 Sam. ch 31. There it was told that Saul, after begging his arms-bearer to kill him, committed suicide by falling on his sword; here, that Saul, after requesting an unknown Amalekite to kill him, died by the hand of that Amalekite. Some scholars explain the discrepancy by assuming two different sources; others contend that the Amalekite lied (to find favor with David). It is quite possible, however, that the two accounts complement each other. The Amalekite does not say that he killed Saul, but that he *finished him off* (v. 10). Perhaps Saul, close to death after falling upon his sword, begged the Amalekite to finish him off (regarding the statement in 31.6 that Saul died, cf. 1 Sam. 17.50–51). According to this interpretation, Saul, who failed to kill all the Amalekites and particularly their king (1 Sam. ch 15), is now dispatched himself by an Amalekite. David, at any rate, believes the Amalekite, who brings Saul's crown and armlet as evidence. The Amalekite expects to be rewarded by David for liquidating his enemy, but David puts him to death, and mourns over Saul and Jonathan. **1:** *After the death of Saul,* cf. Josh. 1.1; Judg. 1.1. This formula motivated the division of Samuel into two books at this particular point. *The Amalekites,* see 1 Sam. ch 30. *Ziklag,* see 1 Sam. 27.6. **2:** *On the third day* may indicate a climactic event (see e.g., Gen. 34.25; Exod. 19.16). *His clothes rent and earth on his head,* conventional signs of mourning as in 1 Sam. 4.12. **4:** The man's account, conveying the bad news in increasing order, is similar to

And he told him how the troops had fled the battlefield, and that, moreover, many of the troops had fallen and died; also that Saul and his son Jonathan were dead. 5 "How do you know," David asked the young man who brought him the news, "that Saul and his son Jonathan are dead?" 6 The young man who brought him the news answered, "I happened to be at Mount Gilboa, and I saw Saul leaning on his spear, and the chariots and horsemen closing in on him. 7 He looked around and saw me, and he called to me. When I responded, 'At your service,' 8 he asked me, 'Who are you?' And I told him that I was an Amalekite. 9 Then he said to me, 'Stand over me, and finish me off, [a-]for I am in agony and am barely alive.'[-a] 10 So I stood over him and finished him off, for I knew that [a-]he would never rise from where he was lying.[-a] Then I took the crown from his head and the armlet from his arm, and I have brought them here to my lord."

11 David took hold of his clothes and rent them, and so did all the men with him. 12 They lamented and wept, and they fasted until evening for Saul and his son Jonathan, and for the soldiers of the LORD[b] and the House of Israel who had fallen by the sword. 13 David said to the young man who had brought him the news, "Where are you from?" He replied, "I am the son of a resident alien, an Amalekite." 14 "How did you dare," David said to him, "to lift your hand and kill the LORD's anointed?" 15 Thereupon David called one of the attendants and said to him, "Come over and strike him!" He struck him down and he died. 16 And David said to him, "Your blood be on your own head! Your own mouth testified against you when you said, 'I put the LORD's anointed to death.' "

17 And David intoned this dirge over Saul and his son Jonathan— 18 [a-]He ordered the Judites to be taught [The Song of the] Bow.[-a] It is recorded in the Book of Jashar.[c]

19 Your glory, O Israel,
Lies slain on your heights;
How have the mighty fallen!
20 Tell it not in Gath,
Do not proclaim it in the streets of Ashkelon,
Lest the daughters of the Philistine rejoice,
Lest the daughters of the uncircumcised exult.

a-a Meaning of Heb. uncertain. *b Septuagint reads "Judah."* *c See note at Josh. 10.13.*

the account given to Eli by the man of Benjamin (1 Sam. 4.16–17). **6:** Saul, weak from his mortal wounds, supported himself on his spear, the symbol of his kingship (see 1 Sam. 26.11 n.). The Philistines had chariots, which carried a charioteer and an archer. **10:** The Amalekite justifies his deed: Not only did he fulfill Saul's explicit wish, but he was also sure that Saul had no chance of recovering. *He would never rise from where he was lying,* lit. "he would not live after his falling" (presumably, upon his sword). *Crown,* actually a coronet or band worn on the forehead. It was a symbol of kingship (2 Kings 11.12); the *armlet* here likely serves a similar function. **13:** David directly confirms the messenger's Amalekite ancestry, already noted in v. 8. Although the text never states this directly, it is possible that the messenger is killed both for killing Saul, and for being from Amalek, thus recalling 1 Sam. chs 15 and 30. **14:** *To lift your hand and kill the LORD's anointed,* cf. 1 Sam. 24.7; 26.9, 11. **16:** This v. chronologically precedes v. 15. *Your blood be on your own head,* idiomatic for the guilt for your death is entirely yours. *I put the LORD's anointed to death:* David's formulation of the Amalekite's confession reflects his own viewpoint.

1.17–27: David's dirge. Like the first part of the ch, the dirge demonstrates David's deep sorrow over Saul and Jonathan's death. The dirge lacks religious or national motifs. It does not mention God, and the expressions of grief relate to the deaths of Saul and Jonathan only, not to Israel's defeat. Prominent among the dirge's many poetical features—parallelism, metaphor, synecdoche, etc.—is the frequent use of apostrophe, the direct addressing of Israel, (virtual) messengers, the hills of Gilboa, the daughters of Israel, and Jonathan. This device is particularly impressive, because the addressees are unable to hear and respond. The two lines of v. 19 recur, in different form, in v. 25, and the second line also recurs in v. 26, forming a refrain that underscores the contrast between the leaders' courage and their fate. Other biblical dirges, but not this one, are characterized by a long line followed by a short one (see e.g., Amos 5.1–2 n.). **18:** The difficult word *Bow* is not in LXX. Regarding David's instruction that the song be taught, cf. Deut. 31.22 and Ps. 60.1. **19:** The v. contrasts heights and depths in a striking manner. *Glory:*

21 O hills of Gilboa—
Let there be no dew or rain on you,
[a]Or bountiful fields,[a]
For there the shield of warriors lay rejected,
The shield of Saul,
Polished with oil no more.

22 From the blood of slain,
From the fat of warriors—
The bow of Jonathan
Never turned back;
The sword of Saul
Never withdrew empty.

23 Saul and Jonathan,
Beloved and cherished,
Never parted
In life or in death!
They were swifter than eagles,
They were stronger than lions!

24 Daughters of Israel,
Weep over Saul,
Who clothed you in crimson and finery,
Who decked your robes with jewels of gold.

25 How have the mighty fallen
In the thick of battle—
Jonathan, slain on your heights!
26 I grieve for you,
My brother Jonathan,
You were most dear to me.
Your love was wonderful to me
More than the love of women.

27 How have the mighty fallen,
The [b]weapons of war[b] perished!

2 Sometime afterward, David inquired of the LORD, "Shall I go up to one of the towns of Judah?" The LORD answered, "Yes." David further asked, "Which one shall I go up to?" And the LORD replied, "To Hebron." 2 So David went up there, along with his two wives, Ahinoam of Jezreel and Abigail wife of

a-a Meaning of Heb. uncertain. Emendation yields "springs from the deep" (cf. Ugaritic shrʿthmtm, *and Gen. 7.11; 8.2).* *b-b I.e., Saul and Jonathan.*

The metaphor refers to Saul. **20:** The towns *Gath* and *Ashkelon* stand for all Philistia. *Daughters:* Women used to celebrate victories with song and dance when their menfolk returned safely from war (Judg. 11.34; 1 Sam. 18.6). *Uncircumcised,* see 1 Sam. 14.6 n. **21:** *Gilboa,* see 1 Sam. 31.1, 8. Instead of *bountiful fields,* the Heb may be translated "fields of heights" (the same Heb root in Judg. 5.18), which parallels *hills of Gilboa.* Shields were made of leather, and had to be oiled regularly. **22:** *From the blood ... from the fat,* i.e., from spilling the blood and the fat; the entire v. depicts Saul and Jonathan as great warriors. **23:** This v. underplays the rift between Saul and Jonathan, ignoring David's alliance with Jonathan. **24:** *Daughters of Israel:* Dirges were conventionally sung by women (Jer. 9.16–19). The clothes and ornaments represent the prosperity brought by Saul as a successful king, though this detail is nowhere recorded in 1 Sam. **26:** This v., wholly dedicated to Jonathan, and formulated in the first and second person, is the most direct and personal one in the dirge. David's statement that Jonathan's *love was wonderful* to him *more than the love of women* (for him) does not hint at homosexual relations, but is an expression of deep friendship (regarding this friendship, see 1 Sam. chs 18–20; 23.15–18). The (literary) claim that Jonathan was his *brother* legitimates David as Saul's son (see also 1 Sam. 24.12 and translators' note, 24.17 and 26.17, 21, 25). **27:** Frequently, biblical poems end with a short verse, breaking the rhythmic patterns of what precedes.

2.1–11: King of Judah. While David reigns over Judah, Ish-bosheth, Saul's son, reigns over parts of Israel, which consisted of the other tribes. **1:** After Saul's death David wants to return home from the land of the Philistines, where he fled from Saul's persecutions (1 Sam. ch 27). *Inquired,* most likely by means of the ephod, which contained the Urim and Thummim (1 Sam. 14.42; 23.6, 11). *Hebron* was the principal city of Judah before Jerusalem. **2:** *Ahinoam, Abigail,* see 1 Sam. 25.42–43. Both Jezreel and Carmel were near Hebron; thus David is related through his wives to the families in

Nabal the Carmelite. 3 David also took the men who were with
him, each with his family, and they settled in the towns about
Hebron. 4 The men of Judah came and there they anointed David king over the House of Judah.

David was told about the men of Jabesh-gilead who buried
Saul. 5 So David sent messengers to the men of Jabesh-gilead
and said to them, "May you be blessed of the LORD because
you performed this act of faithfulness to your lord Saul and
buried him. 6 May the LORD in turn show you true faithfulness;
and I too will reward you generously because you performed
this act. 7 Now take courage and be brave men; for your lord
Saul is dead and the House of Judah have already anointed me
king over them."

8 But Abner son of Ner, Saul's army commander, had taken
Ish-bosheth[a] son of Saul and brought him across to Maha-
naim 9 and made him king over Gilead, the Ashurites,[b] Jezreel,
Ephraim, and Benjamin—over all Israel. 10 Ish-bosheth[a] son of
Saul was forty years old when he became king of Israel, and
he reigned two years. But the House of Judah supported Da-
vid. 11 The length of time that David reigned in Hebron over the
House of Judah was seven years and six months.

12 Once Abner son of Ner and the soldiers of Ish-bosheth
son of Saul marched out from Mahanaim to Gibeon, 13 and
Joab son of Zeruiah and the soldiers of David [also] came
out.[c] They confronted one another at the pool of Gibeon: one
group sat on one side of the pool, and the other group on the
other side of the pool. 14 Abner said to Joab, "Let the young
men come forward and sport[d] before us." "Yes, let them,"
Joab answered. 15 They came forward and were counted off,
twelve for Benjamin and Ish-bosheth son of Saul, and twelve
of David's soldiers. 16 Each one grasped his opponent's head[e]
[and thrust] his dagger into his opponent's side; thus they fell
together. That place, which is in Gibeon, was called Helkath-
hazzurim.[f]

17 A fierce battle ensued that day, and Abner and the men
of Israel were routed by David's soldiers. 18 The three sons of
Zeruiah[g] were there—Joab, Abishai, and Asahel. Asahel was
swift of foot, like a gazelle in the open field. 19 And Asahel ran
after Abner, swerving neither right nor left in his pursuit of Abner. 20 Abner looked back and shouted, "Is that you, Asahel?"
"Yes, it is," he called back. 21 Abner said to him, "Turn to the
right or to the left, and seize one of our boys and strip off his

a *Meaning "Man of Shame," deliberately altered from* Ish-baal, *"man of Baal"; cf. 1 Chron. 8.33; 9.39, and note at 2 Sam. 4.4.*
b *Meaning of Heb. uncertain.*
c *Septuagint adds "from Hebron."*
d *I.e., engage in single combat.*
e *Septuagint adds "with his hand."*
f *Meaning perhaps "the Field of the Flints (or Blades)."*
g *A sister of David, 1 Chron. 2.16.*

the region. **3:** *The men who were with him,* see 1 Sam. 27.2. **4a:** Through the initiative of the men of Judah David is made king over *the House of Judah* only. The gifts he sent to the elders of Judah (1 Sam. 30.26–31) may have contributed to his being chosen. **4b–7:** Besides expressing appreciation for their pious burial of Saul (1 Sam. 31.11–13), David's blessing of the men of *Jabesh-gilead* also has the purpose of persuading them to offer him Saul's throne. **8:** *Abner,* Saul's cousin (1 Sam. 14.50), is the strong man, who dominates *Ish-bosheth.* This is a tendentious and secondary form of the name Ish-baal (NJPS: Eshbaal), Baal-exists, which has been transformed into "there is shame." The original form of the name is preserved in some Gk versions and in 1 Chron. 8.33 and 9.39. *Mahanaim,* east of the Jordan. Most of the land west of the Jordan was under Philistine control after their victory at the battle of Mount Gilboa (1 Sam. ch 31). **9:** Ish-bosheth first reigns over Gilead, in the Transjordan, and then gradually extends his rule to the west and the south, and in the last two years rules over all Israel (except Judah). *Ashurites,* probably Asherites (members of the tribe of Asher). **10:** This is the standard regnal formula used in Samuel and Kings; see 1 Sam. 13.1 n.

2.12–32: Civil war. David's men gain victory over Ish-bosheth's men, signaling the ascent of David versus the descent of the house of Saul (cf. 3.1). **13:** *Joab,* see 1 Sam. 26.6 n. Archeological excavations at Gibeon have revealed a deep pool, hewn in the rock. **14:** Single combat between representatives of two opposing armies is found with Goliath (see 1 Sam. 17.4–7 n.). Its purpose was to avoid comprehensive fighting of the entire armies. **15:** *Benjamin,* Ish-bosheth's tribe. **17:** Since none of the young men prevailed over his opponent a battle between the armies ensues. **18–24:** The account of the battle focuses on two men: Abner and Asahel. Abner, who will figure prominently in the following chs, does not want to kill Asahel, but sees

tunic." But Asahel would not leave off. [22] Abner again begged Asahel, "Stop pursuing me, or I'll have to strike you down. How will I look your brother Joab in the face?" [23] When he refused to desist, Abner struck him in the belly with [a-]a backward thrust[-a] of his spear and the spear protruded from his back. He fell there and died on the spot. And all who came to the place where Asahel fell and died halted; [24] but Joab and Abishai continued to pursue Abner. And the sun was setting as they reached the hill of Ammah, [a-]which faces Giah on the road to the wilderness of Gibeon.[-a]

[25] The Benjaminites rallied behind Abner, forming a single company; and they took up a position on the top of a hill. [26] Abner then called out to Joab, "Must the sword devour forever? You know how bitterly it's going to end! How long will you delay ordering your troops to stop the pursuit of their kinsmen?" [27] And Joab replied, "As God lives, [b-]if you hadn't spoken up, the troops would have given up the pursuit of their kinsmen only the next morning."[-b] [28] Joab then sounded the horn, and all the troops halted; they ceased their pursuit of Israel and stopped the fighting. [29] Abner and his men marched through the Arabah all that night and, after crossing the Jordan, they marched [a-]through all of Bithron[-a] until they came to Mahanaim. [30] After Joab gave up the pursuit of Abner, he assembled all the troops and found nineteen of David's soldiers missing, besides Asahel. [31] David's soldiers, on the other hand, [a-]defeated the Benjaminites and the men under Abner and killed three hundred and sixty men.[-a] [32] They bore Asahel away and buried him in his father's tomb in Bethlehem. Then Joab and his men marched all night; day broke upon them in Hebron.

3 The war between the House of Saul and the House of David was long-drawn-out; but David kept growing stronger, while the House of Saul grew weaker.

[2][c]Sons were born to David in Hebron: His first-born was Amnon, by Ahinoam of Jezreel; [3] his second was Chileab, by Abigail wife of Nabal the Carmelite; the third was Absalom son of Maacah, daughter of King Talmai of Geshur; [4] the fourth was Adonijah son of Haggith; the fifth was Shephatiah son of Abital; [5] and the sixth was Ithream, by David's wife Eglah. These were born to David in Hebron.

[6] During the war between the House of Saul and the House of David, Abner supported the House of Saul. [7] Now Saul had a concubine named Rizpah, daughter of Aiah; and [Ish-bosheth]

a-a Meaning of Heb. uncertain.
b-b Emendation yields "If you had only spoken up, the troops would already have given up the pursuit of their kinsmen this morning."
c The list of David's wives and sons in vv. 2–5 differs somewhat from the parallel list in 1 Chron. 3.1–3. The narrative in v. 1 is resumed in v. 6.

no alternative. **21:** *Strip off his tunic,* see Judg. 14.19. **23:** *A backward thrust,* rather "the back end." The butt of the spear was fitted with a metal blade, which would be stuck in the ground (1 Sam. 26.7). **26:** In order to prevent further bloodshed Abner, who has suffered many more losses than Joab, proposes to end hostilities. *Must the sword devour forever:* A stock metaphor used in Deut. 32.42; 2 Sam. 18.8, and elsewhere. **28:** The sounding of the horn signals the cessation of pursuit. **30–31:** The imbalance in the death toll implicitly reflects divine favoring of David. **32:** Lying unburied on the battlefield and being prey to the wild animals was the greatest horror that a warrior could face (cf. 1 Sam. 17.44, 46). Especially great value was attached to burial in one's father's tomb (see 19.38; 21.14).

3.1–5: Family enlargement, part 1. Through his marriages David enters into relations with many families, one of them a royal one. Numerous wives and children were considered a sign of status. The list mentions only one son, probably the eldest, for each wife. Three of these children, Amnon, Absalom and Adonijah play important roles in the David story. **1:** This v. serves as a link between 2.12–32 and 3.6–39, suggesting that 3.2–5 are a later insertion. Only a few details are told concerning the *long-drawn-out* war. **3:** *Geshur,* a small Aramaic kingdom, east of the Sea of Galilee.

3.6–39: The strong army chief. The first part of the narrative deals with Abner's efforts to transfer rule over Israel from Ish-bosheth to David; the second part is concerned with Abner's death. Both parts aim at proving that Abner's murder *was not by the king's will* (v. 37). David took pains to distance himself from the death of Saul and members of his household; see 4.9–12. Thus the first part stresses (three times) that Abner, after being honorably received by David, went away unharmed; the second part, that David intensely mourned Abner's death. Abner's death was disadvantageous to David, because Abner was in the course

said to Abner, "Why have you lain with my father's concubine?" 8 Abner was very upset by what Ish-bosheth said, and he replied, "Am I a dog's head [a-]from Judah?[-a] Here I have been loyally serving the House of your father Saul and his kinsfolk and friends, and I have not betrayed you into the hands of David; yet this day you reproach me over a woman! 9 May God do thus and more to Abner if I do not do for David as the LORD swore to him—10 to transfer the kingship from the House of Saul, and to establish the throne of David over Israel and Judah from Dan to Beer-sheba." 11 [Ish-bosheth] could say nothing more in reply to Abner, because he was afraid of him.

12 Abner immediately[b] sent messengers to David, saying, [a-]"To whom shall the land belong?" and to say [further],[-a] "Make a pact with me, and I will help you and bring all Israel over to your side." 13 He replied, "Good; I will make a pact with you. But I make one demand upon you: Do not appear before me unless you bring Michal daughter of Saul when you come before me." 14 David also sent messengers to Ish-bosheth son of Saul, to say, "Give me my wife Michal, for whom I paid the bride-price[c] of one hundred Philistine foreskins."[d] 15 So Ish-bosheth sent and had her taken away from [her] husband, Paltiel son of Laish. 16 Her husband walked with her as far as Bahurim, weeping as he followed her; then Abner ordered him to turn back, and he went back.

17 Abner had conferred with the elders of Israel, saying, "You have wanted David to be king over you all along. 18 Now act! For the LORD has said concerning David: [e-]I will deliver[-e] My people Israel from the hands of the Philistines and all its other enemies through My servant David." 19 Abner also talked with the Benjaminites; then Abner went and informed David in Hebron of all the wishes of Israel and of the whole House of Benjamin.

20 When Abner came to David in Hebron, accompanied by twenty men, David made a feast for Abner and the men with him. 21 Abner said to David, "Now I will go and rally all Israel to Your Majesty. They will make a pact with you, and you can reign over all that your heart desires." And David dismissed Abner, who went away unharmed.

22 Just then David's soldiers and Joab returned from a raid, bringing much plunder with them; Abner was no longer with David in Hebron, for he had been dismissed and had gone away unharmed. 23 When Joab and the whole force with him arrived, Joab was told that Abner son of Ner had come to the king, had been dismissed by him, and had gone away unharmed. 24 Joab went to the king and said, "What have you done?

a-a Meaning of Heb. uncertain. *b Meaning of Heb. uncertain.*

c Cf. Exod. 22.15; Deut. 20.7; 22.23–29.

d Cf. 1 Sam. 18.27 (where the number is given as "two hundred").

e-e So many mss. and versions; most mss. and editions have "He has delivered."

of making him king over all Israel, whereas it benefitted Joab, who feared that Abner might take his place. The strong polemics in the text suggest that rumors may have circulated that David was complicit in Abner's death. **7:** Sexual relations with the king's wife or concubine amounted to claiming the throne (see 16.22; 1 Kings 2.22); this action and what follows suggest that Abner, Saul's cousin, was the de facto king of Israel. **8–10:** Ish-bosheth's reproach infuriates Abner, who swears to deprive the king of his rule. **8:** *A dog's head:* Comparison to a dog was a common way of expressing contempt (see 9.8; 16.9). Dogs lived in human society as scavengers, not as pets. Abner does not deny Ish-bosheth's accusation. **9:** *Thus and more,* see 1 Sam. 3.17 n. **10:** *From Dan to Beer-sheba,* greater Israel and Judah, see 1 Sam. 3.19–21 n. **13:** *Michal daughter of Saul:* David's right to succeed Saul as king is based in part on his marriage to Saul's daughter. **14:** See 1 Sam. 18.25–27. The official request for Michal is made to the king, who, in spite of its political implications, must concede, because Abner demands it. **15:** Michal was given to Paltiel by Saul (1 Sam. 25.44). **16:** Paltiel's weeping brings out the fact that nothing is said about Michal's or David's feelings—their reunion being purely political (see 6.20 n.). Michal is a pawn in the struggle between the House of Saul and the House of David. **17:** Abner argues that both the people and God wanted David to be king. Regarding David's popularity, see 1 Sam. 18.16. **18:** Since Saul failed to deliver Israel from the hands of the Philistines (see 1 Sam. 9.16), that task passed to David. The quote attributed to God is not found in Samuel. **19:** Abner even succeeds in persuading *Benjamin,* the tribe of Saul, Ish-bosheth (and Abner himself), to replace their king with a non-Benjaminite. **23:** The repetition that Abner left *unharmed* in three consecutive vv. emphasizes David's innocence. **24–25:** Joab accuses both David and Abner: David, that he let the enemy commander go, and Abner, that he came to spy

Here Abner came to you; why did you let him go? Now he has gotten away! 25 Don't you know that Abner son of Ner came only to deceive you, to learn your comings and goings and to find out all that you are planning?" 26 Joab left David and sent messengers after Abner, and they brought him back from the cistern of Sirah; but David knew nothing about it. 27 When Abner returned to Hebron, Joab took him aside within the gate to talk to him privately;[a] there he struck him in the belly. Thus [Abner] died for shedding the blood of Asahel, Joab's[b] brother.

28 Afterward, when David heard of it, he said, "Both I and my kingdom are forever innocent before the LORD of shedding the blood of Abner son of Ner. 29 May [the guilt] fall upon the head of Joab and all his father's house. May the house of Joab never be without someone suffering from a discharge or an eruption, or [c]a male who handles the spindle,[c] or one slain by the sword, or one lacking bread."—30 Now Joab and his brother Abishai had killed Abner because he had killed their brother Asahel during the battle at Gibeon.—31 David then ordered Joab and all the troops with him to rend their clothes, gird on sackcloth, and make lament before[d] Abner; and King David himself walked behind the bier. 32 And so they buried Abner at Hebron; the king wept aloud by Abner's grave, and all the troops wept. 33 And the king intoned this dirge over Abner,

"Should Abner have died the death of a churl?
34 Your hands were not bound,
Your feet were not put in fetters;
But you fell as one falls
Before treacherous men!"

And all the troops continued to weep over him.

35 All the troops came to urge David to eat something while it was still day; but David swore, "May God do thus to me and more if I eat bread or anything else before sundown." 36 All the troops [e]took note of it[e] and approved, [e]just as all the troops approved everything else the king did.[e] 37 That day all the troops and all Israel knew that it was not by the king's will that Abner son of Ner was killed. 38 And the king said to his soldiers, "You well know that a prince, a great man in Israel, has fallen this day. 39 And today I am weak, even though anointed king; those men, the sons of Zeruiah, are too savage for me. May the LORD requite the wicked for their wickedness!"

4 When [Ish-bosheth] son of Saul heard that Abner had died in Hebron, [f]he lost heart[f] and all Israel was alarmed. 2 The son of Saul [had] two company commanders, one named

a Meaning of Heb. uncertain. b Heb. "his."
c-c I.e., a man fit only for woman's work. d I.e., in the procession.
e-e Meaning of Heb. uncertain. f-f Lit. "his hands weakened"; and so frequently.

on David. *Comings and goings,* a military term (cf. translators' note at 1 Sam. 29.6). **27:** Instead of *privately,* the Heb may be translated "misleadingly" (cf. 2 Kings 4.28). Joab strikes Abner in the belly, enacting measure-for-measure revenge, just as Abner struck Asahel in the belly (2.23). **28–29:** Shedding innocent blood entails punishment by heaven. Therefore David declares that responsibility for the murder does not rest with him, but with Joab. *A discharge,* a venereal disease. *An eruption,* a skin disease. **30:** According to v. 27 Joab alone killed Abner. But instead of the first *killed,* the Dead Sea manuscript 4QSam[a] and LXX read "lay in wait for," i.e., both Joab and Abishai watched for an opportunity to kill Abner. Whereas Asahel was killed *during the battle,* Abner was killed in peacetime (cf. 1 Kings 2.5). **31:** Joab, the murderer, is obliged to participate in the mourning. Rending clothes and wearing sackcloth were signs of grief. **33–34:** The first line of David's dirge parallels the fourth *(died the death/fell as one falls),* and the second line parallels the third *(your hands/your feet; not bound/not put in fetters).* The dirge emphasizes that Abner did not fall in a more dignified fashion, as a prisoner of war, but as a victim of a common crime. **35:** Fasting until evening was an expression of mourning (see 1.12). **39:** David explains why he does not punish Joab and Abishai, leaving that to the LORD.

4.1–12: The weak king. After several introductory remarks the narrative first tells of Ish-bosheth's death, and then of David's reaction to it, which is similar to his reaction to Saul's and Abner's death. Because Ish-bosheth's assassination made the way free for David to become king over all Israel, the narrative aims to clear him of all suspicion of complicity. This continues the theme of the initial chs of 2 Sam. David had no hand in the death of Saul and his family. **1–2:** *Son of Saul:* The omission of the personal name may express contempt (cf. 1 Sam. 20.27, 30, 31). *Benjaminites,*

Baanah and the other Rechab, sons of Rimmon the Beerothite—Benjaminites, since Beeroth too was considered part
of Benjamin. [3] The Beerothites had fled to Gittaim,[a] where
they have sojourned to this day. ([4] Jonathan son of Saul had
a son whose feet were crippled. He was five years old when
the news about Saul and Jonathan came from Jezreel, and
his nurse picked him up and fled; but as she was fleeing in
haste, he fell and was lamed. His name was Mephibosheth.[b])
[5] Rechab and Baanah, sons of Rimmon the Beerothite, started
out, and they reached the home of Ish-bosheth at the heat
of the day, when he was taking his midday rest. [6] [c-]So they
went inside the house, as though fetching wheat, and struck
him in the belly.[-c] Rechab and his brother Baanah slipped by,
[7] and entered the house while he was asleep on his bed in his
bedchamber; and they stabbed him to death. They cut off his
head and took his head and made their way all night through
the Arabah. [8] They brought the head of Ish-bosheth to David
in Hebron. "Here," they said to the king, "is the head of your
enemy, Ish-bosheth son of Saul, who sought your life. This
day the LORD has avenged my lord the king upon Saul and
his offspring."

[9] But David answered Rechab and his brother Baanah, the
sons of Rimmon the Beerothite, and said to them, "As the LORD
lives, who has rescued me from every trouble: [10] The man who
told me in Ziklag that Saul was dead thought he was bringing
good news. But instead of rewarding him for the news, I seized
and killed him. [11] How much more, then, when wicked men
have killed a blameless man in bed in his own house! I will certainly avenge his blood on you, and I will rid the earth of you."
[12] David gave orders to the young men, who killed them; they
cut off their hands and feet and hung them up by the pool in
Hebron. And they took the head of Ish-bosheth and buried it
in the grave of Abner at Hebron.

5 [d]All the tribes of Israel came to David at Hebron and said,
"We are your own flesh and blood. [2] Long before now, when
Saul was king over us, it was you who [e-]led Israel in war;[-e] and
the LORD said to you: You shall shepherd My people Israel; you
shall be ruler of Israel." [3] All the elders of Israel came to the king
at Hebron, and King David made a pact with them in Hebron
before the LORD. And they anointed David king over Israel.

a Gittaim was likewise in Benjamin; cf. Neh. 11.31 ff.
b The original form of the name, Merib-baal, is preserved in 1 Chron. 8.34; 9.40. Cf. Ish-bosheth (Eshbaal) in 2 Sam. 2.8, note a. This subject is resumed in chapter 9.
c-c Meaning of Heb. uncertain. Septuagint reads, "And behold, the woman who kept the door of the house was cleaning wheat. She became drowsy and fell asleep."
d The account in vv. 1–3 and 6–10 is to be found also, with variations, in 1 Chron. 11.1–9. *e-e Lit. "led Israel out and in."*

of the tribe of Ish-bosheth. **3:** After the original inhabitants of Beeroth (see Josh. 9.17ff.) had fled, Benjaminites settled in the town. **4:** Mephibosheth being crippled and therefore considered unfit to be king, no offspring of Saul, except Ish-bosheth, was left who could be king of Israel; Mephibosheth is also introduced here because he will play an important role later in Samuel (chs 9, 16, 19). **6–7:** V. 6 is largely repeated in v. 7 (the Heb verb at its end means "escaped" rather than *slipped by*). Abravanel explains that either v. 7 adds details about the way Ish-bosheth was murdered or that after striking him in the belly the assassins returned to his house in order to finish him off. It seems, however, that v. 6 is corrupt (cf. the different reading of the LXX) and superfluous. V. 7 is a perfect continuation of v. 5. **8:** The *enemy ... who sought your life* is Saul, not Ish-bosheth (in the Heb the word order is "the head of Ish-bosheth son of Saul, your enemy"). Cf. 1 Sam. 20.1; 23.15. **9:** The same phrase, *As the LORD lives, who has rescued me from every trouble,* is repeated at the very end of David's reign (1 Kings 1.29). **10:** See 1.1–16. **12:** Cutting off hands and feet as well as hanging in a public place (after the execution) were considered extremely humiliating (Judg. 1.6–7; Deut. 21.22–23). It is perhaps beneath the king's dignity to kill them himself; cf. 1 Sam. 22.18.

5.1–5: King of Israel. 1–3: Without effort on his part, the kingdom of Israel is offered to David, just as the kingdom of Judah was seven years earlier. The account emphasizes, right from its beginning, that *all the tribes* favored David; *all* is repeated in vv. 1–3 for emphasis and clarity. **2:** No such prophecy is extant in Samuel.

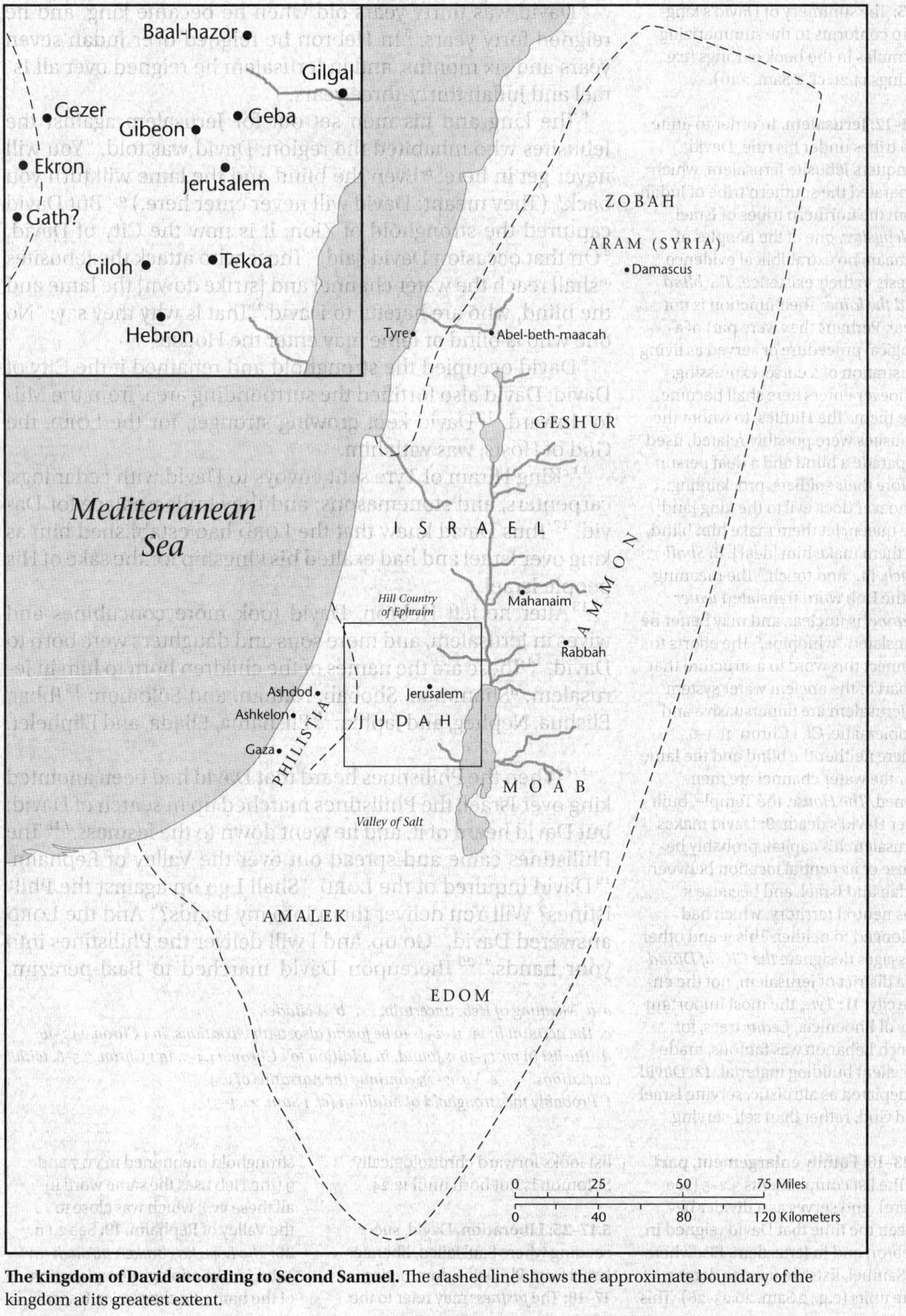

The kingdom of David according to Second Samuel. The dashed line shows the approximate boundary of the kingdom at its greatest extent.

4 David was thirty years old when he became king, and he
reigned forty years. 5 In Hebron he reigned over Judah seven
years and six months, and in Jerusalem he reigned over all Israel and Judah thirty-three years.

6 The king and his men set out for Jerusalem against the
Jebusites who inhabited the region. David was told, "You will
never get in here! [a-]Even the blind and the lame will turn you
back." (They meant: David will never enter here.)[-a] 7 But David
captured the stronghold of Zion; it is now the City of David.
8 On that occasion David said, "Those who attack the Jebusites
[a-]shall reach the water channel and [strike down] the lame and
the blind, who are hateful to David." That is why they say: "No
one who is blind or lame may enter the House."[-a]

9 David occupied the stronghold and renamed it the City of
David; David also fortified the surrounding area, from the Mil-
lo[b] inward. 10 David kept growing stronger, for the LORD, the
God of Hosts, was with him.

11 [c]King Hiram of Tyre sent envoys to David with cedar logs,
carpenters, and stonemasons; and they built a palace for David. 12 Thus David knew that the LORD had established him as
king over Israel and had exalted his kingship for the sake of His
people Israel.

13 After he left Hebron, David took more concubines and
wives in Jerusalem, and more sons and daughters were born to
David. 14 These are the names of the children born to him in Jerusalem: [d]Shammua, Shobab, Nathan, and Solomon; 15 Ibhar,
Elishua, Nepheg, and Japhia; 16 Elishama, Eliada, and Eliphelet.

17 [e]When the Philistines heard that David had been anointed
king over Israel, the Philistines marched up in search of David;
but David heard of it, and he went down to the fastness.[f] 18 The
Philistines came and spread out over the Valley of Rephaim.
19 David inquired of the LORD, "Shall I go up against the Philistines? Will You deliver them into my hands?" And the LORD
answered David, "Go up, and I will deliver the Philistines into
your hands." 20 Thereupon David marched to Baal-perazim,

a-a Meaning of Heb. uncertain. *b A citadel.*
c The account in vv. 11–25 is to be found also, with variations, in 1 Chron. 14.1–16.
d The list in vv. 14–16 is found, in addition to 1 Chron. 14.4–7, in 1 Chron. 3.5–8, with variations. *e Vv. 17–25 continue the narrative of v. 3.*
f Probably the stronghold of Adullam (cf. 1 Sam. 22.4–5).

4–5: The summary of David's kingship conforms to the summarizing formulas in the book of Kings (e.g., 1 Kings 14.21; cf. 2 Sam. 2.10).

5.6–12: Jerusalem. In order to unite the tribes under his rule, David conquers Jebusite Jerusalem, which separated the southern tribe of Judah from the northern tribes of Israel. **6:** *Jebusites,* one of the peoples of Canaan; no extrabiblical evidence attests to their existence. *The blind and the lame:* Their function is not clear. Perhaps they were part of a magical procedure or served as living illustration of a curse, expressing: Whoever enters here shall become like them. The Hittites, to whom the Jebusites were possibly related, used to parade a blind and a deaf person before their soldiers, proclaiming: Whoever does evil to the king [and] the queen, let them make him blind, let them make him [deaf]. **8:** *Shall reach,* lit. "and touch." The meaning of the Heb word translated *water channel* is unclear, and may better be translated "windpipe." The efforts to connect this word to a structure that is part of the ancient water system of Jerusalem are unpersuasive and problematic. Cf. 1 Chron. 11.4–6, where neither the blind and the lame nor the water channel are mentioned. *The House,* the Temple, built after David's death. **9:** David makes Jerusalem his capital, probably because of its central location between Judah and Israel, and because it was neutral territory, which had belonged to neither. This v. and other passages designate *the City of David* as a district of Jerusalem, not the entire city. **11:** *Tyre,* the most important city of Phoenicia. *Cedar* trees, for which Lebanon was famous, made excellent building material. **12:** David is depicted as altruistic, serving Israel and God, rather than self-serving.

5.13–16: Family enlargement, part 2. The list complements 3.2–5 (see there), and serves as a divider between the time that David reigned in Hebron and in Jerusalem. Elsewhere in Samuel, lists are used to demarcate units (e.g., 2 Sam. 20.23–26). This list looks forward chronologically; Solomon is not born until 12.24.

5.17–25: Liberation. David, succeeding where Saul failed, liberates Israel from Philistine domination. **17–18:** The *fastness* may refer to the stronghold mentioned in vv. 7 and 9 (the Heb uses the same word in all these vv.), which was close to the Valley of Rephaim. **19:** See 2.1 n. **20:** *The LORD has broken through my enemies:* An etiological explanation of the name *Baal-perazim.* It seems

and David defeated them there. And he said, "The LORD has broken through my enemies before me as waters break through [a dam]." That is why that place was named Baal-perazim.[a] 21 The Philistines abandoned their idols there, and David and his men carried them off.

22 Once again the Philistines marched up and spread out over the Valley of Rephaim. 23 David inquired of the LORD, and He answered, "Do not go up, but circle around behind them and confront them at the *baca*[b] trees. 24 And when you hear the sound of marching in the tops of the *baca* trees, then go into action, for the LORD will be going in front of you to attack the Philistine forces." 25 David did as the LORD had commanded him; and he routed the Philistines from Geba all the way to Gezer.

6 David again assembled all the picked men of Israel, thirty thousand strong. 2 [c]Then David and all the troops that were with him set out from Baalim[d] of Judah to bring up from there the Ark of God to which the Name was attached, the name LORD of Hosts Enthroned on the Cherubim.

3 They loaded the Ark of God onto a new cart and conveyed it from the house of Abinadab, which was on the hill; and Abinadab's sons, Uzza and Ahio, guided the [e-]new cart. 4 They conveyed it from Abinadab's house on the hill, [Uzzah walking][f] alongside[-e] the Ark of God and Ahio walking in front of the Ark. 5 Meanwhile, David and all the House of Israel danced before the LORD to [g-][the sound of] all kinds of cypress wood [instruments],[-g] with lyres, harps, timbrels, sistrums, and cymbals.

6 But when they came to the threshing floor of Nacon, Uzzah reached out for the Ark of God and grasped it, for the oxen had stumbled.[b] 7 The LORD was incensed at Uzzah. And God struck him down on the spot [h-]for his indiscretion,[-h] and he died there beside the Ark of God. 8 David was distressed because the LORD had inflicted a breach upon Uzzah; and that place was named Perez-uzzah,[i] as it is still called.

a Interpreted as "Baal of Breaches." Cf. 6.8 below, and the name Perez in Gen. 38.29 and note. *b Meaning of Heb. uncertain.*
c Vv. 2–12 are found also in 1 Chron. 13.5–14, with variations.
d Identical with Baalah, another name for Kiriath-jearim, where the Ark had been kept (cf. 1 Sam. 6.21; 1 Chron. 13.6; Josh. 15.9).
e-e Septuagint and 4QSam[a] read "cart alongside." *f Cf. vv. 6–7.*
g-g Cf. Kimhi; the parallel passage 1 Chron. 13.8 reads "with all their might and with songs."
h-h So Targum; 1 Chron. 13.10 reads "because he had laid a hand on the Ark."
i I.e., "the Breach of Uzzah"; cf. 5.20 and note.

that "Baal," lit. "master," but also the name of the main Canaanite deity, is here an epithet for the Israelite God. (Contrast Hos. 2.18.) **21:** It was customary to bring one's gods to the battlefield in order to obtain their help (see 1 Sam. 4.3 n.). David's capture of the Philistine idols is a reversal of the situation of 1 Sam. 4.11, when the Ark of the LORD was captured by the Philistines. These idols were often valuable and gold-covered; they were captured as war-booty, and as sign of the weakness of the deity whom they represented. Mesopotamian documents suggest that they were sometimes returned to the subjugated nation. **23:** *Do not go up,* to the front. **24:** *The sound of marching,* "when a wind will move the tops of the *bacas* so that a sound is heard like the footsteps of marching people" (Ralbag). God is imagined as directly participating in battle (as against Egypt in Exod. 14.25), not even using his "hosts" or other intermediaries, as in Judg. 5.20. This expressed God's great favor for David. **25:** Routing the Philistines to *Gezer,* on the border between Israel and Philistia, amounts to expelling them from Israelite territory.

6.1–23: Holiness. David brings the Holy Ark to Jerusalem, making the city not only his administrative, but also his religious, center. Thus Jerusalem becomes the holy city, first in Judaism, where it is still the direction of prayer, and later also in Christianity and Islam, though for different reasons. Some scholars believe that this ch was part of a larger composition, the Ark narrative, that included sections of 1 Sam. chs 4–7. **1:** *Thirty thousand,* see 1 Sam. 15.4 n. **2:** *The Ark of God to which the Name was attached, the name LORD of Hosts Enthroned on the Cherubim,* see 1 Sam. 4.4 n. **3–4:** *A new cart,* see 1 Sam. 6.7 n. *Abinadab,* see 1 Sam. 7.1. The passage from *new* at the end of v. 3 to *hill* in v. 4 is a dittography, repeating (in exactly the same words in the Heb) what was said in v. 3a. Read: "Uzza and Ahio guided the cart, [Uzzah walking] alongside the Ark of God and Ahio walking in front of the Ark." **5:** *To all kinds of cypress wood* is a corruption of "with all their might and with songs" (1 Chron. 13.8), which is similar in Heb. **6–8:** Touching the sacred object, loaded with awesome divine power, is fraught with danger (cf. Num. 4.15; 1 Sam. 6.19). David is distressed, because Uzzah only intended to prevent the Ark from slipping down. The fact is, however, that Uzzah came in direct contact with the Ark and therefore he is slain by God. The name *Perez-uzzah* is explained etiologically.

9 David was afraid of the LORD that day; he said, "How can
I let the Ark of the LORD come to me?" 10 So David would not
bring the Ark of the LORD to his place in the City of David; instead, David diverted it to the house of Obed-edom the Gittite.
11 The Ark of the LORD remained in the house of Obed-edom
the Gittite three months, and the LORD blessed Obed-edom
and his whole household.

12 It was reported to King David: "The LORD has blessed
Obed-edom's house and all that belongs to him because of
the Ark of God." [a]Thereupon David went and brought up the
Ark of God from the house of Obed-edom to the City of David,
amid rejoicing. 13 When the bearers of the Ark of the LORD had
moved forward six paces, he sacrificed [b]an ox and a fatling.[b]
14 David whirled with all his might before the LORD; David was
girt with a linen ephod. 15 Thus David and all the House of Israel brought up the Ark of the LORD with shouts and with blasts
of the horn.

16 As the Ark of the LORD entered the City of David, Michal
daughter of Saul looked out of the window and saw King David
leaping and whirling before the LORD; and she despised him
for it.

17 They brought in the Ark of the LORD and set it up in its
place inside the tent which David had pitched for it, and David sacrificed burnt offerings and offerings of well-being before the LORD. 18 When David finished sacrificing the burnt
offerings and the offerings of well-being, he blessed the people in the name of the LORD of Hosts. 19 And he distributed
among all the people—the entire multitude of Israel, man
and woman alike—to each a loaf of bread, [c]a cake made in
a pan, and a raisin cake.[c] Then all the people left for their
homes.

20 David went home to greet his household. And Michal
daughter of Saul came out to meet David and said, "Didn't the
king of Israel do himself honor today—exposing himself today
in the sight of the slavegirls of his subjects, as one of the riffraff
might expose himself!" 21 David answered Michal, "It was before the LORD who chose me instead of your father and all his
family and appointed me ruler over the LORD's people Israel! I
will dance before the LORD 22 and dishonor myself even more,
and be low in [d]my own[d] esteem; but among the slavegirls that
you speak of I will be honored." 23 So to her dying day Michal
daughter of Saul had no children.

a Vv. 12b–14 are found, with variations, in 1 Chron. 15.25–27; vv. 15–19a, with variations, in 1 Chron. 15.28–16.3; vv. 19b–20a, with variations, in 1 Chron. 16.43.
b-b 4QSam[a] reads "seven oxen and seven [rams]"; cf. 1 Chron. 15.26.
c-c Meaning of Heb. uncertain.
d-d Septuagint reads "your."

9–10: David now sees the Ark as a liability. **10:** *Obed-edom* may have been one of the Gittites who accompanied David on his way from the Philistine town of Gath (see 15.18). But there were also several places called Gath (meaning "winepress") in Israel. **12:** The report to King David convinces him that the Ark can be a blessing, if only it is handled properly. **13:** This time no cart is mentioned. The bearers may have been priests or Levites (see Num. 7.9; 1 Chron. 15.2). The excessive sacrifices are meant to appease God in case another inadvertent mistake is made (cf. Job 1.5). **14:** The *ephod* was a priestly garment (1 Sam. 2.18–21 n.); 2 Sam. 8.18 suggests that David and his family held priestly roles. **16:** *Michal daughter of Saul* (i.e., daughter of a king) despises her husband *King David,* whose frivolous behavior is unworthy of a king. **17:** The Ark had been in a tent since olden times (Exod. ch 40; Josh. 18.1). **18:** David, sacrificing and blessing *in the name of the LORD of Hosts* (see v. 2, which associates that name with the Ark), exercises priestly functions (see also vv. 13–14). **19:** Women too participated in this religious event. **20:** Honor in Michal's view consists of external dignified behavior; in David's view, of devotion to lofty ideas. But Michal's sarcasm likely springs from pent-up pain and bitterness. In the past she loved David, helped him to escape, and even deceived her father for his sake (1 Sam. 18.20, 28; 19.11–17). Then Saul gave her to Paltiel, who fervently loved her (2 Sam. 3.15–16). After many years David demanded her back, for utilitarian reasons (see 3.13, 16 n.), and she found herself one of his many wives. There is no hint that David ever loved her. **21:** *Instead of your father:* David taunts Michal in return. **22:** Michal's childlessness may be a punishment by God or the result of David's abstaining from sexual relations with her. There is thus no possibility of uniting the house of Saul and the house of David through a child of David and Michal.

7 [a]When the king was settled in his palace and the LORD
had granted him safety from all the enemies around him,
2 the king said to the prophet Nathan: "Here I am dwelling in
a house of cedar, while the Ark of the LORD abides in a tent!"
3 Nathan said to the king, "Go and do whatever you have in
mind, for the LORD is with you."
4 But that same night the word of the LORD came to Nathan:
5 "Go and say to My servant David: Thus said the LORD: Are you
the one to build a house for Me to dwell in? 6 From the day that
I brought the people of Israel out of Egypt to this day I have
not dwelt in a house, but have moved about in Tent and Tabernacle. 7 As I moved about wherever the Israelites went, did I
ever reproach any of the tribal leaders[b] whom I appointed to
care for My people Israel: Why have you not built Me a house
of cedar?
8 "Further, say thus to My servant David: Thus said the LORD
of Hosts: I took you from the pasture, from following the flock,
to be ruler of My people Israel, 9 and I have been with you wherever you went, and have cut down all your enemies before you.
Moreover, I will give you great renown like that of the greatest
men on earth. 10 I will establish a home for My people Israel
and will plant them firm, so that they shall dwell secure and
shall tremble no more. Evil men shall not oppress them any
more as in the past, 11 ever since I appointed chieftains over
My people Israel. I will give you safety from all your enemies.
"The LORD declares to you that He, the LORD, will establish
a house[c] for you. 12 When your days are done and you lie with
your fathers, I will raise up your offspring after you, one of your
own issue, and I will establish his kingship. 13 He shall build a
house for My name, and I will establish his royal throne forever. 14 I will be a father to him, and he shall be a son to Me.
When he does wrong, I will chastise him [d-]with the rod of men
and the affliction of mortals;[-d] 15 but I will never withdraw My
favor from him as I withdrew it from Saul, whom I removed
[e-]to make room for you.[-e] 16 Your house and your kingship shall

a This chapter is found, with variations, also in 1 Chron. 17.
b Understanding shibṭe *as "scepters"; so Kimhi. 1 Chron. 17.6 reads "chieftains"; cf. below, v. 11.* *c I.e., a dynasty; play on "house" (i.e., Temple) in v. 5.*
d-d I.e., only as a human father would. *e-e Lit. "from before you."*

7.1–29: The house. The ch contains a short introduction and two long speeches: one by God and one by David. God, pointing out that He has not previously needed a home, objects to David's plan to build Him a house (temple, Heb "bayit"), and announces instead that He will make a house (dynasty, Heb "bayit") for David and that David's son will build Him a house (temple). David first thanks the LORD and then requests that his house (dynasty) may endure forever. This ch is multi-layered, and atypically for Samuel, contains many Deuteronomistic characteristics. In its final form, it recognizes both judges (see v. 11) and kings, or at least the kingship of Solomon, David's son who will build the Temple. **1:** *Palace,* lit. "house." *All the enemies around him:* Either only the Philistines are meant or the ch is not in its proper chronological place, because in the following chs more wars are reported. The language here is similar to Deut. 12.10, which indeed suggests that the Temple should be built when all the enemies are put down. **2:** *House of cedar,* paneled with precious cedar, imported from Lebanon. **3–7:** Nathan encourages David to carry out his plan, but the LORD objects. Prophets sometimes express their personal feelings, which are not always in accord with God (e.g., Samuel opposed the people's demand for a king, whereas God consented, 1 Sam. 8.6–7). **5:** *Thus said the LORD,* the messenger formula (cf. Gen. 32.4–5), which assures that the following words, spoken by Nathan, are really the LORD's. **6:** *Not dwelt in a house:* In Shiloh, however, there was a House of the LORD (1 Sam. 1.7, 9). But there was also a Tent (Josh. 18.1; 1 Sam. 2.22), which symbolized the idea that the LORD is not restricted to one fixed place. **12:** *Your offspring:* This undoubtedly refers to Solomon, though no clear reason is offered here for why Solomon can do what David cannot (contrast 1 Kings 5.17; 1 Chron. 22.8–9). This v. and the following ones, however, have been interpreted in the postbiblical period as referring to the Messiah, who will be of the house of David and whose reign will last forever. **13:** In this v. the two main themes of the ch, the building of the Temple and the establishment of the eternal Davidic dynasty, are joined together. *My name* (instead of "Me") serves to exclude the possible misunderstanding that God actually dwells in a house; this is a key point of Deuteronomistic theology (see Deut. 12.11; 1 Kings 8.27; contrast Exod. 40.34–35). **14–15:** Like a father his son, the LORD will chastise David's successor but never reject him; this v. suggests that the Davidic king is God's adopted son; cf. Ps. 2.7. **15–16:** The promise that David's dynasty shall last *forever,* repeated several times in the ch, is

ever be secure before you;[a] your throne shall be established
forever."
17 Nathan spoke to David in accordance with all these words
and all this prophecy. 18 Then King David came and sat before
the LORD, and he said, "What am I, O Lord GOD, and what is
my family, that You have brought me thus far? 19 Yet even this,
O Lord GOD, has seemed too little to You; for You have spoken of Your servant's house also for the future. [b-]May that be
the law for the people,[-b] O Lord GOD. 20 What more can David say to You? You know Your servant, O Lord GOD. 21 [b-]For
Your word's sake and of Your own accord[-b] You have wrought
this great thing, and made it known to Your servant. 22 You are
great indeed, O Lord GOD! There is none like You and there is
no other God but You, as we have always heard. 23 And who is
like Your people Israel, a unique nation on earth, whom God
went and redeemed as His people, winning renown for Himself and doing great and marvelous deeds for them[c] [and] for
Your land—[driving out][d] nations and their gods before Your
people, whom You redeemed for Yourself from Egypt. 24 You
have established Your people Israel as Your very own people
forever; and You, O LORD, have become their God.
25 "And now, O LORD God, fulfill Your promise to Your servant and his house forever; and do as You have promised. 26 And
may Your name be glorified forever, in that men will say, 'The
LORD of Hosts is God over Israel'; and may the house of Your
servant David be established before You. 27 Because You, O
LORD of Hosts, the God of Israel, have revealed to Your servant
that You will build a house for him, Your servant has ventured
to offer this prayer to You. 28 And now, O Lord GOD, You are
God and Your words will surely come true, and You have made
this gracious promise to Your servant. 29 Be pleased, therefore,
to bless Your servant's house, that it abide before You forever;
for You, O Lord GOD, have spoken. May Your servant's house
be blessed forever by Your blessing."

8 [e]Some time afterward, David attacked the Philistines and
subdued them; and David took Metheg-ammah[f] from the
Philistines. 2 He also defeated the Moabites. He made them lie
down on the ground and he measured them off with a cord;

a *Septuagint reads "before Me," i.e., "by My favor."*
b-b *Meaning of Heb. uncertain.*
c *Heb. "you," apparently denoting Israel.* d *So 1 Chron. 17.21.*
e *This chapter is reproduced, with some variations, in 1 Chron. 18.*
f *If not a place name, meaning of Heb. uncertain.*

not accompanied by any conditions (contrast 1 Kings 9.4–7). **18:** David's humility is shared by other leaders in the Bible, including Moses (Exod. 3.11), Gideon (Judg. 6.15), and Saul (1 Sam. 9.21). *Family,* lit. "house." The word "house," Heb "bayit," in its various meanings occurs in the ch fifteen times (in the Heb). **21:** *This great thing,* the promise of a lasting dynasty. **22:** The idea of absolute monotheism, that *there is no other God but You,* characterizes Isa. chs 40–66 and other exilic and postexilic biblical books (see Exod. 15.11 n.); indeed, the end of the next v. assumes the existence of many gods, over whom the God of Israel is more powerful. **23:** *Redeemed,* from slavery in Egypt. *[Driving out],* from the land of Canaan. **24:** The idea that Israel is the LORD's people and that He is Israel's God is central in biblical thought (e.g., Exod. 6.7) and in Judaism in general. The repetition of *established* regarding Israel, used above in reference to David (v. 16) ties together God, Israel, and David *forever.* **25–29:** After extolling God and His deeds for Israel, David returns to the subject of his own dynasty and prays that God may fulfill His promise *forever* (because sometimes He changes His mind, e.g., 1 Sam. 2.30–31). These vv. reflect anxiety about the precariousness of the dynasty, and may derive from the exilic period.

8.1–14: Expansion. The summary of David's conquests shows him at the height of his power, ruling over a vast territory, from the Euphrates in the northeast to the Egyptian border in the southwest. His success is attributed to divine help, in recognition of which David consecrates to God the spoils from his wars; the Chronicler builds upon this, and assumes that David used this material to prepare for his son's Temple building (see 1 Chron. 22.16). This ch is the only one in the book that contains no dialogue. **1:** *Some time afterward* is an editorial addition used to stitch various stories together; this v. and what follows contradict 7.1 (see n. there). In 5.25 it was told that David expelled the Philistines from Israelite territory; here it is reported that he subjugated them. **2:** In order to justify David's cruel act the Midrash (*Tanḥuma,* Buber recension, *Vayera'* 25) asserts that the king of Moab

he measured out two lengths of cord for those who were to be
put to death, and one length for those to be spared.[a] And the
Moabites became tributary vassals of David.
3 David defeated Hadadezer son of Rehob, king of Zobah, who
was then on his way to restore his monument[b] at the Euphrates
River. 4 David captured 1,700 horsemen and 20,000 foot soldiers
of his force; and David hamstrung all the chariot horses, except
for 100 which he retained. 5 And when the Arameans of Damascus came to the aid of King Hadadezer of Zobah, David struck
down 22,000 of the Arameans. 6 David stationed garrisons in
Aram of Damascus, and the Arameans became tributary vassals of David. The LORD gave David victory wherever he went.
7 David took the gold shields[c] carried by Hadadezer's retinue
and brought them to Jerusalem; 8 and from Betah and Berothai,
towns of Hadadezer, King David took a vast amount of copper.
9 When King Toi of Hamath heard that David had defeated
the entire army of Hadadezer, 10 Toi sent his son Joram to King
David to greet him and to congratulate him on his military victory over Hadadezer—for Hadadezer had been at war with Toi.
[Joram] brought with him objects of silver, gold, and copper.
11 King David dedicated these to the LORD, along with the other
silver and gold that he dedicated, [taken] from all the nations
he had conquered: 12 from Edom,[d] Moab, and Ammon; from
the Philistines and the Amalekites, and from the plunder of
Hadadezer son of Rehob, king of Zobah.
13 David gained fame [e]when he returned from defeating[e]
Edom[d] in the Valley of Salt, 18,000 in all. 14 He stationed garrisons in Edom—[f]he stationed garrisons in all of Edom[f]—and
all the Edomites became vassals of David. The LORD gave David victory wherever he went.
15 David reigned over all Israel, and David executed true
justice among all his people. 16 Joab son of Zeruiah was commander of the army; Jehoshaphat son of Ahilud was recorder; 17 Zadok son of Ahitub and [g]Ahimelech son of Abiathar[g]
were priests; Seraiah[h] was scribe; 18 Benaiah son of Jehoiada

a *I.e., he repeatedly doomed twice the number he spared.*
b *On* yad *in this sense, cf. 18.18; 1 Chron. 18.3; 1 Sam. 15.12. Others "dominion."*
c *Or "quivers."*
d *So several mss., Septuagint, and 1 Chron. 18.11–13; and cf. v. 14 below. Printed editions and most mss. read "Aram."*
e-e *1 Chron. 18.12 and Ps. 60.1 read differently.*
f-f *This phrase is lacking in 1 Chron. 18.13.*
g-g *Emendation yields "Abiathar son of Ahimelech," cf., e.g., 20.25; 1 Sam. 22.20.*
h *"Sheva" in 20.25; "Shavsha" in 1 Chron. 18.16.*

had killed David's parents, who had been entrusted to his care (1 Sam. 22.4). **3:** *Hadadezer* was David's chief opponent. He not only ruled over the Aramean kingdom of Zobah, but also dominated other Aramean territories (see 10.19). The circumstances of Hadadezer's restoring *his monument* are unclear (1 Chron. 18.3 reads "set up his monument"). But the Heb may also be translated "turn his hand" (the same expression in Isa. 1.25; Ezek. 38.12; Amos 1.8), though it is not said against whom. **4:** The word translated *horsemen* may also mean "horses" (as regards the numbers, cf. 1 Chron. 18.4). David *hamstrung* the horses, making them unfit for military use rather than taking them as booty because Israel did not yet employ chariots in its army. **6:** *Garrisons,* rather "prefects," as the Heb word is translated in 1 Sam. 10.5; 13.3–4. *The LORD gave David victory wherever he went* functions as a mini-refrain with the end of v. 14, summarizing the ch's theme. **8:** *Copper* was of high value for the production of bronze tools and weapons. **9:** *Hamath* was the capital of a Hittite-Canaanite (i.e., non-Aramean) country, adjacent to Zobah. **10:** By sending his son with precious presents King Toi acknowledges David's supremacy and offers to become his vassal. Instead of *Joram,* the Heb form of the name, 1 Chron. 18.10 reads "Hadoram," which is the Canaanite form. **11:** The silver and gold were later deposited in the Temple (1 Kings 7.51). **14:** *Garrisons,* see v. 6 n.

8.15–18: Administration, part 1. After the summary account of David's foreign enterprises, a brief list of his senior officials follows, which shows that he also concerned himself with the organization of his administration at home. The exact role of many of these functionaries is debated. The list marks the conclusion of the first part of 2 Sam., separating David's successes, from what follows, which begins the narration of his personal and political failures. **15:** The execution of justice is considered in the Bible to be the king's foremost duty (1 Kings 10.9; Jer. 22.2–3). David is pictured as the ideal king. **18:** *The Cherethites and the Pelethites,* military units of (Philistine) mercenaries, probably serving as David's bodyguard. The Cherethites—i.e., Cretans—are mentioned together with the Philistines in Ezek. 25.16; Zeph. 2.5. *David's sons were priests:*

was [a]commander of[a] the Cherethites and the Pelethites; and
David's sons were priests.

9

David inquired, "Is there anyone still left of the House of
Saul with whom I can keep faith for the sake of Jonathan?"
[2]There was a servant of the House of Saul named Ziba, and they
summoned him to David. "Are you Ziba?" the king asked him.
[b]"Yes, sir,"[b] he replied. [3]The king continued, "Is there anyone
at all left of the House of Saul with whom I can keep faith as
pledged before God?"[c] Ziba answered the king, "Yes, there is
still a son of Jonathan whose feet are crippled." [4]"Where is he?"
the king asked, and Ziba said to the king, "He is in the house
of Machir son of Ammiel, in Lo-debar." [5]King David had him
brought from the house of Machir son of Ammiel, at Lo-debar;
[6]and when Mephibosheth son of Jonathan son of Saul came
to David, he flung himself on his face and prostrated himself.
David said, "Mephibosheth!" and he replied, "At your service,
sir." [7]David said to him, "Don't be afraid, for I will keep faith
with you for the sake of your father Jonathan. I will give you
back all the land of your grandfather Saul; moreover, you shall
always eat at my table." [8][Mephibosheth] prostrated himself
again, and said, "What is your servant, that you should show
regard for a dead dog like me?"
[9]The king summoned Ziba, Saul's steward, and said to him,
"I give to your master's grandson everything that belonged to
Saul and to his entire family. [10]You and your sons and your
slaves shall farm the land for him and shall bring in [its yield]
to provide food for your master's grandson[d] to live on; but Mephibosheth, your master's grandson, shall always eat at my
table."—Ziba had fifteen sons and twenty slaves.—[11]Ziba said
to the king, "Your servant will do just as my lord the king has
commanded him." [e]"Mephibosheth shall eat at my table[e] like
one of the king's sons."
[12]Mephibosheth had a young son named Mica; and all
the members of Ziba's household worked for Mephibosheth.

a-a So Targum (cf. 20.23; 1 Chron. 18.17); Heb. "and." *b-b Lit. "Your servant is."*
c See 1 Sam. 20.14 and note. *d Septuagint reads "household."*
e-e Septuagint reads "And Mephibosheth ate at David's table."

Apparently David's sons fulfilled priestly functions at the court (cf. 6.18 n. and 20.26), whereas Zadok and Abiathar were the chief priests. Kings often assumed cultic functions in the ancient Near East, though this practice was not recognized later, with the establishment of a professional clergy, tracing its descent from Levi and Aaron, with a monopoly on cultic practice (see 2 Chron. 26.16–21).

Chs 9–20: These chs, with the addition of 1 Kings chs 1–2, are known as the succession narrative, because the succession to David's throne is believed by many biblical scholars to be their principal subject. Only 1 Kings ch 1 is devoted specifically to that subject, however. Most of the other chs (11–19) are concerned with David's sin and its consequences. The calamities in his family, which are interpreted by the prophet Nathan (12.9–12) as punishment for his crimes, convey the message that kings are not above law and morals; nevertheless, because of the promise in 2 Sam. ch 7, David's kingship endures. Chs 9–10 provide the background for the main story.

9.1–13: Faithfulness. David, true to his covenant with Jonathan (1 Sam. 20.14–16), shows kindness to Jonathan's son Mephibosheth. This episode is mentioned here since it provides relevant background material for chs 16 and 19. **1:** The Heb word "ḥesed," translated *faith,* also means "kindness." It is sometimes the term for what the more powerful person in a pact (Heb "berit") does to the less powerful, sometimes a mutual obligation, and reflects the pact that David had with Jonathan (1 Sam. 18.3; 23.18). **2:** Since the courtiers are unable to answer David's question, they summon Ziba, who will become important in ch 16. **3:** *Crippled,* see 4.4 and n. **4:** *Machir son of Ammiel,* one of the notables of Gilead (17.27). **6:** *Mephibosheth:* The original form of the name was "Merib-baal" (see translators' note at 4.4). The element "baal" was changed into "bosheth," meaning "shame" (cf. translators' notes at 2.8 and 11.21). The names of his father and grandfather are mentioned because of their relevance to David's treatment of Mephibosheth (v. 7). His excessive expressions of submissiveness testify to his fear that David is about to put him to death as a potential pretender to the throne (see 1 Sam. 20.15 n.). **7:** Eating at the king's table, i.e., being maintained by the king, was considered a special favor (1 Kings 2.7; 18.19; 2 Kings 25.29–30), though in this case, it allowed David to keep an eye on the one surviving heir of Saul. **8:** *A dead dog,* see 3.8 n. **10:** Though a servant, Ziba is clearly well-to-do, keeping slaves himself; nevertheless, he now has to work for Mephibosheth.

13 Mephibosheth lived in Jerusalem, for he ate regularly at the
king's table. He was lame in both feet.

10 [a]Some time afterward, the king of Ammon died, and his
son Hanun succeeded him as king. 2 David said, "I will
keep faith with Hanun son of Nahash, just as his father kept
faith with me." He sent his courtiers with a message of condo-
lence to him over his father. But when David's courtiers came
to the land of Ammon, 3 the Ammonite officials said to their
lord Hanun, "Do you think David is really honoring your father
just because he sent you men with condolences? Why, David
has sent his courtiers to you to explore and spy out the city, and
to overthrow[b] it." 4 So Hanun seized David's courtiers, clipped
off one side of their beards and cut away half of their garments
at the buttocks, and sent them off. 5 When David was told of
it, he dispatched men to meet them, for the men were greatly
embarrassed. And the king gave orders: "Stop in Jericho until
your beards grow back; then you can return."
6 The Ammonites realized that they had [c]incurred the wrath
of[c] David; so the Ammonites sent agents and hired Arameans of Beth-rehob and Arameans of Zobah—20,000 foot
soldiers—the king of Maacah [with] 1,000 men, and 12,000
men from Tob. 7 On learning this, David sent out Joab and the
whole army—[including] the professional fighters. 8 The Ammonites marched out and took up their battle position at the
entrance of the gate, while the Arameans of Zobah and Rehob
and the men of Tob and Maacah took their stand separately
in the open. 9 Joab saw that there was a battle line against him
both front and rear. So he made a selection from all the picked
men of Israel and arrayed them against the Arameans, 10 and
the rest of the troops he put under the command of his brother
Abishai[d] and arrayed them against the Ammonites. 11 [Joab]
said, "If the Arameans prove too strong for me, you come to
my aid; and if the Ammonites prove too strong for you, I will
come to your aid. 12 Let us be strong and resolute for the sake
of our people and the land[e] of our God; and the LORD will do
what He deems right."
13 Joab and the troops with him marched into battle against
the Arameans, who fled before him. 14 And when the Ammonites saw that the Arameans had fled, they fled before Abishai
and withdrew into the city. So Joab broke off the attack against
the Ammonites, and went to Jerusalem.

a This chapter is found also in 1 Chron. 19.
b Emendation yields "reconnoiter"; cf. Deut. 1.22; Josh. 2.2–3.
c-c See note at 1 Sam. 13.4. *d Heb. "Abshai."* *e Lit. "towns."*

13: Mephibosheth moves to Jerusalem in order to eat at the king's table. **10.1–19: War.** The account of the war with Ammon serves as background to the next story, which deals with David's sin against Bathsheba and Uriah. The first part of the present account explains the cause of the war, the second part tells of its first stage, which involved both the Ammonites and the Arameans, and the third part reports the second stage, which was conducted against the Arameans only (mentioned in ch 8). David did not initiate the war, but through his victory he gained supremacy in the region (the third stage of the war, against the Ammonites only, is related in chs 11–12). These battles conflict with the claim in 7.1 that David was at peace, suggesting that the organization here is thematic rather than chronological. **2:** *Nahash* is mentioned in 1 Sam. 11.1–2. It is unknown of what his *faith* (or "kindness," Heb "ḥesed") to David consisted. Perhaps there was a treaty between David and Nahash; in any case, the use of the term "ḥesed" connects this episode to 9.1, where the same word appears. David's gesture signals that he is willing to continue the good relations with Ammon. **4:** *Hanun,* accepting his officials' opinion, not only expels David's courtiers, but also humiliates them, insulting their dignity. The Lachish reliefs show that at least at a later period, Israelites were bearded. **5:** *Jericho* was on the border between Israel and Ammon. According to the Bible, the city had been (almost) empty since Joshua destroyed it; it was rebuilt only during Ahab's reign (1 Kings 16.34). **6:** The enumeration of the countries and the numbers of the fighting men point to the superiority of the enemy's forces, and thus enhance Joab's victory. **8:** *The gate,* of Rabbah, capital of Ammon. **9:** Joab's position between the Arameans and the Ammonites is extremely hazardous, reflecting his bravado. **11–12:** Joab, in the only speech in the ch, first sets forth his plan of battle based on mutual aid, and then delivers a message of encouragement and faith in God. *Let us be strong and resolute,* lit. "be strong and let us strengthen ourselves."

[15] When the Arameans saw that they had been routed by Israel, they regrouped their forces. [16] [a-]Hadadezer sent for and brought out the Arameans from across the Euphrates; they came to Helam, led by Shobach, Hadadezer's[-a] army commander. [17] David was informed of it; he assembled all Israel, crossed the Jordan, and came to Helam. The Arameans drew up their forces against David and attacked him; [18] but the Arameans were put to flight by Israel. David killed 700 Aramean charioteers and 40,000 horsemen;[b] he also struck down Shobach, Hadadezer's[c] army commander, who died there. [19] And when all the vassal kings of Hadadezer[d] saw that they had been routed by Israel, they submitted to Israel and became their vassals. And the Arameans were afraid to help the Ammonites any more.

11 At the turn of the year, the season when kings go out [to battle], David sent Joab with his officers and all Israel with him, and they devastated Ammon and besieged Rabbah; David remained in Jerusalem. [2] Late one afternoon, David rose from his couch and strolled on the roof of the royal palace; and from the roof he saw a woman bathing. The woman was very beautiful, [3] and the king sent someone to make inquiries about the woman. He reported, "She is Bathsheba daughter of Eliam [and] wife of Uriah the Hittite." [4] David sent messengers to fetch her; she came to him and he lay with her—she had just purified herself after her period—and she went back home. [5] The woman conceived, and she sent word to David, "I am pregnant." [6] Thereupon David sent a message to Joab, "Send Uriah the Hittite to me"; and Joab sent Uriah to David.

[7] When Uriah came to him, David asked him how Joab and the troops were faring and how the war was going. [8] Then David said to Uriah, "Go down to your house and bathe your feet."

a-a Many editions read "Hadarezer ... Hadarezer's."
b 1 Chron. 19.18 reads "foot soldiers." *c Heb. "his."* *d See note a-a.*

16: *Hadadezer,* see 8.3 n. **18:** As elsewhere, the numbers seem exaggerated. **19:** The Arameans were the most powerful city-state, and the v. suggests that even they now feared David; the end of the v. also supplies important information for the following ch, explaining why the Ammonites had to face David without any help.

11.1–27a: Adultery and murder. The narrative of David's adultery and murder is embedded in the account of the war with Ammon (ch 10; 12.26–31), because the events of the story occur against the background of that war. Uriah's absence from home, which paves the way for the adultery and also necessitates creating an explanation for Bathsheba's pregnancy, is occasioned by the war, as is Uriah's death. The narrative does not try to conceal or mitigate David's sins. The outstanding loyalty of the non-Israelite soldier (Uriah) underscores David's perfidy. It is highly unusual for ancient literature to criticize powerful and successful kings. The way David's behavior is depicted and condemned in the Bible shows the overriding importance it assigns to moral values; nevertheless, the story emphasizes that David is forgiven, perhaps because of the eternal covenant in ch 7. Some rabbinic sources tried to clear David from guilt, claiming that he did not commit adultery, since warriors in that period, before setting out to battle, gave their wives (conditional) divorces so that they could remarry in case their husbands should not return; neither was David considered to be guilty of murder, since Uriah was killed in action by the Ammonites (*b. Shab.* 56a). This rereading, from an era when David was idealized and the idea of a Davidic messiah was well-developed, is anachronistic and goes against the gist of the biblical text. **1:** *The season,* the spring, the beginning of the dry season. An alternative and more literal translation of v. 1a would be: "It happened when a year had passed since the time that the kings went out [to battle]," i.e., a year after the war of ch 10 took place. *Rabbah,* modern Amman, the capital of ancient Ammon. **2:** David strolls on the flat roof of his palace in the evening breeze and sees *a woman bathing,* perhaps to purify herself after her period (v. 4). Some modern scholars suggest that the woman knew that this was David's habit, and that she was trying to entice him. **3:** Both Bathsheba's father and her husband are mentioned, suggesting her high status. Uriah was an army officer, and so perhaps was Eliam (see 23.34, 39). David thus commits adultery with the wife of one of his officers and probably the daughter of another. *Hittite,* see 1 Sam. 26.6 n. **4:** *She had just purified herself after her period:* This indicates that at this juncture Bathsheba is not pregnant. **6:** Bathsheba's perspective is not given for the rest of the story, except, in passing, at v. 26. Her pregnancy is David's problem. **7:** David's questions disguise his real intent. The narrator omits Joab's answers, thus hinting that David is not really interested in them. **8:** David commands Uriah to go to his house, expecting

When Uriah left the royal palace, a present from the king followed him. 9 But Uriah slept at the entrance of the royal palace, along with the other officers of his lord, and did not go down to his house. 10 When David was told that Uriah had not gone down to his house, he said to Uriah, "You just came from a journey; why didn't you go down to your house?" 11 Uriah answered David, "The Ark and Israel and Judah are located at Succoth, and my master Joab and Your Majesty's men are camped in the open; how can I go home and eat and drink and sleep with my wife? [a]As you live, by your very life,[a] I will not do this!" 12 David said to Uriah, "Stay here today also, and tomorrow I will send you off." So Uriah remained in Jerusalem that day. The next day, 13 David summoned him, and he ate and drank with him until he got him drunk; but in the evening, [Uriah] went out to sleep in the same place, with his lord's officers; he did not go down to his home.

14 In the morning, David wrote a letter to Joab, which he sent with Uriah. 15 He wrote in the letter as follows: "Place Uriah in the front line where the fighting is fiercest; then fall back so that he may be killed." 16 So when Joab was besieging the city, he stationed Uriah at the point where he knew that there were able warriors. 17 The men of the city sallied out and attacked Joab, and some of David's officers among the troops fell; Uriah the Hittite was among those who died.

18 Joab sent a full report of the battle to David. 19 He instructed the messenger as follows: "When you finish reporting to the king all about the battle, 20 the king may get angry and say to you, 'Why did you come so close to the city to attack it? Didn't you know that they would shoot from the wall? 21 Who struck down Abimelech son of Jerubbesheth?[b] Was it not a woman who dropped an upper millstone on him from the wall at Thebez, from which he died? Why did you come so close to the wall?' Then say: 'Your servant Uriah the Hittite was among those killed.' "

22 The messenger set out; he came and told David all that Joab had sent him to say.[c] 23 The messenger said to David, "First the men prevailed against us and sallied out against us into the open; then we drove them back up to the entrance to the gate. 24 But the archers shot at your men from the wall and some of Your Majesty's men fell; your servant Uriah the Hittite also

a-a Meaning of Heb. uncertain. Emendation yields "As the Lord *lives and as you live" (cf. 1 Sam. 20.3; 25.26; etc.). Lit. "as you live and as your being lives."*
b The earlier form is Jerubbaal (another name for Gideon), Judg. 7.1; on -bosheth/besheth *for* -baal, *see note at 2 Sam. 4.4. For the event at Thebez described here, see Judg. 9.35 ff.*
c Septuagint continues with a recapitulation of vv. 19–21.

that he will sleep with his wife and thus—unwittingly—cover up the adultery. *Bathe your feet,* as usual after a journey (cf. Gen. 18.4). *A present,* victuals. **9:** *Uriah slept,* but not with his wife and not even in his house. **11:** *The Ark* was taken to the battlefield in the belief that God's Presence would ensure victory (cf. 1 Sam. 4.3). *Located at,* lit. "staying in." *Succoth,* the Heb word means "booths." Probably not the town Succoth is meant, but the simple shelters of the soldiers in the *open* (lit. "field"), as opposed to the comfortable *home* of Uriah. Uriah rejects any amenities that are denied his comrades. Uriah's piety (esp. for a Hittite!) and military discipline are remarkable, and they contrast with David's lack of these qualities. **13:** *He got him drunk,* hoping that in that state Uriah would sleep with his wife. The expression *did not go down to his (your) home (house)* occurs four times (vv. 9–13), thus emphasizing Uriah's steadfastness. **14:** David trusts Uriah that he will not open the sealed letter; this suggests that Uriah did not suspect David's motives. **15:** David's order to *fall back* is not carried out, and other officers are killed along with Uriah. **20–21:** Joab knows that he made a fatal mistake, allowing his men to come close to the city wall. In his instructions to the messenger he couches David's anticipated reaction in the form of a series of rhetorical questions. The first and last questions, being similar (ring composition), contain the main argument, whereas the other questions supply the reasons. Joab should have learned from the precedent of Abimelech, who was killed by a (weak) woman (Judg. 9.53). The message that Uriah was one of the killed, however, instead of increasing the king's rage at the unwarranted death of a loyal officer and comrade, will have the (ironic) effect of calming him down. **23–24:** Not understanding why Joab couched his response so carefully, in order to forestall David's anger the messenger explains that the men came close to the gate in the course of driving the enemy back; and, without waiting for the king's expected angry reaction, he immediately adds that Uriah also died.

fell." 25 Whereupon David said to the messenger, "Give Joab this
message: 'Do not be distressed about the matter. The sword
[a]always takes its toll.[a] Press your attack on the city and destroy
it!' Encourage him!"
26 When Uriah's wife heard that her husband Uriah was
dead, she lamented over her husband. 27 After the period of
mourning was over, David sent and had her brought into his
palace; she became his wife and she bore him a son.
12 But the LORD was displeased with what David had done,
1 and the LORD sent Nathan to David. He came to him
and said, "There were two men in the same city, one rich and
one poor. 2 The rich man had very large flocks and herds, 3 but
the poor man had only one little ewe lamb that he had bought.
He tended it and it grew up together with him and his children: it used to share his morsel of bread, drink from his cup,
and nestle in his bosom; it was like a daughter to him. 4 One
day, a traveler came to the rich man, but he was loath to take
anything from his own flocks or herds to prepare a meal for the
guest who had come to him; so he took the poor man's lamb
and prepared it for the man who had come to him."
5 David flew into a rage against the man, and said to Nathan,
"As the LORD lives, the man who did this deserves to die! 6 He
shall pay for the lamb four times over, because he did such a
thing and showed no pity." 7 And Nathan said to David, "That
man is you! Thus said the LORD, the God of Israel: 'It was I who
anointed you king over Israel and it was I who rescued you
from the hand of Saul. 8 I gave you your master's house and
possession of your master's wives; and I gave you the House
of Israel and Judah; and if that were not enough, I would give
you twice as much more. 9 Why then have you flouted the command of the LORD and done what displeases Him? You have
put Uriah the Hittite to the sword; you took his wife and made
her your wife and had him killed by the sword of the Ammonites. 10 Therefore the sword shall never depart from your
House—because you spurned Me by taking the wife of Uriah
the Hittite and making her your wife.' 11 Thus said the LORD:
'I will make a calamity rise against you from within your own
house; I will take your wives and give them to another man before your very eyes and he shall sleep with your wives under

a-a Lit. "consumes the like and the like."

25: Because of Uriah's death, David does not get enraged, and even comforts and encourages Joab. **27a:** *Period of mourning,* see 1 Sam. 31.13 n. Because of Bathsheba's pregnancy David cannot wait long. The subunit ends here; this is one of many places where the ch divisions are inappropriate, and the end of one v. has been incorrectly combined with the beginning of the following one (see e.g., Gen. 2.4 n.).

11.27b–12.25: Repentance. God's stern condemnation of David's crimes induces the king to repent. **27b:** Explicit judgment of the characters or their actions is rare in the book of Samuel. Here it is attributed to God Himself because of the seriousness of the sins and because the sinner is a king. God's authority is above that of the king and from Him nothing can be concealed. **1–4:** Nathan's parable, presented as a legal case, aims at getting David to pass verdict on himself unwittingly (kings used to perform judicial functions, see 15.2–6 n.). Therefore it closely corresponds to the actual events, but not completely (cf. Jotham's parable in Judg. ch 9): e.g., whereas the rich man represents David, the poor man Uriah, and the lamb Bathsheba, nobody corresponds to the traveler; moreover, the lamb is slaughtered, instead of being added to the herd. The parable stresses the social aspect of the robbery, the rich man taking the scant property of the poor man. **1:** *The LORD sent,* as against David's frequent sending (11.1, 3, 6, 14, 27). **3:** Nathan stresses the emotional angle: the poor man's touching attachment to his lamb; noting that the lamb *was like a daughter* (Heb "bat") *to him* is a play on the name of Bathsheba, but David is too oblivious to his crimes to notice. **5:** *Deserves to die,* an outburst of indignation. Israelite law does not impose the death penalty for robbery. **6:** *Four times over,* in accordance with the law in Exod. 21.37 (LXX reads "sevenfold," cf. Prov. 6.31). *Pity:* The same Heb word is translated "loath" in v. 4. It seemed a pity to the rich man to take from his own herd, but he showed no pity for the poor man's only lamb. **7–12:** Nathan's rebuke. **7–9:** David has been ungrateful to the LORD, who gave him everything. **7:** *Thus said the LORD,* the messenger formula (see 7.5 n.), assuring that the following statement derives from God. **8:** *Your master's wives:* Perhaps David took over Saul's wives, though this is nowhere mentioned. **9:** The repetition of *sword* highlights the serious accusation of murder, even if David did so via an agent rather than directly. **10–12:** The punishments correspond to David's sins

this very sun. 12 You acted in secret, but I will make this happen in the sight of all Israel and in broad daylight.' "

13 David said to Nathan, "I stand guilty before the LORD!" And Nathan replied to David, "The LORD has remitted your sin; you shall not die. 14 However, since you have spurned [a]the enemies of[a] the LORD by this deed, even the child about to be born to you shall die."

15 Nathan went home, and the LORD afflicted the child that Uriah's wife had borne to David, and it became critically ill. 16 David entreated God for the boy; David fasted, and he went in and spent the night lying[b] on the ground. 17 The senior servants of his household tried to induce him to get up from the ground; but he refused, nor would he partake of food with them. 18 On the seventh day the child died. David's servants were afraid to tell David that the child was dead; for they said, "We spoke to him when the child was alive and he wouldn't listen to us; how can we tell him that the child is dead? He might do something terrible." 19 When David saw his servants talking in whispers, David understood that the child was dead; David asked his servants, "Is the child dead?" "Yes," they replied.

20 Thereupon David rose from the ground; he bathed and anointed himself, and he changed his clothes. He went into the House of the LORD and prostrated himself. Then he went home and asked for food, which they set before him, and he ate. 21 His courtiers asked him, "Why have you acted in this manner? While the child was alive, you fasted and wept; but now that the child is dead, you rise and take food!" 22 He replied, "While the child was still alive, I fasted and wept because I thought: 'Who knows? The LORD may have pity on me, and the child may live.' 23 But now that he is dead, why should I fast? Can I bring him back again? I shall go to him, but he will never come back to me."

24 David consoled his wife Bathsheba; he went to her and lay with her. She bore a son and she named him Solomon. The LORD favored him, 25 and He sent a message through the prophet Nathan; and he was named Jedidiah[c] at the instance of the LORD.

26 [d]Joab attacked Rabbah of Ammon and captured the royal city. 27 Joab sent messengers to David and said, "I have attacked Rabbah and I have already captured [e]the water city.[e] 28 Now

a-a The phrase is intended to avoid saying "spurned the LORD"; cf. note b-b at 1 Sam. 25.22.
b Some Septuagint mss. and 4QSam[a] add "in sackcloth"; cf. 1 Kings 21.27.
c I.e., "Beloved of the LORD." *d Vv. 26–29 are abridged in 1 Chron. 20.1b.*
e-e Meaning of Heb. uncertain; perhaps the source of the water supply.

in a typical measure-for-measure fashion: Because he put Uriah to the sword, the sword will never depart from his house (alluding to the violent deaths of Amnon, Absalom, and Adonijah in the following chs), and because he took Uriah's wife, his wives will be taken by another man (Absalom). V. 10b gives the reason for the punishment mentioned in vv. 11–12 (see 16.22). **13:** David, without arguing, frankly and immediately admits his guilt (contrary to Saul, 1 Sam. ch 15). His confession is remarkably short—two words in Heb, but it is heeded, unlike the longer confession of Saul in 1 Sam. 15.24–25. This is because David is favored by God, and Saul was not. *Remitted,* better "transferred," namely to the young child (see Exod. 34.7). The sin cannot be forgiven, and someone, either David or one of his descendants, must be punished. **15:** *The child that Uriah's wife had borne to David:* The wording hints at the adultery. **19:** David's cleverness contrasts with his earlier lack of understanding to appreciate Nathan's parable. **20:** *The House of the LORD,* this must be the tent that housed the Ark, though elsewhere this term is reserved for a sanctuary or a temple, as in Shiloh (1 Sam. 1.7), or later in Jerusalem. **21–22:** The courtiers thought that David's fasting and weeping were signs of grief, but David explains that they expressed repentance and supplication, in the hope that the child would yet be saved. **24–25:** Bathsheba is now designated *his* (David's) *wife,* and he is now sensitive to her feelings (contrary to 11.4). The story does not explain why God favored Solomon, though this anticipates the beginning of Kings, where Solomon is chosen to succeed his father. *The LORD favored* (or loved) *him,* is the meaning of the name Jedidiah, but no etymological wordplay is given. The name *Jedidiah* never appears again.

12.26–31: Conquest. The passage concludes the account of the Ammonite war (ch 10; 11.1), into which the David and Bathsheba story has been embedded. **26:** *The royal city,* probably the citadel with the palace. **27:** *Captured the water city,* controlling the water supply. The final conquest of the city would now

muster the rest of the troops and besiege the city and capture it; otherwise I will capture the city myself, and my name will be connected with it." 29 David mustered all the troops and marched on Rabbah, and he attacked it and captured it. 30[a] The crown was taken from the head of their king[b] and it was placed on David's head—it weighed a talent of gold, and [on it][c] were precious stones. He also carried off a vast amount of booty from the city. 31 He led out the people who lived there and set them to work with saws, iron threshing boards, and iron axes, or assigned them to brickmaking; David did this to all the towns of Ammon. Then David and all the troops returned to Jerusalem.

13 This happened sometime afterward: Absalom son of David had a beautiful sister named Tamar, and Amnon son of David became infatuated with her. 2 Amnon was so distraught because of his [half-]sister Tamar that he became sick; for she was a virgin, and it seemed impossible to Amnon to do anything to her. 3 Amnon had a friend named Jonadab, the son of David's brother Shimah; Jonadab was a very clever man. 4 He asked him, "Why are you so dejected, O prince, morning after morning? Tell me!" Amnon replied, "I am in love with Tamar, the sister of my brother Absalom!" 5 Jonadab said to him, "Lie down in your bed and pretend you are sick. When your father comes to see you, say to him, 'Let my sister Tamar come and give me something to eat. Let her prepare the food in front of me, so that I may look on, and let her serve it to me.' "

6 Amnon lay down and pretended to be sick. The king came to see him, and Amnon said to the king, "Let my sister Tamar come and prepare a couple of cakes in front of me, and let her bring them to me." 7 David sent a message to Tamar in the palace, "Please go to the house of your brother Amnon and prepare some food for him." 8 Tamar went to the house of her brother Amnon, who was in bed. She took dough and kneaded it into cakes in front of him, and cooked the cakes. 9 She took the [d]pan and set out [the cakes],[-d] but Amnon refused to eat and ordered everyone to withdraw. After everyone had withdrawn, 10 Amnon said to Tamar, "Bring the food inside and feed me." Tamar took the cakes she had made and brought them to her brother inside. 11 But when she served them to him, he caught hold of her and said to her, "Come lie with me, sister." 12 But she said to him, "Don't, brother. Don't force me. Such things are not done in Israel! Don't do such a vile thing! 13 Where will I carry my shame? And you, you will be like any of the scoundrels in Israel! Please, speak to the king; he will not refuse me

a *Vv. 30–31 are found also in 1 Chron. 20.2–3.*
b *Heb.* "malkam," *perhaps equivalent to "Milcom," the Ammonite deity; cf. 1 Kings 11.5.*
c *So Targum and 1 Chron. 20.2.* *d-d* *Meaning of Heb. uncertain.*

be easy. **30:** *A talent,* more than 34 kg (75 pounds). **31:** Setting captives to forced labor was customary in the ancient Near East. *Returned to Jerusalem,* see 1 Sam. 1.19 n.

13.1–22: Rape. The story of Amnon and Tamar is the first of a trilogy, the other two stories relating Absalom's murder of Amnon and Absalom's return from exile. Tamar's rape is seen as punishment for David, corresponding to his adultery: a sexual offense, followed by murder. Intergenerational punishment is accepted here and thus it is fair that these punishments (see 12.13 n.) are meted out on David's family. **1–3:** The exposition supplies the necessary information about the characters. Absalom is the first character introduced, because of the central role he has in the following narratives, which describe the developments ensuing from the events in the present story. **1:** Tamar was Absalom's full sister and Amnon's half-sister. **2:** *Impossible:* Being a virgin, she was "chaste at home and did not go out" (Rashi). **4:** Heb does not distinguish between *in love with* and to lust after; the latter is the sense here. **5:** Jonadab advises Amnon how to lure Tamar to his home and keep her there for a while, but he does not mention rape. The final idiom, and *let her serve it to me,* is literally "and I will eat it from her hand," may imply intimacy. **7:** Apparently each prince had his own house (cf. v. 20). **8:** The Heb from *in front of him* is "before his eyes"; the reader can feel his lustful gaze. **11:** Amnon tries to persuade Tamar with words, but at the same time he retains his hold of her. **12:** Tamar's long reply, her arguments, her alternative proposal, and her repetitions of *don't,* all attest to her vigorous objection. **13:** Tamar states the shameful consequences of rape for each of them, hoping for her good to evoke Amnon's mercy and to deter him for his own good. Marrying one's half-sister, though forbidden in Lev. 20.17, was apparently possible according to the norms of that time (cf. Gen. 20.12).

to you." 14 But he would not listen to her; he overpowered her
and lay with her by force.

15 Then Amnon felt a very great loathing for her; indeed, his
loathing for her was greater than the passion he had felt for her.
And Amnon said to her, "Get out!" 16 She pleaded with him,
"Please don't [a-]commit this wrong; to send me away would be
even worse[-a] than the first wrong you committed against me."
But he would not listen to her. 17 He summoned his young attendant and said, "Get that woman out of my presence, and
bar the door behind her."—18 She was wearing an ornamented
tunic,[b] for maiden princesses were customarily dressed [c-]in
such garments.[-c]—His attendant took her outside and barred
the door after her. 19 Tamar put dust on her head and rent the
ornamented tunic she was wearing; she put her hands on her
head,[d] and walked away, screaming loudly as she went. 20 Her
brother Absalom said to her, "Was it your brother Amnon[e] who
did this to you? For the present, sister, keep quiet about it; he
is your brother. Don't brood over the matter." And Tamar remained in her brother Absalom's house, forlorn. 21 When King
David heard about all this, he was greatly upset.[f] 22 Absalom
didn't utter a word to Amnon, good or bad; but Absalom hated
Amnon because he had violated his sister Tamar.

23 Two years later, when Absalom was having his flocks
sheared at Baal-hazor near Ephraim, Absalom invited all the
king's sons. 24 And Absalom came to the king and said, "Your
servant is having his flocks sheared. Would Your Majesty and
your retinue accompany your servant?" 25 But the king answered Absalom, "No, my son. We must not all come, or we'll
be a burden to you." He urged him, but he would not go, and
he said good-bye to him. 26 Thereupon Absalom said, "In that
case, let my brother Amnon come with us," to which the king
replied, "He shall not go with you." 27 But Absalom urged him,
and he sent with him Amnon and all the other princes.[g]

28 Now Absalom gave his attendants these orders: "Watch, and
when Amnon is merry with wine and I tell you to strike down
Amnon, kill him! Don't be afraid, for it is I who give you the order. Act with determination, like brave men!" 29 Absalom's attendants did to Amnon as Absalom had ordered; whereupon
all the other princes mounted their mules and fled. 30 They were
still on the road when a rumor reached David that Absalom had
killed all the princes, and that not one of them had survived.

Tamar's suggestion to speak to the king cannot merely be a stratagem to buy time, because it must be plausible in order to serve its end; this is confirmed by v. 16. **15:** *Get out,* lit. "get up, go"—the exact reversal of Amnon's earlier "come, lie" (v. 11). **16:** Sending Tamar away is *even worse* than the rape, because she must then remain unmarried for life. According to Deut. 22.28–29 and ancient Assyrian law, the rapist must marry the raped woman (in order to secure her material and social position). **17:** *That woman,* in Heb only "that one," a contemptuous expression. Amnon's orders are deeply offending. **18:** The story-teller offers explanatory background information that the reader might not know. **19:** Tamar's gestures are all expressions of grief. The rending of *the ornamented tunic* signifies that she is no longer a virgin. **21:** David is *greatly upset,* but he does not act; as the story unfolds, this inaction is a clear criticism of David. **22:** *A word,* about the matter.

13.23–39: Vengeance. Absalom murders Amnon to avenge his sister's rape. The murder is a punishment not only for Amnon, but also for David for his murder of Uriah. **23:** Absalom waits *two years* for the right opportunity to kill Amnon, and for Amnon's suspicions to abate. Sheepshearing was an occasion for celebration (cf. 1 Sam. 25.4ff.). **24–27:** In order to prevent suspicion, Absalom first invites the king, expecting that he will decline, and then asks for the crown prince to come instead. David is weak and yields to Absalom's urging. **28:** *Merry with wine,* drunk. **29:** *Mules* were used by the royal family (18.9; 1 Kings 1.33). The other princes fear that Absalom intends to kill them all as potential threats to his eventual kingship.

a-a *Meaning of Heb. uncertain.*
b *See Gen. 37.3 and note.*
c-c *Meaning of Heb. uncertain. Emendation yields "(thus) in olden times,"* me'olam.
d *A gesture of wild grief; cf. Jer. 2.37.* e *Heb. "Aminon."*
f *Septuagint adds "but he did not rebuke his son Amnon, for he favored him, since he was his first-born"; cf. 1 Kings 1.6.*
g *Septuagint adds "and Absalom made a feast fit for a king."*

[31] At this, David rent his garment and lay down on the ground,
[a-]and all his courtiers stood by with their clothes rent.[-a] [32] But Jonadab, the son of David's brother Shimah, said, "My lord must not
think that all the young princes have been killed. Only Amnon is
dead; for this has been [b-]decided by[-b] Absalom ever since his sister Tamar was violated. [33] So my lord the king must not think for
a moment that all the princes are dead; Amnon alone is dead."
[34] Meanwhile Absalom had fled.
The watchman on duty looked up and saw a large crowd
coming [c-]from the road to his rear,[-c] from the side of the hill.
[35] Jonadab said to the king, "See, the princes have come! It is
just as your servant said." [36] As he finished speaking, the princes came in and broke into weeping; and David and all his courtiers wept bitterly, too.
[37] Absalom had fled, and he came to Talmai son of Ammihud, king of Geshur. And [King David] mourned over his son a
long time. [38] Absalom, who had fled to Geshur, remained there
three years. [39] And [d-]King David[-d] was pining away for Absalom,
for [the king] had gotten over Amnon's death.

14 Joab son of Zeruiah could see that the king's mind was
on Absalom; [2] so Joab sent to Tekoa and brought a clever
woman from there. He said to her, "Pretend you are in mourning; put on mourning clothes and don't anoint yourself with
oil; and act like a woman who has grieved a long time over a
departed one. [3] Go to the king and say to him thus and thus."
And Joab told her what to say.[e]
[4] The woman of Tekoa came[f] to the king, flung herself face
down to the ground, and prostrated herself. She cried out,
"Help, O king!" [5] The king asked her, "What troubles you?" And
she answered, "Alas, I am a widow, my husband is dead. [6] Your
maidservant had two sons. The two of them came to blows out
in the fields where there was no one to stop them, and one of
them struck the other and killed him. [7] Then the whole clan
confronted your maidservant and said, 'Hand over the one
who killed his brother, that we may put him to death for the
slaying of his brother, [g-]even though we wipe out the heir.'[-g]
Thus they would quench the last ember remaining to me, and
leave my husband without name or remnant upon the earth."
[8] The king said to the woman, "Go home. I will issue an order

a-a Septuagint reads "and all his courtiers who were standing by him rent their clothes." *b-b Lit. "determined by the command of."*
c-c Emendation yields "down the slope of the Horonaim road. The watchman came and told the king 'I see men coming from the Horonaim road.'" Cf. Septuagint.
d-d Some Septuagint mss. and 4QSam[a] read "the spirit [ruaḥ] *of the king."*
e Lit. "and he put words into her mouth."
f So many mss. and printed editions. Most mss. and printed editions read "said."
g-g Emendation yields "Thus they would destroy the [last] heir and..."

31: David *lay down on the ground* recalls the death of Bathsheba's first child in 12.16. **32–33:** Jonadab, the instigator, understands that Absalom's purpose was not to put the princes out of the way in order to secure the throne for himself, but to take revenge on Amnon. **37:** *Talmai,* Absalom's maternal grandfather (see 3.3 and n.). It is unclear which *son* David is mourning: the dead Amnon or the crown-prince Absalom, who had fled. **39:** Adopting the superior reading of 4QSam[a], the beginning of the v. should be translated: "and the king's wrath (lit. "spirit," as in Eccl. 10.4) towards Absalom was spent." This translation accords better with the following narrative.

14.1–33: Reconciliation. The first part of the narrative describes the ruse used to persuade David to allow Absalom's return from exile; the second part tells of obtaining David's consent to meeting his son. In both parts it is Joab who endeavors to reconcile father and son. He seems to be acting on behalf of David's best interests, but ultimately causes further difficulties. **2–3:** The woman is to present a judicial case to David in order to get him, unwittingly, to absolve his son from the death penalty. Like Nathan's parable (12.1–4), the case is similar to the real events, but not identical. The woman must not only describe the case, as Nathan did, but actually perform it—including dressing up. Her cleverness is revealed in her acting as well as her speech, which is submissive, polite, and rich in rhetorical means, such as metaphor and simile. The dialogue between the woman and the king is one of the longest in the Bible. Even after being tricked already by Nathan with one simulated legal case, David is taken in by another. **7:** The demand to kill the murderer is rooted in the custom of blood vengeance. But acceding to it would worsen the woman's situation, because instead of one dead son she would have two and be left without an heir. *Without name,* see Deut. 25.6; Ruth 4.10. **8:** This v., and the entire unit, suggests that

in your behalf." 9 And the woman of Tekoa said to the king, "My lord king, may the guilt be on me and on my ancestral house; Your Majesty and his throne are guiltless." 10 The king said, "If anyone says anything more to you, have him brought to me, and he will never trouble you again." 11 She replied, "Let Your Majesty be mindful of the LORD your God and restrain the blood avenger bent on destruction, so that my son may not be killed." And he said, "As the LORD lives, not a hair of your son shall fall to the ground."

12 Then the woman said, "Please let your maidservant say another word to my lord the king." "Speak on," said the king. 13 And the woman said, "Why then have you planned the like against God's people? In making this pronouncement, Your Majesty condemns himself in that Your Majesty does not bring back his own banished one. 14 We must all die; we are like water that is poured out on the ground and cannot be gathered up. [a-]God will not take away the life of one who makes plans so that no one may be kept banished.[-a] 15 And the reason I have come to say these things to the king, my lord, is that the people have frightened me. Your maidservant thought I would speak to Your Majesty; perhaps Your Majesty would act on his handmaid's plea. 16 For Your Majesty would surely agree to deliver his handmaid from the hands of anyone [who would seek to] cut off both me and my son from the heritage[b] of God. 17 Your maidservant thought, 'Let the word of my lord the king provide comfort; for my lord the king is like an angel of God, understanding everything, good and bad.' May the LORD your God be with you."

18 In reply, the king said to the woman, "Do not withhold from me anything I ask you!" The woman answered, "Let my lord the king speak." 19 The king asked, "Is Joab in league with you in all this?" The woman replied, "As you live, my lord the king, [c-]it is just as my lord the king says.[-c] Yes, your servant Joab was the one who instructed me, and it was he who [d-]told your maidservant everything she was to say.[-d] 20 It was to conceal the real purpose of the matter that your servant Joab did this thing. My lord is as wise as an angel of God, and he knows all that goes on in the land."

21 Then the king said to Joab, "I will do this thing. Go and bring back my boy Absalom." 22 Joab flung himself face down on the ground and prostrated himself. Joab blessed the king and said, "Today your servant knows that he has found favor with you, my lord king, for Your Majesty has granted his servant's request." 23 And Joab went at once to Geshur and brought Absalom to Jerusalem. 24 But the king said, "Let him

a-a Meaning of Heb. uncertain. The apparent sense is: God will not punish you for bringing back the banished Absalom. *b I.e., people.*
c-c Lit. "there is no turning to the right or to the left of what my lord the king says."
d-d See v. 3, note e.

the king has a supreme judicial role in Israel. Exactly who could consult and under what circumstances is unclear, though this case, in which a widow has access, is instructive. **9:** *The guilt,* for not expiating the blood of the slain (see Num. 35.33). The woman strives for an explicit and binding pardon for the murderer. **11:** *Be mindful of the LORD,* i.e., mention the LORD (in an oath), so your verdict will be fully binding. *Not a hair ... shall fall to the ground,* see 1 Sam. 14.45 n. **12:** The woman's respectful speech contrasts with the king's curtness. **13:** The woman obliquely explains that all that preceded was a parable; she does not even mention Absalom's name. She suggests that Absalom's death would be harmful to God's people, Israel. *This pronouncement,* pardoning the woman's fictional son. **14:** *Like water ... :* Death is irreversible; executing Absalom will not bring Amnon back. *God will not take away the life,* see v. 9 n. **15–17:** Because the king might get angry and punish her, the woman now explains why she deceived David and presented a fictional case to him. **15:** She misrepresents the truth, claiming *that the people have frightened me.* David knows better, and asks several vv. later if Joab is behind the ruse. **16:** *The heritage of God* may refer to the land of Israel. **17:** *Like an angel of God,* an extreme flattery (see 1 Sam. 29.9 n.). **19:** Though the woman was careful not to betray Joab, David understands that it was all his design. **20:** The woman repeats the flattering comparison of David to an angel. In the Bible, God is omniscient in the sense that He *knows all that goes on in the land,* but does not generally know the future; as the story continues, David's inability to see the future implications of his actions is highlighted. **21:** The woman now leaves the stage, and Joab himself appears. **22:** Joab's excessive expressions of gratitude and politeness testify to his fear of punishment for having deceived David. **24:** The king allowed Absalom to return, but has not forgiven him; the language shows that Absalom obeyed the king

go directly to his house and not present himself to me." So Absalom went directly to his house and did not present himself to the king.

25 No one in all Israel was so admired for his beauty as Absalom; from the sole of his foot to the crown of his head he was without blemish. 26 When he cut his hair—he had to have it cut every year, for it grew too heavy for him—the hair of his head weighed two hundred shekels by the royal weight. 27 Absalom had three sons and a daughter whose name was Tamar; she was a beautiful woman.

28 Absalom lived in Jerusalem two years without appearing before the king. 29 Then Absalom sent for Joab, in order to send him to the king; but Joab would not come to him. He sent for him a second time, but he would not come. 30 So [Absalom] said to his servants, "Look, Joab's field is next to mine, and he has barley there. Go and set it on fire." And Absalom's servants set the field on fire. 31 Joab came at once to Absalom's house and said to him, "Why did your servants set fire to my field?" 32 Absalom replied to Joab, "I sent for you to come here; I wanted to send you to the king to say [on my behalf]: 'Why did I leave Geshur? I would be better off if I were still there. Now let me appear before the king; and if I am guilty of anything, let him put me to death!' " 33 Joab went to the king and reported to him; whereupon he summoned Absalom. He came to the king and flung himself face down to the ground before the king. And the king kissed Absalom.

15 Sometime afterward, Absalom provided himself with a chariot, horses, and fifty outrunners. 2 Absalom used to rise early and stand by the road to the city gates; and whenever a man had a case that was to come before the king for judgment, Absalom would call out to him, "What town are you from?" And when he answered, "Your servant is from [a]such and such a tribe[a] in Israel," 3 Absalom would say to him, "It is clear that your claim is right and just, but there is no one assigned to you by the king to hear it." 4 And Absalom went on, "If only I were appointed judge in the land and everyone with a legal dispute came before me, I would see that he got his rights." 5 And if a man approached to bow to him, [Absalom] would extend his hand and take hold of him and kiss him. 6 Absalom did this to every Israelite who came to the king for judgment. Thus Absalom won away the hearts of the men of Israel.

7 After a period of forty[b] years had gone by, Absalom said to the king, "Let me go to Hebron and fulfill a vow that I made to the LORD. 8 For your servant made a vow when I lived in

a-a Lit. "one of the tribes."

b Some Septuagint mss. and Syriac read "four."

exactly. **25:** Kings were expected to be handsome, so this v. sets up the expectation that Absalom is a very suitable king (see 1 Sam. 9.1–2; 16.12 nn.). **26:** Growing and weighing his hair are signs of Absalom's narcissism; Absalom's long hair will play a key part in his demise. *Two hundred shekels,* more than 2 kg (4.5 pounds). **27:** *Tamar:* Her name is probably mentioned, unlike the sons' names, because she bears the same name as Absalom's sister. We do not know, however, the extent to which children in ancient Israel were named after deceased ancestors. **28:** David's prolonged refusal to see Absalom is humiliating and unbearable to him. **30:** Absalom uses violent means to compel Joab to intervene with the king. **32:** Absalom considers himself free of guilt, because the killing of Amnon was justified. **33:** Though the kiss signifies forgiveness, it should be noted that the v. repeatedly uses the designation *the king* instead of "David" or "his father." In addition, there is no mention of any verbal exchange between father and son—after five years of separation! This suggests that the enforced reconciliation is purely formal, setting the stage for the following episode.

15.1–12: Rebellion. Absalom prepares his rebellion over several years. **1:** The *chariot, horses and fifty outrunners* were signs of kingship (cf. 1 Sam. 8.11). **2–6:** Absalom uses demagogic means to win popular support. Administration of justice was one of the king's main functions (see 12.1–6; 1 Kings 3.16–28; 2 Kings 8.1–6), as seen in the previous ch. **5:** *Kiss,* as in 14.33. **6:** The Heb for *won away* is "stole," a negative value judgment. **7:** *Forty* should be emended to four, following some ancient versions and the retelling of this story in Josephus' *Antiquities. Hebron,* capital of Judah, where David first was king (2.4). Apparently Absalom wanted to go to Hebron because he found among his kinsmen there discontent with David, who became king of all Israel and moved his capital to Jerusalem (cf. 5.9). **8:** Even if he really made the vow in Geshur, he

Geshur of Aram: If the LORD ever brings me back to Jerusalem,
I will worship the LORD."[a] 9 The king said to him, "Go in peace";
and so he set out for Hebron.

10 But Absalom sent agents to all the tribes of Israel to say,
"When you hear the blast of the horn, announce that Absalom has become king in Hebron." 11 Two hundred men of Jerusalem accompanied Absalom; they were invited and went
in good faith, suspecting nothing. 12 Absalom also [b-]sent [to
fetch][-b] Ahithophel the Gilonite, David's counselor, from his
town, Giloh, when the sacrifices were to be offered. The conspiracy gained strength, and the people supported Absalom in
increasing numbers.

13 Someone came and told David, "The loyalty of the men of
Israel has veered toward Absalom." 14 Whereupon David said to
all the courtiers who were with him in Jerusalem, "Let us flee at
once, or none of us will escape from Absalom. We must get away
quickly, or he will soon overtake us and bring down disaster
upon us and put the city to the sword." 15 The king's courtiers said
to the king, "Whatever our lord the king decides, your servants
are ready." 16 So the king left, followed by his entire household,
except for ten concubines whom the king left to mind the palace.
17 The king left, followed by [c-]all the people,[-c] and they
stopped at [d-]the last house.[-d] 18 All [e-]his followers[-e] marched past
him, including all the Cherethites and all the Pelethites; and[f]
all the Gittites, six hundred men who had accompanied him
from Gath, also marched by the king. 19 And the king said to Ittai the Gittite, "Why should you too go with us? Go back and
stay with the [new] king, for you are a foreigner and you are also
an exile from[g] your country. 20 You came only yesterday; should
I make you wander about with us today, when I myself must go
wherever I can? Go back, and take your kinsmen with you, [in]
[h] true faithfulness." 21 Ittai replied to the king, "As the LORD lives
and as my lord the king lives, wherever my lord the king may be,
there your servant will be, whether for death or for life!" 22 And
David said to Ittai, "Then march by." And Ittai the Gittite and all
his men and all the children who were with him marched by.

23 The whole countryside wept aloud as the troops marched
by. The king [i-]crossed the Kidron Valley, and all the troops
crossed by the road to[-i] the wilderness. 24 Then Zadok appeared,

could have fulfilled it long since, yet David, who in the previous ch "is as wise as an angel of God" (14.20), does not become suspicious. **9:** *Go in peace,* but Absalom goes for war. **10–12:** *The blast of the horn* (shofar) and a sacrificial meal including many guests were part of the royal inauguration ceremony (1 Kings 1.18–19, 39). **12:** *Ahithophel* is introduced here; he will play a crucial role later in the story.

15.13–16.14: Flight. David decides not to fortify himself in Jerusalem, but to leave the city. His flight is depicted in a series of scenes, mainly consisting of dialogues. **16:** That David leaves *ten concubines* behind discloses his intention soon to return. He foolishly disregards Nathan's prophecy in 12.11–12. **17:** *The last house,* probably on the boundary of Jerusalem. **18:** The repetition of *all* shows that among his retinue nobody is disloyal. *Cherethites* and *Pelethites,* see 8.18 n. *Gittites,* mercenaries from the Philistine town of Gath, where David stayed sometime in the past (1 Sam. 27.3). **19–20:** David, forgoing his own interest, shows extraordinary consideration for Ittai and his men. Ittai's introduction is ironic: the foreigner stays beside David, while David's own son abandons him. Ittai is introduced here for the role he will later play in ch 18. **21:** The double oath reinforces Ittai's declaration of unlimited loyalty. **22:** *The children:* The Gittites had come with their families. **23:** *The Kidron Valley,* the eastern boundary of biblical Jerusalem. **24–29:** Both Zadok and Abiathar are priests (see 8.17), but *Zadok* appears here to be the principal one, foreshadowing his later role as Solomon's high priest.

a Some Septuagint mss. add "in Hebron."
b-b Some Septuagint mss. and 4QSam[a] read "sent and summoned."
c-c Septuagint reads "his courtiers." *d-d Meaning of Heb. uncertain.*
e-e Septuagint reads "the people." *f Emendation yields "and Ittai and."*
g So one Heb. ms. and several ancient versions; most mss. and editions read "to."
h Meaning of Heb. uncertain. Septuagint reads "and may the LORD show you" (cf., e.g., 2.6).
i-i Meaning of Heb. uncertain. Emendation yields "stopped in the Kidron Valley, while all the people marched on before him by way of the Mount of Olives to…"

with all the Levites carrying the Ark of the Covenant of God; and they set down the Ark of God until all the people had finished marching out of the city. [a-]Abiathar also came up.[-a] [25] But the king said to Zadok, "Take the Ark of God back to the city. If I find favor with the LORD, He will bring me back and let me see it and its abode. [26] And if He should say, 'I do not want you,' I am ready; let Him do with me as He pleases." [27] And the king said to the priest Zadok, [b-]"Do you understand? You return[-b] to the safety of the city with your two sons, your own son Ahimaaz and Abiathar's son Jonathan. [28] Look, I shall linger in the steppes of the wilderness until word comes from you to inform me." [29] Zadok and Abiathar brought the Ark of God back to Jerusalem, and they stayed there.

[30] David meanwhile went up the slope of the [Mount of] Olives, weeping as he went; his head was covered and he walked barefoot. And all the people who were with him covered their heads and wept as they went up. [31] David [was] told that Ahithophel was among the conspirators with Absalom, and he prayed, "Please, O LORD, frustrate Ahithophel's counsel!" [32] When David reached the top, where people would prostrate themselves to God, Hushai the Archite was there to meet him, with his robe torn and with earth on his head. [33] David said to him, "If you march on with me, you will be a burden to me. [34] But if you go back to the city and say to Absalom, 'I will be your servant, O king; I was your father's servant formerly, and now I will be yours,' then you can nullify Ahithophel's counsel for me. [35] You will have the priests Zadok and Abiathar there, and you can report everything that you hear in the king's palace to the priests Zadok and Abiathar. [36] Also, their two sons are there with them, Zadok's son Ahimaaz and Abiathar's son Jonathan; and through them you can report to me everything you hear." [37] And so Hushai, the friend of David, reached the city as Absalom was entering Jerusalem.

16 David had passed a little beyond the summit when Ziba the servant of Mephibosheth came toward him with a pair of saddled asses carrying two hundred loaves of bread, one hundred cakes of raisin, one hundred cakes of figs,[c] and a jar of wine. [2] The king asked Ziba, "What are you doing with these?" Ziba answered, "The asses are for Your Majesty's family to ride on, the bread and figs are for the attendants to eat, and the wine is to be drunk by any who are exhausted in the wilderness." [3] "And where is your master's son?" the king asked. "He is staying in Jerusalem," Ziba replied to the king, "for he thinks

25–28: David expresses the idea that God's favor is not dependent on the presence or veneration of religious objects, though later it becomes clear that he wants Zadok and Abiathar to remain in Jerusalem as his spies. **30:** Covering the head and walking barefoot were signs of grief (Jer. 14.3; Esth. 6.12). **31:** David, aware of Ahithophel's wisdom, greatly dreads his counsel to Absalom. **32:** At the very place *where people would prostrate themselves to God* David's prayer (v. 31) is answered: Hushai appears, who will counteract Ahithophel's counsel. *His robe torn and with earth on his head,* see 1.2 n. **33–36:** David assigns Hushai a twofold task: to nullify Ahithophel's counsel, and to supply information right from the heart of the uprising to David's secret agents. **37:** *Friend,* or perhaps "companion," an official title (1 Kings 4.5). **16.1:** *Ziba,* see 9.2. The detailed list of supplies underscores Ziba's support. **2:** *The attendants,* see 1 Sam. 25.27 n. **3:** *Your master's son,* Mephibosheth, Saul's grandson (9.6).

a-a Meaning of Heb. uncertain.

b-b Meaning of Heb. uncertain. Emendation yields "Look, you and Abiathar return."

c Lit. "summer fruit."

that the House of Israel will now give him back the throne of
his grandfather." 4 The king said to Ziba, "Then all that belongs
to Mephibosheth is now yours!" And Ziba replied, "I bow low.
Your Majesty is most gracious to me."
5 As King David was approaching Bahurim, a member of
Saul's clan—a man named Shimei son of Gera—came out
from there, hurling insults as he came. 6 He threw stones at
David and all King David's courtiers, while all the troops and
all the warriors were at his right and his left. 7 And these are
the insults that Shimei hurled: "Get out, get out, you criminal,
you villain! 8 The LORD is paying you back for all your crimes
against the family of Saul, whose throne you seized. The LORD
is handing over the throne to your son Absalom; you are in
trouble because you are a criminal!"
9 Abishai son of Zeruiah said to the king, "Why let that dead
dog abuse my lord the king? Let me go over and cut off his
head!" 10 But the king said, [a-]"What has this to do with you,[-a] you
sons of Zeruiah? He is abusing [me] only because the LORD told
him to abuse David; and who is to say, 'Why did You do that?' "
11 David said further to Abishai and all the courtiers, "If my son,
my own issue, seeks to kill me, how much more the Benjaminite! Let him go on hurling abuse, for the LORD has told him
to. 12 Perhaps the LORD will look upon my punishment[b] and recompense me for the abuse [Shimei] has uttered today." 13 David and his men continued on their way, while Shimei walked
alongside on the slope of the hill, insulting him as he walked,
and throwing stones at him and flinging dirt. 14 The king and all
who accompanied him arrived[c] exhausted, and he rested there.

15 Meanwhile Absalom and all the people, the men of Israel, arrived in Jerusalem, together with Ahithophel. 16 When
Hushai the Archite, David's friend, came before Absalom,
Hushai said to Absalom, "Long live the king! Long live the
king!" 17 But Absalom said to Hushai, "Is this your loyalty to
your friend? Why didn't you go with your friend?" 18 "Not at
all!" Hushai replied. "I am for the one whom the LORD and this
people and all the men of Israel have chosen, and I will stay
with him. 19 Furthermore, whom should I serve, if not David's[d]
son? As I was in your father's service, so I will be in yours."
20 Absalom then said to Ahithophel, "What do you advise
us to do?" 21 And Ahithophel said to Absalom, "Have intercourse with your father's concubines, whom he left to mind
the palace; and when all Israel hears that you have dared the
wrath of your father, all who support you will be encouraged."

4: David believes Ziba, and, wishing to reward him for his support, gives him all the fields he has previously given to Mephibosheth (9.9). **8:** Shimei accuses David of having murdered Abner and Ish-baal in order to usurp Saul's throne. The initial chs of 2 Sam. deny this accusation. Shimei will reappear in ch 19 and in 1 Kings ch 2, suggesting that the beginning of Kings is the end of the succession narrative in Samuel as well as the beginning of the narratives about the monarchy. **9:** *That dead dog,* see 3.8 n. **10:** *Sons of Zeruiah:* David habitually lumps Abishai and Joab, his sister's sons, together (cf. 3.39; 19.23). **11:** David accepts his profound humiliation with resignation. What his son, his *own issue,* is doing to him is much worse than *the Benjaminite*'s abuse. **14:** *There:* According to 17.21–22, David waited near the Jordan.

16.15–17.14: The counselors' contest. The contest between Ahithophel and Hushai will ultimately decide the battle between David and Absalom. **16–19:** Hushai, though known to be *David's friend* (vv. 16–17), tries to win Absalom's confidence. His statements, however, are equivocal. By *the king* (v. 16) either Absalom or David can be meant, and the same applies to the *chosen* one (v. 18). Similarly, the answer to the question in v. 19 can be Absalom or David himself. Finally, *so* (v. 19) can refer to loyal service either to Absalom or to David even while Hushai is in Absalom's employment. Absalom understands that he is meant, but Hushai probably thinks of David. Absalom's answer is not reported, though he initially turns to Ahithophel for advice. **21:** *Have intercourse,* see 3.7 n. Having possession of the royal concubines signals having possession of the throne. See Esth. 7.8. *To mind the palace,* see 15.16.

a-a Lit. "What have I and you."
b So kethib; qere *"eye." Ancient versions read "suffering."*
c Some Septuagint mss. add "at the Jordan." *d Heb. "his."*

22 So they pitched a tent for Absalom on the roof, and Absalom
lay with his father's concubines [a]with the full knowledge[a] of
all Israel.—23 In those days, the advice which Ahithophel gave
was accepted like an oracle sought from God; that is how all
the advice of Ahithophel was esteemed both by David and by
Absalom.

17 And Ahithophel said to Absalom, "Let me pick twelve
thousand men and set out tonight in pursuit of David.
2 I will come upon him when he is weary and disheartened,
and I will throw him into a panic; and when all the troops with
him flee, I will kill the king alone. 3 And I will bring back all the
people [b]to you; when all have come back [except] the man you
are after,[b] all the people will be at peace." 4 The advice pleased
Absalom and all the elders of Israel. 5 But Absalom said, "Summon Hushai the Archite as well, so we can hear what he too
has to say." 6 Hushai came to Absalom, and Absalom said to
him, "This is what Ahithophel has advised. Shall we follow his
advice? If not, what do you say?"
7 Hushai said to Absalom, "This time the advice that Ahithophel has given is not good. 8 You know," Hushai continued,
"that your father and his men are courageous fighters, and they
are as desperate as a bear in the wild robbed of her whelps.
Your father is an experienced soldier, and he will not spend
the night with the troops; 9 even now he must be hiding in one
of the pits or in some other place. And if any of them[c] fall at the
first attack, whoever hears of it will say, 'A disaster has struck
the troops that follow Absalom'; 10 and even if he is a brave
man with the heart of a lion, he will be shaken—for all Israel
knows that your father and the soldiers with him are courageous fighters. 11 So I advise that all Israel from Dan to Beer-
sheba—as numerous as the sands of the sea—be called up to
join you, and that you yourself march [d]into battle.[d] 12 When
we come upon him in whatever place he may be, we'll descend
on him [as thick] as dew falling on the ground; and no one will
survive, neither he nor any of the men with him. 13 And if he
withdraws into a city, all Israel will bring ropes to that city and
drag [e]its stones[e] as far as the riverbed, until not even a pebble

a-a *Lit. "before the eyes."*
b-b *Meaning of Heb. uncertain. Septuagint reads "to you as a bride comes back to her husband; you seek the life of but one man, and..."*
c *Some Septuagint mss. read "the troops" (i.e., Absalom's).*
d-d *Ancient versions read "among them."* *e-e* *Heb. "it."*

22: Absalom's public intercourse with *his father's concubines,* on the very roof from where David observed Bathsheba (ch 11), is the fulfillment of Nathan's prophecy (12.11–12). **23:** This suggests that Ahithophel may be more wise than David, who, according to the wise woman from Tekoa, is "is as wise as an angel of God" (14.20). **17.1–3:** Ahithophel's second advice is to set out immediately and come upon David while he is weary and not yet organized. Ahithophel, without battle, will kill the king alone and then all the people will turn to Absalom. **1:** *Twelve thousand,* implicitly, one thousand from each tribe, reflecting Absalom's control over all Israel. **3:** *When all have come back* is probably a dittography of *and I will bring back all.* Read: "and I will bring back all the people to you; for you are after one man, and all the people will be at peace." **5–6:** Hushai gets the opportunity to nullify Ahithophel's advice. But achieving this is exceedingly difficult, because Ahithophel's counsel is generally highly esteemed (16.23), his present advice has already been accepted by Absalom and all the elders (v. 4), and Hushai is probably still suspected of allegiance to David. **7:** *This time:* Hushai begins with subscribing to the prevailing opinion concerning Ahithophel's advice—only this piece of advice is an exception. **8–13:** Hushai's aim is to buy time for David to rest, find out Absalom's plans, and organize a defense. In the first part of his speech (vv. 8–10) he shows the shortcomings of Ahithophel's plan: It has no chance of success because of the nature of the opponents, and it is even harmful to Absalom's forces. In the second part (vv. 11–13) he proposes an alternative plan: Thorough preparations must be made, and then Absalom will be able to inflict utter defeat upon David. Hushai's speech excels in the use of rhetorical means, such as metaphor, simile, and hyperbole. **9:** *He must be hiding,* therefore it will be impossible to find him and kill him alone. **10:** Not only Absalom knows his father's courage (v. 8), *all Israel knows* it. **11:** Only quantity can overcome quality—i.e., only by assembling a huge army can Absalom prevail over David's courageous men. Contrary to Ahithophel, who stressed his own role (note the repetitions of "I"), Hushai gives prominence to Absalom's leadership. *Dan to Beer-sheba* represents all Israel (1 Sam. 3.20 n.). **13:** This highly hyperbolic language

of it is left." [14] Absalom and all Israel agreed that the advice of
Hushai the Archite was better than that of Ahithophel.—The
LORD had decreed that Ahithophel's sound advice be nullified,
in order that the LORD might bring ruin upon Absalom.
[15] Then Hushai told the priests Zadok and Abiathar, "This is
what Ahithophel advised Absalom and the elders of Israel; this
is what I advised. [16] Now send at once and tell David, 'Do not
spend the night at the fords of the wilderness, but cross over at
once; otherwise the king and all the troops with him will be annihilated.' " [17] Jonathan and Ahimaaz were staying at En-rogel,
and a slave girl would go and bring them word and they in turn
would go and inform King David. For they themselves dared not
be seen entering the city. [18] But a boy saw them and informed
Absalom. They left at once and came to the house of a man in
Bahurim who had a well in his courtyard. They got down into
it, [19] and the wife took a cloth, spread it over the mouth of the
well, and scattered groats on top of it, so that nothing would be
noticed. [20] When Absalom's servants came to the woman at the
house and asked where Ahimaaz and Jonathan were, the woman told them that they had crossed [a-]a bit beyond the water.[-a]
They searched, but found nothing; and they returned to Jerusalem.
[21] After they were gone, [Ahimaaz and Jonathan] came up
from the well and went and informed King David. They said
to David, "Go and cross the water quickly, for Ahithophel has
advised thus and thus concerning you." [22] David and all the
troops with him promptly crossed the Jordan, and by daybreak
not one was left who had not crossed the Jordan.
[23] When Ahithophel saw that his advice had not been followed, he saddled his ass and went home to his native town.
He set his affairs in order, and then he hanged himself. He was
buried in his ancestral tomb.
[24] David had reached Mahanaim when Absalom and all the
men of Israel with him crossed the Jordan. [25] Absalom had
appointed Amasa army commander in place of Joab; Amasa
was the son of a man named Ithra the [b-]Israelite, who had married Abigal, daughter of Nahash and sister of Joab's mother
Zeruiah.[-b] [26] The Israelites and Absalom encamped in the district of Gilead. [27] When David reached Mahanaim, Shobi son
of Nahash from Rabbath-ammon, Machir son of Ammiel from
Lo-debar, and Barzillai the Gileadite from Rogelim [28] presented[c] couches, basins, and earthenware; also wheat, barley,
flour, parched grain, beans, lentils, [d-]parched grain,[-d] [29] honey,

a-a Meaning of Heb. uncertain. Targum reads "the Jordan."
b-b Some Septuagint mss. and 1 Chron. 2.12–17 read "Ishmaelite" and give a somewhat different genealogy.
c Brought up from v. 29 for clarity.
d-d Lacking in the Septuagint and Syriac.

(so Radak) is a fitting and successful climax to the speech. **14:** Because rejection of Ahithophel's sound advice seemed unthinkable, the narrator ascribes this to the LORD. On the human level, it was Hushai's outstanding rhetorical skill and psychological insight that achieved the rejection of Ahithophel's plan.

17.15–29: Recovery. Hushai's triumph over Ahithophel marks a turning point in David's situation. From now on all developments are in David's favor. **15–17:** Using the intelligence chain set up earlier (15.27–28, 35–36), Hushai reports to David and advises him to cross the Jordan immediately, lest *the elders* after all convince Absalom to adopt Ahithophel's plan. *En-Rogel,* a well in the Kidron Valley, not far from Jerusalem. **18–20:** *Bahurim* belonged to Benjamin, the tribe of Saul, and there Shimei cursed David a short while ago (16.5–8). Now in the same place a woman, believing in David, helps his agents in the same way Rahab once helped Joshua's spies (Josh. 2.3–7). **23:** His advice being rejected, Ahithophel commits suicide, convinced that David will gain the upper hand and execute him as traitor. Now at least he can *set his affairs in order* and be *buried in his ancestral tomb* (see 2.32 n.). No negative value judgment is implied by this decision (see 1 Sam. 31.4 n.). **24:** *Mahanaim,* see 2.8. **25:** *Amasa,* like Joab, David's nephew and Absalom's cousin. *Nahash:* According to 1 Chron. 2.16 *Abigal's* father was Jesse. "Nahash" probably crept in erroneously from v. 27. **27–29:** *Shobi son of Nahash* is probably the brother of Hanun, who was defeated by David (ch 10), *Machir son of Ammiel* accommodated Mephibosheth, Saul's grandson, in his home (9.4–5), and *Barzillai* who makes several more appearances in the continuation of the narrative, is presumably the father of Saul's son-in-law (21.8). These men, though close to the royal houses of Ammon and Saul, display their belief in David's kingship. The long list of their gifts demonstrates the extent of their support. **29:** That David and

[a]curds, a flock,[a] and cheese[b] from the herd for David and the troops with him to eat. For they knew that the troops must have grown hungry, faint, and thirsty in the wilderness.

18 David mustered the troops who were with him and set over them captains of thousands and captains of hundreds. 2 David [c]sent out the troops,[c] one-third under the command of Joab, one-third under the command of Joab's brother Abishai son of Zeruiah, and one-third under the command of Ittai the Gittite. And David said to the troops, "I myself will march out with you." 3 But the troops replied, "No! For if some of us flee, the rest will not be concerned about us; even if half of us should die, the others will not be concerned about us. But [d]you are worth ten thousand of us.[d] Therefore, it is better for you to support us from the town." 4 And the king said to them, "I will do whatever you think best."

So the king stood beside the gate as all the troops marched out by their hundreds and thousands. 5 The king gave orders to Joab, Abishai, and Ittai: "Deal gently with my boy Absalom, for my sake." All the troops heard the king give the order about Absalom to all the officers.

6 The troops marched out into the open to confront the Israelites,[e] and the battle was fought in the forest of Ephraim.[f] 7 The Israelite troops were routed by David's followers, and a great slaughter took place there that day—twenty thousand men. 8 The battle spread out over that whole region, and the forest devoured more troops that day than the sword.

9 Absalom encountered some of David's followers. Absalom was riding on a mule, and as the mule passed under the tangled branches of a great terebinth, his hair got caught in the terebinth; he [g]was held[g] between heaven and earth as the mule under him kept going. 10 One of the men saw it and told Joab, "I have just seen Absalom hanging from a terebinth." 11 Joab said to the man who told him, "You saw it! Why didn't you kill him [h]then and there?[h] I would have owed you ten[i] shekels of silver and a belt." 12 But the man answered Joab, "Even if I had a thousand shekels of silver in my hands, I would not raise a hand against the king's son. For the king charged you and Abishai and Ittai in our hearing, 'Watch over my boy

his men must be *hungry, faint, and thirsty* is true, and highlights the wisdom of Ahithophel's advice (see v. 2), which thanks to Hushai and God, is contravened.

18.1–18: The rebels' downfall. The battle between the armies of David and Absalom results in Absalom's death. **1:** *Thousands ... hundreds,* military units (cf. 1 Sam. 29.2). **2:** *Ittai,* see 15.19. **3–4:** The army understands—just as Ahithophel did (17.2–3)—that David is the rebels' only target and his death will decide the battle. *Ten thousand,* see v. 1 n. **5:** *My boy,* Heb, "the boy," notwithstanding his criminal behavior and adult age. **8:** The image of the *forest devour*ing troops is unique but hints ahead to the next v., concerning Absalom, who is literally devoured by the forest. **9:** Unlike David, Absalom participates in the battle himself, as suggested by Hushai (17.11). *Mule,* see 13.29 n. Absalom, who used to grow his hair and weigh it every year (14.26), is caught by *his hair* (lit. "his head")—indicating that his pride is his undoing. **10–15:** The dialogue between Joab and the man who saw Absalom hanging in the tree underscores Joab's deliberate violation of David's explicit order to deal gently with Absalom. Though Absalom is finally killed by ten arms-bearers, responsibility for his death rests with Joab, who gave the order—just as responsibility for Amnon's death, though carried out by attendants, rested with Absalom (13.28–29), and as David is held responsible for the death of Uriah, which according to the narrative set these actions in motion. Joab may have been driven by concern for the people and the kingdom, but personal feelings—disappointment and anger at Absalom's ingratitude and violence (14.30–31)—may also have been involved. **12:** The commoner's speech highlights Joab's disobeying the king.

a-a *Emendation yields "curds from the flock."* *b* *Meaning of Heb. uncertain.*
c-c *Some Septuagint mss. read "divided the troops into three."*
d-d *So two Heb. mss., Septuagint, and Vulgate; cf. 1 Kings 1.18 and note. Most mss. and the editions read "Now there are ten thousand like us."*
e *The usual term in this narrative for the supporters of Absalom.*
f *Some Septuagint mss. read "Mahanaim"; cf. 17.24.*
g-g *Meaning of Heb. uncertain. Ancient versions and 4QSam[a] read "was left hanging"; cf. v. 10.*
h-h *Lit. "to the ground."* *i* *Some Septuagint mss. and 4QSam[a] read "fifty."*

Absalom, [a-]for my sake.'[-a] 13 If I betrayed myself[b]—and nothing is hidden from the king—you would have stood aloof." 14 Joab replied, [c-]"Then I will not wait for you."[-c] He took three darts in his hand and drove them into Absalom's chest. [Absalom] was still alive in the thick growth of the terebinth, 15 when ten of Joab's young arms-bearers closed in and struck at Absalom until he died. 16 Then Joab sounded the horn, and the troops gave up their pursuit of the Israelites; for Joab held the troops in check. 17 They took Absalom and flung him into a large pit in the forest, and they piled up a very great heap of stones over it. Then all the Israelites fled to their homes.—18 Now Absalom, in his lifetime, had taken the pillar which is in the Valley of the King and set it up for himself; for he said, "I have no son to keep my name alive." He had named the pillar after himself, and it has been called Absalom's Monument to this day.

19 Ahimaaz son of Zadok said, "Let me run and report to the king that the LORD has vindicated him against his enemies." 20 But Joab said to him, "You shall not be the one to bring tidings today. You may bring tidings some other day, but you'll not bring any today; for the king's son is dead!" 21 And Joab said to a Cushite, "Go tell the king what you have seen." The Cushite bowed to Joab and ran off. 22 But Ahimaaz son of Zadok again said to Joab, "No matter what, let me run, too, behind the Cushite." Joab asked, "Why should you run, my boy, when you have no news [d-]worth telling?"[-d] 23 "I am going to run anyway." "Then run," he said. So Ahimaaz ran by way of the Plain, and he passed the Cushite.

24 David was sitting between the two gates.[e] The watchman on the roof of the gate walked over to the city wall. He looked up and saw a man running alone. 25 The watchman called down and told the king; and the king said, "If he is alone, he has news to report." As he was coming nearer, 26 the watchman saw another man running; and he called out to the gatekeeper, "There is another man running alone." And the king said, "That one, too, brings news." 27 The watchman said, "I can see that the first one runs like Ahimaaz son of Zadok"; to which the king replied, "He is a good man, and he comes with good news." 28 Ahimaaz called out and said to the king, "All is well!" He bowed low with his face to the ground and said, "Praised be the LORD your God, who has delivered up the men who raised their hand against my lord the king." 29 The king asked, "Is my boy Absalom safe?" And Ahimaaz answered, "I saw [d-]a large crowd when Your Majesty's servant Joab was sending your servant off,[-d] but I don't know

a-a So some Heb. mss. and ancient versions. Most mss. and editions read "who"—perhaps meaning "whoever you are." *b I.e., by killing Absalom.*

c-c Some Septuagint mss. and Targum read "Therefore, I will begin before you."

d-d Meaning of Heb. uncertain. *e I.e., the inner and outer gateways.*

14: These *darts* (others: spears or javelins) were not lethal. **15:** The death by the hand of *ten* men was especially brutal. **16:** *Sounded the horn,* see 2.28 n.; this horn signals the end of the rebellion, begun in a similar fashion (15.10). *Held ... in check,* lit. "spared." **17:** *Flung him into a large pit,* an act of contempt. A *heap of stones,* a sign of disgrace (see Josh. 7.26; 8.29). **18:** The humiliating pile of stones on his grave is an ironic contrast to the glorious memorial that Absalom had set up for himself in the *Valley of the King. No son:* According to 14.27 Absalom had three sons. Radak resolves the contradiction by assuming that they had died. *Absalom's Monument,* not to be confused with the Roman-period tomb bearing that designation today.

18.19–19.9: The sad victory. Joy over the victory is overshadowed by David's grief over Absalom's death. In spite of what Absalom did to him, David loved his son dearly. This unit is similar to 1.1–16, when David is told of Saul's death. **19–32:** The detailed account concerning the two runners focuses attention on David's reaction to their messages. **19:** *Ahimaaz,* see 15.27. **20:** Joab fully understands the significance of Absalom's death for David. **21:** *Cushite,* a black person from Cush, the region south of Egypt, an anonymous person who is not part of David's close circle. Then, as now, Africans are known to be outstanding runners. **23:** *The Plain,* the Jordan Valley. **24:** The narrative's point of view leaps to Mahanaim, where David is anxiously waiting for news from the battlefield. Cities in biblical times often had two gates connected by a short fortified passageway. **27:** David's reply reflects the view that messenger and message are of the same nature (cf. 1 Kings 1.42). **28:** *All is well:* Ahimaaz thinks of the battle, whereas David is concerned about "the boy" Absalom. **29:** Ahimaaz evades David's question.

what it was about." 30 The king said, "Step aside and stand over
there"; he stepped aside and waited.
31 Just then the Cushite came up; and the Cushite said, "Let
my lord the king be informed that the LORD has vindicated you
today against all who rebelled against you!" 32 The king asked
the Cushite, "Is my boy Absalom safe?" And the Cushite replied,
"May the enemies of my lord the king and all who rose against
19 you to do you harm fare like that young man!" 1[a]The king
was shaken. He went up to the upper chamber of the
gateway and wept, moaning these words as he went,[b] "My son
Absalom! O my son, my son Absalom! If only I had died instead
of you! O Absalom, my son, my son!"

2 Joab was told that the king was weeping and mourning over
Absalom. 3 And the victory that day was turned into mourning
for all the troops, for that day the troops heard that the king was
grieving over his son. 4 The troops stole into town that day like
troops ashamed after running away in battle. 5 The king covered his face and the king kept crying aloud, "O my son Absalom! O Absalom, my son, my son!"
6 Joab came to the king in his quarters and said, "Today you
have humiliated all your followers, who this day saved your
life, and the lives of your sons and daughters, and the lives of
your wives and concubines, 7 by showing love for those who
hate you and hate for those who love you. For you have made
clear today that the officers and men mean nothing to you.
I am sure that if Absalom were alive today and the rest of us
dead, you would have preferred it. 8 Now arise, come out and
placate your followers! For I swear by the LORD that if[c] you do
not come out, not a single man will remain with you overnight;
and that would be a greater disaster for you than any disaster
that has befallen you from your youth until now." 9 So the king
arose and sat down in the gateway; and when all the troops
were told that the king was sitting in the gateway, all the troops
presented themselves to the king.
Now the Israelites had fled to their homes. 10 All the people throughout the tribes of Israel were arguing: Some said,
"The king saved us from the hands of our enemies, and he
delivered us from the hands of the Philistines; and just now
he had to flee the country because of Absalom. 11 But Absalom, whom we anointed over us, has died in battle; why then
do you sit idle instead of escorting the king back?" 12 The
talk of all Israel reached the king in his quarters. So King
David sent this message to the priests Zadok and Abiathar:

32: The Cushite's reply is indirect, but unambiguously suggests that Absalom is dead. **19.1:** David's personal lament, unlike the public laments for Saul and Jonathan (1.19–27) and for Abner (3.33–34), consists mainly of short cries, repeating the beloved's name and the word *my son* over and over again. **5:** *Covered his face,* see 15.30 n. **6–9:** While David the father succumbs to his personal grief, Joab threatingly orders him in language not elsewhere used to a king that he must fulfill his public duties as king. **6:** Joab accuses David of ingratitude to his loyal followers. **7:** Joab's extreme, unjustified accusations are based on half-truths. His aggressive language covers up that he was responsible for killing Absalom. **9:** David yields to Joab, but does not forgive him (see v. 14).

19.10–41: Return. On his flight from Jerusalem David first met his loyal supporters the priests and Hushai, then Mephibosheth's servant Ziba, and finally his opponent Shimei the son of Gera; on his way back the order is reversed—he first meets Shimei, then Mephibosheth himself, and finally his staunch supporter Barzillai. **10–11:** Only the arguments in favor of David are reported. *Israel,* excluding Judah. **12:** *Zadok and Abiathar* were left in Jerusalem as informants (15.27–29). The men of *Judah,* David's own tribe, many of whom supported Absalom (see 15.7 n.).

a Counted as 18.33 in some versions. *b Some Septuagint mss. read "wept."*
c So Septuagint, 4QSam[a], and some other Heb. mss., and an ancient masoretic tradition; ordinary texts omit "if."

“Speak to the elders of Judah and say, ‘Why should you be the
last to bring the king back to his palace? 13 You are my kinsmen, my own flesh and blood! Why should you be the last to
escort the king back?’ 14 And to Amasa say this, ‘You are my
own flesh and blood. May God do thus and more to me if you
do not become my army commander permanently in place
of Joab!’ ” 15 So [Amasa] swayed the hearts of all the Judites as
one man; and they sent a message to the king: “Come back
with all your followers.”

16 The king started back and arrived at the Jordan; and the
Judites went to Gilgal to meet the king and to conduct the king
across the Jordan. 17 Shimei son of Gera, the Benjaminite from
Bahurim, hurried down with the Judites to meet King David,
18 accompanied by a thousand Benjaminites. [a]And Ziba, the
servant of the House of Saul, together with his fifteen sons and
twenty slaves, rushed down to the Jordan ahead of the king
19 while the crossing was being made, to escort the king's family over, and to do whatever he wished. Shimei son of Gera
flung himself before the king as he was about to cross the Jordan. 20 He said to the king, “Let not my lord hold me guilty, and
do not remember the wrong your servant committed on the
day my lord the king left Jerusalem; let Your Majesty give it no
thought. 21 For your servant knows that he has sinned; so here
I have come down today, the first of all the House of Joseph, to
meet my lord the king.” 22 Thereupon Abishai son of Zeruiah
spoke up, “Shouldn't Shimei be put to death for that—insulting the LORD's anointed?” 23 But David said, [b-]“What has this to
do with you,[-b] you sons of Zeruiah, that you should cross me
today? Should a single Israelite be put to death today? Don't I[c]
know that today I am again king over Israel?” 24 Then the king
said to Shimei, “You shall not die”; and the king gave him his
oath.

25 Mephibosheth, the grandson of Saul, also came down to
meet the king. He had not pared his toenails, or trimmed his
mustache, or washed his clothes from the day that the king left
until the day he returned safe. 26 When he [d-]came [from][-d] Jerusalem to meet the king, the king asked him, “Why didn't you
come with me, Mephibosheth?” 27 He replied, “My lord the
king, my own servant[e] deceived me. [f-]Your servant planned to
saddle his ass and ride[-f] on it and go with Your Majesty—for
your servant is lame. 28 [Ziba] has slandered your servant to my
lord the king. But my lord the king is like an angel of the LORD;
do as you see fit. 29 For all the members of my father's family

14: *My own flesh and blood* was used earlier in 5.1, when David was anointed, which is recalled here. Although *Amasa* was Absalom's army commander (17.25), David appoints him—his nephew—as permanent army commander in place of Joab, because of his anger at Joab for killing Absalom. David knows that Amasa has great influence in Judah. **16:** *Gilgal,* near the Jordan. **17:** *Shimei,* who cursed and insulted David on his flight from Jerusalem (16.5–13), now hurries to make amends and save his life. He introduces a section on reconciliation with Benjamin, Saul's tribe. **18:** The *thousand Benjaminites* are meant to show Shimei's power in his tribe. *Ziba,* see 16.1ff. **20–21:** Shimei couches his plea in most deferential language. *House of Joseph,* a designation of northern Israel as opposed to Judah (see Josh. 18.5). The first northern king was Jeroboam, descended from Ephraim, son of Joseph—this reflects that tribe's importance. **22–24:** *Abishai,* Joab's brother. His relentless approach (cf. 1 Sam. 26.8ff.; 2 Sam. 16.9ff.) sets off David's moderate attitude. David swears not to put Shimei to death, probably in order to win the support of Benjamin. He does not, however, forgive Shimei (see 1 Kings 2.8–9). Appropriately, David is called here *the LORD's anointed,* used earlier by David concerning Saul of Benjamin (e.g., 1 Sam. 24.7; 2 Sam. 1.14). **25–29:** *Mephibosheth,* addressing David in most polite language, accuses Ziba of failing to bring his ass and slandering him (16.1–4). He acknowledges the favors David has shown to him (ch 9) and even compares David to an angel of God (see 1 Sam. 29.9 n.), but refrains from mentioning directly that David, unjustly, gave his fields to Ziba.
25: Mephibosheth's physical appearance is a sign of his sorrow.

a Meaning of parts of the rest of vv. 18 and 19 uncertain.
b-b See note at 16.10. *c Some Septuagint mss. read “you.”*
d-d So Septuagint. Heb. “entered.” *e I.e., Ziba (cf. v. 30 and 9.2 ff.).*
f-f Ancient versions read “Your servant said to him, ‘Saddle my ass, that I may ride . . .’ ”

deserved only death from my lord the king; yet you set your
servant among those who ate at your table. What right have I to
appeal further to Your Majesty?" 30 The king said to him, "You
need not speak further. I decree that you and Ziba shall divide
the property." 31 And Mephibosheth said to the king, "Let him
take it all, as long as my lord the king has come home safe."
32 Barzillai the Gileadite had come down from Rogelin and
[a]passed on to the Jordan with the king, to see him off at[a]
the Jordan. 33 Barzillai was very old, eighty years of age; and
he had provided the king with food during his stay at Mahanaim, for he was a very wealthy man. 34 The king said to
Barzillai, "Cross over with me, and I will provide for you in
Jerusalem at my side." 35 But Barzillai said to the king, "How
many years are left to me that I should go up with Your Majesty to Jerusalem? 36 I am now eighty years old. Can I tell the
difference between good and bad? Can your servant taste
what he eats and drinks? Can I still listen to the singing of
men and women? Why then should your servant continue
to be a burden to my lord the king? 37 [a]Your servant could
barely cross the Jordan[a] with your Majesty! Why should
Your Majesty reward me so generously? 38 Let your servant
go back, and let me die in my own town, near the graves of
my father and mother. But here is your servant Chimham; let
him cross with my lord the king, and do for him as you see
fit." 39 And the king said, "Chimham shall cross with me, and
I will do for him as you see fit; and anything you want me to
do, I will do for you."
40 [b]All the troops crossed the Jordan; and when the king was
ready to cross, the king kissed Barzillai and bade him farewell; and [Barzillai] returned to his home. 41 The king passed
on to Gilgal, with Chimham[c] accompanying him; and all the
Judite soldiers and part of the Israelite army escorted the king
across.
42 Then all the men of Israel came to the king and said to the
king, "Why did our kinsmen, the men of Judah, steal you away
and escort the king and his family across the Jordan, along
with all David's men?" 43 All the men of Judah replied to the
men of Israel, "Because the king is our relative! Why should
this upset you? Have we consumed anything that belongs to
the king? Has he given us any gifts?" 44 But the men of Israel
answered the men of Judah, "We have ten shares in the king,
and [d]in David, too, we have more than you.[d] Why then have
you slighted us? Were we not the first to propose that our king
be brought back?" However, the men of Judah prevailed over
the men of Israel.

a-a Meaning of Heb. uncertain. *b Meaning of parts of vv. 40–44 uncertain.*
c Heb. Chimhan. *d-d Septuagint reads "we are the first-born, rather than you."*

30: David understands Mephibosheth's hint. Without investigating who lied, Ziba or Mephibosheth, he decrees that the fields shall be divided. According to the Talmud (*b. Shab.* 56a), David's unjust decision will have repercussions in the future: "When David said to Mephibosheth, you and Ziba shall divide the field, a heavenly voice was heard, saying, Rehoboam and Jeroboam will divide the kingdom." (See 1 Kings ch 12.) **32:** *Barzillai,* see 17.27. **35–38:** Rhetorical questions are characteristic of Barzillai's style. **33:** *Eighty* was exceedingly old in antiquity; see Ps. 90.10: "The span of our life is seventy years, / or, given the strength, eighty years." **36:** *Good and bad,* in the material, not the moral, sense. *Singing ... men and women* were part of the royal court, and were exiled from the Judean court by Sennacherib in 701 BCE according to his inscription. **38:** *Chimham,* probably Barzillai's son. **39:** David does not forget his promise (see 1 Kings 2.7). **41:** *Soldiers, army,* lit. "people" (see vv. 11–12, 16). The contrast between *all the Judite soldiers* and *part of the Israelite army* suggests that trouble lies ahead.

19.42–20.22: Rebellion again. Conflict between Israel and Judah leads to Israel's breaking away from David. Civil war and division of the kingdom are prevented by David's swift action, resulting in the rebel's death. **42:** See v. 16. **44:** *Ten shares,* ten times as much (Rashi: "for we are ten tribes").

20 A scoundrel named Sheba son of Bichri, a Benjaminite, happened to be there. He sounded the horn and proclaimed:

"We have no portion in David,
No share in Jesse's son!
Every man to his tent, O Israel!"

[2] All the men of Israel left David and followed Sheba son of Bichri; but the men of Judah accompanied their king from the Jordan to Jerusalem. [3] David went to his palace in Jerusalem, and the king took the ten concubines he had left to mind the palace and put them in a guarded place; he provided for them, but he did not cohabit with them. They remained in seclusion until the day they died, in living widowhood.

[4] The king said to Amasa, "Call up the men of Judah to my standard, and report here three days from now." [5] Amasa went to call up Judah, but he took longer than the time set for him. [6] And David said to Abishai, "Now Sheba son of Bichri will cause us more trouble than Absalom. So take your lord's servants and pursue him, before he finds fortified towns and [a-]eludes us."[-a] [7] [b-]Joab's men, the Cherethites and Pelethites, and all the warriors, marched out behind him.[-b] They left Jerusalem in pursuit of Sheba son of Bichri. [8] They were near the great stone in Gibeon when Amasa appeared before them. [a-]Joab was wearing his military dress, with his sword girded over it and fastened around his waist in its sheath; and, as he stepped forward, it fell out.[-a] [9] Joab said to Amasa, "How are you, brother?" and with his right hand Joab took hold of Amasa's beard as if to kiss him. [10] Amasa was not on his guard against the sword in Joab's [left] hand, and [Joab] drove it into his belly so that his entrails poured out on the ground and he died; he did not need to strike him a second time.

Joab and his brother Abishai then set off in pursuit of Sheba son of Bichri, [11] while one of Joab's henchmen stood by [c-]the corpse[-c] and called out, "Whoever favors Joab, and whoever is on David's side, follow Joab!" [12] Amasa lay in the middle of the road, drenched in his blood; and the man saw that everyone stopped. And when he saw that all the people were stopping, he dragged Amasa from the road into the field and covered him with a garment. [13] Once he was removed from the road, everybody continued to follow Joab in pursuit of Sheba son of Bichri. [14] [Sheba] had passed through all the tribes of Israel up to Abel of[d] Beth-maacah; and all the Beerites[e] assembled and followed him inside. [15] [Joab's men] came and besieged him in

20.1: *A Benjaminite,* from the tribe of Saul. As in 15.10, the blast of a horn starts a rebellion, but calling *Sheba* a *scoundrel* hints that this rebellion will not succeed. *His tent,* an archaic term for "his home." **2:** Only Judah remains loyal to David. **3:** *The ten concubines,* see 15.16. David does not cohabit with them, because Absalom had slept with them (16.22). **4:** *Amasa,* see 19.14 n. **6:** Because of Amasa's delay in calling up the men of Judah, David, aware of the urgency of action, appoints *Abishai,* Joab's brother, as commander of his personal forces, and not Joab himself, because David is angry with him for killing Absalom. It is unclear if Amasa is simply delayed, or has defected. **7:** *The Cherethites and Pelethites,* see 8.18 n. *Behind him,* behind Abishai. **10:** Usually the sword is held in the right hand. Joab lets it slip out of its sheath and then snatches it with his left hand. He treacherously kills Amasa in the same way he killed Abner, striking him in the belly (3.27). His motive, then and now, was to get rid of a rival. David never forgave him (see 1 Kings 2.5). **11:** The henchman urges Amasa's men to go over to Joab, who assumed command over the troops pursuing Sheba. **12:** *The man*'s concern was practical—facilitating the battle, and not respecting the corpse of Amasa. **14:** *Abel of Beth-maacah,* a town in the extreme north of Israel. **15:** In ancient sieges, a city was surrounded to prevent food and supplies from entering, and a *siegemound* was built to facilitate toppling or scaling the wall.

a-a Meaning of Heb. uncertain.
b-b Emendation yields "Joab, the Cherethites and Pelethites, and all the warriors marched out behind Abishai." *c-c Heb. "him."*
d Heb. "and." Cf. v. 15 (and "Abel-beth-maacah" in 1 Kings 15.20 and 2 Kings 15.29).
e Emendation yields "Bichrites"; cf. Septuagint.

Abel of Beth-maacah; they threw up a siegemound against the city [a]and it stood against the rampart.[-a]

All the troops with Joab were [b]engaged in battering the wall,[-b] [16] when a clever woman shouted from the city, "Listen! Listen! Tell Joab to come over here so I can talk to him." [17] He approached her, and the woman asked, "Are you Joab?" "Yes," he answered; and she said to him, "Listen to what your handmaid has to say." "I'm listening," he replied. [18] And she continued, "In olden times people used to say, [c]'Let them inquire of Abel,'[-c] and that was the end of the matter. [19] I am one of those who seek the welfare of the faithful in Israel. But you seek to bring death upon a mother city in Israel! Why should you destroy the LORD's possession?" [20] Joab replied, "Far be it, far be it from me to destroy or to ruin! [21] Not at all! But a certain man from the hill country of Ephraim, named Sheba son of Bichri, has rebelled against King David. Just hand him alone over to us, and I will withdraw from the city." The woman assured Joab, "His head shall be thrown over the wall to you." [22] The woman came to all the people with her clever plan; and they cut off the head of Sheba son of Bichri and threw it down to Joab. He then sounded the horn; all the men dispersed to their homes, and Joab returned to the king in Jerusalem.

[23] Joab was commander of the whole army [of] Israel; Benaiah son of Jehoiada was commander of the Cherethites and the Pelethites; [24] Adoram[d] was in charge of forced labor; Jehoshaphat son of Ahilud was recorder; [25] Sheva[e] was scribe; and Zadok and Abiathar were priests. [26] Ira the Jairite also served David as priest.

21 There was a famine during the reign of David, year after year for three years. David inquired of the LORD, and the LORD replied, "It is because of the bloodguilt of Saul

a-a Meaning of Heb. uncertain. The phrase would read well in the next verse ("... a clever woman stood on the rampart and shouted ...").
b-b Lit. "destroying, to topple the wall." Septuagint and Targum read "were planning to topple the wall." *c-c Meaning of Heb. uncertain.*
d So in 1 Kings 12.18 and 2 Chron. 10.18 ("Hadoram"); elsewhere "Adoniram."
e See note h at 8.17.

16: The *clever woman* of Abel, like her counterpart of Tekoa (ch 14), is endowed with great power of persuasion. As in Judg. 9.53, where Abimelech is killed when a woman threw an upper millstone on his skull, death by the hand of a woman shames the victim. **18:** *Let them inquire ... the end of the matter:* The town of Abel was apparently famous for its wisdom, and its rulings were invariably accepted. **19:** *Mother city,* metropolis. *The LORD's possession,* the people of Israel. **21:** The *hill country of Ephraim* included parts of Benjamin. **22:** *Clever plan,* lit. "cleverness." The woman persuades her people, thus preventing war. *Sounded the horn,* see 2.28 n. *To the king,* to his service. Beheadings are surprisingly frequent in Samuel (1 Sam. 17.51; 31.9; 2 Sam. 4.7). This beheading is a reminder that in 16.9, Abishai had wanted to behead Shimei; had David heeded him then, this rebellion would not have occurred. *And Joab returned to the king in Jerusalem* is a very anticlimactic ending, suggesting that this story continues at the beginning of 1 Kings, where the crisis over who will succeed David continues.

20.23–26: Administration, part 2. The list of David's senior officials is similar to the list in 8.16–18 (see annotations there), but probably reflects a later stage in David's reign. The list marks the conclusion of the second part of 2 Sam. **24:** *Adoram* still functions under Solomon (see translators' note). Since *forced labor* is not mentioned in the first list, it was apparently instituted later. It aroused fierce opposition, culminating in Adoram's murder (see 1 Kings 12.18). **26:** Cf. 8.18.

Chs 21–24: Appendix. The last four chs of Samuel include diverse materials. These are somewhat different in character, theological outlook, and language from the main body of the book, and were added later as an appendix. They are arranged in chiastic order: (A) a narrative about a national calamity, (B) short accounts of heroic feats, (C) a poem, (C') a poem, (B') short accounts of heroic feats, with a list of David's heroes, and (A') a narrative about a national calamity. The first narrative looks back to the past, to events that occurred before David's reign; the last narrative points to the future, to the period of David's son Solomon. The material in the appendix sometimes contradicts the body of Samuel. This material may supplement the book by offering alternative views.

21.1–14: Vengeance versus charity. The first part of the narrative tells of the Gibeonites' revenge for Saul's violation of the oath promising them preservation of life; the second part describes the acts of charity to the dead performed by Saul's concubine and David. This story is probably imagined to have transpired early in David's reign, soon after Saul's death. It reflects a very different attitude toward Saul's family than that reflected

and [his] house, for he put some Gibeonites to death.” 2 The king summoned the Gibeonites and spoke to them.—Now the Gibeonites were not of Israelite stock, but a remnant of the Amorites, to whom the Israelites had given an oath; and Saul had tried to wipe them out in his zeal for the people of Israel and Judah.—3 David asked the Gibeonites, “What shall I do for you? How shall I make expiation, so that you may bless the LORD's own people?” 4 The Gibeonites answered him, “We have no claim for silver or gold against Saul and his household; and we have no claim on the life of any other man in Israel.” And [David] responded, “Whatever you say I will do for you.” 5 Thereupon they said to the king, “The man who massacred us and planned to [a-]exterminate us, so that we[-a] should not survive in all the territory of Israel—6 let seven of his male issue be handed over to us, and we will impale them before the LORD in [b-]Gibeah of Saul, the chosen of the LORD.”[-b] And the king replied, “I will do so.”

7 The king spared Mephibosheth son of Jonathan son of Saul, because of the oath before the LORD between the two, between David and Jonathan son of Saul. 8 Instead, the king took Armoni and Mephibosheth, the two sons that Rizpah daughter of Aiah bore to Saul, and the five sons that Merab[c] daughter of Saul bore to Adriel son of Barzillai the Meholathite, 9 and he handed them over to the Gibeonites. They impaled them on the mountain before the LORD; all seven of them perished at the same time. They were put to death in the first days of the harvest, the beginning of the barley harvest.

10 Then Rizpah daughter of Aiah took sackcloth and spread it on a rock for herself, and she stayed there from the beginning of the harvest until rain from the sky fell on [d-]the bodies;[-d] she did not let the birds of the sky settle on them by day or the wild beasts [approach] by night. 11 David was told what Saul's concubine Rizpah daughter of Aiah had done. 12 And David went and took the bones of Saul and of his son Jonathan from the citizens of Jabesh-gilead, who had made off with them from the public square of Beth-shan, where the Philistines had hung them up on the day the Philistines killed Saul at Gilboa. 13 He brought up the bones of Saul and of his son Jonathan from there; and he gathered the bones of those who had been impaled. 14 And they buried the bones of Saul and of his son Jonathan[e] in Zela, in the territory of Benjamin, in the tomb of his father Kish. And when all that the king had commanded was done, God responded to the plea of the land thereafter.

a-a Meaning of Heb. uncertain.
b-b Emendation yields “at Gibeon, on the mountain of the LORD” (cf. Septuagint and v. 9).
c So two Heb. mss., many Septuagint mss., and Peshitta; and cf. Targum, Sanhedrin 19b, and 1 Sam. 18.19. Most mss. and the printed editions read “Michal.”
d-d Heb. “them.” *e Septuagint adds “and the bones of those impaled.”*

in the rest of Samuel, and is another illustration in the book of intergenerational punishment (see 12.13 n.) **1:** The famine was the result of drought, regarded in the Bible as divine punishment for bad behavior (see esp. Deut. 11.13–17). *Put some Gibeonites to death,* lit. “killed the Gibeonites.” This act of Saul is mentioned nowhere else. **2:** The *Gibeonites* were a remnant of the *Amorites,* or native Canaanites, who inhabited the country before the Israelite conquest. As a result of a ruse, Joshua swore to them that their lives would be spared (Josh. 9.15). The whole people have to bear, even after many years, the consequences of Saul's sin. *In his zeal:* The narrator explains why Saul broke the oath and *tried* to exterminate the Gibeonites (but did not quite succeed). **3:** The Gibeonites' blessing will annul the curse of the famine. **4:** The Gibeonites, demanding blood vengeance, settle neither for material reparations nor for the death of anyone other than Saul's offspring. **6:** Impaling as a means of propitiating divine anger is only found here and in Num. 25.4. *Gibeah of Saul,* Saul's town (see 1 Sam. 10.5 n.). *The chosen of the LORD,* a sarcastic utterance (but see translators' note). **7:** Contrary to Saul, who violated the oath to the Gibeonites, David keeps the oath to Jonathan (1 Sam. 20.14–15, 42). **8:** *Rizpah,* Saul's concubine (3.7). *Merab ... Adriel,* see 1 Sam. 18.19. **9:** *The mountain before the LORD:* In Gibeah, on the Hill of God, there was a shrine (1 Sam. 10.5). *The barley harvest* began in April. **10:** *Spread it,* pitched it as a tent to protect herself from the scorching sun. *Until rain from the sky fell,* until the beginning of winter. All during the hot summer Rizpah guards the decaying, smelling corpses; contrast the legislation in Deut. 21.23, precisely to avoid this situation. **11:** The noble deed of the simple *concubine* provokes David also to perform an act of charity for the dead. **12:** See 1 Sam. 31.10–13. **14:** *In the tomb of his father Kish:* Great value was attached to being buried in one's forefathers' grave (see 2.32 n.). *God responded to the plea of the land,* or more properly, to the actions of David, and put an end to the famine.

15 Again war broke out between the Philistines and Israel,
and David and the men with him went down and fought the
Philistines; David grew weary, 16 and [a]Ishbi-benob[a] tried to
kill David.—He was a descendant of the Raphah;[b] his bronze
spear weighed three hundred shekels and he wore new armor.—17 But Abishai son of Zeruiah came to his aid; he attacked the Philistine and killed him. It was then that David's
men declared to him on oath, "You shall not go with us into
battle any more, lest you extinguish the lamp of Israel!"
18 [c]After this, fighting broke out again with the Philistines, at
Gob; that was when Sibbecai the Hushathite killed Saph, a descendant of the Raphah.[b] 19 Again there was fighting with the
Philistines at Gob; and Elhanan son of Jaare-oregim[d] the Bethlehemite killed Goliath the Gittite, whose spear had a shaft like
a weaver's bar. 20 Once again there was fighting, at Gath. There
was a [a]giant of a man,[a] who had six fingers on each hand and
six toes on each foot, twenty-four in all; he too was descended
from the Raphah. 21 When he taunted Israel, Jonathan, the son
of David's brother Shimei, killed him. 22 Those four were descended from the Raphah in Gath, and they fell by the hands
of David and his men.

22 [e]David addressed the words of this song to the LORD,
after the LORD had saved him from the hands of all his
enemies and from the hands of Saul. 2 He said:

a-a Meaning of Heb. uncertain. *b Apparently a race of giants.*

c This paragraph is found also in 1 Chron. 20.4–8; in part, also in 1QSam[a], with some variations.

d Perhaps a duplicate of 'oregim *("weavers") at the end of the verse; meaning of Heb. uncertain. 1 Chron. 20.5 reads "And Elhanan son of Jair killed Lahmi, the brother of Goliath the Gittite."*

e This poem occurs again as Ps. 18, with a number of variations, some of which are cited in the following notes.

21.15–22: Heroic feats. The four short accounts of feats performed by David's heroes against Philistine giants resemble each other in content and form. They also show similarities—particularly the third one—with the narrative of David and Goliath (1 Sam. ch 17), though there are significant differences here as well. All of them tell of single combats. They probably were thought to belong to David's early period, though v. 17 assumes he was already king. **15:** This unit's opening, "Again war broke out," suggests that this was a fragment of a longer text dealing with David and the Philistines. *Went down,* from the mountain region to the plain. **16:** *Ishbi-benob,* a peculiar name, probably resulting from textual corruption. *Raphah* is mentioned only in this unit. The connection between this *Raphah* and Heb "repha'im, "shades" or residents of the underworld (e.g., Isa. 26.14, 19) also known from Ugaritic literature, remains unclear. *His bronze spear weighed three hundred shekels,* about 3.5 kg (7.7 pounds). Cf. 1 Sam. 17.7. **17:** *Abishai,* see 1 Sam. 26.6 n. Regarding the declaration of David's men, compare 18.3. *The lamp of Israel* is an honorific term for the king; cf. Ps. 132.17. **19:** According to 1 Sam. ch 17 *Goliath* of Gath (i.e., the Gittite), *whose spear had a shaft like a weaver's bar* (1 Sam. 17.7), was killed by David, the Bethlehemite. To resolve the contradiction 1 Chron. 20.5 reads "brother of Goliath." Rashi assumes that David and Elhanan were one and the same person. Probably, however, the killing of the giant Goliath was initially attributed to Elhanan (perhaps the hero mentioned in 23.24), but later the more famous David was credited with it. This was facilitated by the fact that the Philistine killed by David was originally anonymous (only in 1 Sam. 17.4, 23, where he is introduced, is his name mentioned; otherwise he is simply designated "the Philistine"). **20:** *Six fingers ... six toes,* an extraordinary and perhaps frightening phenomenon. **21:** Several times in 1 Sam. ch 17 Goliath is depicted as *taunt*ing Israel.

22.1–51: A song of thanksgiving. The song, attributed to David, expresses thanks to the LORD, who delivered the author from mortal danger and granted him victory over his enemies. The song's major theme is God's great power. It abounds in poetical devices, includes the following sections: praise of God (vv. 2–4); the author's plight and cry for help (vv. 5–7); God's appearance (vv. 8–16); God's rescue (vv. 17–20); the reward for the author's righteousness (vv. 21–25); God's ways of requital (vv. 26–28); the power of God's help (vv. 29–32); God's equipping the author for battle (vv. 33–37); the victory over the enemies (vv. 38–43); the author ruler of nations (vv. 44–46); praise of God (vv. 47–51). The song's frame—praise of God—defines its purpose. The same poem, with minor variations, which crept in during the process of transmission, is found in Ps. 18; see the more extensive nn. there. **1:** The superscription resembles headings in the book of Psalms (see, e.g., Pss. 3, 34, 51), which were added to the songs to connect them with the events in David's life that occasioned their composition. Given that Saul was David's main enemy, it was natural for this superscription to be

O LORD, my crag, my fastness, my deliverer!
3 O [a-]God, the rock[-a] wherein I take shelter:
My shield, my [b-]mighty champion,[-b] my fortress and refuge!
My savior, You who rescue me from violence!

4 [c-]All praise! I called on the LORD,[-c]
And I was delivered from my enemies.

5 For the breakers of Death encompassed me,
The torrents of Belial[d] terrified me;
6 The snares of Sheol encircled me,
The coils of Death engulfed me.

7 In my anguish I called on the LORD,
Cried out to my God;
In His Abode[e] He heard my voice,
My cry entered His ears.

8 Then the earth rocked and quaked,
The foundations of heaven[f] shook—
Rocked by His indignation.
9 Smoke went up from His nostrils,
From His mouth came devouring fire;
Live coals blazed forth from Him.
10 He bent the sky and came down,
Thick cloud beneath His feet.
11 He mounted a cherub and flew;
[g-]He was seen[-g] on the wings of the wind.
12 He made pavilions of darkness about Him,
Dripping clouds, huge thunderheads;
13 In the brilliance before Him
Blazed fiery coals.
14 The LORD thundered forth from heaven,
The Most High sent forth His voice;
15 He let loose bolts, and scattered them;[h]
Lightning, and put them to rout.
16 The bed of the sea was exposed,
The foundations of the world were laid bare
By the mighty roaring of the LORD,
At the blast of the breath of His nostrils.
17 He reached down from on high, He took me,
Drew me out of the mighty waters;[i]

added. **2–3:** The metaphors, occurring in a long string of epithets, stress God's strength. Such lists are often found in Mesopotamian royal inscriptions of the king, but are found in the Bible only of God. **5–6:** Such hyperbolic language expresses being close to death (see 1 Sam. 2.6 n.), rather than having died and been resurrected. **7:** *Abode:* V. 10 suggests that God's heavenly abode is meant. **8–16:** God's appearance (theophany) is manifested by terrifying natural phenomena: earthquake, volcanic eruption, and thunderstorm (cf. Exod. 19.16–18; Judg. 5.4–5). God is pictured in anthropomorphic terms, though his power is beyond any human's ability. **11:** *Cherub,* see 1 Sam. 4.4 n. **14:** See similarly Amos 1.2, though there God sends *forth His voice* from Zion, namely Jerusalem.

a-a Lit. "the God of my rock"; Ps. 18.3 "my God, my rock."
b-b Lit. "horn of rescue." *c-c Construction of Heb. uncertain.*
d I.e., the netherworld, like "Death" and "Sheol." *e Lit. "Temple."*
f Ps. 18.8 "mountains." *g-g Ps. 18.11 "Gliding."*
h I.e., the enemies in v. 4. *i Cf. v. 5.*

18: Since God is so *strong,* as the previous vv. show, He can save anyone from the strongest enemies. **21–27:** These vv. convey the idea that the deliverance is a reward for merit. **28:** An expansion from the individual to the community. **29:** "The hardship is the darkness and the deliverance is the light" (Radak). God as *lamp* connects this passage to the previous one, where the Davidic king is "the lamp of Israel" (21.17). **32:** A declaration of monotheism typifying later biblical literature (cf. Isa. 44.8). **34:** The singular of the word translated *the heights* also means "my back" and thence in the plural perhaps "my thighs" (parallel to *my legs*).

18 He rescued me from my enemy so strong,
From foes too mighty for me.
19 They attacked me on my day of calamity,
But the LORD was my stay.
20 He brought me out to freedom,
He rescued me because He was pleased with me.
21 The LORD rewarded me according to my merit,
He requited the cleanness of my hands.

22 For I have kept the ways of the LORD
And have not been guilty before my God;
23 I am mindful of all His rules
And have not departed from His laws.
24 I have been blameless before Him,
And have guarded myself against sinning—
25 And the LORD has requited my merit,
According to my purity in His sight.
26 With the loyal You deal loyally;
With the blameless hero,[a] blamelessly.
27 With the pure You act in purity,
And with the perverse You are wily.
28 To humble folk You give victory,
[b]And You look with scorn on the haughty.[b]

29 You, O LORD, are my lamp;
The LORD lights up my darkness.
30 With You, I can rush a barrier,[c]
With my God, I can scale a wall.
31 The way of God is perfect,
The word of the LORD is pure.
He is a shield to all who take refuge in Him.
32 Yea, who is a god except the LORD,
Who is a rock except God—
33 The God, [d]my mighty stronghold,[d]
Who kept[e] my path secure;
34 Who made my legs like a deer's,
And set me firm on the[f] heights;
35 Who trained my hands for battle,
So that my arms can bend a bow of bronze!
36 You have granted me the shield of Your protection
[g]And Your providence has made me great.[g]

a *Ps. 18.26 "man."*
b-b *Lit. "And lower Your eyes on the haughty"; Ps. 18.28 "But haughty eyes You humble."* c *Cf. postbiblical* gedudiyyoth *"walls," Aramaic* gudda, *"wall."*
d-d *Ps. 18.33 "who girded me with might."*
e *Meaning of Heb. uncertain; Ps. 18.33 "made."*
f *Taking* bamothai *as a poetic form of* bamoth; *cf. Hab. 3.19; others "my."*
g-g *Meaning of Heb. uncertain.*

37 You have let me stride on freely,
And my feet have not slipped.
38 I pursued my enemies and wiped them out,
I did not turn back till I destroyed them.
39 I destroyed them, I struck them down;
They rose no more, they lay at my feet.
40 You have girt me with strength for battle,
Brought low my foes before me,
41 Made my enemies turn tail before me,
My foes—and I wiped them out.
42 They looked,[a] but there was none to deliver;
To the LORD, but He answered them not.
43 I pounded them like dust of the earth,
Stamped, crushed them like dirt of the streets.
44 You have rescued me from the strife of peoples,[b]
[c-]Kept me to be[-c] a ruler of nations;
Peoples I knew not must serve me.
45 Aliens have cringed before me,
Paid me homage at the mere report of me.
46 Aliens have lost courage
[d-]And come trembling out of their fastnesses.[-d]

47 The LORD lives! Blessed is my rock!
Exalted be God, the rock
Who gives me victory;
48 The God who has vindicated me
And made peoples subject to me,
49 Rescued me from my enemies,
Raised me clear of my foes,
Saved me from lawless men!
50 For this I sing Your praise among the nations
And hymn Your name:
51 [e-]Tower of victory[-e] to His king,
Who deals graciously with His anointed,
With David and his offspring evermore.

23

These are the last words of David:

[f]The utterance of David son of Jesse,
The utterance of the man [g-]set on high,[-g]

a Ps. 18.42 "cried."
b So some mss. and the Septuagint; most mss. and the printed editions "my people."
c-c Ps. 18.44 "made me."
d-d Meaning of Heb. uncertain.
e-e Kethib *and Ps. 18.51 read "He accords wondrous victories."*
f Meaning of much of this poem (vv. 1–7) uncertain.
g-g *4QSam[a] reads "God raised up."*

39: The vanquisher could stand symbolically on the defeated enemy, who was literally under his *feet.* Placing one's foot upon the neck of the vanquished was a symbol of victory in the ancient Near East. **42:** This psalm even assumes that the enemy is monotheistic (see v. 32 n.); this may explain why it was connected to David's defeat of Saul, rather than other enemies such as the Philistines. **46:** *Lost courage,* lit. "wilted." **47:** *Rock,* a return at the end to the central opening image of vv. 2–3. **51:** *Tower of victory,* cf. Ps. 61.4. But the reading "he accords great victories" (Ps. 18.51) is preferable (in the Heb the difference between the two readings is very slight). *His anointed,* see 1 Sam. 2.10 n. This v. is part of the prayer Grace after Meals. *Evermore* is one common way to end a psalm.

23.1–7: Last words. Poems containing last words are also attributed to Jacob (Gen. ch 49) and Moses (Deut. ch 33). Given that the psalm looks forward to David's successors, it was imagined as his "last words." The present poem, ascribed to David, contrasts the just ruler, who is likened to light and beneficial rain, to the wicked, who are compared to harmful thorns. Contrasts between the righteous and the wicked are common in Proverbs and in some psalms (e.g., Ps. 1). **1:** *Utterance,* cf. Num. 24.3–4, 15 (in the Heb the same word is used). The rendering "the favorite of the Mighty One of Israel" (translators' note *a-a,* next p.) is preferable because it constitutes a parallel to *the anointed of the God of Jacob* (note the parallelisms in vv. 1–3). *Anointed,* see 22.51. The translation *the favorite of the songs of Israel* (see also translators' note *a-a*) helped give rise to the tradition that David composed the entire book of Psalms.

The anointed of the God of Jacob,
[a]The favorite of the songs of Israel:[-a]
2 The spirit of the LORD has spoken through me,
His message is on my tongue;
3 The God of Israel has spoken,
The Rock of Israel said concerning me:
"He who rules men justly,
He who rules in[b] awe of God
4 Is like the light of morning at sunrise,
A morning without clouds—
[c]Through sunshine and rain
[Bringing][-c] vegetation out of the earth."
5 Is not my House established before God?
For He has granted me an eternal pact,
Drawn up in full and secured.
Will He not cause all my success
And [my] every desire to blossom?
6 But the wicked shall all
Be raked aside like thorns;
For no one will take them in his hand.
7 Whoever touches them
Must arm himself with iron
And the shaft of a spear;
And they must be burned up on the spot.

8 These are the names[d] of David's warriors: Josheb-basshebeth, a Tahchemonite, the chief officer—he is Adino the Eznite; [e][he wielded his spear][-e] against eight hundred [f]and slew them[-f] on one occasion.

9 Next to him was Eleazar son of Dodo son of Ahohi. He was one of the three warriors with David when they defied the Philistines gathered there for battle. The Israelite soldiers retreated, 10 but he held his ground. He struck down Philistines until his arm grew tired and his hand stuck to his sword; and the LORD wrought a great victory that day. Then the troops came back to him—but only to strip [the slain].

11 Next to him was Shammah son of Age the Ararite. The Philistines had gathered [c]in force[-c] where there was a plot of ground full of lentils; and the troops fled from the Philistines. 12 But [Shammah] took his stand in the middle of the plot and defended it, and he routed the Philistines. Thus the LORD wrought a great victory.

a-a Or "The favorite of the Mighty One of Israel"; cf. Exod. 15.2. Others "The sweet singer of Israel." *b So many Heb. mss. Most mss. and the printed editions lack "in."*
c-c Meaning of Heb. uncertain.
d A number of these names, with variations, are found in 1 Chron. 11 and 27.
e-e Preserved in 1 Chron. 11.11; similarly some Septuagint mss. of 2 Sam.
f-f Lit. "slain."

2: David presents himself as a prophet; this is not expressed in the rest of the book, where he needed to consult prophets and oracles. Perhaps the sense of prophet here is an inspired singer, as Miriam was (see Exod. 15.20–21 n.). This, too, adds to the later tradition that David was divinely inspired to compose the psalms. **3:** *Rock,* see 22.47. A just ruler (all kings aimed to administer justice) shows himself to be God-fearing. Justice shines light on the world, like the sun. In Mesopotamia, Shamash, the sun god, is also the god of justice. **5:** The *eternal pact* refers to God's promise of an everlasting dynasty for David (7.16). **6:** *The wicked,* here, David's opponents. For a slightly different image of the wicked, see Ps. 1.4.

23.8–39: The heroes. The first part contains short stories, which are similar to the short accounts of 21.15–22. They also relate heroic feats of individual warriors and refer to David's early period. The second part merely contains the names of David's body of heroes, without their actions. The order is hierarchical: First the exploits of the highest in rank, "the three," are recorded, beginning with the chief officer; then those of two heroes who were prominent among "the thirty"—the main body—but did not attain to "the three"; finally the names of "the thirty" are listed. The text of this section is poorly preserved, and many variants are found in the ancient versions and in the parallel text in Chronicles. **8:** *Josheb-basshebeth,* an odd name. LXX reads "Iebosthe," "Ish-bosheth" (or "Ish-baal"). Instead of *he is Adino the Eznite,* 1 Chron. 11.11 reads "he wielded his spear" (see v. 18). Emendation yields "he wielded his ax" (the Semitic word for "ax" is similar in Heb to "the Eznite"). **9:** Instead of *when they defied,* 1 Chron. 11.13 reads "at Pas Dammim when" (note the following *there* and see 1 Sam. 17.1). **11:** Instead of *in force,* mss of LXX read "to Lehi," which is almost identical in Heb (note the following *there* and see Judg. 15.9).

13 [a]Once, during the harvest,[a] three of the thirty chiefs went down to David at the cave[b] of Adullam, while a force of Philistines was encamped in the Valley of Rephaim. 14 David was then in the stronghold,[b] and a Philistine garrison was then at Bethlehem. 15 David felt a craving and said, "If only I could get a drink of water from the cistern which is by the gate of Bethlehem!" 16 So the three warriors got through the Philistine camp and drew water from the cistern which is by the gate of Bethlehem, and they carried it back. But when they brought it to David he would not drink it, and he poured it out as a libation to the LORD. 17 For he said, "The LORD forbid that I should do this! Can [I drink][c] the blood of the men who went at the risk of their lives?" So he would not drink it. Such were the exploits of the three warriors.

18 Abishai, the brother of Joab son of Zeruiah, was head of [d]another three.[d] He once wielded his spear against three hundred [e]and slew them.[e] 19 He won a name among the three;[f] since he was the most highly regarded among the three,[f] he became their leader. However, he did not attain to the three.

20 Benaiah son of Jehoiada, from Kabzeel, was [g]a brave soldier[g] who performed great deeds. He killed the two [a][sons] of Ariel of Moab.[a] Once, on a snowy day, he went down into a pit and killed a lion. 21 He also killed an Egyptian, a huge[h] man. The Egyptian had a spear in his hand, yet [Benaiah] went down against him with a club, wrenched the spear out of the Egyptian's hand, and killed him with his own spear. 22 Such were the exploits of Benaiah son of Jehoiada; and he won a name among the three[f] warriors. 23 He was highly regarded among the thirty, but he did not attain to the three. David put him in charge of his bodyguard.[i]

24 Among the thirty were Asahel, the brother of Joab; Elhanan son of Dodo [from] Bethlehem, 25 Shammah the Harodite, Elika the Harodite, 26 Helez the Paltite, Ira son of Ikkesh from Tekoa, 27 Abiezer of Anathoth, Mebunnai the Hushathite, 28 Zalmon the Ahohite, Maharai the Netophathite, 29 Heleb son of Baanah the Netophathite, Ittai son of Ribai from Gibeah of the Benjaminites, 30 Benaiah of Pirathon, Hiddai of Nahale-gaash, 31 Abialbon the Arbathite, Azmaveth the Barhumite, 32 Eliahba of Shaalbon, sons of [a]Jashen, Jonathan,[a] 33 Shammah the Ararite, Ahiam son of Sharar the Ararite, 34 Eliphelet son of Ahasbai son of the Maacathite, Eliam son of Ahithophel the Gilonite,

13: *During the harvest,* i.e., in the hot, dry season of the summer. *Three,* probably the three heroes mentioned before. **15:** *Bethlehem,* David's hometown. **16:** As in the opening story of 1 Sam., that which is desired and most valuable is dedicated to God. **17:** Drinking the water would be like drinking the blood of the men, who risked their lives. **18:** The reading of Syriac is to be preferred (*another* does not occur in the Heb). **19:** The more plausible "thirty" instead of *three* (twice) is confirmed by v. 23. **20:** *Benaiah,* see 8.18. **24–39:** This list is presented, by and large, in concentric circles: most of the heroes are from Judah, and particularly from the region around Bethlehem, David's hometown. Some are from Benjamin and Ephraim, and the last-named are of foreign origin. **34:** *Ahithophel,* see 15.12.

a-a Meaning of Heb. uncertain. *b See note at 1 Sam. 22.1.*
c So Septuagint and 1 Chron. 11.19.
d-d Two Heb. mss. and Syriac read "the thirty"; cf. vv. 23–24. *e-e Lit. "slain."*
f Emendation yields "thirty." *g-g Heb. "the son of a brave soldier."*
h Meaning of Heb. uncertain. 1 Chron. 11.23 reads "a giant of a man."
i Meaning of Heb. uncertain.

35 Hezrai the Carmelite, Paarai the Arbite, 36 Igal son of Nathan
from Zobah, Bani the Gadite, 37 Zelek the Ammonite, Naharai
the Beerothite—the arms-bearer of Joab son of Zeruiah—38 Ira
the Ithrite, Gareb the Ithrite, 39 Uriah the Hittite: thirty-seven
in all.[a]

24 [b]The anger of the LORD again[c] flared up against Israel;
and He incited David against them, saying, "Go and
number Israel and Judah." 2 The king said to Joab, [d-]his army
commander,[-d] "Make the rounds of all the tribes of Israel, from
Dan to Beer-sheba, and take a census of the people, so that I
may know the size of the population." 3 Joab answered the king,
"May the LORD your God increase the number of the people a
hundredfold, while your own eyes see it! But why should my
lord king want this?" 4 However, the king's command to Joab
and to the officers of the army remained firm; and Joab and the
officers of the army set out, at the instance of the king, to take a
census of the people of Israel.

5 They crossed the Jordan and [e-]encamped at Aroer, on the
right side of the town, which is in the middle of the wadi of
Gad, and[-e] [went on] to Jazer. 6 They continued to Gilead and
to the region of [f-]Tahtim-hodshi, and they came to Dan-jaan
and around to[-f] Sidon. 7 They went onto the fortress of Tyre
and all the towns of the Hivites and Canaanites, and finished
at Beer-sheba in southern Judah. 8 They traversed the whole
country, and then they came back to Jerusalem at the end of
nine months and twenty days. 9 Joab reported to the king the
number of the people that had been recorded: in Israel there
were 800,000 soldiers ready to draw the sword, and the men of
Judah numbered 500,000.

10 But afterward David [g-]reproached himself[-g] for having
numbered the people. And David said to the LORD, "I have
sinned grievously in what I have done. Please, O LORD, remit
the guilt of Your servant, for I have acted foolishly." 11 When
David rose in the morning, the word of the LORD had come to
the prophet Gad, David's seer: 12 "Go and tell David, 'Thus said

a Septuagint and 1 Chron. 11 differ from the foregoing lists in vv. 8–38, and from each other in the number and forms of the names.

b This chapter is also found, with some variations, in 1 Chron. 21.1–7.

c Cf. above 21.1–14.

d-d 1 Chron. 21.2 reads "and to the officers of the army"; cf. below v. 4.

e-e Some Septuagint mss. read "began at Aroer, and from the town, which is ... Gad, they." *f-f Meaning of Heb. uncertain.*

g-g See note at 1 Sam. 24.6.

39: *Uriah,* see ch 11. *Thirty-seven:* Since only 36 names are mentioned, the name of Joab, who is conspicuous by his absence from the list, should probably be added (both his brothers are included). It may have been assumed or lost accidentally, or omitted due to the attitude toward Joab, who was responsible for Absalom's death in the previous stories (ch 18 and esp. 19.14).

24.1–25: Census, plague, and altar. These three topics, which are successively dealt with in the three parts of the narrative, are causally connected. David conducts a census, which is considered a sin. God then punishes Israel with a plague. To put an end to the plague, David erects an altar on the site where later the Temple will be built (according to 2 Chron. 3.1). Though the plague as well as its cessation result from actions by David, they are independently decided upon by God, hinting at both human responsibility and divine sovereignty. **1:** It is unknown what caused God's anger. In order to punish Israel He incites David to number the people; this raises the theological problem of God inciting to sin. The author of 1 Chron. 21.1 solves the problem by replacing God with Satan (a late biblical concept). Radak explains that inciting does not mean commanding, but only putting the idea in David's mind; therefore it remained David's decision whether actually to carry the census out. According to ancient belief counting people exposes them to misfortune. Exod. 30.11–16 requires each counted person to pay expiation money, so "that no plague may come upon them" (Rashi: "for the evil eye rules over counting"). **2:** The census is conducted for military purposes (see v. 9). *From Dan to Beer-sheba,* see 1 Sam. 3.20 n. **3:** Joab's objection serves as counterweight to God's incitement (cf. 1 Chron. 21.3). **5–7:** The census-takers follow the borderline, beginning in the southeast, going up to the north, from there to the west, and finishing in the south. **8:** It took a long time to count the large number of people. **9:** This number is exaggerated; it does not reflect the historical reality of the time of David. **10:** *Remit,* actually transfer (see 2 Sam. 12.13 n.), as the continuation of the text makes clear. **11:** *Gad,* first mentioned at 1 Sam. 22.5. **12:** *Thus said the LORD,* see 7.5 n.

the LORD: I hold three things over you; choose one of them,
and I will bring it upon you.' " 13 Gad came to David and told
him; he asked, "Shall a seven-year famine come upon you in
the land, or shall you be in flight from your adversaries for
three months while they pursue you, or shall there be three
days of pestilence in your land? Now consider carefully what
reply I shall take back to Him who sent me." 14 David said to
Gad, "I am in great distress. Let us fall into the hands of the
LORD, for His compassion is great; and let me not fall into the
hands of men."[a]

15 The LORD sent a pestilence upon Israel from morning [b]until the set time;[b] and 70,000 of the people died, from
Dan to Beer-sheba. 16 But when the angel extended his hand
against Jerusalem to destroy it, the LORD renounced further
punishment and said to the angel who was destroying the people, "Enough! Stay your hand!" The angel of the LORD was then
by the threshing floor of Araunah the Jebusite. 17 When David
saw the angel who was striking down the people, he said to the
LORD, "I alone am guilty, I alone have done wrong; but these
poor sheep, what have they done? Let Your hand fall upon me
and my father's house!"

18 Gad came to David the same day and said to him, "Go and
set up an altar to the LORD on the threshing floor of Araunah
the Jebusite." 19 David went up, following Gad's instructions, as
the LORD had commanded. 20 Araunah looked out and saw the
king and his courtiers approaching him.[c] So Araunah went out
and bowed low to the king, with his face to the ground. 21 And
Araunah asked, "Why has my lord the king come to his servant?" David replied, "To buy the threshing floor from you, that
I may build an altar to the LORD and that the plague against the
people may be checked." 22 And Araunah said to David, "Let
my lord the king take it and offer up whatever he sees fit. Here
are oxen for a burnt offering, and the threshing boards and the
gear of the oxen for wood. 23 All this, [b]O king,[b] Araunah gives
to Your Majesty. And may the LORD your God," Araunah added, "respond to you with favor!"

24 But the king replied to Araunah, "No, I will buy them from
you at a price. I cannot sacrifice to the LORD my God burnt
offerings that have cost me nothing." So David bought the

a *Septuagint adds "So David chose the pestilence. It was the time of the wheat harvest."*

b-b *Meaning of Heb. uncertain.*

c *4QSam^a and 1 Chron. 21.20 add "Araunah (Ornan) was threshing wheat."*

13: Instead of *seven-year,* LXX and 1 Chron. 21.12 read "three-year" (note the recurrence of the number three). These three punishments are imagined as commensurate and suitable expiation for the sin of the census. **14:** The expression *the hands* (lit. "hand") *of the LORD* points to pestilence (cf. Exod. 9.3). **16:** The *angel* is the Destroyer (see Exod. 12.23), who acts on the LORD's orders. The *threshing floor,* a flat area where the grain was removed from the ears and separated from the chaff. It was usually situated outside the city, near the gate. *Araunah,* one of the Jebusites, the Canaanite people who inhabited Jerusalem before David's conquest. It is unclear if the three-day period is over, if Jerusalem is to be spared, or if God has simply relented. **17:** David saw the destroying angel before the LORD ordered him to stop (v. 16). Instead of *I alone have done wrong* the Dead Sea manuscript 4QSam^a, some mss of LXX, and Josephus read: "I the shepherd have caused harm" (cf. 1 Chron. 21.17), in contradistinction to *these poor sheep.* David's pronouncement thus expresses objection to collective punishment, which is felt to be unjust, though he feels his *father's house* may be punished (see Exod. 34.7); though it is clear that wrong, as well as wise, decisions of rulers necessarily have repercussions on their peoples. **19:** *David went up:* Araunah's threshing floor was higher than David's residence, namely, on the mountain to the north of biblical Jerusalem (cf. 2 Chron. 3.1). **20:** The narrative's point of view switches to Araunah, who receives the king with great respect, and the notion that the Jebusites should be proscribed (Deut. 20.17) is absent. **22:** Araunah offers the king everything as a present, a customary part of negotiating in the East (cf. Gen. 23.11). *Threshing boards,* presumably wooden boards, having sharp iron teeth underneath, which were drawn by animals over the ears of grain. **23:** Araunah's exemplary piety also makes the site suitable for the Temple. **24:** The fact that David paid for the threshing floor and the oxen is strongly emphasized, to indicate that the Temple site was acquired by proper transaction and duly paid for (cf. Gen. ch 23). *Fifty shekels,* approximately 0.55 kg (slightly more than 1 pound). 1 Chron. 21.25 considerably magnifies that amount.

threshing floor and the oxen for fifty shekels of silver. [25] And David built there an altar to the LORD and sacrificed burnt offerings and offerings of well-being. The LORD responded to the plea for the land, and the plague against Israel was checked.

25: *The LORD responded to the plea for the land:* Cf. the similar ending of the narrative about the famine (21.14), suggesting that these stories were originally contiguous. According to v. 16 the LORD, acting independently, had already decided to renounce further punishment before David built the altar; either the vv. represent a different tradition, or they are meant to be read as an expansion of v. 16. The book of Samuel concludes with a pious deed of David: the acquisition and sanctification of the site of the Temple. This points ahead to Solomon, who will build the Temple in the following book, 1 Kings.

מלכים א

1 Kings

KINGS, THE LAST BOOK of the "Former Prophets," relates the history of Israel from the declining days of David (10th c.) through the beginning of the Babylonian exile. Its last verses describe the release of Jehoiachin, exiled king of Judah, from prison in Babylonia during the reign of Evil-merodach son of Nebuchadnezzar, an event datable through Babylonian sources to 562–561 BCE.

The division of Kings into two books is first attested in the LXX, the Greek version of the Bible, where it is combined with Samuel into a single four-part composition, *Basileiai* ("kingdoms" or "dynasties" or "reigns"). The division of Kings into two books was later followed in the Latin Vulgate version, and was adopted from there to vernacular Bible translations. Classical Jewish sources through the end of the Middle Ages do not make such a division, and it is first attested in Hebrew printed texts from the early 16th century, where it is noted as a division used by foreign translators. In the course of time, however, the division has been universally adopted by Jews as a matter of convention and convenience. This division splits the book into two more or less equal parts.

The narrative of Kings falls naturally into three sections followed by two brief additions. The first section (1 Kings chs 1–11) narrates the circumstances of Solomon's ascent to the throne and describes the source of his wisdom, his reign over all Israel in a united kingdom, and the building and furnishing of the Temple and other structures; it also evaluates his religious behavior. Solomon's life is represented in greater detail than that of other kings, and the author cites a special document, "the book of the Annals of Solomon" (1 Kings 11.41), whereas in the rest of the book he cites the annals of the kings of Judah and the annals of the kings of Israel. Its beginning is a natural continuation of 2 Samuel 20, and at some point, the two may have been joined. The second section (1 Kings ch 12–2 Kings ch 17) begins by recounting the circumstances under which the northern tribes rejected the authority of Solomon's son, Rehoboam, withdrew from his kingdom (henceforth called Judah), and formed another, called Israel, with a king of their choosing. From that point the narrative provides a synchronistic, overlapping history of the kings of Judah and Israel for almost two centuries until the Northern Kingdom was destroyed by Assyria in 722 BCE. The third section (2 Kings 18.1–25.21) describes the reigns of Davidic dynasts in Judah, the Southern Kingdom, until Babylonia conquered Judah, ruined Jerusalem, destroyed the Temple, and executed some and exiled others from among its leading citizens in 586 BCE. The first brief addition (2 Kings 25.22–26) tells of the appointment and assassination of Gedaliah, a native Israelite appointed administrator of Judah by the Babylonians; the second (2 Kings 25.27–30) adds a notice that Jehoiachin, the exiled king of Judah, was released from a Babylonian prison in the thirty-seventh year of exile.

Kings is not a history in the contemporary sense, that is, a factual description of past events and an explanation for their occurrence. It is, in the main, an extended theological essay written by a person or persons with passionately held beliefs, convinced that the destruction of the Northern Kingdom and the fall of the southern one were due to the misguided policies of their kings. The author described past events selectively, telescoping some and commenting extensively on others, using them as illustrations of the lessons that he believed they taught.

The author maintained that the LORD, the God of history, made His will known to Israel with regard to specific key issues, that punishments are preceded by warnings through prophets, and that people are responsible for the consequences of their choices. He further maintained that kings were responsible for the fate of their people. It was axiomatic for him that those ruling over the tribes of Israel were obligated to maintain the centrality of the Jerusalem Temple as the unique place where offerings acceptable to God might be made and to eliminate the illegitimate worship of any deity other than the LORD. The author's composition demonstrated how all northern and most southern kings failed to meet their obligations and how all adversity, from minor disasters to the final catastrophe, followed as a consequence of this failure. Somewhat contradictorily, he also took pains to note that despite this, the divine promise of an eternal dynasty to David (2 Sam. 7.11) was maintained out of God's love for David ("for the sake of ... David," 1 Kings 11.12; 2 Kings 8.19; 19.34).

The author expressed his axiomatic notions, described Josiah (2 Kings chs 22–23)—whom he regarded as best exemplifying what a king should be—and expressed his theme of the uniqueness of the Jerusalem Temple, in language closely tied to that of Deut. ch 12. Deuteronomy is the only book in the Torah to project an image of the ideal king (Deut. 17.14–20), who bears a striking resemblance to Josiah as depicted in Kings. The author's ideas about how God works in history parallel those of Deut. ch 28. For these reasons, contemporary scholarship refers to the author of Kings as a Deuteronomistic historian, i.e., as one who wrote under the influence of Deuteronomy, reflecting its concerns and ideology. In addition to sharing phrases found in Deuteronomy, the author also developed some unique expressions that are repeatedly used throughout Kings: worshipping foreign gods and serving them (1 Kings 9.6; 16.31; 2 Kings 17.35; 21.3, 21); on every high hill and under every leafy tree (1 Kings 14.23; 2 Kings 16.4; 17.10); idolatry as abhorrent (1 Kings 14.24; 2 Kings 16.3; 21.2, 11); detestable things (1 Kings 11.5, 7; 2 Kings 23.24); the city that the LORD has chosen (1 Kings 8.16, 44, 48; 11.13, 32, 36; 14.21; 2 Kings 21.7; 23.27); to build a House for the name of the LORD (1 Kings 3.2; 5.17, 19; 8.17, 18, 19, 20, 44); to sacrifice and offer at the open shrines (1 Kings 3.2, 3; 22.44; 2 Kings 12.4; 14.4; 15.4, 35; 16.4); to revere the LORD, i.e., serve God from a sense of awe (1 Kings 8.40, 43; 2 Kings 17.32, 33, 34, 39, 41).

The author cites by name three documents to which the original readers might refer for additional information about the kings discussed: Annals of Solomon (1 Kings 11.41); Annals of the Kings of Israel (1 Kings 14.19); Annals of the Kings of Judah (1 Kings 14.29). The formula used to introduce individual kings in the second section of Kings most likely draws regularly on a source that had chronological information about the reigns of the kings, perhaps from the annals mentioned above. He regularly added a formulaic evaluation of the kings reign that reflected his opinion: "In the ______ year of king ______ son of ______ of Israel/Judah, ______ son of ______ became king of Judah/Israel. He was ______ years old when he began to reign, and he reigned for ______ years. He did what was pleasing/displeasing to the LORD." The source also includes the names of the mothers of the kings of Judah (the queen mother).

Although no scholarly consensus exists concerning the nature of these documents, the author, by mentioning them, challenged readers to deny the veracity of the facts that he was evaluating and interpreting. In addition to these, he had access to documents bearing on the Davidic court (1 Kings chs 1–2) and the history of the Temple (1 Kings chs 6–7; 2 Kings ch 23), as well as to some form of edited materials by and about the prophet Isaiah (2 Kings 19.20–20.11), and to collections of prophetic stories that he interspersed in his narratives about the Northern Kingdom: Ahijah (1 Kings 11.29–14.18), Elijah (1 Kings 17.1–2 Kings 2.18), Micaiah (1 Kings

22.1–40), and Elisha (2 Kings 2.1–13.21). Although no copies of these specific sources survive, and we therefore cannot prove they existed, documents that match each type or genre of document are known from other literate, ancient Near Eastern cultures.

The author's sustained lesson about God's justice in history continues through the untimely death of Josiah in 2 Kings 23.25. This death stilled his voice. According to the author's philosophy, Josiah should not have died as he did. The deeds of that good king should have set things right, but did not. Scholars refer to this first author as Dtr^1, the first Deuteronomistic writer.

A second person, writing during the Babylonian exile, completed the book through 2 Kings 25.26. This writer attributed Josiah's death and every bad thing that happened subsequently to the sins of King Manasseh, a 7th-century Judean monarch. He inserted passages expressing this notion, combined with a prophetic idea that Israelites as a people bore collective responsibility for the fate of their kingdoms, into earlier parts of the book, contradicting the first author's original axiom of royal responsibility (2 Kings 21.10–15; 22.16–17). This second writer, called Dtr^2 by scholars, continued the narrative, appending terse notices about the last kings but describing only political events, not religious ones. The Annals of Judah are not cited after 2 Kings 24.5 and were most likely not needed because he was noting current events. This writer made no comments and found no lesson to teach in the destruction of Jerusalem.

The combined efforts of the original author and the second writer produced a document relevant to the post-destruction communities in both Judah and Babylonia. Their situation was explained as the outcome not only of the religious policies of their kings, who had violated ancient revealed teachings, but also of the behavior of their own ancestors. The implication of this didactic text was that the very facts of destruction and exile demonstrated the power of God, the validity of His covenant with Israel, and His meticulousness in maintaining it. Therefore, when the punishment of ruin and exile had run its course, His promises of restoration made in Deut. 30.1–5 and by different prophets could reasonably be expected to come to fruition. This message was especially important because of the viability of an alternate explanation, that Judah was exiled by the Babylonians because the Babylonian gods, headed by Marduk, were stronger than the Israelite God, YHVH.

At least 25 years after the destruction of Jerusalem, a third writer appended a few sentences to the composition, now the last three verses of the book. This person may have hoped that the event recorded, King Jehoiachin's release from prison, was the harbinger of coming changes in the fortunes of his people.

Jewish tradition has maintained, on the basis of statements in the Babylonian Talmud (*b. B. Bat.* 14b–15a), that the prophet Jeremiah, who prophesied from the time of Josiah until the exile, but lived beyond that (Jer. 1.2–3; chs 40–41), wrote Kings. This tradition may be based on the similarities between the final chapter of Kings and Jer. chs 25 and 52. As noted above, however, Kings has a much more complex history, and may not be attributed to a single individual; like most ancient Near Eastern compositions, its author is anonymous.

Even though it is a narrative about the past intended to inculcate religious values, and not an objective, analytical "history" in the modern sense, Kings does present historical data that its authors believed to be true and accurate according to the standards of the time. During the last half of the 20th century, a small group of biblical historians, known as "minimalists," and a few archaeologists challenged the veracity of some or all of its historical references and allusions, including questioning the existence of king David and Solomon as real historical figures.

By the beginning of the 21st century, however, comparative studies of biblical and ancient Near Eastern history writing in combination with new archeological discoveries, confirmed some details previously questioned, leading to a sense that the book as a whole is generally reliable. For example, thirteen foreign rulers mentioned in Kings, from the Egyptian Shishak

(1 Kings 11.40) through the Babylonian Evil-merodach (2 Kings 25.27) appear in their proper chronological order and historical horizon as determined by non-Israelite texts from the ancient world. Moreover, twelve kings from Israel and Judah, from David (1 Kings 1.1) through Jehoiachin (2 Kings 24.8; 25.27) are mentioned in non-Israelite texts in the same chronological order as they appear in Kings. In addition, archaeological finds provide data supporting indirectly the historicity of several narratives. Many of these sources are referred to in the annotations on specific verses. This new evidence does not suggest that all facts mentioned in Kings are historically accurate, but it does suggest that the book can be used as an important source for reconstructing the history of ancient Israel.

Kings was copied many times in the course of its transmission, and as the many differences between the Hebrew text and the LXX concerning number of years that kings reigned indicates, changes were made during this process. Sometimes these were introduced into the text intentionally and sometimes accidentally. This is not surprising, since mistakes inevitably occur in the process of transmission. As a result, the raw historical skeleton that the book provides may be considered dependable, even though it is not perfect. (See the essays and chart at the back of this volume: "The Bible in the Dead Sea Scrolls" [pp. 1850–59]; "Textual Criticism" [pp. 2149–52]; and "Chronological Table of Rulers" [pp. 2226–29].)

[ZIONY ZEVIT]

1 King David was now old, advanced in years; and though
they covered him with bedclothes, he never felt warm. 2 His
courtiers said to him, "Let a young virgin be sought for my lord
the king, to wait upon Your Majesty and be his attendant;[a] and
let her lie in your bosom, and my lord the king will be warm."
3 So they looked for a beautiful girl throughout the territory of
Israel. They found Abishag the Shunammite and brought her
to the king. 4 The girl was exceedingly beautiful. She became
the king's attendant[a] and waited upon him; but the king was
not intimate with her.

5 Now Adonijah son of Haggith [b-]went about boasting,[-b] "I will
be king!" He provided himself with chariots and horses,[c] and an
escort of fifty outrunners. 6 His father had never scolded him:

a Meaning of Heb. uncertain. *b-b Or "presumed to think."*

c Others "horsemen"; meaning of Heb. parash(im) *not always certain.*

1.1–2.46: How Solomon became king of Israel after David. The first two chs detail the turbulent events, most of which transpired in a single day, that resulted in Solomon, one of David's younger sons, ascending the throne of his father. The narrative line continues from 2 Sam. 20.26 and according to many scholars, is the conclusion of the succession narrative, an ancient source partially preserved in 2 Sam. that dealt with who will reign after David.

1.1–4: David weakens with age. David is portrayed as frail and dependent. Others advise him about caring for his essential needs. From 1.1 through 2.10, where his death is mentioned, the narrative implies that David was bedridden; see 1.47. **1:** Reference to a king of "byt dwd," the house or dynasty of David, was discovered in 1993 in an Aram. stele set up at Dan by an Aramean king during the mid-9th c. BCE. **2:** The warmth of a human body could have been provided by any of David's wives or concubines. Malbim suggests that his advisers didn't want him to be weakened further by sexual intercourse so they sought a suitable person with whom he would not have intercourse. **3:** *The Shunammite,* from the town of Shunem, in northern Israel. *Abishag* should not be confused with the woman whose dead son was revived by Elisha in 2 Kings 4.8–37. **4:** *Attendant,* the Heb denotes "caretaker" and nothing more. As a special servant, her presence was ignored by others, e.g., 1.15. Although she was present when David was in undignified circumstances, the author makes a point of indicating that they were not intimate. It is unclear, however, if this was common knowledge.

1.5–53: Adonijah's attempted usurpation of the throne and its aftermath. 5–6: Adonijah outfits himself with royal trappings and embarks on a program modeled after the failed one of his older brother Absalom (see 2 Sam. 15.1), to whom the author compares him, thereby implying that he would fail. After the violent deaths of his older brothers

"Why did you do that?" He was the one born after Absalom[a]
and, like him, was very handsome.
[7] He conferred with Joab son of Zeruiah and with the priest
Abiathar, and they supported Adonijah; [8] but the priest Zadok,
Benaiah son of Jehoiada, the prophet Nathan, Shimei and Rei,
and David's own fighting men did not side with Adonijah.
[9] Adonijah made a sacrificial feast of sheep, oxen, and fatlings
at the Zoheleth stone which is near En-rogel; he invited all his
brother princes[b] and all the king's courtiers of the tribe of Judah; [10] but he did not invite the prophet Nathan, or Benaiah, or
the fighting men, or his brother Solomon.
[11] Then Nathan said to Bathsheba, Solomon's mother, "You
must have heard that Adonijah son of Haggith has assumed
the kingship without the knowledge of our lord David. [12] Now
take my advice, so that you may save your life and the life of
your son Solomon. [13] Go immediately to King David and say
to him, 'Did not you, O lord king, swear to your maidservant:
"Your son Solomon shall succeed me as king, and he shall
sit upon my throne"? Then why has Adonijah become king?'
[14] While you are still there talking with the king, I will come in
after you and confirm your words."
[15] So Bathsheba went to the king in his chamber.—The
king was very old, and Abishag the Shunammite was waiting on the king.—[16] Bathsheba bowed low in homage to
the king; and the king asked, "What troubles you?" [17] She
answered him, "My lord, you yourself swore to your maidservant by the LORD your God: 'Your son Solomon shall
succeed me as king, and he shall sit upon my throne.' [18] Yet
now Adonijah has become king, and you,[c] my lord the king,
know nothing about it. [19] He has prepared a sacrificial feast
of a great many oxen, fatlings, and sheep, and he has invited all the king's sons and Abiathar the priest and Joab

a *Thus, Absalom having died, Adonijah was David's oldest living son.*
b *Lit. "all his brothers sons of the king."*
c *So many mss. and ancient versions; usual editions "now."*

Amnon and Absalom, and perhaps the natural death of Chileab, Adonijah was apparently the oldest of David's living sons and the main heir of his personal property (see 2 Sam. 3.2–5). **5:** *I will be king:* The monarchy was a recent innovation, so there was no tradition of royal primogeniture, nor were there laws governing the transmission of royal authority. Adonijah may have acted not only because he thought that the young Abishag could become pregnant and produce an heir that might be named successor, but also because the incapacitated David was not a reigning presence outside of the palace. **6:** *Was very handsome,* like Saul, he was qualified by his appearance to reign (see 1 Sam. 9.2; 16.12). **7:** *Joab* and *Abiathar,* supporters of David from his earliest days as an outlaw, may have become disaffected because of the erosion of their influence and prestige as some of their authority was assigned to others. See the list of officials in 2 Sam. 20.23–25. **8:** These were the loyalists of David's party who would do what David directed. **9:** En-Rogel, a spring southeast of Jerusalem in the Kidron Valley, out of sight of the city itself (2 Sam. 17.17). The plan calls for Adonijah to be confirmed king by an oligarchy of a priest, a general, princes, and tribal leaders (vv. 19, 25). **10:** By not inviting Solomon and his followers, whom he excludes from the "brother princes" and the "king's courtiers of the tribe of Judah," Adonijah is showing that he knew he was usurping Solomon's throne. **11–27:** Nathan's response to the plan. Nathan's motivation is not clarified by the author, but since he spurs Bathsheba to action by pointing out that her life and that of Solomon are in danger, he may have perceived that his life was in danger also. **12:** *Save your life:* Abravanel proposes that the danger lay in that Adonijah knew about David's promise to Bathsheba (v. 13) and that should he succeed, he would eliminate potential threats to his rule. **13:** The key to Nathan's plan is the oath David swore to her concerning Solomon. There is no earlier mention of this oath. On the basis of 2 Sam. 12.24–25, Radak infers that David swore this oath to Bathsheba after the death of their first child as a way of consoling her. Nathan would subsequently have learned of it from Bathsheba. Some interpreters suggest that Nathan and Bathsheba are taking advantage of David's feebleness to "plant" a memory so that he will act in the manner that they wish. **17–18:** Abravanel highlights the rhetorical flourishes of Bathsheba's calculated presentation: (1) She initiates conversation with an honorific, my lord. (2) Going beyond Nathan's words (v. 13), she states that David swore … *by the LORD your God,* so that his words must be considered not an idle promise to her but an oath to God. (3) She quotes and does not paraphrase David's promise, making it immediate in a historical present. (4) She emphasizes David's promise that Solomon would reign in the future so that it contrasts with her description of Adonijah reigning in the present.

commander of the army; but he has not invited your servant Solomon. 20 And so the eyes of all Israel are upon you, O lord king, to tell them who shall succeed my lord the king on the throne. 21 Otherwise, when my lord the king lies down with his fathers, my son Solomon and I will be regarded as traitors."

22 She was still talking to the king when the prophet Nathan arrived. 23 They announced to the king, "The prophet Nathan is here," and he entered the king's presence. Bowing low to the king with his face to the ground, 24 Nathan said, "O lord king, *a-*you must have said,*-a* 'Adonijah shall succeed me as king and he shall sit upon my throne.' 25 For he has gone down today and prepared a sacrificial feast of a great many oxen, fatlings, and sheep. He invited all the king's sons and the army officers and Abiathar the priest. At this very moment they are eating and drinking with him, and they are shouting, 'Long live King Adonijah!' 26 But he did not invite me your servant, or the priest Zadok, or Benaiah son of Jehoiada, or your servant Solomon. 27 Can this decision have come from my lord the king, without your telling your servant who is to succeed to the throne of my lord the king?"

28 King David's response was: "Summon Bathsheba!" She entered the king's presence and stood before the king. 29 And the king took an oath, saying, "As the LORD lives, who has rescued me from every trouble: 30 The oath I swore to you by the LORD, the God of Israel, that your son Solomon should succeed me as king and that he should sit upon my throne in my stead, I will fulfill this very day!" 31 Bathsheba bowed low in homage to the king with her face to the ground, and she said, "May my lord King David live forever!"

32 Then King David said, "Summon to me the priest Zadok, the prophet Nathan, and Benaiah son of Jehoiada." When they came before the king, 33 the king said to them, "Take *b-*my loyal soldiers,*-b* and have my son Solomon ride on my mule and bring him down to Gihon. 34 Let the priest Zadok and the prophet Nathan anoint him there king over Israel, whereupon you shall sound the horn and shout, 'Long live King Solomon!' 35 Then march up after him, and let him come in and sit on my throne. For he shall succeed me as king; him I designate to be ruler of Israel and Judah." 36 Benaiah son of Jehoiada spoke up and said to the king, "Amen! And may the LORD, the God of my lord the king, so ordain. 37 As the LORD was with my lord the king, so may He be with Solomon; and may He exalt his throne even higher than the throne of my lord King David."

a-a Or (cf. Rashi, Ralbag, Radak) "have you said ...?"
b-b Lit. "your lord's men."

28: *Summon Bathsheba:* Since Bathsheba was already there (v. 22), this is an indication that different accounts, one with Nathan taking the lead, the other with Bathsheba, have been combined. **29:** *Every trouble* refers to the rebellions against David narrated at the end of 2 Sam.; the events narrated here were likely the culmination of that story. **30:** David repeats, with some embellishment, the oath quoted by Bathsheba (v. 17) but purposely misquoted by Nathan (v. 24) to spur David's response. David, changes "the LORD your God" to *the LORD, the God of Israel* and adds *in my stead* at the end, a concluding phrase which, apparently, he remembered but that they had forgotten. Whether or not he ever swore this oath (see vv. 17–18 n.) he makes it appear that he knew he had. Although feeble, he is neither forgetful nor witless. Informed, he proves capable of decisive action. **32–39:** At David's command and under the protection of David's personal guard, *the Cherethites and the Pelethites* (see v. 38 n.), Solomon is confirmed king by an oligarchy of a priest, a general, and a prophet. The anointing ceremony (cf. 1 Sam. 10.1), a performative act whereby a man becomes king (see 1 Sam. 10.1 n.), takes place by the Gihon spring in the Kidron Valley just below the city wall; all the people by their acclamation confirm the choice. **33:** *My mule:* Ancient convention disallowed casual use of royal property. David's provision of his own animal confirms that Solomon's accession to the throne is indeed supported by David and is not a partisan act (see v. 44 and Esth. 6.6–11).

[38] Then the priest Zadok, and the prophet Nathan, and Benaiah son of Jehoiada went down with the Cherethites and the Pelethites. They had Solomon ride on King David's mule and they led him to Gihon. [39] The priest Zadok took the horn of oil from the Tent and anointed Solomon. They sounded the horn and all the people shouted, "Long live King Solomon!" [40] All the people then marched up behind him, playing on flutes and making merry till the earth was split open by the uproar.

[41] Adonijah and all the guests who were with him, who had just finished eating, heard it. When Joab heard the sound of the horn, he said, "Why is the city in such an uproar?" [42] He was still speaking when the priest Jonathan son of Abiathar arrived. "Come in," said Adonijah. "You are a worthy man, and you surely bring good news." [43] But Jonathan replied to Adonijah, "Alas, our lord King David has made Solomon king! [44] The king sent with him the priest Zadok and the prophet Nathan and Benaiah son of Jehoiada, and the Cherethites and Pelethites. They had him ride on the king's mule, [45] and the priest Zadok and the prophet Nathan anointed him king at Gihon. Then they came up from there making merry, and the city went into an uproar. That's the noise you heard. [46] Further, Solomon seated himself on the royal throne; [47] further, the king's courtiers came to congratulate our lord King David, saying, 'May God make the renown of Solomon even greater than yours, and may He exalt his throne even higher than yours!' And the king bowed low on his couch. [48] And further, this is what the king said, 'Praised be the LORD, the God of Israel who has this day provided a successor to my throne, while my own eyes can see it.' " [49] Thereupon, all of Adonijah's guests rose in alarm and each went his own way.

[50] Adonijah, in fear of Solomon, went at once [to the Tent] and grasped the horns of the altar. [51] It was reported to Solomon: "Adonijah is in fear of King Solomon and has grasped the horns of the altar, saying, 'Let King Solomon first swear to me that he will not put his servant to the sword.' " [52] Solomon said, "If he behaves worthily, not a hair of his head shall fall to the ground; but if he is caught in any offense, he shall die." [53] So King Solomon sent and had him taken down from the altar. He came and bowed before King Solomon, and Solomon said to him, "Go home."

2 When David's life was drawing to a close, he instructed his son Solomon as follows: [2] "I am going the way of all the earth; be strong and show yourself a man. [3] Keep the charge of the LORD your God, walking in His ways and following His laws, His commandments, His rules, and His

38: *Cherethites and the Pelethites,* Aegean mercenaries in David's personal service with no ties of loyalty to anybody other than him (see 2 Sam. 8.18; 20.23). The former group may have come from Crete; the origins of the latter are uncertain. **48:** A loose paraphrase of the oath in v. 30. **50:** *Horns of the altar,* projections from each corner of the top surface. Blood of purification sacrifices was usually daubed on the horns. Taking hold of them was a way for an individual who believed himself innocent of a capital crime to claim sanctuary (see Exod. 21.13–14 n.). **51:** *Let King Solomon ... swear:* Adonijah acknowledges not only that Solomon is king, but that he, Adonijah, is his servant.

2.1–46: Solomon guarantees the throne for himself. 1–12: David counsels Solomon to follow the norms established by God to maintain the promise of an everlasting dynasty, and asks Solomon to execute David's vengeance on Joab, act kindly toward descendants of a former benefactor, and kill one who had insulted him, all on David's behalf. These actions would eliminate Solomon's potential enemies and protect his supporters. **1–4:** The author (Dtr^{2}) introduces the theme of a conditional promise to David of a dynasty. There is some tension between this version of the promise and the unconditional promise of Dtr^{1} in 2 Sam. 7.11–16 and the ancient poem in 2 Sam. 23.5. The "Teaching ["torah"] of Moses" refers to Deut. (cf. Deut. 4.44–45), which contains instructions about a future king (Deut. 17.14–20). In general, whenever Kings refers to this teaching, Deut. is meant (see 2 Kings 14.5–6 n.)

admonitions as recorded in the Teaching of Moses, in order that you may succeed in whatever you undertake and wherever you turn. 4 Then the LORD will fulfill the promise that He made concerning me: 'If your descendants are scrupulous in their conduct, and walk before Me faithfully, with all their heart and soul, [a-]your line on the throne of Israel shall never end!'[-a]

5 "Further, you know what Joab son of Zeruiah did to me, what he did to the two commanders of Israel's forces, Abner son of Ner and Amasa son of Jether: he killed them, shedding[b] blood of war in peacetime, staining the girdle of his loins and the sandals on his feet with blood of war.[c] 6 So act in accordance with your wisdom, and see that his white hair does not go down to Sheol in peace.

7 "But deal graciously with the sons of Barzillai the Gileadite, for they befriended me when I fled from your brother Absalom; let them be among those that eat at your table.[d]

8 "You must also deal with Shimei son of Gera, the Benjaminite from Bahurim. He insulted me outrageously when I was on my way to Mahanaim; but he came down to meet me at the Jordan,[e] and I swore to him by the LORD: 'I will not put you to the sword.' 9 So do not let him go unpunished; for you are a wise man and you will know how to deal with him and send his gray hair down to Sheol in blood."

10 So David slept with his fathers, and he was buried in the City of David. 11 The length of David's reign over Israel was forty years: he reigned seven years in Hebron, and he reigned thirty-three years in Jerusalem. 12 And Solomon sat upon the throne of his father David, and his rule was firmly established.

13 Adonijah son of Haggith came to see Bathsheba, Solomon's mother. She said, "Do you come with friendly intent?" "Yes," he replied; 14 and he continued, "I would like to have a word with you." "Speak up," she said. 15 Then he said, "You know that the kingship was rightly mine and that all Israel wanted me to reign. But the kingship passed on to my brother; it came to him by the will of the LORD. 16 And now I have one request to make of you; do not refuse me." She said, "Speak up." 17 He replied, "Please ask King Solomon—for he won't refuse you—to give me Abishag the Shunammite as wife." 18 "Very well," said Bathsheba, "I will speak to the king in your behalf."

19 So Bathsheba went to King Solomon to speak to him about Adonijah. The king rose to greet her and bowed down to her.

5: Joab's murderous self-interested acts could not be addressed at the time (2 Sam. 3.27–39; 20.8–10). **6:** *Sheol* is the underworld, where all the dead go. **7:** *Barzillai* aided David selflessly during Absalom's revolt (2 Sam. 19.32–40). **8–9:** *Shimei* cursed David during Absalom's revolt (2 Sam. 16.5–8; 19.22–24). The import of v. 9 is "You do what I was unable to do owing to an oath that circumstances compelled me to take." **10–12:** David dies, and Solomon, having served as co-regent with his father for an undisclosed period of time, ascends his father's throne as sole monarch, his authority firmly established, but only in principle. **11:** Chronological information about David's reign (see 2 Sam. 5.5) forms an inclusion around the stories about him as king. *Forty years:* Solomon also reigned forty years (11.42). The number may be typological, indicating an indeterminate but ideal, long period of time: The catastrophic rain of the deluge lasted forty days and nights (Gen. 7.12), and Israelites were in the desert forty years. **12:** Solomon is the only king whose *rule was firmly established.* **13–23:** Adonijah's incipient insurrection and its aftermath. **15:** Adonijah paints himself as pious, citing *the will of the LORD.* **17:** Adonijah's request is hardly innocent. He plans to take as wife one who, so far as the public knew, may have been intimate with David. (See 1.4 n.) This is tantamount to usurping the throne, as is clear from Solomon's response in v. 22. Compare Absalom's action in 2 Sam. 16.21–22. **19:** Solomon's actions toward Bathsheba indicate her high staus as queen mother.

a-a Lit. "there shall never cease to be a man of yours on the throne of Israel." Cf. 2 Sam. 7.12–16. *b Meaning of Heb. uncertain.*
c I.e., Joab had thus brought bloodguilt on David's house; see 2 Sam. 3.27 and 20.10.
d I.e., for whose maintenance you provide; see 2 Sam. 19.32 ff.
e See 2 Sam. 16.5 ff; 19.17 ff.

He sat on his throne; and he had a throne placed for the queen
mother, and she sat on his right. 20 She said, "I have one small
request to make of you, do not refuse me." He responded, "Ask,
Mother; I shall not refuse you." 21 Then she said, "Let Abishag
the Shunammite be given to your brother Adonijah as wife."
22 The king replied to his mother, "Why request Abishag the
Shunammite for Adonijah? Request the kingship for him! For
he is my older brother, [a-]and the priest Abiathar and Joab son
of Zeruiah are on his side."[-a]
23 Thereupon, King Solomon swore by the LORD, saying, "So
may God do to me and even more, if broaching this matter
does not cost Adonijah his life! 24 Now, as the LORD lives, who
has established me and set me on the throne of my father David and who has provided him[b] with a house, as he promised,
Adonijah shall be put to death this very day!" 25 And Solomon
instructed Benaiah son of Jehoiada, who struck Adonijah[c]
down; and so he died.
26 To the priest Abiathar, the king said, "Go to your estate at
Anathoth! You deserve to die, but I shall not put you to death at
this time, because you carried the Ark of my Lord GOD before
my father David and because you shared all the hardships that
my father endured." 27 So Solomon dismissed Abiathar from
his office of priest of the LORD—thus fulfilling what the LORD
had spoken at Shiloh[d] regarding the house of Eli.
28 When the news reached Joab, he fled to the Tent of the
LORD and grasped the horns of the altar—for Joab had sided
with Adonijah, though he had not sided with Absalom. 29 King
Solomon was told that Joab had fled to the Tent of the LORD
and that he was there by the altar; so Solomon sent Benaiah
son of Jehoiada, saying, "Go and strike him down." 30 Benaiah
went to the Tent of the LORD and said to him, "Thus said the
king: Come out!" "No!" he replied; "I will die here." Benaiah
reported back to the king that Joab had answered thus and
thus, 31 and the king said, "Do just as he said; strike him down
and bury him, and remove guilt from me and my father's
house for the blood of the innocent that Joab has shed. 32 Thus
the LORD will bring his blood guilt down upon his own head,
because, unbeknown to my father, he struck down with the
sword two men more righteous and honorable than he—Abner son of Ner, the army commander of Israel, and Amasa son
of Jether, the army commander of Judah. 33 May the guilt for
their blood come down upon the head of Joab and his descendants forever, and may good fortune from the LORD be
granted forever to David and his descendants, his house and
his throne." 34 So Benaiah son of Jehoiada went up and struck

22: Solomon sees through the ploy and responds to her ironically at first. Although the meaning of the end of the v. is unclear, Solomon's mention of *Abiathar* and *Joab* indicates that he discerns a potential plot against him. **23–25:** Solomon goes further than his father's advice and has his main rival, Adonijah, killed. **24:** House ("bayit") is an allusion to the dynastic promise in 2 Sam. ch 7, which uses "bayit" as a leitwort. **26–27:** Solomon banishes *Abiathar* to *Anathoth,* a Levitical city north of Jerusalem. The author interprets Solomon's decision as fulfillment of a prophetic oracle delivered against Abiathar's ancestor (1 Sam. 2.30–36). Prophecy and fulfillment is a major theme of the Deuteronomistic History. For the author, human events and divine causality are intertwined. Abravanel suggests that Solomon's reason for not executing Abiathar rings hollow; the true reason, unstated in the text, is that Solomon did not want to call down on himself misfortunes such as those that visited Saul after he executed Abiathar's relatives, the priests at Nob (1 Sam. 22.17–19). **28:** *Horns of the altar,* see 1.50 n. **30–31:** *I will die here:* Solomon cleverly misconstrues Joab's intemperate statement as a request which thereby nullifies the sanctuary of the altar. Ostensibly convinced by Solomon's words, Benaiah returns and kills Joab on the spot. This text is unconcerned with the ritual impurity that would have resulted from a corpse in the sanctuary.

a-a Lit. "And for him and for Abiathar and for Joab son of Zeruiah." Meaning of Heb. uncertain. *b Heb. "me."* *c Heb. "him."* *d Cf. 1 Sam. 3.14.*

him down. And he was buried at his home in the wilderness.
35 In his place, the king appointed Benaiah son of Jehoiada
over the army, and in place of Abiathar, the king appointed
the priest Zadok.
36 Then the king summoned Shimei and said to him, "Build
yourself a house in Jerusalem and stay there—do not ever go
out from there anywhere else. 37 On the very day that you go
out and cross the Wadi Kidron, you can be sure that you will
die; your blood shall be on your own head." 38 "That is fair,"
said Shimei to the king, "your servant will do just as my lord
the king has spoken." And for a long time, Shimei remained in
Jerusalem.
39 Three years later, two slaves of Shimei ran away to King
Achish son of Maacah of Gath. Shimei was told, "Your slaves
are in Gath." 40 Shimei thereupon saddled his ass and went to
Achish in Gath to claim his slaves; and Shimei returned from
Gath with his slaves. 41 Solomon was told that Shimei had gone
from Jerusalem to Gath and back, 42 and the king summoned
Shimei and said to him, "Did I not adjure you by the LORD and
warn you, 'On the very day that you leave and go anywhere
else, you can be sure that you will die,' and did you not say to
me, 'It is fair; I accept'? 43 Why did you not abide by the oath
before the LORD and by the orders which I gave you?" 44 The
king said further to Shimei, "You know all the wrong, which
you remember very well, that you did to my father David. Now
the LORD brings down your wrongdoing upon your own head.
45 But King Solomon shall be blessed, and the throne of David
shall be established before the LORD forever."
46 The king gave orders to Benaiah son of Jehoiada and he
went out and struck Shimei[a] down; and so he died.
Thus the kingdom was secured in Solomon's hands.

3 Solomon allied himself by marriage with Pharaoh king of
Egypt. He married Pharaoh's daughter and brought her to
the City of David [to live there] until he had finished building
his palace, and the House of the LORD, and the walls around
Jerusalem.
2 The people, however, continued to offer sacrifices at the
open shrines, because up to that time no house had been built
for the name of the LORD. 3 And Solomon, though he loved the
LORD and followed the practices of his father David, also sacrificed and offered at the shrines.
4 The king went to Gibeon to sacrifice there, for that was the
largest shrine; on that altar Solomon presented a thousand
burnt offerings. 5 At Gibeon the LORD appeared to Solomon in
a dream by night; and God said, "Ask, what shall I grant you?"

a *Heb. "him."*

36–46: *Shimei,* a Benjaminite (Saul's tribe: 1 Sam. 9.1–2), was not only a former enemy of David but also, therefore, a potential enemy of his dynasty in the future. **37:** *Wadi Kidron,* the valley just to the east of the city wall. A wadi is a seasonal watercourse. **39–40:** Shimei's trip indicates that relationships between Solomon and Achish were such that a man from Jerusalem was able to have his runaway slaves extradited from Philistia. **45:** Immediately before his death, Shimei reaffirms the Davidic covenant of 2 Sam. ch 7. **46:** Through the death and banishment of internal enemies, in partial fulfillment of David's requests, Solomon secured the reins of power over his kingdom.

3.1–4: Introduction. Brief comments introducing themes and ideas developed later in the book. **1:** After consolidating authority among his own people, Solomon turned to establishing strategic political alliances with neighboring kingdoms through diplomatic marriages. Since Egyptian sources indicate it is unlikely that the actual *daughter* of a reigning pharaoh would have been given in marriage to a non-Egyptian, "daughter" may refer to a woman closely related to or descended from the royal family. The names of the pharaoh and the woman are not mentioned. She lived in the *City of David* only until Solomon built her a palace elsewhere. This brief notice anticipates the more detailed versions of Solomon's construction projects (chs 7–8) and also the problems caused by Solomon's foreign wives (ch 11); it may form a frame with 9.24–25, demarcating a unit in which Solomon fulfills God's commands and is blessed. **2–3:** *Open shrines:* The author is apologetic about Solomon's participation in rites at these places (Heb "bamot"), usually translated "high places," even though Deut. did not prohibit their use until after the construction of the Temple (Deut. 12.4–12). In describing events transpiring after the Temple was built, the author condemns worship at such shrines.

6 Solomon said, "You dealt most graciously with Your servant my father David, because he walked before You in faithfulness and righteousness and in integrity of heart. You have continued this great kindness to him by giving him a son to occupy his throne, as is now the case. 7 And now, O LORD my God, You have made Your servant king in place of my father David; but I am a young lad, [a-]with no experience in leadership.[-a] 8 Your servant finds himself in the midst of the people You have chosen, a people too numerous to be numbered or counted. 9 Grant, then, Your servant an understanding mind to judge Your people, to distinguish between good and bad; for who can judge this vast people of Yours?"

10 The Lord was pleased that Solomon had asked for this. 11 And God said to him, "Because you asked for this—you did not ask for long life, you did not ask for riches, you did not ask for the life of your enemies, but you asked for discernment in dispensing justice—12 I now do as you have spoken. I grant you a wise and discerning mind; there has never been anyone like you before, nor will anyone like you arise again. 13 And I also grant you what you did not ask for—both riches and glory all your life—the like of which no king has ever had. 14 And I will further grant you long life, if you will walk in My ways and observe My laws and commandments, as did your father David."

15 Then Solomon awoke: it was a dream! He went to Jerusalem, stood before the Ark of the Covenant of the LORD, and sacrificed burnt offerings and presented offerings of well-being; and he made a banquet for all his courtiers.

16 Later two prostitutes came to the king and stood before him. 17 The first woman said, "Please, my lord! This woman and I live in the same house; and I gave birth to a child while she was in the house. 18 On the third day after I was delivered, this woman also gave birth to a child. We were alone; there was no one else with us in the house, just the two of us in the house. 19 During the night this woman's child died, because she lay on it. 20 She arose in the night and took my son from my side while your maidservant was asleep, and laid him in her bosom; and she laid her dead son in my bosom. 21 When I arose in the morning to nurse my son, there he was, dead; but when I looked at him closely in the morning, it was not the son I had borne."

22 The other woman spoke up, "No, the live one is my son, and the dead one is yours!" But the first insisted, "No, the dead boy is yours; mine is the live one!" And they went on arguing before the king.

a-a Lit. "do not know to go out and come in"; cf. Num. 27.17.

Their mention here introduces the next section.

3.4–15: The dream at the large open shrine at Gibeon, northwest of Jerusalem, and four divine grants. **4–5:** The story may be describing a ritual of incubation attested elsewhere in ancient literature. A person seeking guidance would sleep in a sanctuary or holy spot in the hope of a divine visitation in a dream. The huge number of offerings *(a thousand)* reflects both Solomon's wealth and piety. **9:** *Understanding mind,* Heb "lev shome'a," lit. "listening heart." *Judge,* Heb "lishpot," also connotes leading, guiding, administering, or ruling. **10–14:** The four grants: wisdom, riches, glory, and a long life. A block of narratives, 3.16–10.29, demonstrates how these promises were fulfilled. **11:** *Ask* is repeated five times, emphasizing the wisdom of Solomion's request; by making the right request, he gets both what he asked for, and everything else that a king might need.

3.16–28: The case of the two prostitutes demonstrates Solomon's judicial wisdom. There was no male head of household to adjudicate the case, so it was taken to the king, who also served as a judge.

[23] The king said, "One says, 'This is my son, the live one, and
the dead one is yours'; and the other says, 'No, the dead boy is
yours, mine is the live one.' [24] So the king gave the order, "Fetch
me a sword." A sword was brought before the king, [25] and the
king said, "Cut the live child in two, and give half to one and
half to the other."

[26] But the woman whose son was the live one pleaded with
the king, for she was overcome with compassion for her son.
"Please, my lord," she cried, "give her the live child; only don't
kill it!" The other insisted, "It shall be neither yours nor mine;
cut it in two!" [27] Then the king spoke up. "Give the live child to
her," he said, "and do not put it to death; she is its mother."

[28] When all Israel heard the decision that the king had rendered, they stood in awe of the king; for they saw that he possessed divine wisdom to execute justice.

4 King Solomon was now king over all Israel. [2] These were
his officials:

Azariah son of Zadok—the priest;
3 Elihoreph and Ahijah sons of Shisha—scribes;
Jehoshaphat son of Ahilud—recorder;
4 Benaiah son of Jehoiada—over the army;
Zadok and Abiathar—priests;
5 Azariah son of Nathan—in charge of the prefects;
Zabud son of Nathan the priest—companion of the king;
6 Ahishar—in charge of the palace; and
Adoniram son of Abda—in charge of the forced labor.

[7] Solomon had twelve prefects governing all Israel, who pro-
vided food for the king and his household; each had to provide
food for one month in the year. [8] And these were their names:
Ben-hur, in the hill country of Ephraim; [9] Ben-deker, in Makaz,
Shaalbim, Beth-shemesh, and Elon-beth-hanan; [10] Ben-hesed
in Arubboth—he governed Socho and all the Hepher area;
[11] Ben-abinadab, [in] all of Naphath-dor (Solomon's daughter
Taphath was his wife); [12] Baana son of Ahilud [in] Taanach and
Megiddo and all Beth-shean, which is beside Zarethan, below
Jezreel—from Beth-shean to Abel-meholah as far as the other
side of Jokmeam; [13] Ben-geber, in Ramoth-gilead—he governed the villages of Jair son of Manasseh which are in Gilead,
and he also governed the district of Argob which is in Bashan,
sixty large towns with walls and bronze bars; [14] Ahinadab son
of Iddo, in Mahanaim; [15] Ahimaaz, in Naphtali (he too took a
daughter of Solomon—Basemath—to wife); [16] Baanah son of
Hushi, in Asher and Bealoth;[a] [17] Jehoshaphat son of Paruah,

a Or *"in Aloth."*

23: *One says ... the other says ... :* Solomon discerns a distinctive pattern in each woman's speech: The more loquacious one emphasizes death first while the other emphasizes life. Solomon intuits who is the mother of the living child and announces it circumspectly. **24–26:** Since justice requires a more convincing demonstration of truthfulness, Solomon stages a confrontation in which the passionate public behavior of the mother emphasizing life validates his intuition.

4.1–20: Solomon's bureaucracy for the administration of Israel demonstrates other applications of his wisdom. 2–6: A list of Solomon's high officials. His administration is more complex than that of David (cf. 2 Sam. 20.23–26) and includes new offices. This list contains some obvious inconsistencies: *Azariah son of Zadok* is listed as holding the office of *priest,* as are *Zadok and Abiathar;* the latter was deposed (2.27). It may combine two lists from different periods in Solomon's reign. The exact function of many of these officials is uncertain. **7–19:** Although the *twelve prefects* correspond to the number of tribes, the territories of some prefectures did not follow tribal boundaries. This may have been an attempt by Solomon to weaken the authority of tribal organization in the interest of making Jerusalem more central. Judah is not mentioned in this list unless the first word of v. 20 is considered the last word of v. 19. The last part of v. 19 would then be translated: "and one prefect who was in the land of Judah." See 5.7–8 on the reason for this division of the kingdom. **13:** *The villages of Jair* must have been an important place; two different biblical stories explain the origin of their name (Deut. 3.14 [Num. 32.41] and Judg. 10.4). **19:** On the incorporation of *the country of Sihon ... and Og,* see Num. 32.33. **20:** The author informs readers that despite the bureaucracy, both *Judah*—a term used anachronistically here to refer to what would become the Southern Kingdom—and Israel, the tribes north of Judah, lacked nothing and were content.

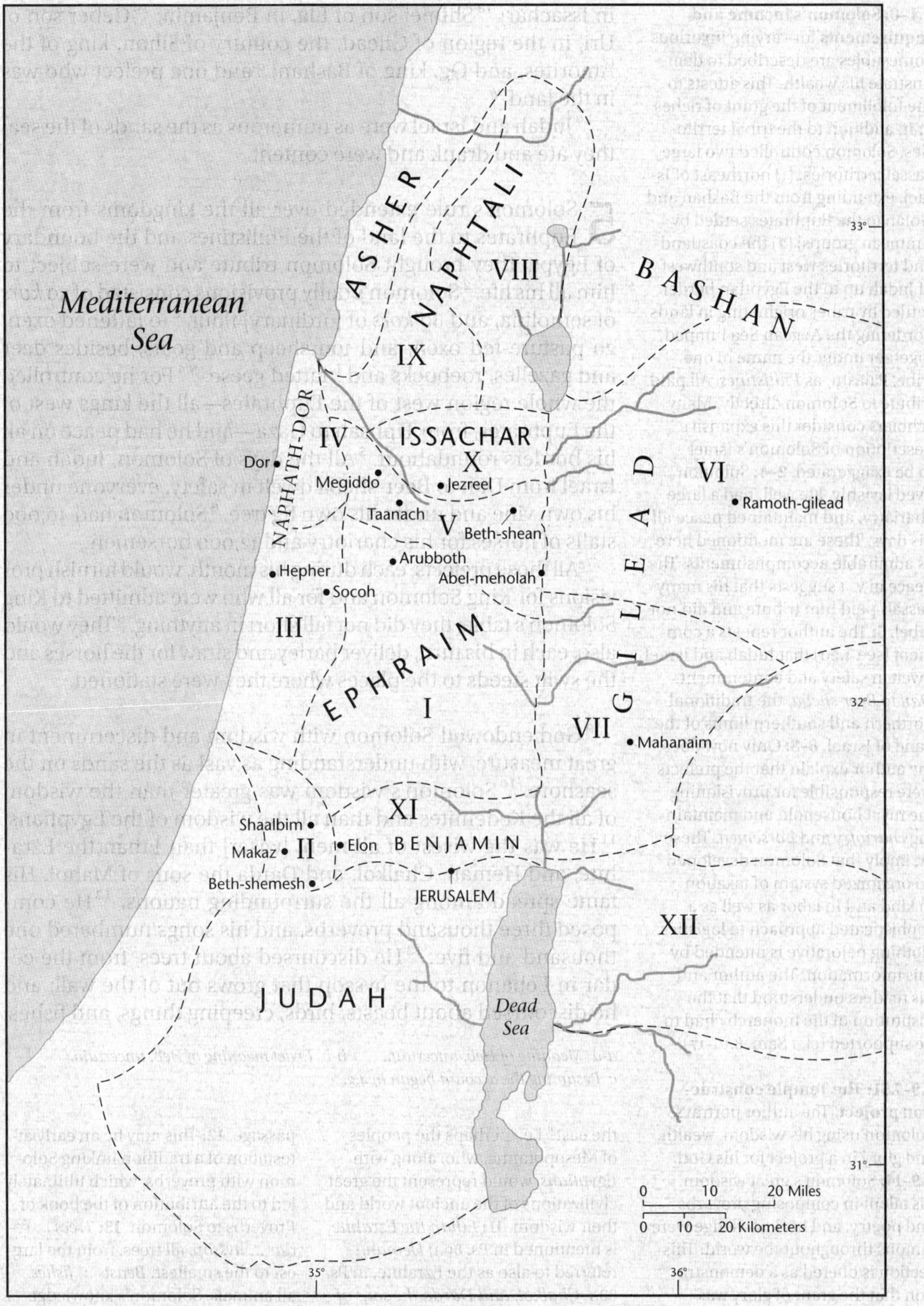

Solomon's twelve administrative districts according to First Kings ch 4

in Issachar; 18 Shimei son of Ela, in Benjamin; 19 Geber son of Uri, in the region of Gilead, the country of Sihon, king of the Amorites, and Og, king of Bashan; [a-]and one prefect who was in the land.[-a]

20 Judah and Israel were as numerous as the sands of the sea; they ate and drank and were content.

5 Solomon's rule extended over all the kingdoms from the Euphrates to the land of the Philistines and the boundary of Egypt. They brought Solomon tribute and were subject to him all his life. 2 Solomon's daily provisions consisted of 30 *kors* of semolina, and 60 *kors* of [ordinary] flour, 3 10 fattened oxen, 20 pasture-fed oxen, and 100 sheep and goats, besides deer and gazelles, roebucks and [b-]fatted geese.[-b] 4 For he controlled the whole region west of the Euphrates—all the kings west of the Euphrates, from Tiphsah to Gaza—and he had peace on all his borders roundabout. 5 All the days of Solomon, Judah and Israel from Dan to Beer-sheba dwelt in safety, everyone under his own vine and under his own fig tree. 6 Solomon had 40,000 stalls of horses for his chariotry and 12,000 horsemen.

7[c] All those prefects, each during his month, would furnish provisions for King Solomon and for all who were admitted to King Solomon's table; they did not fall short in anything. 8 They would also, each in his turn, deliver barley and straw for the horses and the swift steeds to the places where they were stationed.

9 God endowed Solomon with wisdom and discernment in great measure, with understanding as vast as the sands on the seashore. 10 Solomon's wisdom was greater than the wisdom of all the Kedemites and than all the wisdom of the Egyptians. 11 He was the wisest of all men: [wiser] than Ethan the Ezrahite, and Heman, Chalkol, and Darda the sons of Mahol. His fame spread among all the surrounding nations. 12 He composed three thousand proverbs, and his songs numbered one thousand and five. 13 He discoursed about trees, from the cedar in Lebanon to the hyssop that grows out of the wall; and he discoursed about beasts, birds, creeping things, and fishes.

a-a Meaning of Heb. uncertain. *b-b Exact meaning of Heb. uncertain.*
c Resuming the account begun in 4.2.

5.1–8: Solomon's income and requirements for varying luxurious comestibles are described to demonstrate his wealth. This attests to the fulfillment of the grant of riches. **1:** In addition to the tribal territories, Solomon controlled two large vassal territories: (1) northeast of Israel, extending from the Bashan and Golan to the Euphrates settled by Aramean groups; (2) the coastland and territories west and southwest of Judah up to the Egyptian border settled by tribes originating in lands bordering the Aegean Sea lumped together under the name of one tribe, Palastu, as *Philistines*. All paid tribute to Solomon directly. Many scholars consider this expansive description of Solomon's Israel to be exaggerated. **2–4:** Solomon lived lavishly, ate well, had a large chariotry, and maintained peace all his days. These are mentioned here as admirable accomplishments. The peace in v. 4 suggests that his many vassals paid him tribute and did not rebel. **5:** The author repeats a comment (see 4.20) that Judah and Israel dwelt in safety and contentment. *Dan to Beer-sheba,* the traditional northern and southern limits of the Land of Israel. **6–8:** Only now does the author explain that the prefects were responsible for provisioning the royal household and maintaining *chariotry* and *horsemen*. These vv. imply that Solomon developed an organized system of taxation in kind and in labor as well as a sophisticated approach to logistics. Nothing pejorative is intended by this information. The author and his readers understood that the institution of the monarchy had to be supported (cf. 1 Sam. 8.10–17).

5.9–7.51: The Temple construction project. The author portrays Solomon using his wisdom, wealth, and glory in a project for his God. **5.9–14:** Solomon's great wisdom, his talent in composing proverbs and poetry, and his knowledge were famous throughout the world. This section is offered as a demonstration that the grant of glory was fulfilled. **10:** *Kedemites,* "people of the east," i.e., perhaps the peoples of Mesopotamia, who, along with *Egyptians,* would represent the great civilizations of the ancient world and their wisdom. **11:** *Ethan the Ezrahite* is mentioned in Ps. 89.1; *Heman,* referred to also as the Ezrahite, in Ps. 88.1. *Chalkol, and Darda the sons of Mahol* are not known outside of this passage. **12:** This may be an early attestation of a tradition linking Solomon with proverbs, which ultimately led to the attribution of the book of Proverbs to Solomon. **13:** *Trees ... cedar ... hyssop,* all trees, from the largest to the smallest. *Beasts ... fishes,* all animals. Solomon's knowledge was encyclopedic.

14 Men of all peoples came to hear Solomon's wisdom, [sent] by all the kings of the earth who had heard of his wisdom.

15 King Hiram of Tyre sent his officials to Solomon when he heard that he had been anointed king in place of his father; for Hiram had always been a friend of David. 16 Solomon sent this message to Hiram: 17 "You know that my father David could not build a house for the name of the LORD his God because of the enemies[a] that encompassed him, until the LORD had placed them under the soles of his feet. 18 But now the LORD my God has given me respite all around; there is no adversary and no mischance. 19 And so I propose to build a house for the name of the LORD my God, as the LORD promised my father David, saying, 'Your son, whom I will set on your throne in your place, shall build the house for My name.' 20 Please, then, give orders for cedars to be cut for me in the Lebanon. My servants will work with yours, and I will pay you any wages you may ask for your servants; for as you know, there is none among us who knows how to cut timber like the Sidonians."

21 When Hiram heard Solomon's message, he was overjoyed. "Praised be the LORD this day," he said, "for granting David a wise son to govern this great people." 22 So Hiram sent word to Solomon: "I have your message; I will supply all the cedar and cypress logs you require. 23 My servants will bring them down to the sea from the Lebanon; and at the sea I will make them into floats and [deliver them] to any place that you designate to me. There I shall break them up for you to carry away. You, in turn, will supply the food I require for my household." 24 So Hiram kept Solomon provided with all the cedar and cypress wood he required, 25 and Solomon delivered to Hiram 20,000 *kors* of wheat as provisions for his household and [b]20 *kors*[b] of beaten oil. Such was Solomon's annual payment to Hiram.

26 The LORD had given Solomon wisdom, as He had promised him. There was friendship between Hiram and Solomon, and the two of them made a treaty.

27 King Solomon imposed forced labor on all Israel; the levy came to 30,000 men. 28 He sent them to the Lebanon in shifts of 10,000 a month: they would spend one month in the Lebanon and two months at home. Adoniram was in charge of the forced labor. 29 Solomon also had 70,000 porters and 80,000 quarriers in the hills, 30 apart from Solomon's 3,300 officials who were in charge of the work and supervised the gangs doing the work.

a Heb. "war"; cf. Targum. *b-b Septuagint reads, "20,000 baths."*

15: *Hiram of Tyre,* who had supplied wood for David's palace (2 Sam. 5.11–12), was king of the two leading Phoenician city-states, Sidon and Tyre, north of Israel. The Phoenicians were important sea traders, exporting lumber from the Lebanese hinterland east to Mesopotamia and down the coast to Egypt. The following vv. depict Hiram as an equal treaty partner, not a vassal of Solomon. **17:** *David could not build:* According to 2 Sam. 7.5–7, the LORD forbade David to build a Temple. **18:** The respite is referred to in 2 Sam. ch 7, as a precondition for building the Temple. **19:** The Temple is for God's *name,* not God's physical presence; see Deut. 12.5 n. **20–31:** International trade in the ancient Near East was a royal monopoly. Solomon guarantees to provide food for Hiram's household annually for an unspecified number of years (vv. 23, 25) in return for cypress and cedar logs, their transport to a Mediterranean landing place, their manufacture on shore into lumber (vv. 19, 22–23), and, apparently, the loan of master masons and stone cutters (vv. 31–32). **25:** Kor, the largest dry measure used in Israel, is estimated to have been 6.5 bushels or about 230 liters. The tradition preserved in the LXX that Solomon supplied 20,000 "baths" of olive oil, a liquid measure, is preferable to what is found in the MT. A "bath" is estimated to have been 6 gallons or 23 liters. **27–30:** Solomon exploits his prerogative to have *Adoniram* conscript a labor corps of *30,000* workers for work on a rotational basis as lumberjacks in *Lebanon.* (See a different tradition in 9.20–22.) The remaining 150,000 workers may have been paid.

31 The king ordered huge blocks of choice stone to be quarried, so that the foundations of the house might be laid with hewn stones. 32 Solomon's masons, Hiram's masons, and the men of Gebal shaped them. Thus the timber and the stones for building the house were made ready.

6 In the four hundred and eightieth year after the Israelites left the land of Egypt, in the month of Ziv—that is, the second month—in the fourth year of his reign over Israel, Solomon began to build the House of the LORD. 2 The House which King Solomon built for the LORD was 60 cubits long, 20 cubits wide, and 30 cubits high. 3 The portico in front of the Great Hall of the House was 20 cubits long—along the width of the House—and 10 cubits deep to the front of the House. 4 [a]He made windows for the House, recessed and latticed. 5 Against the outside wall of the House—the outside walls of the House enclosing the Great Hall and the Shrine[b]—he built a storied structure; and he made side chambers all around. 6 The lowest story was 5 cubits wide, the middle one 6 cubits wide, and the third 7 cubits wide; for he had provided recesses around the outside of the House so as not to penetrate the walls of the House.

7 When the House was built, only finished stones cut at the quarry were used, so that no hammer or ax or any iron tool was heard in the House while it was being built.

8 The entrance to the middle[c] [story of] the side chambers was on the right side of the House; and winding stairs led up to the middle chambers, and from the middle chambers to the third story. 9 When he finished building the House, [d]he paneled the House with beams and planks of cedar.[-d] 10 He built the storied structure against the entire House—each story 5 cubits high, so that it encased the House with timbers of cedar.

11 Then the word of the LORD came to Solomon, 12 "With regard to this House you are building—if you follow My laws and observe My rules and faithfully keep My commandments, I will fulfill for you the promise that I gave to your father David: 13 I will abide among the children of Israel, and I will never forsake My people Israel."

14 When Solomon had completed the construction of the House, 15 he paneled the walls of the House on the inside with

a Meaning of parts of vv. 4–6 uncertain.
b I.e., the inner sanctuary, designated in v. 16 and elsewhere as the "Holy of Holies."
c Septuagint and Targum read "lowest." *d-d Meaning of Heb. uncertain.*

6.1–38: Building the Temple. **1:** Solomon's fourth year, determined on the basis of the chronology of Tyrian kings provided by Josephus and Assyro-Tyrian synchronisms, was 968 BCE. This would date the exodus to 1448 BCE, a date most scholars consider too early. If, however, 480 years are a figurative way of indicating 12 generations, and an actual generation is 25 years, the exodus would be dated to 1268 BCE. Alternatively, it may be an approximation of the period from Joshua to the beginning of Solomon's reign, based on the chronology found in Joshua-Samuel. The Canaanite month name, Ziv, is the same as "Iyar," the month name adopted by Jews after the Babylonian exile. The second month on a spring-based calendar, it corresponds to April-May. **2:** The *cubit*, an ancient measure of length that contemporary scholars think was equal to approximately 0.5 m or 18 in. **2–36:** The main building was a tripartite, rectangular structure *20 cubits* (perhaps 30 ft) *wide* consisting of a *portico* (v. 3) and a main building entered through a doorway (v. 33) divided into a *40-cubit*-long entrance hall (v. 17) and a *20-cubit*-square inner shrine blocked by chained doors from the hall (vv. 20–21, 31–32). The tripartite floor plan of Solomon's Temple is paralleled by an 8th-c. BCE temple excavated at Tel Tainat, while some of its structural and internal designs have parallels in a temple at Ain Dara, both in Syria. The Temple was a relatively small structure, more of a royal chapel than a large public building. It shares some similarities with the Tabernacle, a much smaller temporary structure that, according to the Torah's Priestly tradition, traveled with Israel in the wilderness, whose construction is described in Exod. chs 25–40. **5–8:** A three-story store building enveloped the main Temple on three sides, buttressing and protecting it as well as providing some massiveness to the sparse structure. **7:** See Deut. 27.5–6; later Jewish legend suggested that Solomon found and employed, the Shamir, perhaps a special worm, to cut the stones of the Temple (*b. Sot.* 48b). **13:** See similarly concerning the construction of the Tabernacle, Exod. 25.8. **15–22:** The interior of the main building was floored, paneled, decorated, and *overlaid ... with gold* (see also vv. 29–30). Although some consider this description to be exaggerated, the study of almost contemporary ancient Near Eastern

planks of cedar. He also overlaid the walls on the inside with
wood, from the floor of the House to the ceiling. And he overlaid the floor of the House with planks of cypress. 16 Twenty
cubits from the rear of the House, he built [a partition] of cedar
planks from the floor to the walls;[a] he furnished its interior to
serve as a shrine, as the Holy of Holies. 17 [b]The front part of the
House, that is, the Great Hall, measured 40 cubits. 18 The cedar
of the interior of the House had carvings of gourds and calyxes;
it was all cedar, no stone was exposed. 19 In the innermost part
of the House, he fixed a Shrine in which to place the Ark of the
LORD's Covenant. 20 [c-]The interior of the[-c] Shrine was 20 cubits
long, 20 cubits wide, and 20 cubits high. He overlaid it with solid gold; he similarly overlaid [its] cedar altar. 21 Solomon overlaid the interior of the House with solid gold; and he inserted
golden chains [d-]into the door of[-d] the Shrine. He overlaid [the

a Septuagint reads "rafters." *b Meaning of vv. 17–22 is unclear in part.*
c-c I.e., the inner sanctuary, designated in v. 16 and elsewhere as the "Holy of Holies."
d-d Heb. "in front of."

culture supports its likelihood. In Mesopotamian documents ranging from about 2400 to 539 BCE different rulers proclaim that they covered the walls and doors of their temples with gold and silver, while Egyptian documents indicate that pharaohs living between 1550 and 1152 did likewise. **19:** Compare the placement of the *Ark* in the Holy of Holies (the Priestly source's name for *the innermost part of the House*) in the Tabernacle (Exod. 40.20–21). **23:** *Cherubim:* The "im" ending is a Heb plural marker; compare the reference to cherubs in the description of the Tabernacle in Exod. 25.18–19. A "cherub" was a mythical, composite animal, often represented with a human face, eagle wings, and a lion's body. Cherubim were considered guardian figures. Solomon not

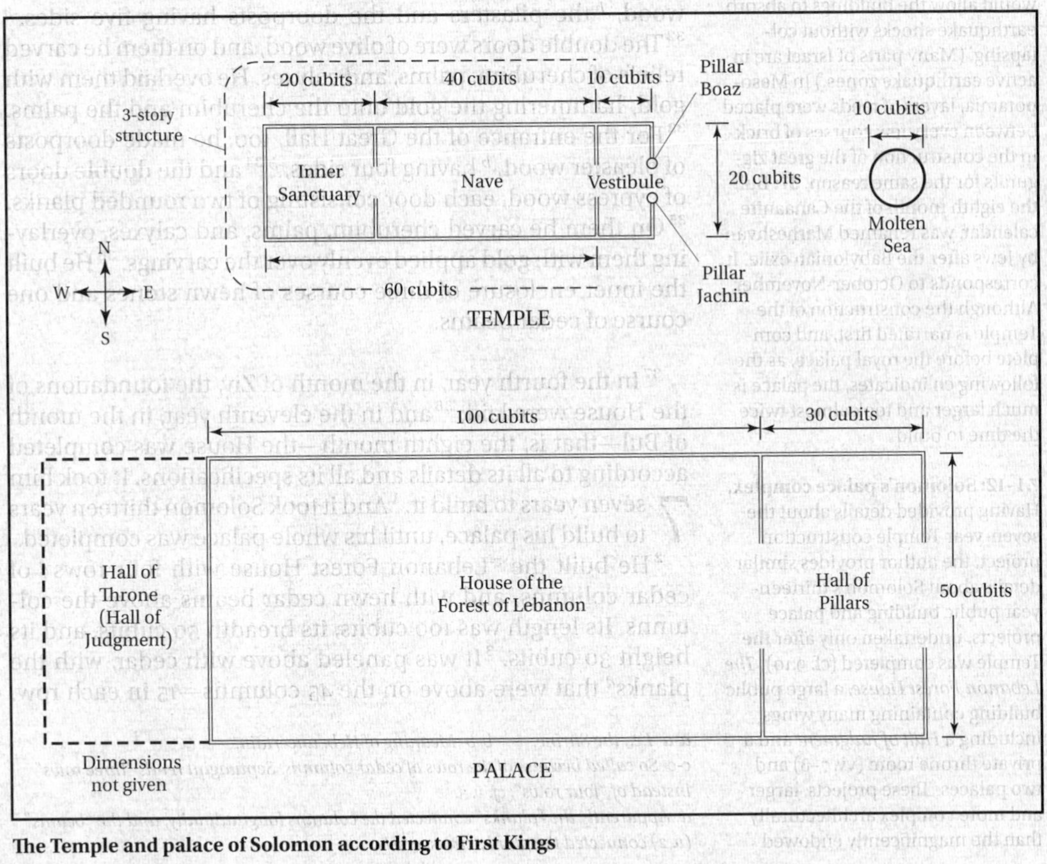

The Temple and palace of Solomon according to First Kings

Shrine] with gold, 22 so that the entire House was overlaid with gold; he even overlaid with gold the entire altar of the Shrine. And so the entire House was completed.

23 In the Shrine he made two cherubim of olive wood, each 10 cubits high. 24 [One] had a wing measuring 5 cubits and another wing measuring 5 cubits, so that the spread from wingtip to wingtip was 10 cubits; 25 and the wingspread of the other cherub was also 10 cubits. The two cherubim had the same measurements and proportions: 26 the height of the one cherub was 10 cubits, and so was that of the other cherub.

27 He placed the cherubim inside the [a]inner chamber.[-a] Since the wings of the cherubim were extended, a wing of the one touched one wall and a wing of the other touched the other wall, while their wings in the center of the chamber touched each other. 28 He overlaid the cherubim with gold. 29 All over the walls of the House, of both the inner area and the outer area, he carved reliefs of cherubim, palms, and calyxes, 30 and he overlaid the floor of the House with gold, both the inner and the outer areas.

31 For the entrance of the Shrine he made doors of olive wood, [b]the pilasters and the doorposts having five sides.[-b] 32 The double doors were of olive wood, and on them he carved reliefs of cherubim, palms, and calyxes. He overlaid them with gold, hammering the gold onto the cherubim and the palms. 33 For the entrance of the Great Hall, too, he made doorposts of oleaster wood, [b]having four sides,[-b] 34 and the double doors of cypress wood, each door consisting of two rounded planks. 35 On them he carved cherubim, palms, and calyxes, overlaying them with gold applied evenly over the carvings. 36 He built the inner enclosure of three courses of hewn stones and one course of cedar beams.

37 In the fourth year, in the month of Ziv, the foundations of the House were laid; 38 and in the eleventh year, in the month of Bul—that is, the eighth month—the House was completed according to all its details and all its specifications. It took him seven years to build it.

7 1 And it took Solomon thirteen years to build his palace, until his whole palace was completed.

2 He built the [c]Lebanon Forest House with four rows[-c] of cedar columns, and with hewn cedar beams above the columns. Its length was 100 cubits, its breadth 50 cubits, and its height 30 cubits. 3 It was paneled above with cedar, with the planks[d] that were above on the 45 columns—15 in each row.

a-a I.e., the Shrine. *b-b Meaning of Heb. uncertain.*
c-c So called because of the rows of cedar columns. Septuagint reads "three rows" instead of "four rows"; cf. v. 3.
d Apparently the "planks" connected the columns longitudinally, and the "beams" (v. 2) connected the planks transversely.

only placed two three-dimensional cherubim in the Holy of Holies, but also had them carved in relief on the two sets of doors in the main building (vv. 32, 35). Cherub images are attested on various ancient Near Eastern artifacts, including carved ivory panels used to decorate furniture from Samaria and on two clay cult stands from excavations at Taanach. They were also carved into the sides of the throne used by Hiram of Tyre, as illustrated on his excavated sarcophagus; this may suggest that in the Temple as well the cherubim served as the throne of (the invisible) God. In Jewish tradition they came to symbolize the Presence of God. **36:** Israeli archeologists have excavated stone structures and fortification walls in which horizontal courses of wood beams were laid intermittently between courses of stones. These would allow the buildings to absorb earthquake shocks without collapsing. (Many parts of Israel are in active earthquake zones.) In Mesopotamia, layers of reeds were placed between every few courses of brick in the construction of the great ziggurats for the same reason. **37:** Bul, the eighth month of the Canaanite calendar, was renamed Marḥeshvan by Jews after the Babylonian exile. It corresponds to October-November. Although the construction of the Temple is narrated first, and complete before the royal palace, as the following ch indicates, the palace is much larger and took almost twice the time to build.

7.1–12: Solomon's palace complex. Having provided details about the seven-year Temple construction project, the author provides similar details about Solomon's thirteen-year public building and palace projects, undertaken only after the Temple was completed (cf. 9.10). *The Lebanon Forest House,* a large public building containing many wings including a *Hall of Judgment* and a private throne room (vv. 7–8) and two palaces. These projects, larger and more complex architecturally than the magnificently endowed

4 And there were three rows of window frames, with three tiers of windows facing each other. 5 All the doorways and doorposts[a] had square frames—with three tiers of windows facing each other.

6 He made the portico of columns 50 cubits long and 30 cubits wide; [b-]the portico was in front of [the columns], and there were columns with a canopy in front of them.[-b] 7 He made the throne portico, where he was to pronounce judgment—the Hall of Judgment. It was paneled with cedar from floor to floor.[c]

8 The house that he used as a residence, in the rear courtyard, back of the portico, was of the same construction. Solomon also constructed a palace like that portico for the daughter of Pharaoh, whom he had married.

9 All these buildings, from foundation to coping and all the way out to the great courtyard, were of choice stones, hewn according to measure, smooth on all sides.[d] 10 The foundations were huge blocks of choice stone, stones of 10 cubits and stones of 8 cubits; 11 and above were choice stones, hewn according to measure, and cedar wood. 12 The large surrounding courtyard had three tiers of hewn stone and a row of cedar beams, the same as for the inner court of the House of the LORD, and for the portico of the House.

13 King Solomon sent for Hiram and brought him down from Tyre. 14 He was the son of a widow of the tribe of Naphtali, and his father had been a Tyrian, a coppersmith. He was endowed with skill, ability, and talent for executing all work in bronze.[e] He came to King Solomon and executed all his work. 15 He cast two columns of bronze; one column was 18 cubits high and measured 12 cubits in circumference, [and similarly] the other column. 16 He made two capitals, cast in bronze, to be set upon the two columns, the height of each of the two capitals being 5 cubits; 17 also nets of meshwork with festoons of chainwork for the capitals that were on the top of the columns, seven for each of the two capitals. 18 He made the columns[f] so that there were two rows [of pomegranates] encircling the top of the one network, to cover the capitals that were on the top of the pomegranates;[g] and he did the same for [the network on] the second capital. 19 The capitals upon the columns of the portico were of lily design, 4 cubits high; 20 so also the capitals upon the two columns extended above and

a Septuagint reads "windows." *b-b Meaning of Heb. uncertain.*
c Syriac reads "rafters." *d Lit. "sawed with a saw in the inside and outside."*
e Heb. neḥosheth *means both copper and bronze. In the translation "copper" is ordinarily used to denote the natural product and "bronze" for the artifacts.*
f Two Heb. mss. read "pomegranates." *g About fifty Heb. mss. read "columns."*

Temple, intending to accommodate large numbers of people, necessitated pillars. In combination, both projects attest to Solomon's skill as a designer-contractor.

7.13–51: Furnishing the Temple. The author returns to the main line of his narrative. **13–14:** *Hiram,* not the king of Tyre. This Hiram, a bronzeworker living in Tyre, is accounted to the northern tribe of *Naphtali* through his deceased father. This artisan plays a role similar to that of Bezalel in the construction of the tent-shrine in the wilderness (Exod. 36.1; 37.1). His specialty appears to have been the ability to cast very large, curved and spherical objects (cf. 7.46). *Bronze,* an alloy (usually) of copper and tin. As translators' note *e* points out, Heb makes no distinction between pure copper and copper alloys such as bronze. Pure copper is too soft, however, to make an effective "pillar." **15–22:** The two specially made bronze pillars, manufactured after the Temple's completion, lacked any structural purpose. Their function may have been symbolically decorative. On the basis of 2 Chron. 3.17, artistic reconstructions often represent them as freestanding either near the entrance of the Temple or at the front edge of the portico. The consonants of the Heb names *Jachin* and *Boaz* (v. 21) may be read as a sentence meaning "May He establish in strength." The pillars may have comprised a visible prayer asking that God care either for the Temple or for the dynasty. (2 Kings 11.14; 23.3 may support the latter interpretation even though they mention only one pillar.) Shrine models excavated in the Levant show such freestanding pillars.

next to the bulge[a] that was beside the network. There were 200 pomegranates in rows around the top of the second capital.[b]
21 He set up the columns at the portico of the Great Hall; he set up one column on the right and named it Jachin, and he set up the other column on the left and named it Boaz. 22 Upon the top of the columns there was a lily design. Thus the work of the columns was completed.

23 Then he made the tank[c] of cast metal, 10 cubits across from brim to brim, completely round; it was 5 cubits high, and it measured 30 cubits in circumference. 24 There were gourds below the brim completely encircling it—ten to a cubit, encircling the tank; the gourds were in two rows, cast in one piece with it. 25 It stood upon twelve oxen: three facing north, three facing west, three facing south, and three facing east, with the tank resting upon them; their haunches were all turned inward. 26 It was a handbreadth thick, and its brim was made like that of a cup, like the petals of a lily. Its capacity was 2,000 *baths*.

27 He made the ten laver stands of bronze. The length of each laver stand was 4 cubits and the width 4 cubits, and the height was 3 cubits. 28 The structure of the laver stands was as follows: They had insets,[d] and there were insets within the frames;
29 and on the insets within the frames were lions, oxen, and cherubim. Above the frames was a stand; and both above and below the lions and the oxen were spirals of hammered metal.
30 Each laver stand had four bronze wheels and [two] bronze axletrees. Its four legs had brackets; the brackets were under the laver, cast [e-]with spirals beyond each.[-e] 31 Its funnel, within the crown, rose a cubit above it; this funnel was round, in the fashion of a stand, a cubit and a half in diameter. On the funnel too there were carvings.

But the insets were square, not round. 32 And below the insets were the four wheels. The axletrees of the wheels were [fixed] in the laver stand, and the height of each wheel was a cubit and a half. 33 The structure of the wheels was like the structure of chariot wheels; and their axletrees, their rims, their spokes, and their hubs were all of cast metal. 34 Four brackets ran to the four corners of each laver stand; the brackets were of a piece with the laver stand. 35 At the top of the laver stand was a round band half a cubit high, and together with the top of the laver stand; its sides and its insets were of one piece with it.
36 [e-]On its surface—on its sides—and on its insets [Hiram] engraved cherubim, lions, and palms, as the clear space on each allowed,[-e] with spirals roundabout. 37 It was after this manner that he made the ten laver stands, all of them cast alike, of the

23–26: The elevated tank provided water under pressure so that the priests could wash conveniently without having to draw water from Temple cisterns (2 Chron. 4.6). The text does not indicate how water was released from the tank or how it was filled. The tank's design, mounted on the back of twelve oxen, actually bulls, facing the cardinal points of the compass, may have been symbolically meaningful. **23:** A comparison of the tank's diameter and circumference indicates that the author used 3 as the value of pi. Assuming the correctness of the diameter, the circumference was almost 31.5 cubits (14.4 m or 47 ft). **27–39:** Hiram also made ten lavers and ten intricately designed rolling stands for the washing of sacrificial parts (cf. 2 Chron. 4.6). The inclusion of mythical cherubs along with bulls and lions in the side frames of the *stands* suggests that they too conveyed some symbolic message (v. 29). Bronze models of such stands have been found in excavations on Cyprus and in Israel.

a Lit. "belly"; exact force of Heb. uncertain. *b I.e., each of the two capitals.*
c Lit. "sea." *d Emendation yields "frames."* *e-e Meaning of Heb. uncertain.*

same measure and the same form. [38]Then he made ten bronze lavers, one laver on each of the ten laver stands, each laver measuring 4 cubits and each laver containing forty *baths*.

[39]He disposed the laver stands, five at the right side of the House and five at its left side; and the tank he placed on the right side of the House, at the southeast [corner].

[40]Hiram also made the lavers, the scrapers, and the sprinkling bowls.

So Hiram finished all the work that he had been doing for King Solomon on the House of the LORD: [41]the two columns, the two globes of the capitals upon the columns; and the two pieces of network to cover the two globes of the capitals upon the columns; [42]the four hundred pomegranates for the two pieces of network, two rows of pomegranates for each network, to cover the two globes of the capitals upon the columns; [43]the ten stands and the ten lavers upon the stands; [44]the one tank with the twelve oxen underneath the tank; [45]the pails, the scrapers, and the sprinkling bowls. All those vessels in the House of the LORD that Hiram made for King Solomon were of burnished bronze. [46]The king had them cast [a-]in earthen molds,[-a] in the plain of the Jordan between Succoth and Zarethan. [47]Solomon left all the vessels [unweighed] because of their very great quantity; the weight of the bronze was not reckoned.

[48]And Solomon made all the furnishings that were in the House of the LORD: the altar, of gold; the table for the bread of display, of gold; [49]the lampstands—five on the right side and five on the left—in front of the Shrine, of solid gold; and the petals, lamps, and tongs, of gold; [50]the basins, snuffers, sprinkling bowls, ladles, and fire pans, of solid gold; and the hinge sockets for the doors of the innermost part of the House, the Holy of Holies, and for the doors of the Great Hall of the House, of gold.

[51]When all the work that King Solomon had done in the House of the LORD was completed, Solomon brought in the sacred donations of his father David—the silver, the gold, and the vessels—and deposited them in the treasury of the House of the LORD.

8 Then Solomon convoked the elders of Israel—all the heads of the tribes and the ancestral chieftains of the Israelites—before King Solomon in Jerusalem, to bring up the Ark of the Covenant of the LORD from the City of David, that is, Zion.

a-a Lit. "in the thick of the earth."

48–49: In contrast to the bronze vessels and implements manufactured for use in the courtyard and on the altar in front of the Temple, those intended for use within the Temple itself were made from or covered with gold. The metals themselves indicated gradations of holiness. **48–49:** These vv. show particular affinity to the Priestly Tabernacle account in Exod. **51:** For *the sacred donations of his father David,* see 2 Sam. 8.9–12.

8.1–66: Dedicating the Temple. The formal dedication ceremonies consisted of moving the Ark and attendant items from a tent where they had been kept since the days of David, joyful celebration, public sacrifices, prayers, and speeches. The dedication ceremonies took place in the seventh month, *Ethanim,* called "Tishri" after the Babylonian exile. It corresponds to September-October and is the month when the high holidays, Rosh Ha-Shanah (New Year) and Yom Kippur (Day of Atonement) are observed, followed immediately by Sukkot (Tabernacles or Booths). The dedication, eleven months after the completion of the Temple (see 6.37), was scheduled for the feast of Booths, Sukkot (v. 2), suggesting that it, and not Rosh Ha-Shanah, was the major festival at that time. **1:** The sacred objects were kept in a tent within the *City of David.* They had to be carried up to the Temple, which had been constructed on a hill north of the city. A broad consensus among historians and archeologists maintains that Solomon's Temple was built beneath the platform around the later Dome of the Rock and in the surrounding area.

2 All the men of Israel gathered before King Solomon at the
Feast,[a] in the month of Ethanim—that is, the seventh month.
3 When all the elders of Israel had come, the priests lifted the
Ark 4 and carried up the Ark of the LORD. Then the priests and
the Levites brought the Tent of Meeting and all the holy vessels that were in the Tent. 5 Meanwhile, King Solomon and the
whole community of Israel, who were assembled with him before the Ark, were sacrificing sheep and oxen in such abundance that they could not be numbered or counted.
6 The priests brought the Ark of the LORD's Covenant to its
place underneath the wings of the cherubim, in the Shrine of
the House, in the Holy of Holies; 7 for the cherubim had their
wings spread out over the place of the Ark, so that the cherubim shielded the Ark and its poles from above. 8 The poles
projected so that the ends of the poles were visible in the sanctuary in front of the Shrine, but they could not be seen outside;
and there they remain to this day. 9 There was nothing inside
the Ark but the two tablets of stone which Moses placed there
at Horeb, when the LORD made [a covenant] with the Israelites
after their departure from the land of Egypt.
10 When the priests came out of the sanctuary—for the cloud
had filled the House of the LORD 11 and the priests were not
able to remain and perform the service because of the cloud,
for the Presence of the LORD filled the House of the LORD—
12 then Solomon declared:

"The LORD has chosen
To abide in a thick cloud:
13 I have now built for You
A stately House,
A place where You
May dwell forever."

14 Then, with the whole congregation of Israel standing, the
king faced about and blessed the whole congregation of Israel.
15 He said:
"Praised be the LORD, the God of Israel, [b-]who has fulfilled
with deeds the promise He made[-b] to my father David. For He
said, 16 'Ever since I brought My people Israel out of Egypt, I
have not chosen a city among all the tribes of Israel for building

a I.e., of Booths. Cf. Lev. 23.34.
b-b Lit. "who spoke with His own mouth ... and has fulfilled with His own hand."

3–7: These vv. show Priestly influence, including the idea that *the priests and the Levites* were two separate groups (contrast Deut. 18.1–8). The description of the cherubim also appears in Priestly texts (Exod. 25.20; 37.9). Although Kings is a Deuteronomistic book, at some crucial points an editor brought it in line with Priestly writings. **8:** *To this day,* an indication that this description was written before the destruction of the Temple in 586 BCE. See also 9.21. **9:** This v. follows Deut. 10.1–5 (note the use of Horeb, which characterizes Deut.); contrast Exod. 16.33 and Num. 17.25. **10:** *The cloud,* a conventional figure indicating divine Presence (Exod. 33.9). The cloud here alludes to earlier Priestly traditions about the Tabernacle (Exod. 40.34–35), suggesting the continuity between the Tabernacle and the Temple. **11:** *The Presence of the LORD:* In Deut., and the continuation of this ch, it is God's name that resides in the Temple. **12–13:** Since God dwells in *a thick cloud,* Solomon has provided a proper house. The Temple building was dimly illuminated by light entering through apertures high on the wall and by ten lamps. The square, back chamber, where the Ark was kept, was blocked off from the long hall, so that it was always dim; it was dangerous to see the Ark, which served as God's throne.

8.13–66: The prayer of Solomon is filled with phrases that echo Deut.: v. 23, *in the heavens above and on the earth below* (Deut. 4.39); v. 23, *keep Your gracious covenant* (Deut. 7.9, 12); v. 24, as is now the case (Deut. 2.30; 4.20; etc.); vv. 30, 39, 43, 49, *Your heavenly abode* (Deut. 26.15); vv. 33, 34, 38, 43, 52, *Your people Israel* (Deut. 21.8; 26.15); v. 36, *which You gave ... as their heritage* (Deut. 4.21; 15.4; etc.); v. 40, *revere* [the LORD] (Deut. 4.10; 5.26; etc.); v. 42, *mighty hand ... outstretched arm* (Deut. 4.34; 5.15; etc.); v. 51, *iron furnace* (Deut. 4.20). It likely is, in part, a later Deuteronomistic composition (Dtr^2).

13: *I have ... built* recurs five additional times in Solomon's speeches (vv. 20, 27, 43, 44, 48), sounding a message of personal piety. *A place where You / May dwell forever:* The concept expressed here that the Temple is the place where God dwells is qualified by a more abstract conception in v. 29, which portrays the Temple as the place where the divine "name" dwells. This suggests that the prayers in vv. 12–13 and 15–53 are two separate compositions; the latter may have a long history of composition. **16–21:** These vv. contain many

a House where My name might abide; but I have chosen David
to rule My people Israel.'
17 "Now my father David had intended to build a House for
the name of the LORD, the God of Israel. 18 But the LORD said to
my father David, 'As regards your intention to build a House for
My name, you did right to have that intention. 19 However, you
shall not build the House yourself; instead, your son, the issue
of your loins, shall build the House for My name.'
20 "And the LORD has fulfilled the promise that He made:
I have succeeded[a] my father David and have ascended the
throne of Israel, as the LORD promised. I have built the House
for the name of the LORD, the God of Israel; 21 and I have set
a place there for the Ark, containing the covenant which the
LORD made with our fathers when He brought them out from
the land of Egypt."
22 Then Solomon stood before the altar of the LORD in the
presence of the whole community of Israel; he spread the
palms of his hands toward heaven 23 and said, "O LORD God
of Israel, in the heavens above and on the earth below there is
no god like You, who keep Your gracious covenant with Your
servants when they walk before You in wholehearted devotion; 24 You who have kept the promises You made to Your
servant, my father David, fulfilling with deeds the promise
You made—as is now the case. 25 And now, O LORD God of Israel, keep the further promise that You made to Your servant,
my father David: 'Your line on the throne of Israel shall never
end, if only your descendants will look to their way and walk
before Me as you have walked before Me.' 26 Now, therefore, O
God of Israel, let the promise that You made to Your servant
my father David be fulfilled.
27 "But will God really dwell[b] on earth? Even the heavens to
their uttermost reaches cannot contain You, how much less
this House that I have built! 28 Yet turn, O LORD my God, to the
prayer and supplication of Your servant, and hear the cry and
prayer which Your servant offers before You this day. 29 May
Your eyes be open day and night toward this House, toward
the place of which You have said, 'My name shall abide there';
may You heed the prayers which Your servant will offer toward this place. 30 And when You hear the supplications which
Your servant and Your people Israel offer toward this place,
give heed in Your heavenly abode—give heed and pardon.

a Lit. "risen in place of." *b 2 Chron. 6.18 adds "with man."*

allusions to 2 Sam. ch 7, concerning the choosing of David and his line, and thus connects the choice of David as God's king and of Jerusalem as God's city; it also modifies 2 Sam. ch 7 by insisting repeatedly that the Temple houses God's *name*, not God. **22:** In the ancient world, the proper posture for petitionary prayer was standing erect with raised hands. In addition to other biblical descriptions (Exod. 9.29; Isa. 1.15) it is represented in drawings from Israel, Assyria, and Egypt. **23:** Prayers in the ancient world typically opened with an invocation of the deity, here *O LORD God of Israel*. **25–26:** Solomon introduces his petition by suggesting that insofar as he has met conditions presented by God in the dream at Gibeon (3.14) by building the Temple, God should fulfill His (conditional) promise to David about his descendants (cf. 2.4) which would include guaranteeing Solomon long life. The conditional promise is a hallmark of Dtr^2, in contrast to the unconditional promise of 2 Sam. ch 7 (Dtr^1). **27–61:** This section begins with a rhetorical question challenging the notion expressed in vv. 12–13 that God now has an actual presence on earth in the Temple (v. 27). Meditative prayers (vv. 28–53) assert that God, truly present in heaven, resides only symbolically on earth in the Temple; nevertheless, prayer should be directed to the Temple (vv. 29, 31, 35, 38, 42). These ideas, couched in phrases and images from Deut.(see Deut. 6.13; 12.4, 11), attempt to harmonize the Deuteronomic notion of divine immanence in the Temple with the contrasting notion of the universal transcendence of God. The whole section may have been inserted into a text that originally continued seamlessly from v. 26 to 62. V. 54 has Solomon praying on his knees, while v. 22 has him standing. V. 55 has him standing to bless the people, something described already in v. 14. In its present context, the section dilutes the aura of God's immanence cast by the materialistic physicality of Solomon's speech (vv. 12–26). V. 34, calling for the restoration of Israel to the land, is most likely an exilic addition to the text. **27:** See esp. the postexilic Isa. 66.1. **30:** Toward this place suggests that even when worshippers could not be in the Temple, they might face it , and it would be the locus of prayer, which would then rise to God in heaven (see Dan. 6.11 n.).

31: This case is obscure. **35:** Drought is a divine reaction to human sin; see esp. Deut. 11.13–17. **39:** For a similar theology, see Prov. 21.2.

31 "Whenever one man commits an offense against another, and the latter utters an imprecation to bring a curse upon him, and comes with his imprecation before Your altar in this House, 32 oh, hear in heaven and take action to judge Your servants, condemning him who is in the wrong and bringing down the punishment of his conduct on his head, vindicating him who is in the right by rewarding him according to his righteousness.

33 "Should Your people Israel be routed by an enemy because they have sinned against You, and then turn back to You and acknowledge Your name, and they offer prayer and supplication to You in this House, 34 oh, hear in heaven and pardon the sin of Your people Israel, and restore them to the land that You gave to their fathers.

35 "Should the heavens be shut up and there be no rain, because they have sinned against You, and then they pray toward this place and acknowledge Your name and repent of their sins, when You answer[a] them, 36 oh, hear in heaven and pardon the sin of Your servants, Your people Israel, after You have shown them the proper way in which they are to walk; and send down rain upon the land which You gave to Your people as their heritage. 37 So, too, if there is a famine in the land, if there is pestilence, blight, mildew, locusts or caterpillars, or if an enemy oppresses them in any of the settlements of the land.

"In any plague and in any disease, 38 in any prayer or supplication offered by any person among all Your people Israel—each of whom knows his own affliction—when he spreads his palms toward this House, 39 oh, hear in Your heavenly abode, and pardon and take action! Render to each man according to his ways as You know his heart to be—for You alone know the hearts of all men—40 so that they may revere You all the days that they live on the land that You gave to our fathers.

41 "Or if a foreigner who is not of Your people Israel comes from a distant land for the sake of Your name—42 for they shall hear about Your great name and Your mighty hand and Your outstretched arm—when he comes to pray toward this House, 43 oh, hear in Your heavenly abode and grant all that the foreigner asks You for. Thus all the peoples of the earth will know Your name and revere You, as does Your people Israel; and they will recognize that Your name is attached to this House that I have built.

44 "When Your people take the field against their enemy by whatever way You send them, and they pray to the LORD in the direction of the city which You have chosen, and of the House which I have built to Your name, 45 oh, hear in heaven their prayer and supplication and uphold their cause.

a *The Septuagint, with a different vocalization, reads "chastise."*

46 "When they sin against You—for there is no man who does
not sin—and You are angry with them and deliver them to the
enemy, and their captors carry them off to an enemy land, near
or far; 47 and then they take it to heart in the land to which they
have been carried off, and they repent and make supplication
to You in the land of their captors, saying: 'We have sinned,
we have acted perversely, we have acted wickedly,' 48 and they
turn back to You with all their heart and soul, in the land of the
enemies who have carried them off, and they pray to You in
the direction of their land which You gave to their fathers, of
the city which You have chosen, and of the House which I have
built to Your name— 49 oh, give heed in Your heavenly abode to
their prayer and supplication, uphold their cause, 50 and pardon Your people who have sinned against You for all the transgressions that they have committed against You. Grant them
mercy in the sight of their captors that they may be merciful to
them. 51 For they are Your very own people that You freed from
Egypt, from the midst of the iron furnace. 52 May Your eyes be
open to the supplication of Your servant and the supplication
of Your people Israel, and may You heed them whenever they
call upon You. 53 For You, O Lord GOD, have set them apart for
Yourself from all the peoples of the earth as Your very own, as
You promised through Moses Your servant when You freed our
fathers from Egypt."

54 When Solomon finished offering to the LORD all this prayer
and supplication, he rose from where he had been kneeling,
in front of the altar of the LORD, his hands spread out toward
heaven. 55 He stood, and in a loud voice blessed the whole congregation of Israel:

56 "Praised be the LORD who has granted a haven to His people Israel, just as He promised; not a single word has failed of
all the gracious promises that He made through His servant
Moses. 57 May the LORD our God be with us, as He was with
our fathers. May He never abandon or forsake us. 58 May He
incline our hearts to Him, that we may walk in all His ways and
keep the commandments, the laws, and the rules, which He
enjoined upon our fathers. 59 And may these words of mine,
which I have offered in supplication before the LORD, be close
to the LORD our God day and night, that He may provide for
His servant and for His people Israel, according to each day's
needs— 60 to the end that all the peoples of the earth may know
that the LORD alone is God, there is no other. 61 And may you be
wholehearted with the LORD our God, to walk in His ways and
keep His commandments, even as now."

62 The king and all Israel with him offered sacrifices before
the LORD. 63 Solomon offered 22,000 oxen and 120,000 sheep
as sacrifices of well-being to the LORD. Thus the king and all

46–50: The Heb plays exquisitely on the roots "shavah" (carry off) and "shuv" (return). **46:** A remarkable statement about human imperfection: *for there is no man who does not sin.* **47:** Confessional prayer including words like *'We have sinned, we have acted perversely, we have acted wickedly,'* become more common in the exilic period, and are the basis for much longer confessional prayers that became central in the Yom Kippur liturgy. **48:** Prayer is efficacious even outside of Jerusalem and Israel, even in exile (see similarly Ezek. 11.16). **58:** People need divine help to follow the divine commandments. **60:** Such statements of absolute monotheism are exilic or later (see Deut. 4.35 n.).

8.62–66: Conclusion of the dedication. The attendance of the entire population, and the huge numbers of sacrifices offered, are intended to express the completeness of participation and consecration. Taken literally, they would have required the abandonment of all activity by the entire people for two weeks, and the rate of sacrifice (even assuming non-stop activity) would have been one oxen and six sheep every minute.

the Israelites dedicated the House of the LORD. 64 That day the king consecrated the center of the court that was in front of the House of the LORD. For it was there that he presented the burnt offerings, the meal offerings, and the fat parts of the offerings of well-being, because the bronze altar that was before the LORD was too small to hold the burnt offerings, the meal offerings, and the fat parts of the offerings of well-being.

65 So Solomon and all Israel with him—a great assemblage, [coming] from Lebo-hamath to the Wadi of Egypt[a]—observed the Feast[b] at that time before the LORD our God, seven days and again seven days, fourteen days in all. 66 On the eighth day[c] he let the people go. They bade the king good-bye and went to their homes, joyful and glad of heart over all the goodness that the LORD had shown to His servant David and His people Israel.

9 When Solomon had finished building the House of the LORD and the royal palace and everything that Solomon had set his heart on constructing, 2 the LORD appeared to Solomon a second time, as He had appeared to him at Gibeon. 3 The LORD said to him, "I have heard the prayer and the supplication which you have offered to Me. I consecrate this House which you have built and I set My name there forever. My eyes and My heart shall ever be there. 4 As for you, if you walk before Me as your father David walked before Me, wholeheartedly and with uprightness, doing all that I have commanded you [and] keeping My laws and My rules, 5 then I will establish your throne of kingship over Israel forever, as I promised your father David, saying, 'Your line on the throne of Israel shall never end.' 6 [But] if you and your descendants turn away from Me and do not keep the commandments [and] the laws which I have set before you, and go and serve other gods and worship them, 7 then I will sweep[d] Israel off the land which I gave them; I will reject[e] the House which I have consecrated to My name; and Israel shall become a proverb and a byword among all peoples. 8 And [f]as for this House, once so exalted,[f] everyone passing by it shall be appalled and shall hiss.[g] And when they ask, 'Why did the LORD do thus to the land and to this House?' 9 they shall be told, 'It is because they forsook the LORD their God who freed them from the land of Egypt, and they embraced other gods and worshiped them and served them; therefore the LORD has brought all this calamity upon them.'"

a I.e., coming from one end of the country to the other.
b I.e., of Booths. Cf. Lev. 23.34.
c I.e., of the second seven-day feast; cf. 2 Chron. 7.8–10.
d Lit. "cut." *e Lit. "dismiss from My presence."*
f-f Targum and some other ancient versions read "and this House shall become a ruin."
g An action performed at the sight of ruin to ward off a like fate from the observer; cf. note at Jer. 18.16.

64: *Burnt offerings* (Lev. 1.3–17), those wholly consumed by fire. They are at the initiative of the donor, and serve to expiate any shortcomings not covered by purification or reparatory offerings. *Meal offerings* (Lev. 2.1–16), portions of grain burnt completely. The meal offering was a burnt offering that even poor people could afford *(Lev. Rab. 8.4)*. *Offerings of well-being* (Lev. 3.1–16), sacrifice of an animal involving burning its inner organs (entrails, kidney, and liver) and the fat (suet) that is attached to them. These are thanksgiving or celebratory offerings, and the worshipper partakes of the meat that is not burnt. **65:** The second *seven days* is absent in some ancient versions. The seven-day festival of Sukkot comports with Deut. 16.13, 15, rather than with Lev. 23.36, where an eighth day is added. 2 Chron. 7.9 speaks of a seven-day festival for the dedication of the altar and another seven-day festival for the Feast (Sukkot; see 2 Chron. 7.8–11 n.). This may be what our v. is referring to also, although it is not clear.

9.1–9: The second revelation. This unit harks back to the revelation at Gibeon (3.4–15). God here responds to the dedicatory prayers of Solomon; the narrative leaves unclear when and where this occurred. At least part of this unit is likely exilic (Dtr^2). **2–3:** God indicates that He had consecrated the *House* in response to Solomon's prayers and supplications. This emphasizes that it is His act of will, not Solomon's, that makes the Temple an effective place. **4–9:** Reaffirming the conditionality of the promise to David and his dynasty, God denies Solomon's request of 8.25–26 for a guarantee. For emphasis, God states also that the existence of the Temple itself depends on the proper behavior of Israel. Vv. 6–9 are intended to anticipate the exile of all Israel, of both the kingdoms of Israel and Judah, that at this point in the narrative have not yet come into existence as separate kingdoms.

[10]At the end of the twenty years[a] during which Solomon
constructed the two buildings, the LORD's House and the
royal palace—[11] since King Hiram of Tyre had supplied Solomon with all the cedar and cypress timber and gold that he
required—King Solomon in turn gave Hiram twenty towns in
the region of Galilee. [12] But when Hiram came from Tyre to
inspect the towns that Solomon had given him, he was not
pleased with them. [13] "My brother," he said, "what sort of
towns are these you have given me?" So they were named the
land of Cabul,[b] as is still the case. [14] However, Hiram sent the
king one hundred and twenty talents of gold.

[15]This was the purpose of the forced labor which Solomon
imposed: It was to build the House of the LORD, his own palace, the Millo,[c] and the wall of Jerusalem, and [to fortify] Hazor, Megiddo, and Gezer. ([16] Pharaoh king of Egypt had come
up and captured Gezer; he destroyed it by fire, killed the Canaanites who dwelt in the town, and gave it as dowry to his
daughter, Solomon's wife.) [17] So Solomon fortified Gezer,
lower Beth-horon, [18] Baalith, and Tamar[d] in the wilderness,
in the land [of Judah], [19] and all of Solomon's garrison towns,
chariot towns, and cavalry towns—everything that Solomon
set his heart on building in Jerusalem and in the Lebanon,
and throughout the territory that he ruled. [20] All the people
that were left of the Amorites, Hittites, Perizzites, Hivites, and
Jebusites who were not of the Israelite stock—[21] those of their
descendants who remained in the land and whom the Israelites were not able to annihilate—of these Solomon made a
slave force, as is still the case. [22] But he did not reduce any Israelites to slavery; they served, rather, as warriors and as his
attendants, officials, and officers, and as commanders of his
chariotry and cavalry.

[23] These were the prefects that were in charge of Solomon's
works and were foremen over the people engaged in the work,
who numbered 550.[e]

[24] As soon as Pharaoh's daughter went up from the City of
David to the palace that he had built for her, he built the Millo.[c]

[25] Solomon used to offer burnt offerings and sacrifices of
well-being three times a year on the altar that he had built for
the LORD, and [f]he used to offer incense on the one that was
before the LORD. And he kept the House in repair.[-f]

a See 6.38–7.1. *b Perhaps taken to mean "as nothing."* *c A citadel.*
d So kethib, *cf. Ezek. 47.19, 48.28;* qere *Tadmor.*
e Their names are not listed in the text. *f-f Meaning of Heb. uncertain.*

9.10–10.29: The rest of the deeds of Solomon. This section presents truncated information about financial and administrative arrangements consequent to Solomon's building projects. **9:10–14:** A final payment for supplies and for *gold*—not mentioned in the earlier contractual arrangements (5.20–31)—to king Hiram was made by Solomon in the form of twenty towns. Despite Hiram's disparaging remark that gave rise to the area being called Cabul ("nothing"), he accepted them and remitted a final gold payment to Solomon to cover the difference between the value of the cities and what was owed him. **11:** Josephus reports that they were near Tyre, in western Galilee. **13:** *My brother:* "Brother" refers to an equal partner in a treaty. **14:** *Talent,* the equivalent of 3,000 shekels (Exod. 38.25–26), weighed approximately 30 kg (66 pounds). **15–23:** Solomon's labor force. Solomon conducted construction projects in many parts of his kingdom and depended on a combination of conscripted workers under a labor tax system as well as partially enslaved populations. The location of sites mentioned suggests that he felt threatened by Arameans northeast of the Sea of Galilee, Philistines from the coastal plain, and Egyptians from the southwest. The author drew this information from the same source as 5.27–31. **19:** One such *garrison town* dated to the 10th c. BCE was first excavated in 2007 at Khirbet Qeiyafa. It is located on a hill overlooking what were Philistine-controlled territories to its west and south and overseeing passes into the central mountains of Judah. **21:** This v. justifies Solomon's nonfulfillment of Deut. 20.16–18. *Slave force* (Heb "mas ʿoved") refers to tax paid in labor. V. 22 suggests that the status of non-Israelites under this system differed from that of Israelites; this contradicts 5.27–28. **23:** The names of the prefects are not presented. In 2 Chron. 8.10, their number is given as 250. **24–25:** These vv. mirror 3.1–2, and may indicate the conclusion of a section arranged thematically that shows Solomon being blessed. What follows shows his violation of Deut. 17.16–17, as Solomon amasses gold, horses, and wives, and is subsequently punished.

26 King Solomon also built a fleet of ships at Ezion-geber,
which is near Eloth[a] on the shore of the Sea of Reeds in the
land of Edom. 27 Hiram sent servants of his with the fleet, mariners who were experienced on the sea, to serve with Solomon's
men. 28 They came to Ophir; there they obtained gold in the
amount of four hundred and twenty talents, which they delivered to King Solomon.

10 The queen of Sheba heard of Solomon's fame, [b-]through
the name of the LORD,[-b] and she came to test him with
hard questions. 2 She arrived in Jerusalem with a very large
retinue, with camels bearing spices, a great quantity of gold,
and precious stones. When she came to Solomon, she asked
him all that she had in mind. 3 Solomon had answers for all
her questions; there was nothing that the king did not know,
[nothing] to which he could not give her an answer. 4 When
the queen of Sheba observed all of Solomon's wisdom, and
the palace he had built, 5 the fare of his table, the seating of his
courtiers, the service and attire of his attendants, and his wine
service, [c-]and the burnt offerings that he offered at[-c] the House
of the LORD, she was left breathless.
6 She said to the king, "The report I heard in my own land
about you and your wisdom was true. 7 But I did not believe
the reports until I came and saw with my own eyes that not
even the half had been told me; your wisdom and wealth surpass the reports that I heard. 8 How fortunate are your men
and how fortunate are these your courtiers, who are always
in attendance on you and can hear your wisdom! 9 Praised be
the LORD your God, who delighted in you and set you on the
throne of Israel. It is because of the LORD's everlasting love for
Israel that He made you king to administer justice and righteousness."
10 She presented the king with one hundred and twenty talents of gold, and a large quantity of spices, and precious stones.
Never again did such a vast quantity of spices arrive as that
which the queen of Sheba gave to King Solomon.— 11 Moreover, Hiram's fleet, which carried gold from Ophir, brought
in from Ophir a huge quantity of *almug* wood[d] and precious
stones. 12 The king used the *almug* wood for decorations in

a Elsewhere called Elath. *b-b The force of the phrase is uncertain.*
c-c 2 Chron. 9.4 reads "... and the procession with which he went up to ..."
d Others "sandalwood."

9.26–10.22: The outcome of Solomon's additional business dealings with Hiram of Tyre. **9.26–28:** Solomon and Hiram undertook a joint venture in a combination of land and sea trade. Hiram provided the seafaring know-how and Solomon granted overland access to the port at *Ezion-geber* on the Gulf of Eilat. From there, both kings had access to the Red Sea and beyond. This land route was of major importance because it provided access to the copper mines, in use during the 10th and 9th centuries BCE, that were discovered and excavated at Khirbet en-Nahas, in the Arabah valley south of the Dead Sea adjacent to the kingdoms of Judah and Edom. They are evidence of large-scale commercial undertakings and complex economies and trade systems at this early period in the history of the monarchy. The site was first excavated in the late 1990s. **28:** *Ophir,* location uncertain. It has been identified with ports or regions in Ethiopia, North Somalia, South Arabia, and even India.

10.1–13: The story of the queen's visit to Solomon continues the theme of wisdom and wealth (3.12–13). It interrupts the report of his trading venture, which continues in 10.14, and was inserted because of its thematic connection to the international business ventures. **1:** *Sheba,* ancient Sabea at the southwest corner of the Arabian peninsula, controlled access into the Sea of Aden from the Red Sea at the Bab el-Mandeb. The story tells that the queen came to meet a potential trading partner. She provided him with her gifts, and he reciprocated. The type of *hard questions* she proposed, unspecified here, is filled in differently by many postbiblical legends. **6–9:** The queen verifies Solomon's wealth and wisdom (confirming God's bestowal of these attributes in 3.11–13) and she praises (Heb "blesses") God for setting Solomon on the throne. These are the only words in the story that are directly quoted; the rest of the story is summarized in the third-person, not dramatized through dialogue. **9:** *To administer justice and righteousness* is the role of a king. **10:** The Arabian peninsula was a well-known source of spices. **11–12:** Information about almug wood and how it was used dates the Ophir venture to within a few years of Solomon's initial arrangement with Hiram. These vv. interrupt the account of the queen's

the House of the LORD and in the royal palace, and for harps and lyres for the musicians. Such a quantity of *almug* wood has never arrived or been seen to this day.—[13] King Solomon, in turn, gave the queen of Sheba everything she wanted and asked for, in addition to what King Solomon gave her out of his royal bounty. Then she and her attendants left and returned to her own land.

[14] The weight of the gold which Solomon received every year was 666 talents of gold, [15] besides what came from tradesmen, from the traffic of the merchants, and from all the kings of Arabia and the governors of the regions. [16] King Solomon made 200 shields of beaten gold—600 shekels of gold to each shield—[17] and 300 bucklers of beaten gold—three *minas* of gold to each buckler. The king placed them in the Lebanon Forest House.

[18] The king also made a large throne of ivory, and he overlaid it with refined gold. [19] Six steps led up to the throne, and the throne had a back with a rounded top, and arms on either side of the seat. Two lions stood beside the arms, [20] and twelve lions stood on the six steps, six on either side. No such throne was ever made for any other kingdom.[a]

[21] All King Solomon's drinking cups were of gold, and all the utensils of the Lebanon Forest House were of pure gold: silver did not count for anything in Solomon's days. [22] For the king had a Tarshish[b] fleet on the sea, along with Hiram's fleet. Once every three years, the Tarshish fleet came in, bearing gold and silver, ivory, apes, and peacocks.

[23] King Solomon excelled all the kings on earth in wealth and in wisdom. [24] All the world came to pay homage to Solomon and to listen to the wisdom with which God had endowed him; [25] and each one would bring his tribute—silver and gold objects, robes, weapons and spices, horses and mules—in the amount due each year.

[26] Solomon assembled chariots and horses. He had 1,400 chariots and 12,000 horses, which he stationed[c] in the chariot towns and with the king in Jerusalem. [27] The king made silver as plentiful in Jerusalem as stones, and cedars as plentiful as sycamores in the Shephelah. [28] Solomon's horses were procured from Mizraim[d] and Kue. The king's dealers would buy them from Kue at a fixed price. [29] A chariot imported from Mizraim[d] cost 600 shekels of silver, and a horse 150; these in turn were exported by them[e] to all the kings of the Hittites and the kings of the Arameans.

a Or "prince"; like Phoenician mamlakt. *b Probably a fleet of large ships.*
c So 2 Chron. 1.14; 9.25; Heb. here "led."
d Usually Egypt, here perhaps Muṣru, a neighbor of Kue (Cilicia).
e I.e., Solomon's dealers.

visit, and likely represent an attempt to integrate the originally separate story about the queen's visit into the previous episode. **13:** As with the initial "hard questions," the story ends with the unspecified *everything she wanted and asked for.*

10.14–29: Solomon's wealth and horses. Extravagant golden furnishings were captured by David from the Aramean king Hadadezer (2 Sam. 8.7). Ancient Near Eastern documents indicate that gold bowls and dishes were given as gifts to royalty while gold shields are mentioned by Assyrian kings as prize spoils of war. Solomon's trade arrangements explain his access to gold. **22:** *A Tarshish fleet* may refer to a type of ship or to the place to which such ships sailed. The fleet was Solomon's, and run independently from ships involved in joint ventures with Hiram. Since the Ophir fleet plied the Red Sea trade, the Tarshish fleet may have competed with Phoenicians around the Mediterranean. Scholars have identified Tarshish with Sardinia or with Tartessus in southern Spain. The gold described here is used for his palace and other possessions, and not for the Temple, whose riches were described in chs 6–7. **23–25:** Solomon's wealth and wisdom helped confer great recognition and honor on him. These vv. reprise God's grants to Solomon in 3.12–13 and what was already narrated in 5.14. **26–29:** Solomon used and traded in chariots from Egypt and horses from two small kingdoms in Anatolia, keeping some (9.19) and reselling others to small Hittite kingdoms in North Syria near the Euphrates and to Aramean kingdoms (cf. 2 Sam. 10.19). Information about his arms trade with Arameans brings to the foreground the brief notice in 11.23–25. The vv. suggest that Solomon violated Deut. 17.16, that the king "shall not keep many horses or send people back to Egypt to add to his horses."

11 King Solomon loved many foreign women in addition
to Pharaoh's daughter—Moabite, Ammonite, Edomite,
Phoenician, and Hittite women, 2 from the nations of which
the LORD had said to the Israelites, "None of you shall join
them and none of them shall join you,[a] lest they turn your
heart away to follow their gods." Such Solomon clung to and
loved. 3 He had seven hundred royal wives and three hundred
concubines; and his wives turned his heart away. 4 In his old
age, his wives turned away Solomon's heart after other gods,
and he was not as wholeheartedly devoted to the LORD his God
as his father David had been. 5 Solomon followed Ashtoreth
the goddess of the Phoenicians, and Milcom the abomination
of the Ammonites.

6 Solomon did what was displeasing to the LORD and did not
remain loyal to the LORD like his father David. 7 At that time,
Solomon built a shrine for Chemosh the abomination of Moab
on the hill near Jerusalem, and one for Molech the abomination of the Ammonites. 8 And he did the same for all his foreign
wives who offered and sacrificed to their gods.

9 The LORD was angry with Solomon, because his heart
turned away from the LORD, the God of Israel, who had appeared to him twice 10 and had commanded him about this
matter, not to follow other gods; he did not obey what the
LORD had commanded. 11 And the LORD said to Solomon,
[b-]"Because you are guilty of this[-b]—you have not kept My covenant and the laws which I enjoined upon you—I will tear the
kingdom away from you and give it to one of your servants.
12 But, for the sake of your father David, I will not do it in your
lifetime; I will tear it away from your son. 13 However, I will not
tear away the whole kingdom; I will give your son one tribe,
for the sake of My servant David and for the sake of Jerusalem
which I have chosen."

14 So the LORD raised up an adversary against Solomon, the
Edomite Hadad, who was of the royal family of Edom. 15 When
David [c-]was in[-c] Edom, Joab the army commander went up to
bury the slain, and he killed every male in Edom; 16 for Joab
and all Israel stayed there for six months until he had killed
off every male in Edom. 17 But Hadad,[d] together with some

a I.e., in marriage; cf. Deut. 7.3–4; 23.4, 8–9. *b-b Lit. "This is with you."*
c-c Emendation yields "defeated"; cf. 2 Sam. 8.13. *d Heb. Adad.*

11.1–43: The dissolution of Solomon's kingdom. Some of what is narrated here occurred simultaneously with what was presented in chs 1–10. For example, Solomon's marriage to an Ammonite princess occurred while David was alive (14.21). This suggests that the material is arranged theologically rather than chronologically; the first part narrates the successes of Solomon while he observes the law, while ch 11 is part of a section which narrates his failures that result from abrogating the law. **1:** Solomon's diplomatic marriages reflect the range of his trading ventures and his attempt to secure alliances with kingdoms on his undefined eastern Transjordanian borders: Ammon, Moab, Edom. Malbim notes that the author's choice of words, *loved many foreign women,* denotes a child's lust after objects rather than an adult's love for a particular woman. This invites a contrast between David, whose impetuous acts were sins of youth, and Solomon, who sinned in his old age. **1–3:** Having many wives violated general instructions to the king (Deut. 17. 17). Foreign wives would introduce their pagan practices into Judah. The author here combines various biblical texts and extends earlier traditions that prohibit intermarriage with specific nations (Exod. 34.11–16; Deut. 7.1–6; 23.4–9). A similar general ban on intermarriage is found in Ezra-Nehemiah, suggesting that this text in Kings is from the latest, exilic edition of the book. **5–8:** Solomon's tolerance of, participation in, and contributions toward foreign worship—corollary activities to his diplomatic marriages—are described and condemned by the author. **9–13:** God's angry reaction to the actual behavior of a properly informed and warned Solomon (cf. 3.5; 9.2). **10:** Alludes to 9.4–7. **11–13:** The final judgment compromises God's promises to David (2 Sam. 7.16). The kingdom will be torn away, but not the whole kingdom as it was from Saul (1 Sam. 15.28; 28.17–18). *For the sake of ... David* is a major subtheme of the book (11.34; 15.4; 2 Kings 8.19; 19.34; 20.6). Here, as in 8.16, the choosing of David and of Jerusalem are intertwined. **14–22:** *Adversary,* Heb "satan," related to later English "Satan." *Hadad* of Edom, also connected to the Egyptian court through marriage, threatened Solomon from the east. **15–16:** No reason is provided for *Joab's* harsh action. Control of the copper mines and trade routes associated with them may be the reason. See 9.26–28 n. Solomon's overland caravans from Eilat most likely followed routes in the eastern Sinai to avoid Edomite raiders.

Edomite men, servants of his father, escaped and headed for Egypt; Hadad was then a young boy. 18 Setting out from Midian, they came to Paran and took along with them men from Paran. Thus they came to Egypt, to Pharaoh king of Egypt, who gave him a house, assigned a food allowance to him, and granted him an estate. 19 Pharaoh took a great liking to Hadad and gave him his sister-in-law, the sister of Queen Tahpenes, as wife. 20 The sister of Tahpenes bore him a son, Genubath. Tahpenes weaned[a] him in Pharaoh's palace, and Genubath remained in Pharaoh's palace among the sons of Pharaoh. 21 When Hadad heard in Egypt that David had been laid to rest with his fathers and that Joab the army commander was dead, Hadad said to Pharaoh, "Give me leave to go to my own country." 22 Pharaoh replied, "What do you lack with me, that you want to go to your own country?" But he said, "Nevertheless, give me leave to go."

23 Another adversary that God raised up against Solomon[b] was Rezon son of Eliada, who had fled from his lord, King Hadadezer of Zobah, 24 when David was slaughtering them. He gathered men about him and became captain over a troop; they went to Damascus and settled there, and they established a kingdom in Damascus. 25 He was an adversary of Israel all the days of Solomon, adding to the trouble [caused by] Hadad; he repudiated [the authority of] Israel and reigned over Aram.

26 Jeroboam son of Nebat, an Ephraimite of Zeredah, the son of a widow whose name was Zeruah, was in Solomon's service; he raised his hand against the king. 27 The circumstances under which he raised his hand against the king were as follows: Solomon built the Millo and repaired the breach of the city of his father, David. 28 This Jeroboam was an able man, and when Solomon saw that the young man was a capable worker, he appointed him over all the forced labor of the House of Joseph.

29 During that time Jeroboam went out of Jerusalem and the prophet Ahijah of Shiloh met him on the way. He had put on a new robe; and when the two were alone in the open country, 30 Ahijah took hold of the new robe he was wearing and tore it into twelve pieces. 31 "Take ten pieces," he said to Jeroboam. "For thus said the LORD, the God of Israel: I am about to tear the kingdom out of Solomon's hands, and I will give you ten tribes. 32 But one tribe shall remain his—for the sake of My servant David and for the sake of Jerusalem, the city that I have chosen out of all the tribes of Israel. 33 For they have forsaken Me; they have worshiped Ashtoreth the goddess of the Phoenicians, Chemosh the god of Moab, and Milcom the god of the

23–25: *Rezon,* a victim of David's victories over the Arameans, eventually wrested Damascus from Israelite control (cf. 2 Sam. 8.6). He may have threatened Israel with the very chariots that had been sold to him by Solomon. **26–40:** According to the author, Ahijah's message fomented Jeroboam's action. Jeroboam's defiance of Solomon on behalf of northern tribes—no details are provided and several words seem to be missing in the Heb text—had the support of a prophet. The full measure of Jeroboam's popularity is indicated in 12.1–6. Ahijah was introduced in 1 Sam. 14.3. **30:** Ahijah's tearing the robe, like Samuel's in 1 Sam. 15.27–28, symbolizes the removal of the kingship from the current king and its bestowal upon a new king. But here, unlike in the Samuel-Saul encounter, the prophet is speaking with the new king-to-be, not with the rejected king. **31–32:** While the robe is torn into twelve pieces, for the twelve tribes, only eleven are enumerated here—ten in the Northern Kingdom and one tribe, Judah, which will remain for Rehoboam. **33:** The LXX and other versions suggest the contextually more appropriate "he has forsaken," rather than *they have forsaken.*

a Septuagint reads "reared." *b Heb. "him."*

Ammonites; they have not walked in My ways, or done what is pleasing to Me, or [kept] My laws and rules, as his father David did. 34 However, I will not take the entire kingdom away from him, but will keep him as ruler as long as he lives for the sake of My servant David whom I chose, and who kept My commandments and My laws. 35 But I will take the kingship out of the hands of his son and give it to you—the ten tribes. 36 To his son I will give one tribe, so that there may be a lamp for My servant David forever before Me in Jerusalem—the city where I have chosen to establish My name. 37 But you have been chosen by Me; reign[a] wherever you wish, and you shall be king over Israel. 38 If you heed all that I command you, and walk in My ways, and do what is right in My sight, keeping My laws and commandments as My servant David did, then I will be with you and I will build for you a lasting dynasty as I did for David. I hereby give Israel to you; 39 and I will chastise David's descendants for that [sin], though not forever."

40 Solomon sought to put Jeroboam to death, but Jeroboam promptly fled to King Shishak of Egypt; and he remained in Egypt till the death of Solomon.

41 The other events of Solomon's reign, and all his actions and his wisdom, are recorded in the book of the Annals of Solomon. 42 The length of Solomon's reign in Jerusalem, over all Israel, was forty years. 43 Solomon slept with his fathers and was buried in the city of his father David; and his son Rehoboam succeeded him as king.

12 Rehoboam went to Shechem, for all Israel had come to Shechem to acclaim him as king. 2 Jeroboam son of Nebat learned of it while he was still in Egypt; for Jeroboam had fled from King Solomon, [b-]and had settled in Egypt.[-b] 3 They sent for him; and Jeroboam and all the assembly of Israel came and spoke to Rehoboam as follows: 4 "Your father made our yoke heavy. Now lighten the harsh labor and the heavy yoke which your father laid on us, and we will serve you." 5 He answered them, "Go away for three days and then come back to me." So the people went away.

a I.e., establish your residence.
b-b 2 Chron. 10.2 reads "So Jeroboam returned from Egypt."

36: The image of a lamp became a special metaphor for David and for the continuity of his line in the language of the author and like-minded people (2 Sam. 21.17; Ps. 132.17). **38:** Unlike the eternal, unconditional promise to David in 2 Sam. ch 7, the promise to Jeroboam was conditional, and his dynasty would be short-lived. **40:** Shishak (Egyptian Shoshenq) was pharaoh 945–924 BCE. His relationship with Jeroboam bore fruit after the death of Solomon. **41–42:** In citing the sources of his information about Solomon and indicating that he has excerpted only parts of them, the author suggests the veracity of the descriptions which he has evaluated theologically. **41:** *The book of the Annals of Solomon* is presented as an actual document available to the author and to his readers. It is unknown aside from this reference to it. Whether or not it actually existed, the reference to it—like a footnote in a scholarly composition—indicates a reliance on written documents as a source of authority. **42:** *Forty years,* a typological number, just like his father David (2.11).

12.1–14.18: The secession of northern tribes from the united kingdom and the creation of the Northern Kingdom of Israel.

12.1–17: The negotiation at Shechem. Although prophets, acting on instructions from God, might anoint individuals as kings, the authority of any persons so anointed had to be publicly acclaimed by those over whom they ruled, as in the case of Saul (1 Sam. 11.14–15), David over Judah (2 Sam. 2.4, 7), David over all the tribes (2 Sam. 5.1–5), and Solomon (1 Kings 1.39–40). The northern tribes were ready to acclaim Rehoboam as their king, but only if he agreed to certain general conditions. The text has a clear pro-Judean polemical slant, and makes Rehoboam look foolish, thereby justifying the establishment of the Northern Kingdom. **1:** *Shechem:* The major city directly north of Jerusalem on the north-south highway, lay near the border of the two largest and most powerful northern tribes, Ephraim and Manasseh. As excavations of the city and the Amarna letters indicate, Shechem was already a significant city in the pre-Israelite period. *All Israel:* The meaning of this phrase changes from 11.42, where it means the entire kingdom, north (Israel) and south (Judah), to 12.16, where it means the north only; in other cases in Kings, the use of Israel is sometimes ambiguous, referring to the north, the north and the south, or the south only. **2–3:** *Jeroboam* (11.26–40), summoned to Shechem from Egypt by a group of tribal leaders *(the assembly of Israel),* takes part in the negotiation.

6 King Rehoboam took counsel with the elders who had
served his father Solomon during his lifetime. He said, "What
answer do you advise [me] to give to this people?" 7 They answered him, "If you will be a servant to those people today
and serve them, and if you respond to them with kind words,
they will be your servants always." 8 But he ignored the advice
that the elders gave him, and took counsel with the young
men who had grown up with him and were serving him.
9 "What," he asked, "do you advise that we reply to the people who said to me, 'Lighten the yoke that your father placed
upon us'?" 10 And the young men who had grown up with him
answered, "Speak thus to the people who said to you, 'Your
father made our yoke heavy, now you make it lighter for us.'
Say to them, 'My little finger is thicker than my father's loins.

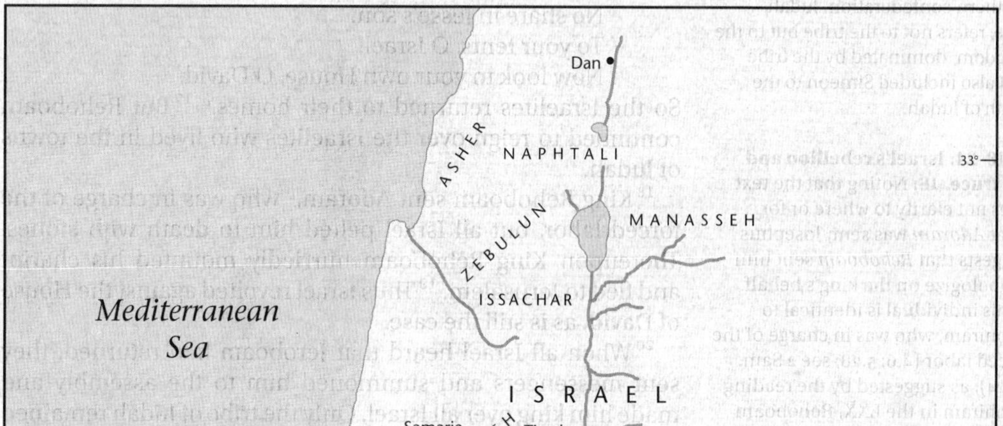

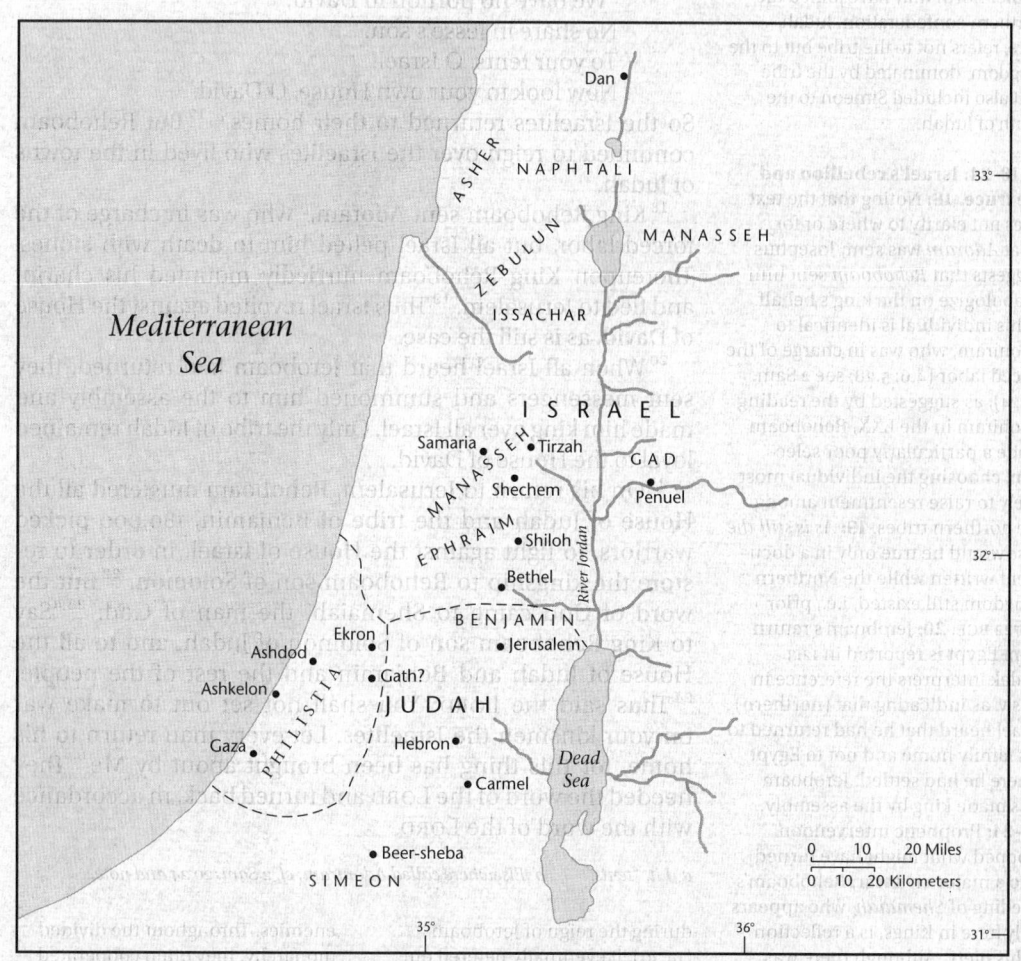

The divided monarchy. The dashed line shows the approximate boundaries between Israel, Judah and Philistia.

11 My father imposed a heavy yoke on you, and I will add to
your yoke; my father flogged you with whips, but I will flog
you with scorpions.' "
12 Jeroboam and all the people came to Rehoboam on the
third day, since the king had told them: "Come back on the
third day." 13 The king answered the people harshly, ignoring
the advice that the elders had given him. 14 He spoke to them
in accordance with the advice of the young men, and said, "My
father made your yoke heavy, but I will add to your yoke; my
father flogged you with whips, but I will flog you with scorpions." 15 (The king did not listen to the people; for the LORD had
brought it about in order to fulfill the promise that the LORD
had made through Ahijah the Shilonite to Jeroboam son of
Nebat.) 16 When all Israel saw that the king had not listened to
them, the people answered the king:

"We have no portion in David,
No share in Jesse's son!
To your tents, O Israel!
Now look to your own House, O David."

So the Israelites returned to their homes.[a] 17 But Rehoboam
continued to reign over the Israelites who lived in the towns
of Judah.
18 King Rehoboam sent Adoram,[b] who was in charge of the
forced labor, but all Israel pelted him to death with stones.
Thereupon King Rehoboam hurriedly mounted his chariot
and fled to Jerusalem. 19 Thus Israel revolted against the House
of David, as is still the case.
20 When all Israel heard that Jeroboam had returned, they
sent messengers and summoned him to the assembly and
made him king over all Israel. Only the tribe of Judah remained
loyal to the House of David.
21 On his return to Jerusalem, Rehoboam mustered all the
House of Judah and the tribe of Benjamin, 180,000 picked
warriors, to fight against the House of Israel, in order to restore the kingship to Rehoboam son of Solomon. 22 But the
word of God came to Shemaiah, the man of God: 23 "Say
to King Rehoboam son of Solomon of Judah, and to all the
House of Judah and Benjamin and the rest of the people:
24 Thus said the LORD: You shall not set out to make war
on your kinsmen the Israelites. Let every man return to his
home, for this thing has been brought about by Me." They
heeded the word of the LORD and turned back, in accordance
with the word of the LORD.

a Lit. "tents." *b Elsewhere called Adoniram; cf. 2 Sam. 20.24 and note.*

11: *Scorpions,* may refer to a particular thorny plant or to some type of whip. **15:** The author's theological comment on the illogical turn of events. All that transpired was a fulfillment of what God told Solomon (11.11) and what Ahijah told Jeroboam (11.31–36); God makes people do unexpected things so the divine plan comes true (see e.g., Judg. 14.4). **16:** Northerners take up the rallying cry of an earlier anti-David rebel, Sheba son of Bichri, whose rebellion had threatened to split the kingdom (2 Sam. 20.1). **17:** Benjaminite clans living within view of Jerusalem may have cast their lot with Judah (v. 21); those farther north may have joined the northern confederation. Judah, here, refers not to the tribe but to the kingdom, dominated by the tribe that also included Simeon to the south of Judah.

12.18–24: Israel's rebellion and the truce. 18: Noting that the text does not clarify to where or for what *Adoram* was sent, Josephus suggests that *Rehoboam* sent him to apologize on the king's behalf. If this individual is identical to Adoniram, who was in charge of the forced labor (4.6; 5.28; see 2 Sam. 20.24), as suggested by the reading Adoniram in the LXX, Rehoboam made a particularly poor selection, choosing the individual most likely to raise resentment among the northern tribes. **19:** *As is still the case* would be true only in a document written while the Northern Kingdom still existed, i.e., prior to 722 BCE. **20:** Jeroboam's return from Egypt is reported in 12.3. Radak interprets the reference in this v. as indicating that (northern) Israel heard that he had returned to his family home and not to Egypt where he had settled. Jeroboam was made king by the assembly. **21–24:** Prophetic intervention stopped what might have turned into a major civil war; Rehoboam's heeding of *Shemaiah,* who appears only here in Kings, is a reflection of his piety. Although there was fighting between the two kingdoms during the reign of Jeroboam (14.30), it eventually petered out as both kingdoms faced common enemies. Throughout the divided monarchy, they often cooperated with each other.

25 Jeroboam fortified Shechem in the hill country of
Ephraim and resided there; he moved out from there and fortified Penuel. 26 Jeroboam said to himself, "Now the kingdom
may well return to the House of David. 27 If these people still
go up to offer sacrifices at the House of the LORD in Jerusalem, the heart of these people will turn back to their master,
King Rehoboam of Judah; they will kill me and go back to King
Rehoboam of Judah." 28 So the king took counsel and made
two golden calves. He said to [a-]the people,[-a] "You have been
going up to Jerusalem long enough. This is your god, O Israel, who brought you up from the land of Egypt!" 29 He set up
one in Bethel and placed the other in Dan. 30 That proved to
be a cause of guilt, for the people went to worship [the calf at
Bethel and] the one at Dan. 31 He also made cult places and
appointed priests from the ranks of the people who were not
of Levite descent.

32 He stationed at Bethel the priests of the shrines that he
had appointed to sacrifice to the calves that he had made.
And Jeroboam established a festival on the fifteenth day of the
eighth month; in imitation of the festival in Judah, he established one at Bethel, and he ascended the altar [there]. 33 On
the fifteenth day of the eighth month—the month in which he
had contrived of his own mind to establish a festival for the
Israelites—Jeroboam ascended the altar that he had made in
Bethel.

13 As he ascended the altar to present an offering, 1 a
man of God arrived at Bethel from Judah at the command of the LORD. While Jeroboam was standing on the altar[b]
to present the offering, the man of God, at the command of
the LORD, cried out against the altar: 2 "O altar, altar! Thus said
the LORD: A son shall be born to the House of David, Josiah
by name; and he shall slaughter upon you the priests of the
shrines who bring offerings upon you. And human bones shall
be burned upon you." 3 He gave a portent on that day, saying, "Here is the portent that the LORD has decreed: This altar
shall break apart, and the ashes on it shall be spilled." 4 When
the king heard what the man of God had proclaimed against
the altar in Bethel, Jeroboam stretched out his arm above the

a-a Heb. "them." *b I.e., at the top of the steps or ramp.*

12.25–33: Jeroboam consolidates his rule. In a highly polemical passage, the author describes a series of cultic actions taken by Jeroboam that he considers spiteful violations of divine will. Consequently, he refers to them throughout Kings as the "sins of Jeroboam" that caused northern tribes to abandon Jerusalem, and are ultimately responsible for the exile of the Northrn Kingdom, a century and a half before the exile of Judah (2 Kings 17.20–21). **28–30:** He set up images, one at *Dan,* the northernmost border city, and one at *Bethel,* the southernmost main center of his kingdom. *Calves,* most likely small images of bulls, which represented the deity, such as have been found in excavations, were held to be in violation of Deut. 5.8–9. The story of Jeroboam's golden calves shares much in common with the episode of fashioning the single golden calf in the wilderness in Exod. ch 32. For example, the phrase "These are your gods, O Israel, who brought you out of the land of Egypt!" is also found though only one calf was made by Aaron (Exod. 32.4 *b-b,* which translates the Heb accurately). **31:** The shrines are held to be in violation of Deut. 12.13–14. **32–33:** Jeroboam celebrated Tabernacles, which was to be celebrated on the fifteenth day of the seventh month (Lev. 23.34), on *the fifteenth day of the eighth month* as determined in Jerusalem, but which was probably what he determined to be the seventh month (cf. 8.2). He may have intercalated a month to align calendared agricultural festivals with the actual harvest patterns of northern tribes, particularly those in Galilee. Tannaitic traditions from the Second Temple period indicate that the year could be intercalated under certain circumstances because of late grain or fruit harvests (*b. Sanh.* 11a–12b). As Solomon had apparently done (9.25), Jeroboam as king officiated on the altar.

13.1–33: Two prophetic stories connected to Bethel. Prophetic stories of unnamed prophets, and later of Elijah and Elisha, play a prominent role in the middle section of Kings. **1–10:** A prophecy against the Bethel altar which is part of a larger miracle story. Specific mention of *Josiah* connects this to the fulfillment narrative associated with that king in 2 Kings 23.15–16. Proof of the validity of long-range prediction is a short-range prediction in v. 3 fulfilled in v. 5. The story cannot have achieved its current form until after the reforms of Josiah, ca. 620 BCE. Like the following story, this narrative emphasizes the importance of divine obedience. **2:** The burning of *human bones* would permanently defile the altar, making it unsuitable for use.

altar and cried, "Seize him!" But the arm that he stretched out
against him became rigid, and he could not draw it back. 5 The
altar broke apart and its ashes were spilled—the very portent
that the man of God had announced at the LORD's command.
6 Then the king spoke up and said to the man of God, "Please
entreat the LORD your God and pray for me that I may be able
to draw back my arm." The man of God entreated the LORD and
the king was able to draw his arm back; it became as it was
before.

7 The king said to the man of God, "Come with me to my
house and have some refreshment; and I shall give you a gift."
8 But the man of God replied to the king, "Even if you give me
half your wealth, I will not go in with you, nor will I eat bread
or drink water in this place; 9 for so I was commanded by the
word of the LORD: You shall eat no bread and drink no water,
nor shall you go back by the road by which you came." 10 So he
left by another road and did not go back by the road on which
he had come to Bethel.

11 There was an old prophet living in Bethel; and his sons[a]
came and told him all the things that the man of God had
done that day in Bethel [and] the words that he had spoken
to the king. When they told it to their father, 12 their father said
to them, "Which road did he leave by?" [b-]His sons had seen[-b]
the road taken by the man of God who had come from Judah.
13 "Saddle the ass for me," he said to his sons. They saddled
the ass for him, and he mounted it 14 and rode after the man
of God. He came upon him sitting under a terebinth and said
to him, "Are you the man of God who came from Judah?" "Yes,
I am," he answered. 15 "Come home with me," he said, "and
have something to eat." 16 He replied, "I may not go back with
you and enter your home; and I may not eat bread or drink
water in this place; 17 the order I received by the word of the
LORD was: You shall not eat bread or drink water there; nor
shall you return by the road on which you came." 18 "I am a
prophet, too," said the other, "and an angel said to me by command of the LORD: Bring him back with you to your house,
that he may eat bread and drink water." He was lying to him.
19 So he went back with him, and he ate bread and drank water
in his house.

20 While they were sitting at the table, the word of the LORD
came to the prophet who had brought him back. 21 He cried
out to the man of God who had come from Judah: "Thus said
the LORD: Because you have flouted the word of the LORD and
have not observed what the LORD your God commanded you,
22 but have gone back and eaten bread and drunk water in
the place of which He said to you, 'Do not eat bread or drink

a Heb. "son." *b-b Septuagint reads "And his sons showed."*

6: The answered prayer of *the man of God* illustrates his great power and prestige. **8:** Compare Num. 22.18; 24.13. **11–32:** A prophetic story in which a Bethel prophet deceptively tests the authenticity of *the man of God* and validates his long-term prediction. The prophet's prediction that *the man of God* would not be buried in a family tomb (vv. 21–22) is fulfilled in vv. 29–30. **22:** Burial outside the ancestoral burial place was perceived as a tragedy.

water [there],' your corpse shall not come to the grave of your
fathers." 23 After he had eaten bread and had drunk, he saddled the ass for him—for the prophet whom he had brought
back. 24 He set out, and a lion came upon him on the road and
killed him. His corpse lay on the road, with the ass standing
beside it, and the lion also standing beside the corpse. 25 Some
men who passed by saw the corpse lying on the road and the
lion standing beside the corpse; they went and told it in the
town where the old prophet lived. 26 And when the prophet
who had brought him back from the road heard it, he said,
"That is the man of God who flouted the LORD's command;
the LORD gave him over to the lion, which mauled him and
killed him in accordance with the word that the LORD had
spoken to him." 27 He said to his sons, "Saddle the ass for me,"
and they did so. 28 He set out and found the corpse lying on the
road, with the ass and the lion standing beside the corpse; the
lion had not eaten the corpse nor had it mauled the ass. 29 The
prophet lifted up the corpse of the man of God, laid it on the
ass, and brought it back; [a]it was brought[a] to the town of the
old prophet for lamentation and burial. 30 He laid the corpse
in his own burial place; and they lamented over it, "Alas, my
brother!" 31 After burying him, he said to his sons, "When I die,
bury me in the grave where the man of God lies buried; lay my
bones beside his. 32 For what he announced by the word of the
LORD against the altar in Bethel, and against all the cult places
in the towns of Samaria, shall surely come true."

33 Even after this incident, Jeroboam did not turn back from
his evil way, but kept on appointing priests for the shrines
from the ranks of the people. He ordained as priests of the
shrines any who so desired. 34 Thereby the House of Jeroboam
incurred guilt—to their utter annihilation from the face of the
earth.

14 At that time, Abijah, a son of Jeroboam, fell sick. 2 Jeroboam said to his wife, "Go and disguise yourself, so
that you will not be recognized as Jeroboam's wife, and go to
Shiloh. The prophet Ahijah lives there, the one who predicted that I would be king over this people. 3 Take with you ten
loaves, some wafers, and a jug of honey, and go to him; he will
tell you what will happen to the boy." 4 Jeroboam's wife did so;
she left and went to Shiloh and came to the house of Ahijah.
Now Ahijah could not see, for his eyes had become sightless
with age; 5 but the LORD had said to Ahijah, "Jeroboam's wife
is coming to inquire of you concerning her son, who is sick.
Speak to her thus and thus. When she arrives, she will be in
disguise."

a-a Lit. "it came."

30: "*Alas my brother!*" was a typical lament (see Jer. 22.18). **31:** The prophet from Bethel believed that the bones of the man of God conveyed magical powers; see 2 Kings 13.21. **33:** This incident refers to the healing event and its aftermath narrated above in vv. 6–10. The story of vv. 11–32 interrupts the flow between vv. 10 and 33, and may have been inserted by a later editor. The Judean author or editor criticizes the Northern practice of appointing priests who were not from Levitical families (Deut. 18.1–8).

14.1–18: A second tale about the prophet Ahijah and Jeroboam inculcating the lesson that the divine retribution is worked out through natural and man-made disasters, and emphasizing the extraordinary power of the prophet. **2:** The continuation of the chs shows the folly of Jeroboam's advice: the prophet is blind (v. 4), but as a prophet, does not need sight to identify the kings's wife. **3:** *Loaves ... wafers ... honey,* as a gift (1 Sam. 9.7–8). The *wafers* (Heb "nikudim," cf. Josh. 9.5, "crumbly") were perhaps a kind of biscuit or hardtack, meant to last longer than regular bread. **4:** *Could not see ... sightless,* so his identification of Jeroboam's wife is due only to God's revelation.

7–11: A prophetic speech serving as a preamble to a prediction. Ahijah alludes to 11.37–38 where conditions which Jeroboam did not meet were set out. **10–11:** The medium-range prediction against Jeroboam's dynasty is fulfilled in 15.29. **12–13:** A short-range prediction that Jeroboam's son Abijah will die is fulfilled in 14.17–18. These vv. originally continued v. 6 in the narrative. The theology of v. 13 is remarkable—the child died young and was given a proper burial because of *some* (undisclosed) *devotion ... to the Lord* that allowed him to avoid the later violent death of Jeroboam's other descendants (15.29). **15:** A long-range prediction that Israel will be destroyed and its people scattered across the Euphrates is fulfilled in 2 Kings 17.5–6. *Sacred posts,* Heb "asherim," were symbols of the goddess Asherah. In northern Canaanite myths she was the wife of El, but in southern Canaanite traditions she was associated with Baal. Heb inscriptions from the 8th and 7th centuries BCE discovered at Khirbet el-Kom near Lachish and at Kuntillet Ajrud in Sinai provide extrabiblical proof that some people in Judah associated her with YHVH, the God of Israel.

14.19–20: A concluding summary used throughout Kings. Jeroboam's reign included other administrative and military accomplishments that the author knows about from the *Annals of the Kings of Israel.* Nearly twenty-two years' worth of royal activites are not mentioned here; he cited only what was useful to him for his purpose.

14.21–31: Rehoboam's reign in Jerusalem, like all accounts in Kings, is presented only in so far as it suits the author's goal. **21:** A formula introduces each Judean king: name, age at beginning of reign, years of reign, name of mother and an evaluation of the reign. These data are followed by some salient facts and sometimes by expansive stories.

6 Ahijah heard the sound of her feet as she came through the
door, and he said, "Come in, wife of Jeroboam. Why are you
disguised? I have a harsh message for you. 7 Go tell Jeroboam:
Thus said the LORD, the God of Israel: I raised you up from
among the people and made you a ruler over My people Israel;
8 I tore away the kingdom from the House of David and gave
it to you. But you have not been like My servant David, who
kept My commandments and followed Me with all his heart,
doing only what was right in My sight. 9 You have acted worse
than all those who preceded you; you have gone and made for
yourself other gods and molten images to vex Me; and Me you
have cast behind your back. 10 Therefore I will bring disaster
upon the House of Jeroboam and will cut off from Jeroboam
every male, [a]bond and free,[a] in Israel. I will sweep away the
House of Jeroboam utterly, as dung is swept away. 11 Anyone
belonging to Jeroboam who dies in the town shall be devoured
by dogs; and anyone who dies in the open country shall be eat-
en by the birds of the air; for the LORD has spoken. 12 As for you,
go back home; as soon as you set foot in the town, the child
will die. 13 And all Israel shall lament over him and bury him;
he alone of Jeroboam's family shall be brought to burial, for in
him alone of the House of Jeroboam has some devotion been
found to the LORD, the God of Israel. 14 Moreover, the LORD will
raise up a king over Israel who will destroy the House of Jeroboam, [b]this day and even now.[b]

15 "The LORD will strike Israel until it sways like a reed in water. He will uproot Israel from this good land that He gave to
their fathers, and will scatter them beyond the Euphrates, because they have provoked the LORD by the sacred posts that
they have made for themselves. 16 He will forsake Israel because
of the sins that Jeroboam committed and led Israel to commit."

17 Jeroboam's wife got up and left, and she went to Tirzah. As
soon as she stepped over the threshold of her house, the child
died. 18 They buried him and all Israel lamented over him, in
accordance with the word that the LORD had spoken through
His servant the prophet Ahijah.

19 The other events of Jeroboam's reign, how he fought and
how he ruled, are recorded in the Annals of the Kings of Israel.
20 Jeroboam reigned twenty-two years; then he slept with his
fathers, and his son Nadab succeeded him as king.

21 Meanwhile, Rehoboam son of Solomon had become king
in Judah. Rehoboam was forty-one years old when he became
king, and he reigned seventeen years in Jerusalem—the city
the LORD had chosen out of all the tribes of Israel to establish

a-a *Meaning of Heb. uncertain; possibly "kinsman and friend," cf. 16.11.*
b-b *Meaning of Heb. uncertain.*

His name there. His mother's name was Naamah the Ammonitess. 22 Judah did what was displeasing to the LORD, and angered Him more than their fathers had done by the sins that
they committed. 23 They too built for themselves shrines, pillars, and sacred posts on every high hill and under every leafy
tree; 24 there were also male prostitutes in the land. [Judah] imitated all the abhorrent practices of the nations that the LORD
had dispossessed before the Israelites.

25 In the fifth year of King Rehoboam, King Shishak of Egypt
marched against Jerusalem 26 and carried off the treasures of
the House of the LORD and the treasures of the royal palace.
He carried off everything; he even carried off all the gold-
en shields that Solomon had made. 27 King Rehoboam had
bronze shields made instead, and he entrusted them to the
officers of the guard[a] who guarded the entrance to the royal
palace. 28 Whenever the king went into the House of the LORD,
the guards would carry them and then bring them back to the
armory of the guards.

29 The other events of Rehoboam's reign, and all his actions,
are recorded in the Annals of the Kings of Judah. 30 There was
continual war between Rehoboam and Jeroboam. 31 Rehoboam slept with his fathers and was buried with his fathers in the
City of David; his mother's name was Naamah the Ammonitess. His son Abijam succeeded him as king.

15 In the eighteenth year of King Jeroboam son of Nebat,
Abijam became king over Judah. 2 He reigned three
years in Jerusalem; his mother's name was [b-]Maacah daughter of Abishalom.[-b] 3 He continued in all the sins that his father
before him had committed; he was not wholehearted with the
LORD his God, like his father David. 4 Yet, for the sake of David, the LORD his God gave him a lamp in Jerusalem, by raising up his descendant after him and by preserving Jerusalem.
5 For David had done what was pleasing to the LORD and never
turned throughout his life from all that He had commanded
him, except in the matter of Uriah the Hittite. 6 There was war
between Abijam[c] and Jeroboam all the days of his life. 7 The
other events of Abijam's reign and all his actions are recorded

a Lit. "runners."

b-b 2 Chron. 13.2 reads "Micaiah daughter of Uriel of Gibeah"; cf. v. 10 below, where Maacah, daughter of Abishalom, appears as mother of Asa.

c So several mss.; most mss. and the editions read "Rehoboam."

22–28: The author first presents a specific summary of what was wrong in the ritual behavior of Judah (vv. 22–24) followed by events that in context are understood as an expression of divine displeasure. **23:** The criticism is that God was worshipped improperly, in many places outside of Jerusalem, and in many ways that were considered illegitimate. The critique is not that Judeans worshipped other gods. **24:** *Male prostitutes* (Heb "kedeshim"), more likely foreign specialists, perhaps poets and musicians, who assisted at rites the author does not approve of. Asa deported them (15.12). By noting the dispossessed nations, the author suggests that Judah should have been similarly punished, and hints at divine grace, for the sake of David. **25–26:** A hieroglyphic inscription on the wall of a temple in Karnak notes that *Shishak* raided the ancient Egyptian province of Canaan, leaving a record of 156 captured cities. Most cities listed were in Israel, the kingdom of Shishak's former protégé, Jeroboam. Abravanel suggested in the early 16th c. that perhaps Jeroboam invited Shishak to attack Jerusalem on his behalf. Although the text seems to imply that Shishak took the plunder by force, it is more likely that Rehoboam despoiled the Temple and palace of all the treasure introduced by Solomon in order to pay ransom to save Jerusalem. This spoil may also have been a bribe to Shishak to finance raids in Israel. Fragments of an inscription with Shishak's name were excavated in Megiddo. **26:** This payment to Shishak despoiled most of the treasure that Solomon had invested in the Temple. Although later generations were able to replace some of the golden decorations of the Temple, later descriptions of the Temple do not refer to its gold plating (2 Kings 14.14; 18.16). This notice, like others in Kings (1 Kings 15.18; 2 Kings 12.19; 14.14; 16.8; 20.13; 24.13), may derive from a Temple accounting book. **29–31:** A standard concluding summary for kings of Judah. Cf. the information about Solomon (11.41–43) and Asa (15.23–24).

15.1–8: The short, undistinguished reign of Abijam son of Rehoboam. **4:** *A lamp*, cf. 11.36. It is used here in the sense of continuity of the line (Jer. 25.10). **5:** *Except in the matter of Uriah the Hittite* is lacking in some LXX mss. **6:** Since border skirmishing continued into the reign of Abijam's son Asa (15.16), the reading adopted in NJPS on the basis of Heb and Gk mss is preferable to the textual tradition preserved in the MT.

15.9–24: Presentation of the reign of Asa follows the regular pattern of formulaic introductory (vv. 9–11) and concluding (vv. 23–24) materials between which selected stories are provided. **12–13:** What earned Asa the author's praise was his abolition of idols, of some wooden object dedicated to Asherah, and what he considered illegitimate places of worship. *Male prostitutes,* see 14.24 n. **13:** The *queen mother* (Heb "gevirah") had some official status and prerogatives; consequently she was accorded respect (2.19; 2 Kings 10.13; Jer. 13.18). Other women mentioned in this role played dominant roles in Israelite history: Jezebel (2 Kings 9.22) and Athaliah (2 Kings 11.1). Asa stripped his mother of her status and prerogatives. **14:** Despite the existence of the Temple, the shrines remained popular places of worship. **17:** *Baasha's* accession is noted later, in v. 33. *Ramah,* a short distance north of Jerusalem, controlled traffic into Jerusalem from the north and from the coast via northwest Benjaminite territories; Benjamin was on the northern border of Judah. **18:** The strong *Aram*ean city state of *Damascus,* to the north of Israel, will play a major role in the politics of the next few centuries. **20:** Asa's bribe to the Arameans cost the Northern Kingdom most of eastern Galilee and all upper Galilee. The tribes of Dan and Naphtali fell under the political domination of Damascus. **22:** Exploiting Israel's weakness while Baasha was rushing to protect his northern borders, Asa literally moved his own northern border past Ramah, about 3.5 km (2 mi) deeper into Benjaminite territory, by fortifying Geba and Mizpah, two villages set on the hill abutting and controlling the main north-south approach to Jerusalem. Excavations at Tel en-Nasbeh, ancient Mizpah, uncovered traces of a rapidly constructed wall that was later replaced by a strongly bonded one. **23:** *In his old age he suffered from a foot ailment* is a very unusual notice. The Talmud (*b. Sanh.* 48b) interprets the ailment as gout.

in the Annals of the Kings of Judah; there was war between
Abijam and Jeroboam. 8 Abijam slept with his fathers; he was
buried in the City of David, and his son Asa succeeded him
as king.
9 In the twentieth year of King Jeroboam of Israel, Asa became king over Judah. 10 He reigned forty-one years in Jerusalem; his mother's name was Maacah daughter of Abishalom.
11 Asa did what was pleasing to the LORD, as his father David
had done. 12 He expelled the male prostitutes from the land,
and he removed all the idols that his ancestors had made.
13 He also deposed his mother Maacah from the rank of queen
mother, because she had made [a]an abominable thing[a] for
[the goddess] Asherah. Asa cut down her abominable thing
and burnt it in the Wadi Kidron. 14 The shrines, indeed, were
not abolished; however, Asa was wholehearted with the LORD
his God all his life. 15 He brought into the House of the LORD all
the consecrated things of his father and [b]his own consecrated
things[b]—silver, gold, and utensils.
16 There was war between Asa and King Baasha of Israel
all their days. 17 King Baasha of Israel advanced against Judah, and he fortified Ramah to prevent anyone belonging to
King Asa from going out or coming in. 18 So Asa took all the
silver and gold that remained in the treasuries of the House
of the LORD as well as the treasuries of the royal palace, and
he entrusted them to his officials. King Asa sent them to King
Ben-hadad son of Tabrimmon son of Hezion of Aram, who
resided in Damascus, with this message: 19 "There is a pact
between you and me, and between your father and my father. I herewith send you a gift of silver and gold: Go and
break your pact with King Baasha of Israel, so that he may
withdraw from me." 20 Ben-hadad responded to King Asa's
request; he sent his army commanders against the towns
of Israel and captured Ijon, Dan, Abel-beth-maacah, and
all Chinneroth, as well as all the land of Naphtali. 21 When
Baasha heard about it, he stopped fortifying Ramah and remained in Tirzah.
22 Then King Asa mustered all Judah, with no exemptions;
and they carried away the stones and timber with which
Baasha had fortified Ramah. With these King Asa fortified
Geba of Benjamin, and Mizpah.
23 All the other events of Asa's reign, and all his exploits, and
all his actions, and the towns that he fortified, are recorded in
the Annals of the Kings of Judah. However, in his old age he
suffered from a foot ailment. 24 Asa slept with his fathers and
was buried with his fathers in the city of his father David. His
son Jehoshaphat succeeded him as king.

a-a Exact meaning of Heb. uncertain. *b-b So* kethib *and 2 Chron. 15.18.*

25 Nadab son of Jeroboam had become king over Israel in the second year of King Asa of Judah, and he reigned over Israel for two years. 26 He did what was displeasing to the LORD; he continued in the ways of his father, in the sins which he caused Israel to commit. 27 Then Baasha son of Ahijah, of the House of Issachar, conspired against him; and Baasha struck him down at Gibbethon of the Philistines, while Nadab and all Israel were laying siege to Gibbethon. 28 Baasha killed him in the third year of King Asa of Judah and became king in his stead. 29 As soon as he became king, he struck down all the House of Jeroboam; he did not spare a single soul belonging to Jeroboam until he destroyed it—in accordance with the word that the LORD had spoken through His servant, the prophet Ahijah the Shilonite—30 because of the sins which Jeroboam committed and which he caused Israel to commit thereby vexing the LORD, the God of Israel.

31 The other events of Nadab's reign and all his actions are recorded in the Annals of the Kings of Israel.

32 There was war between Asa and King Baasha of Israel all their days. 33 In the third year of King Asa of Judah, Baasha son of Ahijah became king in Tirzah over all Israel—for twenty-four years. 34 He did what was displeasing to the LORD; he followed the ways of Jeroboam and the sins which he caused Israel to commit.

16 The word of the LORD came to Jehu son of Hanani against Baasha: 2 "Because I lifted you up from the dust and made you a ruler over My people Israel, but you followed the way of Jeroboam and caused My people Israel to sin, vexing Me with their sins—3 I am going to sweep away Baasha and his house. I will make your house like the House of Jeroboam son of Nebat. 4 Anyone belonging to Baasha who dies in the town shall be devoured by dogs, and anyone belonging to him who dies in the open country shall be devoured by the birds of the sky."

5 The other events of Baasha's reign and his actions and his exploits are recorded in the Annals of the Kings of Israel. 6 Baasha slept with his fathers and was buried in Tirzah. His son Elah succeeded him as king.

7 But the word of the LORD had come through the prophet Jehu son of Hanani against Baasha and against his house, that it would fare like the House of Jeroboam, [a]which he himself had struck down,[a] because of all the evil he did which was displeasing to the LORD, vexing him with his deeds.

8 In the twenty-sixth year of King Asa of Judah, Elah son of Baasha became king over Israel, at Tirzah—for two years.

a-a Syntax of Heb. unclear.

15.25–32: Nadab's reign and Baasha's usurpation. The author considers *Nadab* of Israel irredeemably unworthy because he followed the way of Jeroboam (vv. 26, 30). The extirpation of Jeroboam's family is interpreted as fulfillment of a prophecy and hence a sign of divine providence. Baasha's usurpation, though not backed by a prophet like Ahijah, is considered divinely sanctioned. **32:** This is one of a number of similar notices; see 14.30; 15.6, 16.

15.33–16.7: Baasha's reign is treated sparsely, significant events having been provided in the sketch of Asa's career (15.17–21). The fact that Baasha continued the way of Jeroboam led to his denunciation by a prophet, Jehu son of Hanani. **4:** *Devoured ... dogs ... birds:* The bodies will not receive proper, respectful burial but will be carrion instead. **7:** This v., paraphrasing vv. 3–4, lacks adequate connection to its context. Rashi, perhaps noting the mention of Elah's ascension in v. 6 and the absence of a formulaic condemnation of his reign after v. 8, explains that this v. actually refers to a repetition of Jehu's prophecy during the reign of Elah, already doomed by his father's policies.

16.8–22: The reign of Elah, the usurpation of Zimri, and the struggle between Tibni and Omri. 8–14: The author relates nothing about Elah's brief reign other than the circumstances under which Zimri assassinated him, usurped authority, and murdered his family; such accounts highlight the instability, from Judah's perspective, of northern kingship.

9 His officer Zimri, commander of half the chariotry, committed treason against him while he was at Tirzah drinking
himself drunk in the house of Arza, who was in charge of
the palace at Tirzah. 10 Zimri entered, struck him down, and
killed him; he succeeded him as king in the twenty-seventh
year of King Asa of Judah. 11 No sooner had he become king
and ascended the throne than he struck down all the House of
Baasha; he did not leave a single male of his, nor any kinsman
or friend. 12 Thus Zimri destroyed all the House of Baasha, in
accordance with the word that the LORD had spoken through
the prophet Jehu—13 because of the sinful acts which Baasha
and his son Elah committed, and which they caused Israel to
commit, vexing the LORD, the God of Israel, with their false
gods. 14 The other events of Elah's reign and all his actions are
recorded in the Annals of the Kings of Israel.

15 During the twenty-seventh year of King Asa of Judah,
Zimri reigned in Tirzah for seven days. At the time, the troops
were encamped at Gibbethon of the Philistines. 16 When the
troops who were encamped there learned that Zimri had committed treason and had struck down the king, that very day,
in the camp, all Israel acclaimed the army commander Omri
king over Israel. 17 Omri and all Israel then withdrew from Gibbethon and laid siege to Tirzah. 18 When Zimri saw that the
town was taken, he went into the citadel of the royal palace
and burned down the royal palace over himself. And so he
died—19 because of the sins which he committed and caused
Israel to commit, doing what was displeasing to the LORD and
following the ways of Jeroboam. 20 The other events of Zimri's
reign, and the treason which he committed, are recorded in
the Annals of the Kings of Israel.

21 Then the people of Israel split into two factions: a part of
the people followed Tibni son of Ginath to make him king,
and the other part followed Omri. 22 Those who followed Omri
proved stronger than those who followed Tibni son of Ginath;
Tibni died and Omri became king.

23 In the thirty-first year of King Asa of Judah, Omri became
king over Israel—for twelve years. He reigned in Tirzah six
years. 24 Then he bought the hill of Samaria from Shemer for
two talents of silver; he built [a town] on the hill and named
the town which he built Samaria, after Shemer, the owner of
the hill.

25 Omri did what was displeasing to the LORD; he was worse
than all who preceded him. 26 He followed all the ways of Jeroboam son of Nebat and the sins which he committed and
caused Israel to commit, vexing the LORD, the God of Israel,
with their futilities. 27 The other events of Omri's reign, [and]
his actions, and the exploits he performed, are recorded in the

15–18: Zimri lacked any popular support, even from the chariot troops under his command. Omri, acclaimed king by his army *(all Israel)* while at the Philistine front, withdrew to *Tirzah* in the heart of Israel and captured it. *Zimri,* the assassin, committed suicide. **19:** The author appends a standard condemnation to his summary of Zimri's seven-day reign. So far as he is concerned, had Zimri reversed some of Jeroboam's cultic policies, he would have been lauded. **21–22:** These vv. continue the narrative from v. 18. Despite the army's acclamation of Omri as king, the chronological notices suggest that the northern tribes were divided for almost four years (cf. vv. 15, 23) about who should be elected king: Omri or Tibni (possibly another military figure). Tibni's death resolved the matter. The author, who has no interest in providing any details concerning this civil war, makes no evaluative comment about Tibni because he was never acknowledged officially as king.

16.23–28: The reign of Omri. Aside from formulary types of information, the single event reported for Omri is the construction of a new capital city, *Samaria.* According to an inscription left by Mesha, king of Moab in the mid-9th c. (cf. 2 Kings 3.4), Omri was a powerful king, who conquered and colonized northern Moab. He achieved a level of renown for his exploits such that after his dynasty had been supplanted, an Assyrian inscription called Israel "the house of Omri." The contrast between the biblical account and the ancient Near Eastern account, which indicates Omri's prowess, highlights how little Kings cares to glorify Omri. Omri's dynasty maintained itself through the reigns of three descendants.

Annals of the Kings of Israel. 28 Omri slept with his fathers and
was buried in Samaria; and his son Ahab succeeded him as
king.

29 Ahab son of Omri became king over Israel in the thirty-
eighth year of King Asa of Judah, and Ahab son of Omri reigned
over Israel in Samaria for twenty-two years. 30 Ahab son of Omri
did what was displeasing to the LORD, more than all who preceded him. 31 Not content to follow the sins of Jeroboam son
of Nebat, he took as wife Jezebel daughter of King Ethbaal of
the Phoenicians, and he went and served Baal and worshiped
him. 32 He erected an altar to Baal in the temple of Baal which
he built in Samaria. 33 Ahab also made a sacred post. Ahab did
more to vex the LORD, the God of Israel, than all the kings of
Israel who preceded him.

34 During his reign, Hiel the Bethelite fortified Jericho. He
laid its foundations at the cost of Abiram his first-born, and set
its gates in place at the cost of Segub his youngest, in accordance with the words that the LORD had spoken through Joshua
son of Nun.[a]

17 Elijah the Tishbite, an inhabitant of Gilead, said to Ahab,
"As the LORD lives, the God of Israel whom I serve, there
will be no dew or rain except at my bidding."

a Cf. Josh. 6.26.

16.29–22.40: Stories about the reign of Ahab include a large collection of stories about the charismatic prophet Elijah, who was intimately involved in the religious and political life of the kingdom. **16.29–34:** This section introduces the reign of Ahab in typical formulaic fashion. The concluding formulae are found in 22.39–40. The intervening narratives serve to support the author's extremely negative evaluation of Ahab's reign. **31:** *Jezebel daughter of King Ethbaal of the Phoenicians* (lit. "Sidonians"): Jezebel's name consists of two components, "ʾiy + zebel," which in Phoenician, the language of Tyre and Sidon, mean "where is glory/dominion." Compare Ichabod, Heb "ʾiy + kabod," meaning "where is honor/glory" (1 Sam. 4.21). In Ugaritic mythology, "zebul" is a title of Baal, god of rain and sweet water. Ethbaal's name means "with Baal." His title "king of the Sidonians" indicates that he was king of both Sidon and Tyre. Hiram in the time of David and Solomon held the same authority but used a different title (5.15). Following a common biblical topos, in this passage and elsewhere in the Ahab stories, the wife is blamed for leading the husband astray. **32–33:** In addition to worshipping Baal, Ahab constructed a temple for him in Samaria with a special altar, and he also established an "ʾasherah," a sacred post, the symbol of the goddess Asherah, somewhere in the city, but not in the Baal temple itself (cf. 2 Kings 13.6). **33:** *Vex the LORD* (Heb "lehakhʿis," expressing causality). The author, not believing that anybody could take idolatry seriously, explained that Ahab continued doing such things out of spite in order to anger God. **34:** In another case of the author's prophecy-fulfillment pattern (see e.g., 2.26–27 n.), tragic events in the life of a certain Hiel from Bethel are presented as the actualization of Joshua's curse (Josh. 6.26). Ralbag interprets the placement of this v. as indicating that although Ahab should have understood what happened to Hiel as a warning of what might happen to him, he persisted in his ways.

17.1–19.21: Elijah stories occupy a significant place in the author's composition about the Northern Kingdom. The author, who uses a prediction-fulfillment pattern as a leitmotif (key theme) in Kings, held prophets in high regard and had access to stores of prophetic tales. Some of these presented Elijah as being in contact and conflict with Ahab and Jezebel over religious matters. A zealous champion of God, a radical monotheist, Elijah, whose name means "my God is Yahu (the LORD)," fought for his cause fearlessly and at such personal risk that even Ahab held him in regard. The four major stories about him (17.1–18.46; 19.1–21; 21.1–29; 2 Kings 2.2–2.12) and similar prophets (20.1–43; 22.1–40) are presented because their heroes taught what the author believed and they acted in ways he thought appropriate. These stories, which do not assume the centrality of worship of God in Jerusalem (see esp. ch 18), comprise a source which became incorporated into Kings. Ch 17 seems to begin in the middle of the Elijah story, suggesting that not all of this source was used. Some of the Elijah stories are paralleled in the stories about his prophetic disciple Elisha, described in 2 Kings.

17.1–18.46: The drought. 17.1: Elijah predicts a drought. The mention of dew and rain challenges Ahab's notion that Baal, celebrated as god of fresh water, is responsible for them. Subsequent events suggest that the drought, limited to only Israelite territory and persisting for a long while, came to be seen as unnatural. At a theological level, the author presents this story because Elijah's prediction resonates with Deut. 11.13–17. *Tishbite* may refer to a city of Tishbe, perhaps in Galilee. **2–24:** Miracle stories about Elijah illustrate that God protected and provided for his sustenance and that he in turn provided sustenance for others. They also show that God responded to his prayers. **2:** *Wadi Cherith* in Transjordan may have been in Israelite territory but outside of Ahab's jurisdiction. Later, when the severity of the drought dried up local water, God directed Elijah to Zarephath in Phoenician territory (vv. 7–8).

2 The word of the LORD came to him: 3 "Leave this place; turn
eastward and go into hiding by the Wadi Cherith, which is east
of the Jordan. 4 You will drink from the wadi, and I have commanded the ravens to feed you there." 5 He proceeded to do
as the LORD had bidden: he went, and he stayed by the Wadi
Cherith, which is east of the Jordan. 6 The ravens brought him
bread and meat every morning and every evening, and he
drank from the wadi.
7 After some time the wadi dried up, because there was no
rain in the land. 8 And the word of the LORD came to him: 9 "Go
at once to Zarephath of Sidon, and stay there; I have designated

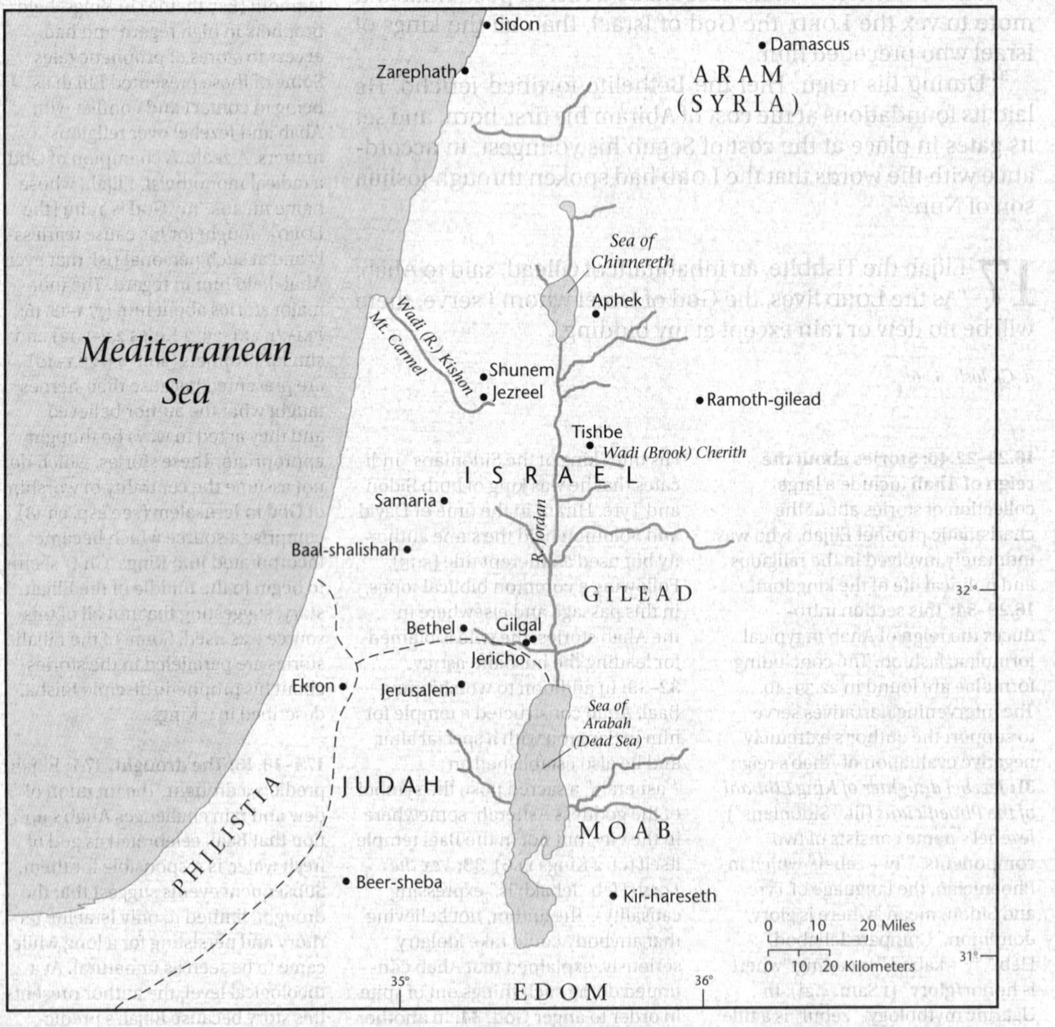

Places associated with the Elijah narratives. The dashed line shows the approximate boundaries between Israel, Judah and Philistia.

a widow there to feed you." [10] So he went at once to Zarephath. When he came to the entrance of the town, a widow was there gathering wood. He called out to her, "Please bring me a little water in your pitcher, and let me drink." [11] As she went to fetch it, he called out to her, "Please bring along a piece of bread for me." [12] "As the LORD your God lives," she replied, "I have nothing baked, nothing but a handful of flour in a jar and a little oil in a jug. I am just gathering a couple of sticks, so that I can go home and prepare it for me and my son; we shall eat it and then we shall die." [13] "Don't be afraid," said Elijah to her. "Go and do as you have said; but first make me a small cake from what you have there, and bring it out to me; then make some for yourself and your son. [14] For thus said the LORD, the God of Israel: The jar of flour shall not give out and the jug of oil shall not fail until the day that the LORD sends rain upon the ground." [15] She went and did as Elijah had spoken, and she and he and her household had food for a long time. [16] The jar of flour did not give out, nor did the jug of oil fail, just as the LORD had spoken through Elijah.

[17] After a while, the son of the mistress of the house fell sick, and his illness grew worse, until he had no breath left in him. [18] She said to Elijah, "What harm have I done you, O man of God, that you should come here to recall my sin and cause the death of my son?" [19] "Give me the boy," he said to her; and taking him from her arms, he carried him to the upper chamber where he was staying, and laid him down on his own bed. [20] He cried out to the LORD and said, "O LORD my God, will You bring calamity upon this widow whose guest I am, and let her son die?" [21] Then he stretched out over the child three times, and cried out to the LORD, saying, "O LORD my God, let this child's life return to his body!" [22] The LORD heard Elijah's plea; the child's life returned to his body, and he revived. [23] Elijah picked up the child and brought him down from the upper room into the main room, and gave him to his mother. "See," said Elijah, "your son is alive." [24] And the woman answered Elijah, "Now I know that you are a man of God and that the word of the LORD is truly in your mouth."

18 Much later, in the third year,[a] the word of the LORD came to Elijah: "Go, appear before Ahab; then I will send rain upon the earth." [2] Thereupon Elijah set out to appear before Ahab.

The famine was severe in Samaria. [3] Ahab had summoned Obadiah, the steward of the palace. (Obadiah revered the LORD greatly. [4] When Jezebel was killing off the prophets of the LORD, Obadiah had taken a hundred prophets and hidden them, fifty to a cave, and provided them with food and drink.)

a *I.e., of the drought; see 17.1.*

10: *A widow:* The story presupposes that there was some external sign that differentiated widows, who were typically poor, from other women, perhaps some item of dress (Gen. 38.14). The widow remains nameless in the two stories about her that follow because the point of the stories is to celebrate the power of the named prophet. Rashi, noting the similarity between Elijah's request for water and that of Abraham's servant in Gen. 24.12–20, suggests that like the servant, Elijah had proposed a test to determine if this particular widow was the one designated by God. **14–16:** Elijah's prediction that as a result of her faith the jars would have an unfailing supply of flour and oil (staple foodstuffs) is fulfilled immediately. **18:** The *sin* is unspecified; Radak suggests that she believes that her son's illness is punishment for her sin. **21:** Elijah attempted what is sometimes described as the first recorded case of artificial respiration on the child, who was critically ill but not dead; then he prayed on the child's behalf. A healing procedure in some Mesopotamian incantations against demons instructs the healer to superimpose his body over that of the patient, head to head, hand to hand, foot to foot. **24:** His success as a wonder-worker is what convinced the widow that he was indeed a prophet. In Israel, the power to intercede with God was considered a prophetic gift (cf. Gen. 20.7). Elijah is here called *a man of God,* a term which in these narratives often emphasizes the prophet's superhuman powers. **18.1:** See 17.1. **4:** The author's parenthetical remark provides important information for this and subsequent narratives: (1) Elijah was not the only prophet in Israel during this time. (2) Jezebel had been persecuting and *killing off* prophets, most likely holding them culpable for the drought. (3) *Obadiah* was part of a coterie of devout people who followed, supported, and protected prophets like Elijah (cf. vv. 12–13).

[5] And Ahab had said to Obadiah, "Go through the land, to all the springs of water and to all the wadis. Perhaps we shall find some grass to keep horses and mules alive, so that we are not left without beasts."

[6] They divided the country between them to explore it, Ahab going alone in one direction and Obadiah going alone in another direction. [7] Obadiah was on the road, when Elijah suddenly confronted him. [Obadiah] recognized him and flung himself on his face, saying, "Is that you, my lord Elijah?" [8] "Yes, it is I," he answered. "Go tell your lord: Elijah is here!" [9] But he said, "What wrong have I done, that you should hand your servant over to Ahab to be killed? [10] As the LORD your God lives, there is no nation or kingdom to which my lord has not sent to look for you; and when they said, 'He is not here,' he made that kingdom or nation swear that you could not be found. [11] And now you say, 'Go tell your lord: Elijah is here!' [12] When I leave you, the spirit of the LORD will carry you off I don't know where; and when I come and tell Ahab and he does not find you, he will kill me. Yet your servant has revered the LORD from my youth. [13] My lord has surely been told what I did when Jezebel was killing the prophets of the LORD, how I hid a hundred of the prophets of the LORD, fifty men to a cave, and provided them with food and drink. [14] And now you say, 'Go tell your lord: Elijah is here.' Why, he will kill me!"

[15] Elijah replied, "As the LORD of Hosts lives, whom I serve, I will appear before him this very day."

[16] Obadiah went to find Ahab, and informed him; and Ahab went to meet Elijah. [17] When Ahab caught sight of Elijah, Ahab said to him, "Is that you, you troubler of Israel?" [18] He retorted, "It is not I who have brought trouble on Israel, but you and your father's House, by forsaking the commandments of the LORD and going after the Baalim. [19] Now summon all Israel to join me at Mount Carmel, together with the four hundred and fifty prophets of Baal and the four hundred prophets of Asherah, [a]who eat at Jezebel's table."[a]

[20] Ahab sent orders to all the Israelites and gathered the prophets at Mount Carmel. [21] Elijah approached all the people and said, "How long will you keep hopping [b]between two opinions?[b] If the LORD is God, follow Him; and if Baal, follow him!" But the people answered him not a word. [22] Then Elijah said to the people, "I am the only prophet of the LORD left, while the prophets of Baal are four hundred and fifty men. [23] Let two young bulls be given to us. Let them choose one bull, cut it up, and lay it on the wood, but let them not apply fire; I will prepare the other bull, and lay it on the wood, and will

a-a I.e., who are maintained by Jezebel.   *b-b Lit. "on the two boughs."*

12: *The spirit of the LORD will carry you off:* One of the supernatural abilities that was attributed to Elijah as a man of God was the ability to travel large distances suddenly. **17:** Ahab attributes the drought to Elijah and his God. **19–46:** The contest between Elijah and the Baal prophets on Mount Carmel pits the Israelite, in the presence of *all Israel,* against *four hundred and fifty prophets of Baal and the four hundred prophets of Asherah* (vv. 19–20). **19:** *Mount Carmel,* at the south end of modern Haifa, is at the seaward end of a range that rises to 530 m (1,600 ft). **21:** Elijah's rhetorical question indicates that Israelites supported both Baal and God. (In 19.18, the author provides a statistic indicating this clearly.) In polytheistic pluralism, this was a valid position. Elijah, however, a radical monotheist, was intolerant of the "both … and" situation; he recasts Israelite options into an "either … or" choice for which they will have to bear consequences. **22–25:** Since Elijah seems to have determined the nature of the contest, he proposes that the Baal prophets select whichever *bull* they wish, perhaps to eliminate any suspicion of fraud.

not apply fire. 24 You will then invoke your god by name, and I will invoke the LORD by name; [a-]and let us agree:[-a] the god who responds with fire, that one is God." And all the people answered, "Very good!"

25 Elijah said to the prophets of Baal, "Choose one bull and prepare it first, for you are the majority; invoke your god by name, but apply no fire." 26 They took the bull that was given them; they prepared it, and invoked Baal by name from morning until noon, shouting, "O Baal, answer us!" But there was no sound, and none who responded; so they performed a hopping dance about the altar that had been set up. 27 When noon came, Elijah mocked them, saying, "Shout louder! After all, he is a god. [b-]But he may be in conversation, he may be detained, or he may be on a journey,[-b] or perhaps he is asleep and will wake up." 28 So they shouted louder, and gashed themselves with knives and spears, according to their practice, until the blood streamed over them. 29 When noon passed, they [c-]kept raving[-c] until the hour of presenting the meal offering. Still there was no sound, and none who responded or heeded.

30 Then Elijah said to all the people, "Come closer to me"; and all the people came closer to him. He repaired the damaged altar of the LORD. 31 Then Elijah took twelve stones, corresponding to the number of the tribes of the sons of Jacob—to whom the word of the LORD had come: "Israel shall be your name"[d]— 32 and with the stones he built an altar in the name of the LORD. Around the altar he made a trench large enough for two *seahs* of seed.[e] 33 He laid out the wood, and he cut up the bull and laid it on the wood. 34 And he said, "Fill four jars with water and pour it over the burnt offering and the wood." Then he said, "Do it a second time"; and they did it a second time. "Do it a third time," he said; and they did it a third time. 35 The water ran down around the altar, and even the trench was filled with water.

36 When it was time to present the meal offering, the prophet Elijah came forward and said, "O LORD, God of Abraham, Isaac, and Israel! Let it be known today that You are God in Israel and that I am Your servant, and that I have done all these things at Your bidding. 37 Answer me, O LORD, answer me, that this people may know that You, O LORD, are God; [b-]for You have turned their hearts backward."[-b]

38 Then fire from the LORD descended and consumed the burnt offering, the wood, the stones, and the earth; and it

24: The nation's support validates the contest. **26:** The words *that was given them* are missing in some LXX mss, and are inappropriate according to v. 25. **26:** The *hopping dance* may reflect a Canaanite ritual, or may simply be mocking the opposition. **27:** The sarcastic comments, ostensibly directed to the Baal prophets, are intended for the ears of the audience. **28:** No extant Canaanite texts reflect such cutting rituals; but cf. Lev. 19.26–28 n. **32–35:** In dousing the ground around and under the altar, and drenching the sacrifice with water, the substance associated with Baal, Elijah indicates that even though Baal failed to ignite his own sacrifice he might be powerful enough to stop God. God's power is also heightened, as God's fire ignites the wet altar and sacrifice. **38:** For a second time, the LORD heeds Elijah (see 17.22). When the divine fire consumed everything, including the water, the message was clear.

a-a Lit. "and it shall be." *b-b Meaning of Heb. uncertain.*

c-c Others "prophesied"; see Num. 11.25–26. *d See Gen. 35.10.*

e I.e., of an area which would require two seahs *of seed if sown. Cf. Lev. 27.16; Isa. 5.10.*

39–40: This cry indicates that they opted for God and monotheism. The same words are found elsewhere in the Bible (e.g., Deut. 4.35, 39), and were later used as the culminating confession of faith at the conclusion of Yom Kippur. Ahab, present through all this (v. 41; 19.1), says and does nothing. The author presents no information about the prophets of Asherah. **41:** Elijah announces the end of the drought. **42–43:** Although the narrative is opaque, it appears that Elijah's posture is somehow responsible for bringing the cloud and the following rain. It is usually assumed that he was praying, but the fetal position is not known to have been adopted for prayer, and no word for prayer appears in the narrative. **46:** The strength and stamina for Elijah's long run came by virtue of the *hand of the Lord* (see also v. 12). Since running before the royal chariot was both an honor and a way of honoring the king (1 Sam. 8.11; 1 Kings 1.5), Elijah's motivation for doing so may have been to show respect to Ahab who he thought had been won over to radical monotheism. Elijah did not enter Jezreel.

19.1–18: Elijah's flight from Jezebel into Judah, and the revelation at Mt. Horeb. 2: Jezebel acts imperiously, warning Elijah of her plan to avenge the deaths of her countrymen. **3:** *Frightened,* he flees south, across Judah and into the wilderness beyond. **4–7:** Again, though Elijah is hiding far from food sources, his needs are provided for (cf. 17.6). The theme of a prophet's wishing for death out of a sense of isolation and failure in v. 4 are mimicked by the request and circumstances of Jonah in Jonah 4.3; that of being provisioned in the wilderness in vv. 5–6 parallels the story of Hagar in Gen. 21.14–19. **8:** *Horeb,* meaning "dry place," is the name preferred by Deut. for the mountain designated Sinai in Exod., Lev., and Num. Information in this v. contributes nothing toward determining its location. Since an unencumbered person used to walking can cover 15–25

licked up the water that was in the trench. [39]When they saw this, all the people flung themselves on their faces and cried out: "The LORD alone is God, The LORD alone is God!"

[40]Then Elijah said to them, "Seize the prophets of Baal, let not a single one of them get away." They seized them, and Elijah took them down to the Wadi Kishon and slaughtered them there.

[41]Elijah said to Ahab, "Go up, eat and drink, for there is a rumbling of [approaching] rain," [42]and Ahab went up to eat and drink. Elijah meanwhile climbed to the top of Mount Carmel, crouched on the ground, and put his face between his knees. [43]And he said to his servant, "Go up and look toward the Sea." He went up and looked and reported, "There is nothing." Seven times [Elijah] said, "Go back," [44]and the seventh time, [the servant] reported, "A cloud as small as a man's hand is rising in the west." Then [Elijah] said, "Go say to Ahab, 'Hitch up [your chariot] and go down before the rain stops you.' " [45]Meanwhile the sky grew black with clouds; there was wind, and a heavy downpour fell; Ahab mounted his chariot and drove off to Jezreel. [46]The hand of the LORD had come upon Elijah. [a-]He tied up his skirts[-a] and ran in front of Ahab all the way to Jezreel.

19 When Ahab told Jezebel all that Elijah had done and how he had put all the prophets[b] to the sword, [2]Jezebel sent a messenger to Elijah, saying, [c-]"Thus and more may the gods do[-c] if by this time tomorrow I have not made you like one of them."

[3]Frightened,[d] he fled at once for his life. He came to Beer-sheba, which is in Judah, and left his servant there; [4]he himself went a day's journey into the wilderness. He came to a broom bush and sat down under it, and prayed that he might die. "Enough!" he cried. "Now, O LORD, take my life, for I am no better than my fathers."

[5]He lay down and fell asleep under a broom bush. Suddenly an angel touched him and said to him, "Arise and eat." [6]He looked about; and there, beside his head, was a cake baked on hot stones and a jar of water! He ate and drank, and lay down again. [7]The angel of the LORD came a second time and touched him and said, "Arise and eat, or the journey will be too much for you." [8]He arose and ate and drank; and with the strength from that meal he walked forty days and forty nights as far as the mountain of God at Horeb. [9]There he went into a cave, and there he spent the night.

a-a Lit. "He bound up his loins." *b Of Baal; see 18.40.*
c-c A formula of imprecation. Many Heb. mss. and Septuagint add "to me."
d So many Heb. mss. and Septuagint; most mss., and the editions, read "And he saw, and."

Then the word of the LORD came to him. He said to him, "Why
are you here, Elijah?" 10 He replied, "I am moved by zeal for the
LORD, the God of Hosts, for the Israelites have forsaken Your
covenant, torn down Your altars, and put Your prophets to the
sword. I alone am left, and they are out to take my life." 11 "Come
out," He called, "and stand on the mountain before the LORD."
And lo, the LORD passed by. There was a great and mighty
wind, splitting mountains and shattering rocks by the power of
the LORD; but the LORD was not in the wind. After the wind—an
earthquake; but the LORD was not in the earthquake. 12 After
the earthquake—fire; but the LORD was not in the fire. And after
the fire—a soft murmuring sound.[a] 13 When Elijah heard it, he
wrapped his mantle about his face and went out and stood at
the entrance of the cave. Then a voice addressed him: "Why are
you here, Elijah?" 14 He answered, "I am moved by zeal for the
LORD, the God of Hosts; for the Israelites have forsaken Your
covenant, torn down Your altars, and have put Your prophets
to the sword. I alone am left, and they are out to take my life."
15 The LORD said to him, "Go back by the way you came,
[and] on to the wilderness of Damascus. When you get there,
anoint Hazael as king of Aram. 16 Also anoint Jehu son of Nimshi as king of Israel, and anoint Elisha son of Shaphat of Abel-
meholah to succeed you as prophet. 17 Whoever escapes the
sword of Hazael shall be slain by Jehu, and whoever escapes
the sword of Jehu shall be slain by Elisha. 18 I will leave in Israel
only seven thousand—every knee that has not knelt to Baal
and every mouth that has not kissed him."
19 He set out from there and came upon Elisha son of Shaphat as he was plowing. There were twelve yoke of oxen ahead
of him, and he was with the twelfth. Elijah came over to him
and threw his mantle over him. 20 He left the oxen and ran after
Elijah, saying: "Let me kiss my father and mother good-by, and
I will follow you." And he answered him, "Go back. What have
I done to you?"[b] 21 He turned back from him and took the yoke
of oxen and slaughtered them; he boiled [c]their meat[c] with the
gear[d] of the oxen and gave it to the people, and they ate. Then
he arose and followed Elijah and became his attendant.

a Others "a still, small voice." *b I.e., I am not stopping you.*
c-c Lit. "them, the flesh." *d I.e., using it as firewood; cf. 2 Sam. 24.22.*

miles a day, depending on the terrain, and Elijah is said to have traveled 40 days, the mountain could be 600–1,000 miles in any direction except north from some point south of Beer-sheba. Cf. Deut. 1.1–2. The *forty days* may suggest Moses, who spent forty days and nights atop Sinai (Exod. 24.18). In both cases, forty may be understood as a formulaic number, not to be taken literally. **9–14:** The combination of a cave and the divine revelation to the dispirited Elijah at Horeb/Sinai parallels thematically the cleft in the rock where God sheltered the overwhelmed Moses when He passed before him (Exod. 33.13–23), and helps to establish Elijah as a new Moses or a prophet like Moses (Deut. 18.15, 18). Elijah repeats in v. 14, after the revelation, what he said in v. 9, but the words ring less urgently. The revelation demonstrated that Elijah was not alone and restored a sense of proportion. The common elements of theophany, wind and thunder are present (see e.g., Exod. ch 19; Hab. ch 3), but here, unlike most theophanies, God is not within these meteorological phenomena. **15–17:** Malbim suggests that each person to be anointed was in response to one of Elijah's complaints: Hazael would punish those who broke down the altars, Jehu would punish those responsible for killing prophets, and Elisha would be a prophet with and after him. No other prophet is recorded to have designated his own prophetic replacement, though here too there may be some echo of Moses choosing Joshua as a replacement in his own lifetime (Num. 27.15–23).

19.19–21: The choice of Elisha. Reassured, Elijah first attends to his third assigned task, appointing Elisha. (The account does not mention completing the first two tasks.) Elijah's call to Elisha consists of the apparently casual but symbolically rich act of throwing his mantle over him and walking on without a word. **20:** The meaning of Elijah's response to Elisha's reasonable request is unclear. Perhaps it means that should he turn back from Elijah, the symbolic act will have lost its significance.

20

20 King Ben-hadad of Aram gathered his whole army;
thirty-two kings accompanied him with horses and
chariots. He advanced against Samaria, laid siege to it, and
attacked it. 2 And he sent messengers to Ahab inside the city
3 to say to him, "Thus said Ben-hadad: Your silver and gold are
mine, and your beautiful wives and children are mine." 4 The
king of Israel replied, "As you say, my lord king: I and all I have
are yours." 5 Then the messengers came again and said, "Thus
said Ben-hadad: When I sent you the order to give me your silver and gold, and your wives and children, 6 I meant that tomorrow at this time I will send my servants to you and they will
search your house and the houses of your courtiers and seize
everything you[a] prize and take it away."
7 Then the king of Israel summoned all the elders of the land,
and he said, "See for yourselves how that man is bent on evil!
For when he demanded my wives and my children, my silver
and my gold, I did not refuse him." 8 All the elders and all the
people said, "Do not obey and do not submit!" 9 So he said
to Ben-hadad's messengers, "Tell my lord the king: All that
you first demanded of your servant I shall do, but this thing
I cannot do." The messengers went and reported this to him.
10 Thereupon Ben-hadad sent him this message: [b-]"May the
gods do thus to me and even more,[-b] if the dust of Samaria will
provide even a handful for each of the men who follow me!"
11 The king of Israel replied, "Tell him: Let not him who girds
on his sword boast like him who ungirds it!"
12 On hearing this reply—while he and the other kings were
drinking together at Succoth—he[c] commanded his followers,
"Advance!" And they advanced against the city. 13 Then a certain prophet went up to King Ahab of Israel and said, "Thus
said the LORD: Do you see that great host? I will deliver it into
your hands today, and you shall know that I am the LORD."
14 "Through whom?" asked Ahab. He answered, "Thus said
the LORD: Through the aides of the provincial governors." He
asked, "Who shall begin the battle?" And he answered, "You."
15 So he mustered the aides of the provincial governors, 232
strong, and then he mustered all the troops—all the Israelites—7,000 strong. 16 They marched out at noon, while Ben-
hadad was drinking himself drunk at Succoth together with the

a Several ancient versions read "they." *b-b See note at 19.2.*
c I.e., Ben-hadad.

1 Kings 20.1–2 Kings 15.18: Throughout the following chs, the chronological notices and narratives present the Arameans, mainly from Damascus, as the major enemies of Israel, while the Trans-jordanian Moabites and Edomites appear mainly as troublers and irritants of Israel and Judah. The author of Kings and the authors of his sources appear to have been unaware that much of the military maneuvering and intrigue from the middle of the 9th through the mid-8th c. was strongly influenced by the military prowess and political strategizing of more distant Assyria, the empire that eventually conquered most of the Levant.

20.1–22.40: Narratives of the life and times of Ahab in which the king is the prime focus of attention and Elijah as well as other prophets appear in significant roles.

20.1–43: Ahab's war with Ben-hadad of Aram originally concerned the city of Samaria alone. Ben-hadad's aggression may have been precipitated after Ahab's closing of Aramean bazaars in the city, an international trade concession granted by Omri to Ben-hadad's father (v. 34). Although his whole army may have been mustered (v. 1), he first threatened the city with a small force, not anticipating a hostile response (vv. 15–20). The anonymous prophet who is the protagonist of the story has many thematic similarities to Elijah and to the nameless prophets earlier in the book. **2–4:** *Ben-hadad* demands payment from Ahab alone and Ahab accedes; this would represent Ahab becoming Ben-hadad's vassal. **5–9:** Hearing Ahab's quick, docile response, Ben-hadad changes the terms and demands the right to loot property from Ahab's courtiers. Ahab, lacking any right to give away what is not his, consults with *the elders of the land,* who instruct him not to comply with the demand. **11:** *Let not* ... was probably a proverb. **13:** An anonymous prophet counsels Ahab on military tactics. The reappearance of the figure bearing messages to Ahab throughout this story (vv. 28, 41) turns the historical narrative into a theological story about how an ungrateful Ahab turned a divinely orchestrated victory—the second battle—into a business opportunity. **14:** *Aides* (Heb "na'ar"), youths who functioned as fighters (cf. Gen. 14.24, where it is translated "servants"; 2 Sam. 2.14, where it is translated "young men"). The prophet counsels

thirty-two kings allied with him. [17] The aides of the provincial governors rushed out first. Ben-hadad sent [scouts], who told him, "Some men have come out from Samaria." [18] He said, "If they have come out to surrender, take them alive; and if they have come out for battle, take them alive anyhow." [19] But the others—the aides of the provincial governors, with the army behind them—had already rushed out of the city, [20] and each of them struck down his opponent. The Arameans fled, and Israel pursued them; but King Ben-hadad of Aram escaped on a horse with other horsemen. [21] The king of Israel came out and attacked the horses and chariots, and inflicted a great defeat on the Arameans. [22] Then the prophet approached the king of Israel and said to him, "Go, keep up your efforts, and consider well what you must do; for the king of Aram will attack you at the turn of the year."

[23] Now the ministers of the king of Aram said to him, "Their God is a God of mountains; that is why they got the better of us. But if we fight them in the plain, we will surely get the better of them. [24] Do this: Remove all the kings from their posts and appoint governors in their place. [25] Then muster for yourself an army equal to the army you lost, horse for horse and chariot for chariot. And let us fight them in the plain, and we will surely get the better of them." He took their advice and acted accordingly.

[26] At the turn of the year, Ben-hadad mustered the Arameans and advanced on Aphek to fight Israel. [27] Now the Israelites had been mustered and provisioned, and they went out against them; but when the Israelites encamped against them, they looked like two flocks[a] of goats, while the Arameans covered the land. [28] Then the man of God approached and spoke to the king of Israel, "Thus said the LORD: Because the Arameans have said, 'The LORD is a God of mountains, but He is not a God of lowlands,' I will deliver that great host into your hands; and you shall know that I am the LORD."

[29] For seven days they were encamped opposite each other. On the seventh day, the battle was joined and the Israelites struck down 100,000 Aramean foot soldiers in one day. [30] The survivors fled to Aphek, inside the town, and the wall fell on the 27,000 survivors.

Ben-hadad also fled and took refuge inside the town, in an inner chamber. [31] His ministers said to him, "We have heard that the kings of the House of Israel are magnanimous kings. Let us put sackcloth on our loins and ropes on our heads, and surrender to the king of Israel; perhaps he will spare your life." [32] So they girded sackcloth on their loins and wound ropes around their heads, and came to the king of Israel and said, "Your servant Ben-hadad says, 'I beg you, spare my life.'" He

him to initiate an attack using the aides as shock troops. **22:** *The turn of the year* is defined in 2 Sam. 11.1 as "the season when kings go out [to battle]." **23:** The narrative shows the folly of the *ministers*—the God of Israel is powerful everywhere, both on *mountains* and on the *plain.* **31–34:** Ben-hadad capitulates totally to Ahab. Following his servants' advice, he humbled himself and referred to himself as Ahab's *servant.* Ahab, however, refers to him by the term *brother,* signaling that he regards the defeated Aramean as an equal partner and inviting him into his chariot where terms for Ben-hadad's freedom must have been discussed. Ahab is given cities lost by his father to the Arameans and market concessions in Damascus. Although victorious in the battle of Aphek, Ahab's negotiating position was weak. Since the days of Baasha, Arameans had retained control of northern Israelite tribal territories in upper Galilee and the eastern part of lower Galilee (cf. 15.20). **32:** They dress like mourners.

a Meaning of Heb. uncertain.

35–42: Ahab had no right to spare those whom he had not defeated. According to the oracle of v. 28, God, not Ahab, defeated Ben-hadad. Consequently, Ben-hadad fell into the category of one doomed (v. 42), i.e., dedicated by God to destruction (see 1 Sam. ch 15). The prophet's use of a parable to get the king to pronounce judgment on himself is similar to Nathan's ploy in the case of Uriah and David (2 Sam. 12.1–12). **35–36:** See 13.1–31 (esp. v. 28); the word of the man of God must be heeded. **42:** *Doomed,* lit. proscribed or banned by the ḥerem, and thus dedicated to God (see 1 Sam. ch 15).

21.1–29: Naboth's vineyard. This story reintroduces Elijah and Jezebel into the narrative. In contrast to the preceding story, in which Ahab profited by not putting to death one who had been doomed by God, here he profits by passively allowing corrupt courts acting in the name of God and king to execute an innocent person. **1–3:** According to the Torah (Lev. 25.29–30), Ahab's request to purchase or trade for Naboth's *vineyard* next to his *palace* was neither unreasonable nor illegal, but Naboth refused because he did not wish to sell his patrimony (v. 3). **4:** *Dispirited and sullen,* as in 20.43; this phrase may have attracted the story of Naboth to its current location, disrupting the narrative concerning the Aramean wars. **6:** Ahab's half-truth to his wife omits Naboth's reason, given in v. 3. Jezebel surmises from Ahab's report to her that Naboth had insulted her husband personally.

replied, "Is he still alive? He is my brother." [33] The men divined
his meaning and quickly [a]caught the word from him,[-a] saying,
"Yes, Ben-hadad is your brother." "Go, bring him," he said. Ben-
hadad came out to him, and he invited him into his chariot.
[34] Ben-hadad said to him, "I will give back the towns that my
father took from your father, and you may set up bazaars for
yourself in Damascus as my father did in Samaria." "And I, for
my part," [said Ahab,] "will let you go home under these terms."
So he made a treaty with him and dismissed him.

[35] A certain man, a disciple of the prophets, said to another,
at the word of the LORD, "Strike me"; but the man refused to
strike him. [36] He said to him, "Because you have not obeyed
the LORD, a lion will strike you dead as soon as you leave me."
And when he left, a lion came upon him and killed him. [37] Then
he met another man and said, "Come, strike me." So the man
struck him and wounded him. [38] Then the prophet, disguised
by a cloth over his eyes, went and waited for the king by the
road. [39] As the king passed by, he cried out to the king and said,
"Your servant went out into the thick of the battle. Suddenly a
man came over and brought a man to me, saying, 'Guard this
man! If he is missing, it will be your life for his, or you will have
to pay a talent of silver.' [40] While your servant was busy here and
there, [the man] got away." The king of Israel responded, "You
have your verdict; you pronounced it yourself." [41] Quickly he
removed the cloth from his eyes, and the king recognized him
as one of the prophets. [42] He said to him, "Thus said the LORD:
Because you have set free the man whom I doomed, your life
shall be forfeit for his life and your people for his people." [43] Dispirited and sullen, the king left for home and came to Samaria.

21 [The following events] occurred sometime afterward:
Naboth the Jezreelite owned a vineyard in Jezreel, adjoining the palace of King Ahab of Samaria. [2] Ahab said to
Naboth, "Give me your vineyard, so that I may have it as a vegetable garden, since it is right next to my palace. I will give you
a better vineyard in exchange; or, if you prefer, I will pay you the
price in money." [3] But Naboth replied, "The LORD forbid that I
should give up to you what I have inherited from my fathers!"
[4] Ahab went home dispirited and sullen because of the answer
that Naboth the Jezreelite had given him: "I will not give up to
you what I have inherited from my fathers!" He lay down on his
bed and turned away his face, and he would not eat. [5] His wife
Jezebel came to him and asked him, "Why are you so dispirited
that you won't eat?" [6] So he told her, "I spoke to Naboth the Jezreelite and proposed to him, 'Sell me your vineyard for money,
or if you prefer, I'll give you another vineyard in exchange'; but

a-a Meaning of Heb. uncertain.

he answered, 'I will not give my vineyard to you.'" 7 His wife
Jezebel said to him, "Now is the time to show yourself king over
Israel. Rise and eat something, and be cheerful; I will get the
vineyard of Naboth the Jezreelite for you."
8 So she wrote letters in Ahab's name and sealed them with
his seal, and sent the letters to the elders and the nobles who
lived in the same town with Naboth. 9 In the letters she wrote as
follows: "Proclaim a fast and seat Naboth at the front of the assembly. 10 And seat two scoundrels opposite him, and let them
testify against him: 'You have reviled God and king!' Then take
him out and stone him to death."
11 His townsmen—the elders and nobles who lived in his
town—did as Jezebel had instructed them, just as was written
in the letters she had sent them: 12 They proclaimed a fast and
seated Naboth at the front of the assembly. 13 Then the two
scoundrels came and sat down opposite him; and the scoundrels testified against Naboth publicly as follows: "Naboth has
reviled God and king." Then they took him outside the town
and stoned him to death. 14 Word was sent to Jezebel: "Naboth
has been stoned to death." 15 As soon as Jezebel heard that
Naboth had been stoned to death, she said to Ahab, "Go and
take possession of the vineyard which Naboth the Jezreelite
refused to sell you for money; for Naboth is no longer alive, he
is dead." 16 When Ahab heard that Naboth was dead, Ahab set
out for the vineyard of Naboth the Jezreelite to take possession
of it.
17 Then the word of the LORD came to Elijah the Tishbite:
18 "Go down and confront King Ahab of Israel who [resides] in
Samaria. He is now in Naboth's vineyard; he has gone down
there to take possession of it. 19 Say to him, 'Thus said the LORD:
Would you murder and take possession? Thus said the LORD:
In the very place where the dogs lapped up Naboth's blood, the
dogs will lap up your blood too.'"
20 Ahab said to Elijah, "So you have found me, my enemy?"
"Yes, I have found you," he replied. "Because you have committed yourself to doing what is evil in the sight of the LORD,
21 I will bring disaster upon you. I will make a clean sweep of
you, I will cut off from Israel every male belonging to Ahab,
[a]bond and free.[a] 22 And I will make your house like the House
of Jeroboam son of Nebat and like the House of Baasha son of
Ahijah, because of the provocation you have caused by leading Israel to sin. 23 And the LORD has also spoken concerning
Jezebel: 'The dogs shall devour Jezebel in the field[b] of Jezreel.
24 All of Ahab's line who die in the town shall be devoured by

a-a See note at 14.10.

b So nine Heb. mss. and the parallel 2 Kings 9.36, as well as Targum and other ancient versions. Most texts read here "rampart."

8–13: Here too, Jezebel is blamed (16.31). In relating how Jezebel corrupted the legal system using two corroborating witnesses (cf. Deut. 17.6; 19.15), the prophetic story reveals that Israel did have a legal system with defined laws and procedures, some of which are found in the Torah. The crime of which Naboth is accused, and its prescribed punishment, is only partially known from the Torah (Lev. 24.15–16). No Torah legislation explicitly criminalizes cursing the king (but see Exod. 22.27). **8:** Jezebel's access to the royal seal reflects her great power.
10: For *reviled,* the Heb uses the word "blessed," not wanting to connect the words "curse" and "God"; Job chs 1–2 employ the same convention. **15–17:** Ahab is portrayed as much weaker than Jezebel (see v. 25). **19–24:** Elijah's denunciation of Ahab flows into a doom-laden series of predictions: *dogs will lap up* [Ahab's] *blood* (fulfilled in 22.38); dogs will *devour Jezebel* (fulfilled in 2 Kings 9.33–36); Ahab's dynasty will be destroyed (cf. 20.42; fulfilled in 2 Kings 10.11, 17). **24:** *Devoured ... dogs ... birds,* see 16.4 n.

dogs, and all who die in the open country shall be devoured by
the birds of the sky.' "
(25 Indeed, there never was anyone like Ahab, who committed himself to doing what was displeasing to the LORD, at the
instigation of his wife Jezebel. 26 He acted most abominably,
straying after the fetishes just like the Amorites, whom the
LORD had dispossessed before the Israelites.)
27 When Ahab heard these words, he rent his clothes and
put sackcloth on his body. He fasted and lay in sackcloth and
walked about subdued. 28 Then the word of the LORD came to
Elijah the Tishbite: 29 "Have you seen how Ahab has humbled
himself before Me? Because he has humbled himself before
Me, I will not bring the disaster in his lifetime; I will bring the
disaster upon his house in his son's time."

22

[a-]There was a lull of[-a] three years, with no war between
Aram and Israel. 2 In the third year, King Jehoshaphat
of Judah came to visit the king of Israel. 3 The king of Israel said
to his courtiers, "You know that Ramoth-gilead belongs to us,
and yet we do nothing to recover it from the hands of the king
of Aram." 4 And he said to Jehoshaphat, "Will you come with
me to battle at Ramoth-gilead?" Jehoshaphat answered the
king of Israel, "I will do what you do; my troops shall be your
troops, my horses shall be your horses." 5 But Jehoshaphat said
further to the king of Israel, "Please, first inquire of the LORD."
6 So the king of Israel gathered the prophets, about four hundred men, and asked them, "Shall I march upon Ramoth-gilead
for battle, or shall I not?" "March," they said, "and the Lord
will deliver [it] into Your Majesty's hands." 7 Then Jehoshaphat
asked, "Isn't there another prophet of the LORD here through
whom we can inquire?" 8 And the king of Israel answered Jehoshaphat, "There is one more man through whom we can
inquire of the LORD; but I hate him, because he never prophesies anything good for me, but only misfortune—Micaiah son

a-a Lit. "They remained."

25–26: The author's comment about Ahab is not anchored in the context of the Naboth story. It addresses Ahab's idolatrous behavior and attributes part of it, at least, to the instigation of his foreign wife. The author used the same device, intended to ameliorate but not forgive the offensive activities, in commenting on Solomon (11.4–5). **27–28:** In view of Ahab's sincere contrition, God tells Elijah—who does not tell Ahab— that the destruction of his dynasty, announced to Ahab in vv. 21–22, will not occur in his lifetime. This qualification of the earlier pronouncement allows the author to maintain congruency between a prediction that was part of an early prophetic story and recorded events. It highlights the power of repentance while emphasizing that misdeeds must at some point be punished.

22.1–40: The battle for Ramoth-gilead. This ch resumes the historical narrative about the Aramean wars from ch 20. Ahab's final war against the Arameans was conducted as a joint undertaking with Jehoshaphat of Judah, with whom he was linked through the marriage of their children (2 Kings 8.18). Possibly their common interest was in weakening the Arameans so that Israel could reassert its authority in Galilee and north Transjordan while Judah could strengthen its influence in Edom and other parts of southern Transjordan. **1:** According to Assyrian sources, Ahab joined a coalition of thirteen kings against Shalmaneser III of Assyria, who planned to conquer territories west of the Euphrates. Shalmaneser's Monolith Inscription, which covers his early western campaigns, notes that Ahab's contribution of 2,000 chariots and 10,000 infantrymen comprised the largest single contingent. At the Battle of Qarqar, near the Orontes River, in 853 BCE, the coalition successfully halted Assyria's advance into western Asia. The author of Kings makes no mention of Ahab's crucial role or of his success at Qarqar. Since the Arameans faced a continual threat from Assyria to their northeast, Ahab may have thought that circumstances afforded him a unique opportunity to reassert his authority easily in territories to which he had claim. **3:** *Ramoth-gilead* in northern Transjordan had been a central city in one of Solomon's prefectures (4.13), a Levitical city (Josh. 21.36), and a city of refuge (Deut. 4.43; Josh. 20.8). **5–28:** The prophetic consultation. **5–6:** Despite the impression left by the Elijah stories that most of the prophets had been killed in Jezebel's pogrom, in this prophetic story the king of Israel—whose name has been suppressed to keep the focus on the prophets and good king *Jehoshaphat*—had no problem arranging a consultation with 400 prophets. **7:** The Judean King Jehoshaphat thinks that this mass of 400 prophets is a sham, since they all agree with the King of Israel. **8:** True prophets generally predict misfortune,; no other biblical passage mentions this *Micaiah*.

of Imlah." But King Jehoshaphat said, "Don't say that, Your
Majesty." 9 So the king of Israel summoned an officer and said,
"Bring Micaiah son of Imlah at once."
10 The king of Israel and King Jehoshaphat of Judah were
seated on their thrones, arrayed in their robes, on the threshing floor at the entrance of the gate of Samaria; and all the
prophets were prophesying before them. 11 Zedekiah son of
Chenaanah had provided himself with iron horns; and he said,
"Thus said the LORD: With these you shall gore the Arameans
till you make an end of them." 12 And all the other prophets
were prophesying similarly, "March upon Ramoth-gilead and
triumph! The LORD will deliver it into Your Majesty's hands."
13 The messenger who had gone to summon Micaiah said
to him: "Look, the words of the prophets are with one accord
favorable to the king. Let your word be like that of the rest of
them; speak a favorable word." 14 "As the LORD lives," Micaiah
answered, "I will speak only what the LORD tells me." 15 When
he came before the king, the king said to him, "Micaiah, shall
we march upon Ramoth-gilead for battle, or shall we not?" He
answered him, "March and triumph! The LORD will deliver
[it] into Your Majesty's hands." 16 The king said to him, "How
many times must I adjure you to tell me nothing but the truth
in the name of the LORD?" 17 Then he said, "I saw all Israel
scattered over the hills like sheep without a shepherd; and the
LORD said, 'These have no master; let everyone return to his
home in safety.' " 18 "Didn't I tell you," said the king of Israel
to Jehoshaphat, "that he would not prophesy good fortune for
me, but only misfortune?" 19 But [Micaiah] said, "I call upon
you to hear the word of the LORD! I saw the LORD seated upon
His throne, with all the host of heaven standing in attendance
to the right and to the left of Him. 20 The LORD asked, 'Who will
entice Ahab so that he will march and fall at Ramoth-gilead?'
Then one said thus and another said thus, 21 until a certain
spirit came forward and stood before the LORD and said, 'I will
entice him.' 'How?' the LORD asked him. 22 And he replied, 'I
will go out and be a lying spirit in the mouth of all his prophets.' Then He said, 'You will entice and you will prevail. Go out
and do it.' 23 So the LORD has put a lying spirit in the mouth of
all these prophets of yours; for the LORD has decreed disaster
upon you."
24 Thereupon Zedekiah son of Chenaanah stepped up and
struck Micaiah on the cheek, and demanded, "Which way did
the spirit of the LORD pass from me to speak with you?" 25 And
Micaiah replied, "You'll find out on the day when you try to
hide in the innermost room." 26 Then the king of Israel said,
"Take Micaiah and turn him over to Amon, the city's governor,
and to Prince Joash, 27 and say, 'The king's orders are: Put this
fellow in prison, and let his fare be scant bread and scant water

10: The Heb for *prophesying* may also be translated as "acting ecstatic," or "acting like prophets," typifying false prophesy. **13:** Micaiah, who has clashed with the king of Israel, most likely Ahab, in the past (v. 8), is coached to deliver a favorable oracle. **15:** The king is suspicious because Micaiah uncharacteristically offers a positive oracle (see v. 8). We may imagine that Micaiah spoke these words sarcastically. **17:** Ancient Near Eastern kings were often called *shepherds,* since they led and protected their people as a shepherd does his flock. **19–23:** A similar scene of the divine retinue is found in Job chs 1–2. Micaiah does not doubt the integrity of the prophets who predicted victory. He explains that they uttered what God wanted the king to hear, a lie intended to lead Ahab to his downfall. Thus, these are true prophets espousing falsehoods so that Ahab will be punished according to God's will. **21–23:** Divine *spirit* ("ruaḥ") is frequently associated with prophecy. **28:** See the similar criteria for a true prophet in Deut. 18.21–22.

29: Jehoshaphat joins Ahab. On the one hand, 400 prophets had predicted success; on the other, nothing Micaiah said threatened him personally. **34:** Ahab was killed by a random arrow, not by the Aramean charioteers searching to kill him. The author includes this piece of information to demonstrate the role of Providence in the fall of an arrow. **38:** This goes beyond the prediction in 21.19. **39:** A standard concluding summary to the reigns of Israelite kings. *Ivory palace,* one with rooms containing rich *ivory inlays,* such as were found in wood panels and furniture excavated at Samaria (cf. Amos 3.15; 6.4).

22.41–51: The reign of Jehoshaphat is presented briefly, omitting details of the Aramean campaign, while inserting a small list of other events into the standard formulary. Chronicles contains an extensive account of Jehoshaphat's judicial initiatives (2 Chron. ch 19), but the historicity of this account is debated. **44:** There was no abatement in the popular practice of sacrificing and offering incense at the shrines. It continued even though the Temple was a well-established institution. The author mentions this as a blemish on the record but not as a fault of the king, who did not promote the open shrines.

until I come home safe.' " 28 To which Micaiah retorted, "If you ever come home safe, the LORD has not spoken through me." [a-]He said further, "Listen, all you peoples!"[-a]

29 So the king of Israel and King Jehoshaphat of Judah marched upon Ramoth-gilead. 30 The king of Israel said to Jehoshaphat, [b-]"Disguise yourself and go[-b] into the battle; but you, wear your robes." So the king of Israel went into the battle disguised. 31 Now the king of Aram had instructed his thirty-two chariot officers: "Don't attack anyone, small or great, except the king of Israel." 32 So when the chariot officers saw Jehoshaphat, whom they took for the king of Israel, they turned upon him to attack him, and Jehoshaphat cried out. 33 And when the chariot officers became aware that he was not the king of Israel, they turned back from pursuing him. 34 Then a man drew his bow at random and he hit the king of Israel between [c-]the plates of[-c] the armor; and he said to his charioteer, "Turn [d-]the horses[-d] around and get me [e-]behind the lines;[-e] I'm wounded." 35 The battle [c-]raged all day long,[-c] and the king remained propped up in the chariot facing Aram; the blood from the wound ran down into the hollow of the chariot, and at dusk he died. 36 As the sun was going down, a shout went through the army: "Every man to his own town! Every man to his own district."

37 So the king died [f-]and was brought[-f] to Samaria. They buried the king in Samaria, 38 and they flushed out the chariot at the pool of Samaria. Thus the dogs lapped up his blood and the whores bathed [in it], in accordance with the word that the LORD had spoken.[g]

39 The other events of Ahab's reign, and all his actions—the ivory palace that he built and all the towns that he fortified—are all recorded in the Annals of the Kings of Israel. 40 Ahab slept with his fathers, and his son Ahaziah succeeded him as king.

41 Jehoshaphat son of Asa had become king of Judah in the fourth year of King Ahab of Israel. 42 Jehoshaphat was thirty-five years old when he became king, and he reigned in Jerusalem for twenty-five years. His mother's name was Azubah daughter of Shilhi. 43 He followed closely the course of his father Asa and did not deviate from it, doing what was pleasing to the LORD. 44 However, the shrines did not cease to function; the people still sacrificed and offered at the shrines.

a-a Perhaps a notation suggesting that Micaiah was identical with Micah, whose prophecies begin, "Listen, all you peoples," Mic. 1.2.
b-b Targum and Septuagint read, "I will disguise myself and go."
c-c Meaning of Heb. uncertain.
d-d Lit. "your hand," because horses are guided by a pull on the appropriate rein; cf. 2 Kings 9.23. *e-e Lit. "outside the camp."* *f-f Lit. "he came."*
g Cf. 21.19.

45 And further, Jehoshaphat submitted to the king of Israel.
46 As for the other events of Jehoshaphat's reign and the valor
he displayed in battle, they are recorded in the Annals of the
Kings of Judah. (47 He also stamped out the remaining male
prostitutes who had survived in the land from the time of his
father Asa.)

48 There was no king in Edom; [a-]a viceroy acted as king.
49 Jehoshaphat[-a] constructed Tarshish[b] ships to sail to Ophir
for gold. But he did not sail because the ships were wrecked at
Ezion-geber. 50 Then Ahaziah son of Ahab proposed to Jehoshaphat, "Let my servants sail on the ships with your servants";
but Jehoshaphat would not agree. 51 Jehoshaphat slept with his
fathers and was buried with his fathers in the city of his father
David, and his son Jehoram succeeded him as king.

52 [Meanwhile,] Ahaziah son of Ahab had become king of Israel, in Samaria, in the seventeenth year of King Jehoshaphat
of Judah; he reigned over Israel two years. 53 He did what was
displeasing to the LORD, following in the footsteps of his father and his mother, and in those of Jeroboam son of Nebat
who had caused Israel to sin. 54 He worshiped Baal and bowed
down to him; he vexed the LORD, the God of Israel, just as his
father had done.

a-a Emendation yields "the viceroy of King Jehoshaphat." *b See note at 10.22.*

45: *Submitted* (Heb "yashlem") is better translated "made peace" or "caused peace." Rashi thinks that it was necessary for the author to mention it because his father Asa had been at war with Baasha, king of Israel. Radak opines that the author intended this to be understood as a second blemish on Jehoshaphat's record, coming, as it does, after the first. **47:** *Male prostitutes,* see 14.24 n. **48–51:** Mention is made of Judah's control over Edom because *Ezion-geber,* from which Jehoshaphat had planned to launch his *Tarshish ships,* was an Edomite port (9.26). Apparently the Red Sea trade had stopped sometime after the death of Solomon.

22.52–54: Ahaziah's reign. Though Ahaziah is ostensibly credited with a two-year reign, the chronological information likely means that he reigned for several months in two different calendar years, which would have been counted as a two-year reign. Radak notes that v. 52 states that he ascended the throne in Jehoshaphat's seventeenth year while 2 Kings 3.1 indicates that Jehoram, Ahaziah's brother, came to power in Jehoshaphat's eighteenth year. Despite this, the author evaluates his reign negatively not only because he followed in the footsteps of Jeroboam, but also because he adopted the practices of his own parents, Ahab and Jezebel, serving and worshipping Baal. His story continues in 2 Kings ch 1.

מלכים ב

2 Kings

FIRST AND SECOND KINGS were originally one book. For information about 2 Kings, see the introduction preceding 1 Kings. [ZIONY ZEVIT]

1 After Ahab's death, Moab rebelled against Israel.
[2] Ahaziah fell through the lattice in his upper chamber at
Samaria and was injured. So he sent messengers, whom he instructed: "Go inquire of Baal-zebub, the god of Ekron, whether
I shall recover from this injury." [3] But an angel of the LORD said
to Elijah the Tishbite, "Go and confront the messengers of the
king of Samaria and say to them, 'Is there no God in Israel that
you go to inquire of Baal-zebub, the god of Ekron? [4] Assuredly,
thus said the LORD: You shall not [a]rise from the bed you are
lying on,[-a] but you shall die.'" And Elijah went.
[5] The messengers returned to Ahaziah;[b] and he asked, "Why
have you come back?" [6] They answered him, "A man came toward us and said to us, 'Go back to the king who sent you, and
say to him: Thus said the LORD: Is there no God in Israel that
you must send to inquire of Baal-zebub, the god of Ekron? Assuredly, you shall not rise from the bed you are lying on, but
shall die.'" [7] "What sort of man was it," he asked them, "who
came toward you and said these things to you?" [8] "A hairy
man," they replied, "with a leather belt tied around his waist."
"That's Elijah the Tishbite!" he said.
[9] Then he sent to him a captain of fifty with his fifty men. He
climbed up to him, and found him sitting at the top of a hill.
"Man of God," he said to him, "by order of the king, come down!"

a-a Lit. "descend from the bed you have mounted." *b Heb. "him."*

1.1–2.12: The final cycle of Elijah stories. 1.1: Moab's rebellion after Ahab's death in the reign of Jehoram (see 3.4–5). It is mentioned here because Ahaziah died, Jehoram came to power, and Moab rebelled in the same calendar year (see 1 Kings 22.52).

1.2–18: The death of Ahaziah. Ahaziah, after being critically injured in Samaria, solicits a prognosis from *Baal-zebub, the god of Ekron.* This evolves into a confrontation with Elijah like the one between Elijah and Ahab, Ahaziah's father (1 Kings 18.16–18). **2:** The *lattice* was probably a window covering made of thin strips of wood or reeds in a loose net in order to let in light and air while still providing some privacy; there were no glass windows in this period. *Baal-zebub,* "Lord of the flies," a god worshipped at Ekron, may have been known as a healer. This form of the name, however, is likely the author's purposeful corruption of an original "Baal-zevul," "Lord of glory/dominion/majesty," understood as a reference to Baal. The word meaning "prince/glory," "zevul," is found as a personal name in Judg. 9.30 and is part of the name of Ahaziah's mother, Jezebel. In the New Testament, Jesus denies that he casts out demons, i.e., heals, in the name of Baal-zevul (see Matt. 12.24–27). The reason that the author or later scribe may have changed the name is that in Solomon's prayer, the Temple is called a "house of zevul" ("A stately House") (1 Kings 8.13). Ekron, the northernmost city of the Philistine pentapolis (see 1 Sam. 5.1 n.), about 37 km (22 mi) west of Jerusalem, may have been under Judah's control at this time. Excavations at the site indicate that its material culture mixed Aegean with local elements. **8:** The identifying physical characteristic of Elijah was most likely his hair. The leather belt around his garment may have been atypical, but was not a rare accoutrement. Ahaziah recognized him not only by the physical description but also through the indictment in the message. **9–15:** The first two groups are destroyed miraculously because their captains failed to respect the *man of God* commanding him imperiously in the name of the king. The third captain humbled himself and made no request. In this story, Elijah does not pray for a miraculous fire; it comes, as if at his bidding. The Heb text is built around the pun between *man of God,* "ʾish ʾelohim," and *fire of God,* "ʾesh ʾelohim." **9–10:** The captain ordered that he come down. Elijah had punishing fire come down instead. A *captain of fifty* commanded a typical military unit. **17:** The fulfillment statement here indicates that the author did not connect Ahaziah's death automatically to his critically injured condition. Had Ahaziah sought forgiveness and healing from the God of Israel, he would not have died. At one and the same time, physical and metaphysical laws of causation were operating in nature. Ahaziah was the third generation of the Omri dynasty. The notice that, in the absence of a son, rule passed to a brother, indicates that in the Northern Kingdom at this time kings were acclaimed according to the customs governing the inheritance of property.

2.1–12: Stories about the death of Elijah show the smooth transition of authority from one prophet to another, and with it, responsibility for groups of disciples living in different communities. Introductory v. 1 mentions the whirlwind, anticipating v. 11. **1:** Elijah did not die. See also the notation about Enoch in Gen. 5.24. His heavenly assumption became the stuff of many legends in Judaism and traditions about him in prophetic circles. These legends, which suggest that Elijah periodically returns to the earth, and is especially associated with the arrival of the Messiah, already have a late biblical precedent (Mal. 3.23–24). **3:** The *disciples of the prophets* were radical monotheists following the teachings of prophets like Elijah, but were not necessarily prophets themselves. Many joined to live together in small communities. Somehow the groups at Bethel and Jericho (v. 5) knew that *the LORD* was about to *take* Elijah. They do not use

10 Elijah replied to the captain of the fifty, "If I am a man of God,
let fire come down from heaven and consume you with your fifty men!" And fire came down from heaven and consumed him
and his fifty men. 11 The king then sent to him another captain
with his fifty men; and he [a]addressed him[a] as follows: "Man
of God, by order of the king, come down at once!" 12 But Elijah
answered him, "If I am a man of God, let fire come down from
heaven and consume you with your fifty men!" And fire of God
came down from heaven and consumed him and his fifty men.
13 Then he sent a third captain of fifty with his fifty men. The
third captain of fifty climbed to the top, knelt before Elijah, and
implored him, saying, "Oh, man of God, please have regard for
my life and the lives of these fifty servants of yours! 14 Already
fire has come from heaven and consumed the first two captains of fifty and their men;[b] I beg you, have regard for my life!"
15 Then the angel of the LORD said to Elijah, "Go down with
him, do not be afraid of him." So he rose and went down with
him to the king. 16 He said to him, "Because you sent messengers
to inquire of Baal-zebub the god of Ekron—as if there were no
God in Israel whose word you could seek—assuredly, you shall
not rise from the bed which you are lying on; but you shall die."
17 And [Ahaziah] died, according to the word of the LORD
that Elijah had spoken. Jehoram[c] succeeded him as king, in the
second year of King Jehoram son of Jehoshaphat of Judah, for
he had no son. 18 The other events of Ahaziah's reign [and] his
actions are recorded in the Annals of the Kings of Israel.

2 When the LORD was about to take Elijah up to heaven in a
whirlwind, Elijah and Elisha had set out from Gilgal. 2 Elijah said to Elisha, "Stay here, for the LORD has sent me on to
Bethel." "As the LORD lives and as you live," said Elisha, "I will
not leave you." So they went down to Bethel. 3 Disciples of the
prophets at Bethel came out to Elisha and said to him, "Do you
know that the LORD will take your master [d]away from you[d] today?" He replied, "I know it, too; be silent."
4 Then Elijah said to him, "Elisha, stay here, for the LORD has
sent me on to Jericho." "As the LORD lives and as you live," said
Elisha, "I will not leave you." So they went on to Jericho. 5 The disciples of the prophets who were at Jericho came over to Elisha
and said to him, "Do you know that the LORD will take your master [d]away from you[d] today?" He replied, "I know it, too; be silent."
6 Elijah said to him, "Stay here, for the LORD has sent me on
to the Jordan." "As the LORD lives and as you live, I will not leave
you," he said, and the two of them went on. 7 Fifty men of the
disciples of the prophets followed and stood by at a distance

a-a *Emendation yields "went up and said to him," cf. v. 9.* b *Lit. "fifties."*
c *Brother of Ahaziah.* d-d *Lit. "from your head."*

from them as the two of them stopped at the Jordan. 8 Thereupon Elijah took his mantle and, rolling it up, he struck the water; it divided to the right and left, so that the two of them crossed over on dry land. 9 As they were crossing, Elijah said to Elisha, "Tell me, what can I do for you before I am taken from you?" Elisha answered, "Let a [a]double portion[a] of your spirit pass on to me." 10 "You have asked a difficult thing," he said. "If

a-a Lit. "two-thirds"; cf. Zech. 13.8.

words indicating death. **4:** In view of 1 Kings 16.34 and Josh. 6.26, the author must have understood that *Jericho* was not a cursed city after its rebuilding. Excavations at Tel es-Sultan, identified with Jericho of the First Temple period, have discovered only sparse finds from the 9th through 7th centuries BCE. **8:** Elijah uses his mantle to perform a miracle at the Jordan similar to Moses' parting of the waters (Exod. 14.21–22). Crossing the Jordan east of Jericho indicates that the place of Elijah's assumption was near Mt. Nebo, where Moses had died (Deut. 34.1–6). Thus, in his death, as in earlier texts, Elijah is patterned after Moses. **9:** *A double portion,* see translators' note *a-a*. Radak (in the name of his father) points out that, according to Deut. 21.17, the eldest

Places associated with the Elisha narratives. The dashed line shows the approximate boundaries between Israel, Judah and Philistia.

you see me as I am being taken from you, this will be granted
to you; if not, it will not." 11 As they kept on walking and talking,
a fiery chariot with fiery horses suddenly appeared and separated one from the other; and Elijah went up to heaven in a
whirlwind. 12 Elisha saw it, and he cried out, "Oh, father, father!
Israel's chariots and horsemen!" When he could no longer see
him, he grasped his garments and rent them in two.

13 He picked up Elijah's mantle, which had dropped from
him; and he went back and stood on the bank of the Jordan.
14 Taking the mantle which had dropped from Elijah, he struck
the water and said, "Where is the LORD, the God of Elijah?" As
he too struck the water, it parted to the right and to the left,
and Elisha crossed over. 15 When the disciples of the prophets
at Jericho saw him from a distance, they exclaimed, "The spirit
of Elijah has settled on Elisha!" And they went to meet him and
bowed low before him to the ground.

16 They said to him, "Your servants have fifty able men with
them. Let them go and look for your master; perhaps the spirit of the LORD has carried him off and cast him upon some
mountain or into some valley." "Do not send them," he replied.
17 But they kept pressing him for a long time, until he said,
"Send them." So they sent out fifty men, who searched for three
days but did not find him. 18 They came back to him while he
was still in Jericho; and he said to them, "I told you not to go."

19 The men of the town said to Elisha, "Look, the town is a
pleasant place to live in, as my lord can see; but the water is bad
and the land causes bereavement." 20 He responded, "Bring me
a new dish and put salt in it." They brought it to him; 21 he went
to the spring and threw salt into it. And he said, "Thus said the
LORD: I heal this water; no longer shall death and bereavement
come from it!" 22 The water has remained wholesome to this
day, in accordance with the word spoken by Elisha.

23 From there he went up to Bethel. As he was going up the
road, some little boys came out of the town and jeered at him,
saying, "Go away, baldhead! Go away, baldhead!" 24 He turned

son inherits a portion twice that of other brothers dividing their father's property. Elisha, therefore, is not asking for twice the spirit of Elijah, but for the larger amount due the eldest. (For the division of the spirit, cf. Num. 11.17, 24–26.) Several rabbinic sources, however, understand double as literal, and suggest that Elijah performed eight miracles, and Elisha sixteen. Many of the miracles performed by Elijah and Elisha are similar, indicating that they shared the same *spirit* (see 1 Kings 22.21–23 n.). **12:** In addition to indicating a biological relationship, *father* indicates a tutorial one: "instructor, counselor, teacher, leader" (Gen. 45.8; Judg. 17.10; Jer. 31.9). *Israel's chariots and horsemen:* The same title, possibly an epithet of Elijah as Israel's defender, is addressed to Elisha when he is about to die in 13.14. In the case of Elisha, it may have been based on the incident recorded in 6.17–18. No similar story is recorded about Elijah. Rending (or tearing) *his garments* was a sign of mourning.

2.13–13.20: The Elisha stories are presented in cycles of varying length interspersed between historical and prophetic narratives, citations from chronicles, and remarks of the author. In contrast to the four major Elijah stories and the story of his death, there are fifteen Elisha stories of varying length. Though many of their activities are similar, Elisha is generally much more sympathetic to the Israelite king than his mentor, Elijah.

2.13–25: The first cycle of stories indicates how Elisha demonstrated that he was a prophet like Elijah and his spiritual heir. **13–14:** Elisha tests himself to determine if he inherited spirit from Elijah. Using his teacher's *mantle* he smites the water, invokes the *God of Elijah,* and smites the water again. The Jordan splits and he crosses on dry land towards Jericho. **15:** The *disciples of the prophets at Jericho* see and declare him heir of Elijah's spirit. He received more than the double portion that he requested (v. 9). **16:** *The spirit of the LORD has carried him off,* see 1 Kings 18.12. **19–22:** A magical "healing" story in which Elisha does and says things that, in combination, produce the desired result. All is done on his own authority, with no prayer for healing. Cf. 1.5–14. A long tradition points to Ein es-Sultan in contemporary Jericho as Elisha's spring. In its present form, the story is etiological, explaining the origin of the freshwater spring in Jericho that makes the whole region agriculturally rich. **21:** The counterintuitive use of salt, which makes water undrinkable, highlights the miracle. **23:** In calling Elisha *baldhead,* the boys seem to be mocking him; they may actually, however, be insulting him as a prophet by comparing him derogatorily to Elijah, who was hairy (1.8). Local tradition places the site of this story near the town of Deir Dibwan, "Lair of the two bears," about 1.5 km (1 mi) east of Bethel. **24:** Here, as in vv. 19–22, Elisha does and says something to produce the desired result. First he turns and looks at the

around and looked at them and cursed them in the name of the LORD. Thereupon, two she-bears came out of the woods and mangled forty-two of the children. 25 He went on from there to Mount Carmel, and from there he returned to Samaria.

3 Jehoram son of Ahab became king of Israel in Samaria in the eighteenth year of King Jehoshaphat of Judah; and he reigned twelve years. 2 He did what was displeasing to the LORD, yet not like his father and mother, for he removed the pillars of Baal that his father had made. 3 However, he clung to the sins which Jeroboam son of Nebat caused Israel to commit; he did not depart from them.

4 Now King Mesha of Moab was a sheep breeder; and he used to pay as tribute to the king of Israel [a]a hundred thousand lambs and the wool of a hundred thousand rams.[-a] 5 But when Ahab died, the king of Moab rebelled against the king of Israel. 6 So King Jehoram promptly set out from Samaria and mustered all Israel. 7 At the same time, he sent this message to King Jehoshaphat of Judah: "The king of Moab has rebelled against me; will you come with me to make war on Moab?" He replied, "I will go. I will do what you do: my troops shall be your troops, my horses shall be your horses." 8 And he asked, "Which route shall we take?" [Jehoram] replied, "The road through the wilderness of Edom."

9 So the king of Israel, the king of Judah, and the king of Edom set out, and they marched for seven days until they rounded [the tip of the Dead Sea]; and there was no water left for the army or for the animals that were with them. 10 "Alas!" cried the king of Israel. "The LORD has brought these three kings together only to deliver them into the hands of Moab." 11 But Jehoshaphat said, "Isn't there a prophet of the LORD here, through whom we may inquire of the LORD?" One of the courtiers of the king of Israel spoke up and said, "Elisha son of Shaphat, who [b]poured water on the hands of[-b] Elijah, is here." 12 "The word of the LORD is with him," said Jehoshaphat. So the king of Israel and Jehoshaphat and the king of Edom went down to him. 13 Elisha said to the king of Israel, "What have you to do with me? Go to your father's

a-a Or "the wool of 100,000 lambs and of 100,000 rams."
b-b I.e., personally attended.

boys, then curses them *in the name of the LORD*. He does not pray that they be punished, although he himself calls down the punishment. The bears did not kill and eat. The large carnage is mentioned to indicate that their behavior was not natural. This story, like the Elijah story in 1.9–16, emphasizes that the man of God must be treated with proper respect.

3.1–27: The Moabite war and Elisha's prophecy initiate the complex of Elisha stories in which the author mixed prophetic tales with archival materials.

3.1–3: Introduction to the reign of Jehoram son of Ahab. The author notes to the king's credit his removal of the pillars of Baal made by his father. This is the first notice that such pillars had been constructed. See also 10.26.

3.4–27: The rebellion of Mesha. The Mesha stele, found in 1868, provides a summary of this king's various achievements arranged in a rough chronological order. It notes the occupation of Moab in the days of Omri and his son, i.e., Ahab. It indicates that Mesha undertook actions against Israelites in occupied northern Moab before the death of Ahab. It may have been only after the death of Ahab that Mesha withheld tribute (1.1; 3.5), slaughtered people from the tribe of Gad in the city of Ataroth (noted on the stele), and moved aggressively north of the Arnon river. **7:** *King Jehoshaphat*'s interest in assisting Jehoram may have been to discourage Judah's vassal, Edom, from seeking its own independence (cf. 1 Kings 22.48). In addition to national interests, Jehoshaphat had married his son Joram to Ahab's daughter (2 Kings 8.18). This contrasts with an earlier period, when Judah and the Northern Kingdom were at war with each other (1 Kings 14.30; 15.6, 16, 32). **8:** Jehoram's strategy was to march through Judah around the southern edge of the Dead Sea and approach Moab from the south. All of Mesha's activities, and presumably the majority of his forces, were north of the Arnon, but the core of his kingdom was south of the river up to the Edomite border. **9–10:** The success of Jehoram's strategy was dependent on an adequate supply of local water. The inadequate supply leads him to think that it is part of a divine plan against his coalition. **11–14:** Jehoshaphat, who wished to consult a prophet (cf. 1 Kings 22.7), knows of Elisha by reputation. Elisha, impolite and rude to the king of Israel (vv. 13–14), responds to the request for an oracle only because Jehoshaphat is also endangered by what may occur.

prophets or your mother's prophets." But the king of Israel said,
"Don't [say that], for the LORD has brought these three kings together only to deliver them into the hands of Moab." [14] "As the
LORD of Hosts lives, whom I serve," Elisha answered, "were it
not that I respect King Jehoshaphat of Judah, I wouldn't look at
you or notice you. [15] Now then, get me a musician."
As the musician played, the hand of the LORD came upon
him, [16] and he said, "Thus said the LORD: This wadi shall be full
of pools. [17] For thus said the LORD: You shall see no wind, you
shall see no rain, and yet the wadi shall be filled with water;
and you and your cattle and your pack animals shall drink.
[18] And this is but a slight thing in the sight of the LORD, for He
will also deliver Moab into your hands. [19] You shall conquer
every fortified town and every splendid city; you shall fell every
good tree and stop up all wells of water; and every fertile field
you shall ruin with stones." [20] And in the morning, when it was
time to present the meal offering, water suddenly came from
the direction of Edom and the land was covered by the water.
[21] Meanwhile, all the Moabites had heard that the kings were
advancing to make war on them; [a-] every man old enough to bear
arms [-a] rallied, and they stationed themselves at the border. [22] Next
morning, when they rose, the sun was shining over the water, and
from the distance the water appeared to the Moabites as red as
blood. [23] "That's blood!" they said. "The kings must have fought
among themselves and killed each other. Now to the spoil, Moab!"
[24] They entered the Israelite camp, and the Israelites arose
and attacked the Moabites, who fled before them. [b-] They advanced, constantly attacking [-b] the Moabites, [25] and they destroyed the towns. Every man threw a stone into each fertile
field, so that it was covered over; and they stopped up every
spring and felled every fruit tree. [c-] Only the walls of [-c] Kir-
hareseth were left, and then the slingers surrounded it and attacked it. [26] Seeing that the battle was going against him, the
king of Moab led an attempt of seven hundred swordsmen to
break a way through to the king of Edom; [d] but they failed. [27] So
he took his first-born son, who was to succeed him as king,
and offered him up on the wall as a burnt offering. A great
wrath came upon Israel, so they withdrew from him and went
back to [their own] land.

4 A certain woman, the wife of one of the disciples of the
prophets, cried out to Elisha: "Your servant my husband is
dead, and you know how your servant revered the LORD. And

a-a *Lit. "from all those old enough to gird on a sword."*
b-b *Meaning of Heb. uncertain.*
c-c *Lit. "Until the stones in"; meaning of Heb. uncertain.*
d *Emendation yields "Aram."*

15: The *musician* helps produce the atmosphere conducive for a divine visitation (cf. 1 Sam. 10.5–6); *the hand of the LORD* refers to prophetic power (1 Kings 18.46). **16:** The *pools* (Heb "gevim") are natural sinkholes and fissures in the limestone floor of the wadis that retain large amounts of water after a runoff (cf. Jer. 14.3). **22:** In the morning, the reflection of red sandstone mountains off the pooled waters is interpreted by the Moabites as *blood*. **24–25:** The three armies pursue Moabites north from the border, destroying fields, stopping wells, and uprooting fruit trees in fulfillment of Elisha's prediction (v. 19). The Moabites take shelter in *Kir-hareseth,* identified with modern el-Kerak, a site on a high hill with deep gorges around its salient. **27:** Mesha sacrifices *his first-born* son in an extreme, powerful act; the text does not say to whom, though as a Moabite, Mesha likely interpreted his losses as punishment for some offense that angered his national deity Chemosh, an offense that could be atoned for through the offering of his son (cf. Mic. 6.7). Although interpreters are unsure what the author meant by *a great wrath came upon Israel,* it suggests that Mesha achieved his objective, and the human sacrifice was efficacious. The coalition abandoned the field and returned home. Although the harsh details related here, told from an Israelite point of view, do not appear on the stele, Mesha's inscription verifies that after a long period of subjugation he overthrew Israelite control.

4.1–6.23: The second cycle of Elisha stories. Perhaps the author inserts them at this point because Elisha was mentioned in the context of the Moabite campaign. The motifs of inadequate provisions and death recur in this cycle of stories, but the main theme is Elisha as a healer.

4.1–7: The miraculous provision of oil. A prophetic story whose central miracle parallels that of Elijah in 1 Kings 17.14–16. This story is atypical of the simple miracle stories in that it provides extraneous details about

now a creditor is coming to seize my two children as slaves."
2 Elisha said to her, "What can I do for you? Tell me, what have
you in the house?" She replied, "Your maidservant has nothing at all in the house, except a jug of oil." 3 "Go," he said, "and
borrow vessels outside, from all your neighbors, empty vessels,
as many as you can. 4 Then go in and shut the door behind you
and your children, and pour [oil] into all those vessels, removing each one as it is filled."
5 She went away and shut the door behind her and her children. They kept bringing [vessels] to her and she kept pouring.
6 When the vessels were full, she said to her son, "Bring me another vessel." He answered her, "There are no more vessels";
and the oil stopped. 7 She came and told the man of God, and
he said, "Go sell the oil and pay your debt, and you and your
children can live on the rest."

8 One day Elisha visited Shunem. A wealthy woman lived
there, and she urged him to have a meal; and whenever he
passed by, he would stop there for a meal. 9 Once she said to
her husband, "I am sure it is a holy man of God who comes this
way regularly. 10 Let us make a small [a]enclosed upper chamber[a] and place a bed, a table, a chair, and a lampstand there
for him, so that he can stop there whenever he comes to us."
11 One day he came there; he retired to the upper chamber and
lay down there. 12 He said to his servant Gehazi, "Call that Shunammite woman." He called her, and she stood before him.
13 He said to him, "Tell her, 'You have gone to all this trouble
for us. What can we do for you? Can we speak in your behalf
to the king or to the army commander?'" She replied, "I live
among my own people." 14 "What then can be done for her?"
he asked. "The fact is," said Gehazi, "she has no son, and her
husband is old." 15 "Call her," he said. He called her, and she
stood in the doorway. 16 And Elisha said, "At this season next
year, you will be embracing a son." She replied, "Please, my
lord, man of God, do not delude your maidservant."
17 The woman conceived and bore a son at the same season the following year, as Elisha had assured her. 18 The child
grew up. One day, he went out to his father among the reapers.
19 [Suddenly] he cried to his father, "Oh, my head, my head!"
He said to a servant, "Carry him to his mother." 20 He picked
him up and brought him to his mother. And the child sat on
her lap until noon; and he died. 21 She took him up and laid
him on the bed of the man of God, and left him and closed
the door. 22 Then she called to her husband: "Please, send me
one of the servants and one of the she-asses, so I can hurry to
the man of God and back." 23 But he said, "Why are you going

a-a Or "upper wall-chamber"; lit. "an upper chamber of wall(s)."

why the woman had some claim to Elisha's help. The story lacks any mention of prayer or divine Presence. The sense of wonderment is thereby focused completely on the only named person in the narrative, Elisha. This story in particular shows signs of remnants of Israelite Hebrew (the dialect of the Northern Kingdom), suggesting that many of these prophetic stories were composed in the north, and later incorporated into the Judean Book of Kings, with their language changed to Judean Hebrew to differing extents. **1:** The woman does not complain about social injustice but about her financial straits. *Seize my two children as slaves:* This was a long-established legal norm; see Exod. 21.2–11; Lev. 25.39–55; Deut. 15.12–15; Neh. 5.1–5. **2:** The fact that the seizure of the children is legal explains why Elisha's first reaction to her statement and implied request for help was to inquire what he could do.

4.8–37: The birth and revivification of the Shunammite's son. The narrative combines prediction and miracle stories in a tale whose chronology spans five to ten years. It is suffused with sufficient background to understand what motivates the actions of all main characters. The expression "one day" introduces each major part of the narrative: in v. 8 it introduces the main characters in the house of the Shunammite, in v. 11 the promise/prediction of the child, in v. 18 the story of the death and revivification of the child. **9:** Elisha traveled a regular circuit, possibly visiting groups of disciples of the prophets (cf. Samuel in 1 Sam. 7.15–17). The woman wanted to help Elisha, believing that his presence as a man of God would benefit her. **12–16:** Elisha begins by speaking to the *woman* indirectly, through *Gehazi,* Elisha's servant, but ends by addressing her directly (see also vv. 26–28, 36). **20–22:** The narrator informs readers that the child *died;* the Shunammite, however, may not have perceived that he was dead, only very ill. She did not tell her husband that the child was dead

to him today? It is neither new moon nor sabbath." She answered, [a-]"It's all right."[-a]
[24] She had the ass saddled, and said to her servant, "Urge [the
beast] on;[b] see that I don't slow down unless I tell you." [25] She
went on until she came to the man of God on Mount Carmel.
When the man of God saw her from afar, he said to his servant
Gehazi, "There is that Shunammite woman. [26] Go, hurry toward
her and ask her, 'How are you? How is your husband? How is
the child?'" "We are well," she replied. [27] But when she came
up to the man of God on the mountain, she clasped his feet.
Gehazi stepped forward to push her away; but the man of God
said, "Let her alone, for she is in bitter distress; and the LORD
has hidden it from me and has not told me." [28] Then she said,
"Did I ask my lord for a son? Didn't I say: 'Don't mislead me'?"
[29] He said to Gehazi, [c-]"Tie up your skirts,[-c] take my staff in
your hand, and go. If you meet anyone, do not greet him; and
if anyone greets you, do not answer him. And place my staff on
the face of the boy." [30] But the boy's mother said, "As the LORD
lives and as you live, I will not leave you!" So he arose and followed her.
[31] Gehazi had gone on before them and had placed the staff
on the boy's face; but there was no sound or response. He
turned back to meet him and told him, "The boy has not awakened." [32] Elisha came into the house, and there was the boy,
laid out dead on his couch. [33] He went in, shut the door behind
the two of them, and prayed to the LORD. [34] Then he mounted
[the bed] and placed himself over the child. He put his mouth
on its mouth, his eyes on its eyes, and his hands on its hands,
as he bent over it. And the body of the child became warm.
[35] He stepped down, walked once up and down the room, then
mounted and bent over him. Thereupon, the boy sneezed sev-
en times, and the boy opened his eyes. [36] [Elisha] called Gehazi and said, "Call the Shunammite woman," and he called
her. When she came to him, he said, "Pick up your son." [37] She
came and fell at his feet and bowed low to the ground; then she
picked up her son and left.

[38] Elisha returned to Gilgal. There was a famine in the land,
and the disciples of the prophets were sitting before him. He
said to his servant, "Set the large pot [on the fire] and cook a
stew for the disciples of the prophets." [39] So one of them went out
into the fields to gather sprouts. He came across a wild vine and
picked from it wild gourds, as many as his garment would hold.
Then he came back and sliced them into the pot of stew, for they

a-a *Heb.* Shalom.

b *The servant runs behind the donkey and urges it on with a stick.*

c-c *Lit. "Gird your loins"; cf. 1 Kings 18.46.*

but proceeded to rush to the person who she believed could heal her child. **23:** Her husband's question assumes that when the Shunammite visited Elisha it was typically for the celebration of either a new month or a Sabbath. **27:** Prophets only knew the future when God revealed it to them; they were not clairvoyants. **29–32:** Gehazi was dispatched to perform a healing using Elisha's staff. Elisha thought that his presence was not actually needed for a healing to occur (cf. 4.5–6). Elisha's initial plan, executed by Gehazi, failed. Malbim suggests that from Gehazi's remark to Elisha in v. 31, it appears that Elisha misdiagnosed the problem on the basis of the Shunammite's information; God had not revealed anything of the matter to him (v. 27). The child was truly dead. **34–35:** The revivification performed here by Elisha is similar to what is described with fewer details about Elijah in 1 Kings 17.21–22.

4.38–41: Elisha neutralizes a poison. 39: *Sprouts:* Radak's opinion that Heb "'orot" refers to herbs, on the basis of Isa. 26.19, is reflected in the translation. Others suggest that it refers to Eruca sativa, a radish-like plant whose bitter leaves are edible. *Wild gourds* (Heb "paku'ot"): Citrullus colocynthis, a melon-like plant, contains seeds in which there is a poisonous substance.

did not know [what they were]; [40] and they served it for the men to eat. While they were still eating of the stew, they began to cry out: "O man of God, there is death in the pot!"[a] And they could not eat it. [41] "Fetch some flour," [Elisha] said. He threw it into the pot and said, "Serve it to the people and let them eat." And there was no longer anything harmful in the pot.

[42] A man came from Baal-shalishah and he brought the man of God some bread of the first reaping—twenty loaves of barley bread, and some fresh grain [b]in his sack.[-b] And [Elisha] said, "Give it to the people and let them eat." [43] His attendant replied, "How can I set this before a hundred men?" But he said, "Give it to the people and let them eat. For thus said the LORD: They shall eat and have some left over." [44] So he set it before them; and when they had eaten, they had some left over, as the LORD had said.

5 Naaman, commander of the army of the king of Aram, was important to his lord and high in his favor, for through him the LORD had granted victory to Aram. But the man, though a great warrior, was a leper.[c] [2] Once, when the Arameans were out raiding, they carried off a young girl from the land of Israel, and she became an attendant to Naaman's wife. [3] She said to her mistress, "I wish Master could come before the prophet in Samaria; he would cure him of his leprosy." [4] [Naaman] went and told his lord just what the girl from the land of Israel had said. [5] And the king of Aram said, "Go to the king of Israel, and I will send along a letter."

He set out, taking with him ten talents of silver, six thousand shekels of gold, and ten changes of clothing. [6] He brought the letter to the king of Israel. It read: "Now, when this letter reaches you, know that I have sent my courtier Naaman to you, that you may cure him of his leprosy." [7] When the king of Israel read the letter, he rent his clothes and cried, "Am I God, to deal death or give life, that this fellow writes to me to cure a man of leprosy? Just see for yourselves that he is seeking a pretext against me!" [8] When Elisha, the man of God, heard that the king of Israel had rent his clothes, he sent a message to the king: "Why have you rent your clothes? Let him come to me, and he will learn that there is a prophet in Israel."

[9] So Naaman came with his horses and chariots and halted at the door of Elisha's house. [10] Elisha sent a messenger to say to him, "Go and bathe seven times in the Jordan, and your flesh shall be restored and you shall be clean." [11] But Naaman

a The wild gourds cause severe cramps.

b-b Or "on the stalk"; perhaps connected with Ugaritic bṣql.

c Cf. note on Lev. 13.3.

4.42–44: Elisha feeds a multitude.

5.1–27: The healing of Naaman the leper. The story of Naaman the Aramean leper is a complex legend. Since only a few main characters are presented by name, the anonymity of the kings of Aram and Israel makes it impossible to attribute the story to a particular period in the life of Elisha. One motif of the story is that people of higher social status are dependent on people of lower status: Naaman on counsel from his wife reporting information from an Israelite slave girl (vv. 2–3); the king of Aram on the king of Israel, and the latter on Elisha (vv. 5–8); Naaman on the advice of his own servants and Elisha (vv. 13–15). **1:** The leprosy of Naaman was some sort of dermatological problem that did not disfigure him or disqualify him from military office or entering temples in his homeland (see v. 18); it is not what we now call leprosy (see annotations on Lev. 13.1–46). **5:** This is an extravagant amount of wealth. **7–8:** In this story, the king of Israel is unaware of Elisha's healing powers although a little girl captured by the Arameans is (vv. 2–3). **10:** Elisha's prescription does not involve divine guidance or prayer.

12: Naaman does not undersand that the Jordan River, as part of the land of Israel, may have special healing powers, though it is a much smaller river than the ones near Damascus. **15–17:** Naaman's experience convinces him of the radical monotheism of Elisha and of the narrator, but he concludes that though God is universal, He may be worshipped only on the soil of His chosen land. A main point of this story, then, is the sanctity of the land of Israel. **18:** *Rimmon,* an alternative name for the Aramean storm-god, Hadad (Zech. 12.11).

was angered and walked away. "I thought," he said, "he would surely come out to me, and would stand and invoke the LORD his God by name, and would wave his hand toward the spot, and cure the affected part.
12 Are not the Amanah and the Pharpar, the rivers of Damascus, better than all the waters of Israel? I could bathe in them and be clean!" And he stalked off in a rage.

13 But his servants came forward and spoke to him. "Sir,"[a] they said, "if the prophet told you to do something difficult, would you not do it? How much more when he has only said to you, 'Bathe and be clean.'"
14 So he went down and immersed himself in the Jordan seven times, as the man of God had bidden; and his flesh became like a little boy's, and he was clean.
15 Returning with his entire retinue to the man of God, he stood before him and exclaimed, "Now I know that there is no God in the whole world except in Israel! So please accept a gift from your servant."
16 But he replied, "As the LORD lives, whom I serve, I will not accept anything." He pressed him to accept, but he refused.
17 And Naaman said, "Then at least let your servant be given two mule-loads of earth; for your servant will never again offer up burnt offering or sacrifice to any god, except the LORD.
18 But may the LORD pardon your servant for this: When my master enters the temple of Rimmon to bow low in worship there, and he is leaning on my arm so that I must bow low in the temple of Rimmon—when I bow low in the temple of Rimmon, may the LORD pardon your servant in this."
19 And he said to him, "Go in peace."

When he had gone some distance from him,
20 Gehazi, the attendant of Elisha the man of God, thought: "My master [b-]has let that Aramean Naaman off without accepting what he brought![-b] As the LORD lives, I will run after him and get something from him."
21 So Gehazi hurried after Naaman. When Naaman saw someone running after him, he alighted from his chariot to meet him and said, "Is all well?"
22 "All is well," he replied. "My master has sent me to say: Two youths, disciples of the prophets, have just come to me from the hill country of Ephraim. Please give them a talent of silver and two changes of clothing."
23 Naaman said, "Please take two talents." He urged him, and he wrapped the two talents of silver in two bags and gave them, along with two changes of clothes, to two of his servants, who carried them ahead of him.
24 When [Gehazi] arrived at the citadel, he took [the things] from them and deposited them in the house. Then he dismissed the men and they went their way.

a *Lit. "[My] father."*

b-b *Lit. "has prevented that Aramean Naaman from having what he brought accepted."*

25 He entered and stood before his master; and Elisha said to him, "Where have you been, Gehazi?" He replied, "Your servant has not gone anywhere." 26 Then [Elisha] said to him, "Did not my spirit[a] go along when a man got down from his chariot to meet you? Is this a time to take money in order to buy clothing and olive groves and vineyards, sheep and oxen, and male and female slaves? 27 Surely, the leprosy of Naaman shall cling to you and to your descendants forever." And as [Gehazi] left his presence, he was snow-white with leprosy.

6 The disciples of the prophets said to Elisha, "See, the place where we live under your direction is too cramped for us. 2 Let us go to the Jordan, and let us each get a log there and build quarters there for ourselves to live in." "Do so," he replied. 3 Then one of them said, "Will you please come along with your servants?" "Yes, I will come," he said; 4 and he accompanied them. So they went to the Jordan and cut timber. 5 As one of them was felling a trunk, the iron ax head fell into the water. And he cried aloud, "Alas, master, it was a borrowed one!" 6 "Where did it fall?" asked the man of God. He showed him the spot; and he cut off a stick and threw it in, and he made the ax head float. 7 "Pick it up," he said; so he reached out and took it.

8 While the king of Aram was waging war against Israel, he took counsel with his officers and said, [b-]"I will encamp[-b] in such and such a place." 9 But the man of God sent word to the king of Israel, "Take care not to pass through that place, for the Arameans are encamped there." 10 So the king of Israel sent word to the place of which the man of God had told him. [c-]Time and again[-c] he alerted [d-]such a place[-d] and took precautions there. 11 Greatly agitated about this matter, the king of Aram summoned his officers and said to them, "Tell me! Who of us is on the side of the king of Israel?" 12 "No one, my lord king," said one of the officers. "Elisha, that prophet in Israel, tells the king of Israel the very words you speak in your bedroom." 13 "Go find out where he is," he said, "so that I can have him seized." It was reported to him that [Elisha] was in Dothan; 14 so he sent horses and chariots there and a strong force. They arrived at night and encircled the town.

15 When the attendant of the man of God rose early and went outside, he saw a force, with horses and chariots, surrounding the town. "Alas, master, what shall we do?" his servant asked him. 16 "Have no fear," he replied. "There are more on our side than on theirs." 17 Then Elisha prayed: "LORD, open his eyes and let him see." And the LORD opened the servant's eyes and he

a Lit. "heart." *b-b Meaning of Heb. uncertain.* *c-c Lit. "not once or twice."* *d-d Heb. "it."*

26: Elisha here has clairvoyant abilities (contrast 4.27). **27:** Gehazi's solicitation had made Elisha appear to be a fee-for-service healer, reducing the miraculous cure to a matter of arcane knowledge. Gehazi's leprosy demonstrated its divine nature.

6.1–7: Elisha makes an ax head float. 1: *Disciples of the prophets:* Elisha much more than Elijah is associated with a prophetic company. *Place where we live:* This seems to imply a regular community *under* Elisha's *direction.* **2:** Trees, and therefore *a log,* would be more readily found near the *Jordan.*

6.8–23: The Aramean raiders are foiled. A prophetic story celebrating how the clairvoyant Elisha, whose skill is known within court circles of the Arameans, captured a contingent of the Aramean army and delivered it to the king of Israel, thereby ending Aramean infiltrations into Israel. The names of the Aramean and Israelite kings are not provided in this story either (cf. 5.1–27). This story concludes the second cycle (see 4.1). **8–13:** The story is set in a period when Aramean troops regularly made incursions deep into Israel, south of the Jezreel Valley, and were even able to attack the city of Dothan. The details, however, are insufficient to place them into a specific chronological setting. **17–18:** Elisha prays twice, once that his servant will see that his master is surrounded and protected by an invisible force and once that the Arameans will be blinded by light so that they cannot see. When Elisha requires miraculous intervention for himself, he prays for it.

saw the hills all around Elisha covered with horses and chariots
of fire. 18 [The Arameans] came down against him, and Elisha
prayed to the LORD: "Please strike this people with a blinding
light." And He struck them with a blinding light, as Elisha had
asked.

19 Elisha said to them, "This is not the road, and that is not
the town; follow me, and I will lead you to the man you want."
And he led them to Samaria. 20 When they entered Samaria,
Elisha said, "O LORD, open the eyes of these men so that they
may see." The LORD opened their eyes and they saw that they
were inside Samaria. 21 When the king of Israel saw them, he
said to Elisha, "Father, shall I strike them down?" 22 "No, do
not," he replied. "Did you take them captive with your sword
and bow that you would strike them down? Rather, set food
and drink before them, and let them eat and drink and return
to their master." 23 So he prepared a lavish feast for them and,
after they had eaten and drunk, he let them go, and they returned to their master. And the Aramean bands stopped invading the land of Israel.

24 Sometime later, King Ben-hadad of Aram mustered his
entire army and marched upon Samaria and besieged it.
25 There was a great famine in Samaria, and the siege continued until a donkey's head sold for eighty [shekels] of silver and
a quarter of a *kab* of [a]doves' dung[a] for five shekels. 26 Once,
when the king of Israel was walking on the city wall, a woman
cried out to him: "Help me, Your Majesty!" 27 "Don't [ask me],"
he replied. "Let the LORD help you! Where could I get help for
you, from the threshing floor or from the winepress? 28 But
what troubles you?" the king asked her. The woman answered,
"That woman said to me, 'Give up your son and we will eat him
today; and tomorrow we'll eat my son.' 29 So we cooked my son
and we ate him. The next day I said to her, 'Give up your son
and let's eat him'; but she hid her son." 30 When the king heard
what the woman said, he rent his clothes; and as he walked
along the wall, the people could see that he was wearing sackcloth underneath.

31 He said, "Thus and more may God do to me if the head
of Elisha son of Shaphat remains on [b]his shoulders[b] today."
32 Now Elisha was sitting at home and the elders were sitting with him. The king had sent ahead one of his men; but
before the messenger arrived, [Elisha] said to the elders, "Do
you see—that murderer has sent someone to cut off my head!
Watch when the messenger comes, and shut the door and hold
the door fast against him. No doubt the sound of his master's
footsteps will follow."

a-a Apparently a popular term for "carob pods," as in Akkadian. *b-b Lit. "him."*

6.24–7.20: The siege of Samaria. 6.24: This introduction, contradicting v. 23, indicates these stories have not been combined in historical order. This siege story may have originally followed the story of the Moabite campaign (3.27). Ralbag's comment on v. 23 suggests how the author may have interpreted the two vv. in a noncontradictory manner by interpreting vv. 23–24 to mean that the Arameans stopped sending in contingents of soldiers and amassed a single army that besieged Samaria. **25:** Even the least desirable, cheapest, foods are sold for a high price. **28:** The motif of cannibalism is associated with sieges also in Deut. 28.53–57; Ezek. 5.10; Lam. 2.20; 4.10, and in other ancient Near Eastern texts. **30:** The king had been wearing sackcloth beneath his normal clothing as a sign of mourning or contrition. **31:** This oath against Elisha indicates that somehow the king held the prophet responsible for the siege. Rashi, Radak, and Joseph Kara suggest that it was because the king thought that Elisha could request relief from God. Ralbag, however, assumes that Elisha provided fair warning of the siege and starvation, just as Elijah had of the drought in 1 Kings 17.1, and that the king thought that it had gone on long enough.

33 While he was still talking to them, the messenger[a] came to
him and said, "This calamity is from the LORD.
7 What more can I hope for from the LORD?" 1 And Elisha replied, "Hear the word of the LORD. Thus said the LORD: This
time tomorrow, a *seah* of choice flour shall sell for a shekel at
the gate of Samaria, and two *seah*s of barley for a shekel." 2 The
aide on whose arm the king was leaning spoke up and said to
the man of God, "Even if the LORD were to make windows in
the sky, could this come to pass?" And he retorted, "You shall
see it with your own eyes, but you shall not eat of it."

3 There were four men, lepers, outside the gate. They said to
one another, "Why should we sit here waiting for death? 4 If we
decide to go into the town, what with the famine in the town,
we shall die there; and if we just sit here, still we die. Come, let
us desert to the Aramean camp. If they let us live, we shall live;
and if they put us to death, we shall but die."
5 They set out at twilight for the Aramean camp; but when
they came to the edge of the Aramean camp, there was no one
there. 6 For the Lord had caused the Aramean camp to hear a
sound of chariots, a sound of horses—the din of a huge army.
They said to one another, "The king of Israel must have hired
the kings of the Hittites and the kings of Mizraim[b] to attack us!"
7 And they fled headlong in the twilight, abandoning their tents
and horses and asses—the [entire] camp just as it was—as they
fled for their lives.
8 When those lepers came to the edge of the camp, they
went into one of the tents and ate and drank; then they carried off silver and gold and clothing from there and buried it.
They came back and went into another tent, and they carried
off what was there and buried it. 9 Then they said to one another, "We are not doing right. This is a day of good news, and
we are keeping silent! If we wait until the light of morning, we
shall incur guilt. Come, let us go and inform the king's palace." 10 They went and called out to the gatekeepers of the city
and told them, "We have been to the Aramean camp. There
is not a soul there, nor any human sound; but the horses are
tethered and the asses are tethered and the tents are undisturbed."
11 The gatekeepers called out, and the news was passed on
into the king's palace. 12 The king rose in the night and said to
his courtiers, "I will tell you what the Arameans have done to us.
They know that we are starving, so they have gone out of camp
and hidden in the fields, thinking: When they come out of the
town, we will take them alive and get into the town." 13 But one
of the courtiers spoke up, "Let a few[c] of the remaining horses

6.33–7.1: The king had a revolutionary change of heart. His messengers, in his name, acknowledge that God is the source of the calamity, and Elisha rewards the confession with a prediction that the famine would end the next day. **7.2:** The cynical aide next to the king challenges Elisha. In response Elisha predicts his death, a prediction fulfilled in vv. 17–20. **3:** As *lepers,* they were excluded from the city. **5–7:** These vv. are a parenthetical explanation of how it happened that the lepers found the Aramean camp empty. **6:** Only Arameans encamped around Samaria heard sounds of the chariots and army. Cf. 6.16–17 that describe the invisible chariots protecting Elisha and 2 Sam. 5.24 that refers to the sounds of an invisible army of God. The reference to *Hittites* and *Mizraim* (probably Egypt) are anachronistic.

a Emendation yields "king." *b Cf. 1 Kings 10.28 and note d there.* *c Lit. "five."*

that are still here be taken—[a]they are like those that are left here
of the whole multitude of Israel, out of the whole multitude of
Israel that have perished[a]—and let us send and find out."
14 They took two teams[b] of horses and the king sent them
after the Aramean army, saying, "Go and find out." 15 They followed them as far as the Jordan, and found the entire road full
of clothing and gear which the Arameans had thrown away in
their haste; and the messengers returned and told the king.
16 The people then went out and plundered the Aramean
camp. So a *seah* of choice flour sold for a shekel, and two *seah*s
of barley for a shekel—as the LORD had spoken.
17 Now the king had put the aide on whose arm he leaned
in charge of the gate; and he was trampled to death in the gate
by the people—just as the man of God had spoken, as he had
spoken when the king came down to him. 18 For when the man
of God said to the king, "This time tomorrow two *seah*s of barley shall sell at the gate of Samaria for a shekel, and a *seah* of
choice flour for a shekel," 19 the aide answered the man of God
and said, "Even if the LORD made windows in the sky, could
this come to pass?" And he retorted, "You shall see it with your
own eyes, but you shall not eat of it." 20 That is exactly what happened to him: The people trampled him to death in the gate.

8 Elisha had said to the woman whose son he revived, "Leave
immediately with your family and go sojourn [c]somewhere
else;[c] for the LORD has decreed a seven-year famine upon the
land, and it has already begun." 2 The woman had done as the
man of God had spoken; she left with her family and sojourned
in the land of the Philistines for seven years. 3 At the end of the
seven years, the woman returned from the land of the Philistines
and went to the king to complain about her house and farm.
4 Now the king was talking to Gehazi, the servant of the man of
God, and he said, "Tell me all the wonderful things that Elisha
has done." 5 While he was telling the king how [Elisha] had revived a dead person, in came the woman whose son he had revived, complaining to the king about her house and farm. "My
lord king," said Gehazi, "this is the woman and this is her son
whom Elisha revived." 6 The king questioned the woman, and
she told him [the story]; so the king assigned a eunuch to her
and instructed him: "Restore all her property, and all the revenue from her farm from the time she left the country until now."

7 Elisha arrived in Damascus at a time when King Ben-hadad
of Aram was ill. [d]The king[d] was told, "The man of God is on his
way here," 8 and he said to Hazael, "Take a gift with you and go

a-a Meaning of Heb. uncertain. *b Meaning of Heb. uncertain.*
c-c Lit. "wherever you may sojourn." *d-d Brought up from v. 8 for clarity.*

8.1–6: A story about Gehazi telling Elisha stories to the king of Israel. The brief tale most likely describes something that occurred after the death of Elisha: (1) the king asks to be told such stories (v. 4) and (2) the woman whose son had been revivified (see 4.8–37) petitions the king on her own, indicating that her husband is dead and that Elisha, who could act on her behalf, is not available (4.13). **1:** The *seven-year famine* may have been a period prior to and during the siege of Samaria narrated in the preceding section.

8.7–15: The prophecy to Hazael, delivered by Elisha, was originally a task assigned to Elijah (1 Kings 19.15–17). **7–9:** Elisha's reputation as a prognosticator was well known among the Arameans, and *Hazael* addresses him in the name of *Ben-hadad* with great respect. Ben-hadad's inquiry of Elisha has no religious implications. As a simple consultation with an acknowledged expert, it was similar to Ahaziah's of Baal-zebub (2 Kings 1.2).

meet the man of God, and through him inquire of the LORD: Will I recover from this illness?" [9] Hazael went to meet him, taking with him as a gift forty camel-loads of all the bounty of Damascus. He came and stood before him and said, "Your son, King Ben-hadad of Aram, has sent me to you to ask: Will I recover from this illness?" [10] Elisha said to him, "Go and say to him, 'You will recover.' However, the LORD has revealed to me that he will die." [11] The man of God [a-]kept his face expressionless[-a] for a long time; and then he wept. [12] "Why does my lord weep?" asked Hazael. "Because I know," he replied, "what harm you will do to the Israelite people: you will set their fortresses on fire, put their young men to the sword, dash their little ones in pieces, and rip open their pregnant women." [13] "But how," asked Hazael, "can your servant, who is a mere dog, perform such a mighty deed?" Elisha replied, "The LORD has shown me a vision of you as king of Aram." [14] He left Elisha and returned to his master, who asked him, "What did Elisha say to you?" He replied, "He told me that you would recover." [15] The next day, [Hazael] took [a-]a piece of netting,[-a] dipped it in water, and spread it over his face. So [Ben-hadad] died, and Hazael succeeded him as king.

[16] In the fifth year of King Joram[b] son of Ahab of Israel—Jehoshaphat had been king of Judah—Joram son of King Jehoshaphat of Judah became king. [17] He was thirty-two years old when he became king, and he reigned in Jerusalem eight years. [18] He followed the practices of the kings of Israel—whatever the House of Ahab did, for he had married a daughter[c] of Ahab—and he did what was displeasing to the LORD. [19] However, the LORD refrained from destroying Judah, for the sake of His servant David, in accordance with His promise to maintain a lamp for his descendants for all time. [20] During his reign, the Edomites rebelled against Judah's rule and set up a king of their own. [21] Joram crossed over to Zair with all his chariotry. [a-]He arose by night and attacked the Edomites, who were surrounding him and the chariot commanders; but[-a] his troops fled to their homes. [22] Thus Edom fell away from Judah, as is still the case. Libnah likewise fell away at that time.

[23] The other events of Joram's reign, and all his actions, are recorded in the Annals of the Kings of Judah. [24] Joram slept with his fathers and was buried with his fathers in the City of David; his son Ahaziah succeeded him as king.

[25] In the twelfth year of King Joram son of Ahab of Israel, Ahaziah son of Joram became king of Judah. [26] Ahaziah was twenty-two

a-a Meaning of Heb. uncertain.

b Throughout this chapter, the name Joram is sometimes written Jehoram.

c Emendation yields "sister"; cf. v. 26.

10–13: Elisha does not lie, but instructs Hazael to do so. He proceeds to inform Hazael that God has foreordained his rise and even his victories over Israel. **15:** According to what may be gleaned from inscriptions of the Assyrian king Shalmaneser III, Hazael usurped the throne in Damascus after 845 but before 841 BCE.

8.16–24: The reign of Joram (Jehoram), king of Judah, paralleled that of his brother-in-law Joram, king of Israel. The author's negative evaluation of his reign cites behaviors modeled after Ahab's dynasty and attributes them directly to the king's wife. **19:** See 1 Kings 15.4. **22:** The growing strength of *Edom* can be discerned by comparing the terminology in this v. with 1 Kings 22.48, where Edomites were controlled through an acting king, and 3.9, where an independent king who was nonetheless a vassal of Judah reigned. The independence of Edom signaled Judah's final loss of control over the central Negev (contiguous with Edom) and all trade through it. The rebellion of *Libnah,* a Levitical city on the western fringe of Judah's territory (Josh. 10.29; 21.13), lacks an adequate explanation.

8.25–29: The short reign of Ahaziah of Judah (not his dead uncle, Ahaziah of Israel) is linked to the fortunes of his living uncle Joram king of Israel. Ahaziah involved Judah in Israel's battle against the Arameans at Ramoth-gilead in Transjordan. His death and burial are noted without the usual formulae in the middle of the account of Jehu's revolt (9.27–29). **26:** In v. 18, Athaliah is referred to as the daughter of Ahab, which would make her Omri's granddaughter. It is possible that the Omrides fashioned all royal descendants as "sons/daughters of Omri," making Omri into the head of a dynasty, as David was for the Southern Kingdom. Jehu, who killed off the Omrides, was identified as "son of Omri" on the Black Obelisk of Shalmaneser III. See also Solomon's wife, "the daughter of Pharaoh," 1 Kings 3.1 n.

9.1–14a: The anointing of Jehu was the last unfinished task of Elijah left for Elisha to carry out (1 Kings 19.15–16). He dispatches one of the disciples of the prophets to carry it out. **3–4:** Elisha gives specific instructions about what the messenger is to do and say, but in fulfilling the instructions, the messenger deviates considerably from his charge (vv. 6–10). A rationale for doing so is provided in v. 4 which when translated literally yields: "And he went, the young man, the young man, the prophet, to Ramoth-gilead." Usually interpreted by both classical and contemporary commentators as "the servant/young man of the prophet," the text indicates that he was a prophet in his own right. Furthermore, Jehu's comment (v. 11) indicates that he was a well-known figure and that people were familiar with his pet concerns. **6:** The anointing is private, as was that of Saul (1 Sam. 10.1). **7–9:** The charge to Jehu is delivered as an oracle of God, not a repetition of something that Elisha said. The prophecy contains an instruction that Jehu become the agent through which the prophecies of Elijah in 1 Kings 21.21–23 are fulfilled. V. 7 also indicates that Jezebel had not only persecuted *prophets* of God, but other *servants of the Lord* as well (see 1 Kings 18.4, 22). Years later, long after the period of the persecutions, there were most likely many descendants of those who had suffered under her hand who were willing to take revenge. **12:** *Thus and thus,* a conventional expression indicating that Jehu repeated everything exactly (see 5.4 where the same Heb expression is translated "just what"). **13:** Other officers acclaim Jehu king, and make noise, typical parts of the coronation ritual (see 1 Kings 1.39–40).

years old when he became king, and he reigned in Jerusalem one year; his mother's name was Athaliah daughter of King Omri of Israel. 27 He walked in the ways of the House of Ahab and did what was displeasing to the LORD, like the House of Ahab, for he was related by marriage to the House of Ahab. 28 He marched with Joram son of Ahab to battle against King Hazael of Aram at Ramoth-gilead, but the Arameans wounded Joram. 29 King Joram retired to Jezreel to recover from the wounds which the Arameans had inflicted upon him at Ramah, when he fought against King Hazael of Aram. And King Ahaziah son of Joram of Judah went down to Jezreel to visit Joram son of Ahab while he was ill.

9 Then the prophet Elisha summoned one of the disciples of the prophets and said to him, "Tie up your skirts,[a] and take along this flask of oil, and go to Ramoth-gilead. 2 When you arrive there, go and see Jehu son of Jehoshaphat son of Nimshi; get him to leave his comrades, and take him into an inner room. 3 Then take the flask of oil and pour some on his head, and say, 'Thus said the LORD: I anoint you king over Israel.' Then open the door and flee without delay."

4 The young man, the servant of the prophet, went to Ramoth-gilead. 5 When he arrived, the army commanders were sitting together. He said, "Commander, I have a message for you." "For which one of us?" Jehu asked. He answered, "For you, commander." 6 So [Jehu] arose and went inside; and [the disciple] poured the oil on his head, and said to him, "Thus said the LORD, the God of Israel: I anoint you king over the people of the LORD, over Israel. 7 You shall strike down the House of Ahab your master; thus will I avenge on Jezebel the blood of My servants the prophets, and the blood of the other servants of the LORD. 8 The whole House of Ahab shall perish, and I will cut off every male belonging to Ahab, [b-]bond and free[-b] in Israel. 9 I will make the House of Ahab like the House of Jeroboam son of Nebat, and like the House of Baasha son of Ahijah. 10 The dogs shall devour Jezebel in the field of Jezreel, with none to bury her." Then he opened the door and fled.

11 Jehu went out to the other officers of his master, and they asked him, "Is all well? What did that madman come to you for?" He said to them, "You know the man and his ranting!" 12 "You're lying," they said. "Tell us [the truth]." Then he replied, "Thus and thus he said: Thus said the LORD: I anoint you king over Israel!" 13 Quickly each man took his cloak and placed it under him,[c] on [d-]the top step.[-d] They sounded the horn and proclaimed, "Jehu is king!" 14 Thus Jehu son of Jehoshaphat son of Nimshi conspired against Joram.

a See note at 4.29. *b-b See note at 1 Kings 14.10.* *c I.e., Jehu.*
d-d Meaning of Heb. uncertain.

Joram and all Israel had been defending Ramoth-gilead against King Hazael of Aram, [15] but King Joram had gone back to Jezreel to recover from the wounds which the Arameans had inflicted on him in his battle with King Hazael of Aram.

Jehu said, "If such is your wish, allow no one to slip out of the town to go and report this in Jezreel." [16] Then Jehu mounted his chariot and drove to Jezreel; for Joram was lying ill there, and King Ahaziah of Judah had gone down to visit Joram. [17] The lookout was stationed on the tower in Jezreel, and he saw the troop of Jehu as he approached. He called out, "I see a troop!" Joram said, "Dispatch a horseman to meet them and let him ask: Is all well?" [18] The horseman went to meet him, and he said, "The king inquires: Is all well?" Jehu replied, "What concern of yours is it whether all is well? Fall in behind me." The lookout reported: "The messenger has reached them, but has not turned back." [19] So he sent out a second horseman. He came to them and said, "Thus says the king: Is all well?" Jehu answered, "What concern of yours is it whether all is well? Fall in behind me." [20] And the lookout reported, "The messenger has reached them, but has not turned back. And it looks like the driving of Jehu son of Nimshi, who drives wildly."

[21] Joram ordered, "Hitch up [the chariot]!" They hitched up his chariot; and King Joram of Israel and King Ahaziah of Judah went out, each in his own chariot, to meet Jehu. They met him at the field of Naboth the Jezreelite. [22] When Joram saw Jehu, he asked, "Is all well, Jehu?" But Jehu replied, "How can all be well as long as your mother Jezebel carries on her countless harlotries and sorceries?" [23] Thereupon Joram turned his horses[a] around and fled, crying out to Ahaziah, "Treason, Ahaziah!" [24] But Jehu drew his bow and hit Joram between the shoulders,[b] so that the arrow pierced his heart; and he collapsed in his chariot.

[25] Jehu thereupon ordered his officer Bidkar, "Pick him up and throw him into the field of Naboth the Jezreelite. Remember how you and I were riding side by side behind his father Ahab, when the LORD made this pronouncement about him: [26] 'I swear, I have taken note of the blood of Naboth and the blood of his sons yesterday—declares the LORD. And I will requite you in this plot—declares the LORD.' So pick him up and throw him unto the plot in accordance with the word of the LORD."

[27] On seeing this, King Ahaziah of Judah fled along the road to Beth-haggan. Jehu pursued him and said, "Shoot him down too!" [And they shot him] in his chariot at the ascent of Gur, which is near Ibleam. He fled to Megiddo and died there. [28] His servants conveyed him in a chariot to Jerusalem, and they buried him in his grave with his fathers, in the City of David.

a Lit. "hands"; see note at 1 Kings 22.34. *b Lit. "arms."*

9.14b–15a: An interpolation. Excavations at Jezreel indicate that it was primarily a fortified administrative center with remains of what may have been a large palace. Two fragments of a victory stele in the Aram. language found in the excavations of Dan attest to Aramean control of the area in the 9th c. as well as to Aramean victories over Israel and success in battle against someone from the Davidic dynasty. One fragment mentions two kings, one whose name ended "-rm" and another whose name ended "-yhw." Historians speculate that these are Jeho**ram** and Ahazy**ahuw**. The only king successful against both Israel and Judah whose respective kings' names match the letters on the fragment was Hazael.

9.15b–37: The battle with Joram of Israel and the death of Jezebel. 15b: This v. appears to pick up from 14a. The interpolation may have been inserted to explain why the news of Jehu's anointing as king should not be reported in *Jezreel.* **17–20:** The author creates the image of a large force moving slowly, even ominously, toward Jezreel. *Jehu* apparently *drives* his chariot *wildly*, perhaps in a zig-zag in front of the advancing troop. They advance so slowly that two different riders are sent out to them and Joram and Ahaziah in their chariots are able to go out to them before they enter Jezreel. The events in this ch, as well as the rise of Hazael in Damascus, are dated to 842 BCE on the basis of correlations between biblical chronological notations and other ancient Near Eastern texts: the Mesha stele, references to Ahab, Jehu, Hazael, and Joash in Assyrian inscriptions, and Aram. inscriptions mentioning Hazael and Ben-hadad. **17:** *Well,* Heb "shalom," is repeated like a dissonant note throughout the scenes of the revolt as death is plotted and executed in vv. 18, 19, 22, 30. **21:** The "chance" meeting *at the field of Naboth the Jezreelite* hints that Naboth's unjust death is about to be avenged. **28:** Although it is mentioned here, Ahaziah's body could only have been

(29 Ahaziah had become king over Judah in the eleventh year
of Joram son of Ahab.)

30 Jehu went on to Jezreel. When Jezebel heard of it, she painted her eyes with kohl and dressed her hair, and she looked out
of the window. 31 As Jehu entered the gate, she called out, "Is all
well, Zimri, murderer of your master?"[a] 32 He looked up toward
the window and said, "Who is on my side, who?" And two or
three eunuchs leaned out toward him. 33 "Throw her down," he
said. They threw her down; and her blood spattered on the wall
and on the horses, and they trampled her.
34 Then he went inside and ate and drank. And he said, "Attend to that cursed woman and bury her, for she was a king's
daughter." 35 So they went to bury her; but all they found of
her were the skull, the feet, and the hands. 36 They came back
and reported to him; and he said, "It is just as the LORD spoke
through His servant Elijah the Tishbite: The dogs shall devour
the flesh of Jezebel in the field of Jezreel; 37 and the carcass of
Jezebel shall be like dung on the ground, in the field of Jezreel,
so that none will be able to say: 'This was Jezebel.'"

10 Ahab had seventy descendants in Samaria. Jehu wrote
letters and sent them to Samaria, to the elders and officials of Jezreel[b] and to the guardians of [the children] of
Ahab, as follows: 2 "Now, when this letter reaches you—since
your master's sons are with you and you also have chariots
and horses, and a fortified city and weapons—3 select the best
and the most suitable of your master's sons and set him on his
father's throne, and fight for your master's house." 4 But they
were overcome by fear, for they thought, "If the two kings could
not stand up to him, how can we?" 5 The steward of the palace
and the governor of the city and the elders and the guardians
sent this message to Jehu: "We are your subjects, and we shall
do whatever you tell us to. We shall not proclaim anyone king;
do whatever you like."
6 He wrote them a second time: "If you are on my side and
are ready to obey me, take the heads of the attendants of your
master's sons and come[c] to me in Jezreel tomorrow at this
time." Now the princes, seventy in number, were with the notables of the town, who were rearing them. 7 But when the letter
reached them, they took the princes and slaughtered all seventy of them; they put their heads in baskets and sent them to
him in Jezreel. 8 A messenger came and reported to him: "They
have brought the heads of the princes." He said, "Pile them
up in two heaps at the entrance of the gate before morning."

a See 1 Kings 16.8–10. *b Emendation yields "of the city."*
c Targum and Septuagint read "and bring them."

removed to Jerusalem later, after the revolt was over. **30–31:** Jezebel is portrayed as a proud, cold, noble woman. After hearing of the deaths of her son and son-in-law, she neither mourns nor tries to flee while Jehu and part of the troop are elsewhere. She pretties herself for a final scene and addresses a perfect barb to Jehu when he enters the palace grounds. **30:** *Kohl:* The English term is a borrowing from Arabic "kuhl," a sulphide of antimony, ground into powder, mixed with oil and applied to the eyelashes, an ancient mascara. **31:** *Zimri,* the assassin of Elah son of Baasha (1 Kings 16.8–14). Zimri eliminated all of the descendants of Baasha, as Baasha had eliminated all of the descendants of Jeroboam (1 Kings 15.27–30). Jehu has eliminated the house of Omri, but if he follows in the footsteps of Zimri his reign will be short (1 Kings 16.15).

10.1–17: The purge of the house of Ahab. 1: *Seventy:* A stereotypical large number. **2–5:** These vv. illustrate that even after the many internal revolutions, the right to proclaim someone king remained vested with certain groups of people or their representatives. Jehu's message affirms the right even as his threat subverts it. **8–9:** Besides being a potent threat, the heads of Ahab's sons arrayed at the entrance of Jezreel proved silently that there was no Ahabite around whom anti-Jehu forces might rally. Jehu used them at Jezreel to argue that he was supported by the people of Samaria, the capital city constructed by Omri, Ahab's father.

9 In the morning he went out and stood there; and he said to
all the people, "Are you blameless?[a] True, I conspired against
my master and killed him; but who struck down all of these?
10 Know, then, that nothing that the LORD has spoken concerning the House of Ahab shall remain unfulfilled, for the LORD
has done what he announced through His servant Elijah."
11 And Jehu struck down all that were left of the House of Ahab
in Jezreel—and all his notables, intimates, and priests—till he
left him no survivor.

12 He then set out for Samaria. On the way, when he was at
Beth-eked of the shepherds, 13 Jehu came upon the kinsmen of
King Ahaziah of Judah. "Who are you?" he asked. They replied,
"We are the kinsmen of Ahaziah, and we have come to pay
our respects to the sons of the king and the sons of the queen
mother." 14 "Take them alive!" he said. They took them alive
and then slaughtered them at the pit of Beth-eked, forty-two of
them; he did not spare a single one.

15 He went on from there, and he met Jehonadab son of Rechab
coming toward him. He greeted him and said to him, "Are you
as wholehearted with me as I am with you?" "I am," Jehonadab
replied. "If so," [said Jehu,] "give me your hand." He gave him his
hand and [Jehu] helped him into the chariot. 16 "Come with me,"
he said, "and see my zeal for the LORD." And he was taken along
in the chariot. 17 Arriving in Samaria, [Jehu] struck down all the
survivors of [the House of] Ahab in Samaria, until he wiped it
out, fulfilling the word that the LORD had spoken to Elijah.

18 Jehu assembled all the people and said to them, "Ahab
served Baal little; Jehu shall serve him much! 19 Therefore, summon to me all the prophets of Baal, all his worshipers, and all
his priests: let no one fail to come, for I am going to hold a great
sacrifice for Baal. Whoever fails to come shall forfeit his life."
Jehu was acting with guile in order to exterminate the worshipers of Baal. 20 Jehu gave orders to convoke a solemn assembly
for Baal, and one was proclaimed. 21 Jehu sent word throughout Israel, and all the worshipers of Baal came, not a single one
remained behind. They came into the temple of Baal, and the
temple of Baal was filled from end to end. 22 He said to the man
in charge of the wardrobe,[b] "Bring out the vestments for all the
worshipers of Baal"; and he brought vestments out for them.
23 Then Jehu and Jehonadab son of Rechab came into the temple of Baal, and they said to the worshipers of Baal, "Search and
make sure that there are no worshipers of the LORD among you,
but only worshipers of Baal." 24 So they went in to offer sacrifices and burnt offerings. But Jehu had stationed eighty of his men
outside and had said, "Whoever permits the escape of a single
one of the men I commit to your charge shall forfeit life for life."

a *Or "You are blameless."* *b* *Meaning of Heb. uncertain.*

11: The killing extends to include those whose position and authority were based on their association with the royal house. The priests in this group may have served at the open shrines or the worship of Baal, or they may have been minor bureaucrats. Priests appear in the lists of royal officials in 2 Sam. 8.18; 20.26; 1 Kings 4.5, and as impoverished appointees (1 Sam. 2.36). These killings go beyond the prophetic charge to Jehu. **12–14:** Jehu extends the purge to a group of men from Judah claiming kinship with the (dead) Ahaziah. However related to Ahaziah, they were also connected to Athaliah, his mother, and through her to Ahab's family. **15–16:** Jehonadab, son of Rechab, founded a small traditionalist group within his clan that adopted a way of life similar to that of the Israelites before their settlement in the land. Rechabites abstained from wine, did not engage in any form of agriculture, and lived in tents (Jer. 35.6–10). Jehu's invitation that Jehonadab join him to see his *zeal for the LORD* (see 1 Kings 19.10, 14) indicates that the Rechabites were also among the radical monotheists. The presence of Jehonadab in Jehu's chariots would have helped rally like-minded people to his support. Their combined *zeal for the LORD* is viewed positively as a continuation of the radical monotheism of Elijah.

10.18–28: The purge of Baalists from Israel. 18: It is unclear why Baalists believed Jehu's proclamation, and why they didn't become suspicious later when Jehonadab appeared with Jehu in the temple (v. 23). The narrative considers it sufficient that he promised to worship Baal more than Ahab. **22:** Some special item of clothing kept in the temple was apparently necessary for the proper worship of Baal.

[25] When Jehu had finished presenting the burnt offering,
he said to the guards and to the officers, "Come in and strike
them down; let no man get away!" The guards and the officers
struck them down with the sword and left them lying where
they were; then they proceeded to the interior[a] of the temple
of Baal. [26] They brought out the pillars[b] of the temple of Baal
and burned them. [27] They destroyed the pillar[c] of Baal, and
they tore down the temple of Baal and turned it into latrines,
as is still the case. [28] Thus Jehu eradicated the Baal from Israel.
[29] However, Jehu did not turn away from the sinful objects by
which Jeroboam son of Nebat had caused Israel to sin, namely,
the golden calves at Bethel and at Dan.
[30] The LORD said to Jehu, "Because you have acted well and
done what was pleasing to Me, having carried out all that I
desired upon the House of Ahab, four generations of your descendants shall occupy the throne of Israel." [31] But Jehu was
not careful to follow the Teaching of the LORD, the God of Israel, with all his heart; he did not turn away from the sins that
Jeroboam had caused Israel to commit.

[32] In those days the LORD began to reduce Israel; and Hazael harassed them throughout the territory of Israel [33] east of
the Jordan, all the land of Gilead—the Gadites, the Reubenites, and the Manassites—from Aroer, by the Wadi Arnon, up
to Gilead and Bashan.
[34] The other events of Jehu's reign, and all his actions, and all
his exploits, are recorded in the Annals of the Kings of Israel.
[35] Jehu slept with his fathers and he was buried in Samaria;
he was succeeded as king by his son Jehoahaz. [36] Jehu reigned
over Israel for twenty-eight years in Samaria.

11 When Athaliah, the mother of Ahaziah, learned that her
son was dead, she promptly killed off all who were of royal
stock. [2] But Jehosheba, daughter of King Joram and sister of Ahaziah, secretly took Ahaziah's son Joash away from among the
princes who were being slain, and [put][d] him and his nurse in a
bedroom. And they[e] kept him hidden from Athaliah so that he
was not put to death. [3] He stayed with her for six years, hidden
in the House of the LORD,[f] while Athaliah reigned over the land.
[4] In the seventh year, Jehoiada sent for the chiefs of the hundreds of the Carites[g] and of the guards, and had them come
to him in the House of the LORD. He made a pact with them,
exacting an oath from them in the House of the LORD, and he

a Lit. "city." *b Emendation yields "sacred posts"; cf. Deut. 12.3.*
c Emendation yields "altar." *d Cf. 2 Chron. 22.11.* *e 2 Chron. 22.11 reads "she."*
f Jehosheba was the wife of the high priest Jehoiada; cf. 2 Chron. 22.11.
g Perhaps the Cherethites (cf. 2 Sam. 20.23) or the Carians. They were members of the king's bodyguard.

10.29–36: The rest of Jehu's reign. **29:** Jehu's commitments did not go so far as to eliminate the institutions established by Jeroboam. No matter what the historical Jehu may have thought, the author considered this sinful. **30:** *Four generations,* signalling the blessing of long life and many progeny; elsewhere, the maximum a person might expect to see in his lifetime (Gen. 50.22 n.; Job 42.16), used in other contexts as well (e.g., Exod. 34.7 and its parallels). **32–33:** Jehu's loss of these territories is verified by the Mesha stele in which the Moabite king boasts that he rebuilt *Aroer*. Mesha may have been allied with the Aramean *Hazael* against Israel.

11.1–20: Athaliah's interregnum (842–836 BCE). **1–3:** Athaliah, with influence and power as queen mother, exploited the death of her son to have all males of royal stock killed, then assumed power. The author did not provide her with the usual opening or closing summary since he does not view her as a legitimate ruler. Jehosheba, who saved Joash's life, was spared since she could not claim the throne. According to the parallel account in 2 Chron. 22.11 she was the wife of Jehoiada the priest. **1:** As the continuation of the story will show, she was not successful, in contrast to Jehu, in killing *off all who were of the royal stock* and the Davidic dynasty would continue. **2:** *Joash* (cf. also 12.19, 20; 13.1) is also called Jehoash (12.1, 5). The difference in the form of the name is due to peculiarities in regional pronunciations of biblical Heb. Both forms are found in Kings because the author tended to write names as he found them in his sources. Joash was the son of Ahaziah by a wife from Beer-sheba (12.2). **3:** *Reigned,* the feminine form of the word used elsewhere for legitimate kings.

showed them the king's son. 5 He instructed them: "This is what you must do: One-third of those who are on duty for the week [a]shall maintain guard[a] over the royal palace; 6 another third shall be [stationed] at the [b]Sur Gate;[b] and the other third shall be at the gate behind [c]the guards; you shall keep guard over the House on every side.[c] 7 The two divisions of yours who are off duty this week shall keep guard over the House of the LORD for the protection of the king. 8 You shall surround the king on every side, every man with his weapons at the ready; and whoever breaks through the ranks shall be killed. Stay close to the king in his comings and goings."

9 The chiefs of hundreds did just as Jehoiada ordered: Each took his men—those who were on duty that week and those who were off duty that week—and they presented themselves to Jehoiada the priest. 10 The priest gave the chiefs of hundreds King David's spears[d] and quivers that were kept in the House of the LORD. 11 The guards, each with his weapons at the ready, stationed themselves—from the south end of the House to the north end of the House, at the altar and the House—to guard the king on every side. 12 [Jehoiada] then brought out the king's son, and placed upon him the crown and the insignia.[e] They anointed him and proclaimed him king; they clapped their hands and shouted, "Long live the king!"

13 When Athaliah heard the shouting of the guards [and] the people, she came out to the people in the House of the LORD. 14 She looked about and saw the king standing by the pillar, as was the custom, the chiefs with their trumpets beside the king, and all the people of the land rejoicing and blowing trumpets. Athaliah rent her garments and cried out, "Treason, treason!" 15 Then the priest Jehoiada gave the command to the army officers, the chiefs of hundreds, and said to them, "Take her out [c]between the ranks[c] and, if anyone follows her, put him to the sword." For the priest thought: "Let her not be put to death in the House of the LORD." 16 They cleared a passageway for her and she entered the royal palace through the horses' entrance: there she was put to death.

17 And Jehoiada solemnized the covenant between the LORD, on the one hand, and the king and the people, on the other—as well as between the king and the people—that they should be the people of the LORD. 18 Thereupon all the people of the land went to the temple of Baal. They tore it down and smashed its altars and images to bits, and they slew Mattan, the priest of Baal, in front of the altars. [Jehoiada] the priest

a-a Heb. "and who keep guard." *b-b 2 Chron. 23.5 reads "Foundation Gate."*
c-c Meaning of Heb. uncertain. *d 2 Chron. 23.9 adds "and shields."*
e Meaning of Heb. uncertain.

5–7: The guards rotated once every three weeks, but were here called together at once to protect the king. **12:** *Insignia* (Heb "'edut") may refer to an identifying object, such as the armband of Saul (2 Sam. 1.10), that marked its wearer as king; these are seen on royal reliefs of Mesopotamian kings. Most medieval and modern commentators interpret the word as "testimony/covenant/teaching" and understand that a document spelling out royal rights and obligations is intended by the word. **14:** The *pillar* may have been one of the two on the porch before the Temple that may have been symbolic of dynastic succession (1 Kings 7.15–22). The *people of the land* is often a technical term in Jeremiah and Ezekiel, prophetic books from the end of the monarchic period, and in 2 Kings and 2 Chron., narrative books dealing with the late monarchy. It refers to an informal coalition of powerbrokers from important clans in Judah concerned with preserving the Davidic dynasty on the throne in Jerusalem (cf. 21.24; 25.19). The significance of their presence at the secret convocation was clear to Athaliah, who cried out *"Treason!"* **15:** She should *not be put to death in the House of the LORD* since a corpse would cause serious ritual contamination to the Temple (see 1 Kings 2.30–31 n.). **17:** After the anointing and public acclamation Jehoiada formalized two covenants. The first, a unique three-party covenant between the *LORD*, the people, and the king; the second, between the people and the king. The word "'edut" in v. 12 may refer to these. **18:** The *temple of Baal* in Jerusalem, mentioned here for the first time, may have been established by Athaliah during the interregnum, or earlier. This passage interrupts the natural flow from v. 17 to 19.

then placed guards over the House of the LORD. 19 He took the chiefs of hundreds, the Carites,[a] the guards, and all the people of the land, and they escorted the king from the House of the LORD into the royal palace by the gate of the guards. And he ascended the royal throne. 20 All the people of the land rejoiced, and the city was quiet. As for Athaliah, she had been put to the sword in the royal palace.

12 Jehoash was seven years old when he became king. 2 Jehoash began his reign in the seventh year of Jehu, and he reigned in Jerusalem forty years. His mother's name was Zibiah of Beer-sheba. 3 All his days Jehoash did what was pleasing to the LORD, as the priest Jehoiada instructed him. 4 The shrines, however, were not removed; the people continued to sacrifice and offer at the shrines.

5 Jehoash said to the priests, "All the money, current money, brought into the House of the LORD as sacred donations—[b]any money a man may pay as the money equivalent of persons,[b] or any other money that a man may be minded to bring to the House of the LORD—6 let the priests receive it, each from his benefactor; they, in turn, shall make repairs on the House, wherever damage may be found."

7 But in the twenty-third year of King Jehoash, [it was found that] the priests had not made the repairs on the House. 8 So King Jehoash summoned the priest Jehoiada and the other priests and said to them, "Why have you not kept the House in repair? Now do not accept money from your benefactors any more, but have it donated for the repair of the House." 9 The priests agreed that they would neither accept money from the people nor make repairs on the House.

10 And the priest Jehoiada took a chest and bored a hole in its lid. He placed it at the right side of the altar as one entered the House of the LORD, and the priestly guards of the threshold deposited there all the money that was brought into the House of the LORD. 11 Whenever they saw that there was much money in the chest, the royal scribe and the high priest would come up and put the money accumulated in the House of the LORD into bags, and they would count it. 12 Then they would deliver the money [c]that was weighed out[c] to the overseers of the work, who were in charge of the House of the LORD. These, in turn, used to pay the carpenters and the laborers who worked on the House of the LORD, 13 and the masons and the stonecutters. They also paid for wood and for quarried stone with which to make the repairs on the House of the LORD, and for every

a Perhaps the Cherethites (cf. 2 Sam. 20.23) or the Carians. They were members of the king's bodyguard. *b-b See Lev. 27.2–8.* *c-c Meaning of Heb. uncertain.*

20: All rejoice at the return of a descendent of King David to the throne.

12.1–22: The reign of Jehoash/Joash began in 836–835 BCE. Both forms of the name are used by the author. **1:** The 40-year reign attributed to him includes the interregnum years of Athaliah, who officially had no reign. Counting his reign as beginning at the death of his father (842), he reigned until 802, though he may actually have reigned for a few more years. In Judah, at this time, the regnal year was counted from the seventh month, Tishri. **5:** Over 140 years had passed since Solomon had completed the Temple, and no major repairs had been undertaken. Jehoash, as royal patron of the Temple, not the priests, launches the project. *Sacred donations* were funds donated to the Temple for use by the clergy (Num. 18.19). These most likely included obligatory offerings of the half-shekel and freewill offerings made in a spirit of generosity. Joash orders that they be collected by the priests, be applied for repairs, and that the priests undertake the repairs themselves. **10–16:** A new system devised by Jehoash removes the priests from all responsibility and labor. Sacred donations are deposited directly into a coffer, counted by two officials, and distributed to special contractors for labor and materials. None of the funds can be used to enhance the Temple treasure and no accounting is demanded from the contractors. Funds deriving from the purification (NJPS sin) and guilt offerings could not be used for Temple repair, but remained priestly income. Income associated with positive feelings and spontaneous acts of kindness went into Temple repair; that associated with negative feelings born out of a sense of obligation or guilt went to the priests. **11:** *The high priest* was the direct descendent of Aaron; the position was hereditary.

other expenditure that had to be made in repairing the House.
14 However, no silver bowls and no snuffers, basins, or trumpets—no vessels of gold or silver—were made at the House of
the LORD from the money brought into the House of the LORD;
15 this was given only to the overseers of the work for the repair
of the House of the LORD. 16 No check was kept on the men to
whom the money was delivered to pay the workers; for they
dealt honestly.
17 Money brought [a]as a guilt offering or as a purification offering[-a] was not deposited in the House of the LORD; it went to
the priests.

18 At that time, King Hazael of Aram came up and attacked
Gath and captured it; and Hazael proceeded to march on Jerusalem. 19 Thereupon King Joash of Judah took all the objects
that had been consecrated by his fathers, Kings Jehoshaphat,
Jehoram, and Ahaziah of Judah, and by himself, and all the
gold that there was in the treasuries of the Temple of the LORD
and in the royal palace, and he sent them to King Hazael of
Aram, who then turned back from his march on Jerusalem.
20 The other events of Joash's reign, and all his actions, are
recorded in the Annals of the Kings of Judah. 21 His courtiers
formed a conspiracy against Joash and assassinated him at
Beth-millo [b]that leads down to Silla.[-b] 22 The courtiers who
assassinated him were Jozacar son of Shimeath and Jehozabad son of Shomer. He died and was buried with his fathers
in the City of David; and his son Amaziah succeeded him as
king.

13 In the twenty-third year of King Joash son of Ahaziah
of Judah, Jehoahaz son of Jehu became king over Israel
in Samaria—for seventeen years. 2 He did what was displeasing to the LORD. He persisted in the sins which Jeroboam son
of Nebat had caused Israel to commit; he did not depart from
them. 3 The LORD was angry with Israel and He repeatedly
delivered them into the hands of King Hazael of Aram and
into the hands of Ben-hadad son of Hazael. 4 But Jehoahaz
pleaded with the LORD; and the LORD listened to him, for He
saw the suffering that the king of Aram inflicted upon Israel.
5 So the LORD granted Israel a deliverer, and they gained their
freedom from Aram; and Israel dwelt in its homes as before.
6 However, they did not depart from the sins which the House
of Jeroboam had caused Israel to commit; they persisted
in them. Even the sacred post stood in Samaria. 7 [c]In fact,
Jehoahaz was left with a force of only fifty horsemen, ten

a-a See Lev. 5.15. *b-b Meaning of Heb. uncertain.*
c This verse would read well after v. 3.

18–19: *At that time* often introduces a new scene or material taken from another source. Hazael's threat to Jerusalem forced Joash to raid the Temple treasury. This provides the background for the author's notation in v. 14 that donated funds were not used for Temple vessels. People donating to the Temple were not obligated to restore treasure withdrawn by the king. Hazael could only have penetrated Judah so deeply because he was in control of Transjordan up to the Jabbok (modern Nahr es-Zerqa) and traversed parts of the kingdom of Israel without fear (see 13.3–7). **21:** The reasons for Joash's assassination are not given. The act was most likely not directed against his family or against the monarchy, but against him directly, perhaps because of his dismal handling of Hazael's incursions deep into the territory of Judah. The two men who killed him did not flee (14.5–6) and, in contrast to what was reported concerning the Northern Kingdom, apparently had no interest in usurping the authority of the Davidic king.

13.1–9: The reign of Jehoahaz. The structure of this section has close parallels to that of the book of Judg., where Israel sins, a foreign nation punishes them, and God sends a savior to help them. Here, however, the additional element of divine prayer to God (v. 4), largely absent in Judg., is added.

chariots, and ten thousand foot soldiers; for the king of Aram
had decimated them and trampled them like the dust under
his feet.
8 The other events of Jehoahaz's reign, and all his actions and
his exploits, are recorded in the Annals of the Kings of Israel.
9 Jehoahaz slept with his fathers and he was buried in Samaria;
his son Joash succeeded him as king.

10 In the thirty-seventh year of King Joash of Judah, Jehoash
son of Jehoahaz became king of Israel in Samaria—for sixteen
years. 11 He did what was displeasing to the LORD; he did not
depart from any of the sins which Jeroboam son of Nebat had
caused Israel to commit; he persisted in them.
12 The other events of Joash's reign, and all his actions, and
his exploits in his war with King Amaziah of Judah, are recorded in the Annals of the Kings of Israel. 13 Joash slept with his
fathers and Jeroboam occupied his throne; Joash was buried
in Samaria with the kings of Israel.

14 Elisha had been stricken with the illness of which he was
to die, and King Joash of Israel went down to see him. He wept
over him and cried, "Father, father! *a*-Israel's chariots and
horsemen!"-*a* 15 Elisha said to him, "Get a bow and arrows"; and
he brought him a bow and arrows. 16 Then he said to the king
of Israel, "Grasp the bow!" And when he had grasped it, Elisha
put his hands over the king's hands. 17 "Open the window toward the east," he said; and he opened it. Elisha said, "Shoot!"
and he shot. Then he said, "An arrow of victory for the LORD!
An arrow of victory over Aram! You shall rout Aram completely
at Aphek." 18 He said, "Now pick up the arrows." And he picked
them up. "Strike the ground!" he said to the king of Israel; and
he struck three times and stopped. 19 The man of God was angry with him and said to him, *b*-"If only you had struck-*b* five or
six times! Then you would have annihilated Aram; as it is, you
shall defeat Aram only three times."
20 Elisha died and he was buried. Now bands of Moabites
used to invade the land *c*-at the coming of every year.-*c* 21 Once a
man was being buried, when the people caught sight of such a
band; so they threw the corpse[d] into Elisha's grave and *e*-made
off.-*e* When the [dead] man came in contact with Elisha's bones,
he came to life and stood up.

22 King Hazael of Aram had oppressed the Israelites throughout the reign of Jehoahaz. 23 But the LORD was gracious and

a-a On Elisha as defender of Israel, see chapters 6–8. *b-b Lit. "to strike."*
c-c Meaning of Heb. uncertain; emendation yields "year by year."
d Heb. "the man." *e-e Heb. "he made off."*

13.10–13: The reign of Joash/ Jehoash of Israel. The highly stereotypical nature of this account of a king who reigned for sixteen years emphasizes that the historian of Kings only included information that fit his theological and ideological interests. Joash of Israel is mentioned in an inscription of the Assyrian Adad-Nariri III—the Tel al-Rimah stele, discovered in 1967— as an active participant in anti-Aramean and anti-Assyrian politics who eventually paid tribute to the Assyrian king. Joash, perhaps, was the unnamed *deliverer* of v. 5 who may have granted Jehoahaz of Judah some respite from the Arameans (vv. 3–5).

13.14–21: The death of Elisha. **14:** *Israel's chariots and horsemen:* Elisha used this title at the assumption of Elijah (2.12). **17–18:** Although both the shooting of the arrows and the hitting of the ground are presented as symbolic prophecies, a closer examination indicates that to be true only of the shooting. According to the prophetic story, Joash's decision on how many times to hit the ground actually determined the future and constituted an act of imitative magic. Elisha could only watch and interpret the significance of Joash's act. **20–21:** The prophetic story of Elisha's final miracle does not refer to something that happened when he was being buried in the ground or in an open grave. Elisha was most likely laid out in a typical Israelite burial cave on a stone bench where his body decomposed. Sometime later, under duress of circumstances, people in the midst of burying a man tossed his body unceremoniously into Elisha's cave where it touched that of Elisha. Elisha's power as a man of God lay not only in his prophetic abilities, but also in his person. Just as his inanimate staff could heal by contact (4.29), so could his bones.

13.22–25: Victory over Aram. **25:** Joash of Israel's minor successes against *Ben-hadad* were possible because Assyrian victory over the Arameans weakened them and drew

merciful to them, and He turned back to them for the sake of
His covenant with Abraham, Isaac, and Jacob. He refrained
from destroying them, and He still did not cast them out from
His presence. 24 When King Hazael of Aram died, his son
Ben-hadad succeeded him as king; 25 and then Jehoash son
of Jehoahaz recovered from Ben-hadad son of Hazael the
towns which had been taken from his father Jehoahaz in war.
Three times Joash defeated him, and he recovered the towns
of Israel.

14 In the second year of King Joash son of Joahaz of Israel, Amaziah son of King Joash of Judah became king.
2 He was twenty-five years old when he became king, and he
reigned twenty-nine years in Jerusalem; his mother's name
was Jehoaddan of Jerusalem. 3 He did what was pleasing to the
LORD, but not like his ancestor David; he did just as his father
Joash had done. 4 However, the shrines were not removed;
the people continued to sacrifice and make offerings at the
shrines. 5 Once he had the kingdom firmly in his grasp, he
put to death the courtiers who had assassinated his father the
king. 6 But he did not put to death the children of the assassins,
in accordance with what is written in the Book of the Teaching
of Moses, where the LORD commanded, "Parents shall not be
put to death for children, nor children be put to death for parents; a person shall be put to death only for his own crime."[a]
7 He defeated ten thousand Edomites in the Valley of Salt,
and he captured Sela in battle and renamed it Joktheel, as is
still the case. 8 Then Amaziah sent envoys to King Jehoash son
of Jehoahaz son of Jehu of Israel, with this message: "Come, let
us confront[b] each other." 9 King Jehoash of Israel sent back this
message to King Amaziah of Judah: "The thistle in Lebanon
sent this message to the cedar in Lebanon, 'Give your daughter to my son in marriage.' But a wild beast in Lebanon went by
and trampled down the thistle. 10 Because you have defeated
Edom, you have become arrogant. Stay home and enjoy your
glory, rather than provoke disaster and fall, dragging Judah
down with you."
11 But Amaziah paid no heed; so King Jehoash of Israel advanced, and he and King Amaziah of Judah confronted each
other at Beth-shemesh in Judah. 12 The Judites were routed by
Israel, and they all fled to their homes. 13 King Jehoash of Israel
captured King Amaziah son of Jehoash son of Ahaziah of Judah
at Beth-shemesh. He marched on Jerusalem, and he made a
breach of four hundred cubits in the wall of Jerusalem, from[c]
the Ephraim Gate to the Corner Gate. 14 He carried off all the
gold and silver and all the vessels that there were in the House

a Deut. 24.16. *b I.e., in battle.* *c Heb. "at."*

forces away from Aram's southern front with Israel to the north. Joash is mentioned on a stele of the Assyrian king Adad-nirari as one who paid him tribute. The author has a narrow, theo-historical perspective, and does not attribute the Israelite victories to these international events.

14.1–22: The reign of Amaziah son of Joash in Judah overlapped that of Joash son of Jehoahaz of Israel. **5–6:** Amaziah restricted his revenge to his father's assassins alone. The author explains that he did so in accordance with a law cited from Deut. 24.16 identified as coming from *the Book of the Teaching* ("torah") *of Moses.* This is a rare case in the Deuteronomistic History where a Torah law (not surprisingly from Deut.) is explicitly cited. Even though it is listed as the first order of his business, avenging his father could not have been the first act of his reign. Since his father had left Judah weak and vulnerable to Aramean attack, the kingdom could not have been *firmly in his grasp* until that threat disappeared thanks to the Assyrians and Joash of Israel. **7–8:** His defeat of the *Edomites in the Valley of Salt* indicates that he was successful in limiting or eliminating their presence in the central Negev. There is a consensus that the sites mentioned are in or near the northern Arava. He did not, however, reestablish control of Edom. **9:** The parable reflects the much greater size and military power of the Northern Kingdom relative to Judah. **11:** That Joash/Jehoash of Israel met his army at *Beth-shemesh,* by the foothills west of Jerusalem, indicates just how weak and unprepared Amaziah was for battle. **13:** The Ephraim Gate through which people went toward the territory of Ephraim was in the north wall of the city. Joash broke the wall here because Jerusalem, surrounded by gorges on its east, south, and west, is most vulnerable from the north. According to 2 Chron. 26.9, the breach was repaired by Amaziah's son.

of the LORD and in the treasuries of the royal palace, as well as
hostages; and he returned to Samaria.
15 The other events of Jehoash's reign, and all his actions and
exploits, and his war with King Amaziah of Judah, are recorded
in the Annals of the Kings of Israel. 16 Jehoash slept with his
fathers, and was buried in Samaria with the kings of Israel; his
son Jeroboam succeeded him as king.
17 King Amaziah son of Joash of Judah lived fifteen years after the death of King Jehoash son of Jehoahaz of Israel. 18 The
other events of Amaziah's reign are recorded in the Annals of
the Kings of Judah. 19 A conspiracy was formed against him in
Jerusalem and he fled to Lachish; but they sent men after him
to Lachish, and they killed him there. 20 They brought back his
body on horses, and he was buried with his fathers in Jerusalem, in the City of David.
21 Then all the people of Judah took Azariah, who was sixteen years old, and proclaimed him king to succeed his father
Amaziah. 22 It was he who rebuilt Elath and restored it to Judah, after King [Amaziah] slept with his fathers.

23 In the fifteenth year of King Amaziah son of Joash of Judah, King Jeroboam son of Joash of Israel became king in Samaria—for forty-one years. 24 He did what was displeasing to
the LORD; he did not depart from all the sins that Jeroboam son
of Nebat had caused Israel to commit. 25 It was he who restored
the territory of Israel from Lebo-hamath to the sea of the Arabah, in accordance with the promise that the LORD, the God of
Israel, had made through His servant, the prophet Jonah son
of Amittai from Gath-hepher. 26 For the LORD saw the very bitter plight of Israel, with neither [a]bond nor free[a] left, and with
none to help Israel. 27 And the LORD resolved not to blot out
the name of Israel from under heaven; and he delivered them
through Jeroboam son of Joash.
28 The other events of Jeroboam's reign, and all his actions
and exploits, how he fought and recovered Damascus and
Hamath [b]for Judah in Israel,[b] are recorded in the Annals of
the Kings of Israel. 29 Jeroboam slept with his fathers, the kings
of Israel, and his son Zechariah succeeded him as king.

15 In the twenty-seventh year of King Jeroboam of Israel,
Azariah son of King Amaziah of Judah became king. 2 He
was sixteen years old when he became king, and he reigned

a-a See note at 1 Kings 14.10. *b-b Emendation yields "for Israel."*

17: If Amaziah reigned 29 years (v. 2), and if he reigned 15 years after the death of Joash/Jehoash of Israel, then their reigns must have overlapped 14 years, not 2 as stated in v. 1. Furthermore, the conspiracy described in vv. 19–20 could not then have taken place immediately after the despoiling of Jerusalem. **21–22:** The *people of Judah,* perhaps the same group as the "people of the land" (11.14), placed Azariah on the throne. (Azariah is also referred to as Uzziah; see 15.13, 30, 32, 34. Both names combine a word meaning "strength" with a short form of the LORD's name, "-iah." This is the same form as in "hallelujah," "hallelu + iah" meaning "praise + the LORD.") Some of Azariah's accomplishments are listed here. *Elath,* an important Red Sea port, would have been under Edomite control.

14.23–28: The reign of Jeroboam II (788–747 BCE) was a long and prosperous one. The author of Kings indicates that, despite doing what displeased the LORD, in the course of his long reign he attained control in the north and in Transjordan of territories lost to the Arameans beginning in the days of Solomon. This author did not have a simplistic theology, where the fate of the people depended on that of the king; see vv. 26–27 n. which speaks of a period of divine sympathy for the north. A somewhat one-sided view of the prosperity and self-confidence that characterized his reign is found in Amos. **25:** The author describes Jeroboam II's military accomplishments as fulfillment of God's promises through a prophet, Jonah son of Amittai. Jeroboam was able to extend Israel's borders deep into the territories once controlled by Arameans and into their kingdoms (v. 28) because the Assyrians had seriously weakened them. This connection between Israel and Assyria helped set the scene for someone in the 5th c. to cast Jeroboam II's prophet as the protagonist in the book of Jonah. **26–27:** The author, who apparently knew the content of Jonah's proclamations in the days of Jeroboam II, suggests that the sinful kingdom of the north was saved because of God's grace, rather than the people's repentance.

15.1–7: The reign of Azariah (Uzziah). Of all that transpired during Azariah's long reign, the author cares to mention only that he became a

fifty-two years in Jerusalem; his mother's name was Jecoliah of Jerusalem. 3 He did what was pleasing to the LORD, just as his father Amaziah had done. 4 However, the shrines were not removed; the people continued to sacrifice and make offerings at the shrines. 5 The LORD struck the king with a plague, and he was a leper until the day of his death; he lived [a-]in isolated quarters,[-a] while Jotham, the king's son, was in charge of the palace and governed the people of the land.

6 The other events of Azariah's reign, and all his actions, are recorded in the Annals of the Kings of Judah. 7 Azariah slept with his fathers, and he was buried with his fathers in the City of David; his son Jotham succeeded him as king.

8 In the thirty-eighth year of King Azariah of Judah, Zechariah son of Jeroboam became king over Israel in Samaria—for six months. 9 He did what was displeasing to the LORD, as his fathers had done; he did not depart from the sins which Jeroboam son of Nebat had caused Israel to commit. 10 Shallum son of Jabesh conspired against him and struck him down [b-]before the people[-b] and killed him, and succeeded him as king. 11 The other events of Zechariah's reign are recorded in the Annals of the Kings of Israel. 12 This was in accord with the word that the LORD had spoken to Jehu: "Four generations of your descendants shall occupy the throne of Israel." And so it came about.[c]

13 Shallum son of Jabesh became king in the thirty-ninth year of King Uzziah of Judah, and he reigned in Samaria one month. 14 Then Menahem son of Gadi set out from Tirzah and came to Samaria; he attacked Shallum son of Jabesh in Samaria and killed him, and he succeeded him as king. 15 The other events of Shallum's reign, and the conspiracy that he formed, are recorded in the Annals of the Kings of Israel.

16 At that time, [a-][marching] from Tirzah,[-a] Menahem subdued Tiphsah and all who were in it, and its territory; and because it did not surrender, he massacred [its people] and ripped open all its pregnant women.

a-a Meaning of Heb. uncertain. *b-b Some Septuagint mss. read "at Ibleam."* *c Cf. 10.30.*

leper. By juxtaposing this fact to his notice that Azariah did nothing about the open shrines, the author may be implying that the leprosy was a punishment. (2 Chron. 26.16–21 provides a different and more explicit explanation for his punishment.) According to the parallel account in Chronicles (2 Chron. 26.3–15), Azariah led successful campaigns against Philistia and established control of areas up to the Egyptian border, collected tribute from the Transjordanian Ammonites (and most likely reestablished influence in Edom; see 14.22), fortified Jerusalem, built towers and excavated cisterns in the wilderness, and undertook varied agricultural projects that increased royal wealth. His sphere of influence in the south was similar to that of Solomon in his day. **1:** Radak, Ralbag, and modern commentators point out that based on this v. and 14.2, 17, 23, the synchronisms between the reigns of kings in Judah and Israel and the years of reign for each king do not work out. The numbers can be reconciled if it is assumed—the Tanakh does not say so explicitly—that Azariah became co-regent with his father at the age of 16 and these years were accounted to both his and his father's credit. **5:** Azariah's particular type of leprosy disqualified him from performing royal duties, so he was retired. (Naaman's leprosy did not disqualify him; cf. 5.1–2.) While he remained king in name, his son Jotham became a co-regent and king in fact. Both Azariah and Jotham were credited with the same years of reign. **7:** An inscribed Aram. marble plaque from the Second Temple period, now in the Israel Museum, reads: "Here were brought the bones of Uzziah, King of Judah. Don't open." The wording suggests that although buried in the City of David, he was buried separately from other kings—perhaps because of the leprosy—whose bones were not reburied during the Second Temple period. It is unknown where the plaque was originally found.

15.8–12: The reign of Zechariah. Zechariah of Israel was the fourth and final ruler of the Jehu dynasty in accordance with the prophecy of 10.30. He was assassinated by *Shallum son of Jabesh. Jabesh* most likely refers to the city of Jabesh in Transjordanian Gilead.

15.13: The reign of Shallum.

15.14–22: Menahem son of Gadi, most likely from the Transjordanian tribe of Gad, assassinated Shallum. **16:** *Tiphsah* was the northernmost city under Solomon's control near the Euphrates (1 Kings 5.4). The location of the city makes it unlikely that Menahem attacked it while engaged in an activity near Tirzah. His brutal reprisal against the people of Tiphsah was not unique (cf. 8.12; Hos. 14.1; Amos 1.13). The incident reported may be connected to the invasion of the Assyrians reported in v. 19. **19:** *Pul* is the Assyrian nickname of King Tiglath-pileser III of Assyria, mentioned by his longer name in v. 29. See 1 Chron. 5.26. Menahem paid tribute for Pul's support in helping him gain control over the kingdom. The tribute is mentioned in the annals of Tiglath-pileser from 738 BCE. The Assyrian may have entered territories claimed by Israel in northern Syria, but not the heartland. In retreating south, Israel effectively gave up control over the Aramean kingdoms.

17 In the thirty-ninth year of King Azariah of Judah, Menahem son of Gadi became king over Israel in Samaria—for ten
years. 18 He did what was displeasing to the LORD; throughout
his days he did not depart from the sins which Jeroboam son of
Nebat had caused Israel to commit. 19 King Pul of Assyria invaded the land, and Menahem gave Pul a thousand talents of silver
that he might support him and strengthen his hold on the kingdom. 20 Menahem exacted the money from Israel: every man of
means had to pay fifty shekels of silver for the king of Assyria.
The king of Assyria withdrew and did not remain in the land.
21 The other events of Menahem's reign, and all his actions, are
recorded in the Annals of the Kings of Israel. 22 Menahem slept
with his fathers, and his son Pekahiah succeeded him as king.

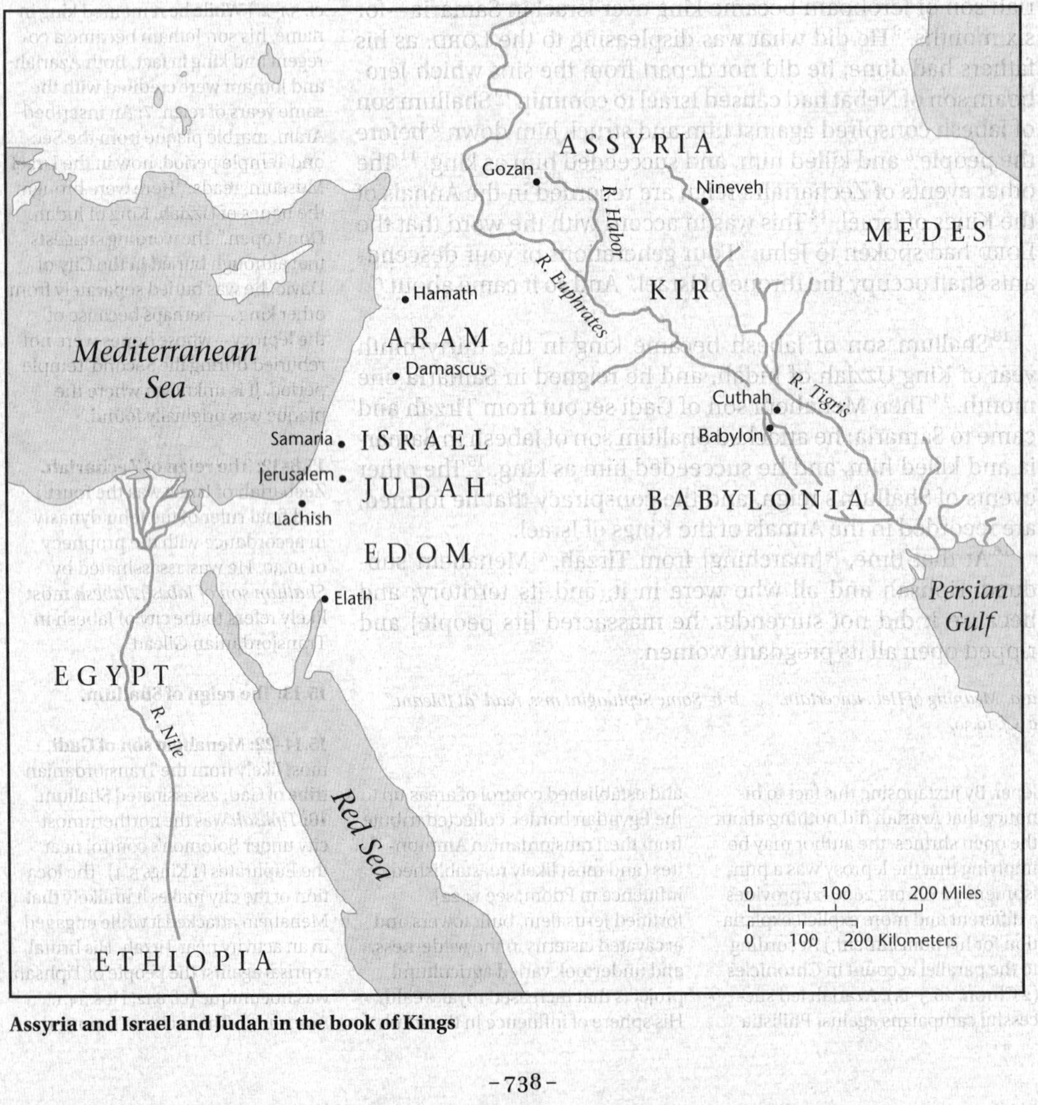

Assyria and Israel and Judah in the book of Kings

23 In the fiftieth year of King Azariah of Judah, Pekahiah son
of Menahem became king over Israel in Samaria—for two
years. 24 He did what was displeasing to the LORD; he did not
depart from the sins which Jeroboam son of Nebat had caused
Israel to commit. 25 His aide, Pekah son of Remaliah, conspired
against him and struck him down in the royal palace in Samaria; with him were fifty Gileadites, [a-]with men from Argob and
Arieh;[-a] and he killed him and succeeded him as king.
26 The other events of Pekahiah's reign, and all his actions,
are recorded in the Annals of the Kings of Israel.

27 In the fifty-second year of King Azariah of Judah, Pekah son
of Remaliah became king over Israel and Samaria—for twenty
years. 28 He did what was displeasing to the LORD; he did not
depart from the sins which Jeroboam son of Nebat had caused
Israel to commit. 29 In the days of King Pekah of Israel, King
Tiglath-pileser of Assyria came and captured Ijon, Abel-beth-
maacah, Janoah, Kedesh, Hazor—Gilead, Galilee, the entire region of Naphtali; and he deported [b-]the inhabitants[-b] to Assyria.
30 Hoshea son of Elah conspired against Pekah son of Remaliah, attacked him, and killed him. He succeeded him as king
in the twentieth year of Jotham son of Uzziah. 31 The other
events of Pekah's reign, and all his actions, are recorded in the
Annals of the Kings of Israel.

32 In the second year of King Pekah son of Remaliah of Israel, Jotham son of King Uzziah of Judah became king. 33 He was
twenty-five years old when he became king, and he reigned
sixteen years in Jerusalem; his mother's name was Jerusha
daughter of Zadok. 34 He did what was pleasing to the LORD,
just as his father Uzziah had done. 35 However, the shrines
were not removed; the people continued to sacrifice and make
offerings at the shrines. It was he who built the Upper Gate of
the House of the LORD. 36 The other events of Jotham's reign,
and all his actions, are recorded in the Annals of the Kings of
Judah. 37 In those days, the LORD began to incite King Rezin
of Aram and Pekah son of Remaliah against Judah. 38 Jotham
slept with his fathers, and he was buried with his fathers in the
city of his ancestor David; his son Ahaz succeeded him as king.

16 In the seventeenth year of Pekah son of Remaliah, Ahaz
son of King Jotham of Judah became king. 2 Ahaz was
twenty years old when he became king, and he reigned sixteen years in Jerusalem. He did not do what was pleasing to
the LORD his God, as his ancestor David had done, 3 but followed the ways of the kings of Israel. He even consigned his

15.23–26: The reign of Pekahiah. Menahem's son, *Pekahiah,* is assassinated by *Pekah,* supported by Transjordanian *Gileadites. Argob* in the Bashan was adjacent to Gilead (Deut. 3.4, 14–15). The catalyst may have been the breakaway of Arameans from Israelite control and a sense among Transjordanian Israelites that the monarch, safe in Samaria, had abandoned them.

15.27–31: The reign of Pekah. **29:** In his campaigns of 733–32 BCE, *Tiglath-pileser* conquered the same block of territories taken by Arameans from Israel in the days of Baasha (1 Kings 15.20) along with Transjordanian Gilead. His annals mention that he took 13,520 people to Assyria. This marks the beginning of the Diaspora of the ten northern tribes.

15.32–38: The reign of Jotham. Little is told about the reign of Jotham in Judah. 2 Chron. 27.1–6 suggests that he maintained the borders of his father's kingdom, extending its control and influence into Ammonite territory. **37:** Rezin and Pekah formed a coalition against Jotham, planning to force him into an anti-Assyrian coalition. Rezin is also known from Assyrian sources.

16.1–20: The reign of Ahaz. Although the author does not evaluate Ahaz highly, his narrative indicates that Ahaz was an astute politician. **3:** *Consigned his son to the fire:* Although usually taken to mean that he sacrificed his son (cf. 3.27), the regular words of sacrifice are not used. It may mean that he had his son undergo some sort of fire ritual, perhaps a ritual singeing.

a-a Meaning of Heb. uncertain. *b-b Heb. "them."*

5–9: The plan of *Rezin* and *Pekah* (15.37) gave rise to what scholars call the Syro-Ephraimitic war (cf. Isa. chs 7–8) in 733–732 BCE. According to Isa. 7.6, they planned to replace Ahaz with a ruler willing to join their coalition. *Ahaz,* learning from the statecraft of Asa (1 Kings 15.18) and Menahem (2 Kings 15.19), bribed the enemy of his enemies to rescue him. **7:** *Your servant and your son:* In the diplomatic context of the ancient Near East, these phrases indicated Ahaz's friendly and voluntary submission to the authority of Tiglath-pileser III, thus becoming his vassal. **9:** The Assyrians responded by eliminating the threat from *Damascus. Kir,* location not known, but according to Amos 9.7, it was the original home of the Arameans. **10–16:** The Damascene type of *altar* introduced by Ahaz into the Jerusalem Temple was acceptable to the author. Ahaz, as Davidic patron of the Jerusalem Temple, could initiate these changes, to which Uriah the priest agreed. The altar that Ezek. 43.13–17 describes and prescribes for a future temple may be a copy of the Ahaz altar that Ezekiel saw in his youth. **17–18:** The removal of the various Temple furnishings was perhaps necessitated in order to meet the required payments to *Assyria.*

son to the fire, in the abhorrent fashion of the nations which the LORD had dispossessed before the Israelites. 4 He sacrificed and made offerings at the shrines, on the hills, and under every leafy tree.

5 Then King Rezin of Aram and King Pekah son of Remaliah of Israel advanced on Jerusalem for battle. They besieged Ahaz, but could not overcome [him]. 6 At that time King Rezin of Aram recovered Elath for Aram;[a] he drove out the Judites from Elath, and Edomites came to Elath and settled there, as is still the case.

7 Ahaz sent messengers to King Tiglath-pileser of Assyria to say, "I am your servant and your son; come and deliver me from the hands of the king of Aram and from the hands of the king of Israel, who are attacking me." 8 Ahaz took the gold and silver that were on hand in the House of the LORD and in the treasuries of the royal palace and sent them as a gift to the king of Assyria. 9 The king of Assyria responded to his request; the king of Assyria marched against Damascus and captured it. He deported [b-]its inhabitants[-b] to Kir and put Rezin to death.

10 When King Ahaz went to Damascus to greet King Tiglath-pileser of Assyria, he saw the altar in Damascus. King Ahaz sent the priest Uriah a sketch of the altar and a detailed plan of its construction. 11 The priest Uriah did just as King Ahaz had instructed him from Damascus; the priest Uriah built the altar before King Ahaz returned from Damascus. 12 When the king returned from Damascus, and when the king saw the altar, the king drew near the altar, ascended it, 13 and offered his burnt offering and meal offering; he poured his libation, and he dashed the blood of his offering of well-being against the altar. 14 As for the bronze altar which had been before the LORD, he moved it from its place in front of the Temple, [c-]between the [new] altar and the House of the LORD,[-c] and placed it on the north side of the [new] altar. 15 And King Ahaz commanded the priest Uriah: "On the great[d] altar you shall offer the morning burnt offering and the evening meal offering and the king's burnt offering and his meal offering, with the burnt offerings of all the people of the land, their meal offerings and their libations. And against it you shall dash the blood of all the burnt offerings and all the blood of the sacrifices. And I will decide[e] about the bronze altar."[f] 16 Uriah did just as King Ahaz commanded.

17 King Ahaz cut off the insets—the laver stands—and removed the lavers from them. He also removed the tank from the bronze oxen that supported it and set it on a stone pavement— 18 on account of the king of Assyria.[g] He also extended

a Emendation yields "Edom." *b-b Heb. "it."* *c-c Meaning of Heb. uncertain.*
d I.e., the new one. *e Meaning of Heb. uncertain.* *f I.e., the old one, cf. v. 14.*
g I.e., because of the metal given him in tribute.

to the House of the LORD [a]the sabbath passage that had been
built in the palace and the king's outer entrance.[a]
19 The other events of Ahaz's reign, and his actions, are recorded in the Annals of the Kings of Judah. 20 Ahaz slept with
his fathers and was buried with his fathers in the City of David;
his son Hezekiah succeeded him as king.

17 In the twelfth year of King Ahaz of Judah, Hoshea son
of Elah became king over Israel in Samaria—for nine
years. 2 He did what was displeasing to the LORD, though
not as much as the kings of Israel who preceded him. 3 King
Shalmaneser marched against him, and Hoshea became his
vassal and paid him tribute. 4 But the king of Assyria caught
Hoshea in an act of treachery: he had sent envoys to King So
of Egypt, and he had not paid the tribute to the king of Assyria,
as in previous years. And the king of Assyria arrested him and
put him in prison. 5 Then the king of Assyria marched against
the whole land; he came to Samaria and besieged it for three
years. 6 In the ninth year of Hoshea, the king of Assyria captured Samaria. He deported the Israelites to Assyria and settled them in Halah, at the [River] Habor, at the River Gozan,
and in the towns of Media.
7 This happened because the Israelites sinned against the
LORD their God, who had freed them from the land of Egypt,
from the hand of Pharaoh king of Egypt. They worshiped other
gods 8 and followed the customs of the nations which the LORD
had dispossessed before the Israelites and the customs which
the kings of Israel had practiced. 9 The Israelites committed[b]
against the LORD their God acts which were not right: They
built for themselves shrines in all their settlements, from
watchtowers to fortified cities; 10 they set up pillars and sacred
posts for themselves on every lofty hill and under every leafy
tree; 11 and they offered sacrifices there, at all the shrines, like
the nations whom the LORD had driven into exile before them.
They committed wicked acts to vex the LORD, 12 and they worshiped fetishes concerning which the LORD had said to them,
"You must not do this thing."
13 The LORD warned Israel and Judah by every prophet
[and] every seer, saying: "Turn back from your wicked ways,
and observe My commandments and My laws, according to
all the Teaching that I commanded your fathers and that I

a-a *Meaning of Heb. uncertain.* *b* *Meaning of Heb. uncertain.*

17.1–23: The end of the Northern Kingdom and the major exile of northern tribes. This ch appears confusing because the author (or a later editor) spliced together several documents in bringing this part of the history to a stirring finish and in driving home some didactic points. **1–3:** *Hoshea* (see 15.30), whose territorially reduced kingdom no longer included Galilee and Transjordan, submitted to Tiglath-pileser's son, *Shalmaneser* V. **4:** There was no pharaoh named So. Some historians consider it an Egyptian word for a high officer of the king; others consider So a reference to the delta city Sais whose kings of the 24th dynasty in the 720s were not friends of Assyria. In any case, the *king of Assyria* believed that *Hoshea ... had sent envoys* to Egypt in order to enlist Egyptian aid in throwing off Assyrian domination. **6:** Cuneiform documents attribute the conquest of *Samaria* to both Shalmaneser V and Sargon II. Possibly, Shalmaneser died just before the capitulation of the city. The author of Kings, however, knows only Shalmaneser (see 18.9–12). Assyrian policy called for dispersing hostile populations throughout its empire, thereby weakening their power. Israelites from Samaria were sent to Gozan on the Upper *Habor* river, to *Halah*, beyond the Tigris northeast of ancient Nineveh (see 15.29), and to towns on the Persian plateau. Large Jewish communities, descendants of these exiles, lived continuously in these or adjacent regions of Syria, Iraq, and Iran until the end of the 20th c. **7–23:** These vv. summarize explicitly the philosophy of sin, covenant violation, and retribution by which the author evaluated all the kings of Israel. Nobody but Israel was responsible for the major calamities that befell the kingdom. This philosophical justification, however, differs from the typical remarks scattered throughout the book in that it holds the people—considered as a collective body—culpable, along with rulers, for the consequences of their choice of religious practices. **7–18:** One explanation for the destruction of Israel is that under the influence of Canaanites and despite warnings, the people—not their rulers—persisted in doing wrong. The author does not agree with this view, regularly condemning the kings for following the ways of Jeroboam son of Nebat. **13:** Punishment is only legitimate after proper prophetic forewarning.

16: The worship instituted in Bethel was illegitimate in the eyes of the Deuteronomistic historian, and is perceived as a continuation of earlier idolatrous practice. **19–20:** A comment from a later historian, after the exile of Judah in 586 BCE, indicates that the contents of vv. 7–18 were applicable also to Judah. Thus, a ch originally about the north was updated and applied to the south as well. **21–23:** A second explanation sketches a brief history of the Northern Kingdom, emphasizing its ignominious beginning and its deserved end. This is in harmony with the running comments and evaluations of the author, and assigns responsibility to Jeroboam's religious policies that were maintained by subsequent rulers.

17.24–41: The practices of the people who were settled in Samaria. **24:** This v. was originally part of the document used by the author for vv. 1–6. The emptied cities of *Samaria* were settled by people exiled there from northern Syria and from southern Mesopotamia, parts of the Assyrian empire. **25–33:** The new immigrants brought with them their own religions, which they tried to accommodate with local practices in order to appease *the God of the land.* In v. 41, which originally concluded this section, the author notes that they never got it quite right and that the hybrid religious practices that they evolved persisted.

transmitted to you through My servants the prophets." 14 But
they did not obey; they stiffened their necks, like their fathers
who did not have faith in the LORD their God; 15 they spurned
His laws and the covenant that He had made with their fathers,
and the warnings He had given them. They went after delusion and were deluded; [they imitated] the nations that were
about them, which the LORD had forbidden them to emulate.
16 They rejected all the commandments of the LORD their God;
they made molten idols for themselves—two calves—and they
made a sacred post and they bowed down to all the host of
heaven, and they worshiped Baal. 17 They consigned their sons
and daughters to the fire; they practiced augury and divination, and gave themselves over to what was displeasing to the
LORD and vexed Him. 18 The LORD was incensed at Israel and
He banished them from His presence; none was left but the
tribe of Judah alone.

19 Nor did Judah keep the commandments of the LORD their
God; they followed the customs that Israel had practiced. 20 So
the LORD spurned all the offspring of Israel, and He afflicted
them and delivered them into the hands of plunderers, and finally He cast them out from His presence.

21 For Israel broke away from the House of David, and they
made Jeroboam son of Nebat king. Jeroboam caused Israel to
stray from the LORD and to commit great sin, 22 and the Israelites persisted in all the sins which Jeroboam had committed;
they did not depart from them. 23 In the end, the LORD removed
Israel from His presence, as He had warned them through all
His servants the prophets. So the Israelites were deported from
their land to Assyria, as is still the case.

24 The king of Assyria brought [people] from Babylon,
Cuthah, Avva, Hamath, and Sephar-vaim, and he settled them
in the towns of Samaria in place of the Israelites; they took possession of Samaria and dwelt in its towns. 25 When they first
settled there, they did not worship the LORD; so the LORD sent
lions against them which killed some of them. 26 They said to
the king of Assyria: "The nations which you deported and resettled in the towns of Samaria do not know the rules of the
God of the land; therefore He has let lions loose against them
which are killing them—for they do not know the rules of the
God of the land."

27 The king of Assyria gave an order: "Send there one of the
priests whom you have deported; let him[a] go and dwell there,
and let him teach them the practices of the God of the land."
28 So one of the priests whom they had exiled from Samaria came
and settled in Bethel; he taught them how to worship the LORD.

a Heb. "them."

29 However, each nation continued to make its own gods and to set them up in the cult places which had been made by the people of Samaria; each nation [set them up] in the towns in which it lived. 30 The Babylonians made Succoth-benoth, and the men of Cuth made Nergal, and the men of Hamath made Ashima, 31 and the Avvites made Nibhaz and Tartak; and the Sepharvites burned their children [as offerings] to Adrammelech and Anamelech, the gods of Sepharvaim. 32 They worshiped the LORD, but they also appointed from their own ranks priests of the shrines, who officiated for them in the cult places. 33 They worshiped the LORD, while serving their own gods according to the practices of the nations from which they had been deported. 34 To this day, they follow their former practices. They do not worship the LORD [properly]. They do not follow the laws and practices, the Teaching and Instruction that the LORD enjoined upon the descendants of Jacob—who was given the name Israel— 35 with whom He made a covenant and whom He commanded: "You shall worship no other gods; you shall not bow down to them nor serve them nor sacrifice to them. 36 You must worship only the LORD your God, who brought you out of the land of Egypt with great might and with an outstretched arm: to Him alone shall you bow down and to Him alone shall you sacrifice. 37 You shall observe faithfully, all your days, the laws and the practices; the Teaching and Instruction that I[a] wrote down for you; do not worship other gods. 38 Do not forget the covenant that I made with you; do not worship other gods. 39 Worship only the LORD your God, and He will save you from the hands of all your enemies." 40 But they did not obey; they continued their former practices. 41 Those nations worshiped the LORD, but they also served their idols. To this day their children and their children's children do as their ancestors did.

18 In the third year of King Hoshea son of Elah of Israel, Hezekiah son of King Ahaz of Judah became king. 2 He was twenty-five years old when he became king, and he reigned in Jerusalem twenty-nine years; his mother's name was Abi[b] daughter of Zechariah. 3 He did what was pleasing to the LORD, just as his father David had done. 4 He abolished the shrines and smashed the pillars and cut down the sacred post. He also broke into pieces the bronze serpent that Moses had made, for until that time the Israelites had been offering sacrifices to it; it was called Nehushtan. 5 He trusted only in the LORD the God of Israel; there was none like him among all the kings of Judah after him, nor among those before him.

a *Heb. "He."* *b* *2 Chron. 29.1 reads "Abijah."*

34–40: Ralbag correctly suggests that these vv. address the behavior of Israelites who had been left in the land; even the experience of the exile of others did not chasten them to return to God. V. 34 likely continued the narrative of v. 23; these are linked together by the same Heb words, translated "as is still the case" in v. 23 and *To this day* in v. 34.

18.1–20.21: The reign of Hezekiah. The author dedicates three chs to selected events from the reign of Hezekiah. He allots as much attention to this king as he did to the house of Ahab, and highlights Isaiah in these narratives as he did Elijah in the earlier ones. Hezekiah is important to the author because he demonstrated that the high standard expected of a king could be and was indeed met. V. 5, which contradicts 23.25, might suggest that an edition of the history originally ended with Hezekiah; this might explain why this section is so long and laudatory. The various sources used by the author to describe Hezekiah's reign are arranged only in a rough chronological order, though the author's thematic interests override the chronology, creating some confusion. 2 Kings 18.9–20.19 is paralleled with variations in 2 Chron. ch 29 and Isa. chs 36–39.

18.1–8: Hezekiah's reforms.
3: *What was pleasing ... as ... David:* Hezekiah is the first king evaluated so positively by the author. The phrase *his father David* is applied also to Asa (1 Kings 15.11) and Josiah (22.2, where NJPS properly renders "father" by "ancestor").
4: Elimination of the open *shrines* concentrated worship in Jerusalem (see v. 22). The author describes *Nehushtan,* a form of the word for serpent, as an ancient relic associated with the miraculous healings in the wilderness (Num. 21.8–9) held sacred by Israelites. Noting that the Heb actually says "he called it" (and not *it was called*), Rashi suggests that Hezekiah, the active subject of the sentence, labeled it "bronze serpent-thing," "neḥushtan" in Heb, as a pejorative.

7–8: Hezekiah planned to revolt against Assyrian control early in his reign, but waited until the opportunity was ripe. The campaign in *Philistia* was intended to bring all coastal cities into an anti-Assyrian coalition. Similarly, his fortification and enhancements around the Gihon spring, the main source of Jerusalem's water, were intended to help the city survive an extended siege (20.20). 2 Chron. ch 32 provides additional information about his preparation of storage facilities, weapons, and fortifications.

18.9–12: The Assyrian invasion of the Northern Kingdom. Cf. 17.1–6. The author abridges information given earlier so as to drive home the lesson learned from history in v. 12.

6 He clung to the LORD; he did not turn away from following
Him, but kept the commandments that the LORD had given to
Moses. 7 And the LORD was always with him; he was successful wherever he turned. He rebelled against the king of Assyria
and would not serve him. 8 He overran Philistia as far as Gaza
and its border areas, from watchtower to fortified town.
9 In the fourth year of King Hezekiah, which was the seventh
year of King Hoshea son of Elah of Israel, King Shalmaneser
of Assyria marched against Samaria and besieged it, 10 and
he[a] captured it at the end of three years. In the sixth year of
Hezekiah, which was the ninth year of King Hoshea of Israel,
Samaria was captured; 11 and the king of Assyria deported
the Israelites to Assyria. He [b-]settled them in[-b] Halah, along
the Habor [and] the River Gozan, and in the towns of Media. 12 [This happened] because they did not obey the LORD
their God; they transgressed His covenant—all that Moses the
servant of the LORD had commanded. They did not obey and
they did not fulfill it.

a So some mss. and ancient versions; most mss. and editions read "they."
b-b Lit. "led them to."

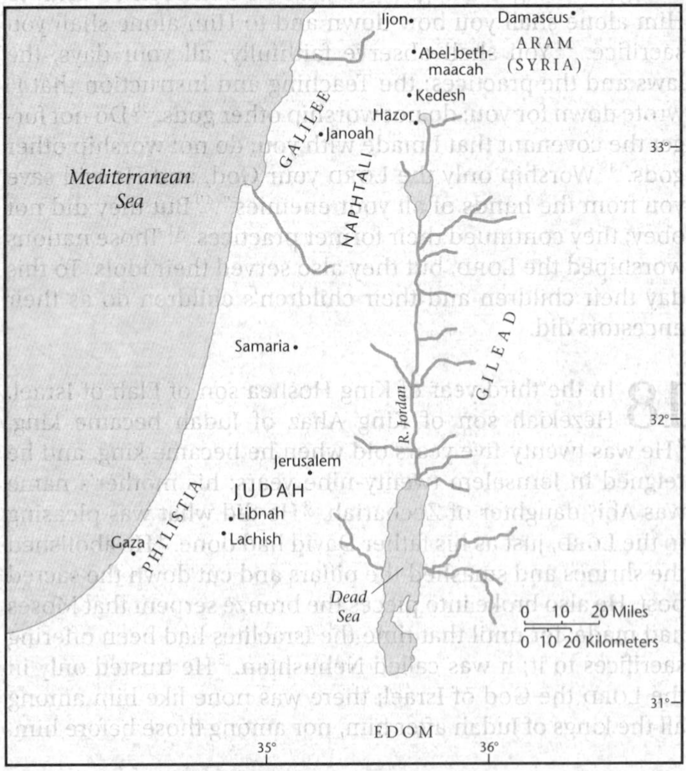

Places associated with Sennacherib's invasion of Judah

13 In the fourteenth year of King Hezekiah, King Sennacherib of Assyria marched against all the fortified towns of Judah and seized them. 14 King Hezekiah sent this message to
the king of Assyria at Lachish: "I have done wrong; withdraw
from me; and I shall bear whatever you impose on me." So the
king of Assyria imposed upon King Hezekiah of Judah a payment of three hundred talents of silver and thirty talents of
gold. 15 Hezekiah gave him all the silver that was on hand in the
House of the LORD and in the treasuries of the palace. 16 At that
time Hezekiah cut down the doors and the doorposts[a] of the
Temple of the LORD, which King Hezekiah had overlaid [with
gold], and gave them to the king of Assyria.
17 But the king of Assyria sent [b]the Tartan, the Rabsaris,
and the Rabshakeh[-b] from Lachish with a large force to King
Hezekiah in Jerusalem. They marched up to Jerusalem; and
when they arrived, they took up a position near the conduit of
the Upper Pool, by the road of the Fuller's Field. 18 They summoned the king; and Eliakim son of Hilkiah, who was in charge
of the palace, Shebna the scribe, and Joah son of Asaph the
recorder went out to them.
19 The Rabshakeh said to them, "You tell Hezekiah: Thus said
the Great King, the King of Assyria: What makes you so confident? 20 You must think that mere talk is counsel and valor
for war! Look, on whom are you relying, that you have rebelled
against me? 21 You rely, of all things, on Egypt, that splintered
reed of a staff, which enters and punctures the palm of anyone
who leans on it! That's what Pharaoh king of Egypt is like to all
who rely on him. 22 And if you tell me that you are relying on
the LORD your God, He is the very one whose shrines and altars Hezekiah did away with, telling Judah and Jerusalem, 'You
must worship only at this altar in Jerusalem.' 23 Come now,
make this wager with my master, the king of Assyria: I'll give
you two thousand horses if you can produce riders to mount
them. 24 So how could you refuse anything even to the deputy of one of my master's lesser servants, relying on Egypt for
chariots and horsemen? 25 And do you think I have marched
against this land to destroy it without the LORD? The LORD
Himself told me: Go up against that land and destroy it."

a Meaning of Heb. uncertain. *b-b Assyrian titles.*

18.13–37: Assyria threatens Judah. 13–16: A brief straightforward description of what happened in Jerusalem. The author may have cited it from a chronicle, and it largely agrees with contemporaneous Assyrian sources. *Sennacherib*'s armies swept through *Judah* in 701 BCE, wreaking great havoc. The author focuses only on what happened at Jerusalem and hints that *Hezekiah* precipitated the Assyrian response (v. 14). Sennacherib's own accounts mention that he conquered 46 strong cities and forts, that he captured over 200,000 people, that he made "Hezekiah a prisoner in Jerusalem, like a bird in a cage," and that Hezekiah paid him a large tribute, including his daughters, palace women, and male and female singers. **14:** Assyrian headquarters were located near *Lachish,* about 45 km (30 mi) southwest of Jerusalem; it was typical for ancient armies to surround the well-fortified enemy capital before attacking it. Wall reliefs from Sennacherib's palace in Nineveh, now in the British Museum, illustrate the siege and fall of Lachish in great detail. These suggest what Hezekiah wished to avoid in Jerusalem. **17:** This is the beginning of the expansive narratives that conclude at 19.37; the name of Hezekiah is spelled differently in the Heb in these stories, indicating that they are not from the same sources as vv. 13–16. They feature prophetic stories about Isaiah concerning the events treated tersely in vv. 13–16; they are not of a single hand, and incorporate legends, and are likely written after the events they describe to show how the God of Israel protected his city, Jerusalem, from the Assyrians. This theme of the inviolability of Jerusalem plays a major role in the work of the prophet Isaiah (chs 1–39). Chronologically, the speeches presented in vv. 17–35, along with some story material in ch 19, belong between the narrative of vv. 13 and 14 above. The three Assyrian titles mean roughly "field marshal," "chief officer" (lit. "chief eunuch"), and "chief administrator" (lit. "chief butler"). The *Rabshakeh* was a highly placed Assyrian official. He was obviously well informed about Hezekiah's political alliances (v. 21), religious activities (v. 22), able to speak the local language, "Judean" (v. 26), and knowledgeable about Israelite religion (v. 25). His speech, although formally directed to the leaders, was intended for the ears of the common folk so that they would pressure their king to give in to Assyria. **19:** *The Great King, the King of Assyria* are actual titles found in the Assyrian annals. **21–25:** Judah's political ally will not save her. Judah's God will not save her either, for Judah has not, says the Rabshakeh, served God properly. The Rabshakeh

26 Eliakim son of Hilkiah, Shebna, and Joah replied to the
Rabshakeh, "Please, speak to your servants in Aramaic, for we
understand it; do not speak to us in Judean in the hearing of
the people on the wall." 27 But the Rabshakeh answered them,
"Was it to your master and to you that my master sent me to
speak those words? It was precisely to the men who are sitting
on the wall—who will have to eat their dung and drink their
urine with you." 28 And the Rabshakeh stood and called out in
a loud voice in Judean: "Hear the words of the Great King, the
King of Assyria. 29 Thus said the king: Don't let Hezekiah deceive you, for he will not be able to deliver you from my[a] hands.
30 Don't let Hezekiah make you rely on the LORD, saying: The
LORD will surely save us: this city will not fall into the hands of
the king of Assyria. 31 Don't listen to Hezekiah. For thus said
the king of Assyria: Make your peace with me and come out to
me,[b] so that you may all eat from your vines and your fig trees
and drink water from your cisterns, 32 until I come and take
you away to a land like your own, a land of grain [fields] and
vineyards, of bread and wine, of olive oil and honey, so that
you may live and not die. Don't listen to Hezekiah, who misleads you by saying, 'The LORD will save us.' 33 Did any of the
gods of other nations save his land from the king of Assyria?
34 Where were the gods of Hamath and Arpad? Where were the
gods of Sepharvaim, Hena, and Ivvah? [And] did they[c] save Samaria from me? 35 Which among all the gods of [those] countries saved their countries from me, that the LORD should save
Jerusalem from me?" 36 But the people were silent and did not
say a word in reply; for the king's order was: "Do not answer
him." 37 And so Eliakim son of Hilkiah, who was in charge of the
palace, Shebna the scribe, and Joah son of Asaph the recorder
came to Hezekiah with their clothes rent, and they reported to
him what the Rabshakeh had said.

19 When King Hezekiah heard this, he rent his clothes,
and covered himself with sackcloth, and went into the
House of the LORD. 2 He also sent Eliakim, who was in charge
of the palace, Shebna the scribe, and the senior priests, covered with sackcloth, to the prophet Isaiah son of Amoz. 3 They
said to him, "Thus said Hezekiah: This day is a day of distress,
of chastisement, and of disgrace. [d-]The babes have reached
the birthstool, but the strength to give birth is lacking.[-d] 4 Perhaps the LORD your God will take note of all the words of the
Rabshakeh, whom his master the king of Assyria has sent to
blaspheme the living God, and will mete out judgment for the

a *So several mss. and ancient versions; most mss. and editions read "his."*
b *I.e., to my representative the Rabshakeh.* *c* *I.e., the gods of Samaria.*
d-d *I.e., the situation is desperate and we are at a loss.*

speaks of Hezekiah's reforms as an affront to God, in his attempt to arouse opposition to Hezekiah's policy of opposing Assyria. **26:** *Aramaic* was the diplomatic language in the southwestern parts of the Assyrian empire. Assyrian reliefs depict two scribes recording events, one on a clay tablet in cuneiform and one on a scroll, in Aramaic. *Judean* refers to the local dialect of Hebrew. Hebrew remained a spoken language, albeit in different dialectal forms, along with Aramaic until the 3rd c. CE. Then it evolved into a liturgical language and a language of learned discourse and writing, like Classical Arabic and Latin. After 1,600 years, Hebrew was conscientiously revived as a mother tongue during the 19th and 20th centuries CE among Jews living in Israel. Aramaic remained an important language in the Middle East until displaced by Arabic in the 7th to 8th centuries CE. Aramaic remains a liturgical language in some Eastern tradition churches. At the end of the 20th century, it was spoken by some Jews in Kurdistan (northern Iraq) and in dialect form by Jews in other parts of Iraq, in Iran, and in a few places in Lebanon. **27:** *Eat ... dung ... urine,* a threat of famine brought about by a siege. **31–32:** As an inducement to surrender, the Rabshakeh offers peace and resettlement in some land of exile described as a wonderful place. **34:** *Hamath ... Ivvah,* cities that the Assyrians had previously conquered.

19.1–37: Hezekiah consults Isaiah. **1–4:** Hezekiah goes directly to the Temple and also sends messengers to Isaiah, attempting to stimulate him to action by emphasizing the words of the Rabshakeh against *the LORD your God.*

words that the LORD your God has heard—if you will offer up
prayer for the surviving remnant."
5 When King Hezekiah's ministers came to Isaiah, 6 Isaiah
said to them, "Tell your master as follows: Thus said the
LORD: Do not be frightened by the words of blasphemy against
Me that you have heard from the minions of the king of Assyria. 7 I will delude[a] him; he will hear a rumor and return to
his land, and I will make him fall by the sword in his land."
8 The Rabshakeh, meanwhile, heard that [the king] had left
Lachish; he turned back and found the king of Assyria attacking
Libnah. 9 But [the king of Assyria] learned that King Tirhakah of
Nubia had come out to fight him; so he again sent messengers
to Hezekiah, saying, 10 "Tell this to King Hezekiah of Judah: Do
not let your God, on whom you are relying, mislead you into
thinking that Jerusalem will not be delivered into the hands of
the king of Assyria. 11 You yourself have heard what the kings
of Assyria have done to all the lands, how they have annihilated them; and can you escape? 12 Were the nations that my
predecessors[b] destroyed—Gozan, Haran, Rezeph, and the
Beth-edenites in Telassar—saved by their gods? 13 Where is the
king of Hamath? And the king of Arpad? And the kings of Lair,
Sepharvaim, Hena, and Ivvah?"
14 Hezekiah took the letter from the messengers and read it.
Hezekiah then went up to the House of the LORD and spread
it out before the LORD. 15 And Hezekiah prayed to the LORD
and said, "O LORD of Hosts, Enthroned on the Cherubim! You
alone are God of all the kingdoms of the earth. You made the
heavens and the earth. 16 O LORD, incline Your ear and hear;
open Your eyes and see. Hear the words that Sennacherib has
sent to blaspheme the living God! 17 True, O LORD, the kings
of Assyria have annihilated the nations and their lands, 18 and
have committed their gods to the flames and have destroyed
them; for they are not gods, but man's handiwork of wood and
stone. 19 But now, O LORD our God, deliver us from his hands,
and let all the kingdoms of the earth know that You alone, O
LORD, are God."
20 Then Isaiah son of Amoz sent this message to Hezekiah:
"Thus said the LORD, the God of Israel: I have heard the
prayer you have offered to Me concerning King Sennacherib
of Assyria. 21 This is the word that the LORD has spoken concerning him:

"Fair Maiden Zion despises you,
She mocks at you;
Fair Jerusalem shakes
Her head at you.

a Lit. "put a spirit in." b Lit. "fathers."

7: Isaiah's prophecy that the king of Assyria would hear a rumor, return to Assyria and be killed there are reported fulfilled in vv. 36–37. **9:** *King Tirhakah* was the last pharaoh of the twenty-fifth (Ethiopian) dynasty. Although he reigned 690–664 BCE, he was active militarily or had armies led in his name years before. He was not a king in 701 when Sennacherib besieged Jerusalem, but was known to have been one when the author wrote. **10–19:** A delegation from Sennacherib, now at Libnah north of Lachish, arrived with essentially the same message as that delivered by the Rabshakeh. **15:** *Enthroned on the Cherubim:* See 1 Sam. 4.4 n. **19:** The assumption of radical monotheism suggests that this is a late text. **20–28:** These vv. are not present in the book of Isaiah, but similar anti-Assyrian passages occur in Isa. 10.12–19; 14.24–27.

23: Lebanon was known for its cedars, which were especially important for the Assyrian's massive building projects that required beams to span large spaces. Here the image is of its high mountains and thick forests. **29:** It will take two years for life to return to normal after the invasion and siege.

22 Whom have you blasphemed and reviled?
Against whom made loud your voice
And haughtily raised your eyes?
Against the Holy One of Israel!
23 Through your envoys you have blasphemed my Lord.
Because you thought,
'Thanks to my vast chariotry,
It is I who have climbed the highest mountains,
To the remotest parts of the Lebanon,
And have cut down its loftiest cedars,
Its choicest cypresses,
And have reached its [a-]remotest lodge,[-a]
[b-]Its densest forest.[-b]
24 It is I who have drawn[c] and drunk the waters of strangers;
I have dried up with the soles of my feet
All the streams of Egypt.'
25 Have you not heard? Of old
I planned that very thing,
I designed it long ago,
And now have fulfilled it.
And it has come to pass,
Laying waste fortified towns
In desolate heaps.
26 Their inhabitants are helpless,
Dismayed and shamed.
They were but grass of the field
And green herbage,
Grass of the roofs that is blasted
Before the [d-]standing grain.[-d]
27 I know your stayings
And your goings and comings,
And how you have raged against Me.
28 Because you have raged against Me,
And your tumult has reached My ears,
I will place My hook in your nose
And My bit between your jaws;
And I will make you go back by the road
By which you came.

29 "And this is the sign for you:[e] This year you eat what grows of
itself, and the next year what springs from that; and in the third
year, sow and reap, and plant vineyards and eat their fruit.

a-a Isa. 37.24 reads "highest peak."
b-b Lit. "Its farmland forest"; exact meaning of Heb. uncertain.
c Or "dug"; meaning of Heb. uncertain.
d-d Emendation yields "east wind"; see note at Isa. 37.27. *e I.e., Hezekiah.*

30 And the survivors of the House of Judah that have escaped
shall regenerate its stock below and produce boughs above.
31 For a remnant shall come forth from Jerusalem,
Survivors from Mount Zion.
The zeal of the LORD of Hosts
Shall bring this to pass.

32 Assuredly, thus said the LORD concerning the king of Assyria:

He shall not enter this city:
He shall not shoot an arrow at it,
Or advance upon it with a shield,
Or pile up a siege mound against it.
33 He shall go back
By the way he came;
He shall not enter this city
—declares the LORD.
34 I will protect and save this city for My sake,
And for the sake of My servant David."

35 That night an angel of the LORD went out and struck down
one hundred and eighty-five thousand in the Assyrian camp,
and the following morning they were all dead corpses.
36 So King Sennacherib of Assyria broke camp and retreated, and stayed in Nineveh. 37 While he was worshiping in the
temple of his god Nisroch, his sons Adrammelech and Sarezer
struck him down with the sword. They fled to the land of Ararat, and his son Esarhaddon succeeded him as king.

20 In those days Hezekiah fell dangerously ill. The prophet
Isaiah son of Amoz came and said to him, "Thus said the
LORD: Set your affairs in order, for you are going to die; you will
not get well." 2 Thereupon Hezekiah turned his face to the wall
and prayed to the LORD. He said, 3 "Please, O LORD, remember
how I have walked before You sincerely and wholeheartedly,
and have done what is pleasing to You." And Hezekiah wept
profusely.
4 Before Isaiah had gone out of the middle court, the word of
the LORD came to him: 5 "Go back and say to Hezekiah, the ruler of My people: Thus said the LORD, the God of your father David: I have heard your prayer, I have seen your tears. I am going
to heal you; on the third day you shall go up to the House of the
LORD. 6 And I will add fifteen years to your life. I will also rescue
you and this city from the hands of the king of Assyria. I will
protect this city for My sake and for the sake of My servant David."—7 Then Isaiah said, "Get a cake of figs." And they got one,
and they applied it to the rash, and he recovered.—8 Hezekiah
asked Isaiah, "What is the sign that the LORD will heal me and

32–34: Known prophecies about the protected status of Jerusalem, combined with the fact that Sennacherib withdrew his forces, gave rise to a sense that the city was inviolable (Isa. 33.20; Zech. 12.8; Ps. 46.5–8). **35:** There is no tradition of such a plague other than here and in Isa. 37.36. **36:** This v. may have originally followed 18.16, concluding a short summary of the siege of 701 BCE, or after the prediction of this event in 19.7. In its present context, the v. leaves the impression that events occurring over many decades actually took place in a short while in fulfillment of the prophecy of 19.7. Sennacherib did hear a rumor (about Tirhakah [v. 9]) and did return to his land (from which he ventured forth in the following years many times on campaigns, primarily against Babylonia), and died by the sword in 681 BCE. **37:** We now know from Assyrian sources that Sennacherib was killed by Arad-Ninlil, rather than his sons Adrammelech and Sarezer; Sennacherib was, however, as stated in the Bible, *succeeded* by *his son Esarhaddon.*

20.1–12: The story of Hezekiah's illness is loosely connected to its context, and is out of chronological order. Ralbag argues that it is not connected to the Sennacherib story. On the basis of v. 6 (= 19.34), with its reference to an Assyrian threat, he proposes that it addresses new threats by Esarhaddon, Sennacherib's son. Merodach-baladan—reading the name correctly as in Isa. 39.1—however, was an anti-Assyrian ruler who usurped the throne of Babylonia twice: the first time, for eleven years after the death of Shalmaneser V in 721 BCE and the second, for nine months in 703 after the death of Sargon II. The time of his envoys' visit in v. 12, then, most likely coincided with his planning to revolt against Assyria in the east, around 705, while Hezekiah was making his own preparations to revolt in the west. **4:** Contrition accompanied by prayer can effect a change in God's decision. **7:** The *cake of figs* was applied as a poultice; the combination

that I shall go up to the House of the LORD on the third day?"
9 Isaiah replied, "This is the sign for you from the LORD that the
LORD will do the thing that He has promised: Shall[a] the shadow advance ten steps or recede ten steps?" 10 Hezekiah said,
"It is easy for the shadow to lengthen ten steps, but not for the
shadow to recede ten steps." 11 So the prophet Isaiah called to
the LORD, and He made the shadow which had descended on
the dial[b] of Ahaz recede ten steps.

12 At that time, King Berodach-[c]baladan son of Baladan of
Babylon sent [envoys with] a letter and a gift to Hezekiah, for
he had heard about Hezekiah's illness. 13 [d]Hezekiah heard
about them-[d] and he showed them all his treasurehouse—the
silver, the gold, the spices, and the fragrant oil—and his armory, and everything that was to be found in his storehouses.
There was nothing in his palace or in all his realm that Hezekiah did not show them. 14 Then the prophet Isaiah came to King
Hezekiah. "What," he demanded of him, "did those men say to
you? Where have they come to you from?" "They have come,"
Hezekiah replied, "from a far country, from Babylon." 15 Next
he asked, "What have they seen in your palace?" And Hezekiah
replied, "They have seen everything that is in my palace. There
was nothing in my storehouses that I did not show them."

16 Then Isaiah said to Hezekiah, "Hear the word of the
LORD: 17 A time is coming when everything in your palace
which your ancestors have stored up to this day will be carried off to Babylon; nothing will remain behind, said the LORD.
18 And some of your sons, your own issue, whom you will have
fathered, will be taken to serve as eunuchs in the palace of the
king of Babylon." 19 Hezekiah declared to Isaiah, "The word of
the LORD that you have spoken is good." For he thought, "It
means that [e]safety is assured for-[e] my time."

20 The other events of Hezekiah's reign, and all his exploits,
and how he made the pool and the conduit and brought the
water into the city, are recorded in the Annals of the Kings of
Judah. 21 Hezekiah slept with his fathers, and his son Manasseh
succeeded him as king.

21 Manasseh was twelve years old when he became king,
and he reigned fifty-five years in Jerusalem; his mother's
name was Hephzibah. 2 He did what was displeasing to the
LORD, following the abhorrent practices of the nations that
the LORD had dispossessed before the Israelites. 3 He rebuilt
the shrines that his father Hezekiah had destroyed; he erected

a Cf. Targum.
b Heb. "steps." A model of a dial with steps has been discovered in Egypt.
c Several mss. and the parallel Isa. 39.1 read "Merodach."
d-d Isa. 39.2 reads "Hezekiah was pleased by their coming."
e-e Lit. "there shall be safety and faithfulness in."

of medicine, prayer, and contrition healed the king. The same medication is prescribed for horses in a text from Ugarit. **9–11:** The sign itself is unclear, but likely refers to *the shadow* of the sun*dial* moving in an unnatural direction.

20.13–21: The prediction of Babylonian conquest and the end of Hezekiah's reign. 18: This is fulfilled in the exiles of 597 and 586 BCE. **19:** *The word of the LORD ... is good* expresses a fatalistic acceptance of what will be in the light of some acknowledged misconduct (cf. 1 Sam. 3.18; 2 Sam. 15.26). **20:** In 1880, the Siloam Tunnel inscription commemorating the completion of the tunneling project was found on the tunnel's wall. This tunnel conveyed water from outside Jerusalem into the city, assuring a water supply even in the time of siege.

21.1–18: Manasseh's long and peaceful reign (698–642 BCE) overlapped those of the three most powerful Assyrian kings: Sennacherib, Esarhaddon, and Ashurbanipal. These absolutely controlled Mesopotamia and, after Esarhaddon defeated Tirhakah in 671, Egypt and everything in between. Manasseh is mentioned as a loyal vassal in Assyrian inscriptions; this explains his peaceful reign. **3–9:** A list of all that Manasseh did wrong (v. 17). According to the author, Manasseh's reign was the worst period of apostasy in Israelite history. Not only did he sin, but he caused others to sin and he introduced illegal cults into the Temple itself. From the author's perspective, Manasseh undid everything that Hezekiah and Asa had achieved and then pressed beyond them to do wrong out of spite (v. 6). The later editor of Kings (Dtr^2) blames the destruction of Jerusalem on the heinous acts of Manasseh; this author, in contrast to the Chronicler, seems undisturbed that this destruction did not take place during the reign of Manasseh, who benefited from a long reign.

altars for Baal and made a sacred post, as King Ahab of Israel
had done. He bowed down to all the host of heaven and worshiped them, 4 and he built altars for them in the House of the
LORD, of which the LORD had said, "I will establish My name
in Jerusalem." 5 He built altars for all the hosts of heaven in the
two courts of the House of the LORD. 6 He consigned his son to
the fire; he practiced soothsaying and divination, and consulted ghosts and familiar spirits; he did much that was displeasing to the LORD, to vex Him. 7 The sculptured image of Asherah
that he made he placed in the House concerning which the
LORD had said to David and to his son Solomon, "In this House
and in Jerusalem, which I chose out of all the tribes of Israel, I
will establish My name forever. 8 And I will not again cause the
feet of Israel to wander from the land that I gave to their fathers,
if they will but faithfully observe all that I have commanded
them—all the Teachings with which My servant Moses charged
them." 9 But they did not obey, and Manasseh led them astray
to do greater evil than the nations that the LORD had destroyed
before the Israelites. 10 Therefore the LORD spoke through His
servants the prophets: 11 "Because King Manasseh of Judah has
done these abhorrent things—he has outdone in wickedness
all that the Amorites did before his time—and because he led
Judah to sin with his fetishes, 12 assuredly, thus said the LORD,
the God of Israel: I am going to bring such a disaster on Jerusalem and Judah that both ears of everyone who hears about
it will tingle. 13 I will [a-]apply to Jerusalem the measuring line
of Samaria and the weights of the House of Ahab;[-a] I will wipe
Jerusalem clean as one wipes a dish and turns it upside down.
14 And I will cast off the remnant of My own people and deliver
them into the hands of their enemies. They shall be plunder
and prey to all their enemies 15 because they have done what is
displeasing to Me and have been vexing Me from the day that
their fathers came out of Egypt to this day."

16 Moreover, Manasseh put so many innocent persons to
death that he filled Jerusalem [with blood] from end to end—
besides the sin he committed in causing Judah to do what was
displeasing to the LORD.

17 The other events of Manasseh's reign, and all his actions,
and the sins he committed, are recorded in the Annals of the
Kings of Judah. 18 Manasseh slept with his fathers and was buried in the garden of his palace, in the garden of Uzza; and his
son Amon succeeded him as king.

19 Amon was twenty-two years old when he became king,
and he reigned two years in Jerusalem; his mother's name was
Meshullemeth daughter of Haruz of Jotbah. 20 He did what

a-a I.e., I will bring the same fate upon it.

4: *Establish My name in Jerusalem:* The quotation here and in v. 7 is from God's speech to Solomon in 1 Kings 9.3; cf. also 1 Kings 8.16. **8–15:** An insertion into the description of Manasseh's culpable acts. These vv. focus attention on the culpability of the king as one who causes others to sin. The emphasis on what the people of Israel did wrong reflects an exilic perspective. **10–15:** According to the author, these vv. are a collage of prophetic pronouncements, but he did not identify any prophet by name. None of the statements are found in any of the canonical prophetic books. They may have been added by the second author. **11:** Amorites, a term referring to pre-Israelite inhabitants of the land who could only be expelled after the measure of their iniquity reached a certain limit (Gen. 15.16 and cf. the imagery in Lev. 18.24–28). **16:** This v. concludes the inventory of Manasseh's wrongs from v. 7. Additional information about Manasseh's religious activities may be inferred from the author's description of Josiah's activities in ch 23. The tradition of killing innocent persons was elaborated in postbiblical works with the idea that he killed the prophet Isaiah (*Ant.* 10.38; *b. Sanh.* 103b). **18:** Manasseh was not buried *with his fathers* in the City of David as were the kings of Judah before him but in *the garden of Uzza* located on the grounds of his palace. Possibly the traditional cave tombs of the Davidic kings were filled and new ones were excavated elsewhere in the city.

21.19–26: The reign of Amon. The author indicates that Amon's short reign (641–640 BCE) did not differ from that of his father with regard to religious policies.

was displeasing to the LORD, as his father Manasseh had done.
21 He walked in all the ways of his father, worshiping the fetishes which his father had worshiped and bowing down to them.
22 He forsook the LORD, the God of his fathers, and did not follow the way of the LORD.
23 Amon's courtiers conspired against him; and they killed
the king in his palace. 24 But the people of the land put to death
all who had conspired against King Amon, and the people of
the land made his son Josiah king in his stead. 25 The other
events of Amon's reign [and] his actions are recorded in the
Annals of the Kings of Judah. 26 He was buried in his tomb in
the garden of Uzza; and his son Josiah succeeded him as king.

22 Josiah was eight years old when he became king, and
he reigned thirty-one years in Jerusalem. His mother's
name was Jedidah daughter of Adaiah of Bozkath. 2 He did
what was pleasing to the LORD and he followed all the ways of
his ancestor David; he did not deviate to the right or to the left.
3 In the eighteenth year of King Josiah, the king sent the
scribe Shaphan son of Azaliah son of Meshullam to the House
of the LORD, saying, 4 "Go to the high priest Hilkiah and let him
weigh[a] the silver that has been deposited in the House of the
LORD, which the guards of the threshold have collected from
the people. 5 And let it be delivered to the overseers of the
work who are in charge at the House of the LORD, that they in
turn may pay it out to the workmen that are in the House of
the LORD, for the repair of the House: 6 to the carpenters, the
laborers, and the masons, and for the purchase of wood and
quarried stones for repairing the House. 7 However, no check
is to be kept on them for the silver that is delivered to them, for
they deal honestly."
8 Then the high priest Hilkiah said to the scribe Shaphan, "I
have found a scroll of the Teaching in the House of the LORD."

a *Meaning of Heb. uncertain. Emendation yields "melt down," cf. v.* 9.

23: The reason for the conspiracy is not mentioned. If political, he may have been killed by an anti-Assyrian group; if religious, by an anti-polytheistic group. **24:** The *people of the land* again stepped into the breech and guaranteed the continuity of the Davidic dynasty; cf. 11.14.

22.1–23.30: The reign of Josiah. In the author's evaluation, Josiah (640–609 BCE) was the most outstanding of all the kings who ruled Judah, with no qualification. His personal piety and righteous zealousness were almost sufficient to avert the disaster which the most heinous of sinners, Manasseh, had sealed for Judah.

22.1–20: The discovery of a scroll. The author's narrative about the discovery of a book in the Temple and the prophetic authentication of its contents is an artfully constructed narrative that emphasizes characteristics in Josiah's personality that the author wished to present to his readers. Unlike the staid narratives in Kings about individuals who lived after Solomon, this contains details approaching the manner of narratives in Samuel and withholds information to create slight tensions in order to achieve its objective: admiration for Josiah. Most, but not all, modern scholars consider this account to be largely historical, reflecting the "(re) discovery" of Deut. in this period. **3:** Josiah was 26 years old in 622 BCE when he instituted a project for the refurbishing of the Temple, approximately 90 years after that of Jehoash (cf. 12.1–7). **4–7:** Josiah's instructions for the administration of the project and his instructions that contractors and suppliers are to be trusted are similar to those of Jehoash in 12.11–16. **4:** Instructions to collect silver for the refurbishing must have been given much earlier. Josiah's order here assumes that what has been deposited suffices to complete the project. **8:** The *scroll of the Teaching* is referred to simply as *a scroll* in v. 10, but in 23.2 as "the covenant scroll" and in 2 Chron. 34.14 as "a scroll of the LORD's teaching given by Moses." Scroll, Heb "sefer," indicates that it was a longish document; teaching, Heb "torah," that it contained instruction; covenant, Heb "berit," that it contained a contract/agreement. Hilkiah's description suggests that what is novel about the find is that *the Teaching*—marked by the definite article as something already known— was found written in a scroll. The contents of this *scroll* and Josiah's and the people's reaction to it suggest that it was some form of the book of Deut. but that it also contained ideas about how improper and illegal rituals and worship contaminated the land and had to be eliminated aggressively. Most medieval Jewish exegetes posit variously that it was unique because either Ahaz or Manasseh had burnt all known scrolls, or—considering the notation in Chronicles—because it was the scroll written by Moses himself (Deut. 31.24–26). Abravanel, however, observing the author's description of Josiah's reaction in v. 11, cites a rabbinic tradition that the scroll was found open to the threat of exile directed against the people and the king in Deut. 28.36.

And Hilkiah gave the scroll to Shaphan, who read it. 9 The scribe
Shaphan then went to the king and reported to the king: "Your
servants have melted down the silver that was deposited in the
House, and they have delivered it to the overseers of the work
who are in charge at the House of the LORD." 10 The scribe Shaphan also told the king, "The high priest Hilkiah has given me
a scroll"; and Shaphan read it to the king.
11 When the king heard the words of the scroll of the Teaching, he rent his clothes. 12 And the king gave orders to the priest
Hilkiah, and to Ahikam son of Shaphan, Achbor son of Michaiah, the scribe Shaphan, and Asaiah the king's minister: 13 "Go,
inquire of the LORD on my behalf, and on behalf of the people,
and on behalf of all Judah, concerning the words of this scroll
that has been found. For great indeed must be the wrath of the
LORD that has been kindled against us, because our fathers did
not obey the words of this scroll to do all that has been prescribed for us."
14 So the priest Hilkiah, and Ahikam, Achbor, Shaphan, and
Asaiah went to the prophetess Huldah—the wife of Shallum
son of Tikvah son of Harhas, the keeper of the wardrobe—who
was living in Jerusalem in the Mishneh,[a] and they spoke to her.
15 She responded: "Thus said the LORD, the God of Israel: Say
to the man who sent you to me: 16 Thus said the LORD: I am
going to bring disaster upon this place and its inhabitants, in
accordance with all the words of the scroll which the king of
Judah has read. 17 Because they have forsaken Me and have
made offerings to other gods and vexed Me with all their
deeds, My wrath is kindled against this place and it shall not be
quenched. 18 But say this to the king of Judah, who sent you to
inquire of the LORD: Thus said the LORD, the God of Israel: As
for the words which you have heard—19 because your heart
was softened and you humbled yourself before the LORD when
you heard what I decreed against this place and its inhabitants—that it will become a desolation and a curse—and because you rent your clothes and wept before Me, I for My part
have listened—declares the LORD. 20 Assuredly, I will gather
you to your fathers and you will be laid in your tomb in peace.
Your eyes shall not see all the disaster which I will bring upon
this place." So they brought back the reply to the king.

23 At the king's summons, all the elders of Judah and Jerusalem assembled before him. 2 The king went up to the
House of the LORD, together with all the men of Judah and all
the inhabitants of Jerusalem, and the priests and prophets—
all the people, young and old. And he read to them the entire
text of the covenant scroll which had been found in the House

a *A quarter in Jerusalem; cf. Zeph. 1.10.*

11: Josiah's reaction to the contents of the scroll is described as a conventional response to hearing bad news (Gen. 37.34; 2 Sam. 1.11; 3.31; 2 Kings 5.7; 19.1). **13:** The message indicates that the scroll taught behaviors which Josiah knows had not been followed and spelled out dire consequences which he knew were about to befall him and his kingdom. **14:** *Huldah,* one of four named women prophets in the Tanakh; the others are Miriam (Exod. 15.20), Deborah (Judg. 4.4), and Noadiah (Neh. 6.14). Huldah lived in the *Mishneh* (cf. Zeph. 1.10), an area of the Old City of Jerusalem now covered by the Jewish and Armenian quarters. It is unknown why Josiah approached her, rather than Jeremiah, who was also living in this period; but Jeremiah is not mentioned in Kings. **16:** Although addressing only the punishments listed in the scroll, Huldah's pronouncement also authenticated the divine source of its teachings. **19–20:** Josiah's remorse postpones the inevitable punishment until after his death. Compare the similar response to the contrite prayers of Ahab (1 Kings 21.27–29) and Hezekiah (2 Kings 20.2–6). Josiah died in battle in 609 BCE (cf. 23.29–30). Huldah's prophecy is mostly fulfilled by the events reported in 25.9–11, 18–21. Rashi and Radak, followed by others, consider the phrase *in peace* applied to Josiah fulfilled in that he did not see the destruction of the Temple implied by the words *your eyes shall not see all the disaster;* most modern scholars think that the violent death of Josiah suggests that this was a real prophecy uttered and recorded before his death.

23.1–25: The reforms of Josiah were instituted in response to Huldah's authentication of the scroll. Initially he mediated a covenant between the people and God and then instituted a course of action to fulfill the conditions of the agreement. **3:** His stand *by the pillar* may have been a symbol of dynastic authority; cf. 11.14. Josiah's role as mediator of the covenant is similar to that of Jehoiada in the days

of the LORD. 3 The king stood [a]by the pillar[a] and solemnized
the covenant before the LORD: that they would follow the LORD
and observe His commandments, His injunctions, and His
laws with all their heart and soul; that they would fulfill all the
terms of this covenant as inscribed upon the scroll. And all the
people [b]entered into[b] the covenant.
4 Then the king ordered the high priest Hilkiah, the priests of
the second rank, and the guards of the threshold to bring out
of the Temple of the LORD all the objects made for Baal and
Asherah[c] and all the host of heaven. He burned them outside
Jerusalem in the fields[d] of Kidron, and he removed the ashes to
Bethel. 5 He suppressed the idolatrous priests whom the kings
of Judah had appointed [e]to make offerings[e] at the shrines in
the towns of Judah and in the environs of Jerusalem, and those
who made offerings to Baal, to the sun and moon and constellations—all the host of heaven. 6 He brought out the [image
of] Asherah from the House of the LORD to the Kidron Valley
outside Jerusalem, and burned it in the Kidron Valley; he beat
it to dust and scattered its dust over the burial ground of the
common people. 7 He tore down the cubicles of the male prostitutes in the House of the LORD, at the place where the women
wove coverings[d] for Asherah.
8 He brought all the priests from the towns of Judah [to Je-
rusalem] and defiled the shrines where the priests had been
making offerings—from Geba to Beer-sheba. He also demolished the shrines of the gates, which were at the entrance of
the gate of Joshua, the city prefect—[f]which were on a person's
left [upon entering] the city gate.[f] 9 [g]The priests of the shrines,
however, did not ascend the altar of the LORD in Jerusalem,
but they ate unleavened bread along with their kinsmen.[g]
10 He also defiled Topheth, which is in the Valley of Ben-
hinnom, so that no one might consign his son or daughter
to the fire of Molech. 11 He did away with the horses that the
kings of Judah had dedicated to the sun, [h]at the entrance[h]
of the House of the LORD, near the chamber of the eunuch
Nathan-melech, which was in the precincts.[d] He burned the
chariots of the sun. 12 And the king tore down the altars made
by the kings of Judah on the roof by the upper chamber of
Ahaz, and the altars made by Manasseh in the two courts of
the House of the LORD. He [i]removed them quickly from there[i]
and scattered their rubble in the Kidron Valley. 13 The king also

a-a Or "on a platform," cf. Targum. *b-b Cf. Targum.*
c For this goddess, cf. 1 Kings 18.19; ordinarily asherah *is rendered "sacred post," e.g., 2 Kings 17.16.* *d Meaning of Heb. uncertain.*
e-e Lit. "and he offered." *f-f Meaning of Heb. uncertain.*
g-g This verse may be understood in connection with vv. 21–23.
h-h Heb. "from entering." *i-i Heb. "ran from there." Emendation yields "smashed them there."*

of Jehoash of Judah (11.17), Joshua at Shechem (Josh. 24.14–25), and particularly Moses at Sinai. Idioms in this v. echo those in Deut.: *follow the LORD* (Deut. 13.5); *observe His commandments, His injunctions, and His laws* (Deut. 4.45 and 40 other vv.); *all their heart and soul* (Deut. 4.29; 6.5); *entered into the covenant* (Deut. 29.11). Cf. 1 Kings 8.22–53. **4–7:** Josiah's purification of the Temple and elimination of shrines outside of Jerusalem illuminate the drastic changes that Manasseh introduced into Judah during his long reign. **4:** *Baal, Asherah,* and the *host of heaven* form a polytheistic triad worshipped in Judah in the days of Ahaz and Manasseh (17.16; 21.3 [NJPS translates Asherah as "sacred post"]). Manasseh must have instituted their worship in the Temple itself. See v. 6. Josiah acts in accord with Deut. 12.2. **5:** *Idolatrous priests* (Heb "kemarim") may refer to foreign-born specialists. Although their activities were discontinued, no action was taken against them. No mention is made of what was done to the native-born priests who served in the Temple. **8:** Shrines outside of Jerusalem where God was worshipped were defiled, restricting all worship to Jerusalem in accord with Deut. 12.4–7. *Geba to Beer-sheba:* These cities designated the northern and southern borders of his kingdom. *Shrines of the gates* have been excavated at Dan, Tirzah, and Geshur (an Aramean city near the northeast shore of the Sea of Galilee). They consisted of a small area in which one or more standing stones were set up. **9:** The priests brought in from the open shrines were denied the right to serve at the altar in Jerusalem, in contrast to the teaching of Deut. 18.6–7. This denial was legitimated about 50 years later by Ezekiel (Ezek. 44.10–14). With this exception, all the other parts of this reform, with their emphasis on cultic purity and centralization in Jerusalem, closely mirror Deut. **13:** Josiah even eliminates monuments attesting the apostasy of Solomon (see 1 Kings 11.1–13). Neither Asa nor Hezekiah, both considered good kings by the

defiled the shrines facing Jerusalem, to the south of the [a]Mount of the Destroyer,[-a] which King Solomon of Israel had built for Ashtoreth, the abomination of the Sidonians, for Chemosh, the abomination of Moab, and for Milcom, the detestable thing of the Ammonites.[b] [14] He shattered their pillars and cut down their sacred posts and covered their sites with human bones.

[15] As for the altar in Bethel [and] the shrine made by Jeroboam son of Nebat who caused Israel to sin—that altar, too, and the shrine as well, he tore down. He burned down the shrine and beat it to dust, and he burned the sacred post.

[16] Josiah turned and saw the graves that were there on the hill; and he had the bones taken out of the graves and burned on the altar. Thus he defiled it, in fulfillment of the word of the LORD foretold by the man of God who foretold these happenings. [17] He asked, "What is the marker I see there?" And the men of the town replied, "That is the grave of the man of God who came from Judah and foretold these things that you have done to the altar of Bethel."[c] [18] "Let him be," he said, "let no one disturb his bones." So they left his bones undisturbed together with the bones of the prophet[d] who came from Samaria.[e]

[19] Josiah also abolished all the cult places in the towns of Samaria, which the kings of Israel had built, vexing [the LORD]. He dealt with them just as he had done to Bethel: [20] He slew on the altars all the priests of the shrines who were there, and he burned human bones on them. Then he returned to Jerusalem. [21] The king commanded all the people, "Offer the passover sacrifice to the LORD your God as prescribed in this scroll of the covenant." [22] Now the passover sacrifice had not been offered in that manner in the days of the chieftains who ruled Israel, or during the days of the kings of Israel and the kings of Judah. [23] Only in the eighteenth year of King Josiah was such a passover sacrifice offered in that manner to the LORD in Jerusalem. [24] Josiah also did away with [f]the necromancers and the mediums,[-f] the idols and the fetishes—all the detestable things that were to be seen in the land of Judah and Jerusalem. Thus

a-a Heb. har ha-mashḥith: *a derogatory play on* har ha-mishḥah *("Mount of Ointment"); Mishnah Middoth 2.4.* *b Cf. 1 Kings 11.5, 7.*
c Cf. 1 Kings 13.2–3. *d See 1 Kings 13.31–32 and note e below.*
e The prophet lived in Bethel, which, in Josiah's time, was part of the Assyrian province of Samaria. *f-f Lit. "the ghosts and the familiar spirits."*

author, had done so. **15–18:** Josiah eliminates structures attesting to the great tragedy of the sundering of Solomon's kingdom at the shrine developed by Jeroboam (1 Kings 12.29). The author relates his activities to the story of an anonymous prophet at Bethel (1 Kings 13.1–2). Josiah's presence in Bethel, north of his political border, indicates that he extended his authority into the former territory of Israel that Assyria had turned into a province, and that Assyrian authority in territories of the former Northern Kingdom had declined considerably. After 629 BCE Assyria's heartland was threatened by a newly powerful Babylonia from the south and by Medes descending from the Persian plateau from the northeast. Some therefore suggest that Josiah's reforms were both political and religious in nature. **16:** See 1 Kings 13.2. **19–20:** Josiah's drive north reaches the towns of Samaria where Assyrians had settled exiles from Syria and Babylonia (17.24). The author's silence about the campaigns themselves indicates that they were successful and that he considered them legitimate. Josiah was acting like a Davidic monarch prior to the formation of the breakaway northern confederacy. **20:** Priests who served at northern shrines are killed, unlike those who served at southern ones (cf. vv. 8–9). The northern priests may have been descendants of the non-Levitical priests appointed by Jeroboam I (1 Kings 12.31). **21–23:** The celebration of Passover in Jerusalem exclusively in accord with the prescription of Deut. 16.5 as understood by the author is possible only because no legitimate clergy and no purified shrine exist anywhere between the cities of Samaria and Beer-sheba except at Jerusalem. **22:** The author may mean that the last such Passover was celebrated in the days before the chieftains/judges, since Judg. 2.7 depicts that period as beginning a time when God was not worshipped properly. Radak considers the point of the author's comment to be that not since the time of the chieftains, among whom he includes Samuel, had the tribes been so dedicated to the LORD (1 Sam. 7.2), rid themselves of idolatrous practices, and served the LORD (1 Sam. 7.4). The Passover celebration of Hezekiah described in 2 Chron. 30.12–27 was not attended by all tribes (2 Chron. 30.10). **24:** This continues the list of Josiah's campaign against illegitimate personnel and activities from v. 20. *Necromancers … mediums,* see Deut. 18.9–14, which formulates compactly legislation found also in Lev. 19.26, 31; 20.27.

he fulfilled the terms of the Teaching recorded in the scroll that
the priest Hilkiah had found in the House of the LORD. 25 There
was no king like him before who turned back to the LORD with
all his heart and soul and might, in full accord with the Teaching of Moses; nor did any like him arise after him.

26 However, the LORD did not turn away from His awesome
wrath which had blazed up against Judah because of all the
things Manasseh did to vex Him. 27 The LORD said, "I will also
banish Judah from My presence as I banished Israel; and I will
reject the city of Jerusalem which I chose and the House where
I said My name would abide."

28 The other events of Josiah's reign, and all his actions, are
recorded in the Annals of the Kings of Judah. 29 In his days,
Pharaoh Neco, king of Egypt, marched against the king of Assyria[a] to the River Euphrates; King Josiah marched toward
him, but when he confronted him at Megiddo, [Pharaoh Neco]
slew him. 30 His servants conveyed his body in a chariot from
Megiddo to Jerusalem, and they buried him in his tomb. Then
the people of the land took Jehoahaz; they anointed him and
made him king in place of his father.

31 Jehoahaz was twenty-three years old when he became
king, and he reigned three months in Jerusalem; his mother's
name was Hamutal daughter of Jeremiah of Libnah. 32 He
did what was displeasing to the LORD, just as his fathers had
done. 33 Pharaoh Neco imprisoned him in Riblah in the region
of Hamath, to keep him from reigning in Jerusalem. And he
imposed on the land an indemnity of one hundred talents of
silver and a talent of gold. 34 Then Pharaoh Neco appointed Eliakim son of Josiah king in place of his father Josiah, changing
his name to Jehoiakim. He took Jehoahaz and [b]brought him[b]
to Egypt, where he died. 35 Jehoiakim gave Pharaoh the silver
and the gold, and he made an assessment on the land to pay
the money demanded by Pharaoh. He exacted from the people
of the land the silver and gold to be paid Pharaoh Neco, according to each man's assessment.

a I.e., the Chaldean Empire; cf. Isa. 52.4 and note.
b-b So 2 Chron. 36.4; Heb. here "he came."

25: *Heart and soul and might* are only here and in Deut. 6.5.

23.26–27: The inevitability of the end. This remark qualifies the high praise lavished on Josiah in the author's evaluation of v. 25. All of his accomplishments were of no avail to his kingdom. Dtr², a later writer, someone other than the author, focuses the reader's attention back to Huldah's declaration (22.17–20) about the inevitability of Judah's end and introduces the twilight of Judah's history. Proper punishment for Manasseh's sins may be delayed (see Exod. 20.5 n.), but not postponed.

23.28–30: The death of Josiah. 29: It is uncertain why *Josiah* confronted *Neco* at *Megiddo*. Nineveh had fallen in 612 BCE to Babylonia, but Assyrians were still fighting in northwest Assyria. Some historians speculate on the basis of 2 Chron. 35.20–24 and a cuneiform document, the Babylonian Chronicle, that Neco was actually moving north to support Assyrian forces against Babylonia and that Josiah acted as part of a Babylonian strategy that would have helped him maintain control over his enlarged kingdom. For the author, this death made no sense and remained unexplained. A later author told the story in a way that provided some theological justification for Josiah's death: He was interfering with a divinely ordained plan (2 Chron. 35.20–27). **30:** The *people of the land* again assure a smooth transition to a legitimate descendant in a period of uncertainty. Cf. 11.14; 14.21–22; 21.24. They decide, however, to skip Josiah's oldest son in favor of a brother at least two years younger (compare the ages at accession in vv. 31, 36).

23.31–33: The brief reign of Jehoahaz son of Josiah. Jeremiah refers to him by the name of Shallum (Jer. 22.11), so Jehoahaz must be a throne name. **33:** Jehoahaz traveled to *Riblah* in northern Syria, most likely to submit formally to Neco as a vassal. Neco arrested him, had him taken to Egypt as a royal hostage, and imposed tribute on Judah. Jehoahaz and the people of the land may have been too closely identified with Josiah's expansionist ambitions for Neco's comfort.

23.34–24.7: Jehoiakim's reign and the collapse of Judah. Jehoiakim's foreign policy assumed that Egypt could be the instrument through which Judah might regain its former glory. **23.34–35:** *Eliakim* was placed on the throne by *Neco,* not the people of the land, and provided by the Egyptian with the throne name *Jehoiakim*. Cf. also 24.17. Eliakim fulfilled his fiscal obligation to Neco, delivering the tribute. **24.1:** According to the Babylonian Chronicle,

[36] Jehoiakim was twenty-five years old when he became king,
and he reigned eleven years in Jerusalem; his mother's name
was Zebudah daughter of Pedaiah of Rumah. [37] He did what
was displeasing to the LORD, just as his ancestors had done.

24 In his days, King Nebuchadnezzar of Babylon came up,
and Jehoiakim became his vassal for three years. Then
he turned and rebelled against him. [2] The LORD let loose against
him the raiding bands of the Chaldeans, Arameans, Moabites,
and Ammonites; He let them loose against Judah to destroy it,
in accordance with the word that the LORD had spoken through
His servants the prophets. [3] All this befell Judah at the command
of the LORD, who banished [them] from His presence because
of all the sins that Manasseh had committed, [4] and also because
of the blood of the innocent that he shed. For he filled Jerusalem
with the blood of the innocent, and the LORD would not forgive.
[5] The other events of Jehoiakim's reign, and all of his actions,
are recorded in the Annals of the Kings of Judah. [6] Jehoiakim
slept with his fathers, and his son Jehoiachin succeeded him
as king. [7] The king of Egypt did not venture out of his country
again, for the king of Babylon had seized all the land that had
belonged to the king of Egypt, from the Wadi of Egypt to the
River Euphrates.

[8] Jehoiachin was eighteen years old when he became king,
and he reigned three months in Jerusalem; his mother's
name was Nehushta daughter of Elnathan of Jerusalem. [9] He
did what was displeasing to the LORD, just as his father had
done. [10] At that time, the troops[a] of King Nebuchadnezzar of
Babylon marched against Jerusalem, and the city came under
siege. [11] King Nebuchadnezzar of Babylon advanced against
the city while his troops were besieging it. [12] Thereupon King
Jehoiachin of Judah, along with his mother, and his courtiers,
commanders, and officers, surrendered to the king of Babylon.
The king of Babylon took him captive in the eighth year of his
reign. [13] He carried off [b-]from Jerusalem[-b] all the treasures of
the House of the LORD and the treasures of the royal palace;
he stripped off all the golden decorations in the Temple of the

a Heb. "servants." *b-b Heb. "from there."*

Babylonians under Nebuchadnezzar defeated Neco's Egyptian forces in Carchemish, in Syria in 605 BCE (cf. Jer. 46.1–2). Nebuchadnezzar's first move against Jerusalem would have happened around the same time (cf. Dan. 1.1), and Jehoiakim became a vassal of Babylonia around 604/3. **2:** Events encouraging rebellion may have developed in 601 after Nebuchadnezzar, unable to conquer Egypt in earlier campaigns, was subsequently forced by local conditions to remain in Babylonia in 600. Jer. 26.22 indicates that Jehoiakim colluded with Egypt and, expecting Egyptian support, may have rebelled. The author's mention that the attacks of *Chaldeans, Arameans, Moabites and Ammonites* came in fulfillment of words *spoken through His servants the prophets* does not reflect any extant prophecies. The *Chaldeans* are a tribe who were powerful in Babylonia in the Neo-Babylonian period, and various biblical and Greek sources use Chaldeans as a a synonym for the Babylonians. **3–7:** The author interprets the political reduction of Judah as the consequence of people reading political maps incompetently as well as the result of God's will after Manasseh's sins. **5:** *Annals of the Kings of Judah:* This last reference to this source in Kings raises the question of what sources were used by the author for descriptions of the final years of Judah. **7:** The author notes that the Babylonians controlled the area that had once comprised the Davidic-Solomonic empire.

24.8–17: Jehoiachin assumed the throne as the Babylonians were positioning themselves to destroy Jerusalem, all that was effectively left of Judah. His surrender in 597 BCE saved the city and led to the first exile from Judah. (The Babylonian Chronicle, first translated in 1956, refers to it as the city of Judah and mentions that Nebuchadnezzar took the [unnamed] king of Judah captive to Babylon.) **12–16:** The objective of the exile was to demilitarize, not punish, Judah by removing the court, high officials, administrators, military officials, and professional soldiers, as well as craftsmen who could manufacture new arms. Unlike the Assyrians, who dispersed populations, the Babylonians allowed them to resettle in exile as organic communities. The extent of the exile is probably exaggerated here; had all of these people been exiled, Judea could not have had the manpower to rebel against the Babylonians again a decade later.

LORD—which King Solomon of Israel had made—as the LORD
had warned. 14 He exiled all of Jerusalem: all the commanders and all the warriors—ten thousand exiles—as well as all
the craftsmen and smiths; only the poorest people in the land
were left. 15 He deported Jehoiachin to Babylon; and the king's
wives and officers and the notables of the land were brought
as exiles from Jerusalem to Babylon. 16 All the able men, to the
number of seven thousand—all of them warriors, trained for
battle—and a thousand craftsmen and smiths were brought
to Babylon as exiles by the king of Babylon. 17 And the king of
Babylon appointed Mattaniah, Jehoiachin's[a] uncle, king in his
place, changing his name to Zedekiah.
18 [b]Zedekiah was twenty-one years old when he became
king, and he reigned eleven years in Jerusalem; his mother's
name was Hamutal daughter of Jeremiah of Libnah. 19 He did
what was displeasing to the LORD, just as Jehoiakim had done.
20 Indeed, Jerusalem and Judah [c-]were a cause of anger for the
LORD, so that[-c] He cast them out of His presence.

25 Zedekiah rebelled against the king of Babylon. 1 And
in the ninth year of his[d] reign, on the tenth day of the
tenth month, Nebuchadnezzar moved against Jerusalem with
his whole army. He besieged it; and they built towers against it
all around. 2 The city continued in a state of siege until the eleventh year of King Zedekiah. 3 By the ninth day [of the fourth
month][e] the famine had become acute in the city; there was no
food left for the common people.
4 Then [the wall of] the city was breached. All the soldiers
[left the city] by night through the gate between the double
walls, which is near the king's garden—the Chaldeans were
all around the city; and [the king] set out for the Arabah.[f] 5 But
the Chaldean troops pursued the king, and they overtook him
in the steppes of Jericho as his entire force left him and scattered. 6 They captured the king and brought him before the
king of Babylon at Riblah; and they put him on trial. 7 They
slaughtered Zedekiah's sons before his eyes; then Zedekiah's
eyes were put out. He was chained in bronze fetters and he was
brought to Babylon.
8 On the seventh day of the fifth month—that was the nineteenth year of King Nebuchadnezzar of Babylon—Nebuzaradan, the chief of the guards, an officer of the king of Babylon,
came to Jerusalem. 9 He burned the House of the LORD, the

a *Heb. "his."* *b* *For the rest of this book cf. Jer. 39 and 52.*
c-c *Meaning of Heb. uncertain.* *d* *I.e., Zedekiah's.* *e* *Cf. Jer. 52.6.*
f *Hoping to escape across the Jordan.*

17: *Mattaniah,* provided with a throne name by Nebuchadnezzar, was the full brother of Jehoahaz (23.31) and the third son of Josiah to rule Judah.

24.18–25.21: The reign of Zedekiah (597–586 BCE) and destruction of the Temple. Much of this material is paralleled in Jer. 39.1–4, Jer. ch 52, and 2 Chron. ch 36. The writer's interest in this king concerns his disastrous international politics, which are given a theological justification in 24.20, not his religious policies. **24.19–20:** The writer again provides a negative assessment and comment, preparing readers for the inevitable (cf. 24.3–7). Zedekiah's acts are likened to those of his half-brother Jehoiakim (23.36). The writer skips over the first nine years of the reign to what interests him. On the basis of remarks in Jer. and Ezek., it is apparent that Zedekiah joined a coalition against Babylonia that included coastal Phoenicians and Transjordanian kingdoms in planning a revolt. Nebuchadnezzar managed to abort it, but then, in 589/8, set out to punish Zedekiah. V. 20 echoes v. 3.

25.1–3: The siege of Jerusalem lasted 17 months. Ultimately, starvation led to the fall of the city; this is a significant theme of Lam. as well (e.g., Lam. 4.10). Jer. 34.7 indicates that a few other cities that might have supported Jerusalem were also besieged. **3–4:** The walls of the city, most likely in the northwest, were breached on the ninth of the month of Tamuz, *the fourth month* (v. 4 and see Jer. 39.2–4; 52.6). Jewish tradition observes the seventeenth of Tamuz as a fast day (see "Biblical Festivals and Fast Days," pp. 2025–34) marking the breaching of the walls. The difference between the day of the breach and the fast is explained by claiming that it was only on the seventeenth that the Babylonians exploited the breach to enter the city. Events narrated in vv. 4–5 occupied them during the intervening days. The fast of the fourth month was known as an old observance two generations after the Temple's destruction (Zech. 7.3; 8.19).

9: Babylonians only gained access to the old part of Jerusalem where the Temple stood in the fifth month, the month of Av, 586 BCE. The Temple,

king's palace, and all the houses of Jerusalem; he burned down
[a]the house of every notable person.[a] 10 The entire Chaldean
force that was with the chief of the guard tore down the walls of
Jerusalem on every side. 11 The remnant of the people that was
left in the city, the defectors who had gone over to the king of
Babylon—and the remnant of the population—were taken into
exile by Nebuzaradan, the chief of the guards. 12 But some of
the poorest in the land were left by the chief of the guards, to be
vinedressers and field hands.
13 The Chaldeans broke up the bronze columns of the House
of the LORD, the stands, and the bronze tank that was in the
House of the LORD; and they carried the bronze away to Babylon. 14 They also took all the pails, scrapers, snuffers, ladles,
and all the other bronze vessels used in the service. 15 The chief
of the guards took whatever was of gold and whatever was of
silver: firepans and sprinkling bowls. 16 The two columns, the
one tank, and the stands that Solomon provided for the House
of the LORD—all these objects contained bronze beyond
weighing. 17 The one column was eighteen cubits high. It had
a bronze capital above it; the height of the capital was three
cubits, and there was a meshwork [decorated] with pomegranates about the capital, all made of bronze. And the like was true
of the other column with its meshwork.

a-a Meaning of Heb. uncertain.

palaces, and a large part of the city were set ablaze on the seventh day of the month, corresponding to August 16, 586. According to Jer. 52.12, they were burnt on the tenth of Av. In the talmudic tractate *Ta'an.* that deals with fasts, the dates were reconciled by explaining that on the seventh, the Babylonians gained access to the Temple, but they only set it afire late on the ninth, just before nightfall, and it burned through the tenth. Jewish tradition and contemporary practice maintains the ninth of Av as a 25-hour fast day commemorating the destruction of both the First Temple by the Babylonians and the Second Temple by the Romans. The fast itself was established early and is mentioned by Zechariah, a prophet who spoke about 60 years after the destruction, referring to the "fast of the fifth month" (Zech. 7.3; 8.19). **11–12:** A second group was taken into exile (see 24.12–16). This one consisted of Jerusalemites who had not fled, people who had defected to the Babylonians during the course of the siege, and a third group not clearly identifiable.

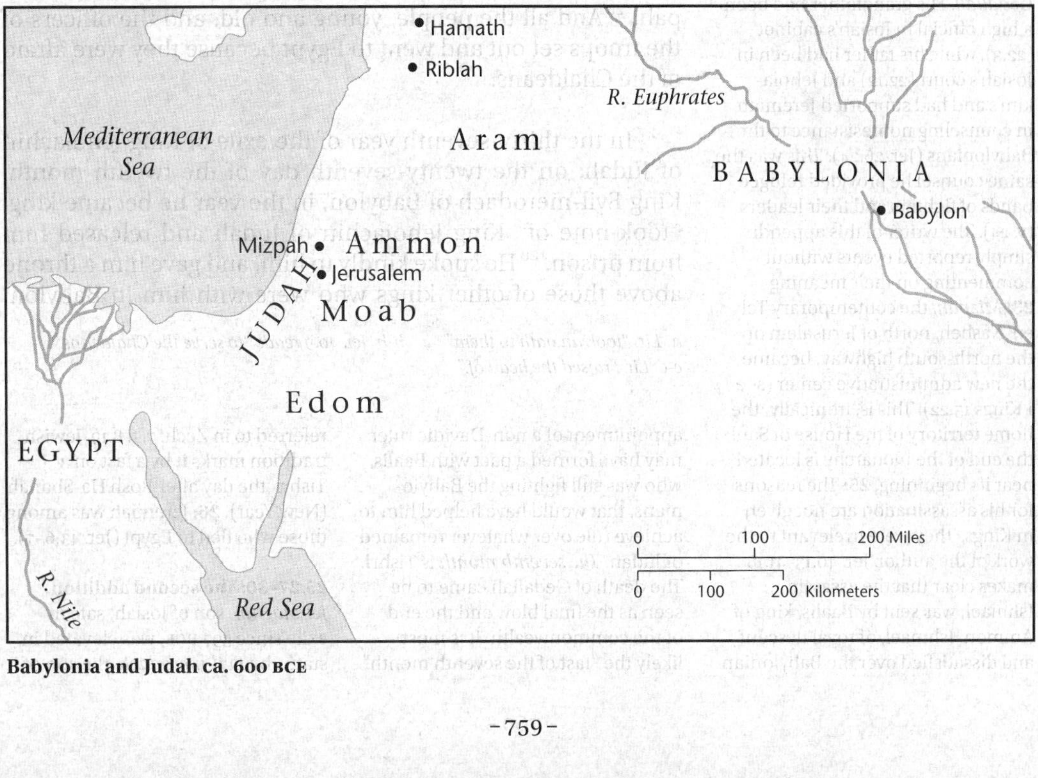

Babylonia and Judah ca. 600 BCE

18 The chief of the guards also took Seraiah, the chief priest,
Zephaniah, the deputy priest, and the three guardians of the
threshold. 19 And from the city he took a eunuch who was in
command of the soldiers; five royal privy councillors who
were present in the city; the scribe of the army commander,
who was in charge of mustering the people of the land; and
sixty of the common people who were inside the city. 20 Nebuzaradan, the chief of the guards, took them and brought them
to the king of Babylon at Riblah. 21 The king of Babylon had
them struck down and put to death at Riblah, in the region of
Hamath.

Thus Judah was exiled from its land. 22 King Nebuchadnezzar of Babylon put Gedaliah son of Ahikam son of Shaphan in
charge of the people whom he left in the land of Judah. 23 When
the officers of the troops and their men heard that the king of
Babylon had put Gedaliah in charge, they came to Gedaliah at
Mizpah with Ishmael son of Nethaniah, Johanan son of Kareah,
Seraiah son of Tanhumeth the Netophathite, and Jaazaniah
son of the Maachite, together with their men. 24 Gedaliah reassured[a] them and their men, saying, "Do not be afraid [b-]of the
servants of the Chaldeans.[-b] Stay in the land and serve the king
of Babylon, and it will go well with you."

25 In the seventh month, Ishmael son of Nethaniah son of
Elishama, who was of royal descent, came with ten men, and
they struck down Gedaliah and he died; [they also killed] the
Judeans and the Chaldeans who were present with him at Mizpah. 26 And all the people, young and old, and the officers of
the troops set out and went to Egypt because they were afraid
of the Chaldeans.

27 In the thirty-seventh year of the exile of King Jehoiachin
of Judah, on the twenty-seventh day of the twelfth month,
King Evil-merodach of Babylon, in the year he became king,
[c-]took note of[-c] King Jehoiachin of Judah and released him
from prison. 28 He spoke kindly to him, and gave him a throne
above those of other kings who were with him in Babylon.

a Lit. "took an oath to them." *b-b Jer. 40.9 reads "to serve the Chaldeans."*
c-c Lit. "raised the head of."

Archeological evidence, however, as well as evidence from Ezra, which depicts significant antagonism between the Judeans who were exiled and those who remained behind in Judah, suggests that the exiles were not as extensive as these vv. suggest. **13–17:** Strikingly, the Ark is not mentioned. Some of the vessels noted were likely warehoused by the Babylonians, and later returned by the Persians in 538 (Ezra 1.7–11). **18–21:** All official perpetrators of the ill-conceived revolt and resistance were executed. Documents from Mesopotamia refer to "a city of the Judahites," indicating that deportees from Jerusalem were settled together in their own communities. Approximately twenty percent of the names in documents from this place discovered in the course of excavation are Yahwistic, that is, they are formed with some element from the name YHVH, indicating that their bearers maintained their national or religious identity in exile.

25.22–26: The first addition. The last administrative overseer of the people of Judah in the land was *Gedaliah.* His grandfather had been a high official in Josiah's cabinet (22.3), while his father had been in Josiah's court (22.12) and Jehoiakim's and had supported Jeremiah in counseling nonresistance to the Babylonians (Jer. 26.24). This was the same counsel he provided refugee bands of fighters and their leaders (v. 24). The writer of this appendix simply reported events without commenting on their meaning. **23:** *Mizpah,* the contemporary Tel en-Nasbeh, north of Jerusalem on the north-south highway, became the new administrative center (see 1 Kings 15.22). This is, ironically, the home territory of the House of Saul; the end of the monarchy is located near its beginning. **25:** The reasons for his assassination are not given in Kings. They were irrelevant to the work of the author. Jer. 40.13–41.18 makes clear that the assassin, Ishmael, was sent by Baalis, king of Ammon. Ishmael, of royal descent and dissatisfied over the Babylonian appointment of a non-Davidic ruler, may have formed a pact with Baalis, who was still fighting the Babylonians, that would have helped him to achieve rule over whatever remained of Judah. *The seventh month* is Tishri. The death of Gedaliah came to be seen as the final blow and the end of the commonwealth. It is most likely the "fast of the seventh month" referred to in Zech. 7.5; 8.19. Jewish tradition marks it by a fast on 3 Tishri, the day after Rosh Ha-Shanah (New Year). **26:** Jeremiah was among those who fled to Egypt (Jer. 43.6–7).

25.27–30: The second addition. *Jehoiachin,* son of Josiah, safe in exile since 597 BCE, was elevated in status by *Evil-merodach,* the son of

[29] His prison garments were removed, and [Jehoiachin] received regular rations by his favor for the rest of his life. [30] A
regular allotment of food was given him at the instance of the
king—an allotment for each day—all the days of his life.

Nebuchadnezzar who reigned 562–560 BCE. **28:** *Spoke kindly:* The Heb translates a technical expression in Babylonian that means to "reach an agreement, conclude a negotiation." The narrative refers to a legal grant recognizing a change in status that had far-reaching implications for Jehoiachin and the exiles. **30:** Lack of any death notice may suggest that this final note was appended before the death of Jehoiachin. The book appears to end with a glimmer of hope for the continuation of the Davidic dynasty. The detail is reported matter-of-factly, without comment. The author, perhaps living too close to the event itself, had no way of determining what significance, if any, it had. Receipts in cuneiform writing excavated in Babylon in the early 20th c. attest that rations were provided by the royal household to a person named Iaukin, identified as a "king," and to "five sons of the king of Judah." Iaukin appears to have been how Jehoiachin's name was pronounced in Babylonian. Some Judeans probably recognized him as king in exile.

ישעיה

Isaiah

ISAIAH IS PERHAPS THE BEST-LOVED of the prophetic books. It is cited more than any other prophetic text in rabbinic literature, and more haftarot are taken from Isaiah than from any other prophetic book containing the work of literary prophets. (Haftarot are the prophetic readings chanted in synagogue on the Sabbath, holidays, and fast days.) In Ashkenazic practice outside the land of Israel, nineteen haftarot are from Isaiah (twenty according to the Reform practice that assigns Isaiah 60.1–22 as the haftarah for Yom Ha-ʿatzmaʾut [Israeli Independence Day] in the Diaspora); by contrast, only nine are from Jeremiah and ten from Ezekiel. Second place goes to the books of Kings, which contributes sixteen haftarot. Isaiah is a major source of prooftexts for some of Judaism's main tenets, such as messianism, the centrality of Jerusalem, and economic and social justice. Not only rabbinic Judaism but also Christianity and Western culture have emphasized the book of Isaiah. First-time readers of Isaiah are often surprised to find that a well-known expression, a famous quotation, or even a favorite song comes from or is based on Isaiah. See, for example, 2.2–4; 6.3; 9.1; 9.5; 11.6–9; 12.3; 22.13; 32.17; 35.10; 40.1; 40.3; 52.2; 53.1–13; 56.7; 60.1; 62.5; 62.6; 66.10. (Some of these vv. will be more familiar to people who attend synagogue, some to people who attend Sabbath meals, some to people who attend performances of Handel's *Messiah*.)

Most passages in this book are poetry, often of a highly complex and elusive sort. It is not always clear where a particular prophecy begins and ends, and, especially in the first half of the book, it is sometimes uncertain whether a given passage intends to comfort or castigate the nation. In many cases, verb forms are ambiguous, and we cannot be sure whether the passage predicts crucial events that will take place in the future or meditates on events that have already occurred. As a result, it is impossible to read quickly through Isaiah the way one might read a biblical book that tells a story, or even a book whose poems or sermons are demarcated in a fairly clear manner (such as the book of Psalms or Jeremiah). A reader will need to read slowly, often re-read a passage several times before its meaning comes through. Rather than reading the whole book from beginning to end, like a novel, it is best to approach the book as a collection of texts or an anthology, in which each passage demands careful attention and contemplation. Keeping in mind the historical setting of each prophecy will also aid the reader greatly, although sometimes its setting, which would influence how we understand the unit, is not specified and is disputed by modern scholars.

The book of Isaiah is one of the most complex prophetic books. It contains at least two distinct sections, dating from two entirely different eras. Chs 1–39 are, in large part, the product of a prophet who lived in Jerusalem during the 8th c. BCE. As early as the Middle Ages, however, the great rabbinic commentator Abraham Ibn Ezra recognized that chs 40 and following reflect another setting altogether, which he identified as the Babylonian exile of the 6th c. BCE. Similarly, Shadal (Samuel David Luzzato, a rabbinic exegete who lived during the 19th c.) maintained that chs 40–66 were addressed to the Judean exiles in Babylonia and were not published until some time after 586 BCE (though Shadal still claimed that the 8th c. Isaiah had written them). All modern scholars share a perspective similar to Ibn Ezra's and believe that chs 40–66 (as well as 34–35) were composed during and after the Babylonian exile in the 6th century. For that reason, chs 1–39 and 40–66 are addressed separately in the introductory comments below.

Isaiah 1–39

THE PROPHET ISAIAH, the son of Amoz, lived in Jerusalem during the last half of the 8th c. BCE. His prophecies are deeply rooted in his time and place, and many of them address current events of his day. Unfortunately, only rarely does he tell us what these events are (his audience, of course, would have known immediately, since they were living through them as well). As a result, scholars frequently need to reconstruct the political or historical settings of his prophecies; some of the major events will be reviewed here. During the 8th c. BCE, the Assyrian empire (located in what we know today as northern Iraq and southeastern Turkey) began to grow in power and influence. It put more and more pressure on the small kingdoms along the eastern coast of the Mediterranean Sea, including Judah and Israel. These countries sometimes accepted Assyria as their overlord, becoming vassals who paid the Assyrian king tribute and relied on him for defense. At other times, they attempted to revolt against Assyria, often relying on Egypt as an ally. Usually, these revolts ended disastrously. In fact, the Northern Kingdom of Israel was destroyed by the Assyrians after one such revolt in 722 BCE, and much of its population was deported and dispersed throughout the Assyrian empire. For Isaiah, the rise of Assyria presented a pressing religious question, central to his recorded prophecies: To what extent should the Judeans attempt to confront their enemies using the usual military and diplomatic means (i.e., entering into alliances with other nations), and to what extent should the Judeans stay free of alliances and rely solely on God to protect them? Isaiah strongly preferred the latter option. A second major trend in Isaiah's day was the growth of large estates owned by aristocrats and the consequent impoverishment of the peasantry. Isaiah, like his contemporaries Micah and Amos, spoke out strongly against the accumulation of great wealth and the haughtiness of the rich.

Several main themes emerge from Isaiah's prophecies. Isaiah believed that Jerusalem, the holy city, would never fall to Judah's enemies. He emphasized social and economic justice. He referred repeatedly to the remnant of Israel, who would survive an enormous catastrophe that God would send to punish the nation for its lack of faith and its hypocrisy. This remnant would serve as the kernel from which a purified Israel would be renewed. (By definition, Jerusalem would be at the core of the remnant, since it would never fall.) He anticipated the dawn of a new era in which all nations would recognize the one true God. Each nation would be satisfied with its own land and would not covet other lands. Consequently empires—and warfare—would exist no more. During this new era the Judean king, a descendant of David, would rule all Israel in perfect justice. (From this set of ideas, later Judaism would construct the idea of the Messiah and the messianic era, though Isaiah never calls the future ideal Davidic king the Messiah.) Common to all these ideas is Isaiah's stress that only God can be great; all other haughty things (whether rich people, large empires, or high mountains) would be reduced to their proper place at the end of days. All sin, for Isaiah, stems from the failure to recognize that God alone can be exalted.

Isaiah's prophecies are remarkable for their lack of oracles of vengeance against Judah's enemies. Assyria and Egypt would be punished in the future for their haughtiness and idolatry, but not for their treatment of Israel and Judah. After all, it was God who sent them to attack Israel and Judah in the first place. Once they had been taken to account for their haughtiness, they would be restored and live in peace, recognizing the one true God. Thus their fate, for worse and then for better, is identical to that of Israel.

Many modern scholars believe that large sections of Isaiah chs 1–33 were written by additional prophets and scribes who lived later than the historical Isaiah in the 8th century. Others, including many leading Jewish biblical critics, attribute most or all of these chs to Isaiah himself. The annotations treat this material as largely dating to the 8th century, with a few possible exceptions (in particular, chs 13, 24–27, and 30.18–26). Chs 34–35 belong to the same time period as chs 40–66. Chs 36–39 narrate certain events in which Isaiah played an important role. They were not written by Isaiah but are taken and modified from the book of Kings.

Isaiah chs 1–39 contains the following subsections: Ch 1: Introductory prophecy, covering Isaiah's main themes. Chs 2–12: Prophecies concerning Judah and Jerusalem. Chs 13–23: Prophecies concerning many nations, including Judah but focusing on foreign peoples. Chs 24–27: Prophecies concerning the end of days, in an apocalyptic style. (These are in all likelihood not by Isaiah.) Chs 28–33: Prophecies concerning the end of days. Chs 34–35: Redemption for Judah. (These too are not by Isaiah.) Chs 36–39: Narratives reworked from the book of Kings concerning the Assyrian invasion of Judah in 701 BCE and Isaiah's role in the events of that time. The book does not always follow a chronological order; the same event is sometimes treated in many different chs.

Isaiah 40–66

THESE CHS, ALONG WITH CHS 34–35, were composed at the end of the Babylonian exile and during the early Persian or postexilic period. Because the name of this prophet is unknown, scholars refer to him (or perhaps her; women served as prophets in ancient Israel, as the examples of Miriam [Exod. 15.20], Deborah [Judg. 4.4–10; 5.1], and Huldah [2 Kings 22.14] show) as Deutero-Isaiah or Second Isaiah. This prophet lived in Babylonia a generation after the Babylonian empire destroyed the Judean state and exiled much of its population. Deutero-Isaiah promised the Judean exiles that the Persians would allow them to return to their homeland and to rebuild their Temple there. Deutero-Isaiah anticipated the victory of the Persian king, Cyrus, over the Babylonian empire. From ch 49 on, the prophet seems to be living in the land of Israel; it is likely that Deutero-Isaiah moved there as soon as the Persians allowed Judean exiles to do so after Cyrus took control of Babylonia. Many scholars believe that chs 56–66 or (more likely) 54–66 were written by yet another prophet, or perhaps a group of prophets, whom they call Trito-Isaiah or Third Isaiah. According to these scholars, Trito-Isaiah was a disciple of Deutero-Isaiah, and in many respects these prophecies resemble those in chs 40–53. These prophecies are set in the land of Israel shortly after the end of the exile, and they often display a sense of disappointment or frustration with the realities of the restoration, rather than the exuberant hope that marks the prophecies in chs 40–53. It is impossible to be sure whether chs 54–66 were written by Deutero-Isaiah, a disciple, or a group of disciples, but it seems clear that chs 34–35 and 40–66 as a whole are a single literary unit: They share many features of poetic style and theological outlook. Because we can analyze them as a block, it will be simplest to refer to their anonymous author or authors as Deutero-Isaiah.

Chs 34–35 and 40–66 are first and foremost persuasive in character. Addressed to a despondent exilic and postexilic audience who have experienced a catastrophe or live in its aftermath, they attempt to convince the Judeans that the God of Israel is still powerful and still loyal to the people Israel. Deutero-Isaiah (that is, the author or authors of chs 34–35 and 40–66) proclaims in an especially insistent manner that only one God exists; this deity alone created the world and brings redemption. The author refers to God using not only masculine metaphors but feminine ones as well (see 42.13–14; 45.10; 49.14–15; 66.13). Deutero-Isaiah is an allusive poet: In every single ch of this work, save ch 34, the prophet borrows vocabulary from earlier biblical texts and reworks it in a very intricate manner, using complex and delightful wordplays, repeating similar-sounding words, or employing alliteration. (This feature is lost in translation.) Like (First) Isaiah, Deutero-Isaiah looks forward to the dawn of a new era, but no mention is made of the expectation that a descendant of King David (or any other human being, for that matter) will reign as king in the rebuilt Jerusalem. Rather, God alone will rule over all creation in that day. Thus Deutero-Isaiah believes in a messianic era, but not in a personal Messiah. Initially, Deutero-Isaiah predicted that the return to Zion at the time of the Persian king Cyrus would usher in the renewal of the Judean commonwealth, the era of peace among all nations, and the end of paganism the world over. In fact, the restoration did not have these far-reaching effects: Judah became not an independent kingdom directly ruled by God but the poor and insignificant Persian province of Yehud; relatively few exiles availed themselves of the opportunity to return to Zion; and the world as a whole remained unchanged. Still, Deutero-Isaiah continued to predict in chs 49 and following that a larger-scale ingathering of exiles would occur and that the new world order would eventually materialize.

These chs contain the following subsections: Chs 40–48: Prophecies delivered to the exiles in Babylonia, predicting the restoration of Zion and the downfall of Babylon; the tone of these is excited and hopeful. Chs 49–57: Prophecies concerning Zion and the renewal of the community there. Their tone remains hopeful, but some disappointment becomes evident. Chs 58–66 and 34–35: Further prophecies concerning the coming of a new age, expressed with a greater sense of frustration at the failure of the earlier prophecies to materialize but with enduring hope in the older predictions (see, e.g., chs 60–62), and also with a notable emphasis on the distinction between faithful Judeans and impious or corrupt ones.

We do not know when, or why, the prophecies of Deutero-Isaiah were combined with those of Isaiah son of Amoz. The strong emphasis in both literary corpora on God's universal kingship, the messianic era, and the future exaltation of Zion may have suggested to ancient editors that these texts belonged together. In fact, there are no extant remnants of two (or three) separate books of Isaianic prophecies. Already at the beginning of the 2nd c. BCE, the Jewish sage Ben Sirach (whose writings are preserved in the Apocryphya, but not in the Jewish Bible) knew a version of the book of Isaiah that combined both blocks of material (see Sirach [Ecclesiasticus] 48.20, 24–25). The great scroll of Isaiah from the Dead Sea Scrolls (dating to the late 2nd c. BCE) also contains the entire book of Isaiah as we know it today.

[BENJAMIN D. SOMMER]

1 The prophecies of Isaiah son of Amoz, who prophesied concerning Judah and Jerusalem in the reigns of Uzziah, Jotham, Ahaz, and Hezekiah, kings of Judah.

2 Hear, O heavens, and give ear, O earth,
For the LORD has spoken:
"I reared children and brought them up—
And they have rebelled against Me!
3 An ox knows its owner,
An ass its master's crib:

1.1: Superscription. Like most prophetic books, this one begins with a title written by an editor indicating the author and the time during which the author works; cf. Jer. 1.1–3, Hos. 1.1, Amos 1.1, Mic. 1.1. It suggests that Isaiah prophesied between about 740 and 700 BCE.

1.2–31: A poem of indictment and hope. Some view this ch as a single speech that is especially

Israel does not know,
My people takes no thought."

4 Ah, sinful nation!
People laden with iniquity!
Brood of evildoers!
Depraved children!
They have forsaken the LORD,
Spurned the Holy One of Israel,
Turned their backs [on Him].

5 Why do you seek further beatings,
That you continue to offend?
Every head is ailing,
And every heart is sick.
6 From head to foot
No spot is sound:
All bruises, and welts,
And festering sores—
Not pressed out, not bound up,
Not softened with oil.
7 Your land is a waste,
Your cities burnt down;
Before your eyes, the yield of your soil
Is consumed by strangers—
A wasteland [a]-as overthrown by strangers!-[a]
8 Fair[b] Zion is left
Like a booth in a vineyard,
Like a hut in a cucumber field,
Like a city beleaguered.
9 Had not the LORD of Hosts
Left us some survivors,
We should be like Sodom,
Another Gomorrah.

a-a Emendation yields "like Sodom overthrown." *b Lit. "Daughter."*

comprehensive in subject matter and biting in tone. Alternatively, it may be a summary of the contents of the book as a whole, written specifically to be an introduction, probably to chs 1–33, but perhaps to the final form of the book (cf. 1.28–31 with 66.24). Much of this ch (vv. 1–27) is read as the haftarah, or prophetic reading, on the Sabbath preceding Tish'ah be'av, which commemorates the destruction of the Temple. This section is thus seen as offering theological justification for that event.

1.2–20: The indictment: complaint, threats, call for repentance. This section is framed by the words, "For the LORD has spoken," which appear in vv. 2 and (with a slight variation) 20. Such framing devices often indicate the extent of a literary unit in biblical literature. **2–4:** The poem consists of a legal complaint concerning covenant violation by the Israelites, who are depicted as ungrateful and also less intelligent than farm animals. In ancient Israelite thinking, heaven and earth serve as witnesses to the covenant between God and Israel (see Deut. 4.26; 32.1). They replace deities who would serve as witnesses in other ancient Near Eastern cultures; hence God calls on them to hear the charges against Israel. **5–9:** A metaphorical description of Israel's punishment (vv. 5–6) leads to a more specific description (vv. 7–8): Judah will be invaded and Jerusalem put under siege (indeed, Assyrians devastated Judah and surrounded Jerusalem in 701; see introductory annotations to chs 36–37 and to ch 29). The phrasing in v. 7 borrows quite precisely from the rhetoric of the Assyrian kings who invaded Judah, which is known from Akkadian documents. From this and other borrowings from Assyrian royal propaganda throughout First Isaiah (see also 8.7–8, 10.13, 14.8, 14.25), it is evident that Isaiah was deeply familiar with the texts that Assyrian imperial officials used to inculcate loyalty and fear among their vassals and especially among elite members of the kingdom's capital cities. A well-educated Jerusalemite, Isaiah was a member of such an elite, and from his frequent reference to Assyrian depictions of their own kings and armies it is clear that he knew these texts and images.

8–9: Zion's inviolability. Here this topic, which will play a large role in chs 1–39, is introduced: Though Judah will be devastated and Jerusalem (also known as Zion) threatened, Isaiah asserts, the city will never fall, according to Isaiah. The same assertion also appears in several of the Psalms (e.g., 46, 48, 87). Jeremiah, who lived in a later period, objected vigorously to this idea, insisting that God would allow Jerusalem to fall if the people's behavior warranted such a severe punishment (see, e.g., Jer. 7.1–20). Later biblical and Jewish writers respond in various ways to the failure of Isaiah's prophecies regarding Jerusalem's eternal status.

10 Hear the word of the LORD,
You chieftains of Sodom;
Give ear to our God's instruction,
You folk of Gomorrah!
11 "What need have I of all your sacrifices?"
Says the LORD.
"I am sated with burnt offerings of rams,
And suet of fatlings,
And blood of bulls;
And I have no delight
In lambs and he-goats.
12 That you come to appear before Me—
Who asked that [a-]of you?
Trample My courts 13 no more;
Bringing oblations is futile,[-a]
Incense is offensive to Me.
New moon and sabbath,
Proclaiming of solemnities,
[b-]Assemblies with iniquity,[-b]
I cannot abide.
14 Your new moons and fixed seasons
Fill Me with loathing;
They are become a burden to Me,
I cannot endure them.
15 And when you lift up your hands,
I will turn My eyes away from you;
Though you pray at length,
I will not listen.
Your hands are stained with crime—
16 Wash yourselves clean;
Put your evil doings
Away from My sight.
Cease to do evil;
17 Learn to do good.
Devote yourselves to justice;
[c-]Aid the wronged.[-c]
Uphold the rights of the orphan;
Defend the cause of the widow.

18 "Come, [c-]let us reach an understanding,"[-c]
—says the LORD.
"Be your sins like crimson,
They can turn snow-white;
Be they red as dyed wool,

a-a Others "To trample My courts? / 13 Bring no more vain oblations."
b-b Septuagint "Fast and assembly"; cf. Joel 1.14.
c-c Meaning of Heb. uncertain.

10–20: Rite and right. The sacrifices and prayers offered by Isaiah's contemporaries are useless because they are not accompanied by ethical action. This is not a condemnation of sacrifices per se, but a critique of the lack of ethical behavior, a claim that sacrifices are not automatically efficacious. This is a common prophetic theme; see esp. Amos 5.21–25; Isa. 58.1–9. **10–15:** God's attitude toward ritual. According to the translation of vv. 12–13, God rejects sacrifice altogether; but according to the alternative in the translators' note *a-a*, God rejects only the vain rituals of unethical people. Both renderings are defensible, but to arrive at the translation in NJPS's main text one must emend the Hebrew text of the MT in several respects, while the alternative in the translators' note renders the MT precisely. Rabbinic commentators prefer the translation in the note (cf. Prov. 21.27). **10:** *Sodom ... Gomorrah:* Isaiah compares Jerusalem's inhabitants to those of the most notorious and sinful Canaanite cities, which were completely destroyed, according to biblical tradition. See Gen. ch 19. **11:** *All* ("rov") *your sacrifices,* more precisely, "the multitude" or "abundance of your sacrifices." Isaiah objects to the idea that offering a larger amount of sacrifices (see Mic. ch 6). is somehow more pious or more praiseworthy than offering a smaller number—which would mean that wealthy or ostentatious people please God more than those who are poor or modest. **15:** *Lift up your hands:* People lifted their hands when praying in ancient Israel; cf. Exod. 9.29, 33; 1 Kings 8.38, 54. *Though you pray at length,* or "pray abundantly" ("tarbu tefillah"). The phrase uses the same verbal root ("r-b-b") found in the word "all your sacrifices/the abundance of sacrifices" in v. 11. For Isaiah, what matters is the quality of prayer and the ethical behavior of the people praying, not the quantity or length of the prayer. Isaiah's attitude towards prayer in this v. is identical to his attitude towards sacrifice in v. 11. According to this passage, God does

They can become like fleece."
19 If, then, you agree and give heed,
You will eat the good things of the earth;
20 But if you refuse and disobey,
[a]You will be devoured [by] the sword.[-a]—
For it was the LORD who spoke.

21 Alas, she has become a harlot,
The faithful city
That was filled with justice,
Where righteousness dwelt—
But now murderers.
22 Your[b] silver has turned to dross;
[c]Your wine is cut with water.[-c]
23 Your rulers are rogues
And cronies of thieves,
Every one avid for presents
And greedy for gifts;
They do not judge the case of the orphan,
And the widow's cause never reaches them.

24 Assuredly, this is the declaration
Of the Sovereign, the LORD of Hosts,
The Mighty One of Israel:
"Ah, I will get satisfaction from My foes;
I will wreak vengeance on My enemies!
25 I will turn My hand against you,
And smelt out your dross [d]as with lye,[-d]
And remove all your slag:
26 I will restore your magistrates as of old,
And your counselors as of yore.
After that you shall be called
City of Righteousness, Faithful City."

27[e] Zion shall be saved in the judgment;
Her repentant ones, in the retribution.[f]
28 But rebels and sinners shall all be crushed,
And those who forsake the LORD shall perish.

29 Truly, you[g] shall be shamed
Because of the terebinths you desired,
And you shall be confounded
Because of the gardens you coveted.

a-a Or "you will be fed the sword." *b I.e., Jerusalem's.*
c-c Meaning of Heb. uncertain. *d-d Emendation yields "in a crucible"; cf. 48.10.*
e Others "Zion shall be saved by justice, / Her repentant ones by righteousness."
f For this meaning cf. 5.16; 10.22. *g Heb. "they."*

not prefer prayer over sacrifice; rather, God rejects both prayer and sacrifice when then the people offering them act with cruelty toward the poor and the weak and with hypocrisy toward God. **16–20:** The unit does not confine itself to complaint but ends with an invitation to repentance and ethical action. Calls to repentance are rare in Isaiah, especially compared with the work of other prophets; they never appear from ch 6 through 31.6. This suggests that Isaiah's main mission was to explain to Judah what was happening, rather than to urge it to change its ways.

1.21–27: Lament and hope. Like the last unit, this unit is defined by a framing device involving repeated vocabulary. In both vv. 21 and 26–27 we hear *faithful city, righteousness* and the root "sh-p-t," meaning *justice* (Heb "mishpat") in v. 21 and both *magistrates* (better, "judges," Heb "shofetayikh") and *justice* in 26–27 (see translators' note *e*). **21–25:** In the ancient Near East, laments for a city typically mourn a destruction that has already occurred, but this lament mourns the city's sinfulness, which will lead to a disaster in the future. **21:** *The faithful city that was filled with ... murderers:* Here Isaiah may allude to the assassinations of three political leaders that took place in Jerusalem in the late 9th c. and early 8th c. (Queen Athaliah [see 2 Kings 11.1–16], King Joash [2 Kings 12.20–21], and King Amaziah [2 Kings 14.19–20]). **26–27:** Having been punished, Zion will again know justice and faithfulness. A new name is given to the reformed Jerusalem; cf. 62.2–4; Ezek. 48.35.

1.28–31: The fiery punishment. Does Isaiah suggest a contrast between the sinners whose end is described here and the reformed Zion described in the preceding vv., since Zion will be spared the sinners' fate? Or are residents of the sinful city as a whole the subject of these vv.? The prophet leaves the answer unclear, perhaps intentionally; it will be given by the inhabitants of Jerusalem themselves; through their behavior, they will lead God to decide whom to punish.

2.1: Another superscription (cf. 1.1), whose presence suggests that the following texts (chs 2–4 or 2–5) were once an independent collection of Isaiah's prophecies. The present book may be built from discrete documents, often several chs long, which presumably preserved Isaiah's speeches. These documents are not organized in chronological order, and the same event is often treated in more than one block of material.

2.2–4.6: The Jerusalem of the future and of the present. This long section begins (2.2–4) and ends (4.2–6) with a description of Jerusalem as it should and will be: a city of peace, equity, and divine Presence. The long middle section (2.6–4.1) focuses on the sinfulness of the current inhabitants and their grim fate. Running throughout this section is imagery relating to height: All that is elevated is brought low, since the LORD alone deserves to be exalted. One modest hill is raised up in 2.2—the hill is the location of the LORD's own Temple.

2.2–4: An eschatological poem. One of the most famous texts in the Bible, this poem is also found, with minor variations, in Mic. 4.1–4. Exactly how these two passages are related is uncertain. **2–3:** *The Mount of the LORD's House* is the Temple Mount (which today is bordered on the west by the Western Wall). *Gaze,* alternatively, "flow towards." *Instruction,* alternatively, "law" (Heb "torah"), or, as in Deut. 17.8–11, Hag. 2.11–13, and Mal. 2.7, "ruling(s)." See further on v. 4. The term *Zion* in the Bible refers to the Temple Mount (and, by extension, more broadly to the whole city of Jerusalem), but never to the hill currently called by that name, which is located immediately south of the present-day Armenian quarter, southwest of the biblical Mount Zion. **4:** The prophet does not imagine a future without borders or distinct nationalities. International conflicts will still occur,

30 For you shall be like a terebinth
Wilted of leaf,
And like a garden
That has no water,
31 [a]Stored wealth[a] shall become as tow,
And he who amassed it a spark;
And the two shall burn together,
With none to quench.

2 The word that Isaiah son of Amoz prophesied concerning Judah and Jerusalem.

2 In the days to come,
The Mount of the LORD's House
Shall stand firm above the mountains
And tower above the hills;
And all the nations
Shall gaze on it with joy.
3 And the many peoples shall go and say:
"Come,
Let us go up to the Mount of the LORD,
To the House of the God of Jacob;
That He may instruct us in His ways,
And that we may walk in His paths."
For instruction shall come forth[b] from Zion,
The word of the LORD from Jerusalem.
4 Thus He will judge among the nations
And arbitrate for the many peoples,
And they shall beat their swords into plowshares[c]
And their spears into pruning hooks:
Nation shall not take up
Sword against nation;
They shall never again know[d] war.

5 O House of Jacob!
Come, let us walk
By the light of the LORD.
6 For you have forsaken [the ways of] your people,
O House of Jacob!
[e]For they are full [of practices] from the East,
And of soothsaying like the Philistines;
They abound in customs [f]of the aliens.[f]

a-a Connecting ḥason *with* ḥasan, *"to store" (23.18), and* ḥosen, *"treasure" (33.6).*
b I.e., oracles will be obtainable.
c More exactly, the iron points with which wooden plows were tipped.
d Cf. Judg. 3.2.
e Emendation yields "For they are full of divination / and have abundance of soothsaying, / Like Philistines / And like alien folk." *f-f Cf. Targum; lit. "children."*

7 Their land is full of silver and gold,
There is no limit to their treasures;
Their land is full of horses,
There is no limit to their chariots.
8 And their land is full of idols;
They bow down to the work of their hands,
To what their own fingers have wrought.
9 But man shall be humbled,
And mortal brought low—
[a]Oh, do not forgive them![a]

10 Go deep into the rock,
Bury yourselves in the ground,
Before the terror of the LORD
And His dread majesty!
11 Man's haughty look shall be brought low,
And the pride of mortals shall be humbled.
None but the LORD shall be
Exalted in that day.

12 For the LORD of Hosts has ready a day
Against all that is proud and arrogant,
Against all that is lofty—so that it is brought low:
13 Against all the cedars of Lebanon,
Tall and stately,
And all the oaks of Bashan;
14 Against all the high mountains
And all the lofty hills;
15 Against every soaring tower
And every mighty wall;
16 Against all the [b]ships of Tarshish[b]
And all the gallant barks.
17 Then man's haughtiness shall be humbled
And the pride of man brought low.
None but the LORD shall be
Exalted in that day.

18 As for idols, they shall vanish completely.
19 And men shall enter caverns in the rock
And hollows in the ground—
Before the terror of the LORD
And His dread majesty,
When He comes forth to overawe the earth.
20 On that day, men shall fling away,
To the [c]flying foxes[c] and the bats,

a-a Meaning of Heb. uncertain. Emendation yields "And their idols with them"; cf. vv. 17–21. *b-b Probably a type of large ship.* *c-c Exact meaning of Heb. uncertain.*

but nations will no longer resolve them through warfare. Instead, they will submit to arbitration at Mount Zion. The Temple will become the headquarters of a divine Security Council with a membership of One and unsurpassed ability to ensure compliance. The nations will flow to Zion in order to receive a "torah" or legal ruling concerning their disputes, with the result that warfare is no longer relevant, since all conflicts will be resolved definitively by the divine pronouncement at the Jerusalem Temple. This text does not explain how the divine pronouncement is given to the nations, but ch 11 suggests that the Davidic king of the ideal future, who is also a prophet, may deliver the oracle to the nations who come to Zion for compulsory arbitration. If so, it is striking that this Davidic king is not mentioned in this passage, which focuses more on a messianic age than on a Davidic messiah.

2.5–22: The current situation and its results. This passage seems to be a warning regarding the future. Alternatively, it may be an attempt to explain the reason for an event that has already occurred, namely the devastating earthquake during the reign of King Uzziah early in Isaiah's career (cf. Amos 1.1 and Zech. 14.5); or it may be both: by alluding back to the events of the earthquake, Isaiah intimates that the future punishment will be on a similar scale. The tense of the verbs in v. 17 is ambiguous; what NJPS renders as the future tense could, linguistically, be the past. **5–9:** Criticism of the nation's sins: magic, amassing extraordinary amounts of wealth, pursuing military power, and idolatry. All these vices embody inappropriate confidence in humanity's own powers. This confidence is not only mistaken, but offensive to God. **10–22:** The fate of the proud. Both in nature and in culture, the high will be brought low, the great will be humbled, and vanity will perish. These vv. utilize and subvert motifs known from Assyrian royal propaganda of the 8th c. BCE to describe

The idols of silver
And the idols of gold
Which they made for worshiping.
21 And they shall enter the clefts in the rocks
And the crevices in the cliffs,
Before the terror of the LORD
And His dread majesty,
When He comes forth to overawe the earth.

22 Oh, cease to glorify man,
Who has only a breath in his nostrils!
For by what does he merit esteem?

3 For lo!
The Sovereign LORD of Hosts
Will remove from Jerusalem and from Judah
Prop and stay,
Every prop of food
And every prop of water:[a]
2 Soldier and warrior,
Magistrate and prophet,
Augur and elder;
3 Captain of fifty,
Magnate and counselor,
Skilled artisan and expert enchanter;[b]
4 And He[c] will make boys their rulers,
And babes shall govern them.
5 So the people shall oppress one another—
Each oppressing his fellow:
The young shall bully the old;
And the despised [shall bully] the honored.

6 For should a man seize his brother,
[d]In whose father's house there is clothing:[d]
"Come, be a chief over us,
And let this ruin[e] be under your care,"
7 The other will thereupon protest,
"I will not be a dresser of wounds,
With no food or clothing in my own house.
You shall not make me chief of a people!"

8 Ah, Jerusalem has stumbled,
And Judah has fallen,

a Emendation yields "clothing"; cf. v. 7; 4.1.
b Emendation yields "craftsman." *c Heb. "I."*
d-d Emendation yields "His father's son, saying ..."
e Meaning of Heb. uncertain. Emendation yields "wound."

the arrogance and folly of those who dare to revolt against the Assyrian empire and their grim fate in the Assyrian campaign against them. (These motifs include opposition to the haughty and lofty, the punishment that involves terrifying the land, the army's movement throughout the whole land, the frightened reaction of the arrogant ones, and the glory and dread majesty of the sovereign.) Isaiah, who was deeply familiar with the Assyrian propaganda of his day (see 1.5–9 n.), uses the same motifs to describe not the temporary victory of the Assyrian empire and the majesty of the Assyrian king but the permanent victory and dread majesty of YHVH. But the object of the campaign remains the same: Israelites and Judeans are the arrogant and foolish ones; Isaiah wants to make clear, however, that their foolishness consists not primarily in only revolting against Assyria but in failing to trust YHVH. **17:** A summary of this section and, arguably, of the message of Isaiah as a whole. **22:** Another summary of the section that states a core message of First Isaiah. *Cease to glorify man:* Alternatively, "Forget about human beings"—i.e., stop paying attention to this species which is weak with respect to the great YHVH; Judah's strength and accomplishments melted away at the earthquake in Uzziah's day and will melt away again in the future.

3.1–4.1: Wealth and woe.
3.1–15: Unworthy leaders and a society in ruins. As in other passages, it is difficult to be sure whether the prophet predicts the future or describes the present. **1–7:** If this is a prediction, then the prophet announces that God will remove Judah's food and its leaders; in their place inexperienced and immature people will rule, and the nation will be desperate for the stability that legitimate authorities bring. If this is a description of the present, then he criticizes the current leadership, asserting that they are like children. Isaiah does not mention the king in this passage; the prophet attacks the

Because by word and deed
They insult the LORD,
Defying His majestic glance.
9 Their partiality in judgment[a] accuses them;
They avow their sins like Sodom,
They do not conceal them.
Woe to them! For ill
Have they served themselves.
10 (Hail[b] the just man, for he shall fare well;
He shall eat the fruit of his works.
11 Woe to the wicked man, for he shall fare ill;
As his hands have dealt, so shall it be done to him.)
12 My people's rulers are babes,
It is governed by women.[c]
O my people!
Your leaders are misleaders;
They have confused the course of your paths.

13 The LORD stands up to plead a cause,
He rises to champion peoples.[d]
14 The LORD will bring this charge
Against the elders and officers of His people:
"It is you who have ravaged the vineyard;
That which was robbed from the poor is in your houses.
15 How dare you crush My people
And grind the faces of the poor?"
—says my Lord GOD of Hosts.

16 The LORD said:
"Because the daughters of Zion
Are so vain
And walk with [e]heads thrown back,[e]
With roving eyes,
And with mincing gait,
Making a tinkling with their feet"—
17 My Lord will bare[f] the pates
Of the daughters of Zion,
The LORD will uncover their heads.

18 In that day, my LORD will strip off the finery[g] of the anklets, the fillets, and the crescents; 19 of the eardrops, the bracelets, and the veils; 20 the turbans, the armlets, and the sashes; of the talismans

a So Targum; cf. Deut. 1.17; 16.19. *b Emendation yields "Happy is."*
c Emendation yields "boys"; cf. v. 4 (and v. 5).
d Septuagint "His people"; cf. vv. 14, 15. *e-e Lit. "throats bent back."*
f So Saadia. To bare a woman's head in public was an intolerable humiliation; cf. Mishnah Baba Kamma 8.6.
g Many of the articles named in vv. 18–24 cannot be identified with certainty.

aristocracy and high government officials and predicts their demise, but he does not look forward to the downfall of the Davidic royal dynasty, which he revered. **1:** *Will remove:* The Heb verb is a participle, which can correspond to any time frame, though the use of the particle "hinneh" earlier in the sentence, in combination with the participle, suggests that the verb refers to an imminent action. **8–15:** The reasons for the crisis: Judah's leaders are corrupt. Here again the theme of hubris appears; rather than depending on divinely ordained standards of equity, they give judgments that magnify their own positions and wealth.

3.16–4.1: The haughtiness of wealthy women, and their downfall. Most passages in Isaiah focus on the misdeeds of men (e.g., in the previous few vv.: the evil man in v. 10, the male leaders ["nogesav"] in v. 12, the elders and princes in v. 14, and note the masculine pronouns in v. 15). This passage is distinctive in that it attends, rather atypically for the prophets, to the sins of women rather than those of men (see also Amos 4.1–3). The vertical imagery in the passage is significant, and quite typical of Isaiah: Women who are metaphorically too high (i.e., too wealthy and too eager to display their wealth) will be brought low. While in vv. 1–15 the prophet starts with punishment and then describes the reason for it, in this passage he describes the ostentatious affluence first (vv. 16–23) and then the punishment (v. 24).

3.25–4.1: The punishment. The two themes of 3.1–23—corrupt and unworthy male leaders and immoral women—combine in a description of a single punishment suitable to both. The men are killed, leaving the women bereaved and impoverished.

4.2–6: Another eschatological poem: redemption in Zion. Very abruptly, the tone changes, and the prophet describes the outcome of the cleansing punishment. The passage closely resembles 2.2–4 in outlook, but it focuses on Israel and Zion rather than on the universal aspect of God's reign. V. 4 mentions *the daughters of Zion,* and thus may be seen as a continuation or response to the previous oracle. **2:** *In that day:* Redemption will come at the same time as, or immediately after, the disaster that will threaten Zion. *Radiance ... splendor,* lit. "branch ... fruit." The former term alludes to the royal line, as indicated by its use elsewhere in the Bible (Jer. 23.5; 33.15; Zech. 3.8; 6.12) and also in Phoenician. Following this sense, the Targum translates it as "Messiah." Some rabbinic commentators interpret it as a reference to King Hezekiah, who reigned at the very end of the 8th c. In the latter interpretation the passage does not deal with the far-away future but with political conditions of the 8th c., and Isaiah may have regarded the ideal future to which it looks forward as close at hand. *The survivors of Israel:* If the passage is closely focused on the situation in the late 8th c., this phrase, and all of the following v., may refer to refugees who fled from northern Israel after its destruction by Assyria late in the 8th c. Archeological evidence suggests that these refugees settled in Jerusalem (which vastly expanded in size then) to escape the Assyrians (translate: "those who survived are in Zion, those who remained, in Jerusalem"). **3:** *Shall be called holy:* With these words Isaiah may be asserting that northern Israelite refugees have a right to settle in Jerusalem, and that Jerusalem is in fact honored to give them a new home. **4–6:** *Cloud* and *smoke* with

and the amulets; 21 the signet rings and the nose rings; 22 of the festive robes, the mantles, and the shawls; the purses, 23 the lace gowns, and the linen vests; and the kerchiefs and the capes.

24 And then—
Instead of perfume, there shall be rot;
And instead of an apron, a rope;
Instead of a diadem of beaten-work,
A shorn head;
Instead of a rich robe,
A girding of sackcloth;
[a-]A burn instead of beauty.[-a]

25 Her[b] men shall fall by the sword,
Her fighting manhood in battle;
26 And her gates shall lament and mourn,
And [c-]she shall be emptied,[-c]
Shall sit on the ground.

4 In that day, seven women shall take hold of one man,
saying,
"We will eat our own food
And wear our own clothes;
Only let us be called by your name—
Take away our disgrace!"
2[d] In that day,
The radiance of the LORD
Will lend beauty and glory,
And the splendor of [e-]the land[-e]
[Will give] dignity and majesty,
To the survivors of Israel.
3 And those who remain in Zion
And are left in Jerusalem—
All who are inscribed for life in Jerusalem—
Shall be called holy.

4 When my Lord has washed away
The filth of [f-]the daughters of Zion,[-f]
And from Jerusalem's midst
Has rinsed out her infamy—

a-a The complete Isaiah scroll from Qumran, hereafter 1QIs[a]*, reads "For shame shall take the place of beauty"; cf. note f at 3.17.*
b I.e., Zion's; cf. vv. 16, 17; Heb. "your."
c-c Meaning of Heb. uncertain. Emendation yields "her wall"; cf. Lam. 2.8.
d For the interpretation of this verse, cf. 28.5. For "radiance," cf. Septuagint and the Syriac ṣemḥa, *and for "splendor," cf. the meaning of* peri *in 10.12.*
e-e Emendation yields "my Lord"; cf. the parallelism (in reverse order) in 3.17.
f-f Emendation yields "Daughter Zion," i.e., Zion personified; cf. 1.8 and note.

In a spirit of judgment
And in a spirit of purging—

5 the LORD will create[a] over the whole shrine and meeting place
of Mount Zion cloud by day and smoke with a glow of flaming
fire by night. Indeed, over [b-]all the glory[-b] shall hang a canopy,
6 which shall serve as a pavilion for shade from heat by day and
as a shelter for protection against drenching rain.

5 Let me sing for my beloved
A song of my lover about his vineyard.

My beloved had a vineyard
[c-]On a fruitful hill.[-c]
2 He broke the ground, cleared it of stones,
And planted it with choice vines.
He built a watchtower inside it,
He even hewed a wine press in it;
For he hoped it would yield grapes.
Instead, it yielded wild grapes.

3 "Now, then,
Dwellers of Jerusalem
And men of Judah,
You be the judges
Between Me and My vineyard:
4 What more could have been done for My vineyard
That I failed to do in it?
Why, when I hoped it would yield grapes,
Did it yield wild grapes?

5 "Now I am going to tell you
What I will do to My vineyard:
I will remove its hedge,
That it may be ravaged;
I will break down its wall,
That it may be trampled.
6 And I will [c-]make it a desolation;[-c]
It shall not be pruned or hoed,
And it shall be overgrown with briers and thistles.
And I will command the clouds
To drop no rain on it."

7 For the vineyard of the LORD of Hosts
Is the House of Israel,

fire indicate the LORD's Presence at the sanctuary; cf. Exod. 40.34–38; Num. 9.15–23; 1 Kings 8.10–12.

5.1–30: A poem of rebuke.
1–7: The song of the vineyard. A parable, in which God is the farmer and Israel the vineyard. At first, the identity of the characters is not evident, and only gradually does the audience realize that it is they themselves who are being rebuked. Nathan's parable and its explanation in 2 Sam. 12.1–12 are structured similarly. The rhetoric is designed to draw in the listeners so that, in the end, they cannot refute the criticism leveled at them. **7:** The English attempts to capture the wordplay of the Heb mishpat-mispaḥ and tzedakah-tze'akah.

a Emendation yields "spread"; cf. Ps. 105.39.
b-b Emendation yields "His whole shrine." *c-c Meaning of Heb. uncertain.*

8–24: A series of divine complaints, each introduced by the word *Ah* (Heb "hoy"). The term may simply be a call for attention ("Hey!"), or it may be an exclamation of woe concerning a punishment that will soon take place ("Warning!"). **8–10:** The first complaint is directed against wealthy landowners who expand their own property at the expense of farmers of modest means. The eviction of peasants and the growth of massive estates was a major problem in the 8th c. (cf. Amos ch 2; Mic. ch 2). In Israelite thought (as reflected in both prophetic literature and the Torah), land was ideally supposed to remain in the hands of the descendants of its original owner in perpetuity, so that both tremendous wealth and penury would become unlikely. The Torah includes several laws to prevent poor or modest families from losing their land (or enabling them to get it back on some guaranteed and regular basis after losing it); see Lev. 25.8; Num. 27.1–11, 35; Deut. 27.17. **11–17:** The second complaint: parties instead of piety. Appropriately, the people whose appetite is insatiable will feed the insatiable appetite of *Sheol,* the underworld (v. 14). See further 14.9–11 n. and 26.19 n. **13:** *Suffer exile* may refer to the fate of northern Israelites in 722 BCE, when the Assyrians destroyed the remnant of the Northern Kingdom and exiled its leadership, or it may refer to the loss of land and small-scale deportations that occurred earlier in the 8th century, when portions of the Northern Kingdom were annexed by Assyria and by Arameans states. This is a possibility if the verb *suffer exile* is in fact a past tense, which is likely. Alternatively, this verb may predict the fate of the southern Judeans, some of whom will be exiled even though Zion will not fall.

And the seedlings he lovingly tended
Are the men of Judah.
[a]And He hoped for justice,
But behold, injustice;
For equity,
But behold, iniquity!

8 Ah,
Those who add house to house
And join field to field,
Till there is room for none but you
To dwell in the land!
9 In my hearing [said] the LORD of Hosts:
Surely, great houses
Shall lie forlorn,
Spacious and splendid ones
Without occupants.
10 For ten acres of vineyard
Shall yield just one *bath,*[b]
And a field sown with a *homer* of seed
Shall yield a mere *ephah.*

11 Ah,
Those who chase liquor
From early in the morning,
And till late in the evening
Are inflamed by wine!
12 [c]Who, at their banquets,
Have[c] lyre and lute,
Timbrel, flute, and wine;
But who never give a thought
To the plan of the LORD,
And take no note
Of what He is designing.
13 Assuredly,
My people will suffer exile
For not giving heed,
Its multitude victims of hunger
And its masses parched with thirst.
14 Assuredly,
Sheol has opened wide its gullet
And parted its jaws in a measureless gape;

a *This sentence contains two word-plays: "And He hoped for* mishpaṭ, *And there is* mispaḥ *[exact meaning uncertain]; / For* ṣedaqah, *But there is* ṣeʿaqah *[lit. 'outcry']."*
b *I.e., of wine. The* bath *was the liquid equivalent of the* ephah; *and the* ḥomer *was ten* baths *or* ephahs *(Ezek. 45.11).*
c-c *Emendation yields "whose interests are"* (mishʿehem, *from* shaʿah *"to turn to," 17.7, 8; 31.1).*

And down into it shall go,
That splendor and tumult,
That din and revelry.
15 Yea, man is bowed,
And mortal brought low;
Brought low is the pride of the haughty.
16 And the LORD of Hosts is exalted by ~~judgment~~, justice
The Holy God proved holy by ~~retribution~~. righteousness
17[a] Then lambs shall graze
As in their meadows,
And strangers shall feed
On the ruins of the stout.

18 Ah,
Those who haul sin with cords of falsehood
And iniquity as with cart ropes!
19 Who say,[b]
"Let Him speed, let Him hasten His purpose,
If we are to give thought;
Let the plans of the Holy One of Israel
Be quickly fulfilled,
If we are to give heed."

20 Ah,
Those who call evil good
And good evil;
Who present darkness as light
And light as darkness;
Who present bitter as sweet
And sweet as bitter!
21 Ah,
Those who are so wise—
In their own opinion;
So clever—
In their own judgment!

22 Ah,
Those who are so doughty—
As drinkers of wine,
And so valiant—
As mixers of drink!
23 Who vindicate him who is in the wrong
In return for a bribe,
And withhold vindication

a Meaning of verse uncertain. Emendation yields "The lambs shall graze / In the pasture of the fat [rams], / And the kids shall feed / On the ranges of the stout [bucks]." The lambs and the kids are the poor and the rams and bucks are the rich oppressors (cf. Ezek. 34.17–22). *b By way of retort to v. 12.*

18–19: The third complaint: The people in v. 19 are guilty in one of two ways. The sinners quoted speak sarcastically and do not believe that God will in fact fulfill His purpose (so according to the translators' note *b*). Or the v. quotes faithful Israelites who impatiently demand that God act immediately. **20–21:** Two brief complaints dealing with sophistry. **22–24:** The last complaint mixes the themes of vv. 8–10 and 11–17. Misplaced abilities are focused on fine tasting wine; officials pervert justice for money. **22:** *Doughty*, or "mighty, heroic" (Heb "gibbor").

24: *Instruction*, Heb "torah," but in this time period, not the Torah as we have it.

25–30: The coming disaster. In this unit, placed here as a response to the woe oracles that indict the nation, God is portrayed as bludgeoning them, both through an earthquake that has already taken place (v. 25) and—in greater detail—a foreign invasion yet to come. **26:** *Ensign:* God acts as commander of the foreign army, showing them the way to Israel. **30:** This seems to belong to the description of the punishment. Elsewhere in Isaiah, however, the portrayal of a devastating invasion suddenly switches to a report of the invaders' defeat (see 28.16 n.; 29.14 n.; 31.5 n.; 32.15–20 n.). If translators' note *d* is correct, this v. may have originally functioned this way. Some have suggested that this passage originally belonged after 10.1–4, with which it has much in common.

6.1–13: Prophetic commissioning. Many read this passage as a description of Isaiah's initiation into prophecy and hence view it as the earliest text of Isaiah's career. They note similarities between this text and others describing the inauguration of prophets (Exod. chs 3–4; Exod. ch 6; Jer. ch 1; Ezek. chs 1–3). Others, pointing out that the ch does not appear at the beginning of the book, suggest that it depicts the beginning of a new stage in Isaiah's career; he receives a new assignment that differs from earlier ones. Supporting this notion is that the first five chs call on the Judeans to repent, but from this ch until the last prophecy of Isaiah son of Amoz, the prophet does not call on the Israelites to repent; 6.9–10 may account for this difference.

1–4: The vision of the divine court. Isaiah sees God and the deity's retinue. This is one of many passages indicating that some biblical authors conceive of God as a physical being whom a few people can see (cf. Exod. 24.11; 33.11; Num. 12.8). On the divine court, cf. 1 Kings 22.19–23; Job chs 1–2.

From him who is in the right.
24 Assuredly,
As straw is consumed by a tongue of fire
And hay [a]-shrivels as it burns,-[a]
Their stock shall become like rot,
And their buds shall blow away like dust.
For they have rejected the instruction of the
LORD of Hosts,
Spurned the word of the Holy One of Israel.

25 That is why
The LORD's anger was roused
Against His people,
Why He stretched out His arm against it
And struck it,
So that the mountains quaked,[b]
And its corpses lay
Like refuse in the streets.
Yet his anger has not turned back,
And His arm is outstretched still.
26 He will raise an ensign to a nation[c] afar,
Whistle to one at the end of the earth.
There it comes with lightning speed!
27 In its ranks, none is weary or stumbles,
They never sleep or slumber;
The belts on their waists do not come loose,
Nor do the thongs of their sandals break.
28 Their arrows are sharpened,
And all their bows are drawn.
Their horses' hoofs are like flint,
Their chariot wheels like the whirlwind.
29 Their roaring is like a lion's,
They roar like the great beasts;
When they growl and seize a prey,
They carry it off and none can recover it.

30 But in that day, a roaring shall resound over him like that
of the sea;[d] and then he shall look below and, behold,
Distressing darkness, with light;
Darkness, [e]-in its lowering clouds.-[e]

6 In the year that King Uzziah died, I beheld my Lord seated
on a high and lofty throne; and the skirts of His robe filled

a-a Emendation yields "is burned by flame"; cf. 33.11–12; 47.14.
b An allusion to the destructive earthquake in the reign of King Uzziah: Amos 1.1; Zech. 14.5; cf. Isa. 9.18a. *c Heb. "nations."*
d I.e., the LORD will intervene and come to his aid. Cf. 29.6–7; 30.27. This verse may constitute a transition between chaps. 8 and 9. *e-e Meaning of Heb. uncertain.*

the Temple. [2] Seraphs stood in attendance on Him. Each of them had six wings: with two he covered his face, with two he covered his legs, and with two he would fly.

3 And one would call to the other,
"Holy, holy, holy!
The LORD of Hosts!
His presence fills all the earth!"

[4] The doorposts[a] would shake at the sound of the one who
called, and the House kept filling with smoke. [5] I cried,
"Woe is me; I am lost!
For I am a man [b-]of unclean lips[-b]
And I live among a people
Of unclean lips;
Yet my own eyes have beheld
The King LORD of Hosts."

[6] Then one of the seraphs flew over to me with a live coal,
which he had taken from the altar with a pair of tongs. [7] He
touched it to my lips and declared,

"Now that this has touched your lips,
Your guilt shall depart
And your sin be purged away."

[8] Then I heard the voice of my Lord saying, "Whom shall I
send? Who will go for us?" And I said, "Here am I; send me."
[9] And He said, "Go, say to that people:
'Hear, indeed, but do not understand;
See, indeed, but do not grasp.'
10 Dull that people's mind,
Stop its ears,
And seal its eyes—

a Meaning of Heb. uncertain.
b-b I.e., speaking impiety; cf. 9.16, and contrast "pure of speech [lit. 'lip']" in Zeph. 3.9.

2: Seraphs, a heavenly being (specifically, a flying asp). Representations of seraphs who surround the heavenly throne appear in Judean art of the 8th c., including a seal presenting a picture almost identical to Isaiah's vision (first published by archaeologists in 1941). The seal belonged to a contemporary of Isaiah's named Ashna, who was a courtier of King Ahaz. Given the relatively small size of Jerusalem in the 8th c. and Isaiah's close connections with the royal court (evident in ch 7 and in chs 36–39), it is highly probable that Isaiah and Ashna knew each other. **3:** Heavenly praise. Along with a v. from Ezekiel's inaugural vision (3.12) and Ps. 146.10, this v. serves as the centerpiece of the *Kedushah* prayer, in which worshippers praise God using angelic liturgy. The *Kedushah* appears in the communal recitation of the "'amidah" (the main statutory prayer in Judaism), which requires a prayer quorum ("minyan") of ten. It is also found in services for all mornings, Sabbath afternoons, and Saturday nights in sections that can be recited in private. These vv. share several features with other biblical and ancient Jewish texts that describe angelic worship (these texts include Pss. 29; 89.6–8; 96.4; 97.7; 103.20–22; and 148.1–3; as well as several texts from the Dead Sea Scrolls, the Apocrypha and Pseudepigrapha (Ben Sirach 42.17–24 and 1 Enoch 47.2 and 61.10–11), and early Jewish mystical texts known as *heikhalot rabbati* literature. The common elements among these texts include God's kingship, glory ("kabod"), and holiness (expressed with the adjective "kadosh"); the three-fold (in some other cases, seven-fold) repetition of key vocabulary; the motif of the heavenly beings singing together or singing antiphonally (here, the seraphim call back and forth to each other).

5–7: Isaiah's reaction and purification. Isaiah fears that he will die, because he is not worthy to see God. The belief was widespread in ancient Israel that a human who saw God would die (see, e.g., Exod. 33.20). Isaiah is informed that he is an exception to this general rule when a *seraph* or angelic being purifies him and reassures him that he is safe.

8–13: The commissioning: repentance is no longer an option. Isaiah is told of his (new) mission. **8–10:** Shockingly, the prophet is not supposed to help the people understand the danger to which their sinfulness exposes them. Cf. 29.9–12. God no longer desires repentance; rather, God wants to vent divine anger on the nation. Some rabbinic commentators, unable to imagine such an interpretation, argue that the imperative verbs must be taken as future-tense verbs. Hence God does not order Isaiah to cause the people to misunderstand; rather, God predicts that they will not achieve understanding in spite of Isaiah's

Lest, seeing with its eyes
And hearing with its ears,
It also grasp with its mind,
And repent and save[a] itself."

[11] I asked, "How long, my Lord?" And He replied:
"Till towns lie waste without inhabitants
And houses without people,
And the ground lies waste and desolate—
12 For the LORD will banish the population—
And deserted sites are many
In the midst of the land.

[13] "But while a tenth part yet remains in it, it shall repent.
It shall be ravaged like the terebinth and the oak, of which
stumps are left even when they are felled: its stump shall be a
holy seed."

7 In the reign of Ahaz son of Jotham son of Uzziah, king of
Judah, King Rezin of Aram and King Pekah son of Remaliah of Israel marched upon Jerusalem to attack it; but they
were not able to attack it.

[2] Now, when it was reported to the House of David that
Aram had allied itself with Ephraim, their hearts and the
hearts of their people trembled as trees of the forest sway before a wind. [3] But the LORD said to Isaiah, "Go out with your
son Shear-jashub[b] to meet Ahaz at the end of the conduit of
the Upper Pool, by the road of the Fuller's Field. [4] And say to
him: Be firm and be calm. Do not be afraid and do not lose
heart on account of those two smoking stubs of firebrands, on
account of the raging of Rezin and his Arameans and the son
of Remaliah.[c] [5] Because the Arameans—with Ephraim and the
son of Remaliah—have plotted against you, saying, [6] 'We will
march against Judah and invade and conquer it, and we will
set up as king in it the son of Tabeel,'[c] [7] thus said my Lord GOD:

It shall not succeed,
It shall not come to pass.
8 For the chief city of Aram is Damascus,
And the chief of Damascus is Rezin;

a *Lit. "heal."*
b *Meaning "[only] a remnant will turn back," i.e., repent; cf. 6.13; 10.21.*
c *To refer to a person only as "the son of—" is slighting; cf. note at 1 Sam. 10.11.*

speeches, because the people do not want to acknowledge the truth. **11–12:** The divine judgment will involve the exile of most of the nation. **13:** According to the NJPS translation (which reads against the cantillation tradition marked by the signs in the Masoretic biblical text which serve as punctuation marks as well as musical notations), a small remnant will repent after the disaster; from this kernel the nation will be renewed. The renewal involves not exiles who return from afar but survivors who remain in the land. Thus Isaiah's notion of renewal differs from the vision of renewal in Ezek., Jer., and Second Isaiah, which involve exile and return from exile. Alternatively (and in accordance with the cantillation), the first half of the v. can be translated much more negatively: "And when a tenth are left, they will again be burned." In this rendering, the few survivors are subject to additional disaster. The second half is also obscure, but it seems to refer to the fact that renewed life can come out of the stump of terebinth and oak trees. Here the notion of the remnant that is saved from a devastating calamity does appear, however subtly.

7.1–8.23: Prophecies delivered during the Syro-Ephraimite crisis. These passages, and perhaps some of the passages following them, deal with a series of events known from both biblical texts (2 Kings ch 16; 2 Chron. ch 28) and ancient Assyrian records. In 735 BCE the leaders of the kingdom of Damascus in Syria (or *Aram*) and of the northern Israelite kingdom (also known as Ephraim) attempted to create a coalition of small states to oppose the Assyrian empire. King Ahaz of Judah did not join their conspiracy, and the Arameans (Syrians) and Israelites (Ephraimites) marched against Judah, intending to depose Ahaz and replace him with an ally of their own, who would join them, the son of Tabeel (his first name is not given, probably to slight him). Ahaz appealed to the Assyrian king, Tiglath-Pileser, for help. The Arameans and Ephraimites did not succeed in their efforts; Damascus was conquered entirely in 732, while Israel lost considerable territory to Assyria. Judah was saved, but it became a vassal of Assyria.

7.1–17: A narrative about Isaiah and King Ahaz. 1: A brief introduction sets the scene by paraphrasing 2 Kings 16.5. **2–9:** Isaiah is sent to reassure Ahaz that the Syro-Ephraimite threat will not succeed. Isaiah's commitment to the Davidic dynasty and his belief in the inviolability of Zion play a crucial role here

9 The chief city of Ephraim is Samaria,
And the chief of Samaria is the son of Remaliah.[a]
[b-]And in another sixty-five years,
Ephraim shall be shattered as a people.[-b]
If you will not believe, for you [c-]cannot be trusted[-c]..."

10 The LORD spoke further to Ahaz: 11 "Ask for a sign from the LORD your God, anywhere down to Sheol or up to the sky." 12 But Ahaz replied, "I will not ask, and I will not test the LORD." 13 "Listen, House of David," [Isaiah] retorted, "is it not enough for you to treat men as helpless that you also treat my God as helpless?[d] 14 Assuredly, my Lord will give you a sign of His own accord! Look, the young woman is with child and about to give birth to a son. Let her name him Immanuel.[e] 15 (By the time he learns to reject the bad and choose the good, people will be feeding on curds and honey.) 16 For before the lad knows to reject the bad and choose the good, the ground whose two kings you dread shall be abandoned. 17 The LORD will cause to come upon you and your people and your ancestral house such days as never have come since Ephraim turned away from Judah—that selfsame king of Assyria![f]

18 "In that day, the LORD will whistle to the flies at the ends of the water channels of Egypt and to the bees in the land of Assyria; 19 and they shall all come and alight in the rugged wadis, and in the clefts of the rocks, and in all the thornbrakes, and in all the watering places.

20 "In that day, my Lord will cut away with the razor that is hired beyond the Euphrates—with the king of Assyria[g]—the hair of the head and [h-]the hair of the legs,[-h] and it shall clip off the beard as well. 21 And in that day, each man shall save alive a heifer of the herd and two animals of the flock. 22 (And he shall obtain so much milk that he shall eat curds.) Thus everyone who is left in the land shall feed on curds and honey.

23 "For in that day, every spot where there could stand a thousand vines worth a thousand shekels of silver[i] shall become a wilderness of thornbush and thistle. 24 One will have to go there with bow and arrows,[j] for the country shall be all thornbushes and thistles. 25 But the perils of thornbush and thistle shall not spread to any of the hills that could only be

a The thought is continued by 8.8b–10; cf. 2 Chron. 13.8–12.
b-b Brought down from v. 8 for clarity.
c-c Others "surely, you shall not be established."
d By insisting on soliciting the aid of Assyria (see 2 Kings 16.7 ff.; cf. below, v. 20). "Treat as helpless" follows the translation of Saadia; cf. Gen. 19.11.
e Meaning "with us is God." *f Cf. note on v. 13.*
g Who was hired by Ahaz; cf. notes on vv. 13 and 17. *h-h I.e., the pubic hair.*
i I.e., all the best farm land, corresponding to the hairiest parts of the body; v. 20.
j Because of dangerous beasts.

(see 1.8–9 n.). **3:** The notion of the remnant that will return is expressed by the name Isaiah gave to his son. **8b:** See translators' note *b-b* (v. 9), an especially obscure v. Why does Isaiah attempt to reassure Ahaz by referring to an event relatively far in the future and therefore not subject to immediate verification? Although it is tempting to view the v. as an addition by a later scribe, Damascus fell to the Assyrians in 733, only three years after the Syro-Ephraimite crisis; a later scribe would not have inserted an inaccurate "prediction." **10–17:** Ahaz chooses to rely on the intervention of the Assyrian king (cf. 2 Kings 16.7–9) rather than on God. **14–17:** The Immanuel passage. Isaiah provides a *sign,* the point of which is either to clarify his message (cf. his sign in ch 20) or to verify it (cf. the sign in Judg. 6.17–23). It is not clear whether the *sign* is the woman's pregnancy, the child's birth, his name, or his diet; nor is it clear when the sign comes to pass—immediately (if the sign is his name), soon (birth), or several years into the future. Similarly ambiguities occur in the case of other biblical signs; cf. Exod. 3.12. This passage, which plays a significant role in Christianity, is of no special importance in Jewish tradition. **14:** *Young woman* (Heb "'almah"). The LXX translates as "virgin," leading ancient and medieval Christians to connect this v. with the New Testament figure of Mary. Modern scholars, however, agree that the Heb merely denotes a young woman of marriageable age, whether married or unmarried, whether a virgin or not. **15–17:** The message the sign represents is twofold: God is with Judah, both to protect it (v. 16) and to punish it (v. 17).

7.18–25: Predictions of disaster for Judah. Ahaz has refused to rely solely on God's promises of enduring kingship for David (cf. 2 Sam. 7.8–16; Ps. 89.20–37) and of Jerusalem's eternal safety (cf. Pss. 46; 48). Consequently (or perhaps as a result of support among Judeans for the attempt to enthrone the son of Tabeel and for the Syro-Ephraimite alliance?), God

tilled with a hoe;[a] and here cattle shall be let loose, and [b]sheep and goats[b] shall tramp about."

8 The LORD said to me, "Get yourself a large sheet and write on it [c]in common script[c] 'For Maher-shalal-hash-baz';[d]
2 and call reliable witnesses, the priest Uriah and Zechariah son of Jeberechiah, to witness for Me." 3 I was intimate with the prophetess,[e] and she conceived and bore a son; and the LORD said to me, "Name him Maher-shalal-hash-baz.[d] 4 For before the boy learns to call 'Father' and 'Mother,' the wealth of Damascus and the spoils of Samaria, [f]and the delights of Rezin and of the son of Remaliah,[f] shall be carried off before the king of Assyria."

5 Again the LORD spoke to me, thus:
6 "Because that people has spurned
The gently flowing waters of Siloam"[g]—
7 Assuredly,
My Lord will bring up against them
The mighty, massive waters of the Euphrates,
The king of Assyria and all his multitude.
It shall rise above all its channels,
And flow over all its beds,
8 And swirl through Judah like a flash flood
Reaching up to the neck.[h]

[i]But with us is God,
Whose wings are spread
As wide as your land is broad!
9 Band together, O peoples—you shall be broken!
Listen to this, you remotest parts of the earth:

a Marginal farm land, too rocky for the plow, corresponding to areas of the body with scant hair. *b-b See note at Exod. 12.3.* *c-c Meaning of Heb. uncertain.*
d I.e., "Pillage hastens, looting speeds," indicating that two cities are to be pillaged at an early date; see v. 4. *e I.e., Isaiah's wife.*
f-f Brought up from v. 6 for clarity.
g The conduit—and later the tunnel—of Siloam conveyed into Jerusalem the waters of Gihon, which symbolize "the LORD of Hosts who dwells on Mount Zion" (v. 18). For the nature of the rejection see note at 7.13.
h I.e., Judah shall be imperiled, but, in contrast to Aram and Ephraim (v. 4), not destroyed. *i See note a at 7.9.*

will use the Assyrians not to rescue Judah but to decimate it. The disaster will not be total, however. Isaiah makes no reference to Jerusalem's capitulation. Agriculture will be curtailed and wild animals will roam in what had been farmland, but those who survive (v. 22) will have food to eat. The reference to *curds and honey* (vv. 15, 22) is unclear: They are either delicacies the survivors are privileged to enjoy (so several rabbinic commentators) or meager provisions left after the punishment. The passage exemplifies the ambivalent tone of Isaiah's doctrine of the surviving remnant: It is unclear whether the description of this future is to be viewed negatively (since only a remnant endure) or positively (since they do in fact endure). The final v. may be a description of the poverty-stricken circumstances after the disaster or of agricultural—hence national—rebirth. In fact the Assyrian invasion Isaiah predicts did not occur during Ahaz's reign, but during the reign of his son, Hezekiah.

8.1–22: Further predictions concerning the Syro-Ephraimite crisis. In the oracles collected here, Isaiah refers to himself in the first person (unlike those in the previous ch, which refer to Isaiah in the third person). They date from the beginning of the crisis through its aftermath. **1–4:** A sign concerning the imminent destruction of Judah's enemies. The thrust of Isaiah's argument, as in ch 7 (with which it is likely to be contemporaneous) is that Ahaz need not rely on Assyrian aid. **5–8:** Isaiah's reaction to Ahaz's lack of faith. Ahaz rejected the God of Zion (symbolized by the waters of the Siloam which flow from the Gihon spring immediately below the Temple Mount) and chose the Assyrians; therefore God will bring Assyrians (represented by the river Euphrates) to punish him. Alternatively, it is possible that v. 6b (printed in NJPS as part of v. 4) should be translated, "And because you rejoiced in Rezin and the son of Remaliah." In this case, these vv. are addressed not to Ahaz but to Judeans who conspire against him on behalf of the Arameans and Israelites; God will punish their infidelity to the Davidic monarch by sending the Assyrians. **7–8:** The comparison of the Assyrian king to a devastating flood appears in Assyrian documents (see 2.10–22 n.). *Multitude* could be translated "glory," a term also used in Assyrian descriptions of their king's terrifying power. **8:** Isaiah expresses the doctrine of Zion's inviolability poetically: The Assyrians will decimate the land of Judah but not Judah's head, which is Jerusalem. **9–10:** Failure awaits the plotters. The identity of the plotters is enigmatic: Are they (1) the Arameans and Israelites who attack Judah; (2) Judeans who support them

Gird yourselves—you shall be broken;
Gird yourselves—you shall be broken!
10 Hatch a plot—it shall be foiled;
Agree on action—it shall not succeed.
For with us is God!

11 For this is what the LORD said to me, when He took me
by the hand[a] and charged me not to walk in the path of that
people:

12[b] "You must not call conspiracy[c]
All that that people calls conspiracy,[c]
Nor revere what it reveres,
Nor hold it in awe.
13 None but the LORD of Hosts
Shall you account holy;
Give reverence to Him alone,
Hold Him alone in awe.
14 He shall be [d]for a sanctuary,
A stone[d] men strike against:
A rock men stumble over
For the two Houses of Israel,
And a trap and a snare for those
Who dwell in Jerusalem.
15 The masses shall trip over these
And shall fall and be injured,
Shall be snared and be caught.
16 Bind up the message,
Seal the instruction with My disciples."

17 So I will wait for the LORD, who is hiding His face from the
House of Jacob, and I will trust in Him. 18 Here stand I and the
children the LORD has given me as signs and portents in Israel
from the LORD of Hosts, who dwells on Mount Zion.
19 Now, should people say to you, "Inquire of the ghosts
and familiar spirits that chirp and moan; for a people may
inquire of its divine beings[e]—of the dead on behalf of the
living—20 for instruction and message," surely, for one who
speaks thus there shall be no dawn. 21 [f]And he shall go about
in it wretched and hungry; and when he is hungry, he shall
rage and revolt against his king and his divine beings.[f] He
may turn his face upward 22 or he may look below, but behold,

a I.e., singled me out; cf. 41.9, 13; 42.6; 45.1; Jer. 31.32 [31].

b The Heb. forms here and in vv. 13 and 19 are plural to include the disciples (v. 16) and the children (v. 18).

c Meaning of Heb. uncertain. Emendation yields "holy"; cf. v. 13.

d-d Emendation yields "... for His holy domain [cf. Ps. 114.2] / A stone ..."

e I.e., the shades of the dead; cf. 1 Sam. 28.13.

f-f This sentence would read well after v. 22.

against King Ahaz; (3) King Ahaz, who creates a conspiracy with the Assyrians against the Arameans and Israelites; or (4) the Assyrians who plan to take over the land of their new Judean ally—or all of these? **11–15:** These vv. are linguistically and interpretively very difficult. They seem to reflect the fact that Isaiah's advice opposes all his contemporaries' perspectives: He advocates joining neither the anti-Assyrian coalition nor the Assyrians themselves. **16–18:** Another obscure passage, perhaps from the end of the crisis. Isaiah's predictions had not come true in the short run: The Assyrians did not invade Judah in Ahaz's day, and Ahaz's policy of turning to them for protection seems to have worked. Nonetheless, the prophet insists that his words would prove valid; he has them written down, bound up, and placed with his disciples for safekeeping. Ultimately it would become clear that the LORD's prophet spoke truly. During the Assyrian invasion three decades later (in the reign of Ahaz's son, Hezekiah), Isaiah's perspective was vindicated, since the Assyrians devastated Judah but did not capture Jerusalem. **19–21:** A polemic against other forms of divination. It is unclear why it is here; perhaps it dates from the period of the Syro-Ephraimite crisis, though it could also fit many other periods. *Ghosts and familiar spirits* are the demigods and deified ancestors to whom some Judeans, following Canaanite and Mesopotamian religious models, turned for guidance. Cf. Lev. 20.27; Deut. 18.9–15; 1 Sam. ch 28.

23: An unusually obscure v. The Assyrian king Tiglath-pileser seized lands belonging to the tribes of *Zebulun* and *Naphtali,* along with parts of *Galilee* and Transjordan, from the Israelite king Pekah son of Remaliah in the aftermath of the Syro-Ephraimite crisis.

9.1–6: The ideal Davidic king. Isaiah describes liberation from some form of adversity (perhaps the Assyrian conquests of Israelite territory described in the previous vv., or Syro-Ephraimite pressures on Judah). The verbs are in the past tense. Some interpreters view them as examples of the "prophetic past," which predicts future events using the past tense because they are as good as done. Thus it is not clear whether the Davidic king whose birth and rule are described (vv. 5–6) has already been born (if the verbs are a regular past tense) or will be born in the future (prophetic past). If the former, the v. probably refers to Ahaz's son Hezekiah, as many modern and rabbinic commentators believe (though other possibilities exist depending on the date of the passage). Most later readers (both Jewish and Christian) understood the passage to describe an ideal future Davidic ruler, i.e., the Messiah. **5:** *"The Mighty God ... ruler":* This long sentence is the throne name of the royal child. Semitic names often consist of sentences that describe God; thus the name Isaiah in Heb means "The LORD saves"; Hezekiah, "The LORD strengthens"; in Akkadian, the name of the Babylonian king Merodach-baladan (Isa. 39.1) means "the god Marduk has provided an heir." These names do not describe that person who holds them but the god whom the parents worship. Similarly, the name given to the child in this v. does not describe that child or attribute divinity to him, but describes God's actions.

Distress and darkness, [a-]with no daybreak;[-a]
Straitness and gloom, [a-]with no dawn.[-a]
23 For [b-]if there were to be[-b] any break of day for that [land]
which is in straits, only the former [king] would have brought
abasement to the land of Zebulun and the land of Naphtali—while the later one would have brought honor to the Way
of the Sea, the other side of the Jordan, and Galilee of the
Nations.[c]

9

[d]The people that walked in darkness
Have seen a brilliant light;
On those who dwelt in a land of gloom
Light has dawned.
2 You have magnified that nation,
Have given it great joy;
They have rejoiced before You
As they rejoice at reaping time,
As they exult
When dividing spoil.

3 For the yoke that they bore
And the stick on their back—
The rod of their taskmaster—
You have broken as on the day of Midian.[e]
4 Truly, all the boots put on [f-]to stamp with[-f]
And all the garments donned in infamy
Have been fed to the flames,
Devoured by fire.
5 For a child has been born to us,
A son has been given us.
And authority has settled on his shoulders.
He has been named
"The Mighty God is planning grace;[g]
The Eternal Father, a peaceable ruler"—
6 In token of abundant authority
And of peace without limit
Upon David's throne and kingdom,
That it may be firmly established
In justice and in equity
Now and evermore.
The zeal of the LORD of Hosts
Shall bring this to pass.

a-a Meaning of Heb. uncertain. *b-b So 1QIs[a]; the others have "there is not."*
c Meaning of verse uncertain. The rendering here assumes that "the former [king]" refers to Pekah (cf. 2 Kings 15.29) and "the later" to Hoshea (ibid. 30). For the construction lu ... ka'eth, *see Judg. 13–23.* *d See note d at 5.30.* *e See Judg. 7–8.*
f-f Meaning of Heb. uncertain; emendation yields "in wickedness"; cf. Targum.
g As in 25.1.

7 My Lord
[a-]Let loose a word[-a] against Jacob
And it fell upon Israel.
8 But all the people noted[b]—
Ephraim and the inhabitants of Samaria—
In arrogance and haughtiness:
9 "Bricks have fallen—
We'll rebuild with dressed stone;
Sycamores have been felled—
We'll grow cedars instead!"
10 So the LORD let [c-]the enemies of Rezin[-c]
Triumph over it
And stirred up its foes—
11 Aram from the east
And Philistia from the west—
Who devoured Israel
With greedy mouths.

Yet His anger has not turned back,
And His arm is outstretched still.

12 For the people has not turned back
To Him who struck it
And has not sought
The LORD of Hosts.
13 So the LORD will cut off from Israel
Head and tail,
Palm branch and reed,
In a single day.
14 Elders [d-]and magnates[-d]—
Such are the heads;
Prophets who give false instruction,
Such are the tails[e]
15 That people's leaders have been misleaders,
So they that are led have been confused.
16 That is why my Lord
Will not spare[f] their youths,
Nor show compassion
To their orphans and widows;
For all are ungodly and wicked,
And every mouth speaks impiety.

9.7–10.4: The fate of the Northern Kingdom, Israel. A repeated refrain in 9.11, 16, 21, and 10.4 structures this poem into four sections. The same refrain is found in 5.25, and scholars speculate that 5.25–30 may originally have been the poem's fifth and final section. The verbs here are in the past tense, but as in the previous unit, their significance is unclear. They may predict disasters to come (in which case the verbs exemplify "the prophetic past" described in 9.1–6 n.); alternatively they may review disasters that God already sent in an unsuccessful attempt to chasten the Northern Kingdom (in which case the prophet does not predict coming events but presents an interpretation of recent history). The verbs in 5.26–30 clearly have a future tense and represent a prediction of the Assyrian invasion that ends the poem. The following remarks assume the verbs in the first four sections refer to the past and are interpretations of recent events, not predictions of upcoming ones. **7–11:** The first section may refer to the earthquake that shook Israel and Judah early in Isaiah's career; cf. Amos 1.1; Zech. 14.5. **12–17:** The second section refers to the chaos in the Northern Kingdom during the coups and massacres described in the mid-740s BCE (see 2 Kings ch 15).

a-a Septuagint reads "Let loose pestilence"; cf. Amos 4.10. In vv. 7–20 Isaiah alludes to and builds upon Amos 4.10–12. *b 1QIs[a] reads "shouted."*
c-c Emendation yields "its enemies."
d-d Emendation yields "who practice partiality."
e Emendation yields "palm branches"; the elders and the prophets are the leaders, the people are the led; cf. 3.1–2, 12. *f Cf. Arabic* samuḥa. *1QIs[a] reads* yḥmw.

17 Already wickedness has blazed forth like a fire
Devouring thorn and thistle.
It has kindled the thickets of the wood,
[a-]Which have turned into billowing smoke.[-a]

[b-]Yet His anger has not turned back,
And His arm is outstretched still.[-b]

18 By the fury of the LORD of Hosts,
The earth was shaken.[c]
Next, the people became like devouring fire:
No man spared his countryman.
19 They snatched on the right, but remained hungry,
And consumed on the left without being sated.
Each devoured the flesh of his [d-]own kindred[-d]—
20 Manasseh Ephraim's, and Ephraim Manasseh's,[e]
And both of them against Judah![f]

Yet His anger has not turned back,
And His arm is outstretched still.

10

Ha!
Those who write out evil writs
And compose iniquitous documents,
2 To subvert the cause of the poor,
To rob of their rights the needy of My people;
That widows may be their spoil,
And fatherless children their booty!
3 What will you do on the day of punishment,
When the calamity comes from afar?
To whom will you flee for help,
And how will you save your carcasses[g]
4 From collapsing under [fellow] prisoners,
From falling beneath the slain?

Yet His anger has not turned back,
And his arm is outstretched still.

a-a Meaning of Heb. uncertain. *b-b Moved down from v. 16 for clarity.*
c Cf. note at 5.25.
d-d Meaning of Heb. uncertain. Emendation yields "fellow"; cf. Targum.
e Alludes to the civil wars of 2 Kings 15.10, 14–16, 25. *f Cf. 7.1–9.*
g Meaning of Heb. uncertain; for "carcasses," compare the rendering of kabod *in v. 16; 22.18.*

18–20: The third section recalls the earthquake, political chaos, and Israel's anti-Judean policies during the Syro-Ephraimite crisis. **10.1–4:** The fourth section. As he comes to the climax of his indictment against the Northern Kingdom, the prophet returns to the theme of the rich who mistreat the poor and pervert justice for their own gain; cf. 1.17; 3.8–15; 5.8–10; 32.7.

10.5–12.6: The earth is the LORD's: from Assyrian conquest through Assyrian collapse to universal peace. This lengthy poem is a literary unit consisting of three stanzas: 10.5–27, 10.28–34, and 11.1–12.16 (it is possible that the third stanza includes some material added later than the 8th c.). The idea of universal history guided by one God comes to the fore in this three-part composition, which describes a divine plan that affects not only Israel but all the world. This plan will manifest itself in three stages. Assyria will serve as God's agent to punish Israel. Assyria's self-promotion will then arouse God's anger, so that Assyria will be punished. Finally, the peaceful era will emerge, in which an ideal Davidic king will reign justly. Repeated images connect the three sections, and each section leads directly into the next. The poem moves between specific geopolitical concerns of the 8th c. and timeless ideals. In the first two stanzas of the poem, the prophet repeatedly weaves language used in Assyrian propaganda (see 2.10–22 n.) into his descriptions of God. In the Assyrian texts, these terms described the god Ashur and the Assyrian emperor, but here the prophet subverts the borrowed language to describe the imminent downfall of the emperor, with the result that the disaster that overcomes him will appear to him as something ironically familiar. In the third stanza the prophet leaves both the Assyrians and their propaganda behind to describe the ideal Judean king in language that recalls specifically Israelite and Judean literary motifs rather than the subverted motifs of the enemy's literature. The passage dates from some time after the destruction of the Northern Kingdom's capital in 722 BCE (see 10.9) but before the Assyrian invasion of 701, which in broad terms it predicts (see note below to 10.28–34). All the cities mentioned in 10.9 were conquered by the Assyrian emperor Sargon in 720, which suggests the possibility that this poem was written in the

5 Ha!
Assyria, rod of My anger,
[a]In whose hand, as a staff, is My fury![a]
6 I send him against an ungodly nation,
I charge him against a people that provokes Me,
To take its spoil and to seize its booty
And to make it a thing trampled
Like the mire of the streets.
7 But he has evil plans,
His mind harbors evil designs;
For he means to destroy,
To wipe out nations, not a few.
8 For he thinks,
"After all, [b]I have kings as my captains![b]
9 Was Calno any different from Carchemish?
Or Hamath from Arpad?
Or Samaria from Damascus?
10 [c]Since I was able to seize
The insignificant kingdoms,
Whose images exceeded
Jerusalem's and Samaria's,[c]
11 Shall I not do to Jerusalem and her images
What I did to Samaria and her idols?"

12 But when my Lord has carried out all his purpose on Mount Zion and in Jerusalem, He[d] will punish the majestic pride and overbearing arrogance of the king of Assyria. 13 For he thought,
"By the might of my hand have I wrought it,
By my skill, for I am clever:
I have erased the borders of peoples;
I have plundered their treasures,
And exiled their vast populations.[e]
14 I was able to seize, like a nest,
The wealth of peoples;
As one gathers abandoned eggs,
So *I* gathered all the earth:
Nothing so much as flapped a wing
Or opened a mouth to peep."

15 Does an ax boast over him who hews with it,
Or a saw magnify itself above him who wields it?
As though the rod raised him who lifts it,
As though the staff lifted the man![f]

a-a Emendation yields "Who is a staff in the hand of my fury."
b-b Emendation yields "all the kingdoms fared alike!"
c-c Emendation yields "Since I was able to seize / those kingdoms and their images, / Why is Jerusalem better than Samaria?" *d Heb. "I."*
e According to vv. 6–7, Assyria was to plunder, but not to exile. *f Lit. "not-wood."*

shadow of the massive Assyrian campaign of that year.

10.5–27: Part I. The Assyrian emperor: lord of lords or pawn of the Lord? This section hearkens back to the names of children earlier in the book: cf. v. 6 with 8.2–4; vv. 20–21 with 7.3 and 9.5. **5–6:** God uses the Assyrian king to punish Israel. **7–15:** The king arrogantly and ignorantly attributes his success to his own might, rather than God's plan. His boasting here recalls inscriptions of the Assyrian kings, with which Isaiah was familiar. Assyrian kings claimed to achieve their conquests with the aid of Ashur, the Assyrian high god, and other gods, but to Isaiah these were human creations, and thus the inscriptions glorified human inventions rather than the God whose bidding Assyrians unknowingly performed. **8:** *Captains* is a bilingual pun: Heb "sar" is cognate to the Akkadian word for king ("sharru"). Vassal kings did serve the Assyrian king as military commanders or captains. **12, 16–19:** The Assyrians' hubris (and not their attack on Israel) leads to their downfall.

18–19: *Scrub,* better, "forest." **19:** *What trees remain of its scrub / Shall be so few ... :* The reference to destruction of trees recalls the wanton destruction of orchards and trees of which Assyrian military records frequently boast. God will use this motif against the Assyrians themselves. According to Deut. 20.19–20, Israelite armies, however, are prohibited from partaking in this practice. *Remain:* The remnant motif is applied here to Assyria rather than to Israel. God treats Assyria like God treats Israel (here, negatively). The implication of this phenomenon is fully spelled out in 19.23–25. **20–27:** Although the Assyrian defeat follows Israel's downfall, it will lead to repentance among those who survive. **26:** The prophet alludes to earlier events in which God saved Israel from more powerful and numerous nations.

16 Assuredly,
The Sovereign LORD of Hosts will send
A wasting away in its[a] fatness;
And under its body[b] shall burn
A burning like that of fire,
[c]Destroying frame and flesh.
It shall be like a sick man who pines away.[-c]
17 The Light of Israel will be fire
And its Holy One flame.
It will burn and consume its thorns
And its thistles in a single day,
18 And the mass of its scrub and its farm land.
19 What trees remain of its scrub
Shall be so few that a boy may record them.

20 And in that day,
The remnant of Israel
And the escaped of the House of Jacob
Shall lean no more upon him that beats it,[d]
But shall lean sincerely
On the LORD, the Holy One of Israel.
21 Only a remnant shall return,
Only a remnant of Jacob,
To Mighty God.
22 Even if your people, O Israel,
Should be as the sands of the sea,
Only a remnant of it shall return.
Destruction is decreed;
Retribution comes like a flood!
23 For my Lord GOD of Hosts is carrying out
A decree of destruction upon all the land.

24 Assuredly, thus said my Lord God of Hosts: "O My people
that dwells in Zion, have no fear of Assyria, who beats you with
a rod and wields his staff over you as did the Egyptians. 25 For
very soon My wrath will have spent itself, and [e]My anger that
was bent on wasting them."[-e] 26 The LORD of Hosts will brandish
a scourge over him as when He beat Midian at the Rock of Oreb,[f]
and will wield His staff as He did over the Egyptians by the sea.

27 And in that day,
His burden shall drop from your back,

a Presumably Israel's. These verses would read well after 9.16. *b Cf. note at v. 3.*
c-c Brought up from v. 18 for clarity.
d I.e., upon Assyria (see v. 24). Ahaz's reliance on Assyria was interpreted by Isaiah as lack of faith in the LORD; see 7.13 with note.
e-e Presumably Assyria; meaning of Heb. uncertain. Emendation yields "My anger against the world shall cease." *f See Judg. 7.25.*

[a]And his yoke from your neck;
The yoke shall be destroyed because of fatness.

28 He advanced upon Aiath,
He proceeded to Migron,
At Michmas he deposited his baggage.
29 They made the crossing;
"Geba is to be our night quarters!"
Ramah was alarmed;
Gibeah of Saul took to flight.
30 "Give a shrill cry, O Bath-gallim!
Hearken, Laishah!
Take up the cry, Anathoth!"
31 Madmenah ran away;
The dwellers of Gebim sought refuge.
32 This same day at Nob
He shall stand and wave his hand.[b]

O mount of Fair Zion!
O hill of Jerusalem!
33 Lo! The Sovereign LORD of Hosts
Will hew off the tree-crowns with an ax:
The tall ones shall be felled,
The lofty ones cut down:
34 The thickets of the forest shall be hacked away with iron,
And the Lebanon trees shall fall [c]in their majesty.[-c]

11 But a shoot shall grow out of the stump of Jesse,
A twig shall sprout from his stock.
2 The spirit of the LORD shall alight upon him:
A spirit of wisdom and insight,
A spirit of counsel and valor,
A spirit of devotion and reverence for the LORD.

a *Emendation yields "And his yoke shall leave your neck. / He came up from Jeshimon / [28]By the ascent of Aiath, / He proceeded to Migron; / At Michmas he commanded his forces: / [29]'Make the crossing; / Geba is to be our night quarters!'" Jeshimon is the southeast corner of the Jordan Valley, Num. 21.20; 23.28; Aiath is elsewhere called Ai.*

b *I.e., the Assyrian king, arriving at Nob (close to Jerusalem), shall beckon his army onward; cf. 13.2.*

c-c *Or "by the bronze," connecting Heb.* 'addir *with Akkadian* urudu, *"bronze."*

10.28–34: Part II. Assyria's near-victory. Isaiah returned constantly to the theme of Jerusalem sorely threatened and suddenly saved, predicting for decades, an event like the one described here. It finally came true when Sennacherib invaded in 701 BCE. (In this passage, however, Isaiah predicts the invader will come from the north, but in fact Sennacherib approached Jerusalem from Lachish, to the southwest; see chs 36–39; 2 Kings chs 18–19; 2 Chron. ch 32.) The events that should follow the defeat of the arrogant empire (see the following ch) have still not come to fruition, even though Isaiah probably thought they would happen in his own lifetime. **28–32:** The invader's route. *He* refers to the leader of the army (probably Assyrian, perhaps Syro-Ephraimite) who comes toward Jerusalem from the north. The locations that are identifiable are all within a few miles of biblical Jerusalem. *Anathoth* is directly across a wadi from today's French Hill neighborhood. *Nob* is probably Mount Scopus, overlooking today's Old City. **33–34:** Just as the invader is about to achieve his goal, he is cut down. Cf. 29.1–8. The prophet uses the term *Lebanon trees* ironically: Assyrian kings boasted in inscriptions that they cut down these mighty cedars on their heroic journeys to despoil the forests of Lebanon to obtain wood for their building projects in Mesopotamia, but here Assyrians themselves become the ax's victim.

11.1–12.6: Part III. The ideal king in the peaceful future: The poem's final section is a messianic and eschatological prophecy comparable to 2.1–4 and 9.1–6. Once vain human striving for empire ends (section II), a perfect Davidic king will reign in Jerusalem, and all the world will enjoy peace and equity. **1–5:** The ideal age as manifested in jurisprudence. The king will be endowed with prophetic insight. **1:** *Jesse* was King David's father; the *shoot ... out of the stump of Jesse* is a king from David's dynasty. The imagery of the previous section continues here, linking the second and third sections of the poem. Whereas the high trees representing Assyria's imperial haughtiness will be cut down to size (10.33–34), real strength will emerge from the lowest part—the *stock* (lit. "roots")—of the humble tree representing David's dynasty. Further, Judah's lasting strength will emerge from within (viz., from a local tree, the family of a small clan in Judah), whereas Assyria's short-lived

3 [a]He shall sense the truth[a] by his reverence for
the LORD:
He shall not judge by what his eyes behold,
Nor decide by what his ears perceive.
4 Thus he shall judge the poor with equity
And decide with justice for the lowly of the land.
He shall strike down a land[b] with the rod of his mouth
And slay the wicked with the breath of his lips.
5 Justice shall be the girdle of his loins,
And faithfulness the girdle of his waist.
6 The wolf shall dwell with the lamb,
The leopard lie down with the kid;
[c]The calf, the beast of prey, and the fatling[c] together,
With a little boy to herd them.
7 The cow and the bear shall graze,
Their young shall lie down together;
And the lion, like the ox, shall eat straw.
8 A babe shall play
Over a viper's hole,
And an infant pass[d] his hand
Over an adder's den.
9 In all of [e]My sacred mount[e]
Nothing evil or vile shall be done;
For the land shall be filled with devotion to the LORD
As water covers the sea.

10 In that day,
The stock of Jesse that has remained standing
Shall become a standard to peoples—
Nations shall seek his counsel
And his abode shall be honored.

11 In that day, my Lord will apply His hand again to redeeming the other part[f] of His people from Assyria—as also from Egypt, Pathros, Nubia, Elam, Shinar, Hamath, and the coastlands.

12 He will hold up a signal to the nations
And assemble the banished of Israel,
And gather the dispersed of Judah
From the four corners of the earth.

a-a Lit. "His sensing [shall be]"; meaning of Heb. uncertain.
b Emendation yields "the ruthless."
c-c 1QIs[a] reads: "The calf and the beast of prey shall feed"; so too the Septuagint.
d Meaning of Heb. uncertain. *e-e I.e., the Holy Land; cf. Exod. 15.17; Ps. 78.54.*
f I.e., the part outside the Holy Land; lit. "the rest that will remain."

strength was based on the Assyrian campaigns far from Assyria itself, in the mountains where they cut down the cedars of Lebanon. Isaiah's insistence on humility and displeasure with human conceit determine the contrast between the images of trees in 11.1 and 10.33–34; cf. 2.2–4.6. If the translation *stump* is correct, then this passage may presume that the Davidic dynasty will (or has) come to an end; this reading would deviate significantly from Isaiah's notion that Davidic kings will reign eternally (cf. 2 Sam. 7.8–16; Ps. 89.20–37). But the Heb "geza'" refers not only to a *stump* of a tree that has been cut down but also to the trunk of a living tree, and thus does not presuppose the dynasty's downfall. **4:** The messianic age will not be perfect; some people will still be *poor,* others ruthless or *wicked.* The difference from the current age will lie, rather, in the king's response to these problems: He will always render accurate and fair judgments. Cf. 2.2–4, where conflicts among nations continue but are settled nonviolently. **6–9:** The ideal age as manifested in nature. **10–16:** The ideal age as manifested in Israel's relationship to other nations. **10:** As in 2.2–4, nations come to Jerusalem to receive instruction. The Davidic king will act as the prophetic conduit through whom responses to the nations' inquiries will come. **11–16:** The ingathering of exiles, which is compared to the exodus from Egypt. Some view this passage as dating to the Babylonian exile (which began in 597 BCE, long after Isaiah's death) or thereafter. Northern Israelites had already been exiled in Isaiah's lifetime, however, and Isaiah predicted that many Judeans outside Jerusalem would be exiled by the Assyrians. **11:** The list of nations is found in Assyrian texts much earlier than 597. Thus some see no reason to deny Isaiah's authorship of vv. 11–16. *The other part,* or "remnant." Elsewhere in Isaiah this term refers to Judeans who, having survived Assyrian invasion, remain in the land of Israel. Its use here to refer to exiles who return to the land of Israel is unique and may support the suggestion that these vv. are a later addition. **12:** *The four corners of the earth* is a central idea in Mesopotamian geography.

13 Then Ephraim's envy shall cease
And Judah's harassment shall end;
Ephraim shall not envy Judah,
And Judah shall not harass Ephraim.
14 They shall pounce on the back of Philistia to the west,
And together plunder the peoples of the east;
Edom and Moab shall be subject to them
And the children of Ammon shall obey them.

15 The LORD will dry up the tongue of the Egyptian sea.—He
will raise His hand over the Euphrates with the might[a] of His
wind and break it into seven wadis, so that it can be trodden
dry-shod. 16 Thus there shall be a highway for the other part[b] of
His people out of Assyria, such as there was for Israel when it
left the land of Egypt.

12 In that day, you shall say:
"I give thanks to You, O LORD!
Although You were wroth with me,
Your wrath has turned back and You comfort me,
2 Behold the God who gives me triumph!
I am confident, unafraid;
For Yah the LORD is my strength and might,[c]
And He has been my deliverance."

3 Joyfully shall you draw water
From the fountains of triumph,
4 And you shall say on that day:
"Praise the LORD, proclaim His name.
Make His deeds known among the peoples;
Declare that His name is exalted.
5 Hymn the LORD,
For He has done gloriously;
Let this be made known
In all the world!
6 Oh, shout for joy,
You who dwell in Zion!
For great in your midst
Is the Holy One of Israel."

13 The "Babylon" Pronouncement, a prophecy of Isaiah son of Amoz.

2 "Raise a standard upon a bare hill,

a Meaning of Heb. uncertain.
b I.e., the part outside the Holy Land; lit. "the rest that will remain."
c Others "song."

13: *Ephraim* and *Judah* refer to the Northern and Southern Kingdoms, whose relationship reached a low point during the Syro-Ephraimite crisis (see 7.1–8.23 n.). **14:** This is one of the only vv. in First Isaiah that anticipates the Israelites and Judeans taking vengeance on their enemies. It contradicts not only the prediction of a nonviolent messianic age earlier in this ch but the consistent rejection of national revenge in Isaiah's prophecies. It may shed additional doubt on Isaianic authorship of vv. 11–16. **12.1–6:** A song of thanksgiving to be recited in the ideal age. Many of these phrases occur in other songs of thanksgiving, especially those associated with the exodus from Egypt. Cf. v. 2 with Exod. 15.2 and Ps. 118.14; cf. v. 4 with Pss. 105.1 and 148.13. Isaiah or a later editor may have capped this section with quotations from these and other well-known hymns.

Chs 13–23: Oracles concerning various nations. Most of the individual oracles within this section begin with the word "masa'," meaning "oracle" or "pronouncement" (others, "burden"). This section includes prophecies by Isaiah supplemented by later texts. Similar collections that draw together prophecies of many nations' downfall appear in other prophetic books, and are often called "oracles against the nations." See Jer. chs 46–51; Ezek. chs 25–32; Amos 1.3–2.6; Zeph. 2.4–15; and Obad.

13.1–22: An oracle concerning the destruction of Babylonia. This oracle assumes that Babylonia, rather than Assyria, is the world power. It must, therefore, have been addressed to an exilic audience in the mid-6th c., not to the 8th c. audience of Isaiah son of Amoz.

13.1: Superscription. The oracle, and hence chs 13–23 as a whole, begins with its own superscription; cf. the superscriptions in 1.1 and 2.1.

13.2–22: The oracle. 2–5: The gathering of the armies that will defeat Babylonia. **6–16:** The Day of the LORD. The upcoming defeat of the Babylonians will be a cosmic event, which Israel's prophets have long anticipated, involving the punishment of God's enemies. Cf., for example, Isa. chs 22 and 34; Ezek. chs 7 and 30; Joel chs 2–3; Amos 5.18–20; Zeph. ch 1. In this oracle, the enemy is Babylonia, while in other Day of the LORD texts Israel is punished. **6:** See the similar material in Joel 1.15. **10:** Darkness is a common theme in Day of the LORD passages; it is uncertain if this is literal or metaphorical.

Cry aloud to them;
Wave a hand, and let them enter
The gates of the nobles!
3 I have summoned My purified guests
To execute My wrath;
Behold, I have called My stalwarts,
My proudly exultant ones."[a]

4 Hark! a tumult on the mountains—
As of[b] a mighty force;
Hark! an uproar of kingdoms,
Nations assembling!
The LORD of Hosts is mustering
A host for war.
5 They come from a distant land,
From the end of the sky—
The LORD with the weapons of His wrath—
To ravage all the earth!

6 Howl!
For the day of the LORD is near;
It shall come like havoc from Shaddai.[c]
7 Therefore all hands shall grow limp,
And all men's hearts shall sink;
8 And, overcome by terror,
They shall be seized by pangs and throes,
Writhe like a woman in travail.
They shall gaze at each other in horror,
Their faces [d-]livid with fright.[-d]

9 Lo! The day of the LORD is coming
With pitiless fury and wrath,
To make the earth a desolation,
To wipe out the sinners upon it.
10 The stars and constellations of heaven
Shall not give off their light;
The sun shall be dark when it rises,
And the moon shall diffuse no glow.

11 "And I will requite to the world its evil,
And to the wicked their iniquity;
I will put an end to the pride of the arrogant
And humble the haughtiness of tyrants.

a The impending slaughter is spoken of as a sacrificial meal, for which the guests were notified to purify themselves ritually; cf. Zeph. 1.7.
b Meaning of Heb. uncertain. *c Traditionally rendered "the Almighty."*
d-d Taking the root lhb *as a variant of* bhl*: others "shall be faces of flame."*

12 I will make people scarcer than fine gold,
And men than gold of Ophir."
13 Therefore [a-]shall heaven be shaken,[-a]
And earth leap out of its place,
At the fury of the LORD of Hosts
On the day of His burning wrath.
14 Then like gazelles that are chased,
And like sheep that no man gathers,
Each man shall turn back to his people,
They shall flee every one to his land.
15 All who remain shall be pierced through,
All who [b-]are caught[-b]
Shall fall by the sword.
16 And their babes shall be dashed to pieces
in their sight,
Their homes shall be plundered,
And their wives shall be raped.

17 "Behold,
I stir up the Medes against them,
Who do not value silver
Or delight in gold.
18 Their bows shall shatter the young;
They shall show no pity to infants,
They shall not spare the children."

19 And Babylon, glory of kingdoms,
Proud splendor of the Chaldeans,
Shall become like Sodom and Gomorrah
Overturned by God.
20 Nevermore shall it be settled
Nor dwelt in through all the ages.
No Arab shall pitch his tent there,
No shepherds make flocks lie down there.
21 But beasts[c] shall lie down there,
And the houses be filled with owls;[c]
There shall ostriches make their home,
And there shall satyrs dance.
22 And jackals[c] shall abide in its castles
And dragons[c] in the palaces of pleasure.
Her hour is close at hand;
Her days will not be long.

17–22: The text becomes more specific, attributing the coming destruction of Babylonia to the *Medes* (v. 17), a people who lived east of Babylonia in today's Iran. The kingdom of the Medes was conquered by the Persian king Cyrus, who became known as king of the Persians and Medes. He conquered Babylon in 539 BCE, but contrary to what vv. 19–22 anticipate, he did not destroy the city. **19:** The *Chaldeans* were an Aramean tribe who became increasingly influential in Babylonia starting in the 8th century; consequently the Bible often uses the term Chaldean as a synonym for Babylonian. *Sodom and Gomorrah* (see Gen. chs 18–19) are a common trope for total destruction in prophetic literature.

a-a Lit. "I will shake heaven."
b-b Meaning of Heb. uncertain; emendation yields "flee."
c Meaning of Heb. uncertain.

14 But the LORD will pardon Jacob, and will again choose
Israel, and will settle them on their own soil. And strangers shall join them and shall cleave to the House of Jacob.
2 For peoples shall take them[a] and bring them to their homeland; and the House of Israel shall possess them[b] as slaves and
handmaids on the soil of the LORD. They shall be captors of
their captors and masters to their taskmasters.
3 And when the LORD has given you rest from your sorrow
and trouble, and from the hard service that you were made
to serve, 4 you shall recite this song of scorn over the king of
Babylon:

How is the taskmaster vanished,
How is oppression[c] ended!
5 The LORD has broken the staff of the wicked,
The rod of tyrants,
6 That smote peoples in wrath
With stroke unceasing,
That belabored nations in fury
In relentless pursuit.

7 All the earth is calm, untroubled;
Loudly it cheers.
8 Even pines rejoice at your fate,
And cedars of Lebanon:
"Now that you have lain down,
None shall come up to fell us."

9 Sheol below was astir
To greet your coming—
Rousing for you the shades
Of all earth's chieftains,
Raising from their thrones
All the kings of nations.
10 All speak up and say to you,
"So you have been stricken as we were,
You have become like us!
11 Your pomp is brought down to Sheol,
And the strains of your lutes!
Worms are to be your bed,
Maggots your blanket!"

12 How are you fallen from heaven,
O Shining One, son of Dawn![d]

a I.e., the House of Jacob. *b I.e., the peoples.*
c Reading marhebah *with 1QIs*[a] *(cf. Septuagint). The traditional reading* madhebah *is of unknown meaning.* *d A character in some lost myth.*

14.1–23: A mock lament concerning Israel's oppressor. The poem in vv. 4b–21 describes the ignominious death of an Assyrian monarch of Isaiah's time, probably Sargon II, who was killed in battle in 705. It was later reinterpreted as predicting the death of a Babylonian monarch. **1–4a:** This introduction, which differs from the surrounding material in style and content, was added to Isaiah's poem by an editor during the time of the Babylonian exile (597–539). **4a–23:** Each Heb line in this poem divides into two halves, the first with three main beats, the second with two. This meter, often called qinah (dirge) meter, is typical of dirges (such as 1.21–27 and the poems in the book of Lamentations); it also occurs, as here, in mock laments (another such mock lament is found in Isa. ch 47). **4b–8:** The whole world is relieved at the death of the Assyrian king, whose brutality was renowned. **8:** In their inscriptions kings of Assyria, which lacked large timber-fields, often boast of their expeditions to cut down *pines* and *cedars* in *Lebanon.* Here, as in 10.7–15 and 10.33–34, Isaiah turns the Assyrians' own rhetoric against them. **9–11:** The king arrives in *Sheol,* or the underworld, and his pretensions to power are mocked by the other kings there; he had ruled over kings, but now he is stuck beneath the earth just as they are. Many ancient Semites and pre-classical Greeks believed that the dead dwelt in unpleasant conditions underground; the fate of the dead there depended in large part on whether the corpse received a proper burial. This conception of a shadowy life after death became a well-known literary motif. On notions of life after death in the Tanakh and ancient Judaism, see 26.19 n. **12–15:** The king's vain aspirations to god-like status are mocked. Isaiah refers ironically to the king as *Shining One, son of Dawn,* applying to him the name of a character from ancient Canaanite myth. (The term *Shining One* is not known from Canaanite texts, but his father, *Dawn,* is described in Canaanite myth from Ugarit as a son

How are you felled to earth,
O vanquisher of nations!
13 Once you thought in your heart,
"I will climb to the sky;
Higher than the stars of God
I will set my throne.
I will sit in the mount of assembly,[a]
On the summit of Zaphon:[b]
14 I will mount the back of a cloud—
I will match the Most High."
15 Instead, you are brought down to Sheol,
To [c-]the bottom of the Pit.[-c]
16 They who behold you stare;
They peer at you closely:
"Is this the man
Who shook the earth,
Who made realms tremble,
17 Who made the world like a waste
And wrecked its towns,
[d-]Who never released his prisoners
to their homes?"
18 All the kings of nations
Were laid, every one, in honor[-d]
Each in his tomb;
19 While you were left lying unburied,
Like loathsome carrion,[e]
Like a trampled corpse
[In] the clothing of slain gashed by the sword
Who sink to the very stones of the Pit.
20 You shall not have a burial like them;
Because you destroyed [f-]your country,
Murdered your people.[-f]

Let the breed of evildoers
Nevermore be named!
21 Prepare a slaughtering block for his sons
Because of the guilt of their father.[g]
Let them not arise to possess the earth!
Then the world's face shall be covered with towns.

of the high god El. The name closely recalls Phaethon son of Eos [or "radiant one" son of "Dawn"] in Greek mythology. Phaethon, a presumptuous young god, was thrown down to earth by Zeus.) This character seems to have attempted to join the head of the pantheon, whether this was El (who was known in Canaanite texts as *Most High*) or Baal (whose palace was located on the *summit of* Mount *Zaphon*); Isaiah seems to mix the characteristics of these two Canaanite deities in his allusion to the myth. Similar references to a Canaanite myth in which an overreaching god is expelled from heaven occur in Ezek. ch 28 and Ps. 82, and possibly in Gen. 6.1–4. Rabbinic commentators identify the term *Shining One* with the morning star (the planet Venus, at certain times visible on the horizon at dawn). Indeed, the mythological figure to whom this poem refers may have been associated with the morning star in ancient Canaanite myth. **16–21:** The fate of the king's body. Denied a proper burial, he is condemned to the most miserable fate in the underworld.

a I.e., the assembly of the gods in council. *b The abode of the gods; cf. Ps. 48.3.*
c-c A region of the netherworld reserved for those who have not received decent burial; cf. Ezek. 32.21 ff.
d-d Emendation yields "Who chained to his palace gate / All the kings of nations? / Yet they were all laid in honor ..." The practice of chaining captive chieftains to gates is attested in Mesopotamia.
e So several ancient versions; cf. postbiblical neṣel, *"putrefying flesh or blood."*
f-f Emendation yields "... countries, / Murdered peoples." *g Heb. "fathers."*

22–23: A later editor added these lines to the original poem by Isaiah to connect it to the hoped-for destruction of Babylon.

14.24–27: A short prophecy on the downfall of Assyria, which Isaiah predicts (wrongly, as it turned out) will occur in a climactic battle to take place in the land of Israel. Cf. the similar prophecies in 10.5–15.

[22] I will rise up against them—declares the LORD of Hosts—
and will wipe out from Babylon name and remnant, kith
and kin—declares the LORD—[23] and I will make it a home of
bitterns,[a] pools of water. I will sweep it with a broom of extermination—declares the LORD of Hosts.

24 The LORD of Hosts has sworn this oath:
"As I have designed, so shall it happen;
What I have planned, that shall come to pass:
25 To break Assyria in My land,
To crush him on My mountain."[b]
And his yoke shall drop off them,
And his burden shall drop from their[c] backs.
26 That is the plan that is planned
For all the earth;
That is why an arm is poised
Over all the nations.
27 For the LORD of Hosts has planned,
Who then can foil it?

a *Meaning of Heb. uncertain.*

b *Heb. "mountains"; for the designation of the entire land of Israel as the* LORD*'s mountain, cf. 11.9.*

c *Heb. "his." The last two lines of this verse would read well after v. 26.*

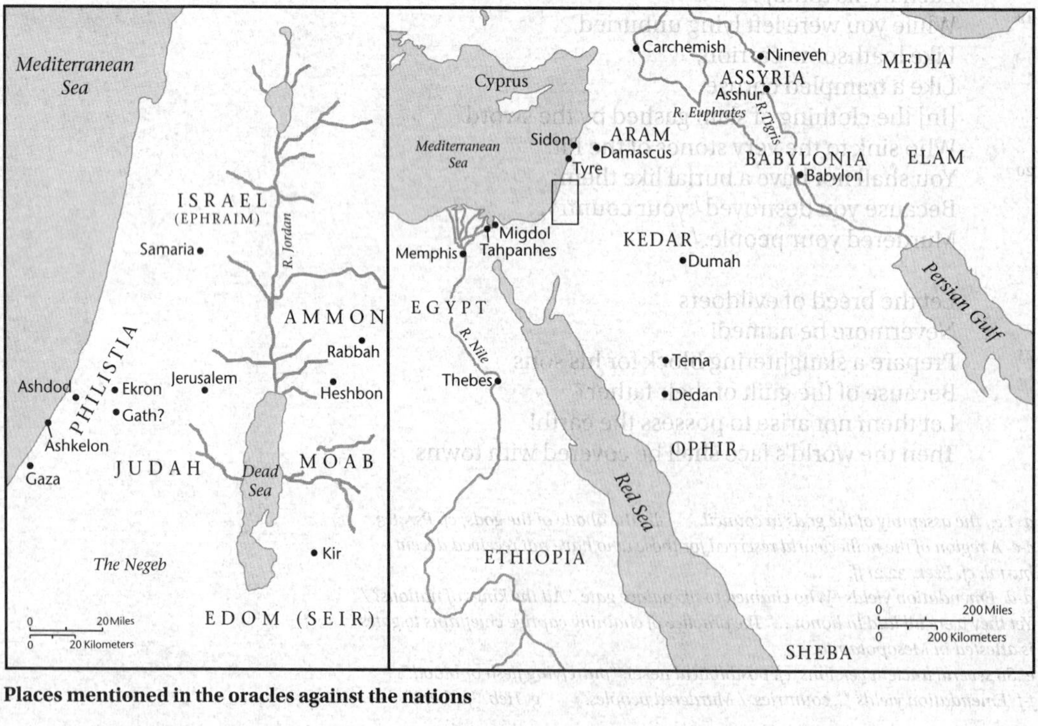

Places mentioned in the oracles against the nations

It is His arm that is poised,
And who can stay it?

28 This pronouncement was made in the year that King Ahaz died:

29 Rejoice not, all Philistia,
Because the staff of him that beat you is broken.
For from the stock of a snake there sprouts an asp,
A flying seraph[a] branches out from it.
30 [b]The first-born of the poor shall graze[-b]
And the destitute lie down secure.
[c]I will kill your stock by famine,[-c]
And it shall slay the very last of you.
31 Howl, O gate; cry out, O city;
Quake, all Philistia!
[d]For a stout one is coming from the north
And there is no straggler in his ranks.[-d]

32 And what will he answer the messengers of
any nation?
That Zion has been established by the LORD:
In it, the needy of His people shall find shelter.

15

The "Moab" Pronouncement.

Ah, in the night Ar was sacked,
Moab was ruined;
Ah, in the night Kir was sacked,
Moab was ruined.

2 He went up to the temple to weep,
Dibon[e] [went] to the outdoor shrines.
Over Nebo and Medeba
Moab is wailing;
On every head is baldness,
Every beard is shorn.
3 In its streets, they are girt with sackcloth;
On its roofs, in its squares,
Everyone is wailing,
Streaming with tears.
4 Heshbon and Elealeh cry out,
Their voice carries to Jahaz.

a Others "fiery serpent"; cf. Num. 21.6, 8.

b-b Emendation yields "The poor shall graze in his pasture." This line and the next would read well after v. 32.

c-c Emendation yields "It shall kill your offspring with its venom (zar'ekh berosho)."

d-d Meaning of Heb. uncertain; the rendering "stout one" is suggested by the Syriac 'ashshīn.

e Regarded as the principal city of Moab.

14.28–32: A short oracle concerning the Philistines. The sad and surprising fate of the Philistines after the death of an Assyrian ruler is contrasted with the security Zion will enjoy.

15.1–16.14: An oracle concerning Moab, with an addendum. *Moab* was the land immediately east of the Dead Sea. The Moabites, according to Gen. 19.36–37, were descended from Abraham's nephew Lot and are thus related to the Israelites, but relations between the two nations were usually tense (see, e.g., Num. 22.1–6; Judg. ch 3; 2 Kings ch 3).

15.1–16.12: A prediction of Moab's imminent defeat. The prediction is expressed in a lament: The author "mourns" over an event that will soon occur. (Alternatively, the poem may have been composed as a real lament after Moab was defeated by some invader, unknown to us.)
15.1–4: The suffering of Moab. *Ar, Kir, Dibon, Nebo,* and *Medeba* are locations in Moab. (Medeba is the location of the much later, famous 6th c. CE mosaic map which focuses on Jerusalem.)

5–9: More descriptions of the distress of the Moabites, who flee toward Edom, the land immediately south of Moab. *Zoar, Luhith, Horonaim,* and *Nimrim* are located in southwestern Moab, near the Edomite border. These vv. seem to trace the path of the Moabite refugees on their way to Edom. **16.1–5:** The Moabite refugees in Edom send a message to the Judean king, seeking haven or aid. *Sela* (which means "rock") is an Edomite city, perhaps now known as Petra (which is Gk for "rock"); cf. Ps. 137.9. **2:** This v. may belong after 15.9; it describes the Moabite refugees lingering at the river Arnon while they were still in Moab on their way to Edom.

Therefore,
[a-]The shock troops of Moab shout,[-a]
His body is convulsed.
5 My heart cries out for Moab—
His fugitives flee down to Zoar,
To Eglath-shelishiyah.
For the ascent of Luhith
They ascend with weeping;
On the road to Horonaim
They raise a cry of anguish.

6 Ah, the waters of Nimrim
Are become a desolation;
The grass is sear,
The herbage is gone,
Vegetation is vanished.

7 Therefore,
The gains they have made, and their stores,
They carry to the Wadi of Willows.

8 Ah, the cry has compassed
The country of Moab:
All the way to Eglaim her wailing,
Even at Beer-elim her wailing!

9 Ah, the waters of Dimon are full of blood[b]
For I pour added [water] on Dimon;
I drench[c] it—for Moab's refugees—
With soil[d] for its remnant.

16 [e]Dispatch as messenger
The ruler of the land,
From Sela in the wilderness
To the mount of Fair Zion:
2 "Like fugitive birds,
Like nestlings driven away,
Moab's villagers linger
By the fords of the Arnon.
3 Give advice,
[f-]Offer counsel.[-f]
At high noon make
Your shadow like night:

a-a Change of vocalization yields "The loins of Moab are trembling."
b Emendation yields "tears." *c Cf. 16.9.*
d Emendation yields "tears"; cf. Ugaritic 'dm't.
e Meaning of vv. 1 and 2 uncertain. *f-f Meaning of Heb. uncertain.*

Conceal the outcasts,
Betray not the fugitives.
4 Let [a]Moab's outcasts[a]
Find asylum in you;
Be a shelter for them
Against the despoiler."

For violence has vanished,
Rapine is ended,
And marauders have perished from this land.
5 And a throne shall be established in goodness
In the tent of David,
And on it shall sit in faithfulness
A ruler devoted to justice
And zealous for equity.[b]

6 "We have heard of Moab's pride—
Most haughty is he—
Of his pride and haughtiness and arrogance,
And of the iniquity in him."[c]

7 Ah, let Moab howl;
Let all in Moab howl!
For the raisin-cakes[d] of Kir-hareseth
You shall moan most pitifully.
8 The vineyards of Heshbon are withered,
And the vines of Sibmah;
[e]Their tendrils spread
To Baale-goiim,[e]
And reached to Jazer,
And strayed to the desert;
Their shoots spread out
And crossed the sea.

9 Therefore,
As I weep for Jazer,
So I weep for Sibmah's vines;
O Heshbon and Elealeh,
I drench you with my tears.
[f]Ended are the shouts
Over your fig and grain harvests.[f]
10 Rejoicing and gladness
Are gone from the farm land;

6: The Judeans respond to the Moabites' request. **7–11:** The lament for the Moabites continues; here as in ch 15 the genuine sympathy of the Judean author (in contrast to the official Judean response in 16.6) is evident. *Heshbon, Jazer,* and *Elealah* are places in Moab; the other locations are not known, but they must lie within Moab as well.

a-a Heb. "my outcasts, Moab." *b 14.32, above, would read well here.*

c Baddaw *is a suffixed form of the preposition* bede: *Nah. 2.13; Hab. 2.13; Job 39.25; with suffixes, Job 11.3, 41.4.*

d Jer. 48.36 has "men." *e-e Meaning of Heb. uncertain.*

f-f Jer. 48.32 reads "A ravager has come down / Upon your fig and grape harvests."

In the vineyards no shouting
Or cheering is heard.
No more does the treader
Tread wine in the presses—
The shouts [a]have been silenced.[-a]

11 Therefore,
Like a lyre my heart moans for Moab,
And my very soul for Kir-heres.

[12] And when it has become apparent that Moab has gained nothing in the outdoor shrine, he shall come to pray in his temple—but to no avail.

[13] That is the word that the LORD spoke concerning Moab long ago. [14] And now the LORD has spoken: In three years, fixed like the years of a hired laborer, Moab's population, with all its huge multitude, shall shrink. Only a remnant shall be left, of no consequence.

17

The "Damascus" Pronouncement.

Behold,
Damascus shall cease to be a city;
It shall become a heap of ruins.
2 [b]The towns of Aroer shall be deserted;[-b]
They shall be a place for flocks
To lie down, with none disturbing.

3 Fortresses shall cease from Ephraim,[c]
And sovereignty from Damascus;
The remnant of Aram shall become
Like the mass of Israelites
—declares the LORD of Hosts.

4 In that day,
The mass of Jacob shall dwindle,
And the fatness of his body become lean:
5 After being like the standing grain
Harvested by the reaper—
Who reaps ears by the armful—
He shall be like the ears that are gleaned
In the Valley of Rephaim.
6 Only gleanings shall be left of him,
As when one beats an olive tree:

a-a Lit. "I have silenced."

b-b Emendation yields (cf. Septuagint) "Its towns shall be deserted forevermore."

c Emendation yields "Aram."

12: This line may be part of the lament that begins in 16.7; or it may be the writer's suggestion regarding the refuge the Moabites request: Allow them to enter Judah, but not to pray at the Temple in Jerusalem (translating: "When Moab appears at the high place, and they weary themselves [there], they will come to His Temple to pray, but they shall not be allowed").

13–14: A later addition, apparently the event predicted in 15.1–16.12 did not come to pass, and Isaiah asserts that the expected defeat of Moab will in fact occur soon. It is possible that 15.1–16.12 were written before Isaiah's time, and that Isaiah reused the text, adding 16.13–14 to relate the older lament or prediction to his own time. Jer. ch 48 is based on 15.1–16.12; there this oracle is expanded and reworked. The older text in 15.1–16.12 is applied to Isaiah's present situation: Moab will be destroyed within three years. *Long ago* means merely "in the past," whether recent or distant. It is even possible that Isaiah himself authored the older text, and that he subsequently composed this addendum when his original prophecy did not come to pass. Cf. 8.16–18, which seems to reflect Isaiah's reaction to the apparent failure of his predictions earlier in chs 7–8.

17.1–14: An oracle concerning Damascus and the Northern Kingdom. This ch addresses the Syro-Ephraimite crisis, which took place in 735 BCE. This crisis is described in 7.1–8.23, and the background provided concerning those chs above should be consulted when reading this ch as well. This ch concerns not only *Damascus* (capital of Syria or Aram) but also their allies, the northern Israelites or Ephraimites, and the Assyrian empire against whom the Arameans (or Syrians) and Ephraimites revolted. **1–6:** As in chs 7–8, the downfalls of Damascus and Ephraim are predicted. The instrument of their destruction, the Assyrian empire, is not specified here. **2:** Several cities called *Aroer* are known in the Bible, but none is

Two berries or three on the topmost branch,
Four or five [a]on the boughs of the crown[-a]
—declares the LORD, the God of Israel.

[7] In that day, men shall turn to their Maker, their eyes look to the Holy One of Israel; [8] they shall not turn to the altars that their own hands made, or look to the sacred posts and incense stands that their own fingers wrought.

[9] In that day, their fortress cities shall be like the deserted sites which [b]the Horesh and the Amir[-b] abandoned because of the Israelites; and there shall be desolation.

10 Truly, you have forgotten the God who saves you
And have not remembered the Rock who shelters you;
That is why, though you plant a delightful[c] sapling,
What you sow proves a disappointing slip.
11 On the day that you plant, you see it grow;
On the morning you sow, you see it bud—
But the branches wither away
On a day of sickness and mortal agony.

12 Ah, the roar of many peoples
That roar as roars the sea,
The rage of nations that rage
As rage the mighty waters—
13 Nations raging like massive waters!
But He shouts at them, and they flee far away,
Driven like chaff before winds in the hills,
And like tumbleweed before a gale.
14 At eventide, lo, terror!
By morning, it is no more.
Such is the lot of our despoilers,
The portion of them that plunder us.

18

Ah,
[d]land in the deep shadow of wings,[-d]
Beyond the rivers of Nubia!

a-a Lit. "on her boughs, the many-branched one."
b-b Septuagint reads "the Amorites and the Hivites."
c Emendation yields "true." So Vulgate (cf. Septuagint); cf. Jer. 2.21.
d-d Or "Most sheltered land"; cf., e.g., 30.2, 3; Pss. 36.8; 57.2; 61.5.

located in Aram, which is the main focus of vv. 1–3. Hence the emendation mentioned in translators' note *c* seems likely. **7–8:** A reflection on the effect these events will have on humanity generally; as elsewhere (2.1–4; 19.19–25), Isaiah maintains that God's intervention in political events will lead to an era in which humans universally acknowledge the one God. The Heb word translated here as *men* is "ha-'adam," which refers to human beings generally, not necessarily limited to males. **9:** A continuation of the prophecy in vv. 1–6 concerning the downfall of Israel and Aram, which will be emptied of their populations. **10–11:** A rebuke specifically directed toward the Israelites, who ally with Arameans rather than depending on God. These vv. also could be directed against Ahaz, the Judean king at the time of the Syro-Ephraimite crisis, who, relied on human saviors (the Assyrians) rather than God. Cf. Isaiah's criticism of Ahaz in 8.5–8. **10:** *Delightful sapling,* alternatively, "gardens for Adonis" or "gardens for the Delightful One." Some believe that this v. describes gardens planted in honor of a Semitic deity of vegetation (variously known as Dumuzi, Tammuz, or Baal, and later called Adonis by the Greeks). Semites believed that this god, like the grass or flowers in the desert, springs to life each year during the fall rainy season and dies during the summer. The Israelites were both unfaithful and self-defeating in their reliance on this false deity. **12–14:** The terrifying arrival and sudden defeat of the enemy. These vv. may refer to the coming arrival of the Syro-Ephraimite forces in Jerusalem; they may also (or alternatively) be intended to predict the arrival of Assyrian forces there. Cf. 8.5–8; 29.1–8. The description matches the surprising withdrawal of Assyrian forces in 701 BCE, three decades after the Syro-Ephraimite crisis (see 10.28–34 n.). Isaiah may have issued the prediction as early as the Syro-Ephraimite crisis in 735, thinking (mistakenly) that the Assyrians would overrun Judah then, though that did not happen until 701. The comparison of an invading army to raging waters appears frequently in Assyrian propaganda of Isaiah's day, while the images in v. 13 are found in other biblical literature (see, e.g., Pss. 1.4; 83.14).

18.1–7: An oracle concerning the Ethiopians. Because this passage lacks a superscription, its setting, background, and meaning are not clear, but the ch suggests that it concerns *Nubia* (Heb "Kush"), the area south of Egypt, sometimes referred to as Ethiopia. In the late 700s and early 600s BCE Egypt was ruled by pharaohs of Ethiopian origin.

This ch probably refers to diplomatic and military moves in which these Ethiopian pharaohs play the central role. **1–3:** Judah sends messengers to the Ethiopians, responding to ambassadors who had been sent to Judah. The Ethiopian ruler of Egypt may have been encouraging a revolt against the Assyrians. At various times, ancient Israel found itself quite literally in the middle of Egyptian and Mesopotamian battles for power. **3–6:** Isaiah encourages the Judeans to send a negative response to the anti-Assyrian overtures: Judah is safe, since the LORD is *calm and confident in* (His) *habitation,* the Temple Mount in Jerusalem. This passage reflects on the Isaianic notion of the inviolability of Zion. Because the LORD is present in His Temple, Jerusalem will never fall, and therefore the Judeans need not depend on alliances with other nations for their safety. Cf. 1.8–9; 7.2–9; 8.8. **4–6:** The imagery describes the defeat of what had seemed a strong and promising empire, probably the Assyrians. *Kites,* a bird of prey; a better translation might be "vultures" or "carrion eaters," since the birds will be devouring the corpses littering the hills. **7:** As elsewhere in Isaiah, the defeat of the enemy will lead to worldwide recognition of the God of Mount Zion.

2 Go, swift messengers,
To a nation [a]far and remote,
To a people thrust forth and away[a]—
A nation of gibber and chatter[b]—
Whose land is cut off by streams;
[c]Which sends out envoys by sea,
In papyrus vessels upon the water![c]

3 [Say this:]
"All you who live in the world
And inhabit the earth,
When a flag is raised in the hills, take note!
When a ram's horn is blown, give heed!"
4 For thus the LORD said to me:
"I rest calm and confident[d] in My habitation—
Like a scorching heat upon sprouts,
[e]Like a rain-cloud in the heat of reaping time."[e]
5 For before the harvest,[f] yet after the budding,
When the blossom has hardened into berries,
He will trim away the twigs with pruning hooks,
And lop off the trailing branches.[g]
6 They shall all be left
To the kites of the hills
And to the beasts of the earth;
The kites shall summer on them
And all the beasts of the earth shall winter
on them.

7 In that time,
Tribute shall be brought to the LORD of Hosts
[From] a people far and remote,
From a people thrust forth and away—
A nation of gibber and chatter,
Whose land is cut off by streams—
At the place where the name of the LORD of Hosts
abides,
At Mount Zion.

a-a Meaning of Heb. uncertain.
b Meaning of Heb. uncertain; cf. 28.10. Biblical writers often characterize distant nations by their unintelligible speech; cf. 33.19; Deut. 28.49; Jer. 5.15.
c-c Brought down from beginning of verse for clarity. The Hebrew verb for "sends" agrees in gender with "nation," not with "land."
d Cf. hibbit *"to rely" (Job 6.19). The related noun* mabbaṭ *occurs with similar meaning in Isa. 20.5, 6.* *e-e I.e., like a threat of disaster; cf. Eccl. 11.4.*
f Emendation yields "vintage." *g A figure of speech for the defeated enemy.*

19 The "Egypt" Pronouncement.

Mounted on a swift cloud,
The LORD will come to Egypt;
Egypt's idols shall tremble before Him,
And the heart of the Egyptians shall sink within them.

2 "I will incite Egyptian against Egyptian:
They shall war with each other,
Every man with his fellow,
City with city
And kingdom with kingdom.[a]
3 Egypt shall be drained of spirit,
And I will confound its plans;
So they will consult the idols and the shades
And the ghosts and the familiar spirits.
4 And I will place the Egyptians
At the mercy of a harsh master,
And a ruthless king shall rule them"
—declares the Sovereign, the LORD of Hosts.
5 Water shall fail from the seas,
Rivers dry up and be parched,
6 Channels turn foul as they ebb,
And Egypt's canals run dry.
Reed and rush shall decay,
7 [b-]And the Nile papyrus by the Nile-side[-b]
And everything sown by the Nile
Shall wither, blow away, and vanish.
8 The fishermen shall lament;
All who cast lines in the Nile shall mourn,
And those who spread nets on the water shall languish.
9 The flax workers, too, shall be dismayed,
Both carders and weavers chagrined.[c]
10[d] Her foundations shall be crushed,
And all who make dams shall be despondent.

11 Utter fools are the nobles of Tanis;
The sagest of Pharaoh's advisers
[Have made] absurd predictions.
How can you say to Pharaoh,
"I am a scion of sages,
A scion of Kedemite kings"?[e]

a I.e., the various districts of Egypt, which in Isaiah's time were governed by hereditary princes. *b-b Meaning of Heb. uncertain.* *c Meaning of Heb. uncertain.*
d Meaning of verse uncertain; emendation yields "Her drinkers shall be dejected, / And all her brewers despondent."
e Or "advisers." The wisdom of the Kedemites was proverbial; cf. 1 Kings 5.10.

19.1–24: A universalist oracle concerning Egypt. Like other oracles concerning the nations, this ch begins by describing the troubles with which God will afflict Egypt. It continues, however, by viewing these troubles as identical to the troubles with which God afflicts Israel: They will lead the Egyptians to recognize the one true God. The ch ends with a remarkably universalist perspective.

1–18: Divine judgment against Egypt. The first section of the ch is negative in tone and poetic in structure. **1–10:** These vv. describe the collapse of Egypt's gods (vv. 1, 3), political stability (vv. 2–4), physical environment (vv. 5–7), and economy (vv. 8–10). **4:** The divine punishment will involve a foreigner coming to rule over Egypt; this v. may refer to the Ethiopian dynasty that took control of Egypt in the late 8th c. (described in the previous ch) or, more likely, to an Assyrian invasion (described in the following ch). **5–6:** *The seas:* Heb is singular and refers to the Nile, which is wide enough to be called a sea during the flood season. In Egypt, agriculture, transportation, and hence life itself depended on the Nile and its canals. **11–15:** The Egyptians rely on their traditional wisdom. Consequently, they fail to understand the cause of their troubles, which come directly from the one God of Israel. *Tanis* and *Memphis* were leading cities in ancient Egypt.

12 Where, indeed, are your sages?
Let them tell you, let them discover
What the LORD of Hosts has planned against Egypt.
13 The nobles of Tanis have been fools,
The nobles of Memphis deluded;
Egypt has been led astray
By the chiefs of her tribes.
14 The LORD has mixed within her
A spirit of distortion,
Which shall lead Egypt astray in all her undertakings
As a vomiting drunkard goes astray;
15 Nothing shall be achieved in Egypt
By either head or tail,
Palm branch or reed.[a]

16 In that day, the Egyptians shall be like women, trembling
and terrified because the LORD of Hosts will raise His hand
against them. 17 And the land of Judah shall also be the dread of
the Egyptians; they shall quake whenever anybody mentions it
to them, because of what the LORD of Hosts is planning against
them. 18 In that day, there shall be several[b] towns in the land of
Egypt speaking the language of Canaan and swearing loyalty to
the LORD of Hosts; one[c] shall be called Town of Heres.[d]
19 In that day, there shall be an altar to the LORD inside the
land of Egypt and a pillar to the LORD at its border.[e] 20 They
shall serve as a symbol and reminder of the LORD of Hosts
in the land of Egypt, so that when [the Egyptians] cry out to
the LORD against oppressors, He will send them a savior and
champion to deliver them. 21 For the LORD will make Himself
known to the Egyptians, and the Egyptians shall acknowledge
the LORD in that day, and they shall serve [Him] with sacrifice
and oblation and shall make vows to the LORD and fulfill them.
22 The LORD will first afflict and then heal the Egyptians; when
they turn back to the LORD, He will respond to their entreaties
and heal them.
23 In that day, there shall be a highway from Egypt to Assyria.
The Assyrians shall join with the Egyptians and Egyptians with
the Assyrians, and then the Egyptians together with the Assyrians shall serve [the LORD].

24 In that day, Israel shall be a third partner with Egypt and
Assyria as a blessing[f] on earth; 25 for the LORD of Hosts will

a I.e., a man of either high or low station; cf. 9.13, 14.
b Lit. "five." *c Or "each one."*
d Meaning uncertain. Many Heb. mss. read ḥeres, *"sun," which may refer to Heliopolis, i.e., Sun City, in Egypt. Targum's "Beth Shemesh" (cf. Jer. 43.13) has the same meaning.* *e As a symbol of the LORD's sovereignty over Egypt.*
f I.e., a standard by which blessing is invoked; cf. Gen. 12.2 with note.

16–17: The Egyptians come to realize that the God of Israel is the source of their troubles, and hence also of their salvation. **16:** *Like women*: It was an insult to a man's virility to be likened to a woman.

18–25: Divine grace toward Egypt. This section, typified by the refrain *in that day*, describes the outcome of the inducements to change with which God afflicted the Egyptians. The style of this section differs from the first one, moving from poetry of rebuke to a series of prose oracles that are positive in nature. **18–22:** These vv. describe how the Egyptians will accept the one God and become His servants, just as the Israelites are. Thus they link up with texts such as 2.1–4 and 11.10. These passages share a vision of a new world order: Ethnicities will remain distinct, but all nations will adopt monotheism and will worship the God of Israel. Some believe these vv. were added by later scribes, and that they refer to Jewish communities in Egypt during the postexilic period, when several Jewish temples existed in Egyptian cities such as Elephantine and Leontopolis. Similarly, the Talmud (*b. Menaḥ.* 109b) understands this section to predict the founding of the Jewish temple in Leontopolis in the 160s BCE, rather than foretelling a temple in which Egyptians worship the LORD. **18:** *The language of Canaan* was the language spoken by the Israelites; Hebrew, a term never found in Tanakh, is a Canaanite dialect, quite different from Egyptian. *Heres* in Heb means "destruction." **23–25:** The universal kingdom of God. Even the archenemies of the Israelites will recognize the one God. Consequently, two empires that perennially fought each other (Egypt and Assyria), and Israel, a small nation between them, variously attacked by either one will be at peace with each other. Some rabbinic commentators (Tg., Rashi) were troubled by v. 25, which puts Israel's enemies on an equal spiritual footing with Israel. They paraphrase as follows: "Blessed be My people Israel, who came out of Egypt and saw

bless them, saying, "Blessed be My people Egypt, My handiwork Assyria, and My very own Israel."

20 It was the year that the Tartan[a] came to Ashdod—being sent by King Sargon of Assyria—and attacked Ashdod
and took it. 2 Previously,[b] the LORD had spoken to Isaiah son of Amoz, saying, "Go, untie the sackcloth from your loins and take your sandals off your feet," which he had done, going naked and barefoot.
3 And now the LORD said, "It is a sign and a portent for Egypt and Nubia. Just as My servant Isaiah has gone naked and barefoot for three years,
4 so shall the king of Assyria drive off the captives of Egypt and the exiles of Nubia, young and old, naked and barefoot and with bared buttocks—to the shame of Egypt!
5 And they shall be dismayed and chagrined because of Nubia their hope and Egypt their boast.
6 In that day, the dwellers of this coastland shall say, 'If this could happen to those we looked to, to whom we fled for help and rescue from the king of Assyria, how can we ourselves escape?' "

21 [c-]The "Desert of the Sea" Pronouncement.[-c]

Like the gales
That race through the Negeb,
It comes from the desert,
The terrible land.
2 A harsh prophecy
Has been announced to me:

a An Assyrian title meaning "General"; cf. 2 Kings 18.17 *and note.*
b Lit. "At that time."
c-c Emendation yields "The 'From the Desert' Pronouncement," agreeing with the phrase farther on in the verse.

My handiwork, which I performed against Assyria." This far-reaching reinterpretation is rejected by other rabbinic authorities (such as Radak), who insist, correctly, the v. carries a strong universal message.

20.1–6: A prophetic sign concerning the Egyptians. In 713, a Greek who usurped the throne of the coastal city-state of *Ashdod* organized a revolt against the Assyrian empire, to whom the various states along the Mediterranean, including Judah, were vassals, obliged to send tribute. Assyrian records tell us that Judah participated in the rebellion. Assyrian historical records indicate that the Assyrians marched against Ashdod, whose Greek usurper fled. Surprisingly, however, they make no reference to military action against Jerusalem at that time. (The Assyrians also took no action against Moab or Edom, who also particpated in the coalition). The rebellious states seem to have appealed to the pharaoh ruling over Egypt (who came from *Nubia,* i.e., Ethiopia) for help at the early stages of the rebellion. In 711, the Assyrian king, *Sargon,* sent his chief-of-staff or *Tartan* to subdue Ashdod. Ashdod and two other cities were besieged, and the Assyrians imprisoned the king of Ashdod. According to this ch, Isaiah argued vigorously against relying on Egyptian help in 713–711, just as he had argued against relying on the Assyrians in 735 (see 7.1–8.23). Isaiah made his point by means of a symbolic action: He imitated the fate that would await the Egyptians (and most likely many Judeans as well) if the situation developed into a full-fledged war against Assyria. Other prophets also used symbolic actions to get their points across; see, for example, Jer. 13.1–14; Ezek. 4.1–5.17. Such actions evoked curiosity among the Judeans, encouraging the prophetic message to be spread more widely in a world that was not highly literate. **6:** *Dwellers of this coastland* refers most likely to the Ashdodites, who instigated the revolt against Assyria; the Philistine city of Ashdod is located on the coast. Many rabbinic commentators suggest, however, that "coastland" refers to the whole land of Israel, including the hill country where the Judeans lived.

21.1–10: An oracle concerning Babylonia. This oracle may date from Isaiah's day, during the reign of the Babylonian king, Merodach-baladan, at the end of the 8th century, when the relatively small kingdom of Babylonia attempted to defeat the larger Assyrian empire. This ultimately futile attempt was relevant to the Judeans, because the Babylonians endeavored to persuade the Judean king, Hezekiah, to join the anti-Assyrian coalition. See ch 39, and also 2 Kings ch 20. If this is the setting of the passage, Isaiah predicts defeat for the Babylonians, in spite of their attempt to create a unified front with the Judeans. Alternatively, this text may date to a century after Isaiah, to a time in which the Babylonians had in fact become the great power of the ancient Near East. In that case, an unnamed prophet later than Isaiah predicts the downfall of the Babylonians. The language of this oracle is unusually obscure. **1:** *Desert of the Sea,* i.e., Babylon. The term may be a Heb translation of an Akkadian term used to refer to southern Mesopotamia, where Babylon was located. (Akkadian was the language of Babylonia and

Assyria.) **2:** *Elam, Media:* These two nations were located to the north of Assyria. Elam joined Merodach-baladan's doomed campaign against Assyria. If this text dates from the 8th c. (that is, the era of Isaiah son of Amoz), then this v. calls on Elam and Media to defend themselves from the coming Assyrian onslaught. Elam and Media eventually became part of the Persian empire, and some late biblical writers seem to equate Elam and Media with Persia. If this text dates from the 6th c. (and is thus much later than Isaiah son of Amoz's prophecies), then these vv. call on Elam and Media to wage war against Babylonia. They thus anticipate the fall of Babylonia to the Persians in 539 BCE, and resemble the prophecies of Deutero-Isaiah (see the intro.). **6–9:** A description of prophetic inspiration: The prophet is like the sentry in a watchtower, who sees the invading armies before anyone else can; see especially the parallels between vv. 8–9 and Hab. 2.1–2.

"The betrayer is [a-]betraying,
The ravager ravaging.[-a]
Advance, Elam!
Lay siege, Media!
[b-]I have put an end
To all her sighing."[-b]
3 Therefore my loins
Are seized with trembling;
I am gripped by pangs
Like a woman in travail,
Too anguished to hear,
Too frightened to see.
4 My mind is confused,
I shudder in panic.
My night of pleasure
He has turned to terror:
5 "Set the table!"
To "Let the watchman watch!"
"Eat and drink!"
To "Up, officers! Grease[c] the shields!"

6 For thus my Lord said to me:
"Go, set up a sentry;
Let him announce what he sees.
7 He will see mounted men,
Horsemen in pairs—
Riders on asses,
Riders on camels—
And he will listen closely,
Most attentively."
8 And [d-][like] a lion he[-d] called out:
[e-]"On my Lord's lookout[-e] I stand
Ever by day,
And at my post I watch
Every night.
9 And there they come, mounted men—
Horsemen in pairs!"
Then he spoke up and said,
"Fallen, fallen is Babylon,
And all the images of her gods
Have crashed to the ground!"
10 [f-]My threshing, the product of my threshing floor:[-f]

a-a Emendation yields "betrayed ... ravaged"; cf. 33.1.
b-b Emendation yields "Put an end to all her merrymaking!"
c Emendation yields "Grasp." *d-d 1QIs[a] reads "The watcher."*
e-e Or "On a lookout, my lord." *f-f Connection of Heb. uncertain.*

What I have heard from the LORD of Hosts,
The God of Israel—
That I have told to you.

11 The "Dumah"[a] Pronouncement.

A call comes to me from Seir:
"Watchman, what of the night?
Watchman, what of the night?"
12 The watchman replied,
"Morning came, and so did night.
If you would inquire, inquire.
Come back again."

13 The "In the Steppe" Pronouncement.

In the scrub, in the steppe, you will lodge,
O caravans of the Dedanites!
14 Meet the thirsty with water,
You who dwell in the land of Tema;
Greet the fugitive with bread.
15 For they have fled before swords:
Before the whetted sword,
Before the bow that was drawn,
Before the stress of war.

16 For thus my Lord has said to me: "In another year, fixed like the years of a hired laborer, all the multitude of Kedar shall vanish; 17 the remaining bows of Kedar's warriors shall be few in number; for the LORD, the God of Israel, has spoken.

22 The [b-]"Valley of Vision"[-b] Pronouncement.

[c]What can have happened to you
That you have gone, all of you, up on the roofs,

a *Name of a people; cf. Gen. 25.14.* b-b *Meaning of Heb. uncertain.*
c *Vv. 1–3 describe a scene of mourning to take place in Jerusalem in the near future. In the ancient Near East, public weeping took place on the low flat roofs as well as in the streets and squares; cf. above, 15.3; Jer. 48.38.*

21.11–12: An oracle concerning Dumah. This oracle is as obscure as it is brief; it is not even clear to whom it is addressed. *Dumah* may be a poetic, short form of the word "Edom," a nation located southeast of Judah. *Seir* was another name for Edom. Alternatively, *Dumah* may refer to a city in northern Arabia. These two explanations are not necessarily exclusive, since the Arabian city in question is due east of Edom. Thus the oracle may address both the Edomites and the Arab tribes with whom they traded. Finally, *Dumah* may be a noun meaning "silence"—an apt title for this oracle, whose meaning is not spoken clearly. In all likelihood, the oracle predicts that Edom and/or the northern Arabs will be defeated in the upcoming upheaval described in the previous ten vv. **12:** This v. may be taken to refer to a real watchman, who is asked whether his watch has passed peacefully; or it may be metaphorical, referring to the night of oppression (of the Edomites and/or the Arabs? or of the Judeans?) at the hands of the conquerors.

21.13–17: An oracle concerning Arabia. Like the previous oracle, these vv. probably describe the defeat of various tribes who were either allied with Babylonia against Assyria (if the oracle dates to the 8th c.) or who were allied with the Babylonian empire that is about to fall (if the oracle dates to the 6th c.). **13:** *In the Steppe:* A more likely translation is "Arabia." *Dedanites,* a nomadic Arab tribe of northern Arabia; they are often mentioned in the Bible along with the Edomites, with whom they seem to have had extensive trade relations. **14:** *Tema,* a city located south of Dumah in Arabia. These vv. seem to assume that the defeated Dedanites will flee south to the caravan oasis of Tema, where they will have to seek refuge. **16:** *Kedar,* a tribe of nomads who traded with the Edomites and other settled peoples; they were located in the extreme north of the Arabian desert.

22.1–25: Oracles concerning Jerusalem and its leadership. Two oracles (in 1–14 and 15–25) are presented under a single rubric in v. 1, which speaks of them as a single *Pronouncement.* They were written, in all likelihood, before the Assyrian invasion in 705–701 BCE. Hezekiah, king of Judah, joined a revolt against the Assyrian king, Sennacherib. Sennacherib's army devastated most of Judah and surrounded Jerusalem but did not conquer it. See 2 Kings 18.13–20.21; Isa. chs 36–39; 2 Chron. ch 32. (Some, however, believe that the ch relates to the events of 713, described in 20.1–6 n.) Isaiah seems to have disapproved of the

2 O you who were full of tumult,
You clamorous town,
You city so gay?
Your slain are not the slain of the sword
Nor the dead of battle.[a]
3 Your officers have all departed,
They fled far away;
Your survivors were all taken captive,
[b-]Taken captive without their bows.[-b]
4 That is why I say, "Let me be,
I will weep bitterly.
Press not to comfort me
For the ruin of [c-]my poor people."[-c]

5 For my Lord GOD of Hosts had a day
Of tumult and din and confusion—
[d-]Kir raged in the Valley of Vision,
And Shoa on the hill;[-d]
6 While Elam bore the quiver
In troops of mounted men,
And Kir bared the shield—
7 And your choicest lowlands
Were filled with chariots and horsemen:
They stormed at Judah's[e] gateway
8 And pressed beyond its screen.[f]
You gave thought on that day
To the arms in the Forest House,[g]
9 And you took note of the many breaches
In the City of David.

[h-]And you collected the water of the Lower Pool;[-h] 10 and you counted the houses of Jerusalem and pulled houses down to fortify the wall; 11 and you constructed a basin between the two walls for the water of the old pool.

a I.e., executed, instead of dying in battle. *b-b Meaning of Heb. uncertain.*
c-c Lit. "the young woman, my people."
d-d Meaning of Heb. uncertain. On Kir see 2 Kings 16.9; Amos 1.5; 9.7; on Shoa see Ezek. 23.23. *e Brought up from 8a for clarity.*
f Judah's gateway is the upper course of the Valley of Elah. The screen is the fortress Azekah, at the mouth of the gateway, which was captured by the Assyrians.
g See 1 Kings 7.2–5; 10.16–17.
h-h This clause would read well after the prose part of v. 11a.

actions taken to fortify Jerusalem (see 2 Kings 20.20; 2 Chron. 32.2–5), perhaps taken under the leadership of the official criticized in 22.25. These preparations betrayed a lack of confidence in the LORD. Alternatively, this ch may have been written after the surprising deliverance of Jerusalem in 701 (or after the surprising failure of the Assyrians to attack Jerusalem in 711, in spite of Judah's participation in the coalition against Assyria organized by the city-state of Ashdod). In that case, the ch expresses Isaiah's disapproval of the tone of the celebrations, which fail to recognize the divine source of deliverance sufficiently. The presence of these oracles in the collection of oracles against foreign nations (chs 13–23) is surprising. Their placement here may suggest that Isaiah regards the Jerusalemites preparations for war and/or their celebrations after the deliverance of 701 (or the failure of the Assyrians to attack Jerusalem in 711) as a sign that Judah differed little from the other nations, for Judah, too, failed to recognize God's plan in directing these events.

22.1–14: The first oracle. 1: *The "Valley of Vision" Pronouncement:* The title is taken from the phrase in v. 5. Jerusalem (or perhaps one particular valley within the hilly city) is referred to as the valley of vision. **1–4:** Isaiah foresees a dramatic turnabout: The city that is festive as it prepares for siege will be surrounded by ruin. **5–7:** The coming calamity. On the theme of the "Day of the LORD," see also Isa. chs 13, 34; Ezek. ch 7; Joel chs 2–3; Amos 5.18–20; Zeph. ch 1. Amos 5.18–20 is especially apposite, since there, as here, the Judeans believe the day will be one of celebration, but it turns out to be one of calamity. **8–14:** The preparations for the upcoming battle, which fail to attend to God's role in salvation. **8:** *The Forest House,* the building housing the royal treasury and weaponry. See 1 Kings 7.2–6; 10.17. **9:** *Breaches,* gaps or weak spots in the wall surrounding the main sector of the city; cf. 2 Kings 32.5. **10–11:** A reference to the waterworks project also mentioned in 2 Kings 20.20. Hezekiah directed workers to build a tunnel (now known as the Siloam Tunnel) to bring water from a spring outside the walls of the city, on the slopes south of the Temple Mount, into a pool known as the Siloam Pool inside the city. The tunnel ensured Jerusalem a safe water supply in the event of a siege. Rediscovered in the 19th c., the tunnel is now accessible to tourists. An inscription found inside the tunnel is perhaps the most famous ancient Heb text outside the Bible; it describes how workmen dug the tunnel from two sides and met in

But you gave no thought to Him who planned it,
You took no note of Him who designed it long before.
12 My Lord GOD of Hosts summoned on that day
To weeping and lamenting,
To tonsuring and girding with sackcloth.
13 Instead, there was rejoicing and merriment,
Killing of cattle and slaughtering of sheep,
Eating of meat and drinking of wine:
"Eat and drink, for tomorrow we die!"
14 Then the LORD of Hosts revealed Himself to my ears:
"This iniquity shall never be forgiven you
Until you die," said my Lord GOD of Hosts.

15 Thus said my Lord GOD of Hosts: Go in to see that steward,
that Shebna, in charge of the palace:
16 What have you here, and whom have you here,
That you have hewn out a tomb for yourself here?—
O you who have hewn your[a] tomb on high;
O you who have hollowed out for yourself[a] an abode
in the cliff!
17 The LORD is about to shake you
[b]Severely, fellow,[b] and then wrap you around Himself.[c]
18 Indeed, He will wind you about Him [d]as a headdress,
a turban.[d]
Off to a broad land!
There shall you die, and there shall be the [e]chariots
bearing your body,[e]
O shame of your master's house!
19 For I will hurl you from your station
And you shall be torn down from your stand.

20 And in that day, I will summon My servant Eliakim son of
Hilkiah, 21 and I will invest him with your tunic, gird him with
your sash, and deliver your authority into his hand; and he
shall be a father to the inhabitants of Jerusalem and the men
of Judah. 22 I will place the keys of David's palace on his shoulders; and what he unlocks none may shut, and what he locks
none may open. 23 He shall be a seat of honor to his father's[f]
household. I will fix him as a peg in a firm place, 24 on which
all the substance of his father's[f] household shall be hung: [g]the
sprouts and the leaves[g]—all the small vessels, from bowls to all
sorts of jars.

a *Heb. "his," "himself."* *b-b* *Emendation yields "as a garment is shaken out."*
c *I.e., and walk off with you; cf. Jer. 43.12.*
d-d *Emendation yields "as a turban is wound about."*
e-e *Emendation yields "abode [cf. v. 16] of your body" [cf. 10.3, 16].*
f *Emendation yields "master's"; cf. v. 18 end.* *g-g* *Meaning of Heb. uncertain.*

the middle. **13:** *Eat and drink ...*, a proverbial expression of fatalism; if Isaiah is not the author, its source is unknown.

22.15–25: An oracle concerning a royal official. Unique among biblical oracles, this text condemns a particular non-royal individual: *Shebna,* who was the royal *steward, in charge of the palace.* These titles are known from other biblical texts and also from ancient Heb inscriptions; they probably denote an office comparable to that of Prime Minister. Isaiah calls for Shebna to be deposed and replaced by a man named *Eliakim son of Hilkiah* (v. 20). In Isa. 36.3; 37.2 and 2 Kings 18.18 Eliakim does in fact have the positions described here, and Shebna has apparently been assigned to a lower-ranking position. Isaiah's audience knew the political background of the conflict at hand, leaving modern readers to speculate as to the reasons that Isaiah objected to Shebna's policies. **16:** A large tomb belonging to a royal official with Shebna's title has been excavated on the eastern edge of the valley of Kidron across from the City of David (in today's Silwan neighborhood), but the inscription in the tomb is damaged, and we do not know the official's name. Archeological evidence points to an 8th c. date for the tomb, suggesting the possibility that it is the tomb described here. If so, Isaiah's prediction that Shebna would never enjoy his magnificent tomb is either incorrect or merely rhetorical, for the owner of that tomb was in fact interred there. **23–24:** The metaphor here depicts Eliakim as a tent peg, ensuring a secure place for his family (the *sprouts and the leaves* and various *vessels* of the metaphor), just as vessels and other objects in a tent would be hung from a rope firmly anchored in the ground. See Ezra 9.8, which uses the same image.

[25][a]In that day—declares the LORD of Hosts—the peg fixed in a firm place shall give way: it shall be cut down and shall fall, and the weight it supports shall be destroyed. For it is the LORD who has spoken.

23

The "Tyre" Pronouncement.

Howl, you [b-]ships of Tarshish![-b]
For havoc has been wrought, not a house is left;
As they came from the land of Kittim,
This was revealed to them.

2 Moan, you coastland dwellers,
You traders of Sidon,
Once thronged by seafarers,
3 Over many waters
Your[c] revenue came:
From the trade of nations,
From the grain of Shihor,
The harvest of the Nile.
4 Be ashamed, O Sidon!
For the sea—this stronghold of the sea—declares,
[d-]"I am as one who has[-d] never labored,
Never given birth,
Never raised youths
Or reared maidens!"
5 When the Egyptians heard it, they quailed
As when they heard about Tyre.

6 Pass on to Tarshish—
Howl, you coastland dwellers!
7 Was such your merry city
In former times, of yore?
Did her feet carry her off
To sojourn far away?

a Apparently continues v. 19. *b-b See note at 2.16.* *c Heb. "her."*
d-d Lit. "I have."

25: The *peg* of this v. seems to refer back to Shebna. Alternatively, if it is the same peg referred to in v. 23, then Eliakim is ultimately subject to the same criticism as the man he replaces.

23.1–18: Oracles concerning the Phoenicians. This passage is a mock lament (see 14.1–23 n.) for *Tyre.* It is not clear whether it was composed as historical reflection after Tyre was attacked by the Assyrian army or as a prophecy beforehand. Throughout the 8th c., the Phoenician city of *Tyre* (located in southern Lebanon) was the capital of a city-state that extended from Acre to *Sidon* and also included colonies elsewhere in the Mediterranean, notably in Cyprus (Heb "Kittim"). Tyre was renowned for its mighty ships; Tyrians grew wealthy from their role as traders and merchants. Indeed the term "Phoenician" or "Canaanite" became a synonym in Heb for "merchant"; see Prov. 31.24. Although Tyre retained some independence from the Assyrian empire, it was required to pay tribute to the Assyrians from the middle of the 8th c. It joined the revolt against Assyria in 705–701, and in 701 the Assyrian king Sennacherib defeated the Tyrians. Tyre's king fled to Cyprus; Sidon and other cities along the coast of Lebanon were removed from Tyrian control; and the Assyrians may have gained some control over parts of Cyprus. Isaiah regards this event favorably, for Tyre, like all wealthy and powerful nations, had grown too great and self-reliant. On the central theme of humility in Isaiah (relevant both for individuals and for nations), cf. 2.5–22; 3.8–15; 10.5–27; 11.1–12.10. Here as in these other passages, Isaiah contrasts the impious self-confidence of human beings with the true grandeur that must be recognized as belonging to God alone. Tyre was located on an island about .8 km (one-half mile) off the coast of Lebanon, and it was never actually conquered during the biblical period, even though its mainland territories were often overrun and its leadership was at times forced to capitulate. Thus it resembles Jerusalem in Isaiah's day: Judah was sorely pressed by the Assyrians (and the Arameans and Ephraimites before them), but the capital never fell. Isaiah may have viewed Tyre as parallel to inviolable Zion and Tyre's experience as especially instructive to the Judeans.

1–14: A lament over the Tyrian empire. 1–5: Phoenician merchant ships, various Tyrian colonies, and Tyre's allies and trading partners learn that Tyre has been subjected to an enemy. **1:** *Tarshish* was a Tyrian trading colony in the western Mediterranean, perhaps located in today's Spain. **6–10:** The Phoenicians are urged to flee to their colonies elsewhere in the Mediterranean, for God is bringing destruction on the Phoenician coastlands. **11–12:** But

8 Who was it that planned this
For crown-wearing Tyre,
Whose merchants were nobles,
Whose traders the world honored?
9 The LORD of Hosts planned it—
To defile all glorious beauty,
To shame all the honored of the world.

10 [a]Traverse your land like the Nile,
Fair Tarshish;[-a]
This is a harbor[b] no more.

11 The LORD poised His arm o'er the sea
And made kingdoms quake;
It was He decreed destruction
For Phoenicia's[c] strongholds,
12 And said,
"You shall be gay no more,
O plundered one, Fair Maiden Sidon.
Up, cross over to Kittim—
Even there you shall have no rest."

13[d] Behold the land of Chaldea—
This is the people that has ceased to be.
Assyria, which founded it for ships,
Which raised its watchtowers,
Erected its ramparts,
Has turned it into a ruin.

14 Howl, O ships of Tarshish,
For your stronghold is destroyed!

15 In that day, Tyre shall remain forgotten for seventy years, equaling the lifetime of one king. After a lapse of seventy years, it shall go with Tyre as with the harlot in the ditty:

16 Take a lyre, go about the town,
Harlot long forgotten;
Sweetly play, make much music,
To bring you back to mind.

a-a Meaning of Heb. uncertain. Emendation yields "Pass on to the land of Kittim, / You ships of Tarshish."
b Meaning of Heb. uncertain; taking mezaḥ *as a by-form of* maḥoz: *cf. Ps. 107.30.*
c Heb. "Canaan's."
d Meaning of verse uncertain. Emendation yields "The land of Kittim itself—/ Which the Sidonian people founded, / Whose watchtowers they raised, / Whose citadels they erected—/ Exists no more; / Assyria has turned it into a ruin."

God's power extends over the seas as well, so that even in exile the Phoenicians will find no rest. Cf. the fate of Israelites and Judeans sent into exile by God in texts such as Deut. 28.64–68. **13:** A very obscure v. Because it mentions the *Chaldea*ns, who took control of Babylonia a century after Isaiah's day, it is most likely a later gloss, but its meaning is unclear. **14:** The conclusion to the lament marks the end of the literary unit by repeating the opening words, "Howl, you ships of Tarshish" from v. 1. Such framing devices often indicate the extent of a literary unit in biblical literature.

15–18: A prophecy of restoration. After a period of subjugation, Tyre will be both religiously purified and politically restored. Its fate closely resembles that of Egypt and Assyria in 19.18–25, as well as that of Israel throughout the Bible. God treats the Phoenicians precisely as God treats the Israelites: They are severely punished, then saved. **15–16:** *Seventy years,* a person's life-span (Ps. 90.10), also the length of Jerusalem's punishment in Jer. 25.11; 29.10. To describe Tyre's renewal, Isaiah quotes a *ditty* or brief song about an aging prostitute who is in effect remembered for her earlier glory.

[17] For after a lapse of seventy years, the LORD will take note
of Tyre, and she shall resume her [a-]"fee-taking" and "play the
harlot"[-a] with all the kingdoms of the world, on the face of the
earth. [18] But her profits and "hire" shall be consecrated to the
LORD. They shall not be treasured or stored; rather shall her
profits go to those who abide before the LORD, that they may
eat their fill and clothe themselves elegantly.

24 Behold,
The LORD will strip the earth bare,
And lay it waste,
And twist its surface,
And scatter its inhabitants.
2 Layman and priest shall fare alike,
Slave and master,
Handmaid and mistress,
Buyer and seller,
Lender and borrower,
Creditor and debtor.
3 The earth shall be bare, bare;
It shall be plundered, plundered;
For it is the LORD who spoke this word.

4 The earth is withered, sear;
The world languishes, it is sear;
[b-]The most exalted people of the earth[-b]
languish.
5 For the earth was defiled
Under its inhabitants;
Because they transgressed teachings,
Violated laws,
Broke the ancient covenant.[c]
6 That is why a curse consumes the earth,
And its inhabitants pay the penalty;
That is why earth's dwellers have dwindled,
And but few men are left.
7 The new wine fails,
The vine languishes;
And all the merry-hearted sigh.
8 Stilled is the merriment of timbrels,
Ended the clamor of revelers,
Stilled the merriment of lyres.
9 They drink their wine without song;
Liquor tastes bitter to the drinker.

a-a I.e., "trading ... trade."
b-b Change of vocalization yields "both sky and earth."
c I.e., the moral law, which is binding on all men (cf. Gen. 9.4–6).

Chs 24–27: Prophecies concerning the end of days. These chs form a distinct section within the book of Isaiah. They refer to no specific historical situation but are concerned instead with a future time in which the world will undergo sweeping devastation, after which redemption will come to survivors from all the nations. They describe humanity as deeply sinful in general terms, but, unlike other Isaianic passages, they do not specify what humanity's sins are, in contrast, for example, to chs 1–3. Like 2.1–4; 4.2–6; 11.1–12.10, they portray the ultimate and lasting divine judgment of the world, but they focus to a greater extent on the break between the end of the old age and the creation of the new world order. These chs share some features with later apocalyptic literature, which is best represented in the Tanakh by the book of Daniel. Consequently, they are often called the Isaiah Apocalypse, and many date chs 24–27 to the Persian or even the Hellenistic period. On the other hand, they also share many features with prophecies of Isaiah, such as the doctrine of the remnant and a thoroughgoing universalism. Whether these Isaianic features result from Isaiah's own authorship of these chs, and they should be considered protoapocalyptic, or from the influence of Isaiah's genuine writings on a later author cannot be determined, but most modern scholars opt for the latter explanation.

24.1–23: Cosmic chaos and divine judgment at the end of time. **1–3:** A summary of the ch as a whole: In the coming destruction God will destroy the social and natural orders. **4–13:** The reason for the upheaval: Humanity is depraved. **4–5:** *The earth* could also be translated as "the land" (i.e., the land of Israel), in which case this section would refer to the Israelites and Judeans, not all humanity. In that case, *the ancient covenant* (or "everlasting commitment") refers to the laws given to Israel through Moses, especially the laws of the Sabbath and sacrifice (cf. Exod. 31.16;

10 Towns are broken,[a] empty;
Every house is shut, none enters;
11 Even over wine, a cry goes up in the streets:
The sun has set on all joy,
The gladness of the earth is banished.
12 Desolation is left in the town
And the gate is battered to ruins.
13 For thus shall it be among the peoples
In the midst of the earth:
As when the olive tree is beaten out,
Like gleanings when the vintage is over.

14 These shall lift up their voices,
Exult in the majesty of the LORD.
They shall shout from the sea:
15 Therefore, honor the LORD with lights
In the coastlands of the sea—
The name of the LORD, the God of Israel.
16 From the end of the earth
We hear singing:
Glory to the righteous!
[b-]And I said:[-b]
[c-]I waste away! I waste away! Woe is me!
The faithless have acted faithlessly;
The faithless have broken faith![-c]

17 [d-]Terror, and pit, and trap[-d]
Upon you who dwell on earth!
18 He who flees at the report of the terror
Shall fall into the pit;
And he who climbs out of the pit
Shall be caught in the trap.
For sluices are opened on high,
And earth's foundations tremble.

19 The earth is breaking, breaking;
The earth is crumbling, crumbling.
The earth is tottering, tottering;
20 The earth is swaying like a drunkard;
It is rocking to and fro like a hut.
Its iniquity shall weigh it down,
And it shall fall, to rise no more.

a Emendation yields "left." *b-b Change of vocalization yields "They shall say."*
c-c Meaning of Heb. uncertain. Emendation yields "Villain [Arabic razīl], *foolish villain! / The faithless who acted faithlessly / Have been betrayed in turn."*
d-d Heb. paḥad wa-paḥath, wa-paḥ.

Lev. 24.8; Num. 18.19, where the same phrase appears in the Heb). But the reference to *the peoples* in v. 13 suggests that this ch is in fact concerned with all humanity and the whole earth, not just Israel and its land. **10:** *Towns,* lit. "the town" (singular). Various proposals regarding the identification of this town (e.g., Jerusalem) have been offered, but it probably refers not to a specific town but to towns as a collective. Hence the NJPS translation. This v. echoes 17.6 and broadens its meaning, the earlier v. referred to the punishment of Israel and this v. (more likely) to the punishment of all humanity. **14–16:** Some group (Judeans who have been saved? human beings generally?) begins to rejoice, thinking the destruction has ended. The prophet laments, however, realizing that the judgment will continue for some time. **16:** *I waste away:* Other commentators, especially rabbinic ones, understand the Heb to mean "I know a secret," i.e., the painful truth about the extent of the coming disaster. (This is based on the understanding of Heb "razi" from the noun "raz," a borrowing into Late Biblical Hebrew from Persian via Aram. [see, e.g., Dan. 2.18 n.].) **17–23:** A vivid description of the inescapable terror that will overtake all creation. God will mete out punishments that affect not only the mighty among humanity but even nature itself. **17–18:** These lines are echoed in Jer. 48.43–44.

21 In that day, the LORD will punish
The host of heaven in heaven
And the kings of the earth on earth.
22 They shall be gathered in a dungeon
As captives are gathered;
And shall be locked up in a prison.
But after many days they shall be remembered.

23 Then the moon shall be ashamed,
And the sun shall be abashed.
For the LORD of Hosts will reign
On Mount Zion and in Jerusalem,
And the Presence will be revealed
to His elders.

25 O LORD, You are my God;
I will extol You, I will praise Your name.
For You planned graciousness[a] of old,
Counsels of steadfast faithfulness.

2 For You have turned a city into a stone heap,
A walled town into a ruin,
The citadel of strangers[b] into rubble,[c]
Never to be rebuilt.
3 Therefore a fierce people must honor You,
A city of cruel nations must fear You.
4 For You have been a refuge for the poor man,
A shelter for the needy man in his distress—
Shelter from rainstorm, shade from heat.
When the fury of tyrants was like a winter[c] rainstorm,
5 The rage of strangers[b] like heat in the desert,
You subdued the heat with the shade of clouds,
The singing[d] of the tyrants was vanquished.

6 The LORD of Hosts will make on this mount[e]
For all the peoples
A banquet of [f]rich viands,
A banquet of choice wines—
Of rich viands seasoned with marrow,
Of choice wines[f] well refined.
7 And He will destroy on this mount[e] the shroud
That is drawn over the faces of all the peoples
And the covering that is spread
Over all the nations:

21: *The host of heaven,* the stars above, or the angels, or both, since the stars were viewed by many ancient peoples as manifestations of divinities. Cf. Jer. 33.22; 1 Kings 22.19; Neh. 9.6. Because the stars were worshipped by many peoples (including misguided Israelites), they too feel the brunt of God's anger.

25.1–12: The end of evil. This ch brings together two or three texts describing God's victory over evil and sorrow. **1–5:** A song of thanksgiving, similar in style and content to many psalms in Psalms, although these vv. seem to refer to some historical event in the past and to have a particular city, unknown to us, in mind. This short song differs from most of chs 24–27. It is possible that these vv. originated as a song of triumph after the downfall of some major city such as the Assyrian capital and were later reused here as an example of the song that will be sung by the faithful remnant that endures after the end of days. **6–9:** Focusing on *this mount,* the rejoicing of the faithful remnant and the end of sorrow in the future. **7:** *Covering:* When the new cosmic order emerges, the illusions that befuddle the nations will disappear, and the survivors from all nations will enjoy access to true teachings, which emanate from the God of Zion. Cf. 2.1–4; 19.18–25; 23.15–18.

a *See 9.5.* *b* *Emendation yields "arrogant men."*
c *Meaning of Heb. uncertain.*
d *Meaning of Heb. uncertain. Emendation yields "rainstorm"; cf. 4d.*
e *I.e., the Holy Land, as in 11.9; 14.25; 57.13.* *f-f* *Meaning of Heb. uncertain.*

8 He will destroy death[a] forever.
My Lord GOD will wipe the tears away
From all faces
And will put an end to the reproach of [b]His people[b]
Over all the earth—
For it is the LORD who has spoken.

9 In that day they shall say:
This is our God;
We trusted in Him, and He delivered us.
This is the LORD, in whom we trusted;
Let us rejoice and exult in His deliverance!

10 For the hand of the LORD shall descend
Upon this mount,[c]
And Moab[d] shall be trampled under Him
As straw is threshed to bits at Madmenah.[e]
11 Then He will spread out His hands in their homeland,[f]
As a swimmer spreads his hands out to swim,
And He will humble their pride
Along with [g]the emblems of their power.[g]
12 Yea, the secure fortification of their[h] walls
He will lay low and humble,
Will raze to the ground, to the very dust.

26 In that day, this song shall be sung
In the land of Judah:
Ours is a mighty city;
He makes victory our inner and outer wall.
2 Open the gates, and let
A righteous nation enter,
[A nation] that keeps faith.
3 The confident mind You guard in safety,
In safety because it trusts in You.

4 Trust in the LORD for ever and ever,
For in Yah the LORD you have an everlasting Rock.
5 For He has brought low those who dwelt high up,
Has humbled the secure city,
Humbled it to the ground,
Leveled it with the dust—

8: *He will destroy death forever:* See 26.19 n. **10–12:** The destruction of Moab. These are the only vv. in chs 24–27 that refer to a specific nation, and they may have originally belonged in the oracles against the nations in chs 13–24; the reference to *this mount* (vv. 6, 7, 10) may have attracted them here. **10:** *Madmenah:* This may refer to a village in Moab; see Jer. 48.2 (where it is called Madmen). Alternatively, the word may be a noun meaning "muddy pit" or "manure pit," with a punning reference to the Moabite village.

26.1–21: A song of thanksgiving and supplication. This ch is highly varied: It begins with a song describing a future act of salvation, moves on to entreaties, and ends with a surprising prediction of triumph over death.

1–7: The thanksgiving song that will be sung in the future. This text resembles psalms of thanksgiving and praise in the book of Psalms, such as Pss. 117; 118. The song contrasts the security of a *mighty city* (v. 1), presumably Jerusalem, and the downfall of a *secure city* (v. 5; better, "exalted city"), likely symbolic of oppressive nations generally.

a *Perhaps an allusion to the mass killings committed by the Assyrians; cf. 10.7; 14.20.*
b-b *Emendation yields "peoples."* *c* *I.e., the Holy Land, as in 11.9; 14.25; 57.13.*
d *Emendation yields "Assyria"; cf. 14.25.*
e *A village near Jerusalem; see 10.31. Emendation yields "As straw gets shredded in the threshing."* *f* *Lit. "midst."*
g-g *Meaning of Heb. uncertain. Emendation yields "their citadels"; cf. the next verse.*
h *Heb. "your."*

6 To be trampled underfoot,
By the feet of the needy,
By the soles of the poor.
7 The path is level for the righteous man;
O Just One, You make smooth the course of the
righteous.

8 For Your just ways, O LORD, we look to You;
We long for the name by which You are called.
9 At night I yearn for You with all my being,
I seek You with all [a]the spirit within me.[-a]
For when Your judgments are wrought on earth,
The inhabitants of the world learn righteousness.
10 But when the scoundrel is spared, he learns not
righteousness;
In a place of integrity, he does wrong—
He ignores the majesty of the LORD.

11 O LORD!
They see not Your hand exalted.
Let them be shamed as they behold
Your zeal for Your people
And fire consuming Your adversaries.
12b O LORD!
May You appoint well-being for us,
Since You have also requited all our misdeeds.

13 O LORD our God!
Lords other than You possessed us,
But only Your name shall we utter.
14 They are dead, they can never live;
Shades, they can never rise;
Of a truth, You have dealt with them and wiped
them out,
Have put an end to all mention of them.
15c When You added to the nation, O LORD,
When You added to the nation,
Extending all the boundaries of the land,[-a]
You were honored.
16 O LORD! In their distress, they sought You;
Your chastisement reduced them
To anguished[d] whispered prayer.
17 Like a woman with child
Approaching childbirth,

a-a *Emendation yields "my spirit in the morning."*
b *Meaning of verse uncertain.* c *Meaning of vv. 15–16 uncertain.*
d *Lit. "anguish"; taking* ṣaqun *as a noun formed like* zadon *and* sason.

8–10: A reflection on divine judgment, whose lessons the evil fail to accept.

11–19: A petition for salvation to the righteous and punishment to the wicked. These vv. move back and forth between confident expectations regarding the future and depressed reflections on the past or present plight of the nation. **11:** The wicked have not yet been shown divine justice and thus do not respect God's power. **12–13:** The Israelites confess their misdeeds, but they claim they have already suffered sufficiently for them.

19: Life after death? This v. and also 25.8 refer to God's triumph over death. Some understand these vv. as metaphors: They portray the surprising vindication of the downtrodden, who are figuratively compared to the dead. According to others, these vv. assert that at least some dead people will return to earth at the end of time, their bodies and spirits restored. Rabbinic Judaism emphasizes the belief in bodily resurrection for all humanity. Indeed, this belief is highlighted in the second paragraph of the "'Amidah" prayer, which is recited three times each day in traditional liturgy and provides a succinct summary of the main points of rabbinic theology. The Tanakh, however, is much more circumspect regarding the possibility of life after death, avoiding discussions of the issue and in some passages apparently denying the possibility (Ps. 115.7; cf. Isa. 38.18–19). Many biblical passages refer to Sheol, where the dead abide (e.g., Gen. 37.25; 42.38; Deut. 32.22; 1 Sam. 2.6; Ps. 88.4; Prov. 15.24), but they do not describe what happens to them there or whether they can be regarded as truly alive. (An exception may be Isa. 14.9–11, 16–21, but that passage is more likely a poetic fantasy. See the comments on these vv.) In Ezek. ch 37 dry bones are reconstituted into bodies and come back to life, but that text presents itself explicitly as a metaphor for national renewal, not as the physical resurrection of

Writhing and screaming in her pangs,
So are we become because of You, O LORD.
18 We were with child, we writhed—
It is as though we had given birth to wind;
We have won no victory on earth;
The inhabitants of the world have not [a-]come to life![-a]
19 Oh, let Your dead revive!
Let corpses[b] arise!
Awake and shout for joy,
You who dwell in the dust!—
For Your dew is like the dew on fresh growth;
You make the land of the shades [a-]come to life.[-a]

20 Go, my people, enter your chambers,
And lock your doors behind you.
Hide but a little moment,
Until the indignation passes.
21 For lo!
The LORD shall come forth from His place
To punish the dwellers of the earth
For their iniquity;
And the earth shall disclose its bloodshed
And shall no longer conceal its slain.

27 In that day the LORD will punish,
With His great, cruel, mighty sword
Leviathan the Elusive[c] Serpent—
Leviathan the Twisting[c] Serpent;
He will slay the Dragon of the sea.[d]

2 In that day,
They shall sing of it:[e]
"Vineyard of Delight."[f]
3 I the LORD keep watch over it,
I water it every moment;
[g-]That no harm may befall it,[-g]
I watch it night and day.
4 There is no anger in Me:
[a-]If one offers Me thorns and thistles,
I will march to battle against him,
And set all of them on fire.[-a]

a-a Meaning of Heb. uncertain. *b Grammar of Heb. unclear.*
c Meaning of Heb. uncertain.
d The monster which the LORD vanquished of old (cf. 51.9; Ps. 74.13–14) was the embodiment of chaos; here it stands for the forces of evil in the present world.
e Apparently the earth; cf. 26.21.
f So some mss. (cf. Amos 5.11); other mss. and the editions have "Wine."
g-g Meaning of Heb. uncertain; emendation yields "My eye is open upon it."

the dead (37.11): The Judeans, having "died" when they lost their land and kingdom, will "come back to life" as they return to their land to reestablish a commonwealth. The metaphor may, however, be based on the idea of personal resurrection. Only in Dan. 12.2–3, 12 does the Tanakh unambiguously endorse the idea that humans will be given life after death. Belief in life after death became central to apocalyptic forms of Judaism (attested to in the book of Dan. and various postbiblical, pre-rabbinic documents). Those modern scholars who emphasize the apocalyptic elements in Isa. chs 24–27 understand 25.8 and 26.19 as a typical apocalyptic statement endorsing the notion of resurrection of the dead. Medieval Jewish philosophers and commentators point to this v. as a biblical warrant for the rabbinic doctrine of life after death. Concerning this whole issue, see 66.24 n.

26.20–27.13: Additional descriptions of the future. The prayer in 26.1–19 has ended, and now the prophet addresses the people. As elsewhere in chs 24–27, the structure of this series of vv. is often loose, with abrupt changes of focus and tone. **26.20–21:** The faithful are instructed to wait patiently and safely until the divine wrath directed against the wicked finishes, suggesting that different units have been combined. **27.1:** Forces of chaos will finally be destroyed at the end of time. *Leviathan ... Dragon:* All these terms occur in Canaanite mythology and elsewhere in the Bible (e.g., Pss. 74.13–15; 89.6–14; Job 26.5–13), where the sea-monsters are destroyed at the beginning of time, when the world is created. In the Canaanite mythology, it is the god Baal who defeats them; in the Bible, it is the LORD. This text moves the event in which chaos is vanquished to the end of time, when the new world order emerges.

2–6: A song of the vineyard. Israel is compared to a vineyard belonging to God, who will tend and protect it at the end of days. This text uses the language of 5.1–7, whose negative thrust it systematically reverses: The earlier text is a song of judgment against Israel, and this text is a song of restoration.

7–11: The purpose of punishment. Israel's suffering and the reasons for it are described. The suffering purges Israel's sins. But those who refuse to repent (the text does not make clear whether this group consists of Jews, Gentiles, or both) will continue suffering.

12–13: Two final prophecies. The end of days will bring terror for God's enemies, restoration for the exiled Israelites, and worship on the Temple Mount in Jerusalem.

5 But if he holds fast to My refuge,
[a]He makes Me his friend;
He makes Me his friend.[a]

6 [In days] to come Jacob shall strike root,
Israel shall sprout and blossom,
And the face of the world
Shall be covered with fruit.

7 Was he beaten as his beater has been?
Did he suffer such slaughter as his slayers?
8 [b]Assailing them[b] with fury unchained,
His pitiless blast bore them off
On a day of gale.

9c Assuredly, by this alone
Shall Jacob's sin be purged away;
This is the only price
For removing his guilt:
That he make all the altar-stones
Like shattered blocks of chalk—
With no sacred post left standing,
Nor any incense altar.
10 Thus fortified cities lie desolate,
Homesteads deserted, forsaken like a
wilderness;
There calves graze, there they lie down
[d]And consume its boughs.
11 When its crown is withered, they break;[d]
Women come and make fires with them.
For they are a people without understanding;
That is why
Their Maker will show them no mercy,
Their Creator will deny them grace.

[12]And in that day, the LORD will beat out [the peoples like grain] from the channel of the Euphrates to the Wadi of Egypt; and you shall be picked up one by one, O children of Israel!

[13]And in that day, a great ram's horn shall be sounded; and the strayed who are in the land of Assyria and the expelled who are in the land of Egypt shall come and worship the LORD on the holy mount, in Jerusalem.

a-a Meaning of Heb. uncertain.

b-b Lit. "Striving with her"; meaning of verse uncertain.

c This verse would read well before v. 6; the thought of vv. 7–8, dealing with the punishment of Israel's enemies, is continued in vv. 10–11.

d-d Meaning of Heb. uncertain. Emendation yields "Or like a terebinth whose boughs / Break when its crown is withered."

28 Ah, the proud crowns of the drunkards of Ephraim,
Whose glorious beauty is but wilted flowers
On the heads of men bloated[a] with rich food,
Who are overcome by wine!

2 Lo, my Lord has something strong and mighty,
Like a storm of hail,
A shower of pestilence.
Something like a storm of massive, torrential rain[b]
Shall be hurled with force to the ground.
3 Trampled underfoot shall be
The proud crowns of the drunkards of Ephraim,
4 The wilted flowers—
On the heads of men bloated[a] with rich food—
That are his glorious beauty.
They shall be like an early fig
Before the fruit harvest;
Whoever sees it devours it
While it is still [c-]in his hand.[-c]

5 In that day, the LORD of Hosts shall become a crown of
beauty and a diadem of glory for the remnant of His people,
6 and a spirit of judgment for him who sits in judgment and of
valor for those who repel attacks at the gate.

7 But these are also muddled by wine
And dazed by liquor:
Priest and prophet
Are muddled by liquor;
They are confused by wine,
They are dazed by liquor;
They are muddled in their visions,
They stumble in judgment.
8 Yea, all tables are covered
With vomit and filth,
So that no space is left.

9 [d]"To whom would he give instruction?
To whom expound a message?

a Ge *is contracted from* ge'e; *cf. Ibn Ezra.* b *Lit. "water."*
c-c *Emendation yields "on the bough."*
d *This is the drunkards' reaction to Isaiah's reproof.*

28.1–29: Judgment against Samaria and against Jerusalem. The various sections of this ch share the central Isaianic theme of haughtiness, which is expressed in the rejection of divine counsel and leads to foolishness and drunkenness. God responds to this haughtiness by sending an enemy to punish Israel and Judah.

1–6: The downfall of Samaria. These vv. are directed against *Ephraim,* or the northern Israelite kingdom, whose capital was located in Samaria. Thus they must date to some time before the final destruction of Samaria by the Assyrians in 722. The wealthy northerners are described as self-indulgent drunkards. Like all humans who are too proud, they will experience a brutal downfall. **1:** *On the heads of men … overcome by wine:* Alternatively, this might be rendered: "Those above the fertile valley are overcome with wine." This sentence refers to the drunken inhabitants of the city of Samaria, which was located on a hill above a valley. **2:** *Something strong and mighty,* the Assyrians, who will come to punish the Northern Kingdom. **4:** *The wilted flowers—on the heads of men bloated with rich food:* This might be rendered, "The wilted flowers that are above the fertile valley"; the wilted flower refers to the ephemeral glory of Samaria. **5–6:** The fate of Samaria is contrasted to the fate of *the remnant of His people,* those Judeans who will enjoy the glory that the northerners haughtily took as their own. Initially one may think that the favored groups described in these vv. consist of the Judeans in Jerusalem, which is the true place of divine manifestation, in contrast to Samaria. Jerusalem, too, however, will be subject to judgment, as the rest of the ch makes clear.

7–22: The judgment against Jerusalem. Surprisingly, Jerusalem is not contrasted with Samaria but compared to it, for the fate of drunken Samaria provides the model for the fate of drunken Jerusalem. **7:** *These are also muddled:* Not only those people (miles away in Samaria) but our people (here in Jerusalem) are guilty of drunken excess. It is not clear whether drunkenness here is literal or refers to the effects of the self-deluding policies with which the Judeans have become inebriated. **9–10:** In these vv. Isaiah summarizes the reaction of the priests and prophets in Jerusalem to his message. *He* in these vv., then, refers to Isaiah himself. **10:** *Murmur … now there:* The Heb consists of repetitive gibberish; Isaiah's audience disregards his poetic warnings as monotonous nonsense. **11–13:** Isaiah's response to those who mock him. **14–22:** The judgment oracle, directed especially against Jerusalem's leaders. **15:** Isaiah again summarizes his opponents, this time sarcastically putting into their mouths words that uncover the folly of their thinking: They believe that their *covenants* (their treaties with foreign powers such as Egypt or Assyria) will protect them. In fact, those covenants will be no more effective than an attempt to defy death, which inevitably comes to all humans. **16:** An oracle of promise suddenly changes the tone in the midst of the oracle of judgment. In spite of the harsh words against the Judeans, Isaiah reiterates the notion of Zion's inviolability (see 1.8–9 n.), which provides a measure of hope even in the midst of this prophecy of divine retribution.

To those newly weaned from milk,
Just taken away from the breast?
10 That same mutter upon mutter,
Murmur upon murmur,
Now here, now there!"

11 Truly, as one who speaks to that people in a stammering
jargon and an alien tongue 12 is he who declares to them, "This is
the resting place, let the weary rest;[a] this is the place of repose."
They refuse to listen. 13 To them the word of the LORD is:
"Mutter upon mutter,
Murmur upon murmur,
Now here, now there."
And so they will march,[b]
But they shall fall backward,
And be injured and snared and captured.

14 Hear now the word of the LORD,
You men of mockery,
[c-]Who govern that people[-c]
In Jerusalem!
15 For you have said,
"We have made a covenant with Death,
Concluded a pact with Sheol.
When the sweeping flood passes through,
It shall not reach us;
For we have made falsehood our refuge,
Taken shelter in treachery."
16 Assuredly,
Thus said the Lord GOD:
"Behold, I will found in Zion,
Stone by stone,
[d-]A tower of precious cornerstones,[-d]
Exceedingly firm;
He who trusts need not fear.
17 But I will apply judgment as a measuring line
And retribution[e] as weights;[f]
Hail shall sweep away the refuge of falsehood,
And flood-waters engulf your shelter.
18 Your covenant with Death shall be annulled,
Your pact with Sheol shall not endure;
When the sweeping flood passes through,
You shall be its victims.

a *I.e., do not embark on any political adventure at this time.*
b *I.e., embark on the political adventure.*
c-c *Or "composers of taunt-verses for that people."*
d-d *Meaning of Heb. uncertain.* *e* *As in 1.27; 5.16; 10.22.*
f *I.e., I will make judgment and retribution My plan of action; cf. 34.11; 2 Kings 21.13.*

19 It shall catch you
Every time it passes through;
It shall pass through every morning,
Every day and every night.
And it shall be sheer horror
To grasp the message."

20 The couch is too short for stretching out,
And the cover too narrow for curling up!

21 For the LORD will arise
As on the hill of Perazim,
He will rouse Himself
As in the vale of Gibeon,
To do His work—
Strange is His work!
And to perform His task—
Astounding is His task![a]
22 Therefore, refrain from mockery,
Lest your bonds be tightened.
For I have heard a decree of destruction
From my Lord GOD of Hosts
Against all the land.

23 Give diligent ear to my words,
Attend carefully to what I say.
24 Does he who plows to sow
Plow all the time,
Breaking up and furrowing his land?
25 When he has smoothed its surface,
Does he not rather broadcast black cumin
And scatter cumin,
Or set wheat in a row,[b]
Barley in a strip,
And emmer in a patch?
26 For He teaches him the right manner,
His God instructs him.
27 So, too, black cumin is not threshed with a
threshing board,
Nor is the wheel of a threshing sledge rolled over
cumin;
But black cumin is beaten out with a stick
And cumin with a rod.
28 It is cereal that is crushed.[c]

a *Instead of giving victory, as at Baal-perazim and Gibeon (cf. 2 Sam. 5.19–25; 1 Chron. 14.9–16), He will inflict punishment.*
b *In some Near Eastern countries, wheat is actually planted rather than scattered.*
c *Emendation yields "threshed."*

20: When the disaster comes, no rest will be possible for the weary nation. This line ironically comments on v. 12. **21:** *Perazim ... vale of Gibeon,* an allusion to the victory God gave to David over the Philistines at two locations near Jerusalem; see 2 Sam. 5.20–25. This time, however, God's might will work against the Judeans.

23–29: A parable concerning God's plan in history. The style and content of this complex passage resemble that of wisdom literature, particularly the book of Proverbs; like many texts in Proverbs and Job, this poem focuses on the depth of divine wisdom. (Wisdom influence has been suggested for Isaiah and a variety of other non-wisdom texts.) When a farmer breaks up soil, overturns it, and levels it, his activities seem destructive but are in fact wise and ultimately life-giving. So too God has a purpose as He breaks up and levels nations. Further, God treats Israel and Judah in different ways, just as the farmer uses different techniques when planting and harvesting various types of grain. The fates of Israel and Judah seem similar, but Jerusalem will never suffer the degree of defeat meted out to Samaria.

29: The sentiments of this v. are common in wisdom literature, especially Job.

29.1–24: Three poems on God's surprising treatment of Jerusalem. This ch contains brief poems that share several characteristics. Each suggests that Jerusalem deserves punishment, but each ultimately predicts salvation.

1–8: The first poem: Jerusalem surrounded, Jerusalem saved. In this short poem, God first announces that He will bring an army to put David's city under siege. Just when disaster seems inevitable, however, the foreign army disappears. Similar predictions of destruction that leads not to defeat but to a sudden and surprising rescue appear often in Isaiah; cf. 3.25–5.6; 8.6–8; 8.22–9.1. The event described here closely resembles the sudden departure of the Assyrian army of Sennacherib during the reign of King Hezekiah in the year 701, which is narrated in chs 36–39; 2 Kings chs 18–19; 2 Chron. ch 32. The same event may form the basis for the prophecy in 22.1–14; see the comments on that passage. A crucial notion underlying this poem is the inviolability of Zion; see 1.8–9 n. **1:** *Ariel:* This poetic name for Jerusalem, found only in this ch, either means "hearth of God" (i.e., altar) or "lion of God."

For [a-]even if[-a] he threshes it thoroughly,
And the wheel of his sledge [b-]and his horses
overwhelm it,[-b]
He does not crush it.
29 That, too, is ordered by the LORD of Hosts;
His counsel is unfathomable,
His wisdom marvelous.

29

1 "Ah, Ariel,[c] Ariel,
City where David camped!
Add year to year,
Let festivals come in their cycles!
2 And I will harass Ariel,
And there shall be sorrow and sighing.
[b-]She shall be to Me like Ariel.[-b]
3 And I will camp against you [d-]round about;[-d]
I will lay siege to you [b-]with a mound,[-b]
And I will set up siegeworks against you.
4 And you shall speak from lower than the ground,
Your speech shall be humbler than the sod;
Your speech shall sound like a ghost's from the ground,
Your voice shall chirp from the sod.
5 And like fine dust shall be
The multitude of [e-]your strangers;[-e]
And like flying chaff,
The multitude of tyrants."

And suddenly, in an instant,
6 She shall be remembered of the LORD of Hosts
With roaring, and shaking, and deafening noise,
Storm, and tempest, and blaze of consuming fire.
7 Then, like a dream, a vision of the night,
Shall be the multitude of nations
That war upon Ariel,
And all her besiegers, and the siegeworks against her,
And those who harass her.
8 Like one who is hungry
And dreams he is eating,
But wakes to find himself empty;
And like one who is thirsty
And dreams he is drinking,
But wakes to find himself faint
And utterly parched—

a-a *Taking* lo *as equivalent to* lu. b-b *Meaning of Heb. uncertain.*
c *A poetic name of Jerusalem; cf.* 33.7.
d-d *Meaning of Heb. uncertain. Septuagint reads "like David"; cf. v.* 1.
e-e *Manuscript* 1QIs[a] *reads "haughty men."*

So shall be all the multitude of nations
That war upon Mount Zion.

9 Act stupid and be stupefied!
Act blind and be blinded!
(They are drunk, but not from wine,
They stagger, but not from liquor.)
10 For the LORD has spread over you
A spirit of deep sleep,
And has shut your eyes, the prophets,
And covered your heads, the seers;
11 So that all prophecy has been to you
Like the words of a sealed document.

If it is handed to one who can read and he is asked to read it,
he will say, "I can't, because it is sealed"; 12 and if the document
is handed to one who cannot read and he is asked to read it, he
will say, "I can't read."

13 My Lord said:
Because that people has approached [Me]
with its mouth
And honored Me with its lips,
But has kept its heart far from Me,
And its worship of Me has been
A commandment of men, learned by rote—
14 Truly, I shall further baffle that people
With bafflement upon bafflement;
And the wisdom of its wise shall fail,
And the prudence of its prudent shall vanish.

15 Ha! Those who would hide their plans
Deep from the LORD!
Who do their work in dark places
And say, "Who sees us, who takes note of us?"
16 [a]How perverse of you!
Should the potter be accounted as the clay?[a]
Should what is made say of its Maker,
"He did not make me,"
And what is formed say of Him who formed it,
[b]"He did not understand"?[b]
17 Surely, in a little while,
Lebanon will be transformed into farm land,
And farm land accounted as mere brush.

a-a Meaning of first line uncertain; emendation yields "Should the potter be accounted / Like the jugs or like the clay?"
b-b Emendation yields "He did not fashion me."

9–14: The second poem: A stubborn people, a surprising God. 9–12: The people fail to understand God's will, because God deliberately misleads them, preventing them from hearing or understanding the prophetic message. Cf. 6.8–10. **13:** The Judeans' hypocritical and useless rituals. Cf. Isa. 58.2; Hos. 7.14; 8.2; 10.1–2; Mic. 3.11; 6.6. **14:** A surprising outcome is predicted, but not described. This may refer to either a punishment that goes beyond what even the wise can imagine in their worst nightmares or a sudden act of forgiveness, or both.

15–24: The third poem: Condemnation and redemption. 15–16: The people's haughtiness: They presume to act as if God were unaware of their actions and to second-guess God's plans. **17–21:** Consequently, evil-doers are punished, but the humble will be made glad.

18: *Deaf ... blind* may refer to the nation as a whole. In the previous poem (vv. 9–12) the people were deaf and blind because God removed their ability to perceive, but now God reverses His earlier action.

30.1–17: Reliance on humanity, disloyalty toward God. Several related poems address the Judeans' reliance on human helpers, which Isaiah sees as a lack of faith in God. Similar prophecies appear in chs 7–8, and a similar idea is found in Ps. 118.6–9.

1–7: Oracles concerning Judah's diplomatic overtures toward Egypt. At some point, perhaps during the reign of Hezekiah (probably in either 714 or 701), the king of Judah sent an embassy to the Egyptians as a potential ally against Assyria. As the other major power of the era, the Egyptians were a natural counterweight to the Assyrian threat. Isaiah opposes this strategy, insisting that Judah take an independent path, neither capitulating to Assyria nor depending on Egyptian aid. **1–5:** The first oracle, apparently composed when the overture to the Egyptians was being considered. **4:** *Zoan ... Hanes,* cities in northern and southern Egypt, respectively.

18 In that day, the deaf shall hear even written words,
And the eyes of the blind shall see
Even in darkness and obscurity.
19 Then the humble shall have increasing joy through
the LORD,
And the neediest of men shall exult
In the Holy One of Israel.
20 For the tyrant shall be no more,
The scoffer shall cease to be;
And those diligent for evil shall be wiped out,
21 Who cause men to lose their lawsuits,
Laying a snare for the arbiter at the gate,
And wronging by falsehood
Him who was in the right.

22 Assuredly, thus said the LORD to the House of Jacob, [a]Who
redeemed Abraham:[a]

No more shall Jacob be shamed,
No longer his face grow pale.

23 For when he—that is, his children—behold what My hands
have wrought in his midst, they will hallow My name.

Men will hallow the Holy One of Jacob
And stand in awe of the God of Israel.
24 And the confused shall acquire insight
And grumblers accept instruction.

30 Oh, disloyal sons!
—declares the LORD—
Making plans
Against My wishes,
Weaving schemes
Against My will,
Thereby piling
Guilt on guilt—
2 Who set out to go down to Egypt
Without asking Me,
To seek refuge with Pharaoh,
To seek shelter under the protection of Egypt.

3 The refuge with Pharaoh shall result in your shame;
The shelter under Egypt's protection,
in your chagrin.
4 Though his officers are present in Zoan,[b]

a-a Emendation yields "Whose fathers He redeemed." *b Or "Tanis."*

And his messengers[a] reach as far as Hanes,
5 They all shall come to shame
Because of a people that does not avail them,
That is of no help or avail,
But [brings] only chagrin and disgrace.

6[b-]The "Beasts of the Negeb" Pronouncement.

Through a[-b] land of distress and hardship,
Of lion and roaring[c] king-beast,
Of viper and flying seraph,[d]
They convey their wealth on the backs of asses,
Their treasures on camels' humps,
To a people of no avail.
7 For the help of Egypt
Shall be vain and empty.
Truly, I call this,
[e-]"They are a threat that has ceased."[-e]

8 Now,
Go, write it down on a tablet
And inscribe it in a record,
That it may be with them for future days,
A witness[f] forever.
9 For it is a rebellious people,
Faithless children,
Children who refused to heed
The instruction of the LORD;
10 Who said to the seers,
"Do not see,"
To the prophets, "Do not prophesy truth to us;
Speak to us falsehoods,
Prophesy delusions.
11 Leave the way!
Get off the path!
Let us hear no more
About the Holy One of Israel!"

12 Assuredly,
Thus said the Holy One of Israel:
Because you have rejected this word,
And have put your trust and reliance
In that which is fraudulent and tortuous—

6–7: The second oracle, apparently composed after the ambassadors set out southward toward Egypt through the *Negeb* desert.

8–17: The rebellious nation. This poem also stresses that depending on humanity amounts to rejection of God, though it is phrased in more general terms than the previous one, not mentioning Egypt specifically. **8–11:** Isaiah is commanded to write his prophecy down, so that when it proves correct, God will be on record as having warned the nation against the Egyptian alliance. That Isaiah is commanded to write this prophecy specifically suggests that he often delivered prophecies as speeches without writing them down. Cf. 8.16. **8:** *On a tablet ... inscribe,* a permanent and durable way to preserve the record. Tablets were used in Mesopotamia as opposed to parchment and papyrus, the typical writing materials in Israel; contrast Jeremiah's writing his prophecy on a scroll (Jer. 36.2). **11:** The people wish to prevent the prophets from speaking the truth because they do not want to hear it. This is another reason for writing down the prophecy—because it could not be delivered orally. **12–17:** Punishment will result from the people's refusal to rely exclusively on God.

a Emendation yields "kings"; cf. 19.2 with note.
b-b Meaning of Heb. uncertain; emendation yields "Through the wasteland of the Negeb / Through a ..." *c Meaning of Heb. uncertain.* *d See note on 14.29.*
e-e Meaning of Heb. uncertain. Emendation yields "Disgrace and chagrin"; cf. v. 5.
f Understanding ʿad, *with Targum, as a variant of* ʿed.

13–14: The metaphor is vivid. The people weakened by iniquity will be broken as easily as a clay vessel; they will be smashed into tiny bits that are useless even for the most menial tasks. **17:** An expression of the remnant that stays faithful (see 6.13).

30.18–33: God's future justice and grace. Two short passages of an eschatological nature.

18–26: Guidance and grace. The first of the passages is similar in outlook and language to chs 24–27, and in all likelihood these vv., like those chs, were written in the postexilic era, several centuries after the life of Isaiah himself. The remarkable change in nature itself (v. 26) is typical of postexilic apocalyptic literature. See intro. to chs 24–27. These vv. are noteworthy for their lack of specific historical reference. They rely heavily on passages from the Torah, especially Deuteronomy. **18–21:** In the ideal future, the nation will finally be fully receptive of divine teaching. Cf. Jer. 31.31–36, a postexilic text with a similar perspective. **22–26:** Idolatry will cease and nature will be gloriously transformed, to humanity's advantage.

13 Of a surety,
This iniquity shall work on you
Like a spreading breach that occurs in a lofty wall,
Whose crash comes sudden and swift.
14 It is smashed as one smashes an earthen jug,
Ruthlessly shattered
So that no shard is left in its breakage
To scoop coals from a brazier,
Or ladle water from a puddle.

15 For thus said my Lord GOD,
The Holy One of Israel,
"You shall triumph by stillness and quiet;
Your victory shall come about
Through calm and confidence."
But you refused.
16 "No," you declared.
"We shall flee on steeds"—
Therefore you shall flee!
"We shall ride on swift mounts"—
Therefore your pursuers shall prove swift!
17 One thousand before the shout of one—
You shall flee at the shout of five;
Till what is left of you
Is like a mast on a hilltop,
Like a pole upon a mountain.

18 Truly, the LORD is waiting to show you grace,
Truly, He will arise to pardon you.
For the LORD is a God of justice;
Happy are all who wait for Him.

19 Indeed, O people in Zion, dwellers of Jerusalem, you shall
not have cause to weep. He will grant you His favor at the sound
of your cry; He will respond as soon as He hears it. 20 My Lord
will provide for you meager bread and scant water. Then your
Guide will no more [a]be ignored,[a] but your eyes will watch
your Guide; 21 and, whenever you deviate to the right or to the
left, your ears will heed the command from behind you: "This
is the road; follow it!" 22 And you will treat as unclean the silver overlay of your images and the golden plating of your idols.
You will cast[b] them away like a menstruous woman. "Out!" you
will call to them.
23 So rain shall be provided for the seed with which you sow the
ground, and the bread that the ground brings forth shall be rich
and fat. Your livestock, in that day, shall graze in broad pastures;

a-a Meaning of Heb. uncertain. *b Change of vocalization yields "keep."*

[24] as for the cattle and the asses that till the soil, they shall partake
of salted fodder that has been winnowed with shovel and fan.
[25] And on every high mountain and on every lofty hill, there
shall appear brooks and watercourses—on a day of heavy
slaughter, when towers topple. [26] And the light of the moon
shall become like the light of the sun, and the light of the sun
shall become sevenfold, like the light of the seven days, when
the LORD binds up His people's wounds and heals the injuries
it has suffered.

27 Behold the [a]LORD Himself[a]
Comes from afar
In blazing wrath,
[b]With a heavy burden[b]—
His lips full of fury,
His tongue like devouring fire,
28 And his breath like a raging torrent
Reaching halfway up the neck—
To set a misguiding yoke[c] upon nations
And a misleading bridle upon the jaws of peoples,

29 For you, there shall be singing
As on a night when a festival is hallowed;
There shall be rejoicing as when they march
With flute, [d]with timbrels, and with lyres[d]
To the Rock of Israel on the Mount of the LORD.

30 For the LORD will make His majestic voice heard
And display the sweep of His arm
In raging wrath,
In a devouring blaze of fire,
In tempest, and rainstorm, and hailstones.
31 Truly, Assyria, who beats with the rod,
Shall be cowed by the voice of the LORD;
32 [e]And each time the appointed staff passes by,
The LORD will bring down [His arm] upon him
And will do battle with him as he waves it.[e]
33 The Topheth[f] has long been ready for him;
He too is destined for Melech[g]—
His firepit has been made both wide and deep,
With plenty of fire and firewood,
And with the breath of the LORD
Burning in it like a stream of sulfur.

a-a Lit. "The name of the LORD."
b-b Presumably with a heavy load of punishment. Meaning of Heb. uncertain.
c Interpreting naphath *like Arabic* nāf; *meaning of line uncertain.*
d-d Brought from v. 32 for clarity. *e-e Meaning of Heb. uncertain.*
f A site near Jerusalem at which human beings were sacrificed by fire in periods of paganizing; see 2 Kings 23.10. *g Cf. Molech, Lev. 18.21; 20.2–5.*

26: The bright *light* contrasts with the terrible darkness in the Day of the LORD passages (see, e.g., 13.10).

27–33: The ultimate defeat of God's enemies. Like the preceding vv., this passage is concerned with the end of days. It has a specific historical setting, however, referring to *Assyria* in v. 31. Further, the literary styles of the passages differ markedly. **27–28:** God arrives on earth to punish the nations who oppressed Judah. **29:** But the Judeans will enjoy a festival of liberation (perhaps comparable to Passover). **30–33:** The downfall of Assyria. **33:** *Topheth ... Melech,* see translators' notes *f, g.*

31.1–32.8: Rebuke, threat, and salvation. Like 30.1–17, this poem begins with a specific historical situation, the Judean strategy of relying on the Egyptians to counter Assyrian hegemony (see 30.1–17 n.). The poem moves on to broader issues, ending with a messianic passage concerning the end of days.

31.1–9: Human help, divine protection. 1–3: The folly of relying on the Egyptians rather than God. The Egyptians would supply *chariots* and the *horses* to pull them, important military equipment, the equivalent of tanks. **4:** As translated in NJPS, this v. contains the oracle of judgment threat that concludes the divine complaint in vv. 1–3: It is God, not Assyria, who really threatens Jerusalem, and the Egyptians will be as useless to defend Zion against God as shepherds are against a lion. Some rabbinic commentators, however, read as follows: "So the LORD ... will descend to make war at Mount Zion" (against the Assyrians who attack Zion). In that case, this v. marks the move from rebuke to consolation. **5:** God defends Zion, saving it suddenly. Cf. 29.1–8. *Protecting* (Heb "pasoaḥ"): The same verb describes God's protection of Israel in Egypt (Exod. 12.13, 23). The noun "pesaḥ" (Passover) is from the same root, and originally meant "to protect," not "to pass over" (see Exod. 12.11 n.). Strikingly, in the Assyrian account of the siege of Jerusalem in 701, king Hezekiah is besieged in Jerusalem "like a bird in cage." **6–7:** This is the first passage in which Isaiah calls on the nation to repent since 6.9, where God ordered Isaiah not to engender penitence among the Judeans (see 6.8–10 n.). As the prophecies of Isaiah draw to their close (ch 33 or 34 is the last ch of the collection of Isaiah's own prophecies), this order in ch 6 seems to be rescinded. The reversal of 6.9–10 is made even more clear later in this poem, in 32.3–4. **8–9:** The fall of Assyria and salvation of Judah, which come due to God's intervention, not Egypt's.

31 Ha!
Those who go down to Egypt for help
And rely upon horses!
They have put their trust in abundance of chariots,
In vast numbers of riders,
And they have not turned to the Holy One of Israel,
They have not sought the LORD.

2 But He too is wise!
He has brought on misfortune,
And has not canceled His word.
So He shall rise against the house of evildoers,
And the allies[a] of the workers of iniquity.
3 For the Egyptians are man, not God,
And their horses are flesh, not spirit;
And when the LORD stretches out His arm,
The helper shall trip
And the helped one shall fall,
And both shall perish together.

4 For thus the LORD has said to me:
As a lion—a great beast—
Growls over its prey
And, when the shepherds gather
In force against him,
Is not dismayed by their cries
Nor cowed by their noise—
So the LORD of Hosts will descend to make war
Against the mount and the hill of Zion.

5 Like the birds that fly, even so will the LORD of Hosts shield
Jerusalem, shielding and saving, protecting and rescuing.
6 [b]-Return, O children of Israel,-[b] to Him to whom they have
been so shamefully false; 7 for in that day everyone will reject
his idols of silver and idols of gold, which your hands have
made for your guilt.

8 Then Assyria shall fall,
Not by the sword of man;
A sword not of humans shall devour him.
He shall shrivel[c] before the sword,
And his young men [d]-pine away.-[d]
9 His rock shall melt with terror,
And his officers shall [e]-collapse from weakness-[e]—

a Lit. "help." *b-b* Emendation yields "Then the children of Israel shall return."
c From root nss; cf. 10.18; others "flee."
d-d From root mss; cf. 10.18; others "become tributary."
e-e Cf. note c; meaning of Heb. uncertain.

Declares the LORD, who has a fire in Zion,
Who has an oven in Jerusalem.[a]

32 Behold, a king shall reign in righteousness,
And ministers shall govern with justice;
2 Every one of them shall be
Like a refuge from gales,
A shelter from rainstorms;
Like brooks of water in a desert,
Like the shade of a massive rock
In a languishing land.

3 Then the eyes of those who have sight shall not be sealed,
And the ears of those who have hearing shall listen;
4 And the minds of the thoughtless shall attend and note,
And the tongues of mumblers shall speak with fluent eloquence.
5 No more shall a villain be called noble,
Nor shall "gentleman" be said of a knave.
6 For the villain speaks villainy
And plots treachery;
To act impiously
And to preach disloyalty against the LORD;
To leave the hungry unsatisfied
And deprive the thirsty of drink.
7 As for the knave, his tools are knavish.
He forges plots
To destroy the poor with falsehoods
And the needy when they plead their cause.
8 But the noble has noble intentions
And is constant in noble acts.

9 You carefree women,
Attend, hear my words!
You confident ladies,
Give ear to my speech!
10 [b]In little more than a year,[b]
You shall be troubled, O confident ones,
When the vintage is over
And no ingathering takes place.
11 Tremble, you carefree ones!
Quake, O confident ones!
Strip yourselves naked,
Put the cloth about your loins!

32.1–8: The final salvation. **1–2:** The ideal ruler in the end of days. Cf. 9.1–6; 11.1–5. **3:** The nation was blind to God's message, initially because they refused to listen to it, and subsequently because God compounded their inability to hear; see 6.9–10. That fateful decision will be reversed in the end of days. **4–8:** True nobility of character will be the mark of the aristocracy of the future.

32.9–20: Another poem of rebuke followed by encouragement. **9–14: The corrupt women of Jerusalem and their downfall.** **9–13:** The women of Jerusalem are condemned. This passage is a counterpart to the condemnation of the (male) political leadership in Jerusalem in 30.1–17; 31.1–3. Cf. 3.16–26, a rebuke of wealthy women which immediately follows a rebuke of (male) political leaders in 3.8–15.

a *Cf. 30.33.* *b-b* *Meaning of Heb. uncertain.*

12–14: The downfall of Judah. **14:** *Citadel* (Heb "'ophel"), the neighborhood just south of the Temple Mount (today's Silwan neighborhood), which was the oldest section of the city. Uniquely in Isa. chs 1–33, this v. foresees the destruction of Jerusalem itself. It contradicts the doctrine of the inviolability of Zion, which is everywhere else central to Isaiah's beliefs. See 1.8–9 n.; 8.8 n.; 18.3–6 n.; 28.16 n.; 29.1–8 n.

15–20: From destruction to renewal. Quite abruptly, the tone changes to one of salvation and comfort. Sudden and surprising changes of tone recur especially frequently in chs 28–33. **15:** Nature itself will be changed in the end of days (see similarly 11.6–8), ending hunger and reducing toil. **17:** *The work of righteousness shall be peace,* alternatively: "The outcome of justice will be peace." This v. is the source of our contemporary saying, "If you want peace, work for justice."

33.1–24: A prayer and a prophecy. This ch includes sections that initially seem unrelated: Some vv. are spoken to God by the Judeans or by Isaiah on the Judeans' behalf, others are descriptions of a disaster, and some include prophecies of salvation. Many of the prayers in the book of Psalms are similarly diverse; see, e.g., Ps. 89. Thus this text is probably a prayer or psalm composed by Isaiah.

1: A denunciation of an enemy. The enemy is not identified, perhaps because in Isaiah's historical context the enemy was obviously Assyria. On the theme of the destruction meted out to the destroyer, cf. chs 13–14.

2–9: The heart of the prayer: the petition. The speakers call out for God's attention, make their request for divine intervention (v. 2), express their confidence in God's ability to save (vv. 3–6), and describe their current lamentable state (vv. 7–9). The combination of these four elements is very common in psalms of lament or petition; cf. Ps. 44.2, 24–27, 4–8, 10–17; Ps. 74.1, 2–3, 12–17, 4–9. **2:** *Arm,* or, "strength." **5:** *Zion ... justice*

12 Lament [a]upon the breasts,[a]
For the pleasant fields,
For the spreading grapevines,
13 For my people's soil—
It shall be overgrown with briers and thistles—
Aye, and for all the houses of delight,
For the city of mirth.
14 For the castle shall be abandoned,
The noisy city forsaken;
Citadel and tower shall become
[b]Bare places[b] forever,
A stamping ground for wild asses,
A pasture for flocks[c]—
15 Till a spirit from on high is poured out on us,
And wilderness is transformed into farm land,
While farm land rates as mere brush.[d]
16 Then justice shall abide in the wilderness
And righteousness shall dwell on the farm land.
17 For the work of righteousness shall be peace,
And the effect of righteousness, calm and confidence
forever.
18 Then my people shall dwell in peaceful homes,
In secure dwellings,
In untroubled places of rest.
19[e] And the brush shall sink and vanish,
Even as the city is laid low.

20 Happy shall you be who sow by all waters,
Who [f]send out cattle and asses to pasture.[f]

33 Ha, you ravager who are not ravaged,
You betrayer who have not been betrayed!
When you have done ravaging, you shall be ravaged;
When you have finished betraying, you shall be
betrayed.

2 O LORD, be gracious to us!
It is to You we have looked;
[g]Be their arm[g] every morning,
Also our deliverance in time of stress.
3 At [Your] roaring, peoples have fled,

a-a *Emendation yields "for the fields."*
b-b *Meaning of Heb. uncertain; emendation yields "Brushland, desert."*
c *Emendation yields "onagers"; cf. Job 39.5.*
d *I.e., the transformed wilderness will surpass in fertility what is now used as farm land.*
e *Meaning of verse uncertain.*
f-f *Lit. "let loose the feet of cattle and asses"; cf. 7.25 end.*
g-g *Emendation yields "You have been our help."*

Before Your majesty nations have scattered;
4 And spoil[a] was gathered as locusts are gathered,
It[b] was amassed[c] as grasshoppers are amassed.[d]

5 The LORD is exalted,
He dwells on high!
[Of old] He filled Zion
With justice and righteousness.
6 Faithfulness to [e]Your charge[e] was [her] wealth,
Wisdom and devotion [her] triumph,
Reverence for the LORD—that was her[f] treasure.

7 Hark! The Arielites[g] cry aloud;
Shalom's[h] messengers weep bitterly.
8 Highways are desolate,
Wayfarers have ceased.
A covenant has been renounced,
Cities[i] rejected
[j]Mortal man[j] despised.
9 The land is wilted and withered;
Lebanon disgraced and moldering,
Sharon is become like a desert,
And Bashan and Carmel are stripped bare.
10 "Now I will arise," says the LORD,
"Now I will exalt Myself, now raise Myself high.
11 You shall conceive hay,
Give birth to straw;
My[k] breath will devour you like fire.
12 Peoples shall be burnings of lime,[l]
Thorns cut down that are set on fire.
13 Hear, you who are far, what I have done;
You who are near, note My might."

14 Sinners in Zion are frightened,
The godless are seized with trembling:
"Who of us can dwell with the devouring fire:
Who of us can dwell with the never-dying blaze?"
15 He who walks in righteousness,
Speaks uprightly,
Spurns profit from fraudulent dealings,
Waves away a bribe instead of grasping it,

and righteousness: This v. echoes 1.21, 27. Ch 33 may be the last ch of the original collection of Isaiah's prophecies (see intro.), and hence the reversal of a complaint from ch 1 may be intended to create a literary frame around the entire collection. **7:** *Arielites,* the inhabitants of Jerusalem; cf. 29.1, 2, 7–8. Alternative understandings of this term abound. According to many rabbinic texts, it refers to a class of angels, who are described here as weeping for Zion. (The Bible uses the same word for angels and *messengers.*) Other possibilities include "valiant men" and "the altar of the Temple." *Shalom's messengers,* see the translators' note *h.* Alternatively, "angels of peace," or, most likely, "messengers of peace," "peace envoys," perhaps referring to ambassadors sent by Hezekiah to the Assyrians at some point during the siege of Jerusalem in 701. (Concerning the events of 701, see 22.1–14 n. and chs 36–39 n.) Apparently, the diplomatic overture was rejected, and the Judeans reacted with dismay. This phrase is one of the sources for the wording of the hymn sung before dinner on Friday nights, "Shalom Aleikhem." **8:** *Covenant,* or, "treaty." The text may refer to an agreement between Judah and some other nation that has been discarded.

a Heb. "your spoil."
b Meaning of Heb. uncertain. Emendation yields "booty"; cf. v. 23.
c Taking šqq *as a cognate of* qšš. *d Apparently for food; cf. Lev. 11.22.*
e-e Meaning of Heb. uncertain. f Heb. "his."
g So a few manuscripts; cf. 29.1. h I.e., Jerusalem's; cf. Salem (Heb. Shalem*), Ps. 76.3. i 1QIs[a] reads "A pact." j-j Emendation yields "an obligation."*
k Heb. "your." l Emendation yields "brambles"; cf. 32.13.

Stops his ears against listening to infamy,
Shuts his eyes against looking at evil—
16 Such a one shall dwell in lofty security,
With inaccessible cliffs for his stronghold,
With his food supplied
And his drink assured.

17 When your eyes behold [a-]a king in his beauty,[-a]
When they contemplate the land round about,
18 Your throat[b] shall murmur in awe,
"Where is one who could count? Where is one
who could weigh?
Where is one who could count [all these] towers?"
19 No more shall you see the barbarian folk,
The people of speech too obscure to comprehend,
So stammering of tongue that they are not understood.
20 When you gaze upon Zion, our city of assembly,
Your eyes shall behold Jerusalem
As a secure homestead,
A tent not to be transported,
Whose pegs shall never be pulled up,
And none of whose ropes shall break.
21 For there the LORD in His greatness shall be for us
Like a region of rivers, of broad streams,
Where no floating vessels can sail
And no mighty craft can travel—
[c-]Their[d] ropes are slack,
They cannot steady the sockets of their masts,
They cannot spread a sail.[-c]
22 For the LORD shall be our ruler,
The LORD shall be our prince,
The LORD shall be our king:
He shall deliver us.
23 Then [e-]shall indeed much spoil be divided,[-e]
Even the lame shall seize booty.
24 And none who lives there shall say, "I am sick";
It shall be inhabited by folk whose sin has been forgiven.

34 Approach, O nations, and listen,
Give heed, O peoples!
Let the earth and those in it hear;

a-a Emendation yields "perfection of beauty"; cf. Ps. 50.2.
b As in 59.13 and elsewhere; others "heart."
c-c Brought up from v. 23 for clarity. The passage means that the LORD will render Jerusalem as inaccessible to enemies as if it were surrounded by an impassable sea.
d Heb. "your."
e-e Meaning of Heb. uncertain; emendation yields "even a blind man shall divide much spoil."

10–16: God's response to the prayer. Responses to a prayer are sometimes found in the text of a psalm. **10–13:** God announces that He will take action. It is not initially clear, however, whether the doomed people are the sinful Judeans or their enemies. **14–16:** The effect of God's announcement. The ambiguity in the previous vv. is resolved: The doomed will include not only the enemies, but also sinners in Zion. On the question of who may dwell in Zion, cf. Ps. 24.3–10; see Ps. 24 n.

17–24: Conclusion: Zion at the end of days. Cf. 2.1–4; 4.2–6; 9.1–6; 11.1–12.10. **17:** *King:* The passage may refer to the future Davidic monarch (as in chs 9, 11, and 32.1–8) or to the LORD (as in v. 22 of this ch). **20–24:** The notion of the inviolability of Zion is repeated. This passage reverses but also echoes ch 1 (e.g., the immovable tent, v. 20, and the broken booth, 1.8), which bitterly condemns Jerusalem's leaders yet describes the city's inviolability. These vv. form a fitting end to the prophecies of Isaiah son of Amoz.

Chs 34–35: Vengeance on Edom and the restoration of Israel. According to most modern scholars, these chs were written after the Babylonian exile, which ended in 538 BCE, probably by the same author responsible for chs 40–66 or 54–66. (On the authorship of Isa. chs 40–66 and 34–35, see intro.) Alternatively, these chs may have been written in the postexilic period as a bridge linking the prophecies of Isaiah in chs 1–33 with the exilic and postexilic prophecies in chs 40–66.

34.1–17: Judgment against the nations and against the Edomites in particular. A disturbing ch, full of bitterness and anger, this text portrays the LORD as wreaking vengeance against the nations, apparently because they opposed Zion. It focuses in particular on Edom, a nation located southeast of Judah between the Dead Sea and the Gulf of Aqaba or Eilat. Relations between Edom and Judah during the

The world, and what it brings forth.
2 For the LORD is angry at all the nations,
Furious at all their host;
He has doomed them, consigned them to slaughter.
3 Their slain shall be left lying,
And the stench of their corpses shall mount;
And the hills shall be drenched with their blood,
4 [a]All the host of heaven shall molder.[a]
The heavens shall be rolled up like a scroll,
And all their host shall wither
Like a leaf withering on the vine,
Or shriveled fruit on a fig tree.

5 For My sword shall [b]be drunk[b] in the sky;
Lo, it shall come down upon Edom,
Upon the people I have doomed,
To wreak judgment.
6 The LORD has a sword; it is sated with blood,
It is gorged with fat—
The blood of lambs and he-goats,
The kidney fat of rams.
For the LORD holds a sacrifice in Bozrah,
A great slaughter in the land of Edom.
7 Wild oxen shall fall [c]with them,[c]
Young bulls with mighty steers;
And their land shall be drunk with blood,
Their soil shall be saturated with fat.
8 For it is the LORD's day of retribution,
The year of vindication for Zion's cause.
9 Its[d] streams shall be turned to pitch
And its soil to sulfur.
Its land shall become burning pitch,
10 Night and day it shall never go out;
Its smoke shall rise for all time.
Through the ages it shall lie in ruins;
Through the aeons none shall traverse it.
11 [e]Jackdaws and owls[e] shall possess it;
Great owls and ravens shall dwell there.
He shall measure it with a line of chaos
And with weights of emptiness.[f]
12 [e]It shall be called, "No kingdom is there,"[e]
Its nobles and all its lords shall be nothing.
13 Thorns shall grow up in its palaces,

preexilic period were often hostile (e.g., 2 Sam. 8.13–14). This hostility is represented in Genesis, in the stories of Esau, the ancestor of the Edomites, who is depicted as Jacob's brother and rival (see Gen. 25.20–34; 27.1–28.9; 33.1–20; Mal. 1.1–5). Other biblical passages suggest that the Edomites were especially antagonistic towards the Judeans when the Babylonians conquered Judah at the end of the 6th c. BCE, and Judean anger towards the Edomites was severe (see Ps. 137.7; Ezek. 25.12; 35.5–10; Obad. 1.10–16). This ch predicts an utter disaster overcoming the Edomites in the strongest possible terms. This is ironic in light of later Jewish history, since the Edomites (then known by their Greek name, Idumeans) converted to Judaism en masse during the late 2nd c. BCE, and were among the most zealous Jews during the conflict with Rome in the 1st c. CE. Rabbinic literature understands Edom in prophetic texts as a symbolic reference to the Roman empire and Christianity, rather than to the historical Edomites, who were in fact Jewish by the time rabbinic literature was composed. See, for example, Targum to v. 9. **1–4:** Judgment against the nations of the world. **5–8:** The slaughter of the Edomites. **9–17:** The everlasting destruction of Edom is depicted through two somewhat contradictory figures: In vv. 9–10, Edom becomes the site of an eternal fire (cf. 66.24); in vv. 11–17, Edom becomes a deserted wasteland, inhabited only by wild beasts.

a-a 1QIs[a] reads "And the valleys shall be cleft, / And all the host of heaven shall wither." *b-b 1QIs[a] reads "be seen"; cf. Targum.*
c-c Emendation yields "with fatted calves." *d I.e., Edom's.*
e-e Meaning of Heb. uncertain.
f I.e., He shall plan chaos and emptiness for it; cf. 28.17; Lam. 2.8.

Nettles and briers in its strongholds.
It shall be a home of jackals,
An abode of ostriches.
14a Wildcats shall meet hyenas,
Goat-demons shall greet each other;
There too the lilith[b] shall repose
And find herself a resting place.
15 There the arrow-snake shall nest and lay eggs,
And shall brood and hatch in its shade.
There too the buzzards shall gather
With one another.
16 Search and read it in the scroll of the LORD:
Not one of these shall be absent,
Not one shall miss its fellow.
For His[c] mouth has spoken,
It is His spirit that has assembled them,
17 And it is He who apportioned it to them by lot,
Whose hand divided it for them with the line.
They shall possess it for all time,
They shall dwell there through the ages.

35 The arid desert shall be glad,
The wilderness shall rejoice
And shall blossom like a rose.[d]
2 It shall blossom abundantly,
It shall also exult and shout.
It shall receive the glory of Lebanon,
The splendor of Carmel and Sharon.
They shall behold the glory of the LORD,
The splendor of our God.

3 Strengthen the hands that are slack;
Make firm the tottering knees!
4 Say to the anxious of heart,
"Be strong, fear not;
Behold your God!
Requital is coming,
The recompense of God—
He Himself is coming to give you triumph."

5 Then the eyes of the blind shall be opened,
And the ears of the deaf shall be unstopped.
6 Then the lame shall leap like a deer,
And the tongue of the dumb shall shout aloud;
For waters shall burst forth in the desert,

a *Most of the creatures in vv. 14–15 cannot be identified with certainty.*
b *A kind of demon.* c *Heb. "My."* d *Lit. "crocus."*

14: *Lilith:* In ancient Semitic belief contemporaneous with the Bible (and also in rabbinic literature), this term referred to a group of female demons, in Akkadian, lilitu. They seduced and then killed single men, and they were especially dangerous to nursing mothers and infants. In later rabbinic and kabbalistic folklore, a character with this name was said to be the first wife of Adam. Their parting was not amicable; he later married Eve, and she embarked on a career killing young children. These legends about Adam and Lilith are postbiblical, however, and have no bearing on the term used here.

35.1–10: The renewal of Israel and the return of the exiles. This ch is the converse of the previous one: In ch 34, a land inhabited by Judah's enemies becomes a desert; in ch 35, the desert is transformed so that Judean exiles in Babylonia can pass through it with ease on their journey to Zion. Normally, travelers from Babylonia to the land of Israel would move northwest along the Euphrates, then southwest through Syria, avoiding the route that went directly west through the impassable desert. But this prophecy insists that the exiles will be able to go directly and quickly through the desert, because the LORD will provide water and safety for them there. This passage borrows extensively from Jeremiah's prediction of the exiles' return in Jer. 31.7–9. It amplifies that prediction, while changing its historical referent from northern (Israelite) exiles in Assyria to southern (Judean) exiles in Babylonia. It also deliberately recalls the vocabulary of Isaiah 32.1–6. **6–10:** The return to Zion is portrayed as a new exodus, a major theme in Deutero-Isaiah: Like the Israelites fleeing slavery in Egypt, the returning exiles will receive water and protection in the desert as they go to the land of Israel. **8:** *No one unclean:* Since God would personally accompany the exiles (v. 4), they would have to be in a state of ritual purity (see "Concepts of Purity," pp. 1998–2005).

Streams in the wilderness.
7 Torrid earth shall become a pool;
Parched land, fountains of water;
The home of jackals, a pasture;[a]
The abode [of ostriches],[b] reeds and rushes.

8 And a highway shall appear there,
Which shall be called the Sacred Way.
No one unclean shall pass along it,
But it shall be for them.[c]
[d-]No traveler, not even fools, shall go astray.[-d]
9 No lion shall be there,
No ferocious beast shall set foot on it—
These shall not be found there.
But the redeemed shall walk it;
10 And the ransomed of the LORD shall return,
And come with shouting to Zion,
Crowned with joy everlasting.
They shall attain joy and gladness,
While sorrow and sighing flee.

36 [e]In the fourteenth year of King Hezekiah, King Sennacherib of Assyria marched against all the fortified towns of Judah and seized them. 2 From Lachish, the king of Assyria sent the Rabshakeh,[f] with a large force, to King Hezekiah in Jerusalem. [The Rabshakeh] took up a position near the conduit of the Upper Pool, by the road of the Fuller's Field; 3 and Eliakim son of Hilkiah who was in charge of the palace, Shebna the scribe, and Joah son of Asaph the recorder went out to him.

4 The Rabshakeh said to them, "You tell Hezekiah: Thus said the Great King, the king of Assyria: What makes you so confident? 5 I suppose[g] mere talk makes counsel and valor for war! Look, on whom are you relying, that you have rebelled against me? 6 You are relying on Egypt, that splintered reed of a staff, which enters and punctures the palm of anyone who leans on it. That's what Pharaoh king of Egypt is like to all who rely on him. 7 And if you tell me that you are relying on the LORD your God, He is the very one whose shrines and altars Hezekiah did

a Meaning of Heb. uncertain; emendation yields "a marsh." *b Cf. 34.13.*
c Emendation yields "for His people." *d-d Meaning of Heb. uncertain.*
e Chaps. 36–39 occur also as 2 Kings 18.13–20.19, with a number of variants, some of which will be cited here in the footnotes.
f An Assyrian title; cf. "Tartan," 20.1. *g 2 Kings 18.20 "You must think."*

Chs 36–39: Historical appendices to the prophecies of Isaiah son of Amoz. These chs closely resemble 2 Kings 18.13–20.19. It seems likely that they were borrowed from 2 Kings, since they consist of historical narratives of the sort found throughout the books of Kings, rather than prophetic pronouncements of the sort found throughout the book of Isaiah. They were probably taken from 2 Kings and inserted into Isaiah (with several variations) because the prophet Isaiah plays an important role in these narratives. The historical narratives from Kings seem to confirm a central point of Isaiah—the inviolability of Jerusalem, and thus may have served as a concluding appendix attesting to the veracity of the book's prophecies, much like the final ch of Jeremiah. For detailed notes, see the relevant section in 2 Kings.

Chs 36–37: The invasion of Sennacherib in 701 BCE. The Assyrian king Sennacherib invaded the western edge of Asia to put down revolts there by his vassals, who were supported by the king of Egypt. This event serves as the backdrop of many prophecies of Isaiah, such as 1.5–9; 10.28–34; 22.1–14; 23.1–18; 29.1–24; 33.1–24, among others. The account here portrays the event as a disaster for Assyria and an impressive victory for Judah, as does 2 Chron. ch 32. The account in 2 Kings is largely identical, but it adds several vv. (2 Kings 18.14–16) which differ considerably, portraying the event as a partial Assyrian victory; it is likely that these sections of Kings were intentionally omitted in Isaiah.

36.1–37.8: The arrival of Assyrian messengers and negotiations between them and the leadership of Judah. 1–3: The arrival of the Assyrians. Assyrian records indicate that Assyrian troops vanquished forty-six Judean cities, but not Jerusalem. Isaiah had been predicting an invasion which would devastate Judah but spare Jerusalem since early in his career; cf. 1.5–9; 8.8; 29.1–24. **4–10:** The Assyrian official's speech to the Judeans. The *Rabshakeh,* or Assyrian general, urges the Judeans to surrender. **6:** Isaiah disapproved of the Judean policy of relying on the Egyptians as a counterbalance against Assyria. See 30.1–11; 31.1–9. **7:** Hezekiah had centralized sacrificial worship in Jerusalem, closing many local temples and shrines throughout Judah. See 2 Kings 18.4–6; 2 Chron. 29.3–31.21. His actions were based on laws of centralization like those found in Deut. ch 12, but the Rabshakeh misinterprets them as blasphemous. **11–22:** The dialogue between the Assyrian official and the Judeans.

away with, telling Judah and Jerusalem, 'You must worship
only at this altar!' 8 Come now, make this wager with my master, the king of Assyria: I'll give you two thousand horses, if you
can produce riders to mount them. 9 So how could you refuse
anything, even to the deputy of one of my master's lesser servants, relying on Egypt for chariots and horsemen? 10 And do
you think I have marched against this land to destroy it without
the LORD? The LORD Himself told me: Go up against that land
and destroy it."

11 Eliakim, Shebna, and Joah replied to the Rabshakeh,
"Please, speak to your servants in Aramaic, since we understand it; do not speak to us in Judean in the hearing of the
people on the wall." 12 But the Rabshakeh replied, "Was it to
your master and to you that my master sent me to speak those
words? It was precisely to the men who are sitting on the wall—
who will have to eat their dung and drink their urine with you."
13 And the Rabshakeh stood and called out in a loud voice in
Judean: 14 "Hear the words of the Great King, the king of Assyria! Thus said the king: Don't let Hezekiah deceive you, for he
will not be able to save you. 15 Don't let Hezekiah make you rely

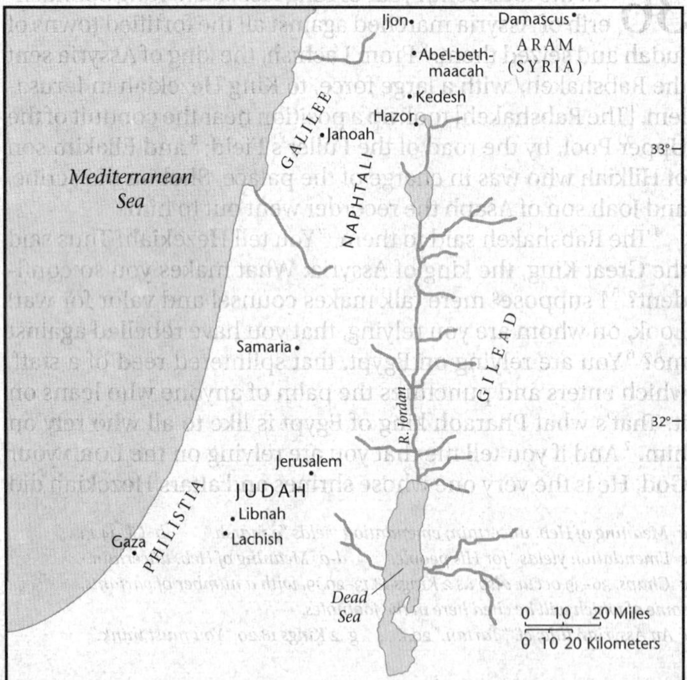

Places associated with Sennacherib's invasion of Judah

on the LORD, saying, 'The LORD will surely save us; this city will
not fall into the hands of Assyria!' 16 Don't listen to Hezekiah.
For thus said the king of Assyria: Make your peace with me and
come out to me,[a] so that you may all eat from your vines and
your fig trees and drink water from your cisterns, 17 until I come
and take you away to a land like your own, a land of bread and
wine, of grain [fields] and vineyards. 18 Beware of letting Hezekiah mislead you by saying, 'The LORD will save us.' Did any
of the gods of the other nations save his land from the king of
Assyria? 19 Where were the gods of Hamath and Arpad? Where
were the gods of Sepharvaim? And did they[b] save Samaria
from me? 20 Which among all the gods of those countries saved
their countries from me, that the LORD should save Jerusalem
from me?" 21 But they were silent and did not answer him with
a single word; for the king's order was: "Do not answer him."
22 And so Eliakim son of Hilkiah who was in charge of the
palace, Shebna the scribe, and Joah son of Asaph the recorder
came to Hezekiah with their clothes rent, and they reported to
him what the Rabshakeh had said.

37 When King Hezekiah heard this, he rent his clothes
and covered himself with sackcloth and went into the
House of the LORD. 2 He also sent Eliakim, who was in charge
of the palace, Shebna, the scribe, and the senior priests, covered with sackcloth, to the prophet Isaiah son of Amoz. 3 They
said to him, "Thus said Hezekiah: This day is a day of distress,
of chastisement, and of disgrace. [c-]The babes have reached
the birthstool, but the strength to give birth is lacking.[-c] 4 Perhaps the LORD your God will take note of the words of the
Rabshakeh, whom his master the king of Assyria has sent to
blaspheme the living God, and will mete out judgment for the
words that the LORD your God has heard—if you will offer up
prayer for the surviving remnant."
5 When King Hezekiah's ministers came to Isaiah, 6 Isaiah
said to them, "Tell your master as follows: Thus said the LORD:
Do not be frightened by the words of blasphemy against Me
that you have heard from the minions of the king of Assyria. 7 I
will delude[d] him: He will hear a rumor and return to his land,
and I will make him fall by the sword in his land."
8 The Rabshakeh, meanwhile, heard that [the King] had left
Lachish; he turned back and found the king of Assyria attacking
Libnah. 9 But [the king of Assyria] learned that King Tirhakah of
Nubia had come out to fight him; and when he heard it, he sent
messengers to Hezekiah, saying, 10 "Tell this to King Hezekiah of
Judah: Do not let your God, on whom you are relying, mislead

19–20: Cf. the similar speech put into the mouth of the Assyrian king in 10.8–11. **37.1–7:** The reaction of the Judeans. Hezekiah, the king of Judah, is dismayed. He seeks advice from Isaiah, who emphasizes that God has vowed to protect Jerusalem. **8:** The Assyrian general leaves.

37.9–36: Assyrian messengers to the Judeans, and Judean reactions. The narrative sequence of vv. resembles that of the preceding ones, and they may present another version of the same events rather than a second series of negotiations between the Assyrians and Judeans. **9–13:** The Assyrians' message to the Judeans. Cf. 36.4–22.

a *I.e., to my representative the Rabshakeh.* b *I.e., the gods of Samaria.*
c-c *I.e., the situation is desperate, and we are at a loss.* d *Lit. "put a spirit in."*

11–13: Cf. 36.11–22; 10.8–11. **14–20:** King Hezekiah's reaction is portrayed as more faithful and less lacking in confidence than it was in 37.1–7. **21–35:** Isaiah's reaction. The poem attributed to Isaiah here resembles his prophecies throughout chs 1–33; note especially the emphasis on Zion (v. 22), the criticism of haughtiness of the foreign empire (v. 23), the phrase *Holy One of Israel* (v. 23; cf. e.g., 1.4; 5.19; 10.20), the use of imagery taken from Assyrian propaganda (vv. 24–25; cf. 10.7–15; 10.33–34; 14.8; 17.12–14), the notion of the remnant of Judah from whom Israel will be renewed (vv. 31–32; cf. 6.13; 7.3) and especially the doctrine of the inviolability of Zion (vv. 33–35).

you into thinking that Jerusalem will not be delivered into the
hands of the king of Assyria. 11 You yourself have heard what
the kings of Assyria have done to all the lands, how they have
annihilated them; and can you escape? 12 Were the nations that
my predecessors[a] destroyed—Gozan, Haran, Rezeph, and the
Bethedenites in Telassar—saved by their gods? 13 Where is the
king of Hamath? and the king of Arpad? and the kings of Lair,
Sepharvaim, Hena, and Ivvah?"

14 Hezekiah received the letter from the messengers and
read it. Hezekiah then went up to the House of the LORD and
spread it out before the LORD. 15 And Hezekiah prayed to the
LORD: 16 "O LORD of Hosts, enthroned on the Cherubim! You
alone are God of all the kingdoms of the earth. You made the
heavens and the earth. 17 O LORD, incline Your ear and hear,
open Your eye and see. Hear all the words that Sennacherib
has sent to blaspheme the living God! 18 True, O LORD, the
kings of Assyria have annihilated all the nations[b] and their
lands 19 and have committed their gods to the flames and have
destroyed them; for they are not gods, but man's handwork of
wood and stone. 20 But now, O LORD our God, deliver us from
his hands, and let all the kingdoms of the earth know that You,
O LORD, alone [are God]."[c]

21 Then Isaiah son of Amoz sent this message to Hezekiah:
"Thus said the LORD, the God of Israel, to whom you have
prayed, concerning King Sennacherib of Assyria—22 this is the
word that the LORD has spoken concerning him:

Fair Maiden Zion despises you,
She mocks at you;
Fair Jerusalem shakes
Her head at you.
23 Whom have you blasphemed and reviled?
Against whom made loud your voice
And haughtily raised your eyes?
Against the Holy One of Israel!
24 Through your servants you have blasphemed my Lord.
Because you thought,
'Thanks to my vast chariotry,
It is I who have climbed the highest mountains,
To the remotest parts of the Lebanon,
And have cut down its loftiest cedars,
Its choicest cypresses,
And have reached its highest peak,
[d]Its densest forest.[d]

a Lit. "fathers."

b So 2 Kings 19.17, and 13 mss. here; most mss. and editions read "lands."

c Supplied from 2 Kings 19.19.

d-d Lit. "Its farmland forest"; exact meaning of Heb. uncertain.

25 It is I who have drawn[a]
And drunk water.
I have dried up with the soles of my feet
All the streams of Egypt.'
26 Have you not heard? Of old
I planned that very thing,
I designed it long ago,
And now have fulfilled it.
And it has come to pass,
Laying fortified towns waste in desolate heaps.
27 Their inhabitants are helpless,
Dismayed and shamed.
They were but grass of the field
And green herbage,
Grass of the roofs [b-]that is blasted
Before the east wind.[-b]
28 I know your stayings
And your goings and comings,
And how you have raged against Me,
29 Because you have raged against Me,
And your tumult has reached My ears,
I will place My hook in your nose
And My bit between your jaws;
And I will make you go back by the road
By which you came.

30 "And this is the sign for you:[c] This year you eat what grows
of itself, and the next year what springs from that, and in the
third year sow and reap and plant vineyards and eat their fruit.
31 And the survivors of the House of Judah that have escaped
shall renew its trunk below and produce boughs above.

32 For a remnant shall come forth from Jerusalem,
Survivors from Mount Zion.
The zeal of the LORD of Hosts
Shall bring this to pass.

33 "Assuredly, thus said the LORD concerning the king of Assyria:

He shall not enter this city;
He shall not shoot an arrow at it,
Or advance upon it with a shield,
Or pile up a siegemound against it.

a Or "dug"; meaning of Heb. uncertain.
b-b So ms. 1QIs[a]; cf. 2 Kings 19.26. The usual reading in our passage means, literally, "and a field [?] before standing grain." *c I.e., Hezekiah.*

36: The miraculous disappearance of the army that threatened Zion. Cf. 2 Chron. 32.21–23. In 2 Kings 18.14–16, the Assyrians leave only after having been offered tribute. **37–38:** The withdrawal of the Assyrians and the death of Sennacherib. According to Assyrian records, Sennacherib was assassinated in 681 BCE, two decades after the events described here; history has been telescoped to make a theological point.

Chs 38–39: The illness of Hezekiah and the overtures of the Babylonian empire. The events described in chs 38–39 preceded the events described in chs 36–37 by at least ten years. Because chs 38–39 end with a prediction of the Babylonian exile, however, they were placed (both here and respectively in 2 Kings) after chs 36–37. The result in Isaiah is that the prediction of the Babylonian exile would immediately precede ch 40, whose subject is the return from that exile.

38.1–8: Hezekiah's illness and prayer.

9–20: Hezekiah's psalm of thanksgiving. This text does not appear in the parallel version in 2 Kings ch 20. It is typical of psalms of thanksgiving found in the book of Ps. Similar elements appear, for example, in Ps. 118 and in Jonah ch 2. **10–13:** A description of the crisis that the speaker overcame. Cf. Ps. 118.5–7, 10–16; Jonah 2.4–7.

34 He shall go back
By the way he came,
He shall not enter this city
—declares the LORD;
35 I will protect and save this city for My sake
And for the sake of My servant David."

36 [That night][a] an angel of the LORD went out and struck
down one hundred and eighty-five thousand in the Assyrian
camp, and the following morning they were all dead corpses.
37 So King Sennacherib of Assyria broke camp and retreated, and stayed in Nineveh. 38 While he was worshiping in the
temple of his god Nisroch, he was struck down with the sword
by his sons Adrammelech and Sarezer. They fled to the land of
Ararat, and his son Esarhaddon succeeded him as king.

38 In those days Hezekiah fell dangerously ill. The prophet
Isaiah son of Amoz came and said to him, "Thus said
the LORD: Set your affairs in order, for you are going to die;
you will not get well." 2 Thereupon Hezekiah turned his face
to the wall and prayed to the LORD. 3 "Please, O LORD," he
said, "remember how I have walked before You sincerely and
wholeheartedly, and have done what is pleasing to You." And
Hezekiah wept profusely.
4 Then the word of the LORD came to Isaiah: 5 "Go and tell
Hezekiah: Thus said the LORD, the God of your father David:
I have heard your prayer, I have seen your tears. I hereby add
fifteen years to your life. 6 I will also rescue you and this city
from the hands of the king of Assyria. I will protect this city.
7 And this is the sign for you from the LORD that the LORD will
do the thing that He has promised: 8 I am going to make the
shadow on the steps, which has descended on the dial[b] of Ahaz
because of the sun, recede ten steps." And the sun['s shadow]
receded ten steps, the same steps as it had descended.
9 A poem by King Hezekiah of Judah when he recovered
from the illness he had suffered:

10[c] I had thought:
I must depart in the middle of my days;
I have been consigned to the gates of Sheol
For the rest of my years.
11 I thought, I shall never see Yah,[d]
Yah in the land of the living,

a Supplied from 2 Kings 19.35.
b Heb. "steps." A model of a dial with steps has been discovered in Egypt.
c Meaning of verse uncertain in part.
d I.e., visit His Temple. For "Yah" see 12.2; 26.4.

Or ever behold men again
Among those who inhabit the earth.
12 My dwelling is pulled up and removed from me
Like a tent of shepherds;
My life is rolled up like a web
And cut from the thrum.

[a]-Only from daybreak to nightfall
Was I kept whole,
13 Then it was as though a lion
Were breaking all my bones;
I cried out until morning.
(Only from daybreak to nightfall
Was I kept whole.)-[a]
14 I piped like a swift or a swallow,
I moaned like a dove,
As my eyes, all worn, looked to heaven:
"My Lord, I am in straits;
Be my surety!"
15 What can I say? [a]-He promised me,-[a]
And He it is who has wrought it.
[a]-All my sleep had fled
Because of the bitterness of my soul.
16 My Lord, for all that and despite it
My life-breath is revived;-[a]
You have restored me to health and revived me.
17 Truly, it was for my own good
That I had such great bitterness:
You saved my life
From the pit of destruction,
For You have cast behind Your back
All my offenses.
18 For it is not Sheol that praises You,
Not [the Land of] Death that extols You;
Nor do they who descend into the Pit
Hope for Your grace.
19 The living, only the living
Can give thanks to You
As I do this day;
Fathers[b] relate to children
Your acts of grace:
20 "[It has pleased] the LORD to deliver us,[b]
That is why we offer up music[c]

a-a Meaning of Heb. uncertain. *b Heb. singular.*
c Neginothai *is a poetic form of* neginoth.

14: A reference to a lament or petition the speaker uttered during the crisis. Cf. Ps. 118.5; Jonah 2.3. **15–20:** God's faithfulness: The speaker has been saved. Cf. Ps. 118.8–9; Jonah 2.7–8.

All the days of our lives
At the House of the LORD."

[21] When Isaiah said, "Let them take a cake of figs and apply it
to the rash, and he will recover," [22] Hezekiah asked, "What will
be the sign that I shall go up to the House of the LORD?"

39 At that time, Merodach-baladan son of Baladan, the
king of Babylon, sent [envoys with] a letter and a gift
to Hezekiah, for he had heard about his illness and recovery.
[2] Hezekiah was pleased by their coming, and he showed them
his treasure house—the silver, the gold, the spices, and the fragrant oil—and all his armory, and everything that was to be
found in his storehouses. There was nothing in his palace or
in all his realm that Hezekiah did not show them. [3] Then the
prophet Isaiah came to King Hezekiah. "What," he demanded
of him, "did those men say to you? Where have they come to
you from?" "They have come to me," replied Hezekiah, "from
a far country, from Babylon." [4] Next he asked, "What have they
seen in your palace?" And Hezekiah replied, "They have seen
everything there is in my palace. There was nothing in my
storehouses that I did not show them."
[5] Then Isaiah said to Hezekiah, "Hear the word of the LORD
of Hosts: [6] A time is coming when everything in your palace,
which your ancestors have stored up to this day, will be carried off to Babylon; nothing will be left behind, said the LORD.
[7] And some of your sons, your own issue, whom you will have
fathered, will be taken to serve as eunuchs in the palace of the
king of Babylon." [8] Hezekiah declared to Isaiah, "The word of
the LORD that you have spoken is good." For he thought, "It
means that [a-]safety is assured for[-a] my time."

40 Comfort, oh comfort My people,
Says your God.
2 Speak tenderly to Jerusalem,
And declare to her
That her term of service is over,

a-a *Lit. "there shall be safety and faithfulness in."*

21–22: The healing of Hezekiah. In 2 Kings 20.6–7, these vv. follow immediately on the prediction that God will add fifteen years to Hezekiah's life and protect him from the Assyrians (see Isa. 38.5–6). Thus in 2 Kings ch 20, these vv. lead naturally into the sign oracle, which appears here in 38.7–8.

39.1–4: The ambassadors from Babylon. *Merodach-baladan* was king of Babylonia in the 710s BCE. He attempted to lead a revolt against the Assyrians, and his messengers tried to entice Hezekiah to join the revolt. Ultimately, the revolt did not succeed; see 21.1–10 n. Here as in 21.1–10 Isaiah counsels against relying on the Babylonians. **5–8:** A prediction of the Babylonian exile. It is unlikely that this prophecy was in fact uttered by the historical Isaiah son of Amoz, who believed that Jerusalem would never fall, and he does not seem to have anticipated any break in the reign of Davidic kings, even though he predicted that Judah would be punished and the Davidic family sorely pressed. This prediction was probably attributed to Isaiah by the author of 2 Kings, and the whole passage was added to the book of Isaiah from Kings. It now provides a link with the next section of the book of Isaiah, the prophecies of an anonymous prophet who lived in the Babylonian exile. See the intro.

Chs 40–48: The first prophecies of Deutero-Isaiah. On the authorship of chs 40–66, see intro. The first of the three sections within chs 40–66 was written by the anonymous exilic prophet in Babylonia, shortly before or immediately after the fall of Babylonia to the Persians led by Cyrus in 539 BCE, but before Cyrus issued his decree allowing the Judean exiles to return to Zion in 538 (see Ezra 6.3–5; 2 Chron. 36.22–23). Chs 40–48 consist of several long speeches. In each, Deutero-Isaiah marshals evidence to show the depressed exiles that (1) God is genuinely powerful, and the Babylonian conquest does not indicate that God was defeated by some other alleged god or some other force; (2) God continues to love the nation Israel, and the Babylonian conquest does not indicate that God has abandoned Israel; (3) God is reliable, and what God promises God does; and therefore (4) the exiles can be sure that they will soon return to their land. The prophet frequently seems to be responding to specific complaints, doubts, and expressions of hopelessness among the exiles. A few of these statements made by Deutero-Isaiah's listeners are cited explicitly (e.g., 40.27; 49.14; 50.1; 50.2). Each speech appearing in these chs moves through several types of reasoning to support these assertions; then the speech ends, and another one begins. It is often

That her iniquity is expiated;
For she has received at the hand of the LORD
Double for all her sins.

3 A voice rings out:
"Clear in the desert
A road for the LORD!
Level in the wilderness
A highway for our God!
4 Let every valley be raised,
Every hill and mount made low.
Let the rugged ground become level
And the ridges become a plain.
5 The Presence of the LORD shall appear,
And all flesh, as one, shall behold—
For the LORD Himself has spoken."

6 A voice rings out: "Proclaim!"
[a-]Another asks,[-a] "What shall I proclaim?"
"All flesh is grass,
All its goodness like flowers of the field:
7 Grass withers, flowers fade
When the breath of the LORD blows on them.
Indeed, man is but grass:
8 Grass withers, flowers fade—
But the word of our God is always fulfilled!"

a-a 1QIs[a] and Septuagint read "And I asked."

difficult (and, ultimately, unimportant) to delineate the precise beginning and end of each speech, since each one presents the same argument using the same types of evidence. This first section of Deutero-Isaiah's prophecies focuses on several themes that are absent in chs 49–66: the uniqueness of the LORD, who is the only God; the Persian king Cyrus is the individual through whom God brings salvation to Israel; and the "former things" that God had done are compared with "new things" that God is about to do. Since the major message of this prophet is reconciliation and comfort, eight sections from these chs are read as the haftarah, or prophetic readings, on the Sabbaths following Tish'ah be'av (July or August), which commemorates the destruction of the Temple.

40.1–11: An introduction to the prophecies of Deutero-Isaiah. Vv. 1–11 introduce the main themes and motifs of the following chs: God comforts the nation, assures them that their term of punishment in the Babylonian exile has ended, and promises that they will soon return to Zion. This introductory passage echoes elements of the prophetic initiation scene (see ch 6 nn.): God announces that God has a message that the prophet should convey to the nation Israel (vv. 1–5); the prophet objects and is reassured (vv. 6–9). This section also introduces a special feature of Deutero-Isaiah's work: This prophet frequently borrows and revises material from older biblical texts. This tendency to allude to earlier compositions is especially evident in these eleven vv., which use terms and images from ch 6; 28.1–2; Exod. 32.14–15; Jer. 16.16–18; 31.15; Ezek. 21.2–12; Lam. 1.2, 9, 16, 21. **1–2:** God's initial message of consolation. These initial two vv. summarize the main themes of chs 40–66 in their entirety. The verbs *(comfort, speak, declare)* are in the plural, indicating that God addresses not only Deutero-Isaiah but other messengers as well, probably angelic messengers in the heavenly court. As in ch 6 and 2 Kings ch 22, the prophet overhears and to some extent participates in the deliberations of God's angelic staff. *Double for all her sins:* The exiles may feel that they deserve punishment, and therefore salvation is remote. The prophet assures them that the punishment they have suffered is more than enough, and there is no impediment to their salvation. Cf. Isa. 61.7 and Jer. 16.18. **3–5:** God's highway. The *Presence* of God left the land of Israel along with the exiles (cf. Ezek. chs 8–11); now it will return with them (cf. Ezek. 43.1–5). On the motif of the *road* through the *desert,* see 35.1–10 n. (Chs 34 and 35 were also written by Deutero-Isaiah.) **6–8:** Objection and reassurance. A heavenly voice gives an order to issue a proclamation; another voice (probably that of the prophet, esp. if the alternate version in translators' note *a-a* is correct) asks what should be proclaimed, and the first voice answers this question. According to the quotation marks added by the NJPS translation, the prophet's question is brief, and the answer takes up most of v. 6 and all of vv. 7–8. Thus the prophet must proclaim that humans are weak (and therefore the Babylonian conquerors will disappear), but God's strength is enduring. It is also possible, however, that the prophet's question continues through the end of v. 7. In that case, these vv. are an objection to acting as conduit for the divine word: As a mere human, the prophet fears that he will be overcome by the powerful and destructive *breath of the LORD* (lit. "wind" or "Spirit" of the LORD a technical term denoting the God-given capability to serve as a prophet). V. 8 contains the divine response: Even though the task of conveying God's words is

9 Ascend a lofty mountain,
O herald of joy to Zion;
Raise your voice with power,
O herald of joy to Jerusalem—
Raise it, have no fear;
Announce to the cities of Judah:
Behold your God!
10 Behold, the Lord GOD comes in might,
And His arm wins triumph for Him;
See, His reward[a] is with Him,
His recompense before Him.
11 Like a shepherd He pastures His flock:
He gathers the lambs in His arms
And carries them in His bosom;
Gently He drives the mother sheep.

12 Who measured the waters with the hollow of His hand,
And gauged the skies with a span,
And meted earth's dust with a measure,[b]
And weighed the mountains with a scale
And the hills with a balance?
13 Who has plumbed the mind of the LORD,
What man could tell Him His plan?
14 Whom did He consult, and who taught Him,
Guided Him in the way of right?
Who guided Him in knowledge
And showed Him the path of wisdom?

15 The nations are but a drop in a bucket,
Reckoned as dust on a balance;
The very coastlands He lifts like motes.
16 Lebanon is not fuel enough,
Nor its beasts enough for sacrifice.
17 All nations are as naught in His sight;
He accounts them as less than nothing.

18 To whom, then, can you liken God,
What form compare to Him?
19 The idol? A woodworker shaped it,
And a smith overlaid it with gold,
[c]Forging links of silver.[c]
20 As a gift, he chooses the mulberry[d]—
A wood that does not rot—

a *The reward and recompense to the cities of Judah; cf. Jer. 31.14, 16.*
b *Heb.* shalish *"third," probably a third of an* ephah.
c-c *Meaning of Heb. uncertain.*
d *Heb.* mesukkan; *according to a Jewish tradition, preserved by Jerome, a kind of wood; a similar word denotes a kind of wood in Akkadian.*

frightening, it must be completed. **6:** *Goodness,* or, "loyalty, reliability." **9–11:** God's arrival in Jerusalem. Messengers are told to announce to Jerusalem that the LORD will soon arrive. Normally, a *herald* would inform a city that an enemy army was arriving, but here God arrives as a gentle *shepherd,* not to destroy but to protect.

40.12–31: The incomparable God. In this speech, Deutero-Isaiah focuses on God's unique power. Because the LORD is the only true God, the Creator of the world and sovereign over all of it, the LORD will be able to defeat the Babylonians and restore Zion. Some Judeans probably believed that Babylonia's gods defeated their God, but the prophet insists that in fact no other being in the universe could do so. **12–17:** Divine grandeur. No entity in heaven or earth compares to God, in size or in power or in wisdom, and therefore none can prevent God from acting. **12:** God created the world from cosmic materials which, compared to Him, were small and easily manipulated. Likewise, in v. 15, the nations are like specks of dust. **16:** The great cedar forests of Lebanon cannot provide enough wood to fuel a proper sacrifice to God, nor enough animals to offer as sacrifices. **18–20:** A brief argument against idolatry: Certainly the God who created the world is mightier than the gods worshipped by most humans. Those gods, after all, are created, not creators. See 44.9–20 n., concerning Isaiah's misrepresentation of the place of divine images in Mesopotamian religion.

Then seeks a skillful woodworker
To make a firm idol,
That will not topple.

21 Do you not know?
Have you not heard?
Have you not been told
From the very first?
Have you not discerned
[a]How the earth was founded?[a]
22 It is He who is enthroned above the vault of
the earth,
So that its inhabitants seem as grasshoppers;
Who spread out the skies like gauze,
Stretched them out like a tent to dwell in.
23 He brings potentates to naught,
Makes rulers of the earth as nothing.
24 Hardly are they planted,
Hardly are they sown,
Hardly has their stem
Taken root in earth,
When He blows upon them and they dry up,
And the storm bears them off like straw.

25 To whom, then, can you liken Me,
To whom can I be compared?
—says the Holy One.
26 Lift high your eyes and see:
Who created these?
He who sends out their host by count,
Who calls them each by name:
Because of His great might and vast power,
Not one fails to appear.

27 Why do you say, O Jacob,
Why declare, O Israel,
"My way is hid from the LORD,
My cause is ignored by my God"?
28 Do you not know?
Have you not heard?
The LORD is God from of old,
Creator of the earth from end to end,
He never grows faint or weary,
His wisdom cannot be fathomed.
29 He gives strength to the weary,
Fresh vigor to the spent.

a-a Meaning of Heb. uncertain.

21–26: God's incomparable might as manifest in nature and in history. **22:** The divine perspective is so much larger than the human perspective. In size, distance, and time (v. 24) God's scale of measurement vastly surpasses the human scale. **26:** God knows each individual star, which to humans appear to be infinite in number, and He controls the appearance in the sky of each one. This may be a pointed polemic against Babylonian astral worship. **27–31:** Deutero-Isaiah arrives at the point of the arguments marshaled in vv. 12–26. The Judean exiles have lamented that God no longer pays attention to them (v. 27). But God is still able to listen to them, for God never grows tired (vv. 28–31). **28:** Possibly a clarification of Gen. 2.1–3, noting that the LORD did not rest because of tiredness at the conclusion of creation.

30 Youths may grow faint and weary,
And young men stumble and fall;
31 But they who trust in the LORD shall renew
their strength
As eagles grow new plumes:[a]
They shall run and not grow weary,
They shall march and not grow faint.

41 Stand silent before Me, coastlands,
And let nations [b-]renew their strength.[-b]
Let them approach to state their case;
Let us come forward together for argument.
2 Who has roused a victor[c] from the East,
Summoned him to His service?
Has delivered up nations to him,
And trodden sovereigns down?
Has rendered their[d] swords like dust,
Their[d] bows like wind-blown straw?
3 He pursues them, he goes on unscathed;
No shackle[e] is placed on his feet.
4 Who has wrought and achieved this?
He who announced the generations from
the start—
I, the LORD, who was first
And will be with the last as well.

5 The coastlands look on in fear,
The ends of earth tremble.

They draw near and come;
6 Each one helps the other,
Saying to his fellow, "Take courage!"
7 The woodworker encourages the smith;
He who flattens with the hammer
[Encourages] him who pounds the anvil.
He says of the riveting, "It is good!"
And he fixes it with nails,
That it may not topple.

8 But you, Israel, My servant,
Jacob, whom I have chosen,
Seed of Abraham My friend—
9 You whom I drew from the ends of the earth
And called from its far corners,

a Alluding to a popular belief that eagles regain their youth when they molt; cf. Ps. 103.5. *b-b Connection of Heb. uncertain.* *c Lit. "victory."*
d Heb. "his." *e ʾrḥ has this meaning in Old Aramaic.*

31: *Trust,* or, "wait with patience and hope."

41.1–42.17: The divine ruler and His servants. A lengthy speech that moves through several lines of reasoning to persuade the audience that God can and will redeem Israel. A theme uniting the whole passage is service to God: Cyrus acts as God's servant by defeating Babylonia (41.2, 25); Israel is God's servant and hence enjoys divine protection (41.8; 42.1).

41.1–7: A mock dialogue with the nations. God calls on the nations to show whether they and their gods can match the true deity's power. Unable to respond, they are terrified. **1–4:** God asks whether any other nation or its gods has accomplished what the LORD has. **2:** *A victor from the East,* alternatively, "A righteous one from the east." This refers to Cyrus, king of the Persians, who lived east of Babylonia and achieved great victories over all the *nations* and *sovereigns* of the ancient Near East. The Targum takes this to refer to Abraham, the righteous man (see Gen. 15.6), whom God brought from Mesopotamia in the east to Canaan and connects it to Abraham's military victory in Gen. ch 14. **4:** The LORD takes responsibility for Cyrus's (and perhaps also Abraham's) victories. The prophet refers especially to Cyrus's defeat of the Babylonian empire. This v. recalls earlier prophecies according to which the great Mesopotamian empire that defeated Judah would itself fall; see Isa. 10.5–27; 13.1–14.27; 21.1–10; Jer. 29.10; 30.11; Zeph. 2.15. Because the God of Israel correctly predicted the downfall of Babylonia in these prophetic passages, which were written years earlier, the God of Israel is clearly the true lord of history. **5–7:** The nations are unable to rely on their gods, who have not demonstrated such mastery over events as the God of Israel. Consequently, they are frightened, but rather than acknowledge the one true God, they foolishly rush to construct a new idol to save themselves.

To whom I said: You are My servant;
I chose you, I have not rejected you—
10 Fear not, for I am with you,
Be not frightened, for I am your God;
I strengthen you and I help you,
I uphold you with My victorious right hand.
11 Shamed and chagrined shall be
All who contend with you;
They who strive with you
Shall become as naught and shall perish.
12 You may seek, but shall not find
Those who struggle with you;
Less than nothing shall be
The men who battle against you.
13 For I the LORD am your God,
Who grasped your right hand,
Who say to you: Have no fear;
I will be your help.
14 Fear not, O worm Jacob,
O [a]men of[a] Israel:
I will help you
—declares the LORD—
I your Redeemer, the Holy One of Israel.
15 I will make of you a threshing board,
A new thresher, with many spikes;
You shall thresh mountains to dust,
And make hills like chaff.
16 You shall winnow them
And the wind shall carry them off;
The whirlwind shall scatter them.
But you shall rejoice in the LORD,
And glory in the Holy One of Israel.

17 The poor and the needy
Seek water,[b] and there is none;
Their tongue is parched with thirst.
I the LORD will respond to them.
I, the God of Israel, will not forsake them.
18 I will open up streams on the bare hills
And fountains amid the valleys;
I will turn the desert into ponds,
The arid land into springs of water.
19 I will plant cedars in the wilderness,
Acacias and myrtles and oleasters;
I will set cypresses in the desert,

a-a Emendation yields "maggot."
b I.e., on the homeward march through the desert.

8–20: Encouragement to Israel, God's servant. The nations in vv. 5–7 are frightened, but the Israelites are told that they should fear no more. **8–16:** Israel's fortunes are reversed. The defeated nation will be able to defeat its enemies; the great nations that tormented Israel will lose power. **9:** *I have not rejected you,* a direct address to the exiles, who wonder whether the covenant between God and Israel came to an end with the destruction of the Temple in 586 BCE. **15:** Mighty nations are compared to mountains, which Israel will be able to destroy. The theme of the haughty mountains and empires that will disappear at the end of days is central to the earlier Isaiah son of Amoz, cf. 2.10–22. **17–20:** Return from exile. The poor and thirsty nation will march through the desert, where God will fulfill all their needs. Here as in ch 35 Deutero-Isaiah compares the upcoming return to Zion with the exodus from Egypt and wandering in the Sinai wilderness, where God provided water and food for the Israelites as they marched to the land of Canaan.

21–29: Another mock debate emphasizing God's sovereignty. As in vv. 1–4, the setting is a courtroom or contest; God speaks, but the other side in the debate simply has nothing to say in its defense and remains silent. **21–23a:** The LORD argues against other gods and their believers, asking them to step forward and announce what great acts they have committed or what predictions they have successfully made. **23b:** God asks the other gods to do anything at all, so that at least their mere existence will be made clear. **24:** The inevitable conclusion: The other gods simply do not exist. **25–26:** The LORD, by contrast, has raised up Cyrus (*him from the north*—Persia is northeast of Babylonia) to defeat Babylonia, just as in the past the LORD brought the Mesopotamian rulers from the north to defeat Israel and Judah and predicted the downfall of Babylonia successfully. Cf. v. 4 in this ch. **27:** *The things once predicted to Zion* refers both to predictions of Zion's defeat (e.g., in prophecies throughout the book of Jeremiah) and also the predictions of Zion's renewal (e.g., Jer. chs 29–33). Because the former prophecies came true, one can be sure that the latter will come true as well—the LORD is reliable. **28–29:** *And there is not a man,* better: "and there is no one." God has asked other gods to come stake their claims to divinity, but none has come forward. This compels the conclusion that *they are all nothingness. See,* or, "Here is" (Heb "hen").

42.1–9: God's servant. The identification of the servant in these vv. and in other related chs is hotly debated. Possibilities include Cyrus (according to Saadia Gaon), the prophet himself (so Ibn Ezra), the Messiah (so Tg. and Radak), and the Israelite nation as a whole (so LXX and Rashi). See 52.13–53.12 n. The term "servant" in most other passages in chs 40–66 clearly refers to the nation Israel or to the faithful within Israel, and that is the most likely explanation here as well. This passage borrows vocabulary and ideas

Box trees and elms as well—
20 That men may see and know,
Consider and comprehend
That the LORD's hand has done this,
That the Holy One of Israel has wrought it.

21 Submit your case, says the LORD;
Offer your pleas, says the King of Jacob.
22 Let them approach[a] and tell us what will happen.
Tell us what has occurred,[b]
And we will take note of it;
Or announce to us what will occur,
That we may know the outcome.
23 Foretell what is yet to happen,
That we may know that you are gods!
Do anything, good or bad,
That we may be awed and see.[c]
24 Why, you are less than nothing,
Your effect is less than nullity;
One who chooses you is an abomination.

25 I have roused him from the north, and he has come,
From the sunrise, one who invokes My name;
And he has trampled rulers like mud,
Like a potter treading clay.
26 Who foretold this from the start, that we may note it;
From aforetime, that we might say, "He is right"?
Not one foretold, not one announced;
No one has heard your utterance!
27 [d-]The things once predicted to Zion—
Behold, here they are![-d]
And again I send a herald to Jerusalem.
28 But I look and there is not a man;
Not one of them can predict
Or can respond when I question him.
29 See, they are all nothingness,
Their works are nullity,
Their statues are naught and nil.

42 This is My servant, whom I uphold,
My chosen one, in whom I delight.
I have put My spirit upon him,
He shall teach the true way to the nations.
2 He shall not cry out or shout aloud,

a *Taking* yaggishu *intransitively; cf.* hiqriv. *Exod. 14.10.*
b *I.e., former prophecies by your gods which have been fulfilled.*
c *Change of vocalization yields "fear"; cf. v. 10.* d-d *Meaning of Heb. uncertain.*

Or make his voice heard in the streets.
3 [a-]He shall not break even a bruised reed,
Or snuff out even a dim wick.[-a]
He shall bring forth the true way.
4 He shall not grow dim or be bruised
Till he has established the true way on earth;
And the coastlands shall await his teaching.

5 Thus said God the LORD,
Who created the heavens and stretched them out,
Who spread out the earth and what it brings forth,
Who gave breath to the people upon it
And life to those who walk thereon:
6 I the LORD, in My grace, have summoned you,
And I have grasped you by the hand.
I created you, and appointed you
A [b-]covenant people,[-b] [c-]a light of nations[-c]—
7 [d-]Opening eyes deprived of light,[-d]
Rescuing prisoners from confinement,
From the dungeon those who sit in darkness.
8 I am the LORD, that is My name;
I will not yield My glory to another,
Nor My renown to idols.
9 See, the things once predicted have come,
And now I foretell new things,
Announce to you ere they sprout up.
10 Sing to the LORD a new song,
His praise from the ends of the earth—
[e-]You who sail the sea and you creatures in it,
You coastlands[-e] and their inhabitants!
11 Let the desert and its towns cry aloud,
The villages where Kedar dwells;
Let Sela's inhabitants shout,
Call out from the peaks of the mountains.

a-a Or "A bruised reed, he shall not be broken; / A dim wick, he shall not be snuffed out." *b-b Lit. "covenants of a people"; meaning of Heb. uncertain.*
c-c See 49.6 and note.
d-d An idiom meaning "freeing the imprisoned"; cf. 61.1.
e-e Emendation yields "Let the sea roar and its creatures, / The coastlands ..." Cf. Ps. 98.7.

from both ch 11 and Jer. 31.31–36. Like those passages, this text looks forward to the ideal world of the future, in which justice will reign and the covenant between Israel and God will be observed perfectly. The servant in this passage is parallel to, though not identical with, the ideal Davidic king described in ch 11; promises made to the king there are transferred to the whole nation here, since the future ideal Davidic king has no place in Deutero-Isaiah (cf. 55.3 n.; 60.1–22 n.; 65.25 n.). **1–4:** God introduces the servant, whose gentle nature is emphasized. In these lines God addresses the nations of the world while pointing to the servant, the nation Israel. **1:** *This,* or, "Here is" (Heb "hen"). The term deliberately contrasts God's servant with the pagan gods and their worshippers introduced with the same term in the previous v. (see 41.28–29 n.). **4:** *Coastlands:* Even nations far away will know God as a result of God's treatment of Israel. This idea is further developed in v. 6. *His teaching,* or, "his law" (Heb "torah"). **5–7:** God addresses the servant directly and describes the reason that the servant has been chosen. **6:** *Created,* or "guarded." *A covenant people,* i.e., a nation that continues to exist by virtue of the covenant God formed with their ancestors long ago. In spite of their sins and in spite of the exile, the people Israel is assured of restoration because of the covenant. *A light of nations:* The nations of the world will witness God's faithfulness to the covenant when Israel is redeemed. Consequently, the people will be the tool through which God becomes known to all nations as mighty, just, and reliable. In contrast to many modern uses of this passage, the Israelites here are a light to the nations by virtue of what happens to them, not because of what they do. **7:** *Opening ... Rescuing:* The subject of the verbs may be either the people or God.

8–9: God's guarantee to the servant. The servant is guaranteed salvation because his sponsor is the Creator. **9:** *Things once predicted,* lit. "the former things." Cf. 41.4.

42.10–17: A concluding hymn. The speech that began in 41.1 concludes with a song describing God's might and Israel's restoration. **10–12:** As in 42.1–4, the whole world witnesses God's saving power. **11:** *Kedar,* an area in the north of the Arabian desert, inhabited by nomads. *Sela,* an Edomite city, probably the city now known as Petra in the kingdom of Jordan.

12 Let them do honor to the LORD,
And tell His glory in the coastlands.

13 The LORD goes forth like a warrior,
Like a fighter He whips up His rage.
He yells, He roars aloud,
He charges upon His enemies.
14 "I have kept silent [a]far too long,[-a]
Kept still and restrained Myself;
Now I will scream like a woman in labor,
I will pant and I will gasp.
15 Hills and heights will I scorch,
Cause all their green to wither;
I will turn rivers into isles,[b]
And dry the marshes up.
16 I will lead the blind
By a road they did not know,
And I will make them walk
By paths they never knew.
I will turn darkness before them to light,
Rough places into level ground.
These are the promises—
I will keep them without fail.
17 Driven back and utterly shamed
Shall be those who trust in an image,
Those who say to idols,
'You are our gods!'"

18 Listen, you who are deaf;
You blind ones, look up and see!
19 Who is so blind as My servant,
So deaf as the messenger I send?
Who is so blind as the chosen[c] one,
So blind as the servant of the LORD?
20 Seeing many things, [d]he gives[-d] no heed;
With ears open, he hears nothing.
21[e] The LORD desires His [servant's] vindication,
That he may magnify and glorify [His] Teaching.

22 Yet it is a people plundered and despoiled:
All of them are trapped in holes,
Imprisoned in dungeons.
They are given over to plunder, with none to rescue them;

a-a Lit. "from of old." *b Emendation yields "desert."*
c Meaning of Heb. uncertain. *d-d Heb. "you give."*
e Meaning of verse uncertain; cf. 43.9–12.

13–17: God goes to war on behalf of Israel. This passage deliberately mixes two types of images of God, as warrior fighting enemies and as mother giving birth, which are united by the extraordinary energy each involves. A bloody process ends with new creation.

42.18–44.5: God's loyalty, which is unshaken even by Israel's sins. This long speech comforts the exiles, assuring them that God is able and willing to redeem them, regardless of the sins they and their forebears committed.

42.18–43.8: The servant, who deserves punishment, will ultimately be redeemed. 18–21: The nation Israel will serve God by becoming an object lesson for God's loyalty and ability to save (cf. 42.1–9 n.). Thus Israel is a *messenger;* through Israel's experiences, the world will come to know the one God. Israel is blind, however, and has not yet understood its own purpose in history. **21:** *His vindication:* This might refer to the vindication of the servant Israel or of God, or perhaps both; the former brings about the latter. *Teaching,* Heb "torah." **22–25:** The tone of these vv. seems bleak, but they in fact comfort the exiles. Deutero-Isaiah recalls Israel's sins (e.g., those described in 30.9–14, whose vocabulary is repeated here) in order to explain to the people why they are in their current state. They need not doubt the LORD's attention or power to save; the nation's plight is fully understandable and justifiable. Hence the exile gives no reason for despair.

To despoilment, with none to say "Give back!"
23 If only you would listen to this,
Attend and give heed from now on!
24 Who was it gave Jacob over to despoilment
And Israel to plunderers?
Surely, the LORD against whom they[a] sinned
In whose ways they would not walk
And whose Teaching they would not obey.
25 So He poured out wrath upon them,
His anger and the fury of war.
It blazed upon them all about, but they heeded not;
It burned among them, but they gave it no thought.

43 But now thus said the LORD—
Who created you, O Jacob,
Who formed you, O Israel:
Fear not, for I will redeem you;
I have singled you out by name,
You are Mine.
2 When you pass through water,
I will be with you;
Through streams,
They shall not overwhelm you.
When you walk through fire,
You shall not be scorched;
Through flame,
It shall not burn you.
3 For I the LORD am your God,
The Holy One of Israel, your Savior.
I give Egypt as a ransom for you,
Ethiopia and Saba in exchange for you.
4 Because you are precious to Me,
And honored, and I love you,
I give men in exchange for you
And peoples in your stead.

5 Fear not, for I am with you:
I will bring your folk from the East,
Will gather you out of the West;
6 I will say to the North, "Give back!"
And to the South, "Do not withhold!
Bring My sons from afar,
And My daughters from the end of the earth—
7 All who are linked to My name,
Whom I have created,
Formed, and made for My glory—

a Heb. "we."

43.1–7: Just as the negative prophecies of the past were fulfilled, so too the people can have confidence that the new, positive ones will come true. **1–2:** Israel belongs to God, and therefore God will not abandon her, even though God punishes her. **3–4:** God will reward Cyrus with the conquest of far-off lands including *Egypt,* because his work allows the exiles to return home. In fact, Cyrus never conquered Egypt, but his son, Cambyses, did. **5–8:** The ingathering of the exiles, not only from Babylonia (which was *East* of the land of Israel) but from other areas as well. Some Judean refugees fled to Egypt and other areas after the Babylonian conquest; see Jer. chs 43–44.

43.9–21: The arguments from prophecy and from history. **9–15:** The fulfillment of prophecies concerning Babylonia. As in other speeches (41.4, 27; 42.9; 44.6–8, 24–26; 45.21; 46.10–11; 48.3), Deutero-Isaiah argues that one should believe in the God of Israel because God's predictions come true. Long ago the LORD foretold the downfall of the Mesopotamian empire that defeated Judah; see 10.5–27; 13.1–14.27; 21.1–10; Jer. 29.10; 30.11. Now that Babylonia has indeed fallen (or perhaps is about to fall), it is clear that the God of Israel alone rules. **14:** *I send* Cyrus *to Babylon* to conquer it. *Chaldeans:* The Chaldeans were a leading tribe in Babylonia from the 7th c. on, and the last kings of Babylonia stemmed from this group. As a result the term "Chaldean" became a synonym for Babylonian. **16–21:** Long ago God took Israel out of slavery and defeated the mighty Egyptians. The liberation from Babylonian exile will prove even more impressive than the exodus from Egypt. **16–17:** A reference to the parting of the Reed Sea and the defeat of Pharaoh's army there; see Exod. chs 14–15.

8 Setting free that people,
Blind though it has eyes
And deaf though it has ears."

9 All the nations assemble as one,
The peoples gather.
Who among them declared this,
Foretold to us the things that have happened?
Let them produce their witnesses and be vindicated,
That men, hearing them, may say, "It is true!"[a]
10 My witnesses are *you*
—declares the LORD—
My servant, whom I have chosen.
To the end that you[b] may take thought,
And believe in Me,
And understand that I am He:
Before Me no god was formed,
And after Me none shall exist—
11 None but me, the LORD;
Beside Me, none can grant triumph.
12 I alone foretold the triumph
And I brought it to pass;
I announced it,
And no strange god was among you.
So you are My witnesses
—declares the LORD—
And I am God.
13 Ever since day was, I am He;
None can deliver from My hand.
When I act, who can reverse it?

14 Thus said the LORD,
Your Redeemer, the Holy One of Israel:
For your sake [c-]I send to Babylon;
I will bring down all [her] bars,
And the Chaldeans shall raise their voice in
lamentation.[-c]
15 I am your Holy One, the LORD,
Your King, the Creator of Israel.

16 Thus said the LORD,
Who made a road through the sea
And a path through mighty waters,
17 Who destroyed[d] chariots and horses,

a *I.e., that the other nations' gods are real.* b *Emendation yields "they."*
c-c *Meaning of Heb. uncertain.*
d *Understanding* hoṣi, *here, as equivalent to Aramaic* sheṣi.

And all the mighty host—
They lay down to rise no more,
They were extinguished, quenched like a wick:
18 Do not recall what happened of old,
Or ponder what happened of yore!
19 I am about to do something new;
Even now it shall come to pass,
Suddenly you shall perceive it:
I will make a road through the wilderness
And rivers[a] in the desert.
20 The wild beasts shall honor Me,
Jackals and ostriches,
For I provide water in the wilderness,
Rivers in the desert,
To give drink to My chosen people,
21 The people I formed for Myself
That they might declare My praise.

22 But you have not worshiped Me, O Jacob,
That you should be weary of Me, O Israel.
23 You have not brought Me your sheep for burnt offerings,
Nor honored Me with your sacrifices.
I have not burdened you with meal offerings,
Nor wearied you about frankincense.
24 You have not bought Me fragrant reed with money,
Nor sated Me with the fat of your sacrifices.
Instead, you have burdened Me with your sins,
You have wearied Me with your iniquities.
25 It is I, I who—for My own sake[b]—
Wipe your transgressions away
And remember your sins no more.
26 Help me remember!
Let us join in argument,
Tell your version,
That you may be vindicated.
27 Your earliest ancestor sinned,
And your spokesmen transgressed against Me.
28 So I profaned [c]the holy princes;[-c]
I abandoned Jacob to proscription[d]
And Israel to mockery.

a 1QIs[a] reads "paths"; cf. v. 16.
b I.e., in order to put an end to the profanation of My holy name; cf. 48.9–11.
c-c Emendation yields "My holy name"; see preceding note.
d Emendation yields "insult."

43.22–44.5: Israel's sin and redemption. As in 42.22–25, God recalls the sins of the Israelites (esp. of the exiles' ancestors), focusing on their failure to conduct proper sacrifices. The passage underscores the justice of their punishment and hence emphasizes that God is neither uncaring toward Israel nor too weak to save it. Once the punishment has been completed, there is no impediment to Israel's restoration. **22–24:** The passage is obscure. Deutero-Isaiah may maintain that the Israelites' sacrifices to the LORD were not accompanied by the proper intentions, and hence they really did not constitute worship of the LORD at all. (Cf. this prophet's criticism of the Israelites' fasts in 58.3–7; and see also other prophetic critiques of sacrifice as the Israelites practiced it, such as Isa. 1.11–13; Jer. 7.21–22; Amos 5.21–25.) Alternatively, the prophet may accuse them of neglecting the sacrificial cult and of worshipping other gods instead. Finally, this passage may simply take note of the fact that the exiles did not offer sacrifices, since they no longer had a legitimate Temple in which they could do so. **22:** *But you have not worshipped Me,* better: "It is not Me whom you have worshipped." The Heb emphasizes the word *Me.* **25:** The Israelites' failure or inability to offer proper sacrifices to the LORD is inconsequential; the LORD will redeem them not due to their righteousness but for the sake of God's own reputation. Unlike other cases where God transfers sins away from the sinner (see 2 Sam. 12.13 n.), or passes them over (e.g., Mic. 7.18), here God totally wipes our transgressions away. **43.26–44.5:** The Israelites' forebears were sinful, and hence they deserved punishment. But the punishment has run its course, and redemption is now called for. **27:** *Your earliest ancestor,* Jacob, who is depicted in very ambiguous terms in Gen. *Spokesmen,* the priests and Levites; or, the kings of Israel and Judah and their advisers.

44.1: See 43.1–2 n., which applies here as well. **3–4:** In the land of Israel, plants wither and remain brown for long periods until they are revived by rainfall. Israel in exile resembles these plants, which had looked dead but in fact were merely dormant. **5:** Possibly a reference to non-Jews who would adopt Jewish beliefs, practices, and ethnicity, which in fact did occur during the exilic and postexilic periods. This phenomenon is one of Deutero-Isaiah's particular concerns; see 56.3–6 n.; 56.7 n.

44.6–28: The persuasive power of monotheism and the folly of idolatry. This shorter speech focuses on the argument from prophecy and the ridiculous nature of idolatry. It gives particular emphasis to one of Deutero-Isaiah's main themes: the insistence that no other gods in fact exist. As with all of the speeches in chs 40–66, the main point is that the one true God can and will redeem Israel. The speech reaches its climax with the identification of the person through whom God brings redemption, the Persian king Cyrus.

6–8: The argument from prophecy. The LORD is clearly unique, since only the LORD predicted so far in advance events that in fact came to be. Cf. 43.9–15.

44 But hear, now, O Jacob My servant,
Israel whom I have chosen!
2 Thus said the LORD, your Maker,
Your Creator who has helped you since birth:
Fear not, My servant Jacob,
Jeshurun[a] whom I have chosen,
3 Even as I pour water on thirsty soil,
And rain upon dry ground,
So will I pour My spirit on your offspring,
My blessing upon your posterity.
4 And they shall sprout like[b] grass,
Like willows by watercourses.
5 One shall say, "I am the LORD's,"
Another shall use the name of "Jacob,"
Another shall mark his arm "of the LORD"[c]
And adopt the name of "Israel."

6 Thus said the LORD, the King of Israel,
Their Redeemer, the LORD of Hosts:
I am the first and I am the last,
And there is no god but Me.
7[d] Who like Me can announce,
Can foretell it—and match Me thereby?
Even as I told the future to an ancient
people,
So let him foretell coming events to them.
8 Do not be frightened, do not be shaken!
Have I not from of old predicted to you?
I foretold, and you are My witnesses.
Is there any god, then, but Me?
"There is no other rock; I know none!"

9 The makers of idols
All work to no purpose;
And the things they treasure
Can do no good,
As they themselves can testify.
They neither look nor think,
And so they shall be shamed.
10 Who would fashion a god
Or cast a statue
That can do no good?
11 Lo, all its adherents shall be shamed;
They are craftsmen, are merely human.

a A name for Israel; see note on Num. 23.10; cf. Deut. 32.15; 33.5, 26.
b Lit. "in among." *c It was customary to mark a slave with the owner's name.*
d Meaning of verse uncertain.

Let them all assemble and stand up!
They shall be cowed, and they shall be shamed.

12[a] The craftsman in iron, with his tools,
Works it[b] over charcoal
And fashions it by hammering,
Working with the strength of his arm.
Should he go hungry, his strength would ebb;
Should he drink no water, he would grow faint.

13 The craftsman in wood measures with a line
And marks out a shape with a stylus;
He forms it with scraping tools,
Marking it out with a compass.
He gives it a human form,
The beauty of a man, to dwell in a shrine.
14 For his use he cuts down cedars;
He chooses plane trees and oaks.
He sets aside trees of the forest;
Or plants firs, and the rain makes them grow.
15 All this serves man for fuel:
He takes some to warm himself,
And he builds a fire and bakes bread.
He also makes a god of it and worships it,
Fashions an idol and bows down to it!
16 Part of it he burns in a fire:
On that part he roasts[c] meat,
He eats[c] the roast and is sated;
He also warms himself and cries, "Ah,
I am warm! I can feel[d] the heat!"
17 Of the rest he makes a god—his own carving!
He bows down to it, worships it;
He prays to it and cries,
"Save me, for you are my god!"

18 They have no wit or judgment:
Their eyes are besmeared, and they see not;
Their minds, and they cannot think.
19 They do not give thought,
They lack the wit and judgment to say:
"Part of it I burned in a fire;
I also baked bread on the coals,
I roasted meat and ate it—
Should I make the rest an abhorrence?
Should I bow to a block of wood?"

a The meaning of parts of vv. 12–13 is uncertain. *b I.e., the image he is making.*
c Transposing the Heb. verbs for clarity. *d Lit. "see."*

9–20: A comic portrayal of an idolater. The prophet mercilessly lampoons people who make their own gods to worship, implicitly contrasting them with people who worship the true God. The former worship their own creation; the latter, much more sensibly, worship their Creator. Deutero-Isaiah to some extent misrepresents, or misunderstands, the actual nature of idolatry as practiced in the ancient Near East, however. Pagans did not believe that idols really were gods, but they believed that the presence of the god entered the idol as the result of complex rituals used to activate the idol after it had been made. **9–11:** The pointlessness of idol-worship. **12–13:** This description of how idols are made shows detailed familiarity with this ancient Near Eastern industry. Some idols were made of metal (v. 12), some of wood (v. 13). **14–20:** The most biting, and humorous, section of the passage. For Deutero-Isaiah, the fact that the same piece of wood can be put to mundane and religious (idolatrous) uses shows the idiocy of idolatry.

21–28: The result of rejecting idolatry. The recognition that idolatry is false leads to several practical conclusions. **21–22:** God formed Israel; in contrast pagans form their gods. Therefore Israel should serve, and trust, its God. Further it follows that God will forgive Israel. **22:** See 43.25 n. **23–28:** God tells the heavens to announce that God takes specific action to save Israel: God brings Cyrus, the Persian king who conquered Babylonia, to rebuild Jerusalem and its Temple. **24–26:** The monotheistic theme, with its argument from prophecy, is repeated; cf. vv. 6–8. God had earlier predicted the rebuilding of Jerusalem and the Temple in Jer. 30.18; 31.6–40; 33.10–18; Ezek. chs 40–48.

45.1–25: The universal God. This speech focuses on the Persian king Cyrus as the tool through whom God brings salvation not only to Israel but to the whole world. After Cyrus allows the exiles to return to Jerusalem, peoples the world over will recognize the LORD's faithfulness to the covenant made with Israel, and consequently they will join Israel in worshipping the one true God.

1–8: An address to Cyrus, the liberator. God is presented as speaking directly to Cyrus, who does not understand the true nature of his role. **1–3:** Cyrus's victories are summarized. **1:** *His anointed one,* Heb "mashiaḥ," often translated as "Messiah." It is striking that this term is used of Cyrus, and not of the ideal Davidic king, but according to Deutero-Isaiah, a Davidic king does not play a significant role in the expected restoration (see 55.3 n.). In the Bible, Messiah always refers to the present king, never to the future ideal one.

20 He pursues ashes![a]
A deluded mind has led him astray,
And he cannot save himself;
He never says to himself,
"The thing in my hand is a fraud!"
21 Remember these things, O Jacob
For you, O Israel, are My servant:
I fashioned you, you are My servant—
O Israel, never forget Me.[b]
22 I wipe away your sins like a cloud,
Your transgressions like mist—
Come back to Me, for I redeem you.

23 Shout, O heavens, for the LORD has acted;
Shout aloud, O depths of the earth!
Shout for joy, O mountains,
O forests with all your trees!
For the LORD has redeemed Jacob,
Has glorified Himself through Israel.

24 Thus said the LORD, your Redeemer,
Who formed you in the womb:
It is I, the LORD, who made everything,
Who alone stretched out the heavens
And unaided[c] spread out the earth;
25 Who annul the omens of diviners,
And make fools of the augurs;
Who turn sages back
And make nonsense of their knowledge;
26 But confirm the word of My[d] servant
And fulfill the prediction of My[d] messengers.
It is I who say of Jerusalem, "It shall be inhabited,"
And of the towns of Judah, "They shall be rebuilt;
And I will restore their ruined places."
27 [I,] who said to the deep, "Be dry;
I will dry up your floods,"
28 Am the same who says of Cyrus, "He is My shepherd;[e]
He shall fulfill all My purposes!
He shall say of Jerusalem, 'She shall be rebuilt,'
And to the Temple: 'You shall be founded again.' "

45 Thus said the LORD to Cyrus, His anointed one—
Whose right hand [f]He has[f] grasped,

a Lit. "He shepherds ashes." *b Emendation yields "them," these things.*
c Lit. "with none beside me," or (following many Heb. mss., kethib, *and ancient versions) "who was with me?"* *d Heb. "His."*
e I.e., the king whom I have designated. *f-f Heb. "I have." Cf. note at 8.11.*

Treading down nations before him,
[a]Ungirding the loins of kings,[a]
Opening doors before him
And letting no gate stay shut:
2 I will march before you
And level [b]the hills that loom up;[b]
I will shatter doors of bronze
And cut down iron bars.
3 I will give you treasures concealed in the dark
And secret hoards—
So that you may know that it is I the LORD,
The God of Israel, who call you by name.
4 For the sake of My servant Jacob,
Israel My chosen one,
I call you by name,
I hail you by title, though you have not known Me.
5 I am the LORD and there is none else;
Beside Me, there is no god.
I engird you, though you have not known Me,
6 So that they may know, from east to west,
That there is none but Me.
I am the LORD and there is none else,
7 I form light and create darkness,
I make weal and create woe—
I the LORD do all these things.
8 Pour down, O skies, from above!
Let the heavens rain down victory!
Let the earth open up and triumph sprout,
Yes, let vindication spring up:
I the LORD have created it.

9 Shame on him who argues with his Maker,
Though naught but a potsherd of earth!
Shall the clay say to the potter, "What are you doing?
[c]Your work has no handles"?[c]
10 Shame on him who asks his father, "What are you begetting?"
Or a woman, "What are you bearing?"

11 Thus said the LORD,
Israel's Holy One and Maker:
[d]Will you question Me[d] on the destiny of My children,
Will you instruct Me about the work of My hands?

a-a I.e., I made them helpless; one who wished to move freely belted his garment around the waist; cf. "engird," v. 5. *b-b Meaning of Heb. uncertain.*
c-c Emendation yields "To its maker, 'You have no hands'?"
d-d Heb. imperative.

4–8: God did not give Cyrus these great victories for Cyrus's sake. Rather, the purpose of Cyrus's rise to power is twofold: to liberate Israel, and thus to spread the fame of the one true God of Israel throughout the world. **7:** This v. is quoted at the beginning of the morning service (immediately after the *Barekhu* or call to prayer), where the word *woe* (or "evil") is replaced with the euphemism, "everything."

9–13: Objection and response. People (either the Judeans themselves or perhaps the nations of the world) are surprised by God's plan to bring salvation to the exiles by means of a Persian king. God rebukes them for their chutzpah in questioning the means through whom God chose to work. Cf. Isa. 10.15; 29.14–21.

13: The exiles will not have to pay any price to Cyrus to gain their liberation. Rather (as the next v. makes clear) God will personally reward the Persian king.

14–17: Cyrus's reward. God again addresses Cyrus (so Ibn Ezra), describing the vast territories he will receive for restoring Zion. Cf. 43.3. **14:** *Nubia* is the area south of Egypt, often referred to as Ethiopia in most Bible translations (it was probably closer to today's Sudan). *Sabaites* were residents of an area south of Egypt. *Only among you is God,* better, "Indeed, through you God [has worked]." Even far-off nations realize that the God who worked through Cyrus, the God of Israel, is the one true deity. Alternatively (and contrary to the quotation marks in NJPS), these words may be spoken by God to Cyrus, rather than by the African nations.

18–25: Universal recognition of the LORD. The vv. again rely on the argument from prophecy, which Deutero-Isaiah uses to show the whole world that the LORD is the true master of history. The predictions made to earlier Israelite prophets were not secret, but were made public long ago. **18:** This v. alludes to the first creation story in Gen. ch 1.

12 It was I who made the earth
And created man upon it;
My own hands stretched out the heavens,
And I marshaled all their host.
13 It was I who roused him[a] for victory
And who level all roads for him.
He shall rebuild My city
And let My exiled people go
Without price and without payment
—said the LORD of Hosts.

14 Thus said the LORD:
Egypt's wealth and Nubia's gains
And Sabaites, [b-]long of limb,[-b]
Shall pass over to you and be yours,
Pass over and follow you in fetters,
Bow low to you
And reverently address you:
"Only among you is God,
There is no other god at all!
15 You are indeed a God who concealed
Himself,
O God of Israel, who bring victory!
16 Those who fabricate idols,
All are shamed and disgraced;
To a man, they slink away in disgrace.
17 But Israel has won through the LORD
Triumph everlasting.
You shall not be shamed or disgraced
In all the ages to come!"

18 For thus said the LORD,
The Creator of heaven who alone is God,
Who formed the earth and made it,
Who alone established it—
He did not create it a waste,
But formed it for habitation:
I am the LORD, and there is none else.
19 I did not speak in secret,
At a site in a land of darkness;
I did not say to the stock of Jacob,
"Seek Me out in a wasteland"—
I the LORD, who foretell reliably,
Who announce what is true.

a I.e., Cyrus.
b-b Emendation yields "bearing tribute." For "tribute" cf. Ezra 4.20; 6.8; Neh. 5.4.

20 Come, gather together,
Draw nigh, you remnants of the nations!
No foreknowledge had they who carry their
wooden images
And pray to a god who cannot give success.
21 Speak up, compare testimony—
Let them even take counsel together!
Who announced this aforetime,
Foretold it of old?
Was it not I the LORD?
Then there is no god beside Me,
No God exists beside Me
Who foretells truly and grants success.
22 Turn to Me and gain success,
All the ends of earth!
For I am God, and there is none else.
23 By Myself have I sworn,
From My mouth has issued truth,
A word that shall not turn back:
To Me every knee shall bend,
Every tongue swear loyalty.
24 [a]They shall say: "Only through the LORD
Can I find victory and might.[a]
When people [b]trust in[b] Him,
All their adversaries are put to shame.
25 It is through the LORD that all the offspring of Israel
Have vindication and glory."

46 Bel[c] is bowed, Nebo[c] is cowering,
Their images are a burden for beasts and cattle;
The things you[d] would carry [in procession]
Are now piled as a burden
On tired [beasts].
2 They cowered, they bowed as well,
They could not rescue the burden,[e]
And they themselves went into captivity.

3 Listen to Me, O House of Jacob,
All that are left of the House of Israel,
Who have been carried since birth,
Supported since leaving the womb:
4 Till you grow old, I will still be the same;
When you turn gray, it is I who will carry;

a-a Emendation yields "Only in the LORD / Are there victory and might for man."
b-b Lit. "come to"; for this idiom cf. Ps. 65.3; Job 6.20.
c Babylonian deities. *d Emendation yields "they."*
e Emendation yields "him who carried [them]"; cf. Targum.

23: The nations of the world are invited to share in the worship of the true God and the benefits it brings. **25:** Israel's vindication leads other nations to worship the LORD as well. The mixture of nationalism and universalism here is noteworthy: A universalist outcome results from a particularist victory.

46.1–15: The gods of Babylonia vs. the God of Israel. This short speech contrasts the LORD, who is capable of mighty acts, and the gods of Babylonia, who are shown to be illusions.

1–4: The essential contrast between a God who carries His faithful and gods who must be carried by theirs. 1: *Bel* is another name for Marduk, the chief deity of Babylon. His son, *Nebo* (Akkadian Nabû), became an increasingly important deity during the last century of Babylonian independence. *Carry [in procession]:* The Babylonians paraded the statues of their gods through the city on major holidays, such as the Akitu or New Year festival. **3–4:** The maternal image of the LORD is significant here; God is so concerned with Israel, whom He protects in the divine womb until their old age. Cf. 42.13–14; 45.10; 49.14–15; 66.13.

5–7: The folly of idolatry. Cf. 40.18–20; 44.9–20; Ps. 115.4–8.

8–13: The former and latter things. The listeners are urged to recall what God did in the past (specifically, God saved and made accurate predictions). These demonstrate the salvation that God will bring in the near future. The reliability of earlier prophets also demonstrates the trustworthiness of Deutero-Isaiah himself. **8:** *Sinners:* God addresses the exiles as rebellious because their forebears' misdeeds caused the exile, but perhaps also because many of them failed to believe in Deutero-Isaiah's message. **10–11:** The argument from prophecy.

47.1–15: A mock lament over Babylon, or Babylonia (the Heb term "bavel" is used for Babylon, the capital city, and for Babylonia, the country). This poem personifies Babylon as a haughty young woman of great wealth and prestige who has suddenly lost everything. It focuses on the surprising reversal of fortune meted out to the seemingly invincible empire that tormented the Judeans. Taunting songs directed against enemies appear several times in the Bible; see Isa. ch 14; Ezek. chs 27–28.

1–5: Babylon's reversal of fortune. Once a princess, Babylon now must work as a lowly slave-girl. **1:** *Chaldea,* a synonym for Babylonia in this period; see 43.14 n. **2–3:** See similarly Ezek. 16.37; 23.26.

I was the Maker, and I will be the Bearer;
And I will carry and rescue [you].

5 To whom can you compare Me
Or declare Me similar?
To whom can you liken Me,
So that we seem comparable?
6 Those who squander gold from the purse
And weigh out silver on the balance,[a]
They hire a metal worker to make it into a god,
To which they bow down and prostrate themselves.
7 They must carry it on their backs and transport it;
When they put it down, it stands,
It does not budge from its place.
If they cry out to it, it does not answer;
It cannot save them from their distress.
8 Keep this in mind, and [b-]stand firm![-b]
Take this to heart, you sinners!
9 Bear in mind what happened of old;
For I am God, and there is none else,
I am divine, and there is none like Me.
10 I foretell the end from the beginning,
And from the start, things that had not occurred.
I say: My plan shall be fulfilled;
I will do all I have purposed.
11 I summoned that swooping bird from the East;[c]
From a distant land, the man for My purpose.
I have spoken, so I will bring it to pass;
I have designed it, so I will complete it.
12 Listen to Me, you [d-]stubborn of heart,[-d]
Who are far from victory:
13 I am bringing My victory close;
It shall not be far,
And My triumph shall not be delayed.
I will grant triumph in Zion
To Israel, in whom I glory.

47 Get down, sit in the dust,
Fair Maiden Babylon;
Sit, dethroned, on the ground,
O Fair Chaldea;
Nevermore shall they call you
The tender and dainty one.
2 Grasp the handmill and grind meal.
Remove your veil,

a Lit. "beam [of the balance]." b-b Meaning of Heb. uncertain.
c I.e., Cyrus; cf. 41.2–3; 44.28–45.1. d-d Septuagint reads, "who have lost heart."

Strip off your train, bare your leg,
Wade through the rivers.
3 Your nakedness shall be uncovered,
And your shame shall be exposed.
I will take vengeance,
[a-]And let no man intercede.
4 Our Redeemer—LORD of Hosts is His name—
Is the Holy One of Israel.[-a]
5 Sit silent; retire into darkness,
O Fair Chaldea;
Nevermore shall they call you
Mistress of Kingdoms.

6 I was angry at My people,
I defiled My heritage;
I put them into your hands,
But you showed them no mercy.
Even upon the aged you made
Your yoke exceedingly heavy.
7 You thought, "I shall always be
The mistress still."
You did not take these things to heart,
You gave no thought to the end of it.

8 And now hear this, O pampered one—
Who dwell in security,
Who think to yourself,
"I am, and there is none but me;
I shall not become a widow
Or know loss of children"—
9 These two things shall come upon you,
Suddenly, in one day:
Loss of children and widowhood
Shall come upon you in full measure,
Despite your many enchantments
And all your countless spells.
10 You were secure in your wickedness;
You thought, "No one can see me."
It was your skill and your science
That led you astray.
And you thought to yourself,
"I am, and there is none but me."
11 Evil is coming upon you
Which you will not know how to [b-]charm away;[-b]

a-a Meaning of Heb. uncertain; emendation yields "And not be appeased, / Says our Redeemer, whose name is LORD of Hosts, / The Holy One of Israel."
b-b Meaning of Heb. uncertain. Emendation yields "bribe."

6–7: Babylonia's hubris. Babylonia never was as strong and self-sufficient as she believed. Her victory resulted only from the LORD's decision to punish Judah. Babylonia took this commission too far, however, and now she must be punished as well. On the hubris of the foreign conqueror who unknowingly does God's work, cf. 10.5–15.

8–15: Babylon is sentenced. God speaks directly to Babylon (cf. 45.1, of Cyrus), informing her of her fate. **8:** The line spoken here by Babylon is a precise quotation of a line spoken by Nineveh, the capital of Assyria, in Zeph. 2.13. For Deutero-Isaiah, statements that earlier prophets made concerning Assyria should be understood as referring to the Babylonians, who inherited the Assyrians' empire and their role as Israel's oppressors. **9–13:** Deutero-Isaiah makes frequent reference to the famed magicians and soothsayers of Babylonia, whose skills turn out to be illusions.

48.1–22: Rebuke and consolation. The concluding speech in the first section of Deutero-Isaiah's prophecies (see chs 40–48 n.). It focuses attention on the sins that Israel had committed in the past. By reviewing the reasons Israel deserved punishment, the prophet explains why the exile had to occur and hence reassures the people that the LORD is neither weak nor fickle. The passage may also criticize the faithlessness of the Judean exiles in Babylonia, who were not as receptive to Deutero-Isaiah's message as they should have been.

1–16: The argument from prophecy. In previous passages (43.9–15; 44.6–8, 24–26; 45.18–25; 46.10–11) the prophet directed this argument (at least rhetorically) to foreigners or their gods; Deutero-Isaiah contrasted the illusion in which the Babylonians believed with the reliable LORD of the Israelites and thus rebuked the former. But here the rebuke is directed against the Israelites, who have prayed to idols and have failed to recognize their own God's power.

Disaster is falling upon you
Which you will not be able to appease;
Coming upon you suddenly
Is ruin of which you know nothing.
12 Stand up, with your spells and your many enchantments
On which you labored since youth!
Perhaps you'll be able to profit,
Perhaps you [a]will find strength.[a]
13 You are helpless, despite all your art.
Let them stand up and help you now,
The scanners[b] of heaven, the star-gazers,
Who announce, month by month,
Whatever will come upon you.
14 See, they are become like straw,
Fire consumes them;
They cannot save themselves
From the power of the flame;
This is no coal for warming oneself,
No fire to sit by!
15 This is what they have profited you—
The traders you dealt with since youth—
Each has wandered off his own way,
There is none to save you.

48 Listen to this, O House of Jacob,
Who bear the name Israel
And have issued from the waters[c] of Judah,
Who swear by the name of the LORD
And invoke the God of Israel—
Though not in truth and sincerity—
2 For you[d] are called after [e]the Holy City[e]
And you[d] do lean on the God of Israel,
Whose name is LORD of Hosts:

3 Long ago, I foretold things that happened,
From My mouth they issued, and I announced them;
Suddenly I acted, and they came to pass.
4 Because I know how stubborn you are
(Your neck is like an iron sinew
And your forehead bronze),
5 Therefore I told you long beforehand,
Announced things to you ere they happened—
That you might not say, "My idol caused them,
My carved and molten images ordained them."

a-a Taking ʿaraṣ *as a variant of* ʿaṣar; *cf. 2 Chron. 20.37.*
b Meaning of Heb. uncertain. *c Emendation yields "loins."*
d Heb. "they." *e-e Emendation yields "the holy people."*

6 You have [a]heard all this; look, must you not
acknowledge it?[a]
As of now, I announce to you new things,
Well-guarded secrets you did not know.
7 Only now are they created, and not of old;
[a]Before today[a] you had not heard them;
You cannot say, "I knew them already."
8 You had never heard, you had never known,
Your ears were not opened of old.

Though I know that you are treacherous,
That you were called a rebel from birth,
9 For the sake of My name I control My wrath;
To My own glory, [a]I am patient[a] with you,
And I will not destroy you.
10 See, I refine you, but not as silver;
I test you in the furnace of affliction.
11 For My sake, My own sake, do I act—
Lest [My name][b] be dishonored!
I will not give My glory to another.

12 Listen to Me, O Jacob,
Israel, whom I have called:
I am He—I am the first,
And I am the last as well.
13 My own hand founded the earth,
My right hand spread out the skies.

I call unto them, let them stand up.
14 Assemble, all of you, and listen!
Who among you[c] foretold these things:
[a]"He whom the LORD loves
Shall work His will against Babylon,
And, with His might, against Chaldea"?[a]
15 I, I predicted, and I called him;
I have brought him and he shall succeed in his
mission.
16 Draw near to Me and hear this:
From the beginning, I did not speak in secret;
From the time anything existed, I was there.[d]

"And now the Lord GOD has sent me, [e]endowed
with His spirit."[e]

9–11: In light of the people's sins, the exiles may wonder why God wants to save them. The prophet answers this potential question: God will save the people for God's own sake, for the nation Israel is linked to God's reputation (see similarly Ezek. 36.22, 32). Deutero-Isaiah lists several different reasons that the exiles are sure to be saved (see 40.1; 43.4), some of which contradict each other on a strictly literal level. The prophet's goal, however, is not to present a philosophical argument but to convince the exiles of their imminent return to Zion, using various lines of reasoning. These vv. utilize language from Jer. 9.6, and they confirm the accuracy of Jeremiah's predictions. **10:** Better, "I purchase you, but not for silver; / I choose you in the furnace of affliction." **14:** A reference to Cyrus, the Persian king. *Chaldea,* a synonym for Babylonia; see 43.14 n.

a-a *Meaning of Heb. uncertain.*
b *These words are supplied in some ancient versions; cf. v. 9.*
c *Heb. "them."*
d *I.e., I foretold it through prophets.*
e-e *Lit. "and His spirit."*

17 Thus said the LORD your Redeemer,
The Holy One of Israel:
I the LORD am your God,
Instructing you for your own benefit,
Guiding you in the way you should go.
18 If only you would heed My commands!
Then your prosperity would be like a river,
Your triumph like the waves of the sea.
19 Your offspring would be as many as the sand,
Their issue as many as its grains.[a]
Their name would never be cut off
Or obliterated from before Me.

20 Go forth from Babylon,
Flee from Chaldea!
Declare this with loud shouting,
Announce this,
Bring out the word to the ends of the earth!
Say: "The LORD has redeemed
His servant Jacob!"
21 They have known no thirst,
Though He led them through parched places;
He made water flow for them from the rock;
He cleaved the rock and water gushed forth.

22 There is no safety—said the LORD—for the wicked.

49 Listen, O coastlands, to me,
And give heed, O nations afar:
The LORD appointed me before I was born,
He named me while I was in my mother's womb.
2 He made my mouth like a sharpened blade,
He hid me in the shadow of His hand,
And He made me like a polished arrow;
He concealed me in His quiver.
3 And He said to me, "You are My servant,
Israel in whom I glory."
4 I thought, "I have labored in vain,
I have spent my strength for empty breath."

a Meaning of Heb. uncertain.

17–19: An explanation for the exile. Language used to described the exodus from Egypt in Ps. 81.6–17 is applied to the upcoming exodus from Babylonia.

20–22: Conclusion: The return to Zion is at hand. Deutero-Isaiah demands that the exiles leave Babylonia. The prophet took this exhortation seriously: From the beginning of the next ch on, Deutero-Isaiah seems no longer to be located in Babylonia but in Jerusalem. **22:** The same words appear—and make more sense—in 57.21, which marks the end of the second section within Deutero-Isaiah's prophecies. They have been copied here to indicate that this v. also marks the end of a section.

Chs 49–57: Prophecies of Zion. The second of the three sections within chs 40–66 seems to have been written in Jerusalem after the first wave of exiles returned there from Babylonia in 538 BCE. Like chs 40–48, it consists of several long speeches, each of which attempts to convince the city of Jerusalem (usually referred to as Zion) or the returned exiles that their current wretched state will be transformed to a glorious one. Many of the arguments the prophet sets forth resemble those found in chs 40–48, but several characteristic themes of that first section no longer appear in chs 49–57: Cyrus, Babylonia, the new exodus, and the theme of the former and latter things. These are replaced by a stronger emphasis on Zion and the servant of the LORD, and convey disappointment at the reality of conditions in the restored Zion (cf. Ezra chs 1–3; Haggai; Zech. chs 1–8). This sense of disappointment leads the prophet to condemn the people for certain misdeeds toward the end of this section, in language somewhat harsher than the rebukes found in chs 40–48.

49.1–26: The role of the servant and encouragement for Zion. The first speech in this section divides into two parts, each of which comforts the people and assures them that Zion's full restoration is not far off.

1–13: The servant of the LORD and universal recognition of God. The motif of God's servant or servants appeared briefly in chs 40–48, especially in 42.1–9. **1–6:** The servant speaks to the nations of the world as well as the Israelites. The identity of the servant has generated much debate. Most rabbinic commentators and some modern scholars argue that Deutero-Isaiah speaks here in the first person and that these vv. describe the prophet's own mission. Others argue that the whole nation

But my case rested with the LORD,
My recompense was in the hands of my God.
5 And now the LORD has resolved—
He who formed me in the womb to be His servant—
To bring back Jacob to Himself,
That Israel may be restored to Him.
And I have been honored in the sight of the LORD,
My God has been my strength.
6 For He has said:
"It is too little that you should be My servant
In that I raise up the tribes of Jacob
And restore the survivors of Israel:
I will also make you a light[a] of nations,
That My salvation may reach the ends of the earth."

7 Thus said the LORD,
The Redeemer of Israel, his Holy One,
[b-]To the despised one,
To the abhorred nations,[-b]
To the slave of rulers:
Kings shall see and stand up;
Nobles, and they shall prostrate themselves—
To the honor of the LORD, who is faithful,
To the Holy One of Israel who chose you.
8 Thus said the LORD:
In an hour of favor I answer you,
And on a day of salvation I help you—
I created you and appointed you [c-]a covenant people[-c]—
Restoring the land,
Allotting anew the desolate holdings,
9 Saying to the prisoners, "Go free,"
To those who are in darkness, "Show yourselves."
They shall pasture along the roads,
On every bare height shall be their pasture.
10 They shall not hunger or thirst,
Hot wind and sun shall not strike them;
For He who loves them will lead them,
He will guide them to springs of water.
11 I will make all My mountains a road,
And My highways shall be built up.
12 Look! These are coming from afar,
These from the north and the west,
And these from the land of Sinim.[d]

Israel is the servant, and some suggest that an ideal Israel or a faithful subset of the nation is the servant. **5:** *To bring:* The subject of the Heb verb may be either God or the servant. **7–13:** The servant announces that all the world will recognize the one God when the whole Israelite nation returns to its land. At this early stage of Cyrus's reign, only a few Judean exiles took the opportunity to return to Zion. See Ezra chs 1–3. **8:** *A covenant people,* see 42.6 n. **12:** *Sinim,* Aswan, in southern Egypt, where a colony of Israelite soldiers lived during the Persian period and before.

a I.e., the agent of good fortune; cf. 42.1–4; 51.4–5.
b-b Meaning of Heb. uncertain. Emendation yields "Whose being is despised, / Whose body is detested"; cf. 51.23. *c-c See note b-b at 42.6.*
d 1QIs[a] reads "the Syenians"; cf. Ezek. 30.6.

14–26: Consolation for Zion. Zion (i.e., Jerusalem) serves as a metaphor for the nation as a whole; the despair she feels (v. 14) is Israel's, and God speaks words of comfort to Israel through her. **14–23:** A dialogue between God and Zion, which is personified as a bereaved woman. Her "children"—the Judeans—have died or been sent into exile. Jerusalem's population fell after the Babylonians destroyed the city in 586 BCE, and it remained small even when the Persian king Cyrus allowed exiled Judeans to return there. **14–18:** These vv. recall, and reverse, God's complaint in Jer. 2.32. **15–16:** God is portrayed as the perfect mother. **19–20:** A recollection and reversal of the prophecy of doom in 6.10–12. **22–23:** The reversal of fortune for Zion and the Israelites. The text repeats the promises found in Isa. 11.10–12.3 and Pss. 2; 72. **24–26:** Israel's conqueror must give Israel back to God, and Israel's redemption brings knowledge of the one God to all humanity.

13 Shout, O heavens, and rejoice, O earth!
Break into shouting, O hills!
For the LORD has comforted His people,
And has taken back His afflicted ones in love.

14 Zion says,
"The LORD has forsaken me,
My Lord has forgotten me."
15 Can a woman forget her baby,
Or disown the child of her womb?
Though she might forget,
I never could forget you.
16 See, I have engraved you
On the palms of My hands,
Your walls are ever before Me.
17 Swiftly your children are coming;
Those who ravaged and ruined you shall leave you.
18 Look up all around you and see:
They are all assembled, are come to you!
As I live
—declares the LORD—
You shall don them all like jewels,
Deck yourself with them like a bride.
19 As for your ruins and desolate places
And your land laid waste—
You shall soon be crowded with settlers,
While destroyers stay far from you.
20 The children [a]you thought you had lost[a]
Shall yet say in your hearing,
"The place is too crowded for me;
Make room for me to settle."
21 And you will say to yourself,
"Who bore these for me
When I was bereaved and barren,
Exiled and disdained[b]—
By whom, then, were these reared?
I was left all alone—
And where have these been?"

22 Thus said the Lord GOD:
I will raise My hand to nations
And lift up My ensign to peoples;
And they shall bring your sons in their bosoms,
And carry your daughters on their backs.
23 Kings shall tend your children,
Their queens shall serve you as nurses.

a-a Lit. "of your bereavement." *b Meaning of Heb. uncertain.*

They shall bow to you, face to the ground,
And lick the dust of your feet.
And you shall know that I am the LORD—
Those who trust in Me shall not be shamed.

24 Can spoil be taken from a warrior,
Or captives retrieved from a victor?
25 Yet thus said the LORD:
Captives shall be taken from a warrior
And spoil shall be retrieved from a tyrant;
For *I* will contend with your adversaries,
And *I* will deliver your children.
26 I will make your oppressors eat their own flesh,
They shall be drunk with their own blood
as with wine.
And all mankind shall know
That I the LORD am your Savior,
The Mighty One of Jacob, your Redeemer.

50 Thus said the LORD:
[a]Where is the bill of divorce
Of your mother whom I dismissed?
And which of My creditors was it
To whom I sold you off?
You were only sold off for your sins,
And your mother dismissed for your crimes.
2 Why, when I came, was no one there,
Why, when I called, would none respond?
Is my arm, then, too short to rescue,
Have I not the power to save?
With a mere rebuke I dry up the sea,
And turn rivers into desert.
Their fish stink from lack of water;
They lie dead [b-]of thirst.[-b]
3 I clothe the skies in blackness
And make their raiment sackcloth.

4 [c-]The Lord GOD gave me a skilled tongue,
To know how to speak timely words to the weary.[-c]
Morning by morning, He rouses,
He rouses my ear
To give heed like disciples.
5 The Lord GOD opened my ears,

a The mother (the country) has not been formally divorced, nor the children (the people) sold because of poverty. Therefore there is no obstacle to their restoration.
b-b Change of vocalization yields "on the parched ground"; cf. 44.3.
c-c Meaning of Heb. uncertain.

50.1–51.8: A response to the nation's tribulations. God addresses the Israelites' despair at their plight. The previous section described Deutero-Isaiah's own prophetic mission (which is ultimately the mission of the whole nation) and proceeded to relay God's message to the city of Jerusalem. Similarly, this passage describes Deutero-Isaiah's mission (which is a model for all Israel) while relaying a divine message to the nation.

50.1–3: The relationship between God and Israel endures. 1: The Israelites viewed themselves metaphorically as God's wife and also as God's children. If the former, they worry that God has divorced them and therefore cannot take them back (cf. Jer. 3.1; Deut. 24.1–4). If the latter, then God has sold them away (cf. Exod. 21.7–11; 2 Kings 4.1). But God insists that no divorce has taken place, and that the children remain God's own property. **2:** Behind God's frustrated words here may lie the failure of the exiles to accept the message of consolation. Only a small number of exiles took the opportunity to return to Zion after Cyrus (the Persian king who conquered Babylonia) allowed them to do so. *Dry up the sea,* an allusion to the splitting of the Reed Sea (see Exod. chs 14–15) and also to stories of divine combat at the time of the world's creation (see 51.9–11; Hab. 2.8–9; Pss. 74.13–15; 89.6–14; Job 26.5–13).

4–11: The mission of the prophet and of the nation. As in 49.1–6, Deutero-Isaiah speaks in the first person. By doing so the prophet sets a model that the nation as a whole should follow, since the whole nation has a prophetic role to the world at large. **4–5:** The prophet is a disciple of older prophets, constantly borrowing their words and noting how their predictions proved true.

6–9: Deutero-Isaiah, like all Judeans, suffered in the exile, but the prophet knows the punishment meted out to the exiles was just, accepts it, and awaits the vindication that surely follows. **10–11:** Israel's response: Some of Deutero-Isaiah's listeners will accept both divine punishment and divine reward, but others will continue to reject God's word, to their own detriment.

51.1–8: An exhortation to Judeans who despair. Four brief statements, each opening with an imperative verb addressed to the Judeans, explain why the nation's current state is not a cause for hopelessness. **1–3:** The example of *Abraham* and *Sarah*: they, like the current Israelites, were few in number, yet God multiplied their descendants. The divine promise to Abraham of great progeny is still in force. As in previous sections that alluded to the creation stories in Gen., this too assumes the audience's familiarity with traditional stories. **3:** God's comforting Zion is a reversal of the book of Lam., where Zion received no comfort. **4–5:** God is the source of teaching, and thus God can indeed save. **4:** *Teaching,* Heb "torah." Cf. Isa. 2.3. **6–8:** Two metaphors (v. 6) by contrast emphasize the enduring nature of the salvation that God brings; these are matched by two metaphors in v. 8.

And I did not disobey,
I did not run away.
6 I offered my back to the floggers,
And my cheeks to those who tore out my hair.
I did not hide my face
From insult and spittle.
7 But the Lord GOD will help me—
Therefore I feel no disgrace;
Therefore I have set my face like flint,
And I know I shall not be shamed.
8 My Vindicator is at hand—
Who dares contend with me?
Let us stand up together![a]
Who would be my opponent?
Let him approach me!
9 Lo, the Lord GOD will help me—
Who can get a verdict against me?
They shall all wear out like a garment,
The moth shall consume them.

10 Who among you reveres the LORD
And heeds the voice of His servant?—
Though he walk in darkness
And have no light,
Let him trust in the name of the LORD
And rely upon his God.
11 But you are all kindlers of fire,
[b]Girding on[b] firebrands.
Walk by the blaze of your fire,
By the brands that you have lit!
This has come to you from My hand:
[c]You shall lie down in pain.[c]

51 Listen to Me, you who pursue justice,
You who seek the LORD:
Look to the rock you were hewn from,
To the quarry you were dug from.
2 Look back to Abraham your father
And to Sarah who brought you forth.
For he was only one when I called him,
But I blessed him and made him many.

3 Truly the LORD has comforted Zion,
Comforted all her ruins;
He has made her wilderness like Eden,

a I.e., as opponents in court; cf. Num. 35.12. *b-b Emendation yields "Lighters of."*
c-c Meaning of Heb. uncertain.

Her desert like the Garden of the LORD.
Gladness and joy shall abide there,
Thanksgiving and the sound of music.

4 Hearken to Me, [a]My people,[a]
And give ear to Me, O [a]My nation,[a]
For teaching shall go forth[b] from Me,
My way for the light of peoples.
In a moment I will bring it:
5 The triumph I grant is near,
The success I give has gone forth.
My arms shall [c]provide for[c] the peoples;
The coastlands shall trust in Me,
They shall look to My arm.

6 Raise your eyes to the heavens,
And look upon the earth beneath:
Though the heavens should melt away like smoke,
And the earth wear out like a garment,
And its inhabitants die out [d]as well,[d]
My victory shall stand forever,
My triumph shall remain unbroken.

7 Listen to Me, you who care for the right,
O people who lay My instruction to heart!
Fear not the insults of men,
And be not dismayed at their jeers;
8 For the moth shall eat them up like a garment,
The worm[e] shall eat them up like wool.
But My triumph shall endure forever,
My salvation through all the ages.

9 Awake, awake, clothe yourself with splendor,
O arm of the LORD!
Awake as in days of old,
As in former ages!
It was you that hacked Rahab[f] in pieces,
That pierced the Dragon.[f]
10 It was you that dried up the Sea,
The waters of the great deep;
That made the abysses of the Sea
A road the redeemed might walk.
11 So let the ransomed of the LORD return,

a-a Several mss. read "O peoples ... O nations"; cf. end of this verse and v. 5.
b I.e., through My servant Israel; cf. 42.1–4; 49.6. *c-c Lit. "judge."*
d-d Emendation yields "like gnats." *e Heb. sas, another word for "moth."*
f Names of primeval monsters.

51.9–52.12: Lament and response. In the first part of this composition, the people pray for deliverance, bemoaning God's apparent abandonment of them. In the second part, God responds at length, assuring them that they have not been forgotten.

9–11: The people's entreaty. These vv. contain the people's words to God. As in many psalms of lament, the people recall God's glorious victories in the past in an attempt to goad the LORD to action now. **9:** *Arm of the LORD,* referring to God's strength. **9–10:** *Rahab ... Dragon ... abysses of the Sea:* These refer to mythical beings whom God defeated to create the world; cf. 50.2 n. The people argue that the God who defeated the forces of evil at the beginning of time and who split the Reed Sea to liberate the Israelites from Egyptian bondage should use the same divine power to liberate Israel now.

51.12–52.6: God's positive response. The divine answer echoes the language of the request; see esp. 51.17; 52.1, which echo 51.9. This section borrows vocabulary from several older prophecies: Isa. 29.9–10; Jer. 4.20; 15.2–5. Those passages predicted disaster for Zion and her people; now Deutero-Isaiah at once confirms the accuracy of the older predictions and reverses their message, telling Zion that the period of suffering is coming to an end. This passage also reverses the description of Zion's suffering found in Lam. 2.13–19. This highly allusive passage became the source for another highly allusive poem written 2,000 years later: "Lekha Dodi" (the hymn recited in Jewish liturgy at the outset of the Sabbath) borrows phrasing from these vv. **51.12–16:** God speaks to the nation Israel. Language that described the prophet Jeremiah in Jer. 1.9–10; 11.19–21 is applied to the nation as a whole here. **17–23:** God addresses Jerusalem. Zion, portrayed as a bereaved mother, gets her children back. **17:** The *cup of... wrath* is a metaphoric cup of poisonous wine that symbolizes divine punishment. See, e.g., Jer. 25.15–26; Lam. 4.21 n.

And come with shouting to Zion,
Crowned with joy everlasting.
Let them attain joy and gladness,
While sorrow and sighing flee.

12 I, I am He who comforts you!
What ails you that you fear
Man who must die,
Mortals who fare like grass?
13 You have forgotten the LORD your Maker,
Who stretched out the skies and made firm
the earth!
And you live all day in constant dread
Because of the rage of an oppressor
Who is aiming to cut [you] down.
Yet of what account is the rage of an oppressor?
14*a* Quickly the crouching one is freed;
He is not cut down and slain,
And he shall not want for food.
15 For I the LORD your God—
Who stir up the sea into roaring waves,
Whose name is LORD of Hosts—
16 [b]Have put My words in your mouth
And sheltered you with My hand;[b]
I, who planted[c] the skies and made firm the earth,
Have said to Zion: You are My people!
17 Rouse, rouse yourself!
Arise, O Jerusalem,
You who from the LORD's hand
Have drunk the cup of His wrath,
You who have drained to the dregs
The bowl, the cup of reeling!
18 She has none to guide her
Of all the sons she bore;
None takes her by the hand,
Of all the sons she reared.[d]
19 These two things have befallen you:
Wrack and ruin—who can console you?
Famine and sword—[e]how shall I[e] comfort you?
20 Your sons lie in a swoon
At the corner of every street—
Like an antelope caught in a net—

a Meaning of verse uncertain. Emendation yields (cf. Jer. 11.19; Job 14.7–9) "Quickly the tree buds anew; / It does not die though cut down, / And its sap does not fail."
b-b I.e., I have chosen you to be a prophet-nation; cf. 49.2; 59.21.
c Emendation yields "stretched out"; cf. Syriac version and v. 13.
d To guide a drunken parent home was a recognized filial duty in ancient Canaan and Egypt. *e-e Several ancient versions render "who can."*

Drunk with the wrath of the LORD,
With the rebuke of your God.
21 Therefore,
Listen to this, unhappy one,
Who are drunk, but not with wine!
22 Thus said the LORD, your Lord,
Your God who champions His people:
Herewith I take from your hand
The cup of reeling,[a]
The bowl, the cup of My wrath;
You shall never drink it again.
23 I will put it in the hands of your tormentors,
Who have commanded you,
"Get down, that we may walk over you"—
So that you made your back like the ground,
Like a street for passersby.

52 Awake, awake, O Zion!
Clothe yourself in splendor;
Put on your robes of majesty,
Jerusalem, holy city!
For the uncircumcised and the unclean
Shall never enter you again.
2 Arise, shake off the dust,
Sit [on your throne], Jerusalem!
Loose the bonds from your neck,
O captive one, Fair Zion!

3 For thus said the LORD:
You were sold for no price,
And shall be redeemed without money.
4 For thus said the Lord GOD:
Of old, My people went down
To Egypt to sojourn there;
But Assyria has robbed them,
Giving nothing in return.[b]
5 What therefore do I gain here?
—declares the LORD—
For My people has been carried off for nothing,
Their mockers howl
—declares the LORD—
And constantly, unceasingly,
My name is reviled.
6 Assuredly, My people shall learn My name,

a A figure of speech for a dire fate; cf. Jer. 25.15 ff.

b Whereas the Israelites themselves sought hospitality in Egypt, Assyria (i.e., the Chaldean Empire) has exiled them by force.

52.1–6: God speaks again to Zion, telling her that her nightmare is over; the opening language is similar to 51.17. **2:** *Shake off the dust:* As a captive, the city sat in dirt, humiliated. **3:** God did not sell Judah to a creditor (cf. 50.1), and hence Judah still belongs to God. There is no impediment to Judah's redemption. **4:** *Robbed them, giving nothing in return,* or, "oppressed them, gaining nothing." The Assyrians acquired no rights to Israel, who still belong to the LORD. Emendation yields, "oppressed them due to My anger"; cf. 10.5. **5:** *Therefore,* rather, "But now." The current exile in Babylonia is contrasted with the people's earlier exiles in Egypt and in Assyria. *My name is reviled:* God's own reputation is harmed by the Babylonian exile since people may think that this represents the triumph of the Babylonian gods over the God of Israel, and for this reason God is sure to liberate the nation. **6:** *I ... am now at hand,* Heb "hineni." Elsewhere in the Bible this word is used by human beings responding to a divine call (e.g., Gen. 22.1, 11; Exod. 3.4). Only in Deutero-Isaiah does God call "here I am" to humans (see also 58.9; 65.1).

Assuredly [they shall learn] on that day
That I, the One who promised,
Am now at hand.

7 How welcome on the mountain
Are the footsteps of the herald
Announcing happiness,
Heralding good fortune,
Announcing victory,
Telling Zion, "Your God is King!"
8 Hark!
Your watchmen raise their voices,
As one they shout for joy;
For every eye shall behold
The LORD's return to Zion.
9 Raise a shout together,
O ruins of Jerusalem!
For the LORD will comfort His people,
Will redeem Jerusalem.
10 The LORD will bare His holy arm
In the sight of all the nations,
And the very ends of earth shall see
The victory of our God.

11 Turn, turn away, touch naught unclean
As you depart from there;
Keep pure, as you go forth from there,
You who bear the vessels of the LORD![a]
12 For you will not depart in haste,
Nor will you leave in flight;

a Cf. Ezra 1.7–8; 5.14–15.

7–12: A concluding prophecy of restoration. God's response to the nation's prayer ended in v. 6, and now the prophet sums up the message: Redemption is at hand. **7–10:** God's own Presence will return to Jerusalem; the prophet imagines that the lookouts in Jerusalem's higher buildings or fortifications will see God's Presence as it comes toward the city. Cf. 40.3–5 n. This passage was composed after some Judeans had already returned to Jerusalem but before the full-fledged redemption that Deutero-Isaiah anticipated had come to pass. **11–12:** An exhortation to exiles still in Babylonia to come to Jerusalem, bearing the Temple vessels that the Babylonians had taken from the Temple. Because they will accompany the divine Presence in Its journey, they must maintain ritual purity. **12:** The earlier exodus from Egypt is contrasted with the imminent exodus from Babylonia. The former took place in haste and confusion (see Exod. 12.11; Deut. 16.3), but the new exodus will be more stately.

52.13–53.12: The servant. One of the most difficult and contested passages in the Bible, these fifteen vv. have attracted an enormous amount of attention from ancient, medieval, and modern scholars. In particular the identity of the servant is vigorously debated. Although the servant is spoken of as an individual, the reference may well be to the collective nation (or the remnant). Thus, many argue that the servant symbolizes the entire Jewish people. The passage, then, describes the nation's unjust tribulations at the hands of the Babylonians (and later oppressors) as well as the nation's salvific role for the world at large. Others maintain that the passage describes a pious minority within the Jewish people; this minority suffers as a result of the sins committed by the nation at large. (Bolstering these interpretations is the fact that the term "servant" in Deutero-Isaiah generally refers to the nation as a whole or an idealized representation of the nation; cf. 42.1–9 n.; 42.18–21 nn.; 49.1–13 n.). Other scholars argue that the servant in this passage is a specific individual (cf. 50.4–11 n.). Targum and various midrashim identify the servant as the Messiah, but this suggestion is unlikely, since nowhere else does Deutero-Isaiah refer to the Messiah, and the absence of a belief in an individual Messiah is one of the hallmarks of Deutero-Isaiah's outlook (in contrast to that of First Isaiah). Because of marked similarities between the language describing the servant and Jeremiah's descriptions of himself (see Jer. 10.18–24; 11.19), Saadia Gaon argued that the text refers to Jeremiah, while the Talmud (*b. Sot.* 14a) records the opinion that it describes Moses. Both opinions have been echoed by modern scholars. On the other hand, equally impressive parallels between the servant and First Isaiah can be observed (see ch 6). Furthermore, many passages in Deutero-Isaiah view the prophet Jeremiah as a model for the nation as a whole without equating the nation and that prophet. Christians have argued that this passage in fact predicts the coming of Jesus. Medieval rabbinic commentators devoted considerable attention to refuting this interpretation. The passage is deeply allusive, drawing on the texts from Jeremiah and Isaiah noted above and also on Isa. 1.5–6; 2.12–14; 11.1–10; Ps. 91.15–16.

For the LORD is marching before you,
The God of Israel is your rear guard.

13 "Indeed, My servant shall prosper,
Be exalted and raised to great heights.
14 Just as the many were appalled at him[a]—
So marred was his appearance, unlike that of man,
His form, beyond human semblance—
15 Just so he shall startle[b] many nations.
Kings shall be silenced because of him,
For they shall see what has not been told them,
Shall behold what they never have heard."

53 "Who can believe what we have heard?
Upon whom has [c]the arm of the LORD[-c] been revealed?
2 For he has grown, by His favor, like a tree crown,
Like a tree trunk out of arid ground.
He had no form or beauty, that we should look at him:
No charm, that we should find him pleasing.
3 He was despised, [d]shunned by men,[-d]
A man of suffering, familiar with disease.
[e]As one who hid his face from us,[-e]
He was despised, we held him of no account.
4 Yet it was our sickness that he was bearing,
Our suffering that he endured.
We accounted him plagued,
Smitten and afflicted by God;
5 But he was wounded because of our sins,
Crushed because of our iniquities.
He bore the chastisement that made us whole,
And by his bruises we were healed.
6 We all went astray like sheep,
Each going his own way;
And the LORD visited upon him
The guilt of all of us."

7 He was maltreated, yet he was submissive,
He did not open his mouth;
Like a sheep being led to slaughter,
Like a ewe, dumb before those who shear her,
He did not open his mouth.
8 By oppressive judgment he was taken away,
[d]Who could describe his abode?[-d]

a Heb. "you." *b* Meaning of Heb. uncertain.
c-c I.e., the vindication which the arm of the LORD effects.
d-d Meaning of Heb. uncertain. *e-e* I.e., as a leper; cf. Lev. 13.45 ff.

52.12–15: God's first speech. God describes the servant, who will ultimately, and surprisingly, achieve great things. **14:** *So marred ... semblance,* rather, "His appearance was more disfigured than any man's, / his form, more than any person's."

53.1–11a: The surprised observers' speech. The identity of the speakers who express their shock at the career of the servant is unclear. Are they the kings and nations of the world (cf. 52.15)? If so, then the servant is probably the nation Israel, and the nations are stunned that such an insignificant and lowly group turns out to have been so important to the divine plan. (Cf. Deut. 7.7.) Alternatively, the speakers may be the Judeans themselves, in which case the servant is either a pious minority (the ideal Israel, in contrast to the mass of Judeans whose faith and behavior miss the mark God set for them) or some individual within the Israelite community. **4–6:** Either the servant suffered on behalf of the speakers (i.e., the guilty were not punished at all), or he suffered along with the guilty, even though he himself did not share in the guilt of his fellow Israelites. The former idea (i.e., the notion of vicarious suffering) would be unusual for the Bible; the latter idea (the idea of corporate guilt) is not. **8–9:** *Cut off from the land of the living .... grave:* Scholars debate whether these lines describe the literal death of the servant or the severe straits he was in. Exaggerated descriptions of one's plight as equivalent to death are common in ancient Near Eastern literature, including the Bible; see Pss. 18.5–6; 30.4; Jonah 2.2, 8.

10b–11a: The servant is vindicated. Either he is saved from a fate like death, or he is actually described as being resurrected. In the latter case, his resurrection is probably a metaphor for the renewal of the nation at the end of the exile. Similarly, in Ezek. ch 37 Israel in exile is described as dead; the nation is brought back to life when the exile ends.

11b–12: God's concluding speech. God describes the vindication of the servant, echoing and confirming the themes of the spectators' speech.

54.1–17: Zion, rebuilt and secure. As in several earlier speeches, the city of Jerusalem or Zion is portrayed as a woman; cf. 49.14–26; 50.1–3. She is childless (i.e., without inhabitants) and apparently forsaken by her husband (i.e., the LORD). This passage assures her, however, that God remains her husband and protector and that she will soon have abundant children; in other words, the exiles will soon return to Judah. The passage as a whole recalls Hos. ch 1, where similar metaphors convey the message that God will punish but not abandon Israel. Deutero-Isaiah at once confirms the accuracy of Hosea's prophecy of doom while repeating Hosea's assurance that the covenant between God and Israel will endure.

1–5: The prophet comforts Zion. Due to the exile, Zion seemed empty and in ruins. Deutero-Isaiah assures Zion that not only will she have a tent to live in, she will need to enlarge it to accommodate her abundant offspring. The theme of Zion abundantly repopulated also appears in 49.17–21. This passage is based on Jer. 10.17–25, where the Judeans who are about to be exiled lament the loss of their children and the destruction of their tent (symbolizing the Temple), their city and kingdom, and their social structures generally.

For he was cut off from the land of the living
Through the sin of my people, who deserved
the punishment.
9 And his grave was set among the wicked,
[a]And with the rich, in his death[a]—
Though he had done no injustice
And had spoken no falsehood.
10 But the LORD chose to crush him [b]by disease,
That, if he made himself an offering for guilt,[b]
He might see offspring[c] and have long life,
And that through him the LORD's purpose might prosper.
11 Out of his anguish he shall see it;[d]
He shall enjoy it to the full through his devotion.[e]

"My righteous servant makes the many righteous,
It is their punishment that he bears;
12 Assuredly, I will give him the many as his portion,
He shall receive the multitude as his spoil.
For he exposed himself to death
And was numbered among the sinners,
Whereas he bore the guilt of the many
And made intercession for sinners."

54 Shout, O barren one,
You who bore no child!
Shout aloud for joy,
You who did not travail!
For the children of the wife forlorn
Shall outnumber those of the espoused
—said the LORD.

2 Enlarge the site of your tent,
[f]Extend the size of your dwelling,[f]
Do not stint!
Lengthen the ropes, and drive the pegs firm.
3 For you shall spread out to the right and the left;
Your offspring shall dispossess nations[g]
And shall people the desolate towns.

4 Fear not, you shall not be shamed;
Do not cringe, you shall not be disgraced.
For you shall forget

a-a Emendation yields "And his tomb with evildoers."
b-b Meaning of Heb. uncertain.
c Emendation yields "His arm," i.e., His vindication; cf. v. 1 with note.
d I.e., the arm of the LORD; see preceding note. *e For this sense of* da'ath *see 11.2, 9.*
f-f Lit. "Let the cloths of your dwelling extend."
g I.e., the foreigners who had occupied regions from which Israelites had been exiled; cf. 2 Kings 17.24.

The reproach of your youth,
And remember no more
The shame of your widowhood.
5 For He who made you will espouse you—
His name is "LORD of Hosts."
The Holy One of Israel will redeem you—
He is called "God of all the Earth."

6 The LORD has called you back
As a wife forlorn and forsaken.
Can one cast off the wife of his youth?
—said your God.
7 For a little while I forsook you,
But with vast love I will bring you back.
8 In slight anger, for a moment,
I hid My face from you;
But with kindness everlasting
I will take you back in love
—said the LORD your Redeemer.
9 For this to Me is like the waters[a] of Noah:
As I swore that the waters of Noah
Nevermore would flood the earth,
So I swear that I will not
Be angry with you or rebuke you.
10 For the mountains may move
And the hills be shaken,
But my loyalty shall never move from you,
Nor My covenant of friendship be shaken
—said the LORD, who takes you back in love.

11 Unhappy, storm-tossed one, uncomforted!
I will lay carbuncles[b] as your building stones
And make your foundations of sapphires.
12 I will make your battlements of rubies,
Your gates of precious stones,
The whole encircling wall of gems.
13 And all your children shall be disciples of the LORD,
And great shall be the happiness of your children;
14 You shall be established through righteousness.
You shall be safe from oppression,
And shall have no fear;
From ruin, and it shall not come near you.
15[c] Surely no harm can be done
Without My consent:

a Other Heb. mss. and the ancient versions read "days."
b Taking pukh *as a byform of* nophekh; *so already Rashi.*
c Meaning of verse uncertain.

6–10: God addresses Zion directly. 6–8: God assures Zion that He has not divorced her (cf. 50.1–3). God's anger was brief and brought about a temporary separation; the reconciliation will last forever. **9–10:** God switches from a marital metaphor to a simile based on the story of Noah (Gen. chs 8–9). The former metaphor implied that the covenant between God and Israel is one of mutual obligation; the allusion to Noah recalls the notion of a covenant of grace, which God unilaterally grants to human beings. Deutero-Isaiah often moves back and forth between portrayals of Israel as God's spouse and God's child, hence insisting that both covenant models are valid; see 49.14–21; 50.1–3. The reference to the flood (*the waters of Noah*) is apt because the flood is a return to chaos, an undoing of creation; likewise the destruction of the Temple was conceptually equated with the destruction of the world. The prophet again invokes a story now found in Gen. (see Isa. 51.2 for the previous story). **10:** On the steadfast nature of the covenant, see also Jer. 31.33–35, whose vocabulary and ideas Deutero-Isaiah borrows here. *Friendship,* or, "peace."

11–17: An eternal structure. God promises that Zion will be rebuilt as a beautiful and enduring city, secure due to God's incomparable protection. **13:** As in Jer. 31.33–35, the people in the restored community will learn God's teaching successfully, thus ensuring the eternal nature of the covenant. *All your children ... your children,* alternatively: "All those who build you [O Zion] will be learned in the ways of the LORD, / and great shall be the well-being of your inhabitants, endowed with understanding." The Heb letters "bnyk" appear twice in this v., implying at once the idea of "children," "builders," and "those who understand," each of which fits the context of ch 54 (cf. *b. Ber.* 64a). Deutero-Isaiah frequently puns on various meanings of a single word.

Whoever would harm you
Shall fall because of you.
16 It is I who created the smith
To fan the charcoal fire
And produce the tools for his work;
So it is I who create
The instruments of havoc.
17 No weapon formed against you
Shall succeed,
And every tongue that contends with you at law
You shall defeat.
Such is the lot of the servants of the LORD,
Such their triumph through Me
—declares the LORD.

55 Ho, all who are thirsty,
Come for water,
Even if you have no money;
Come, buy food and eat:
Buy food without money,
Wine and milk without cost.
2 Why do you spend money for what is not bread,
Your earnings for what does not satisfy?
Give heed to Me,
And you shall eat choice food
And enjoy the richest viands.
3 Incline your ear and come to Me;
Hearken, and you shall be revived.
And I will make with you an everlasting covenant,
The enduring loyalty promised to David.
4 [a-]As I made him a leader[b] of peoples,
A prince and commander of peoples,
5 So you shall summon a nation you did not know,
And a nation that did not know you
Shall come running to you[-a]—
For the sake of the LORD your God,
The Holy One of Israel who has glorified you.

6 Seek the LORD while He can be found,
Call to Him while He is near.

a-a Cf. 2 Sam. 22.44–45 (Ps. 18.44–45). *b Cf. Targum; others "witness."*

55.1–13: An invitation to redemption. This passage differs from many earlier Deutero-Isaianic speeches because of its general nature. It contains few references to the exile or the trek through the desert to Judah, instead couching its description of the upcoming redemption in broad terms that are less anchored in a specific historical situation. Isa. chs 40–66 progress from concrete language that reflects the situation of the Babylonian exiles toward phrasing that could apply to any historical era. Also noteworthy is the plea that people abandon sinful behavior, which is absent in the first division of Deutero-Isaiah's work (chs 40–48) but increasingly common in the second and third divisions (chs 49–57, 58–66).

1–5: God's invitation. It is unclear whether these lines are addressed specifically to Judeans (which is implied by vv. 3–5, 12) or to any person who wants to recognize the one God (so Ibn Ezra, Radak). *Water,* understood by rabbinic commentators as a metaphor for Torah. **3:** *The enduring loyalty promised to David:* In 2 Sam. 7.8–16 and Ps. 89.4, 20–37, God promised David that his descendants would rule Israel forever as an enduring royal dynasty. Here, Deutero-Isaiah reframes that promise to apply to the nation as a whole. The restored Judean commonwealth will have no one human king, for all its members will have royal status. Thus Deutero-Isaiah transforms the older Davidic covenant by democratizing it. (Cf. Deutero-Isaiah's democratizing of the priesthood in 61.5–6 and n.) The prophet also saves the Davidic promise by means of this transformation, for the more natural reading of the Davidic promise in 2 Sam. ch 7 and Ps. 89 proved incorrect in light of the fall of the Davidic dynasty to the Babylonians in 586 BCE. This transformation explains why the idea of a future ideal Davidic king (a messiah) is absent from Deutero-Isaiah's thought. On Deutero-Isaiah's attitude toward the monarchy, see also 42.1–9; 60.1–22; 65.25. **5:** Israel's royal status yields benefits for all humanity, who come to recognize, as a result of her redemption, the one true God.

6–7: A call to repentance. The haftarah for the afternoon of fast days (including, but not limited to, Tish'ah be'av) begins here and continues through 56.8. This selection contains two sections, 55.6–13 and 56.1–8. The first section emphasizes repentance, an appropriate theme for fast days, during which Jews afflict themselves

7 Let the wicked give up his ways,
The sinful man his plans;
Let him turn back to the LORD,
And He will pardon him;
To our God,
For he freely forgives.
8 For My plans are not your plans,
Nor are My ways[a] your ways[a]
—declares the LORD.
9 But as the heavens are high above the earth,
So are My ways[a] high above your ways[a]
And My plans above your plans.
10 For as the rain or snow drops from heaven
And returns not there,
But soaks the earth
And makes it bring forth vegetation,
Yielding [b-]seed for sowing and bread for eating,[-b]
11 So is the word that issues from My mouth:
It does not come back to Me unfulfilled,
But performs what I purpose,
Achieves what I sent it to do.
12 Yea, you shall leave[c] in joy and be led home secure.
Before you, mount and hill shall shout aloud,
And all the trees of the field shall clap their hands.
13 Instead of the brier, a cypress shall rise;
Instead of the nettle, a myrtle shall rise.
These shall stand as a testimony to the LORD,
As an everlasting sign that shall not perish.

56 Thus said the LORD:
Observe what is right and do what is just;
For soon My salvation shall come,
And my deliverance be revealed.

a Emendation yields "words"; cf. v. 11 and 40.8.
b-b Lit. "seed for the sower and bread for the eater."
c I.e., leave the Babylonian exile.

with hunger as a sort of purificatory sacrifice. The second section focuses on two themes: the importance of Sabbath observance and the inclusion in the covenant community of willing foreigners who are monotheists and Sabbath-observers. The Sabbath is an appropriate theme for the exilic situation that calls for the fast days (all of which relate historically in some way to the fall of Jerusalem or to the exile): in the absence of the Temple destroyed at the outset of the exile, the Sabbath becomes (as the theologian Abraham Joshua Heschel phrases it) "a palace in time" that can take the place of the Temple. The Sabbath provides an opportunity for the Jewish community to come together in sacred time even when they no longer possess their sacred space. The theme of bringing foreigners into the covenant community is appropriate for the liturgical reading in the afternoon of a fast day, when the liturgical mood moves from sorrow to hope. The fact that foreigners will want to join into the covenant community provides a sense of relief to the community that is completing its fast: far from being eternally downtrodden and despised, the community of Israel and its teachings are sufficiently appealing to attract converts.

8–11: The trustworthiness of God's words. Deutero-Isaiah picks up the metaphor of water from v. 1 in a new way to emphasize a favorite theme: God's promises and the prophecies God issued through the prophets never fail to come true. Cf. 45.23. The metaphor is significant: God sends rain, which inevitably falls to the ground; then it is absorbed by soil and nourishes vegetation. Humans in turn harvest the vegetation and transform it into food. Similarly, God's word is sure to have a series of effects, the most important of which are indirect and involve human input.

12–13: The exodus from Babylonia. The prophet again calls on the exiles to leave Babylonia. Cf. 48.20–23; 49.13; 52.11–12. The LORD's promise of glorious restoration will be fulfilled, but as the preceding vv. imply, the nature of their fulfillment may be indirect and will depend on human response to God's invitation. The prophet may be responding to the failure of most Judeans to move back to Zion after the Persian king Cyrus allowed them to do so, beginning in 538 BCE.

56.1–8: Covenant and community. The prophet addresses the role that observance of the commandments plays in forming Judean identity. Not only does it bring happiness for Judeans (v. 2), but it allows foreigners to become members of the community as well (vv. 6–7).

1–2: The importance of observing the law. The passage focuses in particular on the laws of the Sabbath, which may have attained particular importance during the exile, as sacred time replaced sacred space. Cf. 58.13–14.

2 Happy is the man who does this,
The man who holds fast to it:
Who keeps the sabbath and does not profane it,
And stays his hand from doing any evil.

3 Let not the foreigner say,
Who has attached himself to the LORD,
"The LORD will keep me apart from His people";
And let not the eunuch say,
"I am a withered tree."
4 For thus said the LORD:
"As for the eunuchs who keep My sabbaths,
Who have chosen what I desire
And hold fast to My covenant—
5 I will give them, in My House
And within My walls,
A monument and a name
Better than sons or daughters.
I will give them an everlasting name
Which shall not perish.
6 As for the foreigners
Who attach themselves to the LORD,
To minister to Him,
And to love the name of the LORD,
To be His servants—
All who keep the sabbath and do not profane it,
And who hold fast to My covenant—
7 I will bring them to My sacred mount
And let them rejoice in My house of prayer.
Their burnt offerings and sacrifices
Shall be welcome on My altar;
For My House shall be called
A house of prayer for all peoples."
8 Thus declares the Lord GOD,
Who gathers the dispersed of Israel:
"I will gather still more to those already
gathered."

9 All you wild beasts, come and devour,
All you beasts of the forest!

3–6: Foreigners and eunuchs. The prophet responds to feelings of exclusion among these groups, emphasizing that Torah observance renders them complete members of the community. Formal conversion did not exist in the biblical period. **Foreigners.** During the period of the exile and the return to Zion, some foreigners became attracted to the monotheism of the Judeans. Further, non-Judeans mixed with the Judean population in the land of Israel (a topic that receives a great deal of attention in the books of Ezra and Neh.). Deutero-Isaiah assures the foreigners that through full observance of the covenant they can become like members of the Judean community. This passage shows, by verbs such as *keep, hold fast,* and *attach,* the beginnings of the religious institution that later came to be called conversion, and rabbinic commentators understand the passage as referring to converts. The rhetoric in the books of Ezra and Neh. seems less welcoming to foreigners (see Ezra ch 9), but the policy reflected by those books is in fact identical to that advocated by this prophet: Outsiders become insiders if they embrace the covenant (see Ezra 6.21). **Eunuchs.** Some officials at the Babylonian court (including some exiled Judeans) were castrated. Judeans subject to this fate (and also perhaps foreigners attracted to monotheism) felt cut off from the Judean people in the sense that they would have no descendants; the nation in the future would not include their seed. Further, Lev. 21.16–23 disqualified eunuchs from priestly service; see also Deut. 23.2. Deutero-Isaiah reassures eunuchs that they nonetheless have an enduring future in the sacred community. **5:** *A monument and a name,* a memorial, lit. "a hand and a name" (Heb "yad vashem," the name of the Holocaust Museum in Jerusalem). **7:** According to the Torah, foreigners' offerings are welcome at the Temple; see Num. 15.14–16; Lev. 22.18–25 (cf. 1 Kings 8.41–43). This text goes a step further, moving toward the institution of conversion.

8: Ingathering of exiles. The first wave of exiles who returned to the land of Israel when the Persian king Cyrus allowed them to do so in the 530s was disappointingly small. The prophet looks forward to further, and more impressive, waves of "'aliyah."

56.9–57.21: Castigation and consolation. This section contains Deutero-Isaiah's harshest denunciation of the Judeans' behavior, and in many ways it resembles the rebukes found in First Isaiah, Jeremiah, and other preexilic prophets more than the bulk of the prophecies in

10 The[a] watchmen are blind, all of them,
They perceive nothing.
They are all dumb dogs
That cannot bark;
They lie sprawling,[b]
They love to drowse.
11 Moreover, the dogs are greedy;
They never know satiety.
[c]As for the shepherds, they know not
What it is to give heed.[c]
Everyone has turned his own way,
Every last one seeks his own advantage.
12 "Come, I'll get some wine;
Let us swill liquor.
And tomorrow will be just the same,
Or even much grander!"

57 The righteous man perishes,
And no one considers;
Pious men are taken away,
And no one gives thought
That because of evil
The righteous was taken away.
2 Yet he shall come to peace,
[d]He shall have rest on his couch[d]
Who walked straightforward.

3 But as for you, come closer,
You sons of a sorceress,
You offspring of an adulterer and a harlot![e]
4 With whom do you act so familiarly?
At whom do you open your mouth
And stick out your tongue?
Why, you are children of iniquity,
Offspring of treachery—
5 You who inflame[f] yourselves
Among the terebinths,
Under every verdant tree;
Who slaughter children in the wadis,
Among[g] the clefts of the rocks.
6 [h]With such[i] are your share and portion,[h]
They, they are your allotment;

a Heb. "his." *b Meaning of Heb. uncertain.*
c-c Meaning of Heb. uncertain. Emendation yields "Neither do the shepherds ever know sufficiency (hon)*." Cf.* hon *in Prov. 30.15, 16.*
d-d Heb. "They shall have rest on their couches." *e Lit. "she acts the harlot."*
f I.e., in some frenzied idolatrous rite. *g Heb. "under."*
h-h Meaning of Heb. uncertain. *i The cult-trees referred to above in v. 5.*

chs 40–66. It ends, however, on a typically Deutero-Isaianic note, assuring the faithful among the Judean population that peace and salvation will eventually arrive. The description of the Judeans' sins focuses on Canaanite-influenced idolatry of the sort known from the preexilic era. Some suggest that idolatry became common in the period of the restoration as Judeans intermarried with the local population, a practice repeatedly condemned in the books of Ezra and Neh. Others argue that this passage refers in fact to the sins of the exiles' ancestors and thus does not predict a new disaster but explains the reason for the exile that has already occurred. The whole passage is heavily allusive, borrowing vocabulary and literary motifs from 2.6–21; 6.1–10; 30.9–14; Jer. 2.23–25; 3.12–14; 6.13–14; 12.8–12.

56.9–57.2: Denunciation of Israel's corrupt leaders. *Wild beasts* (v. 9)—i.e., foreign nations—are invited to devour Israel. Some argue that *dogs* (v. 10) and *shepherds* (v. 11) refer to false prophets, while others view them as political leaders.

57.3–13a: Idolatry. A condemnation of pagan practices among the Judeans, whether past or present. Sexual imagery pervades this passage, not because the idolatrous worship involved lewd practices but because idolatry among Israelites is compared to adultery (see, e.g., Jer. 3.1; Ezek. 6.9; 16.15; Hos. 2.7; 4.15; and cf. Isa. 1.21): The LORD is Israel's husband, and thus any worship of other gods by Israelites is an act of marital infidelity. **5–7:** Israelite pagan religious ceremonies are often depicted as taking place under leafy trees and on hilltops. Cf. 1 Kings 14.13; 2 Kings 17.10; Jer. 2.20; 3.6–13; Ezek. 6.13; Hos. 4.13.

13b–21: Salvation. Not all Judeans are guilty of these crimes, however, and God recognizes the Judeans' weaknesses and will help them overcome them. The faithful and the penitent will enjoy well-being, even as the inveterate sinners are punished. **57.14–58.15:** These vv. are the haftarah for the morning of Yom Kippur. Its focus is on the nature of the true fast, which is not merely ritual in nature but also leads to ethical action towards downtrodden, (58.3–7). It also emphasizes that in spite of God's punishments, God is ready to comfort and heal the truly penitent (57.16–19). **14:** Cf. 40.3–5. **15:** God, the highest of all beings, desires to dwell among the lowest. Deutero-Isaiah often portrays the LORD as voluntarily accepting human roles out of love for the people. Cf. 52.6; 58.9; 65.1.

To them you have poured out libations,
Presented offerings.
Should I relent in the face of this?

7 On a high and lofty hill
You have set your couch;
There, too, you have gone up
To perform sacrifices.
8 Behind the door and doorpost
You have directed your thoughts;
[a]Abandoning Me, you have gone up
On the couch you made so wide.
You have made a covenant with them,[b]
You have loved bedding with them;[c]
You have chosen lust.[d]
9 You have approached[a] the king[e] with oil,
You have provided many perfumes.
And you have sent your envoys afar,
Even down to the netherworld.[f]
10 Though wearied by much travel,
You never said, "I give up!"
You found gratification for your lust,
And so you never cared.
11 [g]Whom do you dread and fear,
That you tell lies?[g]
But you gave no thought to Me,
You paid no heed.
It is because I have stood idly by [h]so long[h]
That you have no fear of Me.
12 I hereby pronounce [i]judgment upon your deeds:[i]
[j]Your assorted [idols][j] shall not avail you,
13 Shall not save you when you cry out.
They shall all be borne off by the wind,
Snatched away by a breeze.
But those who trust in Me shall inherit the land
And possess My sacred mount.
14 [The LORD] says:
Build up, build up a highway!
Clear a road!
Remove all obstacles
From the road of My people!

a-a Meaning of Heb. uncertain. *b The cult-trees referred to above in v. 5.*
c I.e., with the objects behind door and doorpost.
d Like Ugaritic yd, *from root* ydd, *"to love."* *e Or "Molech."*
f I.e., you have brought tribute to alien cults as to a king.
g-g Emendation yields "Them you dreaded and feared, / And so you gave them thought." *h-h Emendation yields "and shut My eyes."*
i-i Lit. "your retribution and your deeds." *j-j Brought up from v. 13 for clarity.*

15 For thus said He who high aloft
Forever dwells, whose name is holy:
I dwell on high, in holiness;
Yet with the contrite and the lowly in spirit—
Reviving the spirits of the lowly,
Reviving the hearts of the contrite.
16 For I will not always contend,
I will not be angry forever:
Nay, I [a-]who make spirits flag,[-a]
Also create the breath of life.
17 For their[b] sinful greed I was angry;
I struck them and turned away in My wrath.
[c-]Though stubborn, they follow the way of their hearts,[-c]
18 I note how they fare and will heal them:
I will guide them and mete out solace to them,
And to the mourners among them 19 heartening,[d]
comforting[e] words:
It shall be well,
Well with the far and the near
—said the LORD—
And I will heal them.
20 But the wicked are like the troubled sea
Which cannot rest,
Whose waters toss up mire and mud.
21 There is no safety
—said my God—
For the wicked.

58 Cry with full throat, without restraint;
Raise your voice like a ram's horn!
Declare to My people their transgression,
To the House of Jacob their sin.

a-a Meaning of Heb. uncertain. *b I.e., Israel's. Cf. "My people," v. 14.*
c-c Meaning of Heb. uncertain. Emendation yields "When they have walked broken in the contrition of their hearts."
d Lit. "the vigor of"; cf. Eccl. 12.1 and postbiblical bori.
e The Heb. nib *is otherwise unknown; its meaning is inferred from that of* nid *(cf. the verb* nad *"to condole") in the parallel expression in Job 16.5.*

19–21: The prophet divides the nation into two groups: the true or faithful Israel for whom *it shall be well* (or, "there will be peace," Heb "shalom," v. 19), and the wicked, for whom *there is no safety* (or, "there will be no peace," v. 21). **19:** *The far and the near,* respectively, Israelites who remain in exile and those who already live in the land of Israel.

Chs 58–66: Further denunciations and promises. The third section of Deutero-Isaiah's prophetic collection. Chs 34–35 in all likelihood were originally part of this section as well. Like the second section (chs 49–57), these chs were composed in Jerusalem after the initial, somewhat disappointing, restoration had taken place in 538 BCE (see intro. to the book of Isaiah, section on chs 40–66). Several characteristics that begin to emerge in chs 49–57 become more pronounced here. The prophet rebukes the nation for moral and religious shortcomings. Further, Deutero-Isaiah responds to complaints regarding the full redemption's delay, and the theme of the cleavage between faithful and unfaithful Judeans becomes a main focus of attention. On the other hand, several chs, especially 60–62 and parts of 65–66, recall the most exuberant prophecies of chs 40–48; these chs insist that the full redemption predicted in the earliest chs of Deutero-Isaiah's collection will indeed take place. All the exiles will return to the land of Israel, the nations of the world will join Israel in worshipping the one true God, and the Presence of God will journey back to Jerusalem, bringing great joy to the faithful within Israel and among the nations.

58.1–15: True piety and false piety. The prophet denounces the Judeans, focusing not on pagan practices (as in ch 57) but on apparently proper religious practices that the Judeans perform hypocritically. Lying behind the passage is an implied question: Why have the predictions of glorious restoration found in chs 40–48 not come true? Exiles had indeed returned to Jerusalem, but—contrary to the expectations raised in the opening chs of Deutero-Isaiah's work—the land remained under foreign control (the Persians having replaced the Babylonians as overlords), conditions were difficult, and God's Presence was not manifest there. (On the difficulties facing the early postexilic community, see Ezra chs 4–6; Hag. chs 1–2; Zech. chs 1, 3.) Deutero-Isaiah maintains that it is now the people's sins that prevent the full-fledged restoration from taking place.

1–7: Fasting and justice. The Judeans observe rituals such as fasting, but they do so only for their own benefit, not out of true devotion. Real humility toward God would engender a desire for justice toward

2 To be sure, they seek Me daily,
Eager to learn My ways.
Like a nation that does what is right,
That has not abandoned the laws of its God,
They ask Me for the right way,
They are eager for the nearness of God:
3 "Why, when we fasted, did You not see?
When we starved our bodies, did You pay no heed?"
Because on your fast day
You see to your business
And oppress all your laborers!
4 Because you fast in strife and contention,
And you strike with a wicked fist!
Your fasting today is not such
As to make your voice heard on high.
5 Is such the fast I desire,
A day for men to starve their bodies?
Is it bowing the head like a bulrush
And lying in sackcloth and ashes?
Do you call that a fast,
A day when the LORD is favorable?
6 No, this is the fast I desire:
To unlock fetters of wickedness,
And untie the cords of [a]the yoke[a]
To let the oppressed go free;
To break off every yoke.
7 It is to share your bread with the hungry,
And to take the wretched poor into your home;
When you see the naked, to clothe him,
And not to ignore your own kin.

8 Then shall your light burst through like the dawn
And your healing spring up quickly;
Your Vindicator shall march before you,
The Presence of the LORD shall be your rear guard.
9 Then, when you call, the LORD will answer;
When you cry, He will say: Here I am.
If you banish [a]the yoke[a] from your midst,
[b]The menacing hand,[b] and evil speech,
10 And you offer your compassion[c] to the hungry
And satisfy the famished creature—
Then shall your light shine in darkness,
And your gloom shall be like noonday.
11 The LORD will guide you always;

a-a *Change of vocalization yields "lawlessness"; cf.* muṭṭeh, *Ezek.* 9.9.
b-b *Lit. "Extending the finger."*
c *Some Heb. mss. and ancient versions read "bread."*

the weak, compassion toward the downtrodden, and charity toward the poor. Then fasting would involve a willingness to give up one's own things rather than the hope to acquire salvation. These vv. borrow ideas and vocabulary from Mic. 3.6–12. **2:** *The right way,* alternatively, "victorious judgments." People pray for divine intervention in their quarrels against others; their prayers and fasts have selfish purposes, not sacred ones.

8–9a: The result of true righteousness. Cf. 40.3; 52.12. Deutero-Isaiah repeats the earlier predictions that God's own Presence will return to Zion. Here, however, the prophecy is conditional: Only when the Judeans' behavior warrants divine Presence will God arrive. **9a:** *Here I am,* Heb "hineni." See 52.6 n.

9b–12: Righteousness and restoration. Although some exiles returned to Zion after the Persians defeated the Babylonians in 538, the land of Israel remained for the most part in ruins. The prophet attempts to explain why the rebuilding of the cities destroyed by the Babylonians has been delayed.

He will slake your thirst in [a]parched places[a]
And give strength to your bones.
You shall be like a watered garden,
Like a spring whose waters do not fail.
12 Men from your midst shall rebuild ancient ruins,
You shall restore foundations laid long ago.
And you shall be called
"Repairer of fallen walls,
Restorer of lanes for habitation."
13 If you [b]refrain from trampling[b] the sabbath,
From pursuing your affairs on My holy day;
If you call the sabbath "delight,"
The LORD's holy day "honored";
And if you honor it and go not your ways
Nor look to your affairs, nor strike bargains—
14 Then you [c]can seek the favor of the LORD.[c]
I will set you astride the heights of the earth,
And let you enjoy the heritage of your
father Jacob—
For the mouth of the LORD has spoken.

59 No, the LORD's arm is not too short to save,
Or His ear too dull to hear;
2 But your iniquities have been a barrier
Between you and your God,
Your sins have made Him turn His face away
And refuse to hear you.
3 For your hands are defiled with crime[d]
And your fingers with iniquity.
Your lips speak falsehood,
Your tongue utters treachery.
4 No one sues justly
Or pleads honestly;
They rely on emptiness and speak falsehood,
Conceiving wrong and begetting evil.

5 They hatch adder's eggs
And weave spider webs;
He who eats of those eggs will die,
And if one is crushed, it hatches out a viper.
6 Their webs will not serve as a garment,
What they make cannot serve as clothing;
Their deeds are deeds of mischief,
Their hands commit lawless acts,
7 Their feet run after evil,

a-a *Meaning of Heb. uncertain.* b-b *Lit. "turn back your foot from."*
c-c *Cf. Ps. 37.4; Job 22.26–27; 27.10.* d *Or "blood."*

13–14: The Sabbath. Deutero-Isaiah does not reject ritual in favor of ethical action but calls on the nation to attend to both, and focuses especially on the observance of the Sabbath. On the increasing importance of the Sabbath in the exilic and postexilic periods, see 56.1–2 n. These vv. highlight delight of Shabbat, rather than focus on capital punishment required by Exod. 31.14–15 for not observing it. Cf. 56.6. These vv. borrow vocabulary from Deut. 32.9–13.

59.1–21: Rebuke, confession, and reconciliation. This ch presents a three-part dialogue. The prophet reprimands the nation; the nation, or at least the faithful among them, acknowledge their misdeeds; and then the prophet announces that God will bring justice and mercy to the people. God speaks directly to the faithful in the last v. This ch, like the previous one, attributes the delay of the redemption predicted in chs 40–48 to the people's sins.

1–8: Sin and its consequences. **1–2:** Here, as in 40.27; 49.14; 50.1–2, Deutero-Isaiah implicitly responds to specific complaints uttered by contemporaries. The Babylonians have been defeated, as Deutero-Isaiah and earlier prophets predicted, but the new age has failed to materialize: The exiles have not all returned to Zion, and the land remains mostly desolate. Consequently, some Judeans speculated that the LORD was not able to save them, or that God did not listen to their prayers. The prophet retorts that Israel's sins, not God's abilities, are the root of the problem. Earlier, Deutero-Isaiah seemed to think that sins were only a part of Israel's past, and that God would automatically treat the nation with grace after their punishment in Babylon (40.2; 43.25; 48.11), but now that an imperfect restoration has taken place, the prophet recognizes the continuing existence of sin and its unhappy consequences. **2:** *Your iniquities ... Your sins:* The Heb word order emphasizes these nouns. Therefore, translate: "It is your *iniquities* that have been a barrier ... It is your *sins* that have made Him turn ..."

9–15a: Confession. 9–11: The Judeans lament their fate. They thought that *vindication* (v. 9) was at hand, only to be disappointed. **11:** *Hope,* or, "anticipate." **12–15a:** The faithful confess their sins. Rather than distancing themselves from those responsible for the misdeeds, they acknowledge that they share culpability for their neighbors' sins.

15b–20: God's response. God brings justice, which is good news for the faithful and dreadful news for everyone else. The phrasing here is often used of foreign nations in the Bible; here the guilty among Israel bear the brunt of divine wrath along with evildoers from other nations.

They hasten to shed the blood of the innocent.
Their plans are plans of mischief,
Destructiveness and injury are on their roads.
8 They do not care for the way of integrity,
There is no justice on their paths.
They make their courses crooked,
No one who walks in them cares for integrity.

9 "That is why redress is far from us,
And vindication does not reach us.
We hope for light, and lo! there is darkness;
For a gleam, and we must walk in gloom.
10 We grope, like blind men along a wall;
Like those without eyes we grope.
We stumble at noon, as if in darkness;
[a-]Among the sturdy, we are[-a] like the dead.
11 We all growl like bears
And moan like doves.
We hope for redress, and there is none;
For victory, and it is far from us.
12 For our many sins are before You,
Our guilt testifies against us.
We are aware of our sins,
And we know well our iniquities:
13 Rebellion, faithlessness to the LORD,
And turning away from our God,
Planning fraud and treachery,
Conceiving lies and uttering them with the throat.[b]
14 And so redress is turned back
And vindication stays afar,
Because honesty stumbles in the public square
And uprightness cannot enter.
15 Honesty has been lacking,
He who turns away from evil is despoiled."

The LORD saw and was displeased
That there was no redress.
16 He saw that there was no man,
He gazed long, but no one intervened.
Then His own arm won Him triumph,
His victorious right hand[c] supported Him.
17 He donned victory like a coat of mail,
With a helmet of triumph on His head;
He clothed Himself with garments of retribution,
Wrapped himself in zeal as in a robe.

a-a *Meaning of Heb. uncertain. Emendation yields "In the daytime ..."*
b *Lit. "heart"; see note at 33.18 and frequently elsewhere.* c *Cf. Ps. 98.1–2.*

18 [a-]According to their deserts,
So shall He repay[-a] fury to His foes;
He shall make requital to His enemies,
Requital to the distant lands.
19 From the west, they shall revere[b] the name of
the LORD,
And from the east, His Presence.
For He shall come like a hemmed-in stream
Which the wind of the LORD drives on;
20 He shall come as redeemer to Zion,
To those in Jacob who turn back from sin
—declares the LORD.

21 And this shall be My covenant with them, said the LORD: My spirit[c] which is upon you, and the words which I have placed in your mouth, shall not be absent from your mouth, nor from the mouth of your children, nor from the mouth of your children's children—said the LORD—from now on, for all time.[d]

60 Arise, shine, for your light has dawned;
The Presence of the LORD has shone upon you!
2 Behold! Darkness shall cover the earth,
And thick clouds the peoples;
But upon you the LORD will shine,
And His Presence be seen over you.
3 And nations shall walk by your light,
Kings, by your shining radiance.

4 Raise your eyes and look about:
They have all gathered and come to you.
Your sons shall be brought from afar,
Your daughters like babes on shoulders.

a-a Meaning of Heb. uncertain.
b Or (with a number of mss. and editions) "see."
c I.e., the gift of prophecy; cf., e.g., 61.1.
d Israel is to be a prophet-nation; cf. 51.16.

20: *Those in Jacob who turn back from sin:* It is the penitent Israelites, not the whole nation, who will enjoy the salvation long predicted and thus far delayed.

21: The eternal covenant. God speaks directly to the penitent. Cf. Jer. 31.31.

Chs 60–62: Encouragement to Zion. This lengthy poem portrays Jerusalem (Zion) as a bereaved woman. In this respect it resembles many passages encountered in the previous section of Deutero-Isaiah's work, chs 49–57. Its enthusiasm and optimism recall the prophecies in chs 40–48, and like them it heralds the dawn of a new age. The restored Zion will be home for a righteous nation newly returned to its land and its God; universal recognition of the one God will lead all the nations to enrich Zion and her inhabitants. Unlike the prophecies in chs 40–48, however, this passage puts relatively little emphasis on the return from the exile and does not mention the fall of Babylonia, suggesting that it was composed after the Persians under Cyrus defeated the Babylonians in 539 BCE, and allowed the Jews to return home one year later. The restoration of Zion that followed proved in most ways disappointing (see chs 49–57 n.). Rather than giving up hope, the prophet repeats the earlier message, insisting that the LORD will become manifest to humanity and that Jerusalem will eventually achieve peace, security, wealth, and glory. The prophet focuses less on the return to Zion, since it has already begun.

60.1–22: Royal city, royal nation. Throughout these vv., the prophet uses vocabulary and motifs associated with royalty in biblical and ancient Near Eastern literature. In particular, Deutero-Isaiah borrows royal vocabulary from texts that are concerned with the Davidic dynasty, including Isa. ch 11; Ps. 72. Here, however, the motifs are not applied to a Davidic king. Instead, they are transferred to the city of Zion and to the Israelite nation as a whole; the text makes no mention of the Davidic family. This prophet does not look forward to the arrival of a human Messiah to liberate the Israelites or a human king to govern them. Rather, God will rule the nation directly in the future, and the whole nation will enjoy royal status. Cf. 55.3 n. and also the democratization of the priesthood in 61.5–6.

60.1–3: Light shines in the darkness. The prophet speaks to Zion, which literally becomes a light to the nations. Cf. 42.6; 49.6.

60.4–16: Zion and the nations. Because the nations of the world will recognize and fear God, they will bring tribute to Zion. This passage deliberately echoes Isa. 2.1–4, but Deutero-Isaiah offers a different picture of what the nations will do: They will transport Judean exiles to Jerusalem and add to the city's wealth. Isaiah's universalism gives way to a more national set of concerns. **6:** *Midian,* an area in the Sinai, inhabited by nomadic traders. *Ephah,* a Midianite tribe. *Sheba,* Yemen, the southwest corner of the Arabian peninsula, renowned for its wealth and exotic goods. **7:** *Kedar,* a tribe of nomadic traders located in the extreme north of the Arabian desert. *Nebaioth,* the Nabateans, an Arabian tribe located east of the Dead Sea. *Rams:* The Heb term could refer to animals or to political leaders. *They shall be welcome offerings:* If "rams" refers to animals, then translate, "They will go up willingly on My altar." If "rams" refers to leaders, then translate "They will offer acceptable offerings on My altar." The latter translation may suggest that foreigners will be able to serve in priestly roles in the Temple of the future. Cf. 54.7; 66.21. The issue is debated in the Babylonian Talmud (*b. A. Z.* 23b). **11:** Jerusalem will be secure and therefore the city gates will be kept open continuously; there will be no need for the usual practice of closing and bolting the city gates at night for security. **13:** The rebuilt Temple, like the First Temple, will be constructed with wood from Lebanon; cf. 1 Kings 5.15–25. **14–16:** A reversal of fortune.

5 As you behold, you will glow;
Your heart will throb and thrill—
For the wealth of the sea[a] shall pass on to you,
The riches of nations shall flow to you.
6 Dust clouds of camels shall cover you,
Dromedaries of Midian and Ephah.
They all shall come from Sheba;
They shall bear gold and frankincense,
And shall herald the glories of the LORD.
7 All the flocks of Kedar shall be assembled for you,
The rams of Nebaioth shall serve your needs;
They shall be welcome offerings on My altar,
And I will add glory to My glorious House.

8 Who are these that float like a cloud,
Like doves to their cotes?
9 [b-]Behold, the coastlands await me,[-b]
With [c-]ships of Tarshish[-c] in the lead,
To bring your sons from afar,
And their[d] silver and gold as well—
For the name of the LORD your God,
For the Holy One of Israel, who has glorified you.
10 Aliens shall rebuild your walls,
Their kings shall wait upon you—
For in anger I struck you down,
But in favor I take you back.
11 Your gates shall always stay open—
Day and night they shall never be shut—
To let in the wealth of the nations,
With their kings in procession.

12 For the nation or the kingdom
That does not serve you shall perish;
Such nations shall be destroyed.

13 The majesty of Lebanon shall come to you—
Cypress and pine and box—
To adorn the site of My Sanctuary,
To glorify the place where My feet rest.

14 Bowing before you, shall come
The children of those who tormented you;
Prostrate at the soles of your feet
Shall be all those who reviled you;

a *Emendation yields "coastlands."*
b-b *Emendation yields "The vessels of the coastlands are gathering."*
c-c *See note at 2.16.* *d* *I.e., of the people of the coastlands.*

And you shall be called
"City of the LORD,
Zion of the Holy One of Israel."
15 Whereas you have been forsaken,
Rejected, with none passing through,
I will make you a pride everlasting,
A joy for age after age.
16 You shall suck the milk of the nations,
Suckle at royal breasts.[a]
And you shall know
That I the LORD am your Savior,
I, The Mighty One of Jacob, am your Redeemer.
17 Instead of copper I will bring gold,
Instead of iron I will bring silver;
Instead of wood, copper;
And instead of stone, iron.
And I will appoint Well-being as your government,
Prosperity as your officials.
18 The cry "Violence!"
Shall no more be heard in your land,
Nor "Wrack and ruin!"
Within your borders.
And you shall name your walls "Victory"
And your gates "Renown."

19 No longer shall you need the sun
For light by day,
Nor the shining of the moon
For radiance [by night[b]];
For the LORD shall be your light everlasting,
Your God shall be your glory.
20 Your sun shall set no more,
Your moon no more withdraw;
For the LORD shall be a light to you forever,
And your days of mourning shall be ended.
21 And your people, all of them righteous,
Shall possess the land for all time;
They are the shoot that I planted,
My handiwork in which I glory.
22 The smallest shall become a clan;
The least, a mighty nation.
I the LORD will speed it in due time.

60.17–22: The city transformed. Jerusalem and its inhabitants will be secure and prosperous, and God's Presence will dwell in the city once again. **19–20:** A return to the opening theme of light in v. 1. According to biblical writers, the divine Presence consists of or is surrounded by an extraordinarily bright light (see Exod. 24.16–17; Isa. 4.5; Ezek. 1.26–28; 10.4; 43.2; Ps. 104.2). Because God's Presence will dwell on Zion, neither the sun nor the moon will be visible, much less necessary. **22:** The few become many. Deutero-Isaiah reverses the theme of the remnant found in the prophecies of First Isaiah (e.g., 6.13; 7.3; 11.11; 28.5–6; 30.17).

a *Lit. "breasts of kings" or "breasts of kingdoms."*
b *So 1QIs[a], Septuagint, and Targum.*

61.1–9: Jubilee for Jerusalem. The identity of the speaker in these vv. is debated. It is possible that Zion speaks, but in the next passage, the speaker addresses Zion. Hence it is more likely that the speaker is the prophet. The text describes the prophet's divine inspiration and God-given mission. **1:** *Proclaim release:* The phrasing comes from Lev. 25.10, which discusses Israelite farmers who lost their land and were forced into indentured servitude. Leviticus rules that they may leave their servitude and regain their land every fifty years. Deutero-Isaiah applies this concept to the nation as a whole: In 586 it lost its land and was forced to live elsewhere. Fifty years later, its period of service ended when the Edict of Cyrus allowed them to leave Babylonia and to regain their ancestral land. **5–6:** The nations serve the Judeans (cf. 60.4–16), and the Judeans in turn serve the nations as priests. The priestly role that once belonged to the descendants of Aaron alone (i.e., the "Kohanim"; see Num. ch 18) is now extended to the whole nation. This is similar to the idea of the democratization of the monarchy, discussed in 55.3 n.; 60.1–22 n.

61.10–62.7: Triumph for Zion. The prophet speaks on behalf of the people. Royal motifs are applied to the prophet, to Zion, and thus to the whole nation; cf. Ps. 132.9–18.

61.10–62.2: The nations witness the surprising vindication of Israel.

61 The spirit of the Lord GOD is upon me,
Because the LORD has anointed me;
He has sent me as a herald of joy to the humble,
To bind up the wounded of heart,
To proclaim release to the captives,
Liberation to the imprisoned;
2 To proclaim a year of the LORD's favor
And a day of vindication by our God;
To comfort all who mourn—
3 [a]To provide for[a] the mourners in Zion—
To give them a turban instead of ashes,
The festive ointment instead of mourning,
A garment of splendor instead of a drooping spirit.
They shall be called terebinths of victory,
Planted by the LORD for His glory.
4 And they shall build the ancient ruins,
Raise up the desolations of old,
And renew the ruined cities,
The desolations of many ages.
5 Strangers shall stand and pasture your flocks,
Aliens shall be your plowmen and vine-trimmers;
6 While you shall be called "Priests of the LORD,"
And termed "Servants of our God."
You shall enjoy the wealth of nations
And revel[b] in their riches.
7 Because your shame was double—
[c]Men cried, "Disgrace is their portion"[c]—
Assuredly,
They shall have a double share in their land,
Joy shall be theirs for all time.
8 For I the LORD love justice,
I hate [d]robbery with a burnt offering.[d]
I will pay them their wages faithfully,
And make a covenant with them for all time.
9 Their offspring shall be known among
the nations,
Their descendants in the midst of the peoples.
All who see them shall recognize
That they are a stock the LORD has blessed.

10 I greatly rejoice in the LORD,
My whole being exults in my God.
For He has clothed me with garments of triumph,
Wrapped me in a robe of victory,

a-a Meaning of Heb. uncertain. *b Meaning of Heb. uncertain.*
c-c Emendation yields "They inherited disgrace as their portion."
d-d Emendation yields "the robbing of wages."

Like a bridegroom adorned with a turban,
Like a bride bedecked with her finery.
11 For as the earth brings forth her growth
And a garden makes the seed shoot up,
So the Lord God will make
Victory and renown shoot up
In the presence of all the nations.

62 For the sake of Zion I will not be silent,
For the sake of Jerusalem I will not be still,
Till her victory emerge resplendent
And her triumph like a flaming torch.
2 Nations shall see your victory,
And every king your majesty;
And you shall be called by a new name
Which the LORD Himself shall bestow.
3 You shall be a glorious crown
In the hand of the LORD,
And a royal diadem
In the palm of your God.

4 Nevermore shall you be called "Forsaken,"
Nor shall your land be called "Desolate";
But you shall be called "I delight in her,"
And your land "Espoused."
For the LORD takes delight in you,
And your land shall be espoused.
5 As a youth espouses a maiden,
[a-]Your sons[-a] shall espouse you;
And as a bridegroom rejoices over his bride,
So will your God rejoice over you.

6 Upon your walls, O Jerusalem,
I have set watchmen,
Who shall never be silent
By day or by night.
O you, the LORD's remembrancers,[b]
Take no rest
7 And give no rest to Him,
Until He establish Jerusalem
And make her renowned on earth.

8 The LORD has sworn by His right hand,
By His mighty arm:
Nevermore will I give your new grain

62.2–6: The prophet addresses Jerusalem and informs her of the reversal of her sad plight. **6–7:** The postexilic setting is crucial for understanding these vv. The full redemption predicted for Zion has not yet arrived, even though some exiles have returned. Therefore the watchmen remind God that Jerusalem still awaits aid, for the city is not yet firmly established.

8–12: God addresses Zion. Responding to the prophet's entreaties in vv. 6–7, God speaks directly to Zion. The LORD confirms the prophet's words, assuring the city that redemption will indeed come. **8–9:** Those who farm will enjoy the fruit of their own labor. Contrast Deut. 28.30–34.

a-a Change of vocalization yields "He who rebuilds you."
b I.e., the watchmen just mentioned.

10: The road is for the use not only of Judeans who remain in exile but also for the divine Presence (v. 11). Cf. 40.3; 49.11. *Raise an ensign* or flag to guide the exiles back to the land of Israel.

63.1–6: The divine warrior. A short and disturbing passage concerning divine vengeance against God's enemies, symbolized especially by the Edomites. This passage is closely connected with ch 34, which also belongs to the Deutero-Isaianic collection; there, too, the prophet predicted a great slaughter in the land of Edom. On the Edomites and the background of this ch, see 34.1–17 n. **1:** God comes from the south, covered with the blood of enemies. A speaker (perhaps the prophet, perhaps the inhabitants or watchmen of Jerusalem) notices a figure approaching from the south and asks who it is; God replies in the second half of the v. *Edom* is the land southeast of Judah. *Bozrah* is a city in Edom. **2–6:** The speaker asks another question, and God gives a lengthier response.

To your enemies for food,
Nor shall foreigners drink the new wine
For which you have labored.
9 But those who harvest it shall eat it
And give praise to the LORD;
And those who gather it shall drink it
In My sacred courts.
10 Pass through, pass through the gates!
Clear the road for the people;
Build up, build up the highway,
Remove the rocks!
Raise an ensign over the peoples!
11 See, the LORD has proclaimed
To the end of the earth:
Announce to Fair Zion,
Your Deliverer is coming!
See, his reward is with Him,
His recompense before Him.[a]
12 And they shall be called, "The Holy People,
The Redeemed of the LORD,"
And you shall be called, "Sought Out,
A City Not Forsaken."

63 Who is this coming from Edom,
In crimsoned garments from Bozrah—
Who is this, majestic in attire,
[b-]Pressing forward[-b] in His great might?
"It is I, who contend victoriously,
Powerful to [c-]give triumph."[-c]

2 Why is your clothing so red,
Your garments like his who treads grapes?[d]
3 "I trod out a vintage alone;
[e-]Of the peoples[-e] no man was with Me.
I trod them down in My anger,
Trampled them in My rage;
Their life-blood[f] bespattered My garments,
And all My clothing was stained.
4 For I had planned a day of vengeance,
And My year of redemption arrived.
5 Then I looked, but there was none to help;
I stared, but there was none to aid—
So My own arm wrought the triumph,

a *See note at 40.10.* *b-b* *Meaning of Heb. uncertain; emendation yields "striding."*
c-c *Change of vocalization yields "Who contest triumphantly"; cf. 19.20.*
d *Lit. "in a press."* *e-e* *Emendation yields "Peoples, and ..."*
f *Meaning of Heb. uncertain.*

And [a-]My own rage[-a] was My aid.
6 I trampled peoples in My anger,
[b-]I made them drunk with[-b] My rage,
And I hurled their glory to the ground."

7 I will recount the kind acts of the LORD,
The praises of the LORD—
For all that the LORD has wrought for us,
The vast bounty to the House of Israel
That He bestowed upon them
According to His mercy and His great kindness.
8 He thought: Surely they are My people,
Children who will not play false.
[c-]So He was their Deliverer.
9 In all their troubles He was troubled,
And the angel of His Presence delivered them.[-c]
In His love and pity
He Himself redeemed them,
Raised them, and exalted them
All the days of old.
10 But they rebelled, and grieved
His holy spirit;
Then He became their enemy,
And Himself made war against them.
11 Then they[d] remembered the ancient days,
[e-]Him, who pulled His people[-e] out [of the water]:
"Where is He who brought them up from the Sea
Along with the shepherd[f] of His flock?
Where is He who put
In their midst His holy spirit,
12 Who made His glorious arm
March at the right hand of Moses,
Who divided the waters before them
To make Himself a name for all time,
13 Who led them through the deeps
So that they did not stumble—
As a horse in a desert,
14 Like a beast descending to the plain?"
'Twas the spirit of the LORD [g-]gave them rest;[-g]

a-a *Many mss. read* weṣidqathi *"My victorious [right hand]"; cf. 59.16.*
b-b *Many mss. and Targum read "I shattered them in"; cf. 14.25.*
c-c *Ancient versions read "So He was their Deliverer / [9]In all their troubles. / No* [*so* kethib] *angel or messenger, / His own Presence delivered them." Cf. Deut. 4.37 and note.* d *Heb. "he."*
e-e *Heb.* moshe ʿammo, *a play on the name Moshe (Moses).*
f *So many mss. and ancient versions; other texts "shepherds."*
g-g *Emendation yields "guided them."*

63.7–64.11: A psalm of lament. A communal complaint, this text is spoken by the nation and addressed to God; it may also include lines spoken by God in response, which is a typical feature of a lament. The lament follows the pattern of similar prayers found in the book of Psalms (e.g., 3, 6, 13, 44). The presence of a psalm in prophetic literature is not unusual; see Isa. 33.1–9; Jonah ch 2. As is normal in laments, the description of the nation's current plight and the request for help are preceded by a review of God's mighty acts in the past. Deutero-Isaiah may have composed this prayer, or the prophet may have included (and perhaps modified) a psalm already in use.

63.7–14: God's mighty acts recalled. Before outlining the complaint and the request for divine aid, the prayer calls God's kind deeds to mind. It is because God acted successfully and graciously in the past that the nation expects that God will intervene now. These vv. at once bolster the Judeans' confidence and goad the LORD to live up to the divine reputation. **9:** As rendered in the NJPS, this v. reflects an important tendency of Deutero-Isaiah's theology: God participates in the suffering of the nation. Cf. 57.15. But many regard the translation in translators' note *c-c* as more accurate. **10:** Here again the prophet mentions God's pain. **11:** *They* (Heb "he") *remembered:* The subject of this verb is not clear: "He" may refer to God or to the nation as a collective. It is also possible to translate, "He who pulled his people out [of the water] remembered the ancient days," but even then it is not clear whether "He who pulled ..." refers to God or to Moses. *Where is He who brought ... :* The identity of the speaker here through v. 14a is not clear. Perhaps the Judeans speak, wondering where their savior is (so most rabbinic commentators). Alternatively, God may ask these questions, as if saying, "Long ago I saved Israel—whatever became of that side of Me?" In that case, vv. 11b–14 mark the beginning of God's movement from wrath to grace. *Along with,*

Thus did You shepherd Your people
To win for Yourself a glorious name.

15 Look down from heaven and see,
From Your holy and glorious height!
Where is Your zeal, Your power?
Your yearning and Your love
Are being withheld from us![a]
16 Surely You are our Father:
Though Abraham regard us not,
And Israel recognize us not,
You, O LORD, are our Father;
From of old, Your name is "Our Redeemer."
17 Why, LORD, do You make us stray from Your ways,
And turn our hearts away from revering You?
Relent for the sake of Your servants,
The tribes that are Your very own!
18 Our foes have trampled Your Sanctuary,
Which Your holy people [b-]possessed but
a little while.[-b]
19 We have become as a people You never ruled,
To which Your name was never attached.

If You would but tear open the heavens and
come down,
64 So that mountains would quake before You—
[c]As when fire kindles brushwood,
And fire makes water boil—
To make Your name known to Your adversaries
So that nations will tremble at Your Presence,
2 When You did wonders we dared not hope for,
You came down
And mountains quaked before You.
3 Such things had never been heard or noted.
No eye has seen [them], O God, but You,
Who act for those who trust in You.[d]
4 Yet you have struck him who would gladly do justice,
And remember You in Your ways.
It is because You are angry that we have sinned;
[e-]We have been steeped in them from of old,
And can we be saved?[-e]
5 We have all become like an unclean thing,
And all our virtues like a filthy rag.

a Heb. "me." Emendation yields "[Where are] Your yearning and Your love? / Let them not be restrained!" *b-b Meaning of Heb. uncertain.*
c Meaning of vv. 1–4 uncertain. *d Heb. "Him."*
e-e Emendation yields "Because You have hidden Yourself we have offended." For the thought cf. 63.17.

alternatively, "Specifically." *Shepherd of His flock:* The flock is the nation Israel; the shepherd is either Moses or God. (If the translation "shepherds" found in translators' note *f* is correct, then this word refers to Moses and Aaron and perhaps also to Miriam.)

63.15–64.11: Complaint and request for help. Having expressed confidence in God's ability to save, the speaker now calls out for God's attention (63.15; 64.8), describes their current lamentable state (63.18–19a; 64.8–10), and requests divine intervention (63.19b–64.1; 64.8; 64.11). The combination of these four elements is very common in psalms of lament; see 33.2–9 n. **63.16:** *Israel:* Here this name refers not to the nation as a whole but to the patriarch Jacob; see Gen. 32.29; 35.9. **63.17–64.4:** These vv. are remarkable and rather daring for their assertion that God, too, must accept some responsibility for the Judeans' sins. Their continuing hardships have worn away their hope (so Radak). If the LORD would intervene more quickly on their behalf, they would have clear reason to abandon their misdeeds and adopt a firm belief in God's authority. God's response to the nation's sins has created a cycle: Crime leads to punishment, punishment to disbelief, disbelief to more crime. Some rabbinic commentators reject this interpretation, however, arguing that only Israel is responsible for its sins, and that these vv. do not attribute responsibility to God. **63.18:** As this v. indicates, the surrounding passage was written before the Temple was completed in 516 BCE (see also 64.9–10).

We are all withering like leaves,
And our iniquities, like a wind, carry us off.
6 Yet no one invokes Your name,
Rouses himself to cling to You.
For You have hidden Your face from us,
And [a]made us melt because of[a] our iniquities.
7 But now, O LORD, You are our Father;
We are the clay, and You are the Potter,
We are all the work of Your hands.
8 Be not implacably angry, O LORD,
Do not remember iniquity forever.
Oh, look down to Your people, to us all!
9 Your holy cities have become a desert:
Zion has become a desert,
Jerusalem a desolation.
10 Our holy Temple, our pride,
Where our fathers praised You,
Has been consumed by fire:
And all that was dear to us is ruined.
11 At such things will You restrain Yourself,
O LORD,
Will You stand idly by and let us suffer so
heavily?

65 [b]I responded to[b] those who did not ask,
I was at hand to those who did not seek Me;
I said, "Here I am, here I am,"
To a nation that did not invoke My name.
2 I constantly spread out My hands
To a disloyal people,
Who walk the way that is not good,
Following their own designs;
3 The people who provoke My anger,
Who continually, to My very face,
Sacrifice in gardens and burn incense on tiles;
4 Who sit inside tombs
And pass the night in secret places;
Who eat the flesh of swine,
With broth of unclean things in their bowls;
5 Who say, "Keep your distance! Don't come closer!
[c]For I would render you consecrated."[c]
Such things make My anger rage,
Like fire blazing all day long.

a-a Emendation yields "delivered us into the hands of ..."
b-b Lit. "I let Myself be inquired of ..."
c-c Taking qedashtikha *as equivalent to* qiddashtikha, *cf. Ezek. 44.19; others "For I am holier than thou."*

65.1–66.24: Blessing and doom. Earlier Deutero-Isaiah alluded to a distinction between faithful and sinful Judeans, intimating that the final act of salvation will benefit only the former; see 57.19–21, 59.1–21, and passages which contrast the ideal servant nation and the blind servant, such as 42.1–9, and 42.18–43.8. Here the prophet sharpens this distinction. The nation includes both those who patiently wait for the LORD's salvation and those who have taken up the worship of other deities in addition to or in place of the true God. The latter will suffer the sort of punishment often associated in the Bible with Assyrians, Babylonians, and Edomites. Conversely, the righteous from other nations will enjoy the privilege of worshipping at Zion.

65.1–16: The faithful and the apostates within Israel. The opening vv. set up the contrast at the heart of this unit by describing the behavior and fate of each group. **1–2:** God responds to the nation, even though it includes sinners, and even though it may not seek God. **1:** This initial v. seems to respond directly to the last v. of the previous ch. *Here I am,* Heb "hineni"; see 52.6 n. **2:** *Spread out My hands:* Normally, humans pray to God by spreading out their hands (Exod. 9.29, 33; 1 Kings 8.22, 38; Isa. 1.15), but here, in an extraordinary gesture, the LORD stretches hands out to human beings. Cf. 52.6 n.; 57.15 n.; 63.9 n. **3–5:** A description of pagan practices adopted by some Israelites. **4:** *Who sit inside tombs:* Worship of deceased ancestors was common among Canaanites, and the Bible often warns Israelites against any such rite. See Lev. 19.31; 20.6, 27; Deut. 18.11. In related rites among the Hittites and some inhabitants of Canaan, pigs were sacrificed to underworld deities or the gods of the dead; pig bones have in fact been found in tombs in Canaanite sites. Such practices explain why eating pork is mentioned specifically here, as opposed to other foods prohibited in biblical dietary law.

6–7: The punishment for these sins. **8–10:** The righteous remnant. Some Judeans reject the sins just described, and they will receive the promises of salvation. **10:** *Sharon,* the coastal plain from Jaffa to Haifa, a very fertile area marking the western extreme of the land of Israel. *Achor,* a valley near Jericho, a desolate area marking the land's eastern extreme. **11–16:** The prophet contrasts the fates of loyal and sinful Israelites.

6 See, this is recorded before Me;
I will not stand idly by, but will repay,
Deliver [a-]their[b] sins[-a] into their bosom,
7 And the sins of their fathers as well
—said the LORD—
For they made offerings upon the mountains
And affronted Me upon the hills.
I will count out their recompense in full,[c]
Into their bosoms.
8 Thus said the LORD:
As, when new wine is present in the cluster,
One says, "Don't destroy it; there's good in it,"
So will I do for the sake of My servants,
And not destroy everything.
9 I will bring forth offspring from Jacob,
From Judah heirs to My mountains;
My chosen ones shall take possession,
My servants shall dwell thereon.
10 Sharon[d] shall become a pasture for flocks,
And the Valley of Achor a place for cattle to
lie down,
For My people who seek Me.

11 But as for you who forsake the LORD,
Who ignore My holy mountain,
Who set a table for Luck[e]
And fill a mixing bowl for Destiny:[e]
12 I will destine you for the sword,
You will all kneel down, to be slaughtered—
Because, when I called, you did not answer,
When I spoke, you would not listen.
You did what I hold evil,
And chose what I do not want.

13 Assuredly, thus said the Lord GOD:
My servants shall eat, and you shall hunger;
My servants shall drink, and you shall thirst;
My servants shall rejoice, and you shall be shamed;
14 My servants shall shout in gladness,
And you shall cry out in anguish,
Howling in heartbreak.
15 You shall leave behind a name
By which My chosen ones shall curse:

a-a Brought up from v. 7 for clarity. *b Heb. "your."*

c Taking rishonah *as equivalent to* beroshah; *cf. Lev. 5.24; Jer. 16.18. Meaning of Heb. uncertain.*

d Emendation yields "Jeshimon," the bleak southeast corner of the Jordan Valley; cf. Num. 21.20; 23.8. *e Names of heathen deities.*

"So may the Lord GOD slay you!"
But His servants shall be given a
[a-]different name.[-a]
16 For whoever blesses himself in the land
Shall bless himself by the true God;
And whoever swears in the land
Shall swear by the true God.
The former troubles shall be forgotten,
Shall be hidden from My eyes.

17 For behold! I am creating
A new heaven and a new earth;
The former things shall not be remembered,
They shall never come to mind.
18 Be glad, then, and rejoice forever
In what I am creating.
For I shall create Jerusalem as a joy,
And her people as a delight;
19 And I will rejoice in Jerusalem
And delight in her people.
Never again shall be heard there
The sounds of weeping and wailing.
20 No more shall there be an infant or graybeard
Who does not live out his days.
He who dies at a hundred years
Shall be reckoned a youth,
And he who fails to reach a hundred
Shall be reckoned accursed.
21 They shall build houses and dwell in them,
They shall plant vineyards and enjoy their fruit.
22 They shall not build for others to dwell in,
Or plant for others to enjoy.
For the days of My people shall be
As long as the days of a tree,
My chosen ones shall outlive[b]
The work of their hands.
23 They shall not toil to no purpose;
They shall not bear children [c-]for terror,[-c]
But they shall be a people blessed by the LORD,
And their offspring shall remain with them.
24 Before they pray, I will answer;
While they are still speaking, I will respond.
25 The wolf and the lamb shall graze together,
And the lion shall eat straw like the ox,
And the serpent's food shall be earth.

a-a I.e., a name to be used in blessing. *b Lit. "wear out."*
c-c Emendation yields "in vain."

17–25: The renewal of creation. This passage recalls the initial prophecies of Deutero-Isaiah in its exuberant tone and literary style, but the nature of the prediction goes beyond those found in chs 40–48: The world itself will be transformed in the new age that God brings. **20–23:** While the new age will be one of extraordinary longevity, these vv. do not predict eternal life or the resurrection of the dead, in contrast to rabbinic notions of the messianic era. **24:** In 51.9–11 and chs 63–64, the people wondered whether God listens to their prayers. God answers this question here: In the future, God will answer prayers before the people even utter them. **25:** This v. quotes two lines from 11.6–9. In that passage First Isaiah predicted a new era ushered in by an ideal Davidic king, but Deutero-Isaiah leaves the human king out of this re-prediction. Cf. 42.1–9 n.; 55.3 n.; 60.1–22 n.

66.1–4: Temple and sacrifice. Deutero-Isaiah takes up an old prophetic theme. Although God commanded the nation to offer sacrifices, God does not need them. Neither generous attention to the Temple nor punctilious observance of cultic ritual grants Judeans license to sin. **1:** The Temple plays an important role in the prophet's thinking (see 44.28; 56.5–7; 64.10; 66.20). Nonetheless, the prophet recognizes that God hardly needs that particular building; the Temple exists for the sake of humanity, not for the benefit of God. Cf. 1 Kings 8.27. **2:** Cf. 57.15. **3:** This v. presents four lines in which a legitimate action is paired with an illegitimate one. The prophet condemns people who participate in legitimate or even sacred actions but also commit sins, whether by acting immorally toward other human beings or by practicing idolatrous rites in addition to worshipping the true God. The prophet fights not only outright apostasy but also pious hypocrisy. Cf. 1.10–20; 29.13; 58.1–14.

5–18a: Deliverance and destruction. In highly emotional tones, the prophet lashes out against those disloyal to the LORD and predicts vindication for the faithful. This section passes abruptly from one subject to the other. **5–6:** The fate of the foes. **5:** *Your kinsmen ... joy:* According to the NJPS, the enemies (who reject the LORD) mock the faithful, sarcastically saying, *"Let the LORD manifest His Presence...."* Another translation, which more closely follows the Heb cantillation (see 6.13 n.), reads, "Your brothers who hate you and reject you say [self-righteously], 'For my sake the LORD will manifest His Presence!' But we [the truly righteous] will see their joy discomfited." In this translation both groups, the prophets and the enemies, regard themselves as followers of the LORD, but the other group will be unmasked as hypocritical when the LORD appears. **7–14:** Jerusalem consoled. As in previous passages, Jerusalem is portrayed as a bereaved woman (see 49.14–26; 50.1–3; 51.23; 54.1–17;

In all My sacred mount[a]
Nothing evil or vile shall be done
—said the LORD.

66 Thus said the LORD:
The heaven is My throne
And the earth is My footstool:
Where could you build a house for Me,
What place could serve as My abode?
2 All this was made by My hand,
And thus it all came into being
—declares the LORD.

Yet to such a one I look:
To the poor and brokenhearted,
Who is concerned about My word.

3[b] As for those who slaughter oxen and slay humans,
Who sacrifice sheep and immolate[c] dogs,
Who present as oblation the blood of swine,
Who offer[d] incense and worship false gods—
Just as they have chosen their ways
And take pleasure in their abominations,
4 So will I choose to mock them,
To bring on them the very thing they dread.
For I called and none responded,
I spoke and none paid heed.
They did what I deem evil
And chose what I do not want.

5 Hear the word of the LORD,
You who are concerned about His word!
Your kinsmen who hate you,
Who spurn you because of Me,[e] are saying,
"Let the LORD manifest His Presence,
So that we may look upon your joy."
But theirs shall be the shame.
6 Hark, tumult from the city,
Thunder from the Temple!
It is the thunder of the LORD
As He deals retribution to His foes.

7 Before she labored, she was delivered;
Before her pangs came, she bore a son.

a *See note at 11.9.*
b *Vv. 3–4 refer to practitioners of idolatrous rites; cf. v. 17 and 57.5–8; 65.1–12.*
c *Lit. "break the necks of."*
d *Heb.* mazkir *refers to giving the "token portion"* ('azkarah); *cf. Lev. 2.2, etc.*
e *Lit. "My name."*

8 Who ever heard the like?
Who ever witnessed such events?
Can a land pass through travail
In a single day?
Or is a nation born
All at once?
Yet Zion travailed
And at once bore her children!
9 Shall I who bring on labor not bring
about birth?
—says the LORD.
Shall I who cause birth shut the womb?
—said your God.
10 Rejoice with Jerusalem and be glad for her,
All you who love her!
Join in her jubilation,
All you who mourned over her—
11 That you may suck from her breast
Consolation to the full,
That you may draw from her bosom[a]
Glory to your delight.

12 For thus said the LORD:
I will extend to her
Prosperity like a stream,
The wealth of nations
Like a wadi in flood;
And you shall drink of it.
You shall be carried on shoulders
And dandled upon knees.
13 As a mother comforts her son
So I will comfort you;
You shall find comfort in Jerusalem.
14 You shall see and your heart shall rejoice,
Your limbs shall flourish like grass.
The power of the LORD shall be revealed
In behalf of His servants;
But He shall rage against His foes.

15 See, the LORD is coming with fire—
His chariots are like a whirlwind—
To vent His anger in fury,
His rebuke in flaming fire.
16 For with fire will the LORD contend,
With His sword, against all flesh;
And many shall be the slain of the LORD.

a Cf. Akkadiam zīzu, *Arabic* zīzat, *"udder."*

chs 60–62). She will suddenly, without pain, bear children and become a bustling city, full of life. **11:** The Israelites, as Zion's children, take consolation from the city's breasts. **13:** The metaphor suddenly changes, and God is portrayed as the nation's mother. Cf. the feminine images of God in 42.13–14; 45.10; 49.14–15. **14b–18a:** Attention switches to the apostates within Israel, who will be punished rather than comforted.

17 Those who sanctify and purify themselves to enter the groves, [a]imitating one in the center,[a] eating the flesh of the swine, the reptile, and the mouse, shall one and all come to an end—declares the LORD. 18[b]For I [know] their deeds and purposes.

[The time] has come to gather all the nations and tongues; they shall come and behold My glory. 19 I will set a sign among them, and send from them survivors to the nations: to Tarshish, Pul, and Lud—that draw the bow—to Tubal, Javan, and the distant coasts, that have never heard My fame nor beheld My glory. They shall declare My glory among these nations. 20 And out of all the nations, said the LORD, they shall bring all your brothers on horses, in chariots and drays, on mules and dromedaries, to Jerusalem My holy mountain as an offering to the LORD—just as the Israelites bring an offering in a pure vessel to the House of the LORD. 21 And from them likewise I will take some to be [c]levitical priests,[c] said the LORD.

22 For as the new heaven and the new earth
Which I will make
Shall endure by My will
—declares the LORD—
So shall your seed and your name endure.
23 And new moon after new moon,
And sabbath after sabbath,
All flesh shall come to worship Me
—said the LORD.

24 They shall go out and gaze
On the corpses of the men who rebelled
against Me:
Their worms shall not die,

a-a Meaning of Heb. uncertain.
b Exact construction of this verse uncertain; for the insertions in brackets, cf. Kimhi.
c-c Some Heb. mss. read "priests and Levites."

17: Another description of pagan rites among the Israelites, or perhaps simply of the flouting of the dietary laws distinctive to the Israelites. If the former, these rites may be identical with the sacrifices to the dead or to underworld deities described in 65.3–6, parts of which, like the rites described here, took place in *groves* (the same terms is translated in 65.3 as *gardens*). See 65.4 n.

18b–21: Universal recognition of the LORD and the ingathering of exiles. All nations will come to know the one God and will travel to the Temple in Jerusalem. This passage repeats the prophecy of First Isaiah and Micah found in Isa. 2.1–4 and Mic. 4.1–4, though Deutero-Isaiah adds that the nations of the world will bring exiled Israelites back to the land of Israel. **18:** *Behold My glory,* or "My Presence." This line repeats a prediction with which Deutero-Isaiah began this collection; see 40.5. **19:** *Set a sign among them,* i.e., God will perform a miracle that will convince them that the LORD is the only true God. *Survivors,* i.e., of the disaster described in v. 15. *Tarshish,* possibly an area west of Gibraltar in Spain. *Pul,* possibly a scribal error for "Put," an area in Libya. *Lud, Tubal,* areas in Asia minor (present-day Turkey). *Javan,* Greece. **21:** *From them likewise ...* : This v. allows two interpretations: (1) members of these other nations, having recognized the true God, will serve as priests in Jerusalem (a radical departure from Num. ch 18, which limits the priesthood to descendants of Moses' brother Aaron); or (2) some of the exiled Israelites whom the nations bring back to the land of Israel will serve as priests alongside the priests who are already in Jerusalem. Cf. 61.5–6.

22–24: Reward and punishment. A final description of the fates awaiting those who accept the LORD and those who reject the LORD. The distinction between Judeans and non-Judeans is not mentioned here; the worshippers of the LORD in v. 23 include *all flesh,* not just Israelites; and *the men who rebelled* against God in v. 24 include Israelites, as the preceding two chs make clear. Thus the book ends on a highly universal note. **24:** After worshipping (vv. 22–23), the righteous will pass by the Valley (Heb "Gei") of Hinnom, immediately south of the Temple Mount, and there they will see the burning corpses of those who rebelled against God. Many medieval rabbinic commentators take this v. as a reference to Gehinnom or hell, where sinners suffer punishment forever (or, according to Tg., until the righteous take pity on them and ask that the punishment cease). It is not clear, however, that Deutero-Isaiah imagines the sinners as remaining cognizant or in any sense alive; rather, the eternal fire burns but does not consume their corpses as a sign to those who pass by. Nonetheless, the later Jewish belief of punishment after death in a location called

Nor their fire be quenched;
They shall be a horror
To all flesh.

And new moon after new moon,
And sabbath after sabbath,
All flesh shall come to worship Me
—said the LORD.

Gehinnom developed out of this v. On the idea of life after death in the Bible see 14.9–11 n.; 26.19 n.; Dan. 12.2–3 n. The connection in this v. between burning bodies and the Hinnom Valley may allude to the child sacrifices that had taken place there, which earlier biblical authors bitterly condemn; see 2 Kings 23.10; Jer. 7.30–34; 32.35; 2 Chron. 28.3; 33.6. *And new moon ... the LORD:* In Jewish practice, v. 23 is always printed again after v. 24, so that the book ends on a positive note. Cf. the end of Mal., Eccl., and Lam. Because the new moon and the sabbath are mentioned together in v. 23, this ch is read as the haftarah when Rosh Ḥodesh (the beginning of the month) occurs on a Sabbath.

ירמיה

Jeremiah

THE BOOK OF JEREMIAH is the second book of the latter prophets, following Isaiah and preceding Ezekiel. Rabbinic literature, however, reflects a different order: Kings, Jeremiah, Ezekiel, and Isaiah, based on the principle of "approximating destruction to destruction and consolation to consolation" (*b. B. Bat.* 14b). According to this tradition, the book of Kings ends with destruction and Jeremiah is entirely focused on destruction, Ezekiel starts with the destruction and moves to consolation, and Isaiah is entirely focused on consolation.

Jeremiah is, however, about much more than destruction. Written in poetry and prose, it contains different genres and themes: prophecies of judgment to Israel (most of chs 1–25), and judgment prophecies to the nations (chs 46–51), prophecies of consolation to Israel (chs 30–33), disputations (such as 32.36–41), covenant speeches (as in 7.1–15; 11.1–14; etc.), symbolic actions (13.1–9; 18.1–12), prophetic visions (as in 25.15–29), prose sermons (as in 34.8–22), poetic individual and communal laments (chs 11–20), and also biographical stories about the prophet and his activity (chs 26–37; 40–44), and historiographical reports that are similar to Kings (chs 39; 52). Like other prophetic literature, this collection was written down by various authors over time. The book purports to present the prophet's words that were collected, transmitted orally, and preserved in written form by his followers (called also "disciples," "tradents") within the prophet's life and beyond, in both Judah and Babylonia.

The interpretation proffered here assumes that most of the book contains the prophecies of Jeremiah. The prophet from Anathoth (1.1) is said to have started his prophetic mission by 627 BCE, and continued probably until the late eighties of the 6th c. BCE. This dramatic period of over forty years had seen the fall of the Neo-Assyrian empire, a short period of Egyptian control, and the Neo-Babylonian regime turning Judah into a vassal state. The Babylonians besieged Jerusalem twice, and led large parts of its population into exile in several deportations (597, 586, 582 BCE). In its evolution over the 6th c. BCE, the book of Jeremiah reflects unprecedented theological crises in face of the loss of political independence and of the final fall and destruction of Jerusalem and the Kingdom of Judah (588–586 BCE). These events shook the most central conceptions of Israelite religion, particularly challenging the role of God in the destruction and in its aftermath, divine justice, and the divine covenant with Israel. Along with changes in theology, the national-religious identity of the Judeans as the people of God (in Judah and in Babylon) was also refashioned. This period, including the prophet's activity and two or three generations of his followers, with its rapid changes from destruction and exile to the early period of restoration, raised questions of survival and of continuity, brought the re-evaluation of the basic theological and ideological concepts, and reformulated them under harsh circumstances. Hence, Jeremiah, the prophet and his book, reflect the theological, social, and ideological conflicts that Judean society experienced and survived over the 6th c. BCE. Jeremiah was not only a prophet of destruction; he also played a significant role in creating hope for those he considered to be the remnant of Judah. Jeremiah and his book had a remarkable role in building bridges from destruction to restoration.

The annotations that follow focus on five major topics in Jeremiah.

The Prophet in His Place

THE BOOK OF JEREMIAH includes many more biographical details about the prophet than any other prophetic book (though our knowledge of his private life is still very limited). He was a priest, from Anathoth, 5 km (3 mi) northeast of Jerusalem (a Levitical town according to Josh. 21.18; 1 Chron. 6.60). The Anathoth area, the narrow geographical belt between the central Jerusalem-Benjamin mountains and the border of the Judean Desert, plays a significant role in Jeremiah's prophecies; desert images (plants, animals, water sources, and landscape) inform much of his metaphorical language.

The Prophet and His Book in Their Social Contexts of the 6th Century BCE Judean Society(ies)

THE IDENTIFICATION OF JEREMIAH as "of the priests of Anathoth" (1.1) led early commentators to assume that he was a descendant of the Elide priest Abiathar, expelled by King Solomon from Jerusalem to Anathoth (1 Kings 2.26–27; see also 1 Sam. chs 22–23; 2 Sam. 8.17; 1 Kings ch 1). This biographical note suggests that, in contrast to Ezekiel, his younger, contemporary prophet, Jeremiah was not of the mainstream, aristocratic priestly family branch of Jerusalem. Nevertheless, the prophet was active in Jerusalem, supported by the Shaphanide family of royal scribes (chs 26; 29; 40–41), and in constant contact with the kings and the royal courts of Jehoiakim and Zedekiah over the last two decades of Jerusalem and after its destruction (chs 21–23; 26; 36; 37–38).

Jeremiah is famous for his struggles with his contemporaries. No other prophet is recorded as having suffered such conflicts with his hometown fellows (as in 11.18–23), and having debated with officials, priests, and prophets in Jerusalem (chs 26; 36–39; cf. Amos 7.10–17). More than any other prophet, Jeremiah quotes (or puts words into the mouths of) his contemporaries: kings, officials, peace prophets, priests, and anonymously the "people." Jeremiah's theological view was very close to the historiographical Deuteronomistic circle, and he constantly refutes perspectives we recognize as held by poets and the people he quotes. Thus, he remains at the mainstream of the Judean worldviews.

Society and ideology are further intertwined on another cluster of questions. What was Jeremiah's initial ideological orientation, and who were the prophet's "followers" in both Judah and in Babylonia? Did they all belong to one specific authorial circle? Was the prophet himself a member of the Deuteronomistic literary school? Or were only his "followers" members of that powerful authorial group, as so often assumed in the Jeremiah scholarship?

Finally, following the exile of Jehoiachin (597 BCE, 2 Kings 24.8–17), Jeremiah reveals his pro-land (or pro-Judean) position, and builds his theo-political conceptions when he was in Mizpah and subsequently in Egypt (chs 27–29; 40–44). These perspectives emerge in his prophecies of judgment and consolation that are aimed at the people who remained in Jerusalem under Zedekiah (32.6–15) and under Gedaliah (chs 40–43). Yet, the book of Jeremiah expresses also a diametrically opposite perspective, that supports those exiled with Jehoiachin, finding them to be the true people of God, the surviving remnant (ch 24; 29.16–20; 32.36–41). This internal contradiction suggests that two distinct circles of authors were involved in the evolution of the book of Jeremiah: the prophet and his Judean tradents versus Babylonian tradents (of the Jehoiachin exiles and the 586 exiles and their descendants).

It seems that the editors of Jeremiah, who were of the Babylonian exiles (or repatriates) not only collected the prophet's words, but also added prophecies of their own in his name. Therefore, the current form of the book of Jeremiah introduces Babylonian-exilic ideologies that are similar to the Deuteronomistic historiography of the last chs of Kings, to Ezekiel, and to Deutero-Isaiah.

The Intellectual World of Jeremiah

THE POETRY AND PROSE of the book of Jeremiah are acclaimed for their poetic-literary qualities. The writing is allusive, drawing on literary traditions and specific compositions now found in the Hebrew Bible; it also borrows genres and patterns, themes and conceptions, style, and phrases. Examples include traditions from the Torah (Pentateuch) (such as Jer. 4.23–28 and Gen. ch 1; Sodom in Jer. 5.1 and Gen. 18.23–32; Jacob in Jer. 9.3–5 and Gen. 25.26; 27.36; 31.7) as well as from the historiographical corpus (as in the reference to Shiloh and its destruction, Jer. 7.1–15, told at 1 Sam. ch 4, and otherwise mentioned in Ps. 78.59–64).

Jeremiah also uses legal traditions from the Torah, alluding to the law of theft of the Covenant Collection (Jer. 2.26; see Exod. 22.6–7, as possibly also to Prov. 6.30–31) and some of the divine epithets of Exod. 34.6–7 (see Jer. 32.18–19; 30.10–11). Laws and terminology from the Priestly material in the Torah are utilized more often than was previously recognized (as in Jer. 2.20–25 and Num. 5.11–31; Jer. 3.1–5 and Num. 35.33), and even more allusions may be from the Holiness Legislation (as in Jer. 2.2 and Lev. 22.14–16; Jer. 32.6–15 and Lev. 25.39–44). Most prevalent are allusions to Deuteronomy (as in Jer. 3.1–5 and Deut. 24.1–4; segments of the Decalogue in Jer. 7.9; including the Sabbath, 17.19–27; the rebellious son in Jer. 5.20–25 and Deut. 21.18–21). These legal allusions serve as major tools to admonish the people for breaching the covenant with God. Jeremiah cites exemplary sins from these legal references to accuse his contemporaries in Jerusalem and Judah of offending God by their infidelity. Oftentimes, the prophet brings together several legal traditions in one context, usually combining allusions to Holiness Code or Priestly sources with Deuteronomic laws and concepts (such as Jer. 2.2–3; 3.1–5; 34.8–22). The use of pentateuchal traditions (of Deuteronomy or Priestly sources) seems to characterize Jeremiah's prophecy. Just as this usage of legal traditions and concepts characterizes also the prophet's followers (e.g., the conception of exile in 16.14–15; 23.7–8, echoing exilic Deuteronomic conceptions found in Deut. 4.29–31; 30.1–10). Hence, it cannot be taken as a reliable marker to distinguish between levels of evolution within the book, and should not serve as a valid criterion to differentiate between the prophet and his followers.

Furthermore, Jeremiah utilizes more of the same allusive techniques when he invokes other segments of the biblical literature. He is familiar with early poetry (as in 46.8 alluding to Exod. 15.5, 10; and the many allusions to Deut. ch 32, such as Jer. 12.14 and Deut. 32.20), and with different genres within the psalmodic literature (individual laments, as in Jer. 12.1–4 with its possible allusions to both Pss. 1 and 5; or 139.1–2, 23–24; and communal laments brought in Jer. 14.7–9, 19–21).

Jeremiah is steeped in prophetic traditions. He is familiar with the genre of visions (1.11–12, 13–19; cf. Amos 7.1–9), symbolic actions (Jer. 13.1–11), and oracles against the nations (ch 48 concerning Moab; cf. Isa. chs 15 and 24; see Jer. 48.43 and Isa. 24.17; to Edom in Jer. 49.7–22 and Obad.), and various other prophetic genres. He ties himself to the prophetic tradition, mostly influenced by 8th c. prophets: possibly Hosea (as, for instance, in his use of the marital metaphor for the covenant between God and His people, in Hos. chs 1–2 and Jer. chs 2–3), Amos, and Micah (mentioned explicitly in Jer. 26.18); and to a different extent the book shows connections with other prophets of the Twelve. Jeremiah's "followers" contribute similarities to Ezekiel and to Deutero-Isaiah (as in Jer. 32.36–41).

Finally, Jeremiah utilizes wisdom literature as well, referring specifically to Proverbs (as in Jer. 9.3 and Prov. 11.13; 20.19, conflated with allusion to Lev. 19.16); and Job (as in Jer. 12.1 and Job 9.32; 13.18; etc.), alluding to specific sayings, but more so bringing into his prophecies wisdom conceptions.

Jeremiah (and possibly his "followers" as well) uses all these diverse biblical materials in a free fashion. The prophet coins his own Jeremian phraseology which is clearly influenced by his sources, yet idiosyncratic. He borrows, transforms, expands, or specifies, analogizes or reverses the materials at hand to shape his message in the most efficient way.

Theology

THE BOOK OF JEREMIAH contains the prophet's ad hoc reactions addressing the theological challenges through four decades, and further retrospective reactions that may be connected to his "followers" later on within the exilic period and the early Persian period, in both Judah (then Yehud) and in Babylonia. This complex literary and theological growth of the book explains the polyphonic nature of its prophetic proclamations, although even the prophet himself did not have a consistent position on the theological issues at stake.

Jeremiah believes that God has sent him, and he dramatically fights his contemporaries (and at times even himself) to justify God in His harsh judgment against His city, His house, His kingdom and the Davidic kings, His people, and His land. Although he rarely explicitly calls God "king," he constantly treats God as king in his anthropomorphic metaphoric imagery and language. YHVH the God of Israel appears as the great Sovereign King who controls the entire world, overpowering even the Babylonian emperor (27.1–8). The metaphor of God as King governs the prophet's descriptions of God's roles on the different events.

God as King subsumes within it the divine role of warrior, and as such He may be either a foe or a savior; both options are used by Jeremiah. In judgment prophecies, God is the true Foe of His people, thus minimizing the role of the Babylonian king (21.1–7). The prophet interchangeably describes the roles of God in the destruction as a sole warrior (as in 15.5–9), or as the One that summons human foes (as in 25.15–29). In consolation prophecies, God's skills as warrior are just as omnipotent, when He is His people's sole savior (as in 30.8–9).

As King, God plays the role of judge (11.20; 12.1; see 32.18–19), and the prophet is compelled to justify His judgment over Judah (as in 2.35; or the *riv* pattern, see 2.4–13 nn.) and over the nations (as in 25.31). The issue of the divine justice in this time of destruction is unusually complex, comprised of the following issues:

(1) Jeremiah invested great energy to explain why God inflicted punishment on Judah. He needed to substantiate the people's guilt, opposing the voices that claimed innocence (such as 2.23, 35; and see Ps. 44.18). Jeremiah demonstrates the people's misconduct in various ways, mostly by alluding to pentateuchal legal traditions (see above), and by proclaiming lists of sins to prove the people's guilt (as in Jer. 1.16).

(2) The struggle to justify God's actions against Judah leads the prophet to emphasize repeatedly that the destruction was the deserved judgment, following the principle of "measure-for-measure" (as in 14.15–16; 16.10–13; 28.15–16). An exceptional perspective is proclaimed in 16.16–18: "I will pay them in full—/ Nay, doubly for their iniquity and their sins—" (and see 17.18).

Following the traditional retribution concept, as illustrated in God's epithet "visiting the guilt of the parents upon the children, upon the third and upon the fourth generations" (Exod. 20.5), the prophet addresses another question: Did this specific generation that suffered the destruction deserve its judgment? Protests against this were recorded, for instance, in the same quotation brought by Ezekiel (Ezek. 18.2) and Jeremiah (31.29; and see Lam. 5.7). Jeremiah suggests different answers. First, the current generation has followed the steps of their fathers, and thus is responsible for its own fate (as in 11.6–8); second, the present generation has surpassed earlier generations in its sins, thus they clearly deserved punishment (as in 7.26; 16.12); third, the destruction is an immediate judgment brought upon this specific generation for its own sins. This immediate (and collective) retribution stands against the concept of transgenerational retribution. Like Ezekiel (though not in that schematic way Ezekiel suggested in Ezek. ch 18), Jeremiah is also familiar with the individual and immediate retribution (17.9–10; 32.19). Jeremiah detaches the fathers' sins from their sons' retribution, and he even allows the change of behavior by this generation and the subsequent immediate change in their fate (as in 3.12; 4.3–4).

The third major role of God as King is His role as LORD of His people. As such, God is the initiator of the covenant with His people, and His Presence, care, and involvement (the components of what is later called "providence") are put into question during the period of the destruction and in its aftermath. Jeremiah uses two interchangeable covenant metaphors: the political sovereign-vassal metaphor and the familial metaphors of adoption and marriage (where God is portrayed as father or husband). The two metaphors are used in different contexts. The political metaphor serves to explain the judgment as the deserved punishment inflicted upon a rebellious people. This same metaphor of God as the sovereign King is the basis for reinstituting the covenant in the days to come as "a new covenant" (31.31–34). The marital metaphor (chs 2–3), on the other hand, is used to present the calamitous end of the relationship between God and the people. The disobedient people is sentenced to total annihilation, with no hope of restoration, like the adulteress woman (2.20–25; 3.1–5; contrast Hos. ch 2). Future consolation is portrayed only through the adoption metaphor of God as Father (Jer. 31.6–8, 19).

Composition and Transmission

IT IS UNCERTAIN AND DEBATED how this literarily rich book was collected and ordered. In its overall order, the book divides into three large units: chs 1–24, 25–45, and 46–51, with ch 1 as an introduction, ch 25 as a bridge between the first two units, and ch 52 as an appendix. This formal division, however, only partially reveals the actual structure and internal order of the prophecies within each of these three units. While each unit accords with the three elements in other prophetic books: prophecies of judgment against Judah (chs 1–24), prophecies of consolation to Israel and Judah (chs 30–33), and prophecies against the nations (chs 46–51); there are additional smaller collections or independent prophecies that show this schematic division. Genre, content, theme and chronological superscripts in places help determine the placement of smaller or larger units within Jeremiah. Three units in the book are possibly arranged chronologically (chs 27–29; 32–34; 35–44), while other segments in the book seem to be compiled by theme or literary proximation (chs 21–22, for the kings of the House of Judah; 23.9–40, for the prophets; chs 30–31, the book of consolation; chs 36–44, biographical [and historiographical] chapters; chs 46–51, prophecies against the nations). This lack of clarity in the internal order of the prophecies is found in most of the larger prophetic books. (Ezek., which is largely arranged chronologically, is an exception.)

Jeremiah ch 36 tells of the divine command to write down God's words spoken to the prophet over two decades. Hence, the first scroll was a prophetic writing of judgment prophecies to Israel, to Judah, and to the nations (36.2). The ch highlights the divine motivation to warn the people and allow them to change their ways, so that God may refrain from bringing the judgment He threatened (v. 3). As King Jehoiakim burnt this initial scroll, the prophet got a second command to take another scroll, and dictate it all to Baruch, his scribe, for the second time. This second scroll now contained all that was written on the first, with many more things added to the latter (v. 32). Hence, this story suggests Jeremiah's personal involvement in the initial collection and transmission of his own prophecies, at least to the very last years of the 7th c. BCE.

The book seems to have gained its overall shape in Babylonia by Deuteronomistic tradents, who among other things have set the book's chronological frame through its opening and the closing chs. Jeremiah ch 52 (like 2 Kings ch 25) closes with the release of Jehoiachin, which not only supplies the date (561 BCE), but reveals that the editors who gave the book its current shape accepted the Babylonian exilic ideology. This explains why other prophecies in the book support the Jehoiachin exiles; evidence suggests that these prophecies were products of anonymous exiles in Babylonia (ch 24; 32.36–41). We do not know how Jeremiah's scrolls or materials arrived in Babylonia or how they were completed by the repatriates in Yehud by the early Persian period.

The Greek translation (the Septuagint [LXX]) of Jeremiah was produced in Alexandria, Egypt by the 2nd c. BCE; it is recognized already in 116 BCE (by Ben-Sirach's grandson). That translation represents a collation of the work of at least two translators (chs 1–28; 29–52, in the LXX's order). The LXX orders the chs differently from the Masoretic Text (MT) (the prophecies against the nations are located after 25.13, and not at the end of the book, chs 46–51), and lacks phrases, verses, or full passages found in the standard Hebrew version (see e.g., 33.14–26; 39.4–13; 52.2–3, 15, 28–30). As a consequence, the LXX version of Jeremiah is almost one-sixth shorter than the MT.

Jeremiah scholarship has long been divided over the relationship between these two texts. The majority of scholars think the LXX reflects an earlier, more original, more reliable Hebrew text and the MT a later, secondary, and elaborative revision of it. They assume that the LXX and the MT reflect two different Hebrew revisions of the same book of Jeremiah from the late Persian period, a shorter one and a longer one. The shorter version was the text used by the Greek translators in Alexandria, while the longer one continued its literary development until (at least) the 4th c. BCE (and possibly later), and subsequently was accepted by the mainstream Jewish scribes as the official MT. Over the last two decades, however, a growing number of scholars have concluded that the LXX is a secondary shortening of a longer Hebrew text, close to the MT. Another theory, bolstered by one of the Dead Sea Scrolls ($4QJer^b$), suggests that the two versions or recensions reflect two different independent ancient texts, neither of which should be considered superior.

The following annotations, based on the longer Masoretic version translated here, accepts the independence of each of the textual versions of Jeremiah. Some textual variants in the LXX will be highlighted.

[DALIT ROM-SHILONI]

1 The words of Jeremiah son of Hilkiah, one of the priests at
Anathoth in the territory of Benjamin. 2 The word of the
LORD came to him in the days of King Josiah son of Amon of
Judah, in the thirteenth year of his reign, 3 and throughout the
days of King Jehoiakim son of Josiah of Judah, and until the
end of the eleventh year of King Zedekiah son of Josiah of Judah, when Jerusalem went into exile in the fifth month.

4 The word of the LORD came to me:

5 Before I created you in the womb, I selected you;
Before you were born, I consecrated you;
I appointed you a prophet concerning the nations.

6 I replied:
Ah, Lord GOD!
I don't know how to speak,
For I am still a boy.
7 And the LORD said to me:
Do not say, "I am still a boy,"
But go wherever I send you
And speak whatever I command you.
8 Have no fear of them,
For I am with you to deliver you
—declares the LORD.

9 The LORD put out His hand and touched my mouth, and
the LORD said to me: Herewith I put My words into your mouth.

1.1–19: Superscription and commissioning prophecy. Jer. 1.1–2.3 and 2.4–28; 3.4 (or 4.1–2) serve as the first two of the three haftarot of rebuke prior to the Ninth of Av, which commemorates the destruction of the Jerusalem Temple. In addition, Sephardic communities read 1.1–2.3 as the haftarah for Shemot (Exod. 1.1–6.1) because Moses and Jeremiah are the two prophets who initially refuse the divine call. **1–3:** The superscription resembles those introducing the prophetic books of Isa., Ezek., Hos., Amos, Mic., Zeph., Hag., and Zech. Jeremiah's superscription is, nevertheless, unique in its mention of his place of birth (cf. to only Amos 1.1) and his family affiliation. *Of the priests at Anathoth:* Jeremiah is not of the Jerusalem priesthood but from an excluded priestly family and from *the territory of Benjamin* (see intro.). **2–3:** The time span of Jeremiah's prophetic mission is dated precisely (cf. to Isa. 1.1; Hos. 1.1; Amos 1.1), from the thirteenth year of Josiah (627 BCE) until the fifth month (Av) of Zedekiah's eleventh year, the date of Jerusalem's destruction (586 BCE). Josiah and two of his sons Jehoiakim and Zedekiah are mentioned, while two other kings of Judah mentioned in Jeremiah's prophecies, are here omitted: Jehoahaz/Shallum (2 Kings. 23.31–35; Jer. 22.11–12) and Jehoiachin/Coniah (2 Kings 24.8–17; 25.27–30; Jer. 22.24–30; 52.31–34). The two reigned only three months each, and were captured and exiled, and their kingship was transferred to other descendants of Josiah (Jehoiakim and Zedekiah, respectively). The timeframe of the superscription is problematic, since few prophecies in Jer. may be dated to Josiah's reign, and the book contains biographical and prophetic materials past Av 586 BCE (chs 40–44). **4–19:** The prophet's commission presents him as God's messenger, and establishes Jeremiah's legitimacy as a true prophet of God in a time of abundant prophetic activity (see chs 23; 27–29; and Ezek. ch 13), though not all of his prophecies were fulfilled. It is constructed on the common pattern of calls to prophecy, also present in the call story of Moses (Exod. ch 3; cf. the judge Gideon, Judg. ch 6), Isaiah (Isa. ch 6), and Ezekiel (Ezek. 1.1–3.15). **4:** In contrast to these other prophetic call narratives, Jeremiah's commissioning lacks a vision, suggesting that Jeremiah only heard God's words (cf. Samuel in 1 Sam. ch 3). The prophetic formula, *The word of the LORD came to me* (vv. 4, 11, 13; and common in Jer.; see also 1 Sam. 14.10; 1 Kings 6.11; Ezek. 6.1; etc.), governs all the prophetic proclamations throughout the book, emphasizing that the message that the prophet delivers derives from God. The prophet is chosen before birth (otherwise typical of political leaders, such as Moses and Sargon of Akkad) and is sent to the widest audiences as *a prophet concerning the nations* (v. 5), and *over nations and kingdoms* (v. 10). More than other call narratives, this prophecy portrays Jeremiah as Moses. **6:** Like Moses, Jeremiah initially declines his prophetic assignment (cf. Exod. 3.11; 4.1, 10; and 6.12, 30). **7:** God, however, reaffirms the call and sends him, to go, and speak (see Exod. 3.10, 12; 4.11–12). Jeremiah's prophetic role follows the law of the prophet in Deut. 18.9–22, where Moses is the role-model. Jeremiah is instructed to speak all that he will be ordered to speak (alluding to Deut. 18.18). **8:** God promises protection, and strengthens the prophet in face of his opponents (see vv. 17–19; Exod. 3.12). **9:** The divine words are put into the prophet's mouth (Deut. 18.18), here graphically and even more graphically in Ezek. 3.1–3. Nevertheless, the prophet and God recognize that prophecy requires human rhetorical skills (vv. 6, 7).

10 See, I appoint you this day
Over nations and kingdoms:
To uproot and to pull down,
To destroy and to overthrow,
To build and to plant.

11 The word of the LORD came to me: What do you see, Jeremiah? I replied: I see a branch of an almond tree.[a]
12 The LORD said to me:
You have seen right,
For I am watchful[b] to bring My word to pass.

13 And the word of the LORD came to me a second time: What
do you see? I replied:
I see a steaming pot,
[c]Tipped away from the north.[-c]
14 And the LORD said to me:
From the north shall disaster break loose
Upon all the inhabitants of the land!
15 For I am summoning all the peoples
Of the kingdoms of the north
—declares the LORD.
They shall come, and shall each set up a throne
Before the gates of Jerusalem,
Against its walls roundabout,
And against all the towns of Judah.
16 And I will argue My case against them[d]
For all their wickedness:
They have forsaken Me
And sacrificed to other gods
And worshiped the works of their hands.

17 So you, gird up your loins,
Arise and speak to them
All that I command you.
Do not break down before them,
Lest I break you before them.
18 I make you this day
A fortified city,

a Heb. shaqed. *b Heb.* shoqed. *c-c Meaning of Heb. uncertain.*
d I.e., against Jerusalem and Judah.

10: The prophet's mission is characterized by six terms, four of destruction and two of restoration. These phrases recur in judgment proclamations (12.14–17; 18.5–10), and even more so in proclamations of consolation (24.6; 31.28, 40; 42.10; 45.4). **11–16:** Two symbolic visions. These visions are similar to the earlier symbolic visions in Amos (of the 8th c. BCE, see Amos 7.7–9; 8.1–14) and later in Zech. (late 6th c., Zech. chs 1; 4–5). Their interpretations are based on puns involving the name of the object seen. **11–12:** The staff or stick from an *almond tree* ("shaqed"), means that God is watching ("shoqed") for the opportunity to fulfill His (destructive) words. The verb "sh-q-d" stands for "to watch for an opportunity to act," or "to take advantage of and act immediately." **13–16:** The second vision, a pot steaming on a fire that gets its air supply from the north, enflaming the fire greatly (see Ezek. 22.21), plays on the idea of "north," the direction from which military disaster will arrive against Jerusalem. The threat of the north is both local and more distant; enemies approached Jerusalem from the north, since the city was protected by valleys to the east, south, and west, but most vulnerable to attacks from the north, and the enemy will come from the far north, from Mesopotamia via Aram, though the identity of this northern enemy is not specified until later in the book (25.9). **15:** The northern kingdoms summoned by God to Jerusalem form a coalition. The *thrones* of those northern kingdoms may symbolize laying siege over the city (see 39.3; see Kimḥi [Rabbi David Kimḥi, also known as RaDaK]). **16:** The subject is again the people of Judah, who are accused of rejecting God in favor of man-made objects (idols). In light of v. 16, the placing of thrones in front of the city gates in the previous v. may represent the foreign kings witnessing the divine trial against Jerusalem. In sum, the kings from the north, the imperial forces of the time, will witness the way God as sovereign judges His rebellious people, and they will help to execute the divine judgment. This symbolic vision encapsulates Jeremiah's conceptions of history and of war. **17–19:** Returning to the commissioning of vv. 11–12, and repeating the words of v. 8, this final component encourages the prophet to stand firm against his internal opponents, the kings of Judah, its officials, priests, and the entire people (see Ezek. 2.6; 3.8). **17:** *Gird up your loins,* partakes in the image of a warrior preparing for battle.

And an iron pillar,
And bronze walls
Against the whole land—
Against Judah's kings and officers,
And against its priests and citizens.[a]
19 They will attack you,
But they shall not overcome you;
For I am with you—declares the LORD—to save you.

2 The word of the LORD came to me, saying, 2 Go proclaim to
Jerusalem: Thus said the LORD:
I accounted to your favor
The devotion of your youth,
Your love as a bride—
How you followed Me in the wilderness,
In a land not sown.
3 Israel was holy to the LORD,
The first fruits of His harvest.
All who ate of it were held guilty;
Disaster befell them —declares the LORD.

4 Hear the word of the LORD, O House of Jacob,
Every clan of the House of Israel!
5 Thus said the LORD:
What wrong did your fathers find in Me
That they abandoned Me
And went after delusion and were deluded?

a Lit. "the people of the land."

2.1–10.25: Prophecies of judgment against Jerusalem and Judah. The first unit of Jer., constructed of the two symbolic visions (1.11–16), builds towards the gradual understanding that God aims to bring total destruction upon Judah as punishment for the people's stubborn disobedience and their consistent rejections of His call to repent. The following collection of independent prophecies seems to reflect Jeremiah's early career: A unique superscription ties a prophetic passage to the days of Josiah (3.6). Calls to repent are addressed to the Israelites of the former Northern Kingdom (3.12; 4.1). The political threat is as yet only a vague enemy "of the north" (4.5–7; 6.1, 22; 10.22; otherwise mentioned in 25.9, 26; and in reference to Egypt's judgment, 46.24; 47.2). Babylon will be first mentioned only in Jer. 20.4. Hence, this unit is likely from Jeremiah's first scroll, said to be written by 605 BCE (36.1–3); the additional materials (still relatively early) are part of the second scroll, written in 604 BCE (36.27–29, 32).

2.1–4.2: The relationship between God and the people is in jeopardy. Ch 2 uses two major metaphors to portray the crisis in the relationship between God and Judah. The ch divides into two parts (vv. 1–19, 20–37); each opens and closes (forming an "inclusio") with the marriage metaphor of God as a Husband and the people (and/or Jerusalem) as His wife (2.1–3, 17–19, and vv. 20–25, 33–37). It accentuates the great gap between the beginning of this marriage, at the time of the exodus, when God guided and cared for His people and they were faithful to Him (v. 2), and the relationship's rapid deterioration into infidelity (vv. 17, 20–22, 36–37). The second metaphor derived from the political sphere, which depicts God as Sovereign and the people as subservient vassals, is intertwined with the marriage metaphor, adding to the disappointment at the people's disloyalty and preference of other gods (2.4–9, 10–13, 14–16, 26–28, 29–32). Both metaphors are connected, representing different types of relationships between a superior party, here God, to whom the subservient party, here Israel, owes obedience. **2.1–3:** Treating the wilderness wanderings as an ideal bridal love illustrating the people's complete loyalty to God, is exceptional and contrasts sharply with the murmuring and the rebellious stories in Exod.–Num. (Exod. chs 15–16, etc.). The people's full confidence in God is further exemplified by the imagery of a flock led by a shepherd through the wilderness, another image important as this ch develops (vv. 6, 13, 31–32). **3:** The designation of the people *Israel* as *holy to* [/of] *the LORD,* draws an analogy to the priestly restrictions concerning eating sacred donations (e.g., Lev. 22.14–16). This designation is based on a Deuteronomic conception of Israel as holy (e.g., Deut. 7.6), and guarantees constant divine protection from enemies that will be held responsible for "consuming" Israel. This oracle, even though it depicts Israel positively, should not be seen as an oracle of consolation (these are found predominantly in chs 30–31), but as the background for the admonitions that follow. **4–9:** The people's abandonment of God is incomprehensible; their preference for *delusion,* preferring vain idols over the God whose great act in saving His people from *Egypt,* leading them *through the wilderness* (described by six phrases that stress its dryness and danger (v. 7; cf. v. 31), and bringing them to the good land, has been totally disregarded by the people (vv. 5–7) and also by society's leaders: the *priests,* who were the "torah" *guardians* (18.18), the leaders, and the *prophets* (v. 8). This disobedient behavior constitutes a breaking of the covenant and leads to the proclamation that God will initiate a lawsuit ("riv") against His people, the current generation and also their descendants (v. 9). The lawsuit (vv. 10–19) portrays God as both Advocate and Judge, first setting forth the accusation (vv. 10–13) and then the irrefutable judgment (vv. 14–19; see Isa. 1.2–4; Mic. 6.1–8). **7:** Serious moral sins defiled the land of Israel (see essay on "Concepts of Purity," pp. 1998–2005), making it unsuitable for habitation by Israel. **10–13:** No other nation has abandoned its gods as Israel abandoned God. Even though, in the prophet's view, those nations worship non-gods (called earlier, lit. "vain, futile, delusion" [v. 5] or "unhelpful, no good gods" [v. 8], "no-gods" [v. 11]), they remained faithful to them. **10:** *Kittim,* to the west, the islands of the Aegean. *Kedar,* to the east, in Transjordan. **11:** *But My people has exchanged its glory:* Israel's glory is God. *Its glory* is written instead of "my glory" (see also Hos. 4.7; Ps. 106.19–20), as a scribal correction; this is one of eighteen examples of "tiqqun soferim" (scribal corrections mentioned in *Sifre Zuta,* 12; *Tanḥ.* Exod. 15.7). "Kavod," *glory,* is used frequently in Priestly literature to refer to God's manifestation in the Temple (see e.g., Exod. 40.34–35). **13:** Another wilderness image, precious water sources. God is like a fountain *of living waters,* a natural water source (as for instance, Ein Perat, in Wadi Qelt, the closest water resource to Anathoth) but the other gods are like the man-made *cisterns* that gather seasonal-rain waters and tend to leak if their plaster cracks. Israel has wrongly chosen the inferior source of sustenance over the superior one. **14–16:** Another rhetorical question conveys Judah's prospective penalty: it will be given *to plunder* (v. 14), attacked by invaders who turn its land into total desolation (v. 15). Jeremiah in particular favors such rhetorical questions.

6 They never asked themselves, "Where is the LORD,
Who brought us up from the land of Egypt,
Who led us through the wilderness,
A land of deserts and pits,
A land of drought and darkness,
A land no man had traversed,
Where no human being had dwelt?"
7 I brought you to this country of farm land
To enjoy its fruit and its bounty;
But you came and defiled My land,
You made My possession abhorrent.
8 The priests never asked themselves,
"Where is the LORD?"
The guardians of the Teaching ignored Me;
The rulers[a] rebelled against Me,
And the prophets prophesied by Baal
And followed what can do no good.

9 Oh, I will go on accusing you
—declares the LORD—
And I will accuse your children's children!
10 Just cross over to the isles of the Kittim and look,
Send to Kedar and observe carefully;
See if aught like this has ever happened:
11 Has any nation changed its gods
Even though they are no-gods?
But My people has exchanged its glory
For what can do no good.
12 Be appalled, O heavens, at this;
Be horrified, utterly dazed! —says the LORD.
13 For My people have done a twofold wrong:
They have forsaken Me, the Fount of living waters,
And hewed them out cisterns, broken cisterns,
Which cannot even hold water.

14 Is Israel a bondman?
Is he a home-born slave?
Then why is he given over to plunder?
15 Lions have roared over him,
Have raised their cries.
They have made his land a waste,
His cities desolate, without inhabitants.
16 Those, too, in Noph and Tahpanhes[b]
[c]Will lay bare[c] your head.

a *Lit. "shepherds"; cf. 3.15; 23.1 ff.*
b *Cities in Egypt. The Egyptians, like the Assyrians, will prove a disappointment; cf. v. 36.*
c-c *Meaning of Heb. uncertain.*

17 See, [a-]that is the price you have paid
For forsaking the LORD your God[-a]
[b-]While He led you in the way.[-b]
18 What, then, is the good of your going to Egypt
To drink the waters of the Nile?
And what is the good of your going to Assyria
To drink the waters of the Euphrates?
19 Let your misfortune reprove you,
Let your afflictions rebuke you;
Mark well how bad and bitter it is
That you forsake the LORD your God,
That awe for Me is not in you
—declares the Lord GOD of Hosts.
20 For long ago you[c] broke your yoke,
Tore off your yoke-bands,
And said, "I will not work!"[d]
On every high hill and under every verdant tree,
You recline as a whore.
21 I planted you with noble vines,
All with choicest seed;
Alas, I find you changed
Into a base, an alien vine!
22 Though you wash with natron
And use much lye,
Your guilt is ingrained before Me
—declares the Lord GOD.
23 How can you say, "I am not defiled,
I have not gone after the Baalim"?
Look at your deeds in the Valley,[e]
Consider what you have done!
Like a lustful she-camel,
[b-]Restlessly running about,[-b]
24 Or like a wild ass used to the desert,
Snuffing the wind in her eagerness,
Whose passion none can restrain,
None that seek her need grow weary—
In her season, they'll find her!

25 Save your foot from going bare,
And your throat from thirst.
But you say, "It is no use.
No, I love the strangers,[f]
And after them I must go."

a-a *Lit. "that is what your forsaking the* LORD *your God is doing to you."*
b-b *Meaning of Heb. uncertain.*
c *For the form, cf.* shaqqamti, *Judg. 5.7; others "I."*
d *Following the* kethib; qere *"transgress."*
e *I.e., of Hinnom; cf. 7.31–32; 32.35.*
f *I.e., other gods.*

17–19: The marital metaphor intrudes on the political one. The image of walking after/on the way of (vv. 2, 6) is further developed here into admonishing the people for asking political assistance from the imperial forces of Egypt and Assyria, an image that also concludes the ch (v. 36). The two are the typological enemies of Judah, from the southwest and the northeast (see Isa. 7.18; 19.25; 52.4; Hos. 7.11; 9.3; 11.5; Zech. 10.10; Lam. 5.6).

2.20–25: The denunciation. The second half of the ch opens with the harsh accusation, for the first time in Jeremiah, that Israel is a whore. **20:** Infidelity is portrayed as a great betrayal of God, who had broken the people's *yoke* and *yoke-bands,* alluding to the paradigmatic salvation from Egypt. Yet the people did not accept God's sovereignty, saying in rebellion: *"I will not work!"* ("qere," "I will not transgress," see translators' note *d*), which suggests loyalty (see Tg., followed by Rashi and Kara). **21:** The prophet continues to express God's surprise at the people's ungrateful behavior (as already in vv. 4–9, 10–13). The image of Israel as a failed vineyard is developed more powerfully in the earlier Isa. 5.1–7. **22:** See the similar use of *wash*ing imagery in Isa. 1.16. **23–25:** The designation of the people as adulterous gains extra force from the allusion to the priestly trial of the suspected adulteress (*m. Sot.* 1.5, referring to Num. 5.5–31), referred to in v. 23, *I am not defiled* ("lo nitmeʾti," cf. Num. 5.13–14, 19–20, 27). The thematic allusion to going astray ("s-t-h" in Num. 5.12, 20) is further developed through the metaphor of the *she-camel* in sexual heat, that while *restlessly running about* is nevertheless sought and found by her lovers, and by various references to "walking" and to "path(s)" repeated in these vv. The third allusive marker is in the divine conclusion: "Your guilt is ingrained before Me" (v. 22; see Num. 5.31). This literary allusion emphasizes that while the people at first denied the suspicion/the accusation of infidelity (v. 23), their sin is exposed and they finally confess it and even cling willingly to it (v. 25). This unit then stands in diametrical opposition to the bridal love of v. 2.

2.26–28: Denunciation of the rulers. Turning to the political metaphor, the people as a whole, including their rulers of different types—kings, officials, priests, and prophets—are quoted as holding a syncretistic belief, worshipping man-made idols of wood and stone (see Deut. 4.28; 28.36, 64), but appealing to God in times of military distress (v. 27). The unit ends with a rhetorical exaggeration, suggesting that Israel has as many *gods* as *towns.*

2.29–37: Conclusion. Two rhetorical questions (vv. 31, 32), that utilize the imagery of the wilderness (v. 31) and of the people as a bride (v. 32), close the ch. The two metaphoric components of obedience in v. 2 have turned into symbols of disobedience. Yet the people still maintain their innocence (v. 35; see Num 5.22, 28). **31:** An ironic return to the image of the *desert,* here negative, building upon the initial image of the ch of God's beneficent care for Israel there. **32:** The conclusion picks up on the initial marital metaphor.

26 Like a thief chagrined when he is caught,
So is the House of Israel chagrined—
They, their kings, their officers,
And their priests and prophets.
27 They said to wood, "You are my father,"
To stone, "You gave birth to me,"
While to Me they turned their backs
And not their faces.
But in their hour of calamity they cry,
"Arise and save us!"
28 And where are those gods
You made for yourself?
Let them arise and save you, if they can,
In your hour of calamity.
For your gods have become, O Judah,
As many as your towns!
29 Why do you call Me to account?
You have all rebelled against Me
—declares the LORD.
30 To no purpose did I smite your children;
They would not accept correction.
Your sword has devoured your prophets
Like a ravening lion.
31 [a-]O generation, behold[-a] the word of the LORD!
Have I been like a desert to Israel,
Or like a land of deep gloom?
Then why do My people say, "We have broken loose,
We will not come to You any more?"
32 Can a maiden forget her jewels,
A bride her adornments?
Yet My people have forgotten Me—
Days without number.

33 How skillfully you plan your way
To seek out love!
Why, you have even taught
The worst of women your ways.
34 Moreover, on your garments is found
The lifeblood of the innocent poor—
You did not catch them breaking in.[b]
[a-]Yet, despite all these things,[-a]
35 You say, "I have been acquitted;
Surely, His anger has turned away from me."
Lo, I will bring you to judgment
For saying, "I have not sinned."

a-a Meaning of Heb. uncertain.

b In which case there might have been an excuse for killing them; cf. Exod. 22.1.

36 How you cheapen yourself,
By changing your course!
You shall be put to shame through Egypt,
Just as you were put to shame through Assyria.
37 From this way, too, you will come out
[a]With your hands on your head;[-a]
For the LORD has rejected those you trust,
You will not prosper with them.

3 [The word of the LORD came to me] as follows: If a man
divorces his wife, and she leaves him and marries another
man, can he ever go back to her? Would not such a land be
defiled?[b] Now you have whored with many lovers: can you return to Me?—says the LORD.

2 Look up to the bare heights, and see:
Where have they not lain with you?
You waited for them on the roadside
Like a bandit[c] in the wilderness.
And you defiled the land
With your whoring and your debauchery.
3 And when showers were withheld
And the late rains did not come,
You had the brazenness[d] of a street woman,
You refused to be ashamed.
4 Just now you called to Me, "Father!
You are the Companion of my youth.
5 Does one hate[e] for all time?
Does one rage[e] forever?"
That is how you spoke;
You did wrong, and [f]had your way.[-f]

6 The LORD said to me in the days of King Josiah: Have you
seen what Rebel Israel did, going to every high mountain and
under every leafy tree, and whoring there? 7 I thought: After
she has done all these things, she will come back to Me. But
she did not come back; and her sister, Faithless Judah, saw it.

a-a *A gesture of wild grief; cf. 2 Sam. 13.19.* b *Cf. Deut. 24.1–4.* c *Lit. "Arab."* d *Lit. "forehead."* e *Cf. Akkadian parallels* nadāru and shamāru. f-f *Meaning of Heb. uncertain.*

36: See vv. 17–19 n. **37:** God has rejected those the people trusted, and not the people themselves.

3.1–5: Irreversible divorce. The prophet paraphrases the Deuteronomic law of divorce (Deut. 24.1–4) as a precedent to the pivotal rhetorical question: *can he ever go back to her?* The Deuteronomic law is given additional force by the principle "from the minor to the major" ("qal vaḥomer"). The law speaks of one man, one woman, and her subsequent marriage to another, whereas the metaphorical situation projects the woman/people to have whored with *many lovers* (v. 1). As the law forbids the man to re-marry his former wife, how much more decisive it is in excluding the possibility that God will return to His people, that is, the woman who has been constantly and repeatedly disloyal to Him with many lovers. Using this civil-personal law, known to the prophet and to his audience, the prophet presents an extreme view of the God-Israel covenant relationship as irredeemable because of the woman's/the people's sins (cf. to Hos. 2.4–15, but see also vv. 16–24). Various shared phrases (e.g., "'ish 'et 'ishto" / "'ish 'isha"; "shilah, vehayta l'ish 'aher, shuv") make it clear that Jeremiah is alluding to this Deuteronomic law. This prophecy refutes the people's words (vv. 4–5), which express obedience to God by using familial metaphors of adoption and marriage (*Father! You are the Companion of my youth,* v. 4; see 2.23, 35). The prophet, however, considers these proclamations of faithfulness to be hypocritical and deceptive, in the face of the people's continuous disobedience to God.

3.6–4.2: Five responses. Here are five different reactions to the breakdown in relations between God and the people. Each (3.6–11, 12–13, 14–18, 19–25; 4.1–2) adds an independent response to 3.4–5 or to the prophet's insistence that the relationship between God and Israel is severed (vv. 1–5), returning to the marital metaphor introduced in ch 2. **3.6–11:** This prophetic proclamation is set in *the days of ... Josiah,* and follows the prophetic accusation of infidelity (vv. 6, 9, 10, in comparison to vv. 1b–2). This is the only prophecy in the book explicitly attributed to the time of *King Josiah* (see 1.2–3 n.); given the highly positive description of that king as a monotheistic reformer in 2 Kings chs 22–23, this negative prophecy is surprising, as there is a total absence of reference to Josiah's reforms. These vv. add *the bill of divorce* (v. 8; see Deut. 24.1, 3), which further enforces God's initiative in severing the relationship. Yet, in justifying God's seemingly harsh reaction, they

8 I noted: Because Rebel Israel had committed adultery, I cast her off and handed her a bill of divorce; yet her sister, Faithless Judah, was not afraid—she too went and whored. 9 Indeed, the land was defiled by her casual immorality, as she committed adultery with stone and with wood.[a] 10 And after all that, her sister, Faithless Judah, did not return to Me wholeheartedly, but insincerely—declares the LORD.

11 And the LORD said to me: Rebel Israel has shown herself more in the right than Faithless Judah. 12 Go, make this proclamation toward the north, and say: Turn back, O Rebel Israel—declares the LORD. I will not look on you in anger, for I am compassionate—declares the LORD; I do not bear a grudge for all time. 13 Only recognize your sin; for you have transgressed against the LORD your God, and scattered your favors[b] among strangers under every leafy tree, and you have not heeded Me—declares the LORD.

14 Turn back, rebellious children—declares the LORD. Since I have espoused[c] you, I will take you, one from a town and two from a clan, and bring you to Zion. 15 And I will give you shepherds[d] after My own heart, who will pasture you with knowledge and skill.

16 And when you increase and are fertile in the land, in those days—declares the LORD—men shall no longer speak of the Ark of the Covenant of the LORD, nor shall it come to mind. They shall not mention it, or miss it, or make another. 17 At that time, they shall call Jerusalem "Throne of the LORD," and all nations shall assemble there, in the name of the LORD, at Jerusalem. They[e] shall no longer follow the willfulness of their evil hearts. 18 In those days, the House of Judah shall go with the House of Israel; they shall come together from the land of the north to the land I gave your fathers as a possession.

19 I had resolved to adopt you as My child, and I gave you a desirable land—the fairest heritage of all the nations; and

a *She deserted her God for idols of stone and wood.* b *Lit. "ways."*
c *Meaning of Heb.* ba'alti *uncertain; compare 31.32.*
d *Meaning of Heb. uncertain.* e *I.e., Israel and Judah.*

introduce a previous call to repent, which contradicts the analogy drawn in 3.1 to the law of divorce; God is not bound by the laws He has given for Israel. (The same is true for the law of intergenerational punishment; contrast Deut. 5.9; 24.16.) Finally, this passage distinguishes between Israel and Judah, comparing the two sisters, and portraying Judah as even worse than her rebellious sister, who was exiled a century earlier (v. 11; such distinctions appear in 2 Kings 17.18–20; and within the marital metaphor, Ezek. 16.44–58, esp. v. 51; ch 23). **6:** "Meshuvah Israel" (NJPS: *Rebel Israel*): The root "shuv" appears seventeen times in 3.1–4.2 with "meshuvah" (vv. 6, 8, 11, 12, 22; already 2.19) and "shovavim" (vv. 14, 22) that are almost unique to Jer. While all occurrences draw on the basic meaning of "turn back" (as in Jer. 31.16; 42.12; 50.19), Jeremiah uses it to call for repentance (thus *come back to* [God], v. 7; 4.1), but also for turning away from God, (vv. 19–20; see 32.40), or to return and repeat evil and disobedience (11.10; with "meshuvah," 8.5; 14.7). He even brings together the two opposite uses of the root in the highly alliterative phrases "shuva meshuva Israel," *Turn back, O Rebel Israel* (v. 12), and "shuvu banim shovavim," *Turn back, rebellious children* (v. 14). Another cluster of "shuv" occurs in the consolations of chs 30–31. **12–13:** In response to the earlier question, lit. in Heb, "Shall He keep His hate/anger for all time?" (v. 5; NJPS: *Does one hate for all time?*), the prophet is commanded to call the Northern Kingdom of Israel to repent, for God promises not to afflict His people *for all time*, and characterizes Himself as "ḥasid" (exceptional in reference to God, see Ps. 145.17) *compassionate*, the one who activates "ḥesed," a key biblical theological term referring to God's beneficence toward Israel (see Exod. 34.6; Ps. 103.8–9). **14–18:** The *rebellious children* are called to repent, and consolation is promised in the return and reunification of the *House of Israel* and the *House of Judah* from their exile in *the land of the north* to Zion (vv. 14, 18), new leadership (v. 15), procreation in the land (v. 16), and transformation of the conceptions of the city as the locus of divine Presence (vv. 16b–17). **15:** *Shepherds,* may refer to kings; the image of the king as the people's shepherd is widespread in the ancient Near East, found already in Hammurabi, and widespread in the Bible (see e.g., 23.1–6). **16:** The *Ark of the Covenant,* constructed in the wilderness at the time of the exodus to hold the tablets of the covenant (Exod. 25.10–22; 37.1–9; Deut. 10.1–5; cf. Num. 10.35–36), symbolized divine Presence in Solomon's Temple (see 1 Kings 8.1–13; 2 Chron. 5.1–14). When the Temple was destroyed, no mention was made of the fate of the Ark (see 2 Kings ch 25; Jer. ch 52), suggesting that it had disappeared earlier, perhaps during the reign of Manasseh. According to 2 Macc. 2.1–8, Jeremiah hid the Ark in a cave

I thought you would surely call Me "Father," and never cease
to be loyal to Me. [20] Instead, you have broken faith with Me,
as a woman breaks faith with a paramour, O House of Israel—
declares the LORD.

21 Hark! On the bare heights is heard
The suppliant weeping of the people of Israel,
For they have gone a crooked way,
Ignoring the LORD their God.

22 Turn back, O rebellious children,
I will heal your afflictions!

"Here we are, we come to You,
For You, O LORD, are our God!
23 [a]Surely, futility comes from the hills,
Confusion from the mountains.[a]
Only through the LORD our God
Is there deliverance for Israel.
24 But the Shameful Thing[b] has consumed
The possessions of our fathers ever since our youth—
Their flocks and herds,
Their sons and daughters.
25 Let us lie down in our shame,
Let our disgrace cover us;
For we have sinned against the LORD our God,
We and our fathers from our youth to this day,
And we have not heeded the LORD our God."

4 If you return, O Israel —declares the LORD—
If you return to Me,
If you remove your abominations from My presence
And do not waver,
2 And [c]swear, "As the LORD lives,"[c]
In sincerity, justice, and righteousness—
Nations shall bless themselves by you[d]
And praise themselves by you.[d]

[3] For thus said the LORD to the men of Judah and to Jerusalem:

Break up the untilled ground,
And do not sow among thorns.
4 Open[e] your hearts to the LORD,
Remove the thickening about your hearts—

a-a I.e., the pagan rites celebrated on the hills are futile; exact force of Heb. uncertain.
b Heb. Bosheth, *a contemptuous substitute for Baal.*
c-c I.e., profess the worship of the LORD.
d Heb. "him."
e Lit. "circumcise"; cf. Deut. 10.16 and 30.6.

on Mt. Nebo or Pisgah in Moab, where Moses was buried (Deut. 32.49–52; 34.1–8). Rabbinic tradition maintains that Josiah hid the Ark so that it would not be taken to Babylon (*b. Yoma* 53b; *y. Shek.* 6:1, 49c). The ark that houses Torah scrolls in synagogues symbolizes the ancient Ark of the Covenant. **19–25:** This passage gives up the marital metaphor altogether (v. 20), preferring the adoption metaphor, which indeed allows reinstitution of the God-people relationship (vv. 21–22). **22:** The alliteration of the first half of the v. is very striking: "shuvu banim shovavim erpah meshuvotekhem." **25:** *We and our fathers:* A recognition of the people's transgenerational disobedience to God (v. 24; cf. to 2.23, 35; Lam. 5.7). **4.1–2:** God's response closes this prophetic unit. Each of the conditions enumerated closes with the promised result: repentance *(If you return to Me),* no exile ("you will not wander," see 50.3), and political greatness (*Nations shall bless themselves by you / And praise themselves by you,* see Gen. 22.18; 26.4).

4.3–4: Judgment and repentance. Addressing his audience for the first time as the *men of Judah and ... inhabitants of Jerusalem* (see 11.9; 17.25; 35.13; etc.), this passage opens a new collection of judgment prophecies with a call to repent. Unlike the conditional yet hopeful prospect of vv. 1–2, this call is coupled with an implicit threat (v. 3), that turns explicit (v. 4), and then further develops into a concrete military menace (vv. 5–10). **3:** The agricultural imagery builds on the direct connection of an act and its consequence: sowing the field leads to collecting its product (Hos. 10.12). Jeremiah emphasizes the need to prepare the field (NJPS: *untilled ground*) before seeds are spread (by early autumn), in order to prevent the growth of thorns in place of wheat during the rainy season (Prov. 24.30; Job 31.38–40). The image calls the people to take preventative action, i.e., to repent, prior to the divine judgment (v. 4) and the arrival of the enemies' troops (vv. 5–10; see Rashi and Kara).

O men of Judah and inhabitants of Jerusalem—
Lest My wrath break forth like fire,
And burn, with none to quench it,
Because of your wicked acts.

5 Proclaim in Judah,
Announce in Jerusalem,
And say:
"Blow the horn in the land!"
Shout aloud and say:
"Assemble, and let us go
Into the fortified cities!"
6 Set up a signpost: To Zion.
Take refuge, do not delay!
For I bring evil from the north,
And great disaster.
7 The lion has come up from his thicket:
The destroyer of nations has set out,
Has departed from his place,
To make your land a desolation;
Your cities shall be ruined,
Without inhabitants.
8 For this, put on sackcloth,
Mourn and wail;
For the blazing anger of the LORD
Has not turned away from us.
9 And in that day —declares the LORD—
The mind of the king
And the mind of the nobles shall fail,
The priests shall be appalled,
And the prophets shall stand aghast.

10 *a-*And I said:*-a* Ah, Lord GOD! Surely You have deceived this people and Jerusalem, saying:
It shall be well with you—
Yet the sword threatens the very life!

11 At that time, it shall be said concerning this people and Jerusalem:
The conduct of *b-*My poor people*-b* is like searing wind
From the bare heights of the desert—
It will not serve to winnow or to fan.
12 A full blast from them comes against Me:
Now I in turn will bring charges against them.

a-a Septuagint reads "And they shall say."
b-b Lit. "the daughter that is My people"; so, frequently, in poetry.

4: Circumcision (see translators' note *e*) of the hearts draws on Deut. 10.16; 30.6; cf. circumcision as the physical sign of the covenant with God, in the Priestly covenant, Gen. ch 17, both of which Jeremiah may have known.

4.5–31: Judgment and lament. This unit masterfully intertwines judgment prophecies (vv. 6–7, 23–28) with the people's physical reactions (vv. 8–9, 29–31). Their communal laments over the perceived distress (vv. 13b, 20–21, 31) are coupled with the prophet's own cries (vv. 10, 19–21), or perhaps it is God that cries out at this total destruction (vv. 20–22). **5–9:** The concrete military-political threat, still not specified by name (see 1.14), is portrayed as *evil from the north* (v. 6; 6.1), or a nation coming from the land of the north (6.22). Several identifications of this enemy have been suggested (the Scythians, following the Greek historian, Herodotus, A:104–106; or the Babylonians, who were the imperial ruling force from 605 BCE forward); the prophecies may describe both, having been updated over time; or perhaps the north stands for diverse enemies, see 25.26. The descriptions of enemy troops invading the land are highly conventional (as also in vv. 13–18; 5.15–17; 6.1–8, 22–26; 10.22), and the enemy remains anonymous, even though Jeremiah and those responsible for preserving his oracles had experienced destruction by the Babylonians. The *north* in Jeremiah is the source of military threat also to Egypt (46.6, 10, 24), Philistia (47.2), and even Babylonia itself (50.3, 9, 41). **5–6:** Anxiety is produced by calling the people into walled cities (so also 6.1; and quoting the enemy in such instructions, 6.4–5). **7:** Terror rises with the enemy as a metaphorical lion pursuing its prey, that is, destroying the land (see "a ravening lion," 2.30; and Joel 1.6). **8–9:** Agony results as the people realize that the political events designate divine wrath that affects all the leadership: the king, officials, priests, and prophets. **10:** Jeremiah, more than any other prophet, talks to God. Here taking the side of the

13 Lo, he[a] ascends like clouds,
His chariots are like a whirlwind,
His horses are swifter than eagles.
Woe to us, we are ruined!
14 Wash your heart clean of wickedness,
O Jerusalem, that you may be rescued.
How long will you harbor within you
Your evil designs?

15 Hark, one proclaims from Dan
And announces calamity from Mount Ephraim!
16 Tell the nations: Here they are!
Announce concerning Jerusalem:
Watchers[a] are coming from a distant land,
They raise their voices against the towns of Judah.
17 Like guards of fields, they surround her on every side.
For she has rebelled against Me
—declares the LORD.
18 Your conduct and your acts
Have brought this upon you;
This is your bitter punishment;
It pierces your very heart.

19 Oh, my suffering,[b] my suffering!
How I writhe!
Oh, the walls of my heart!
My heart moans within me,
I cannot be silent;
For [c]I hear[c] the blare of horns,
Alarms of war.
20 Disaster overtakes disaster,
For all the land has been ravaged.
Suddenly my tents have been ravaged,
In a moment, my tent cloths.
21 How long must I see standards
And hear the blare of horns?

22 For My people are stupid,
They give Me no heed;
They are foolish children,
They are not intelligent.
They are clever at doing wrong,
But unable to do right.

a *I.e., the invader of v. 7.* *b* *Lit. "entrails."*
c-c *Lit. "you, O my being, hear." Change of vocalization yields "I hear the blare of horns, / My inner being, alarms of war."*

people, as prophets sometimes do, Jeremiah protests that God has deceived the people, promising peace when total defeat is approaching (cf. Isa. 6.9–13). This protest has usually been interpreted as referring to Jeremiah's struggle with the false prophets (see Tg. and Rashi); on God seducing ("pth") false prophets, see Ezek. 14.9. But theologically, all these are not quite the same as what Jeremiah here proclaims. **13–18:** A second passage on the enemy's approach, this time using weather images (*clouds* and *whirlwind*) and fauna (*horses* and *eagles,* see Hab. 1.8). **14, 18:** These two vv. frame the prophetic rebuke. **14:** Another call to repent, with the prophet's acknowledgement that Jerusalem chooses sin over repentance. With "kibbes" (*wash*ing the *heart*) and "lyn" (*harbor*ing *evil designs*/thoughts), the prophet transforms Priestly terminology about defilement and purification into the realm of sin and repentance. Purification rituals require washing the clothes and at times washing the body; defilement remains only until sundown (see Lev. 11.25; 17.15–16; Num. 19.7–8; etc.). Jeremiah reverses this purification procedure to admonish Jerusalem for clinging to its sins overnight, hence permanently. **18:** A clear accusation justifies the divine judgment, putting the blame on Jerusalem, whose evil has reached its innermost organ, her *heart,* the organ she was asked to wash (v. 14).

23–28: Jeremiah envisions a full reversal of creation (see 24.1; Ezek. 1.4, 15; 2.9; Amos 7.1, 4, 7; Zech. 1.8; 2.1, 5; etc.). The return to chaos (the phrase *unformed and void* [v. 23] is used in this form only here and in Gen. 1.2), to no-light, no-man, no-birds of the sky alludes to Gen. ch 1 in wording and order, from cosmic substances to living creatures. The choice of bird migration is appropriate, since thousands of birds disappear from sight in a short time. **24:** The trembling *mountains* and *hills* seem closer either to mythic reminiscence (as in Ps. 104.5–10, 32), or, less likely, to descriptions of theophanies (as in Jer. 10.10; Joel 2.10; Nah. 1.2–9). **26:** The fourth and closing element of this vision draws this prophecy to its local geographical context of the (Judean) Desert and the Carmel, the cultivated land, including the very region where Jeremiah was born and raised in the area of Anathoth. The Carmel is a narrow geographical strip from north to south of about 5–10 km (3–6 mi) between the Jerusalem high hills and the Judean Desert (it is not the Carmel near Haifa). This area still supports agriculture and permanent settlement; though years of drought could turn the Carmel into desert, that is, transform its geographical conditions into complete desolation. **27:** *But I will not make an end of it,* pulls back from the total calamity (see vv. 26b, 28b). This is one of three modifications of desolation (see also 5.10, 18) that shows that Jeremiah's preliminary message was one of total destruction that evolved over time. These modifications accord with consolation prophecies like 30.11 and 46.28 and the common prophetic theme of a remnant (e.g., Isa. 6.13).

5.1–31: The refusal to repent. Instead of further calls for repentance, this ch recognizes that the people refuse to repent (v. 3). To deepen this painful recognition, it is the entire people that cling to sin: the sinners are both the *poor folk* (v. 4) and the *wealthy* and powerful (v. 5); both *the House of Israel and the House of Judah* betray God (vv. 11–12); the entire people are designated as *foolish*

23 I look at the earth,
It is unformed and void;
At the skies,
And their light is gone.
24 I look at the mountains,
They are quaking;
And all the hills are rocking.
25 I look: no man is left,
And all the birds of the sky have fled.
26 I look: the farm land is desert,
And all its towns are in ruin—
Because of the LORD,
Because of His blazing anger.
27 (For thus said the LORD:
The whole land shall be desolate,
But I will not make an end of it.)
28 For this the earth mourns,
And skies are dark above—
Because I have spoken, I have planned,
And I will not relent or turn back from it.

29 At the shout of horseman and bowman
The whole city flees.
They enter the thickets,
They clamber up the rocks.
The whole city is deserted,
Not a man remains there.
30 And you, who are doomed to ruin,
What do you accomplish by wearing crimson,
By decking yourself in jewels of gold,
By enlarging your eyes with kohl?
You beautify yourself in vain:
Lovers despise you,
They seek your life!
31 I hear a voice as of one in travail,
Anguish as of a woman bearing her first child,
The voice of Fair Zion
Panting, stretching out her hands:
"Alas for me! I faint
Before the killers!"

5 Roam the streets of Jerusalem,
Search its squares,
Look about and take note:
You will not find a man,
There is none who acts justly,
Who seeks integrity—
That I should pardon her.

2 Even when they say, "As the LORD lives,"
They are sure to be swearing falsely.
3 O LORD, Your eyes look for integrity.
You have struck them, but they sensed no pain;
You have consumed them, but they would accept
no discipline.
They made their faces harder than rock,
They refused to turn back.

4 Then I thought: These are just poor folk;
They act foolishly;
For they do not know the way of the LORD,
The rules of their God.
5 So I will go to the wealthy
And speak with them:
Surely they know the way of the LORD,
The rules of their God.
But they as well had broken the yoke,
Had snapped the bonds.
6 Therefore,
The lion of the forest strikes them down,
The wolf of the desert ravages them.
A leopard lies in wait by their towns;
Whoever leaves them will be torn in pieces.
For their transgressions are many,
Their rebellious acts unnumbered.

7 Why should I forgive you?
Your children have forsaken Me
And sworn by no-gods.
When I fed them their fill,
They committed adultery
And went trooping to the harlot's house.
8 They were [a]well-fed, lusty[a] stallions,
Each neighing at another's wife.
9 Shall I not punish such deeds?
—says the LORD—
Shall I not bring retribution
On a nation such as this?
10 Go up among her vines[b] and destroy;
Lop off her trailing branches,
For they are not of the LORD.
(But do not make an end.)
11 For the House of Israel and the House of Judah
Have betrayed Me —declares the LORD.
12 They have been false to the LORD

a-a *Meaning of Heb. uncertain.* b *Lit. "rows."*

... *devoid of intelligence* (v. 21), they have *a wayward and defiant heart* (v. 23, see Deut. 21.18–21); and finally, the three parts of the community, *prophets, priests* and *My people* (v. 31), all contribute to the disobedience that calls for judgment. **1–6:** The call to *roam* through *the streets of Jerusalem* in search of a single righteous resident, so that God could forgive, alludes to the Sodom and Gomorrah tradition (Gen. 18.20–33), although the theme of that story is modified through the Priestly term "salaḥ l-" ("forgive," as for instance in Lev. 4.20). **2:** Taking an oath in God's name represents obedience (as in 4.2); whereas swearing to the "sheqer" (NJPS: *falsely*) stands for taking an oath in the name of other gods (see v. 7; 12.16). "Sheqer" in Jer. refers to other gods. **6:** *Lion, wolf* and *leopard* are the three predators God summons against his people (see Ezek. 14.21), attacking the people in all ecological regions, in the *forest,* in the *desert* and out of the walls of *towns.* **7–8:** God's first desire to forgive Jerusalem (v. 3), switches to the rhetorical question: *Why should I forgive you?* and opens a new list of iniquities, this time using sexual metaphors. **9:** This formula is repeated in v. 29 and 9.8, and serves as a refrain, bridging passages. God's revenge is typical of His actions against His people's enemies (Num. 31.2; Deut. 32.43; Josh. 10.13; 2 Kings 9.7; Isa. 1.24; and in the personal sphere, 1 Sam. 24.13). Jeremiah coins a special phrase with "nqm" *(bring retribution)* in which God acts just as fiercely against His own people. This transformation from rescuer to foe occurs with other phrases already in Isa. (see Isa. 5.25; 9.16; etc.). **10–14:** God summons the human enemies to destroy Jerusalem. God's instructions use verbs that assure total calamity, which is justified by the people's extreme sins of betrayal ("bagad") and denial of His involvement in causing the military distress. The phrase *but do not make an end* (v. 10) may be a revision or addition to soften the verb "kalah," *end* (as earlier 4.27; 5.18; 30.11; NJPS reverses the order of the clauses).

15–17: The arrival of foreign troops is announced by the repetition (four times) of "goy," *nation;* each adds a frightening attribute: this enemy is *from afar, enduring, ancient,* and unintelligible. The description proceeds to its weapons (v. 16), and then goes into its devouring deeds, again repeating the term *devour* four times (v. 17). Isa. 5.26–30 portrays a similar enemy's approach but Jeremiah's description more closely alludes to Deut. 28.49–53. **18–19:** These two vv., a prose insertion in the poetry, designate a third stage in the growth of this collection. They soften the annihilation prophecy (vv. 10–14) by noting "but do not make an end" (v. 10b). In v. 19, in dialogue form, the people ask for a theological explanation for the distress. God presents exile in a measure-for-measure (talion) fashion: for worshipping foreign deities, Israel will be subjugated by *foreigners.* These may refer to foreign nations, and may even reflect the conception that in exile, Israel will worship foreign deities (see Deut. 4.28; 28.64; 1 Sam. 19.26). "Zarim," rendered by NJPS as *foreigners,* may mean other gods (see Deut. 32.16) or foreign rulers (as in Jer. 30.8, so Kimḥi); the Tg. conflates the two: "you shall be subjugated to peoples who worship other gods." **20–25:** The play between other gods and human behavior characterizes this passage as well, which first addresses the people's foolish behavior, in terms that are otherwise used concerning other gods (Deut. 4.28; Ps. 115.5–6). **22:** The rhetorical question brings out the absurdity of the people's disobedience, as they do not revere the God of creation (the concept returns in v. 24, a closure referring to God as LORD of nature and agriculture). The reference to psalmodic-mythic traditions of creation in combat is clear (see Ps. 104.9), and shows that Jeremiah's acquaintance with creation traditions extends beyond Gen. ch 1 (see 4.23–28). His usage of "hoq 'olam," *a limit for all time,* is clearly borrowed from Priestly terminology, where it typically is translated "throughout

And said: "[a]It is not so![a]
No trouble shall come upon us,
We shall not see sword or famine.
13 The prophets shall prove mere wind
For the Word is not in them;
Thus-and-thus shall be done to them!"

14 Assuredly, thus said the LORD,
The God of Hosts:
Because they[b] said that,
I am putting My words into your mouth as fire,
And this people shall be firewood,
Which it will consume.
15 Lo, I am bringing against you, O House of Israel,
A nation from afar —declares the LORD;
It is an enduring nation,
It is an ancient nation;
A nation whose language you do not know—
You will not understand what they say.
16 [c]Their quivers[c] are like a yawning grave—
They are all mighty men.
17 They will devour your harvest and food,
They will devour your sons and daughters,
They will devour your flocks and herds,
They will devour your vines and fig trees.
They will batter down with the sword
The fortified towns on which you rely.

18 But even in those days—declares the LORD—I will not make
an end of you. 19 And when they[b] ask, "Because of what did the
LORD our God do all these things?" you shall answer them, "Because you forsook Me and served alien gods on your own land,
you will have to serve foreigners in a land not your own."

20 Proclaim this to the House of Jacob
And announce it in Judah:
21 Hear this, O foolish people,
Devoid of intelligence,
That have eyes but can't see,
That have ears but can't hear!
22 Should you not revere Me —says the LORD—
Should you not tremble before Me,
Who set the sand as a boundary to the sea,
As a limit for all time, not to be transgressed?
Though its waves toss, they cannot prevail;

a-a Or "Not He"; cf. Deut. 32.39; Isa. 43.13. *b Heb. "you."*
c-c Emendation yields "Whose mouths."

Though they roar, they cannot pass it.
23 Yet this people has a wayward and defiant heart;
They have turned aside and gone their way.
24 They have not said to themselves,
"Let us revere the LORD our God,
Who gives the rain,
The early and late rain in season,
Who keeps for our benefit
The weeks appointed for harvest."
25 It is your iniquities that have diverted these things,
Your sins that have withheld the bounty from you.
26 For among My people are found wicked men,
[a]Who lurk, like fowlers lying in wait;[a]
They set up a trap to catch men.
27 As a cage is full of birds,
So their houses are full of guile;
That is why they have grown so wealthy.
28 They have become fat and sleek;
They [b]pass beyond the bounds of wickedness,[b]
And they prosper.
They will not judge the case of the orphan,
Nor give a hearing to the plea of the needy.
29 Shall I not punish such deeds
—says the LORD—
Shall I not bring retribution
On a nation such as this?
30 An appalling, horrible thing
Has happened in the land:
31 The prophets prophesy falsely,
And the priests [a]rule accordingly;[a]
And My people like it so.
But what will you do at the end of it?

6

Flee for refuge, O people of Benjamin,
Out of the midst of Jerusalem!
Blow the horn in Tekoa,
Set up a signal at Beth-haccerem!
For evil is appearing from the north,
And great disaster.
2 [a]Fair Zion, the lovely and delicate,
I will destroy.[a]

a-a Meaning of Heb. uncertain.
b-b Some ancient versions read "have transgressed My words for evil."

the ages," and is used in reference to donations given to Aaron and his descendants (Exod. 29.28; 30.21; Lev. 6.11, 15; 7.34; 10.15; 24.9; Num. 18.8, 11, 19). **23:** *A wayward and defiant heart:* "lev sorer umoreh" is another Jeremianic pun, on Deut. 21.18–21, the law of the wayward and defiant son. The following passage also uses both Priestly and Deuteronomic traditions, together with psalmodic and wisdom conventions. **26–28:** Echoing psalmodic-wisdom poetry, these vv. refer to a portion of the people, *wicked men* that set traps against others (Pss. 9.8–10; 35.7); their richness only excels their sins (see Ps. 73.3–8). Jeremiah typically deals with idolatry and ritual sins, and rarely mentions moral misconduct. **29–31:** A summary denunciation.

6.1–30: Judgment and exhortation. This tapestry of prophetic proclamations extends the feeling of the coming disaster over the entire sinful people (vv. 10, 13, 21, 28) by weaving together description of judgment (vv. 1–6a, 9, 11–12, 22–26) with prophetic exhortations that justify it (vv. 6b–8, 10, 13–21). The people's continued rebellion is accentuated by their refusal to listen to the prophetic warning (vv. 10, 17, 19). V. 8 still calls on Jerusalem to accept the divine rebuke, yet the threat of total annihilation awaits the city (vv. 8, 9, 15, 21). **1–9:** A dramatic opening calls the *people of Benjamin* to *flee* out of Jerusalem, then moves further south to *Tekoa,* hometown of the prophet Amos (Amos 1.1), located in Judah, about 20 km (12 mi) south of Jerusalem and 10 km (6 mi) south of Bethlehem. The prophet is punning here, using the verb "taka'" *(blow the horn)* which plays on the name place *Tekoa. Set up a signal,* light hilltop signal fires over *Beth-haccerem* to warn all Judah of the approaching enemy. *Beth-haccerem* is either the village 'Ain Karem to the west of modern Jerusalem or more likely is Ramat Raḥel, 5 km (3 mi) south of the city. It means "the house of the vineyard," and thus puns on the vineyard imagery used earlier (2.21), and anticipates v. 9. **2:** *Fair Zion, the lovely and delicate:* Oblivious to the imminent danger surrounding her; the prospect of her destruction thus comes as a total surprise (see 8.14; 25.37; 47.5; Hos. 4.6; so Tg. and Rashi), or is portrayed as such (Kimḥi), see Deut. 28.56.

3 Against her come shepherds with their flocks,
They pitch tents all around her;
Each grazes [a]the sheep under his care.[a]
4 [b]Prepare for[b] battle against her:
"Up! we will attack at noon."
"Alas for us! for day is declining,
The shadows of evening grow long."
5 "Up! let us attack by night,
And wreck her fortresses."

6 For thus said the LORD of Hosts:
Hew down her trees,
And raise a siegemound against Jerusalem.
[c]She is the city destined for punishment;[c]
Only fraud is found in her midst.
7 As a well flows with water,
So she flows with wickedness.
Lawlessness and rapine are heard in her;
Before Me constantly are sickness and wounds.
8 Accept rebuke, O Jerusalem,
Lest I come to loathe you,
Lest I make you a desolation,
An uninhabited land.

9 Thus said the LORD of Hosts:
[d]Let them glean[d] over and over, as a vine,
The remnant of Israel.
Pass your hand again,
Like a vintager,
Over its branches.

10[e] To whom shall I speak,
Give warning that they may hear?
Their ears are blocked
And they cannot listen.
See, the word of the LORD has become for them
An object of scorn; they will have none of it.
11 But I am filled with the wrath of the LORD,
I cannot hold it in.

Pour it on the infant in the street,
And on the company of youths gathered together!
Yes, men and women alike shall be captured,
Elders and those of advanced years.

a-a Understanding yado *as in Ps. 95.7.* *b-b Lit. "Consecrate."*
c-c Emendation yields "She is the city of falseness."
d-d Emendation yields "Glean" (singular). *e The prophet speaks.*

3–6: Instructions for the military attack; v. 3 uses the metaphor of *shepherds* for kings (see 3.15 n.), in this case foreign kings, and of *flocks* grazing, and thus decimating the pasture land. **7–8:** Moral sin justifies this disaster. *Sickness and wounds:* While the context makes these two elements part of the city's sins (so Kimḥi), they are usually part of the punishment (see 10.19; Deut. 28.59, 61; and so Tg.). Moral sins as reasons for the destruction are very unusual in Jer. (see vv. 12–14, 28), and when they are mentioned they are often linked to religious offenses (as in 5.1, 20–25, 26–29; 7.5–6). **8:** This is the only call for repentance in this ch. The threat that God will *come to loathe you* appears otherwise in Ezek. 23.18 (and twice in Ezek. ch 23 with Jerusalem [Oholibah] as agent, vv. 22, 28). **9:** The agricultural imagery adds to the force of the threat of destruction. Grapes were picked several times during the harvest, and Israel will be like a grapevine picked over and over, left bare, and not even the gleanings, which are supposed to be left for the poor (Lev. 19.10; Deut. 24.21), will remain. **10:** The prophet feels that he is speaking to people who have made themselves deaf; no one listens to him. *Their ears are blocked:* Heb "their ears are uncircumcised"; they are not in a condition to hear (see 4.4, "circumcise your hearts"). **11:** The prophet is filled to overflowing with the divine wrath (see 20.9), and so he pours his words out on the entire community, even upon the innocent *infant in the street.*

12 Their houses shall pass to others,
Fields and wives as well,
For I will stretch out My arm
Against the inhabitants of the country
—declares the LORD.
13 For from the smallest to the greatest,
They are all greedy for gain;
Priest and prophet alike,
They all act falsely.
14 They offer healing offhand
For the wounds of My people,
Saying, "All is well, all is well,"
When nothing is well.
15 They have acted shamefully;
They have done abhorrent things—
Yet they do not feel shame,
And they cannot be made to blush.
Assuredly, they shall fall among the falling,
They shall stumble at the time when I
punish them
—said the LORD.

16 Thus said the LORD:
Stand by the roads and consider,
Inquire about ancient paths:
Which is the road to happiness?
Travel it, and find tranquillity for yourselves.
But they said, "We will not."
17 And I raised up watchmen[a] for you:
"Hearken to the sound of the horn!"
But they said, "We will not."
18 Hear well, O nations,
And know, [b]O community, what is in store for them.[b]
19 Hear, O earth!
I am going to bring disaster upon this people,
The outcome of their own schemes;
For they would not hearken to My words,
And they rejected My Instruction.
20 What need have I of frankincense
That comes from Sheba,
Or fragrant cane from a distant land?
Your burnt offerings are not acceptable
And your sacrifices are not pleasing to Me.
21 Assuredly, thus said the LORD:
I shall put before this people stumbling blocks
Over which they shall stumble—

a I.e., prophets. b-b *Meaning of Heb. uncertain.*

12–15: Parallel to 8.10–12. Initially, the entire community sins, hence the entire community suffers (see 5.1–8); only in vv. 13b–14 does the prophet specify that the *priests* and the *prophets* acted *falsely,* assuring the people falsely that *all is well.* Jeremiah is later accused of the opposite, of demoralizing the people (38.4 and see v. 24). **15:** Justifications of judgment on the entire community, using the root "b-w-sh," to shame, three times in the Heb. **17:** The image of prophets as *watchmen* is also found in Ezek. (see esp. Ezek. 3.17). **20:** The people continue to go through the motions of their religious practice, despite their disobedience to God. God rejects *sacrifices* if they are accompanied by immoral behavior. This is not a rejection of sacrifices per se, but of the thinking that performing a ritual sacrifice will allow God to ignore wrong behavior. *Frankincense* and *fragrant cane* are aromatic spices used in sacrificial worship (see "cane" in Exod. 30.23 and "frankincense" in Exod. 30.34; frankincense accompanies various offerings, Lev. 2.1–2, 15–16; 5.11; 6.8; 24.7). *Your burnt offerings are not acceptable,* echoes Priestly language (see Exod. 28.38; Lev. 1.3; and esp. Lev. 22.17–33) where "acceptance" is said of burnt offerings (Lev. 22.19–20; Isa. 60.7) and well-being offerings; Jeremiah reverses the Priestly conception that seems to suggest that sacrifices by themselves automatically atone. Arguing that the burnt offerings are not acceptable and that the *sacrifices are not pleasing* suggests that God cannot be made to reverse His judgment to carry out the evil judgment (v. 19a).

22–26: The foe from the north. As in 4.5–8, 13–18; 5.15–17; 6.1–8; 10.22 (see 4.5–31), the enemy's approach is described in colorful imagery. **23:** *Like the roaring sea,* the sound of their galloping horses. **24:** *Agony like a woman in childbirth,* an evocative biblical image suggesting pain, screaming, and powerlessness. **25:** The idiom *Terror on every side* typifies Jeremiah (see esp. 20.3). **27–30:** God appoints the prophet to *assay* and refine the people, as one does to metal, to see if impurities remain in it. **28:** *Stubbornly defiant,* strongly alliterative in Heb, "sarei sorerim." **30:** *Rejected silver* (cf. Prov. 8.19; 10.20) is of no use; the same is true of Israel.

Fathers and children alike,
Neighbor and friend shall perish.

22 Thus said the LORD:
See, a people comes from the northland,
A great nation is roused
From the remotest parts of the earth.
23 They grasp the bow and javelin;
They are cruel, they show no mercy;
The sound of them is like the roaring sea.
They ride upon horses,
Accoutered like a man for battle,
Against you, O Fair Zion!

24 "We have heard the report of them,
Our hands fail;
Pain seizes us,
Agony like a woman in childbirth.
25 Do not go out into the country,
Do not walk the roads!
For the sword of the enemy is there,
Terror on every side."

26 [a-]My poor people,[-a]
Put on sackcloth
And strew dust on yourselves!
Mourn, as for an only child;
Wail bitterly,
For suddenly the destroyer
Is coming upon us.

27 I have made you an assayer of My people
—A refiner[b]—
You are to note and assay their ways.
28 They are copper and iron:
They are all stubbornly defiant;
They [c-]deal basely[-c]
All of them act corruptly.
29 [d-]The bellows puff;
The lead is consumed by fire.[-d]
Yet the smelter smelts to no purpose—
The dross[b] is not separated out.
30 They are called "rejected silver,"
For the LORD has rejected them.

a-a Lit. "Daughter that is My people"; so, frequently, in poetry. See 4.11 and note.
b Meaning of Heb. uncertain. *c-c See note at Lev. 19.16.*
d-d Meaning of Heb. uncertain.

7 The word which came to Jeremiah from the LORD: [2]Stand
at the gate of the House of the LORD, and there proclaim
this word: Hear the word of the LORD, all you of Judah who enter these gates to worship the LORD!
[3]Thus said the LORD of Hosts, the God of Israel: Mend your
ways and your actions, and I will [a]let you dwell[a] in this place.
[4]Don't put your trust in illusions and say, "The Temple of the
LORD, the Temple of the LORD, the Temple of the LORD are
these [buildings]." [5]No, if you really mend your ways and your
actions; if you execute justice between one man and another;
[6]if you do not oppress the stranger, the orphan, and the widow;
if you do not shed the blood of the innocent in this place; if
you do not follow other gods, to your own hurt—[7]then only
will I [a]let you dwell[a] in this place, in the land that I gave to
your fathers for all time. [8]See, you are relying on illusions that
are of no avail. [9]Will you steal and murder and commit adultery and swear falsely, and sacrifice to Baal, and follow other
gods whom you have not experienced,[b] [10]and then come and
stand before Me in this House which bears My name and say,
"We are safe"?—[Safe] to do all these abhorrent things! [11]Do
you consider this House, which bears My name, to be a den of
thieves? As for Me, I have been watching—declares the LORD.
[12]Just go to My place at Shiloh, where I had established My
name formerly, and see what I did to it because of the wickedness of My people Israel. [13]And now, because you do all these
things—declares the LORD—and though I spoke to you persistently, you would not listen; and though I called to you, you
would not respond—[14]therefore I will do to the House which

a-a Meaning of Heb. uncertain. Change of vocalization yields "dwell with you"; so Aquila and Vulgate. *b See note at Deut. 11.28.*

7.1–8.3: The threat of destruction at the gates of the House of the LORD. This judgment prophecy consists of four prose passages; it opens with an admonition that threatens destruction but still calls to repent (vv. 1–15); is followed by accusations that specify the people's sins (vv. 16–20, 21–29); and closes with the prospect of destruction (7.30–8.3). A shortened version of the Temple sermon is found in a parallel passage in the narrative account in ch 26, which shows its immediate impact on the Jerusalem audience and the great fury it enflamed against the prophet (see 26.1–6 n.). **7.1–15:** The Temple would not save the disobedient people. This is the first of five covenant speeches in Jer., all characterized by a repeated pattern (see 11.1–14; 17.19–27; 22.1–5; 25.1–14). These are often called "sermons," but are better termed judgment prophecies; the references to the people's covenant obligations to obey God and His commandments serve as the accusation (vv. 1–11), followed by the judgment (vv. 12–15). **2:** The prophet as the covenant mediator is instructed to announce his words publicly, in the court of the Temple. **3:** Imperatives and idioms of rebuke characterize the demand for the people's obedience to God. The call *mend your ways and your actions* (see also v. 5), promises that God will guarantee the people's continuous existence in the land (a similar promise is in 11.5; 17.25; 25.5; see also 22.4) if they are obedient, in line with God's eternal promise to the forefathers of v. 7. **4:** The Temple, that is, the locus of God's Presence, cannot in itself save the people from destruction. The Temple is not inviolable (see Pss. 46; 48; 78.68–69). *The Temple of the LORD,* also used of the sanctuary at Shiloh (1 Sam. 1.9); the link between the Jerusalem Temple and the Shiloh sanctuary is the core of this speech in vv. 12–15. The threefold repetition of *the Temple of the LORD* is for emphasis, as in Isa. 6.3. **5–6:** The divine demands are structured so one may recognize the legal collections of the Torah, often reworded by the prophet. *If you do not oppress the stranger, the orphan, and the widow,* for instance, collates the Deuteronomic triad and the social concept behind it (as in Deut. 14.29, etc.) with "'shaq," *oppress,* that never comes with this triad, but with "a needy and destitute laborer" (Deut. 24.14, "abuse"). The list combines social-moral demands with religious edicts that exemplify the general request for obedience. **9:** The Decalogue, the text that more than any other illustrates the covenant obligations placed on the people at Sinai, is alluded to as six of its ten statements are explicitly or implicitly alluded to (per NJPS, numbers 8, 6, 7, 9, 2, 1). Here again, the first three are social, the others are in the religious sphere. **10:** Having done evil, the people come to the Temple, thinking that it will save them. This v. joins 2.27 in presenting syncretistic worship. *House which bears My name,* clearly alludes to the Deuteronomic phrase and conception of the one place that God had selected for His name to dwell (see Deut. 12.5, etc.). **12–14:** The Jerusalem Temple will be destroyed just as the Shiloh sanctuary was. (see Ps. 78.59–67). This reference to the northern historical tradition is unique and is often understood as part of Jeremiah's personal background among the priests in Anathoth, presumably a descendant of the Elide priests of Shiloh. **14:** *The place which I gave you:* The

bears My name, on which you rely, and to the place which I gave you and your fathers, just what I did to Shiloh. 15 And I will cast you out of My presence as I cast out your brothers, the whole brood of Ephraim.

16 As for you, do not pray for this people, do not raise a cry of prayer on their behalf, do not plead with Me; for I will not listen to you. 17 Don't you see what they are doing in the towns of Judah and in the streets of Jerusalem? 18 The children gather sticks, the fathers build the fire, and the mothers knead dough, to make cakes for the Queen of Heaven,[a] and they pour libations to other gods, to vex Me. 19 Is it Me they are vexing?—says the LORD. It is rather themselves, to their own disgrace. 20 Assuredly, thus said the Lord GOD: My wrath and My fury will be poured out upon this place, on man and on beast, on the trees of the field and the fruit of the soil. It shall burn, with none to quench it.

21 Thus said the LORD of Hosts, the God of Israel: Add your burnt offerings to your other sacrifices and eat the meat! 22 For when I freed your fathers from the land of Egypt, I did not speak with them or command them concerning burnt offerings or sacrifice. 23 But this is what I commanded them: Do My bidding, that I may be your God and you may be My people; walk only in the way that I enjoin upon you, that it may go well with you. 24 Yet they did not listen or give ear; they followed their own counsels, the willfulness of their evil hearts. They have gone backward, not forward, 25 from the day your fathers left the land of Egypt until today. And though I kept sending all My servants, the prophets, to them[b] daily and persistently, 26 they would not listen to Me or give ear. They stiffened their necks, they acted worse than their fathers.

27 You shall say all these things to them, but they will not listen to you; you shall call to them, but they will not respond to you. 28 Then say to them: This is the nation that would not obey the LORD their God, that would not accept rebuke. Faithfulness has perished, vanished from their mouths.

29 Shear your locks and cast them away,
Take up a lament on the heights,
For the LORD has spurned and cast off
The brood that provoked His wrath.

a I.e., the mother goddess (Ishtar, Astarte) in whose honor these cakes were baked.
b Heb. "you."

prophecy ties together the Temple and the land; the destruction of the House is the destruction of the land. According to ancient belief, once a deity abandons a temple, that site and the entire country are open to destruction. **15:** Exile is the result of destruction. The analogy shifts slightly from the fate of Shiloh of the 11th c. BCE (where there is no record of exile), to the exile of the *brood of Ephraim,* the Northern Kingdom, in the 8th c. (see 2 Kings 17.18, 23; cf. 2 Kings 13.23; 24.20). Jeremiah could not have used the later Northern Kingdom temple at Bethel as a precedent for temple destruction since that temple was illegitimate in the eyes of the Judeans. **16–20:** Praying on behalf of the people recognizes that a major role of the prophet was as intercessor for the nation, and ties Jeremiah to Moses (see Num. 21.7; Deut. 9.20) and Samuel (1 Sam. 12.18, 23), as in Jer. 15.1. **17–19:** *Queen of heaven,* an epithet of the Assyrian-Babylonian goddess Ishtar (worshipped also in Egypt, see ch 44), whose worship is conducted within the family, and not as an official national cult. **20:** Judgment is presented as reversal of creation (see Gen. 1.26; 2.20; and Jer. 21.6; 27.5; and it might reverse again to consolation, 32.43; 33.10, 12; etc.). **21:** *Add your burnt offerings to your other sacrifices and eat the meat!* This has become one of Jeremiah's most famous rebukes. **22–23:** The opposition between the sacrifices that were not commanded at the time of the exodus, and the clear demand of obedience, which dates from the exodus (the stipulation of the covenant at Sinai); obedience is more ancient and more important than sacrifices. Amos 5.25 makes a similar claim; in contrast, the Priestly tradition traces the origin of sacrifices to Sinai (Lev. 7.37–38). **23:** *That I may be your God and you may be My people,* see 11.4; otherwise in consolation prophecies, 24.7; 30.22; 31.33. **24–28:** *Yet they did not listen* [to me], a refrain, emphasizing disobedience (vv. 24, 26, 27, 28). **26:** The retrospective overview makes the current generation those who *acted worse than their fathers.* This implies that despite continuity of sin, Jeremiah's generation is responsible for their own fate. **29:** This poetic v. connects the two passages.

30 For the people of Judah have done what displeases Me—
declares the LORD. They have set up their abominations in the
House which is called by My name, and they have defiled it.
31 And they have built the shrines of Topheth in the Valley of
Ben-hinnom to burn their sons and daughters in fire—which I
never commanded, which never came to My mind.
32 Assuredly, a time is coming—declares the LORD—when
men shall no longer speak of Topheth or the Valley of Ben-
hinnom, but of the Valley of Slaughter; and they shall bury in
Topheth until no room is left. 33 The carcasses of this people
shall be food for the birds of the sky and the beasts of the earth,
with none to frighten them off. 34 And I will silence in the towns
of Judah and the streets of Jerusalem the sound of mirth and
gladness, the voice of bridegroom and bride. For the whole
land shall fall to ruin.

8 At that time—declares the LORD—the bones of the kings of
Judah, of its officers, of the priests, of the prophets, and of
the inhabitants of Jerusalem shall be taken out of their graves
2 and exposed to the sun, the moon, and all the host of heav-
en which they loved and served and followed, to which they
turned and bowed down. They shall not be gathered for reburi-
al; they shall become dung upon the face of the earth. 3 And
death shall be preferable to life for all that are left of this wicked
folk, in all the other places to which I shall banish them—declares the LORD of Hosts.

4 Say to them: Thus said the LORD:
When men fall, do they not get up again?
If they turn aside, do they not turn back?
5 Why is this people—Jerusalem—rebellious
With a persistent rebellion?
They cling to deceit,
They refuse to return.
6 I have listened and heard:
They do not speak honestly.
No one regrets his wickedness
And says, "What have I done!"
They all persist in their wayward course
Like a steed dashing forward in the fray.

7.30–8.3: Religious sins and their punishment. 7.30–31: The offenses were conducted in the Temple and nearby, in *the Valley of Ben-hinnom,* where sacrifices of *sons and daughters* took place, arguably to YHVH. See also 19.5; 32.35; Ezek. 20.25–26, 30–31; and Mic. 6.7. **32–34:** The punishment concerns death, and the place of sacrifice that caused death of a few will turn into *the Valley of Slaughter,* where the multitude of dead will be brought, though they will not receive a decent burial (see 9.21; 14.16; 15.3; 16.3–4, 6; 19.7; 22.18–19). The curses are borrowed from the context of Neo-Assyrian political treaties (see Esarhaddon's Vassal Treaty, §§56, 59), and also cited in Deut. 28.26; Ps. 79.2. The Heb *Valley of Ben-hinnom,* underlies the terms "geihinnom" or "gehenna," which designates hell in later Jewish tradition (see *b. 'Eruv.* 19a; *b. Tamid* 32b). **34:** The phrase *the sound of mirth and gladness, the voice of bridegroom and bride,* found only in Jer. (16.9; 25.10; 33.11) is used in the Jewish wedding ceremony. **8.1–3:** The horrible description of the vast death in Jerusalem moves to the burial areas, where the *bones* of the dead will be desecrated, dug up but not reburied to lie exposed to the very astral deities that were wrongly worshipped (see Deut. 17.2–7; 2 Kings 23.5). **3:** Choosing death over life follows the curses of Deut. 28.64–68: see Jer. 22.10–12.

8.4–9.25: A cluster of judgment prophecies against Jerusalem. This unit lacks a superscription that dates it; it is in poetry, and thus separate from the previous unit, and distinct from 10.1ff., which opens with a formula calling the people to attention ("Hear the word ..."), marking a new unit. **8.4–7:** Opening this cluster of prophecies are three vv. with six occurrences of "shuv" *(turn)* in its special Jeremian forms of "shovevah" and "meshuvah," and in its opposite meanings of *turn aside* from God and *turn back* to God (see 3.6 n.). **6–7:** *I have listened and heard:* It is unclear if God or Jeremiah is speaking; LXX reads the verbs here in the plural, "listen and hear." To illustrate the persistence of iniquity, Jeremiah introduces two animal images. The first is war-horses *(steeds)* famous for their speed (6.23; 50.42); the second is four species of migratory birds, the *stork, turtledove, swift,* and *crane,* which are famous for returning each year at the exact time to the same places to nest. Bird migration is a seasonal phenomenon in the landscape of Israel, in the autumn and in the spring (the stork passes over Israel twice a year). Israel is more stupid than these birds—it does not return to God, its source.

8–9: Quoting the wise with a critical tone (see 2.23), Jeremiah presents a counter-argument. Those wise people in Jerusalem claim to own "torat-YHVH." The words "torah," "teaching" or "instruction," or "torat-YHVH," *the Instruction of the LORD* occurs eleven times in Jer., more than in any other prophetic book, in both poetry (2.8; 6.19; 8.8; 9.12) and in prose passages (16.11; 18.18; 26.4; 31.33; 32.23; 44.10, 23). For Jeremiah, the "torah," whose extent is uncertain, is a formal authoritative work, perhaps written, available to (at least) two professional circles: priests (18.18, and presumably, 2.8), and the wise (8.8). The current context illustrates the struggle between Jeremiah as a prophet (with priestly origins) and others who also claim to gain their ideological support from the Torah. While Jeremiah as a prophet proclaims the word (18.18), he often bases his words on traditions now found in the Torah. Thus, this text reflects a polemic about who owns the Torah and has the right to interpret it (see intro., "The Intellectual World of Jeremiah"). **10–12:** Parallels 6.13–15. **13:** *I will make an end of them:* The Heb puns on "'asaf" (to gather) and "swf" (to bring an end to, cut); it can be translated as both the pessimistic *I will make an end of them* and as the optimistic "I will gather them." Context makes it clear that the first is intended. **14–17:** A second pun is built on the nuances of the verb "dmm," "silent" in its various forms, which can mean "to be silenced, cease to exist, destroyed" as well "to be *doomed.*" "Rosh" *(bitter draft)* is a poisonous plant, see 9.14; 23.15 (cf. Amos 6.12). **15:** See 14.19.

7 Even the stork in the sky knows her seasons,
And the turtledove, swift, and crane
Keep the time of their coming;
But My people pay no heed
To the law of the LORD.
8 How can you say, "We are wise,
And we possess the Instruction of the LORD"?
Assuredly, for naught has the pen labored,
For naught the scribes!
9 The wise shall be put to shame,
Shall be dismayed and caught;
See, they reject the word of the LORD,
So their wisdom amounts to nothing.

10 Assuredly, I will give their wives to others,
And their fields to dispossessors;
For from the smallest to the greatest,
They are all greedy for gain;
Priest and prophet alike,
They all act falsely.
11 They offer healing offhand
For the wounds of My poor people,
Saying, "All is well, all is well,"
When nothing is well.
12 They have acted shamefully;
They have done abhorrent things—
Yet they do not feel shame,
They cannot be made to blush.
Assuredly, they shall fall among the falling,
They shall stumble at the time of their doom
—said the LORD.

13 [a]I will make an end of them[a]
—declares the LORD:
No grapes left on the vine,
No figs on the fig tree,
The leaves all withered;
[b]Whatever I have given them is gone.[b]
14 Why are we sitting by?
Let us gather into the fortified cities
And meet our doom there.
For the LORD our God has doomed us,
He has made us drink a bitter draft,
Because we sinned against the LORD.
15 We hoped for good fortune, but no happiness came;

a-a Meaning of Heb. uncertain; change of vocalization yields "Their fruit harvest has been gathered in." b-b Meaning of Heb. uncertain.

For a time of relief—instead there is terror!
16 The snorting of their horses was heard from Dan;
At the loud neighing of their steeds
The whole land quaked.
They came and devoured the land and what was in it,
The towns and those who dwelt in them.

17 Lo, I will send serpents against you,
Adders that cannot be charmed,
And they shall bite you —declares the LORD.

18 [a]When in grief I would seek comfort,[a]
My heart is sick within me.

19[b] "Is not the LORD in Zion?
Is not her King within her?
Why then did they anger Me with their images,
With alien futilities?"

Hark! The outcry of my poor people
From the land far and wide:
20 "Harvest is past,
Summer is gone,
But we have not been saved."
21 Because my people is shattered I am shattered;
I am dejected, seized by desolation.
22 Is there no balm in Gilead?
Can no physician be found?
Why has healing not yet
Come to my poor people?
23 Oh, that my head were water,
My eyes a fount of tears!
Then would I weep day and night
For the slain of my poor people.

9 Oh, to be in the desert,
At an encampment for wayfarers!
Oh, to leave my people,
To go away from them—
For they are all adulterers,
A band of rogues.

2 They bend their tongues like bows;
They are valorous in the land
For treachery, not for honesty;
They advance from evil to evil.

a-a Meaning of Heb. uncertain. *b Here God is speaking.*

18–20: Doubt and protest characterize the quotation in vv. 19a, 20: *Is not the LORD in Zion? / Is not her king within her? / Why ... Harvest is past, / summer is gone, / but we have not been saved.* Formed in a three-part rhetorical question, this cry suits the desperate feelings on the eve of destruction. The sentence of rebuke, *Why then did they anger Me with their images, / With alien futilities?* (v. 19), intrudes. This intrusion may very well be of the prophet himself, who is stating that God has not arbitrarily abandoned Zion, but has punished His people for idolatry. The idea that God had abandoned Jerusalem is found explicitly in 12.7, but in most other places, the prophet accentuates God's Presence and His involvement in the destruction (e.g., 21.3–7). **21–23:** This second lament, in the first person singular, may be a quotation of the people, perhaps from a late stage in the fall of Jerusalem, when the city was already filled with *the slain of my poor people* (v. 23). Alternatively, it may use the medical imagery as an alternative metaphor for the same point in vv. 19–20, concerning divine absence. Medical imagery as metaphor for military defeat appears also in 14.18; 51.8–9; and God as a physician is found in Exod. 15.26; Hos. 5.13; 6.1; 7.1; 11.3; 14.4. This second lament, unlike the first, does not accuse the people of any crime, and does not see God as involved in causing distress, but is a desperate call for salvation. **9.1–8:** The people are so evil; living in the desert is preferable. **1–2:** As in 8.18–19a, 21, 23, the initial voice is the prophet's; God interrupts, justifying Jeremiah's attitude, and further noting that *they advance from evil to evil,* but last, and most important, they neglect God Himself *(and they do not heed Me).*

And they do not heed Me
—declares the LORD.
3 Beware, every man of his friend!
Trust not even a brother!
For every brother takes advantage,
Every friend [a]-is base in his dealings.-[a]
4 One man cheats the other,
They will not speak truth;
They have trained their tongues to speak falsely;
[b]-They wear themselves out working iniquity.
5 You dwell in the midst of deceit.
In their deceit,-[b] they refuse to heed Me
—declares the LORD.

6 Assuredly, thus said the LORD of Hosts:
Lo, I shall smelt and assay them—
[b]-For what else can I do because of My poor people?-[b]
7 Their tongue is a sharpened arrow,
They use their mouths to deceive.
One speaks to his fellow in friendship,
But lays an ambush for him in his heart.
8 Shall I not punish them for such deeds?
—says the LORD—
Shall I not bring retribution
On such a nation as this?

9 For the mountains I take up weeping and wailing,
For the pastures in the wilderness, a dirge.
They are laid waste; no man passes through,
And no sound of cattle is heard.
Birds of the sky and beasts as well
Have fled and are gone.

10 I will turn Jerusalem into rubble,
Into dens for jackals;
And I will make the towns of Judah
A desolation without inhabitants.

11 What man is so wise
That he understands this?
To whom has the LORD's mouth spoken,
So that he can explain it:
Why is the land in ruins,
Laid waste like a wilderness,
With none passing through?

a-a See note at Lev. 19.16. *b-b Meaning of Heb. uncertain.*

3–5: The prophet now warns the people about each other. These vv. refer to Jacob's deceit, drawing the analogy from the forefather to the present behavior of his descendants, the people of Israel of the 6th c. BCE. Jeremiah reuses specific language (more easily seen in the Heb) found in the Gen. story to make his point: "'ah" (*brother,* see Gen. 25.26), "'aqav" / "Yaakov" (lit. "to follow," Gen. 25.26; 27.36), and "hittel b-" (*cheats, deceit;* see Gen. 31.7); he combines Jacob's trickster behavior toward Esau (Gen. chs 25–27) and Laban (Gen. chs 29–31). Jeremiah combines the Gen. story with Priestly terminology from the Holiness Legislation (see Lev. 19.16–18, "deal basely with" and the interchange between "friend" and "brother"). **5:** Once again God interrupts the prophet's words, putting neglect of God under the broader accusation of cheating. **6–8:** Judgment on this unfaithful behavior again involves *smelt*ing; see 6.27, 29. **8:** See 5.9, 29. **9–10:** Lament over the destruction of both rural and urban areas. **9:** Destruction is portrayed as a profound ecological disaster that affects *the mountains* and *the pastures in the wilderness;* all become desolate and empty of their fauna. The picture of their sudden and complete disappearance reuses the imagery of bird migration (see 8.7). **10:** *Rubble,* lit. "heaps of stones" (see 51.37 concerning Babylon), and *dens for jackals* (see 10.22; 49.22, Hazor; 51.37, Babylon); the cities of Judah shall become desolate and empty. *Dens for jackals,* a very powerful image since jackals enter human habitations only if they are fully deserted. In these two laments God is the sole agent of destruction; there is no mention of a human foe. As a result, the land is left empty of man and beast (vv. 9, 11; 32.43) and in complete ruin (see also 6.8; 12.10). **11–15:** The following vv., couched as question-and-answer, explain in detail why the destruction is taking place, allowing those who survived to understand the theological reasons for God's judgment. The setting calls (again—see 8.8) for the wise to supply their own explanation, while the prophet is to tell the people God's reasons.

[12]The LORD replied: Because they forsook the Teaching I
had set before them. They did not obey Me and they did not
follow it, [13]but followed their own willful heart and followed
the Baalim, as their fathers had taught them. [14]Assuredly, thus
said the LORD of Hosts, the God of Israel: I am going to feed
that people wormwood and make them drink a bitter draft. [15]I
will scatter them among nations which they and their fathers
never knew; and I will dispatch the sword after them until I
have consumed them.

16 Thus said the LORD of Hosts:
Listen!
Summon the dirge-singers, let them come;
Send for the skilled women, let them come.
17 Let them quickly start a wailing for us,
That our eyes may run with tears,
Our pupils flow with water.

18 For the sound of wailing
Is heard from Zion:
How we are despoiled!
How greatly we are shamed!
Ah, we must leave our land,
Abandon[a] our dwellings!

19 Hear, O women, the word of the LORD,
Let your ears receive the word of His mouth,
And teach your daughters wailing,
And one another lamentation.
20 For death has climbed through our windows,
Has entered our fortresses,
To cut off babes from the streets,
Young men from the squares.

21 Speak thus—says the LORD:
The carcasses of men shall lie
Like dung upon the fields,
Like sheaves behind the reaper,
With none to pick them up.

22 Thus said the LORD:
Let not the wise man glory in his wisdom;
Let not the strong man glory in his strength;
Let not the rich man glory in his riches.
23 But only in this should one glory:
In his earnest devotion to Me.

a *Lit. "They abandoned."*

12–13: Forsaking God's Torah is considered apostasy, equivalent to worshipping other gods. **14–15:** Judgment is total annihilation in two different locations. Death by two poisonous plants is to occur in the land of Judah (see 8.14), and death will be the fate of those deported into exile as God will send his *sword* against them until they are fully *consumed*. **16–21:** A call to lament over the destruction. This passage is an example of the inclusion of communal laments within judgment prophecies (see also 4.8b, 13b, 19–21, 29–31). **18:** Professional mourning women are called to produce *the sound of wailing* in *Zion*. Women were known for performing rituals of mourning in the ancient world. **20:** The personification of death that cannot be stopped (see Joel 2.9) may also recall Mot, the Canaanite god of death. **21:** The image of lack of burials is repeated in Jer. (7.33; 8.2; etc.). It is added here to an image of harvest, *like sheaves behind the reaper, / with none to pick them up.* **22–23:** Drawing on the polemic with the wise (8.8–9; 9.11, see Rashi and Kara), these vv. use wisdom style to rebuke three typically arrogant characters: the *wise*, the hero *(strong man)*, and the *rich* (see 1 Kings 20.11; Pss. 49.7; 52.3). Better than wisdom, strength, and riches, is *devotion* to God. God's attributes of *kindness, justice, and equity in the world* (see 17.5–8; Ps. 33.5) seem totally detached from the painful theological struggles in chs 8–9 so far, reflecting God's desertion and impotence.

For I the LORD act with kindness,
Justice, and equity in the world;
For in these I delight —declares the LORD.

24 Lo, days are coming—declares the LORD—when I will take
note of everyone [a-]circumcised in the foreskin:[-a] 25 of Egypt,
Judah, Edom, the Ammonites, Moab, and all the desert dwellers who have the hair of their temples clipped. For all these
nations are uncircumcised, but all the House of Israel are
[b-]uncircumcised of heart.[-b]

10

Hear the word which the LORD has spoken to you, O House of Israel!

2 Thus said the LORD:
Do not learn to go the way of the nations,
And do not be dismayed by portents in the sky;
Let the nations be dismayed by them!
3 For [c-]the laws of the nations[-c] are delusions:
For it is the work of a craftsman's hands.
He cuts down a tree in the forest with an ax,
4 He adorns it with silver and gold,
He fastens it[d] with nails and hammer,
So that it does not totter.
5 They are like a scarecrow in a cucumber patch,
They cannot speak.
They have to be carried,
For they cannot walk.
Be not afraid of them, for they can do no harm;
Nor is it in them to do any good.

6 O LORD, there is none like You!
You are great and Your name is great in power.
7 Who would not revere You, O King of the nations?
For that is Your due,
Since among all the wise of the nations
And among all their royalty
There is none like You.

a-a Force of Heb. uncertain.
b-b I.e., their minds are blocked to God's commandments.
c-c Emendation yields "the objects that the nations fear." *d Heb. "them."*

24–25: Circumcision and circumcision of the heart. Jeremiah, following Deut. 10.16, is the only prophet who mentions circumcision at all. The translation *when I will take note of everyone circumcised in the foreskin* (NJPS) implies that all those neighboring nations were circumcised. This, however, is beyond our knowledge. There is only limited information about circumcision in Egypt, and it seems to be restricted to priests (and see Josh. 5.2–9). Furthermore, this unit seems to posit that the *nations are* physically *uncircumcised,* while Israel the physically circumcised, appears to suffer from the metaphoric uncircumcision of the heart (as in 4.4). Thus, vv. 24–25b may be corrupt, and may have originally referred to the non-circumcised foreign nations.

10.1–16: The way of the nations in comparison to the true God. This passage, unique in Jer., contains no rebuke against Israel, no threats of judgment, not even threats against the nations who worship idols. It may have been placed here at the close of the first unit of chs 2–10 with a broad religious message, or because it refers to ideas found in the previous ch (see 9.22–23, 24–25; cf. 10.2, 6, 12–14). **1–3a:** This prophecy calls on Israel not to *learn* from *the way of the nations,* not to fear *portents in the sky* (lit. "astral signs") or follow *the laws of the nations.* The three phrases are euphemisms for other gods (and their idols), echoing Lev. 18.1–5 in the Holiness Legislation. **3b–5:** Deutero-Isaiah (Isa. 40.18–20, 28; 41.6–7; 44.9–20; 45.16–17, 20–22; 46.5–7) similarly mocks the worship of idols as worship of hand-made artifacts that are useless, powerless, unable to harm or to assist (cf. Ps. 115.4–8). This reflects a misunderstanding of ancient polytheists, who saw such images as a way that a powerful deity might dwell among them, without compromising that deity's power or ability to live in heaven. **6–10:** This hymn opens and closes (vv. 6, 10) by praising God's incomparable greatness. **6–7:** *O LORD, there is none like You!* which speaks to God's great power, is an inclusio to these two vv. (see 2 Sam. 7.22; 1 Kings 8.23; and in an elaborated form, Isa. 46.9; Ps. 86.8). **7:** God is called *King of the nations;* see v. 10, lit. "king of the world" (NJPS: *The everlasting King*). These are the only explicit references to God as King in Jer., though the metaphor of God as King governs the entire portrayal of God in the book, presented implicitly in his roles as Warrior, Judge and LORD.

8 But they are both dull and foolish;
[a-][Their] doctrine is but delusion;[-a]
It is a piece of wood,
9 Silver beaten flat, that is brought from Tarshish,
And gold from Uphaz,
The work of a craftsman and the goldsmith's hands;
Their clothing is blue and purple,
All of them are the work of skilled men.
10 But the LORD is truly God:
He is a living God,
The everlasting King.
At His wrath, the earth quakes,
And nations cannot endure His rage.

11[b]Thus shall you say to them: Let the gods, who did not make heaven and earth, perish from the earth and from under these heavens.

12 He made the earth by His might,
Established the world by His wisdom,
And by His understanding stretched out the skies.
13 [c-]When He makes His voice heard,[-c]
There is a rumbling of water in the skies;
He makes vapors rise from the end of the earth,
He makes lightning for the rain,
And brings forth wind from His treasuries.
14 Every man is proved dull, without knowledge;
Every goldsmith is put to shame because of the idol,
For his molten image is a deceit—
There is no breath in them.
15 They are delusion, a work of mockery;
In their hour of doom, they shall perish.
16 Not like these is the Portion of Jacob;
For it is He who formed all things,
And Israel is His very own tribe:
LORD of Hosts is His name.

17 Gather up your bundle[d] from the ground,
You who dwell under siege!
18 For thus said the LORD: I will fling away the inhabitants of the land this time: I will harass them so that they shall [e-]feel it.[-e]

19 Woe unto me for my hurt,
My wound is severe!

a-a Meaning of Heb. uncertain. *b This verse is in Aramaic.*
c-c Lit. "At the sound of His making." *d Meaning of Heb. uncertain.*
e-e Emendation yields "have to leave."

8–9: The craftsmen, *skilled men,* not the foreign gods, are mocked here. **10:** Three epithets: *the LORD is truly* [better: a true] *God: He is a living God, the everlasting King.* God's sovereignty (announced already in vv. 6–7), is demonstrated by His *wrath*ful rule over the *earth,* and all *nations.* **11:** This is the only v. in Jer. written in Aram., and it combines Old Aram. with Middle Aram. orthography (see "'arqa'" and "'ar'a'"). Aram. had become the lingua franca of the Near Eastern world by the time of the Neo-Assyrian empire, by the 8th c. BCE. This v. seems to have been interpolated into this hymnic passage for at least two reasons: it introduces a polemic against the nations over the identity of the true God, and highlights the importance of the issue of creation. It is likely addressed to the nations, and thus is in Aram. **12–16:** The passage is parallel to 51.15–19, and the last three lines of v. 13 are parallel to Ps. 135.7. Returning to the hymnic style, these vv. further emphasize the role of God as King of the world (see v. 10). **16:** Israel is different, alluding to Deut. 32.9. The thematic similarities to Deutero-Isaiah identify this entire passage as non-Jeremian, composed by a Babylonian-exilic author (see ch 24 nn.), with the additional Aram. note in v. 11 added still later. **17–25:** Five miscellaneous and independent passages close this ch, and present a sample of admonitions (vv. 17, 22), judgment oracle (v. 18), a lament (v. 19–21), a confession and an individual plea (vv. 23–24), and a communal plea for revenge (v. 25). **17–18:** Jerusalem *under siege* is called to *gather* its *bundle,* or load (a hapax term). The passage puns, juxtaposing the *siege* ("matzor") with God *harass*ing ("hezzar") the besieged people. This passage may have been composed during the first siege of Jerusalem in 597 BCE. **19–21:** A lament over destruction and dispersion, strikingly recited by Jerusalem herself. (Cf. Isa. 33.20; 49.17; 54.1–2.)

I thought, "This is but a sickness
And I must bear it."
20 My tents are ravaged,
All my tent cords are broken.
My children have gone forth from me
And are no more;
No one is left to stretch out my tents
And hang my tent cloths.
21 For the shepherds[a] are dull
And did not seek the LORD;
Therefore they have not prospered
And all their flock is scattered.
22 Hark, a noise! It is coming,
A great commotion out of the north,
That the towns of Judah may be made a desolation,
A haunt of jackals.

23 I know, O LORD, that man's road is not his [to choose],
That man, as he walks, cannot direct his own steps.
24 Chastise me, O LORD, but in measure;
Not in Your wrath, lest You reduce me to naught.
25 Pour out Your wrath on the nations who have not
heeded You,
Upon the clans that have not invoked Your name.
For they have devoured Jacob,
Have devoured and consumed him,
And have laid desolate his homesteads.

11

The word which came to Jeremiah from the LORD:

2 "Hear the terms of this covenant, and recite them to the
men of Judah and the inhabitants of Jerusalem! 3 And say to
them, Thus said the LORD, the God of Israel: Cursed be the
man who will not obey the terms of this covenant, 4 which I

a I.e., rulers; cf. note at 2.8.

21: The prophet responds to the lament, specifying the leaders as responsible for the dispersion; see 23.1–2. **22:** The foe of the *north;* see 6.22. **23–25:** This individual lament (vv. 23–24) turns into a communal plea (v. 25). This cluster of psalmodic sayings is exceptional among the individual laments in Jer. (see 11.18–23). **23:** Unparalleled elsewhere in Jer. is this wisdom conception that *man's road is not his [to choose], / that man, as he walks, cannot direct his own steps* (see Prov. 16.9); it is uncertain why it was inserted here. **24:** This request for a just judgment and yet limited wrath, so as to spare the speaker's life (Pss. 6.2; 107.38–39), does not accord with either Jeremiah's conviction that he is blameless (as in 12.3; 17.16–18), nor with his common theodicy, in which a righteous God had afflicted the people measure-for-measure (12.1; 20.12). **25:** Borrowed from Ps. 79.6–7 with minor variants, this v. reflects the destruction of Jerusalem. After the Christian persecution of Jews in the medieval period, this v. has been recited during the Passover Seder when the door is opened to admit the prophet Elijah, to express the hope for ultimate divine justice in the world and for divine protection for His people.

11.1–17: The evil of Judah, covenant breaking, and its hazardous consequences. Two passages, vv. 1–14, 15–17, are tied together by the proximity of passages illustrating the people's evil behavior of cultic disobedience. See the repetition of *House of* ["Beit"] *Israel and the House of* ["Beit"] *Judah* (vv. 10, 17), "raʿah" (or "evil," *disaster,* vv. 11, 12, 14, 17), and "qitter laBaʿal" (or "to other gods," vv. 12, 13, 17). The first, vv. 1–14, is a prosaic covenant speech, the second a poetic passage closed by prose (v. 17). The harsh consequence in these two passages is the divine decision to bring evil upon the House of Israel and the House of Judah, to disregard their pleas for help (v. 11), even to close the gates of prayer to the prophet (v. 14), to drop God's obligations to the covenant in retaliation for the people's annulment of His covenant. **1–14:** This second covenant speech (see 7.1–15 n.), a judgment prophecy (the accusation in vv. 1–10; and the judgment, vv. 11–14), explicitly focuses on the covenant between God and His people. **2:** The speech opens with a public call to the people of Judah and the residents of Jerusalem to listen (and obey, see 7.1–2; 17.19–20). The plural form may be part of the call itself (see 7.2b), though according to *Pesik. Rab.,* this statement is addressed to the three prophets active at this time: the prophetess Huldah (2 Kings 22.14–20; 2 Chron. 34.22–28); a relative of Jeremiah, who spoke to the women while Jeremiah spoke to the men on the streets (see v. 6); and Jeremiah's teacher, Zephaniah (Zeph. 1.1), who preached in the synagogue. **3–5:** The threat of an "ʾarur"-curse with the prophet's closing response: *Amen* (v. 5), the key verbs "shamʿ" and "ʿasah" (vv. 3, 4, and also vv. 6–8), all refer to Deut. 27.8–26. The blessing and the curse on Mt. Gerizim and Mt. Ebal is the

enjoined upon your fathers when I freed them from the land of
Egypt, the iron crucible, saying, 'Obey Me and observe them,[a]
just as I command you, that you may be My people and I may
be your God'—5 in order to fulfill the oath which I swore to
your fathers, to give them a land flowing with milk and honey,
as is now the case." And I responded, "Amen, LORD."

6 And the LORD said to me, "Proclaim all these things through
the towns of Judah and the streets of Jerusalem: Hear the terms
of this covenant, and perform them. 7 For I have repeatedly and
persistently warned your fathers from[b] the time I brought them
out of Egypt to this day, saying: Obey My commands. 8 But they
would not listen or give ear; they all followed the willfulness
of their evil hearts. So I have brought upon them all the terms[c]
of this covenant, because they did not do what I commanded
them to do."

9 The LORD said to me, "A conspiracy exists among the men of
Judah and the inhabitants of Jerusalem. 10 They have returned
to the iniquities of their fathers of old, who refused to heed My
words. They, too, have followed other gods and served them.
The House of Israel and the House of Judah have broken the
covenant that I made with their fathers."

11 Assuredly, thus said the LORD: I am going to bring upon
them disaster from which they will not be able to escape. Then
they will cry out to me, but I will not listen to them. 12 And the
townsmen[d] of Judah and the inhabitants of Jerusalem will go
and cry out to the gods to which they sacrifice; but they will not
be able to rescue them in their time of disaster. 13 For your gods
have become as many as your towns, O Judah, and you have
set up as many altars to Shame[e] as there are streets in Jerusalem—altars for sacrifice to Baal.

14 As for you, do not pray for this people, do not raise a cry of
prayer on their behalf; for I will not listen when they call to Me
on account of their disaster.

a I.e., the terms of the covenant. *b Lit. "at."*
c I.e., the punishments prescribed for violation. *d Lit. "towns."*
e See note at 3.24.

ceremony that designates the reinstitution of the covenant with God, a covenant that is based on "every word of this Teaching" (Deut. 27.8). Jeremiah here draws a clear analogy to the early covenant(s), whence the people had become God's people (cf. Jer. 11.4 and Deut. 27.9–10). In his prophecy, Jeremiah ratifies the constitution of the covenant (or actually its early reinstitution) with his contemporary Judean audience, who, he hopes will recommit to the covenant. **5:** This is an exceptional reference to God's obligations towards His people, a reference to the promise (the divine *oath*) to *your fathers, to give them a land* (the common phenomenon is to focus on the people's obligations, and this is well contextualized in the political treaties between the Assyrian emperor and his vassals). **8:** *The terms* (lit. "words," i.e., penalties for violation; see translators' note *c*) *of this covenant* ("Diveri haberit hazot") means first (v. 3) the commitments by the people to obey, but here it stands for the curses of that treaty obligation. The words of the covenant are for Jeremiah the actual written commandments that gain their authority from that constitutive covenant, and are still relevant by the last decades of Judah. Disobedience to any of those regulations is, therefore, a profound action against the covenant and against God; it thus initiates the covenant stipulations. This matter of theodicy is of paramount importance in this covenant speech as in others, leading to the harshest accusation. **9–10:** A conspiracy among the people (leaders?) of Judah and Jerusalem leaves the people's current behavior full of blame (see 34.15–16). This portrayal of reverting to a period of sin has suggested that this v. hints at the Josiah cultic reform as the period of obedience, and thus perceive it as a complete failure. But this is doubtful. The fact remains, Jeremiah does not refer explicitly to the reform (ca. 622 BCE) that presumably took place during his years of activity. **10:** Returning to their forefathers' sins, the people are accused of annulling the covenant. The demonstration of this betrayal is worshipping other gods. **11–14:** In retaliation, at the point where the people are said to have withdrawn from their part of the treaty, God threatens to bring total *disaster* upon them, which would not leave room for salvation (the people are ironically called to address the multiple other gods they worship, in vain; see 2.27–28). Furthermore, God chooses to be deaf to their cries (cf. the constant divine response in other eras, as in the book of Judg. 3.7–9, and passim; and the penitential declarations in Neh. 9.26–31). Theologically, this extreme presentation leaves God present and active, hard and unrelenting not in the salvation of His people, but in inflicting disaster upon them. The covenant speech frames these extreme theological perspectives in a justified and explicable scheme: God has acted according to the words of the covenant, and in line with its stipulations.

15 Why should My beloved be in My House,
[a]Who executes so many vile designs?
The sacral flesh will pass away from you,
For you exult while performing your evil deeds.[-a]
16 The LORD named you
"Verdant olive tree,
Fair, with choice fruit."
But with a great roaring sound
He has set it on fire,
And its boughs are broken.[b]

17 The LORD of Hosts, who planted you, has decreed disaster for you, because of the evil wrought by the House of Israel and the House of Judah, who angered Me by sacrificing to Baal.

18 The LORD informed me, and I knew—
Then You let me see their deeds.
19 For I was like a docile lamb
Led to the slaughter;
I did not realize
That it was against me
They fashioned their plots:
"Let us destroy the tree with its fruit,[c]
Let us cut him off from the land of the living,
That his name be remembered no more!"
20 O LORD of Hosts, O just Judge,
Who test the thoughts and the mind,
Let me see Your retribution upon them,
For I lay my case before You.

21 Assuredly, thus said the LORD of Hosts concerning the men of Anathoth who seek your life and say, "You must not prophesy any more in the name of the LORD, or you will die

a-a Meaning of Heb. uncertain. Emendation yields "Who does such vile deeds? / Can your treacheries be canceled by sacral flesh / That you exult while performing your evil deeds?" *b Emendation yields "burned."* *c Or "sap."*

15–17: The poetic vv. are difficult, as it is hard to define the speaker and the beloved (see S. D. Luzzatto). An overly simple explanation takes the beloved to refer to the people (Tg. and Rashi); Kimḥi finds the prophet calling God his beloved, and this is just as improbable. **16:** The fresh *olive tree* symbolizes the good divine benevolence over the people or the individual (Hos. 14.7; Ps. 52.10). Here it follows the disastrous transformation from a fresh, permanently green, and beautiful tree, to a tree set on fire, whose branches were brutally broken (Rashi). **17:** Indeed, the people who were God's plant, are now to suffer His affliction due to their cultic misbehavior.

11.18–20.18: Laments and further prophetic passages. In this section seven passages are typical individual laments (common in Psalms): 11.18–23; 12.1–6; 15.10–21; 17.14–18; 18.18–23; 20.7–13; 20.14–18. The laments are unique in that they reverse the direction of speech. While prophecy is the word of God spoken via His messengers to the people, the laments are the words of the prophet (the individual) addressed to God. Unattested in any other prophetic collection (but with some similarities in Second Isaiah), these laments shed light on the prophetic mission, the personal distress in which the prophet was trapped, his struggles with different enemies, and just as fierce, his protests against God, his sender (cf. with communal laments in ch 14, below, where the perspective is national). The name "confessions," given to these passages in Christian exegesis, is thus inappropriate. In addition, these passages, while "personal," can hardly serve to reconstruct any biographical details of the prophet's life, except for the general impression of his being hounded, scrutinized, and very lonely. The laments illustrate conventional style and phraseology found in many other individual prayers of lament in the HB, with clear influences of wisdom literature. Similar to Jeremiah's usage of pentateuchal traditions, the prophet has worked phrases or even passages of poetry in his own idiosyncratic ways. He created a unique voice, illustrating his knowledge of biblical literature and his exceptional rhetorical skills to make them his own.

11.18–23: Jeremiah's first lament. **19:** No less than three figurative complaints are brought in this v. to arouse God to act on the prophet's behalf: being a *lamb led to the slaughter,* the victim of a conspiracy, and a tree that is cut down. **20:** The prophet approaches God, the *just Judge* (see Isa. 11.4; Pss. 9.5, 9; 35.24; 50.6), setting his case before Him, expecting revenge (see Jer. 15.15; 20.12). **21–23:** But, differing from individual laments, the one brought by the prophet suggests a full dialogue, in which Jeremiah raises his complaint (vv. 18–20), and is immediately answered by divine words of judgment against his enemies, who are identified as his hometown residents, the people of *Anathoth.*

by our hand"—[22] Assuredly, thus said the LORD of Hosts: "I am going to deal with them: the young men shall die by the sword, their boys and girls shall die by famine. [23] No remnant shall be left of them, for I will bring disaster on the men of Anathoth, the year of their doom."

12 You will win,[a] O LORD, if I make claim against You,
Yet I shall present charges against You:
Why does the way of the wicked prosper?
Why are the workers of treachery at ease?
2 You have planted them, and they have taken root,
They spread, they even bear fruit.
You are present in their mouths,
But far from their thoughts.
3 Yet You, LORD, have noted and observed me;
You have tested my heart, and found it with You.
Drive them out like sheep to the slaughter,
Prepare them for the day of slaying!

4 How long must the land languish,
And the grass of all the countryside dry up?
Must beasts and birds perish,
Because of the evil of its inhabitants,
Who say, "He will not look upon our future"?[b]
5[c] If you race with the foot-runners and they exhaust you,
How then can you compete with horses?
If you are [d]secure only[d] in a tranquil land,
How will you fare in the jungle of the Jordan?
6 For even your kinsmen and your father's house,
Even they are treacherous toward you,
They cry after you as a mob.
Do not believe them
When they speak cordially to you.

7 I have abandoned My House,
I have deserted My possession,
I have given over My dearly beloved
Into the hands of her enemies.
8 My own people[e] acted toward Me
Like a lion in the forest;
She raised her voice against Me—
Therefore I have rejected her.

a Lit. "be in the right." *b Septuagint reads "ways."*
c God here replies to Jeremiah's plea in vv. 1–3.
d-d Some Septuagint mss. read "not secure."
e Lit. "possession"; the land as well as the people, as is clear in v. 14.

The total judgment on the people of Anathoth is phrased in great resemblance to other prophecies of judgment (see 14.15, etc.).

12.1–6: Jeremiah's second lament is also structured in two parts: the prophet's protest (vv. 1–4) and the divine response (vv. 5–7), though this time only confirming his suffering and calling on him to be strong; there are no promises of salvation. **1:** The prophet recognizes God as righteous (see Pss. 11.7; 116.5; 119.137, etc.; and among the prophets only Zeph. 3.5), and yet puts his complaints to Him, as does Job (Job 13.18; 33.13) in a way that challenges the conventional epithets, such as in Jer. 17.10. **1–2:** The success of the *wicked* is depicted metaphorically as the fruitful tree planted by water, the ultimate emblem of righteousness and its reward; see Ps. 1.3 and Jer. 17.5–8. Jeremiah uses this image for denunciation, as he protests against God who has planted and nurtured those who least deserve His help (see Ps. 73.3–12; divine planting as a metaphor on the national sphere, see Ps. 80.9–13; Jer. 2.21; 11.17). In his portrayal of the wicked, Jeremiah uses the opposite ideas of outer *(mouths)* and inner *(thoughts)* and near *(present)* and distant *(far)*. For such hypocrisy on the national level, see Isa. 29.13. **3:** Implicitly, the prophet depicts himself as righteous, one whom God had known inside-out (see Ps. 139.1, 23–24), who deserves divine justice and protection. He demands revenge and *slaughter*.

12.7–13: God's lament over the destruction of Judah. 7: This is one of the exceptional statements where God confesses He has deserted His people and land ("'azav," "natash"; see 23.33). Cf. Jer. 8.18–19; 14.7–9; Ezek. 8.12; 9.9 (and Lam. 5.20), where the people protest against the divine abandonment, and the prophets each in their own way refute the protests. God's desertion is otherwise admitted retrospectively by Second Isaiah (Isa. 54.6–7; 60.15; 62.4, 12).

9 [a]My own people acts toward Me
Like a bird of prey [or] a hyena;
Let the birds of prey surround her![a]
Go, gather all the wild beasts,
Bring them to devour!
10 Many shepherds have destroyed My vineyard,
Have trampled My field,
Have made My delightful field
A desolate wilderness.
11 [b]They have[b] made her a desolation;
Desolate, she pours out grief to Me.
The whole land is laid desolate,
But no man gives it thought.
12 Spoilers have come
Upon all the bare heights of the wilderness.
For a sword of the LORD devours
From one end of the land to the other;
No flesh is safe.
13 They have sown wheat and reaped thorns,
They have endured pain to no avail.
Be shamed, then, by your harvest—
By the blazing wrath of the LORD!

14 Thus said the LORD: As for My wicked neighbors who encroach on the heritage that I gave to My people Israel—I am going to uproot them from their soil, and I will uproot the House of Judah out of the midst of them. 15 Then, after I have uprooted them, I will take them back into favor, and restore them each to his own inheritance and his own land. 16 And if they learn the ways of My people, to swear by My name—"As the LORD lives"—just as they once taught My people to swear by Baal, then they shall be [c]built up in the midst of[c] My people. 17 But if they do not give heed, I will tear out that nation, tear it out and destroy it—declares the LORD.

13 Thus the LORD said to me: "Go buy yourself a loincloth of linen, and put it around your loins, but do not dip it into water." 2 So I bought the loincloth in accordance with the LORD's command, and put it about my loins. 3 And the word

a-a Meaning of Heb. uncertain. *b-b Heb. "He has."*
c-c Or "incorporated into."

9–12: Total destruction is brought by predators (*birds* and *beasts*), by *shepherds* grazing their flocks in *vineyard* and *field* (see Isa. 5.5; Ps. 80.9–14), and finally by human invaders who turn the land to total desolation. Was it a divine judgement? Did God summon them all? **12b:** A possible interpolation to clarify that this is God's doing. On the redactional level, the first two laments by the prophet (11.18–23; 12.1–6) and the third by God (12.7–13), share both their feelings of betrayal by those who were supposed to be the closest (see the triad "My House," "My possession," "My dearly beloved," v. 7), painful acknowledgment of the alliance and physical distance from their habitat, and finally the total annihilation in prospect for all. 12.14–17 is connected to this context by the reference to "nahalah" ("My possession," vv. 7, 8, and 14; and possibly also the close tone of "natash" "desert," v. 7 and "natash" "uproot," vv. 14, 15, 17 ["tear out"]).

12.14–17: A prophecy of destruction and restoration. This prophecy is distinct from its current context, and shows resemblances to editorial and late strands of the book's evolution. **14:** *Uproot ... soil* ("natash me'al 'dmatam"), exile, a judgment not mentioned in the previous three passages of this ch, which deal only with death and desolation within the land (11.22; 12.3b–4, 10–13). **15:** Judgment over the neighboring enemy nations that transforms into restoration occurs in 46.26; 48.47; 49.6, 39, all editorial comments of restoration added to prophecies against the nations. But in distinction from those, and unique in Jeremiah, this passage sees "conversion" of those foreigners and their incorporation within God's people.

13.1–14: Two enigmatic images (vv. 1–11, 12–14), are tied together by style (prose), by structure—quite mysterious divine instructions or saying (vv. 1–7, 12) that require divine explanations (vv. 8–11, 13–14), and by phrase ("shahat," vv. 7, 9, 14). The linkage indicates that the second passage is an elaboration of the first. **1–11:** The *loincloth of linen* buried in the desert. This is the first of several symbolic actions the prophet is ordered to perform using artifacts from his daily environment (see further 18.1–18; 19.1–15). **1–7:** The prophet acts in silence and with full obedience, as he follows instructions: first, to purchase and wear it. **3–5:** Second, to go to *Perath,* the nearby, familiar Wadi (known today as Nahal Perat, Wadi Qelt), which supplies fresh water to Anathoth

of the LORD came to me a second time: 4 "Take the loincloth
which you bought, which is about your loins, and go at once to
Perath[a] and cover it up there in a cleft of the rock." 5 I went and
buried it at Perath, as the LORD had commanded me. 6 Then,
after a long time, the LORD said to me, "Go at once to Perath
and take there the loincloth which I commanded you to bury
there." 7 So I went to Perath and dug up the loincloth from the
place where I had buried it; and found the loincloth ruined; it
was not good for anything.
8 The word of the LORD came to me: 9 Thus said the LORD:
Even so will I ruin the overweening pride of Judah and Jerusalem. 10 This wicked people who refuse to heed My bidding,
who follow the willfulness of their own hearts, who follow
other gods and serve them and worship them, shall become
like that loincloth, which is not good for anything. 11 For as the
loincloth clings close to the loins of a man, so I brought close to
Me the whole House of Israel and the whole House of Judah—
declares the LORD—that they might be My people, for fame,
and praise, and splendor. But they would not obey.
12 And speak this word to them: Thus said the LORD, the God
of Israel: "Every jar should be filled with wine." And when they
say to you, "Don't we know that every jar should be filled with
wine?" 13 say to them, "Thus said the LORD: I am going to fill
with drunkenness all the inhabitants of this land, and the kings
who sit on the throne of David, and the priests and the prophets, and all the inhabitants of Jerusalem. 14 And I will smash
them one against the other, parents and children alike—declares the LORD; no pity, compassion, or mercy will stop Me
from destroying them."

15 Attend and give ear; be not haughty,
For the LORD has spoken.
16 Give honor to the LORD your God
Before He brings darkness,
Before your feet stumble
On the mountains in shadow—
When you hope for light,
And it is turned to darkness
And becomes deep gloom.
17 For if you will not give heed,
My inmost self must weep,

a *Or "the Euphrates"; cf. "Parah," Josh. 18.23.*

(there is no reason to identify the *Perath* with the Euphrates River, as do LXX, and Kimḥi). The prophet is to bury the loincloth in one of the cliffs in the wadi. **6–7:** Third, *after a long time,* a third divine word instructs the prophet to dig up the loincloth, only to discover it was *ruined; it was not good for anything.* Whether it was wet or dry, in the very hot climate of the Judean Desert, the flexible cloth has become useless. **8–11:** God explains this symbolic action in two comparisons between the linen loincloth and God's people, presented in a chiastic order. **9–10:** The *ruined* loincloth symbolizes, first, the fate of *Judah and Jerusalem,* which are to be ruined and useless (referring back to vv. 6–7). **11:** Only then the prophet draws back on the initial step (vv. 1–2), the purchase of a perfect loincloth that symbolizes God's basic intentions to make the *House of Israel* and the *House of Judah … My people, for fame, and praise, and splendor* (see Deut. 26.19); alas, a symbol to God's great disappointment in the people's disobedience. **12–14:** Smashed jars of wine. **12:** The divine words are so simple they form a riddle: surely *jars* are made to contain *wine* (1 Sam. 1.24; 10.3; 25.18; 2 Sam. 16.1). In distinction to the earlier passage, this one is built on common knowledge, and does not involve symbolic action. **13–14:** The imagery is unique, in that the vessels, not the contents, are the focus (cf. 48.11–12). In contradistinction to the real vessels, which are not affected by the fluid they hold, these human containers will be filled with *drunkenness* (metonymy). God will *smash* these clay vessels (see Lam. 4.2) *one against the other,* declaring that *compassion* is not going to play its role (see 21.7; and only the first two verbs, in Ezek. 5.11, etc.); God is determined to destroy them all ("shahat," as in vv. 7, 9).

13.15–27: Three independent passages emphasizing Judah's judgment affected by hubris (vv. 15–17, 18–19, 20–27). These may be seen as elaborations on v. 9, where God threatens to ruin "the overweening pride of Judah and Jerusalem" (it may also be that the linkage to v. 9 explains why the three are together; see "ga'on"); see also the "fame," "praise, and splendor" of his initial plans for the people, v. 11. **15:** *Be not haughty* ("gavah") calls for obedience and humility (so Kimḥi), since it is God who should be given honor.

18: The king and his mother, probably Jehoiachin and Nehushta (see 2 Kings 24.8, 12), are called to humiliate themselves in face of the catastrophe that reached their *glorious crowns.* **20:** The entire people are called *the flock you took pride in,* a flock that was captured and dispersed. In addition, all three passages mention deportation, captivity (v. 16), Judah's complete exile (v. 19), and the divine dispersion (v. 24). **20–27:** The feminine imagery of Jerusalem alternates between the city as shepherd responsible for the flock given her to guard (v. 20), as a caring mother, even in labor (v. 21), and as God's adulterous consort (vv. 25–27); see chs 2–3. **23:** Interrupting the imagery of Jerusalem as a woman, this v. has two rhetorical questions that have become well-known: *Can the Cushite change his skin, / Or the leopard his spots?*—claiming ironically that the people cannot avoid their deeply ingrained sinful behavior, as if it is part of their defining identity (see 4.22; cf. Jeremiah's calls to repent, as in 3.12; 4.1–2). **27:** The ch closes with a cry over Jerusalem (otherwise over Moab, 48.46; see Ezek. 16.23). Accused of adulterous behavior, Jerusalem will not be able to be purified, a possible echo of the menstruation law of purification (Lev. 15.28; also 12.4, 6–8; see Jer. 2.20–25).

Because of your arrogance;
My eye must stream and flow
With copious tears,
Because the flock of the LORD
Is taken captive.

18 Say to the king and the queen mother,
"Sit in a lowly spot;
For your diadems are abased,
Your glorious crowns."
19 The cities of the Negeb are shut,
There is no one to open them;
[a]Judah is exiled completely,
All of it exiled.[a]
20 Raise your eyes and behold
Those who come from the north:
Where are the sheep entrusted to you,
The flock you took pride in?
21 [b]What will you say when they appoint as your heads
Those among you whom you trained to be tame?[b]
Shall not pangs seize you
Like a woman in childbirth?
22 And when you ask yourself,
"Why have these things befallen me?"
It is because of your great iniquity
That your skirts are lifted up,
Your limbs exposed.

23 Can the Cushite change his skin,
Or the leopard his spots?
Just as much can you do good,
Who are practiced in doing evil!
24 So I will scatter you[c] like straw that flies
Before the desert wind.
25 This shall be your lot,
Your measured portion from Me
—declares the LORD.
Because you forgot Me
And trusted in falsehood,
26 I in turn will lift your skirts over your face
And your shame shall be seen.
27 I behold your adulteries,
Your lustful neighing,
Your unbridled depravity, your vile acts
On the hills of the countryside.

a-a *I.e., most of Judah has been annexed by an alien people.*
b-b *Meaning of Heb. uncertain.* c *Heb. "them."*

Woe to you, O Jerusalem,
Who will not be clean!
How much longer shall it be?

14 The word of the LORD which came to Jeremiah concerning the droughts.

2 Judah is in mourning,
Her settlements languish.
Men are bowed to the ground,
And the outcry of Jerusalem rises.
3 Their nobles sent their servants for water;
They came to the cisterns, they found no water.
They returned, their vessels empty.
They are shamed and humiliated,
They cover their heads.
4 [a]Because of the ground there is dismay,[a]
For there has been no rain on the earth.
The plowmen are shamed,
They cover their heads.
5 Even the hind in the field
Forsakes her new-born fawn,
Because there is no grass.
6 And the wild asses stand on the bare heights,
Snuffing the air like jackals;
Their eyes pine,
Because there is no herbage.

7 Though our iniquities testify against us,
Act, O LORD, for the sake of Your name;
Though our rebellions are many
And we have sinned against You.
8 O Hope of Israel,
Its deliverer in time of trouble,
Why are You like a stranger in the land,
Like a traveler who stops only for the night?

a-a Meaning of Heb. uncertain.

14.1–15.4: Concerning the drought (and the military defeat). This unit has two symmetric parts (14.1–16; 14.17–15.4) with four components in each: description of distress (vv. 2–6, 17–18), communal lament (vv. 7–9, 19–22), prohibition to pray for the people (vv. 11–12; 15.1), and God's response (vv. 10, 13–16; 15.2–4). **14.1:** The title specifies drought as its thematic focus (see 46.1; 47.1; 49.34). However, as of 14.7 the six passages (vv. 7–9, 10, 11–16, 17–18, 19–22; 15.1–4) do not refer to ecological conditions. Rather, the prophet, the people, and God in His responses discuss the horrors of a military-political threat, and the expectation for God's involvement and possible salvation is challenged. **2–6:** Drought and its dire consequences. Starting from the city of Jerusalem, the prophet moves out to the rural area east of the city, to the Judean desert, the area so familiar to Jeremiah with its water resources (see 2.13 n.). **3:** *Cisterns* (Heb "gevim") are natural open rock-basins, often on the bottom of wadis, where flood waters gather. They hold water only for a limited time depending on the rain (2 Kings 3.16–17), and are the first to dry out when the area lacks precipitation. **3–4:** Desperation concerning both shepherds and peasants who cannot cultivate their lands *(they are shamed ..., they cover their heads)*. **5–6:** Even wild animals on the border of the desert cannot find green lawn to sustain themselves in their vicinity (as the *hind* after labor), and no hope is seen even from afar (for the larger, more powerful animals, such as *wild asses* and *jackals*). This is an overwhelming description of drought, which is a steady phenomenon in the land of Israel, and particularly in the border area between Carmel and the western ridge of the Jerusalem mountains. **7–9:** A partial communal lament is proclaimed, starting with confession of sins and moving on to pleas of salvation. Formally, these two components leave vv. 2–6 as the description of the distress. However, vv. 8b–9 illustrate a disaster of a military threat, where divine assistance as a warrior is expected. This communal lament, like vv. 19–22 below, holds phrases and themes otherwise unknown in Jer. (e.g., *for the sake of Your name* [v. 7], otherwise in Isa. 66.5; Ezek. 20.9, 14, 22; 36.22; and mostly within psalmodic literature, as in Pss. 79.9; 106.8; and in individual laments, such as Ps. 23.3). **8–9:** Two epithets of God—"miqveh Israel" (see 17.13, in its double meaning of "water source" and "hope," this epithet connects the two arenas of this prophecy) and God as savior in times of need (see 2 Sam. 22.42; Isa. 43.3, 11; Pss. 18.42; 106.21; etc.)—set the context for two rhetorical questions. In using the imagery of a *stranger* and a passing guest (LXX: "citizen," seems harmonistic, employing here the known pair "ger" / "ezrah," as in Lev.

9 Why are You like a man who is stunned,
Like a warrior who cannot give victory?
Yet You are in our midst, O LORD,
And Your name is attached to us—
Do not forsake us!

10 Thus said the LORD concerning this people: "Truly, they
love to stray, they have not restrained their feet; so the LORD
has no pleasure in them. Now He will recall their iniquity and
punish their sin."
11 And the LORD said to me, "Do not pray for the benefit of this
people. 12 When they fast, I will not listen to their outcry; and
when they present burnt offering and meal offering, I will not accept them. I will exterminate them by war, famine, and disease."
13 I said, "Ah, Lord GOD! The prophets are saying to them,
'You shall not see the sword, famine shall not come upon you,
but I will give you unfailing security in this place.' "
14 The LORD replied: It is a lie that the prophets utter in My
name. I have not sent them or commanded them. I have not
spoken to them. A lying vision, an empty divination, the deceit of their own contriving—that is what they prophesy to you!
15 Assuredly, thus said the LORD concerning the prophets who
prophesy in My name though I have not sent them, and who
say, "Sword and famine shall not befall this land"; those very
prophets shall perish by sword and famine. 16 And the people
to whom they prophesy shall be left lying in the streets of Jerusalem because of the famine and the sword, with none to bury
them—they, their wives, their sons, and their daughters. I will
pour out upon them [the requital of] their wickedness.

17 And do you speak to them thus:
Let my eyes run with tears,
Day and night let them not cease,
For [a-]my hapless people[-a] has suffered
A grievous injury, a very painful wound.
18 If I go out to the country—
Lo, the slain of the sword.
If I enter the city—
Lo, [b-]those who are sick with[-b] famine.
Both priest and prophet roam[c] the land,
They know not where.

a-a Lit. "the maiden daughter, My people." *b-b Lit. "the sicknesses of."*
c Meaning of Heb. uncertain.

17.15), the first question challenges God's Presence, and the imagery of a stunned man and *a warrior who cannot give victory* questions God's omnipotence (cf. Zeph. 3.17, where both Presence and salvation occur together). The two questions are answered by the proclamation *You are in our midst, O LORD, / and Your name is attached to us*—expressing confidence in God, the people declare that God is present among them, and is thus expected to be involved on their behalf, yet the historical reality they face puts in jeopardy those religious conventions, and they need to make their plea: *do not forsake us* (for similar feelings of desertion and lack of salvation, see 8.19–22). These theological expressions of doubt typify communal laments, whereas Jeremiah in his prophecies refutes them vigorously, when he distinguishes Presence from salvation (as for instance 21.1–7). It seems, therefore, that Jeremiah had taken well known laments produced in his time, and woven them into his prophecy, adding minimal phrases of his own ("meshuvot" and "miqve Israel"), in order to illustrate the immensity of destruction. **10–12:** Two divine reactions on the above show God's determination to bring total judgment on the people. **11–12:** Prohibition to pray for the people; see 7.16. **13–16:** Referring to the harsh judgment God proclaimed against the people, and for the first time in this book, the prophet introduces his struggle with the peace prophets, those who from Jeremiah's point of view prophesy in the name of God, though they were never sent by Him (see 23.9–40; chs 27–29). These prophets are quoted as saying no sword or famine shall come upon the people; rather God will guarantee "shelom 'emet" *(unfailing security)* in this place, see Lev. 26.6 (for "shalom" and "'emet," see Jer. 33.6). **15–16:** Judgment is to come upon those prophets, as also upon the entire people, repeating the pair *sword* and *famine,* but now in a chiastic order. **17–18:** Opening the second part of this prophetic unit (14.17–15.4), the prophet draws on the closing description of judgment by sword and famine. For God (or the prophet) as weeping over the disaster, see 8.23. As in vv. 2–6, Jeremiah observes both rural and urban areas to present the entirety of the prospective calamity.

19 Have You, then, rejected Judah?
Have You spurned Zion?
Why have You smitten us
So that there is no cure?
Why do we hope for happiness,
But find no good;
For a time of healing,
And meet terror instead?
20 We acknowledge our wickedness, O LORD—
The iniquity of our fathers—
For we have sinned against You.
21 For Your name's sake, do not disown us;
Do not dishonor Your glorious throne.
Remember, do not annul Your covenant with us.
22 Can any of the false gods of the nations give rain?
Can the skies of themselves give showers?
Only You can, O LORD our God!
So we hope in You,
For only You made all these things.

15 The LORD said to me, "Even if Moses and Samuel were to [a]intercede with Me,[a] I would not be won over to that people. Dismiss them from My presence, and let them go forth! 2 And if they ask you, 'To what shall we go forth?' answer them, 'Thus said the LORD:
Those destined for the plague, to the plague;
Those destined for the sword, to the sword;
Those destined for famine, to famine;
Those destined for captivity, to captivity.

3 And I will appoint over them four kinds[b] [of punishment]—declares the LORD—the sword to slay, the dogs to drag, the birds of the sky, and the beasts of the earth to devour and destroy. 4 I will make them a horror to all the kingdoms of the earth, on account of King Manasseh son of Hezekiah of Judah, and of what he did in Jerusalem.' "

a-a *Lit. "stand before Me," as Jeremiah is doing now; cf. 18.20.*
b *Meaning of Heb. uncertain.*

19–22: A second fragment of a communal lament introduces by a rhetorical question the most difficult issue: Do these catastrophic events illustrate that God had rejected Judah and spurned His city? The third component of this question conveys the understanding that it is God who has afflicted Judah (see 8.15). "Ma'as" and "ga'al nephesh" occur only here and three times in Lev. ch 26 (vv. 15, 43, 44, plus "ga'al nephesh" alone in vv. 11, 30). In Lev. ch 26, this phrase designates the conditional divine Presence with the people (26.11, 15–16), and threatens the detestation that will bring destruction of their cultic sites (26.30), just as it marks the restoration of the covenant relationship in exile with the deported community (26.43–44). This fragment of lament seems to draw an analogy from the blessing and curses of Lev. ch 26 to the current events in Jerusalem on the eve of destruction. **20:** Confession of sins occurs also in v. 7, and only at some of the communal laments, as for instance Ps. 79.8, but cf. with Ps. 44. Here the poet laments transgenerational sins (as in 3.25). **21:** The motivation *for Your name's sake* is another non-Jeremian phrase (see v. 7); as also the call *remember, do not annul Your covenant with us.* Such a call is heard in Ps. 74.20, for instance, but almost never in the prophecies of Jeremiah, which consistently blame the people for their betrayal of the covenant that God has struggled to maintain (as in 11.1–14; see Deut. 31.20; for the exceptional status of Jer. 3.1–5, see n.). **22:** The prayer concludes with the people's declaration of faith in God's cosmic sovereignty, and with the people's announcement of complete obedience (see 21.2, for another quotation of obedience in Jerusalem on the eve of destruction).

15.1–4: God's response, as in 14.10, 11–12, annuls any hope. **1:** Jeremiah stands in the line of tradition with Moses and Samuel (Ps. 96.6), who had plead for the people and succeeded in appeasing God (Exod. 32.11–14; Num. 14.13–20; 1 Sam. 7.7–14). Yet, terms of salvation from the exodus (*Dismiss them from My presence, and let them go forth,* see Exod. 3.10, 12) are reversed to proclaim lack of rescue. This extreme reaction follows God's repeated prevention of Jeremiah from serving in the role of mediator (vv. 11–12; 11.14; etc.). **2–4:** Judgment is complete, and the irony of choice is between four deadly options: *plague, sword, famine,* and *captivity* (see 43.11); on top of these, four procedures of killing and abusing the corpses are added, with no mention of burying the dead (see 7.33; 16.4; 19.7; 34.20). **4:** *I will make them a horror to all the kingdoms of the earth:* This proclamation uses the curse of Deut. 28.25. For the first and only time in Jer., the burden of the destruction is laid on Manasseh, king of Judah (2 Kings ch 21; 23.26; 24.3–4).

5 But who will pity you, O Jerusalem,
Who will console you?
Who will turn aside to inquire
About your welfare?
6 You cast Me off —declares the LORD—
You go ever backward.
So I have stretched out My hand to destroy you;
I cannot relent.
7 I will scatter them as with a winnowing fork
Through the settlements of the earth.
I will bereave, I will destroy My people,
For they would not turn back from their ways.
8 Their widows shall be more numerous
Than the sands of the seas.
I will bring against them—
[a-]Young men and mothers together[-a]—
A destroyer at noonday.
I will bring down suddenly upon them
Alarm[b] and terror.
9 She who bore seven is forlorn,
Utterly disconsolate;
Her sun has set while it is still day,
She is shamed and humiliated.
The remnant of them I will deliver to the sword,
To the power of their enemies
—declares the LORD.

10 Woe is me, my mother, that you ever bore me—
A man of conflict and strife with all the land!
I have not lent,
And I have not borrowed;
Yet everyone curses me.

11 The LORD said:
[a-]Surely, a mere remnant of you
Will I spare for a better fate![-a]
By the enemy [c-]from the north[-c]
In a time of distress and a time of disaster,
Surely, I will have you struck down!
12 [d-]Can iron break iron and bronze?[-d]

a-a Meaning of Heb. uncertain. *b Meaning of Heb. uncertain.*
c-c Moved up from v. 12 for clarity.
d-d Emendation yields "He shall shatter iron—iron and bronze!"

15.5–9: God's lament over Jerusalem's total destruction is expressed by the very One who destroyed the city. This agony of the destroyer also characterizes laments over the destruction of foreign nations; see 48.34–39. **5:** To illustrate the catastrophe, cries of empathy emphasize that there are none to show pity, to console, or to inquire about Jerusalem's welfare (see Isa. 51.19; Jer. 48.17; Nah. 3.7; Ps. 69.9; Lam. 2.13). God certainly does not feel pity for Jerusalem (see Lam. 2.17, 21; 3.34). **6:** Judgment steps taken against Jerusalem were justified retaliation for disobedience. Throughout this poem, God is the sole agent of its annihilation, and the entire world is at His command (including human foes, but not only them); note the first-person verbal phrases of war, very common throughout the book. **8:** The statement that *Their widows shall be more numerous/ Than the sands of the seas* is an ironic reference to God's promise of many descendants to Abraham (Gen. 22.17) and Jacob (Gen. 32.13; cf. 1 Kings 4.20; Isa. 10.22; Hos. 2.1). **9:** The theme is later developed in 2 Macc. ch 7 in relation to the martyrs of the Maccabean period.

15.10–21: Jeremiah's third lament (see 11.18–23 nn.). In its four passages, this lament is a dialogue, alternating between the prophet's protests (vv. 10, 15–18) and God's immediate answers (vv. 11–14, 19–21). In contrast to Psalms, the prophet's role allows a divine response to his complaints. Nevertheless, the connections between these complaints and their responses are not complete, and might be a result of only a secondary editorial ordering. **10–14:** Lamenting his own birth (cf. with cursing the day of birth, 20.14–18), the prophet portrays himself by a cluster of negative attributes (see further, vv. 15, 17). *A man of conflict and strife with all the land!* is borrowed from the wisdom literature (see Prov. 15.18; 16.28). Yet the themes in conflict were clearly not common: *I have not lent, / And I have not borrowed; / Yet everyone curses me;* see 1 Sam. 12.3–5. **11–14:** Very difficult vv., though they clearly introduce a judgment prophecy to Israel (see Deut. 28.36, 48; 32.22); thus they suggest a different and broader spectrum than that required as a response to v. 10, which makes the dialogic pattern on vv. 10–21 look artificial.

13 [a-]I will hand over your wealth and your treasures
As a spoil, free of charge,
Because of all your sins throughout your territory.
14 And I will bring your enemies
By way of a land you have not known.[-a]
For a fire has flared in My wrath,
It blazes against you.

15 O LORD, you know—
Remember me and take thought of me,
Avenge me on those who persecute me;
Do not yield to Your patience,
[b-]Do not let me perish![-b]
Consider how I have borne insult
On Your account.
16 When Your words were offered, I devoured them;
Your word brought me the delight and joy
Of knowing that Your name is attached to me,
O LORD, God of Hosts.
17 I have not sat in the company of revelers
And made merry!
I have sat lonely because of Your hand upon me,
For You have filled me with gloom.
18 Why must my pain be endless,
My wound incurable,
Resistant to healing?
You have been to me like a spring that fails,
Like waters that cannot be relied on.

19 Assuredly, thus said the LORD:
If you turn back, I shall take you back
And you shall stand before Me;
If you produce what is noble
Out of the worthless,
You shall be My spokesman.
They shall come back to you,
Not you to them.
20 Against this people I will make you
As a fortified wall of bronze:
They will attack you,
But they shall not overcome you,
For I am with you to deliver and save you
—declares the LORD.
21 I will save you from the hands of the wicked
And rescue you from the clutches of the violent.

a-a Meaning of Heb. uncertain. *b-b Lit. "Do not take me away."*

15–18: These poetic vv. open with a request for revenge, based on the prophet's bearing insult on God's account (see Ps. 69.8). **16:** Surprisingly, and as a symbol of the emotional storm the prophet experiences, God's words that he has eaten brought joy and happiness to his heart (see Ps. 40.17; cf. with Ezek. 3.1–3, where the scroll of judgment words becomes sweet as honey in the prophet's mouth). **17:** Here happiness changes to loneliness and fury; the phrase *sat lonely* (lit. "dwell apart") is borrowed from Lev. 13.46, the separation inflicted on a person with a leprous affliction. **18:** *You have been to me like a spring that fails, / Like waters that cannot be relied on:* Jeremiah's accurate use of water imagery in the desert gives extra force to this image of unreliable waters (see 2.10–13; 17.13). No other than God is portrayed here as unreliable. "'Aman" "be firm, trustworthy" (NJPS *relied on*) (as in Num.12.7; Deut. 1.32; etc.) is a quality otherwise limited to man; "kazav" "tell a lie, prove to be a liar" (NJPS *fails*) is negated as immoral behavior (in Zeph. 3.13); and defines a very clear border between human and God. When referring to God, "kazav" is negated, arguing repeatedly that God cannot be considered unreliable (see Num. 23.19; Hab. 2.3; Ps. 89.36; and in reference to other gods, Isa. 28.15). The unreliability of the desert wadis is in the continual change of route caused by each flood, or the unpredictable noisy flood itself, which depends on precipitation in the Jerusalem mountains; see Job 6.15. **19–21:** God empowers the prophet. **19:** In two conditional clauses God promises the prophet to continue standing before God, and to be His spokesman. The demand is that the people should make the change, not the prophet, which will still leave him lonely. **20:** See commission, 1.18–19.

16 The word of the LORD came to me:
2 You are not to marry and not to have sons and daughters in this place. 3 For thus said the LORD concerning any sons
and daughters that may be born in this place, and concerning
the mothers who bear them, and concerning the fathers who
beget them in this land: 4 They shall die gruesome deaths. They
shall not be lamented or buried; they shall be like dung on the
surface of the ground. They shall be consumed by the sword
and by famine, and their corpses shall be food for the birds of
the sky and the beasts of the earth.

5 For thus said the LORD:
Do not enter a house of mourning,[a]
Do not go to lament and to condole with them;
For I have withdrawn My favor from that people
—declares the LORD—
My kindness and compassion.
6 Great and small alike shall die in this land,
They shall not be buried; men shall not lament them,
Nor gash and tonsure themselves for them.
7 They shall not break bread[b] for a mourner[c]
To comfort him for a bereavement,
Nor offer one a cup of consolation
For the loss of his father or mother.
8 Nor shall you enter a house of feasting,
To sit down with them to eat and drink.

9 For thus said the LORD of Hosts, the God of Israel: I am going
to banish from this place, in your days and before your eyes, the
sound of mirth and gladness, the voice of bridegroom and bride.
10 And when you announce all these things to that people,
and they ask you, "Why has the LORD decreed upon us all this
fearful evil? What is the iniquity and what the sin that we have

a Lit. "religious gathering."
b So a few mss. Most mss. and editions read "to them." *c Lit. "mourning."*

16.1–9: Three symbolic actions, three prohibitions destine Jeremiah to loneliness, and illustrate the horrors of destruction. Jeremiah may not marry and have children (vv. 1–4), he may not attend mourning feasts and lament the dead (vv. 5–7), and he may not participate in any joyful feasts (vv. 8–9). Each prohibition is explained in a judgment prophecy. The first two elaborate on the atrocities concerning the great numbers of dead, parents and children (v. 3), adults and young ones alike (v. 6), to the point of no burial, to the point of no mourning customs practiced (vv. 3–4, 6; see 7.33; etc.). The third unit widens the spectrum to every other daily, private feast occasion, such as marriage ceremonies, that will cease completely (v. 9). The three units perceive calamity in the land, with no survivors, and no mention of exile (see Kimḥi, who challenged this totality, limited it to Anathoth, and brought Ezek. 14.22 to show that there were sons and daughters that survived and were deported). **5:** *A house of mourning,* ("beit marzeah") occurs otherwise only in Amos 6.4–7, where it involves hedonistic pleasures. Known from Ugaritic, Akkadian, Aram. and Gk texts and inscriptions, "marzeah" is a gathering for both joy and mourning. *For I have withdrawn My favor from that people—declares the LORD—/ My kindness and compassion:* God gathering His ("'asaf") "shalom," "hesed," and "rahamim" (security or well-being, *favor,* and *compassion*) from His people is a powerful agricultural image (see Isa. 16.10; Jer. 48.33), that leaves the people devoid of those three essential divine roles (or responsibilities) when facing the hazardous era of destruction. Jeremiah perceives the current period as a time when God was present (in almost all of his prophecies God did not leave the city or the land, cf. 12.7–13), but had actively chosen to withhold these aspects of His activity. God is LORD of History, but is intentionally closing the curtain on His qualities of favor and compassion (for lack of compassion, see also 13.14; 21.7). Compassion in Jer. is only a future hope (see 12.15; 30.18; 31.20; 33.26; 42.12). **6:** The mourning customs mentioned are forbidden according to Deut. 14.1 (see Kimḥi; as also Lev. 19.27–28; 21.5), probably due to their foreign religious background (1 Kings 18.28). **9:** See 7.34.

16.10–13: Question and answer. *Why has the LORD decreed upon us all this fearful evil?* This does not follow up on the previous passage, but stands as an independent one (for a similar pattern, see 5.19). One great difference between the two passages is their different portrayal of the distress. While vv. 1–9 refer to calamity in the land, vv. 10–13 do not mention death and destruction at all, but focus only on deportation. This passage presents two important theodicy arguments to justify the Judean deportation. First, it is a proper judgment by the principle of "measure-for-measure." This principle even governs the form of this passage, opening with a quoted question, by which the prophet

committed against the LORD our God?" 11 say to them, "Because your fathers deserted Me—declares the LORD—and followed other gods and served them and worshiped them; they
deserted Me and did not keep My Instruction. 12 And you have
acted worse than your fathers, every one of you following the
willfulness of his evil heart and paying no heed to Me. 13 Therefore I will hurl you out of this land to a land that neither you nor
your fathers have known, and there you will serve other gods,
day and night; for I will show you no mercy."

14 Assuredly, a time is coming—declares the LORD—when it
shall no more be said, "As the LORD lives who brought the Israelites out of the land of Egypt," 15 but rather, "As the LORD lives
who brought the Israelites out of the northland, and out of all
the lands to which He had banished them." For I will bring
them back to their land, which I gave to their fathers.

16 Lo, I am sending for many fishermen
—declares the LORD—
And they shall haul them out;
And after that I will send for many hunters,
And they shall hunt them
Out of every mountain and out of every hill
And out of the clefts of the rocks.
17 For My eyes are on all their ways,
They are not hidden from My presence,
Their iniquity is not concealed from My sight.
18 I will pay them in full[a]—
Nay, doubly for their iniquity and their sins—
Because they have defiled My land
With the corpses of their abominations,[b]
And have filled My own possession
With their abhorrent things.

a See note to Isa. 65.7. *b I.e., their lifeless idols.*

constructs his answer (cf. "'al meh," v. 10, and "'al 'asher ...," v. 11); and it follows in v. 13. **11–12:** A second theodicy argument addresses the question of "our sins": Was the affliction justified at the time it occurred? Although forsaking God was the forefathers' sin, Jeremiah insists on the additional burden of evil added by the current generation, who is even worse than their predecessors (see 7.26). This statement seems implicitly to argue with prevailing sayings such as Ezek. 18.2; Lam. 5.7, as also Jer. 31.27. **13:** Retaliation is going to be analogical to the major sin. Since they have been worshipping other gods in God's land, exile to a foreign land is the proper judgment, where worshipping other gods is expected. Jeremiah here follows the Deuteronomic conception of exile (Deut. 4.27–28; 28.36, 64), by which he foresees total calamity, with no mercy, to the exiles (for this conception of exile in Jer., see 22.10–12, 24–30; 27.12–13; 42.7–17). "Haninah" *(mercy)* is a hapax, see "hanan" designating (lack of) mercy in war in Deut. 28.50. LXX reads the verb in the plural: "they shall not give you mercy," thus suggesting the subject to be the other gods, and theologically "cleaning" God from the notion of lack of mercy. Addressing the exiles, this prospect follows vv. 1–9 as another prophecy of complete annihilation, but this time aimed at the exiles (and possibly the Jehoiachin exiles of 597 BCE).

16.14–15: Consolation prophecy to the exiles. This passage (parallel to 23.7–8) is brought here to correct the earlier message of total annihilation in exile. It is restricted to the deported Judeans, and it projects restoration in two stages: ingathering the dispersed from a northern land and from all other lands of expulsion; and re-establishment in the land given to the forefathers. This passage seems to belong to the Babylonian-exilic level of Jer. (see ch 24). While the exodus in Jer. appears only as part of the historical retrospective on the God-people relationship (as in 7.21–23), the analogy to a future, second exodus from the north is a central component of consolation in Babylonian-exilic prophecy (see Isa. 48.20–21; 52.11–12; Ezek. 20.32–38).

16.16–18: A judgment prophecy, possibly against Israel, portrays the enemy forces as many fishermen and many hunters that God spreads around with the mission to capture them; note that the addressees are not explicitly identified. **17:** God's role is to locate those to be punished, for He is omniscient; see 32.19. **18:** God declares that He brings judgment twice as much, doubled in proportion to the sin (see Job 42.10; and the double portion of judgment and consolation, Isa. 61.7). For double judgment, see Isa. 40.2; and in Jeremiah's individual lament it appears as a legitimate request, Jer. 17.18. This is then another distinct perception of retribution in comparison with the measure-for-measure judgment of 16.10–13. *The corpses of their abominations, / and ... / their abhorrent things:* The combination of "shiqutsim" and "to'evot" is hapax in Jer., but typical of Ezek. (5.11; 7.20;

19 O LORD, my strength and my stronghold,
My refuge in a day of trouble,
To You nations shall come
From the ends of the earth and say:
Our fathers inherited utter delusions,
Things that are futile and worthless.
20 Can a man make gods for himself?
No-gods are they!
21 Assuredly, I will teach them,
Once and for all I will teach them
My power and My might.
And they shall learn that My name is LORD.

17 The guilt of Judah is inscribed
With a stylus of iron,
Engraved with an adamant point
On the tablet of their hearts,
[a-]And on the horns of their altars,
2 While their children remember[-a]
Their altars and sacred posts,
By verdant trees,
Upon lofty hills.
3 [b-]Because of the sin of your shrines
Throughout your borders,
I will make your rampart a heap in the field,
And all your treasures a spoil.[-b]
4 [c-]You will forfeit,[-c] by your own act,
The inheritance I have given you;
I will make you a slave to your enemies
In a land you have never known.
For you have kindled the flame of My wrath
Which shall burn for all time.

5 Thus said the LORD:
Cursed is he who trusts in man,
Who makes mere flesh his strength,
And turns his thoughts from the LORD.

a-a Meaning of Heb. uncertain. Emendation yields "Surely the horns of their altars / Are as a memorial against them." *b-b Meaning of Heb. uncertain.* *c-c Meaning of Heb. uncertain. Emendation yields "Your hand must let go."*

11.18, 21), though Jeremiah does use each of them separately (see 7.30; 13.27; etc.; and 6.15; etc.).

16.19–21: A hymn of confidence in God that recognizes His important status among foreigners, just as it confesses worshipping other gods in vain. **21:** A divine response to this earlier recognition approves God's might and the general acknowledgement of His name (see Isa. 42.8).

17.1–4: Judah's cultic sins are inscribed, and will lead to total exile. This passage is not in LXX. **1:** *A stylus of iron* and *an adamant point* attest to the hardest devices (iron, Job 19.23–24; and "shamir," as also in Ezek. 3.9; Zech. 7.12, identified as the hard stone of corundum), used to inscribe letters on hard surfaces (cf. with writing in ink on parchment and papyri, Jer. 36.18). This metaphor gains its power from the two different "writing surfaces" which are brought together in the case of Judah. First, *the tablet of their hearts,* which in diametric opposition to fidelity (Prov. 3.3; 7.3) has sins inscribed upon it. A tough heart symbolizes disobedience (Ezek. 2.4; 3.7), and Jeremiah's prophecy for the new covenant suggests a full transformation of the heart (31.33). Second, *the horns of their altars* echoes expiation rituals where blood of the purification offering was poured on the horns of the altar (see Lev. 4.1–7; 13–20, etc.). Yet, here instead of reparation blood, the very stones of the altar have the sins of Judah inscribed upon them, hence no room for expiation or forgiveness (Lev. 4.20, 26, 31, 35). **2–4:** Jeremiah uses this Priestly ritual to illustrate the profound guilt of Judah, which he describes in broken Deuteronomic phrases referring to the worship of other gods on high hills and under luxuriant trees (Deut. 12.2; and see Jer. 2.20; 3.6, 13). This accusation concerning illegitimate worship in cultic sites throughout Judah challenges what we know of Josiah's cultic reform (2 Kings chs 22–23), which should have been reflected in Jer. (see 11.9–10 n.). Perhaps this passage is earlier than the reform, or the reform failed. **4:** Judgment includes two distinct Deuteronomic references. The first is complicated by the textual difficulty of *You will forfeit, by your own act, / the inheritance.* "Uvecha," suggested as a corruption of "yadcha" "your hand," refers to Deut. 15.2, which concerns remission of debts. Jer. 17.4 transforms this monitory-social context into giving up land property, the land given by God to His people. This in turn raises another allusion to the curses of Deut. 28.48, and suggests that exile to an unknown land will be the proper retaliation (see 15.13–14; 16.13).

6 He shall be like a bush[a] in the desert,
Which does not sense the coming of good:
It is set in the scorched places of the wilderness,
In a barren land without inhabitant.
7 Blessed is he who trusts in the LORD,
Whose trust is the LORD alone.
8 He shall be like a tree planted by waters,
Sending forth its roots by a stream:
It does not sense the coming of heat,
Its leaves are ever fresh;
It has no care in a year of drought,
It does not cease to yield fruit.

9 Most devious is the heart;
It is perverse—who can fathom it?
10 I the LORD probe the heart,
Search the mind—
To repay every man according to his ways,
With the proper fruit of his deeds.

11 [b-]Like a partridge hatching what she did not lay,[-b]
So is one who amasses wealth by unjust means;
In the middle of his life it will leave him,
And in the end he will be proved a fool.
12 O Throne of Glory exalted from of old,
Our Sacred Shrine!
13 O Hope of Israel! O LORD!
All who forsake You shall be put to shame,
Those in the land who turn from You[c]
Shall be doomed[d] men,
For they have forsaken the LORD,
The Fount of living waters.

14 Heal me, O LORD, and let me be healed;
Save me, and let me be saved;
For You are my glory.
15 See, they say to me:
"Where is the prediction of the LORD?
Let it come to pass!"

a Or "tamarisk"; exact meaning of Heb. uncertain.
b-b Meaning of Heb. uncertain. *c Lit. "Me."*
d Lit. "inscribed"; meaning of line uncertain.

17.5–13: Wisdom and prophecy coalesce, on retribution and divine justice. 5–8: Cursed be the one man, and blessed be the other. The opposition is between trust in man and trust in God, and in both theme and style is very close to wisdom literature (see Pss. 37.3; 56.12; Prov. 3.5; 16.20; 22.19; see also Ps. 1). LXX lacks the prophetic formula, and thus presents these vv. as a selection of wisdom sayings. Theologically, however, they go beyond the wisdom phraseology, as they foresee one confidently turning away from God (Deut. 5.32; 7.4; and see Jer. 5.23), a move that according to this Deuteronomic conception initiates divine curse (Deut. 11.21). **6–8:** The natural imagery uses two trees, one in the Arabah, the desert, the salty soil; the other planted by flowing water, bringing growth, green leaves, and constant fruit. While the latter is elaborately described, it remains unspecified, as no tree is named (one may think of the large fig trees in the Judean Desert wadies). The "ʿArʿar," perhaps the Calotropis procera (so n. HaReuveni, an Israeli botanist), is a tree that grows on the Judean Desert and has relatively large, green fruit, though completely dry (called by the Bedouins "the cursed Lemon"). This suggestion aptly complements the comparison between the trees, which says nothing of the fruits produced by the dry tree. **9–10:** The internal organs, and mostly the heart (and kidneys), are the residence of thoughts (Prov. 16.9) and piety (Pss. 7.10; 26.2). V. 9 opens with the human limitations to fathom those human complexities, only to set the stage for the divine self-statement that praises God's ability to conduct full justice for each person according to his conduct. This is one example of Jeremiah's view of individual retribution (see 32.19). **12–13:** These vv. either have no connection to retribution or only an oblique one. **13:** Following on the water imagery, the v. plays with the double meanings of both "qawah" *(hope)*, "miqor" *(waters)* and "bosh," *(put to shame)*, "borot," ("cisterns," see Jer. 2.13). God is a source of living water, and thus a reliable hope for Israel. Hence, those who desert him suffer shame, dismay, and mostly drought.

17.14–18: Jeremiah's fourth lament (see 11.18–23 nn.). This opens with a plea for health (cf. Ps. 6.3), joined to a request for salvation (3.8), and closes

16 But I have not [a-]evaded
Being a shepherd in your service,[-a]
Nor have I longed for the fatal day.
You know the utterances of my lips,
They were ever before You.
17 Do not be a cause of dismay to me;
You are my refuge in a day of calamity.
18 Let my persecutors be shamed,
And let not me be shamed;
Let them be dismayed,
And let not me be dismayed.
Bring on them the day of disaster,
And shatter them with double destruction.

[19] Thus said the LORD to me: Go and stand in the People's
Gate, by which the kings of Judah enter and by which they go
forth, and in all the gates of Jerusalem, [20] and say to them: Hear
the word of the LORD, O kings of Judah, and all Judah, and all
the inhabitants of Jerusalem who enter by these gates!
[21] Thus said the LORD: Guard yourselves for your own sake
against carrying burdens[b] on the sabbath day, and bringing
them through the gates of Jerusalem. [22] Nor shall you carry out
burdens from your houses on the sabbath day, or do any work,
but you shall hallow the sabbath day, as I commanded your
fathers. ([23] But they would not listen or turn their ear; they stiffened their necks and would not pay heed or accept discipline.)
[24] If you obey Me—declares the LORD—and do not bring in
burdens through the gates of this city on the sabbath day, but

a-a Exact force of Heb. uncertain. Emendation yields "urged you to [bring] misfortune." *b Or "merchandise."*

with praise (Deut. 10.21; Ps. 119.171). This general psalmodic opening develops into a complaint on the prophetic mission. **17–18:** As typical of individual laments, the pleas call God to evince His protection over the prophet (see Pss. 14.6; 91.2, 9; 94.22), and bring dismay over his enemies (Prov. 10.29). *A day of calamity,* has personal reference (Ps. 41.2; Prov. 16.4), but may also set this individual complaint in a national context; see the prophecy against Babylon as its day of calamity (Jer. 51.2).

17.19–27: The Sabbath and the fate of Jerusalem. This third covenant speech takes the Sabbath as the paradigmatic commandment the people of Judah and Jerusalem have breached. **19–20:** Once again, the prophet as the covenant mediator is instructed to announce his words publicly, at the gates of the city (see 7.1; 11.1). His first address, in the imperative, demands listening, that is, obedience ("shama'," as in 7.2; 11.2; 22.2). **21–23:** "Hishamru benafshotechem" *(Guard yourselves),* while it sounds like the "shamor" of Deut. 5.12, it brings to this context the Deuteronomic (and Deuteronomistic) rebuke to be faithful to God and to His covenant (see Deut. 4.15; Josh. 23.11). Along the same lines, Jeremiah expands the Deuteronomic Sabbath law, as he presents a specific case. It is not only the general ban on work (Deut. 5.14), but the further prohibition of commercial transactions. **22:** Closing with *as I commanded your fathers,* gives the entire expansion divine legitimation, an early implementation of the rabbinic principle of "Torah leMoshe MiSinai." **23:** But as before, past generations had already disobeyed this demand (see 11.8, 10), which leaves room for the current generation to change and be saved. **24–27:** A full condition (v. 24: *if you obey ...,* and v. 27: *if you do not obey ...*) marks the last segment of the speech, promising to the present people of Jerusalem, if obedient, the continuous existence of Davidic rulership in Jerusalem, no less than the city's eternal existence (v. 25), and the continued worship in the House of God (v. 26). **27:** Disobedience will bring total annihilation of the city by *fire* (see 4.4; 21.12), burning all of its *fortresses* (a prophetic symbol of destruction; see Hos. 8.14; Amos 1.4, 7, 10, 12, 14; 2.2, 5). Of the various Sabbath laws within the Pentateuch, Jeremiah uses the Deuteronomic Ten Commandment's Sabbath passage (Deut. 5.12–15; the other pentateuchal passages are not echoed in this passage; cf. to Exod. 20.8–11; and Priestly references: Gen. 2.1–3; Exod. 23.12; 31.12–17; 35.2–3; Lev. 23.3). Neh. 13.15–22 stands as a further expansion, broadening the prohibition to any agricultural work and trade (vv. 15–16). Nehemiah grounds his order in the 5th c. BCE on the historical lesson that should have been learned from Jer. 17.19–27, from the destruction of the early 6th c. BCE, and he further adds Priestly legal terminology which is beyond the references adduced by Jeremiah in the present passage (see "halal" in Neh. 13.17, 18 and Exod. 31.14). Hence, relative chronology based on diachrony of the intertextual relationships sets Jer. 17.19–27 within its preexilic context, where the Sabbath was already recognized as part of the Yahvistic ritual (see Amos 8.5; Isa. 1.13), and clearly prior to Nehemiah. As in the other covenant speeches, Jeremiah picks the Sabbath as part of the inventory of specific sins of the people that breach God's covenant. He thus lays an additional burden

hallow the sabbath day and do no work on it, 25 then through
the gates of this city shall enter kings who sit upon the throne
of David, with their officers—riding on chariots and horses,
they and their officers—and the men of Judah and the inhabitants of Jerusalem. And this city shall be inhabited for all time.
26 And people shall come from the towns of Judah and from
the environs of Jerusalem, and from the land of Benjamin, and
from the Shephelah, and from the hill country, and from the
Negeb, bringing burnt offerings and sacrifices, meal offerings
and frankincense, and bringing offerings of thanksgiving to
the House of the LORD. 27 But if you do not obey My command
to hallow the sabbath day and to carry in no burdens through
the gates of Jerusalem on the sabbath day, then I will set fire
to its gates; it shall consume the fortresses of Jerusalem and it
shall not be extinguished.

18 The word which came to Jeremiah from the LORD: 2 "Go
down to the house of a potter, and there I will impart My
words to you." 3 So I went down to the house of a potter, and
found him working at the wheel. 4 [a-]And if the vessel he was
making was spoiled, as happens to clay in the potter's hands,[-a]
he would make it into another vessel, such as the potter saw fit
to make.

5 Then the word of the LORD came to me: 6 O House of Israel,
can I not deal with you like this potter?—says the LORD. Just like
clay in the hands of the potter, so are you in My hands, O House
of Israel! 7 At one moment I may decree that a nation or a kingdom shall be uprooted and pulled down and destroyed; 8 but
if that nation against which I made the decree turns back from
its wickedness, I change My mind concerning the punishment
I planned to bring on it. 9 At another moment I may decree that
a nation or a kingdom shall be built and planted; 10 but if it does
what is displeasing to Me and does not obey Me, then I change
My mind concerning the good I planned to bestow upon it.

a-a So some mss. and one early edition. Most mss. and editions read "And if the vessel that he was making with clay in the potter's hands was spoiled."

on the Sabbath as being the reason for Jerusalem's destruction.

18.1–23: Three prophecies. Ch 18 brings three different prophecies together: a symbolic act (vv. 1–12), a judgment prophecy (vv. 13–17), and an individual lament (vv. 18–23). Each has its own literary characteristics and its distinct themes. Possible connections behind this compilation are the repetition of several words in the first and in the third passages: the root "hashav" ("made, devise, plan") as verb and noun (vv. 8, 11, 12, 18); the root "shuv" ("turns") (vv. 4, 8, 11, 20); the antonyms "tovah" ("good") and "ra'ah" ("evil") (vv. 10, 11, 20; and 8, 10, 11, 20, respectively). Such connections may be drawn between the first and the second passages as well; see: "goy" ("nation") (vv. 7, 8, 9, 13); "natash" ("uproot") (vv. 7, 14); "derekh" ("path, ways") (vv. 11, 15); as also between the second and third: the root "kashal" ("stumble") (vv. 15, 23); the motif of walking in dangerous paths (vv. 15, 22); the motif of the enemy (vv. 16–17, 21–22). Still, all these draw but very loose threads between independent prophecies.

18.1–12: The potter. Like clay in the potter's hand, the people are under God's sovereignty. The prophecy is a symbolic action (vv. 1–4), applied to the status of Judah (vv. 5–12). **1–4:** The symbolic action is part of the regular daily work of the *potter* (cf. with other symbolic acts that focus on a procedure done by the prophet himself faced with specific, unusual, often unclear requests, as in 13.1–11; Ezek. chs 4–5; 24.15–27); just as it is a regular scene, which is not presented as a vision (cf. with 1.11, 13, where the regular scene calls for a divine interpretation). The *potter* working on the *wheel* is dynamic, forming new products, always able to change them as long as they are still wet clay, "homer." "Yatzar" (v. 4, *make*) is the verb used to designate God's creation of man (Gen. 2.7, 8; and see Jer. 1.5) and animals (2.19; compare to "bara'" of Gen. ch 1), as well as the people of Israel (Isa. 43.21; 44.2, 21; Amos 4.13), and the entire cosmos (Isa. 45.7, 18; as also with "bara'," Isa. 42.5, etc.; and Jer. 33.2; 51.19). **5–6:** Answering the rhetorical question, the prophecy emphasizes the complete freedom of the Creator to handle His own creation. A medieval liturgical poem ("piyyut"), recited on the high holidays, extends the metaphor of God as Creator and man as inanimate vessel (see Isa. 45.9), to include the stone in the hand of the stoneworker, the ax in the hand of the smith, the tiller in the hand of the sailor, and other images. **7–10:** God may speedily change His earlier decisions on account of any people's behavior, changing evil-destructive thoughts (vv. 7–8), or drawing back from good-restorative plans (vv. 9–10). In both cases "niham 'al" ("regret," NJPS: *change My mind*) serves in the sense of transforming the divine plans for better or worse (see Gen. 6.6–7; Judg. 2.18; 2 Sam. 24.16; Ezek.

24.14; as also in Jer. 20.16; 26.13, 19). This suggests clear, systematic, organized, even compulsory procedures by which God changes His mind; He is driven by a known and just retribution conception. Hence God is still completely sovereign over the fate of all nations, but this prophecy illustrates the limits even on the sovereign God. Theodicy requires explanation, by which God's deeds in history might be justified, and not perceived as simply caprice. **11–12:** Addressing the people of *Judah* and *Jerusalem,* God is said to be the creator of *disaster,* the *planner* of the (destructive) thought, yet repentance is still an option (see Jer. ch 3). But the people are quoted to respond in continued rebellion.

18.13–17: Scandalous and absurd is Maiden Israel's religious behavior. 13: Technically, "lakhen" *(Assuredly)* ties this prophecy to its previous passage, suggesting judgment (a component that indeed was not introduced in vv. 1–12). Israel's religious behavior is compared with that of the nations, as in 2.10–13, and likewise introduced with rhetorical questions to raise amazement. **15:** The great absurdity: the people are accused of forgetting God (as in 2.32; 13.25; 23.27), a first step to disobedience (as in Deut. 8.11) and worshipping other gods (as in Deut. 8.19; Judg. 3.7). Cf., however, to repeated complaints in non-prophetic sources that it was God who forgot His people (Pss. 10.11; 42.10; 44.25; 74.18, 23; Lam. 5.20; and in individual laments, Ps. 13.2). Forgetting God in Jer. 18.15 is illustrated by worshipping *a delusion,* leading the people to unpaved roads. **16–17:** Desolation is presented as a consequence of the people's straying (Kimḥi), not mentioning God's role as causing it (as regularly in Jer., see 6.8; 25.12, etc.).

18.18–23: Jeremiah's fifth lament (see 11.18–23 nn.). **18:** Quoting his opponents, Jeremiah mentions two kinds of threats: the first may indeed be life-threatening, plotting against him, taking physical action against his source of power, his tongue, or

11 And now, say to the men of Judah and the inhabitants of
Jerusalem: Thus said the LORD: I am devising[a] disaster for you
and laying plans against you. Turn back, each of you, from your
wicked ways, and mend your ways and your actions! 12 But they
will say, "It is no use. We will keep on following our own plans;
each of us will act in the willfulness of his evil heart."

13 Assuredly, thus said the LORD:
Inquire among the nations:
Who has heard anything like this?
Maiden Israel has done
A most horrible thing.
14[b] Does one forsake Lebanon snow
From the mountainous rocks?
Does one abandon cool water
Flowing from afar?
15 Yet My people have forgotten Me:
They sacrifice to a delusion:
They are made to stumble in their ways—
The ancient paths—
And to walk instead on byways,
On a road not built up.
16 So their land will become a desolation,
An object of hissing[c] for all time.
Every passerby will be appalled
And will shake his head.[c]
17 Like the east wind, I will scatter them
Before the enemy.
[d-]I will look upon their back, not their face,[-d]
In their day of disaster.

18 They said,[e] "Come let us devise a plot against Jeremiah—
for instruction shall not fail from the priest, nor counsel from
the wise, nor oracle from the prophet. Come, let us strike him
with the tongue, and we shall no longer have to listen to all
those words of his."

19 Listen to me, O LORD—
And take note of[f-] what my enemies say![-f]
20 Should good be repaid with evil?
Yet they have dug a pit for me.
Remember how I stood before You

a The same Hebrew word as is used above for "potter."
b Meaning of verse uncertain; cf. 2.13, 17.13.
c These actions were performed at the sight of ruin to ward off a like fate from the observer; cf. Lam. 2.15.
d-d Change of vocalization yields "I will show them [My] back and not [My] face."
e Cf. 20.10. f-f Emendation yields "my case."

To plead in their behalf,
To turn Your anger away from them!
21 Oh, give their children over to famine,
Mow them down by the sword.
Let their wives be bereaved
Of children and husbands,
Let their men be struck down by the plague,
And their young men be slain in battle by the sword.
22 Let an outcry be heard from their houses
When You bring sudden marauders against them;
For they have dug a pit to trap me,
And laid snares for my feet.
23 O LORD, You know
All their plots to kill me.
Do not pardon their iniquity,
Do not blot out their guilt from Your presence.
Let them be made to stumble before You—
Act against them in Your hour of wrath!

19 Thus said the LORD: Go buy a jug of potter's ware. And
[take] some of the elders of the people and the priests,
2 and go out to the Valley of Ben-hinnom—[a]at the entrance of
the Harsith Gate[a]—and proclaim there the words which I will
speak to you.
3 Say: "Hear the word of the LORD, O kings of Judah and inhabitants of Jerusalem! Thus said the LORD of Hosts, the God of
Israel: I am going to bring such disaster upon this place that the
ears of all who hear about it will tingle. 4 For they and their fathers and the kings of Judah have forsaken Me, and have made
this place alien [to Me]; they have sacrificed in it to other gods
whom they have not experienced,[b] and they have filled this
place with the blood of the innocent. 5 They have built shrines
to Baal, to put their children to the fire as burnt offerings to

a-a Others "by way of the Potsherd Gate"; meaning of Heb. uncertain.
b See note at Deut. 11.28.

with the Tg. only a verbal insult of false witness; the second is the call to ignore him. *Instruction ... priest, nor counsel ... wise, nor oracle ... prophet:* Three kinds of sayings, three professional circles, and their continued functioning seems to be guaranteed (but see 8.8; Ezek. 7.26; Lam. 2.9). **19–23:** The individual lament responds to the plot organized against the prophet (vv. 20, 23), giving it much harsher colors and taking it as a clear physical threat (vv. 22–23). God is called to act as a judge that listens to the prophet and to his opponents (see Ps. 35.1; and applied to the nation, Isa. 49.25). **20:** *Remember how I stood before You:* In his own defense, Jeremiah recalls his service on behalf of the people, in his prayers to God (Jer. 15.1; and designating the prophetic service, 1 Kings 17.1; 2 Kings 3.14). *To turn Your anger away from them,* echoes the story of Phinehas son of Eleazar who has turned the divine anger from the people (Num. 25.11; Ps. 106.23). **21–23:** Against his opponents, the prophet asks for the most severe actions using phrases of war and total annihilation. **23:** Jeremiah's request for a permanent punishment without any option of reparation (drawing upon the Priestly rituals of reparation, Lev. ch 5), is the most extreme request within these individual laments. *Act against them in Your hour of wrath!* Closes the lament and ch, giving room to God's acting out of great anger (see Jer. 23.20), and yet doing justice to His loyal servant.

19.1–20.6: The symbolic act and its effect. This prophetic cluster contains three episodes, in three different locations. A symbolic act to take place in the Valley of Ben-hinnom (vv. 1–13), its repetition in the court of the Temple (vv. 14–15), and Pashhur's violent reaction against the prophet and his prophecy, which arouses Jeremiah to further proclaim not only the city's judgment, but also Pashhur's personal fate (20.1–6).

19.1–15: The symbolic act of the broken jug. In accordance with other symbolic actions (13.1–11; 18.1–12), the prophet is asked to perform a casual daily deed, to purchase a *jug of potter's ware* which he should take along with him, stand at the Valley of Ben-hinnom and proclaim God's words (vv. 3–9), before he continues with the symbolic action and shatters the vessel irreparably (v. 10). This symbolic action thus combines an artifact and a place, a story and a prophecy (vv. 1–2, 3–9, 10, 11–13), and they are all intertwined in vv. 10–13. **4–5:** To illustrate the people's misconduct, the prophet presents a string of cultic sins (as in 1.16); the worst is child sacrifice, which in MT is presented in two contradictory ways: they are *burnt offerings to Baal* (lacking in LXX), but if that is so, why should the v. emphasize that *I never commanded, never decreed, and which never came to My mind?* Ezek. 20.25–26, 30–31; Mic. 6.7; and also pentateuchal laws concerning the firstborn (Exod. 13.1–13; 34.19–20; Num. 3.11–13, 40–41) substantiate the notion that even by

Baal—which I never commanded, never decreed, and which never came to My mind. 6 Assuredly, a time is coming—declares the LORD—when this place shall no longer be called Topheth or Valley of Ben-hinnom, but Valley of Slaughter.

7 "And I will frustrate[a] the plans of Judah and Jerusalem in this place. I will cause them to fall by the sword before their enemies, by the hand of those who seek their lives; and I will give their carcasses as food to the birds of the sky and the beasts of the earth. 8 And I will make this city an object of horror and hissing;[b] everyone who passes by it will be appalled and will hiss over all its wounds. 9 And I will cause them to eat the flesh of their sons and the flesh of their daughters, and they shall devour one another's flesh—because of the desperate straits to which they will be reduced by their enemies, who seek their life."

10 Then you shall smash the jug in the sight of the men who go with you, 11 and say to them: "Thus said the LORD of Hosts: So will I smash this people and this city, as one smashes a potter's vessel, which can never be mended. And they shall bury in Topheth until no room is left for burying. 12 That is what I will do to this place and its inhabitants—declares the LORD. I will make this city like Topheth: 13 the houses of Jerusalem and the houses of the kings of Judah shall be unclean, like that place Topheth—all the houses on the roofs of which offerings were made to the whole host of heaven and libations were poured out to other gods."

14 When Jeremiah returned from Topheth, where the LORD had sent him to prophesy, he stood in the court of the House of the LORD and said to all the people: 15 "Thus said the LORD of Hosts, the God of Israel: I am going to bring upon this city and upon all its villages all the disaster which I have decreed against it, for they have stiffened their necks and refused to heed My words."

20 Pashhur son of Immer, the priest who was chief officer of the House of the LORD, heard Jeremiah prophesy these things. 2 Pashhur thereupon had Jeremiah flogged and put in the cell[c] at the Upper Benjamin Gate in the House of the LORD. 3 The next day, Pashhur released Jeremiah from the cell.

But Jeremiah said to him, "The LORD has named you not Pashhur, but Magor-missabib.[d] 4 For thus said the LORD: I am going to deliver you and all your friends over to terror: they will fall by the sword of their enemies while you look on. I will deliver all Judah into the hands of the king of Babylon; he will

a *Lit. "empty," Heb.* u-baqqothi, *a play on* baqbuq, *"jug" in v. 1.*
b *See note at 18.16.* c *Meaning of Heb. uncertain.*
d *I.e., "Terror all around"; cf. v. 10.*

the early 6th c. BCE, people in Judah had thought this was a Yahvistic commandment; see 7.30–8.3. The prophets and the pentateuchal legislation are unanimous in their struggle against this perception. **6:** The *Topheth* in the *Valley of Ben-hinnom* is to be called the *Valley of Slaughter* (see 7.31–33, that seems to take phrases from 19.5–7). **7:** *And I will frustrate the plans of Judah and Jerusalem in this place:* "Bqq" is a pun on "baqbuq" ("jug," v. 1; see translators' note *a*), though it is only here and in Isa. 19.3 that this verb appears in an abstract context; cf. with Isa. 24.1, 3; Jer. 51.2. **7–9:** Judgment is described bringing together various conventions, already known in Jer., concerning defeat (21.7; 22.25; 34.20–21; 44.30), lack of burial (7.33; 16.4; 34.20; based on Deut. 28.26; and see Ps. 79.2), turning the land into desolation (Jer. 2.15; 18.16); the new convention introduced here borrows Deut. 28.53, 55, 57 (and Lev. 26.29) to illustrate the famine horrors of parents eating the flesh of sons and daughters under siege conditions (see Lam. 2.20; 4.10). **14–15:** Standing at the court of the Temple, Jeremiah repeats his earlier prophecy; cf. v. 15a and v. 3.

20.1–6: Pashhur as "magor" all around. 1: Pashhur the priest held a special official role in the Temple; and in 21.1 he is one of the two officials Zedekiah had sent to the prophet. **3–6:** The prophecy opens and closes with a personal prediction against Pashhur (vv. 3, 6), coupling a judgment prophecy against all of Judah for defeat and exile (vv. 4–5). **3–4:** *Magor-missabib,* lit. "terror all around" (see translators' note *d*), comes from "gur" "be frightened," and is commonly used by Jeremiah. It is possibly borrowed from Ps. 31.14, lit. repeated in Jer. 20.10, and see 6.25; 46.5; 49.29. **4:** This is the first explicit occurrence of the Babylonian king, and of Babylon as the destination of exile, in the book of Jeremiah; up to this point there has only been vague language about the nation from the north (see 4.6, etc.).

exile them to Babylon or put them to the sword. [5] And I will deliver all the wealth, all the riches, and all the prized possessions of this city, and I will also deliver all the treasures of the kings of Judah into the hands of their enemies: they shall seize them as plunder and carry them off to Babylon. [6] As for you, Pashhur, and all who live in your house, you shall go into captivity. You shall come to Babylon; there you shall die and there you shall be buried, and so shall all your friends to whom you prophesied falsely."

7 You enticed me, O LORD, and I was enticed;
You overpowered me and You prevailed.
I have become a constant laughingstock,
Everyone jeers at me.
8 For every time I speak, I must cry out,
Must shout, "Lawlessness and rapine!"
For the word of the LORD causes me
Constant disgrace and contempt.
9 I thought, "I will not mention Him,
No more will I speak in His name"—
But [His word] was like a raging fire in my heart,
Shut up in my bones;
I could not hold it in, I was helpless.
10 I heard the whispers of the crowd—
Terror all around:
"Inform! Let us inform against him!"
All my [supposed] friends
Are waiting for me to stumble:
"Perhaps he can be entrapped,
And we can prevail against him
And take our vengeance on him."
11 But the LORD is with me like a mighty warrior;
Therefore my persecutors shall stumble;
They shall not prevail and shall not succeed.
They shall be utterly shamed
With a humiliation for all time,
Which shall not be forgotten.
12 O LORD of Hosts, You who test the righteous,
Who examine the heart and the mind,
Let me see Your retribution upon them,
For I lay my case before You.
13 Sing unto the LORD,
Praise the LORD,
For He has rescued the needy
From the hands of evildoers!

14 Accursed be the day
That I was born!

6: According to Jeremiah's conception of exile as dislocation with no return, Pashhur is to die in exile (see 22.10–12, 24–30; 42.10–17). In contradistinction to this prophecy, descendants of Pashhur and his priestly family, Immer, are mentioned as part of the repatriate community back in Persian Yehud (Ezra 2.37; 10.20–22; Neh. 7.40–41, etc.).

20.7–17: Jeremiah's sixth and seventh laments (see 11.18–23 nn.). At the close of the prose section of 19.1–20.6, this poetic section suggests two independent individual laments; see 18.18–23. **7–13:** While this poem shows similarities in phrase and theme to the psalmodic literature, there is a unique dimension to this lament that reflects on Jeremiah's status as God's prophet (see also 15.15–16). **7:** Enticed by God (see Ezek. 14.9), the prophetic mission is an obligation the prophet could not refuse, and ever since he has suffered laughter, mockery, disgrace and contempt. **9:** Unable to be released from his prophetic mission, the prophet discovers that prophecy is an existential issue for him, it is like a burning fire in his body (see 23.29). **10:** The prophet is torn between his obligations to God and his human hostile audience (20.7, 13). **11–13:** As typical of individual laments, the prophet closes this poem with declarations of confidence in God's assistance (though v. 13 shows similarities with thanksgiving poems and not with individual laments; see Pss. 33.1–4; 117.1). Jeremiah literarily repeats 11.20 in v. 12, stating that the just (omniscient) Judge will surely take vengeance on his opponents (Lam. 3.60; and also Jer. 12.3; 15.15). As before, Jeremiah places himself at the side of the "'evion," the poor, oppressed by evil doers (see 12.1–3). **14–18:** Cursing the day he was born, cursing the messenger who brought the happy note to his father (see Kimḥi, who suggested the messenger was Pashhur), Jeremiah refrains from cursing his parents (see Deut. 27.16). This curse shows only typological similarities with Job 3.3–26.

21.1–24.10: Oracles against political and religious leaders, kings and prophets. Two collections are at the core of this unit: prophecies *to the House of the king of Judah* (21.11–22.30) and prophecies to *the prophets* (23.9–40). These are framed by prophecies of total annihilation to Zedekiah and Jerusalem (21.1–7, 8–10), and a prophecy that distinguishes between the fortune of the Jehoiachin exiles for the better, and the fate of Zedekiah and those who remained with him in Jerusalem for the worse (ch 24). Hence, at the redaction level, this frame around chs 21–24 sees the prospect of the end of one community and the restoration of the other.

21.1–10: Would God make wonders? Zedekiah sends a delegation of two officials to the prophet with a special plea for divine help. While undated, based on the officials' request *(for King Nebuchadrezzar of Babylon is attacking us),* this prophecy fits with the final Babylonian siege of Jerusalem (see 32.1–5; 34.1–7; 37.1–11, probably summer of 588 BCE). **1:** This is a different *Pashhur* than the one mentioned in 10.1; perhaps this unit was placed here by association, connecting episodes about different individuals with the same name. **2:** God's *wonders* refer to the exodus, leading the people in the desert, and settling them in the land (see Exod. 3.19–20; and, in prophecy and poetry, Mic. 7.15; Pss. 106.22; 136.4, 22–24; Neh. 9.17, etc.). Recalling this earlier deliverance from Egypt as God's paradigmatic act on behalf of His people, the officials hope that God will resolve the current crisis similarly, and the Babylonians will withdraw from the city (for another delegation see 37.1–10; and cf. with Hezekiah's delegation to Isaiah son of Amoz facing the Assyrian threat of Sennacherib's third campaign by 701 BCE, Isa. 37.1–7). **3–7:** Jeremiah fully understood the plea but was determined to refute it boldly. **4:** *Chaldeans,* a name for the Babylonians in the period, based on an Aramean tribe that became especially significant then. **5:** Giving the most famous

Let not the day be blessed
When my mother bore me!
15 Accursed be the man
Who brought my father the news
And said, "A boy
Is born to you,"
And gave him such joy!
16 Let that man[a] become like the cities
Which the LORD overthrew without relenting!
Let him hear shrieks in the morning
And battle shouts at noontide—
17 Because he did not kill me before birth
So that my mother might be my grave,
And her womb big [with me] for all time.
18 Why did I ever issue from the womb,
To see misery and woe,
To spend all my days in shame!

21 The word which came to Jeremiah from the LORD, when
King Zedekiah sent to him Pashhur son of Malchiah
and the priest Zephaniah, son of Maaseiah, to say, 2 "Please
inquire of the LORD on our behalf, for King Nebuchadrezzar of
Babylon is attacking us. Perhaps the LORD will act for our sake
in accordance with all His wonders, so that [Nebuchadrezzar]
will withdraw from us."
3 Jeremiah answered them, "Thus shall you say to Zedekiah: 4 Thus said the LORD, the God of Israel: I am going to turn
around the weapons in your hands with which you are battling
outside the wall against those who are besieging you—the king
of Babylon and the Chaldeans—and I will take them into the
midst of this city; 5 and I Myself will battle against you with an
outstretched mighty arm, with anger and rage and great wrath.
6 I will strike the inhabitants of this city, man and beast: they
shall die by a terrible pestilence. 7 And then—declares the
LORD—I will deliver King Zedekiah of Judah and his courtiers
and the people—those in this city who survive the pestilence,

a Emendation yields "day."

exodus phrase an intentional twist, the prophet turns God into Jerusalem's major foe: *and I Myself will battle against you with an outstretched mighty arm* (see Deut. 5.15; 11.2; Ps. 136.12). The small change of phraseology, having "yad netuyah," "an outstretched hand" (instead of the expected "yad ḥazakah," "strong hand"), echoes the war that God conducts against His enemies, and at times, against His own people (see Isa. 5.25; 9.11, 16, 20; 10.4; 14.26). This explicit portrayal of God as an enemy (see Lam. 2.4–5) is further developed through phrases in the first person that illustrate God as warrior (vv. 3–7), leaving only a minor role to the Babylonian emperor, who does not act independently, but is God's tool for punishing Israel (see earlier of Assyrian emperor in Isa. 10.5).

the sword, and the famine—into the hands of King Nebuchadrezzar of Babylon, into the hands of their enemies, into the
hands of those who seek their lives. He will put them to the
sword without pity, without compassion, without mercy.
8 "And to this people you shall say: Thus said the LORD: I
set before you the way of life and the way of death. 9 Whoever
remains in this city shall die by the sword, by famine, and by
pestilence; but whoever leaves and goes over to the Chaldeans
who are besieging you shall live; [a]he shall at least gain his life.[-a]
10 For I have set My face against this city for evil and not for
good—declares the LORD. It shall be delivered into the hands
of the king of Babylon, who will destroy it by fire."

11 To the House of the king of Judah: Hear the word of the
LORD! 12 O House of David, thus said the LORD:

Render just verdicts
Morning by morning;
Rescue him who is robbed
From him who defrauded him.
Else My wrath will break forth like fire
And burn, with none to quench it,
Because of your wicked acts.
13 I will deal with you, [b]O inhabitants of the valley,
O rock of the plain[-b]—declares the LORD—
You who say, "Who can come down against us?
Who can get into our lairs?"
14 I will punish you according to your deeds
—declares the LORD.

I will set fire to its forest;[c]
It shall consume all that is around it.

a-a Lit. "he shall have his life as booty." *b-b Force of Heb. uncertain.*
c Perhaps a reference to the royal palace; cf. 1 Kings 7.2.

8–10: A second and initially independent prophecy is attached here, addressing the entire people. Unlike the earlier threat of total annihilation for the king, his officials, and everyone who remained in the city (vv. 6–7), this passage offers a choice of life or death (Deut. 30.19). Surrendering to the Babylonians promises life (see 27.11, 12–13). **10:** In a further contrast with vv. 1–7, God summons the Babylonians and gives the city into their king's hand, who then burns it (so also 37.6–10).

21.11–23.8: Various royal prophecies. This collection discusses the royal obligations in general terms (21.11–12; 22.1–9); treats separately the last kings of Judah, the sons of Josiah one by one (22.10–30); excluding the final king, Zedekiah (?); and closes with two general passages for a hopeful future when a Davidic king will rule Judah and Israel as of old and the exiles will be returned (23.1–8).

21.11–14: To the House of the king of Judah. 11–12: These vv. provide the theological justification absent in the earlier two passages. The call for the *House of David* to do justice follows the royal ideology (2 Sam. 8.15; 1 Kings 10.9; Ps. 72.2; see Jer. 22.1–5). **11:** *To the House of the king of Judah,* may serve as a title for the entire unit that ends in 23.8, similar to "Concerning the prophets" in 23.9. Prophetic oracles could be arranged topically, as here and in various collections of oracles against the nations in different prophetic books, by association (see v. 1 n.), or chronologically, as in Ezek. **12:** The threat is that the divine wrath will consume unceasingly (see 4.4; 7.20; all echoing Lev. 6.5). Judgment by fire is a connecting thread in this ch (see vv. 10, 12, 14). **13–14:** Only when observed from the east, from Mt. Scopus and Mt. of Olives (826 m and 815 m [2700 ft and 2675 ft] above sea level), may Jerusalem be seen as the one that dwells in *the valley,* the *rock of the plain;* the Temple Mount is only 743 m (2440 ft) high. This northeast orientation reflects where Jeremiah had regularly passed on his way from his hometown of Anathoth to Jerusalem. **13:** The hubris of the people of Jerusalem is shown in their reliance on the city's supposed inviolability (see Ps. 46). "Yeḥat" in the first question *(Who can come down against us?)* is from the verb "naḥat" (*come down against,* see Ps. 38.3, so Kimḥi; Luzzatto recognized its Aram. origin), but is also playing on "ḥatat" ("be filled with terror," as Isa. 30.31 [NJPS "shall be cowed"]; and repeatedly in Jer. 1.17; 8.9; 17.18).

22 Thus said the LORD: Go down to the palace of the king of
Judah, where you shall utter this word. 2 Say: "Hear the
word of the LORD: O king of Judah, you who sit on the throne
of David, and your courtiers and your subjects who enter these
gates! 3 Thus said the LORD: Do what is just and right; rescue
from the defrauder him who is robbed; do not wrong the stranger, the fatherless, and the widow; commit no lawless act, and
do not shed the blood of the innocent in this place. 4 For if you
fulfill this command, then through the gates of this palace
shall enter kings of David's line who sit upon his throne, riding
horse-drawn chariots, with their courtiers and their subjects.
5 But if you do not heed these commands, I swear by Myself—
declares the LORD—that this palace shall become a ruin."
6 For thus said the LORD concerning the royal palace of Judah:

You are as Gilead to Me,
As the summit of Lebanon;
But I will make you a desert,
Uninhabited towns.
7 I will appoint destroyers against you,
Each with his tools;
They shall cut down your choicest cedars
And make them fall into the fire.

8 And when many nations pass by this city and one man asks
another, "Why did the LORD do thus to that great city?" 9 the reply will be, "Because they forsook the covenant with the LORD
their God and bowed down to other gods and served them."

10 Do not weep for the dead[a]
And do not lament for him;

a I.e., Josiah; see 2 Kings 23.29–30.

22.1–5: A covenant speech addressed to the House of the king of Judah. This prose passage (unique in this context of poetic prophecies) follows the major characteristics of the covenant speeches, a special genre within judgment prophecies in Jer. (see 7.1–15; 11.1–14; 17.19–27; 25.1–14). **1:** The prophet is instructed to call the king at "these gates" (NJPS: *the palace;* either the gates of the royal palace, the city, as in 17.19, or the Temple, as in 7.1). Unlike the other prophecies to the House of the king of Judah, this public speech is addressed broadly to the king, his officials, and the people. **2:** The call opens with *Hear the word of the LORD ... !*, as in 7.2; 11.2 ("Hear the terms of this covenant"); 17.20. **3:** The speech is introduced as a legal demand to keep specific moral laws, as part of the king's particular responsibility (see vv. 15–17, and 21.12; 33.15; as part of the Davidic ideology, see 1 Sam. 8.15; Ps. 72.2, etc.), and in accordance with the general demands on the entire people (7.5–6; and see 4.2). **4–5:** A conditional sentence introduces a promise of continuous Davidic rule in case of obedience (for similar promises of continuity, see 7.5–7; 11.4–5; 17.25–26); and threatens destruction of the royal house (as in 7.12–15; 11.11–14; 17.27). Thus, the unconditional promise for the Davidic dynasty of 2 Sam. 7.13–15 is viewed as conditional, as in 1 Kings 89.4–9.

22.6–7: Gilead and Lebanon as metaphors. Another prophecy against the House of the king of Judah that also condemns Jerusalem (see also 21.13–14; 22.20–23). Exceptionally, this text refers to the city as male. The combination of *Gilead* and *Lebanon* otherwise occurs only in Zech. 10.10; Jer. 50.19 refers to the Carmel and Bashan, Mt. Ephraim and Gilead as a merism for south to north, and west and east. The destruction imagery in v. 6b occurs elsewhere in reference to a city and region, as in the transformation from the Carmel to the desert, in 4.26. The Gilead area in Cisjordan, famous for herds (Num. 32.1, 26), was on the border of the desert, and will indeed turn into such. It is uncertain what Gilead represents metaphorically; Rashi suggested that it refers to the Temple (so the Tg. and *Pesik. Rab.* 33), while Kimḥi identifies it with the king (and so Luzzatto). **7:** Lebanon was famous for its high mountains and tall cedars (2 Kings 19.23), that became a symbol of the king (and the royal house, see 22.15; as also in the allegory, in Ezek. 17.3, 12). The metaphor here may address the city (see 22.23), as suggested by the following vv. 8–9, or the king, the crown of Lebanon (see Ezek. 17.3–4). The fact that all of the city's royal institutions (including the Temple) were built and decorated with cedar (see 1 Kings 5.20; 7.2), might have led to the use of cedars as symbols for the city.

22.8–9: The general reaction to the city's destruction. Quoting passersby amazed at the destruction's severity, a common trope, intensifies its horror (see Deut. 29.23–25; 1 Kings 9.8–9). Even foreigners can see that God dealt justly with His people (see 2.11). For the question and answer form, see Jer. 5.19; 9.11–13; 16.10–13.

22.10–12: Lament over Shallum son of Josiah. *Shallum,* otherwise known by his regnal name, Jehoahaz, was deposed and exiled to Egypt by Pharaoh Neco three

Weep rather for [a]him who is leaving,[-a]
For he shall never come back
To see the land of his birth!

11 For thus said the LORD concerning [a]Shallum son of King
Josiah of Judah,[-a] who succeeded his father Josiah as king, but
who has gone forth from this place: He shall never come back.
12 He shall die in the place to which he was exiled, and he shall
not see this land again.

13 Ha! he who builds his house with unfairness
And his upper chambers with injustice,
Who makes his fellow man work without pay
And does not give him his wages,
14 Who thinks: I will build me a vast palace
With spacious upper chambers,
Provided with windows,
Paneled in cedar,
Painted with vermilion!
15 Do you think you are more a king
Because you compete in cedar?
Your father [b]ate and drank[-b]
And dispensed justice and equity—
Then all went well with him.
16 He upheld the rights of the poor and needy—
Then all was well.
[c]That is truly heeding Me[-c]
—declares the LORD.
17 But your eyes and your mind are only
On ill-gotten gains,
On shedding the blood of the innocent,
On committing fraud and violence.

a-a *I.e., the king called by his throne name Jehoahaz in 2 Kings 23.31 ff., and by his private name Shallum here in v. 11 and in 1 Chron. 3.15.*
b-b *I.e., he was content with the simple necessities of life.*
c-c *Or "That is the reward for heeding Me."*

months after the latter killed his father Josiah at Megiddo (609 BCE, see 2 Kings 23.28–35; 2 Chron. 35.20–36.4). *Do not weep for the dead* refers to Josiah. Weep for *him who is leaving* refers to Jehoahaz, who died in exile in Egypt (so Luzzatto). This lament, presented first as a general poetic dirge (v. 10), elaborated by a prose oracle (v. 11), illustrates Jeremiah's conception of exile as a final judgment with no return (see 22.24–30; and chs 27–28). Neither Shallum/Jehoahaz nor Jehoiachin are mentioned in the superscription (1.1–3).

22.13–23: Against King Jehoiakim son of Josiah. Placed on the throne by Pharaoh Neco of Egypt, Jehoiakim reigned for eleven years, as a vassal first to Egypt, then to Babylonia (609–598 BCE; 2 Kings 23.36–24.7; 2 Chron. 36.5–8). In Jehoiakim's fourth year Judah was forced to accept Nebuchadnezzar's Babylonian sovereignty (604 BCE), and three years later Jehoiakim rebelled. Jeremiah's prophecy against Jehoiakim, however, reveals nothing of the political-international circumstances Jehoiakim and Judah faced, nor anything of the internal conflicts with Jeremiah (cf. ch 36). Rather, in line with 21.11–12; 22.1–5, Jeremiah's critique accuses the king of failing to do justice on behalf of the people as his office requires. **13–17:** *Ha!* (Heb "hoy") is best translated "Woe!" an exclamation of mourning (v. 18). The exclamation frequently appears in prophetic oracles of judgment (as in Isa. 5.8–24; chs 28–33; Amos 5.18–20; Nah. 3.1; Hab. 2.6–20; 3.1), and also signals a warning of coming danger (Zech. 2.10). Jehoiakim is said to *build* (better: refurbish) his *house* (both "palace" and "dynasty") with *unfairness* and *injustice* (see Lev. 19.15; Deut. 16.18); accusations accumulate and culminate in the murder of innocents (see 2 Kings 24.4, shared also by Manasseh, 21.16; for such an accusation addressed to the people, see Jer. 2.34; 7.6; 19.4; 26.15; and to the kings, 22.3). This behavior is denigrated as hubris, especially in comparison to the great image of his father, the true cedar. **15–16:** Only here in the book is Josiah mentioned *(Your father);* he is highly appreciated, or rather mourned, as a just and pious king (see 2 Chron. 35.25). Full silence is kept about his tragic death (even if possibly hinted at in vv. 10–12; see 2 Kings 23.29–31) or his religious reform.

[18] Assuredly, thus said the LORD concerning Jehoiakim son
of Josiah, king of Judah:
[a-]They shall not mourn for him,
"Ah, brother! Ah, sister!"
They shall not mourn for him,
"Ah, lord! Ah, his majesty!"[-a]
19 He shall have the burial of an ass,
Dragged out and left lying
Outside the gates of Jerusalem.

20[b] Climb Lebanon and cry out,
Raise your voice in Bashan,
Cry out from Abarim,
For all your lovers are crushed.
21 I spoke to you when you were prosperous;
You said, "I will not listen."
That was your way ever since your youth,
You would not heed Me.
22 All your shepherds[c] shall be devoured by the wind,
And your lovers shall go into captivity.
Then you shall be shamed and humiliated
Because of all your depravity.
23 You who dwell in Lebanon,
Nestled among the cedars,
[d-]How much grace will you have[-d]
When pains come upon you,
Travail as in childbirth!

[24] As I live—declares the LORD—[e-]if you, O King Coniah,
son of Jehoiakim, of Judah, were[-e] a signet on my right hand,
I would tear you off even from there. [25] I will deliver you into
the hands of those who seek your life, into the hands of those

a-a They shall express neither sorrow at the loss of a relative nor grief at the death of a ruler. *b Israel is addressed.*
c Change of vocalization yields "paramours."
d-d Septuagint reads "How you will groan."
e-e Heb. "If Coniah ... were ..."; Coniah (Jeconiah in 24.1) is identical with Jehoiachin, 2 Kings 24.8 ff.

18–23: The admonition turns into judgment—a disgraceful death with no mourning or burial awaits this arrogant king of Judah (see 7.33; 8.1–2; 16.4). In contradistinction to this harsh prophecy, Jehoiakim is said to have died peacefully in his palace, and was buried with his forefathers, probably during the Babylonian siege of Jerusalem, at the end of which Jehoiachin was captured and exiled (2 Kings 24.5–6; 8–12, and see below). **20–23:** Cries for political assistance and moaning are all around. These vv. address Jerusalem as an adulterous woman (cf. 2.14–19, 20–25, 33–37; Ezek. chs 16; 23), caught by surprise. Following the mention of the highest mountains, serving as metaphors for Jerusalem (v. 6), the prophet opens and closes this poem with *Lebanon,* to which he adds the *Bashan* (the Golan Heights region, between the Hermon and the Yarmuk river, v. 20), and then recalls the common pair of Lebanon and its cedars, now as the place to nestle (v. 23; see Ezek. 31.6). **22:** It is unclear if this refers to the 597 BCE crisis (with Luzzatto) or to the 586 BCE one. **23:** The active adulterous woman (v. 20) is turned into a powerless woman in childbirth.

22.24–30: Lament over King Coniah son of Jehoiakim. Coniah (as also 37.1; otherwise known as Jehoiachin, Jer. 52.31; or Jeconiah, 27.20; 28.4; 29.2; see translators' note *e-e*) came to power following Jehoiakim's death (2 Kings 24.6, 8), ruled only three months, presumably during a Babylonian campaign against his father, the rebellious vassal (2 Kings 24.1). Following a first siege of Jerusalem the king, his mother, and his court surrendered to the Babylonians and were taken to Babylonia (2 Kings 24.8–17); Jehoiachin resided in the Babylonian court. Food ration lists from Nebuchanezzar's palace mention food given to Jehoiachin and his five sons in 592 BCE, and 2 Kings 25.27–30; Jer. 52.31–34 (2 Kings 25.27–30) tell of his release from prison on Evil-merodach's regnal year, by 562 BCE. Thirty-seven years after his short three months of reign, Jehoiachin still kept his title, King of Judah, though it is unclear if he had contacts with the Babylonian deportees (see 52.31–34 nn.). As with Shallum (Jehoahaz), Coniah is not mentioned in the superscription (1.1–3), and Jeremiah's perspective on him and his community of exiles appears further in chs 28, 29 (see below; for a favorable attitude toward them, see ch 24). **24:** *A signet on my right hand,* a symbol of royal authority, an expression of the closeness between the Davidic king and God (see 2 Sam. 7.14; Pss. 2.6; 110.1). This anti-Jehoiachin prophecy was reversed by Haggai in support of Zerubbabel, a fifth generation heir to Jehoiachin (Hag. 2.23; 1 Chron. 3.17–19; see v. 30 n.). **26:** Exile to a land you were not born in, or to an unknown land (v. 28), namely Babylonia, ties this

you dread, into the hands of King Nebuchadrezzar of Babylon
and into the hands of the Chaldeans. [26] I will hurl you and the
mother who bore you into another land, where you were not
born; there you shall both die. [27] They shall not return to the
land that they yearn to come back to.

28 Is this man Coniah
A wretched broken pot,
A vessel no one wants?
Why are he and his offspring hurled out,
And cast away in a land they knew not?
29 O land, land, land,
Hear the word of the LORD!
30 Thus said the LORD:
Record this man as without succession,
One who shall never be found acceptable;
For no man of his offspring shall be accepted
To sit on the throne of David
And to rule again in Judah.

23 Ah, shepherds who let the flock of My pasture stray and
scatter!—declares the LORD. [2] Assuredly, thus said the
LORD, the God of Israel, concerning the shepherds who should
tend My people: It is you who let My flock scatter and go astray.
You gave no thought to them, but I am going to give thought to
you, for your wicked acts—declares the LORD. [3] And I Myself
will gather the remnant of My flock from all the lands to which
I have banished them, and I will bring them back to their pasture, where they shall be fertile and increase. [4] And I will appoint over them shepherds who will tend them; they shall no
longer fear or be dismayed, and none of them shall be missing—declares the LORD.
[5] See, a time is coming—declares the LORD—when I will
raise up a true branch of David's line. He shall reign as king
and shall prosper, and he shall do what is just and right in the
land. [6] In his days Judah shall be delivered and Israel shall
dwell secure. And this is the name by which he shall be called:
"The LORD is our Vindicator."
[7] Assuredly, a time is coming—declares the LORD—when it
shall no more be said, "As the LORD lives, who brought the Israelites out of the land of Egypt," [8] but rather, "As the LORD lives,

lament/oracle to the Deuteronomic conception of exile (see Deut. 28.33, 36, 64; as also Jer. 5.15). Accordingly, Jeremiah prophesies death in exile to Jehoachin, annulling any hopes for return (contrast 28.1–4; 29.1–7). Luzzatto considered this to be the background for the later Jewish custom to die within the land of Israel, so as to be buried in it. **28–30:** The three-part (see 7.4) rhetorical question portrays Coniah as a worthless pottery vessel (man-made, like an idol; see Hos. 8.4; Job 10.8), thrown away and broken (see Hos. 8.8). **30:** Coniah is cursed to have no successor (Gen. 15.2), explained as an unacceptable king who cannot produce offspring to carry on his rule. In contradistinction to this harsh curse, the Davidic lineage did continue with Jehoiachin (see v. 24 n.).

23.1–8: Woe to the shepherds of My people. 1–4: *Shepherds,* the political leaders (Num. 27.17; 2 Sam. 7.8; and see Ezek. ch 34, where the alternative is a divine shepherd, God Himself, 34.11–16). By placing this passage here, the redactor of Jeremiah used this prophecy to conclude the unit concerning the kings of the House of Judah (21.11–22.30) and as a bridge to broader observations on leaders, who in ch 23, include false prophets and priests (23.11, 33, 34). The puns on various uses of the Heb root letters "resh" and "'ayin," as it moves from the "ro'im" (*shepherds,* in vv. 1–4) to the "ra'ah" (*evil,* vv. 10, 11, 12, 14, 17, 22), "mere'im" (*evildoers,* v. 14), and "re'im" (*each other,* vv. 27, 30, 35). **5–8:** These vv. join two separate prophecies of consolation that appear separately elsewhere in the book (16.14–15; 33.14–16). **5–6:** A promise of a new Davidic king, who is righteous and a true branch of the Davidic line, to be called *The LORD is our Vindicator.* This prophecy puns on the name of Zedekiah (Heb "Zidkiyahu"), insisting instead that God will raise up a true ("zedek") branch; if so, it implicitly criticizes Zedekiah, the king not mentioned so far in the oracles against the House of the King of Judah (so Luzzatto; and see 33.14–16). This prophecy builds on the previous unit, which noted that God will appoint better shepherds (v. 4) by describing the raising up of an ideal Davidic king. The same Heb word is used for "appoint" in v. 4 and *raise up* here. **7–8:** Restoration is promised to the exiles, particularly to those residing in the land of the north (see 3.18), the area known as the source of judgment and destruction (see 6.22; 10.22); only in the most general terms are other diasporas mentioned (see v. 3). This passage is secondary to the current context; while it provides a hopeful tone to

who brought out and led the offspring of the House of Israel from the northland and from all the lands to which I have banished them." And they shall dwell upon their own soil.

9 Concerning the prophets.

My heart is crushed within me,
All my bones are trembling;[a]
I have become like a drunken man,
Like one overcome by wine—
Because of the LORD and His holy word.
10 For the land is full of adulterers,
The land mourns because of [b-]a curse;[-b]
The pastures of the wilderness are dried up.
[c-]For they run to do evil,
They strain to do wrong.[-c]
11 For both prophet and priest are godless;
Even in My House I find their wickedness
—declares the LORD.
12 Assuredly,
Their path shall become
Like slippery ground;
They shall be thrust into darkness
And there they shall fall;
For I will bring disaster upon them,
The year of their doom —declares the LORD.
13 In the prophets of Samaria
I saw a repulsive thing:
They prophesied by Baal
And led My people Israel astray.
14 But what I see in the prophets of Jerusalem
Is something horrifying:
Adultery and false dealing.
They encourage evildoers,
So that no one turns back from his wickedness.
To Me they are all like Sodom,
And [all] its inhabitants like Gomorrah.

15 Assuredly, thus said the LORD of Hosts concerning the prophets:

a Meaning of Heb. uncertain. *b-b A few Heb. mss. and Septuagint read "these."*
c-c Lit. "Their running is wickedness, / Their straining is iniquity."

conclude the earlier unit against the kings of the House of Judah, it raises a much broader topic.

23.9–40: Against the prophets. For this type of title, see 21.11; 46.2; 48.1, etc. More than any other prophetic book, Jeremiah characterizes his era as having intense prophetic activity. Prophets are found among the leading circles together with officials, wise men, and priests (2.8, 26; 4.9; 5.31; 6.13; 8.1, 10; 13.13; 14.18; 18.18; 26.7, 8, 11; 27.16). Jeremiah is but one of many voices that looked to the future in those critical years. He portrays himself alone in projecting disaster (ignoring his slightly younger contemporary Ezekiel, who similarly prophesized disaster), a counter-voice to the many who offered calming prophecies for peace (5.12–13; 14.13, 15; 23.17; 27.9, 14; 28.1–4; 37.19). This collection of six prophecies against the prophets (vv. 9–12; 13–15, 16–17, 18–24, 25–32, 33–40) brings various accusations to delegitimize them, and set clear distinctions between the true and the false. These judgment prophecies in poetry and prose are collected by theme, and reflect diverse prophetic pronouncements proclaimed during Jeremiah's long prophetic activity, though mainly in the last two decades of Jerusalem. See further chs 26–29. **9–12:** Jeremiah describes his overwhelming prophetic experience as an internal physical reaction with outer symptoms, like drunkenness (see 15.17). The *trembling* might be due to the iniquity in the land (v. 10), specifically perpetrated by *prophet* and *priest* in God's *House* (v. 11), or by the divine *curse* of the prospective destruction (v. 10). MT opens with a general statement *for the land is full of adulterers* (v. 10; see v. 14; 22.20), which is absent in the LXX. **13–15:** Jeremiah distinguishes two groups of false prophets: those in Samaria, and those in Jerusalem. The Samaria prophets prophesy in the name of the Baal, thus leading the people astray (v. 32; 50.6; see Mic. 3.5; cf. Deut. 13.7–12); their conduct is *repulsive* (Heb "tiflah," "foolishness, nonsense"). **14:** The Jerusalem *prophets,* however, are accused of "shaʿrurah" (*something horrifying;* see 5.30), moral misbehavior (see also 6.13; 8.10), bringing the people to the level of *Sodom* and *Gomorrah,* implying that they will be similarly punished. **15:** As often in prophetic literature, *Assuredly* introduces the punishment. *Godlessness* reflected the hapax "ḥannupah." The related

I am going to make them eat wormwood
And drink a bitter draft;
For from the prophets of Jerusalem
Godlessness has gone forth to the whole land.

16 Thus said the LORD of Hosts:
Do not listen to the words of the prophets
Who prophesy to you.
They are deluding you,
The prophecies they speak are from their own minds,
Not from the mouth of the LORD.
17 They declare to men who despise Me:
The LORD has said:
"All shall be well with you";
And to all who follow their willful hearts they say:
"No evil shall befall you."
18 But he who has stood in the council of the LORD,
And seen, and heard His word—
He who has listened to His word must obey.[a]
19 [b]Lo, the storm of the LORD goes forth in fury,
A whirling storm,
It shall whirl down upon the heads of the wicked.
20 The anger of the LORD shall not turn back
Till it has fulfilled and completed His purposes.[b]
In the days to come
You shall clearly perceive it.

21 I did not send those prophets,
But they rushed in;
I did not speak to them,
Yet they prophesied.
22 If they have stood in My council,
Let them announce My words to My people
And make them turn back
From their evil ways and wicked acts.

23 Am I only a God near at hand
—says the LORD—
And not a God far away?
24 If a man enters a hiding place,
Do I not see him? —says the LORD.
For I fill both heaven and earth
—declares the LORD.

a Change of vocalization yields "announce it"; cf. vv. 22, 28.
b-b This section constitutes the word of God to which Jeremiah refers.

verb "ḥanaf" occurs five times in Jer. (out of eleven times in the entire HB); three of them designate pollution of the land as the consequence of idolatry (metaphorically, adultery; Jer. 3.1, 2, 9; echoing the Priestly conception of polluting the land by blood, Num. 35.33–35), and the other two are in Jer. 23.11, 15, in contexts that give additional emphasis to sexual misconduct (see the resemblance to "na'af," vv. 10, 14). **16–17:** The major accusation against the prophets is that they were never commissioned by God; as noted in 14.14, they speak instead from "the deceit of their own contriving" (see v. 21 below). **18–24:** Jeremiah sets clear distinctive characteristics to identify a true prophet. A true prophet has stood within *the council of the LORD* ("Sod YHVH," vv. 18, 22), that is among the celestial beings to whom God regularly speaks (see 1 Kings 22.19–23; Isa. 6.1–8; Ps. 68; and see Deut. 5.31; 10.10). **19–21:** Standing in the council allows the prophet to witness the horrors of the divine wrath, a swirling *storm* to afflict the wicked; he also witnesses God saying He had never sent those false prophets and had never spoken to them, yet they ran and prophesied (cf. with 1.7). Vv. 19–20 are duplicated at 30.23–24. **22:** The true prophet has thus heard God's words to His people, and can then strive to bring the people back from their iniquities (see Ezek. 22.28–30). **23–24:** The true prophet recognizes the God who is all-encompassing. In spatial terms, God is both *near* and *far away*, but nevertheless, omniscient, for He is in both heaven and earth (Amos 9.1–6; Ps. 138.6). These vv. challenge the distinction between immanence and transcendence by arguing that God's Presence does not require proximity, and His involvement is active even from a distance (see also Ezek. chs 8–11).

25 I have heard what the prophets say, who prophesy falsely
in My name: "I had a dream, I had a dream." 26 [a-]How long will
there be[-a] in the minds of the prophets who prophesy falsehood—the prophets of their own deceitful minds—27 the plan
to make My people forget My name, by means of the dreams
which they tell each other, just as their fathers forgot My name
because of Baal? 28 Let the prophet who has a dream tell the
dream; and let him who has received My word report My word
faithfully! How can straw be compared to grain?—says the
LORD. 29 Behold, My word is like fire—declares the LORD—and
like a hammer that shatters rock!

30 Assuredly, I am going to deal with the prophets—declares
the LORD—who steal My words from one another. 31 I am going
to deal with the prophets—declares the LORD—who wag[b] their
tongues and make oracular utterances. 32 I am going to deal
with those who prophesy lying dreams—declares the LORD—
who relate them to lead My people astray with their reckless
lies, when I did not send them or command them. They do this
people no good—declares the LORD.

33 And when this people—or a prophet or a priest—asks you,
"What is the burden[c] of the LORD?" you shall answer them,
[d-]"What is the burden?[-d] I will cast you off"— declares the LORD.
34 As for the prophet or priest or layman who shall say "the
burden of the LORD," I will punish that person and his house.
35 Thus you shall speak to each other, every one to his fellow,
"What has the LORD answered?" or "What has the LORD spoken?" 36 But do not mention "the burden of the LORD" any
more. [a-]Does a man regard his own word as a "burden,"[-a] that
you pervert the words of the living God, the LORD of Hosts, our
God? 37 Thus you shall speak to the prophet: "What did the
LORD answer you?" or "What did the LORD speak?" 38 But if you
say "the burden of the LORD"—assuredly, thus said the LORD:
Because you said this thing, "the burden of the LORD," whereas
I sent word to you not to say "the burden of the LORD," 39 I will
utterly [e-]forget you[-e] and I will cast you away from My presence,
together with the city that I gave to you and your fathers. 40 And
I will lay upon you a disgrace for all time, shame for all time,
which shall never be forgotten.

a-a *Meaning of Heb. uncertain.* b *Meaning of Heb. uncertain.*
c *I.e., pronouncement; cf. Isa. 13.1, 15.1, etc., where the word rendered "pronouncement" can also mean "burden."*
d-d *Septuagint and other versions read "You are the burden!"*
e-e *Some Heb. mss., Septuagint, and other versions read "lift you up," a word from the same root as "burden."*

25–32: In the ancient world, *dreams* were a legitimate vehicle for divine communication, but this is mocked here by Jeremiah. **27:** Derogatory phrases accumulate. In addition to these accusations (and see vv. 16–17), the prophets are blamed for their *plan to make My people forget My name* (see Ps. 44.21), namely to worship other gods. This harsh accusation is thematically connected with Deut. 13.2–6 (see Jer. 29.8). **28–29:** These vv. use two different proverbs. *Straw ... grain,* emphasizes the difference in value between the dream (straw) and the true word of God (the seed), devaluing any dream (see Zech. 10.2; cf. Joel 3.1), not only one that brings the people to forget God (v. 27). *My word is like fire ... a hammer that shatters rock!* These similes express the effectiveness, the totality, and the great power of the word of God (see Kimḥi; Jer. 5.14). By its nature, God's word consumes like fire, and shatters like the strongest hammer. In rabbinic tradition, this phrase was cited to suggest that God's words are multivalent, may be interpreted in a wide variety of legitimate ways (*b. Sanh.* 34a). **33–40:** A wordplay on "massa'" in its two senses: *burden* (as in 17.24, 27; metaphorically, Deut. 1.12) and "prophetic pronouncement." "Massa'" is common in prophecies against the nations, particularly in Isa. (13.1; 15.1, etc.; Nah. 1.1; Hab. 1.1; Mal. 1.1); and is seldom used about Israel (only in Isa. 22.1; Zech. 9.1; 12.1). Jeremiah ridicules this saying, which may be connected to the peace prophets, who might have pronounced prophecies of retribution against the nations (see Jer. 28.1–4). A talion (measure-for-measure) judgment will be brought upon those false prophets, priests, and the entire people, whom God will cast away (as fitting for a burden) and be punished. **35–40:** Jeremiah broadens his scope and applies this admonition and judgment to the entire people and city. **39:** *I will utterly forget you and I will cast you away from My presence.* "Nasha'" as *forget* is unique in Jer. (but see Job 11.6; 39.7; Lam. 3.17), and a unique proclamation by God (see its refutation in Isa. 44.21). Though formally it may have been chosen to play on the words "nasa'" and "massa'" (LXX translates it as "take, seize"), theologically it makes an even more extreme declaration, suspending the relationship between God and the people.

24 The LORD showed me two baskets of figs, placed in front
of the Temple of the LORD. This was after King Nebuchadrezzar of Babylon had exiled King Jeconiah son of Jehoiakim of Judah, and the officials of Judah, and the craftsmen
and smiths, from Jerusalem, and had brought them to Babylon.
2 One basket contained very good figs, like first-ripened figs,
and the other basket contained very bad figs, so bad that they
could not be eaten.
3 And the LORD said to me, "What do you see, Jeremiah?" I
answered, "Figs—the good ones are very good, and the bad
ones very bad, so bad that they cannot be eaten."
4 Then the word of the LORD came to me:
5 Thus said the LORD, the God of Israel: As with these good
figs, so will I single out for good the Judean exiles whom I have
driven out from this place to the land of the Chaldeans. 6 I will
look upon them favorably, and I will bring them back to this
land; I will build them and not overthrow them; I will plant
them and not uproot them. 7 And I will give them the understanding to acknowledge Me, for I am the LORD. And they shall
be My people and I will be their God, when they turn back to
Me with all their heart.
8 And like the bad figs, which are so bad that they cannot be
eaten—thus said the Lord—so will I treat King Zedekiah of Judah and his officials and the remnant of Jerusalem that is left
in this land, and those who are living in the land of Egypt: 9 I
will make them a horror—an evil—to all the kingdoms of the
earth, a disgrace and a proverb, a byword and a curse[a] in all the
places to which I banish them. 10 I will send the sword, famine,

a I.e., a standard by which men curse; cf. Gen. 12.2 and note; Zech. 8.13.

24.1–10: The good and the bad figs. The symbolic vision represents two groups within the Judean people: those exiled, destined for restoration, vs. those who remain in Judah, who will be annihilated. **1–4:** This vision may build on 1.11–14 and Amos 7.1, 7; 8.1. As happens in biblical parables and allegories, there is only general thematic connection between the vision (the good figs proper to be brought as gifts to the Temple, and the bad figs not to be eaten) and its elaborate interpretation (restoration for the one vs. total calamity for the other). The good basket stands for "galut Yehuda," those exiled with Jehoiachin. **5–7:** These exiles are the only group that will continue the national-religious existence of Judah. This community gained God's favor (vv. 5, 6), they will be delivered *back to this land;* and will go through profound and obligatory transformation, which will lead to reinstitution of the covenant relationship with them; this will all take place following the people's return to God *with all their heart* (see Deut. 30.10; 1 Kings 8.48). Conceptions of covenant, land, and the trajectory of exile-redemption are thus applied exclusively to that one community of exiles with Jehoiachin in 597. **6:** *Build … overthrow … plant … uproot:* Using terms from Jeremiah's dedication prophecy in 1.10. **8–10:** The bad basket, on the other hand, contains those who have not gone into Babylonian exile. This group is composed of the royalty that remains in Judah and the lay people—some of whom also fled to Egypt. *The remnant of Jerusalem* is called in chs 40–44 the remnant of Judah. All the groups in the "bad basket" date back to the period immediately prior to the destruction (597–586 BCE), or shortly after it, and they are all destined to total annihilation. The phraseology used in vv. 9–10 accumulates several otherwise independent curse motifs in order to denigrate this community as doomed both in the land and in Egypt. This judgment inaccurately portrays the land of Judah as completely empty once the extermination is implemented against the remnant of Jerusalem, in all of their places of residence (v. 10). The Judean exiles, "galut yehudah," in Babylonia, now represents the entire people of God; it is the only community that God will return to the land, the only community with whom God will reinstitute the covenant relationship. These vv. do not explain why the remnant of Jerusalem (including those settled in Egypt) is cursed (see similarly 29.16–20). This prophecy is not Jeremian, but derives from a secondary level composed during the Babylonian-exilic origin (see intro.). It resembles Ezekiel and Deutero-Isaiah (see also 32.36–41), and contradicts Jeremiah's pro-Judah/land orientation throughout (see ch 27) and his antagonism toward Jehoiachin (22.24–30). Ch 24 is thus of paramount importance for understanding the initial stages of the internal polemic prior to the destruction and immediately after it, as different communities understood themselves as God's chosen, in contradistinction to others. Like Ezekiel (see esp. Ezek. 11.6), the author of ch 24 emphasized that while the exiles of 597 had indeed been removed from the land, only they should be considered the recipients of the promise of future restoration; they (and they alone) are the (entire) people of God, those with whom God will reinstitute the covenant relationship.

and pestilence against them until they are exterminated from
the land that I gave to them and their fathers.

25 The word which came to Jeremiah concerning all the
people of Judah, in the fourth year of King Jehoiakim son
of Josiah of Judah, which was the first year of King Nebuchadrezzar of Babylon. 2 This is what the prophet Jeremiah said to
all the people of Judah and to all the inhabitants of Jerusalem:

3 From the thirteenth year of King Josiah son of Amon of Judah, to this day—these twenty-three years—the word of the
LORD has come to me. I have spoken to you persistently, but
you would not listen. 4 Moreover, the LORD constantly sent all
his servants the prophets to you, but you would not listen or
incline your ears to hear 5 when they said, "Turn back, every
one, from your evil ways and your wicked acts, that you may
remain throughout the ages on the soil which the LORD gave to
you and your fathers. 6 Do not follow other gods, to serve them
and worship them. Do not vex Me with what your own hands
have made,[a] and I will not bring disaster upon you." 7 But you
would not listen to Me—declares the LORD—but vexed Me
with what your hands made, to your own hurt.
8 Assuredly, thus said the LORD of Hosts: Because you would
not listen to My words, 9 I am going to send for all the peoples
of the north—declares the LORD—and for My servant, King
Nebuchadrezzar of Babylon, and bring them against this land
and its inhabitants, and against all those nations roundabout.
I will exterminate them and make them a desolation, an object
of hissing[b]—ruins for all time. 10 And I will banish from them
the sound of mirth and gladness, the voice of bridegroom
and bride, and the sound of the mill and the light of the lamp.
11 This whole land shall be a desolate ruin.

a I.e., idols. *b Cf. note at 18.16.*

25.1–38: This ch stands at a central place. The first part of the ch opens with a summary covenant speech (see 7.1–15 n.) that reviews twenty-three years of prophetic service (vv. 1–13), and concludes with an introduction to the prophecies against the nations (v. 14). This is the point where MT and LXX differ drastically. In MT, a symbolic act concerning God's judgment executed on those nations, the enemies of His people follows (vv. 15–38). In MT the two parts of this ch close the section of the judgment prophecies against Israel (chs 1–24), and introduce the prophecies dated to the early years, specifically the fourth and fifth years of Jehoiakim (chs 26–36), opening with the conflict concerning the subjugation to Babylon (chs 25–29). LXX, on the other hand, has a very different order of the second half of the book, and uses the introduction of this ch as a bridge to the prophecies against the nations (chs 1–24; 25.1–13; chs 46–51; 25.15–38; chs 26–45, 52).

25.1–14: Jeremiah's retrospective speech. 1: *The fourth year of King Jehoiakim* and *the first year of King Nebuchadrezzar . . . :* Synchronizing this date with the Babylonian king's regnal years occurs also in 32.1, and is followed in the list of deportations (52.28–30) and in Jehoiachin's release (52.31), as it is also shared by 2 Kings 24.12; 25.8 (LXX lacks the dating synchronism in 25.1; 52.12). The year is 605 BCE, the year that Nebuchadrezzar defeated Egypt at Carchemish and about a year later is assumed to have gained control over Judah. **2–4:** In a public address the prophet is instructed to summarize twenty-three years of prophetic activity (referring to Jer. 1.1–3). Sent daily (every morning) to speak to the people, he was met with constant disobedience (v. 4 draws heavily on 7.25–26, which addresses a transgenerational disobedience to generations of prophets). **5–7:** As in the other covenant speeches (7.1–15; 11.1–14; 17.19–27; 22.1–5), there is a call to repent (see 7.3, 7), accompanied by a conditional promise of continued existence in the land (7.3, 5–7; 11.5; 17.24–25; 22.4); and the mention of a specific sin to illustrate the people's disobedience, in this case the making of divine images (see Deut. 5.8–9). **8–14:** Disobedience leads to judgment, described as an invasion of a northern political coalition headed by Babylonia. Destruction means complete desolation, afflicting the ecological systems of life (Jer. 18.16; 19.8; etc.), and cessation of routine activities like marriage, grinding grain (supposedly by the early morning), and lighting candles by night. **11:** *Those nations,* Judah and its neighbors. *Seventy years:* This time period stands for subjugation (so also 29.10), roughly equal to three generations under the Babylonian king, his son, and his grandson (27.7), when the empire was at its peak, (Isa. 23.15, 17; seventy years is also mentioned in Mesopotamian sources as a term of long duration, as for instance Babylonia's destruction in royal inscriptions of Esarhaddon). The seventy years run roughly from 605 to 539 BCE, when the Persians conquered Babylonia (see Kimḥi for his detailed calculation). This hopeful prospect on the fall of Babylonia is transformed into

And those nations shall serve the king of Babylon seventy
years. 12 When the seventy years are over, I will punish the king
of Babylon and that nation and the land of the Chaldeans for
their sins—declares the LORD—and I will make it a desolation
for all time. 13 And I will bring upon that land all that I have decreed against it, all that is recorded in this book—that which Jeremiah prophesied against all the nations. 14 For they too shall
be enslaved by many nations and great kings; and I will requite
them according to their acts and according to their conduct.

15 For thus said the LORD, the God of Israel, to me: "Take
from My hand this cup of wine—of wrath—and make all the
nations to whom I send you drink of it. 16 Let them drink and
retch and act crazy, because of the sword that I am sending
among them."

17 So I took the cup from the hand of the LORD and gave
drink to all the nations to whom the LORD had sent me: 18 Jerusalem and the towns of Judah, and its kings and officials, to
make them a desolate ruin, an object of hissing and a curse[a]—
as is now the case; 19 Pharaoh king of Egypt, his courtiers, his
officials, and all his people; 20 all [b-]the mixed peoples;[-b] all the
kings of the land of Uz; all the kings of the land of the Philistines—Ashkelon, Gaza, Ekron, and what is left of Ashdod;
21 Edom, Moab, and Ammon; 22 all the kings of Tyre and all
the kings of Sidon, and all the kings of the coastland across
the sea; 23 Dedan, Tema, and Buz, and all those who have
their hair clipped; 24 all the kings of Arabia, and all the kings
of [b-]the mixed peoples[-b] who live in the desert; 25 all the kings
of Zimri[c] and all the kings of Elam and all the kings of Media;
26 all the kings of the north, whether far from or close to each
other—all the [b-]royal lands which are on the earth.[-b] And last
of all, the king of Sheshach[d] shall drink.

27 Say to them: "Thus said the LORD of Hosts, the God of Israel: Drink and get drunk and vomit; fall and never rise again,
because of the sword that I send among you." 28 And if they refuse to take the cup from your hand and drink, say to them,
"Thus said the LORD of Hosts: You must drink! 29 If I am bringing the punishment first on the city that bears My name, do
you expect to go unpunished? You will not go unpunished, for
I am summoning the sword against all the inhabitants of the
earth—declares the LORD of Hosts."

a *Cf. note at* 24.9. b-b *Meaning of Heb. uncertain.*
c *Meaning of Heb. uncertain.* d *A cipher for* Babel, *Babylon.*

seventy years of exile, of dislocation from the land, before restoration. Such an interpretive-adaptive explanation occurs already in the early Persian period prophecy, where Jeremiah's prophecy was expected to be fulfilled, as the seventy years were counted between destruction and return (538–520 BCE), or between the destruction of the First Temple (587 BCE) and the dedication of the Second (516 BCE; see Zech. 1.12; 7.5; the great gap between Jeremiah's consolation prophecies and reality seems to be the background to the people's despair in Hag. chs 1–2; but cf. 2 Chron. 36.21; and Dan. 9.2). **13:** *All that is recorded in this book,* as in Jer. 51.63 might refer to a specific prophecy against Babylon; LXX understood this to be the heading of the prophecies against the nations, in line with v. 13b.

25.15–29: The cup of wrath, a vision report. The prophet is instructed to symbolically make all the nations drink the wine of wrath, a poisonous drink (see 49.12; 51.7; Isa. 51.17, 22; Ezek. 23.31–34; Obad. 1.16; Hab. 2.15–16; Pss. 11.6; 75.9; Lam. 4.21). This is a vivid portrayal of an imaginary scene where the prophet is to be active among the nations, and to create havoc (1.5; for a universalistic divine sovereignty, see 18.1–13). **17–26:** A long list of twenty-six nations, all the nations of the known world, starting with *Jerusalem* and the cities of *Judah,* going south to *Egypt,* east to the Cisjordan nations and then from the Arab kingdoms of the desert, west to the *Philistines* and then to the Phoenician cities, closing with the northern kingdoms of *Elam* and *Media;* the king of Babylonia is saved for last (see translators' note *d*). The movement back and forth between east and west recalls the behavior of the intoxicated; those who have drunk from the cup. **26:** *Sheshach* is a coded reference to Babylonia, using a technique called "atbash," in which the last letter of the alphabet is substituted for the first, the penultimate letter for the second, and so forth. (Thus "b" becomes "sh" and "l" becomes "k."). The need to speak in codes concerning Babylonia is puzzling (see 51.41); perhaps it was unsafe to speak directly against Babylonia during the exile. **27–29:** Drunk as the nations are, God will send the sword among them. "Shalaḥ" (Qal [the basic form of the verb] here, vv. 16, 27, but commonly Piel [the third of the verb forms, indicating here an intensification]), "shillaḥ ḥerev," as if it was an epidemic (see 9.15; 24.10; 49.37; and see "shillaḥ dever," pestilence, in Lev. 26.25); thus as an epidemic.

25.30–38: Three pictures of destruction. 30–31: God as a lion, who roars from His holy residence in heaven (not in the Temple; cf. Joel 4.16; Amos 1.2). Great noise and tumult symbolize this war and it goes from one side of the world to the other. The war is further couched as a divine trial that delivers punishment to the wicked. **32–33:** Destruction is a great storm, leaving in its wake the earth strewn with unburied corpses that disintegrate into dung (as in 8.2; 9.21; 16.4; Ps. 79.2–3). **34–38:** Noise of war turn into wails over the disaster, leading to complete silence, complete desolation, because of God's wrath. This desolation brings God to abandon His earthly lair (cf. with v. 30; and see Pss. 10.9; 76.3). This is one of the rare instances where the prophet is proclaiming that God had deserted, left ("'azav"), His city and people (see 12.7); cf. the common accusation of the people who deserted God (as in 5.19; 9.12; 16.11, etc.). The prophecy complements the ch's universal perspective, which accentuates God's sovereignty as King of the world. Under the great power of Babylonian rule, Jeremiah presents a theological point of view where God is in control and the emperor of the world is but His vassal (25.9; 27.6).

26.1–24: Jeremiah's trial and death sentence, early in Jehoiakim's reign (609–608 BCE, or any time before his fourth year, 36.1). A full biographical report on the prophet's intense relationship with his audience in Jerusalem: priests, prophets, officials, and the entire people (cf. with 20.1–6). Such accounts, occasional anecdotes of the prophet's life and activity, are unique to Jeremiah in the prophetic literature; they occur in 20.1–6; chs 26 and 36–38; 40.1–6; 42.1–6; 43.1–7. They recount the antagonism Jeremiah had raised among the people, threats to his life, imprisonment,

30 You are to prophesy all those things to them, and then say
to them:

The LORD roars from on high,
He makes His voice heard from His holy dwelling;
He roars aloud over His [earthly] abode;
He utters shouts like the grape-treaders,
Against all the dwellers on earth.
31 Tumult has reached the ends of the earth,
For the LORD has a case against the nations,
He contends with all flesh.
He delivers the wicked to the sword
—declares the LORD.
32 Thus said the LORD of Hosts:
Disaster goes forth
From nation to nation;
A great storm is unleashed
From the remotest parts of earth.

33 In that day, the earth shall be strewn with the slain of the
LORD from one end to the other. They shall not be mourned, or
gathered and buried; they shall become dung upon the face of
the earth.

34 Howl, you shepherds, and yell,
Strew [dust] on yourselves, you lords of the flock!
For the day of your slaughter draws near.
[a]I will break you in pieces,[a]
And you shall fall like a precious vessel.
35 Flight shall fail the shepherds,
And escape, the lords of the flock.
36 Hark, the outcry of the shepherds,
And the howls of the lords of the flock!
For the LORD is ravaging their pasture.
37 The peaceful meadows shall be wiped out
By the fierce wrath of the LORD.
38 Like a lion, He has gone forth from His lair;
The land has become a desolation,
Because of the oppressive[b] wrath,
Because of His fierce anger.

26 At the beginning of the reign of King Jehoiakim son of
Josiah of Judah, this word came from the LORD:
2 "Thus said the LORD: Stand in the court of the House of the
LORD, and speak to [the men of] all the towns of Judah, who
are coming to worship in the House of the LORD, all the words

a-a *Meaning of Heb. uncertain.* b *Meaning of Heb. uncertain.*

which I command you to speak to them. Do not omit anything.
3 Perhaps they will listen and turn back, each from his evil way,
that I may renounce the punishment I am planning to bring
upon them for their wicked acts.

4 "Say to them: Thus said the LORD: If you do not obey Me,
abiding by the Teaching that I have set before you, 5 heeding the words of My servants the prophets whom I have been
sending to you persistently—but you have not heeded—6 then
I will make this House like Shiloh, and I will make this city a
curse[a] for all the nations of earth."

7 The priests and prophets and all the people heard Jeremiah
speaking these words in the House of the LORD. 8 And when
Jeremiah finished speaking all that the LORD had commanded
him to speak to all the people, the priests and the prophets and
all the people seized him, shouting, "You shall die! 9 How dare
you prophesy in the name of the LORD that this House shall
become like Shiloh and this city be made desolate, without inhabitants?" And all the people crowded about Jeremiah in the
House of the LORD.

10 When the officials of Judah heard about this, they went
up from the king's palace to the House of the LORD and held a
session at the entrance of the New Gate of [b-]the House of[-b] the
LORD. 11 The priests and prophets said to the officials and to all
the people, "This man deserves the death penalty, for he has
prophesied against this city, as you yourselves have heard."

12 Jeremiah said to the officials and to all the people, "It was
the LORD who sent me to prophesy against this House and this
city all the words you heard. 13 Therefore mend your ways and
your acts, and heed the LORD your God, that the LORD may renounce the punishment He has decreed for you. 14 As for me, I
am in your hands: do to me what seems good and right to you.
15 But know that if you put me to death, you and this city and its
inhabitants will be guilty of shedding the blood of an innocent
man. For in truth the LORD has sent me to you, to speak all
these words to you."

16 Then the officials and all the people said to the priests and
prophets, "This man does not deserve the death penalty, for he
spoke to us in the name of the LORD our God."

17 And some of the elders of the land arose and said to the
entire assemblage of the people, 18 "Micah the Morashtite, who
prophesied in the days of King Hezekiah of Judah, said to all
the people of Judah: 'Thus said the LORD of Hosts:

Zion shall be plowed as a field,
Jerusalem shall become heaps of ruins
And the Temple Mount a shrine in the woods.'[c]

a Cf. note at 24.9. b-b So many mss. and ancient versions; other mss. and the editions omit these words. c Cf. Mic. 3.12.

but nevertheless his protection by allies of the Shaphan scribal family in Jerusalem. **1–6:** A brief summary of the Temple prophecy (see 7.1–15): the public oration, the call to repent (with implicit promise of salvation), in standard Deuteronomic form. **6:** A significant change in the prospective judgment(s). The fortune of the *House* is compared to *Shiloh* (7.14), but instead of referring to the vague "the place" (7.14, and repeatedly there, vv. 3, 7, 12) this v. focuses on the city, and uses a curse formula (see 24.9; 25.18; see v. 9). Furthermore, 26.6 does not mention exile (see 7.15). **7–15:** Prophecy against the government could be considered treasonous (Amos 7.10–11) since it can demoralize the people and undermine government policy. Caught and brought to trial (v. 10), the prophet is threatened with a death sentence for his judgment prophecy (v. 11). **12–15:** Jeremiah's words of defense make clear that the struggle involves Jeremiah's legitimacy as a prophet. The opening and closing words, *It was the LORD who sent me to prophesy .... For in truth the LORD has sent me to you,* introduce chs 27–29, where the struggle between Jeremiah and the peace prophets, who are denounced as false prophets, becomes the main issue. The narrative clearly shows that at that time in Jerusalem there was much prophetic activity and no criteria to decide who was a true prophet (see chs 27–28). **16–24:** At the trial other voices defend Jeremiah: anonymous *officials and all the people,* who recognize his status as a true prophet. Two precedents are given; in one case the prophet was not put to death and in the second case he was. **17–19:** The first, brought by *the elders of the land,* recalls that *Micah the Morashtite,* a prophet of the 8th c. during the reign of Hezekiah, delivered a message of destruction but was not executed. His message influenced Hezekiah and ultimately saved the nation. This is the only place in the prophetic literature where another prophet's words (Mic. 3.12) are explicitly quoted.

19 "Did King Hezekiah of Judah, and all Judah, put him to death? Did he not rather fear the LORD and implore the LORD, so that the LORD renounced the punishment He had decreed against them? We are about to do great injury to ourselves!"

20 There was also a man prophesying in the name of the LORD, Uriah son of Shemaiah from Kiriath-jearim, who prophesied against this city and this land the same things as Jeremiah. 21 King Jehoiakim and all his warriors and all the officials heard about his address, and the king wanted to put him to death. Uriah heard of this and fled in fear, and came to Egypt. 22 But King Jehoiakim sent men to Egypt, Elnathan son of Achbor and men with him to Egypt. 23 They took Uriah out of Egypt and brought him to King Jehoiakim, who had him put to the sword and his body thrown into the burial place of the common people. 24 However, Ahikam son of Shaphan protected Jeremiah, so that he was not handed over to the people for execution.

27 At the beginning of the reign of King Jehoiakim[a] son of Josiah of Judah, this word came to Jeremiah from the LORD:

2 Thus said the LORD to me: Make for yourself thongs and bars of a yoke, and put them on your neck. 3 [b-]And send them[-b] to the king of Edom, the king of Moab, the king of the Ammonites, the king of Tyre, and the king of Sidon, by envoys who have come to King Zedekiah of Judah in Jerusalem; 4 and give them this charge to their masters: Thus said the LORD of Hosts, the God of Israel: Say this to your masters:

a Emendation yields "Zedekiah"; so a few mss. and Syriac; cf. vv. 3 and 12.
b-b Emendation yields "And send," i.e., a message.

20–23: The second precedent is the case of *Uriah son of Shemaiah* of *Kiriath-jearim* ("Qiriat Yearim"), a prophet active during Jeremiah's time but otherwise unknown, who might be mentioned in the Lachish ostracon 3.13–21. Uriah, also a true prophet, also spoke of destruction but fled to Egypt to escape being put to death by King Jehoiakim. (Note that Jeremiah did not flee, but stood his ground, daring the people to wrongly kill a prophet of God; vv. 14–15). Uriah was captured and brought back to the king and put to death. This episode gives a negative perspective on Jehoiakim, who is very far from righteous Hezekiah (see 22.13–19). Uriah was not even given a trial. Nevertheless, the case of Uriah provides a precedent for executing Jeremiah. **24:** *Ahikam son of Shaphan,* (see 2 Kings 22.12; and the father of Gedaliah, Jer. 40.5) saved Jeremiah from potential execution.

27.1–29.32: Conflicts with other prophets. Chs 27–29 form a special unit within Jeremiah, addressing theological and political issues between Jeremiah and other prophets whom he (and his followers) considered false prophets (this is a continuation of ch 26, where Jeremiah himself is accused of being a false prophet). In this unique account these opponent prophets have names (cf. to Ezek. ch 13), and they are active in Jerusalem (Jer. ch 28), or already in Babylonia (29.8–9, 15–32). The unifying theme is the false hope that the Jehoiachin exiles will soon be returning back home (27.9, 14–15, 17; 28.1–4; 29.1–8, 24–32), and that the Babylonian regime is only a short-lived threat (27.5–11, 16; 28.14; 29.4–7, 10, 28). Formal characteristics also unify these chs: personal names end with "-yah" (not "-yahu"), thus Jeremiah, Hananiah, Gemariah, Hilkiah, Maaseiah, Zedekiah, Zephaniah, Kolaiah, and Shemaiah (exceptions appear only in ch 29); Nebuchadnezzar (instead of the form Nebuchadrezzar elsewhere in the book, as in 21.2, 7; 22.25; 25.19; 32.1; with but one exception, 29.21); emphasis on the title "the prophet" accompanying Jeremiah (eight times in chs 28 and 29; six times for Hananiah, in ch 28; and relatively much more than in other parts of the book, where it is used altogether twenty-three times for Jeremiah).

27.1–28.17: The subjugation to Babylon fiercely disputed in Jerusalem. Ch 27 introduces the prophet's theological view of the international-political relationships between the Neo-Babylonian empire and its vassal states, including Judah. To emphasize his call to accept Babylonian rule, the prophet addresses three separate audiences in three different circles on presumably three occasions: first, he addresses a universal message to foreign kings who sent envoys to Jerusalem (vv. 4–11); second, the prophet asks Zedekiah to spare the people of Judah (vv. 12–15); finally, the prophet addresses the priests and the people of Jerusalem about their continuous existence in Jerusalem and the fate of the Temple vessels (vv. 16–22). To dramatize his words, the prophet places a yoke on his neck to illustrate the Babylonian

5 "It is I who made the earth, and the men and beasts who
are on the earth, by My great might and My outstretched arm;
and I give it to whomever I deem proper. 6 I herewith deliver
all these lands to My servant, King Nebuchadnezzar of Babylon; I even give him the wild beasts to serve him. 7 All nations
shall serve him, his son and his grandson—until the turn of
his own land comes, when many nations and great kings shall
subjugate him. 8 The nation or kingdom that does not serve
him—King Nebuchadnezzar of Babylon—and does not put its
neck under the yoke of the king of Babylon, that nation I will
visit—declares the LORD—with sword, famine, and pestilence,
until I have destroyed it by his hands. 9 As for you, give no heed
to your prophets, augurs, dreamers,[a] diviners, and sorcerers,
who say to you, 'Do not serve the king of Babylon.' 10 For they
prophesy falsely to you—with the result that you shall be banished from your land; I will drive you out and you shall perish.
11 But the nation that puts its neck under the yoke of the king of
Babylon, and serves him, will be left by Me on its own soil—declares the LORD—to till it and dwell on it."

12 I also spoke to King Zedekiah of Judah in just the same
way: "Put your necks under the yoke of the king of Babylon;
serve him and his people, and live! 13 Otherwise you will die
together with your people, by sword, famine, and pestilence,
as the LORD has decreed against any nation that does not serve
the king of Babylon. 14 Give no heed to the words of the prophets who say to you, 'Do not serve the king of Babylon,' for they
prophesy falsely to you. 15 I have not sent them—declares the
LORD—and they prophesy falsely in My name, with the result
that I will drive you out and you shall perish, together with the
prophets who prophesy to you."

a Lit. "dreams."

subjugation (27.2, and vv. 8, 12; and see Deut. 28.48; for other symbolic actions see 13.1–11; 18.1–12). Subsequently, the yoke is the symbol of Jeremiah's conflict with the prophet Hananiah son of Azzur in ch 28 (vv. 1–4, 10–11, 13–14); just as the Temple vessels taken during the Jehoiachin exile (27.18–22) are of great importance in Hanaiah's prophecy (28.1–4). LXX and MT differ in ch 27: LXX is forty-two percent shorter than MT (the average is seventeen percent). Most of the differences would seem to be intentional corrections (usually omitting phrases), interpretive harmonizations (see v. 6) from the earlier Heb version, and transmission mistakes (mostly of haplography [omission of partial phrases with the same opening words] or homoioteleuton [which results in omitting a phrase between two occurrences of the same word], as for instance vv. 12–13).

27.1–11: Babylonian international rule under God's sovereignty. Envoys from Edom, Moab, Ammon, Tyre, and Sidon come to Zedekiah in his fourth year (594 BCE). This coalition against Babylonia under Zedekiah's leadership is a unique witness to Zedekiah's international power, since he is otherwise portrayed as wicked (see 37.17; 38.14–27). Zedekiah's revolt might have been the background to the delegation sent to Babylon (51.59–64), but there are no further indications as to whether this initiative ever went further. **5–7:** This presentation of divine sovereignty combines two very different traditions: the creation tradition, which in Gen. ch 1 is not creation by combat, and the exodus tradition, highlighting the power and outstretched arm by which God rules in history (see Deut. 9.29; 2 Kings 17.36; and Jer. 32.17). The combination depicts God as LORD of the universe. This leaves Nebuchadnezzar, the great emperor, as a mere servant of God (see also Jer. 25.9; 43.10), who allots his reign for three generations. **9:** The false prophecy not to *serve the king of Babylon* occurs in all three passages (v. 14, indirectly in v. 17). **11:** Serving the Babylonians guarantees continual residence in the land (see also Gedaliah's words to the remnant, 40.9).

27.12–15: The plea to Zedekiah to accept Babylon's rule and live (see also v. 17) accords with Jeremiah's conception of the land and of exile, in which he follows Deuteronomic preexilic conceptions that treat expulsion from the land as calamity (see "'avad" in vv. 10, 15 and in Deut. 6.15; 8.19–20; 28.20–26). Accordingly, Jeremiah prophesies against Shallum (22.10–12) and Jehoiachin (22.24–30), chooses to remain in the land following the destruction (40.1–6), and calls the remnant of Judah to hold on to this land as well (42.10–17). This is a clear pro-land (pro-Judean) perspective; there is no justification to the claim that Jeremiah was pro-Babylonian (see ch 37).

27.16–22: Prophecy to priests and people. This third passage addresses priests and people jointly, excluding the prophets (cf. the regular cluster of prophets and priests, with or without the people, in 26.7, 8, 11, 16; also 8.10; 23.11, 33, 34). **18–22:** The remaining vessels of the Temple, those that were not looted by 597 BCE, are to be taken away in a further deportation (see 52.17–23). **22:** This prophecy foresees restoration of the vessels, but note the difference in comparison to Ezra 1.11 (where only small vessels of gold and silver are mentioned).

28.1–17: Two prophets struggling over the true word of God. Hananiah son of Azzur of Gibeon (north of Jerusalem), who is called regularly in this ch *the prophet* (LXX argues: "false-prophet"), opens a public debate with Jeremiah at the Temple in front of the priests and the entire people. **2–4:** In a remarkably styled prophecy, with an inclusio (v. 2: *I hereby break the yoke of the king of Babylon;* v. 4: *Yes, I will break the yoke of the king of Babylon*), using the prophetic formula so typical of Jeremiah (see for instance, 9.14; 16.9; 27.21, and in Jeremiah's response, 28.14), he promises the return of three things dearly missed in Jerusalem: the *vessels* of the Temple, the king of Judah, *Jeconiah* (Jehoiachin), and the entire exiled community. Hananiah, furthermore, illustrates his words with a symbolic act, in which he breaks the yoke that Jeremiah still wears and prophesies deliverance (vv. 10–11, see 30.8–9). **6–9:** Jeremiah opens his response with an ironic *Amen,* meaning "O, I only wish you are right but you are not." He then cites the long tradition of prophets of woe, who are, it is implied, to be considered true prophets. But if a prophet prophesies good fortune, as Hananiah did, he can only be judged a true prophet if his word comes to pass. Jeremiah invokes Deut. 18.21–22 only on this favorable prophecy for peace. The prophecy of doom is accepted at face value. But these criteria for judging true and false prophecy are hardly practical.

16 And to the priests and to all that people I said: "Thus said
the LORD: Give no heed to the words of the prophets who
prophesy to you, 'The vessels of the House of the LORD shall
shortly be brought back from Babylon,' for they prophesy falsely to you. 17 Give them no heed. Serve the king of Babylon, and
live! Otherwise this city shall become a ruin. 18 If they are really
prophets and the word of the LORD is with them, let them intercede with the LORD of Hosts not to let the vessels remaining
in the House of the LORD, in the royal palace of Judah, and in
Jerusalem, go to Babylon!
19 "For thus said the LORD of Hosts concerning the columns,
the tank,[a] the stands, and the rest of the vessels remaining in
this city, 20 which King Nebuchadnezzar of Babylon did not
take when he exiled King Jeconiah son of Jehoiakim of Judah,
from Jerusalem to Babylon, with all the nobles of Judah and
Jerusalem; 21 for thus said the LORD of Hosts, the God of Israel,
concerning the vessels remaining in the House of the LORD,
in the royal palace of Judah, and in Jerusalem: 22 They shall be
brought to Babylon, and there they shall remain, until I take
note of them—declares the LORD of Hosts—and bring them up
and restore them to this place."

28 That year, early in the reign of King Zedekiah of Judah,
in the fifth month of the fourth year, the prophet Hananiah son of Azzur, who was from Gibeon, spoke to me in the
House of the LORD, in the presence of the priests and all the
people. He said: 2 "Thus said the LORD of Hosts, the God of Israel: I hereby break the yoke of the king of Babylon. 3 In two
years, I will restore to this place all the vessels of the House of
the LORD which King Nebuchadnezzar of Babylon took from
this place and brought to Babylon. 4 And I will bring back to
this place King Jeconiah son of Jehoiakim of Judah, and all the
Judean exiles who went to Babylon—declares the LORD. Yes, I
will break the yoke of the king of Babylon."
5 Then the prophet Jeremiah answered the prophet Hananiah in the presence of the priests and of all the people who
were standing in the House of the LORD. 6 The prophet Jeremiah said: "Amen! May the LORD do so! May the LORD fulfill
what you have prophesied and bring back from Babylon to this
place the vessels of the House of the LORD and all the exiles!
7 But just listen to this word which I address to you and to all
the people: 8 The prophets who lived before you and me from
ancient times prophesied war, disaster, and pestilence against
many lands and great kingdoms. 9 So if a prophet prophesies
good fortune, then only when the word of the prophet comes
true can it be known that the LORD really sent him."

a *Lit. "sea"; cf. 1 Kings 7.23 ff.*

10 But the prophet Hananiah removed the bar from the neck
of the prophet Jeremiah, and broke it; 11 and Hananiah said in
the presence of all the people, "Thus said the LORD: So will I
break the yoke of King Nebuchadnezzar of Babylon from off
the necks of all the nations, in two years." And the prophet Jeremiah went on his way.
12 After the prophet Hananiah had broken the bar from off
the neck of the prophet Jeremiah, the word of the LORD came
to Jeremiah: 13 "Go say to Hananiah: Thus said the LORD: You
broke bars of wood, but [a]you shall[-a] make bars of iron instead.
14 For thus said the LORD of Hosts, the God of Israel: I have put
an iron yoke upon the necks of all those nations, that they may
serve King Nebuchadnezzar of Babylon—and serve him they
shall! I have even given the wild beasts to him."
15 And the prophet Jeremiah said to the prophet Hananiah,
"Listen, Hananiah! The LORD did not send you, and you have
given this people lying assurances. 16 Assuredly, thus said the
LORD: I am going to banish you from off the earth. This year
you shall die, for you have urged disloyalty to the LORD."
17 And the prophet Hananiah died that year, in the seventh
month.

29 This is the text of the letter which the prophet Jeremiah
sent from Jerusalem to the priests, the prophets, the rest
of the elders of the exile community, and to all the people whom
Nebuchadnezzar had exiled from Jerusalem to Babylon—2 after
King Jeconiah, the queen mother, the eunuchs, the officials of
Judah and Jerusalem, and the craftsmen and smiths had left Jerusalem. 3 [The letter was sent] through Elasah son of Shaphan
and Gemariah son of Hilkiah, whom King Zedekiah of Judah
had dispatched to Babylon, to King Nebuchadnezzar of Babylon.

4 Thus said the LORD of Hosts, the God of Israel, to the whole
community which I exiled from Jerusalem to Babylon: 5 Build
houses and live in them, plant gardens and eat their fruit. 6 Take
wives and beget sons and daughters; and take wives for your

a-a Septuagint reads "I will."

In fact, even Jeremiah prophesied peace and consolation (see chs 30–31). **12–17:** Having left the place in silence (maybe in embarrassment), Jeremiah receives another prophecy, this time enforcing the national message of subjugation to Babylonia (see 28.14, and cf. 27.6). On the personal level, Hananiah is doomed to talion retaliation—having never been sent by God to the people and yet having prophesied to them, now Hananiah will be sent away by God, but this time for good, that is, he will die. Indeed Hananiah died two months later (see 28.1). This is another indication of the bitter struggles among members of the religious and the political leadership in Jerusalem.

29.1–33: Further conflict. This ch not only carries on the peculiarities in theme and form of chs 27–29, it also illustrates the antagonistic perspectives on the crucial issue of Judean identity, on the status of each of the communities, the Jeconiah/Jehoiachin (and Babylonian) exiles vs. those who remained in Judah.

29.1–7: Jeremiah's letter to the exiles. The time is after the Jehoiachin exile (597 BCE, see 2 Kings 24.8–17; 2 Chron. 36.9–10). The officials mentioned are *Elasah son of Shaphan,* who was the brother of Ahikam son of Shaphan (26.24) and the son of Josiah's scribe (2 Kings 22.3, 12). *Gemariah son of Hilkiah* may be the son of Josiah's high priest (2 Kings 22.4). **3:** The two officials were part of the political delegation sent by Zedekiah to Babylon, presumably to appease the emperor following the rebellious initiative mentioned in 27.1–11 (594/93 BCE; this was also suggested for 51.59–64, where another official is named). The mission these officials were given by the prophet is, however, by no means political. Addressed to the exiles' leadership and to the entire community, it reflects Jeremiah's ongoing involvement in the theological crisis these exiles faced, now that they were displaced from the land of Israel. The prophet sends his practical advice to cope with the new circumstances or dislocation, advice based on the Deuteronomic conception of exile, and its reflection in prophetic tradition. **5–6:** Building houses and planting vineyards, like marriage and procreation, designate permanent settlement in Deut. 20.5–7, where they form orderly events of life and of the agricultural routine; all these crash down in the event of divine punishment in Deut. 28.30–32. This imagery appears in prophecies of judgment (Amos 5.11; Zeph. 1.13); and in reverse, it plays a role in prophecies of consolation and restoration (Isa. 65.21–23; Jer. 29.5–6; Ezek. 28.25–26). Hence, Jeremiah applies these Deuteronomic conceptions of disobedience and its consequences of war, subjugation, and exile to the current crisis. **6:** Multiply there, do not decrease,

sons, and give your daughters to husbands, that they may bear
sons and daughters. Multiply there, do not decrease. 7 And seek
the welfare of the city to which I have exiled you and pray to the
LORD in its behalf; for in its prosperity you shall prosper.
8 For thus said the LORD of Hosts, the God of Israel: Let not
the prophets and diviners in your midst deceive you, and pay
no heed to the dreams they[a] dream. 9 For they prophesy to you
in My name falsely; I did not send them—declares the LORD.
10 For thus said the LORD: When Babylon's seventy years are
over, I will take note of you, and I will fulfill to you My promise
of favor—to bring you back to this place. 11 For I am mindful of
the plans I have made concerning you—declares the LORD—
plans for your welfare, not for disaster, to give you a hopeful future. 12 When you call Me, and come and pray to Me, I will give
heed to you. 13 You will search for Me and find Me, if only you
seek Me wholeheartedly. 14 I will be at hand for you—declares
the LORD—and I will restore your fortunes. And I will gather
you from all the nations and from all the places to which I have
banished you—declares the LORD—and I will bring you back
to the place from which I have exiled you.
15 But you say, "The LORD has raised up prophets for us in
Babylon."[b]
16 Thus said the LORD concerning the king who sits on the
throne of David, and concerning all the people who dwell in this
city, your brothers who did not go out with you into exile— 17 thus
said the LORD of Hosts: I am going to let loose sword, famine,

a *Heb. "you."* b *This verse is continued in vv. 20 ff.*

adds a third Deuteronomic allusion, thematically reversing the Deuteronomic conception of exile as expressed in Deut. 4.27: "The LORD will scatter you among the peoples, and only a scant few of you shall be left among the nations to which the LORD will drive you." Emphasizing marriage and progeny (v. 6a), the prophet calls the exiles to be active to prevent this danger of physical decrease. **7:** Jeremiah's main message to the Jehoiachin/Jeconiah exiles is to settle down permanently in their new exilic locations, seeking the peace of their relocation city, Babylon, *for in its prosperity you shall prosper.* While Jeremiah reverses the Deuteronomic conception of exile from calamity to prosperity, he urges the Jehoiachin exiles to accept their deportation as a permanent position, with no prospect of return. Hence, although Jeremiah's letter to the exiles is far from being a consoling letter of restoration, the reversal of the Deuteronomic conception of exile is significant. The prophet, nevertheless, maintains his basic conception of exile as a situation of no return (see 22.10–12, 24–30). Yet, his letter clearly differs from other prophecies of judgment (as in 9.14–15), which take exile as sheer annihilation. This message thus differs from chs 27–28—from the struggle within Jerusalem concerning the political question of rebellion against Babylonia—though it does follow the mutual hope in both Jerusalem and in Babylonia for a short exile and a quick return of the Jehoiachin exiles (see 28.1–4; 29.21–32).

29.8–9: The call to disregard the deceiving words of the prophets, who prophesy lies and were never sent by God (Jer. 14.14; 23.32; 27.15; 28.15; 29.31), does not seem to be related to the previous letter, where the prophets were one of the groups addressed (v. 1; cf. with 27.16 where the prophet divides between the groups). It might be an opening statement tied to v. 15, and then vv. 21ff., thus leaving two interpolated passages, vv. 10–14 and vv. 16–20.

29.10–14: A consolation prophecy of restoration to the exiles. In contradistinction to Jeremiah's message in his letter (vv. 1–7), these vv. promise *a hopeful future* (v. 11). This future and hope is specified as before the end of seventy years (see 25.11). But note the difference: in 25.12–14 and 27.7, seventy years or three generations refer to the Babylonian regime and prophesy its eventual destruction; it is only here that this timespan sets the bounds of exile and the time of return and restoration in the land (see Zech. 1.12; 7.5; Dan. 9.2; 2 Chron. 36.21–22). **12–14:** Following the Deuteronomic conception of exile (Deut. 4.29–31; 30.1–10), the people are the ones who reinstitute the relationship with God (cf. Jer. 31.31–34). God's attendance to the people's prayers follows Deut. 4.29 and 1 Kings 8.28–53, but clearly deviates from Jeremiah's judgment prophecies (see 7.16; 11.14; 14.11).

29.15–32: Other prophets. 15: *The LORD has raised up prophets for us in Babylon* opens the second part of this ch (vv. 15–32), which focuses on several prophets mentioned by name. Once again, inexplicably, Ezekiel goes unmentioned, though he is the one true prophet God had commissioned in Babylonia (Ezek. 1.1–3). **16–20:** Interpolated between vv. 15 and 21ff., this unit seems to be a fragment of another non-Jeremian prophecy. **16:** Addressed to the reigning king of Jerusalem, though not mentioning Zedekiah by name, and all the residents of the city, these vv. foresee total annihilation of those who were not exiled. **17:** In similar imagery to 24.2, 8, they are the *loathsome figs, so bad that they cannot*

and pestilence against them and I will treat them as loathsome figs, so bad that they cannot be eaten.[a] 18 I will pursue them with the sword, with famine, and with pestilence; and I will make them a horror to all the kingdoms of the earth, a curse and an object of horror and hissing[b] and scorn among all the nations to which I shall banish them, 19 because they did not heed My words—declares the LORD—when I persistently sent to them My servants, the prophets, and they[c] did not heed—declares the LORD.

20 But you, the whole exile community which I banished from Jerusalem to Babylon, hear the word of the LORD! 21 Thus said the LORD of Hosts, the God of Israel, concerning Ahab son of Kolaiah and Zedekiah son of Maaseiah, who prophesy falsely to you in My name: I am going to deliver them into the hands of King Nebuchadrezzar of Babylon, and he shall put them to death before your eyes. 22 And the whole community of Judah in Babylonia shall use a curse derived from their fate: "May God make you like Zedekiah and Ahab, whom the king of Babylon consigned to the flames!"—23 because they did vile things in Israel, committing adultery with the wives of their fellows and speaking in My name false words which I had not commanded them. I am He who knows and bears witness—declares the LORD.

24 Concerning Shemaiah the Nehelamite you[d] shall say: 25 Thus said the LORD of Hosts, the God of Israel: Because you sent letters in your own name to all the people in Jerusalem, to Zephaniah son of Maaseiah and to the rest of the priests, as follows, 26 "The LORD appointed you priest in place of the priest Jehoiada, [e-]to exercise authority[-e] in the House of the LORD over every madman who wants to play the prophet, to put him into the stocks[f] and into the pillory.[f] 27 Now why have you not rebuked Jeremiah the Anathothite, who plays the prophet among you? 28 For he has actually sent a message to us in Babylon to this effect: It will be a long time. Build houses and live in them, plant gardens and enjoy their fruit."—

29 When the priest Zephaniah read this letter in the hearing of the prophet Jeremiah, 30 the word of the LORD came to Jeremiah: 31 Send a message to the entire exile community: "Thus said the LORD concerning Shemaiah the Nehelamite: Because Shemaiah prophesied to you, though I did not send him, and made you false promises, 32 assuredly, thus said the LORD: I am going to punish Shemaiah the Nehelamite and his offspring. There shall be no man of his line dwelling among this people or seeing the good things I am going to do for My

a *Cf. 24.1 ff.* b *Cf. note at 18.16.* c *Heb. "you."* d *I.e., Jeremiah.*
e-e *Lit. "that there might be officials."* f *Meaning of Heb. uncertain.*

be eaten, the disobedient people who suffer calamity in similar ways (see 24.9–10). **20:** The prophecy here moves to its target audience, which is either the Jehoiachin/Jeconiah exiles, or the entire people deported from Jerusalem to Babylonia. The dichotomy between those who remained and the Babylonian exiles is brought out once again, and the prophecy clearly delegitimizes the former. Yet the passage is cut short and the prophet's words, which were probably consoling ones for the Babylonian exiles (as in 24.3–7) are missing. **21–23:** In response to the people's claim that God had raised prophets in Babylon, two are named and designated as false prophets, to be smitten by Nebuchadrezzar (see *b. Sanh.* 93a; on this exceptional form of the Babylonian name, see 27.1–29.32 n.). Their deaths will remain a *curse* ("qelalah") to the entire Judean exile in Babylonia: Playing on the name *Kolaiah,* the king of Babylon had consumed (NJPS: *consigned to*) ("qalam") them with fire, and with *Maaseiah* their judgment was a retaliation *because they did* ("'asu") *vile things in Israel.* (The LXX omits their names, and thus the puns.) They are accused of diverse moral and religious sins, and only then of their false prophecy (see 23.10, 14). **24–32:** *Shemaiah the Nehelamite* is recognized as another false prophet active among the exiles in Babylonia (v. 31). But the passage starts by quoting the letter Shemaiah had sent to the priest *Zephaniah son of Maaseiah* and the Jerusalem priests (lacking in LXX) rebuking his (their) negligence in treating Jeremiah. **26:** The authority to imprison *every madman who wants to play the prophet* suggests Jeremiah used ecstatic activity, which is seldom connected with the classical prophets, but see Hos. 9.7; and Jer. 23.9 (in reference to Elisha, 2 Kings 9.11). **27–28:** The major complaint against Jeremiah is his message to the exiles (see v. 5), with the addition of but two significant Heb words: *It will be a long time.* **30–32:** Only through the denunciation of *Shemaiah* can one reconstruct his comforting message of

people—declares the LORD—for he has urged disloyalty toward the LORD."

30

The word which came to Jeremiah from the LORD:
2 Thus said the LORD, the God of Israel: Write down in
a scroll all the words that I have spoken to you. 3 For days are
coming—declares the LORD—when I will restore the fortunes
of My people Israel and Judah, said the LORD; and I will bring
them back to the land that I gave their fathers, and they shall
possess it. 4 And these are the words that the LORD spoke concerning Israel and Judah:

5 Thus said the LORD:
We have heard cries of panic,
Terror without relief.
6 Ask and see:
Surely males do not bear young!
Why then do I see every man
With his hands on his loins
Like a woman in labor?
Why have all faces turned pale?
7 Ah, that day is awesome;
There is none like it!
It is a time of trouble for Jacob,
But he shall be delivered from it.

salvation very soon. Jeremiah's judgment prophecy against Shemaiah is transferred to his descendants; cf. with the judgments of Hananiah, Ahab and Zedekiah, who suffered immediate death themselves (28.17; 29.21–22). *For he has urged disloyalty toward the LORD* echoes Deut. 13.6; and is the same accusation against Hananiah in Jer. 28.16.

30.1–31.40: The book of consolation. Consolation prophecies are collected in these two chs, but additional proclamations of hope are sporadically placed within the book (see 3.14–17; 16.14–15; 23.7–8; ch 24; 29.10–14; chs 32, 33, and passages within chs 50–51). The prophecies of consolation in general, and specifically here, comprise several layers of prophetic pronouncements; three major ones may be identified. First, there are prophecies assumed to be Jeremian in origin, or at least Judean in their geographical location. They may reflect some of the earliest prophecies of Jeremiah, at the end of the 7th c., calling for a reunion with northern Israel, and following up on the Neo-Babylonian era down to Judah's destruction: 30.4–9, 10–11; 31.2–6, 7–9, 10–14, 15–22. A second layer may have been the product of the prophet's Babylonian followers and editors of the book, thus reflecting Babylonian exilic ideology (as ch 24), and may be dated to the Neo-Babylonian period (and into the early Persian era); here: 30.12–17. The third layer, which is even harder to identify, contains a mix of Jeremian earlier proclamations composed in Judah, which were adapted, expanded and re-read by authors from the repatriate Babylonian community (as also 33.10–13). These prophecies are thus hard to date, as they contain both an early layer and elaborations that may be dated to the early Persian period, and are thus among the latest levels of the book; here: 30.18–22, 23–24; 31.23–26, 27–30, 31–34, 35–37, 38–40. The book of consolation, therefore, is an accumulation of at least three generations in Judah, Babylonia, and back to Judah. Thematically, restoration in Jeremiah is presented as an actual historical fate in the coming future, not an eschatological universal event. Rich in different themes (which will be unfolded below), Jeremiah does not raise the demand of repentance on the side of the people, and it is clearly not a precondition to deliverance (cf. with Deut. 4.30–31; 30.1–6).

30.1–3: Introduction to the book of consolation. God had already delivered to Jeremiah the command to write down a collection of prophecies; this repeats the ones concerning prophecies against the nations (25.1; and see 51.60), and judgment prophecies against Israel, Judah, and the nations (36.2; 45.1). The extent of the original collection and all that had accumulated later on is unclear; just as the question whether these prophecies were ever proclaimed publicly or written down and kept for later generations to read remains open (see Kimḥi).

3: The introduction offers two positive prospects for the future, distinguished semantically in two formulae: consolation refers to the restoration of both Israel and Judah, since both comprise *My people;* and, for the exiles, consolation means regathering the dispersed back to the promised land. The first formula ("shav shvut," that is: *I will restore the fortunes of My people*) signifies restoration within the land (see 33.7); the second refers to regathering the people from exile ("heshiv" ["shevit"], that is: *and I will bring them back to the land that I gave their fathers;* see 29.14).

30.4–31.1: Five prophecies. The prophecies start with references to anxiety during *a time of trouble* (vv. 5–7, so also vv. 12–15), but gradually modulate into words of deliverance. **30.4–9:** The first oracle is nearly all concerned with distress. Only the last two Heb words of v. 7 promise a change: *But he shall be*

[8] In that day—declares the LORD of Hosts—I will break the yoke from off your neck and I will rip off your bonds. Strangers shall no longer make slaves of them; [9] instead, they shall serve the LORD their God and David, the king whom I will raise up for them.

10 But you,
Have no fear, My servant Jacob
—declares the LORD—
Be not dismayed, O Israel!
I will deliver you from far away,
Your folk from their land of captivity.
And Jacob shall again have calm
And quiet with none to trouble him;
11 For I am with you to deliver you
—declares the LORD.
I will make an end of all the nations
Among which I have dispersed you;
But I will not make an end of you!
I will not leave you unpunished,
But will chastise you in measure.

12 For thus said the LORD:
Your injury is incurable,
Your wound severe;
13 [a]No one pleads for the healing of your sickness,[a]
There is no remedy, no recovery for you.
14 All your lovers have forgotten you,
They do not seek you out;
For I have struck you as an enemy strikes,
With cruel chastisement,
Because your iniquity was so great
And your sins so many.
15 Why cry out over your injury,
That your wound is incurable?
I did these things to you
Because your iniquity was so great
And your sins so many.

16 Assuredly,
All who wanted to devour you shall be devoured,
And every one of your foes shall go into captivity;
Those who despoiled you shall be despoiled,
And all who pillaged you I will give up to pillage.
17 But I will bring healing to you
And cure you of your wounds
—declares the LORD.

a-a Meaning of Heb. uncertain.

delivered from it. The following vv. elaborate on this deliverance. Note that there is no mention of a geographical change of location, which means this prophecy belongs to the earlier stage of this collection, to the Judean layer (see 30.1–31.40 n.). **8–9:** Release from political subjugation turns into worshipping God. This prophecy is semantically and thematically close to Hananiah son of Azzur's prophecy (see 28.2–4), and both are part of a shared prophetic tradition, known from the prophecies of Isaiah (9.3; 10.27), Ezekiel (34.27–28), and Nahum (1.13); all seem to be based on the concluding blessing of Lev. 26.13. God's portrayal as deliverer of His people from human subjugation echoes the paradigmatic salvation from Egypt (Exod. 20.2–5; Deut. 6.12–13). Restoration of Davidic rule may thus be a later addition to this original tradition. **10–11:** The second oracle focuses on deliverance of Jacob from afar. Addressing Jacob (see also Israel, 31.2; "betulat" Israel, 31.6; Ephraim, 31.9, 18, 20), this prophecy calls for reincorporation of the remnant from the past Northern Kingdom into Zion (see 31.7–9). The statements *have no fear* and *I am with you to deliver you* are typical features of the prophetic oracle of reassurance in Israel (cf. Gen. 15.1; 2 Kings 6.16; Isa. 7.4–9; 10.24–37; 37.6–7; 40.9; 41.10) and Mesopotamia. **11:** Deliverance from among the nations is coupled with judgment God will inflict on the subjugating nations (see also 30.16–17, 23). **12–17:** A third oracle focuses on Zion, afflicted and deserted because of her sins (cf. vv. 14–15 to Isa. 42.24). **13, 17:** The metaphors of sickness and wounds for Israel's judgment are reversed in this portrayal of consolation (see 8.21–22; 14.19), according to the conception that God can both inflict sickness (Deut. 28.27, 35) and heal and cure (Deut. 32.39). **17:** Restoration reinstitutes Zion after a period of neglect (see 32.36). Reversal of her fortune accords with Deutero-Isaiah (Isa. 49.14–26), and is expressed by renaming it, another clear tie to Deutero-Isaiah (Isa. 60.14; 62.4, 12). These similarities to

Though they called you "Outcast,
That Zion whom no one seeks out,"
18 Thus said the LORD:
I will restore the fortunes of Jacob's tents
And have compassion upon his dwellings.
The city shall be rebuilt on its mound,[a]
And the fortress in its proper place.
19 From them shall issue thanksgiving
And the sound of dancers.
I will multiply them,
And they shall not be few;
I will make them honored,
And they shall not be humbled.
20 His children shall be as of old,
And his community shall be established by My grace;
And I will deal with all his oppressors.
21 His chieftain shall be one of his own,
His ruler shall come from his midst;
I will bring him near, that he may approach Me
—declares the LORD—
For who would otherwise dare approach Me?
22 You shall be My people,
And I will be your God.

23 Lo, the storm of the LORD goes forth in fury,
A raging tempest;
It shall whirl down upon the head of the wicked.
24 The anger of the LORD shall not turn back
Till it has fulfilled and completed His purposes.
In the days to come
You shall perceive it.

31 [b]At that time—declares the LORD—I will be God to all the clans of Israel, and they shall be My people.

2 Thus said the LORD:
The people escaped from the sword,
Found favor in the wilderness;
When Israel was marching homeward

a I.e., on the mound of ruins left after its previous destruction.
b In some editions this verse is 30.25.

Deutero-Isaiah suggest a Babylonian-exilic authorship of this passage (see second layer, 30.1–31.40 n.). **30.18–31.1:** The fourth oracle brings together several themes of restoration, a mix that is typical of the third layer in the consolation prophecies, which is recognized as Judean in its geographical reference. **30.18–22:** Rebuilding the rural and urban settlements, Zion foremost. This aspect of restoration concerns the revival of pastoral life (as in 31.24; 33.13), and the physical rebuilding of the city and its fortresses. Note the lack of reference to exile and return; restoration is within the land of Judah. **19:** Increasing the number of the people reverses Deut. 28.27; see Jer. 29.6. **20–21:** Restoration gains a national aspect, though no mention of a Davidic king (cf. with vv. 8–9). **22:** Another reversal theme concerns the reinstitution of the relationship between God and Israel, illustrated by the covenant formula, *You shall be My people, / And I will be your God* (see 7.23; 11.4; and otherwise in consolation prophecies: 31.33; 32.38). **23–24:** Duplicated from 23.19–20. **24:** The statement that *The anger of the LORD shall not turn back / Till it has fulfilled and completed His purposes* recalls Isaiah's earlier prophecies (Isa. 5.25; 9.11, 16, 20; 10.4) and anticipates Second Isaiah (Isa. 40.8; 55.11). **31.1:** A paraphrase on v. 22.

31.2–40: The second part of the book of consolation contains several poetic prophecies from the earliest layer, concerning the restoration of the Northern Kingdom (vv. 2–21), and prose passages from the third mixed layer (vv. 22–40).

31.2–22: The sixth to the ninth oracles of consolation focus on the return of the Northern Kingdom (Samaria) exiles to Zion (vv. 2–6, 7–9, 10–14, 15–22; there is no mention of the kingdom of Judah). Samaria had been a Neo-Assyrian province for about a hundred years already, since 722 (2 Kings ch 17), thus this prophecy may reflect the political hopes for reunification associated with Josiah in the last years of his reign, during the decline of the Neo-Assyrian empire. Hence, these prophecies may be among the earliest materials in Jeremiah. 31.2–20 is the haftarah for the second day of Rosh Ha-Shanah. Its optimism, and especially its focus on the restoration of Rachel's lost children as a metaphor for the restoration of Israel corresponds to the deliverance of Isaac in the Torah portion (Gen. 22.1–24). **2–6:** This sixth prophecy calls for restoration of the remnant from the Northern Kingdom to Zion. **2–3:** God's words to Israel draw on exodus traditions,

3 The LORD revealed Himself to me[a] of old.
Eternal love I conceived for you then;
Therefore I continue My grace to you.
4 I will build you firmly again,
O Maiden Israel!
Again you shall take up your timbrels
And go forth to the rhythm of the dancers.
5 Again you shall plant vineyards
On the hills of Samaria;
Men shall plant and live to enjoy them.
6 For the day is coming when watchmen
Shall proclaim on the heights of Ephraim:
Come, let us go up to Zion,
To the LORD our God!

7 For thus said the LORD:
Cry out in joy for Jacob,
Shout at the crossroads[b] of the nations!
Sing aloud in praise, and say:
[c-]Save, O LORD, Your people,[-c]
The remnant of Israel.
8 I will bring them in from the northland,
Gather them from the ends of the earth—
The blind and the lame among them,
Those with child and those in labor—
In a vast throng they shall return here.
9 They shall come with weeping,
And with compassion[d] will I guide them.
I will lead them to streams of water,
By a level road where they will not stumble.
For I am ever a Father to Israel,
Ephraim is My first-born.

10 Hear the word of the LORD, O nations,
And tell it in the isles afar.
Say:
He who scattered Israel will gather them,
And will guard them as a shepherd his flock.
11 For the LORD will ransom Jacob,
Redeem him from one too strong for him.
12 They shall come and shout on the heights of Zion,
Radiant over the bounty of the LORD—
Over new grain and wine and oil,
And over sheep and cattle.

a Emendation yields "him." *b Lit. "head."*
c-c Emendation yields "The LORD has saved His people."
d For this meaning, cf. Zech. 12.10.

and adapt the initial love of God to Israel of Jer. 2.2 into *eternal love* (see Hos. ch 2, esp. vv. 21–24). *Of old:* Heb "meraḥok," lit. "from afar"; this term usually refers to spatial distance (as in 23.23), but in this pairing with "ʿolam," *eternal,* it may be used temporally (as in Isa. 22.3; 23.7). **5–6:** Restoration brings back routine cycles of life and growth; this is a reversal of Deut. 28.30, and 20.6. The return to Zion reflects a religious and ritual return to God (see Gen. 35.1, 3; Deut. 17.8; Judg. 20.18; Ps. 24.3). **7–9:** The seventh passage tells of ingathering *Jacob,* the *remnant of Israel* from the north and from the ends of the earth to Zion (as in v. 6, and see v. 12). Jeremiah's address to Samaria is quite general in tone, and is silent about the political expectations of this return and the north's relation with the political entity of Judah (so also vv. 7–9, 12). The *remnant of Israel,* designated as *Your people,* is called by its ancient patronymic names: *Israel* and *Ephraim* (as also vv. 18, 20; see *Jacob* ("Yaakov"), 30.10; 31.11; "Maiden Israel," 31.4, 21; and the reference to "Rachel," v. 15). These designations invite this community, whether still in exile or remaining in Samaria, to be incorporated into the dominant Judean community, which the prophet considers the current people of God (v. 14). The v. concludes with an unusual explicit reference to God as Israel's *Father;* though this metaphor is frequent in the Bible, it is rarely explicit, usually taking the form of calling Israel "son" or "child" (e.g., Hos. 11.1). **10–14:** The eighth passage opens with an address to the nations that observe this miraculous regathering. *He who scattered Israel will gather them:* This first image reverses the language of exile (see Lev. 26.33; Jer. 15.7; 49.32, 36; 51.2; Ezek. 5.2, 10; etc.). The image of scattering (seeds) depicts the restoration as something out of the ordinary, since there is no way to gather seeds that are scattered for sowing. The second complementary image, of God as a shepherd of His people, follows 23.3 (and cf. Ezek. 34.11–16).

15–22: The ninth oracle opens with a portrayal of Israel as *Rachel weeping* for her lost children, drawing upon the tragic tradition of Rachel, Jacob's beloved wife, who died while giving birth to Benjamin. Although Gen. 35.16–21 places her tomb on the road to Bethlehem, in the south (where the current structure stands), 1 Sam. 10.2 suggests that her tomb was on the road to *Ramah* (near modern Ramallah), toward the north. Here Rachel weeps not for herself, but for her lost children who have gone into exile. **16–17:** *For there is a reward for your labor .... And there is hope for your future:* These vv. do not echo Gen. traditions, but reward the mother for her long-standing care. The midrashic tradition in *Gen. Rab.* 82.10 suggests that Jacob deliberately buried Rachel by the road because he knew that his descendants would pass by as they went into exile; she would then weep and intercede for their return. This oracle provides an answer for Rachel's weeping by promising the return of her children. **18–19:** God hears *Ephraim* (the son of Joseph, one of the strongest northern tribes) *lamenting,* a lament that contains a confession and a plea for deliverance. **20:** God responds with a rhetorical question that confirms His special feelings toward Ephraim (see v. 9), feelings of parental love and compassion. **21–22:** The final imagery again refers to *Maiden Israel* (see v. 4), calling for the return to the very cities that were left. **22:** *O rebellious daughter,* (see 3.22) along with v. 19 are the only references to the iniquities of the past. Restoration brings new customs that reverse the known ones (Isa. 43.19): *A woman courts a man,* lit. "a woman surrounds a man." The gender reversal calls upon Maiden Israel to initiate her return to God (cf. with Deut. 4.29–31; 30:1–6, where it is required). The Bible elsewhere presents brides as passive rather than as active, as they are brought to the man (Gen. 2.22; ch 24; 29.23). This statement, taken literally as "surrounds" provides a basis for the custom of a bride circling the groom seven times at a Jewish wedding.

They shall fare like a watered garden,
They shall never languish again.
13 Then shall maidens dance gaily,
Young men and old alike.
I will turn their mourning to joy,
I will comfort them and cheer them in their grief.
14 I will give the priests their fill of fatness,
And My people shall enjoy My full bounty
—declares the LORD.

15 Thus said the LORD:
A cry is heard [a]in Ramah[a]—
Wailing, bitter weeping—
Rachel weeping for her children.
She refuses to be comforted
For her children, who are gone.
16 Thus said the LORD:
Restrain your voice from weeping,
Your eyes from shedding tears;
For there is a reward for your labor
—declares the LORD:
They shall return from the enemy's land.
17 And there is hope for your future
—declares the LORD:
Your children shall return to their country.

18 I can hear Ephraim lamenting:
You have chastised me, and I am chastised
Like a calf that has not been broken.
Receive me back, let me return,
For You, O LORD, are my God.
19 Now that I have turned back, I am filled with remorse;
Now that I am made aware, I strike my thigh.[b]
I am ashamed and humiliated,
For I bear the disgrace of my youth.
20 Truly, Ephraim is a dear son to Me,
A child that is dandled!
Whenever I have turned[c] against him,
My thoughts would dwell on him still.
That is why My heart yearns for him;
I will receive him back in love
—declares the LORD.
21 Erect markers,
Set up signposts;[d]
Keep in mind the highway,
The road that you traveled.

a-a Or "on a height." *b I.e., as a gesture of self-reproach.* *c Lit. "spoken."*
d Meaning of Heb. uncertain.

Return, Maiden Israel!
Return to these towns of yours!
22 How long will you waver,
O rebellious daughter?
(For the LORD has created something new on earth:
A woman courts[a] a man.)

23 Thus said the LORD of Hosts, the God of Israel: They shall
again say this in the land of Judah and in its towns, when I restore their fortunes:
"The LORD bless you,
Abode of righteousness,
O holy mountain!"
24 Judah and all its towns alike shall be inhabited by the
farmers and [b]such as move about[b] with the flocks. 25 For I will
give the thirsty abundant drink, and satisfy all who languish.

26 At this I awoke and looked about, and my sleep[c] had been
pleasant to me.

27 See, a time is coming—declares the LORD—when I will
sow the House of Israel and the House of Judah with seed of
men and seed of cattle; 28 and just as I was watchful over them
to uproot and to pull down, to overthrow and to destroy and to
bring disaster, so I will be watchful over them to build and to
plant—declares the LORD. 29 In those days, they shall no longer
say, "Parents have eaten sour grapes and children's teeth are
blunted."[d] 30 But every one shall die for his own sins: whoso-
ever eats sour grapes, his teeth shall be blunted.
31 See, a time is coming—declares the LORD—when I will
make a new covenant with the House of Israel and the House of
Judah. 32 It will not be like the covenant I made with their fathers,
when I took them by the hand to lead them out of the land of
Egypt, a covenant which they broke, though I espoused[e] them—
declares the LORD. 33 But such is the covenant I will make with
the House of Israel after these days—declares the LORD: I will

a *Meaning of Heb. uncertain.* b-b *Lit. "they shall travel."*
c *I.e., the vision in the preceding verses.* d *Others "set on edge."*
e *Meaning of Heb. uncertain; compare 3.14.*

31.23–40: Five prose oracles present the mixture of components typical of the third layer in the prophecies of consolation in Jeremiah (vv. 23–26, 27–30, 31–34, 35–37, 38–40). Their main characteristic is their omission of any mention of exile, of any period of separation from the land, and thus, of the need to gather the dispersed and return to Zion. They are completely Judean in their geographic outlook. **23–26:** The tenth oracle provides the words to be said when the people in Judah are restored. *Restore their fortunes* means "to restore to its former status," namely, a restoration within the land designated as *the land of Judah* (see "Judah and Israel" in 33.7–9), "Jacob's tents" (30.18), or simply "the land" (33.11). None of these passages mentions exile as the point of departure, nor describes the journey back to the land. This third layer of prophecies uses the word "again" (see 30.8–9; 31.2–6; as also 32.15; 33.10, 12). **24:** The great change is the resettlement of the cities, the revival of pastoral life, peasants and shepherds together (see 33.13). **27–30:** This prophecy reverses the prophet's commissioning (1.10). The formula *just as ... so ...* draws an analogy from the previous judgments to the hope of complete fulfillment of the restoration. **29–30:** Introducing a current quotation, the prophet foresees its reversal in the future (so 3.16; 23.7; and with a slight change, 31.34). The quoted proverb, also known from Ezek. 18.2, is based on the natural phenomenon of eating unripe fruit; the eater immediately feels bitterness in the mouth, especially in the front teeth and tongue. The proverb builds upon what is improbable in real life: if a father eats unripe fruit, he himself, and not his descendants, tastes the sourness. This shows the absurdity of the concept of vicarious retribution, when a father sins and his descendants are punished (see Exod. 20.5–6; Deut. 5.9–10). By invoking this proverb, Jeremiah accepts the unnatural character of divine justice, and looks forward to its change into an individual and immediate retribution. Ezek. 18.2–20, which uses the same proverb, suggests that intergenerational retribution is already not applied by God. According to Deut. 24.16, humans may not perpetrate intergenerational punishment (cf. 2 Kings 14.6). **31–34:** The twelfth oracle introduces the *new covenant with the House of Israel and the House of Judah.* The great change foreseen is in obedience, as the first covenant was time and again betrayed, and God was forced to assert lordship and enforce punishment (NJPS: *espoused them,* see 3.14). The term "new covenant" was understood in the early church as a reference to Jesus (see esp. Hebrews 8.7–13), and thus the term

put My Teaching into their inmost being and inscribe it upon
their hearts. Then I will be their God, and they shall be My people. 34 No longer will they need to teach one another and say to
one another, "Heed the LORD"; for all of them, from the least of
them to the greatest, shall heed Me—declares the LORD.

For I will forgive their iniquities,
And remember their sins no more.

35 Thus said the LORD,
Who established the sun for light by day,
The laws of moon and stars for light by night,
Who stirs up the sea into roaring waves,
Whose name is LORD of Hosts:
36 If these laws should ever be annulled by Me
—declares the LORD—
Only then would the offspring of Israel cease
To be a nation before Me for all time.

37 Thus said the LORD: If the heavens above could be measured, and the foundations of the earth below could be fathomed, only then would I reject all the offspring of Israel for all
that they have done—declares the LORD.

38 See, a time is coming—declares the LORD—when the city
shall be rebuilt for the LORD from the Tower of Hananel to the
Corner Gate; 39 and the measuring line shall go straight out to
the Gareb Hill, and then turn toward Goah. 40 And the entire Valley of the Corpses and Ashes, and all the fields as far as the Wadi
Kidron, and the corner of the Horse Gate on the east, shall be holy
to the LORD. They shall never again be uprooted or overthrown.

32 The word which came to Jeremiah from the LORD in the
tenth year of King Zedekiah of Judah, which was the
eighteenth year of Nebuchadrezzar. 2 At that time the army of
the king of Babylon was besieging Jerusalem, and the prophet
Jeremiah was confined in the prison compound attached to
the palace of the king of Judah. 3 For King Zedekiah of Judah
had confined him, saying, "How dare you prophesy: 'Thus said

"New Testament" (= Covenant), introduced by the patristic theologian Tertullian, for the books of the Christian Bible. **33–34:** In the new covenant, God's "torah" *(Teaching)* will be internalized into the *hearts* and minds of the people, an internal transformation that will remove the option of disobedience. This kind of internal transformation is a figurative interpretation of the Deuteronomic conception (see Deut. 6.6), and a clear reversal to the investment of the people in their sins (Jer. 17.1–4). This same idea of transformation is also found in Ezekiel's prophecies of consolation (Ezek. 11.17–21; 36.25–28). Here in vv. 31–34, what starts as a forced and comprehensive divine initiative becomes the foreground for reinstitution of the covenant relationship (see the covenant formula, 30.22; 31.1), and for the general acknowledgement of God by all, from young to old (NJPS: *from the least of them to the greatest*). The use of the word "torah," *teaching,* emphasizes that Jeremiah's new covenant stands in complete continuity with the former one (for "torah," see 8.8–9 n.). **35–37:** In the thirteenth passage, two oaths guarantee the eternal existence of Israel as the people of God, this time as commitments taken by God (see 33.25–26). **35–36:** God is the Creator of the world, the One who established the celestial bodies and control over the waters. Just as He fixed the natural order for all time, so has He made Israel His nation for all time. **37:** If the immeasurable heaven and earth could ever be measured, only then would God reject Israel, although they had sinned (see 2 Sam. 7.14–16; Ps. 89.29–38). **38–40:** In the fourteenth and final passage, Jerusalem will be rebuilt (see 30.18–22), and is specifically designated as holy to God. This terminology of holiness draws on the Priestly terminology of restricting and sanctifying to God (see Exod. 28.36; 31.15; Lev. 27.30). This prophecy extends holiness to the entire city, not only to the Temple (see also Joel 4.17; and see "the holy city," Isa. 48.2; 52.1; Neh. 11.1, 18). By specifying its geographical extent, concluding with the promise it will never be deserted and destroyed, the prophecy offers another reversal of Jeremiah's first prophecy (1.10).

32.1–44: From defeat to consolation. The core of the ch describes another symbolic action the prophet is required to perform (vv. 6–15; see 13.1–11; 18.1–12), purchasing land in Anathoth during the final siege over Jerusalem, when the city and king were given *into the hands of the Chaldeans* (v. 28). It is followed by the prophet's prayer (vv. 16–25), and a divine judgment response (vv. 26–35). The ch ends, however, with two different prophecies of consolation (vv. 36, 42–44; 37–41), one for the residents who remained in the land, the other for the restoration of the Babylonian

the LORD: I am delivering this city into the hands of the king of Babylon, and he shall capture it. 4 And King Zedekiah of Judah shall not escape from the Chaldeans; he shall be delivered into the hands of the king of Babylon, [a-]and he shall speak to him face to face and see him in person.[-a] 5 And Zedekiah shall be brought to Babylon, there to remain until I take note of him—declares the LORD. When you wage war against the Chaldeans, you shall not be successful.'"

6 Jeremiah said: The word of the LORD came to me: 7 Hanamel, the son of your uncle Shallum, will come to you and say, "Buy my land in Anathoth, [b-]for you are next in succession to redeem it by purchase."[-b] 8 And just as the LORD had said, my cousin Hanamel came to me in the prison compound and said to me, "Please buy my land in Anathoth, in the territory of Benjamin; for the right of succession is yours, and you have the duty of redemption. Buy it." Then I knew that it was indeed the word of the LORD.

9 So I bought the land in Anathoth from my cousin Hanamel. I weighed out the money to him, seventeen shekels of silver. 10 I wrote a deed, sealed it, and had it witnessed; and I weighed out the silver on a balance. 11 I took the deed of purchase, the sealed text and the open one [c-]according to rule and law,[-c] 12 and gave the deed to Baruch son of Neriah son of Mahseiah in the presence of my kinsman Hanamel, of the witnesses [d-]who were named[-d] in the deed, and all the Judeans who were sitting in the prison compound. 13 In their presence I charged Baruch as follows: 14 Thus said the LORD of Hosts, the God of Israel: "Take these documents, this deed of purchase, the sealed text and the

a-a *Lit. "and his mouth shall speak with his mouth, and his eyes shall see his eyes."*
b-b *Lit. "for yours is the procedure of redemption by purchase."*
c-c *Force of Heb. uncertain.*
d-d *With many mss. and ancient versions; so ancient Near Eastern practice. Other mss. and the editions read "who wrote" (i.e., signed their names).*

exiles. The words *deliver(ing) ... into the hands of the king of Babylon/Chaldeans* (vv. 3, 4, 28, 36, 43) unify the ch.

32.1–15: Redemption and possession of the land in Anathoth. 1–5: A long and complex introduction (for a similar structure, see 34.8–11). **1:** The prophecy is dated to 587 BCE, the final siege of Jerusalem, when the prophet was already in prison (38.1–13). **3–5:** The exposition quotes several of Jeremiah's earlier prophecies against the city (see 21.19; 34.2; 38.3); and against Zedekiah (34.3). **5:** LXX is shorter, ending with *there to remain* (as in 22.12, 26). MT adds two additional clauses: *until I take note of him* may suggest an exceptional, hopeful message about this last king of Judah (see 28.22), or further judgment of death as was indeed Zedekiah's fate according to chs 39, 52 (see 5.9; 15.3; 21.14, and Rashi, Kimḥi, and others). The other added note concerns the war against the Chaldeans said to culminate in defeat (see 37.3–10; and see 2 Chron. 13.12). **6–15:** This story of Jeremiah's purchase of his uncle or cousin's field in Anathoth in Benjamin (see 37.12) is symbolic; the action of an individual has national significance and divine authority. **7–8:** *The right of succession ... the duty of redemption:* The inheritance law in Num. 27.11 had been harmonized or conflated with the land redemption law in Lev. ch 25 (the law mandating that a close relative should buy back land that his kinsman was forced to sell, so as not to alienate it from the family). While redemption and inheritance are two different legal institutions, they share the concept that land is inalienable and should remain close to its original owner, during his lifetime (redemption) and after his death (inheritance). Actually, though, Jeremiah's action constitutes neither a redemption nor an inheritance. While the terminology is drawn from two Torah laws, Jeremiah's land purchase does not fit either one (just as the levirate cum redemption in Ruth ch 4 does not exactly fit Torah law); Hanamel was not selling his land because he was impoverished (redemption) and he was not dead (inheritance). This is an ordinary out-and-out sale, under the guise of a redemption cum inheritance. Jeremiah pays money to the original owner and receives a witnessed deed, and the land now belongs to Jeremiah, apparently never to be returned to Hanamel or his descendants (the deed was given to Baruch for safe-keeping for a long time, hinting that Jeremiah's ownership would be of long duration). In fact, this is a symbolic act whose stated purpose is to show that in the restoration that will follow the exile, ordinary real estate transactions will resume, for the land will regain any value it might have lost in the face of the Babylonian conquest (vv. 43–44). The thematic connections to Lev. ch 25 have motivated the choice of Jer. 32.6–27 as the haftarah for the parashah of Be-har (Lev. 25.1–26.2). **9–14:** The transaction is described in detail. *The deed of purchase* in two copies is signed by Jeremiah in public (as in Ruth ch 4) in the presence of witnesses (the Jews, that is the Judeans; see Jer. 34.9; 38.19; 40.11, etc.), who were imprisoned with Jeremiah at the *prison compound.* The deeds were stored and sealed in a *jar,* for long preservation, indicating

open one, and put them into an earthen jar, so that they may
last a long time." [15] For thus said the LORD of Hosts, the God of
Israel: "Houses, fields, and vineyards shall again be purchased
in this land."

[16] But after I had given the deed to Baruch son of Neriah, I
prayed to the LORD: [17] "Ah, Lord GOD! You made heaven and
earth with Your great might and outstretched arm. Nothing is
too wondrous for You! [18] You show kindness to the thousandth
generation, but visit the guilt of the fathers upon their children
after them. O great and mighty God whose name is LORD of
Hosts, [19] wondrous in purpose and mighty in deed, whose eyes
observe all the ways of men, so as to repay every man according to his ways, and with the proper fruit of his deeds! [20] You
displayed signs and marvels in the land of Egypt [a-]with lasting effect,[-a] and won renown in Israel and among mankind to
this very day. [21] You freed Your people Israel from the land of
Egypt with signs and marvels, with a strong hand and an outstretched arm, and with great terror. [22] You gave them this land
that You had sworn to their fathers to give them, a land flowing with milk and honey, [23] and they came and took possession
of it. But they did not listen to You or follow Your Teaching;
they did nothing of what You commanded them to do. Therefore you have caused all this misfortune to befall them. [24] Here
are the siegemounds, raised against the city to storm it; and
the city, because of sword and famine and pestilence, is at the
mercy of the Chaldeans who are attacking it. What You threatened has come to pass—as You see. [25] Yet You, Lord GOD, said
to me: Buy the land for money and call in witnesses—when the
city is at the mercy of the Chaldeans!"

[26] Then the word of the LORD came to Jeremiah:
[27] "Behold I am the LORD, the God of all flesh. Is anything
too wondrous for Me? [28] Assuredly, thus said the LORD: I am
delivering this city into the hands of the Chaldeans and of King
Nebuchadrezzar of Babylon, and he shall capture it. [29] And
the Chaldeans who have been attacking this city shall come

a-a Lit. "to this day."

continuous and eternal ownership of the property, and evoking optimism that the land will revert to Jeremiah's family in the future. **15:** *Houses, fields, and vineyards shall again be purchased in this land.* This may be a short-term prospect (as in Zech. 1.16, 17; including threats of immediate judgment, as in Ezek. 8.6, 13, 14; Jer. 2.9), or a long-term forecast that includes exile (Isa. 49.20; 56.8; Zech. 8.20–23), though the ch's emphasis on the law of redemption and the divine permission to possess the land with no interruption, implies that this promise of possession has current significance: it applies to those who remained in Judah, Jeremiah's immediate audience. Jeremiah's position validates the Jerusalem perspective that those who remain in the land are the true Israel, a perspective that Ezekiel quotes and harshly refutes (Ezek. 11.15; 33.24). The two prophets and their respective communities were engaged in a live polemical exchange with high theological and political stakes.

32.16–25: Jeremiah's prayer. This prayer differs from individual laments (see 11.18–23), and from communal laments (see 14.7–9) seen previously in the book. It opens with a hymn, recalling God as Creator and as just judge (vv. 17–19), and reviews God's past deeds of salvation: the exodus and the settlement in the land, followed by the people's disobedience, and therefore their judgment (vv. 20–24). Jeremiah ultimately challenges the logic behind God's instructions and message, pointing to discord between current events leading to inevitable and justified defeat (v. 24, see v. 5), and the previous symbolic action that promises continuity within the land (v. 15). **16:** Ch 36 describes *Baruch* as Jeremiah's official scribe. **18:** The beginning of the v. is similar to the formula in Exod. 34.7, the end of the v. to Deut. 10.17. **19:** Jer. 17.10 is similar.

32.26–35: God's response to the prophet's prayer suggests an exceptional, complete, and immediate dialogue between the prophet and God (v. 27 responds to v. 17; see also 14.7–15.4). **27:** The epithet *the LORD, the God of all flesh* is unique. **28:** The prophecy, however, does not address the prophet's query (v. 25), but once again justifies the divine judgment against Jerusalem, thus referring only to this key phrase that closes the prophet's prayer: "the city is at the mercy of the Chaldeans" (v. 25). **30–31:** The people's continuous misconduct is presented in two ways: the people's sins from *their youth,* from the beginning of the relationship with God (see 3.24–25; perhaps since the exodus, 7.25; 11.7); and Jerusalem has sinned *from the day it was built* (44.9, 17, 21, due to the sins of the kings of Judah). Elsewhere the book suggests a third point when

and set this city on fire and burn it down—with the houses on whose roofs they made offerings to Baal and poured out libations to other gods, so as to vex Me. 30 For the people of Israel and Judah have done nothing but evil in My sight since their youth; the people of Israel have done nothing but vex Me by their conduct—declares the LORD. 31 This city has aroused My anger and My wrath from the day it was built until this day; so that it must be removed from My sight 32 because of all the wickedness of the people of Israel and Judah who have so acted as to vex Me—they, their kings, their officials, their priests and prophets, and the men of Judah and the inhabitants of Jerusalem. 33 They turned their backs to Me, not their faces; though I have taught them persistently, they do not give heed or accept rebuke. 34 They placed their abominations in the House which bears My name and defiled it; 35 and they built the shrines of Baal which are in the Valley of Ben-hinnom, where they offered up their sons and daughters to Molech—when I had never commanded, or even thought [of commanding], that they should do such an abominable thing, and so bring guilt on Judah.

36 But now, assuredly, thus said the LORD, the God of Israel, concerning this city of which you say, "It is being delivered into the hands of the king of Babylon through the sword, through famine, and through pestilence": 37 See, I will gather them from all the lands to which I have banished them in My anger and wrath, and in great rage; and I will bring them back to this place and let them dwell secure. 38 They shall be My people, and I will be their God. 39 I will give them a single heart and a single nature to revere Me for all time, and it shall be well with them and their children after them. 40 And I will make an everlasting covenant with them that I will not turn away from them and that I will treat them graciously; and I will put into their hearts reverence for Me, so that they do not turn away from Me. 41 I will delight in treating them graciously, and I will plant them in this land faithfully, with all My heart and soul.

42 For thus said the LORD: As I have brought this terrible disaster upon this people, so I am going to bring upon them the vast good fortune which I have promised for them. 43 And fields shall again be purchased in this land of which you say, "It is a desolation, without man or beast; it is delivered into the hands of the Chaldeans."

44 Fields shall be purchased, and deeds written and sealed, and witnesses called in the land of Benjamin and in the environs of Jerusalem, and in the towns of Judah; the towns of the hill country, the towns of the Shephelah, and the towns of the Negeb. For I will restore their fortunes—declares the LORD.

sin began, with the settlement in the land (2.7; 32.23). The general emphasis here on continuous sin is typical in Jer. (7.25; 25.4; 26.5; 29.19; 35.15; 44.4). **32:** Furthermore, the sins are comprehensive: they include *kings, officials, priests, prophets,* and the entire people. **34–35:** The sins resemble those of Manasseh, king of Judah, upon whom the author of Kings blames the exile (2 Kings 21.1–17).

32.36–44: Restoration to the land. The passage combines two distinct prophecies of restoration, that of the exiles and that of the people who remained in the land. Vv. 42–44 draw on the prophet's symbolic action (vv. 6–15, and 25) in relation to those who remain in Judah. But vv. 36–41 interpolate an altogether different message of restoration, limited to the Babylonian exiles. **37–41:** Restoration of the Babylonian exiles is secondary, as reflected in its content, genre and style. It does not refer back to v. 36, which recalls the fall of the city (in line with the key theme of vv. 3, 25, and 43). Rather it uses two distinct sayings of Jeremiah (see 38.3; and the three disasters of 14.12 and elsewhere) as an anchor for a promise of restoration for the exiles. **38–40:** These vv. contain phrases that are known from various sources, some of them later than Jeremiah, including Ezekiel's prophecies of consolation to the Jehoiachin exiles (see Ezek. 11.17–21; 18.31; 36.24–28) and phrases shared by both Ezekiel and Second Isaiah (*an everlasting covenant,* as also Jer. 50.5; see Isa. 61.8; Ezek. 16.60; 37.26, drawing on Priestly and Holiness Legislation phrases in the Torah) and also from Deut. Jer. 32.36–41 is an independent Babylonian exilic prophetic passage, not composed by Jeremiah the prophet in Judah. **42:** The *terrible disaster,* emphasized so far in this ch as the siege (vv. 1–5, assuming the subsequent destruction), becomes the great source of hope (see 31.28). **43–44:** There is neither reference to time and circumstance for when this prophecy will be fulfilled, nor mention of exile and return. The vv. are likely a later addition from the followers of Jeremiah who remained in Judah (see 33.12–13).

33 The word of the LORD came to Jeremiah a second time, while he was still confined in the prison compound, as follows:

2 Thus said the LORD who is planning it,
The LORD who is shaping it to bring it about,
Whose name is LORD:
3 Call to Me, and I will answer you,
And I will tell you wondrous things,
Secrets you have not known.

4 For thus said the LORD, the God of Israel, concerning the
houses of this city and the palaces of the kings of Judah that were
torn down [a]for [defense] against the siegemounds and against
the sword, 5 and were filled by those who went to fight the
Chaldeans,-[a]—with the corpses of the men whom I struck down
in My anger and rage, hiding My face from this city because of all
their wickedness: 6 I am going to bring her relief and healing. I
will heal them and reveal to them abundance[b] of true favor. 7 And
I will restore the fortunes of Judah and Israel, and I will rebuild
them as of old. 8 And I will purge them of all the sins which they
committed against Me, and I will pardon all the sins which they
committed against Me, by which they rebelled against Me. 9 And
she shall gain through Me renown, joy, fame, and glory above
all the nations on earth, when they hear of all the good fortune
I provide for them.[c] They will thrill and quiver because of all the
good fortune and all the prosperity that I provide for her.
10 Thus said the LORD: Again there shall be heard in this
place, which you say is ruined, without man or beast— in the
towns of Judah and the streets of Jerusalem that are desolate,
without man, without inhabitants, without beast— 11 the sound
of mirth and gladness, the voice of bridegroom and bride, the
voice of those who cry, "Give thanks to the LORD of Hosts, for
the LORD is good, for His kindness is everlasting!" as they bring
thanksgiving offerings to the House of the LORD. For I will restore the fortunes of the land as of old—said the LORD.

a-a Meaning of Heb. uncertain. *b Meaning of Heb. uncertain.*
c I.e., for Judah and Israel.

33.1–26: The closing collection of consolation prophecies begins with a hymnic introduction (vv. 1–3) and closes with a disputation speech (vv. 23–26), framing four passages of consolation: 4–9, 10–11, 12–13, 14–22. It repeats the key theme of the previous ch: *I will restore their fortunes and take them back in love* (v. 26; vv. 7, 11; 32.44). **2–3:** This hymnic introduction repeats the divine name three times, tying together creation and Israel's deliverance (see 31.35–37; 32.17–25). **4–9:** As in the previous ch, the besieged city is in ruins, overrun by *Chaldeans* with God fighting alongside them—the catastrophe of war is a divine deed (often in Jer.; see 21.1–7). It is unclear how this depiction of divine action fits with God's *hiding* His *face from this city,* which draws on Deut. (Deut. 31.17–18; 32.20) and is found only here in Jer., and generally refers to perceived divine neglect (see esp. in Pss. 69.18; 88.15; 143.7; Job 13.24). Perhaps here it refers to God's lack of acknowledgement of Judah's distress. **6:** Picking up on previous language (30.17) that reverses his earlier prospects of doom (see 8.15; and in the communal lament, 14.19). **7:** Vv. 6–10, 11–13, do not mention exile, nor do they describe the journey back to the land; their context is the restoration of the population of Judah who was not exiled. In addition to restoration of material culture (houses, including the royal buildings, v. 4), the reversal will also bring about changes in the human beings, and the reinstitution of the God-people relationship (see v. 11). **8:** A cluster of Priestly reparation terms; see Lev. ch 16 (esp. vv. 16, 19, 21, 30); and for *pardon* ("salaḥ," a hapax in Jer.) as part of the reparation, see Lev. 4.31, 35. **10–11:** Desolation is replaced by *mirth and gladness* (see 32.43), and by transforming a previous prophecy of doom (see 7.34). It is formally illustrated by five repetitions of *without* in the Heb (four in the NJPS), matched with five repetitions of *voice* in the Heb (two in the NJPS). A more literal translation that reflects this would read: "without man, without beast, ... without man, without inhabitants, without beast ... the voice of mirth, the voice of gladness, the voice of bridegroom, the voice of bride, the voice of those who cry .... " This shows how the empty and desolate land becomes a place of lively voices of joy, of marriage, and of renewal of worship within the House of YHVH (see Isa. 65.19). *"Give thanks to the LORD of Hosts, for the LORD is good, for His kindness is everlasting!"* is a late liturgical phrase (e.g., Pss. 106.1; 107.1, 8, 15, 21, 31; 118.1, 29; Ezra 3.11; 1 Chron. 16.34, 41). An abbreviated form of these vv., *Again there shall be heard ... in the towns of Judah and the streets of Jerusalem ... the sound of mirth and gladness, the voice of bridegroom and bride,* is frequently sung at contemporary Jewish weddings.

12 Thus said the LORD of Hosts: In this ruined place, without
man and beast, and in all its towns, there shall again be a pasture
for shepherds, where they can rest their flocks. 13 In the towns of
the hill country, in the towns of the Shephelah, and in the towns
of the Negeb, in the land of Benjamin and in the environs of Jerusalem and in the towns of Judah, sheep shall pass again under
the hands of one who counts them—said the LORD. 14 See, days
are coming—declares the LORD—when I will fulfill the promise
that I made concerning the House of Israel and the House of Judah. 15 In those days and at that time, I will raise up a true branch
of David's line, and he shall do what is just and right in the land.
16 In those days Judah shall be delivered and Israel shall dwell
secure. And this is what she shall be called: "The LORD is our Vindicator." 17 For thus said the LORD: There shall never be an end
to men of David's line who sit upon the throne of the House of
Israel. 18 Nor shall there ever be an end to the line of the levitical
priests before Me, of those who present burnt offerings and turn
the meal offering to smoke and perform sacrifices.

19 The word of the LORD came to Jeremiah: 20 Thus said the
LORD: If you could break My covenant with the day and My
covenant with the night, so that day and night should not come
at their proper time, 21 only then could My covenant with My
servant David be broken—so that he would not have a descendant reigning upon his throne—or with My ministrants,
the levitical priests. 22 Like the host of heaven which cannot be
counted, and the sand of the sea which cannot be measured,
so will I multiply the offspring of My servant David, and of the
Levites who minister to Me.

23 The word of the LORD came to Jeremiah: 24 You see what this
people said: "The two families which the LORD chose have now
been rejected by Him." Thus they despise My people, [a-]and regard them as no longer a nation.[-a] 25 Thus said the LORD: As surely as I have established My covenant with day and night—the
laws of heaven and earth—26 so I will never reject the offspring of

a-a Meaning of Heb. uncertain.

12–13: Another description of return to normal life, throughout Jerusalem and Judah (see 32.44; 17.26). The two passages postdate the destruction of Jerusalem, offering a hopeful message of restoration within the land. **14–22:** These prophecies of consolation, addressed to the houses of Israel and Judah, focus on divine commitments given by oath to the Davidic king, to the city and kingdom (see 23.5–6), most especially to two of the leading groups: the Davidic king and the Levitical priests. David is mentioned in each of the four sections (14–16, 17–18, 19–22, 23–26). This entire section does not appear in LXX. **15–16:** This passage modifies 23.5–6 in two significant ways: deliverance is promised to Judah and Jerusalem (the translation substitutes *Israel* for "Jerusalem" in Heb.; cf. with 23.6: Israel), and it refers to the city (23.6: to him, that is, the king). V. 15 nevertheless reintroduces *a true branch of David's line,* referring to either the last king of Judah, Zedekiah, or a general messianic hope for a future Davidic king. **17–18:** There will be no end to the Davidic monarchy or to Levitical priesthood. The covenants are that with David (see 1 Kings 2.4; 9.5; Jer. 35.19), and with Phinehas (Num. 25.10–13; Ps. 106.30–31). Kingship and priesthood are here joined, as in the exilic Zech. chs 3–4. **19–22:** The covenant with David and the Levitical priests is equated with the covenant that ensures the stability of the cosmos (see also Jer. 31.35–36; and Gen. 9.8–17; cf. Exod. 31.16–17; Ps. 89.20–38). **23–26:** A disputation speech closes these consolation prophecies. It may have been an independent speech, since unlike the the previous passages (vv. 14–22), which focused on the city, the king, and the Levitical priests, this one focuses on the status of the covenant between God and His people. The people, in despair, accuse God of rejecting/despising His people, divided into two nations (see v. 14). Israel and Judah were first the chosen (united) people of God, but with Judah's defeat, they now are joined in divine neglect. The prophet reflects on the danger of such a thought: *Thus they despise My people, and regard them as no longer a nation.* This passage is listed among the scribal corrections ("tiqqun sofrim" see 2.11 n.), and thus presumably originally ended with the first person pronoun, "before Me." If this perception that God *rejected* and despised Judah had gained acceptance by the people, they would have severed their relation with God. The prophet therefore states the divine oath that guarantees the covenant to be as stable as the day and night, as *the laws of heaven and earth.* V. 26 includes five addressees of divine covenants: the descendants of Jacob, of David, together with those of Abraham, Isaac, and Jacob—all past promises are relevant and valid.

Jacob and My servant David; I will never fail to take from his offspring rulers for the descendants of Abraham, Isaac, and Jacob. Indeed, I will restore their fortunes and take them back in love.

34 The word which came to Jeremiah from the LORD, when King Nebuchadrezzar of Babylon and all his army, and all the kingdoms of the earth and all the peoples under his sway, were waging war against Jerusalem and all its towns:
[2] Thus said the LORD, the God of Israel: Go speak to King Zedekiah of Judah, and say to him: "Thus said the LORD: I am going to deliver this city into the hands of the king of Babylon, and he will destroy it by fire. [3] And you will not escape from him; you will be captured and handed over to him. [a-]And you will see the king of Babylon face to face and speak to him in person;[-a] and you will be brought to Babylon. [4] But hear the word of the LORD, O King Zedekiah of Judah! Thus said the LORD concerning you: You will not die by the sword. [5] You will die a peaceful death; and as incense[b] was burned for your ancestors, the earlier kings who preceded you, so they will burn incense[b] for you, and they will lament for you 'Ah, lord!' For I Myself have made the promise—declares the LORD."
[6] The prophet Jeremiah spoke all these words to King Zedekiah of Judah in Jerusalem, [7] when the army of the king of Babylon was waging war against Jerusalem and against the remaining towns of Judah—against Lachish and Azekah, for they were the only fortified towns of Judah that were left.

[8] The word which came to Jeremiah from the LORD after King Zedekiah had made a covenant with all the people in Jerusalem to proclaim a release[c] among them—[9] that everyone should set free his Hebrew slaves, both male and female, and that no one should keep his fellow Judean enslaved.
[10] Everyone, officials and people, who had entered into the covenant agreed to set their male and female slaves free and not keep them enslaved any longer; they complied and let them go. [11] But afterward they turned about and brought back the men and women they had set free, and forced them into slavery again. [12] Then it was that the word of the LORD came to Jeremiah from the LORD:

[13] Thus said the LORD, the God of Israel: I made a covenant with your fathers when I brought them out of the land of Egypt,

a-a For the idiom see note at 32.4. *b Lit. "burnings."* *c Others "liberty."*

34.1–7: Zedekiah's fate. 1: As in the previous two chs, the prophecy is set within the final stages of the Babylonian campaign against Judah, and the prophet predicts a Babylonian victory. **3:** Zedekiah will be captured and brought to the Babylonian king. **4–5:** Surprisingly, these vv. foresee a hopeful twist (as in 32.5): Zedekiah will die in peace (like his father, Josiah, 2 Kings 22.30), and the typical royal burial rituals will be performed (2 Chron. 16.14). Jer. 39.5–7 and 52.10–11 suggest that this prophecy was not fulfilled. This motivated the Tg. (followed by Rashi among others) to translate v. 4 as a conditional. This is impossible grammatically, and thus these vv. join a small number of other unfulfilled prophecies in Jer. **6–7:** The mention of the specific names of *Lachish* (60 km, 35 mi west of Jerusalem) and *Azekah* (25 km, 15 mi) is remarkable, as otherwise Jeremiah focuses on Jerusalem, and treats only generally "the cities of Judah" (as in 4.16). Ostraca found in Lachish add epigraphic information about these last months of Judah.

34.8–22: Reenslaving Judean slaves was the cause of Jerusalem's destruction. The accusation of this judgment prophecy (vv. 8–16) specifies a violation of a cluster of legal traditions concerning manumission of slaves, for which Jerusalem is punished in measure-for-measure (vv. 17–22). It thus joins other passages that use legal issues as paradigms for the people's sins, illustrating the people's violation of the covenant to justify the destruction. **8–11:** The exact circumstances and motives behind the manumission are unclear, though it is associated with the final siege of Jerusalem (vv. 1–7). This event involves a ceremony held in the Temple, perhaps a reinstitution of the covenant with God (v. 15; see 2 Kings 23.1–3). **9–11:** Phraseology known from both the Deuteronomic manumission law (Deut. 15.1, 12–17) and from the Holiness Legislation manumission law (Lev. 25.10, 39–56) is brought together in the style of later rabbinic midrash (see "Inner-biblical Interpretation," pp. 1835–41).

13–14: Drawing on the constituting covenant with the fathers, *when I brought them out of the land of Egypt,* Deut. 15.1, 12 are paraphrased (for the neglect of Sinai, see 7.22; 11.7, etc.). *The house of bondage,* another Deuteronomic phrase (see Deut. 5.6; 6.12; etc.; see also Exod. 13.3, 14; 20.2),

the house of bondage, saying: 14 "In the seventh year[a] each of you must let go any fellow Hebrew [b]who may be sold[b] to you; when he has served you six years, you must set him free." But your fathers would not obey Me or give ear. 15 Lately you turned about and did what is proper in My sight, and each of you proclaimed a release to his countrymen; and you made a covenant accordingly before Me in the House which bears My name. 16 But now you have turned back and have profaned My name; each of you has brought back the men and women whom you had given their freedom, and forced them to be your slaves again.

17 Assuredly, thus said the LORD: You would not obey Me and proclaim a release, each to his kinsman and countryman. Lo! I proclaim your release—declares the LORD—to the sword, to pestilence, and to famine; and I will make you a horror to all the kingdoms of the earth. 18 I will make the men who violated My covenant, who did not fulfill the terms of the covenant which they made before Me, [like] the calf which they cut in two so as to pass between the halves:[c] 19 The officers of Judah and Jerusalem, the officials, the priests, and all the people of the land who passed between the halves of the calf 20 shall be handed over to their enemies, to those who seek to kill them. Their carcasses shall become food for the birds of the sky and the beasts of the earth. 21 I will hand over King Zedekiah of Judah and his officers to their enemies, who seek to kill them—to the army of the king of Babylon which has withdrawn from you. 22 I hereby give the command—declares the LORD—by which I will bring them back against this city. They shall attack it and capture it, and burn it down. I will make the towns of Judah a desolation, without inhabitant.

35 The word which came to Jeremiah from the LORD in the days of King Jehoiakim son of Josiah of Judah:

2 Go to the house of the Rechabites and speak to them, and bring them to the House of the LORD, to one of the chambers, and give them wine to drink.

3 So I took Jaazaniah son of Jeremiah son of Habazziniah, and his brothers, all his sons, and the whole household of the Rechabites; 4 and I brought them to the House of the LORD, to the chamber of the sons of Hanan son of Igdaliah, the man of God, which is next to the chamber of the officials and above the chamber of Maaseiah son of Shallum, the guardian of the threshold. 5 I set bowls full of wine and cups before the men of the house of the Rechabites, and said to them, "Have some wine."

a I.e., of servitude. Lit. "After a period of seven years"; cf. Deut. 14.28 and 15.1.
b-b Or "who sells himself." *c Cf. Gen. 15.9–10, 17–21.*

ties the two covenants together, the old and the new, thus exemplifying the people's betrayal of their commitment. This passage may know the Covenant Collection as well, the only legal collection that opens with manumission of slaves (Exod. 21.2–6). This connection led the Rabbis to choose Jer. 34.8–22; 33.25, 26 as the haftarah for the parashah of Mishpatim (Exod. 21.1–24.18). Here, as in the case of the purchase of Hanamel's field (ch 32), the passage reflects a combination of various Torah laws while departing from their precise application. **17–22:** *Proclaim a release* is turned on its head, as it refers to the release of *sword, pestilence,* and *famine* rather than to the manumission of slaves. **18:** Jeremiah cites the practice of passing *between the halves* of a slaughtered calf, attested in Gen. 15.7–21 and in ancient Near Eastern treaties, to make (lit. "cut") a covenant. The parties to an agreement pass between the two halves of slaughtered animals that represent what will happen to them if they violate the terms of the agreement, thereby formally ratifying the treaty or covenant. **20–22:** Jerusalem's judgment is depicted in language known elsewhere in Jer. (see 21.1–10; 32.24, 29; 37.8, 10). *The army of the king of Babylon which has withdrawn from you,* see 37.5.

35.1–19: Covenant obedience and disobedience. The Rechabite example. The Rechabite clan, which adheres to its traditional way of life, is a counter-example to Israel; the example illustrates that obedience is rewarded and disobedience is punished (for other symbolic actions see 13.1–11). The superscription suggests that this ch transpired before the events of the previous chs. **1–11:** The Rechabites were an ancient group, founded in the 9th c. by Jonadab son of Rechab, who assisted Jehu in his successful revolt against the house of Omri (842 BCE; 2 Kings 10.15–28). A different tradition identifies them as Kenites (1 Chron. 2.55), descended from Moses' Kenite father-in-law, Jethro (Judg. 1.16; Exod. 3.1; 18.1; so midrash

6 They replied, "We will not drink wine, for our ancestor, Jonadab son of Rechab, commanded us: 'You shall never drink wine, either you or your children. 7 Nor shall you build houses or sow fields[a] or plant vineyards, nor shall you own such things; but you shall live in tents all your days, so that you may live long upon the land where you sojourn.' 8 And we have obeyed our ancestor Jonadab son of Rechab in all that he commanded us: we never drink wine, neither we nor our wives nor our sons and daughters. 9 Nor do we build houses to live in, and we do not own vineyards or fields for sowing; 10 but we live in tents. We have obeyed and done all that our ancestor Jonadab commanded us. 11 But when King Nebuchadrezzar of Babylon invaded the country, we said, 'Come, let us go into Jerusalem because of the army of the Chaldeans and the army of Aram.' And so we are living in Jerusalem."

12 Then the word of the LORD came to Jeremiah:

13 Thus said the LORD of Hosts, the God of Israel: Go say to the men of Judah and the inhabitants of Jerusalem: "You can learn a lesson [here] about obeying My commands—declares the LORD. 14 The commands of Jonadab son of Rechab have been fulfilled: he charged his children not to drink wine, and to this day they have not drunk, in obedience to the charge of their ancestor. But I spoke to you persistently, and you did not listen to Me. 15 I persistently sent you all My servants, the prophets, to say: 'Turn back, every one of you, from your wicked ways and mend your deeds; do not follow other gods or serve them. Then you may remain on the land that I gave to you and your fathers.' But you did not give ear or listen to Me. 16 The family of Jonadab son of Rechab have indeed fulfilled the charge which their ancestor gave them; but this people has not listened to Me. 17 Assuredly, thus said the LORD, the God of Hosts, the God of Israel: I am going to bring upon Judah and upon all the inhabitants of Jerusalem all the disaster with which I have threatened them; for I spoke to them, but they would not listen; I called to them, but they would not respond."

a Lit. "seed."

Mek., Jethro-Amalek 2; followed by medieval commentators). **6–7:** In response to the prophet's offering wine, the Rechabites recall their forefather's commandments never to drink wine, which they obey completely. Five restrictions are set in apodictic phrases, stylistically echoing the Decalogue: *You shall never drink wine ... nor shall you build houses or sow fields or plant vineyards, nor shall you own such things.* The prohibitions turn into a sixth positive instruction and a promise: *but you shall live in tents all your days, so that you may live long upon the land where you sojourn.* Accordingly, keeping to a nomadic way of life, moving from place to place, is ironically here the condition for continuous residence in the land. **8–10:** These prohibitions seem not to be connected to the Nazirite vow, which also prohibited drinking wine; Nazirites sanctified themselves for divine service for the duration of the vow by refraining from wine, contact with the dead, and cutting the hair (Num. 6.1–21; cf. Judg. chs 13–16; 1 Sam. ch 1; *m. Naz.*; *b. Naz.*). The Rechabite customs have no cultic context and are equally binding on men, women and children. As a resident of Anathoth, on the border of the Judean Desert, Jeremiah was exposed to the tensions between nomads and city-dwellers. **11:** A note on the circumstances that had brought these nomads to town, though conflicting with v. 1. For the forces of *Chaldeans* and *Aram* (Edom, according to the Peshitta—Aram and Edom are written very similarly), see 2 Kings 24.2. **12–19:** The entire symbolic action takes place in the Temple, and the prophet speaks to the residents of Judah and Jerusalem, as he often does (4.3, 4; 11.2, 9; 17.25; 18.11; 36.31). *You can learn a lesson* is another instance of wisdom influence on Jeremiah (see 5.3; 7.28; 17.23; 32.33; otherwise in the prophetic literature only in Zeph. 3.2, 7; and frequently Prov. 1.3; 8.10; 24.32). **14–16:** Opening and closing with the historical lesson of the Rechabites, who obeyed their father and thus safely survived (vv. 14, 16), the prophet draws a "qal vahomer" (from the minor to the major) argument, emphasizing the different attitudes these groups have shown toward their God. Though He constantly sent prophets to the broad population with calls to repent and to obey, to guarantee continuous settlement in the land given to their forefathers, this people did not pay attention, did not listen. (This form of admonition is typical of the covenant speeches; see 7.1–15; 11.1–14; 17.19–27, and in accordance with those, the prophecy concludes with judgment.) **17–19:** Although punishment in Jer. is generally viewed as corporate and total, i.e., all Israel is to be punished for the sins of its members (and thus the entire ecological system suffers as well), these vv. exempt the extremely righteous Rechabites from the full fury of the impending disaster. (Elsewhere, such a distinction otherwise

18 And to the family of the Rechabites Jeremiah said: "Thus
said the LORD of Hosts, the God of Israel: Because you have
obeyed the charge of your ancestor Jonadab and kept all his
commandments, and done all that he enjoined upon you,
19 assuredly, thus said the LORD of Hosts, the God of Israel:
There shall never cease to be a man of the line of Jonadab son
of Rechab standing before Me."

36 In the fourth year of King Jehoiakim son of Josiah of Judah, this word came to Jeremiah from the LORD:
2 Get a scroll and write upon it all the words that I have spoken to you—concerning Israel and Judah and all the nations—
from the time I first spoke to you in the days of Josiah to this
day. 3 Perhaps when the House of Judah hear of all the disasters I intend to bring upon them, they will turn back from their
wicked ways, and I will pardon their iniquity and their sin. 4 So
Jeremiah called Baruch son of Neriah; and Baruch wrote down
in the scroll, at Jeremiah's dictation, all the words which the
LORD had spoken to him.
5 Jeremiah instructed Baruch, "I am in hiding; I cannot go to
the House of the LORD. 6 But you go and read aloud the words of
the LORD from the scroll which you wrote at my dictation, to all
the people in the House of the LORD on a fast day; thus you will
also be reading them to all the Judeans who come in from the
towns. 7 Perhaps their entreaty will be accepted by the LORD, if
they turn back from their wicked ways. For great is the anger
and wrath with which the LORD has threatened this people."
8 Baruch son of Neriah did just as the prophet Jeremiah had
instructed him, about reading the words of the LORD from the
scroll in the House of the LORD. 9 In the ninth month of the fifth

is only for individual supporters of Jeremiah, namely Ebed-melech, 39.15–19; and Baruch, 45.2, 5.)

36.1–32: Writing down Jeremiah's prophecies. This is a unique report on the preservation of Jeremiah's words, written for the first time and burnt by king Jehoiakim, and then rewritten, updating the first version (v. 32). This story is concerned both with Jeremiah and the scroll. Jeremiah faces another threat on his life due to his prophetic message (see 20.1–6; ch 26; chs 37–38). He is *in hiding* (v. 5), but then is instructed by the king's officials to hide with his scribe Baruch (v. 19). The major interest, however, is in the scroll, the written form of Jeremiah's prophecies (vv. 1–4), read to the people (vv. 5–13), to the officials (vv. 14–19), and finally to the king who burns it to ashes (vv. 20–26). At that critical point, the prophet is instructed to produce a second scroll (vv. 27–28), and to proclaim judgment on Jehoiakim (vv. 29–31). The ch closes with this second scroll being written, noting that it was an elaborated version of the first. The ch provides the most complete information we have about the copying of prophetic texts, though it is unknown if the process it describes should be generalized to all prophetic writings. The events in the ch are set at approximately the same time as the previous ch. **1–8:** Writing the first scroll, and reading it aloud at the Temple. **1:** Jehoiakim's fourth year, 605, the year Nebuchadnezzar gained control over the Levant following his victory at Carchemish (Jer. 25.1–14 n.; 46.2; 2 Chron. 35.20; 2 Kings 24.7). **2–4:** The divine order to write down the prophecies proclaimed over about two decades, against Israel, Judah and the nations, has a clear didactic motivation, when they are seen cumulatively, *Perhaps ... they will turn back from their wicked ways, and I will pardon their iniquity and their sin.* **4:** *Baruch son of Neriah,* Jeremiah's devoted scribe (see 32.12–16; 43.6; 45.1–5), appears here to be both scribe, who wrote down Jeremiah's words from dictation, and the person who read the words aloud in public. Such dictation is important evidence for the move from oral proclamation to written prophecies. This story legitimizes the first, and actually the second scroll, as the one (the only) legitimate scroll, that reflects the words God had spoken to the prophet, that he himself dictated to his one and only scribe (vv. 6, 17–18, 27, 32). The book of Jeremiah, however, contains much more than only this layer, and presumably many more scribes were involved in its compilation. Two bullae (pieces of clay inscribed with a seal) reading "belong to Berachyahu [a variant form of Baruch] son of Neriyahu the scribe" appeared on the antiquities market in 1975 and 1996; if not forgeries, these may belong to the scribe Baruch, or to someone else bearing that name. Some have suggested that Baruch played an especially important role for the prophet because Jeremiah was illiterate. **5–8:** A second instruction concerns the recitation of these words, repeating the hope for the people's repentance (see v. 3). **5:** Jeremiah may have been *in hiding* because he felt endangered as a result of the antagonist prophecies he offered against Jehoiakim. **8:** Baruch accurately executes his master's instructions. Precise execution of commandments typifies this entire ch (see vv. 15, 27 and 32).

year of King Jehoiakim son of Josiah of Judah, all the people in Jerusalem and all the people coming from Judah proclaimed a fast before the LORD in Jerusalem. 10 It was then that Baruch—in the chamber of Gemariah son of Shaphan the scribe, in the upper court, near the new gateway of the House of the LORD—read the words of Jeremiah from the scroll to all the people in the House of the LORD.

11 Micaiah son of Gemariah son of Shaphan heard all the words of the LORD [read] from the scroll, 12 and he went down to the king's palace, to the chamber of the scribe. There he found all the officials in session: Elishama the scribe, Delaiah son of Shemaiah, Elnathan son of Achbor, Gemariah son of Shaphan, Zedekiah son of Hananiah, and all the other officials. 13 And Micaiah told them all that he had heard as Baruch read from the scroll in the hearing of the people.

14 Then all the officials sent Jehudi son of Nethaniah son of Shelemiah son of Cushi to say to Baruch, "Take that scroll from which you read to the people, and come along!" And Baruch took the scroll and came to them.

15 They said, [a-]"Sit down and read it[-a] to us." And Baruch read it to them. 16 When they heard all these words, they turned to each other in fear; and they said to Baruch, "We must report all this to the king."

17 And they questioned Baruch further, "Tell us how you wrote down all these words [b-]that he spoke."[-b] 18 He answered them, "He himself recited all those words to me, and I would write them down in the scroll in ink."

19 The officials said to Baruch, "Go into hiding, you and Jeremiah. Let no man know where you are!" 20 And they went to the king in the court, after leaving the scroll in the chamber of the scribe Elishama. And they reported all these matters to the king.

21 The king sent Jehudi to get the scroll and he fetched it from the chamber of the scribe Elishama. Jehudi read it to the king and to all the officials who were in attendance on the king. 22 Since it was the ninth month, the king was sitting in the winter house, with a fire burning in the brazier before him. 23 And every time Jehudi read three or four columns, [the king] would cut it up with a scribe's knife and throw it into the fire in the brazier, until the entire scroll was consumed by the fire in the brazier. 24 Yet the king and all his courtiers who heard all these words showed no fear and did not tear their garments; 25 moreover, Elnathan, Delaiah, and Gemariah begged the king not to burn the scroll, but he would not listen to them.

a-a Change of vocalization yields "Read it again"; cf. Targum and Septuagint.
b-b Force of Heb. uncertain.

9–13: A special fast is attested to only here, during Kislev of Jehoiakim's fifth year, December 604 BCE. The Babylonian Chronicles report Nebuchadnezzar's capture of Ashkelon that year, which might have caused fear in Judah. The story goes into great detail enumerating no less than nine officials by name, or *all the officials* in general (vv. 12, 19), and one of Jehoiakim's sons (Jerahmeel, v. 26). **14–20:** Baruch reads the scroll for the second time to the officials within the royal palace, raising fear among the officials (cf. with vv. 24–25). **17–18:** Curious as to *how* (LXX: "from where") this scroll was produced, what exactly was Baruch's role in it, the officials illustrate the relationship between the prophet and his scribe. Baruch assures the officials of his limited technical role: he only copied down what the prophet told him; the prophet was responsible for its content. **21–26:** The scroll is read aloud to the king. The setting is Jerusalem on a cold December day with the fire lit in the brazier, in which the king burns the scroll. **24:** The general reaction is surprising, clearly contrasting with Josiah's and his officials' reaction hearing "the scroll of the Teaching" (2 Kings chs 22–23; see 22.10–20). **25:** Nevertheless, several officials tried to prevent the king from burning the scroll, but in vain (cf. with 26.16–24). The king was determined to annul the words by burning them, and orders the arrest of Baruch and Jeremiah, who produced the scroll.

26 The king ordered Jerahmeel, the king's son, and Seraiah
son of Azriel, and Shelemiah son of Abdeel to arrest the scribe
Baruch and the prophet Jeremiah. But the LORD hid them.

27 The word of the LORD came to Jeremiah after the king had
burned the scroll containing the words that Baruch had written at Jeremiah's dictation: 28 Get yourself another scroll, and
write upon it the same words that were in the first scroll that
was burned by King Jehoiakim of Judah. 29 And concerning
King Jehoiakim of Judah you shall say: Thus said the LORD: You
burned that scroll, saying, "How dare you write in it that the
king of Babylon will come and destroy this land and cause man
and beast to cease from it?" 30 Assuredly, thus said the LORD
concerning King Jehoiakim of Judah: He shall not have any of
his line sitting on the throne of David; and his own corpse shall
be left exposed to the heat by day and the cold by night. 31 And
I will punish him and his offspring and his courtiers for their
iniquity; I will bring on them and on the inhabitants of Jerusalem and on all the men of Judah all the disasters of which I
have warned them—but they would not listen.
32 So Jeremiah got another scroll and gave it to the scribe
Baruch son of Neriah. And at Jeremiah's dictation, he wrote in
it the whole text of the scroll that King Jehoiakim of Judah had
burned; and more of the like was added.

37 Zedekiah son of Josiah became king instead of Coniah
son of Jehoiakim, for King Nebuchadrezzar of Babylon
set him up as king over the land of Judah. 2 Neither he nor his
courtiers nor the people of the land gave heed to the words
which the LORD spoke through the prophet Jeremiah.

3 Yet King Zedekiah sent Jehucal son of Shelemiah and
Zephaniah son of the priest Maaseiah to the prophet Jeremiah, to say, "Please pray on our behalf to the LORD our God."

26: *But the LORD hid them,* cf. 26.24. According to the MT, God hid the two; LXX reads "and they were hidden." **27–32:** The second scroll. Repeating the divine instruction and its accurate execution, a second scroll is produced like the first one, written again by Baruch from Jeremiah's dictation (see vv. 4, 6, 17–18). **29–31:** Jehoiakim's judgment. Jehoiakim's will be punished severely for burning the scroll. Strikingly, neither of his punishments is fulfilled. Jehoiachin/Coniah was Jehoiakim's son and king of Judah (2 Kings 24.6, 8–17; Jer. 22.24–30) and Jehoiakim died in his royal house and was probably buried with his forefathers (see some LXX mss of 2 Kings 24.6, in contrast also to Jer. 22.18–19). **29:** Jehoiakim quotes Jeremiah's prophecy: *the king of Babylon will come and destroy this land and cause man and beast to cease from it.* This is a summary note (as in 29.28). It does not quote any specific prophecy, and clearly does not reflect all that was presumably in the first scroll. It reflects instead the current political distress (see vv. 1, 9–13 nn.), and it treats Jeremiah's prophecy as only a short-term future prediction. **31:** A second cluster of judgment, addressed to the king, his descendants and servants, and including the entire people, is formulated theologically to justify the disaster, as a fulfillment of God's words which they all had not heeded (see 11.17; 16.10; 18.8; 19.15; 26.13, 19; 35.17, etc.). **32:** The second scroll is presumably an early edition of the present book. The story closes with further important information about the evolution of the prophetic collection, *and more of the like was added,* reflecting awareness of the cumulative nature of the prophetic words that constantly undergo additions and updates. These additions do not minimize the legitimacy of the words of God spoken to the prophet, transmitted in writing through Baruch to the people.

37.1–38.28: Jeremiah's personal fortune during the final siege and his secret connections with Zedekiah on the eve of destruction. While the two are intertwined, there are difficulties in the narrative flow, indicating that they are distinct stories combined, or different versions of one story. They are now part of a larger account in chs 37–44 that narrate the final days of the siege of Jerusalem, the city's fall, Gedaliah's murder, and Jeremiah's sojourn in Egypt. The content of 45.1 suggests that it once followed 36.32, and thus chs 37–44 were inserted as a block here.

37.1–21: Three episodes. The following events— the official delegation to the prophet (vv. 3–10), the prophet's capture and imprisonment (vv. 11–16), and Zedekiah's private consultation with Jeremiah (vv. 17–21)—are only loosely connected. This ordering suggests a causal sequence whereby Jeremiah's harsh prophecy raises the officials' anxiety, leading them to accuse him of treason, and then the king eventually rescinds his imprisonment. **1–2:** This summary note accuses Zedekiah of not listening to *the words which the LORD spoke through the prophet Jeremiah* (see 50.1), a phrase unique to this context, but widely used elsewhere. **3–10:** Another delegation of two

4 (Jeremiah could still go in and out among the people, for they had not yet put him in prison. 5 The army of Pharaoh had set out from Egypt; and when the Chaldeans who were besieging Jerusalem heard the report, they raised the siege of Jerusalem.)

6 Then the word of the LORD came to the prophet Jeremiah: 7 Thus said the LORD, the God of Israel: Thus shall you say to the king of Judah who sent you to Me to inquire of Me: "The army of Pharaoh, which set out to help you, will return to its own land, to Egypt. 8 And the Chaldeans will come back and attack this city and they will capture it and destroy it by fire."

9 Thus said the LORD: Do not delude yourselves into thinking, "The Chaldeans will go away from us." They will not. 10 Even if you defeated the whole army of the Chaldeans that are fighting against you, and only wounded men were left lying in their tents, they would get up and burn this city down!

11 When the army of the Chaldeans raised the siege of Jerusalem on account of the army of Pharaoh, 12 Jeremiah was going to leave Jerusalem and go to the territory of Benjamin *a-*to share in some property there*-a* among the people. 13 When he got to the Benjamin Gate, there was a guard officer there named Irijah son of Shelemiah son of Hananiah; and he arrested the prophet Jeremiah, saying, "You are defecting to the Chaldeans!" 14 Jeremiah answered, "That's a lie! I'm not defecting to the Chaldeans!" But Irijah would not listen to him; he arrested Jeremiah and brought him to the officials. 15 The officials were furious with Jeremiah; they beat him and put him into prison, in the house of the scribe Jonathan—for it had been made into a jail. 16 Thus Jeremiah came to the *a-*pit and the cells,*-a* and Jeremiah remained there a long time.

17 Then King Zedekiah sent for him, and the king questioned him secretly in his palace. He asked, "Is there any word from the LORD?" "There is!" Jeremiah answered, and he continued, "You will be delivered into the hands of the king of Babylon." 18 And Jeremiah said to King Zedekiah, "What wrong have I done to you, to your courtiers, and to this people, that you have put me in jail? 19 And where are those prophets of yours who prophesied to you that the king of Babylon would never move

a-a Meaning of Heb. uncertain.

officials is sent to the prophet with a plea for a prayer (see 21.1–10). *Jehucal son of Shelemiah* is called Jucal in 38.1. *Zephaniah son of the priest Maaseiah* was one of the two officials in the delegation of 21.1–2. He was the deputy priest of the Temple who had earlier read a letter from the exiles demanding that Jeremiah be rebuked (29.24–28); he is later executed by the Babylonians (52.24). **4–5:** The narrator offers general background: the prophet is still free, not yet imprisoned (see vv. 15ff.), and the final siege of Jerusalem is suddenly, though temporarily lifted as a result of the military intervention of Pharaoh Hophra (also known as Apries; 589–570 BCE; cf. Jer. 44.30). The Babylonian withdrawal from Jerusalem raised hopes in Jerusalem for permanent deliverance, as in the Assyrians' sudden withdrawal in 701 BCE (2 Kings 19.35–36). **6–10:** Two oracles inform the officials that the relief is temporary; the Babylonians will return to wage war again, capturing and burning the city (vv. 8, 10). **11–16:** During the period of Babylonian withdrawal, Jeremiah among others escaped from the city northward, to the area of Benjamin. **12:** *To share in some property there:* The Heb is difficult, and the versions (LXX, Vg, Tg. and Peshitta), and commentators connect this incident of escape to Jer. 32.6–15. Yet, based on Akkadian, this phrase means "to escape, desert," though as Jeremiah insists in v. 14, he has not engaged in treason or cooperation with the Babylonian as others have accused. Most of those who escaped Jerusalem to the north were probably saved from the war; archeological evidence from the territory of Benjamin shows that the region did not suffer destruction. Those who submitted to the Babylonians were treated better: they were exiled to Babylonia rather than killed on the spot (38.19; 39.9; 52.15; as also 2 Kings 19.30). Jeremiah thus suggested surrender to the populace (Jer. 21.8–10; quoted in 38.2) and to Zedekiah (38.17–23) as part of his repeated call to accept Babylonian subjugation and continue living in the land (27.12–13). **13–16:** Accused of treason, Jeremiah is beaten and jailed, and the following episodes depict his imprisonment in different places. According to v. 20, this first place was the worst. **17–21:** A first confrontation between the king and the prophet takes place in the palace, in secret. Zedekiah is interested in hearing a divine oracle, and the prophet repeats his earlier message (21.7; 32.4; 34.3; see also 22.25; and concerning the city and the kingdom, Judah, 20.4; 21.10; 32.3, 28, 36; 34.2). This passage draws a clear distinction between the king

against you and against this land? 20 Now, please hear me, O lord king, and grant my plea: Don't send me back to the house of the scribe Jonathan [a-]to die there.”[-a]

21 So King Zedekiah gave instructions to lodge Jeremiah in the prison compound and to supply him daily with a loaf of bread from the Bakers' Street—until all the bread in the city was gone. Jeremiah remained in the prison compound.

38 Shephatiah son of Mattan, Gedaliah son of Pashhur, Jucal son of Shelemiah, and Pashhur son of Malchiah heard what Jeremiah was saying to all the people: 2 “Thus said the LORD: Whoever remains in this city shall die by the sword, by famine, and by pestilence; but whoever surrenders to the Chaldeans shall live; [b-]he shall at least gain his life[-b] and shall live. 3 Thus said the LORD: This city shall be delivered into the hands of the king of Babylon's army, and he shall capture it.”

4 Then the officials said to the king, “Let that man be put to death, for he disheartens[c] the soldiers, and all the people who are left in this city, by speaking such things to them. That man is not seeking the welfare of this people, but their harm!” 5 King Zedekiah replied, “He is in your hands; the king cannot oppose you in anything!”

6 So they took Jeremiah and put him down in the pit of Malchiah, the king's son, which was in the prison compound; they let Jeremiah down by ropes. There was no water in the pit, only mud, and Jeremiah sank into the mud.

7 Ebed-melech the Cushite, a eunuch who was in the king's palace, heard that they had put Jeremiah in the pit. The king was then sitting at the Benjamin Gate; 8 so Ebed-melech left the king's palace, and spoke to the king: 9 “O lord king, those men have acted wickedly in all they did to the prophet Jeremiah; they have put him down in the pit, to die there of hunger.” For there was no more bread in the city.

10 Then the king instructed Ebed-melech the Cushite, “Take with you thirty[d] men from here, and pull the prophet Jeremiah up from the pit before he dies.” 11 So Ebed-melech took the men with him, and went to the king's palace, to [e-]a place below[-e] the treasury. There they got worn cloths and rags, which they let down to Jeremiah in the pit by ropes. 12 And Ebed-melech the Cushite called to Jeremiah, “Put the worn cloths and rags under your armpits, inside the ropes.” Jeremiah did so, 13 and they pulled Jeremiah up by the ropes and got him out of the pit. And Jeremiah remained in the prison compound.

and his officials; only the latter will continue to be the prophet's fiercest opponents. The king was attentive, even pious, yet frightened and weak, in contrast to his much stronger image in ch 27. **21:** Jeremiah is put in *the prison compound,* from where he purchases Hanamel's land (32.6–15), and from where he will be taken to Gedaliah after the city's surrender (39.14).

38.1–13: Jeremiah in great jeopardy but rescued. An alternative account of Jeremiah's imprisonment in 37.11–16. He never escaped, and his prophecy offended the nation's morale, leading to the accusation of treason. **5–6:** The king admits his weakness, and Jeremiah is thrown into a *pit* (cistern). Cf. Joseph in Gen. 37.19–24. **7–9:** *Ebed-melech* approaches the king on Jeremiah's behalf. **10–12:** Jeremiah is rescued by a large company under the leadership of Ebed-melech; the account concludes with him back in *the prison compound* (37.21). Jeremiah is silent throughout.

a-a *Lit. “and let me not die there.”* *b-b* *Lit. “he shall have his life as booty”; cf.* 21.9.
c *Lit. “weakens the hands of.”* *d* *One ms. reads “three.”*
e-e *Emendation yields “the wardrobe of.”*

38.14–28: A second secret meeting between Zedekiah and Jeremiah. This is a follow-up of the first meeting in 37.17–21. It starts with guaranteeing Jeremiah's safety, then turns to the main issue—King Zedekiah's desire to know the immediate future. Jeremiah again tells the king (and again, vv. 21–23) to surrender to the Babylonian officials, which will save him, his royal house, and the city. **19:** In these hazardous circumstances, Zedekiah expresses personal anxiety about his own subjects. **22:** The short poem is in qinah (or dirge) meter, reflecting its content. **24–27:** King Zedekiah is frightened by his own officials, and offers Jeremiah advice about assuring his personal safety (vv. 15–16), and disregards the prophet's advice about surrender.

14 King Zedekiah sent for the prophet Jeremiah, and had him brought to him at the third entrance of the House of the LORD. And the king said to Jeremiah, "I want to ask you something; don't conceal anything from me."

15 Jeremiah answered the king, "If I tell you, you'll surely kill me; and if I give you advice, you won't listen to me."

16 Thereupon King Zedekiah secretly promised Jeremiah on oath: "As the LORD lives who has [a]given us this life,[a] I will not put you to death or leave you in the hands of those men who seek your life."

17 Then Jeremiah said to Zedekiah, "Thus said the LORD, the God of Hosts, the God of Israel: If you surrender to the officers of the king of Babylon, your life will be spared and this city will not be burned down. You and your household will live. 18 But if you do not surrender to the officers of the king of Babylon, this city will be delivered into the hands of the Chaldeans, who will burn it down; and you will not escape from them."

19 King Zedekiah said to Jeremiah, "I am worried about the Judeans who have defected to the Chaldeans; that they [the Chaldeans] might hand me over to them to abuse me."

20 "They will not hand you over," Jeremiah replied. "Listen to the voice of the LORD, to what I tell you, that it may go well with you and your life be spared. 21 For this is what the LORD has shown me if you refuse to surrender: 22 All the women who are left in the palace of the king of Judah shall be brought out to the officers of the king of Babylon; and they shall say:

The men who were your friends
Have seduced you and vanquished you.
Now that your feet are sunk in the mire,
They have turned their backs [on you].

23 They will bring out all your wives and children to the Chaldeans, and you yourself will not escape from them. You will be captured by the king of Babylon, and [b]this city shall be burned down."[b]

24 Zedekiah said to Jeremiah, "Don't let anyone know about this conversation, [c]or you will die.[c] 25 If the officials should hear that I have spoken with you, and they should come and say to you, 'Tell us what you said to the king; hide nothing from us, [d]or we'll kill you.[d] And what did the king say to you?' 26 say to them, 'I was presenting my petition to the king not to send me back to the house of Jonathan to die there.'"

27 All the officials did come to Jeremiah to question him; and he replied to them just as the king had instructed him. So they

a-a *Meaning of Heb. uncertain.*
b-b *So Targum and Septuagint and some mss. Most mss. and the editions read "you will burn down this city by fire."* *c-c* *Lit. "that you may not die."*
d-d *Lit. "that we may not kill you."*

stopped questioning him, for the conversation had not been
overheard. 28 Jeremiah remained in the prison compound until the day Jerusalem was captured.
When Jerusalem was captured ... [a]

39 In the ninth year of King Zedekiah of Judah, in the tenth
month, King Nebuchadrezzar of Babylon moved against
Jerusalem with his whole army, and they laid siege to it. 2 And
in the eleventh year of Zedekiah, on the ninth day of the fourth
month, the [walls of] the city were breached. 3 All the officers of
the king of Babylon entered, and took up quarters at the middle
gate—Nergal-sarezer, Samgar-nebo, Sarsechim the Rab-saris,[b]
Nergal-sarezer the Rab-mag,[b] and all the rest of the officers of
the king of Babylon.
4 When King Zedekiah of Judah saw them, he and all the soldiers fled. They left the city at night, by way of the king's garden, through the gate between the double walls; and he set
out toward the Arabah.[c] 5 But the Chaldean troops pursued
them, and they overtook Zedekiah in the steppes of Jericho.
They captured him and brought him before King Nebuchadrezzar of Babylon at Riblah in the region of Hamath; and he
put him on trial. 6 The king of Babylon had Zedekiah's children

a *This clause would read well before 39.3.* *b* *Titles of officers.*
c *Hoping to escape across the Jordan.*

28: Jeremiah is back in *the prison* (as in 37.21; 38.13).

39.1–44.30: Jerusalem's destruction and the fate of the remnant of Judah. This section combines general historical information (39.1–10; 40.7–41.18; 43.4–7), biographical notes about Jeremiah (39.11–14; 40.1–6; 43.1–7), and prophecies (39.15–18; chs 42–44). This section uniquely offers the perspectives of the people who remained in Judah; other biblical texts give voice only to the Babylonian exiles. In their final form, these chs edited by writers in the Babylonian exile, depict two clear and antagonistic strands: reflecting a group that suggests staying in exile, and another that depicts the community who survived the Babylonian exile as the ideal Israel.

39.1–14: The fall of Jerusalem. The king was captured, the city burnt down, but the prophet is saved and released. This section is a revision of 2 Kings 25.1–12; minor changes include the list of names and titles of the Babylonian officials (vv. 3, 13),

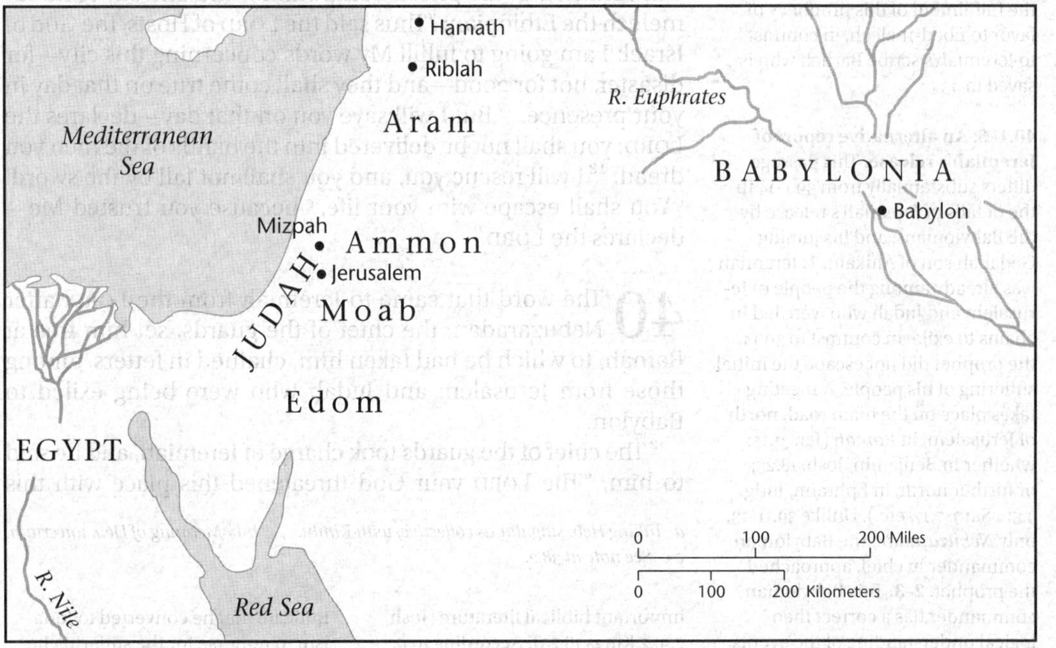

Babylonia and Judah ca. 600 BCE

slaughtered at Riblah before his eyes; the king of Babylon had
all the nobles of Judah slaughtered. 7 Then the eyes of Zedekiah were put out and he was chained in bronze fetters, that he
might be brought to Babylon.
8 The Chaldeans burned down the king's palace and the
houses[a] of the people by fire, and they tore down the walls of
Jerusalem. 9 The remnant of the people that was left in the city,
and the defectors who had gone over to him—the remnant
of the people that was left—were exiled by Nebuzaradan, the
chief of the guards, to Babylon. 10 But some of the poorest people who owned nothing were left in the land of Judah by Nebuzaradan, the chief of the guards, and he gave them vineyards
and fields at that time.
11 King Nebuchadrezzar of Babylon had given orders to
Nebuzaradan, the chief of the guards, concerning Jeremiah:
12 "Take him and look after him; do him no harm, but grant
whatever he asks of you." 13 So Nebuzaradan, the chief of the
guards, and Nebushazban the Rab-saris, and Nergal-sarezer
the Rab-mag, and all the commanders of the king of Babylon
sent 14 and had Jeremiah brought from the prison compound.
They committed him to the care of Gedaliah son of Ahikam
son of Shaphan, [b-]that he might be left at liberty in a house.[-b]
So he dwelt among the people.

15 The word of the LORD had come to Jeremiah while he was
still confined in the prison compound: 16 Go and say to Ebed-
melech the Ethiopian: "Thus said the LORD of Hosts, the God of
Israel: I am going to fulfill My words concerning this city—for
disaster, not for good—and they shall come true on that day in
your presence. 17 But I will save you on that day—declares the
LORD; you shall not be delivered into the hands of the men you
dread. 18 I will rescue you, and you shall not fall by the sword.
[c-]You shall escape with your life,[-c] because you trusted Me—
declares the LORD."

40

The word that came to Jeremiah from the LORD, after
Nebuzaradan, the chief of the guards, set him free at
Ramah, to which he had taken him, chained in fetters, among
those from Jerusalem and Judah who were being exiled to
Babylon.
2 The chief of the guards took charge of Jeremiah, and he said
to him, "The LORD your God threatened this place with this

a Taking Heb. singular as collective, with Kimhi. *b-b Meaning of Heb. uncertain.*
c-c See note at 38.2.

and the omission of the destruction of the Temple (cf. 2 Kings 25.9; and see Jer. 52.4–16). LXX does not include vv. 4–13, and thus leaves only vv. 1–3 as introduction. Jeremiah is completely absent until v. 11. **11–14:** Jeremiah's fate is determined by personal intervention of the Babylonian king and his highest officials. **13:** The same officials who were responsible for the disaster take action to save the prophet. The vv. present the officials' differing behavior toward the prophet, those of Judah who were persecuting the prophet and ready to kill him (chs 37–38), and those Babylonian officials who saved Jeremiah from prison and handed him over to Gedaliah son of Ahikam son of Shaphan, the Babylonian appointee over the remnant (40.5, 7). The passage illustrates the fulfillment of Jeremiah's main message to the king in chs 37–38: surrender and be saved, or rebel and die (38.17–23; cf. ch 27).

39.15–18: Ebed-melech is rewarded for his personal care for the prophet (38.7–13). The book never narrates the fulfillment of this prophecy of favor to Ebed-melech, in contrast to Jeremiah's scribe Baruch who is saved in 43.6.

40.1–6: An alternative report of Jeremiah's release. This passage differs substantially from 39.1–14 in the details of Jeremiah's release by the Babylonians, and his joining Gedaliah son of Ahikam. **1:** Jeremiah was already among the people of Jerusalem and Judah who were led in chains to exile. In contrast to 39.14, the prophet did not escape the initial suffering of his people. A meeting takes place on the main road, north of Jerusalem, in *Ramah* (Jer. 31.15; whether in Benjamin, Josh. 18.25; or further north, in Ephraim, Judg. 4.5; 1 Sam. 7.17, etc.). Unlike 39.11–13, only *Nebuzaradan,* the Babylonian commander in chief, approached the prophet. **2–3:** This Babylonian commander has a correct theological understanding of the events (Deut. 29.23–27), and knows other important biblical literature (Josh. 2.9; 2 Kings 18.25). According to *b. Git.* 57a, Nebuzaradan's statements indicate that he converted to Judaism in remorse for the suffering he caused. **4–6:** Nebuzaradan removes

disaster; 3 and now the LORD has brought it about. He has acted as He threatened, because you sinned against the LORD and did not obey Him. That is why this has happened to you. 4 Now, I release you this day from the fetters which were on your hands. If you would like to go with me to Babylon, come, and I will look after you. And if you don't want to come with me to Babylon, you need not. See, the whole land is before you: go wherever seems good and right to you."—5 [a]But [Jeremiah] still did not turn back.[a]—"Or go to Gedaliah son of Ahikam son of Shaphan, whom the king of Babylon has put in charge of the towns of Judah, and stay with him among the people, or go wherever you want to go."

The chief of the guards gave him an allowance of food, and dismissed him. 6 So Jeremiah came to Gedaliah son of Ahikam at Mizpah, and stayed with him among the people who were left in the land.

7 The officers of the troops in the open country, and their men with them, heard that the king of Babylon had put Gedaliah son of Ahikam in charge of the region, and that he had put in his charge the men, women, and children—of the poorest in the land—those who had not been exiled to Babylon. 8 So they with their men came to Gedaliah at Mizpah—Ishmael son of Nethaniah; Johanan and Jonathan the sons of Kareah; Seraiah son of Tanhumeth; the sons of Ephai the Netophathite; and Jezaniah son of the Maacathite. 9 Gedaliah son of Ahikam son of Shaphan reassured[b] them and their men, saying, "Do not be afraid to serve the Chaldeans. Stay in the land and serve the king of Babylon, and it will go well with you. 10 I am going to stay in Mizpah to attend upon the Chaldeans who will come to us. But you may gather wine and figs[c] and oil and put them in your own vessels, and settle in the towns you have occupied." 11 Likewise, all the Judeans who were in Moab, Ammon, and Edom, or who were in other lands, heard that the king of Babylon had let a remnant stay in Judah, and that he had put Gedaliah son of Ahikam son of Shaphan in charge of them. 12 All these Judeans returned from all the places to which they had

a-a Meaning of Heb. uncertain. *b Lit. "swore to."* *c Lit. "summer fruit."*

Jeremiah from his group, allowing him to choose one of three options: to continue *to go* to Babylon, released from chains and promised this official's protection; to remain in the land as a free man who may go wherever he wishes (see Gen. 13.9); or to return to *Gedaliah son of Ahikam,* already settled in *Mizpah,* located in Benjamin, about 13 km (8 mi) north of Jerusalem (Judg. 20.1; probably Tel en-Nasbeh). **6:** As in 38.7–13, Jeremiah's verbal reaction is not given; the narrator notes that he chose to join Gedaliah and remain in the land *among the people who were left in the land.* This choice accords with Jeremiah's call to remain in Judah under the Babylonians (27.12–13) and his concept of exile as dislocation with no return (22.10–12, 24–30; 29.1–7; 42.10–17).

40.7–41.18: Gedaliah's assassination. A second historiographical story (see 39.1–14) tells of Gedaliah's leadership and his assassination, which led to the escape of the remnant (the remaining Judeans) from *Mizpah* to the *Bethlehem* region, on their way to Egypt (41.16–17). The story is not mentioned elsewhere among the episodes in Jer. that deal with the destruction of 586 BCE and its aftermath (39.1–11; ch 52). The year is uncertain; the account may depict events during a few months in 586 BCE, or over several years, in which case it might be connected with the latest deportation wave of 582 BCE (52.30). This elaborate story is summarized in 2 Kings 25.22–26 in order to present the entire Judean remnant's descent to Egypt, thus leaving the land of Judah empty, in keeping with Kings' ideological stance. This same intention governs Jer. chs 40–44, also written by Babylonian exiles. **40.7–8:** The main characters are: *Gedaliah,* the Babylonian appointee (he is not even given an official title) over the impoverished Judean community who remained in the land; several army officers, two of whom will have destructive and restorative roles in the coming story; *Ishmael son of Nethaniah,* only later identified as belonging to the royal house (41.1)—his connections to Baalis, king of the Ammonites, inspire the thought that he had ambitions to gain control over the remnant as a Davidide heir (v. 14, and so Rashi, Kimḥi, and others); *Johanan and Jonathan the sons of Kareah* and other officers, otherwise unknown, though *Johanan* will play a particularly important role in sparing the remnant from extinction. **9–10:** Gedaliah begins his administration with confidence, calling for the restoration of agriculture in the land under the Babylonians. His call is similar to Jeremiah's (27.12–13, 17). **11–12:** A small "return to Zion" from the countries

scattered. They came to the land of Judah, to Gedaliah at Mizpah, and they gathered large quantities of wine and figs.[a]
13 Johanan son of Kareah, and all the officers of the troops in
the open country, came to Gedaliah at Mizpah 14 and said to him,
"Do you know that King Baalis of Ammon has sent Ishmael son
of Nethaniah to kill you?" But Gedaliah son of Ahikam would
not believe them. 15 Johanan son of Kareah also said secretly to
Gedaliah at Mizpah, "Let me go and strike down Ishmael son of
Nethaniah before anyone knows about it; otherwise he will kill
you, and all the Judeans who have gathered about you will be
dispersed, and the remnant of Judah will perish!"
16 But Gedaliah son of Ahikam answered Johanan son of Kareah, "Do not do such a thing: what you are saying about Ishmael is not true!"

41 In the seventh month, Ishmael son of Nethaniah son
of Elishama, who was of royal descent and one of the
king's commanders, came with ten men to Gedaliah son of
Ahikam at Mizpah; and they ate together there at Mizpah.
2 Then Ishmael son of Nethaniah and the ten men who were
with him arose and struck down Gedaliah son of Ahikam son
of Shaphan with the sword and killed him, because the king
of Babylon had put him in charge of the land. 3 Ishmael also
killed all the Judeans who were with him—with Gedaliah in
Mizpah—and the Chaldean soldiers who were stationed there.
4 The second day after Gedaliah was killed, when no one yet
knew about it, 5 eighty men came from Shechem, Shiloh, and
Samaria, their beards shaved, their garments torn, and their
bodies gashed, carrying meal offerings and frankincense to
present at the House of the LORD. 6 Ishmael son of Nethaniah
went out from Mizpah to meet them, weeping as he walked.
As he met them, he said to them, "Come to Gedaliah son of
Ahikam." 7 When they came inside the town, Ishmael son of
Nethaniah and the men who were with him slaughtered them
[and threw their bodies] into a cistern.
8 But there were ten men among them who said to Ishmael,
"Don't kill us! We have stores hidden in a field—wheat, barley,
oil, and honey." So he stopped, and did not kill them along
with their fellows.— 9 The cistern into which Ishmael threw all
the corpses of the men he had killed [b-]in the affair of Gedaliah was the one that[-b] King Asa had constructed on account of
King Baasha of Israel. That was the one which Ishmael son of

a *Lit. "summer fruit."* *b-b* *Septuagint reads "was a large cistern, which ... "*

immediately surrounding Judah. The gathering of *wine and figs* (summer fruits: grapes and figs) is a first step in re-cultivating the fields that were deserted. This may have inspired the hopes of restoration expressed in Jeremiah's consolation prophecies (as in 32.42–44; 33.10–13). **13–16:** These high hopes are jeopardized by rumors that are brought twice by Johanan and the other officers explicitly to Gedaliah. **15:** *And all the Judeans:* The danger of which Johanan warns here is more than the personal threat against Gedaliah; it is a second dispersion and the end of the *remnant,* the small group that was supposed to be the basis for growth and renewal (e.g., 23.3).

41.1–10: Ishmael kills Gedaliah, the Judeans, and the Babylonian soldiers in Mizpah. The assassination of Gedaliah represented the end of even limited restoration of Judean autonomy in the land. It is the culmination of events associated with the destruction of the Temple and the exile, which is thus portrayed as a total desertion of the land (2 Kings 25.26; and so Jer. 43.4–7). **1:** The exact day of *the seventh month,* Tishri, is not specified, but it is likely that this is "the fast of the seventh month" mentioned in Zech. 8.19. The Fast of Gedaliah is still observed on the third of Tishri, among the four fasts commemorating the destruction. **2–3:** Ishmael's betrayal takes advantage of Gedaliah's hospitality. Those killed include not only the official Babylonian appointee, but all the Judeans and the Babylonian guards in Mizpah, which thus portrays the entire action as a revolt. **4–9:** A second massacre kills eighty men arriving from the northern cities of Shechem, Shiloh, and Samaria, approaching Mizpah as part of their mourning over the destroyed Temple. Of the eighty, ten were spared; the seventy killed are among the worst general political massacres in Israel and Judah (see Judg. 9.5, 24; 2 Kings 10.6–7). Strikingly, they are bringing to the Temple site only *meal offerings and frankincense,* but not animal sacrifices. **9:** King Asa's cistern is not mentioned elsewhere, although he did build up Geba (between Mizpah and Jerusalem) and Mizpah (1 Kings 15.22; 2 Chron. 16.6). The reference may only echo an earlier internal struggle (so Tg.).

Nethaniah filled with corpses.—10 Ishmael carried off all the
rest of the people who were in Mizpah, including the daughters of the king—all the people left in Mizpah, over whom
Nebuzaradan, the chief of the guards, had appointed Gedaliah son of Ahikam. Ishmael son of Nethaniah carried them
off, and set out to cross over to the Ammonites.
11 Johanan son of Kareah, and all the army officers with him,
heard of all the crimes committed by Ishmael son of Nethaniah. 12 They took all their men and went to fight against Ishmael son of Nethaniah; and they encountered him by the great
pool in Gibeon. 13 When all the people held by Ishmael saw
Johanan son of Kareah and all the army officers with him, they
were glad; 14 all the people whom Ishmael had carried off from
Mizpah turned back and went over to Johanan son of Kareah.
15 But Ishmael son of Nethaniah escaped from Johanan with
eight men, and went to the Ammonites.
16 Johanan son of Kareah and all the army officers with him
took all the rest of the people whom [a]he had rescued from
Ishmael son of Nethaniah[a] from Mizpah after he had murdered Gedaliah son of Ahikam—the men, soldiers, women,
children, and eunuchs whom [Johanan] had brought back
from Gibeon. 17 They set out, and they stopped at Geruth[b]
Chimham, near Bethlehem, on their way to go to Egypt 18 because of the Chaldeans. For they were afraid of them, because Ishmael son of Nethaniah had killed Gedaliah son of
Ahikam, whom the king of Babylon had put in charge of the
land.

42 Then all the army officers, with Johanan son of Kareah,
Jezaniah son of Hoshaiah, and all the rest of the people, great and small, approached 2 the prophet Jeremiah and
said, "Grant our plea, and pray for us to the LORD your God,
for all this remnant! For we remain but a few out of many, as
you can see. 3 Let the LORD your God tell us where we should
go and what we should do."
4 The prophet Jeremiah answered them, "Agreed: I will pray
to the LORD your God as you request, and I will tell you whatever response the LORD gives for you. I will withhold nothing
from you."
5 Thereupon they said to Jeremiah, "Let the LORD be a true
and faithful witness against us! We swear that we will do exactly as the LORD your God instructs us through you—6 Whether
it is pleasant or unpleasant, we will obey the LORD our God to
whom we send you, in order that it may go well with us when
we obey the LORD our God."

a-a Emendation yields "Ishmael son of Nethaniah had carried off."
b Aquila reads "the sheepfolds of."

10: Ishmael captures the entire community, including the king's daughters; this too suggests Ishmael's royal pretensions (see 2 Sam. 16.20–23). **11–15:** Johanan and the other officers rescue the remnant. It is not stated where Johanan was, but apparently the region of Benjamin was re-populated, or continued with limited rural life after the destruction. The confrontation occurs in Gibeon, 8 km (5 mi) southwest of Mizpah. *The great pool,* see 2 Sam. 2.12–17 (so Tg.). In contrast to the previous scene, no further blood is shed at Gibeon, and even Ishmael escapes penalty, as he flees to his supporters in Ammon. **16–18:** The entire community of the remnant was led safely by Johanan and the officers to *Geruth Chimham,* in the region of *Bethlehem.* This southern point in Judah, a region that was unaffected by the destruction, was a stop on their way to Egypt, as the group feared Babylonian reprisals.

42.1–43.7: Jeremiah among the remnant of Judah, and the decision to flee to Egypt. This unit opens and closes with the negotiations between the remnant community and the prophet, mentioned here for the first time, although 40.6 earlier placed him at Mizpah. It thus becomes clear that the events in the previous chs were by and large background for understanding the prophet's mission. The opening plea expresses respect and obedience (42.1–6), but the closing one notes conflict and disobedience (43.1–7). In between (42.7–22), Jeremiah repetitively proclaims promises and threats aimed at preventing the people from executing their plan to *go* [to Egypt] *and sojourn there* (see the repetition in 42.15, 17, 22; 43.2). **42.1–3:** The remnant approach the prophet with a request for guidance from his God (see v. 4: *your God;* LXX harmonizes, reading "our God"). Jeremiah is asked to continue his role as mediator between the people and God (see 21.1–2; 37.3–4; and the divine prohibitions to do so, 7.16; 11.14; 14.11). **5–6:** The people pledge obedience to God. Their oath piously echoes the

7 After ten days, the word of the LORD came to Jeremiah.
8 He called Johanan son of Kareah and all the army officers,
and the rest of the people, great and small, 9 and said to them,
"Thus said the LORD, the God of Israel, to whom you sent me to
present your supplication before Him: 10 If you remain in this
land, I will build you and not overthrow, I will plant you and
not uproot; for I regret the punishment I have brought upon
you. 11 Do not be afraid of the king of Babylon, whom you fear;
do not be afraid of him—declares the LORD—for I am with you
to save you and to rescue you from his hands. 12 I will dispose
him to be merciful to you: he shall show you mercy and [a]bring
you back to[a] your own land.
13 "But if you say, 'We will not stay in this land'—thus disobeying the LORD your God—14 if you say, 'No! We will go to
the land of Egypt, so that we may not see war or hear the sound
of the horn, and so that we may not hunger for bread; there
we will stay,' 15 then hear the word of the LORD, O remnant of
Judah! Thus said the LORD of Hosts, the God of Israel: If you
turn your faces toward Egypt, and you go and sojourn there,
16 the sword that you fear shall overtake you there, in the land
of Egypt, and the famine you worry over shall follow at your
heels in Egypt too; and there you shall die. 17 All the men who
turn their faces toward Egypt, in order to sojourn there, shall
die by the sword, by famine, and by pestilence. They shall have
no surviving remnant of the disaster that I will bring upon
them. 18 For thus said the LORD of Hosts, the God of Israel: As
My anger and wrath were poured out upon the inhabitants of
Jerusalem, so will My wrath be poured out on you if you go to
Egypt. You shall become [b]an execration of woe, a curse[b] and
a mockery; and you shall never again see this place. 19 The
LORD has spoken against you, O remnant of Judah! Do not go

a-a Change of vocalization yields "let you dwell in."
b-b I.e., a standard by which men execrate and curse; cf. note at 24.9.

"na'aseh venishma'" ("All that the LORD has spoken we will faithfully do!" see Exod. 24.7) of the earliest covenant. Their disobedience is highlighted in the following vv.

42.7–22: Jeremiah's prophecies to the entire community (cf. v. 8 to v. 1). Six proclamations are noted (vv. 9–11a, 11b–12, 13–15a, 15b–16, 17–18, 19–22), suggesting repeated efforts by Jeremiah to persuade his audience to back off from their plans, which were presumably still open (v. 3). These chs present the Judean return to Egypt as a reversal of the exodus narrative. **7:** *Ten days:* It is quite remarkable that God does not immediately answer the prophet. Abravanel therefore understands the ten days to be reckoned from the first of Tishri when Gedaliah was assassinated (41.1). Yom Kippur (the Day of Atonement) falls on the tenth of Tishri (Lev. 23.26–32; Num. 29.7–11). Jeremiah's oracle would therefore have come immediately following Yom Kippur (cf. Ezek. 40.1, which places Ezekiel's vision of the Temple on Yom Kippur). Such a reckoning of the date would emphasize the theme of the people's repentance, which of course does not take place in the following vv. However, there is no explicit indication that Yom Kippur was observed in this period. **10–17:** In Deuteronomic language (see Deut. 11.13–17; 28.1, 15), these vv. demand that the remnant remain in the land, arguing that God's punishment is complete (vv. 9–11a) and God is with the remnant (vv. 11b–12). **9–11a:** The divine judgment is completed, and God promises to build and plant the remnant (cf. 1.10), as He changes His plan from destruction to restoration (as in 2 Sam. 24.16; Ezek. 5.13). There is thus no reason to fear the king of Babylonia, but this is predicated upon the people's commitment to an ongoing settlement in the land. **11b–12:** God proclaims His Presence and promises His assistance, salvation, and mercy. The Heb is ambiguous about whether God directly, or the Babylonian king, will *show you mercy.* **13–16:** If the people will not remain, fearing war or famine, the prophet responds measure-for-measure (talion): God will bring sword and famine upon the remnant of Judah in their new place of residence, in Egypt. Jeremiah draws on the Deuteronomic concept of exile as a final and comprehensive judgment of annihilation (see Deut. 4.25–28; and the covenant speeches in Jer. 7.3–7; 11.3–5; 17.22–17; 25.5–7). **17:** The *sword ... famine, and ... pestilence* (see 14.12; 21.7; etc.) are a separate threat, adding a complete analogy between the residents of Jerusalem prior to the destruction and this remnant now descending to Egypt. Both communities are to be afflicted by the divine anger (see 7.20; 44.6), and are to suffer the same total calamity (29.18; 44.12). **18–22:** The prophecy closes with another plea and a set of threats to the remnant of Judah, admonishing them for earlier deceiving the prophet (vv. 3, 5–6), and even more so for their disobedience to the divine word. Therefore, as in v. 17, *sword, famine* and *pestilence* will be their judgment. These vv. are from a Babylonian exilic editorial strand added to an earlier pro-remnant line

to Egypt! Know well, then—for I warn you this day [20] that you
were deceitful at heart when you sent me to the LORD your
God, saying, 'Pray for us to the LORD our God; and whatever
the LORD our God may say, just tell us and we will do it.' [21] I
told you today, and you have not obeyed the LORD your God
in respect to all that He sent me to tell you—[22] know well, then,
that you shall die by the sword, by famine, and by pestilence in
the place where you want to go and sojourn."

43 When Jeremiah had finished speaking all these words
to all the people—all the words of the LORD their God,
with which the LORD their God had sent him to them—[2] Azariah son of Hoshaiah and Johanan son of Kareah and all the
arrogant men said to Jeremiah, "You are lying! The LORD our
God did not send you to say, 'Don't go to Egypt and sojourn
there'! [3] It is Baruch son of Neriah who is inciting you against
us, so that we will be delivered into the hands of the Chaldeans
to be killed or to be exiled to Babylon!"
[4] So Johanan son of Kareah and all the army officers and the
rest of the people did not obey the LORD's command to remain
in the land of Judah. [5] Instead, Johanan son of Kareah and all
the army officers took the entire remnant of Judah—those who
had returned from all the countries to which they had been
scattered and had sojourned in the land of Judah, [6] men, wom-
en, and children; and the daughters of the king and all the people whom Nebuzaradan the chief of the guards had left with
Gedaliah son of Ahikam son of Shaphan, as well as the prophet
Jeremiah and Baruch son of Neriah—[7] and they went to Egypt.
They did not obey the LORD.

They arrived at Tahpanhes, [8] and the word of the LORD came
to Jeremiah in Tahpanhes: [9] Get yourself large stones, and embed them in mortar in the brick structure at the entrance to
Pharaoh's palace in Tahpanhes, with some Judeans looking
on. [10] And say to them: "Thus said the LORD of Hosts, the God
of Israel: I am sending for My servant King Nebuchadrezzar of
Babylon, and I[a] will set his throne over these stones which I
have embedded. He will spread out his pavilion[b] over them.
[11] He will come and attack the land of Egypt, delivering

> Those destined for the plague, to the plague,
> Those destined for captivity, to captivity,
> And those destined for the sword, to the sword.

[12] And I[a] will set fire to the temples of the gods of Egypt; he
will burn them down and carry them[c] off. He shall wrap himself up in the land of Egypt, as a shepherd wraps himself up

a Septuagint reads "he." *b Meaning of Heb. uncertain.* *c I.e., the gods.*

of Jeremian prophecies. This late strand presented the positive prospects of restoration as an opportunity the remnant had rejected in their continuous disobedience, which will lead to their complete annihilation, following the Deuteronomic concepts of exile (see v. 19 and Deut. 4.26); this will leave the Babylonian exiles as the only remnant.

43.1–7: Delegitimizing Jeremiah's prophecy. 2: As a reaction to Jeremiah's clear message against descending to Egypt, the entire people accuse the prophet of false prophecy, claiming that Baruch incited him to prophesy against the people (see Deut. 13.7), a unique attestation to Baruch's influence on Jeremiah. "Shalakh," "to send" serves as the key verb (as in 23.9–40, 27–29), challenging the status of Jeremiah as God's messenger, as in ch 26. **4–7:** The vv. describe the general descent to Egypt that takes all the remnant, including Jeremiah and Baruch—*all,* a word repeated several times, arrived in Egypt, suggesting that they all disobeyed God. Following 24.8–10, this presents the land of Judah as completely empty of any Judeans, and emphasizes the calamitous fortune that awaits those who had remained once they arrived in Egypt. This description leaves the Babylonian exiles as the only legitimate remnant of Judah, a perspective also known in Ezek., Deutero-Isaiah, and among the prophets and historians of the Persian period. *Tahpanhes,* "the fortress of Panhes," was an Egyptian stronghold in the northeast Nile Delta (Tel Deffeneh) that was intended to defend the Delta against foreign invasion.

43.8–13: Jeremiah prophesies in Egypt concerning a Babylonian victory over it. 9: In a symbolic action (see 13.1–11), the prophet is to build a *structure* at the gates of the *Pharaoh's palace.* Unlike other symbolic actions, this act is not explained, but it clearly symbolizes the Babylonian king's future control over the king of Egypt, which was not accomplished; Egypt was invaded and

in his garment. And he shall depart from there in safety. 13 He shall smash the obelisks of the Temple of the Sun which is in the land of Egypt, and he shall burn down the temples of the gods of Egypt.

44 The word which came to Jeremiah for all the Judeans living in the land of Egypt, living in Migdol, Tahpanhes, and Noph, and in the land of Pathros:

2 Thus said the LORD of Hosts, the God of Israel: You have seen all the disaster that I brought on Jerusalem and on all the towns of Judah. They are a ruin today, and no one inhabits them, 3 on account of the wicked things they did to vex Me, going to make offerings in worship of other gods which they had not known—neither they nor you nor your fathers. 4 Yet I persistently sent to you all My servants the prophets, to say, "I beg you not to do this abominable thing which I hate." 5 But they would not listen or give ear, to turn back from their wickedness and not make offerings to other gods; 6 so My fierce anger was poured out, and it blazed against the towns of Judah and the streets of Jerusalem. And they became a desolate ruin, as they still are today.

7 And now, thus said the LORD, the God of Hosts, the God of Israel: Why are you doing such great harm to yourselves, so that every man and woman, child and infant of yours shall be cut off from the midst of Judah, and no remnant shall be left of you? 8 For you vex me by your deeds, making offering to other gods in the land of Egypt where you have come to sojourn, so that you shall be cut off and become a curse[a] and a mockery among all the nations of earth. 9 Have you forgotten the wicked acts of your forefathers, of the kings of Judah and their[b] wives, and your own wicked acts and those of your wives, which were committed in the land of Judah and in the streets of Jerusalem? 10 No one has shown contrition to this day, and no one has shown reverence. You[c] have not followed the Teaching and the laws that I set before you and before your fathers.

11 Assuredly, thus said the LORD of Hosts, the God of Israel: I am going to set My face against you for punishment, to cut off all of Judah. 12 I will take the remnant of Judah who turned their faces toward the land of Egypt, to go and sojourn there,

a See note at 24.9; 42.18. *b Heb. "his."* *c Heb. "They."*

conquered only by the Persian Cambyses (525 BCE). **10:** Nebuchadrezzar is called once again *My servant* (vassal, see 25.9; 27.6). **13:** *The obelisks of the Temple of the Sun,* may refer to the city of On or Heliopolis, which was known for its obelisks and was a center for the worship of the sun god, Re. It is identified with Tel Hisn and Matariyeh, about 7 km (7 mi) northeast of Cairo (cf. Isa. 19.18).

44.1–30: Jeremiah's oracle to the Judeans settled in Egypt. The ch contains two judgment prophecies (vv. 1–14, 20–30), with the people's refutation in between (vv. 15–19). It went through significant modifications over time and is a retrospective on the fate of the remnant in Egypt (see vv. 29–30). **1:** Four place names, two of which are located at the eastern branches of the Nile Delta. *Migdol,* possibly Tel el-Hier (or a close-by settlement) on the coastal road; *Tahpanhes,* an Egyptian stronghold in the northeast Nile Delta; see 43.4–7 n.); both places were intended to defend the Delta against foreign invasion (see 2.16; 43.7, 8–13). *Noph,* Memphis, south of the Delta (see 2.16); these three places appear together in 46.14. *The land of Pathros,* Upper [southern] Egypt, the area of Aswan, mentioned in Isa. 11.11. Excavations on the island of Elephantine (Yeb), located in the Nile opposite Aswan, demonstrate the existence of Persian period (6th c. BCE and later) Jewish settlements in Egypt that originated in earlier times. The Aram. papyri found there describe a community that communicated with authorities in Jerusalem, although their religious practice was somewhat syncretistic. These four locations may refer to the actual places where Judeans settled in Egypt, or they may represent a north to south list, emphasizing that Jeremiah addressed them all (see v. 15). The following dialogue, in which the community as a whole responds in unified disobedience, is a literary convention. **2–6:** Using Deuteronomic language, Jeremiah bases his admonition on a retrospective of the destruction brought on Jerusalem and the cities of Judah, which are currently (*today,* v. 2) still completely desolate. Once again (see 7.21–28; 25.4–7; 26.5; 29.16–19), the prophet recalls the divine warnings and the people's stubbornness (see 7.20). **7–10:** *And now,* why have you, the remnant of Judah, not learned the lesson of the destruction? Although Jeremiah is speaking to an audience that presumably experienced those atrocities, the speech uses conventional phrases known from Jeremiah's earlier prophecies (see v. 9), abruptly adding to the evils of the current generation the earlier ones. **11–14:** The judgment part of this prophecy follows the two

and they shall be utterly consumed in the land of Egypt. They shall fall by the sword, they shall be consumed by famine; great and small alike shall die by the sword and by famine, and they shall become an execration[a] and a desolation, a curse[a] and a mockery. 13 I will punish those who live in the land of Egypt as I punished Jerusalem, with the sword, with famine, and with pestilence. 14 Of the remnant of Judah who came to sojourn here in the land of Egypt, no survivor or fugitive shall be left to return to the land of Judah. Though they all long to return and dwell there, none shall return except [a few] survivors.

15 Thereupon they answered Jeremiah—all the men who knew that their wives made offerings to other gods; all the women present, a large gathering; and all the people who lived in Pathros in the land of Egypt: 16 "We will not listen to you in the matter about which you spoke to us in the name of the LORD. 17 On the contrary, we will do [b-]everything that we have vowed[-b]—to make offerings to the Queen of Heaven and to pour libations to her, as we used to do,[c] we and our fathers, our kings and our officials, in the towns of Judah and the streets of Jerusalem. For then we had plenty to eat, we were well-off, and suffered no misfortune. 18 But ever since we stopped making offerings to the Queen of Heaven and pouring libations to her, we have lacked everything, and we have been consumed by the sword and by famine. 19 And when we make offerings to the Queen of Heaven and pour libations to her, is it without our husbands' approval that we have made cakes [d-]in her likeness[-d] and poured libations to her?"

20 Jeremiah replied to all the people, men and women—all the people who argued with him. He said, 21 "Indeed, the offerings you presented in the towns of Judah and the streets of Jerusalem—you, your fathers, your kings, your officials, and the people of the land—were remembered by the LORD and brought to mind! 22 When the LORD could no longer bear your evil practices and the abominations you committed, your land became a desolate ruin and a curse,[a] without inhabitant, as is still the case. 23 Because you burned incense and sinned against the LORD and did not obey the LORD, and because you did not follow His Teaching, His laws, and His exhortations, therefore this disaster has befallen you, as is still the case."

24 Jeremiah further said to all the people and to all the women: "Hear the word of the LORD, all Judeans in the land of Egypt! 25 Thus said the LORD of Hosts, the God of Israel: You and your wives have [e-]confirmed by deed what you spoke in words:[-e]

earlier components of the accusation, announcing complete calamity in the fiercest phrases: *no survivor or fugitive shall be left* (v. 14, see 22.27). The prophecy refers back to chs 42–43 concerning the improper intention *to go* [to the land of Egypt] *and sojourn there* (v. 12, and see v. 28; 42.15, 17, 19, 22; 43.2). **14:** *Except [a few] survivors* is absent in LXX, and may be an added gloss. **15–19:** Illustrating their disobedience, and quite exceptionally in prophetic literature in general, the audience responds to the prophet's words. Striking as well is the focus on women's religion. **16:** Differing from 43.1–3, they do not question Jeremiah's status as God's prophet, they simply disagree. **17:** The accusation of worshipping other gods (vv. 3, 8) here refers specifically to the worship of *the Queen of Heaven,* probably Ishtar, the Mesopotamian goddess of passion in war and love. Identified with the North Star or Venus, she represents stability in the world of creation. Here and 7.18 suggests that women in particular were involved in this worship. The same cult of the Queen of Heaven ("mlkt shmyn") is mentioned in an Aram. papyrus from Hermopolis in the Delta, dated to the 5th c. **18:** Although not stated, scholars have connected the discontinuance of this form of worship to Josiah's reforms (622 BCE, 2 Kings 23.4–20), shortly after which Josiah was killed, and Judah became a vassal of Babylonia. **20–30:** The prophet's next response is well calculated and serves as the final verdict on the community. **20–25:** This retrospective view precedes Jeremiah's proclamation of judgment.

a *See note at 24.9; 42.18.*
b-b *Lit. "everything that has gone forth from our mouth."* c *Cf. 7.18.*
d-d *Meaning of Heb. uncertain.*
e-e *Lit. "spoken with your mouth and fulfilled by your hands."*

'We will fulfill the vows which we made, to burn incense to the Queen of Heaven and to pour libations to her.' So fulfill your vows; perform your vows!

26 "Yet hear the word of the LORD, all Judeans who dwell in the land of Egypt! Lo, I swear by My great name—said the LORD—that none of the men of Judah in all the land of Egypt shall ever again invoke My name, saying, 'As the Lord GOD lives!' 27 I will be watchful over them to their hurt, not to their benefit; all the men of Judah in the land of Egypt shall be consumed by sword and by famine, until they cease to be. 28 Only the few who survive the sword shall return from the land of Egypt to the land of Judah. All the remnant of Judah who came to the land of Egypt to sojourn there shall learn whose word will be fulfilled—Mine or theirs!

29 "And this shall be the sign to you—declares the LORD—that I am going to deal with you in this place, so that you may know that My threats of punishment against you will be fulfilled: 30 Thus said the LORD: I will deliver Pharaoh Hophra, king of Egypt, into the hands of his enemies, those who seek his life, just as I delivered King Zedekiah of Judah into the hands of King Nebuchadrezzar of Babylon, his enemy who sought his life."

45 The word which the prophet Jeremiah spoke to Baruch son of Neriah, when he was writing these words in a scroll at Jeremiah's dictation, in the fourth year of King Jehoiakim son of Josiah of Judah:

2 Thus said the LORD, the God of Israel, concerning you, Baruch: 3 You say, "Woe is me! The LORD has added grief to my pain. I am worn out with groaning, and I have found no rest." 4 Thus shall you speak to him: "Thus said the LORD: I am going to overthrow what I have built, and uproot what I have planted—[a-]this applies to the whole land.[-a] 5 And do you expect great things for yourself? Don't expect them. For I am going to bring disaster upon all flesh—declares the LORD—but I will [b-]at least grant you your life[-b] in all the places where you may go."

46 The word of the LORD to the prophet Jeremiah concerning the nations.

2 Concerning Egypt, about the army of Pharaoh Neco, king of Egypt, which was at the river Euphrates near Carchemish, and which was defeated by King Nebuchadrezzar of Babylon, in the fourth year of King Jehoiakim son of Josiah of Judah.

a-a Meaning of Heb. uncertain. *b-b Cf. note at 21.9.*

26–28: God's judgment is of total annihilation (cf. with 5.2; 12.16). **29–30:** The sign is the death of *Pharaoh Hophra* (Apries), who ruled 589–570 BCE. He was assassinated by Amasis (570–526 BCE), a former court official who served as co-regent during the last three years of his reign; the ch thus gained its final shape after 570. The ch ends by connecting the remnant in Egypt and Zedekiah; see 24.8–10, and chs 42–43.

45.1–5: Jeremiah's words to Baruch, his scribe. This ch might be a colophon, a concluding note to the biographical accounts of Jeremiah, or to the historical reports on the last siege, the fall, and its aftermath. Alternatively, it may serve as an introduction to the oracles against the nations (so MT, introducing chs 46–51), or an end to the entire book (so LXX, placing ch 45 just before 52). **1–2:** Moving backwards chronologically to the fourth year of Jehoiakim (605 BCE) and on the event of writing the scroll (ch 36), this prophecy rebukes the scribe. **3–5:** Baruch's lament of v. 3 provokes God's critical response of vv. 4–5, conveyed by Jeremiah. The lament shares many characteristics of individual laments in Psalms (cf. e.g., *I am worn out with groaning* with Ps. 6.7). While his suffering might be due to Jeremiah's judgment prophecies against Judah, the unit suggests that it is nothing compared with the general hazards awaiting all in the land (1.10), though hope is guaranteed to Baruch wherever he might find himself going (see Ebed-melech, 39.15–18; and even Jeremiah's fate, 1.13–19), turning a lament into a promise of salvation. The Tg. (followed by Rashi, Kimḥi, Kara) understands the motivation of lament differently, suggesting Baruch was lamenting his status as scribe rather than as prophet.

46.1–51.64: Jeremiah's oracles concerning the nations. A collection of oracles concerning the nations (see 30.1–2; and 25.13) of Egypt (46.2–28), Philistia (47.1–7), Moab (48.1–47), the Ammonites (49.1–6), Edom (49.7–22), Damascus (49.23–27), Kedar and Hazor (49.28–33), Elam (49.34–39), and Babylonia (50.1–51.64). The collection comprises two circles of nations, opening and closing with the more distant ones, Egypt in the south, and then east and north: Kedar, Hazor, Elam and Babylonia. In the inner circle are the neighboring nations: Philistia, Edom, Moab,

3 Get ready buckler and shield,
And move forward to battle!
4 Harness the horses;
Mount, you horsemen!
Fall in line, helmets on!
Burnish the lances,
Don your armor!
5 Why do I see them dismayed,
Yielding ground?
Their fighters are crushed,
They flee in haste
And do not turn back—
Terror all around! —declares the LORD.
6 [a]The swift cannot get away,
The warrior cannot escape.[-a]
In the north, by the river Euphrates,
They stagger and fall.

7 Who is this that rises like the Nile,
Like streams whose waters surge?
8 It is Egypt that rises like the Nile,

a-a Lit. "Let not the swift get away, / Let not the warrior escape."

Ammon, and Damascus. Similar collections of oracles concerning the nations appear in other prophetic books: Isa. chs 13–23; Ezek. chs 25–32; Amos 1.2–2.16; Obad.; Nah.; Zeph. 2.4–15; and Zech. 9.1–8. Like Isa. chs 13–23, the oracles in Jer. chs 46–51 include nations that were conquered by the Persian empire beginning in 539 BCE; this reflects an effort to claim that God's judgment against Babylonia was carried out by the Persians. LXX has these oracles after Jer. 25.13, and their internal order differs. **46.1:** These oracles are *concerning the nations* but are not addressed to the nations. They emphasize a central point made from the beginning of classical prophecy: the God of Israel is a universal God, controlling the destiny of all nations. In some cases, there are significant similarities between oracles against the nations recited by different prophets (see esp. Jer. 49.9–16; Obad. 1.1–6), suggesting that prophets or editors of prophetic books borrowed from one another.

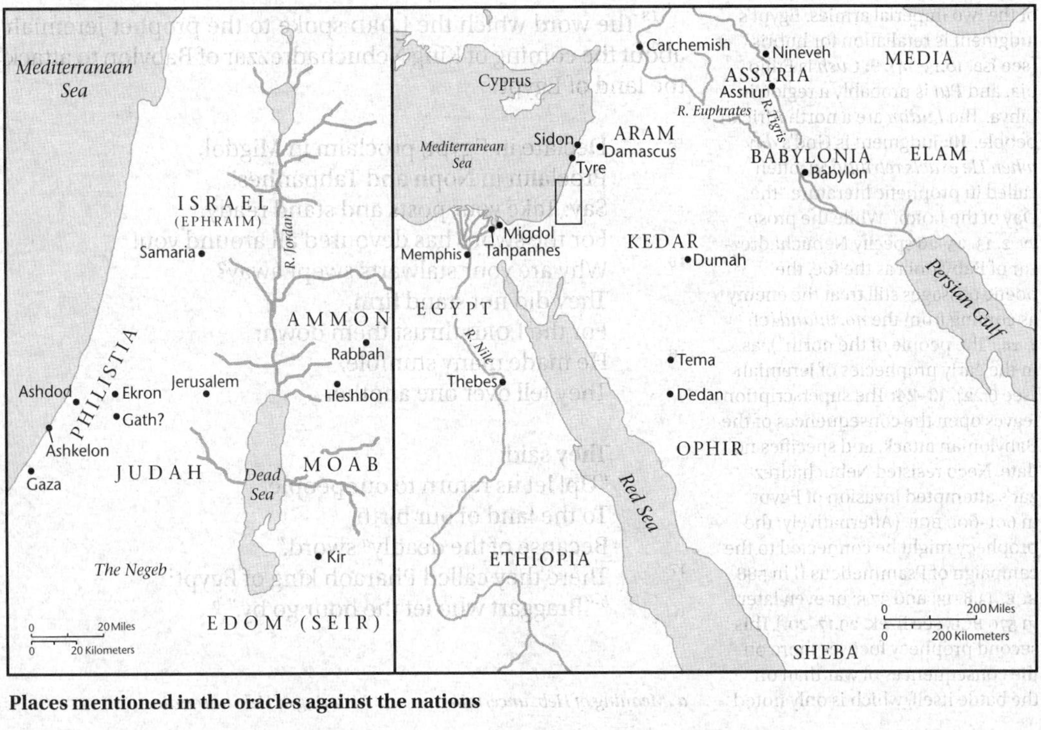

Places mentioned in the oracles against the nations

Like streams whose waters surge,
That said, "I will rise,
I will cover the earth,
I will wipe out towns
And those who dwell in them.
9 Advance, O horses,
Dash madly, O chariots!
Let the warriors go forth,
Cush and Put, that grasp the shield,
And the Ludim who grasp and draw the bow!"

10 But that day shall be for the Lord GOD of Hosts a day when
He exacts retribution from His foes. The sword shall devour; it
shall be sated and drunk with their blood. For the Lord GOD
of Hosts is preparing a sacrifice in the northland, by the river
Euphrates.

11 Go up to Gilead and get balm,
Fair Maiden Egypt.
In vain do you seek many remedies,
There is no healing for you.
12 Nations have heard your shame;
The earth resounds with your screams.
For warrior stumbles against warrior;
The two fall down together.

13 The word which the LORD spoke to the prophet Jeremiah
about the coming of King Nebuchadrezzar of Babylon to attack
the land of Egypt:

14 Declare in Egypt, proclaim in Migdol,
Proclaim in Noph and Tahpanhes!
Say: Take your posts and stand ready,
For the sword has devoured all around you!
15 Why are your stalwarts swept away?
They did not stand firm,
For the LORD thrust them down;
16 He made many stumble,
They fell over one another.

They said:
"Up! let us return to our people,
To the land of our birth,
Because of the deadly[a] sword."
17 There they called Pharaoh king of Egypt:
[b-]"Braggart who let the hour go by."[-b]

a Meaning of Heb. uncertain. *b-b Meaning of Heb. uncertain.*

46.2–28: Against Egypt (see 21.11; 23.9; 49.1). Three passages against Egypt, two poetic (vv. 2–12, 13–24) and one in prose (vv. 25–26), precede Israel, which will not suffer Egypt's fate (vv. 27–28). **2–12:** *Pharaoh Neco* (610–595 BCE) was the son of Psammetichus (664–610 BCE), the founder of the Twenty-sixth Saite Egyptian dynasty (664–525 BCE), which supported Assyria in its campaign to control Egypt and defeat the Twenty-fifth Ethiopian dynasty. Neco's defeat by the Babylonian monarch *Nebuchadrezzar* at *Carchemish* (on the west bank of the Upper Euphrates) in 605 forced Egypt to withdraw from Judah, and enabled Babylonia to take control of the Levant, following the collapse of the Neo-Assyrian empire (see 2 Kings 24.7). The Saite dynasty came to an end in 525 when the Persians conquered Egypt. **3–12:** The description alternates between military instructions calling the Egyptian army to war (vv. 3–4, 7–9) and proclaiming its defeat (vv. 5–6, 10–12). **6–8:** Water plays a central role in this imagery; the Euphrates and the Nile are symbols of the two imperial armies. Egypt's judgment is retaliation for hubris (see Isa. 10.13–14). **9:** *Cush* is Ethiopia, and *Put* is probably a region in Libya. The *Ludim* are a north African people. **10:** Judgment is God's *day when He exacts retribution,* often called in prophetic literature "the Day of the LORD." While the prose vv. 2, 13, 25–26 specify Nebuchadrezzar of Babylonia as the foe, the poetic passages still treat the enemy as coming from the *northland* (cf. v. 24, "the people of the north"), as in the early prophecies of Jeremiah (see 6.22). **13–24:** The superscription leaves open the consequences of the Babylonian attack, and specifies no date. Neco resisted Nebuchadrezzar's attempted invasion of Egypt in 601–600 BCE. (Alternatively, the prophecy might be connected to the campaign of Psammeticus II in 588 BCE, 43.8–13; and 37.5; or even later, in 570 BCE, see Ezek. 29.17–20.) This second prophecy focuses more on the consequences of war than on the battle itself, which is only noted

18 As I live—declares the King,
Whose name is LORD of Hosts—
[a]As surely as Tabor is among the mountains
And Carmel is by the sea,
So shall this come to pass.[a]
19 Equip yourself for exile,
Fair Egypt, you who dwell secure!
For Noph shall become a waste,
Desolate, without inhabitants.
20 Egypt is a handsome heifer—
A gadfly[b] from the north [c]is coming, coming![c]
21 The mercenaries, too, in her midst
Are like stall-fed calves;
They too shall turn tail,
Flee as one, and make no stand.
Their day of disaster is upon them,
The hour of their doom.
22 [a]She shall rustle away like a snake[a]
As they come marching in force;
They shall come against her with axes,
Like hewers of wood.
23 They shall cut down her forest
—declares the LORD—
Though it cannot be measured;
For they are more numerous than locusts,
And cannot be counted.
24 Fair Egypt shall be shamed,
Handed over to the people of the north.

25 The LORD of Hosts, the God of Israel, has said: I will inflict punishment on Amon[d] of No and on Pharaoh—on Egypt, her gods, and her kings—on Pharaoh and all who rely on him. 26 I will deliver them into the hands of those who seek to kill them, into the hands of King Nebuchadrezzar of Babylon and into the hands of his subjects. But afterward she shall be inhabited again as in former days, declares the LORD.

27 But you,
Have no fear, My servant Jacob,
Be not dismayed, O Israel!
I will deliver you from far away,
Your folk from their land of captivity;
And Jacob again shall have calm
And quiet, with none to trouble him.

a-a *Meaning of Heb. uncertain.* *b* *Or "butcher"; meaning of Heb. uncertain.*
c-c *Many mss. read "will come upon her."*
d *Tutelary deity of the city No (Thebes); cf. Nah. 3.8.*

briefly in vv. 14–16. Vv. 13–28 serve as the haftarah for the parashah Bo' (Exod. 10.1–13.16), which relates the plagues of locusts, darkness, and the slaying of the first-born of Egypt. **18–23:** The landscape descriptions of the landscape, specifically *mountains* (v. 18) and *forest* (v. 23), do not match Egypt. **25–26:** These vv. identify Nebuchadrezzar king of Babylonia as that nation of the north (vv. 10, 24), and add a new theme: the Egyptian gods, not only the Pharaoh and his allies, will be punished. LXX lacks v. 26. *But afterward she shall be inhabited again as in former days, declares the LORD:* This closing formula that promises restoration to Egypt *afterwards* (or "in the days to come") occurs also in the prophecies against Moab, Ammon, and Elam (48.47; 49.6, 39), and might be a late editorial addition. **27–28:** A prophecy of consolation to Israel, taken from 30.10–11, and missing from LXX.

28 But you, have no fear,
My servant Jacob —declares the LORD—
For I am with you.
I will make an end of all the nations
Among which I have banished you,
But I will not make an end of you!
I will not leave you unpunished,
But I will chastise you in measure.

47 The word of the LORD that came to the prophet Jeremiah concerning the Philistines, before Pharaoh conquered Gaza.

2 Thus said the LORD:
See, waters are rising from the north,
They shall become a raging torrent,
They shall flood the land and its creatures,
The towns and their inhabitants.
Men shall cry out,
All the inhabitants of the land shall howl,
3 At the clatter of the stamping hoofs of his stallions,
At the noise of his chariots,
The rumbling of their wheels,
Fathers shall not look to their children
Out of [a]sheer helplessness[a]
4 Because of the day that is coming
For ravaging all the Philistines,
For cutting off every last ally
Of Tyre and Sidon.
For the LORD will ravage the Philistines,
The remnant from the island of Caphtor.
5 Baldness[b] has come upon Gaza,
Ashkelon is destroyed.
O remnant of [c]their valley,[c]
How long will you [d]gash yourself?[d]

6 "O sword of the LORD,
When will you be quiet at last?
Withdraw into your sheath,
Rest and be still!"

a-a Lit. "weakness of hands."
b Shaving the head and gashing the body were expressions of mourning; cf. Deut. 14.1. *c-c Septuagint reads "the Anakites"; cf. Josh. 11.22.*
d-d Shaving the head and gashing the body were expressions of mourning; cf. Deut. 14.1.

47.1–7: Jeremiah's oracle concerning Philistia. The Philistines were descended from the Sea Peoples who advanced by land and sea from the Greek islands through Asia Minor and the eastern Mediterranean beginning in the 14th c. BCE. They destroyed the ancient Hittite empire in Asia Minor, and continued down the eastern Mediterranean coast, where they destroyed the city of Ugarit in Syria and attacked Egypt during the reign of Rameses III (1182–1152 BCE). Following their defeat by Rameses III, some groups of the Sea Peoples settled along the Mediterranean coast of Canaan, where they merged with the local population to become the Philistines. The Philistine coalition was organized into five major cities (a pentapolis): Ashkelon, Ashdod, Ekron, Gaza, and Gath (only two of them are mentioned here, in vv. 5, 7). Although the Philistines play a major role in texts describing the rise of the monarchy, they are hardly mentioned later. Herodotus reports that Neco conquered Gaza, at the border of the desert on the way to Egypt, after his battle with Josiah at Megiddo (2.159). This view also appears in the rabbinic work *Seder Olam* 26. Nebuchadnezzar's invasion of Philistia in 604 and his subsequent deportation of major elements of the population brought an end to Philistia as a cohesive ethnic and national group, though archeological finds and various texts confirm that the Philistines remained important and active through the period of Jeremiah. **1:** *Before Pharaoh conquered Gaza,* lacking in the LXX, is unusual in this context, which is about a foe from the north affecting the coastal cities down to Gaza; this phrase provides a link to the previous ch. **2–6:** Two major images characterize the destructive forces in this prophecy: a flood of great waters coming from the north (see 46.10, 24) and God's sword that would *be quiet* and *withdraw into* [its] *sheath.* **4:** No explanation is given for the divine judgment on the *Philistines* or on their coastal allies, *Tyre* and *Sidon,* cities of Phoenicia (modern Lebanon). Such an alliance is not noted in any extrabiblical source. *Caphtor* is the island of Crete, which Amos 9.7 identifies as the original home of the Philistines.

7 How can it[a] be quiet
When the LORD has given it orders
Against Ashkelon and the seacoast,
Given it assignment there?

48 Concerning Moab.[b]

Thus said the LORD of Hosts, the God of Israel:
Alas, that Nebo should be ravaged,
Kiriathaim captured and shamed,
[c-]The stronghold[-c] shamed and dismayed!
2 Moab's glory is no more;
In Heshbon they have planned[d] evil against her:
"Come, let us make an end of her as a nation!"
You too, O Madmen, shall be silenced;[e]
The sword is following you.
3 Hark! an outcry from Horonaim,
Destruction and utter ruin!

4 Moab is broken;
[f-]Her young ones cry aloud;[-f]
5 They climb to Luhith
Weeping continually;
On the descent to Horonaim
A distressing cry of anguish is heard:
6 Flee, save your lives!
[g-]And be like Aroer in the desert.[-g]

7 Surely, because of your trust
In your wealth and in your treasures,
You too shall be captured.
And Chemosh shall go forth to exile,
Together with his priests and attendants.
8 The ravager shall come to every town;
No town shall escape.
The valley shall be devastated
And the tableland laid waste
—because the LORD has spoken.
9 Give [g-]wings to Moab,
For she must go hence.[-g]
Her towns shall become desolate,
With no one living in them.

a *Heb. "you."* *b* *A number of parallels to this chapter occur in Isa. 15–16.*
c-c *Or "Misgab."* *d* *Heb.* ḥashebu, *play on Heshbon.*
e *Heb.* tiddommi, *play on Madmen, the name of a town.*
f-f *Emendation yields "They cry aloud as far as Zoar"; cf. Isa. 15.5.*
g-g *Meaning of Heb. uncertain.*

48.1–47: Concerning Moab. Moab was situated east of the Dead Sea to the north of Edom and southwest of Ammon, in what is now the central part of modern Jordan. Israel's relationship with Moab was generally tense (see e.g., Num. ch 22 and Deut. 2.8–9). The mid-9th c. Moabite Stone (Mesha Stele) reports that the Moabite King Mesha (cf. 2 Kings 3.4) conquered Israel's land in the Transjordan, including the territories of Reuben and Gad. The Moabites were allies of the Assyrians, but the Babylonians apparently destroyed Moab in the mid-6th c. Jeremiah's prophecies against Moab combine different types of materials: descriptions of mourning (vv. 3–5, 32, 37–38), descriptions of the destruction and desolation of the land and its agriculture (vv. 8–9, 18, 32–33, 34–39, 45), divine admonitions and theological notes on the disaster (vv. 7, 14, 26, 29, 42), and references to *Chemosh,* its patron god (vv. 7, 13, 46). These combine to highlight Moab's panic and helplessness, the lengthy ch's main theme, reflecting the great antipathy felt toward them. These prophecies share imagery, phrases, and themes with Isa. chs 15–16 and Num. 21.27–30, and may rely on an early Moabite lament; their exact historical context cannot be reconstructed. **1–10:** The prophecy opens with judgment on cities and regions, where cries and wails are heard: *Moab is broken* (v. 4, see a similar structure in vv. 21–25). In total, quite remarkably twenty-four place names are mentioned; *Moab* occurs thirty-four times in forty-seven vv. **7:** Moab is repeatedly blamed for pride and complacency, presented as offenses against YHVH (see also vv. 14, 26, 29, 42). *Chemosh* was the chief god of Moab (as in Num. 21.29; 1 Kings 11.7, 33; and the epigraphic Moabite materials). In all of its references here, *Chemosh* is captured (the ancient custom was to exile the statues of foreign deities) and is dislocated together with *his priests* and officials. The patron god has lost power, place, and people, a theme repeated in several other oracles against the nations (see concerning Ammon, 49.3; Babylonia, 50.2; 51.44; and Isa. 46.1–2).

10: A call to Moab's enemies, cursing the ones who fail YHVH's instructions, who withhold the sword. **11–17:** The image of wine jars that have never been moved, thereby allowing the sediment *(lees)* to settle, depicts Moab as good old wine kept stable to maintain its value; this image makes the impending destruction, expressed through *smash*ing its wine-*jars,* more powerful (see 13.12–14). **13:** The disappointment in *Chemosh* is parallel to that of Israel's in *Bethel, on whom they relied.* If Bethel is a place name, it might mean northern Israel relying on King Jeroboam's temple at Bethel (see 1 Kings chs 12–13; 2 Kings ch 17). This cultic center was destroyed in 622 by Josiah (2 Kings 23.15–16); this may show that at least parts of the oracles concerning the nations were among Jeremiah's earliest proclamations, even though they are collected in MT at the end of the book. Here, however, the comparison with Chemosh may suggest that Bethel was a deity, as attested clearly in the Elephantine Papyri and some earlier sources.

10 Cursed be he who is slack in doing the LORD's work!
Cursed be he who withholds his sword from blood!

11 Moab has been secure from his youth on—
He is settled on his lees
And has not been poured from vessel to vessel—
He has never gone into exile.
Therefore his fine flavor has remained
And his bouquet is unspoiled.

12 But days are coming—declares the LORD—when I will
send men against him to tip him over; they shall empty his vessels and smash his jars. 13 And Moab shall be shamed because
of Chemosh, as the House of Israel were shamed because of
Bethel, on whom they relied.

14 How can you say: We are warriors,
Valiant men for war?
15 Moab is ravaged,
His towns have been entered,
His choice young men
Have gone down to the slaughter
—declares the King whose name is
LORD of Hosts.

16 The doom of Moab is coming close,
His downfall is approaching swiftly.
17 Condole with him, all who live near him,
All you who know him by name!
Say: "Alas, the strong rod is broken,
The lordly staff!"

18 Descend from glory
And sit in thirst,[a]
O inhabitant of Fair Dibon;
For the ravager of Moab has entered your town,
He has destroyed your fortresses.
19 Stand by the road and look out,
O inhabitant of Aroer.
Ask of him who is fleeing
And of her who is escaping:
Say, "What has happened?"
20 Moab is shamed and dismayed;
Howl and cry aloud!
Tell at the Arnon
That Moab is ravaged!

a *Meaning of Heb. uncertain.*

[21] Judgment has come upon the tableland—upon Holon, Jahzah, and Mephaath; [22] upon Dibon, Nebo, and Beth-
diblathaim; [23] upon Kiriathaim, Beth-gamul, and Beth-meon;
[24] upon Kerioth and Bozrah—upon all the towns of the land of
Moab, far and near.

25 The might of Moab has been cut down,
His strength is broken —declares the LORD.
26 Get him drunk
For he vaunted himself against the LORD.
Moab shall vomit till he is drained,
And he too shall be a laughingstock.
27 Wasn't Israel a laughingstock to you?
Was he ever caught among thieves,
That you should [a-]shake your head[-a]
Whenever you speak of him?
28 Desert the cities
And dwell in the crags,
O inhabitants of Moab!
Be like a dove that nests
In the sides of a pit.

29 We have heard of Moab's pride—
Most haughty is he—
Of his arrogance and pride,
His haughtiness and self-exaltation.
[30] I know his insolence—declares the LORD—the wickedness
that is in him,[b] the wickedness [c-]he has[-c] committed.
31 Therefore I will howl for Moab,
I will cry out for all Moab,
I[d] will moan for the men of Kir-heres.
32 With greater weeping than for Jazer
I weep for you, O vine of Sibmah,
Whose tendrils crossed the sea,
Reached to the sea,[e] to Jazer.
A ravager has come down
Upon your fig and grape harvests.
33 Rejoicing and gladness
Are gone from the farm land,
From the country of Moab;
I have put an end to wine in the presses,
No one treads [the grapes] with shouting—
[f-]The shout is a shout no more.[-f]
34 There is an outcry from Heshbon to Elealeh,
They raise their voices as far as Jahaz,

a-a I.e., in mockery. *b Cf. note at Isa. 16.6.* *c-c Heb. "they have."*
d Heb. "He." *e Meaning of Heb. uncertain.* *f-f Meaning of Heb. uncertain.*

21–25: *Judgment* (Heb "mishpat") *has come upon the tableland:* Use of this word for judgment upon a foreign nation is very unusual (see v. 47; and in reference to Babylonia, 51.9). See vv. 1–10 n. **26:** *For he vaunted himself against the LORD,* pride by trusting in its wealth and treasures (v. 7), or in its military forces (v. 14). This accusation (cf. v. 42), sees this pride as aimed against YHVH (cf. Ezek. 35.13; Zeph. 2.8–10). **32–34:** *Vine of Sibmah,* a city in the region of Jazer (Num. 32.38), symbolizes here Moab's profound destruction. Picking up on the wine imagery in vv. 11–17, Jeremiah depicts the destruction as geographically widespread as the vine branches in their grandeur, producing abundant wine. Harvesting grapes and producing wine were equated with joy and gladness; the destruction brings an end to the lively and joyous agricultural life in Moab (see Isa. 16.10).

35–38: A funerary lament over Moab, comprised of phrases and themes from Isa. 15.2–3, 7a, and 16.11. **36:** *My heart moans for Moab like a flute,* cf. Isa. 16.11, which mentions a lyre. The flute and the lyre were associated with happy occasions (1 Kings 1.40; Isa. 5.12; 30.29). **40–41:** The enemy is like a soaring eagle that dives onto its prey, a stock image (see 49.22; Hab. 1.8; Job 9.26; Lam. 4.19). **42–46:** *And Moab shall be destroyed as a people .... The people of Chemosh are undone,* this is expressed using verbs from Deut. (e.g., Deut. 4.26; 9.3; 28.20, 51) that designate total annihilation. **46:** *People* [Heb "'am"] *of Chemosh,* "'am" here is unique, paralleling the use of Israel as called "the people of YHVH" (e.g., Num. 11.29; 17.6; Judg. 5.11). This v. closes the curtain over Moab, treating exile as total calamity. **47:** A consolation to Moab (see similarly 49.39, and phrased differently, 46.26; 49.6), a secondary addition. *Thus far is the judgment on Moab,* another editorial comment, as in 51.64.

From Zoar to Horonaim and Eglath-shelishiah.
The waters of Nimrim
Shall also become desolation.
35 And I will make an end in Moab
—declares the LORD—
Of those who offer at a shrine
And burn incense to their god.
36 Therefore,
My heart moans for Moab like a flute;
Like a flute my heart moans
For the men of Kir-heres—
[a]Therefore,
The gains they have made shall vanish[a]—
37 For every head is bald
And every beard is shorn;
On all hands there are gashes,
And on the loins sackcloth.
38 On all the roofs of Moab,
And in its squares
There is naught but lamentation;
For I have broken Moab
Like a vessel no one wants
—declares the LORD.
39 How he is dismayed! Wail!
How Moab has turned his back in shame!
Moab shall be a laughingstock
And a shock to all those near him.

40 For thus said the LORD:
See, he soars like an eagle
And spreads out his wings against Moab!
41 Kerioth shall be captured
And the strongholds shall be seized.
In that day, the heart of Moab's warriors
Shall be like the heart of a woman in travail.
42 And Moab shall be destroyed as a people,
For he vaunted himself against the LORD.
43 [b]Terror, and pit, and trap[b]
Upon you who dwell in Moab!
—declares the LORD.
44 He who flees from the terror
Shall fall into the pit;
And he who climbs out of the pit
Shall be caught in the trap.
For I will bring upon Moab
The year of their doom —declares the LORD.

a-a Meaning of Heb. uncertain. *b-b See note at Isa. 24.17.*

45 In the shelter of Heshbon
Fugitives halt exhausted;
For fire went forth from Heshbon,
Flame from the midst[a] of Sihon,
Consuming the brow of Moab,
The pate of the people of Shaon.[b]
46 Woe to you, O Moab!
The people of Chemosh are undone,
For your sons are carried off into captivity,
Your daughters into exile.

47 But I will restore the fortunes of Moab in the days to come—
declares the LORD.

Thus far is the judgment on Moab.

49 Concerning the Ammonites.

Thus said the LORD:
Has Israel no sons,
Has he no heir?
Then why has Milcom[c] dispossessed Gad,
And why have his people settled in Gad's[d]
towns?
2 Assuredly, days are coming
—declares the LORD—
When I will sound the alarm of war
Against Rabbah of the Ammonites;
It shall become a desolate mound,
And its villages shall be set on fire.
And Israel shall dispossess
Those who dispossessed him —said the LORD.
3 Howl, O Heshbon, for Ai is ravaged!
Cry out, O daughters of Rabbah!
Gird on sackcloth, lament,
[e]And run to and fro in the sheepfolds.[e]
For Milcom shall go into exile,
Together with his priests and attendants.

4 [f]Why do you glory in strength,
Your strength is drained,[f]
O rebellious daughter,
You who relied on your treasures,
[Who said:] Who dares attack me?

a Emendation yields "house." *b Or "tumult."*
c The name of the Ammonite deity; vocalized Malcam here and in v. 3.
d Heb. "his." *e-e Meaning of Heb. uncertain.*
f-f Meaning of Heb. uncertain; for "strength" cf. Akkadian emuqu.

49.1–6: Concerning the Ammonites. Ammon was centered on the city of Rabbath-Ammon, modern Amman, east of the Jordan River and north of Moab. Long and complicated relationships characterize Ammon and Israel. The Ammonites were at times foes (Amos 1.13; Zeph. 2.8; and earlier, Judg. 11.12–28; 1 Sam. ch 11; 2 Sam. ch 10; 12.26–31) and at times allies of Israel and Judah (as in Jer. 27.3). The Ammonites supported Ishmael son of Nethaniah, a member of the Davidic family, in his revolt against Gedaliah (40.7–41.18). Nebuchadnezzar's invasion put an end to the ancient Ammonite state (contrast v. 6). **1–2:** Exceptional among the prophecies against the nations in Jer., this passage focuses on Ammon's crimes against Israel, its constant effort to gain control over Israel's territory (see Ezek. 25.3). The prophecy opens with a three-part rhetorical question, a common structure in Jer. (see partially in v. 7; and 2.14; 8.19, 22). In this case, by its double use of "yarash" *(heir, settled in)* these three parts form a semantic pun. The first two components of the rhetorical question use "yarash" in the sense of "legitimate inheritance of a property by the nearest kin," a meaning known from Priestly inheritance laws, when the deceased has no sons (Num. 27.8–11). The third, climactic component of the rhetorical question uses "yarash" in its more common Deuteronomic meaning, "to take possession of a territory by force / in war" (see Deut. 2.21, 22; 11.31; 12.29; 17.14; 19.1; 26.1; Josh. 21.43). Through this double use of "yarash," the prophet harmonizes Priestly and Deuteronomic material. **2:** Israel will once again become the possessor of the land, even its legitimate inheritor, and Ammon, the dispossessed. The prophet passes judgment on Ammon as measure-for-measure, lex talionis (see 30.16). **2–3:** *Milcom,* the chief god of Ammon is written in ancient Heb, before the introduction of vowels, as "mlkm," which may also be read as "malkam," "their king"; LXX takes it as *Milcom,* the chief god of the Ammonites (1 Kings 11.5, 33), preferred also by Vg and Peshitta; see

5 I am bringing terror upon you
—declares the Lord GOD of Hosts—
From all those around you.
Every one of you shall be driven [a-]in every direction,[-a]
And none shall gather in the fugitives.
6 But afterward I will restore the fortunes of the Ammonites—
declares the LORD.

7 Concerning Edom.

Thus said the LORD of Hosts:
Is there no more wisdom in Teman?
Has counsel vanished from the prudent?
Has their wisdom gone stale?
8 Flee, turn away, sit down low,
O inhabitants of Dedan,
For I am bringing Esau's doom upon him,
The time when I deal with him.
9 [b-]If vintagers were to come upon you,
Would they leave no gleanings?
Even thieves in the night
Would destroy only for their needs![-b]
10 But it is I who have bared Esau,
Have exposed his place of concealment;
He cannot hide.
His offspring is ravaged,
His kin and his neighbors—
[c-]He is no more.[-c]
11 "Leave your orphans with me,
I will rear them;
Let your widows rely on me!"
12 For thus said the LORD: If they who rightly should not
drink of the cup must drink it, are you the one to go unpunished? You shall not go unpunished: you will have to drink!
13 For by Myself I swear—declares the LORD—Bozrah shall become a desolation, a mockery, a ruin, and a curse;[d] and all its
towns shall be ruins for all time.

14 I have received tidings from the LORD,
And an envoy is sent out among the nations:
Assemble, and move against her,
And rise up for war!

a-a Lit. "each man straight ahead."

b-b Obad. 1.5 reads: "If thieves were to come to you, / Marauders by night, / They would steal no more than they needed. / If vintagers came to you, / They would surely leave some gleanings."

c-c Some Septuagint mss. read "And there is none to say."

d Cf. note at 24.9 and 42.18.

Rashi. MT, however, prefers "their king," at the end of v. 3. **3–5:** Ammon's destruction and dispersion is described through mourning cries heard from its different cities, as in 48.1–4, 21–25. **6:** In contrast to judgment, the passage closes with consolation (see 48.47 n.).

49.7–22: Concerning Edom. The Edomites were located to the southeast of the Dead Sea and east of the Arabah or Jordan rift that extends to the Gulf of Aqabah. Gen. chs 25–35 identifies the Edomites as the descendants of Jacob's brother Esau; see v. 10. Other biblical passages suggest that the Edomites joined the Babylonian assault against Jerusalem (see Ps. 137.7; Obad. 1.10–16; Lam. 4.21–22). Following the destruction of Jerusalem, Edomites moved into the Negev region and established themselves in Hebron; these were known as the Idumeans in Hellenistic and Roman times. This passage collects several independent poems, and offers no clear historical context. Much of the prophecy is composed of prophetic proclamations from other parts of Jer. and Obad.: cf. v. 8 with 49.30; vv. 9–10 with Obad. 1.5–6; vv. 12–13 with Jer. 25.29; vv. 14–16 with Obad. 1.1–3; v. 17 with Jer. 50.13; vv. 18–21 with Jer. 50.40–46; v. 22 with Jer. 48.40, 41. **7:** *Edom* is elsewhere associated with wisdom (Job 1.3; Prov. 30.1; 31.1). **13:** *Bozrah,* the chief city and fortress of northern Edom, 13 km (8 mi) south of modern Tefileh.

15 For I will make you least among nations,
Most despised among men.
16 [a]Your horrible nature,[a]
Your arrogant heart has seduced you,
You who dwell in clefts of the rock,
Who occupy the height of the hill!
Should you nest as high as the eagle,
From there I will pull you down
—declares the LORD.

17 And Edom shall be a cause of appallment; whoever
passes by will be appalled and will hiss[b] at all its wounds. 18 It
shall be like the overthrow of Sodom and Gomorrah and their
neighbors—said the LORD: no man shall live there, no human
shall sojourn there. 19 It shall be as when a lion comes up out
of the jungle of the Jordan against a secure pasture: in a moment [c]I can harry him out of it and appoint over it anyone I
choose.[c] Then who is like Me? Who can summon Me? Who is
the shepherd that can stand up against Me? 20 Hear, then, the
plan which the LORD has devised against Edom, and what He
has purposed against the inhabitants of Teman:

Surely the shepherd boys
Shall drag them away;
Surely the pasture shall be
Aghast because of them.
21 At the sound of their downfall
The earth shall shake;
The sound of screaming
Shall be heard at the Sea of Reeds.
22 See, like an eagle he flies up,
He soars and spreads his wings against Bozrah;
And the heart of Edom's warriors in that day
Shall be like the heart of a woman in travail.

23 Concerning Damascus.

Hamath and Arpad are shamed,
For they have heard bad news.
They shake with anxiety,
Like[d] the sea which cannot rest.
24 Damascus has grown weak,
She has turned around to flee;

a-a Meaning of Heb. uncertain. *b Cf. note at 18.16.*
c-c Emendation yields "he can harry them [i.e., the sheep] out of it; and what champion could one place in charge of them?"
d So a few mss. Most mss. and editions read "In."

17–18: *The overthrow of Sodom and Gomorrah,* totally destroyed and uninhabited (Gen. 19.23–29; cf. Jer. 50.40 and Isa. 13.19).

49.23–27: Concerning Damascus. Damascus was the ancient capital of Aram (modern Syria). It was destroyed in 734–732 BCE by the Assyrians, who later employed it as an administrative center. Hence, this prophecy against Damascus in Jeremiah is puzzling. **23:** *Hamath* is modern Hama. *Arpad* was located 40 km (25 mi) north of Aleppo. Both were destroyed by the Assyrians (2 Kings 18.34; 19.13; Isa. 10.9; 36.19; 37.13).

27: The concluding statement of the oracle is drawn from Amos 1.4, 14. *Ben-hadad* is the name of several Aramean kings (1 Kings 15.18, 20; 2 Kings 13.24).

49.28–33: Concerning Kedar and Hazor, struck by Nebuchadrezzar. For the first time in this ch, the Babylonians are explicitly named (cf. 46.2, 10, 13, 24, and 26). **28:** *Kedar* refers to a coalition of Arab tribes in the north Arabian Desert. *Hazor* is not the northern Israelite city (Josh. ch. 11), but an unknown site associated with Arab tribes. Arab tribes frequently served with the Babylonians, esp. in the 7th c. when they were used to harass the Assyrians. Babylonian records note Nebuchadnezzar's campaigns against Arab tribes by 599 BCE. **29–31:** The description suits nomadic groups, attacked at their settlements, which are not walled; they are looted and will be scattered. *Terror all around* appears frequently in Jer. (e.g., 20.10). **33:** *Hazor* as *a lair of jackals* is unusual; the image usually refers to deserted walled cities, as in 9.10.

49.34–39: Concerning Elam. Though Elam is mentioned in the prophetic literature, there is no other oracle against it within the collections of oracles against the nations. Ancient Elam, with its capital Shushan (Susa), was located east of the Tigris River and Babylonia. The Assyrians sacked Susa in 646 BCE, and Elamite archers joined in Assyrian attacks against Judah (Isa. 21.2; 22.6). The Elamites were later controlled by Babylonia and Persia, and the Persian monarch Darius established his winter palace in Susa. **34:** This prophecy, dated to the early years of Zedekiah (597–586), accords with Babylonian records depicting Nebuchadnezzar's expulsion of the Elamite invaders into the Tigris region by 596 BCE. As far as is known, Elam had only indirect contact with Judah.

Trembling has seized her,
Pain and anguish have taken hold of her,
Like a woman in childbirth.
25 [a]How has the glorious city not been deserted,[a]
The citadel of my joy!
26 Assuredly, her young men shall lie fallen in her squares.
And all her warriors shall be stilled in that day
—declares the LORD of Hosts.
27 I will set fire to the wall of Damascus,
And it shall consume the fortresses of Ben-hadad.

28 Concerning Kedar and the kingdoms of Hazor, which King Nebuchadrezzar of Babylon conquered.

Thus said the LORD:
Arise, march against Kedar,
And ravage the Kedemites!
29 They will take away their tents and their flocks,
Their tent cloths and all their gear;
They shall carry off their camels,
And shall proclaim against them:
Terror all around!
30 Flee, wander far,
Sit down low, O inhabitants of Hazor
—says the LORD.
For King Nebuchadrezzar of Babylon
Has devised a plan against you
And formed a purpose against you:
31 Rise up, attack a tranquil nation
That dwells secure —says the LORD—
That has no barred gates,
That dwells alone.
32 Their camels shall become booty,
And their abundant flocks a spoil;
And I will scatter to every quarter
Those who have their hair clipped;
And from every direction I will bring
Disaster upon them —says the LORD.
33 Hazor shall become a lair of jackals,
A desolation for all time.
No man shall live there,
No human shall sojourn there.

34 The word of the LORD that came to the prophet Jeremiah concerning Elam, at the beginning of the reign of King Zedekiah of Judah:

a-a Emendation yields "How has the glorious city been deserted"; so Vulgate.

35 Thus said the LORD of Hosts: I am going to break the bow
of Elam, the mainstay of their strength. 36 And I shall bring four
winds against Elam from the four quarters of heaven, and scatter them to all those winds. There shall not be a nation to which
the fugitives from Elam do not come. 37 And I will break Elam
before their enemies, before those who seek their lives; and
I will bring disaster upon them, My flaming wrath—declares
the LORD. And I will dispatch the sword after them until I have
consumed them.

38 And I will set My throne in Elam,
And wipe out from there king and officials
—says the LORD.

39 But in the days to come I will restore the fortunes of Elam—
declares the LORD.

50

The word which the LORD spoke concerning Babylon, the land of the Chaldeans, through the prophet Jeremiah:

2 Declare among the nations, and proclaim;
Raise a standard, proclaim;
Hide nothing! Say:
Babylon is captured,
Bel[a] is shamed,
Merodach[a] is dismayed.
Her idols are shamed,
Her fetishes dismayed.
3 For a nation from the north has attacked her,
It will make her land a desolation.
No one shall dwell in it,
Both man and beast shall wander away.

4 In those days and at that time—declares the LORD—the
people of Israel together with the people of Judah shall come,
and they shall weep as they go to seek the LORD their God.
5 They shall inquire for Zion; in that direction their faces shall
turn; [b-]they shall come[-b] and attach themselves to the LORD by

a Names of the city god of Babylon. *b-b Heb. "come ye."*

36: Dividing the world into *four* compass points is borrowed from Mesopotamia, where it first developed. **38:** In setting His *throne in Elam,* God expresses sovereignty, even over this distant area; see 43.10 (and in the political arena, Ps. 89.30; Esth. 3.1). **39:** An eschatological restoration is promised to Elam, as with prophecies concerning Egypt, Moab, and Ammon.

50.1–51.58: The prophecies concerning Babylonia. This final collection of the oracles concerning the nations, originally concluding the book, intertwines prophecies about Babylonia's total destruction (e.g., 50.2–3, 8–14, 21–32) with prospects for Judah's restoration (e.g., 50.4–7, 19–20, 33–34). Unlike the prophecies that foresee the restoration of Egypt, Moab, Ammon, and Elam, there is no such hope for Babylonia. Restoration here is for Israel alone. More than any other of Jeremiah's prophecies against the nation, these against Babylonia accentuate its accountability, especially for acting against Judah and its God (see 50.14b, 15b, 17–18, 24b, 28b; 51.5–10, 24, 33–36, 49–51, 56b). The two chs combine independent poetic and prose oracles, and fragments of what might have been longer pieces. These were compiled over time, but before the bloodless fall of the Neo-Babylonian empire to the Persians by 539 BCE, which contradicts the bloody fall of Babylonia predicted throughout. **50.2–3:** *Bel* ("master," cognate to "Baal") is Marduk's (*Merodach*'s) main epithet in the Neo-Babylonian period. *Idols* (Heb "'etzev") a clay figure; see 22.28; it describes worship of other gods in Hos. 8.4. *Fetishes,* (Heb "gillulim") is unique here in Jer. but common in Ezek. (e.g., Ezek. 6.4; 8.10; 14.3). The capture of Babylonia will involve the physical shattering of its idols, which points to the powerlessness, dismay, fear, and shame of its major gods. **3:** Ironically, the *nation from the north* is again the source of threat (see 6.22–26; and repeatedly, 50.9, 41). This does not accord with the historical Persian-Elamite foe, which had come from the east. Following another convention, Babylonia's destruction is total, just as Jeremiah prophesied (9.9). **4–5:** This first reference to restoration is exceptional in phraseology and theme. *The people of Israel,* the Northern Kingdom that had been exiled almost a century and a half earlier, and *the people of Judah* gather together and walk in tears (see 31.9). They both seek their God and ask for Zion, as they reinstitute their attachment to God and to His eternal covenant. This prophecy uniquely combines several elements otherwise known separately: *attach themselves to the LORD* (Heb "nilvu 'el YHVH") is otherwise known only as a step taken by foreigners who associate themselves with the Jewish community (Isa. 14.1; 56.3, 6; Zech. 2.15); seeking God as a first step of restoration is

a covenant for all time, which shall never be forgotten. [6] My
people were lost sheep: their shepherds led them astray, they
drove them out to the mountains, they roamed from mount to
hill, they forgot their own resting place. [7] All who encountered
them devoured them; and their foes said, "We shall not be held
guilty, because they have sinned against the LORD, the true
Pasture, the Hope of their fathers—the LORD."

8 Flee from Babylon,
Leave the land of the Chaldeans,
And be like he-goats that lead the flock!
9 For see, I am rousing and leading
An assemblage of great nations against Babylon
From the lands of the north.
They shall draw up their lines against her,
There she shall be captured.
Their arrows are like those of [a]a skilled warrior[a]
Who does not turn back without hitting the mark.
10 Chaldea shall be despoiled,
All her spoilers shall be sated
—declares the LORD.

11 For you rejoiced, you exulted,
You who plundered My possession;
You stamped like a heifer treading grain,
You neighed like steeds.
12 So your mother will be utterly shamed,
She who bore you will be disgraced.
Behold the end of the nations—
Wilderness, desert, and steppe!
13 Because of the LORD's wrath she shall not be
inhabited;
She shall be utterly desolate.
Whoever passes by Babylon will be appalled
And will hiss at all her wounds.

14 Range yourselves roundabout Babylon,
All you who draw the bow;
Shoot at her, don't spare arrows,
For she has sinned against the LORD.
15 Raise a shout against her all about!
[b]She has surrendered;[b]
Her bastions have fallen,
Her walls are thrown down—
This is the LORD's vengeance.

a-a So many mss., editions, and versions; other mss. and editions read "a warrior who bereaves."

b-b Lit. "She has given her hand"; meaning of Heb. uncertain.

a Deuteronomic conception (Deut. 4.29; 30.1–10); the eternal covenant is mentioned in Jer. 32.40 (and likewise in Ezek. 37.26); the demand not to forget the covenant follows Deut. 4.23 (and 2 Kings 17.38). The eternal covenant is elsewhere characterized as unforgettable since it follows a genuine transformation or a divine guarantee of obedience (Jer. 31.31–34; 32.37–41; Ezek. 37.23; for a reversal within Jer., cf. 20.11; 23.40). **6–7:** A retrospective on the fate of God's people and their leaders, who are largely responsible for their straying, *lost sheep* with faithless *shepherds* (see 23.1–4). The epithets *the true Pasture, the Hope* [water source] *of their fathers* partake in the metaphor of shepherding in the desert of Jer. 17.13. **8–10:** The image of Israel as a *flock* ties this passage to the previous one. *He-goats that lead the flock,* perhaps Israel (Judah) as leading the exodus of other peoples (see Kimḥi and Kara). **10:** The people in Babylonia will be part of the spoil; that is why the Judeans must flee beforehand. **11–13:** Divine anger empowers total destruction (see 10.10). Similar descriptions of the amazement of onlookers at the extent of crisis are also found in 19.8 (Jerusalem) and 49.17 (Edom). **14–16:** Babylonia is to suffer a measure-for-measure, talionic judgment—it is to be besieged and devastated as it besieged and devastated others. God summons Babylonia's human enemies against her and instructs them to lay siege and fight against the city and its rural surroundings (vv. 14, 16; see 50.9). **15:** The revenge is *the LORD's vengeance* in retaliation for Babylonia's military steps against her foes, and is further described in v. 28.

Take vengeance on her,
Do to her as she has done!
16 Make an end in Babylon of sowers,
And of wielders of the sickle at harvest time.
Because of the deadly[a] sword,
Each man shall turn back to his people,
They shall flee every one to his land.

17 Israel are scattered sheep, harried by lions. First the king
of Assyria devoured them, and in the end King Nebuchadrezzar of Babylon crunched their bones. 18 Assuredly, thus said
the LORD of Hosts, the God of Israel: I will deal with the king of
Babylon and his land as I dealt with the king of Assyria. 19 And
I will lead Israel back to his pasture, and he shall graze in Carmel and Bashan, and eat his fill in the hill country of Ephraim
and in Gilead.

20 In those days and at that time
—declares the LORD—
The iniquity of Israel shall be sought,
And there shall be none;
The sins of Judah,
And none shall be found;
For I will pardon those I allow to survive.

21 Advance against her—[b]the land of Merathaim[-b]—
And against the inhabitants of Pekod;
Ruin and destroy after them to the last
—says the LORD—
Do just as I have commanded you.
22 Hark! War in the land
And vast destruction!
23 How the hammer of the whole earth
Has been hacked and shattered!
How Babylon has become
An appallment among the nations!
24 I set a snare for you, O Babylon,
And you were trapped unawares;
You were found and caught,
Because you challenged the LORD.
25 The LORD has opened His armory
And brought out the weapons of His wrath;
For that is the task
Of my Lord GOD of Hosts
In the land of the Chaldeans.

a Meaning of Heb. uncertain. *b-b Meaning of Heb. uncertain.*

17–20: Another passage centered on (northern) Israel; it is unclear if people identifying themselves as northern Israelites were living in Babylonia at this point, long after their deportation. **17–18:** In v. 6 Israel was a flock of sheep led astray by their leaders; here Israel is *scattered sheep* (Heb is singular), that is, a sheep separated from the rest of the flock and therefore easy prey for the two lions, the two major empires that conquered her: first Assyria *devoured* them, then Babylonia *crunched their bones.* Just as Assyria was destroyed (by the Babylonians in the late 7th c.), so will Babylonia, in turn, be destroyed. **19–20:** The prophecy of restoration includes the return of both the Northern and Southern Kingdoms. *Pasture:* its land, and also, according to v. 7, its God. *Carmel and Bashan, ... Ephraim and in Gilead:* These mountains were all in the Northern Kingdom prior to its destruction. Each pair consists of one mountain west of the Jordan and the other east, starting north and going south. **20:** Absence of *iniquity* and *sin* is a reversal of the judgment (see 2.22; 16.18; 30.14–15). Forgiveness here and in other consolation prophecies (31.34; 33.8; 36.3) reflects Priestly language and concepts. The LXX places the two words opening v. 21, "on the land," as the conclusion of v. 20; thus the object of forgiveness is the remnant left in the land. This disagrees with v. 19, which depicts gathering the dispersed exiles back to the land. **21–32:** God perpetrates the war against Babylonia. **23:** The prophet intensifies his cries over the destruction of Babylonia with *how,* typical in laments and dirges (2 Sam. 1.25, 27; Isa. 14.12; Jer. 9.18), also used in other prophecies against the nations in Jer. (47.7; 48.14, 39; 49.25; 51.41). The masculine of the first sentence (cities and countries are feminine) might refer specifically to the Babylonian king, the now broken hammer of all the land; see 51.20–24. **25:** One of the Bible's most graphic portrayals of God as Warrior, who has His own *armory* that includes *the weapons of His wrath* (see Isa. 13.4–6).

28–29: Among the horrors of war are the voices of those who flee, including those who flee back to Zion; they explain Babylonia's defeat in two ways: as God's revenge for His Temple (see 50.14), and as retaliation for Babylonia's presumptuous behavior against God. *Holy One of Israel* (Heb "Kedosh Yisrael") is common in Isa. (5.24; 10.20; 41.14; 55.5; 60.9, etc.), but in Jer. only here and in 51.5. **31–32:** This insolent behavior (perhaps over-confidence or disobedience; see Deut. 1.43; 17.13; 18.20; Neh. 9.10, 16, 29) becomes Babylonia's, or rather its king's, nickname: "zadon," *Insolence.* This portrayal of Babylonia builds upon the way Isaiah presents Assyria's hubris as its central sin against God (Isa. 10.5–19). Jeremiah's more common accusation concerns Babylonia's cruel rule over Judah and others, which is to be repaid by total annihilation (50.10, 14–16, 23). **33–34:** God as Judge and Advocate of His people champions His people's cause (see also 25.31; 31.11). Second Isaiah uses "Redeemer" (Heb "go'el") often as a divine epithet (e.g., Isa. 54.5, 8; cf. Jer. 31.11). **35–38:** *Sword* ("ḥerev"), repeated five times, is a synecdoche for war. The culmination of the poem in v. 38 plays on this word, describing a *drought* (Heb "ḥorev"; see translators' note *a*). The war will affect all: the *inhabitants* of Babylonia, its *officials* and *wise men,* its *diviners* (see Isa. 44.25; Jer. 48.30), its *warriors,* its *horses and chariots,* its entire mixed population, and its *treasuries.* All these will become powerless, "become women" (see 48.41; 49.22, 24; 51.30). The climax of the punishment will be a drought afflicting all of Babylonia's water sources, the mighty and dependable Tigris and Euphrates.

26 Come against her [a]from every quarter;[a]
Break open her granaries,
[a]Pile her up like heaps of grain,[a]
And destroy her, let her have no remnant!
27 [b]Destroy all[b] her bulls,
Let them go down to slaughter.
Alas for them, their day is come,
The hour of their doom!
28 Hark! fugitives are escaping
From the land of Babylon,
To tell in Zion of the vengeance of the LORD our God,
Vengeance for His Temple.

29 Summon archers against Babylon,
All who draw the bow!
Encamp against her roundabout,
Let none of her people escape.
Pay her back for her actions,
Do to her just what she has done;
For she has acted insolently against the LORD,
The Holy One of Israel.
30 Assuredly, her young men shall fall in her squares,
And all her warriors shall perish in that day
—declares the LORD.
31 I am going to deal with you, O Insolence
—declares the Lord GOD of Hosts—
For your day is come, the time when I doom you:
32 Insolence shall stumble and fall,
With none to raise her up.
I will set her cities on fire,
And it shall consume everything around her.

33 Thus said the LORD of Hosts:
The people of Israel are oppressed,
And so too the people of Judah;
All their captors held them,
They refused to let them go.
34 Their Redeemer is mighty,
His name is LORD of Hosts.
He will champion their cause—
So as to give rest to the earth,
And unrest to the inhabitants of Babylon.

35 A sword against the Chaldeans
—declares the LORD—

a-a Meaning of Heb. uncertain.
b-b Emendation yields "A sword against"; cf. vv. 35 ff.

And against the inhabitants of Babylon,
Against its officials and its wise men!
36 A sword against the diviners, that they be made fools of!
A sword against the warriors, that they be dismayed!
37 A sword against its horses and chariots,
And against all the motley crowd in its midst,
That they become like women!
A sword against its treasuries, that they be pillaged!
38 A drought[a] against its waters, that they be dried up!
For it is a land of idols;
They are besotted by their [b-]dread images.[-b]
39 Assuredly,
[b-]Wildcats and hyenas[-b] shall dwell [there],
And ostriches shall dwell there;
It shall never be settled again,
Nor inhabited throughout the ages.

40 It shall be as when God overthrew Sodom and Gomorrah and their neighbors—declares the LORD; no man shall live there, no human shall sojourn there.

41 Lo, a people comes from the northland;
A great nation and many kings are roused
From the remotest parts of the earth.
42 They grasp the bow and javelin,
They are cruel, they show no mercy;
The sound of them is like the roaring sea.
They ride upon horses,
Accoutered like a man for battle,
Against you, O Fair Babylon!
43 The king of Babylon has heard the report of them,
And his hands are weakened;
Anguish seizes him,
Pangs like a woman in childbirth.

44 It shall be as when a lion comes out of the jungle of the Jordan against a secure pasture: in a moment [c-]I can harry them out of it and appoint over it anyone I choose.[-c] Then who is like Me? Who can summon Me? Who is the shepherd that can stand up against Me? 45 Hear, then, the plan that the LORD has devised against Babylon, and has purposed against the land of Chaldea:
Surely the shepherd boys
Shall drag them away;
Surely the pasture shall be
Aghast because of them.

a Ḥoreb, *play on* ḥereb, *"sword" in preceding verses.*
b-b Meaning of Heb. uncertain. *c-c See note at* 49.19.

39–40: Similar references to *Sodom* and *Gomorrah* are in 20.16, concerning Judah, and 49.18 regarding Edom (cf. Isa. 13.19–20, regarding Babylonia). **41–43:** 6.22–23 are modified to address *Fair Babylon.* **43:** Modifying 6.24 where panic captures the entire (Judean) population, this v. depicts only the king (feminized to show his weakness) as afraid. **44–46:** An adaptation of two oracles against Edom (see 49.19–21). Surprisingly the text describes the Jordan rather than the more impressive great rivers of Babylonia, the Tigris and the Euphrates.

46 At the sound of Babylon's capture
The earth quakes,
And an outcry is heard among the nations.

51 Thus said the LORD:
See, I am rousing a destructive wind
Against Babylon and the inhabitants of Leb-kamai.[a]
2 I will send strangers[b] against Babylon, and they shall
winnow her.
And they shall strip her land bare;
They shall beset her on all sides
On the day of disaster.
3 Let[c] the archer draw his bow,
And let him stand ready in his coat of mail!
Show no pity to her young men,
Wipe out all her host!
4 Let them fall slain in the land of Chaldea,
Pierced through in her streets.

5 For Israel and Judah were not bereft[d]
Of their God the LORD of Hosts,
But their land was filled with guilt
Before the Holy One of Israel.

6 Flee from the midst of Babylon
And save your lives, each of you!
Do not perish for her iniquity;
For this is a time of vengeance for the LORD,
He will deal retribution to her.

7 Babylon was a golden cup in the LORD's hand,
It made the whole earth drunk;
The nations drank of her wine—
That is why the nations are mad.
8 Suddenly Babylon has fallen and is shattered;
Howl over her!
Get balm for her wounds:
Perhaps she can be healed.
9 We tried to cure Babylon
But she was incurable.
Let us leave her and go,
Each to his own land;
For her punishment reaches to heaven,
It is as high as the sky.

a A cipher for Kasdim, *"Chaldea."* *b Change of vocalization yields "winnowers."*
c Some Heb. mss. and ancient versions read "Let not" here and in next line.
d Lit. "widowed."

51.1–5: Other *destructive winds* are found in judgment prophecies against Judah (13.24; 18.17), and against Elam (49.36), though the Heb term used here is unique. **1:** *Leb-kamai* ("the heart of those who rise against me") is an "'atbash" for Kasdim, Chaldea, a late name for Babylonia (see translators' note *a;* so the LXX: Chaldeans); see Jer. 25.26 n.; and 51.41. **5:** *For Israel and Judah were not bereft* [lit. "widowed"; see translators' note *d*] *of their God:* The people as widower uniquely places God as wife. Thematically, the image stands for either the divine protection over His people (for a widow in need of protection, see 7.6), or for the divine Presence (opposite of the absence of the dead partner, so Tg.). **6–10:** Babylonia as a *golden cup* picks up the image of Jer. 25.15, 17, 28 (cf. 49.12). **6:** The command to *flee* from Babylonia is a saving action from total destruction (see Ezek. 21.8). This is unlike God's deliverance in Egypt, where Israel was spared the disasters that afflicted Egypt (Exod. 8.18–19; 9.4, 25–26; 10.23; 12.12–13). **8–9:** Babylonia's destruction is sudden, and with great irony passersby mourn over her and supply healing herbs and balm (see 8.22). Yet Babylonia is not redeemable.

10 The LORD has proclaimed our vindication;
Come, let us recount in Zion
The deeds of the LORD our God.

11 Polish the arrows,
Fill the quivers!
The LORD has roused the spirit of the kings of Media,
For His plan against Babylon is to destroy her.
This is the vengeance of the LORD,
Vengeance for His Temple.

12 Raise a standard against the walls of Babylon!
Set up a blockade; station watchmen;
Prepare those in ambush.
For the LORD has both planned and performed
What He decreed against the inhabitants of Babylon.

13 O you who dwell by great waters,
With vast storehouses,
Your time is come, [a]the hour of your end.[-a]
14 The LORD of Hosts has sworn by Himself:
I will fill you with men like a locust swarm,
They will raise a shout against you.

15 He made the earth by His might,
Established the world by His wisdom,
And by His understanding stretched out the skies.
16 [b]When He makes His voice heard,[-b]
There is a rumbling of waters in the skies;
He makes vapors rise from the end of the earth,
He makes lightning for the rain,
And brings forth wind from His treasuries.
17 Every man is proved dull, without knowledge;
Every goldsmith is put to shame because of the idol,
For his molten image is a deceit—
There is no breath in them.
18 They are delusion, a work of mockery;
In their hour of doom, they shall perish.
19 Not like these in the Portion of Jacob,
For it is He who formed all things;
And [Israel is] His very own tribe.
LORD of Hosts is His name.

20 You are My war club, [My] weapons of battle;
With you I clubbed nations,
With you I destroyed kingdoms;

10: The prophecy ends with a hymnic proclamation of the Judean exiles, grateful to God who saved them (see Isa. 56.1). The call to flee has now turned into a pilgrimage to Zion to tell of God's salvific deeds (see 50.28; and Ps. 105.1–5). **11–14:** The destructive wind is revealed as the kings of the Medes (see Isa. 13.17), who were the great threat for the Neo-Babylonian empire. In 550 BCE, Cyrus the Mede gained control over the entire Persian kingdom. **12:** *For the LORD has both planned and performed / What He decreed against the inhabitants of Babylon:* In Lam. 2.17 this refers to Jerusalem and Judah. **15–19:** The hymn opens a new theme: God, the Creator of the world, is supreme over idols. It is not well integrated into this context, and is a reworking of Jer. 10.12–16. Cf. Second Isaiah, e.g., Isa. ch 40.

a-a Meaning of Heb. uncertain. *b-b Lit. "At the sound of His making."*

20–24: The earlier image of Babylonia as a hammer (50.23; see Isa. 10.5–7) is reworked into Babylonia as a *war club.* The verb or noun *club* is used ten times; the *club* was the tool used to breach city walls. **21–23:** Eight pairs, each expressing completeness, cumulatively illustrate the totality of the Babylonian destruction. **24–26:** Now Babylonia itself will be *a desolation for all time.* **24:** *Before your eyes:* This prophecy (likely all others) was addressed to a Judean audience. It is unknown, however, when they were each proclaimed. **25–26:** Babylonia that was the *mountain of the destroyer* (or "the destroying mountain") is to be transformed into *a burnt-out mountain* (perhaps a volcano). Not only will it suffer this profound ecological disaster, it will end up useless, unable to supply basic building materials. **27–33:** This poem vividly portrays the capture of Babylonia by nations of the north and northeast (*Ararat, Minni, and Ashkenaz*—the Scythians, [but in later Jewish literature the term refers to Franco-Germany]), which will bring annihilation over its land. None of these prophecies was fulfilled, as Babylonia surrendered peacefully to Cyrus the Persian.

21 With you I clubbed horse and rider,
With you I clubbed chariot and driver,
22 With you I clubbed man and woman,
With you I clubbed graybeard and boy,
With you I clubbed youth and maiden;
23 With you I clubbed shepherd and flock,
With you I clubbed plowman and team,
With you I clubbed governors and prefects.
24 But I will requite Babylon and all the inhabitants
of Chaldea
For all the wicked things they did to Zion before
your eyes —declares the LORD.
25 See, I will deal with you, O mountain of the
destroyer —declares the LORD—
Destroyer of the whole earth!
I will stretch out My hand against you
And roll you down from the crags,
And make you a burnt-out mountain.
26 They shall never take from you
A cornerstone or foundation stone;
You shall be a desolation for all time
—declares the LORD.
27 Raise a standard on earth,
Sound a horn among the nations,
Appoint nations against her,
Assemble kingdoms against her—
Ararat, Minni, and Ashkenaz—
Designate a marshal against her,
Bring up horses like swarming[a] locusts!
28 Appoint nations for war against her—
The kings of Media,
Her governors and all her prefects,
And all the lands they rule!

29 Then the earth quakes and writhes,
For the LORD's purpose is fulfilled against Babylon,
To make the land of Babylon
A waste without inhabitant.
30 The warriors of Babylon stop fighting,
They sit in the strongholds,
Their might is dried up,
They become women.
Her dwellings are set afire,
Her bars are broken.
31 Runner dashes to meet runner,
Messenger to meet messenger,

a *Meaning of Heb. uncertain.*

To report to the king of Babylon
That his city is captured, from end to end.
32 The fords are captured,
And the swamp thickets[a] are consumed in fire;
And the fighting men are in panic.

33 For thus said the LORD of Hosts, the God of Israel:
Fair Babylon is like a threshing floor
Ready to be trodden;
In a little while her harvesttime will come.

34 "Nebuchadrezzar king of Babylon
Devoured me and discomfited me;
He swallowed me like a dragon,
He filled his belly with my dainties,
And set me down like an empty dish;
Then he [b]rinsed me out.[-b]
35 Let the violence done me and my kindred
Be upon Babylon,"
Says the inhabitant of Zion;
"And let my blood be upon the inhabitants of
Chaldea,"
Says Jerusalem.

36 Assuredly, thus said the LORD:
I am going to uphold your cause
And take vengeance for you;
I will dry up her sea
And make her fountain run dry.
37 Babylon shall become rubble,
A den for jackals,
An object of horror and hissing,[c]
Without inhabitant.
38 Like lions, they roar together,
They growl like lion cubs.
39 [d]When they are heated, I will set out their drink
And get them drunk, that they may become hilarious[-d]
And then sleep an endless sleep,
Never to awake —declares the LORD.
40 I will bring them down like lambs for slaughter,
Like rams and he-goats.
41 How has Sheshach[e] been captured,
The praise of the whole earth been taken!

33: The poem closes with a summary that combines two agricultural similes concerning the fall of Babylonia, as *a threshing floor ready to be trodden* and as the *harvesttime.* **34–44:** Babylonia's capture. **34–35:** A dialogue between Jerusalem and God (vv. 36–44). **36–44:** Rich with images of landscape and fauna, these vv. mention *jackals, lions, lion cubs, lambs, rams,* and *he-goats.*

a Meaning of Heb. uncertain. *b-b Meaning of Heb. uncertain.*
c See note at 18.16.
d-d Emendation yields "With poison [so Syriac] will I set out their drink / And get them drunk till they fall unconscious" (so ancient versions). *e See note at 25.26.*

44: The prophecy presents a confrontation between YHVH and *Bel,* i.e., Marduk, who is foreseen as devoid of his powers, even of his ability to protect his own city. This passage must precede the reign of Nabunaid (Nabonidus, 556–539), the last king of Babylonia, who established the god Sin as its major deity. **45–58:** Ravaging Babylonia. **45:** Direct call to God's people to leave Babylonia (see 51.6). **48:** *Heavens and earth* rejoice at Babylonia's fall, caused by plunderers or devastators ("shodedim"). In judgment prophecies against Judah, the word "shadad" is frequent (Jer. 4.13, 20, 30; 5.6; 6.26; 9.18; 10.20; 12.12; 15.8; 25.36), and it is used in oracles against other nations (47.4; 48.1, 8, 20, 32; 49.3, 10, 28). **50–51:** Another call for the exiles to leave Babylonia (so Rashi and Kimḥi). They are once again refugees, but here called to leave Babylonia, and to remember God and Jerusalem *from afar* (see Ps. 137.5–6). Remembering God from afar is part of the promise of a future regathering (see Isa. 43.6; 49.12; 60.4). **51:** The exiles' response to God's words, in which they express reproach and disgrace that foreigners, the Babylonians, entered the Temple (see Pss. 42.11; 44.16–17; 79.1–5). (The surprising plural forms, *the sacred areas of the LORD's House,* appear also in Pss. 74.8; 84.2.) **52–58:** This last passage on the fall of Babylonia responds to the disgrace it brought to Judah (v. 51; see also vv. 47–49 as a response to v. 46). God acts as *a God of requital, / He deals retribution* (v. 56, see 51.6; Ps. 137.8). **52–55:** God alone will act against its idols, and will punish Babylonia for its hubris (see 49.16; and elaborately, Isa. 14.12–20). He will leave the execution of Babylonia's destruction to those human plunderers ("shodedim"), who acting on earth, will sound like roaring waters (see v. 42, and 6.23), causing total devastation.

How has Babylon become
A horror to the nations!
42 The sea has risen over Babylon,
She is covered by its roaring waves.
43 Her towns are a desolation,
A land of desert and steppe,
A land no man lives in
And no human passes through.
44 And I will deal with Bel in Babylon,
And make him disgorge what he has swallowed,
And nations shall no more gaze on him with joy.
Even the wall of Babylon shall fall.

45 Depart from there, O My people,
Save your lives, each of you,
From the furious anger of the LORD.
46 Do not be downhearted or afraid
At the rumors heard in the land:
A rumor will come one year,
And another rumor the next year
Of violence in the land,
And of ruler against ruler.
47 Assuredly, days are coming,
When I will deal with Babylon's images;
Her whole land shall be shamed,
And all her slain shall fall in her midst.
48 Heavens and earth and all that is in them
Shall shout over Babylon;
For the ravagers shall come upon her from the north
—declares the LORD.
49 Yes, Babylon is to fall
[For] the slain of Israel,
As the slain of all the earth
Have fallen through Babylon.
50 You fugitives from the sword,
Go, don't delay!
Remember the LORD from afar,
And call Jerusalem to mind.
51 "We were shamed, we heard taunts;
Humiliation covered our faces,
When aliens entered
The sacred areas of the LORD's House."
52 Assuredly, days are coming
—declares the LORD—
When I will deal with her images,
And throughout her land the dying shall groan.

53 Though Babylon should climb to the skies,
Though she fortify her strongholds up to heaven,
The ravagers would come against her from Me
—declares the LORD.
54 Hark! an outcry from Babylon,
Great destruction from the land of the
Chaldeans.
55 For the LORD is ravaging Babylon;
He will put an end to her great din,
Whose roar is like waves of mighty waters,
Whose tumultuous noise resounds.
56 For a ravager is coming upon Babylon,
Her warriors shall be captured, their bows shall
be snapped.
For the LORD is a God of requital,
He deals retribution.
57 I will make her officials and wise men drunk,
Her governors and prefects and warriors;
And they shall sleep an endless sleep,
Never to awaken
—declares the King whose name is
LORD of Hosts.
58 Thus said the LORD of Hosts:
Babylon's broad wall shall be knocked down,
And her high gates set afire.
Peoples shall labor for naught,
And nations have wearied themselves for fire.

59 The instructions that the prophet Jeremiah gave to Seraiah son of Neriah son of Mahseiah, when the latter went with[a] King Zedekiah of Judah to Babylonia, in the fourth year of [Zedekiah's] reign. Seraiah was quartermaster.[b]
60 Jeremiah wrote down in one scroll all the disaster that would come upon Babylon, all these things that are written concerning Babylon.
61 And Jeremiah said to Seraiah, "When you get to Babylon, see that you read out all these words.
62 And say, 'O LORD, You Yourself have declared concerning this place that it shall be cut off, without inhabitant, man or beast; that it shall be a desolation for all time.'
63 And when you finish reading this scroll, tie a stone to it and hurl it into the Euphrates.
64 And say, 'Thus shall Babylon sink and never rise again, because of the disaster that I will bring upon it. And [nations] shall have wearied themselves [for fire].' "[c]

Thus far the words of Jeremiah.

a Emendation yields "at the instance of." *b Meaning of Heb. uncertain.*
c Cf. v. 58, last line.

57: Drunkenness closes this prophecy against Babylonia, drawing on the image of 25.14–29 (cf. 51.39).

51.59–64: Jeremiah's colophon to the prophecies concerning Babylonia. A symbolic action for Zedekiah's official delegation to Babylonia (593 BCE). **60–61:** Jeremiah commands Seraiah, lit. "the official of the resting place," (NJPS: *quartermaster*) who may have been from a scribal family (perhaps Baruch's brother; see 32.12), to read out loud the scroll the prophet had written, which contains all his prophecies against Babylonia. It is plausible, though not made explicit, that the parchment or papyrus scroll was similar to some version of 50.1–51.58, perhaps copied by Seraiah before leaving. **63–64:** A symbolic action, or a performative curse; the sinking of the scroll enacts the curse: *Thus shall Babylon sink and never rise again.* The passage says nothing of the circumstances that led Zedekiah to send officials to Babylonia in his fourth year, a time of his rebellious initiatives against Babylonia (chs 27–28, or 29.1–7), just as we know nothing of any other members in this delegation, its goals, and its achievements. **64b:** *Thus far the words of Jeremiah,* designates the close of this prophetic collection. This is unique in prophetic literature, though Ps. 72.20 closes a collection of psalms.

52 [a]Zedekiah was twenty-one years old when he became
king, and he reigned in Jerusalem for eleven years. His
mother's name was Hamutal, daughter of Jeremiah of Libnah.
2 He did what was displeasing to the LORD, just as Jehoiakim
had done. 3 Indeed, Jerusalem and Judah [b-]were a cause of anger for the LORD, so that[-b] He cast them out of His presence.
Zedekiah rebelled against the king of Babylon. 4 And in the
ninth year of his[c] reign, on the tenth day of the tenth month,
King Nebuchadrezzar moved against Jerusalem with his whole
army. They besieged it and built towers against it all around.
5 The city continued in a state of siege until the eleventh year
of King Zedekiah. 6 By the ninth day of the fourth month, the
famine had become acute in the city; there was no food left for
the common people.
7 Then [the wall of] the city was breached. All the soldiers
fled; they left the city by night through the gate between the
double walls, which is near the king's garden—the Chaldeans
were all around the city—and they set out for the Arabah.[d]
8 But the Chaldean troops pursued the king, and they overtook
Zedekiah in the steppes of Jericho, as his entire force left him
and scattered. 9 They captured the king and brought him before the king of Babylon at Riblah, in the region of Hamath;
and he put him on trial. 10 The king of Babylon had Zedekiah's
sons slaughtered before his eyes; he also had all the officials of
Judah slaughtered at Riblah. 11 Then the eyes of Zedekiah were
put out, and he was chained in bronze fetters. The king of Babylon brought him to Babylon and put him in prison, [where he
remained] to the day of his death.

12 On the tenth day of the fifth month—that was the nineteenth year of King Nebuchadrezzar, the king of Babylon—
Nebuzaradan, the chief of the guards, came [e-]to represent[-e]
the king of Babylon in Jerusalem. 13 He burned the House of
the LORD, the king's palace, and all the houses of Jerusalem;

a For this chapter cf. chap. 39 above and 2 Kings 24–25.
b-b Meaning of Heb. uncertain. *c I.e., Zedekiah's.* *d See note at 39.4.*
e-e Lit. "he stood before."

52.1–34: Historical summary. After the close of Jeremiah's words, this ch (largely a duplication of 2 Kings 24.18–25.30—see nn. there) provides a historiographical report on the last siege of Jerusalem until its fall (vv. 6–7); the tragic fortune of the last Davidic king of Judah, his descendants and his officials (vv. 8–11); the destruction, including the burning of the Temple, the palace, and the entire city (vv. 12–14); the fate of the exiles, as opposed to the poorest people who remained (vv. 15–16). The description continues with the looting of the Temple's bronze vessels (vv. 17–23); the capture, exile, and execution of the high priests and other officials in Riblah (vv. 24–27); and closes with this summary: "Thus Judah was exiled from its land" (v. 27). As in 2 Kings ch 25, the description continues with two separate appendices, but unlike its source does not mention those who remained behind, containing instead a list of the three deportations and the numbers of the deportees (vv. 28–30, though lacking in the LXX). The closing passage, similar to 2 Kings ch 25, tells of Jehoiachin's release from jail and his personal good fortune till his death (52.31–34). Jeremiah is not mentioned at all, and this description is theologically silent, illustrating the catastrophe in the human plane only. The exceptionally detailed description (shared by 2 Kings ch 25 and Jer. ch 52) seems to cover over the historian's inability to cope with the theological crisis these events raised. This ch was not part of the Jeremian-Judean compilation of the prophecies, but rather part of the Babylonian editorial Deuteronomistic framework given to the book, completed before Babylonia's conquest by Cyrus (539 BCE). It was copied here from (some form of) Kings to show that Jeremiah was a true prophet, whose prophecies concerning the destruction were fulfilled. **1–3:** See 2 Kings 24.18–25.2, which likewise suggest that Babylonia's actions against Judah reflect God's justified divine judgment against Judah for its religious-cultic disobedience. Only here in this entire ch is God mentioned. **4–11:** As in 2 Kings 25.1–7 (but differing from Jer. chs 27–29), the historiographer jumps directly to Zedekiah's ninth year (588 BCE), to the Babylonian siege, dated to the tenth of the tenth month, Tevet (Zech. 8.19); such selectivity typifies the biblical historians. **6:** By the ninth day of the fourth month (Tamuz) the city walls were breached (so also 39.2). *B. Taʿan.* 28b notes a fast on the seventeenth of Tamuz, which accords with Titus' breach of the walls of the Second Temple. The list of the four fasts in Zech. 8.19 does not specify precise dates within each of the four months. **11:** The *prison* is not mentioned in 2 Kings 25.7 or Jer. 39.7. The LXX suggests that Zedekiah was in the millhouse, namely he underwent forced labor (see Lam. 5.13; Judg. 16.21). **12–16:** *The tenth day of the fifth month* seems to correct the sequence suggested by 2 Kings 25.3, 8; cf. *b. Taʿan.* 29a

he burned down the house of [a-]every notable person.[-a] [14]The entire Chaldean force that was with the chief of the guards tore down all the walls of Jerusalem on every side. [15]The remnant of the people left in the city, the defectors who had gone over to the king of Babylon, and what remained of the craftsmen[b] were taken into exile by Nebuzaradan, the chief of the guards. But some of the poorest elements of the population—[16]some of the poorest in the land—were left by Nebuzaradan, the chief of the guards, to be vine-dressers and field hands.

[17]The Chaldeans broke up the bronze columns of the House of the LORD, the stands, and the bronze tank that was in the House of the LORD; and they carried all the bronze away to Babylon. [18]They also took the pails, scrapers, snuffers, sprinkling bowls, ladles, and all the other bronze vessels used in the service. [19]The chief of the guards took whatever was of gold and whatever was of silver: basins, fire pans, sprinkling bowls, pails, lampstands, ladles, and jars. [20]The two columns, the one tank and the twelve bronze oxen which supported it, and the stands, which King Solomon had provided for the House of the LORD—all these objects contained bronze beyond weighing. [21]As for the columns, each was eighteen cubits high and twelve cubits in circumference; it was hollow, and [the metal] was four fingers thick. [22]It had a bronze capital above it; the height of each capital was five cubits, and there was a meshwork [decorated] with pomegranates about the capital, all made of bronze; and so for the second column, also with pomegranates. [23]There were ninety-six pomegranates [a-]facing outward;[-a] all the pomegranates around the meshwork amounted to one hundred.

[24]The chief of the guards also took Seraiah the chief priest and Zephaniah, the deputy priest, and the three guardians of the threshold. [25]And from the city he took a eunuch who was in command of the soldiers; seven royal privy councilors, who were present in the city; the scribe of the army commander, who was in charge of mustering the people of the land; and sixty of the common people who were inside the city. [26]Nebuzaradan, the chief of the guards, took them and brought them to the king of Babylon at Riblah. [27]The king of Babylon had them struck down and put to death at Riblah, in the region of Hamath.

Thus Judah was exiled from its land. [28]This is the number of those whom Nebuchadrezzar exiled in the seventh year: 3,023 Judeans. [29]In the eighteenth year of Nebuchadrezzar, 832 persons [were exiled] from Jerusalem. [30]And in the twenty-third year of Nebuchadrezzar, Nebuzaradan, the chief of the guards, exiled 745 Judeans. The total amounted to 4,600 persons.

a-a Meaning of Heb. uncertain.

b Apparently after the deportation of 2 Kings 24.14; meaning of Heb. uncertain.

that reconciles these different dates. **15–16:** See 2 Kings 24.14. The *poorest* in v. 16 contrasts to the prestigious Babylonian deportees of 597 (2 Kings 24.14). **27:** *Thus Judah was exiled from its land,* from 2 Kings 25.21 (lacking in the LXX of Jer.), was the original ending of one form of Kings. Following this statement, 2 Kings ch 25 appends a passage on the fortune of the remnant (vv. 22–26), while Jer. ch 52 adds different material. **28–30:** *This is the number of those whom Nebuchadrezzar exiled* begins an archival list of three deportations assigned by the regnal years of the Babylonian king (597, 586, 582 BCE) and specifying numbers of deportees *(3,023, 832, 745),* totalling *4,600.* These numbers are significantly lower than the Jehoiachin exile (597 BCE) that is described in 2 Kings 24.14, 16 through the round numbers of 10,000, 7,000 and 1,000. The numbers listed here for 586 seem too low to reflect the extent of that exile.

31–34: See 2 Kings 25.27–30 nn. **31–32:** These vv. contrast Jehoiachin's fortune ("diber 'itto tovim," *He spoke kindly to him)* with that of Zedekiah, with whom the Babylonian king "diber 'itto mishpatim," "and he spoke with [NJPS: put] him on trial," v. 9. **33–34:** Perhaps in 2 Kings these concluding vv. are meant to provide some hope (see 2 Kings 25.30 n.), but in Jeremiah, who did not see any hope for Jehoiachin or his descendants (Jer. 22.24–30), they merely conclude an era.

31 In the thirty-seventh year of the exile of King Jehoiachin of
Judah, on the twenty-fifth day of the twelfth month, King Evil-
merodach of Babylon, in the year he became king, [a]took note
of[a] King Jehoiachin of Judah and released him from prison.
32 He spoke kindly to him, and gave him a throne above those
of other kings who were with him in Babylon. 33 He removed
his prison garments and [Jehoiachin] ate regularly in his presence the rest of his life. 34 A regular allotment of food was given
him by order of the king of Babylon, an allotment for each day,
to the day of his death—all the days of his life.

a-a Lit. "raised the head of."

יחזקאל

Ezekiel

THE PROPHETIC BOOK OF EZEKIEL spans a critical twenty-two year period in Jewish history: from 593 BCE, the fifth year of the exile of King Jehoiachin, to 571 BCE, twenty-seven years after Jehoiachin was exiled and fifteen years after the destruction of the First Temple. Two unprecedented circumstances confronted the Judeans: the coexistence of two separate communities, one in Judah and the other in Babylonia, each with its distinct identity; and the destruction of the Temple and the exile, which challenged the exiles to preserve their national identity outside the land of Israel, without a Temple, its sacrificial worship and the leadership of the priests, and without a Davidic king.

Ezekiel's oracles comprise the sole indisputable biblical evidence for prophecy delivered in Babylonia after the destruction of the Temple and before the proclamation of Cyrus in the restoration era (538 BCE). Although other biblical passages—from Jeremiah, Lamentations, Isaiah chs 40–66, and maybe even Joel and Obadiah—relate to the period of exile (586–538 BCE), Ezekiel differs from them in one major respect: they speak about the events of the destruction from within the land of Israel, while Ezekiel delivered his prophecies in the Babylonian exile. Ezekiel's response from Babylonia to events in the land of Israel exhibits a unique, organized worldview, making this prophetic book a significant touchstone for comprehending this crisis and its ramifications for the shaping of Jewish identity in exile to the present.

Ezekiel stands out from other prophetic books in its chronological organization. It has three main divisions: chs 1–24, which predate the destruction; chs 33–48, which postdate the destruction; and chs 25–32, a topically but not chronologically ordered collection of oracles in the middle of the book. Within each division, much of the material is also arranged chronologically. A broad summary of the topics covered in each division is:

I. Predestruction oracles (chs 1–24)
   A. Vision of the divine chariot and the journeys of the divine Presence (1.1–28)
   B. Description of Ezekiel's task and prophetic mission (2.1–3.21)
   C. Symbolic acts and their interpretation (3.22–5.17)
   D. Sins of the people that caused the destruction (6.1–7.27)
   E. Acts of the people in the Temple (8.1–18)
   F. Departure of the divine Presence from the Temple (9.1–11.25)
   G. Two symbolic actions concerning the exile (12.1–20)
   H. Prophecy and prophets (12.21–14.11)
   I. Oracle concerning individual righteousness (14.12–23)
   J. The vine parable (15.1–8)
   K. The allegory of Jerusalem as God's adulterous wife (16.1–63)
   L. The allegory of the eagles, the vine, and the cedar (17.1–24)

M. Individual responsibility and reward (18.1–32)
N. End of the Judean monarchy (19.1–14)
O. Destruction of Judah and Jerusalem (20.1–24.27)

II. Oracles concerning the nations (chs 25–32)
A. Oracles condemning Israel's neighbors: Ammon, Moab, Edom, Philistia (25.1–17)
B. Oracles against Tyre (26.1–28.26)
C. Oracles against Egypt (29.1–32.32)

III. Postdestruction oracles (chs 33–48)
A. Restoration Prophecies (chs 33–39)
1. Response to the destruction of the Temple (33.1–33)
2. The shepherds of Israel (34.1–31)
3. Divine preference for Israel over Edom and the purification of the people (35.1–36.38)
4. Vision of the dry bones and the future of the kingdom of Israel (37.1–28)
5. Vision of the eschatological war with Gog from the land of Magog (38.1–39.29)
B. The vision of the future Temple (chs 40–48)
1. Vision of the future Temple (40.1–43.27)
2. Temple functionaries and sacrificial rites (44.1–46.24)
3. A stream that emerges from the Temple; the division of the land (47.1–48.35)

Because the central themes of the Temple, acts of the leadership, sins of the people, and divine theophanies appear in both the predestruction and postdestruction oracles (1.3, 12–15, 22–24; 8.2–3; 10.11, 22–23; 40.1, 2; 43.1–5), Ezekiel's oracles merit both sequential and topical study.

Historical Background

EZEKIEL IS NOT MENTIONED elsewhere in the Bible, though 2 Kings 24.10–17 (and 2 Chron. 36.9–10 and Jer. 27.19–20, 29) offers important background for understanding the book's historical context. In 597 BCE King Nebuchadnezzar of Babylonia exiled the Judean elite; Ezekiel son of Buzi, priest and prophet, was among these exiles. The centrality of this event for Ezekiel is clear from the date formulas in the book, all of which relate to the exile of Jehoiachin, including the oracle prophesying the destruction of the Temple and those uttered after its destruction. This exile of the king, royal family, warriors, and artisans and the emptying of the Temple and royal treasuries undermined the political and economic status of the Judeans.

The exile by King Nebuchadnezzar of King Jehoiachin and the appointment of Zedekiah in his place demanded Judean recognition of Babylonian control over their country. These administrative measures were, for the purpose of such recognition, as important as the destruction of the Temple eleven years later. The final administrative fait accompli, which left the Judeans with no official leadership, came after the murder of the non-Davidic Babylonian appointee Gedaliah, likely several years after Jerusalem's destruction and the exile of some of the remaining population to Egypt. As long as the Temple remained standing, the residents of Judah took the view that the situation was neither hopeless nor final. Past events, mainly Sennacherib's failed campaign against Jerusalem in 701, as reflected in Isaiah ch 37, still reverberated in their memory: "Assuredly, thus said the LORD concerning the king of Assyria: He shall not enter this city; / He shall not shoot an arrow at it, / Or advance upon it with a shield, / Or pile up a siegemound against it. / He shall go back / By the way he came, / He shall not enter this city / —declares the LORD; / I will protect and save this city for My sake / And for the sake of My servant David" (vv. 33–35). The expectation of a miraculous divine salvation in the last moments of the siege, alongside the confidence that the Temple would stand forever, were deeply engraved in Judean consciousness.

Theological Worldview

EZEKIEL'S PROPHECIES WERE DELIVERED to the exiles who accompanied Jehoiachin to Babylonia. The predestruction oracles aimed to inform the people that God had departed the Jerusalem Temple; this is the underlying purpose of Ezekiel's description of the divine chariot and the journeys of the divine Presence outside the Temple (mainly ch 1 and chs 10–11). Moreover, Ezekiel stresses that the physical destruction of the Temple was simply a matter of time since Jerusalem has already been defiled, and therefore the divine Presence (Heb *kavod*) has already departed the city (1.28–3.15; 24.15–27). Because he expected that his tidings would not be accepted, the prophet's main function is to be a "watchman" (3.17–21; 33.1–9) rather than to convince the nation to repent. In addition to his oracles to those who enter his house (8.1; 14.1; 20.1), Ezekiel's symbolic acts (primarily chs 4–5) underscore this message, which culminates in a description of the sins of the people and the destruction of the city (primarily chs 8–11; 16; 23).

The primary messages of Ezekiel's oracles of rage, from the vision in the valley (3.22) until the escapee reached the prophet with word of the fall of Jerusalem (33.21) are the destruction of the Temple, Jerusalem, and Judah. The book suggests that at the beginning of his prophetic career, God commanded Ezekiel to shut himself up in his house, as if bound with cords, and to be silent until released; perhaps this means that other than uttering prophetic oracles, Ezekiel was silent. In this speechlessness, which passed with the destruction of Jerusalem, the prophet served as an exemplary model for the people (24.27; 33.22). Ezekiel equates the abominations of Judah, the destruction of the Temple, and the exile with the status of Jerusalem in the past and in the present; Jerusalem is both an independent entity, the city of the Temple, and a representation, or stand-in, for all of Judah. Like other prophets, Ezekiel compares Judah to the bride of God's youth, who has prostituted herself (see esp. chs 16 and 23).

The catastrophic destruction of the Temple and the exile of the people sparked additional questions: What is the view of individual reward (as opposed to the national guilt) (chs 14; 18; 33)? What is the desirable attitude toward Babylonia (ch 17)? What is the status of the covenant between God and Israel after it has been broken by Israel and the Temple has been destroyed (mainly chs 20; 36)? The prophetic reply to these questions includes the oracles against the nations (chs 25–32), and lays the foundation for understanding Ezekiel's view of the future redemption of Israel (chs 34–39), which includes many of the best-known chs of the book. These encompass the divine promise to restore the people to their land, purification of the people and flowering of their wasteland (ch 36), the vision of the dry bones (ch 37), and the chs describing the war of Gog from the land of Magog (chs 38–39). The book concludes with the vision of the future Temple with its rich detail, including its dimensions, the number of sacrifices, the division of the land, and that a stream that will issue forth from within the Temple (chs 40–48).

The theme of the book is holiness: of the people of Israel, the land of Israel, the Temple, the Sabbath, and the divine name. It was the people's task to preserve their sanctity, but, according to Ezekiel the sins of the people, primarily idolatry, throughout their history, have desecrated the people, the Temple, and the divine name, and have ritually defiled the city of Jerusalem, here termed "the city of blood" (22.2 ["bloodshed"]; 24.6, 9). In order to attain to their sanctity, the people must be purified and all impurity must be removed from the land upon their return, the Temple must be built according to an entirely new model, and only after the ingathering of the people in their land will the divine name be sanctified.

Nowhere in the book of Ezekiel do we find a description of an ideal past, a time when Israel preserved its sanctity or purity. For Ezekiel, from the moment that Israel became a nation in Egypt to his day, the period of the destruction of the First Temple, the people failed to meet divine demands, thus they were never holy or pure. Additionally, in contrast to other prophets, for Ezekiel the future restoration is entirely divorced from the people's behavior or repentance, and is instead an act of divine grace, where God has become "concerned for My holy name, which the House of Israel have caused to be profaned among the nations to which they have come" (36.21).

Literary Style

EZEKIEL USES A RICH, evocative and elegant prose style, incorporating parables and allegories to convey his prophetic message. The boundary between the divine message to the prophet and the associated concrete reality is often unclear, blurring the distinction between deed and vision, and between parable and message. This is seen in the description of the prophet's silence (3.26–27), in his many symbolic acts (4.1–6, 9–12; chs 21; 24; 27), and in his metaphorical language, with its mixture of image and reality (chs 15; 16; 19; among others).

In addition, Ezekiel's style is penetratingly harsh: the Heb expressions for "spare," "have pity," "assuage" appear only in strongly negative contexts (5.11–13). Ezekiel unhesitatingly accuses the leadership and the people of sin, and has no compunctions about criticizing their most sacred symbols, namely the Temple and Jerusalem. In none of the oracles does God take pity, have mercy on, comfort, or forgive his people, thereby underscoring the irreversible, singular reality of the destruction of the Temple. At times, Ezekiel uses emphatic repetition to highlight his message; for example, in ch 7 in speaking of the impending destruction, the words "doom" and "coming" recur repeatedly, along with the phrases "the day is near," "very soon," and "the day has arrived." Ezekiel's rich language contains many unique words and also employs highly developed metaphor, comparing the people to prostitutes, and its leaders to shepherds, and a grapevine.

Relationship to Other Biblical Texts

TORAH: THE INFLUENCE of both Ezekiel's priestly background and the Priestly sources are in evidence throughout the book and Ezekiel has been linked, linguistically and topically, to Leviticus, chs 17–26 in particular. Some linguistic links may suggest dependence on Deuteronomy, but these are less definitive. Ezekiel's oracles also contain many allusions to Torah traditions, including the story of the Garden of Eden (chs 28; 31; 47); Noah (ch 14, alongside Daniel and Job); Abraham, as the father of the nation (ch 33); the sin of the Sodomites (ch 16); and the exodus from Egypt (ch 20).

PROPHETS: Although there are many linguistic parallels between Ezekiel's language and that of Isaiah, Hosea, Joel, Amos, and Zephaniah, it is difficult to determine the direction of the influence. Ezekiel shows some affinities to his contemporary Jeremiah (e.g., Jer. 31.29 and Ezek. 18.2, which treat the question of divine recompense), although the two use very different language, contain dissimilar descriptions of the future consolation and restoration, and a different attitude toward those who remain in the land of Israel after the destruction. Some of these differences may perhaps be attributed to their target audiences: Jeremiah was speaking to those remaining in the land of Israel, who witnessed the horrors of the destruction, while Ezekiel was addressing the Babylonian exiles far from the land of Israel, whose culture has been influenced by the local Babylonian one. Ezekiel's links to the local culture are discernible in the Akkadian loanwords interspersed in his oracles, in the description of the rite of divination by liver (21.16), a well-known Babylonian rite, and other connections.

The Importance of Ezekiel within Judaism

FOUR PROPHECIES IN THE BOOK of Ezekiel have evoked special interest throughout the generations. The first is referred to as the vision of the "divine chariot," even though the word chariot does not appear in this divine theophany (ch 1). Later designated *maʿaseh merkabah,* "the episode of the chariot," it achieved prominence because the Rabbis prohibited a person to study it alone (*y. Ḥag.* 13a). This prohibition seems to have aroused curiosity among many who took an interest in the description of the divine figure. In addition, the Rabbis pointed to this ch as signifying the first step in the departure of the divine Presence from the Temple in "ten stages" (*Lam. Rab., petiḥta* 15; *b. Rosh Hash.* 31a). At a later date, the phrase *maʿaseh merkabah* came to connote more generally mystical doctrines or philosophical literature treating God.

The second pericope is the "vision of the dry bones," as Ezek. 37.1–14 is usually designated. Linked in rabbinic literature to an actual description of the future resurrection of the people, as in "The dead whom Ezekiel revived went up to Palestine" (*b. Sanh.* 92b), this prophecy, which remained a metatemporal oracle in Jewish awareness, has been quoted throughout the generations. Thus, for example, its echoes are found in the *Kuzari* (2:34), but also in modern Zionist poetry.

The third prophecy is the "Gog and Magog oracles" (chs 38–39). Maimonides points to this war as marking the beginning of the messianic age (*Code: Book of Judges,* "Laws of Kings and Their Wars," 12:2). Accordingly, there is in Jewish consciousness an eternal aspiration that the words of this prophecy will be realized and the phrase "Gog and Magog" is commonly used to refer to the culminating battle of the eschatological age.

Finally, Ezekiel is the sole prophet to impart laws to the people, including the regulations governing the sacrificial rites in his vision of the future Temple, priestly laws, and others. In some instances, these laws contradict their Torah parallels. The Babylonian Talmud attributes to these contradictions a rabbinic attempt to suppress the book of Ezekiel (*b. Menaḥ.* 45a; *b. Shab.* 13b; *b. Ḥag.* 13a), even stating "this ... will be interpreted by Elijah in the future."

The Relationship between the Prophet and the Book

STARTING IN THE 18TH CENTURY, biblical scholars questioned the literary unity of the book of Ezekiel from the perspective of language, sequence, time, and place of composition. Some proposed that chs 40–48, the vision of the new Temple, were not written by Ezekiel and were a later addition; others argued that the oracles against the nations were not authored by Ezekiel. Most scholars currently recognize the unity of the book but are divided as to the time of its composition. Some propose that the book was composed in the Persian period or later, after Ezekiel putatively lived. As opposed to the books of Isaiah and Jeremiah, the prevailing consensus is that the book of Ezekiel displays unity in language and in the ordering of its pericopes and that none of its parts should be seen as foreign to the book. In the absence of more precise data, we can surmise that Ezekiel, or perhaps his disciples, recorded his oracles, and that those preserved in the book of Ezekiel largely reflect his words. (1.2 was added by a redactor who sought to establish the prophet's name and location, and this may not have been the only addition.) The notion that the book achieved its final form after Ezekiel lived may also be reflected in the rabbinic dictum that "the Men of the Great Assembly [a group who according to the Rabbis functioned in the period of the return and beyond] wrote Ezekiel" (*b. B. Bat.* 15a).

[TOVA GANZEL]

1 In the thirtieth year,[a] on the fifth day of the fourth month,
when I was in the community of exiles by the Chebar Canal, the heavens opened and I saw visions of God. 2 On the fifth
day of the month—it was the fifth year of the exile of King Jehoiachin— 3 the word of the LORD came to the priest Ezekiel
son of Buzi, by the Chebar Canal, in the land of the Chaldeans.
And the hand of the LORD came upon him there.
4 I looked, and lo, a stormy wind came sweeping out of the
north—a huge cloud and flashing fire, surrounded by a radiance; and in the center of it, in the center of the fire, a gleam
as of amber. 5 In the center of it were also the figures of four
creatures. And this was their appearance:
They had the figures of human beings. 6 However, each had
four faces, and each of them had four wings; 7 the legs of each
were [fused into] a single rigid leg, and the feet of each were

a We do not know the 30th of what.

1.1–3: Time, place and date of the prophecy of Ezekiel. The book begins with a date formula, which places the prophet's oracles *in the thirtieth year, on the fifth day of the fourth month,* i.e., 5 Tammuz, 593 BCE (see 1.1–3 n.). The introduction includes a series of five narratives in 1.1–28a; 1.28b–3.21; 3.22–5.17; 6.1–14; 7.1–27, each of which begins with a version of God addressing Ezekiel. These narrate his initial prophetic experiences in which God commissioned him to speak as a prophet. **1:** *The thirtieth year:* The reference point is not provided. It may refer to the thirtieth year after Josiah's reform (622 BCE), or as *Seder 'Olam Rab.*, followed by Rashi, has suggested, to thirty years since the previous Jubilee, or to Ezekiel's age at the time of his commissioning, though there are no parallel examples to any of these proposals. The dated oracles of the book extend from the fifth (1.2) to the twenty-seventh year of the exile (29.17) *The fifth day of the fourth month* would be 5 Tammuz, in June. The river *Chebar* is a canal known in Akkadian sources as "nar Kabari" referred to in the 5th c. BCE Murashu family archives; it passes next to the city of Nippur, southeast of the city of Babylon. *The heavens opened and I saw visions of God.* The opening of the heavens to see a divine vision is found only here. **2:** *On the fifth day of the month—it was the fifth year of the exile of King Jehoiachin,* 593 BCE. Jehoiachin was exiled to Babylonia in 597 at the age of eighteen after only three months on the throne (2 Kings 24.8–17; cf. 2 Chron. 36.9–10). Throughout the book Ezekiel dates his oracles to the exile of Jehoiachin, whom many viewed as the last legitimate Davidic king. **3:** The formula, *the word of the LORD came to the priest Ezekiel,* is based on the typical formula for introducing prophetic oracles (see 1 Sam. 15.10; 1 Kings 6.11; Jer. 1.4; Hos. 1.1), and is the first of two occurrences (the other is in 24.24) not written in the first person. *The land of the Chaldeans:* Babylonia, so named after the Chaldeans, a tribe related to the Arameans that had become especially prominent in Babylonia by this time.

1.4–28a: Vision of the divine chariot and the journeys of the divine Presence. Although commonly described as the divine chariot, the word "chariot" is absent here. The prophet describes God's throne, anchored by four mythological creatures, one on each side, that is set upon wheels and moves in all directions. The prophet views this vision from the bottom to the top, as his eyes move upward to where God would be seated. The imagery of God's throne chariot (see 1 Chron. 28.18) is based on the Holy of Holies in the Tabernacle and Temple where the Ark of the Covenant was kept under the cherubim (Exod. 25.10–22; 37.1–9; 1 Kings 6.19–28). For examples of the frequent biblical references to "the Ark of the Covenant of the LORD of Hosts enthroned on the Cherubim" see 1 Sam. 4.4; 2 Sam. 6.2; 1 Chron. 13.6. Cherubim are composite creatures combining features of different types of animals and human beings, e.g., the body of a lion or a bull, the wings of an eagle, and the head of a human being. Similar creatures frequently appear in ancient Near Eastern art and architecture as the guardians of royal thrones, temples, and city gates, and Ezekiel, who lived in Babylonia, probably saw them. Ezek. 10.1 later refers to the four creatures of this vision as cherubim. **4:** *Wind, cloud,* and *fire* appear frequently in depictions of theophany or divine appearance in the world (Exod. ch 19; 1 Kings ch 19). The imagery of radiance reflects the gleaming gold with which the Ark and other Temple implements were overlaid (Exod. 25.10–22; 37.1–9) as well as a type of halo that was imagined to surround Mesopotamian deities. The exact meaning of the term "ḥashmal," translated here as *a gleam as of amber,* is uncertain. It may be derived from Akkadian or Egyptian terms for polished bronze. Talmudic tradition (*b. Ḥag.* 13.1–2) identifies it as a name for a combination of terms "ḥayot" ("living creatures"), "'esh" ("fire"), or a combination of "ḥashot" ("silent") and "mimalelot" ("speaking"). The modern Heb "ḥashmal," "electricity," derives from this passage. **5:** *Figures of four creatures* are seen vaguely. **7:** *Like:* The use of similes throughout this vision emphasizes that the prophet can only attempt to describe the divine Presence indirectly, as the limits of human understanding permit. This passage thus takes a middle position concerning the corporeality of God's representation; some texts describe God as having a human body (Exod. 24.10–11; Dan. 7.9), while others insist otherwise (Deut. 4.15).

like a single calf's hoof;[a] and their sparkle[b] was like the luster of burnished bronze. [8] They had human hands below their wings. The four of them had their faces and their wings on their four sides. [9] Each one's wings touched those of the other. They did not turn when they moved; each could move in the direction of any of its faces.

[10] Each of them had a human face [at the front]; each of the four had the face of a lion on the right; each of the four had the face of an ox on the left; and each of the four had the face of an eagle [at the back]. [11] Such were their faces. As for their wings, they were separated: above, each had two touching those of the others, while the other two covered its body. [12] And each could move in the direction of any of its faces; they went wherever the spirit impelled them to go, without turning when they moved.

[13] Such then was the appearance of the creatures. With them was something that looked like burning coals of fire. This fire, suggestive of torches, kept moving about among the creatures; the fire had a radiance, and lightning issued from the fire. [14][c-]Dashing to and fro [among] the creatures was something that looked like flares.[-c]

[15] As I gazed on the creatures, I saw one wheel on the ground next to each of the four-faced creatures. [16] As for the appearance and structure of the wheels, they gleamed like beryl. All four had the same form; the appearance and structure of each was as of two wheels cutting through each other. [17] And when they moved, each could move in the direction of any of its four quarters; they did not veer when they moved. [18] Their rims were tall and frightening, for the rims of all four were covered all over with eyes. [19] And when the creatures moved forward, the wheels moved at their sides; and when the creatures were borne above the earth, the wheels were borne too. [20] Wherever the spirit impelled them to go, they went—wherever the spirit impelled them—and the wheels were borne alongside them; for the spirit of the creatures was in the wheels. [21] When those moved, these moved; and when those stood still, these stood still; and when those were borne above the earth, the wheels were borne alongside them—for the spirit of the creatures was in the wheels.

[22] Above the heads of the creatures was a form: an expanse, with an awe-inspiring gleam as of crystal, was spread out above their heads. [23] Under the expanse, each had one pair of wings extended toward those of the others; and each had another pair covering its body. [24] When they moved, I could hear the sound of their wings like the sound of mighty waters, like the sound of Shaddai,[d] a tumult like the din of an army. When they

a I.e., cleft in front. *b Or "plumage."* *c-c Meaning of Heb. uncertain.*
d Traditionally "the Almighty"; see Gen. 17.1.

10: The four faces are *human, lion, ox,* and *eagle.* **13–14:** The *burning coals of fire* are constantly moving. **15–21:** The *wheels* depict divine motion in all four directions. **16:** The *wheels cutting through each other* represent either a wheel with a hub or wheels that could travel in any direction. **22:** *An expanse, with an awe-inspiring gleam as of crystal:* The priest Ezekiel is drawing on the Priestly Gen. 1.6–8, which uses the same term, "rakiʿa" (*expanse,* "firmament"), to depict the distinction between heaven and earth. **24:** *The sound of mighty waters* portrays the vision as both auditory and visual.

stood still, they would let their wings droop. 25 [a]From above the expanse over their heads came a sound.[a] When they stood still, they would let their wings droop.

26 Above the expanse over their heads was the semblance of a throne, in appearance like sapphire; and on top, upon this semblance of a throne, there was the semblance of a human form. 27 From what appeared as his loins up, I saw a gleam as of amber—[a]what looked like a fire encased in a frame;[a] and from what appeared as his loins down, I saw what looked like fire. There was a radiance all about him. 28 Like the appearance of the bow which shines in the clouds on a day of rain, such was the appearance of the surrounding radiance. That was the appearance of the semblance of the Presence of the LORD. When I beheld it, I flung myself down on my face. And I heard the voice of someone speaking.

2 And He said to me, "O mortal, stand up on your feet that I may speak to you." 2 As He spoke to me, a spirit entered into me and set me upon my feet; and I heard what was being spoken to me. 3 He said to me, "O mortal, I am sending you to the people of Israel, that nation of rebels, who have rebelled against Me.—They as well as their fathers have defied Me to this very day; 4 for the sons are brazen of face and stubborn of heart. I send you to them, and you shall say to them: 'Thus said the Lord GOD'— 5 whether they listen or not, for they are a rebellious breed—that they may know that there was a prophet among them.

6 "And you, mortal, do not fear them and do not fear their words, though thistles and thorns [b]press against[b] you, and you sit upon scorpions. Do not be afraid of their words and do not be dismayed by them, though they are a rebellious breed; 7 but speak My words to them, whether they listen or not, for they are rebellious.

8 "And you, mortal, heed what I say to you: Do not be rebellious like that rebellious breed. Open your mouth and eat what I am giving you." 9 As I looked, there was a hand stretched out to me, holding a written scroll. 10 He unrolled it before me, and it was inscribed on both the front and the back; on it were written lamentations, dirges, and woes.

a-a Meaning of Heb. uncertain. *b-b Lit. "are with."*

26: *Sapphire* (possibly lapis lazuli), see Exod. 24.10, which employs the imagery of blue sapphire or lapis to depict the pavement under God's feet, which humans see as the sky. **27:** *Gleam as of amber* and *fire* convey the power of the divine Presence. **28a:** The rainbow here may also symbolize God's covenant with creation (Gen. 9.8–17). *The Presence of the LORD,* a Priestly term for God's glory (Exod. 16.6–7; 40.34–38), the manner in which God is revealed on the earth.

1.28b–3.21: Description of Ezekiel's task and prophetic mission. **1.28b:** *I flung myself down ... the voice of someone speaking:* Ezekiel, in a sign of reverence and fear, bows very low before God. **2.1–2:** *And He said to me, "O mortal, stand up on your feet that I may speak to you":* God addresses Ezekiel as "mortal," lit. "son of Adam/man" meaning "human being," ninety-three times in the book. "Son of man" conveys Ezekiel's mortal status in contrast to God. This message is further demonstrated in these vv., by emphasizing four times, in these three vv. (1.28b–2.2), that he hears a human voice. **3–7:** The charge of Israel's rebellion against God is a constant theme throughout the prophets and is the reason for Israel's exile and the destruction of the Temple as acts of divine punishment. This common theme is mixed with phrases unique to Ezekiel, including *that nation of rebels, who have rebelled against Me; brazen of face and stubborn; rebellious breed.* These phrases used here to address the nation (rebels, rebelled) are repeated in the prophecies of destruction, unlike the prophecies of restoration where the nation is called "people of Israel." **3:** The reference to *that nation of rebels* is plural ("those nations of rebels"), underscoring the sinfulness of the entire nation. **4:** The messenger formula, *Thus said the Lord GOD,* typical of Ezekiel, indicates Ezekiel's role as God's representative. **6:** *Do not fear,* a formula of encouragement, repeated here four times, is said to Jeremiah in his dedication as well (1.8). *Though thistles and thorns ... and you sit upon scorpions:* Israel will harass you like thorns, and hurt you like scorpions. **2.8–3.3:** Ezekiel eats the scroll to symbolize his internalizing the divine message. This action is even more dramatic than the preparation of both Isaiah's and Jeremiah's mouth, through which each delivers his message, in Isa. 6.6–7 and Jer. 1.9; it may be the formal call and commissioning for Ezekiel. **3.3:** Although the scroll is inscribed with *lamentations, dirges,*

3 He said to me, “Mortal, eat what is offered you; eat this scroll, and go speak to the House of Israel.” [2] So I opened my mouth, and He gave me this scroll to eat, [3] as He said to me, “Mortal, feed your stomach and fill your belly with this scroll that I give you.” I ate it, and it tasted as sweet as honey to me.

[4] Then He said to me, “Mortal, go to the House of Israel and repeat My very words to them. [5] For you are sent, not to a people of unintelligible speech and difficult language, but to the House of Israel—[6] not to the many peoples of unintelligible speech and difficult language, whose talk you cannot understand. If I sent you to them, they would listen to you. [7] But the House of Israel will refuse to listen to you, for they refuse to listen to Me; for the whole House of Israel are brazen of forehead and stubborn of heart. [8] But I will make your face as hard as theirs, and your forehead as brazen as theirs. [9] I will make your forehead like adamant, harder than flint. Do not fear them, and do not be dismayed by them, though they are a rebellious breed.”

[10] Then He said to me: “Mortal, listen with your ears and receive into your mind all the words that I speak to you. [11] Go to your people, the exile community, and speak to them. Say to them: Thus says the Lord God—whether they listen or not.” [12] Then a spirit carried me away, and behind me I heard a great roaring sound: [a-]“Blessed is the Presence of the Lord, in His place,”[-a] [13] with the sound of the wings of the creatures beating against one another, and the sound of the wheels beside them—a great roaring sound. [14] A spirit seized me and carried me away. I went in bitterness, in the fury of my spirit, while the hand of the Lord was strong upon me. [15] And I came to the exile community that dwelt in Tel Abib by the Chebar Canal, and I remained where they dwelt. And for seven days I sat there stunned among them.

[16] After those seven days, the word of the Lord came to me: [17] “O mortal, I appoint you watchman for the House of Israel; and when you hear a word from My mouth, you must warn them for Me. [18] If I say to a wicked man, ‘You shall die,’ and you do not warn him—you do not speak to warn the wicked man of his wicked course in order to save his life—he, the wicked man, shall die for his iniquity, but I will require a reckoning for his blood from you. [19] But if you do warn the wicked man, and he does not turn back from his wickedness and his wicked course, he shall die for his iniquity, but you will have saved your own life. [20] Again, if a righteous man abandons his righteousness and does wrong, when I put a stumbling block before him, he shall die. He shall die for his sins; the righteous deeds that he did shall not be remembered; but because you did not warn him, I will require a reckoning for his blood from you.

a-a Emendation yields “as the Presence of the Lord rose from where it stood.”

and woes (2.10), Ezekiel states that *it tasted as sweet as honey,* suggesting that the prophet is happy to accept his commission. **3.4–11:** Ezekiel's mission is outlined. **6:** *Many peoples of unintelligible speech and difficult language:* God stresses that the message is for Israel, not the nations. **12–15:** The prophet relates his bitterness at being compelled to speak such a harsh message of judgment, yet he does not seem ambivalent about his prophetic role. **12:** *“Blessed is the Presence of the Lord, in His place,”* is significant in later Jewish liturgy, especially in the *Kedushah.* **15:** *Tel Abib,* likely derives from the Babylonian expression “til abubi,” “mound of the flood.” In the view of the ancient residents this mound was an ancient settlement that was destroyed in the days of the flood. (The name was given to the new city of Tel Aviv, founded in 1909, to symbolize the rebirth of the land of Israel.) As a result of this experience, Ezekiel sits stunned for seven days prior to speaking his oracles in the following passage. **16–21:** God appoints Ezekiel as the *watchman for the House of Israel,* who is responsible to warn them of the approaching destruction (as seen in Jer. 6.17;). This function corresponds to the knowledge of the nation that there was a prophet among them (2.5). The prophet's responsibility to warn the people about their wickedness is illustrated in various permutations. The general rule is that if the prophet fails to warn the person, then he, the prophet, is held responsible. If the person is warned, however, and fails to act righteously or abandons righteousness, then the person is responsible. But not all options are mentioned; the examples do not include a sinner who corrected his ways. In addition, only the current generation is discussed; the question of children being punished for their father's sin is not addressed. (For both of these scenarios, see ch 18.) Therefore, it seems that along with the message that everyone is responsible for his or her actions, Ezekiel is describing the inhabitants of Jerusalem of his generation as sinners that did not change their

21 If, however, you warn the righteous man not to sin, and he, the righteous, does not sin, he shall live because he took warning, and you will have saved your own life."

22 Then the hand of the LORD came upon me there, and He said to me, "Arise, go out to the valley, and there I will speak with you." 23 I arose and went out to the valley, and there stood the Presence of the LORD, like the Presence that I had seen at the Chebar Canal; and I flung myself down on my face. 24 And a spirit entered into me and set me upon my feet. And He spoke to me, and said to me: "Go, shut yourself up in your house. 25 As for you, O mortal, cords have been placed upon you, and you have been bound with them, and you shall not go out among them.[a] 26 And I will make your tongue cleave to your palate, and you shall be dumb; you shall not be a reprover to them, for they are a rebellious breed. 27 But when I speak with you, I will open your mouth, and you shall say to them, 'Thus says the Lord GOD!' He who listens will listen, and he who does not will not—for they are a rebellious breed."

4 "And you, O mortal, take a brick and put it in front of you, and incise on it a city, Jerusalem. 2 Set up a siege against it, and build towers against it, and cast a mound against it; pitch camps against it, and bring up battering rams roundabout it. 3 Then take an iron plate and place it as an iron wall between yourself and the city, and set your face against it. [b]Thus it shall be under siege, you shall besiege it. This shall be an omen for the House of Israel.

4 "Then lie on your left side, and let it bear the punishment of the House of Israel;[c] for as many days as you lie on it you shall bear their punishment. 5 For I impose upon you three hundred and ninety days, corresponding to the number of the years of their punishment; and so you shall bear the punishment for the House of Israel. 6 When you have completed these, you shall lie another forty days on your right side, and bear the punishment of the House of Judah.[c] I impose on you one day for each year.

7 "Then, with bared arm, set your face toward besieged Jerusalem and prophesy against it. 8 Now I put cords upon you, so that you cannot turn from side to side until you complete your days of siege.

a I.e., the people. *b I.e., in hostility.*
c Since left and right also denote north and south (e.g., 16.46), the left side represents Israel, the northern kingdom, and the right side Judah, the southern kingdom.

actions. The prophetic mission in this case is only to warn, and does not affect the acts of people. This watchman role is developed more fully in ch 33.

3.22–5.17: Symbolic acts and their interpretation. This section presents oracles and symbolic actions that are concerned with the destruction of Jerusalem and fall of Judah. Chs 4–5 continue the divine instruction speech that begins in 3.16–21. **3.22–27:** The conditions of Ezekiel's mission: isolation and silence. This prophecy is part of a series of symbolic acts Ezekiel is commanded to do: eating the scroll (ch 3), withdrawal in his home while tied up (ch 3), restrictions on his movements and his food over time (ch 4), shaving his hair (ch 5), forging the chains (7. 23) and finally avoiding mourning the death of his wife (ch 24). **26:** God prevents Ezekiel from carrying out his role of warning Israel. The meaning of this silence is unclear, and different suggestions have been offered, including that Ezekiel must be silent except when he is speaking the divine word, that this was a metaphoric or a symbolic act, or that he spoke only to the elders that came to his house and not to the public.

4.1–5.17: God instructs Ezekiel to perform symbolic actions. Classical prophets perform symbolic actions to dramatize their statements and to enable the prophecy to take effect. **4.1–2:** God instructs Ezekiel to build a model of Jerusalem under siege. **3:** This symbolic act uses an iron pan, symbolizing the barrier between the prophet, representing God, and besieged Jerusalem. **4–8:** The basis for calculating *three hundred and ninety* years for the sin of Israel and *forty* years for the sin of Judah is uncertain. The different LXX version that states that Ezekiel shall lie on his left side for one hundred ninety days is no clearer; what is certain is that Ezekiel symbolically bears the punishment of the people. *Seder 'Olam* (26) states that we learn from here that "Israel sinned for three hundred ninety years from the time that Israel entered the land until the exile of the ten tribes [the Northern Kingdom]." The various suggestions that have explained the number of years mentioned include from the formation of the nation in Egypt, or from the time of the establishment of the united monarchy of Israel under Saul until the destruction. After the descriptions of the siege, the withdrawal of God, and the sins of the people using symbolic acts, the following symbolic act was intended to illustrate the famine during the siege.

9 “Further, take wheat, barley, beans, lentils, millet, and emmer. Put them into one vessel and bake them into bread. Eat it
as many days as you lie on your side: three hundred and ninety.
10 The food that you eat shall be by weight, twenty shekels a day;
this you shall eat in the space of a day. 11 And you shall drink
water by measure; drink a sixth of a *hin* in the space of a day.

12 “Eat it as a barley[a] cake; you shall bake it on human excrement before their eyes. 13 So,” said the LORD, “shall the people
of Israel eat their bread, unclean, among the nations to which
I will banish them.” 14 Then I said, “Ah, Lord GOD, my person
was never defiled; nor have I eaten anything that died of itself
or was torn by beasts from my youth until now, nor has foul
flesh entered my mouth.” 15 He answered me, “See, I allow you
cow's dung instead of human excrement; prepare your bread
on that.”

16 [b]And He said to me, “O mortal, I am going to break the staff
of bread in Jerusalem, and they shall eat bread by weight, in
anxiety, and drink water by measure, in horror, 17 so that, lacking bread and water, they shall stare at each other, heartsick
5 over their iniquity. 1 And you, O mortal, take a sharp knife;
use it as a barber's razor and pass it over your head and
beard. Then take scales and divide the hair.[c] 2 When the days of
siege are completed, destroy a third part in fire in the city, take
a third and strike it with the sword all around [d]the city,[-d] and
scatter a third to the wind and unsheathe[e] a sword after them.

3 “Take also a few [hairs] from there and tie them up in your
skirts. 4 And take some more of them and cast them into the
fire, and burn them in the fire. From this a fire shall go out
upon the whole House of Israel.”

5 Thus said the Lord GOD: I set this Jerusalem in the midst
of nations, with countries round about her. 6 But she rebelled
against My rules and My laws, acting more wickedly than the nations and the countries round about her; she[f] rejected My rules
and disobeyed My laws. 7 Assuredly, thus said the Lord GOD: Because you have outdone the nations that are round about you—
you have not obeyed My laws or followed My rules, nor have you
observed the rules of the nations round about you—8 assuredly,
thus said the Lord GOD: I, in turn, am going to deal with you, and
I will execute judgments in your midst in the sight of the nations.
9 On account of all your abominations, I will do among you what
I have never done, and the like of which I will never do again.

10 Assuredly, parents shall eat their children in your midst, and
children shall eat their parents. I will execute judgments against
you, and I will scatter all your survivors in every direction.

a *Meaning of Heb. uncertain.* b *Resuming the thought of v. 11.* c *Lit. “them.”*
d-d *Heb. “it.”* e *Cf. v. 12; lit. “I will unsheathe.”* f *Heb. “they.”*

9–12: God instructs Ezekiel to perform a fourth symbolic act that requires him to bake bread composed of a mixture of grains that grow under siege conditions; this was to be eaten during the time the prophet was lying down. The amounts of food and water were barely enough to sustain the prophet. Ezekiel mixes a variety of grains, including those not normally used to make bread, to demonstrate that there is insufficient grain to make an entire loaf of bread. *Twenty shekels,* about 225 gm (10 oz). *A sixth of a hin* (v. 11), about six-tenths of a liter (two-thirds of a quart). In order to demonstrate the difficult and impure conditions of the coming siege, God commands Ezekiel to use human dung as fuel. When he protests, God allows him to use cow's dung, which was typically used as fuel, especially when wood was not available. The bread cooked over human feces was impure according to Ezekiel's norms, and as a priest, he would not have eaten it. **16–17:** The coming disaster will result in the people lacking food, so that they and the priests will be compelled to violate their food restrictions, and will have to eat impure food when Jerusalem and the Temple are under seige and ultimately destroyed. **5.1–4:** The last symbolic act describes what is to be expected by the inhabitants of Jerusalem after the siege. One-third of the hair is burned to represent those who die when the city is burned; one-third is struck with the sword to symbolize those killed around the city; and one-third is scattered to symbolize those who flee. The hairs tied to the prophet's clothes may represent those pursued by the Babylonians. Some of the hair is burned once again to symbolize the suffering of the people. **5–17:** God concludes the instruction speech to Ezekiel by summing up the significance of the punishment and impurity that Ezekiel's symbolic actions illustrate. Charging that Israel acts like the nations by defiling the Temple, God suggests that the people will be treated like the nations. **10:** Parents shall eat their children, children shall

11 Assuredly, as I live—said the Lord GOD—because you
defiled My Sanctuary with all your detestable things and all
your abominations, I in turn will shear [you] away[a] and show
no pity. I in turn will show no compassion: 12 One-third of
you shall die of pestilence or perish in your midst by famine,
one-third shall fall by the sword around you, and I will scatter one-third in every direction and will unsheathe the sword
after them. 13 I will vent all My anger and satisfy My fury upon
them; and when I vent all My fury upon them, they shall know
that I the LORD have spoken in My passion. 14 I will make you a
ruin and a mockery among the nations roundabout you, in the
sight of every passerby. 15 And when I execute judgment upon
you in anger and rage and furious chastisement, you[b] shall be
a mockery and a derision, a warning and a horror, to the nations roundabout you: I the LORD have spoken. 16 When I loose
the deadly arrows of famine against those doomed to destruction, when I loose them against you to destroy you, I will heap
more famine upon you and break your staff of bread. 17 I will
let loose against you famine and wild beasts and they shall bereave you; pestilence and bloodshed shall sweep through you,
and I will bring the sword upon you. I the LORD have spoken.

6 The word of the LORD came to me: 2 O mortal, turn your face
toward the mountains of Israel and prophesy to them 3 and
say: O mountains of Israel, hear the word of the Lord GOD. Thus
said the Lord GOD to the mountains and the hills, to the streams
and the valleys: See, I will bring a sword against you and destroy your shrines. 4 Your altars shall be wrecked and your incense stands smashed, and I will hurl down your slain in front
of your fetishes. 5 I will cast the corpses of the people of Israel
in front of their fetishes, and scatter your bones around your
altars 6 in all your settlements. The towns shall be laid waste
and the shrines shall be devastated. Thus your altars shall be
laid waste and [c]bear their punishment;[c] your fetishes shall be
smashed and annihilated, your incense stands cut down, and
your handiwork wiped out; 7 and the slain shall fall in your
midst. Then you shall know that I am the LORD. 8 Yet I will leave a
remnant, in that some of you shall escape the sword among the
nations and be scattered through the lands. 9 And those of you
that escape will remember Me among the nations where they
have been taken captive, [d]how I was brokenhearted through[d]
their faithless hearts which turned away from Me, and through
their eyes which lusted after their fetishes. And they shall loathe
themselves for all the evil they committed and for all their

a *Cf. Isa. 15.2 and Jer. 48.37; here an allusion to the symbolism in v. 1.*
b *Heb. "she."* c-c *Targum and other ancient versions read "shall be devastated."*
d-d *Emendation yields "how I broke."*

eat their parents. Cannibalism is a known trope in biblical war literature (Lam. 2.20; 4.10) but this is an extreme form. The people will suffer war and exile, ultimately perishing by pestilence, famine, and sword. **14:** God's threat to make Israel *a ruin and a mockery among the nations roundabout you* and to unleash famine, wild animals, etc., against the people recalls threats made in the roughly contemporaneous Jer. 24.9–10. If the chronological order of the chs represents the prophets actions then this is the first prophecy that Ezekiel delivered to the nation. **17:** *I the LORD have spoken* is another phrase that typifies Ezekiel, and is used by him elsewhere to end a unit.

6.1–7.27: Sins of the people that caused the destruction. 6.1–10: Oracle against the mountains of Israel. 1: The passage begins with the prophetic word formula, *the word of the LORD came to me* (see 1.3; 3.16; 7.1). Ezekiel addresses the entire land and people of Israel. **2:** *The mountains of Israel,* the biblical homeland of Israel (see ch 36 nn.). **3–7:** The similarity of these vv. to Lev. 26.30–33 suggests that this prophecy may have been an application of the curses in Lev. Ezekiel identifies the cause of punishment in the various altars and high places where the people worship, which compromise the sanctity of the land. An example of such a sanctuary was excavated at the site of 7th-c. Arad, where a "matzevah" or cultic pillar was found in the Holy of Holies of the temple located there. **5:** The scattering of dead corpses around the altars renders the land impure (Num. ch 19; see also Lev. 21.10–12). **7:** Ezekiel employs the so-called "proof saying," *then you shall know that I am the LORD,* throughout the book to identify God as the source of his prophetic words. It is extremely common in Ezek., appearing over fifty times, four times in this ch alone (vv. 7, 10 [obscured in translation], 13, 14). **8–10:** Ezekiel emphasizes that God's power to destroy and punish will leave only a portion of the people to be scattered among the nations; the

abominable deeds. 10 Then they shall realize it was not without
cause that I the LORD resolved to bring this evil upon them.
11 Thus said the Lord GOD: Strike your hands together and
stamp your feet and cry: Aha! over all the vile abominations
of the House of Israel who shall fall by the sword, by famine,
and by pestilence. 12 He who is far away shall die of pestilence,
and he who is near shall fall by the sword, and he who survives and is protected shall die of famine. Thus I will spend
My fury upon them. 13 And you shall know that I am the LORD,
when your slain lie among the fetishes round about their altars, on every high hill, on all the mountaintops, under every
green tree, and under every leafy oak—wherever they presented pleasing odors to all their fetishes.
14 I will stretch out My hand against them, and lay the land
waste and desolate in all their settlements, from the wilderness
as far as Diblah;[a] then they shall know that I am the LORD.

7 The word of the LORD came to me: 2 You, O mortal, [say:]
Thus said the Lord GOD to the land of Israel: Doom! Doom
is coming upon the four corners of the land. 3 Now doom is
upon you! I will let loose My anger against you and judge you
according to your ways; I will requite you for all your abominations. 4 I will show you no pity and no compassion; but I will
requite you for your ways and for the abominations in your
midst. And you shall know that I am the LORD.
5 Thus said the Lord GOD: [b-]A singular disaster; a disaster[-b]
is coming. 6 Doom is coming! The hour of doom is coming! It
stirs against you; there it comes! 7 [c-]The cycle has come around
for you, O inhabitants of the land; the time has come; the day is
near. There is panic on the mountains, not joy.[-c] 8 Very soon I will
pour out My wrath upon you and spend My anger on you; I will
judge you according to your ways, and I will requite you for all
your abominations. 9 I will show you no pity and no compassion;
but I will requite you for your ways, and for the abominations in
your midst. And you shall know it was I the LORD who punished.
10 Here is the day! See, the [c-]cycle has come round; it has appeared. The rod has blossomed; arrogance has budded, 11 lawlessness has grown into a rod of wickedness. Nothing comes of
them, nor of their abundance, nor of their wealth; nor is there
preeminence among them.[-c] 12 The time has come, the day has

a *A few Heb. mss. read "Riblah"; cf. 2 Kings 23.33; 25.6 ff.*
b-b *A number of mss. and editions, as well as Targum, read "Disaster after disaster."*
c-c *Meaning of Heb. uncertain.*

idea of a *remnant* typifies classical prophecy; if all are destroyed, God will have no covenant partner. **6.11–14:** Ezekiel returns to the imagery of sword, pestilence, and famine (5.1–17) to tie his oracles against Israel to the fate of Jerusalem. **13:** *Altars, on every high hill, on all the mountaintops, under every green tree, and under every leafy oak,* a common Deuteronomic formulaic description of pagan worship (Deut. 12.2; Jer. 2.20). **14:** The *wilderness* designates the Negev desert in southern Judah. *Diblah:* Some mss read *Riblah* (see translators' note *a;* Heb letters "resh" and "dalet" are similar and sometimes confused; see "Reuel" in Num. 2.14, but "Deuel" in Num. 1.14). Since Riblah is situated on the northern border of Israel (Num. 34.11), this emendation is likely, indicating the borders of the country, from the desert in the south to Riblah in the north. As elsewhere, *then they shall know that I am the LORD* is the climactic conclusion of Ezekiel's prophecy.

7.1–27: Prophecy of doom. The passage begins with the prophetic "word" formula, *the word of the LORD came to me.* This passage is the culmination of the first chs of the book, presenting the doom of Israel as the outcome of God's initial revelation to Ezekiel in 1.1–3.15. The culminating prophecy is poetic in style. The unit is typified by repetition: the word "doom" is repeated five times in vv. 2–12, and "come" nine times in these vv. These are joined by the combinations: *the time has come, very soon,* and *here is the day,* all of which relate to the same semantic field. The "Day of the LORD" motif functioned as an announcement of God's defense of Israel, or as an announcement of God's punishment against Israel and Judah (see e.g., Amos 5.18–20; Zeph. 1.7–18; 2.1–3). **1–4:** The first oracle announces the doom of Israel. **2:** *The four corners of the land,* that is all the land in the four cardinal directions, known from Mesopotamian texts, indicates the complete destruction of the land. **5–9:** Ezekiel again employs the statement *doom* (lit. "the end") *is coming,* but shifts his language to that of the "Day of the LORD" traditions. **10–27:** The third oracle elaborates upon the imagery of the land's destruction on the "Day of the LORD." **10–11:** The blossoming *rod:* The reference to the budding *arrogance* may indicate Ezekiel's view that the priestly rod is now employed for the punishment of Israel, just as Moses' rod punished Egypt (Exod. chs 7–11). **12–13:** Normal commercial life will end. Radak maintains that the buyer is happy with a purchase whereas the seller mourns for that which is sold. *The buyer* may not *rejoice* because he will soon be exiled and therefore lose what he has bought. *The seller* may not *mourn* because he is going into exile and would have lost the property anyway. **14–17:** Ezekiel again takes up the imagery of *sword, pestilence,* and *famine* (chs 5–6). **20:** *An unclean thing:* Heb "nidah," menstrual flow, considered ritually impure (Lev. 15.19–30; 18.19; 20.18), serves as a metaphor for the impurity of idols. See also Zeph. 1.18; Lam. 1.17. **22:** God will withdraw His protection from the people. *My treasures,* Heb is singular ("tzafun"), lit. "hidden," referring to the Holy of Holies in the Temple, which shall be defiled when Jerusalem is taken. **23–27:** In the last part of the ch Ezekiel predicts for the first time that the Temple will be desecrated by strangers, and then makes it clear that the leaders (vv. 26–27: *prophet, priest, elders, king, prince, the people* [the landed gentry]) are responsible for this punishment because of their own actions. It is to this new condition, perceived as impossible in the eyes of the Judeans, that Ezekiel speaks in the following prophecies. Since these leaders did not act properly in the past, they will be unable to fulfill their roles at the time of disaster when the people will need them the most. This idea is further developed in chs 40–48 where Ezekiel maintains that just as they did not act properly in the past, so they will be unable to fulfill their proper roles in the future. **27:** *They shall know that I am the* L*ORD*, brings the oracle to a close.

8.1–11.13: Vision of the destruction of Jerusalem. The account of Ezekiel's vision depicts the departure of the divine Presence employing the imagery of priestly sacrifice as an act that purges the city from impurity. The people who have committed

arrived. Let not the buyer rejoice nor the seller mourn—for divine wrath shall overtake all her multitude. 13 For the seller shall
not return to what he sold so long as they remain among the living. For the vision concerns all her multitude, it shall not be revoked. And because of his guilt, no man shall hold fast to his life.
14 They have sounded the horn, and all is prepared; but no
one goes to battle, for My wrath is directed against all her multitude. 15 The sword is outside and pestilence and famine are
inside; he who is in the open shall die by the sword, he who is
in the town shall be devoured by famine and pestilence. 16 And
if any survive, they shall take to the mountains; they shall be
[a-]like doves of the valley, moaning together[-a]—every one for
his iniquity. 17 All hands shall grow weak, and all knees shall
turn to water. 18 They shall gird on sackcloth, and horror shall
cover them; every face shall betray shame, and every head
shall be made bald.
19 They shall throw their silver into the streets, and their gold
shall be treated as something unclean. Their silver and gold
shall not avail to save them in the day of the LORD's wrath—to
satisfy their hunger or to fill their stomachs. Because they made
them stumble into guilt—20 for out of their beautiful adornments, in which they took pride, they made their images and
their detestable abominations—therefore I will make them[b] an
unclean thing to them. 21 I will give them as spoil to strangers,
and as plunder to the wicked of the earth; and they shall defile
them. 22 I will turn My face from them, and My treasures shall
be defiled; ruffians shall invade it and defile it.
23 [c-]Forge the chain,[-c] for the land is full of bloody crimes, and
the city is full of lawlessness. 24 I will bring in the worst of the nations to take possession of their houses; so shall I turn to naught
the pride of the powerful, and their sanctuaries shall be defiled.
25 Horror[d] comes, and they shall seek safety, but there shall
be none. 26 Calamity shall follow calamity, and rumor follow
rumor. Then they shall seek vision from the prophet in vain;
instruction shall perish from the priest, and counsel from the
elders. 27 The king shall mourn, the prince shall clothe himself with desolation, and the hands of the people of the land
shall tremble. I will treat them in accordance with their own
ways and judge them according to their deserts. And they shall
know that I am the LORD.

8 In the sixth year, on the fifth day of the sixth month, I was sitting at home, and the elders of Judah were sitting before me,
and there the hand of the Lord GOD fell upon me. 2 As I looked,

a-a *Emendation yields "like moaning doves. All of them shall perish."*
b *I.e., their adornments.* c-c *Meaning of Heb. uncertain.*
d *Meaning of Heb. uncertain.*

there was a figure that had the appearance of fire:[a] from what appeared as his loins down, [he was] fire; and from his loins up, his appearance was resplendent and had the color of amber. 3 He stretched out the form of a hand, and took me by the hair of my head. A spirit lifted me up between heaven and earth and brought me in visions of God to Jerusalem, to the entrance of the Penimith[b] Gate that faces north; that was the site of the infuriating image that provokes fury. 4 And the Presence of the God of Israel appeared there, like the vision that I had seen in the valley.[c]

5 And He said to me, "O mortal, turn your eyes northward." I turned my eyes northward, and there, [d]north of the gate of the altar, was[-d] that infuriating image on the approach.[b] 6 And He said to me, "Mortal, do you see what they are doing, the terrible abominations that the House of Israel is practicing here, [e]to drive Me far[-e] from My Sanctuary? You shall yet see even greater abominations!"

7 Then He brought me to the entrance of the court;[f] and I looked, and there was a hole in the wall. 8 He said to me, "Mortal, break through the wall"; so I broke through the wall and found an entrance. 9 And He said to me, "Enter and see the vile abominations that they are practicing here." 10 I entered and looked, and there all detestable forms of creeping things and beasts and all the fetishes of the House of Israel were depicted over the entire wall. 11 Before them stood seventy men, elders of the House of Israel, with Jaazaniah son of Shaphan standing in their midst. Everyone had a censer in his hand, and a thick cloud of incense smoke ascended. 12 Again He spoke to me, "O mortal, have you seen what the elders of the House of Israel are doing

a Septuagint "a man." *b Meaning of Heb. uncertain.*
c See chap. 1 and 3.22–23. *d-d Meaning of Heb. uncertain; emendation yields "north of the gate was the altar of."* *e-e Or "at a distance."*
f I.e., the outer court of the Temple.

sins are to be purged themselves as part of the overall scenario for God's destruction of Jerusalem and the Temple. The cultic infractions "observed" by Ezekiel most probably did not take place contemporaneously; it is more likely that he is being shown a set of infractions that transpired over a long period of time which have cumulatively caused the divine Presence to leave the Temple.

8.1–18: Acts of the people in the Temple. This ch and chs 9–11 focus on Ezekiel's vision of God's departure from the Jerusalem Temple and the following oracles that elaborate upon the significance of this event. **1:** *In the sixth year, on the fifth day of the sixth month,* 5 ʾElul, 592 BCE, fourteen months after Ezekiel's inaugural vision. The presence of the elders in Ezekiel's home indicates that the Jewish community in Babylonian exile was organized with recognized leadership and that Ezekiel enjoyed a high status in that society (cf. 14.1). Many older interpreters have seen this v. as evidence for the origins of the synagogue, but there is no evidence for the development of this institution for several centuries (see 11.16 n.). **2:** Ezekiel returns to the imagery of his inaugural vision to describe a human-like being. The LXX reads the expression *a figure that had the appearance of fire* as "the appearance (or likeness) of a man," apparently based upon the similarity of the Heb term "ʾesh" (fire) with "ʾish" ("man"), which would have been written the same way in his period. The language employed here, *fire* and *resplendent and had the color of amber,* describe a being that cannot be defined in earthly terms. **3:** The exact meaning of *the entrance of the Penimith Gate that faces north,* is uncertain, although it may refer to a gate to the inner court of the Temple on the north side. This would place the prophet at the entry of the most sacred areas of the Temple. **4:** *The Presence of the God of Israel* indicates that the divine throne chariot from ch 1 has once again appeared. **5–6:** *That infuriating image* north of the altar indicates the presence of a pagan idol that would defile the holy Temple precincts. **7–13:** The portrayal of the prophet breaking or digging through the walls of the Temple suggests the later Babylonian attempts to breach the walls of Jerusalem or it may apply to a hiding place. **10:** *Detestable forms ... fetishes:* Such depictions violated the command (Deut. 4.15–18) against images. In addition, *creeping things* are ritually impure (see Lev. 20.25) and would defile the Temple. **11:** The *seventy men, elders of the House of Israel* and *Jaazaniah son of Shaphan* indicate that the highest leaders of the nation are involved in pagan worship inside the Temple. The institution of Israel's seventy elders is mentioned in Exod. 24.1 and Num. 11.16; they later played a role in selecting and advising kings (2 Sam. 5.3; cf. 1 Kings 12.6; 20.7). Shaphan, from a prominent family, played a major role in Josiah's reform (2 Kings ch 22). **12:** The claim that *the LORD has abandoned the country* indicates the belief that God would no longer protect Jerusalem from Babylon. The quotation and refutation of a folk-saying by the prophet is especially characteristic of Ezekiel (see 11.2, 15; 18.2).

in the darkness, everyone in his image-covered chamber? For
they say, 'The LORD does not see us; the LORD has abandoned
the country.'" 13 And He said to me, "You shall see even more
terrible abominations which they practice."
14 Next He brought me to the entrance of the north [a]gate of
the House of the LORD;[a] and there sat the women bewailing
Tammuz.[b] 15 He said to me, "Have you seen, O mortal? You
shall see even more terrible abominations than these."
16 Then He brought me into the inner court of the House of
the LORD, and there, at the entrance to the Temple of the LORD,
between the portico and the altar, were about twenty-five men,
their backs to the Temple of the LORD and their faces to the
east; they were bowing low to the sun in the east. 17 And He said
to me, "Do you see, O mortal? Is it not enough for the House of
Judah to practice the abominations that they have committed
here, that they must fill the country with lawlessness and provoke Me still further and [c]thrust the branch to their nostrils?[c]
18 I in turn will act with fury, I will show no pity or compassion;
though they cry aloud to Me, I will not listen to them."

9 Then He called loudly in my hearing, saying, "Approach,
you men in charge of the city, each bearing his weapons of
destruction!" 2 And six men entered by way of the upper gate
that faces north, each with his club in his hand; and among
them was another, clothed in linen, with a writing case at his
waist. They came forward and stopped at the bronze altar.
3 Now the Presence of the God of Israel had moved from the
cherub on which it had rested to the platform[d] of the House.
He called to the man clothed in linen with the writing case at
his waist; 4 and the LORD said to him, "Pass through the city,
through Jerusalem, and put a mark on the foreheads of the men
who moan and groan because of all the abominations that are
committed in it." 5 To the others He said in my hearing, "Follow
him through the city and strike; show no pity or compassion.

a-a I.e., the gate of the inner court. *b A Babylonian god.*
c-c Apparently meaning "goad Me to fury"; "their" is a euphemism for "My."
d The raised platform on which the Temple stood; cf. 47.1.

14–15: This is a pagan practice taking place at the Temple itself. Women weep for *Tammuz,* the Babylonian vegetation god who dies at the onset of the dry season and must be brought back to life to inaugurate the rains. According to Babylonian mythology, the goddess Ishtar descends to the underworld each year to return Tammuz to the world of the living for the six months of the rainy season. Mourning rituals by women for the dead Tammuz play a role in bringing the god back to life. **16–18:** Ezekiel sees *twenty-five men* engaged in sun worship. The sun god Shamash was the Babylonian god of law and justice. The worshippers apparently turn their backs to the Temple to face the east where the sun rises. Traditional interpreters understand this as an expression of their rejection of God, since Jewish worshippers face the Temple and the Holy of Holies. The meaning of the expression, *thrust the branch to their nostrils,* is unknown, although it is generally understood to refer to some noxious idolatrous practice. Radak follows the *Mek.* to Exod. 15.7 in maintaining that this statement is one of the eighteen "emendations of the scribes" that originally read, "thrust the branch to my (God's) nostrils." The various actions described in this narrative indicate that the Temple has been profaned, and must be purified to restore its sacred character.

9.1–11.25: Departure of the divine Presence from the Temple.

9.1–11: The slaughter of Jerusalem. Ezekiel's depiction of the killing of the people of Jerusalem employs the imagery of sacrificial slaughter combined with the images of the Babylonian soldiers slaughtering the defenders of Jerusalem. **1:** The verb "karevu" *(approach)* may be used to refer to the presentation of an offering to God (Exod. 29.4; 40.12; Lev. 3.6; 7.35; 8.6; Num. 8.9; 16.5); it may also refer to drawing near for battle (Exod. 14.20; Judg. 20.24). **2–3:** The *six men* come from the upper gate to the north with weapons in their hands to begin the slaughter, since the Babylonian army will enter from the north (see 26.7; 38.6, 15; 39.2). **3:** The *man clothed in linen* carries a writing case to record the sacrifices. **4:** God commands that a *mark* (the ancient form of the Heb letter "tav," here translated mark, looks like an "X") be placed on the foreheads of *the men who moan and groan because of all the abominations* to protect them from death. The mark presumably indicates someone who is to be spared. All who lack the mark are to die, defiling the sanctuary. But the meaning of this v. is not entirely certain as the ch subsequently depicts the slaughter of all Jerusalem's inhabitants except for Ezekiel (see vv. 8–10); Ezekiel often simultaneously describes complete destruction, while suggesting that some would be spared. Interpreters therefore debate whether the mark indicates those who are guilty or innocent.

6 Kill off graybeard, youth and maiden, women and children;
but do not touch any person who bears the mark. Begin here
at My Sanctuary." So they began with the elders who were in
front of the House. 7 And He said to them, "Defile the House
and fill the courts with the slain. Then go forth." So they went
forth and began to kill in the city. 8 When they were out killing, and I remained alone, I flung myself on my face and cried
out, "Ah, Lord GOD! Are you going to annihilate all that is left of
Israel, pouring out Your fury upon Jerusalem?" 9 He answered
me, "The iniquity of the Houses of Judah and Israel is very very
great, the land is full of crime and the city is full of corruption.
For they say, 'The LORD has forsaken the land, and the LORD
does not see.' 10 I, in turn, will show no pity or compassion; I will
give them their deserts." 11 And then the man clothed in linen
with the writing case at his waist brought back word, saying, "I
have done as You commanded me."

10 I looked, and on the expanse over the heads of the cherubs, there was something like a sapphire stone; an appearance resembling a throne could be seen over them. 2 He
spoke to the man clothed in linen and said, "Step inside the
wheelwork, under the cherubs, and fill your hands with glowing coals from among the cherubs, and scatter them over the
city." And he went in as I looked on. 3 Now the cherubs were
standing on the south side of the House when the man entered, and the cloud filled the inner court. 4 But when the Presence of the LORD moved from the cherubs to the platform[a] of
the House, the House was filled with the cloud, and the court
was filled with the radiance of the Presence of the LORD. 5 The
sound of the cherubs' wings could be heard as far as the outer
court, like the voice of El Shaddai[b] when He speaks.
6 When He commanded the man dressed in linen: "Take
fire from among the cherubs within the wheelwork," he went
in and stood beside a wheel. 7 And a cherub stretched out his
hand among the cherubs to the fire that was among the cherubs; he took some and put it into the hands of him who was
clothed in linen, who took it and went out. 8 The cherubs appeared to have the form of a man's hand under their wings.
9 I could see that there were four wheels beside the cherubs,
one wheel beside each of the cherubs; as for the appearance
of the wheels, they gleamed like the beryl stone. 10 In appearance, the four had the same form, as if there were two wheels
cutting through each other. 11 And when they moved, each
could move in the direction of any of its four quarters; they
did not veer as they moved. The [cherubs] moved in the direction in which one of the heads faced, without turning as they

a *See note at 47.1.* *b* *See note at Gen. 17.1.*

8–9: Unlike most prophets, who emphasize repentance, the theology of Ezekiel is that the people's sin is so great that repentance at this point is impossible (see also Jer. ch 25, an alteration in Jeremiah's mission [see vv. 5–7 n.]). The purpose of Ezekiel's prophecies is thus to explain the disaster, not to try to avert it. Radak states that the executioners are to begin at the Temple with the seventy elders because they engaged in idolatry (Ezek. 8.11), though he cites Rashi who maintains that they were the men who kept Torah from "alef" to "tav," (first to last).

10.1–11.13: The LORD's departure from Jerusalem. God's throne chariot will return in 43.1–12 when the city is purified and the Temple reestablished. Once God's Presence has left the Temple, the city is open to foreign invasion and destruction; this theme of divine abandonment is common in Mesopotamian literature. **10.1:** The *expanse over the heads of the cherubs* is associated with *sapphire.* Cf. 1.26. **2:** God commands the *man clothed in linen* to take *glowing coals from among the cherubs, and scatter them over the city.* Insofar as Ezekiel envisions the restoration of the Temple (see 11.14–21; chs 40–48) at some time following its destruction, the sacrificial imagery of this act also likens it to the purification and guilt offerings presented in the Temple (Lev. chs 4–5; 7.1–10). Such sacrifices play a role in atoning for iniquity and impurity so that the offender can "return" as a member of the community. **2–7:** This act demonstrates that not only the city is defiled from within the Temple, but also that the burning of the city is from fire that originated from the Temple. **4:** God's Presence is signified by the *cloud* (Exod. 19.9; 1 Kings 8.10–11) and the *radiance of the Presence of the LORD* as it moves about the Temple complex. **6–7:** Because of the sanctity of the throne chariot or Ark the man clothed in linen approaches and stands in front of the wheel. **8–22:** Ezekiel's detailed description of the cherubim (not mentioned in

moved. 12 Their entire bodies—backs, hands, and wings—and the wheels, the wheels of the four of them, were covered all over with eyes. 13 It was these wheels that I had heard called "the wheelwork."[a] 14 Each one had four faces: One was a cherub's face, the second a human face, the third a lion's face, and the fourth an eagle's face.

15 The cherubs ascended; those were the creatures that I had seen by the Chebar Canal. 16 Whenever the cherubs went, the wheels went beside them; and when the cherubs lifted their wings to ascend from the earth, the wheels did not roll away from their side. 17 When those stood still, these stood still; and when those ascended, these ascended with them, for the spirit of the creature was in them.

18 Then the Presence of the LORD left the platform[b] of the House and stopped above the cherubs. 19 And I saw the cherubs lift their wings and rise from the earth, with the wheels beside them as they departed; and they[c] stopped at the entrance of the eastern gate of the House of the LORD, with the Presence of the God of Israel above them. 20 They were the same creatures that I had seen below the God of Israel at the Chebar Canal; so now I knew that they were cherubs.[d] 21 Each one had four faces and each had four wings, with the form of human hands under the wings. 22 As for the form of their faces, they were the very faces that I had seen by the Chebar Canal—their appearance and [e-]their features[-e]—and each could move in the direction of any of its faces.

11 Then a spirit lifted me up and brought me to the east gate of the House of the LORD, which faces eastward; and there, at the entrance of the gate, were twenty-five men, among whom I saw Jaazaniah son of Azzur and Pelatiah son of Benaiah, leaders of the people. 2 [The LORD] said to me, "O mortal, these are the men who plan iniquity and plot wickedness in this city, 3 who say: 'There is no need now to build houses; this [city] is the pot, and we are the meat.'[f] 4 I adjure you, prophesy against them; prophesy, O mortal!"

5 Thereupon the spirit of the LORD fell upon me, and He said to me, "Speak: Thus said the LORD: Such are your thoughts, O House of Israel; I know what comes into your mind. 6 Many have you slain in this city; you have filled its streets with corpses. 7 Assuredly, thus says the Lord GOD: The corpses that you have piled up in it are the meat for which it is the pot; but you shall be taken out of it. 8 You feared the sword, and the sword I will bring upon you—declares the Lord GOD. 9 I will take you

ch 1) and the wheels differs from that in ch 1 in that one of their four faces is a cherub rather than an ox. **19:** *The Presence of the God of Israel* above *the entrance of the eastern gate of the House of the LORD* is the main or processional entrance to the Temple and from there God is to return to the Temple in the future (43.1–2). **20–22:** These vv. emphasize that although they are depicted somewhat differently, these are the images Ezekiel saw in ch 1 in Babylonia. Ezekiel, but not the Judeans who are still living in Judah, see that God has left the Temple before its destruction.

11.1–13: After completing the description of God's leaving the Temple, Ezekiel returns to describe the people's actions. **1–4:** The *spirit* or "wind" transports Ezekiel to the *east gate* of the Temple where he sees twenty-five officials. He is at the eastern gate, and can see their faces. Ezekiel's recognition of two ministers may signal the responsibility of the leaders for the sins; it also contributes information regarding Ezekiel's high status before the exile. **3:** Their statement, *there is no need now to build houses,* indirectly rejects Jeremiah's call to build and to plant (Jer. 1.10; 31.28). Their statement, *this [city] is the pot, and we are the meat,* indicates their incorrect belief that Jerusalem will protect them. **7:** In stating that the dead will become *the meat* and the city *the pot,* God turns their statement against them and injects a metaphorical portrayal of the destruction of Jerusalem with sacrificial imagery.

a *See v. 2.* *b* *See note at 47.1.* *c* *Lit. "it."*
d *Because they had been called "cherubs" (cf. v. 2).* *e-e* *Lit. "themselves."*
f *I.e., the exiles will not return.*

out of it and deliver you into the hands of strangers, and I will
execute judgments upon you. 10 You shall fall by the sword; I
will punish you at the border of Israel. And you shall know that
I am the LORD. 11 This [city] shall not be a pot for you, nor you
the meat in it; I will punish you at the border of Israel. 12 Then
you shall know that I am the LORD, whose laws you did not follow and whose rules you did not obey, acting instead according to the rules of the nations around you."

13 Now, as I prophesied, Pelatiah son of Benaiah dropped
dead. I threw myself upon my face and cried out aloud, "Ah,
Lord GOD! You are wiping out the remnant of Israel!"

14 Then the word of the LORD came to me: 15 "O mortal, [I will
save] your brothers, your brothers, the men of your kindred,[a]
all of that very House of Israel to whom the inhabitants of Jerusalem say, 'Keep far from the LORD; the land has been given
as a heritage to us.' 16 Say then: Thus said the Lord GOD: I have
indeed removed them far among the nations and have scattered them among the countries, and I have become to them
a diminished sanctity in the countries whither they have gone.
17 Yet say: Thus said the Lord GOD: I will gather you[a] from the
peoples and assemble you out of the countries where you have
been scattered, and I will give you the Land of Israel. 18 And they
shall return there, and do away with all its detestable things
and all its abominations. 19 I will give them one heart and put a
new spirit in them;[b] I will remove the heart of stone from their
bodies and give them a heart of flesh, 20 that they may follow

a I.e., the exiles. *b Heb. "you."*

13: The immediate death of *Pelatiah son of Benaiah* confirms both Ezekiel's worries that there will be no survivors, and proves that he is a true prophet.

11.14–21: Oracle concerning the restoration of Israel. Following the initial presentation of his second vision in 8.1–11.13, a series of fourteen oracle accounts follow in 11.14–25; 12.1–7; 12.8–16; 12.17–20; 12.21–25; 12.26–28; 13.1–23; 14.1–11; 14.12–23; 15.1–8; 16.1–63; 17.1–10; 17.11–24; 18.1–19.14. Whereas the vision account begins with the formula, "and there the hand of the Lord GOD fell upon me" (8.1), the oracle accounts each begin with a version of the typical prophetic formula, *the word of the LORD came to me.* Many scholars group the prophet's vision of God's departure in chs 8–11 with the account of his inaugural vision in chs 1–7, but the presence of the date formulas and the prophetic formulas indicates an interest in setting out the prophet's vision, and then providing oracles that elaborate upon its significance or meaning. Overall, the oracles prompt the reader to consider the means by which Jerusalem will be purified later so that the restoration of Israel and God's Presence to Jerusalem may take place. The exiles will be gathered from the places to which they have been scattered and will be returned to the land of Israel, where they will follow God's laws. The covenant between God and Israel will be reinstated. Most such prophecies of consolation are concentrated in the final section of the book. **15:** The reference to *your brothers, the men of your kindred* can also be read as "your brothers, the men of your redemption." The Heb term "ge'ulatekha" has a background in the Priestly laws of redemption whereby a family member, "go'el," must redeem land sold to pay a debt in the jubilee year (Lev. 25.23–55). Ezekiel apparently envisions that those exiled from the land of Israel will redeem the land following the death of those who defiled it. In contrast, those who remain in the land claim incorrectly that the exiles (which would include Ezekiel) are far from God because they are no longer entitled to the land. **16:** God claims to be *a diminished sanctity in the countries whither they have gone.* God's Presence with the exiles confirms Ezekiel's prophetic messages regarding the future. Jewish tradition anachronistically reads into "mikdash me'at," "a little sanctuary," a reference to the origins of synagogues; this is especially reflected in the translation of *Tg. Jon.*, "and I have become for them synagogues, second to My Temple." Although the origins of synagogues are obscure, they can first be traced to the 3rd c. BCE, and only emerged as the primary Jewish centers for study and worship following the destruction of the Second Temple by the Romans in 70 CE. **17:** God promises to gather the people from exile, to give them *the Land of Israel* and then to remove their abominations. This is the first of three prophecies devoted to the nation's restoration within chs 1–24, in addition to 16.59–63 and 20.22–44. **19:** The promise of *one heart* (some mss read "a new heart") and *a new spirit in them* ("you") can be compared with Jeremiah (Jer. 31.33–34; 32.39; and Ezek. 18.31; 36.26). These chs offer a radical solution to prevent Israel from sinning again and experiencing another exile: Free choice is replaced by a new heart which is pre-programmed for obedience. *Tg. Jon.* expresses this idea in translating vv. 19–20 as, "and I will break the heart of wickedness, which is as strong as stone, from their flesh, and I shall give them a fearing heart before Me to perform My will." **20:** *They shall be My people and I will be their God,* a formulation which characterizes the covenant between God and Israel.

11.22–24: The Presence of the LORD departs from the city. 22: With the departure of the *Presence,* the city is no longer protected from the Babylonians. **23:** Rabbinic tradition identifies *the hill east of the city* as the Mount of Olives, (Pesik. Rav Kah. 13, 1; cf. Zech. 14.4: "the Mount of Olives, near Jerusalem on the east"). **24:** Ezekiel is returned to *Chaldea* (Babylonia) to report to the exiles; their reaction is not recorded since it is ultimately irrelevant to the book in its current form, intended for later generations.

12.1–20: Two symbolic actions concerning the exile. God instructs Ezekiel to perform a symbolic act that depicts the exile of the House of Israel. **1:** Like the other oracles that follow Ezekiel's vision, the passage begins with the formula, *the word of the LORD came to me.* **2:** God calls Israel *the rebellious breed,* but adds *they have eyes to see but see not, ears to hear but hear not.* These vv. demonstrate that Ezekiel's prophetic message did not convince his stubborn audience. **3–7:** Ezekiel is to prepare his baggage *(gear for exile),* dig through the wall, and depart with his face covered so that all may see that the exile of Israel is taking place. Ezekiel is told to act *before their eyes* in each of these vv. (seven times altogether) in contrast to the people's *eyes to see but see not. By day:* Ezekiel may have done this act a few times.

12.8–16: The first symbolic action: Ezekiel's explanation for his symbolic action. God instructs Ezekiel to explain his action to satisfy the questions that it provokes. He relates the symbolic action to the exile of the prince, which strikes at the foundation of Judean identity and the promise of God's protection of Jerusalem. **10:** He calls the action a *pronouncement.* **12–13:** Ezekiel's scenario of the prince's escape and capture reflects Zedekiah's capture near Jericho and blinding at Riblah

My laws and faithfully observe My rules. Then they shall be My
people and I will be their God. 21 But as for them whose heart is
set upon their detestable things and their abominations, I will
repay them for their conduct—declares the Lord GOD."
22 Then the cherubs, with the wheels beside them, lifted their
wings, while the Presence of the God of Israel rested above
them. 23 The Presence of the LORD ascended from the midst of
the city and stood on the hill east of the city. 24 A spirit carried
me away and brought me in a vision by the spirit of God to the
exile community in Chaldea. Then the vision that I had seen
left me, 25 and I told the exiles all the things that the LORD had
shown me.

12 The word of the LORD came to me: 2 O mortal, you dwell
among the rebellious breed. They have eyes to see but
see not, ears to hear but hear not; for they are a rebellious
breed. 3 Therefore, mortal, get yourself gear for exile, and go
into exile by day before their eyes. Go into exile from your
home to another place before their very eyes; perhaps they
will take note, even though they are a rebellious breed. 4 Carry
out your gear as gear for exile by day before their very eyes;
and go out again in the evening before their eyes, as one who
goes out into exile. 5 Before their eyes, break through the wall
and carry [the gear] out through it; 6 before their eyes, carry it
on your shoulder. Take it out in the dark, and cover your face
that you may not see the land; for I make you a portent to the
House of Israel.
7 I did just as I was ordered: I took out my gear by day as gear
for exile, and in the evening I broke through the wall [a-]with my
own hands.[-a] In the darkness I carried [the gear] out on my
shoulder, carrying it before their eyes.
8 In the morning, the word of the LORD came to me: 9 O
mortal, did not the House of Israel, that rebellious breed, ask
you, "What are you doing?" 10 Say to them: "Thus said the Lord
GOD: This pronouncement concerns the prince in Jerusalem
and all the House of Israel who are in it." 11 Say: "I am a portent for you: As I have done, so shall it be done to them; they
shall go into exile, into captivity. 12 And the prince among
them shall carry his gear on his shoulder as he goes out in the
dark. He[b] shall break through the wall in order to carry [his
gear] out through it; he shall cover his face, because he himself shall not see the land with his eyes." 13 I will spread My net
over him, and he shall be caught in My snare. I will bring him
to Babylon, the land of the Chaldeans, but he shall not see it;[c]
and there he shall die. 14 And all those around him, his helpers
and all his troops, I will scatter in every direction; and I will

a-a Lit. "by hand." *b Heb. "They."* *c Cf. 2 Kings 25.7.*

unsheathe the sword after them. 15 Then, when I have scattered them among the nations and dispersed them through the countries, they shall know that I am the LORD. 16 But I will spare a few of them from the sword, from famine, and from pestilence, that they may recount all their abominable deeds among the nations to which they come; and they shall know that I am the LORD!

17 The word of the LORD came to me: 18 O mortal, eat your bread in trembling and drink your water in fear and anxiety. 19 And say to the people of the land: Thus said the Lord GOD concerning the inhabitants of Jerusalem in the land of Israel: They shall eat their bread in anxiety and drink their water in desolation, because their land will be desolate of its multitudes on account of the lawlessness of all its inhabitants. 20 The inhabited towns shall be laid waste and the land shall become a desolation; then you shall know that I am the LORD.

21 The word of the LORD came to me: 22 O mortal, what is this proverb that you have in the land of Israel, that you say, "The days grow many and every vision comes to naught?" 23 Assuredly, say to them, Thus said the Lord GOD: I will put an end to this proverb; it shall not be used in Israel any more. Speak rather to them: The days draw near, and the fulfillment of every vision. 24 For there shall no longer be any false vision or soothing divination in the House of Israel. 25 But whenever I the LORD speak what I speak, that word shall be fulfilled without any delay; in your days, O rebellious breed, I will fulfill every word I speak—declares the Lord GOD.

26 The word of the LORD came to me: 27 See, O mortal, the House of Israel says, "The vision that he sees is far ahead, and he prophesies for the distant future." 28 Assuredly, say to them: Thus said the Lord GOD: There shall be no more delay; whenever I speak a word, that word shall be fulfilled—declares the Lord GOD.

13 The word of the LORD came to me: 2 O mortal, prophesy against the prophets of Israel who prophesy; say to those who prophesy out of their own imagination: Hear the word of the LORD! 3 Thus said the Lord GOD: Woe to the degenerate prophets, who follow their own fancy, without having had a vision! 4 Your prophets, O Israel, have been like jackals among ruins. 5 You did not enter the breaches and repair the walls for the House of Israel, that they might stand up in battle in the

prior to imprisonment in Babylon (2 Kings 25.1–7; Jer. 52.4–11). Rashi and Radak quote a midrashic source indicating that Zedekiah tunneled out of Jerusalem to Jericho, but God caused a gazelle to run along the top of the tunnel pursued by Babylonian soldiers, who then captured him as he emerged. **15:** Since the destruction is predicted in advance, it reflects divine power rather than divine apathy or weakness. **16:** *But I will spare a few of them* reflects the tradition of a remnant that is common in prophetic literature. Yet the view of this remnant is bleak, in contrast to other prophetic passages.

12.17–20: The second symbolic action concerning eating and drinking. Eating meals in fear dramatizes the realities of exile. The effectiveness of this symbolic action assumes that members of the exile community are visiting Ezekiel, and the purpose of this message delivered before *the inhabited towns shall be laid waste* was to convince the exiles that this was the appropriate destination for the Jerusalemites.

12.21–14.11: Prophecy and Prophets. 12.21–28: Oracles concerning the fulfillment of prophecy. 21–25: Ezekiel's oracle builds upon the idea that prophecies often lack specific dates for fulfillment. He thus affirms the imminent fulfillment of God's visions and challenges those prophets and prophetesses who proclaim false messages of peace. Ezekiel responds to those who claim that his vision will not be fulfilled or materialized in the near future. **22:** *Proverb* here refers to a common saying among the people; Ezekiel cites these elsewhere. *Vision* refers to both visual and auditory experience. **26–28:** Prophetic visions often do not have a clear time-period associated with them. In this context, Ezekiel responds to the charge that his visions will be fulfilled only in the distant future by stating that they are about to be realized.

13.1–16: Oracle concerning false prophets. 2: Ezekiel charges that they *prophesy out of their own imagination* rather than speaking the word of God. **4:** He compares them to "foxes", animals associated with ruins. Instead of helping to prevent the destruction, the prophets encourage it through their false prophecies.

10: God is against those prophets who announce *"It is well* [shalom]," *when nothing is well.* The expression may be translated, "saying, 'peace,' when there is no peace." Ezekiel compares these prophecies to *daubing with plaster* [a] *flimsy wall* that is then destroyed by rain, hail, and wind. Walls made of sun-dried brick are frequently destroyed by heavy rain and wind. Heb "tafel" *(plaster)* also means "folly" (cf. Lam. 2.14), and may here function as a pun with "yipol/tipol" *(it shall collapse).* Such wordplays are common in prophetic speeches; cf. Amos 7.7–9. **13:** These vv. apply the ancient image of God as a storm God to this specific situation, where a severe storm is especially damaging.

13.17–23: Oracle continues concerning women who prophesy falsely. Though according to biblical texts a predominantly male institution, several female prophets are noted elsewhere in Israel and Judah: Miriam (Exod. 15.20–21), Deborah (Judg. chs 4–5), the wife of Isaiah (Isa. 8.1–4), Huldah (2 Kings 22.14–20), and Noadiah (Neh. 6.14). The women condemned here are false prophets who *prophesy out of their own imagination.* **18:** Ezekiel points to the divinatory side of their activities in which they employ wristbands and veils, and he indicates that they are paid for their services. The exact identity and function of these devices are unclear, and they are depicted in detail to mock these female prophets, who unlike Ezekiel require special accessories to receive the divine word. **19:** Prophecy is a profession in the ancient world for which payment may be received (1 Sam. 9.7; but see Amos 7.10–17); Ezekiel reproaches them for delivering life and death prophecies for negligible compensation. *Death of persons ... survival of persons:* The false prophetesses and diviners apparently play a role in deciding capital cases in which a person's life is at stake. **20:** God will tear the bands from their hands and let the lives of such people go free like birds.

day of the LORD. 6 They prophesied falsehood and lying divination; they said, "Declares the LORD," when the LORD did not
send them, and then they waited for their word to be fulfilled.
7 It was false visions you prophesied and lying divination you
uttered, saying, "Declares the LORD," when I had not spoken.
8 Assuredly, thus said the Lord GOD: Because you speak falsehood and prophesy lies, assuredly, I will deal with you—declares the Lord GOD. 9 My hand will be against the prophets who
prophesy falsehood and utter lying divination. They shall not
remain in the assembly of My people, they shall not be inscribed
in the lists of the House of Israel, and they shall not come back to
the land of Israel. Thus shall you know that I am the Lord GOD.
10 Inasmuch as they have misled My people, saying, "It is
well," when nothing is well, daubing with plaster the flimsy
wall which [a-]the people[-a] were building, 11 say to those daubers
of plaster: It shall collapse; a driving rain shall descend—and
you, O great hailstones, shall fall—and a hurricane wind shall
rend it. 12 Then, when the wall collapses, you will be asked,
"What became of the plaster you daubed on?"
13 Assuredly, thus said the Lord GOD: In My fury I will let
loose hurricane winds; in My anger a driving rain shall descend, and great hailstones in destructive fury. 14 I will throw
down the wall that you daubed with plaster, and I will raze it to
the ground so that its foundation is exposed; and when it falls,
you shall perish in its midst; then you shall know that I am the
LORD. 15 And when I have spent My fury upon the wall and
upon those who daubed it with plaster, I will say to you: Gone
is the wall and gone are its daubers, 16 the prophets of Israel
who prophesy about Jerusalem and see a vision of well-being
for her when there is no well-being—declares the Lord GOD.
17 And you, O mortal, set your face against the women of your
people, who prophesy out of their own imagination. Prophesy
against them 18 and say: Thus said the Lord GOD: Woe to those
who sew pads[b] on all arm-joints and make bonnets[b] for the
head of every person, in order to entrap! Can you hunt down
lives among My people, while you preserve your own lives?
19 You have profaned [c-]My name[-c] among My people in return for
handfuls of barley and morsels of bread; you have announced
the death of persons who will not die and the survival of persons
who will not live—lying to My people, who listen to your lies.
20 Assuredly, thus said the Lord GOD: I am going to deal with
your pads,[b] [d-]by which[-d] you hunt down lives like birds, and I
will tear them from your arms and free the persons whose lives
you hunt down like birds. 21 I will tear off your bonnets[b] and
rescue My people from your hands, and they shall no longer

a-a Heb. "it." *b Meaning of Heb. uncertain.* *c-c Heb. "Me."*
d-d Heb. "where."

be prey in your hands; then you shall know that I am the LORD. 22 Because you saddened the heart of the innocent with lies, when I would not inflict suffering on him, and encouraged the wicked not to repent of his evil ways and so gain life— 23 assuredly, you shall no longer prophesy lies or practice divination! I will save My people from your hands, and you shall know that I am the LORD.

14 Certain elders of Israel came to me and sat down before me. 2 And the word of the LORD came to me: 3 O mortal, these men have turned their thoughts upon their fetishes and set their minds upon the sin through which they stumbled: Shall I respond to their inquiry? 4 Now speak to them and tell them: Thus said the Lord GOD: If anyone of the House of Israel turns his thoughts upon his fetishes and sets his mind upon the sin through which he stumbled, and yet comes to the prophet, I the LORD will respond to him [a]as he comes with[a] his multitude of fetishes. 5 Thus I will hold the House of Israel to account for their thoughts, because they have all been estranged from Me through their fetishes.

6 Now say to the House of Israel: Thus said the Lord GOD: Repent, and turn back from your fetishes and turn your minds away from all your abominations. 7 For if any man of the House of Israel, or of the strangers who dwell in Israel, breaks away from Me and turns his thoughts upon his fetishes and sets his mind upon the sins through which he stumbled, and then goes to the prophet to inquire of Me through him, I the LORD will respond to him directly. 8 I will set My face against that man and make him a sign and a byword, and I will cut him off from the midst of My people. Then you shall know that I am the LORD.

9 And if a prophet is seduced and does speak a word [to such a man], it was I the LORD who seduced that prophet; I will stretch out My hand against him and destroy him from among My people Israel. 10 Thus they shall bear their punishment: The punishment of the inquirer and the punishment of the prophet shall be the same, 11 so that the House of Israel may never again stray from Me and defile itself with all its transgressions. Then they shall be My people and I will be their God—declares the Lord GOD.

12 The word of the LORD came to me: 13 O mortal, if a land were to sin against Me and commit a trespass, and I stretched out My hand against it and broke its staff of bread, and sent famine against it and cut off man and beast from it, 14 even if these three men—Noah, Daniel, and Job—should be in it, they would by their righteousness save only themselves—declares

a-a Emendation yields "directly, because of"; cf. v. 7.

14.1–11: Threats against false prophets and diviners. Here and in the following section, Ezekiel uses the form of case law, familiar from ancient Near Eastern and biblical law collections, to frame his address. Divination is prohibited in the Bible because it is associated with idolatry and apostasy (Deut. 13.2–6). **1:** See 8.1 n. **3:** God states that the elders *have turned their thoughts upon their fetishes and set their minds upon the sin through which they stumbled,* apparently a reference to their consulting pagan diviners or a charge that other Judean prophets are false. The coarse term for fetishes, lit. "dung balls," demonstrates the use of harsh terminology. Such diviners are not worthy of an answer. **4:** In response to those who consult idols or false prophets, God states, *"I the LORD will respond to him."* **7:** *The strangers who dwell in Israel* are non-Israelites. **9–11:** In this last case both the idolater and the prophet who *is seduced* by *the LORD* (!) into being his accomplice will be held accountable; why such a prophet was seduced, and deserves this punishment, is not clarified, though the story of Micaiah ben Imlah, notes a divine command to send a lying spirit to the prophets of Ahab (1 Kings ch 22). God's commission to Isaiah similarly asserts that the people should not repent and be saved (Isa. ch 6). **11:** The covenant formula (see 11.14–21 n.), *they shall be My people and I will be their God,* conveys God's intention to convince the people to remain loyal. Formulae are often used to end oracles in Ezek., and emphasize God's everlasting relationship with Israel even in the most difficult times.

14.12–23: Oracle concerning individual righteousness. The following prophecy discusses the existence of survivors, and is repeated four times with slight variations. This may echo the rhetorical uses of the prophet and repeated efforts to persuade the recipients of his prophecy. The prophet, reusing sections of the curses in the Priestly Lev. ch 26, describes the hunger expected to come to the city, the beast walking through

the Lord GOD. 15 Or, if I were to send wild beasts to roam the land and they depopulated it, and it became a desolation with none passing through it because of the beasts, 16 as I live—declares the Lord GOD—those three men in it would save neither sons nor daughters; they alone would be saved, but the land would become a desolation. 17 Or, if I were to bring the sword upon that land and say, "Let a sword sweep through the land so that I may cut off from it man and beast," 18 if those three men should be in it, as I live—declares the Lord GOD—they would save neither sons nor daughters, but they alone would be saved. 19 Or, if I let loose a pestilence against that land, and poured out My fury upon it in blood, cutting off from it man and beast, 20 should Noah, Daniel, and Job be in it, as I live—declares the Lord GOD—they would save neither son nor daughter; they would save themselves alone by their righteousness.

21 Assuredly, thus said the Lord GOD: How much less [should any escape] now that I have let loose against Jerusalem all four of My terrible punishments—the sword, famine, wild beasts, and pestilence—to cut off man and beast from it! 22 Yet there are survivors left of it, [a]sons and daughters who are being brought out.[a] They are coming out to you; and when you see their ways and their deeds, you will be consoled for the disaster that I brought on Jerusalem, for all that I brought on it. 23 You will be consoled through them, when you see their ways and their deeds and realize that not without cause did I do all that I did in it—declares the Lord GOD.

15 The word of the LORD came to me: 2 O mortal, how is the wood of the grapevine better than the wood of any branch to be found among the trees of the forest? 3 Can wood be taken from it for use in any work? Can one take a peg from it to hang any vessel on? 4 Now suppose it was thrown into the fire as fuel and the fire consumed its two ends and its middle was charred—is it good for any use? 5 Even when it was whole it could not be used for anything; how much less when fire has consumed it and it is charred! Can it still be used for anything?

a-a Several ancient versions read "who are bringing out sons and daughters."

the country, the sword and finally the pestilence. These descriptions lead to the question of whether righteous people will remain, and if so, whether their families will be saved on their behalf. Ezekiel prophesizes that individual people are responsible for their own moral actions and that the wicked will not be saved because of the few among them who are righteous; retribution functions only on the level of the individual, not the community. Abraham (Gen. ch 18) argued with God to save Sodom if there could be found in it the minimum number of righteous people; Ezekiel argues that Jerusalem could not be saved even for the three most righteous. **13:** The form imitates the casuistic law collections, "if a man...." **14:** *Noah, Daniel, and Job* were exemplary righteous persons who had the capacity to save others. Noah saved his family during the flood (Gen. chs 6–9), and Job saved his three friends who spoke wrongly about God (Job 42.7–9). Daniel probably refers not to the Daniel in the book of Daniel, but to Dan-El in the Canaanite legend of Aqhat, found among the Ugaritic tablets. The righteous Dan-El saves his son Aqhat from death. It is noteworthy that Dan-El in Ezek. is spelled according to the Canaanite pattern (see 28.3). In a similar vein, Jeremiah argues that the wicked would suffer punishment even if Moses and Samuel were present (Jer. 15.1). The theme of this section, individual rather than communal responsibility and retribution, is the topic of ch 18 as well. **21:** The same punishments are applied to Jerusalem. **22–23:** These vv. (like 12.16), contrary to the extreme rhetoric of what precedes, emphasize that there will be survivors, sons and daughters. However, these survivors are undeserving and their evil deeds will prove that the destruction was warranted. The "consolation" that they bring is the justification that God acted correctly.

The prophecies in chs 15–24 include a sequence of parables and metaphors concerning the fate of Jerusalem, its inhabitants and its leaders. These parables (meshalim; sing. mashal) often do not include a clear explanation at their end, and at times they cannot be correlated accurately with historical events. Therefore their message is sometimes unclear, though their wording often offers clues to their interpretation.

15.1–8: The vine parable. Ezekiel uses the genre of riddles, known in ancient Near Eastern wisdom literature, to compare the inhabitants of Jerusalem to the wood of a grapevine, which is entirely useless except for burning **3:** The wood of the vine cannot be used to make anything, since vine branches are twisted and weak. **4–5:** Even when burned, the charred ends are useless; they do not produce useful charcoal.

6 Assuredly, thus said the Lord GOD: Like the wood of the
grapevine among the trees of the forest, which I have designated to be fuel for fire, so will I treat the inhabitants of Jerusalem.
7 I will set My face against them; they escaped from fire, but
fire shall consume them. When I set my face against them, you
shall know that I am the LORD. 8 I will make the land a desolation, because they committed trespass—declares the Lord
GOD.

16 The word of the LORD came to me: 2 O mortal, proclaim
Jerusalem's abominations to her, 3 and say: Thus said the
Lord GOD to Jerusalem: By origin and birth you are from the land
of the Canaanites—your father was an Amorite and your mother a Hittite. 4 As for your birth, when you were born your navel
cord was not cut, and you were not bathed in water to [a]smooth
you;[a] you were not rubbed with salt, nor were you swaddled.
5 No one pitied you enough to do any one of these things for you
out of compassion for you; on the day you were born, you were
left lying, rejected, in the open field. 6 When I passed by you and
saw you wallowing in your blood, I said to you: "Live in spite of
your blood." [b]Yea, I said to you: "Live in spite of your blood."[b]
7 I let you grow like the plants of the field; and you continued to
grow up until you attained [a]to womanhood,[a] until your breasts
became firm and your hair sprouted.

You were still naked and bare 8 when I passed by you [again]
and saw that your time for love had arrived. [c]So I spread My
robe over you[c] and covered your nakedness, and I entered into
a covenant with you by oath—declares the Lord GOD; thus you
became Mine. 9 I bathed you in water, and washed the blood off
you, and anointed you with oil. 10 I clothed you with embroidered garments, and gave you sandals of [a]dolphin leather[a]
to wear, and wound fine linen about your head, and dressed
you in silks. 11 I decked you out in finery and put bracelets on
your arms and a chain around your neck. 12 I put a ring in your
nose, and earrings in your ears, and a splendid crown on your
head. 13 You adorned yourself with gold and silver, and your

a-a Meaning of Heb. uncertain.
b-b This sentence is missing from some ancient versions and a few Heb. mss.
c-c An act symbolizing espousal; cf. note at Deut. 23.1, Ruth 3.9.

6–8: Like vine branches, useless Jerusalem will be burned. Trespasses is frequently used in Priestly literature.

16.1–63: The allegory of Jerusalem as God's adulterous wife. Prophets often employ the metaphor of marriage to portray the relationship between God, the husband, and Israel, the bride (Isa. 8.5–8; chs 49–54; 66.7–14; Jer. chs 2–3; Hos. chs 1–3; Zeph. 3.14–20). This ch describes Jerusalem as a foundling of non-Israelite parentage, abandoned at birth. God cared for her and raised her to adulthood, fell in love with her and married her, and bestowed upon her the finest clothing, jewelry, and food. She was beautiful, but she misused her beauty to seduce other men, and misused God's gifts to entice them. Her harlotry, representing idolatry, led her to despicable pagan acts. As punishment, God will gather her lovers (the other nations) against her. They will shame her and destroy her. Ultimately, though, God will honor His covenant with her and restore her, but as elsewhere in Ezek., it will be for God's sake, not because Israel is deserving. R. Eliezer rules that this ch should not be read as a haftarah portion (*m. Meg.* 4.10); this was not accepted, and Maimonides read it as the haftarah for Shemot (Exod. 1.1–6.1) and the Yemenites follow this custom, reading vv. 16.1–14 then. Along with ch 23, which is similar, it has been the subject of much recent feminist interpretation. **1–5:** Ezekiel portrays Jerusalem as an unwanted baby who is abandoned to die at birth. **3:** *Your father was an Amorite and your mother a Hittite:* The indigenous inhabitants of Canaan were idolaters and these were Jerusalem's cultural (if not genealogical) fathers, and Ezekiel is thus suggesting that Jerusalem has idolatrous antecedents and is therefore predisposed to sin. **4–5:** A catalogue of activities typically performed on the newborn. **6–7:** God wills the abandoned infant to live. She lives and grows to puberty. *Live in spite of your blood* may also be rendered "live because of your blood," and with this understanding this phrase is incorporated into the circumcision ceremony. **8:** Upon reaching puberty, she is ready for marriage. *I spread My robe over you and covered your nakedness* indicates God's marriage to the young woman; a similar metaphor expresses Boaz's desire to marry Ruth (Ruth 3.9). God is depicted in strikingly anthropomorphic terms (contrast ch 1). **9:** With her "marriage" to God comes Jerusalem's washing and anointing—that is, her purification and beautification. **10–13:** The description of fine clothing, jewelry, and food demonstrates God's overabundant generosity to the unwanted Jerusalem, who is treated as a queen.

apparel was of fine linen, silk, and embroidery. Your food was
choice flour, honey, and oil. You grew more and more beautiful, and became fit for royalty. [14] Your beauty won you fame
among the nations, for it was perfected through the splendor
which I set upon you—declares the Lord God.
[15] But confident in your beauty and fame, you played the
harlot: you lavished your favors on every passerby; [a-]they were
his.[-a] [16] You even took some of your cloths and made yourself
[a-]tapestried platforms[-a] and fornicated on them—not in the
future; not in time to come. [17] You took your beautiful things,
made of the gold and silver that I had given you, and you made
yourself phallic images and fornicated with them. [18] You took
your embroidered cloths to cover them; and you set My oil and
My incense before them. [19] The food that I had given you—the
choice flour, the oil, and the honey, which I had provided for
you to eat—you set it before them for a pleasing odor.[b] And so
it went—declares the Lord God. [20] You even took the sons and
daughters that you bore to Me and sacrificed them to those
[images] as food—as if your harlotries were not enough, [21] you
slaughtered My children and presented them as offerings to
them! [22] In all your abominations and harlotries, you did not
remember the days of your youth, when you were naked and
bare, and lay wallowing in your blood.
[23] After all your wickedness (woe, woe to you!)—declares
the Lord God—[24] you built yourself an eminence and made
yourself a mound in every square. [25] You built your mound
at every crossroad; and you sullied your beauty and spread
your legs to every passerby, and you multiplied your harlotries. [26] You played the whore with your neighbors, the lustful[c] Egyptians—you multiplied your harlotries to anger Me.
[27] Now, I will stretch out My arm against you and withhold
your maintenance; and I will surrender you to the will of your
enemies, the Philistine women, who are shocked by your lewd
behavior.
[28] In your insatiable lust you also played the whore with the
Assyrians; you played the whore with them, but were still un-
sated. [29] You multiplied your harlotries with Chaldea, that land
of traders; yet even with this you were not satisfied.
[30] [d-]How sick was your heart[-d]—declares the Lord God—
when you did all those things, the acts of a self-willed whore,
[31] building your eminence at every crossroad and setting your
mound in every square! Yet you were not like a prostitute, for
you spurned fees; [32] [you were like] the adulterous wife who

15–29: God's charge that Jerusalem used the gifts to become a whore describes Israel's religious unfaithfulness; since these are imagined as influenced by foreigners, the metaphor then shifts to political and trade alliances with foreign nations. Israel is throughout depicted as a lascivious and unfaithful woman; (the Heb is even more graphic than the translation). **27:** *The Philistine women* are imagined as sexually loose, yet even they *are shocked.* **29:** *Chaldea, that land of traders:* The Heb reads, "Chaldea, that land of Canaan." The Heb term "Canaan" sometimes signifies merchants or traders and is translated as such (Isa. 23.8; cf. Ezek. 17.4; Hos. 12.8; Prov. 31.24). **30–34:** Ezekiel charges that Jerusalem, contrary to the expectations of a prostitute, pays her lovers! This may reflect Nebuchadnezzar stripping the Temple of its wealth when he first conquered Jerusalem (2 Kings 24.10–17).

a-a Meaning of Heb. uncertain. *b I.e., as a sacrifice; cf. Lev. 2.2.*
c Lit. "big of phallus"; cf. 23.20.
d-d Change of vocalization yields "How furious I was with you"; lit. "How I was filled with your fury" (libbat, *as in Akkadian and Old Aramaic).*

welcomes strangers instead of her husband. [33] Gifts are made
to all prostitutes, but you made gifts to all your lovers, and
bribed them to come to you from every quarter for your harlotries. [34] You were the opposite of other women: you solicited
instead of being solicited; you paid fees instead of being paid
fees. Thus you were just the opposite!
[35] Now, O harlot, hear the word of the LORD. [36] Thus said the
Lord GOD: Because of your brazen effrontery, offering your nakedness to your lovers for harlotry—[a]just like the blood of your
children, which you gave to all your abominable fetishes:[a]
—[37] I will assuredly assemble all the lovers to whom you gave
your favors, along with everybody you accepted and everybody you rejected. I will assemble them against you from every
quarter, and I will expose your nakedness to them, and they
shall see all your nakedness. [38] I will inflict upon you the punishment of women who commit adultery and murder, and I
will direct bloody and impassioned fury against you. [39] I will
deliver you into their hands, and they shall tear down your eminence and level your mounds; and they shall strip you of your
clothing and take away your dazzling jewels, leaving you naked and bare. [40] Then they shall assemble a mob against you to
pelt you with stones and pierce you with their swords. [41] They
shall put your houses to the flames and execute punishment
upon you in the sight of many women; thus I will put a stop to
your harlotry, and you shall pay no more fees. [42] When I have
satisfied My fury upon you and My rage has departed from
you, then I will be tranquil; I will be angry no more.
[43] Because you did not remember the days of your youth,
but infuriated Me with all those things, I [a]will pay you back for
your conduct[a]—declares the Lord GOD.
Have you not committed depravity on top of all your other
abominations? [44] Why, everyone who uses proverbs applies
to you the proverb "Like mother, like daughter." [45] You are the
daughter of your mother, who rejected her husband and children. And you are the sister of your sisters, who rejected their
husbands and children; for you are daughters of a Hittite mother and an Amorite father. [46] Your elder sister was Samaria, who
lived with her daughters to the north of you; your younger sister
was Sodom, who lived with her daughters to the south of you.
[47] Did you not walk in their ways and practice their abominations? Why, you were almost[b] more corrupt than they in all your
ways. [48] As I live—declares the Lord GOD—your sister Sodom
and her daughters did not do what you and your daughters
did. [49] Only this was the sin of your sister Sodom: arrogance!
She and her daughters had plenty of bread and untroubled
tranquillity; yet she did not support the poor and the needy.

35–43: God states that all of Jerusalem's lovers, the nations with whom she was allied, will come to punish her. She is punished measure for measure including multiple deaths: stoning, fire and sword. As in many prophetic oracles, the punishment is introduced with the word *Now* ("lakhen"). **38:** No Torah text describes this as *the punishment of women who commit adultery,* though this may reflect some extra-legal practice. **44–58:** Charging that Jerusalem is like her mother *who rejected her husband and children,* God points to the sexual "abominations" of the nations who possessed the land before Israel (Lev. 18.24–30; 20.23), as the proverb (v. 44) notes: the daughter behaves like her mother. **46:** God compares Jerusalem to *Samaria,* the *elder sister ... to the north,* destroyed in 722 BCE, and *Sodom,* the *younger sister ... to the south,* completely destroyed according to common lore long ago. **47:** According to biblical tradition (Gen. chs 18–19; 2 Kings ch 17), both cities were destroyed for their sins, but God states that Jerusalem's sins are even worse and therefore her destruction is inevitable. **49:** Sodom's sin mentioned here differs from the sins described in Gen. chs 18–19. **53:** God intends to *restore ... the fortunes* of both Sodom and Samaria and their *daughters,* a reference to cities allied with each. Similarly, God will restore Jerusalem.

a-a Construction of Heb. uncertain. *b Meaning of Heb. uncertain.*

54: God intends to punish or cleanse Israel from sins so it will continue to experience the shame of its past actions. **57:** Jerusalem has become a mockery to *Aram* (Peshitta reads "Edom"; the letters "dalet" and "resh" are graphically similar) and *Philistia,* Judah's surviving neighbors. **60–61:** The *everlasting covenant* with Jerusalem alludes to God's eternal protection for Jerusalem. The covenant is not "new"; God "remembers" the covenant, and calls upon Jerusalem to do the same. Jerusalem and not God is charged with violating the "eternal covenant," according to which Jerusalem is destroyed. Samaria and Sodom were sisters, but they will become Jerusalem's daughters, indicating Jerusalem's premier status. **62:** *I will establish My covenant with you, and you shall know that I am the LORD* restates the covenant formula. **63:** God's remembering (vv. 60–61) has as its ultimate goal making Israel *remember. When I have forgiven you for all that you did* is unique, stressing that even these most grave sins, which deserved such harsh punishment, will not disconnect God from Israel.

17.1–24: The allegory of the eagles, the vine, and the cedar. The allegory most likely describes Jehoiachin's exile to Babylonia, the installation of his uncle Zedekiah as king, and Zedekiah's demise when he allied himself with Egypt and revolted against Babylonia (see 2 Kings chs 24–25; Jer. ch 52; 2 Chron. ch 36). **1–2:** God instructs Ezekiel to speak a *riddle* and *an allegory* (elsewhere translated "proverb" [12.22], "theme" [Job 27.1], "byword" [Ps. 69.12]; the basic meaning is "likeness" or "comparison"). **3–10:** The allegory proceeds in three stages. **3–4:** The first describes an eagle, later identified as Nebuchadnezzar, who breaks off the *top* shoot of the *cedar* and carries it *to the land of traders* (lit. "to the land of Canaan"; cf. 16.29;) and *a city of merchants.* Lebanon was known for "the cedars of Lebanon" (Ps. 92.13).

50 In their haughtiness, they committed abomination before
Me; and so I removed them, as you saw.[a] 51 Nor did Samaria
commit even half your sins. You committed more abominations than they, and by all the abominations that you committed you made your sisters look righteous. 52 Truly, you must
bear the disgrace of serving as your sisters' advocate: Since you
have sinned more abominably than they, they appear righteous in comparison. So be ashamed and bear your disgrace,
because you have made your sisters look righteous.
53 I will restore their fortunes—the fortunes of Sodom and
her daughters and the fortunes of Samaria and her daughters—
and your fortunes along with theirs. 54 Thus you shall bear your
disgrace and feel your disgrace for behaving in such a way that
they could take comfort. 55 Then your sister Sodom and her
daughters shall return to their former state, and Samaria and
her daughters shall return to their former state, and you and
your daughters shall return to your former state. 56 Was not
your sister Sodom a byword in your mouth in the days of your
pride, 57 before your own wickedness was exposed? So must
you now bear the mockery of the daughters of Aram[b] and all
her neighbors, the daughters of Philistia who jeer at you on
every side. 58 You yourself must bear your depravity and your
abominations—declares the LORD.
59 Truly, thus said the Lord GOD: I will deal with you as you
have dealt, for you have spurned the pact and violated the covenant. 60 Nevertheless, I will remember the covenant I made
with you in the days of your youth, and I will establish it with
you as an everlasting covenant. 61 You shall remember your
ways and feel ashamed, when you receive your older sisters
and your younger sisters, and I give them to you as daughters, though they are not of your covenant. 62 I will establish
My covenant with you, and you shall know that I am the LORD.
63 Thus you shall remember and feel shame, and you shall be
too abashed to open your mouth again, when I have forgiven
you for all that you did—declares the Lord GOD.

17 The word of the LORD came to me: 2 O mortal, propound
a riddle and relate an allegory to the House of Israel.
3 Say: Thus said the Lord GOD: The great eagle with the great
wings and the long pinions, [c]with the full plumage and the
brilliant colors,[c] came to the Lebanon range and seized the
top of the cedar. 4 He plucked off its topmost bough and carried it off to the land of traders[d] and set it in a city of merchants.

a *Construed as second-person feminine; cf.* qere, *vv. 47 and 51; and see above vv. 13, 18, 22, 31, 43.* b *Many Heb. mss. and editions read "Edom."*
c-c *This description suggests the golden eagle; the vulture, called by the same word in Heb.* (nesher) *has a bald head (Mic. 1.16) and dark feathers.*
d *Cf. 16.29.*

5 He then took some of the seed of the land[a] and planted it in a
fertile field; [b]he planted and set it like a willow[b] beside abundant waters. 6 It grew and became a spreading vine of low stature; it became a vine, produced branches, and sent out boughs.
[He had intended] that its twigs should turn to him, and that its
roots should stay under him.

7 But there was another great eagle with great wings and full
plumage; and this vine now bent its roots in his direction and
sent out its twigs toward him, that he might water it more than
the bed where it was planted—8 though it was planted in rich
soil beside abundant water—so that it might grow branches
and produce boughs and be a noble vine.

9 Say: Thus said the Lord God: Will it thrive? Will he[c] not
tear out its roots and rip off its crown, so that its entire foliage
withers? It shall wither, despite any strong arm or mighty army
[that may come] to remove it from its roots. 10 And suppose it
is transplanted, will it thrive? When the east wind strikes it, it
shall wither—wither upon the bed where it is growing.

11 Then the word of the Lord came to me: 12 Say to the rebellious breed: Do you not know what these things mean? Say:
The king of Babylon came to Jerusalem, and carried away its
king and its officers and brought them back with him to Babylon. 13 He took one of the seed royal and made a covenant
with him and imposed an oath on him, and he carried away
the nobles of the land—14 so that it might be a humble kingdom and not exalt itself, but keep his covenant and so endure.

15 But [that prince] rebelled against him and sent his envoys
to Egypt to get horses and a large army. Will he succeed? Will
he who does such things escape? Shall he break a covenant
and escape? 16 As I live—declares the Lord God—in the very
homeland of the king who made him king, whose oath he
flouted and whose covenant he broke—right there, in Babylon,
he shall die. 17 Pharaoh will not fight at his side with a great
army and with numerous troops in the war, when mounds
are thrown up and siege towers erected to destroy many lives.
18 He flouted a pact and broke a covenant; he gave his promise and did all these things—he shall not escape. 19 Assuredly,
thus said the Lord God: As I live, I will pay him back for flouting My pact and breaking My covenant. 20 I will spread My net
over him and he shall be caught in My snare; I will carry him to
Babylon and enter with him into judgment there for the trespass which he committed against Me. 21 And all the fugitives[d]
of all his battalions shall fall by the sword, and those who remain shall scatter in every direction; then you will know that I
the Lord have spoken.

a Emendation yields "cedar." b-b Meaning of Heb. uncertain.
c I.e., the first eagle. d Many mss. read "picked men."

5–6: The second stage describes the planting of seed that becomes a vine, which is later identified as Zedekiah. **7–8:** The third stage describes the second *great eagle,* generally identified as the Egyptian Pharaoh Psammetichus II, to whom Zedekiah turned for support in his revolt against Nebuchadnezzar (Jer. ch 27). **9–10:** The rhetorical questions portray the destruction of the vine. The first eagle, Nebuchadnezzar, will destroy the vine (Zedekiah). **11–21:** The allegory is explained; the realpolitik of the situation is detailed. **20:** God identifies with the Babylonian king by referring to Zedekiah's revolt against Babylonia as *the trespass which he committed against Me.* In 2 Chron. 36.13 Zedekiah is punished for not upholding his oath of vassaldom to Babylonia and in 2 Kings 25.7, he is eventually brought to *Babylon.* It is now known that the future of Israel's kingship is with Jehoiachin in Babylonia, and not with Zedekiah in Jerusalem.

[22] Thus said the Lord GOD: Then I in turn will take and set [in the ground a slip] from the lofty top of the cedar; I will pluck a tender twig from the tip of its crown, and I will plant it on a tall, towering mountain. [23] I will plant it in Israel's lofty highlands, and it shall bring forth boughs and produce branches[a] and grow into a noble cedar. Every bird of every feather shall take shelter under it, shelter in the shade of its boughs. [24] Then shall all the trees of the field know that it is I the LORD who have abased the lofty tree and exalted the lowly tree, who have dried up the green tree and made the withered tree bud. I the LORD have spoken, and I will act.

18 The word of the LORD came to me: [2] What do you mean by quoting this proverb upon the soil of Israel, "Parents eat sour grapes and their children's teeth are blunted"?[b] [3] As I live—declares the Lord GOD—this proverb shall no longer be current among you in Israel. [4] Consider, all lives are Mine; the life of the parent and the life of the child are both Mine. The person who sins, only he shall die.

[5] Thus, if a man is righteous and does what is just and right: [6] If he has not eaten on the mountains[c] or raised his eyes to the fetishes of the House of Israel; if he has not defiled another man's wife or approached a menstruous woman; [7] if he has not wronged anyone; if he has returned the debtor's pledge to him and has taken nothing by robbery; if he has given bread to the hungry and clothed the naked; [8] if he has not lent at advance interest or exacted accrued interest;[d] if he has abstained from wrongdoing and executed true justice between man and man; [9] if he has followed My laws and kept My rules and acted honestly—he is righteous. Such a man shall live—declares the Lord GOD.

[10] Suppose, now, that he has begotten a son who is a ruffian, a shedder of blood, who [e-]does any of these things,[-e] [11] whereas he himself did none of these things. That is, [the son] has eaten on the mountains,[c] has defiled another man's wife, [12] has wronged the poor and the needy, has taken by robbery, has not returned a pledge, has raised his eyes to the fetishes, has

a Others "fruit." *b Others "set on edge."*
c I.e., in idolatry. Emendation yields "with the blood"; cf. 33.25; Lev. 17.10–11, 19.26.
d I.e., interest deducted in advance or interest added at the time of repayment; cf. Lev. 25.36. *e-e Meaning of Heb. uncertain.*

22–24: God employs the allegory of *the cedar* to promise restoration. The cedar, the grandest of trees, will tower over all the other trees (nations), and all will see the power of God. Radak, maintains that these statements refer to Zerubbabel son of Shealtiel, the grandson of King Jehoiachin whom Haggai declared to be God's "signet ring" or regent (Hag. 2.20–23;), and who commenced the building of the Second Temple. **24:** The ch is brought to a close by a modified, expanded version of formulae used throughout Ezek.

18.1–32: Individual responsibility and reward. This ch states the principle of individual responsibility, a topic also dealt with in 3.16–21; 14.12–23; 33.1–20. The prophet disputes the view that Israel's punishment is due to the sins of past generations; instead, each individual is responsible for his or her own actions. In contrast the Decalogue (Exod. 20.5; Deut. 5.9), indicates that God visits "the guilt of the parents upon the children, upon the third and upon the fourth generations of those who reject Me" (cf. Exod. 34.7). **2:** The opposing view is quoted as a proverb, *"Parents eat sour grapes and their children's teeth are blunted."* Jeremiah takes up the same proverb to argue for individual moral responsibility in the future (see Jer. 31.29–30), but for Ezekiel this principle of individual responsibility is currently operative. It allows the exiles in Babylon to feel that the impending destruction does not suggest that they are unredeemable. **5–20:** Ezekiel describes four cases. **5–8:** The righteous man's deeds include refraining from idolatry, sexual, and social wrong doings. **6:** *Eaten on the mountains,* found only in Ezek.; the exact meaning is unclear. *Raised his eyes to the fetishes of the House of Israel,* improper worship of God; *defiled another man's wife,* adultery (Lev. 19.20–22; 20.10); *approached a menstruous woman,* had relations with a woman during her menstrual period (Lev. 15.19–24). **7:** *Wronged anyone,* economic oppression is unholy (Lev. 19.13); *has returned the debtor's pledge to him and has taken nothing by robbery ... has given bread to the hungry and clothed the naked,* a person's only cloak could be taken in pledge for a loan, but it had to be returned if the debtor needed it (Exod. 22.25–27). **8:** *Has not lent at advance interest or exacted accrued interest* (Exod. 22.25; Lev. 25.35–38); *executed true justice between man and man,* in a court of law (Lev. 19.15–19). **9:** The righteous person shall live. **10–13:** If a righteous person's child sins, that child is responsible for his or her own sins and shall die and does not inherit

committed abomination, 13 has lent at advance interest, or exacted accrued interest—shall he live? He shall not live! If he has committed any of these abominations, he shall die; he has forfeited his life.

14 Now suppose that he, in turn, has begotten a son who has seen all the sins that his father committed, but has taken heed and has not imitated them: 15 He has not eaten on the mountains[a] or raised his eyes to the fetishes of the House of Israel; he has not defiled another man's wife; 16 he has not wronged anyone; he has not seized a pledge or taken anything by robbery; he has given his bread to the hungry and clothed the naked; 17 he has [b]refrained from oppressing the poor;[-b] he has not exacted advance or accrued interest; he has obeyed My rules and followed My laws—he shall not die for the iniquity of his father, but shall live. 18 To be sure, his father, because he practiced fraud, robbed his brother, and acted wickedly among his kin, did die for his iniquity; 19 and now you ask, "Why has not the son shared the burden of his father's guilt?" But the son has done what is right and just, and has carefully kept all My laws: he shall live!

20 The person who sins, he alone shall die. A child shall not share the burden of a parent's guilt, nor shall a parent share the burden of a child's guilt; the righteousness of the righteous shall be accounted to him alone, and the wickedness of the wicked shall be accounted to him alone.

21 Moreover, if the wicked one repents of all the sins that he committed and keeps all My laws and does what is just and right, he shall live; he shall not die. 22 None of the transgressions he committed shall be remembered against him; because of the righteousness he has practiced, he shall live. 23 Is it my desire that a wicked person shall die?—says the Lord GOD. It is rather that he shall turn back from his ways and live.

24 So, too, if a righteous person turns away from his righteousness and does wrong, practicing the very abominations that the wicked person practiced, shall he live? None of the righteous deeds that he did shall be remembered; because of the treachery he has practiced and the sins he has committed—because of these, he shall die.

25 Yet you say, "The way of the Lord is unfair." Listen, O House of Israel: Is My way unfair? It is your ways that are unfair! 26 When a righteous person turns away from his righteousness and does wrong, he shall die for it; he shall die for the wrong he has done. 27 And if a wicked person turns back from the wickedness that he practiced and does what is just and right, such

the parent's righteousness. The list of offenses abridges and rearranges vv. 6–9. **14–18:** Conversely, if a sinner's child behaves righteously, that child shall be spared. **19–20:** Ezekiel concludes this section by emphasizing that each individual is to take responsibility for his or her own actions alone. **21–24:** Ezekiel contends that a wicked person who repents shall be saved, but a righteous person who sins shall be condemned. Even a person's own past actions do not determine his fate, if he changes his course of action. This concluding section of the ch in a sense takes the previous part metaphorically, understanding the father and children as the actions of single indviduals at different times of their lives. **25–29:** Ezekiel restates the preceding principle about repentance, to answer those living in Babylonia who think that all is lost and who might object, thinking that they are now being punished for sins of past generations.

a *I.e., in idolatry. Emendation yields "with the blood"; cf. 33.25; Lev. 17.10–11, 19.26.*
b-b *Lit. "turned his hand back from the poor." Emendation yields "abstained from wrongdoing"; cf. v. 8.*

30–32: *A new heart and a new spirit* These vv., addressed primarily to residents of Judah and Jerusalem before the destruction, are remarkable since there is no additional call for repentance in the book, because its underlying assumption is that no change will prevent the destruction of the Temple.

19.1–14: End of the Judean monarchy. Ezekiel illustrates his messages regarding the leaders' responsibility with two allegories, concerning the demise of the Judean kings, styled as dirges or songs of mourning, and they refer to events recounted in 2 Kings chs 23–24 and 2 Chron. ch 36. As here, in biblical dirges the first part of each half-verse is usually longer than the second. **1:** *And you are to intone a dirge over the princes of Israel:* A dirge, or lament (Heb "qinah") was recited at the death of an individual (e.g., 2 Sam. ch 1; 2 Chron. 35.25) but the prophets use it metaphorically to signal the demise of the people (Jer. 9.9; Amos 5.1). Ezekiel refers to the kings as "princes," thereby expressing the king's diminished status in relation to the priests (34.24; 45.7–8). **2–9:** The lion symbolizes the tribe of the Davidic king, Judah. **2:** *A lioness was your mother* refers to Judah or all Israel. **4:** The first cub who is brought *with hooks to the land of Egypt* is King Jehoahaz son of Josiah, who was exiled to Egypt by Pharaoh Neco after Josiah's death (2 Kings 23.31–34; 2 Chron. 36.1–4). **6:** The second cub who *learned to hunt prey ... devoured men* might be King Jehoiakim son of Josiah, whom Pharaoh Neco placed on the throne after exiling Jehoahaz. Jeremiah condemns Jehoiakim for his injustice (Jer. 21.11–22.19). Other possible identifications include Zedekiah and Jehoiachin.

a person shall save his life. 28 Because he took heed and turned
back from all the transgressions that he committed, he shall
live; he shall not die.

29 Yet the House of Israel say, "The way of the Lord is unfair."
Are My ways unfair, O House of Israel? It is your ways that are
unfair! 30 Be assured, O House of Israel, I will judge each one
of you according to his ways—declares the Lord GOD. Repent
and turn back from your transgressions; let them not be a
stumbling block of guilt for you. 31 Cast away all the transgressions by which you have offended, and get yourselves a new
heart and a new spirit, that you may not die, O House of Israel.
32 For it is not My desire that anyone shall die—declares the
Lord GOD. Repent, therefore, and live!

19 And you are to intone a dirge over the princes of Israel,
2 and say:

What a lioness was your mother
Among the lions!
Crouching among the great beasts,
She reared her cubs.
3 She raised up one of her cubs,
He became a great beast;
He learned to hunt prey—
He devoured men.
4 Nations heeded [the call] against him;
He was caught in their snare.
They dragged him off with hooks
To the land of Egypt.
5 When she saw herself frustrated,
Her hope defeated,
She took another of her cubs
And set him up as a great beast.
6 He stalked among the lions,
He was a great beast;
He learned to hunt prey—
He devoured men.
7 He [a]ravished their widows,[a]
Laid waste their cities;
The land and all in it were appalled
At the sound of his roaring.
8 Nations from the countries roundabout
Arrayed themselves against him.
They spread their net over him,
He was caught in their snare.
9 With hooks he was put in a cage,

a-a *Emendation yields "ravaged their castles."*

They carried him off to the king of Babylon
And confined him in a fortress,
So that never again should his roar be heard
On the hills of Israel.

10 Your mother was like a vine [a]in your blood,[-a]
Planted beside streams,
With luxuriant boughs and branches
Thanks to abundant waters.
11 And she had a mighty rod[b]
Fit for a ruler's scepter.[b]
It towered highest [c]among the leafy trees,[-c]
It was conspicuous by its height,
By the abundance of its boughs.
12 But plucked up in a fury,
She was hurled to the ground.
The east wind withered her branches,
They broke apart and dried up;
And her mighty rod was consumed by fire.
13 Now she is planted in the desert,
In ground that is arid and parched.
14 Fire has issued from her twig-laden branch
And has consumed her boughs,
She is left without a mighty rod,
A scepter to rule with.

This is a dirge, and it has become a [familiar] dirge.

20 In the seventh year, on the tenth day of the fifth month,
certain elders of Israel came to inquire of the LORD, and
sat down before me. [2] And the word of the LORD came to me:
[3] O mortal, speak to the elders of Israel and say to them: Thus
said the Lord GOD: Have you come to inquire of Me? As I live, I
will not respond to your inquiry—declares the Lord GOD.

a-a Meaning of Heb. uncertain; emendation yields "in a vineyard."
b Heb. plural. *c-c Meaning of Heb. uncertain.*

9: *Carried him off to the king of Babylon and confined him in a fortress* refers to King Jehoiachin son of Jehoiakim, who was exiled to Babylon following Jehoiakim's failed revolt and death (2 Kings 24.8–17; 2 Chron. 36.9–10). **10–14:** This poem employs the imagery of the vine (see chs 15; 17). It is hard to identify the poem's imagery with specific individuals or countries though Radak identifies King Zedekiah son of Josiah, who is not referred to in the preceding vv., as the subject of the allegory. **12:** *The east wind withered her branches:* The "Sharav" or "Hamsin," a dry and destructive desert wind is frequently employed as a symbol of God's power (Exod. 14.21; 15.8–10; Isa. 11.15). **13:** *Now she is planted in the desert:* Zedekiah was captured in the desert (better: "wilderness"); this may be referring to the exile in Babylonia (2 Kings ch 25; Jer. ch 52).

20.1–24.27: Destruction of Judah and Jerusalem. This section begins with the introductory date formula, *In the seventh year, on the tenth day of the fifth month,* 10 Av, 591 BCE, approximately two years before the siege on Jerusalem. Once again, the formula *and the word of the LORD* marks the various oracle reports that comprise this section, including 20.1–44; 21.1–5; 21.6–12; 21.13–22; 21.23–37; 22.1–16; 22.17–22; 22.23–31; 23.1–49. The sequence begins with an examination of Israel's past in the wilderness, which provides a basis for returning the nation to the wilderness so that it might be purged. It continues with prophecies against the Negev desert, oracles concerning God's sword, and the allegory of Oholah and Oholibah which outlines the sins of Samaria and Jerusalem.

20.1–44: Ezekiel's assessment of Israel's past and future. The ch begins with Ezekiel's overview of Israel's history in the wilderness, which unfolds in four stages: in Egypt (vv. 5–9), the first generation in the wilderness (vv. 10–17), the second generation in the wilderness (vv. 18–26), and in the land of Israel (vv. 27–29). In its second part, God refuses to respond to the inquiry, because of the people's sins (vv. 30–31); and God plans a new exodus and judgment in the wilderness (vv. 32–44). The historical précis in vv. 5–29 is very selective, and presents the past in terms of Israel's rebellion, God's punishment, and divine compassion. Ezek. 20.2–20 serves as the haftarah for the parashah of Kedoshim (Lev. 19.1–20.27) in the Sephardi and Yemenite tradition. **1–2:** *The seventh year ... tenth day ... fifth month,* 10 Av, 591 BCE. The content of the elders' inquiry is unknown; it is irrelevant, since the main point is that God will not answer them. **3–4:** *Inquire of* the LORD is a technical term for seeking a divine oracle. God refuses to answer *the elders,* and instead calls upon Ezekiel to judge them. Cf. vv. 30–31.

4 [a]Arraign, arraign them, O mortal![a] Declare to them the
abhorrent deeds of their fathers. 5 Say to them: Thus said the
Lord GOD:

On the day that I chose Israel, I [b]gave My oath[b] to the stock
of the House of Jacob; when I made Myself known to them in
the land of Egypt, I gave my oath to them. When I said, "I the
LORD am your God," 6 that same day I swore to them to take
them out of the land of Egypt into a land flowing with milk and
honey, a land which I had sought out for them, the fairest of
all lands.

7 I also said to them: Cast away, every one of you, the detestable things [c]that you are drawn to,[c] and do not defile yourselves with the fetishes of Egypt—I the LORD am your God.
8 But they defied Me and refused to listen to Me. They did not
cast away the detestable things they were drawn to, nor did
they give up the fetishes of Egypt. Then I resolved to pour out
My fury upon them, to vent all My anger upon them there, in
the land of Egypt. 9 But I acted for the sake of My name, that it
might not be profaned in the sight of the nations among whom
they were. For it was before their eyes that I had made Myself
known to Israel[d] to bring them out of the land of Egypt.

10 I brought them out of the land of Egypt and I led them
into the wilderness. 11 I gave them My laws and taught them
My rules, by the pursuit of which a man shall live. 12 Moreover,
I gave them My sabbaths to serve as a sign between Me and
them, that they might know that it is I the LORD who sanctify them. 13 But the House of Israel rebelled against Me in the
wilderness; they did not follow My laws and they rejected My
rules—by the pursuit of which a man shall live—and they
grossly desecrated My sabbaths. Then I thought to pour out
My fury upon them in the wilderness and to make an end of
them; 14 but I acted for the sake of My name, that it might not
be profaned in the sight of the nations before whose eyes I had
led them out. 15 However, I swore[e] to them in the wilderness
that I would not bring them into the land flowing with milk
and honey, the fairest of all lands, which I had assigned [to
them], 16 for they had rejected My rules, disobeyed My laws,
and desecrated My sabbaths; their hearts followed after their
fetishes. 17 But I had pity on them and did not destroy them; I
did not make an end of them in the wilderness.

18 I warned their children in the wilderness: Do not follow
the practices of your fathers, do not keep their ways, and do
not defile yourselves with their fetishes. 19 I the LORD am your
God: Follow My laws and be careful to observe My rules. 20 And

a-a Lit. "Will you arraign them, will you arraign, O mortal?"
b-b Lit. "raised My hand." *c-c Lit. "of his eyes."* *d Lit. "them."*
e Lit. "raised My hand."

5–32: God rehearses the history of Israel's rebellion during the exodus and wilderness periods (see Ps. 106, which also views Israel's history in a negative manner). **5–6:** *I the LORD am your God ... I swore to them to take them out of the land of Egypt,* see also Exod. 20.2. **7–8:** Apostasy in Egypt; actually, immediately during and following the exodus, presented here in a way unknown from the description in Exod. **9:** *I acted for the sake of My name,* a key issue in Ezek. (20.14, 22; 36.22). **10–26:** Apostasy in the wilderness, this too is presented in a manner not found in the Torah's descriptions. See Exod. chs 32–34; Num. chs 14; 25. **11–12:** The Sabbath is the foundational sign of the covenant (Exod. 20.8–11; 31.12–17). Scholars have suggested that the Sabbath became particularly significant in the exile, as holy time replaced the vacuum of holy space (the Temple); this might explain why the Sabbath plays such a significant role here. As in Exod. 31.13, 17 (from the Priestly tradition), it is viewed as a sign, namely a symbol acknowledging God as Creator. **13–17:** The rebellion of the first generation is the golden calf incident and the reaction to the report of the spies in which Moses persuaded God not to destroy the entire people (Exod. 33.12–33; Num. 14.13–25). **18–26:** Following Israel's rebellion, God condemned the people to death in the wilderness.

hallow My sabbaths, that they may be a sign between Me and
you, that you may know that I the LORD am your God.
21 But the children rebelled against Me: they did not follow
My laws and did not faithfully observe My rules, by the pursuit of which man shall live; they profaned My sabbaths. Then
I resolved to pour out My fury upon them, to vent all My anger
upon them, in the wilderness. 22 But I held back My hand and
acted for the sake of My name, that it might not be profaned
in the sight of the nations before whose eyes I had led them
out. 23 However, I swore[a] to them in the wilderness that I would
scatter them among the nations and disperse them through
the lands, 24 because they did not obey My rules, but rejected
My laws, profaned My sabbaths, and looked with longing to
the fetishes of their fathers. 25 Moreover, I gave them laws that
were not good and rules by which they could not live: 26 When
they set aside every first issue of the womb, I defiled them by
their very gifts[b]—that I might render them desolate,[c] that they
might know that I am the LORD.
27 Now, O mortal, speak to the House of Israel and say to
them: Thus said the Lord GOD: By this too your fathers affronted Me and committed trespass against Me: 28 When I brought
them to the land that I had sworn[a] to give them, and they saw
any high hill or any leafy tree, they slaughtered their sacrifices
there and presented their offensive offerings there; there they
produced their pleasing odors and poured out their libations.
29 Then I said to them, "What is this shrine which you visit?"
(Therefore such [a shrine] is called *bamah*[d] to this day.)
30 Now say to the House of Israel: Thus said the Lord GOD:
If you defile yourselves as your fathers did and go astray after their detestable things, 31 and if to this very day you defile
yourselves in the presentation of your gifts by making your
children pass through the fire to all your fetishes, shall I respond to your inquiry, O House of Israel? As I live—declares
the Lord GOD—I will not respond to you. 32 And what you have
in mind shall never come to pass—when you say, "We will
be like the nations, like the families of the lands, worshiping
wood and stone." 33 As I live—declares the Lord GOD—I will
reign over you with a strong hand, and with an outstretched
arm, and with overflowing fury. 34 With a strong hand and an
outstretched arm and overflowing fury I will bring you out
from the peoples and gather you from the lands where you are
scattered, 35 and I will bring you into the wilderness of the peoples; and there I will enter into judgment with you face to face.
36 As I entered into judgment with your fathers in the wilderness of the land of Egypt, so will I enter into judgment with

a Lit. "raised My hand." *b See v. 31.* *c Emendation yields "guilty."*
d As if from ba *"visit" and* mah *"what."*

25: This refers to acts of apostasy following the incident of the spies (e.g., Meribah, Num. ch 20; Baal Peor, Num. ch 25). One option is that since the people disobeyed God's good laws, He gave them bad laws instead, exemplified by child sacrifice. Alternatively, some Israelites interpreted Exod. 22.28; 34.19 as literally requiring sacrifice of the first-born. (It is unclear if at an early point in Israelite religion sacrifice of the first-born was regularly practiced in some circles, though it seems that some believed that God approved of child sacrifice [Deut. 12.29; Jer. 7.31; 19.5; 32.25].) The notion that God misled the people so that He could then condemn them for it is found also in 14.9. **27–31:** Apostasy in the land of Israel. **29:** See translators' note *d* for Ezekiel's pun; this is a mocking etymology of the term bamah, high-place. **32:** *We will be like the nations,* see Deut. 17.14; 1 Sam. 8.4–5 concerning the institution of kingship. **33–44:** God returns Israel to the wilderness to purge and to restore the nation. *A strong hand, and ... an outstretched arm,* typically used of God liberating Israel from Egypt (e.g., Deut. 4.34), are here reversed and used of God punishing Israel. **33:** *I will reign over you,* one of God's fundamental claims to kingship. **35:** *Wilderness of the peoples* associates Israel's exile among the nations with the wilderness tradition. **36:** The past was sometimes imagined as cyclical.

you—declares the LORD GOD. 37 I will make you pass under the
shepherd's staff,[a] and I will bring you into the bond[b] of the covenant. 38 I will remove from you those who rebel and transgress
against Me; I will take them out of the countries where they
sojourn, but they shall not enter the land of Israel. Then you
shall know that I am the LORD.
39 As for you, O House of Israel, thus said the Lord GOD: Go,
every one of you, and worship his fetishes and continue,[b] if you
will not obey Me; but do not profane My holy name any more
with your idolatrous gifts. 40 For only on My holy mountain, on
the lofty mount of Israel—declares the Lord GOD—there, in
the land, the entire House of Israel, all of it, must worship Me.
There I will accept them, and there I will take note of your contributions and the choicest offerings of all your sacred things.
41 When I bring you out from the peoples and gather you from
the lands in which you are scattered, I will accept you as a
pleasing odor; and I will be sanctified through you in the sight
of the nations. 42 Then, when I have brought you to the land
of Israel, to the country that I swore[c] to give to your fathers,
you shall know that I am the LORD. 43 There you will recall your
ways and all the acts by which you defiled yourselves; and
you will loathe yourselves for all the evils that you committed.
44 Then, O House of Israel, you shall know that I am the LORD,
when I deal with you for My name's sake—not in accordance
with your evil ways and corrupt acts—declares the Lord GOD.

21 The word of the LORD came to me: 2 O mortal, set your
face toward Teman,[d] and proclaim to Darom,[d] and
prophesy against the brushland of the Negeb.[d] 3 Say to the
brushland of the Negeb: Hear the word of the LORD. Thus said
the Lord GOD: I am going to kindle a fire in you, which shall
devour every tree of yours, both green and withered. Its leaping flame shall not go out, and every face from south to north
shall be scorched by it. 4 Then all flesh shall recognize that I the
LORD have kindled it; it shall not go out. 5 And I said, "Ah, Lord
GOD! They say of me: He is just a riddlemonger."
6 Then the word of the LORD came to me: 7 O mortal, set your
face toward Jerusalem and proclaim against her sanctuaries and prophesy against the land of Israel. 8 Say to the land
of Israel: Thus said the LORD: I am going to deal with you! I
will draw My sword from its sheath, and I will wipe out from
you both the righteous and the wicked. 9 In order to wipe out
from you both the righteous and the wicked, My sword shall
assuredly be unsheathed against all flesh from south to north;

a I.e., to be counted; see Lev. 27.32. *b Meaning of Heb. uncertain.*
c Lit. "raised My hand."
d Teman, Darom, Negeb are three terms for "the south." The allusion is to Jerusalem (v. 7), which was always approached from Babylon by way of the north.

37: *Pass under the shepherd's staff,* by the shepherd culling the flock. God uses this metaphor to portray the purge of Israel that will take place when the Temple is destroyed. This image is developed more extensively in ch 34. **40–44:** *My holy mountain,* the Jerusalem Temple where the people will present their offerings to God. As in the conclusion to ch 23, Ezekiel emphasizes that Israel's restoration is for God's sake only, and that Israel will fully understand its shame in the future.

21.1–5: A prophecy against the Negeb. The *Negeb* (Negev) is the desert region of southern Judah. **2:** *Teman* designates the location of the Edomites (25.13), who are condemned for assisting Babylonia in Judah's destruction (25.12–14). Both *Teman* and *Darom* refer to the south; the repetition is for emphasis. **5:** *Riddlemonger,* Heb "memashal meshalim," "an allegorizer of allegories," here pejorative, but see 17.2.

21.6–37: Oracles concerning God's sword. The oracles concerning God's sword may be subdivided into three sections: 21.6–12; 21.13–22; and 21.23–37. **21.6–12:** Ezekiel speaks toward the Jerusalem sanctuary as the holy center of the nation. **8:** God's threat to *wipe out from you both the righteous and the wicked* contradicts Ezekiel's concept of individual moral responsibility (ch 18), and instead conforms to the portrayal of wholesale slaughter in ch 9.

10 and all flesh shall know that I the LORD have drawn My sword from its sheath, not to be sheathed again.

11 And you, O mortal, sigh; with tottering limbs and bitter grief, sigh before their eyes. 12 And when they ask you, "Why do you sigh?" answer, "Because of the tidings that have come." Every heart shall sink and all hands hang nerveless; every spirit shall grow faint and all knees turn to water because of the tidings that have come. It is approaching, it shall come to pass—declares the Lord GOD.

13 The word of the LORD came to me: 14 O mortal, prophesy and say: Thus said the Lord GOD: A sword! A sword has been whetted and polished. 15 It has been whetted to wreak slaughter; [a-][therefore] it has been ground to a brilliant polish.[-a] [b-]How can we rejoice? My son, it scorns[-b] the rod and every stick. 16 It has been given to be polished and then grasped in the hand; for this has the sword been whetted, for this polished—to be put into the hand of a slayer. 17 Cry and wail, O mortal, for this shall befall My people, this shall befall all the chieftains of Israel: they shall be cast before the sword together with My people; oh, strike the thigh [in grief]. 18 [b-]Consider: How shall it fail to happen, seeing that it even scorns the rod?[-b]—says the Lord GOD.

19 Further, O mortal, prophesy, striking hand against hand. Let the sword strike a second time and yet a third time; it is a sword for massacre, a sword for great carnage, that presses[c] upon them. 20 Thus hearts shall lose courage and many shall fall. At all their gates I have appointed slaughter[c] by the sword. Ah! it is made to flash brilliantly, it is honed[c] for slaughter. 21 Be united,[d] go to the right, turn left; whither are you bound? 22 I, too, will strike hand against hand and will satisfy My fury upon you; I the LORD have spoken.

23 The word of the LORD came to me: 24 And you, O mortal, choose two roads on which the sword of the king of Babylon may advance, both issuing from the same country; and select a spot, select it where roads branch off to [two] cities. 25 Choose a way for the sword to advance on Rabbah of the Ammonites or on fortified Jerusalem in Judah. 26 For the king of Babylon has stood at the fork of the road, where two roads branch off, to perform divination: He has shaken arrows, consulted teraphim, and inspected the liver.[e] 27 In his right hand came up the omen against Jerusalem—to set battering rams, to proclaim murder, to raise battle shouts, to set battering rams against the gates, to cast up mounds, to erect towers.

21.13–22.15: *My son, it scorns the rod and every stick:* a deadly instrument is required. **19:** The third strike of the sword is enigmatic, although the commentators understand it as a reference to Zedekiah's disaster, which was far greater than Jehoiakim's or Jehoiachin's. **21.23–37:** The sword of Babylonia. **23–28:** When the Babylonian king reaches a fork in the road, he employs divination, a technique widely used by the Babylonians, to decide which route to take. His alternatives are Jerusalem and Rabbah (the modern city of Amman, Jordan), the capital of Ammon. Ammon is one of Judah's allies against Babylonia (Jer. 27.3). Jerusalem is a former ally of Babylonia (2 Kings 20.12–19; Isa. ch 39), but Judah's revolt justifies the protracted siege. **26:** *He has shaken arrows, consulted teraphim, and inspected the liver,* reflecting Ezekiel's familiarity with common techniques of divination. *Teraphim,* family gods (Gen. 31.19; Judg. 17.5; 18.17, 20).

a-a Lit. "it has been polished in order that it may have lightning."
b-b Meaning of Heb. uncertain. *c Meaning of Heb. uncertain.*
d Meaning of Heb. uncertain; Targum reads "Be whetted." Cf. vv. 14–16.
e I.e., of a sacrificed animal.

28 [a]In their eyes, the oaths they had sworn to them were like
empty divination; but this shall serve to recall their guilt, for
which they shall be taken to task. 29 Assuredly, thus said the
Lord GOD: For causing your guilt to be recalled, your transgressions to be uncovered, and your sins to be revealed—all
your misdeeds—because you have brought yourselves to [My]
mind, you shall be taken to task.

30 And to you, O dishonored wicked prince of Israel, whose
day has come—the time set for your punishment—31 thus
said the Lord GOD: Remove the turban and lift off the crown!
This shall not remain as it is; exalt the low and abase the high.
32 Ruin, an utter ruin I will make it. [b-]It shall be no more[-b] until
he comes to whom it rightfully belongs; and I will give it to him.

33 Further, O mortal, prophesy and say: Thus said the Lord
GOD concerning the Ammonites and their blasphemies: Proclaim: O sword! O sword unsheathed for slaughter, polished
to the utmost, to a flashing brilliance! 34 Because they have
prophesied falsely about you and have divined deceitfully
concerning you, you shall be wielded over the necks of the dishonored wicked ones, for their day has come, the time [b-]set for
their punishment.[-b]
35 [c-]Return it to its sheath![-c] In the place where you were created, in the land of your origin, I will judge you. 36 I will pour
out My indignation upon you, I will blow upon you with the
fire of My wrath; and I will deliver you into the hands of bar-
barians, craftsmen of destruction. 37 You shall be fuel for the
fire, your blood shall sink into the earth, you shall not be remembered, for I the LORD have spoken.

22 The word of the LORD came to me: 2 Further, O mortal,
[d-]arraign, arraign[-d] the city of bloodshed; declare to her
all her abhorrent deeds! 3 Say: Thus said the Lord GOD: O city
in whose midst blood is shed, so that your hour is approaching; within which fetishes are made, so that you have become
unclean! 4 You stand guilty of the blood you have shed, defiled
by the fetishes you have made. You have brought on your day;
[e-]you have reached your year.[-e] Therefore I will make you the
mockery of the nations and the scorn of all the lands. 5 Both
the near and the far shall scorn you, O besmirched of name, O
laden with iniquity!

30: *The dishonored wicked prince of Israel,* Zedekiah. **33–37:** The sword will be wielded against Ammon, but it will be destroyed in Babylonia where it was created; in other words, Babylonian domination will not last long.

22.1–16: Oracle concerning bloodshed in Jerusalem. Ezek. 22.1–19 (22.1–16 in the Sephardi tradition) serves as the haftarah for the parashah of ʾAḥarei Mot (Lev. 16.1–18.30), which focuses on the atonement of Yom Kippur, the proper treatment of blood, and incestuous sexual relations. As in ch 18, the catalogue of crimes listed here is closely related to Lev. chs 17–26. **2–6:** *Bloodshed* (Lev. 19.26).

a The inhabitants of Jerusalem disregarded their oaths to the Babylonians; cf. 17.13 ff.
b-b Meaning of Heb. uncertain.
c-c Emendation yields "Return to your scabbard!" In this and the following verses, the prophet describes the future punishment of Babylon, still symbolized by the sword.
d-d Lit. "will you arraign, arraign."
e-e Some Babylonian mss. and ancient versions read "the time of your years has come."

[6] Every one of the princes of Israel in your midst used his strength for the shedding of blood. [7] Fathers and mothers have been humiliated within you; strangers have been cheated in your midst; orphans and widows have been wronged within you. [8] You have despised My holy things and profaned My sabbaths.

[9] Base[a] men in your midst were intent on shedding blood; in you they have eaten [b-]upon the mountains;[-b] and they have practiced depravity in your midst. [10] In you they have uncovered their fathers' nakedness;[c] in you they have ravished women during their impurity. [11] They have committed abhorrent acts with other men's wives; in their depravity they have defiled their own daughters-in-law; in you they have ravished their own sisters, daughters of their fathers. [12] They have taken bribes within you to shed blood. You have taken advance and accrued interest;[d] you have defrauded your countrymen to your profit. You have forgotten Me—declares the Lord GOD.

[13] Lo, I will strike My hands over the ill-gotten gains that you have amassed, and over the bloodshed that has been committed in your midst. [14] Will your courage endure, will your hands remain firm in the days when I deal with you? I the LORD have spoken and I will act. [15] I will scatter you among the nations and disperse you through the lands; I will consume the uncleanness out of you. [16] You shall be dishonored in the sight of nations, and you shall know that I am the LORD.

[17] The word of the LORD came to me: [18] O mortal, the House of Israel has become dross to Me; they are all copper, tin, iron, and lead. [e-]But in a crucible, the dross shall turn into silver.[-e] [19] Assuredly, thus said the Lord GOD: Because you have all become dross, I will gather you into Jerusalem. [20] As silver, copper, iron, lead, and tin are gathered into a crucible to blow the fire upon them, so as to melt them, so will I gather you in My fierce anger and cast you [into the fire] and melt you. [21] I will gather you and I will blow upon you the fire of My fury, and you shall be melted in it. [22] As silver is melted in a crucible, so shall you be melted in it. And you shall know that I the LORD have poured out My fury upon you.

[23] The word of the LORD came to me: [24] O mortal, say to her: You are an uncleansed land, [e-]not to be washed with rain[-e] on the day of indignation. [25] [f-]Her gang of prophets[-f] are like roaring lions in her midst, rending prey. They devour human

a Meaning of Heb. uncertain.
b-b I.e., in idolatry. Emendation yields "with the blood"; cf. Lev. 19.26.
c I.e., have cohabited with a former wife of the father; cf. Lev. 18.7–8.
d Cf. note at 18.8. *e-e Meaning of Heb. uncertain.*
f-f Septuagint reads "Whose chieftains."

7: Contempt for parents (Exod. 21.17; Lev. 20.9); extortion of the aliens, orphans, and widows (Exod. 22.21–22; Lev. 19.33–34; Deut. 14.29). **8:** *Despised ... holy things ... sabbaths,* see Lev. 19.30. **9:** *Base men* employs a term commonly used for slander (Lev. 19.16). **10:** *Uncovered their fathers' nakedness,* see Lev. 18.8; 20.11. See also regarding relations with menstruating women (Lev. 18.19). **11:** Incest (Lev. chs 18; 20). **12:** Bribery (Lev. 19.15; Deut. 16.19); interest on loans (Lev. 25.36–37); extortion of a neighbor (Lev. 19.15–18, 35–36). **13–16:** The punishment, whose main point is to *consume the uncleanness out of you:* Ezekiel's Priestly perspective is especially visible here.

22.17–22: Oracle concerning the smelting of Jerusalem. Just as precious metals are smelted to remove *dross,* Israel will be purified in fire to remove its sins and impurities. As in smelting, only a small amount of the original will remain.

22.23–31: Oracle condemning the leadership of Jerusalem. The oracle focuses on the wrongdoing of Jerusalem's leaders and the people at large. The emphasis is on the ritual impurity created through these actions; as in the Holiness Collection, Ezekiel believes that both cultic infractions and ethical violations create ritual impurity. **25–29:** The prophet names all types of leaders in Jerusalem, including *her ... prophets ... priests ... officials ... the people of the land* (a technical term for the landed gentry).

beings; they seize treasure and wealth; they have widowed many women in her midst. 26 Her priests have violated My Teaching: they have profaned what is sacred to Me, they have not distinguished between the sacred and the profane, they have not taught the difference between the unclean and the clean, and they have closed their eyes to My sabbaths. I am profaned in their midst. 27 Her officials are like wolves rending prey in her midst; they shed blood and destroy lives to win ill-gotten gain. 28 Her prophets, too, daub the wall for them with plaster:[a] They prophesy falsely and divine deceitfully for them; they say, "Thus said the Lord GOD," when the LORD has not spoken. 29 And the people of the land have practiced fraud and committed robbery; they have wronged the poor and needy, have defrauded the stranger without redress. 30 And I sought a man among them to repair the wall or to stand in the breach before Me in behalf of this land, that I might not destroy it; but I found none. 31 I have therefore poured out My indignation upon them; I will consume them with the fire of My fury. I will repay them for their conduct—declares the Lord GOD.

23 The word of the LORD came to me: 2 O mortal, once there were two women, daughters of one mother. 3 They played the whore in Egypt; they played the whore while still young. There their breasts were squeezed, and there their virgin nipples were handled. 4 Their names were: the elder one, Oholah;[b] and her sister, Oholibah.[c] They became Mine, and they bore sons and daughters. As for their names, Oholah is Samaria, and Oholibah is Jerusalem.

5 Oholah whored while she was Mine, and she lusted after her lovers, after the Assyrians, warriors[d] 6 clothed in blue, governors and prefects, horsemen mounted on steeds—all of them handsome young fellows. 7 She bestowed her favors upon them—upon all the pick of the Assyrians—and defiled herself with all their fetishes after which she lusted. 8 She did not give up the whoring she had begun with the Egyptians; for they had lain with her in her youth, and they had handled her virgin nipples and had poured out their lust upon her. 9 Therefore I delivered her into the hands of her lovers, into the hands of the Assyrians after whom she lusted. 10 They exposed her nakedness; they seized her sons and daughters, and she herself was put to the sword. And because of the punishment inflicted upon her, she became a byword among women.

11 Her sister Oholibah saw this; yet her lusting was more depraved than her sister's, and her whoring more debased. 12 She lusted after the Assyrians, governors and prefects, warriors[d]

a Cf. 13.10 ff. *b I.e., "Tent."* *c I.e., "My Tent Is in Her."*
d Meaning of Heb. uncertain.

31: The divine fire here is more consuming than that of the previous oracle.

23.1–49: Oholah and Oholibah. Presupposing the portrayal of Israel as God's wife (cf. Jer. chs 2–3; Hos. chs 1–3), Ezekiel employs the metaphor of harlotry to describe Samaria and Jerusalem. Here as elsewhere, adultery is equated with idolatry. The punishment for adultery is death, and so the adulterous cities are destroyed. This ch has much in common with ch 16. **3:** In contrast to modern sensibilities, Israel is blamed for its own abuse. **4:** *Oholah,* "her tent," refers to Samaria. The name Oholah alludes to the Presence of God, who dwells in a tent (Heb "'ohel"). *Oholibah,* "my tent is in her," refers to Jerusalem, home to the Temple (Rashi, Radak). **5–10:** Oholah's or Samaria's relations with the officers of Assyria presuppose its earlier alliance with Assyria under the Jehu dynasty. Ezekiel portrays this alliance as harlotry, and argues that it led to Israel's destruction (in 722 BCE). The reference to *the Assyrians, warriors* deliberately employs the ambiguous Heb term "kerovim," lit. "those who draw near," which may be used for war, sacrifice, sex, etc. **11–21:** Ezekiel charges that *Oholibah,* Jerusalem, was even worse than her sister in pursuing both the Assyrians and the Chaldeans, or Babylonians. King Ahaz of Judah requested Assyrian assistance against Israel in the Syro-Ephraimitic War (2 Kings ch 16), and Hezekiah later made an alliance with Babylonia against Assyria (2 Kings 20.11–19; Isa. ch 39). The reference to relations with Egypt may recall Solomon's early alliance with Egypt (1 Kings 3.1) and Jehoiakim's support from Pharaoh Neco before he turned to Babylonia (2 Kings 23.31–24.7).

gorgeously clad, horsemen mounted on steeds—all of them
handsome young fellows. 13 And I saw how she had defiled
herself. Both of them followed the same course, 14 but she carried her harlotries further. For she saw men sculptured upon
the walls, figures of Chaldeans drawn in vermilion, 15 girded
with belts round their waists, and with flowing turbans on their
heads, all of them looking like officers—a picture of Babylonians whose native land was Chaldea. 16 At the very sight of
them she lusted after them, and she sent messengers for them
to Chaldea. 17 So the Babylonians came to her for lovemaking
and defiled her with their whoring; and she defiled herself with
them until she turned from them in disgust. 18 She flaunted her
harlotries and exposed her nakedness, and I turned from her
in disgust, as I had turned disgusted from her sister. 19 But she
whored still more, remembering how in her youth she had
played the whore in the land of Egypt; 20 she lusted for concubinage with them, whose members were like those of asses
and whose organs[a] were like those of stallions. 21 Thus you reverted to the wantonness of your youth, remembering[b] your
youthful breasts, when the men of Egypt handled your nipples.

22 Assuredly, Oholibah, thus said the Lord GOD: I am going
to rouse against you the lovers from whom you turned in disgust, and I will bring them upon you from all around—23 the
Babylonians and all the Chaldeans, [the people of] Pekod,
Shoa, and Koa, and all the Assyrians with them, all of them
handsome young fellows, governors and prefects, officers and
warriors,[a] all of them riding on horseback. 24 They shall attack
you with fleets[a] of wheeled chariots and a host of troops; they
shall set themselves against you on all sides with bucklers,
shields, and helmets. And I will entrust your punishment to
them, and they shall inflict their punishments on you. 25 I will
direct My passion against you, and they shall deal with you in
fury: they shall cut off your nose and ears. The last of you shall
fall by the sword; they[c] shall take away your sons and daughters, and your remnant shall be devoured by fire. 26 They shall
strip you of your clothing and take away your dazzling jewels.
27 I will put an end to your wantonness and to your whoring in
the land of Egypt, and you shall not long for them or remember
Egypt any more.

28 For thus said the Lord GOD: I am going to deliver you
into the hands of those you hate, into the hands of those from
whom you turned in disgust. 29 They shall treat you with hate,
and they shall take away all you have toiled for, and leave you
naked and bare; your naked whoredom, wantonness, and harlotry will be exposed. 30 These things shall be done to you for

22–35: As in ch 16, Ezekiel declares that Oholibah's *lovers,* the Babylonians and their allies, will strip and conquer Jerusalem. **23:** *Pekod, Shoa,* and *Koa,* Aramean tribes allied with Babylonia.

a *Meaning of Heb. uncertain.* *b* *Lit. "for the sake of."*
c *I.e., the former lovers, vv. 22 ff.*

32: Drinking from the *sister's cup,* a common motif in Judean prophecy (Isa. 51.17, 22; Jer. 25.15–29; 51.7; Hab. 2.16). As in other contexts, the cup contains strong wine that ultimately poisons the drinker. **38:** *They defiled My Sanctuary,* see ch 8; *and profaned My sabbaths,* see 20.12–24. **39:** *They slaughtered their children,* see 20.26. **40:** *Moreover, they sent for men to come from afar,* a reference to Judean attempts to find allies (cf. Jer. 27.3). **46–47:** Stoning is the punishment for an adulterous woman (Lev. 20.10) or a person who profanes God (Lev. 20.2–5).

your harlotries with the nations, for defiling yourself with their
fetishes. 31 You walked in your sister's path; therefore I will put
her cup into your hand.
32 Thus said the Lord GOD:

You shall drink of your sister's cup,
So deep and wide;
It shall cause derision and scorn,
It holds so much.
33 You shall be filled with drunkenness and woe.
The cup of desolation and horror,
The cup of your sister Samaria—
34 You shall drink it and drain it,
[a-]And gnaw its shards;[-a]
And you shall tear your breasts.
For I have spoken—declares the Lord GOD.

35 Assuredly, thus said the Lord GOD: Because you have forgotten Me and cast Me behind your back, you in turn must suffer for your wanton whoring.
36 Then the LORD said to me: O mortal, arraign[b] Oholah and
Oholibah, and charge them with their abominations. 37 For
they have committed adultery, and blood is on their hands;
truly they have committed adultery with their fetishes, and
have even offered to them as food the children they bore to Me.
38 At the same time they also did this to Me: they defiled My
Sanctuary and profaned My sabbaths. 39 On the very day that
they slaughtered their children to their fetishes, they entered
My Sanctuary to desecrate it. That is what they did in My House.
40 Moreover, they sent for men to come from afar, [men] to
whom a messenger was sent; and they came. For them, [Oholi-
bah,] you bathed, painted your eyes, and donned your finery;
41 and you sat on a grand couch with a set table in front of it—and
it was My incense and My oil you laid upon it. 42 And the noise
of a carefree multitude was there, [a-]of numerous men brought
drunk from the desert;[-a] and they put bracelets on their arms
and splendid crowns upon their heads. 43 Then I said, [a-]"To destruction with adultery! Look, they are still going on with those
same fornications of hers."[-a] 44 And they would go to her as one
goes to a prostitute; that is how they went to Oholah and Oholibah, wanton women. 45 But righteous men shall punish them
with the punishments for adultery and for bloodshed, for they
are adulteresses and have blood on their hands.
46 For thus said the Lord GOD: Summon an assembly against
them, and make them an object of horror and plunder. 47 Let
the assembly pelt them with stones and cut them down with
their swords; let them kill their sons and daughters, and burn

a-a Meaning of Heb. uncertain. *b Lit. "will you arraign"; cf. 22.2.*

down their homes. [48] I will put an end to wantonness in the land; and all the women shall take warning not to imitate your wantonness. [49] They shall punish you for your wantonness, and you shall suffer the penalty for your sinful idolatry. And you shall know that I am the Lord GOD.

24 In the ninth year, on the tenth day of the tenth month, the word of the LORD came to me: [2] O mortal, record this date, this exact day; for this very day the king of Babylon has laid siege to Jerusalem. [3] Further, speak in an allegory to the rebellious breed and say to them: Thus said the Lord GOD:
Put the caldron [on the fire], put it on,
And then pour water into it.
4 Collect in it the pieces [of meat].
Every choice piece, thigh and shoulder;
Fill it with the best cuts[a]—
5 Take the best of the flock.
Also pile the cuts[b] under it;
Get it boiling briskly,
And cook the cuts in it.
6 Assuredly, thus said the Lord GOD:
Woe to the city of blood—
A caldron whose scum[c] is in it,
Whose scum has not been cleaned out!
Empty it piece by piece;
[d-]No lot has fallen upon it.[-d]
7 For the blood she shed is still in her;
She set it upon a bare rock;
She did not pour it out on the ground
To cover it with earth.
8 She[e] set her blood upon the bare rock,
So that it was not covered,
So that it may stir up [My] fury
To take vengeance.
9 Assuredly, thus said the Lord GOD:
Woe to the city of blood!
I in turn will make a great blaze.
10 Pile on the logs,
Kindle the fire,
Cook the meat through
And[f-]stew it completely,[-f]
And let the bones be charred.
11 Let it stand empty on the coals,
Until it becomes so hot

a Lit. "limbs." *b Emendation yields "wood"; cf. v. 10.*
c Or "rust." *d-d Meaning of Heb. uncertain.* *e Heb. "I."*
f-f Emendation yields "Pour out the broth."

48: The metaphorical nature of the image is forgotten, and is here literalized in this aside—real women are to learn proper sexual behavior from this metaphor. **49:** The prophecy is brought to a close, like so many others, with the stereotypical *And you shall know that I am the Lord GOD.*

24.1–27: Further symbolic actions. The prophetic word formula in this ch introduces two oracles that comprise this section, including the allegory of the pot (24.1–14), and the death of Ezekiel's wife (24.15–27). The oracles take up symbolic actions concerning the destruction of Jerusalem.

24.1–14: The allegory of the pot. 1–2: *The ninth year, on the tenth day of the tenth month* would be 10 Tevet, 589–588 BCE, which is identified as the day that the Babylonian king Nebuchadnezzar laid siege to Jerusalem (see also 2 Kings 25.1; Jer. 52.4). The day is marked as a public fast day in Judaism (cf. Zech. 8.19). **4:** *Thigh and shoulder:* The choicest meat, given to the priests, symbolizing the elite of the nation. **6–8:** The imagery of the corroded bottom of the pot symbolizes the bloody crimes of Jerusalem. Blood must be covered when shed (Lev. 17.13–16). **7:** Rabbinic interpretation relates this v. to the murder of Zechariah son of Jehoiada, the prophet and priest, during the reign of King Joash son of Ahaziah (2 Chron. 24.20–22). His blood had not been requited (2 Chron. 24.22), but lay seething on the pavement when Nebuchadnezzar's commander Nebuzaradan entered the Temple courts. Nebuzaradan therefore killed thousands of people in order to appease it (*b. Git.* 57b; *Pesik. Rav Kah.* 122a; *Lam. Rab.* 23). **9–14:** As a cauldron is cleansed by fire, Ezekiel calls for the "cleansing" of Jerusalem by fire.

24.15–27: The death of Ezekiel's wife. The death of Ezekiel's wife symbolizes the destruction of Jerusalem, and in his treatment of it, Ezekiel makes it a radical symbolic action. The regular rituals of mourning are insufficient for the cataclysmic destruction of the Temple, and are thus not practiced. Similarly, in Jer. 16.6–7, the observance of mourning and consolation will break down in the face of national destruction. **15–18:** Ezekiel's action may draw upon priestly sanctity (see Lev. 21.1–3) to symbolize the inability of God and the people of Judah to mourn the loss of Jerusalem when in exile. **16:** *The delight of your eyes:* The same term will be used for the Temple in v. 21. **17:** *Turban,* a headdress worn by priests (Exod. 39.28; Ezek. 44.18) as well as by wealthy women (Isa. 3.20) and bridegrooms (Isa. 61.10). Rabbinic tradition reads this v. as an instruction for proper mourning. A mourner does not wear tefillin or shoes; he wraps his head; and others serve him food (*b. Mo'ed Kat.* 15, 27b). **21:** *I am going to desecrate My Sanctuary* by allowing foreigners to enter it; only the high priest could enter the Holy of Holies. **23:** The people are to be fully dressed, with *turbans* and *sandals,* as they go into exile. **24:** Usually a divine action is a *portent;* here Ezekiel the person is a portent (see 12.5, 11; Zech. 3.8 ["sign"]). **25–27:** When the Temple is destroyed, Ezekiel will be able to speak again. The arrival of the *fugitive* is recorded in 33.21, in a ch immediately following the oracles concerning the nations (chs 25–32). The placement of these oracles here thus disrupts the flow of the book, but also emphasizes God's capability to act at a time that His Temple is destroyed, emphasizing that the Temple was destroyed by God, not because of God's weakness.

That the copper glows.
Then its uncleanness shall melt away in it,
And its rust be consumed.
12 [a]It has frustrated all effort,
Its thick scum will not leave it—
Into the fire with its scum![a]
13 For your vile impurity—because I sought to cleanse you
of your impurity, but you would not be cleansed—you shall
never be clean again until I have satisfied My fury upon you.
14 I the LORD have spoken: It shall come to pass and I will do it.
I will not refrain or spare or relent. You shall be punished according to your ways and your deeds—declares the Lord GOD.

15 The word of the LORD came to me: 16 O mortal, I am about
to take away the delight of your eyes from you through pestilence; but you shall not lament or weep or let your tears flow.
17 Moan softly; observe no mourning for the dead: Put on your
turban and put your sandals on your feet; do not cover over
your upper lip, and do not eat the bread of comforters."[b]
18 In the evening my wife died, and in the morning I did as
I had been commanded. And when I spoke to the people that
morning, 19 the people asked me, "Will you not tell us what
these things portend for us, that you are acting so?" 20 I answered them, "The word of the LORD has come to me: 21 Tell
the House of Israel: Thus said the Lord GOD: 'I am going to desecrate My Sanctuary, your pride and glory, the delight of your
eyes and the desire of your heart; and the sons and daughters
you have left behind shall fall by the sword. 24 [c]And Ezekiel shall
become a portent for you: you shall do just as he has done,
when it happens; and you shall know that I am the Lord GOD.'
22 Accordingly, you shall do as I have done: you shall not cover
over your upper lips or eat the bread of comforters;[b] 23 and your
turbans shall remain on your heads, and your sandals upon
your feet. You shall not lament or weep, but you shall be heartsick because of your iniquities and shall moan to one another."[c]

25 You, O mortal, take note: On the day that I take their stronghold from them, their pride and joy, the delight of their eyes and
the longing of their hearts—their sons and daughters—26 on
that day a fugitive will come to you, to let you hear it with your
own ears. 27 On that day your mouth shall be opened to the fugitive, and you shall speak and no longer be dumb. So you shall
be a portent for them, and they shall know that I am the LORD.

25 The word of the LORD came to me: 2 O mortal, set your
face toward the Ammonites and prophesy against them.

a-a Meaning of Heb. uncertain. b Lit. "men." c V. 24 moved up for clarity.

3 Say to the Ammonites: Hear the word of the Lord GOD! Thus
said the Lord GOD: Because you cried "Aha!" over My Sanctuary when it was desecrated, and over the land of Israel when it
was laid waste, and over the House of Judah when it went into
exile—4 assuredly, I will deliver you to the Kedemites as a possession. They shall set up their encampments among you and
pitch their dwellings in your midst; they shall eat your produce
and they shall drink your milk. 5 I will make Rabbah a pasture
for camels and Ammon a place for sheep to lie down. And you
shall know that I am the LORD.
6 For thus said the Lord GOD: Because you clapped your hands
and stamped your feet and rejoiced over the land of Israel with
such utter scorn—7 assuredly, I will stretch out My hand against
you and give you as booty to the nations; I will cut you off from
among the peoples and wipe you out from among the countries
and destroy you. And you shall know that I am the LORD.

8 Thus said the Lord GOD: Because Moab [a]and Seir[a] said,
"See, the House of Judah is like all other nations"—9 assuredly,
I will lay bare the flank of Moab, all its towns to the last one—
Beth-jeshimoth, Baal-meon, and Kiriathaim, the glory of the

a-a Lacking in some Septuagint mss.

25.1–32.32: Oracles concerning the nations. Like other prophetic books (Isa. chs 13–23; Jer. chs 46–51; Amos 1.3–2.3), Ezek. contains a section of oracles concerning foreign nations. These oracles are rhetorical; they are not literally spoken to the other nations but to Israel, and demonstrate that God is not merely a national God, concerned only with His people and land, but with the entire world, over which He has control. These prophecies lay the groundwork for Israel's restoration, and demonstrate the nations' future recognition of Israel's God, in contrast to the desecration of God's name among the nations, which reached its peak during the destruction. The nations and cities included here are Ammon, Moab (and Seir), Edom, Philistia, Tyre, Sidon, and Egypt. Ezekiel, like Jeremiah, identifies the projected expansion of Babylonia as an act of God. (Similarly Isaiah saw God use Assyria, esp. in Isa. 10.5–11). In contrast to Jer. chs 50–51, however, Ezekiel does not prophesy against

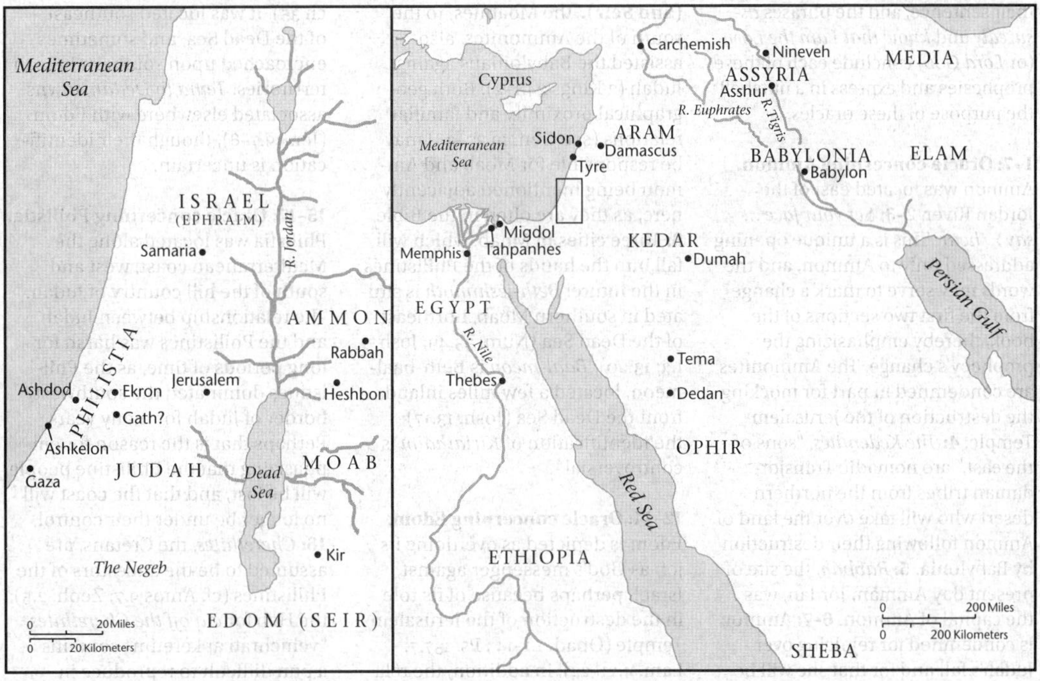

Places mentioned in the oracles against the nations

country. 10 I will deliver it, together with Ammon, to the Kedemites as their possession. Thus Ammon shall not be remembered among the nations, 11 and I will mete out punishments
to Moab. And they shall know that I am the LORD.

12 Thus said the Lord GOD: Because Edom acted vengefully
against the House of Judah and incurred guilt by wreaking
revenge upon it—13 assuredly, thus said the Lord GOD: I will
stretch out My hand against Edom and cut off from it man
and beast, and I will lay it in ruins; from Tema to Dedan they
shall fall by the sword. 14 I will wreak My vengeance on Edom
through My people Israel, and they shall take action against
Edom in accordance with My blazing anger; and they shall
know My vengeance—declares the Lord GOD.

15 Thus said the Lord GOD: Because the Philistines, in their
ancient hatred, acted vengefully, and with utter scorn sought
revenge and destruction—16 assuredly, thus said the Lord GOD:
I will stretch out My hand against the Philistines and cut off the
Cherethites and wipe out the last survivors of the seacoast. 17 I
will wreak frightful vengeance upon them by furious punishment; and when I inflict My vengeance upon them, they shall
know that I am the LORD.

Babylonia. From the appearance of the date formulas in 24.1; 26.1; 29.1, 17; 30.20; 31.1; 32.1, 17, we learn that these chs are organized in thematic order, as opposed to the chronological order of the rest of the prophecies in the book. One prophecy against Egypt (29.1) is given before the prophecy to Tyre (26.1), while another prophecy against Egypt (29.17; the 27th year) is the latest of the dated prophecies to the nations. These prophecies are arranged geographically rather than chronologically, with the nations mentioned moving generally from north to south (ch 25: Ammon, Moab, and Edom and Philistia; chs 26–28: Tyre and Sidon; chs 29–32: Egypt).

25.1–17: Oracles condemning Israel's neighbors: Ammon, Moab, Edom, Philistia. The oracles against Israel's immediate neighbors Ammon, Moab, Edom, and Philistia are grouped together. The entire ch is formulated as an instruction speech in which God tells Ezekiel what to say. The details of sin follow the word *because,* the description of their sentence, and the phrases *assuredly* and *know that I am the LORD* (or *Lord GOD*) conclude each of these prophesies and express in a nutshell the purpose of these oracles.

1–7: Oracle concerning Ammon. Ammon was located east of the Jordan River. **2–3:** *Set your face ... say ... hear:* This is a unique opening addressed only to Ammon, and the words may serve to mark a change from the first two sections of the book, thereby emphasizing the prophecy's change. The Ammonites are condemned in part for mocking the destruction of the Jerusalem Temple. **4:** *The Kedemites,* "sons of the east," are nomadic Transjordanian tribes from the northern desert who will take over the land of Ammon following their destruction by Babylonia. **5:** *Rabbah,* the site of present day Amman, Jordan, was the capital of Ammon. **6–7:** Ammon is condemned for rejoicing over Judah's fall and for that she will be destroyed herself.

8–11: Oracle concerning Moab (and Seir). The Moabites, to the south of the Ammonites, also assisted the Babylonians against Judah (2 Kings 24.1–2). Both geographical proximity and familial relations (see Gen. 19.37–38) may be responsible for Moab and Ammon being mentioned adjacently here, as they are often in the Bible. **9:** Three cities in Moab, which will fall into the hands of the Philistines in the future: *Beth-jeshimoth* is situated in southern Moab, northeast of the Dead Sea (Num. 33.49; Josh. 1.3; 13.20); *Baal-meon* is Beth-baal-meon, located a few miles inland from the Dead Sea (Josh. 13.17); the identification of *Kiriathaim* is controversial.

12–14: Oracle concerning Edom. Edom is depicted as overdoing its job as God's messenger against Israel, perhaps because of its role in the destruction of the Jerusalem Temple (Obad. 1.1–14 ; Ps. 137.7; Lam. 4.21–22); in addition, the relationship between Israel and Edom had been continuously hostile (see ch 35). It was located southeast of the Dead Sea, and sometimes encroached upon southern Judean territories. *Tema to Dedan,* towns associated elsewhere with Edom (Jer. 49.7–8), though their identification is uncertain.

15–17: Oracle concerning Philistia. Philistia was located along the Mediterranean coast, west and south of the hill country of Judah. The relationship between Judah and the Philistines was harsh for long periods of time, as the Philistines dominated the southwest border of Judah for many years. Perhaps that is the reason for emphasizing that the Philistine people will be lost, and that the coast will no longer be under their control. **16:** *Cherethites,* the Cretans, are assumed to be the ancestors of the Philistines (cf. Amos 9.7; Zeph. 2.5); the Heb for *cut off the Cherethites,* "vehichrati at keretim" contains a pun difficult to reproduce in English.

26 In the eleventh year, on the first of the month,[a] the
word of the LORD came to me: 2 O mortal, because Tyre
gloated over Jerusalem, "Aha! The gateway[b] of the peoples is
broken, it has become mine; I shall be filled, now that it is laid
in ruins"—3 assuredly, thus said the Lord GOD:

I am going to deal with you, O Tyre!
I will hurl many nations against you,
As the sea hurls its waves.
4 They shall destroy the walls of Tyre
And demolish her towers;
And I will scrape her soil off her
And leave her a naked rock.
5 She shall be in the heart of the sea
A place for drying[c] nets;
For I have spoken it —declares the Lord GOD.
She shall become spoil for the nations,
6 And her daughter-towns in the country
Shall be put to the sword.
And they shall know that I am the LORD.

7 For thus said the Lord GOD: I will bring from the north,
against Tyre, King Nebuchadrezzar of Babylon, a king of kings,
with horses, chariots, and horsemen—a great mass of troops.

8 Your daughter-towns in the country
He shall put to the sword;
He shall erect towers against you,
And cast up mounds against you,
And raise [a wall of] bucklers against you.
9 He shall turn the force of his battering rams
Against your walls
And smash your towers with his axes.[d]
10 From the cloud raised by his horses
Dust shall cover you;
From the clatter of horsemen
And wheels and chariots,
Your walls shall shake—
When he enters your gates
As men enter a breached city.

a The month is not indicated. *b Targum reads "trafficker"; cf. 27.3.*
c Lit. "spreading out." *d Lit. "swords."*

26.1–28.19: Oracles against Tyre. The initial date formula identifies the oracles concerning the Phoenician city of Tyre in 26.1–28.19. The prophetic word formula introduces four oracles in chronological order against Tyre: 26.1–21; 27.1–36; 28.1–10, 11–19. Tyre, the preeminent maritime power of the ancient world, joined Judah in revolt against Babylonia (Jer. 27.3). Tyre was an island until its conquest in 332 BCE by Alexander the Great, who built an earthen corridor through the water to assault the city by land. Shortly after his conquest of Jerusalem, Nebuchadrezzar laid siege to Tyre for thirteen years. Although he was not able to conquer the city, it finally submitted to him. The large number of oracles about Tyre reflects both its economic significance at this time and the theological difficulty that it presented by thwarting Nebuchadrezzar, when Jerusalem was captured. This prophecy, like previous prophecies in the book, interweaves parable and explanation, and establishes links between the content and the form of the prophetic message regarding Tyre's downfall. The passage uses imagery that distinctively characterizes Tyre.

26.1–21: First oracle concerning Tyre. 1: *The eleventh year, on the first of the month,* the month name may have fallen out. The year is 586 BCE, and the prophecy may date from shortly after the fall of Jerusalem (2 Kings 25.1–2; Jer. 52.4–5). **2–6:** Ezekiel's indictment and sentencing of Tyre presupposes that the city was a commercial rival to Judah. **2:** *The gateway of the peoples,* lit. "gateways," indicates Judah's role in controlling inland trade routes. **4:** *Naked rock,* "sela'" or rock in Heb, plays upon the Heb name "Tzor," *Tyre,* which is another word for rock. **6:** *Daughter-towns* designates nearby towns (suburbs) that were subsidiary to Tyre; they will be destroyed as well. **7–14:** Nebuchadrezzar conquered Tyre using cavalry and chariots surrounding the city, and embankments placed against the city walls. When the walls collapsed, the destruction of the city was complete: the city was sacked and covered with water and eventually the structures on the island were destroyed. In contrast, Ezekiel's description presupposes the tactics and weapons of land warfare, which were useless against an island state. **7:** As in some sections of Jeremiah, *Nebuchadrezzar,* (= Nebuchadnezzar) is spelled here as in the Akkadian (a language of ancient Mesopotamia) name, Nabu-kudurri-utzur ("May Nebo [the name of a Babylonian god] protect my labor").

16: *Rulers of the sea,* an allusion to Tyre's trading partners and allies. **17:** *They shall intone a dirge over you,* see 19.1 n.; the vv. here also represent qinah meter (a dirge or lament meter where the second line is a beat shorter than the first line, displaying a "limping" or "falling" rhythm). **19–21:** Ezekiel employs mythological language to portray Tyre's fall. **19:** *I bring the deep over you* reverses the imagery of creation in which dry land emerges from the waters (Gen. ch 1). **20:** *Go down to the Pit,* descend into the underworld at death (see 32.18–22). This was a characteristic motif of Babylonian mythology, in which the fertility god Tammuz had to be rescued from the underworld each year by the goddess Ishtar.

11 With the hoofs of his steeds
He shall trample all your streets.
He shall put your people to the sword,
And your mighty pillars shall crash to the ground.
12 They shall plunder your wealth
And loot your merchandise.
They shall raze your walls
And tear down your splendid houses,
And they shall cast into the water
Your stones and timber and soil.
13 I will put an end to the murmur of your songs,
And the sound of your lyres shall be heard no more.
14 I will make you a naked rock,
You shall be a place for drying[a] nets;
You shall never be rebuilt.
For I have spoken —declares the Lord GOD.

[15] Thus said the Lord GOD to Tyre: The coastlands shall quake
at the sound of your downfall, when the wounded groan, when
slaughter is rife within you. [16] All the rulers of the sea shall descend from their thrones; they shall remove their robes and
strip off their embroidered garments. They shall clothe themselves with trembling, and shall sit on the ground; they shall
tremble every moment, and they shall be aghast at you. [17] And
they shall intone a dirge over you, and they shall say to you:

How you have perished, [b-]you who were peopled[-b]
from the seas,
O renowned city!
Mighty on the sea were she and her inhabitants,
Who cast their terror on all [c-]its inhabitants.[-c]
18 Now shall the coastlands tremble
On the day of your downfall,
And the coastlands by the sea
Be terrified at your end.

[19] For thus said the Lord GOD: When I make you a ruined
city, like cities empty of inhabitants; when I bring the deep
over you, and its mighty waters cover you, [20] then I will bring
you down, with those who go down to the Pit, to the people
of old. I will install you in the netherworld, with those that go
down to the Pit, like the ruins of old, so that you shall not be
inhabited and shall not radiate[d] splendor in the land of the living. [21] I will make you a horror, and you shall cease to be; you
shall be sought, but shall never be found again—declares the
Lord GOD.

a Lit. "spreading out." *b-b Septuagint reads "vanished."*
c-c I.e., of the sea. Emendation yields "the dry land."
d Understanding nathatti *as second-person singular feminine; cf. 16.50 and note. But meaning of Heb. uncertain.*

27 The word of the LORD came to me: 2 Now you, O mortal,
intone a dirge over Tyre. 3 Say to Tyre:

O you who dwell at the gateway of the sea,
Who trade with the peoples on many coastlands:
Thus said the Lord GOD:
[a]O Tyre, you boasted,
I am perfect in beauty.[a]
4 Your frontiers were on the high seas,
Your builders perfected your beauty.
5 From cypress trees of Senir
They fashioned your planks;
They took a cedar from Lebanon
To make a mast for you.
6 From oak trees of Bashan
They made your oars;
Of boxwood from the isles of Kittim,
Inlaid with ivory,
They made your decks.
7 Embroidered linen from Egypt
Was the cloth
That served you for sails;
Of blue and purple from the coasts of Elishah
Were your awnings.
8 The inhabitants of Sidon and Arvad
Were your rowers;
[b]Your skilled men, O Tyre,[b] were within you,
They were your pilots.
9 Gebal's elders and craftsmen were within you,
Making your repairs.

All the ships of the sea, with their crews,
Were [c]in your harbor[c]
To traffic in your wares.
10 Men of Paras, Lud, and Put
Were in your army,
Your fighting men;
They hung shields and helmets in your midst,
They lent splendor to you.
11 Men of Arvad and Helech
Manned your walls all around,
And men of Gammad were stationed in your towers;
They hung their quivers all about your walls;
They perfected your beauty.

a-a *Emendation yields: "O Tyre, you are a ship / Perfect in beauty."*
b-b *Emendation yields "The skilled men of Zemar"; cf. Gen. 10.18.*
c-c *Lit. "in you."*

27.1–36: Lamentation over Tyre. The ch begins as a eulogy for the commercial beauty and prominence of Tyre, a vibrant center of trade, where people from distant and exotic lands came to exchange their wares. The ch describes in detail Tyre as a ship built from luxury goods (the best wood, ivory, linen) and piloted by the most skillful crew (vv. 3–9); she is an international harbor, defended by military strength (vv. 10–11), enabling it to trade with many countries; she is in a key position in international trade (vv. 12–25). **3–9:** Ezekiel portrays Tyre as a well-built ship, symbolizing the way in which Tyre achieved wealth through maritime trade. Parts of these vv. exhibit qinah meter (see 26.17 n.). **4:** Unlike the previous ch, here Tyre is recognized as an island. **5:** *Senir,* Mt. Hermon in the Golan Heights. **6:** *Bashan,* the region east of the Sea of Galilee. The *isles of Kittim,* likely the Greek islands. **7:** *Elishah,* Cyprus (cf. Gen. 10.4). **8:** *Sidon* is a city-state north of Tyre (Gen. 10.15). *Arvad,* Phoenicia (Gen. 10.18). *Zemar* (see translators' note *b-b*), "Tyre" in Heb. **9:** *Gebal,* Byblos (1 Kings 5.32), a major center of papyrus production in antiquity. **10–11:** Tyre's defenders include mercenary troops. *Paras,* Persia. *Lud,* Lydia. *Put,* Libya. *Helech* may mean "your army" in Heb or may refer to a place (Hilakku in Southeast Asia). *Gammad* is uncertain, although *Tg. Jon.* identifies it with Cappodocia (Turkey).

12–25: A prose section contains a catalogue of Tyre's extensive and far-flung commercial relations. **12:** *Tarshish,* Tartessos in southern Spain. **13:** *Javan,* Ionians or Greeks. *Tubal, and Meshech,* Asia Minor (Gen. 10.2). **14:** *Beth-togarmah,* Armenia (Gen. 10.3). **15:** *Dedan,* an Arabian people south of Israel in central Arabia. **16:** *Turquoise, purple stuff, embroidery:* Phoenicia was known for trade in purple dye derived from a shellfish. The names for the country, Phoenicia (Gk, "Phoinikos") and Canaan, both mean "purple." **17:** *Minnith,* in Ammonite territory (Judg. 11.33). *Pannag:* Otherwise unknown. It may be understood as related to Akkadian "pannigu," meaning "pastries." (Radak considers this to be a place name.) **18:** *Helbon,* 22 km (13 mi) north of Damascus. **19:** *Vedan and Javan from Uzal,* place names whose identifications are controversial. **20:** *Dedan,* in central Arabia (Jer. 25.23). **21:** *Kedar,* in Arabia (Gen. 25.13). **22:** *Sheba,* in Arabia (Gen. 25.3). *Raamah* may be near the Persian Gulf. **23:** *Haran, Canneh, and Eden,* cities in Syria. *Assyria,* the ancient Assyrian empire in northern Iraq. *Chilmad,* Media. **25:** *The ships of Tarshish* may refer to long-haul vessels, able to complete the trip to distant Tarsus. **26–27:** The description of Tyre as a great ship is abruptly changed to a ship floundering in a tempest, lit. "the east wind," a common symbol of God's power. **28–36:** As the city-ship sinks into the sea, losing all her precious cargo, all those around her mourn and lament. Many of these laments are expressed in the qinah or dirge meter (see 26.17 n.).

12 Tarshish traded with you because of your wealth of all
kinds of goods; they bartered silver, iron, tin, and lead for your
wares. 13 Javan, Tubal, and Meshech—they were your merchants; they trafficked with you in human beings and copper
utensils. 14 From Beth-togarmah they bartered horses, horsemen, and mules for your wares. 15 The people of Dedan were
your merchants; many coastlands traded under your rule and
rendered you tribute in ivory tusks and ebony. 16 Aram traded
with you because of your wealth of merchandise, dealing with
you in turquoise, purple stuff, embroidery, fine linen, coral,
and agate.[a] 17 Judah and the land of Israel were your merchants;
they trafficked with you in wheat of [b]Minnith and Pannag,[b]
honey, oil, and balm. 18 Because of your wealth of merchandise, because of your great wealth, Damascus traded with you
in Helbon wine and white wool. 19 [c]Vedan and Javan from Uzal
traded for your wares; they trafficked with you in polished iron,
cassia, and calamus. 20 Dedan was your merchant in saddle-
cloths for riding.[c] 21 Arabia and all Kedar's chiefs were traders
under your rule; they traded with you in lambs, rams, and goats.
22 The merchants of Sheba and Raamah were your merchants;
they bartered for your wares all the finest spices, all kinds of
precious stones, and gold. 23 Haran, Canneh, and Eden, the
merchants of Sheba, Assyria, and Chilmad traded with you.
24 [c]These were your merchants in choice fabrics, embroidered
cloaks of blue, and many-colored carpets tied up with cords
and preserved with cedar—among your wares.[c] 25 The ships of
Tarshish were in the service of your trade.

[d]So you were full and richly laden
On the high seas.
26 Your oarsmen brought you out
Into the mighty waters;
The tempest wrecked you
On the high seas.
27 Your wealth, your wares, your merchandise,
Your sailors and your pilots,
The men who made your repairs,
Those who carried on your traffic,
And all the fighting men within you—
All the multitude within you—
Shall go down into the depths of the sea
On the day of your downfall.
28 At the outcry of your pilots
The billows shall heave;

a *The exact identity of these stones is uncertain.*
b-b *Meaning of Heb. uncertain; cf. "Minnith," Judg. 11.33.*
c-c *Meaning of Heb. uncertain.*
d *Resuming the description of Tyre as a ship, as in vv. 3b–9a.*

29 And all the oarsmen and mariners,
All the pilots of the sea,
Shall come down from their ships
And stand on the ground.
30 They shall raise their voices over you
And cry out bitterly;
They shall cast dust on their heads
And strew ashes on themselves.
31 On your account, they shall make
Bald patches on their heads,
And shall gird themselves with sackcloth.
They shall weep over you, brokenhearted,
With bitter lamenting;
32 They shall intone a dirge over you as they wail,
And lament for you thus:

Who was like Tyre when she was silenced
In the midst of the sea?
33 When your wares were unloaded from the seas,
You satisfied many peoples;
With your great wealth and merchandise
You enriched the kings of the earth.
34 But when you were wrecked on the seas,
In the deep waters sank your merchandise
And all the crew aboard you.
35 All the inhabitants of the coastlands
Are appalled over you;
Their kings are aghast,
Their faces contorted.[a]
36 The merchants among the peoples hissed[b] at you;
You have become a horror,
And have ceased to be forever.

28 The word of the LORD came to me: 2 O mortal, say to the prince of Tyre: Thus said the Lord GOD:

Because you have been so haughty and have said, "I am a god; I sit enthroned like a god in the heart of the seas," whereas you are not a god but a man, though you deemed your mind equal to a god's[c]—
3 Yes, you are wiser than Daniel;
In no hidden matter can anyone
Compare to you.
4 By your shrewd understanding
You have gained riches,

a Meaning of Heb. uncertain.

b I.e., to ward off the calamity from the viewer; cf. Jer. 18.16, 49.17; Job 27.23; Lam. 2.15.

c This sentence is continued in v. 6; vv. 3–5 are parenthetical.

28.1–10: Oracle concerning the ruler of Tyre. 2: Self-deification was a claim of some ancient Near Eastern rulers, but in this case, says Ezekiel, the ruler has gone too far and is guilty of hubris. **3:** *Yes, you are wiser than Daniel:* Ezekiel apparently holds the Tyrian king in high regard and compares him to Dan-El, the wise ruler of Canaanite mythology who may stand behind the figure of Daniel in biblical tradition (see 14.12–20).

5: Ezekiel charges that the king has overstepped his bounds. **8:** The mythological language of descent into the sea and the *Pit* reappears. **10:** *The uncircumcised:* While the Phoenicians (Tyrians) practiced circumcision (see Jer. 9.24–25, for additional nations who practiced circumcision), they are threatened with the death of the uncircumcised; that is, a death that uncircumcised peoples would be subjected to, clearly a worse death than that of the circumcised.

28.11–19: Dirge for the king of Tyre. While it was the "ruler" who was condemned in vv. 1–10, here the lament is for the *king.* This prophecy is to be understood against the background of the king of Tyre being in a bejeweled Garden of Eden. References to the Garden of Eden are very rare outside of Gen. chs 2–3. The king boasts of his wisdom and beauty, qualities that that ancient Near Eastern kings were expected to have. **12:** *Seal of perfection,* a unique expression, here a sign of royal authority. **13–15:** Ezekiel employs the imagery of the Garden of Eden story to describe the Tyrian king's downfall. **14:** He employs the imagery of the *cherub* to stress the Tyrian king's power and high position. The once perfect creature is shown to have sinned and therefore was struck down.

And have amassed gold and silver
In your treasuries.
5 By your great shrewdness in trade
You have increased your wealth,
And you have grown haughty
Because of your wealth.

6 Assuredly, thus said the Lord GOD: Because you have
deemed your mind equal to a god's,

7 I swear I will bring against you
Strangers, the most ruthless of nations.
They shall unsheathe their swords
Against your prized shrewdness,
And they shall strike down[a] your splendor.
8 They shall bring you down to the Pit;
In the heart of the sea you shall die
The death of the slain.
9 Will you still say, "I am a god"
Before your slayers,
When you are proved a man, not a god,
At the hands of those who strike you down?
10 By the hands of strangers you shall die
The death of the uncircumcised;[b]
For I have spoken —declares the Lord GOD.

11 The word of the LORD came to me: 12 O mortal, intone a
dirge over the king of Tyre and say to him: Thus said the Lord
GOD:

You were the seal of perfection,
Full of wisdom and flawless in beauty.
13 You were in Eden, the garden of God;
Every precious stone was your adornment:
Carnelian, chrysolite, and amethyst;
Beryl, lapis lazuli, and jasper;
Sapphire, turquoise, and emerald;
And gold [c]beautifully wrought for you,
Mined for you, prepared the day you were created.[c]
14 [d]I created you as a cherub
With outstretched shielding wings;[d]
And you resided on God's holy mountain;
You walked among stones of fire.
15 You were blameless in your ways,
From the day you were created
Until wrongdoing was found in you.

a Meaning of Heb. uncertain.
b According to popular belief, those who die uncircumcised and those left unburied are relegated to the lower level of the netherworld; cf. 31.18; 32.19 ff.
c-c Meaning of Heb. uncertain. On the stones, see note at Exod. 28.17.
d-d Meaning of Heb. uncertain.

16 By your far-flung commerce
You were filled with lawlessness
And you sinned.
So I have struck you down
From the mountain of God,
And I have destroyed you, O shielding cherub,
From among the stones of fire.
17 You grew haughty because of your beauty,
You debased your wisdom for the sake of your splendor;
I have cast you to the ground,
I have made you an object for kings to stare at.
18 By the greatness of your guilt,
Through the dishonesty of your trading,
You desecrated your sanctuaries.
So I made a fire issue from you,
And it has devoured you;
I have reduced you to ashes on the ground,
In the sight of all who behold you.
19 All who knew you among the peoples
Are appalled at your doom.
You have become a horror
And have ceased to be, forever.

20 The word of the LORD came to me: 21 O mortal, set your
face toward Sidon and prophesy against her. 22 Say: Thus said
the Lord GOD:

I am going to deal with you, O Sidon.
I will gain glory in your midst;
And they shall know that I am the LORD,
When I wreak punishment upon her
And show Myself holy through her.
23 I will let pestilence loose against her
And bloodshed into her streets.
And the slain shall fall in her midst
When the sword comes upon her from all sides.
And they shall know that I am the LORD.

24 Then shall the House of Israel no longer be afflicted with
prickling briers and lacerating thorns from all the neighbors
who despise them; and they shall know that I am the Lord GOD.
25 Thus said the Lord GOD: When I have gathered the House
of Israel from the peoples among which they have been dispersed, and have shown Myself holy through them in the sight
of the nations, they shall settle on their own soil, which I gave
to My servant Jacob, 26 and they shall dwell on it in security.
They shall build houses and plant vineyards, and shall dwell
on it in security, when I have meted out punishment to all
those about them who despise them. And they shall know that
I the LORD am their God.

16: The prophet charges the king with corrupt trade practices. **18:** *You desecrated your sanctuaries,* a unique reference; there is no other evidence in Ezek. for the existence of foreign sanctuaries. **19:** This prophecy was not fulfilled, as the city eventually became subservient to Nebuchadnezzar, but he did not destroy it.

28.20–24: Oracle concerning Sidon. 21: *Sidon,* another Phoenician port city-state, 40 km (25 mi) north of Tyre. One of the ancient cities of Canaan that shared a common past with Israel. Joshua noted Sidon as the northern border of Israel when the Israelites entered the land (Josh. 11.8; 19.27–28), but it was never settled by Israelites. Sidon joined the revolt (Jer. 27.3) and probably fell to Nebuchadrezzar.

25–26: A contrasting oracle concerning Judah. Once the nations that treated Israel with contempt are destroyed, the exiles will return to the land of Israel sworn to Jacob (Gen. 28.13; 35.12) and rebuild their community; thus will they manifest God's holiness in the world. *And they shall know that I the LORD am their God,* the self-identification formula.

29 In the tenth year, on the twelfth day of the tenth month,
the word of the LORD came to me: 2 O mortal, turn your
face against Pharaoh king of Egypt, and prophesy against him
and against all Egypt. 3 Speak these words:

Thus said the Lord GOD:
I am going to deal with you, O Pharaoh king of Egypt,
Mighty monster, sprawling in your[a] channels,
Who said,
My Nile is my own;
I made it for myself.
4 I will put hooks in your jaws,
And make the fish of your channels
Cling to your scales;
I will haul you up from your channels,
With all the fish of your channels
Clinging to your scales.
5 And I will fling you into the desert,
With all the fish of your channels.
You shall be left lying in the open,
Ungathered and unburied:
I have given you as food
To the beasts of the earth
And the birds of the sky.
6 Then all the inhabitants of Egypt shall know
That I am the LORD.
Because you[b] were a staff of reed
To the House of Israel:
7 When they grasped you with the hand, you would
splinter,
And wound all their shoulders,[c]
And when they leaned on you, you would break,
And make all their loins unsteady.[d]

8 Assuredly, thus said the Lord GOD: Lo, I will bring a sword
against you, and will cut off man and beast from you, 9 so that
the land of Egypt shall fall into desolation and ruin. And they
shall know that I am the LORD—because he boasted, "The Nile
is mine, and I made it." 10 Assuredly, I am going to deal with you
and your channels, and I will reduce the land of Egypt to utter ruin and desolation, [e]from Migdol to Syene, all the way to
the border of Nubia.[-e] 11 No foot of man shall traverse it, and no
foot of beast shall traverse it; and it shall remain uninhabited

a *Lit. "its."* b *Lit. "they."*
c *Septuagint and Syriac read "palms"; cf. 2 Kings 18.21; Isa. 36.6.*
d *Taking* ʿamad *as a byform of* maʿad; *cf. Syriac translation.*
e-e *I.e., the length of Egypt, from north to south. Syene is modern Aswan.*

29.1–32.32: Oracles against Egypt. 29.1–16: The first oracle of seven concerning Egypt. The initial date formula marks this as the first of the oracles against Egypt and its rulers. Ezek. 28.25–29.21 constitutes the haftarah reading for the parashah of Va-ʾeraʾ (Exod. 6.2–9.35), which relates the plagues against Egypt at the time of the exodus. Egypt played a role in instigating the revolt against its enemy Babylonia. When Pharaoh Hophra (Apries) attempted to relieve Jerusalem from the Babylonian siege in 588 BCE, he was repulsed. **1:** The initial date formula, *in the tenth year, on the twelfth day of the tenth month,* 12 Tevet, 588–587 BCE, is not in chronological sequence, since the prophecies to the nations are arranged thematically and not chronologically. Radak states that the oracle concerning Tyre appears first because it was fulfilled first, i.e., whereas Tyre submitted to Nebuchadnezzar in 573 BCE after thirteen years of siege, Egypt was conquered by the Persian king Cambyses in 525. Although it is not clear in the English translation, this particular date formula lacks the verb "vayehi" ("and it came to pass") that appears in the other chronological formulae of the book (except 40.1). When considered in relation to the disruption of the book's chronological sequence, this suggests that the oracles concerning Egypt may have once circulated independently, and were combined here as a group. **2–7:** God instructs Ezekiel to address Pharaoh, probably Hophra (ruled 589–570) after his failed attempt to rescue Jerusalem. **3:** *Mighty monster,* lit. "the great dragon." This comparison is sarcastic, and contains a hidden polemic against Egyptian beliefs; the crocodile was an Egyptian symbol. The Nile river forms the natural "backbone" of Egypt and serves as the source of Egypt's life. **6:** *A staff of reed to the House of Israel* symbolizes an unreliable support (cf. 2 Kings 18.21 || Isa. 36.6). **8–12:** Egypt's judgment results from Pharaoh's claim that the Nile is his and not God's (28.2). **10:** *From Migdol to Syene,* cities that define the northern and southern borders of Egypt; Syene is modern Aswan. **11:** *Forty years,* a common number for a complete and lengthy period of time (Ps. 95.10).

for forty years. 12 For forty years I will make the land of Egypt the
most desolate of desolate lands, and its cities shall be the most
desolate of ruined cities. And I will scatter the Egyptians among
the nations and disperse them throughout the countries.
13 Further, thus said the Lord GOD: After a period of forty
years I will gather the Egyptians from the peoples among
whom they were dispersed. 14 I will restore the fortunes of the
Egyptians and bring them back to the land of their origin, the
land of Pathros,[a] and there they shall be a lowly kingdom. 15 It
shall be the lowliest of all the kingdoms, and shall not lord it
over the nations again. I will reduce the Egyptians,[b] so that they
shall have no dominion over the nations. 16 Never again shall
they be the trust of the House of Israel, recalling its guilt in having turned to them. And they shall know that I am the Lord GOD.

17 In the twenty-seventh year, on the first day of the first
month, the word of the LORD came to me: 18 O mortal, King
Nebuchadrezzar of Babylon has made his army expend vast
labor on Tyre; every head is rubbed bald and every shoulder
scraped. But he and his army have had no return for the labor
he expended on Tyre. 19 Assuredly, thus said the Lord GOD: I
will give the land of Egypt to Nebuchadrezzar, king of Babylon.
He shall carry off her wealth and take her spoil and seize her
booty; and she shall be the recompense of his army. 20 As the
wage for which he labored, for what they did for Me, I give him
the land of Egypt—declares the Lord GOD.
21 On that day I will [c]endow the House of Israel with strength,
and you shall be vindicated[-c] among them. And they shall
know that I am the LORD.

30 The word of the LORD came to me: 2 O mortal, prophesy
and say: Thus said the Lord GOD:

Wail, alas for the day!
3 For a day is near;
A day of the LORD is near.
It will be a day of cloud,
An hour of [invading] nations.
4 A sword shall pierce Egypt,
And Nubia shall be seized with trembling,

a I.e., southern Egypt. *b Heb. "them."*
c-c Lit. "cause a horn to sprout for the House of Israel, and I will grant you opening of the mouth."

13–16: Egypt will be restored to its land as a minor kingdom rather than a great empire rivaling the Babylonians. The prophet clearly has in mind Egypt's failure to aid Israel in its time of need. **14:** *Pathros,* Upper Egypt, the southern portion of the kingdom. In Egypt, "up" is south (upstream on the Nile) and "down" is north (downstream on the Nile). **16:** The oracle ends with the self-identification formula, but it is applied to Egypt rather than to Israel. (This oracle is similar to the theme of Isa., that Israel must trust God alone, rather than depending on foreign nations).

29.17–21: The second oracle concerning Egypt. The prophetic word formula, *the word of the LORD came to me,* in 29.17 and 30.1 marks the two oracle reports that appear in this section. **17:** *The twenty-seventh year, on the first day of the first month,* 1 Nisan 571–570 BCE. This date is the latest date in the book. *Seder 'Olam Rab.* 26 maintains implausibly that this refers to the twenty-seventh year (578 BCE) of Nebuchadnezzar's reign when Egypt fell into his hands. Nebuchadrezzar reigned for forty-three years, 605–562, but he never conquered Egypt. Modern commentators maintain that this date was written at a later time, following the delayed fulfillment of the oracle concerning Tyre. **18:** Ezekiel may be referring to Nebuchadrezzar's failure to conquer Tyre as a basis for his campaign against Egypt. Following the conclusion of his siege against Tyre in 573 BCE, Nebuchadrezzar attacked Egypt in 668 but failed to conquer the land. Although Tyre submitted to him, the failure to conquer the city meant that his troops would receive little booty. **21:** *I will endow the House of Israel with strength,* lit. "I will cause a horn to sprout for the house of Israel": the restoration of the Davidic monarchy in the aftermath of Egypt's collapse (see Isa. 11.1–16; Ps. 132.17). This phrase plays a prominent role in the daily "'Amidah" prayer concerning the restoration of Davidic kingship.

30.1–19: The third oracle concerning Egypt. After its opening this section contains four oracles (vv. 2–5, 6–9, 10–12, 13–19), each identified by the prophetic messenger formula, *thus said the Lord GOD.* **2–5:** God instructs Ezekiel to lament for Egypt and her supporters. The prophet

When men fall slain in Egypt
And her wealth is seized
And her foundations are overthrown.
5 Nubia, Put, and Lud, and all [a]the mixed populations,[a] and
Cub, and the inhabitants of the allied countries shall fall by the
sword with them.
6 Thus said the LORD:
Those who support Egypt shall fall,
And her proud strength shall sink;
There they shall fall by the sword,
From Migdol to Syene
—declares the Lord GOD.
7 They shall be the most desolate of desolate lands, and her
cities shall be the most ruined of cities, 8 when I set fire to Egypt
and all who help her are broken. Thus they shall know that I
am the LORD.
9 On that day, messengers shall set out at My bidding to
strike terror into confident Nubia. And they shall be seized
with trembling on Egypt's day [of doom]—for it is at hand.
10 Thus said the Lord GOD: I will put an end to the wealth
of Egypt through King Nebuchadrezzar of Babylon. 11 He, together with his troops, the most ruthless of the nations, shall
be brought to ravage the land. And they shall unsheathe the
sword against Egypt and fill the land with the slain.
12 I will turn the channels into dry ground, and I will deliver
the land into the hands of evil men. I will lay waste the land
and everything in it by the hands of strangers. I the LORD have
spoken.

13 Thus said the Lord GOD: I will destroy the fetishes and
make an end of the idols in Noph; and no longer shall there
be a prince in the land of Egypt; and I will strike the land
of Egypt with fear. 14 I will lay Pathros waste, I will set fire
to Zoan, and I will execute judgment on No. 15 I will pour
out my anger upon Sin, the stronghold of Egypt, and I will
destroy the wealth of No. 16 I will set fire to Egypt; Sin shall
writhe in anguish and No shall be torn apart; [a]and Noph
[shall face] adversaries in broad daylight.[a] 17 The young men
of Aven[b] and Pi-beseth shall fall by the sword, and those
[towns] shall go into captivity. 18 In Tehaphnehes[c] daylight
shall be withheld,[d] when I break there the power of Egypt,
and there her proud strength comes to an end. [The city] itself shall be covered with cloud, and its daughter towns shall
go into captivity.

a-a Meaning of Heb. uncertain. *b Elsewhere called "On"; cf. Gen. 41.45, 50; 46.20.*
c Elsewhere vocalized "Tahpanhes"; e.g., Jer. 2.16; 44.1.
d Some Heb. mss. and editions read "darkened."

employs the "Day of the LORD" motif to express the overthrow of Egypt. **5:** *Put, and Lud,* see 27.10–11 n. *Cub* is unknown. **13–19:** The many place names that Ezekiel cites demonstrate that destruction will encompass the entire land. The description of Egypt's destruction in these vv. is highlighted by a cluster of verbs repeated here thirteen times in seven vv.: *destroy, make an end, no longer shall there be, I will lay, I will set fire, I will execute judgment, I will pour out my anger, I will destroy, I will set fire, writhe, torn apart, fall by the sword, go into captivity, I will execute judgment.* **13:** *Noph* is Memphis, the early capital south of Cairo. **14:** *Pathros,* (see 29.14). *Zoan,* also called Rameses, Tanis, and Avaris, the site where the Heb slaves worked in the Nile Delta according to Num. 13.22 and Ps. 78.12, 43. *No* is Thebes, Egypt's capital throughout much of Israel's history (Jer. 46.25). **15:** *Sin* is Pelusium, near Zoan in the northeastern Delta. **17:** *Aven* is "On" or Heliopolis, 10 km (6 mi) northeast of Cairo. *Pi-beseth,* Bubastis in the eastern Delta. **18:** *Tehaphnehes,* by the north shore of the Gulf of Suez (Jer. 2.16; 46.14).

19 Thus I will execute judgment on Egypt;
And they shall know that I am the LORD.

20 In the eleventh year, on the seventh day of the first month,
the word of the LORD came to me: 21 O mortal, I have broken
the arm of Pharaoh king of Egypt; it has not been bound up
to be healed nor firmly bandaged to make it strong enough to
grasp the sword. 22 Assuredly, thus said the Lord GOD: I am going to deal with Pharaoh king of Egypt. I will break his arms,
both the sound one and the injured, and make the sword drop
from his hand. 23 I will scatter the Egyptians among the nations
and disperse them throughout the countries. 24 I will strength-
en the arms of the king of Babylon and put My sword in his
hand; and I will break the arms of Pharaoh, and he shall groan
before him with the groans of one struck down. 25 I will make
firm the arms of the king of Babylon, but the arms of Pharaoh
shall fail. And they shall know that I am the LORD, when I put
My sword into the hand of the king of Babylon, and he lifts it
against the land of Egypt. 26 I will scatter the Egyptians among
the nations and disperse them throughout the countries. Thus
they shall know that I am the LORD.

31 In the eleventh year, on the first day of the third month,
the word of the LORD came to me: 2 O mortal, say to
Pharaoh king of Egypt and his hordes:

Who was comparable to you in greatness?
3 Assyria was a cedar in Lebanon
With beautiful branches and [a]-shady thickets,-[a]
Of lofty stature,
With its top among [b]-leafy trees.-[b]
4 Waters nourished it,
The deep made it grow tall,
Washing with its streams
The place where it was planted,
Making its channels well up
[c]-To all-[c] the trees of the field.
5 Therefore it exceeded in stature
All the trees of the field;
Its branches multiplied and its boughs grew long
Because of the abundant water
That welled up for it.
6 In its branches nested
All the birds of the sky;
All the beasts of the field

a-a Meaning of Heb. uncertain. *b-b Septuagint reads "clouds."*
c-c Meaning of Heb. uncertain; emendation yields "more than for all."

19: The *judgment* executed against Egypt recalls language of the exodus tradition (e.g., Exod. 6.6), and suggests a reenactment of the plagues of the exodus.

30.20–26: The fourth oracle concerning Egypt. 20: *In the eleventh year, on the seventh day of the first month,* 7 Nisan, 587–586 BCE, approximately four months before the destruction. **21:** The broken arm of Pharaoh refers to Nebuchadrezzar's defeat of Hophra, who attempted to relieve Jerusalem under siege. **22–26:** The prophet anticipates an even more devastating defeat of Egypt by Babylonia, but this did not transpire. **26:** As elsewhere, this destruction is not for vengeance, but so *they shall know that I am the LORD,* a common ending formula of Ezekiel's oracles; most often it refers to Israel, but it is used here of the Egyptians.

31.1–18: The fifth oracle concerning Egypt. The imagery of a fallen cedar of Lebanon portrays Pharaoh's downfall; this oracle shares many elements with the oracles against Tyre. The fall of Assyria forms the precedent and model for the fall of Egypt. Isa. 14.3–23 likewise portrays the downfall of the Babylonian king, and relates it to the downfall of Assyria (Isa. 14.24–27). Thematically, this oracle is similar to those against Tyre in chs 27 and 28. **1:** *In the eleventh year, on the first day of the third month,* 1 Sivan, 587–586 BCE, about two months prior to the destruction of the Temple. **2–9:** The tradition of the well-watered tree in the garden of Eden, here called *the garden of God* (v. 8).

10–14: Because of its height and arrogance, the tree is cut down. **11:** *The mightiest of nations,* lit. "the ram of the nations," Nebuchadrezzar. The Babylonians boasted of the trees they took from Lebanon. **14:** *Pit,* the underworld. **15–18:** *Sheol,* the Heb name for the underworld.

Bore their young under its boughs,
And in its shadow lived
All the great nations.
7 It was beautiful in its height,
In the length of its branches,
Because its stock stood
By abundant waters.
8 Cedars in the garden of God
Could not compare with it;
Cypresses could not match its boughs,
And plane trees could not vie with its branches;
No tree in the garden of God
Was its peer in beauty.
9 I made it beautiful
In the profusion of its branches;
And all the trees of Eden envied it
In the garden of God.

[10] Assuredly, thus said the Lord GOD: Because it[a] towered
high in stature, and thrust its top up among the [b-]leafy trees,[-b]
and it was arrogant in its height, [11] I delivered it into the hands
of the mightiest of nations. They treated it as befitted its wickedness. I banished it. [12] Strangers, the most ruthless of nations, cut it down and abandoned it; its branches fell on the
mountains and in every valley; its boughs were splintered in
every watercourse of the earth; and all the peoples of the earth
departed from its shade and abandoned it. [13] Upon its fallen
trunk all the birds of the sky nest, and all the beasts of the field
lodge among its boughs—[14] so that no trees by water should
exalt themselves in stature or set their tops among the [b-]leafy
trees,[-b] and that no well-watered tree may reach up to them in
height. For they are all consigned to death, to the lowest part
of the netherworld,[c] together with human beings who descend
into the Pit.
[15] Thus said the Lord GOD: On the day it went down to Sheol, I closed[d] the deep over it and covered it; I held back its
streams, and the great waters were checked. I made Lebanon
mourn deeply for it, and all the trees of the field languished
on its account. [16] I made nations quake at the crash of its fall,
when I cast it down to Sheol with those who descend into
the Pit; and all the trees of Eden, the choicest and best of
Lebanon, all that were well watered, were consoled in the
lowest part of the netherworld. [17] They also descended with
it into Sheol, to those slain by the sword, together with its

a Heb. "you." *b-b Septuagint reads "clouds."*
c To which popular belief relegated those who died uncircumcised or by the sword; cf. v. 18. *d Cf. Aramaic* 'abulla, *"gate."*

supporters,[a] they who had lived under its shadow among the nations.

18 [Now you know] who is comparable to you in glory and greatness among the trees of Eden. And you too shall be brought down with the trees of Eden to the lowest part of the netherworld; you shall lie among the uncircumcised and those slain by the sword. Such shall be [the fate of] Pharaoh and all his hordes—declares the Lord GOD.

32 In the twelfth year, on the first day of the twelfth month, the word of the LORD came to me: 2 O mortal, intone a dirge over Pharaoh king of Egypt. Say to him:

[b]O great beast among the nations,[b] you are doomed!
You are like the dragon in the seas,
Thrusting through their[c] streams,
Stirring up the water with your feet
And muddying their streams!
3 Thus said the Lord GOD:
I will cast My net over you
In an assembly of many peoples,
And you shall be hauled up in My toils.
4 And I will fling you to the ground,
Hurl you upon the open field.
I will cause all the birds of the sky
To settle upon you.
I will cause the beasts of all the earth
To batten on you.
5 I will cast your carcass upon the hills
And fill the valleys with your [b]rotting flesh.[b]
6 I will drench the earth
With your oozing blood upon the hills,
And the watercourses shall be filled with your [gore].
7 When you are snuffed out,
I will cover the sky
And darken its stars;
I will cover the sun with clouds
And the moon shall not give its light.
8 All the lights that shine in the sky
I will darken above you;
And I will bring darkness upon your land
—declares the Lord GOD.
9 I will vex the hearts of many peoples
When I bring your [d]shattered remnants[d] among the nations,
To countries which you never knew.

32.1–16: The sixth oracle concerning Egypt. This particular oracle is characterized by animal imagery at its beginning and end. **1:** *In the twelfth year, on the first day of the twelfth month,* 1 Adar, 585 BCE, the year following the destruction of the Temple. The oracle is in the form of a dirge. **2–15:** The portrayal of Pharaoh's defeat by God draws upon the mythological traditions of God's defeat of the sea dragon Leviathan at creation (Isa. 11.15; 27.1; Pss. 74.12–17; 104.7–9; Job 38.8–11; see also Exod. ch 15). In addition, it evokes the crocodiles of the Nile; Pharaoh is a monster crocodile. The motif of oozing blood (v. 6) recalls the plague of blood (Exod. 7.19–24); the motif of darkness recalls the plague of darkness against Egypt (Exod. 10.21–29) and also the Day of the LORD traditions (Joel 2.1–2; 3.15; Zeph. 1.15).

a Heb. "arm." *b-b* Meaning of Heb. uncertain. *c* Heb. "your."
d-d Septuagint reads "captives."

11: *The sword of the king of Babylon,* Nebuchadrezzar. The nations will witness God's victory (Exod. 15.13–18). **16:** Women served as mourners in the ancient Near East (see Jer. 9.17–18).

32.17–32: The seventh and last oracle concerning Egypt. 17: *In the twelfth year, on the fifteenth day of the month,* 15 Adar, 585 BCE. Although the month is not specified, it likely follows from the reference to the twelfth month in 32.1 (see translators' note *a* on v. 17). The association highlights the motif of coming restoration. This final oracle alludes to the previous destruction of Israel's other enemies, depicting Egypt as joining them in the underworld. **18:** God instructs Ezekiel to wail for Egypt as its people descend into the underworld. **19–32:** Egypt will join the nations that have been destroyed. **22:** *Assyria* was conquered by Babylonia and Media during the period 627–609, and was thus representative of a once great nation now totally destroyed.

10 I will strike many peoples with horror over your fate;
And their kings shall be aghast over you,
When I brandish My sword before them.
They shall tremble continually,
Each man for his own life,
On the day of your downfall.
11 For thus said the Lord GOD:
The sword of the king of Babylon shall come upon you.
12 I will cause your multitude to fall
By the swords of warriors,
All the most ruthless among the nations.
They shall ravage the splendor of Egypt,
And all her masses shall be wiped out.
13 I will make all her cattle vanish from beside
abundant waters;
The feet of man shall not muddy them any more,
Nor shall the hoofs of cattle muddy them.
14 Then I will let their waters settle,
And make their rivers flow like oil
—declares the Lord GOD:
15 When I lay the land of Egypt waste,
When the land is emptied of [the life] that filled it,
When I strike down all its inhabitants,
And they shall know that I am the LORD.
16 This is a dirge, and it shall be intoned;
The women of the nations shall intone it,
They shall intone it over Egypt and all her multitude
—declares the Lord GOD.

17 In the twelfth year, on the fifteenth day of the month,[a] the
word of the LORD came to me: 18 [b]O mortal, wail [the dirge]—
along with the women of the mighty nations—over the masses
of Egypt, accompanying their descent to the lowest part of the
netherworld, among those who have gone down into the Pit.
19 [c]-Whom do you surpass in beauty? Down with you, and be
laid to rest with the uncircumcised! 20 They shall lie amid those
slain by the sword,-[c] [b][amid those slain by] the sword [Egypt]
has been dragged and left with all her masses.
21 From the depths of Sheol the mightiest of warriors speak to
him and his allies; the uncircumcised, the slain by the sword,
have gone down and lie [there]. 22 Assyria is there with all her
company, their graves round about, all of them slain, fallen by
the sword. 23 Their graves set in the farthest recesses of the Pit,
all her company are round about her tomb, all of them slain,

a *Presumably the twelfth month; cf. v. 1.*
b *Construction of these verses uncertain.*
c-c *Cf. 31.18 ff. and note c on 31.14.*

fallen by the sword—they who struck terror in the land of the living. 24 There too is Elam and all her masses round about her tomb, all of them slain, fallen by the sword—they who descended uncircumcised to the lowest part of the netherworld, who struck terror in the land of the living—now they bear their shame with those who have gone down to the Pit. 25 They made a bed for her among the slain, with all her masses; their graves are round about her. They are all uncircumcised, slain by the sword. Though their terror was once spread over the land of the living, they bear their shame with those who have gone into the Pit; they are placed among the slain. 26 Meshech and Tubal and all their masses are there; their graves are round about. They are all uncircumcised, pierced through by the sword—they who once struck terror in the land of the living. 27 And they do not lie with the fallen uncircumcised warriors, who went down to Sheol with their battle gear, who put their swords beneath their heads and their iniquities[a] upon their bones—for the terror of the warriors was upon the land of the living. 28 And you too shall be shattered amid the uncircumcised, and lie among those slain by the sword. 29 Edom is there, her kings and all her chieftains, who, for all their might, are laid among those who are slain by the sword; they too lie with the uncircumcised and with those who have gone down to the Pit. 30 All the princes of the north and all the Sidonians are there, who went down in disgrace with the slain, in spite of the terror that their might inspired; and they lie, uncircumcised, with those who are slain by the sword, and bear their shame with those who have gone down to the Pit.

31 These Pharaoh shall see, and he shall be consoled for all his masses, those of Pharaoh's men slain by the sword and all his army—declares the Lord GOD. 32 [b-]I strike terror into the land of the living; Pharaoh[-b] and all his masses are laid among the uncircumcised, along with those who were slain by the sword—said the Lord GOD.

33 The word of the LORD came to me: 2 O mortal, speak to your fellow countrymen and say to them: When I bring the sword against a country, the citizens of that country take one of their number and appoint him their watchman. 3 Suppose he sees the sword advancing against the country, and he blows the horn and warns the people. 4 If anybody hears the sound of the horn but ignores the warning, and the sword comes and dispatches him, his blood shall be on his own head. 5 Since he heard the sound of the horn but ignored the warning, his bloodguilt shall be upon himself; had he taken

a Emendation yields "shields."

b-b Emendation yields "because he struck terror in the land of the living, Pharaoh."

24: *Elam* was destroyed by the Assyrians in the mid-7th c. BCE. **26:** *Meshech and Tubal,* two unidentified kingdoms in Asia Minor that perhaps were destroyed by Assyria. **29:** *Edom* was conquered by Babylonia. **30:** *The princes of the north,* probably the Phoenicians, as indicated by the reference to the Sidonians.

33.1–48.35: Postdestruction Oracles. 33.1–39.29: Restoration Prophecies. This section is the first part of the last major division of Ezek.

33.1–20: Response to the destruction of the Temple and Ezekiel's appointment as Israel's watchman. This is a transitional section in the book, bridging the oracles concerning the fall of Jerusalem (chs 1–24) and the oracles to the nations (chs 25–32) and the end of the book, mostly comprised of prophecies of restoration. This short section contains many echoes of earlier portions of Ezekiel. The role of a prophet is like that of a watchman who stands watch over a city; this picks up on the earlier use of the image (see 3.9–21). The watchman is not responsible for the fate of the people if he warns them, but he is fully responsible if he does not. The passage presupposes that the threat of death for the wicked can be reversed if they change their ways.

10–20: This paraphrases many sections of 18.21–32, which emphasize that people are judged for their current actions only. Ezekiel debates those who believe that past righteousness can deliver someone who commits wrongdoing later in life and that past wrongdoing will still condemn those who have turned to righteousness.

33.21–33: Once the prophet is informed of the fall of Jerusalem (33.21–22), he emphasizes restoration for Israel (33.21–39.29) and the Temple (chs 40–48). Many of the prophecies of restoration use images from the earlier prophecies of retribution and overturn them.

the warning, he would have saved his life. [6] But if the watchman sees the sword advancing and does not blow the horn, so that the people are not warned, and the sword comes and destroys one of them, that person was destroyed for his own sins; however, I will demand a reckoning for his blood from the watchman.

[7] Now, O mortal, I have appointed you a watchman for the House of Israel; and whenever you hear a message from My mouth, you must transmit My warning to them. [8] When I say to the wicked, "Wicked man, you shall die," but you have not spoken to warn the wicked man against his way, he, that wicked man, shall die for his sins, but I will demand a reckoning for his blood from you. [9] But if you have warned the wicked man to turn back from his way, and he has not turned from his way, he shall die for his own sins, but you will have saved your life.

[10] Now, O mortal, say to the House of Israel: This is what you have been saying: "Our transgressions and our sins weigh heavily upon us; we are sick at heart about them. How can we survive?" [11] Say to them: As I live—declares the Lord GOD—it is not My desire that the wicked shall die, but that the wicked turn from his [evil] ways and live. Turn back, turn back from your evil ways, that you may not die, O House of Israel!

[12] Now, O mortal, say to your fellow countrymen: The righteousness of the righteous shall not save him when he transgresses, nor shall the wickedness of the wicked cause him to stumble when he turns back from his wickedness. The righteous shall not survive through [a]his righteousness[a] when he sins. [13] When I say of the righteous "He shall surely live," and, relying on his righteousness, he commits iniquity, none of his righteous deeds shall be remembered; but for the iniquity that he has committed he shall die. [14] So, too, when I say to the wicked, "You shall die," and he turns back from his sinfulness and does what is just and right—[15] if the wicked man restores a pledge, makes good what he has taken by robbery, follows the laws of life,[b] and does not commit iniquity—he shall live, he shall not die. [16] None of the sins that he committed shall be remembered against him; since he does what is just and right, he shall live.

[17] Your fellow countrymen say, "The way of the Lord is unfair." But it is their way that is unfair! [18] When a righteous man turns away from his righteous deeds and commits iniquity, he shall die [c]for it.[c] [19] And when a wicked man turns back from his wickedness and does what is just and right, it is he who shall live by virtue of these things. [20] And will you say, "The way of the Lord is unfair"? I will judge each one of you according to his ways, O House of Israel!

a-a Heb. "it." *b Cf. Lev. 18.5.* *c-c Or "in spite of them," i.e., his righteous deeds.*

21 In the twelfth year of our exile, on the fifth day of the tenth
month, a fugitive came to me from Jerusalem and reported,
"The city has fallen." 22 Now the hand of the LORD had come
upon me the evening before the fugitive arrived, and He
opened my mouth before he came to me in the morning; thus
my mouth was opened and I was no longer speechless.
23 The word of the LORD came to me: 24 O mortal, those who
live in these ruins in the land of Israel argue, "Abraham was
but one man, yet he was granted possession of the land. We
are many; surely, the land has been given as a possession to
us." 25 Therefore say to them: Thus said the Lord GOD: You eat
with the blood, you raise your eyes to your fetishes, and you
shed blood—yet you expect to possess the land! 26 You have
relied on your sword, you have committed abominations, you
have all defiled other men's wives—yet you expect to possess
the land!
27 Thus shall you speak to them: Thus said the Lord GOD: As
I live, those who are in the ruins shall fall by the sword, and
those who are in the open I have allotted as food to the beasts,
and those who are in the strongholds and caves shall die by
pestilence. 28 I will make the land a desolate waste, and her
proud glory shall cease; and the mountains of Israel shall be
desolate, with none passing through. 29 And they shall know
that I am the LORD, when I make the land a desolate waste on
account of all the abominations which they have committed.
30 Note well, O mortal: your fellow countrymen who converse
about you by the walls and in the doorways of their houses and
say to each other and propose to one another, "Come and hear
what word has issued from the LORD." 31 They will come to you
[a-]in crowds and sit before you in throngs[-a] and will hear your
words, but they will not obey them. For [b-]they produce nothing
but lust with their mouths;[-b] and their hearts pursue nothing
but gain. 32 To them you are just a singer of bawdy songs, who
has a sweet voice and plays skillfully; they hear your words, but
will not obey them. 33 But when it[c] comes—and come it will—
they shall know that a prophet has been among them.

34 The word of the LORD came to me: 2 O mortal, prophesy
against the shepherds[d] of Israel. Prophesy, and say to
them:
To the shepherds: Thus said the Lord GOD: Ah, you shepherds
of Israel, who have been tending yourselves! Is it not the flock
that the shepherds ought to tend? 3 You partake of the fat,[e] you

a-a Meaning of Heb. uncertain. Lit. "as a people come, and sit before you as My people." *b-b Meaning of Heb. uncertain.*
c I.e., the punishment predicted. *d I.e., rulers.*
e Septuagint and Vulgate, reading the Hebrew consonants with different vowels, translate "milk."

21–22: *In the twelfth year of our exile, on the fifth day of the tenth month,* 5 Sivan, 585 BCE. The prophet first receives word of Jerusalem's fall some seven months after the event; the previous night, as a sign that the announcement was about to come, he was released from his speechlessness (3.26–27), as was predicted in 24.27. **23–29:** Ezekiel counters the claim that *those who live in these ruins,* desert nomads, will take control of the land. Ezekiel argues that they will be destroyed because they do not observe God's requirements for holy life in the land. For the crimes enumerated here, see ch 18. This section also highlights that the exiles in Babylon will fare better than those who remain behind in Israel. **29:** In many ways, this v. summarizes the main point of Ezek.: Contrary to what many people believed, the destruction of Jerusalem does not indicate that God is powerless and has abandoned the Israelites, but that He is powerfully and legitimately punishing them for their deeds. **30–33:** God charges that people come to hear Ezekiel, but will not do as he says. That attitude, however, will change with the destruction of the Temple, when Ezekiel is fully legitimated as a true prophet.

34.1–31: The shepherds of Israel. Ezekiel contends that Israel's kings have acted improperly and must be replaced. The ch is complex, first suggesting that God will function as the people's shepherd, and then proposing that David will return, subject to God's authority. As a prophecy of redemption, the emphasis is not on the condemnation of the kings, but on the establishment of a better monarchy. **1–10:** The image of the shepherd is commonly used to portray monarchs in biblical and ancient Near Eastern literature (e.g., David, 1 Sam. 16.11; ch 17; and much earlier, Hammurabi of Babylon). God charges that the "shepherds" have not taken care of the "flock" so that they are "scattered" or sent into exile. **2:** *Ah,* lit. "woe (to)!" **3:** The metaphors of this v. are explained in the following vv.

clothe yourselves with the wool, and you slaughter the fatlings;
but you do not tend the flock. [4] You have not sustained the weak,
healed the sick, or bandaged the injured; you have not brought
back the strayed, or looked for the lost; but you have driven them
with harsh rigor, [5] and they have been scattered for want of anyone to tend them; scattered, they have become prey for every
wild beast. [6] My sheep stray through all the mountains and over
every lofty hill; My flock is scattered all over the face of the earth,
with none to take thought of them and none to seek them. [7] Hear
then, O shepherds, the word of the LORD! [8] As I live—declares
the Lord GOD: Because My flock has been a spoil—My flock has
been a prey for all the wild beasts, for want of anyone to tend
them since My shepherds have not taken thought of My flock,
for the shepherds tended themselves instead of tending the
flock—[9] hear indeed, O shepherds, the word of the LORD: [10] Thus
said the Lord GOD: I am going to deal with the shepherds! I will
demand a reckoning of them for My flock, and I will dismiss them
from tending the flock. The shepherds shall not tend themselves
any more; for I will rescue My flock from their mouths, and it
shall not be their prey. [11] For thus said the Lord GOD: Here am
I! I am going to take thought for My flock and I will seek them
out. [12] As a shepherd seeks out his flock when some [animals] in
his flock have gotten separated, so I will seek out My flock, I will
rescue them from all the places to which they were scattered on
a day of cloud and gloom. [13] I will take them out from the peoples and gather them from the countries, and I will bring them
to their own land, and will pasture them on the mountains of
Israel, by the watercourses and in all the settled portions of the
land. [14] I will feed them in good grazing land, and the lofty hills
of Israel shall be their pasture. There, in the hills of Israel, they
shall lie down in a good pasture and shall feed on rich grazing
land. [15] I Myself will graze My flock, and I Myself will let them
lie down—declares the Lord GOD. [16] I will look for the lost, and I
will bring back the strayed; I will bandage the injured, and I will
sustain the weak; and the fat and healthy ones I will destroy.[a] I
will tend them rightly.

[17] And as for you, My flock, thus said the Lord GOD: I am going to judge between one animal and another.

To the rams and the bucks: [18] Is it not enough for you to graze
on choice grazing ground, but you must also trample with your
feet what is left from your grazing? And is it not enough for you
to drink [b-]clear water,[-b] but you must also muddy with your feet
what is left? [19] And must My flock graze on what your feet have
trampled and drink what your feet have muddied? [20] Assuredly, thus said the Lord GOD to them: Here am I, I am going to
decide between the stout animals and the lean. [21] Because you

a *Several ancient versions read "guard."* *b-b* *Lit. "water that has settled."*

7: As elsewhere in prophetic literature, the inevitable punishment is introduced by "lakhen," "therefore," omitted in the translation. **11–16:** God acts as the ideal "shepherd" (Ps. 23) who will return the sheep/people who have been scattered and will shepherd them under idyllic conditions. **12:** *As a shepherd seeks out his flock* is reused with a different nuance in the "unetaneh tokef" prayer of the high holidays (the prayer known by its opening as "Let us now tell the power of this day's holiness"), as part of the image of God's annual judgment of each Jew. **16:** *The fat and healthy ones I will destroy:* They will be destroyed because they neglected the people. Heb reads "'ashmid" *(I will destroy)*, the LXX reads "I will tend them rightly" (presumably based on Heb "'eshmor," ["resh" looks like "dalet" and the two are often confused]; see translators' note *a*). **17–22:** Ezekiel portrays the leaders as stronger sheep who trample the pasture and dirty the water that others must use, and who push the weaker aside. Thus, some of the flock must be destroyed. The image relates to ch 18, where each person is judged individually, according to his or her merit.

pushed with flank and shoulder against the feeble ones and
butted them with your horns until you scattered them abroad,
22 I will rescue My flock and they shall no longer be a spoil. I
will decide between one animal and another.
23 Then I will appoint a single shepherd over them to tend
them—My servant David. He shall tend them, he shall be
a shepherd to them. 24 I the LORD will be their God, and My
servant David shall be a ruler among them—I the LORD have
spoken. 25 And I will grant them a covenant of friendship. I will
banish vicious beasts from their land, and they shall live secure in the wasteland, they shall even sleep in the woodland.
26 I will make [a]these and the environs of My hill[a] a blessing: I
will send down the rain in its season, rains that bring blessing.
27 The trees of the field shall yield their fruit and the land shall
yield its produce. [My people] shall continue secure on its own
soil. They shall know that I am the LORD when I break the bars
of their yoke and rescue them from those who enslave them.
28 They shall no longer be a spoil for the nations, and the beasts
of the earth shall not devour them; they shall dwell secure and
untroubled. 29 I shall establish for them [a]a planting of renown;[a]
they shall no more be carried off by famine, and they shall not
have to bear again the taunts of the nations.[b] 30 They shall know
that I the LORD their God am with them and they, the House of
Israel, are My people—declares the Lord GOD.
31 For you, My flock, flock that I tend, are men; and I am your
God—declares the Lord GOD.

35 The word of the LORD came to me: 2 O mortal, set your
face against Mount Seir and prophesy against it. 3 Say to
it: Thus said the Lord GOD: I am going to deal with you, Mount
Seir: I will stretch out My hand against you and make you an
utter waste. 4 I will turn your towns into ruins, and you shall
be a desolation; then you shall know that I am the LORD. 5 Because you harbored an ancient hatred and handed the people
of Israel over to the sword in their time of calamity, the time set
for their punishment—6 assuredly, as I live, declares the Lord
GOD, [a]I will doom you with blood; blood shall pursue you; I
swear that, for your bloodthirsty hatred, blood shall pursue
you.[a] 7 I will make Mount Seir an utter waste, and I will keep

a-a Meaning of Heb. uncertain. *b Cf.* 36.30.

23–31: God's rule will be manifested in the establishment of a descendant of David as *ruler* ("nasi" rather than "melekh," king). **24:** It is likely that the title *ruler* given here and in chs 40–48 to the king represents a diminution of royal power: He is a ruler, but not a full-fledged king. **25:** *A covenant of friendship,* the idyllic situation for those whom God will return to the land. Contrary to those who assert that "those who live in these ruins" will take over the land (33.23–29), Ezekiel maintains that God will protect the people of Israel. **27–29:** The references to *trees* and *beasts of the earth* together with the threat of enemies overturn the curses of Lev. ch 26 and recall God's role as Creator of the natural world and protector in the human world. **31:** *For you, My flock, flock that I tend, are men; and I am your God,* a variation of the covenant formula (11.20; 14.11) that emphasizes that God will be Israel's ultimate shepherd-king.

35.1–36.38: Divine preference for Israel over Edom and the purification of the people.

35.1–36.15: Edom and Israel. Ezekiel delivers contrasting oracles to *Mount Seir,* which personifies Edom, concerning judgment against Edom (see Isa. ch 34; Jer. 49.7–22; Obad.) and to the *mountains of Israel* (36.1) concerning the restoration of Israel. The restoration here, as elsewhere in prophetic literature, envisions the restoration of both kingdoms, Israel and Judah. The oracles presuppose Edom's actions against Jerusalem at the time of the Babylonian assault (see Obad. 1.11–14; Joel 4.19; Ps. 137.7–9). This may explain their placement here, (rather than with the earlier collection of oracles concerning the nations). In the Bible, Edom is descended from Isaac's son and Jacob's/Israel's brother; the point of this section is that even though they are closely related, Edom will not benefit from the restoration, which will affect Israel alone. **35.1–15:** The prophecy concerning Edom begins with an initial oracle in vv. 3–4, followed by "proof sayings" in vv. 5–9, 10–13 that establish the grounds for punishment. **2:** *Mount Seir,* the mountain range extending south from the Dead Sea and east of the Arabah that was Edom's homeland. **3–4:** The initial oracle calls for Edom's destruction. **5–9:** The first "proof saying" indicates that Edom played a role in Israel's destruction; it has Edom's desolation as its theme, and repeats words from the root "sh-m-m" (rendered as *waste* and *desolation*). **5:** *Ancient hatred* likely alludes to the feud between Esau (father of the Edomites) and

all passersby away from it. 8 I will cover its mountains with the
slain; men slain by the sword shall lie on your hills, in your valleys, and in all your watercourses. 9 I will make you a desolation for all time; your towns shall never be inhabited. And you
shall know that I am the LORD.

10 Because you thought "The two nations and the two lands
shall be mine and we shall possess them"—[a]although the
LORD was there[a]— 11 assuredly, as I live, declares the Lord GOD,
I will act with the same anger and passion that you acted with
in your hatred of them. And I will make Myself known through
them when I judge you. 12 You shall know that I the LORD have
heard all the taunts you uttered against the hills of Israel: "They
have been laid waste; they have been given to us as prey." 13 And
you spoke arrogantly against Me and [b]multiplied your words[b]
against Me: I have heard it.

14 Thus said the Lord GOD: When the whole earth rejoices, I
will make you a desolation. 15 As you rejoiced when the heritage of the House of Israel was laid waste, so will I treat you: the
hill country of Seir and the whole of Edom, all of it, shall be laid
waste. And they shall know that I am the LORD.

36 And you, O mortal, prophesy to the mountains of Israel
and say: O mountains of Israel, hear the word of the
LORD:
2 Thus said the Lord GOD: Because the enemy gloated over
you, "Aha! Those ancient heights have become our possession!" 3 therefore prophesy, and say: Thus said the Lord GOD:
Just because [c]they eagerly lusted to see you become a possession of the other nations round about, so that you have become the butt of gossip in every language and of the jibes from
every people[c]— 4 truly, you mountains of Israel, hear the word
of the Lord GOD: Thus said the Lord GOD to the mountains and
the hills, to the watercourses and the valleys, and to the desolate wastes and deserted cities which have become a prey and
a laughingstock to the other nations round about:
5 Assuredly, thus said the Lord GOD: I have indeed spoken
in My blazing wrath against the other nations and against all
of Edom which, [c]with wholehearted glee and with contempt,
have made My land a possession for themselves for pasture
and for prey.[c] 6 Yes, prophesy about the land of Israel, and say
to the mountains and the hills, to the watercourses and to the
valleys, Thus said the Lord GOD: Behold, I declare in My blazing
wrath: Because you have suffered the taunting of the nations,
7 thus said the Lord GOD: I hereby swear that the nations which
surround you shall, in their turn, suffer disgrace. 8 But you, O

a-a Meaning of Heb. uncertain; emendation yields "and the LORD heard it."
b-b Emendation yields "and spoke arrogantly." *c-c Meaning of Heb. uncertain.*

Jacob or the long history of conflict between Israel and Edom (Num. 20.14–21). **10–13:** The second "proof saying." **10:** *The two nations and the two lands:* In addition to the conflict between Esau and Jacob, there is a tradition of God's self-revelation from Seir (Deut. 33.2; Judg. 5.4). **14–15:** Edom disappeared following the 6th c. as it was overrun by Arab nomads who later became known as the Nabateans.

36.1–15: The oracle concerning the restoration of the mountains of Israel is a deliberate contrast with that against Mount Seir; it also reverses some of the imagery of the prophecy of retribution in ch 6. **2:** God begins by citing *the enemy's,* most likely Edom's, intentions to take control of Israel. **3–12:** The oracle presupposes the depopulation and desolation of the entire land, which must now be replenished; texts from the period of the return suggest that the land was not entirely abandoned. **3, 5:** *The other nations,* lit. "the remnant of the nations"; Edom elsewhere is a symbol for nations that threaten Israel (Isa. ch 34; 63.1–6).

mountains of Israel, shall yield your produce and bear your
fruit for My people Israel, for their return is near. 9 For I will care
for you: I will turn to you, and you shall be tilled and sown. 10 I
will settle a large population on you, the whole House of Israel;
the towns shall be resettled, and the ruined sites rebuilt. 11 I
will multiply men and beasts upon you, and they shall increase
and be fertile, and I will resettle you as you were formerly, and
will make you more prosperous than you were at first. And you
shall know that I am the LORD. 12 I will lead men—My people
Israel—to you, and they shall possess you. You shall be their
heritage, and you shall not again cause them to be bereaved.
13 Thus said the Lord GOD: Because they say to you,
"You are [a land] that devours men, you have been a be-
reaver of your nations,"[a] 14 assuredly, you shall devour men
no more, you shall never again bereave your nations—
declares the Lord GOD. 15 No more will I allow the jibes of the
nations to be heard against you, no longer shall you suffer the
taunting of the peoples; and never again shall you cause your
nations to stumble[b]—declares the Lord GOD.

16 The word of the LORD came to me: 17 O mortal, when the
House of Israel dwelt on their own soil, they defiled it with
their ways and their deeds; their ways were in My sight like the
uncleanness of a menstruous woman. 18 So I poured out My
wrath on them for the blood which they shed upon their land,
and for the fetishes with which they defiled it. 19 I scattered
them among the nations, and they were dispersed through
the countries: I punished them in accordance with their ways
and their deeds. 20 But when they came [c-]to those nations,[-c]
they caused My holy name to be profaned,[d] in that it was said
of them, "These are the people of the LORD, yet they had to
leave His land." 21 Therefore I am concerned for My holy name,
which the House of Israel have caused to be profaned among
the nations to which they have come.
22 Say to the House of Israel: Thus said the Lord GOD: Not for
your sake will I act, O House of Israel, but for My holy name,
which you have caused to be profaned among the nations to
which you have come. 23 I will sanctify My great name which
has been profaned among the nations—among whom you
have caused it to be profaned. And the nations shall know that
I am the LORD—declares the Lord GOD—when I manifest My
holiness before their eyes through you. 24 I will take you from
among the nations and gather you from all the countries, and
I will bring you back to your own land. 25 I will sprinkle clean

a *I.e., Israel and Judah; cf. 37.15–22.* b *Many mss. read "be bereaved"; cf. vv. 13–14.*
c-c *Lit. "the nations they came to."*
d *I.e., the exile of Israel was taken by the nations to be evidence of the LORD's weakness.*

11: *They shall increase and be fertile,* reflecting the blessings of the Priestly creation story (Gen. 1.22), later applied to Israel as a whole (e.g., Gen. 48.4). **13–15:** The prophet promises that the land will no longer be open to the accusation of devouring *the peoples* and the attendant shame.

36.16–38: The purification and restoration of Israel and the sanctification of God's name. Ezek. 36.16–38 speaks of the purification of the defiled people and their land, and is followed by 37.1–14, a separate unit that portrays the resuscitation of the dead bones, representing the coming back to life of the people Israel. This section, 36.16–38 (Sephardi lectionary, 36.16–36), serves as the haftarah on Shabbat Parah, the third of the four special Shabbats preceding Passover (m. Meg. 3.4). **16–22:** The prophet initially employs the imagery of menstrual blood (see 18.6 and Lev. 15.19–30) to portray the impurity of the land. The impurity resulted from the *blood which they shed upon their land,* another metaphor for idolatrous practices. The exile of the people profanes God's name since it may suggest to others that the Israelite God is weaker than their gods, and did not have the power to prevent their exile. **22–32:** In order to reclaim God's name, Israel must be restored. As the vv. make clear, this is done for God's sake, not because Israel is deserving. **25:** God intends to purify Israel with *clean water,* which is a standard procedure for purification (Lev. 15.7, 11–12, etc.; Num. 19.17).

26–27: Once the land and people are cleansed, God will provide *a new heart* and *a new spirit* (11.19; 18.31) that will force the people to live in accordance with God's commandments. **28:** The covenant formula signifies the restoration of Israel's relationship with God and the fertility of the land. **33–36:** Replenishing of the land to resemble *the garden of Eden* (see 28.13–15 n.) reveals God to the nations. **37–38:** Along with the agricultural plenty comes the image of pastoral plenty, which is then related to the abundance of sacrificial sheep that fill Jerusalem during festivals, suggesting that these festivals will once again be celebrated in Jerusalem and prefiguring chs 40–48, with the reconstructed Jerusalem and the Temple.

37.1–28: Vision of the dry bones and the future of the kingdom of Israel. 37.1–14: The valley of dry bones. Ezekiel's vision of the dry bones symbolizes the restoration of the people Israel. Ezekiel is speaking metaphorically in this vision. When, in postbiblical times, the doctrine of resurrection took hold, Ezekiel's vision was interpreted literally. **1–10:** God instructs him to prophesy. **1–2:** Valley, or "plain," the location of his initial visions (1.22–27). **5, 8, 9:** *Breath,* lit. "wind," elsewhere called "breath (wind) of life" (e.g., Gen. 6.17). On the *four winds,* see similarly the 7.2 n.

water upon you, and you shall be clean: I will cleanse you from
all your uncleanness and from all your fetishes. 26 And I will
give you a new heart and put a new spirit into you: I will remove the heart of stone from your body and give you a heart of
flesh; 27 and I will put My spirit into you. Thus I will cause you
to follow My laws and faithfully to observe My rules. 28 Then
you shall dwell in the land which I gave to your fathers, and
you shall be My people and I will be your God.

29 And when I have delivered you from all your uncleanness,
I will summon the grain and make it abundant, and I will not
bring famine upon you. 30 I will make the fruit of your trees and
the crops of your fields abundant, so that you shall never again
be humiliated before the nations because of famine. 31 Then
you shall recall your evil ways and your base conduct, and
you shall loathe yourselves for your iniquities and your abhorrent practices. 32 Not for your sake will I act—declares the Lord
GOD—take good note! Be ashamed and humiliated because of
your ways, O House of Israel!

33 Thus said the Lord GOD: When I have cleansed you of all
your iniquities, I will people your settlements, and the ruined
places shall be rebuilt; 34 and the desolate land, after lying
waste in the sight of every passerby, shall again be tilled. 35 And
men shall say, "That land, once desolate, has become like the
garden of Eden; and the cities, once ruined, desolate, and ravaged, are now populated and fortified." 36 And the nations that
are left around you shall know that I the LORD have rebuilt the
ravaged places and replanted the desolate land. I the LORD
have spoken and will act.

37 Thus said the Lord GOD: Moreover, in this I will respond
to the House of Israel and act for their sake: I will multiply
their people like sheep. 38 As Jerusalem is filled with sacrificial
sheep during her festivals, so shall the ruined cities be filled
with flocks of people. And they shall know that I am the LORD.

37 The hand of the LORD came upon me. He took me out
by the spirit of the LORD and set me down in the valley.
It was full of bones. 2 He led me all around them; there were
very many of them spread over the valley, and they were very
dry. 3 He said to me, "O mortal, can these bones live again?"
I replied, "O Lord GOD, only You know." 4 And He said to me,
"Prophesy over these bones and say to them: O dry bones,
hear the word of the LORD! 5 Thus said the Lord GOD to these
bones: I will cause breath to enter you and you shall live again.
6 I will lay sinews upon you, and cover you with flesh, and form
skin over you. And I will put breath into you, and you shall live
again. And you shall know that I am the LORD!"

7 I prophesied as I had been commanded. And while I was
prophesying, suddenly there was a sound of rattling, and the

bones came together, bone to matching bone. 8 I looked, and
there were sinews on them, and flesh had grown, and skin had
formed over them; but there was no breath in them. 9 Then He
said to me, "Prophesy to the breath, prophesy, O mortal! Say
to the breath: Thus said the Lord God: Come, O breath, from
the four winds, and breathe into these slain, that they may live
again." 10 I prophesied as He commanded me. The breath entered them, and they came to life and stood up on their feet, a
vast multitude.

11 And He said to me, "O mortal, these bones are the whole
House of Israel. They say, 'Our bones are dried up, our hope is
gone; we are doomed.' 12 Prophesy, therefore, and say to them:
Thus said the Lord God: I am going to open your graves and lift
you out of the graves, O My people, and bring you to the land
of Israel. 13 You shall know, O My people, that I am the Lord,
when I have opened your graves and lifted you out of your
graves. 14 I will put My breath into you and you shall live again,
and I will set you upon your own soil. Then you shall know that
I the Lord have spoken and have acted"—declares the Lord.

15 The word of the Lord came to me: 16 And you, O mortal,
take a stick and write on it, "Of Judah and the Israelites associated with him"; and take another stick and write on it, "Of
Joseph—the stick of Ephraim—and all the House of Israel associated with him." 17 Bring them close to each other, so that they
become one stick, joined together in your hand. 18 And when
any of your people ask you, "Won't you tell us what these actions of yours mean?" 19 answer them, "Thus said the Lord God:
I am going to take the stick of Joseph—which is in the hand of
Ephraim—and of the tribes of Israel associated with him, and
I will place the stick of Judah [a]upon it[a] and make them into
one stick; they shall be joined in My hand." 20 You shall hold
up before their eyes the sticks which you have inscribed, 21 and
you shall declare to them: Thus said the Lord God: I am going
to take the Israelite people from among the nations they have
gone to, and gather them from every quarter, and bring them to
their own land. 22 I will make them a single nation in the land,
on the hills of Israel, and one king shall be king of them all.
Never again shall they be two nations, and never again shall
they be divided into two kingdoms. 23 Nor shall they ever again
defile themselves by their fetishes and their abhorrent things,
and by their other transgressions. I will save them in all their
settlements where they sinned, and I will cleanse them. Then
they shall be My people, and I will be their God.

24 My servant David shall be king over them; there shall be
one shepherd for all of them. They shall follow My rules and

a-a Meaning of Heb. uncertain.

11–14: The image symbolizes the restoration of Israel to its own land. **11:** As elsewhere, Ezekiel refutes a popular proverb (see 8.12 n.).

37.15–28: The future of the kingdom of Israel. Ezekiel's symbolic action represents the unification of Israel and Judah under the rule of a Davidic king. These vv. serve as the haftarah for the parashah of Vayiggash (Gen. 44.18–47.27), in which Joseph reveals himself to his brothers, thereby reuniting the twelve sons of Jacob. Ezekiel's prophecy may be highly idealized, since it is unlikely that significant remnants of the ten northern tribes survived until this period, but the reunification of the Northern Kingdom, along with Judah, figures in several prophecies of restoration (Jer. ch 31; Ps. 133 [see v. 1 n.]). **15–19:** On the use of a stick or staff to represent a tribe, see Num. 17.1–26. **16:** *Judah* is the Southern Kingdom, and *Joseph* is the father of *Ephraim,* the central tribe of the Northern Kingdom, Israel. *Stick,* lit. "tree" or "wood." **20–28:** Just as one gathers sticks for a fire, God will gather the exiles to establish them as one nation, with David as their king, undoing the damage caused after the death of Solomon with the division of the monarchy. As in ch 34, King David, however, is clearly subservient to God: He is God's *servant* (v. 24) and is called a *prince* (v. 25) rather than a full-fledged king.

faithfully obey My laws. 25 Thus they shall remain in the land which I gave to My servant Jacob and in which your fathers dwelt; they and their children and their children's children shall dwell there forever, with My servant David as their prince for all time. 26 I will make a covenant of friendship with them—it shall be an everlasting covenant with them—I will establish[a] them and multiply them, and I will place My Sanctuary among them forever. 27 My Presence[b] shall rest over them; I will be their God and they shall be My people. 28 And when My Sanctuary abides among them forever, the nations shall know that I the LORD do sanctify Israel.

38 The word of the LORD came to me: 2 O mortal, turn your face toward Gog of the land of Magog, the chief prince of Meshech and Tubal. Prophesy against him 3 and say: Thus said the Lord GOD: Lo, I am coming to deal with you, O Gog, chief prince of Meshech and Tubal! 4 I will turn you around and put hooks in your jaws, and lead you out with all your army, horses, and horsemen, all of them clothed in splendor, a vast assembly, all of them with bucklers and shields, wielding swords. 5 Among them shall be Persia, Nubia, and Put, everyone with shield and helmet; 6 Gomer and all its cohorts, Beth-togarmah [in] the remotest parts of the north and all its cohorts—the many peoples with you.[c] 7 Be ready, prepare yourselves, you and all the battalions mustered about you, and hold yourself in reserve for them.[d] 8 After a long time you shall be summoned; in the distant future you shall march against the land [of a people] restored from the sword, gathered from the midst of many peoples—against the mountains of Israel, which have long lain desolate—[a people] liberated from the nations, and now all dwelling secure. 9 You shall advance, coming like a storm; you shall be like a cloud covering the earth, you and all your cohorts, and the many peoples with you.

10 Thus said the Lord GOD: On that day, a thought will occur to you, and you will conceive a wicked design. 11 You will say, "I will invade a land of open towns, I will fall upon a tranquil people living secure, all of them living in unwalled towns and lacking bars and gates, 12 in order to take spoil and seize plunder"—to turn your hand against repopulated wastes, and against a people gathered from among nations, acquiring livestock and possessions, living at the center of the earth. 13 Sheba and Dedan, and the merchants and all the magnates of Tarshish will say to

a Meaning of Heb. uncertain. *b Lit. "dwelling place."* *c I.e., with Gog.*
d Septuagint reads "Me."

26: Ezekiel draws upon the tradition of permanent Davidic rule (2 Sam. ch 7; Pss. 89; 132), the eternal *covenant of friendship,* lit. "covenant of peace," and upon the role of the Temple as the center of both Israel and the nations. **27:** As the translators' note indicates, *My Presence,* lit. "dwelling place" (Heb "mishkan") is the word used for the Tabernacle constructed at the end of Exod. **28:** Here the more expected word for "Temple" *(Sanctuary),* "mikdash," is used.

38.1–39.29: Vision of the eschatological war with Gog from the land of Magog. Ezekiel's oracles against Gog, ruler from the land of Magog, express an apocalyptic scenario of God's victory over the nations that threaten Israel. The original identity of Gog is uncertain, although some have identified him with Gyges, a 7th-c. ruler of Lydia in Asia Minor. The land of *Magog* appears together with *Meshech, Tubal, Gomer* (Cimmerians in central Asia Minor), and Togarmah (cf. *Beth-togarmah,* in Armenia), apparently in reference to lands in Asia Minor and Greece. Gomer, Magog, Meshech, and Tubal were sons of Japheth (Gen. 10.2), who is associated with Europe and Asia beyond the Middle East. Later interpreters have understood him to be a transnational symbol of evil. Ezek. 38.18–39.16 is the haftarah for the Middle Days of Sukkot when Exod. 33.12–34.26 and the relevant day's passage from Num. ch 29 are read as the Torah portion. Exod. 33.12–34.26 relates God's revelation to Moses and the restoration of the two tablets of the covenant after the golden calf incident, which corresponds to the focus on Israel's restoration in Ezek. 38.1–39.16. **38.1–9:** God's initial instructions to Ezekiel present Gog as the leader of a host of nations that threaten Israel, reusing a wellknown motif in the tradition about Zion as an invincible fortress. **5:** *Persia, Nubia* (or Ethiopia), and *Put* (Libya) are distant lands from throughout the ancient Near Eastern world, suggesting that only God could prevent mass devastation. **10–13:** God portrays Gog's intentions to plunder unsuspecting nations. **13:** *Sheba,* southern Arabia. *Dedan,* central Arabia, although some identify it as Rhodes. *Tarshish,* Tartessos in Spain.

you, "Have you come to take spoil? Is it to seize plunder that you
assembled your hordes—to carry off silver and gold, to make off
with livestock and goods, to gather an immense booty?"
14 Therefore prophesy, O mortal, and say to Gog: Thus said
the Lord GOD: Surely, on that day, when My people Israel are
living secure, you will [a]take note,[a] 15 and you will come from
your home in the farthest north, you and many peoples with
you—all of them mounted on horses, a vast horde, a mighty
army—16 and you will advance upon My people Israel, like a
cloud covering the earth. This shall happen on that distant day:
I will bring you to My land, that the nations may know Me when,
before their eyes, I manifest My holiness through you, O Gog!
17 Thus said the Lord GOD: Why, you are the one I spoke of
in ancient days through My servants, the prophets of Israel,
who prophesied for years in those days that I would bring you
against them!
18 On that day, when Gog sets foot on the soil of Israel—declares the Lord GOD—My raging anger shall flare up. 19 For I
have decreed in My indignation and in My blazing wrath: On
that day, a terrible earthquake shall befall the land of Israel.
20 The fish of the sea, the birds of the sky, the beasts of the field,
all creeping things that move on the ground, and every human being on earth shall quake before Me. Mountains shall
be overthrown, cliffs shall topple, and every wall shall crumble to the ground. 21 [b]I will then summon the sword against
him throughout My mountains[b]—declares the Lord GOD—
and every man's sword shall be turned against his brother.
22 I will punish him with pestilence and with bloodshed; and
I will pour torrential rain, hailstones, and sulfurous fire upon
him and his hordes and the many peoples with him. 23 Thus
will I manifest My greatness and My holiness, and make Myself
known in the sight of many nations. And they shall know that
I am the LORD.

39 And you, O mortal, prophesy against Gog and say: Thus
said the Lord GOD: I am going to deal with you, O Gog,
chief prince of Meshech and Tubal! 2 I will turn you around
and [b]drive you on,[b] and I will take you from the far north and
lead you toward the mountains of Israel. 3 I will strike your bow
from your left hand and I will loosen the arrows from your right
hand. 4 You shall fall on the mountains of Israel, you and all
your battalions and the peoples who are with you; and I will
give you as food to carrion birds of every sort and to the beasts
of the field, 5 as you lie in the open field. For I have spoken—
declares the Lord GOD. 6 And I will send a fire against Magog
and against those who dwell secure in the coastlands. And

14–16: God portrays Gog's advance with a mighty army against Israel. **16:** *That distant day* (others "in the latter days") normally refers to the future, and many believe the expression to have eschatological meaning in contexts such as this one. *That the nations may know Me* draws upon earlier traditions in which the nations recognize God's power and sovereignty. **17–23:** *The Lord GOD* portrays the defeat of Gog as a cosmic event that was announced by the prophets. This suggests that by the period of Ezekiel, prophetic works were available to be studied. No single prophecy among those extant in the Bible stands out as the likely referent; the vv. likely refer to the many Day of the LORD prophecies that depict cataclysmic events of the type developed here. **19–20:** The cosmic dimensions of the defeat appear in the quaking of the land, including *the fish of the sea, the birds of the sky, the beasts of the field, all creeping things,* and *every human being,* alluding to the created order as described in the Priestly creation story of Gen. ch 1. **21–22:** Likewise, the defeat of Gog by the sword and natural elements, such as *torrential rain, hailstones,* and *sulfurous fire,* appeals to God's role as Creator as well as to the tradition about the destruction of Sodom and Gomorrah (Gen. chs 18–19). This is logical in this context, which suggests the universal acknowledgment of God. **39.4–5:** Unburied corpses on the mountains recall the imagery of the vision of dry bones (37.1–14), the death of the Babylonian king in the open, and the defeat of Assyria on the mountains of Israel. Lying unburied reflected serious shame in antiquity, and created serious ritual impurity, which is why the remainder of the ch focuses on ritual purification.

a-a *Septuagint reads "rouse yourself."* *b-b* *Meaning of Heb. uncertain.*

they shall know that I am the LORD. [7] I will make My holy name known among My people Israel, and never again will I let My holy name be profaned. And the nations shall know that I the LORD am holy in Israel. [8] Ah! it has come, it has happened—declares the Lord GOD: this is that day that I decreed.

[9] Then the inhabitants of the cities of Israel will go out and make fires and feed them with the weapons—shields and bucklers, bows and arrows, clubs and spears; they shall use them as fuel for seven years. [10] They will not gather firewood in the fields or cut any in the forests, but will use the weapons as fuel for their fires. They will despoil those who despoiled them and plunder those who plundered them—declares the Lord GOD.

[11] On that day I will assign to Gog a burial site there in Israel—the Valley of the Travelers, east of the Sea. It shall block the path of travelers, for there Gog and all his multitude will be buried. It shall be called the Valley of Gog's Multitude. [12] The House of Israel shall spend seven months burying them, in order to cleanse the land; [13] all the people of the land shall bury them. [a-]The day I manifest My glory shall bring renown to them[-a]—declares the Lord GOD. [14] And they shall appoint men to serve permanently, to traverse the land and bury any invaders who remain above ground, in order to cleanse it. The search shall go on for a period of seven months. [15] As those who traverse the country make their rounds, any one of them who sees a human bone shall erect a marker beside it, until the buriers have interred them in the Valley of Gog's Multitude. [16] [a-]There shall also be a city named Multitude.[-a] And thus the land shall be cleansed.

[17] And you, O mortal, say to every winged bird and to all the wild beasts: Thus said the Lord GOD: Assemble, come and gather from all around for the sacrificial feast that I am preparing for you—a great sacrificial feast—upon the mountains of Israel, and eat flesh and drink blood. [18] You shall eat the flesh of warriors and drink the blood of the princes of the earth: rams, lambs, he-goats, and bulls—fatlings of Bashan all of them. [19] You shall eat fat to satiety and drink your fill of blood from the sacrificial feast that I have prepared for you. [20] And you shall sate yourselves at My table with horses, charioteers,[b] warriors, and all fighting men—declares the Lord GOD. [21] Thus will I manifest My glory among the nations, and all the nations shall see the judgment that I executed and the power that I wielded against them.

[22] From that time on, the House of Israel shall know that I the LORD am their God. [23] And the nations shall know that the House of Israel were exiled only for their iniquity, because they

a-a Meaning of Heb. uncertain. *b Lit. "chariots"; Septuagint reads "riders."*

9: The victory fires that burn for *seven years* throughout the land represent the vast amount of weaponry that could not defeat Israel, protected by its God. It also recalls the sabbatical (seven-year) agricultural and economic cycle. **11:** The burial of Gog marks the final stage of the cleansing of the land of Israel prior to its restoration. *The Valley of the Travelers* or the "Valley of those who pass by" may be a word play on the Valley of Abarim east of the Dead Sea. Heb for "travelers, passers-by" is "ha'orim." *The Valley of Gog's Multitude* (Heb "gei' hamon gog"), a wordplay on the Valley of Hinnom, southwest of Jerusalem, which was known for idolatry, the burning of children, and dead bodies (2 Kings 23.10; Jer. 7.30–34). **12–13:** The *seven months* of burial purify the land so that God's *glory* or Presence may appear. The length of time again emphasizes the vast number of people who were defeated by God. **16:** *A city named Multitude* (Heb "Hamonah"), see v. 11 n. **17–29:** The feast of the birds and wild animals recalls the covenant curses (e.g., Deut. 28.16–44) in which Israel is fed to the birds and animals, but they are now applied to Israel's enemies. **17:** The *sacrificial feast* reverses the image of usual sacrifices, for here animals and birds feast on human flesh. **18–21:** These actions enable God to display the divine glory to the nations. **23–24:** The image of God hiding His face, namely turning away from Israel and choosing not to help them, is common in the Bible (e.g., Deut. 31.17–18; Jer 33.4–5).

trespassed against Me, so that I hid My face from them and delivered them into the hands of their adversaries, and they all
fell by the sword. 24 When I hid My face from them, I dealt with
them according to their uncleanness and their transgressions.
25 Assuredly, thus said the Lord GOD: I will now restore the
fortunes of Jacob and take the whole House of Israel back
in love; and I will be zealous for My holy name. 26 They will
bear[a] their shame and all their trespasses that they committed against Me, when they dwell in their land secure and untroubled, 27 when I have brought them back from among the
peoples and gathered them out of the lands of their enemies
and have manifested My holiness through them in the sight
of many nations. 28 They shall know that I the LORD am their
God when, having exiled them among the nations, I gather
them back into their land and leave none of them behind. 29 I
will never again hide My face from them, for I will pour out My
spirit upon the House of Israel—declares the Lord GOD.

40 In the twenty-fifth year of our exile,[b] the fourteenth
year after the city had fallen, at the beginning of the
year, the tenth day of the month—on that very day—the hand
of the LORD came upon me, and He brought me there. 2 He
brought me, in visions of God, to the Land of Israel, and He set
me down on a very high mountain[c] on which there seemed to
be the outline of a city [d-]on the south.[-d] 3 He brought me over
to it, and there, standing at the gate, was a man who shone like
copper. In his hand were a cord of linen and a measuring rod.
4 The man spoke to me: "Mortal, look closely and listen attentively and note well everything I am going to show you—for
you have been brought here in order to be shown—and report
everything you see to the House of Israel."
5 Along the outside of the Temple [area] ran a wall on every
side. The rod that the man held was six cubits long, plus one

a *Change of diacritical point yields "forget."*
b *I.e., the exile of King Jehoiachin; see 1.2.*
c *Cf. Isa. 2.1; Mic. 4.1.*
d-d *Septuagint reads "in the distance."*

25: *Restore the fortunes of Jacob* recalls God's promise to remember the covenant of Jacob if the people confess their iniquity. **27–28:** As elsewhere in Ezek., Israel is not restored for its own sake, but so its God is magnified. **29:** *I will never again hide My face from them:* In the future the relationship of God with His people will change, and all Israel will have the spirit of God, which will enable them to manifest God's holiness.

40.1–48.35: The Vision of the Future Temple. *In the twenty-fifth year ... at the beginning of the year, the tenth day of the month* (40.1), 10 Nisan , 573–572 BCE. Ezekiel's vision of the Temple complements God's earlier prophecies to make a covenant with Israel and to place the sanctuary among them forever. This vision provides a literary and conceptual envelope for the book that complements the visions of God's departure and the Temple's destruction in chs 1–7; 9–11 with one of the Temple's restoration and God's return. Ezek. 40.1–43.12 relates instruction concerning the building of the Temple and the return of God's glory; 43.13–47.12 provides instruction concerning the associated structures and activities of the Temple complex; and 47.13–48.35 guides the reestablishment of the land and people of Israel around the Temple. The details of the Temple, its courts, furnishings, and laws and the technical terminology presented here differ in many respects from those for the wilderness Tabernacle (see esp. Exod. chs 25–30; 35–45), Solomon's Temple (1 Kings chs 6–7; 2 Chron. chs 3–4), and the Second Temple (*m. Mid.* 5). Indeed, the differences in the portrayal of the Temple were, according to the Rabbis, a major discrepancy that Hananiah son of Hezekiah reconciled so that Ezek. could be included in the biblical canon (*b. Shab.* 13b). Because of the discrepancies, there is a strand in Jewish tradition that regards these chs as Ezekiel's vision of the Third Temple to be built in future days (*Seder 'Olam Rab.* 26; Rashi; Radak).

40.1–43.12: The Temple and the return of God's Presence. 40.1: The date is 10 Nisan, 573–572 BCE. *The beginning of the year:* This date is unique (with one exception in Ezekiel's prophecies to Egypt). The following prophecies explicitly mentioned in the Bible depict the days of the return to Zion, about thirty-five to fifty years after this prophecy of Ezekiel (Hag. 1.1; Ezra 1.1) **2:** Ezekiel is transported to the site of the Temple. Note that the city of Jerusalem is not mentioned explicitly here as in chs 40–48, although the prophet does describe the place using different terms: *the Land of Israel, a very high mountain, the outline of a city.* **3–4:** Ezekiel's guide recalls the bronze-colored living creatures that supported God's throne chariot (1.5–14; see also 8.2). The Heb root "ra'ah," *look* is repeated five times in these two vv., in addition to the mention of eyes, probably to emphasize the importance of this prophecy. The *cord of linen* and the *measuring rod* enable the guide to instruct Ezekiel in the dimensions of the Temple structures.

5–47: The Temple walls, gates, and courtyards. 5–16: The walls and the outer gate. 5: *Six cubits long, plus one handbreadth for each cubit,* over 3 m (10 ft). Whereas the normal cubit is five handbreadths, the cubit used for the construction of the Temple is six handbreadths. The long cubit is about 518 mm or 20.68 in. **6–7:** The *gate that faced eastward* is the main gate of the Temple complex, which faces east toward the sun. It is built according to the basic pattern of the fortified Solomonic gates at Gezer, Hazor, and Megiddo, with an initial *threshold of the gate,* three recessed chambers on either side, and the *inner vestibule of the gate.* **9:** *Its supports,* projecting columns that may have served as a door jamb. Windows provide light for the recessed chambers and the vestibule. **14:** *And the gate next to the support on every side of the court:* There were five gates to the women's courtyard of the Second Temple, the two Huldah gates to the south, the Kiponos gate to the west, the Tadi gate to the north, and the eastern gate (*m. Mid.* 1.3). **17–19: The outer court.** The *30 chambers* that line the *outer court* were used by the Levites for various activities. *The lower court* and *the inner gate* rearrange the nouns and adjectives so that they will agree in gender (see translators' note *j-j*). They likely refer to the "inner court" in Heb, and "the lower gate," that would allow entry.

handbreadth for each cubit; and when he applied it to that
structure, it measured one rod deep[a] and one rod high.
6 He went up to the gate that faced eastward and mounted
its steps. He measured the threshold of the gate; it was one rod
deep[a]—[b-]the one threshold was one rod deep.[-b] 7 Each recess
was one rod wide and one rod deep, with [a partition of] 5
cubits between recesses; and the threshold of the gate, at the
inner vestibule of the gate, was one rod deep. 8 [b-]For when he
measured it at the inner vestibule of the gate, it was one rod
[deep].[-b] 9 Next he measured the vestibule of the gate, and it
measured 8 cubits and its supports 2 cubits; the vestibule of
the gate was at its inner end. 10 [c]On either side of this eastern gate there were three recesses, all three of the same size;
of identical sizes were also the supports[d] on either side. 11 He
measured the opening of the gate and found it 10 cubits wide,
while the gate itself measured 13 cubits across.[e] 12 At the fronts
of the recesses on either side were [b-]barriers of one cubit;[-b] the
recesses on either side were 6 cubits [deep]. 13 Their openings
faced each other directly across the gate passage, so that when
he measured from rear[f] of recess to rear[f] of recess he obtained
a width of 25 cubits.[g] 14 [b-]He made the vestibule[h]—60 cubits—
and the gate next to the support on every side of the court.[-b]
15 And [the distance] from the front of the outer[f] gate to the
front of the inner vestibule of the gate was 50 cubits. 16 The recesses—and their supports—had windows [b-]with frames[-b] on
the interior of the gate complex on both sides, and the interiors
of the vestibules also had windows on both sides; and the supports were adorned with palms.
17 He took me into the outer court. There were chambers
there, and there was a pavement laid out all around the court.
There were 30 chambers on the pavement. 18 The pavements
flanked the gates; the depth of the lower[i] pavements paralleled that of the gates. 19 Then he measured the width of [j-]the
lower[i] court, from in front of the inner gate to in front of the
outer gate[-j]—100 cubits.

a In this description, the Hebrew word which ordinarily corresponds to English "width" sometimes designates a measurement from an opening or outer surface inward, and so corresponds to the English "depth"; and the word which ordinarily corresponds to English "length" designates the distance from side to side of a vestibule or a passage, and so corresponds to the English "width."
b-b Meaning of Heb. uncertain. *c This verse would read well before v. 7.*
d In connection with recesses, the "supports" are partitions.
e The opening was perhaps narrowed by a stone on each side for receiving the hinge of a door-leaf. *f Meaning of Heb. uncertain.*
g Since each of the recesses was 6 cubits deep (v. 7a) and the passage in the middle was 13 cubits wide (v. 11). *h* Elim *here is the same as* elam *in vv. 16, 21, 22, etc.*
i The outer court and its gates were 8 steps lower than the inner ones: v. 34.
j-j In this rendering, the adjectives "lower" and "inner" are construed, not with the nouns they stand next to in the Hebrew, but with those with which they agree in gender.

[a-]After the east [gate], the north [gate].[-a] 20 Next he measured the gate of the outer court that faced north: its length and its width, 21 its three recesses on either side and its supports, as also its vestibule. It measured, like the first gate, 50 cubits in length and 25 cubits in width. 22 Its windows and [those of] its vestibule, as also its palm trees, corresponded to those of the gate that faced east. [From the outside] one had to climb 7 steps to reach it, and its vestibule was [b-]ahead of them.[-b] 23 Like the east gate, the north gate faced a gate leading into the inner forecourt; and when he measured the distance from gate to gate, it was 100 cubits.

24 Then he took me to the south side. There was also a gate on the south side, and he got the same measurements as before for its supports and its vestibule. 25 Both it and its vestibule had windows like the aforementioned ones. It was 50 cubits long and 25 cubits wide. 26 Its staircase consisted of 7 steps; its vestibule was [b-]ahead of them,[-b] and its supports were decorated on both sides with palm trees. 27 The inner court likewise had a gate facing south; and on the south side, too, he measured a distance of 100 cubits from the [outer] gate to the [inner] gate.

28 He now took me into the inner forecourt through its south gate. When he measured this south gate, it had the same measurements as the foregoing. 29 Its recesses, its supports, and its vestibule had the same measurements. Both it and its vestibule had windows on both sides; it was 50 cubits long and 25 cubits wide—30 [c-]vestibules on both sides, 25 cubits long, 5 cubits wide.[-c] 31 Its vestibule, however, gave on the outer court.[d] Its supports were adorned on either side with palms, and its staircase consisted of 8 steps.

32 Then he took me to the eastern side of the inner forecourt; and when he measured the gate there, he got the same measurements: 33 its recesses, supports, and vestibule had the above measurements. Both it and its vestibule had windows on both sides; it was 50 cubits long and 25 cubits wide, 34 and its vestibule gave on the outer court. Its supports were decorated on both sides with palm trees, and its staircase consisted of 8 steps.

35 Then he took me to the north gate, and found its measurements to be identical, 36 with the same recesses, supports, vestibule, windows on both sides, and a length of 50 cubits and a width of 25 cubits. 37 Its supports[e] gave on the outer court; its supports were decorated on both sides with palm trees; and its staircase consisted of 8 steps.

20–27: The north gate and the south gate. The gates for the outer court to the north and south are similar to the eastern gate. There is no western gate mentioned here as the Temple occupies the western side of the compound (contra *m. Mid.* 1.3, which mentions the western gate, but states that the northern gate was not used). Each of the three gates faces corresponding gates to the inner court. **28–37: The inner court gates.** The south, east, and north gates to the *inner forecourt* (lit. "the inner court," [or later the "court of the Israelites"; *m. Mid.* 2.6]) are similar to those for the outer court. The Second Temple had seven gates to this court (*m. Mid.* 1.4–5).

a-a Meaning of Heb. uncertain. *b-b Septuagint reads "at its inner end."*
c-c Connection unclear; wanting in some Heb. mss. and versions.
d I.e., in the inner gates the vestibules were situated at their entrances, and so they were true vestibules, in contrast to the "inner vestibules" of the outer gates.
e Septuagint reads "vestibules"; cf. vv. 31, 34.

38–46: The functions of the northern inner gate. Chambers were built by the vestibule of the gate to prepare sacrificial animals for the *burnt offering* (Lev. 1.3–17), the *purification offering* (Lev. 4.1–5.13), and the *guilt offering* (Lev. 5.14–6.7). **44:** Chambers were placed by the sides of the north and east (LXX reads "south") for the priests who have charge of the Temple and the altar. (The measurements of the inner court of the Second Temple differ from the 100 square cubit figure given here). **47:** The inner court.

40.48–41.26: The Temple plan. The Temple is constructed according to a three-room pattern, like that of Solomon's Temple (1 Kings ch 6) and other examples of temples and royal palaces from Babylonia and elsewhere. The detail offered here is excessive. This great concern with detail reflects the notion that God's house must be custom-built to its exact specification so God will be able to dwell in there amidst Israel. **40.48:** The *portico* (Heb, "'ulam," 20 by 11 cubits [about 10 m by 6 m, 30 ft by 17 ft]) was an entry or reception room. **41.1:** The great hall (Heb, "heikhal," 40 by 20 cubits [about 20 m by 10 m, 60 ft by 30 ft]) was the main hall where the Temple furnishings are placed.

38 A chamber opened into the gate;[a] there the burnt offering would be washed. 39 And inside the vestibule of the gate,
there were two tables on each side, at which the burnt offering, the purification offering, and the guilt offering were to
be slaughtered; 40 while outside—[b]as one goes up toward[b]
the opening of the north gate—there were two tables on one
side, and there were two tables on the other side of the gate's
vestibule. 41 Thus there were four tables on either flank of the
gate—eight tables in all—at which [the sacrifices] were to be
slaughtered. 42 As for the four tables for the burnt offering[c]—
they were of hewn stone, one and a half cubits long, one and
a half cubits wide, and one cubit high—[d]on them were laid
out the instruments with which burnt offerings and sacrifices
were slaughtered.[d] 43 Shelves,[e] one handbreadth wide, were
attached all around the inside; and the sacrificial flesh was
[laid] on the tables.
44 There were [f]chambers for singers[f] in the inner forecourt:
[one] beside the north gate facing south, and one beside the
east[g] gate facing north. 45 [The man] explained to me: "The
chamber that faces south is for the priests who perform the
duties of the Temple; 46 and the chamber that faces north is for
the priests who perform the duties of the altar—they are the
descendants of Zadok, who alone of the descendants of Levi
may approach the LORD to minister to Him."

47 He then measured the forecourt: 100 cubits long and 100
cubits broad—foursquare. In front of the Temple stood the
altar. 48 He took me into the portico of the Temple and measured it. The jambs[h] of the portico were 5 cubits deep on either
side. The width of the gate-opening was [i][14 cubits, and the
flanking wall of the gate was][i] 3 cubits on either side. 49 The
portico was 20 cubits wide[j] and 11[k] cubits deep, and [l]it was by
steps that it was reached.[l] There were columns by the jambs
on either side.

41 He then led me into the great hall. He measured the
jambs, 6 cubits on either side; such was the depth[m] of
each jamb.[n] 2 The entrance was 10 cubits wide, and the flanking
walls of the entrance were each 5 cubits wide. Next he measured the depth [of the hall], 40 cubits, and the width, 20 cubits.

a Heb. "gates"; the reference is apparently to the north gate; cf. v. 40 and Lev. 1.11; 4.24; 7.2. *b-b Emendation yields "the vestibule at."* *c See v. 39.*
d-d This clause would read well after v. 43. *e Meaning of Heb. uncertain.*
f-f Septuagint reads "two chambers." *g Septuagint reads "south."*
h I.e., the edges of the flanking walls. *i-i Preserved in the Septuagint.*
j See note on v. 5. *k Septuagint reads "12"; see note i on 41.13.*
l-l Septuagint reads "it was reached by ten steps." *m See note on 40.5.*
n This sense is demanded by the context; usually, ohel *means "tent."*

3 And then he entered the inner room. He measured each jamb of the entrance, 2 cubits [deep]; the entrance itself, 6 cubits across; and the width of [a]-[the flanking wall on either side of]-[a] the entrance, 7 cubits. 4 Then he measured the depth, 20 cubits; and the width at the inner end of the great hall was also 20 cubits. And he said to me, "This is the Holy of Holies."

5 Then he measured the wall of the Temple. [It was] 6 cubits [thick] on every side of the Temple, and the side-chamber measured 4 cubits [across].[b] 6 The side chambers were arranged one above the other, in 33 sections.[c] All around, there were projections in the Temple wall to serve the side chambers as supports, so that [their] supports should not be the Temple wall itself. 7 The [d]-winding passage-[d] of the side chambers widened from story to story; [e]-and since the structure was furnished all over with winding passages from story to story, the structure itself became wider from story to story.-[e] It was by this means that one ascended from the bottom story to the top one by way of the middle one.

8 I observed that the Temple was surrounded by a raised pavement—the foundations of the side chambers; its elevation was a rod's length, or 6 cubits. 9 The outer wall of the side chamber was 5 cubits thick, and that which served as a walk between the Temple's side chambers 10 and the chamber complexes[f] was 20 cubits wide all around the Temple. 11 Of entrances to the side chambers giving on the walk, there was one entrance on the north side and one entrance on the south side; and the space[g] of the walk was 5 cubits thick all around. 12 And the structure that fronted on the vacant space at the [Temple's] western end was 70 cubits deep;[h] the walls of the structure were 5 cubits thick on every side; and it was 90 cubits wide.[h]

13 He measured the [total] depth of the Temple, 100 cubits;[i] and the depth of the vacant space and of the structure, with its walls, also came to 100 cubits.[j] 14 The front side of the Temple, like the vacant space on the east, was 100 cubits wide.[k] 15 He also

3: The 2 cubit (1 m, 3 ft) measurement for the entrance conflicts with the 1 cubit (.5 m, 18 in) mentioned in *m. Mid.* 4.7. **4:** The *Holy of Holies* (20 by 20 cubits [10 m by 10 m, 30 ft by 30 ft]) was God's throne room, which according to Kings housed the Ark of the Covenant in Solomon's Temple. Ezekiel does not enter the Holy of Holies. **5–11:** Three stories of chambers with thirty chambers each line the walls of the Temple. They have an independent support structure so that they are not supported by the Temple itself. **12–15a:** The unidentified building is behind the Temple to the west.

a-a Preserved in the Septuagint. *b I.e., on the ground level; cf. v. 7.*
c Lit. "times." Emendation yields "in three sections of three tiers each," i.e., one section next to each of the two side walls of the Temple and one next to its rear wall; cf. v. 7. *d-d So Targum; cf. Mishnah Tamid 1.1.* *e-e Exact meaning of Heb. uncertain, but for the general sense cf. 1 Kings 6.6a, 8b.* *f See 42.1 ff.*
g Emendation yields "parapet." *h See note on 40.5.*
i Comprising the 5 cubits of 40.48, the 12 of 40.49 (see note there), the 6 of 41.1, the 40 of 41.2, the 2 of 41.3, the 20 of 41.4, the 6 of 41.5a, the 4 of 41.5b, and the 5 of 41.9.
j The structure was 70 cubits deep and its front and rear walls each 5 cubits thick (v. 12). The remaining 20 cubits are accounted for by the vacant space; cf. 42.1–2.
k To the inside width of 20 cubits (40.49; 41.2–4) must be added on each side: one Temple wall of 6 cubits equals 12; one side-chamber wall of 5 cubits equals 10; one side chamber's inner depth of 4 cubits equals 8; a walk's width of 20 cubits (40.9–10) equals 40; and a parapet's thickness of 5 cubits (v. 11) equals 10; totaling 100 cubits.

15b–21: The interior decoration of the Temple. **18–19:** The *cherubs* and *palm trees* carved into the wainscoting or paneling of the interior walls. **21–22:** Something resembling a wooden altar, the table for the presentation of rows of "showbread." *The table that stands before the* L*ORD*, i.e., the altar.

measured the width[a] of the structure facing the vacant space in the rear, inclusive of its ledges,[b] 100 cubits.

Both the great hall inside and the portico next to the court—[16] [c-]the thresholds[-c]—and the windows [d-]with frames[-d] and the ledges[e] at the threshold, all over the three parts of each, were completely overlaid[f] with wood. There was wainscoting from the floor to the windows, including the window [frame]s [17] and extending above the openings, [g-]both in the inner Temple and outside.[-g] And all over the wall, [g-]both in the inner one and in the outer,[-g] ran a pattern.[f] [18] It consisted of cherubs and palm trees, with a palm tree between every two cherubs. Each cherub had two faces: [19] a human face turned toward the palm tree on one side and a lion's face turned toward the palm tree on the other side. This was repeated all over the Temple; [20] the cherubs and the palm trees were carved on[h] the wall from the floor to above the openings.

As regards the great hall, [21] the great hall had four doorposts; and before the Shrine was something resembling [22] a wooden altar 3 cubits high and 2 cubits long and having inner corners;[i] and its length[j] and its walls were of wood. And he said to me, "This is the table[k] that stands before the LORD." [23] The great hall had a double door, and the Shrine likewise had [24] a double door, and each door had two [d-]swinging leaves:[-d] two for the one door and two [d-]such leaves[-d] for the other. [25] Cherubs and palm trees were carved on these—on the doors of the hall—just as they were carved on the walls; and there was a lattice[f] of wood outside in front of the portico. [26] And there were windows [d-]with frames[-d] and palm trees on the flanking walls of the portico on either side [of the entrance] [d-]and [on] the Temple's side chambers and [on] the lattices.[-d]

42 He took me out, by way of the northern gate, into the outer court, and he led me [westward] up to a [l-]complex of chambers[-l] that ran parallel to the northern ends of the vacant space and the structure. [2] The width[m] of its façade—[n-]its north side, the one from which it was entered[-n]—was 100 cubits, and its depth[m] was 50 cubits. [3] At right angles to the 20 cubits[o]

a See note on 40.5. *b Emendation yields "walls"; cf. v. 12.*
c-c Septuagint reads "were paneled." *d-d Meaning of Heb. uncertain.*
e Here perhaps designating the door frames, since it is these that (as required by the continuation of the verse) are situated at the threshold and consist of three parts (a lintel and two doorposts). *f Meaning of Heb. uncertain.*
g-g Meaning perhaps the great hall and the vestibule; cf. v. 5. *h Heb. "and."*
i Apparently meaning that it had a rim around the top, like the table of Exod. 25.25; see the final note on the present verse. *j Septuagint reads "base."*
k Serving to hold the bread of display; cf. Exod. 25.30; 40.22–23; 1 Kings 7.48.
l-l Heb. simply "chambers," and so elsewhere.
m See note a at 40.6. *n-n Lit. "the north entrance"; but cf. v. 4.*
o I.e., the vacant space; cf. 41.13 with note j.

of the inner court and to the pavement of the outer court,[a] the
complex rose ledge by ledge[b] in three tiers. 4 There was an are-
away, 10 cubits wide and [c]a road of one cubit,[c] running along
the inner-court side of the chamber complex, but its entrances were on its north side. 5 Here its upper chambers were cut
back, because ledges took away from them as construction
proceeded backward from the bottom ones and then from the
middle ones. 6 For they were arranged in three tiers, and they
had no columns like those of the chambers in the courts.[d] That
is why the rise proceeded by stages: from the ground, from the
bottom ones, and from the middle ones. 7 In the outer court,
a wall 50 cubits long ran parallel to the chamber complex up
to the chambers in the outer court;[d] 8 for the chambers in the
outer court were themselves 50 cubits deep, thus completing
100 cubits alongside the edifice.[e] 9 Thus, at the foot of that complex of chambers ran a passage[f]—[g]of a width set by the wall in
the outer court[g]—which one entered from the east in order to
gain access to them from the outer court.

10 There was another chamber complex to the east[h] of the
vacant space and the structure, 11 likewise with a passage in
front—just like the complex on the north side, with which this
one agreed in width[i] and depth[i] and in the exact layout of its
exits and entrances. 12 Accordingly, the entrances to the chamber complex on the south side were approached from the east
by the entrance at the head of [j]the corresponding passage
along the matching wall.[j]

13 And he said to me, "The northern chambers and the southern chambers by the vacant space are the consecrated chambers
in which the priests who have access to the LORD shall eat the
most holy offerings. There they shall deposit the most holy offerings—the meal offerings, the purification offerings, and the guilt
offerings, for the place is consecrated. 14 When the priests enter,
they shall not proceed from the consecrated place to the outer
court without first leaving here the vestments in which they minister; for the [vestments] are consecrated. Before proceeding to
the area open to the people,[k] they shall put on other garments."

15 When he had finished the measurements of the inner Temple [area], he led me out by way of the gate which faces east, and
he measured off the entire area. 16 He measured the east side

42.1–14: The Chambers between the outer and inner courts. **13–14:** The priests use the chambers to store and eat *the most holy offerings*. In these chambers the priests left their holy vestments before entering the outer court.

42.15–20: The Scope of Temple Mount and the Temple wall. The Temple complex is 500 rods square. Based on Ezek. 40.5, a rod is 6 cubits so that the Temple complex is 3,000 cubits square (Rashi), or about 1,500 m (4,500 ft) on a side. This is an extremely large area. Based on Ezek. 45.2, Radak argues that it is 500 cubits square, but does not explain the term *rods*. (This interpretation, giving an area of about 250 m [750 ft] on a side, or about 14 acres, is the one followed in the NJPS.)

a *Cf. 40.17.*
b *Because this part of the inner court was considerably higher than the outer; 40.28–31 and 41.8, 9b–10.*
c-c *Septuagint and Syriac read "and 100 cubits long"; cf. vv. 2–3.*
d *See vv. 8–9 referring to chambers along the west wall.*
e *Apparently meaning the chamber complex of v. 1.*
f *So* kethib; qere *"thing giving access."* g-g *Brought up from v. 10 for clarity.*
h *Septuagint reads "south"; cf. v. 13.* i *See note a at 40.6.*
j-j *Exact meaning of Heb. uncertain; the phrase apparently refers to vv. 7–8.*
k *Cf. 44.19 and note b.*

20: The outer wall marks the separation between the holy Temple and the profane world.

43.1–12: The divine Presence returns to the Temple complex through the eastern gate from which it had earlier departed (chs 1; 8–11; 10.19). **5:** Ezekiel recalls his inaugural vision, and reports that he is transported to the inner court where he sees *the Presence of the Lord* filling the Temple (Exod. 40.34–35; 1 Kings 8.11). **7:** God informs him that this will be *the place of My throne. The corpses of their kings* refers to burials of kings near the Temple, which defile it (2 Kings 21.18, 26). **10–12:** God instructs Ezekiel to teach the people the plan for the Temple so they will recognize their sins.

with the measuring rod, 500 [cubits]—in rods, by the measuring
rod. He turned [17] [and] measured the north side: 500 [cubits]—
in rods, by the measuring rod. He turned [18] [and] measured the
south side: 500 [cubits]—in rods, by the measuring rod. [19] Then
he turned to the west side [and] measured it: 500 cubits—in
rods, by the measuring rod. [20] Thus he measured it on the four
sides; it had a wall completely surrounding it, 500 [cubits] long
[a-]on each side,[-a] to separate the consecrated from the unconsecrated.

43 Then he led me to a gate, the gate that faced east. [2] And
there, coming from the east with a roar like the roar of
mighty waters, was the Presence of the God of Israel, and the
earth was lit up by His Presence. [3] The vision was like the vision I
had seen when I[b] came to destroy the city, the very same vision
that I had seen by the Chebar Canal. Forthwith, I fell on my face.
[4] The Presence of the Lord entered the Temple by the gate
that faced eastward. [5] A spirit carried me into the inner court,
and lo, the Presence of the Lord filled the Temple; [6] and I
heard speech addressed to me from the Temple, though [the]
man[c] was standing beside me. [7] It said to me:

O mortal, this is the place of My throne and the place for
the soles of My feet, where I will dwell in the midst of the people Israel forever. The House of Israel and their kings must not
again defile My holy name by their apostasy and by the corpses of their kings [d-]at their death.[-d] [8] When they placed their
threshold next to My threshold and their doorposts next to My
doorposts with only a wall between Me and them,[e] they would
defile My holy name by the abominations that they committed, and I consumed them in My anger. [9] Therefore, let them
put their apostasy and the corpses of their kings far from Me,
and I will dwell among them forever.

[10] [Now] you, O mortal, describe the Temple to the House
of Israel,[f] and let them measure its design. But let them be
ashamed of their iniquities: [11] When they are ashamed of all
they have done, make known to them the plan of the Temple
and its layout, its exits and entrances—its entire plan, and all
the laws and instructions pertaining to its entire plan. Write it
down before their eyes, that they may faithfully follow its entire

a-a Lit. "and 500 wide." *b Six mss. and two ancient versions read "He."*
c I.e., the guide of 40.3 ff.
d-d So with a number of Heb. mss. The usual vocalization yields "their shrines."
e The south wall of the First Temple enclosure was also the north wall of the royal enclosure; the two communicated by the Gate of the Guard (2 Kings 11.19). Thus Temple and palace could be regarded as a single dwelling ("tent") in the sense of Num. 19.14, and the death of a king in the palace would defile the Temple. Hence the zoning provisions of 45.2 ff.
f In accordance with the three preceding chapters; cf. 40.4.

plan and all its laws. 12 Such are the instructions for the Temple on top of the mountain: the entire area of its enclosure shall be most holy. Thus far the instructions for the Temple.

13 [a]And these are the dimensions of the altar, in cubits where each is a cubit and a handbreadth. The trench[b] shall be a cubit deep and a cubit wide, with a rim one span high around its edge. And the height[c] shall be as follows: 14 From the trench in the ground to the lower ledge, which shall be a cubit wide: 2 cubits; from the [d]lower ledge to the upper[d] ledge, which shall likewise be a cubit wide: 4 cubits; 15 and the height of the altar hearth shall be 4 cubits, with 4 horns projecting upward from the hearth: 4 cubits. 16 Now the hearth shall be 12 cubits long and 12 broad, square, with 4 equal sides. 17 Hence, the [upper] base[e] shall be 14 cubits broad, with 4 equal sides. The surrounding rim shall be half a cubit [high],[f] and the surrounding trench shall measure one cubit. And the ramp[g] shall face east.

18 Then he[h] said to me: O mortal, thus said the Lord GOD: These are the directions for the altar on the day it is erected, so that burnt offerings may be offered up on it and blood dashed against it. 19 You shall give to the levitical priests who are of the stock of Zadok, and so eligible to minister to Me—declares the Lord GOD—a young bull of the herd for a purification offering. 20 You shall take some of its blood and apply it to [i]the four horns [of the altar],[i] to the four corners of the base, and to the surrounding rim; thus you shall purge it and perform purification upon it. 21 Then you shall take the bull of purification offering and burn it in the [j]designated area[j] of the Temple, outside the Sanctuary.

22 On the following day, you shall offer a goat without blemish as a purification offering; and the altar shall be purged [with it] just as it was purged with the bull. 23 When you have completed the ritual of purging, you shall offer a bull of the herd without blemish and a ram of the flock without blemish. 24 Offer them to the LORD; let the priests throw salt on them and offer them up as a burnt offering to the LORD. 25 Every day, for seven days, you shall present a goat of purification offering, as well as a bull of the herd and a ram of the flock; you[k] shall present unblemished ones. 26 Seven days they shall purge the altar and cleanse it; [l]thus shall it be consecrated.[l]

43.13–27: The altar. 13: The *trench,* also rendered "base," lit. "bosom of the earth," is 18 cubits (about 9 m, 27 ft) square. **14:** The *lower ledge* is 16 cubits (about 8 m or 24 ft) square. The *upper ledge* is 14 cubits (about 7 m or 21 ft) square. **15:** The *hearth* (Heb "harar'el," may be referring to the "mountain of God" or "God appeared") with *4 horns,* (see Exod. 27.1–2; 28.2). **17:** Its *ramp* faces the eastern gate. **18–26:** Dedication of the altar. The seven-day consecration of the altar is performed and resembles the ordination of priests (Exod. 29.1–37; Lev. ch 8). **20:** The *purification* of the altar with blood is analogous to the sprinkling of blood on the altar (see Exod. 29.12 n.). **22–25:** The use of a *goat* as a *purification offering* for the dedication is uniquely done in the first day. **24:** *Salt* is offered with grain offerings but in Ezek. is mentioned only with this sacrifice. Ezek. 43.10–27 is the haftarah for the parashah of Tetsavveh (Exod. 27.20–30.10).

a *Some of the terms and details in vv. 13–17 are obscure.* b *Lit. "bosom."*
c *Lit. "bulge."* d-d *Lit. "lesser ledge to the greater."*
e *Heb.* 'azarah, *which in v. 14 means "ledge." The altar consists of 3 blocks, each smaller than the one below it.* f *Half a cubit is identical with the one span of v. 13.*
g *Leading up to the altar; cf. Exod. 20.23.* h *I.e., the guide of 40.3 ff.*
i-i *Heb. "its four horns."*
j-j *Meaning of Heb. uncertain. Emendation yields "burning place"; cf. Lev. 6.2; Isa. 33.14; Ps. 102.4 (for the word), and Lev. 4.12; 6.4 (for the place).*
k *Heb. "they."* l-l *Lit. "they shall fill its hands"; cf. note at Exod. 28.41.*

44.1–46.24: Temple functionaries and sacrificial rites. 44.1–3: The eastern gate remains closed because God enters the Temple through this eastern gate. The *prince* eats here. This leader is not a king. His name and his responsibilities differ from the Israelite king's responsibilities. **4–14:** Those who have engaged in idolatry or abominations are to be excluded from the Temple. **9:** Foreigners shall not enter. **10–14:** Unlike the practice in the First Temple where Levites served at the altar, they are disenfranchised here for idolatrous behavior and allowed to perform only secondary service.

27 And when these days are over, then from the eighth day
onward the priests shall offer your burnt offerings and your offerings of well-being on the altar; and I will extend My favor to
you—declares the Lord GOD.

44 Then he led me back to the outer gate of the Sanctuary
that faced eastward; it was shut. 2 And the LORD said to
me: This gate is to be kept shut and is not to be opened! No
one shall enter by it because the LORD, the God of Israel, has
entered by it; therefore it shall remain shut. 3 Only the prince
may sit in it and eat bread before the LORD, since he is a prince;
he shall enter by way of [a-]the vestibule of the gate,[-a] and shall
depart by the same way.
4 Then he led me, by way of the north gate, to the front of the
Temple. I looked, and lo! the Presence of the LORD filled the
Temple of the LORD; and I fell upon my face. 5 Then the LORD
said to me: O mortal, mark well, look closely and listen carefully to everything that I tell you regarding all the laws of the
Temple of the LORD and all the instructions regarding it. Note
well who may enter the Temple and all who must be excluded
from the Sanctuary. 6 And say to the rebellious House of Israel: Thus said the Lord GOD: Too long, O House of Israel, have
you committed all your abominations, 7 admitting aliens, uncircumcised of spirit and uncircumcised of flesh, to be in My
Sanctuary and profane My very Temple, when you offer up My
food—the fat and the blood. You[b] have broken My covenant
with all your abominations. 8 You have not discharged the duties concerning My sacred offerings, but have appointed them
to discharge the duties of My Sanctuary for you.
9 Thus said the Lord GOD: Let no alien, uncircumcised in
spirit and flesh, enter My Sanctuary—no alien whatsoever
among the people of Israel. 10 But the Levites who forsook
Me when Israel went astray—straying from Me to follow their
fetishes—shall suffer their punishment: 11 They shall be servitors in My Sanctuary, appointed over the Temple gates, and
performing the chores of My Temple; they shall slaughter the
burnt offerings and the sacrifices for the people. They shall
attend on them and serve them. 12 Because they served the
House of Israel in the presence of their fetishes and made
them stumble into guilt, therefore—declares the Lord GOD—
I have sworn concerning them that they shall suffer their
punishment: 13 They shall not approach Me to serve Me as
priests, to come near any of My sacred offerings, the most
holy things. They shall bear their shame for the abominations that they committed. 14 I will make them watchmen of

a-a *This does not contradict v. 2 because the vestibule is at the inner end of the gate; cf. 40.9.* b *Heb. "They."*

the Temple, to perform all its chores, everything that needs to be done in it.

15 [a-]But the levitical priests descended from Zadok,[-a] who maintained the service of My Sanctuary when the people of Israel went astray from Me—they shall approach Me to minister to Me; they shall stand before Me to offer Me fat and blood—declares the Lord GOD. 16 They alone may enter My Sanctuary and they alone shall approach My table to minister to Me; and they shall keep My charge. 17 And when they enter the gates of the inner court, they shall wear linen vestments: they shall have nothing woolen upon them when they minister inside the gates of the inner court. 18 They shall have linen turbans on their heads and linen breeches on their loins; they shall not gird themselves with anything that causes sweat. 19 When they go out to the outer court—the outer court where the people are—they shall remove the vestments in which they minister and shall deposit them in the sacred chambers;[b] they shall put on other garments, lest they make the people consecrated[c] by [contact with] their vestments. 20 They shall neither shave their heads nor let their hair go untrimmed; they shall keep their hair trimmed. 21 No priest shall drink wine when he enters into the inner court. 22 They shall not marry widows[d] or divorced women; they may marry only virgins of the stock of the House of Israel, or widows who are widows of priests.

23 They shall declare to My people what is sacred and what is profane, and inform them what is clean and what is unclean. 24 In lawsuits, too, it is they who shall act as judges; they shall decide them in accordance with My rules. They shall preserve My teachings and My laws regarding all My fixed occasions; and they shall maintain the sanctity of My sabbaths.

25 [A priest] shall not defile himself by entering [a house] where there is a dead person. He shall defile himself only for father or mother, son or daughter, brother or unmarried sister. 26 After he has become clean, seven days shall be counted off for him; 27 and on the day that he reenters the inner court of the Sanctuary to minister in the Sanctuary, he shall present his purification offering—declares the Lord GOD.

28 This shall be their portion, for I am their portion; and no holding shall be given them in Israel, for I am their holding. 29 The meal offerings, purification offerings, and guilt offerings shall be consumed by them. Everything proscribed[e] in Israel shall be theirs. 30 All the choice first fruits of every kind, and all the gifts of every kind—of all your contributions—shall go to the priests. You shall further give the first of the

15–31: This passage serves as the haftarah for the parashah of 'Emor (Lev. 21.1–24.23), which relates regulations concerning the sanctity and roles of the priests. **15–16:** The Levites of the Zadokite line (1 Kings 2.26–27) shall enter the sanctuary and serve at the altar. **17–31:** They shall wear only linen (cf. Exod. 28.39–40, 42); they shall not wear holy garments outside of the inner court (Ezek. 42.14); they shall trim their hair, but not shave it (contrast Lev. 21.5); they shall not drink wine in the inner court (Lev. 10.9); they shall marry only virgins or the widows of other priests (contrast Lev. 21.7, 13–14); they shall instruct the people concerning holiness and purity; they shall act as judges (Deut. 17.8–13; 19.17; 21. 5); they shall observe the festivals; they shall avoid contact with the dead and mourning, except for parents and siblings (Lev. 21.1); they shall receive no inheritance other than a share of the first fruits and offerings at the Temple (Num. ch 18); and they shall not eat meat that was not properly slaughtered (Lev. 22.8).

a-a *By contrast with the Levite-priests whose demotion has just been announced.*
b *Cf. 42.13–14.* c *Thereby rendering the people unfit for ordinary activity.*
d *I.e., of laymen.* e *See Lev. 27.28.*

yield of your baking[a] to the priest, that a blessing may rest upon your home.

31 Priests shall not eat anything, whether bird or animal, that died or was torn by beasts.

45 When you allot the land as an inheritance, you shall set aside from the land, as a gift sacred to the LORD, an area[b] 25,000 [cubits] long and 10,000[c] wide: this shall be holy through its entire extent. 2 Of this, a square measuring a full 500 by 500 shall be reserved for the Sanctuary,[d] and 50 cubits for an open space all around it. 3 Of the aforesaid area, you shall measure off, as most holy and destined to include the Sanctuary, [a space] 25,000 long by 10,000 wide; 4 it is a sacred portion of the land; it shall provide space for houses for the priests, the ministrants of the Sanctuary who are qualified to minister to the LORD, as well as holy ground for the Sanctuary. 5 Another [space], 25,000 long by 10,000 wide, shall be the property of the Levites, the servants of the Temple—[e-]twenty chambers.[-e] 6 Alongside the sacred reserve, you shall set aside [a space] 25,000 long by 5,000 wide, as the property of the city; it shall belong to the whole House of Israel. 7 And to the prince shall belong, on both sides of the sacred reserve and the property of the city and alongside the sacred reserve and the property of the city, on the west extending westward and on the east extending eastward, a portion[b] corresponding to one of the [tribal] portions that extend from the western border to the eastern border 8 of the land.[f] That shall be his property in Israel; and My princes shall no more defraud My people, but shall leave the rest of the land to the several tribes of the House of Israel.

9 Thus said the Lord GOD: Enough, princes of Israel! Make an end of lawlessness and rapine, and do what is right and just! Put a stop to your evictions of My people—declares the Lord GOD. 10 Have honest balances, an honest *ephah,* and an honest *bath.*[g] 11 The *ephah* and the *bath* shall comprise the same volume, the *bath* a tenth of a *ḥomer* and the *ephah* a tenth of a *ḥomer;* their capacity shall be gauged by the *ḥomer.* 12 And the shekel shall weigh 20 *gerahs.* [h-]20 shekels, 25 shekels [and] 10 plus 5 shekels shall count with you as a *mina.*[-h]

13 This is the contribution you shall make: One-sixth of an *ephah* from every *ḥomer* of wheat and one-sixth of an *ephah* from every *ḥomer* of barley, 14 while the due from the oil—[i-]the oil being measured by the *bath*[-i]—shall be one-tenth of a *bath*

a *See Num. 15.20–21.* b *Lit. "length."* c *Septuagint reads 20,000; cf. vv. 3–5.*
d *Cf. 42.15 ff.* e-e *Septuagint reads "for towns to dwell in."*
f *Cf. for all the foregoing 48.1 ff.*
g *The* ephah *is used for dry measure and the* bath *for liquid measure.*
h-h *The Mesopotamian* mina *of 60 shekels; but meaning of Heb. uncertain.*
i-i *Meaning of Heb. uncertain.*

45.1–9: The size and distribution of the *gift sacred to the LORD* in the land for the use of the priests, the Levites, Israel, and the prince. **1:** According to the Heb text, *10,000* [cubits] *wide,* the combined land area is 250,000,000 square cubits, slightly more than 13,000 acres. The priestly portion includes the area for the sanctuary. **5–6:** The Levites' portion equals that of the priests, but the portion for the rest of Israel is half of that. **7–9:** The portion of the *prince* is not included in the *sacred reserve* or *city;* he may not evict Israel. **10–12:** The leaders are in charge of providing just and standardized measures. The *ḥomer* equals 229.7 liters (6.524 bushels); the *ephah* is a dry measure that equals 22.9 liters (20.878 quarts); the *bath* is a liquid measure that equals 23 liters (6.073 gal); the *shekel* is a measure of weight equivalent to 11.42 gm (176.29 grains); in standard usage, 50 *shekels* constitute a *mina* equivalent to 571.2 gm (20.148 oz); if this passage refers to the Mesopotamian mina (see translators' note *h-h*), it is then equivalent to 685.44 gm (24.178 oz). **13–17:** The people give a percentage of wheat (1.7 percent), barley (1.7 percent), oil (possibly 1 percent; the kor measurement changes), and sheep (0.5 percent) for offerings *to make expiation for them.*

from every *kor.*—As 10 *baths* make a *ḥomer,* so 10 *baths* make a *ḥomer.*[a]— 15 And [the due] from the flock shall be one animal from every 200. [All these shall be contributed] from Israel's products[b] for meal offerings, burnt offerings, and offerings of well-being, to make expiation for them—declares the Lord GOD. 16 In this contribution, the entire population must join with the prince in Israel.

17 But the burnt offerings, the meal offerings, and the libations on festivals, new moons, sabbaths—all fixed occasions—of the House of Israel shall be the obligation of the prince; he shall provide the purification offerings, the meal offerings, the burnt offerings, and the offerings of well-being, to make expiation for the House of Israel.

18 Thus said the Lord GOD: On the first day of the first month, you shall take a bull of the herd without blemish, and you shall cleanse the Sanctuary. 19 The priest shall take some of the blood of the purification offering and apply it to the doorposts of the Temple, to the four corners of the ledge[b] of the altar, and to the doorposts of the gate of the inner court. 20 You shall do the same [c-]on the seventh day of the month[-c] to purge the Temple from uncleanness caused by unwitting or ignorant persons.

21 On the fourteenth day of the first month you shall have the passover sacrifice; and during a festival of seven days unleavened bread shall be eaten. 22 On that day, the prince shall provide a bull of purification offering on behalf of himself and of the entire population; 23 and during the seven days of the festival, he shall provide daily—for seven days—seven bulls and seven rams, without blemish, for a burnt offering to the LORD, and one goat daily for a purification offering. 24 He shall provide a meal offering of an *ephah*[d] for each bull and an *ephah* for each ram, with a *hin* of oil to every *ephah.* 25 So, too, during the festival of the seventh month, for seven days from the fifteenth day on, he shall provide the same purification offerings, burnt offerings, meal offerings, and oil.

46 Thus said the Lord GOD: The gate of the inner court which faces east shall be closed on the six working days; it shall be opened on the sabbath day and it shall be opened on the day of the new moon. 2 The prince shall enter by way of the vestibule outside the gate, and shall attend at the gatepost while the priests sacrifice his burnt offering and his offering of well-being; he shall then bow low at the threshold of the gate and depart. The gate, however, shall not

a *The Vulgate reads* "kor"; ḥomer *and* kor *are synonyms.*
b *Meaning of Heb. uncertain.* c-c *Septuagint reads "in the seventh month."*
d *Of choice flour.*

16–17: The people pay their *contribution* to the *prince.* The prince in turn is obligated to provide *the burnt offerings, the meal offerings, and the libations on festivals* on behalf of the people at all *festivals, new moons, sabbaths,—all fixed occasions.* Ezek. 45.16–46.18 (Sephardi lectionary 45.18–46.15) serves as the haftarah for Shabbat Ha-Ḥodesh (the Shabbat prior to 1 Nisan or 1 Nisan if it is Shabbat). **18–25: The position of the prince in sanitization of the Temple and on holidays. 18–20:** The prescribed ritual on the first day in Nisan is not attested elsewhere and may be seen as a replacement for the atonement ceremony performed on the 10th of Tishri, Yom Kippur (Lev. ch 16). **19:** The blood of a *purification offering* purifies the Temple, altar, and inner court on the first day of the first month. **21–25: The Passover Festival of Matzot and Sukkot Sacrifices. 22:** Here is one of the changes in the sacrifices in Ezek. since there is no precedent for the offering of a *bull* on 14 Nisan. **23:** The offering of *seven bulls and seven rams* daily conflicts with Num. 28.19. Here the same number of sacrifices are on Passover as are on Sukkot.

46.1–18: The prince and the regulations concerning his offerings and property. 1–8: The eastern gate is opened on Sabbaths and new moons so that the prince may enter to present his offerings. **2:** The prince *shall attend at the gatepost* and bow down at the *threshold of the gate.*

3: The people bow down at the same gate entrance. **4:** The sacrifice of *six lambs* and *one ram* conflicts with Num. 28.9–10. **9–10:** The people enter by the north and south gates, but exit by the opposite gates. **11–15:** The freewill and daily offerings of the prince are specified. **16–18:** The prince may pass property on to his sons, but property passed to servants reverts to the prince at the *year of release* (like the jubilee year found in Lev. 25.8–17). The prince may not pass property of the people to his own sons. **19–24:** Areas for the preparation of sacrifices for consumption by the priests are located in the northwestern area of the inner court. Kitchens for the people are located at the four corners of the outer court.

be closed until evening. 3 The common people[a] shall worship
before the LORD on sabbaths and new moons at the entrance
of the same gate.
4 The burnt offering which the prince presents to the LORD
on the sabbath day shall consist of six lambs without blemish and one ram without blemish—5 with a meal offering of
an *ephah* for the ram, a meal offering of as much as he wishes
for the lambs, and a *hin* of oil with every *ephah.* 6 And on the
day of the new moon, it shall consist of a bull of the herd without blemish, and six lambs and a ram—they shall be without
blemish. 7 And he shall provide a meal offering of an *ephah* for
the bull, an *ephah* for the ram, and as much as he can afford for
the lambs, with a *hin* of oil to every *ephah.*
8 When the prince enters, he shall come in by way of the vestibule of the gate, and he shall go out the same way.
9 But on the fixed occasions, when the common people
come before the LORD, whoever enters by the north gate to
bow low shall leave by the south gate; and whoever enters by
the south gate shall leave by the north gate. They shall not go
back through the gate by which they came in, but shall go out
[b]by the opposite one.[b] 10 And as for the prince, he shall enter
with them when they enter and leave when they leave.
11 On festivals and fixed occasions, the meal offering shall be
an *ephah* for each bull, an *ephah* for each ram, and as much as
he wishes for the lambs, with a *hin* of oil for every *ephah.*
12 The gate that faces east shall also be opened for the prince
whenever he offers a freewill offering—be it burnt offering or
offering of well-being—freely offered to the LORD, so that he
may offer his burnt offering or his offering of well-being just as
he does on the sabbath day. Then he shall leave, and the gate
shall be closed after he leaves.
13 Each day you shall offer a lamb of the first year without
blemish, as a daily burnt offering to the LORD; you shall offer
one every morning. 14 And every morning regularly you shall
offer a meal offering with it: a sixth of an *ephah,* with a third
of a *hin* of oil to moisten the choice flour, as a meal offering to
the LORD—a law for all time. 15 The lamb, the meal offering,
and oil shall be presented every morning as a regular burnt
offering.

16 Thus said the Lord GOD: If the prince makes a gift to any
of his sons, it shall become the latter's inheritance; it shall pass
on to his sons; it is their holding by inheritance. 17 But if he
makes a gift from his inheritance to any of his subjects, it shall
only belong to the latter until the year of release.[c] Then it shall

a I.e., those other than the priests, the Levites, and the prince; lit. "the people of the land." *b-b Lit. "straight before him."* *c Cf. Lev. 25.10.*

revert to the prince; his inheritance must by all means pass on to his sons.

18 But the prince shall not take property away from any of the people and rob them of their holdings. Only out of his own holdings shall he endow his sons, in order that My people may not be dispossessed of their holdings.

19 Then he led me into the passage at the side of the gate to the sacred chambers of the priests, which face north, and there, at the rear of it, in the west, I saw a space. 20 He said to me, "This is the place where the priests shall boil the guilt offerings and the purification offerings, and where they shall bake the meal offerings, so as not to take them into the outer court and [a]make the people consecrated."[-a] 21 Then he led me into the outer court and led me past the four corners of the court; and in each corner of the court there was an enclosure. 22 These unroofed[b] enclosures, [each] 40 [cubits] long and 30 wide, were in the four corners of the court; the four corner enclosures had the same measurements. 23 [On the inside,] running round the four of them, there was a row of masonry, equipped with hearths under the rows all around. 24 He said to me, "These are the kitchens where the Temple servitors shall boil the sacrifices of the people."

47 He led me back to the entrance of the Temple, and I found that water was issuing from below the platform[c] of the Temple—eastward, since the Temple faced east—but the water was running out at the [d]south of the altar,[-d] under the south wall of the Temple. 2 Then he led me out by way of the northern gate and led me around to the outside of the outer gate that faces in the direction of the east;[e] and I found that water was gushing from [under] the south wall. 3 As the man went on eastward with a measuring line in his hand, he measured off a thousand cubits and led me across the water; the water was ankle deep. 4 Then he measured off another thousand and led me across the water; the water was knee deep. He measured off a further thousand and led me across the water; the water was up to the waist. 5 When he measured yet another thousand, it was a stream I could not cross; for the water had swollen into a stream that could not be crossed except by swimming. 6 "Do you see, O mortal?" he said to me; and he led me back to the bank of the stream.

7 As I came back, I saw trees in great profusion on both banks of the stream. 8 "This water," he told me, "runs out to

a-a See note c at 44.19. *b So Mishnah Middoth 2.5; emendation yields "small."*
c See note at 9.3. *d-d Connection unclear. Emendation yields "southeast."*
e The end of the verse explains why he could not have made the detour by way of the south gate. For the reasons why he could not have proceeded to his present position directly by way of the east gate, see 43.1–2; 44.1–2.

47.1–48.35: A stream that emerges from the Temple; the division of the land. 47.1–12: Once the Temple is reestablished, water streams up from *below the platform of the Temple—eastward* to water the land of Israel. This indicates the role of the Temple as the center of creation (the garden of Eden, Gen. 2.10–14; Ps. 46.4). The water flows into the *eastern region* (v. 8) and eventually into the *Arabah* (the Jordan rift where the Dead Sea is located) to transform salty waters into fresh water. The fresh water supports and heals all those sheltered by the river, and waters the everlasting fruit trees that have leaves that can be used to cure.

11: *Its swamps and marshes ... will serve to [supply] salt:* The waters of the swamps and marshes around the river will stay salty as a source for salt.

47.13–48.35: The reestablishment of the land and people of Israel. The reconstruction of the Temple provides the basis for the reestablishment of the land and people of Israel. **47.13–23:** The boundaries of the land are similar to those found in Num. 34.1–15.

the eastern region, and flows into the Arabah; and when it
comes into the sea, into [a-]the sea of foul waters,[-a] the water
will become wholesome. 9 Every living creature that swarms
will be able to live wherever this stream goes; the fish will
be very abundant once these waters have reached there. It
will be wholesome, and everything will live wherever this
stream goes. 10 Fishermen shall stand beside it all the way
from En-gedi to En-eglaim; it shall be a place for drying nets;
and the fish will be of various kinds [and] most plentiful,
like the fish of the Great Sea. 11 But its swamps and marshes
shall not become wholesome; they will serve to [supply] salt.
12 All kinds of trees for food will grow up on both banks of the
stream. Their leaves will not wither nor their fruit fail; they
will yield new fruit every month, because the water for them
flows from the Temple. Their fruit will serve for food and their
leaves for healing."

13 Thus said the Lord GOD: These shall be the boundaries of
the land that you shall allot to the twelve tribes of Israel. Joseph shall receive two portions, 14 and you shall share the rest

a-a I.e., the Dead Sea.

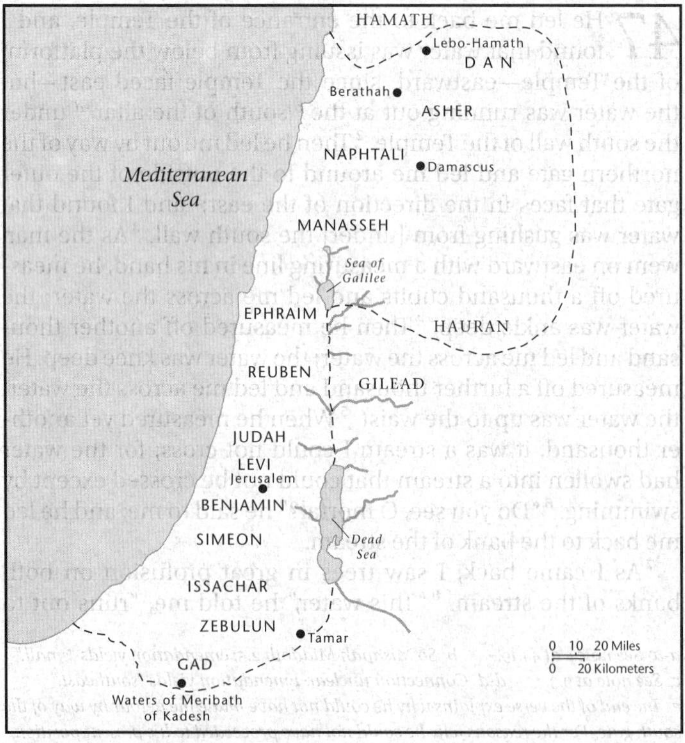

Tribal territories in the restored Israel

equally. As I swore to give it to your fathers, so shall this land fall to you as your heritage. [15] These are the boundaries of the land:

As the northern limit: From the Great Sea by way of Hethlon, Lebo-[a]hamath,-[a] Zedad, [16] Berathah, Sibraim—which lies between the border of Damascus and the border of Hamath—[down to] Hazer-hatticon, which is on the border of Hauran. [17] Thus the boundary shall run from the Sea to [b]Hazar-enon,-[b] to the north of the territory of Damascus, with the territory of Hamath to the north of it. That shall be the northern limit.

[18] As the eastern limit: A line between Hauran and Damascus, and between Gilead and the land of Israel: with the Jordan as a boundary, you shall measure down to the [c]Eastern Sea.-[c] That shall be the eastern limit.

[19] The southern limit shall run: A line from Tamar to the waters of Meriboth-kadesh, along the Wadi [of Egypt and] the Great Sea. That is the southern limit.

[20] And as the western limit: The Great Sea shall be the boundary up to a point opposite Lebo-hamath. That shall be the western limit.

[21] This land you shall divide for yourselves among the tribes of Israel. [22] You shall allot it as a heritage for yourselves and for the strangers who reside among you, who have begotten children among you. You shall treat them as Israelite citizens; they shall receive allotments along with you among the tribes of Israel. [23] You shall give the stranger an allotment within the tribe where he resides—declares the Lord GOD.

48 These are the names of the tribes:
At the northern end, along the Hethlon road, [from] Lebo-hamath to Hazar-enan—which is the border of Damascus, with Hamath to the north—from the eastern border to the Sea: Dan—one [tribe].

[2] Adjoining the territory of Dan, from the eastern border to the western border: Asher—one.

[3] Adjoining the territory of Asher, from the eastern border to the western border: Naphtali—one.

[4] Adjoining the territory of Naphtali, from the eastern border to the western border: Manasseh—one.

[5] Adjoining the territory of Manasseh, from the eastern border to the western border: Ephraim—one.

[6] Adjoining the territory of Ephraim, from the eastern border to the western border: Reuben—one.

[7] Adjoining the territory of Reuben, from the eastern border to the western border: Judah—one.

15–17: The northern border runs from the Mediterranean east to *Hazar-enon,* between Hamath (modern Hama) to the north and Damascus to the south (Num. 34.7–9). **19:** The eastern border runs south through the Jordan Valley to *Tamar* just south of the Dead Sea (Num. 34.10–12). The southern border runs through the Negev to the *Wadi [of Egypt ...]* (see Num. 34.3–5). **20:** The western border runs along the Mediterranean coast (Num. 34.6). **22:** *The strangers who reside among you* (Heb "gerim," "sojourners") are those who joined the Jewish community during the exile. They live according to the same laws as Israelites (Exod. 12.49). **48.1–35:** The tribes are assigned equal portions of land and are arrayed along the length of the land from north to south. **1–7:** The northern tribes are listed from north to south as *Dan, Asher, Naphtali, Manasseh, Ephraim, Reuben,* and *Judah.*

a-a Brought up from v. 16 for clarity.
b-b Apparently identical with Hazer-hatticon in v. 16. *c-c I.e., the Dead Sea.*

8–22: The *sacred reserve,* or Levitical allotment (45.1–9), is defined in detail. The priests are placed in the north, and the sanctuary is assigned to their portion; the Levites are placed to the south of the priests; and the portion reserved for Israel, which contains the city, is to the south of the Levites. The portion allotted to the prince is on either side of the sacred reserve.

8 Adjoining the territory of Judah, from the eastern border to the western border, shall be the reserve that you set aside: 25,000 [cubits] in breadth and in length equal to one of the portions from the eastern border to the western border; the Sanctuary shall be in the middle of it. 9 The reserve that you set aside for the LORD shall be 25,000 long and 10,000[a] wide. 10 It shall be apportioned to the following: The sacred reserve for the priests shall measure 25,000 [cubits] on the north, [b]10,000 on the west, 10,000 on the east, and 25,000 on the south,[-b] with the LORD's Sanctuary in the middle of it. 11 This consecrated area shall be for the priests of the line of Zadok, who kept My charge and did not go astray, as the Levites did when the people of Israel went astray. 12 It shall be a special reserve for them out of the [total] reserve from the land, most holy, adjoining the territory of the Levites. 13 Alongside the territory of the priests, the Levites shall have [an area] 25,000 long by 10,000 wide; the total length shall be 25,000 and the breadth 10,000.[c] 14 None of it—the choicest of the land—may be sold, exchanged, or transferred; it is sacred to the LORD.

15 The remaining 5,000 in breadth by 25,000 shall be for common use—serving the city for dwellings and pasture. The city itself shall be in the middle of it; 16 and these shall be its measurements: On the north side 4,500 cubits, on the south side 4,500, on the east side 4,500, and on the west side 4,500. 17 The pasture shall extend 250 cubits to the north of the city, 250 to the south, 250 to the east, and 250 to the west. 18 As for the remaining 10,000 to the east and 10,000 to the west, adjoining the long side[d] of the sacred reserve, the produce of these areas adjoining the sacred reserve shall serve as food for the workers in the city; 19 the workers in the city from all the tribes of Israel shall cultivate it. 20 The entire reserve, 25,000 square, you shall set aside as the sacred reserve plus the city property. 21 What remains on either side of the sacred reserve and the city property shall belong to the prince. The prince shall own [the land] from the border of the 25,000 [e]of the reserve[-e] up to the eastern boundary, and from the border of the 25,000 on the west up to the western boundary, corresponding to the [tribal] portions. The sacred reserve, with the Temple Sanctuary in the middle of it 22 and the property of the Levites and the city property as well, shall be in the middle of the [area belonging] to the prince; [the rest of the land] between the territory of Judah and the territory of Benjamin shall belong to the prince.

a Emendation yields "25,000"; cf. 45.3–6.

b-b Lit. "10,000 in breadth on the west; 10,000 in breadth on the east; and 25,000 in length on the south."

c Septuagint reads "20,000"; cf. note a.

d I.e., the south side.

e-e Emendation yields "on the east."

23 As for the remaining tribes:[a] From the eastern border to
the western border: Benjamin—one.
24 Adjoining the territory of Benjamin, from the eastern border to the western border: Simeon—one.
25 Adjoining the territory of Simeon, from the eastern border
to the western border: Issachar—one.
26 Adjoining the territory of Issachar, from the eastern border
to the western border: Zebulun—one.
27 Adjoining the territory of Zebulun, from the eastern border
to the western border: Gad—one.
28 The other border of Gad shall be the southern boundary.
This boundary shall run from Tamar to the waters of Meribath-
kadesh, to the Wadi [of Egypt], and to the Great Sea.
29 That is the land which you shall allot as a heritage to the
tribes of Israel, and those are their portions—declares the Lord
GOD.
30 And these are the exits from the city: On its northern side,
measuring 4,500 cubits, 31 the gates of the city shall be—three
gates on the north—named for the tribes of Israel: the Reuben
Gate: one; the Judah Gate: one; the Levi Gate: one. 32 On the
eastern side, [measuring] 4,500 cubits—there shall be three
gates: the Joseph Gate: one; the Benjamin Gate: one; and the
Dan Gate: one. 33 On the southern side, measuring 4,500 cubits,
there shall be three gates: the Simeon Gate: one; the Issachar
Gate: one; and the Zebulun Gate: one. 34 And on the western
side, [measuring] 4,500 cubits—there shall be three gates: the
Gad Gate: one; the Asher Gate: one; the Naphtali Gate: one.
35 Its circumference [shall be] 18,000 [cubits]; and the name
of the city from that day on shall be "The LORD Is There."

a The tribes not provided for in vv. 1–7, and lying south of the sacred gift.

23–29: The southern tribes are listed from north to south as *Benjamin, Simeon, Issachar, Zebulun,* and *Gad.* **30–35:** There are three gates allotted to the tribes on each side of the square city. The northern gates include Reuben, Judah, and Levi; the eastern gates include Joseph, Benjamin, and Dan; the southern gates include Simeon, Issachar, and Zebulun; and the western gates include Gad, Asher, and Naphtali. The name of the city is *The LORD Is There* to signify the return of God's Presence, reversing the divine abandonment that was the theme of the prophecies of retribution in the first twenty-four chs of the book.

תרי עשר

The Twelve

THE TWELVE IS A COLLECTION of twelve separate prophetic books, each associated with and evoking a particular prophetic personage of the past (e.g., Hosea, Micah, Haggai). The books present themselves as YHVH's word or communication and thus, all of these books claim to communicate to the readers authoritative knowledge about the LORD. Some of these prophetic books are explicitly set in a particular time period in Israel's past, somewhere between the 8th and the 5th centuries BCE. According to the Talmud, "the Men of the Great Assembly [whom they believed lived in the Persian period] wrote the Twelve" (*b. B. Bat.* 15a). Today, many scholars think that all or most of the prophetic books in the Twelve—at least in their present form—were either composed or edited after the fall of the monarchy (586 BCE) and probably during the Persian period (539–332). Many scholars argue also that forerunners (or earlier editions) of some of the books may date to monarchic times, or that the scribes who composed or edited the prophetic books as we know them had access to textual sources and traditions from periods earlier than their own.

There were substantial differences between the monarchic and the postmonarchic periods. Judah was a relatively prosperous kingdom during the late monarchic period (the last decades before the destruction of the Temple in 586). Jerusalem was at the time an important city whose population (about 25,000 people) was about a third of that of the kingdom as a whole (about 75,000). Postmonarchic Judah, the Persian province of Yehud, was much smaller and poorer. For instance, the population of Jerusalem in the second half of the Persian period (450–332) was likely around 1,500 inhabitants; the highest estimate in historical circles today is 4,500. Likewise, the province of Yehud after the restoration, which began in 538 reached a population peak of probably only 17,000.

An analysis of the material culture shows similar differences between late monarchic Judah and Yehud. The once independent Davidic kingdom has become a relatively small and peripheral province in a large empire. Moreover, the fall of Jerusalem and Judah in 586 had more than just political, demographic, and economic impact. From an insider's religious perspective, when the monarchic period came to a close, Jerusalem (= the LORD's city), the Temple (= the LORD's house), and the Davidic dynasty (= the LORD's chosen dynasty) all fell. There is no doubt that the events of 586 represent a watershed in the history of Judah and ancient Israel, and were understood as such by those who lived after these events. Postmonarchic Judahites attempted to understand them in terms of divine justice and tried to understand themselves within a world in which their community, from their perspective the LORD's people, was so powerless compared to other nations and compared to their memory of monarchic Judah. These issues loomed large in the postmonarchic communities within which the prophetic books were written or reached their present form, and certainly were of great concern to the people for whom they were written. Reflections on these issues are evident in many of the prophetic books, and assume two forms: condemnations of monarchic

Judah for sins so great that they justified the LORD's destruction of Jerusalem, and messages of hope and restoration that reassured the postmonarchic community that their present situation was not the "end of the road" but only a minor stop in a journey that led to an ideal and glorious future for Israel—and at times, for the nations too.

Prophetic books were written texts meant to be read or more properly, to be re-read and studied. Like other works intended for rereading, they tend to show more than passing instances of ambiguity or multiple meanings (as the annotations will show). Traditional Jewish interpreters maintained that the prophetic books were given to Israel to convince them to return to Torah norms, to call for repentance and to provide guidance, that is, to affect, not merely to inform, their readers. We know that already in the late biblical period prophetic works were read, re-read, and studied in order to find such guidance.

Reading and rereading the prophetic books influenced and shaped the world of the community in complementary ways. Prophetic books, including those included in the Twelve—along with some other biblical books, e.g., Genesis, Kings, Chronicles—were books of memory. The socially shared activity of reading and rereading the prophetic books made the past and the future present in the community. In fact, these books served, *inter alia* ("among other things"), to bring the past and the future to the reading community, to give it immediacy, such that the community could vicariously experience Israel's past and future. This process was one of both "remembering" and "shaping memories."

The memories evoked by, and shaped and reflected by, these books concerned (for the most part) the sinful late monarchic past that led to the destruction of Jerusalem and the monarchic polity, of the destruction and its aftermath. Reflected also is the beginning of the process of restoration and above all, the glorious future the LORD has promised and which the writers believed would certainly come. These prophetic books evoked memories of multiple ideal futures (e.g., God or [a descendent of] David as the ideal king). These multiple memories and hopes allowed the prophetic books to become a shared, communal meeting place in which the community evoked and negotiated memories of utopia and what utopia should be.

In terms of the past, the evoked memories were structured to convey a narrative of decline, a constant slide towards the catastrophe of 586 BCE. It is not an accident that the books within the Twelve that are explicitly set in monarchic times tend to concentrate around either the late northern Israelite period and its chronological counterpart in Judah under Hezekiah (Hosea, Amos, Micah; cf. Isaiah), or the period of the late Judahite monarchy (Zephaniah; cf. Jeremiah; Ezekiel). The periods that were systemically selected shared one central quality: They were imagined, from the perspective of the later readers of the books, as directly leading to the destruction of the monarchic polities and above all leading Israel to exile and to the destruction of Jerusalem. Within this mnemonic narrative, the late monarchic prophets had to be imagined, for the most part, as being, first, aware of the incoming and justified catastrophe; second, as warning voices; third, as on the whole unsuccessful in terms of their generation, since the catastrophe did happen; fourth, successful in the sense that their words as written in the prophetic books remained to teach later Israel; and fifth, as voices of hope, since through them, at the worst moment of Israel, the LORD promised it a great future.

Prophets associated with the period of the rebuilding of the Temple focus on the Temple (see Haggai and Zechariah), but as the book of Zechariah demonstrates, they were also similar to the prophets of old. The book of Malachi reminded the community that the presence of the Temple itself provides no warranty that Israel will behave in accordance with the will of God; people may, did, and will fail, and so there is a need of prophets and of prophetic books and above all for *torah*.

The prophetic books included in the collection of the Twelve contributed much to the comprehensive social memory of the community; the paradox is that often in these books the divine or human utterances that the books reveal are not directly associated with particular historical events. Six out of twelve books have a superscription that lacks any explicit reference to the temporal setting for the book (Joel, Obadiah, Jonah, Nahum, Habakkuk, Malachi), and in the majority of those books set in the late monarchic era, the superscription refers to a *general* period of several decades as the time in which the world of the book is set (see Hosea, Micah, and Zephaniah). Most of the Twelve, then, do not ask their readers to read the prophet within a constrained set of historical circumstances, or to strongly historicize it through emphatic mimesis (this is most obvious in Joel).

The twelve prophetic books shaped a collection in which, as a whole, there are two main characters: trans-temporal God and trans-temporal (though not atemporal) Israel. Manifestations of the latter included, among others, the Israel of the exodus, Sinai, the monarchic polities, exilic Israel and of course the community centered around Jerusalem in the Persian period, and most significantly, the authors and readers of the books themselves. By remembering events and characters in a way that allowed also for their trans-temporality, the community could identify more easily with the Israel, the prophets and the God that emerged from their twelve prophetic books. (The book of Haggai is an exception, as it reported oracles that were narrowly dated, both explicitly and emphatically [see Hag. 1.1, 15; 2.1, 10, 20]. The association of Haggai with the beginning of the establishment of the [Second] Temple may be the reason for the different pattern.)

Eventually, some reported prophetic utterances became detached from their original context and therefore available for more general application. Thus, for instance, brief texts from the twelve prophetic books could be removed from their context in their respective books and placed in the mouth of other "prophetic voices" in periods that preceded the one to which the original prophet was associated (e.g., in Azariah's speech: 2 Chron. 15.3 [cf. Hos. 3.4], 5 [cf. Zech. 8.10 and Amos 3.9–10], 6 [cf. Zech. 11.6], 7 [cf. Jer. 31.16; Zeph. 3.16]). Thus, a-contextualized prophetic words became sites of memory by themselves and the door opened to the type of biblical interpretation that eventually became attested in the *pesharim* (the later interpretive tradition).

Prophetic books were, as mentioned above, about God and Israel, but also about prophetic characters; they evoked the "person" of the particular prophet. The prophet that readers imagined through their readings symbolized, and embodied, as it were, the contents and messages of the book. The book served thus as means to encounter such a "person," identify with and learn from him, and to identify with the deity whose word was associated with such a person. Since reading the prophetic book brought such a "person" from the past into the present of the remembering community, this social (and mnemonic) process may have facilitated redactional activities in the prophetic books, including those comprising the collection of the Twelve. After all, if each book was meant to encode the proper memory of the prophet for the present community, there would be a tendency to shape the book consistently with what the community thought to be the character of the prophet and his message. After all, the book had to evoke the proper memory of the prophet and conversely, what the community considered to be the proper memory of the prophet had to be reflected in the book. When redactional activity on the texts of the prophetic books became impossible, in later Jewish and Christian communities interpretation played a similar role, and it reshaped the message of the prophet to fit what the reading/remembering community thought it to be.

Many readers of the prophetic books, including scholars, wish to encounter, as it were, "the (true) prophet." Today, more often than not, this means to encounter the "historical" prophet.

This is consistent with a "historicist" turn in Western societies that has become dominant since at least the early 19th century. Of course, to reconstruct and thus shape a memory of the historical prophet involves abstracting from the relevant book everything that may be considered by the scholar or groups of scholars the words relating to or attesting to the "historical prophet." By combining these texts into a new text and interpreting it in terms of a construction of the circumstances of the putative time of the "historical prophet," an image of the latter emerges and a memory of him is created. Some of these memories had actually a strong impact well beyond academic circles, on both Jewish and non-Jewish circles for decades (e.g., Amos as the prophet of social justice). Scholars have also created images as well of a number of "historical redactors" who worked in each of the prophetic books (or collections of them) and contributed sequentially to a proposed historical process that through various stages led the putative original prophetic texts attributed to the "historical prophet" to the eventual prophetic book attested in the Hebrew Bible.

To be sure, the images and memories of the historical prophets are based, in most cases, on only parts of the texts included in the prophetic books. And the historical circumstances in which the historical prophets are supposed to have existed differed substantially from those that existed within the socially shared memory of the the Israel of the period in which the prophetic books as we know them emerged. It is thus the case that the "historical prophets" mentioned above are substantially different from the memories of the twelve prophets evoked by the twelve prophetic books within the context in which they emerged in their present form. This form (and the related prophets it creates) is the text that subsequent generations of readers studied and discussed.

There are fifteen prophetic books in the Bible: the collection called "the Twelve," plus Isaiah, Jeremiah, and Ezekiel. (Unlike Christian Bibles, the Jewish Bible does not include Daniel in the Prophets section of the canon, but among the Kethuvim, or Writings.) Each of the fifteen prophetic books is associated with a single prophetic personage. In the Twelve, each book displays distinctive language and themes that set it apart from the other books. Thus the human speaker in each book has his own voice. Even the divine speaker, God, is distinctive in each book, with a voice that is similar to (and at times blends with) that of the particular human speaker.

There are no prophetic books associated with women prophets, although there were female prophets in ancient Israel (see, e.g., 2 Kings 2.14; Neh. 6.14). There are also no prophetic books associated with men who were remembered as born and educated in a diasporic setting. These are not random or minor omissions, but reflect and reinforce a certain worldview that existed at the time on matters of gender and land.

The lengths of the books in this collection range from one chapter to fourteen. Their relative length reflects, in part, the relative importance that the community assigned to particular prophets. Even the longest of the Twelve, however, is short compared to any of the three books associated with the major prophets, Isaiah, Jeremiah, and Ezekiel. Since a scroll can hold about fifty to sixty chapters, each of the major prophets was most likely written on one scroll. Smaller books, like those in the Twelve, were at some point collected and copied together on one scroll, so as not to waste expensive writing material. The total length of the Twelve approximates the length of one of the major prophetic books. Nevertheless, they have been read as separate books (and are counted that way in Christian Bibles) rather than as sections of a single book. Even though they are counted as one book in Jewish Bibles (because they were written on one scroll), they are perceived in Jewish tradition as well as twelve separate books.

We do not know when the twelve prophetic books were first collected onto one scroll. The practice is probably implied in Sirach 49.10 (early 2nd c. BCE): "May the bones of the Twelve

Prophets / send forth new life from where they lie, / for they comforted the people of Jacob / and delivered them with confident hope." (Sirach refers here and elsewhere in this poem to prophets not to the prophetic books, attesting to the importance of the character of the prophets as embodying the book's teaching.)

The oldest extant manuscript of the Twelve is among the Dead Sea Scrolls (4Q XII[a]) and dates from the middle of the 2nd c. BCE. In this manuscript the book of Jonah follows (most likely) that of Malachi. In fact, the individual and separate character of each book in the collection allowed their order in the scroll to remain fluid for a relatively long period (as was also the case with the later collection called the Kethuvim/Writings; see pp. 1263–64). Eventually the Septuagint (LXX), the ancient Greek translation of the Hebrew Bible, and the Hebrew text tradition finalized the order of these books, though in slightly different ways. To some extent a chronological principle governs the present order in the Masoretic Text (and in the LXX). For instance, Hosea is the first because he was probably considered the earliest of four prophets who prophesied at one particular, early period, the others being Isaiah, Amos, and Micah (see *b. B. Bat.* 14a). The books of Haggai, Zechariah, and Malachi, who "came at the end of the prophets," close the collection. But chronological concerns were not the only consideration. It seems that an emphatic focus on Jerusalem and Judah was either a main concern for those who ordered the books in the Masoretic tradition or was a background belief reflected in their final ordering in this tradition.

A significant clue for understanding the prophetic books within their historical setting stands at the conclusion of Hos. 14.10, which may be translated as follows: "Those who are wise understand these things [i.e., the prophetic readings included in the book]; those who are discerning know them. For the ways of the LORD are right, and the upright walk in them, but transgressors stumble in them."

Beyond the theological language used here, the passage reflects the social reality that, since the prophetic books were written texts, only those able to read could approach them directly and thus the literate minority served as brokers of divine knowledge to the vast majority who could not read. These ancient scholars studied the texts, and read and interpreted them to others. Since the texts were considered to communicate (authoritative) knowledge about God, early interpretations of what they meant had to be consistent with what was known about God from other sources.

This put certain limitations on the kinds of interpretations that were acceptable. It is likely that the earliest extant summary of the message of the Twelve in Sirach 49.10 reflects a predominant way in which they were read in antiquity. The very basic message that they conveyed to their ancient readership is well summarized in that passage: "They [these Twelve Prophets] comforted the people of Jacob and delivered them with confident hope." This is quite remarkable, since these books devote many more words and chapters to divine punishment than consolation.

The last book of the Twelve and, accordingly the entire section of Nevi'im/Prophets in the Tanakh, concludes—whether by design or fortuitously with a passage that includes the following sentence: "Remember the Torah of Moses, my servant, which I commanded him at Horeb for all of Israel—its decrees and statutes" (Mal. 3.22; author's translation). This verse gives a clear sense that The Prophets is subordinate to the Torah of Moses. Maimonides in the *Mishneh Torah* (*Hilchot Yesodei Hatorah* 9.2 in the version in the Bar Ilan Response ed. and 9.3 in Snunit's) quoted a portion of this verse as a proof that prophets are not supposed to bring a new Torah, but to warn people not to trespass the Torah—a position central to traditional Judaism. Critical biblical scholarship, however, has seen the Torah and The Prophets as separate corpora originating in the same time period, with some differing and some similar norms and beliefs. There is no doubt that each of these two separate sections influenced, and were influenced by, the other section and some scholars are now emphasizing that the two sections together reflected the worldview of the community.

The very end of the prophetic collection reads: "Lo, I will send the prophet Elijah to you before the coming of the awesome, fearful day of the LORD" (Mal. 3.23–24). In other words, it keeps a tension and balance between the activities of the scholars and of all Israel in their present circumstances and their hopes for a positive change in the future, a change that was later understood in messianic terms (see the *Mishneh Torah* of Maimonides, *hilchot melachim* 12.2 in the version of Bar Ilan's Response and 12.3 in Snunit's version). Significantly, the entire Christian Old Testament concludes with Mal. 3.23–24 and calls as it were for the realization of that messianic time. The Tanakh, however, moves from these verses directly to the Writings, to either Ps. 1, whose spirit may be understood as consonant with Hos. 14.10 and Mal. 3.22 or in the Leningrad Codex, for instance, to Chronicles, which recounts and reinterprets the history of Israel in a way that is deeply informed by the Torah.

[EHUD BEN ZVI]

הושע

Hosea

THE FIRST VERSE SERVES as both the superscription and the introduction of the book to the readers. It communicates to them that the following text is YHVH's word to a prophet from the past, Hosea. The book's main themes are Israel's abandoning of the LORD, the LORD's punishment of Israel for that abandonment, calls for Israel's repentance, and hope for an ideal future of reconciliation between YHVH and Israel.

Israel's abandoning of the LORD is expressed in terms of cultic, religious, social, sexual, and political offenses. Horrifying imagery, along with references to Israel's destruction in the land and its exile from it, as well as to the fall of the Northern Kingdom, express the theme of the YHVH's punishment of Israel. To be sure, no prophetic book concerns itself only with condemnation and punishment. All of them convey hope for the future. Hosea does so in highly poetic language. Yet hope for the future, for a restoration of the ideal relation between YHVH and Israel, requires that Israel turn from its ways and return to the LORD, so the call for repentance is an important theme in the book.

It is precisely the element of hope—hope against a background of apparent hopelessness—that has led to the book's wide use in Jewish liturgy. Thus Hos. 14.2–10 is read in the afternoon service of Tish'ah be'av (Sephardic and Yemenite traditions; others read Isa. 55.6–56.8) and on Shabbat Shuvah, the Sabbath between Rosh Ha-Shanah (the New Year) and Yom Kippur (the Day of Atonement). Hos. 2.1–22 is read as the haftarah for the parashah of Be-midbar (Num. 1.1–4.20). Hos. 2.21–22 are recited as part of the ritual for donning tefillin (phylacteries).

Like other prophetic books, Hosea often employs sexual and family metaphors to express the relationship between YHVH and Israel. Within the book's metaphorical world, the deity takes the role of an angry husband who condemns, severely punishes, and publicly dishonors his unfaithful wife, who fails to recognize how good he had been to her. After his violent and shaming punishment is carried out, he will be willing to accept her back. This basic imagery is quite common in the society that produced the prophetic books (see also Ezek. chs 16, 23), and in the ancient Near East as a whole. To be sure, the text was not written to glorify or justify family violence or violence against women in general, but rather to dramatize and explain the reasons for the disasters that befell Israel, to persuade the readers to live their lives in a way consistent with the will of YHVH, and to give them hope for the future. Nevertheless, this imagery is very troublesome for many contemporary readers, and especially painful for those who associate their reading of the text with their or their acquaintances' personal experiences (see chs 1–3, and particularly 2.3–15). The book is set in the last period of political strength of the Northern Kingdom of Israel, in the middle 8th c. BCE, through the time of its destruction by Assyria in 722 (see 1.1 n.). While the threat of Assyrian invasion hovers in the background, the book focuses on the behavior of Israel, which it condemns in very sharp terms. It depicts the period as a time of apostasy, of social disintegration, of wrongful leadership, of failed alliances, in sum a time when knowledge of (and reverence for) YHVH are lacking.

The time period portrayed in the book of Hosea is one of the earliest among the book of the Twelve, and this may be one of the reasons for its place at the beginning of the collection (for a traditional Jewish text on the matter, see *b. B. Bat.* 14b).

The book contains an introduction (1.1), and a very significant conclusion that provides a key for its interpretation (14.10; see intro. to the Twelve). The rest of the book consists of two main sections: 1.2–3.5, in which narrative and imageries of whoredom are prominent, and 4.1–14.9, which consists of a set of readings that report prophetic announcements associated with Hosea. An alternative subdivision of 1.2–14.9 is: (1) chs 1–3; (2) chs 4–11; and (3) chs 12–14.

[EHUD BEN ZVI]

1 The word of the LORD that came to Hosea son of Beeri, in
the reigns of Kings Uzziah, Jotham, Ahaz, and Hezekiah
of Judah, and in the reign of King Jeroboam son of Joash of
Israel.

2 When the LORD first spoke to Hosea, the LORD said to Hosea, "Go, get yourself [a-]a wife of whoredom and children of
whoredom; for the land will stray[b] from following the LORD."[-a]

a-a Force of Heb. uncertain. *b Lit. "whore away."*

1.1: Superscription. The v. characterizes the book as a particular instance of the LORD's word (that is, as a prophetic book), set in a particular time and associated with a prophetic character from the past, Hosea. Although the setting for the book is the Northern Kingdom of Israel, its intended readers are the Judahites who may constructively reflect upon the demise of the Northern Kingdom in 722 BCE. References to the kings of Judah precede, and are more elaborate than, the reference to the Israelite king. Further, since *Jeroboam* (II) died during the reign of *Uzziah* (2 Kings 15.8), the temporal references do not match. From the Israelite perspective, the book is anchored in the last period of strength of the Northern Kingdom; from the Judahite perspective it is anchored in a period in which Israel moves from a political position of strength to the beginning of its demise in the days of *Hezekiah.* This double perspective is no mistake, but a rhetorical clue for the reading of the book.

1.2–3.5: Between "proper marriage" and "whoredom." A set of readings that develops a sharp contrast between Israel's reported abandonment of the LORD and the future reconciliation between the two. Punishment, however, is presented as a kind of bridge that leads from one situation to another. These passages are built around images of "whoredom" and "(proper) marriage." **2–8:** Was Hosea's marriage real or a figurative symbol that was not enacted? Some traditional Jewish commentators opted for a literal reading (e.g., *b. Pes.* 87a; Rashi, Abravanel) while others maintained that this is an account of a prophetic vision (Ibn Ezra, Radak, Maimonides). The Tg.'s understanding that these vv. are figurative becomes clear in its rendition of 2.2–4: "The beginning of the word of the LORD with Hosea: The LORD said to Hosea: Go (and) speak a prophecy against the inhabitants of the idolatrous city, who continue to sin. For the inhabitants of the land surely go astray from the worship of the LORD. So he went and prophesied concerning them that, if they repented, they would be forgiven; but, if not, they would fall as the leaves of a fig-tree fall. But they continued to do wicked deeds. And the LORD said to him, 'Call their name "scattered ones" [pun on *Jezreel,* see below] for in a little while I will avenge the blood.…' " As for the biblical text itself, the main concern (see the final clause of v. 2) is not the reported sexual sins and marital life of Gomer (or of the unnamed woman in ch 3), but rather that *the land will [whore away]* (see translators' note). The words symbolize the harlotry (idolatry) of the land and its inhabitants. Here, as frequently in the Bible, harlotry represents worship of gods other than YHVH—the deity and Israel were imagined to be in a monogamous relationship. (The image of God married to Israel that predominates here also occurs elsewhere, e.g., in the books of Jer. and Ezek.) Moreover, within their larger context in chs 1–3, or even 1–14, these references point toward the possibility of repentance and return to the proper relation between the LORD and Israel (see 2.20–25 for one expression of that proper relation; 3.5 for another). The Tg. (quoted above), although departing from the literal meaning, captures the book's theological message. **2:** A literal translation is "Go take for yourself a wife of whoredom and children of whoredom, for the land whores, whores away from following the LORD." The motif of "whoredom" and "committing whoredom" is emphasized by the quadruple repetition at the center of the v. Around the center are the references to the woman and the land, i.e., to those

3 So he went and married Gomer daughter of Diblaim. She
conceived and bore him a son, 4 and the LORD instructed him,
"Name him Jezreel; for, I will soon punish the House of Jehu[a]
for the [b]bloody deeds at Jezreel[b] and put an end to the monarchy of the House of Israel. 5 In that day, I will break the bow of
Israel in the Valley of Jezreel."

6 She conceived again and bore a daughter; and He said
to him, "Name her Lo-ruhamah;[c] for I will no longer accept
the House of Israel [d]or pardon them.[d] (7 But I will accept the
House of Judah. And I will give them victory through the LORD
their God; I will not give them victory with bow and sword and
battle, by horses and riders.)"

8 After weaning Lo-ruhamah, she conceived and bore a son.
9 Then He said, "Name him Lo-ammi;[e] for you[f] are not My people, and [g]I will not be your [God]."[g]

2 [h]The number of the people of Israel shall be like that of the
sands of the sea, which cannot be measured or counted;
and instead of being told, "You are Not-My-People,"[i] they shall
be called Children-of-the-Living-God. 2 The people of Judah
and the people of Israel shall assemble together and appoint
one head over them; and they shall rise from the ground[j]—for
marvelous shall be [k]the day of Jezreel![k]

3 Oh, call[l] your brothers "My People,"
And your sisters "Lovingly Accepted!"

a Emendation yields "Israel"; cf. next note.
b-b See 1 Kings 21.1–24; 2 Kings 9.21–35. Emendation yields "the Baal days"; cf. 2.15.
c I.e., "Not-accepted"; cf. 2.3, 6, and 25.
d-d Meaning of Heb. uncertain; emendation yields "but will disown them"; cf. 9.15 and elsewhere.
e I.e., "Not-My-People." *f I.e., you and your fellow countrymen.*
g-g Cf. 2.25. *h Vv. 1–3 anticipate the conclusion of the chapter.* *i See 1.9.*
j Meaning, perhaps, "from their wretched condition," or "to ascendancy over the land."
k-k I.e., the day when the name Jezreel will convey a promise (2.23–25) instead of a threat (1.4–5).
l The LORD addresses Hosea and his fellow North Israelites; see 1.9. The mother is the nation; her children the individual North Israelites.

who commit adultery/"whoredom", and at the beginning of the v., are the "wronged husbands," namely YHVH and Hosea. The imagery also suggests that the people of Israel are metaphorically the children of the land of Israel and of her husband (YHVH). Even if the father clearly acknowledges that the children are his, he can justifiably reject them because of the behavior of the mother (cf. 2.6). **4:** *Jezreel* is a plain in central Israel and a city on its perimeter. The allusion is likely to the events described in 1 Kings 21.1–24; 2 Kings 9.21–35, involving the murder of Naboth at the instance of Ahab and Jezebel in order to seize his property, and the consequent assassination of their son at the same location. The name *Jezreel* means "El/God sows," and has numerous positive connotations; still, "sowing" means "scattering seed." More important, ancient Heb poets played with the similarly sounding "zr'" (sow seed) and "zrh" (scatter)—see Ps. 106.27; Mal. 2.3, and the Tg. (see above). *The House of Jehu* was the last stable dynasty of the Northern Kingdom of Israel (ca. 842–747 BCE). After the lengthy rule of Jeroboam II (ca. 788–747), his son Zechariah reigned only six months. He was murdered, and so were almost all the kings who followed him in rapid succession (2 Kings 15.8–25). The reference in this v. to the future punishment of the House of Jehu explains why only Jeroboam is mentioned among the kings of Israel in v. 1. **6–9:** *Lo-ruhamah* may also be translated "Unpitied" and *Lo-ammi* means "not my people" (see translators' note *e*); these symbolic names signify the rejection of Israel, but they carry a very suggestive potential for reversal; see 2.1–3. **7:** The mention of Judah reflects the Judahite readership of the book of Hos. in its final form.

2.1–25: Denunciations and promises. Condemnations and judgments are interspersed with announcements of future restoration and hope (e.g., Mic. 2.12–13). Readers are made aware of seeds and promises of hope and contemplate their eventual blooming even as they read the most difficult texts about their past sinful deeds. These deeds are "their" deeds, because they identify—at least in part—with the Israel of the book. **1:** A reversal of the name and fate given in 1.9. The language here and in the promises to the patriarchs (Gen. 22.17; 32.13) echo each other. **2–3:** The motif of a future reunification of (northern) Israel and Judah appears elsewhere in prophetic literature (cf. Ezek. 37.15–28), though it was never fulfilled. *Jezreel,* a place of bloody deeds and divine punishment (see 1.4 n.), here becomes a place of future redemption. Similarly, the names of the other two children will have their meanings reversed, turning separation from the LORD into future closeness to Him.

4: *Rebuke,* or "remonstrate." The word carries a legal connotation of arguing against someone in a court of law, while at the same time it means "reprove" in the hope of correcting the behavior of someone (cf. Radak and Tg.). This "someone" is metaphorically both the community of Israel and the land. *For she is not My wife* may be the legal language used in a declaration of divorce. **5:** As in Ezek. ch 16, the punishment for the reported sexual promiscuity is sexual shaming. The image of the woman then becomes the image of the land, punished by drying up, losing its fertility. **6:** The land/woman will lose her children, the population of the land. Disown (Heb "will not pity") is another play on the name Lo-ruhamah. (Cf. 1.2, 6.) **7:** *Lovers,* male providers whom she loved; a reference to rulers of other nations and particularly to their gods. **8:** Heb reads, "your roads ..." (see translators' note *b*). The second person conveys direct face-to-face address meant to have an affective impact. **9–15:** The other male providers are worthless. The wife (Israel) sought material benefits from other males, all the while ignorant of the fact that it was her husband (YHVH) who provided for her. But now her husband will remove His provisions, including food and clothing. Without the clothing, she (Israel) will be naked and shamed. Her joy will disappear and none of her lovers will be able to help her against her angry husband.

4 Rebuke[a] your mother, rebuke her—
For she is not My wife
And I am not her husband—
And let her put away her harlotry from her face
And her adultery from between her breasts.
5 Else will I strip her naked
And leave her as on the day she was born:
And I will make her like a wilderness,
Render her like desert land,
And let her die of thirst.
6 I will also disown her children;
For they are now a harlot's brood,
7 In that their mother has played the harlot,
She that conceived them has acted shamelessly—
Because she thought,
"I will go after my lovers,
Who supply my bread and my water,
My wool and my linen,
My oil and my drink."

8 Assuredly,
I will hedge up her[b] roads with thorns
And raise walls against her,
And she shall not find her paths.
9 Pursue her lovers as she will,
She shall not overtake them;
And seek them as she may,
She shall never find them.
Then she will say,
"I will go and return
To my first husband,
For then I fared better than now."
10 And she did not consider this:
It was I who bestowed on her
The new grain and wine and oil;
I who lavished silver on her
And gold—which they used for Baal.
11 Assuredly,
I will take back My new grain in its time
And My new wine in its season,
And I will snatch away My wool and My linen
That serve to cover her nakedness.
12 Now will I uncover her shame
In the very sight of her lovers,
And none shall save her from Me.

a The LORD addresses Hosea and his fellow North Israelites; see 1.9. The mother is the nation; her children the individual North Israelites.
b Heb. "your." Vv. 8–9 would read well after v. 15.

13 And I will end all her rejoicing:
Her festivals, new moons, and sabbaths—
All her festive seasons.
14 I will lay waste her vines and her fig trees,
Which she thinks are a fee
She received from her lovers;
I will turn them into brushwood,
And beasts of the field shall devour them.
15 Thus will I punish her
For the days of the Baalim,
On which she brought them offerings;
When, decked with earrings and jewels,
She would go after her lovers,
Forgetting Me —declares the LORD.

16 Assuredly,
I will speak coaxingly to her
And lead her through the wilderness[a]
And speak to her tenderly.
17 I will give her her vineyards from there,
And the Valley of Achor[b] as a [c]plowland of hope.[c]
There she shall respond as in the days of her youth,
When she came up from the land of Egypt.
18 And in that day —declares the LORD—
You will call [Me] Ishi,[d]
And no more will you call Me Baali.[d]
19 For I will remove the names of the Baalim from her mouth,
And they shall nevermore be mentioned by name.

20 In that day, I will make a covenant for them with the beasts of the field, the birds of the air, and the creeping things of the ground; I will also banish[e] bow, sword, and war from the land. Thus I will let them lie down in safety.

a *I.e., her ravaged land (see vv. 5, 10–11, 14); so Ibn Ezra.*
b *A desolate region; cf. Isa. 65.10; see further Josh. 7.25–26.*
c-c *Connecting* pethaḥ *with* pittaḥ *"to plow" (see Isa. 28.24). Meaning of Heb. uncertain; others "door of hope."*
d *Both* Ishi *and* Baali *mean "my husband," but the latter also means "my Baal."*
e *Lit. "break."*

15: *Days of the Baalim,* festivals and other occasions in which offerings were sacrificed to different Baals (Baalim is the plural of the deity Baal). "Baal" means "lord" or "owner" and in the Bible often refers to a Phoenician or Canaanite god of the same name. The term was also used as a title for YHVH (see 2 Sam. 5.20; 1 Chron. 14.11), though the book of Hos. does not support that practice (2.18). This ch (see esp. v. 18 below) is playing on the meaning of "Baal" as "husband" and the related verb meaning "marry" or "take a woman as a sexual partner [the active subject is here always the man]." Baals stand for the unidentified "lovers" mentioned before, and all the terms' connotations suit well the general atmosphere permeating the text. **16–25: Marital reconciliation.** The husband will bring the wife (Israel) back. The wife will be faithful forever. She is endowed with attributes such as righteousness and faithfulness (the crucial preposition in vv. 21–22 carries the meanings of "with" and "in"). The husband (YHVH) will provide (for her), i.e., the fertility of the land will return. All of nature participates in the renewal of the marital covenant. **17:** *Valley of Achor,* see Josh. 7.24–26; 15.7; Isa. 65.10. The name may be translated as "Valley of Trouble." Significantly, this valley will be transformed into a "Door of Hope" (see translators' note *c-c*), Heb "Petach Tikvah," the name of a city in modern Israel. **18:** "You will call Me 'my Man' (or husband), and no more will you call Me 'my Baal' (or husband)." (See v. 15 n.) Although the two terms can both mean "husband," their connotations are very different. The wordplay projects an image of a future rejection of the cult of Baal (i.e., a Phoenician and Canaanite god) and Israel's acceptance of YHVH as her "Man."

21 And I will espouse you forever:
I will espouse you [a-]with righteousness and justice,
And with goodness and mercy,
22 And I will espouse you with faithfulness;[-a]
Then you shall be devoted to the LORD.
23 In that day,
I will respond —declares the LORD—
I will respond to the sky,
And it shall respond to the earth;
24 And the earth shall respond
With new grain and wine and oil,
And they shall respond to Jezreel.[b]
25 I will sow her in the land as My own;
And take Lo-ruhamah back in favor;
And I will say to Lo-ammi, "You are My people,"
And he will respond, "[You are] my God."

3 The LORD said to me further, "Go, [c-]befriend a woman who,
while befriended by a companion, consorts with others,
just as the LORD befriends the Israelites,[-c] but they turn [d-]to
other gods and love the cups of the grape."[-d]
2 Then I hired her for fifteen [shekels of] silver, a *ḥomer* of
barley, and [e-]a *lethech* of barley;[-e] 3 and I stipulated with her,
[f-]"In return,[-f] you are to go a long time without either fornicating or marrying; even I [shall not cohabit] with you."
4 For the Israelites shall go a long time without king and
without officials, without sacrifice[g] and without cult pillars,
and without ephod and teraphim. 5 Afterward, the Israelites
will turn back and will seek the LORD their God and David their
king—and they will thrill over the LORD and over His bounty in
the days to come.

4 Hear the word of the LORD,
O people of Israel!
For the LORD has a case
Against the inhabitants of this land,
Because there is no honesty and no goodness
And no obedience to God in the land.
2 [False] swearing, dishonesty, and murder,
And theft and adultery are rife;
Crime follows upon crime!

a-a As the bride-price which the bridegroom will pay, He will confer these qualities on her, so that she will never offend again.
b I.e., "God sows." The names of Hosea's children (1.3–8) are applied here to Israel.
c-c For "befriend," see Deut. 10.19. For God's befriending Israel, see Hos. 2.10.
d-d Meaning of Heb. uncertain; emendation yields "'to other gods.' And so I befriended a woman of lust." *e-e Septuagint reads "a jar of wine."*
f-f Lit. "for me." *g Emendation yields "altar."*

21–22: These vv. are well known from Jewish liturgy. They are usually translated more literally, "And I will betroth you [i.e., Israel] to Me for ever; I will betroth you to Me in/with righteousness and in justice, in/with kindness and in mercy. I will betroth you to Me in/with faithfulness; and you shall know the LORD." Traditional Jews say these vv. when winding the straps of the tefillin [phylacteries] three times round the middle finger. **23–25:** These vv. emphasize that the Israelites were wrong to assume that Baal was the fertility god—the LORD controls fertility. **3.1–5:** Another marriage metaphor. **1:** An alternative translation is: "Go again, love a woman who has a lover and is an adulteress. [This is just] as the love of YHVH for the Children of Israel, who turn to other gods." Scholars disagree on whether it refers to Gomer (1.3) or to another woman. Because she is unnamed, both options are open. Clearly, though, Hosea's relationship to this woman symbolizes again God's relationship to Israel. **2:** A *ḥomer* is probably about 230 liters (6.5 bushels), and a *lethech* is half a homer. **5:** References to YHVH and (human) kings occur elsewhere in the Tanakh. Still it is important to note that the book in its final form tells its readers of a northern (Israelite) prophet who, even though the Israelite monarchy is at its political zenith, not only perceives that its end is near, but also that the *Israelites will turn back* to *David their king,* the dynasty of the Southern Kingdom. (See similarly the final version of the conclusion of Amos.)

4.1–14.9: Reports of prophetic announcements associated with Hosea. The remainder of the book consists of a collection of prophetic speeches that accuse monarchic Israel and Judah of unfaithfulness, announce the judgment that will be passed on the people, but also foreshadow the hope of restoration and return. Most of this material (4.1–12.1; 12.7–14.9) deals with Israel; 12.3–7 focuses on Judah.

3 For that, the earth is withered:
Everything that dwells on it languishes—
Beasts of the field and birds of the sky—
Even the fish of the sea perish.

4 "Let no man rebuke, let no man protest!"
[a]For this your people has a grievance against [you],
O priest![a]
5 So you shall stumble by day,
And by night [b]a prophet[b] shall stumble as well,
And I will destroy your kindred.[c]
6 My people is destroyed because of [your]
disobedience!
Because you have rejected obedience,
I reject you as My priest;
Because you have spurned the teaching of your God,
I, in turn, will spurn your children.
7 The more they increased, the more they sinned
against Me:
I will change their dignity to dishonor.
8 They feed on My people's sin offerings,
And so they desire its iniquity.
9 Therefore, the people shall fare like the priests:
I will punish it for its conduct,
I will requite it for its deeds.
10 Truly, they shall eat, but not be sated;
They shall swill,[d] but not be satisfied,
Because they have forsaken the LORD
To practice[e] 11 lechery.
Wine[f] and new wine destroy
The mind of 12 My people:
It consults its stick,[g]
Its rod[g] directs it!
A lecherous impulse has made them go wrong,
And they have strayed[h] from submission to their God.

a-a *For failing to reprove; but meaning of Heb. uncertain.*
b-b *Emendation yields "your children"; cf. v. 6 end.* c *Lit. "mother."*
d *For this meaning of* hiznah *cf. v. 18.* e *Cf. 12.7.*
f *Emendation yields "New grain"; cf. 7.14; 9.1–2.*
g *I.e., its phallus, meaning "its lust."* h *See note b at 1.2.*

4.1–19: On Israel's corruption, rejection of divine teaching and worship, harlotry, and divine punishment. 1: *Hear the word of the LORD:* This phrase or variants of it, used in several prophetic books, conveys the legitimacy and importance of what follows. In addition, it often marks the beginning of a new section (cf. 5.1). In the world of the book, people are supposed to hear "this word," but in the actual world the book's (later) readers are asked to read and study "the word of the LORD" and to convey it to those who cannot read it by themselves. **2:** A portion of the Decalogue may be paraphrased here (Exod. 20.13–14; Deut. 5.17–18 (note also Exod. 20.7; Deut. 5.11). **5:** The v. ends with "I will destroy your mother" (see translators' note *c*), which may refer to the mother of the priest (possibly all priests?), and the land (Gomer) as the mother of Israel; see the opening of v. 6. The former would point to the punishment of the mother for the sin of her children. The text carries both meanings, which are complementary. **6:** *Teaching* translates Heb "torah." Many later Jewish readers and commentators understood the term "torah" as "the Torah," i.e., a reference to the traditional Jewish Torah. This notion of Torah is, however, much later than the time of the composition of the book of Hos. The association of *teaching* and priests here is common in prophetic literature (Jer. 18.18; Ezek. 7.26; 22.26; Zeph. 3.4; Hag. 2.11; Mal. 2.7). Within this context, "torah" or *teaching* points at the divine instructions that the priests were responsible for keeping and transmitting. **10:** The text imparts, at least by connotation, the following meaning: "... but not be sated; they shall play the whore, but not multiply." The image of sexual promiscuity is linked to the idea that since these sexual relations were illicit, they would "bear no fruit." (The text implies that the desired fruit of all sexual relations, even "illicit relations," is to have children.) **11:** A rendering of the first word as "whoredom" instead of *lechery* better reflects the emphatic repetition of terms (from the root "z-n-h") and the images they evoke that characterizes the Heb here, and that closely links it to chs 1–3. **12:** The same holds true for "spirit of whoredom" instead of *lecherous impulse.* The conclusion may also be translated more literally: "they have played the whore, forsaking their God," again hammering away at the root for "whore." The explanation in the translators' note at 1.2 in the NJPS reflects only one of the possible interpretations of the v.

13 They sacrifice on the mountaintops
And offer on the hills,
Under oaks, poplars, and terebinths
Whose shade is so pleasant.
That is why their[a] daughters fornicate
And their daughters-in-law commit adultery!
14 I will not punish their daughters for fornicating
Nor their daughters-in-law for committing adultery;
For they themselves [b]turn aside[-b] with whores
And sacrifice with prostitutes,
And a people that is without sense[c] must stumble.
15 If you are a lecher, Israel—
Let not Judah incur guilt—
Do not come to Gilgal,[d]
Do not make pilgrimages to Beth-aven,[e]
And do not swear by the LORD![f]

16 Ah, Israel has balked
Like a stubborn cow;
Therefore,
The LORD will graze him
On the range, like a sheep.[g]
17[h] Ephraim is addicted to images—
Let him be.
18 They drink to excess—
Their liquor turns against them.
They "love" beyond measure—
Disgrace is the "gift"
19 Which the wind [i]is bringing;[-i]
They shall garner shame from their sacrifices.

5 Hear this, O priests,
Attend, O House[j] of Israel,
And give ear, O royal house;
For right conduct is your responsibility!
But you have been a snare to Mizpah
And a net spread out over Tabor;
2 [b]For when trappers dug deep pitfalls,
I was the only reprover of them all.[-b]

a Heb. "your," here and through v. 14. *b-b Meaning of Heb. uncertain.*
c Cf. vv. 11–12.
d One who participates in the debaucheries of the open-air shrines is not fit to visit a temple building. *e Lit. "House of Delusion," substituted for Bethel (cf. Amos 4.4).*
f I.e., you are not fit to profess His religion; see Jer. 12.16.
g Instead of giving them fodder in return for their work; cf. Isa. 30.23–24.
h Meaning of vv. 17–19 uncertain in part.
i-i Lit. "has bound up in the corners of its garment"; see note at Mal. 3.20.
j Emendation yields "prophets."

14: Similarly, "I will not punish your daughters when they play the whore, nor your daughters-in-law when they commit adultery; for the men themselves go aside with whores, and sacrifice with prostitutes." **15:** Bethel and *Gilgal* were two main cultic centers in the Northern Kingdom of Israel (cf. Amos 4.4). *Beth-aven* (namely, "House of Iniquity" or "Delusion"; see translators' note *e*) is a sarcastic way of referring to Bethel. See also 12.12 ("if Gilgal is iniquity"—NJPS, "as for Gilead, it is worthless") and cf. 9.15. **16:** *On the range,* i.e., in a "broad pasture." The image of God as a shepherd is a common biblical and ancient Near Eastern image. It is very open-ended, and may refer to the munificent care of the ideal shepherd (Ps. 23), or the punishment of the straying sheep by the harsh shepherd (Ezek. ch 34). **17:** *Ephraim:* An alternative name for the Northern Kingdom that is widely used in the book of Hos. The first king and founder of the kingdom came from the tribe of Ephraim, and the territory of Ephraim remained at the heart of the kingdom until its very end. **18:** The second half of the v. connotes, "they surely fornicate (or commit acts of whoredom)."

5.1–15: Further denunciations of monarchic Israel and Judah and announcements of their punishment. 1: For the readership of the book, *Tabor* is symbolic of a high mountain (see Jer. 46.18; Ps. 89.13; cf. Tg.), which is a necessary feature for the literary gradation of height in the text from *Mizpah* (a city that evokes the image of a "watchtower") to Tabor and the eventual contrast in "dug deep" in v. 2a.

3 Yes, I have watched Ephraim,
Israel has not escaped my notice:
Behold, you have fornicated, O Ephraim;
Israel has defiled himself!
4 Their habits do not let them
Turn back to their God;
Because of the lecherous impulse within them,
They pay no heed to the LORD.
5 [a-]Israel's pride shall be humbled before
his very eyes,
As Israel and Ephraim fall because of their sin
(And Judah falls with them).
6 Then they will go with their sheep and cattle
To seek the LORD, but they will not find Him.[-a]

[b-]He has cast them off:[-b]
7 [Because] they have broken faith with the LORD,
Because [c-]they have[-c] begotten
Alien children.
Therefore, [b-]the new moon
Shall devour their portion.[-b]

8 Sound a ram's horn in Gibeah,
A trumpet in Ramah;
Give the alarm in Beth-aven;[d]
[e-]After you,[-e] Benjamin!
9 Ephraim is stricken with horror
On a day of chastisement.

Against the tribes[f] of Israel
I proclaim certainties:
10 The officers of Judah have acted
Like shifters of field boundaries;
On them I will pour out
My wrath like water.
11 Ephraim is defrauded,
Robbed of redress,
Because he has witlessly
Gone after futility.[g]
12 For it is I who am like rot to Ephraim,
Like decay to the House of Judah;[h]

a-a This passage would read well after 5.15; cf. 5.6 with 6.6.
b-b Meaning of Heb. uncertain. *c-c Emendation yields "He has."*
d The three towns named, in the territory of Benjamin, are now being wrested from Israel by Judah; see v. 10. *e-e Emendation yields "Stir up."*
f I.e., the kingdoms of Judah and Israel (Ephraim).
g Cf. Targum and Septuagint; but meaning of Heb. uncertain.
h Emendation yields "Israel."

4: *Lecherous impulse,* see 4.12 n. **5:** References to Judah are not minor parenthetical remarks, but major markers of where the interest of the present book lies (see, among others, 1.7; 3.5; 4.15; 5.5, 10, 12, 14; 6.11; 12.3). **6:** This echoes a common prophetic motif: Sacrifices alone are not sufficient to assure divine Presence (see esp. Isa. 1.10–17). **7:** *They have broken faith ... children:* Another translation, "They have been unfaithful to the LORD, for they have brought bastards to birth." *The new moon shall devour their portion:* The second half of the v. probably means that a "new time [namely, a new period] will destroy them with their lands." **8–14:** Some scholars argue that the passage may reflect the circumstances of the Syro-Ephraimitic war in 734–733 BCE, when Israel (Ephraim) and Aram (Syria) were allied in trying to force Judah to join them in a revolt against Assyria (see "History of Israel," pp. 2107–19), but this runs counter to the gist of the text, since at that time Israel stood against Assyria, rather than as her ally. **8:** The ram's horn (shofar) was used to call troops to war or to sound an alarm. *Beth-aven* (i.e., Bethel; see 4.15 n.), *Gibeah,* and *Ramah* are all close to each other in the territory of Benjamin (see map on p. 541). **10:** *Shifters of field boundaries:* Moving the boundary marker of a field, which was equivalent to stealing property, was a severe violation of proper behavior (see Deut. 19.14; 27.17; Prov. 22.28; admonitions against moving boundary markers occur elsewhere in the ancient Near East).

15: The idea of *seek*ing God *in their distress* is found in Deut. 4.29–30 as well. In general, there are many vocabulary links between Hos. and Deut. Some scholars attribute these links to the fact that Deut. was originally a northern work, and thus shares the vocabulary of the northern Hos. Others think the final form of Hos. was particularly influenced by Deut.

6.1–7.16: The LORD is reluctant to hear the people's appeal. Further condemnations of monarchic Israel and Judah. 6.1–3: The book quotes a human voice urging repentance, saying that just as God wounded, He will heal. The appearance of God is as assured as the daybreak, as refreshing as rain. **4:** A divine response to the earlier speech. Here and in the following vv. the images of daybreak and rain are turned on their head as they apply to monarchic Israel. YHVH is probably presented here in the image of a father who laments his inability to help a wayward son: *what can I do for you?* or, as others read, "what can I do with you?" The implied answer is "nothing." *Morning clouds ... dew,* both of which evaporate at the first warmth of day. Israel's good intentions do not last. **6:** Not a condemnation of sacrifice but rather a statement about the primacy of morality over sacrifices. Needless to say, sacrifices offered by those unworthy of bringing an offering to the deity are not efficacious (cf. 5.6; 8.13).

13 Yet when Ephraim became aware of his sickness,
Judah[a] of his sores,
Ephraim repaired to Assyria—
He sent envoys to a patron[b] king!
He will never be able to cure you,
Will not heal you of your sores.
14 No, I will be like a lion to Ephraim,
Like a great beast to the House of Judah;[a]
I, I will attack and stride away,
Carrying the prey that no one can rescue;
15 And I will return to My abode—
Till they realize their guilt.
In their distress, they will seek Me
And beg for My favor.

6 [c]"Come, let us turn back to the LORD:
He attacked, and He can heal us;
He wounded, and He can bind us up.
2 In two days He will make us whole again;
On the third day He will raise us up,
And we shall be whole by His favor.
3 Let us pursue obedience to the LORD,
And we shall become obedient.
His appearance is as sure as daybreak,
And He will come to us like rain,
Like latter rain that refreshes[d] the earth."

4 What can I do for you, Ephraim,
What can I do for you, Judah,[e]
When your goodness is like morning clouds,
Like dew so early gone?
5 That is why I have hewn down [f]the prophets,[-f]
Have slain them with the words of My mouth:
[g-]And the day that dawned [brought on] your punishment.[-g]
6 For I desire goodness, not sacrifice;
Obedience to God, rather than burnt offerings.
7[h] But they, to a man, have transgressed the Covenant.
This is where they have been false to Me:

a Emendation yields "Israel."
b Compare the verb ryb *in the sense of "to champion, uphold the cause of," in Isa. 1.17; 3.13; 19.20 end; 51.22.*
c As anticipated at the end of chapter 5, Israel seeks the LORD's favor; His answer begins with v. 4. *d Taking* yoreh *as equivalent of* yarweh.
e Emendation yields "Israel"; cf. "Ephraim ... Israel" in v. 10.
f-f Emendation yields "your children"; cf. 9.13.
g-g Cf. v. 3; but meaning of Heb. uncertain.
h Meaning of vv. 7–11 unclear in part.

8 Gilead is a city of evildoers,
Tracked up with blood.
9 The gang of priests is
Like the ambuscade of bandits
Who murder on the road to Shechem,
For they have encouraged[a] depravity.
10 In [b-]the House of Israel[-b] I have seen
A horrible thing;
Ephraim has fornicated there,
Israel has defiled himself.
11 [c-](Even Judah has reaped a harvest of you!)[-c]

7 When I would restore My people's fortunes,
1 When I would heal Israel,
The guilt of Ephraim reveals itself
And the wickedness of Samaria.
For they have acted treacherously,
With thieves breaking in
And bands raiding outside.
2 And they do not consider
That I remembered all their wickedness.
Why, their misdeeds have been all around them,[d]
They have been ever before Me.

3[e] In malice they make a king merry,
And officials in treachery.
4 They [f-]commit adultery,[-f] all of them,
Like an oven fired by a baker,
Who desists from stoking only
From the kneading of the dough to its leavening.
5 The day they made our king sick
[And] officials with the poison of wine,
[g-]He gave his hand to traitors.[-g]
6 [h-]For they approach their ambush
With their hearts like an oven:[-h]
Through the night
Their baker[i] has slept;
In the morning, it flares up
Like a blazing fire.
7 They all get heated like an oven
And devour their rulers—
None of them calls to Me.
All their kings have fallen [by their hand].

7.1: *Samaria,* the capital of the Northern Kingdom, and therefore another synonym for it (like *Ephraim;* see 4.17 n.). **5–6:** These vv. are difficult. NRSV renders them: "On the day of our king the officials/ became sick with the heat of wine;/ he stretched out his hand with mockers./ For they are kindled like an oven, their heart burns within them;/ all night their anger smolders;/ in the morning it blazes like a flaming fire."

a Heb. "done"; cf. 5.1–3. b-b Emendation yields "Beth-shean."
c-c Cf. 5.9–10; but meaning of clause uncertain. d Emendation yields "Me."
e Vv. 3–6 would read well in the order 4, 6, 3, 5. f-f Emendation yields "rage."
g-g I.e., he trusted traitors; but meaning of verse uncertain.
h-h Meaning of Heb. uncertain. i Emendation yields "rage."

11: Relying on other nations is viewed as tantamount to rebelling against God, a view governing other biblical texts, especially Isa. and Chron. (e.g., Isa. 31.1; 2 Chron. 16.7–9). The *silly dove* (*Ephraim*) will be caught in God's net (v. 12). *Egypt* and *Assyria* (cf. 11.5; 12.2) were the main powers of the period in which the book is set, and particularly toward the end of that period. They remained the two main powers until Babylonia replaced Assyria as the main northern power in the late 7th c. BCE. Reliance on Egypt vs. Assyria (later Babylonia) is a common theme in prophetic literature. Historically, however, the debacle of the Northern Kingdom followed its disastrous alliance with Aram, the main regional power that opposed Assyria at the time. Egypt's intervention in these events was quite marginal. But references to the Aram vs. Assyria conflict that predominated in the time period noted in the superscription of the book (1.1) is found nowhere in Hos. **16:** On Egyptian as a foreign or strange language, see Ps. 114.1.

8 [a-]Ephraim is among the peoples;
He is rotting away.
Ephraim is like a cake—
Incapable of turning.[-a]
9 Strangers have consumed his strength,
But he has taken no notice;
Also, mold[b] is scattered over him,
But he has taken no notice.
10 Though Israel's pride has been humbled
Before his very eyes,
They have not turned back
To their God the LORD;
They have not sought Him
In spite of everything.
11[c] Instead, Ephraim has acted
Like a silly dove with no mind:
They have appealed to Egypt!
They have gone to Assyria!
12 When they go, I will spread
My net over them,
I will bring them down
Like birds of the sky;
[a-]I will chastise them
When I hear their bargaining.[-a]
13 Woe to them
For straying from Me;
Destruction to them
For rebelling against Me!
For I was their Redeemer;
Yet they have plotted treason against Me.

14[c] But they did not cry out to Me sincerely
As they [d-]lay wailing.[-d]
They debauch[e] over new grain and new wine,
They are faithless[f] to Me.

15 *I* braced, *I* strengthened their arms,
And they plot evil against *Me!*
16 They come back;
They have been of no use,[g]
Like a slack bow.
Their officers shall fall by the sword,
Because of the stammering[h] of their tongues.

a-a Meaning of Heb. uncertain. *b Like Akkadian* shību; *others "gray hairs."*
c This verse would read well after 8.2. *d-d I.e., in penitence; cf. Isa.* 58.5.
e Cf. Aramaic gar/yegur *"to commit adultery"; for the thought, cf.* 4.11.
f Taking yasuru *as equivalent to* yasoru, *from* sarar; *cf.* 9.15 *end.*
g Meaning of Heb. uncertain. *h Cf. Arabic* zaghūm *and* zughmūm *"a stammerer."*

Such shall be [the results of] their jabbering[a]
In the land of Egypt.

8 [Put] a ram's horn to your mouth—
[b-]Like an eagle[-b] over the House of [c-]the LORD;[-c]
Because they have transgressed My covenant
And been faithless to My teaching.
2 Israel cries out to Me,
"O my God, we are devoted to You."[d]

3 Israel rejects what is good;
[e-]An enemy shall pursue him.[-e]
4 They have made kings,
But not with My sanction;
They have made officers,
But not of My choice.
Of their silver and gold
They have made themselves images,
To their own undoing.
5 [f-]He rejects[-f] your calf, Samaria!
I am furious with them!
Will they never be capable of [g-]purity?
6 For it was Israel's doing;[-g]
It was only made by a joiner,
It is not a god.
No, the calf of Samaria shall be
Reduced to splinters!

7 They sow wind,
And they shall reap whirlwind—
Standing stalks devoid of ears
And yielding no flour.
If they do yield any,
Strangers shall devour it.
8 Israel is bewildered;[h]
They have now become among the nations
Like an unwanted vessel,
9 [Like] a lonely wild ass.
For they have gone up to Assyria,
[i-]Ephraim has[-i] courted friendship.

a I.e., the negotiations conducted in the Egyptian language.
b-b Meaning of Heb. uncertain. *c-c Emendation yields "Israel."*
d See note c at 7.14. *e-e Emendation yields "They pursue delusion."* *f-f Emendation yields "I reject."*
g-g Emendation yields "understanding, / That House of Israel?"
h A play on words: The Heb. root bala', *which means "bewildered" here (cf. Isa. 28.7), means "devour" in the preceding verse.*
i-i Emendation yields "In Egypt they have."

8.1–14: On Israel's unfaithfulness to the LORD. 1: Traditional Jewish interpreters associated the *eagle* with Nebuchadnezzar (cf. Ezek. ch 17) who destroyed the Temple in 586; this association implies an identification of the House of the LORD with the Temple in Jerusalem. *The House of the LORD:* The reference to the legitimate House of the LORD was most likely understood as pointing to the Temple in Jerusalem by the Judahite readership of the book of Hos. For them, therefore, Israel in v. 3 must carry two meanings: Israel in the sense of the Northern Kingdom and Israel as the people in a covenantal relationship with the LORD, which includes both the Northern and Southern Kingdoms, as well as the intended readership of the book (later Jews). *My teaching* (Heb "torah") here and in 8.12 was later understood by many Jewish readers as "My Torah" (i.e., a reference to the traditional Jewish Torah). **4–6:** The mention of illegitimate *kings* may point to the rapid succession of kings in the last twenty-five years of the Northern Kingdom (see 1.4 n.), but in the light of 3.5 may well point to all northern kings, from Jeroboam I on, who from a Judahite perspective were illegitimate. The reference to the *images* (i.e., idols) and the *calf* (a young bull, usual representation of strength and fertility) seem to reinforce the latter interpretation (see 1 Kings 12.25–33). **8:** The beginning of the v. may be translated as "Israel is devoured"; cf. the last line of the previous v. and translators' note *h*.

12: The *teachings* (singular in Heb) of the LORD is conceived as a written document, just as "the word of the LORD that came to Hosea" (1.1) is the book of Hos., a written text too. See also 8.1 n. **13:** *Back to Egypt,* or more literally, "they shall go back to Egypt." The v. may have carried more than one meaning, either referring to the exile to Egypt or to a reversal of the exodus. Cf. Deut. 28.68, and see also 9.3. **14:** *Judah*'s sin is not the setting up of multiple religious centers or the calf statues, as *Israel* had done; but Judah had also sinned, perhaps by not relying sufficiently on God to defend them (see 7.11 n.) The expression *I will set fire to* ... / *and it shall consume* ... appears also in Amos 1.4, 7, 10, 12; 2.2, 5 (compare in particular the text here with Amos 2.5. When readers read one text, they were reminded of the other).

9.1–17: On the results of divine punishment. 1: *You have strayed away,* lit. "For you [male] have committed deeds of whoredom" (cf. 1.2; 2.7; 3.3; 4.10, 12, 13, 14, 15, 18; 5.3; and see previous nn.). **1–2:** The *threshing floor* and the *winepress,* along with the references to joy, create an image of agricultural festivals (e.g., the harvest festival). The mention of the threshing floor under these circumstances (cf. Ruth ch 3) and the explicit reference to a *harlot's fee* and the statement *you have strayed* (lit. "you committed deeds of whoredom") all contribute to the atmosphere of illicit sexual activity. In the book of Hos. these images are associated with the theme of Israel's abandoning YHVH. The precise metaphor here was already a matter of debate among traditional Jewish interpreters. Is the male worshipping other gods, as *other peoples* do, and so presented as abandoning the LORD, a husband figure, and therefore compared to a female prostitute (a common image in the book; cf. Radak)? Or is the male happy to receive his grain as a present from his gods—not YHVH, and therefore compared to a prostitute coming to pick up her fees (Rashi)? The two

10 And while they are courting among the nations,
[a]-There I will hold them fast;-[a]
[b]-And they shall begin to diminish in number
From the burden of king [and] officers.-[b]

11 For Ephraim has multiplied altars—for guilt;
His altars have redounded to his guilt:
12 The many teachings I wrote for him
Have been treated as something alien.
13 [b]-When they present sacrifices to Me,-[b]
It is but flesh for them to eat:
The LORD has not accepted them.
Behold, He remembers their iniquity,
He will punish their sins:
Back to Egypt with them!
14 Israel has ignored his Maker
And built temples
(And Judah has fortified many cities).
So I will set fire to his cities,
And it shall consume their fortresses.

9

Rejoice not, O Israel,
As other peoples exult;
For you have strayed
Away from your God:
[c]-You have loved a harlot's fee
By every threshing floor of new grain.
2 Threshing floor and winepress
Shall not join them,
And the new wine shall betray her.-[c]
3 They shall not be able to remain
In the land of the LORD.
But Ephraim shall return to Egypt
And shall eat unclean food in Assyria.[d]
4 It shall be for them like the food of mourners,
All who partake of which are defiled.
They will offer no libations of wine to the LORD,
And no sacrifices of theirs will be
    pleasing to Him;
But their food will be only for their hunger,
It shall not come into the House of the LORD.
5 What will you do about feast days,
About the festivals of the LORD?

a-a Cf. 9.6; but meaning of Heb. uncertain. *b-b Meaning of Heb. uncertain.*
c-c Emendation and rearrangement yield: "You have loved fornication / By every threshing floor and press; / The new grain shall not join them, / And the new wine shall fail them."
d The lands of the heathen and the food there are unclean; cf. Ezek. 4.13; Amos 7.17.

6 Behold, they have gone [a-]from
destruction[-a]
[With] the silver they treasure.
Egypt shall [b-]hold them fast,[-b]
Moph[c] shall receive them in burial.
Weeds are their heirs;
Prickly shrubs occupy their [old] homes.
7 The days of punishment have come
For your heavy guilt;
The days of requital have come—
Let Israel know it!

The prophet was distraught,
The inspired man driven mad
By constant harassment.
8 Ephraim watches for [d-]my God.
As for the prophet,[-d]
Fowlers' snares are on all his paths,
Harassment in the House of his God.
9 They have been as grievously corrupt
As in the days of Gibeah;[e]
He will remember their iniquity,
He will punish their sins.

10 I found Israel [as pleasing]
As grapes in the wilderness;
Your fathers seemed to Me
[f-]Like the first fig to ripen on a fig tree.[-f]
But when they came to Baal-peor,
They turned aside to shamefulness;[g]
[h-]Then they became as detested
As they had been loved.[-h]
11 From birth, from the womb, from
conception
Ephraim's glory shall be
Like birds that fly away.[i]
12 Even if they rear their infants,
I will bereave them of men.
[j-]Woe to them indeed
When I turn away from them![-j]

a-a Emendation yields "to Assyria." *b-b Cf. 8.10.*
c Believed to be Memphis, elsewhere called Noph.
d-d Emendation yields "the prophet of my God." *e See Judg. 19–20.*
f-f Emendation yields "like a ripe fig in a waterless waste"; cf. 13.5.
g Cf. Num. 25.1–3. *h-h Meaning of Heb. uncertain.*
i V. 16 would read well after v. 11.
j-j Emendation yields: "Even if they wean their babes, / They shall be dismayed because of them."

readings may be complementary. In any case, although the peoples may rejoice, Israel will have no reason for joy since the threshing floor and the winepress will not join them, i.e., they will not provide them with food or drink. Even the *new wine* will disappoint them. In sum, the text plays again with the motif of God as the Provider, who ceases to provide for His sinful, whoring wife. Israel is first represented as a male (v. 1), and then the image shifts to a female character *(her)* when the theme of the provider who ceases to provide is fully developed (v. 2). For proposed emendations of the text see translators' note *c-c* on p. 1144. **6:** *Moph,* Memphis, one of the most important cities in Egypt. **9:** *The days of Gibeah,* see Judg. chs 19–20; Hos. 10.9. **10:** Although there are idyllic elements in the depiction of Israel's past (cf. Jer. 2.2; 31.2), it is viewed as fundamentally problematic, as in Ps. 106. The positive elements serve here to enhance the negative description of Israel's past. *Baal-peor,* see Num. ch 25; Deut. 4.3–4. In the stories alluded to, sinful sexual behavior is associated with the two places. **11–12:** Illicit sexual relations do not provide offspring (cf. 4.10 n.).

13: *Tyre,* a major Phoenician city-port and an important regional power. The area under its control bordered on Israel; it was often, but not always, an ally of Israel. **15:** *My House,* see 8.1 n.

10.1–15: The vine and the heifer: Agricultural images show Israel's failure and consequent ruin.
1: *Cult pillars:* Pillars and altars were part of a cultic site (cf. Exod. 24.4–5); many have been excavated in Israel. During the monarchic period pillars were also involved in the worship of the LORD. Several biblical texts command the destruction of altars and pillars used in the worship of gods other than the LORD (e.g., Exod. 34.13; Deut. 7.5; 12.3); others condemn the making and use of pillars in general (Lev. 26.1).

13 [a-]It shall go with Ephraim
As I have seen it go with Tyre,
Which was planted in a meadow;[-a]
Ephraim too must bring out
His children to slayers.
14 Give them, O LORD—give them what?
Give them a womb that miscarries,
And shriveled breasts!
15 All their misfortune [began] at Gilgal,
For there I disowned them.[b]
For their evil deeds
I will drive them out of My House.
I will accept them no more;
[c-]All their officials are[-c] disloyal.

16[d] Ephraim[e] is stricken,
Their stock is withered;
They can produce no fruit.
Even if they do bear children,
I will slay their cherished offspring.

17 My God rejects them
Because they have not obeyed Him,
And they shall go wandering
Among the nations.

10 Israel is a ravaged vine
And its fruit is like it.
When his fruit was plentiful,
He made altars aplenty;
When his land was bountiful,
Cult pillars abounded.
2 Now that his boughs[f] are broken up,
He feels his guilt;
He himself pulls apart his altars,
Smashes his pillars.

3 Truly, now they say,
"We have no king;
For, since we do not fear the LORD,
What can a king do to us?"
4 So they conclude agreements and make
covenants
With false oaths,

a-a *Meaning of Heb. uncertain.* b *The specific allusion is uncertain.*
c-c *Emendation yields "They are all."* d *V. 16 would read well after v. 11.*
e *Targum reads "Their crown," i.e., of a tree.*
f *Cf. 2 Sam. 18.14, where the word is rendered "thick growth."*

And justice [a]degenerates into poison weeds,
Breaking out[a] on the furrows of the fields.

5 The inhabitants of Samaria fear
For the calf of Beth-aven;[b]
Indeed, its people and priestlings,
[c]Whose joy it once was,[c]
Mourn over it for the glory
That is departed from it.
6 It too shall be brought to Assyria
As tribute to a patron[d] king;
Ephraim shall be chagrined,
Israel shall be dismayed
Because of his plans.[e]
7 Samaria's monarchy[f] is vanishing
Like foam upon water,
8 Ruined shall be the shrines of [Beth-]aven,[b]
That sin of Israel.
Thorns and thistles
Shall grow on their altars.
They shall call to the mountains, "Bury us!"
To the hills, "Fall on us!"

9 You have sinned more, O Israel,
Than in the days of Gibeah.[g]
[c]There they stand [as] at Gibeah!
Shall they not be overtaken
By a war upon scoundrels
10 As peoples gather against them?[c]

When I chose [them], I broke them in,
Harnessing them for two furrows.
11 Ephraim became a trained heifer,
But preferred to thresh;
I [h]placed a yoke
Upon her sleek neck.[h]
I will make Ephraim [i]do advance plowing;[i]
Judah[j] shall do [main] plowing!
Jacob shall do final plowing!
12 "Sow righteousness for yourselves;
Reap [k]the fruits of[k] goodness;

5: *Priestlings,* a derogatory term for the priests of Samaria, who were condemned before (see ch 4; cf. Zeph. 1.4 in reference to Judah). *Beth-aven,* see 4.15 n. **9:** *Gibeah,* see 9.9 n. **11–15:** Instead of plowing correctly, Israel, the trained heifer, plows wickedness. **11:** *Ephraim ... Judah ... Jacob,* together, the totality of Israel. The three kinds of *plowing* suggest the initial breaking up of the ground, then plowing to cover the seed, then plowing (or "harrowing" [cf. NRSV]) to clear the ground for the next cycle. **12:** Cf. 8.7. The text is difficult, and can also be translated as: "Sow righteousness for yourselves; / reap according to [divine] kindness; / break up for yourselves fallow ground; / for it is time to seek the LORD / till He comes and teaches you righteousness" (or perhaps, "rains righteousness upon you" [cf. NRSV]).

a-a Cf. Amos 6.12; lit. "breaks out like poison weeds." *b See note e at 4.15.*
c-c Meaning of Heb. uncertain. *d See note b at 5.13.*
e Emendation yields "image," referring to the calf.
f The Heb. verb agrees with this word, not with "Samaria." *g See note at 9.9.*
h-h Lit. "passed over the comeliness of its neck."
i-i Taking rkb *in the sense of the Arabic* krb.
j Emendation yields "Israel." *k-k Lit. "according to."*

14: *Shalman* is probably a reference to Shalmaneser V (727–722 BCE), king of Assyria, who attacked and defeated Israel. The imagery regarding the fate of women and children is relatively common; see 2 Kings 8.12; Isa. 13.16; Hos. 14.1; Nah. 3.10; Ps. 137.9.

11.1–11: On consistent paternal love for a rebellious son. 1–4: The father-child relationship is used often in prophetic books as a metaphor for the relation between God and Israel. The child is often stubborn and rebellious and is chastised by the father, but the father nonetheless loves the child. As in the case of the husband-wife metaphor, many of today's readers may find the image of a father severely punishing his son troublesome, even if the father is presented as loving. (Corporal punishment was assumed to be beneficial in Israel, as in much of the pre-modern world; see e.g., Prov. 13.24.) The paternal metaphor, however, was commonly used in the ancient Near East to express the relation between ruler and ruled, sovereign and subject. It is not incongruous for prophets to mix metaphors, such as Israel as God's wife and as God's child.

Break for yourselves betimes fresh ground
Of seeking the LORD,
So that you may obtain [a-]a teacher[-a]
of righteousness."
13 You have plowed wickedness,
You have reaped iniquity—
[And] you shall eat the fruits of treachery—
Because you relied on your way,[b]
On your host of warriors.
14 But the din of war shall arise in your
own people,
And all your fortresses shall be ravaged
As Beth-arbel was ravaged by Shalman[c]
On a day of battle,
When mothers and babes were dashed to death
together.
15 This [d-]is what Bethel has done to you[-d]
For your horrible wickedness:
[e-]At dawn[-e] shall Israel's monarchy
Utterly perish.

11 I fell in love with Israel
When he was still a child;
And I have called [him] My son
Ever since Egypt.
2[f] Thus were they called,
But they went their own way;
They sacrifice to Baalim[g]
And offer to carved images.
3 I have pampered Ephraim,
Taking them in My[h] arms;
But they have ignored
My healing care.
4 I drew them with human ties,
With cords of love;
But I seemed to them as one
Who imposed a yoke on their jaws,
Though I was offering them food.
5 No!
They return to the land of Egypt,

a-a Meaning of Heb. uncertain; Septuagint reads "the fruits."
b Septuagint reads "chariots."
c Perhaps identical with the Shallum of 2 Kings 15.10 ff.; cf. the atrocities of Shallum's rival, ibid., v. 16.
d-d Emendation yields "will I do to you, O House of Israel."
e-e Meaning, perhaps, "swiftly as the dawn"; cf. v. 7 above, "like foam upon water."
f Meaning of parts of vv. 2–7 uncertain.
g Emendation yields "calves"; cf. 8.4–6; 13.2. *h Heb. "his."*

And Assyria is their king.
Because they refuse to repent,
6 A sword shall descend upon their towns[a]
And consume their limbs
And devour [b-][them] because of their designs.[-b]
7 [c-]For My people persists
In its defection from Me;
When it is summoned upward,
It does not rise at all.[-c]

8 How can I give you up, O Ephraim?
How surrender you, O Israel?
How can I make you like Admah,
Render you like Zeboiim?[d]
I have had a change of heart,
All My tenderness is stirred.
9 I will not act on My wrath,
Will not turn to destroy Ephraim.
For I am God, not man,
[c-]The Holy One in your midst:
I will not come in fury.[-c]

10 The LORD will roar like a lion,
And they shall march behind Him;
When He roars, His children shall come
Fluttering out of the west.
11 They shall flutter from Egypt like sparrows,
From the land of Assyria like doves;
And I will settle them in their homes
—declares the LORD.

12 Ephraim surrounds Me with deceit,
The House of Israel with guile.[e]
[c-](But Judah stands firm with God
And is faithful to the Holy One.)[-c]
2 Ephraim tends the wind
And pursues the gale;
He is forever adding
Illusion to calamity.[f]
Now they make a covenant with Assyria,
Now oil is carried to Egypt.[g]

8: *Admah* and *Zeboiim,* examples of cities that were utterly destroyed (see, among others, Deut. 29.22). **9:** God's change of heart and the decision not to obliterate Ephraim (cf. Jonah ch 3) are associated with the phrase *For I am God, not man.* The very same language is used to convey the opposite meaning in Num. 23.19.

a Emendation yields "bodies," lit. "skins"; cf. Job 18.13.
b-b Emendation yields "their bones." *c-c Meaning of Heb. uncertain.*
d Admah and Zeboiim were destroyed with neighboring Sodom and Gomorrah; cf. Gen. 10.19; 14.2, 8; Deut. 29.22.
e I.e., the deceit and guile they practice on each other (below vv. 8–9) is constantly noted by the LORD. *f Septuagint reads "futility."*
g I.e., they foolishly depend on alliances instead of on the LORD; cf. 5.13; 7.10–11.

12.1–14.1: Further condemnation of Israel and its consequences. 12.3: Here Judah is singled out, rather than being the poetic parallel of Israel. **4–5:** See Gen. 25.26; 27.36; 32.23–33. Such recollections of ancestral traditions (see also v. 13) are relatively rare in prophetic discourse. **11:** The reference to the LORD speaking in *parables* to the prophets helps us to understand how prophetic words were understood in antiquity. **13:** An allusion to Gen. ch 29, the story of Jacob's flight to Laban and his marriage to Leah and Rachel. Sections of Hos. that retell these ancestral stories are used as the haftarah for the corresponding portions of Gen. **14:** The *prophet* is Moses, who is considered to be the greatest prophet (see, e.g., Deut. 34.10; Exod. 23.20; Num. 20.16). The text carries three complementary meanings: (1) through a prophet (i.e., Moses), YHVH brought Israel from Egypt, and by a prophet (i.e., Moses) it was guarded (cf. Deut. 4.14–19); (2) through a prophet (i.e., Moses), YHVH brought Israel from Egypt, and by a prophet (i.e., someone other than Moses and in a period later than the exodus and purposefully not identified in the text) it was guarded and (3) through a prophet YHVH brought Israel up from Egypt (Moses), and by a prophet it has *guarded* itself. The second and third reading conveyed an association between the foundational prophet (Moses) and the prophetic office and the actual prophets necessary for Israel to guard itself after Moses.

3 The LORD once indicted Judah,[a]
And punished Jacob for his conduct,
Requited him for his deeds.
4 In the womb he tried to supplant his brother;
Grown to manhood, he strove with a
divine being,[b]
5 He strove with an angel and prevailed—
The other had to weep and implore him.
At Bethel [Jacob] would meet him,
There to commune with him.[c]
6 Yet the LORD, the God of Hosts,
Must be invoked as "LORD."[d]
7 You must return to your God!
Practice goodness and justice,
And constantly trust in your God.

8 A trader who uses false balances,
Who loves to overreach,
9 Ephraim thinks,
"Ah, I have become rich;
I have gotten power!
[e-]All my gains do not amount
To an offense which is real guilt."[-e]
10 I the LORD have been your God
Ever since the land of Egypt.
I will let you dwell in your tents[f] again
As in the days of old,[g]
11 When I spoke to the prophets;
For I granted many visions,
[e-]And spoke parables through the prophets.
12 As for Gilead, it is worthless;
And to no purpose[-e] have they
Been sacrificing oxen in Gilgal:
The altars of these are also
Like stone heaps upon a plowed field.[h]

13 Then Jacob had to flee[i] to the land of Aram;
There Israel served for a wife,
For a wife he had to guard [sheep].
14 But when the LORD
Brought Israel up from Egypt,

a *Presumably the patriarch Judah. Emendation would yield "Israel"; cf. next note.*
b *Cf. Gen. 25.26 and 32.29.* *c* *Heb. "us."*
d *I.e., one should not invoke any of the angelic hosts.*
e-e *Meaning of Heb. uncertain.* *f* *I.e., securely; see 2 Kings 13.5.*
g *Lit. "fixed season."*
h *I.e., the cults of Gilead and Gilgal are as worthless as that of Bethel.*
i *This is the punishment mentioned in 12.3.*

It was through a prophet;[a]
Through a prophet[a] they were guarded.
15b Ephraim gave bitter offense,
And his Lord cast his crimes upon him
And requited him for his mockery.

13 When Ephraim spoke piety,
He was exalted in Israel;
But he incurred guilt through Baal,[c]
And so he died.
2 And now they go on sinning;
They have made them molten images,
Idols, by their skill, from their silver,
Wholly the work of craftsmen.
[d-]Yet for these they appoint men to sacrifice;[-d]
They are wont to kiss calves!
3 Assuredly,
They shall be like morning clouds,
Like dew so early gone;
Like chaff whirled away from the threshing floor.
And like smoke from a lattice.
4 Only I the LORD have been your God
Ever since the land of Egypt;
You have never known a [true] God but Me,
You have never had a helper other than Me.
5 I looked after you in the desert,
In a thirsty land.
6 When they grazed, they were sated;
When they were sated, they grew haughty;
And so they forgot Me.
7 So I am become like a lion to them,
Like a leopard I lurk on the way;
8 Like a bear robbed of her young I attack them
And rip open the casing of their hearts;
[e-]I will devour them there like a lion,[-e]
The beasts of the field shall mangle them.

9 [d-]You are undone, O Israel!
You had no help but Me.[-d]
10 Where now is your king?
Let him save you!
Where are the chieftains in all your towns
From whom you demanded:
"Give me a king and officers"?

a I.e., not through an angel. *b Meaning of 12.15–13.1 uncertain.*
c I.e., Baal-peor; cf. 9.10. *d-d Meaning of Heb. uncertain.*
e-e Emendation yields "There dogs shall devour them"; cf. Septuagint.

13.2–4: As elsewhere in the Bible, the book is assuming that the calves are not alternate ways of depicting the LORD, as many northern Israelites likely believed, but represent foreign deities. **3:** *Morning clouds ... dew,* see 6.4 n. *Chaff ... smoke,* further images of evanescence. **7:** The image of the LORD as a *lion* is common in the prophetic books (cf. Amos 3.8). In Hos. it is clearly a double-edged image. It may point to restoration and hope (11.10–11) or horrifying punishment (5.14; 13.7–8). God is powerful to punish and to restore. A reader who understands the described punishment as a past event and sees the restoration as still standing in the future can find much solace in this imagery. **10:** The institution of human kingship is viewed negatively here, as a rejection of God's kingship, as in some of the narratives concerning the origins of the monarchy (see, e.g., 1 Sam. 10.17–19).

11 I give you kings in my ire,
And take them away in My wrath.

12 Ephraim's guilt is bound up,
His sin is stored away.[a]
13 Pangs of childbirth assail him,
[b-]And the babe is not wise—
For this is no time to survive
At the birthstool of babes.[-b]

14c From Sheol itself I will save them,
Redeem them from very Death.
Where, O Death, are your plagues?
Your pestilence where, O Sheol?
[d-]Revenge shall be far from My thoughts.[-d]
15 For though he flourish among reeds,
A blast, a wind of the LORD,
Shall come blowing up from the wilderness;
His fountain shall be parched,
His spring dried up.
That [wind] shall plunder treasures,
Every lovely object.

14

Samaria must bear her guilt,
For she has defied her God.
They shall fall by the sword,
Their infants shall be dashed to death,
And their women with child ripped open.

2 Return, O Israel, to the LORD your God,
For you have fallen because of your sin.
3 Take words with you
And return to the LORD.
Say to Him:
[b-]"Forgive all guilt
And accept what is good;
Instead of bulls we will pay
[The offering of] our lips.[-b]
4 Assyria shall not save us,
No more will we ride on steeds;[e]
Nor ever again will we call
Our handiwork our god,
Since in You alone orphans find pity!"

a I.e., for future retribution. *b-b Meaning of Heb. uncertain.*
c This verse would read well before 14.5.
d-d Lit. "Satisfaction (for this meaning of nḥm *see Deut. 32.36; Isa. 1.24) shall be hidden from My eyes."*
e I.e., we will no longer depend on an alliance with Egypt; cf. 2 Kings 18.24 (Isa. 36.9); Isa. 30.16.

13: *The babe is not wise … birthstool of babes,* a metaphor in which the son is partially compared to a woman in labor. The son will suffer the pains associated with childbirth. This child is so unwise that "at the right time he does not come to the birthstool (author's translation)," i.e., he resists birth, endangering himself and the one who gives birth and prolonging her (and here, his) pain. The birth here symbolizes the turning of the heart necessary for a new beginning. In other words, if Ephraim repents soon it will end its suffering and begin a new era of divine blessing, but Ephraim, a foolish son, does not do so. **14:** *Sheol,* the netherworld, the land of the dead. The LORD will save Israel even from Sheol, if Israel repents. **15:** *Though he flourish among reeds,* a double word-play: Ephraim and *flourish* sound similar in Heb, but more importantly so do *reeds* or "marshes" and "brothers" (Rashi favors the first meaning, Radak, the second). *Reeds* might be an allusion to Egypt; "brothers," a reference to the place of Ephraim at the head of his brothers (the other northern tribes; cf. Gen. 48.19). *A blast, a wind,* Heb "an east wind." The east wind is a dry, scorching wind and is often associated with disaster and/or God's power (Exod. 14.21; Isa. 27.8; Jer. 18.17; cf. Gen. 41.6). If the reference to reeds is an allusion to Egypt, then this wind may be reminiscent of the east wind at the Reed Sea (Exod. 14.21; 15.8). **14.1:** Cf. 10.14. **2–9:** *Return, O Israel:* Because of the powerful call for repentance and hope it conveys and the high poetic languages it uses, 14.1–10 eventually became a classical text in Jewish tradition and liturgy. As mentioned in the intro., it is read on Shabbat Shuvah (the Shabbat that precedes Yom Kippur) and in the afternoon service of Tish'ah be'av (Sephardic and Yemenite traditions). As in Deut. ch 30, once Israel returns, God returns to take them back. **4:** *Find pity* recalls "Lo-ruhamah" of 1.8 and its reversal in 2.3. The v. as a whole is a rejection by Israel of its past behavior, rejecting improper political alliances and foreign deities.

5 I will heal their affliction,[a]
Generously will I take them back in love;
For My anger has turned away from them.[b]
6 I will be to Israel like dew;
He shall blossom like the lily,
He shall strike root like a [c]Lebanon tree.[-c]
7 His boughs shall spread out far,
His beauty shall be like the olive tree's,
His fragrance like that of Lebanon.
8 They who sit in his shade shall be revived:
They shall bring to life new grain,
They shall blossom like the vine;
His scent shall be like the wine of Lebanon.[d]
9 Ephraim [shall say]:
"What more have I to do with idols?
When I respond and look to Him,
I become like a verdant cypress."
[e]Your fruit is provided by Me.[-e]

10 He who is wise will consider these words,
He who is prudent will take note of them.
For the paths of the LORD are smooth;
The righteous can walk on them,
While sinners stumble on them.

6–7: With God bringing nourishment to Israel like the dew brings water to the land, Israel will flourish like the best trees—beautiful like the lily in bloom and like the olive tree, strongly rooted and fragrant like the cedars of Lebanon. **8:** Contrast with 9.1–2. **10:** The prophetic word should not merely be heard once, but must be carefully studied (see intro. to the Twelve).

a For this meaning of meshubah *see Jer. 2.19; 3.22.* *b Heb. "him."*
c-c Emendation yields "poplar." *d Emendation yields "Helbon"; cf. Ezek. 27.18.*
e-e Meaning of Heb. uncertain.

יואל

Joel

THE BOOK OF JOEL is an unusual prophetic book. Although it contains readings in the form of oracles, announcements of judgment against the nations, and promises of an ideal future, it does not follow the structure of most prophetic books, where prophets deliver divine oracles of doom or consolation. Instead, the readers of the book of Joel are asked to imagine a terrifying plague of locusts and its horrifying impact on society and the natural environment. Then the locusts become a mighty army sent by the LORD against Judah. As the text leads the readers to sense that human society and culture in Judah are at the brink of obliteration, it asks them to identify with a prophetic voice that calls on them to return to the LORD, to fast and lament. The book concludes with Judah's salvation and a range of passages describing the ideal future, in which the fate of the nations figures prominently.

Unlike many other prophetic books (e.g., Hosea, Amos, Micah, Zechariah) the book is not set in any particular era of Israel's past. There is no mention in Joel 1.1 of any particular king or any datable event. References to an invasion by an enemy are not specific. The lack of specificity regarding events in Israel's past (locust plagues were not uncommon) and the overall imagery of the book encourage its readers to understand it against the background of Israel's past in general.

In the view of most scholars, the book of Joel dates to the Persian period (539–332 BCE), and most likely the period around 400–350. The reference to *Ionians* (Greek inhabitants from Ionia, a region in western Asia Minor, today's Turkey) in 4.6 is often mentioned among the grounds for this dating. More important, the book of Joel has an "anthological quality." In a relatively large number of cases, the book seems to be quoting, commenting on, or elaborating on other biblical, mainly prophetic, texts. This adds prestige to the human speaker of the book, whom the readers would have imagined as a learned individual—a living depository or an embodiment of godly texts and a re-shaper of them.

The book shows apocalyptic concerns. Some scholars think that it represents some form of transitional or hybrid work that stands between prophetic and apocalyptic writings; given its likely date of composition, this is quite possible. Certainly, the book conveys images and reassurances of "once and for all" actions of the LORD on behalf of Judah and Jerusalem, and against those who persecuted them. Moreover, it implies that this future is already known to those able to read the book of Joel (i.e., the scribes of Yehud) and to those to whom they may read the book (i.e., the vast majority of the people of Yehud who did not know how to read).

There are several possible ways to understand the structure of Joel. Each points to a particular but partial reading that emphasizes certain aspects of the book and de-emphasizes others. These partial readings inform each other, and all together create a much richer meaning. The following is one of these possible outlines:

I. Superscription (1.1).
II. A set of prophetic readings that concerns mostly divine judgment against Judah and its response (1.2–2.17).

III. A set of prophetic readings that concerns mostly divine forgiveness and future restoration for Judah along with judgment and calamity for its enemies (2.18–4.21).

Standard Christian translations divide the book into three chapters: 1.1–20 (as here); 2.1–32 (including the current text's 2.1–27, plus 3.1–5); and 3.1–21 (corresponding to the current text's 4.1–21). The division of biblical books into chapters dates to medieval times and originated within Christianity. The first rabbinic Bible (1517) shows the then popular division of the text of Joel in three chapters, but the second rabbinic Bible and all subsequent Hebrew Bibles, including the NJPS divide the book into four chapters.

Joel 2.15–27 is included in the haftarah for Shabbat Shuvah (the Shabbat that precedes Yom Kippur) in several Jewish traditions (e.g., Ashkenazi, Conservative) because of its theme of repentance, lamentation, divine forgiveness, and restoration. The theme is certainly appropriate for the ʿAseret Yemei Teshuvah ("Ten Days of Repentance" from Rosh Ha-Shanah to Yom Kippur). Note especially the conclusion of the reading, 2.27.

[EHUD BEN ZVI]

1 The word of the LORD that came to Joel son of Pethuel.

2 Listen to this, O elders,
Give ear, all inhabitants of the land.
Has the like of this happened in your days
Or in the days of your fathers?
3 Tell your children about it,
And let your children tell theirs,
And their children the next generation!
4 What the cutter[a] has left, the locust has devoured;
What the locust has left, the grub has devoured;
And what the grub has left, the hopper has devoured.
5 Wake up, you drunkards, and weep,
Wail, all you swillers of wine—
For the new wine that is [b]denied you![b]
6 For a nation has invaded my land,
Vast beyond counting,
With teeth like the teeth of a lion,
With the fangs of a lion's breed.
7 They have laid my vines waste
And splintered my fig trees:
They have stripped off their bark and thrown [it] away;
Their runners have turned white.

a The Heb. terms translated "cutter, locust, grub, and hopper" are of uncertain meaning; they probably designate stages in the development of the locust.
b-b Lit. "cut off from your mouth."

1.1: Superscription. The superscription introduces the book and characterizes it as YHVH's word, as a prophetic book. As mentioned above, Joel is not set in any particular period. Readers, beginning in ancient times, have suggested various settings. In Jewish tradition, Joel is associated with at least three different periods: (1) the days of Jehoram, the son of Ahab (*b. Taʿan.* 5a), (2) the time of Samuel (Joel is the son of Samuel, who eventually repented and turned into a prophet, according to Rashi and others), and (3) the time of Manasseh *(Seder ʿOlam)*. *Joel,* like its inverted form Elijah, probably means "the LORD is God."

1.2–2.17: On divine judgment against Judah and its response. **1.2–3: A call to read the text.** This call emphasizes the link between generations, and thus the everlasting truth and relevance of what follows.

1.4–2.17: On the plague of locusts and the corresponding communal cry (or lamentation) to the LORD. **4:** *Cutter ... locust ... grub ... hopper:* There are many references to locusts in ancient Near Eastern texts and some associate the imagery of swarms of locusts with that of large invading armies or troops. The use of these four terms may represent an attempt to convey a sense of completeness, rather than express a biological, detailed focus. Abravanel understands the text as metaphorical: The four kinds of locusts stand for four nations that will rule over Israel—Babylonia, Persia, Greece, and Rome. **7:** *Vines ... fig trees,* a reversal of a traditional image of agrarian peace (cf. Mic. 4.4; Zech. 3.10).

8 Lament—like a maiden girt with sackcloth
For the husband of her youth!
9 Offering and libation have ceased
From the House of the LORD;
The priests must mourn
Who minister to the LORD.
10 The country is ravaged,
The ground must mourn;
For the new grain is ravaged,
The new wine is dried up,
The new oil has failed.
11 Farmers are dismayed
And vine dressers wail
Over wheat and barley;
For the crops of the field are lost.
12 The vine has dried up,
The fig tree withers,
Pomegranate, palm, and apple—
All the trees of the field are sear.
And joy has dried up
Among men.

13 Gird yourselves and lament, O priests,
Wail, O ministers of the altar;
Come, spend the night in sackcloth,
O ministers of my God.
For offering and libation are withheld
From the House of your God.
14 Solemnize a fast,
Proclaim an assembly;
Gather the elders—all the inhabitants of the land—
In the House of the LORD your God,
And cry out to the LORD.

15 Alas for the day!
For the day of the LORD is near;
It shall come like havoc from Shaddai.[a]
16 For food is cut off
Before our very eyes,
And joy and gladness
From the House of our God.
17 [b-]The seeds have shriveled
Under their clods.[-b]
The granaries are desolate,
Barns are in ruins,
For the new grain has failed.

a Traditionally "the Almighty"; see Gen. 17.1. *b-b Meaning of Heb. uncertain.*

The speaker is presented as one who owns vines and fig trees. **8:** *Maiden,* Heb "betulah," means a young woman of marriageable age; here, a newly married woman. *Husband of her youth,* an emotive counterpart to the expression "wife of his youth" (cf. Isa. 54.6; Mal. 2.14–15; Prov. 1.5). The association of Judah in distress with a powerless, lamenting (young) woman is common in the Bible, and parallels exist in other ancient Near Eastern literature. Such imagery suggests, or creates an expectation for, a redemptive action by a caring (male) patron, who in this case would be YHVH. Usually such references to women point directly at or seem to suggest some negatively valued behavior on the part of the woman, here Judah, which within the world of the text justifies her present situation. The last part of the v. appears in a well-known poetic lament ("qinah") recited on the Ninth of Av, the traditional day of fasting and mourning for the destruction of the Temple. **9:** The text shifts from the young woman in one v. to an indirect reference to the LORD in the next, and to the (male) *priests* who are (partially) responsible for keeping an effective and positive interaction between the people and God. **12:** *Among men* (Heb "min-bnei 'adam"), "among the people." **13:** The priests and many others believed that the daily offerings were a prerequisite to divine beneficence; the plague would thus be viewed as an extreme disaster. **14:** *Fast … cry out,* cf. 2.15. The actions are a typical response to an upcoming disaster (cf. Jonah 3.6–8). This v. serves in *b. Ta'an.* 12b to explain that work is prohibited on a fast day, because it should be treated as a day of a solemn assembly, on which work is forbidden.

1.15–20: The cry. 15: *Day of the LORD* (cf. Isa. 13.6; Ezek. 30.2, 3; Obad. 1.15; Zeph. 1.14–15, among others), a relatively common term in prophetic literature. It points to a time when the LORD dramatically alters the normal order of things. In many places it refers to an extraordinary day of judgment for the wicked (e.g., Isa. 13.9), and it is often associated with images of darkness and cosmic upheaval (e.g., 2.1–2; Amos 5.18–20; Zeph. 1.14–15). Here the images stress the absence and lack of what is necessary for life. **20:** If God is not to pity the (sinful) people, He should at least pity the blameless animals (similarly Jonah 4.11).

2.1–11: On the mighty army of the Lord. Military imagery is pervasive in this section; in this context, the army is a personification of the locusts (see Prov. 6.6–7); this is made explicit in 2.25. **1:** Cf. 1.15 and 2.15; Hos. 5.8. *Sound an alarm,* usually the task of the guards on the wall. **2:** Cf. Zeph. 1.14–15; Zech. 8.22. **3:** Cf. Isa. 51.3; Ezek. 36.35. **6:** Cf. Nah. 2.11.

18 How the beasts groan!
The herds of cattle are bewildered
Because they have no pasture,
And the flocks of sheep are dazed.[a]

19 To You, O Lord, I call.
For fire[b] has consumed
The pastures in the wilderness,
And flame[b] has devoured
All the trees of the countryside.
20 The very beasts of the field
Cry out to You;
For the watercourses are dried up,
And fire has consumed
The pastures in the wilderness.

2 Blow a horn in Zion,
Sound an alarm on My holy mount!
Let all dwellers on earth tremble,
For the day of the Lord has come!
It is close—
2 A day of darkness and gloom,
A day of densest cloud
Spread like soot over the hills.
A vast, enormous horde—
Nothing like it has ever happened,
And it shall never happen again
Through the years and ages.

3 Their vanguard is a consuming fire,
Their rear guard a devouring flame.
Before them the land was like the Garden of Eden,
Behind them, a desolate waste:
Nothing has escaped them.
4 They have the appearance of horses,
They gallop just like steeds.
5 With a clatter as of chariots
They bound on the hilltops,
With a noise like a blazing fire
Consuming straw;
Like an enormous horde
Arrayed for battle.
6 Peoples tremble before them,
All faces [c-]turn ashen.[-c]
7 They rush like warriors,

a Meaning of Heb. uncertain. *b I.e., scorching heat.*
c-c Meaning of Heb. uncertain; cf. Nah. 2.11.

They scale a wall like fighters.
And each keeps to his own track.
Their paths never cross;[a]
8 No one jostles another,
Each keeps to his own course.
[b-]And should they fall through a loophole,
They do not get hurt.[-b]
9 They rush up the wall,
They dash about in the city;
They climb into the houses,
They enter like thieves
By way of the windows.
10 Before them earth trembles,
Heaven shakes,
Sun and moon are darkened,
And stars withdraw their brightness.
11 And the LORD roars aloud
At the head of His army;
For vast indeed is His host,
Numberless are those that do His bidding.
For great is the day of the LORD,
Most terrible—who can endure it?
12 "Yet even now"—says the LORD—
"Turn back to Me with all your hearts,
And with fasting, weeping, and lamenting."
13 Rend your hearts
Rather than your garments,
And turn back to the LORD your God.
For He is gracious and compassionate,
Slow to anger, abounding in kindness,
And renouncing punishment.
14 Who knows but He may turn and relent,
And leave a blessing behind
For meal offering and drink offering
To the LORD your God?[c]

15 Blow a horn in Zion,
Solemnize a fast,
Proclaim an assembly!
16 Gather the people,
Bid the congregation purify themselves.[d]
Bring together the old,
Gather the babes
And the sucklings at the breast;

a Meaning of Heb. uncertain. *b-b Meaning of Heb. uncertain.*
c When the locusts depart, there will again be yield enough for offerings; see 1.9.
d Cf. Exod. 19.10; Zeph. 1.7.

2.12–17: On the need to turn back to the LORD, and for a communal lamentation. This must be done before the arrival of the Day of the LORD, which is near or close (1.15; 2.1), otherwise Israel too will be the victim of God's power. **13:** Cf. Exod. 34.6; Num. 14.18; Jonah 4.2; Nah. 1.3; Pss. 86.15; 103.8; 145.8; Neh. 9.17, 31; 2 Chron. 30.9. Some of these have a more complete list of YHVH's attributes, which include intergenerational punishment. As in Jonah 4.2, this is lacking here. Also cf. *m. 'Avot* 2.13. **14:** Cf. Jonah 3.9. The v. implies uncertainty about divine response to human repentance; this idea was disturbing to many classical readers of the text, who filled it in to read "He [who] knows [that he has sins], he should return and repent" (so Tg. and Rashi, but not, e.g., Ibn Ezra). **15:** *Blow a horn:* The same phrase used to give the alarm of war in v. 1 is here used to call the people for a communal lamentation. The latter here, and elsewhere, includes calls to repentance and requires their repentance to be effective (cf. Jonah 3.5–10). **16:** The entire community must assemble.

Let the bridegroom come out of his chamber,
The bride from her canopied couch.
17 Between the portico and the altar,
Let the priests, the LORD's ministers, weep
And say:
"Oh, spare Your people, LORD!
Let not Your possession become a mockery,
To be taunted by nations!
Let not the peoples say,
'Where is their God?'"

18 Then the LORD was roused
On behalf of His land
And had compassion
Upon His people.
19 In response to His people
The LORD declared:
"I will grant you the new grain,
The new wine, and the new oil,
And you shall have them in abundance.
Nevermore will I let you be
A mockery among the nations.
20 I will drive the northerner[a] far from you,
I will thrust it into a parched and desolate land—
Its van to the Eastern Sea[b]
And its rear to the Western Sea;[c]
And the stench of it shall go up,
And the foul smell rise."
For [the LORD] shall work great deeds.

21 Fear not, O soil, rejoice and be glad;
For the LORD has wrought great deeds.
22 Fear not, O beasts of the field,
For the pastures in the wilderness
Are clothed with grass.
The trees have borne their fruit;
Fig tree and vine
Have yielded their strength.
23 O children of Zion, be glad,
Rejoice in the LORD your God.

a *I.e., the locusts. Emendation yields "My multitude"; cf. "nation" (1.6), "horde," "army," and "host" (2.2, 5, 11, and 25).*
b *The Dead Sea.* c *The Mediterranean Sea.*

17: Cf. Ps. 79.10. Similar arguments are made in the Torah, e.g., Exod. 32.12. The emphasis is on God's concern for His image rather than Israel's guiltlessness.

2.18–4.21: Forgiveness and restoration for Judah, divine judgment against their enemies. 2.19: Cf. 1.10; Deut. 7.13; 11.14; 14.23; 33.28; Jer. 31.12; Hos. 2.10. **20:** *Parched and desolate:* The description of the land to which the *northerner* will be driven may be compared to that in Zeph. 2.13 (there "arid," Heb "parched"). The reference points on the surface to the locust, but also to a mighty invading army sent by the LORD, evoking the common imagery of a powerful and at times mythic enemy coming from the north (see, among others, Jer. 1.13–15; 4.6; Ezek. 38.6, 15; 39.2; cf. Isa. 5.26–30). The Tg. reads: "I will remove the people who come from the north far from you, ... for they have done much evil." The Tg. understands the "northerners" as referring to an enemy army. The second part of the Tg.'s statement reflects one of the two possible understandings of the Heb text. The text does not specify the subject of the verb *work* or "do." The most likely subject is *the northerner,* in which case the Tg. adds the obvious, that the northerner has done great evil, perhaps overstepped its bounds by inflicting too great a punishment (see Isa. 10.5–11). But, particularly in the light of v. 21, it is possible to understand a secondary connotation in this phrase, "the LORD has done great deeds," namely that God has restored the land's vegetation. This "turning point" v. in Joel carries two instances of multiple meanings conveyed by a careful choice of words or their omission at critical places in the text. A later, talmudic interpretation is based on a slight revocalization of the term for northerner and sets the v. in a different sphere. According to *b. Sukk.* 52a, the relevant section of the v. reads "but I will remove far off from you the hidden one" (i.e., instead of "northerner") and then it goes on and explains that this hidden one is "yetzer ha-ra'," that is, "the evil inclination" which is constantly hidden in the heart of humans. The v. is thus understood as stating that in an ideal future, God will drive this basic inclination away from humanity into a land barren and desolate. **21:** Cf. Ps. 126.3. **23:** *For He has given you the early rain in [His] kindness:* Other

For He has given you the early rain in [His] kindness,
Now He makes the rain fall [as] formerly—
The early rain and the late—
24 And threshing floors shall be piled with grain,
And vats shall overflow with new wine and oil.

25 "I will repay you [a]for the years[a]
Consumed by swarms and hoppers,
By grubs and locusts,
The great army I let loose against you.
26 And you shall eat your fill
And praise the name of the LORD your God
Who dealt so wondrously with you—
My people shall be shamed no more.
27 And you shall know
That I am in the midst of Israel:
That I the LORD am your God
And there is no other.
And My people shall be shamed no more."

3 After that,
I will pour out My spirit on all flesh;
Your sons and daughters shall prophesy;
Your old men shall dream dreams,
And your young men shall see visions.
2 I will even pour out My spirit
Upon male and female slaves in those days.

3 [b]Before the great and terrible day of the LORD comes,[b]
I will set portents in the sky and on earth:
Blood and fire and pillars of smoke;
4 The sun shall turn into darkness
And the moon into blood.

5 But everyone who invokes the name of the LORD shall escape; for there shall be a remnant on Mount Zion and in Jerusalem, as the LORD promised. [c]Anyone who invokes the LORD
will be among the survivors.[c]

a-a Emendation yields "double what was." *b-b Brought up from v. 4 for clarity.* *c-c Meaning of Heb. uncertain.*

possible meanings of this phrase include: "For He has given you the early rain in its season"; "For He has given you the early rain for your vindication"; "For He has given you back your teacher in righteousness"; "For He has given you a teacher for righteousness"; "For He has given you a righteous teacher." The word translated *rain* ("moreh," the same as in Ps. 84.7) is usually "yoreh," and "moreh" can mean "teacher." If the word is understood as "teacher," then who is the teacher? YHVH? Furthermore, it is possible that this is another case of a main denoted meaning (probably "the early rain in its season") along with a connoted meaning ("teacher"). The Qumran community derived the term "the teacher of righteousness," an early leader of the group, from this v. **27:** Cf. Isa. 45.5, 6, 18.

3.1–5: A glorious future for the faithful. Men and women, male and female slaves, all are included. **1:** Cf. Ezek. 39.29. Prophecy, *dreams,* and *visions* were the three recognized ways in which human beings received communications from God. God will once again reveal himself to people. **3–4:** *Before the great and terrible ... comes,* in the Heb at the conclusion of v. 4. *Portents ... blood ... fire ... pillars of smoke:* The language evokes the plagues preceding the exodus (Exod. chs 7–11) and the Presence of the LORD during the exodus (Exod. 13.21). For this reason the expression "I will set portents in the sky and on the earth; blood, fire and pillars of smoke" is included in the Passover Haggadah before the recitation of the ten plagues. **5:** For the first section of the v., cf. Obad. 1.17. The conclusion of the v. is often translated "and among survivors whom the LORD calls."

4.1–21: Judgment and calamity for the nations; restoration for Israel. The text reflects the motif of the enemy gathering massive forces against Jerusalem but being finally destroyed. Cf. Ezek. chs 32, 38, 39; Zech. ch 14. Towards the end, the ch presents a view of the restoration of Israel in terms of agricultural plenty and peace. **1:** Cf. Jer. 33.15; 50.4, 20. As is typical, the time period when this will transpire is not specified. **2:** Cf. Isa. 66.18; Zech. 14.2. Here and in v. 12 there is wordplay on the name of the valley, based on whether the meaning of the Heb word is "contend" or "judge" (see translators' notes *a* and *d*). **3:** Note the relation between the two "sale prices." **6:** *Ionians,* see intro. to Joel. **8:** The nations are punished measure-for-measure, a typical prophetic punishment. **10:** A reversal of the well-known image of Isa. 2.4 and Mic. 4.3.

4 For lo! in those days
And in that time,
When I restore the fortunes
Of Judah and Jerusalem,
2 I will gather all the nations
And bring them down to the Valley of Jehoshaphat.[a]
There I will contend with them
Over My very own people, Israel,
Which they scattered among the nations.
For they divided My land among themselves
3 And cast lots over My people;
And they bartered a boy for a whore,
And sold a girl for wine, which they drank.

4 What is this you are doing to Me, O Tyre, Sidon, and all the
districts of Philistia? Are you requiting Me for something I have
done, or are you doing something for My benefit? Quick as a
flash, I will pay you back; 5 for you have taken My gold and My
silver, and have carried off My precious treasures to your palaces; 6 and you have sold the people of Judah and the people
of Jerusalem to the Ionians, so that you have removed them far
away from their homeland. 7 Behold, I will rouse them to leave
the place you have sold them to, and I will pay you back: 8 I will
deliver your sons and daughters into the hands of the people
of Judah, and they will sell them into captivity to a distant nation—for the LORD has spoken.

9 Proclaim this among the nations:
Prepare for battle!
Arouse the warriors,
Let all the fighters come and draw near!
10 Beat your plowshares[b] into swords,
And your pruning hooks into spears.
Let even the weakling say, "I am strong."
11 [c-]Rouse yourselves[-c] and come,
All you nations;
Come together
From roundabout.
There [c-]bring down[-c]
Your warriors, O LORD!
12 Let the nations rouse themselves and march up
To the Valley of Jehoshaphat;[d]
For there I will sit in judgment
Over all the nations roundabout.

a Here understood as "The LORD contends"; contrast v. 12.
b See note at Isa. 2.4. *c-c Meaning of Heb. uncertain.*
d Here understood as "The LORD judges"; contrast v. 2.

13 Swing the sickle,
For the crop is ripe;
Come and tread,
For the winepress is full,
The vats are overflowing!
For great is their wickedness.

14 Multitudes upon multitudes
In the Valley of Decision!
For the day of the LORD is at hand
In the Valley of Decision.
15 Sun and moon are darkened,
And stars withdraw their brightness.
16 And the LORD will roar from Zion,
And shout aloud from Jerusalem,
So that heaven and earth tremble.
But the LORD will be a shelter to His people,
A refuge to the children of Israel.
17 And you shall know that I the LORD your God
Dwell in Zion, My holy mount.
And Jerusalem shall be holy;
Nevermore shall strangers pass through it.
18 And in that day,
The mountains shall drip with wine,
The hills shall flow with milk,
And all the watercourses of Judah shall flow with water;
A spring shall issue from the House of the LORD
And shall water the Wadi of the Acacias.
19 Egypt shall be a desolation,
And Edom a desolate waste,
Because of the outrage to the people of Judah,
In whose land they shed the blood of the innocent.
20 But Judah shall be inhabited forever,
And Jerusalem throughout the ages.
21 Thus [a]-I will treat as innocent their blood
Which I have not treated as innocent;-[a]
And the LORD shall dwell in Zion.

a-a Emendation yields "their unavenged blood shall be avenged."

16: See Amos 1.2. The book of Amos follows Joel in the Masoretic order of the prophetic books within the Twelve, though not in that of the LXX, in which Joel is preceded by Mic. and followed by Obad. It is possible that, among other considerations, the presence of a phrase at the ending of Joel and the beginning of Amos influenced the position of Joel in the Masoretic order of the Twelve. **17:** Cf. Ezek. 39.28 and passim; also cf. Joel 2.27. Other prophetic texts suggest that the Temple would be open to certain foreigners (Isa. 56.6–7). **18:** Cf. Amos 9.13. **19:** *Edom* is elsewhere condemned for joining in with the Babylonians at the destruction of the First Temple (see Obad. 1.10–11). A late antique and medieval Jewish interpretation associated Edom first with the Roman empire and later with Christendom. **21:** The first section of this v. is unclear, and may be understood as (1) "I will avenge their blood, yet unavenged," (2) "I will avenge their blood, and I will not clear the guilty," or (3) "though I cleanse their blood(shed), I will not cleanse." The final words of the book are a fitting conclusion given the centrality of *Zion,* which is mentioned seven times in this short book.

עמוס

Amos

THE FIRST VERSE OF THE BOOK sets the text in the days of Uzziah, king of Judah, and Jeroboam, king of Israel—the 8th c. BCE. The book is set in the monarchic period, when the sanctuary at Bethel served as a central place of worship for the Northern Kingdom. Some scholars propose that the book of Amos was written (wholly or in the main) in the 8th century; others that it is the result of a lengthy process of redaction that spanned centuries; still others focus on the present text of Amos and date it to the postmonarchic period, since it implies the fall of the monarchy (9.11–15).

Even a cursory reading of the book shows that it deals mainly with the malady of Israel, its condemnation, and the future restoration and glory of Israel within a friendly, renewed physical world. When it condemns Israel, it repeatedly stresses social and political ills. (Contrast Hosea, which largely concerns religious ills.) As expected in a prophetic book meant to be read again and again, and meditated upon—as all prophetic books are—these social and political ills are described in relatively general terms, making them eternally relevant. Thus, the critique becomes applicable to different historical and social circumstances. It is thus not surprising that a substantial number of readers in the 20th c. considered either the book or the prophet it describes an inspiring source for their endeavors in social reform. For instance, Labor/socialist parties in the first decades of the State of Israel and its leaders (e.g., David Ben Gurion) considered Amos a source of inspiration, and it is quoted (Amos 5.24) in Martin Luther King, Jr.'s "I Have a Dream" speech. Some advocates of "liberation theology" in Latin America see the book as a source of support for their theological and social positions.

The book also makes an unequivocal but somewhat implicit claim about the absolute primacy of Jerusalem/Zion, linked to a strong condemnation of the sanctuary of Bethel. The theme of repentance is important in the book, and so is the distinctive relationship between the LORD and Israel along with its limitations; for example, not only that the LORD executes judgment against Israel like all other nations (2.6–3.2), but also explicitly states, "To Me, O Israelites, you are/ Just like the Ethiopians" (9.7) and yet says "You [Israel] alone have I singled out / Of all the families of the earth" (3.2). The book also restates a common prophetic position about the primacy of morality over sacrifices.

The book includes a superscription or title that serves as an introduction (1.1), a clear motto that communicates one of the most significant messages of the book (1.2), and a series of prophetic readings of which the last two encapsulate much of the book: The LORD announces a severe, future punishment for the condemned nation, then an ideal and plentiful future to follow the deserved punishment (9.7–15). The series of prophetic readings begins with announcements of judgment against the nations, including Judah and Israel (1.3–2.16) and continues with reports of prophetic speeches and visions of the fate of Israel, along with a biographical vignette in 7.10–17.

Amos 2.6–3.8 is read as the haftarah for the parashah of Va-yeshev (Gen. 37.1–40.23), and in the Ashkenazi tradition 9.7–15 as the haftarah for the parashah of 'Aḥarei Mot (Lev. 16.1–18.30).

[EHUD BEN ZVI]

1 The words of Amos, a sheepbreeder from Tekoa, who prophesied concerning Israel in the reigns of Kings Uzziah of Judah and Jeroboam son of Joash of Israel, two years before the earthquake.[a]

2 He proclaimed:
The LORD roars from Zion,
Shouts aloud from Jerusalem;
And the pastures of the shepherds shall languish,
And the summit of Carmel shall wither.

3 Thus said the LORD:
For three transgressions of Damascus,
For four, I will not revoke it:[b]
Because they threshed Gilead
With threshing boards of iron.
4 I will send down[c] fire upon the palace of Hazael,
And it shall devour the fortresses of Ben-hadad.[d]
5 I will break the gate bars of Damascus,
And wipe out the inhabitants from the Vale of Aven
And the sceptered ruler of Beth-eden;
And the people of Aram shall be exiled to Kir
—said the LORD.

a See Zech. 14.5. *b I.e, the decree of punishment.* *c Cf. Lam. 1.13.* *d Cf. 2 Kings 13.22–25.*

1.1: Superscription. The superscription introduces the book and characterizes it as a prophetic book. It associates the book with *Amos,* sets its world in the monarchic period, specifically in the days of *Uzziah* and *Jeroboam* of the 8th c. BCE, and provides additional information about Amos. The v. tells the readers that Amos was a herdsman, a sheep and cattle breeder (see also 7.14). As such, Amos was a relatively wealthy man (cf. Mesha, 2 Kings 3.4), and not a poor shepherd, as is at times erroneously claimed. He was from Tekoa, a Judahite town about 8 km (5 mi) south of Bethlehem. He *prophesied concerning Israel:* The meaning is ambiguous; it certainly points to the Northern Kingdom to the exclusion of Judah, but particularly from the perspective of a postmonarchic readership, it points to "the LORD's people" (e.g., 9.14) who have a covenantal relationship with the LORD, and as such to both the former kingdoms, northern and southern, as well as to the much later intended readership of the book. The temporal reference to *two years before the earthquake* (cf. Zech. 14.5) enhances the verisimilitude, that is, the quality of appearing to be true or real, of the temporal frame and the reliability of the authorial voice in the book, since the imagery in 9.1–6 may be understood as earthquake imagery. Further, since earthquakes were seen as acts of God, it suggests an additional divine validation of the message of the book.

1.2: Motto and theophany. The book is unique in opening with a motto, a short, general thematic statement that is meant to (re)focus how the book should be understood. Its general imagery follows that of many theophanic reports. These reports frequently depict a manifestation of the deity's power as leading to an upheaval in the natural world. Further, the LORD is likened to a lion (cf. Hos. 5.14; 11.10; 13.7), a relatively common motif of strength in the ancient Near East. But one detail in the text is of utmost importance: The lion *roars from Zion.* The Jerusalem-centric message is abundantly clear, as the book presents itself as a work that conveys the message of that roaring lion from Zion, namely Jerusalem. *Carmel* is a fertile, mountainous area in the Northern Kingdom (southeast of modern Haifa), but the Heb word "carmel" refers also to farmland (cf. Isa. 32.15) or an orchard (and particularly to a vineyard). The general character of *the pastures of the shepherds* supports and plays on the broader meaning. The geographical reference does not restrict the horizon of the text to the particular region of the Northern Kingdom.

1.3–2.16: Reports of announcements of judgment against the nations. The unit is kept coherent not only by its unifying theme, but also by a careful balance between repetition and differentiation among the subunits. Nations other than Israel and Judah are condemned for transgressions against other nations; Judah for the rejection of YHVH's teaching and Israel for actions against YHVH's teaching. (The nations mentioned here are immediate neighbors of Israel/Judah. Assyria and Egypt, for instance, are not mentioned.) Rhetorically, the readers are sucked into this passage, eagerly anticipating the punishment of their neighbors, until the prophecy is turned against them as well. While Judah and Israel are condemned for covenant infractions, their neighbors are condemned for violating basic norms of decency. **1.3:** The "it" in *I will not revoke it* is anticipatory, i.e., it points to the following decree of punishment. **4–5:** *Hazael* and *Ben-hadad* are the names of two kings of Aram Damascus (see 2 Kings 8.7–15; 13.22–25). The territory of the kingdom of Aram Damascus (or simply Aram, as often in the Bible) partially overlaps that of Syria today. *Vale of Aven* and *Beth-eden:*

6 Thus said the LORD:
For three transgressions of Gaza,
For four, I will not revoke it:
Because they exiled[a] an entire population,
Which they delivered to Edom.[b]
7 I will send down fire upon the wall of Gaza,
And it shall devour its fortresses;
8 And I will wipe out the inhabitants of Ashdod
And the sceptered ruler of Ashkelon;
And I will turn My hand against Ekron,
And the Philistines shall perish to the last man
—said the Lord GOD.

9 Thus said the LORD:
For three transgressions of Tyre,
For four, I will not revoke it:
Because they handed over
An entire population to Edom,[c]
Ignoring the covenant of brotherhood.[d]

Although Beth-eden points to an area near the Euphrates River, the wordplay is clear; the first name means "valley of disaster, nothingness" (or valley of delusion; cf. 5.5), the second "house of bliss." Within the book of Amos, *Kir* is the place of origin for the Arameans (see 9.7). Its whereabouts are unknown, but 2 Kings 16.9 reports that the Assyrians deported the Arameans to Kir, after they put an end to the kingdom of Aram. **6–8:** *Gaza* here stands for all the Philistine cities. Three others are mentioned by name, *Ashdod, Ashkelon,* and *Ekron.* The same four cities are mentioned in the same order in Zeph. 2.4. **9:** *Tyre,* situated in Lebanon of today, along with Sidon, two of the most important Phoenician cities for many centuries.

a *I.e., they cooperated in the annexation of Israelite territory; cf. Jer. 13.19 with note.*
b *Emendation yields "Aram"; cf. Isa. 9.11.* c *Emendation yields "Aram."*
d *Cf. 1 Kings 5.26; 9.12–13.*

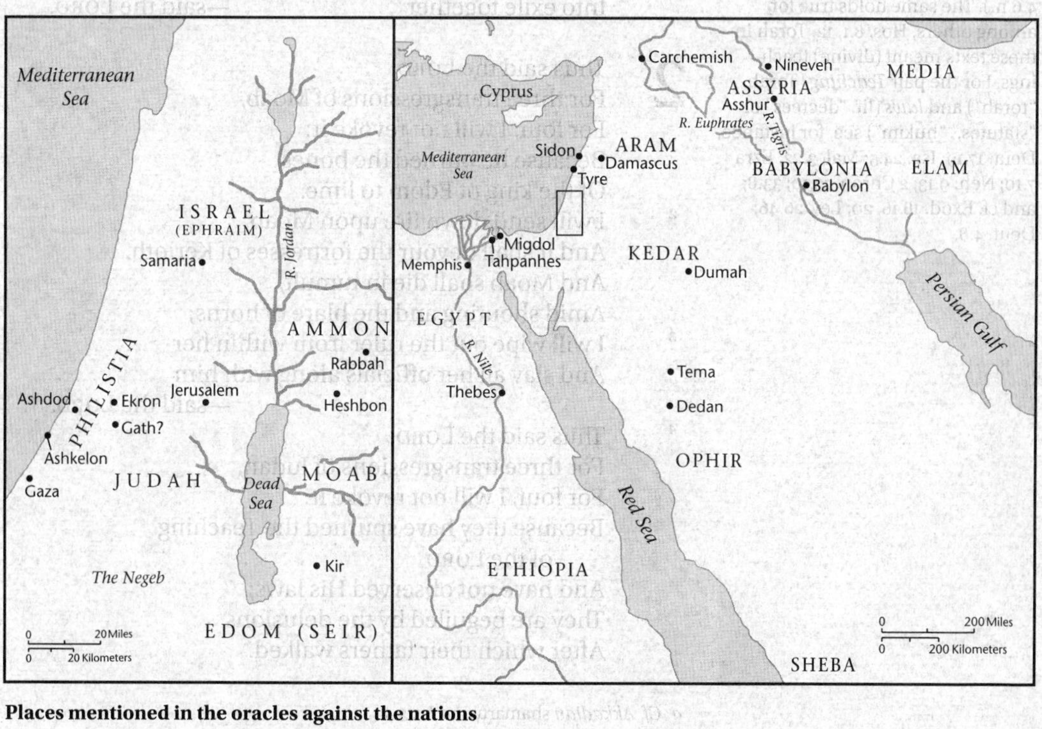

Places mentioned in the oracles against the nations

10 I will send down fire upon the wall of Tyre,
And it shall devour its fortresses.

11 Thus said the LORD:
For three transgressions of Edom,
For four, I will not revoke it:
Because he pursued his brother with the sword
And repressed all pity,
Because his anger raged unceasing
And his fury stormed[a] unchecked.
12 I will send down fire upon Teman,
And it shall devour the fortresses of Bozrah.

13 Thus said the LORD:
For three transgressions of the Ammonites,
For four, I will not revoke it:
Because they ripped open the pregnant women of Gilead
In order to enlarge their own territory.
14 I will set fire to the wall of Rabbah,
And it shall devour its fortresses,
Amid shouting on a day of battle,
On a day of violent tempest.
15 Their king and his officers shall go
Into exile together —said the LORD.

2 Thus said the LORD:
For three transgressions of Moab,
For four, I will not revoke it:
Because he burned the bones
Of the king of Edom to lime.
2 I will send down fire upon Moab,
And it shall devour the fortresses of Kerioth.
And Moab shall die in tumult,
Amid shouting and the blare of horns;
3 I will wipe out the ruler from within her
And slay all her officials along with him
—said the LORD.
4 Thus said the LORD:
For three transgressions of Judah,
For four, I will not revoke it:
Because they have spurned the Teaching of the LORD
And have not observed His laws;
They are beguiled by the delusions
After which their fathers walked.

11: Cf. Obad. 1.10–14. *Edom* was located in the area south of the Dead Sea. The last lines of the v. translated by author, "and destroyed his womenfolk, because his anger raged unceasing and he kept his wrath forever." **12:** *Teman* and *Bozrah* are elsewhere situated in Edomite territory (cf. Isa. 34.6; 63.1; Jer. 49.7; Obad. 1.9). **13–14:** *Gilead* was a region north of Ammon. It was a disputed area that changed hands several times in the monarchic period. From the perspective of the Bible it was Israelite territory, though not always under Israelite control. *Rabbah,* the capital of Ammon, is within the area of today's Amman. On the imagery, cf. 2 Kings 8.12; Isa. 13.16; Hos. 10.14; 14.1; Nah. 3.10; Ps. 137.9.

2.1–2: The kingdom of *Moab* was east of the Dead Sea, within the territory of present-day Jordan. Ruth, for instance, was a Moabite woman (see book of Ruth). **4:** Traditional Jewish interpreters understood *the Teaching* [Heb "torah"] *of the LORD* as a reference to the Torah (see Hos. 4.6 n.). The same holds true for, among others, Hos. 8.1, 12. Torah in these texts meant (divine) teachings. For the pair *Teaching* (Torah, "torah") and *laws* (lit. "decrees" or "statutes," "ḥukim") see, for instance, Deut. 17.19; Isa. 24.5; Mal. 3.22; Ezra 7.10; Neh. 9.13; 2 Chron. 19.10; 33.8; and cf. Exod. 18.16, 20; Lev. 26.46; Deut. 4.8.

a *Cf. Akkadian* shamaru *and Jer. 3.5.*

5 I will send down fire upon Judah,
And it shall devour the fortresses of
Jerusalem.

6 Thus said the LORD:
For three transgressions of Israel,
For four, I will not revoke it:
Because they have sold for silver
Those whose cause was just,
And the needy for a pair of sandals.
7 [Ah,] you [a-] who trample the heads of the poor
Into the dust of the ground,
And make the humble walk a twisted course![-a]
Father and son go to the same girl,
And thereby profane My holy name.
8 They recline by every altar
On garments taken in pledge,
And drink in the House of their God
Wine bought with fines they imposed.
9 Yet I
Destroyed the Amorite before them,
Whose stature was like the cedar's
And who was stout as the oak,
Destroying his boughs above
And his trunk below!
10 And I
Brought you up from the land of Egypt
And led you through the wilderness
forty years,
To possess the land of the Amorite!
11 And I raised up prophets from among your sons
And nazirites from among your young men.
Is that not so, O people of Israel?
—says the LORD.
12 But you made the nazirites drink wine
And ordered the prophets not to prophesy.
13 [b-]Ah, I will slow your movements
As a wagon is slowed
When it is full of cut grain.[-b]
14 Flight shall fail the swift,
The strong shall find no strength,
And the warrior shall not save his life.
15 The bowman shall not hold his ground,

a-a *Understanding* sho'afim *as equivalent to* shafim. *Emendation yields: "Who crush on the ground / The heads of the poor, / And push off the road / The humble of the land"; cf. Job 24.4.*

b-b *Meaning of verse uncertain; alternatively: "I will slow your movements / As a threshing sledge (cf. Isa. 28.27–28) is slowed / When clogged by cut grain."*

6–16: Who is Israel here? Does Israel mean only the Northern Kingdom? On the surface, the answer seems positive; for Israel is set as a nation other than Judah, see vv. 5–6. V. 10, however, which refers to the exodus, suggests a broad understanding of Israel. The text plays with the ambiguity of the term Israel and allows and even encourages the readership of the book—which lives in the post-monarchic period (that is, the Jews, the "remnant of Judah")—to identify with the Israel of the book; they are their ancestors and their fate is important to them. The main transgressions are of a social nature and involve the oppression of the powerless. Sexual and cultic behaviors are also explicitly mentioned. **6:** This begins the haftarah (prophetic reading) for the Torah portion concerned with the sale of Joseph, most likely reflecting an interpretive tradition that Joseph was the *just* person sold *for* [the price of] *a pair of sandals.* **8:** *On garments taken in pledge,* cf. Deut. 4.17; Job 22.6; 24.3–4, 9 and contrast this element and the entire description of the sinners here with the one of the pious son in Ezek. 18.15–17. **9–11:** The summary of the LORD's dealings with Israel is meant to contrast the faithfulness of the patron of Israel (i.e., the LORD) with the long history of unfaithfulness of the patron's client (i.e., Israel). The readers of the book know that such a pattern of behavior calls for the punishment of the client (Israel) and provides just grounds for punishment of the latter. Nevertheless, the book of Amos communicates that the LORD is not going to revoke the status of Israel. **12:** *Nazirites drink wine:* The Nazirite vow forbade the consumption of wine or any derivation of grapes (Num. 6.3; Judg. 13.7). **14–16:** The description of the warrior men points at an upside-down order caused by divine intervention. It parallels the one caused by human intervention (i.e., prophets who do not talk, Nazirites who drink wine). The term translated as *unarmed* means lit. "naked" (see translators' note at v. 16).

And the fleet-footed shall not escape,
Nor the horseman save his life.
16 Even the most stouthearted warrior
Shall run away unarmed[a] that day
—declares the LORD.

3 Hear this word, O people of Israel,
That the LORD has spoken concerning you,
Concerning the whole family that I brought up
from the land of Egypt:
2 You alone have I singled out
Of all the families of the earth—
That is why I will call you to account
For all your iniquities.

3 Can two walk together
Without having met?
4 Does a lion roar in the forest
When he has no prey?
Does a great beast let out a cry from its den
Without having made a capture?
5 Does a bird drop on the ground—in a trap—
With no snare there?
Does a trap spring up from the ground
Unless it has caught something?
6 When a ram's horn is sounded in a town,
Do the people not take alarm?
Can misfortune come to a town
If the LORD has not caused it?
7 Indeed, my Lord GOD does nothing
Without having revealed His purpose
To His servants the prophets.
8 A lion has roared,
Who can but fear?

a Lit. "naked."

3.1–6.14: Three readings about judgment. The readers are presented with a set of three units, each beginning with the phrase *Hear this word* (3.1; 4.1; 5.1), a phrase that serves also to mark the book into subunits, just as the phrase ending the previous ch, *declares the LORD,* typically expresses the end of a subunit. Each of these units shows internal subdivisions that are marked at times by the repetition of another phrase, such as "Assuredly" (or "therefore") units (5.13, 16) and "Ah" (or "Woe") units (see 5.18; 6.1). In ancient times there were no paragraph markers, but the repetition of an important word, particularly at the beginning of a section, served approximately the same purpose. But ancient writers and readers did not think of units as we do, and often weakened the boundaries between what we consider to be formally demarcated literary subunits. For instance, they created links that cut across different units within the book (e.g., there is a fourth "Hear" unit in 8.4–14, which is linked to the surrounding text in the book and to these three units at the same time). Moreover, particularly in prophetic books, the way in which texts were written permits various ways of subdividing them. Each subdivision may be a partial reading, but the readings can inform each other, and all together create a meaning much richer than any of them separately. In the world portrayed in the book, people are supposed to hear "this word," but in the "actual" world, the readers of the book are asked to read and study "this word" and to read it to those who cannot read by themselves. Each of these units (3.1–15; 4.1–13; 5.1–6.14) deals with judgment (see below), and each of them is presented as a reliable report of "this word," that is, of a "prophetic word" (Heb "davar") from the monarchic past. Each of them addresses the matter in a different way, and all together provide the reader with a multifaceted image of Israel and of its impending judgment.

3.1–15: First report of a prophetic word in the monarchic period announcing judgment against Israel. 1: *The whole family:* This inclusive reference to Israel allows and encourages the identification of the readership with Israel, though, as expected, vv. 9, 12 point to Israel as the Northern Kingdom. The text shifts its references to the LORD from the third to the first person, and accordingly human and divine speech become interwoven and their respective limits blurred. Shifts like these are common in prophetic books. **2:** The LORD states that this unique relationship carries obligations, and punishment will result if the obligations are not fulfilled (see 2.9–11 n.). **3–8:** A series of rhetorical questions, invoking cause-and-effect situations, serves didactic purposes. The questions lead up to the implicit question: How is it that the prophet warns of the impending doom to be caused by God, but the people do not pay any attention?

My Lord GOD has spoken,
Who can but prophesy?
9 Proclaim in the fortresses of Ashdod[a]
And in the fortresses of the land of Egypt!
Say:
Gather on the hill[b] of Samaria
And witness the great outrages within her
And the oppression in her midst.
10 They are incapable of doing right
—declares the LORD;
They store up lawlessness and rapine
In their fortresses.
11 Assuredly,
Thus said my Lord GOD:
An enemy, all about the land!
He shall strip you of your splendor,
And your fortresses shall be plundered.
12 Thus said the LORD:
As a shepherd rescues from the lion's jaws
Two shank bones or the tip of an ear,
So shall the Israelites escape
Who dwell in Samaria—
With the leg[c] of a bed or the head[c] of a couch.

13 Hear [this], and warn the House of Jacob
—says my Lord GOD, the God of Hosts—
14 That when I punish Israel for its transgressions,
I will wreak judgment on the altar[d] of Bethel,
And the horns of the altar shall be cut off
And shall fall to the ground.
15 I will wreck the winter palace
Together with the summer palace;
The ivory palaces shall be demolished,
And the great houses shall be destroyed
—declares the LORD.

4 Hear this word, you cows of Bashan
On the hill of Samaria—
Who defraud the poor,
Who rob the needy;
Who say to your[e] husbands,
"Bring, and let's carouse!"
2 My Lord GOD swears by His holiness:
Behold, days are coming upon you

a Septuagint reads "Assyria." *b Heb. plural; but cf. 4.1; 6.1.*
c Meaning of Heb. uncertain. *d Heb. plural, but cf. "altar" in next line.*
e Heb. "their."

12: The lion imagery emerges again (cf. 1.2; 3.4, 8), this time with sarcasm. Just as two bones or the tip of an ear are useless remnants of an attack, so the small material remains of the Northern Kingdom will be useless, serving only as tokens and reminders of what had been before. Yet, following a theme that would be developed later in this book, and is developed in other prophetic books, there would be some kind of remnant. **14:** *Bethel,* a city and one of the main centers of worship in the Northern Kingdom. It plays an important role in the book of Amos; see 4.4; 5.5; 7.10, and in numerous biblical traditions (e.g., Gen. 12.8; Judg. 21.2; 1 Kings 12.29; Hos. 10.15; 12.5). **15:** *Winter palace ... summer palace,* perhaps a reference to the wealthy (including the king) who can afford two houses, but also a merism, i.e., a reference to extremes (e.g., "young and old") to convey totality ("all your houses"). *Ivory palaces,* ornamented with, not made of, ivory. Since ivory was costly, this is an extravagantly luxurious house. Pieces of well-crafted ivory inlay have been excavated from Samaria.

4.1–13: Second report of a prophetic word in the monarchic period announcing judgment against Israel. Israel is here given many warnings and chances; the phrase *Yet you did not turn back to Me—declares the LORD* (vv. 6b, 8b, 9b, 10b, 11b) repeats as a litany, justifying the punishment of Israel, but also emphasizing that repenting or returning is efficacious. **1:** *Cows of Bashan,* well-fed, plump cows, in this context, elite women. According to the text these women oppressed the poor and encouraged their husbands to do so for their benefit. Although today it is clearly offensive to call a woman "a fat cow," it is uncertain if this was an insult at the time of the composition of the book. **2–3:** The precise meaning of the vv. is uncertain, but they surely point to deportation. The identity of the enemy that will exile the people is not mentioned, nor is it anywhere in the book, though exile is announced repeatedly (e.g., 5.5, 27; 6.7; 7.11, 17; cf. 9.4). **4–5:** The sarcasm is striking. *Gilgal,* a main center of worship in the Northern Kingdom (cf. Josh. 4.20–22; Hos. 4.15; 9.15; 12.2). **6:** *Cleanness of teeth,* a euphemism for famine. Since there will be nothing to eat, the teeth will be very clean. **7:** The LORD's micromanagement of rain to express reward and punishment explicitly contradicts the obvious expectation, based on empiric observation, that when it rains in an area, it rains on the fields of both the pious and the sinners. Thus this micromanagement carries not only its basic message in terms of an economy of judgment/punishment, but by being in itself a "miracle" or a "sign," because nature deviates from its normal path, it reinforces the message that it communicates. **10:** *In the manner of Egypt,* an allusion to the plagues (Exod. chs 7–12).

[a]When you will be carried off in baskets,
And, to the last one, in fish baskets,
3 And taken out [of the city]—
Each one through a breach straight ahead—
And flung on the refuse heap[a]
—declares the LORD.

4 Come to Bethel and transgress;
To Gilgal, and transgress even more:
Present your sacrifices the next morning
And your tithes on the third day;
5 And burn a thank offering of leavened bread;[b]
And proclaim freewill offerings loudly.
For you love that sort of thing, O Israelites
—declares my Lord GOD.

6 I, on My part, have given you
Cleanness of teeth in all your towns,
And lack of food in all your settlements.
Yet you did not turn back to Me
—declares the LORD.

7 I therefore withheld the rain from you
Three months before harvesttime:
I would make it rain on one town
And not on another;
One field would be rained upon
While another on which it did not rain
Would wither.
8 So two or three towns would wander
To a single town to drink water,
But their thirst would not be slaked.
Yet you did not turn back to Me
—declares the LORD.

9 I scourged you with blight and mildew;
Repeatedly[c] your gardens and vineyards,
Your fig trees and olive trees
Were devoured by locusts.
Yet you did not turn back to Me
—declares the LORD.

10 I sent against you pestilence
In the manner of Egypt;[d]
I slew your young men with the sword,
Together with your captured horses,
And I made the stench of your armies

a-a Meaning of Heb. uncertain.
b Cf. Lev. 7.12–14; where, however, the bread is not to be burned.
c Meaning of Heb. uncertain.
d Alluding to the plagues at the time of the Exodus.

Rise in your very nostrils.
Yet you did not turn back to Me
—declares the LORD.

11 I have wrought destruction among you
As when God destroyed Sodom and Gomorrah;
You have become like a brand plucked
from burning.
Yet you have not turned back to Me
—declares the LORD.

12 Assuredly,
[a]Because I am doing that to you,[a]
Even so will I act toward you, O Israel—
Prepare to meet your God, O Israel!

13 Behold,
He who formed the mountains,
And created the wind,
And has told man what His wish[b] is,
Who turns blackness[c] into daybreak,
And treads upon the high places of the earth—
His name is the LORD, the God of Hosts.

5 Hear this word which I intone
As a dirge over you, O House of Israel:
2 Fallen, not to rise again,
Is Maiden Israel;
Abandoned on her soil
With none to lift her up.
3 For thus said my Lord GOD
About the House of Israel:
The town that marches out a thousand strong
Shall have a hundred left,
And the one that marches out a hundred
strong
Shall have but ten left.
4 Thus said the LORD
To the House of Israel:
Seek Me, and you will live.
5 Do not seek Bethel,
Nor go to Gilgal,
Nor cross over[d] to Beer-sheba;
For Gilgal shall go into exile,
And Bethel shall become a delusion.

a-a Emendation yields "Because you are acting thus toward Me."
b Meaning of Heb. uncertain. *c Cf. Joel 2.2. Emendation yields "darkness"; cf. 5.8.*
d I.e., into Judah; cf. 1 Kings 19.3.

11–12: The list of ever-increasing calamities seems to reach its peak with the reference to *Sodom and Gomorrah,* which were traditional, conventional examples of cities destroyed because of immorality, but there is even more. V. 12 may be translated, "Therefore, thus I am about to do to you (sing.), O Israel: because this is what I will do to you—Prepare to meet your God, O Israel." The exact punishment, narrated to Israel in the second-person singular, in contrast to the previous second-person plurals, is meant to increase its affective appeal, though the exact punishment is left to the reader's imagination. **13:** Compare with, for instance, Amos 5.8–9; 9.5–6; Mic. 1.3 and see also Job ch 38 and passim in Psalms.

5.1–6.14: Third report of a prophetic word in the monarchic period announcing judgment against Israel. This section concludes with two expanded "Ah" (or "Woe") units (see 5.18–27; 6.1–14). **1–2:** Amos uses the funeral "qinah" or dirge (used to lament the death of individuals) metaphorically to show that the nation is "dead." **3:** Again, the idea of a remnant (see 3.12 n.). **4–6:** The emphasis must be on seeking God, which cannot be accomplished by seeking out the traditional sites where He is worshipped. **5:** The Heb is punning: *For Gilgal shall go into exile* ("galoh yigleh").

6: *House of Joseph,* the Northern Kingdom. **7:** *Wormwood,* an aromatic plant that yields a bitter extract and tastes bitter (cf. Deut. 29.7; Jer. 9.14; 23.15; Prov. 5.4; Lam. 3.15, 19). Justice is supposed to be sweet, but they turn it bitter and thereby they embitter the life of the poor; cf. 6.12. **8:** Allusions to creation are often invoked to show God's power. **11:** The image of building houses and establishing vines but being denied the ability to enjoy them points to the futility of human activities in the face of divine judgment (cf. Deut. 28.39; Mic. 6.15; Zeph. 1.13). Later (9.4) the image is turned around to exemplify the bliss that results from human activity under divine blessing. **12:** *In the gate,* where justice was dispensed (cf. Deut. 16.18; 17.8; Zech. 8.10, among others). Again, the infractions are ethical rather than cultic. **14–15:** This picks up on the theme of seeking, developed in vv. 4–6. The emphasis on ethical behavior here and in similar vv. (e.g., Mic. 6.8) contributed much to an understanding of the prophets as bearers of ethical monotheism. These vv. are much cherished for this reason in modern liberal streams in Judaism. Within its ancient context, the v. claims that a sharp turn toward ethical behavior may influence God to revoke the divine decree against Israel. Still, whereas repentance is necessary for the annulment of the decree, the book claims that repentance by itself is not sufficient. God decides whether to revoke or not. On this understanding of ethical monotheism, see also 5.21–25.

6 Seek the LORD, and you will live,
[a]Else He will rush like fire upon[a] the House of Joseph
And consume Bethel[b] with none to quench it.

7 [Ah,] you who turn justice into wormwood
And hurl righteousness to the ground!
[Seek the LORD,]
8 Who made the Pleiades and Orion,
Who turns deep darkness into dawn
And darkens day into night,
Who summons the waters of the sea
And pours them out upon the earth—
His name is the LORD!
9 [a]It is He who hurls destruction upon strongholds,
So that ruin comes upon fortresses![a]

10 They hate the arbiter in the gate,
And detest him whose plea is just.
11 Assuredly,
Because you [a]impose a tax[a] on the poor
And exact from him a levy of grain,
You have built houses of hewn stone,
But you shall not live in them;
You have planted delightful vineyards,
But shall not drink their wine.
12 For I have noted how many are your crimes,
And how countless your sins—
You enemies of the righteous,
You takers of bribes,
You who subvert in the gate
The cause of the needy!

13 Assuredly,
At such a time the prudent man keeps silent,
For it is an evil time.

14 Seek good and not evil,
That you may live,
And that the LORD, the God of Hosts,
May truly be with you,
As you think.
15 Hate evil and love good,
And establish justice in the gate;
Perhaps the LORD, the God of Hosts,
Will be gracious to the remnant of Joseph.

a-a Meaning of Heb. uncertain. *b Septuagint reads "the House of Israel."*

16 Assuredly,
Thus said the LORD,
My Lord, the God of Hosts:
In every square there shall be lamenting,
In every street cries of "Ah, woe!"
And the farm hand shall be
Called to mourn,
And those skilled in wailing
To lament;
17 For there shall be lamenting
In every vineyard, too,
When I pass through your midst
—said the LORD.

18 Ah, you who wish
For the day of the LORD!
Why should you want
The day of the LORD?
It shall be darkness, not light!—
19 As if a man should run from a lion
And be attacked by a bear;
Or if he got indoors,
Should lean his hand on the wall
And be bitten by a snake!
20 Surely the day of the LORD shall be
Not light, but darkness,
Blackest night without a glimmer.

21 I loathe, I spurn your festivals,
I am not appeased by your solemn assemblies.
22 If you offer Me burnt offerings—or your meal
offerings—
I will not accept them;
I will pay no heed
To your gifts of fatlings.
23 Spare Me the sound of your hymns,
And let Me not hear the music of your lutes.
24 But let justice well up like water,
Righteousness like an unfailing stream.
25 Did you offer sacrifice and oblation to Me
Those forty years in the wilderness,
O House of Israel?

26a And you shall carry off your "king"—
Sikkuth[b] and Kiyyun,[b]

a Vv. 26–27 would read well after 6.14.
b Two Akkadian names applied to Saturn, here deliberately pointed with the vowels of Heb. shiqquṣ, *"detestable thing."*

18–20: On *the day of the LORD* here and elsewhere, see Joel 1.15 n. As the context suggests, the popular understanding of this Day was a day in which Israel would be saved through God's great power, while the prophetic suggestion is that God will use His power against His enemies, here Israel. If this v. is authentic to the prophet Amos, it is the earliest reference to the Day of the LORD. **21–25:** The text does not state that sacrifices—or any other cultic rituals—are wrong per se, but rather that those brought by people who behave in a manner offensive to God are unacceptable to God. From the perspective of the intended readers of the book, the time in the wilderness is comparable to the time between the destruction of the First and the building of the Second Temple, since there was no Temple at either time. **25:** This contradicts the Priestly tradition reflected in the Torah, which suggests that offerings were a crucial part of the wilderness experience. **26:** The passage has a strong satiric tone. Their *"king"—Sikkuth,* is a Mesopotamian, astral deity. *Kiyyun* refers to Saturn, *your astral deity.* The god Sikkuth is mentioned here because of the aural pun created by his name and "shikutz" (detestable things). The people are satirically depicted carrying their images as in a (ritual) procession, but they walk into exile!

6.2: *Calneh ... Great Hamath ... Gath,* cities and territories that were conquered by the Assyrians. The author or authors and the intended readers of the book were either unaware or thought it irrelevant that these cities and territories were actually conquered years after the period in which the book is set (see 1.1). **5:** The tradition of David as the archetypal musician is reflected in later Jewish tradition, which attributes the entire book of Psalms to him. **7:** *Festive meals* stands for "mrzḥ," a term referring to social and cultic banquets. The term is often associated with funerary meals in the ancient Near East and see Jer. 16.5, the only other text in the HB in which "mrzḥ" appears. **8:** The reference to *the Pride of Jacob* points to the arrogance of the people. It also ridicules one of the most positive self-descriptions of Israel (see Ps. 47.5). Note the strong contrast between the text there and this v. Ironically, in 8.7, God swears by this pride which He here condemns.

The images you have made for yourselves
Of your astral deity—
27 As I drive you into exile beyond Damascus
—Said the LORD,
whose name is God of Hosts.[a]

6 Ah, you who are at ease in Zion[b]
And confident on the hill of Samaria,
You notables of the leading nation
On whom the House of Israel [c-]pin their hopes:[-c]
2 Cross over to Calneh and see,
Go from there to Great Hamath,
And go down to Gath of the Philistines:
Are [you] better than those kingdoms,
[d-]Or is their territory larger than yours?[-d]
3 [e-]Yet you ward off [the thought of] a day of woe
And convene a session of lawlessness.[-e]
4 They lie on ivory beds,
Lolling on their couches,
Feasting on lambs from the flock
And on calves from the stalls.
5 [e-]They hum snatches of song
To the tune of the lute—
They account themselves musicians[-e] like David.
6 They drink [straight] from the wine bowls
And anoint themselves with the choicest oils—
But they are not concerned about the ruin of Joseph.
7 Assuredly, right soon
They shall head the column of exiles;
They shall loll no more at festive meals.

8 My Lord GOD swears by Himself:
I loathe [f-]the Pride of Jacob,[-f]
And I detest his fortresses.
I will declare forfeit city and inhabitants alike
—declares the LORD, the God of Hosts.
9 If ten people are left in one house, they shall die. 10 [e-]And if
someone's kinsman—who is to burn incense for him—comes
to carry the remains out of a house,[-e] and he calls to the one at
the rear of the house, "Are there any alive besides you?" he will
answer, "No, none." And he will say, "Hush!"—so that no one
may utter the name of the LORD.

a I.e., who is Lord of all the astral bodies.
b Emendation yields "Joseph," cf. v. 6, and 5.6, 15, where "Joseph" denotes the northern kingdom.
c-c Taking ba' l- *as synonymous with* ba' 'ad; *see Isa. 45.24 and note b-b.*
d-d Emendation yields "Or is your territory larger than theirs?"
e-e Meaning of Heb. uncertain.
f-f A poetic designation of the northern kingdom.

11 For the LORD will command,
And the great house shall be smashed to bits,
And the little house to splinters.
12 Can horses gallop on a rock?
[a]Can it be plowed with oxen?[a]
Yet you have turned justice into poison weed
And the fruit of righteousness to wormwood.
13 [Ah,] those who are so happy about Lo-dabar,[b]
Who exult, "By our might
We have captured Karnaim"![b]
14 But I, O House of Israel,
Will raise up a nation against you
—declares the LORD, the God of Hosts—
Who will harass you from Lebo-Hamath
To the Wadi Arabah.

7 This is what my Lord GOD showed me: He was creating [a
plague of] locusts at the time when the late-sown crops
were beginning to sprout—[c]the late-sown crops after the
king's reaping.[c] 2 When it had finished devouring the herbage
in the land, I said, "O Lord GOD, pray forgive. How will Jacob
survive? He is so small." 3 The LORD relented concerning this.
"It shall not come to pass," said the LORD.
4 This is what the Lord GOD showed me: Lo, my Lord GOD
was summoning [d]to contend by[d] fire which consumed the
Great Deep and was consuming the fields. 5 I said, "Oh, Lord
GOD, refrain! How will Jacob survive? He is so small." 6 The
LORD relented concerning this. "That shall not come to pass,
either," said my Lord GOD.
7 This is what He showed me: He was standing on a wall
[e]checked with a plumb line[e] and He was holding a plumb
line.[f] 8 And the LORD asked me, "What do you see, Amos?" "A
plumb line,"[f] I replied. And my Lord declared, "I am going to
apply a plumb line[f] to My people Israel; I will pardon them no
more. 9 The shrines of Isaac shall be laid waste, and the sanctuaries of Israel reduced to ruins; and I will turn upon the House
of Jeroboam with the sword."

a-a Meaning of Heb. uncertain; emendation yields "Can one plow the sea with oxen?"

b Two towns east of the Jordan recovered for Israel by Jeroboam II (see 2 Kings 14.25). For Lo-dabar, cf. 2 Sam. 9.4, 5; 17.27; for Karnaim, cf. Gen. 14.5.

c-c Meaning of Heb. uncertain. The king's reaping of fodder apparently occurred near the end of the rainy season, and whatever the locust destroyed after that could not be replaced for another year.

d-d Emendation yields "flaming."

e-e Or "destined for the pickax"; meaning of Heb. uncertain.

f Or "pickax"; meaning of Heb. uncertain.

13: The reference to *Lo-dabar* points to a city east of the Jordan (and so does *Karnaim*). At the same time, it conveys a pun on the basic meaning of "lo-davar," that is, "not a thing," nothing. Similarly, Karnaim suggests to the readers a pun on "keren," horn, a symbol of strength. Wordplays are common in prophetic books.

7.1–9: Three reports of prophetic visions of judgment. These are the first three of five reports about prophetic visions (7.1–3, 4–6, 7–9; 8.1–3; 9.1–6); the narrative of 7.10–17 disrupts their continuity. The series leads up to the vision of the destruction in 9.1–6. In the first two of the three cases, the LORD relents. **1–3:** Judgment by locusts (cf. Joel). **4–6:** Judgment by fire. **7–9:** *The House of Jeroboam* refers to Jeroboam II or better, the "House of Jehu," the last stable dynasty of the Northern Kingdom. The term refers also—at least by connotation—to the Northern Kingdom as a whole.

10 Amaziah, the priest of Bethel, sent this message to King
Jeroboam of Israel: "Amos is conspiring against you within the
House of Israel. The country cannot endure the things he is
saying. 11 For Amos has said, 'Jeroboam shall die by the sword,
and Israel shall be exiled from its soil.'"

12 Amaziah also said to Amos, "Seer, off with you to the land
of Judah! [a-]Earn your living[-a] there, and do your prophesying
there. 13 But don't ever prophesy again at Bethel; for it is a king's
sanctuary and a royal palace." 14 Amos answered Amaziah: "I
am not a prophet,[b] and I am not a prophet's disciple. I am a cattle breeder[c] and a tender of sycamore figs. 15 But the LORD took
me away from following the flock, and the LORD said to me, 'Go,
prophesy to My people Israel.' 16 And so, hear the word of the
LORD. You say I must not prophesy about the House of Israel or
preach about the House of Isaac; 17 but this, I swear, is what the
LORD said: Your wife shall [d-]play the harlot[-d] in the town, your
sons and daughters shall fall by the sword, and your land shall
be divided up with a measuring line. And you yourself shall die
on unclean soil;[e] for Israel shall be exiled from its soil."

8 This is what my Lord GOD showed me: There was a basket
of figs.[f] 2 He said, "What do you see, Amos?" "A basket of
figs," I replied. And the LORD said to me: "The [g-]hour of doom[-g]
has come for My people Israel; I will not pardon them again.
3 And the singing women of the palace shall howl on that day—
declares my Lord GOD:

So many corpses
Left lying everywhere!
Hush!"

4 Listen to this, you [h-]who devour the needy, annihilating the
poor of the land,[-h] 5 saying, "If only the new moon were over,
so that we could sell grain; the sabbath, so that we could offer
wheat for sale, [i-]using an *ephah* that is too small, and a shekel
that is too big,[-i] tilting a dishonest scale, 6 and selling grain refuse as grain! We will buy the poor for silver, the needy for a
pair of sandals." 7 The LORD swears by[j] the Pride of Jacob: "I
will never forget any of their doings."

8 Shall not the earth shake for this
And all that dwell on it mourn?

a-a Lit. "eat bread." *b I.e., by profession.*
c Meaning of Heb. uncertain; emendation yields "sheep breeder"; cf. the next verse and 1.1. *d-d Emendation yields "be ravished"; cf. Lam. 5.11.*
e Cf. Hos. 9.3 and note. *f Heb.* qayiṣ, *lit. "summer fruit."* *g-g Heb.* qeṣ.
h-h Emendation yields "who on every new moon devour the needy, and on every sabbath the humble of the land"; cf. v. 5.
i-i Giving short measures of grain, but using oversize weights for the silver received in payment. *j Or "concerning"; cf. 6.8 with note.*

7.10–17: Narrative about Amos and the priest Amaziah. In some cases the term "Israel" here points only to the Northern Kingdom, but in others it may evoke a more inclusive idea of Israel to the postmonarchic readers of the book and accordingly allow them to identify with that Israel. Although this section disrupts the narrative of "This is what my Lord GOD showed me," it is placed here, because it is contextually appropriate, immediately following the oracle against Jeroboam in v. 9. **11:** Amos's prophecy was considered treasonous because it would demoralize the people and set them against their leaders. **12:** The prophet is a Judahite, and so Amaziah wants to send him back to Judah. **14:** Amos maintains that he is not a professional prophet, who may be hired for his services (see 1 Sam. 9.7) and thus "bought"; rather, God took him away from his job to perform a particular task (cf. 2 Sam. 7.8). This being so, he has no alternative but to prophesy (see 3.8). Amos's reply enhances the authority associated with his message.

8.1–3: Fourth report of a prophetic vision of judgment: the basket of summer fruit. *Figs,* lit. "summer basket" or "basket of summer fruit," plays on the words "kayitz" and "the end" ("ketz"). V. 2 may be translated "The end has come upon My people Israel."

8.4–14: Report of a prophetic word in the monarchic period. Another "Hear" unit (cf. 3.1–6.14). **4–5:** *New moon,* the beginning of a month, traditionally observed as a holiday. The text clearly implies that days of religious observance (Shabbat, new moon) are supposed to be kept, though observance of the new moon by ceasing from work is nowhere recorded in Torah legislation. The book of Amos is certainly not against cultic observance. The problem here is that people are eager for the holiday to be over so they can get on with employing dishonest means to make money. The text associates lack of reverence for these

Shall it not all rise like the Nile
And surge and subside like the Nile of Egypt?
9 And in that day —declares my Lord GOD—
I will make the sun set at noon,
I will darken the earth on a sunny day.
10 I will turn your festivals into mourning
And all your songs into dirges;
I will put sackcloth on all loins
And tonsures on every head.
I will make it[a] mourn as for an only child,
All[b] of it as on a bitter day.

11 A time is coming—declares my Lord GOD—when I will
send a famine upon the land: not a hunger for bread or a thirst
for water, but for hearing the words of the LORD. 12 Men shall
wander from [c-]sea to sea[-c] and from north to east to seek the
word of the LORD, but they shall not find it.

13 In that day, the beautiful maidens and the young men
shall faint with thirst—
14 Those who swear by the guilt of Samaria,
Saying, "As your god lives, Dan,"[d]
And "As the way to Beer-sheba lives"[e]—
They shall fall to rise no more.

9 I saw my LORD standing by the altar, and He said: [f-]Strike the
capitals so that the thresholds quake, and make an end of the
first of them all.[-f] And I will slay the last of them with the sword;
not one of them shall escape, and not one of them shall survive.
2 If they burrow down to Sheol,
From there My hand shall take them;
And if they ascend to heaven,
From there I will bring them down.
3 If they hide on the top of Carmel,
There I will search them out and seize them;
And if they conceal themselves from My sight
At the bottom of the sea,
There I will command
The serpent to bite them.
4 And if they go into captivity
Before their enemies,
There I will command
The sword to slay them.
I will fix My eye on them for evil
And not for good.

a I.e., the earth; cf. vv. 8 and 9d. *b Lit. "the end."*
c-c Emendation yields "south to west." *d See 1 Kings 12.28–29.*
e See 5.5 with note. *f-f Meaning of Heb. uncertain.*

religious observances and dishonest trade (see Lev. 19.35–37); cf. Amos 5.21–25 n. *Ephah ... small ... shekel ... big:* The measure with which the corrupt merchants sell grain is smaller than it should be, allowing them to sell less than an ephah (a unit of dry measure of perhaps 23 liters) for the full price; on the other hand, the weight with which they buy grain is larger than it should be, allowing them to get more for the shekel (about 11.4 g) than they should. **9:** A solar eclipse is a portent of doom and a reversal of the natural order. Compare the description of the Day of the LORD in 5.18–20. **10:** The idea of reversal continues. The festivals, which the people do not respect, will be turned into times of *mourning.* **11–14:** *Famine,* which is one of the ways God punishes the people's sins, and which often accompanies destruction, is here used metaphorically. **11–12:** The people will be hungry and thirsty for God's word. Rabbinic sources understand this text as pointing to a time in which the Torah *(the words of the LORD)* will be forgotten: "Our Rabbis taught: When our Masters entered the vineyard at Yabneh, they said, The Torah is destined to be forgotten in Israel, as it is said, Behold, the days come, saith the Lord GOD, that I will send a famine in the land ..." *b. Shab.* 138b [Soncino Press, English Talmud]; and see also *t. 'Ed.* 1.1).

9.1–6: Fifth report of a prophetic vision of judgment: the LORD at the altar. Which altar? The text carefully avoids an explicit reference to the altar at Bethel, which would have constrained the intended readers of the book. The text may use the imagery of an earthquake (cf. 1.1) **2:** *Sheol,* the place of the dead. The nadir of the earth; the opposite of heaven. **3:** *Carmel,* a peak in northern Israel. Here it serves as both a reference to the highest point on earth that an Israelite may think of reaching and as a symbol of the highest point on earth in cosmic terms (cf. 1.2); the opposite of the bottom of the sea. *Serpent,* here a mythical sea-creature.

5 It is my Lord the GOD of Hosts
At whose touch the earth trembles
And all who dwell on it mourn,
And all of it swells like the Nile
And subsides like the Nile of Egypt;
6 Who built His chambers in heaven
And founded His vault on the earth,
Who summons the waters of the sea
And pours them over the land—
His name is the LORD.

7 To Me, O Israelites, you are
Just like the Ethiopians —declares the LORD.
True, I brought Israel up
From the land of Egypt,
But also the Philistines from Caphtor
And the Arameans from Kir.
8 Behold, the Lord GOD has His eye
Upon the sinful kingdom:
I will wipe it off
The face of the earth!

But, I will not wholly wipe out
The House of Jacob —declares the LORD.
9 For I will give the order
And shake the House of Israel—
Through all the nations—
As one shakes [sand] in a sieve,[a]
And not a pebble falls to the ground.
10 All the sinners of My people
Shall perish by the sword,
Who boast,
"Never shall the evil
Overtake us or come near us."

11 In that day,
I will set up again the fallen booth of David:
I will mend its breaches and set up its ruins anew.
I will build it firm as in the days of old,
12 [b-]So that they shall possess the rest of Edom
And all the nations once attached to My name[-b]
—declares the LORD
who will bring this to pass.

a A coarse sieve used for cleansing grain of straw and stones, or sand of pebbles and shells.

b-b I.e., the House of David shall reestablish its authority over the nations that were ruled by David.

5–6: Theophanic (cf. 1.2) and creation imagery is used to emphasize God's power. Such descriptions, called doxologies (praises of God) are interspersed throughout Amos, and characterize this prophetic book.

9.7–10: The final account of judgment provides also a glimmer of hope. 7: Israel is not granted special privileges by the LORD, even if He took them out of Egypt (see 3.2). **8–9:** The severe condemnation and punishment of Israel in the past (from the viewpoint of the readership) shifts now to a promise of restoration and ideal conditions for Israel in the future.

9.11–15: Hope: restoration and an ideal future are promised. 11: Rabbinic sources understood the setting up the *fallen booth of David* as pointing to the messianic era (e.g., *b. Sanh.* 96b–97a). Some Jewish medieval commentators understood the booth as a reference to the Temple, but the majority saw it as the Davidic kingdom. Most modern scholars associate the image of the fallen booth of David with the fall of monarchic Judah and the exile. Ibn Ezra associates the v. with Hezekiah's successful stand against Sennacherib (see 2 Kings 18.13–19.37; Isa. 36.1–37.38; 2 Chron. 32.1–23). (The majority of contemporary historians agree that Hezekiah was not successful against Sennacherib, either militarily or politically [see 2 Kings chs 18–20]. But the image of Hezekiah's success had already become central to the way Israel understood its past.) As for the particular reference to Edom, see Obad. and nn. there.

13 A time is coming —declares the LORD—
When the plowman shall meet the reaper,[a]
And the treader of grapes
Him who holds the [bag of] seed;
When the mountains shall drip wine
And all the hills shall wave [with grain].

14 I will restore My people Israel.
They shall rebuild ruined cities and inhabit them;
They shall plant vineyards and drink their wine;
They shall till gardens and eat their fruits.
15 And I will plant them upon their soil,
Nevermore to be uprooted
From the soil I have given them
—said the LORD your God.

a Cf. Lev. 26.5.

13: Cf. Lev. 26.5. The produce will be so abundant that the harvesting will continue through the time for planting new seeds. **15:** The book concludes with a highly optimistic, unconditional promise: *Nevermore* will the foretold disaster, which, from the perspective of the post-monarchic community had already actually transpired, be repeated.

עֹבַדְיָה

Obadiah

OBADIAH IS THE SHORTEST BOOK in the Bible, containing only 291 Heb words. Nonetheless, like all prophetic books, it is meant to be read, read again, and studied. The book's main topic is the destruction of Jerusalem in 586 BCE, and the putative actions of Edom against Judah at the time. The Edomites, the central characters of the book, were regarded as kin to the Israelites, since they were supposedly descended from Esau, Jacob's brother (see Gen. 25.30; 36.8; Num. 20.14; Deut. 2.4, 8, passim). In Obadiah, Edom serves both as a reference to the nation of that name that was considered to be Israel's brother—a motif explicitly mentioned in Obad. 1.10—and also to the nations in general. Subsequently, Jews identified Edom with Rome and later with Christendom. For them, the book of Obadiah referred at least in part to the events associated with the destruction of the Second Temple (cf. Radak), or to future events associated with the coming of the messianic era (e.g., Abravanel). Of course, ancient and medieval Christian readers were convinced that they were not Edom but rather (the true) Israel (cf. Rom. 9.6–13).

According to the book, the Edomites did not behave as brothers to the people of Judah in their worst hour but rather joined the enemy forces (cf. Ps. 137.7; Lam. 4.21–22). The book of Obadiah presents therefore a major confrontation between the LORD and Edom (and the nations it represents) that is in sharp contrast to God's relation with Judah/Israel, which will enjoy an eventual utopian future that will be consistent with God's kingdom on earth.

Some scholars differentiate between an original book of Obadiah and the present book, which they view as an expansion around an earlier core. Others emphasize the coherence of the book as it stands. The present book was composed in the postmonarchic period, as the references to the fall of Jerusalem, the exile, and the exilic community in Sardis (a city in modern Turkey that was the capital of the ancient kingdom of Lydia) demonstrate.

There are clear similarities between Obad. 1.1–7 and Jer. 49.7–22 (or more precisely Jer. 49.7a, 14–16, 9–10). According to some, the author of the book of Obadiah borrowed from Jeremiah; according to others the opposite happened. More likely, however, the author of both texts borrowed from a common text whose full length and precise wording are unrecoverable.

The book of Obadiah is read as the haftarah for the parashah of Va-yishlaḥ (Gen. 32.4–36.43) in the Sephardic and Yemenite traditions; the Ashkenazic traditions read Hos. 11.7–12.12 instead of, or in addition to, Obadiah. Gen. chs 32–33 tells of the meeting between Jacob and Esau after Jacob's sojourn with Laban.

The book begins with an introduction (v. 1), then moves to a set of passages each of which deals with Edom's condemnation and judgment (vv. 2–4, 5–7, 8–15). By the end it becomes clear that Edom also stands for all the nations other than Israel. The theme of the judgment of the nations, and of Edom as a paradigm for the nations, is intertwined with that of Zion's glorious future in vv. 15b–18. The book concludes (vv. 19–21), like many prophetic books (e.g., Amos) with an image of an ideal future in which Israel is restored and the dominion is the LORD's (v. 21).

[EHUD BEN ZVI]

1 The prophecy of Obadiah.

We have received tidings from the LORD,
And an envoy has been sent out among the nations:
"Up! Let us rise up against her for battle."

Thus said my Lord GOD concerning Edom:
2 I will make you least among nations,
You shall be most despised.
3 Your arrogant heart has seduced you,
You who dwell in clefts of the rock,
In your lofty abode.
You think in your heart,
"Who can pull me down to earth?"
4 Should you nest as high as the eagle,
Should your eyrie be lodged 'mong the stars,
Even from there I will pull you down
—declares the LORD.

5 If thieves were to come to you,
Marauders by night,
They would steal no more than they needed.
If vintagers came to you,
They would surely leave some gleanings.
How utterly you are destroyed!
6 How thoroughly rifled is Esau,
How ransacked his hoards!
7 All your allies turned you back
At the frontier;
Your own confederates
Have duped and overcome you;
[Those who ate] your bread
Have planted snares under you.

1: Introduction to the book. **1a:** NJPS follows the Tg. and translates the title of the book as *The prophecy of Obadiah.* This translation is preferable to the usual, more etymological "The vision of Obadiah" (e.g., NRSV), because visual elements do not figure prominently in the book (the same holds true for Isa. 1.1). The title, however, should be not understood as meaning that the ensuing text contains only a report of God's words to Obadiah. God is surely not the only speaker in the book. It is unusual to introduce a biblical character by one name only, without a patronymic or name of a father (contrast Isa. 1.1; Jer. 1.1; Hos. 1.1; etc.). The lack of a more precise reference to Obadiah allowed the readers of the book to wonder whether the Obadiah of this book was the same Obadiah who figures prominently in 1 Kings ch 18. **1b:** *Thus said my Lord GOD concerning Edom:* The Heb is better translated, "Thus said the Lord GOD concerning Edom." More importantly, the four lines of the translation that follow the title of the book (1a) are rearranged. The Heb text places "Thus said the Lord GOD concerning Edom" before *We have received tidings from the LORD.* Those who favor the rearrangement of the text adopted in NJPS maintain that it makes more contextual sense to have *thus said ...* just before v. 2. But others claim that the presence of the expression at the beginning of the book points to an important theological claim, namely that the entire prophetic book—including words uttered by God but also by a human prophetic speaker—is to be considered the LORD's word, and as such shares divine origin and authority.

2–4: First condemnation of Edom: its foolishness and self-deluding reliance on its own terrain. These vv. use well-known rhetorical techniques to characterize Edom as foolish while it claims to be wise. They represent Edom as one who inanely claims that the LORD is unable to reach it because of its mountainous territory, and at the same time considers scaling into the celestial realm. This type of characterization of the "enemy" is common in the ancient Near East. Edom was associated with wisdom in the Bible (v. 8; Jer. 49.7). **3:** *Rock* (Heb "sela'") is a pun on the name "Sela," one of the important cities of Edom (perhaps near the ancient city of Petra).

5–7: Second condemnation of Edom: its foolishness and self-deluding reliance on human allies. Edom is presented as one who inanely trusts unreliable allies, who will turn against it and utterly destroy it. The section leads up to the obvious conclusion: *He* [Edom] *is bereft of understanding.* This type of characterization of the "enemy" is also common in the ancient Near East. **5:** *Vintagers* (Heb "botzrim") evokes the name of another main Edomite city, "Botzrah" (Bozrah). **7:** Another possible, and perhaps more likely, understanding of the first part of the v. is: "All your allies have deceived you, / they have driven you to the border" (NRSV). In any case, it is clear that the trusted allies of Edom contributed to its downfall. Eating *bread* together was a sign of close relationship.

He is bereft of understanding.
8 In that day —declares the LORD—
I will make the wise vanish from Edom,
Understanding from Esau's mount.
9 Your warriors shall lose heart, O Teman,
And not a man on Esau's mount
Shall survive the slaughter.

10 For the outrage to your brother Jacob,
Disgrace shall engulf you,
And you shall perish forever.
11 On that day when you stood aloof,
When aliens carried off his goods,
When foreigners entered his gates
And cast lots for Jerusalem,
You were as one of them.
12 [a]How could you[-a] gaze with glee
On your brother that day,
On his day of calamity!
How could you gloat
Over the people of Judah
On that day of ruin!
How could you loudly jeer
On a day of anguish!
13 How could you enter the gate of My people
On its day of disaster,
Gaze in glee with the others
On its misfortune
On its day of disaster,
And lay hands on its wealth
On its day of disaster!
14 How could you stand at the passes[b]
To cut down its fugitives!
How could you betray those who fled
On that day of anguish!
15 As you did, so shall it be done to you;
Your conduct shall be requited.

Yea, against all nations
The day of the LORD is at hand.
16 That same cup that you[c] drank on
My Holy Mount
Shall all nations drink evermore,[d]

8–15: Judgment over Edom: the two days of destruction. Edom and the nations (other than Israel). The last passage in the set focuses on the actions of Edom against his brother *on that day* of Jerusalem's destruction and directly relates it to the future day of Edom's destruction (notice the repetition of "on that day"). The motto of this section is to a large extent *as you did, so shall it be done to you* (v. 15, and contrast with Prov. 24.29). But as the unit concludes, the object of the divine wrath shifts from Edom to *all nations* (that is, nations other than Israel), suggesting to the readers that Edom also symbolizes all the nations. Edom's actions, behavior, and future judgment are not an aberration, but rather paradigmatic for those of the nations. **8:** *In that day,* Heb "on that day," just as all other "on ... day" in this unit. **9:** *Teman,* a grandson of Esau (Edom, Gen. 36.11), here, as often in prophetic literature, a synonym for Edom (e.g., Jer. 49.7, 20; Ezek. 25.13). The name itself means "South"; Edom was south of Judah. **10:** *Your brother Jacob,* i.e., Israel. Jacob and Esau were brothers (Gen. 25.20–34).

15b–18: On salvation for post-monarchic Israel/Zion and judgment over Edom/the nations. 15b: This line is shared by the previous unit and this one. (Sharing expressions or lines between two neighboring units within a literary text is not uncommon in prophetic literature.) The feature brings here the two units together; this makes the book more cohesive, and contributes to the flow of the reading. **16–17:** The text creates both a temporal differentiation between Israel that already drank the cup (see Jer. 25.15–29), and the nations that shall drink it, and a spatial one between holy Mt. Zion and the rest of the world.

a-a Lit. "Do not," and so through v. 14. *b Meaning of Heb. uncertain.*
c I.e., the Israelites.
d Emendation yields "at My hand," cf. Isa. 51.17; Jer. 25.15; Ps. 75.9.

Drink till their speech grows thick,
And they become as though they had never been.
17 But on Zion's mount a remnant shall survive,
And it shall be holy.[a]
The House of Jacob shall dispossess
Those who dispossessed them.
18 The House of Jacob shall be fire,
And the House of Joseph flame,
And the House of Esau shall be straw;
They shall burn it and devour it,
And no survivor shall be left of the House of Esau
—for the LORD has spoken.

19[b] Thus they shall possess the Negeb and Mount Esau as well,
the Shephelah and Philistia. They shall possess the Ephraimite country and the district of Samaria,[c] and Benjamin[d] along
with Gilead. 20 And that exiled force of Israelites [shall possess]
what belongs to the Phoenicians as far as Zarephath,[e] while
the Jerusalemite exile community of Sepharad[f] shall possess
the towns of the Negeb. 21 For [g]liberators shall march up[g] on
Mount Zion to wreak judgment on Mount Esau; and dominion
shall be the LORD's.

a I.e., inviolate; cf. Jer. 2.3. *b Meaning of parts of vv. 19–21 uncertain.*
c After the exile of the northern tribes, the city and district of Samaria were occupied mainly by non-Israelites. *d Emendation yields "the land of the Ammonites."*
e A town in southern Phoenicia; see 1 Kings 17.9. *f Probably Asia Minor, called Saparda in Persian cuneiform inscriptions.*
g-g Several ancient versions read, "they [the exiles from Jerusalem named in the preceding verse] shall march up victorious."

17: The Heb clearly states that it is *Zion's mount* that *shall be holy,* not the *remnant.* **18:** *And no survivor shall be left of the House of Esau:* This claim has later been understood as pointing to the world to come and to the place of "those whose evil deeds are like to those of Esau" rather than specifically to Romans (or non-Jews in general). See *b. A. Z.* 10b.

19–21: The concluding note of the book: a particular image of, and a divine promise for, the ideal future. As the translators' note *b* in NJPS suggests, the text is somewhat difficult. V. 19 is probably better understood as follows: "Those of the Negev (South) will and should inherit/possess [the whole of] Mt. Esau (the mountain of Esau); those of the Shephelah (the coastal plain) will and should inherit/possess the [whole of (the land of) the] Philistines; they (i.e., those of the Shephelah) will and should inherit/possess [all of] the land/highland of Ephraim and [all of] the land/highland of Samaria; and the Benjaminites, [all of the Gilead]"; cf. the Tg. Alternative readings and understandings of v. 20 have been advanced. Among them, "The exiles (exilic community) of this territory who are (consist of) the Israelites who are among the Canaanites (i.e., Phoenicians) will and should inherit/possess [what belongs to the Canaanites/Phoenicians] as far as Zarephath, while the Jerusalemite exiles (exilic community) who are in Sepharad will and should inherit/possess the towns of the Negev/South." Although all agree that the text communicates that Israel will repossess the land, the question at stake is which social and geographical structure is envisioned for that Israel. *Sepharad* was identified in the Tg. as Spain. (It is more likely to be Sardis, a main city in Asia Minor.) The equation Sepharad = Spain, however, became a cornerstone in Jewish self-identification for centuries. The Jews of Spain and their descendants are called, and call themselves, Sepharadim (or Sefaradim). Some scholars prefer to translate "saviors" instead of *liberators* and "to judge" rather than *to wreak judgment on Mount Esau.* The conclusion of the book originally evoked the language associated with the time of the Judges, who are sometimes called deliverers or liberators (see, e.g., Judg. 3.9). In later Jewish tradition, some understood the text as pointing to a messianic time. Such an understanding raises questions about the identity of the mentioned saviors (see Radak on Mic. 5.4; Ibn Ezra; Abravanel). The final sentence may be translated as "the kingdom will be the LORD's" or even better, "the kingship (i.e., the office of the king) will be the LORD's." In other words, at that time the LORD will be manifest (in Israel and in the entire world) as the king. In this case, Obadiah, like Deutero-Isaiah, is imagining an ideal future in which a Davidic messiah plays no role.

יונה

Jonah

THE BOOK OF JONAH was included in "the Twelve," among the other prophetic books, because it was accepted as a prophetic book. Yet it is unlike all the other prophetic books in many and diverse ways. For one thing, the book of Jonah is a narrative, whereas the others are not, though they may include some narrative sections. Prophetic books tend to allocate a large share of their text to reports of divine announcements (or "oracles") and of prophetic addresses to a public other than the LORD or the prophet alone. This is clearly not the case in Jonah. Further, none of the other eleven prophets rebels against God, as Jonah does, and takes practical steps to preempt the fulfillment of the explicit divine will as communicated to the prophet. The motif of Jonah's active opposition to the LORD's command and will, and accordingly his reluctance to show honor and reverence to his Master, is overtly emphasized in the text by contrasting him with various non-Israelites, including the inhabitants of Nineveh. Despite the typically negative view of Assyria in the Bible, the book characterizes the entire population of Nineveh (the capital of Assyria; a fact well-known to the intended readership of the book), including its elite, the sailors, and even all creation, as clearly responsive to the LORD. Finally, according to this book, this extremely atypical prophet is the most successful in the Bible (see the annotations).

The book itself has been characterized in different ways, among them: as a satire, a story that presents an implicit ideal by means of an exaggerated portrait of its opposite; as a parable, which makes its theological, spiritual, or moral point implicitly through narrative; and as didactic fiction, perhaps a narrative philosophical tractate. It is perhaps better to understand it as a meta-prophetic book, that is, a book that probes the role of the prophet, and as a book that is to be studied as the LORD's word or teaching (see below). As such it uses humor and elements of satire and parody and it carries a strong didactic message.

Some have argued that the principal theme of the book of Jonah concerns the power of repentance; others that its main focus and message contrast a doctrine of retributive justice to one of divine grace. Still others maintain that the main issue in Jonah is a conflict between God's universalist approach and Jonah's nationalistic tendencies. Another group of scholars is convinced that the focus of the book is the contrast or conflict between an understanding of God as constrained by particular rules known to human beings and another that stresses the radical independence of such a being. None of these and similar approaches to the book have commanded overwhelming assent because the book cannot be reduced to one main theme.

At one level, the basic narrative is quite simple, but at another, it shows much sophistication and polyvalence (that is, multiple meanings). For instance, in the basic story Nineveh is saved from destruction because, as the LORD states, "And should not I care about Nineveh, that great city, in which there are more than a hundred and twenty thousand persons who do not yet know their right hand from their left, and many beasts as well!" (4.11). But if so, what are the readers of the book supposed to make of the well-known fact in their time that historical Nineveh had long been totally destroyed and never rebuilt? Surely, they thought, such destruction must have been a manifestation of God's will. But if so, are some of God's words, as recorded in the prophetic books, valid at one time but not another, even if God's explicit argument seems universal? Are prophetic words contingent on a set of particular historical circumstances and therefore of no absolute value and general scope? Is it possible to distinguish between those that can apply more generally, and those that are tied to a particular historical event? Or in other words, between contingent and the noncontingent words, and if so how? Or are all prophetic/YHVH's words contingent? The book raises many other issues concerning the role of prophets, the question of if and when prophecies will be fulfilled, and the limitations of human knowledge based on reading Scripture. It bears noting that Jonah is depicted as one who knows Scripture well (see the multiple biblical references in the prayer in ch 2 and see also 4.2); nevertheless, his understanding of the role of prophecy and of God's will is presented as defective.

The language of the book, and its use of earlier biblical books, suggests that it was written in the Persian period. No critical scholar today advocates the historicity of the prophet and his fantastic misadventures.

The book is read in the afternoon service of Yom Kippur, the Day of Atonement (see *b. Meg.* 31a) because of the theme of repentance. On that day Jews are supposed to identify with the Ninevites and their plea (certainly not with Jonah; and cf. already *m. Ta'an.* 2.1; on the completeness and truthfulness of the Ninevites' repentance see, for instance, *b. Ta'an.* 16a, cf. Rambam, *Mishneh Torah, b. Ta'an.* 4.2; the Jerusalem Talmud, however, shows other voices, e.g., R. Yohanan in *y. Ta'an.* 9a; perek b, halakhah a).

The basic structure of the book of Jonah is clear and quite symmetrical. There are two divine calls to Jonah, both worded in a similar manner. In the first case, Jonah disobeys the divine command; in the second, he obeys (cf. 1.1–3 and 3.1–3). In both cases he interacts with non-Israelites who show fear of the LORD, and in both he stands in sharp contrast to them (cf. 1.4–15 and 3.5–10). Both interactions lead Jonah to address the LORD in distress (2.2–10 and 4.1–3). The main difference is that in the concluding case, the LORD responds in words and enters into a didactic dialogue with Jonah (4.4–11).

[EHUD BEN ZVI]

1 The word of the LORD came to Jonah[a] son of Amittai: 2 Go
at once to Nineveh, that great city, and proclaim judgment
upon it; for their wickedness has come before Me.
3 Jonah, however, started out to flee to Tarshish from the
LORD's service. He went down to Joppa and found a ship going
to Tarshish. He paid the fare and went aboard to sail with the
others to Tarshish, away from the service of the LORD.

a Mentioned in 2 Kings 14.25.

1.1–16: Jonah's first call from God and his response. Contrast between Jonah and the sailors. 1: The opening of the book, *the word of the LORD came to Jonah,* is a common one for a prophetic narrative that is embedded in a book, but it does not occur elsewhere as the opening of a book, so from the start, Jonah is different. This opening suggests to the readers that the book begins, as it were, "in the middle," and that much of the background of the story is not told in the book. It is up to them to fill the gap. *Jonah son of Amittai:* The name of the prophet is identical with that of a prophet mentioned in 2 Kings 14.25, who prophesied in the days of Jeroboam II, king of Israel and foretold territorial conquests for Israel. It seems possible and even likely that the text here serves to encourage its readers to identify the two, or at least to fill the mentioned gap with their knowledge about the prophet Jonah mentioned in Kings. **2:** *Nineveh* was the capital of Assyria, the conqueror of Samaria in 722 BCE; it was destroyed by the Babylonians and their allies in 612. Numerous prophetic texts characterize the Assyrians as extremely cruel and savage. Although this unflattering characterization pervaded much of biblical literature, the book of Jonah, which calls them Ninevites, never Assyrians, describes them as sinners who fully repented. The choice of words for this (first) call of Jonah reverberates in the second divine call (3.1–2). **3:** *To flee to Tarshish,* from the perspective of the readers a faraway place (cf. Isa. 66.19) in the opposite

4 But the LORD cast a mighty wind upon the sea, and such a great tempest came upon the sea that the ship was in danger of breaking up. 5 In their fright, the sailors cried out, each to his own god; and they flung the ship's cargo overboard to make it lighter for them. Jonah, meanwhile, had gone down into the hold of the vessel where he lay down and fell asleep. 6 The captain went over to him and cried out, "How can you be sleeping so soundly! Up, call upon your god! Perhaps the god will be kind to us and we will not perish."

7 The men said to one another, "Let us cast lots and find out on whose account this misfortune has come upon us." They cast lots and the lot fell on Jonah. 8 They said to him, "Tell us, you who have brought this misfortune upon us, what is your business? Where have you come from? What is your country, and of what people are you?" 9 "I am a Hebrew," he replied. "I worship the LORD, the God of Heaven, who made both sea and land." 10 The men were greatly terrified, and they asked him, "What have you done?" And when the men learned that he was fleeing from the service of the LORD—for so he told them—11 they said to him, "What must we do to you to make the sea calm around us?" For the sea was growing more and more stormy. 12 He answered, "Heave me overboard, and the sea will calm down for you; for I know that this terrible storm came upon you on my account." 13 Nevertheless, the men rowed hard to regain the shore, but they could not, for the sea was growing more and more stormy about them. 14 Then they cried out to the LORD: "Oh, please, LORD, do not let us perish on account of this man's life. Do not hold us guilty of killing an innocent person! For You, O LORD, by Your will, have brought this about." 15 And they heaved Jonah overboard, and the sea stopped raging.

16 The men feared the LORD greatly; they offered a sacrifice to the LORD and they made vows.

2 The LORD provided a huge fish to swallow Jonah; and Jonah remained in the fish's belly three days and three nights. 2 Jonah prayed to the LORD his God from the belly of the fish. 3 He said:

direction from Nineveh. Tarshish may have been in the Tarsus region on the southern coast of Turkey, but many other places have been suggested including Tartessus in Spain. *Joppa* was just outside Israelite territory, on the Mediterranean at the northern border of Philistia. Its modern name is Jaffa/Yafo (adjacent to Tel Aviv in modern Israel), and it is still a port. Jonah found a ship "coming from Tarshish" rather than *going to Tarshish,* as usually translated. Many scholars accept the translation *he paid the fare* but there is good reason to prefer "he paid its hire" (that is, he hired the ship and its sailors; cf. already *b. Ned.* 38a). In other words, he was "lucky" to find a ship just coming to port and hastened so much that he hired everyone so as to leave for the sea, on the spot. Jonah first *went down* to the port, and then *went aboard* (lit. "down to") the ship. **5:** Once in the ship he went *down into the hold of the vessel.* Eventually he will go down into the deep of the sea. Jonah *fell asleep,* but his was a "deep sleep," perhaps akin to a trance. **7:** *Cast lots,* a way to determine the divine will that is mentioned multiple times in the Bible (e.g., Lev. 16.8–10; Josh. 18.8–10; 1 Sam. 10.20–24; Obad. 1.11). The Heb term for *lot,* i.e., "gôral" appears more than seventy times in the Bible; cleromancy, i.e., divination through casting of lots, was widely attested in the ancient Near East. **9:** Jonah speaks to the sailors in terms they can relate to. He tells them he is a Hebrew, a term sometimes used when speaking to non-Israelites, and he identifies God as the Creator of the sea and land, putting the sea first, since that is the important element to the sailors. **10–16:** The sailors' reverence for and fear of the LORD is explicitly emphasized by the expanded repetition of v. 10 in v. 16, and by the description of their actions. They seem convinced that the storm was due to Jonah's presence, but they are more than reluctant to murder a prophet even if he is a fugitive servant of the LORD. In fact, the LORD has to force them to heave Jonah overboard, a point that is emphasized and embellished in *Midr. Tanḥ.* and *Pirqe R. El.* Even then they are afraid of being held responsible for the death of the prophet. To be sure, God knows that their action will not lead to Jonah's death, but rather serves as a necessary step for the completion of Jonah's mission and of God's overall intention. But the sailors do not know that. As for Jonah, he probably thought that death was the best available way out of his mission. Had he died, he would have successfully escaped from God's call. Of course, the readers know that God will not let this happen. As soon as Jonah is thrown overboard, they expect a divine action aimed at saving Jonah from death. Their expectations are fulfilled.

2.1–11: Jonah in the big fish. The fish (never called a whale) rescues Jonah from the sea. Most of this section of the book consists of Jonah's prayer. **3–10:** The prayer of Jonah is a pastiche of different vv. taken

In my trouble I called to the LORD,
And He answered me;
From the belly of Sheol I cried out,
And You heard my voice.
4 You cast me into the depths,
Into the heart of the sea,
The floods engulfed me;
All Your breakers and billows
Swept over me.
5 I thought I was driven away
Out of Your sight:
Would I ever gaze again
Upon Your holy Temple?
6 The waters closed in over me,
The deep engulfed me.
Weeds twined around my head.
7 I sank to the base of the mountains;
The bars of the earth closed upon me
forever.
Yet You brought my life up from the pit,
O LORD my God!
8 When my life was ebbing away,
I called the LORD to mind;
And my prayer came before You,
Into Your holy Temple.
9 They who cling to empty folly
Forsake their own welfare,[a]
10 But I, with loud thanksgiving,
Will sacrifice to You;
What I have vowed I will perform.
Deliverance is the LORD's!

11 The LORD commanded the fish, and it spewed Jonah out upon dry land.

3 The word of the LORD came to Jonah a second time: 2 "Go at once to Nineveh, that great city, and proclaim to it what I tell you." 3 Jonah went at once to Nineveh in accordance with the LORD's command.

Nineveh was [b-]an enormously large city[-b] a three days' walk across. 4 Jonah started out and made his way into the city the distance of one day's walk, and proclaimed: "Forty days more, and Nineveh shall be overthrown!"

a Meaning of Heb. uncertain. *b-b Lit. "a large city of God."*

from Psalms (see v. 3 and cf. Pss. 18.7; 30.3; 118.5; 120.1; 130.1, 2; v. 4 and cf. Ps. 42.8; v. 5 and cf. Ps. 31.23; v. 6 and cf. Pss. 18.5–6 and 69.2; v. 7 and cf. Pss. 30.4 and 71.20; v. 8a and cf. Pss. 142.4 and 143.4; v. 8b and cf. Pss. 5.8; 18.7 and 88.3; v. 9 and cf. Ps. 31.7; v. 10a and cf. Pss. 42.5; 50.14, 23 and 66.13; v. 10b and cf. Ps. 3.9). Jonah is thereby presented as a person well versed in the language of Psalms and able to compose a sophisticated prayer on their basis (cf. David or Solomon as described in Chronicles). In contrast to the rest of the book, which is a prose narrative, this is poetry. The verbs translated here in the past tense are probably better translated in the present. They point to events that are either happening or will happen (thus, "In my trouble I call to the LORD" rather than *In my trouble I called to the LORD*). **3:** *Sheol,* the Pit or the netherworld. It is the utter bottom of the world (in this case the depths of the sea) and also the land of the dead. **5:** *Would I ever gaze again* reflects a minor emendation, and may be understood as "Nevertheless I shall gaze again" (cf. Tg.). **9:** The final line of the v. conveys more than one meaning. *Forsake their own welfare,* "forsake their (true) loyalty," "forsake their bounty" are all possible understandings. Further, since *empty folly* can be understood as a reference to idols, and since *cling to* connotes worshipping, then the final line may be understood also as "forsake their idols," as some medieval Jewish commentators interpreted it.

3.1–10: Jonah's second call and the repentance of the Ninevites. **1–2:** Jonah's call to prophesy from ch 1 is replayed, but this time Jonah accepts his commission. **3:** *An enormously large city,* another case of double meaning. The text also means "a large city that belongs to God" (cf. translators' note *b-b*). This translation states that the city was a three-day walk across, an impossibly large distance for an ancient city. The text may be stating that the city was at a distance of three days' walk from Jonah's place. **4:** What Jonah means and what he is saying are not exactly the same. Jonah means to say, "Forty days more, and Nineveh is undone" but the readers notice that he is actually saying, "Forty days more, and Nineveh is overturned."

[5] The people of Nineveh believed God. They proclaimed a fast, and great and small alike put on sackcloth. [6] When the news reached the king of Nineveh, he rose from his throne, took off his robe, put on sackcloth, and sat in ashes. [7] And he had the word cried through Nineveh: "By decree of the king and his nobles: No man or beast—of flock or herd—shall taste anything! They shall not graze, and they shall not drink water! [8] They shall be covered with sackcloth—man and beast—and shall cry mightily to God. Let everyone turn back from his evil ways and from the injustice of which he is guilty. [9] Who knows but that God may turn and relent? He may turn back from His wrath, so that we do not perish."

[10] God saw what they did, how they were turning back from their evil ways. And God renounced the punishment He had planned to bring upon them, and did not carry it out.

4 This displeased Jonah greatly, and he was grieved. [2] He prayed to the LORD, saying, "O LORD! Isn't this just what I said when I was still in my own country? That is why I fled beforehand to Tarshish. For I know that You are a compassionate and gracious God, slow to anger, abounding in kindness, renouncing punishment. [3] Please, LORD, take my life, for I would rather die than live." [4] The LORD replied, "Are you that deeply grieved?"

[5] Now Jonah had left the city and found a place east of the city. He made a booth there and sat under it in the shade, until he should see what happened to the city. [6] The LORD God provided a ricinus plant,[a] which grew up over Jonah, to provide

a *Meaning of Heb. uncertain; others "gourd."*

Jonah chooses language that is reminiscent of God's destruction of Sodom and Gomorrah in Gen. ch 19. But the careful readers of the book notice the irony of the situation: Jonah's words potentially carry two, opposite meanings: (1) "Nineveh is undone," and (2) "Nineveh turns over (i.e., reforms itself)." One feature of his proclamation is unambiguous: Jonah's proclamation is extremely short and includes no call to repentance, unlike many other prophetic proclamations. **5–9:** Still it is the most effective, since the entire city immediately turns from its ways and repents. (*Sackcloth, ashes,* and fasting are typical signs of repentance.) Jonah does not wish to be a prophetic voice calling for repentance, and does not ask for the divine judgment to be turned into mercy (contrast Abraham in the case of Sodom and Gomorrah, Gen. 18.16–32), but he is still the most successful prophet in the Bible who achieves both in an unparalleled, complete, and immediate way—even the animals repent! The message is that the success of the prophet is not dependent on his attributes or rhetorical power, but on the will of God. And yet, there is a second reading. Jonah's message "Nineveh is undone" was fulfilled in history, as the readers of the book know well. If so, Jonah's understanding of his prophecy was fulfilled too. The problem was then that Jonah erred by believing that his prophecy must be fulfilled in his own days. The latter may well be an important message for readers of prophetic books in the Persian period: Prophetic words, especially those concerning the ideal status of the restored Israel, will be fulfilled, in their due time—but even prophets do not know when.

4.1–11: Jonah and the LORD discuss the matter. Jonah is upset, because his proclamation did not come true, from his perspective (see Deut. 18.21–22). He associates this lack of fulfillment with God's attributes (in v. 3 he is using Joel 2.13; Pss. 86.15; 103.8; 145.8 as key interpretative texts for Exod. 34.6–7 and Num. 14.18), and by doing so he is raising a theological confrontation between himself and God. One has to infer that Jonah thought that God should behave according to the paradigm advanced in another set of biblical texts (see Num. 23.19, 1 Sam. 15.29), but he was sure that God's behavior would not follow this paradigm. So God was in the wrong, from his perspective. Some interpreters, both Jewish and non-Jewish, have supported a different understanding. According to them, Jonah was upset that God relented from punishment only because those who were to be punished were not Israelites. A variant of this interpretation posits that the issue was not that they were not Israelites per se, but that they were Ninevites, i.e., the same people who will later oppress Israel and Judah. Those for whom Jonah is a stern chauvinist text—and there are still some contemporaneous readers who think so—tend to maintain that the book was a theological attack against those who may identify with this jingoist Jonah and his positions. The problem with this approach is that Jonah never says that he wants the Ninevites destroyed because they are not Israelites. Furthermore, there is not even a hint of the tension between Israel and the nations in the book of Jonah. **6–8:** This scene may be based on Elijah in 1 Kings 19.4. If so, Jonah is being parodied as an anti-Elijah figure. **6:** *The LORD God provided:* The repetition of this

shade for his head and save him from discomfort. Jonah was
very happy about the plant. 7 But the next day at dawn God
provided a worm, which attacked the plant so that it withered.
8 And when the sun rose, God provided a sultry[a] east wind;
the sun beat down on Jonah's head, and he became faint. He
begged for death, saying, "I would rather die than live." 9 Then
God said to Jonah, "Are you so deeply grieved about the plant?"
"Yes," he replied, "so deeply that I want to die."
10 Then the LORD said: "You cared about the plant, which you
did not work for and which you did not grow, which appeared
overnight and perished overnight. 11 And should not I care
about Nineveh, that great city, in which there are more than a
hundred and twenty thousand persons who do not yet know
their right hand from their left, and many beasts as well!"[b]

a Meaning of Heb. uncertain.
b Infants and beasts are not held responsible for their actions.

language links the fish (2.1), the plant here, the successful *worm* in v. 7, and the extremely scorching *wind* in v. 8. All of them are provided or appointed by God. *Ricinus plant* (see translators' note *a* on p. 1191): There is no general agreement on the botanical identification of the plant. More important, the particular plant described here belongs to the realm of the fantastic (like the beanstalk in "Jack and the Beanstalk") that is provided only by God, just as was the "great fish" in whose belly a man can be accommodated. This plant suddenly grows to provide shade over Jonah's head and just as suddenly it withers. **8:** The *east wind* is a dry, scorching wind and is often associated with disaster and/or God's power (Exod. 14.21; Isa. 27.8; Jer. 18.17; cf. Gen. 41.6). **10:** There is an additional underlying dissymmetry in the comparison advanced in 4.6–11 that makes Jonah's position even more difficult. God cared about the fate of God's creation, but Jonah did not really care for the plant, but rather for himself, for the shade that the plant provided him. **11:** Midr. Yonah adds the following: "At this moment he (Jonah) fell upon his face and said: Guide Your world by the attribute of mercy, as it is written: 'To the LORD our God belong mercy and forgiveness ... ' [Dan. 9.9]." The biblical book of Jonah, however, does not end with Jonah's acceptance of God's position. It rather leaves the question open, asking the reader to fill the gap. Some modern readers who imagine Jonah as a prophet who knew too well what Assyria will do (later) to Israel think that Jonah remained unconvinced, and praise him for that, especially in the light of holocaust theology. Many other readers point out that the future actions of Assyria are not mentioned in the text at all, and are introduced into the text by the readers themselves. The translation "yet" in *who do not yet know,* is not present in most English translations; it is an interpretation of the v. rather than a reflection of any necessity of the Heb. The reference to the *many beasts* at the end of the book has become an anchor for theological thought about care and protection for animals among some Christian and Jewish thinkers.

מיכה

Micah

THE FIRST VERSE OF THE BOOK sets the text in the days of Kings Jotham, Ahaz, and Hezekiah of Judah—in modern chronology the latter half of the 8th and the early years of the 7th c. BCE (1.1), approximately the same time as Isaiah (see Isa. 1.1). The book is associated in 1.1 with the figure of the prophet Micah, who is characterized as a Morashtite prophet, from a town in Judah. (The same identification appears in the reference to Mic. 3.12 in Jer. 26.18.) The intended readers of the book were, however, Jerusalemites.

Many scholars attribute much (but not all) of the book of Micah to the historical prophet or to someone close to the time mentioned in 1.1. Others note that the text includes, among other references, an explicit mention of the Babylonian exile (4.10), and therefore date it to the postmonarchic period (cf. 7.11–13), at least in its final form.

After the introduction or superscription the book moves to sets of prophecies. The first (1.2–2.13) concerns mostly divine judgment, exile, and social ethics, but—as is typical—also provides hope for the future (2.5, 12–13). The second (3.1–12) explains the fall of Jerusalem as due to wrongful leadership. The third one (4.1–5.14) raises diverse images of a utopian future and touches on aspects of the relations between Israel and the nations at that time. The book concludes with a didactic prophecy (6.1–8), another explanation for the judgment that befell monarchic Jerusalem (6.9–16), an expression of trust in the LORD in spite of and as a response to social disintegration (7.1–7), and finally a confirmation of the LORD's distinct relationship with Zion and Judah (7.7–20); this leads to an upbeat conclusion of the entire book (7.18–20).

Mic. 5.6–6.8 is the haftarah (prophetic reading) for the parashah of Balak (Num. 22.2–25.9), since 6.5 explicitly mentions Balak and Balaam. Mic. 7.18–20 has been incorporated into the supplication that follows the reading of the story of Abraham's sacrifice (Gen. 22.1–19) in the morning service. The reference to "hurl" (Heb "tashlikh") in v. 19 has been associated with tashlikh (a ritual on the first day of Rosh Ha-Shanah symbolizing a desire to get rid of sins, to "hurl them away," and be forgiven by God). In the Sepharadic and Yemenite traditions, Mic. 7.18–20 is read after Hos. 14.2–10 on Shabbat Shuvah (the Shabbat preceding Yom Kippur), following Jonah in the Minḥah service of Yom Kippur, and also in the Minḥah service of Tishʿah beʾav (commemorating the destruction of the Temple). Conservative Judaism reads Hos. 14.2–10; Mic. 7.18–20; Joel 2.15–27 on Shabbat Shuvah.

[EHUD BEN ZVI]

1 The word of the LORD that came to Micah the Morashtite, who prophesied concerning Samaria and Jerusalem in the reigns of Kings Jotham, Ahaz, and Hezekiah of Judah.

2 Listen, all you peoples,
Give heed, O earth, and all it holds;
And let my Lord GOD be your accuser—
My Lord from His holy abode.
3 For lo! the LORD
Is coming forth from His dwelling-place,
He will come down and stride
Upon the heights of the earth.
4 The mountains shall melt under Him
And the valleys burst open—
Like wax before fire,
Like water cascading down a slope.

5 All this is for the transgression of Jacob,
And for the sins of the House of Israel.
What is the transgression of Jacob
But Samaria,
And what the shrines[a] of Judah
But Jerusalem?
6 So I will turn Samaria
Into a ruin in open country,
Into ground for planting vineyards;
For I will tumble her stones into the valley
And lay her foundations bare.
7 All her sculptured images shall be smashed,
And all her harlot's wealth be burned,
And I will make a waste heap of all her idols,
For they were amassed from fees for harlotry,
And they shall become harlots' fees again.

8 Because of this I will lament and wail;
I will go stripped and naked!
I will lament as sadly as the jackals,
As mournfully as the ostriches.
9 For her[b] wound is incurable,
It has reached Judah,

a Emendation yields "sins." *b I.e., the nation's.*

1.1: Superscription. The v. characterizes the book as a particular instance of the LORD's word (that is, as a prophetic book), sets it in a particular time, and associates it with a prophetic character from the past, Micah (see intro.). The word of the LORD concerned both *Samaria* and *Jerusalem*, the capitals of the Northern and Southern Kingdoms respectively. But most of this "word" (i.e., the book of Mic.) deals with the fate of Jerusalem and Judah. In this book references to Samaria serve only to preface and sharpen the message concerning Judah.

1.2–2.13: A set of readings about divine judgment, exile, social ethics, and divine hope. The set consists of four main sections: 1.2–16; 2.1–5; 2.6–11; 2.12–13. **1.2–16: About divine judgment and exile.** The punishment moves from Israel to Judah, reflecting the situation of the exile of Israel, which was followed by that of Judah. **2:** On literary units in prophetic books that begin with "hear" or *listen* (Heb "shim'u") see Amos 3.1–6.14 n. *Listen, all you peoples:* The Heb is more emphatic: "Hear, O peoples, all of them." *My Lord GOD:* Heb "Adonai YHVH" vocalized (MT) as "Adonai Elohim" as in Amos 1.8, Obad. 1.1, and many other places. In most instances YHVH is vocalized in the MT with the vowels of "Adonai," but when it appears alongside "Adonai," as here, YHVH is vocalized with the vowels of "Elohim," and the translation indicates this by "GOD." These rules of vocalization are later than the original text. Although *be your accuser* is a possible reading—it is based on an interpretation of the phrase as "be a witness against you"—so is "be a witness among you." The text encourages this ambiguity. **3, 5:** A wordplay: *Heights* is echoed in *shrines* (same word in the Heb). The latter could also be translated "high places." **7:** *Harlot's wealth* (or hire) ... *idols* ... *harlotry:* The metaphorical association of sinful worship with prostitution is common in the prophetic books; see esp. Hos. chs 1–3. Many readers today raise the question of the problematic ways in which this metaphorical association may have colored the way in which gender roles are viewed in society (e.g., "the worshipper" is male and he is at risk of going astray because of enticing females whose job is to snare him). See nn. on the book of Hos. **8:** *I will lament:* The speaker in v. 7 is the LORD, as it is in v. 9, but most readers think that here it must be a human character, most likely the prophet (see Radak, Ibn

It has spread to the gate of my people,
To Jerusalem.

10[a] Tell it not in Gath,
Refrain from weeping;[b]
In Beth-leaphrah,
Strew dust[c] over your [head].
11 Pass on, inhabitants of Shaphir!
Did not the inhabitants of Zaanan
Have to go forth naked in shame?
There is lamentation in Beth-ezel—
It will withdraw its support from you.
12 Though the inhabitants of Maroth
Hoped for good,
Yet disaster from the LORD descended
Upon the gate of Jerusalem.
13 Hitch the steeds to the chariot,
Inhabitant of Lachish!
It is the beginning
Of Fair Zion's guilt;
Israel's transgressions
Can be traced to you!
14 Truly, you must give a farewell gift
To Moresheth-gath.
[d-]The houses of Achzib are[-d]
To the kings of Israel
Like a spring that fails.
15 A dispossessor will I bring to you
Who dwell in Mareshah;
At Adullam the glory
Of Israel shall set.
16 [e]Shear off your hair and make yourself bald
For the children you once delighted in;
Make yourself as bald as a vulture,
For they have been banished from you.

a *Meaning of much of vv. 10–13 uncertain. They may refer to the transfer of part of western Judah to Philistine rule by Sennacherib of Assyria in the year 701* B.C.E.
b *So that enemies may not gloat; cf. 2 Sam. 1.20.*
c *Heb.* ʿaphar, *a play on Beth-leaphrah; vv. 10–15 contain several similar puns.*
d-d *Emendation yields "Fair Achzib is."*
e *A common rite of mourning; cf. Jer. 7.29.*

Ezra). The Tg. has "they" instead of "I" and represents an understanding of the speaker as the people of Israel. The subject of these actions in the Heb is, however, ambiguous. The image of the LORD lamenting and grieving, and even metaphorically going *stripped and naked* because of the fate of His people, may have been unthinkable to the Tg. and medieval commentators, but not necessarily so to biblical writers, who stressed the divine pathos (e.g., Isa. 63.10; Hos. 11.8–9), a point often emphasized by the American rabbi and philosopher, Abraham Joshua Heschel. **10–16:** In some places it is difficult to understand the Heb. All agree however that the most salient feature of this text is its concentration of wordplays on the names of towns, each of which substantially contribute to the meaning of the unit. (Towns and their inhabitants are represented by female imagery.) English renderings of some of these wordplays and the connoted message they communicate would be as follows: **10:** "In Dusthouse I will roll myself in dust." **11:** "Pass on your way, girl of Pretty-town, in shameful nakedness." **12:** "The girl of Bitterness-town aches for good, yet evil has come down from the LORD to the gate of Jerusalem." **14:** "The houses of Deception-ville shall be a deception to the kings of Israel." Whereas in all these instances the name of the town is constructed as an omen about its future, no such claim is made for Jerusalem. Jerusalem stands in a category of its own, as its name does not convey an omen. Some scholars maintain that the list may reflect the results of military campaigns in the area either in 734–732, 722, 712, or for the most part, 701 BCE, i.e., the victorious campaign against Judah by Sennacherib, the Assyrian king. The text itself does not identify the disaster described with any particular military campaign; the name Sennacherib does not occur anywhere, the disaster is not particularly associated with the name of any Judahite king, nor is any chronological information provided (contrast Isa. 7.1; 20.1; Jer. 32.1; 46.1–2; Hag. 1.1). This is intentional. The book of Mic. does not set any of its literary units in a narrowly marked historical period. The result is a literary work that may be read in general terms, because it downplays particular historical situations. **15:** The text is equivocal: *Dispossessor* may also be understood as (rightful) inheritor; *the glory* (or honor) *of Israel* may refer to Israel's wealth, might, or army, or to the LORD; the name of the town *Adullam* evokes a possible association with Heb "ʿolam," "forever." **16:** *For they have been banished from you* may be translated also as "for they have gone from you into exile." The readers of the book who were aware of the exile to Babylonia (see 4.10, and intro.) identified such exile with the Babylonian exile.

2.1–5: On social ethics, divine judgment, and hope. 1–3: Another wordplay with a strong message. Elite people within society *design* (or, "work") *evil;* the LORD plans (Heb) "evil" *(misfortune)* against them. Moreover, members of this group are able to do so because *they have the power;* the LORD certainly has the power to carry "evil" *(misfortune),* and God's might is infinitely superior to that of these people (cf. Prov. 17.5; 22.23). **5:** The descendants of the transgressors will not be part of *the assembly of the LORD.* This v. suggests a transgenerational aspect in the divine punishment.

2.6–11: On social ethics, divine character, mistaken positions, and judgment. 7: The speaker is the LORD. Thus the first three lines point at the LORD's representation of the theological thought of the evildoers described above. Given their actions, the LORD will not refrain from acting against them. **8:** It is possible to understand the v. as stating, "but yesterday My people rose as an enemy (i.e., of the LORD)." If so, the text maintains that the evildoers, despite their deeds, remain Jacob, the LORD's people. To be sure, these evildoers attack and dispossess Israelites too—who, of course, are also God's people (cf. v. 9). The continued reference to the evildoers in the second person following this phrase stresses the affective element of the condemnation. Several scholars have advanced proposals for emending this line to mean, "But you rise against my people as an enemy."

2

Ah, those who plan iniquity
And design evil on their beds;
When morning dawns, they do it,
For they have the power.
2 They covet fields, and seize them;
Houses, and take them away.
They defraud men of their homes,
And people of their land.

3 Assuredly, thus said the LORD: I am planning such a misfortune against this clan that you will not be able to free your necks from it. You will not be able to walk erect; it will be such a time of disaster.

4 In that day,
One shall recite a poem about you,
And utter a bitter lament,
And shall say:
[a-]"My people's portion changes hands;
How it slips away from me!
Our field is allotted to a rebel.[b]
We are utterly ravaged."[-a]
5 Truly, none of you
Shall cast a lot cord[c]
In the assembly of the LORD!

6 "Stop preaching!" they preach.
"That's no way to preach;
[a-]Shame shall not overtake [us].
7 Is the House of Jacob condemned?[-a]
Is the LORD's patience short?
Is such His practice?"

To be sure, My words are friendly
To those who walk in rectitude;
8 But [d-]an enemy arises against[-d] My people.
You strip the mantle [e-]with the cloak[-e]
Off such as pass unsuspecting,
[a-]Who are turned away from war.[-a]
9 You drive the women of My people away
From their pleasant homes;
You deprive their infants
Of My glory forever.
10 Up and depart!
This is no resting place

a-a Meaning of Heb. uncertain. *b Emendation yields "ravager."*
c On a piece of land, thus acquiring title to it; cf. Josh. 18.6 and Ps. 16.6.
d-d Meaning of Heb. uncertain; emendation yields "you arise as enemies against."
e-e Meaning of Heb. uncertain; emendation yields "off peaceful folk."

[a]Because of [your] defilement.
Terrible destruction shall befall.[-a]

11 If a man were to go about uttering
Windy, baseless falsehoods:
"I'll preach to you in favor of wine and liquor"—
He would be a preacher [acceptable] to that people.

12b I will assemble Jacob, all of you;
I will bring together the remnant of Israel;
I will make them all like sheep [c-]of Bozrah,[-c]
Like a flock inside its pen[d]—
They will be noisy with people.
13 One who makes a breach
Goes before them;
They enlarge it to a gate
And leave by it.
Their king marches before them,
The LORD at their head.

3 I said:
Listen, you rulers of Jacob,
You chiefs of the House of Israel!
For you ought to know what is right,
2e But you hate good and love evil.
3 You have devoured My people's flesh;
You have flayed the skin off them,
And their flesh off their bones.
[f-]And after tearing their skins off them,
And their flesh off their bones,[-f]
And breaking their bones to bits,
You have cut it up [g-]as into[-g] a pot,
Like meat in a caldron.
4 Someday they shall cry out to the LORD,
But He will not answer them;

a-a *Meaning of Heb. uncertain.*
b *Vv. 12–13 may be an example of such "acceptable" preaching.*
c-c *Emendation yields "in a fold* [Arabic *sīrah*]." d *Meaning of Heb. uncertain.*
e *Syntax of vv. 2–3 uncertain.* f-f *Brought down from v. 2 for clarity.*
g-g *Meaning of Heb. uncertain; Septuagint and Syriac read "like flesh in."*

2.12–13: A promise of hope following judgment. The set of readings has dealt mainly with judgment; they end with a reassuring statement of hope. These vv. interweave the related images of shepherd and king. The image of God as shepherd, however, is ambiguous in the Bible: The shepherd may lead his flock gently (Ps. 23), or may punish those who are out of step (Ezek. ch 34). Most interpreters (including the Tg.) understand these vv. as an announcement of future well-being, of Jacob's return from exile. A minority considers them as one of punishment (e.g., Radak who thinks that the king referred to is Zedekiah). Ibn Ezra (and a few modern scholars) relate these vv. to the false prophets (cf. translators' note *b*). According to *Pesik. Rav Kah.* 24.14, the reference in v. 13 to "their king" is a reference to the Shekhinah (a Jewish concept that might be translated as "the divine presence"), and the entire v. points at the return of the exiles of Israel. **12:** *Sheep* ("flock") *of Bozrah:* Wordplays and multiple, complementary meanings; the Heb carries two basic meanings: "flock in a fenced place," and *sheep of Bozrah* (an Edomite city; see Amos 1.12). *Sheep of Bozrah,* evoking the quality or quantity of the flock, connotes a sense of plenty. "Flock in a fenced place" completes the metaphor of the good shepherd (the LORD) who leads the flock to safety. **13:** It is unclear if a human king is meant, or whether the LORD here is the King.

3.1–12: The failures of leadership that led to the fall of Jerusalem. The destruction of Jerusalem is explained as due to the failures of its leaders. The high value attached to the loss of Jerusalem demands a highly negative description of the leadership (cf. *b. Yoma* 9b). The structure of the unit is ABA: The rulers and chiefs are condemned in the first and third sections (A: 1–4, 9–12), and the prophets in the middle section (B: 5–8). (Condemnations of prophets are not rare in prophetic literature; see, for instance, Isa. 28.7; Jer. 14.14–15; 23.9–40; Ezek. 13.4–16; Hos. 4.5; Mic. 2.6–11; Zech. 13.2–6.) The issue of wrong, "hopeful" theology is also revisited (3.11; cf. 2.6–7). **2–3:** The translation rearranges the Heb, but this does not affect the main picture: the incredible violence perpetrated by the rulers of Jacob against Jacob, or in the theological term advanced in the book, "My people." **4:** The Tg. understands *He will hide His face from them* as "He will remove His Shekhinah from them." On the concept of the LORD's hiding the divine face, see Deut. 31.17. The concept, common in biblical texts, was developed later in Judaism and served to bridge the tension between

At that time He will hide His face from them,
In accordance with the wrongs they have done.

5 Thus said the LORD to the prophets
Who lead My people astray,
Who cry "Peace!"
When they have something to chew,
But launch a war on him
Who fails to fill their mouths:
6 Assuredly,
It shall be night for you
So that you cannot prophesy,
And it shall be dark for you
So that you cannot divine;
The sun shall set on the prophets,
And the day shall be darkened for them.
7 The seers shall be shamed
And the diviners confounded;
They shall cover their upper lips,[a]
Because no response comes from God.
8 But I,
I am filled with strength by the spirit of the LORD,
And with judgment and courage,
To declare to Jacob his transgressions
And to Israel his sin.

9 Hear this, you rulers of the House of Jacob,
You chiefs of the House of Israel,
Who detest justice
And make crooked all that is straight,
10 Who build Zion with crime,
Jerusalem with iniquity!
11 Her rulers judge for gifts,
Her priests give rulings for a fee,
And her prophets divine for pay;
Yet they rely upon the LORD, saying,
"The LORD is in our midst;
No calamity shall overtake us."
12 Assuredly, because of you
Zion shall be plowed as a field,
And Jerusalem shall become heaps of ruins,
And the Temple Mount
A shrine in the woods.

a As a sign of mourning; cf. Ezek. 24.17, 22; Lev. 13.45.

divine goodness and acute suffering. **5:** *When they have something to chew,* or more literally, "when they have something to bite with their teeth." The point is not so much that prophets received gifts from their "clients." This behavior seems to have been widely accepted (see 1 Sam. 9.8; 1 Kings 14.3; 2 Kings 4.42; 8.8–9; Amos 7.12), and the prophets needed their bread too. Rather, these prophets shaped or announced their prophecies to please their clients, so as to increase the gifts they received from them. By doing so they perverted their office (and the LORD's trust) for material gain. The precise choice of words in the Heb implies additional powerful connotations. The expression "bite with their teeth" allows not only the wordplay between teeth and *mouths,* but also a description of the behavior of the prophets that evokes the animal behavior of other leaders (v. 3). The verb "nashakh," "to bite," has a sound reminiscent to that of "naḥash," "snake." The same verb "nashakh" means in other contexts "to charge interest" and carries negative connotations (cf. Hab. 2.7; Deut. 23.20). To some extent, the text suggests that they are like beastly creditors or snakes that bite the flesh of Israel with their teeth (cf. v. 3). **8:** The beginning of the v. offers an emphatic contrast between the true and the false prophet. Heb has no term for a false prophet; thus, in v. 5 they are called "nevi'im," the same term that would be used of true prophets. In many such cases, the LXX translation clarifies the meaning, by inserting the word "false" ("pseudo"). **11:** The image (and the implied concept) of YHVH's hiding (or hiding His face) in v. 4 does not appear again in Mic., but it is present in many other texts in the HB (e.g., Deut. 31.17–18; Isa. 8.17; 45.15; 54.8; Ps. 89.47). (The image and concept of the "hidden face of God" played, though in a different way, a substantial role in the thought of Martin Buber, millennia later.) **12:** Cf. Jer. 26.18. This is a rare instance of a quotation of a prophetic character by another prophetic character in a different book, and it indicates that prophetic books were studied in antiquity. Some scholars slightly emend the last phrase of this v. so as to read, "the Temple mountain shall belong to the wild animals." The motif of wild animals taking control of

4 [a]In the days to come,
The Mount of the LORD's House shall stand
Firm above the mountains;
And it shall tower above the hills.
The peoples shall gaze on it with joy,
2 And the many nations shall go and shall say:
"Come,
Let us go up to the Mount of the LORD,
To the House of the God of Jacob;
That He may instruct us in His ways,
And that we may walk in His paths."
For instruction shall come forth[b] from Zion,
The word of the LORD from Jerusalem.
3 Thus He will judge among the many peoples,
And arbitrate for the multitude of nations,
However distant;
And they shall beat their swords into plowshares[c]
And their spears into pruning hooks.
Nation shall not take up
Sword against nation;
They shall never again know[d] war;
4 But every man shall sit
Under his grapevine or fig tree
With no one to disturb him.
For it was the LORD of Hosts who spoke.
5 Though all the peoples walk
Each in the names of its gods,
We will walk
In the name of the LORD our God
Forever and ever.

6 In that day —declares the LORD—
I will assemble the lame [sheep]
And will gather the outcast
And those I have treated harshly;

a For vv. 1–3 cf. Isa. 2.2–4. *b I.e., oracles will be obtainable.*
c More exactly, the iron points with which wooden plows were tipped.
d Cf. Judg. 3.2.

destroyed cities is relatively common in ancient Near Eastern literature, including the Bible.

4.1–5.14: A series of texts about the future. This section consists of six different subunits (4.1–5; 4.6–8; 4.8–5.1; 5.1–5; 5.6–8; 5.9–15). Each of these literary subunits presents a portrait of a future. These images of the future are widely different from one another, allowing each one to inform and balance the other. One of the most significant differences among these images of an ideal future concerns the fate of the nations other than Israel: Are they going to flow to Jerusalem to learn divine teachings coming from Jerusalem and its religious elite (4.2), or are they going to be crushed (5.14)? **4.1–5:** In this portrait of the future, Jerusalem and the Temple Mount are the center of the world. Vv. 1–3 are nearly identical with Isa. 2.2–4; the exact literary relationship between these two units is debated. **2:** *Instruction,* Heb "torah." The text clearly associates "torah" with "the word of the LORD." In Jewish liturgy this portion of the v., *For instruction shall come forth from Zion, / The word of the LORD from Jerusalem,* is read when the Torah scroll is taken out of the Ark to be read. **3:** *He will judge:* The one who will judge is the LORD. Some medieval commentators, however, identified the judge with the Messiah (Ibn Ezra, Radak) and thus reformulated to some extent the image of the ideal period. In its biblical context, however, this passage depicts a messianic age without a personal messiah. *They shall beat their swords into plowshares ... they shall never again know* [others translate, "train for"] *war* is one of the most popular, condensed descriptions of an ideal future. (Contrast it with Joel 4.10.) **5:** This v. has been considered "narrowly particularistic" or "nationalistic" (as opposed to "universalistic") and has certainly been read in such a fashion (cf. Tg., Rashi, *Exod. Rab.* 15.15). In its context in Mic., however, the v. rejects the imperial model of everyone becoming Israel, supporting instead the concept that non-Israelites may accept the word of the LORD from Jerusalem and still maintain their non-Israelite identity and worship (as the sailors in Jonah ch 1).

8: *Migdal-eder,* "tower of the flock," reinforces the previous image of Israel as "flock" whose shepherd is the LORD. *Outpost of Fair Zion* may be translated as "Ophel (or stronghold) of the daughter of Zion." **10:** The explicit reference to the Babylonian exile of Judah shows the authorship's awareness of both the historical event and its importance for postmonarchic Israel. The writer cannot be Micah, because the latter lived—according to the book—more than a century before the destruction of Jerusalem and the exile to Babylonia. Quite remarkably, this v. views the Babylonian exile as a positive experience, and along with other vv. helps to explain why those who returned to Yehud (Judah) after the exile felt superior to those who remained behind, a major theme of Ezra-Neh.

7 And I will turn the lame into a remnant
And the expelled[a] into a populous nation.
And the LORD will reign over them on Mount Zion
Now and for evermore.

8 And you, O Migdal-eder,[b]
[c-]Outpost of Fair Zion,
It shall come to you:[-c]
The former monarchy shall return—
The kingship of [d-]Fair Jerusalem.[-d]

9 Now why do you utter such cries?
Is there no king in you,
Have your advisors perished,
That you have been seized by writhing
Like a woman in travail?
10 Writhe and scream,[e] Fair Zion,
Like a woman in travail!
For now you must leave the city
And dwell in the country—
And you will reach Babylon.
There you shall be saved,
There the LORD will redeem you
From the hands of your foes.
11 Indeed, many nations
Have assembled against you
Who think, "Let our eye
[c-]Obscenely gaze[-c] on Zion."
12 But they do not know
The design of the LORD,
They do not divine His intent:
He has gathered them
Like cut grain to the threshing floor.
13 Up and thresh, Fair Zion!
For I will give you horns of iron
And provide you with hoofs of bronze,
And you will crush the many peoples.
You[f] will devote their riches to the LORD,
Their wealth to the Lord of all the earth.

14 Now you gash yourself [c-]in grief.[-c]
They have laid siege to us;

a *Meaning of Heb. uncertain; emendation yields "weaklings"; cf. Ezek. 34.4.*
b *Apparently near Bethlehem; see Gen. 35.19–21.*
c-c *Meaning of Heb. uncertain.*
d-d *Emendation yields "the House of Israel"; cf. 5.1–2.*
e *Meaning of Heb. uncertain.* *f* *Heb.* -ti *serves here as the ending of the second-person singular feminine; cf. Judg. 5.7 and note; Jer. 2.20; etc.*

They strike the ruler of Israel
On the cheek with a staff.

5 And you, O Bethlehem of Ephrath,[a]
Least among the clans of Judah,
From you one shall come forth
To rule Israel for Me—
One whose origin is from of old,
From ancient times.
2 [b]Truly, He will leave them [helpless]
Until she who is to bear has borne;[c]
Then the rest of his countrymen
Shall return to the children of Israel.[-b]
3 He shall stand and shepherd
By the might of the LORD,
By the power of the name
Of the LORD his God,
And they shall dwell [secure].
For lo, he shall wax great
To the ends of the earth;
4 And that shall afford safety.
Should Assyria invade our land
And tread upon our fortresses,[d]
We will set up over it[e] seven shepherds,
Eight princes of men,
5 Who will shepherd Assyria's land with swords,
The land of Nimrod [f]in its gates.[-f]
Thus he will deliver [us]
From Assyria, should it invade our land,
And should it trample our country.

6 The remnant of Jacob shall be,
In the midst of the many peoples,
Like dew from the LORD,
Like droplets on grass—
Which do not look to any man
Nor place their hope in mortals.

7 The remnant of Jacob
Shall be among the nations,
In the midst of the many peoples,
Like a lion among beasts of the wild,
Like a fierce lion among flocks of sheep,

5.1: The reference is to David, from *Bethlehem* in *Judah.* **2:** *Until she who is to bear has borne:* Traditional Jewish interpretations of this v. tend to focus on comparisons between the birth pangs of a woman and the hardship of Israel prior to the coming of the Messiah. The following is one example: "Rab said: 'The son of David will not come until the [Roman] power enfolds Israel for nine months, as it is written, Therefore will he give them up, until the time that she which travaileth hath brought forth: then the remnant of his brethren shall return unto the children of Israel.' Ulla said: 'Let him [The Messiah] come, but let me not see him.' Rabbah said likewise: 'Let him come, but let me not see him ... ' Abaye enquired of Rabbah: 'What is your reason [for not wishing to see him]? Shall we say, because of the birth pangs [preceding the advent] of the Messiah?' But it has been taught, R. Eleazar's disciples asked him: 'What must a man do to be spared the pangs of the Messiah?' [He answered,] 'Let him engage in study and benevolence; and you Master do both.' " (*b. Sanh.* 98b [Soncino Press, English Talmud]). **5:** *The land of Nimrod,* Assyria (cf. Gen. 10.8–12). *Nimrod* is chosen because might was associated with him (Gen. 10.8), but this image is ironically turned against him.

a The clan to which the Bethlehemites belonged; see 1 Sam. 17.12; Ruth 1.2; 4.11.
b-b Meaning of Heb. uncertain.
c I.e., a ruler, shepherd (v. 3), to deliver Israel from the Assyrians (vv. 4–5).
d Septuagint and Syriac read "soil"; cf. v. 5. *e I.e., Assyria.*
f-f Emendation yields "with drawn blades"; cf. Ps. 37.14; 55.22.

9–14: A divine purge of Israel and the nations that serves to emphasize the importance of obedience to the LORD. The rhetorically powerful repetitions of "you/your" and "I will" stress the main point of the text, namely the relation between the LORD and Israel in the future envisioned in these vv., as the destruction of sinful elements of Judah is transformed at the last moment to *retribution on the nations.*

6.1–8: A didactic section about divinely ordained behavior. The text advances the legal metaphor of a lawsuit, so as to address the relationship between God and Israel. Of course, this is not a usual lawsuit. Mountains, hills, and the very foundations of the earth are summoned. The Heb of vv. 1–2 abounds in multiple (possible) meanings, but the message of vv. 3–5 is unequivocal: Israel had no reason to abandon God, for God has done no wrong, but rather many *gracious acts* for Israel. The acts explicitly mentioned relate to the exodus from Egypt, the period of wandering in the desert, including the Balak-Balaam story (see Num. chs 22–24), and the crossing of the Jordan (see Josh. chs 3–4). **4:** Miriam here plays a role equal to her brothers, in contrast to the Torah narrative.

Which tramples wherever it goes
And rends, with none to deliver.
8 Your hand shall prevail over your foes,
And all your enemies shall be cut down!
9 In that day —declares the LORD—
I will destroy the horses in your midst
And wreck your chariots.
10 I will destroy the cities of your land
And demolish all your fortresses.
11 I will destroy the sorcery you practice,
And you shall have no more soothsayers.
12 I will destroy your idols
And the sacred pillars in your midst;
And no more shall you bow down
To the work of your hands.
13 I will tear down the sacred posts in your midst
And destroy your cities.[a]
14 In anger and wrath
Will I wreak retribution
On the nations[b] that have not obeyed.

6 Hear what the LORD is saying:
Come, present [My] case before the mountains,
And let the hills hear you pleading.

2 Hear, you mountains, the case of the LORD—
[c-]You firm[-c] foundations of the earth!
For the LORD has a case against His people,
He has a suit against Israel.

3 "My people!
What wrong have I done you?
What hardship have I caused you?
Testify against Me.
4 In fact,
I brought you up from the land of Egypt,
I redeemed you from the house of bondage,
And I sent before you
Moses, Aaron, and Miriam.

5 "My people,
Remember what Balak king of Moab
Plotted against you,
And how Balaam son of Beor
Responded to him.

a *Emendation yields "idols."* *b* *Emendation yields "arrogant."*
c-c *Emendation yields "Give ear, you."*

[Recall your passage]
From Shittim to Gilgal[a]—
And you will recognize
The gracious acts of the LORD."

6 With what shall I approach the LORD,
Do homage to God on high?
Shall I approach Him with burnt offerings,
With calves a year old?
7 Would the LORD be pleased with
thousands of rams,
With myriads of streams of oil?
Shall I give my first-born for my transgression,
The fruit of my body for my sins?

8 "He has told you, O man, what is good,
And what the LORD requires of you:
Only to do justice
And to love goodness,
And [b-]to walk modestly with your God;[-b]
9 [c-]Then will your name achieve wisdom."[-c]

Hark! The LORD
Summons the city:
[d-]Hear, O scepter;
For who can direct her 10 but you?[-d]
Will I overlook,[e] in the wicked man's house,
The granaries of wickedness
And the accursed short *ephah?*[f]
11 Shall he[g] be acquitted despite wicked balances
And a bag of fraudulent weights?—
12[h] Whose rich men are full of lawlessness,
And whose inhabitants speak treachery,
With tongues of deceit in their mouths.

13 I, in turn, have beaten you sore,
Have stunned [you] for your sins:
14 You have been eating without getting your fill,
[d-]And there is a gnawing at your vitals;
You have been conceiving without bearing young,[-d]
And what you bore I would deliver to the sword.

a I.e., the crossing of the Jordan; see Josh. 3.1, 14–4.19.
b-b Or "It is prudent to serve your God."
c-c Emendation yields "And it is worthwhile to revere His name."
d-d Meaning of Heb. uncertain.
e Taking ish *as from* nashah *"to forget"; cf. Deut. 32.18.*
f Cf. Amos 8.4–5. *g Heb. "I"; change of vocalization yields "Will I acquit him."*
h This v. would read well after "city" in v. 9.

6–8: The text here does not communicate a rejection of Temple offerings; rather it expresses the common biblical and ancient Near Eastern concept of the primacy of morality over sacrifices (e.g., 1 Sam. 15.22; Prov. 21.3). **7:** This v. seems to assume that human sacrifice, at least in extreme circumstances, was thought to have been acceptable and efficacious (see Gen. ch 22; 2 Kings 3.27). **8:** This didactic saying is one of the most influential and often quoted sayings in prophetic literature. It was considered as a possible compendium of all the "mitzvot." "R. Simlai when preaching said: Six hundred and thirteen precepts were communicated to Moses, three hundred and sixty-five negative precepts ... Micah came and reduced them to three [principles], as it is written, He has told you, O human, what is good, and what the Lord requires of you: only to do justice, and to love goodness, and to walk humbly with your God. 'To do justice,' this concerns justice; 'and to love goodness,' this concerns "gemilut hasadim" (acts of kindness); 'and to walk humbly with your God,' this concerns walking in funeral and bridal processions" (*b. Mak.* 23b–24a; cf. *b. Sukk.* 49b and Radak). *To walk modestly with your God* (cf. Tg.) is usually translated as "to walk humbly with your God," but its original meaning is likely to be "to walk wisely (or perhaps carefully/completely) with your God" (and cf. v. 9).

6.9–16: Another explanation for the fall of Jerusalem. 9: The text is difficult and some emendations have been suggested. The rendition of this v. reflects one such emendation; the MT may be translated as: "The voice of the LORD cries out to the city—it is sound wisdom to fear Your name—'Hear, O tribe and city assembly!' " If so, the expression within dashes serves as a comment made by the narrator that is easily understood by the readership of the book.

16: *Omri ... Ahab,* the most notorious kings of the dynasty of Omri/Ahab. The text reflects the common characterization of the House of Ahab as the primary example of a sinful royal house of northern Israel; see 2 Kings 8.18; 21.3, 13; 2 Chron. 21.13; 22.4; 1 Kings 16.23–22.40; 2 Kings chs 10–28. Likewise, 2 Kings 17.19, 22, and other texts condemn Judah for following the ways of Israel.

7.1–7: A text about trust in the LORD despite and in response to social disintegration. The book teaches the readers that the response to social disintegration must be trust in the LORD (see v. 7 to which the text leads up). **6:** The situation envisioned here is reversed in the eschatological image of Mal. 3.24. **7:** *Yet I will look to the LORD* may be translated "As for me, I will look to the LORD." The "me" is the pious speaker in the text with whom the readers are supposed to identify.

7.8–20: A concluding note of hope. A confirmation that the relationship between the LORD and Judah and Jerusalem is maintained, that the LORD forgives and Israel will be restored.

15 You have been sowing, but have nothing to reap;
You have trod olives, but have no oil for rubbing,
And grapes[a] but have no wine to drink.
16 Yet [b]you have kept[b] the laws of Omri,
And all the practices of the House of Ahab,
And have followed what they devised.
Therefore I will make you an object of horror
And [c]her inhabitants[c] an object of hissing;[d]
And you shall bear the mockery of peoples.[e]

7

Woe is me![f]
I am become like leavings of a fig harvest,
Like gleanings when the vintage is over,
There is not a cluster to eat,
Not a ripe fig I could desire.
2 The pious are vanished from the land,
None upright are left among men;
All lie in wait to commit crimes,
One traps the other in his net.
3 [g]They are eager to do evil:
The magistrate makes demands,
And the judge [judges] for a fee;
The rich man makes his crooked plea,
And they grant it.[g]
4 The best of them is like a prickly shrub;
The [most] upright, worse than a barrier of thorns.
[g]On the day you waited for,[g] your doom has come—
Now their confusion shall come to pass.
5 Trust no friend,
Rely on no intimate;
Be guarded in speech
With her who lies in your bosom.
6 For son spurns father,
Daughter rises up against mother,
Daughter-in-law against mother-in-law—
A man's own household
Are his enemies.
7 Yet I will look to the LORD,
I will wait for the God who saves me,
My God will hear me.

8 Do not rejoice over me,
O my enemy![h]

a *Lit. "new wine."* *b-b* *Heb. "is kept."*
c-c *I.e., those of the city of v. 9, apparently Samaria.* *d* *See note at Jer. 18.16.*
e *Heb. "My people."* *f* *The speaker is feminine (cf.* 'elohayikh, *v. 10), probably Samaria personified; cf. note c-c at 6.16.* *g-g* *Meaning of Heb. uncertain.*
h *Heb. feminine, apparently referring to Damascus.*

Though I have fallen, I rise again;
Though I sit in darkness, the LORD is my light.
9 I must bear the anger of the LORD,
Since I have sinned against Him,
Until He champions my cause
And upholds my claim.
He will let me out into the light;
I will enjoy vindication by Him.
10 When my enemy[a] sees it,
She shall be covered with shame,
She who taunts me with "Where is He,
The LORD your God?"
My eyes shall behold her [downfall];
Lo, she shall be for trampling
Like mud in the streets.
11 A day for mending your walls[b]—
That is a far-off day.
12 This is rather a day when to you
[Tramplers] will come streaming
From Assyria and the towns of Egypt—
From [every land from] Egypt to the Euphrates,
From sea to sea and from mountain to mountain—
13 And your[c] land shall become a desolation—
Because of those who dwell in it—
As the fruit of their misdeeds.

14 Oh, shepherd Your people with Your staff,
Your very own flock.
May they who dwell isolated
[d-]In a woodland surrounded by farmland[-d]
Graze[e] Bashan and Gilead
As in olden days.
15 [f-]I will show him[-f] wondrous deeds
As in the days when You sallied forth from the land of Egypt.
16 Let nations behold and be ashamed
Despite all their might;
Let them put hand to mouth;
Let their ears be deafened!
17 Let them lick dust like snakes,
Like crawling things on the ground!
[g-]Let them come trembling out of their strongholds[-g]

14: *Bashan and Gilead,* fertile lands in Transjordan. **15:** As elsewhere in prophetic literature, particularly in Deutero-Isaiah (Isa. chs 40ff.), the exodus is paradigmatic for restoration and salvation. **18–20:** These vv. provide an upbeat, extremely hopeful conclusion of the book. Such conclusions are expected in prophetic books (see intro. to The Twelve). Because of their assurance of God's forgiveness, these vv. are used in the liturgy for Rosh Ha-Shanah and Yom Kippur (see intro. to Mic.).

a *Heb. feminine, apparently referring to Damascus.*
b *To keep out tramplers (end of preceding verse); cf. Isa. 5.5; Ps. 80.13–14.*
c *Heb. "the."*
d-d *I.e., the land west of the Jordan, which is represented as far less fertile than adjacent regions.* e *Emendation yields "possess."*
f-f *Emendation yields "Show us."* g-g *Meaning of Heb. uncertain.*

18: *Who is a God like You* is a rhetorical question that prompts among the readers the response that none is like God (i.e., incomparability; cf. Exod. 15.11). *Forgiving iniquity / And remitting transgression,* cf. and contrast with Exod. 34.7; Num. 14.18. A partial (and only a partial) echo of these texts is required by the message of the text. **19:** On "tashlikh," see the intro. to Mic. **20:** Cf., among others, Deut. 7.8; Ps. 105.9–10. The ancestors stand here for the people. The reversal of the common pair Abraham-Jacob is related to that of "hesed" (NJPS *loyalty*) and "emet" (NJPS *faith*); see Gen. 24.49, "true loyalty," and passim. The text plays on these reversals to create a less than common ending to the book. Prophetic books tend to end with less than common expressions.

To the LORD our God;
Let them fear and dread You!

18 Who is a God like You,
Forgiving iniquity
And remitting transgression;
Who has not maintained His wrath forever
Against the remnant of His own people,
Because He loves graciousness!
19 He will take us back in love;
He will cover up our iniquities,
You will hurl all our[a] sins
Into the depths of the sea.
20 You will keep faith with Jacob,
Loyalty to Abraham,
As You promised on oath to our fathers
In days gone by.

a Heb. *"their."*

נחום

Nahum

THE DOUBLE TITLE OF THE BOOK of Nahum (1.1) points to its main characteristics. It is a written prophetic book associated with Nahum. It is also, in the main, a pronouncement against Nineveh. From the readers' viewpoint Nineveh was both a historical city, the capital of the Assyrian empire, and a symbol of a sinful, overbearing, exceedingly oppressive political structure that was totally destroyed in the late 7th c. BCE and never rebuilt. From the perspective of a readership well aware of the fall of Nineveh, such a descent from the pinnacle of glory and might becomes a paradigmatic example for the fate of worldly, powerful oppressors and, above all, of the even greater power of the LORD who brings them down. As such, the book provides a message of hope and trust in YHVH to those who saw themselves as oppressed by their own "Nineveh."

The book is not set in any particular period. Thus from the perspective of the intended readership, the only restriction was that Nahum must have lived before the destruction of the city, because prophetic characters in a prophetic book are supposed to prophesy about what will be, not what has already happened. The date of the composition of the book is another matter. Some scholars argue that the vivid description of the destruction of Nineveh (612 BCE) indicates that the book (or a portion of it) must have been written soon after the events. Other scholars strongly disagree. The reference to the conquest and sack of the Egyptian capital of Thebes (No-amon) as a past event in 3.8 indicates that the book was composed later than this event (663). The question of how much later remains open. *Seder Olam Rabbah* and other Jewish traditional sources claim that Nahum prophesied in the days of Manasseh, that is, sometime in the first half of the 7th c. BCE.

The book may be subdivided in different ways. One possibility is that there are three main sections or readings. After the superscription (1.1), the first section (1.2–14) deals mainly with the LORD's character and responses to opponents (symbolized by Assyria) and to Israel's plight. The second (2.1–14) first links the actions of the LORD to Judah's joy, restoration, and freedom from oppressive scoundrels and marauders (vv. 1–3). The reference to the end of the latter flows into a vivid description of the fall of Nineveh (2.4–14). The last (3.1–19) dwells on Nineveh's hubris—which is understood as a challenge to the LORD—and the fall of the city. Indirectly, it returns to God's character and attributes. Other divisions of the text are possible. The multiple ways in which the book may be structured contributes to the ability of the community to read, re-read, and continually study the prophetic book, and to emphasize one aspect of the book in one reading and another in a different reading.

[EHUD BEN ZVI]

1 A pronouncement on Nineveh: The Book of the Prophecy of Nahum the Elkoshite.

2 The LORD is a passionate, avenging God;
The LORD is vengeful and fierce in wrath.
The LORD takes vengeance on His enemies,
He rages against His foes.
3 The LORD is slow to anger and of great forbearance,
But the LORD does not remit all punishment.
He travels in whirlwind and storm,
And clouds are the dust on His feet.
4 He rebukes the sea and dries it up,
And He makes all rivers fail;
Bashan and Carmel languish,
And the blossoms[a] of Lebanon wither.
5 The mountains quake because of Him,
And the hills melt.
The earth heaves[b] before Him,
The world and all that dwell therein.
6 Who can stand before His wrath?
Who can resist His fury?
His anger pours out like fire,
And rocks are shattered because of Him.
7 The LORD is good to [those who hope in Him],
A haven on a day of distress;
He is mindful of those who seek refuge in Him.
8 And with a sweeping flood
He makes an end of [c-]her place,[-c]
And chases His enemies into darkness.
9 Why will you plot against the LORD?
He wreaks utter destruction:
No adversary[d] opposes Him twice!
10 [e-]For like men besotted with drink,
They are burned up like tangled thorns,
Like straw that is thoroughly dried.[-e]

11[f] The base plotter
Who designed evil against the LORD
Has left you.
12 Thus said the LORD:
[e-]"Even as they[g] were full and many,
Even so are they over and gone;
As surely as I afflicted you,
I will afflict you no more."[-e]

a Lit. "bud." *b Meaning of Heb. uncertain.*
c-c Meaning of Heb. uncertain; emendation yields "those who oppose Him."
d Cf. Ugaritic ṣrt. *e-e Meaning of Heb. uncertain.*
f Vv. 11–14 would read well after 2.1. *g I.e., the days of your affliction.*

1.1: Superscription. This is an unusual double title, emphasizing the central theme of the book, the fall of Nineveh. *Elkoshite:* There is no known location that corresponds to this town. Some scholars doubt that the reference is to a town at all and others (cf. Tg.) have suggested that the writer may have invented it as wordplay (Heb "God is harsh"; cf. Isa. 19.4).

1.2–14: The LORD responds to Assyria and to Israel's plight. There are remnants of an acrostic in these vv., but it has been disrupted in the transmission of the passage, and can no longer be reconstructed, esp. after v. 8. These initial vv. are extremely traditional, quoting common themes and phrases. **2–3:** These vv. offer an interpretation and elaboration of Exod. 34.6–7 (cf. Num. 14.18; Jonah 4.2; Ps. 145.8); also cf. Josh. 24.19; Jer. 3.5, 12. **4:** *The sea,* often considered a mythological place of chaos (cf. Isa. 27.1). *Dries it up,* as during the exodus (Exod. 14.21; Ps. 106.9). **5:** For similar theophanic imagery, see Mic. 1.5; Isa. 13.13; Jer. 4.24; 2 Sam. 22.8 || Ps. 18.8, among many others. **7:** As the community reads about the LORD's power and the ridiculousness of any attempt to withstand God's fury, this v. serves to reassure them that not all need be afraid of such fury and power. **8:** If *her place* is correct, it refers to Nineveh. The same consonants may be read "His opposition" (see translators' note *c-c*). **11:** The v. may be translated as: "From you has come forth a plotter of evil against the LORD, a lawless counselor." This counselor is identified as an Assyrian king, or as an "archetypal Assyrian king," and in the Jewish tradition in particular, as Sennacherib (see 2 Kings 18.13–19.37). Readers would associate the figure of this counselor with that of the leader of whatever group they are opposing.

13 And now
I will break off his yoke bar from you
And burst your cords apart.
14 The LORD has commanded concerning him:[a]
[b]No posterity shall continue your name.[b]
I will do away with
The carved and graven images
In the temples of your gods;
I will make your grave
[b]Accord with your worthlessness.[b]

2 Behold on the hills
The footsteps of a herald
Announcing good fortune!
"Celebrate your festivals, O Judah,
Fulfill your vows.
Never again shall scoundrels invade you,
They have totally vanished."

2[c] A shatterer has come up against you.
Man the guard posts,
Watch the road;
Steady your loins,
Brace all your strength!

3 For the LORD has restored [d]the Pride[e] of Jacob
As well as the Pride[e] of Israel,[d]
Though marauders have laid them waste
And ravaged their branches.

4 His warriors' shields are painted red,
And the soldiers are clothed in crimson;
The chariots are like flaming torches,[f]
On the day they are made ready.
[g]The [arrows of] cypress wood are poisoned,[g]
5 The chariots dash about frenzied in the fields,
They rush through the meadows.
They appear like torches,
They race like streaks of lightning.

2.1–14: The two poles: Judah's joy and peace and the conquest and destruction of Nineveh. 1: Cf. Isa. 52.7. **3:** The pride of Jacob as well as the pride of Israel; or "the pride of Jacob, yea, the pride of Israel." Here Jacob and Israel are likely to be synonyms that stand for all Israel or, given that the passage as a whole focuses on Judah, on Judah as its legitimate representative. **4–10:** A narrative account of the destruction of Nineveh begins with the siege and defense and concludes with the plunder of the city, and the confused and terrified response of those who survived. The precise wording of the narrative sets a tempo that conveys a sense of the intensity, chaos, and confusion of the battle scene; much of this is lost in translation. **4:** *His warriors' shields,* the shields of those attacking Nineveh. Note that the beginning of the narrative has no clear antecedent.

a Heb. "you." *b-b Meaning of Heb. uncertain.*
c This verse would read well after v. 3.
d-d "Jacob" refers to the northern kingdom (cf. Amos 6.8; 8.7); Israel refers to the southern kingdom, regarded as the remnant of Israel after the fall of the northern kingdom (cf. Mic. 1.13–15).
e Emendation yields "vine."
f Understanding peladoth *as equivalent to* lappidoth.
g-g Meaning of Heb. uncertain. Emendation yields "The horsemen charge"; cf. 3.3.

6: The v. may be translated: "He calls (or assigns) his mighty men (or commanders); / they stumble as they go; / they hurry to her wall [Nineveh's wall], / and the siege shelters [to protect the troops from the weaponry of the besieged] are set up." The language of the v. stresses the speed of the actions. 7: The *floodgates* refer to the gates of the canals and dams. This reflects the physical environment of Nineveh and is a metaphorical reference to the conquering flood of the enemy. The fall of the *palace* is the beginning of the end of Nineveh. 8: The reference to *Huzzab* is unclear. Given the reference to her maidservants, one may assume that the v. portrays an Assyrian woman of high status, either metaphorically or not. The Tg., Rashi, and other medieval interpreters understood the term as "queen." 11: The alliteration in the Heb is striking: "bukah umevukah umevulakah." 12: The language resembles a lament. This sharpens the message by heightening the irony and prepares the reader for the next passage (3.1–19). The repetition of *lion* may play on the common motif of lions in Assyrian palace reliefs, where the king slays lions; here the lion imagery is ironically turned against the Assyrians.

6 [a]He commands his burly men;
They stumble as they advance,
They hasten up to her wall,
Where [b]wheeled shelters[b] are set up.[a]
7 [c]The floodgates are opened,
And the palace is deluged.[c]
8 [d]And Huzzab is exiled and carried away,[d]
While her handmaidens [e]escort [her][e]
As with the voices of doves,
Beating their breasts.
9 Nineveh has been like a [placid] pool of water
[a]From earliest times;[a]
Now they flee.
"Stop! Stop!"—
But none can turn them back.
10 "Plunder silver! Plunder gold!"
There is no limit to the treasure;
It is a hoard of all precious objects.

11 Desolation, devastation, and destruction!
Spirits sink,
Knees buckle,
All loins tremble,
All faces [f]turn ashen.[f]
12 What has become of that lions' den,
That pasture[g] of great beasts,
Where lion and lion's breed walked,
And lion's cub—with none to disturb them?
13 [Where is] the lion that tore victims for his cubs
And strangled for his lionesses,
And filled his lairs with prey
And his dens with mangled flesh?
14 I am going to deal with you
—declares the LORD of Hosts:
I will burn down [h]her chariots in smoke,[h]
And the sword shall devour your great beasts;
I will stamp out your killings from the earth,
And the sound of your messengers[i]
Shall be heard no more.

a-a Meaning of Heb. uncertain.
b-b To protect the crews that swung the battering rams.
c-c I.e., the walls are breached and the palace is overrun.
d-d Meaning of Heb. uncertain. Emendation yields "And its mistress is led out and exiled." *e-e Emendation yields "moan."*
f-f Meaning of Heb. uncertain; cf. note at Joel 2.6.
g Emendation yields "cave." *h-h Emendation yields "your thicket in fire."*
i Emendation yields "devouring."

3 Ah, city of crime,
Utterly treacherous,
Full of violence,
Where killing never stops!
2 Crack of whip
And rattle of wheel,
Galloping steed
And bounding chariot!
3 Charging horsemen,
Flashing swords,
And glittering spears!
Hosts of slain
And heaps of corpses,
Dead bodies without number—
They stumble over bodies.
4 Because of the countless harlotries of the harlot,
The winsome mistress of sorcery,
Who ensnared[a] nations with her harlotries
And peoples with her sorcery,
5 I am going to deal with you
—declares the LORD of Hosts.
I will lift up your skirts over your face
And display your nakedness to the nations
And your shame to kingdoms.
6 I will throw loathsome things over you
And disfigure you
And make a spectacle of you.
7 All who see you will recoil from you
And will say,
"Nineveh has been ravaged!"
Who will console her?
Where shall I look for
Anyone to comfort you?
8 Were you any better than No-amon,[b]
Which sat by the Nile,
Surrounded by water—
Its rampart a river,[c]
Its wall [d-]consisting of sea?[-d]
9 Populous Nubia
And teeming Egypt,
Put and the Libyans—
They were her[e] helpers.

3.1–19: On Nineveh's pride and its fall. The passage begins *Ah* (v. 1) and concludes with the clapping of hands (v. 19), from an ironic imitation of a lament to universal joy. The entire section explains the fall of the city in terms of its behavior. **1:** This is an instance of the typical "Ah" (Heb "hoy") formula. Usually "ah" is followed by a noun phrase (or a participle) that not only identifies for whom the exclamation is due, but also explains their fate in terms of just punishment (e.g., Zeph. 3.1). *City of crime* (more lit. "city of blood[shed]") follows this pattern. The NJPS translation of the v. is not fully literal. **4–7:** On the general imagery, cf. Lam. ch 1. **4:** The association of a female metaphor for the city with the negative, female imagery of *harlotries* and *sorcery* is obvious. Such metaphors were common in the societies in which biblical texts were written and first read, though problematic to many readers today. **8:** *No-amon,* Thebes, the Egyptian capital, one of the most impressive and wealthy cities of the ancient Near East. It was conquered by Assyria in the days of Ashurbanipal (663 BCE). The main enemy of the Assyrians at the time was an Ethiopian dynasty that ruled over Egypt. The pun on words and historical background is clear.

a Meaning of Heb. uncertain.
b Amon was the tutelary deity of No (Thebes; cf. Jer. 46.25), which the Assyrians had sacked in 663 B.C.E. *c Heb. "sea."*
d-d Change of vocalization yields "water." *e Heb. "your."*

10: On the image of smashed babies, cf. 2 Kings 8.12; Isa. 13.16; Hos. 10.14; 14.1; Ps. 137.9. **11:** The *you* (feminine) refers back to Nineveh. The metaphor is one of a drunken woman; see v. 12. **13:** The language reflects a worldview in which women are seen as weak and defenseless; to compare a man to a woman is an insult. The relevant section of the v. may be understood not only as *the troops within you are women* but also as "Behold! Your people: women in your midst!" Cf. Isa. 19.16; Jer. 30.57; 51.30. **15, 17:** The text plays on two common associations of the locust, with troops and with being a multitude (cf. Joel). Some translations have "locust" or "chewing locust" instead of *grub* in v. 15. The point is that the locust (enemy) will devour Assyria whereas its multitude (locust) of troops, merchants, scribes, and the like will not be able to save Assyria. The word translated *marshals* may also be translated "scribes."

10 Yet even she was exiled,
She went into captivity.
Her babes, too, were dashed in pieces
At every street corner.
Lots were cast for her honored men,
And all her nobles were bound in chains.
11 You too shall be drunk
And utterly overcome;[a]
You too shall seek
A refuge from the enemy.
12 All your forts are fig trees
With[b] ripe fruit;
If shaken they will fall
Into the mouths of devourers.
13 Truly, the troops within you are women;
The gates of your land have opened themselves
To your enemies;
Fire has consumed your gate bars.

14 Draw water for the siege,
Strengthen your forts;
Tread the clay,
Trample the mud,
Grasp the brick mold!
15 There fire will devour you,
The sword will put an end to you;
It will devour you like the grub.
[c-]Multiply like grubs,
Multiply like locusts![-c]

16 You had more traders
Than the sky has stars—
The grubs cast their skins and fly away.
17 Your guards were like locusts,
Your marshals like piles of hoppers
Which settle on the stone fences
On a chilly day;
When the sun comes out, they fly away,
And where they are nobody knows.
18 Your shepherds are slumbering,
O king of Assyria;
Your sheepmasters are [d-]lying inert;[-d]
Your people are scattered[a] over the hills,
And there is none to gather them.

a *Meaning of Heb. uncertain.*
b *Emendation yields "Your troops are"; cf. next verse.*
c-c *Meaning of Heb. uncertain.* d-d *Lit. "dwelling"; emendation yields "asleep."*

19 There is no healing[a] for your injury;
Your wound is grievous.
All who hear the news about you
Clap their hands over you.
For who has not suffered
From your constant malice?

19: On clapping hands for joy, cf. Ps. 47.2. Everyone has suffered because of Assyria and now rejoices in its permanent destruction.

a Heb. kehah, *a variant of* gehah; *see Prov. 17.22.*

חבקוק

Habakkuk

THE BOOK OF HABAKKUK consists of a report of a dialogue between the prophet and the LORD (chs 1–2) and a prayer or psalm (ch 3). It is particularly significantly that a book that contains mainly human speech is considered to be "the (prophetic) pronouncement that Habakkuk, the prophet, saw (i.e., perceived in a revelation/vision)." In other words, the written report of the words of a prophet to God becomes a revelation or divinely originated vision. (The same process may have led to the consideration of the book of Psalms, for instance, as Scripture.)

From the perspective of the intended readers, the text presents Habakkuk's vision as preceding the fall of Babylon. Needless to say, nothing about the date of composition of the book or a historical Habakkuk can be learned from this observation. The most that can be said is that the book presumes the situation that began with the rise of Babylonian power around 612 BCE, and therefore is not earlier. The text assumes a readership (and authorship) that was aware that Babylonia was the main power in the area at some point. Readers who lived after the fall of the Babylonian (or Chaldean) empire in 539 BCE likely read the book as a meditation on living under injustice, wondering how to relate the known attributes of the LORD to an international system in which the dominant imperial power "slays nations without pity," or "seizes homes not their own" and which surely does not place its trust in the LORD, and how a pious person is supposed to deal with this situation. From the perspective of such readers the fact that Babylonia has already fallen makes a prominent contribution to the persuasive power of the book and its message.

Following the superscription, the book contains a report of a dialogue between the prophet and the LORD that may be divided into four parts: (1) Habakkuk's first complaint (1.2–4), (2) the LORD's response (1.5–11), (3) Habakkuk's second complaint (1.12–17), and (4) Habakkuk's report of the LORD's response (ch 2). The book concludes with the prayer or psalm of Habakkuk (ch 3). This section has its own title or subtitle (see 3.1) and contains a short, human petition to God to manifest God's power (3.2), a lengthy report about an appearance of the LORD in the world (a theophany) (vv. 3–15), and above all concludes with an expression of human confidence in the LORD (vv. 16–19). Many scholars maintain this prayer is secondary to the book, and it is lacking in the *Pesher Habakkuk* (see below). The book as it stands (whether in the MT or in any of the ancient versions, e.g., the LXX), however, presents all three chapters as "the (prophetic) pronouncement that Habakkuk, the prophet, saw (i.e., perceived in a revelation/vision)."

A long commentary on the first two chapters of Habakkuk has been preserved among the Dead Sea Scrolls. This commentary, called by scholars *Pesher Habakkuk* (1QpHab), understands this prophetic work as being actualized in its author's own day, centuries after Habakkuk was written. Specifically, it identifies Habakkuk's Chaldeans, a name for the Babylonians, with the Kittim, almost certainly the Romans. This offers clear proof of how prophetic works were read and studied within a Jewish group that lived in the late Maccabean period in the 1st c. BCE as works that contain information about the life of their community of readers rather than arcane reports of past historical periods.

[EHUD BEN ZVI]

1 The pronouncement made by the prophet Habakkuk.

2 How long, O LORD, shall I cry out
And You not listen,
Shall I shout to You, "Violence!"
And You not save?
3 Why do You make me see iniquity
[a-][Why] do You look[-a] upon wrong?—
Raiding and violence are before me,
Strife continues and contention [b-]goes on.[-b]
4 That is why decision fails
And justice never emerges;
For the villain hedges in the just man—
Therefore judgment emerges deformed.

5 "Look among the nations,
Observe well and be utterly astounded;
For a work is being wrought in your days
Which you would not believe if it were told.
6 For lo, I am raising up the Chaldeans,
That fierce, impetuous nation,
Who cross the earth's wide spaces
To seize homes not their own.
7 They are terrible, dreadful;
[c-]They make their own laws and rules.[-c]
8 Their horses are swifter than leopards,
Fleeter than wolves of the steppe.[d]
Their steeds gallop—[e-]their steeds[-e]
Come flying from afar.
Like vultures rushing toward food,
9 They all come, bent on rapine.
The thrust[f] of their van is forward,
And they amass captives like sand.
10 Kings they hold in derision,
And princes are a joke to them;
They laugh at every fortress,
They pile up earth and capture it.

a-a Targum and Syriac "So that I look." *b-b Meaning of Heb. uncertain.*
c-c Lit. "Their law and majesty proceed from themselves."
d Understanding 'ereb *as synonymous with* 'arabah; *cf. Jer. 5.6.*
e-e The Qumran Habakkuk commentary (hereafter 1QpHab) reads "and spread [wings]." *f Meaning of Heb. uncertain.*

1.1: Superscription. A more literal translation of the v. would be "the (prophetic) pronouncement that Habakkuk, the prophet, saw (i.e., perceived in a revelation/vision)." Some scholars consider this title to refer only to chs 1 and 2, because ch 3 has its own title. It is more likely, however, that 3.1 served as a subtitle, whereas 1.1 performs the usual role of title and introduction to the entire book.

1.2–2.20: A dialogue between Habakkuk and the LORD.
1.2–4: This is the beginning of the dialogue between the LORD and a prophetic voice (Habakkuk). The human speaker initiates the dialogue with a series of pointed, rhetorical questions. The issue at stake is not simply theodicy but the very order and possibility of existence of the world (see below). Nothing in the text directly anchors the questions to a particular historical situation. The speaker implicitly identifies himself with the righteous, but not much about them is told. The text is written in general terms so readers may identify with the speaker and the speaker's questions. **4:** *That is why decision fails,* probably better, "therefore torah slacks." The word "torah" here points to the divine teaching that maintains the order of the world, and that was later understood by traditional Jewish commentators as "the Torah." **5–11:** These vv. present the divine response to the human complaint. Initially, it seems incongruous, since it announces that the LORD gives victory to the Babylonians, who are described by the same divine voice in the most terrifying terms. So not only will the wicked prosper and have dominion, but even the righteous in Judah will continue to suffer at the hands of a dread and fierce, wicked power. The divine response, in fact, strengthens rather than weakens the case advanced in the human complaint. **7:** *They make their own laws and rules,* they take upon themselves a role that is the LORD's (see translators' note *c-c*). Still, despite their arrogance, the LORD raises them up. **8:** The Chaldean troops are compared and declared swifter and more menacing than the swiftest wild animals. The point is not only "de-humanizing" but also "de-naturalizing" them, that is, portraying them as beyond the scope of the natural world in terms of their ferocity and the menace they constitute.

11 [a-]Then they pass on like the wind,
They transgress and incur guilt,
For they ascribe their might to their god."[-a]

12 You, O LORD, are from everlasting;
My holy God, You[b] never die.
O LORD, You have made them a subject of contention;
O Rock, You have made them a cause for complaint.
13 You whose eyes are too pure to look upon evil,
Who cannot countenance wrongdoing,
Why do You countenance treachery,
And stand by idle
While the one in the wrong devours
The one in the right?
14 You have made mankind like the fish of the sea,
Like creeping things [c-]that have no ruler.[-c]
15 He has fished them all up with a line,
Pulled them up in his trawl,
And gathered them in his net.
That is why he rejoices and is glad.
16 That is why he sacrifices to his trawl
And makes offerings to his net;
For through them his portion[d] is rich
And his nourishment fat.
17 Shall he then keep [e-]emptying his trawl,[-e]
And slaying nations without pity?

2 I will stand on my watch,
Take up my station at the[f] post,
And wait to see what He will say to me,
What He[g] will reply to my complaint.

2 The LORD answered me and said:
Write the prophecy down,
Inscribe it clearly on tablets,
So that it can be read easily.

a-a *Meaning of Heb. uncertain.* b *Heb. "we," a change made by a pious scribe.*
c-c *1QpHab "[for him] to rule over"; cf. Gen. 1.28; Ps. 8.7–9.*
d *Emendation yields "bread"; cf. Gen. 49.20.* e-e *1QpHab "drawing his sword."*
f *1QpHab reads "my."* g *Taking* 'ashib *as equivalent to* yashib.

11: There is an ongoing debate on how to translate this textually difficult v. Although several substantially different proposals have been advanced, the general gist of the text is clear: The Babylonians do not think that their power is established and maintained by the LORD. **12–17:** The reaction of the prophetic voice to such a reply is—as one may expect—a second complaint, one that takes into account the divine response and the aggravating circumstances that it describes. **12:** The Heb actually says something akin to "we shall not die" or "let us not die." There is a tradition that the original text read, "You [i.e., the LORD] never die," and that scribes changed it because of its embarrassing content. (These emendations are called "Tikkunei Soferim.") There is a considerable debate on how to evaluate this tradition concerning v. 12, and accordingly, about the wording of the original text of the v. It seems more likely that the v. read, "let us not die" or the like. **13:** The meaning of the last two lines in the v. is something like "[why do you] remain silent when the wicked swallow those more righteous than they?" The question is not why one who is more righteous would suffer, but why the hierarchy of people in the spectrum of righteousness-wickedness runs opposite to that of power in the "real world." **14:** This is a reversal of people's role as described in Gen. 1.26, 28. **2.1–20:** At this point, the reader waits to see how the LORD will respond. The response comes in the form of the speaker's report of a revelation. **1:** *I will stand on my watch … and wait to see what He will say to me.* Is he patiently or defiantly waiting? The text does not answer this question. But later readers did. Thus, for instance, *b. Ta'an.* 23a reflects a memory of him as a defiant character who would not move until he receives a response to his complaint and evaluates this attitude positively as it imagines Habakkuk as a forerunner of Ḥoni ha-Me'agel (the circle-maker), a kind of "miracle-maker" figure who saved Israel from severe draught (see also Rashi). Compare and contrast with Jonah 4.5. **2:** YHVH answers the prophet. *Inscribe it clearly on tablets,* cf. Deut. 27.8. The divine message is to be written, but significantly, the text of that message is not reported in the book.

3 For [a-]there is yet a prophecy[-a] for a set term,
A truthful witness for a time that will come.
Even if it tarries, wait for it still;
For it will surely come, without delay:
4 [b-]Lo, his spirit within him is puffed up, not upright,
But[-b] the righteous man is rewarded with life
For his fidelity.
5 How much less then shall the defiant[c]
go unpunished,
The treacherous, arrogant man
Who has made his maw as wide as Sheol,
Who is as insatiable as Death,
Who has harvested all the nations
And gathered in all the peoples!
6 Surely all these shall pronounce a satire against him,
A pointed epigram concerning him.
They shall say:
Ah, you who pile up what is not yours—
How much longer?—
And make ever heavier your load of indebtedness!
7 Right suddenly will your creditors[d] arise,
And those who remind[e] you will awake,
And you will be despoiled by them.
8 Because you plundered many nations,
All surviving peoples shall plunder you—
For crimes against men and wrongs against lands,
Against cities and all their inhabitants.

9 Ah, you who have acquired gains
To the detriment of your own house,
[f-]Who have destroyed many peoples[-f]
In order to set your nest on high
To escape disaster!
10 You have plotted shame for your own house,
And guilt for yourself;
11 For a stone shall cry out from the wall,
And a rafter shall answer it from the woodwork.

12 Ah, you who have built a town with crime,
And established a city with infamy,
13 So that peoples have had to toil for the fire,[g]

a-a Emendation yields "the prophecy is a witness."
b-b Meaning of Heb. uncertain. Emendation yields "Lo, there is a reward for the upright—/ the life breath within him—/ And . . . "
c Connecting hyyn *(1QpHab* hwn*) with the root* hwn, *Deut. 1.41; for the thought cf. Prov. 11.31. Meaning of rest of line uncertain.* *d Lit. "usurers."*
e Lit. "shake"; the same verb means "to call to mind" in Samaritan Aramaic. *f-f Brought up from v. 10 for clarity.* *g I.e., without profit.*

3: This v. is associated in Jewish tradition with the coming of the Messiah and is reflected in the language of the twelfth principle of the thirteen principles of faith of Maimonides. **4:** *But the righteous man is rewarded with life / For his fidelity,* often translated "the righteous one lives (or shall live) by his faith" or "the righteous one shall live through (or is sustained by) his faith." According to one of the Rabbis in *b. Mak.* 23b, this saying encapsulates all the commandments. The saying also had an important influence in Christianity, and in particular in the doctrine of justification through faith (see Rom. 1.17; Gal. 3.11; Hebrews 10.38–39). In its original context the saying is clearly interwoven with the first part of the v. The saying there focuses on a person whose life is swollen and crooked. Then the v. moves to the opposite pole, a pious person who keeps his or her trust in the LORD under the dire circumstances described in the book, i.e., when the righteous are asked to wait while those who do not deserve worldly power wield it over them. The text does not identify such persons with any particular characters, thereby facilitating different identifications and accordingly, diverse readings of the text. Given the general focus in the book on Babylonia and its wickedness, readers may have understood the negative character in the first line as pointing to the king of Babylonia, as an archetypal representative of both the Babylonian empire and any proud people who rely on their own power. **5:** *Sheol,* the Pit (Ps. 6.6 and many other places) or the netherworld, where all people descend upon death, it is the nadir of the world. Human attributes are associated with Sheol here. It has a *maw* and, of course, the "maw of Sheol" is surely *insatiable,* like that of Death (see also Isa. 5.14, cf. Ps. 141.7). **6a:** *A pointed epigram concerning him. / They shall say: . . . ,* or "Shall not all these take up a parable about him and a metaphor, and riddles regarding him? One will say: . . . " **6b–20:** What this "one" will say is presented as a series of five

And nations to weary themselves for naught!
[a]Behold, it is from the LORD of Hosts:
14 [b-]For the earth shall be filled
With awe for the glory of the LORD
As water covers the sea.[-b]

15 Ah, you who make others drink to intoxication
[c-]As you pour out[-c] your wrath,
In order to gaze upon their nakedness![d]
16 You shall be sated with shame
Rather than glory:
Drink in your turn and stagger![e]
The cup in the right hand of the LORD
Shall come around to you,
And [f-]disgrace to[-f] your glory.
17 [g-]For the lawlessness against Lebanon shall cover you,
The destruction of beasts shall overwhelm you[-g]—
For crimes against men and wrongs against lands,
Against cities and all their inhabitants.
18[h] What has the carved image availed,
That he who fashioned it has carved it
For an image and a false oracle—
That he who fashioned his product has trusted in it,
Making dumb idols?
19 Ah, you who say, "Wake up" to wood,
"Awaken," to inert stone!
Can that give an oracle?
Why, it is encased in gold and silver,
But there is no breath inside it.
20 But the LORD in His holy Abode—
Be silent before Him all the earth!

3 A prayer of the prophet Habakkuk. In the mode of *Shigionoth.*[i]

2 O LORD! I have learned of Your renown;
I am awed, O LORD, by Your deeds.
Renew them in these years,
Oh, make them known in these years!
Though angry, may You remember compassion.

a Connection with the next four lines uncertain; they might read better after v. 20.
b-b Cf. Isa. 11.9.
c-c Meaning of Heb. uncertain. Emendation yields "from the bowl of."
d Cf. Gen. 9.21–22.
e Emendation yields "uncover yourself"; cf. Lam. 4.21.
f-f Or "vomit of disgrace upon." *g-g Meaning of Heb. uncertain.*
h This verse would read well after v. 19.
i Meaning uncertain; perhaps "psalms of supplication"; cf. Ps. 7.1.

Ah or "woe" passages marked by the formula, *Ah, you* (vv. 6b, 9, 12, 15, 19). The enemy is now denounced as a spoiler, greedy, unjust, lawless, and idolatrous. (On the structure of these *Ah* oracles, see Nah. 3.1 n.) **14:** This is nearly identical with the second half of Isa. 11.9. A more literal translation would be, "for the earth shall be filled with the knowledge of the glory of the LORD, as water covers the sea." In other words, just as there is no place in the sea without water, there will be no place on the earth that will not be filled with the knowledge of the glory of the LORD. Some traditional commentators have suggested that the text is elliptic and means "... shall be filled "by the will" to know the glory." The Tg. seems to assume that people cannot really know the glory of the LORD, so it translates and reinterprets the text to mean, "... to know the fear of the LORD." **18–19:** For similar polemical texts, see Isa. 40.19–20; 44.9–20; 46.6–7; Pss. 115.4–8; 135.15–18. **20:** When the LORD is present in the Temple, silence is required (cf. Zeph. 1.7; Zech. 2.17). Some scholars argue that the sacrificial service was conducted in silence.

3.1–19: The psalm of Habakkuk. The prayer/psalm contains a title (v. 1), a petition to God to manifest His power (v. 2), a lengthy report about a theophany (vv. 3–15), an expression of confidence by the human speaker (vv. 16–19), and musical instructions (v. 19). There are several instructions for performance in ch 3. They include three occurrences of *Selah* (vv. 3, 9, 13) and the concluding phrase (v. 19); these are otherwise only attested in the book of Ps., and for this reason many consider this to be a psalm that became part of Hab. It is abundantly clear that ch 3 asks its intended readers to envision it not only as a prophetic reading, but also as a composition to be performed. At points, the language of this ch is very difficult, and perhaps archaic. **1:** The exact meaning of *Shigionoth* is unclear, but it has something to do with a musical aspect of the performance

3 God is coming from Teman,
The Holy One from Mount Paran. *Selah.*[a]
His majesty covers the skies,
His splendor fills the earth:
4 [b]It is a brilliant light
Which gives off rays on every side—
And therein His glory is enveloped.[b]
5 Pestilence marches before Him,
And plague comes forth at His heels.
6 When He stands, He makes the earth shake;[c]
When He glances, He makes nations
tremble.
The age-old mountains are shattered,
The primeval hills sink low.
[b]His are the ancient routes:
7 As a scene of havoc I behold[b]
The tents of Cushan;
Shaken are the pavilions
Of the land of Midian!

8 Are You wroth, O LORD, with Neharim?
Is Your anger against Neharim,
Your rage against Yam[d]—
That You are driving Your steeds,
Your victorious chariot?
9 All bared and ready is Your bow.
[b]Sworn are the rods of the word.[b] *Selah.*
You make the earth burst into streams,
10 The mountains rock at the sight of You,
A torrent of rain comes down;
Loud roars the deep,
[b]The sky returns the echo.[b]
11 Sun [and] moon stand still on high
As Your arrows fly in brightness,
Your flashing spear in brilliance.
12 You tread the earth in rage,
You trample nations in fury.
13 You have come forth to deliver Your
people,
To deliver Your anointed.[e]

of the psalm (cf. Ps. 7.1; Radak). According to a certain traditional Jewish interpretation, this phrase is not a musicological note, but should be translated, "... for erroneous speech/utterances." This reading reflects a particular understanding of the claims made by the human speaker in these dialogues (contrast with Job 42.8). The Tg. offers a different interpretation of the title of the prayer: "The prayer which Habakkuk the prophet prayed when it was revealed to him concerning the extension of time which he gives to the wicked, that if they return to the law with a perfect heart they shall be forgiven and all their sins ... shall be as sins of ignorance." **3–15:** The theophanic description emphasizes the awesome power of God and reassures the readers that the LORD will vanquish their enemies, in judgment. Mythological references (vv. 5, 8), images of shaking in the natural and human world (vv. 6–7, 10), and of destruction of enemies (vv. 12–15) are common in theophanic reports. **3:** In this theophany, the LORD is coming from the south: Both *Teman* and *Mount Paran* are in the south from a Judahite perspective (cf. Deut. 33.2; Judg. 5.4). **5:** *Pestilence,* some translate "plague" or "Plague" since it is personified. The personification contributes to the mythological atmosphere of this passage. The Tg. identifies "Plague" with the angel of death. *Plague,* some translate "Fever" (Heb "reshef"), a West-Semitic mythological figure. **7:** *Cushan ... Midian,* two tent-dwellers, "nomadic" groups south, or southeast, of Judah. As mentioned above, the LORD is presented as coming from the south in this theophany (see v. 3). **8:** *Neharim,* or "River" or "Floods" or "rivers." *Neharim* is another West-Semitic mythological figure (cf. "reshef" in v. 5 n.) and so is *Yam,* "Sea" or "sea." See translators' note *d.*

a A musical direction of uncertain meaning.
b-b Meaning of Heb. uncertain. *c Cf. Targum and Septuagint.*
d Neharim (lit. "Floods") and Yam (lit. "Sea") were marine monsters vanquished by the LORD in hoary antiquity. On Yam see Ps. 74.13; Job 7.12. A being called both Yam and Nahar figures in early Canaanite literature.
e I.e., the king of Judah.

[a-]You will smash the roof of the villain's house,
Raze it from foundation to top. *Selah.*
14 You will crack [his] skull with Your[b] bludgeon;
Blown away shall be his warriors,
Whose delight is to crush me suddenly,
To devour a poor man in an ambush.[-a]
15 [c-]You will make Your steeds tread the sea,
Stirring the mighty waters.
16 I heard and my bowels quaked,
My lips quivered at the sound;
Rot entered into my bone,
I trembled where I stood.
Yet I wait calmly for the day of distress,
For a people to come to attack us.
17 Though the fig tree does not bud
And no yield is on the vine,
Though the olive crop has failed
And the fields produce no grain,
Though sheep have vanished from the fold
And no cattle are in the pen,[-c]
18 Yet will I rejoice in the LORD,
Exult in the God who delivers me.
19 My Lord GOD is my strength:
He makes my feet like the deer's
And lets me stride upon the heights.

[d-]For the leader; with instrumental music.[-d]

a-a Emendation yields: You will strike the heads of men of evil, / Smash the pates of Your adversaries. Selah. */ You will crack their skulls with Your bludgeon; / Dispersed, blown like chaff shall be they / Who lie in wait to swallow the innocent, / To devour the poor in an ambush.* *b Heb. "His."*

c-c Or: [15]You will make Your steeds tread the sea, / Stirring the mighty waters, / [16]That I may have rest on a day of distress, / When a people come up to attack us. / But this report made my bowels quake, / These tidings made my lips quiver; / Rot entered into my bone, / I trembled where I stood: / [17]That the fig tree does not bud, / And no yield is on the vine; / The olive crop has failed, / And the fields produce no grain; / The sheep have vanished from the fold, / And no cattle are in the pen.

d-d Meaning of Heb. uncertain.

16–19: The text here advances the normative position that the readers of the book should take to heart, namely that despite all worldly circumstances (v. 17), the righteous rejoice and exult in a God that delivers them, who is their strength (v. 19). **19:** Cf. 2 Sam. 22.34; Ps. 18.34.

צפניה

Zephaniah

THE BOOK OF ZEPHANIAH claims to be a particular instance of the LORD's word, namely that associated with Zephaniah, the son of Cushi (see 1.1 and n.). The book is set in the time of Josiah (late 7th c. BCE), the last great king of Judah according to the books of Kings and Chronicles. Judah as described in Zephaniah (and elsewhere in prophetic literature) is quite an ungodly place. This is to be expected: Prophetic books that include divine announcements of judgment and destruction against Judah tend for obvious reasons to describe the social and religious situation in monarchic Judah in harsh, negative terms. Most scholars date the present book of Zephaniah to the postmonarchic period, but many of them maintain that a forerunner or a previous version of the book existed in the monarchic period and contained much (but not all) of the present text.

Some scholars attempted to harmonize the positive image of Josianic times in the historical books and its negative characterization here by assigning the circumstances described in the book to a time when Josiah was still a minor and consequently did not actually rule over the land, or to a time after his death. But this is not the claim of the book of Zephaniah. To be sure, the king is not explicitly criticized when all the leadership of Judah is condemned, but the same can be said of other prophetic books (e.g., Micah) and it is difficult to reach historical conclusions on this basis. Some scholars associate the oracles against the nations in ch 2 with a presumed plan for territorial expansion that was advanced by King Josiah, but either never materialized or did so to only a very small extent, but this is speculative.

The book uses wordplay and ambiguity to channel the attention of the readers and contribute to the possibility of multiple readings. These features are typical in prophetic books, and facilitate the continuous reading and study of these texts.

The book begins like most prophetic books with an introduction or superscription and then moves to sets of prophetic pronouncements. The book announces severe judgment against Judah and nations other than Israel, and, as do all other prophetic books, Zephaniah includes reports of prophecies of hope. Even the announcements of doom against Judah serve, in part, to emphasize hope from the perspective of the postmonarchic readers of the book of Zephaniah, because for them the fact that the announcements of doom were fulfilled in the past, as written, reassured them that those of hope will also be fulfilled in the future.

There are several possible ways to outline the book of Zephaniah, each pointing to a particular but partial reading that emphasizes certain aspects of the book and de-emphasizes others. These partial readings inform each other, and all together create a meaning much richer than any of them separately. This is a common situation in prophetic books. The following is one of these possible outlines:

I. Announcement of doom (1.2–9)
II. Description of doom (1.10–18)

III. The last chance to repent (2.1–3)
IV. Against the nations and their gods (2.4–15)
V. Against the overbearing city (3.1–13)
VI. Joy to Jerusalem (3.14–20)

[EHUD BEN ZVI]

1 The word of the LORD that came to Zephaniah son of Cushi son of Gedaliah son of Amariah son of Hezekiah, during the reign of King Josiah son of Amon of Judah.

2 I will sweep everything away
From the face of the earth
—declares the LORD.
3 I will sweep away man and beast;
I will sweep away the birds of the sky
And the fish of the sea.
[a]I will make the wicked stumble,[-a]
And I will destroy mankind
From the face of the earth
—declares the LORD.

4 I will stretch out My arm against Judah
And against all who dwell in Jerusalem;
And I will wipe out from this place
Every vestige of Baal,
And the name of the priestlings[b]
along with the priests;
5 And those who bow down on the roofs
To the host of heaven;
And those who bow down and swear to the LORD
But also swear by Malcam;[c]
6 And those who have forsaken the LORD,
And those who have not sought the LORD
And have not turned to Him.

a-a Meaning of Heb. uncertain.
b Heb. kemarim, *a term used only of priests of heathen gods.*
c Apparently identical with "Milcom the abomination of the Ammonites"; cf. 1 Kings 11.5.

1.1: Superscription. *Cushi,* in principle, may also mean "Cushite" (i.e., Ethiopian). Because of the context in which it appears, however, it can only be a personal name. The last of the ancestors mentioned in the list is Hezekiah. Some interpreters maintained that this Hezekiah was the famous king of Judah (Ibn Ezra, but contrast with Radak), but such a claim is not advanced in the text. (The Sages understood the list as pointing at Zephaniah as a righteous man who is himself a son of a righteous man; see *b. Meg.* 15a.) On the reference to the reign of Josiah, see intro.

1.2–9: Announcement of doom. 2–3: The translation suggests a universal scenario of destruction. The Heb is more ambiguous. It can certainly be understood in such a way, but also as pointing to the total destruction of a particular area. **3:** *I will make the wicked stumble* reflects an emendation of the MT. The latter may be translated as "[I will sweep away] the stumbling blocks along with the wicked" or "[I will sweep away] the stumbling blocks of the wicked" or "[I will sweep away] what makes the wicked stumble." The text does not identify these stumbling blocks, but readers throughout generations filled this gap from the perspective of their worldview and particular circumstances. For instance, many associated them with the animals previously mentioned in the text. But if so, why do the animals make people stumble? *Gen. Rab.* hints that this is because they provide abundance, and abundance may lead to sin (see *Gen. Rab.* 28.6). According to many others, this is because they may lead to idolatrous worship (*b. A. Z.* 55a). **5:** *Those who bow down on the roofs / To the host of heaven:* A reference to astral worship (cf. Jer. 19.13; 2 Kings 17.16; 21.3). *Malcam,* or "their king." Medieval Jewish interpretation tends to follow the Tg. and to associate "their king" with "false deities" (Rashi, Radak), a rendering supported by the poetic parallelism of the v. Similarly, some modern interpreters see here Milcom, the head of the pantheon of Ammon (1 Kings 11.5, 33; 2 Kings 23.13); or Molech, a deity to whom children were sacrificed or passed through fire (see Lev. 18.21; 20.2; 2 Kings 23.10; cf. 1 Kings 11.7). Other modern scholars maintain that "their king" means just "their king" (cf. Exod. 22.27; 1 Kings 21.10; Isa. 8.21), while some suggest that "their king" points to the LORD,

7 Be silent before my Lord GOD,
For the day of the LORD is approaching;
For the LORD has prepared a [a]sacrificial feast,[-a]
Has bidden His guests purify themselves.
8 And on the day of the LORD's sacrifice
I will punish the officials
And the king's sons,[b]
[c]And all who don a foreign vestment.
9 I will also punish on that day
Everyone who steps over the threshold,[-c]
Who fill their master's[d] palace
With lawlessness and fraud.
10 In that day there shall be
—declares the LORD—
A loud outcry from the Fish Gate,
And howling from the Mishneh,[e]
And a sound of great anguish from the hills.
11 The dwellers of the Machtesh[f] howl;
For all the tradesmen have perished,
All who weigh silver are wiped out.

12 At that time,
I will search Jerusalem with lamps;
And I will punish the men
Who rest untroubled on their lees,
Who say to themselves,
"The LORD will do nothing, good or bad."
13 Their wealth shall be plundered
And their homes laid waste.
They shall build houses and not dwell in them,
Plant vineyards and not drink their wine.
14 The great day of the LORD is approaching,
Approaching most swiftly.
[g]Hark, the day of the LORD!
It is bitter:
There a warrior shrieks![-g]
15 That day shall be a day of wrath,
A day of trouble and distress,
A day of calamity and desolation,
A day of darkness and deep gloom,

wrongly worshipped. **7:** The last two lines in the v. can be translated as "the LORD has prepared a sacrifice; He has consecrated those He has invited." This translation communicates the likely intentional ambiguity of the Heb, where it is unclear if the guests are consecrated so they can take part in the sacrificial meal or, are consecrated because they are about to be slaughtered for the meal. **8:** *King's sons* refers to the royal family in general, and perhaps even to royal officers; in other words, to the elite of the kingdom, which was understood as the "king's house(hold)" over which the king rules as a "father." **9:** *Everyone who steps over the threshold* may refer to an imitation of the ways of "idolaters" in general or Philistines (see 1 Sam. 5.4–5) in particular (e.g., Tg., and most of recent scholarship) or it may point to social injustice, oppression, and thievery (e.g., Radak; Ibn Ezra). The reference to *their master's palace* is ambiguous: It may refer to the Temple of the LORD or to the palace of the king, or to both.

1.10–18: Description of doom. **10:** The *Mishneh* or "Second Quarter" is probably the Upper City of Jerusalem, the Western Hill, where the upper social strata of Jerusalem dwelled. **12:** It is God who will be searching Jerusalem with lamps. The Tg., and some later interpreters, reinterpreted the v. to avoid the anthropomorphism that this image involves. **13:** The text sounds like a reverberation of the curse in Deut. 28.30, and it points to the futility of human actions contrary to divine will. **14–18:** The traditional prophetic Day of the LORD imagery is employed to reflect the great disaster (see Joel 1.15 n.).

a-a *I.e., a slaughter of sinners.*
b *Apparently brothers of King Amon, who exercised influence during the minority of King Josiah (2 Kings 22.1).*
c-c *Apparently references to two customs of heathen worship; cf. 2 Kings 10.22 and 1 Sam. 5.5.* d *I.e., King Josiah's.*
e *A quarter of Jerusalem; cf. 2 Kings 22.14.* f *Another quarter of Jerusalem.*
g-g *Emendation yields: "The day of the LORD is faster than a runner, / Fleeter than a warrior"; cf. Ps. 19.6.*

2.1–4: The last chance to repent. **1:** The Heb term translated as *without shame* may be understood as "not desiring [God]" or as "not desired [by God]." The context indicates that this nation is (Josianic) Judah. **4:** English translations are unable to convey the puns on the terms *Gaza* and *Ekron* that feature prominently in the Heb text. Something like "Powertown shall be powdered" or "Gaza shall be ghastful," and "Rootville—or perhaps Uprootville—will be uprooted" suggest the force of the pun. The towns mentioned, including *Ashkelon* and *Ashdod,* were Philistine cities.

2.5–15: Against the nations and their gods. Such oracles against the nations are typical of prophetic books. They emphasize that YHVH's control is universal. **5:** *Nation of Cherethites,* people of Crete (an island in the eastern Mediterranean Sea). The *Cherethites* are associated with Philistines in Ezek. 25.16. Another wordplay: The main three letters of *Cherethites* in Heb connote a sense of "cut off" (cf. v. 6).

A day of densest clouds,
16 A day of horn blasts and alarms—
Against the fortified towns
And the lofty corner towers.
17 I will bring distress on the people,
And they shall walk like blind men,
Because they sinned against the LORD;
Their blood shall be spilled like dust,
And their fat[a] like dung.
18 Moreover, their silver and gold
Shall not avail to save them.
On the day of the LORD's wrath,
In the fire of His passion,
The whole land shall be consumed;
For He will make a terrible end
Of all who dwell in the land.

2 Gather together, gather,
[b-]O nation without shame,
2 Before the day the decree is born—
The day flies by like chaff[-b]—
Before the fierce anger
Of the LORD overtakes you,
Before the day of anger
Of the LORD overtakes you.
3 Seek the LORD,
All you humble of the land
Who have fulfilled His law;
Seek righteousness,
Seek humility.
Perhaps you will find shelter
On the day of the LORD's anger.

4 Indeed, Gaza shall be deserted
And Ashkelon desolate;
Ashdod's people shall be expelled in broad daylight,
And Ekron shall be uprooted.
5 Ah, nation of Cherethites
Who inhabit the seacoast!
There is a word of the LORD against you,
O Canaan,[c] land of the Philistines:
I will lay you waste
Without inhabitants.

a *Or "marrow"; meaning of Heb. uncertain.*
b-b *Meaning of Heb. uncertain. Emendation yields: "O straw [Aramaic* gel*] not gathered in, / Before you are driven like flying chaff"; cf. Ps. 35.5.*
c *Or "Phoenicia," of which Philistia is regarded as an extension southward.*

6 The seacoast Cheroth[a] shall become
An abode for shepherds and folds for flocks,
7 And shall be a portion for the remnant of the House
of Judah;
On these [pastures] they shall graze [their flocks],
They shall [b-]lie down[-b] at eventide
In the houses of Ashkelon.
For the LORD their God will take note of them
And restore their fortunes.

8 I have heard the insults of Moab
And the jeers of the Ammonites,
Who have insulted My people
And gloated over their country.
9 Assuredly, as I live
—declares the LORD of Hosts,
the God of Israel—
Moab shall become like Sodom
And the Ammonites like Gomorrah:
Clumps[a] of weeds and patches[a] of salt,
And desolation evermore.
The remnant of My people shall plunder them,
The remainder of My nation shall possess them.
10 That is what they'll get for their haughtiness,
For insulting and jeering
At the people of the LORD of Hosts.
11 The LORD will show Himself terrible against them,
Causing all the gods on earth to shrivel;[a]
And all the coastlands of the nations
Shall bow down to Him—
Every man in his own home.

12 You Cushites too—
[c-]They shall be slain by My sword.[-c]
13 And He will stretch out His arm against the north
And destroy Assyria;
He will make Nineveh a desolation,
Arid as the desert.
14 In it flocks shall lie down,
Every [d-]species of beast,
While jackdaws and owls roost on its capitals,
The great owl hoots in the window,
And the raven [croaks] on the threshold.
For he has stripped its cedarwork bare.[-d]

a Meaning of Heb. uncertain. b-b Change of vocalization yields "rest [them]"; cf. Song of Songs 1.7. c-c Emendation yields "shall be slain by the sword of the LORD." d-d Meaning of Heb. uncertain.

11: The v. may be translated "The LORD is awesome against them, for He shrivels [or weakens] all the gods of the earth." The text does not claim that the *gods on earth* do not exist (cf. Exod. 15.11), or that the LORD will or has destroyed them (cf. Ps. 82.6–7). It claims, rather, that the LORD is superior to them and that this superiority will be manifested so that people from far away countries ("all the islands/coastlands of the nations") will bow down to the LORD, each in his or her place. This v. stands in the midst of an announcement of judgment against the nations as a central text and a theologically driven explanatory note on this type of announcement. It maintains that the purpose of the LORD is not to destroy nation after nation—as might be suggested by a plain reading of a sequence of announcements against nations—but to bring these nations to bow to the LORD (cf. Zeph. 3.9). The contents, and often the language, of this v. are reminiscent of those in many psalms that depict the LORD as King (e.g., Pss. 29.1; 82.2, 6; 95.3; 96.4–10; 97.6–9). **14–15:** The language points to the image of a wilderness retaking a place of culture and city (cf. 2.6–7). The characterization of Nineveh in v. 15 is almost identical to that of Babylon in Isa. 47.8. The message is not so much that the historical Ninevites or Babylonians actually thought that way and thus deserve punishment—other reasons could have been adduced—but rather that such proud thinking is fully unacceptable and those who indulge in it will be punished by an active God who can bring good (or blessing) but also evil (or judgment); cf. 1.12.

15 Is this the gay city
That dwelt secure,
That thought in her heart,
"I am, and there is none but me"?
Alas, she is become a waste,
A lair of wild beasts!
Everyone who passes by her
Hisses and gestures with his hand.[a]

3 Ah, sullied, polluted,
Overbearing[b] city!
2 She has been disobedient,
Has learned no lesson;
She has not trusted in the LORD,
Has not drawn near to her God.
3 The officials within her
Are roaring lions;
Her judges are wolves [c]of the steppe,
They leave no bone until morning.[-c]
4 Her prophets are reckless,
Faithless fellows;

a To ward off a like fate from himself; cf. Jer. 18.16 and note.
b Meaning of Heb. uncertain. Emendation yields "harlot"; cf. Isa. 1.21.
c-c Meaning of Heb. uncertain.

3.1–13: Against the overbearing city. 1–2: The Heb exudes ambiguity. It is uncertain whether the city is Nineveh or Jerusalem. *Sullied* can be understood as "revered or feared"; *polluted* as "redeemed"; and *overbearing* (or "oppressing") as "the dove city" (i.e., a powerless city). In this particular case the ambiguities are unequivocally resolved within the context of the text. V. 2 clarifies that the city is not powerless and redeemed, but polluted and oppressing. The descriptions of wrongdoing in the following vv. show that the city is Jerusalem. This type of ambiguity shows the artistry of the book's composition and also points to the use of ambiguity as a rhetorical device to capture the readers' attention, and then lead them to a central issue: the identity and main characteristics of the city, which is eventually identified as the polluted, sinful, late monarchic (Josianic) Jerusalem. **3–4:** Compare the language with Ezek. 22.25, 27, 26 and for similar descriptions, cf. Mic. 3.1–7.

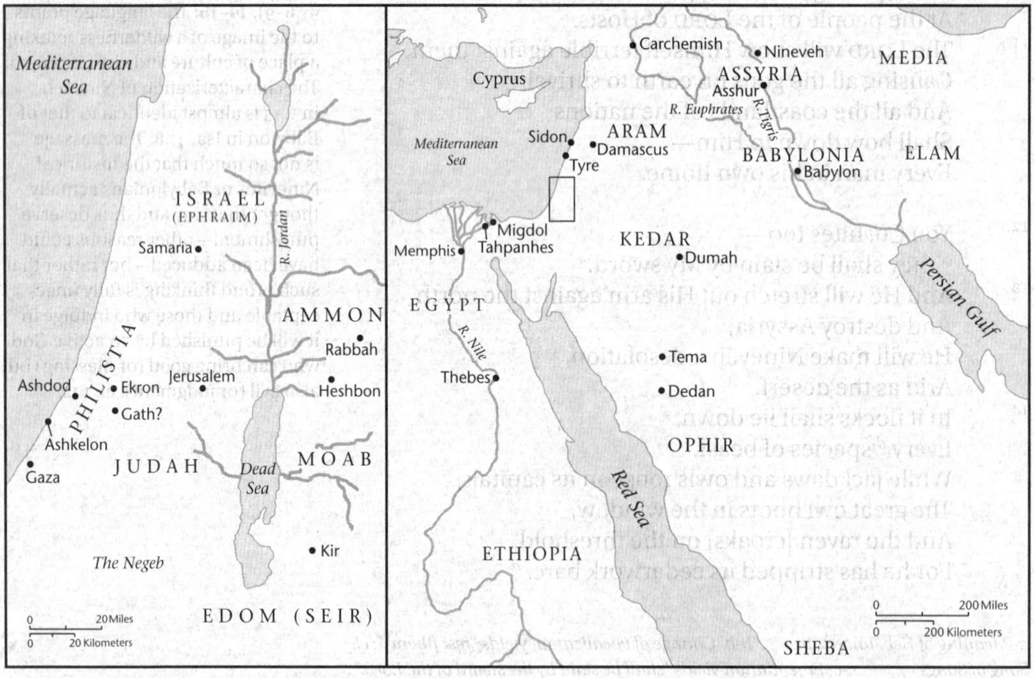

Places mentioned in the oracles against the nations

Her priests profane what is holy,
They give perverse rulings.
5 But the LORD in her midst is righteous,
He does no wrong;
He issues judgment every morning,
As unfailing as the light.

The wrongdoer knows no shame!
6 I wiped out nations:
Their corner towers are desolate;
I turned their thoroughfares into ruins,
With none passing by;
Their towns lie waste without people,
Without inhabitants.
7 And I thought that she[a] would fear Me,
Would learn a lesson,
And that the punishment I brought on them[b]
Would not be [c]lost on her.[c]
Instead, all the more eagerly
They have practiced corruption in all their deeds.

8 But wait for Me—says the LORD—
For the day when I arise as an accuser;[d]
When I decide to gather nations,
To bring kingdoms together,
To pour out My indignation on them,
All My blazing anger.
Indeed, by the fire of My passion
All the earth shall be consumed.
9 For then I will make the peoples pure of speech,
So that they all invoke the LORD by name
And serve Him with one accord.[e]
10 From beyond the rivers of Cush, My suppliants[f]
Shall bring offerings to Me in Fair Puzai.[g]
11 In that day,
You will no longer be shamed for all the deeds
By which you have defied Me.
For then I will remove
The proud and exultant within you,
And you will be haughty no more
On My sacred mount.[h]
12 But I will leave within you
A poor, humble folk,

a *Heb. "you."* *b* *Heb. "her."* *c-c* *Lit. "cut off [from] her vision."*
d *Understanding* 'ad *as equivalent to* 'ed, *with Septuagint and Syriac.*
e *Lit. "back," i.e., like beasts of burden.* *f* *Meaning of Heb. uncertain.*
g *Emendation yields "Zion." For the thought, cf. Isa. 18.1, 7.*
h *I.e., in My holy land; cf. Isa. 11.9; 57.13; 65.25.*

5: *Every morning as unfailing as the light* (or dawn) (but) *the wrongdoer knows no shame.* The text addresses the implied question: why do the wicked do evil in spite of YHVH's continuous presence and actions (issuing judgments day by day)? Because they know no shame. The reference to the light/dawn and to mornings communicates permanent, continuous presence, day after day and at the same time reflects a common ancient Near Eastern background in which justice is associated with the solar deity (Shamash) and with his light. Solar imagery is associated with YHVH in other texts (e.g., Isa. 60.1). **10:** There are three main understandings of this difficult v. They are represented by the following translations: (1) "From beyond the rivers of Cush (i.e., from far, far away) my suppliants, / Fair scattered (i.e., Israel in exile), shall bring my offering"; (2) "From beyond the rivers of Cush (i.e., from far, far away) my suppliants, / Fair Puzai (i.e., a faraway nation), shall bring my offering"; and (3) "From beyond the rivers of Cush (i.e., from far, far away) my suppliants, / Fair scattered (i.e., Israel in exile), they (i.e., the nations) shall bring as my offering" (cf. Isa. 66.20). The text plays again with ambiguity, and this time one that is not resolved by its context.

13: The *remnant* is a central prophetic idea (see Isa. 6.13 n.).

3.14–20: Joy to Jerusalem. 15: As in some other prophetic texts, here God is active as King (Sovereign), obviating the need for an ideal human king (a "messiah"). **18:** The Heb is extremely difficult. Tentative and at times quite divergent translations have been proposed. One possibility is: "Those who are afflicted because they are deprived of the festivals, I [i.e., the LORD] have gathered, they were from you, (they were) a sign on her, (they were) a (source of) mockery." **20:** The book concludes with a strong announcement of hope for the readers of the book; such positive conclusions typify prophetic books. The fortunes of Israel/Judah will be restored, and this restoration includes the gathering of the exiles (on this point, cf. Amos 9.14–15—though in Amos the image of restoration is agrarian). Because of its tone this v. has been included in Jewish liturgy (in the morning service, at the conclusion of an important section, just before the section that opens with a recitation of Exod. 30.17–21).

And they shall find refuge
In the name of the LORD.
13 The remnant of Israel
Shall do no wrong
And speak no falsehood;
A deceitful tongue
Shall not be in their mouths.
Only such as these shall graze and lie down,
With none to trouble them.

14 Shout for joy, Fair Zion,
Cry aloud, O Israel!
Rejoice and be glad with all your heart,
Fair Jerusalem!
15 The LORD has annulled the judgment against you,
He has swept away your foes.
Israel's Sovereign the LORD is within you;
You need fear misfortune no more.

16 In that day,
This shall be said to Jerusalem:
Have no fear, O Zion;
Let not your hands droop!
17 Your God the LORD is in your midst,
A warrior who brings triumph.
He will rejoice over you and be glad,
He will shout over you with jubilation.
He will [a]soothe with His love
18 Those long disconsolate.[a]
I will take away from you [b]the woe
Over which you endured mockery.[b]
19 At that time I will make [an end]
Of all who afflicted you.
And I will rescue the lame [sheep]
And gather the strayed;
And I will exchange their disgrace
For fame and renown in all the earth.
20 At that time I will gather you,
And at [that] time I will bring you [home];
For I will make you renowned and famous
Among all the peoples on earth,
When I restore your fortunes
Before their[c] very eyes —said the LORD.

a-a Meaning of Heb. uncertain. Emendation yields "renew His love / As in the days of old." *b-b Meaning of Heb. uncertain.* *c Heb. "your."*

חגי
Haggai

THE REBELLION OF JUDAH against the Babylonian empire led to the fall of Jerusalem (586 BCE), the destruction of the Temple, a severe decrease in the population of Judah due to death and deportation, and the end of the monarchy in Judah. The Babylonian empire fell at the hands of a Persian dynasty (the Achaemenid dynasty) in 539. As a result, the Babylonian province of Judah became the Persian or Achaemenid province of Yehud. According to 2 Chron. 36.22–23, the Persian conqueror of Babylon, Cyrus II (reigned 559–530) issued a proclamation in his first year after the conquest of Babylon (538) that stated, "The LORD, God of Heaven, has given me all the kingdoms of the earth and He has commanded me to build Him a Temple in Jerusalem, which is in Judah. Whoever is among you of his entire people, may the LORD be with him, and let him go up [to Jerusalem, to build the Temple]" (cf. Ezra 1.1–4). The book of Haggai is set about eighteen years later, in the second year of the Persian king Darius I, that is, 520 BCE, and clearly implies that the Temple was still not rebuilt at that time. The book contains reports of theologically based exhortations to undertake the work of reconstruction and discusses the central role of the Temple in the life of the community. (Historians agree that the construction of the Jerusalem Temple was encouraged or even mandated by the Persian imperial center.)

The book of Haggai consists of four narrative reports about four particular divine communications and their circumstances. These communications are set in a precise historical timeframe: namely, the second year of Darius (520), and specifically, the first day of the sixth month, the twenty-first day of the seventh month, and the twenty-fourth day of the ninth month (this last date has two reports). Such specific dating, beyond what is found in other prophetic books (except for the beginning of the following book, Zechariah), creates an important temporal framework within the narrative, and, in addition, strengthens the rhetorical claim for the reliability of the account.

The four reports are integrated into a tight literary unit. They are kept together by the figure of Haggai, with whom they are explicitly and repeatedly associated, by their common introduction, structure, and even choice of words. Each of the reports provides a kind of snapshot, and all together they address the restoration of the Temple, Judah, and Jerusalem in the Persian period. The main focus of the book as a whole is the Temple, or to be more precise, the necessary character, centrality, and legitimacy of the Second Temple. The book of Haggai, in its present form, must have been written later than the last date mentioned in the text (24th of Kislev, 520 BCE), at some point within the Persian period. The matters mentioned above, however, remained central in the discourse of Judah throughout the Persian and Hellenistic period, and thereafter. Questions of leadership in the Second Temple polity are also addressed in this book.

Some Jewish sources understand the prophets Haggai, Zechariah and Malachi to represent the end prophecy (e.g., *b. Yoma* 9b; *b. Sot.* 48b; *y. Sot.* 9:13); others that Jeremiah was the last prophet (see *Pesik. Rav Kah.* 13.14). Josephus and other sources from later in the Second

Temple period assume that prophecy continued beyond that time. The leading tradition within rabbinic Judaism is that prophecy ceased after Haggai, Zechariah, and Malachi. This tradition includes them among the members of the "Great Assembly," a group that was the precursor of the Sanhedrin. After the death of these prophets, according to this tradition, the Holy Spirit departed from Israel, though "bat kol" (lit. the "daughter of the voice," or echo) remained available to Israel (see *b. Yoma* 9b; *b. Sot.* 48b; *b. Sanh.* 11a). This "echo" of the voice of God is sometimes available to the Rabbis in their deliberations about legal interpretation (halakhah), but it is not on the same level as prophecy, and the "echo" cannot overrule legal decisions arrived at by the established methods (*b. B. M.* 59b). As the final representatives of the prophetic tradition, Haggai, Zechariah, and Malachi represent the link in the transmission of the oral Torah between prophets and sages. Certain sages in the Talmud mention rulings and sayings by Haggai, or Haggai, Zechariah, and Malachi (e.g., *b. Yebam.* 16a; *b. Kid.* 43a; *b. Ḥul.* 137b). Further, according to talmudic traditions, not only the books included in the Twelve were written by the members of the Great Assembly (*b. B. Bat.* 15a) but the Tg. of the prophets was written under the guidance of these three prophets (*b. Meg.* 3a). The Haggai of the biblical book of Haggai, however, is not characterized in these terms.

[EHUD BEN ZVI]

1 In the second year of King Darius, on the first day of the sixth month, this word of the LORD came through the prophet Haggai to Zerubbabel son of Shealtiel, the governor of Judah, and to Joshua son of Jehozadak, the high priest:

1.1–15a: A report of a divine announcement or exhortation and the people's response to it. This first report includes an introduction of the divine announcement (v. 1), the divine announcement itself (vv. 2–11), and a report of the reception of the announcement (vv. 12–15a). **1:** The beginning of the book serves as an introduction to the entire book. *In the second year of King Darius, on the first day of the sixth month:* The year is 520 BCE, and the day is the 1st of 'Elul (= 29 August, 520 BCE). This date refers to the first divine message reported in the book. The month is the last before the seventh month—i.e., Tishri—with all its appointed festivals and sacred occasions (see Lev. ch 23, esp. vv. 23–36; Num. ch 29), the month associated with the building and dedication of the first Temple (see 1 Kings ch 8); it may have connoted a sense of a new beginning to the readers. The second year of Darius, 520, is when he consolidated his control over the empire, after a difficult civil war. This year is mentioned as the time of the renewed beginning of the building of the Second Temple in Ezra 4.24; according to Ezra 6.15, the house was completed in the sixth year of Darius. The second year of Darius is also associated with divine messages reported in the book of Zech. The divine message here is not directed to all the people, but to the two leaders, *Zerubbabel son of Shealtiel, the governor of Judah* and the high priest, *Joshua.* Thus the book already conveys and legitimates a model of dual leadership. (This was the model of local government of Yehud during the Persian period. It replaced that of the monarchic period that came to an end when the Babylonian king Nebuchadnezzar abolished the kingdom of Judah, and in turn it was replaced by one in which the high priest became the local ruler by the early Hellenistic period.) The divine message reported here concerns building the Temple. Building temples is the prerogative and obligation of kings. The book recognizes that the king at the time was Darius (see Hag. 1.1, 15; 2.10). Still, the text does not relate the construction of the Temple to Darius, or to any Persian king for that matter (contrast Ezra 1.2; 5.13; 6.14 and see the tone of Ezra ch 6). In Hag., the dual leadership of a *high priest* and a *governor* fulfills the expected role of a king. The claim in the text that the LORD encouraged them to build the Temple conveys necessary legitimacy to their leadership and their role as temple builders, as well as to the fruit of their work, the Second Temple. Conversely, the building of the Temple certainly conferred some kingly imagery on the two leaders. Still, the text here unequivocally refers to one as the high priest (see also 1.12, 14; 2.2, 4) and the other as the governor (see also 1.14; 2.2, 21). On the role of the personage Zerubbabel, see also Ezra chs 3–4; Zech. ch 4 and following nn. Some Jewish traditions claimed that the Darius mentioned here is the son of Esther and Ahasuerus (see Rashi; Ibn Ezra; cf. *Lev. Rab.* 13.4). From a historical perspective, this claim is impossible, but the value of this interpretation does not rest in its historicity, but rather in the way it expresses beliefs and worldviews and responds to questions that reading the text may raise. Here

2 Thus said the LORD of Hosts: These people say, [a]"The time
has not yet come[a] for rebuilding the House of the LORD."
3 And the word of the LORD through the prophet Haggai continued:
4 Is it a time for you to dwell in your paneled houses, while
this House is lying in ruins? 5 Now thus said the LORD of Hosts:
Consider how you have been faring! 6 You have sowed much
and brought in little; you eat without being satisfied; you drink
without getting your fill; you clothe yourselves, but no one gets
warm; and he who earns anything earns it for a leaky purse.

7 [b]Thus said the LORD of Hosts: Consider how you have fared:
8 Go up to the hills and get timber, and rebuild the House; then
I will look on it with favor and I will [c]be glorified[c]—said the
LORD.
9 You have been expecting much and getting little; and
when you brought it home, I would blow on it![d] Because of
what?—says the LORD of Hosts. Because of My House which
lies in ruins, while you all hurry to your own houses! 10 That
is why the skies above you have withheld [their] moisture and
the earth has withheld its yield, 11 and I have summoned fierce
heat upon the land—upon the hills, upon the new grain and
wine and oil, upon all that the ground produces, upon man
and beast, and upon all the fruits of labor.

12 Zerubbabel son of Shealtiel and the high priest Joshua
son of Jehozadak and all the rest of the people gave heed to
the summons of the LORD their God and to the words of the
prophet Haggai, when the LORD their God sent him; the people feared the LORD. 13 And Haggai, the LORD's messenger,
fulfilling the LORD's mission, spoke to the people, "I am with
you—declares the LORD."

14 Then the LORD roused the spirit of Zerubbabel son of
Shealtiel, the governor of Judah, and the spirit of the high priest
Joshua son of Jehozadak, and the spirit of all the rest of the
people: They came and set to work on the House of the LORD
of Hosts, their God, 15 on the twenty-fourth day of the sixth
2 month. In the second year of King Darius, 1 on the twenty-
first day of the seventh month, the word of the LORD came
through the prophet Haggai:
2 Speak to Zerubbabel son of Shealtiel, the governor of Judah, and to the high priest Joshua son of Jehozadak, and to the
rest of the people: 3 Who is there left among you who saw this

a-a Lit. "It is not time for the coming of the time."
b Vv. 7–8 would read well after v. 11. *c-c Emendation yields "glorify it"; see 2.7–9.*
d Meaning, perhaps, cast a curse on.

this interpretation directly links the ruler who allowed and encouraged the building of the Temple with the Jewish people in general, and in particular their heroine, Esther (cf. Tamar, Ruth, Hannah). **2:** The text implies that the people thought that there was a correct, prescribed time for rebuilding the Temple, and that such a time had not yet come (cf. 2 Chron. 36.20–23; Ezra 1.1–2). In the ancient Near East, temples were not supposed to be built by anyone except royal figures (see v. 1 n.), and they were not supposed to be built at any random time, but at the time favored by the gods. The people's attitude is facilitated by the success they felt in Babylonia, where God's presence was not expressed through the building of a temple. **4–10:** The basic message is that the presence of the Temple is a necessary condition for the prosperity of the land and the people. Of course, the Temple, to be effective, must be a proper one from a divine perspective. The passages that follow in the book deal with that matter. **13:** *The LORD's messenger,* prophets were considered to be YHVH's messengers; see Isa. 44.26; Mal. 1.1; 2 Chron. 36.15–16. *I am with you;* cf. 2.5; Isa. 40.10; 43.5; Ps. 118.6 and passim. **14:** Cf. 2 Chron. 36.22; Hag. 1.2 n. **15:** According to the text, the two leaders and the people set to work on the Temple on the 24th of 'Elul, just before the beginning of the seventh month. In a relatively unusual case, the v. includes both the final sentence of the first report and the introduction of the second one *(In the second ...).*

1.15b–2.9: A report of a divine announcement: The new Temple will be an appropriate "house of the LORD." The divine message here is addressed to both the two leaders and all the people. It is set on the 21st of Tishri, about a month since the leaders and the people took action, and in the last day of a festival, Sukkot. The text leaves for the book's readers to discern the potential significance of this time of the year for the narrative. The divine message reported here does not deal with

House in its former splendor? How does it look to you now?
It must seem like nothing to you. 4 But be strong, O Zerubbabel—says the LORD—be strong, O high priest Joshua son
of Jehozadak; be strong, all you people of the land—says the
LORD—and act! For I am with you—says the LORD of Hosts. 5 So
I promised you when you came out of Egypt, and My spirit is
still in your midst. Fear not!
6 For thus said the LORD of Hosts: In just a little while longer I
will shake the heavens and the earth, the sea and the dry land;
7 I will shake all the nations. And the precious things of all the
nations shall come [here], and I will fill this House with glory,
said the LORD of Hosts. 8 Silver is Mine and gold is Mine—says
the LORD of Hosts. 9 The glory of this latter House shall be greater than that of the former one, said the LORD of Hosts; and in
this place I will grant prosperity—declares the LORD of Hosts.

10 On the twenty-fourth day of the ninth [month], in the second year of Darius, the word of the LORD came to the prophet
Haggai:
11 Thus said the LORD of Hosts: Seek a ruling from the priests,
as follows: 12 If a man is carrying sacrificial flesh in a fold of
his garment, and with that fold touches bread, stew, wine, oil,
or any other food, will the latter become holy? In reply, the
priests said, "No." 13 Haggai went on, "If someone defiled by a
corpse touches any of these, will it be defiled?" And the priests
responded, "Yes."
14 Thereupon Haggai said: That is how this people and that is
how this nation looks to Me—declares the LORD—and so, too,
the work of their hands: Whatever they offer there is defiled.

the construction of the Temple per se, but with the question of whether the new Temple is an appropriate Temple for the LORD. The underlying issue is the incongruity between the expected glory of the house of a king who is sovereign over all and the absolute lack of splendor of a relatively small temple of a minor, poor province (cf. Ezra 3.12–13). The people must have wondered if such a temple would be pleasing to the LORD, even if it has not received the type of legitimating sign seen at the completion of the first Temple (1 Kings 8.10–11), and if it would secure the divine Presence. The report serves to allay these concerns of both the people described in the book and, above all, the later readers for whom the book was written, since the incongruity characterized their days too. Further, according to the book, it was the LORD who answered these questions and legitimized the readership's Temple. Still the text recognizes the incongruity and maintains that in the future it will eventually be rectified (vv. 7–8). Here the text assumes common, ancient Near Eastern concepts, namely that the wealth of a dominion should flow to the house of the ruler of the dominion, and that the manifestation of the glory of a king relates to the wealth flowing to him from the different nations and places under his dominion. **6:** This v. is quite remarkable within the prophetic worldview. Usually consolation is predicted for some vague future time, rather than *In just a little while longer.* **8:** The expression *silver is Mine and gold is Mine* was taken by the Rabbis as teaching that gaining silver or gold is not an appropriate goal for mortals. Instead they stressed that Torah and good deeds are such goals. See *m. 'Avot* 6.9. **9:** The LXX concludes the v. with a sentence that may be translated as "and peace of soul as a possession for all who build, to erect this temple."

2.10–19: Report of divine announcement: The Temple will be effective and the LORD will secure blessings on the people. The divine communication is set three months later than the day which the two leaders and the people set to build the Temple (1.15). It seems to imply that some cultic facility, including an altar, has already been used and that it has its own personnel. The text emphasizes again that an effective Temple is a precondition for the prosperity of people and land (cf. 1.2–11). Lack of defilement is an obvious precondition for an effective Temple, and for the divine presence. But it is a difficult precondition. To be sure, purity requires—within the discourse of the period—an appropriate cultic facility, which suggests that the people and their produce are impure in its absence. If the latter are impure, then they cannot come or be brought to a sacred place, lest they defile it. This logic leads to a breakdown of any hope of a new, untarnished beginning. This portion of the book of Hag. informs the readers that the LORD can overcome these circumstances and accordingly, a new beginning and the establishment of an effective cultic facility become a possible and actual reality (v. 19). This divine communication concerning the possibility of purification and of a new Temple that overcomes earlier defilement is dated to the 24th of Kislev (cf. the later (postbiblical) festival of Hanukkah, which begins on 25 Kislev). **11:** Purity and the avoidance of the defilement of the cultic facility is possible only if there are priests who know how to differentiate between holy and defiled, and teach and rule accordingly (cf. Lev. 10.10–11).

[15] And now take thought, from this day backward:[a] As long as
no stone had been laid on another in the House of the LORD,
[16] if one came to a heap of twenty measures,[b] it would yield only
ten; and if one came to a wine vat to skim off fifty measures, the
press would yield only twenty. [17] I struck you—all the works of
your hands—with blight and mildew and hail, but [c]you did
not return[c] to Me—declares the LORD. [18] Take note, from this
day forward—from the twenty-fourth day of the ninth month,
from the day when the foundation was laid for the LORD's Temple—take note [19] while the seed is still in the granary, and the
vine, fig tree, pomegranate, and olive tree have not yet borne
fruit. For from this day on I will send blessings.

[20] And the word of the LORD came to Haggai a second time
on the twenty-fourth day of the month: [21] Speak to Zerubbabel
the governor of Judah: I am going to shake the heavens and the
earth. [22] And I will overturn the thrones of kingdoms and destroy the might of the kingdoms of the nations. I will overturn
chariots and their drivers. Horses and their riders shall fall,
each by the sword of his fellow. [23] On that day—declares the
LORD of Hosts—I will take you, O My servant Zerubbabel son
of Shealtiel—declares the LORD—and make you as a signet;[d]
for I have chosen you—declares the LORD of Hosts.

a *Or "forward."* b *I.e., of grain.*
c-c *Lit. "there was not with you to Me"; cf. Amos 4.9.*
d *I.e., bring you close to Me; contrast Jer. 22.24–30.*

2.20–23: The coming of the ideal age. The last report is different from the others. It focuses on a future event, carries some apocalyptic tones, and a large geographical horizon. Moreover, it does not directly relate to the matter of building a legitimate, efficacious temple, or turning material lack into prosperity. The readers are invited, however, to associate the divine communication reported here with the preceding one because the text assigns them to the same date (*a second time,* v. 20). As mentioned above, since the two leaders of the project were involved in a kind of kingly role—i.e., the building of the Temple—one may expect the development of some form of royal imagery in their characterization in the texts of the community (cf. Zech. chs 3–4; see also 1 Chron. 3.19), though not an overtly explicit one. **21–22:** The language of these vv. is as vivid as it is open-ended. If they point to the fall of the Persian empire, then they remained unfulfilled as far as the Persian period is concerned. If they refer to the revolts in the first two years of Darius, then the date associated with the message reflects a lack of awareness or interest in the precise chronology of the events. Unlike other sections of the book of Hag., the text here is very general (e.g., no nation, ruler, or particular time is mentioned), and accordingly it encourages multiple readings. **23:** The characterization of the present governor of Judah as a personage who will become *a signet* of the LORD at some point in the future evokes the royal imagery of Jer. 22.24 (see Maimonides, *Mishneh Torah, Sefer ha-Mada* 7.7; cf. Ezek. 28.12), suggesting that earlier prophetic books were studied in the Persian period, but it is overtly open-ended. Just as a signet represents the power of an earthly king, the signet here may represent the power of the divine King. The metaphor may also play on the idea that a person never leaves his (or her) signet. Similarly, the language *I have chosen you* (cf. 1 Chron. 28.6) or *My servant* may evoke Davidic, royal connotations, but not necessarily so (e.g., Num. 17.20; Isa. 44.1; Job 1.8; 2.3; 42.8). (Significantly, in Chronicles—but nowhere else in the Bible—Zerubbabel is explicitly associated with the Davidic line.) Had the language been more unequivocal, readers would have seen the concluding statement not only as unfulfilled, but unfulfillable after the death of Zerubbabel. Conversely, the fact that the Temple was built may have led the readers to accept that at least in some sense Zerubbabel actually served as a "signet of the LORD," even if he was not crowned king of Judah.

זכריה

Zechariah

THE BOOK OF ZECHARIAH is set in the same period as the book of Haggai: the early years of Darius I (reigned 522–486 BCE). The book of Ezra associates Haggai and Zechariah (Ezra 5.1; 6.14) and the building of the Temple; rabbinic sources associate these two prophets with Malachi, and so they create the triad of last prophets (see introductions to Haggai and Malachi).

The first part of the book of Zechariah (chs 1–8) deals with issues similar to those in the book of Haggai: the restoration of the community in the Persian period. Like Haggai, it legitimizes the rebuilding of the Temple and the dual leadership under which it was built. It emphasizes repentance and exhorts the community directly addressed within the book, and above all, that of the readership to behave in accordance with the divine will, so as to avoid the fate of their ancestors (see, e.g., 1.2–6; 7.8–13; 8.13–17).

The book also addresses the dissonance between the actual status and power of the community and the Temple and what they should be according to the theological beliefs of the readership. This dissonance is solved in a way that conveys hope and reaffirms the beliefs of the community about its own place in the divine plan. The text communicates divine, unequivocal assertions about an ideal future in which the remnant of Israel will grow and prosper, Jerusalem will take its proper place, the Temple will become the focal point of worship for the entire world, and the kingship of the LORD will be recognized by all nations.

The book as a whole shows a strong orientation toward the future, particularly the ideal future. Not only does it communicate promises of a future glory for Zion, but it also provides some scenarios that would lead to its realization. These scenarios directly address the question of the relations between Zion (and Judah) and the nations in the future, ideal world. They also involve direct action by the LORD, much conflict and stern divine judgment. The conclusion of the book brings to the readers vivid images of the nations' final attack against Jerusalem and a cosmic upheaval that leads to the creation of a new landscape for Jerusalem and for the land as a whole (ch 14). The book has eschatological and even apocalyptic overtones.

Although there are clear temporal and thematic links between Zechariah and Haggai, the two books, as they stand today, are markedly different in style, structure, and tone. Zechariah opens with a superscription (1.1) that along with the following passage (1.2–6) introduces the book as a whole. The rest of the book consists of a series of prophetic texts about divine communications associated with Zechariah. At the heart of the first set of texts (1.7–8.23) are eight visions mediated by an angelic figure (see 1.7–6.15) that have no parallel in Haggai, even if the issues they address are similar to those in Haggai. The next sets, 9.1–11.17 and 12.1–14.21, are obviously different from Haggai. Ch 9 opens with "a pronouncement," separating the chs that follow from those that precede.

Many scholars have argued that the book of Zechariah originally included only chs 1–8, and that only at a later stage were chs 9–14, written in the late Persian or the Hellenistic period, attached to them. This is likely, but the book of Zechariah in its present form associates all its texts with the prophet Zechariah mentioned in 1.1.

Many ancient readers found in Zechariah numerous references to messianic times, and, some early Christian readers understood them in christological terms (see, for instance, Mark 14.27 and Zech. 13.7; Matt. 27.9 and Zech. 11.12–13; John 19.37 and Zech. 12.10; John 12.15 and Zech. 9.9). Rabbinic Judaism interpreted many of these texts in relation to a messianic time still to come (e.g., Zech. 3.8; 6.12 in the Tg.; in relation to Zech. 6.12 see *Num. Rab.* 18.21; for Zech. 9.9 see *Gen. Rab.* 56.2, 98.9; and for Zech. 12.10 as pointing to the Messiah from the House of Joseph, see *b. Sukk.* 52a).

Some vv. of Zechariah have been included in Jewish liturgy. The best-known example is 14.9, which concludes the ʿ*Aleinu* prayer. Zech. 14.1–21 is the haftarah for the first day of Sukkot since that festival is mentioned there; Zech. 2.14–4.7 for the first shabbat of Hanukkah and for the parashah of Be-haʿalotekha (Num. 8.1–12.16), since the lampstand ("menorah") plays a central role in this passage.

[EHUD BEN ZVI]

1 In the eighth month of the second year of Darius, this word
of the LORD came to the prophet Zechariah son of Berechiah son of Iddo:[a] 2 The LORD was very angry with your fathers.
3 Say to them further:

Thus said the LORD of Hosts: Turn back to me—says the
LORD of Hosts—and I will turn back to you—said the LORD
of Hosts. 4 Do not be like your fathers! For when the earlier
prophets called to them, "Thus said the LORD of Hosts: Come,
turn back from your evil ways and your evil deeds, they did
not obey or give heed to Me—declares the LORD. 5 Where are
your fathers now? And did the prophets live forever? 6 But the
warnings and the decrees with which I charged My servants
the prophets overtook your fathers—did they not?—and in the
end they had to admit, 'The LORD has dealt with us according
to our ways and our deeds, just as He purposed.' "

7 On the twenty-fourth day of the eleventh month of the second year of Darius—the month of Shebat—this word of the

a A clause like "Say to the people" is here understood; cf. 7.5.

1.1–6: Superscription, introduction, and call to repentance. The text assumes that the words of the earlier prophets are available and are being studied. **1:** The month is Marḥeshvan (October-November), in fall 520 BCE. This divine communication is set slightly later than those reported in Hag. 1.1, 15; 2.1, but slightly earlier than those in Hag. 2.10, 20. This temporal note suggests to the readers of the book that they are supposed to read 1.2–6 in the light of the texts in Hag. and vice versa. **2:** The story and explanation of the exile and the destruction of Jerusalem, including the Temple, in just four (separate) words (in Heb). The v. begins with YHVH angry and concludes with the word "anger" strongly making the point. **3:** Cf. Mal. 3.7; for a similar mutual interaction, but this time on its negative side, see Zech. 7.13. **4:** Since the sins of the monarchic period were considered the cause of the calamity, the monarchic period prophets had to be remembered as unsuccessful in their attempts to bring the people back to YHVH. This characterization of the prophets of old is very common (see 7.7, 13; 2 Kings 17.13–14; Jer. 25.4–5; 2 Chron. 24.19; 36.15–16; cf. Neh. 9.26) and only one of these prophets was remembered as successful, namely Isaiah, due to his association with the divine deliverance of Jerusalem in the days of Hezekiah of Judah and Sennacherib of Assyria. These memories of prophets warning Israel to turn to YHVH, calling for repentance before the execution of divine judgment, provide an excellent example of the basic principle of warning before punishment (e.g., 2 Kings 17.13; Ezek. 3.16–21; Neh. 9.29; passim in Chronicles). The principle of "warning" ("azharah") is widely attested in rabbinic (and later Jewish) literature as well (e.g., *b. Rosh Hash.* 21b; *b. Ketub.* 9a). **6:** *He purposed* may also be understood as "He considered [doing]," thereby conveying a conditional element from the outset in God's plans: If the (monarchic period) Israelites had heard their prophets, the punishment would not have come.

1.7–6.15: Reports of eight visions. The visions are described in graphic, and highly symbolic, detail, as are most apocalyptic visions. The "tour" by an angelic being is also typical of apocalypse, as is the use of specific numbers. Unlike most later apocalyptic visions, however, the mediating angel is here anonymous.

1.7–17: The first vision: the horsemen. 7: Within the world of the

LORD came to the prophet Zechariah son of Berechiah son of Iddo:

8 In the night, I had a vision. I saw a man, mounted on a bay horse, standing [a]among the myrtles[a] in the Deep, and behind him were bay,[b] sorrel,[c] and white horses. 9 I asked, "What are those, my lord?" And the angel who talked with me answered, "I will let you know what they are." 10 Then the man who was standing [a]among the myrtles[a] spoke up and said, "These were sent out by the LORD to roam the earth."

11 And in fact, they reported to the angel of the LORD who was standing [a]among the myrtles,[a] "We have roamed the earth, and have found all the earth dwelling in tranquility."[d] 12 Thereupon the angel of the LORD exclaimed, "O LORD of Hosts! How long will You withhold pardon from Jerusalem and the towns of Judah, which You placed under a curse seventy years ago?"

13 The LORD replied with kind, comforting words to the angel who talked with me.

14 Then the angel who talked with me said to me: "Proclaim! Thus said the LORD of Hosts: I am very jealous for Jerusalem—for Zion—15 and I am very angry with those nations that are at ease; for I was only angry a little, but they overdid the punishment. 16 Assuredly, thus said the LORD: I graciously return to Jerusalem. My House shall be built in her—declares the LORD of Hosts—the measuring line is being applied to Jerusalem. 17 Proclaim further: Thus said the LORD of Hosts: My towns shall yet overflow with bounty. For the LORD will again comfort Zion; He will choose Jerusalem again."

2 I looked up, and I saw four horns.[e] 2 I asked the angel who talked with me, "What are those?" "Those," he replied, "are the horns that tossed Judah, Israel, and Jerusalem."[e] 3 Then the LORD showed me four smiths. 4 "What are they coming to do?" I asked. He replied: "Those are the horns that tossed Judah, so that no man could raise his head; and these men have come [f]to throw them into a panic,[f] to [g]hew down[g] the horns of the nations that raise a horn against the land of Judah, to toss it."

a-a Septuagint reads "between the mountains"; cf. 6.1. In 6.1 ff. four teams of horses leave the LORD's abode to roam the four quarters of the earth; in 1.8 ff. they are about to reenter His abode after such a reconnaissance.

b Septuagint adds "dappled"; cf. 6.3.

c Meaning of Heb. uncertain. Emendation yields "black"; cf. 6.2.

d Upheavals at the start of Darius' reign had encouraged hopes of an early restoration of the Davidic dynasty (cf. Hag. 2.21 ff.). Now these hopes were dashed.

e The four horns correspond to the four winds of v. 10.

f-f Meaning of Heb. uncertain; emendation yields "to sharpen ax heads."

g-g Meaning of Heb. uncertain.

present book, this date seems to apply to 1.7–6.15, i.e., the entire series of eight visions. The date is just two months after the divine communications in Hag. 2.10, 20. **9–10:** The term *angel* here and elsewhere in the book (e.g., vv. 11, 12; 4.1; 5.10) may be translated as "messenger," in the sense of a divine messenger. The text leaves open the question of whether this messenger is the same as the *man* mentioned in these vv., as Ibn Ezra and others think. **11:** *Tranquility* carries here a negative connotation, because it is associated with a status quo in which Judah and Jerusalem have not been restored. The implicit connotation is that their (full) restoration necessitates much turmoil and probably judgment against the nations (see v. 15 and cf. ch 14). Some scholars associate this tranquility with the imperial peace achieved by Darius I in his second year, though Darius plays no active role whatsoever in the book of Zech. **12:** *Seventy years* is a reference to Jer. 25.11 (cf. 29.10), another clear indication that prophetic works were being studied at this period. That text also plays a crucial role in Dan. ch 9.

2.1–4: The second vision: the four horns. 2–3: *Horns* are symbols of power. Here they represent politico-military agents, nations. The number *four* connotes a sense of totality, rather than four specific nations; it points to the four points of the compass (a concept that originated in Mesopotamian literature); see also 2.10.

5 I looked up, and I saw a man holding a measuring line.
6 "Where are you going?" I asked. "To measure Jerusalem," he
replied, "to see how long and wide it is to be." 7 But the angel
who talked with me came forward, and another angel came
forward to meet him. 8 The former said to him, "Run to that
young man and tell him:
"Jerusalem shall be peopled as a city without walls, so many
shall be the men and cattle it contains. 9 And I Myself—declares the LORD—will be a wall of fire all around it, and I will be
a glory inside it.
10 "Away, away! Flee from the land of the north—says the
LORD—though I swept you [there] like the four winds of heav-
en—declares the LORD."
11 Away, escape, O Zion, you who dwell in Fair Babylon!
12 For thus said the LORD of Hosts—He [a-]who sent me after
glory[-a]—concerning the nations that have taken you as spoil:
"Whoever touches you touches the pupil of [b-]his own[-b] eye.
13 For I will lift My hand against them, and they shall be spoil
for those they enslaved."—Then you shall know that I was sent
by the LORD of Hosts.

14 Shout for joy, Fair Zion! For lo, I come; and I will dwell in
your midst—declares the LORD. 15 In that day many nations
will attach themselves to the LORD and become His[c] people,
and He[d] will dwell in your midst. Then you will know that I was
sent to you by the LORD of Hosts.
16 The LORD will [e-]take Judah to Himself as His portion[-e] in
the Holy Land, and He will choose Jerusalem once more.
17 Be silent, all flesh, before the LORD!
For He is roused from His holy habitation.

3 He further showed me Joshua, the high priest, standing
before the angel of the LORD, and the Accuser[f] standing at
his right to accuse him. 2 But [the angel of] the LORD said to the
Accuser, "The LORD rebuke you, O Accuser; may the LORD who
has chosen Jerusalem rebuke you! For this is a brand plucked

a-a Emendation yields "whose Presence sent me."
b-b According to ancient Jewish tradition, a scribal change for "My."
c Heb. "My." *d Heb. "I."*
e-e Emendation yields "allot to Judah its portion"; cf. Num. 34.17.
f Others "Satan."

2.5–9: The third vision: the man with the measuring line. 5–6: Questions of the type "who are those?" (1.9; 2.2) are omitted now. The prophet is described as getting more and more acquainted with his (and God's) visionary world. Ezek. 48.15–20 describes the size of ideal Jerusalem also in terms of length and width (see also Ezek. 45.1–6). **7–9:** There is no need to measure Jerusalem, for it will be or grow without any material limit, such as the one created by a city wall. Of course, a city without walls might evoke the image of a defenseless city, but the LORD will serve as its wall.

2.10–17: The establishment of ideal Zion, from the departure from Babylonia to an ideal future. 10: *Away, away! Flee from the land of the north ... four winds of heaven:* The return from Zion is given some cataclysmic dimensions. The text does not say "return" or the like, but *Away, away! Flee* as if from a disaster about to happen. There is also the explicit comparison with the *four winds,* and Babylonia is referred to as *the land of the north,* a place often imagined as a source of chaos or chaotic forces (cf. Isa. 14.31; Jer. 1.14–15; 4.6; 10.22). **12:** The v. may be translated "For thus said the LORD of Hosts (after [the/His] glory sent me) concerning ..." According to *Mek.,* (Shirata 6.10), the original text read, "the pupil of My own eye," and was changed by the soferim (scribes) so as to avoid the obvious anthropomorphism. **15:** The Heb reads "and become My people, and I will dwell in your midst." (Cf. "I will dwell in your midst" with v. 14; 8.3; Exod. 25.8; 29.45; 1 Kings 6.13; Ezek. 43.9.) The shift to direct divine speech might have conveyed some emphasis on the part of the LORD. The unique relation between Zion and the LORD is not diminished, but to the contrary, re-emphasized by the vision of many nations becoming God's people (cf. 8.22; Isa. 2.2–4; 56.3–8; Mic. 4.1–4; Hag. 2.7).

3.1–10: The fourth vision: the high priest Joshua is purified. 1: NJPS correctly translates the Heb "ha-satan," as the *Accuser* instead of the common, but erroneous, "Satan." (On the development of this notion in the Persian period, see Job 1.6 n.) The high priest assumes here a central position of leadership. In fact, the text seems to explore the issue of dual leadership (see Hag. 2.2). Eventually, during the Hellenistic period the high priest became the only leader. The process leading to the further empowerment of the high priest already began in the late Persian period. But the text here explores, in the main, a future, hoped

from the fire."[a] 3 Now Joshua was clothed in filthy garments when he stood before the angel. 4 The latter spoke up and said to his attendants, "Take the filthy garments off him!" And he said to him, "See, I have removed your guilt from you, and you shall be clothed in [priestly] robes." 5 Then he[b] gave the order, "Let a pure[c] diadem be placed on his head." And they placed the pure diadem on his head and clothed him in [priestly] garments,[d] as the angel of the LORD stood by.

6 And the angel of the LORD charged Joshua as follows: 7 "Thus said the LORD of Hosts: If you walk in My paths and keep My charge, you in turn will rule My House and guard My courts, and I will permit you to move about among these attendants. 8 Hearken well, O High Priest Joshua, you and your fellow priests sitting before you! For those men are a sign that I am going to bring My servant the Branch.[e] 9 For mark well this stone which I place before Joshua, a single stone with seven eyes.[f] I will execute its engraving—declares the LORD of Hosts—and I will remove that country's guilt in a single day. 10 In that day—declares the LORD of Hosts—you will be inviting each other to the shade of vines and fig trees."

4 The angel who talked with me came back and woke me as a man is wakened from sleep. 2 He said to me, "What do you see?" And I answered, "I see a lampstand all of gold, with a bowl above it. The lamps on it are seven in number, and the [g]lamps above it have[g] seven pipes; 3 and by it are two olive trees, one on the right of the bowl and one on its left." 4 I, in turn, asked the angel who talked with me, "What do those things mean, my lord?" 5 "Do you not know what those things mean?" asked the angel who talked with me; and I said, "No, my lord." 6 Then he explained to me as follows:[h]

"This is the word of the LORD to Zerubbabel:[i] Not by might, nor by power, but by My spirit[j]—said the LORD of Hosts. 7 Whoever you are, O great mountain in the path of Zerubbabel, turn into level ground! For he shall produce that

a Joshua's father (Hag. 1.1; 1 Chron. 5.40–41) was exiled and his grandfather executed (2 Kings 25.18–21) by the Babylonians, but Joshua returned. *b Heb. "I."*
c I.e., ritually pure.
d Joshua has now been rendered fit to associate with the heavenly beings (v. 7); cf. Isa. 6.6–8.
e I.e., the future king of David's line. See 6.12; Jer. 23.5–6; 33.15–16; cf. Isa. 11.1.
f Meaning of Heb. uncertain. The stone apparently symbolizes the God-given power of the future Davidic ruler; see below 4.6–7.
g-g Emendation yields "bowl above it has."
h The explanation is given in the last sentence of v. 10. *i A grandson of King Jehoiachin (1 Chron. 3.17–19) and the secular head of the repatriated community (Hag. 1.1; etc.).*
j I.e., Zerubbabel will succeed by means of spiritual gifts conferred upon him by the LORD; cf. Isa. 11.2. ff.

for Branch (see v. 8 n.). **5:** *Then he gave the order:* The Heb reads, "Then I gave the order." See translators' note *b*. **8:** *The Branch* (or "the Sprout") has been understood as a Davidic, most often messianic figure based on Jer. 23.5–6; 33.15–16 (cf. Isa. 11.1—again, earlier prophetic material is being studied and interpreted). According to 6.12–13, the Sprout will build the Temple and assume majesty. Many medieval Jewish commentators (e.g., Rashi, Ibn Ezra) and many modern scholars maintain that the reference to the Branch was meant to be understood as pointing to Zerubbabel (see 4.8, and the reference to his partner in the leadership, the high priest Joshua in 6.11), whose name means "the seed of Babylon." Even if there is a lionization of Zerubbabel (see 4.6–7), the book of Zech. does not explicitly state that he is the expected Sprout. Moreover, it is unlikely that the later readers of the book as a whole would have understood references to a messianic king (cf. Jer. 23.5–6; 33.15–16) as being actually fulfilled in the person of Zerubbabel or by the time he built the Temple. Some of the utopian futures expressed in the HB figure a Davidic personage, as in this case; others do not and some among them even hint that there is no room for any human king over Israel in the ideal future, because YHVH will rule over them (and the world) directly (see Isa. chs 40–66 [esp. Isa. 55.3]; Jer. 50.4–5, 19–20; Ezek. 16.60; Hos. 2.18–22; 14.6–9; Obad.; Zeph. ch 3).

4.1–14: The fifth vision: the lampstand and the olive trees. 2: *Lampstand,* Heb "menorah." (This menorah is not to be confused with the eight-branched menorah used at Hanukkah.) **6–7:** See 3.8 n. **6:** This v. has often played a significant role within Judaism, which has felt small and powerless, yet comforted by its reliance on God. It is inscribed on the front of the Synagogue of Cologne reconstructed after World War II.

excellent stone; it shall be greeted with shouts of 'Beautiful!
Beautiful!' "
8 And the word of the LORD came to me: 9 "Zerubbabel's
hands have founded this House and Zerubbabel's hands shall
complete it. Then you shall know that it was the LORD of Hosts
who sent me to you. 10 Does anyone scorn a day of small beginnings? When they see [a]the stone of distinction[a] in the hand of
Zerubbabel, they shall rejoice.
"Those seven are the eyes of the LORD, ranging over the
whole earth."
11 "And what," I asked him, "are those two olive trees, one on
the right and one on the left of the lampstand?" 12 And I further
asked him, "What are the two tops[b] of the olive trees that feed
their gold[c] through those two golden tubes?"[d] 13 He asked me,
"Don't you know what they are?" And I replied, "No, my lord."
14 Then he explained, "They are the two [e]anointed dignitaries[e]
who attend the Lord of all the earth."

5 I looked up again, and I saw a flying scroll. 2 "What do you
see?" he asked. And I replied, "A flying scroll, twenty cubits
long and ten cubits wide." 3 "That," he explained to me, "is the
curse which goes out over the whole land. [f]For everyone who
has stolen, as is forbidden on one side [of the scroll], has gone
unpunished; and everyone who has sworn [falsely], as is forbidden on the other side of it, has gone unpunished.[f] 4 [But] I
have sent it forth—declares the LORD of Hosts—and [the curse]
shall enter the house of the thief and the house of the one who
swears falsely by My name, and it shall lodge inside their houses and shall consume them to the last timber and stone."
5 Then the angel who talked with me came forward and said,
"Now look up and note this other object that is approaching."
6 I asked, "What is it?" And he said, "This tub[g] that is approaching—this," said he, "is their eye[h] in all the land." 7 And behold,
a disk of lead was lifted, revealing a woman seated inside the

a-a *Meaning of Heb. uncertain; others "plummet."*
b *Meaning of Heb. uncertain; literally "ears" (as of grain).*
c *Emendation yields "oil"; cf. v. 14.*
d *Or "funnels"; through them the oil runs from the olive trees into the bowl of vv. 2 and 3.*
e-e *I.e., the high priest and the king (cf. 3.8–9 with note); lit. "sons of oil."*
f-f *Meaning of Heb. uncertain.* g *Heb.* ephah, *a measure of capacity.*
h *Septuagint and Syriac read "guilt."*

10: The expression *the stone of distinction* may be translated as "the stone of the plumb" or "the plummet." The text implies and criticizes a sentiment akin to the one expressed in Hag. 2.3. *Those seven are the eyes of the LORD,* probably the answer to the question in v. 4 regarding the meaning of the seven lamps of the lampstand. Cf. 3.9. **14:** The two *anointed dignitaries,* lit. "sons of oil." The term is different from the one translated as "anointed" in Lev. 4.3; 1 Sam. 2.10, 35; 26.9; Ps. 2.2, and passim. The two "sons of oil" represent Joshua, the high priest, and Zerubbabel, the nonpriestly ruler who shares some royal responsibilities. It is not by chance that the text coins a unique expression rather than using a very common one. Most likely, the point is to avoid depicting Zerubbabel as a significant royal or messianic figure. Unlike in the book of Hag., Zerubbabel is not called "governor" in Zech., but neither is he called "king," nor is it stated explicitly anywhere in the book that he is from Davidic lineage, nor can we assume that he was anointed. The openness of the text in this matter is remarkable, and hardly unintentional. (The high priest was presumably anointed—see Num. 3.3, 25—but his anointing did not carry any kingly attributes.)

5.1–4: The sixth vision: the flying scroll. 2: The *scroll* stands for the contents of the writing on it—i.e., the curse against wrongdoers—and for the implementation of the curse. In other words, the curse (i.e., the written scroll) curses, or carries out the curse. *Twenty cubits ... ten cubits:* approx. 10 m by 5 m (30 ft by 15 ft), the size of the portico of the Great Hall of Solomon's Temple (1 Kings 6.3). **3:** *Over the whole land ... who has stolen ... who has sworn [falsely]: Over the whole land* is a possible translation, but so is "over the whole earth" as the same Heb phrase has been translated in 1.11; 4.14; 6.5; 14.9 (but not in 14.10, and with good reason there). The flying scroll or curse creates an ideal society in which there will be no social transgressors such as those mentioned above. If v. 3 is rendered "over the whole earth" (rather than *land*), this society is not restricted to Judah or Jerusalem, but will cover the entire world (cf. 14.9).

5.5–11: The seventh vision: the woman in the tub. This is an odd vision, even when compared with other texts within the same literary genre. **6:** The *tub* (Heb "ephah") suggests a container of that capacity, 23 liters (21 quarts), dimensions too

tub. 8 "That," he said, "is Wickedness"; and, thrusting her down
into the tub, he pressed the leaden weight into its mouth.
9 I looked up again and saw two women come soaring with
the wind in their wings—they had wings like those of a stork—
and carry off the tub between earth and sky. 10 "Where are they
taking the tub?" I asked the angel who talked with me. 11 And
he answered, "To build a shrine for it in the land of Shinar;[a]
[a stand] shall be erected for it, and it shall be set down there
upon the stand."

6 I looked up again, and I saw: Four chariots were coming out from between the two mountains; the mountains
were of copper. 2 The horses of the first chariot were bay, the
horses of the second chariot were black; 3 the horses of the
third chariot were white, and the horses of the fourth chariot
were spotted—dappled. 4 And I spoke up and asked the angel
who talked with me: "What are those, my lord?" 5 In reply, the
angel said to me, "Those are the four winds of heaven coming out after presenting themselves to the Lord of all the earth.
6 The one with the black horses is going out to the region of the
north; the white ones [b-]have gone out[-b] to [c-]what is to the west
of them;[-c] the spotted ones [b-]have gone out[-b] to the region of
the south; 7 and [d-]the dappled ones have gone out..."[-d] They
were ready to start out and range the earth, and he gave them
the order, "Start out and range the earth!" And they ranged the
earth. 8 Then he alerted me, and said to me, "Take good note!
Those that went out to the region of the north have [e-]done my
pleasure[-e] in the region of the north."[f]

9 The word of the LORD came to me: 10 Receive from[g] the exiled community—from Heldai, Tobijah, and Jedaiah, who have
come from Babylon—and you, in turn, proceed the same day
to the house of Josiah son of Zephaniah. 11 Take silver and gold
and make crowns. Place [one] on the head of High Priest Joshua son of Jehozadak, 12 and say to him, "Thus said the LORD
of Hosts: Behold, a man called the Branch[h] shall branch out
from the place where he is, and he shall build the Temple of
the LORD. 13 He shall build the Temple of the LORD and shall
assume majesty, and he shall sit on his throne and rule. And

small for what is inside it. **8:** *Wickedness* is represented by a female figure, and her mouth is to be shut with the *leaden weight.* **9–11:** Further, female figures take Wickedness to the *land of Shinar,* namely Babylonia. The text reflects (and contributes to shape) gendered constructions.

6.1–8: The eighth vision: the four chariots. The *horses, winds,* etc., symbolize all directions and therefore cover the earth. It is unknown if the further details (e.g., the colors of the horses) are symbolic, or are given merely to add vividness to the description.

6.9–15: The coronation of the high priest. 11–12: One would expect that the king would be crowned, but only the high priest Joshua is crowned; not Zerubbabel. Ibn Ezra, Radak, Rashi, and others consider Zerubbabel to be the Branch, and the person for whom the other crown was meant. The Tg., however, reflects a different understanding: "And you shall take silver and gold and make a large crown and set it upon the head of Joshua, son of Jehozadak, the high priest. And you shall speak to him, saying, 'Thus speaks the LORD of hosts, saying, behold, the man whose name is Anointed will be revealed and he shall be raised up, and shall build the Temple of the LORD.' " It is likely that the text read "crown" in vv. 11 and 14 (see some of the Gk mss and the Peshitta; NRSV) rather than *crowns.* If this is the case, then there was only one crown in the world of the book, and it was Joshua's. **13:** In the ideal future, both the Branch and the priest will *sit,* each on his own *throne.*

a I.e., Babylonia; cf. Gen. 10.10; 11.2, 9. *b-b Change of vocalization yields "will go out."*
c-c Cf. 'aḥor, *"west," Isa. 9.11. Emendation yields "the region of the west."*
d-d Emendation yields "the bay ones will go out to the region of the east."
e-e Cf. postbiblical naḥath ruaḥ, *"gratification." Emendation yields, "done the LORD's pleasure."*
f I.e., Babylonia, whose communication with Judah was via North Mesopotamia and Syria; cf. 2.10–11.
g Emendation yields "the gift of." *h See note at 3.8.*

15: The concluding words *if only you will obey* are an almost exact quotation of Deut. 28.1 and may allude to that ch; at this point in history, Deut. was well known.

7.1–14: A passage about fasting and true obedience. 2–3: The fifth month is the month of Av. The events described in 2 Kings 25.8–12 are the reason for the weeping and abstinence. V. 2 may also be translated: "When the people of Bethel had sent Sharezer and Regem-melech and his (or their) men, to entreat ..." If this is the case, the text emphasizes that the people from Bethel, the place of the ancient sanctuary of northern Israel, recognize now the authority of Jerusalem and ask its priests and prophets for instructions. **5:** The fifth month is Av and the seventh month is Tishri. The reference is to the commemoration of destruction of the First Temple. No dates of the month are given. Rabbinic literature and subsequent Jewish practice commemorate the destruction on 9 Av. The mention of the seventh month could be an early reference to the Fast of Gedaliah (2 Kings 25.25; Jer. 41.1–3; the Fast of Gedaliah on 3 Tishri marks the end of the independence of Judah, and is still observed as a fast day). **10:** The offenses include plotting evil in one's heart, not just the actual commission of evil against another.

8.1–23: A set of divine announcements of hope dealing with an ideal future for Jerusalem and Judah. 3: The ideal Jerusalem is also renamed in Isa. 1.26; 62.2; Ezek. 48.35.

there shall also be a priest [a-]seated on his throne,[-a] and harmonious understanding shall prevail between them."
14 The crowns shall remain in the Temple of the LORD as a memorial to Helem,[b] Tobijah, Jedaiah, and Hen[c] son of Zephaniah.
15 Men from far away shall come and take part in the building of the Temple of the LORD, and you shall know that I have been sent to you by the LORD of Hosts—if only you will obey the LORD your God!

7

1 In the fourth year of King Darius, on the fourth day of the ninth month, Kislev, the word of the LORD came to Zechariah—
2 when Bethel-sharezer [d-]and Regem-melech and his men sent[-d] to entreat the favor of the LORD,
3 [and] to address this inquiry to the priests of the House of the LORD and to the prophets: "Shall I weep and practice abstinence in the fifth month,[e] as I have been doing all these years?"
4 Thereupon the word of the LORD of Hosts came to me:
5 Say to all the people of the land and to the priests: When you fasted and lamented in the fifth and seventh months all these seventy years, did you fast for my benefit?
6 And when you eat and drink, who but you does the eating, and who but you does the drinking?
7 Look, this is the message that the LORD proclaimed through the earlier prophets, when Jerusalem and the towns about her were peopled and tranquil, when the Negeb and the Shephelah were peopled.
8 And the word of the LORD to Zechariah continued:
9 Thus said the LORD of Hosts: Execute true justice; deal loyally and compassionately with one another.
10 Do not defraud the widow, the orphan, the stranger, and the poor; and do not plot evil against one another.—
11 But they refused to pay heed. They presented a balky back and turned a deaf ear.
12 They hardened their hearts like adamant against heeding the instruction and admonition that the LORD of Hosts sent to them by His spirit through the earlier prophets; and a terrible wrath issued from the LORD of Hosts.
13 Even as He called and they would not listen, "So," said the LORD of Hosts, "let them call and I will not listen."
14 I dispersed them among all those nations which they had not known, and the land was left behind them desolate, without any who came and went. They caused a delightful land to be turned into a desolation.

8

1 The word of the LORD of Hosts came [to me]:
2 Thus said the LORD of Hosts: I am very jealous for Zion, I am fiercely jealous for her.
3 Thus said the LORD: I have returned

a-a Septuagint reads "on his right side." *b The Syriac version reads "Heldai"; cf. v. 10.*
c In v. 10, "Josiah." *d-d Emendation yields "sent Regem-melech and his men."*
e Because of the destruction of the Temple and Jerusalem; cf. 2 Kings 25.8 ff.

to Zion, and I will dwell in Jerusalem. Jerusalem will be called the City of Faithfulness, and the mount of the LORD of Hosts the Holy Mount.

4 Thus said the LORD of Hosts: There shall yet be old men and women in the squares of Jerusalem, each with staff in hand because of their great age. 5 And the squares of the city shall be crowded with boys and girls playing in the squares. 6 Thus said the LORD of Hosts: Though it will seem impossible to the remnant of this people in those days, shall it also be impossible to Me?—declares the LORD of Hosts. 7 Thus said the LORD of Hosts: I will rescue My people from the lands of the east and from the lands of the west, 8 and I will bring them home to dwell in Jerusalem. They shall be My people, and I will be their God—in truth and sincerity.

9 Thus said the LORD of Hosts: Take courage, you who now hear these words which the prophets spoke when the foundations were laid for the rebuilding of the Temple, the House of the LORD of Hosts.

10 [a]For before that time, the earnings of men were nil, and profits from beasts were nothing. It was not safe to go about one's business on account of enemies; and I set all men against one another. 11 But now I will not treat the remnant of this people as before—declares the LORD of Hosts—12 but what it sows shall prosper: The vine shall produce its fruit, the ground shall produce its yield, and the skies shall provide their moisture. I will bestow all these things upon the remnant of this people. 13 And just as you were a curse[b] among the nations, O House of Judah and House of Israel, so, when I vindicate you, you shall become a blessing.[b] Have no fear; take courage!

14 For thus said the LORD of Hosts: Just as I planned to afflict you and did not relent when your fathers provoked Me to anger—said the LORD of Hosts—15 so, at this time, I have turned and planned to do good to Jerusalem and to the House of Judah. Have no fear! 16 These are the things you are to do: Speak the truth to one another, render true and perfect justice in your gates. 17 And do not contrive evil against one another, and do not love perjury, because all those are things that I hate—declares the LORD.

18 And the word of the LORD of Hosts came to me, saying, 19 Thus said the LORD of Hosts: The fast of the fourth month, the fast of the fifth month, the fast of the seventh month, and the fast of the tenth month[c] shall become occasions for joy and gladness, happy festivals for the House of Judah; but you must love honesty and integrity.

4: According to a well-known story in *b. Mak.* 24b, the certainty that this announcement will be fulfilled was the reason of R. Akiva's joy at the sight of painful markers of the Roman destruction of Jerusalem. He thought that just as the announced judgment was fulfilled, so will be the announced future glory of the city. **8:** *They shall be My people, and I will be their God:* Cf. Jer. 24.7; 32.38; Ezek. 11.20; 14.11; 36.28; 37.23, 27; cf. also Exod. 29.45. **13:** Cf. Gen. 12.12. **14:** See 1.6 n. **16–17:** Cf. 8.9–11. **17:** Lit. "do not devise evil in your hearts" (NRSV). The text reiterates the message of 7.10; plotting evil in one's heart, not just the actual commission of evil against another is a serious offense. **19:** This divine announcement returns to the question posed at the beginning of ch 7, but incorporates the intervening material, noting that only when the ideal restoration is completed will these fast days be transformed. It served as a basis for the traditional Jewish belief that present days of fast and lamentation will become days of joy in the messianic era; see, e.g., Maimonides, *Mishneh Torah, Ta'an.* 5.19. **23:** Cf. 2.15.

a Cf. Hag. 1.6. *b I.e., a standard by which men curse or bless; cf. Gen. 12.2 and note.*
c Commemorating, respectively, the events of 2 Kings 25.3 ff. (Jer. 52.6 ff.); 2 Kings 25.8 ff. (Jer. 52.12 ff.); 2 Kings 25.25 ff. (Jer. 41); 2 Kings 25.1 ff. (Jer. 52.4).

[20] Thus said the LORD of Hosts: Peoples and the inhabitants of many cities shall yet come—[21] the inhabitants of one
shall go to the other and say, "Let us go and entreat the favor
of the LORD, let us seek the LORD of Hosts; I will go, too." [22] The
many peoples and the multitude of nations shall come to seek
the LORD of Hosts in Jerusalem and to entreat the favor of the
LORD. [23] Thus said the LORD of Hosts: In those days, ten men
from nations of every tongue will take hold—they will take
hold of every Jew by a corner of his cloak and say, "Let us go
with you, for we have heard that God is with you."

9 A pronouncement: The word of the LORD.

He will reside in the land of Hadrach and Damascus;
For all men's eyes will turn to the LORD—
Like all the tribes of Israel—
2 Including Hamath, which borders on it,[a]
And Tyre and Sidon, though they are very wise.
3 Tyre has built herself a fortress;
She has amassed silver like dust,
And gold like the mud in the streets.
4 But my Lord will impoverish her;
He will defeat her forces at sea,
And she herself shall be consumed by fire.

5 Ashkelon shall see it and be frightened,
Gaza shall tremble violently,
And Ekron, at the collapse of her hopes.
Kingship shall vanish from Gaza,
Ashkelon shall be without inhabitants,
6 And [b-]a mongrel people[-b] shall settle in Ashdod.
I will uproot the grandeur of Philistia.

7 But I will clean out the blood from its mouth,
And the detestable things from between its teeth.
Its survivors, too, shall belong to our God:
They shall become like a clan in Judah,
And Ekron shall be like the Jebusites.

8 And I will encamp in My House [c-]against armies,[-c]
Against any that come and go,
And no oppressor shall ever overrun them again;
For I have now taken note [d-]with My own eyes.[-d]

a I.e., on the land of Hadrach and Damascus.
b-b Heb. mamzer; *cf. note at Deut. 23.3.*
c-c Change of vocalization yields "as a garrison."
d-d Emendation yields "of their suffering"; cf. 1 Sam. 1.11.

9.1–11.17: A divine pronouncement: another word of the LORD associated with Zechariah. See also 12.1. This section of the book of Zech. has its own intro. (9.1a) that characterizes the following text as a divine pronouncement (Heb "massa'"; the precise meaning of the term in Heb is a matter of debate). A set of announcements of judgment against the nations and of a glorious restoration for Jerusalem and Judah follows the intro. The section contains numerous descriptions of an ideal future, but also of the period that leads up to such an ideal future (see 11.4–17). The issue of leadership, good and bad, figures prominently in 9.1–11.17. **9.1:** The *land of Hadrach* is in Aram (today, Syria), north of Damascus. The v. may be translated also as, "the word of the LORD is against Hadrach and its resting place, Damascus, for to the LORD belongs the spring of humanity/humankind [that is, all humanity], as do all the tribes of Israel." **2:** *Hamath,* an important city and kingdom in the territory of today's Syria. *Tyre and Sidon,* two of the most important eastern Mediterranean city ports and capital cities of two Phoenician kingdoms. The cities are located in today's Lebanon. **5–6:** *Ashkelon ... Gaza ... Ekron ... Ashdod,* Philistine cities. **7:** *Jebusites,* former inhabitants of Jerusalem (cf. Judg. 19.10; 2 Sam. 5.6, 8; 24.16, 18; 1 Kings 9.20; 1 Chron. 11.4).

9 Rejoice greatly, Fair Zion;
Raise a shout, Fair Jerusalem!
Lo, your king is coming to you.
He is victorious, triumphant,
Yet humble, riding on an ass,
On a donkey foaled by a she-ass.
10 He[a] shall banish chariots from Ephraim
And horses from Jerusalem;
The warrior's bow shall be banished.
He shall call on the nations to surrender,[b]
And his rule shall extend from sea to sea
And from ocean to land's end.

11[c] You, for your part, have released[d]
Your prisoners from the dry pit,[e]
For the sake of the blood of your covenant,
12 [Saying], "Return to Bizzaron,[f]
You prisoners of hope."
In return [I] announce this day:
I will repay you double.
13 For I have drawn Judah taut,
And applied [My hand] to Ephraim as to a bow,
And I will arouse your sons, O Zion,
Against your sons, O Javan,
And make you like a warrior's sword.

14 And the LORD will manifest Himself to them,[g]
And His arrows shall flash like lightning;
My Lord GOD shall sound the ram's horn
And advance in a stormy tempest.[h]
15 The LORD of Hosts will protect them:
[i][His] slingstones shall devour and conquer;
They shall [j-]drink, shall rage as with[-j] wine,
And be filled [with it] like a dashing bowl,
Like the corners of an altar.
16 The LORD their God shall prosper them
On that day;
[He shall pasture] His people like sheep.
[They shall be] like crown jewels glittering on His soil.

9: *Fair Zion:* Personification of Jerusalem (see Jer. 6.2, 23; Mic. 4.8, 10; Zeph. 3.14; Lam. 2.1, 4, 8, 13, 18; 4.22). This image of the ideal future king (Messiah) has been very influential in Jewish tradition, and has influenced the depiction of Jesus in the Gospels (see intro. to Zech.). **10:** The Heb has "I shall banish/cut off." See 2.15 n. Cf. the conclusion of this v. with Ps. 72.8. The phrase is often translated in English by "his dominion" rather than "his rule." The phrase inspired the Canadian "Fathers of the Confederation" to give the new country its official title, Dominion of Canada. **11:** An alternative translation of the v. reads, "As for you [fem.] also, because of the blood of My covenant with you, I will set your [fem.] prisoners free from the waterless pit/dungeon." The feminine "you" is most likely "Fair Zion" (see v. 9). **12:** *Bizzaron* may mean "Fortress" or "a fortress." **14:** Another possible translation of the v. is, "and advance in the storm-winds of the south."

a *Heb. "I."* b *Cf. Deut. 20.10–12 and note.*
c *Exact meaning and connection of vv. 11–12 uncertain.*
d *Taking* shillaḥti *as a second-person singular feminine form, with Septuagint; cf. Judg. 5.7 with note.*
e *I.e., a pit that serves as a dungeon rather than a cistern (both are called* bor *in Heb.).*
f *Perhaps a nickname ("fortress") for Samaria (Heb.* Shomeron*).* g *I.e., Judah.*
h *Lit. "tempests of wind"; for* teman *in the sense of wind, cf. Job 9.9; 39.26.*
i *The meaning of much of the rest of the chapter is uncertain.*
j-j *Some Septuagint mss. read "drink blood like."*

17: There are a number of alternative translations of this verse: (1) "For what goodness and beauty are His! Grain shall make the young men flourish, and new wine the young women" (NRSV); (2) "For what is His goodness and His beauty? Grain that makes the young men flourish, and new wine that makes the young women flourish (author's translation)." In any case, the cultural association of grain with males and new wine with females is noteworthy. **10.2:** For *teraphim* see, among others, Gen. 31.19; Judg. 17.5; 1 Sam. 15.23; Ezek. 21.26. Here it points to images that were consulted for the purpose of divination. False prophets continued into the Persian period (Neh. 6.14). **3:** There were *shepherds* (cf. v. 2), but they failed. These failed, oppressive leaders are also characterized as rams (cf. Jer. 50.8; Ezek. 39.18).

17 How lovely, how beautiful they shall be,
Producing young men like new grain,
Young women like new wine!

10 Ask the LORD for rain
In the [a-]season of late rain.[-a]
It is the LORD who causes storms;[b]
And He will provide rainstorms [c-]for them,
Grass in the fields for everyone.[-c]

2 For the teraphim[d] spoke delusion,
The augurs predicted falsely;
And dreamers speak lies
And console with illusions.
That is why My people have strayed[b] like a flock,
They suffer[b] for lack of a shepherd.
3 My anger is roused against the shepherds,
And I will punish the he-goats.[e]

For the LORD of Hosts has taken thought
In behalf of His flock, the House of Judah;
He will make them like majestic chargers in battle.
4 From them shall come [f-]cornerstones,
From them tent pegs,[-f]
From them bows of combat,
And every captain shall also arise from them.
5 And together they shall be like warriors in battle,
Tramping in the dirt of the streets;
They shall fight, for the LORD shall be with them,
And they shall put horsemen to shame.
6 I will give victory to the House of Judah,
And triumph to the House of Joseph.
I will restore them, for I have pardoned them,
And they shall be as though I had never disowned them;
For I the LORD am their God,
And I will answer their prayers.
7 [g-]Ephraim shall be like a warrior,
And they[-g] shall exult as with wine;
Their children shall see it and rejoice,

a-a Septuagint reads "in its season / The early rain and the late." Cf. Deut. 11.14.
b Meaning of Heb. uncertain.
c-c Emendation yields "[producing] food for men, / Grass in the fields for cattle." Cf. Deut. 11.14–15.
d Idols consulted for oracles; cf. 1 Sam. 15.23; Ezek. 21.26.
e I.e., oppressive leaders; cf. Ezek. 34.17 ff.
f-f Emendation yields "shields and bucklers."
g-g Emendation yields "And when Ephraim is victorious, / They ..."

They shall exult in the LORD.
8 I will whistle to them and gather them,
For I will redeem them;
They shall increase [a]-and continue increasing.-[a]
9 For though I sowed them among the nations,
In the distant places they shall remember Me,
They shall escape with their children and shall return.
10 I will bring them back from the land of Egypt
And gather them from Assyria;
And I will bring them to the lands of Gilead and
Lebanon,
And even they shall not suffice for them.
11 [a]-A hemmed-in force shall pass over the sea
And shall stir up waves in the sea;-[a]
And all the deeps of the Nile shall dry up.
Down shall come the pride of Assyria,
And the scepter of Egypt shall pass away.
12 But I will make them[b] mighty through the LORD,
And they shall [c]-march proudly-[c] in His name
—declares the LORD.

11 Throw open your gates, O Lebanon,
And let fire consume your cedars!
2 Howl, cypresses, for cedars have fallen!
How the mighty are ravaged!
Howl, you oaks of Bashan,
For the stately forest is laid low!
3 Hark, the wailing of the shepherds,
For their [a]-rich pastures-[a] are ravaged;
Hark, the roaring of the great beasts,
For the jungle of the Jordan is ravaged.

4 Thus said my God the LORD: Tend the sheep meant for
slaughter, 5 whose buyers will slaughter them with impunity,
whose seller will say, "Praised be the LORD! I'll get rich," and
whose shepherd will not pity them. 6 For I will pity the inhabitants of the land no more—declares the LORD—but I will place
every man at the mercy of every other man and at the mercy
of his king; they shall break the country to bits, and I will not
rescue it from their hands.
7 So I tended the sheep meant for slaughter, [d]-for those poor
men of the sheep.-[d] I got two staffs, one of which I named Favor
and the other Unity, and I proceeded to tend the sheep. 8 But
I lost [e]-the three shepherds-[e] in one month; then my patience

a-a Meaning of Heb. uncertain. *b I.e., Judah and Ephraim.*
c-c Meaning of Heb. uncertain. Emendation yields "have glory"; cf. Isa. 45.25.
d-d Emendation yields "for the sheep dealers"; cf. the word rendered "trader" in 14.21.
e-e Emendation yields "a third of the flock."

11.1–17: The readers of this literary subunit learn much about the worthless shepherds and their fate. Building upon common ancient Near Eastern and biblical imagery, these shepherds are political leaders, but significantly their identity is never revealed, nor even hinted at to encourage multiple interpretations.

with them was at an end, and they in turn were disgusted with
me. 9 So I declared, "I am not going to tend you; let the one that
is to die die and the one that is to get lost get lost; and let the
rest devour each other's flesh!"

10 Taking my staff Favor, I cleft it in two, so as to annul the
covenant I had made with all the peoples;[a] 11 and when it was
annulled that day, [b-]the same poor men of the sheep[-b] who
watched[c] me realized that it was a message from the LORD.
12 Then I said to them, "If you are satisfied, pay me my wages;
if not, don't." So they weighed out my wages, thirty shekels of
silver— 13 [d-]the noble sum that I was worth in their estimation.[-d]
The LORD said to me, "Deposit it in the treasury."[e] And I took
the thirty shekels and deposited it in the treasury in the House
of the LORD. 14 Then I cleft in two my second staff, Unity, in order to annul the brotherhood between Judah and Israel.[f]

15 The LORD said to me further: Get yourself the gear of a
foolish shepherd. 16 For I am going to raise up in the land a
shepherd who will neither miss the lost [sheep], nor seek the
strayed,[e] nor heal the injured, nor sustain the frail,[e] but will
feast on the flesh of the fat ones and [d-]tear off their hoofs.[-d]

17 Oh, the worthless shepherd
Who abandons the flock!
Let a sword descend upon his arm
And upon his right eye!
His arm shall shrivel up;
His right eye shall go blind.

12

A pronouncement: The word of the LORD concerning
Israel.

The utterance of the LORD,
Who stretched out the skies
And made firm the earth,
And created man's breath within him:

2 Behold, I will make Jerusalem a bowl of reeling for the peoples all around. Judah shall be caught up in the siege upon Jerusalem, 3 when all the nations of the earth gather against her.
In that day, I will make Jerusalem a stone for all the peoples
to lift; all who lift it shall injure themselves. 4 In that day—declares the LORD—I will strike every horse with panic and its
rider with madness. But I will [g-]watch over the House of Judah
while I strike every horse of[-g] the peoples with blindness. 5 And

a Perhaps alluding to the prediction of 14.1–3.
b-b Emendation yields "the sheep dealers." *c Emendation yields "hired."*
d-d Meaning of Heb. uncertain. *e Meaning of Heb. uncertain.*
f Two mss. of the Septuagint have "Jerusalem"; cf. 12.2–3; 14.14.
g-g Emendation yields "open the eyes of Judah while I strike all."

13: See the intro.

12.1–14.21: Another divine pronouncement associated with Zechariah: The word of the LORD concerning Israel. This section is set apart from the preceding one (9.1–11.17) by an unmistakable, composite subtitle that serves as an introduction to the unit in 12.1 (see 9.1). The repetition of the expression *in that day* (vv. 3, 4, 6, 8, etc.) provides much cohesion and structure to this literary unit within the book. The section as a whole is meant to bridge the gap between the actual world of the authorship and readership of the book and an expected future in which the kingship of the LORD over all the earth will be clearly manifested and acknowledged by all. Thus the unit reports a divine communication about the process that will lead to that future and about that future itself. Following earlier prophetic traditions, this process involves political and military turmoil, as well as cosmic disturbances and the transformation of the landscape of Jerusalem. **12.1:** The v. reaffirms the authority and legitimacy of the following text three times: (prophetic) *pronouncement, the word of the LORD,* and *the utterance of the LORD.* This v. asks the readers to interpret the ensuing text (12.2–14.21) as a divine pronouncement concerning Israel, even if the nations play a major role in it. **2:** *Bowl of reeling:* The metaphor of a divinely induced, incapacitating drunkenness under judgment occurs elsewhere in the prophets (see esp. Jer. 25.15–29 and Isa. 51.17–23). Here, however, the nations, rather than Jerusalem, are incapacitated.

the clans of Judah will say to themselves, [a-]"The dwellers of Jerusalem are a task set for us by[-a] their God, the LORD of Hosts."
6 In that day, I will make the clans of Judah like a flaming brazier among sticks and like a flaming torch among sheaves.
They shall devour all the besieging peoples right and left; and
Jerusalem shall continue on its site, in Jerusalem.[b]

7 The LORD will give victory to the tents of Judah first, so that
the glory of the House of David and the glory of the inhabitants
of Jerusalem may not be too great for Judah. 8 In that day, the
LORD will shield the inhabitants of Jerusalem; and the feeblest
of them shall be in that day like David, and the House of David
like a divine being—like an angel of the LORD—at their head.
9 In that day I will [c-]all but annihilate[-c] all the nations that
came up against Jerusalem. 10 But I will fill the House of David and the inhabitants of Jerusalem with a spirit of pity and
compassion; and they shall lament[d] to Me about those who
are slain, wailing over them as over a favorite son and showing bitter grief as over a first-born. 11 In that day, the wailing in
Jerusalem shall be as great as the wailing at Hadad-rimmon
in the plain of Megiddon.[e] 12 The land shall wail, each family
by itself: The family of the House of David by themselves, and
their womenfolk by themselves; the family of the House of
Nathan by themselves, and their womenfolk by themselves;
13 the family of the House of Levi by themselves, and their
women-folk by themselves; the family of the Shimeites by
themselves, and their womenfolk by themselves; 14 and all the
other families, every family by itself, with their womenfolk by
themselves.[f]

13 In that day a fountain shall be open to the House of David and the inhabitants of Jerusalem for purging and
cleansing.
2 In that day, too—declares the LORD of Hosts—I will erase
the very names of the idols from the land; they shall not be uttered any more. And I will also make the "prophets" and the
[g-]unclean spirit[-g] vanish from the land. 3 If anyone "prophesies"
thereafter, his own father and mother, who brought him into
the world, will say to him, "You shall die, for you have lied in
the name of the LORD"; and his own father and mother, who
brought him into the world, will put him to death when he

10: An alternative and more common translation, which is at home in christological interpretation, is represented by "And I will pour out a spirit of compassion and supplication on the house of David and the inhabitants of Jerusalem, so that, when they look on the one whom they have pierced, they shall mourn for him, as one mourns for an only child, and weep bitterly over him, as one weeps over a firstborn" (NRSV). The Heb is ambiguous, because it may refer to a person or a group whom they have pierced. Although the identity of the pierced one/ones is unclear, if the text is read as the continuation of v. 9—as the structure of the section set by the "in that day" openings suggests—it more likely points to an individual or group from within the nations. For an understanding of the v. as pointing to the Messiah from the House of Joseph, see *b. Sukk.* 52a. Radak reads the text differently; for him it describes such a salvation that if even one person of Israel were killed in the battle, they will be astonished.

13.2–6: Away with the prophets. Although the removal of the idols is mentioned, the main emphasis is on the removal of the prophets. It is likely that a particular group or type of prophets is meant.

a-a Emendation yields "We will save the dwellers of Jerusalem with the help of."
b Emendation yields "safety."
c-c For the idiom cf. Gen. 43.30; it is also attested in postbiblical Hebrew.
d Meaning of Heb. uncertain. e Usually "Megiddo."
f In this way, apparently, they will prevail upon the LORD to spare the remnant of the besieging nations; cf. v. 10.
g-g To which abnormal human behavior was attributed.

"prophesies." 4 In that day, every "prophet" will be ashamed of
the "visions" [he had] when he "prophesied." In order to deceive, he[a] will not wear a hairy mantle,[b] 5 and he will declare,
"I am not a 'prophet'; [c-]I am a tiller of the soil;[-c] you see, [d-]I
was plied with the red stuff[-d] from my youth on." 6 And if he is
asked, "What are those [e-]sores on your back?"[-e] he will reply,
"From being beaten in the homes of my friends."[f]

7[g] O sword!
Rouse yourself against My shepherd,
The man [h-]in charge of My flock[-h]
—says the LORD of Hosts.
Strike down the shepherd
And let the flock scatter;
And I will also turn My hand
Against all the shepherd boys.
8 Throughout the land —declares the LORD—
Two-thirds shall perish, shall die,
And one-third of it shall survive.
9 That third I will put into the fire,
And I will smelt them as one smelts silver
And test them as one tests gold.
They will invoke Me by name,
And I will respond to them.
I will declare, "You are My people,"
And they will declare,
"The LORD is our God!"

14 Lo, a day of the LORD is coming when your[i] spoil shall
be divided in your very midst! 2 For I will gather all the
nations to Jerusalem for war: The city shall be captured, the
houses plundered, and the women violated; and a part of the
city shall go into exile. But the rest of the population shall not
be uprooted from the city.
3 Then the LORD will come forth and make war on those nations as He is wont to make war on a day of battle. 4 On that day,
He will set His feet on the Mount of Olives, near Jerusalem on
the east; and the Mount of Olives shall split across from east to
west, and one part of the Mount shall shift to the north and the

a *Heb. "They."* *b* *In imitation of Elijah; cf. 2 Kings 1.8.*
c-c *I.e., I was addicted to wine like Noah, the tiller of the soil (cf. Gen. 9.20–21), hence my hallucinations and ravings; cf. Prov. 23.33.*
d-d *Connecting* 'adam *with* 'adom *"red" (cf. Prov. 23.31); but meaning of Heb. uncertain.*
e-e *Lit. "sores between your arms"; cf. 2 Kings 9.24. Sores are sometimes symptoms of hysteria.*
f *Presumably for making drunken scenes; cf. Prov. 23.35.*
g *Vv. 7–9 would read well after 11.17.* *h-h* *Meaning of Heb. uncertain.*
i *Jerusalem is addressed.*

4: The *hairy mantle* is an allusion to Elijah (see 2 Kings 1.8). **5:** The language seems to allude to Amos 7.14, but with a most significant shift that results in a possible association with Cain (see Gen. 4.2). **6:** Possibly a reference to ecstatic prophecy. **7–9:** YHVH attacks His *shepherd* and His *flock* suffers. Suffering, however, refines the *one-third* that remains and eventually YHVH and this refined group come together. In *b. Rosh Hash.* 16b–17a, v. 7 is understood in terms of the (rabbinic) Day of Judgment. In that day, there will be three groups of people. The first two, the pious and the wicked are respectively "inscribed and sealed" for eternal life or Gehenna. The middle group goes down to Gehenna where they scream v. 7 (among a few other vv.) and as they do they identify with the third mentioned here and hope for their fate.

14.1–21: Earth-shaking events lead to the establishment of Jerusalem as the center of the world and the place from which the LORD reigns over all. 4–5: *Mount of Olives,* a mount east of, and in the vicinity of, Jerusalem. *Valley in the Hills,* perhaps, "valley in/between the hills." The Heb word for "hill" is often translated "mount" or "mountain." *And the Valley ... shall be stopped up:* Heb reads "you shall flee by the valley of My hills/mountains" (i.e., the new valley created by the LORD). *Azal,* an unknown location in the area. Some scholars assume that the original text read "'etzel," i.e., "side" and, accordingly, that the text read: "the valley between the hills reached to each side (of the now split Mount of Olives)."

other to the south, a huge gorge. 5[a]And the Valley in the Hills shall be stopped up, for the Valley of the Hills shall reach only to Azal; it shall be stopped up as it was stopped up as a result of the earthquake in the days of King Uzziah of Judah.—And the LORD my God, with all the holy beings, will come to you.

6[b]In that day, there shall be neither sunlight nor cold moonlight, 7 but there shall be a continuous day—only the LORD knows when—of neither day nor night, and there shall be light at eventide.

8 In that day, fresh water shall flow from Jerusalem, part of it to the Eastern Sea[c] and part to the Western Sea,[d] throughout the summer and winter.

9 And the LORD shall be king over all the earth; in that day there shall be one LORD with one name.[e]

10 Then the whole country shall become like the Arabah,[f] [g]from Geba to Rimmon south of Jerusalem.[g] The latter, however, shall perch high up where it is, and [h]shall be inhabited[h] from the Gate of Benjamin to the site of the Old Gate, down to the Corner Gate, and from the Tower of Hananel to the king's winepresses. 11 Never again shall destruction be decreed, and Jerusalem shall dwell secure.

12 As for those peoples that warred against Jerusalem, the LORD will smite them with this plague: Their flesh shall rot away while they stand on their feet; their eyes shall rot away in their sockets; and their tongues shall rot away in their mouths.

13 In that day, a great panic from the LORD shall fall upon them, and everyone shall snatch at the hand of another, and everyone shall raise his hand against everyone else's hand. 14 Judah shall join the fighting in Jerusalem, and the wealth of all the nations roundabout—vast quantities of gold, silver, and clothing—shall be gathered in.

15 The same plague shall strike the horses, the mules, the camels, and the asses; the plague shall affect all the animals in those camps.

16 All who survive of all those nations that came up against Jerusalem shall make a pilgrimage year by year to bow low to the King LORD of Hosts and to observe the Feast of Booths. 17 Any of the earth's communities that does not make the pilgrimage

a *Vocalizing* [we] nistam *with Targum, Septuagint, and an old Heb. ms. Other mss. and printed editions read, "You [pl.] shall flee [to] the Valley in the Hills, for the Valley of the Hills shall reach up to Azal. You shall flee as you fled because of the earthquake ... "*

b *Meaning of verse uncertain; cf. Job 21.26.*

c *I.e., the Dead Sea; cf. Joel 2.20.*

d *I.e., the Mediterranean Sea; cf. Joel 2.20.*

e *I.e., the* LORD *alone shall be worshiped and shall be invoked by His true name.*

f *I.e., shall be depressed like the Jordan Valley.*

g-g *I.e., from the northern border of the Kingdom of Judah (1 Kings 15.22; 2 Kings 23.8) to the southern border (Josh. 15.32; 19.7).*

h-h *Brought up from v. 11 for clarity.*

8: *In that day, fresh water shall flow from Jerusalem ...,* cf. 13.1. A reflection of the ancient near eastern motif of the (cosmic) temple as a source of living water and of the related idea of Jerusalem/Temple as a watered and water providing garden (cf. the imagery of the garden of Eden). YHVH's future Presence in the Temple in Jerusalem is associated with fertilizing waters emerging from the place in Ezek. 47.1–12 and also with the image of a future "fountain" in the Temple or Jerusalem which occurs in texts as different as Joel 4.18; Zech. 13.1 and Ps. 46.5–6 (cf. Isa. 33.21). YHVH Himself was imagined as "the fountain of living water" (see Jer. 2.13; cf. Ps. 36.10 and also Jer. 2.13; 17.13. Earthly Jerusalem was a relatively water-poor city whose only source was the Gihon. Many utopian texts (imaginatively) reconfigure the geography of the land (e.g., Isa. 2.2; Ezek. ch 47). **9:** See intro. The v. evokes the language of Deut. 6.4, the beginning of what became the Shema prayer in later Judaism, and, given its context, it most likely means that in that day all humanity will acknowledge and worship the LORD alone and invoke the LORD's name alone. (Contrast the different vision in Mic. 4.5.) **10:** *Like the Arabah* means as low and plain as the Jordan Valley. *From Geba to Rimmon south of Jerusalem* refers to the territory of Judah. Jerusalem will be higher than its surroundings; cf. Mic. 4.1; Isa. 2.2. The expression it *shall be inhabited,* placed in our translation in v. 10 for clarity, stands in v. 11 in the Heb. V. 11 then reads, "And it [Jerusalem] shall be inhabited, for never again shall destruction be decreed, Jerusalem shall dwell secure." **16–17:** The *Feast of Booths,* Sukkot, comes at the beginning of the rainy season and is the time for petitioning rain from the LORD (see Rashi); that is why it is singled out here. As in other biblical calendars, Sukkot rather than Rosh Ha-Shanah (the New Year) or Yom Kippur (the Day of Atonement) is the central festival.

18: Egypt's agriculture was not dependent on rain, but on the Nile. **21:** Holiness will be so pervasive that every mundane household object will be holy, and therefore there will be no need for merchants to sell ritually pure vessels.

to Jerusalem to bow low to the King LORD of Hosts shall receive
no rain. 18 However, if the community of Egypt does not make
this pilgrimage, it shall not be visited by the same affliction
with which the LORD will strike the other nations that do not
come up to observe the Feast of Booths.[a] 19 Such shall be the
punishment of Egypt and of all other nations that do not come
up to observe the Feast of Booths.

20 In that day, even the bells on the horses shall be inscribed
"Holy to the LORD." The metal pots in the House of the LORD
shall be like the basins before the altar; 21 indeed, every metal pot in Jerusalem and in Judah shall be holy to the LORD of
Hosts. And all those who sacrifice shall come and take of these
to boil [their sacrificial meat] in; in that day there shall be no
more traders[b] in the House of the LORD of Hosts.

a *Because Egypt is not dependent on rain, it will suffer some other punishment, presumably that described in v. 12.* b *To sell ritually pure vessels.*

מלאכי

Malachi

THE BOOK OF MALACHI is set in a time when the Second Temple was rebuilt and sacrificial worship was resumed, thus later than the bulk of Haggai and Zechariah. It was composed in the Persian period, and is addressed originally to the inhabitants of the Persian province of Yehud (Judah). Because of the reference to intermarriage (2.11), some modern scholars assume that it belongs to a time closely preceding that of Ezra's actions on the matter (cf. *b. Meg.* 15a).

Some scholars have argued that the book was composed to provide an appropriate closing to the book of the Twelve, or that its conclusion (3.22–24, or a portion thereof) was written as a conclusion to the Twelve rather than to Malachi, or that substantial portions of the book were originally associated with some form of the book of Zechariah. None of these proposals is compelling.

Since Malachi means "my messenger," it has been thought from early times that it was not the name of the prophet, but an appellation, perhaps based on 3.1, "Behold, I am sending My messenger to clear the way before Me"; the LXX translates it as "His messenger." There is a tradition in the Tg. that Malachi is Ezra; a similar tradition is brought to bear in *b. Meg.* 15a; an alternate tradition of R. Naḥman claims that Malachi was Mordecai. Still the Rabbis (and later Ibn Ezra, Radak, and Maimonides) maintained that Malachi is the name of the prophet. Haggai, Zechariah, and Malachi are all understood by the Rabbis as the last of the prophets, at the time of the transition from prophets to sages, and the Talmud mentions rulings and sayings by this prophet that seem to characterize him as an early sage, in addition to his being a prophet (see intro. to Haggai). Despite these traditions, it is likely that Malachi should be understood as a personal name.

The readers of the book of Malachi are asked to look at some pitfalls in everyday life and in the cult at the Temple, and particularly at how they affect the relationship between YHVH and Israel, resulting in a lack of prosperity. Issues concerning proper offerings, marriage practices, and tithes are especially prominent in the book.

Messages of cultic reform and proper worship are deeply interwoven with the conviction of the coming of a future day in which the LORD will trample all evildoers. Such optimism about an ideal future is typical in prophetic works.

As a whole, the book is aimed at persuading its readers to follow the Torah of Moses, or at strengthening their resolve to continue to do so. This message must be understood within the book's historical setting. The book presents a prophetic voice that ultimately asserts the superiority of Torah over prophecy.

The use of a disputation format in much of the book contributes rhetorically to that purpose, for it allows the arguments of evildoers to be heard, in order to be countered and neutralized. Further, it allows the readers some limited form of self-identification with the actions of the evildoers, and as such serves as a call for them to examine themselves and repent.

The book uses imagery that refers to the structure of ancient patriarchal family groups. The LORD, as the main power figure, is imagined as a father, and at times (given the tone of the book) as an infuriated patriarchal figure. To be sure, this figure loves Israel/Judah, but within this world, the loved one should fulfill its role and obligations as the father figure envisages them. This metaphor is common in an ancient context, but it is difficult for many contemporary readers because our understanding of family life differs significantly from the one presumed in the book. Certainly modern readers who have had a damaging experience of an overbearing father find the message of such texts difficult to accept (cf. the book of Hosea). Other aspects of the imagery of the book of Malachi, and particularly its ending, have brought much hope and comfort. In fact, the reference to Elijah in 3.23–24 was often understood as an affirmation of hope for a final liberation, one even greater than the exodus from Egypt, for after Israel's first liberation it eventually becomes enslaved, but it will not after the one promised in Malachi (see *Pesik. Rab.* 4.3). Similarly the language of 3.4 is repeated often in traditional Jewish liturgy as an expression of hope about the restoration of appropriate worship in a future, third Temple.

Mal. 1.1–2.7 is read as the haftarah for the parashah of Toledot (Gen. 25.19–28.9), since these share the themes of Jacob and Esau, and Mal. 3.4–24 as that of Shabbat Ha-Gadol, the Sabbath preceding Passover, most likely because of the association of Elijah and the forthcoming messianic liberation, which is traditionally connected to Passover. (In the Yemenite tradition Mal. 1.1–3.4 is read with the parashah of Toledot.)

[EHUD BEN ZVI]

1 A pronouncement: The word of the LORD to Israel through Malachi.

2 I have shown you love, said the LORD. But you ask, "How
have You shown us love?" After all—declares the LORD—Esau
is Jacob's brother; yet I have accepted Jacob 3 and have rejected
Esau. I have made his hills a desolation, his territory [a-]a home
for beasts[-a] of the desert. 4 If Edom thinks, "Though crushed,
we can build the ruins again," thus said the LORD of Hosts: They
may build, but I will tear down. And so they shall be known as
the region of wickedness, the people damned forever of the
LORD. 5 Your eyes shall behold it, and you shall declare, "Great
is the LORD beyond the borders of Israel!"

6 A son should honor his father, and a slave[b] his master. Now
if I am a father, where is the honor due Me? And if I am a master, where is the reverence due Me?—said the LORD of Hosts to
you, O priests who scorn My name. But you ask, "How have we
scorned Your name?" 7 You offer defiled food on My altar. But

a-a Meaning of Heb. uncertain.

b Septuagint and Targum add "should reverence"; cf. next part of verse.

1.1: Superscription. The book has a double title, *a* (prophetic) *pronouncement* and *the word of the* LORD. It is addressed *to Israel,* meaning here Israel as a people with a particular relation to the LORD (see, e.g., 2.16), a particular history, and a particular obligation to follow the Torah of Moses (cf. 3.22) and to worship in Jerusalem. This conception of Israel is especially associated with the Persian period Yehud (or Judah), and it assumes a partial overlap between the concepts of "Israel" and "Judah" (a more geographico-political term). Thus references to Judah in 2.11 and 3.4 are identical with Israel in 1.1. The ancient readers of the book in ancient Yehud most likely identified themselves with both Judah and Israel.

1.2–5: The LORD loves Jacob. This section is meant to persuade or remind the readers of the LORD's special relationship with them. This is shown in the divine preference of Jacob over Esau. Esau stands both for Edom and for all the other nations. The contrast between the fates of the siblings (Esau/Edom and Jacob/Israel) is a central motif in the book of Obad. (On the later identifications of Esau/Edom, see nn. on Obad.) In the book of Mal., however, the issue is not central; rather it is used for rhetorical purposes within an argument developed against a particular group in Israel. The central point is that Israel is beloved, even if certain of its members are acting improperly.

1.6–14: Improper cultic practices at the Temple. 6–8: The logic of the argument is that if an animal cannot

you ask, "How have we defiled You?"[a] By saying, "The table of
the LORD can be treated with scorn." 8 When you present a blind
animal for sacrifice—it doesn't matter! When you present a lame
or sick one—it doesn't matter! Just offer it to your governor: Will
he accept you? Will he show you favor?—said the LORD of Hosts.
9 And now implore the favor of God! Will He be gracious to us?
This is what you have done—will He accept any of you?
The LORD of Hosts has said: 10 If only you would lock My
doors, and not kindle fire on My altar to no purpose! I take no
pleasure in you—said the LORD of Hosts—and I will accept no
offering from you. 11 For from where the sun rises to where it
sets, My name is honored among the nations, and everywhere
incense and pure oblation are offered to My name; for My
name is honored among the nations—said the LORD of Hosts.
12 But you profane it when you say, "The table of the Lord is
defiled and the meat,[b] the food, can be treated with scorn."
13 You say, "Oh, what a bother!" And so you degrade[b] it—said
the LORD of Hosts—and you bring the stolen, the lame, and
the sick; and you offer such as an oblation. Will I accept it from
you?—said the LORD.
14 A curse on the cheat who has an [unblemished] male in
his flock, but for his vow sacrifices a blemished animal to the
Lord! For I am a great King—said the LORD of Hosts—and My
name is revered among the nations.

2 And now, O priests, this charge is for you: 2 Unless you obey
and unless you lay it to heart, and do honor to My name—
said the LORD of Hosts—I will send a curse and turn your
blessings into curses. (Indeed, I have turned them into curses,
because you do not lay it to heart.) 3 I will [c-]put your seed under
a ban,[-c] and I will strew dung upon your faces, the dung of your
festal sacrifices, and you shall be carried out to its [heap].
4 Know, then, that I have sent this charge to you that My covenant with Levi may endure—said the LORD of Hosts. 5 I had
with him a covenant of life and well-being, which I gave to
him, and of reverence, which he showed Me. For he stood in
awe of My name.

6[d] Proper rulings were in his mouth,
And nothing perverse was on his lips;
He served Me with complete loyalty
And held the many back from iniquity.
7 [e-]For the lips of a priest guard knowledge,
And men seek rulings from his mouth;[-e]
For he is a messenger of the LORD of Hosts.

a Septuagint "it." *b Meaning of Heb. uncertain.*
c-c Meaning of Heb. uncertain. *d See Hag. 2.10–13; cf. Lev. 10.8–11, Deut. 33.8, 10.*
e-e Or: For the lips of a priest are observed; / Knowledge and ruling are sought from his mouth.

be offered to a provincial governor without risking punishment, it is certainly not a suitable offering for the King of Kings (cf. vv. 13–14). From the LORD's perspective, the fact that these offerings are still brought demonstrates the priests' disrespect for, and lack of fear of, the LORD, as proven by the validity of the previous statement of the LORD, *O priests who scorn My name* (v. 6). Several laws in the Bible state that blemished animals were not acceptable for sacrifice (e.g., Exod. 12.5; 29.1; Lev. 1.3, 10; 3.1; 22.22, passim). **10:** The first sentence may be translated as, "Oh, that someone among you would shut the temple doors, so that you would not kindle fire on my altar in vain" (NRSV). YHVH prefers no sacrifices at all, and even the closing of the Temple, over the improper situation described in these vv. **14:** *[Unblemished] male:* Blemished animals, which were not fit for sacrifice (cf. Lev. 1.3), were offered even by those who had unblemished animals. The main opposition is not between female and male offerings, but between blemished and unblemished male animals. In Israel, as in other agrarian societies, the most common sacrifice was that of a male animal; female sacrifices were rarer and more expensive, since each female is potentially a separate breeding animal.

2.1–9: The improper behavior of the priest. The readers overhear, as it were, the LORD's speech to the priests as reported in these vv. The speech reminds the readers of the importance of the rulings/torah/teachings of the priests (cf. Hag. 2.10–13), and of their role as "the LORD's messengers" (see v. 7 and notice the pun on the name Malachi, "My messenger"). To be sure, unless the priests perform their duty as the LORD expects them to, there cannot be proper worship, with all the consequences that this might entail. **4:** Cf. 2.8; Neh. 13.29. **5:** *Life and well-being* (life and peace), cf. Prov. 3.2. Are the famous "Vulcan salutes" a late reflection of this text? **7:** The *priest* is the *messenger* of YHVH. Usually prophets are the

8 But you have turned away from that course: You have made
the many stumble through your rulings;[a] you have corrupted
the covenant of the Levites—said the LORD of Hosts. 9 And I, in
turn, have made you despicable and vile in the eyes of all the
people, because you disregard My ways and show partiality in
your rulings.

10 Have we not all one Father? Did not one God create us?
Why do we break faith with one another, profaning the covenant of our ancestors? 11 Judah has broken faith; abhorrent things have been done in Israel and in Jerusalem. For
Judah has profaned what is holy to the LORD—what He desires—and espoused daughters of alien gods. 12 May the LORD
leave to him who does this [b-]no descendants[-b] dwelling in the
tents of Jacob and presenting offerings to the LORD of Hosts.
13 And this you do [c-]as well:[-c] You cover the altar of the LORD
with tears, weeping, and moaning, so that He refuses to regard the oblation any more and to accept [d-]what you offer.[-d]

a *By ruling falsely that an act was licit or an object ritually pure.*
b-b *Meaning of Heb. uncertain.*
c-c *Lit. "a second time"; Septuagint reads "which I detest"; cf. v. 16.*
d-d *Lit. "from your hand."*

messengers of YHVH. Since both communicate divine instructions, both can be characterized as "messengers of YHVH." Cf. the association of "the word of the LORD" and "torah" ("instruction") in Isa. 2.3; Mic. 4.2. Conversely, the prophets were imagined as teachers of Torah (e.g., Moses, the prophet par excellence). Later in rabbinic Judaism the prophets are forerunners of the Torah Sages and the three "last prophets" were members of the Great Assembly. **9:** *Show partiality in your rulings* seems to point to the priests' acceptance of unacceptable offerings brought by powerful members of society (e.g., Radak; cf. Prov. 18.5); this refers back to 1.8. (The Heb idiom translated as "show ... favor" in 1.8 is the same as *show partiality* here.) The point of the v. is that the priests' privileged status is conditional and can be overturned.

2.10–16: On marriage. The improper behavior of (male) Israel. This passage condemns male Judah because of intermarriage and because they "acted treacherously" against their Judahite wives. It concludes with another reported speech of the LORD (v. 6) supporting the message conveyed by the preceding vv. Scholars have debated whether the language of intermarriage should be taken literally or symbolically, as a reference to idolatry. The majority of scholars support the first alternative, but the text may have more than one level of meaning. **10–11:** *Have we not all one Father? Did not one God create us?* These words have been used numerous times to point to the unity (or, brotherhood or siblinghood) of all humanity (see *b. Ta'an.* 18a) and to advance ethical claims about the treatment of different groups on that basis. Within Mal., however, these expressions carry a different meaning. Because *we* equals Israel, which in turn was identified with Persian Yehud (see intro.), they refer to inner Israelite responsibilities to "keep faith" with one another and to honor the covenant of their fathers. If this understanding of the text is accepted, then the term *Father* has two meanings: (1) the LORD as father of Israel; and (2) the patriarchs of Israel, and esp. Jacob (e.g., Ibn Ezra). The first meaning relates this v. to other sections in Mal. in which the LORD is characterized as father. The second meaning emphasizes the border between Israel and the nations, which is an important issue in the unit, and directly links the reference to the ancestral fathers at the conclusion of the v. (and perhaps even alludes to the reference to Jacob and Esau in 1.2–3). (The use of the capital "F" for *Father,* indicating the deity, is a translational and interpretative choice; Heb does not mark a distinction between common and proper nouns in these cases.) There is an alternative tradition of reading these expressions within their context in the book of Mal. Within this tradition *Have we not all one Father? Did not one God create us?* actually points at the unity of humanity, but it is said by the (sinful) Judahites to justify their actions. To them, the prophetic voice in the text answers, *Judah has broken faith.* (It is also possible to understand *father* as referring to Adam.) The expression translated *break faith with one another* may also be translated "act treacherously, a man to his brother." If the latter translation is followed, then v. 11 should be translated, "Judah has acted treacherously." The text clearly conveys to the readers that marrying daughters of alien gods (i.e., foreign women) is tantamount to profaning what is holy to the LORD and committing abominations; Judah acting treacherously is the equivalent of a Judahite man breaking faith with his brothers. Thus, within the book intermarriage is presented here not only as a husband-wife affair, but as a brother-brother affair, and a son-patriarch affair (since the latter's covenant is breached), and a matter between Israel and the LORD, with grave cultic and covenantal implications (see vv. 12–13). The precise language chosen to describe the women, namely not as "foreign women" but rather as *daughters of alien gods,* is rhetorically significant. **13–16:** Judahite men failed on another account. They "have acted treacherously"

14 But you ask, "Because of what?" Because the LORD is a witness between you and the wife of your youth with whom you
have broken faith, though she is your partner and covenanted
spouse. 15 Did not the One make [all,] [a-]so that all remaining
life-breath is His? And what does that One seek but godly
folk? So be careful of your life-breath,[-a] and let no one break
faith with the wife of his youth. 16 For I detest divorce—said
the LORD, the God of Israel—[a-]and covering oneself with lawlessness as with a garment[-a]—said the LORD of Hosts. So be
careful of your life-breath and do not act treacherously.

17 You have wearied the LORD with your talk. But you ask,
"By what have we wearied [Him]?" By saying, "All who do evil
are good in the sight of the LORD, and in them He delights," or
else, "Where is the God of justice?"

3 Behold, I am sending My messenger to clear the way before Me, and the Lord whom you seek shall come to His
Temple suddenly. As for the angel of the covenant[b] that you
desire, he is already coming. 2 But who can endure the day of
his coming, and who can hold out when he appears? For he
is like a smelter's fire and like fuller's lye. 3 He shall act[c] like a
smelter and purger of silver; and he shall purify the descendants of Levi and refine them like gold and silver, so that they
shall present offerings in righteousness. 4 Then the offerings
of Judah and Jerusalem shall be pleasing to the LORD as in
the days of yore and in the years of old. 5 But [first] I will step
forward to contend against you, and I will act as a relentless
accuser against those who have no fear of Me: Who practice
sorcery, who commit adultery, who swear falsely, who cheat
laborers of their hire, and who subvert [the cause of] the widow,
orphan, and stranger, said the LORD of Hosts.

a-a *Meaning of Heb. uncertain.*
b *Apparently the messenger of the previous sentence is regarded as Israel's tutelary angel.* c *Lit. "sit."*

against (or *broken faith* with) their Judahite wives whom they married in their *youth.* Their actions not only caused great pain to these women, but also involved covenant breaking, and as such they carried grave cultic implications: The LORD rejected the offerings of those Judahites and of Judah. The sentence translated *I detest* [or "hate"] *divorce—said the LORD, the God of Israel* has attracted much attention in the last decades. The Heb is difficult. Moreover, a text of the v. in a Dead Sea Scrolls ms may be translated "But if you hate [your wife] divorce [her]!" (4Q12ᵃ). Significantly, this is also the way in which the Tg., the Vg, and (likely) the LXX understood the v. (cf. *b. Git.* 80b). This reading is consistent with the liberal attitude toward divorce of the House of Hillel and R. Akiva (*m. Git.* 9.10); cf. Deut. 24.1–2; Sir. 25.26. Even if the MT version of the v. represents the original text, different interpretations and versions of it already existed in ancient times. Controversies about its meaning are also well attested in medieval times.

2.17–3.21: The coming day: judgment for the doers of evil and a "sun of righteousness" for those who revere the LORD's name. Although there is some debate about the scope of the different units included in these vv., it is clear that they address issues such as theodicy, a response to those who claim that the LORD is either unjust or unable to provide justice in this world, strong affirmations of a great day of judgment to come, a reference to a long history of Israel turning away from the LORD, and calls for repentance. As a whole, the emphasis on the future, and the general tone of hope, sets ch 3 apart from the previous chs in Malachi. Mal. 3.6–12, however, is closely related to 1.2–5. **2.17:** Despite the present division according to chs, the v. is to be read as directly linked to the following vv. The scribal tradition of the MT has a break after 2.16 reflected in the paragraph division in NJPS. **3.1–2:** Cf. Isa. 40.3. Much of the discussion on the "messianic" tone of Mal. centers on 3.23 and this v. The identity of the messenger in 3.1 has been highly debated. Is *My messenger* (Heb "malakhi") Malachi? Or is there at least a pun on the name of the prophet? Is the messenger the *angel of the covenant,* a zealous, powerful enforcer of the covenant who is *like a smelter's fire and like fuller's lye* (i.e., a purifying, caustic treatment)? Is he Elijah (see v. 23)? Or is Elijah the *angel of the covenant?* Does the text indicate an expectation of a priestly Messiah? There is a very long history of interpretation on this v., with multiple meanings already in antiquity. The New Testament merges this v. with Isa. 40.3 and identifies the expected messenger as John the Baptist (Matt. 11.10; Mark 1.2; Luke 7.27). Moreover, it is uncertain what "covenant" means in this context—does it refer to a specific earlier covenant, or does it refer to the "covenanted people," that is, to Israel (cf. also Dan. 11.22, 28, 30)? **4:** See intro.

8–9: The repeated use of terms translated as *defraud* and the like (Heb "kabaʿ") is a pun on the name Jacob ("Yaʿakob") and its negative connotations (cf. Gen. 27.36; Jer. 9.3; Hos. 12.4). See translators' note *b.* **10:** Cf. Neh. 13.10–11; Dan. 1.2. **16:** This *scroll of remembrance* is found elsewhere in the Bible (e.g., Exod. 32.32); it is a Mesopotamian concept that becomes especially developed in the idea of the book of life associated with the Jewish high holiday liturgy. **19–24:** In most English translations these vv. appear as Mal. 4.1–6. **20:** *A sun of victory,* lit. and in most translations, "a sun of righteousness." *To bring healing,* lit. and in most translations, "with healing in its wings." The background of the imagery is mythological. The rising of "a sun of righteousness" is a metaphor for the dawn of a new "day," i.e., era of history.

6 [a]For I am the LORD—I have not changed; and you are the children of Jacob—you have not ceased to be. 7 From the very days of your fathers you have turned away from My laws and have not observed them. Turn back to Me, and I will turn back to you—said the LORD of Hosts. But you ask, "How shall we turn back?" 8 Ought man to defraud[b] God? Yet you are defrauding Me. And you ask, "How have we been defrauding You?" In tithe and contribution.[c] 9 You are suffering under a curse, yet you go on defrauding Me—the whole nation of you. 10 Bring the full tithe into the storehouse,[d] and let there be food in My House, and thus put Me to the test—said the LORD of Hosts. I will surely open the floodgates of the sky for you and pour down blessings on you; 11 and I will banish the locusts[e] from you, so that they will not destroy the yield of your soil; and your vines in the field shall no longer miscarry—said the LORD of Hosts. 12 And all the nations shall account you happy, for you shall be the most desired of lands—said the LORD of Hosts.

13 You have spoken hard words against Me—said the LORD. But you ask, "What have we been saying among ourselves against You?" 14 You have said, "It is useless to serve God. What have we gained by keeping His charge and walking in abject awe of the LORD of Hosts? 15 And so, we account the arrogant happy: they have indeed done evil and endured; they have indeed dared God and escaped." 16 In this vein have those who revere the LORD been talking to one another. The LORD has heard and noted it, and a scroll of remembrance has been written at His behest concerning those who revere the LORD and esteem His name. 17 And on the day that I am preparing, said the LORD of Hosts, they shall be My treasured possession; I will be tender toward them as a man is tender toward a son who ministers to him. 18 And you shall come to see the difference between the righteous and the wicked, between him who has served God and him who has not served Him.

19 For lo! That day is at hand, burning like an oven. All the arrogant and all the doers of evil shall be straw, and the day that is coming—said the LORD of Hosts—shall burn them to ashes and leave of them neither stock nor boughs. 20 But for you who revere My name a sun of victory shall rise [f]to bring healing.[f] You shall go forth and stamp like stall-fed calves, 21 and you shall trample the wicked to a pulp, for they shall be

a Vv. 6–12 resume the thought of 1.2–5.

b Heb. qabaʿ, *a play on the name of Jacob (v. 6); cf. Gen. 27.36.*

c I.e., the contributions to the priests from the new grain, oil, and wine; see Num. 18.12.

d I.e., the public storehouse; see Neh. 13.10–13. *e Lit. "devourer."*

f-f Lit. "with healing in the folds of its garments"; others "with healing in its wings."

dust beneath your feet on the day that I am preparing—said
the LORD of Hosts.
22 Be mindful of the Teaching of My servant Moses, whom I
charged at Horeb with laws and rules for all Israel.
23 Lo, I will send the prophet Elijah to you before the coming
of the awesome, fearful day of the LORD. 24 He shall reconcile
parents with children and children with their parents, so that,
when I come, I do not strike the whole land with utter destruction.

Lo, I will send the prophet Elijah to you before the coming of the awesome, fearful day of the LORD.

22–24: At its conclusion, Mal. asserts the dominance of Mosaic Torah over the prophetic tradition. See intro. to Mal. and intro. to the Twelve. **23:** Since Elijah did not die, but ascended to heaven (2 Kings 2.11), he can return. There is a long tradition of interpretation of this v. expanding on the role of Elijah, the herald of the messianic era; see, e.g., *b. Shab.* 118a; *b. ʿEruv.* 43b; *y. Shab.* 1.3 and the Passover Haggadah. The *awesome, fearful day of the LORD* is associated with the "travails of the messiah" in *b. Shab.* 118a; *Mishneh Torah,* Kings 12.3. It is traditional in Jewish liturgy to repeat v. 23 after v. 24 (written in a smaller font in NJPS) so as to conclude the public reading on a strong, hopeful note, rather than the threat of destruction in the final phrase of v. 24. (The same holds true for the conclusion of Isa., Lam., and Eccl.) **24:** The connection between intergenerational reconciliation and Elijah is enigmatic.

כתובים

KETHUVIM

Terminology and Content

THE BROAD TERM KETHUVIM, "WRITINGS," reflects the variety of material collected in this canonical division, including works about Israel's past (e.g., Chronicles), prayers (Psalms), wisdom literature (e.g., Job, Proverbs and Ecclesiastes; on this genre see the essay on "Religion of the Bible," pp. 1978–97), and apocalyptic prophecy (the second half of Daniel). It is likely that the various books now in this section became part of the Bible for quite different reasons: Psalms, for example, was used for prayers, while the book Proverbs was used in educating the young. Most likely the books now in Kethuvim came together and were ultimately canonized toward the end of the Second Temple period, after the canonical section Nevi'im was closed, and thus the books now comprising Kethuvim were assembled together, despite their different natures, into a single group (see the essay on "Canonization," on pp. 2153–58). The wide variety of the ordering of these books found in manuscripts and canonical lists reflects the fact that Kethuvim was canonized later than Torah, which has a fixed order, and Nevi'im, where there is only slight variation in the order of the books.

An early order, where the books are largely arranged in what the Rabbis understood to be their chronological sequence (from Ruth to Chronicles), is found in the Babylonian Talmud (*b. B. Bat.* 15a). No surviving manuscript, however, has this order. Most sources divide Kethuvim into three parts; however, unlike "the former prophets" and "the latter prophets," no names are extant for each part.

The first section of Kethuvim is composed of the three large books Psalms, Proverbs, and Job, either in that order, or in the order Psalms, Job, and Proverbs. In Jewish tradition, these three books are often called *sifrei ʾemet,* books of truth, an acronym for Job *(ʾiyov),* Proverbs *(mishlei)* and Psalms *(tehilim).* These books are also distinguished by the use of special trope, cantillation or chanting marks. Psalms is always the first book, suggesting that in some early sources (e.g., Luke 24.44) Psalms may be the title for the entire collection of Kethuvim.

These three long books are typically followed by five shorter books—Song of Songs, Ruth, Lamentations, Ecclesiastes, and Esther— called *ḥamesh megillot,* "the five scrolls" ; see the intro. to "The Five Megillot (Scrolls)," on p. 1557. The last collection is of three narrative texts: Daniel, which contains diaspora stories set in the royal court and also apocalyptic prophecy, Ezra-Nehemiah, which narrates the partial history of the return to Judah in the early postexilic period, and Chronicles, which very selectively retells events from Adam through the Cyrus declaration of 538 BCE. This is the order found in the NJPS translation, which follows some manuscripts and most printed editions. It is a strange order, since Ezra-Nehemiah is a logical continuation of Chronicles, beginning where Chronicles ends, with the Cyrus declaration. It is thus not surprising that most manuscripts have Ezra-Nehemiah as the final book of the Bible. Chronicles and Ezra-Nehemiah are each viewed by Jewish tradition as a single book. Like Samuel and Kings (see the intro. to Nevi'im, pp. 429–38), only under the influence of the

Septuagint (LXX) did some manuscripts and early printed versions of the Bible divide these books into two.

These books come from widely diverse time periods. Many show clear linguistic signs of postexilic composition; for example, Ecclesiastes was influenced by Aramaic, and Daniel by Greek (see the introductions to these books). Moreover, historical references in Daniel would place its composition in the 2nd c. BCE. Lamentations is clearly from the exilic period (586–538 BCE) or very shortly thereafter. Ruth is most likely a postexilic work. Psalms is a collection, containing some poems which are considered among the earliest of biblical literature (e.g., Ps. 68), and others that are dated on the basis of language or content to the exilic or postexilic periods (Pss. 135; 145). Rabbinic literature, in some cases following earlier traditions, attributes many of the works now found in Kethuvim to biblical figures; thus Jeremiah is considered the author of Lamentations, David composed Psalms, and Solomon authored Proverbs and Ecclesiastes. These attributions, which are not historically accurate, reflect a late biblical and early rabbinic desire to enhance the authority of these books by connecting them to figures who are central in tradition, indeed, who are considered to have been divinely inspired. Linguistic and other internal evidence, which is investigated in the introductions to each of the books in Kethuvim, is the basis for the modern dating of these books.

Kethuvim as a Collection

THE OBSERVATIONS ABOVE SHOW THAT KETHUVIM is the most diverse collection of the three canonical divisions. Even though various texts may be grouped together, e.g., as wisdom literature or as historical texts, the individual works that comprise these categories (e.g., Job and Proverbs) have little in common. Kethuvim has no central theme or idea, in the way that the Torah (or Hexateuch) might have the land promise and its fulfillment as its center, or the Prophets as a whole might illustrate the significance of heeding the mediated divine word. In fact, with the exception of Psalms and the five scrolls, which have significant liturgical uses, Kethuvim has received less attention than the other biblical books within Jewish tradition.

This diminished attention is quite unfortunate, for these books are among the most interesting biblical books, and also among the most significant for understanding the Bible as a whole and for following the development of Jewish thought in Second Temple times. Since this collection contains some of the latest books in the Bible (Chronicles, Ezra-Nehemiah, Daniel, Ecclesiastes), it shows us how classical biblical ideas evolved and changed in the late biblical period, as they began to develop into notions that would be much more familiar to readers of Jewish texts beginning with the Hellenistic period (Apocrypha, Pseudepigrapha, and Dead Sea Scrolls) and continuing in early rabbinic literature.

[MARC ZVI BRETTLER]

תהלים

Psalms

THE BOOK OF PSALMS IS THE FIRST BOOK of Kethuvim, or Writings—probably because of its size and significance and also perhaps because it was the first book in Kethuvim to become authoritative. Its early importance may be reflected in a text from the Dead Sea Scrolls, 4QMMT[d] (4Q397: 14–21; C.9–10, slightly reconstructed), which speaks of "the books of Moses and the books of the Prophets and David," thus indicating its status. (For "David" as a locution for Psalms, see below.) It was not always the first book of Kethuvim—a rabbinic tradition concerning the order of this section puts Ruth in first place (probably because it imagines Ruth to be written earlier than Psalms), followed by Psalms (*b. B. Bat.* 14b).

Psalms is a collection, actually a collection of collections, of poetic prayers. (Prose prayers are also found throughout the Bible, but they are ad hoc, private prayers of individuals.) The origin of most of these poetic prayers is lost in obscurity, but they were preserved because they were likely used liturgically in ancient Israel, certainly in the Second Temple and in some cases, perhaps in the First Temple. The Hebrew name of the book, *Tehilim,* "songs of praise," is found often in rabbinic literature and is also attested in one of the Dead Sea Scrolls, in a Psalms scroll (11QPs[a], lines 4–5) which says that David wrote 3,600 *tehilim* plus other compositions (see below for David as the author of Psalms). The English title "Psalms" derives from the Greek *psalmos,* a translation of Hebrew *mizmor,* "a song with the accompaniment of a stringed instrument."

There are 150 chs or psalms in the Masoretic Text of the Hebrew Bible; some chapters may contain two separate psalms (e.g., Ps. 40), while in other cases one composition has been split into two chapters (e.g., Pss. 9–10 and 42–43). The book crystallized in several different forms in different communities: The LXX contains an additional psalm at the end of the book, and the Syriac Peshitta Bible translation contains five additional psalms. Several of these, as well as some previously unknown compositions, have been found in the Qumran Psalm scroll (11QPs[a]), suggesting that the collection of psalms in the early Psalter was fluid. 11QPs[a] also often arranges the psalms in a different order from our Psalter, suggesting that there was no fixed order for the psalms in the late Second Temple period.

The book of Psalms is subdivided into five "Books": I, chs 1–41 (most of the "Psalms of David" are in this collection); II, chs 42–72 (containing some psalms of Korah and Asaph); III, chs 73–89 (almost exclusively the psalms of Korah and Asaph); IV, chs 90–106 (mostly untitled psalms); V, chs 107–150 (mostly liturgical psalms for pilgrimages to the Temple and for festivals). The division into books is marked by the insertion of doxologies, short hymnic praises of God, at the end of each book. The doxologies to Books I–IV all begin with the words "Blessed is the LORD." The last psalm, Ps. 150, serves as the concluding doxology for Book V and for the book of Psalms as a whole (just as Ps. 1 may be viewed as an introduction to the entire book). The division into five books of psalms is designed to parallel the five books of the Torah. As the Rabbis put it: "Moses gave the five books of the Torah to Israel and David gave the five books of Psalms to

Israel" (*Midrash Shoḥer Tov,* 1.2). This arrangement into five books is artificial and relatively late, and reflects the development from Psalms as a liturgical collection of prayers that were recited to a Torah-like book to be studied. Strong evidence for the existence of separate collections is: (1) the end of one collection, Ps. 72.20, is clearly marked by the words "End of the prayers of David son of Jesse"; and (2) some psalms were included in two different collections, as is seen by the fact that Pss. 14 and 53 are nearly identical, as are Ps. 18 and 2 Sam. ch 22; Ps. 70 is comprised of Ps. 40.14–18. The first three books seem to have been in place before the last two were added, judging from the fact that 28 out of 33 untitled psalms are found in Books IV and V, and that the differences between the Dead Sea Psalms text and the Masoretic Text occur mostly in Books IV and V. Within the present collections are smaller collections, for example, the Songs of Ascents (the ascent of pilgrims to the Temple Mount; Pss. 120–134), so named from their opening words. Modern scholars speak of the Elohist Psalter, Pss. 42–83, in which God is typically referred to as Elohim rather than as LORD (YHVH). Some scholars see clusters of psalms that begin or end with "hallelujah" as subcollections (Pss. 105–106; 111–113; 115–117; 146–150). Other collections have been isolated as well. It remains unclear, however, if the psalms within each collection, and the collections themselves, were arranged according to any overarching principle. Perhaps an original collection of Psalms 2–89 focused on David, and was expanded with the addition of Psalm 1 and 90–150, which then created a structure that begins with petitions and laments and concludes with hymns. It is clear, though, that Psalms, even at 150 chapters, is not the single definitive collection of ancient Israel's psalms, since similar poems are also found outside of the Psalter (e.g., 1 Sam. 2.1–10; 2 Sam. 23.1–7; Jonah ch 3; Hab. ch 3).

An ancient and pervasive tradition, going back to the Bible itself, attributes the authorship of Psalms to David. David is "the favorite of the songs of Israel" (2 Sam. 23.1), the one who soothed Saul with music (1 Sam. 16.17–23), the classic example of a musician (Amos 6.5), and the founder of Temple singing (2 Chron. 23.18). Deriving from and reinforcing this tradition are the many psalm superscriptions or titles that contain "a psalm of David." This may imply Davidic authorship; or perhaps it meant that the psalms were dedicated to David or were composed in what may have been perceived as the style of David, the arch-musician. Other superscriptions link a psalm with a specific event in the life of David (Pss. 3; 18; 34; 51; 56). These superscriptions are not original to these psalms, but reflect early interpretive additions that derive from the notion of David as author of the psalms. Early extrabiblical sources show that ancient Jewish and Christian tradition also assumed that David wrote all or most of Psalms. As mentioned above, a Psalms scroll from the Dead Sea Scrolls attributes 3,600 psalms to David (a tradition based on the analogy of the Bible's attribution of 3,000 proverbs and 1,005 songs to Solomon in 1 Kings 5.12). Additionally, Davidic superscriptions occur in that scroll in Pss. 104 and 123, although they are lacking in the Masoretic Text. Along the same lines, the author of Acts, the 1st c. CE New Testament book, assigns Ps. 2 to David (Acts 4.25), even though the psalm itself has no such ascription. This evidence suggests that there was widespread acceptance of the Davidic authorship of the entire Psalter, a tradition that is echoed in rabbinic literature and has continued until modern times in both Jewish and Christian circles. Davidic authorship, however, on the basis of linguistic and contextual evidence, is not accepted as historical fact by modern scholars, but is viewed as a way the ancients linked biblical writings with the appropriate inspired well-known biblical figure, thereby confirming the divine inspiration and the authority of those writings (as is the case in the ascription of Proverbs to Solomon, Lamentations to Jeremiah, and so forth). Not all psalms are specifically attributed to David; some are attributed to the sons of Korah (e.g., Ps. 42), to Asaph (e.g., Ps. 50), to Ethan the Ezrahite (Ps. 89), to Heman the Ezrahite (Ps. 88), to Solomon (Ps. 72), and to Moses (Ps. 90)—and others bear no ascription at all.

Dating the psalms is notoriously difficult, partly because they contain few explicit references to specific historical events or personages (as noted above, the superscriptions are not useful in this regard). While many modern scholars believe that at least some, perhaps even many, of the psalms are from the preexilic period (before 586 BCE), none can be dated on linguistic grounds to the 10th c. BCE, the period of David. There is little consensus on the dating of preexilic psalms, or even on which psalms are preexilic. Linguistic analysis can, in general, differentiate between preexilic and postexilic Hebrew, but the analysis is not always refined enough to be definitive. For one thing, poetry is often archaizing, so the presence of older-sounding phrases does not, in itself, prove an early date. Moreover, the hints to specific events that scholars find in the psalms often have more than one possible reference. Dating of psalms is subject to trends in biblical scholarship: At one time many psalms were thought to have originated in the Maccabean era (2nd c. BCE), then in the preexilic period, and now more are being seen as products of the exilic or postexilic period. Some psalms clearly date from exilic or postexilic times, as we know from their references to events or their linguistic usages (e.g., Pss. 137; 145). It is also likely that some psalms have an ancient core that was reshaped after the exile into a new psalm. Nevertheless, linguistic and other evidence suggests that most of the psalms in Books I–III are preexilic, and those in Books IV–V are exilic or postexilic. The bane of historical critics may be the virtue of the book of Psalms: The absence of specific historical references results in the poems being seen as timeless, appropriate to many recurring occasions in the life of the individual or the community.

Many of the psalms have superscriptions containing information other than a personal name. Their terms are not well understood, but some are thought to be musical directions or instruments; for example, *sheminith* (Ps. 12); *ayyeleth ha-shaḥar* (Ps. 22); *maskil* (Ps. 32). The *menatzeaḥ* or "leader" often referred to is presumably a choir-leader or chief musician. (The meaning of the frequent musical term "Selah," which occurs often in the middle of a psalm, is also not known. See note at 3.3.) It is likely that the psalms were sung or recited to musical accompaniment. Psalm 150 indicates that music was a form of praise to God, and terms for praise include "sing ... a new song" (96.1; 98.1; 149.1), "chant hymns" (147.1), and "sing joyously" (95.1). Unfortunately, the acoustic dimension, known in part from contemporaneous cultures, has been lost, but it must have been an important component of the performance of psalms.

While no psalm is exactly identical with another and many show considerable creativity, all the psalms have similar style, vocabulary, and forms of expression. They share these features with other ancient Near Eastern prayers as well; Israel's borrowing from its neighbors included forms of religious expression. Like all biblical poetry, the psalms make much use of repetition, parallelism, and imagery (see essay on "Biblical Poetry," pp. 2184–91). They also have recourse to many of the same themes found elsewhere in the Bible, for these themes were central to the identity of Israel. Included are the themes of creation (which shows God's supreme power over everything in the world); the promise to Abraham of land and progeny (esp. important after the exile); the exodus (the foundational experience in the formation of the people of Israel and their covenant with God); the exile (the key event in the formation of Jewish identity after 586 BCE); the Davidic monarchy (symbol of the continuity of Judah); the centrality of Jerusalem, Zion, and the Temple. (Striking in its absence is the giving of the Decalogue or Torah at Sinai.) These themes generally do not appear in a form identical to the Torah and Prophets, since some psalms may antedate the completed Torah or books of the Prophets. Even when psalms know earlier written works, they often elaborate upon them or re-interpret them. In addition, psalms borrow Canaanite mythological motifs known from Ugarit and elsewhere in the ancient Near East, such as God the warrior defeating Israel's enemies, the conquest of the primeval waters (the forces of chaos), and God as king enthroned amid a heavenly court. The book is a broad collection, representing a variety of different, even contradictory, religious views, (cf. e.g., 44.24 with 121.4). Not surprisingly, the psalms draw heavily on the religious concepts of ancient Israel; for modern scholars they are a window into the religious experience that the Bible chose to preserve (see essay on the "Religion of the Bible," pp. 1978–97).

Based on the literary structure or "form" of each psalm, modern form-critical scholars have been concerned to assign to each psalm a genre and a specific social setting (the German term *Sitz im Leben* is often used) in the religious practice of ancient Israel. This is often conjectural, based on interpreting hints contained in the psalms (see, e.g., Ps. 67.7–8 n.). It is surprising that the psalms contain so few hints (but see 118.27 n.). Like dates, and for much the same reasons, modern genre labels must be assigned tentatively. Most psalms fall into three general categories (sometimes a psalm partakes of more than one category): hymns of praise; complaints or pleas for help (sometimes called laments); and thanksgiving psalms. Other subcategories, like wisdom psalms (see Ps. 1) or royal psalms (see Ps. 2) have also been discerned. Several do not address God at all, and can only with great difficulty be classified as prayers. These psalms, as well as the others, serve to unify the community by creating and reinforcing a common notion of its God and its beliefs. Psalms may be written in the first-person singular, called a psalm of the individual, or in the first-person plural, communal psalms. The speaking voice should not be understood as a sign of authorship, but rather as a literary persona through whom the psalm is conveyed. In fact, psalms often move from an individual speaker to a communal speaker (this is frequently accomplished through brief additions at a psalm's conclusion; and all psalms, by their inclusion in the Psalter, are property of the community). As is the case in later prayer, a psalm may be recited privately by an individual or publicly by an individual or by a group.

The annotations offered below are eclectic. Where we find that modern scholars have suggested compelling dates for psalms, or explanations for a psalm's origin, we note that. We believe that Psalms contains some of the most beautiful poetry in the Bible, and we try to give the reader, especially the person reading in English, a sense of how this poetry works, how it functions as moving liturgy. As it is relevant, we also incorporate insights from the Jewish interpretive tradition. That tradition, with a few exceptions, saw Psalms as a Davidic composition—an assumption that we do not share—but nevertheless traditional insights into meaning and structure often foreshadow modern observations.

The book of Psalms occupies a prominent place in Jewish liturgy; some entire psalms are recited as part of the regular service or on special occasions, and many individual vv. or passages have found their way into later prayers (see list in "The Bible in the Liturgy," pp. 2057–67). Additionally, psalms are recited publicly or privately at times of joy or danger. Some individuals or groups take upon themselves the recitation of all the psalms on a weekly basis.

Praise is the quintessential nature of psalms, and hymns of praise are the most common type of psalm in the Psalter. In the words of Ps. 106.1: "Hallelujah. Praise the LORD for He is good; His steadfast love is eternal" (see also 107.1; 118.1, 29; 136.1). Most psalms are, in one way or another, aimed at praising God—for His power and beneficence, for His creation of the world, and for His past acts of deliverance to Israel. Often the praise comes after the psalmist has prayed for help from sickness or enemies (the typical subject of complaints) and his prayer has been answered. As part of his complaint, he promises to praise God when he has been delivered from trouble. Thanksgiving for God's help or beneficence is another form of praise. According to the outlook of Psalms, the main religious function of human beings is to offer praise to God, to proclaim His greatness throughout the world. Thus, the psalms enjoin others to praise God, and they envision a world in which everyone and everything will praise God (see esp. Ps. 150). This implies a relationship between God and humans, another important dimension of Psalms. God is called upon to hear prayers and to respond; this is one of His attributes. Worst of all is when He "hides His face" and refuses to pay attention to the psalmist (see e.g., 30.8), because this puts into question the efficacy of prayer. If there is one primary underlying assumption of the book of Psalms, it is the potential efficacy of prayer. This is expressed beautifully in the following two vv. from Psalms: "The LORD is close to the broken-hearted; / those crushed in spirit He delivers" (34.19), and "The LORD is near to all who call Him, / to all who call Him with sincerity" (145.18).

[ADELE BERLIN AND MARC ZVI BRETTLER]

BOOK ONE

1

Happy is the man who has not followed the
counsel of the wicked,
or taken the path of sinners,
or joined the company of the insolent;
2 rather, the teaching of the LORD is his delight,
and he studies[a] that teaching day and night.
3 He is like a tree planted beside streams of water,
which yields its fruit in season,
whose foliage never fades,
and whatever [b-]it produces thrives.[-b]

4 Not so the wicked;
rather, they are like chaff that wind blows away.

a *Or "recites"; lit. "utters."* *b-b* *Or "he does prospers."*

Ps. 1: This psalm (along with Ps. 2) serves as an introduction to the Psalter, as is suggested by the absence of a superscription or title mentioning David, unlike most psalms in Book I (Pss. 1–41). It depicts a straightforward system of personal retribution that stands behind many psalms (see also Ezek. ch 18). It features "torah" (v. 2), translated as "teaching," but perhaps understood as Torah ("Teaching"), the five books of Moses, as the guide and nourishment of the righteous man. By placing a reference to Torah at the beginning of the Psalter, the centrality of the Torah, presumably already considered authoritative by the time the Psalter was compiled, is reinforced (see similarly Josh. 1.7–8). The mention of Torah here may also be connected to the fact that the Psalter is divided into five books (see intro. to Psalms), and the intent may have been to advocate the study of the Psalter by analogy with the study of the Torah. Many scholars consider Ps. 1 to be a wisdom psalm, based on its contrast between the righteous and the wicked as seen in Prov., Job, and Eccl. (see the discussion of "wisdom literature" in the intro. to "Kethuvim," pp. 1263–64). Ps. 1, however, does not share extensive terminology with these books, and scholars now question the usefulness of the designation "wisdom psalms." **1–3:** Conventional biblical imagery (e.g., Jer. 17.8 for a tree image and Josh. 1.8 for reciting "torah" day and night) is used to develop the picture of the ideal righteous person. This person is first described through what he does not do (v. 1), then through what he does (v. 2), and then via a simile. *Followed ... taken ... joined ...* does not fully capture the imagery of location and movement in the Heb "walk, stand, sit." **1:** *Happy:* in a good state of being. *Man:* Heb "'ish" is often gender neutral but here may refer to a male since women probably did not study Torah in biblical times. **2:** *Day and night* is figurative for "always," though the Dead Sea Scroll community took it literally, suggesting that "[I]n the place in which the Ten assemble there should not be missing a man to interpret the law day and night, always relieving each other" (1QS 6.6–7, as translated in Florentino García Martínez and Eibert J.C. Tigchelaar, *The Dead Sea Scrolls Study Edition* [Leiden: Brill, 1997], vol. 1, p. 83). This psalm is unusual in its stress on Torah study rather than on observance based on Torah study (see Josh. 1.7–8); it thus approaches the rabbinic ideal of "torah lishmah," Torah study for its own sake, as an end in itself, though the psalm strongly suggests that Torah study keeps people away from *the wicked* and *sinners. The teaching of the LORD* is often a late biblical term (e.g., Ezra 7.10; 1 Chron. 16.40). **3:** Living to a ripe old age and having many children is the biblical ideal for a successful life. *And whatever it produces thrives* may refer either to the *tree* or the righteous individual. **4–5:** The depiction of the wicked is much shorter, and in the plural, whereas the righteous person was spoken of in the singular. In contrast to the deeply rooted tree, the wicked are insubstantial *chaff,* the light outside husk of grain that flies away during winnowing.

5 Therefore the wicked will not survive judgment,
nor will sinners, in the assembly of the righteous.
6 For the LORD cherishes the way of the righteous,
but the way of the wicked is doomed.

2 Why do nations assemble,
and peoples plot[a] vain things;
2 kings of the earth take their stand,
and regents intrigue together
against the LORD and against His anointed?
3 "Let us break the cords of their yoke,
shake off their ropes from us!"
4 He who is enthroned in heaven laughs;
the Lord mocks at them.
5 Then He speaks to them in anger,
terrifying them in His rage,
6 "But I have installed My king
on Zion, My holy mountain!"
7 Let me tell of the decree:
the LORD said to me,
b-"You are My son,
I have fathered you this day.-b
8 Ask it of Me,
and I will make the nations your domain;
your estate, the limits of the earth.
9 You can smash them with an iron mace,
shatter them like potter's ware."

a Lit. "utter." *b-b Compare 2 Sam. 7.14, and Ps. 89.27 ff.*

5: *Judgment* refers to a court case. Medieval Jewish interpretation traditionally understands this judgment as occurring in the afterworld (e.g., Ibn Ezra and Radak), but belief in the afterworld is largely a postbiblical development (see Dan. 12.2–3 n.). **6:** The final v. sums up the fate of both *the righteous* of vv. 1–3 and *the wicked* of vv. 4–5. Echoing the structure of the psalm as a whole, this v. dedicates more words to the righteous than to the wicked, again emphasizing the insubstantial nature of the wicked. God approves of the behavior of the righteous. The psalm does not say that God punishes the wicked, suggesting that they doom themselves.

Ps. 2: Some traditions see this psalm as a continuation of Ps. 1. (A variant in the New Testament quotes from this psalm, calling it "the first," and the Talmud in *b. Ber.* 9b–10a notes that Pss. 1–2 are a single psalm, enclosed by the inclusio "happy" [1.1 and 2.12]). These psalms share some vocabulary, but the differences in their style, tone, and theme outweigh the verbal similarities, suggesting that the medieval tradition, which sees them as separate psalms, is correct. Modern scholars often call it a "royal psalm," because it features a king (see also Pss. 18; 20; 21; 45; 72; 89; 101; 110; 132; 144). Its original context is obscure, and it may refer to a war against Judah or be part of a ritual imagining such a war. Its present location near the beginning of the Psalter, serving as a second introduction (like Ps. 1, it lacks a superscription), calls attention to the royal-Davidic nature of the Psalter and may also hint at a possible eschatological dimension of the Psalter, its hope for the future Davidic king. This is especially likely if this psalm was placed here after the destruction of the Temple in 586 BCE, as is likely. **1–2:** The attack depicted is extreme and hyperbolic. **2:** Since anointing was the major performative ritual to denote kingship (e.g., 1 Sam. 10.1), *His anointed* likely refers to the king. The same term "mashiaḥ" is used in postbiblical literature (but never in the Bible) to refer to the ideal future Davidic king, and is the origin of the term "Messiah." The relationship between God and king is very close; the attack *against the LORD* is equated with that *against His anointed,* suggesting that the (Davidic) king was viewed by some as God's earthly representative. (See also the striking filial language in v. 7 and Ps. 45.) This idea recurs in many depictions of the ideal future Davidic king, called Messiah in postbiblical texts. **3:** Similar animal yoke imagery is found later in rabbinic expressions: "the yoke of commandments," "the yoke of the Torah," and "the yoke of the kingdom of heaven." **4:** The Bible contains various conceptions of where God resides. 1 Kings 8.32 similarly argues that God dwells *in heaven;* for two different conceptions see 1 Kings 8.13 and 27. **6:** *Zion,* a synonym for Jerusalem, is typically depicted as *holy* (e.g., Isa. 52.1; Ps. 20.3); Zion and Davidic kingship are often connected in the Bible. God is here envisaged as present both in heaven (v. 4) and in Jerusalem (see 1 Kings 8.13), perhaps where this mountain and heaven meet. **7:** Adoption language metaphorically expresses the close kinship between God and the king, and is common in the ancient Near East. The *son* language here has played a significant role in medieval Jewish-Christian polemic (e.g., the final comment of Radak on this psalm). The *decree* may reflect 2 Sam. 7.14, where God says to David concerning his heir: "I will be a father to him, and he shall be a son to Me."

10 So now, O kings, be prudent;
accept discipline, you rulers of the earth!
11 Serve the LORD in awe;
[a]tremble with fright,[a]
12 [b]pay homage in good faith,[b]
lest He be angered, and your way be doomed
in the mere flash of His anger.
Happy are all who take refuge in Him.

3 A psalm of David when he fled from his son Absalom.

2 O LORD, my foes are so many!
Many are those who attack me;
3 many say of me,
"There is no deliverance for him through God."
Selah.[c]
4 But You, O LORD, are a shield about me,
my glory, He who holds my head high.
5 I cry aloud to the LORD,
and He answers me from His holy mountain.
Selah.
6 I lie down and sleep and wake again,
for the LORD sustains me.
7 I have no fear of the myriad forces
arrayed against me on every side.

8 Rise, O LORD!
Deliver me, O my God!
For You slap all my enemies in the face;[d]
You break the teeth of the wicked.

a-a Meaning of Heb. uncertain; others "rejoice with trembling."
b-b Meaning of Heb. uncertain.
c A liturgical direction of uncertain meaning. *d Lit. "cheek."*

10–12: In a rhetorical flourish, God is depicted as speaking directly to the foreign monarchs. A similar depiction of the centrality of God and Zion for all nations is also found in Isa. 2.2–4, but is there in an eschatological setting. **11:** Contrast how Israel is told to worship God in Ps. 100.2, "worship the LORD in gladness; / come into His presence with shouts of joy." **12:** As noted, the translation *in good faith* is uncertain. The Heb word "bar" can also mean "son," especially in Aram., and this has sometimes been connected to the divinely adopted son ("ben") in v. 7.

Ps. 3: This may have originally been the first psalm (see introductory n. to Pss. 1 and 2); it is the first of many psalms with a superscription or title mentioning David. **1:** Several psalms have introductions that connect their content to the life of David as depicted in Samuel (e.g., Pss. 18; 51); the superscription here refers to events narrated in 2 Sam. chs 15–19. These historical superscriptions reflect a type of inner-biblical interpretation (see "Inner-biblical Interpretation," pp. 1835–41, and "Midrash," pp. 1879–91) in which individual psalms are connected to the life of David. The Heb and Gk (LXX) texts show significant variation in these superscriptions, indicating that they are a late, secondary element. The phrase *of David* may mean written by David, or in the style of David (cf. a Miltonic Ode); already in early postbiblical tradition, the former was assumed, in support of other traditions that see David as the author of Psalms (see introduction). The word *psalm,* translating Heb "mizmor," is a borrowing from Gk. Both words mean a song sung to the accompaniment of a stringed instrument (see esp. 33.2; 92.4; 144.9). **2–3:** A description of the psalmist's numerous troubles; this is highlighted by the threefold repetition of *many.* **3:** The psalmist dramatizes his call for God's help by quoting his enemy's words, *There is no deliverance for him through God.* He then contradicts his enemy's words in v. 4. *Selah* is most likely a musicological term, of uncertain meaning and etymology, typically appearing at major disjunctures in a psalm. The LXX translates it as "an interlude," while another ancient Gk translation, the early Church father Jerome, and some medieval commentators render it as "always." Radak understands it as "with a raised voice," from the Heb root "s-l-l," "to raise." Some modern scholars view it as an abbreviation, though it is uncertain to what extent abbreviations were used in ancient Israel. *Selah* is found only in the Psalter and in the psalm in Hab. ch 3. **4–7:** The contrast is between the many enemies and the single God, more powerful than the lot of them. **5:** It is unclear exactly how God *answers me from His holy mountain,* whether the psalmist saw or heard some clear sign of God's attention. **6–7:** This confidence motif is central to many psalms that call upon God for help. (See also 6.9–11 n.) **8–9:** These vv. have an odd mixture of tenses and moods not fully conveyed in the English: God is commanded to act, but the defeat of the enemies is depicted in the past. This may reflect the certainty of the psalmist that his petition has been heeded. Such mixing of tenses

9 Deliverance is the LORD's;
Your blessing be upon Your people! *Selah.*

4

[a-]For the leader; with instrumental music.[-a]
A psalm of David.

2 Answer me when I call,
O God, my vindicator!
You freed me from distress;
have mercy on me and hear my prayer.
3 You men, how long will my glory be mocked,
will you love illusions,
have recourse to frauds? *Selah.*
4 Know that the LORD singles out the faithful for Himself;
the LORD hears when I call to Him.
5 So tremble, and sin no more;
ponder it on your bed, and sigh.[b]
6 Offer sacrifices in righteousness
and trust in the LORD.

7 Many say, "O for good days!"
[c-]Bestow Your favor on us,[-c] O LORD.
8 You put joy into my heart
when their grain and wine show increase.
9 Safe and sound, I lie down and sleep,
[d-]for You alone, O LORD, keep me secure.[-d]

5

[a-]For the leader; on *neḥiloth*.[-a] A psalm of David.

2 Give ear to my speech, O LORD;
consider my utterance.
3 Heed the sound of my cry,
my king and God,
for I pray to You.

a-a Meaning of Heb. uncertain. *b Others "be still."*
c-c Lit. "Lift up the light of Your countenance upon us"; cf. Num. 6.25 f.
d-d Or "for You, O LORD, keep me alone and secure."

is frequent at the conclusion of individual petitions. **9:** The psalm concludes, as many others do, by moving from the individual to the community, *upon Your people.*

Ps. 4: Although a petition, the emphasis is more on the psalmist's confidence in God than on his troubles, and it focuses more on others than on the psalmist. Radak, followed by some early modern commentators, connects this psalm to the previous one and understands "them" as those allied with Absalom and his rebellion against David. V. 6, however, *Offer sacrifices in righteousness,* suggests a Temple setting. **1:** The meaning of the two terms translated as *leader* and *instrumental music* is uncertain; it was already lost in antiquity, as reflected in the divergent renditions found in the ancient biblical translations. **2:** The Heb, followed in this translation, reflects an imperative, a past, and two imperatives, suggesting that based on a past experience of salvation, the psalmist, again in straits, wants to be saved again; other ancient translations reflect different tenses. **3–7:** The psalmist's adversaries are addressed; they are called (mere) *men* (v. 3) and *many* (v. 7). **4:** *Faithful* translates "ḥasid." In most psalms "ḥasid" is a generic term for the righteous individual, though in some Second Temple writings, it may refer to a specific group of Jews (see 2 Macc. 14.6, where the Gk "asidaioi" refers to the followers of Judah the Maccabee). **6:** The Heb tolerates both *sacrifices in righteousness* (Ibn Ezra, Radak) and *sacrifices of righteousness* (Rashi). The former may be connected to Isa. 1.10–17, which stresses that sacrifices are not automatically efficacious, while the latter idea may be connected to Ps. 51.19, "True sacrifice to God is a contrite spirit." In either case, the word *righteousness* ("tzedek") recalls God's title in v. 2 as *my vindicator,* lit. "of my righteousness" ("tzidki")—a righteous deity must be offered righteous offerings. **7:** *Bestow Your favor on us* is lit. "lift up for us the light of your face." As in the priestly blessing in Num. 6.25, the striking anthropomorphism of God's shining face refers to divine blessing. **9:** Anxiety causes sleeplessness (6.7–8), while full confidence in God allows for untroubled *sleep,* even in distress, as in 3.6.

Ps. 5: Petitions to God are structured like petitions to humans: The one petitioned is invoked; a request, typically in the imperative, is offered; and motivation for why this request should be heard is provided. Here, God is invoked as *O LORD* (v. 2) with the imperatives *Give ear, consider, Heed,* and *Hear* (vv. 2–4). The psalmist's need in this case is vague; this allows the psalm to be reused in a wide variety of situations. Several reasons are given for why God should heed the petition: God despises evildoers (vv. 5–7), *because of my watchful foes*

4 Hear my voice, O LORD, at daybreak;
at daybreak I plead before You, and wait.

5 For You are not a God who desires wickedness;
evil cannot abide with You;
6 wanton men cannot endure in Your sight.
You detest all evildoers;
7 You doom those who speak lies;
murderous, deceitful men the LORD abhors.

8 But I, through Your abundant love, enter Your house;
I bow down in awe at Your holy temple.
9 O LORD, [a]lead me along Your righteous [path][a]
because of my watchful foes;
make Your way straight before me.
10 For there is no sincerity on their lips;[b]
their heart is [filled with] malice;
their throat is an open grave;
their tongue slippery.
11 Condemn them, O God;
let them fall by their own devices;
cast them out for their many crimes,
for they defy You.
12 But let all who take refuge in You rejoice,
ever jubilant as You shelter them;
and let those who love Your name exult in You.
13 For You surely bless the righteous man, O LORD,
encompassing him with favor like a shield.

6

[c]For the leader; with instrumental music on the *sheminith.*[c] A psalm of David.

2 O LORD, do not punish me in anger,
do not chastise me in fury.

a-a Or "as You are righteous, lead me." *b Lit. "mouth."*
c-c Meaning of Heb. uncertain.

(vv. 9–11), and because rectification of the situation will encourage the already faithful (vv. 12–13). The poetic diction of the psalm is quite standard, often using parallelism (see "Biblical Poetry," pp. 2184–91), as in v. 2: *Give ear* || *consider* and *my speech* || *my utterance.* **3:** The psalmist's view of God is highly personal, as *my king and* (my) *God.* The image of God as king, frequent in the psalms, esp. in Pss. 93–100, here expresses God's responsibility for His subjects and His ability to help them. In the words of Radak: "I am crying out to you just as one cries out to a king." **4:** *Daybreak* may reflect the time of such prayers, or the expected time of divine deliverance (see 46.6; Lam. 3.23). **5–8:** These vv. express the idea that sinners were not welcome at the Jerusalem Temple (see intro. to Ps. 15; the Heb for *abide* in v. 5 is the same word rendered "sojourn" in Ps. 15.1). **6:** The *evildoers* ("poʿalei ʾaven") are often mentioned in Psalms, always in the plural, and may represent a particular group of maleficent individuals. **8:** *But I,* as opposed to the evildoers mentioned in the preceding vv. It is uncertain if this is a description of the individual worshipping in Jerusalem, as in this translation, or if it should be read as a wish, " … may I enter … may I bow." *Love* here translates "ḥesed," a frequent attribute of God in the Bible. "Ḥesed," a common biblical term, describes a relationship of mutuality between individuals or groups, and between God and human beings, especially Israel. It expresses both an attitude and actions devolving from that attitude; English "loyalty" best approximates its sense, which reflects kindness or favor. When used of God toward Israel, it may be related to the covenant, and it expresses God's faithfulness, goodness, and graciousness. **10:** *Heart,* Heb "qerev," better rendered as innards, puns on the following "qever," "grave." **12–13:** As in 3.9, the conclusion moves from the individual to the community. **13:** Since the theme of the psalm is divine protection from enemies, it concludes with the simile of God as *a shield.*

Ps. 6: This psalm has entered the Jewish liturgy as the daily prayer for supplication ("taḥanun"), recited every weekday morning. It is the typical individual petition (see intro. to Ps. 5), opening with a divine invocation (v. 2, *O LORD*), followed by imperatives describing the petitioner's condition and problems (vv. 2–3), and offering a set of motivations for divine intervention: God's "ḥesed" (see 5.8 n.), and the fact that if God kills the petitioner, He will no longer hear his praise (v. 6). It also plays on God's emotions (v. 7). The psalm is tightly structured, in balanced vv. It uses repetition very effectively, as seen in "b-h-l" in vv. 3 *(shake with terror),* 4 *(stricken with terror),* and 11 *(stricken with terror).* The Heb expresses the turn in fortunes through an anagram: God's turning ("shuv" v. 5) is transposed into the enemies becoming frustrated ("bush" v. 11); these are combined at the psalm's conclusion "yashuvu yevoshu," *they will turn back … frustrated.* The

3 Have mercy on me, O LORD, for I languish;
heal me, O LORD, for my bones shake with terror.
4 My whole being is stricken with terror,
while You, LORD—O, how long!
5 O LORD, turn! Rescue me!
Deliver me as befits Your faithfulness.
6 For there is no praise of You among the dead;
in Sheol, who can acclaim You?

7 I am weary with groaning;
every night I drench my bed,
I melt my couch in tears.
8 My eyes are wasted by vexation,
worn out because of all my foes.
9 Away from me, all you evildoers,
for the LORD heeds the sound of my weeping.
10 The LORD heeds my plea,
the LORD accepts my prayer.
11 All my enemies will be frustrated and stricken with terror;
they will turn back in an instant, frustrated.

7

[a-]*Shiggaion* of David,[-a] which he sang to the LORD, concerning Cush, a Benjaminite.

2 O LORD, my God, in You I seek refuge;
deliver me from all my pursuers and save me,
3 lest, like a lion, they tear me apart,
rending in pieces, and no one save me.
4 O LORD, my God, if I have done such things,
if my hands bear the guilt of wrongdoing,
5 if I have dealt evil to my ally—
[b-]I who rescued my foe without reward[-b]—

a-a Meaning of Heb. uncertain.
b-b Meaning of Heb. uncertain; others "or stripped my foe clean."

psalmist is ill (v. 3), scared (v. 4), and is being persecuted by enemies (v. 11). These typical elements in petitions or complaints to God in Psalms allow the psalm to be used on multiple occasions. **1:** The *sheminith* may be a type of musical instrument, perhaps with eight strings (from Heb "shemoneh"). **2–4:** The plea, *O, how long,* found in other psalms as well (e.g., 74.10; 80.5), is part of the Near Eastern prayer tradition; see, for example, a Mesopotamian prayer to the goddess Ishtar, which includes: "How long, O my Lady, will you be angered so that your face is turned away? How long, O my Lady, will you be infuriated so that your spirit is enraged?" (modified translation from *ANET,* p. 385). **2:** This psalm contains no confession of guilt, suggesting that the psalmist believes he has done nothing to deserve such grave punishment. **4–5:** The elliptical *O, how long!* is connected to the following *turn;* the psalmist is saying, "How long will You neglect me, hiding Your face from me?" (see introduction; Deut. 31.18). On God's *faithfulness* ("ḥesed"), see 5.8. **6:** Biblical Israel knew of no afterlife with reward and punishment—everyone, irrespective of behavior or social status, descended to "She'ol," the dark underworld where one was cut off from God's Presence, and lived a quasi-life there. *Among the dead* may also be translated "in the place of death," paralleling "She'ol." **9–11:** The Heb tenses are better reflected by rendering: "Away ... has heard ... has heeded ... will be frustrated." The back-and-forth movement may express the psalmist's religious conviction that God will hear his prayer, and thus he simultaneously expresses hope and certainty. Alternatively, psalms like this may have been recited after the individual's position improved, and he entered the Temple in thanksgiving, reciting his past afflictions.

Ps. 7: This psalm, like the previous one, is a petition of an individual, but differs in structure and tone. Ps. 7, unlike Ps. 6, contains a protestation of innocence (vv. 4–6), emphasizes God's role as a warrior (see v. 7 n.), and concludes with the wisdom idea that evil will befall the one who initiates it (vv. 13–17). **1:** In contrast to other superscriptions that refer to events mentioned in Samuel, the reference to *Cush* is puzzling; no such name occurs in Samuel. Rabbinic interpreters (e.g., Tg., but rejected by Ibn Ezra) took *Cush* as a reference to "Saul, son of Kish." The superscription may refer to a story about David that was not incorporated into Samuel. **4–6:** This short section, concluded by *Selah* (see 3.3 n.), is a protestation of innocence in the form of a self-imprecation. A much longer self-imprecation is found in Job ch 31; in Pss. 17 and 26 the psalmists likewise insist that they are punished unfairly by God. **3:** *Lion*s are found frequently in biblical images. **7:** In the previous psalm, the individual feels that God is unjustly using his *anger* against him; our psalmist wants God to use his *anger* justly against his enemies. The demand to *rise* (Heb "kumah") may recall God's role as warrior, as

6 then let the enemy pursue and overtake me;
let him trample my life to the ground,
and lay my body in the dust. *Selah.*

7 Rise, O LORD, in Your anger;
assert Yourself [a-]against the fury of my foes;[-a]
bestir Yourself on my behalf;
You have ordained judgment.
8 [b-]Let the assembly of peoples gather about You,
with You enthroned above, on high.[-b]
9 The LORD judges the peoples;
vindicate me, O LORD,
for the righteousness and blamelessness that are mine.
10 Let the evil of the wicked come to an end,
but establish the righteous;
he who probes the mind and conscience[c] is God the righteous.
11 [d-]I look to God to shield me;[-d]
the deliverer of the upright.
12 God vindicates the righteous;
God [e-]pronounces doom[-e] each day.
13 [f-]If one does not turn back, but whets his sword,
bends his bow and aims it,
14 then against himself he readies deadly weapons,
and makes his arrows sharp.[-f]
15 See, he hatches evil, conceives mischief,
and gives birth to fraud.
16 He has dug a pit and deepened it,
and will fall into the trap he made.
17 His mischief will recoil upon his own head;
his lawlessness will come down upon his skull.
18 I will praise the LORD for His righteousness,
and sing a hymn to the name of the LORD Most High.

8

[b-]For the leader; on the *gittith.*[-b] A psalm of David.

2 O LORD, our Lord,
How majestic is Your name throughout the earth,
[g-]You who have covered the heavens with Your splendor![-g]

a-a Or "in Your fury against my foes." *b-b Meaning of Heb. uncertain.*
c Lit. "kidneys." *d-d Cf. Ibn Ezra and Kimhi; lit. "My Shield is upon God."*
e-e Others "has indignation."
f-f Meaning of vv. 13–14 uncertain; an alternate rendering, with God as the main subject, is: [13]If one does not turn back, He whets His sword, / bends His bow and aims it; / [14]deadly weapons He prepares for him, / and makes His arrows sharp.
g-g Meaning of Heb. uncertain; or "You whose splendor is celebrated all over the heavens!"

in Num. 10.35, "Advance (or rise: Heb "kumah"), O LORD! / May Your enemies be scattered, / And may Your foes flee before You!" *Bestir Yourself* (Heb "ʿurah") is more literally "awake." Some psalms imagine God as sleeping, as in 44.24, "Rouse Yourself (Heb "ʿurah"); why do You sleep, O Lord? / Awaken, do not reject us forever!" while 121.4 states categorically: "See, the guardian of Israel / neither slumbers nor sleeps!" **9–10:** Through the punishment of the *wicked,* the psalmist is *vindicated.* **11:** As in 5.13, God is a shield, protecting the supplicant from his enemies. **15–17:** A similar notion predominates in wisdom texts, e.g., Prov. 26.27: "He who digs a pit will fall in it, / And whoever rolls a stone, it will roll back on him." **18:** God's *righteousness* here reflects proper recompense of the innocent and punishment of the guilty. A common motif in petitions is that if the plea is heeded, the psalmist will utter praise and thanksgiving to God. *Most High* (Heb "ʿelyon") is an ancient Canaanite divine epithet used for the deities Baal and El; it was taken over by Israel, and used of God.

Ps. 8: This psalm is pure praise, without any request, and like other hymns from the Bible and the ancient Near East expresses the religious moment when the individual stands before the deity and appreciates the greatness and power of the divine, especially as reflected in creation. Like Pss. 19 and 104, its hymnic focus is on creation, a motif that shows God's power over the entire world. Specifically here, the psalmist marvels at the place of honor humans have been accorded in the creation. This psalm is tightly structured, framed by the inclusio (vv. 2, 10): "O LORD, our Lord, / How majestic is Your name throughout the earth." **2:** The parallelism highlights the complete extent of God's power *(name)* and splendor, on *the earth* and in *the heavens.*

3 [a-]From the mouths of infants and sucklings
You have founded strength on account of Your foes,
to put an end to enemy and avenger.[-a]
4 When I behold Your heavens, the work of Your fingers,
the moon and stars that You set in place,
5 what is man that You have been mindful of him,
mortal man that You have taken note of him,
6 that You have made him little less than divine,[b]
and adorned him with glory and majesty;
7 You have made him master over Your handiwork,
laying the world at his feet,
8 sheep and oxen, all of them,
and wild beasts, too;
9 the birds of the heavens, the fish of the sea,
whatever travels the paths of the seas.
10 O LORD, our Lord, how majestic is Your name
throughout the earth!

9

[c-]For the leader; *ʿalmuth labben.*[-c] A psalm of David.

2 I will praise You, LORD, with all my heart;
I will tell all Your wonders.
3 I will rejoice and exult in You,
singing a hymn to Your name, O Most High.

4 When my enemies retreat,
they stumble to their doom at Your presence.
5 For You uphold my right and claim,
enthroned as righteous judge.
6 You blast the nations;
You destroy the wicked;
You blot out their name forever.
7 [a-]The enemy is no more—
ruins everlasting;
You have torn down their cities;
their very names are lost.[-a]

a-a Meaning of Heb. uncertain. *b Or "the angels."*
c-c Meaning of Heb. uncertain; some mss. and ancient versions, ʿal muth labben, *as though "over the death of the son."*

3: Though somewhat obscure, this seems to say that even very young children recognize God's majesty. The *enemy and avenger* likely refer to sea-monsters, whom God subdued while creating the world. Though not explicit in Gen. (yet see Gen. 1.21 n.), the creation motif wherein God subdues the sea, is known from Ugarit and is found throughout the Bible and in rabbinic literature (see 74.12–17; Job 26.12; Isa. 51.9–10 n.). **4:** The finery of God's creation is not just handiwork, but *the work of Your fingers.* As noted by Ibn Ezra and Radak, the sun is lacking; this may be to discourage sun-worship, or because the psalm was recited at night. **6–9:** As in Gen. 1.26–30, humans are the climax of creation (contrast Job 17.17–18 and ch 26). "ʾElohim" is properly translated as *divine;* this explains why people are *adorned ... with glory and majesty,* typically divine qualities. The tradition that "ʾelohim" should be rendered here as angels (LXX, Tg., Radak) is the result of the discomfort of depicting humans as too God-like—a discomfort not shared by this psalmist.

Ps. 9: As v. 2 suggests *(I will praise You, LORD, with all my heart),* this is a psalm of thanksgiving. Ps. 9 does not stand by itself; rather Pss. 9–10 were originally a single psalm. The LXX treats them as a single psalm. Ps. 10 is the only psalm between Pss. 3 and 32 lacking a superscription, a sign that it is the second half of Ps. 9. Finally, the beginning and ending of an acrostic is preserved in the combined Pss. 9–10 (the first two letters are found in 9.2, 4, while the last two are found in 10.15, 17; certain elements of the original acrostic were lost during transmission. More complete acrostics occur in Pss. 25; 34; 37; 111; 112; 119; 145; and Lam. chs 1–4). **1:** This superscription is especially difficult, and many medieval commentators struggled to understand the possible historical context of "over the death of the son," if that is the correct translation (see translators' note). **2–3:** Each of the four lines opens with "alef," the first letter of the Heb alphabet, anchoring the acrostic.

3: On *Most High,* see 7.18 n. **4–7:** The finality of the vanquishing of the enemy *(forever, no more, everlasting, are lost)* is hyperbolic, since the enemies reappear in vv. 20–21. **5:** The main image is God *enthroned* as king; like the ancient Israelite king, He is judge and warrior, but He carries out these roles with greater power and equity than human monarchs. **8–9:** Parts of these vv., with slight variants, are found elsewhere (v. 8: Pss. 29.10; 102.13; Lam. 5.19; v. 9: Pss. 96.13; 98.9); such repetitions may offer hints about the composition of the psalms, suggesting that authors copied from other compositions or used traditional phrases.

8 But the LORD abides forever;
He has set up His throne for judgment;
9 it is He who judges the world with righteousness,
rules the peoples with equity.
10 The LORD is a haven for the oppressed,
a haven in times of trouble.
11 Those who know Your name trust You,
for You do not abandon those who turn to You, O LORD.
12 Sing a hymn to the LORD, [a-]who reigns in Zion;[-a]
declare His deeds among the peoples.
13 [b-]For He does not ignore the cry of the afflicted;
He who requites bloodshed is mindful of them.[-b]
14 Have mercy on me, O LORD;
see my affliction at the hands of my foes,
You who lift me from the gates of death,
15 so that in the gates of [c-]Fair Zion[-c]
I might tell all Your praise,
I might exult in Your deliverance.
16 The nations sink in the pit they have made;
their own foot is caught in the net they have hidden.
17 The LORD has made Himself known:
He works judgment;
the wicked man is snared by his own devices.
Higgaion.[d] *Selah.*
18 Let the wicked be[e] in Sheol,
all the nations who ignore God!
19 Not always shall the needy be ignored,
nor the hope of the afflicted forever lost.
20 Rise, O LORD!
Let not men have power;
let the nations be judged in Your presence.
21 [f-]Strike fear into them,[-f] O LORD;
let the nations know they are only men. *Selah.*

10

Why, O LORD, do You stand aloof,
heedless in times of trouble?
2 The wicked in his arrogance hounds the lowly—
[g-]may they be caught in the schemes they devise![-g]
3 [f-]The wicked crows about his unbridled lusts;
the grasping man reviles and scorns the LORD.
4 The wicked, arrogant as he is,
in all his scheming [thinks],[-f]

a-a Or "O You who dwell in Zion."
b-b Order of Heb clauses inverted for clarity. *c-c Lit. "the Daughter of Zion."*
d Meaning of Heb. uncertain. *e Others "return to."*
f-f Meaning of Heb. uncertain.
g-g Or "they (i.e., the lowly) are caught by the schemes they devised."

8: *Abides* is better rendered "is enthroned," continuing the main theme of God's kingship. **10–13:** As in many other places in the Bible, Psalms shows great concern for *the oppressed, afflicted,* and poor. **12–15:** The call to others to praise God and the explicit mention of *the gates of Fair Zion* suggest that psalms such as this were recited publicly, though not always at the Temple. **12:** God reigns in Zion, enthroned in the Temple (see Exod. 25.21–22). **14:** Images such as *lift me from the gates of death* or "You brought me up from Sheol" (30.4) are always metaphorical in the Bible, which by and large lacks a concept of personal resurrection; similar phrases are used in Akkadian literature to express rescue from severe illness or danger. **16:** See 7.15–17. **17:** *Higgaion* is probably a musical notation, related to the Heb root "h-g-h" meaning to utter (quietly) or recite. **18:** A way of saying "may *the wicked* die" (see 6.6 n.). **19–21:** Beginning with an acknowledgment that God is *not always* or immediately fair in doling out retribution, the psalmist calls upon God to *rise,* namely to immediately show Himself as a warrior (see 7.7 n. and Ps. 13). The psalmist's claim that God should do this for His own sake, for the sake of His reputation (rather than for the psalmist or for Israel), is a major theme of Ezek. (e.g., 5.13; 20.9). **20:** The conception of humanity here is in stark contrast to the previous psalm (see vv. 6–9), a striking reminder of the number of different religious moods encompassed in the Psalter.

Ps. 10: A continuation of the previous psalm (see Ps. 9 n.). The calls to God to act (vv. 1, 12, 15) continue 9.20–21. The repeated 9.20 and 10.12 beginning, *Rise, O LORD!,* further suggests the unity of these two psalms. **1:** The psalmist continues, wanting to know why God hides His face (see v. 11 and 6.4–5 n.). **2:** Continuing a previous theme, the persecution of *the lowly* (see also vv. 9, 10, 14, 18). **3–5:** These vv. are unusually obscure. The acrostic of Pss. 9–10 is

“He does not call to account;
*a-*God does not care.”*-a*
5 His ways prosper at all times;
Your judgments are far beyond him;
he snorts at all his foes.
6 He thinks, “I shall not be shaken,
through all time never be in trouble.”
7 His mouth is full of oaths, deceit, and fraud;
mischief and evil are under his tongue.
8 He lurks in outlying places;
from a covert he slays the innocent;
his eyes spy out the hapless.
9 He waits in a covert like a lion in his lair;
waits to seize the lowly;
he seizes the lowly as he pulls his net shut;
10 he stoops, he crouches,
*b-*and the hapless fall prey to his might.*-b*
11 He thinks, “God is not mindful,
He hides His face, He never looks.”
12 Rise, O Lord!
*c-*Strike at him,*-c* O God!
Do not forget the lowly.
13 Why should the wicked man scorn God,
thinking You do not call to account?
14 You do look!
You take note of mischief and vexation!
*b-*To requite is in Your power.*-b*
To You the hapless can entrust himself;
You have ever been the orphan’s help.
15 O break the power of the wicked and evil man,
so that when You *d-*look for*-d* his wickedness
You will find it no more.

16 The Lord is king for ever and ever;
the nations will perish from His land.
17 You will listen to the entreaty of the lowly, O Lord,
You will make their hearts firm;
You will incline Your ear
18 to champion the orphan and the downtrodden,
*b-*that men who are of the earth tyrannize
no more.*-b*

a-a Lit. “There is no God.”
b-b Meaning of Heb. uncertain.
c-c Lit. “Lift Your hand.”
d-d A play on darash, *which in vv. 4 and 13 means “to call to account.”*

not apparent here, suggesting that the vv. are corrupt. **4:** The translation of Heb “There is no God” as *God does not care* is based on the assumption that atheism did not exist in antiquity (see also 14.1). People could, however, believe in a deity who created the world, but then absented himself from running it. **7:** Here and elsewhere in Psalms there is tremendous concern for what is in the mouth of the wicked person. Some modern scholars therefore conjecture that the evildoers of the Psalms are evil magicians, casting spells upon the hapless. Alternatively, these are the psalmist’s adversaries who speak against him publicly or whose positions are antithetical to his. **8–9:** The emphasis is on *covert* places; the wicked are not seen in their activities and cannot be punished by human courts, so the psalmist needs to rely on God to find them out (Radak to v. 1). **11–12:** The Heb root “sh-kḥ,” “to forget, ignore, pay no heed to,” joins these two vv. together: the wicked believes that God has forgotten (translated *God is not mindful*), but the psalmist tells God *“Do not forget the lowly,”* attend to the lowly. **13-15:** As elsewhere, the psalmist invokes God’s nature and power in order to convince Him to act. **16:** The image of God as king (and thus judge and warrior) that stands behind these two psalms is made explicit here. *The Lord is king for ever and ever* recalls the earlier (9.6), “You blot out their name forever.” **17:** The Heb ends with a past tense, “you have heeded,” expressing a pattern of confidence seen at the conclusion of many psalms (see 3.6–7 n.); the translation *You will listen,* which sees the tense as less significant, follows Radak.

11 For the leader. Of David.

In the LORD I take refuge;
how can you say to me,
"Take to [a-]the hills like a bird![-a]
2 For see, the wicked bend the bow,
they set their arrow on the string
to shoot from the shadows at the upright.
3 [b-]When the foundations are destroyed,
what can the righteous man do?"[-b]

4 The LORD is in His holy palace;
the LORD—His throne is in heaven;
His eyes behold, His gaze searches mankind.
5 The LORD seeks out the righteous man,
but loathes the wicked one who loves injustice.
6 He will rain down upon the wicked blazing coals and sulfur;
a scorching wind shall be [c-]their lot.[-c]
7 For the LORD is righteous;
He loves righteous deeds;
the upright shall behold His face.

12 For the leader; on the *sheminith.* A psalm of David.

2 Help, O LORD!
For the faithful are no more;
the loyal have vanished from among men.
3 Men speak lies to one another;
their speech is smooth;
they talk with duplicity.
4 May the LORD cut off all flattering lips,
every tongue that speaks arrogance.
5 They say, "By our tongues we shall prevail;
with lips such as ours, who can be our master?"

a-a Meaning of Heb. uncertain; lit. "your hill, bird!"
b-b Or "For the foundations are destroyed; what has the Righteous One done?" Or "If the foundations are destroyed, what has the righteous man accomplished?"
c-c Lit. "the portion of their cup."

Ps. 11: Though this psalm contains standard motifs of the Psalter, it is oddly structured and several of its phrases are difficult to grasp. It invokes divine punishment (vv. 4–7), but God is referred to in the third person, not the second person that typifies other petitions. Perhaps the psalmist is speaking from the Temple to his friends, rejecting their advice that he flee from the persecution of the evildoers (see comments below). **1–3:** Though *taking refuge* in God is frequently used metaphorically in the Psalms, it is best construed as literal here, as in 61.5, "O that I might dwell in Your tent forever, / take refuge under Your protecting wings." The psalmist is thus seeking refuge at the Temple (see 1 Kings 1.50 n.) and rejecting his friends' advice to flee. **4–5:** Many medieval and modern commentators understand *holy palace* and *heaven* as synonymous, referring to God's heavenly temple. More likely, the point of the psalmist is that (paradoxically) God is located both in the Jerusalem Temple *(His holy palace),* where He can offer protection, and *in heaven,* from where *His eyes behold* and *seek out* and punish evildoers. **6:** These are extreme supernatural punishments, like that of Sodom (Gen. 19.24). **7:** *The LORD is righteous* in the sense of being fair in retribution: this is emphasized through the word-repetition *For the LORD is righteous; / He loves righteous deeds. Behold His face:* This may refer to being in God's Presence or to seeing a manifestation of God at the Temple, yet another hint that this psalmist is praying at the Temple, and wants to remain there. Other biblical texts suggest that the worshipper could *behold* the *face* of God at a temple (see Exod. 23.17 n.).

Ps. 12: This psalm has an unusual structure: after the superscription (v. 1) it contains a standard petition (vv. 2–5), but this is followed by the divine response (v. 6) and the psalmist's answer (vv. 7–9). It is difficult to understand how this psalm was used liturgically—perhaps since the divine response is positive, a supplicant might recite it as a way of "assuring" a positive hearing. The main theme has to do with words—the false and arrogant words of the wicked against the righteous, in contrast with God's pure words, likened to ultra-refined *silver.* Unusually, the focus is on an undefined group who needs help, rather than on the individual psalmist. **2:** *Faithful* translates "ḥasid"; see 4.4 n. This v. compactly contains the three crucial parts of the petition: the invocation *(O LORD),* the plea in the imperative *(Help),* and the motivation *(for the faithful . . .).* **3–5:** The emphasis here is only on the danger of the word, which may reflect slander, a false oath, or magic (see 10.7 n.); no physical harm is described. *Smooth* and *flattering* (vv. 3-4) are the same word in Heb: *ḥalaqot,* "slippery, slick."

6 "Because of the groans of the plundered poor and needy,
I will now act," says the LORD.
[a-]"I will give help," He affirms to him.[-a]
7 The words of the LORD are pure words,
silver purged in an earthen crucible,
refined sevenfold.
8 You, O LORD, will keep them,
guarding each [a-]from this age[-a] evermore.
9 On every side the wicked roam
[a-]when baseness is exalted among men.[-a]

13

For the leader. A psalm of David.

2 How long, O LORD; will You ignore me forever?
How long will You hide Your face from me?
3 How long will I have cares on my mind,
grief in my heart all day?
How long will my enemy have the upper hand?
4 Look at me, answer me, O LORD, my God!
Restore the luster to my eyes,
lest I sleep the sleep of death;
5 lest my enemy say, "I have overcome him,"
my foes exult when I totter.
6 But I trust in Your faithfulness,
my heart will exult in Your deliverance.
I will sing to the LORD,
for He has been good to me.

14

[b]For the leader. Of David.

The benighted man thinks,
[c-]"God does not care."[-c]

a-a Meaning of Heb. uncertain. *b Cf. Ps. 53.* *c-c Lit. "There is no God"; cf. Ps. 10.4.*

6: The divine speech reflects response to the underclasses (see 9.10–13 n.). **7:** *Sevenfold* is a typologically large number (see Ibn Ezra and Radak). **8–9:** Unfortunately, the psalm's conclusion is likely corrupt and defies precise translation, though the general sense of God preserving the faithful from the evildoers is clear.

Ps. 13: In this poignant individual petition, the petitioner feels abandoned, as in the more famous 22.2: "My God, my God, / why have You abandoned me?" The typical elements for the petition are all found: the invocation, *O LORD* (v. 2), the petition, which here takes up most of the psalm (vv. 2–4a), and a short, double motivation, *lest I sleep the sleep of death; / lest my enemy* ... (vv. 4b–5). A typical expression of divine confidence concludes the psalm (v. 6). **2–3:** The four-fold repetition of *How long* forms a refrain, emphasizing the psalmist's long-standing sense of abandonment. The paradoxical *How long ... will You ignore* (lit. "forget") *me forever?* heightens the petitioner's pain. On God hiding His face, see 6.4–5 n. In Torah and prophetic contexts, God's hidden face, his refusal to attend to humans, is typically a result of punishment; in many psalms, including this one, the psalmist suggests that this hiddenness is instead the result of divine neglect. **4:** If God *looks,* he *answers,* and is no longer hiding his face (see Ibn Ezra and Radak). *Restore the luster to my eyes,* restore my strength, vigor (see 1 Sam. 14.27). *The sleep of death* represents the ultimate and permanent separation between God and humans, for in death one cannot praise God (Ps. 6.6). **5:** If the psalmist dies, the enemies will think that they are more powerful than God. Implicit in this psalm, as in many others, is the argument that God cares about his reputation in the world. **6:** As in other petitions, the tenses are confusing (see 3.8–9 n.; 6.9–11 n.), and a more literal rendering would be: "But I trust(ed) in your faithfulness ('ḥesed,' see 5.8 n.), / may my heart exult in Your deliverance. / May I sing to the LORD / because He has been good to me."

Ps. 14: Because this psalm does not address God but speaks about Him in the third person, some modern scholars view it as a psalm of instruction. Ps. 53, from the Elohistic Psalter (see intro., p. 1266) is a variant of this psalm. The variations both small (e.g., 14.3 *All have turned bad* ["hkl sr"]; 53.4 "Everyone is dross" ["klw sg"]) and large (e.g., 14.5b–6, *for God is present in the circle of the righteous. / You may set at naught the counsel of the lowly, / but the LORD is his refuge;* 53.6, "There they will be seized with fright /—never was there such a fright—/ for God has scattered the bones of your besiegers; / you have put them to shame, / for God has rejected them"), offer important data about the transmission of psalms in antiquity. The medieval commentators, influenced by the Davidic superscriptions to both psalms, viewed both as Davidic compositions. Rashi, for example, viewed Ps. 14 as David's words concerning the destruction of the First Temple (586 BCE), while Ps. 53, which is so similar, is about the destruction of the Second Temple (70 CE). Radak much more prosaically

Man's deeds are corrupt and loathsome;
no one does good.
2 The LORD looks down from heaven on mankind
to find a man of understanding,
a man mindful of God.
3 All have turned bad,
altogether foul;
there is none who does good,
not even one.
4 Are they so witless, all those evildoers,
who devour my people as they devour food,
and do not invoke the LORD?
5 There they will be seized with fright,
for God is present in the circle of the righteous.
6 You may set at naught the counsel of the lowly,
but the LORD is his refuge.

7 O that the deliverance of Israel might come from Zion!
When the LORD restores the fortunes of His people,
Jacob will exult, Israel will rejoice.

15

A psalm of David.

LORD, who may sojourn in Your tent,
who may dwell on Your holy mountain?
2 He who lives without blame,
who does what is right,
and in his heart acknowledges the truth;
3 [a]whose tongue is not given to evil;[a]
who has never done harm to his fellow,

a-a Meaning of Heb. uncertain; or "who has no slander upon his tongue."

suggests in his intro. to Ps. 53: "and now he [David] repeated himself here in slightly different words." **1:** Heb "naval," *benighted,* is a very strong term that can carry moral overtones; see esp. 2 Sam. 13.13, in relation to Amnon's rape of his half-sister Tamar. On *God does not care,* see 10.4. The claim of this *benighted* individual would invalidate two of the basic assumptions of Psalms: the ability of God to hear prayers, and the ability of God to punish the human wrongs that various psalmists lament. **2:** On God in *heaven,* see 2.6 n. Being *mindful of God* ("doresh 'et 'elohim") may also be understood as praying to God (see esp. Ps. 77.3); note the prayer language in v. 4, *invoke the LORD.* **6:** The wicked are spoken to in the second person *(You),* rather than in the third person as earlier in the psalm (e.g., v. 5 *they*). Such changes in person are frequent in biblical poetry (e.g., Isa. 1.2–9). **7:** Many modern scholars see this final v. as secondary, since it does not fit the theme or tone of the psalm, and generalizes to all Israel. Many other individual petitions conclude with general vv. about the community (e.g., 3.9). (In antiquity, it was easiest to make additions at the end of a composition.) The phrase *restores the fortunes* is ambiguous; it may refer to personal restoration (see esp. Job 42.10), or more specifically to the return from the Babylonian exile (see esp. Ps. 126.4). The latter sense explains why many medieval commentators (e.g., Rashi, Radak) view the psalm as a Davidic prophecy concerning the Babylonian exile.

Ps. 15: Perhaps like the previous psalm, this may be considered a psalm of instruction, teaching the listener to become an individual who *shall never be shaken* (v. 5). In Jewish ritual, the psalm is often used as a eulogy, expressing the ideal human qualities that assure the deceased a place in the afterlife (see Radak to v. 5: "Even at his death he *shall never be shaken,* since his soul will rest in the place of glory"); this is, however, a postbiblical notion. Many modern scholars take v. 1 literally, and suggest that the psalm functioned as an entrance liturgy for the Temple, where *who may sojourn in Your tent, / who may dwell on Your holy mountain?* is the beginning of a dialogue between the priest and the worshipper who wishes to enter the Temple precincts, and vv. 2–5 are a type of liturgical password recited by the worshipper. Such liturgies are suggested by Egyptian and Mesopotamian texts, and may also stand behind Ps. 24.3–4: "Who may ascend the mountain of the LORD? / Who may stand in His holy place?—/ He who has clean hands and a pure heart, / who has not taken a false oath by My life or sworn deceitfully." The psalm, like much prophetic literature, emphasizes moral, rather than cultic, characteristics. As in the Decalogue and later medieval lists of precepts, these are listed in groupings of positive and negative qualities. The qualities listed in this psalm are included among epitomes of the commandments (e.g., Isa. 33.14–16; Mic. 6.8) listed in *b. Mak.* 24a. **1:** *Tent* may refer to a temple or sanctuary (see 1 Kings 2.28). **2:** The list begins with very general positive qualities *(He who lives without blame, who does what is right),* followed by a more specific positive quality *(and in his heart acknowledges the truth),* which is to be connected to the following v. **3–4:** Three qualities, all expressed as negatives, balanced by

or borne reproach for [his acts toward]
his neighbor;
4 for whom a contemptible man is abhorrent,
but who honors those who fear the LORD;
who stands by his oath even to his hurt;
5 who has never lent money at interest,
or accepted a bribe against the innocent.
The man who acts thus shall never be shaken.

16 A *michtam*[a] of David.

Protect me, O God, for I seek refuge in You.
2 I say to the LORD,
"You are my Lord, [b]my benefactor;
there is none above You."[-b]
3 [c]As to the holy and mighty ones that are in the land,
my whole desire concerning them is that
4 those who espouse another [god]
may have many sorrows![-c]
I will have no part of their bloody libations;
their names will not pass my lips.
5 The LORD is my allotted share and portion;[d]
You control my fate.
6 Delightful country has fallen to my lot;
lovely indeed is my estate.
7 I bless the LORD who has guided me;
my conscience[e] admonishes me at night.
8 I am ever mindful of the LORD's presence;
He is at my right hand; I shall never be shaken.
9 So my heart rejoices,
my whole being exults,
and my body rests secure.
10 For You will not abandon me to Sheol,
or let Your faithful one see the Pit.
11 You will teach me the path of life.
In Your presence is perfect joy;
delights are ever in Your right hand.

a Meaning of Heb. uncertain. *b-b Others "I have no good but in You."*
c-c Meaning of Heb. uncertain; "holy and mighty ones" taken as epithets for divine beings; cf. qedoshim *in Ps. 89.6, 8, and* 'addirim *in 1 Sam. 4.8.*
d Lit. "cup." *e Lit. "kidneys."*

three positive qualities. **5:** Two negative qualities conclude the list. To *be shaken* or to totter is the opposite of the ideal of remaining firm. The person whose conduct is moral will sojourn in God's Presence, under His protection, always.

Ps. 16: Though this does not share much vocabulary with Ps. 15, it may have been placed here as its thematic sequel, suggesting a petition for God's protection by someone who expects, even deserves, to be in God's Presence. The psalmist is entirely loyal to God and utterly opposed to those who follow other gods. He delights in having God as his portion and is confident that God will protect him. **1:** The obscure term *michtam* is found only here and in a cluster of Psalms (56–60); the LXX translates it as "a stele or pillar inscription." **2:** Alternately, this may be understood as the individual praying citing his earlier prayer, *"I have said to the LORD ..."* **3–4:** These are among the most obscure vv. in the Psalter. **5–6:** With the exception of *portion* (lit. "cup"), it is striking and unusual that all the nouns used of God refer to the land and land allocation *(allotted share and portion, Delightful country, my estate).* A similar idea, that God is the portion of the deceased, is found in the "'el male' raḥamim" prayer for the dead. The reversal, that Israel is God's portion or estate, is in Deut. 32.9. **7–11:** The conclusion of the psalm is unified through references to body parts. The psalmist speaks of his kidneys (the seat of his *conscience*), *right hand, heart,* and *body* (lit. "flesh"; *my whole being,* "kevodi," might also be a play on "kevedi," my liver); this is matched (v. 11) by God's face (translated here as *presence)* and *right hand.* **8:** The phrase *I am ever mindful of the LORD's presence* was frequently used for meditation within the kabbalistic tradition and is often inscribed on the Ark or at the front of the synagogue, reminding the congregation that they are standing before God. *At my right hand,* protecting me, as in Ps. 121.5. *Never be shaken,* see 15.5. **10:** On *Sheol,* see 6.6 n.; on *faithful* ("ḥasid"), see 4.4 n. **11:** The first word allows for both the translation *You will teach me,* followed here (so Rashi), as well as "May you teach me," as a prayer or request (so Radak). God's right hand symbolizes his power, as in 118.16, "The right hand of the LORD is exalted! / The right hand of the LORD is triumphant!" (see Exod. 15.6). As elsewhere in the Bible (see esp. Exod. 24.10–11), God is depicted anthropomorphically.

17

A prayer of David.

Hear, O LORD, what is just;
heed my cry, give ear to my prayer,
uttered without guile.
2 My vindication will come from You;
Your eyes will behold what is right.
3 You have visited me at night, probed my mind,
You have tested me and found nothing amiss;
[a]I determined that my mouth should not
transgress.
4 As for man's dealings,
in accord with the command of Your lips,[-a]
I have kept in view the fate[b] of the lawless.
5 My feet have held to Your paths;
my legs have not given way.

6 I call on You;
You will answer me, God;
turn Your ear to me,
hear what I say.
7 Display Your faithfulness in wondrous deeds,
You who deliver with Your right hand
those who seek refuge from assailants.
8 Guard me like the apple of Your eye;
hide me in the shadow of Your wings
9 from the wicked who despoil me,
[c]my mortal enemies who[-c] encircle me.
10 [a]Their hearts are closed to pity;[-a]
they mouth arrogance;
11 now they hem in our feet on every side;
they set their eyes roaming over the land.
12 He is like a lion eager for prey,
a king of beasts lying in wait.

13 Rise, O LORD! Go forth to meet him.
Bring him down;
rescue me from the wicked with Your sword,
14 [a]from men, O LORD, with Your hand,
from men whose share in life is fleeting.
But as to Your treasured ones,
fill their bellies.[-a]
Their sons too shall be satisfied,
and have something to leave over for their
young.

a-a Meaning of Heb. uncertain. *b Cf. Prov. 1.19; lit. "paths."*
c-c Or "from my enemies who avidly."

Ps. 17: This individual petition, like Ps. 7, is also characterized by a protestation of innocence (see esp. 7.4–6). The word "tzedek," *just,* occurs in the first and last v., framing the psalm and its theme that a just God may not let the just suffer. **1:** *Prayer* ("tefilah") is the most general, all-encompassing word for a prayer (see 72.20), though etymologically it refers to intercessory prayer. The poetry of the v. is very striking: after demanding three times, through typical biblical poetic synonyms, that God hear, the pattern is broken by introducing the next sub-theme of the petitioner's innocence: *uttered without guile.* **2–5:** The protestation of innocence. **2:** The psalmist's acknowledgment of God's role as judge is really a demand that the psalmist be adjudicated fairly. **6–12:** The second section of the psalm is introduced by another call for divine justice; this section emphasizes the enemies and their evil activities. **7:** On God's faithfulness ("ḥesed"), see 5.8 n. **8:** *The apple of Your eye* is the pupil. The second half of the v. uses a stereotypical image of God as a protective bird (36.8; 57.2; 63.8). **11:** The psalmist suddenly speaks in the plural *(our feet);* this and similar cases have led some scholars to suggest that the "I" of the individual petitions may be the king or some other significant individual who speaks on behalf of the entire community. **12:** Lions roamed the countryside of ancient Israel, and are mentioned frequently in the Bible. They were symbols of great power; this is why a standard scene of the Assyrian royal reliefs depicts the king killing a lion. Compare David's statement in 1 Sam. 17.34–35. **13–16:** This final section is also introduced by a set of imperatives. **13:** *Rise* may have a military sense (see Ibn Ezra, "to show your strength," and 7.7 n.), carefully playing against the enemies who are brought *down,* or it may refer to the judge standing during the verdict.

15 Then I, justified, will behold Your face;
awake, I am filled with the vision of You.

18

[a]For the leader. Of David, the servant of the LORD, who addressed the words of this song to the LORD after the LORD had saved him from the hands of all his enemies and from the clutches of Saul.

2 He said:
[b-]I adore you, O LORD, my strength,[-b]
3 O LORD, my crag, my fortress, my rescuer,
my God, my rock in whom I seek refuge,
my shield, my [c-]mighty champion,[-c] my haven.
4 [d-]All praise! I called on the LORD[-d]
and was delivered from my enemies.
5 Ropes[e] of Death encompassed me;
torrents of Belial[f] terrified me;
6 ropes of Sheol encircled me;
snares of Death confronted me.
7 In my distress I called on the LORD,
cried out to my God;
in His temple He heard my voice;
my cry to Him reached His ears.
8 Then the earth rocked and quaked;
the foundations of the mountains shook,
rocked by His indignation;
9 smoke went up from His nostrils,
from His mouth came devouring fire;
live coals blazed forth from Him.

a This poem occurs again at 2 Sam. 22, with a number of variations, some of which are cited in the following notes. *b-b Not in 2 Sam. 22.2.*
c-c Lit. "horn of rescue." *d-d Construction of Heb. uncertain.*
e 2 Sam. 22.5, "breakers." *f I.e., the netherworld, like "Death" and "Sheol."*

15: This v. is better taken as expressing a wish or desire ("may I behold ... ; may I be filled ... "), perhaps a wish to see God at the Temple (see 11.7 n.), or even expressing a type of mystical yearning to see God, as in the vision in Ezek. ch 1. Many medieval interpreters (e.g., Rashi, Radak) understand this as a reference to seeing God in heaven after death, but as noted (see 6.6 n.), the conception of a heavenly afterworld is absent from the Bible.

Ps. 18: Linguistic and stylistic evidence suggest that this may be one of the older psalms in the Psalter. It is also one of the longest psalms, and its flow is not entirely clear. It is nearly identical to 2 Sam. ch 22, which, based on linguistic evidence, is older than the psalm, though it is unclear if Ps. 18 was copied from 2 Sam. ch 22, or if they were both copied from a common source. As in Ps. 14, which is parallel to Ps. 53, the many types of differences are illustrative of the process of textual transmission. A major difference is the extra v. found in the psalm but not in Samuel (v. 2), which frames that version in a different fashion. Sometimes synonyms or near synonyms are used (e.g., Ps. 18.5, *Ropes of Death;* 2 Sam. 22.5, "breakers of Death"); a singular in place of a plural (e.g., *lightning* in v. 15 is singular in 2 Sam. ch 22 ["brk"] and plural in Ps. 18 ["brkym"]); word order may vary (e.g., Ps. 18.50, *among the nations, LORD;* 2 Sam. 22.50, "LORD, among the nations"); and graphically similar letters are confused (e.g., Ps. 18.11, "vyd'," *gliding,* vs. 2 Sam. 22.11, "vyr'," "He was seen"). Some medieval commentators understood the variants in Ps. 18 as reflecting David's divinely inspired reworking of his earlier composition for inclusion in the Psalter (see esp. I. Abravanel to 2 Sam. ch 22), while others paid less attention to the variants, believing that they reflect the same meaning (Radak at Ps. 18.1). **1:** David's troubles are described in 1 Sam. ch 18–2 Sam. ch 20. As elsewhere in the Psalter, this superscription is secondary, reflecting an attempt to understand the psalms in the context of David's biography (see 3.1 n.); the superscription here, however, is unique in its reference to a broad set of events, rather than to one particular event—this long and general psalm has been assigned to a long period of general troubles. *The servant of the LORD* is lacking in the parallel in Samuel; for similar phrases concerning David, see, e.g., 2 Sam. 7.8; 1 Kings 8.66; Jer. 33.26; Pss. 4; 21; 89. Its use in the superscription likely reflects the notion that David was very close to God. **2:** Lacking in 2 Sam. ch 22. **3:** Slightly shorter than the parallel in Samuel, a list of divine attributes connected to God's strength, highlighting the theme of the psalm, God the warrior. The Samuel parallel is the longest such list of divine qualities in the Bible. **5–7:** Highly mythological underworld imagery is used to express the psalmist's former dire straits. Given that God descends (v. 10), the psalmist's *cry* is likely ascending to God's heavenly *temple* (see Isa. 6.1–4). As elsewhere, death imagery refers to the psalmist's sense of a near-death experience (see 9.14 n.). **8–16:** A description of a divine theophany. These descriptions often emphasize God as a thunderstorm deity, probably imitating descriptions of the Canaanite deity, Baal.

10 He bent the sky and came down,
thick cloud beneath His feet.
11 He mounted a cherub and flew,
gliding on the wings of the wind.
12 He made darkness His screen;
dark thunderheads, dense clouds of the sky
were His pavilion round about Him.
13 Out of the brilliance before Him,
hail and fiery coals [a]pierced His clouds.[a]
14 Then the LORD thundered from heaven,
the Most High gave forth His voice—
[b]hail and fiery coals.[b]
15 He let fly His shafts and scattered them;
He discharged lightning and routed them.
16 The ocean bed was exposed;
the foundations of the world were laid bare
by Your mighty roaring, O LORD,
at the blast of the breath of Your nostrils.
17 He reached down from on high, He took me;
He drew me out of the mighty waters;
18 He saved me from my fierce enemy,
from foes too strong for me.
19 They confronted me on the day of my calamity,
but the LORD was my support.
20 He brought me out to freedom;
He rescued me because He was pleased with me.

21 The LORD rewarded me according to my merit;
He requited the cleanness of my hands;
22 for I have kept to the ways of the LORD,
and have not been guilty before my God;
23 for I am mindful of all His rules;
I have not disregarded His laws.
24 I have been blameless toward Him,
and have guarded myself against sinning;
25 and the LORD has requited me according to my merit,
the cleanness of my hands in His sight.

26 With the loyal, You deal loyally;
with the blameless man, blamelessly.
27 With the pure, You act purely,
and with the perverse, You are wily.
28 It is You who deliver lowly folk,
but haughty eyes You humble.
29 It is You who light my lamp;
the LORD, my God, lights up my darkness.

10: *He bent the sky:* Cf. 144.5; Isa. 63.19. **11:** *A cherub* is a winged composite figure, combining various human and animal elements. God is enthroned on cherubs in 80.2 and 99.1. **14:** *Hail and fiery coals,* absent in 2 Sam., may reflect the hail plague (Exod. 9.23–24; Ps. 105.32). **15:** *His shafts* represent both arrows thrust against the enemies, as well as *lightning* mentioned later in the v. **16:** The description of the theophany in Hab. ch 3 likewise emphasizes the fear of the primordial waters. **17–20:** A single powerful deity saves a single deserving individual against many enemies because of that person's righteousness. This act of deliverance takes on cosmic proportions. **18:** Mighty waters are associated with chaos that was vanquished by God in some biblical creation stories (see 8.3 n.). Theophany imagery blends with creation imagery. **21–25:** Vv. 21 and 25 are almost identical, insisting on a clear measure-for-measure retribution, and framing the intervening protestation of innocence. As in Ps. 15, no cultic activities are mentioned. **26–31:** These vv. show particular affinity to wisdom texts; see esp. v. 31 and Prov. 30.5, "Every word of God is pure, / A shield to those who take refuge in Him." **26–27:** God works in a fair, measure-for-measure manner. **28:** The psalmist steps beyond himself, using the plural. **29:** The v. partakes in the general metaphor of light as good, darkness as bad. Elsewhere, the Bible associates light with the righteous and darkness with evil (e.g., Job 18.5–6; 21.17).

a-a *2 Sam. 22.13, "blazed."* *b-b* *Not in 2 Sam. 22.14.*

30 With You, I can rush a barrier;[a]
with my God I can scale a wall;
31 the way of God is perfect;
the word of the LORD is pure;
He is a shield to all who seek refuge in Him.
32 Truly, who is a god except the LORD,
who is a rock but our God?—
33 the God who girded me with might,
who made my way perfect;
34 who made my legs like a deer's,
and let me stand firm on the[b] heights;
35 who trained my hands for battle;
my arms can bend a bow of bronze.
36 You have given me the shield of Your protection;
Your right hand has sustained me,
Your care[c] has made me great.
37 You have let me stride on freely;
my feet have not slipped.
38 I pursued my enemies and overtook them;
I did not turn back till I destroyed them.
39 I struck them down,
and they could rise no more;
they lay fallen at my feet.
40 You have girded me with strength for battle,
brought my adversaries low before me,
41 made my enemies turn tail before me;
I wiped out my foes.
42 They cried out, but there was none to deliver;
[cried] to the LORD, but He did not answer them.
43 I ground them fine as windswept dust;
I trod them flat as dirt of the streets.
44 You have rescued me from the strife of people;
You have set me at the head of nations;
peoples I knew not must serve me.
45 At the mere report of me they are submissive;
foreign peoples cower before me;
46 foreign peoples lose courage,
[d-]and come trembling out of their strongholds.[-d]

47 The LORD lives! Blessed is my rock!
Exalted be God, my deliverer,
48 the God who has vindicated me
and made peoples subject to me,

a *Cf. note to 2 Sam. 22.30; or "troop."*
b *Taking* bamothai *as a poetic form of* bamoth; *cf. Hab. 3.19; others "my."*
c *Meaning of Heb. uncertain; others "condescension."*
d-d *Meaning of Heb. uncertain.*

32: Vv. declaiming the absolute exclusivity of God are typically found in later biblical literature (cf. Exod. 15.11 n. and Isa. 44.6). **33–49:** It is God the warrior who helps the psalmist to totally and completely annihilate the enemy. **34:** An image of swiftness and stability. **35–44:** Human success in war depends on divine assistance. **40:** Bringing *adversaries low* may be a literal reference to stepping on the necks of enemies (see v. 39, "they lay fallen at [lit. under] my feet"). **47:** *The LORD lives!* A similar statement about the Canaanite deity Baal is found in the Ugaritic epics after he defeats his enemies. When used in biblical literature, "living" with respect to God often carries the connotation of power. *Rock* continues the main image of God as a stronghold, but may also refer to God's divine justice, as in Deut. 32.4: "The Rock!—His deeds are perfect, / Yea, all His ways are just." **48–49:** The psalmist restates his main point—that victory comes only with divine help.

49 who rescued me from my enemies,
who raised me clear of my adversaries,
saved me from lawless men.
50 For this I sing Your praise among the nations, LORD,
and hymn Your name:
51 [a-]He accords great victories[-a] to His king,
keeps faith with His anointed,
with David and his offspring forever.

19

For the leader. A psalm of David.

2 The heavens declare the glory of God,
the sky proclaims His handiwork.
3 Day to day makes utterance,
night to night speaks out.
4 There is no utterance,
there are no words,
[b-]whose sound goes unheard.[-b]
5 Their voice[c] carries throughout the earth,
their words to the end of the world.
He placed in them[d] a tent for the sun,
6 who is like a groom coming forth from the chamber,
like a hero, eager to run his course.
7 His rising-place is at one end of heaven,
and his circuit reaches the other;
nothing escapes his heat.

8 The teaching of the LORD is perfect,
renewing life;
the decrees of the LORD are enduring,
making the simple wise;

a-a *2 Sam. 22.51, "Tower of victory."*
b-b *With Septuagint, Symmachus, and Vulgate; or "their sound is not heard."*
c *Cf. Septuagint, Symmachus, and Vulgate; Arabic* qawwah, *"to shout."*
d *Viz., the heavens.*

49: As the psalm moves to a close, it returns to the word *rescue,* found also in v. 3. **50:** *Sing*ing God's *praise* is a major theme of the Psalter, appearing in over sixty vv. **51:** *Anointed,* Heb "mashiaḥ"; see 2.2 n. The final v. suggests that this psalm was recited by or on behalf of a Davidic king, and that the king is the "I" of the psalm.

Ps. 19: This psalm is recited in the preliminary morning service on Sabbath and festivals. It divides into three sections: Vv. 2–7, a hymn focusing on creation, specifically on the sun; vv. 8–11, a hymn focusing on torah; and vv. 12–15, which are connected to the immediately preceding section (see v. 12, *them*), a petition to be saved from sin, and for prayers to be heard. Some scholars believe that either two psalms have been combined (vv. 2–7 and 8–15), or that a later psalmist who composed vv. 8–15 incorporated the earlier vv. 2–7, which have a different topic, style, and poetic structure. It has been suggested that vv. 2–7 may have been adapted from a non-Israelite hymn praising the sun. Vv. 8–15 show significant connections to wisdom ideas and vocabulary (see below). The difference between vv. 2–7 and vv. 8–15 was realized already by the medieval Jewish interpreters, who suggested various ways that creation, the sun, and torah may be connected. The discovery of ancient Near Eastern texts, where justice is often part of the sun god's realm (so, e.g., Shamash, the Mesopotamian sun god) since he traverses the earth seeing wrongdoings, has offered a new way of understanding the psalm's unity. In fact, recent commentators stress the psalm's unity, noting that the poem as a whole is focused on God's revelation in heaven and on the earth (Radak is similar), or that torah is associated with light (e.g., Prov. 6.23). The wording unifies the two parts by using terms for light (normally associated with creation) in connection with torah, and words for speaking (associated with torah) in reference to creation. The message is, then, that God reveals Himself both through His creation and through His torah or teaching, that is, His revelation to humans, later formulated in writing in the books of the Torah. **2–4:** The cosmos praises God; the creation testifies to God's greatness. It is unclear if the *sound* is metaphorical, or if some Israelites believed in the music of the spheres, an idea later associated with Pythagoras, or if this refers to the praise of God by the heavenly beings (see e.g., Isa. 6.3). An Ugaritic epic speaks of "Speech of tree and whisper of stone, converse of heaven with earth" (*ANET,* p. 136). An alternative rendering of v. 4, "their sound is not heard," means that the celestial bodies "speak" soundlessly; they convey their message simply by their being. **5–7:** The sun was typically associated with a major deity in the ancient Near East, and cylinder seals with winged sundisks have been found in Israel, and 2 Kings 23.11 and other sources offer evidence for solar worship in ancient Israel. **6–7:** The sun, shining and eager, traverses the sky. **8–11:** This section is suffused with wisdom terminology, including

9 The precepts of the LORD are just,
rejoicing the heart;
the instruction of the LORD is lucid,
making the eyes light up.
10 The fear of the LORD is pure,
abiding forever;
the judgments of the LORD are true,
righteous altogether,
11 more desirable than gold,
than much fine gold;
sweeter than honey,
than drippings of the comb.
12 Your servant pays them heed;
in obeying them there is much reward.
13 Who can be aware of errors?
Clear me of unperceived guilt,
14 and from [a]-willful sins-[a] keep Your servant;
let them not dominate me;
then shall I be blameless
and clear of grave offense.
15 May the words of my mouth
and the prayer of my heart[b]
be acceptable to You,
O LORD, my rock and my redeemer.

20

For the leader. A psalm of David.

2 May the LORD answer you in time of trouble,
the name of Jacob's God keep you safe.
3 May He send you help from the sanctuary,
and sustain you from Zion.
4 May He receive the tokens[c] of all your meal
offerings,
and approve[d] your burnt offerings. *Selah.*

a-a Or "arrogant men"; cf. Ps. 119.51.
b For leb *as a source of speech, see note to Eccl. 5.1.*
c Reference to azkara, *"token portion" of meal offering; Lev. 2.2, 9, 16, etc.*
d Meaning of Heb. uncertain.

simple, wise, fear of the LORD, and wisdom or torah being compared to *gold* (of great value, and in this case, also the color of the sun). The highly stylized, repetitive form of vv. 8–10 is very striking, though in Heb, v. 10 is slightly different in structure from the previous vv.; v. 11 concludes this section by breaking the structure altogether. Heb "torah" is here translated as *instruction,* on the assumption that this psalm was written before the Torah was canonized; traditional Jewish interpretation, which assumes that this is a Davidic composition from the period after a Mosaic Torah, understands "torah" as the Torah. **13:** The v. assumes that human sinning is inevitable (see similarly 1 Kings 8.46). In Heb, *unperceived guilt* ("nistarot") plays with v. 7, "escapes" ("nistar"), lending additional unity to the psalm. (See similarly v. 9, "light up," which as Rashi points out [v. 8], connects back to the sun.) **14:** *Willful sins* are distinguished from inadvertent ones. **15:** This v. appears as a coda at the conclusion of the "'Amidah," the main daily prayer. In its original context, it is unclear if *the words of my mouth / and the prayer of my heart* refer to the immediately preceding vv., asking forgiveness from sins, or if this entire psalm served as an introduction to a larger liturgical complex.

Ps. 20: This is a prayer for the king before battle. A very close parallel to this psalm from the Egyptian Papyrus Amherst 63 was published in 1983. That version, however, was written in Aram. in Demotic script (late Egyptian characters) and opens: "May Horus [an Egyptian deity]/the master answer us in our straits; send your messenger from the temple of Arash" (translation from Ziony Zevit, *The Religions of Ancient Israel: A Synthesis of Parallactic Approaches* [London: Continuum, 2001], p. 669). Initially, it was thought that this Aram. text was a paganized version of the biblical psalm, but more recently it has been suggested that both the Aram. Egyptian text and Ps. 20 derive from a common non-Israelite poem, most likely to Baal (see intro. to Ps. 29). Ps. 20 is now recited toward the conclusion of the morning weekday service. **2:** The reference to "His anointed" in v. 7 makes it clear that the *you* is the king. *The name of Jacob's God* is an odd appellation for LORD, perhaps used so that both verse-halves would be of approximately the same length. There may be an allusion here to Gen. 35.3, where Jacob builds an altar to "the God who answered me when I was in distress"; alternatively, it stresses, like Deut. (e.g., 12.5), that only God's name is present on the earth. **3:** God is envisioned as enthroned in the *sanctuary* in *Zion.* **4:** This may reflect a ritual of sacrificing before going to battle (1 Sam. 7.9–10).

5 May He grant you your desire,
and fulfill your every plan.
6 May we shout for joy in your victory,
arrayed by standards in the name of our God.
May the LORD fulfill your every wish.

7 Now I know that the LORD will give victory to His anointed,
will answer him from His heavenly sanctuary
with the mighty victories of His right arm.
8 They [call] on chariots, they [call] on horses,
but we call on the name of the LORD our God.
9 They collapse and lie fallen,
but we rally and gather strength.
10 [a]-O LORD, grant victory!
May the King answer us when we call.-[a]

21 For the leader. A psalm of David.

2 O LORD, the king rejoices in Your strength;
how greatly he exults in Your victory!
3 You have granted him the desire of his heart,
have not denied the request of his lips. *Selah.*
4 You have proffered him blessings of good things,
have set upon his head a crown of fine gold.
5 He asked You for life; You granted it;
a long life, everlasting.
6 Great is his glory through Your victory;
You have endowed him with splendor and majesty.
7 You have made him blessed forever,
gladdened him with the joy of Your presence.
8 For the king trusts in the LORD;
Through the faithfulness of the Most High
he will not be shaken.
9 Your hand is equal to all Your enemies;
Your right hand overpowers Your foes.
10 You set them ablaze like a furnace
[b]-when You show Your presence.-[b]
The LORD in anger destroys them;
fire consumes them.
11 You wipe their offspring from the earth,
their issue from among men.

a-a Or in the light of v. 7, "O LORD, grant victory to the king; may He answer us when we call."
b-b Or "at the time of Your anger."

6: The Davidic king and God are tightly bound together. **7:** *Now I know* may reflect a positive answer to a ritual; see Ps. 6.9–11 n.; 1 Sam. 28.6; 30.8. **8:** The strength of divine Presence over military might is a central biblical theme. **10:** As noted, it is unclear where this v. should be divided. This translation (following the Tg.) takes the king to be the divine *King,* God. The LXX read it as: "O LORD grant victory to the king; answer us when we call"; this is the origin of the expression, "God save the king!" The psalm begins as it ends, with a request for an *answer.*

Ps. 21: A blessing for the king, who will lead his nation to victory. A companion hymn to Ps. 20 sharing vocabulary and theme (cf. 20.5 and 21.3; 20.7c and 21.9b). Vv. 1–7 rejoice in God's beneficence to the king; vv. 8–13 express trust that God will grant victory. The psalm is replete with superlatives expressing the king's power. The reference to the king using *you* (vv. 9–10) may suggest a ritual in which the king was present. (NJPS translation takes "you" as referring to God.) **2:** An introduction to the psalm's theme: the fate of the king depends on God. **3:** *Selah,* see 3.3 n. **4:** *A crown of fine gold:* Remarkably, this term for crown is never used in the historical texts depicting an Israelite king (but see 2 Sam. 12.30, the crowns of a foreign king). **5:** A past request for the long life of the king was granted (1 Kings 3.14; Ps. 61.6). **6:** *Glory ... splendor and majesty,* the nimbus of light surrounding gods and kings (Ps. 8.6). Through the victory that God grants, the king is enhanced. **7:** Perhaps the king is envisioned as having special access to God. **8:** This abundant royal blessing is here predicated on royal obedience. **9:** The blessing is complete; *all ... enemies* are obliterated. **10:** For the fiery wrath of God, see Isa. 29.6; 66.15–16. The image of God's blazing fury burning up the enemy is common, and may reflect the reality of war in which cities were set ablaze. **11:** See Ps. 37.38.

12 For they schemed against You;
they laid plans,
but could not succeed.
13 [a]For You make them turn back[a]
by Your bows aimed at their face.
14 Be exalted, O LORD, through Your strength;
we will sing and chant the praises of Your mighty
deeds.

22

For the leader; on [a]*ayyeleth ha-shaḥar.*[a]
A psalm of David.

2 My God, my God,
why have You abandoned me;
why so far from delivering me
and from my anguished roaring?
3 My God,
I cry by day—You answer not;
by night, and have no respite.

4 [b]But You are the Holy One,
enthroned,
the Praise of Israel.[b]
5 In You our fathers trusted;
they trusted, and You rescued them.
6 To You they cried out
and they escaped;
in You they trusted
and were not disappointed.

7 But I am a worm, less than human;
scorned by men, despised by people.

a-a Meaning of Heb. uncertain.
b-b Or "But You are holy, enthroned upon the praises of Israel."

12: The plots against Israel are perceived as plots against God; cf. Ps. 83.5–6. **14:** God's strength frames the psalm (see v. 2) and is the source of the king's strength. The conclusion moves from the fact of God's power to a wish for God's exaltation by virtue of that power.

Ps. 22: The psalm opens with a plea from a person in dire straits, apparently a serious illness. His prayers having been answered, he brings the offerings he vowed and gives public acclaim to God as he promised. God is praised for His care of all people, and all people, now and in the future, should praise God. It contains a striking maternal image (vv. 10–11), and contains fewer male images than most psalms; some therefore attribute it to a female author, but that seems unlikely (male authors also use feminine imagery). The structure of the psalm is uncertain. Calls for God not to abandon the psalmist (vv. 2, 12, and 20) suggest one way to divide the psalm. NJPS has made four subdivisions based on the contents. Another possibility is to see two main parts: vv. 2–22, the petition in time of trouble, and 23–31, the vow to praise God. The first of these sections is framed by *You answer not* (v. 3) and "answer me" (v. 22; NJPS main translation: *rescue me*). The second is framed by *will I proclaim* (v. 23) and *shall be proclaimed* (v. 31). This psalm does not have the same significant place in Jewish tradition that it has within Christianity, where the beginning words of v. 2, partially in Aram. translation, are the last words of Jesus on the cross according to some gospel traditions. Jewish tradition interprets this psalm as a lament by David over the future exile (Rashi), more specifically the threat against the Jews by Haman in the book of Esth. (various Rabbis). For that reason there is a custom to read it on Purim (Sephardic custom reads it on the Fast of Esther and on Purim). **1:** *Ayyeleth ha-shaḥar* (perhaps "Deer of the Dawn"; see translators' note *a-a*), a musical term, which may indicate the melody to which the words were sung. **2–12:** Why does God, who cared for the ancestors (vv. 5–6) and the psalmist (vv. 10–11) in the past, not do so now? **2:** Divine abandonment is a major theme of the Psalter; see Ps. 10.1. The first part of this v. occurs in the New Testament, uttered by Jesus when he is being crucified (Matt. 27.46; Mark 15.34). **3:** It is unclear if *by day … by night* is a merism, indicating the palmist's unceasing prayer, or if he is praying twice daily. **4:** *Praise of Israel:* Cf. Exod. 15.11. According to the alternate translation, which understands the syntax of the Heb differently, prayers form the throne upon which God sits—a lovely metaphor stressing the importance of prayer. **5–6:** God's heeding Israel's past prayers is the major theme of Ps. 107. **7–8:** The psalmist feels less than human. He is scorned by those who think that God will not help him. The commonalities between this v. and the suffering servant passage in Isa. ch 53, which was understood by the early Christians as referring to Jesus, may have facilitated placing v. 2 in Jesus' mouth in

8 All who see me mock me;
[a]they curl their lips,[a]
they shake their heads.
9 "Let him commit himself to the LORD;
let Him rescue him,
let Him save him,
for He is pleased with him."
10 You [b]drew me[b] from the womb,
made me secure at my mother's breast.
11 I became Your charge at birth;
from my mother's womb You have been my God.
12 Do not be far from me,
for trouble is near,
and there is none to help.
13 Many bulls surround me,
mighty ones of Bashan encircle me.
14 They open their mouths at me
like tearing, roaring lions.
15 [c]My life ebbs away:[c]
all my bones are disjointed;
my heart is like wax,
melting within me;
16 my vigor dries up like a shard;
my tongue cleaves to my palate;
You commit me to the dust of death.
17 Dogs surround me;
a pack of evil ones closes in on me,
[d]like lions [they maul] my hands and feet.[d]
18 I take the count of all my bones
while they look on and gloat.
19 They divide my clothes among themselves,
casting lots for my garments.

20 But You, O LORD, be not far off;
my strength, hasten to my aid.
21 Save my life from the sword,
my precious life[e] from the clutches of a dog.
22 Deliver me from a lion's mouth;
from the horns of wild oxen rescue[f] me.
23 Then will I proclaim Your fame to my brethren,
praise You in the congregation.

24 You who fear the LORD, praise Him!
All you offspring of Jacob, honor Him!
Be in dread of Him, all you offspring of Israel!

a-a Lit. "they open wide with a lip." *b-b Meaning of Heb. uncertain.*
c-c Lit. "I am poured out like water." *d-d With Rashi; cf. Isa. 38.13.*
e Lit. "only one." *f Lit. "answer."*

the New Testament. *Curl their lips,* gestures of derision. **9:** The scorners open their mouths to mock and to devour (v. 14). **10–12:** The psalmist hopes that God who was with him since conception will not abandon him now; these vv. contain several of the very few maternal images in the Psalter. **13–22:** The psalmist's opponents as animal predators (Ps. 17.12). The mixing of conflicting metaphors and similes (the enemies are *bulls, lions,* and *dogs)* is common in the Bible. **13:** *Bashan,* a region in northern Transjordan famous for its fat, strong cattle, which are here predators. **15–19:** A graphic description of mortal illness depicted in highly original language. The psalmist feels his body stop working and disintegrating. He sees himself die, his body so dried up that it turns to dust. The scorners are like *dogs* (and *lions,* according to NJPS) hunting prey (cf. v. 14). They gloat at his death and are eager to take his possessions. **20–23:** At his lowest point, the psalmist calls on God to save him from what has just been described. **20:** *My strength* puns with the Heb word "ram," continuing the animal images. **22:** *Rescue me* in the Heb is "you rescued me," reflecting the common motif of certainty that God will heed the call of the psalmist (see 6.9–11 n.). **23–24:** See Ps. 35.18–19. **24–31:** The psalmist's recovery is a sign of God's power and mercy, an example for all, and an occasion for praise. With his reintegration into the community, all Israel is invited to join him in praise. **24:** *You who fear the LORD:* YHVH-fearers is a term that occurs elsewhere in Psalms; sometimes it is a general designation for those who worship the God of Israel and at other times it seems to be a group within Israel—proselytes, according to some scholars. Here it is the former, as the v. moves from a smaller to a larger group (see the reverse in Ps. 135.19–20).

25 For He did not scorn, He did not spurn
the plea[a] of the lowly;
He did not hide His face from him;
when he cried out to Him, He listened.
26 [b-]Because of You I offer praise[-b] in the great
congregation;
I pay my vows in the presence of His worshipers.
27 Let the lowly eat and be satisfied;
let all who seek the LORD praise Him.
Always be of good cheer!
28 Let all the ends of the earth pay heed and turn to the
LORD,
and the peoples of all nations prostrate themselves
before You;
29 for kingship is the LORD's
and He rules the nations.
30 [c-]All those in full vigor shall eat and prostrate
themselves;
all those at death's door, whose spirits flag,
shall bend the knee before Him.[-c]
31 Offspring shall serve Him;
the Lord's fame shall be proclaimed to the
generation to come;
they shall tell of His beneficence to people yet to be
born,
for He has acted.

23 A psalm of David.

The LORD is my shepherd;
I lack nothing.
2 He makes me lie down in green pastures;
He leads me to [d-]water in places of repose;[-d]
3 He renews my life;
He guides me in right paths
as befits His name.
4 Though I walk through [e]a valley of deepest darkness,[-e]
I fear no harm, for You are with me;
Your rod and Your staff—they comfort me.

a *Or "plight."* *b-b* *Lit. "From You is my praise."*
c-c *Meaning of Heb. uncertain; others "All the fat ones of the earth shall eat and worship; / All they that go down to the dust shall kneel before Him, / Even he that cannot keep his soul alive."*
d-d *Others "still waters."*
e-e *Others "the valley of the shadow of death."*

28–30: The praise of God, king of all, is universalized to the nations; see Pss. 47.10; 67.3–5; 86.9; 117.1. **30:** The healthy and the sick should praise God. *Those at death's door,* Heb "those who go down to dust," usually a reference to the dead or the almost dead. If the reference is to the dead, it would contradict the predominant belief that the dead do not praise God (Ps. 6.6); but it is perhaps a poetic way to reinforce the idea of the surrounding vv. that everyone, in every time and every place, should praise God. **31:** God's power to cure will be proclaimed to future generations. Such sentiments are common in petitions, and serve as a motivation for God to improve the lot of the petioner.

Ps. 23: God, the divine shepherd-king, leads his people to nourishment and safety (vv. 1–4), keeping them alive and protecting them. In vv. 5–6 the image shifts, as the psalmist is hosted by God and hopes to remain in His presence all his life. Some scholars interpret the psalm as an exilic or postexilic portrait of a new exodus, from the exile to the return in the land of Israel (cf. Isa. 40.3–5; 49.8–13; Ps. 78.43–55—the exodus is a common exilic trope for the return). This interpretation helps to see the psalm's two parts as a unity: God guides the people through the difficult journey from Babylonia and then hosts them at His own table, the rebuilt Temple. Alternatively, as elsewhere in the Bible, a single psalm combines two diverse images. **1–4:** The shepherd-sheep metaphor for God and Israel (see also Ps. 95.7). The shepherd leads the sheep to pasture, to water, and through difficult terrain. *Shepherd* is a frequent biblical and ancient Near Eastern metaphor for royalty (Isa. 40.11; Ezek. ch 34; Ps. 80). This is the case with David (and Moses); the Babylonian king Hammurabi is called "the shepherd" (*ANET,* p. 164). **2:** The alternate reading "still waters" (translators' note *d-d)* means that the waters are not turbulent and hence are easy to drink from. **3:** See Ps. 31.4.

4: The shepherd's *rod* and *staff,* implements that prod and guide the sheep, here provide the comfort that comes from divine guidance.

5 You spread a table for me in full view of my enemies;
You anoint my head with oil;
my drink is abundant.
6 Only goodness and steadfast love shall pursue me
all the days of my life,
and I shall dwell in the house of the LORD
for many long years.

24

Of David. A psalm.

The earth is the LORD's and all that it holds,
the world and its inhabitants.
2 For He founded it upon the ocean,
set it on the nether-streams.

3 Who may ascend the mountain of the LORD?
Who may stand in His holy place?—
4 He who has clean hands and a pure heart,
who has not taken a false oath by My[a] life
or sworn deceitfully.
5 He shall carry away a blessing from the LORD,
a just reward from God, his deliverer.
6 Such is the circle[b] of those who turn to Him,
Jacob, who seek Your presence. *Selah.*

7 O gates, lift up your heads!
Up high, you everlasting doors,
so the King of glory may come in!
8 Who is the King of glory?—
the LORD, mighty and valiant,
the LORD, valiant in battle.
9 O gates, lift up your heads!
Lift them up, you everlasting doors,
so the King of glory may come in!

a Ancient versions and some mss. read "His." *b Lit. "generation."*

5–6: The shepherd metaphor is replaced by a banquet metaphor: God's luxurious care of the psalmist. **5:** God hosts with luxury. A set or spread *table* (cf. Ezek. 23.41; Prov. 9.2) and *oil* on the head (cf. Eccl. 9.8; Ps. 92.11) are signs of luxury. Oil was used to wash away the grime of a long journey and was placed on the heads of guests at banquets. Ps. 78.19 speaks of the preparation of *a table* in the wilderness for the first exodus generation. This may lend support for seeing our psalm as a reference to the (second) exodus. **6:** *Goodness and steadfast love,* covenant blessings, rather than curses (Deut. 28.3, 15, 45). Notice that such blessings, rather than enemies, are personified as pursuing the psalmist. *The house of the LORD,* the Temple (Ps. 27.4). The psalmist hopes to be in God's Presence at the Temple (have access to God) throughout his long life. If this is an exilic psalm, it implies the return to the land of Israel. *For many long years:* lit. "for length of days." This refers to one's natural life (to live a long life was a blessing), but it has traditionally been understood as referring to the next life (after death), and hence this psalm is customarily recited at funerals or on occasions commemorating the dead. V. 3, *He renews my life,* has also facilitated this use.

Ps. 24: A hymn celebrating God, Creator and victor, with an "entrance liturgy" (vv. 3–6; Pss. 5; 15). After an introduction celebrating God as the Creator, the psalm has two parts; in the first (vv. 3–6), pilgrims enter the Temple, and in the second (vv. 7–10), the Ark enters. The two are separated by "Selah." Each part has rhetorical questions and their answers; perhaps they were recited antiphonally. The psalm is used in Jewish liturgy on festivals, when the Torah is returned to the ark. **1–2:** God tamed the primeval waters and founded the earth upon them (Ps. 136.6); He is therefore to be acknowledged as the supreme sovereign of the world. The Temple is a microcosm of the world (cf. Gen. 2.1–3; Exod. 39.32, 42–43) and thus God's act of creation form an appropriate introduction to this Temple liturgy. **3–6:** The requirements for participation in Temple worship are predominantly moral, signifying obedience to God; see Ps. 15.2–5. **3:** *The mountain of the LORD:* The Temple mount, perhaps also echoing Mt. Sinai. **4:** As in 15:4 and the Decalogue (see Exod. 20.7 n.), swearing falsely is viewed with utmost seriousness. **6:** *Jacob:* Israel, the congregation present at the ceremony. *Selah* (also v. 10), see Ps. 3.3 n. **7–10:** God, as it were, enters the Temple. The Temple gates open for the Ark, symbolizing God's Presence, to enter. The gates "lift up their heads," a metaphoric expression for joyously welcoming God, pictured as a victorious king returning home to his palace; a slight emendation (she'arim to sho'arim) suggests that the gatekeepers open the gates.

10 Who is the King of glory?—
the LORD of hosts,
He is the King of glory! *Selah.*

25

Of David.

א O LORD, I set my hope on You;
2 ב my God, in You I trust;
may I not be disappointed,
may my enemies not exult over me.
3 ג O let none who look to You be disappointed;
let the faithless be disappointed, empty-handed.
4 ד Let me know Your paths, O LORD;
teach me Your ways;
5 הו guide me in Your true way and teach me,
for You are God, my deliverer;
it is You I look to at all times.
6 ז O LORD, be mindful of Your compassion
and Your faithfulness;
they are old as time.
7 ח Be not mindful of my youthful sins and transgressions;
in keeping with Your faithfulness consider what is in my favor,
as befits Your goodness, O LORD.
8 ט Good and upright is the LORD;
therefore He shows sinners the way.
9 י He guides the lowly in the right path,
and teaches the lowly His way.
10 כ All the LORD's paths are steadfast love
for those who keep the decrees of His covenant.
11 ל As befits Your name, O LORD,
pardon my iniquity though it be great.
12 מ Whoever fears the LORD,
he shall be shown what path to choose.
13 נ He shall live a happy life,
and his children shall inherit the land.
14 ס The counsel[a] of the LORD is for those who fear Him;
to them He makes known His covenant.
15 ע My eyes are ever toward the LORD,
for He will loose my feet from the net.
16 פ Turn to me, have mercy on me,
for I am alone and afflicted.

a Or *"secret."*

10: *The LORD of hosts,* a relatively infrequent divine epithet in Psalms, emphasizes God's role in leading the heavenly hosts in battle, and is associated with the Ark, which could precede Israel in battle (see 1 Sam. ch 4). A plausible setting for this section of the psalm might be the return from battle of the Ark, a symbol of (v. 8) "the LORD, mighty and valiant, / the LORD, valiant in battle."

Ps. 25: An individual's petition in acrostic form: the first line begins with the first letter of the Heb alphabet, the first word of the second line with the second letter of the alphabet, and so on to the final letter (see Ps. 9 n.). Two letters are missing and two are doubled, likely reflecting changes that the psalm has undergone in its transmission. The psalm is made up of alternating petitions and expressions of trust. It resembles wisdom literature in its concern with learning and finding the right path, but has the religious concerns of Psalms in its hope for forgiveness and for deliverance from distress. **1:** *Set my hope on You,* lit. "lift my soul to You" (cf. 86.4; 143.8), i.e., "turn to You for protection." **2–3:** The plea for the "shaming" of one's enemies is frequent in complaints (6.11; 35.4, 26; 40.15–16). **4–5:** Prayer for (moral) guidance, with a wisdom cast; cf. vv. 8–10, 12. **6–7:** Prayer for divine mercy and forgiveness of sins. A key word is "z-kr," "remember," found three times in these two vv., and translated as *be mindful* and *consider.* God should remember that He is merciful and not remember (take into account) the psalmist's sins. *Youthful sins:* From the time when the psalmist might be accountable for his sins (see similarly Jer. 3.25). **8:** This unusual sentiment is stronger than Ezek. ch 18; God not only does not want sinners to die, but actively helps them find the right way, assistance that they are free to ignore. **11:** The request for forgiveness of sins closes the first half of the psalm; *name* here means essence. *Pardon my iniquity* echoes Moses' words in Exod. 34.9. **12–13:** Those who fear the LORD and their children shall be blessed (Ps. 37.28–29). Possession of *the land* is a major theme of Ps. 37. **15:** *Net,* frequently in the Bible, is used by hunters and soldiers to capture and kill something or someone. **16:** Strikingly, this is the only psalm where the psalmist claims to be *alone* (though see 142.5).

17 צ [a]My deep distress[a] increases;
deliver me from my straits.
18 ר Look at my affliction and suffering,
and forgive all my sins.
19 See how numerous my enemies are,
and how unjustly they hate me!
20 ש Protect me and save me;
let me not be disappointed,
for I have sought refuge in You.
21 ת May integrity and uprightness watch over me,
for I look to You.
22 O God, redeem Israel
from all its distress.

26 Of David.

Vindicate me, O LORD,
for I have walked without blame;
I have trusted in the LORD;
I have not faltered.
2 Probe me, O LORD, and try me,
test my [b]heart and mind;[b]
3 [c]for my eyes are on Your steadfast love;
I have set my course by it.[c]
4 I do not consort with scoundrels,
or mix with hypocrites;
5 I detest the company of evil men,
and do not consort with the wicked;
6 I wash my hands in innocence,
and walk around Your altar, O LORD,
7 raising my voice in thanksgiving,
and telling all Your wonders.
8 O LORD, I love Your temple abode,
the dwelling-place of Your glory.
9 Do not sweep me away with sinners,
or [snuff out] my life with murderers,
10 who have schemes at their fingertips,
and hands full of bribes.
11 But I walk without blame;
redeem me, have mercy on me!
12 My feet are on level ground.
In assemblies I will bless the LORD.

a-a Lit. "The distress of my heart." *b-b Lit. "kidneys and heart."*
c-c Or "I am aware of Your faithfulness, and always walk in Your true [path]."

17: *Increases,* Heb "broadens," the opposite of *distress* and *straits,* with their meaning of narrowness. **19:** Here as elsewhere, *enemies* need not be literal but stands for trouble in general. **21:** *Integrity and uprightness,* characteristics of Job (1.1), here personified as protecting guardians provided by God. **22:** As in many psalms, the end of a prayer of an individual becomes a prayer for the community. A v. beginning with the letter "pe" follows the acrostic (see also Ps. 34.23). It has been suggested that this arrangement makes the first letter "alef," the middle letter "lamed," and the last letter "pe"—spelling the word "to learn, teach" and thereby emphasizing the instructional nature of the psalm.

Ps. 26: A prayer for divine justice. The bulk of the psalm is a protestation of innocence, where the psalmist insists that he has conducted his life as God requires and therefore should not be punished like the wicked. His plea is based on the assumption that the righteous are rewarded and the wicked punished, yet in his case this expectation seems not yet to have been fulfilled. Like Ps. 25 and Ps. 1, this psalm uses some language of wisdom literature. **1–3:** The psalmist prays that God adjudicate him and find him righteous (7.9; 17.2–5); the Heb of v. 2 reflects metal refining language. **4–5:** See 1.1–2. **6–8:** The mention of the *altar* and *temple* suggests to some that the psalmist is a priest, but he may be an ordinary person who delights in coming to the Temple. Clean hands (literally or metaphorically) are required for entrance to the Temple (Ps. 24.4). **8:** *Glory,* the light streaming from the deity (63.3). **9–10:** If the psalmist is swept away with the evildoers, he will not be able to come to the Temple, which he loves (v. 8). **11–12:** *I walk without blame* forms an inclusio, with a change of tense, with v. 1; the psalmist was blameless in the past and continues to be. *My feet are on level ground,* Heb "my foot stands on level ground" recalls the walking in vv. 1, 3; the psalm is especially rich in its use of parts of the body and physical actions. Heb *without blame* and *level ground* echoes the words "tam" and "yashar," "to have integrity and be upright," the desired traits of the righteous person (cf. 25.21). A slightly different form of the conclusion is in 68.27.

Ps. 27: A psalm of trust; the psalmist has no fear of enemies in the protective refuge of the Temple. This psalm is recited from 1 'Elul (in the late summer) through Hoshanah Rabbah in the early fall, the period of seeking forgiveness from God surrounding Rosh Ha-Shanah and Yom Kippur. Like the previous psalm, it focuses on being present in the Temple and reflects a self-assured psalmist; v. 11 is similar to 26.12. **1:** *My light,* see 36.10; Mic. 7.8; Job 33.30. *Light* is used in other psalms as well (e.g., "favor," in 31.17; 80.4), where it suggests that seeing the light/favor from God's beneficent face assures deliverance (see Num 6.25). **2:** *Devour my flesh,* an idiom for harmful, malicious speech (cf. English "backbite"; see translators' note *a-a); it can also refer to enemies as predators. **4–6:** The Temple as a place of eternal refuge, clearly hyperbolic, where the psalmist can experience God's Presence. **4:** *Live in the house of the Lord,* the psalmist hopes to visit the Temple on pilgrimages throughout his life (23.6; 84.5). **5:** *Pavilion* (Heb "sukkah") and *tent* are terms for the Temple (cf. 76.3; 15.1; 61.5). **7–13:** The psalmist seeks God, worried that God will abandon him (see 6.4–5 n.). **10:** Even if his parents abandon him, through death or otherwise, the psalmist will have a divine "parent" who will protect and instruct him. The motif of the god as a parent of the king is familiar from Mesopotamian hymns and elsewhere in biblical literature, where God is the superlative parent (see esp. Isa. 49.15 and Ps. 103.13).

27

Of David.

The LORD is my light and my help;
whom should I fear?
The LORD is the stronghold of my life,
whom should I dread?
2 When evil men assail me
[a]to devour my flesh[a]—
it is they, my foes and my enemies,
who stumble and fall.
3 Should an army besiege me,
my heart would have no fear;
should war beset me,
still would I be confident.

4 One thing I ask of the LORD,
only that do I seek:
to live in the house of the LORD
all the days of my life,
to gaze upon the beauty of the LORD,
[b]to frequent[b] His temple.
5 He will shelter me in His pavilion
on an evil day,
grant me the protection of His tent,
raise me high upon a rock.
6 Now is my head high
over my enemies roundabout;
I sacrifice in His tent with shouts of joy,
singing and chanting a hymn to the LORD.

7 Hear, O LORD, when I cry aloud;
have mercy on me, answer me.
8 [b]In Your behalf[b] my heart says:
"Seek My face!"
O LORD, I seek Your face.
9 Do not hide Your face from me;
do not thrust aside Your servant in anger;
You have ever been my help.
Do not forsake me, do not abandon me,
O God, my deliverer.
10 Though my father and mother abandon me,
the LORD will take me in.
11 Show me Your way, O LORD,
and lead me on a level path
because of my watchful foes.

a-a *Or "to slander me"; cf. Dan. 3.8; 6.25.*
b-b *Meaning of Heb. uncertain.*

12 Do not subject me to the will of my foes,
for false witnesses and unjust accusers
have appeared against me.
13 Had I not the assurance
that I would enjoy the goodness of the LORD
in the land of the living...

14 Look to the LORD;
be strong and of good courage!
O look to the LORD!

28 Of David.

O LORD, I call to You;
my rock, do not disregard me,
for if You hold aloof from me,
I shall be like those gone down into the Pit.
2 Listen to my plea for mercy
when I cry out to You,
when I lift my hands
toward Your inner sanctuary.
3 Do not [a]count me[-a] with the wicked and evildoers
who profess goodwill toward their fellows
while malice is in their heart.
4 Pay them according to their deeds,
their malicious acts;
according to their handiwork pay them,
give them their deserts.
5 For they do not consider the LORD's deeds,
the work of His hands.
May He tear them down,
never to rebuild them!
6 Blessed is the LORD,
for He listens to my plea for mercy.
7 The LORD is my strength and my shield;
my heart trusts in Him.
I was helped,[b] and my heart exulted,
so I will glorify Him with my song.
8 The LORD is [c]their strength;[-c]
He is a stronghold for the deliverance of His anointed.
9 Deliver and bless Your very own people;
tend them and sustain them forever.

a-a Or "drag me off"; Meaning of Heb. uncertain.
b Or "strengthened."
c-c Septuagint, Saadia, and others render, and some mss. read, 'oz le'ammo, *"the strength of His people."*

12: The foes are here lying witnesses testifying against the psalmist (similarly 35.11, 19). **13:** *The land of the living,* as opposed to the land of the dead, where there is no access to God. **14:** Possibly an encouraging response to the psalmist's prayer, this sums up the psalm's message.

Ps. 28: A plea for deliverance from enemies; likely a royal psalm (cf. vv. 8–9). God is described in terms of military strength: a *rock, strength, shield, stronghold,* as in Ps. 18. Like the previous psalms, it focuses upon the Temple. In vv. 1–5 the psalmist prays for God's response, arguing that he should not be grouped with the wicked (see Ps. 26), whom God correctly distances from Himself, punishing them with death. Vv. 6–9 follow God's (implicit) response; the psalmist praises Him and encourages others to do likewise. As is frequent at the conclusion, v. 9 moves from the personal to the national, praying for God's ongoing protection of Israel. **1:** *Disregard,* lit. "be deaf" to my call. *The Pit,* a synonym for Sheol, the abode of the dead. One not heard by God is like the dead, who were permanently cut off from God. **2:** To *lift* one's *hands* was the typical position of biblical prayer (see, e.g., 1 Kings 8.22; cf. Ps. 44.21 n.). *Toward Your inner sanctuary,* the holy of holies, where God was imagined as being present. **3:** The deceitful, untrustworthy speech of the wicked is commonplace (Ps. 27.12), but if this is a royal psalm, as some think (cf. vv. 8–9), it may refer to conspiracy against the king. **4:** Prayer for measure-for-measure retribution (Ps. 94.2; Deut. 19.19). **6–7:** The characteristic move from complaint and petition to praise, with expressions of trust (see 6.9–11). **8–9:** The mention of *His anointed* (a Davidic king) and the prayer for the people (cf. 3.9) suggest that the speaker is a king or that the psalm was recited on behalf of the king.

29

A psalm of David.

Ascribe to the LORD, O divine beings,
ascribe to the LORD glory and strength.
2 Ascribe to the LORD the glory of His name;
bow down to the LORD, majestic in holiness.
3 The voice of the LORD is over the waters;
the God of glory thunders,
the LORD, over the mighty waters.
4 The voice of the LORD is power;
the voice of the LORD is majesty;
5 the voice of the LORD breaks cedars;
the LORD shatters the cedars of Lebanon.
6 [a-]He makes Lebanon skip like a calf,[-a]
Sirion, like a young wild ox.
7 The voice of the LORD kindles flames of fire;
8 the voice of the LORD convulses the wilderness;
the LORD convulses the wilderness of Kadesh;
9 the voice of the LORD causes hinds to calve,
[b-]and strips forests bare;[-b]
while in His temple all say "Glory!"
10 The LORD sat enthroned at the Flood;
the LORD sits enthroned, king forever.

a-a *Lit. "He makes them skip like a calf, Lebanon and Sirion, etc."*
b-b *Or "brings ewes to early birth."*

Ps. 29: A hymn celebrating God's awesome power over nature. Cf. Pss. 46–48; 96–99. God is portrayed as a storm, an earthquake—a theme associated with theophany (cf. *b. Zevaḥ.* 116a where a link is made with the giving of the Torah at Sinai). More commonly, the psalm is considered a prayer for rain. According to the Talmud, *b. Sukk.* 55a, the psalm was recited in the Temple on the first of the intermediate days of Sukkot; LXX associates it with the end of Sukkot ("Shemini ʿAtzeret"), the time for the prayer for rain; *b. Rosh Hash.* 32a and *b. Meg.* 17b link it with the paragraph about rain in the "Shemoneh ʿEsrei" prayer. A number of themes and linguistic usages that are also found in Ugaritic literature, as well as the mention of northern locations (Lebanon and Sirion, v. 6), have led modern scholars to see this psalm as an adaptation of a Ugaritic hymn to Baal (or to Hadad, the storm-god). Others see the psalm as part of a more generally shared ancient Near Eastern tradition rather than as a direct borrowing. Either way, the basic theme is built on the "combat-myth," known in Ugarit and Mesopotamia and reflected in other biblical passages, in which the hero-god defeats the forces of chaos and is then acclaimed by the other gods as their leader. The psalm shares with Ps. 24 the themes of God's triumph over the forces of chaos (primeval waters) and God enthroned as king in His Temple. Ps. 29 is used liturgically on the Sabbath when the Torah, seen as God's embodiment or representative in later Judaism, is returned to the ark. **1–2:** Cf. 96.7–9; 1 Chron. 16.28–30. **1:** *Divine beings,* lit. "sons of God," or "sons of gods," subordinate deities in the heavenly assembly. In Israelite thought these divine beings are part of God's retinue, His heavenly court (Exod. 15.11; Pss. 82.1; 89.6–8; Job chs 1–2). Probably because of its polytheistic overtones, Ps. 96.7 substitutes "families of the peoples" for this term. *Glory and strength,* key qualities of God, cf. Ps. 63.3. *Glory,* Heb "kavod," which is sometimes seen (Exod. 33.18; Isa. 40.5; Ps. 63.3) may refer to the divine radiance, the visual manifestation of God. **2:** *Majestic in holiness,* "behadrat kodesh," an odd phrase but cf. 110.3, "behadrei kodesh." LXX and Peshitta (Syriac) render "in His holy court." Cf. *b. Ber.* 30b. **3–9:** *The voice of the LORD* (claps of thunder), signifying God's power over the natural world, occurs seven times in these vv. **3:** The LORD battles the *mighty waters,* the primeval forces of chaos (cf. 24.2). **5:** The *cedars of Lebanon:* "Lebanon" is a name meaning whiteness, referring to the snow-covered mountain range in the modern country of Lebanon. Its cedars were famous for their height and strength. **6–8:** Earthquake is a traditional accompaniment of a theophany or divine manifestation (18.8; 114.7). **6:** *Sirion,* Mount Hermon (see Deut. 3.9), at the southern border of *Lebanon.* For mountains skipping, or more likely rearing up, see also 114.4. **8:** *The wilderness of Kadesh,* in western Syria; or if meant to express God's Presence over all Israel, the wilderness of Zin at Qadesh, to the south of Israel, where the Israelites encamped during their wanderings (Num. 20.1; 33.36). **9:** Reading with translators' note *b-b* makes a closer parallelism. An alternate emendation of *causes hinds* ("ʾayalot") *to calve* yields "causes ʾelotʾ (oak trees) to tremble." *In His temple,* praise from the subordinate deities in the heavenly temple, as in Isa. 6.3. **10:** The LORD's enthronement as king at *the Flood* (see Ps. 93) may be a double entendre, signifying that God defeated the waters (forces of chaos) and that He reigned since the time of the Flood, and will reign forever. Strikingly, God is not depicted as king since the creation, but rather since the Flood, the destruction that preceded the re-creation of the world.

11 May the LORD grant strength to His people;
may the LORD bestow on His people wellbeing.

30 A psalm of David. A song for the dedication of the House.[a]

2 I extol You, O LORD,
for You have lifted me up,
and not let my enemies rejoice over me.
3 O LORD, my God,
I cried out to You,
and You healed me.
4 O LORD, You brought me up from Sheol,
preserved me from going down into the Pit.

5 O you faithful of the LORD, sing to Him,
and praise His holy name.
6 For He is angry but a moment,
and when He is pleased there is life.
[b-]One may lie down weeping at nightfall;[-b]
but at dawn there are shouts of joy.

7 When I was untroubled,
I thought, "I shall never be shaken,"
8 for You, O LORD, when You were pleased,
made [me][c] firm as a mighty mountain.
When You hid Your face,
I was terrified.
9 I called to You, O LORD;
to my LORD I made appeal,
10 "What is to be gained from my death,[d]
from my descent into the Pit?
Can dust praise You?
Can it declare Your faithfulness?
11 Hear, O LORD, and have mercy on me;
O LORD, be my help!"

a I.e., the Temple. *b-b Or "Weeping may linger for the night."*
c Following Saadia, R. Isaiah of Trani; cf. Ibn Ezra. *d Lit. "blood."*

11: A prayer that God, supremely powerful and enthroned forever, will grant well-being to Israel; the psalm moves from powerful God to national peace.

Ps. 30: The superscription reinterprets the hymn, perhaps originally a thanksgiving hymn upon recovering from illness, as a prayer about the sickness of the community—i.e., national calamity—and its recovery, the restoration from exile and the rebuilding of the Temple (from 520–516 BCE; cf. Ezra 6.15–18). An older view sees the occasion as the rededication of the Temple in 164 BCE, following the victory of Judah Maccabee (cf. 1 Macc. 4.36–59). Following tractate *Soferim,* this psalm is read on Hanukkah. It is also part of the introductory liturgy for the morning service. **1:** The translation inverts the words, which in Heb are clumsy, reflecting the likely development of the superscription over time: "A psalm, a song of dedication of the House; of David." The mention of David in connection with the dedication of the Temple is anachronistic, since it occurred under Solomon (1 Kings ch 8; 2 Chron. chs 5–7); see Ps. 3.1 n. **2:** *Lifted me up,* lit. "drew me up" (like water from a well); it complements the idea of being raised from the Pit (v. 4). *Let my enemies rejoice* is a common biblical motif (e.g., Ps. 89.43; Prov. 24.17). **4:** God brought the psalmist back from a near-death state, from imminent death; he did not let the psalmist actually die. As in Mesopotamian literature, the image of being brought up from death (*Sheol* and *the Pit;* 28.1 n.) reflects recovery from serious illness, and not resurrection from death. **5–6:** The ritual of thanksgiving in the Temple, involving family and friends celebrating the psalmist's reintegration into the community. God is angry only momentarily (cf. Isa. 54.7–8); His (normal) favor is life-sustaining. An alternative meaning: God is angry for but a moment; His favor lasts a lifetime. **7–8:** The psalmist was apparently in God's favor for a long time, as evidenced by his good health; he complacently expected to remain so indefinitely. He was terrified when God *hid* His *face,* was no longer accessible and supportive. **9–11:** The psalmist quotes his earlier appeal for divine help. **10:** *Dust,* the dead, who have returned to dust. On the inability of the dead to praise God, see 6.5–6; 88.4–6, 11–13; 115.7; 118.17; Isa. 38.18–19. The psalmist argues that God should keep him alive so he can praise God (cf. v. 13).

12: God replaces the psalmist's *lament* (mourning) with *dancing,* and his *sackcloth* with a festal robe, signifying that God has brought him back from near-death into God's Presence. *Dancing* is also a form of praising God (149.3; 150.4). **13:** The Heb is difficult—literally, so that my glory ("kavod"—the same word at the end of 29.9) might sing songs; a slight emendation yields "kaved," liver, the source of emotions (see Lam. 2.11 translators' note).

Ps. 31: An anthological psalm, drawing on vv. from other psalms and Jer.: it calls on God for help and affirms the psalmist's trust in God. **1–5:** God is a refuge, described in terms connoting physical strength and protection *(rock, stronghold, citadel, fortress).* **1–3:** Cf. 18.3; 71.1–3. **5:** The *net* is a military weapon used to capture prisoners. **6:** The language of commercial borrowing and lending. The psalmist entrusts to God his *spirit,* the animating force that keeps him alive (this is not the "body" and "soul" dichotomy), as one would give a valuable object as a pledge. He is sure that his pledge will be redeemed, returned to him and not forfeited. God will return his life to him, because He is a *faithful God.* He keeps faith with those who trust in Him. In the later Jewish poem "Adon Olam," the beginning of the v. is quoted in a different sense, of entrusting the soul to God while sleeping, where sleep is viewed as a mini-death. **7:** *Empty folly* (see the poem in Jonah 2:9) is the opposite of the *faithful God* (v. 6). **9:** The psalmist is not entrapped in an enemy's *net* (v. 5), but finds a "broad place" in the care of God (25.15). **10–11:** Physical wasting away, perhaps by illness or perhaps a metaphor for the psalmist's distress. Because of illness the psalmist is shunned by all (38.12; 88.9)—this may be the result of natural fear from the illness, and/or the notion that such illness reflects divine disfavor. Cf. 6.3, 8 for similar phraseology. **12–13:** The scorn or shame felt by the petitioner is a major theme of Psalms (e.g., 22.7), and of the Bible as a whole (e.g., Jer. 23.40; Job 19.19), reflecting the fact that ancient Israel was a shame culture. **13:** Cf. Eccl. 9.5.

12 You turned my lament into dancing,
you undid my sackcloth and girded me with joy,
13 that [my] whole being might sing hymns to You
endlessly;
O LORD my God, I will praise You forever.

31

For the leader. A psalm of David.

2 I seek refuge in You, O LORD;
may I never be disappointed;
as You are righteous, rescue me.
3 Incline Your ear to me;
be quick to save me;
be a rock, a stronghold for me,
a citadel, for my deliverance.
4 For You are my rock and my fortress;
You lead me and guide me as befits Your name.
5 You free me from the net laid for me,
for You are my stronghold.
6 Into Your hand I entrust my spirit;
You redeem me, O LORD, faithful God.
7 I detest those who rely on empty folly,
but I trust in the LORD.
8 Let me exult and rejoice in Your faithfulness
when You notice my affliction,
are mindful of my deep distress,
9 and do not hand me over to my enemy,
but [a]grant me relief.[a]

10 Have mercy on me, O LORD,
for I am in distress;
my eyes are wasted by vexation,
[b]my substance and body too.[b]
11 My life is spent in sorrow,
my years in groaning;
my strength fails because of my iniquity,
my limbs waste away.
12 Because of all my foes
I am the particular butt of my neighbors,
a horror to my friends;
those who see me on the street avoid me.
13 I am put out of mind like the dead;
I am like an object given up for lost.

a-a *Lit. "make my feet stand in a broad place."* b-b *Meaning of Heb. uncertain.*

14 I hear the whisperings of many,
intrigue[a] on every side,
as they scheme together against me,
plotting to take my life.

15 But I trust in You, O LORD;
I say, "You are my God!"
16 My fate is in Your hand;
save me from the hand of my enemies and pursuers.
17 Show favor to Your servant;
as You are faithful, deliver me.
18 O LORD, let me not be disappointed when I call You;
let the wicked be disappointed;
let them be silenced in Sheol;
19 let lying lips be stilled
that speak haughtily against the righteous
with arrogance and contempt.
20 How abundant is the good
that You have in store for those who fear You,
that You do in the full view of men
for those who take refuge in You.
21 You grant them the protection of Your presence
[b-]against scheming men;[-b]
You shelter them in Your pavilion
from contentious tongues.
22 Blessed is the LORD,
for He has been wondrously faithful to me,
a veritable bastion.
23 Alarmed, I had thought,
"I am thrust out of Your sight";
yet You listened to my plea for mercy
when I cried out to You.
24 So love the LORD, all you faithful;
the LORD guards the loyal,
and more than requites
him who acts arrogantly.
25 Be strong and of good courage,
all you who wait for the LORD.

32

Of David. [b-]A *maskil.*[-b]

Happy is he whose transgression is forgiven,
whose sin is covered over.
2 Happy the man whom the LORD does not hold guilty,
and in whose spirit there is no deceit.

a Others "terror." *b-b Meaning of Heb. uncertain.*

14: Likely citing Jer. 20.10. **15:** In the preceding vv., the psalmist was the object of other people's thoughts or actions. Now he is the grammatical subject, expressing his own beliefs. The opening words, *But I,* contrast the psalmist's trust in God with his troubled condition. **17:** See Ps. 4.7. **18–21:** Counterpoised to Sheol, the abode of the silent dead, is the Temple, residence of the living God. The psalmist prays that the wicked will *be silenced in Sheol,* while he, like all God-fearers, will be granted *the protection of Your presence* and will be sheltered *in Your pavilion* (the Temple). The disappointment of the wicked is also juxtaposed to his lack of disappointment. **18:** Let the wicked suffer the fate that the psalmist almost suffered. The sin of the wicked is their arrogant speech against the righteous; cf. v. 21. **21:** Cf. Ps. 76.3. **22:** *A veritable bastion:* According to this reading, God is a bastion; cf. v. 3. Heb reads "in the besieged city," which might mean "while the psalmist felt himself under siege." **23:** *Thrust out of Your sight,* separated from the Presence of God in the Temple (Hos. 9.15; Jonah 2.5; 2 Chron. 26.21). Like v. 15, this v. begins in Heb with "but I," this time contrasting the "before" and the "after." **24–25:** A ritual of public thanksgiving with the psalmist's community (30.12–13). The psalmist's deliverance in vv. 22–23 validates the principle of trusting in God and encourages others to do so.

Ps. 32: The happiness, or good fortune, of the sinner who is forgiven. The psalm has some affinity to wisdom texts (vv. 1–2, 8–9; cf. Ps. 1). The term *maskil,* of unknown meaning, resonates with "'askilkha," "let me enlighten you" (v. 8). **1:** *Forgiven ... covered over,* divine passives; as the continuation makes clear, it is God who forgives sin. This v. uses two different images for forgiveness—lifting the sin (or its burden) from the individual (translated here metaphorically as *forgiven*) and having it *covered over* (i.e., put out of sight).

3–5: The psalmist's silence (not confessing his sin) brought on illness; acknowledgment of sin brought healing and forgiveness. **4:** *Your hand lay heavy* is an idiom for divine punishment (1 Sam. 5.6, 11). *Selah* (also vv. 5, 7), see Ps. 3.3 n. **7:** *You preserve me from distress* in Heb is a soundplay, "mitzar" and "titzreni." **8–9:** A teacher's instruction, promising guidance for life. *Senseless horse . . .* , cf. Prov. 26.3. **10–11:** The varying fates of the wicked and the upright (1.6). Sickness and pain are punishment for sin. *Favor,* Heb "ḥesed," God's faithful care (cf. 5.8 n.). *Surrounded with favor* picks up on v. 7, *You surround me with the joyous shouts of deliverance,* implying that deliverance reflects divine favor. The psalm ends on a communal high note of joyful praise (see 97.12), using phrases that lead into the next psalm.

Ps. 33: A call to praise God's faithful care and the joy of trusting in God. The Creator of the world maintains control of it; in contrast to Him, all human power pales in significance. Pss. 33 and 34 are thematically similar, and have been incorporated into the introductory prayers to the morning service on Sabbath and festivals. **1–3:** For music as a form of worship, see 81.2–4; 92.2–4; 150.3–5. **3:** God is so magnificent that he deserves *a new song.* **4–5:** The world that God created by his *word,* which is right, is full of God's faithful care. The world is, as a result of how it was created, a place of rightness, justice, and "ḥesed," and thus God loves these attributes when practiced by people.

3 As long as I said nothing,
my limbs wasted away
from my anguished roaring all day long.
4 For night and day
Your hand lay heavy on me;
my vigor waned
as in the summer drought. *Selah.*
5 Then I acknowledged my sin to You;
I did not cover up my guilt;
I resolved, "I will confess my transgressions to the LORD,"
and You forgave the guilt of my sin. *Selah.*
6 Therefore let every faithful man pray to You
[a-]upon discovering [his sin],[-a]
that the rushing mighty waters
not overtake him.
7 You are my shelter;
You preserve me from distress;
You surround me with the joyous shouts of deliverance. *Selah.*

8 Let me enlighten you
and show you which way to go;
let me offer counsel; my eye is on you.
9 Be not like a senseless horse or mule
[b-]whose movement must be curbed by bit and bridle;[-b]
[c-]far be it from you![-c]
10 Many are the torments of the wicked,
but he who trusts in the LORD
shall be surrounded with favor.
11 Rejoice in the LORD and exult, O you righteous;
shout for joy, all upright men!

33

Sing forth, O you righteous, to the LORD;
it is fit that the upright acclaim Him.
2 Praise the LORD with the lyre;
with the ten-stringed harp sing to Him;
3 sing Him a new song;
play sweetly with shouts of joy.
4 For the word of the LORD is right;
His every deed is faithful.
5 He loves what is right and just;
the earth is full of the LORD's faithful care.

a-a Meaning of Heb. uncertain; others "in a time when You may be found."
b-b Meaning of Heb. uncertain.
c-c Meaning of Heb. uncertain; for this rendering cf. Ibn Ezra.

6 By the word of the LORD the heavens were made,
by the breath of His mouth, all their host.
7 He heaps up the ocean waters like a mound,
stores the deep in vaults.

8 Let all the earth fear the LORD;
let all the inhabitants of the world dread Him.
9 For He spoke, and it was;
He commanded, and it endured.
10 The LORD frustrates the plans of nations,
brings to naught the designs of peoples.
11 What the LORD plans endures forever,
what He designs, for ages on end.

12 Happy the nation whose God is the LORD,
the people He has chosen to be His own.
13 The LORD looks down from heaven;
He sees all mankind.
14 From His dwelling-place He gazes
on all the inhabitants of the earth—
15 He who fashions the hearts of them all,
who discerns all their doings.

16 Kings are not delivered by a large force;
warriors are not saved by great strength;
17 horses are a false hope for deliverance;
for all their great power they provide no escape.
18 Truly the eye of the LORD is on those who fear
Him,
who wait for His faithful care
19 to save them from death,
to sustain them in famine.
20 We set our hope on the LORD,
He is our help and shield;
21 in Him our hearts rejoice,
for in His holy name we trust.
22 May we enjoy, O LORD, Your faithful care,
as we have put our hope in You.

34

Of David, [a]when he feigned madness in the presence of Abimelech, who turned him out, and he left.[a]

2 א I bless the LORD at all times;
praise of Him is ever in my mouth.
3 ב I glory in the LORD;
let the lowly hear it and rejoice.

a-a *Cf. 1 Sam. 21.14 ff.*

6–9: As in Gen. ch 1, creation is by the divine *word:* the making of the *heavens,* the confinement of the chaotic *waters,* and the peopling of the earth (Gen. 1.6–10). **7:** Cf. Exod. 15.8 where the water of the Sea of Reeds is piled in a heap, though here this image refers to creation. **8–11:** All inhabitants of the world must be in awe of the powerful Creator. Human plans can easily come to naught, but God's plans are eternal. **12:** Israel is special because of its relationship with this God. **13–14:** For God residing in heaven, cf. Deut. 26.15; 1 Kings 8.30, 39; Pss. 14.2; 53.3; 102.20; 113.4–6; Lam. 3.50. **16–17:** Human armies and military equipment, however strong, are no match for God's power. *Horses* pulled war-chariots. **18:** God has a special relationship with *those who fear Him,* though they may need to *wait.* **19:** *Death* and *famine* were common results of war and siege. **20:** *Shield* is an apt metaphor in this military context. **22:** The psalm ends with the hope of God's continued care and protection, for which the psalm has been praising Him.

Ps. 34: Praise of God for deliverance from trouble. An acrostic psalm (see Ps. 9 n.) with the sixth letter "vav" missing. (Aside from the conjunction "and," Heb *ve,* almost no Heb words start with this letter.) As in Ps. 25, an additional v., also beginning with the letter "pe," follows the acrostic. The psalm can be divided into two sections, vv. 2–11 and 12–22; the second half in particular has wisdom affinities. Frequent reference is made to parts of the body: *mouth, tongue, lips, eyes, ears, face, bones;* and to actions associated with them: seeing, hearing, tasting, shouting. **1:** See 1 Sam. 21.12–15, where the king, who is here called *Abimelech,* is referred to as Achish; see also Ps. 3. **2:** *At all times* (Heb "tamid") is often used hyperbolically in Ps. (e.g., 16.8, "ever"; 71.6, "always"). **3:** *The lowly,* those completely dependent on God.

4: This v. is used liturgically in the synagogue when the Torah scroll, seen as the representation of God, is removed from the ark. **6:** *Radiant,* the external manifestation of happiness, a bright, smiling face. **7:** The psalmist may see himself as a personal example for others. **8:** Protection by a guardian angel, a member of the heavenly court or a manifestation of God (Gen. 24.4; 48.16; Ps. 35.5–6). **10–11:** Predatory carnivores (metaphors for the proud and arrogant) suffer want, while the humble are sustained by God. **12–15:** A sage's address to students, teaching fear of the LORD (Prov. 1.7; Job 28.28) is incorporated here. In order to achieve a good life, one should guard one's tongue, etc. Questions and riddles were among the ancient pedagogic techniques. **16–18:** The LORD's benevolent gaze on the righteous, and His angry face, glaring at evildoers. If we follow the order of the alphabet found in Lam. chs 2, 3, and 4 and some ancient Heb abecedaries, and read v. 17 after v. 18, the vv. flow more smoothly. **19:** *Brokenhearted ... crushed in spirit,* the depressed and despondent who call on God. **20–21:** An admission that the righteous do encounter misfortune but that it is temporary; God will remove it before grave harm ensues. **20–23:** The varying fates of *the righteous* and *the wicked.* **23:** This v. stands outside the acrostic and provides a happy ending for the psalm. See 25.22 n.

4 ג Exalt the LORD with me;
let us extol His name together.
5 ד I turned to the LORD, and He answered me;
He saved me from all my terrors.
6 ה Men look to Him and are radiant;
ו let their faces not be downcast.
7 ז Here was a lowly man who called,
and the LORD listened,
and delivered him from all his troubles.
8 ח The angel of the LORD camps around those who fear Him
and rescues them.
9 ט Taste and see how good the LORD is;
happy the man who takes refuge in Him!
10 י Fear the LORD, you His consecrated ones,
for those who fear Him lack nothing.
11 כ Lions have been reduced to starvation,
but those who turn to the LORD shall not lack any good.
12 ל Come, my sons, listen to me;
I will teach you what it is to fear the LORD.
13 מ Who is the man who is eager for life,
who desires years of good fortune?
14 נ Guard your tongue from evil,
your lips from deceitful speech.
15 ס Shun evil and do good,
seek amity[a] and pursue it.
16 ע The eyes of the LORD are on the righteous,
His ears attentive to their cry.
17 פ The face of the LORD is set against evildoers,
to erase their names from the earth.
18 צ They[b] cry out, and the LORD hears,
and saves them from all their troubles.
19 ק The LORD is close to the brokenhearted;
those crushed in spirit He delivers.
20 ר Though the misfortunes of the righteous be many,
the LORD will save him from them all,
21 ש Keeping all his bones intact,
not one of them being broken.
22 ת One misfortune is the deathblow of the wicked;
the foes of the righteous shall be ruined.
23 The LORD redeems the life of His servants;
all who take refuge in Him shall not be ruined.

a Or "integrity."
b Viz., the righteous of v. 16.

35

Of David.

O LORD, strive with my adversaries,
give battle to my foes,
2 take up shield and buckler,
and come to my defense;
3 ready the spear and javelin
against my pursuers;
tell me, "I am your deliverance."
4 Let those who seek my life
be frustrated and put to shame;
let those who plan to harm me
fall back in disgrace.
5 Let them be as chaff in the wind,
the LORD's angel driving them on.
6 Let their path be dark and slippery,
with the LORD's angel in pursuit.
7 For without cause they hid a net to trap me;
without cause they dug a pit[a] for me.
8 Let disaster overtake them unawares;
let the net they hid catch them;
let them fall into it when disaster [strikes].
9 Then shall I exult in the LORD,
rejoice in His deliverance.
10 All my bones shall say,
"LORD, who is like You?
You save the poor from one stronger than he,
the poor and needy from his despoiler."

11 Malicious witnesses appear
who question me about things I do not know.
12 They repay me evil for good,
[seeking] my bereavement.
13 Yet, when they were ill,
my dress was sackcloth,
I kept a fast—
[b-]may what I prayed for happen to me![-b]
14 I walked about as though it were my friend or my brother;
I was bowed with gloom, like one mourning for his mother.
15 But when I stumble, they gleefully gather;
wretches gather against me,

Ps. 35: The speaker presents himself as a military leader, possibly the king, who prays for deliverance from his enemies. In vv. 1–10 the enemies are portrayed as foreign countries with armies; in vv. 11–16 they are false witnesses and treacherous friends, that is, allies who proved untrustworthy. V. 19, *treacherous* (lit. "lying") *enemies* ties these two themes together. **1–3:** Prayer that God, the Divine Warrior, arm Himself for battle against the psalmist's foes; elsewhere God as warrior is rarely depicted as fully armed like a human. **4–6:** Traditional invective against enemies (40.15–16); punishment by God's angelic forces. **5:** As in the previous psalm (v. 8), the focus moves to *the LORD's angel,* a manifestation of God. This commonality may explain the adjacent placement of these two psalms. *Chaff* is easily blown away (Ps. 1.4; Isa. 17.13). **7–8:** By the law of talion or equivalent retribution (see 3.8), *net* and *pit* entrap those who used them to ensnare others. **8:** *Disaster,* Heb "sho'ah," the term now used for the Holocaust. *Unawares:* Just as the enemy plotted to catch the psalmist without warning, so their measure-for-measure punishment will come without warning. **10:** *All my bones,* my whole being. **13–18:** The supplicant feels betrayed by those he prayed for. When they were weak he prayed for them but they do not reciprocate; rather they hope for his downfall. **13:** Typical mourning practices.

a Transferred from first clause for clarity.
b-b Meaning of Heb. uncertain; lit. "my prayer returns upon my bosom."

18: A return to the theme of v. 10. **19–21:** The language of conspiracy. **21:** *Aha, aha,* a common exclamation (see Pss. 40.16; 70.4). **22–25:** Appeal to God to intervene; the psalmist assumes that God has *seen* (v. 22), but for unknown reasons, has not acted. **27–28:** In place of the enemies' damaging speech (vv. 11–12, 20–21), the psalmist's tongue and that of his friends tell of the LORD's victory (see vv. 10, 18).

Ps. 36: Rejoicing in the Temple, protected from evildoers. The poem consists of instruction about the wicked (vv. 2–5), a hymn lauding the Temple (vv. 6–10), and a prayer for God's care of the righteous and the fall of the wicked (vv. 11–13). **1:** *Servant of the LORD,* 18.1. **2–5:** The wicked have no dread of God, nothing to motivate them to desist from evil thoughts and speech, which occupy them privately *(in bed)* and publicly *(on a path)*. **2:** Transgression, remarkably personified, speaks in oracular form (like a prophet). To the wicked, this voice is authoritative. The Rabbis identified it with the evil inclination.

I know not why;
[a]-they tear at me without end.
16 With impious, mocking grimace-[a]
they gnash their teeth at me.

17 O Lord, how long will You look on?
Rescue me [a]-from their attacks,-[a]
my precious life, from the lions,
18 that I may praise You in a great congregation,
acclaim You in a mighty throng.
19 Let not my treacherous enemies rejoice over me,
or those who hate me without reason wink their
eyes.
20 For they do not offer amity,
but devise fraudulent schemes against harmless folk.
21 They open wide their mouths at me,
saying, "Aha, aha, we have seen it!"

22 You have seen it, O LORD;
do not hold aloof!
O Lord, be not far from me!
23 Wake, rouse Yourself for my cause,
for my claim, O my God and my Lord!
24 Take up my cause, O LORD my God, as You are
beneficent,
and let them not rejoice over me.
25 Let them not think,
"Aha, just what we wished!"
Let them not say,
"We have destroyed him!"
26 May those who rejoice at my misfortune
be frustrated and utterly disgraced;
may those who vaunt themselves over me
be clad in frustration and shame.
27 May those who desire my vindication
sing forth joyously;
may they always say,
"Extolled be the LORD
who desires the well-being of His servant,"
28 while my tongue shall recite Your beneficent acts,
Your praises all day long.

36 For the leader. Of the servant of the LORD, of David.

2 [b]-I know-[b] what Transgression says to the wicked;
he has no sense of the dread of God,

a-a Meaning of Heb. uncertain. *b-b Lit. "In my heart is."*

3 [a]because its speech is seductive to him
till his iniquity be found out and he be hated.[-a]
4 His words are evil and deceitful;
he will not consider doing good.
5 In bed he plots mischief;
he is set on a path of no good,
he does not reject evil.

6 O LORD, Your faithfulness reaches to heaven;
Your steadfastness to the sky;
7 Your beneficence is like the high mountains;
Your justice like the great deep;
man and beast You deliver, O LORD.
8 How precious is Your faithful care, O God!
Mankind shelters in the shadow of Your wings.
9 They feast on the rich fare of Your house;
You let them drink at Your refreshing stream.
10 With You is the fountain of life;
by Your light do we see light.
11 Bestow Your faithful care on those devoted to You,
and Your beneficence on upright men.
12 Let not the foot of the arrogant tread on me,
or the hand of the wicked drive me away.
13 There lie the evildoers, fallen,
thrust down, unable to rise.

37

Of David.

א Do not be vexed by evil men;
do not be incensed by wrongdoers;
2 for they soon wither like grass,
like verdure fade away.
3 ב Trust in the LORD and do good,
abide in the land and remain loyal.
4 Seek the favor of the LORD,
and He will grant you the desires of your heart.
5 ג Leave all[b] to the LORD;
trust in Him; He will do it.

a-a Meaning of Heb. uncertain. *b Lit. "your way."*

6–11: Contrasted with the wicked are those who seek God in his Temple. **6–7:** Though God is worshipped at the Temple, His beneficent justice is of cosmic proportion, reaching everywhere, as expressed through the merism *high mountains ... great deep.* **7–9:** These vv. are recited when donning the tallit (prayer shawl), as the worshipper imagines being enveloped not merely by the tallit, but by God's beneficence. **8–10:** A remarkable mixture of images of sustenance: shade, food, water, and light. The Temple protects and its sacrificial meals provide *rich fare,* the meat and fat eaten by the sacrificer. *Refreshing stream,* the river of life-giving water that goes out from the Temple; cf. Ezek. 47.1–2; Joel 4.18; Zech. 14.8; Ps. 46.5. Heb for "refreshing" is "ʿadanekha," forming a nexus with the rivers of Eden (Gen. 2.10); Eden is also known as the Garden of God. These waters are the *fountain* (source) *of life. Light* signifies life. **12–13:** The psalmist hopes to be safe from the wicked, *arrogant* in that they do not recognize a higher power. The wicked will be made permanently powerless. **13:** *There,* at Mt. Zion, where the wicked cannot come. Alternatively, it may mean the underworld (cf. Job 3.17) or be an adverb of time ("then"); a slight emendation (from "sham" to "shamemu") yields "are ruined/devastated."

Ps. 37: An alphabetic acrostic psalm (see Pss. 9 n.; 25 n.) whose themes, structure, and vocabulary are characteristic of Prov. "Wisdom" is mentioned explicitly in v. 30, and thus the psalm should be considered a wisdom psalm, written by someone who was part of the wisdom movement or heavily influenced by it. It expresses the certainty that ultimately the righteous will succeed and will inherit the land, and the wicked will fail. Inheriting the land is a major theme, repeated six times. The authors of the Dead Sea Scrolls wrote a "pesher" (a type of commentary) on this psalm in which they apply it to their own situation (4Q171 = 4QpPs[a]). They see "Ephraim" and "Manasseh" (their code words for Pharisees and Sadducees) as the wicked and themselves as the people who will, in the future, inherit the land. Like the previous psalms, it focuses on the contrast between the righteous and the wicked. **1–2:** *Do not be vexed* by the success of *evil men,* which is brief: Repeated in vv. 7–8; see Prov. 23.17–18; 24.1, 19–20. **2:** *Like grass,* the evanescence of the wicked (90.5–6; 102.5, 12; 103.15; Job 8.12–13), especially apt in the context of "the land"; cf. vv. 20, 35. **3:** The first occurrence of the refrainlike promise of possessing the land (vv. 9, 11, 22, 29, 34).

7: A repetition of the psalm's initial theme—that the wicked may prosper, albeit briefly. **9–10:** *Cut off,* separated from the land (cf. vv. 28, 38; Prov. 2.21–22). **13:** God laughs derisively at the wicked because He knows they will be punished (2.4; 59.9). **14–15:** The weapons of the wicked "backfire" and are broken, as are their arms (v. 17). **16:** *Better ... than,* characteristic wording of wisdom literature (e.g., Prov. 15.16–17). **17:** A chiastic explanation of the previous v. **18–20:** The varying fates of the righteous and the wicked. **18:** *Concerned,* Heb lit. "knows," translated as "cherishes" in 1.6. **23–24:** The world is not run in an impersonal fashion, as some wisdom texts may suggest, but with deep involvement by God.

6 He will cause your vindication to shine forth like the light,
the justice of your case, like the noonday sun.
7 ד Be patient and wait for the LORD,
do not be vexed by the prospering man
who carries out his schemes.

8 ה Give up anger, abandon fury,
do not be vexed;
it can only do harm.
9 For evil men will be cut off,
but those who look to the LORD—
they shall inherit the land.
10 ו A little longer and there will be no wicked man;
you will look at where he was—
he will be gone.
11 But the lowly shall inherit the land,
and delight in abundant well-being.
12 ז The wicked man schemes against the righteous,
and gnashes his teeth at him.
13 The Lord laughs at him,
for He knows that his day will come.
14 ח The wicked draw their swords, bend their bows,
to bring down the lowly and needy,
to slaughter [a]upright men.[-a]
15 Their swords shall pierce their own hearts,
and their bows shall be broken.
16 ט Better the little that the righteous man has
than the great abundance of the wicked.
17 For the arms of the wicked shall be broken,
but the LORD is the support of the righteous.
18 י The LORD is concerned for the needs[b] of the blameless;
their portion lasts forever;
19 they shall not come to grief in bad times;
in famine, they shall eat their fill.
20 כ But the wicked shall perish,
and the enemies of the LORD shall be consumed,
like meadow grass[c] consumed in smoke.
21 ל The wicked man borrows and does not repay;
the righteous is generous and keeps giving.
22 Those blessed by Him shall inherit the land,
but those cursed by Him shall be cut off.
23 מ The steps of a man are made firm by the LORD,
when He delights in his way.

a-a Lit. "those whose way is upright." *b Lit. "days."*
c Meaning of Heb. uncertain.

24 Though he stumbles, he does not fall down,
for the LORD gives him support.
25 נ I have been young and am now old,
but I have never seen a righteous man abandoned,
or his children seeking bread.
26 He is always generous, and lends,
and his children are held blessed.
27 ס Shun evil and do good,
and you shall abide forever.
28 For the LORD loves what is right,
He does not abandon His faithful ones.
They are preserved forever,
while the children of the wicked will be cut off.
29 The righteous shall inherit the land,
and abide forever in it.
30 פ The mouth of the righteous utters wisdom,
and his tongue speaks what is right.
31 The teaching of his God is in his heart;
his feet do not slip.
32 צ The wicked watches for the righteous,
seeking to put him to death;
33 the LORD will not abandon him to his power;
He will not let him be condemned in judgment.
34 ק Look to the LORD and keep to His way,
and He will raise you high that you may inherit the land;
when the wicked are cut off, you shall see it.
35 ר I saw a wicked man, powerful,
well-rooted like a robust native tree.
36 Suddenly he vanished and was gone;
I sought him, but he was not to be found.
37 ש Mark the blameless, note the upright,
for there is a future for the man of integrity.
38 But transgressors shall be utterly destroyed,
the future of the wicked shall be cut off.
39 ת The deliverance of the righteous comes from the LORD,
their stronghold in time of trouble.
40 The LORD helps them and rescues them,
rescues them from the wicked and delivers them,
for they seek refuge in Him.

38 A psalm of David. *Lehazkir.*[a]

2 O LORD, do not punish me in wrath;
do not chastise me in fury.

a *Meaning of Heb. uncertain.*

25: A remarkable claim concerning theodicy, this v. is recited toward the end of the grace after meals. **27:** Traditional advice; see v. 3; Ps. 34.15; Prov. 13.19. **28:** A word or phrase may have dropped out here since the letter "ayin" is missing in the acrostic; an emendation for *They are preserved forever,* restoring the missing letter would read "sinners ("avalim") are destroyed forever." **33:** A repeated insistence of divine justice, which serves as a motivation to be just (v. 34). **35–38:** The varying fates of the righteous (v. 25) and of the transgressors; this type of contrast also typifies wisdom literature. Wisdom literature often employs empirical observation, as in vv. 25 and 35 "to see." This word occurs eighteen times in Eccl. **40:** *Helps ... rescues ... delivers* highlights the power of God to completely (albeit eventually) save the righteous.

Ps. 38: A sinner prays for healing, and forgiveness of sins. Though similar to Ps. 6, this psalm depicts the psalmist openly admitting his sins. The psalm contains an extensive description of physical illness and mental anguish (see Pss. 6; 13; 22; 31). The list of ailments—which includes the entire body racked with pain, festering wounds, inability to stand erect, fever, dull eyes, lack of strength—sounds like a catalogue of all possible maladies, suggesting that the illness may be metaphoric. Burdened by his sins, the psalmist is in mental and physical anguish. The psalm is thus more a prayer for forgiveness (see esp. v. 19) than a prayer for healing. **2:** Sickness was thought to be the punishment for sin. **3:** The punishing illness is described as arrows sent by God (Job 6.4; 16.12–13).

4–6: Sin as the cause of the psalmist's malady (Isa. 1.5–6). Most psalms of complaint lack such confessions. **9:** *I roar* introduces a set of verbs that play a key role in the continuation of the psalm. **11:** *My eyes too have lost their luster,* a biblical expression for loss of strength (see e.g., 1 Sam. 14.27). **12–13:** Friends and family distance themselves from the psalmist, showing indifference (see 31.10–13 nn.), while enemies speak against him. **14–18:** The psalmist does not respond to his foes, pretending that he does not hear them, preferring to wait for God's response, without which he will die. He worries that if his death occurs, his foes will rejoice, a common theme of Psalms (e.g., 13.5). As a sinner, the psalmist has no way to withstand evildoers by himself. **14:** *Deaf,* i.e., ignorant of the plotting of his foes in v. 13. **19:** Confession of sin (32.5). **22–23:** Like the opening, highly stereotypical language; see 22.12, 20; 40.14.

3 For Your arrows have struck me;
Your blows have fallen upon me.
4 There is no soundness in my flesh because of Your rage,
no wholeness in my bones because of my sin.
5 For my iniquities have [a]overwhelmed me;[a]
they are like a heavy burden, more than I can bear.
6 My wounds stink and fester
because of my folly.
7 I am all bent and bowed;
I walk about in gloom all day long.
8 For my sinews are full of fever;
there is no soundness in my flesh.
9 I am all benumbed and crushed;
I roar because of the turmoil in my mind.

10 O Lord, You are aware of all my entreaties;
my groaning is not hidden from You.
11 My mind reels;
my strength fails me;
my eyes too have lost their luster.
12 My friends and companions stand back from my affliction;
my kinsmen stand far off.
13 Those who seek my life lay traps;
those who wish me harm speak malice;
they utter deceit all the time.
14 But I am like a deaf man, unhearing,
like a dumb man who cannot speak up;
15 I am like one who does not hear,
who has no retort on his lips.
16 But I wait for You, O LORD;
You will answer, O Lord, my God.
17 For I fear they will rejoice over me;
when my foot gives way they will vaunt themselves against me.
18 For I am on the verge of collapse;
my pain is always with me.
19 I acknowledge my iniquity;
I am fearful over my sin;
20 for my mortal enemies are numerous;
my treacherous foes are many.
21 Those who repay evil for good
harass me for pursuing good.

22 Do not abandon me, O LORD;
my God, be not far from me;

a-a *Lit. "passed over my head."*

23 hasten to my aid,
O Lord, my deliverance.

39 For the leader; for *Jeduthun.* A psalm of David.

2 I resolved I would watch my step
lest I offend by my speech;
I would keep my mouth muzzled
while the wicked man was in my presence.
3 I was dumb, silent;
I was very[a] still
while my pain was intense.
4 My mind was in a rage,
my thoughts were all aflame;
I spoke out:
5 Tell me, O LORD, what my term is,
what is the measure of my days;
I would know how fleeting my life is.
6 You have made my life just handbreadths long;
its span is as nothing in Your sight;
[b-]no man endures any longer than a breath.[-b]
Selah.
7 Man walks about as a mere shadow;
mere futility is his hustle and bustle,
amassing and not knowing who will gather in.
8 What, then, can I count on, O Lord?
In You my hope lies.
9 Deliver me from all my transgressions;
make me not the butt of the benighted.
10 I am dumb, I do not speak up,
for it is Your doing.
11 Take away Your plague from me;
I perish from Your blows.
12 You chastise a man in punishment for his sin,
consuming like a moth what he treasures.
No man is more than a breath. *Selah.*

13 Hear my prayer, O LORD;
give ear to my cry;
do not disregard my tears;
for like all my forebears
I am an alien, resident with You.
14 Look away from me, [b-]that I may recover,[-b]
before I pass away and am gone.

a *Cf. use of* ṭwb *in Hos. 10.1; Jonah 4.4.* b-b *Meaning of Heb. uncertain.*

Ps. 39: An atypical psalm, meditating in an anguished manner on the brevity of human life (cf. Pss. 90; 102), and the inevitability of sin. The psalmist hopes that the short time he has to live will be spent in God's favor. Emphasis is placed on restraining one's speech against God, accepting one's fate. Nevertheless, the psalmist questions God, trying to understand God's plan for him. This is a quiet yet effective protest against the human condition. This psalm has some commonality with Ps. 38 (admission that suffering is the result of sin, being "dumb," that is keeping silent), but it does not emphasize physical suffering. It also shares major themes with Eccl.: the idea of the brevity of life, expressed by the term "hevel," "a breath," (see the refrain in vv. 6 and 12), a questioning of the purpose of life, and the conclusion that people should use their time in the service of God. In terms of its conception of humanity, the psalm offers a marvelous counterpoint to Ps. 8. **1:** *Jeduthun* was a famous Temple musician; see Pss. 62; 77; 1 Chron. 16.42; 25.6. **2–5:** Avoidance of sins of speech is a common concern of Psalms. Here, speech would challenge God or express anger at His actions against the psalmist, so the psalmist keeps silent as long as he can (cf. v. 10); but at last he speaks out, asking God how long he has to live, that is, how long he must bear his suffering. (Cf. Job, who does not hesitate to challenge God.) **6:** *Selah* (also v. 11), see 3.3 n. **7:** For the theme of one's wealth left for others, see 49.17–18; Eccl. 2.18–19. **8–9:** Given that life is short and unpredictable, the only durable hope is faith in God, which the psalmist professes. This faith should lead God to forgive his sins and remove his punishment. **12:** Here and in v. 7 the suffering seems to be financial loss rather than illness. A *breath,* "hevel," as in Eccl. 1.2, there translated "futility." **13:** *An alien, resident,* a resident alien, a legal term (see Lev. 25.23; 1 Chron. 29.15) used metaphorically to mean that the psalmist resides only temporarily and conditionally with God. **14:** *Look away from me,* stop punishing me. *Am gone,* there is no thought of an afterlife in Psalms. The v. is similar to Job 10.20.

40 For the leader. A psalm of David.

2 I put my hope in the LORD;
He inclined toward me,
and heeded my cry.
3 He lifted me out of the miry pit,
the slimy clay,
and set my feet on a rock,
steadied my legs.
4 He put a new song into my mouth,
a hymn to our God.
May many see it and stand in awe,
and trust in the LORD.
5 Happy is the man who makes the LORD his trust,
who turns not to the arrogant or to followers of
falsehood.
6 [a]You, O LORD my God, have done many things;
the wonders You have devised for us
cannot be set out before You;[a]
I would rehearse the tale of them,
but they are more than can be told.
7 [b]You gave me to understand that[b]
You do not desire sacrifice and meal offering;
You do not ask for burnt offering and purification
offering.
8 Then I said,
[b]"See, I will bring a scroll recounting what befell me."[b]
9 To do what pleases You, my God, is my desire;
Your teaching is in my inmost parts.
10 I proclaimed [Your] righteousness in a great
congregation;
see, I did not withhold my words;
O LORD, You must know it.

a-a Or "You, O LORD my God, have done many things—/ the wonders You have devised for us; / none can equal You." *b-b Meaning of Heb. uncertain.*

Ps. 40: The psalmist seeks a public and permanent venue for praising God, to acknowledge God's past favors and in anticipation of the current favor he now requests. This balance between anticipatory praise and a request for deliverance is not unusual (cf. Ps. 22), but here the emphasis is on praise rather than on complaint about misfortune. This psalm is perhaps a combination of two psalms, the second of which (vv. 14–18) is preserved as Ps. 70. (NJPS makes the break after v. 12.) Alternatively, the psalm was one composition and Ps. 70 has lost the first part. **2:** *Inclined* introduces a series of verbs of movement in vv. 2–3. **3:** *Pit ... slimy clay,* synonyms for the abode of the dead; as in 30.4, death is used to refer to grave illness. The terra firma image of *a rock* contrasts with the slippery and sinking image of *slimy clay.* **4:** *A new song,* cf. Ps. 33.3. **5:** Ps. 34.9; Prov. 16.20. *Arrogant,* a striking word, used elsewhere for the sea monster, Rahab, that threatened God at creation (e.g., Ps. 89.11). **6:** *Cannot be set out before you,* or, "cannot be compared to you"—the biblical God is incomparable, but not, as some later theologians claimed, "wholly other." **7–9:** Difficult to interpret. A general statement about sacrifice is illustrated by listing several main types: *sacrifice,* a nonspecific term for animal offerings; *meal offering,* a grain offering accompanying animal sacrifice; *burnt offering,* in which the entire sacrifice is consumed by fire; *purification offering,* a sin offering. This is not a critique of the sacrificial system, but rather a notice that sacrifice is not required in this instance and does not satisfy the psalmist's desire *to do what pleases ... God.* God is pleased if people follow his *teaching,* his torah, written in a scroll (cf. Deut. 31.26). Doing what pleases God is preferable to sacrifice (1 Sam. 15.22; Jer. 7.21–23; Mic. 6.6–7). For the idea that a psalm or prayer may please God more than a sacrifice or may take the place of (unavailable) sacrifice, cf. Pss. 69.30–32; 141.2. **8:** This v. is a crux. NJPS interprets a scroll as the psalmist's hymn or a record of his experience. Other interpretations are: the Torah (Jer. 31.31–34); or the book of life, which appears elsewhere in the Bible (e.g., Exod. 32.32; Pss. 69.29; 139.16; Dan. 12.1)—this idea is further developed in later Judaism, especially in the Rosh Ha-Shanah liturgy; or, if the psalmist is a king, the law of the king (Deut. 17.14–20). *Recounting what befell me* translates Heb "katuv ʿalay," "written on/about me." According to this translation, the psalmist brings a written, and therefore permanent, account of his experience in place of a sacrifice—a very literary touch by a man of words. Others understand "written of me" to mean "prescribed to me," that is, the Torah is prescribed to the psalmist. It is unlikely, however, that this v. refers to the Torah as we now have it. **9:** The v.'s image of the internalization of God's teaching, *in my inmost parts,* lit. "in my abdomen," is very striking. **10:** *Great congregation,* the psalmist's community, participants in the thanksgiving ceremony (cf. Pss. 22.26; 35.18). Praise is only meaningful if it is public, encouraging others to follow God.

11 I did not keep Your beneficence to myself;
I declared Your faithful deliverance;
I did not fail to speak of Your steadfast love in a great congregation.
12 O LORD, You will not withhold from me Your compassion;
Your steadfast love will protect me always.

13 For misfortunes without number envelop me;
my iniquities have caught up with me;
I cannot see;
they are more than the hairs of my head;
[a-]I am at my wits' end.[-a]
14[b] O favor me, LORD, and save me;
O LORD, hasten to my aid.
15 Let those who seek to destroy my life
be frustrated and disgraced;
let those who wish me harm
fall back in shame.
16 Let those who say "Aha! Aha!" over me
be desolate because of their frustration.
17 But let all who seek You be glad and rejoice in You;
let those who are eager for Your deliverance always say, "Extolled be the LORD!"
18 But I am poor and needy;
may the Lord devise [deliverance] for me.
You are my help and my rescuer;
my God, do not delay.

41 For the leader. A psalm of David.
2 Happy is he who is thoughtful of the wretched;
in bad times may the LORD keep him from harm.
3 May the LORD guard him and preserve him;
and may he be thought happy in the land.
Do not subject him to the will of his enemies.
4 The LORD will sustain him on his sickbed;
[c-]You shall wholly transform his bed of suffering.[-c]
5 I said, "O LORD, have mercy on me,
heal me, for I have sinned against You."
6 My enemies speak evilly of me,
"When will he die and his name perish?"
7 If one comes to visit, he speaks falsely;
his mind stores up evil thoughts;
once outside, he speaks them.

a-a Or "my courage fails me." *b With vv. 14–18, cf. Ps. 70.*
c-c Meaning of Heb. uncertain.

13: The psalmist's misfortunes are too many to list, paralleling God's deeds that are too numerous to recount (v. 6). **15–17:** The psalmist prays that the enemy be repulsed and shamed, and that those who seek God join the psalmist in praise, a typical trope in Psalms. **17:** *"Extolled be the LORD!"* is a cultic cry in 35.27 and Mal. 1.5 as well. **18:** The righteous are often called *poor and needy* (cf. Ps. 86.1). *Do not delay,* lit. "do not be late," as though only a short time remains.

Ps. 41: A prayer for healing, with similarities to Pss. 38 and 39. It opens with *the wretched* (or poor), connecting it to the end of the previous psalm. **2–4:** God's protection of the ill. **5–9:** The psalmist moves from third person (him) to first person (I), and then contrasts what he says to what the enemies have said. **5:** The petitioner believes that sin is the cause of the illness (39.12). **6–9:** The psalmist's enemies are guilty of insincere and damaging speech (38.13). **6:** *His name perish,* people could gain immortality through the deeds associated with their name (see Isa. 56.5), but not so for the psalmist, whose enemies want his body and memory to perish.

8 All my enemies whisper together against me,
imagining the worst for me.
9 "Something baneful has settled in him;
he'll not rise from his bed again."
10 My ally in whom I trusted,
even he who shares my bread,
[a]has been utterly false to me.[-a]
11 But You, O LORD, have mercy on me;
let me rise again and repay them.
12 Then shall I know that You are pleased with me:
when my enemy cannot shout in triumph over me.
13 You will support me because of my integrity,
and let me abide in Your presence forever.

14 Blessed is the LORD, God of Israel,
from eternity to eternity.
Amen and Amen.

BOOK TWO

42 For the leader. A *maskil* of the Korahites.
2 Like a hind crying for water,[b]
my soul cries for You, O God;
3 my soul thirsts for God, the living God;
O when will I come to appear before God!

a-a Meaning of Heb. uncertain. *b Lit. "watercourses."*

8: *Whisper together* suggests a curse or spell against the sick person, quoted in v. 9. **10:** Cf. 35.11–16. **11:** *Let me rise,* "raise me up," in contrast to the words of the enemies: "he'll not rise ..." *Repay* in the sense of repay their evil intentions and actions. **12–13:** In the context of a plea for healing, these vv. may suggest that, once prevented by his illness from coming to the Temple (cf. 2 Chron. 26.21), the psalmist is confident that he will be healed and readmitted to God's Presence. **13:** *Integrity* and being in God's *presence forever* are found elsewhere at the close of a psalm (e.g., 23; 26). *Forever* means here (as elsewhere) for my entire life—the Bible nowhere partakes of the notion that the righteous live forever before God in a literal sense. **14:** The doxology or blessing that closes Book I of the Psalter is not originally part of the psalm, but reflects the editing of the Psalter into five books. Similar doxologies are found at the end of the other book divisions (72.19; 89.53; 106.48); *Amen and Amen* is only found in the first three doxologies in Psalms (here; 72.19; and 89.53).

Ps. 42: Although written as two separate psalms in the Heb ms tradition, Pss. 42–43 are a single psalm, as indicated by their shared refrain (42.6, 12; 43.5), and common theme of the desire to come to the Temple despite enemy persecution (42.3; 43.3–4; cf. Pss. 9–10, also thought to have been one psalm). Ps. 42 begins a collection called the Elohistic Psalter. Comprised of Pss. 42–83, this section much prefers the Heb "ʾelohim," "God" (sometimes translated "god") to LORD (Heb "YHVH"), in sharp contrast to the rest of the Psalter. Phrases like (Ps. 43.4) "O God, my God" are awkward in Heb, and may reflect a revision of the more common and expected, "O LORD, my God" (e.g., Jonah 2.7). Likewise, the use of "God" throughout Ps. 82 is confusing, and is likely secondary (see 82.1 n.). Scholars suggest that most of the references to God in this grouping are secondary, and were originally LORD ("YHVH"); these were changed by an editor who preferred to call the deity "ʾelohim," God. A similar phenomenon is the use of "ʾelohim" in the E source in the Torah. Ps. 42 also introduces the collection of Korahite psalms. These are found in Pss. 42(–43); 44–49; 84–85; 87–88, in other words in two collections, one in the Elohistic Psalter (42–49), one outside it (84–88). The separation of this collection in two sections of Psalms is one of many indications of the complexity of the editing of the Psalter. As indicated by 2 Chron. 20.19, "Levites of the sons of Kohath and of the sons of Korah got up to extol the LORD God of Israel at the top of their voices," the Korahites had a special role in Temple singing. (Contrast the negative depiction of the Korahites in Num. ch 16.) There are some common phrases in the collection (e.g., Pss. 42.3 and 84.3, "the living God"; 42.3 and 84.8, "appear[ing] before God"), but attempts at finding strong thematic similarities between them are not compelling. Similarly unconvincing are attempts to read the Korahite collection as a whole, especially as stages of a ritual. **1:** On *maskil,* see 32 n.; a disproportionate number of psalms with this word appear in the Elohistic Psalter. **2–3:** The imagery is very striking (see also 63.2). God is the basic nourishment for the psalmist. **3:** On *the living God,* see 18.47 n. Some ancient biblical translations render *to appear before God* as "to see God"; the consonantal Heb text allows this translation. This may reflect an idea that God could actually be seen at a temple, manifest through an image (see 11.7 n.). The vocalization in the MT, however, which is later than the consonantal text, construes the verb "to see" in the passive so as to avoid saying that one can see

4 My tears have been my food day and night;
I am ever taunted with, "Where is your God?"
5 When I think of this, I pour out my soul:
how I [a]walked with the crowd, moved with them,[a]
the festive throng, to the House of God
with joyous shouts of praise.
6 Why so downcast, my soul,
why disquieted within me?
Have hope in God;
I will yet praise Him
[b]for His saving presence.[b]

7 O my God, my soul is downcast;
therefore I think of You
in this land of Jordan and Hermon,
in Mount Mizar,
8 where deep calls to deep
in the roar of [a]Your cataracts;[a]
all Your breakers and billows have swept over me.
9 By day may the LORD vouchsafe His faithful care,
so that at night a song to Him may be with me,
a prayer to the God of my life.
10 I say to God, my rock,
"Why have You forgotten me,
why must I walk in gloom,
oppressed by my enemy?"
11 [a]Crushing my bones,[a]
my foes revile me,
taunting me always with, "Where is your God?"
12 Why so downcast, my soul,
why disquieted within me?
Have hope in God;
I will yet praise Him,
my ever-present help, my God.

43 [c]Vindicate me, O God,
champion my cause
against faithless people;
rescue me from the treacherous, dishonest man.
2 For You are my God, my stronghold;
why have You rejected me?

a-a Meaning of Heb. uncertain.
b-b Several ancient versions and Heb. mss. connect the first word in v. 7 with the end of 6, reading yeshuʿot panai weʾElohai, *"my ever-present help, my God," as in vv. 12 and Ps. 43.5.* *c A continuation of Ps. 42.*

God. Zion plays a disproportionately significant role in the Korah psalms; see esp. Ps. 48. **4:** Instead of divine nourishment, the psalmist's food and drink is his tears (see Job 3.24 for similar imagery). The taunt of the enemies is that his God is powerless to relieve his current predicament. **5–6:** This psalm is remarkable for the inner dialogues it relates. *Soul* reflects the inner being; the Bible does not partake in the (Greek) notion of a bipartite being, comprised of body and soul. **5:** The opening words of the v. are reused in a later midrash which is part of the Yom Kippur liturgy, depicting the martyrizing of leading Jewish figures during the Hadrianic persecutions (132–135 CE). **6:** A refrain (see also v. 12 and 43.5). God's *saving presence* refers back to seeing God in v. 3 (the word "face" [Heb "panim"] is used in both vv.). **7:** The northern geographical locations (Mount Mizar is probably near Hermon) mentioned suggest that the psalmist is distant from Jerusalem, either physically or psychologically; some have suggested that this psalm, and perhaps all of the Korahite psalms, are northern in origin. **8:** A mythological reference, alluding to the cosmic waters of creation, and perhaps also to the sources of the Jordan River in northern Israel. The psalmist feels overwhelmed by these waters; cf. Jonah 2.4. **9:** *The God of my life* refers back to v. 3; this psalm has an unusual number of refrains and cross-references. **10–11:** *My rock,* a common metaphor for divine reliability. *Foes* are finally revealed to be the main topic of this petition. *Taunting me always with, "Where is your God?"* serves as a refrain with v. 4. **12:** See v. 6 n., although here the context offers a deeper meaning to the refrain: in v. 11, the foes asked where the psalmist's God is—a reasonable question in a polytheistic world, but here he responds that there is a single *God,* who is also *my God.*

Ps. 43: Pss. 42–43 form a single unit (see above). It is unclear when and how they became separated; perhaps the fact that Ps. 42 nostalgically focuses on the past, while Ps. 43 is more concerned with the future, promoted this division. In addition, Ps. 43 opens with the common initial elements of an individual petition (e.g., 5.2–3). **1–2:** These reflect the

Why must I walk in gloom,
oppressed by the enemy?
3 Send forth Your light and Your truth;
they will lead me;
they will bring me to Your holy mountain,
to Your dwelling-place,
4 that I may come to the altar of God,
God, my delight, my joy;
that I may praise You with the lyre,
O God, my God.
5 Why so downcast, my soul,
why disquieted within me?
Have hope in God;
I will yet praise Him,
my ever-present help, my God.

44

For the leader. Of the Korahites. A *maskil.*

2 We have heard, O God,
our fathers have told us
the deeds You performed in their time,
in days of old.
3 With Your hand You planted them,
displacing nations;
You brought misfortune on peoples,
and drove them out.
4 It was not by their sword that they took the land,
their arm did not give them victory,
but Your right hand, Your arm, and Your goodwill,
for You favored them.
5 You are my king, O God;
decree victories for Jacob!
6 Through You we gore our foes;
by Your name we trample our adversaries;
7 I do not trust in my bow;
it is not my sword that gives me victory;
8 You give us victory over our foes;
You thwart those who hate us.
9 In God we glory at all times,
and praise Your name unceasingly. *Selah.*

10 Yet You have rejected and disgraced us;
You do not go with our armies.
11 You make us retreat before our foe;
our enemies plunder us at will.

typical features of a petition: invocation *(O God),* petition in the imperative or related forms *(vindicate, champion, rescue),* and motivation *(For You ...). Why must I walk in gloom ...*, see 42.10. **3–4:** The main theme, the desire to visit the Temple, is reiterated (see 42.3 n.). *Dwelling-place* is the plural of the word for "Tabernacle" ("mishkan") in Priestly literature. It is not entirely clear how God's *light and ... truth* will save the psalmist from his enemies. Ibn Ezra and Radak note that the *light* is a countermeasure to the gloom, lit. darkness, that the psalmist felt in v. 2. **5:** A concluding refrain; see 42.6 n.

Ps. 44: This is a community petition; it begins with a hymn about God's past deliverance (vv. 2–9), followed by a complaint about the current situation (vv. 10–17). A protestation of innocence (vv. 18–23) and the petition itself (vv. 24–27) conclude the psalm. Although the dating is contested, the theme and language of the psalm, similar to Pss. 74, 79, and Lam., may suggest an exilic composition. God, who in the past championed Israel, has now *rejected and disgraced* them (v. 10) by letting the enemy conquer them and *disperse* them (v. 12). The usual biblical explanation for the destruction and exile is that Israel sinned by being unfaithful to God. Yet the psalmist insists (vv. 18–23) that at least now, in exile, the people remain loyal to Him. The psalm calls upon God to rescue them. **2:** On parents teaching children, see, e.g., Deut. 6.20–25. **3:** On planting as a metaphor for possessing the land of Israel, see Exod. 15.17. **4:** Even Rahab the foreign prostitute acknowledges that it is through divine help that Israel succeeds militarily (Josh. 2.9–11). **5:** In the ancient Near Eastern world, the king led his people in battle; thus God's role as warrior is part of His role as *king. Decree:* God determines to whom He will grant victory (Pss. 7.6; 71.3). **9:** This is a typical case where *Selah* appears at a main division of a psalm (see 3.3 n.), in this case, demarcating the hymn from the complaint. **10:** *You do not go with our armies* may be a play on God's role as LORD of hosts, who is supposed to lead His heavenly hosts or armies in Israel's defense.

12 You let them devour us like sheep;
You disperse us among the nations.
13 You sell Your people for no fortune,
You set no high price on them.
14 You make us the butt of our neighbors,
the scorn and derision of those around us.
15 You make us a byword among the nations,
a laughingstock[a] among the peoples.
16 I am always aware of my disgrace;
I am wholly covered with shame
17 at the sound of taunting revilers,
in the presence of the vengeful foe.

18 All this has come upon us,
yet we have not forgotten You,
or been false to Your covenant.
19 Our hearts have not gone astray,
nor have our feet swerved from Your path,
20 though You cast us, crushed, to where the [b]sea
monster[b] is,
and covered us over with deepest darkness.
21 If we forgot the name of our God
and spread forth our hands to a foreign god,
22 God would surely search it out,
for He knows the secrets of the heart.
23 It is for Your sake that we are slain all day long,
that we are regarded as sheep to be slaughtered.

24 Rouse Yourself; why do You sleep, O Lord?
Awaken, do not reject us forever!
25 Why do You hide Your face,
ignoring our affliction and distress?
26 We lie prostrate in the dust;
our body clings to the ground.
27 Arise and help us,
redeem us, as befits Your faithfulness.

45

For the leader; [c]on *shoshannim.*[c] Of the Korahites.
A *maskil.* A love song.

2 My heart is astir with gracious words;
I speak my poem to a king;
my tongue is the pen of an expert scribe.

a *Lit. "a wagging of the head."* b-b *Heb.* tannim = tannin, *as in Ezek. 29.3 and 32.2.*
c-c *Meaning of Heb. uncertain.*

12: God abandons His role as the ideal shepherd (see e.g., Ps. 23), and instead allows His sheep, Israel, to disperse, defeated, as in 1 Kings 22.17: "I saw all Israel scattered over the hills like sheep without a shepherd." **18:** *Covenants* are mutual obligations; the psalmist is saying that even though God has broken His side, the community continues to maintain its obligations. **19:** Israel has remained faithful in thought (*heart*) and action (*feet*). **20:** A reference to the chaos that preceded creation. The destruction of the Temple, implied but not explicitly stated, is likened to a return to chaos. **21–22:** See the similar self-imprecation at 7.4–6 and the extended self-imprecations in Job ch 31. *Spread forth our hands* refers to praying; this was the typical prayer gesture in the ancient Near East, and a stele from Hazor shows two upraised hands, representing the supplicant. On God knowing people's secret thoughts, see Jer. 17.10. **23:** *Sheep,* a return to the simile of v. 12. **24–27:** This section contains the typical elements of a petition: the invocation *(O Lord),* imperatives *(rouse, awaken, arise, help),* and a motivation *(as befits Your faithfulness).* This motivation goes beyond the ideas expressed in vv. 21–23, suggesting that even if the people are culpable, they must be forgiven; an idea found also in Lam. **24:** On God sleeping, see 7.7 n. **25:** On God hiding His face, see 6.4–5 n. **26:** These represent military subjugation (see Josh. 10.24). **27:** *Arise* may have military connotations; see 7.7 n. On God's *faithfulness,* his covenant obligation, see 5.8 n.

Ps. 45: A unique psalm, commemorating a royal wedding. It mentions the name of neither king nor queen, and thus could be reused for other royal weddings. Scholars have speculated on the psalm's original setting. Ahab is a leading contender since he married Jezebel, a Phoenician princess (see v. 13), and built a palace inlaid with ivory (see v. 9 and 1 Kings 22.39); some have even suggested the verb (v. 8) *You love* ("'ahavta") is a play on the name Ahab. Medieval commentators read the psalm about David (Ibn Ezra, first opinion) or about the Messiah (Ibn Ezra, second opinion, Radak). See especially vv. 7–8, which suggests that the king's throne is divine

3 You are fairer than all men;
your speech is endowed with grace;
rightly has God given you an eternal blessing.
4 Gird your sword upon your thigh, O hero,
in your splendor and glory;
5 [a-]in your glory, win success;
ride on in the cause of truth and meekness and right;
and let your right hand lead you to awesome deeds.[-a]
6 Your arrows, sharpened,
[b-][pierce] the breast of the king's enemies;
peoples fall at your feet.[-b]
7 Your [c-]divine throne[-c] is everlasting;
your royal scepter is a scepter of equity.
8 You love righteousness and hate wickedness;
rightly has God, your God, chosen to anoint you
with oil of gladness over all your peers.
9 All your robes [are fragrant] with
myrrh and aloes and cassia;
from ivoried palaces
lutes entertain you.
10 Royal princesses are your favorites;
the consort stands at your right hand,
decked in gold of Ophir.

11 Take heed, lass, and note,
incline your ear:
forget your people and your father's house,
12 and let the king be aroused by your beauty;
since he is your lord, bow to him.
13 O Tyrian lass,
the wealthiest people will court your favor with gifts,
14 [a-]goods of all sorts.

The royal princess,
her dress embroidered with golden mountings,
15 is led inside to the king;[-a]

a-a *Meaning of Heb. uncertain.* b-b *Order of Heb. clauses inverted for clarity.* c-c *Cf. 1 Chron. 29.23.*

and everlasting. In the Christian community, this was typically read Christologically, and Radak concludes his commentary with a long polemic against this reading. Although the psalm is singular as a royal wedding psalm, it shares the following motifs with Ps. 72, another royal psalm: the king's might, his justice, and a conclusion that all nations shall praise him. **1:** A unique superscription with many attributes. *Shoshannim* (lilies?) predominate in the Song of Songs, and are seen as erotic (e.g., Song 5.13); this connects to the attribute *A love song.* **2:** This too is unique—no other psalm has this type of introduction, speaking to an audience about the following psalm *(my poem to a king).* **3:** Exceptional beauty was a royal attribute (see 1 Sam. 9.2 of Saul and 1 Sam. 16.12 of David); Egyptian kings are also described as very handsome. **4–6:** Israelite kings led their nation in battle and were expected to be warriors; here the king is depicted as an ideal, successful warrior. **4:** *Splendor and glory* are elsewhere divine attributes (e.g., 104.1); this raises the possibility that the king is here viewed as divine (see v. 7 n.). **7–8:** Justice was an important royal quality; see esp. 1 Kings 3.4–14 (of Solomon) and the description of the ideal future king in Isa. 11.3–5. **7:** This may also be translated "Your throne, O God ("'elohim"), is everlasting" (so LXX), where the king is referred to as God. If this is taken literally, this psalm would be unique in the entire Bible in explicitly depicting the king as divine (see v. 4 and v. 18 nn.), a notion that existed at times in other ancient Near Eastern cultures but is otherwise absent in biblical thought. Other modern scholars render the v. as "Your throne is like God's throne" (so already Ibn Ezra) or "Your throne is supreme." The Tg. and Saadia add the words "will establish," reading "God will establish your throne," while Rashi understands "'elohim" as judges (see Exod. 21.6, translators' note). These medieval and modern translations, including NJPS *(Your divine throne),* make this v. fit typical biblical texts, which do not view the biblical king as divine. **8:** *Anoint*ing is the central ritual of kingship (see 2.2 n.), though *oil of gladness* is only used here with kings, referring to the joy that accompanied the coronation. **9–10:** A description of the pomp and ceremony of the wedding. **10:** The psalmist avoids the usual word for queen, choosing *consort* ("shegal"), a rare loanword from Akkadian. **11–12:** In the ancient Near East, wives were subservient to their husbands, and abandoned the practices and religion of their birth family for those of their husbands; even queens must do so. **13:** Others, rejecting the idea that the psalm refers to the marriage of Ahab to Jezebel, assume that a Tyrian woman from Phoenicia was part of the wedding party, though not necessarily the bride. **14–17:** A continuation of the description of the wedding

maidens in her train, her companions,
are presented to you.
16 They are led in with joy and gladness;
they enter the palace of the king.
17 Your sons will succeed your ancestors;
you will appoint them princes throughout the land.

18 I commemorate your fame for all generations,
so peoples will praise you forever and ever.

46

For the leader. Of the Korahites; [a-]on *alamoth.*[-a]
A song.

2 God is our refuge and stronghold,
a help in trouble, very near.
3 Therefore we are not afraid
though the earth reels,
though mountains topple into the sea—
4 its waters rage and foam;
in its swell mountains quake. *Selah.*

5 There is a river whose streams gladden God's city,
the holy dwelling-place of the Most High.
6 God is in its midst, it will not be toppled;
by daybreak God will come to its aid.
7 Nations rage, kingdoms topple;
at the sound of His thunder the earth dissolves.
8 The LORD of hosts is with us;
the God of Jacob is our haven. *Selah.*

9 Come and see what the LORD has done,
how He has wrought desolation on the earth.
10 He puts a stop to wars throughout the earth,
breaking the bow, snapping the spear,
consigning wagons to the flames.
11 "Desist! Realize that I am God!
I dominate the nations;
I dominate the earth."

a-a Meaning of Heb. uncertain.

ceremony. **14:** The Heb is difficult; in classical Jewish sources, the first part of the v. sanctions female modesty, and is understood as suggesting that a woman's place is in her house rather than in public (e.g., *b. Yebam.* 67a and *b. Git.* 12a). **18:** A remarkable conclusion, where the king is praised in language typically reserved for God; the royal Ps. 72.17 offers a similar conclusion.

Ps. 46: This psalm expresses the community's confidence in God; the extensive military language suggests to some that it may have been recited before a battle. Some modern commentators connect it to the deliverance of Jerusalem from Sennacherib in 701 (see 1 Kings chs 18–20), but there is nothing specific in the psalm to support this. Like Ps. 48, another Korahite psalm, its focus is on Jerusalem, called here "God's city" (v. 5). A refrain occurs in vv. 8 and 12. **1:** The meaning of *alamoth* is uncertain, though some connect it to the same word meaning "maidens," perhaps referring to a tune that started with that word. **2:** Similar imagery is in 18.3. **3–4:** Mythological language going back to Canaanite traditions (see 8.3 n.). It signals the end of the world, the undoing of creation, and in this context may refer to a catastrophic battle. Before these myths were recovered, the psalm was often connected to the eschatological battles (so Rashi and Radak). **5:** As in 104.6–13, the waters of chaos are domesticated. This description is imaginative, since the Gihon Spring, the main water source of Jerusalem, is too small to fit the depiction of the v. There may be a hint here of the city likened to the Garden of Eden, watered in a positive way (as opposed to the waters of chaos in v. 4); cf. Isa. 51.3; Ezek. 36.35, referring to Judah and Jerusalem (and Ezek. 28.13; 31.8, describing the once glorious Tyre and Assyria). Others suggest that this psalm was originally northern (see the Korahite psalm 42.8 n.) but in the Korahite psalm 87.3 "city of God" clearly refers to Jerusalem. **6:** As in Ps. 2.6, God is envisioned as dwelling in Jerusalem. *Daybreak,* when dangerous night ends, is traditionally seen as an auspicious time, a time when deliverance comes. **7:** The *kingdoms topple,* matching the defeat of chaos ("mountains topple") in v. 3; the same word *rage* is used here and in v. 4. For the power of God's thunderous roar, see Amos 1.2. **8:** *LORD of hosts,* associated with God as warrior (see 24.10 n.), is infrequent in Psalms, but is used here as contextually appropriate. **9:** *Wrought desolation* is a pun in Heb: "sam shamot." **10:** God is so great a warrior that He can end all war (see Isa. 2.4 || Mic. 4.3). **11:** God is quoted in a number of psalms (e.g., 2.6; 89.4–5; 110.1; 132.11–12) in content and style (note the imperatives) God's words match the psalmist's in v. 9.

12 The LORD of hosts is with us;
the God of Jacob is our haven. *Selah.*

47

For the leader. Of the Korahites. A psalm.

2 All you peoples, clap your hands,
raise a joyous shout for God.
3 For the LORD Most High is awesome,
great king over all the earth;
4 He subjects peoples to us,
sets nations at our feet.
5 He chose our heritage for us,
the pride of Jacob whom He loved. *Selah.*

6 God ascends midst acclamation;
the LORD, to the blasts of the horn.
7 Sing, O sing to God;
sing, O sing to our king;
8 for God is king over all the earth;
sing a hymn.[a]
9 God reigns over the nations;
God is seated on His holy throne.
10 The great of the peoples are gathered together,
the retinue of Abraham's God;
for the guardians of the earth belong to God;
He is greatly exalted.

48

A song. A psalm of the Korahites.

2 The LORD is great and much acclaimed
in the city of our God,
His holy mountain—

a *Heb.* maskil, *a musical term of uncertain meaning.*

12: A refrain (see Ps. 42.6 n.) with v. 8.

Ps. 47: Pss. 47; 93; 96–99 are called kingship psalms because they all explicitly refer to God as king. Ps. 47, in the Korahite collection, shares many elements with the other kingship psalms; it is uncertain if they all functioned together in a ritual commemorating God's kingship or enthronement. If such a ritual existed in the biblical period, it may have been associated with the new year (postbiblical Rosh Ha-Shanah, early biblical Sukkot; see Exod. 23.16 n.), which in the rabbinic period has the kingship of God as one of its major themes. (See also introduction to Ps. 93.) This understanding of the psalm developed in the early 20th c., when an attempt was made to understand the ritual background of each psalm; most traditional Jewish interpreters understood the psalm eschatologically (see esp. Radak to v. 9, who connects the theme of universal acknowledgment of God to Zech. 14.9). In the Middle Ages, Ps. 47 began to be recited on Rosh Ha-Shanah before the blowing of the shofar (ram's horn), most likely under the influence of v. 6. **2:** It is unclear how the nations are being invoked. V. 10 seems to suggest that their representatives were actually present, though more likely they are invoked rhetorically, much as the prophets offer prophecies to other nations. In either case, the theme is God's universal kingship. This psalm may then be seen as an actualization of the immediately preceding Ps. 46.11, "Desist! Realize that I am God! I dominate the nations; I dominate the earth." Great noise and *a joyous shout* are part of the human coronation ritual (e.g., 1 Kings 1.39–40), here projected onto God. This suggests that this psalm may be viewed as an enthronement psalm, and that through a set of rituals, God was (re)enthroned annually. **3:** The epithet *great king,* a popular epithet of Mesopotamian kings, is used of no Israelite king, perhaps because it was reserved for God as King. **5:** *The pride of Jacob* seems to be a nickname of Israel or Jerusalem. **6:** *Ascends* ("ʿalah") refers back to God as "Most High" (v. 3, "ʿelyon"; the Heb root is the same), and most likely refers to God ascending the royal throne. **7–8:** *Sing* is repeated five times; perhaps the human king had a group of singers who entertained him. Angelic singing, or at least chanting to God as king, is described in Isa. 6.1–5; indeed, the beginning of the v. could alternatively be translated as "Sing, O celestial beings, sing." The structure of these vv., an imperative followed by *for,* mirrors vv. 2–3. **8:** *God is* (or "has become") *king* mirrors the human enthronement declaration; see, e.g., "Absalom has become king" (2 Sam. 15.10). **9:** *God is seated on His holy throne* describes God's re-enthronement (see Ps. 48.2 n.). In contrast to the human throne, only God's is *holy.* This throne may be in His heavenly or His earthly palace (see Ps. 2.4, 6 nn.). **10:** Most likely this reflects a wish rather than a reality; it is difficult to believe that at any time *the great of the peoples* gathered to acknowledge the universal sovereignty of God. The final word, *exalted* ("naʿaleh"), reflects the theme of the psalm, echoing the usage of the root "ʿ-l-h" in vv. 3 and 6 (see v. 6 n.).

3 fair-crested, joy of all the earth,
Mount Zion, summit of Zaphon,[a]
city of the great king.
4 Through its citadels, God has made Himself known as
a haven.
5 See, the kings joined forces;
they advanced together.
6 At the mere sight of it they were stunned,
they were terrified, they panicked;
7 they were seized there with a trembling,
like a woman in the throes of labor,
8 as the Tarshish fleet was wrecked
in an easterly gale.[b]
9 The likes of what we heard we have now witnessed
in the city of the LORD of hosts,
in the city of our God—
may God preserve it forever! *Selah.*

10 In Your temple, God,
we meditate upon Your faithful care.
11 The praise of You, God, like Your name,
reaches to the ends of the earth;
Your right hand is filled with beneficence.
12 Let Mount Zion rejoice!
Let the towns[c] of Judah exult,
because of Your judgments.

13 Walk around Zion,
circle it;
count its towers,
14 take note of its ramparts;
[d]go through[-d] its citadels,
that you may recount it to a future age.

a A term for the divine abode. *b See 1 Kings 22.49.*
c Or "women." *d-d Meaning of Heb. uncertain.*

Ps. 48: This communal hymn has strong thematic connections to the previous two psalms: it too focuses on Jerusalem as God's city, and is primarily concerned with a conflict between Israel and the nations, where God ultimately saves Israel. It reworks certain old myths (see v. 3 n.), but historicizes them. The battle envisioned in vv. 5–6 is most likely ideal rather than real; several medieval commentators read it eschatologically (see, e.g., Rashi and Radak). There are also hints of a ritual (see vv. 13–14 n.), suggesting that the psalm as a whole reflects a ritualized commemoration of a divine victory. More than any other psalm it focuses on the greatness of Jerusalem, but its primary focus is on God, and on Jerusalem as God's city (vv. 2, 9). **2:** *His holy mountain,* a reference to Mount Zion (which is actually more like a hill), mirrors the previous psalm's "holy throne" (47.9). **3:** The centrality of Jerusalem is likewise expressed in the eschatological Isa. 23.2–3, but in this psalm, it is imagined as happening in the present. *Zaphon* refers to the mountain where Baal resided according to the Ugaritic myths (see, e.g., *ANET,* p. 136, "my mount Godly Zaphon"). Some believe that this psalm therefore originally referred to a northern city (see 42.8 and 46.5 nn.); more likely, this is a remarkable reuse of old mythological material, where the Israelite God has absorbed qualities of Baal (see Ps. 29 n.), including even his place of residence! In this context, it is likely that the *great king* is God (see 47.3), rather than the Davidic king. **7:** The image of a woman in labor is common in prophetic literature (e.g., Isa. 13.8; Jer. 4.31) to describe the trembling before a defeat. **8:** The identification of Tarshish is uncertain; biblical texts suggest that it is a faraway place in the western Mediterranean, reachable by boat (see esp. Jonah 1.3). Thus, the Tarshish fleet represents well-built boats, capable of long journeys. The east wind, or sirocco, is a destructive wind (see Ezek. 27.26–27 n.). **9:** It is God's physical presence in Jerusalem (see Ps. 2.3 n.) that makes Jerusalem inviolable. The beginning of Ezek. describes the divine Presence leaving the Temple, which allows the city's conquest (Ezek. 10.18; 11.23). Conversely, this psalm hopes that Jerusalem will forever remain God's city, *may God preserve it forever!* **10:** God's *faithful care* ("ḥesed"; see 5.8 n.) is localized in the Temple, where God resides. **11:** Names express essence in ancient Israel (see 1 Sam. 25.25). God's *right hand* is often associated with his power as warrior (e.g., Exod. 15.6); here this is replaced with *beneficence* or justice. **12:** *Mount Zion* rejoices at God's *judgments* of retribution against the assembled enemies. Either *Mount Zion* is personified (see Isa. 35.1), or the words "inhabitants of" is elided or assumed (Radak raises both options). **13–14:** A ritual of circumambulating the city walls stands behind this description; see Neh. 12.27–43. The ramparts and citadels (see v. 4) signify the beauty and the protection of the city.

15 For God—He is our God forever;
He will lead us [a]evermore.[a]

49 For the leader. Of the Korahites. A psalm.

2 Hear this, all you peoples;
give ear, all inhabitants of the world,
3 men of all estates,
rich and poor alike.
4 My mouth utters wisdom,
my speech[b] is full of insight.
5 I will turn my attention to a theme,
set forth my lesson to the music of a lyre.

6 In time of trouble, why should I fear
the encompassing evil of those who would supplant me—
7 men who trust in their riches,
who glory in their great wealth?
8 [c]Ah, it[c] cannot redeem a man,
or pay his ransom to God;
9 the price of life is too high;
and so one ceases to be, forever.
10 Shall he live eternally,
and never see the grave?
11 For one sees that the wise die,
that the foolish and ignorant both perish,
leaving their wealth to others.
12 Their grave[d] is their eternal home,
the dwelling-place for all generations
of those once famous on earth.
13 Man does not abide in honor;
he is like the beasts that perish.

14 Such is the fate of those who are self-confident,
[a]the end of those pleased with their own talk.[a]
Selah.

15 Sheeplike they head for Sheol,
with Death as their shepherd.

a-a *Meaning of Heb. uncertain.*
b *Lit. "utterance of my heart"; on* leb, *cf.* Ps. 19.15. c-c *Or "A brother."*
d *Taken with ancient versions and medieval commentators as the equivalent of* qibram.

15: *Evermore* follows the tradition of the LXX, Menachem ben Saruq (quoted in Rashi), Ibn Ezra, Radak, and others (Heb ʿolamot); the Heb reads "over death" ("ʿal mavet"). Most likely, this is a corruption of the word "ʿalamot" used in the superscription to Ps. 46; it probably was misplaced from the beginning of Ps. 49 to the end of Ps. 48.

Ps. 49: This is an unusual and difficult psalm. Unlike most psalms, it is addressed to the (human) community, and not to God. It also is very difficult textually; for example, it is unclear if the refrain in vv. 13 and 21 differs intentionally or as a result of scribal error. In vocabulary (see vv. 4–5 n.) and in theme the psalm, especially its first few vv., shares much with wisdom literature. It is highly didactic, teaching that the wealthy should not be envied, a common theme of parts of Prov. (e.g., 28.6) and Eccl. (e.g., 10.6). **2:** As elsewhere in the Korahite psalms, foreigners are the (imagined) audience (see 47.10 n.), giving a universal flavor. **4–5:** The numerous wisdom terms *(wisdom, insight, theme, lesson),* are integrated into the psalm through the mention of *the music of a lyre,* a psalm formula. **6–13:** The wealthy cannot take their wealth with them to Sheol, the biblical underworld. Proverbs often has a more positive, pragmatic attitude toward wealth (e.g., 14.20; 18.11); the attitude here more closely resembles Eccl. (e.g., 2.1–11; 5.9, 12–13; 6.1–6). **8–9:** In certain cases, according to various texts, a *ransom* might be taken by a human to *redeem* a person from a capital offense (see Exod. 21.30; Prov. 6.35), but even the great wealth of the rich cannot buy them eternal life from God. **13:** See Eccl. 3.19, "For in respect of the fate of man and the fate of beast, they have one and the same fate: as the one dies so dies the other, and both have the same lifebreath; man has no superiority over beast, since both amount to nothing." The Heb contains a clever pun—with a slight change *in honor* ("biqar") would read "is cattle" ("baqar"). **14:** It is unclear if this refers to the wealthy, or if a new subject is being (briefly) introduced. **15:** Textually very difficult. It is possible that *Death* ("Mot") here recollects the Canaanite deity of the same name, known from Ugarit.

The upright shall rule over them at daybreak,
[a]and their form shall waste away in Sheol
till its nobility be gone.[a]
16 But God will redeem my life from the clutches of Sheol,
for He will take me. *Selah.*

17 Do not be afraid when a man becomes rich,
when his household goods increase;
18 for when he dies he can take none of it along;
his goods cannot follow him down.
19 Though he congratulates himself in his lifetime
—[a]"They must admit that you did well by yourself"[a]—
20 yet he must join the company of his ancestors,
who will never see daylight again.
21 Man does not understand honor;
he is like the beasts that perish.

50

A psalm of Asaph.

[b]God, the LORD God[b] spoke
and summoned the world from east to west.
2 From Zion, perfect in beauty,
God appeared
3 —let our God come and not fail to act!
Devouring fire preceded Him;
it stormed around Him fiercely.
4 He summoned the heavens above,
and the earth, for the trial of His people.
5 "Bring in My devotees,
who made a covenant with Me over sacrifice!"
6 Then the heavens proclaimed His righteousness,
for He is a God who judges. *Selah.*

a-a Meaning of Heb. uncertain. *b-b Heb.* ʼEl ʼElohim YHWH.

16: It is uncertain if the psalmist wishes to be saved (temporarily) from death (see Ps. 30.4 n.), or if he desires to be like Enoch or Elijah who do not die (Gen. 5.24; 2 Kings 2.11), or if this psalm partakes of the notion of personal resurrection, expressed clearly only in Dan. 12.2. The medieval period knew a much more developed notion of heaven and hell, and the v. is thus traditionally understood in reference to the afterworld reward of the righteous. **20:** Sheol, underground, is a dark place (88.13; Job 17.13); light signifies life (Job 3.20). **21:** A refrain; see v. 13.

Ps. 50: This is the first psalm of an Asaphite collection; it is separated from the other eleven Asaphite psalms, found in Pss. 73–83. The "sons (or guild) of Asaphites" were Levites who served as Temple singers in the Second Temple (Neh. 7.44), though 1 Chron. 16.7 traces the connection between Asaph and Temple music back to Davidic times. Second Chron. 29.30 refers to "Asaph the seer," suggesting that for some, the liturgical poetry produced by this clan was understood to be divinely inspired. More than other psalms, several of the Asaphite psalms have prophetic echoes, refer to past historical events, and reflect northern Israel (see esp. Pss. 80; 81). The collection also often characterizes the relation between God and Israel as that between a shepherd and his flock, and it has an unusually large number of allusions to the Song of the Sea (Exod. ch 15). Ps. 50 is not addressed to God, but is an admonition from God. As such, it shares much with prophetic oracles, and it is unclear if this is modeled after such oracles, or reflects a prophetic utterance within a ritual context (a cultic prophet). After an introduction (vv. 1–6), the main admonition is addressed to the community (vv. 7–15), a special admonition is addressed to the wicked (vv. 16–21), and a general conclusion is offered (vv. 22–23). **1–6:** God appears in a theophany, preceded by *fire* (so, e.g., 18.8; 97.3) and *storm* (see esp. Job 38.1; 40.6). As *judge* indicting His people in a "riv" (covenantal lawsuit), He calls upon *heavens above, and the earth* as witnesses (so, e.g., Isa. 1.2). **2:** On *Zion,* Jerusalem, as beautiful, see Ps. 48.3; the rabbis extended this notion, claiming: "There are ten measures of beauty in the Universe, nine belong to Jerusalem, and one to the rest of the world" (*b. Kid.* 49b). **5:** Perhaps the heaven and earth (so, e.g., Rashi), or other divine beings are addressed. On *devotees,* translated elsewhere as "faithful ones" (Heb "ḥasid"), see 4.4 n.

7–15: Like the prophetic texts in Isa. 1.10–17 and Mic. 6.6–8, these vv. polemicize against the Priestly notion that sacrifices by themselves are efficacious. The psalm does not object to sacrifices per se, and in fact endorses them (see esp. vv. 14, 23), but insists that (1) they must be understood symbolically, rather than as actual food for the deity; if God were hungry, He could take any bird or animal He liked, but He does not need food (contrast, e.g., the "pleasing odor" in Lev. 1.13), and (2) they are not sufficient, but must be accompanied by correct behavior (vv. 14–15, 22–23). A more negative attitude toward hollow sacrifices is reflected in the following psalm (51.18–21). **7:** *I am God, your God* may be citing the opening of the Decalogue (Exod. 20.2; Deut. 5.6), and may be referring to the Decalogue as a whole through its opening words; see v. 18 n. The substitution of "'elohim" for the Tetragrammaton, YHVH, is especially noticeable. **10–12:** Of God as owner of all, see Deut. 10.14. In style and content, the psalm is similar to Deut. **14:** The *thank offering* is partially eaten by the person who brings it, usually as a result of a *vow* (see Lev. 7.12–15; 2 Sam. 15.7). **16–17:** The *wicked* person is accused of hypocrisy. The empty spouting of God's laws, like empty sacrifices, does not compensate for wrong behavior. **18:** Citing part of the Decalogue (Exod. 20.13; Deut. 5.17). **19–20:** For the prohibition against slander, see, e.g., Lev. 19.16. **22–23:** The conclusion is chiastic, mentioning first the wicked (vv. 16–21), and then returning to the righteous (vv. 7–15).

Ps. 51: An individual complaint expressing an extreme sense of guilt. Although written in good classical Heb, internal evidence suggests that this psalm may be exilic or early postexilic (see vv. 5, 9, 11, 12, 20–21 nn.). **2:** See 2 Sam. ch 12, where Nathan rebukes David for two grave offenses: committing adultery with Bathsheba, and having her husband, Uriah, murdered. Given the tremendous guilt expressed in the psalm, and the specific request

7 "Pay heed, My people, and I will speak,
O Israel, and I will arraign you.
I am God, your God.
8 I censure you not for your sacrifices,
and your burnt offerings, made to Me daily;
9 I claim no bull from your estate,
no he-goats from your pens.
10 For Mine is every animal of the forest,
the beasts on [a]a thousand mountains.[a]
11 I know every bird of the mountains,
the creatures of the field are subject to Me.
12 Were I hungry, I would not tell you,
for Mine is the world and all it holds.
13 Do I eat the flesh of bulls,
or drink the blood of he-goats?
14 Sacrifice a thank offering to God,
and pay your vows to the Most High.
15 Call upon Me in time of trouble;
I will rescue you, and you shall honor Me."

16 And to the wicked, God said:
"Who are you to recite My laws,
and mouth the terms of My covenant,
17 seeing that you spurn My discipline,
and brush My words aside?
18 When you see a thief, you fall in with him,
and throw in your lot with adulterers;
19 you devote your mouth to evil,
and yoke your tongue to deceit;
20 you are busy maligning your brother,
defaming the son of your mother.
21 If I failed to act when you did these things,
you would fancy that I was like you;
so I censure you and confront you with charges.
22 Mark this, you who are unmindful of God,
lest I tear you apart and no one save you.

23 He who sacrifices a thank offering honors Me,
[a]and to him who improves his way[a]
I will show the salvation of God."

51

For the leader. A psalm of David, [2]when Nathan the prophet came to him after he had come to Bathsheba.[b]

3 Have mercy upon me, O God,
as befits Your faithfulness;

a-a Meaning of Heb. uncertain. *b Cf.* 2 Sam. 12.

in keeping with Your abundant compassion,
blot out my transgressions.
4 Wash me thoroughly of my iniquity,
and purify me of my sin;
5 for I recognize my transgressions,
and am ever conscious of my sin.
6 Against You alone have I sinned,
and done what is evil in Your sight;
so You are just in Your sentence,
and right in Your judgment.
7 Indeed I was born with iniquity;
with sin my mother conceived me.
8 [a]-Indeed You desire truth about that which is hidden;
teach me wisdom about secret things.-[a]

9 Purge me with hyssop till I am pure;
wash me till I am whiter than snow.
10 Let me hear tidings of joy and gladness;
let the bones You have crushed exult.
11 Hide Your face from my sins;
blot out all my iniquities.
12 Fashion a pure heart for me, O God;
create in me a steadfast spirit.
13 Do not cast me out of Your presence,
or take Your holy spirit away from me.
14 Let me again rejoice in Your help;
let a vigorous spirit sustain me.
15 I will teach transgressors Your ways,
that sinners may return to You.

16 Save me from bloodguilt,
O God, God, my deliverer,
that I may sing forth Your beneficence.
17 O Lord, open my lips,
and let my mouth declare Your praise.
18 You do not want me to bring sacrifices;
You do not desire burnt offerings;
19 True sacrifice to God is a contrite spirit;
God, You will not despise
a contrite and crushed heart.

a-a Meaning of Heb. uncertain.

to be saved "from bloodguilt" (v. 16), it is understandable that tradition would explicitly connect this psalm to those events. **3–4:** The complaint in a nutshell, containing four imperatives (*Have mercy, blot out, purify, Wash me thoroughly,* lit. "be thorough; wash me"), an invocation *(O God),* and the motivations *(as befits Your faithfulness; in keeping with Your abundant compassion).* God is asked to act according to His faithfulness, "ḥesed," since the supplicant feels himself guilty (contrast Ps. 6); see 5.8 n. **5:** Elaborate confessions are not typical of psalms; they develop more extensively in late biblical literature (see Dan. 9.4; Ezra 10.1; Neh. 9.2; 2 Chron. 30.22). A few psalms, however, mention confession or the acknowledgement of sin (32.3–5; 41.5). **7:** So extreme are the psalmist's guilt feelings that he sees himself as sinful even before birth; in other words, he is, by nature, a sinful being. The idea of the inherent sinfulness of humans is rarely expressed in the Bible, though see Gen. 8.21: "the devisings of man's mind are evil from his youth" (see also Job 25.4). Christianity developed the notion of original sin. **9:** God, rather than the impure individual, uses the hyssop for the purification ritual (contrast Num. 19.6, 18), perhaps because the Temple is not standing and the Temple-bound purification ritual cannot be performed. **11:** In a remarkable reversal of the standard idiom, the psalmist asks God to *hide* His *face*—not from the supplicant (see 6.4–5 n.), but from *sins.* Unlike 2 Sam. ch 12, the supplicant does not request that the sin and punishment be transferred (see 2 Sam. 12.13 n.), but rather that it be *blot*ted *out,* an idea found in the exilic Deutero-Isaiah (Isa. 43.25; 44.22). **12:** See similarly the exilic Ezek. 36.26. **13–14:** A poetic request not to be killed by God. **15–16:** The motivation for that request. *Bloodguilt* has severe consequences for the individual and the community (see Ezek. 9.9). **17–19:** Prayer is more effective than sacrifices; this stands in stark contrast to the Priestly tradition, which emphasizes the efficacy of sacrifices, largely ignoring prayer, and differs in perspective from the previous psalm, which also concerns prayer and sacrifice. The content of v. 17 has made it appropriate for the introduction to the standard statutory prayer (the "'Amidah"). **19:** God, "who probes the mind (lit. hearts)" (Ps. 7.10), knows, appreciates, and rewards internal behavior.

20–21: The psalm's conclusion suggests that the acceptability of prayer instead of sacrifices is due to a catastrophe, which has made access to the Temple impossible. Many modern scholars see these vv. as an addition, an opinion already cited in Ibn Ezra in the name of "one of the Spanish scholars."

Ps. 52: Although sharing many motifs with other psalms, this is an atypical psalm, addressed not to God, but to a particular "brave fellow" (v. 3). **2:** Given the tendency to identify psalms with events in David's life as recorded in Samuel, it is logical to equate the treacherous brave fellow of the psalm with *Doeg the Edomite* (see 1 Sam. 22.9–11). **3–5:** The emphasis is on damaging speech (see 10.7 n.). **7:** This sets up two contrasts with v. 10: the wicked will be removed from his *tent,* while the righteous will live "in God's house"; and the wicked will be *root*ed ... *out,* while the righteous psalmist is "like a thriving olive tree." **8:** The Heb is punning: the *righteous see* ("veyir'u") and are *awestruck* ("veyira'u"). **10–11:** The psalmist will express God's *faithfulness* ("ḥesed") *in the presence of ... faithful ones* ("ḥasid"). **10:** Olive trees were of great significance for the oil they produced, which was used in the Temple. It is uncertain if the psalmist is a religious official in the Temple *(God's house),* or is a lay Israelite who wants to enjoy God's proximity at the Temple (see Ps. 23.6 n.). **11:** *Forever* means "as long as I live," as is frequent in the Bible.

Ps. 53: This is the Elohistic Psalter's (see introduction to Ps. 42) version of Ps. 14; see annotations there.

20 May it please You to make Zion prosper;
rebuild the walls of Jerusalem.
21 Then You will want sacrifices offered in righteousness,
burnt and whole offerings;
then bulls will be offered on Your altar.

52

For the leader. A *maskil* of David, 2 when Doeg the Edomite came and informed Saul, telling him, "David came to Ahimelech's house."[a]

3 Why do you boast of your evil, brave fellow?
God's faithfulness [b]never ceases.[b]
4 Your tongue devises mischief,
like a sharpened razor that works treacherously.
5 You prefer evil to good,
the lie, to speaking truthfully. *Selah.*
6 You love all pernicious words,
treacherous speech.
7 So God will tear you down for good,
will break you and pluck you from your tent,
and root you out of the land of the living. *Selah.*
8 The righteous, seeing it, will be awestruck;
they will jibe at him, saying,
9 "Here was a fellow who did not make God his refuge,
but trusted in his great wealth,
relied upon his mischief."

10 But I am like a thriving olive tree in God's house;
I trust in the faithfulness of God forever and ever.
11 I praise You forever, for You have acted;
[c]I declare that Your name is good[c]
in the presence of Your faithful ones.

53

[d]For the leader; on *mahalath.*[e] A *maskil* of David.

2 The benighted man thinks,
[f]"God does not care."[f]
Man's wrongdoing is corrupt and loathsome;
no one does good.
3 God looks down from heaven on mankind
to find a man of understanding,
a man mindful of God.
4 Everyone is dross,
altogether foul;

a Cf. 1 Sam. 22.9 ff. *b-b Lit. "is all the day."*
c-c Meaning of Heb. uncertain; others "I will wait for Your name for it is good."
d Cf. Ps. 14. *e Meaning of Heb. unknown.* *f-f Lit. "There is no God"; cf. Ps. 10.4.*

there is none who does good,
not even one.
5 Are they so witless, those evildoers,
who devour my people as they devour food,
and do not invoke God?
6 There they will be seized with fright
—[a]never was there such a fright—
for God has scattered the bones of your besiegers;
you have put them to shame,[-a]
for God has rejected them.

7 O that the deliverance of Israel might come from Zion!
When God restores the fortunes of His people,
Jacob will exult, Israel will rejoice.

54 For the leader; with instrumental music. A *maskil* of David, 2 when the Ziphites came and told Saul, "Know, David is in hiding among us."[b]

3 O God, deliver me by Your name;
by Your power vindicate me.
4 O God, hear my prayer;
give ear to the words of my mouth.
5 For strangers have risen against me,
and ruthless men seek my life;
they are unmindful of God. *Selah.*

6 See, God is my helper;
the Lord is my support.
7 He will repay the evil of my watchful foes;
by Your faithfulness, destroy them!
8 Then I will offer You a freewill sacrifice;
I will praise Your name, LORD, for it is good,
9 for it has saved me from my foes,
and let me gaze triumphant upon my enemies.

55 For the leader; with instrumental music.
A *maskil* of David.

2 Give ear, O God, to my prayer;
do not ignore my plea;
3 pay heed to me and answer me.
I am tossed about, complaining and moaning
4 at the clamor of the enemy,
because of the oppression of the wicked;

Ps. 54: A typical individual petition. It is stylistically simplistic, with standard parallelisms. It contains neither a confession (see e.g., Ps. 51) nor a protestation of innocence (see e.g., Ps. 7). **2:** The psalm is secondarily connected to 1 Sam. 23.15–20; this is thematically appropriate, though not compelling. **3–5:** The petition, with an invocation *(O God),* four imperatives expressing the urgent request of the supplicant, and a motivation *(For strangers ...).* **3:** On God's *name,* see 48.11 n. **6–9:** As in other such prayers, the tense and tone change, reflecting the psalmist's certainty of salvation (see Ps. 6.9–11 n.). **8:** For the freewill sacrifice, see Lev. 22.18–25; Num. 15.1–16. *Praise ... name, LORD* often appear together, esp. in Psalms (see e.g., Ps. 92.2: "It is good to praise the LORD, to sing hymns to Your name, O Most High").

Ps. 55: Although an individual petition like the previous psalm (cf. esp. 55.2 and 54.4), this psalm is as innovative as the previous one is standard. The structure of Ps. 55 is unusually complex; the psalmist's complaint, for example, is found in three different sections (vv. 4–9, 11–12, 21–22), meant to evoke God's sympathy for the supplicant. Additionally, the vocabulary of the psalm is unique and quite difficult.

a-a Meaning of Heb. uncertain. *b Cf. 1 Sam. 23.19.*

5–9: The description of the psalmist's troubles is unusually long and flowery, and functions to motivate God to heed his petition. The image in vv. 7–9 of finding sanctuary in the wilderness is unusual; elsewhere the Psalter emphasizes the Jerusalem Temple as a sanctuary (e.g., 23.6). **10–12:** These vv. emphasize both the geographical and chronological *(day and night)* ubiquity of the *evil,* employing a large number of synonyms: *lawlessness, strife, evil, mischief, malice, fraud and deceit.* **10:** On improper speech as a psalmist's problem, see 10.7 n. **13–16:** As in Job, the great tragedy is that friends have turned into enemies. **16:** The phrase to *go down alive into Sheol,* also used in Num. 16.33, expresses sudden death. **17:** It is unclear if this and the following vv. express certainty of deliverance, as in other such prayers, or if instead of *the* L*ORD will deliver me,* we should translate "may the LORD deliver me." **18:** This v. suggests that the liturgical day began at or after sunset, as in postbiblical Jewish practice. Prayer three times daily may be suggested here; this was normative in rabbinic times, and is already expressed in a late biblical text, Dan. 6.10.

for they bring evil upon me
and furiously harass me.
5 My heart is convulsed within me;
terrors of death assail me.
6 Fear and trembling invade me;
I am clothed with horror.
7 I said,
"O that I had the wings of a dove!
I would fly away and find rest;
8 surely, I would flee far off;
I would lodge in the wilderness; *selah*
9 I would soon find me a refuge
from the sweeping wind,
from the tempest."

10 O Lord, confound their speech, confuse it!
For I see lawlessness and strife in the city;
11 day and night they make their rounds on its walls;
evil and mischief are inside it.
12 Malice is within it;
fraud and deceit never leave its square.

13 It is not an enemy who reviles me
—I could bear that;
it is not my foe who vaunts himself against me
—I could hide from him;
14 but it is you, my equal,
my companion, my friend;
15 sweet was our fellowship;
we walked together in God's house.
16 Let Him incite death against them;
may they go down alive into Sheol!
For where they dwell,
there evil is.

17 As for me, I call to God;
the LORD will deliver me.
18 Evening, morning, and noon,
I complain and moan,
and He hears my voice.
19 He redeems me unharmed
from the battle against me;
[a]it is as though many are on my side.[a]
20 God who has reigned from the first,
who will have no successor,

a-a *Meaning of Heb. uncertain.*

hears and humbles those who have no fear of
God. *Selah.*

21 He[a] harmed his ally,
he broke his pact;
22 his talk was smoother than butter,
yet his mind was on war;
his words were more soothing than oil,
yet they were drawn swords.

23 Cast your burden on the LORD and He will sustain you;
He will never let the righteous man collapse.
24 For You, O God, will bring them down to the
nethermost Pit—
those murderous, treacherous men;
they shall not live out half their days;
but I trust in You.

56

For the leader; [b]on *yonath elem reḥokim.*[-b] Of David.
A *michtam;* when the Philistines seized him in Gath.

2 Have mercy on me, O God,
for men persecute me;
all day long my adversary oppresses me.
3 My watchful foes persecute me all day long;
many are my adversaries, O Exalted One.
4 When I am afraid, I trust in You,
5 in God, whose word I praise,
in God I trust;
I am not afraid;
what can mortals[c] do to me?
6 All day long [b]they cause me grief in my affairs,[-b]
they plan only evil against me.
7 They plot, they lie in ambush;
they watch my every move, hoping for my death.
8 Cast them out for their evil;
subdue peoples in Your anger, O God.

9 [b]You keep count of my wanderings;
put my tears into Your flask,
into Your record.[-b]
10 Then my enemies will retreat when I call on You;
this I know, that God is for me.
11 In God, whose word I praise,
in the LORD, whose word I praise,
12 in God I trust;

a I.e., the friend of v. 14. *b-b Meaning of Heb. uncertain.* *c Lit. "flesh."*

21–24: As in vv. 13–16, the friend turned enemy is referred to in both the singular and the plural. **23:** This is likely a quotation but the speaker is uncertain. Ibn Ezra and Radak suggest that the psalmist is speaking to himself or to the righteous; modern suggestions vary, including the idea that this was a prophetic oracle. **24:** The psalm concludes with a return to the theme of v. 16.

Ps. 56: This individual petition emphasizes the great confidence or trust of the psalmist. In expressing his trust in God rather than humans, it shares certain phrases with Pss. 116–118 (see vv. 5, 14 nn.). **1:** An extremely long, multilayered and complex superscription. On *michtam,* found in Pss. 56–60 and 16, see 16.1 n. A time *when the Philistines seized him* [David] *in Gath* is never recorded in Samuel; it might be inferred from 1 Sam. 21.11–16, or the superscription may reflect another story about David that was not preserved in the canonical Samuel (see introduction to Ps. 7). **2:** The psalm proper begins with the typical imperative *(Have mercy on me),* invocation *(O God),* and motivation *(for ...).* **4–5:** The repetition of *I trust* highlights the psalm's theme. **4:** The Heb more literally reads "when I fear by day." **5:** Cf. 118.6, "The LORD is on my side, / I have no fear; / what can man do to me?" **6:** *All day long,* picking up on the lit. mention of "day" in v. 4. **9:** God's *record* may refer to divine ledgers, where He keeps track of human activities (see Exod. 32.32 and Mal. 3.16). These are well known from earlier Mesopotamia, and later rabbinic tradition, especially concerning the ledger books that are open and written on Rosh Ha-Shanah. The Heb has a wordplay on *my wanderings,* "nodi," and *Your flask,* "no'dekha." Additionally, the root "s-pr" is repeated in *You keep count* and *into Your record.* **11:** This v., unusual in its repetition of two identical words in a parallelism, forms a quasi-refrain with v. 5. **12:** The refrain continues; see v. 5.

I am not afraid;
what can man do to me?
13 I must pay my vows to You, O God;
I will render thank offerings to You.
14 For You have saved me from death,
my foot from stumbling,
that I may walk before God in the light of life.

57 For the leader; [a-]*al tashḥeth.*[-a] Of David. A *michtam;* when he fled from Saul into a cave.

2 Have mercy on me, O God, have mercy on me,
for I seek refuge in You,
I seek refuge in the shadow of Your wings,
until danger passes.
3 I call to God Most High,
to God who is good to me.
4 He will reach down from heaven and deliver me:
God will send down His steadfast love;
my persecutor reviles. *Selah.*

5 As for me, I lie down among man-eating lions
whose teeth are spears and arrows,
whose tongue is a sharp sword.
6 Exalt Yourself over the heavens, O God,
let Your glory be over all the earth!
7 They prepared a net for my feet [b-]to ensnare me;[-b]
they dug a pit for me,
but they fell into it. *Selah.*

8c My heart is firm, O God;
my heart is firm;
I will sing, I will chant a hymn.

a-a Meaning of Heb. uncertain.
b-b Cf. Mishnaic Heb. kefifah, *a wicker basket used in fishing.*
c With vv. 8–12, cf. Ps. 108.2–6.

13: See 50.14. **14:** Cf. 116.8–9: "You have delivered me from death, / my eyes from tears, / my feet from stumbling. / I shall walk before the LORD / in the lands of the living." As is common in these petitions, the certainty of hearing is presented in the past tense, reflecting the supplicant's certainty of a positive divine answer.

Ps. 57: The psalmist's confidence in God's salvation is less prominent in this personal petition, which instead is full of urgent cries for divine help, including the refrain (vv. 6, 12), *Exalt Yourself over the heavens, O God, / let Your glory be over all the earth!* **1:** An unusually long, multi-part superscription, likely reflecting various layers of composition. *Al tashḥeth* means "do not destroy." It may be the incipit (first words) of a different song to whose melody this psalm was recited; alternately, Pss. 57; 58; 59; 75, all of which contain *al tashḥeth,* served together in a ritual petitionary context. (These four psalms, like the Asaph or the Korah psalms [see introductions to Pss. 42; 50], likely were once a mini-collection that was broken up in the process of editing of Psalms.) *When he fled from Saul into a cave,* probably the latest element in this superscription, reflecting the application of Psalms to the biography of David, may refer to events in 1 Sam. chs 24 or 26. This cannot be the original context of the psalm, which does not fit these chs precisely: In Samuel, David's main protagonist is Saul alone, while this psalm mentions many enemies. However, the Heb of v. 5 mentions a spear in the singular (translated here generically as "spears"); this may have reminded a creative editor, drawing on his traditions, of the story in 1 Sam. ch 26, which highlights the role of Saul's spear, taken by David while Saul slept "a deep sleep from the LORD" (v. 12; on the "spear" see vv. 7, 8, 11, 12, 16, 22). **2:** The exact repetition of *Have mercy on me* (see also Ps. 123.3), rather than use of a synonym, is unusual, but may reflect the psalmist's desperation (see Radak), though exact verbal repetition characterizes this psalm in general. *The shadow of Your wings* is a standard Psalms image, of God as a large protective bird (17.8; 36.8; 63.8), though the ultimate origin may be of the protection by the winged sun god. **3:** On *Most High* ("elyon"), see 7.18 n. **4:** On God in *heaven,* see 2.4 n. The Heb for *God will send down His steadfast love,* lit. "His faithfulness and His steadfastness," may retain echoes of God controlling minor deities who serve His will. **5:** A striking double metaphor, where the enemies are *lions,* and their *teeth* are weapons. **6:** The psalmist wants God, though residing in *the heavens* (see v. 4), to be manifest on *the earth.* God is exalted and His *glory* is expressed by granting victory to the supplicant. **7:** A fulfillment of Prov. 26.27, "He who digs a pit will fall in it." Nets appear in a surprising number of psalms (9; 10; 25; 31; 35; 37; 57; 140); this may simply reflect the realities of ancient Israelite trapping techniques, although others suggest that this refers to magical practices. **8–10:** The psalmist is implying that he should be saved so that God will

9 Awake, O my soul!
Awake, O harp and lyre!
I will wake the dawn.
10 I will praise You among the peoples, O Lord;
I will sing a hymn to You among the nations;
11 for Your faithfulness is as high as heaven;
Your steadfastness reaches to the sky.
12 Exalt Yourself over the heavens, O God,
let Your glory be over all the earth!

58

For the leader; *al tashḥeth.* Of David. A *michtam.*

2 [a]O mighty ones,[a] do you really decree what is just?
Do you judge mankind with equity?
3 In your minds you devise wrongdoing in the land;
[a]with your hands you deal out lawlessness.[a]
4 The wicked are defiant from birth;
the liars go astray from the womb.
5 Their venom is like that of a snake,
a deaf viper that stops its ears
6 so as not to hear the voice of charmers
or the expert mutterer of spells.

7 O God, smash their teeth in their mouth;
shatter the fangs of lions, O LORD;
8 let them melt, let them vanish like water;
let Him aim His arrows that they be cut down;
9 [a]like a snail that melts away as it moves;[a]
like a woman's stillbirth, may they never see the sun!
10 Before [a]the thorns grow into a bramble,
may He whirl them away alive in fury.[a]

11 The righteous man will rejoice when he sees revenge;
he will bathe his feet in the blood of the wicked.
12 Men will say,
"There is, then, a reward for the righteous;
there is, indeed, divine justice on earth."

59

For the leader; *al tashḥeth.* Of David. A *michtam;* when Saul sent men to watch his house in order to put him to death.[b]

2 Save me from my enemies, O my God;
secure me against my assailants.
3 Save me from evildoers;
deliver me from murderers.

a-a *Meaning of Heb. uncertain.* b *Cf.* 1 *Sam.* 19.11.

continue to hear his praises; see more explicitly 30.13. **8:** The first half of the v. is a protestation of innocence, justifying divine intervention. **10:** On the presence of nations, see Ps. 47. **11:** A recasting of v. 4, returning to *heaven, faithfulness,* and *steadfastness.*

Ps. 58: The language of the psalm is very difficult, and it is likely that it has been imperfectly preserved. Though it does not begin with an address to God, and initially looks like a psalm of instruction (see Ps. 14), the second half of the psalm, including the long curse of the wicked (vv. 7–10), makes it clear that it is a petition, although it does not follow the typical form of that genre—indeed, the problems of the petitioner are never noted, keeping with the general instructional nature of the psalm. The psalm is unusually rich in animal imagery. **2:** Many scholars suggest that "ʾelem" *(mighty ones)* refers to minor deities, and that this psalm, like Ps. 82, originally referred to the demotion of these deities due to their malfeasance. **6:** *Charmers ... spells,* a rare explicit mention of magic in Psalms, though some scholars believe that many individual petitioners feel cursed by magical charms. **7–10:** This may be a seven-fold curse, with seven functioning as a magical number. Petitions of the individual are characterized by imperatives, typically asking God to save the petitioners (e.g., 57.2, "have mercy on me"); here these are transformed with requests to punish the wicked. **11–12:** Like v. 11, Isa. 63.1–6 similarly revels in bloody gore. But the point is not pure *revenge,* but highlighting the power of *divine justice,* thereby encouraging others to be righteous. **12:** *Divine justice* translates the anomalous "gods who judge" ("ʾelohim shoftim"—see v. 2 n.), perhaps a textual error.

Ps. 59: This individual petition has clearly grown over time, as it is quite diffuse in content and style; it suggests, for example, that the supplicant is hounded by both personal (vv. 2–4) and national (v. 6) enemies. As noted by Ibn Ezra and Radak, the psalm incorporates a significant number of words from the root "ʿ-z-z," "strong, fierce": this

4 For see, they lie in wait for me;
fierce men plot against me
for no offense of mine,
for no transgression, O LORD;
5 for no guilt of mine
do they rush to array themselves against me.
Look, rouse Yourself on my behalf!
6 You, O LORD God of hosts,
God of Israel,
bestir Yourself to bring all nations to account;
have no mercy on any treacherous villain.
Selah.

7 They come each evening growling like dogs,
roaming the city.
8 They rave with their mouths,
[a]sharp words[a] are on their lips;
[they think,] "Who hears?"
9 But You, O LORD, laugh at them;
You mock all the nations.

10 O my[b] strength, I wait for You;
for God is my haven.
11 My faithful God will come to aid me;
God will let me gloat over my watchful foes.
12 Do not kill them lest my people be unmindful;
with Your power make wanderers of them;
bring them low, O our shield, the Lord,
13 because of their sinful mouths,
the words on their lips.
Let them be trapped by their pride,
and by the imprecations and lies they utter.
14 In Your fury put an end to them;
put an end to them that they be no more;
that it may be known to the ends of the earth
that God does rule over Jacob. *Selah.*

15 They come each evening growling like dogs,
roaming the city.
16 They wander in search of food;
and whine if they are not satisfied.
17 But I will sing of Your strength,
extol each morning Your faithfulness;
for You have been my haven,
a refuge in time of trouble.

helps to unify it. **1:** An unusually complex superscription that, like the psalm it introduces, likely grew over time. *To watch his house in order to put him to death* is a near quotation of 1 Sam. 19.11, where Saul sent men to kill David, but David's wife Michal saved him. The content of the psalm, where the individual is surrounded and is worried about being killed (v. 3), suggests this context; it is also possible that the Heb for "fierce men" (v. 4, "'azim") suggested the household idol covered with goat's hair (1 Sam. 19.13, "'izim") that Michal used to impersonate David, fooling Saul's men. **3:** On *evildoers,* see Ps. 5.6 n. **4–5:** A protestation of innocence; see 7.4–6 n. **5:** On *rouse Yourself* (Heb "'urah"), see 7.7 n. **6:** *Hosts* refers to God's role as leader of divine armies; see 46.8 n. **7:** This serves as a refrain with v. 15; the reference is to packs of wild *dogs* (see Ps. 22.17). **9:** Cf. 2.4. **10:** As the translators' note suggests, two similar letters were confused; the Heb reads His *strength,* which is contextually very difficult. **12–14:** Usually the petitioner requests the death of his persecutors (see esp. the immediately preceding 58.11), but here punishment is a vehicle for education; see Exod. 9.16. **17–18:** As in 57.8–10, the psalmist wants to be kept alive in order to praise God. **17:** Perhaps morning was a standard time of prayer (though see Ps. 92.3, which adds "night"); alternately, the supplicant prayed after surviving the difficulties of the night.

a-a Lit. "swords."
b With several mss.; cf. v. 18; lit. "His."

18 O my strength, to You I sing hymns;
for God is my haven, my faithful God.

60 For the leader; on [a]-*shushan eduth.*-[a] A *michtam* of David (to be taught), [2] when he fought with Aram-Naharaim and Aram-Zobah, and Joab returned and defeated Edom—[an army] of twelve thousand men—in the Valley of Salt.[b]

3 O God, You have rejected us,
You have made a breach in us;
You have been angry;
restore us!
4 You have made the land quake;
You have torn it open.
Mend its fissures,
for it is collapsing.
5 You have made Your people suffer hardship;
[c]-You have given us wine that makes us reel.-[c]
6 [a]-Give those who fear You because of Your truth
a banner for rallying.-[a] *Selah.*
7[d] That those whom You love might be rescued,
deliver with Your right hand and answer me.

8 God promised [e]-in His sanctuary-[e]
that I would exultingly divide up Shechem,
and measure the Valley of Sukkoth;
9 Gilead and Manasseh would be mine,
Ephraim my chief stronghold,
Judah my scepter;
10 Moab would be my washbasin;
on Edom I would cast my shoe;
acclaim me, O Philistia!

a-a Meaning of Heb. uncertain. *b Cf. 2 Sam. 8; 1 Chron. 18.*
c-c Or "You have sated Your people with a bitter draft."
d Cf. Ps. 108.7–14. *e-e Or "by His holiness."*

18: This conclusion is an expanded reworking of v. 10 and the beginning of v. 11. *My haven* ("misgav") returns to the opening of the psalm, "secure me" ("tesagveni"); on God as *faithful,* see 5.8 n.

Ps. 60: This communal petition is unusual in mentioning so many specific geographical locations (vv. 8–10); only 83.7–12 is comparable. **1:** In the superscription, *on shushan eduth* and *to be taught* are unique and obscure. **2:** David's wars against Aram (Syria) are narrated in 2 Sam. 8.3–8; 10.6–18; it is likely that the editor who added this superscription was referring to 2 Sam. ch 8, which opens with references to the Philistines and Moabites (see Ps. 60.10). The second half of the v. is based on 2 Sam. 8.13, "David gained fame when he returned from defeating Edom in the Valley of Salt, 18,000 in all." The number of casualties has changed in transmission, as has the city-state; in Heb, Edom ("ʼdm") and Aram ("ʼrm") are nearly identical, and in many cases the letters "dalet" and "resh" are confused due to their similarity in both the old and new Heb script. (Traditional attempts at reconciling these different accounts, as in Radak, are forced.) The content of the psalm, a communal lament, however, does not conform to the story in Samuel. Although these historical superscriptions are secondary and not relevant for dating the psalms, the content of the psalm suggests the Northern Kingdom did not exist as a separate entity, which would date the psalm to the period either before the development (ca. 922 BCE), or after the destruction, of the Northern Kingdom (ca. 722 BCE). **3:** Divine anger leads to divine abandonment. Punishment as a result of divine anger is a common ancient Near Eastern idea; the Moabite Mesha Inscription describes Moab's military losses "because Chemosh [the Moabite national god] was angry at his land" (*ANET,* p. 320), using the same root for "angry" as this v. **5:** On the poison cup of God, see esp. Isa. 51.17; Jer. 25.15–29. **7:** The motivation for God to act. *Answer me* may reflect a call for a divine oracle, which is delivered in the following vv. **8–10:** In contrast to the surrounding vv., these are formed as tricola, vv. with three sections, instead of the typical two (bicola). **8:** From *His sanctuary,* the Temple, God provides a positive answer (so Ibn Ezra, Radak), perhaps through a cultic prophet; the word *that* is lacking in Hebrew, and *I would* may introduce a direct quotation. *Shechem* and *Sukkoth* are two cities in central Israel, to the west and east of the Jordan. **9:** *Gilead* is treated as a tribe, as in the early Song of Deborah (Judg. 5.17). *Judah my scepter* recalls the enigmatic blessing of Jacob (Gen. 49.10), "The scepter shall not depart from Judah, Nor the ruler's staff from between his feet." **10:** *Moab … Edom … Philistia,* city-states surrounding Israel on the east, south, and west. *Casting a shoe* may reflect ownership (Ruth 4.7).

11 Would that I were brought to the bastion!
Would that I were led to Edom!

12 But You have rejected us, O God;
God, You do not march with our armies.
13 Grant us Your aid against the foe,
for the help of man is worthless.
14 With God we shall triumph;
He will trample our foes.

61 For the leader; with instrumental music. Of David.

2 Hear my cry, O God,
heed my prayer.
3 From the end of the earth I call to You;
when my heart is faint,
You lead me to a rock that is high above me.
4 For You have been my refuge,
a tower of strength against the enemy.
5 O that I might dwell in Your tent forever,
take refuge under Your protecting wings. *Selah.*

6 O God, You have heard my vows;
grant the request[a] of those who fear Your name.
7 Add days to the days of the king;
may his years extend through generations;
8 may he dwell in God's presence forever;
appoint[b] steadfast love to guard him.
9 So I will sing hymns to Your name forever,
as I fulfill my vows day after day.

62 For the leader; on *Jeduthun.* A psalm of David.

2 Truly my soul waits quietly for God;
my deliverance comes from Him.
3 Truly He is my rock and deliverance,
my haven; I shall never be shaken.
4 How long will all of you attack[b] a man,
to crush[b] him, as though he were
a leaning wall, a tottering fence?
5 They lay plans to topple him from his rank;
they delight in falsehood;

a Taking the noun yršt *as an alternate form of* ʾršt; *cf. Ps. 21.3.*
b Meaning of Heb. uncertain.

11: Perhaps the human response to the divine oracle. **12:** The psalmist is suggesting that God is not fulfilling His role as LORD of hosts (see 44.10 n.). **13–14:** As often in historiographical and prophetic literature (e.g., Zech. 4.6), a single God is more effective than any number of human fighters.

Ps. 61: The beginning of the psalm is a personal petition (vv. 2–5), while the second half (vv. 6–9) is a prayer for the king; "Selah" divides the psalm in half (see 3.3 n.). It is unclear if two separate psalms have been combined, or if, as in Mesopotamia, an individual might incorporate a royal prayer into a petition. **2–5:** The supplicant is hyperbolically at *the end of the earth,* distant from the Temple (*Your tent;* so Ibn Ezra and Radak; see 15.1 n.), where he wants to reside under divine protection (see 57.2 n.), as reflected in *rock ... refuge ... tower of strength ... tent ... refuge ... protecting wings.* This petition includes the typical elements: imperatives *(Hear ... heed),* an invocation *(O God),* and a motivation *(For you ...).* **6–9:** This second unit is framed by the mention of the *vow.* **7–8:** Similar hyperbolic language about the king is reflected in Pss. 21.5; 72.5, and reflects notions of the king being (close to) divine (see 45.7 n.). **9:** Ps. 30.13 concludes in a similar fashion.

Ps. 62: This is an oblique form of an individual petition. It lacks that genre's usual pattern of invocation, imperatives, and motivation, but instead indirectly notes expected deliverance from God (vv. 2–3) and highlights God's great power. Except for the last v., it is addressed to the community rather than to God. The Heb is unique in its sixfold repetition of "ʾakh," "truly" (vv. 2, 3, 5, 6, 7, 10; NJPS does not translate all of them), expressing the petitioner's great certainty. The psalm shares some of the same refuge language as the previous psalm (esp. 61.3 and 62.7). **1:** On *Jeduthun,* see 39.1. **2–3:** The repetition of *deliverance* and the surrounding imagery suggest persecution by enemies. **4:** *A leaning wall, a tottering fence* unique images in the Bible. **5:** As in other contexts, this persecution is connected to false speech (see 10.7 n.).

they bless with their mouths,
while inwardly they curse. *Selah.*

6 Truly, wait quietly for God, O my soul,
for my hope comes from Him.
7 He is my rock and deliverance,
my haven; I shall not be shaken.
8 I rely on God, my deliverance and glory,
my rock of strength;
in God is my refuge.
9 Trust in Him at all times, O people;
pour out your hearts before Him;
God is our refuge. *Selah.*

10 Men are mere breath;
mortals, illusion;
placed on a scale all together,
they weigh even less than a breath.
11 Do not trust in violence,
or put false hopes in robbery;
if force bears fruit pay it no mind.
12 One thing God has spoken;
two things have I heard:
that might belongs to God,
13 and faithfulness is Yours, O Lord,
to reward each man according to his deeds.

63 A psalm of David, when he was in the Wilderness of Judah.

2 God, You are my God;
I search for You,
my soul thirsts for You,
my body yearns for You,
as a parched and thirsty land that has no water.
3 I shall behold You in the sanctuary,
and see Your might and glory,
4 Truly Your faithfulness is better than life;
my lips declare Your praise.
5 I bless You all my life;
I lift up my hands, invoking Your name.

6–7: A slight variant of vv. 2–3, functioning as a refrain. **9:** The psalmist moves from his personal trust, exhorting the listeners to do the same: God moves from being *my refuge* (v. 8) to becoming *our refuge.* **10:** This may reflect the weighing of people's deeds or hearts, well attested in ancient Egypt, especially in illustrations accompanying the Book of the Dead. **12:** Numbers are paralleled by x || x+1; this explains why *one* is paralleled by *two.* Thus, God has spoken, perhaps via an oracle answering the psalmist, one thing only: *that might belongs to God.* This is a direct answer to the psalmist's indirect request for deliverance (see vv. 2–3). This parallelism is one of the classic texts expounded in rabbinic culture to mean that God's word is multivalent and needs to be interpreted in a variety of special ways—quite literally, God has spoken once, but people hear two equally legitimate things (see, e.g., *b. Sanh.* 34a). It is also used to explain why the Decalogue versions in Exod. ch 20 and Deut. ch 5 differ: God spoke once, but people heard two different utterances (*Mek., In the Month,* section 7 and parallels, cited by Rashi). **13:** This is the psalmist's response to the divine oracle; on divine *faithfulness* ("ḥesed"), see 5.8 n. It functions as an oblique request that he will be *reward*ed ... *according to his deeds,* in other words, saved from the enemies.

Ps. 63: This psalm defies classification; it is characterized by a deep spiritual, almost mystical sense. In theme and vocabulary Pss. 42–43; 73; 84 are similar. **1:** The superscription is likely based on the "parched and thirsty land" described in v. 2. David was in the wilderness on various occasions when fleeing from Saul and Absalom. **2:** Ps. 42 opens with a similar image. **3:** This derives from the idea of seeing the cult statue at a temple; see 11.7 n. It is easy to imagine that such a statue could artistically express God's *might and glory,* especially since *glory* may represent the glow of the metal image. It is uncertain if this v. represents a wish *(I shall behold)* or a past or present action ("I beheld; I behold"). **4:** *Faithfulness* reflects "ḥesed"; see 5.8 n. This is a remarkable notion—God's "ḥesed" is better than human life itself. **5:** On lifting up *hands* as the ancient prayer position, see 44.21–22 n.

6 I am sated as with a [a]rich feast,[a]
I sing praises with joyful lips
7 when I call You to mind upon my bed,
when I think of You in the watches of the night;
8 for You are my help,
and in the shadow of Your wings
I shout for joy.
9 My soul is attached to You;
Your right hand supports me.

10 May those who seek to destroy my life
enter the depths of the earth.
11 May they be gutted by the sword;
may they be prey to jackals.
12 But the king shall rejoice in God;
all who swear by Him shall exult,
when the mouth of liars is stopped.

64

For the leader. A psalm of David.

2 Hear my voice, O God, when I plead;
guard my life from the enemy's terror.
3 Hide me from a band of evil men,
from a crowd of evildoers,
4 who whet their tongues like swords;
they aim their arrows—cruel words—
5 to shoot from hiding at the blameless man;
they shoot him suddenly and without fear.
6 [b]They arm themselves with an evil word;
when they speak, it is to conceal traps;[b]
they think, "Who will see them?"
7[c] Let the wrongdoings [d]they have concealed,[d]
each one inside him, his secret thoughts,
be wholly exposed.
8 God shall shoot them with arrows;
they shall be struck down suddenly.
9 Their tongue shall be their downfall;
all who see them shall recoil in horror;
10 all men shall stand in awe;
they shall proclaim the work of God
and His deed which they perceived.
11 The righteous shall rejoice in the LORD,
and take refuge in Him;
all the upright shall exult.

a-a Lit. "suet and fat." b-b Meaning of Heb. uncertain.
c Meaning of verse uncertain.
d-d Reading ṭamnu *with some mss. (cf. Minḥat Shai) and Rashi; most printed editions* tamnu, *traditionally rendered "they have accomplished."*

6: This v. conceptually joins prayer and sacrifice (see the translators' note "suet and fat"), as in Pss. 50 and 51. **7:** Night is a typical time for reflection and meditation (4.5; 16.7; 119.55). Nighttime was divided into three or four *watches.* **8:** See 57.2 n. **9:** The Heb for *attached* ("davkah") is very intense, showing close proximity and longing. **10–11:** Such requests typify individual petitions. **12:** Compare the ending of Ps. 61. It is uncertain if the people are swearing by God (this translation) or by the king (see, e.g., 1 Sam. 17.55), or possibly by both (see, e.g., 2 Sam. 15.21).

Ps. 64: A prayer for deliverance from evildoers, whose words are the means of their wickedness. Military metaphors make the wicked into enemies and their speech into weapons of war: *swords, arrows, traps,* and ambushes, but in measure-for-measure fashion; God punishes them with *arrows* and *their tongue.* **4:** For the metaphor of *tongues* as *swords* (damaging speech), cf. Pss. 57.5; 59.8. **5:** The psalmist obliquely suggests that he is a *blameless man,* and thus must be spared. **6:** *"Who will see them?,"* the confidence of the evildoers that their activity goes unnoticed (Pss. 10.11; 59.8). This is a less extreme idea than Ps. 14.1 (and Ps. 53.2), "God does not care," lit. "there is no God." **7:** The *secret thoughts* may be a reference to sorcery (see 10.7 n.); or it may simply be plotting in one's mind. **8:** Just as the wicked shoot arrows at others, so will God shoot arrows at them (Ibn Ezra). Cf. Pss. 7.13–14; 38.3. The enemies are described at length while God's action is instantaneous. **9–11:** Vengeance is not the motive; rather the defeat of the wicked causes *all men* (human beings) to *stand in awe* and *proclaim the work of God,* and causes the *upright* to *exult.*

65

For the leader. A psalm of David. A song.

2 Praise befits You in Zion, O God;
vows are paid to You;
3 all mankind[a] comes to You,
You who hear prayer.
4 When all manner of sins overwhelm me,
it is You who forgive our iniquities.
5 Happy is the man You choose and bring near
to dwell in Your courts;
may we be sated with the blessings of Your
house,
Your holy temple.

6 Answer us with victory through awesome deeds,
O God, our deliverer,
in whom all the ends of the earth
and the distant seas
put their trust;
7 who by His power fixed the mountains firmly,
who is girded with might,
8 who stills the raging seas,
the raging waves,
and tumultuous peoples.
9 Those who live at the ends of the earth are awed by
Your signs;
You make the lands of sunrise and sunset shout
for joy.
10 You take care of the earth and irrigate it;
You enrich it greatly,
with the channel of God full of water;
You provide grain for men;
for so do You prepare it.
11 Saturating its furrows,
leveling its ridges,
You soften it with showers,
You bless its growth.
12 You crown the year with Your bounty;
fatness is distilled in Your paths;

a *Lit. "flesh."*

Ps. 65: The beginning of the psalm celebrates God and the Temple, the place where vows are paid (vv. 2–5). The psalmist is thankful for the privilege of entering the Temple—i.e., coming into God's Presence—in order to pay his vow (present an offering). The payment is made possible by the bounteous harvest that God has provided. The vow may have been to bring a special offering for a good harvest. This connects to the body of the psalm that praises God for His power over the sources of water and His beneficence in providing water for irrigation. It is possible that this psalm was sung during Sukkot, the Feast of Tabernacles, which marks the end of the harvest and the beginning of the rainy season. In postbiblical times it featured prayers for rain for the coming rainy season. **2:** *Zion,* sometimes a synonym for Jerusalem or, as here, the site of the Temple. On the paying of vows at the Temple, see Ps. 66.13. **3:** The translation reverses the clauses in this v. *All mankind* gives a more universal flavor to the psalm, as does v. 9, "Those who live at the ends of the earth." Zech. 14.17 envisions survivors of all nations making a pilgrimage to Jerusalem on Sukkot. **4:** Divine forgiveness of sin is the precondition for winter rains and an abundant harvest (Deut. 11.13–17). **5:** *The blessings of Your house* may refer to general prosperity, or specifically to the rain that God will send. Alternatively, it may refer to the sacrificial meal at the Temple or the general goodness that derives from being proximate to God. **6–10:** The hope for adequate rainfall is couched in descriptions of God as the supreme power of the world, especially over the cosmic water: *seas, waves,* and water *channel. Awesome deeds,* God's acts of creation by His victory over the forces of primeval chaos (*the ... seas;* Pss. 29; 93), and His provision of rain. **10:** *The channel of God,* the conduit that brings rain to the earth (Job 38.25–26), perhaps associated with the Temple (see Ps. 36.9). The repetition *You provide grain for men; for so do you prepare it* (Heb uses the same word for *provide* and *prepare*) emphasizes that this is not a psalm about God as creator, but as provider through His beneficent creation. **11–14:** The potentially destructive cosmic water forces are tamed by God and become the gentle rain and run-off that irrigates the earth, providing vegetation and flocks with their nourishment. All the creatures who are thus nourished join humankind in the praise of the beneficent God (Pss. 69.35; 96.11–12; 98.7–8). The picture of the harvest sounds eschatological; cf. Joel 4.18; Amos 9.13.

Ps. 66: The theme of this psalm is not obvious; it offers a picture of God's wonders that differs from the previous psalm, though some themes are echoed (victory through God's awesome deeds, universal blessing of God, bringing offerings to the Temple). It is unclear at times whether the psalmist is speaking of events in the past or the present. The psalm begins and ends with praise, surrounding passages of communal and individual thanksgiving. The date of the psalm is unknown and its context is quite general. It may be interpreted as praise to God for the return from exile and the rebuilding of the Temple. All peoples of the world witnessed this event, which redounds to God's praise. **1:** This v. is formulaic; cf. 98.4; 100.1. **2–4:** Universal acclamation for God for His deliverance of Israel (Josh. 2.9–11). **4:** *Selah* (also vv. 7, 15), see Ps. 3.3 n. This term may divide sections of the psalm. **5–7:** The world is invited to consider God's acts, which are epitomized by His splitting of the sea during the exodus and the drying up of the Jordan when the Israelites entered the promised land (Exod. 14.21–22; Josh. 4.23). The parallelism between sea and Jordan in Ps. 114.3–5 suggests that *river* refers to the Jordan. The exodus-conquest theme may hint at the theme of the return from exile and re-entrance to Judah (the exodus was a common symbol for the return in postexilic times, esp. in Second Isaiah). **8–9:** All peoples should praise Israel's God for His beneficence to them (see Ps. 117). **10–12:** A recent event in which Israel has been threatened but delivered from harm parallels the exodus. This may be a reference to the exile, expressed in terms of the exodus from Egypt, the arduous trek through the wilderness *(fire),* and the crossing of the Jordan *(water);* cf. Isa. 43.2. **10:** The refining process is arduous but purifies that which is refined. **13–15:** Abundant thanksgiving sacrifices in the Temple—most of the nouns reflecting the sacrifices are in the plural. The psalmist can now deliver the sacrifices he vowed to bring if God would rescue him from his distress (cf. Ps. 65.2).

13 the pasturelands distill it;
the hills are girded with joy.
14 The meadows are clothed with flocks,
the valleys mantled with grain;
they raise a shout, they break into song.

66

For the leader. A song. A psalm.

Raise a shout for God, all the earth;
2 sing the glory of His name,
make glorious His praise.
3 Say to God,
"How awesome are Your deeds,
Your enemies cower before Your great strength;
4 all the earth bows to You,
and sings hymns to You;
all sing hymns to Your name." *Selah.*

5 Come and see the works of God,
who is held in awe by men for His acts.
6 He turned the sea into dry land;
they crossed the river on foot;
we therefore rejoice in Him.
7 He rules forever in His might;
His eyes scan the nations;
let the rebellious not assert themselves. *Selah.*

8 O peoples, bless our God,
celebrate His praises;
9 who has granted us life,
and has not let our feet slip.

10 You have tried us, O God,
refining us, as one refines silver.
11 You have caught us in a net,
[a]caught us in trammels.[a]
12 You have let men ride over us;
we have endured fire and water,
and You have brought us through to prosperity.

13 I enter Your house with burnt offerings,
I pay my vows to You,
14 [vows] that my lips pronounced,
that my mouth uttered in my distress.

a-a *Lit. "put a trammel on our loins."*

15 I offer up fatlings to You,
with the odor of burning rams;
I sacrifice bulls and he-goats. *Selah.*

16 Come and hear, all God-fearing men,
as I tell what He did for me.
17 I called aloud to Him,
glorification on my tongue.
18 Had I an evil thought in my mind,
the Lord would not have listened.
19 But God did listen;
He paid heed to my prayer.
20 Blessed is God who has not turned away my prayer,
or His faithful care from me.

67

For the leader; with instrumental music.
A psalm. A song.

2 May God be gracious to us and bless us;
may He show us favor, *selah*
3 that Your way be known on earth,
Your deliverance among all nations.

4 Peoples will praise You, O God;
all peoples will praise You.
5 Nations will exult and shout for joy,
for You rule the peoples with equity,
You guide the nations of the earth. *Selah.*
6 The peoples will praise You, O God;
all peoples will praise You.

7 May the earth yield its produce;
may God, our God, bless us.
8 May God bless us,
and be revered to the ends of the earth.

68

[a]For the leader. Of David. A psalm. A song.

2 God will arise,
His enemies shall be scattered,
His foes shall flee before Him.

a The coherence of this psalm and the meaning of many of its passages are uncertain.

16–20: The psalmist's experience serves as proof to all God-fearers that God hears people's prayers. (It is unclear who these God-fearers were.) Strikingly, the psalmist speaks here in the singular, although the previous vv. (vv. 8–12) speak of Israel in the plural; perhaps a representative individual is speaking here. **20:** Final benediction (2 Sam. 7.15). On *faithful care* ("ḥesed"), see 5.8 n.

Ps. 67: A prayer that good harvests continue, with a refrain in vv. 4, 6. The psalm uses the root "b-r-k," "to bless," three times at its beginning and end (vv. 2, 7, 8). It bears some resemblance to Ps. 65 and continues the theme of blessing found in the conclusion of Ps. 66. All three psalms speak of the universal acknowledgment of God; this is especially appropriate in the context of God as provider of rain and sustenance to all humanity. **2:** An echo of the Aaronic (priestly) blessing (Num. 6.24–26; Ps. 4.6). *Show ... favor,* lit. "make His face shine." The shining face of God is the visible expression of His benevolence; the opposite is God's hiding His face. *Selah* (also vv. 4, 7), see Ps. 3.3 n. **5:** See Pss. 96.10–13; 98.7–9. **7–8:** *May God ... bless us,* with copious winter rain (Lev. 26.4; Deut. 11.17; Ezek. 34.27). The hymn may be associated with the fall festival of Sukkot (Tabernacles). **8:** The conclusion, like the entire psalm, balances particularistic *(us)* and universal *(ends of the earth)* concerns.

Ps. 68: A hymn describing God's victory over His foes and His choice of Jerusalem as the place of His dominion. It draws on an ancient tradition, found also in the very old poem in Judg. ch 5, about the southern origins (Sinai) of Israel's God. It invokes themes from the exodus and the conquest. Because the psalm appears disjointed, some scholars see it as a combination of numerous psalms or a list of their opening lines. Its vocabulary includes fifteen words found nowhere else in the Bible, plus other rare words, adding to the difficulty of interpreting it. Indeed, much of it remains obscure, and many consider it to be the most difficult psalm in the Psalter. **2:** Num. 10.35 is similar, suggesting that the psalm was perhaps associated with the Ark. The Ark was taken out to battle at the head of the troops (1 Sam. ch 4).

3 Disperse them as smoke is dispersed;
as wax melts at fire,
so the wicked shall perish before God.
4 But the righteous shall rejoice;
they shall exult in the presence of God;
they shall be exceedingly joyful.

5 Sing to God, chant hymns to His name;
extol Him who rides the clouds;
the LORD is His name.
Exult in His presence—
6 the father of orphans, the champion of widows,
God, in His holy habitation.
7 God restores the lonely to their homes,
sets free the imprisoned, safe and sound,
while the rebellious must live in a parched land.

8 O God, when You went at the head of Your army,
when You marched through the desert, *selah*
9 the earth trembled, the sky rained because of God,
yon Sinai, because of God, the God of Israel.
10 You released a bountiful rain, O God;
when Your own land languished, You sustained it.
11 Your tribe dwells there;
O God, in Your goodness You provide for the needy.

12 The Lord gives a command;
the women who bring the news are a great host:
13 "The kings and their armies are in headlong flight;
housewives are sharing in the spoils;
14 even for those of you who lie among the sheepfolds
there are wings of a dove sheathed in silver,
its pinions in fine gold."
15 When Shaddai scattered the kings,
it seemed like a snowstorm in Zalmon.

16 O majestic mountain, Mount Bashan;
O jagged mountain, Mount Bashan;
17 why so hostile, O jagged mountains,
toward the mountain God desired as His dwelling?
The LORD shall abide there forever.

3: God will make the enemies (= *the wicked*) disappear in such a way that they will no longer exist; like smoke or melted wax, they will have no substance. For another smoke metaphor in connection with the wicked, see Ps. 37.20. **4:** Joy is equated, in a ritual sense, with being in God's Presence. The enemies cannot be in God's Presence. The v. abounds in "joy" language. **5:** *Who rides the clouds,* God's stormcloud chariot (v. 34; Ps. 65.12). The image and language are found in Ugaritic writings. **6:** As often in psalms, God uses His power to care for the downtrodden. **7:** *Restores the lonely to their homes,* a difficult phrase, perhaps better translated "he sets individuals (who are not part of a family) in households"; cf. Ps. 113.7–9. It is parallel to the rest of the v., which is concerned with assigning befitting living-places to prisoners and to rebellious people. If this v. is a late addition, *the imprisoned* may refer to the captives of the exile (cf. Ps. 69.34), who will be returned home. **8–9:** A likely allusion, with changes, to Judg. 5.4–5. A reference to the exodus. **8:** *Selah* (also vv. 20, 33), see Ps. 3.3 n. **9:** One of the few references to *Sinai* outside of the Torah; it is not, however, connected here to the giving of the Torah. **10–11:** The mention of rain in the allusion provokes further description of God's bountiful rain, by which He cares for His people. This is a major theme of the three previous psalms. **11:** *Needy,* not simply the underprivileged mentioned in vv. 6–7, but all the people who need rain to survive. The community often calls itself "needy" ("'ani," or a synonym; cf. Pss. 18.28; 74.21). **12–15:** God *gives a command* for war; women announce the good *news* of God's victory (Exod. 15.20; 1 Sam. 18.6–7). **13:** *Sharing in the spoils,* Judg. 5.30. **14:** *Among the sheepfolds,* Judg. 5.16. *Wings of a dove ...*, presumably some treasure found among the spoil. **15:** The specific incident referred to cannot be identified. *Zalmon* may be the same mountain mentioned in Judg. 9.48. Another possibility is Zalmonah, in the south (Num. 33.41–42). **16–24:** God's move from Mount Sinai (v. 9) to Mount Zion, God's choice for his royal residence (Isa. 2.3). For unclear reasons, Mount Bashan looks upon this move with hostility—perhaps the northern mountain does not want God to dwell forever in Jerusalem, in Judah to the south. **16:** *Bashan,* a region in northern Transjordan. The specific mountain referred to is unknown. **17:** *Mountain ... His dwelling,* cf. Exod. 15.17; Ps. 132.13–14.

18 God's chariots are myriads upon myriads,
thousands upon thousands;
the Lord is among them as in Sinai in holiness.

19 You went up to the heights, having taken captives,
having received tribute of men,
even of those who rebel
against the LORD God's abiding there.

20 Blessed is the Lord.
Day by day He supports us,
God, our deliverance. *Selah.*
21 God is for us a God of deliverance;
GOD the Lord provides an escape from death.
22 God will smash the heads of His enemies,
the hairy crown of him who walks about in his guilt.
23 The Lord said, "I will retrieve from Bashan,
I will retrieve from the depths of the sea;
24 that your feet may wade through blood;
that the tongue of your dogs may have its portion of your enemies."

25 Men see Your processions, O God,
the processions of my God, my king,
into the sanctuary.
26 First come singers, then musicians,
amidst maidens playing timbrels.
27 In assemblies bless God,
the LORD, O you who are from the fountain of Israel.
28 There is little Benjamin who rules them,
the princes of Judah who command them,
the princes of Zebulun and Naphtali.

29 Your God has ordained strength for you,
the strength, O God,
which You displayed for us
30 from Your temple above Jerusalem.
The kings bring You tribute.
31 Blast the beast of the marsh,
the herd of bulls among the peoples, the calves,
till they come cringing with pieces of silver.
Scatter the peoples who delight in wars!
32 Tribute-bearers shall come from Egypt;
Cush shall hasten its gifts to God.

33 O kingdoms of the earth,
sing to God;
chant hymns to the Lord, *selah*

18: Cf. Deut. 33.2. **19:** An unusually obscure v. in an unusually obscure psalm—it is unclear how it relates contextually, though some understand *the heights* as a reference to Sinai of the preceding v. **23:** *Bashan,* see v. 16. **24:** *Feet ... blood,* see 58.11. *Dogs,* for dogs lapping up the blood of the dead, cf. 1 Kings 21.19; 22.38. **25–28:** Processions into the Temple (Ps. 24.7–10). **25:** *Men* is missing in the Heb, and the subject is uncertain. **26:** Elsewhere women are not depicted as having a role in Temple music. **28:** Cf. Judg. 5.14–18. *Little Benjamin who rules them* sounds like a reference to King Saul, who was from the tribe of Benjamin. **29–36:** International praise for God and tribute from all the kings of the world—a theme of the three previous psalms, and a scene like that pictured in Isa. 2.2–4 and Mic. 4.1–3, where Mt. Zion is the religious center of the world. Cf. Zeph. 3.9–10. **32:** *Cush,* Ethiopia, the farthest south from Israel's perspective. **33–36:** Cf. 29.1–3, 11. God's power at the end of the psalm forms an inclusio with its beginning. The final three vv. mention "might" (Heb "ʿoz") four times, highlighting a main theme of the psalm.

34 to Him who rides the ancient highest heavens,
who thunders forth with His mighty voice.
35 Ascribe might to God,
whose majesty is over Israel,
whose might is in the skies.
36 You are awesome, O God, in Your holy places;
it is the God of Israel who gives might and power to the people.
Blessed is God.

69 For the leader. On *shoshannim.*[a] Of David.

2 Deliver me, O God,
for the waters have reached my neck;
3 I am sinking into the slimy deep
and find no foothold;
I have come into the watery depths;
the flood sweeps me away.
4 I am weary with calling;
my throat is dry;
my eyes fail
while I wait for God.
5 More numerous than the hairs of my head
are those who hate me without reason;
many are those who would destroy me,
my treacherous enemies.
Must I restore what I have not stolen?
6 God, You know my folly;
my guilty deeds are not hidden from You.
7 Let those who look to You,
O Lord, GOD of hosts,
not be disappointed on my account;
let those who seek You,
O God of Israel,
not be shamed because of me.
8 It is for Your sake that I have been reviled,
that shame covers my face;
9 I am a stranger to my brothers,
an alien to my kin.
10 My zeal for Your house has been my undoing;
the reproaches of those who revile You have fallen upon me.
11 When I wept and fasted,
I was reviled for it.
12 I made sackcloth my garment;
I became a byword among them.

a *Meaning of Heb. uncertain.*

34: *To Him who rides* returns to v. 5, toward the beginning. **36:** *Blessed is God* (or "the Lord") is typically a beginning rather than concluding formula, but see Gen. 26.29.

Ps. 69: An individual complains that he is drowning, figuratively, from the hatred of his enemies: members of his own society and even his family. He calls to God for help, trusting that God will accept his prayer with favor. While this seems like a very general prayer by an individual hoping for the return to Zion and the rebuilding of Judah (v. 36), it is best interpreted as a petition by a person lamenting the destruction of the Temple—one of the "mourners for Zion" (see v. 10 n.). The psalmist's troubles stem from his public mourning for the lost Temple, acts for which his friends and family taunt him (vv. 10–13). The idea of exile and mourning is suggested at numerous points in the psalm. **1:** *Shoshannim,* "lilies," perhaps a melody or a musical instrument; see Ps. 45.1. **2–3:** The drowning metaphor is well developed (cf. Ps. 130.1). We can see the speaker sinking further and further into the water until he is swept away. **4:** *My throat is dry* is ironic, given that the psalmist is surrounded by water. **5–6:** The friends' hatred for the psalmist takes the form of false accusations, which the psalmist denies. But he does not claim to be innocent; God knows his errors. **5:** The image *More numerous than the hairs of my head* is found only here and in 40.13. **7–13:** The psalmist is criticized by his society for what he considers his pious devotion, especially in regard to Jerusalem. **9:** The language is stereotypical; see see Ps. 38.12; Job 19.13–15. **10:** *My zeal for Your house:* Like the mourners for Zion in Isa. 61.2–3 and Zech. 7.3, the psalmist mourns for the destroyed Temple by weeping (that is, crying out in lament), fasting, and wearing sackcloth. This behavior causes everyone to revile him. **13:** *Those who sit in the gate:* The gate was the main public meeting-place, where business and

13 Those who sit in the gate talk about me;
I am the taunt of drunkards.

14 As for me, may my prayer come to You, O LORD,
at a favorable moment;
O God, in Your abundant faithfulness,
answer me with Your sure deliverance.
15 Rescue me from the mire;
let me not sink;
let me be rescued from my enemies,
and from the watery depths.
16 Let the floodwaters not sweep me away;
let the deep not swallow me;
let the mouth of the Pit not close over me.
17 Answer me, O LORD,
according to Your great steadfastness;
in accordance with Your abundant mercy
turn to me;
18 do not hide Your face from Your servant,
for I am in distress;
answer me quickly.
19 Come near to me and redeem me;
free me from my enemies.

20 You know my reproach,
my shame, my disgrace;
You are aware of all my foes.
21 Reproach breaks my heart,
I am in despair;[a]
I hope for consolation, but there is none,
for comforters, but find none.
22 They give me gall for food,
vinegar to quench my thirst.
23 May their table be a trap for them,
a snare for their allies.
24 May their eyes grow dim so that they cannot see;
may their loins collapse continually.
25 Pour out Your wrath on them;
may Your blazing anger overtake them;
26 may their encampments be desolate;
may their tents stand empty.
27 For they persecute those You have struck;
they talk about the pain of those You have
felled.
28 Add that to their guilt;
let them have no share of Your beneficence;

a Meaning of Heb. uncertain.

legal transactions took place. Those who sit in the gate are the leading officials of the city. At the other end of the spectrum of those who congregate publicly are the *drunkards.* **14:** *At a favorable moment,* at a time when God is most disposed to accept his prayer. Human beings do not know when these times are, and indeed many psalms call upon God to wake up or to listen or not to hide His face (see v. 18 below). This v. is recited during the Torah service on festivals in conjunction with God's attributes (see Exod. 34.6–7). **16:** *The Pit:* The usual word for the Pit is "bor," "cistern," and it symbolizes the grave, or death (cf. Pss. 28.1; 30.4; 88.5; 143.7), although the similar-sounding "be'er," "well," as here, can be used in the same sense (Ps. 55.24). The use of "be'er" in the context of the other water imagery is apt, for a cistern may be full or empty but a well always contains water. The picture of a person in a well or cistern brings to mind Joseph, who was held in a dry cistern (Gen. 37.24), and Jeremiah, who was in a muddy one (Jer. 38.6). A cistern or well is, then, a place of imprisonment. Cf. Lam. 3.53–54, which can be interpreted as an individual imprisoned in a full cistern with its lid being closed, and Lam. 3.55, a call to be saved from the Pit. See also Ps. 40.3. Exilic literature often uses prison (real or metaphoric) as a symbol of exile, and this v.—and indeed all the drowning imagery—symbolizes the exile in which the psalmist feels himself to be. **17–19:** The psalmist prays that God will not *hide* His *face* (be inattentive to the psalmist's prayers). *Answer me* occurs in vv. 17 and 18, harking back to v. 14. **19:** *From my enemies,* better "for the sake of my enemies," namely so they will recognize your power. The psalmist is guilty (v. 6), so cannot ask to be saved due to his innocence. **22:** *My thirst* returns to the image of the parched throat in v. 4. **27:** *Those You have struck* and *those You have felled* refer to the punishment of exile. The psalmist's friends make light of his sense of being in exile.

29 may they be erased from the book of life,
and not be inscribed with the righteous.

30 But I am lowly and in pain;
Your help, O God, keeps me safe.
31 I will extol God's name with song,
and exalt Him with praise.
32 That will please the LORD more than oxen,
than bulls with horns and hooves.
33 The lowly will see and rejoice;
you who are mindful of God, take heart!
34 For the LORD listens to the needy,
and does not spurn His captives.
35 Heaven and earth shall extol Him,
the seas, and all that moves in them.
36 For God will deliver Zion
and rebuild the cities of Judah;
they shall live there and inherit it;
37 the offspring of His servants shall possess it;
those who cherish His name shall dwell there.

70

For the leader. Of David. *Lehazkir.*[a]

2[b] Hasten, O God, to save me;
O LORD, to aid me!
3 Let those who seek my life
be frustrated and disgraced;
let those who wish me harm,
fall back in shame.
4 Let those who say, "Aha! Aha!"
turn back because of their frustration.

5 But let all who seek You be glad and rejoice in You;
let those who are eager for Your deliverance
always say,
"Extolled be God!"
6 But I am poor and needy;
O God, hasten to me!

a Meaning of Heb. uncertain. *b Cf. Ps. 40.14–18.*

29: *The book of life* in which God inscribes the righteous; see 56.9 n. **32:** The animal sacrifices could not take place without the Temple; prayer was the substitute for sacrifice until the Temple could be rebuilt (cf. Pss. 51.17–19; 141.2). **34:** *Captives,* Heb "'asirim," is another reference to the exiles (as in Pss. 79.11; 102.21; 107.10, 14). **35:** The focus on *all that moves in them* [the seas] is odd, and may recall the creation story or the myth that God subjugated the sea monsters (see 8.3 n.). **36:** The psalmist derives comfort and the strength to persist in his mourning from his firm belief that God will rebuild the Temple, Jerusalem, and the country of Judah, and will return the exiles to it. They will not only live in Judah, but will *inherit it,* possess ownership that can be bequeathed as an inheritance to their children. **37:** *Offspring of His servants* are the descendants of those the Bible calls God's servants. Psalms applies this designation to Abraham (Ps. 105.6, 42), Jacob (Ps. 136.22), Moses (Ps. 105.26), and David (Ps. 78.70). The psalmist is underlining the continuity between the returnees from exile who *cherish His name* and their ancient ancestors. Only at its conclusion does the psalm move from the individual, who represents the suffering community (see Lam. ch 3) to explicit mention of the broader community.

Ps. 70: This psalm expresses a great sense of urgency in calling on God to save the speaker from those who threaten his life. It contrasts the disgrace that will come to the psalmist's opponents ("those who seek my life") with the joy of those who trust in God ("all who seek You"). These two groups are characterized by the words they say (vv. 4–5). The psalm is framed by the idea of urgency—that God should hasten (v. 2) and that he should not delay (v. 6). The psalm repeats with minor variations Ps. 40.14–18; as in Pss. 14 || 53, these vv. were included in two different subcollections within the Psalter. "The Lord" in Ps. 40.14, 17 is here *God* (vv. 2, 5, 6), typical of the Elohist psalms, suggesting that this psalm copied a section of Ps. 40 or a similar composition. The translation inverts the order of the phrases in vv. 1–5. **1:** The unusual term *Lehazkir* in the superscription is found also in Ps. 38.1. **3–4:** The public shaming (shame is the opposite of honor) of the psalmist's opponents will prove God's power to protect His faithful ones. *Aha! Aha!* expresses derisive joy; cf. 35.21; 40.16. It is matched by the repetitive *be glad and rejoice* in the following v. **5:** *Those who are eager for,* lit. "those who love." **6:** *Poor and needy,* typical language for the

You are my help and my rescuer;
O LORD, do not delay.

71 I seek refuge in You, O LORD;
may I never be disappointed.
2 As You are beneficent, save me and rescue me;
incline Your ear to me and deliver me.
3 Be a sheltering rock for me to which I may always
repair;
decree my deliverance,
for You are my rock and my fortress.
4 My God, rescue me from the hand of the wicked,
from the grasp of the unjust and the lawless.
5 For You are my hope,
O Lord GOD,
my trust from my youth.
6 While yet unborn, I depended on You;
in the womb of my mother, You were my support;[a]
I sing Your praises always.
7 I have become an example for many,
since You are my mighty refuge.
8 My mouth is full of praise to You,
glorifying You all day long.
9 Do not cast me off in old age;
when my strength fails, do not forsake me!

10 For my enemies talk against me;
those who wait for me are of one mind,
11 saying, "God has forsaken him;
chase him and catch him,
for no one will save him!"
12 O God, be not far from me;
my God, hasten to my aid!
13 Let my accusers perish in frustration;
let those who seek my ruin be clothed in reproach
and disgrace!

14 As for me, I will hope always,
and add to the many praises of You.
15 My mouth tells of Your beneficence,
of Your deliverance all day long,
though I know not how to tell it.
16 I come with praise of Your mighty acts, O Lord GOD;
I celebrate Your beneficence, Yours alone.
17 You have let me experience it, God, from my youth;
until now I have proclaimed Your wondrous deeds,

a *Meaning of Heb. uncertain.*

psalmist and his community. The poor have no protector in society; the psalmist is figuratively poor in that he has no protector and calls on God to protect him.

Ps. 71: The psalmist presents himself as an individual, now aged and infirm (vv. 9, 18), who has been faithful to God all his life, even from the womb (v. 6), and now prays that God not forsake him as he reaches the end of his life. Central to this psalm, and to psalms in general, is the idea that the purpose of human life is to offer praise to God, and that if one dies, that praise will cease. If praise for God is to continue (that is, if God is to be known throughout the world), God must keep people alive and in good health. The psalm has a number of refrainlike repetitions (vv. 9, 18; vv. 8, 15, 24). The thematic similarity to Ps. 70 and the lack of superscription in Ps. 71 have led some to suggest that these two psalms were once one psalm. **1:** The psalm opens with the image of God as *refuge,* a central theme of the psalm. **3:** *Sheltering rock,* "tzur maʿon," perhaps suggests the Temple (see 76.3), where the psalmist may be praying for healing. *My rock and my fortress,* similarly 18.3. **5–9:** Divine care for the psalmist, from birth to old age (Ps. 22.10–11). The psalmist has always depended on God, even before he was born (v. 6), and has not yet been disappointed. **7:** *Example,* in a positive sense, that others see how God protects the psalmist. **9:** Perhaps implied is that the psalmist wishes not to be abandoned even when he no longer has the strength to serve God. **10–11:** When others see that God does not protect the psalmist, they take advantage of him. **10:** These vv. are quoting enemies, as in 41.6. **12:** See Ps. 22.2, 12, 20. **14–16:** The psalmist looks forward to praising God, most likely in the Temple. **15:** *Though I know not how to tell it:* Though I do not know their number, that is, praise to God is infinite.

18 and even in hoary old age do not forsake me, God,
until I proclaim Your strength to the next generation,
Your mighty acts, to all who are to come,
19 Your beneficence, high as the heavens, O God,
You who have done great things;
O God, who is Your peer!
20 You who have made me undergo many troubles and misfortunes
will revive me again,
and raise me up from the depths of the earth.
21 You will grant me much greatness,
You will turn and comfort me.
22 Then I will acclaim You to the music of the lyre
for Your faithfulness, O my God;
I will sing a hymn to You with a harp,
O Holy One of Israel.
23 My lips shall be jubilant, as I sing a hymn to You,
my whole being, which You have redeemed.
24 All day long my tongue shall recite Your beneficent acts,
how those who sought my ruin were frustrated and disgraced.

72

Of Solomon.

O God, endow the king with Your judgments,
the king's son with Your righteousness;
2 that he may judge Your people rightly,
Your lowly ones, justly.
3 Let the mountains produce well-being for the people,
the hills, the reward of justice.
4 Let him champion the lowly among the people,
deliver the needy folk,
and crush those who wrong them.
5 Let them fear You as long as the sun shines,
while the moon lasts, generations on end.
6 Let him be like rain that falls on a mown field,
like a downpour of rain on the ground,
7 that the righteous may flourish in his time,
and well-being abound, till the moon is no more.
8 Let him rule from sea to sea,
from the river to the ends of the earth.

18: The psalmist does not have many years of life left to praise God; he wants to perpetuate the praise of God beyond his own lifetime, passing it on to the next generation. **20:** *Depths of the earth,* Sheol, the abode of the dead, where there is no praising God (Ps. 6.6). The psalmist prays that God will *revive* him, keep him alive (cure his malady). This image contrasts with *high as the heavens* in the previous v. **22:** When his illness is cured, the psalmist will perform a thanksgiving ritual in the Temple (Pss. 50.14; 56.13–14). The *lyre* and *harp* are the typical instruments that accompanied hymns in Psalms (e.g., 33.2; 57.9). **24:** The psalm's conclusion returns to its introduction with the word "bosh," translated *frustrated* here, and *disappointed* in v. 1.

Ps. 72: A prayer for the success of the king, perhaps a coronation ode. The king's greatness will be known forever (as long as the sun and moon shine) and throughout the world. The psalm shows how close God-language and king-language are. Only Pss. 72 and 127 are headed by *Of Solomon.* Ps. 72 is probably ascribed to Solomon because it emphasizes qualities and events for which he was known: judicial wisdom (1 Kings 3.16–28), the great extent of the kingdom and the gifts and tribute he collected (1 Kings 5.1–3), including from Tarshish (cf. 1 Kings 10.22), and from Sheba (cf. 1 Kings 10.10); he is also the first king who may be called (v. 1) "the king's son." The psalm combines a wide variety of ideal royal attributes, especially justice (see also Isa. 11.3–5, of the future ideal Davidic king), wealth, and military power. **1–2:** The king's responsibility to uphold and administer justice (2 Sam. 8.15; Jer. 22.15–16), with divine assistance. *The king's son,* the dynastic successor, a reference to the Davidic covenant. Rashi attributes this psalm to David, who prayed it on behalf of his son Solomon when David foresaw that Solomon would ask God for wisdom. **3–4:** Moral order (justice for the poor and oppressed) in the world brings about cosmic order (fertility and bounty). **5:** Let the wrongdoers fear the king's punishment; or, let the people fear, that is, respect, the king. **6:** A good king ensures the prosperity of his people. **7:** The Heb for *the righteous* is singular, and not collective; a slight emendation yields "justice" (from "tzadik" to "tzedek"). **8:** The extent of the king's dominion *from sea to sea,* from the Mediterranean Sea to the Persian Gulf, and from *the river,* the Euphrates (1 Kings 5.4). This is hyperbolic court

9 Let desert-dwellers kneel before him,
and his enemies lick the dust.
10 Let kings of Tarshish and the islands pay tribute,
kings of Sheba and Seba offer gifts.
11 Let all kings bow to him,
and all nations serve him.

12 For he saves the needy who cry out,
the lowly who have no helper.
13 He cares about the poor and the needy;
He brings the needy deliverance.
14 He redeems them from fraud and lawlessness;
[a]the shedding of their blood weighs heavily upon him.[-a]

15 So let him live, and receive gold of Sheba;
let prayers for him be said always,
blessings on him invoked at all times.
16 [b]Let abundant grain be in the land, to the tops of the mountains;
let his crops thrive like the forest of Lebanon;
and let men sprout up in towns like country grass.
17 May his name be eternal;
while the sun lasts, may his name endure;[-b]
let men invoke his blessedness upon themselves;
let all nations count him happy.

18 Blessed is the LORD God, God of Israel,
who alone does wondrous things;
19 Blessed is His glorious name forever;
His glory fills the whole world.
Amen and Amen.

20 End of the prayers of David son of Jesse.

BOOK THREE

73 A psalm of Asaph.

God is truly good to Israel,
to those whose heart is pure.
2 As for me, my feet had almost strayed,
my steps were nearly led off course,
3 for I envied the wanton;
I saw the wicked at ease.

a-a Or "their life is precious in his sight."
b-b Meaning of some Heb. phrases in these verses uncertain.

style; or, alternatively, the language is mythic, signifying that the king reigns over the entire universe (cf. Ps. 89.26; Zech. 9.10). **10–11:** Homage to the Israelite monarch by distant kings (1 Kings 4.21); a reflection of the king's great power. *Tarshish,* the city of Tarsus on the southern coast of Turkey, or Tartessus in southern Spain; see 1 Kings 10.22. *The islands,* the islands of the eastern Aegean Sea. *Sheba,* in southwestern Arabia; cf. 1 Kings 10.1. *Seba,* probably also southwestern Arabia, or perhaps Ethiopia; cf. Isa. 43.3. **12–14:** This king is served not because of his military power, but because of his righteousness. **16:** Extremely difficult; it apparently deals with agricultural bounty in hyperbolic terms, as in v. 3. **17:** The king's *name* means both his fame (1 Kings 3.14) and his progeny. *All nations ... happy,* the promises to the ancestors (Gen. 12.3) fulfilled in the Davidic realm and dynasty. **18–19:** Not a part of the psalm, but the concluding doxology of Book II of the Psalter (see 41.14; 89.53; 106.48). **20:** Important evidence for the gradual editing of the Psalter; contrast the "Davidic" psalms found later, e.g., 86; 101; 103.

Ps. 73: The psalm invokes typical wisdom themes (as in Prov. and Eccl.) about God's justice in the world and His punishment of evil. The psalmist, seeing how wicked people prosper and how they have no fear of punishment, almost abandoned his belief that God rewards the good and punishes the evil. But a visit to the Temple (v. 17), with its aura of being in God's Presence, caused the psalmist to reconsider. His faith was strengthened and he renews his praise of God. Much of the psalm's language is very difficult. **1–3:** The psalmist affirms God's goodness to the upright, although he came close to rejecting this idea when he saw the good fortune of the wicked. **1:** This psalm begins a collection attributed to *Asaph* (Pss. 73–83), a Levite who established a guild of Temple singers (1 Chron. ch 25); see also Ps. 50 n. *Whose heart is pure,* see Ps. 24.4.

4 Death has no pangs for them;
their body is healthy.
5 They have no part in the travail of men;
they are not afflicted like the rest of mankind.
6 So pride adorns their necks,
lawlessness enwraps them as a mantle.
7 [a]Fat shuts out their eyes;
their fancies are extravagant.[a]
8 They scoff and plan evil;
from their eminence they plan wrongdoing.
9 They set their mouths against heaven,
and their tongues range over the earth.
10 [a]So they pound His people again and again,
until they are drained of their very last tear.[a]
11 Then they say, "How could God know?
Is there knowledge with the Most High?"
12 Such are the wicked;
ever tranquil, they amass wealth.

13 It was for nothing that I kept my heart pure
and washed my hands in innocence,
14 seeing that I have been constantly afflicted,
that each morning brings new punishments.
15 Had I decided to say these things,
I should have been false to the circle of Your disciples.
16 So I applied myself to understand this,
but it seemed a hopeless task
17 till I entered God's sanctuary
and reflected on their fate.

18 You surround them with flattery;
You make them fall through blandishments.
19 How suddenly are they ruined,
wholly swept away by terrors.
20 [a]When You are aroused You despise their image,
as one does a dream after waking, O Lord.[a]

21 My mind was stripped of its reason,
[b]my feelings were numbed.[b]
22 I was a dolt, without knowledge;
I was brutish toward You.

23 Yet I was always with You,
You held my right hand;

a-a Meaning of Heb. uncertain.
b-b Lit. "I was pierced through in my kidneys."

4–10: The prosperity and contentment of the wicked. The wicked are successful, arrogant, materialistic, and they doubt God's power—contrast e.g., Ps. 1. **4–5:** Illness and early death were thought to be punishments for sin, yet the wicked do not suffer these things nor do they worry about suffering them. They seem to have it easy in life, without the cares of ordinary people. **7:** Eyes and heart (here translated as *fancies)* are commonly paired and represent the external and the internal aspects of a person. Other parts of the body, "mouths" and "tongues," are mentioned in v. 9. **9:** The evildoers' activities span the entire world. **11:** See Pss. 10.11; 64.6; 94.7. There was no atheism in ancient times, only the notion that God, who once created the world, lacked knowledge and power. **13–15:** In contrast to the prosperous wicked, the psalmist found no material benefit in his righteousness. He hesitated to utter his doubts publicly, and sought to understand his observations. **16–17:** Reason alone could not solve the psalmist's dilemma or quiet his doubts. The Heb for hopeless task, "'amal," is a key word of the pessimistic book Eccl. It is not philosophical exploration, but a religious experience in *God's sanctuary* that provided our psalmist with an answer. *Sanctuary* is plural in Heb, perhaps referring to the Temple. **18–20:** The wicked may look successful but ruin will come upon them suddenly (cf. Ps. 37; Job 4.8–9). A *dream* is insubstantial, passing away quickly. **21–22:** The psalmist apologizes for his earlier doubts, characterizing himself as lacking understanding. **22:** *Brutish,* lit. like (an) animal(s). **23–24:** Yet despite his boorishness, God has helped the psalmist in the past, and he looks forward to similar help now.

24 You guided me by Your counsel
[a-]and led me toward honor.[-a]
25 Whom else have I in heaven?
And having You, I want no one on earth.
26 My body and mind fail;
but God is the stay[b] of my mind, my portion forever.
27 Those who keep far from You perish;
You annihilate all who are untrue to You.
28 As for me, nearness to God is good;
I have made the Lord GOD my refuge,
that I may recount all Your works.

74

A *maskil* of Asaph.

Why, O God, do You forever reject us,
do You fume in anger at the flock that You tend?
2 Remember the community You made Yours long ago,
Your very own tribe that You redeemed,
Mount Zion, where You dwell.
3 [c-]Bestir Yourself[-c] because of the [d-]perpetual tumult,[-d]
all the outrages of the enemy in the sanctuary.
4 Your foes roar inside Your meeting-place;
they take their signs for true signs.
5 [d-]It is like men wielding axes
against a gnarled tree;
6 with hatchet and pike
they hacked away at its carved work.[-d]
7 They made Your sanctuary go up in flames;
they brought low in dishonor the dwelling-place of
Your presence.
8 They resolved, "Let us destroy them altogether!"
They burned all God's tabernacles in the land.
9 No signs appear for us;
there is no longer any prophet;
no one among us knows for how long.

10 Till when, O God, will the foe blaspheme,
will the enemy forever revile Your name?
11 Why do You hold back Your hand, Your right hand?
[d-]Draw it out of Your bosom![-d]

12 O God, my King from of old,
who brings deliverance throughout the land;
13 it was You who drove back the sea with Your might,
who smashed the heads of the monsters in the waters;

a-a Meaning of Heb. uncertain; others "And afterward receive me with glory."
b Lit. "rock." *c-c Lit. "Lift up Your feet."* *d-d Meaning of Heb. uncertain.*

25: God is his only help, in heaven or on earth. Having God, he has no need of another source of help. **26:** *My portion,* see Ps. 16.5. **27:** *Untrue* in Heb is "zoneh," the same word for "to prostitute oneself"; prostitution or infidelity was the common term for idolatry (see e.g., Num. 15.39). **28:** The psalmist favors *nearness to God,* as opposed to *those who keep far from You* (v. 27).

Ps. 74: An exilic lament for the destruction of Jerusalem (see v. 7 and also Ps. 79). The psalmist calls upon God to end the exile. God, the Creator of the world and the vanquisher of the mythic forces of chaos, is called upon to vanquish the Babylonians, who are identified with the forces of chaos. Vv. 3–18 resemble Lam. in the way they make the destruction of Jerusalem vivid. The psalmist worries that God may have rejected Israel for eternity, or what seems like an eternity; the word "forever" (Heb "netzaḥ") is repeated four times (1, 3 [perpetual], 10, 19). It is a common trope in laments of destruction; see Ps. 79.5; Lam. 5.20. **1:** *Asaph,* see Ps. 73.1 n. **1–2:** Experiencing disaster and exile, the psalmist recalls the early history of the relationship between God and Israel. This special relationship, the fact that God chose Judah and dwelled on Zion, are the reasons that He should restore Judah and Zion (cf. also v. 20). *The flock that You tend,* in the exodus (Exod. 15.13, 16–17). The shepherd metaphor, a common way of portraying the relationship between Israel and God (cf. Ps. 79.13), emphasizes the deep care that Israel expects from God. *The community You made Yours,* through the covenant at Sinai. *Your very own tribe,* Judah, the tribe in which Jerusalem was located. **5:** For the Babylonians coming as woodcutters with *axes,* see Jer. 46.22–23. **7:** *Your presence,* better, "Your name," fitting the ideology of Deut. (e.g., 12.5). **9–10:** There is no reliable prophet to tell them how long the exile will last (see Amos 8.11). **11:** A plea to God to take action against the enemy. **12–17:** The classic example of God's power is the creation of the world, here retold in a mythological

14 it was You who crushed the heads of Leviathan,
who left him as food for [a]the denizens of the desert;[-a]
15 it was You who released springs and torrents,
who made mighty rivers run dry;
16 the day is Yours, the night also;
it was You who set in place the orb of the sun;
17 You fixed all the boundaries of the earth;
summer and winter—You made them.

18 Be mindful of how the enemy blasphemes the LORD,
how base people revile Your name.
19 Do not deliver Your dove to the wild beast;
do not ignore forever the band of Your lowly ones.
20 Look to the covenant!
For the dark places of the land are full of the haunts of lawlessness.
21 Let not the downtrodden turn away disappointed;
let the poor and needy praise Your name.
22 Rise, O God, champion Your cause;
be mindful that You are blasphemed by base men all day long.
23 Do not ignore the shouts of Your foes,
the din of Your adversaries that ascends all the time.

75
For the leader; *al tashḥeth.*
A psalm of Asaph, a song.

2 We praise You, O God;
we praise You;
Your presence is near;
men tell of Your wondrous deeds.

3 "At the time I choose,
I will give judgment equitably.
4 Earth and all its inhabitants dissolve;
it is I who keep its pillars firm. *Selah.*
5 To wanton men I say, 'Do not be wanton!'
to the wicked, 'Do not lift up your horns!' "

6 Do not lift your horns up high
[b]in vainglorious bluster.[-b]

a-a Or "seafaring men"; meaning of Heb. uncertain.
b-b Lit. "with arrogant neck you speak."

way (different from Gen. chs 1–3) so as to emphasize God's might over the forces of chaos. A God as powerful as this can certainly defeat the Babylonians. Cf. also Ps. 89.9–14. **14:** *Leviathan,* the forces of chaos represented as a sea monster (Job 3.8; 26.12–13; 41.1; Isa. 27.1), also mentioned in the myths from Ugarit. **16–17:** Just as God fixed the spatial boundaries of the world, confining the waters and making them flow where he wanted, so he fixed the temporal boundaries, creating day and night, and the seasons. **17:** See Deut. 32.8. **19:** *Your dove,* sacrificial animal of the poor (e.g., Lev. 5.7); here a metaphor for those slaughtered by Babylonia like sacrificed animals (Isa. 34.6–7). **20:** Despite the destruction and exile, God's covenant with Israel is still in force. For the author, the covenant must be eternal, and implies that God must protect Israel. *Look to the covenant,* rather than the more usual "remember the covenant." "Look" parallels "remember" in Lam. 5.1 and Isa. 64.8. **23:** Here the *foes* and *adversaries* are both the Babylonians and the forces of chaos (vv. 12–17). The Babylonians are made to look as dangerous as the forces of chaos; indeed, the destruction of the Temple represents a return to chaos, with the implication that God must once again destroy the forces of chaos so that the world will continue to exist as God created it.

Ps. 75: Praise for God, who renders justice. The wicked should not be arrogant because God will judge them as they deserve. V. 2, *wondrous deeds,* connects this psalm to the mention of creation in the preceding one. **1:** *Al tashḥeth,* perhaps "do not destroy"; see Ps. 57.1. *Asaph,* see Ps. 73.1 n. **2:** *Your presence,* Heb "Your name"; see 74.7 n. God is accessible. **3–5:** Heb has no quotation marks, but it is likely that the psalmist is quoting God in these vv. **3:** *At the time,* the time God sets for judging. Humans do not know when God will render judgment but they should rest assured that the time will come. God's justice is equitable, though not immediate. **4:** Just as the earth has "pillars" to keep it firm, so justice keeps society firm. *Pillars,* see 1 Sam. 2.8. *Selah,* see Ps. 3.3 n. If God's words continue in the next v., this does not seem to be the place for subdividing the psalm. Ibn Ezra suggests that v. 5 begins the words of the psalmist. **5:** *Lift up your horns,* an idiom meaning to be victorious. The

7 For what lifts a man comes not from the east
or the west or the wilderness;[a]
8 for God it is who gives judgment;
He brings down one man, He lifts up another.
9 There is a cup in the LORD's hand
with foaming wine fully mixed;
from this He pours;
all the wicked of the earth drink,
draining it to the very dregs.
10 As for me, I will declare forever,
I will sing a hymn to the God of Jacob.

11 "All the horns of the wicked I will cut;
but the horns of the righteous shall be lifted up."

76

For the leader; with instrumental music.
A psalm of Asaph, a song.

2 God has made Himself known in Judah,
His name is great in Israel;
3 Salem became His abode;
Zion, His den.
4 There He broke the fiery arrows of the bow,
the shield and the sword of war. *Selah.*

5 You were resplendent,
glorious, on the mountains of prey.
6 The stout-hearted were despoiled;
they were in a stupor;
the bravest of men could not lift a hand.
7 At Your blast, O God of Jacob,
horse and chariot lay stunned.

a Reading midbār *with many mss.*

wicked lift their horns in arrogance, as if they have won, but ultimately their horns will be cut (they will be deprived of power) and the horns of the righteous will be lifted up in victory over evil (v. 11 and cf. Ibn Ezra on v. 11). **7:** *Wilderness:* The v. is difficult. If the word "harim" is read, it may mean "mountains," signifying the north (the opposite of "wilderness," referring to the south), or it may be a verb, "to raise up." **8:** *He brings down one man, He lifts up another,* see similarly 1 Sam. 2.7. **9:** The *cup* (of the LORD's wrath in Isa. 51.17; Jer. 25.15) signifies punishment. **11:** The *horn* language continues from v. 6. Heb has no quotation marks; this translation assumes that God is again speaking (after the psalmist's speech in v. 10).

Ps. 76: A hymn praising God, the victorious warrior, who resides in Jerusalem. Attempts have been made to identify the specific battle that may have occasioned the psalm, but there is no consensus. An ancient tradition, reflected in the LXX, rabbinic midrashim, and Rashi, connects it with the defeat of Sennacherib (2 Kings 19.35). Others interpret the battle as eschatological. In either case, as elsewhere in the Bible, God is depicted as the divine warrior. The two aspects of God highlighted here are His strength as a warrior and as a judge; these are the attributes of successful kings and God is envisioned as the supreme King, known to Israel and Judah at the beginning of the psalm and acknowledged by all the kings of the earth at the end. The psalm's main theme is God's awe, expressed explicitly in vv. 8 and 13, and hinted at elsewhere through plays on the word "awesome" (Heb "nora'," e.g., v. 2, "noda'"; v. 5, "na'or"). The text is difficult at points. **1:** *Asaph,* see Ps. 73.1 n. **2:** *Judah ... Israel:* If *Israel* is the Northern Kingdom, this would date the psalm to the time of the divided monarchy. Alternatively, "Israel" may be a general designation that was used to parallel Judah after the fall of the Northern Kingdom in 722 BCE (see Ps. 114.2). **3:** *Salem,* variant name for Jerusalem (Gen. 14.18). *His abode ... His den:* Heb "sukkah" and "ma'on" have two sets of associations, God's protective pavilion (the Temple or the sky) and a lion's den. For "sukkah" as the Temple, cf. Pss. 27.5; 31.21; cf. Exod. 40.3; for a lion's den, Ps. 10.9. For "ma'on" as the Temple, cf. Ps. 26.8; for a den, Amos 3.4; Nah. 2.12; Song 4.8. "Ma'on" and "sukkah" are used in parallelism for a lion's den in Job 38.39–40. God as a lion is an image of fearsome strength. Jer. 25.30 also invokes this association: God roars from his holy "ma'on" (see also Amos 1.2). **4:** *There:* Some commentators see this as referring to David's conquest of Jerusalem. For the breaking of the (enemies') weapons, see Ps. 46.10. God is so powerful, he destroys both offensive and defensive weapons. *Selah* (also v. 10), see Ps. 3.3 n. **5:** *Mountains of prey,* a strange phrase, variously interpreted as "mountains of booty," "mountains rich with game," or, with an emendation, "everlasting mountains." If taken as *mountains of prey* it connects with the image of God as a lion (v. 3); for *prey* associated with a "ma'on" of a lion, cf. Amos 3.4; Nah. 2.13; Job 38.40. **7:** *At your blast,* better "roar", God's war-cry which is sufficiently terrifying to assure the enemies' defeats.

8 O You! You are awesome!
Who can withstand You
when You are enraged?
9 In heaven You pronounced sentence;
the earth was numbed with fright
10 as God rose to execute judgment,
to deliver all the lowly of the earth. *Selah.*

11 [a]-The fiercest of men shall acknowledge You,
when You gird on the last bit of fury.-[a]
12 Make vows and pay them to the LORD your God;
[a]-all who are around Him shall bring tribute to the
Awesome One.-[a]
13 He curbs the spirit of princes,
inspires awe in the kings of the earth.

77

For the leader; on *Jeduthun.* Of Asaph. A psalm.

2 I cry aloud to God;
I cry to God that He may give ear to me.
3 In my time of distress I turn to the Lord,
[a]-with my hand [uplifted];
[my eyes] flow all night without respite;-[a]
I will not be comforted.
4 I call God to mind, I moan,
I complain, my spirit fails. *Selah.*

5 You have held my eyelids open;
I am overwrought, I cannot speak.
6 My thoughts turn to days of old,
to years long past.
7 I recall at night their jibes at me;
I commune with myself;
my spirit inquires,
8 "Will the Lord reject forever
and never again show favor?
9 Has His faithfulness disappeared forever?
Will His promise be unfulfilled for all time?
10 Has God forgotten how to pity?
Has He in anger stifled His compassion?" *Selah.*

a-a *Meaning of Heb. uncertain.*

9–10: As in Ps. 75, God is a powerful judge. When God pronounces and executes his judgment, the world is terrified. **11:** Very difficult; *the fiercest of men* may be Israel's enemies. Some read "'edom" (Edom, a kingdom south of Judah) instead of "'adam," "men," and "ḥamat" (Hamath, a kingdom to the north) instead of *fury,* Heb "ḥemot," suggesting that nations both south and north of Israel fear God. **12:** Tribute is brought to God by the kings of the earth (Ps. 72.10–11), showing that God is recognized by all as the supreme king.

Ps. 77: An individual calls upon God in his time of trouble, connecting his personal plight to the nation's past, specifically to the exodus, the paradigm for the return from the exile; like Rashi, we may see this psalm as lamenting the exile and hoping for a new exodus. The God of the exodus is known for His faithfulness and mercy, yet now God seems to have lost these characteristics. "Has God changed?" wonders the psalmist. "How long will he ignore me?" The psalm climaxes in a paean of praise in which the exodus, specifically the splitting of the sea, is couched in terms of the victory over chaos at the time of the creation. The implication is that the return from exile will not only be a new exodus, but also a new creation. The psalm's theme is memory—the psalmist remembers God, and in so doing, asks God to remember and reenact his great acts in the past; the root "z-k-r," "to remember," appears four times in the psalm (vv. 4, 7, 12 [twice]). **1:** *Jeduthun,* see Ps. 39.1. *Asaph,* see Ps. 73.1 n. **2–4:** Initial appeal for divine help (Ps. 142.2–4). **2:** The repetition in the parallelism is unusual; the first three Heb words (lit. "My voice is to God") begin each part of the v. **3:** *Night* is the time when pain and trouble seem most unbearable; cf. Ps. 6.7; Lam. 1.2. Rashi equates *night* with the exile. **4:** *I call ... to mind ... moan ... complain:* These verbs connote uttering aloud. *Selah* (also vv. 10, 16), see Ps. 3.3 n. **5–7:** The speaker, who cannot sleep at night, ponders the past and his present situation. **5:** *Eyelids open,* watchful, as in night vigils (Rashi). **6:** *Days of old,* the time of the exodus, the paradigmatic act of divine liberation (vv. 20–21). **7:** *Recall ... commune:* These are the same verbs, "z-kr" and "s-yḥ," that occur in v. 4: *call ... to mind* and *complain.* **8–10:** God, who is known for His faithfulness, for keeping His promise, and for His mercy (cf. Exod. 34.6), is not manifesting these qualities. The psalmist is appealing to God's mercy, and wonders if God's nature has changed.

11 And I said, [a]"It is my fault
that the right hand of the Most High has changed."[-a]

12 I recall the deeds of the LORD;
yes, I recall Your wonders of old;
13 I recount all Your works;
I speak of Your acts.
14 O God, Your ways are holiness;
what god is as great as God?
15 You are the God who works wonders;
You have manifested Your strength among the peoples.
16 By Your arm You redeemed Your people,
the children of Jacob and Joseph. *Selah.*
17 The waters saw You, O God,
the waters saw You and were convulsed;
the very deep quaked as well.
18 Clouds streamed water;
the heavens rumbled;
Your arrows flew about;
19 Your thunder rumbled like wheels;
lightning lit up the world;
the earth quaked and trembled.
20 Your way was through the sea,
Your path, through the mighty waters;
Your tracks could not be seen.
21 You led Your people like a flock
in the care of Moses and Aaron.

78

A *maskil* of Asaph.

Give ear, my people, to my teaching,
turn your ear to what I say.

a-a Meaning of Heb. uncertain.

12–21: The psalmist recalls ("z-kr") the classic demonstration of God's power on behalf of Israel, the exodus and the splitting of the sea, which is likened to the mythical victory over the forces (waters) of chaos. **12:** Just as he voiced his complaint in vv. 4 and 7, the psalmist voices praise for God here. **14:** As in many biblical texts, the author is imaging the possibility of other deities, but highlighting God's incomparability (see e.g., Exod. 15.11). **16:** *Jacob and Joseph,* the ancestors immediately preceding the exodus who brought their families to Egypt and from whom Israel descended. **17–21:** The sea of the exodus is identified with the *waters* of chaos, defeated by God (Isa. 51.9–10; cf. Pss. 18.8–16; 114.3–6). **18–19:** Language of theophany; God appeared on Sinai amidst thunder and lightning. *Your arrows* are flashes of lightning and also the weapons God uses against the enemy, as in: "He let fly His shafts and scattered them; He discharged lightning and routed them" (Ps. 18.15). *Your thunder rumbled like wheels:* On the noise of chariot wheels, see Jer. 47.3; Ezek. 26.10. The mention of wheels may recall the chariots of the pursuing Egyptians (cf. Exod. 14.9, 23–25), the topic of this section. **21:** God as the shepherd of Israel is a common image (e.g., Pss. 74.1; 79.13). The mention of *Aaron* along with *Moses* is somewhat surprising, but see Ps. 105.26.

Ps. 78: This is the second-longest psalm, after Ps. 119. It retells Israel's past in a poetic precis, mainly the exodus and the wandering in the wilderness (as do Pss. 105 and 106; cf. also 136). It is didactic in that it uses a narrative about the past to teach about the present; and it is a psalm of praise in that the recitation of God's past acts on behalf of Israel constitute praise of God. The psalm is addressed to the public (v. 1, "Give ear, my people") rather than to God (several psalms are addressed to a human audience, e.g., 1, 49, 105). Its introduction suggests that its purpose is to encourage the listeners to be obedient, in contrast to previous generations, especially those of the exodus generation (vv. 6–7). The psalm concludes, however, with a justification for the destruction of the Northern Kingdom (722 BCE), and praise for Davidic kingship centered in the chosen city of Zion. Like many psalms, this one may have gone through a process of revision; in any case, it needs to be dated in its final form after the fall of the Northern Kingdom in 722, if not to exilic times (the return from exile is often viewed as a new exodus). The events as recounted in the psalm differ from their Torah version (e.g., the wilderness wandering precedes the plagues and the exodus, and the order and number of the plagues is different). This is in part because of the specific focus of the psalm and also its need for poetic terseness, and also because it seems to contain later interpretations or reinterpretations of the earlier biblical traditions. It is based on non-Priestly narrative traditions (esp. the sources J and D). Traditional Jewish interpretation, which assumes that this psalm follows the authoritative Torah, expends much effort in reconciling these texts. **1–2:** These vv. show affinities to the

2 I will expound a theme,
hold forth on the lessons of the past,
3 things we have heard and known,
that our fathers have told us.
4 We will not withhold them from their
children,
telling the coming generation
the praises of the LORD and His might,
and the wonders He performed.
5 He established a decree in Jacob,
ordained a teaching in Israel,
charging our fathers
to make them known to their children,
6 that a future generation might know
—children yet to be born—
and in turn tell their children
7 that they might put their confidence in God,
and not forget God's great deeds,
but observe His commandments,
8 and not be like their fathers,
a wayward and defiant generation,
a generation whose heart was inconstant,
whose spirit was not true to God.

9 Like the Ephraimite bowmen
who played false in the day of battle,
10 they did not keep God's covenant,
they refused to follow His instruction;
11 they forgot His deeds
and the wonders that He showed them.
12 He performed marvels in the sight of their
fathers,
in the land of Egypt, the plain of Zoan.
13 He split the sea and took them through it;
He made the waters stand like a wall.
14 He led them with a cloud by day,
and throughout the night by the light of fire.
15 He split rocks in the wilderness
and gave them drink as if from the great deep.
16 He brought forth streams from a rock
and made them flow down like a river.

17 But they went on sinning against Him,
defying the Most High in the parched land.
18 To test God was in their mind
when they demanded food for themselves.
19 They spoke against God, saying,
"Can God spread a feast in the wilderness?

didactic aspect of wisdom literature, and to Deut., which itself is influenced by wisdom traditions. **4–7:** The concern is that future generations will know the Torah traditions, the *decree* and *teaching,* and hence obey God's commandments (see Deut. 4.9; 6.1–2, 7, 20–25). **4:** *Might, and the wonders* are emphasized since the psalmist wants God to repeat them. **5:** *Teaching:* Heb "torah," which eventually came to mean the Torah or Pentateuch. **7–8:** These vv. emphasize that knowing these traditions of the past is important because they foster obedience to God's *commandments.* The psalmist does not want present or future generations to repeat the mistakes of their ancestors. **9:** The reference is obscure; much traditional Jewish interpretation (so, e.g., Rashi, Radak) connects it to an (otherwise unknown) abortive first exodus organized by the Ephraimites. Or perhaps the psalmist, or a later reviser who inserted this v. here, is criticizing Ephraim in anticipation of the rejection of the Northern Kingdom (see v. 67). **11:** In contrast to *wonders, deeds* is not an important term of the exodus tradition. **12:** *Zoan,* also in v. 43, is in the Nile Delta, and is not mentioned in association with the exodus tradition in the Torah. **13:** *Like a wall* quotes Exod. 15.8, suggesting that the Song of the Sea was among this psalmist's sources. **14:** See Exod. 13.21 (J). **15–31:** These traditions are similar to Exod. chs 17 (water from the rock) and 16 (manna and birds; see also Num. ch 11), but their order is reversed. **17:** Similar notices (e.g., vv. 21, 32) create a type of refrain, emphasizing the main point: Israel's past sinfulness despite God's beneficence. **19–20:** Comparable sentiments are attributed to Moses in Num. 11.21–22.

20 True, He struck the rock and waters flowed,
streams gushed forth;
but can He provide bread?
Can He supply His people with meat?"
21 The LORD heard and He raged;
fire broke out against Jacob,
anger flared up at Israel,
22 because they did not put their trust in God,
did not rely on His deliverance.
23 So He commanded the skies above,
He opened the doors of heaven
24 and rained manna upon them for food,
giving them heavenly grain.
25 Each man ate a hero's meal;
He sent them provision in plenty.
26 He set the east wind moving in heaven,
and drove the south wind by His might.
27 He rained meat on them like dust,
winged birds like the sands of the sea,
28 making them come down inside His camp,
around His dwelling-place.
29 They ate till they were sated;
He gave them what they craved.
30 They had not yet wearied of what they craved,
the food was still in their mouths
31 when God's anger flared up at them.
He slew their sturdiest,
struck down the youth of Israel.
32 Nonetheless, they went on sinning
and had no faith in His wonders.
33 He made their days end in futility,
their years in sudden death.
34 When He struck[a] them, they turned to Him
and sought God once again.
35 They remembered that God was their rock,
God Most High, their Redeemer.
36 Yet they deceived Him with their speech,
lied to Him with their words;
37 their hearts were inconstant toward Him;
they were untrue to His covenant.
38 But He, being merciful, forgave iniquity
and would not destroy;
He restrained His wrath time and again
and did not give full vent to His fury;
39 for He remembered that they were but flesh,
a passing breath that does not return.

22: The psalm's main theme: the importance of obedience, and the implications of disobedience. **25:** Exod. 16.17–18, in contrast, emphasizes the moderate, though sufficient quantity of manna. Many scholars understand *hero's meal* as food of the angels, and so does ancient interpretation. **27–31:** See Num. ch 11 (J), though the psalmist nowhere calls the meat specifically quail. **35:** *Rock* implies strength and reliability. **38:** This v., an important theological exposition of divine mercy, is reused in several later Jewish penitential contexts. **39:** Clearly this author, as is typical of the biblical period, does not believe in resurrection.

a *Lit. "killed."*

40 How often did they defy Him in the wilderness,
did they grieve Him in the wasteland!
41 Again and again they tested God,
vexed[a] the Holy One of Israel.
42 They did not remember His strength,
or the day He redeemed them from the foe;
43 how He displayed His signs in Egypt,
His wonders in the plain of Zoan.
44 He turned their rivers into blood;
He made their waters undrinkable.
45 He inflicted upon them swarms of insects to devour them,
frogs to destroy them.
46 He gave their crops over to grubs,
their produce to locusts.
47 He killed their vines with hail,
their sycamores [b-]with frost.[-b]
48 He gave their beasts over to hail,
their cattle to lightning bolts.
49 He inflicted His burning anger upon them,
wrath, indignation, trouble,
a band of deadly messengers.
50 He cleared a path for His anger;
He did not stop short of slaying them,
but gave them over to pestilence.
51 He struck every first-born in Egypt,
the first fruits of their vigor in the tents of Ham.
52 He set His people moving like sheep,
drove them like a flock in the wilderness.
53 He led them in safety; they were unafraid;
as for their enemies, the sea covered them.
54 He brought them to His holy realm,[c]
the mountain His right hand had acquired.
55 He expelled nations before them,
[d-]settled the tribes of Israel in their tents,
allotting them their portion by the line.[-d]

56 Yet they defiantly tested God Most High,
and did not observe His decrees.
57 They fell away, disloyal like their fathers;
they played false like a treacherous bow.
58 They vexed Him with their high places;
they incensed Him with their idols.
59 God heard it and was enraged;
He utterly rejected Israel.

a *Or "set a limit to."* *b-b* *Meaning of Heb. uncertain.*
c *Or "hill" with Septuagint and Saadia.* *d-d* *Inverted for clarity.*

41: Num. 14.22, which states that the people "have tried Me these many times and have disobeyed Me," has a similar understanding of the wilderness period. **42–43:** The terms *redeemed* from Egypt and *signs* and *wonders* are characteristic of Deut. (e.g., 7.8, 19). **44–51:** Rather than ten plagues, as in Exod., seven plagues are described: blood (44), swarms of frogs (45), locusts (46), hail affecting agriculture (47), hail affecting livestock (48), pestilence (50), and death of the first-born (51). The missing plagues from the perspective of the Torah include darkness (contrast Ps. 105.28, where it is the first plague), and lice, which is only mentioned in the Priestly source. **44:** As in Exod. ch 7, *blood* is the first plague. **45:** The Heb is simply *swarms* ("'arov"), and here refers to *swarms* of frogs. In Exod. 9.16–28, "'arov" is a free-standing plague of either swarms of insects or animals. **48:** *Lightening bolts,* Heb "reshaphim," is also the name of a Canaanite deity. **49:** This v. is an interlude, describing no plague in particular; it plays a major role in a midrash quoted in the Passover Haggadah, where it serves to multiply the number of plagues. For Radak, it alludes to the plagues mentioned in Exod. but not explicit in this psalm, so that Psalms may be reconciled with Exod. *Messengers* (angels, minor deities) do not play a significant role in the plague narrative in Exod. **50:** The expression *gave them over to pestilence* may suggest the pestilence was viewed as a minor deity (see also "a band of deadly messengers" in the previous v.). **51:** In all the plague traditions the death of the *first-born* is the final, climactic plague. **52–53:** The wanderings in the desert, alluded to earlier in the psalm, are summarized briefly here. **54:** Another echo of the Song of the Sea (Exod. 15.17); one of the few explicit references to the land of Israel as holy. **55:** A remarkably concise summary of Josh., suggesting that the nations of Canaan were *expelled* rather than exterminated. **56–64:** The destruction of Shiloh because of the idolatry of the Northern tribes. **58:** This v. is suffused with the terminology of Deut.

60 He forsook the tabernacle of Shiloh,
the tent He had set among men.
61 He let His might[a] go into captivity,
His glory into the hands of the foe.
62 He gave His people over to the sword;
He was enraged at His very own.
63 Fire consumed their young men,
and their maidens [b]remained unwed.[-b]
64 Their priests fell by the sword,
and their widows could not weep.

65 The Lord awoke as from sleep,
like a warrior [c]shaking off[c] wine.
66 He beat back His foes,
dealing them lasting disgrace.
67 He rejected the clan of Joseph;
He did not choose the tribe of Ephraim.
68 He did choose the tribe of Judah,
Mount Zion, which He loved.
69 He built His Sanctuary like the heavens,
like the earth that He established forever.
70 He chose David, His servant,
and took him from the sheepfolds.
71 He brought him from minding the nursing ewes
to tend His people Jacob, Israel, His very own.
72 He tended them with blameless heart;
with skillful hands he led them.

79

A psalm of Asaph.

O God, heathens have entered Your domain,
defiled Your holy temple,
and turned Jerusalem into ruins.
2 They have left Your servants' corpses
as food for the fowl of heaven,
and the flesh of Your faithful for the wild beasts.

a I.e., the Ark; cf. Ps. 132.8. *b-b Lit. "had no nuptial song."*
c-c Meaning of Heb. uncertain.

(see esp. Deut. 32.16, 21) and related books. **60:** The destruction of *Shiloh,* the central site in the period of Samuel, is never narrated in Samuel, and is assumed to have been accomplished by the Philistines. **61:** The Ark was captured by the Philistines (1 Sam. ch 4.). **64:** They did *not weep* due to the huge magnitude of the catastrophe. **65:** On God awaking, see 7.7 n. **67:** *The clan of Joseph* and *the tribe of Ephraim* were the dominant groups in the Northern Kingdom and stand for the Northern Kingdom as a whole. **68–72:** The choosing of Jerusalem as a royal city and of David as the first king are here tightly linked in what modern scholars call "the Royal Zion theology"(see also Ps. 132); the order of these events here is the reverse of the Samuel version, where first David, and then Jerusalem, was chosen. Although if read in context, these vv. also suggest that Judah was only chosen after the rejection of the Northern Kingdom; the following vv. suggest otherwise. Indeed, much of this psalm is not in chronological order, as is the case in other biblical poetic retellings of past events. **70–72:** The image of the king as the shepherd of his people is a common ancient Near Eastern topos; here it also echoes David's biography as rendered in 1 Sam. **72:** The depiction of David is highly idealized, more like Chronicles than Samuel. In fact the phrase *led them,* used of David here, was earlier used of God (vv. 14, 53), suggesting that David served as God's representative.

Ps. 79: A powerfully accusatory exilic lament for the destruction of Jerusalem and the Temple, like Ps. 74 and Lam. The psalm sees the destruction as an affront to God rather than to the people of Judah, and calls upon God to redress the heinous act for the sake of His name (v. 9). The psalm draws on a common stock of phrases and motifs of lament. This psalm is recited at the Western Wall on Friday evenings and on the Ninth of Av. **1:** *Asaph,* see Ps. 73.1 n. *Heathens,* Heb "goyim," is used in a neutral sense of other nations; here it refers to Babylonia and its allies (Ps. 137.7–8). *Your domain,* God's "naḥalah," the land of Israel, or in this case, Judah. The parallel terms, *Your holy Temple* and *Jerusalem* narrow and intensify the focus. *Ruins* ("ʿiyim") is a rare word, possibly alluding to the well-known prophecy of Mic. 3.12 (see Jer. 26.18), "Jerusalem shall become heaps of ruins ("ʿiyim")." **2–3:** *Heaven, wild beasts* (lit. beasts of the land), and *water* reflects the ancient idea of the tripartite cosmos—heaven, earth, water—and is another way of saying that the defilement of the Temple is a defilement of the universe. To be left unburied and exposed to scavengers is in the ancient Near East a terrible disgrace (Josh. 10.27; 2 Kings 9.25–26). For

3 Their blood was shed like water around Jerusalem,
with none to bury them.
4 We have become the butt of our neighbors,
the scorn and derision of those around us.

5 How long, O LORD, will You be angry forever,
will Your indignation blaze like fire?
6 Pour out Your fury on the nations that do not know
You,
upon the kingdoms that do not invoke Your name,
7 for they have devoured Jacob
and desolated his home.
8 Do not hold our former iniquities against us;
let Your compassion come swiftly toward us,
for we have sunk very low.
9 Help us, O God, our deliverer,
for the sake of the glory of Your name.
Save us and forgive our sin,
for the sake of Your name.
10 Let the nations not say, "Where is their God?"
Before our eyes let it be known among the nations
that You avenge the spilled blood of Your servants.
11 Let the groans of the prisoners reach You;
reprieve those condemned to death,
as befits Your great strength.
12 Pay back our neighbors sevenfold
for the abuse they have flung at You, O Lord.
13 Then we, Your people,
the flock You shepherd,
shall glorify You forever;
for all time we shall tell Your praises.

variations on this image, see Ezek. 32.4–6; Zeph. 1.17. When sacrifices of meat were offered in the Temple, the blood was to be poured out like water (Deut. 12.24, 27), so there is an ironic element here, in that Judah was a sacrifice whose blood was poured out. In addition, blood defiles, as does a corpse. So the heathens have defiled Jerusalem not only by entering God's holy precinct (which according to some views was off-limits to them; see Lam. 1.10), but further by contaminating it with corpses, which create the most serious ritual impurity. Concerning *Your faithful,* see Ps. 4.4 n. **4:** Ps. 44.14. The scorn heaped upon the defeated Judah is a conventional motif. **5:** Cf. Ps. 89.47. The question about the duration of divine wrath, which seems endless, is typical of laments (Ps. 74.9–10). *Indignation,* Heb "kin'ah," is a strong term, often expressing uncontrollable wrath. **6–7:** Jer. 25.10. These vv. were added to the end of the Passover Haggadah during the Middle Ages, reacting to Jewish persecution; they are part of the hope for the redemption of Israel. **8–9:** One of the few communal laments that contains an admission of Israel's sins. *Former iniquities* may mean the earlier (preexilic) iniquities of the speakers that, according to the Deuteronomic idea assumed here, led to the destruction. Another interpretation is "iniquities of former generations," which would refer to the idea of intergenerational punishment (see Exod. 34.7, but contrast Ezek. ch 18). The emphasis, however, is not on Israel's guilt, but on God's future actions. Various prophetic texts ask for communal forgiveness *for the sake of ... Your name,* in other words for God's reputation (see e.g., Isa. 48.9; Jer. 14.7; Ezek. 20.9). **10:** Incremental movement from the admission of sins and the hope that they will not be held against the community (v. 8), to a plea that God forgive the sins (v. 9), to the idea that God avenge *the spilled blood of Your servants,* that is, punish the enemy for the destruction, which is an affront to God (also v. 12). This v. is a generalization of Exod. 21.12. **11:** *Prisoners,* exiles. *Those condemned to death:* Being denied access to the Temple is like death, for one cannot praise God (cf. Ps. 137.4). When the restoration has taken place, the people will be able to praise God (v. 13). Cf. Ps. 142.8. **12:** The psalmist appeals for *sevenfold* retribution on Babylonia's allies. Many laments end with a plea for retribution against the enemy; this is not to be taken as simple revenge, but as a way of expressing the hope for the return of the right world order, where evil has no place and all acknowledge God. *Pay back ... sevenfold,* a stereotypical number that may evoke the vengeance of Cain (Gen. 4.15). Like Cain, Israel was banished from its land/soil and from God's Presence. *For the abuse they have flung at You:* An attack on God's Temple and His people is an affront to God since it may imply God's powerlessness. **13:** Like Pss. 77 and 78, Ps. 79 ends with the image of the divine shepherd; Ps. 80 begins with the same image, thereby joining together this cluster of Asaphite psalms. The psalm concludes with a promise to tell God's *praises,* the focus of the previous psalm (see esp. v. 4).

80

For the leader; on *shoshannim, eduth.*
Of Asaph. A psalm.

2 Give ear, O shepherd of Israel
who leads Joseph like a flock!
Appear, You who are enthroned on the cherubim,
3 at the head of Ephraim, Benjamin, and Manasseh!
Rouse Your might and come to our help!
4 Restore us, O God;
show Your favor that we may be delivered.

5 O LORD, God of hosts,
how long will You be wrathful
toward the prayers of Your people?
6 You have fed them tears as their daily bread,
made them drink great measures of tears.
7 You set us at strife with our neighbors;
our enemies mock us at will.
8 O God of hosts, restore us;
show Your favor that we may be delivered.

9 You plucked up a vine from Egypt;
You expelled nations and planted it.
10 You cleared a place for it;
it took deep root and filled the land.
11 The mountains were covered by its shade,
mighty cedars by its boughs.
12 Its branches reached the sea,
its shoots, the river.
13 Why did You breach its wall
so that every passerby plucks its fruit,
14 wild boars gnaw at it,
and creatures of the field feed on it?

15 O God of hosts, turn again,
look down from heaven and see;
take note of that vine,
16 the stock planted by Your right hand,
the stem[a] you have taken as Your own.
17 For it is burned by fire and cut down,
perishing before Your angry blast.
18 Grant Your help[b] to the man at Your right hand,
the one You have taken as Your own.

a *Lit. "son."* *b* *Lit. "hand."*

Ps. 80: Its references to the Northern Kingdom suggest that this may originally have been a lament for the fall of the Northern Kingdom (722 BCE), but its placement after Ps. 79, with which it shares phraseology, indicates that the psalm was reworked and in its present form serves as a lament for the destruction of Judah. In addition to the mention of the northern tribes (Joseph, Ephraim, Benjamin, Manasseh), there are echoes of the time before the reign of Saul (cf. v. 5). A refrain of sorts occurs in vv. 4, 8, 20; in each case it is expanded slightly from the previous use. **1:** *Shoshannim* ("lilies"), see Ps. 45.1.; cf. Ps. 60.1. *Asaph,* see Ps. 73.1 n. **2:** *Shepherd of Israel:* Pastoral imagery is found in other Asaph psalms (74.1; 78.52; 79.13). Cf. Gen. 48.14–15; 49.24. *Appear* (lit. "shine"), theophany (divine manifestation) language (Pss. 50.2; 94.1). **2–3:** *Israel … Joseph … Ephraim, Benjamin, and Manasseh,* the Northern Kingdom. More specifically, the sons of Rachel (Joseph and Benjamin), and grandsons (Joseph's sons: Ephraim and Manasseh). The tribes of Ephraim, Manasseh, and Benjamin were encamped under one banner according to the list in Num. 2.18–24. Benjamin's tribal territory lay just south of Ephraim. **4:** *Show Your favor* (Heb "light up your face"), expressing God's benevolence; see Num. 6.24–26; Pss. 4.7; 67.2. **5:** These epithets of God along with *enthroned on the cherubim* (v. 2) suggest God's Presence in the Ark that went out to battle (1 Sam. 4.4; 2 Sam. 6.2). *Be wrathful toward the prayers:* Reject the prayers, prevent them from reaching you. Cf. Lam. 3.44. **6:** See Pss. 42.4; 102.10. **9–17:** The pastoral imagery of Israel as God's sheep (v. 2) shifts to an agricultural metaphor of Israel as a *vine* (cf. Isa. 5.1–7; Jer. 2.21; Ezek. 17.1–10), plucked from Egypt and planted in the Promised Land where it took root and flourished. But then God in His anger allowed its protecting wall to be breached, and the vine was destroyed by human and animal forces. **12:** *The river,* the Euphrates. **17:** See Ps. 74.5–7. According to Ezek. ch 15, grape vines were especially combustible. **18:** *The man at Your right hand,* a reference to the king (Ps. 110.1). *The one You have taken as Your own,* a reference to the Davidic dynasty. In its present version, the psalmist's main concern is not the north but Judah, threatened with

19 We will not turn away from You;
preserve our life that we may invoke Your name.
20 O LORD, God of hosts, restore us;
show Your favor that we may be delivered.

81

For the leader; on the *gittith.* Of Asaph.
2 Sing joyously to God, our strength;
raise a shout for the God of Jacob.
3 Take up the song,
sound the timbrel,
the melodious lyre and harp.
4 Blow the horn on the new moon,
on the full moon for our feast day.
5 For it is a law for Israel,
a ruling of the God of Jacob;
6 He imposed it as a decree upon Joseph
when [a]he went forth from[a] the land of Egypt;
I heard a language that I knew not.

7 I relieved his shoulder of the burden,
his hands were freed from the basket.
8 In distress you called and I rescued you;
I answered you from the [b]secret place of thunder[b]
I tested you at the waters of Meribah. *Selah.*
9 Hear, My people, and I will admonish you;
Israel, if you would but listen to Me!
10 You shall have no foreign god,
you shall not bow to an alien god.
11 I the LORD am your God
who brought you out of the land of Egypt;
open your mouth wide and I will fill it.

12 But My people would not listen to Me,
Israel would not obey Me.

a-a Or "He went forth against." *b-b Meaning of Heb. uncertain.*

defeat in the 8th c. by the Assyrians and subsequently conquered by the Babylonians in 586 BCE. **19:** *Preserve our life,* or revive us, the same image as Ezek. 37.1–14, concerning the dry bones. The reference is to national, not personal resurrection.

Ps. 81: A call to praise God with music; perhaps a hymn for the festivals (v. 4). God speaks in the first person in vv. 7–16, 17b, reviewing the exodus and wandering, with emphasis on Israel's disobedience. If Israel is obedient, God will subdue its enemies and grant agricultural abundance. This psalm shares themes with Ps. 95 but reflects a strong interest in the Northern Kingdom, as do Pss. 78 and 80. This psalm is recited in the morning service on Thursdays. **1:** *The gittith,* see Ps. 8.1. *Asaph,* see Ps. 73.1 n. **2:** *The God of Jacob,* repeated in v. 5 is not necessarily a sign of northern origin (see Pss. 84.9; 94.7; 114.7; 146.5); but "Israel" (vv. 5, 9, 12, 14) and "Joseph" (v. 6; a term for the Northern Kingdom) indicate northern provenance. **4:** *New moon,* observed as a holiday in ancient Israel; here it likely refers to the New Year, announced with loud blasts (Lev. 23.23–25; Num. 29.1). *Full moon,* when Passover and Sukkot begin. *Our feast day,* likely the festival of Sukkot (Lev. 23.33–34), also called "the feast," "he-ḥag" (1 Kings 8.2; Neh. 8.14; and in rabbinic literature). Rabbinic interpretation understands "keseh" as "new moon," (instead of *full moon*), and takes the entire v. as referring to Rosh Ha-Shanah, the New Year. The practice of reciting this v. to introduce the daytime kiddush (blessing over wine) on Rosh Ha-Shanah derives from this rabbinic interpretation. **5:** Praising God with song and music is connected with the exodus and the giving of the Torah. **6:** *A language that I knew not,* the language of Egypt; cf. Ps. 114.1. **7:** Deliverance from slavery and oppression in Egypt (Exod. 6.6–7). The *basket* is the workbasket that symbolizes subjugated people (often captives of war). **8:** *Meribah,* the place where Israel tested God (Exod. 17.7; Num. 20.13; Ps. 95.8–9), but here seen as a test of Israel (as in Deut. 33.8, where God tested the Levites); it epitomizes Israel's rebellion. *Selah,* see Ps. 3.3 n. **9:** It is uncertain who is speaking here, or if an old oracle is quoted. **10–11:** An allusion to the beginning of the Decalogue (Exod. 20.1–2; Deut. 5.6). It is cited in reverse order *(You shall have no foreign god ... I the LORD am your God).* Instead of "other gods" as in the commandment, the psalm has "foreign ... alien gods." *Foreign god,* see Deut. 32.12, where the reference is presumably to Egyptian gods. Cf. Ps. 44.21 where Babylonian gods are meant. The reference here is to Canaanite gods. **11:** God fills the mouths of the obedient people with food (v. 17); strikingly, no reward for obedience is offered at the beginning of the Decalogue. **12–13:** The infidelity of the wilderness generation

13 So I let them go after their willful heart
that they might follow their own devices.
14 If only My people would listen to Me,
if Israel would follow My paths,
15 then would I subdue their enemies at once,
strike their foes again and again.
16 Those who hate the LORD shall cower before Him;
their doom shall be eternal.
17 He fed them[a] the finest wheat;
I sated you with honey from the rock.

82

A psalm of Asaph.

God stands in the divine assembly;
among the divine beings He pronounces judgment.
2 How long will you judge perversely,
showing favor to the wicked? *Selah.*
3 Judge the wretched and the orphan,
vindicate the lowly and the poor,
4 rescue the wretched and the needy;
save them from the hand of the wicked.

5 They neither know nor understand,
they go about in darkness;
all the foundations of the earth totter.
6 I had taken you for divine beings,
sons of the Most High, all of you;
7 but you shall die as men do,
fall like any prince.

8 Arise, O God, judge the earth,
for all the nations are Your possession.

a Lit. "him," i.e., Israel.

(Ps. 78.17, 40), a warning to the psalmist's contemporaries. **13:** God does not compel obedience (see Deut. 30.19). **14–17:** Israel's obedience would mean victory over foes and agricultural bounty. **17:** The v. switches abruptly from third person to first person. *Finest wheat,* see Deut. 32.14; Ps. 147.14. *Honey from the rock,* see Deut. 32.13.

Ps. 82: A vision of a heavenly court scene where God condemns those who judge unfairly. The psalm plays on the word "'elohim," which means "God" as well as "gods" or "divine beings." The notion that other divine beings exist is found elsewhere in the Bible, although they are never equal to God. (see v. 1 n.). In later biblical thought these beings serve as God's ministering angels (cf. Ps. 89.5–8). An earlier view is reflected, and then rejected, in this psalm, according to which the divine beings each represent one nation, serving as that nation's protector, a remnant of the idea that the world was populated by many gods, each assigned to a different nation (cf. Deut. 4.19 and 32.8, according to LXX and the Dead Sea Scrolls). This psalm forcefully rejects the idea of other gods; God deprives them of their divinity and He alone has dominion over all nations. In content and language, the psalm resembles prophetic criticisms of the oppression of the poor, including the denial of access to the judicial system and the disadvantages faced by the poor in obtaining just verdicts. Through the scenario of the heavenly tribunal, the psalm speaks to the issue of a just society, without which the world cannot exist. It also speaks to the universality of God, the supreme judge over all nations. **1:** *Asaph,* see Ps. 73.1 n. *God,* "'elohim," as is the preference in Pss. 42–83, rather than the Tetragrammaton (YHVH); this substitution creates some confusion in the Heb. *Stands,* rises to render a verdict. Cf. Isa. 3.13–14. *Divine assembly,* Heb could also be rendered "the assembly of El," referring to the head of the Ugaritic pantheon. Perhaps originally a separate deity in early Israelite religion, the name "El" became synonymous with YHVH. *Divine beings,* the celestial council. Cf. Isa. ch 6; 1 Kings ch 22; Job 1.6. Some commentators prefer to interpret this use of "'elohim" as human judges, but this is less likely. **2:** *Selah,* see Ps. 3.3 n. **3–4:** Let the cases of the poor be heard and, when they bring a case against the rich, make it possible for them to win it if they are in the right. Cf. Isa. 1.23. **5:** Without justice the world is in danger of collapse (Jer. 4.23–26). Justice is a cornerstone of the cosmos. **6:** *Sons of the Most High,* members of God's heavenly court. "Elyon" is an ancient Canaanite epithet for Baal, here applied to God (7.18 n.). **7:** Divine beings are immortal but humans are subject to death. Unjust divine beings are unmasked as not being divine. The gods of the other nations are not real gods. **8:** God alone is the true judge; He does not pervert justice. Cf. Isa. 3.13–14; Ps. 76.9. He is therefore called upon to judge the world, including the nations thought to belong to other gods or divine beings, which here are shown to be God's possessions. God's justice is universal. *Arise* returns to the psalm's opening, where "God stands."

83

A song, a psalm of Asaph.

2 O God, do not be silent;
do not hold aloof;
do not be quiet, O God!
3 For Your enemies rage,
Your foes [a]assert themselves.[a]
4 They plot craftily against Your people,
take counsel against Your treasured ones.
5 They say, "Let us wipe them out as a nation;
Israel's name will be mentioned no more."
6 Unanimous in their counsel
they have made an alliance against You—
7 the clans of Edom and the Ishmaelites,
Moab and the Hagrites,
8 Gebal, Ammon, and Amalek,
Philistia with the inhabitants of Tyre;
9 Assyria too joins forces with them;
they give support to the sons of Lot. *Selah.*

10 Deal with them as You did with Midian,
with Sisera, with Jabin,
at the brook Kishon—
11 who were destroyed at En-dor,
who became dung for the field.
12 Treat their great men like Oreb and Zeeb,
all their princes like Zebah and Zalmunna,
13 who said, "Let us take the meadows of God as our
possession."
14 O my God, make them like thistledown,
like stubble driven by the wind.
15 As a fire burns a forest,
as flames scorch the hills,
16 pursue them with Your tempest,
terrify them with Your storm.
17 Cover[b] their faces with shame
so that they seek Your name, O LORD.
18 May they be frustrated and terrified,
disgraced and doomed forever.

a-a Lit. "lift up the head." *b Lit. "Fill."*

Ps. 83: A plea to be saved from all the enemies surrounding Israel. Psalms rarely refer overtly to specific historical events, and in any case it is doubtful that an actual military campaign provoked this psalm; the list of hostile nations is better understood as a composite of the traditional enemies encircling Israel. The list begins with countries to the east and south of Israel, and moves to the west and north, returning in v. 9 to the sons of Lot, Moab and Edom (previously mentioned in v. 7). Assyria is the largest nation, and comprised an empire that conquered the northern kingdom of Israel. Babylonia and Egypt are not mentioned, leading some scholars to date the original form of this psalm to the preexilic period, perhaps originating in the north. Alternatively, Assyria stands for any great world power, whichever country it was at the time. Vv. 10–13 allude to the defeat of enemies in the book of Judg., viewed as an idealized period of divine intervention, hoping that the current enemies will suffer the same fate. The psalm presents all these nations not as Israel's enemies, but as God's, provoking Him to act since He has been directly assaulted. See also Ps. 79. **1:** *Asaph,* see Ps. 73.1 n. **2–5:** The silence of God is contrasted with the *rage* and speech of the enemies against Israel and its God. **3:** Israel's enemies are, according to this psalmist, by definition *Your* (God's) *enemies.* Cf. vv. 5–6. **5–6:** The threat against Israel is a threat against God. If Israel's name is no longer mentioned, God's name will be forgotten. Cf. v. 19. **7–9:** Enemies of Israel. *Hagrites,* descendants of Hagar; a tribe of pastoralists in northern Transjordan (1 Chron. 5.10, 18–22). *Gebal,* later Byblos, north of Beirut on the coast of Lebanon. Alternatively, a place near Edom. *The sons of Lot,* Moab and Edom (Gen. 19.36–38). *Selah,* see Ps. 3.3 n. **10–13:** See Judg. chs 4–8. **11:** *En-dor* is not mentioned in Judges, which locates these events at En- (the spring of) harod (Judg. 7.1); *dor* and "harod" share several letters. **14–16:** See Isa. 17.13–14. *Thistledown* and *stubble* are easily burnt up. Here the psalm shifts from the analogy of past human events to metaphors from the world of nature. **15–16:** Combining fire imagery and tempest imagery, the picture that emerges is of enemies being burnt up as if in a forest fire by God's powerful windstorm that will fan the flames into a huge conflagration. **17–19:** The confounding of the enemies' plans, and by implication the power of their own gods, will cause them to recognize God's name and His supremacy over the earth. As in Ps. 82, the theme of Ps. 83 is God's supremacy over all nations. Cf. Pss. 47.2; 97.9. It is odd that this v.,

19 May they know
that Your name, Yours alone, is the LORD,
supreme over all the earth.

84 For the leader; on the *gittith.* Of the Korahites.
A psalm.

2 How lovely is Your dwelling-place,
O LORD of hosts.
3 I long, I yearn for the courts of the LORD;
my body and soul shout for joy to the living God.
4 Even the sparrow has found a home,
and the swallow a nest for herself
in which to set her young,
near Your altar, O LORD of hosts,
my king and my God.
5 Happy are those who dwell in Your house;
they forever praise You. *Selah.*

6 Happy is the man who finds refuge in You,
whose mind is on the [pilgrim] highways.
7 They pass through the Valley of Baca,
[a]regarding it as a place of springs,
as if the early rain had covered it with blessing.[-a]
8 They go from [b]rampart to rampart,[-b]
appearing before God in Zion.
9 O LORD, God of hosts,
hear my prayer;
give ear, O God of Jacob. *Selah.*
10 O God, behold our shield,
look upon the face of Your anointed.

11 Better one day in Your courts than a thousand
[anywhere else];
I would rather stand at the threshold of God's house
than dwell in the tents of the wicked.
12 For the LORD God is sun[c] and shield;
the LORD bestows grace and glory;
He does not withhold His bounty from those who
live without blame.
13 O LORD of hosts,
happy is the man who trusts in You.

a-a *Meaning of Heb. uncertain.* b-b *Others "strength to strength."*
c *Or "bulwark," with Targum; cf. Isa. 54.12.*

concluding the Elohistic Psalter (see Ps. 42 n.), emphasizes the importance of the name *the LORD.*

Ps. 84: A celebration of the pilgrimage to the Temple. The psalmist yearns to be in God's Presence and rehearses every step of the way to Jerusalem. It is one of the psalms that glorifies Zion (see also Pss. 46; 48; 76; 87; 122), and mentions the Davidic king, enthroned there (v. 10). It is slightly disjointed and diffuse, and may have developed over time. **1:** *Gittith,* see Ps. 8.1. *Korahites,* see Ps. 42.1. **2:** *Lovely,* Heb "yedidot," is not just "beautiful" but "beloved." There is almost a mystical quality in the intensity of the psalmist's desire (with his entire being, v. 3) to be in God's Presence (see similarly Ps. 42). **3:** *The courts,* the outer parts of the Temple complex. *My body and soul:* lit. "my heart and flesh," my physical and mental being, or my insides and outside. The later theological distinction between body and soul is not implied here. Cf. 147.3: "He heals their broken hearts, / and binds up their wounds." **4:** The movement progresses from the courts to the *altar,* near which birds find a home, much as the psalmist wishes to find a home near God. The image implies naturalness—it is just as natural for a person to be in the Temple as it is for a bird to be in its nest. **5:** *Selah* (also v. 9), see Ps. 3.3 n. **6:** *Happy,* in a fortunate state; cf. vv. 6, 13. It is doubtful if anyone actually *dwell*ed (v. 5) in the Temple, though Ps. 23.6 is similar. **7:** *Valley of Baca* is an unknown place on the way to the Temple. Some interpret this as the valley of Rephaim, where the baca trees grow (2 Sam. 5.22–24). The *early rain* falls in the land of Israel in mid-fall. This reference suggests that the pilgrimage is for the festival of Sukkot, just before the start of the rainy season, when prayers for rain are offered. **9:** *God of hosts* is a substitute for "LORD of hosts" (cf. v. 4). **10:** *Shield* and *anointed* refer to the king, whom God is asked to look upon with favor. **11:** The psalmist prefers to stand at God's threshold, merely setting his foot at the entrance and not fully entering the Temple, rather than to dwell, to reside fully, in the tents of the wicked (Heb "tents of wickedness"). **12:** *Shield,* the same word used of the Davidic king in v. 10. *His bounty,* rain; cf. v. 7.

Ps. 85: An exilic or postexilic psalm, praying for the restoration of Israel to its land. The land is mentioned in vv. 2, 10, 13. Depending on how the tense of the verbs in vv. 1–4 is interpreted, the Jews have already returned, or the return is in the future. If the former, the plea is for an additional favor of restoration, perhaps because of the problems encountered by the returnees. (See also Ps. 126.) The hope is for a moral and prosperous society. **1:** *Korahites,* see Ps. 42 n. **2:** *Restore Jacob's fortune,* a common phrase for the return from exile (Jer. 30.3, 18; Amos 9.14). **3–7:** Forgiveness of Israel's sin is necessary for the restoration. **3:** For the images behind *forgive* and *pardon,* see 32.1. *Selah,* see Ps. 3.3 n. **7:** *Revive,* see 80.19. If the nation returns and the Temple is rebuilt, the people may *rejoice in* God, that is, be in His presence and in His favor. **8:** God's *faithfulness* ("ḥesed," see Ps. 5.8 n.) to His covenant with Israel remains constant despite the exile, and is invoked here. **9:** Introducing an oracle from a temple prophet. **11–14:** A personification of the divine attributes of *faithfulness, truth,* and *justice* (see 89.15 n.). **13:** *Bounty* (lit. "the good"), rain (Lev. 26.1–6; Deut. 28.12; Ps. 67.6).

Ps. 86: An individual calls on God's help. The "I" and "You" of the psalm is strongly felt. The psalm is anthological, reusing language and motifs occurring elsewhere in the Bible. The psalmist feels that God is absent (v. 16) or not hearing (vv. 1, 6, 7), and, by means of the psalm, tries to convince God to be present, to hear, and to help. He *calls to* God *all day long* (v. 3) in an attempt to get God's attention, and hopes that God will give him a *sign* (v. 17) that he has been heard. **1:** *A prayer,* cf. Pss. 90; 102. *Poor and needy* are common terms for the psalmist and his community. While these terms may refer to a low socioeconomic status, it is just as likely that they function as literary tropes to signify the absence of protection that the psalmist feels. **4:** *Servant,* another term related to v. 1, *poor and needy,*

85

For the leader. Of the Korahites. A psalm.

2 O LORD, You [a]will favor[a] Your land,
restore[b] Jacob's fortune;
3 You [c]will forgive[c] Your people's iniquity,
pardon[d] all their sins; *selah*
4 You [e]will withdraw[e] all Your anger,
turn[f] away from Your rage.
5 Turn again, O God, our helper,
revoke Your displeasure with us.
6 Will You be angry with us forever,
prolong Your wrath for all generations?
7 Surely You will revive us again,
so that Your people may rejoice in You.
8 Show us, O LORD, Your faithfulness;
grant us Your deliverance.

9 Let me hear what God, the LORD, will speak;
He will promise well-being to His people,
His faithful ones;
may they not turn to folly.
10 His help is very near those who fear Him,
to make His glory dwell in our land.
11 Faithfulness and truth meet;
justice and well-being kiss.
12 Truth springs up from the earth;
justice looks down from heaven.
13 The LORD also bestows His bounty;
our land yields its produce.
14 Justice goes before Him
as He sets out on His way.

86

A prayer of David.

Incline Your ear, O LORD,
answer me,
for I am poor and needy.
2 Preserve my life, for I am steadfast;
O You, my God,
deliver Your servant who trusts in You.
3 Have mercy on me, O Lord,
for I call to You all day long;
4 bring joy to Your servant's life,
for on You, Lord, I set my hope.

a-a *Or "have favored."* *b* *Or "have restored."*
c-c *Or "have forgiven."* *d* *Or "have pardoned."*
e-e *Or "have withdrawn."* *f* *Or "have turned."*

5 For You, Lord, are good and forgiving,
abounding in steadfast love to all who call on You.
6 Give ear, O LORD, to my prayer;
heed my plea for mercy.
7 In my time of trouble I call You,
for You will answer me.

8 There is none like You among the gods, O Lord,
and there are no deeds like Yours.
9 All the nations You have made
will come to bow down before You, O Lord,
and they will pay honor to Your name.
10 For You are great and perform wonders;
You alone are God.
11 Teach me Your way, O LORD;
I will walk in Your truth;
let my heart be undivided in reverence for Your
name.
12 I will praise You, O Lord, my God, with all my heart
and pay honor to Your name forever.
13 For Your steadfast love toward me is great;
You have saved me from the depths of Sheol.

14 O God, arrogant men have risen against me;
a band of ruthless men seek my life;
they are not mindful of You.
15 But You, O Lord, are a God
compassionate and merciful,
slow to anger, abounding in steadfast love and
faithfulness.
16 Turn to me and have mercy on me;
grant Your strength to Your servant
and deliver the son of Your maidservant.
17 Show me a sign of Your favor,
that my enemies may see and be frustrated
because You, O LORD, have given me aid and
comfort.

87

[a]1-2 Of the Korahites. A psalm. A song.

[b-]The LORD loves the gates of Zion,
His foundation on the holy mountains,[-b]
more than all the dwellings of Jacob.
3 Glorious things are spoken of you,
O city of God. *Selah.*

a The meaning of many passages in this psalm is uncertain.
b-b Order of lines inverted for clarity.

though adding the dimension of subservience to God. **5:** The first of two references (also v. 15) to Exod. 34.6–7. This v. is part of the High Holy Day liturgy. As in Jonah 4.2, only the "forgiveness" aspects of the divine attributes are cited in this psalm. **8:** Divine incomparability is here an expression of Israel's monotheism (Pss. 40.6 [see note *a-a*]; 71.19; cf. Exod. 15.11)—see the end of v. 10, *You alone are God.* **9:** God created all the nations although they do not yet recognize that; but soon they will. See Ps. 22.28. **11:** See Ps. 27.11, a similar request for divine help. **13:** *Sheol,* the abode of the dead. **14:** See Ps. 54.5. **15:** An exact quotation of Exod. 34.6. **16:** *Turn to me and have mercy on me,* a paraphrase of the middle of the priestly blessing (Num. 6.25). *Son of Your maidservant,* parallel to *Your servant* (see v. 2), but expressing even more humility. **17:** *Show me a sign:* Give me an indication that You will help me; or, when You help me, that will be a sign to my enemies of Your power.

Ps. 87: A textually difficult hymn celebrating Zion as God's specially chosen city, the center of the world, to which all nations will come (cf. Isa. 2.2–4). The psalm is structured around "(in) you/her" ("bakh, bah") = Zion and "there" ("sham") = the other nations. The nations are thereby contrasted with Zion and at the same time drawn into her orbit. **1–2:** *Korahites,* see Ps. 42 n. *All the dwellings of Jacob,* the places in Israel that were considered holy sites before the Temple, like Shiloh. Another interpretation: the northern temples (Bethel, Dan) that God rejected in favor of Zion (Ps. 78.67–69). **3:** *City of God* in direct address is unique to this context, but see city of the LORD (e.g., Ps. 48.9)—both idioms express the idea that God physically resided in the Temple in Jerusalem. *Selah* (also v. 6), see Ps. 3.3 n.

4 I mention Rahab[a] and Babylon among those who
acknowledge Me;
Philistia, and Tyre, and Cush—each was born there.
5 Indeed, it shall be said of Zion,
"Every man was born there."
[b-]He, the Most High, will preserve it.[-b]
6 The LORD will inscribe in the register of peoples
that each was born there. *Selah.*
7 Singers and dancers alike [will say]:
"All my roots[c] are in You."

88 A song. A psalm of the Korahites. For the leader; [d-]on *maḥalath leannoth.*[-d] A *maskil* of Heman the Ezrahite.

2 O LORD, God of my deliverance,
[e-]when I cry out in the night[-e] before You,
3 let my prayer reach You;
incline Your ear to my cry.
4 For I am sated with misfortune;
I am at the brink of Sheol.
5 I am numbered with those who go down to the
Pit;
I am a helpless man
6 abandoned[f] among the dead,
like bodies lying in the grave
of whom You are mindful no more,
and who are cut off from Your care.
7 You have put me at the bottom of the Pit,
in the darkest places, in the depths.
8 Your fury lies heavy upon me;
You afflict me with all Your breakers. *Selah.*
9 You make my companions shun me;
You make me abhorrent to them;
I am shut in and do not go out.
10 My eyes pine away from affliction;
I call to You, O LORD, each day;
I stretch out my hands to You.

a A primeval monster; here, a poetic term for Egypt; cf. Isa. 30.7.
b-b Or "He will preserve it supreme." *c Lit. "sources."*
d-d Meaning of Heb. uncertain. *e-e Or "by day I cry out [and] by night."*
f Lit. "released."

4–6: The LORD records the names of those from the Gentiles who have adopted Judaism; they are now part of God's people (Isa. 44.5). **4:** *Rahab,* a mythical monster, here designates Egypt; see Isa. 30.7. Egypt and Babylonia were the great world powers after the fall of Assyria in 612 BCE. *Philistia ... Tyre ... Cush,* smaller countries to the west, north, and south of Judah. Cush is Ethiopia or Nubia. **5–7:** Everyone will recognize Zion as the primary place in the world, the source of all nations; all peoples will think of themselves as citizens of Zion. **7:** *Roots* (Heb "sources"; see translators' note *c)* perhaps springs of water, the source of life. See Ezek. 47.1–12; Pss. 36.8; 46.4.

Ps. 88: A desperate complaint by a person mortally ill; perhaps to be interpreted as symbolizing the national catastrophe, the destruction and exile (Sheol may represent the exile), which could potentially sever the connection between Israel and God. Prolonged thoughts of death dominate, with many synonyms for the place of the dead: *Sheol, Pit, grave, depths, place of perdition,* darkness (the *netherworld), land of oblivion.* In the realm of the dead, humankind is cut off from God and completely forgotten; the sense of isolation and finality is overwhelming. The psalm ends without hope or resolution; unlike most such complaints in Psalms, there is no expectation that God will cure the psalmist and no promise to praise God upon recovery. **1:** *Korahites,* see Ps. 42 n. *Maḥalath leannoth,* probably a melody. The term "maḥalath" may be related to the word "maḥalah," "illness," making this a sad melody or a melody for the sick (cf. Ps. 53.1). Alternatively, it may derive from "ḥalil," "flute." *Heman,* a famous Temple musician (1 Chron. 25.5–6), mentioned only here in the Psalter. **3:** Connecting this psalm to the previous one. **4–6:** The psalmist is near death, on the *brink of Sheol,* the abode of the dead, separated from and forgotten by God. **5:** *Helpless man,* a man lacking the vigor to live. **6:** *Abandoned,* or "released, freed." Cf. Job 3.19. The dead are released from the socioeconomic hierarchy of the living. According to traditional Jewish interpretation, the dead are free of their obligation to God. **7–8:** The psalmist's troubles come from God, suggesting that God can remedy them as well. **8:** *Breakers,* death (2 Sam. 22.5; Pss. 42.8; 69.2–3). *Selah* (also v. 11), see Ps. 3.3 n. **9:** His illness made him a recluse, abandoned by friends. See v. 19; 31.12–14; Job 19.13; 30.10.

11 Do You work wonders for the dead?
Do the shades rise to praise You? *Selah.*
12 Is Your faithful care recounted in the grave,
Your constancy in the place of perdition?
13 Are Your wonders made known in the netherworld,[a]
Your beneficent deeds in the land of oblivion?

14 As for me, I cry out to You, O LORD;
each morning my prayer greets You.
15 Why, O LORD, do You reject me,
do You hide Your face from me?
16 From my youth I have been afflicted
and near death;
I suffer Your terrors [b-]wherever I turn.[-b]
17 Your fury overwhelms me;
Your terrors destroy me.
18 They swirl about me like water all day long;
they encircle me on every side.
19 You have put friend and neighbor far from me
and my companions out of my sight.[c]

89 A *maskil* of Ethan the Ezrahite.

2 I will sing of the LORD's steadfast love forever;
to all generations I will proclaim Your faithfulness
with my mouth.
3 I declare, "Your steadfast love is confirmed forever;
there in the heavens You establish Your faithfulness."

4 "I have made a covenant with My chosen one;
I have sworn to My servant David:
5 I will establish your offspring forever,
I will confirm your throne for all generations."
Selah.

a Lit. "darkness." *b-b Following Saadia; meaning of Heb. uncertain.*
c Lit. "into darkness."

11–13: The psalmist tries to convince God to save him from death by reminding God that once dead, he will remain dead, and then cannot praise God (see e.g., 6.6). **12:** *Place of perdition,* Heb "'abadon," "destruction, loss," another name for the abode of the dead. **14–19:** A replay of previous thoughts at a higher pitch. **14:** *As for me:* In contrast to the dead, the psalmist still can and does call out to God. *Morning* is the time God is expected to answer prayers (cf. Ps. 90.14). **16–17:** His troubles are not recent; his entire life has been one of misery, a victim of God's *fury* (cf. v. 8); there is no admission that his own sin caused this punishment. **18:** *Like water,* cf. *breakers,* v. 8. **19:** The psalmist is shunned by his community (v. 9). Another interpretation of *my companions out of my sight* is "my companions are (those of) darkness," i.e., the other residents of Sheol.

Ps. 89: An exilic or postexilic psalm praying for the restoration of the Davidic dynasty, that is, for the end of the exile and the restoration of the Jews to their land as an independent people, as they were before the exile. After a brief introduction (vv. 2–5), God is proclaimed king (vv. 6–19); He then proclaims David and his dynasty king (vv. 20–38); the psalm ends with a lament for the loss of the Davidic dynasty and the hope for its return (vv. 39–52). The psalm consists largely of a poetic reinterpretation of the promise to David in 2 Sam. 7.11–17. But whereas 2 Sam. ch 7 is concerned with the building of the Temple and the establishment of the dynastic succession, Ps. 89 omits references to the Temple and focuses on the permanence of Davidic kingship; it reflects royal rather than priestly interests. This is a striking departure from most exilic psalms, which are more concerned with the Temple than with the dynasty. Keywords connecting these chs include *steadfast love, forever, faithfulness, covenant, throne.* Of these, the most important is *steadfast love,* Heb "ḥesed," which opens the psalm in Heb, and refers to both God's general beneficence, as well as His covenant with David, which is a reflection of that beneficence (vv. 2, 3, 15, 25, 34, 50). **1:** *Ethan,* a Temple musician (1 Chron. 15.17, 19), mentioned only here in Psalms. The third book of the Psalter ends with two psalms attributed to figures mentioned only once, forming a type of miscellany after the longer Korah collection. **2–5:** The psalmist's praise of God's *steadfast love* and *faithfulness,* his choice of *David* and his establishment of the Davidic dynasty, which is eternal (the word *forever* appears seven times in the psalm, in vv. 2, 3, 5, 30, 37, 38, 53) and unconditional (cf. 2 Sam. 7.15–16; contrast Ps. 132.12). The faithfulness with which the dynastic promise was made is the main theme of the psalm. At the end (v. 50), the psalmist will remind God of it. **4:** Cf. Ps. 132.11–12. **5:** The wording of the covenant. *Selah* (also vv. 38, 46, 49), see Ps. 3.3 n.

6 Your wonders, O LORD, are praised by the heavens,
Your faithfulness, too, in the assembly of holy beings.
7 For who in the skies can equal the LORD,
can compare with the LORD among the divine beings,
8 a God greatly dreaded in the council of holy beings,
held in awe by all around Him?
9 O LORD, God of hosts,
who is mighty like You, O LORD?
Your faithfulness surrounds You;
10 You rule the swelling of the sea;
when its waves surge, You still them.
11 You crushed Rahab; he was like a corpse;
with Your powerful arm You scattered Your enemies.
12 The heaven is Yours,
the earth too;
the world and all it holds—
You established them.
13 North and south—
You created them;
Tabor and Hermon sing forth Your name.
14 Yours is an arm endowed with might;
Your hand is strong;
Your right hand, exalted.
15 Righteousness and justice are the base of Your throne;
steadfast love and faithfulness stand before You.

16 Happy is the people who know the joyful shout;
O LORD, they walk in the light of Your presence.
17 They rejoice in Your name all day long;
they are exalted through Your righteousness.
18 For You are their strength in which they glory;
our horn is exalted through Your favor.
19 Truly our shield is of the LORD,
our king, of the Holy One of Israel.

20 Then[a] You spoke to Your faithful ones in a vision
and said, "I have conferred power upon a warrior;
I have exalted one chosen out of the people.

a *Referring to vv. 4–5; cf. 2 Sam. 7.1–17.*

6–9: The heavenly council, in whose presence God announces his decree, praises the incomparable and awesome God; cf. Pss. 29.1; 82.1; Exod. 15.11; Jer. 23.18, 21–22. **8:** *Holy beings,* cf. Job 5.1. **10–14:** God's power as reflected in creation; having defeated the mythical chaotic waters, God is the victorious Creator of the universe, over which He has dominion (see Ps. 74.12–17). **11:** *Rahab,* a name for the primeval chaos monster; Isa. 51.9; Job 26.12. **13:** *Tabor and Hermon,* two prominent mountains; Tabor is south of the Sea of Galilee (Ps. 68; Hos. 5.1) and Hermon is to the north, in Syria (Pss. 42.6; 133.3). The mountains, like the heavenly court, sing praise to God. **15:** God's reign is founded upon the principles of *righteousness* and *justice;* He is heralded by *steadfast love* and *faithfulness.* These abstract principles are personified as parts of God's heavenly installation and His servants (see 85.11). Mesopotamian tradition also associates justice and righteousness ("kittu" and "mesharu") as attributes and as metaphorical guardians of gods and kings. The emphasis on the moral attributes of God's rule stresses that God does not break His promise; cf. vv. 34–35. **16–19:** Like the cosmos, the people will also proclaim loudly that God is king. The psalm here moves from the cosmic to the national. **16:** *Joyful shout,* Heb "teruʿah" is also a blast of the ram's horn, proclaiming God king. Vv. 16–18 are part of the Rosh Ha-Shanah liturgy, before the blowing of the shofar. **18–19:** *Horn* (also v. 25), a metaphor for *strength. Horn* and *shield:* the king protects his people and leads them to victory. Depending on the interpretation, v. 19 is the climax of the expression of the kingship of God, or it is a transition to the idea of David as king. The first interpretation takes the Heb letter "lamed"—rendered as *of* in *of the* LORD and *of the Holy One*—to be an emphatic particle: "our shield is indeed the LORD ... our king is indeed the Holy One." The second interpretation yields "our shield belongs to the LORD, our king to the Holy One" (so NRSV). **20–38:** The covenant with David and his descendants ("David" represents the Davidic dynasty), which will be eternal (vv. 29–30, 36–38) even in the face of human sin (vv. 31–35). This is a poetic reformulation and expansion of 2 Sam. 7.11–17, which like that text assumes an eternal, unbreakable Davidic covenant; contrast Ps. 132.11–12; 1 Kings 9.4–9. **20:** *In a vision,* through a prophet, Nathan (see 2 Sam. 7.17).

21 I have found David, My servant;
anointed him with My sacred oil.
22 My hand shall be constantly with him,
and My arm shall strengthen him.
23 No enemy shall [a]oppress him,[a]
no vile man afflict him.
24 I will crush his adversaries before him;
I will strike down those who hate him.
25 My faithfulness and steadfast love shall be with him;
his horn shall be exalted through My name.
26 I will set his hand upon the sea,
his right hand upon the rivers.
27 He shall say to Me,
'You are my father, my God, the rock of my
deliverance.'
28 I will appoint him first-born,
highest of the kings of the earth.
29 I will maintain My steadfast love for him always;
My covenant with him shall endure.
30 I will establish his line forever,
his throne, as long as the heavens last.
31 If his sons forsake My Teaching
and do not live by My rules;
32 if they violate My laws,
and do not observe My commands,
33 I will punish their transgression with the rod,
their iniquity with plagues.
34 But I will not take away My steadfast love from him;
I will not betray My faithfulness.
35 I will not violate My covenant,
or change what I have uttered.
36 I have sworn by My holiness, once and for all;
I will not be false to David.
37 His line shall continue forever,
his throne, as the sun before Me,
38 as the moon, established forever,
an enduring witness in the sky." *Selah.*

39 Yet You have rejected, spurned,
and become enraged at Your anointed.
40 You have repudiated the covenant with Your servant;
You have dragged his dignity in the dust.
41 You have breached all his defenses,
shattered his strongholds.
42 All who pass by plunder him;
he has become the butt of his neighbors.

a-a Meaning of Heb. uncertain.

25–26: *His horn shall be exalted through My name,* creating a parallel to v. 18, of God, *our horn is exalted through Your favor,* another indication that the Davidic king is viewed as God's ideal representative on earth. Thus, in v. 26, the powers associated with God in vv. 10–11 are bestowed upon David. **27–28:** A widespread ancient Near Eastern tradition sees the king as the adopted son of a god who ordained that he should rule (2 Sam. 7.14; Ps. 2.7). This king, however, is also the *first-born,* specially privileged. **28–30:** The promise of an eternal dynasty. **31–38:** If the Davidic kings sin, they will be punished, but the dynasty will never come to an end. It will endure as long as the *sun* and the *moon* endure. This idea is emphasized through the extensive repetition in these vv. These celestial bodies are *an enduring witness* testifying to God's promise. **31:** Depending on the date of this ch, *My Teaching,* "torati," might mean My Torah, which, as the continuation of this v. and the next notes, is comprised of *rules, laws,* and *commands* (see Neh. 1.7), though the referent may also be the book of Deut., which is closely associated to Samuel and the promise to David (see Deut. 26.16–17). **39–52:** The destruction of Jerusalem and the end of the Davidic dynasty is seen as a betrayal of God's promise, a repudiation of His covenant. These vv. echo many terms in vv. 2–38; at the same time, they share thoughts and language with Lam. **39:** *Anointed,* the Davidic king (v. 21). The king symbolizes the kingship or the people in the following vv. **40:** *Dragged his dignity in the dust,* lit. "desecrated his crown [by making it fall] to the ground," signifying the besmirching of the kingship.

43 You have exalted the right hand of his adversaries,
and made all his enemies rejoice.
44 You have turned back the blade of his sword,
and have not sustained him in battle.
45 You have brought [a]his splendor[a] to an end
and have hurled his throne to the ground.
46 You have cut short the days of his youth;
You have covered him with shame. *Selah.*
47 How long, O LORD; will You forever hide Your face,
will Your fury blaze like fire?
48 O remember [a]how short my life is;[a]
why should You have created every man in vain?
49 What man can live and not see death,
can save himself from the clutches of Sheol?
Selah.

50 O Lord, where is Your steadfast love of old
which You swore to David in Your faithfulness?
51 Remember, O Lord, the abuse flung at Your servants
[a]that I have borne in my bosom [from] many peoples,[a]
52 how Your enemies, O LORD, have flung abuse,
abuse at Your anointed at every step.

53 Blessed is the LORD forever;
Amen and Amen.

BOOK FOUR

90

A prayer of Moses, the man of God.

O Lord, You have been our refuge in every generation.
2 Before the mountains came into being,
before You brought forth the earth and the world,
from eternity to eternity You are God.

3 You return man to dust;[b]
You decreed, "Return you mortals!"
4 [a]For in Your sight a thousand years
are like yesterday that has passed,
like a watch of the night.
5 You engulf men in sleep;[a]
at daybreak they are like grass that renews itself;
6 at daybreak it flourishes anew;
by dusk it withers and dries up.
7 So we are consumed by Your anger,
terror-struck by Your fury.

46: The kingship or nation has been cut off in its prime. This is not necessarily a reference to the age of a particular king. As is often the case, *Selah* ends a subunit; at this point the psalm moves from a description to an accusation. **49:** *Sheol,* the abode of the dead and a metaphor for the exile. **51–52:** *Abuse* is repeated three times, highlighting the dimensions of the God-wrought catastrophe. **53:** A doxology closing Book III of the Psalter (cf. Pss. 41.14; 72.18–19; 106.48).

Ps. 90: Human mortality and God's eternity. Words for time figure prominently: *years, watch of the night, daybreak, days, span of our life.* They are used to contrast God's eternity and human beings' transience and fragility. Human life is perceived as, by its nature, difficult and sorrowful. The psalmist asks for divine compassion to make human life satisfying and joyful. This psalm and Ps. 91 are recited in the introductory prayers of the morning service on Shabbat and festivals. **1–2:** God is eternal; He was a *refuge* even before there was a physical habitat. The language of birth, rather than the language of creating, is used of the world; quite exceptionally, God gave birth to the world. **1:** This psalm alone is associated with *Moses,* perhaps because, on one hand, he died prematurely, before entering the land, and on the other hand, he lived until 120, the ideal life span, with eyes undimmed and vigor unabated (Deut. 34.7). *The man of God,* the prophet. **3:** *To dust,* see Gen. 2.7; 3.19. **4:** An observation that human time is in a different scale from divine time. *A watch of the night,* less than one day. The night was divided into three or four watches of three to four hours each, depending on the time of year. **5:** *Grass* grows and withers quickly (Isa. 40.6–8; Ps. 102.25–28).

a-a Meaning of Heb. uncertain. *b Or "contrition."*

8 You have set our iniquities before You,
our hidden sins in the light of Your face.
9 All our days pass away in Your wrath;
we spend our years like a sigh.
10 The span of our life is seventy years,
or, given the strength, eighty years;
but the [a-]best of them[-a] are trouble and sorrow.
They pass by speedily, and we [b-]are in darkness.[-b]
11 Who can know Your furious anger?
Your wrath matches the fear of You.
12 Teach us to count our days rightly,
that we may obtain a wise heart.

13 Turn, O LORD!
How long?
Show mercy to Your servants.
14 Satisfy us at daybreak with Your steadfast love
that we may sing for joy all our days.
15 Give us joy for as long as You have afflicted us,
for the years we have suffered misfortune.
16 Let Your deeds be seen by Your servants,
Your glory by their children.
17 May the favor of the Lord, our God, be upon us;
let the work of our hands prosper,
O prosper the work of our hands!

91 O you who dwell in the shelter of the Most High
and abide in the protection of Shaddai—
2 I say of the LORD, my refuge and stronghold,
my God in whom I trust,
3 that He will save you from the fowler's trap,
from the destructive plague.
4 He will cover you with His pinions;
you will find refuge under His wings;
His fidelity is an encircling shield.
5 You need not fear the terror by night,
or the arrow that flies by day,

a-a Meaning of Heb. uncertain. *b-b Or "fly away."*

8–10: Human lives are brief and troubled. Trouble was thought to result from sin, which God, in his anger, punished. **10:** *Seventy years:* Seventy (like seven) represents completion and perfection. Most people in ancient times did not reach this age, but some did. The ideal life span of 120 years (Gen. 6.3) is not realistic; a life span of 70 is. **13–17:** Darkness ends and daybreak comes; sorrow is mitigated by joy. **13:** *Turn .... Show mercy:* God is called upon to repent, or relent—to stop bringing punishment; and to be comforted—not to be angry any longer. The words are similar to Moses' plea after the golden calf incident (Exod. 32.12)—another reason that the psalm is called the prayer of Moses. *Turn* and "return" (v. 3) are the same verb in Heb. **14:** *Daybreak:* Morning is the time of renewal, the time that God answers prayers (Pss. 30.6; 46.6; 143.8), and when flowers bloom (v. 6). **15:** The psalmist prays for parity between days of joy and days of affliction. **16–17:** The limited "immortality" of human beings is in their children and their achievements, *the work of our hands.* The psalmist prays that his own generation and his children's will be able to rejoice in God's deeds and that their own deeds will prosper, with God's help.

Ps. 91: God protects from all harm those who trust Him. The many terms for protection, shelter, refuge, and the like emphasize the theme. A speaker in the first person addresses an audience, encouraging them to trust God so no harm will befall them (vv. 1–13); God responds (vv. 14–16), reinforcing the speaker's words. According to some commentators, *the shelter of the Most High* (v. 1) is the Temple, and the psalm was part of the liturgy for entering or departing from the Temple. It is not clear how metaphorical the language is or whether it reflects various magical ideas from popular religion and superstition; whether the dangers are from demons or from the ordinary dangers of plague, war, and wild animals. **1–2:** *Shelter ... protection ... refuge and stronghold:* For the Temple as a place of protection see Pss. 27.5; 31.21. *Most High* ("elyon") and *Shaddai* are old epithets for God, borrowed from the Canaanites, who applied them to the head of their pantheon. **1:** *O you who dwell,* lit. "the one who dwells"; Heb lacks the pronoun "you." It may be speaking in the third person or the psalmist may be referring to himself (see the opening of v. 2, though there the Gk [LXX] is in third person). **3:** God saves the individual from all danger, ranging from *the fowler's trap* to *the destructive plague.* The word for *plague* may also refer to a minor deity. **4:** *Wings* may be a metaphor for divine protection, the outspread wings of a bird (Pss. 17.8; 36.8), or may refer to the wings of the cherubim on either side of the Ark (Exod. 25.17–22). **5–6:** God

6 the plague that stalks in the darkness,
or the scourge that ravages at noon.
7 A thousand may fall at your left side,
ten thousand at your right,
but it shall not reach you.
8 You will see it with your eyes,
you will witness the punishment of the wicked.
9 Because you took the LORD—my refuge,
the Most High—as your haven,
10 no harm will befall you,
no disease touch your tent.
11 For He will order His angels
to guard you wherever you go.
12 They will carry you in their hands
lest you hurt your foot on a stone.
13 You will tread on cubs and vipers;
you will trample lions and asps.

14 "Because he is devoted to Me I will deliver him;
I will keep him safe, for he knows My name.
15 When he calls on Me, I will answer him;
I will be with him in distress;
I will rescue him and make him honored;
16 I will let him live to a ripe old age,
and show him My salvation."

92

A psalm. A song; for the sabbath day.
2 It is good to praise the LORD,
to sing hymns to Your name, O Most High,
3 To proclaim Your steadfast love at daybreak,
Your faithfulness each night
4 With a ten-stringed harp,
with voice and lyre together.
5 You have gladdened me by Your deeds, O LORD;
I shout for joy at Your handiwork.
6 How great are Your works, O LORD,
how very subtle[a] Your designs!

a Or *"profound."*

protects at all times: *night* and *day*, *darkness* (when there is no light), and *noon* (the brightest light). The two typical dangers in Psalms are enemies and sickness, and they may be represented here as *terror* and *arrows* (enemies) and *plague* and *scourge* (disease). Alternatively, *terror by night* is perhaps an attack by demonic forces (Song 3.8) and *plague* and *scourge* may also be demons. **7–9:** Even if all those who do not have God's protection fall (the numbers are exaggerated), the one who trusts in God will be safe. **8:** *The wicked,* those who lack trust in God. **11–12:** The psalmist's "guardian angels" (Exod. 23.20; Pss. 34.8; 103.20); perhaps the protectors against the demonic forces mentioned in vv. 5–6. According to vv. 12–13, the angels will metaphorically lift him up, protecting him from the rugged or stony path (v. 12) and from predatory and poisonous animals which he will be able to trample into submission (v. 13). **14–16:** God, speaking in the first person, perhaps through a cultic prophet, responds to the psalmist, reassuring him of God's protection. **16:** *A ripe old age,* length of days is a sign of God's favor, and is especially welcome after Ps. 90, which dwells on the shortness of human life.

Ps. 92: A hymn praising God; to be recited on the Sabbath, according to the superscription. According to early rabbinic tradition, particular psalms were recited each day of the week by the Levites at the Temple (*m. Tamid* 7.4 and parallels; see list in "The Bible in the Liturgy," pp. 2057–67), but the Bible indicates a psalm only for the "sabbath day." The psalm contains seven uses of the Tetragrammaton (YHVH), suggesting a link with the seventh day of creation (see *b. Ber.* 4.3 and parallels); The wonders of creation is a subtheme of the psalm. (The psalm's main theme is God's wondrous retribution.) It is uncertain when the psalm became connected with the Sabbath and when in the Sabbath liturgy in the Temple it was recited. Rabbinic and much medieval tradition understand the psalm eschatologically (*b. Rosh Hash.* 31a; Rashi). **1:** An unusual superscription, with no ascription of authorship; midrashic tradition suggests that Adam recited it (*Shoḥer Tov* to Ps. 92). **2:** The *praise* may be related to the frequent liturgical formula: "Praise the LORD for He is good; His steadfast love is eternal" (see 106.1 n.). On *Most High,* see 7.18 n. **3:** It is uncertain if this refers to two specific times *(daybreak, night)* at which God was praised in the Temple service, or is a merism for "always." **4:** The characteristics of a "mizmor" or psalm: a melody sung to the accompaniment of a stringed instrument (see 3.1 n.). **5:** On *handiwork* referring to creation, see 8.4 n., though here it may also refer to God's

7 A brutish man cannot know,
a fool cannot understand this:
8 though the wicked sprout like grass,
though all evildoers blossom,
it is only that they may be destroyed forever.

9 But You are exalted, O LORD, for all time.

10 Surely, Your enemies, O LORD,
surely, Your enemies perish;
all evildoers are scattered.
11 You raise my horn high like that of a wild ox;
I am soaked in freshening oil.
12 I shall see the defeat of my watchful foes,
hear of the downfall of the wicked who beset me.
13 The righteous bloom like a date-palm;
they thrive like a cedar in Lebanon;
14 planted in the house of the LORD,
they flourish in the courts of our God.
15 In old age they still produce fruit;
they are full of sap and freshness,
16 attesting that the LORD is upright,
my rock, in whom there is no wrong.

93

The LORD is king,
He is robed in grandeur;
the LORD is robed,
He is girded with strength.
The world stands firm;
it cannot be shaken.
2 Your throne stands firm from of old;
from eternity You have existed.
3 The ocean sounds, O LORD,
the ocean sounds its thunder,
the ocean sounds its pounding.

ongoing wonders. **6:** On *works* as the objects of creation, see 104.24; they may also refer to retribution. **8–9:** A strong contrast between the temporary flourishing of the wicked and God's permanence. **8:** A variant on the imagery of Ps. 1: here the wicked may prosper, but only for a short time. **9:** This v. is also an introduction to the following, since according to the Canaanite mythological tradition that Israel shared (see v. 10 n.), the high God ascended as king *for all time* only after his enemies had been vanquished. **10:** A reuse and revision of the material known from the Baal epic, where Baal defeats the rebellious Sea, a myth that is reflected in much of the Bible (see 8.3 n.): "Now your enemy, O Baal, Now your enemy will you smite; Now will you cut off your adversaries" (*ANET,* p. 131, slightly modified). In style as well as in contents the biblical v. resembles its Canaanite predecessor. Here God's enemies are not mythological creatures but human evildoers (cf. v. 8). **11:** Symbols of victory; see 75.5 n. Others translate this and the following v. in the past tense, and view the psalm as having elements of thanksgiving. **13–15:** The psalmist again uses agricultural imagery (cf. v. 8). **13:** *Cedars* of *Lebanon* were known for strength; they were used in constructing the Temple, and thus offer a subtle segue into the following v. **14:** For the desire to remain in the Temple, proximate to God, see 23.6; 27.5. **16:** *Attesting,* lit. "to proclaim," forming a frame with v. 3.

Ps. 93: This enthronement psalm (see introduction to Ps. 47) narrates God's ascent to the throne after defeating the powers of chaos, represented in vv. 3–4 as the ocean. It is an Israelite adoption and transformation of the Canaanite myth about Baal's kingship (see 92.10 n.). In classical rabbinic (see *b. Rosh Hash.* 31a) and later liturgical tradition, it is recited on Friday nights. Like the previous psalm, it concerns creation, and thus is connected to the Sabbath, which commemorates the completion of creation; a superscription in the LXX also connects it to the Sabbath. The kingship psalms grouped together (93–99) may have been seen as a subcollection in antiquity; none has a Davidic superscription. **1:** Heb may be translated as *The LORD is king* or "The LORD has become king"; context favors the latter, though in other psalms, which lack this psalm's explicit mythological background, the former may be preferable. (This translation difference determines whether these should be called enthronement psalms, those commemorating God's ascent to the throne, or kingship psalms that celebrate His ongoing role as king.) This v. narrates God's creation after defeating His mythological enemies. *Robed,* an image of an enthronement ceremony; God becomes king. God enrobed in His creation is an image known also from 104.1–2, where God's enthronement is by means of His creation. **2:** From the time of creation (in mythological terms, from the time of the defeat of the mythological enemies) God's *throne stands firm.* **3–4:** God successfully vanquishes

4 Above the thunder of the mighty waters,
more majestic than the breakers of the sea
is the LORD, majestic on high.
5 Your decrees are indeed enduring;
holiness befits Your house,
O LORD, for all times.

94

God of retribution, LORD,
God of retribution, appear!
2 Rise up, judge of the earth,
give the arrogant their deserts!
3 How long shall the wicked, O LORD,
how long shall the wicked exult,
4 shall they utter insolent speech,
shall all evildoers vaunt themselves?
5 They crush Your people, O LORD,
they afflict Your very own;
6 they kill the widow and the stranger;
they murder the fatherless,
7 thinking, "The LORD does not see it,
the God of Jacob does not pay heed."

8 Take heed, you most brutish people;
fools, when will you get wisdom?
9 Shall He who implants the ear not hear,
He who forms the eye not see?
10 Shall He who disciplines nations not punish,
He who instructs men in knowledge?
11 The LORD knows the designs of men to be futile.

12 Happy is the man whom You discipline, O LORD,
the man You instruct in Your teaching,
13 to give him tranquillity in times of misfortune,
until a pit be dug for the wicked.
14 For the LORD will not forsake His people;
He will not abandon His very own.
15 Judgment shall again accord with justice
and all the upright shall rally to it.

16 Who will take my part against evil men?
Who will stand up for me against wrongdoers?

the rebellious *oceans* below, and then resides *on high.* **5:** This defeat has theological implications for the validity of the Temple *(Your house)* as the place of worship and for the validity of God's *decrees.*

Ps. 94: This psalm, a request for the destruction of evildoers, does not explicitly deal with God's kingship like the surrounding Pss. 93–99. The image of God as judge may, however, be subsumed under God's kingship (see esp. 96.13; 99.4), and it is possible that v. 20, which mentions a (human) throne, draws a contrast with the divine throne. There are additional thematic and lexical similarities to the surrounding psalms. The psalm has several affinities to wisdom literature, including interest in educating the fool (v. 8; see also vv. 11, 12 nn.). The destruction of the wicked is a major theme of prophetic eschatology, and thus Radak, citing Mal. 3.19, understands this psalm as a request for the arrival of the eschaton. **1:** *Retribution* (Heb "nekamot"), some translate "vengeance," fostering a picture of a vengeful "Old Testament" deity (versus a loving God of the New Testament). Though "n-km" may have this sense elsewhere in the Bible, in this psalm fair retribution and not vengeance is being sought. Verbal repetition characterizes the opening (*God of retribution;* v. 3, "how long") and the closing (v. 23, "annihilate") of the psalm. **2:** *Rise up* may reflect human institutions, where the judge may have stood up to offer his verdict (cf. 82.1 n.). **3–6:** The focus here is on internal rather than external enemies; it is impossible to determine whether a specific group is meant. **6:** *Widow, stranger,* and *fatherless* are the defenseless in society; Deut. commands their protection (e.g., 10.18; 14.29). **7:** Similar quotations are in 10.11 and 73.11. Heb uses the root "ʾ-m-r" to indicate both verbal and internal speech (thought); the translation could be *thinking* or "saying," though v. 11 suggests the former. **11:** Although couched as a general statement, the v. refers to the wicked fools; perhaps a wisdom epigram is quoted here ("hevel," *futile,* is a characteristic term in Eccl., a wisdom text). **12:** This v. shares the wisdom notion (see esp. Prov. 3.11–12; Job 5.17) that divine chastisement is beneficial. Heb "Torah" likely here reflects general *teaching,* as in much wisdom literature (e.g., Prov. 1.8), though traditional Jewish commentary understands it as Torah on the assumption that the Mosaic Torah was canonical for David, the author of Psalms. **16:** A protestation of innocence; the psalmist is opposed by the *wrongdoers* or evil men ("poʿalei

17 Were not the LORD my help,
I should soon dwell in silence.
18 When I think my foot has given way,
Your faithfulness, O LORD, supports me.
19 When I am filled with cares,
Your assurance soothes my soul.

20 Shall the seat of injustice be Your partner,
that frames mischief by statute?
21 They band together to do away with the righteous;
they condemn the innocent to death.
22 But the LORD is my haven;
my God is my sheltering rock.
23 He will make their evil recoil upon them,
annihilate them through their own wickedness;
the LORD our God will annihilate them.

95 Come, let us sing joyously to the LORD,
raise a shout for our rock and deliverer;
2 let us come into His presence with praise;
let us raise a shout for Him in song!
3 For the LORD is a great God,
the great king of all divine beings.
4 In His hand are the depths of the earth;
the peaks of the mountains are His.
5 His is the sea, He made it;
and the land, which His hands fashioned.

6 Come, let us bow down and kneel,
bend the knee before the LORD our maker,
7 for He is our God,
and we are the people He tends, the flock in His care.
O, if you would but heed His charge this day:
8 Do not be stubborn as at Meribah,
as on the day of Massah, in the wilderness,
9 when your fathers put Me to the test,
tried Me, though they had seen My deeds.
10 Forty years I was provoked by that generation;
I thought, "They are a senseless people;
they would not know My ways."
11 Concerning them I swore in anger,
"They shall never come to My resting-place!"

'aven"; see 5.6 n.) of v. 4. **18:** On God's "ḥesed," see 5.8 n. **22:** Compare the extensive fortress language applied to God in 18.13. **23:** As frequently occurs, especially at the end of personal petitions, the tenses are unclear; the first verb is in the past ("he has"), while *annihilate* is in the future.

Ps. 95: A kingship psalm (see v. 3, *the great king*), which, after an introductory call to worship (vv. 1–3), focuses on God as creator of the world (vv. 4–5) and creator of Israel (vv. 6–7). Just as human kings were responsible for major building projects, God as king has created the world and Israel. Like Ps. 81, to which it is thematically similar, it concludes with a rebuke (vv. 8–11; cf. 81.9–17). The psalm can also be understood as having two calls to worship (vv. 1–2, 6), each followed by the impetus for that call, introduced by "ki," *for;* a similar structure is found in the early Song of the Sea recited by Miriam in Exod. 15.21, "Sing to the LORD, for ("ki") He has triumphed gloriously." This psalm (and those that follow through Ps. 99) is recited during the Friday night service. **1–2:** The *shout* is modeled after the acclaim for the new king at his enthronement (see 47.2 n.; 98.4, 6). **1:** *Rock* connects to the conclusion of the previous psalm (94.22). **3:** God is incomparable. As in Exod. 15.11 and elsewhere, the existence of other, less powerful deities is acknowledged; they serve to show God's superiority even over other divine beings. Medieval interpreters understand the divine beings as "angels" (Ibn Ezra, Radak). **7:** The image of God as shepherd is frequent in Psalms, and part of royal imagery; see 23.1–4 n. **8–11:** This is an unusual case where divine speech, perhaps spoken through a religious official, is quoted in psalms. (See also 91.14–16.) The tradition offered, like Ps. 78.32, stands in stark contrast with other traditions that see the wilderness period as ideal (esp. Jer. 2.2). The traditions about *Meribah* and *Massah* are in Exod. 17.7 and Deut. 33.8 (cf. Num. 20.1–13 about Meribah alone). This psalm connects the forty years of wandering to rebellion at these sites, in contrast to Num. 14.33–34; 32.13, which connect the forty years to the sin of the spies (but see Deut. 8.2; Josh. 5.6). These vv. function as an admonition, telling the people what to do if they want to remain in God's favor as His *people.* **9:** Like Exod. 17.2, this v. explains the etymology of Massah by the root "n-sh," to *put ... to the test.* **11:** *Resting-place* refers to the land of Israel (Deut. 12.9).

96

[a]Sing to the LORD a new song,
sing to the LORD, all the earth.
2 Sing to the LORD, bless His name,
proclaim His victory day after day.
3 Tell of His glory among the nations,
His wondrous deeds, among all peoples.
4 For the LORD is great and much acclaimed,
He is held in awe by all divine beings.
5 All the gods of the peoples are mere idols,
but the LORD made the heavens.
6 Glory and majesty are before Him;
strength and splendor are in His temple.

7 Ascribe to the LORD, O families of the peoples,
ascribe to the LORD glory and strength.
8 Ascribe to the LORD the glory of His name,
bring tribute and enter His courts.
9 Bow down to the LORD majestic in holiness;
tremble in His presence, all the earth!
10 Declare among the nations, "The LORD is king!"
the world stands firm; it cannot be shaken;
He judges the peoples with equity.
11 Let the heavens rejoice and the earth exult;
let the sea and all within it thunder,
12 the fields and everything in them exult;
then shall all the trees of the forest shout for joy
13 at the presence of the LORD, for He is coming,
for He is coming to rule the earth;
He will rule the world justly,
and its peoples in faithfulness.

97

The LORD is king!
Let the earth exult,
the many islands rejoice!

a Cf. 1 Chron. 16.23–33.

Ps. 96: This kingship psalm is similar in structure to the previous one, also containing two calls to worship, beginning in vv. 1 and 7. Like Ps. 95, it emphasizes God as creator; like Ps. 94, it emphasizes God as judge. It is, however, more universal in outlook, demanding that all nations acknowledge God (vv. 1, 7); perhaps there is a progression or intensification as we move through the kingship psalms. A variant of this psalm appears in 1 Chron. 16.23–33, where it is combined with different psalms (see annotations there), and is used in connection with the installation of the Ark in Jerusalem. A similar tradition is related in the LXX superscription to Ps. 96: "when the house was being rebuilt after the captivity"; these pieces of evidence suggest particular roles for the psalm in the Second Temple. The psalm (and several other kingship psalms) shares significant elements with Deutero-Isaiah (see vv. 4–5 n. below); the psalm may be exilic or later. **1–3:** It is unclear what new song (see Isa. 42.10) is meant—perhaps the psalm as a whole, or perhaps part of v. 10, "The LORD is king!" The rhetorical presence of other *nations* (see 47.10 n.) shows that God's glory is worldwide. **4–5:** God is depicted as more incomparable than in 95.3. The depiction of other deities as mere idols is a major theme of Deutero-Isaiah (e.g., Isa. 40.18–20). **6:** *Glory and majesty* (as well as *strength)* are typically royal attributes (21.6; 45.4), here shared by God as King in his palace, namely the *temple.* **7–8:** A reworked citation of Ps. 29.1–2; there the "divine beings" offer the praise that here is to be offered by the *families of the peoples.* Ascribing *to the LORD* and bringing *tribute* (offerings) to *His courts* (at the Temple) may be a single action, or two coordinated actions of song and sacrifice. **10:** The formula to be recited *among the nations* may either end with *king,* or may extend until the end of the v. In contrast to 93.1, this and the following psalms do not imagine an enthronement of God—God is king—so the phrase "YHVH malakh" is best translated in these psalms as *The LORD is king!* **11–13:** Here the entire natural world plays the role of the populace at the coronation, rejoicing loudly (see 47.2 n.). **13:** The verb "ba'" may be translated as *is coming* or "has come." The phrase is repeated, following a usage in Semitic poetry; as Radak notes: "the second *[is coming]* explains the first, and the doubling functions to strengthen [the rhetoric]." The end of the v. paraphrases the end of v. 10 and returns to the theme of justice, a central royal task emphasized in this collection. Human kings did not always mete out justice fairly, so these psalms express a desire for an ideal, divine royal judge.

Ps. 97: Thematically, this is similar to the previous two kingship psalms, emphasizing God's justice and power (though not His role as creator). Structurally it is quite different; it contains no call to worship, and rather than beginning with imperatives, it concludes with them. It builds upon the earlier kingship psalms, moving the declaration *The LORD is king!* to the psalm's beginning. As in other

2 Dense clouds are around Him,
righteousness and justice are the base of His throne.
3 Fire is His vanguard,
burning His foes on every side.
4 His lightnings light up the world;
the earth is convulsed at the sight;
5 mountains melt like wax at the LORD's presence,
at the presence of the Lord of all the earth.
6 The heavens proclaim His righteousness
and all peoples see His glory.
7 All who worship images,
who vaunt their idols,
are dismayed;
all divine beings bow down to Him.
8 Zion, hearing it, rejoices,
the towns[a] of Judah exult,
because of Your judgments, O LORD.
9 For You, LORD, are supreme over all the earth;
You are exalted high above all divine beings.

10 O you who love the LORD, hate evil!
He guards the lives of His loyal ones,
saving them from the hand of the wicked.
11 Light is sown for the righteous,
radiance[b] for the upright.
12 O you righteous, rejoice in the LORD
and acclaim His holy name!

98 A psalm.

Sing to the LORD a new song,
for He has worked wonders;
His right hand, His holy arm,
has won Him victory.
2 The LORD has manifested His victory,
has displayed His triumph in the sight of the nations.
3 He was mindful of His steadfast love and faithfulness
toward the house of Israel;
all the ends of the earth beheld the victory of our God.

a *Or "women."* *b* *Others "joy."*

kingship psalms, a utopian world is depicted; this motivates Radak to say: "many similar psalms were written to strengthen the hearts of people who despaired of redemption due to the length of the exile." **1:** See 96.11–13. *Islands* are far-off places. **2–5:** God appears as powerful and just in a theophany (see introduction to Ps. 29). **6:** Both the natural and human world react. **7:** This degrades the other deities even more than 96.4–5, showing progression in these psalms. **8:** God's *judgments,* either against other nations, or in the sense of divine justice (see v. 2, "righteousness and justice are the base of His throne") are the cause for *Zion*'s rejoicing. **9:** Ps. 47.3, another kingship psalm, is similar. **10–12:** A concluding call to the righteous. Calls seem to be part of this genre, though here the call itself is different from the surrounding psalms. **10:** The status of God has moral implications. On *loyal ones* ("ḥasid"), see 12.2 n. **11–12:** Heb "simḥah," the opening word of the second line, is a pun, meaning both *radiance* and joy. *And acclaim His holy name,* namely praise Him, may be a stock psalm phrase; see 30.5. The psalm concludes with a call to *rejoice,* echoing joy, a major theme of the psalm. Since the righteous are properly rewarded by God, it thus asserts that joy rather than fear is the proper reaction to God's great power.

Ps. 98: This kingship psalm highlights the military victory of God. It is closely related to Ps. 96: Both open with the same formula, *Sing to the LORD a new song,* and the conclusion of this psalm is a variant of the conclusion of 96. Both emphasize the role of nature in praising God, and both mention God's kingship in the middle rather than at the beginning. In fact, Ps. 98 can be seen as an actualized version of Ps. 96. Ps. 96.3 commands: "Tell of His glory among the nations, / His wondrous deeds, among all peoples," and 98.3 claims (in the past): "all the ends of the earth beheld the victory of our God." **1:** The short superscription, *A psalm,* is unique in Psalms and probably an error (a word dropped out); the LXX introduces all of the kingship psalms with "A psalm of David." This psalm collapses the typically longer summons to worship and motivation (introduced by "ki," *for)* into a single v.; see introductory n. to Ps. 95. Like many of the other kingship psalms, this too shows affinities to Deutero-Isaiah, and is likely based on it; compare vv. 1–2 with Isa. 52.10: "The LORD will bare His holy arm / In the sight of all the nations, / And the very ends of earth shall see / The victory of our God." **3:** *Steadfast love* and *faithfulness* are often connected

4 Raise a shout to the LORD, all the earth,
break into joyous songs of praise!
5 Sing praise to the LORD with the lyre,
with the lyre and melodious song.
6 With trumpets and the blast of the horn
raise a shout before the LORD, the King.
7 Let the sea and all within it thunder,
the world and its inhabitants;
8 let the rivers clap their hands,
the mountains sing joyously together
9 at the presence of the LORD,
for He is coming to rule the earth;
He will rule the world justly,
and its peoples with equity.

99

[a]-The LORD, enthroned on cherubim, is king,
peoples tremble, the earth quakes.-[a]
2 The LORD is great in Zion,
and exalted above all peoples.
3 They praise Your name as great and awesome;
He is holy!

4 [b]-Mighty king-[b] who loves justice,
it was You who established equity,
You who worked righteous judgment in Jacob.
5 Exalt the LORD our God
and bow down to His footstool;
He is holy!

6 Moses and Aaron among His priests,
Samuel, among those who call on His name—
when they called to the LORD,
He answered them.
7 He spoke to them in a pillar of cloud;
they obeyed His decrees,
the law He gave them.

a-a Clauses transposed for clarity. *b-b Meaning of Heb. uncertain.*

to covenant obligations. **4–8:** These mirror the noisy acclaim of the new king (see 47.2 n.), a common motif in the kingship psalms. **6:** The mention of the *horn* ("shofar") is especially significant given 1 Kings 1.39, concerning the coronation of Solomon: "They sounded the horn ("shofar") and all the people shouted, 'Long live King Solomon!'" This and other affinities to the coronation ritual may suggest that these psalms celebrate the (re)enthronement of God, perhaps during an annual ritual. The central significance of the shofar or ram's horn in the Rosh Ha-Shanah (New Year) celebration may be a remnant of this biblical ritual. **7–8:** See 96.11–12. These vv. possibly allude to the myth concerning the rebellion of the waters (see Ps. 93), in which case they suggest that the *sea* and *rivers* have been totally subdued, and are now paying homage to God. Thus, this v. may not merely be a personification of the sea (so Rashi, Radak), but may contain a recollection of the Sea as a deity. **8:** Another strong connection to Deutero-Isaiah; see Isa. 55.12: "Yea, you shall leave in joy and be led home secure. / Before you, mount and hill shall shout aloud, / And all the trees of the field shall clap their hands." **9:** A variant of 96.13.

Ps. 99: The final kingship psalm, though it does not serve as an obvious climax. Much of vv. 1–4 is similar to the previous kingship psalms, while vv. 5–9, framed by a refrain and focused on prophetic intercession and divine response, are unique. **1:** Quaking of people and nature accompanies theophanies (Exod. 19.16, 18). *Enthroned on cherubim* refers to God's Presence in the Temple, where the Ark serves as His throne (see 1 Sam. 4.4 n.). This kingship psalm, more than the others, focuses on God's Presence in the Jerusalem Temple (vv. 5, 9) in Zion (v. 2). **2:** God is exalted over *all peoples,* rather than greater than other gods, as in 95.3; 96.4; 97.9. **3:** *Great* and *awesome* are also paired in the kingship psalms 47.3 and 96.4. *He is holy!* may be the actual words of praise; see Isa. 6.3, where the seraphs declare: "Holy, holy, holy! / The LORD of Hosts! / His presence fills all the earth!" **4:** Similar themes and vocabulary are used in 97.2 and 98.9 of God the righteous judge. **5:** A typical call to worship. Several LXX mss suggest that "ki," "for" has been lost before *He is holy* (see the parallel in v. 9); this would fit the typical pattern (see introduction to Ps. 95). The *footstool* is the Ark (see 1 Chron. 28.2); the phrase is only known in exilic and later literature (Isa. 66.1; Lam. 2.1). **6:** In contrast to the Priestly tradition, *Moses* is viewed as a priest. The singling out of *Samuel* as an intercessor is somewhat surprising, though he sometimes has that role in Samuel (e.g., 1 Sam. 19.5, 9). Priests and prophets, but no king is mentioned; perhaps this reflects the postexilic era and highlights the incomparable nature of God's kingship. **7:** This v. is puzzling; it seems

8 O LORD our God, You answered them;
You were a forgiving God for them,
but You exacted retribution for their misdeeds.

9 Exalt the LORD our God,
and bow toward His holy hill,
for the LORD our God is holy.

100

A psalm [a]-for praise.-[a]

Raise a shout for the LORD, all the earth;
2 worship the LORD in gladness;
come into His presence with shouts of joy.
3 Acknowledge that the LORD is God;
He made us and [b]-we are His,-[b]
His people, the flock He tends.
4 Enter His gates with praise,
His courts with acclamation.
Praise Him!
Bless His name!
5 For the LORD is good;
His steadfast love is eternal;
His faithfulness is for all generations.

101

Of David. A psalm.

I will sing of faithfulness and justice;
I will chant a hymn to You, O LORD.

a-a Traditionally "for the thanksgiving offering."
b-b So qere; kethib *and some ancient versions "not we ourselves."*

to telescope, with some changes, the traditions preserved elsewhere in the Bible. Moses and Samuel also appear together as intercessors in Jer. 15.1. God does not appear in *a pillar of cloud* to Samuel. *Decrees* in reference to Samuel may mean laws pertaining to the monarchy (1 Sam. 8.9, 11; 10.25). **8:** This v. seems to be an oblique request for a divine answer for the psalmist. It is one of many biblical reuses of the divine attributes of Exod. 34.6–7; specifically *You were a forgiving God for them* reflects "forgiving iniquity, transgression, and sin," while *but You exacted retribution for their misdeeds* reworks "yet He does not remit all punishment." **9:** A slight variant of v. 5, functioning as a refrain. Although the phrase *holy hill* is found in Psalms (e.g., 15.1), it predominates in Deutero-Isaiah (e.g., 56.7), offering a final connection between that prophet and the kingship psalms.

Ps. 100: This psalm is formally distinct from the kingship psalm collection (93–99): it nowhere mentions the kingship of God, and unlike 93–99, it has a superscription. Nevertheless, as noted below, it shares many themes and words with these psalms. The reference in v. 3 recalls the royal shepherd image. It even has the same structure as Pss. 95–97: a call to worship followed by a reason introduced by "ki," *for.* The many similarities between Ps. 100 and the previous psalms suggest that Ps. 100 serves as an concluding anthology or summary for the collection. It may also be understood as a general call to worship, and may have functioned as an introduction to larger liturgical works; it serves a similar role now when recited in the daily morning service. It is universalistic like Deutero-Isaiah in the sense that *all the earth* is expected to *acknowledge that the LORD is God.* **1:** It is uncertain if "todah," used uniquely here in a superscription, should be translated *for praise,* specifying the genre of the psalm (see Radak), or if it refers to the thanksgiving offering (so Rashi; see 50.14 n.), suggesting a liturgy to be recited in conjunction with the sacrifice. On shouting, see 47.2 n., and 95.1–2; 98.4, 6. **2:** On *gladness,* see 97.11; contrast 2.11: "Serve the LORD in awe; / tremble with fright." **3:** The LORD (YHVH) as sole or most powerful God is emphasized in Pss. 96–98. On *the flock,* see 95.7. As the translators' note in NJPS indicates, there is a difference between the "qere" (how the text is to be read aloud) and the "ketiv ["kethib"]" (how the text is written). NJPS adopts the "qere," which is preferred. The "ketiv" writes "lo'," "not" in place of "lo," "His, to Him." **4:** This type of call to worship typifies 95–99; on *courts* see 96.8. *With praise* may also be rendered "with a thanksgiving offering." **5:** On the formula *For the LORD is good; / His steadfast love is eternal,* see 106.1 n. For *steadfast love* and *faithfulness,* see 98.3.

Ps. 101: While any individual could have recited this psalm, the speaker sounds like a ruler (see esp. v. 8) and therefore many scholars consider it a royal psalm, perhaps sung at a coronation. Cf. Pss. 2 and 110. In the first part (vv. 1–4), the speaker promises to conduct himself with honesty and uprightness; compare this declaration with the instructions for a king in Deut. 17.18–20 and the farewell speech of Samuel in 1 Sam. 12.2–5. In the second part (vv. 5–8) the speaker might be addressing his courtiers, explaining how he will ensure that his royal court will meet the highest moral standards. **1:** *Faithfulness and justice,* likely a reference to God's loyalty to the Davidic monarchy.

2 I will study the way of the blameless;
when shall I attain it?
I will live without blame within my house.
3 I will not set before my eyes anything base;
I hate crooked dealing;
I will have none of it.
4 Perverse thoughts will be far from me;
I will know nothing of evil.
5 He who slanders his friend in secret I will destroy;
I cannot endure the haughty and proud man.
6 My eyes are on the trusty men of the land,
to have them at my side.
He who follows the way of the blameless
shall be in my service.
7 He who deals deceitfully
shall not live in my house;
he who speaks untruth
shall not stand before my eyes.
8 Each morning I will destroy
all the wicked of the land,
to rid the city of the LORD
of all evildoers.

102

A prayer of the lowly man when he is faint and pours forth his plea before the LORD.

2 O LORD, hear my prayer;
let my cry come before You.
3 Do not hide Your face from me
in my time of trouble;
turn Your ear to me;
when I cry, answer me speedily.
4 For my days have vanished like smoke
and my bones are charred like a hearth.
5 My body is stricken and withered like grass;
[a]too wasted[a] to eat my food;
6 on account of my vehement groaning
my bones [b]show through my skin.[b]
7 I am like a great owl in the wilderness,
an owl among the ruins.
8 I lie awake; I am like
a lone bird upon a roof.
9 All day long my enemies revile me;
my deriders use my name to curse.
10 For I have eaten ashes like bread
and mixed my drink with tears,

a-a Others "I forget." *b-b Lit. "cling to my flesh."*

Cf. 89.2–5. This v. is interpreted in Jewish traditional sources (Tg., Rashi) to mean that whether God acts with favor ("ḥesed") or with justice ("mishpat"), the psalmist will always praise him. **2:** *My house* may refer to the palace (also v. 7). **3–5:** The king's protestation of innocence (18.22–24) for nonassociation with evildoers, see 1.1; 26.4–5. **5:** *Haughty,* lit. "high of eyes"; *proud,* lit. "wide of heart"; the psalm contains an unusual focus on body parts. **8:** *Each morning:* Morning is the time that justice is rendered (Jer. 21.12) and the time that deliverance is expected (46.6; Isa. 37.36; Lam. 3.23). *The city of the LORD* (also 48.9), Jerusalem (Tg.), the capital of the Davidic dynasty.

Ps. 102: A psalm lamenting the destruction of Jerusalem and praying for its restoration. Rabbinic tradition (*m. Ta'an.* 2.3) assigns this psalm to fast days. A prayer for personal restoration (vv. 2–12, 24–29) frames the prayer for the rebuilding of Zion (Jerusalem) after the exile (vv. 13–23). **1:** The *lowly man* of the superscription is one of the exiles. **3:** See the similar 69.18; God's hiding His face ("hester panim"; see 6.4–5 n.) became a theological concept in later Jewish thought. It represents God's withdrawal of His presence from the world. **4–8:** The psalmist describes his trouble as a physical illness; he is stricken with pain and weakness. **7–8:** The bird similes suggest loneliness and shrieks of pain which are calls for help. The birds mentioned are perceived negatively, as inhabiting ruins (Zeph. 2.14). **9:** Taunting from enemies is a common usage in the psalms and need not be taken literally. The psalmist feels socially isolated as well as physically ill. **10:** These actions indicate extreme mourning and lamenting; cf. 42.4; 80.6.

11 because of Your wrath and Your fury;
for You have cast me far away.
12 My days are like a lengthening shadow;
I wither like grass.

13 But You, O LORD, are enthroned forever;
Your fame endures throughout the ages.
14 You will surely arise and take pity on Zion,
for it is time to be gracious to her;
the appointed time has come.
15 Your servants take delight in its stones,
and cherish its dust.
16 The nations will fear the name of the LORD,
all the kings of the earth, Your glory.
17 For the LORD has built Zion;
He has appeared in all His glory.
18 He has turned to the prayer [a]of the destitute[a]
and has not spurned their prayer.
19 May this be written down for a coming
generation,
that people yet to be created may praise the
LORD.
20 For He looks down from His holy height;
the LORD beholds the earth from heaven
21 to hear the groans of the prisoner,
to release those condemned to death;
22 that the fame of the LORD may be recounted
in Zion,
His praises in Jerusalem,
23 when the nations gather together,
the kingdoms, to serve the LORD.

24 He drained my strength in mid-course,
He shortened my days.
25 I say, "O my God, do not take me away
in the midst of my days,
You whose years go on for generations on end.
26 Of old You established the earth;
the heavens are the work of Your hands.
27 They shall perish, but You shall endure;
they shall all wear out like a garment;
You change them like clothing and they pass
away.
28 But You are the same, and Your years never end.
29 May the children of Your servants dwell securely
and their offspring endure in Your presence."

a-a Meaning of Heb. uncertain.

11: Like Lam. ch 2, God's anger rather than human sin is blamed for the destruction. **12–13:** The transitory nature of humankind (*grass;* cf. Isa. 40.6) contrasted with the eternity of God (see Ps. 90.1–6). See also vv. 24–28. **12:** The psalmist feels he is nearing the end of his life. Cf. v. 24. **13:** Cf. Lam. 5.19, from the same period: "But You, O LORD, are enthroned forever, / Your throne endures through the ages." **14–17:** The psalmist prays that God will rebuild Zion and that the divine glory will again appear there (Ezek. 43.1–5); foreign kings will come to acknowledge God's supremacy (Isa. 60.1–3; Jer. 30.18). **14:** *The appointed time* may be unspecified or the psalmist may have known of a specific prophecy, like Jeremiah's prophecy (Jer. 25.11–12; 29.10–14) that Babylonia would be overthrown in seventy years. **16:** God's concern for his *name* is frequent in Psalms; see e.g., 79.9, where *name* and *glory* are similarly connected. **20–21:** God hears the groaning of the exiles (79.11), as he looks down from heaven (11.4–5; 14.2). **22–23:** The reinstitution of Temple worship will lead to the further glorification of God's *fame* (lit. "name" in Heb). All peoples will gather there to serve God, an idea similar to Isa. 2.2–3; Mic. 4.1–2; Ps. 117. **24–25:** The psalmist prays that he not suffer premature death (55.23; 89.45). Perhaps the psalmist is expressing regret that he will not live to see the restoration, but in v. 29 he hopes that his children will. **26:** Isa. 48.13; Ps. 104.5; Prov. 8.29; Job 38.4. **27–29:** The permanence of God is contrasted with the most permanent objects in the world, heaven and earth, usually thought of as existing forever (Eccl. 1.4). God created them and God will let them perish, but God will continue to exist for eternity, beyond all measure of time. The permanence of God gives hope that He will, at some time in the future, restore Israel. **28:** This v. is part of the liturgy for Rosh Ha-Shanah and Yom Kippur. **29:** There is hope of restoration for a future generation. To endure in God's Presence is the opposite of God's hiding His face.

Ps. 103: A hymn of praise for God's nature (divine attributes) and for His acts on behalf of Israel; it contains quotations from and allusions to Exod. and Isa. It is thematically similar to the previous psalm, and shares the same opening word with the following psalm. **1–2:** A double self-invitation to praise God. *Bless the Lord, O my soul* was likely a stock introduction to a psalm (104.1). *Soul* means one's being. There is as yet no concept of the soul as distinct from the body. **3–4:** Among God's blessings are the forgiveness of sin and the healing of mortal illness (32.1–5), which might have been thought of as punishment for sin. **3:** *He forgives all your sins,* see Exod. 34.7. **4:** *The Pit,* a poetic term for Sheol, the abode of the dead. **7–8:** See Exod. 33.13; 34.6. **9–13:** Interpreting or elaborating on the meaning and current application of Exod. 34.6, quoted in v. 8. This is a rare reference to the idea of a Mosaic Torah in Psalms, though it is uncertain if its contents were identical to our Torah. **9:** Cf. Isa. 57.16. **11:** Cf. Isa. 55.9. **13:** The relationship between God and His worshippers is portrayed as that between a father and a son (cf. Jer. 31.20; Mal. 3.16–17). **14–17:** The creaturely and ephemeral status of humanity (Gen. 2.7; Ps. 90.3–6), and the permanence of God's covenant with those who fear Him. **15–16:** Cf. Isa. 40.6–8. **19–22:** God is lauded by His heavenly council, and by all He has created (cf. Ps. 148); thus human praise of God mimics angelic praise, a significant theme of later Jewish prayer.

103 Of David.

Bless the LORD, O my soul,
all my being, His holy name.
2 Bless the LORD, O my soul
and do not forget all His bounties.
3 He forgives all your sins,
heals all your diseases.
4 He redeems your life from the Pit,
surrounds you with steadfast love and mercy.
5 He satisfies you with good things in [a]the prime of life,[-a]
so that your youth is renewed like the eagle's.

6 The LORD executes righteous acts
and judgments for all who are wronged.
7 He made known His ways to Moses,
His deeds to the children of Israel.
8 The LORD is compassionate and gracious,
slow to anger, abounding in steadfast love.
9 He will not contend forever,
or nurse His anger for all time.
10 He has not dealt with us according to our sins,
nor has He requited us according to our iniquities.
11 For as the heavens are high above the earth,
so great is His steadfast love toward those who fear Him.
12 As east is far from west,
so far has He removed our sins from us.
13 As a father has compassion for his children,
so the LORD has compassion for those who fear Him.
14 For He knows how we are formed;
He is mindful that we are dust.

15 Man, his days are like those of grass;
he blooms like a flower of the field;
16 a wind passes by and it is no more,
its own place no longer knows it.
17 But the LORD's steadfast love is for all eternity
toward those who fear Him,
and His beneficence is for the children's children
18 of those who keep His covenant
and remember to observe His precepts.
19 The LORD has established His throne in heaven,
and His sovereign rule is over all.

a-a Meaning of Heb. uncertain.

20 Bless the LORD, O His angels,
mighty creatures who do His bidding,
ever obedient to His bidding;
21 bless the LORD, all His hosts,
His servants who do His will;
22 bless the LORD, all His works,
through the length and breadth of His realm;
bless the LORD, O my soul.

104 Bless the LORD, O my soul;
O LORD, my God, You are very great;
You are clothed in glory and majesty,
2 wrapped in a robe of light;
You spread the heavens like a tent cloth.
3 He sets the rafters of His lofts in the waters,
makes the clouds His chariot,
moves on the wings of the wind.
4 He makes the winds His messengers,
fiery flames His servants.
5 He established the earth on its foundations,
so that it shall never totter.
6 You made the deep cover it as a garment;
the waters stood above the mountains.
7 They fled at Your blast,
rushed away at the sound of Your thunder,
8 —mountains rising, valleys sinking—
to the place You established for them.
9 You set bounds they must not pass
so that they never again cover the earth.

10 You make springs gush forth in torrents;
they make their way between the hills,
11 giving drink to all the wild beasts;
the wild asses slake their thirst.
12 The birds of the sky dwell beside them
and sing among the foliage.
13 You water the mountains from Your[a] lofts;
the earth is sated from the fruit of Your work.
14 You make the grass grow for the cattle,
and herbage for man's labor
that he may get food out of the earth—

a Lit. "His."

20–21: These council members are not independent, but *do His bidding* and *His will.* **22:** The psalm ends as it began, forming an inclusio.

Ps. 104: In praise of the Creator of a perfect world. The creation, an ecological harmony in which all are provided for, is an ideal world in which evil has no place. Structured on Gen. ch 1, but incorporating various other creation traditions, the description is highly poetic. It resembles both the divine catalogue of creation in Job chs 38–39 (which is more exotic and less idyllic) and the Egyptian "Hymn to Aten (the sun god)" (*ANET,* pp. 369–71), from which some scholars think it was adapted. This hymn is recited on the new moon. **1–4:** God is clothed in the glory of His creation; He is housed in it; He is transported by it. **2:** The creation of light and of the firmament. *Spread the heavens,* Isa. 40.22; 42.5; Zech. 12.2; Job 9.8. **3:** *Moves on ... the wind,* Pss. 18.11; 68.5. **4:** See 148.8: "fire and hail, snow and smoke, / storm wind that executes His command." **5:** See 102.26. **6–9:** God created the primordial *waters* (which Gen. 1.2 says were there at the beginning of creation), and then separated them from the dry land. God's *blast* put the chaotic waters to flight (29.3; Jer. 5.22). In their flight they ran up and down the *mountains* (v. 8), which had been submerged before (v. 6). *Never again* will the waters of chaos *cover the earth* (v. 9). These vv. incorporate recollections of the Canaanite mythological tradition attested at Ugarit and also found elsewhere in the Bible (cf. Prov. 8.29; Job 38.8–10). **10–18:** The emergence of the ideal, ordered, habitable world, where God provides water and food to all his creatures. **10–11:** Instead of the waters of chaos, God made *springs* that meander among the hills so that animals would have drink. **12:** Near the springs the *birds* live. **13–15:** The mention of the sky leads to the mention of rain, which waters the vegetation and enables herding and agricultural production. **13:** See 36.9; 65.10. **14:** Cf. 147.9. *Get food out of the earth:* The blessing over bread before meals uses this wording to bless God for bringing bread out of the earth. (In later Heb, the word "leḥem," "food," has the more restrictive meaning of "bread.") Here it is humans, through God's planning, who get food from the earth.

15: The three main crops of the agricultural year: grain (for *bread,* May-June), grapes (for *wine,* August-September), and olives (for *oil,* October). Wine is associated with pleasure and oil with luxury (oil was a cosmetic). **16–18:** The *trees,* also nourished by the water God provides, were created for *birds* to live in; *mountains* and caves were made to be homes for wild animals. **19–23:** The creation of the celestial bodies (Gen. 1.14–18) sets in motion the diurnal cycle. Each creature has its place in this cycle. Predators seek their food at night, and people labor during the day. **19:** Although the (full) moon marks the seasons—actually the celebration of the seasonal festivals (Sukkot and Passover)—it is better to render *to mark the seasons* as "to mark the set times," that is, the time for day and night. Cf. Gen. 1.16. **21:** Job 38.39. **24–26:** Both the land and the sea are marvels of God's creation. **26:** Oddly, manmade *ships* are seen as part of God's creations in the sea. They are accompanied by the *Leviathan,* elsewhere the great marine chaos monster (74.14; Job ch 41). In Ugaritic literature, Leviathan (Lotan) was also a "beloved" of the deity El, a plaything, and that idea may be reflected here. Another quite different interpretation, not mythological, understands "Leviathan" in its literal sense of "the escort"—the dolphins or large fish often found near ships. **27–30:** God maintains His providential care of the world. According to Gen. 2.7 (cf. Ps. 103.14), God formed the human from dust and breathed life into him, but here God's *breath* animates all living things and without it they return to dust. **29:** *Hide Your face,* see 102.3. **31–32:** The creation is a theophany, accompanied by convulsions of the earth (114.7) and the mountains surrounded with smoke (144.5). **33–34:** The implication of this wonder is that the psalmist must praise God.

15 wine that cheers the hearts of men
[a]oil that makes the face shine,[a]
and bread that sustains man's life.
16 The trees of the LORD drink their fill,
the cedars of Lebanon, His own planting,
17 where birds make their nests;
the stork has her home in the junipers.
18 The high mountains are for wild goats;
the crags are a refuge for rock-badgers.

19 He made the moon to mark the seasons;
the sun knows when to set.
20 You bring on darkness and it is night,
when all the beasts of the forests stir.
21 The lions roar for prey,
seeking their food from God.
22 When the sun rises, they come home
and couch in their dens.
23 Man then goes out to his work,
to his labor until the evening.

24 How many are the things You have made, O LORD;
You have made them all with wisdom;
the earth is full of Your creations.
25 There is the sea, vast and wide,
with its creatures beyond number,
living things, small and great.
26 There go the ships,
and Leviathan that You formed to sport with.
27 All of them look to You
to give them their food when it is due.
28 Give it to them, they gather it up;
open Your hand, they are well satisfied;
29 hide Your face, they are terrified;
take away their breath, they perish
and turn again into dust;
30 send back Your breath, they are created,
and You renew the face of the earth.

31 May the glory of the LORD endure forever;
may the LORD rejoice in His works!
32 He looks at the earth and it trembles;
He touches the mountains and they smoke.
33 I will sing to the LORD as long as I live;
all my life I will chant hymns to my God.

a-a *Lit. "to make the face shine from oil."*

34 May my prayer be pleasing to Him;
I will rejoice in the LORD.
35 May sinners disappear from the earth,
and the wicked be no more.
Bless the LORD, O my soul.
Hallelujah.

105 Praise the LORD;
call on His name;
proclaim His deeds among the peoples.
2 Sing praises to Him;
speak of all His wondrous acts.
3 Exult in His holy name;
let all who seek the LORD rejoice.
4 Turn to the LORD, to His might;[a]
seek His presence constantly.
5 Remember the wonders He has done,
His portents and the judgments He has pronounced,
6 O offspring of Abraham, His servant,
O descendants of Jacob, His chosen ones.

7 He is the LORD our God;
His judgments are throughout the earth.
8 He is ever mindful of His covenant,
the promise He gave for a thousand generations,
9 that He made with Abraham,
swore to Isaac,
10 and confirmed in a decree for Jacob,
for Israel, as an eternal covenant,
11 saying, "To you I will give the land of Canaan
as your allotted heritage."

12 They were then few in number,
a mere handful, sojourning there,
13 wandering from nation to nation,
from one kingdom to another.

a I.e., the Ark; cf. Pss. 78.61; 132.8.

35: There is no place in this harmonious creation for *sinners.* As in the previous psalm, this concludes as it began. *Hallelujah,* "Praise the LORD." These words occur at the end and sometimes at the beginning of a number of psalms from this point on (see 105; 106; 111–113; 115–117; 135; 146–150); these may have been part of one or more subcollections.

Ps. 105: Like Pss. 78, 106, 135, and 136, this psalm invokes selected authoritative traditions now found in the Torah along with exegetical comments on them in praise of God. The main theme is God's covenant with Abraham to give him the promised land. This covenant, a popular theme in postexilic times (e.g., Isa. 41.8; 51.2; 63.16; Neh. 9.7), was eternal and unconditional, and therefore still in effect (v. 8) despite the exile and the fact that Jews both in and outside the land of Israel lived under Persian rule. It provides encouragement and assurance to the postexilic audience (most likely those who had returned to the land of Israel) that they are entitled to the land of Israel by divine right. Vv. 1–15 are quoted in 1 Chron. 16.8–22. **1–2:** God's *deeds* and *wondrous acts* are those recorded in the Torah, which the psalm goes on to recite and reinterpret. The psalmist knew some form of the Torah traditions, which had already become authoritative. **4:** *Seek His presence,* in the Temple. **5:** *Portents* recalls the wonders in Egypt, the focus of much of the psalm, and *judgments He has pronounced* may recall the giving of the law at Sinai (Exod. 21.1). **6:** The audience is addressed as the offspring (seed) of Abraham, thereby making them the fulfillment of God's promise to give Abraham many offspring (Gen. 15.3–6). *Descendants of Jacob* (lit. "children of Jacob") again emphasizes the continuity between the patriarchs and the audience. *His chosen ones,* the present generation is just as "chosen" as the forefathers. **9–11:** The covenant with Abraham was reiterated for Isaac and Jacob (Gen. ch 15; 17.7–8; 28.13–14). The wording of v. 11 is similar to Gen. 17.8, with the addition of "your allotted heritage" from Deut. 32.9, further strengthening the bond between Israel and its land. **12–15:** The story of the ancestors before they possessed the land highlights their wanderings in and out of Canaan, making them "exiles" just like the audience. The use of allusions and phrases associated with exile strengthen this theme that the patriarchs experienced exile like the contemporary audience. They, like their ancestors, will be redeemed and brought to the promised land. **12:** The wording alludes to Deut. 4.27; 28.62, and most closely to Deut. 26.5. In all these cases "few in number" is associated with being in exile.

14 He allowed no one to oppress them;
He reproved kings on their account,
15 "Do not touch My anointed ones;
do not harm My prophets."

16 He called down a famine on the land,
destroyed every staff of bread.
17 He sent ahead of them a man,
Joseph, sold into slavery.
18 His feet were subjected to fetters;
an iron collar was put on his neck.
19 Until his prediction came true
the decree of the LORD purged him.
20 The king sent to have him freed;
the ruler of nations released him.
21 He made him the lord of his household,
empowered him over all his possessions,
22 to discipline his princes at will,
to teach his elders wisdom.
23 Then Israel came to Egypt;
Jacob sojourned in the land of Ham.

24 He made His people very fruitful,
more numerous than their foes.
25 [a]He changed their heart[a] to hate His people,
to plot against His servants.
26 He sent His servant Moses,
and Aaron, whom He had chosen.
27 They performed His signs among them,
His wonders, against the land of Ham.
28 He sent darkness; it was very dark;
[b]did they not defy His word?[b]
29 He turned their waters into blood
and killed their fish.
30 Their land teemed with frogs,
even the rooms of their king.
31 Swarms of insects came at His command,
lice, throughout their country.
32 He gave them hail for rain,
and flaming fire in their land.
33 He struck their vines and fig trees,
broke down the trees of their country.
34 Locusts came at His command,
grasshoppers without number.
35 They devoured every green thing in the land;
they consumed the produce of the soil.

a-a Or "Their heart changed." *b-b Meaning of Heb. uncertain.*

14–15: Cf. Gen. ch 20, where God *reproved* King Abimelech, and where Abraham is called a *prophet.* Cf. also Gen. 12.10–20; 26.1–2. *Anointed ones,* a synonym for "prophets," who were sometimes anointed (1 Kings 19.16; Isa. 61.1). Cf. Damascus Document 2.12; 6.1 (a Dead Sea Scroll text). **16–22:** The *Joseph* story (Gen. chs 37–50) retold with interpretive additions, ending with Joseph as a wisdom teacher (Gen. 41.39). **16:** *Staff of bread,* a phrase used in connection with the famine that results from enemy sieges (Lev. 26.26; Ezek. 4.16; 5.16; 14.13), forming another link between the forefathers' experience and that of the exiles. **18:** This treatment is not recounted in Gen.; it is an exegetical addition making Joseph into a prisoner of war, like the deportees after the destruction. **19:** As in later traditions, Joseph's righteousness is emphasized. **23–38:** The exodus story. Its telling emphasizes the destruction of the land of Egypt, showing God's power over that land. The exodus is a common metaphor for the return from captivity. **23–25:** Israel in *Egypt,* oppressed yet fruitful (Exod. ch 1). *Ham,* Egypt; see 78.51. **26–36:** The plagues (Exod. chs 7–12). The number and order of plagues differs from the Exod. account (see Ps. 78.43–51). **28:** *Darkness* is here the first, not the penultimate plague, as in Exod. **30:** *Their king,* Heb "kings" (plural), reflecting an ancient tradition that also appears in Wisdom of Solomon 10.16 and Sir. 45.3. **31:** In Exod., *swarms* and *lice* appear as two separate plagues. **33:** *Vines and fig trees,* an exegetical comment elaborating on the hail plague. Cf. 78.47 for a similar elaboration.

36 He struck down every first-born in the land,
the first fruit of their vigor.
37 He led Israel[a] out with silver and gold;
none among their tribes faltered.
38 Egypt rejoiced when they left,
for dread of Israel[a] had fallen upon them.

39 He spread a cloud for a cover,
and fire to light up the night.
40 They asked and He brought them quail,
and satisfied them with food from heaven.
41 He opened a rock so that water gushed forth;
it flowed as a stream in the parched land.
42 Mindful of His sacred promise
to His servant Abraham,
43 He led His people out in gladness,
His chosen ones with joyous song.
44 He gave them the lands of nations;
they inherited the wealth of peoples,
45 that they might keep His laws
and observe His teachings.
Hallelujah.

106 Hallelujah.
Praise the LORD for He is good;
His steadfast love is eternal.
2 Who can tell the mighty acts of the LORD,
proclaim all His praises?

3 Happy are those who act justly,
who do right at all times.
4 Be mindful of me, O LORD, when You favor Your
people;
take note of me when You deliver them,
5 that I may enjoy the prosperity of Your chosen
ones,
share the joy of Your nation,
glory in Your very own people.

a *Lit. "them."*

37: Exod. 12.33–36. *None among their tribes,* an interpretation of Exod. 6.26 and 12.51, where God took out the Israelites "troop by troop." This interpretation is found in Josephus (*Ant.* 14.6) and in traditional Jewish commentaries. Exegetical additions justify the taking of the *silver and gold;* this episode has a long history of interpretation, going back at least to this psalm and Exod. 3.22. **39–44:** The wandering in the wilderness and the coming to the promised land is discussed in highly positive terms, omitting the stories of murmuring and of wandering for forty years. **39:** The pillar of *cloud* that led the Israelites (Exod. 13.21) takes on a protective function (Exod. 14.19) and is easily conflated with the cloud of the theophany that protects the people from direct contact with the divine (which would be fatal); cf. Exod. 33.1–10; Lev. 16.2; Num. 14.14. Isa. 4.5–6 applies the image to Mt. Zion. **40:** The provision of Israel with *food* (Exod. 16.1–17.7). No mention is made of the people's complaints (Exod. ch 16 and Num. ch 11); the point is that God takes care of Israel's needs. **42–44:** An inclusio (cf. vv. 8–11) returns to the promise to Abraham, which God remembers and will now act upon. **45:** The community is enjoined to obey the Torah traditions, the same traditions that the psalmist has utilized and reinterpreted to give the community encouragement.

Ps. 106: This postexilic psalm presents a history of Israel in a very different manner from the preceding one; it highlights Israel's sins that culminates in idolatrous practices that polluted the land of Israel and led to the destruction and exile. The catalogue of sins shows how forbearing and forgiving God has been throughout the past, and, by implication, how forgiving He will continue to be, since He maintains His covenant and is merciful (vv. 43–45). The past history of God and Israel is presented as a model for God's future behavior. The exile of 586 BCE, says the psalmist, is no different from earlier punishments, after which God took Israel back into His favor. The psalm is both a praise to God and a request to be gathered from among the nations, that is, returned from exile. Like Ps. 105, this psalm invokes Torah traditions along with interpretive comments. It adopts the Deuteronomic view that the exile was caused by Israel's sins. **1:** *Praise the LORD for He is good; His steadfast love is eternal* was a ritual exclamation in the exilic period; see 107.1; 118.1, 29; 136.1; 1 Chron. 16.41; 2 Chron. 7.6. **3:** See the concluding v. of the previous psalm. **4–5:** The psalmist wishes to be included in the national favor that God will grant.

6: The present generation joins itself to past generations of sinners, implicitly suggesting that it should be forgiven, as they were. Cf. Lam. 5.7. This three-part confession is long by biblical standards, but becomes more developed and longer in later tradition. **8–12:** God's rescue of Israel at the sea and Israel's initial obedience (Exod. 14.26–15.19). **13–33:** Rebellion in the wilderness. **14–15:** The feeding of Israel and their testing of God (Exod. chs 16–17; Num. ch 11). **15:** *Then made them waste away,* see Num. 11.33. **16–18:** The rebellion of Dathan and Abiram (Num. ch 16). The rebellion of Korah, also noted in Num. ch 16, is absent. **19–20:** The making of the golden calf (Exod. 32.1–10). **19:** *Horeb,* an alternate name for Sinai favored by Deut. **20:** *Their glory,* God. *That feeds on grass,* an interpretive comment belittling the molten calf. **22:** *Ham,* Egypt; see 78.51. **23:** The intercession of Moses (Exod. 32.11–14). **24–27:** The Israelites' wish to return to Egypt rather than to enter Canaan, *the desirable land,* God's anger at them, and Moses' plea on their behalf (Num. 14.1–35). V. 27 is clearly a reference to the author's period, when Israel was *disperse*d and *scattere*d, rather than to the period of the wilderness.

6 We have sinned like our forefathers;
we have gone astray, done evil.
7 Our forefathers in Egypt did not perceive Your wonders;
they did not remember Your abundant love,
but rebelled at the sea, at the Sea of Reeds.
8 Yet He saved them, as befits His name,
to make known His might.
9 He sent His blast against the Sea of Reeds;
it became dry;
He led them through the deep as through a wilderness.
10 He delivered them from the foe,
redeemed them from the enemy.
11 Water covered their adversaries;
not one of them was left.
12 Then they believed His promise,
and sang His praises.
13 But they soon forgot His deeds;
they would not wait to learn His plan.
14 They were seized with craving in the wilderness,
and put God to the test in the wasteland.
15 He gave them what they asked for,
then made them waste away.
16 There was envy of Moses in the camp,
and of Aaron, the holy one of the LORD.
17 The earth opened up and swallowed Dathan,
closed over the party of Abiram.
18 A fire blazed among their party,
a flame that consumed the wicked.
19 They made a calf at Horeb
and bowed down to a molten image.
20 They exchanged their glory
for the image of a bull that feeds on grass.
21 They forgot God who saved them,
who performed great deeds in Egypt,
22 wondrous deeds in the land of Ham,
awesome deeds at the Sea of Reeds.
23 He would have destroyed them
had not Moses His chosen one
confronted Him in the breach
to avert His destructive wrath.
24 They rejected the desirable land,
and put no faith in His promise.
25 They grumbled in their tents
and disobeyed the LORD.
26 So He raised His hand in oath
to make them fall in the wilderness,

27 to disperse[a] their offspring among the nations
and scatter them through the lands.
28 They attached themselves to Baal Peor,
ate sacrifices offered to the dead.
29 They provoked anger by their deeds,
and a plague broke out among them.
30 Phinehas stepped forth and intervened,
and the plague ceased.
31 It was reckoned to his merit
for all generations, to eternity.
32 They provoked wrath at the waters of Meribah
and Moses suffered on their account,
33 because they rebelled against Him
and he spoke rashly.

34 They did not destroy the nations
as the LORD had commanded them,
35 but mingled with the nations
and learned their ways.
36 They worshiped their idols,
which became a snare for them.
37 Their own sons and daughters
they sacrificed to demons.
38 They shed innocent blood,
the blood of their sons and daughters,
whom they sacrificed to the idols of Canaan;
so the land was polluted with bloodguilt.
39 Thus they became defiled by their acts,
debauched through their deeds.
40 The LORD was angry with His people
and He abhorred His inheritance.
41 He handed them over to the nations;
their foes ruled them.
42 Their enemies oppressed them
and they were subject to their power.
43 He saved them time and again,
but they were deliberately rebellious,
and so they were brought low by their iniquity.
44 When He saw that they were in distress,
when He heard their cry,
45 He was mindful of His covenant
and in His great faithfulness relented.
46 He made all their captors kindly disposed toward them.

47 Deliver us, O LORD our God,
and gather us from among the nations,

28–31: The worship of Baal of Peor and the episode of the Midianite woman (Num. 25.1–9). **28:** *Ate sacrifices offered to the dead,* the sacrifices of foreign gods (Ibn Ezra). Some modern scholars associate Canaanite worship with worship of the dead—the "marzeaḥ" feast. **30–31:** Num. 25.6–9. The Zadokite priests, who ministered during the Judean monarchy, traced themselves to Phinehas (1 Chron. 5.30–41). **32–33:** *The waters of Meribah,* where Moses hit the rock in order to get water from it and was therefore not permitted to enter the Land of Israel (Num. 20.2–13; cf. Exod. 17.1–7). **34–36:** Because they left the holy war (extermination of their enemies) incomplete, the Israelites learned their practices (Deut. 20.18), and the land was polluted with idolatry. **37–39:** The passing of children through fire as a form of sacrifice to foreign gods is often condemned in the Bible (Deut. 12.31; 2 Kings 16.3; 21.6; Jer. 19.5; Ezek. 20.31; 23.37). **37:** No mention is made here of passing the children through fire; rather, the pagan practice is called sacrificing *to demons*—a later interpretation of a practice that was no longer current (and which remains incompletely understood by modern scholars). **40–42:** The destruction and exile resulted from the people's accumulated sins of idolatry, which God could no longer leave unpunished. **44–47:** As God saved the people in the past, the exiles ask for a new act of deliverance, the regathering of the people from their captivity (v. 27; 1 Chron. 16.35–36).

a *Cf. Targum, Kimhi.*

to acclaim Your holy name,
to glory in Your praise.

48 Blessed is the LORD, God of Israel,
From eternity to eternity.
Let all the people say, "Amen."
Hallelujah.

BOOK FIVE

107 "Praise the LORD, for He is good;
His steadfast love is eternal!"
2 Thus let the redeemed of the LORD say,
those He redeemed from adversity,
3 whom He gathered in from the lands,
from east and west,
from the north and from the sea.

4 Some lost their way in the wilderness,
in the wasteland;
they found no settled place.
5 Hungry and thirsty,
their spirit failed.
6 In their adversity they cried to the LORD,
and He rescued them from their troubles.
7 He showed them a direct way
to reach a settled place.
8 Let them praise the LORD for His steadfast love,
His wondrous deeds for mankind;
9 for He has satisfied the thirsty,
filled the hungry with all good things.

10 Some lived in deepest darkness,
bound in cruel irons,
11 because they defied the word of God,
spurned the counsel of the Most High.
12 He humbled their hearts through suffering;
they stumbled with no one to help.
13 In their adversity they cried to the LORD,
and He rescued them from their troubles.

48: The doxology ending Book IV of the Psalter (cf. 41.14; 72.18–19; 89.53). *Amen,* an affirmation of the words just spoken. In its final form, the psalm ends with *Hallelujah,* forming an inclusio.

Ps. 107: The division between Books IV and V of the Psalter is late and improperly placed: Ps. 107, with its allusions to earlier traditions, belongs with Pss. 103–106. Furthermore, the opening of Ps. 107, *"Praise the LORD, for He is good; / His steadfast love is eternal!"* connects it to Pss. 105 and 106; the connection is even more striking if the word "Hallelujah" is restored at the beginning of the psalm, following the LXX. The last v. clarifies the psalm's purpose: *The wise man will take note of these things; / he will consider the steadfast love of the LORD,* namely that these beneficent events reflect God's *steadfast love* or "ḥesed" (see 5.8 n.). The psalm may be divided into two large units: vv. 1–32 and 33–43; several scholars believe that two originally separate psalms have been combined. In contrast to the latter unit, the former, after an introduction (vv. 1–3), can be divided into stanzas (vv. 4–9; 10–16; 17–22; 23–32), each of which has the double refrain *In their adversity they cried to the LORD, / and He rescued them from their troubles* (vv. 6, 13, 19, 28) and *Let them praise the LORD for His steadfast love, / His wondrous deeds for mankind* (vv. 8, 15, 21, 31), followed in each stanza by a single, concluding v. This section shares many motifs with Job. The psalm shows some signs of late biblical Heb, and vv. 1–2 are likely influenced by Isa. 62.12 and 43.5; it is thus a postexilic psalm. The Rabbis used this psalm as the basis for requiring a special blessing thanking God from those who survived the desert, those released from prison, seafarers, and those who were seriously ill (*b. Ber.* 54b). **1–2:** Compare the opening of Ps. 118. **2–3:** A reference to the return from the Babylonian exile. **4–9:** Deliverance in the wilderness after the exodus, here conflated with and symbolizing the difficulties of the exile and the return. The theme of God's care in the wilderness became particularly important in the early postexilic period as the return from Babylonia was viewed by Deutero-Isaiah as a second exodus (see Isa. 43.16–21 n.). The Tg. through its additions (v. 4, "He [David, author of Psalms] is prophesying concerning His nation Israel"; cf. v. 10, "concerning Zedekiah ... ") makes it clear that this psalm is to be read in reference to specific events in Israel's past. **10–16:** V. 10 is a reference to the exile; v. 14 to a release from exile. **17–22:** Two general

14 He brought them out of deepest darkness,
broke their bonds asunder.
15 Let them praise the LORD for His steadfast love,
His wondrous deeds for mankind,
16 For He shattered gates of bronze,
He broke their iron bars.
17 There were fools who suffered for their sinful way,
and for their iniquities.
18 All food was loathsome to them;
they reached the gates of death.
19 In their adversity they cried to the LORD
and He saved them from their troubles.
20 He gave an order and healed them;
He delivered them from the pits.[a]
21 Let them praise the LORD for His steadfast love,
His wondrous deeds for mankind.
22 Let them offer thanksgiving sacrifices,
and tell His deeds in joyful song.

23 Others go down to the sea in ships,
ply their trade in the mighty waters;
24 they have seen the works of the LORD
and His wonders in the deep.
25 By His word He raised a storm wind
that made the waves surge.
26 Mounting up to the heaven,
plunging down to the depths,
disgorging in their misery,
27 they reeled and staggered like a drunken man,
all their skill to no avail.
28 In their adversity they cried to the LORD,
and He saved them from their troubles.
29 He reduced the storm to a whisper;
the waves were stilled.
30 They rejoiced when all was quiet,
and He brought them to the port they desired.
31 Let them praise the LORD for His steadfast love,
His wondrous deeds for mankind.
32 Let them exalt Him in the congregation of the
people,
acclaim Him in the assembly of the elders.

33 He turns the rivers into a wilderness,
springs of water into thirsty land,
34 fruitful land into a salt marsh,
because of the wickedness of its inhabitants.

descriptions of those who are being punished for misdeeds; they too will be forgiven. **21–26, 40:** Each of these vv. begins with an inverted Heb letter "nun," adapted from a sign used in Gk ms editing, to indicate that lines are isolated or separated from the surrounding material (the same indication occurs at Num. 10.35–36), but their use here is enigmatic. **23–32:** This stanza, longer than the others, deals with the dangers of sailing (see Jonah chs 1–2). **32:** This clarifies that "praise" must be public; although the Temple is a natural site for this, an *assembly of the elders* is not elsewhere associated with the Temple. **33–36:** These vv., concerning the return to Israel, hark back to vv. 4–9, and show close affinities to Deutero-Isaiah.

a *Viz., of death.*

37–39: Blessings in the land. **40–42:** A qualifier, using typical psalmic language, noting that only the *needy* and *upright* prosper. **43:** In several places, *the steadfast love of the Lord* seems to be a technical term for the past beneficent acts of God in history (89.2; Isa. 63.7). This final v. is similar to the final v. of Hos. (Hos. 14.10).

Ps. 108: After a unique superscription, vv. 2–6 duplicate 57.8–12 and vv. 7–14 duplicate 60.7–14. As in other cases (see Ps. 31 intro.), there are slight variations in these duplicates, suggesting that there was some flexibility in the transmission of passages. It is not clear why these two passages should be joined in this fashion, but it is noteworthy that v. 7, the first v. from the second passage, serves as a logical continuation of v. 6; v. 6 is a request, and in its new home, v. 7 offers the motivation or justification for that request. The result of the join fits the structure of communal petitions. The reuse of sections from one passage to create a new passage was accepted practice in the ancient world (see Isa. 2.2–4 n.). For medieval commentators, the problem of repeated passages was more severe. Radak, for example glosses: "and he [David] repeated it here, and we do not know why." On specific vv., see the annotations to Pss. 57 and 60.

35 He turns the wilderness into pools,
parched land into springs of water.
36 There He settles the hungry;
they build a place to settle in.
37 They sow fields and plant vineyards
that yield a fruitful harvest.
38 He blesses them and they increase greatly;
and He does not let their cattle decrease,
39 after they had been few and crushed
by oppression, misery, and sorrow.
40 He pours contempt on great men
and makes them lose their way in trackless deserts;
41 but the needy He secures from suffering,
and increases their families like flocks.

42 The upright see it and rejoice;
the mouth of all wrongdoers is stopped.
43 The wise man will take note of these things;
he will consider the steadfast love of the LORD.

108

A song. A psalm of David.

2a My heart is firm, O God;
I will sing and chant a hymn with all my soul.
3 Awake, O harp and lyre!
I will wake the dawn.
4 I will praise You among the peoples, O LORD,
sing a hymn to You among the nations;
5 for Your faithfulness is higher than the heavens;
Your steadfastness reaches to the sky.
6 Exalt Yourself over the heavens, O God;
let Your glory be over all the earth!
7b That those whom You love may be rescued,
deliver with Your right hand and answer me.

8 God promised [c]in His sanctuary[c]
that I would exultingly divide up Shechem,
and measure the Valley of Sukkoth;
9 Gilead and Manasseh would be mine,
Ephraim my chief stronghold,
Judah my scepter;
10 Moab would be my washbasin;
on Edom I would cast my shoe;
I would raise a shout over Philistia.

a With vv. 2–6, cf. Ps. 57.8–12. *b With vv. 7–14, cf. Ps. 60.7–14.*
c-c Or "by His holiness."

11 Would that I were brought to the bastion!
Would that I were led to Edom!

12 But You have rejected us, O God;
God, You do not march with our armies.
13 Grant us Your aid against the foe,
for the help of man is worthless.
14 With God we shall triumph;
He will trample our foes.

109

For the leader. Of David. A psalm.

O God of my praise,
do not keep aloof,
2 for the wicked and the deceitful
open their mouth against me;
they speak to me with lying tongue.
3 They encircle me with words of hate;
they attack me without cause.
4 They answer my love with accusation
[a]and I must stand judgment.[a]
5 They repay me with evil for good,
with hatred for my love.

6 Appoint a wicked man over him;
may an accuser stand at his right side;
7 may he be tried and convicted;
may he be judged and found guilty.
8 May his days be few;
may another take over [b]his position.[b]
9 May his children be orphans,
his wife a widow.
10 May his children wander from their hovels,
begging in search of [bread].
11 May his creditor seize all his possessions;
may strangers plunder his wealth.
12 May no one show him mercy;
may none pity his orphans;
13 may his posterity be cut off;
may their names be blotted out in the next
generation.
14 May God be ever mindful of his father's iniquity,
and may the sin of his mother not be blotted out.
15 May the LORD be aware of them always
and cause their names to be cut off from the earth,

a-a Or "but I am all prayer"; meaning of Heb. uncertain, but see v. 7.
b-b Meaning of Heb. uncertain.

Ps. 109: This individual petition has the expected structure: it opens with an invocation *(O God of my praise)*, followed by a petition in the imperative *(Do not keep aloof)*, and it contains a variety of motivations, reasons why this petition should be answered (esp. vv. 30–31). In other ways, however, it is unusual: the wording of the invocation is unique, and the center of the psalm, vv. 6–19, is a long vituperative curse of the enemies. The psalm, particularly this section, resembles the Mesopotamian "namburbi," lit. "untying," a type of prayer intended to undo a magical spell. It is thus noteworthy that vv. 2–4 emphasize the harmful words of the enemy (see 10.7 n.). **1:** The unique invocation, *O God of my praise,* here functions as a motivation, alluding to the psalm's conclusion (vv. 30–31): God must save the supplicant so He will continue to be praised (see 6.6). *Do not keep aloof,* lit. "do not be silent," fitting the psalm's context of evil words. **2–5:** The complaint focuses on the evil words rather than the actions of the enemies; for this reason, many scholars posit that here and elsewhere the enemies are magicians. **6–20:** Although other psalms have short and powerful curses (see esp. 139.9), this is by far the longest curse in the Psalter. Some scholars understand this to be the curse of the enemy, and understand v. 20 as a declarative statement, rather than a wish: "This is the action of my accusers." The curses themselves are rather typical of the Bible and the ancient Near East. **6:** *Accuser,* Heb "satan," which later came to mean the Satan. **14:** An allusion to intergenerational punishment; see Exod. 34.7 and 2 Sam. 12.13–14.

16: Concern for the *poor and needy man* is a major concern of the Psalter. **21–29:** This section, marked off from what precedes by *Now You, O God,* highlights the reasons that God should respond positively. The psalmist does not claim to be innocent (contrast, e.g., Pss. 7; 17), but offers a wide variety of arguments meant to motivate God. These are all found elsewhere in Psalms and in other biblical literature: God should act for the sake of his *name* (v. 21; see 23.3 n.), for his "ḥesed" (vv. 21, 26; see 5.8 n.), because of the supplicant's lowly status (v. 22; see also v. 16) and pain (vv. 23–24), and so that the enemies will appreciate God's power (v. 27; see, e.g., 1 Sam. 17.46; 2 Kings 19.19; Isa. 41.20). **28:** Curses are not self-effectuating, but are affected by God, who can subvert them (see Deut. 23.6). **30–31:** A final reason why God should save this *needy* person: so He will be praised. This type of argument concludes the individual petitions 7.18 and 52.11 as well.

Ps. 110: A royal psalm (see Ps. 2 intro.). It is quite difficult because v. 3 is totally obscure, and the psalm changes speakers often. In Christian interpretation, it is understood as a reference to Jesus, as a messianic and sometimes eschatological psalm; Radak polemicizes against this view. **1:** Here, God is speaking to the king, called *my lord;* perhaps these are the words spoken by a prophet. The king is very proximate to God, in a position of privilege, imagined as being on His right in the divine council. (The second-in-command was seated to the right of the king in the ancient Near East.) Such images are rare in Psalms, but see 45.7 n. If the king trods on the back of his *enemies* (see Josh. 10.24), they poetically become his *footstool.* **2:** In contrast to v. 1, God is spoken of in the third person. The Zion tradition (see Isa. 2.1–4; 60.1–22) and royal tradition are here connected. While vv. 1–2 express the great power of the king, they also emphasize that it comes from God.

16 because he was not minded to act kindly,
and hounded to death the poor and needy man,
one crushed in spirit.
17 He loved to curse—may a curse come upon him!
He would not bless—may blessing be far from him!
18 May he be clothed in a curse like a garment,
may it enter his body like water,
his bones like oil.
19 Let it be like the cloak he wraps around him,
like the belt he always wears.
20 May the LORD thus repay my accusers,
all those who speak evil against me.

21 Now You, O GOD, my Lord,
act on my behalf as befits Your name.
Good and faithful as You are, save me.
22 For I am poor and needy,
and my heart is pierced within me.
23 I fade away like a lengthening shadow;
I am shaken off like locusts.
24 My knees give way from fasting;
my flesh is lean, has lost its fat.
25 I am the object of their scorn;
when they see me, they shake their head.
26 Help me, O LORD, my God;
save me in accord with Your faithfulness,
27 that men may know that it is Your hand,
that You, O LORD, have done it.
28 Let them curse, but You bless;
let them rise up, but come to grief,
while Your servant rejoices.
29 My accusers shall be clothed in shame,
wrapped in their disgrace as in a robe.

30 My mouth shall sing much praise to the LORD;
I will acclaim Him in the midst of a throng,
31 because He stands at the right hand of the needy,
to save him from those who would condemn him.

110

Of David. A psalm.

The LORD said to my lord,
"Sit at My right hand
while I make your enemies your footstool."
2 The LORD will stretch forth from Zion your mighty scepter;
hold sway over your enemies!

3 [a]Your people come forward willingly on your day of battle.
In majestic holiness, from the womb,
from the dawn, yours was the dew of youth.[a]

4 The LORD has sworn and will not relent,
"You are a priest forever, [b]a rightful king by My decree."[b]
5 The Lord is at your right hand.
He crushes kings in the day of His anger.

6 He works judgment upon the nations,
heaping up bodies,
crushing heads far and wide.
7 He drinks from the stream on his way;
therefore he holds his head high.

111

Hallelujah.
א I praise the LORD with all my heart
ב in the assembled congregation of the upright.
2 ג The works of the LORD are great,
ד [a]within reach of all who desire them.[a]
3 ה His deeds are splendid and glorious;
ו His beneficence is everlasting;
4 ז He has won renown for His wonders.
ח The LORD is gracious and compassionate;

a-a Meaning of Heb. uncertain. *b-b Or "after the manner of Melchizedek."*

3: Though extremely obscure and likely corrupt, this v., like 2.7, may refer to the king as the child of God. Some find in *the dawn,* Heb "shaḥar," a reference to the deity Shaḥar known from Ugarit and elsewhere, also the morning star (thus *dawn*). **4:** A second divine quotation, mirroring v. 1; this, however, is likely a citation of an old oracle; note 1 Sam. 15.11, where God repents that he made Saul king. David and Solomon often perform priestly roles (e.g., 2 Sam. 6.14; 1 Kings ch 8), and 2 Sam. 8.18 concludes: "David's sons were priests." The translation of the second half of the v. (see translators' note) depends on whether "malki-tzedek" is understood as two common nouns *(a rightful king)* or a personal name (Melchizedek). If the latter is correct, this is likely an allusion to Gen. 14.18: "And King Melchizedek of Salem [most likely an abbreviated form of Jerusalem] brought out bread and wine; he was a priest of God Most High." (This v. influences some classical rabbis [*b. Ned.* 32b], followed by Rashi, to interpret this psalm in relation to Abraham.) Melchizedek, having the double role of priest and king at Jerusalem, is seen as offering precedent for the similar roles of Davidic kings. Melchizedek played a significant role in a Dead Sea Scroll and in early Jewish and Christian literature, and it is likely that a variety of stories no longer preserved in the Bible circulated about him in the biblical period. **5:** *The Lord is at your right hand,* a reversal of places with v. 1. Here the idea is that God stands ready to assist the king, or, more specifically, is the king's weapon (the right hand held the weapon); cf. 16.8; 18.36; 109.31. **7:** Perhaps this reflects part of the coronation ritual, held near the Gihon Spring (1 Kings 1.38–40); alternately, it refers to the king and army drinking water from faraway streams, a practice often mentioned in Mesopotamian royal inscriptions. In the words of Ibn Ezra: "The enemies were so afraid of them because when they went along the roads they would drink from their streams, and they were powerless to stop them." Holding one's *head high* is a symbol of triumph, the opposite of being a footstool (v. 1).

Ps. 111: This is the first of two acrostic psalms introduced by "Hallelujah," comprised of similary structured short lines that often quote traditional expressions (see some examples below), and containing wisdom ideas. Stylistically, the two are so similar that they have been characterized as "twins." It is likely that 111 was composed first and was used as a model by the author of 112. The two psalms are of different genres and have different foci. In the words of Rashi (to 111.1): "The first tells of the praise of God [i.e., it is a hymn], while the second tells of the praise of the righteous individual." V. 1 suggests that Ps. 111 was a hymn recited publicly, *in the assembled congregation of the upright,* though the identity of this group is unknown. God's wonders are at first expressed in the most general terms, but as the psalm progresses it becomes clear that God's works refer to His just laws (v. 7). **1:** Cf. Ps. 9.2: "I will praise You, LORD, with all my heart." **3:** *Splendid and glorious* are a frequent pair concerning God (e.g., 96.6). *His beneficence is everlasting* is a refrain joining Pss. 111–112 (see 112.3, 9). **4:** *Gracious and compassionate* are a common pair of divine epithets; see Exod. 34.6 (in the opposite order). The word order here is common in late texts (e.g., Neh. 9.17). The beginning of the v. might also be rendered "He fashioned a remembrance for his wonders," referring to the Torah.

5 ט He gives food to those who fear Him;
י He is ever mindful of His covenant.
6 כ He revealed to His people His powerful works,
ל in giving them the heritage of nations.
7 מ His handiwork is truth and justice;
נ all His precepts are enduring,
8 ס well-founded for all eternity,
ע wrought of truth and equity.
9 פ He sent redemption to His people;
צ He ordained His covenant for all time;
ק His name is holy and awesome.
10 ר The beginning[a] of wisdom is the fear of the LORD;
ש all who practice it gain sound understanding.
ת Praise of Him is everlasting.

112

Hallelujah.
א Happy is the man who fears the LORD,
ב who is ardently devoted to His commandments.
2 ג His descendants will be mighty in the land,
ד a blessed generation of upright men.
3 ה Wealth and riches are in his house,
ו and his beneficence lasts forever.
4 ז [b-]A light shines[-b] for the upright in the darkness;
ח he is gracious, compassionate, and beneficent.
5 ט All goes well with the man who lends generously,
י who conducts his affairs with equity.
6 כ He shall never be shaken;
ל the beneficent man will be remembered forever.
7 מ He is not afraid of evil tidings;
נ his heart is firm, he trusts in the LORD.
8 ס His heart is resolute, he is unafraid;
ע in the end he will see the fall of his foes.
9 פ He gives freely to the poor;
צ his beneficence lasts forever;
ק his horn is exalted in honor.
10 ר The wicked man shall see it and be vexed;
ש he shall gnash his teeth; his courage shall fail.
ת The desire of the wicked shall come to nothing.

113

Hallelujah.
O servants of the LORD, give praise;
praise the name of the LORD.
2 Let the name of the LORD be blessed
now and forever.

a Or "chief part." *b-b Or "He shines as a light."*

5: Such an eternal *covenant* (see also v. 9) typifies Priestly thinking (see Gen. 17.7) and is found elsewhere in Psalms (105.8, 10). **7:** *His precepts,* as found in the Torah. **9:** *His covenant,* here a name for the Torah. *Holy and awesome* are found in the opposite order in 99.3. **10:** See Prov. 1.7: "The fear of the LORD is the beginning of knowledge"; this line is picked up in the following psalm, which focuses on the righteous individual. *Sound understanding* ("sekhel tov"), a wisdom phrase, is in the Heb of Prov. 3.4 and 13.15.

Ps. 112: A didactic poem, actually more of a catalogue, about the righteous man; see the intro. to Ps. 111. The poem's subject, the "tzadik," the "righteous" or *beneficent man,* appears at the center of the poem in v. 6. The psalm is a derivative of Ps. 111. **1:** Compare the opening of Ps. 1, and esp. 128.1, "Happy are all who fear the LORD." The fear of the LORD is a major wisdom theme in Prov.; see Prov. 1.7. **2–4:** These vv. outline the wide-ranging recompense of the righteous man. **3:** *Wealth* is a major concern of wisdom literature. *And his beneficence lasts forever* (see also v. 6) quotes Ps. 111 (see v. 3); this refrain equates God's and the righteous man's *beneficence.* **4:** On *he is gracious, compassionate,* see 111.4 n. In 112, however, these clauses are abrupt, suggesting that they are copied from the previous psalm. **5:** Lending generously is a major theme of wisdom literature. **6:** Compare the conclusion of the catalogue of qualities of the individual who may enter the Temple precincts in 15.5: "The man who acts thus shall never be shaken." **7:** *His heart is firm,* see 57.8 and 108.2. **10:** Like Ps. 1, the depiction of the righteous gains force through comparison with *the wicked,* though here even less attention is given to the wicked than in Ps. 1. This v. in particular is based on other sources; see 37.12, "The wicked man schemes against the righteous, / and gnashes his teeth at him" and Prov. 10.28, "But the hope of the wicked is doomed" (the Heb of these vv. differs by one letter only). Radak's paraphrase clarifies this v.: "When the wicked sees the honor accorded to the righteous, he will be vexed from jealousy ... and if he had the power to kill him, he would."

3 From east to west
the name of the LORD is praised.
4 The LORD is exalted above all nations;
His glory is above the heavens.
5 Who is like the LORD our God,
who, enthroned on high,
6 sees what is below,
in heaven and on earth?
7 He raises the poor from the dust,
lifts up the needy from the refuse heap
8 to set them with the great,
with the great men of His people.
9 He sets the childless woman among her household
as a happy mother of children.
Hallelujah.

114
When Israel went forth from Egypt,
the house of Jacob from a people of strange speech,
2 Judah became His [a]holy one,[a]
Israel, His dominion.
3 The sea saw them and fled,
Jordan ran backward,
4 mountains skipped like rams,
hills like sheep.

a-a Or "sanctuary."

Pss. 113–118 are known in Jewish liturgy as the Egyptian Hallel, or just Hallel (praise), named for the reference to the exodus from Egypt in Ps. 114.1. The Egyptian Hallel is recited in the synagogue at the end of the morning service on the three pilgrimage festivals (Passover, Shavuʿot, Sukkot), and on Hanukkah, and it has been incorporated into the Passover Seder. In many synagogues it is also recited on Yom Haʿatzmaʾut, Israel Independence Day. Beginning with the second day of Passover, and on Rosh Ḥodesh (the new moon) the Half Hallel, omitting the first parts of Pss. 115 and 116, is recited. These psalms lack superscriptions and most, but not all, begin or end with *Hallelujah,* "Praise the LORD" (cf. also Pss. 111–112), but it is not certain that these were an ancient collection prior to the compilation of the Psalter. While praise for God is the dominant theme, other themes or genres of psalms are represented.

Ps. 113: Praise for God, who is exalted above all in the cosmos, should extend throughout the world because God is everywhere in the world. The psalm is pure praise; there is no hint of petition. It was perhaps recited antiphonally, at least in part. V. 1 calls on the worshippers to praise God; v. 2 may contain their response. Various word repetitions form a kind of echo throughout the psalm: *praise* (vv. 1, 3), *name of the LORD* (vv. 1, 2, 3), *heaven* (vv. 4, 6), *enthroned/sets* ("lashevet," v. 5; "lehoshiv," v. 8; "moshivi," v. 9), *exalted/lifts up* ("ram," v. 4; "yarim," v. 7). **1:** *Servants,* either a specific group in the Temple, or general worshippers. The idea of worshipping is serving God, as a servant serves a master. **2–3:** Praise for God at all times and in all places. **3:** *From east to west* (Heb "from sun's rising to setting"), globally. **4–6:** God is above the cosmos, above the sky, and looks down to see it. Cf. v. 6 and Ps. 18.10. **7–9:** The extremes on the vertical axis are brought together as God, the highest being imaginable, raises up the lowest human beings. Vv. 7–8 echo 1 Sam. 2.8 and v. 9 bears a resemblance to 1 Sam. 2.5. **7:** *Poor* and *needy* are terms often used of the psalmist's group, i.e., righteous Israelites, although in this instance the description may suggest the more literal meaning of those with low social status. *The refuse heap* is where the homeless live; cf. Lam. 4.5. **9:** Like the poor, a woman without children had no social standing. As the final climactic v., v. 9 may suggest that the psalm was recited by a previously childless woman after giving birth; this would also explain several similarities between the psalm and 1 Sam. 2.1–10.

Ps. 114: The exodus and its aftermath is celebrated not only as the liberation of Israel, but as an event through which all of nature came to see the power of God. The exodus is a cosmic theophany that alters the course of nature. The poem is structured on events involving water: the splitting of the sea, the crossing of the Jordan, and the supplying of water in the wilderness. The language suggests that this is a late psalm, and is commemorating the new exodus, namely the return from Babylonian exile. (See introductions to Pss. 77 and 78.) **1–2:** In v. 1, *Israel* is the entire nation, *the house of Jacob;* in v. 2, *Judah* and *Israel* refer to the Southern and Northern Kingdoms. **1:** *Strange speech,* ancient peoples were categorized not by race but by language; cf. Gen. ch 10. Foreignness is conveyed in similar, but not identical, terms in Deut. 28.49; Isa. 33.19; Jer. 5.15. **2:** *His holy one … His dominion:* The parallelism breaks up a single thought and distributes it over two lines; the meaning is that Judah and Israel are His holy dominion. Cf. Exod. 19.6; Jer. 2.3. **3–6:** The passage through the sea (Exod. 14.29) is paralleled by the crossing of the Jordan (Josh. 3.14–17), the beginning and end of the exodus. These waters are personified and their splitting is imagined as their flight from the awe of God. The *mountains* and *hills* hark

5 What alarmed you, O sea, that you fled,
Jordan, that you ran backward,
6 mountains, that you skipped like rams,
hills, like sheep?
7 Tremble, O earth, at the presence of the Lord,
at the presence of the God of Jacob,
8 who turned the rock into a pool of water,
the flinty rock into a fountain.

115 Not to us, O LORD, not to us
but to Your name bring glory
for the sake of Your love and Your faithfulness.
2 Let the nations not say,
"Where, now, is their God?"
3 when our God is in heaven
and all that He wills He accomplishes.
4*a* Their idols are silver and gold,
the work of men's hands.
5 They have mouths, but cannot speak,
eyes, but cannot see;
6 they have ears, but cannot hear,
noses, but cannot smell;
7 they have hands, but cannot touch,
feet, but cannot walk;
they can make no sound in their throats.
8 Those who fashion them,
all who trust in them,
shall become like them.
9 O Israel, trust in the LORD!
He is their help and shield.
10 O house of Aaron, trust in the LORD!
He is their help and shield.
11 O you who fear the LORD, trust in the LORD!
He is their help and shield.

12 The LORD is mindful of us.
He will bless us;
He will bless the house of Israel;
He will bless the house of Aaron;

a With vv. 4–11, cf. Ps. 135.15–20.

back to Mount Sinai (so Radak), but here the theophany takes on cosmic proportions. Compare the sea fleeing in terror from God (104.7), and the theophanous quaking of the earth (68.9; Judg. 5.4–5). **8:** Water in the desert (Exod. 17.6; Num. 20.11). On the cosmic level, God has power over all the material of the earth and can alter it as He wishes.

Ps. 115: The power of God is contrasted with the impotence of idols. Pss. 114–115 are written as one psalm in the LXX, the Aleppo Codex and the Leningrad Codex, and in R. Saadia Gaon's translation. Understood as one unit, Ps. 114 speaks of God's past acts of deliverance and Ps. 115 asks for God's help in the present. Yet the different style of the psalms suggest that they were not originally a single composition. **1:** God is not asked to do favors for Israel on account of their merit, but in order to glorify His name; a typical thought in Psalms. God's *love* ("ḥesed") and *faithfulness* to Israel are often connected in Psalms and elsewhere; they bring Him glory. **2:** *Let the nations not say,* Heb is phrased as a rhetorical question: "Why should the nations say." *Where, now, is their God?:* While Israel glorifies the divine name, the nations question God's effective Presence (42.4; Ezek. 36.22–32). **3–7:** The existence of Israel's God is contrasted with the gods of the nations. Israel's God dwells in the heavens (that is, He is real but invisible), while the nations' gods are not real at all but are visible as impotent representations. **4:** *Silver and gold,* elsewhere idols are called "wood and stone." The idol-worshippers adorned their idols with precious metals, making them into a valuable commodity; this is ironic mockery since the idols are worthless. *The work of men's hands,* the idols are no different from other objects of human manufacture; there is nothing divine about them. **5–7:** Unlike the God of Israel, who has no physical representation but can act in the world, the idols have physical features but cannot act. **8–9:** Those who make and worship idols will be as powerless as their idols (Deut. 4.28; 2 Kings 17.15); cf. Ps. 135.15–18. By contrast, Israel is urged to believe in the true God who has the power to help them. **10:** *House of Aaron,* the priestly leaders of the postexilic community. **11:** *You who fear the LORD,* possibly non-Jews who attached themselves to the Jewish community (cf. Ezra 6.21; Neh. 10.28; Rashi: "proselytes"). Some modern scholars think the LORD-fearers here refer to special champions of YHVH over all other gods; others suggest they were a subset of the priests (cf. 135.19–20). **12–13:** The same groups

13 He will bless those who fear the LORD,
small and great alike.

14 May the LORD increase your numbers,
yours and your children's also.
15 May you be blessed by the LORD,
Maker of heaven and earth.
16 The heavens belong to the LORD,
but the earth He gave over to man.
17 The dead cannot praise the LORD,
nor any who go down into silence.
18 But we will bless the LORD
now and forever.
Hallelujah.

116 [a-]I love the LORD
for He hears[-a] my voice, my pleas;
2 for He turns His ear to me
whenever I call.
3 The bonds of death encompassed me;
the torments of Sheol overtook me.
I came upon trouble and sorrow
4 and I invoked the name of the LORD,
"O LORD, save my life!"

5 The LORD is gracious and beneficent;
our God is compassionate.
6 The LORD protects the simple;
I was brought low and He saved me.
7 Be at rest, once again, O my soul,
for the LORD has been good to you.
8 You[b] have delivered me from death,
my eyes from tears,
my feet from stumbling.
9 I shall walk before the LORD
in the lands of the living.
10 [c-]I trust [in the LORD];
out of great suffering I spoke[-c]
11 and said rashly,
"All men are false."

12 How can I repay the LORD
for all His bounties to me?
13 I raise the cup of deliverance
and invoke the name of the LORD.

as noted in vv. 9–11. **14:** A blessing of prosperity and progeny. **15:** *Maker of heaven and earth,* the idols are made by people; God made the world. This is a late phrase, found in the Psalter only in Book V. **16–17:** The cosmos is envisioned as having three levels: heaven is the abode of God, earth is the domain God assigned to human beings, and Sheol, below the earth, is the realm of the dead. Those who *go down into silence* are the dead, for those in Sheol do not praise God. By implication, those who do not praise God, that is, the idolatrous nations, are like the dead. Israel, ever alive, continues its vocal praise of God (cf. 30.13).

Ps. 116: Thanksgiving for healing. A thanksgiving psalm of anthological character, quoting from other psalms (e.g., 18.2–7; 56.13–14). **1–4:** God has answered the psalmist's cry for help in the past, and now he calls on God's help again. **3:** *Sheol,* the abode of the dead. A common symbol for dire sickness or trouble. **5:** An echo of God's attributes in Exod. 34.6. **6–7:** Expressions of trust, characteristic of laments and thanksgivings. The psalmist is here self-identifying as a *simple* person, whom God should save. **8–9:** To remain alive is to have the opportunity to be in God's Presence; the dead are cut off from God. See 56.14. **12–14:** The psalmist vows a public thanksgiving offering if God will help him. **13:** *Cup of deliverance,* a libation celebrating the psalmist's deliverance. This may be taken literally, as referring to the libation accompanying the thanksgiving offering, or metaphorically, as a kind of "toast" to God invoking His name to publicize His great deeds. Just as the psalmist invoked God's name when asking for His help (v. 4), he invokes His name when offering thanks.

a-a Heb. transposed for clarity; others "I would love that the LORD hear," etc.
b I.e., God. *c-c Meaning of Heb. uncertain.*

14 I will pay my vows to the LORD
in the presence of all His people.
15 The death of His faithful ones
is grievous in the LORD's sight.

16 O LORD,
I am Your servant,
Your servant, the son of Your maidservant;
You have undone the cords that bound me.
17 I will sacrifice a thank offering to You
and invoke the name of the LORD.
18 I will pay my vows to the LORD
in the presence of all His people,
19 in the courts of the house of the LORD,
in the midst of[a] Jerusalem.
Hallelujah.

117

Praise the LORD, all you nations;
extol Him, all you peoples,
2 for great is His steadfast love toward us;
the faithfulness of the LORD endures forever.
Hallelujah.

118

Praise the LORD, for He is good,
His steadfast love is eternal.
2 Let Israel declare,
"His steadfast love is eternal."
3 Let the house of Aaron declare,
"His steadfast love is eternal."
4 Let those who fear the LORD declare,
"His steadfast love is eternal."

5 In distress I called on the LORD;
the LORD answered me and brought me relief.
6 The LORD is on my side,
I have no fear;
what can man do to me?

a Others "of you."

14: The vow made in time of trouble was not fulfilled earlier but can now be paid (cf. Jonah 2.10) in an exaggerated fashion, before *all.* This use mimics *all His bounties* (v. 12); the psalmist cannot truly repay God for everything, and the thank offering (v. 17) is a token of this payment. **15:** *Grievous,* Heb "yakar," "precious," is difficult but is traditionally interpreted as here. As Radak says, "Their blood is precious in his sight" (72.14). The v. is best taken as a rhetorical question: God does not wish His adherents to die; therefore, the psalmist is reassured that God will keep him alive. **16:** *Servant ... maidservant,* an epithet of extreme humility; see 86.16. *Cords that bound me,* perhaps a reference to an illness; or a general description of being constricted, being in trouble. Cf. the similar *bonds of death* (v. 3). **17–19:** The *thank offering* will be offered in the Temple in Jerusalem. **18:** Repeating v. 14, creating a mini-refrain.

Ps. 117: The shortest psalm in the Psalter, calling on all the nations to praise God (Pss. 67; 100). **2:** God's *steadfast love* and *faithfulness* (the same terms as in 115.1) to Israel are divine attributes—what gives God His special identity in the world—and are worthy of universal praise. God is not expected to work on behalf of other nations, but only on behalf of Israel. *For great ... toward us:* Heb "gavar 'alenu," "prevailed over us" in the sense that God's faithfulness to Israel is manifest in His heroic acts ("gevurah"), which usually refers to His saving Israel from its enemies. There is a certain irony in universal praise deriving from God's particularistic acts. Radak, who sees this psalm as applying to the future, at the time of the coming of the messiah, explains that the other nations will feel compelled to praise God when He frees Israel from their control, in recognition of God's fidelity to Israel throughout the long period of the Diaspora.

Ps. 118: The mention of the nations and the battle imagery (vv. 10–16) suggest that this is a victory song, possibly reformulated to celebrate the return from exile and the rebuilding of the Temple. The psalm gives the impression that it was recited in a ceremony upon entering the Temple. It is anthological (like Pss. 116 and 135) with numerous quotations of other texts. **1–4:** Praise from Israel, the Aaronic priesthood, and the LORD-fearers (possibly proselytes); see 115.9–11. V. 1 may be formulaic; see 1 Chron. 16.34. **5:** *Distress,* lit. a narrow, constricted space; correspondingly, a *relief,* Heb "a broad space," connotes deliverance, release (4.2; 18.20). **6–8:** No human can harm the psalmist as long as God is on his side; conversely, no human is as reliable as God. **6:** See 56.5, 12.

7 With the LORD on my side as my helper,
I will see the downfall of my foes.

8 It is better to take refuge in the LORD
than to trust in mortals;
9 it is better to take refuge in the LORD
than to trust in the great.

10 All nations have beset me;
by the name of the LORD I will surely [a-]cut them
down.[-a]
11 They beset me, they surround me;
by the name of the LORD I will surely cut them
down.
12 They have beset me like bees;
they shall be extinguished like burning thorns;
by the name of the LORD I will surely cut them
down.

13 You[b] pressed me hard,
I nearly fell;
but the LORD helped me.
14 The LORD is my strength and might;[c]
He has become my deliverance.
15 The tents of the victorious[d] resound with joyous shouts
of deliverance,
"The right hand of the LORD is triumphant!
16 The right hand of the LORD is exalted!
The right hand of the LORD is triumphant!"

17 I shall not die but live
and proclaim the works of the LORD.
18 The LORD punished me severely,
but did not hand me over to death.

19 Open the gates of victory[e] for me
that I may enter them and praise the LORD.
20 This is the gateway to the LORD—
the victorious[d] shall enter through it.

21 I praise You, for You have answered me,
and have become my deliverance.
22 The stone that the builders rejected
has become the chief cornerstone.

8–9: See 146.3. **10–13:** The attack of the nations, cf. v. 7; the one praying is perhaps a kingly persona, or the psalmist on behalf of the nation. **10–12:** The four-fold repetition of *beset* and *surround* (the same word in Heb) emphasizes the grave nature of the former disaster, and may suggest a siege. Military imagery recurs in v. 15, *tents of the victorious.* The enemy swarms around the psalmist *like bees,* numerous and about to attack. Note the involvement of sound in the buzzing bees and the crackling thorns. **12:** *Thorns* are easily consumed by fire. **14–16:** A quotation of Exod. 15.2, 6; cf. Isa. 12.2. **16:** *The right hand* with which God defends Israel against the enemy. **19–20:** An allusion to entrance rituals whereby the righteous gain admittance to the Temple (Pss. 15; 24.3–6). **22:** A metaphor of reversal of expectations (cf. 113.7–9); once rejected, Israel is now the keystone. The architectural imagery links with *gates* and *gateway* in vv. 19–20.

a-a Meaning of 'amilam *in this and the following two verses uncertain.*
b I.e., the enemy. *c Others "song."* *d Or "righteous."*
e Or "righteousness."

23 This is the LORD's doing;
it is marvelous in our sight.
24 This is the day that the LORD has made—
let us exult and rejoice on it.

25 O LORD, deliver us!
O LORD, let us prosper!

26 May he who enters be blessed in the name of the LORD;
we bless you from the House of the LORD.
27 The LORD is God;
He has given us light;
[a]bind the festal offering to the horns of the altar with cords.[-a]
28 You are my God and I will praise You;
You are my God and I will extol You.
29 Praise the LORD for He is good,
His steadfast love is eternal.

119

א Happy are those whose way is blameless,
who follow the teaching of the LORD.
2 Happy are those who observe His decrees,
who turn to Him wholeheartedly.
3 They have done no wrong,
but have followed His ways.
4 You have commanded that Your precepts
be kept diligently.
5 Would that my ways were firm
in keeping Your laws;
6 then I would not be ashamed
when I regard all Your commandments.
7 I will praise You with a sincere heart
as I learn Your just rules.
8 I will keep Your laws;
do not utterly forsake me.

a-a Meaning of Heb. uncertain.

23–28: A thanksgiving ritual in the Temple amid the psalmist's friends and family (*us ... we* in vv. 23–26). The shift to first-person plural suggests that vv. 23–27 may have been recited by all those assembled. Certainly vv. 25–26 sound like public proclamations. **24:** *The day,* a play on the notion of the day of the LORD, a technical term, especially in prophetic literature, for when God comes and fights on Israel's behalf (see e.g., Isa. 13.6, 9). **27:** *Bind the festal ...,* likely the instructions for a ritual accompanying the sacrifice that entered the text of the psalm. **29:** This v. forms a frame or inclusio with v. 1. The second part of the v., or perhaps the entire v., was recited by the congregation. Cf. 136.1.

Ps. 119: This is the longest psalm, indeed the longest ch in the Bible. It is comprised of an eight-fold alphabetic acrostic. Comparable to it is an Akkadian text, the "Babylonian Theodicy," an eleven-fold acrostic of 297 lines, not alphabetic—Akkadian had no alphabet—but spelling out the author's name and occupation. Many earlier critical scholars considered this psalm monotonous and devalued its emphasis on "law." More recently, the skill of the poet in composing this tour de force has been appreciated. For example, there are eight main words used for "torah" (their English translations include: *word, laws, commandments, rules, decrees, precepts, teaching*), corresponding to the eight-fold acrostic; approximately 176 of these synonyms for Torah are found in the 176 vv. of the psalm (noted as early as Ibn Ezra and Radak). Why the author chose eight, rather than a more common number like seven, is unknown. It is difficult to know exactly how to translate "torah" and its synonyms in this psalm. The psalm is postexilic (even Ibn Ezra hints that it is non-Davidic in authorship), and certainly may know a canonized Torah; on the other hand, it is closely connected to wisdom texts, where "torah" often means the teaching of the wise (see, e.g., Prov. 28.7, "An intelligent son heeds instruction ['torah']"). Neither of these understandings of "torah" quite fits: the origin of torah in the psalm is clearly with God, yet it does not come from Sinai, and Moses as intermediary is never explicitly mentioned (though see 103.9–13 n.).

The psalm is often seen as anthological, i.e., quoting earlier vv. (see Pss. 111–112), especially from Isa., Jer., Prov., and Job. In echoing Torah texts and ideas, it is much closer to Deut. than to the Priestly tradition, yet certain core ideas of Deut.—the centrality of Moses, the Torah as a book, and covenant—are lacking. It also shows certain affinities to the nonbiblical wisdom book of Ben Sirach.

The psalmist's depiction of "torah" is unique and verges on the mystical. He *clings* ("d-bk") to it—a very strong term, often with sexual

9 ב How can a young man keep his way pure?—
by holding to Your word.
10 I have turned to You with all my heart;
do not let me stray from Your commandments.
11 In my heart I treasure Your promise;
therefore I do not sin against You.
12 Blessed are You, O LORD;
train me in Your laws.
13 With my lips I rehearse
all the rules You proclaimed.
14 I rejoice over the way of Your decrees
as over all riches.
15 I study Your precepts;
I regard Your ways;
16 I take delight in Your laws;
I will not neglect Your word.

17 ג Deal kindly with Your servant,
that I may live to keep Your word.
18 Open my eyes, that I may perceive
the wonders of Your teaching.
19 I am only a sojourner in the land;
do not hide Your commandments from me.
20 My soul is consumed with longing
for Your rules at all times.
21 You blast the accursed insolent ones
who stray from Your commandments.
22 Take away from me taunt and abuse,
because I observe Your decrees.
23 Though princes meet and speak against me,
Your servant studies Your laws.
24 For Your decrees are my delight,
my intimate companions.

25 ד My soul clings to the dust;
revive me in accordance with Your word.
26 I have declared my way, and You have answered me;
train me in Your laws.
27 Make me understand the way of Your precepts,
that I may study Your wondrous acts.

connotations (see, e.g., Gen. 2.24; 34.3, and compare the later Jewish conception of "devekut," "clinging" to God). What is most remarkable is that a close relationship to Torah replaces a close relationship with God, and that in general, "torah" as a manifestation of the deity supplants God. For example, the "torah" rather than God is the source of life (vv. 50, 93). In Ps. 18.29 and its parallel in 2 Sam. 22.29, God is the psalmist's "light" ("ner"), but in v. 105, "Your word is a lamp to my feet, a light for my path." God's "deliverance" is not understood as coming from divine intervention to save the psalmist, but from God's words (v. 123): "My eyes pine away for Your deliverance, for Your righteous words" (author's translation). Other examples of this transformation from God to "torah" are noted below. V. 135 captures the psalm's unique and innovative understanding of Torah. Like the priestly blessing (Num. 6.25), it is interested in having God shine His face, but this is expressed not through God's shining face, but through Torah (v. 135): "Show favor to Your servant [lit. "shine Your Face upon Your servant"], and teach me Your laws." The psalm thus expresses a worldview in which God is distant, and most manifest to Jews through His Torah, a view that informed much of later Judaism.

The celebration of "torah" ends with a final stanza in which the psalmist petitions to be granted understanding of the very "torah" that he has been extolling throughout the poem. Though they predominate at the end, petitionary elements are interspersed throughout the psalm (vv. 8, 10, 17, etc.), which from a formal perspective should be considered a petitionary psalm. **1:** *Happy are,* common in Psalms, is sometimes used to open a psalm (e.g., 1; 41; 112). It declares the blameless to be in a fortunate state. **4:** The absence of Sinai in this context is striking. **8:** The plea *do not ... forsake me* typifies individual petitions (27.9; 38.22; 71.9, 18). **12:** The formula *Blessed are You, O LORD,* a postexilic phrase (see 1 Chron. 29.10), is later expanded with "our God, king of the universe" to become the standard rabbinic blessing formula. **14:** Comparison of wisdom or "torah" to riches typifies wisdom literature (cf. v. 72). In this psalm, joy rather than fear typifies torah observance. **19:** In contrast to the conventional request that God not hide His face (see Ps. 10.1 n.), the psalmist requests *do not hide Your commandments from me.* **25:** Another element typifying laments.

28 I am racked with grief;
sustain me in accordance with Your word.
29 Remove all false ways from me;
favor me with Your teaching.
30 I have chosen the way of faithfulness;
I have set Your rules before me.
31 I cling to Your decrees;
O LORD, do not put me to shame.
32 I eagerly pursue Your commandments,
for You broaden my understanding.

33 ה Teach me, O LORD, the way of Your laws;
I will observe them [a]-to the utmost.-[a]
34 Give me understanding, that I may observe Your teaching
and keep it wholeheartedly.
35 Lead me in the path of Your commandments,
for that is my concern.
36 Turn my heart to Your decrees
and not to love of gain.
37 Avert my eyes from seeing falsehood;
by Your ways preserve me.
38 Fulfill Your promise to Your servant,
which is for those who worship You.
39 Remove the taunt that I dread,
for Your rules are good.
40 See, I have longed for Your precepts;
by Your righteousness preserve me.

41 ו May Your steadfast love reach me, O LORD,
Your deliverance, as You have promised.
42 I shall have an answer for those who taunt me,
for I have put my trust in Your word.
43 Do not utterly take the truth away from my mouth,
for I have put my hope in Your rules.
44 I will always obey Your teaching,
forever and ever.
45 I will walk about at ease,
for I have turned to Your precepts.
46 I will speak of Your decrees,
and not be ashamed in the presence of kings.
47 I will delight in Your commandments,
which I love.
48 I reach out for Your commandments, which I love;
I study Your laws.

a-a Meaning of Heb. uncertain.

30: Compare *I have set Your rules before me* ("shiviti") with the more typical "I am ever mindful ("shiviti") of the LORD's presence" (16.8). **32:** *Pursu*ing the *commandments* replaces pursuing (lit. "running after") God (Ps. 18.30). **33:** *Teach me, O LORD, the way of Your laws* is a revision of 27.11: "Show me Your way, O LORD," and 86.11. Once again, God is replaced by His laws. **39:** God's *rules,* rather than God, are *good.* **45:** God's commandments are not restrictive, but allow the individual to *walk about at ease,* lit "in a broad place." **48:** Lit. "I will stretch out my palms," an allusion to the prayer position of outstretched arms to God (see 44.21–22 n.), but here God has been replaced by *commandments.*

49 ז Remember Your word to Your servant
through which You have given me hope.
50 This is my comfort in my affliction,
that Your promise has preserved me.
51 Though the arrogant have cruelly mocked me,
I have not swerved from Your teaching.
52 I remember Your rules of old, O LORD,
and find comfort in them.
53 I am seized with rage
because of the wicked who forsake Your teaching.
54 Your laws are [a]a source of strength to me[a]
wherever I may dwell.
55 I remember Your name at night, O LORD,
and obey Your teaching.
56 This has been my lot,
for I have observed Your precepts.

57 ח The LORD is my portion;
I have resolved to keep Your words.
58 I have implored You with all my heart;
have mercy on me, in accordance with Your
promise.
59 I have considered my ways,
and have turned back to Your decrees.
60 I have hurried and not delayed
to keep Your commandments.
61 Though the bonds of the wicked are coiled
round me,
I have not neglected Your teaching.
62 I arise at midnight to praise You
for Your just rules.
63 I am a companion to all who fear You,
to those who keep Your precepts.
64 Your steadfast love, O LORD, fills the earth;
teach me Your laws.

65 ט You have treated Your servant well,
according to Your word, O LORD.
66 Teach me good sense and knowledge,
for I have put my trust in Your commandments.
67 Before I was humbled I went astray,
but now I keep Your word.
68 You are good and beneficent;
teach me Your laws.
69 Though the arrogant have accused me falsely,
I observe Your precepts wholeheartedly.

52: Again, rules replace God; compare 77.4: "I call God to mind (z-kr)." **53:** Unlike most of Psalms, which does not imagine a single book that tells individuals what God's norms are, here the *wicked* are defined as those *who forsake Your teaching* (torah). **62:** The mystical custom of offering special prayers at midnight ("tikun ḥatzot") derives from this v. **68:** God's goodness and beneficence are not expressed through His compassion, as elsewhere (e.g., 145.9), but through *teach*ing of *laws.* **69:** False accusations typify petitions.

a-a Or "songs for me."

71: On the positive value of rebuke by God, see Prov. 3.12. **72:** Comparison to *gold and silver* typify wisdom literature (e.g., Prov. 22.1). The order "silver and gold" is more common in earlier biblical books, while *gold and silver* is often found in later texts (cf. 2 Sam. 8.10 and 1 Chron. 18.10). **75:** The emphasis is on *just rulings,* rather than on a just God. **80:** Not coming to *grief* (or "shame") is a frequent focus of petitions (see e.g., Ps. 6). **81:** Hoping or longing ("y-ḥ-l") for God's *word* (see also vv. 43, 81, 114, 147) rather than for God (e.g., 31.25; 38.16) typifies the psalmist's attitude. **84–88:** Typical themes concerning *persecutors* from the individual petition are mixed with praise for the "torah." **88:** The psalmist invokes God's *steadfast love* ("ḥesed"), a frequent motif of the Psalter. **89:** God's eternal existence is compared to the eternal existence of His *word.*

70 Their minds are thick like fat;
as for me, Your teaching is my delight.
71 It was good for me that I was humbled,
so that I might learn Your laws.
72 I prefer the teaching You proclaimed
to thousands of gold and silver pieces.

73 י Your hands made me and fashioned me;
give me understanding that I may learn Your
commandments.
74 Those who fear You will see me and rejoice,
for I have put my hope in Your word.
75 I know, O LORD, that Your rulings are just;
rightly have You humbled me.
76 May Your steadfast love comfort me
in accordance with Your promise to Your servant.
77 May Your mercy reach me, that I might live,
for Your teaching is my delight.
78 Let the insolent be dismayed, for they have wronged
me without cause;
I will study Your precepts.
79 May those who fear You,
those who know Your decrees,
turn again to me.
80 May I wholeheartedly follow Your laws
so that I do not come to grief.

81 כ I long for Your deliverance;
I hope for Your word.
82 My eyes pine away for Your promise;
I say, "When will You comfort me?"
83 Though I have become like a water-skin dried in smoke,
I have not neglected Your laws.
84 How long has Your servant to live?
when will You bring my persecutors to judgment?
85 The insolent have dug pits for me,
flouting Your teaching.
86 All Your commandments are enduring;
I am persecuted without cause; help me!
87 Though they almost wiped me off the earth,
I did not abandon Your precepts.
88 As befits Your steadfast love, preserve me,
so that I may keep the decree You proclaimed.

89 ל The LORD exists forever;
Your word stands firm in heaven.
90 Your faithfulness is for all generations;
You have established the earth, and it stands.

91 They stand this day to [carry out] Your rulings,
for all are Your servants.
92 Were not Your teaching my delight
I would have perished in my affliction.
93 I will never neglect Your precepts,
for You have preserved my life through them.
94 I am Yours; save me!
For I have turned to Your precepts.
95 The wicked hope to destroy me,
but I ponder Your decrees.
96 I have seen that all things have their limit,
but Your commandment is broad beyond measure.

97 מ O how I love Your teaching!
It is my study all day long.
98 Your commandments make me wiser than my enemies;
they always stand by me.
99 I have gained more insight than all my teachers,
for Your decrees are my study.
100 I have gained more understanding than my elders,
for I observe Your precepts.
101 I have avoided every evil way
so that I may keep Your word.
102 I have not departed from Your rules,
for You have instructed me.
103 How pleasing is Your word to my palate,
sweeter than honey.
104 I ponder Your precepts;
therefore I hate every false way.

105 נ Your word is a lamp to my feet,
a light for my path.
106 I have firmly sworn
to keep Your just rules.
107 I am very much afflicted;
O LORD, preserve me in accordance with Your word.
108 Accept, O LORD, my freewill offerings;
teach me Your rules.
109 Though my life is always in danger,
I do not neglect Your teaching.
110 Though the wicked have set a trap for me,
I have not strayed from Your precepts.
111 Your decrees are my eternal heritage;
they are my heart's delight.
112 I am resolved to follow Your laws
[a]to the utmost[a] forever.

94: This expresses the essence of the psalm's theology: Devotion to God is expressed by following his *precepts. Save me!,* typified petitions in the Psalter. **97:** The Deuteronomic ideal of loving God (e.g., Deut. 6.5) is replaced by loving His *teaching.* **99–100:** He is wisest since, unlike his teachers, only divine teaching, as opposed to secular wisdom, is his guide. **105:** Compare 2 Sam. 22.29, where God is a lamp ("ner"). **110:** *Traps* are mentioned elsewhere in personal petitions (e.g., 140.6).

a-a Meaning of Heb. uncertain.

115: Compare the petition in 6.9. **117:** In contrast to those who bless God always (34.2), or always hope for Him (71.14), this psalmist *will always muse upon Your laws.* **126:** In postbiblical legal literature, this v. is decontextualized and translated as "When it is time to act for the LORD, you may abrogate the Torah," in other words in extremis, one may violate a precept to preserve the Torah as a whole. **132:** Another typical element of petitions (see e.g., 25.16).

113 ס I hate men of divided heart,
but I love Your teaching.
114 You are my protection and my shield;
I hope for Your word.
115 Keep away from me, you evildoers,
that I may observe the commandments of
my God.
116 Support me as You promised, so that I may live;
do not thwart my expectation.
117 Sustain me that I may be saved,
and I will always muse upon Your laws.
118 You reject all who stray from Your laws,
for they are false and deceitful.
119 You do away with the wicked as if they were dross;
rightly do I love Your decrees.
120 My flesh creeps from fear of You;
I am in awe of Your rulings.

121 ע I have done what is just and right;
do not abandon me to those who would
wrong me.
122 Guarantee Your servant's well-being;
do not let the arrogant wrong me.
123 My eyes pine away for Your deliverance,
for Your promise of victory.
124 Deal with Your servant as befits Your steadfast love;
teach me Your laws.
125 I am Your servant;
give me understanding,
that I might know Your decrees.
126 It is a time to act for the LORD,
for they have violated Your teaching.
127 Rightly do I love Your commandments
more than gold, even fine gold.
128 Truly [a]by all [Your] precepts I walk straight;[a]
I hate every false way.

129 פ Your decrees are wondrous;
rightly do I observe them.
130 [b]The words You inscribed give[b] light,
and grant understanding to the simple.
131 I open my mouth wide, I pant,
longing for Your commandments.
132 Turn to me and be gracious to me,
as is Your rule with those who love Your name.

a-a *Or "I declare all [Your] precepts to be just."*
b-b *With Targum; or "The exposition of Your words gives"; meaning of Heb. uncertain.*

133 Make my feet firm through Your promise;
do not let iniquity dominate me.
134 Redeem me from being wronged by man,
that I may keep Your precepts.
135 Show favor to Your servant,
and teach me Your laws.
136 My eyes shed streams of water
because men do not obey Your teaching.

137 צ You are righteous, O LORD;
Your rulings are just.
138 You have ordained righteous decrees;
they are firmly enduring.
139 I am consumed with rage
over my foes' neglect of Your words.
140 Your word is exceedingly pure,
and Your servant loves it.
141 Though I am belittled and despised,
I have not neglected Your precepts.
142 Your righteousness is eternal;
Your teaching is true.
143 Though anguish and distress come upon me,
Your commandments are my delight.
144 Your righteous decrees are eternal;
give me understanding, that I might live.

145 ק I call with all my heart;
answer me, O LORD,
that I may observe Your laws.
146 I call upon You; save me,
that I may keep Your decrees.
147 I rise before dawn and cry for help;
I hope for Your word.
148 My eyes greet each watch of the night,
as I meditate on Your promise.
149 Hear my voice as befits Your steadfast love;
O LORD, preserve me, as is Your rule.
150 Those who pursue intrigue draw near;
they are far from Your teaching.
151 You, O LORD, are near,
and all Your commandments are true.
152 I know from Your decrees of old
that You have established them forever.

153 ר See my affliction and rescue me,
for I have not neglected Your teaching.
154 Champion my cause and redeem me;
preserve me according to Your promise.

135: See Num. 6.25. **136:** The same image is used about the destruction in 586 BCE (Lam. 3.48): "My eyes shed streams of water / Over the ruin of my poor people." "Torah" is thus equated with Temple, monarchy, and the land of Israel, all of which were lost in 586. **141:** It is doubtful that this can be taken literally, suggesting that the psalmist is young, as some have suggested; it is likely a formula of self-abasement (see Gen. 47.9). **146:** Contrast other individual petitions that plea for deliverance so *that* the supplicant may praise God (e.g., 57.10). **149:** *Hear my voice* is typical petition language (e.g., 28.9). **153:** Typical psalmic language; see 9.14; 25.18.

161–169: At least by late medieval times, the twenty-first letter of the alphabet was pronounced in two ways, distinguished by a dot over the left or right side of that letter ("sin" and "shin," pronounced "s" and "sh"). These two sounds are mixed in these vv., as in the biblical period this difference was not marked. **159:** Rather than asking God to *see* his affliction (e.g., 25.18), the psalmist asks Him to observe how he *loved Your precepts.* **163, 167:** As in v. 97, and elsewhere in this psalm, *love* of "torah" replaces love of God. **164:** *Seven* is a formulaic number expressing completeness. **169–176:** As noted, elements of the personal petition predominate here. **169:** The psalmist asks not for deliverance, but for *understanding.* He assumes that if he understands and follows God's torah, he will be rewarded with a good life. **175:** Consistent with the psalm's focus, the psalmist wishes that God's *rules* rather than God will be his *help.*

155 Deliverance is far from the wicked,
for they have not turned to Your laws.
156 Your mercies are great, O LORD;
as is Your rule, preserve me.
157 Many are my persecutors and foes;
I have not swerved from Your decrees.
158 I have seen traitors and loathed[a] them,
because they did not keep Your word in mind.
159 See that I have loved Your precepts;
O LORD, preserve me, as befits Your steadfast love.
160 Truth is the essence of Your word;
Your just rules are eternal.

161 ש Princes have persecuted me without reason;
my heart thrills at Your word.
162 I rejoice over Your promise
as one who obtains great spoil.
163 I hate and abhor falsehood;
I love Your teaching.
164 I praise You seven times each day
for Your just rules.
165 Those who love Your teaching enjoy well-being;
they encounter no adversity.
166 I hope for Your deliverance, O LORD;
I observe Your commandments.
167 I obey Your decrees
and love them greatly.
168 I obey Your precepts and decrees;
all my ways are before You.

169 ת May my plea reach You, O LORD;
grant me understanding according to Your word.
170 May my petition come before You;
save me in accordance with Your promise.
171 My lips shall pour forth praise,
for You teach me Your laws.
172 My tongue shall declare Your promise,
for all Your commandments are just.
173 Lend Your hand to help me,
for I have chosen Your precepts.
174 I have longed for Your deliverance, O LORD;
Your teaching is my delight.
175 Let me live, that I may praise You;
may Your rules be my help;

a Or *"have contended with."*

176 I have strayed like a lost sheep;
search for Your servant,
for I have not neglected Your commandments.

120 A song of ascents.[a]

In my distress I called to the LORD
and He answered me.
2 O LORD, save me from treacherous lips,
from a deceitful tongue!
3 What can you profit,
what can you gain,
O deceitful tongue?
4 A warrior's sharp arrows,
with hot coals of broom-wood.

a *A term of uncertain meaning.*

176: It is God's *commandments,* the embodiment of "torah," that must not be *neglected* or forgotten (sh-kḥ); contrast 44.18: "yet we have not forgotten (sh-kḥ) You."

Ps. 120: Pss. 120–134 all begin "A song of [or 'for'] ascents," forming the clearest collection of psalms in the Psalter; while other collections were included in the book, they are not found in a single block (see introductions to Pss. 42 and 50 on the Korahite and Asaphite psalms.), but are identified by common ascription or style. It is likely that these fifteen psalms already existed as a unit when they were incorporated into the Psalter (although the large Qumran Psalter, 11QPs[a], disconnected Pss. 133 and 134 from the first thirteen and located them elsewhere, not adjacent to each other). These short psalms are exilic or postexilic and speak to the issue of the return from exile, the re-establishment of the community in Judah, the centrality of Jerusalem, Zion, and the Temple, and the future of the Davidic dynasty. In this they resemble a number of other psalms, especially in Books IV and V, whose themes pertain to the main concerns of postexilic biblical literature, but these themes are more concentrated here. The terms *Jerusalem* and *Zion,* and also *Israel* (the people) occur frequently. There is a notable focus on blessings, esp. blessings of peace, on God's help, and a general attitude of hope for the future. The Songs of Ascents are, by and large, prayers for God's blessing on the people of Israel, blessings on or emanating from Jerusalem/Zion. Peace for Jerusalem and prosperity for the people are dominant themes. In the modern liturgical practice, Ashkenazic Jews recite the Songs of Ascents after minʿund'hah (the afternoon service) on the sabbaths between Sukkot and Passover, and on Tu Bshevat (the fifteenth day of the month of Shevat, when trees are planted).

The meaning of the superscription has been elusive from rabbinic times and remains so. Interpretations can be categorized as relating to (1) the poetic or musical structure or performance of the psalms, or (2) the place or occasion on which the psalms were recited. For example, Saadia Gaon suggested that "song of ascents" is the name of a particular melody "sung in a loud and high voice." He is followed by Ibn Ezra, and Radak. Several modern commentators have suggested that the "ascents" or "steps" refer to the verbal structure in which a word or phrase at the end of one verse is repeated near the beginning of the next, creating a kind of steppingstone from one verse to the next. The Midrash on Psalms takes "ascents" to mean the going up out of exile. Some modern scholars (apparently independently from the Midrash), basing themselves on Ezra 7.9 where the phrase "ascent ("maʿaleh") from Babylonia" is found, and on their own understanding of the psalms' contents, also see the occasion as the return from Babylonian exile. The Mishnah (*m. Sukk.* 5.4; *m. Mid.* 2.5) explains that these fifteen songs were sung by the Levites on the steps ("maʿalot") of the Temple, which, according to Ezek. 40.26, 31, numbered fifteen; one psalm for each step. A number of medieval Jewish commentaries share this view. The most widely held modern explanation is that these are pilgrimage psalms (so Radak). The 1st-century allegorist Philo understood them as expressing the ascent of the individual to God.

Ps. 120, the first of the collection, is an individual petition. It is characterized by repetitions of the same phrase in contiguous vv. ("deceitful tongue" in vv. 2, 3; "dwell/dwelt" in vv. 5, 6; "peace" in vv. 6, 7), a frequent stylistic aspect of this collection (see intro. above). **1:** A unique introduction to the individual petition, saying at the beginning that it was effective. **2–4:** Two of the typical elements of the petition are the invocation *(O LORD),* and the petition itself in the imperative *(save me).* As in many other psalms, the emphasis is on the danger of speech (see 10.7 n.). The typical motivation—why God should hear this petition—is absent here. **4:** The image is of an *arrow* with a sharp arrowhead that was as hot as *broom-wood* coals. Or, perhaps the metal arrowhead was forged in a very hot flame to make it extra sharp. The metaphor may describe the sharpness and dangerousness of wrong speech, or it may be the punishment that awaits the lips and tongue.

5 Woe is me, that I live with Meshech,
that I dwell among the clans of Kedar.
6 Too long have I dwelt with those who hate peace.
7 I am all peace;
but when I speak,
they are for war.

121 A song for ascents.

I turn my eyes to the mountains;
from where will my help come?
2 My help comes from the LORD,
maker of heaven and earth.
3 He will not let your foot give way;
your guardian will not slumber;
4 See, the guardian of Israel
neither slumbers nor sleeps!
5 The LORD is your guardian,
the LORD is your protection
at your right hand.
6 By day the sun will not strike you,
nor the moon by night.
7 The LORD will guard you from all harm;
He will guard your life.
8 The LORD will guard your going and coming
now and forever.

5: *Meshech* is near the Caspian Sea (Gen. 10.2; Ezek. 32.26; 38.2-3; 39.1–3), and the *clans of Kedar* are in the Arabian Peninsula (Gen. 25.13). Taken together, the two locations symbolize barbarian peoples on the fringes of the civilized world, thought of as warmongers (Isa. 21.16–17). The psalmist feels as if he lives, metaphorically, among these far-away, militant people (v. 6); he is alienated from his own society.

Ps. 121: This psalm expresses confidence in God as a constant guardian; the root "sh-mr," "to guard," appears six times. In many contemporary Jewish communities, it is recited at times of trouble to offer comfort and assurance. As in the previous psalm, words are often repeated in adjacent vv. (vv. 1–2, "my help"; vv. 3–4, "slumber"; vv. 7–8, "guard"). **1:** Uniquely, the opening is *A song for ascents* rather than "to ascents." The psalmist looks to the mountains because "it is the custom of anyone in straits to lift his eyes to see if help will come to repel the enemy" (Ibn Ezra). If this psalm is written in the voice of a pilgrim, he looks up as he approaches Jerusalem or the Temple Mount. Some have suggested that this is a polemic against deities on the mountains (see esp. Ezek. 18.6). **2:** The psalm recounts the psalmist's inner dialogue. The psalmist answers himself confidently either "through prophecy or expressing hope" (Ibn Ezra). The epithet *maker of heaven and earth* is found three times in the Songs of Ascents (here, 124.8; 134.3), and twice outside them (115.5; 146.6). It is likely that this epithet became popular in postexilic times (see 2 Chron. 2.11). Scholars associate this liturgical phrase with the Jerusalem tradition. In this context, raising the eyes to the mountains, as if to appreciate the heaven and the earth, takes on additional meaning. **3–4:** This is polemicizing against the notion that God does sleep, or stands by doing nothing; see, e.g., 44.24, "Rouse Yourself; why do You sleep, O LORD? / Awaken, do not reject us forever!" (see 7.7 n.). **3:** *He will not let your foot give way:* Cf. Ps. 66.9, where the idiom is parallel to "grant life." The idiom may be used in a general sense of keeping one secure but here, in the context of a journey, it is even more concrete. **5:** *Protection* ("tzel") refers to shade or refuge from the hot sun (see v. 6); note the biblical personal name (e.g., Exod. 31.2) Bezalel, "in the protection of God." *Right hand* expresses proximity, at your side (cf. 110.5); God will function as the psalmist's weapon. **6:** It is unclear how *the moon by night* might afflict a person: the notion of being moonstruck is postbiblical. Most likely, the parallelism of "day" and "night" requires a term to parallel "sun." Taken together, day and night are a merism for all the time. **8:** *Going and coming* means daily work (Deut. 31.2; 2 Kings 11.8). If this is a pilgrimage song, it may refer more specifically to setting out on the journey to the Temple and returning home. In sum, the psalm says that God guards the individual at all times everywhere. *Now and forever,* a liturgical phrase (Pss. 113.2; 115.18; 125.2; 131.3; Isa. 9.6 ["Now and evermore"]; 59.21 ["From now on, for all time"]; Mic. 4.7 ["Now and for evermore"]), that projects the thought into the continuous future so that it becomes permanent.

Ps. 122: The psalmist presents himself as a pilgrim to the Temple in Jerusalem and addresses Jerusalem, describing the city as it once was when it was the capital of the united kingdom: the home of the Temple, and the seat of the Davidic monarchy (the place where justice was dispensed). More specifically, the (postexilic) psalmist is expressing his hope for pilgrimage by picturing himself as a preexilic pilgrim who went regularly to the Temple before its destruction. As Radak says: "This psalm quotes the exiles, who in their

122 A song of ascents. Of David.

I rejoiced when they said to me,
"We are going to the House of the LORD."
2 Our feet stood inside your gates, O Jerusalem,
3 Jerusalem built up, a city knit together,
4 to which tribes would make pilgrimage,
the tribes of the LORD,
—as was enjoined upon Israel—
to praise the name of the LORD.
5 There the thrones of judgment stood,
thrones of the house of David.
6 Pray for the well-being of Jerusalem;
"May those who love you be at peace.
7 May there be well-being within your ramparts,
peace in your citadels."
8 For the sake of my kin and friends,
I pray for your well-being;
9 for the sake of the house of the LORD our God,
I seek your good.

123 A song of ascents.

To You, enthroned in heaven,
I turn my eyes.
2 As the eyes of slaves follow their master's hand,
as the eyes of a slave-girl follow the hand of her mistress,

great desire to build the Temple remembered Israel's pilgrimages, and spoke about their ancestors at the time that the Temple was standing." A wish for the well-being of Jerusalem, upon which the community and the Temple depend, forms the climax of the psalm. The psalm is, then, an expression of hope for the restoration and reunification of the country and the rebuilding of the Temple. Various linguistic clues (e.g., the spelling of David, "dvyd" with a "yod" rather than "dvd" in v. 5) as well as its nostalgic attitude toward the preexilic past (v. 5, "there") suggest that the psalm is postexilic. The psalm is full of echoes of the sounds in the name "Yerushalayim," "Jerusalem"—the letter "resh" (corresponding to "r") is overrepresented, along with the word "shalom" (peace) and "sham" (there), esp. in vv. 4–8. Jerusalem, whose original meaning is likely connected to the Canaanite deity Shalem, is thus re-etymologized as the city of peace. **1:** Like Pss. 124, 131, and 133, *A song of ascents* is augmented with *Of David* (lacking in some Heb mss and in the LXX, though as noted above, Davidic authorship is most unlikely. **1–2:** The psalmist moves from the singular to the plural (v. 1, *I,* to v. 2, *our*); it is unclear who is addressed, perhaps the pilgrims joining the psalmist. *"We are going to the House of the LORD"* is likely formulaic; cf. Isa. 2.3, "Come, Let us go up to the Mount of the LORD." **3:** *Jerusalem* was built up before the exile and again in the time of Nehemiah (mid-5th c. BCE). *A city knit together:* Heb *ḥuberah* has been explained as an architectural term—the city is built up with the appearance of a compact block of buildings—or built with a wall surrounding it to protect its inhabitants (v. 7, *ramparts* and *citadels*), or as a reference to the bond between all the tribes and the city (see v. 4), since it was the capital. **4:** The period of the united monarchy, when all the tribes made pilgrimages to Jerusalem, is recalled with nostalgia. *The tribes of the LORD*, the tribes who are the LORD's possession, i.e., the tribes of Israel. The first half of the v. alliteratively recalls Jerusalem (Heb "Yerushalayim"): *"shesham ʿalu shevatim shivtei yah."* The end of the v., where *the name of the LORD* rather than God Himself is praised, follows the norms of Deut. (see Deut. 12.5 n.). **5:** Administration of justice was a primary function of the king, as highlighted in the stories about Solomon as a just king (1 Kings 3.16–28; see also 2 Sam. 15.2, 6) and prophecies such as Jer. 21.12, "O House of David, thus said the LORD: Render just verdicts / Morning by morning." **6:** The alliteration of the first four words is striking: "shaʾalu shelom Yerushalayim yishlayu." The v. is a reversal of Jer. 29.7, "And seek the welfare of the city to which I have exiled you," insisting that one must pray for Babylon, not for Jerusalem. **7:** *Well-being* ("shalom") and *peace* ("shalvah") both play on the name Jerusalem, "Yerushalayim." **8:** The psalmist identifies himself with his community (see v. 2). **9:** The climax refers to the Temple, *the house of the LORD our God,* which makes Jerusalem so significant; this forms an inclusio with v. 1.

Ps. 123: An expression of dependence on God (vv. 1–2) introduces a communal petition for deliverance from scorn and contempt, perhaps from opponents whose speech causes harm (see v. 3), as in Ps. 120. An individual perspective (v. 1) quickly shifts to the plural (vv. 2–4), as in Ps. 122. Like Pss. 120 and 121, adjacent vv. use the same words (vv. 1–2, "eyes"; vv. 2–3, "favor"; vv. 3–4, "contempt, enough"). **1:** *I turn my eyes,* cf. Ps. 121.1. On God *in heaven,* see 2.4 n. **2:** The imagery expresses the subordination

so our eyes are toward the LORD our God,
awaiting His favor.
3 Show us favor, O LORD,
show us favor!
We have had more than enough of contempt.
4 Long enough have we endured
the scorn of the complacent,
the contempt of the haughty.

124 A song of ascents. Of David.

Were it not for the LORD, who was on our side,
let Israel now declare,
2 were it not for the LORD, who was on our side
when men assailed us,
3 they would have swallowed us alive
in their burning rage against us;
4 the waters would have carried us off,
the torrent would have swept over us;
5 over us would have swept
the seething waters.
6 Blessed is the LORD, who did not let us
be ripped apart by their teeth.
7 We are like a bird escaped from the fowler's trap;
the trap broke and we escaped.
8 Our help is the name of the LORD,
maker of heaven and earth.

and dependence of both men and women on God; and God himself is metaphorized as male and female. The parallelism also invokes plural (*slaves*) and singular (*a slave-girl*). *Follow ... hand:* The master indicates his command and the granting of his favor with his hand—more concretely, his hand distributes food. Request for divine *favor,* here and in v. 3, is a major theme of individual petitions (see e.g., "mercy," 6.3; 9.14). **3:** *More than enough:* lit. "we have been over-satiated"—with contempt rather than with nourishment. **4:** Viewed from the perspective of postexilic Judah, *the complacent* may be opposing factions with the country or neighbors who oppose the restoration of Judah.

Ps. 124: The beginning of this psalm, expressing the congregation's acknowledgement of God's beneficent action, contains repetition of lines, like many Songs of Ascents. **1:** Alternately, this may be understood as "May Israel now declare [or, 'sing'] the song that begins with the words / 'Were it not for the LORD, who was on our side' "—namely the song that begins in v. 2. In ancient Semitic cultures, compositions were typically known by their first words, so, e.g., what we call *The Epic of Gilgamesh* was known as *He who Saw Everything.* The same holds for the books of the Torah, whose Heb names are the opening words of each. Liturgical instructions are also found in later prayers, e.g., in the Kaddish prayer: "Say 'Amen'" and at the end of Yikum Purkan: "let us say 'Amen.'" The Barekhu prayer opens with a call by the leader to bless the Lord, "Bless the Lord, the blessed one," followed by the congregation's response blessing the Lord, "Blessed is the Lord, the blessed one, for ever and ever." Cf. Ps. 135.20–21. *Were it not for the LORD, who was on our side:* An alternative translation is "Were it not (or: had it not been) the LORD who was on our side," that is, if it had been a less powerful god. **2:** The event referred to is not made explicit, as is often the case in psalms, so the psalm lent itself to many new situations. But the psalm's imagery seems to be referring to the destruction of Judah, which this psalm sees as almost, but not quite, the end of Israel. *Men,* Heb "'adam," "human beings." **3–7:** The mixing of images—being swallowed, drowned, hunted—is odd to modern sensibilities, but biblical poems often use a variety of intersecting images to strengthen their point. The images here combine to picture the exile as a cosmic event of destruction. **3:** *Swallowed us alive,* as Sheol swallows its victims (Num. 16.30, 32; Prov. 1.12). "Swallow" is commonly used for an enemy's destruction of Israel (Jer. 51.34; Hos. 8.7–8 ["devour"]; Ps. 35.25 ["destroyed"]) but "swallowed alive" is more cosmic. **4–5:** Three escalating terms for the waters that wash over Israel: waters washing over, a torrential stream, and seething waters. *Seething waters:* "Zeydonim," literally "insolent," describes uncontrollable water. A form of this word is used in Jer. 50.29, 31 to characterize Babylonia. See Ps. 69.2, 16 for a more extensive description of being overtaken by water, which is synonymous with the Deep and the Pit, another way of referring to Sheol or the waters of chaos. The destruction of Jerusalem and the Temple is a comic destruction, like the Flood. **7:** *The fowler's trap,* a pit covered with a net, is a common image (Pss. 31.5; 35.7–8; 91.3; Prov. 7.23). The combination of drowning and being trapped like a bird is found in Lam. 3.52–54, suggesting that the topic is the exile. **8:** Cf. Ps. 121.2 and annotation.

125 A song of ascents.

Those who trust in the LORD
are like Mount Zion
that cannot be moved,
enduring forever.
2 Jerusalem, hills enfold it,
and the LORD enfolds His people
now and forever.
3 [a]The scepter of the wicked shall never rest
upon the land allotted to the righteous,
that the righteous not set their hand to wrongdoing.[a]
4 Do good, O LORD, to the good,
to the upright in heart.
5 [a]But those who in their crookedness act corruptly,[a]
let the LORD make them go the way of evildoers.
May it be well with Israel!

126 A song of ascents.

When the LORD restores the fortunes of Zion
—[b]we see it as in a dream[b]—
2 our mouths shall be filled with laughter,
our tongues, with songs of joy.

a-a Meaning of Heb. uncertain. *b-b Lit. "we are veritable dreamers."*

Ps. 125: Though the psalm is disjointed, its message is that "those who trust in the LORD" (v. 1) will be secure. God will reward them and will remove the wicked. While this psalm shares the idea of retribution with Ps. 1, this psalm speaks on a national level. Its imagery focuses on Mount Zion and Jerusalem, and it ends with a blessing for Israel. **1:** *Trusting in the LORD* (= the righteous) is a significant biblical theme (Pss. 32.10; 37.3–4; Prov. 16.20; 29.25); it implies action, not merely belief. On *Mount Zion,* see Ps. 48. Before the exile, Jerusalem was thought to be inviolable. But in this postexilic psalm, it is not a question of whether Jerusalem can be destroyed, but rather the idea that God's throne remains on Mount Zion (the Temple). Cf. Lam. 5.18–19, which says that although Zion is desolate, God's throne endures forever. The idea of God's cosmic mountain, eternally stable and unmovable, resonates here (cf. Ps. 93), as does the stability of the righteous person in Ps. 15.5. **2:** The order of the nouns in vv. 1–2 *(LORD, Zion, Jerusalem, LORD)* is reversed as the same point is emphasized: the stability of Jerusalem and Israel. The imagery moves from the cosmic to the topographic: the mountains surrounding Jerusalem that offer protection from enemies who would march against it. *Now and forever,* see 121.8 n. **3:** The Heb is difficult. *The scepter of the wicked,* or "the scepter of wickedness," means the rule of wickedness, an unjust governmental power. Perhaps a reference to foreign occupiers or to the Persian empire, of which Judah was part. In contrast, see God's scepter or rule, which is just (Ps. 45.7). **5:** *The way of evildoers* is doomed, as in 1.4; the ultimate result of their annihilation is the end of the conflict between those who are good and those who are evil; thus the concluding expression, which became popular in postexilic times: "Peace/well-being over Israel." This expression is found in the famous Byzantine (6th to 7th c. CE) synagogue at Jericho, where it is incorporated into a mosaic below a menorah (candelabrum) flanked by a shofar (ram's horn) and a lulav (palm frond).

Ps. 126: This psalm is about the return from Babylonian exile and the rejoicing that accompanied it, although whether the return has already occurred or whether it lies in the future is uncertain. Many medieval and modern commentators have read this as a pre-restoration psalm, looking forward hopefully to the return, but recent interpreters tend to see the return as having already begun, although not yet complete. The historical return from exile fell short of the way it had been imagined; Judah was not independent, the Davidic dynasty was not reinstituted, and the economic and political problems of re-establishing the community were many. So the idea of the return became idealized as a future hope. This psalm is recited before grace after meals on Sabbath and festivals; its weekday counterpart is Ps. 137. **1:** *Restores the fortunes,* may refer to the return from Babylonian exile (so, e.g., Rashi), or may be a general term for improvement of one's lot (see 14.7 n.). *We see it as in a dream:* Literally, "we became like dreamers." In ancient Israel, dreams were considered a form of divine revelation (1 Sam. 28.6), but could alternatively signify something that passes quickly or is insubstantial (Ps. 73.20; Job 20.8). Perhaps both senses of dreaming are at play here: those who had experienced the restoration had received, as it were, a divine revelation, a preview of things to come, but at the same time the restoration proved to be fleeting, not yet complete or permanent. The Tg. reads differently, "like the sick who are cured," taking the word from the root meaning "to be healthy" (cf. Isa. 38.16). This reading may also be reflected in the Dead Sea Scroll 11QPs[a]. The LXX reads "like people comforted." **2–3:** These vv. are framed by *laughter* and *rejoicing,*

Then shall they say among the nations,
"The LORD has done great things for them!"
3 The LORD will do great things for us
and we shall rejoice.

4 Restore our fortunes, O LORD,
like watercourses in the Negeb.
5 They who sow in tears
shall reap with songs of joy.
6 Though he goes along weeping,
carrying the seed-bag,
he shall come back with songs of joy,
carrying his sheaves.

127 A song of ascents. Of Solomon.

Unless the LORD builds the house,
its builders labor in vain on it;
unless the LORD watches over the city,
the watchman keeps vigil in vain.
2 In vain do you rise early
and stay up late,
you who toil for the bread you eat;
[a]He provides as much for His loved ones while they sleep.[a]

3 Sons are the provision[b] of the LORD;
the fruit of the womb, His reward.
4 Like arrows in the hand of a warrior
are sons born to a man in his youth.
5 Happy is the man who fills his quiver with them;
they shall not be put to shame
when they contend with the enemy in the gate.

a-a Meaning of Heb. uncertain. *b Lit. "heritage."*

with *the LORD* doing *great things* doubled in the middle. That expression is otherwise only found in Joel (2.20, 21), an exilic or postexilic book, which has other affinities to this psalm (see v. 1 and Joel 4.1). **2:** *Our mouths shall be filled:* The grammar permits a translation in the future or in the past, "our mouths were filled." **4:** V. 1 is recapitulated, but as an imperative. *Watercourses in the Negeb:* The wadis in the Negeb are empty of water during the summer and refill during the winter rains. The image here implies the cyclical renewal of life-giving water or a sudden and complete restoration, like a positive flash-flood. Rashi notes that, just as the water revives the land and makes it fertile, so God's restoration will enable the people to thrive. Ibn Ezra and Radak say that the Negeb—hot, dry, and lacking water—is a metaphor for the exile. **5–6:** The mentions of watery *tears,* and the agricultural cycle of sowing and reaping reinforces the cycle of the Negeb watercourses as images of the restoration of the people to their land (cf. Amos 9.11–15). The medieval Jewish exegetes explain that the sower is crying because he is in the exile, in the dry lifeless land (the Negeb = Babylonia) that yields little produce; the reaper is a returnee from exile, happy because now God has brought water to assure the plentiful harvest.

Ps. 127: This didactic psalm teaches that God controls all things and without Him nothing can be accomplished. Vv. 1–2 focus on "house" and "city," and vv. 3–5 focus on sons. The two parts are connected, however, since "house" may be a metaphor for family (see esp. 2 Sam. 7.11), and the "quiver" of v. 5 is likely a metaphor for the "house" that is filled with "arrows," namely "sons" (Radak). Like Pss. 128 and 131, the images are familial. As in other Songs of Ascents, the same words are repeated in consecutive vv. **1–2:** The attribution *of Solomon* is due to the understanding of the *house* as the Temple, but more likely the psalm is addressed to Israelites in general, and *house* and *city* have no specific referent (cf. 128.5–6 n.). Many medieval commentators (including Rashi, Ibn Ezra, and Radak) assume that this is a Davidic psalm, recited about *(of)* Solomon. The second half of v. 2 is hopelessly difficult and probably poorly preserved, yet as a whole, these vv. express an idea especially common in wisdom texts, that God ultimately controls all (e.g., Prov. 21.31: "The horse is readied for the day of battle, / But victory comes from the LORD"). **3–5:** The view is very military and masculine. The term "gever" *(man)* in v. 5 is clearly male. Children are a man's means to success in life. Having many children is considered a blessing, especially in wisdom literature (see Ps. 1.3; Job 1.2). The importance of a large family is also a major theme of the ancestral narratives in Gen. By using phrases such as "the LORD opened her womb" or "the LORD remembered her" (see esp. Gen. 30.22), those narratives emphasize the same point as these vv.: these children are God's gift.

128 A song of ascents.

Happy are all who fear the LORD,
who follow His ways.
2 You shall enjoy the fruit of your labors;
you shall be happy and you shall prosper.
3 Your wife shall be like a fruitful vine within your house;
your sons, like olive saplings around your table.
4 So shall the man who fears the LORD be blessed.

5 May the LORD bless you from Zion;
may you share the prosperity of Jerusalem
all the days of your life,
6 and live to see your children's children.
May all be well with Israel!

129 A song of ascents.

Since my youth they have often assailed me,
let Israel now declare,
2 since my youth they have often assailed me,
but they have never overcome me.
3 Plowmen plowed across my back;
they made long furrows.
4 The LORD, the righteous one,
has snapped the cords of the wicked.

5 Let all who hate Zion
fall back in disgrace.
6 Let them be like grass on roofs
that fades before it can be pulled up,
7 that affords no handful for the reaper,
no armful for the gatherer of sheaves,

Ps. 128: This is thematically similar to the previous psalm, emphasizing that God is the source of blessing to those who "fear the LORD." **1:** The structure of this v. makes it clear that *fearing the LORD* is not an abstract attitude, but involves *following His ways.* Although it seems to be addressed to *all,* vv. 3–4 narrow the focus to male addressees; see also v. 4, "man" ("gever"), as in 127.5. **2:** Contrast Gen. 3.19, "By the sweat of your brow / Shall you get bread to eat," which is a curse there, but a blessing here. **3:** Lit. "Your wife shall be like a fruitful vine in the depths/corner/innermost parts of your house," perhaps a reference to the kitchen, typically located in the back corner of the ancient Israelite house. (See Radak: "Even in her house she should be modest ... she should be in the corner of the house so that only her husband and household will see her.") **4:** A summary v., framing vv. 1–4 and emphasizing that prosperity and family are God's blessings. **5–6:** These vv. extend the original blessing to all *Israel,* and note that this blessing comes from God's dwelling-place, *Zion.* The psalmist may here be using traditional formulae; on *May the LORD bless you from Zion,* see 134.3 (and possibly 135.21); on *May all be well with Israel!,* see the identical 125.5. *Children's children,* an extension of the children in v. 3, signifies a blessing of long life and great progeny—the ideal in ancient Israel. Given average life expectancy, living to see grandchildren was a special blessing; seeing great-grandchildren was an exceptional blessing (see Job 42.16). With this psalm in its present position, after Ps. 127, it is easy to understand how "city" in 127.1 came to be understood as Jerusalem.

Ps. 129: This psalm has two parts: vv. 1–4 tell of the psalmist's past persecution by the wicked, and his deliverance by God, and vv. 5–8 are an imprecation against "all who hate Zion" (v. 5). The link between the two parts is not obvious, except that here, as elsewhere, the personal becomes the communal. As in other Songs of Ascents, phrases repeat in consecutive vv. (see vv. 1–2). **1–2:** The pronoun *they* is not defined until v. 4, *the wicked.* As usual, the referents are vague, allowing the psalm to apply to a wide variety of situations. **1:** See 124.1; this v. may also be translated "May Israel now declare [or, 'sing'] the song that begins with the words 'Since my youth they have often assailed me.'" **2:** Compare Gen. 32.29. **3:** A unique and graphic biblical metaphor, sharing the agricultural world of the previous psalm and several other Songs of Ascents. **4:** A new metaphor is introduced with *cords;* such mixing of metaphors is common in biblical poetry (see 124.3–7 n.). **5:** *Zion* is disproportionately mentioned in the Songs of Ascents (125.1; 126.1; 128.5; 129.5; 132.13; 133.3; 134.3). **6–7:** The image, again taken from the agricultural world (see v. 3), is of the insubstantial grass that grows on roofs that are covered with a small coating of soil. This grass fades quickly and is of no value.

8 no exchange with passersby:
"The blessing of the LORD be upon you."
"We bless you by the name of the LORD."

130 A song of ascents.

Out of the depths I call You, O LORD.
2 O Lord, listen to my cry;
let Your ears be attentive
to my plea for mercy.
3 If You keep account of sins, O LORD,
Lord, who will survive?
4 Yours is the power to forgive
so that You may be held in awe.

5 I look to the LORD;
I look to Him;
I await His word.
6 I am more eager for the Lord
than watchmen for the morning,
watchmen for the morning.

7 O Israel, wait for the LORD;
for with the LORD is steadfast love
and great power to redeem.
8 It is He who will redeem Israel from all their iniquities.

131 A song of ascents. Of David.

O LORD, my heart is not proud
nor my look haughty;
I do not aspire to great things
or to what is beyond me;
2 [a-]but I have taught myself to be contented
like a weaned child with its mother;
like a weaned child am I in my mind.[-a]

a-a Meaning of Heb. uncertain.

8: A continuation of the image of the preceding v., since blessings were part of the reaping process (see Ruth 2.4, cited by Radak). It is uncertain whether *The blessing of the LORD be upon you. We bless you by the name of the LORD* is a single blessing, or a blessing and its response, as in Ruth 2.4: "He greeted the reapers, 'The LORD be with you!' And they responded, 'The LORD bless you!' " Like Pss. 128 and 134, this Song of Ascents ends with a blessing.

Ps. 130: A plea for forgiveness and mercy that moves from the personal (vv. 1–6) to the national (vv. 7–8), as many psalms do. The link between the two parts is the idea that God forgives sins (vv. 3–4, 7–8). **1:** *Depths,* elsewhere in Psalms only in 69.3, 15; perhaps here a reference to the underworld, of being in a state near death (see Jonah 2.3–7). **2:** A stereotypical v. in personal petitions; see, e.g., 86.6: "Give ear, O LORD, to my prayer; / heed my plea for mercy." **3–4:** The theological notion expressed is that if God did not forgive sins, all people would be doomed to punishment since everyone sins (see Job ch 7). God's forgiving nature causes people to hold God *in awe.* On God's writing off of Israel's sins see Jer. 50.20, "The iniquity of Israel shall be sought, / And there shall be none; / The sins of Judah, / And none shall be found; / For I will pardon those I allow to survive." *Yours is the power to forgive,* lit. "with you is the forgiveness," the same structure as "with the LORD is steadfast love ["ḥesed"]" (v. 7). The combination of the two phrases suggests that forgiveness is part of God's "ḥesed," his covenant obligation to Israel. **5:** Perhaps the psalmist is awaiting an oracle of deliverance (see 3.5 n.). **6:** The psalmist waits expectantly for God's deliverance, which elsewhere comes in the morning (56.6). **7:** On steadfast love ("ḥesed"), see 5.8 n. **8:** Sinners or their descendants normally need to be punished (see Exod. 34.7), but here God *redeems* or ransoms them *from all their iniquities,* or, better, "from all their punishments" (Heb can mean either), that is, He forgives them and cancels their punishment.

Ps. 131: Like the previous psalm, this too starts in the singular (vv. 1–2) and moves to concerns about the community (v. 3); in fact, the last vv. of these two psalms share the phrase, "O Israel, wait for the LORD." **1:** An initial protestation of innocence (see Pss. 7; 17; 26). The psalmist claims to be "lowly," an ideal in Psalms (e.g., 10.17). As such, he does not *aspire to great things,* or *what is beyond;* these are, as Radak notes, "divine concerns" (e.g., Pss. 86.10; 136.4; Job 5.9). **2:** The v. is textually difficult but the best explanation is that the relationship between a child and his mother is equated with the relationship between the psalmist and God.

3 O Israel, wait for the LORD
now and forever.

132 A song of ascents.

O LORD, remember in David's favor
his extreme self-denial,
2 how he swore to the LORD,
vowed to the Mighty One of Jacob,
3 "I will not enter my house,
nor will I mount my bed,
4 I will not give sleep to my eyes,
or slumber to my eyelids[a]
5 until I find a place for the LORD,
an abode for the Mighty One of Jacob."

6 We heard it was in Ephrath;
we came upon it in the region of Jaar.[b]
7 Let us enter His abode,
bow at His footstool.
8 Advance, O LORD, to Your resting-place,
You and Your mighty Ark!
9 Your priests are clothed in triumph;
Your loyal ones sing for joy.
10 For the sake of Your servant David
do not reject Your anointed one.
11 The LORD swore to David
a firm oath that He will not renounce,
"One of your own issue I will set upon your
throne.

a Lit. "eyes." *b Cf. 1 Sam. 7.1–2; 1 Chron. 13.5–6.*

Once weaned, the child no longer receives milk from its mother, suggesting that the psalmist can rely less on God for nourishment. For that reason, several commentators prefer "a nursed child" or a child who has just finished nursing and is satisfied (Rashi). Only here in Psalms is God viewed as a mother, though this maternal image is found elsewhere in the Bible (e.g., Isa. 49.14–16). **3:** See 121.8; 125.2; 130.7.

Ps. 132: A prayer for the restoration of the Davidic dynasty, along with the Temple, or, more generally, for the restoration of the kingdom of Judah. Like several other Songs of Ascents, this psalm emphasizes the significance of Zion, but it is significantly longer, and stylistically different. The psalm liberally recasts material found in Samuel and Chronicles (1 Sam. 6.21–7.2; 2 Sam. chs 5–7; re-formulated later in 1 Chron. chs 13–17), emphasizing the choice of David as the Judean dynast and its corollary, the choice of Zion as God's permanent place. The hope is that this retelling will foreshadow the replaying of these events, the return of the Ark to Zion (that is, the rebuilding of the Temple) and the re-institution of the Davidic dynasty. **1–2:** *Self-denial,* David's refusal to sleep (vv. 3–4), or the hardship he encountered in transferring the Ark (1 Kings 2.26; cf. 1 Chron. 22.14). This self-denial is not found in Samuel, nor is David's desire to build a Temple expressed as an oath there. *The Mighty One of Jacob* is thought to be an old divine epithet, used only here and in v. 5 in the Psalter (cf. Gen. 49.24; Isa. 49.26; 60.16). **3–5:** An exaggerated poetic rendition of 2 Sam. 7.2: "Here I am dwelling in a house of cedar, while the Ark of the LORD abides in a tent!" *My house,* literally, "my tent-house." The psalm omits David's request to build the Temple, focusing rather on the return of the Ark and its installation at the site upon which the Temple would stand. A postexilic audience would have equated the Ark with the Temple. **4:** A king's depriving himself of sleep until he has built a new temple is a known motif in Egyptian and Mesopotamian literature. **6:** Alternatively: "We heard it in Ephrath," or "We heard about it in Ephrath"—that is, we heard in Ephrath that the Ark was in Kiriath-jearim *(region of Jaar)* and that is where we found it. The referent of *it* (feminine in Heb) is uncertain, though it likely refers to traditions about the Ark (masculine!) wandering. **7:** On *abode* ("mishkanot") and *footstool,* see 43.3–4 and 99.5 n. **8–9:** See 2 Chron. 6.41–42, which were probably taken from our psalm (no parallel in 1 Kings ch 8); as noted by Radak, "there are slight changes between these vv., but they have the same meaning." **8:** *Advance* (lit. "Arise," "kumah"), is often used to rouse God into battle—note *Your mighty Ark* (Num. 10.35; cf. Ps. 68.2; see Ps. 7.7 n.). **9:** It is unclear if *loyal ones* (ḥasidim) is a general term, or refers to a specific group, similar to *priests.* **10:** On David as God's *servant,* see 18.1 n.; on *anointed one,* see 2.2 n. This refers to a Davidic king or potential king in the time of the psalmist or the future. **11:** The divine oath is a response to David's oath (v. 2), creating symmetry in the psalm. *One of your own issue* is a poetic restatement of 2 Sam. 7.12.

12 If your sons keep My covenant
and My decrees that I teach them,
then their sons also,
to the end of time,
shall sit upon your throne."
13 For the LORD has chosen Zion;
He has desired it for His seat.
14 "This is my resting-place for all time;
here I will dwell, for I desire it.
15 I will amply bless its store of food,
give its needy their fill of bread.
16 I will clothe its priests in victory,
its loyal ones shall sing for joy.
17 There I will make a horn sprout for David;
I have prepared a lamp for My anointed one.
18 I will clothe his enemies in disgrace,
while on him his crown shall sparkle."

133 A song of ascents. Of David.

How good and how pleasant it is
that brothers dwell together.
2 It is like fine oil on the head
running down onto the beard,
the beard of Aaron,
that comes down over the collar of his robe;

12: In 2 Sam. ch 7 and related literature (see esp. Ps. 89), the promise is of an eternal ("'olam") dynasty; here, as in 1 Kings 9.4–9 and Chronicles, the promise is conditional (see annotations to 1 Kings ch 9 and intro. to that book). **13:** *For* connects the choosing of David and of Zion (see 78.68–72 n.). **14:** *Resting-place:* See v. 8, of the *Ark,* God's throne or footstool. **15:** The *needy* are a frequent concern of Psalms. **16:** A slight recasting of v. 9. **17:** *Horn* often expresses military victory. In 2 Sam. 21.17, David is called "the lamp of Israel"; in 1 Kings 11.36 it is Solomon's son and in 2 Kings 8.19 it is Joram, son of Jehoshaphat. **18:** *Disgrace,* defeat. Ancient Israel was a shame-oriented society. This image reverses v. 16, *"I will clothe* its priests *in* victory" (Radak). The *crown* is a symbol of royalty (2 Sam. 1.10), given to the king at his enthronement (2 Kings 11.12; 2 Chron. 23.11).

Ps. 133: Like other Songs of Ascents, this one focuses on Zion. The psalm is celebrating the restoration, the rebuilding of the Temple, the reconsecration of the priesthood, and the renewal of sacrificial worship, all of which bring prosperity to the restored community. It may have been recited by pilgrims as they approached Mt. Zion or as they partook of a sacrificial meal in the Temple, but we cannot know for sure what its liturgical setting was. Like several other of these poems, phrases in one line are repeated in the next (vv. 1–2, "tov," *good, fine;* vv. 2–3, "y-rd," *running down, comes down, falls*). The images used combine to produce a picture of great blessing in Zion. This psalm, together with the previous one, mentions rituals concerning the king and high priest, who shared power in the postexilic period (see Zech. 6.13). **1:** While often taken to refer to brotherly harmony in a general sense, the v. is better understood as a hope for the reunification of the Northern and Southern Kingdoms (see Ezek. 37.15–28). *Brothers dwell together:* "Brothers" often designates members of a group, or all Israel. "To dwell together" is a legal term for joint tenancy of land, undivided land holdings (Gen. 13.6 ["staying together; remain together"]; 36.7; Deut. 25.5). It is here used metaphorically, for the reunited kingdom, a hope found also in prophetic literature (e.g., Jer. 31.20, 24). **2–3:** The NJPS translation (and many others) analyzes these vv. as two similes describing how pleasant living together is: it is *like fine oil on the head* and *like the dew of Hermon.* But it is better to disconnect the oil and dew images from v. 1 and link them to each other: oil on Aaron's head is like dew on Hermon. The syntax of "like X, like Y" equates the two items (see also Ps. 139.12). Both oil and dew signify prosperity; here the consecration of the priest is like the dew, a symbol of God's blessing. On the oil used for anointing Aaron, see Exod. 30.22–33; Lev. 8.12; our psalm adds the depiction of the overflowing, effulgent nature of this anointing. Mt. *Hermon,* on the northern tip of Israel, was very high, and therefore received much *dew.* The mention of Hermon, in the far north, and Mt. *Zion* in the south, reinforces the idea that the northern and southern kingdoms are pictured as one, with the dew flowing down from the geologically-distinctive mountain in the far north to the religiously-distinctive mountain in the south, covering the entire land with blessing. Some scholars suggest that *Zion* might here be associated with Mt. *Hermon,* as one of the northern mountains, as in 48.3 (see n. there). This is the only reference to *mountains* (plural!) *of Zion*—perhaps the hills surrounding Jerusalem are meant, though the Dead Sea Psalms scroll reads the more expected "mountain." *Blessing* refers to fertility, as in Lev. 25.21, and anticipates the theme of the following psalm. *Everlasting life* is hyperbolic for a long and prosperous life for

3 like the dew of Hermon
that falls upon the mountains of Zion.
There the LORD ordained blessing,
everlasting life.

134

A song of ascents.

Now bless the LORD,
all you servants of the LORD
who stand nightly
in the house of the LORD.
2 Lift your hands toward the sanctuary
and bless the LORD.
3 May the LORD,
maker of heaven and earth,
bless you from Zion.

135

Hallelujah.
Praise the name of the LORD;
give praise, you servants of the LORD
2 who stand in the house of the LORD,
in the courts of the house of our God.
3 Praise the LORD, for the LORD is good;
sing hymns to His name, for it is pleasant.
4 For the LORD has chosen Jacob for Himself,
Israel, as His treasured possession.

5 For I know that the LORD is great,
that our Lord is greater than all gods.
6 Whatever the LORD desires He does
in heaven and earth,
in the seas and all the depths.
7 He makes clouds rise from the end of the earth;
He makes lightning for the rain;
He releases the wind from His vaults.

individuals and permanent security for the homeland. Some commentators say this refers to life in the next world. The Dead Sea Psalms scroll instead concludes this psalm: "There the LORD ordained blessing forever; / May all be well with Israel" (see Pss. 125.5; 128.6).

Ps. 134: This psalm, the last of the Songs of Ascents, is about blessing: the people's blessing of God (vv. 1–2) and God's blessing of the people (v. 3). The root "b-rk," "to bless," occurs in every v. **1:** This v. shows clear affinities to the contiguous 135.2. It serves as an appropriate conclusion to this collection. *Servants of the LORD* may refer to those present in the Temple (see 135.1–2 n.), or they may be a special group of Temple functionaries. The Heb for *stand* also has a technical sense of "minister," which may be its sense here. It is uncertain what activity is performed *nightly,* other than guard duty by the Levites (1 Chron. 9.23–27). **2:** Lifting of *hands* typically accompanies prayer (see 44.21–22 n.), though here it may indicate blessing, as in Lev. 9.22. Since God rather than the people is being blessed, the hands are lifted in the direction of the sanctuary. **3:** These formulae occur elsewhere in this collection: see 121.2; 124.8; 128.5. Their juxtaposition emphasizes that a universal God, who made heaven and earth, is centered at *Zion.* The collection's conclusion emphasizes Zion, a major theme of the Songs of Ascents, and also shows close connections with the conclusion of the following psalm (135.21). Perhaps an editor placed adjacently psalms that shared certain similarities, or phrases moved from one psalm to an adjacent one, making the Psalter into a more coherent book.

Ps. 135: The greatness of God—as demonstrated by His creation of the world, freeing His people from Egypt, and leading them safely to the promised land—is contrasted with the impotent gods of other nations. This psalm resembles others that review the traditions found in the Torah in order to show God's power (Pss. 78; 105; 106; 136). Here the traditions are more abbreviated. The psalm is an anthology of several other psalms and reworks some Torah traditions. This psalm appears in the liturgy for the introductory morning service for Sabbath and festivals. Like the previous Songs of Ascents, it highlights Zion (v. 21). Pss. 135–136 are known in Jewish liturgy as The Great Hallel, parallel to the Egyptian Hallel (Pss. 113–118); see *m. Taʿan.* 3.9. **1–2:** *Servants of the LORD* are all those who show allegiance to Him. The psalm is directed to those who have come to the Temple (cf. 113.1 and 134.1). **3:** Cf. 136.3. **4:** All gods have their peoples and Israel is the LORD's special people (cf. Deut. 32.8–9). **5:** Israel's God is superior to all other gods (cf. Exod. 18.11; Ps. 96.4–5). **6:** As elsewhere in the Bible (cf. 115.16–17), the cosmos is perceived as having three strata: the sky, the earth, and the water below the earth. **7:** A poetic rendering of the first stages of creation and a portrait of God's control of the natural world.

8 He struck down the first-born of Egypt,
man and beast alike;
9 He sent signs and portents against[a] Egypt,
against Pharaoh and all his servants;
10 He struck down many nations
and slew numerous kings—
11 Sihon, king of the Amorites,
Og, king of Bashan,
and all the royalty of Canaan—
12 and gave their lands as a heritage,
as a heritage to His people Israel.

13 O LORD, Your name endures forever,
Your fame, O LORD, through all generations;
14 for the LORD will champion His people,
and obtain satisfaction for His servants.

15[b] The idols of the nations are silver and gold,
the work of men's hands.
16 They have mouths, but cannot speak;
they have eyes, but cannot see;
17 they have ears, but cannot hear,
nor is there breath in their mouths.
18 Those who fashion them,
all who trust in them,
shall become like them.

19 O house of Israel, bless the LORD;
O house of Aaron, bless the LORD;
20 O house of Levi, bless the LORD;
you who fear the LORD, bless the LORD.
21 Blessed is the LORD from Zion,
He who dwells in Jerusalem.
Hallelujah.

136

Praise the LORD; for He is good,
His steadfast love is eternal.
2 Praise the God of gods,
His steadfast love is eternal.
3 Praise the Lord of lords,
His steadfast love is eternal;

a Others "against you." *b With vv. 15–20, cf. Ps. 115.4–11.*

8–12: A shortened version of 136.10–22. **8:** The poet singles out the last plague against Egypt, the one that finally convinced Pharaoh to let the Israelites leave; the others are summarized in v. 9. **11:** *Sihon* and *Og* were the first Canaanite kings defeated by Israel (Num. 21.21–35). **13:** A reuse of Exod. 3.15. **15–18:** Similar to 115.4–8 (with the omission of 115.7). **19–20:** Cf. 115.11 (omitting "house of Levi"). The psalm emphasizes that the fitting reaction to God's great acts on Israel's behalf is that all Israel should praise Him.

Ps. 136: This psalm is sometimes called in Jewish liturgy the Great Hallel (along with Ps. 135) and has been incorporated into the Passover Seder. Like 135, it is part of the introductory prayers to the morning service on Sabbath and festivals. The psalm is probably written to be chanted responsively, with the assembly chanting the refrain after each line. *His steadfast love,* Heb "ḥesed" means a favor done out of loyalty (see 5.8 n.). God's "ḥesed" to Israel is eternal. The word "ki," left untranslated in NJPS, does not here mean "because" but rather "indeed"; thus the meaning is "Indeed his steadfast love is eternal." The psalm recounts in chronological order the many acts of "ḥesed" that God did for Israel in the past, and the refrain confirms that these acts of "ḥesed" will continue. Like 78, 105, 106, and 135, this psalm utilizes Torah traditions for its recitation of the mighty acts of God that constitute praise of God. The division of heaven and earth and the creation of the celestial bodies (vv. 5–9) is followed by the tenth plague against the Egyptians (cf. 135.8), the exodus from Egypt, the splitting of the Reed Sea, and the travels in the wilderness (vv. 10–20). The recitation of past marvels concludes with the acquisition of the promised land (vv. 21–22). Since God *took note of us in our degradation* and *rescued us from our enemies* in the past (vv. 23–24), there is assurance that He will do so again. These vv. bespeak the exilic condition, the probable time of this psalm's composition. The psalm shares some phrases with the previous psalm, but the suggestion that they are twins, by the same author (see Ps. 111 intro.) has little merit. It ends on a note of the universality of God's care. **2–3:** *God of gods ... Lord of lords,* an allusion to Deut. 10.17. This is a superlative form, like "Song of Songs."

4 Who alone works great marvels,
His steadfast love is eternal;
5 Who made the heavens with wisdom,
His steadfast love is eternal;
6 Who spread the earth over the water,
His steadfast love is eternal;
7 Who made the great lights,
His steadfast love is eternal;
8 the sun to dominate the day,
His steadfast love is eternal;
9 the moon and the stars to dominate the
night,
His steadfast love is eternal;
10 Who struck Egypt through their first-born,
His steadfast love is eternal;
11 and brought Israel out of their midst,
His steadfast love is eternal;
12 with a strong hand and outstretched arm,
His steadfast love is eternal;
13 Who split apart the Sea of Reeds,
His steadfast love is eternal;
14 and made Israel pass through it,
His steadfast love is eternal;
15 Who hurled Pharaoh and his army into the Sea of
Reeds,
His steadfast love is eternal;
16 Who led His people through the wilderness,
His steadfast love is eternal;
17 Who struck down great kings,
His steadfast love is eternal;
18 and slew mighty kings—
His steadfast love is eternal;
19 Sihon, king of the Amorites,
His steadfast love is eternal;
20 Og, king of Bashan—
His steadfast love is eternal;
21 and gave their land as a heritage,
His steadfast love is eternal;
22 a heritage to His servant Israel,
His steadfast love is eternal;
23 Who took note of us in our degradation,
His steadfast love is eternal;
24 and rescued us from our enemies,
His steadfast love is eternal;
25 Who gives food to all flesh,
His steadfast love is eternal.
26 Praise the God of heaven,
His steadfast love is eternal.

4: Any notion of the presence of other gods in vv. 2–3 is banished by the fact that God *alone* works great marvels. **6:** Some vocabulary is shared with Gen. 1.6, 9, though the psalm has a more mythological conception, like that in 24.2, in which the earth is set upon the waters (forces of chaos), which are thereby immobilized. The word for "spreads" is "roka'," the same root as "rakia'," "expanse," in Gen. 1.6–8. **12:** *A strong hand and outstretched arm,* cf. Deut. 4.34; 5.15; 7.19. **19:** Cf. Num. 21.21–35 and Ps. 135.11. **23–25:** A recapitulation of the exodus theme: God took note of the people (Exod. 2.24), rescued them (Exod. chs 14–15), and fed them bread from heaven (Exod. 16.4, 15). **22:** In contrast to expectations and to the previous psalm, 136 does not note the entry into the land of Israel but confines itself to the traditions in the Torah, rather than looking ahead and including Josh. **26:** The phrase *God of heaven* is unique, and comports with an exilic date, when God was not imagined as localized at the Temple.

137

By the rivers of Babylon,
there we sat,
sat and wept,
as we thought of Zion.
2 There on the poplars
we hung up our lyres,
3 for our captors asked us there for songs,
our tormentors,[a] for amusement,
"Sing us one of the songs of Zion."
4 How can we sing a song of the LORD
on alien soil?
5 If I forget you, O Jerusalem,
let my right hand wither;[b]
6 let my tongue stick to my palate
if I cease to think of you,
if I do not keep Jerusalem in memory
even at my happiest hour.

7 Remember, O LORD, against the Edomites
the day of Jerusalem's fall;
how they cried, "Strip her, strip her
to her very foundations!"
8 Fair Babylon, you predator,[c]
a blessing on him who repays you in kind
what you have inflicted on us;
9 a blessing on him who seizes your babies
and dashes them against the rocks!

138

Of David.

I praise You with all my heart,
sing a hymn to You before the divine beings;

a Meaning of Heb. uncertain. *b Others "forget its cunning."*
c With Targum; others "who are to be destroyed."

Ps. 137: A lament for Jerusalem, from the postexilic era. It is conveyed through the persona of a Temple singer, or Levite, now in exile (Ibn Ezra). The main theme is remembering Zion. This psalm is often recited on the Ninth of Av, the day that commemorates the destruction of the Temple, and before the grace after meals on weekdays. **1:** *Rivers of Babylon:* Babylonia was known for its network of irrigation canals, in contrast to Israel where the seasonal rainfall provided irrigation. *There we sat:* Some interpreters think that "there" indicates that the speaker is now somewhere else; not in Babylonia but (most likely) in the land of Israel. *There,* along with *alien soil* (v. 4), stresses the otherness of the place of exile. **2–4:** The Babylonian captors demand musical entertainment but the captive Temple singers, who can only cry, hang up their instruments and refuse to make music. They cannot express joy as long as they are in exile. Joy, which is synonymous with being in God's Presence, is no longer possible when the Temple is destroyed. Exile is equated with descent into the world of the dead; like the dead, the exiles are unable to praise God (30.10; 88.11–13). **2:** The *poplars,* or willows, grow along the canals. **3–4:** *Songs of Zion:* Some scholars identify Zion songs as specific types of hymns about the Temple (46; 48) or as the pilgrimage psalms (84; 120–134). More likely, the Babylonians are asking for any native Judean song. The psalmist equates them with *a song of the LORD,* that is, any song sung in the Temple, and therefore they can no longer be sung. **5–6:** An oath never to forget Jerusalem. This is a central idea in Jewish tradition, enshrined in the later practice of leaving an interior wall facing Jerusalem undecorated or with a "mizraḥ" (plaque indicating the east), and in the breaking of the glass at the conclusion of the wedding ceremony (which symbolizes, according to one explanation, placing the memory of the destruction of Jerusalem above one's greatest joy, that of being wed). *Right hand wither,* or become useless, paralyzed. *My tongue stick to my palate,* be unable to utter a sound (Ezek. 3.26; Lam. 4.4). The paralysis of the *right hand* and *tongue* make it impossible to play the lyre and to sing (Radak). **7:** The tone changes dramatically, but the two parts of the psalm are connected: Just as Israel must remember Jerusalem, God must remember who destroyed it. The *Edomites,* who joined Babylonia in the attack on Jerusalem (Obad. 1.11–14) are cursed. **8–9:** Thoughts of retribution are commonly found in laments (5.11; 35.4–8; 69.23–28; 79.10; Lam. 1.21–22; 3.64–66; 4.21–22). On dashing babies against rocks, see 2 Kings 8.12; Isa. 13.16; Hos. 14.1; Nah. 3.10. *Against the rocks,* Heb "ha-sela'," "the Rock" (possibly Petra), the fortress-city of Edom and also an epithet for Edom (2 Kings 14.7). The gist of this gruesome pun is that the rock-fortress protecting Edom will become the vehicle for Edom's punishment.

Ps. 138: This is the first of a collection of hymns (138–145) that concludes the Psalter. Petitions characterize the Psalter's opening, and many see an intentional movement from petitions

2 I bow toward Your holy temple
and praise Your name for Your steadfast love and faithfulness,
because You have exalted [a]Your name, Your word, above all.[-a]
3 When I called, You answered me,
[a]You inspired me with courage.[-a]
4 All the kings of the earth shall praise You, O LORD,
for they have heard the words You spoke.
5 They shall sing of the ways of the LORD,
"Great is the majesty of the LORD!"
6 High though the LORD is, He sees the lowly;
lofty, He perceives from afar.
7 Though I walk among enemies,
You preserve me in the face of my foes;
You extend Your hand;
with Your right hand You deliver me.
8 The LORD will settle accounts for me.
O LORD, Your steadfast love is eternal;
do not forsake the work of Your hands.

139

For the leader. Of David. A psalm.

O LORD, You have examined me and know me.
2 When I sit down or stand up You know it;
You discern my thoughts from afar.
3 [a]You observe[-a] my walking and reclining,
and are familiar with all my ways.
4 There is not a word on my tongue
but that You, O LORD, know it well.
5 You hedge me before and behind;
You lay Your hand upon me.
6 It is beyond my knowledge;
it is a mystery; I cannot fathom it.
7 Where can I escape from Your spirit?
Where can I flee from Your presence?
8 If I ascend to heaven, You are there;
if I descend to Sheol, You are there too.
9 If I take wing with the dawn
to come to rest on the western horizon,
10 even there Your hand will be guiding me,
Your right hand will be holding me fast.
11 If I say, "Surely darkness [b]will conceal me,
night will provide me with cover,"[-b]

a-a *Meaning of Heb. uncertain.*
b-b *Cf. Rashi, Ibn Ezra; meaning of Heb. uncertain.*

to hymns as part of the structure that the editor intended. The book of Psalms would then reflect a movement from lament to praise. The psalmist praises God, certain that God protects individuals and will not fail to protect the psalmist. **1:** *Before the divine beings,* the divine council (82.1; 89.7–8; 95.3). **2:** In Deuteronomic theology, the name of the LORD resides in the Temple (Deut. 12.11). The Temple is the place where humans come into ritual contact with God, but God, or the divine Presence, does not reside there (contrast Exod. 25.8). **4–5:** Foreign kings praise God (cf. 67.4–6; 117; 126.2); praise for God extends well beyond the psalmist, becoming universal. *The words You spoke:* Medieval commentators explain that these were the words of the Torah or the prophets. **7–8:** See 23.4. *The work of Your hands,* your creatures, including the psalmist.

Ps. 139: God knows all that can be known; He is present in all places; no one can escape His reach. These divine attributes (vv. 1–18), which at first seem threatening to the psalmist (since God will discern his faults), become the basis for the psalmist's plea for God to destroy his enemies, who are also God's enemies (vv. 19–24); the psalmist is convinced of his relative innocence. The text is difficult in vv. 3, 11, 16, and 20. **1–18:** An exquisitely detailed and poetic description of divine omniscience. **2:** *Sit down ... stand up,* an expression comprising the whole of one's life and activity (Deut. 6.7). **5:** The *hand* of the LORD is an expression for divine control and assistance (v. 10). **6:** Similar statements that God's wonders are unknowable are found in Job. **8:** *Sheol,* the abode of the dead, below the ground; here it is the nadir of the earth. Unlike other usages of Sheol, to signify being cut off from God, here the psalmist says, perhaps in a rhetorical overstatement, that one cannot escape from God even in Sheol. **9:** V. 8 gives the vertical axis, from apex to nadir; v. 9 gives the horizontal axis, from east to west. **11–12:** *Darkness,* where humans can hide from each other, is no hiding place from God. **13–16:** The mysteriously wonderful process of gestation. God saw the psalmist even in the womb (cf. Jer. 1.5). **15:** Only here are people imagined to be *knit together.* **16:** *Recorded in Your book:* According to Rashi, this is the book containing a list of all people ever to be born, which God showed to Adam. According to Ibn Ezra, it is the blueprint according to which the person is formed. No such book is mentioned in Gen., though a common rabbinic tradition based on Prov. 3.19 imagines that the Torah served as the divine blueprint during creation. **17–18:** God's thoughts are unfathomable (cf. Isa. 55.8–9). The image of counting thoughts is strikingly original. **21–22:** The psalmist shows his solidarity with God by declaring hatred for God's enemies. **23–24:** A return to the theme of knowledge: An all-knowing God surely knows the psalmist's righteousness.

Ps. 140: A prayer for deliverance from enemies, evil and lawless people whose wrongful speech is likened to weapons. **4:** Sins of speech of the psalmist's foes (v. 12). *Serpents* and *spiders* are dangerous creatures that sting and poison their victims. For the metaphor of *tongues* and *poison* used of damaging speech, see 57.5; 58.5–7. *Selah* (also vv. 6, 9), see 3.3 n.

12 darkness is not dark for You;
night is as light as day;
darkness and light are the same.
13 It was You who created my conscience;[a]
You fashioned me in my mother's womb.
14 I praise You,
for I am awesomely, wondrously made;
Your work is wonderful;
I know it very well.
15 My frame was not concealed from You
when I was shaped in a hidden place,
knit together in the recesses of the earth.
16 Your eyes saw my unformed limbs;
they were all recorded in Your book;
in due time they were formed,
[b]to the very last one of them.[-b]
17 How weighty Your thoughts seem to me,
O God,
how great their number!
18 I count them—they exceed the grains of sand;
I end—but am still with You.

19 O God, if You would only slay the wicked—
you murderers, away from me!—
20 [b]who invoke You for intrigue,
Your enemies who swear by You falsely.[-b]
21 O LORD, You know I hate those who hate You,
and loathe Your adversaries.
22 I feel a perfect hatred toward them;
I count them my enemies.

23 Examine me, O God, and know my mind;
probe me and know my thoughts.
24 See if I have vexatious ways,
and guide me in ways everlasting.

140

For the leader. A psalm of David.

2 Rescue me, O LORD, from evil men;
save me from the lawless,
3 whose minds are full of evil schemes,
who plot war every day.
4 They sharpen their tongues like serpents;
spiders' poison is on their lips. *Selah.*

a Lit. "kidneys."
b-b Meaning of Heb. uncertain.

5 O LORD, keep me out of the clutches of the wicked;
save me from lawless men
who scheme to [a]make me fall.[-a]
6 Arrogant men laid traps with ropes for me;
they spread out a net along the way;
they set snares for me. *Selah.*

7 I said to the LORD: You are my God;
give ear, O LORD, to my pleas for mercy.
8 O GOD, my Lord, the strength of my deliverance,
You protected my head on the day of battle.[b]
9 O LORD, do not grant the desires of the wicked;
do not let their plan succeed,
[c]else they be exalted. *Selah.*

10 May the heads of those who beset me
be covered with the mischief of their lips.[-c]
11 may coals of fire drop down upon them,
and they be cast into pits, never to rise again.
12 Let slanderers have no place in the land;
let the evil of the lawless man drive him into
corrals.
13 I know that the LORD will champion
the cause of the poor, the right of the needy.
14 Righteous men shall surely praise Your name;
the upright shall dwell in Your presence.

141

A psalm of David.

I call You, O LORD, hasten to me;
give ear to my cry when I call You.
2 Take my prayer as an offering of incense,
my upraised hands as an evening sacrifice.
3 O LORD, set a guard over my mouth,
a watch at the door of my lips;
4 let my mind not turn to an evil thing,
to practice deeds of wickedness
with men who are evildoers;
let me not feast on their dainties.
5[d] Let the righteous man strike me in loyalty,
let him reprove me;
let my head not refuse such choice oil.
My prayers are still against their[e] evil deeds.
6 May their judges slip on the rock,
but let my words be heard, for they are sweet.

a-a *Lit. "push my feet."* *b* *Lit. "arms."* *c-c* *Meaning of Heb. uncertain.*
d *Meaning of vv. 5–7 uncertain.* *e* *I.e., the evildoers of v. 4.*

5–6: The psalmist is hunted down by his foes; the metaphors come from the realm of warfare. V. 5 is an expansion of v. 2. **7:** Stereotypic language; see 22.11; 86.6. **10–12:** The evildoers will suffer retribution equal to their deeds ("lex talionis"): They will be overcome by their own venomous words (v. 3) and will be hunted and entrapped permanently (v. 4–5). **13–14:** The psalmist's assurance of divine justice. For *poor* and *needy,* see 86.1 n.

Ps. 141: A prayer requesting that prayer be efficacious. Like Ps. 140, the psalm asks for deliverance from enemies (evildoers) in a way that emphasizes the importance of correct speaking. The text of vv. 5–7 is difficult. **2:** Prayer is seen metaphorically as sacrifice, with the hope that the prayer will rise up to God and be accepted just like incense and offerings. This does not mean that the psalmist sees prayer as a replacement for sacrifice, as was the case in post-Temple rabbinic times and afterwards, though it may suggest that prayer accompanied the evening incense offering. **3–4:** The psalmist wants God to prevent him from wrongful speech and from association with the wicked (1.1; 26.4). The ideas in these vv. are similar to those in Prov., where there is also concern with proper speech, with avoiding evildoers, and with the contrast between the righteous and the wicked.

7 As when the earth is cleft and broken up
our bones are scattered at the mouth of Sheol.
8 My eyes are fixed upon You, O GOD my Lord;
I seek refuge in You, do not put me in jeopardy.
9 Keep me from the trap laid for me,
and from the snares of evildoers.
10 Let the wicked fall into their nets
while I alone come through.

142

A *maskil* of David, while he was in the cave.[a] A prayer.

2 I cry aloud to the LORD;
I appeal to the LORD loudly for mercy.
3 I pour out my complaint before Him;
I lay my trouble before Him
4 when my spirit fails within me.
You know my course;
they have laid a trap in the path I walk.
5 Look at my right and see—
I have no friend;
there is nowhere I can flee,
no one cares about me.
6 So I cry to You, O LORD;
I say, "You are my refuge,
all I have in the land of the living."
7 Listen to my cry, for I have been brought very low;
save me from my pursuers,
for they are too strong for me.
8 Free me from prison,
that I may praise Your name.
The righteous [b-]shall glory in me[-b]
for Your gracious dealings with me.

143

A psalm of David.

O LORD, hear my prayer;
give ear to my plea, as You are faithful;
answer me, as You are beneficent.
2 Do not enter into judgment with Your servant,
for before You no creature is in the right.

3 My foe hounded me;
he crushed me to the ground;
he made me dwell in darkness
like those long dead.

7: A graphic picture of *Sheol,* the abode of the dead. **9–10:** Retribution. As in the previous psalm, planning to entrap the psalmist, the evildoers are themselves entrapped (35.7–8; 140.5), an idea especially common in wisdom literature.

Ps. 142: 1: For a similar superscription see 57.1. The incident referred to is in 1 Sam. 24.3–4, when David was fleeing from Saul. These superscriptions are the ancient editor's way of linking particular psalms to incidents in the life of David, the traditional author of Psalms. Some modern commentators see *the cave* as a reference to prison (see v. 8) and attribute the psalm to a person confined in a prison. The psalmist feels utterly alone; only God cares for him (vv. 5–6). The psalm uses much stereotyped imagery. **2:** See Ps. 3.5. **3:** See 102.1. **4:** See 140.6; 141.9–10. **5:** See 25.16. **8:** *Prison,* a metaphor for Sheol, the abode of the dead, where praising God is not possible (30.4–5; 115.17–18). *For your gracious dealings with me,* see 13.6, also concluding a psalm.

Ps. 143: This psalm contrasts the dead, who have no access to God, with the living, who do. The psalmist pleads to remain among the living. "Enemies" and "illness" are typical threats to the psalmist's well-being. The psalm uses stereotypical language, and contains thematic and verbal connections with the previous psalm; see especially v. 4. **2:** *For before You no creature is in the right* is an idea also expressed by Job's friends (Job 4.17–21). **3:** *Darkness,* the realm of the dead. *Long dead,* better "eternally dead." The idea is that the dead can never live again (see Lam. 3.6).

a *Cf. 1 Sam. 24.3–4.* b-b *Meaning of Heb. uncertain.*

4 My spirit failed within me;
my mind was numbed with horror.
5 Then I thought of the days of old;
I rehearsed all Your deeds,
recounted the work of Your hands.
6 I stretched out my hands to You,
longing for You like thirsty earth. *Selah.*

7 Answer me quickly, O LORD;
my spirit can endure no more.
Do not hide Your face from me,
or I shall become like those who descend into the Pit.
8 Let me learn of Your faithfulness by daybreak,
for in You I trust;
let me know the road I must take,
for on You I have set my hope.
9 Save me from my foes, O LORD;
[a]to You I look for cover.[a]
10 Teach me to do Your will,
for You are my God.
Let Your gracious spirit lead me
on level ground.
11 For the sake of Your name, O LORD, preserve me;
as You are beneficent, free me from distress.
12 As You are faithful, put an end to my foes;
destroy all my mortal enemies,
for I am Your servant.

144

Of David.

Blessed is the LORD, my rock,
who trains my hands for battle,
my fingers for warfare;
2 my faithful one, my fortress,
my haven and my deliverer,
my shield, in whom I take shelter,
who makes peoples[b] subject to me.

3 O LORD, what is man that You should care about him,
mortal man, that You should think of him?
4 Man is like a breath;
his days are like a passing shadow.
5 O LORD, bend Your sky and come down;
touch the mountains and they will smoke.
6 Make lightning flash and scatter them;
shoot Your arrows and rout them.

a-a Meaning of Heb. uncertain. *b So Targum, Saadia; others "my people."*

5–6: In his darkest days, the psalmist remembers God's past deeds. In a move that is the opposite of being dead, he stretches out his hand in prayer, seeking access to God. See 63.2; 77.12–13. **6:** *Selah,* see 3.3 n. **7:** *Hide Your face,* see 102.1. *The Pit,* a poetic term for Sheol, the abode of the dead. Compare 28.1 **8:** *Daybreak,* in contrast to the darkness of death, morning brings a response from God. See 101.8 n. **10:** *Your gracious* (lit. "good") *spirit,* an expression for divine power, contrasted with the weakness of the psalmist (vv. 4, 7). **11:** A common theme in Psalms is that God should preserve the life of the psalmist not because the psalmist is worthy but so that others may see God's power and beneficence and so that the psalmist can offer praise. *For the sake of Your name,* so that the psalmist can praise God, which he cannot do if he dies (see e.g., 6.6). *You are beneficent,* God's beneficence, "tzedakah," frames the psalm and contrasts with the fact that (v. 2) "no human is in the right" ("yitzdak").

Ps. 144: A royal psalm, perhaps recited on the eve of battle by a king who lived after David and who looks to him and other Judean kings as precedents of kings who were saved from danger by God (v. 10). Its theme is that humans, without divine help, cannot win at war. The psalm is anthological, containing language found in a number of other psalms, esp. 18 and 143. It concludes with a prayer for blessings on the people (vv. 12–15). **1–2:** The king as warrior (18.2–3). God is portrayed in military terms as a strong sheltering fortress. **3:** The language resembles 8.5, but the emphasis is different. Here humans are helpless without God. **4–7:** Humans are transient and weak; God is an all-powerful cosmic force (39.6, 7; 109.23). **5:** As frequently in the psalms, God is imagined as dwelling in heaven (see e.g., 2.4). Here, in words with affinities to the language of theophany, He is asked to come down to rescue the supplicant.

7: *Mighty waters,* of the cosmos. *Foreigners,* the human foes, perhaps the Babylonians (if this is an exilic psalm) or the non-Judeans living in Judah at the time of the return (if the psalm is postexilic). **5–7:** See 18.10–17 for a fuller expression of this section. **8:** If "right hand" is meant (see translators' note in NJPS), only God's right hand assures victory (see e.g., 18.36; 118.15–16). **10:** *David* is paralleled with *kings,* suggesting that *David* represents the Davidic dynasty (as does "Your anointed one" in 132.10). **11:** A repetition of elements in v. 8, a type of refrain. **12–14:** The picture is of a well-structured society, youthful and vigorous, with abundance of food and wealth. This is the psalm's wish for the people. **15:** Such *happy* ("'ashrei") statements typically occur at the beginnings of psalms (e.g., Ps. 1) rather than at their ends, but see Ps. 137. Perhaps because it is characteristic of an opening, in Jewish liturgical practice, this v. is read as part of an introduction to Ps. 145.

Pss. 145–150: The Daily Hallel, recited every day in the preliminary morning service. Psalm 145 serves as the introduction to this collection; the following psalms all begin and conclude with *Hallelujah* in the Heb textual tradition.

Ps. 145: An alphabetic acrostic (see Pss. 9–10), with the "nun" (between vv. 13 and 14) omitted (it is supplied, most likely secondarily, in the LXX, the Peshitta, and the Qumran Psalter). The psalm focuses on praise for the kingship of God. This psalm is recited in the three daily prayer services (cf. *b. Ber.* 4b). The alternation between speaking to God and speaking about Him in the third person is typical of many psalms. **1–2:** Eternal blessing of the divine *name* recurs in v. 21. **3:** See 147.5. God is not merely king, but an incomparable king. **4:** God is known through His *acts,* and proclaiming them is a form of praise. **5:** See 77.13; 105.2; 119.27.

7 Reach Your hand down from on high;
rescue me, save me from the mighty waters,
from the hands of foreigners,
8 whose mouths speak lies,
and whose oaths[a] are false.

9 O God, I will sing You a new song,
sing a hymn to You with a ten-stringed harp,
10 to You who give victory to kings,
who rescue His servant David from the deadly sword.
11 Rescue me, save me from the hands of foreigners,
whose mouths speak lies,
and whose oaths[a] are false.

12[b] For our sons are like saplings,
well-tended in their youth;
our daughters are like cornerstones
trimmed to give shape to a palace.
13 Our storehouses are full,
supplying produce of all kinds;
our flocks number thousands,
even myriads, in our fields;
14 our cattle are well cared for.
There is no breaching and no sortie,
and no wailing in our streets.

15 Happy the people who have it so;
happy the people whose God is the LORD.

145

A song of praise. Of David.

א I will extol You, my God and king,
and bless Your name forever and ever.
2 ב Every day will I bless You
and praise Your name forever and ever.
3 ג Great is the LORD and much acclaimed;
His greatness cannot be fathomed.
4 ד One generation shall laud Your works to another
and declare Your mighty acts.
5 ה The glorious majesty of Your splendor
[c]and Your wondrous acts[c] will I recite.
6 ו Men shall talk of the might of Your awesome deeds,
and I will recount Your greatness.

a With Rashi; lit. "right hand."
b The meaning of several phrases in vv. 12–14 is uncertain.
c-c A Qumran Pss. scroll reads: "they will speak of, and Your wonders."

7 ז They shall celebrate Your abundant goodness,
and sing joyously of Your beneficence.
8 ח The LORD is gracious and compassionate,
slow to anger and abounding in kindness.
9 ט The LORD is good to all,
and His mercy is upon all His works.
10 י All Your works shall praise You, O LORD,
and Your faithful ones shall bless You.
11 כ They shall talk of the majesty of Your kingship,
and speak of Your might,
12 ל to make His mighty acts known among men
and the majestic glory of His kingship.
13 מ Your kingship is an eternal kingship;
Your dominion is for all generations.
14 ס The LORD supports all who stumble,
and makes all who are bent stand straight.
15 ע The eyes of all look to You expectantly,
and You give them their food when it is due.
16 פ You give it openhandedly,
feeding every creature to its heart's content.
17 צ The LORD is beneficent in all His ways
and faithful in all His works.
18 ק The LORD is near to all who call Him,
to all who call Him with sincerity.
19 ר He fulfills the wishes of those who fear Him;
He hears their cry and delivers them.
20 ש The LORD watches over all who love Him,
but all the wicked He will destroy.
21 ת My mouth shall utter the praise of the LORD,
and all creatures[a] shall bless His holy name forever
and ever.

146 Hallelujah.
Praise the LORD, O my soul!
2 I will praise the LORD all my life,
sing hymns to my God while I exist.

3 Put not your trust in the great,
in mortal man who cannot save.
4 His breath departs;
he returns to the dust;
on that day his plans come to nothing.

5 Happy is he who has the God of Jacob for his
help,
whose hope is in the LORD his God,

a *Lit. "flesh."*

8: The creed of Exod. 34.6 (Ps. 86.5). **10:** The things that God has created will offer praise to Him (cf. v. 21 and Ps. 148) since he treats them beneficently; or, by their very existence they serve as praise of Him. **11:** Cf. 19.2 where the heavens speak of God's glory. **12:** These are all royal qualities. **13:** Royal dynasties may be long-lived, and subjects may wish their kings long lives, but God as king is truly eternal. **14–16:** As the ideal king, God sustains the oppressed and starving (104.27–28; 146.7–8). **17:** This v. leaves no doubts about God's absolute justice and His ḥesed. **18–19:** True prayer is efficacious. **20:** *Who love Him,* who are loyal to Him; cf. v. 10. Many psalms end with the destruction of the wicked (cf. 1; 146.9). **21:** An inclusio (*praise, bless, forever and ever*) extends the praise of the first-person speaker (vv. 1–2) with that of *all creatures,* all human beings.

Ps. 146: Pss. 146–150 form the concluding doxology of the Psalter; the psalms in this subcollection all begin with *Hallelujah.* Ps. 146 praises God as creator (v. 6) and redeemer (vv. 7–9). Its style is anthological; many of the thoughts and phrases appear elsewhere in the Psalter. **1:** *Praise the LORD, O my soul,* cf. "Bless the LORD, O my soul" (103.1; 104.1). **2:** See 104.33. **3–4:** *Mortal man,* even a prince *(the great),* cannot be relied upon because his life is limited, but God reigns forever (v. 10)—see 118.9. **4:** An allusion to the creation of man from the earth (Gen. 3.19; Ps. 104.29; cf. Eccl. 12.7).

6 maker of heaven and earth,
the sea and all that is in them;
who keeps faith forever;
7 who secures justice for those who are wronged,
gives food to the hungry.
The LORD sets prisoners free;
8 The LORD restores sight to the blind;
the LORD makes those who are bent stand straight;
the LORD loves the righteous;
9 The LORD watches over the stranger;
He gives courage to the orphan and widow,
but makes the path of the wicked tortuous.

10 The LORD shall reign forever,
your God, O Zion, for all generations.
Hallelujah.

147

Hallelujah.
It is good to chant hymns to our God;
it is pleasant to sing glorious praise.

2 The LORD rebuilds Jerusalem;
He gathers in the exiles of Israel.
3 He heals their broken hearts,
and binds up their wounds.
4 He reckoned the number of the stars;
to each He gave its name.
5 Great is our Lord and full of power;
His wisdom is beyond reckoning.
6 The LORD gives courage to the lowly,
and brings the wicked down to the dust.

7 Sing to the LORD a song of praise,
chant a hymn with a lyre to our God,
8 who covers the heavens with clouds,
provides rain for the earth,
makes mountains put forth grass;

6–8: God is not only the creator of the world long ago, but He continues to relieve oppression and hunger and to restore health to His creatures. **7:** *Sets prisoners free,* as a reference to the exiles, cf. Isa. 49.9. **9:** *Stranger ... orphan and widow,* those in society who lack human family protectors. See Deut. 24.17; 27.19; Jer. 7.5–6; Zech. 7.10; Ps. 94.6. **10:** A wish for the eternal kingship of God, and the benefits it would bring. The conclusion recalls and supplements Exod. 15.18. *Zion,* Jerusalem.

Ps. 147: A postexilic psalm praising God, the redeemer of Israel, who restored the exiles and rebuilt Jerusalem. As in Isa. ch 40, upon which this psalm seems to have drawn, God's power to bring about the restoration derives from His being the creator of the world, over which He has continuing control. Much of the psalm, then, describes God as the creator. This divine power is specifically invoked for the benefit of Israel, making it secure and prosperous (vv. 13–14; cf. Ps. 144). In the last part of the psalm, vv. 15–20, God's word, through which He created the world, coalesces with His commandments that He revealed to Israel. This nexus of creation and revelation is found also in Ps. 19, in a different form. The implication is that Judah is restored in order to observe God's commandments (cf. Ps. 105.42–45). More significant, reference to the revelation that initiated the covenantal relationship between God and Israel affirms that the postexilic restoration signals the resumption of this covenantal relationship. **2:** Here and elsewhere in the psalm, God's *rebuild*ing of Jerusalem is idealized. **3:** God heals those broken in spirit and in body, that is, the exiles. *Broken hearts,* those who are contrite or pentitent (51.19). The sick body is best understood as a metaphor for the suffering of the people in exile, now healed by God. Compare Isa. 1.5–6 where the injured body represents the sinful people experiencing their punishment. **4–5:** An allusion to Isa. 40.26. The vast number of the *stars,* which to humans seems infinite, are to God individually countable and recognizable. What is infinite, by contrast, is God's *wisdom.* Mention of the stars is especially meaningful to the exiles living in Babylonia in Second Isaiah's time, where the celestial bodies were revered as gods by the Babylonians and where astral worship was an important part of the religion. By saying that God created the stars, the psalm not only credits God with the masterful creation of the world but also implies that he created the Babylonian gods and retains power over them. **8–9:** God created an ecologically harmonious world in which creatures are cared for (cf. 104.10–16); the psalm stresses God's ongoing care for His creatures. The span of creatures is captured in the merism of domestic animals (*beasts,* "behemah") who eat grass and wild birds of prey (*the raven's*

9 who gives the beasts their food,
to the raven's brood what they cry for.
10 He does not prize the strength of horses,
nor value the fleetness[a] of men;
11 but the LORD values those who fear Him,
those who depend on His faithful care.

12 O Jerusalem, glorify the LORD;
praise your God, O Zion!
13 For He made the bars of your gates strong,
and blessed your children within you.
14 He endows your realm with well-being,
and satisfies you with choice wheat.

15 He sends forth His word to the earth;
His command runs swiftly.
16 He lays down snow like fleece,
scatters frost like ashes.
17 He tosses down hail like crumbs—
who can endure His icy cold?
18 He issues a command—it melts them;
He breathes—the waters flow.
19 He issued His commands to Jacob,
His statutes and rules to Israel.
20 He did not do so for any other nation;
of such rules they know nothing.
Hallelujah.

148

Hallelujah.
Praise the LORD from the heavens;
praise Him on high.
2 Praise Him, all His angels,
praise Him, all His hosts.
3 Praise Him, sun and moon,
praise Him, all bright stars.
4 Praise Him, highest heavens,
and you waters that are above the heavens.
5 Let them praise the name of the LORD,
for it was He who commanded that they be created.
6 He made them endure forever,
establishing an order that shall never change.
7 Praise the LORD, O you who are on earth,
all sea monsters and ocean depths,

a *Lit. "thighs."*

brood) who eat meat. **10–11:** Those who survive are not necessarily the swiftest or most powerful, but those who *fear* the LORD (see esp. Prov. 21.31). *Fear* of the LORD, i.e., respect for God that leads to following His ways, is a major principle in wisdom teachings. *Fleetness of men:* The mention of horses and men suggests horse-drawn war chariots and foot-soldiers (in ancient warfare, horses pulled war-chariots, with the rider standing in the chariot; soldiers did not ride on horseback). **12:** Jerusalem is personified as a mother praising God, overturning images such as Lam. ch 1 where she is personified as a widow, mourning and lamenting. **13–14:** *The bars of your gates,* the locks of the city gates that prevented the enemy from entering the walled city. God brings to Jerusalem security and prosperity. **15–19:** Just as God gave commands to nature, so He gave *commands* (commandments) to Israel. Just as the world is operated by God's command, so Israel should conduct itself by God's commandments, which are a special gift to Israel.

Ps. 148: God is praised for His creation by all that He created, from celestial beings to all the world's rulers and people, including the animate and inanimate (mountains, trees). Praise emanates from the sky and its creations (vv. 1–6) and from the earth (including the sea) and its creations (vv. 7–12), for God's splendor is over earth and sky (v. 13). The psalm shares some elements with the previous psalm; it echoes part of the story of creation in Gen. ch 1 but includes exotic meteorological phenomena (cf. Job ch 38). **2:** The word translated as "angel" is "mal'akh," "messenger." This may refer to the idea that God is surrounded by an entourage of angels or divine beings (8.6; Job 1.6), or that the celestial bodies (v. 3) are God's messengers (cf. 104.4). **4:** For *waters that are above the heavens,* cf. Gen. 1.7. **5:** Creation by God's word, as in Gen. ch 1, but not in Gen. chs 2–3. **6–7:** A reference to the mythological destruction of the sea monster (cf. 74.13–14; Isa. 51.9–10), suppressed and neutralized, as it is in Gen. 1.21, to which this is an allusion. For *ocean depths,* that is, "creatures of the deep," cf. Isa. 42.10. **6:** For God's setting limits to the water, cf. Jer. 5.22.

8 fire and hail, snow and smoke,
storm wind that executes His command,
9 all mountains and hills,
all fruit trees and cedars,
10 all wild and tamed beasts,
creeping things and winged birds,
11 all kings and peoples of the earth,
all princes of the earth and its judges,
12 youths and maidens alike,
old and young together.
13 Let them praise the name of the LORD,
for His name, His alone, is sublime;
His splendor covers heaven and earth.
14 He has exalted the horn of His people
for the glory of all His faithful ones,
Israel, the people close to Him.
Hallelujah.

149

Hallelujah.
Sing to the LORD a new song,
His praises in the congregation of the faithful.
2 Let Israel rejoice in its maker;
let the children of Zion exult in their king.
3 Let them praise His name in dance;
with timbrel and lyre let them chant His praises.
4 For the LORD delights in His people;
He adorns the lowly with victory.
5 Let the faithful exult in glory;
let them shout for joy upon their couches,
6 with paeans to God in their throats
and two-edged swords in their hands,
7 to impose retribution upon the nations,
punishment upon the peoples,
8 binding their kings with shackles,
their nobles with chains of iron,
9 executing the doom decreed against them.
This is the glory of all His faithful.
Hallelujah.

150

Hallelujah.
Praise God in His sanctuary;
praise Him in the sky, His stronghold.

8: For *hail* and *snow,* cf. Job 38.22–30. For *wind* and *fire* as God's messengers, cf. 104.4. **9:** *Cedars* are the stateliest of trees and were used in the construction of the Temple. **10:** See 147.8–9 n. **11–12:** Various merisms—*kings* and commoners, male and female, *old and young.* **13–14:** These vv. are included in the liturgy for returning the Torah to the Ark since the Torah may be seen as representing God (see Ps. 119). They proclaim that God alone is sublime and that He raises *the horn,* the power, of His people Israel. God's *name* is His essence. The entire world is to praise God for the victory He has given to His people. Cf. 117.2.

Ps. 149: An exilic or postexilic psalm, depending on whether the event envisioned has already taken place or is yet to come. The psalm celebrates God's deliverance of His people from exile and their restoration to Judah. The psalm envisions a reversal whereby Israel is the victor and its enemies the vanquished—God again takes delight in his people (v. 4). The music, dancing, joy, and shouting are elements shared by Temple worship and also a victory song, celebrating the conquering hero. The threefold repetition of the *faithful* ("ḥasid," vv. 1, 5, 9; see 4.4 n.) emphasizes loyalty to God. **1:** *A new song,* in the eschatological future. Cf. Isa. 42.10; Pss. 96.1; 144.9. **2:** *Their king,* God. Judah is no longer independent and therefore has no human king. **3:** Cf. 150.3–5; Exod. 15.20; 2 Sam. 6.5. **5:** *Upon their couches,* at night in private (Ibn Ezra). Some emend to "their clans." **6:** *Two-edged swords* may be a metaphor for the power of the words of praise; they can achieve the retribution of the following vv. Ancient swords generally had only one edge, for hacking the enemy, rather than two edges, for stabbing; but see Judg. 3.16. **7:** The idea of retribution against those who harmed Israel is common (Lam. 3.34–66; 4.22). It signifies that God maintains power over the enemy and that His relationship with Israel is still in force. **8:** The treatment received by prisoners of war. The kings who were victorious over Israel are, in turn, defeated and taken captive. **9:** God has already decreed the fate of the enemy, even if it has not yet been fully enacted.

Ps. 150: Praise for God is limitless, to be performed in all places, in all ways, and by all people. The command to *praise,* "hallelu," occurs in every v. This psalm concludes the section and the book of Psalms as

2 Praise Him for His mighty acts;
praise Him for[a] His exceeding greatness.
3 Praise Him with blasts of the horn;
praise Him with harp and lyre.
4 Praise Him with timbrel and dance;
praise Him with lute and pipe.
5 Praise Him with resounding cymbals;
praise Him with loud-clashing cymbals.
6 Let all that breathes praise the LORD.
Hallelujah.

a Or "as befits."

a whole, capturing the essence of the book. The entire ch serves as a doxology (the other four books within Psalms end with a doxological v. **1:** *His sanctuary,* lit. "His holy (place)," which may mean the Temple—where formal or ritual praise took place and where psalms were sung—and/or, as the following line suggests, the heavens. *The sky, His stronghold,* the site of praise is enlarged to include the whole world. The psalm may be contrasting the earthly sanctuary and heavenly sanctuary, or, more likely, may be equating them, speaking of the Temple as a microcosm of the world which God rules from the heavens. Indeed, the psalm seems to be using earthly Temple worship as a metaphor for the universal praise of God. For similar thought and language see 11.4: "The LORD is in His holy palace; / the LORD—His throne is in heaven." *His stronghold,* Heb "ʿuzo" sometimes refers to the Ark (78.61; 105.4; 132.8) or is an attribute of God or His Temple (29.2; 63.3; 96.6). **2:** *His mighty acts,* all the great deeds He did for His people (see 106.2). Praising God for His deeds pays tribute to His nature; God is known by His deeds. Another interpretation is "Praise Him 'with' (the recitation of) His mighty acts." The preposition "b" before *His mighty acts* is the same preposition as before *with harp* (v. 3) and the other musical instruments, and may be construed as the means by which God is to be praised: with words of His deeds and with music. **3–5:** A symphony of praise, where each v. is slightly longer than the previous one, evoking ever-increasing praise. This catalogue-like section (the catalogue was a known ancient literary form) emphasizes the music that accompanies the recitation of God's mighty acts. The list includes wind, percussion, and stringed instruments (cf. Ps. 98.5–6 which lists wind and stringed instruments) and presumably stands for all the known musical instruments. Many of these instruments were used in the Temple. **3:** *Horn:* The ram's horn served in both ritual and secular contexts in biblical times, as an alarm, a call to war, or signal of victory; and in connection with the transfer of the Ark (2 Sam. 6.15). It was also used on the Day of Atonement and the New Moon, in connection with the theophany (Exod. 19.13; Ps. 47.6), and as a cultic instrument (as here). **4:** *Dance:* Dancing accompanied certain cultic rituals, like the return of the Ark (2 Sam. 6.16, 20) and at the sanctuary (Ps. 87.7). Ps. 149.3, like our psalm, speaks of dance, timbrel, and lyre as forms of praise. Miriam and the other women went out dancing, with drums (Exod. 15.20). An alternative explanation takes "mahol" as a musical instrument, related to "halil," as in 1 Sam. 10.5, "lyres, timbrels, flutes, and harps." **6:** *All that breathes,* perhaps all animate creation, though more likely all humans, to all whom God gave the breath of life (Gen. 2.7; Isa. 42.5; 57.16). Similarly, Ps. 145.21, where all human beings are to praise God; contrast Ps. 148 where the divine beings and all things that God created praise him. Here, the eschatological hope for universal human praise for God climactically concludes the psalm and the Psalter as a whole. It looks beyond the collection of Israel's songs of praise contained in the book to the time in the future when all will praise God.

משלי

Proverbs

Setting and Major Themes

THE BOOK OF PROVERBS opens a window to a realm of ancient Israelite experience little seen elsewhere in the Bible: everyday life. Proverbs guides individuals (not the nation) in how to do what is wise in their day-to-day lives. It teaches the attitudes and courses of actions that are right, just, and pious, and the ways of behavior that facilitate and strengthen personal relationships, the forms of communication and commerce that make the life of the community congenial and secure, and the types of prudence and industry that help one achieve financial security.

The English title of the book, Proverbs, based on the Heb title *mishlei,* is a misnomer, since the book contains more than proverbs. The Heb word *mashal,* of which *mishlei,* proverbs, is a form of the plural, can also mean a comparison. The book, however, contains a variety of genres beyond the short proverb and comparison, incorporating a diversity of material that reflects on daily life.

Proverbs is a paean to the power of the human mind. Its authors are convinced that all who attend to the wisdom of the past and employ their powers of rational thinking have the ability to know what to do and what to avoid. These powers and the knowledge that goes with them are called wisdom. Wisdom—Heb *ḥokhmah*—is the great virtue that, for Proverbs, entails all others. No divine revelation is necessary, for God gave humanity the faculty of wisdom, and people need only listen to her call (ch 8). Thus, there is a certain tension between Proverbs and Torah books, which insist on the significance of revealed law.

Authorship

THE BOOK OF PROVERBS, Heb *Mishlei* (for *Mishlei Shlomo,* "Proverbs of Solomon"), is one of three biblical books ascribed to Solomon. According to tradition, he wrote the love lyrics of the Song of Songs when he was young, the wisdom of Proverbs in his midlife, and the disillusioned complaints of Ecclesiastes when he was old (*Song Rab.* §10). Some sections of the book are ascribed to other sages (24.23; 30.1–14; 31.1–9; and probably 22.17—see the n. to that v.). In fact, actual Solomonic authorship of any part of the book is doubtful. Neither the language nor the content, which hardly deals with royal matters, fits Solomon's time. Proverbs is a collective work, holding the wisdom of mostly anonymous wise men (and women, who could make up sayings as well as men; see 31.1) from many walks of life and different periods.

Wisdom Literature

THE WISDOM TEXTS IN THE BIBLE are Proverbs, Job, and Ecclesiastes, which need to be read within the framework of an international Near Eastern wisdom tradition (see intro. to Kethuvim, pp. 1263–64; "Religion of the Bible, 'The Wisdom Tradition,'" pp. 1994–96). Proverbs and the postbiblical book of Sirach belong to the genre of didactic wisdom. They offer instructions and observations directing the reader in the formation of ethical character and in leading a successful and happy life. Ecclesiastes, in spite of its sometimes unorthodox ideas, belongs in this group. Compositions very similar in character and content were written in Egypt and Mesopotamia, starting in the late third millennium BCE and extending to the Hellenistic period, as late as the 3rd c. BCE.

Egyptian wisdom books in particular are close in form and content to Proverbs. Most important is the *Instruction of Amenemope* (probably dating from the 13th or 12th c.), which is the source of much of Prov. 22.17–23.11 (see 22.17–23.11 n.). Foreign wisdom books provide the intellectual context of Proverbs and clarify its ideas and goals. In the annotations, reference will be made primarily to the translations of Egyptian wisdom in Miriam Lichtheim's *Ancient Egyptian Literature (AEL),* vols. 1–3 (Berkeley: University of California).

Proverbs in Jewish Thought

THE HEBREW WORD "TORAH" MEANS "instruction." In Proverbs, this *torah* is human wisdom, the wise man's teachings. Likewise *ḥokhmah* ("wisdom") is human wisdom. Later Jewish sages would understand *torah* as the Torah of Moses and equate "wisdom" with this Torah. (This is first explicitly attested in the 2nd-c. BCE wisdom work, Ben Sira [Ben]Sirach, sometimes also called Ecclesiasticus.) All that is said about "torah" and "wisdom" in Proverbs was understood in this way. For example, Prov. 8.22 was read to mean that Torah was created before the rest of the world, and 3.17–18, which refers to wisdom, became incorporated in the Torah service in the synagogue in reference to the Torah.

Proverbs is widely quoted in the midrash and in subsequent homiletic literature, such as medieval sermons. It was also a foundational text of the Musar movement, a pietistic movement among European Jews in the 18th to 19th centuries.

Reading Proverbs

THE BOOK IS BEST READ WITH ATTENTION to the different genres it contains. Collection I, chs 1–9, is made up of relatively long, carefully structured and interrelated poems, probably fifteen in number. Collection VI, chs 30 and 31, holds four relatively long poems. Collection I should be read as a unit, and each of the four poems in Collection VI should be read as a unit. Very different are the four middle collections, in chs 10–29. These are composed of short sayings, mostly of two lines, though there are occasionally epigrams of several lines, such as 24.30–34. There is no overall organization, and few literary units extend beyond the single-verse couplet. Often, however, one saying continues the general theme of the preceding one or repeats its key terms, thus producing proverb strings. Here it does not matter much in what order they are read. One way of reading them is sequentially, with an attempt to grasp the ideas that unite them all. Another valid approach is to dip into them at random, reading a few at a time and thinking about the ones with striking ideas, metaphors, or imagery. Another approach looks for proverbs from different chapters that share common elements or repeat the same theme.

Proverbs is an anthology, and the sayings in it should be judged individually. Not all sayings will speak to every reader, but each reader should find many sayings and poems that pack insight and good sense into brief and memorable forms.

Major Units of the Book and Their Titles

I. 1.1–9.18 "The proverbs of Solomon son of David, king of Israel" (1.1)
II. 10.1–22.16 "The proverbs of Solomon" (10.1)
III. 22.17–24.22 "Words of the Sages" (22.17, emended)

IV.	24.23–34	"These also are by the sages" (24.23)
V.	25.1–29.27	"These too are proverbs of Solomon, which the men of King Hezekiah of Judah copied" (25.1)
VI.	30.1–31.31	Appendices
A.	30.1–14	"The words of Agur" (30.1)
B.	30.15–33	Numerical epigrams
C.	31.1–9	"The words of Lemuel" (31.1)
D.	31.10–31	The Woman of Strength

[MICHAEL V. FOX]

1 The proverbs of Solomon son of David, king of Israel:

2 For learning wisdom and discipline;
For understanding words of discernment;
3 For acquiring the discipline for success,
Righteousness, justice, and equity;
4 For endowing the simple with shrewdness,
The young with knowledge and foresight.
5 —The wise man, hearing them, will gain more wisdom;
The discerning man will learn to be adroit;
6 For understanding proverb and epigram,
The words of the wise and their riddles.

7 The fear of the LORD is the beginning[a] of knowledge;
Fools despise wisdom and discipline.

8 My son, heed the discipline of your father,
And do not forsake the instruction of your mother;
9 For they are a graceful wreath upon your head,
A necklace about your throat.

a Or "best part."

1.1–9.18: Collection I. Though chs 1–9 serve as an introduction to the book, the section was probably written later as a guide to interpreting the old sayings in chs 10–29. After the prologue (1.1–7), there are two distinct series of poems, the ten "Lectures" (I–X) and the five "Interludes" (A–E). The Lectures are formulated as father-to-son instruction, and each develops a single topic in a three-part structure: (1) A Call to Attention, in which the speaker exhorts his son to hear his wisdom and remember it, because thus he will receive great rewards; e.g., 1.8–9. (2) A Lesson, which is the main body of the teaching; e.g., 1.10–18. (3) A Conclusion, which is a statement of the general principle underlying the Lesson; e.g., 1.19. Sometimes the conclusion is missing. Of the five Interludes, C is a collection of four epigrams that stands apart from the rest of the unit, while A, B, D, and E are interpretive additions in praise of wisdom, which portray wisdom as a nearly divine woman who represents a power transcending the individual teachings (see 1.20–33 n.).

1.1–7: The prologue, added at a late stage in the book's growth, was written as an introduction to the book, to explain its use and to commend it to readers. **1: The title** ascribes the book to King Solomon, the archetypal wise man. See 1 Kings 3.4–28; 5.10–14. On the historical veracity of this inscription, see intro. **2–6: The statement of purpose** defines the twofold purpose of the book: first, to inculcate the basic virtues of wisdom and ethical behavior in the young, and, second, to enable the mature wise man to increase his wisdom and hone his skills in interpreting literary wisdom. In both cases, the assumed audience is male. Like many other lectures, this one is typified by the use of many synonyms and near-synonyms. **7:** *Fear of the LORD* is the ground for wisdom to grow in; it is essentially conscience. In its most basic form, in the untutored child, it is unreflective fear of consequences. As wisdom develops, fear of God becomes a cognitive awareness of what God wants and does, and this type of fear is equivalent to knowledge of the LORD (2.5). Fear of God is effective in keeping one from evil even in secret deeds and even in spheres of behavior where the law does not apply. *Beginning of knowledge:* The commentators debated whether "re'shit" (here translated "beginning") means first in time or first in quality, that is, the best part. The variant of this v. in 9.10 uses a word that definitely means "beginning."

1.8–19: Lecture I: Avoid gangs. In vv. 8–9, the father, who speaks throughout the Lectures in chs 1–9, identifies the instruction he is about to deliver as both his own and his wife's (similarly 6.20), even though the specific words are his.

10 My son, if sinners entice you, do not yield;
11 If they say, "Come with us,
Let us set an ambush to shed blood,
Let us lie in wait for the innocent
(Without cause!)
12 Like Sheol, let us swallow them alive;
Whole, like those who go down into the Pit.
13 We shall obtain every precious treasure;
We shall fill our homes with loot.
14 Throw in your lot with us;
We shall all have a common purse."
15 My son, do not set out with them;
Keep your feet from their path.
16 For their feet run to evil;
They hurry to shed blood.
17 In the eyes of every winged creature
The outspread net means nothing.
18 But they lie in ambush for their own blood;
They lie in wait for their own lives.
19 Such is the fate of all who pursue unjust gain;
It takes the life of its possessor.

20 Wisdom[a] cries aloud in the streets,
Raises her voice in the squares.
21 At the head of the busy streets she calls;
At the entrance of the gates, in the city, she speaks out:
22 "How long will you simple ones love simplicity,
You scoffers be eager to scoff,
You dullards hate knowledge?
23 You are indifferent to my rebuke;
I will now speak my mind to you,
And let you know my thoughts.
24 Since you refused me when I called,
And paid no heed when I extended my hand,
25 You spurned all my advice,
And would not hear my rebuke,

a In Proverbs, wisdom is personified as a woman.

Elsewhere in wisdom literature there is occasional allusion to mothers as teachers. For example, the Egyptian Duachety concludes his instruction with the words, "Praise God for your father and your mother, who set you on the way of life!" (*AEL* 2.191). Also, 31.1–9 is spoken by a woman. **10–14:** *My son,* many scholars understand the "son" to be a student in a school and "father" to be a schoolteacher, but there is no evidence for this. Egyptian instructions are consistently presented as a father's words to his actual son, and the mention of the mother in 1.8; 4.3; 6.20 points to a family context, at least as the fictional setting of wisdom instruction. The texts could secondarily be used in schools, as they were in Egypt, along with works of many other types. In the following annotations, "pupil" means the youth to whom the teaching is directed, without presumption of a school setting. *Come with us,* the invitation a gang of thugs might use to entice a young man to join them in plotting a murderous mugging. They have grandiose notions of their power. They think that they are as powerful as *Sheol,* the netherworld. They hold out promises of comradeship and a share of the wealth. **15–18:** Even a bird has enough sense to avoid a trap laid out in plain sight, but the criminals are too stupid even for that. *They hurry to shed blood,* not realizing that it is *their own.* **19:** Conclusion: Evildoers destroy themselves by means of the evil that they themselves create. This text does not explicitly state that God is involved in this process; contrast 5.21–23.

1.20–33: Interlude A: Lady Wisdom chastises the foolish. In Interludes A, D, and E, wisdom is described as a woman. (In Heb, the word for wisdom, "ḥokhmah," is a feminine abstract noun.) Such personification is briefly suggested in 2.3; 3.13–20; 4.8–9; 7.4. There are various theories to account for the origins of the wisdom personification. Some commentators believe that it derives from a goddess, such as a Canaanite wisdom goddess (though no such deity is known) or the Egyptian Ma'at, goddess of truth and justice, or the Egyptian Isis, goddess of wisdom. Lady Wisdom does bear some similarities to ancient Near Eastern goddesses, but in Prov. she is a literary figure created as a vivid and memorable way of speaking about human wisdom. **20–21:** Wisdom is by no means secret or esoteric. She is public, frequenting the busiest parts of the town (*the gates* of a city were the location of much public and private business) and calling to all to accept her. Cf. 8.1.

1.22–30: Wisdom castigates fools. They spurned her warning, in other words, ignored the teachings and warnings of their elders. In return, Wisdom will scorn the fools when they most need her, when they find

26 I will laugh at your calamity,
And mock when terror comes upon you,
27 When terror comes like a disaster,
And calamity arrives like a whirlwind,
When trouble and distress come upon you.
28 Then they shall call me but I will not answer;
They shall seek me but not find me.
29 Because they hated knowledge,
And did not choose fear of the LORD;
30 They refused my advice,
And disdained all my rebukes,
31 They shall eat the fruit of their ways,
And have their fill of their own counsels.
32 The tranquillity of the simple will kill them,
And the complacency of dullards will destroy them.
33 But he who listens to me will dwell in safety,
Untroubled by the terror of misfortune."

2 My son, if you accept my words
And treasure up my commandments;
2 If you make your ear attentive to wisdom
And your mind open to discernment;
3 If you call to understanding
And cry aloud to discernment,
4 If you seek it as you do silver
And search for it as for treasures,
5 Then you will understand the fear of the LORD
And attain knowledge of God.
6 For the LORD grants wisdom;
Knowledge and discernment are by His decree.
7 He reserves ability for the upright
And is a shield for those who live blamelessly,
8 Guarding the paths of justice,
Protecting the way of those loyal to Him.
9 You will then understand what is right, just,
And equitable—every good course.
10 For wisdom will enter your mind
And knowledge will delight you.
11 Foresight will protect you,
And discernment will guard you.
12 It will save you from the way of evil men,
From men who speak duplicity,
13 Who leave the paths of rectitude
To follow the ways of darkness,
14 Who rejoice in doing evil
And exult in the duplicity of evil men,
15 Men whose paths are crooked
And who are devious in their course.

themselves in trouble and are in desperate need of clear and effective thinking. **31–33:** The punishment threatened here, as so often in Prov., is presented as the natural consequence of the evil action.

2.1–22: Lecture II: The path to wisdom. The entirety of ch 2 is a single Lecture. The extended Call to Attention (vv. 1–11) says that if you (the pupil) attend to my (the father's) words and seek for wisdom diligently, you will, with God's help, gain true wisdom and piety. The Lesson says that wisdom will protect you from the wicked man (vv. 12–15) and the wicked woman (vv. 16–20). The Conclusion (vv. 21–22) recapitulates the two paths that people must choose between. **5:** *The fear of the LORD* is both the starting point of wisdom (1.7; 9.10) and its goal. The wise man attains a deeper, cognitive conscience, and this is linked to *knowledge of God.* This is not theological knowledge, namely an understanding of the nature of God, but rather a constant awareness of God's will. **6:** God is the ultimate source of the faculty of wisdom, though not the specific words. **12–15:** One grave danger facing a youth is *evil men.* These men are inherently corrupt and crooked. Their values are perverted, so that they do not merely do evil as a means, they positively *rejoice* in it.

16 It will save you from the forbidden[a] woman,
From the alien woman whose talk is smooth,
17 Who forsakes the companion of her youth
And disregards the covenant of her God.
18 Her house sinks down to Death,
And her course leads to the shades.
19 All who go to her cannot return
And find again the paths of life.

20 So follow the way of the good
And keep to the paths of the just.
21 For the upright will inhabit the earth,
The blameless will remain in it.
22 While the wicked will vanish from the land
And the treacherous will be rooted out of it.

3 My son, do not forget my teaching,
But let your mind retain my commandments;
2 For they will bestow on you length of days,
Years of life and well-being.
3 Let fidelity and steadfastness not leave you;
Bind them about your throat,
Write them on the tablet of your mind,
4 And you will find favor and approbation
In the eyes of God and man.
5 Trust in the LORD with all your heart,
And do not rely on your own understanding.
6 In all your ways acknowledge Him,
And He will make your paths smooth.
7 Do not be wise in your own eyes;
Fear the LORD and shun evil.
8 It will be a cure for your body,[b]
A tonic for your bones.
9 Honor the LORD with your wealth,
With the best of all your income,

a Lit. "strange." *b Lit. "navel."*

16–20: The second danger is the wicked woman, the sexually predatory female, lit. "the strange woman." Warnings against the "strange woman" appear in 2.16–22; 5.1–23; 6.20–35; 7.1–27, and more briefly in 22.14; 23.27. She is in some ways contrasted with Dame Wisdom and she provides the traits for the personification of folly in 9.13–18. The "strange woman" has been interpreted in various ways, including: (1) a symbol of folly and wicked counsels; (2) a figure for heresy, in medieval Jewish interpretation, and particularly Christianity; (3) foreign wisdom, such as Greek philosophy; (4) a foreign love goddess (Aphrodite-Ishtar); (5) a devotee of the love goddess; (6) a prostitute; (7) the "Other," the repository or symbol of lust, chaos, and evil; (8) a human adulteress, another man's wife. The last is most likely; see v. 16 n. **16:** "Strange" (see translators' note *a*) means an outsider, in this case, one who does not belong in the context of a particular marriage. *Alien* has the same meaning. The strange woman in Prov. is married to another man (see 2.17; 6.26, 29, 34; 7.19; possibly 5.10 as well). The strange woman's allure lies less in her looks (mentioned only in 6.25) than in her words (5.3; 6.24; 7.5, 21; Cf. 22.14). Her speech is *smooth,* lit. "slippery"—flattering, tricky, and ingratiating. Ch 7 is an extended demonstration of her verbal powers. **17:** The *covenant of her God* is often understood (esp. by traditional Jewish commentators) as the covenant at Sinai, whose law forbids adultery, but this is unlikely in wisdom contexts, which never mention the covenant between God and Israel and focus on the individual. It probably means the covenant of marriage, which is made before God. See Mal. 2.14 and Hos. 2.18–22. **18:** Going to the strange woman's house puts one on the slopes to the underworld; the equation between the foreign woman and death is a common theme of these poems. **21–22:** Many traditional Jewish interpreters understood *earth* ("'eretz") to refer to eternal life, a postbiblical notion. Others explained it as the land of Israel. More likely, *earth* is this world. The righteous will *inhabit* it insofar as they will be blessed with a long life, while the wicked will die prematurely.

3.1–12: Lecture III: The wisdom of piety. The Lesson (vv. 5–12), composed of distinct sayings, teaches humility, faith in God, fulfillment of cultic duties, and submission to divine chastisement. Unusually for Prov., it does not insist on the importance of wisdom, nor does it equate wisdom and religious virtues. **3:** Wear the teachings close to your body so that you will always have them with you (1.9; 4.9; 6.21 n.). *Write them on the tablet of your mind* ("heart"), hold them permanently in memory. **9:** *Honor the LORD* by bringing sacrificial donations to the Temple.

10 And your barns will be filled with grain,
Your vats will burst with new wine.
11 Do not reject the discipline of the LORD, my son;
Do not abhor His rebuke.
12 For whom the LORD loves, He rebukes,
As a father the son whom he favors.

13 Happy is the man who finds wisdom,
The man who attains understanding.
14 Her value in trade is better than silver,
Her yield, greater than gold.
15 She is more precious than rubies;
All of your goods cannot equal her.
16 In her right hand is length of days,
In her left, riches and honor.
17 Her ways are pleasant ways,
And all her paths, peaceful.
18 She is a tree of life to those who grasp her,
And whoever holds on to her is happy.

19 The LORD founded the earth by wisdom;
He established the heavens by understanding;
20 By His knowledge the depths burst apart,
And the skies distilled dew.
21 My son, do not lose sight of them;
Hold on to resourcefulness and foresight.
22 They will give life to your spirit
And grace to your throat.
23 Then you will go your way safely
And not injure your feet.
24 When you lie down you will be unafraid;
You will lie down and your sleep will be sweet.
25 You will not fear sudden terror
Or the disaster that comes upon the wicked,
26 For the LORD will be your trust;
He will keep your feet from being caught.

27 Do not withhold good from one who deserves it
When you have the power to do it [for him].
28 Do not say to your fellow, "Come back again;
I'll give it to you tomorrow," when you have it
with you.
29 Do not devise harm against your fellow
Who lives trustfully with you.

11–12: Sometimes suffering can be interpreted as divine discipline, a warning intended to spare one greater punishments. On the basis of vv. 11–12 and Ps. 94.12, the Talmud develops the concept of "afflictions of love" (*b. Ber.* 8a, etc.).

3.13–20: Interlude B: In praise of wisdom. 14–15: Wisdom is precious beyond price. **16:** In the background of this passage may be the Egyptian practice of depicting gods holding the symbols of their powers and blessings (particularly "life" and "prosperity"). **17–18:** These vv. are recited in the Torah service, when the Torah is returned to the Ark. The subject of the sentences is wisdom, which is consistently understood in Jewish interpretation to designate Torah. **18:** The *tree of life* was a widespread ancient Near Eastern mythological symbol, which is especially popular in Mesopotamian palace reliefs. It represented a divine source of well-being and life, sometimes meaning eternal life. In Prov., the symbol has lost its mythological connections and is a metaphor for a source of life and health. Based on the present v., the Rabbis identified the *tree of life* with Torah. **19–20:** The highest praise of wisdom is that God Himself possesses it, used it in creating the world, and continues to use it. The welling up of springs and the descent of dew belong to both original creation and ongoing providence.

3.21–35: Lecture IV: The wisdom of honesty. The Lesson, vv. 27–31, comprises five admonitions, all beginning with *do not.* The general theme of the Lecture is the importance of honesty in social relations. **21:** *Them:* "My words" may have once stood in the Heb, or perhaps there was once a couplet like 4.20a before this v. **22:** *Grace to your throat* suggests the necklace metaphor, used in 1.9 and 3.3b. **24:** God will protect you when you sleep (Ps. 4.9) and spare you nightmares (such as Job suffered; see Job 7.14). **25:** Cf. 1.27. **28:** When someone comes to claim something rightly his—a loan, for example, or property left in your safekeeping—do not dawdle in restoring it to him. **29:** It is especially unethical to scheme to injure someone who trusts you.

30: You may not quarrel for no cause. Sometimes, however, a quarrel is justifiable and unavoidable; see 25.9. **31:** Do not envy or imitate a prospering sinner, because his downfall is inevitable. This is the message of Pss. 37 and 73 as well. **32:** *Abomination* refers to something that causes disgust. In Prov., it is used particularly with reference to falsity in thought and words. It is most often used with regard to sins which are not easily detected or which are not formally illegal. **33–35:** The Conclusion consists of three aphorisms contrasting the consequences of wisdom and folly.

4.1–9: Lecture V: Loving wisdom, hating evil. 1–4: The speaker recounts how he received instruction from his own father and quotes his teaching (vv. 4b–9). The message is: get wisdom. **6:** It is not enough to obey wisdom; you must *love* it. **7:** The first step in attaining wisdom is to *acquire* (absorb) the teachings of wisdom, to hear and assimilate them, even before you can properly understand and apply them.

4.10–19: Lecture VI: The two paths. The person who chooses the right course of behavior will naturally find himself going in the right direction and will prosper and be safe. One must avoid the twisted and murky path of the wicked, for the wicked live in turmoil and anxiety. Throughout Prov., the ideal is walking *straight,* while crooked routes are condemned. **13:** *Discipline,* Heb "musar," is one way wisdom is conveyed. It generally implies physical chastisement of some sort. Even this kind of teaching must be embraced passionately.

30 Do not quarrel with a man for no cause,
When he has done you no harm.
31 Do not envy a lawless man,
Or choose any of his ways;
32 For the devious man is an abomination to the LORD,
But He is intimate with the straightforward.
33 The curse of the LORD is on the house of the wicked,
But He blesses the abode of the righteous.
34 At scoffers He scoffs,
But to the lowly He shows grace.
35 The wise shall obtain honor,
But dullards get disgrace as their portion.

4 Sons, heed the discipline of a father;
Listen and learn discernment,
2 For I give you good instruction;
Do not forsake my teaching.

3 Once I was a son to my father,
The tender darling of my mother.
4 He instructed me and said to me,
"Let your mind hold on to my words;
Keep my commandments and you will live.
5 Acquire wisdom, acquire discernment;
Do not forget and do not swerve from my words.
6 Do not forsake her and she will guard you;
Love her and she will protect you.
7 The beginning[a] of wisdom is—acquire wisdom;
With all your acquisitions, acquire discernment.
8 Hug her to you and she will exalt you;
She will bring you honor if you embrace her.
9 She will adorn your head with a graceful wreath;
Crown you with a glorious diadem."

10 My son, heed and take in my words,
And you will have many years of life.
11 I instruct you in the way of wisdom;
I guide you in straight courses.
12 You will walk without breaking stride;
When you run, you will not stumble.
13 Hold fast to discipline; do not let go;
Keep it; it is your life.
14 Do not enter on the path of the wicked;
Do not walk on the way of evil men.
15 Avoid it; do not pass through it;
Turn away from it; pass it by.

a Or "best part."

16 For they cannot sleep unless they have done evil;
Unless they make someone fall they are robbed of sleep.
17 They eat the bread of wickedness
And drink the wine of lawlessness.
18 The path of the righteous is like radiant sunlight,
Ever brightening until noon.
19 The way of the wicked is all darkness;
They do not know what will make them stumble.

20 My son, listen to my speech;
Incline your ear to my words.
21 Do not lose sight of them;
Keep them in your mind.
22 They are life to him who finds them,
Healing for his whole body.
23 More than all that you guard, guard your mind,
For it is the source of life.
24 Put crooked speech away from you;
Keep devious talk far from you.
25 Let your eyes look forward,
Your gaze be straight ahead.
26 Survey the course you take,
And all your ways will prosper.
27 Do not swerve to the right or the left;
Keep your feet from evil.

5 My son, listen to my wisdom;
Incline your ear to my insight,
2 That you may have foresight,
While your lips hold fast to knowledge.
3 For the lips of a forbidden[a] woman drip honey;
Her mouth is smoother than oil;
4 But in the end she is as bitter as wormwood,
Sharp as a two-edged sword.
5 Her feet go down to Death;
Her steps take hold of Sheol.
6 She does not chart a path of life;
Her course meanders for lack of knowledge.
7 So now, sons, pay heed to me,
And do not swerve from the words of my mouth.
8 Keep yourself far away from her;
Do not come near the doorway of her house
9 Lest you give up your vigor to others,
Your years to a ruthless one;
10 Lest strangers eat their fill of your strength,
And your toil be for the house of another;

a Lit. "strange."

17: The values of the wicked are twisted. They live on *wickedness* and *lawlessness;* see 2.12–15.

4.20–27: Lecture VII: The straight path. Whereas Lecture VI spoke of the two paths of life, good and evil, this one pictures a single path, which is a person's mode of behavior, for better or worse. One must walk straight, for evil and dangers lurk on either side, and look straight ahead, because temptations beckon all around. In biblical literature, "straight" is a common metaphor for correct behavior.

5.1–23: Lecture VIII: Stick to your own wife. This is the first of three Lectures on the "strange woman" (5.1–23; 6.20–35; 7.1–27). See 2.16–20 n. The adulteress is deadly (vv. 3–6), and every man must keep away from her, or he will pay a severe price (vv. 7–14). Instead, a man should enjoy his sexual pleasures with his own wife (vv. 15–20). God sees everything and sin is inevitably punished (vv. 21–23). **3–6:** The strange woman's words are sweet and seductive (2.16), but they leave a bitter aftertaste, and her dulcet speech turns out to be deadly. **9–10:** *Vigor* and *strength* may refer to the adulterer's property, which he will waste on the woman, or to his sexual potency (see 31.3), which he will *give up* in the sense that the son he begets will be reckoned as belonging to the cheated husband, who will benefit from the adulterer's "labor." The *ruthless one* is the enraged husband (see 6.34–35). The *others* may be his family.

11 And in the end you roar,
When your flesh and body are consumed,
12 And say,
"O how I hated discipline,
And heartily spurned rebuke.
13 I did not pay heed to my teachers,
Or incline my ear to my instructors.
14 Soon I was in dire trouble
Amidst the assembled congregation."
15 Drink water from your own cistern,
Running water from your own well.
16 Your springs will gush forth
In streams in the public squares.
17 They will be yours alone,
Others having no part with you.
18 Let your fountain be blessed;
Find joy in the wife of your youth—
19 A loving doe, a graceful mountain goat.
Let her breasts satisfy you at all times;
Be infatuated with love of her always.
20 Why be infatuated, my son, with a forbidden[a] woman?
Why clasp the bosom of an alien woman?
21 For a man's ways are before the eyes of God;
He surveys his entire course.
22 The wicked man will be trapped in his iniquities;
He will be caught up in the ropes of his sin.
23 He will die for lack of discipline,
Infatuated by his great folly.

6 My son, if you have stood surety for your fellow,
Given your hand for another,[b]
2 You have been trapped by the words of your mouth,
Snared by the words of your mouth.
3 Do this, then, my son, to extricate yourself,
For you have come into the power of your fellow:
Go grovel—and badger your fellow;
4 Give your eyes no sleep,
Your pupils no slumber.

a *Lit. "strange."* *b* *Or "a stranger."*

11–14: The fornicator will be forced to publicly confess his folly. V. 11 seems to refer to venereal disease. *The assembled congregation* may be a judicial tribunal, or more likely, the community. Public shaming is a powerful means of social control, especially in Prov. **15–19:** This is the only passage in the Bible that explicitly celebrates the pleasures of marital sex. Your wife alone (the father tells his son) is yours, and she is more attractive than anyone else. The author is seeking to dissuade young men from following a fierce and anarchic urge and so depicts the delights of sanctioned sex as no less intense than those of "stolen waters" (9.17). The metaphors in vv. 15–18 speak of a man's wife as his well, a source of refreshment that slakes (sexual) thirst. Compare the "well" and "drinking" metaphors in 7.18; 9.17, and Song 4.12, 15. V. 16 may be read in several ways, but as translated here it seems to promise a reward—many progeny—for sexual fidelity. **17–18:** Enjoy erotic pleasures with your wife alone. Then her "fountain"—i.e., her womb—will be fruitful (vv. 16–17). **19:** The *doe* connotes grace, tenderness, and affection in the Song of Songs. *Loving* (Heb "'ahavim") has strong sexual connotations. *Breasts* (Heb "dadim") should probably be vocalized "dodim," "lovemaking," as in 7.18, yielding better parallelism with *love;* but there may be a play on the two words. **20:** *Infatuated* (Heb "tishgeh"), lit. "go astray," a negative value judgment. Rather than going astray with a forbidden woman, the young man should "lose himself" in his wife's love.

6.1–19: Interlude C: Four Epigrams on folly and evil. This four-part passage does not follow the structure of the Lectures and differs in subject matter, and it likely a late addition to the book. Epigrams i and ii (vv. 1–5 and 6–11) concern folly, and iii and iv (vv. 12–15 and 16–19) concern evil. The first two epigrams are especially humorous and facetious.

6.1–5: Epigram i. Do not go surety for another's loan. If you have done so, do your best to get released from your promise. (20.16 tells what happens to one who gets himself into this mess.) Rather than putting up his own property as collateral, a borrower could have the loan underwritten by someone else, whose possessions would then be liable to seizure. Going surety is always risky, but doing so for a stranger (which one might do for a fee) is tantamount to loss; see 27.13. See also 11.15; 17.18; 22.26–27. The tone and practical main message of this epigram differs significantly from the emphasis on helping the

5 Save yourself like a deer out of the hand [of a hunter],
Like a bird out of the hand of a fowler.

6 Lazybones, go to the ant;
Study its ways and learn.
7 Without leaders, officers, or rulers,
8 It lays up its stores during the summer,
Gathers in its food at the harvest.
9 How long will you lie there, lazybones;
When will you wake from your sleep?
10 A bit more sleep, a bit more slumber,
A bit more hugging yourself in bed,
11 And poverty will come [a-]calling upon you,[-a]
And want, like a man with a shield.

12 A scoundrel, an evil man
Lives by crooked speech,
13 Winking his eyes,
Shuffling his feet,
Pointing his finger.
14 Duplicity is in his heart;
He plots evil all the time;
He incites quarrels.
15 Therefore calamity will come upon him without warning;
Suddenly he will be broken beyond repair.

16 Six things the LORD hates;
Seven are an abomination to Him:
17 A haughty bearing,
A lying tongue,
Hands that shed innocent blood,
18 A mind that hatches evil plots,
Feet quick to run to evil,
19 A false witness testifying lies,
And one who incites brothers to quarrel.

20 My son, keep your father's commandment;
Do not forsake your mother's teaching.
21 Tie them over your heart always;
Bind them around your throat.

a-a Meaning of Heb. uncertain.

poor found in some Torah texts (e.g., Deut. 15.9).

6.6–11: Epigram ii: Sloth and industry. Cf. 24.30–34. In vv. 6–8, the ant is held up as a model of industry and self-motivation. (Cf. 30.25.) In vv. 9–11, the lazy man is rebuked in humorous tones. **11:** Better, "and penury will come upon you like a vagabond, and poverty like a man of arms." In this vivid trope, a poor man is used as a metaphor for poverty. The vagabond here is not an indigent begging for alms, but is a potentially dangerous armed wanderer.

6.12–15: Epigram iii: The good-for-nothing. The scoundrel's speech is crooked and dishonest. He betrays his nature by certain body gestures. The enumeration of the outward signs of villainy implies a warning to avoid people thus marked. The passage draws together phrases and ideas from 16.27–30, 24.22b, and 29.1b. **13:** *Winking* (more precisely, squinting) the eye was considered a symptom of secretive, hostile thoughts; see Ps. 35.19. *Shuffling* the feet was probably considered symptomatic of an unquiet soul. *Pointing his finger* seems to be a sign of derision (Isa. 58.9).

6.16–19: Epigram iv: What God loathes. Seven abominable things are described. Like Epigram iii, Epigram iv makes the incitement of quarrels the ultimate offense. The use of ascending numbers ("six and seven" or "three and four") for listing items serves a didactic and rhetorical purpose. See 30.15–31 n. and Amos 1.3, 6, 9, 11, 13; 2.1, 4, 6. This is a feature of biblical parallelism (see "Biblical Poetry," pp. 2184–91), and the final number, in this case *seven,* is meaningful in the context.

6.20–35: Lecture IX: Adultery kills. Even though an adulterer might think that his is the most secretive of sins, he cannot evade punishment. The speaker argues the point in a logical fashion, using analogies to other kinds of self-inflicted harm. The message is blunt and memorable: Keep away from another man's wife or he will kill you. **20:** *Mother,* see 1.8–19 n. **21:** *Bind* the teachings (figuratively) like a pendant on a cord about your neck, so that they will rest over your heart. These are metaphors for keeping a valuable object close to oneself always, and they stress the beauty and worth of the teachings. Cf. 3.3; Exod. 28.29; and Song 8.6. Possibly

22 When you walk it will lead you;
When you lie down it will watch over you;
And when you are awake it will talk with you.
23 For the commandment is a lamp,
The teaching is a light,
And the way to life is the rebuke that disciplines.
24 It will keep you from an evil woman,
From the smooth tongue of a forbidden[a] woman.
25 Do not lust for her beauty
Or let her captivate you with her eyes.
26 The last loaf of bread will go for a harlot;
A married woman will snare a person of honor.
27 Can a man rake embers into his bosom
Without burning his clothes?
28 Can a man walk on live coals
Without scorching his feet?
29 It is the same with one who sleeps with his fellow's wife;
None who touches her will go unpunished.
30 A thief is not held in contempt
For stealing to appease his hunger;
31 Yet if caught he must pay sevenfold;
He must give up all he owns.
32 He who commits adultery is devoid of sense;
Only one who would destroy himself does such a thing.
33 He will meet with disease and disgrace;
His reproach will never be expunged.
34 The fury of the husband will be passionate;
He will show no pity on his day of vengeance.
35 He will not have regard for any ransom;
He will refuse your bribe, however great.

7 My son, heed my words;
And store up my commandments with you.
2 Keep my commandments and live,
My teaching, as the apple of your eye.
3 Bind them on your fingers;
Write them on the tablet of your mind.
4 Say to Wisdom, "You are my sister,"
And call Understanding a kinswoman.

a *Lit. "alien."*

the pendant originally was a protective amulet. **22–23:** The relationship between these two vv. is clearer when they are read in reverse order. **23:** The *commandment* ("mitzvah") and the *teaching* ("torah") are here the parental teachings, or perhaps wisdom teachings generally. In the traditional Jewish reading, they are God's commandments and his Torah. **24:** The *forbidden woman*'s first means of seduction is speech; see 2.16; 5.3–6. **25–33:** The punishment for adultery is inherent in the crime. It comes naturally, without any direct intervention by God or a court. **26:** Better, "For a harlot costs but a loaf of bread, but a married woman hunts for a precious life." Harlotry costs money (29.3); adultery kills. **27–29:** As surely as burning coals will scorch the clothes of the man who holds them or the feet of one who walks on them, so too will the man who fools with the fire of adultery inevitably suffer his punishment. **30–33:** If even he who steals out of necessity, and therefore deserves some public sympathy, is forced to pay heavy penalties when caught, how much more will an adulterer, who lacks any excuse for his crime, be severely punished. Unlike the thief, he will not be able to buy his way out of trouble (v. 35). *Sevenfold* in v. 31 may be a way of saying "greatly," though some LXX manuscript readings at 2 Sam. 12.6 suggest that sevenfold compensation for theft was known in ancient Israel. The maximum compensation stipulated in the Torah is fivefold, for an animal that is stolen and killed (Exod. 21.37). The adulterer will suffer "wounds" (not *disease*), namely those inflicted on him by the enraged husband. No such punishment by the husband is known in the Torah, though private vengeance is likely. **34–35: The conclusion.** Sometimes, the payment of *ransom*—monetary gifts and compensation—can appease the wronged party (21.14; Exod. 21.30), but not in the case of adultery.

7.1–27: Lecture X: Beware the seductress. On the *forbidden* or "strange" woman, see 2.16–20 n. In this lecture, the speaker tells how he once witnessed a woman approaching a young man in the dark street and luring him to her house for a night of sex. Her words were silky, brazen, and lewd, and the dupe followed after her like an animal going to slaughter. **3:** These are metaphors for memory, though traditionally Jews have given the reminders concrete form in the practice of tefilin. **4:** *My sister,* some commentators say that "sister" is a term of (erotic) affection, as in the Song of Songs. But "sister" and "kinswoman" may just connote intimacy.

5 She will guard you from a forbidden[a] woman;
From an alien woman whose talk is smooth.

6 From the window of my house,
Through my lattice, I looked out
7 And saw among the simple,
Noticed among the youths,
A lad devoid of sense.
8 He was crossing the street near her corner,
Walking toward her house
9 In the dusk of evening,
In the dark hours of night.
10 A woman comes toward him
[b-]Dressed like a harlot, with set purpose.[-b]
11 She is bustling and restive;
She is never at home.
12 Now in the street, now in the square,
She lurks at every corner.
13 She lays hold of him and kisses him;
Brazenly she says to him,
14 "I had to make a sacrifice of well-being;
Today I fulfilled my vows.
15 Therefore I have come out to you,
Seeking you, and have found you.
16 I have decked my couch with covers
Of dyed Egyptian linen;
17 I have sprinkled my bed
With myrrh, aloes, and cinnamon.
18 Let us drink our fill of love till morning;
Let us delight in amorous embrace.
19 For the man of the house is away;
He is off on a distant journey.
20 He took his bag of money with him
And will return only at mid-month."

21 She sways him with her eloquence,
Turns him aside with her smooth talk.
22 Thoughtlessly he follows her,
Like an ox going to the slaughter,
[b-]Like a fool to the stocks for punishment[-b]—
23 Until the arrow pierces his liver.
He is like a bird rushing into a trap,
Not knowing his life is at stake.
24 Now, sons, listen to me;
Pay attention to my words;

a Lit. "strange."
b-b Meaning of Heb. uncertain.

6: *Window ... lattice:* The window was enclosed with a lattice or trelliswork, through which one could peer without being seen. **10:** *Dressed like a harlot:* Harlots may have worn a heavy veil (Gen. 38.14). The strange woman is dressed as if she were a harlot, perhaps to conceal her identity, but she does not offer herself for money. *With set purpose,* better, "with hidden intent," lit. "with guarded heart." **11–13:** Rather like the scoundrel with his nervous gesticulations (6.13), this woman is afflicted by a constant disquiet. She *lurks* or "lies in ambush" *at every corner,* like a beast of prey—or the muggers in 1.11. Then she pounces. **14:** The woman explains why she has meat available for a fine meal. Meat was very costly and was eaten mostly on special occasions, as when bringing a sacrifice to the Temple (most of the meat would be kept by the worshipper, the rest given to the priest) or when repaying vows. **15:** This seems to be a parodic reversal of the woman in the Song of Songs (3.1–4), who goes forth at night in search of her beloved, finds him, and embraces him. **16–18:** These vv. share much language with the Song of Songs (see esp. 4.14). In them, the sexual innuendo becomes clear, then explicit. **19–20:** She reassures the boy that her husband is away. Since the scene takes place in the deep darkness, when the moon has waned (v. 9), the full moon *(mid-month)* is two weeks off. **22–23:** The teacher does not have to witness the outcome. He already knows what this must be: death. **22:** By a minor emendation the end of the v. reads, "like a stag bounding to bonds." **23:** This v. makes better sense if we place the third line at the beginning of the v. Its sexual imagery is transparent. **24–27:** The speaker warns all young men *(sons)* to avoid the path to the strange woman's house, for it is really the way to death.

25 Let your mind not wander down her ways;
Do not stray onto her paths.
26 For many are those she has struck dead,
And numerous are her victims.
27 Her house is a highway to Sheol
Leading down to Death's inner chambers.

8 It is Wisdom calling,
Understanding raising her voice.
2 She takes her stand at the topmost heights,
By the wayside, at the crossroads,
3 Near the gates at the city entrance;
At the entryways, she shouts,
4 "O men, I call to you;
My cry is to all mankind.
5 O simple ones, learn shrewdness;
O dullards, instruct your minds.
6 Listen, for I speak noble things;
Uprightness comes from my lips;
7 My mouth utters truth;
Wickedness is abhorrent to my lips.
8 All my words are just,
None of them perverse or crooked;
9 All are straightforward to the intelligent man,
And right to those who have attained
knowledge.
10 Accept my discipline rather than silver,
Knowledge rather than choice gold.
11 For wisdom is better than rubies;
No goods can equal her.

12 "I, Wisdom, live with Prudence;
I attain knowledge and foresight.
13 To fear the LORD is to hate evil;
I hate pride, arrogance, the evil way,
And duplicity in speech.
14 Mine are counsel and resourcefulness;
I am understanding; courage is mine.
15 Through me kings reign
And rulers decree just laws;
16 Through me princes rule,
Great men and all the [a-]righteous judges.[-a]
17 Those who love me I love,
And those who seek me will find me.
18 Riches and honor belong to me,
Enduring wealth and success.

a-a According to some Heb. mss. and printed editions, "judges of the earth."

8.1–36: Interlude D: Wisdom's self-praise. Whereas the strange woman of ch 7 is to be shunned, wisdom, here personified, is to be pursued and embraced. The structure of this well-designed ch is as follows: I. Introduction: the setting and call (1–3); II. Call to Attention (4–11); III. Wisdom's present state (12–21); IV. Wisdom's past (22–31); V. Call to Attention renewed (32–36). Wisdom is personified as a woman of nearly divine stature; see 1.20–33 n. There may be subtle erotic connotations (e.g., vv. 17, 35) that suggest the power of Wisdom's attractiveness. Wisdom calls to human beings, praises herself, promises rewards to her devotees, and tells mankind to listen to her, that is to say, the wisdom in this book and wherever it may be found. **1–5:** Wisdom calls for attention. In naturalistic terms, this is the voice of reason, heard in wisdom teachings and in the individual mind. Wisdom calls to people in the most prominent public places, including the city gates, where many of the city's commercial and legal transactions take place. Wisdom is international, offering her teachings to *all mankind.* She is even available to the simple and dullards, if they would just listen to her. **6–9:** Just as the father in the Lectures extols the wisdom he is teaching, so does Lady Wisdom praise her own teachings. **10–11:** Cf. 3.14–15 and 16.16. **12–14:** *Prudence ... knowledge and foresight,* better, "cunning ... knowledge of shrewdness." The virtues in question are practical savvy and good sense. These useful faculties come with wisdom, as do *resourcefulness* and *courage.* **15–16:** Insofar as rulers govern justly, they do so through wisdom. **17:** To gain wisdom, one must *love* it, eagerly desiring to grasp its message. Without this love, even superficial learning is unlikely, and knowledge cannot be translated into action. Later, this was interpreted as love of Torah study, a principle inculcated in the postexilic Ps. 119. **18–21:** Wisdom promises material rewards, but she also emphasizes that she is superior to gold and silver (as in 3.14–15) and that she bestows wealth only

19 My fruit is better than gold, fine gold,
And my produce better than choice silver.
20 I walk on the way of righteousness,
On the paths of justice.
21 I endow those who love me with substance;
I will fill their treasuries.

22 "The LORD created me at the beginning of His course
As the first of His works of old.
23 In the distant past I was fashioned,
At the beginning, at the origin of earth.
24 There was still no deep when I was brought forth,
No springs rich in water;
25 Before [the foundation of] the mountains were sunk,
Before the hills I was born.
26 He had not yet made earth and fields,
Or the world's first clumps of clay.
27 I was there when He set the heavens into place;
When He fixed the horizon upon the deep;
28 When He made the heavens above firm,
And the fountains of the deep gushed forth;
29 When He assigned the sea its limits,
So that its waters never transgress His command;
When He fixed the foundations of the earth,
30 I was with Him as a confidant,
A source of delight every day,
Rejoicing before Him at all times,
31 Rejoicing in His inhabited world,
Finding delight with mankind.
32 Now, sons, listen to me;
Happy are they who keep my ways.
33 Heed discipline and become wise;
Do not spurn it.
34 Happy is the man who listens to me,
Coming early to my gates each day,
Waiting outside my doors.

in honest ways. **22–26:** Wisdom recounts her creation and her presence during the creation of the world. She was the very first of God's creations. An important Jewish interpretation, starting with *Gen. Rab.* 1.2, 5 and found in the Rashi to Gen. 1.1, uses Prov. ch 8 to argue that the Torah (identified by the rabbis with wisdom) was created before the world and was used by God in creating it. **22:** *Created me:* Since ancient times, interpreters have disputed whether the verb "kanah" means "created" or "acquired." The latter allows for the possibility that wisdom existed from eternity and was coeval with God. Some Christian groups preferred this, since they identified wisdom with the Logos, which was in turn identified with the Christ. V. 23 implies that wisdom is a created being, and the verb "kanah" refers to acquisition by any means, including creation, as here. **24:** According to Gen. 1.2, the *deep* (the primordial sea) existed before creation began. Wisdom insists that she preceded in existence even this most primordial of entities. *I was brought forth:* This word is usually used of birth. The background metaphor of divine parenthood is reinforced by v. 30. **25:** The mountains were thought to rest on foundations or on pillars set (miraculously, see Job 38.6) in the abyss or the underworld. **27–31:** Wisdom declares that she was present when God produced the physical universe. **27:** The *horizon* is pictured as a circle engraved at the join of heaven and earth, as appears to be the case when one is at sea. **28:** *Heavens,* actually, "clouds." The paradox of God "firming up" the clouds (so that they stay in the sky) heightens the wonder of His deed. **29:** In several creation traditions found outside of Gen. (and based on Canaanite antecedents), the sea is ever trying to break forth and flood the earth, but God set its boundary (Ps. 104.9), namely the beach (Jer. 5.22), which may also be imagined as a barred door (Job 38.8, 10). **30:** This is one of the most disputed vv. in the Bible and has weighty theological implications. The word translated *confidant* is "'amon." There are three basic ways of interpreting this word: (1) "Artisan" (which is elsewhere "'oman"). This translation implies that wisdom aided God in creation. In a similar vein, a midrash likens wisdom (equated with Torah) to a tool God used in creation, as an architect looks at a blueprint when constructing a palace (*Gen. Rab.* 1.2). (2) "Constant(ly), faithful(ly)"; "confidant." (3) "Ward" or "nursling" (or as a verb, "growing up"). Wisdom was with God as His ward, like a child He was caring for. This fits the context best. Nowhere does the ch imply that Lady Wisdom helped God create the earth. On the contrary, vv. 30–31 emphasize that she was at play while God worked. Wisdom's playing before God represents the "play" of the wise, which is study. Cf. Ps. 119.92. **31:** Just as God gets pleasure from wisdom, so does she delight in humankind. **32–36:** Having established her

35 For he who finds me finds life
And obtains favor from the LORD.
36 But he who misses me destroys himself;
All who hate me love death."

9 Wisdom has built her house,
She has hewn her seven pillars.
2 She has prepared the feast,
Mixed the wine,
And also set the table.
3 She has sent out her maids to announce
On the heights of the town,
4 "Let the simple enter here";
To those devoid of sense she says,
5 "Come, eat my food
And drink the wine that I have mixed;
6 Give up simpleness and live,
Walk in the way of understanding."

7 To correct a scoffer,
[a-]Or rebuke a wicked man for his blemish,
Is to call down abuse on oneself.[-a]
8 Do not rebuke a scoffer, for he will hate you;
Reprove a wise man, and he will love you.
9 Instruct a wise man, and he will grow wiser;
Teach a righteous man, and he will gain in
learning.
10 The beginning of wisdom is fear of the LORD,
And knowledge of the Holy One is understanding.
11 For through me your days will increase,
And years be added to your life.
12 If you are wise, you are wise for yourself;
If you are a scoffer, you bear it alone.
13 The stupid woman bustles about;
She is simple and knows nothing.
14 She sits in the doorway of her house,
Or on a chair at the heights of the town,

a-a *Clauses transposed for clarity.*

unparalleled credentials, Lady Wisdom speaks as a mature lady and addresses her "sons." Fortunate is he who obeys wisdom and eagerly goes to her house, which is any place where wisdom is taught. **35–36:** The vital importance of loving wisdom. The finding of wisdom recalls the finding of a beloved woman; cf. 18.22. V. 36 states the principle that the evildoer is harmed by the evil he creates; cf. 1.19. Those who hate wisdom are not just stupid, they are depraved. Their values are twisted. They may not realize it, but the things they love are really deadly.

9.1–18: Interlude E: Two banquets. This poem elaborates the motif of Wisdom's invitation to her house (8.34) into a figure of two contrary invitations: Lady Wisdom's (vv. 1–6, 11) and Lady Folly's (vv. 13–18). Life offers two "feasts": one is rich yet prudent, the other is enticing but poisonous. Vv. 7–10 and v. 12 do not fit in either vignette and are probably later insertions. It is best to first read the ch without them, then to consider them separately. **1–6, 11:** Lady Wisdom builds a house (v. 1), prepares a feast (v. 2), and issues an open invitation (vv. 3–5). She then explains the meaning of her invitation (v. 6) and reinforces her exhortation (v. 11). **1:** Some consider wisdom's *house* to be a mythological allusion, but this identification is uncertain. *Seven* connotes completeness or expansiveness. **2–3:** Like a noble woman, Wisdom prepares a rich banquet and sends out her maids to invite guests. **4–6:** Wisdom is the sustenance of the soul. (Cf. Deut. 8.3.) Wisdom's wine is *mixed,* probably with water and fragrant spices, as was typical of fine wine in antiquity. **7–10:** Someone has inserted these vv. in a cautionary reaction to Wisdom's invitation to the simple. The insertion says that there are some people who are constitutionally unable to learn wisdom. Wisdom requires the right attitude, namely the fear of God. See 1.7. **11:** The continuation of v. 6. **12:** This seems to be an addition identifying the recipient of wisdom's benefits. Wisdom profits its holder while impudence and arrogance hurt their possessor alone. **13–18: Lady Folly's "feast." 13:** The *stupid woman,* lit. "woman of folly." In this ch, where the "woman of folly" is contrasted with personified Lady Wisdom, the woman in question is best understood as a personification as well. *Bustles about* is better translated "is boisterous" (cf. her human counterpart, 7.11a), for unlike Lady Wisdom, Folly does not put effort into the feast. She just sits at her door or in a public place calling out to passers-by. The underlying picture may reflect the deportment of a prostitute.

15 Calling to all the wayfarers
Who go about their own affairs,
16 "Let the simple enter here";
And to those devoid of sense she says,
17 "Stolen waters are sweet,
And bread eaten furtively is tasty."
18 He does not know that the shades are there,
That her guests are in the depths of Sheol.

10

The proverbs of Solomon:

A wise son brings joy to his father;
A dull son is his mother's sorrow.
2 Ill-gotten wealth is of no avail,
But righteousness saves from death.
3 The LORD will not let the righteous go hungry,
But He denies the wicked what they crave.
4 Negligent hands cause poverty,
But diligent hands enrich.
5 He who lays in stores during the summer is a capable son,
But he who sleeps during the harvest is an incompetent.
6 Blessings light upon the head of the righteous,
But lawlessness covers the mouth of the wicked.
7 The name of the righteous is invoked in blessing,
But the fame of the wicked rots.
8 He whose heart is wise accepts commands,
But he whose speech is foolish comes to grief.
9 He who lives blamelessly lives safely,
But he who walks a crooked path will be found out.

16: Folly mimics Wisdom's call, but to opposite effect. **17:** Lady Folly is telling the truth. The wise recognize in her invitation an unintended warning to beware of her. The foolish hear it as an inducement to enjoy the forbidden, titillating sweets of illegitimate pleasures. Waters can allude to sexual pleasures, as in 5.15–20, but the statement applies to other pleasures as well. **18:** The nitwits who take Folly's bait are blithely unaware that they are about to enter the domain of death, the netherworld, where the *shades* (ghosts) reside. Like the previous two units, the death of the fool ends the passage, effecting closure (7.26–27; 8.36).

10.1–22.16: Collection II. This collection holds mostly antithetical poetic couplets, in which the second line restates basically the same idea in reversed terms (e.g., *wise son ... joy* is echoed by *dull son ... sorrow*). Although they are mostly similar stylistically, they reflect a wide variety of situations and attitudes. They differ from many popular proverbs embedded in other biblical books, which do not have the same poetic structure (e.g., 1 Sam. 24.14, "Wicked deeds come from wicked men"). The proverbs in 10.1–15.33 typically contrast two character types: the wise and the foolish, or the righteous and the wicked. These pairs are not identical, as they typically are in postbiblical literature; the wise are versed in applying secular wisdom as well as in religious virtues, while righteousness is solely a religious value. As a whole, the proverbs create a paradigm of the wise and the righteous person, on which the pupil (and reader) can model his own actions; this facilitated, in part, the identification of the wise and the righteous, and of torah and wisdom in postbiblical literature. Like proverbs in any language, the proverbs that follow are extremely terse and dense, and often ambiguous, and their full meaning does not emerge in translation.

10.1–12.15: Contrasts between the wise and the foolish, the upright and the wicked. Several proverbs speak about a son's merits or faults in terms of the effect they have on his parents. The same message is addressed to the son in 27.11a. Cf. 15.20; 17.21, 25; 19.13; 23.24–25; 28.7. **10.1:** The beginning of the opening proverb continues two main themes of the previous section: the *son* as the recipient of the message, and the importance of being *wise.* **2:** The *ill-gotten wealth* or "treasures of wickedness" are riches gained by wicked means. *Saves from death* does not suggest immortality but rather (as comparison with 11.4 shows) protection in the day of general disaster. In such circumstances, wealth will not help. **3:** This proverb is not a statement of fact but a declaration of faith in a principle: Eventually people will receive the material rewards due them. Cf. Ps. 37.25. **4:** The Sages believed that negligence causes poverty and diligence brings wealth. They did not, however, interpret poverty as a sign of negligence or wealth as a sign of diligence, since these conditions can have other causes as well. **5:** The word translated *incompetent* means, more precisely, "disappointing [one]" or "disgraceful [one]." This proverb is concerned with the effects of diligence and laziness on one's parents. Cf. 10.1. **6:** As translated here, the second line means that the evildoer's own lawlessness, which he covers up, destroys him. **7:** For examples of these two fates, see Gen. 48.20; Jer. 29.22. **9:** *Lives,* lit. "walks." There are two ways of walking through life: straight and honestly, or crookedly and deviously

10 He who winks his eye causes sorrow;
He whose speech is foolish comes to grief.
11 The mouth of the righteous is a fountain of life,
But lawlessness covers the mouth of the wicked.
12 Hatred stirs up strife,
But love covers up all faults.
13 Wisdom is to be found on the lips of the intelligent,
But a rod is ready for the back of the senseless.
14 The wise store up knowledge;
The mouth of the fool is an imminent ruin.
15 The wealth of a rich man is his fortress;
The poverty of the poor is his ruin.
16 The labor of the righteous man makes for life;
The produce of the wicked man makes for want.
17 He who follows discipline shows the way to life,
But he who ignores reproof leads astray.
18 He who conceals hatred has lying lips,
While he who speaks forth slander is a dullard.
19 Where there is much talking, there is no lack of transgressing,
But he who curbs his tongue[a] shows sense.
20 The tongue of a righteous man is choice silver,
But the mind of the wicked is of little worth.
21 The lips of the righteous sustain many,
But fools die for lack of sense.
22 It is the blessing of the LORD that enriches,
And no toil can increase it.
23 As mischief is sport for the dullard,
So is wisdom for the man of understanding.
24 What the wicked man plots overtakes him;
What the righteous desire is granted.
25 When the storm passes the wicked man is gone,
But the righteous is an everlasting foundation.
26 Like vinegar to the teeth,
Like smoke to the eyes,
Is a lazy man to those who send him on a mission.
27 The fear of the LORD prolongs life,
While the years of the wicked will be shortened.
28 The righteous can look forward to joy,
But the hope of the wicked is doomed.
29 The way of the LORD is a stronghold for the blameless,
But a ruin for evildoers.
30 The righteous will never be shaken;
The wicked will not inhabit the earth.
31 The mouth of the righteous produces wisdom,
But the treacherous tongue shall be cut off.

a Lit. "lips."

(see 4.10–19 n.). **10:** See 6.13 and 16.30. **12:** Love can and should cover up others' offenses against oneself, but not one's own offenses. **13:** The parallelism suggests that *rod* here is probably the intelligent man's verbal rebukes. **15:** This is a blunt observation of social realities (contrast v. 2). But by stating the misery of the destitute the observation teaches a moral lesson, stated explicitly elsewhere: the need of the poor for special protection. Cf. 14.20–21, 31; 19.17; 22.22–23; 23.10–11; 28.27. **18–21:** Wise speech and foolish speech. **22:** This proverb reminds a person to give credit for his successes to God, not to his own talents. It also teaches that, although diligence and energetic work are prized, excessive straining for wealth is useless. **23:** The fool enjoys causing trouble. The sensible man gets his pleasure from wisdom. Wisdom is a source of delight to God Himself (8.30). **24:** Cf. 1.27. **26:** Messengers—meaning anyone who is sent out on a task for someone else—were crucial in the ancient world. Communication at a distance, including business and diplomatic dealings, required sending messengers on one's behalf. See also 13.17; 22.21; 25.13; 26.6. **28:** Cf. 10.24. **29:** God's *way*—His characteristic behavior—has a two-pronged effect, protecting the innocent and ruining evildoers (cf. Hos. 14.10). **30:** See 2.21–22.

32 The lips of the righteous know what is pleasing;
The mouth of the wicked [knows] duplicity.

11 False scales are an abomination to the LORD;
An honest[a] weight pleases Him.
2 When arrogance appears, disgrace follows,
But wisdom is with those who are unassuming.
3 The integrity of the upright guides them;
The deviousness of the treacherous leads them to ruin.
4 Wealth is of no avail on the day of wrath,
But righteousness saves from death.
5 The righteousness of the blameless man smooths his way,
But the wicked man is felled by his wickedness.
6 The righteousness of the upright saves them,
But the treacherous are trapped by their malice.
7 At death the hopes of a wicked man are doomed,
And the ambition of evil men comes to nothing.
8 The righteous man is rescued from trouble
And the wicked man takes his place.
9 The impious man destroys his neighbor through speech,
But through their knowledge the righteous are rescued.
10 When the righteous prosper the city exults;
When the wicked perish there are shouts of joy.
11 A city is built up by the blessing of the upright,
But it is torn down by the speech of the wicked.
12 He who speaks contemptuously of his fellowman is devoid of sense;
A prudent man keeps his peace.
13 A base fellow gives away secrets,
But a trustworthy soul keeps a confidence.
14 For want of strategy an army falls,
But victory comes with much planning.
15 Harm awaits him who stands surety for another;[b]
He who spurns pledging shall be secure.
16 A graceful woman obtains honor;
Ruthless men obtain wealth.
17 A kindly man benefits himself;
A cruel man makes trouble for himself.
18 The wicked man earns illusory wages,
But he who sows righteousness has a true reward.
19 Righteousness is a prop of life,
But to pursue evil leads to death.
20 Men of crooked mind are an abomination to the LORD,
But those whose way is blameless please Him.

a Lit. *"whole."* b Or *"a stranger."*

11.1: By nicking off a bit of the balance stone when measuring grain, a merchant could inflate the payment he was receiving, and by using a heavier stone when measuring the silver, he could make the payment seem less than it was really worth. The stability of commerce depends on reliable weights. God demands them (20.10). In fact, He is the source of the standards of weights and measures (16.11). Cf. Lev. 19.36; Deut. 25.15; Amos 8.5; Mic. 6.11; Amenemope §§16, 17 (*AEL* 2.156–57). **2:** Cf. 13.10; 16.6, 18; 29.23. **4:** Cf. 10.2 and Ezek. 7.19a. **7:** *Ambition of evil men,* rather, "expectation of (procreative) strength." The threat implied in this proverb, then, is the loss of family continuity and the sort of permanence this was thought to provide. **8:** This returns to the theme of vv. 4–6. The traditional Jewish commentators often adduce Haman (Esth. 7.10; 9.24–25) as a satisfying instance of this doctrine. **10–12:** The effect people have on their fellow citizens, particularly by their speech. **14:** Cf. 20.18. These appreciative assessments of the value of advisers and planners must come from one of their number. **15:** See 6.1–5 n.; 20.16 n. **16:** We should probably emend *ruthless* ("ʿaritzim") to "diligent" ("ḥarutzim"), following the ancient Gk translation. **20:** See 3.32.

21 Assuredly,[a] the evil man will not escape,
But the offspring of the righteous will be safe.
22 Like a gold ring in the snout of a pig
Is a beautiful woman bereft of sense.
23 What the righteous desire can only be good;
What the wicked hope for [stirs] wrath.
24 One man gives generously and ends with more;
Another stints on doing the right thing and incurs a loss.
25 A generous person enjoys prosperity;
He who satisfies others shall himself be sated.
26 He who withholds grain earns the curses of the people,
But blessings are on the head of the one who dispenses it.
27 He who earnestly seeks what is good pursues what is pleasing;
He who is bent on evil, upon him it shall come.
28 He who trusts in his wealth shall fall,
But the righteous shall flourish like foliage.
29 He who makes trouble for his household shall inherit the wind;
A fool is a slave to the wise-hearted.
30 The fruit of the righteous is a tree of life;
A wise man captivates people.
31 If the righteous on earth get their deserts,
How much more the wicked man and the sinner.

12 He who loves discipline loves knowledge;
He who spurns reproof is a brutish man.
2 A good man earns the favor of the LORD,
A man of intrigues, His condemnation.
3 A man cannot be established in wickedness,
But the root of the righteous will not be shaken loose.
4 A capable wife is a crown for her husband,
But an incompetent one is like rot in his bones.
5 The purposes of the righteous are justice,
The schemes of the wicked are deceit.
6 The words of the wicked are a deadly ambush,
But the speech of the upright saves them.
7 Overturn the wicked and they are gone,
But the house of the righteous will endure.
8 A man is commended according to his intelligence;
A twisted mind is held up to contempt.
9 Better to be lightly esteemed and have a servant
Than to put on airs and have no food.

a *Lit. "Hand to hand"; meaning of Heb. uncertain.*

22: Like an elegant ornament, beauty—fine in itself—becomes ludicrous when attached to a foolish woman. This may be applied to anything which is externally attractive but intrinsically of low value. **24:** Literally: "There is one who scatters yet gets more, and one who saves out of honesty yet ends up in need." The point of this paradox is that we should not admire the rich or despise the poor, because sometimes deeds and efforts do not produce the expected reward. The NJPS translation reflects a traditional moralizing interpretation, which understood the first line to refer to a man who gives charity *(Midr. Prov.)*. **26:** One who withholds grain in time of famine (as Joseph did, Gen. 47.13–26) in order to keep its price high will be despised by his countrymen. **27:** A summary of vv. 24a, 25–26. **28:** Cf. 10.2 and 11.4. **29:** A trouble-making son will inherit nothing. The family slave will do better than him; cf. 17.2. **12.1:** Sometimes even the wise require reproof, but they, unlike the fools, know enough to appreciate it. **4:** The capable woman is praised at length in 31.10–31. **6:** The scenario in 1.8–19 illustrates this v. **7:** When disaster strikes, the wicked are the first to disappear; cf. 10.25a. **9:** In some circumstances, material debasement is worse than lack of prestige.

10 A righteous man knows the needs of his beast,
But the compassion of the wicked is cruelty.
11 He who tills his land shall have food in plenty,
But he who pursues vanities is devoid of sense.
12 [a-]The wicked covet the catch of evil men;
The root of the righteous yields [fruit].[-a]
13 Sinful speech is a trap for the evil man,
But the righteous escapes from trouble.
14 A man gets his fill of good from the fruit of his speech;
One is repaid in kind for one's deeds.
15 The way of a fool is right in his own eyes;
But the wise man accepts advice.
16 A fool's vexation is known at once,
But a clever man conceals his humiliation.
17 He who testifies faithfully tells the truth,
But a false witness, deceit.
18 There is blunt talk like sword-thrusts,
But the speech of the wise is healing.
19 Truthful speech abides forever,
A lying tongue for but a moment.
20 Deceit is in the minds of those who plot evil;
For those who plan good there is joy.
21 No harm befalls the righteous,
But the wicked have their fill of misfortune.
22 Lying speech is an abomination to the LORD,
But those who act faithfully please Him.
23 A clever man conceals what he knows,
But the mind of a dullard cries out folly.
24 The hand of the diligent wields authority;
The negligent are held in subjection.
25 If there is anxiety in a man's mind let him quash it,
And turn it into joy with a good word.
26 A righteous man [a-]gives his friend direction,[-a]
But the way of the wicked leads astray.
27 A negligent man never has game to roast;
[a-]A diligent man has precious wealth.[-a]
28 The road of righteousness leads to life;
By way of its path there is no death.

13 A wise son—it is through the discipline of his father;
A scoffer—he never heard reproof.
2 A man enjoys good from the fruit of his speech;
But out of the throat of the treacherous comes
lawlessness.
3 He who guards his tongue[b] preserves his life;
He who opens wide his lips, it is his ruin.

10: The Bible shows concern for animals. See also Exod. 22.29; 23.19; 34.26; Lev. 22.27–28; Deut. 14.21; 22.6; 25.4. **11:** Cf. 28.19. **15:** It is wise to take counsel (v. 15b). The fool is too smug to do so (v. 15a).

12.16–23: Proverbs on speech, advocating restraint, honesty, and gentleness. **18:** Though truth, even when critical, is essential (v. 22), it should be cushioned in gentle terms (15.1). **21:** An assertion about how things usually work, not an absolute statement.

12.24–16.9: More contrasts. **12.24:** Cf. 17.2. **25–26:** Obscure. **27:** The deceitful man may cheat and "hunt" others, but he will get no benefit from his gains. **28:** The second line was traditionally understood as affirming immortality. But the Heb is obscure, and even if this translation is correct, it could imply the avoidance of a premature death. **13.2–3:** *Speech,* lit. "mouth." *Throat,* Heb "nefesh," also means "person" or "emotion." Cf. 12.14a and 18.20a.

a-a Meaning of Heb. uncertain. *b Lit. "mouth."*

4 A lazy man craves, but has nothing;
The diligent shall feast on rich fare.
5 A righteous man hates lies;
The wicked man is vile and disgraceful.
6 Righteousness protects him whose way is blameless;
Wickedness subverts the sinner.
7 One man pretends to be rich and has nothing;
Another professes to be poor and has much wealth.
8 Riches are ransom for a man's life,
The poor never heard a reproof.
9 The light of the righteous is radiant;
The lamp of the wicked is extinguished.
10 [a]Arrogance yields nothing but strife;[a]
Wisdom belongs to those who seek advice.
11 Wealth may dwindle to less than nothing,
But he who gathers little by little increases it.
12 Hope deferred sickens the heart,
But desire realized is a tree of life.
13 He who disdains a precept will be injured thereby;
He who respects a command will be rewarded.
14 The instruction of a wise man is a fountain of life,
Enabling one to avoid deadly snares.
15 Good sense wins favor;
The way of treacherous men is unchanging.[b]
16 Every clever man acts knowledgeably,
But a dullard exposes his stupidity.
17 Harm befalls a wicked messenger;
A faithful courier brings healing.
18 Poverty and humiliation are for him who spurns discipline;
But he who takes reproof to heart gets honor.
19 Desire realized is sweet to the soul;
To turn away from evil is abhorrent to the stupid.
20 He who keeps company with the wise becomes wise,
But he who consorts with dullards comes to grief.
21 Misfortune pursues sinners,
But the righteous are well rewarded.
22 A good man has what to bequeath to his grandchildren,
For the wealth of sinners is stored up for the righteous.
23 The tillage of the poor yields much food;
But substance is swept away for lack of moderation.
24 He who spares the rod hates his son,
But he who loves him disciplines him early.
25 The righteous man eats to his heart's content,
But the belly of the wicked is empty.

a-a Meaning of Heb. uncertain. *b Or "harsh."*

7: This insight into human character derides phonies and indirectly warns the reader to avoid pretensions. **8:** Contrary to 11.4, people sometimes can save themselves by money. A "ransom" is money paid to get out of trouble. V. 8b is puzzling. **9:** *Light* or *lamp* are metaphors for life itself but also for the quality of life; cf. Job 18.5–6. Darkness is misery. **11:** It is a mistake to try to get rich too quickly; see 10.22; 20.21; 28.20, 22. **12:** The tree of life represents a source of health and vitality (see 3.18 n.). **13–14:** *Precept* (lit. "word") and *command* refer to the teachings of the wise. These save lives by steering people away from deadly temptations. **17:** See 10.26 n. **23:** *Moderation*, rather, "justice" (Heb "mishpat"). A poor man's plot of land can supply his needs, but this is lost when injustice is rife. **24:** A paradox: a harshness inspired by love, a leniency motivated by hatred. A lax parent is treating his son as if he hated him. See also 23.13–14; 29.17. **25:** Cf. 10.3; 13.2, 4, 12, 19. Harsh corporal punishment was standard in the pre-modern world.

14 The wisest of women builds her house,
But folly tears it down with its own hands.
2 He who maintains his integrity fears the LORD;
A man of devious ways scorns Him.
3 In the mouth of a fool is a rod of haughtiness,
But the lips of the wise protect them.
4 If there are no oxen the crib is clean,
But a rich harvest comes through the strength of the ox.
5 An honest witness will not lie;
A false witness testifies lies.
6 A scoffer seeks wisdom in vain,
But knowledge comes easily to the intelligent man.
7 Keep your distance from a dullard,
For you will not learn wise speech.
8 It is the wisdom of a clever man to understand his course;
But the stupidity of the dullard is delusion.
9 Reparations mediate between fools,
Between the upright, good will.
10 The heart alone knows its bitterness,
And no outsider can share in its joy.
11 The house of the wicked will be demolished,
But the tent of the upright will flourish.
12 A road may seem right to a man,
But in the end it is a road to death.
13 The heart may ache even in laughter,
And joy may end in grief.
14 An unprincipled man reaps the fruits of his ways;
[a]A good man, of his deeds.[a]
15 A simple person believes anything;
A clever man ponders his course.
16 A wise man is diffident and shuns evil,
But a dullard rushes in confidently.
17 An impatient man commits folly;
A man of intrigues will be hated.
18 Folly is the lot of the simple,
But clever men [b]glory in knowledge.[b]
19 Evil men are brought low before the good,
So are the wicked at the gates of the righteous.
20 A pauper is despised even by his peers,
But a rich man has many friends.
21 He who despises his fellow is wrong;
He who shows pity for the lowly is happy.
22 Surely those who plan evil go astray,
While those who plan good earn steadfast love.

14.1: *Folly,* a foolish woman. **3:** The speech of *the wise* can protect them against the pain caused by haughty, arrogant words. Cf. 12.6. **4:** *Clean,* that is, devoid of produce. It is a good idea to invest in farming "equipment." **6:** A scoffer might desire wisdom in the sense of learning or cunning, but he does not have the ability to acquire it. Only one with the right mind-set can do so. **9:** Better: "Fools scorn a guilt offering, but the upright find acceptance." Fools lack the humility to admit their guilt and to bring an offering to expiate it. **10:** No one can truly understand what another is feeling. This is restated in v. 13a. **16–17:** Exercise caution and avoid impulsiveness; similarly v. 29. **20–21:** V. 21 seems to respond to the rather cynical observation of v. 20.

a-a Taking ʽal *as from* ʽll; *cf. Hos.* 12.3. *b-b Meaning of Heb. uncertain.*

23 From all toil there is some gain,
But idle chatter is pure loss.
24 The ornament of the wise is their wealth;
The stupidity of dullards is stupidity.
25 A truthful witness saves lives;
He who testifies lies [spreads] deceit.
26 Fear of the LORD is a stronghold,
A refuge for a man's children.
27 Fear of the LORD is a fountain of life,
Enabling one to avoid deadly snares.
28 A numerous people is the glory of a king;
Without a nation a ruler is ruined.
29 Patience results in much understanding;
Impatience gets folly as its portion.
30 A calm disposition gives bodily health;
Passion is rot to the bones.
31 He who withholds what is due to the poor affronts his
Maker;
He who shows pity for the needy honors Him.
32 The wicked man is felled by his own evil;
The righteous man finds security in his death.
33 Wisdom rests quietly in the mind of a prudent man,
But among dullards it makes itself known.
34 Righteousness exalts a nation;
Sin is a reproach to any people.
35 The king favors a capable servant;
He rages at an incompetent one.

15 A gentle response allays wrath;
A harsh word provokes anger.
2 The tongue of the wise produces much
knowledge,
But the mouth of dullards pours out folly.
3 The eyes of the LORD are everywhere,
Observing the bad and the good.
4 A healing tongue is a tree of life,
But a devious one makes for a broken spirit.
5 A fool spurns the discipline of his father,
But one who heeds reproof becomes clever.
6 In the house of the righteous there is much treasure,
But in the harvest of the wicked there is trouble.
7 The lips of the wise disseminate knowledge;
Not so the minds of dullards.
8 The sacrifice of the wicked is an abomination to the
LORD,
But the prayer of the upright pleases Him.
9 The way of the wicked is an abomination to the LORD,
But He loves him who pursues righteousness.

26: A man's righteousness benefits his children as well; cf. 20.6. **27:** For a contrasting notion, see 13.14, "The instruction of a wise man *is a fountain of life, enabling one to avoid deadly snares.*" The difference between these two proverbs highlights the way that the book has ultimately combined largely secular ("the instruction of a wise man") and religious notions ("Fear of the LORD"). **30:** *Passion,* rather, "jealousy." **31:** The poor too are God's handiwork (22.2). As such they are worthy of respect, and mistreating them is an affront to their Creator. **32:** In the second line, we should probably read "betumo," "in his innocence," for "bemoto," *in his death.* **33:** The wise man's wisdom is evident even when he is in a crowd of fools. **15.3:** This v. attributes "geographical omniscience" to God, namely that He sees everything everywhere, but does not suggest that God is omniscient in the sense that He knows the future. **4:** *A healing tongue,* see 15.1. *Tree of life,* see 3.18 n. A *devious* tongue disheartens others. Dishonesty is depressing. **5:** The humility to accept chastisement is crucial to learning. See 1.7; 5.12; 6.23; 8.33. **6:** The righteous get rich. The wicked too might get rich, but their prosperity will be tainted by strife and worry; see 10.24. **8:** Sacrifices and prayers are not automatically efficacious, and must be accompanied by ethical behavior; see, e.g., 21.3; 1 Sam. 15.22b; Isa. 1.10–17; 29.12; Amos 5.21–25; Mic. 6.6–8.

10 Discipline seems bad to him who forsakes the way;
He who spurns reproof will die.
11 Sheol and Abaddon lie exposed to the LORD,
How much more the minds of men!
12 The scoffer dislikes being reproved;
He will not resort to the wise.
13 A joyful heart makes a cheerful face;
A sad heart makes a despondent mood.
14 The mind of a prudent man seeks knowledge;
The mouth of the dullard pursues folly.
15 All the days of a poor man are wretched,
But contentment is a feast without end.
16 Better a little with fear of the LORD
Than great wealth with confusion.
17 Better a meal of vegetables where there is love
Than a fattened ox where there is hate.
18 A hot-tempered man provokes a quarrel;
A patient man calms strife.
19 The way of a lazy man is like a hedge of thorns,
But the path of the upright is paved.
20 A wise son makes his father happy;
A fool of a man humiliates his mother.
21 Folly is joy to one devoid of sense;
A prudent man walks a straight path.
22 Plans are foiled for want of counsel,
But they succeed through many advisers.
23 A ready response is a joy to a man,
And how good is a word rightly timed!
24 For an intelligent man the path of life leads upward,
In order to avoid Sheol below.
25 The LORD will tear down the house of the proud,
But He will establish the homestead of the widow.
26 Evil thoughts are an abomination to the LORD,
But pleasant words are pure.
27 He who pursues ill-gotten gain makes trouble for his household;
He who spurns gifts will live long.
28 The heart[a] of the righteous man rehearses his answer,
But the mouth of the wicked blurts out evil things.
29 The LORD is far from the wicked,
But He hears the prayer of the righteous.
30 What brightens the eye gladdens the heart;
Good news puts fat on the bones.
31 He whose ear heeds the discipline of life
Lodges among the wise.

11: God sees everything, even hidden thoughts; see v. 3. These vv. imply a type of divine omniscience, but do not suggest that God knows all future events. *Abaddon,* lit. "place of destruction," a term found only in wisdom literature (e.g., Job 26.6; 31.12; Ps. 88.12 [translated "place of perdition"]); see also 27.20. Synonymous with Sheol, it is the realm of the dead. **13:** One's emotions are visible on his face and in his demeanor (*mood,* lit. "spirit"). **15:** To be sure, the days of a poor man are (objectively) wretched—that is a fact of life—but if he has inner happiness, he enjoys, as it were, an unending feast. This is confirmed by the next v. **16–17:** This pair of sayings probably derives from the Egyptian sage Amenemope, who said, "Better is poverty in the hand of the god than wealth in the storehouse. Better is bread with a happy heart than wealth with vexation" (§6; *AEL* 2.152). **20:** See 10.1. **21:** The perverse values of the fool; see 9.7–8. **22:** This saying shows an appreciation of collective, cooperative wisdom; see 24.6. **23:** *A word rightly timed* (lit. "a word in its time"), which meets the needs of the particular situation, is satisfying to both speaker and listener. **24:** See 2.18–19; 7.27; 15.19. **25:** *Homestead,* lit. "boundary." God will protect the widow's property from encroachments by the greedy. At the same time, it is forbidden to attempt such encroachments (22.28; 23.10). A widow without grown sons had a precarious legal status in ancient Israel because only adult males had independent access to the courts. **30:** *What brightens the eye,* lit. "brightness of eye," an event or report that makes one happy. *Fat* or "moist" bones were identified with health. **31–33:** The importance of being receptive to correction; see 3.11–12.

a For leb *as a source of speech, see note to Eccl. 5.1.*

32 He who spurns discipline hates himself;
He who heeds reproof gains understanding.
33 The fear of the LORD is the discipline of wisdom;
Humility precedes honor.

16 A man may arrange his thoughts,
But what he says depends on the LORD.
2 All the ways of a man seem right to him,
But the LORD probes motives.
3 Entrust your affairs to the LORD,
And your plans will succeed.
4 The LORD made everything for a purpose,
Even the wicked for an evil day.
5 Every haughty person is an abomination to the
LORD;
Assuredly,[a] he will not go unpunished.
6 Iniquity is expiated by loyalty and faithfulness,
And evil is avoided through fear of the LORD.
7 When the LORD is pleased with a man's conduct,
He may turn even his enemies into allies.
8 Better a little with righteousness
Than a large income with injustice.
9 A man may plot out his course,
But it is the LORD who directs his steps.

10 There is magic on the lips of the king;
He cannot err in judgment.
11 Honest scales and balances are the LORD's;
All the weights in the bag are His work.
12 Wicked deeds are an abomination to kings,
For the throne is established by righteousness.
13 Truthful speech wins the favor of kings;
They love those who speak honestly.
14 The king's wrath is a messenger of death,
But a wise man can appease it.
15 The king's smile means life;
His favor is like a rain cloud in spring.

16 How much better to acquire wisdom than gold;
To acquire understanding is preferable to silver.
17 The highway of the upright avoids evil;
He who would preserve his life watches his way.
18 Pride goes before ruin,
Arrogance, before failure.
19 Better to be humble and among the lowly
Than to share spoils with the proud.

a Lit. "Hand to hand"; meaning of Heb. uncertain.

16.1: Though one may plan what he wants to say, God determines what will actually come out; cf. v. 9. These vv. highlight divine omnipotence rather than divine omniscience. **2:** *Motives,* lit. "hearts," that is, thoughts. One may smugly imagine that all his deeds are pure (14.12), but God sees deeper. Cf. 21.2; 1 Sam. 16.7. **3:** Once one has done his work and applied his wisdom to his practical affairs, he should leave the outcome to God and trust that the results will be appropriate. **4:** We would expect a proverb to say that God made the *evil day* (that is, a time of troubles) for the purpose of punishing the wicked. This v. turns things around and says that God made the evil man so that the *evil day* will have someone to punish. **7:** God protects a righteous man by encompassing him in a sphere of peace. **8:** Cf. 15.16. **9:** Whatever a man's plans, it is God who determines the outcome. See v. 1.

16.10–15: The king's powers and responsibilities. The concern with royal matters is a very significant theme in some Egyptian wisdom books, which often focus on training royal officials, but it is highlighted less in Prov. Sayings that declare the king's powers and righteousness hold a mirror up to the monarch and set forth an ideal for him to emulate. On the king's power, see 19.12; 20.2; 24.21. On his righteousness, see 20.8, 26, 28; 22.11; 29.4, 14. Though Prov. holds kings and rulers in highest esteem, it does not assume that they are inevitably righteous (see 28.15). **10b:** Rather: "No one can defy his command." **11:** See 11.1. **12:** This proverb seems meant for the attention of a king or prince. **14–15:** These proverbs speak to someone, such as a royal scribe, who might find himself close enough to the king to dread his wrath or benefit from his favor. Cf. Eccl. 8.1–5; 10.4.

16.16–17.26: Further maxims. **16.16:** See 8.10. **17–20:** Pride versus trust in God. **18:** *Goes before* means "precedes." An arrogant overconfidence in one's abilities to control his fate prepares the way for disaster.

20 He who is adept in a matter will attain success;
Happy is he who trusts in the LORD.
21 The wise-hearted is called discerning;
One whose speech is pleasing gains wisdom.
22 Good sense is a fountain of life to those who have it,
And folly is the punishment of fools.
23 The mind of the wise man makes his speech effective
And increases the wisdom on his lips.
24 Pleasant words are like a honeycomb,
Sweet to the palate and a cure for the body.
25 A road may seem right to a man,
But in the end it is a road to death.
26 The appetite of a laborer labors for him,
Because his hunger[a] [b]-forces him on.-[b]

27 A scoundrel plots[c] evil;
What is on his lips is like a scorching fire.
28 A shifty man stirs up strife,
And a querulous one alienates his friend.
29 A lawless man misleads his friend,
Making him take the wrong way.
30 He closes his eyes while meditating deception;
He purses his lips while deciding upon evil.

31 Gray hair is a crown of glory;
It is attained by the way of righteousness.
32 Better to be forbearing than mighty,
To have self-control than to conquer a city.
33 Lots are cast into the lap;
The decision depends on the LORD.

17 Better a dry crust with peace
Than a house full of feasting with strife.
2 A capable servant will dominate an incompetent son
And share the inheritance with the brothers.
3 For silver—the crucible;
For gold—the furnace,
And the LORD tests the mind.
4 An evildoer listens to mischievous talk;
A liar gives ear to malicious words.
5 He who mocks the poor affronts his Maker;
He who rejoices over another's misfortune will not go unpunished.
6 Grandchildren are the crown of their elders,
And the glory of children is their parents.

a Lit. "mouth." *b-b Meaning of Heb. uncertain.*
c Meaning of Heb. uncertain.

21–24: Wise and gracious behavior is also effective. **21:** *Gains wisdom,* or "increases learning," i.e., teaches others effectively. **25:** People can be deluded about the quality of their own behavior. See 16.2. **26:** *Hunger,* lit. "mouth." Cf. Eccl. 6.7. **27–30:** Three types of evildoers and their harmful speech. **27:** The word translated *plots* is "koreh," lit. "digs," or "mines." The metaphor is of a smelting furnace, which is hot and dangerous. **29–30:** Compare the body language of the scoundrel in 6.13. His intentions are supposedly readable in his facial expression. **31:** Righteousness is supposed to be the path to a long life. Hence old age is an indicator of virtue, though not an absolute one. **33:** The casting of lots was a widespread means of divination in the ancient world. In one form, names, or "yes" and "no," would be written on stones, which were shaken till one fell out. This was thought to indicate what God wanted. Some suggest that the priestly Urim and Thummim (see Exod. 28.30) were lots, and the answering of yes-no questions by God in texts like Judg. 20.28 likely reflects the casting of lots. **17.1:** *A house full of feasting with strife,* lit. "a house full of sacrifices of strife." When people took an animal to the Temple as a sacrifice, they brought most of the meat back home for feasting. Better a crust of bread than a luxurious banquet at which there is quarreling. See 15.16–17 n. **2:** *Servant* is more precisely rendered "slave," since such a person was typically owned by his master, though a long-term indenture was possible. A capable slave could rise to a position of responsibility in a large household, in spite of his legal inferiority. **3:** A furnace *tests* or assays and purifies ore by heating it until the pure silver or gold melts and rises, where it can be separated from the heavier dross. The analogy, then, implies more than God's just looking into the heart. Like 3.12, it implies a painful test to prove the purity of the sufferer's faithfulness. **4:** Liars and slanderers not only speak lies and slanders, they like to hear them. **5:** See 14.31 n. **6:** One generation can take pride in another.

7 Lofty words are not fitting for a villain;
Much less lying words for a great man.
8 A bribe seems like a charm to him who uses it;
He succeeds at every turn.
9 He who seeks love overlooks faults,
But he who harps on a matter alienates his friend.
10 A rebuke works on an intelligent man
More than one hundred blows on a fool.
11 An evil man seeks only to rebel;
A ruthless messenger will be sent against him.
12 Sooner meet a bereaved she-bear
Than a fool with his nonsense.
13 Evil will never depart from the house
Of him who repays good with evil.
14 To start a quarrel is to open a sluice;
Before a dispute [a]flares up,[a] drop it.
15 To acquit the guilty and convict the innocent—
Both are an abomination to the LORD.
16 What good is money in the hand of a fool
To purchase wisdom, when he has no mind?
17 A friend is devoted at all times;
A brother is born to share adversity.
18 Devoid of sense is he who gives his hand
To stand surety for his fellow.
19 He who loves transgression loves strife;
He who builds a high threshold invites broken bones.
20 Man of crooked mind comes to no good,
And he who speaks duplicity falls into trouble.
21 One begets a dullard to one's own grief;
The father of a villain has no joy.
22 A joyful heart makes for [b]good health;[b]
Despondency dries up the bones.
23 The wicked man draws a bribe out of his bosom
To pervert the course of justice.
24 Wisdom lies before the intelligent man;
The eyes of the dullard range to the ends of the earth.
25 A stupid son is vexation for his father
And a heartache for the woman who bore him.
26 To punish the innocent is surely not right,
Or to flog the great for their uprightness.
27 A knowledgeable man is sparing with his words;
A man of understanding is reticent.
28 Even a fool, if he keeps silent, is deemed wise;
Intelligent, if he seals his lips.

a-a Meaning of Heb. uncertain.
b-b Or "a cheerful face"; meaning of Heb. uncertain.

7: *Lofty,* better, "excessive." **8:** This seems to praise bribes, but it probably describes a course of behavior that seems valuable but is really destructive (14.12; 16.2). **9:** That is, faults or offenses of others toward oneself. **10:** This proverb counterbalances the preceding by reminding us of the importance of a rebuke. See 19.11. **11:** The *ruthless messenger* may be an angel, called "messenger" ("mal'akh") in Heb. **12:** Fools are not only a nuisance, they are dangerous. **16:** The fool might think he can buy wisdom—whose prestige and practical advantages he might covet—but he lacks the wits (or the attitude) to receive it. **18:** On the dangers of guaranteeing another's loan, see 6.1–5 n. **19:** Perhaps building a tall portal (not *threshold*) to one's house is a metaphor for displaying arrogance. **21:** See 10.1 n. **22:** See 15.30. **23:** The Heb probably refers to the wicked man's taking a *bribe.* What is condemned is not gift giving (see 18.16) but its misuse. **24:** Wisdom is near at hand, and the intelligent person sees it. The dullard, in contrast, looks for wisdom (which he might value in the form of practical cleverness) everywhere except right in front of him. **25:** See 10.1. **26:** The second line is better translated: "Or to strike the noble man for his honesty," i.e., for speaking frankly. "Noble" can refer to a generous character.

17.27–18.8: Maxims on speech and its potentials. 17.27–28: The value of reserve in speech. *Reticent,* actually, "cool of spirit." The wise man (in Egyptian wisdom too) is "cool," retaining his repose and controlling his mouth even under provocation.

18 [a-]He who isolates himself pursues his desires;
He disdains all competence.[-a]
2 The fool does not desire understanding,
But only to air his thoughts.
3 Comes the wicked man comes derision,
And with the rogue, contempt.
4 The words a man speaks are deep waters,
A flowing stream, a fountain of wisdom.
5 It is not right to be partial to the guilty
And subvert the innocent in judgment.
6 The words of a fool lead to strife;
His speech invites blows.
7 The fool's speech is his ruin;
His words are a trap for him.
8 The words of a querulous man are bruising;[b]
They penetrate one's inmost parts.
9 One who is slack in his work
Is a brother to a vandal.
10 The name of the LORD is a tower of strength
To which the righteous man runs and is safe.
11 The wealth of a rich man is his fortress;
[a-]In his fancy[-a] it is a protective wall.
12 Before ruin a man's heart is proud;
Humility goes before honor.
13 To answer a man before hearing him out
Is foolish and disgraceful.
14 A man's spirit can sustain him through illness;
But low spirits—who can bear them?
15 The mind of an intelligent man acquires knowledge;
The ears of the wise seek out knowledge.
16 A man's gift eases his way
And gives him access to the great.
17 The first to plead his case seems right
Till the other party examines him.
18 The lot puts an end to strife
And separates those locked in dispute.
19 A brother offended is more formidable than a stronghold;
Such strife is like the bars of a fortress.
20 A man's belly is filled by the fruit of his mouth;
He will be filled by the produce of his lips.
21 Death and life are in the power of the tongue;
Those who love it will eat its fruit.
22 He who finds a wife has found happiness
And has won the favor of the LORD.

a-a *Meaning of Heb. uncertain.* *b* *Meaning of Heb. uncertain.*

18.1: Obscure. **4:** Human speech has the potential to be a deep fount of wisdom. **5–8:** The fool's speech incites strife and thus harms both himself and others.

18.9–22.16: Further maxims.
18.9: An idler causes damage not only to himself but also to those who work with him and depend on his contribution to the enterprise. **10–11:** The juxtaposition of these two antithetical proverbs contrasts real (v. 10) and delusive (v. 11) fortresses. **12:** Pride leads to destructive overconfidence, whereas humility precedes and opens the way to wisdom and prudence. **14:** One's frame of mind has powerful psychosomatic effects. **15:** One who is truly wise continues to seek for knowledge beyond what he already has. **16:** This proverb just gives practical advice. While bribes to subvert justice are condemned (17.23; Deut. 10.17; 16.19), other sorts of gifts and payments (to gain access to an official, e.g.) are acceptable (Prov. 18.16; 21.14). **17:** A cautionary message to judges and officials: do not jump to conclusions, but wait until all the facts are before you. **18:** See 16.33 n. **20–21:** One bears the effects of his own words. **22:** Marriage is a blessing. There may be exceptions (e.g., 19.13; 21.9, 19), but this is the rule. Several ancient sources and translations have "good woman," making it clear that only the good woman is a blessing (*b. Ber.* 8a; *b. Yebam.* 63b; *Mid. Shoḥer Tov* 151ab).

23: This is the way things are, not the way they should be. **24:** Two levels of friendship.

19.3: People blame God for troubles they bring on themselves. **4, 6–7:** Further observations on social realities, which are not always fair. A line seems to be missing before 7c, which is not balanced. **8:** *Wisdom,* lit. "heart." "Acquiring a heart"—gaining the right mind-set—is a prerequisite to gaining wisdom. **10:** The Sages had a conservative view of society. While they demanded fair and compassionate treatment of the lower classes, they assumed that the structure of society as they knew it was fundamentally the right one. Hence it was thought unseemly for a *servant* (more precisely "slave") to *rule over princes* (see 30.21–22). **11:** This refers to overlooking an offense against oneself (cf. 10.12). **12:** An expression of awe at the power of the king; see 16.14–15; cf. 20.2. **13:** This proverb does not condemn all women any more than it condemns all sons. Like the entirety of Prov., however, it does evaluate relationships from the standpoint of the adult male. There is no comparable criticism about a vexatious husband, except in a general way in 11.29. **14:** Counterbalancing v. 13, this proverb declares the value of a (good) wife. Cf. 31.10–31. *Efficient:* better, "intelligent" or "insightful." **18:** See 13.24 n.

23 The poor man speaks beseechingly;
The rich man's answer is harsh.
24 There are companions to keep one company,
And there is a friend more devoted than a brother.

19 Better a poor man who lives blamelessly
Than one who speaks perversely and is a dullard.
2 A person without knowledge is surely not good;
He who moves hurriedly blunders.
3 A man's folly subverts his way,
And his heart rages against the LORD.
4 Wealth makes many friends,
But a poor man loses his last friend.
5 A false witness will not go unpunished;
He who testifies lies will not escape.
6 Many court the favor of a great man,
And all are the friends of a dispenser of gifts.
7 All the brothers of a poor man despise him;
How much more is he shunned by his friends!
[a]He who pursues words—they are of no avail.[a]
8 He who acquires wisdom is his own best friend;
He preserves understanding and attains happiness.
9 A false witness will not go unpunished;
He who testifies falsely is doomed.
10 Luxury is not fitting for a dullard,
Much less that a servant rule over princes.
11 A man shows intelligence by his forebearance;
It is his glory when he overlooks an offense.
12 The rage of a king is like the roar of a lion;
His favor is like dew upon the grass.
13 A stupid son is a calamity to his father;
The nagging of a wife is like the endless dripping of water.
14 Property and riches are bequeathed by fathers,
But an efficient wife comes from the LORD.
15 Laziness induces sleep,
And a negligent person will go hungry.
16 He who has regard for his life pays regard to commandments;
He who is heedless of his ways will die.
17 He who is generous to the poor makes a loan to the LORD;
He will repay him his due.
18 Discipline your son while there is still hope,
And[b] do not [c]set your heart on his destruction.[c]

a-a Meaning of Heb. uncertain. *b Or "But."*
c-c Or "pay attention to his moaning."

19 A hot-tempered man incurs punishment;
[a]-If you try to save him you will only make it worse.-[a]
20 Listen to advice and accept discipline
In order that you may be wise in the end.
21 Many designs are in a man's mind,
But it is the LORD's plan that is accomplished.
22 [a]-Greed is a reproach to a man;-[a]
Better be poor than a liar.
23 He who fears the LORD earns life;
[a]-He shall abide in contentment,-[a]
Free from misfortune.
24 The lazy man buries his hand in the bowl;
He will not even bring it to his mouth.
25 Beat the scoffer and the simple will become clever;
Reprove an intelligent man and he gains knowledge.
26 A son who causes shame and disgrace
Plunders his father, puts his mother to flight.
27 My son, cease to stray from words of knowledge
And receive discipline.
28 A malicious witness scoffs at justice,
And the speech of the wicked conceals mischief.
29 Punishments are in store for scoffers
And blows for the backs of dullards.

20 Wine is a scoffer, strong drink a roisterer;
He who is muddled by them will not grow wise.
2 The terror of a king is like the roar of a lion;
He who provokes his anger risks his life.
3 It is honorable for a man to desist from strife,
But every fool [a]-becomes embroiled.-[a]
4 In winter the lazy man does not plow;
At harvesttime he seeks, and finds nothing.
5 The designs in a man's mind are deep waters,
But a man of understanding can draw them out.
6 He calls many a man his loyal friend,
But who can find a faithful man?
7 The righteous man lives blamelessly;
Happy are his children who come after him.
8 The king seated on the throne of judgment
Can winnow out all evil by his glance.
9 Who can say, "I have cleansed my heart,
I am purged of my sin"?
10 False weights and false measures,
Both are an abomination to the LORD.

a-a Meaning of Heb. uncertain.

24: A humorous picture of extreme sloth. **25:** A "simple" or uneducated boy may take warning from seeing the scoffer beaten. (The scoffer himself is probably hopeless.) But verbal rebukes are enough to straighten out an intelligent person. **28:** *Conceals,* better, "gobbles up." *Mischief* (or "iniquity") is the wicked person's "food." See 4.17. **29:** Implicit threats like these suggest that the intended audience of the collection (but not necessarily of the individual proverbs) is a boy, a son or pupil.
20.1: *Wine* and *strong drink* (more likely, "beer") are personified, as if they were drunken men. **3:** Conflicts often revolve on questions of "honor," but the true honor belongs to him who refrains from strife.
5: *Deep,* concealed and hard to discover. *Draw ... out* or "draw up," as one draws water. **6:** *He,* indefinite: "a man." **8:** The royal ideal. **9:** No human is free of inner sins. This may respond to the perhaps too reverent view of the king in v. 8. **10:** See 11.1 and cf. Deut. 25.13. An ephah was the most common dry measure, about 23 liters (21 quarts).

11 A child may be dissembling in his behavior
Even though his actions are blameless and proper.
12 The ear that hears, the eye that sees—
The LORD made them both.
13 Do not love sleep lest you be impoverished;
Keep your eyes open and you will have plenty of
food.
14 "Bad, bad," says the buyer,
But having moved off, he congratulates himself.
15 Gold is plentiful, jewels abundant,
But wise speech is a precious object.
16 Seize his garment, for he stood surety for another;[a]
Take it as a pledge, [for he stood surety] for an
unfamiliar woman.
17 Bread gained by fraud may be tasty to a man,
But later his mouth will be filled with gravel.
18 Plans laid in council will succeed;
Wage war with stratagems.
19 He who gives away secrets is a base fellow;
Do not take up with a garrulous man.
20 One who reviles his father or mother,
Light will fail him when darkness comes.
21 An estate acquired in haste at the outset
Will not be blessed in the end.
22 Do not say, "I will requite evil";
Put your hope in the LORD and He will deliver you.
23 False weights are an abomination to the LORD;
Dishonest scales are not right.
24 A man's steps are decided by the LORD;
What does a man know about his own way?
25 It is a snare for a man [b]to pledge a sacred gift rashly[b]
And to give thought to his vows only after they have
been made.
26 A wise king winnows out the wicked,
And turns the wheel upon them.
27 The lifebreath of man is the lamp of the LORD
Revealing all his inmost parts.
28 Faithfulness and loyalty protect the king;
He maintains his throne by faithfulness.
29 The glory of youths is their strength;
The majesty of old men is their gray hair.
30 Bruises and wounds are repayment[c] for evil,
Striking at one's inmost parts.

a *Or "a stranger."* *b-b* *Meaning of Heb. uncertain.*
c *Meaning of Heb. uncertain.*

11: An observation of human nature. **12:** God gave humans these faculties, which are the sources of wisdom, so He certainly wants them used. **14:** Dissembling is common both in the market and in life in general. **16:** These are the words the lender might say when a man guaranteed the loan of a stranger, who then defaulted. See 6.1–5. The *garment* is a large cloak that people wore in the cold by day and wrapped themselves in at night. Its importance is shown by the fact that Torah (Exod. 22.25–26; Deut. 24.12–13) requires that a garment given in pledge be returned each evening so its owner could use it. **17:** Stolen pleasures have a special—and deceptive—tang; see 9.17b. **18:** Better, "Plans made with counsel." Plans made in group deliberation are more effective. See 11.14; 24.6. **20:** *Light will fail* may imply that such a man will leave no children of his own when he dies. **21:** See 10.22. **24:** Expressions of humility such as this saying counterbalance the confident assumption, expressed in numerous proverbs, that humans can determine the course of their lives by choosing the right path. The notion of divine inscrutability informs other ancient Near Eastern wisdom literature as well, and it is an important theme in the LORD's speeches in Job chs 38–41. **25:** Vows were taken very seriously; see Lev. 27.28–29; Eccl. 5.3–5. The Rabbis discouraged the making of vows but also developed legal means, beyond Num. ch 30, for releasing people from precipitous vows. One medieval formula for this is retained in the Kol Nidre ("All vows," an early medieval prayer on the eve of Yom Kippur for the nullification of vows). **26:** *Winnows:* A heavy wheel was rolled over grain to crack the husk and then the wheat was thrown in the air so that the wind would blow away the useless chaff and leave the good grain. See Ps. 1.4. **27:** The breath that gives man life illuminates the depths of the human soul. The concept behind this is not clear. **29:** This expresses appreciation for the glories of both youth and old age, the sign of which is *gray hair.* Old age was something to take pride in, for it implied (in the Sages' view) both a successful life and the wisdom of years.

21 Like channeled water is the mind of the king in
the LORD's hand;
He directs it to whatever He wishes.
2 All the ways of a man seem right to him,
But the LORD probes the mind.
3 To do what is right and just
Is more desired by the LORD than sacrifice.
4 Haughty looks, a proud heart—
The tillage of the wicked is sinful.
5 The plans of the diligent make only for gain;
All rash haste makes only for loss.
6 Treasures acquired by a lying tongue
[a]-Are like driven vapor, heading for extinction.-[a]
7 The violence of the wicked sweeps them away,
For they refuse to act justly.
8 The way of a man may be tortuous and strange,
Though his actions are blameless and proper.
9 Dwelling in the corner of a roof is better
Than a contentious wife in a [a]-spacious house.-[a]
10 The desire of the wicked is set upon evil;
His fellowman finds no favor in his eyes.
11 When a scoffer is punished, the simple man is
edified;
When a wise man is taught, he gains insight.
12 The Righteous One observes the house of the
wicked man;
He subverts the wicked to their ruin.
13 Who stops his ears at the cry of the wretched,
He too will call and not be answered.
14 A gift in secret subdues anger,
A present in private, fierce rage.
15 Justice done is a joy to the righteous,
To evildoers, ruination.
16 A man who strays from the path of prudence
Will rest in the company of ghosts.
17 He who loves pleasure comes to want;
He who loves wine and oil does not grow rich.
18 The wicked are the ransom of the righteous;
The traitor comes in place of the upright.
19 It is better to live in the desert
Than with a contentious, vexatious wife.
20 Precious treasure and oil are in the house of the
wise man,
And a fool of a man will run through them.
21 He who strives to do good and kind deeds
Attains life, success, and honor.

a-a Meaning of Heb. uncertain.

21.1: The king's intentions are under God's control and thus express his will. *Channeled water* is used in irrigation and is productive. This proverb expresses great esteem for kingship. See 16.10–15 n. **2:** God perceives a human's subconscious intentions, finding (and judging) unworthy attitudes that even their possessor may be unaware of. **3:** Cf. 15.8; contrast 21.27. **4:** *The tillage of the wicked*—what they produce—is "sin" (rather than *sinful*). **5:** Cf. 19.2; 28.20. **6:** Wealth acquired dishonestly is both ephemeral and deadly. *Heading for extinction* should be emended to "deadly snares." **8:** Strange and even circuitous behavior is not always immoral. **11:** *He* in the second line is probably the *simple man* (actually "simple one," probably meaning a boy). The simple, callow boy can learn by observing how others are "taught," each in his own way; cf. 19.25. **13:** Those who ignore the suffering of others, will be ignored by God when they get into trouble. **14:** *Present,* more precisely, "bribe." Gifts or bribes were acceptable, even recommended, if the intention was good; see 18.16 n. Gifts might be used to placate an angry official or a man who considered himself wronged. **17:** *Pleasure* refers to feasting. One who loves sybaritic pleasures too much will squander his time and his money. **18:** The underlying notion is that when God is angry (at a nation, e.g.), His anger is assuaged by the punishment of the wicked. They take the place of the upright, who might otherwise have suffered in the general catastrophe. Cf. 11.8. **19:** See 19.13.

22 One wise man prevailed over a city of warriors
And brought down its mighty stronghold.
23 He who guards his mouth and tongue
Guards himself from trouble.
24 The proud, insolent man, scoffer is his name,
Acts in a frenzy of insolence.
25 The craving of a lazy man kills him,
For his hands refuse to work.
26 All day long he is seized with craving
While the righteous man gives without stint.
27 The sacrifice of the wicked man is an
abomination,
The more so as he offers it in depravity.
28 A false witness is doomed,
But one who really heard will testify with success.
29 The wicked man is brazen-faced;
The upright man discerns his course.
30 No wisdom, no prudence, and no counsel
Can prevail against the LORD.
31 The horse is readied for the day of battle,
But victory comes from the LORD.

22 Repute is preferable to great wealth,
Grace is better than silver and gold.
2 Rich man and poor man meet;
The LORD made them both.
3 The shrewd man saw trouble and took cover;
The simple kept going and paid the penalty.
4 The effect of humility is fear of the LORD,
Wealth, honor, and life.
5 Thorns and snares are in the path of the
crooked;
He who values his life will keep far from them.
6 Train a lad in the way he ought to go;
He will not swerve from it even in old age.
7 The rich rule the poor,
And the borrower is a slave to the lender.
8 He who sows injustice shall reap misfortune;
His rod of wrath shall fail.
9 The generous man is blessed,
For he gives of his bread to the poor.
10 Expel the scoffer and contention departs,
Quarrel and contumely cease.
11 A pure-hearted friend,
His speech is gracious;
He has the king for his companion.
12 The eyes of the LORD watch the wise man;
He subverts the words of the treacherous.

22: The power of wisdom in war; see 16.32; 24.6; contrast 21.31. **23:** The importance of controlling one's speech, to avoid blurting out offensive or stupid things; see 4.23. **25–26:** These sayings are linked by the word *craving,* but they are independent thoughts. The lazy man is wracked with his appetites, but he refuses to work to satisfy them. In contrast to a greedy man, the righteous man is generous. **27:** See 15.8. **30–31:** No intellectual skills are effective if they are used contrary to God's will. *Prudence,* better, "understanding." **22.1:** *Grace,* "good favor," the favor or esteem which others have for oneself. **2:** When rich and poor come together, their differences are accentuated, and the sage does not blur them (v. 7). But they are both God's handiwork, and the rich man should keep this in mind. **6:** Others render the beginning of the v. "Train a lad according to his way," suggesting that education must be individualized. This type of interpretation goes back at least to Saadia. **7:** A warning against borrowing money. In antiquity, money was typically lent for short periods at very high interest rates. **8:** *Rod,* a flail used in threshing grain. The power of the unjust man's anger will prove ineffective. **10:** The *scoffer,* arrogant and contemptuous of others (21.24), provokes quarrels wherever he goes. **11:** The king wants honest, gracious men for his intimates. Compare Ps. 101, esp. v. 6. This proverb seems to be directed to someone who spends his time in the royal court. **12:** *The wise man,* rather, "knowledge." God protects authentic knowledge and gives it success, whereas He foils the deceits of the treacherous.

13 The lazy man says, "There's a lion in the street;
I shall be killed [a]-if I step outside."-[a]
14 The mouth of a forbidden[b] woman is a deep pit;
He who is doomed by the LORD falls into it.
15 If folly settles in the heart of a lad,
The rod of discipline will remove it.
16 To profit by withholding what is due to the poor
Is like making gifts to the rich—pure loss.

17 Incline your ear and listen to the words of the sages;
Pay attention to my wisdom.
18 It is good that you store them inside you,
And that all of them be constantly on your lips,
19 That you may put your trust in the LORD.
I let you know today—yes, you—
20 Indeed, I wrote down for you [c]-a threefold lore,-[c]
Wise counsel,
21 To let you know truly reliable words,
That you may give a faithful reply to him who sent you.
22 Do not rob the wretched because he is wretched;
Do not crush the poor man in the gate;
23 For the LORD will take up their cause
And despoil those who despoil them of life.
24 Do not associate with an irascible man,
Or go about with one who is hot-tempered,
25 Lest you learn his ways
And find yourself ensnared.
26 Do not be one of those who give their hand,
Who stand surety for debts,
27 Lest your bed be taken from under you
When you have no money to pay.
28 Do not remove the ancient boundary stone
That your ancestors set up.

a-a Lit. "in the square." *b Lit. "strange."* *c-c Meaning of Heb. uncertain.*

13: The lazy man finds the silliest excuses to beg off work; cf. 26.13. **14:** The strange woman (see 2.16) works her seduction above all by her slippery speech. Falling into her trap is so deadly it must be reckoned a sign of divine anger. **16:** Better, "There is one who oppresses the poor, yet makes him (the poor man) profit, and there is one who gives to a rich man, yet he (the rich man) ends up lacking." This is a paradox like 13.7a, and shows that humans do not always realize or control the effects of their actions.

22.17–24.22: Collection III. These are mostly admonitions ("Do not ..."), and in contrast to the previous collection, are often longer than a single two-part verse. Many are particularly relevant to a young man looking forward to his career. They emphasize the inner virtues of humility, compassion, and serenity. Three sections (A–C) are discernible.

22.17–23.11: Collection III, section A. Since 1923 it has been recognized that 22.17–23.11 is based on the Egyptian "Instruction of Amenemope." The relationship is close, and the sayings in this unit follow the order of the parallel sayings in Amenemope. In the following, the parallel passages in Amenemope are indicated by ch number (§) and can be found for example in *AEL* 2.146–63. **22.17:** We should read, "The words of the sages. Incline your ear and listen, pay attention to my words." By this reading (based on the LXX), this unit too has a title, "Words of the Sages." Cf. 24.23. **17b–21:** The prologue. This is similar to the prologue of Amenemope (*AEL* 2.148) and a sentence from its conclusion, §30. It also resembles the Calls to Attention in Prov. chs 1–9. **20:** *A threefold lore,* Heb "shalishim" means "officers," which was traditionally construed to mean "excellent things." But at the end of his book, Amenemope tells his son, "Look to these thirty chapters. They inform; they educate" (*AEL* 2.162). This suggests that we change the vowels of the Heb word to read "sheloshim," "thirty." There is disagreement on identifying thirty proverbs in the present form of section A, but most counts are in agreement on most components. **21:** Amenemope's prologue promises to teach the reader "To reply to one who sends a message." Proper "replies" are a topic of special concern in Egyptian wisdom, though not in Prov. 22.17–23.11, in spite of the promise of the present v. It seems that the author of this unit took the theme from Amenemope without really integrating it in his own instructions. **22–23:** The wretched man's wretchedness is a reason *not* to cheat him. The city gate was where disputes and legal cases were adjudicated. The poor may lack a human protector, but they have a divine one. **24:** Cf. Amenemope §9. **26–27:** See 6.1–5 n. *Bed* refers to a blanket or garment a person would roll up in. Though a debtor had some legal protection in this regard (see 20.16 n.), a guarantor did not. **28:** Moving a boundary stone between your land and your neighbor's was a grave offense, because it was easily done and hard to detect. See 23.10; Deut. 19.14; Amenemope §6.

29 See a man skilled at his work—
He shall attend upon kings;
He shall not attend upon [a]obscure men.[-a]

23 When you sit down to dine with a ruler,
Consider well who is before you.
2 Thrust a knife into your gullet
If you have a large appetite.
3 Do not crave for his dainties,
For they are counterfeit food.

4 Do not toil to gain wealth;
Have the sense to desist.
5 You see it, then it is gone;
It grows wings and flies away,
Like an eagle, heavenward.

6 Do not eat of a stingy man's food;
Do not crave for his dainties;
7 He is like one keeping accounts;
"Eat and drink," he says to you,
But he does not really mean it.
8 The morsel you eat you will vomit;
You will waste your courteous words.

9 Do not speak to a dullard,
For he will disdain your sensible words.
10 Do not remove ancient boundary stones;
Do not encroach upon the field of orphans,
11 For they have a mighty Kinsman,
And He will surely take up their cause with you.

12 Apply your mind to discipline
And your ears to wise sayings.
13 Do not withhold discipline from a child;
If you beat him with a rod he will not die.
14 Beat him with a rod
And you will save him from the grave.

15 My son, if your mind gets wisdom,
My mind, too, will be gladdened.
16 I shall rejoice with all my heart[b]
When your lips speak right things.
17 Do not envy sinners in your heart,
But only God-fearing men, at all times,

a-a Meaning of Heb. uncertain.
b Lit. "kidneys."

29–30: This unit aims to train young men who would likely become officials, and, if very successful, might even land a job in the royal court. Cf. Amenemope §30. **23.1–3:** Proper comportment at a ruler's table: When dining with a ruler, control your appetite. *A ruler* may be any superior. Egyptian writings give similar instructions and show that formal dinners headed by a superior official had a role in professional life (Cf. Amenemope §23). The official showed whom he favored among his underlings by giving them different size portions (see Gen. 43.34). **1:** *Consider well,* that is, look at the portion you receive and not what others get. **2–3:** *Thrust a knife into your gullet,* control your appetite at all costs. *His dainties* are *counterfeit food* in the sense that if you fill up on them, you may find the result dissatisfying. **4–5:** An extension of the principle of vv. 1–3: Do not be greedy. If you strain for wealth, it disappears. Cf. 28.20; Amenemope §7. **6–8:** Dinner with a stingy man is an occasion of hypocrisy on all sides and is nauseating. **9:** Some people just cannot learn; see 9.7–10. **10–11:** See 22.28. *Kinsman,* rather, "redeemer" ("go'el"), one who will punish the transgressor. The redeemer was originally a kinsman who could sue on behalf of the widow and orphan in the city gate; see 22.22–23.

23.12–35: Collection III, section B. Advice addressed to a son in an affectionate tone, emphasizing the joy parents get from wise and upright children and the misery they suffer from foolish ones. **13–14:** Corporal punishment can save a child from sins that will lead to his death; see 13.24. **17–18:** Admire the God-fearing.

18 For then you will have a future,
And your hope will never fail.

19 Listen, my son, and get wisdom;
Lead your mind in a [proper] path.
20 Do not be of those who guzzle wine,
Or glut themselves on meat;
21 For guzzlers and gluttons will be impoverished,
And drowsing will clothe you in tatters.

22 Listen to your father who begot you;
Do not disdain your mother when she is old.
23 Buy truth and never sell it,
And wisdom, discipline, and understanding.
24 The father of a righteous man will exult;
He who begets a wise son will rejoice in him.
25 Your father and mother will rejoice;
She who bore you will exult.
26 Give your mind to me, my son;
Let your eyes watch my ways.
27 A harlot is a deep pit;
A forbidden[a] woman is a narrow well.
28 She too lies in wait as if for prey,
And destroys the unfaithful among men.

29 Who cries, "Woe!" who, "Alas!";
Who has quarrels, who complaints;
Who has wounds without cause;
Who has bleary eyes?
30 Those whom wine keeps till the small hours,
Those who gather to drain the cups.
31 Do not ogle that red wine
As it lends its color to the cup,
As it flows on smoothly;
32 In the end, it bites like a snake;
It spits like a basilisk.
33 Your eyes will see strange sights;
Your heart[b] will speak distorted things.
34 You will be like one lying in bed on high seas,
Like one lying [c-]on top of the rigging.[-c]
35 "They struck me, but I felt no hurt;
They beat me, but I was unaware;
As often as I wake,
I go after it again."

20–21: A life of dissolution and indulgence will lead to poverty. **22:** Cf. 30.17. **27–28:** Avoid harlots. There is a pun here: A woman's sexuality is a *pit* and a *well*. With the wrong woman, these are pitfalls (22.14). The sexuality of a man's own wife, however, is a blessed, joyous, productive well (5.15–18). **29–35:** A humorous and caustic portrayal of the drunkard. He acts like a fool, staggers around in inebriation, and has a horrible hangover. But he starts all over again the next day.

a *Lit. "alien."*
b *See note to 15.28.*
c-c *Meaning of Heb. uncertain.*

24.1–22: Collection III, section C. Maxims mostly praising wisdom and condemning the schemes of the wicked. **1–2:** Of the various dangers that evil people present, Prov. emphasizes their bad influence on those who consort with them rather than the harm they inflict directly. **3–6:** True prosperity (vv. 3–4) and strength (vv. 5–6) come from wisdom, not from nefarious schemes and crude exercise of power. **7:** The fool *does not*—or rather, "cannot"—*open his mouth* insofar as no one will pay attention to him. *Gate,* see 1.20–21 n. **8–9:** Like folly, scheming is held in contempt. **10–12:** The obligation to fight injustice: It is not enough to refrain from committing injustices; you must actively try to prevent them. *Rescuing* may refer to standing up for an unjustly accused defendant in a capital case. **13–14:** Learning wisdom is not just a matter of hard work and harsh discipline. If pursued with love, learning is a joy. Ps. 119.103 uses similar language about Torah. **15:** *Wicked man* looks like a pointless addition. **16:** The righteous have a "future" (v. 14b) because they can recover from misfortune, but wickedness is a dead-end road (vv. 19–20). Like many other biblical passages, it assumes that the righteous will ultimately prosper, though they may fare poorly in the interim. **17–19:** God resents it when you gloat at another's suffering, even if deserved, and might punish you by failing to punish him. Cf. 25.21–22; contrast 11.10b.

24 Do not envy evil men;
Do not desire to be with them;
2 For their hearts[a] talk violence,
And their lips speak mischief.

3 A house is built by wisdom,
And is established by understanding;
4 By knowledge are its rooms filled
With all precious and beautiful things.

5 A wise man is strength;
A knowledgeable man exerts power;
6 For by stratagems you wage war,
And victory comes with much planning.

7 Wisdom is too lofty for a fool;
He does not open his mouth in the gate.
8 He who lays plans to do harm
Is called by men a schemer.
9 The schemes of folly are sin,
And a scoffer is an abomination to men.

10 If you showed yourself slack in time of trouble,
Wanting in power,
11 If you refrained from rescuing those taken off to
death,
Those condemned to slaughter—
12 If you say, "We knew nothing of it,"
Surely He who fathoms hearts will discern
[the truth],
He who watches over your life will know it,
And He will pay each man as he deserves.
13 My son, eat honey, for it is good;
Let its sweet drops be on your palate.
14 Know: such is wisdom for your soul;
If you attain it, there is a future;
Your hope will not be cut off.

15 Wicked man! Do not lurk by the home of the righteous
man;
Do no violence to his dwelling.
16 Seven times the righteous man falls and gets up,
While the wicked are tripped by one misfortune.

17 If your enemy falls, do not exult;
If he trips, let your heart not rejoice,

a *See note to 15.28.*

18 Lest the LORD see it and be displeased,
And avert His wrath from him.

19 Do not be vexed by evildoers;
Do not be incensed by the wicked;
20 For there is no future for the evil man;
The lamp of the wicked goes out.

21 Fear the LORD, my son, and the king,
And do not mix with dissenters,
22 For disaster comes from them suddenly;
The doom both decree who can foreknow?

23 These also are by the sages:

It is not right to be partial in judgment.
24 He who says to the guilty, "You are innocent,"
Shall be cursed by peoples,
Damned by nations;
25 But it shall go well with them who decide justly;
Blessings of good things will light upon them.

26 Giving a straightforward reply
Is like giving a kiss.
27 Put your external affairs in order,
Get ready what you have in the field,
Then build yourself a home.
28 Do not be a witness against your fellow without good cause;
Would you mislead with your speech?
29 Do not say, "I will do to him what he did to me;
I will pay the man what he deserves."

30 I passed by the field of a lazy man,
By the vineyard of a man lacking sense.
31 It was all overgrown with thorns;
Its surface was covered with chickweed,
And its stone fence lay in ruins.
32 I observed and took it to heart;
I saw it and learned a lesson.
33 A bit more sleep, a bit more slumber,
A bit more hugging yourself in bed,
34 And poverty will come [a]calling upon you,[a]
And want, like a man with a shield.

21: The striking parallelism between *the LORD* and *the king* suggests that the Sages held kingship in awe and believed in the fundamental rightness of the social order as they knew it. See 16.10–15 n.

24.23–34: Collection IV. This short collection, introduced by a superscription, is ascribed to anonymous sages. **23–24, 28:** Honesty in judgment. **25–26:** *Them who decide justly,* or, "those who give reproof." Honest words, like kisses, are an expression of love (v. 26) and one who reproves others, though ostensibly harsh, will receive praise and good wishes in the end. **27:** Lay the right groundwork for your home, and for major projects generally. **29:** Do not seek revenge on your own; rather rely on God to execute justice (see 24.12b). **30–34:** A little narrative illustrating the consequences of sloth. The sage passed by the field of the lazy man and saw it had gone wild. He draws a lesson by applying a proverb, vv. 33–34, which is found also in 6.10–11 (see 6.11 n.).

a-a Meaning of Heb. uncertain.

25 These too are proverbs of Solomon, which the men of King Hezekiah of Judah copied:

2 It is the glory of God to conceal a matter,
And the glory of a king to plumb a matter.
3 Like the heavens in their height, like the earth in its
depth,
Is the mind of kings—unfathomable.
4 The dross having been separated from the silver,
A vessel emerged for the smith.
5 Remove the wicked from the king's presence,
And his throne will be established in justice.
6 Do not exalt yourself in the king's presence;
Do not stand in the place of nobles.
7 For it is better to be told, "Step up here,"
Than to be degraded in the presence of the great.

Do not let what your eyes have seen
8 Be vented rashly in a quarrel;
Think[a] of what it will effect in the end,
When your fellow puts you to shame.
9 Defend your right against your fellow,
But do not give away the secrets of another,
10 Lest he who hears it reproach you,
And your bad repute never end.

11 Like golden apples in silver showpieces[b]
Is a phrase well turned.
12 Like a ring of gold, a golden ornament,
Is a wise man's reproof in a receptive ear.
13 Like the coldness of snow at harvesttime
Is a trusty messenger to those who send him;
He lifts his master's spirits.
14 Like clouds, wind—but no rain—
Is one who boasts of gifts not given.
15 Through forbearance a ruler may be won over;
A gentle tongue can break bones.
16 If you find honey, eat only what you need,
Lest, surfeiting yourself, you throw it up.
17 Visit your neighbor sparingly,
Lest he have his surfeit of you and loathe you.

a Lit. "Lest." *b Meaning of Heb. uncertain.*

25.1–29.27: Collection V. Characteristic of this collection are proverbial comparisons in which an image (e.g., "Like clouds, wind—but no rain—" in v. 14a) is followed by the phenomenon being described (e.g., "one who boasts of gifts not given," v. 14b). Like collections I, III and IV, but unlike II, most of the vv. are not self-standing, but parts of short units. **25.1:** *Copied,* better, "transmitted" or "collected." This shows that the royal court in Israel, as elsewhere in the ancient Near East, was one place where traditional wisdom was collected and put in writing. Hezekiah reigned from 715 to 687 BCE. *These too* of this superscription refers back to the superscription of the book in 1.1. **2–7:** Kings and their courts. These proverbs seem to be directed at a scribe or future scribe who might work in the royal court but would not necessarily be of noble rank (v. 6). The proverbs speak of kings and their vast wisdom with reverence, even sycophancy. See 16.10–15 n. **2:** It redounds to God's glory to create mysteries in the world and to the king's to investigate mysteries—not necessarily the same ones. The king would investigate matters when sitting in judgment. **3:** The king's wisdom is vast and his intentions cannot be fully understood. **4–5:** Just as removing dross from silver ore leaves pure silver, which can be made into a fine vessel, so does removing the wicked from the royal court allow the king's reign to be founded firmly on righteousness. **6–7b:** This proverb instructs a young man who might become a royal scribe or official to remember his rank and not to put himself forward too boldly. **7c–10:** This maxim, whose text and meaning is uncertain, apparently warns against blurting out something you know about someone else when you are in an argument with him. Preserve his secrets even when angry. If you violate his confidence, your own reputation will be harmed. **11–15:** Four comparisons concerning speech. **11–12:** Eloquent words—even reprimands—are like precious, well-crafted works of art. **13:** The *harvesttime* in question is probably the wheat harvest in May–June, when it can be quite hot. It is refreshing to have a reliable messenger. **15:** *Won over,* more precisely, "beguiled" or "tempted." Subtle, gentle speech has real power, even over the mighty. The second line is a paradox. **16–17:** Do not overdo good things. If you wear out your welcome, you will be like honey that your neighbor gorges on and throws up.

18 Like a club, a sword, a sharpened arrow,
Is a man who testifies falsely against his fellow.
19 Like a loose tooth and an unsteady leg,
Is a treacherous support in time of trouble.
20 Disrobing on a chilly day,
Like vinegar on natron,
Is one who sings songs to a sorrowful soul.

21 If your enemy is hungry, give him bread to eat;
If he is thirsty, give him water to drink.
22 You will be heaping live coals on his head,
And the LORD will reward you.

23 A north wind produces rain,
And whispered words, a glowering face.
24 Dwelling in the corner of a roof is better
Than a contentious woman in [a-]a spacious house.[-a]
25 Like cold water to a parched throat
Is good news from a distant land.
26 Like a muddied spring, a ruined fountain,
Is a righteous man fallen before a wicked one.
27 It is not good to eat much honey,
[a-]Nor is it honorable to search for honor.[-a]
28 Like an open city without walls
Is a man whose temper is uncurbed.

26 Like snow in summer and rain at harvesttime,
So honor is not fitting for a dullard.
2 As a sparrow must flit and a swallow fly,
So a gratuitous curse must backfire.[b]
3 A whip for a horse and a bridle for a donkey,
And a rod for the back of dullards.
4 Do not answer a dullard in accord with his folly,
Else you will become like him.
5 Answer a dullard in accord with his folly,
Else he will think himself wise.
6 He who sends a message by a dullard
Will wear out legs and [c-]must put up with[-c] lawlessness.
7 As legs hang limp on a cripple,
So is a proverb in the mouth of dullards.
8 Like a pebble in a sling,
So is paying honor to a dullard.

a-a Meaning of Heb. uncertain. b Kethib, *"fail."* c-c *Lit. "drink."*

18–20: Four comparisons describing hurtful behaviors. **20:** The text of this v. is in doubt, and the first line might be very corrupt. As it stands, the proverb offers two images: undressing in the cold and pouring acid on a base. To these are compared the effect that cheerful music has on a melancholy person. The first action causes a chill, the second causes fizzing and hissing, which may suggest irritation and incompatibility. Without the first analogy (which many scholars excise), "vinegar on natron" might imply neutralization of the sorrow. **21–22:** Rather than seeking vengeance, treat a vulnerable enemy kindly. Then he will be ashamed and God will reward your kindness. Amenemope (§2) advises that when the wicked man is in trouble, "Fill his belly with bread of your own, that he be sated and weep." **23:** Enigmatic. **24:** V. 24 = 21.9. Prov. is a collection of collections, so it is not surprising to see a proverb repeated in different sections. **25–26:** Comparisons to "good" and "bad" water. In Heb these vv. (and v. 28) lack the word *like,* and are striking metaphors rather than similes. The defeat of a righteous person is a scandal, fouling the quality of a society. **28:** Like a city wall, self-control holds in one's *temper* (lit. "spirit" or "wind") and also protects its possessor. An angry man's wall is breached and leaves him vulnerable. **26.1:** *Honor,* better, "prestige." **2:** Better, "So a gratuitous [that is, undeserved] insult will not arrive." It will not reach and hurt the person it is sent against.

26.3–12: Sayings on the dullard. The *dullard* (Heb "kesil") is not merely a man of low intelligence. He is the kind of fool who is obtuse because of smug overconfidence. See, e.g., 1.32b. **4–5:** Two contradictory proverbs. The second one seems like a rejoinder to the more standard message of the first. If you answer the fool in kind (that is, in a crude and harsh fashion), you will resemble him, but if you do not, he will think that he has impressed or confounded you. Some interpreters think that this juxtaposition suggests the paradoxical difficulties of being wise. **6:** Better, "cuts off his own legs and drinks poison." **7, 9:** The *dullard* is a verbal cripple. To be effective, a proverb must be spoken at the right time (15.23) and in the right fashion (25.11). **8, 10:** Obscure.

11: A deliberately disgusting characterization of the way some people repeat stupid behavior. Dogs for some reason often lick up their vomit, giving the impression they like it. **12:** A climactic conclusion, observing that as bad as the dullard is, far worse is the man who thinks he is wise (but is not), for he has no hope of improving.

26.13–29.27: Further maxims. **26.13–16:** Humorous characterizations of the sluggard. **14:** See 22.13. **15:** See 19.24. **16:** The sluggard, like the dullard (v. 12) is smug and conceited. **17–22:** The dangers of strife. **20, 22:** *Querulous man,* or "slanderer." **23–28:** The hypocrite hides his hatred and hostile schemes under a cheap sheen of unctuous words. V. 27 states the principle that the schemer is preparing his own punishment.

9 As a thorn comes to the hand of a drunkard,
So a proverb to the mouth of a dullard.
10 [a-]A master can produce anything,[-a]
But he who hires a dullard is as one who hires transients.[b]
11 As a dog returns to his vomit,
So a dullard repeats his folly.
12 If you see a man who thinks himself wise,
There is more hope for a dullard than for him.

13 A lazy man says,
"There's a cub on the road, a lion in the squares."
14 The door turns on its hinge,
And the lazy man on his bed.
15 The lazy man buries his hand in the bowl;
He will not even bring it to his mouth.
16 The lazy man thinks himself wiser
Than seven men who give good advice.

17 A passerby who gets embroiled in someone else's quarrel
Is like one who seizes a dog by its ears.
18 Like a madman[b] scattering deadly firebrands, arrows,
19 Is one who cheats his fellow and says, "I was only joking."

20 For lack of wood a fire goes out,
And without a querulous man contention is stilled.
21 Charcoal for embers and wood for a fire
And a contentious man for kindling strife.
22 The words of a querulous man are bruising;[b]
They penetrate one's inmost parts.

23 Base silver laid over earthenware
Are ardent lips with an evil mind.
24 An enemy dissembles with his speech,
Inwardly he harbors deceit.
25 Though he be fair-spoken do not trust him,
For seven abominations are in his mind.
26 His hatred may be concealed by dissimulation,
But his evil will be exposed to public view.

27 He who digs a pit will fall in it,
And whoever rolls a stone, it will roll back on him.
28 A lying tongue hates [a-]those crushed by it;[-a]
Smooth speech throws one down.

a-a Meaning of Heb. uncertain. *b Meaning of Heb. uncertain.*

27 Do not boast of tomorrow,
For you do not know what the day will bring.
2 Let the mouth of another praise you, not yours,
The lips of a stranger, not your own.
3 A stone has weight, sand is heavy,
But a fool's vexation outweighs them both.
4 There is the cruelty of fury, the overflowing of
anger,
But who can withstand jealousy?
5 Open reproof is better than concealed love.
6 Wounds by a loved one are long lasting;
The kisses of an enemy are profuse.
7 A sated person disdains honey,
But to a hungry man anything bitter seems sweet.
8 Like a sparrow wandering from its nest
Is a man who wanders from his home.
9 Oil and incense gladden the heart,
And the sweetness of a friend is better than one's own
counsel.
10 Do not desert your friend and your father's friend;
Do not enter your brother's house in your time of
misfortune;
A close neighbor is better than a distant brother.
11 Get wisdom, my son, and gladden my heart,
That I may have what to answer those who taunt me.
12 The shrewd man saw trouble and took cover;
The simple kept going and paid the penalty.
13 Seize his garment, for he stood surety for another;[a]
Take it as a pledge, [for he stood surety] for an
unfamiliar woman.
14 He who greets his fellow loudly early in the morning
Shall have it reckoned to him as a curse.
15 An endless dripping on a rainy day
And a contentious wife are alike;
16 As soon repress her as repress the wind,
Or declare one's right hand to be oil.
17 As iron sharpens iron
So a man sharpens the wit[b] of his friend.
18 He who tends a fig tree will enjoy its fruit,
And he who cares for his master will be honored.
19 As face answers to face in water,
So does one man's heart to another.
20 Sheol and Abaddon cannot be satisfied,
Nor can the eyes of man be satisfied.
21 For silver—the crucible, for gold—the furnace,
And a man is tested by his praise.

27.1: Do not praise yourself for future achievements. **5:** Friendship often takes the form of forthright rebuke for faults. **6:** *Long lasting,* or "trustworthy." The *wounds* are verbal, as in v. 5, and they are intended to be beneficial. In contrast, an enemy feigns friendship, but this, of course, means nothing. **8:** The wanderer and the bird are imagined as hapless and lonely. **9:** The word translated *sweetness* may mean "counsel." It is more satisfying to discuss something with another person than to deliberate on it alone. **10:** Three one-line sayings on friends and relations. Together they suggest that friends can be a better support than relatives in a time of difficulty and should be held precious. **11:** When one is being taunted, if his son is smart, he can brag about him. The background circumstances are unclear. **12:** See 22.3. **13:** See 20.16. **14:** People tend to be irritated by loud cheeriness too early in the morning. **15–16:** A nagging wife is like a drizzle—irritating and unrelenting. See 19.13 n. **17:** If this translation of the difficult v. is correct, it means that good conversation sharpens the wits. **18:** This should be read as a comparison. **19:** *Answers* is not in the Heb. The saying is obscure. **20:** The human eye (desire) is insatiable; see Eccl. 1.8. *Abaddon,* see 15.11 n. **21:** *By his praise,* perhaps read "his praisers." To see what a man is really like, consider what sort of person praises him; see 28.4.

a Or "a stranger." *b* Lit. "face."

22 Even if you pound the fool in a mortar
With a pestle along with grain,
His folly will not leave him.

23 Mind well the looks of your flock;
Pay attention to your herds;
24 For property does not last forever,
Or a crown for all generations.
25 Grass vanishes, new grass appears,
And the herbage of the hills is gathered in.
26 The lambs will provide you with clothing,
The he-goats, the price of a field.
27 The goats' milk will suffice for your food,
The food of your household,
And the maintenance of your maids.

28

The wicked flee though no one gives chase,
But the righteous are as confident as a lion.
2 When there is rebellion in the land, many are its rulers;
[a]But with a man who has understanding and
knowledge, stability will last.[a]
3 A poor man who withholds what is due to the
wretched
Is like a destructive rain that leaves no food.
4 Those who forsake instruction praise the wicked,
But those who heed instruction fight them.
5 Evil men cannot discern judgment,
But those who seek the LORD discern all things.
6 Better is a poor man who lives blamelessly
Than a rich man whose ways are crooked.
7 An intelligent son heeds instruction,
But he who keeps company with gluttons disgraces his
father.
8 He who increases his wealth by loans at discount or
interest
Amasses it for one who is generous to the poor.
9 He who turns a deaf ear to instruction—
His prayer is an abomination.
10 He who misleads the upright into an evil course
Will fall into his own pit,
But the blameless will prosper.
11 A rich man is clever in his own eyes,
But a perceptive poor man can see through him.
12 When the righteous exult there is great glory,
But when the wicked rise up men make themselves
scarce.

a-a Meaning of Heb. uncertain.

23–27: An epigram on the advantages of animal husbandry as a livelihood. (*Property* and *a crown* in v. 24 refer to other kinds of wealth and power.) *Grass* (unlike, say, silver) renews itself and feeds the flocks, whose yield provides for many needs. Unlike other sections of Prov., addressed to the wise or those serving the kings, this is addressed to farmers. Its inclusion indicates what a wide-ranging collection Prov. is. **28.1:** The wicked live in constant fear (1.26–27; 10.24), knowing that punishment is approaching but being ignorant of when it will arrive. The righteous enjoy a sense of security; see 1.33; 3.23–26. **2:** *Rebellion* (or "crime") brings anarchy, and with it an oppressive multiplicity of *rulers.* The second line is obscure. **4–5:** These proverbs emphasize the bond between the intellectual power of wisdom and the quality of one's values. *All things* means all things relevant to wisdom teachings. He who seeks God finds wisdom; see 2.4–5. **7:** A variant of 29.3. The *gluttons* are probably guilty of generally licentious and dissolute behavior. **8:** Profit-taking on a loan to a distressed Israelite is forbidden in Exod. 22.24; Lev. 25.36; Deut. 23.20. Such loans are to be given interest free, as an act of charity. **9:** If one does not listen to *instruction* ("torah"), God will not listen to him. It is possible that "torah" here and in 29.18, unlike other occurrences in Prov. (where it usually means parental instructions), means God's Torah. **10:** If one leads someone onto a bad path, he himself will fall. **12:** *Men make themselves scarce,* lit. "a man is sought for." "A man" ("'adam") can mean a worthy man. Compare the use of "'adam" in Eccl. 7.28. People seek for a worthy man but (it may be implied) cannot find one.

13 He who covers up his faults will not succeed;
He who confesses and gives them up will find mercy.
14 Happy is the man who is anxious always,
But he who hardens his heart falls into misfortune.
15 A roaring lion and a prowling bear
Is a wicked man ruling a helpless people.
16 A prince who lacks understanding is very oppressive;
He who spurns ill-gotten gains will live long.
17 A man oppressed by bloodguilt will flee to a pit;
Let none give him support.
18 He who lives blamelessly will be delivered,
But he who is crooked in his ways will fall all at once.
19 He who tills his land will have food in plenty,
But he who pursues vanities will have poverty in plenty.
20 A dependable man will receive many blessings,
But one in a hurry to get rich will not go unpunished.
21 To be partial is not right;
A man may do wrong for a piece of bread.
22 A miserly man runs after wealth;
He does not realize that loss will overtake it.
23 He who reproves a man will in the end
Find more favor than he who flatters him.
24 He who robs his father and mother and says, "It is no offense,"
Is a companion to vandals.
25 A greedy man provokes quarrels,
But he who trusts the LORD shall enjoy prosperity.
26 He who trusts his own instinct is a dullard,
But he who lives by wisdom shall escape.
27 He who gives to the poor will not be in want,
But he who shuts his eyes will be roundly cursed.
28 When the wicked rise up, men go into hiding,
But when they perish the righteous increase.

29

One oft reproved may become stiffnecked,
But he will be suddenly broken beyond repair.
2 When the righteous become great the people rejoice,
But when the wicked dominate the people groan.
3 A man who loves wisdom brings joy to his father,
But he who keeps company with harlots will lose his wealth.
4 By justice a king sustains the land,
But a fraudulent man tears it down.
5 A man who flatters his fellow
Spreads a net for his feet.
6 An evil man's offenses are a trap for himself,
But the righteous sing out joyously.

14: Here, *is anxious* (lit. "fears") means fearing one's own sins and being willing to repent of them. **17:** Text and sense very uncertain. **19:** See 12.11. **20:** See 23.4. **21:** Perhaps: Although partiality in judgment is not right, not even toward a poor man (Exod. 23.3), a judge should remember that a man may commit a crime for bread (6.30–31) and show some mercy. **23:** Cf. 27.5–6. **24:** Those who convince themselves that exploiting their parents' wealth is no crime, since they will be inheriting it eventually, are no better than ordinary thugs. **26:** *Instinct,* rather, "heart," meaning one's own mind, even if untutored and callow. One must rely on a mind infused with the principles and attitudes taught by wisdom. **28:** Cf. v. 12. When the wicked come to power, people hunker down and try to make themselves inconspicuous. When these rulers perish, the moral level of the society rises. See 29.2. **29.3:** A variant of 28.7. One who goes to whores will *lose his wealth* because he wastes his money on them (cf. 31.3) or because his father will diminish his inheritance. **5:** Flattery or "slippery speech" is the device by which the strange woman too lays her trap (2.16; 7.5).

7 A righteous man is concerned with the cause of the wretched;
A wicked man cannot understand such concern.
8 Scoffers inflame a city,
But the wise allay anger.
9 When a wise man enters into litigation with a fool
There is ranting and ridicule, but no satisfaction.
10 Bloodthirsty men detest the blameless,
But the upright seek them out.
11 A dullard vents all his rage,
But a wise man calms it down.
12 A ruler who listens to lies,
All his ministers will be wicked.
13 A poor man and a fraudulent man meet;
The LORD gives luster to the eyes of both.
14 A king who judges the wretched honestly,
His throne will be established forever.
15 Rod and reproof produce wisdom,
But a lad out of control is a disgrace to his mother.
16 When the wicked increase, offenses increase,
But the righteous will see their downfall.
17 Discipline your son and he will give you peace;
He will gratify you with dainties.
18 For lack of vision a people lose restraint,
But happy is he who heeds instruction.
19 A slave cannot be disciplined by words;
Though he may comprehend, he does not respond.
20 If you see a man hasty in speech,
There is more hope for a fool than for him.
21 A slave pampered from youth
[a-]Will come to a bad end.[-a]
22 An angry man provokes a quarrel;
A hot-tempered man commits many offenses.
23 A man's pride will humiliate him,
But a humble man will obtain honor.
24 He who shares with a thief is his own enemy;
He hears the imprecation and does not tell.[b]
25 A man's fears become a trap for him,
But he who trusts in the LORD shall be safeguarded.
26 Many seek audience with a ruler,
But it is from the LORD that a man gets justice.
27 The unjust man is an abomination to the righteous,
And he whose way is straight is an abomination to the wicked.

a-a Meaning of Heb. uncertain.
b Cf. Lev. 5.1.

7: Rather, "A righteous man knows the just claim of the wretched"—what is theirs by right. The wicked man is ignorant of this. **8–13:** Proverbs on deceit and anger. **9:** Translation uncertain. Apparently: It is a mistake to enter into litigation (or just "argue") with fools. Nothing will be resolved. Cf. 26.5. **10:** *Seek them out,* lit. "seek his life." This elsewhere means to try to kill someone, but here the sense may be reversed: They seek his life in order to protect it. **11:** *Rage,* lit. "wind." He lets forth a storm, which the wise man can pacify. Contrast v. 9. **12:** Corruption starts at the top of the regime and inevitably spreads downwards. **13:** *Fraudulent man,* meaning uncertain; possibly "contentious man." God "gives their eyes light" (rather than *luster)* means that he gives life to all. **14–21:** Proverbs on discipline and anarchy, both domestic and social. **14:** Cf. 20.28; 25.5. **17:** Raise your son strictly and he will take care of you when you are old. **18:** *Vision* means prophecy, which was a source of discipline and reproof for Israelite society. *Instruction* is "torah," which in Prov. usually means parental instruction. Here it possibly refers to God's Torah (see 28.9 n.). **19, 21:** Since a *slave* was deprived of material interests of his own, it was assumed that he had to be treated like a child and beaten into submission. Pampering would spoil him. According to Exod. 21.20–21, 26–27, a male or female slave could be beaten at will though not killed or permanently injured. **24:** Upon the discovery of a crime, a proclamation was issued requiring everyone who knew about it to come forward and testify; see Lev. 5.1. *Tell* (as in Lev.) means "testify." The proclamation was accompanied by an *imprecation,* a conditional curse that would fall on whoever had information and failed to come forward. **25:** *A man's fears* may mean "what he fears." These, in the case of the evildoer, will be precisely the punishment he suffers (10.24). Alternatively, this may mean that excessive fears can impel anyone to rash steps. **27:** Values, right and perverse. See 28.4.

30 The words of Agur son of Jakeh, [man of] Massa; The speech of the man to Ithiel, to Ithiel and Ucal:

2 I am brutish, less than a man;
I lack common sense.
3 I have not learned wisdom,
Nor do I possess knowledge of the Holy One.
4 Who has ascended heaven and come down?
Who has gathered up the wind in the hollow of his hand?
Who has wrapped the waters in his garment?
Who has established all the extremities of the earth?
What is his name or his son's name, if you know it?

5 Every word of God is pure,
A shield to those who take refuge in Him.
6 Do not add to His words,
Lest He indict you and you be proved a liar.

7 Two things I ask of you; do not deny them to me before I die:
8 Keep lies and false words far from me;
Give me neither poverty nor riches,
But provide me with my daily bread,
9 Lest, being sated, I renounce, saying,
"Who is the LORD?"
Or, being impoverished, I take to theft
And profane[a] the name of my God.
10 Do not inform on a slave to his master,
Lest he curse you and you incur guilt.

a *Meaning of Heb. uncertain.*

30.1–31.31: Collection VI. Appendices. The book ends with a number of miscellaneous poems and epigrams. In style and sometimes in content they are quite different from the earlier chs and from each other.

30.1–6: Agur. This mysterious poem is ascribed to an otherwise unknown, apparently foreign, sage. Its message is the overriding importance of piety, which does not require wisdom to possess. The poem seems like a cautionary response to the rest of the book of Prov., which makes wisdom a value of the highest order. Such is the poem's difficulty that other commentators read it as an expression of skepticism or as a claim to a superhuman or mystical knowledge superior to human wisdom. **1:** The text and meaning of the title of this poem, after the word *Jakeh,* are very uncertain. It is usually thought that *Agur* was a Massaite, a member of the North Arabian tribe of Massa. 1 Kings 5.10 shows that the Israelites had respect for the wisdom of "the sons of the East," of which this passage might preserve an example. The ascription to a foreign sage may be a fiction, however, intended to show that even a foreigner can see the plain truth that pious obedience to God's word supersedes all human wisdom. Agur calls his *speech* a "ne'um," an "oracle," a communication from God. Compare the way the foreign prophet Balaam introduces his oracle ("ne'um") in Num. 24.3–4. Perhaps *Ithiel* and *Ucal* are Agur's sons. With a slight change in vocalization, these words can, however, also be read as a sentence: "I am weary, God, and perishing." Possibly a double entendre is intended. **2–3:** Agur declares that he has not learned wisdom, meaning the lore and learning of the ancients. *Common sense,* better, "human knowledge." Agur disavows even ordinary human wisdom. In v. 3b, NJPS continues the negative from 3a, but it is not in the text, and an affirmative translation is possible:, "but I do possess knowledge of the Holy One." Similarly, the seer Balaam claimed to have "knowledge of the Most High" (Num. 24.15–19). Knowledge of God (see 2.5; 9.10) is awareness of His will and ways. **4:** These provocative questions may be answered in different ways: (1) God, and He alone, has done these things. As in Job chs 38–41, human wisdom consists in recognizing God's infinite and incomparable powers. (2) No one—no human, that is—has done them. Either way, the point is that God is infinitely powerful and wise and man lowly and limited. Human intellect, therefore, must bow before God's word. **5:** This statement is found also in Ps. 18.31 (= 2 Sam. 22.31). **6:** This is also said of the Torah in Deut. 4.2 and 13.1 and is well-known in other ancient Near Eastern texts.

30.7–9: Agur's prayer. The implied addressee is God, making this the only prayer in Prov. **8–9:** Agur asks, first, to be kept from lies and, second, to be given possessions in moderation. Excess wealth may make one overconfident, and poverty too can corrupt. *Profane,* lit. "grab." If arrested, a thief might profane the name of the LORD by using it in a false vow of innocence.

30.10: Denouncing a slave. A lone couplet. *Incur guilt,* or "be punished."

11 There is a breed of men that brings a curse on its fathers
And brings no blessing to its mothers,
12 A breed that thinks itself pure,
Though it is not washed of its filth;
13 A breed so haughty of bearing, so supercilious;
14 A breed whose teeth are swords,
Whose jaws are knives,
Ready to devour the poor of the land,
The needy among men.

15 The leech has two daughters, "Give!" and "Give!"
Three things are insatiable;
Four never say, "Enough!":
16 Sheol, a barren womb,
Earth that cannot get enough water,
And fire which never says, "Enough!"

17 The eye that mocks a father
And disdains the homage due a mother—
The ravens of the brook will gouge it out,
Young eagles will devour it.

18 Three things are beyond me;
Four I cannot fathom:
19 How an eagle makes its way over the sky;
How a snake makes its way over a rock;
How a ship makes its way through the high seas;
How a man has his way with a maiden.
20 Such is the way of an adulteress:
She eats, wipes her mouth,
And says, "I have done no wrong."

21 The earth shudders at three things,
At four which it cannot bear:
22 A slave who becomes king;
A scoundrel sated with food;

30.11–14: Four breeds of men, each with its own type of corruption. The word translated *breed,* Heb "dor," usually means "generation," and that may be applicable here. There is a notion that certain generations, such as the generation of the flood (Gen. 6.5–12) and the generation of the Tower of Babel (Gen. 11.1–9), are characterized by a certain failing. The failings in the present passage are contempt of parents (v. 11), self-righteousness (v. 12), arrogance (v. 13), and rapaciousness (v. 14). Perhaps this list, and some of those that follow, were answers to riddles whose questions are no longer preserved. Although these vv. contain no numerals, they are similar to the numerical sayings that follow.

30.15–31: Numerical sayings, which associate things sharing a certain feature. When two numbers are mentioned in parallel, the second number is usually what is really meant. Sometimes the numbered items are followed by a supernumerary item which represents the extreme or surprising case. Numerical sayings are common in the Bible (e.g., Amos chs 1–2; Prov. 6.16–19) and other Canaanite literature. **15a:** The *leech* is a bloodsucker. Her *daughters* are like her, greedy and demanding. The message: Watch out. Your children will be like you. The image can be extended to other greedy things. A midrash in the Talmud (*b. A. Z.* 17a) says that the daughters are heresy and government.

30.15b–16: Four insatiable things. *Sheol,* the underworld, the realm of the dead (see 27.20). *A barren womb,* a barren woman, who yearns endlessly for a child. The *earth* always needs more rain. *Fire* always "needs"—can consume—more fuel.

30.17: Parental treatment. An isolated saying excoriating the person who treats his parents with contempt.

30.18–19: Four amazing "ways." The word translated *how* is literally "the way of." The wonder of the "ways" or movement of the eagle, the snake, and the ship may lie in the fact that they do not leave traces or that they are smooth and graceful. As for the way of *a man* with *a maiden,* love is a mystery, but just how it is mysterious is left to the imagination.

30.20: The additional wonder. This v. seems mechanically tacked on and inappropriate, but it might be intended as a shocking climax. The four "ways" are mysterious and graceful and leave no trace. The *way*—that is, behavior—of the adulteress too is especially amazing: She is unbelievably smug and thinks she can wipe her sin away as if wiping the crumbs off her face.

30.21–23: Four things the earth cannot bear, so unnatural are they. (1) *A slave who becomes king* violates the social hierarchy, which the sages of Prov. assumed was the

23 A loathsome woman who gets married;
A slave-girl who supplants her mistress.

24 Four are among the tiniest on earth,
Yet they are the wisest of the wise:
25 Ants are a folk without power,
Yet they prepare food for themselves in summer;
26 The badger is a folk without strength,
Yet it makes its home in the rock;
27 The locusts have no king,
Yet they all march forth in formation;
28 You can catch the lizard[a] in your hand,
Yet it is found in royal palaces.

29 There are three that are stately of stride,
Four that carry themselves well:
30 The lion is mightiest among the beasts,
And recoils before none;
31 [b-]The greyhound, the he-goat,
The king whom none dares resist.[-b]

32 If you have been scandalously arrogant,
If you have been a schemer,
Then clap your hand to your mouth.
33 As milk under pressure produces butter,
And a nose under pressure produces blood,
So patience under pressure produces strife.

31 The words of Lemuel, king of Massa, with which his mother admonished him:

2 No, my son!
No, O son of my womb!
No, O son of my vows!
3 Do not give your strength to women,
Your vigor,[c] [b-]to those who destroy kings.[-b]
4 Wine is not for kings, O Lemuel;
Not for kings to drink,
Nor any strong drink for princes,

a Or "spider." *b-b Meaning of Heb. uncertain.* *c Lit. "ways."*

right and natural order. (See 19.10 n.) *Becomes king,* lit. "rules," with the sense dominates, controls. Perhaps this line implies that one should not let his slave become the master of his household (as Potiphar did to Joseph, though to good effect; Gen. 39.4). (2) *A scoundrel*—a disobedient slave or son, perhaps—should not be indulged, but should be punished by deprivation (cf. 19.10). (3) *A loathsome woman,* lit. "hated woman," has (the author presumes) done something deserving of disgust and is unworthy of marriage. Perhaps the point is that one should not force his son to marry a woman he dislikes. The word for "hated" seems to mean "unloved" or "dispreferred" in Gen. 29.30–31 and Deut. 21.15–17. (4) *A slave-girl* should be kept in her place and not *supplant* or, more precisely, "disinherit" *her mistress.* This would happen if a man favored his concubine and made her children his heirs. A well-to-do Egyptian, Djefai-hapi, boasts, "I did not let a slave woman be valued above her mistress" (M. Lichtheim, *Maat in Egyptian Autobiographies and Related Studies* [1992], p. 38). The four items may thus have messages for a head of a household.

30.24–28: Four small (or "weak") but clever creatures. *Ants* work without a leader (6.6–8). *Badgers*—meaning rock badgers—are clever enough to live in fortress-like cliffs. *Locusts,* also leaderless, move like an army. The *lizard* can slip into the greatest of houses. All these exemplify the superiority of wisdom over size and strength.

30.29–31: Four animals who move in a majestic fashion. *Greyhound,* better "cock." The real point of the epigram lies in the fourth item: the king's incomparability.

30.32–33: Avoid strife. If you are *arrogant* or scheming, at least keep your mouth shut. Just as squeezing (or "churning") *milk* or a *nose* produces *butter* or *blood,* so does squeezing someone's *patience* produce conflict. There is a wordplay in v. 33: Heb "'af," *nose,* also means "anger" in certain idioms and Heb "'apayim," *patience,* also means "nose."

31.1–9: Lemuel's mother. Like Agur (30.1), Lemuel is from the North Arabian nation of Massa. The present passage has several Aramaisms and probably is foreign in origin. Though the passage is called *words of Lemuel,* meaning a teaching he would repeat, it was composed by his mother. See 1.8–19 n. This unit and the next (31.10–31) share the theme of a wise mother. The passage is an instruction for a king, showing a fine sense of

5 Lest they drink and forget what has been ordained,
And infringe on the rights of the poor.
6 Give strong drink to the hapless
And wine to the embittered.
7 Let them drink and forget their poverty,
And put their troubles out of mind.
8 Speak up for the dumb,
For the rights of all the unfortunate.
9 Speak up, judge righteously,
Champion the poor and the needy.

10 א What a rare find is a capable wife!
Her worth is far beyond that of rubies.
11 ב Her husband puts his confidence in her,
And lacks no good thing.
12 ג She is good to him, never bad,
All the days of her life.
13 ד She looks for wool and flax,
And sets her hand to them with a will.
14 ה She is like a merchant fleet,
Bringing her food from afar.
15 ו She rises while it is still night,
And supplies provisions for her household,
The daily fare of her maids.
16 ז She sets her mind on an estate and acquires it;
She plants a vineyard by her own labors.
17 ח She girds herself with strength,
[a]And performs her tasks with vigor.[a]
18 ט She sees[b] that her business thrives;
Her lamp never goes out at night.
19 י She sets her hand to the distaff;
Her fingers work the spindle.
20 כ She gives generously to the poor;
Her hands are stretched out to the needy.
21 ל She is not worried for her household because of snow,
For her whole household is dressed in crimson.

a-a Lit. "And exerts her arms." *b Lit. "tastes."*

social responsibility. In the first part, vv. 3–7, Lemuel's mother first admonishes her son to avoid dissipating his strength on wine and women, for wine may make him forget his duties to the poor and women waste his strength. Rather, one should give strong drink or wine to the poor, to let them drown their troubles in alcohol. Such advice is not found elsewhere. The warning about women is countered by the book's concluding poem in vv. 10–31. In the second part (vv. 8–9), Lemuel's mother exhorts him to give justice to the needy.

31.10–31: The woman of strength. So far, the book of Prov. has been devoted to inculcating the ideal of a wise man. It now concludes with a poem describing a wise woman, praising her energy, her economic talents, and her personal virtues. This is not one specific woman but a paragon of ideal female virtues. These are shared by the ideal man described elsewhere. She is a proud and splendid woman, mistress of a prosperous manor. Contrary to a common notion of woman's status in the ancient world, this woman has considerable independence in interacting with outsiders and conducting business, even in acquiring real estate; this may reflect the reality of women in the Persian period. Her activities allow her husband to spend his time sitting in the city gates, presumably conducting civic business and serving as a judge. Some commentators have interpreted the passage as an allegory, with the wise woman representing wisdom itself. But this woman has a husband and children and is very much a human being, though an ideal one. The poem is traditionally recited by Jewish men to their wives on Sabbath evening, before the Kiddush (the sanctification of the Sabbath over wine). It is also often recited at funerals of women and sometimes sung to the bride at her wedding. The poem is an acrostic, with each line beginning with a letter of the Heb alphabet in sequence. **10:** *What a rare find,* lit. "who can find," as in 20.6. This is an exclamation of value, not of rarity. Cf. 18.22; 19.14. *Capable wife,* Heb "'eshet ḥayil," is commonly translated "woman of valor." Heb "ḥayil" refers to strength of all sorts, whether in physical or military prowess, in social influence, in general competence, in wealth, or in personal ethical and intellectual powers, as here. Ruth is called an "'eshet ḥayil" by her devotion to her mother-in-law and the thoughtful way she carries through her purposes (Ruth 3.11). The woman in the present passage is characterized by the deep and solid strength of her character. **19:** *Distaff* and *spindle,* implements used in hand spinning of flax or wool. Providing cloth for a household would require incessant spinning. **20:** Strikingly, only this v. and the end of v. 26 highlight her pious behavior.

22 מ She makes covers for herself;
Her clothing is linen and purple.
23 נ Her husband is prominent in the gates,
As he sits among the elders of the land.
24 ס She makes cloth and sells it,
And offers a girdle to the merchant.
25 ע She is clothed with strength and splendor;
She looks to the future cheerfully.
26 פ Her mouth is full of wisdom,
Her tongue with kindly teaching.
27 צ She oversees the activities of her household
And never eats the bread of idleness.
28 ק Her children declare her happy;
Her husband praises her,
29 ר "Many women have done well,
But you surpass them all."
30 ש Grace is deceptive,
Beauty is illusory;
It is for her fear of the LORD
That a woman is to be praised.
31 ת Extol her for the fruit of her hand,
And let her works praise her in the gates.

30: The v.'s beginning explains why this woman is not described as beautiful. *Fear of the LORD:* This is the culminating virtue of the woman of strength, just as it is wisdom's starting point (9.10) and high point (2.5), as emphasized in the book's first unit (1.7).

איוב

Job

Introduction

THE BOOK OF JOB IS WIDELY KNOWN in general, though much less known in its specifics. It is usually regarded as the paradigmatic literary case of the innocent sufferer, afflicted by the Deity through no fault of his own, and forever kept in the dark concerning the actual cause of his misery. At first Job rails at his presumed treatment by God, but in the end, having been privileged to a lengthy divine discourse, he retracts his criticism and his losses are restored. And yet, a good deal of this traditional understanding, which assumes that God is ultimately just and that Job, who is praised in the end, must have accepted that premise, is open to serious challenge. For most of its history of interpretation, readers have superimposed on the book of Job hermeneutical and theological frameworks that presuppose and circumscribe its sense. For classical Christian interpreters, taking their cue from the Epistle of James 5.11, Job was a paragon of patience, a characterization that suits Job only in the narrative prologue. As a thoroughly righteous sufferer, the character Job was taken by Christians as a prefigured type of Jesus, beloved of God, sacrificed to atone for other people's sins. The Qur'an (Sura 21:83; cf. 38:41) thinks of Job as one who entreated the Deity in his distress—a move the biblical Job never made.

The Rabbis, on the other hand, had mixed views of Job (e.g., *b. B. Bat.* 15a–16b; *y. Sot.* 5:7–8; *Gen. Rab.* 57:4). For some, he was the most righteous of Gentiles; for others, a Jew. For some, a hero of faithfulness on the level of Abraham; for others, a flawed believer, who revered God out of fear, not devotion. For some, Job spoke honestly and pardonably out of profound pain; for others, he blasphemed. Medieval Jewish thinkers like Saadia Gaon (*Book of Theodicy;* 10th c.) and Maimonides (*Guide* III, 22–23; 12th c.) tend to interpret the arguments of Job and his companions as the controversies of different philosophical schools. Each of the speakers, including Job, represents a different doctrinal position; for them, only Elihu (see below) represents an acceptable one.

Moderns have inherited these conventional understandings of Job, fixed by accepted translations based in crucial parts on guesswork and whimsy. Ironic statements were taken as earnest; and parody was hardly heard. Not until the mid-20th c., following the Shoah (Holocaust), did some interpreters seek to challenge those conventional understandings, suggesting that the book might be more subversive than was generally allowed. Job is a very complicated work, and for that reason different interpreters, even learned ones, will sometimes diverge widely in their understanding of the details—and of the whole. My interpretation of this difficult book is especially indebted to my teacher, Professor H. L. Ginsberg of blessed memory.

Composition

THE BOOK OF JOB is a complex and composite work. The book includes a traditional story about a totally righteous man who was afflicted by God. In Ezek. 14.14, 20 he is cited together with the non-Israelite figures of old, Noah, the hero of the flood story (Gen. chs 6–9); and

Danel (traditionally read "Daniel"), now known (from an Ugaritic epic discovered in the 1930s) as a pious Canaanite judge. The common thread would seem to be that each was doomed to lose his children, but by virtue of his righteousness, the children were saved or replaced. The framework of the book of Job (chs 1–2; 42.7–17) presents an evolved version of that story in a prose similar to classical biblical narrative, albeit in a late biblical Hebrew. There are signs that the tale of Job as we have it may have been based on a folktale or even a verse epic on which the author drew. There are also signs that the prose narrative before us combines two texts: an earlier one without the role of the Satan ("the Adversary"), and a later one introducing him (see 1.13 n.). The prose tale is fairly complete in itself. This prose narrative was incorporated secondarily into the larger book, creating the book as we know it.

The core of the book is a series of discourses, written in poetic verse. In the Bible all verse is speech—words addressed to someone (but not all speech is in verse). Job, in the opening prose tale, is visited by three companions—Eliphaz the Temanite, Bildad the Shuhite, and Zophar the Naamathite—who have come to comfort him, having heard of the death of his children. After sitting with them in silence for seven days, Job cries out (ch 3 and 4.12–21; see further below). Job's outcry and the dialogues that follow are the work of a poet who composed an early form of the book of Job by reshaping the prose narrative and melding it with the poetic core. In this version, Job's bitter complaint against living in pain provokes his friends, and they each speak in turn. Job answers every one; and this pattern recurs for three rounds (chs 4–27). The last round is incomplete. In the text as it stands it lacks the final speech of Zophar, but there is strong reason to suspect that the text fell into some disarray and that the curtailing of the third speech cycle was not intentional. Job then makes a lengthy final brief (chs 29–31)—but the matter does not end there.

In addition to provoking his companions with his irreverent claims of divine unfairness, Job has also all along been challenging God (see below on the lawsuit). Job's final brief (ch 31) was meant to elicit a response from the Deity, in which He would explain to Job the grounds for his affliction. And the Deity does indeed respond, at glorious length (chs 38–41). However, before the Deity speaks out of the "tempest," another character emerges, Elihu the Buzite, and he both anticipates the God speeches and adds another dimension to them—in defense of divine providence and a moral order (chs 32–37 and perhaps ch 28—see below). It is now widely thought that the Elihu speeches were added to the preexisting book of Job. Not only does Elihu figure nowhere in the prose tale, but his arguments are clearly meant to compensate for the deficiencies in the divine discourse. It has been suggested that the Elihu speeches were composed by an early reader of Job distressed that the human protagonist had not received a sufficient answer from the Deity.

The text of Job is in disarray between chs 25 and 28, probably caused by the secondary insertion of the Elihu speeches. There are good reasons to think ch 28, which is not clearly assigned to any known speaker, is the completion of the Elihu speeches and therefore belongs after ch 37 (see the annotations). Chs 25 and 26 are truncated, and it seems that both chs 26 and 27 contain the arguments of two different speakers, perhaps including the missing third speech of Zophar. The annotations that follow offer one possible arrangement for these chs that can give them a more logical order in the narrative.

Structure and Arrangement

THE STRUCTURE OF THE complete book is:

Prologue (prose narrative)—chs 1–2
Job's complaint—ch 3 and 4.12–21 (see below)
The first round of speeches (Eliphaz, Job, Bildad, Job, Zophar, Job)—4.1–11 and chs 5–14

The second round of speeches (same order as above)—chs 15–21
The third round of speeches—ch 22 (Eliphaz), chs 23–24 (Job), chs 25–26 (Bildad), ch 27 (Job [vv.1–7] and Zophar [vv. 8–23])
Job's concluding brief—chs 29–31
Elihu's speeches—chs 32–37 with ch 28
God's speeches—chs 38–41
Job's reply—42.1–6
God's address to Job's companions (prose narrative)—42.7–9
Epilogue (prose narrative)—42.10–17

Although the book of Job, like many ancient literary works, was composed in stages, it is now an integrated composition, and it will be treated as such in the annotations. Nevertheless, passages that are believed to have accidentally fallen out of sequence will be interpreted in what is taken to be their proper place. Aside from ch 28, mentioned above, there is one other passage that will need to be slightly moved. That is 4.12–21, in which the speaker reports a nocturnal revelation from a divine spirit. In the received text of Job, the passage is embedded in the first speech of Eliphaz. However, 4.12–21 properly belongs right after ch 3 and before 4.1–11, and is the original conclusion to Job's first speech. Several references within the book indicate that the words were originally a part of Job's speech rather than Eliphaz's. For example, Eliphaz parodically paraphrases the words of the divine spirit and quotes them as Job's (see ch 15 nn.); Elihu in his rebuttal of Job cites only statements made by him, and he quotes from 4.12–21 in 33.15, implying he knew it as Job's; Eliphaz berates Job for invoking a divine spirit (5.1)—if 4.12–21 is not Job's, the reproach makes no sense; moreover, in another ancient work about a pious sufferer ("Let Me Praise the Lord of Wisdom"—see below), it is the sufferer who enjoys a divine revelation—and note that God appears to Job near the end of the book.

Job's Literary Genealogy

THE BOOK OF JOB may well be the most exquisite work of ancient Near Eastern literature, but it has a literary pedigree. On the one side, Job belongs to a tradition of poems dealing with the suffering of a pious man, known from Mesopotamia, ancient Syria, and Egypt. On the other side, Job draws repeatedly on themes, motifs, and language found in earlier texts that have been incorporated into the Hebrew Bible.

Ancient Mesopotamia produced a number of compositions concerning a pious (not necessarily righteous) sufferer. These include a Sumerian poem of a man trying to understand and do right by his god, and an Old Babylonian poem of a similar nature. Toward the end of the second millennium BCE a long Babylonian poem of over 600 lines presented the complaints of a man suffering from ailments and social alienation reminiscent of Job's and his effort to discover in what way he might have offended the gods. In the course of the account, he is healed by the god Marduk, leading him to praise his "Lord." The text is known by its first line, "Let Me Praise the Lord of Wisdom." A brief variation on this work, or a similar work, was found at Ugarit, in northern Syria, leading to the conclusion that Canaanite scribes, and their Israelite successors, would have been familiar with the pious sufferer type. From a formal perspective, an even closer parallel to Job is an early first millennium BCE poem now called "The Babylonian Theodicy." It features a dialogue between a despondent sufferer and his encouraging friend. Their exchanges are reminiscent of arguments and images from Job. An Egyptian text that is structurally similar to the book of Job contains a prose narrative framework relating the tale of a poor peasant who is swindled out of his goods, but this "Eloquent Peasant" appears before a magistrate and fascinates his audience with a series of highly poetic orations in his demand for justice. Unlike Job, this Egyptian text treats a case of human injustice, whereas Job treats an instance of apparent divine injustice.

Curiously, nowhere in the ancient Near East is there a story like the one that opens the book of Job, in which the depth of a man's devotion to his god is tested by ordeal. The closest parallel is the ʿAkedah narrative in which God demands of Abraham that he offer up his beloved son Isaac as a sacrifice (Gen. ch 22). Folktales from farther afield, such as India, tell how a man's love is tried by seeing how much affliction he can endure. The story of Job is similar. Job appears to have inspired the apocryphal story of Tobit (3rd–2nd c. BCE), a Jew who retained his piety in the face of several personal tragedies.

The prose tale of Job alludes to parts of the Torah, and is familiar with several of the prophetic texts, especially Hosea, Isaiah, and Jeremiah, and with parts of Proverbs and Psalms. Parodies of some of those texts and borrowings of their language not only place the book of Job within the stream of the Hebrew literary tradition but also establish its relative lateness.

Date and Place of Composition

ONE RABBINIC TRADITION ATTRIBUTES the composition of Job to Moses. It was perhaps thought that only someone as intimate with God as he could have dared to be so critical of God's ways; or that only a prophet on the level of Moses could have experienced the magnificent revelation toward the end of the book. However, a lengthy rabbinic midrash on Job finds verbal and thematic connections between Job and virtually every stage in Israelite history from the time of Abraham to the period of the Persian king Ahasuerus and on that basis ascribes the book to every one of those periods (*b. B. Bat.* 15–16; *Gen. Rab.* 57:4). The point of the midrash is that the situation of Job, of a righteous man who suffers, is unfortunately endemic to every time and place. Yet, from the perspective of literary history— the book of Job seems to know texts as late as or later than Second Isaiah (Isa. chs 40–66)—, and of language— a familiarity with Aramaic is taken for granted—, the Sage who pegged Job to the Persian period is correct. It should be noted, in addition, that the Satan ("Adversary") begins to appear as an individual personality only in the Persian period (Zech. 3.1; 1 Chron. 21.1).

The poet who probably shaped the prose tale as well as the dialogues that comprise the core of the book wrote in a very learned Hebrew but knew Aramaic and, it would seem, some Phoenician, Egyptian, Babylonian, and possibly ancient Arabic as well (see further below). He is a polymath, who employs a great deal of legal vocabulary and draws on many areas of natural science and astronomy. He displays knowledge of the geography and nature of Edom and the southern part of Israel. Some phrases exhibit an Israel-centered point of view (e.g., 40.23, see translators' note *b*), and since the center of Jewish culture in the Persian province of Yehud (Judea) was Jerusalem, it is likely that the author of Job was a Jerusalem intellectual.

Setting and Language

THE STORY OF JOB IS SET in the Land of Uz, associated in the Bible with the Transjordan—Aram (Gen. 22.21) and Edom (Lam. 4.21). The name "Uz" (*ʿUtz*) suggests a Hebrew term for "counsel" (*ʿetzah*—see e.g., Prov. 19.20; Job 1.1 n.; 12.13), a fact that reinforces the reputation of Edom and Kedem, the location of Uz in the "East" (Job 1.3), for wisdom (see 1 Kings 5.10; Obad. 1.8). Job and his friends are portrayed as Oriental sages. The names of Job's companions all derive from the names of Edomites enumerated in Gen. ch 36 (see the nn.), and Job's name is identified in the early postbiblical tradition with Jobab, another Edomite name found in that ch

(Gen. 36.32–33). Because Job and his friends are meant to be Easterners, the poet colors their dialogue—and that of the Deity in the end—with Transjordanian, identifiably Aramaic, words, sounds, syntax. Thus, instead of using Hebrew *dabar* "word," the poet will often use the Aramaic loan word *millim*, "words," even in its Aramaic form, *millin*. Moreover, even though the Jewish author uses the name of Israel's God, YHVH, in relating the narrative and in introducing the Deity toward the end; when presenting the discourse of the Kedemite characters—Job and his companions—he uses only generic names for God, like *El, Eloah,* and *Elohim,* and the pre-Mosaic name *Shaddai*.

The story is set in the time of the Hebrew patriarchs. Job is depicted, like the patriarchs, as the head of a rustic household, with many herds of large and small cattle and many servants. The very strong resemblance of a v. such as Job 1.3 to vv. such as Gen. 26.13–14 (concerning Isaac) is a clear allusion to the patriarchal milieu. The token of exchange "kesitah" is found only in Job 42.11 and in Jacob's purchase of Canaanite land (Gen. 33.19; Josh. 24.32). And, as noted above, the only ancient Near Eastern precedent for the testing of Job is the trial of Abraham, the ʿAkedah. In order to evoke that ancient milieu, the poetry of Job is replete with archaic words and forms and "defective" spelling (a tendency to omit the *matres lectionis*—letters written to indicate vowels—which in the later stages of Hebrew are used more and more).

Genre and Forms

THE GENRE OF JOB is quite a mix. The framework is a prose narrative that resembles a folktale. The perfect moral hero, Job, is introduced with the biblical equivalent of "Once upon a time ...": "There was a man in the land of Uz ..." (cf. 2 Sam. 12.1). He has seven sons and three daughters, and his wealth is described in multiples of the round numbers seven and three, as well as five. His unnamed critical wife corresponds to a type. The sole-surviving messenger is also a type (e.g., Gen. 14.13), and Job is visited by one messenger after the other, in conformity with a biblical pattern (e.g., 1 Kings 1.14). The testing of Job reflects the folktale category of a man who must prove his love by suffering physical abuse. The test emerges out of a contest between the Deity and His loyal opponent, the Satan ("Adversary"). The mode of contest, one of the earliest known literary genres in the ancient Near East, characterizes the poetic dialogues that follow—the argument between Job and his companions and the legal challenge that Job presents to God.

In the course of the dialogues, Job entertains the idea, earlier considered by Jeremiah (12.1), of suing the Deity for justice. Job's initial musings (ch 9) turn into an actual lawsuit (ch 13). In accordance with the legal process, Job takes what modern scholars call an oath of innocence, in which he swears that he has committed no trespass that could possibly warrant the punishment he believes he is receiving from God (ch 31). And, compelled to respond or otherwise forfeit the suit, the Deity replies (ch 38); but, instead of answering Job's demand to see the charges he imagines are being held against him, God dismisses Job for lack of standing—for lacking the esoteric knowledge that would put him in a position to challenge divine justice. What does Job know of how God governs the world?

Within the Joban dialogues are additional genres, which will be indicated as they are encountered: curse, complaint, proverb, praise, parody, reverie, and more.

Subject and Theme

THE THEMES OF JOB are most clearly expressed in the dialogues. The dialogues deal with the case of Job, who claims to be an innocent sufferer, and how that case might support or undermine the theological principle of just retribution—that a just and powerful God maintains a world in which the righteous are rewarded and the wicked afflicted. The Rabbis recognized that in this world there can be "a *tzaddik* (righteous person) whose life is bad, and a *rasha*ʿ (wicked person) whose life is good" because they believed that true justice could be obtained only in a truer world, in the World to Come *(ʿolam ha-baʾ),* the Afterlife. Job's companions, however, did not profess belief in an afterlife, and so they insisted that God renders good to the good and bad to the bad. In the first cycle of dialogues, the friends barely blame Job for his condition, and they urge him to preserve his erstwhile piety so that he will ultimately receive the reward he deserves. Job not only maintains that he is innocent and that God is corrupt, but that the well-known fact that the wicked may prosper is incontrovertible evidence of his claim.

Most readers of Job have taken the subject of innocent suffering, or theodicy—the existence of evil combined with a belief in an all-good and all-powerful Deity—as the main theme of the book. It is frustrating to many such readers that, in His speech from the whirlwind, God does not provide an explicit explanation of evil; He would seem to sidestep it. Accordingly, many readers assume that the answer lies between the lines, and so they interpret the Deity's response as a demonstration of divine providence—in the way that God maintains an order in nature, so does God maintain a moral order, difficult as it may often be to discern it. Or they deduce, from the Deity's demonstration to Job of how little he comprehends of the world, that God's justice is as mysterious as the rest of creation. These answers are not satisfactory, since the readers familiar with chs 1–2 know the cause of Job's afflictions—there is no mystery about it.

There is no resolution to the problem of evil in Job because that is not the theme of the book. Although the problem of innocent suffering, the search for an explanation for a case like that of Job, is the topic of discussion among the participants in the dialogues, it is not the theme of Job. Instead, Job incorporates two main themes. First, the book presents a philosophical argument about how our knowledge is warranted or justified. Job's companions stubbornly cling to the claim that all worthwhile knowledge has been transmitted and learned from tradition. "Ask the generation past," Bildad tells Job; "Study what their fathers have searched out— / For we are of yesterday and know nothing" (8.8–9a). Job, on the other hand, bases his claims on his personal observation—knowledge can be transformed by new experience, such as what has happened to him—and on his experience of a revelation from a divine spirit (see 4.12–21 and ch 16). Job's unconventional understanding of God is only confirmed by the theophany from the "tempest," in which the Deity passes over, and possibly tramples, the principle of just retribution (see the nn.).

A second, and arguably even more prevalent, theme in Job is that of honesty in talking about God. The book examines and tests the limits of appropriate speech. The test of Job is all about speech—will Job, severely afflicted with anguish and physical distress, "blaspheme [God] to [His] face" (1.11)? The dialogues, it goes without saying, consist only of speech—there is no action within them. Job's companions continually denigrate the way he talks (e.g., 11.2–4), and he feels he must beg to be heard (13.13). Their view is shared by readers such as the Talmudic Sage Rav, who suggests that "dirt be put in Job's mouth" to silence him. But while the friends regard Job's discourse as no more than hot air, "useless talk" (e.g., 15.2–3), Job takes pride in his absolute commitment to speaking only truth (see 27.3–4). The radical turning point in the book comes at its conclusion: God turns to Job's companions and reproves them for not speaking "truthfully" (*nekhonah* is adverbial) about Him as Job "My servant" had done (42.7–8). Job may not have arrived at the truth, but he had reason to believe in what he was saying, as it came to him honestly, unlike the words of the companions, who merely repeated uncritically the wisdom they had received. Seen this way, the book of Job promotes honesty in theological discourse and rejects a blind reliance on tradition.

Place in the Canon and the Liturgy

AS AN INTELLECTUALLY AND LINGUISTICALLY challenging work, the book probably circulated in narrow circles before, and with the addition of the Elihu chs (see above), it became part of the biblical corpus. By the beginning of the 2nd c. BCE, when Job was cited by the Wisdom of ben Sirach (49.9), it was accepted as part of the sacred tradition. That it was held in high regard may be surmised by the fact that it was translated early into Aramaic (the Qumran Tg.) and Greek (the Old Greek) and written in archaic script otherwise confined to Torah texts in one Qumran manuscript. Although the piety of Job is debated already among the Rabbis of the Mishnaic period (*m. Sot.* 5:5; *b. B. Bat.* 16a), there is no tradition (as there is for Eccl.) that anyone ever tried to suppress it. It is remarkable that of the three biblical books devoted to wisdom—Proverbs, Job, and Ecclesiastes *(Qohelet)*—the latter two raise serious questions about traditional pieties. Some Second Temple literature related to Job—the translations and the pseudepigraphal Testament of Job—tone down the hero's stridency and portray him as far more conventionally pious than in the biblical book.

Readings from the book of Job are used in traditional Christian burials and during Lent. It is customary in Jewish funerals to quote from Job 1.21: "The LORD has given, and the LORD has taken away; blessed be the name of the LORD." On the evening of the Day of Atonement the Mishnah says (*Yoma* 1:6) that Job was to be read to the high priest, but the book does not have a regular place in Jewish liturgy. Together with Psalms and Proverbs, Job in the Palestinian (as opposed to the Babylonian) tradition is marked for chant according to a different system from the rest of the Tanakh; in the Babylonian tradition, the poetic sections, but not the prose framework, use the special system found in Psalms and Proverbs.

The Text

THE TANAKH TRANSLATION closely hews to the Masoretic Text. Rarely does it resolve a difficulty by appealing to the ancient textual versions or translations or to a Masoretic manuscript. Even less does it allow that the received text had been somewhat corrupted and was in need of emendation. The annotations assume in places that the received text is in error and that there is a probable restoration. Occasionally, such reconstructions will find support among the ancient versions and medieval manuscripts. But this method must be used with caution here, since the ancient translators and scribes often resort to paraphrase and conjecture when facing their own difficulties in understanding the text. The language of Job, with its rare vocabulary and archaisms, foreign forms, and newly minted words, is hard to comprehend. (Ibn Ezra, 12th c. Spain and elsewhere, theorized that the difficulty of the language bespeaks a foreign origin; but the book is essentially Hebrew.) It seems likely that by the time the book was accepted and widely copied, it was already less than fully understood. Allowing for textual readjustment is a mostly modern effort, although there are medieval precedents (such as Saadia and the tosafot commentary on the Talmud) for understanding the text differently from the way it is written (see 4.6 n.). The present annotations aim to interpret Job as it might have been understood when it was first transmitted, and not necessarily the way it came to be understood later; it thus rearranges the text at points, and emends the Masoretic Text, both based on the ancient versions and through conjecture. An effort has also been made to indicate some of the passages from Job that have figured significantly in later Jewish interpretation.

[EDWARD L. GREENSTEIN]

1 There was a man in the land of Uz named Job. That man
was blameless and upright; he feared God and shunned
evil. 2 Seven sons and three daughters were born to him; 3 his
possessions were seven thousand sheep, three thousand camels, five hundred yoke of oxen and five hundred she-asses, and
a very large household. That man was wealthier than anyone
in the East.
4 It was the custom of his sons to hold feasts, each on his set
day in his own home. They would invite their three sisters to
eat and drink with them. 5 When a round of feast days was over,
Job would send word to them to sanctify themselves, and, rising early in the morning, he would make burnt offerings, one
for each of them; for Job thought, "Perhaps my children have
sinned and blasphemed God in their thoughts." This is what
Job always used to do.

1.1–2.13: Prologue in prose. This narrative (together with the Epilogue, 42.10–17) frames the poetic dialogues, providing the background and introducing the participants. No other pious sufferer composition from the ancient Near East contains a background story. The folktale-like quality of the story of Job (see the intro.) was suggested already in the Talmud: "Job never was and was never created; he was a fiction (or parable)" (*b. B. Bat.* 15a). While Maimonides and others likewise took Job as a parable, many Talmudic sages and traditional interpreters, like Zerahiah Ḥen of Barcelona (13th c.), pointed to biographical and other details and insisted the narrative is historical. Nevertheless, the Job story resembles other tales of men who must prove their devotion to another, and the contest between God and the Satan has many folktale parallels as well. The scenes in the Prologue alternate between earth and heaven: 1.1–5: Job and his family; 1.6–12: YHVH in His heavenly court; 1.13–22: disasters befalling Job's household and estate and his pious response; 2.1–6: YHVH in His heavenly court; 2.7–10: the affliction of Job himself and his pious response; 2.11–13: Job's friends come to console him.

1.1–3: Job is introduced as a patriarchal figure like Abraham (see intro.). The text does not state whether Job's wealth came to him after he had demonstrated his upright conduct and reverence, in which case it could be interpreted as a reward from God; or whether his behavior followed and was unconnected to his wealth, in which case Job may be one who "serves the Master without an expectation of reward" (*m. ʾAvot* 1:6).

1: *Uz,* possibly connected to Khirbet el-ʿIs, 88 km (55 miles) south-southeast of the Dead Sea, in the territory of Edom. It is significant for its association with the Aramean branch of Abraham's family (Gen. 22.21) and the genealogy of Edom (Gen. 36.28) and its evocation of the Heb verb "yaʿatz" "to give, take counsel" (see intro.). *Job:* Heb "ʾiyyov" evolved from the earlier form "ʾay ʾabu," meaning "Where is the Father (i.e., God)?" The Transjordanian city of Ashtarot was governed by a man named ʾAyyabu in the 14th c. BCE and it is possible that he or someone like him might have been the hero of a Canaanite legend from which the biblical story grew (see Ezek. 14.14, 20, and the intro.). Job will perform a most serious play on his name in 13.24 (see n. there). *Blameless:* Heb "tam," "perfect, having integrity"; a related word ("tamim") describes the lamb "without blemish" offered for the Passover meal (Exod. 12.5). *He feared God,* fear of God in the Bible moral conscience rather than reverence (see e.g., Gen. 20.11; Exod. 1.17). It is the prime virtue in conventional wisdom literature (e.g., Prov. 1.7; 3.7; and see Job 28.28). **2–3:** The round numbers *seven* and *three* (equal ten) and *five* and *five* (equal ten), suggest wholeness. The description of Job's wealth alludes to that of the Hebrew patriarchs; see esp. Gen. 26.13–14, where the word "gadol," "great" connotes *wealth* and the rare collective term for "servants"—"ʿabuddah"—here translated *household*—is found. The typical pious sufferer is a once prosperous man who has lost his wealth and status; see further ch 29.

1.4–5: Job and his family. Job demonstrates his concern for his family and for correctness in speaking of God. **4:** In the patriarchal society being described, the brothers hold the festivities and invite their sisters. In the Epilogue, a radical inversion of status will occur; see 42.15 n. *On his set day,* lit. "his day"—his birthday; the same phrase is translated "the day of his birth" at 3.1. For birthday celebrations in the biblical world, see Gen. 40.20. **5:** *When a round ... was over,* rather, when a period of feasting came around; see Isa. 29.1. *Would send:* Job's use of messengers anticipates the horrific arrival of the messengers below (vv. 14–19). *To sanctify,* to purify themselves for the ritual; see 1 Sam. 16.5. *Rising early,* a possible allusion to Abraham (Gen. 21.14; 22.3). Job makes *burnt offerings* as a precautionary measure, to atone for any sins his children might commit in their time of levity (*eat*ing *and drink*ing, v. 4); see Lev. 1.4. Ironically, Job's friends, who accuse him of impiety, will have to make *burnt offerings* for themselves in the Epilogue (42.8). *Blasphemed ... in their thoughts:* Job does not suspect that his well-reared children would misspeak aloud—only *in their thoughts.* The term for *blaspheme* is "bless," used here and elsewhere in this narrative as a euphemism for cursing God. By using the euphemism (cf. e.g., Ps. 10.3), the narrator mirrors Job's cautious use of language with respect to the Deity. Job and his wife

6 One day the divine beings presented themselves before the
LORD, [a]and the Adversary[a] came along with them. 7 The LORD
said to the Adversary, "Where have you been?" The Adversary
answered the LORD, "I have been roaming all over the earth."
8 The LORD said to the Adversary, "Have you noticed My servant Job? There is no one like him on earth, a blameless and
upright man who fears God and shuns evil!" 9 The Adversary
answered the LORD, "Does Job not have good reason to fear
God? 10 Why, it is You who have fenced him round, him and
his household and all that he has. You have blessed his efforts
so that his possessions spread out in the land. 11 But lay Your
hand upon all that he has and he will surely blaspheme You to
Your face." 12 The LORD replied to the Adversary, "See, all that
he has is in your power; only do not lay a hand on him." The
Adversary departed from the presence of the LORD.
13 One day, as his sons and daughters were eating and
drinking wine in the house of their eldest brother, 14 a messenger came to Job and said, "The oxen were plowing and

a-a *Heb.* ha-satan.

do not participate in their children's celebrations, perhaps suggesting that the parents do not engage in frivolity; but maintaining a distance between the children and Job is necessary for the ensuing drama (vv. 13–19).

1.6–12: The heavenly court. Like a monarch in court, the LORD in His abode in the sky receives His agents, *the divine beings* (lit. "sons of God"), the angels, periodically to receive their reports and give them assignments; cf. the scene in 1 Kings 22.19–22. God singles out the Satan ("Adversary"), whose role, He knows, is to "descend [to earth] and lead [people] astray, and then ascend [to heaven] and arouse [the Deity's] wrath" (*b. B. Bat.* 16a). God incites the Satan to question Job's sincerity and propose a plan to test whether Job's piety can withstand a series of sufferings. Apparently the Deity wants to gauge the depth of His servant's devotion, using the Satan as His ready agent. The Satan is given a free hand, so long as Job himself is not physically affected. **6:** *One day,* not just any day, but one that was anticipated (cf. 1 Sam. 1.4; 2 Kings 4.8). The scene shifts and the action begins. *The Adversary:* The Satan's epithet is derived from a Heb term for an "opponent" ("adversary" in 1 Kings 11.14, 23) or "obstructer" ("adversary" in Num. 22.22). He tries to trip up humanity and raises objections to God's way of thinking. The Heb cannot be rendered as a personal name, Satan, since in Heb personal names cannot be preceded by the definite article ("the"). **7:** *I have been roaming:* The use of this verb ("shut"), which may pun on "Satan," accords with its attribution to the eyes of God, which reconnoiter the earth, like spies in the service of the emperor (see Zech. 4.10; 2 Chron. 16.9). The Satan has been fulfilling his mission, the surveillance of human behavior and reporting on any punishable activity. **8:** *My servant,* a term of endearment, used of the Deity's most trusted devotees; see, e.g., Isa. 41.8, said of Jacob and Abraham, and often of Moses. By claiming *there is no one like* [Job] *on earth,* God is prompting the Satan to object. **9:** *Good reason:* The Satan asks whether Job maintains his piety "for no reason," disinterestedly (more literally, "for free"). He assumes that no one would behave well without being rewarded for doing so. God would like to think that disinterested devotion is possible, and that Job exemplifies it. **10:** *Fenced:* The image of "hedging" someone about is a recurrent motif in Job. The Satan gives expression to a widespread ancient Near Eastern belief: People prosper and come to no harm when a personal god protects them (cf. 5.19). If the "hedge" is removed, the person is vulnerable. *His possessions,* rather, "his cattle"; Heb "miqneh" alone always indicates cattle. The usage with *spread out* ("parats") seems to derive from Gen. 30.30 and may allude to the patriarchal setting. **11:** *Lay Your hand:* The Satan ascribes the power to harm to God. **12:** *In your power,* lit. "in your hand"—the hand that will soon inflict harm upon Job's cattle, servants, and children.

1.13–22: The afflictions and Job's response. Four blows are brought down indirectly on Job, and they are each reported by one sole-surviving messenger, in rapid sequence; for the literary conventions involved, see the intro. Job is given no time to react. The blows alternate between acts of human marauders and acts of God—raid, fire, raid, wind. In the first three attacks Job loses a group of animals and their attendants; in the fourth he loses all his children. The scene is a grotesque instance of irony: all the disasters occur during the birthday celebration of Job's eldest son, while the siblings are all *drinking wine* (v. 13). **13:** *One day,* see v. 6 n. *His sons and daughters:* In normal biblical syntax, the antecedent of the pronoun "his" would be the last named subject, in this case the Satan (see v. 12). However, the reference is clearly to Job, who was last mentioned in v. 5. This is one reason to surmise that the intervening scene of dialogue between God and the Satan belongs to a later literary layer of the story. This is further supported by the fact that the calamities are not expressly ascribed to Satan—or even to God. Laying direct responsibility on God and the Satan is a later development in the history of the tale, and the Satan is also absent from the Epilogue. In the present context,

the she-asses were grazing alongside them 15 when Sabeans
attacked them and carried them off, and put the boys to the
sword; I alone have escaped to tell you." 16 This one was still
speaking when another came and said, "God's fire fell from
heaven, took hold of the sheep and the boys, and burned them
up; I alone have escaped to tell you." 17 This one was still speaking when another came and said, "A Chaldean formation of
three columns made a raid on the camels and carried them
off and put the boys to the sword; I alone have escaped to tell
you." 18 This one was still speaking when another came and
said, "Your sons and daughters were eating and drinking wine
in the house of their eldest brother 19 when suddenly a mighty
wind came from the wilderness. It struck the four corners of
the house so that it collapsed upon the young people and they
died; I alone have escaped to tell you."
20 Then Job arose, tore his robe, cut off his hair, and threw
himself on the ground and worshiped. 21 He said, "Naked came
I out of my mother's womb, and naked shall I return there; the
LORD has given, and the LORD has taken away; blessed be the
name of the LORD."
22 For all that, Job did not sin nor did he cast reproach on
God.

2 One day the divine beings presented themselves before
the LORD. The Adversary came along with them to present
himself before the LORD. 2 The LORD said to the Adversary,
"Where have you been?" The Adversary answered the LORD,
"I have been roaming all over the earth." 3 The LORD said to the
Adversary, "Have you noticed My servant Job? There is no one
like him on earth, a blameless and upright man who fears God
and shuns evil. He still keeps his integrity; so you have incited

the reader traces the antecedent of *his sons and daughters* to Job and integrates the scene of the Deity and His agent into the story, implicating them more directly in the disasters. **15:** *Sabeans,* raiders from the South, from Sheba in Arabia, home of the Queen of Sheba who visited King Solomon (1 Kings ch 10). Sabeans are ordinarily known in the Bible as merchants in precious stones and metals and incense (e.g., Isa. 60.6; Ezek. 27.22). *The boys,* a term for "attendants," as in Gen. 22.3, 5. **16:** *God's fire,* or "a great fire"; cf. Jonah 3.3: "Nineveh was an enormously large city," lit. "a city great (even) for God." **17:** *Chaldean* (Heb "Kasdim"): The Chaldeans were a West Semitic group living in southern Mesopotamia that ascended to power in Babylonia in the late 7th c. BCE; Nebuchadnezzar, the Babylonian king who destroyed Jerusalem and its temple in 586, was Chaldean. They are associated with the Arameans from Syria, and their eponymous ancestor Chesed is said, like Aram, the eponymous ancestor of the Arameans, to be a son of Abraham's brother Nahor (Gen. 22.22). Some passages in Gen. (11.28; 15.7) give Ur of the Chaldeans as Abraham's birthplace. To attack Job's herds, the Chaldeans would come from the north. **19:** *A mighty wind:* Cf. the storm from God that threatened the ship in Jonah 1.4. *Young people:* Job's children are described with the same term used to designate his attendants ("the boys" in v. 15). A similar ironic association is made in the ʿAkedah, where Isaac ("the boy") and "the servants" are designated by the same term (Gen. 22.5). The killing of Job's children was perceived as so horrible that Naḥmanides (13th c. Spain and Palestine) insisted they were not really killed but sequestered until they could be returned to Job at the end of the story (42.13). **20–22:** Job reacts in grief and performs acts of mourning. Tearing the garment is customary in Jewish mourning even at the present day. For the significance of mourning practices, see 2.12 n. **20:** *Cut off his hair,* more precisely, "sheared his head," an act that evokes the sheep and other livestock he has lost. *And worshiped,* rather, "prostrated himself" in homage, in acceptance of his fate. **21:** *Naked ... out of my mother's womb:* When Job cries out, he will refer to the womb as his own (see 3.10 n.). There seems to be an allusion to the Garden of Eden story, where the first man and woman are at first "naked" (Gen. 2.25) and the first human was made of "the dust of the earth" (Gen. 2.7). *Return there,* not to the *womb* but to earth. *Blessed be the name:* Job "blesses," not "curses," the Deity, thus supporting God's claim against the Satan. Traditionally, Jews suffering a loss recite, "Blessed is the True Judge." **22:** The narrator reiterates the piety of Job's response.

2.1–6: Second heavenly scene. The divine entourage assembles again, and God again addresses the Satan, indicating that He had won their contest—Job *stills keeps his integrity*—and blaming the Satan for *inciting* Him *for no good reason* (v. 3). This provokes the Satan to ratchet up the test and afflict Job's body, a sadistic plan that wins a confident God's approval. **3:** *Integrity,* from the same Heb stem as *blameless* ("tam"), more literally "whole." Job will continually insist that he has always been "whole"; e.g., 9.20–21; 27.5–6. *You have incited Me:* It was, of course, God who incited the Satan to test Job's reverence, so that His blame

Me against him to destroy him for no good reason." 4 The Adversary answered the LORD, [a]"Skin for skin[a]—all that a man
has he will give up for his life. 5 But lay a hand on his bones and
his flesh, and he will surely blaspheme You to Your face." 6 So
the LORD said to the Adversary, "See, he is in your power; only
spare his life." 7 The Adversary departed from the presence of
the LORD and inflicted a severe inflammation on Job from the
sole of his foot to the crown of his head. 8 He took a potsherd
to scratch himself as he sat in ashes. 9 His wife said to him,
"You still keep your integrity! Blaspheme God and die!" 10 But
he said to her, "You talk as any shameless woman might talk!
Should we accept only good from God and not accept evil?"
For all that, Job said nothing sinful.

11 When Job's three friends heard about all these calamities
that had befallen him, each came from his home—Eliphaz the
Temanite, Bildad the Shuhite, and Zophar the Naamathite.
They met together to go and console and comfort him. 12 When
they saw him from a distance, they could not recognize him,
and they broke into loud weeping; each one tore his robe and
threw dust into the air onto his head. 13 They sat with him on
the ground seven days and seven nights. None spoke a word to
him for they saw how very great was his suffering.

a-a Apparently a proverb whose meaning is uncertain.

of the Satan is disingenuous. The idea that the Deity could be *incited* to act against His own inclination was regarded as outrageous by the Talmud (*b. B. Bat.* 16a) and would be incredible "were it not written" here. God admits that He is responsible for acting *to destroy* [Job] *for no good reason*—an ironic treatment of a man who has conducted himself impeccably for no reason (see 1.9). **4:** *Skin for skin:* Perhaps a trader's expression: Job will trade the "skins" of his servants and children in order to preserve his own; or "there is skin beneath the skin" (the preposition is most often used in the sense of "behind"; see 3.23 n.)—meaning that by destroying Job's household only his outer skin has been affected; he will only fall apart if his "deeper skin" is afflicted. For *skin* as a metonymic reference to life, see 19.20.

2.7–10: Job's affliction of disease. Job is afflicted with a terrible and chronic skin ailment that covers his entire body. Suddenly his wife appears and advises him to do the normal thing—to *blaspheme God and die* (v. 9)—which is what the Satan had expected Job to do all along. In the face of the additional challenge from his wife, Job maintains his piety. **7:** *And inflicted,* the subject of the verb may be the Satan, but it just as well may be God (so, e.g., Saadia Gaon). The ambiguity underscores the sense that God stands behind whatever the Satan does. *Severe inflammation,* the same term used for the sixth plague brought upon the Egyptians (Exod. 9.8–10) and a terrible curse (Deut. 28.35). **8:** *Ashes:* In the postbiblical tradition, based on the LXX, Job sat on a "dungheap." **9:** *His wife,* her contrariness conforms to a type—e.g., Eve (Gen. ch 3), Sarah (Gen. ch 21), Jezebel (1 Kings ch 21). Her advice makes sense, if one accepts the ordinary thinking exemplified by the Satan: there is no point to behaving well unless you are rewarded for it. Job, like God, believes in disinterested piety. On account of her bitterness, Job's wife is identified in some postbiblical works (e.g., *L.A.B.*) with Jacob and Leah's daughter Dinah (Gen. ch 34). In *T. Job* she is given the name Sitidos, possibly from the Arabic for "Lady" or from the Gk for "food," and, as in most rabbinic interpretations, she is regarded benignly for trying to relieve her husband of suffering and cared for his needs. There is a tendency in classical Christian interpretation to depict her as the devil's ally, trying to tempt him to sin as Eve had done to Adam. *And die:* Blasphemy is punishable by death (Lev. 24.13–16). **10:** Here Job dismisses his wife's suggestion but apparently continues to ponder it as he erupts in a critical outcry after the mourning period is over (ch 3). *Said nothing sinful,* lit. "did not commit a sin with his lips," allowing skeptical readers to understand that he sinned in his heart (beginning with Rava in *b. B. Bat.* 16a).

2.11–13: The visit from the friends. *Job's three friends* come to *comfort him,* and they sit in silence for *seven days.* Their relationship to Job, and how they managed to meet, is not explained. They are, like Job (1.3), men of the East. **11:** As mentioned in the intro., the friends' names are derived in artificial combinations from Gen. ch 36: *Eliphaz the Temanite* (see Gen. 36.11); *Bildad the Shuhite* (see Gen. 36.35: "Bedad" expanded with "l" and "Husham" with the first two consonants reversed); *Zophar the Naamathite* (see Gen. 36.11–12: "Zepho" expanded with "r" and "Timna" with reordering of the consonants). **12:** *Tore his robe,* like Job (1.20). *Threw dust into the air:* Placing dust on the head is an ancient mourning rite (known already in the Ugaritic myth of Baal), but throwing the dust into the air, lit. "toward the sky," is an allusion to the plague of "inflammation" in Egypt (see v. 7 n.), where Moses brings it on by "throwing soot," turning into "dust," "toward the sky." By this gesture, Job's companions identify with his abject situation. In general, mourning rites have the survivors identify temporarily with the condition of

3

[a]Afterward, Job began to speak and cursed the day of his birth. 2 Job spoke up and said:

3 Perish the day on which I was born,
And the night it was announced,
"A male has been conceived!"
4 May that day be darkness;
May God above have no concern for it;
May light not shine on it;
5 May darkness and deep gloom reclaim it;
May a pall lie over it;
May [b]what blackens[b] the day terrify it.
6 May obscurity carry off that night;
May it not be counted among the
days of the year;
May it not appear in any of its months;
7 May that night be desolate;
May no sound of joy be heard in it;

a There are many difficulties in the poetry of Job, making the interpretation of words, verses, and even chapters uncertain. The rubric "Meaning of Heb. uncertain" in this book indicates only some of the extreme instances.
b-b Meaning of Heb. uncertain.

the dead. **13:** *Sat ... on the ground,* cf. Job (v. 8). The ancient practice of sitting on the ground (known already in Ugaritic) continues in Jewish tradition, as mourners sit on the ground or on low seats. *None spoke:* From here derives the Jewish custom of not addressing a mourner until spoken to (*b. Mo'ed Kat.* 28b; *b. Sem.* 6.2). *Seven days:* The seven-day period of mourning ("Shiv'ah") in Jewish tradition has its precedent in Gen. 50.10.

3.1–26: Job's curse. After a brief transition and introduction (vv. 1–2), Job's outcry comprises three parts: a curse on his having been born (vv. 3–10), a complaint over suffering in life (vv. 11–26), and the report of a revelation, according to which humanity deserves suffering (4.12–21). The third part has been displaced, and will be discussed in ch 4 nn. Job's strident complaint follows a period of silent sitting, making it all the more jolting. The transition is also marked by a switch in style—from narrative to discourse—and in language—from classic prose to very intense poetry. What transforms Job from acquiescence to protest? Perhaps he has pondered his wife's suggestion (2.9); perhaps he questions the faith of his friends, who found nothing to say to him (2.13). He finds his literary inspiration in Jeremiah, who had lamented the accursed day of his birth (Jer. 20.14–18; cf. 15.10) and had challenged divine justice (Jer. 12.1–2). In this discourse, however, Job does not protest divine injustice but focuses on the fairness of a life of suffering. He does not yet address the Deity; feeling alienated, he refers to Him little and only in the third person.

3.1–10: Job curses the day of his birth (vv. 4–5) and the night of his conception (vv. 6–9). He wishes he had never been born, for then he would not have suffered. It may seem impossible to erase time that has already passed, but when reality is unbearable, people turn to the surreal. In the ancient world, women would have incantations recited to conceive or to prevent difficulties in childbirth; Job here overturns that convention by seeking to reverse his having been born. **1:** *Day of his birth,* see 1.4 n. The Satan had predicted Job would curse the Deity; instead he curses his own life. **2:** *Spoke up and said:* This recurrent rubric for introducing the speeches in Job has its origins in ancient rhetoric (e.g., Deut. 26.5). Like the similar one-line introductions to discourse in Ugaritic epic, such lines belong to the poem proper, even if in the text this v. is its own line. **3:** *Perish,* the rhetoric of curse; cf. e.g., Judg. 5.31. *It was announced,* rather, the personified night, performing the role of the cursed messenger in Jeremiah's complaint (Jer. 20.15) makes the announcement. *A male,* rather, "a man." The same term ("gever") is used of the sufferer in Lam. 3.1, and Ps. 94.14; and of Job himself in v. 23. In contrast, Jeremiah refers to himself as a son (20.15); Job excludes all the participants of his birth from his account, including himself as a child (see v. 12 n. below). **4–5:** Since day is light (Gen. 1.3–5), shrouding the day in darkness eliminates it. **4:** *That day,* echoing Gen. 1.3, Job seeks to undo the creation of that one day. *Have no concern,* rather, "not summon it" to appear from among the aggregate of days, the way God calls out the stars one by one (Isa. 40.26); and see v. 6. **5:** *Reclaim it,* rather, "cancel it"; "ga'al" means "to disqualify" in Persian period Heb (Ezra 2.62 = Neh. 7.64). **6–10:** Night appears between twilight and dawn, so the way to eliminate the night of Job's conception is to eradicate the signs of its inception and its end (see v. 9). **6:** *Not be counted:* The translation tacitly emends the verb "yiḥadd" (a root meaning "to rejoice") to "yeḥad." The night would be removed from the calendar. **7:** *Desolate* (Heb "galmud"), a double meaning: "sterile" (Isa. 49.21) and "a solitary rock" (cf. Arabic "julmud")—the night on which procreation *(sound of joy)* was to have taken place should be both sterile and isolated from the

8 May those who cast spells upon the day[a] damn it,
Those prepared to disable Leviathan;
9 May its twilight stars remain dark;
May it hope for light and have none;
May it not see the glimmerings of the dawn—
10 Because it did not block my mother's womb,
And hide trouble from my eyes.

11 Why did I not die at birth,
Expire as I came forth from the womb?
12 Why were there knees to receive me,
Or breasts for me to suck?
13 For now would I be lying in repose, asleep and at rest,
14 With the world's kings and counselors who rebuild
ruins for themselves,
15 Or with nobles who possess gold and who fill their
houses with silver.
16 Or why was I not like a buried stillbirth,
Like babies who never saw the light?
17 There the wicked cease from troubling;
There rest those whose strength is spent.
18 Prisoners are wholly at ease;
They do not hear the taskmaster's voice.
19 Small and great alike are there,
And the slave is free of his master.

20 Why does He give light to the sufferer
And life to the bitter in spirit;
21 To those who wait for death but it does not come,
Who search for it more than for treasure,
22 Who rejoice to exultation,
And are glad to reach the grave;
23 To the man who has lost his way,
Whom God has hedged about?

24 My groaning serves as my bread;
My roaring pours forth as water.

a Or "sea," taking Heb. yom *as equivalent of* yam; *compare the combination of sea with Leviathan in Ps. 74.13, 14 and with Dragon in Job 7.12; cf. also Isa. 27.1.*

rest of the year. **8:** Well into the first millennium CE sorcerers continue to invoke spells strong enough to neutralize the primeval chaos monsters, "Yam" (pronounced "Yom" in Phoenician, the same as the Heb word for "day," used throughout this poem) and his doppelganger *Leviathan. To disable,* rather, "to curse" (cognate to "ʿariri," "shamed" in Jer. 22.30 and elsewhere). **10:** Job explains the reason for his complaint: his life has been one of suffering. He forgets the many years of prosperity and family he had enjoyed. *My mother's womb,* rather, "the doors of my womb," that is, the womb where I was gestated. The image of a womb sealed with bolted doors prior to birth is found already in old Mesopotamian incantations.

3.11–26: Life is filled with suffering. Job pursues a line of argument similar to Jeremiah's (Jer. 20.16–18): If I had to have been born, better to have died right away. Contrary to ordinary thinking, Job romanticizes death, as he gives voice to his complaint: God gives life to people and then ignores what befalls them (see v. 23 n.). In conclusion, Job expresses his fear—that God is indeed as callous as he surmises—thereby vv. 25–26 transition to 4.12–21. **12:** *Knees,* of the paterfamilias, who acknowledges the child as his own (cf. Gen. 48.12 and the Hittite story of Appu). *Breasts,* of his mother. In contrast to Jeremiah, Job relates only to the disembodied limbs of his parents (cf. v. 3 n. and v. 10 n.). **17–19:** Death is a release from the troubles of life. **17:** Job is not introducing the subject of evil here; the focus on *the wicked* is that they are nervous, always looking over their shoulders (cf. Ibn Ezra). **20:** *Why does He:* In the Heb the subject is not expressed—Job avoids mentioning the Deity. *Bitter in spirit,* in the Heb in the plural, in contrast to the beginning of the v.; Job extrapolates from his own suffering *(the sufferer)* to that of others. **22:** *To exultation,* more likely, "upon (reaching) the tombstone" that covers the grave ("golel" in the Mishnah). **23:** *Man who has lost his way,* rather, "a man (i.e., Job; see v. 3 n.) whose way is hidden" (from God; see Isa. 40.27); contrast Prov. 5.21. *God has hedged about,* rather, "whom God has screened off" from His view (cf. Eliphaz's paraphrase in 22.13–14 and Lam. 3.44); an ironic contrast with the positive nuance of the same term in 1.10. In ch 1 the term refers to divine protection, here, to divine neglect. **24:** *Serves as my bread:* Job experiences groaning as often as others enjoy food. Job's *roar* are like those of a hungry wild beast (cf. Ps. 104.21).

25 For what I feared has overtaken me;
What I dreaded has come upon me.
26 I had no repose, no quiet, no rest,
And trouble came.

4 Then Eliphaz the Temanite said in reply:

2 If one ventures a word with you, will it be too much?
But who can hold back his words?
3 See, you have encouraged many;
You have strengthened failing hands.
4 Your words have kept him who stumbled from falling;
You have braced knees that gave way.
5 But now that it overtakes you, it is too much;
It reaches you, and you are unnerved.
6 Is not your piety your confidence,
Your integrity your hope?
7 Think now, what innocent man ever perished?
Where have the upright been destroyed?
8 As I have seen, those who plow evil
And sow mischief reap them.
9 They perish by a blast from God,
Are gone at the breath of His nostrils.
10 The lion may roar, the cub may howl,
But the teeth of the king of beasts [a]-are broken.-[a]
11 The lion perishes for lack of prey,
And its whelps are scattered.

12 A word came to me in stealth;
My ear caught a whisper of it.
13 In thought-filled visions of the night,
When deep sleep falls on men,
14 Fear and trembling came upon me,
Causing all my bones to quake with fright.
15 A wind passed by me,
Making the hair of my flesh bristle.
16 It halted; its appearance was strange to me;
A form loomed before my eyes;

a-a Meaning of Heb. uncertain.

25: Many have understood Job's *fear*s to refer to the disasters he has experienced (e.g., Rashi). However, a comparison with the language of 4.14 shows that the *fear* is what he is about to describe in 4.12–21.

4.1–11 and 5.1–27: First response: Eliphaz. Eliphaz, presumably the eldest companion (cf. 15.10), is provoked to speak. The case of Job rattles the traditional belief in just retribution, and Eliphaz cannot grapple with the profundity of Job's suffering. He does not yet accuse Job of having sinned (as he will in the second round), but he cautions him against losing a grip on his erstwhile faith. He suggests two possible causes for Job's suffering: (1) it is part of life and must be patiently endured—in the end the righteous will find blessing and the wicked will deteriorate; (2) God may discipline people with a measure of affliction to remind them of what is in store for those who transgress (5.17–18). **4.3:** *Encouraged many,* the primary meaning is "steadied the trembling"; for Heb "rob," "trembling," see 4.14 and 33.19. The secondary meaning is "instructed many." **6:** The second line is literally "Your hope and your integrity," but even traditional commentators like Saadia Gaon and the tosafists (*b. B. M.* 58b) move the conjunction "and" in order to make proper sense of the v. **8:** *As I have seen,* a formula for introducing traditional wisdom; e.g., Ps. 37.25. Neither Eliphaz nor his colleagues ever shares any actual experience with Job. The combined terms *evil* and *mischief* for the most part indicate "pain" and "suffering" in Job. **9:** Conventional wisdom; e.g., Prov. 22.8. **10–11:** The *lion*s metaphorically represent the wicked (e.g., Prov. 28.15), who thrive for a time but ultimately break down. Analogously, Eliphaz suggests, the righteous may suffer for a time but will ultimately flourish. *Are broken,* a nice example of a Heb word given an Aram. coloring by substituting the "ts" with "ʿ" (cf. Heb "ʾerets" = Aram. "ʾarʿa," "land").

4.12–21: The night vision. This passage describing a disclosure by a renegade spirit from the divine assembly (cf. 15.8) is the continuation of Job's discourse in ch 3 (see the intro.). The spirit reveals a frightening thought about the Deity: since He finds fault even with the angels, He finds even greater deficiencies in fragile humanity. Whereas in the Prologue it is the Satan who is portrayed as an excessive fault finder, here it is God who is portrayed as such. **14:** *Fear ... came upon me:* Job's language links his reported experience to his earlier apprehensions (3.25). *Causing ... to quake:* The verb "hipḥid," "frighten" should be read "hirḥip," "cause to shudder" based on an expression in Jer. 23.9. **15:** *Wind,* rather, "a spirit." **16:** *A murmur, a voice,* a play on the

I heard a murmur, a voice,
17 "Can mortals be acquitted by God?
Can man be cleared by his Maker?
18 If He cannot trust His own servants,
And casts reproach[a] on His angels,
19 How much less those who dwell in houses of clay,
Whose origin is dust,
Who are crushed like the moth,
20 Shattered between daybreak and evening,
Perishing forever, unnoticed.
21 Their cord is pulled up
And they die, and not with wisdom."

5 Call now! Will anyone answer you?
To whom among the holy beings will you turn?
2 Vexation kills the fool;
Passion slays the simpleton.
3 I myself saw a fool who had struck roots;
Impulsively, I cursed his home:
4 May his children be far from success;
May they be oppressed in the gate with none to deliver them;
5 May the hungry devour his harvest,
[b-]Carrying it off in baskets;
May the thirsty swallow their wealth.[-b]
6 Evil does not grow out of the soil,
Nor does mischief spring from the ground;
7 For man is born to [do] mischief,
Just as sparks fly upward.

8 But I would resort to God;
I would lay my case before God,
9 Who performs great deeds which cannot be fathomed,
Wondrous things without number;
10 Who gives rain to the earth,
And sends water over the fields;
11 Who raises the lowly up high,
So that the dejected are secure in victory;
12 Who thwarts the designs of the crafty,
So that their hands cannot gain success;
13 Who traps the clever in their own wiles;
The plans of the crafty go awry.
14 By day they encounter darkness,
At noon they grope as in the night.
15 But He saves the needy from the sword of their mouth,
From the clutches of the strong.

a Meaning of Heb. uncertain. *b-b Meaning of Heb. uncertain.*

"soft, murmuring sound" in which God appeared to Elijah (1 Kings 19.12). In the "U-netaneh tokep" prayer ("Let us now relate ...," the phrase that introduces a prayer concerning the Day of Judgment), the prayer of the Days of Awe (Rosh Ha-Shanah and Yom Kippur), the "still, small voice" of God is contrasted with the blast of the shofar. **19–20:** *Like the moth,* more likely, "before evening" (cf. Arabic "ʿasha"). The human lifespan is analogized to a day, from morning till evening; cf. Ps. 90.5–6. *Unnoticed,* rather, "while it is not yet evening" (cf. Arabic "masa," Akkadian "mushu"). *Perishing forever:* The phrase echoes the beginning of Job's discourse ("Perish the day" [3.3]), bringing it toward closure.

5.1–27: Continuation of Eliphaz's response. Eliphaz mocks Job's claim to have had a revelation from one of the *holy beings* (v. 1), the angels (see 15.15). Putting no stock in the angels, Eliphaz recommends that Job turn directly to God (v. 8). Ironically, that is what Job will do, when he pursues his lawsuit against the Deity. **3–4:** *I myself saw,* see 4.8 n. *I cursed:* The text is apparently misread; Eliphaz is describing the miserable fate of the fool and his children, not cursing them; the syntax of v. 5 makes this fairly clear. One should probably read "petaʾim," "fools" (a synonym of "ʾewil" in the preceding clause; cf. v 2) for "pitʾom," "suddenly" and interpret something like: "And I have seen the estate of fools. The fool's children find no relief at the city-gate, the site of ancient justice" (e.g., Amos 5.15). Prov. (22.22) admonishes specifically against such oppression. **6:** *Evil ... mischief,* see 4.8 n. **7:** *Sparks,* more likely "arrows," lit. "sons of Resheph," the Canaanite god of pestilence whose afflictions were symbolized by arrows. Job apparently reacts to this image in 6.4. **8:** *Lay my case:* Eliphaz would seem to be using this phrase neutrally; but Job will ironically pick up on its connotation of a lawsuit. **9–15:** A doxology affirming God's many beneficences, proverbial wisdom serving as background for Eliphaz's advice in vv. 19–23. Job will later parody this passage (9.4–10 and ch 12). **15:** *Saves the needy:* The translation expands the text without correcting it. For "mi-pihem," "from their mouths" read "mi-pi ham," "(He saves the swordless) from

16 So there is hope for the wretched;
The mouth of wrongdoing is stopped.

17 See how happy is the man whom God reproves;
Do not reject the discipline of the Almighty.
18 He injures, but He binds up;
He wounds, but His hands heal.
19 He will deliver you from six troubles;
In seven no harm will reach you:
20 In famine He will redeem you from death,
In war, from the sword.
21 You will be sheltered from the scourging tongue;
You will have no fear when violence comes.
22 You will laugh at violence and starvation,
And have no fear of wild beasts.
23 For you will have a pact with the rocks in the field,
And the beasts of the field will be your allies.
24 You will know that all is well in your tent;
When you visit your wife[a] you will never fail.
25 You will see that your offspring are many,
Your descendants like the grass of the earth.
26 You will come to the grave [b]in ripe old age,[-b]
As shocks of grain are taken away in their season.
27 See, we have inquired into this and it is so;
Hear it and accept it.

6 Then Job said in reply:

2 If my anguish were weighed,
My full calamity laid on the scales,
3 It would be heavier than the sand of the sea;
That is why I spoke recklessly.[c]
4 For the arrows of the Almighty are in me;
My spirit absorbs their poison;
God's terrors are arrayed against me.
5 Does a wild ass bray when he has grass?
Does a bull bellow over his fodder?

a *Lit. "home."* *b-b* *Meaning of Heb. uncertain.* *c* *Meaning of Heb. uncertain.*

the oppressor" (cf. 36.16); "ham" is derived from the verb "to stun, discomfit" and cognate to the name Haman in Esth. **17–18:** Eliphaz draws on traditional wisdom; e.g., Deut. 32.39; Ps. 94.12; Prov. 3.11–12. **19–23:** Eliphaz enumerates seven types of distress from which God will rescue Job. Two *(famine-starvation, violence-violence)* are duplicated in the received text, but seven can be reconstructed by reading "shed," "demon" for "shod," *violence* in v. 22 (see Ps. 91.6) and "kepin," "stones" (in Aram.; cf. 30.6) for "kapan" "famine" in v. 22. The latter reading is fairly assured from the recapitulation of "stones" and *beasts* from v. 22 in v. 23. The seven disasters are: *famine,* "plague" (a better rendering of "mawet" [*death*] in v. 20), *sword, the scourging tongue, violence,* "demons," and *wild beasts. Rocks:* People were vulnerable to stumbling on stones in the road (see Ps. 91.12–13). **24–25:** Eliphaz assures Job that the loss of all his property and family will be restored. Although his faith-based reasoning will be said to be wrong (42.7–8), Job will in the end receive double his possessions and another ten children. **24:** *Your wife,* rather, "(when you take account of) your estate (you will not be lacking anything)." **25–26:** Having many offspring and living to a ripe old age is the biblical ideal for a successful life; see e.g., Deut. 4.40; Pss. 1.3; 128.6. **26:** The Heb is difficult, but the imagery should illustrate the point of v. 25, that Job will renew his family. He will be like a stalk of grain that produces many seeds (offspring) in its season. **27:** Eliphaz reiterates the basis of his—and his companions'—contentions: tradition.

6.1–7.21: Job's answer. Job responds esp. to two of Eliphaz's arguments—that he is being disciplined by God and that if he would only be patient, he will enjoy a happy future. To the first point he explains that his pain is more profound than mere discipline (6.2–5). To the second he replies that he lacks both the strength to endure and the time to wait (6.11–13; 7.1–2). After addressing his companions, and a transitional passage, he appeals directly to the Deity for the first time, asking why, even if he had sinned, he should be treated so cruelly (7.7–21). **6.1–5:** Job explains the magnitude of his distress. **2:** *Calamity,* rather, "vexation, distress"; note that in Prov. 19.13 "havvah" corresponds to "ka'as" in Prov. 17.25, and that "havvah" is parallel to "ka'as" here. **3:** *I spoke recklessly,* rather, "my words are a stammer"—irrational to you; for the cognate verb "to stammer" in a context of drunkenness, see Obad. 1.16 (with Rashi and Ibn Ezra). **4:** *Arrows,* see 5.7 n. The divine afflictions are figured as arrows; cf. Ps. 38.3. For the punishing Deity as an archer, see e.g., Lam. 2.4. For additional militant images of God, see Job 19.6, 12. **5:** Compare

6 Can what is tasteless be eaten without salt?
Does [a-]mallow juice[-a] have any flavor?
7 I refuse to touch them;
They are like food when I am sick.

8 Would that my request were granted,
That God gave me what I wished for;
9 Would that God consented to crush me,
Loosed His hand and cut me off.
10 Then this would be my consolation,
[a-]As I writhed in unsparing[-a] pains:
That I did not [b-]suppress my words against the Holy
One.[-b]
11 What strength have I, that I should endure?
How long have I to live, that I should be patient?
12 Is my strength the strength of rock?
Is my flesh bronze?
13 Truly, I cannot help myself;
I have been deprived of resourcefulness.

14 [a-]A friend owes loyalty to one who fails,
Though he forsakes the fear of the Almighty;[-a]
15 My comrades are fickle, like a wadi,
Like a bed on which streams once ran.
16 [a-]They are dark with ice;
Snow obscures them;[-a]
17 But when they thaw, they vanish;
In the heat, they disappear where they are.
18 Their course twists and turns;
They run into the desert and perish.
19 Caravans from Tema look to them;
Processions from Sheba count on them.
20 They are disappointed in their hopes;
When they reach the place, they stand aghast.
21 So you are as nothing:[c]
At the sight of misfortune, you take fright.
22 Did I say to you, "I need your gift;
Pay a bribe for me out of your wealth;
23 Deliver me from the clutches of my enemy;
Redeem me from violent men"?
24 Teach me; I shall be silent;
Tell me where I am wrong.
25 [a-]How trenchant honest words are;[-a]
But what sort of reproof comes from you?

the "roar" of the lion (here *bellow*) as a complaint of hunger in 3.24. **6–7:** Job's proverbial rhetoric turns to the friends: their arguments lack *flavor,* which has a secondary meaning of "reason." **8–9:** Job expresses his death wish—let the afflicting Deity go all the way and put him out of his misery. **10:** Job's *consolation* is that he "did not suppress the words of the holy being"—not the Deity, who is never called "Holy One," (contra the NJPS translation) but the spirit who spoke to him in 4.17–21; see 5.1–27 n. **15–20:** Job had expected empathy and support from his friends; but he has heard only pious platitudes. He compares his friends' fickleness, their undependability, to a wadi that runs with water in the winter and spring but dries up in the summer. Job borrows the image from Jer. 15.18, where the prophet accosts God of being like a wadi that failed, like waters that cannot be relied on. **16:** *Snow obscures them,* rather, "snow accumulates on them." **17:** *When they thaw,* rather, "when they are scorched." **19:** The geographical orientation remains Arabian or Edomite. **21–24:** Job spells out the meaning of the analogy to his companions; he expresses his dismay at their lack of empathy—he has never asked them for anything. **25–26:** Job berates the friends for dismissing his argument. **25:** *Trenchant,* rather, "provocative." *Honest words,* Job refers to his own words. The companions are upset when Job speaks straight from the heart.

a-a Meaning of Heb. uncertain.
b-b Meaning of Heb. uncertain; others "deny the words of the Holy One."
c Following kethib, *with Targum; meaning of Heb. uncertain.*

26 Do you devise words of reproof,
But count a hopeless man's words as wind?
27 You would even cast lots over an orphan,
Or barter away your friend.
28 Now be so good as to face me;
I will not lie to your face.
29 Relent! Let there not be injustice;
Relent! I am still in the right.
30 Is injustice on my tongue?
Can my palate not discern evil?

7 Truly man has a term of service on earth;
His days are like those of a hireling—
2 Like a slave who longs for [evening's] shadows,
Like a hireling who waits for his wage.
3 So have I been allotted months of futility;
Nights of misery have been apportioned to me.
4 When I lie down, I think,
"When shall I rise?"
Night [a]drags on,[a]
And I am sated with tossings till morning twilight.
5 My flesh is covered with maggots and clods of earth;
My skin is broken and festering.
6 My days fly faster than a weaver's shuttle,
And come to their end [b]without hope.[b]
7 Consider that my life is but wind;
I shall never see happiness again.
8 The eye that gazes on me will not see me;
Your eye will seek me, but I shall be gone.
9 As a cloud fades away,
So whoever goes down to Sheol does not come up;
10 He returns no more to his home;
His place does not know him.

11 On my part, I will not speak with restraint;
I will give voice to the anguish of my spirit;
I will complain in the bitterness of my soul.
12 Am I the sea or the Dragon,[c]
That You have set a watch over me?
13 When I think, "My bed will comfort me,
My couch will share my sorrow,"
14 You frighten me with dreams,
And terrify me with visions,

a-a Meaning of Heb. uncertain. *b-b Or "when the thread runs out."*
c See note at 3.8.

26: The Old Gk shows that the text was unclear. Read probably "ha-le-ruaḥ" for "ha-le-hokaḥ" and understand: "Do you consider (my) words as (mere) wind?" **27:** Job in his distress exaggerates his friends' level of disloyalty. **28:** *I will not lie:* The verb for *lie* ("kizzev") connotes "disappoint" and echoes the term for a failing wadi in Jer. 15.18 ("'akzav"). Job will not do to them what he perceives they have done to him. **30:** Job reiterates his commitment to honesty (see the intro.). *Evil,* or rather, "false speech" (e.g., Ps. 5.10).

7.1–2: Job continues. Job in his distress views life as *a term of service* (cf. Isa. 40.2) and the human as a laborer who only wants to finish the day and receive his *wages,* which are meant to be paid at the end of each work day (Lev. 19.13; Deut. 24.15). **3–6:** Job is miserable by day and sleepless at night. **6:** In this brilliant metaphor, life is a thread pulled through a loom by a shuttle, and it comes to a predetermined end when the "thread," i.e., the *hope,* runs out. The same word ("tikvah") denotes both the figurative meaning "hope" and the literal meaning "cord" (see Josh. 2.18, 21). **7–21:** Job now turns to God, trying to make sense of why God would want to afflict him so when he poses no threat. **8:** *The eye that gazes,* or: "O eye of My Observer, You will see me no more"; a reference to God in Gen. 16.13. **9:** *Sheol:* Job has described the peaceful existence of the dead in the Netherworld in ch 3. He now makes the point, widely accepted in the ancient Near East, that there is no return from the realm of death. A person disappears, is of no consequence, and does not merit the negative attention of the Deity. Cf. Ps. 6.6; in Sheol there is no access to God. The sage Rava disparaged Job for denying the (rabbinic) belief in resurrection (*b. B. Bat.* 16a). **10:** *His place does not know him:* Compare Ps. 103.16 on the ephemeral nature of life. **12:** *Sea* and *Dragon* are proper names of the primeval monsters of watery chaos that God had to subdue in order to put the world in order; see, e.g., Ps. 74.13–17. Job is hyperbolically asking "why" (not *that*) he must be placed under such close *watch* when he is not the Deity's archenemy.

15 Till I prefer strangulation,
Death, to my wasted frame.
16 I am sick of it.
I shall not live forever;
Let me be, for my days are a breath.

17 What is man, that You make much of him,
That You fix Your attention upon him?
18 You inspect him every morning,
Examine him every minute.
19 Will You not look away from me for a while,
Let me be, till I swallow my spittle?
20 If I have sinned, what have I done to You,
Watcher of men?
Why make of me Your target,
And a burden to myself?
21 Why do You not pardon my transgression
And forgive my iniquity?
For soon I shall lie down in the dust;
When You seek me, I shall be gone.

8 Bildad the Shuhite said in reply:

2 How long will you speak such things?
Your utterances are a mighty wind!
3 Will God pervert the right?
Will the Almighty pervert justice?
4 If your sons sinned against Him,
He dispatched them for their transgression.
5 But if you seek God
And supplicate the Almighty,
6 If you are blameless and upright,
He will protect you,
And grant well-being to your righteous home.
7 Though your beginning be small,
In the end you will grow very great.

8 Ask the generation past,
Study what their fathers have searched out—
9 For we are of yesterday and know nothing;
Our days on earth are a shadow—
10 Surely they will teach you and tell you,
Speaking out of their understanding.
11 Can papyrus thrive without marsh?
Can rushes grow without water?

14: *Terrify me with visions,* perhaps an allusion to the nocturnal vision Job reports in 4.12–21. **15:** *My wasted frame,* lit. "my bones." We should probably read "ʿatsbotai," "(death is preferable to) my pain"; see 9.28. **17–18:** Job parodies Ps. 8.5–6, where God's attention to humanity is complimentary. Job regards God's *attention* as hounding. Here Job takes a position opposite the one he took in 3.23. *Every morning … every minute:* The intensification in the frequency of divine attentiveness is noted in the Talmud (*b. Rosh Hash.* 16a). **20:** Job admits he might have sinned—but not to the degree that it should deeply affect God! *Watcher of men,* sarcastic. *Burden to myself:* This is a scribal euphemism ("tikkun soferim," "emendations [repairs] of the scribes") for "burden to Yourself" (so read in the Gk).

8.1–22: Bildad's speech. The second companion, Bildad, attributes the death of Job's children not to him but to his children (v. 4). Job will continue to receive divine protection if he will *seek* and *supplicate* God (vv. 5–7). Invoking traditional wisdom, Bildad uses imagery to depict the withering of the wicked (vv. 11–15) and the flourishing of the righteous (vv. 16–19). Assuming Job will choose to remain pious, Bildad, like Eliphaz, promises a happy future for Job and discomfiture for his enemies (vv. 20–22). **3:** Job has not yet accused the Deity of jettisoning the principle of just retribution, but Bildad chastens Job as though he had. **6:** Bildad allows that Job may still be *blameless and upright. Protect,* a rare verb drawn from Deut. 32.11, where it describes the eagle's care for its young—a figure for God's care for Israel. **8:** *Their fathers,* probably a scribal error for "your fathers." *Study,* reading apparently "bonen" for "konen." **10:** *Speaking out of their understanding,* rather, "producing words from their hearts"; the heart is a seat of speech (e.g., Pss. 19.15; 49.4; Prov. 24.2). This is a formula introducing a quotation, in this case of proverbs (see 15.13 n.). What follows is traditional wisdom. Bildad may have been inspired by Job's use of proverbs in 6.5–6. **11–13:** The wicked are likened to plants growing without water and drying up.

12 While still tender, not yet plucked,
They would wither before any other grass.
13 Such is the fate of all who forget God;
The hope of the impious man comes to naught—
14 Whose confidence is a [a]thread of gossamer,[a]
Whose trust is a spider's web.
15 He leans on his house—it will not stand;
He seizes hold of it, but it will not hold.
16 He stays fresh even in the sun;
His shoots spring up in his garden;
17 [a]His roots are twined around a heap,
They take hold of a house of stones.[a]
18 When he is uprooted from his place,
It denies him, [saying,]
"I never saw you."
19 Such is his happy lot;
And from the earth others will grow.
20 Surely God does not despise the blameless;
He gives no support to evildoers.
21 He will yet fill your mouth with laughter,
And your lips with shouts of joy.
22 Your enemies will be clothed in disgrace;
The tent of the wicked will vanish.

9 Job said in reply:

2 Indeed I know that it is so:
Man cannot win a suit against God.
3 If he insisted on a trial with Him,
He would not answer one charge in a thousand.
4 Wise of heart and mighty in power—
Who ever challenged Him and came out whole?—
5 Him who moves mountains without their knowing it,
Who overturns them in His anger;
6 Who shakes the earth from its place,
Till its pillars quake;
7 Who commands the sun not to shine;
Who seals up the stars;

a-a *Meaning of Heb. uncertain.*

13: *Fate,* apparently reading "ʾaḥarit" for "ʾorḥot," "paths." **14–15:** The "stronghold" *(confidence)* of the wicked is nothing more substantial than a *spider's web* that collapses when it is leaned upon. *Thread of gossamer,* rather, "a spider's web" (as Saadia Gaon had divined, now corroborated by Akkadian). **16–19:** The lot of the righteous is figuratively described without any introduction, like a riddle. Unlike the wicked, who perish for lack of water, the righteous are well-watered. Elsewhere in the Bible God is imaged as a water source (e.g., Jer. 2.13; 17.13) and the righteous as flourishing plants (e.g., Ps. 1.3). **17:** *Take hold,* more likely, "cut through" (a pseudo-Aramaization of "yeḥzeh"). **18–19:** The sense is more likely that if the righteous is *uprooted* (v. 18), he will move (a form of the verb "mush") to another place from which he can grow (v. 19). **20:** Bildad makes his point explicit and provides a transition to his advice to Job. **22:** Job had not complained of *enemies,* but the statement is a cliché (Ps. 35.26). *Will vanish,* lit. "is no more"—a response to Job's assertion that he would soon "be no more" (7.8, 21). Like Eliphaz (4.7–9), Bildad maintains that the wicked perish before their time, not the righteous, among whom Bildad still counts Job.

9.1–10.22: Job's answer. Job responds not only to Bildad but expands his response to Eliphaz as well. To their advice that he address God directly (5.8; 8.5), Job explains how difficult it is to summon a God who is both severe and unfair. Even if he were to get a hearing, he would be falsely incriminated (9.20, 30–31). With this bold claim, Job disputes Bildad's contention that God would never corrupt justice (8.3). Thus emboldened, Job turns to the Deity and asks, using an ancient argument developed further by Philo of Alexandria, and in conformity with the words of the spirit in 4.17–19, why He would be so strict in finding fault with a creature that He had Himself made (ch 10). If God would be unforgiving, the least He could do is allow His creature to move painlessly from womb to tomb (10.18–19). Several of Job's remarks drew criticism from the Talmudic sages (*b. B. Bat.* 16a). **9.4–13:** In the midst of Job's explanation of why one cannot litigate with God, he presents a parody of Eliphaz's doxology (5.9–16); the allusion to Eliphaz is made certain by repeating 5.9 in 9.10. Job's version lays emphasis on divine anger (v. 5) and brute power. **4:** *Challenged,* a parody on the Deity's ability to "stiffen [the] will and harden [the] heart" (Deut. 2.30). **6:** *Pillars:* In biblical cosmography, the earth rests on pillars, like a building (e.g., Ps. 75.4).

8 Who by Himself spread out the heavens,
And trod on the back of the sea;
9 Who made the Bear[a] and Orion,
Pleiades, and the chambers of the south wind;
10 Who performs great deeds which cannot be fathomed,
And wondrous things without number.
11 He passes me by—I do not see Him;
He goes by me, but I do not perceive Him.
12 He snatches away—who can stop Him?
Who can say to Him, "What are You doing?"
13 God does not restrain His anger;
Under Him Rahab's[b] helpers sink down.
14 How then can I answer Him,
Or choose my arguments against Him?
15 Though I were in the right, I could not speak out,
But I would plead for mercy with my judge.
16 If I summoned Him and He responded,
I do not believe He would lend me His ear.
17 For He crushes me [c]for a hair;[c]
He wounds me much for no cause.
18 He does not let me catch my breath,
But sates me with bitterness.
19 If a trial of strength—He is the strong one;
If a trial in court—who will summon Him for me?
20 Though I were innocent,
My mouth would condemn me;
Though I were blameless, He would prove me crooked.
21 I am blameless—I am distraught;
I am sick of life.
22 It is all one; therefore I say,
"He destroys the blameless and the guilty."
23 When suddenly a scourge brings death,
He mocks as the innocent fail.
24 The earth is handed over to the wicked one;
He covers the eyes of its judges.
If it is not He, then who?

25 My days fly swifter than a runner;
They flee without seeing happiness;
26 They pass like reed-boats,
Like an eagle swooping onto its prey.
27 If I say, "I will forget my complaint;
Abandon my sorrow[d] and be diverted,"
28 I remain in dread of all my suffering;
I know that You will not acquit me.

a Meaning of Heb. uncertain. *b A primeval monster.*
c-c With Targum and Peshitta; or "with a storm." *d Lit. "face."*

8: *Trod ... :* The Deity is described like the Canaanite storm-god Baal symbolizing his victory over the sea-god Yam *(sea)* by treading on his *back.* Job has implied that God is treating him similarly (7.12). **9:** *Chambers,* in context, probably the name of another constellation. **10:** This v. has been incorporated into the evening service liturgy. **11–15:** The passage is more precisely an "If ... then ..." construction ("hen ... ʾap ki ..."), like 4.18–19: seeing that the Deity cannot be restrained, how can I summon Him to judgment? (as Rashi). **15:** *My judge,* or "my co-litigant." **17:** *Crushes me for a hair,* rather, "he pushes me on the hair"—a gesture of dismissal similar to one known in ancient Syria—or "he crushes me with a tempest." The Talmud (ibid.) finds a measure-for-measure response in God's appearance to Job "from the whirlwind" (38.1). *For no cause,* an ironic counter-claim against the Deity, who wanted to know if Job revered Him "for no reason" (1.9). **18:** *Bitterness,* or "poison" (cf. Lam. 3.15); cf. the poisoned arrows in 6.4. **20:** *My mouth:* From the parallel line and what follows (vv. 30–31) it is clear that we should understand *my mouth* as a scribal correction of "Your mouth." *Prove me crooked,* with a slight metathesis ("yaʿashkeni"), "do me wrong" (e.g., 10.3). **22:** *One,* the same. Contrary to what Abraham had assumed (Gen. 18.23), Job contends—evidently based on his own case—that God does not differentiate between the fates of the righteous and the wicked; cf. Eccl. 7.5; 8.14. **23:** *As the innocent fail,* rather, "(He mocks) the trial of the innocent." **24:** *The wicked one:* Through the ages interpreters have differed over whether the reference is to God—in which case it is blasphemous—or to the Satan, or simply to wicked people. While some Rabbis charged Job with blasphemy, others defended him, understanding him to protest the sway held by evil forces. **25–26:** Job interrupts his reflections on suing the Deity with another rumination on the brevity of life (cf. 7.6–10).

29 It will be I who am in the wrong;
Why then should I waste effort?
30 If I washed with soap,
Cleansed my hands with lye,
31 You would dip me in muck
Till my clothes would abhor me.
32 He is not a man, like me, that I can answer Him,
That we can go to law together.
33 No arbiter is between us
To lay his hand on us both.
34 If He would only take His rod away from me
And not let His terror frighten me,
35 Then I would speak out without fear of Him;
For I know myself not to be so.

10 I am disgusted with life;
I will give rein to my complaint,
Speak in the bitterness of my soul.
2 I say to God, "Do not condemn me;
Let me know what You charge me with.
3 Does it benefit You to defraud,
To despise the toil of Your hands,
While smiling on the counsel of the wicked?
4 Do You have the eyes of flesh?
Is Your vision that of mere men?
5 Are Your days the days of a mortal,
Are Your years the years of a man,
6 That You seek my iniquity
And search out my sin?
7 You know that I am not guilty,
And that there is none to deliver from Your hand.

8 "Your hands shaped and fashioned me,
Then destroyed every part of me.
9 Consider that You fashioned me like clay;
Will You then turn me back into dust?
10 You poured me out like milk,
Congealed me like cheese;
11 You clothed me with skin and flesh
And wove me of bones and sinews;
12 You bestowed on me life and care;
Your providence watched over my spirit.

27–35: Job is seeking a way to overcome the intimidation that prevents him from summoning God. **29:** Job means to say that if he does succeed in receiving a divine judgment, "I will be found in the wrong" by the court. Cf. Jer. 12.1: Jeremiah realizes that were he to sue God for justice, God would be found in the right. **30–31:** In Heb parlance and in Job in particular, innocence is often conveyed by the metaphor of cleanliness; guilt is dirt. Underneath Job remains innocent, but he is made to look guilty by a corrupt Deity who covers him with a film of grit. (For the reverse image, see Ps. 51.9.) Job's suffering seems to others like divine punishment, implying that he had sinned. This stigma has social repercussions that are detailed in chs 19 and 29. In this image, only his *clothes ... abhor* him; later (19.17, 19) family and friends will shun him. **31:** *Muck,* lit. "a pit," which also connotes the grave (e.g., Ps. 30.10; Job 33.18). **33:** *No arbiter:* Many ancient versions and commentators read "lu" for "lo'" and interpret: "Would there were an arbiter between us!" See also 2 Sam. 19.7. **35:** The sense of this enigmatic v. is more likely, "For I am not being honest with myself."

10.1–2: Job continues. In the NJPS translation Job expresses himself in the indicative: *I will ... I say ...* The extended verb forms in v. 1 and the context favor the subjunctive: "if I would confront the Deity, this is what I would say." The purpose of suing God is to compel Him to disclose the charges Job assumes are being held over his head. **4:** Job questions whether God does indeed see differently from a human, as has been claimed, e.g., in 1 Sam. 16.7. **5–6:** Since God is not mortal, why should He be threatened by any sin of Job's? Cf. 7.19–21. **7:** Rava in the Talmud (*b. B. Bat.* 16a) understands Job to be saying: If it were your will ("daʿtkha"), I would not act wickedly—an extreme version of Job's argument. Accordingly, there is no reason to judge and punish anything in the world, since You created it the way it is. **8–9:** The description here evokes the formation of the first human out of the ground in Gen. 2.7. **10–11:** The images here analogize human creation to the *congeal*ing of *milk* into *cheese*—probably connected to the transformation of semen into flesh; and the fleshing out of a skeleton (*cloth*ing a body)—the reverse of decomposition, a state that Job has been experiencing since being afflicted with a severe

13 Yet these things You hid in Your heart;
I know that You had this in mind:
14 To watch me when I sinned
And not clear me of my iniquity;
15 Should I be guilty—the worse for me!
And even when innocent, I cannot lift my head;
So sated am I with shame,
And drenched in my misery.
16 [a]It is something to be proud of[a] to hunt me
like a lion,
To [b]show Yourself wondrous through[b] me time and
again!
17 You keep sending fresh witnesses against me,
Letting Your vexation with me grow.
[a]I serve my term and am my own replacement.[a]

18 "Why did You let me come out of the womb?
Better had I expired before any eye saw me,
19 Had I been as though I never was,
Had I been carried from the womb to the grave.
20 My days are few, so desist!
Leave me alone, let me be diverted a while
21 Before I depart—never to return—
For the land of deepest gloom;
22 A land whose light is darkness,
All gloom and disarray,
Whose light is like darkness."

11 Then Zophar the Naamathite said in reply:
2 Is a multitude of words unanswerable?
Must a loquacious person be right?
3 Your prattle may silence men;
You may mock without being rebuked,
4 And say, "My doctrine is pure,
And I have been innocent in Your sight."
5 But would that God might speak,
And talk to you Himself.
6 He would tell you the secrets of wisdom,
[a]For there are many sides to sagacity;
And know that God has overlooked for you some of
your iniquity.[a]

a-a Meaning of Heb. uncertain.
b-b Or "make sport of"; cf. Pal. Aram. ʾafli.

skin disease (see 7.5). Compare another image of formation in utero in Ps. 139.13–16. **13–14:** Job claims to have esoteric knowledge of God—that He keeps close track of people's transgressions in order to punish them; cf. 7.17–21. **16:** *It is something to be proud of,* rather, "And (if) it (my head—see v. 15) does surge"—then You *hunt me like a lion. Show Yourself wondrous,* performing extreme acts. **17:** *Fresh witnesses:* The plural *witnesses* is more likely a collective denoting "prosecution": "You renew your prosecution of me." *Replacement,* as a plural, the term more likely denotes military reinforcements that the Deity arrays against Job; note that the most common meaning of "tsavaʾ" (here rendered *term*) is "army troops." **18–19:** A reprise of 3.10–23. **18:** *Any eye,* esp. the unrelenting eye of God; see 7.17–21. **21–22:** The place of the dead is dark—and desirable to Job (ch 3)—where in Job's topsy-turvy reality *light is darkness. Whose light is like darkness,* a brilliant oxymoron, lit. "That shines like the dark" (cf. Saadia Gaon).

11.1–20: Zophar's speech. Zophar is the first companion to assume that Job has committed a sin; but he also believes that Job thinks he is blameless. His original solution to the paradox is that God has made him forget his sin (see v. 5–6 n.). There is much that is mysterious about the divine and divine wisdom, and Job would do well to accept that fact (vv. 6–11). With this idea, Zophar anticipates Elihu and God's speech from the whirlwind. Since Job is basically a good man, he is advised to supplicate God and maintain righteousness (v. 14). This will bring him peace of mind and a good life (vv. 15–19). Just like Eliphaz and Bildad, Zophar contrasts the dismal fate of the wicked. **3:** The sense is more like: people (the two preceding companions) have been silent when you have spoken; none has refuted you. *Mock,* the verb "l-ʿ-g" may be metathesized from "ʿ-l-g," "to prattle" (see Isa. 32.4). **5–6:** Job's sin is known only to God, and Job will learn of it only if God chooses to reveal it to him. *God has overlooked …,* rather, "God has caused you to forget your sin"; cf. 39.17 ("hishah," "deprived her," i.e., "He made her forget").

7 Would you discover the mystery of God?
Would you discover the limit of the Almighty?
8 Higher than heaven—what can you do?
Deeper than Sheol—what can you know?
9 Its measure is longer than the earth
And broader than the sea.
10 [a]Should He pass by, or confine,
Or call an assembly, who can stop Him?[a]
11 For He knows deceitful men;
When He sees iniquity, does He not discern it?
12 [a]A hollow man will get understanding,
When a wild ass is born a man.[a]

13 But if you direct your mind,
And spread forth your hands toward Him—
14 If there is iniquity with you, remove it,
And do not let injustice reside in your tent—
15 Then, free of blemish, you will hold your
head high,
And, [b]when in straits,[b] be unafraid.
16 You will then put your misery out of mind,
Consider it as water that has flowed past.
17 [a]Life will be brighter than noon;[a]
You will shine, you will be like the morning.
18 You will be secure, for there is hope,
[a]And, entrenched,[a] you will rest secure;
19 You will lie down undisturbed;
The great will court your favor.
20 But the eyes of the wicked pine away;
Escape is cut off from them;
They have only their last breath to look forward to.

12 Then Job said in reply:

2 Indeed, you are the [voice of] the people,
And wisdom will die with you.
3 But I, like you, have a mind,
And am not less than you.
Who does not know such things?

a-a Meaning of Heb. uncertain.
b-b Heb. muṣaq; *other Heb. editions* muṣṣaq, *"you will be firm."*

7: *Would you,* or: "Can you … ?" **8:** *Higher … deeper … :* That humanity cannot reach the sky or the netherworld is a widespread maxim in the ancient Near East and the Bible (e.g., Amos 9.2). **9:** *Its measure,* wisdom's (v. 6). **10:** *Pass by,* many moderns read "yaḥtop," "snatch." *Call an assembly,* "sequester" would make more sense. **12:** Probably a proverbial saying. **15:** *When in straits:* The alternative reading (see translators' note *b-b)* is preferable: "And you will be firm." **16:** *Put … out of mind,* more precisely, "you will forget your suffering"—just as God has made Job forget his transgression (v. 6). **17:** Job in his first discourse (ch 3) had hoped for darkness and death; Zophar foresees for him life and light. *Life,* more precisely, "an enduring life"—in opposition to Job's repeated contentions that life is fleeting. **18:** *Entrenched,* rather, "you will burrow in" like an animal; cf. "lie down," used of animals, in v. 19. **20:** *Their last breath,* rather, "their chagrin" (cf. "to cause chagrin" in 31.38–39).

12.1–14.22: Job's answer. Job responds at length to all he has heard. He begins by addressing his companions, demonstrating that he is, no less than they are, familiar with the traditional wisdom. He parodies their wisdom by reciting wisdom sayings, real and mock (ch 12). Job proceeds to denigrate his friends as false comforters (13.4) and begs them to remain silent and neutral as he begins to realize his notion, laid out only hypothetically in chs 9–10, of summoning the Deity to court (13.5–19). Having readied his companions to witness the proceedings, Job challenges God to appear and to refrain from intimidating him (13.20–24). Job demands to know the charges against him (13.23). Job reminds God that there is little sense in persecuting him, since human existence is frail (13.25–27)—recalling the words of the spirit in 4.19–21. This provides a transition to Job's protracted and highly figurative meditation on the way a human deteriorates—unlike a tree that can renew its growth (13.38–14.22). **12.2–3:** Job's compliment to his companions may be sarcastic; cf. 13.3. On the other hand, he seeks to demonstrate that he is no less wise than they. *Such things:* The use of the pronoun (lit. "these"), which depends for its referent on the context in which it appears, serves formulaically to introduce a quotation—or, in this case, pseudo-quotation (see also v. 9). The parodic character of

4 I have become a laughingstock to my friend—
“One who calls to God and is answered,
Blamelessly innocent”—a laughingstock.
5 [a]In the thought of the complacent there is contempt
for calamity;
It is ready for those whose foot slips.[-a]
6 Robbers live untroubled in their tents,
And those who provoke God are secure,
[a]Those whom God’s hands have produced.[-a]

7 But ask the beasts, and they will teach you;
The birds of the sky, they will tell you,
8 Or speak to the earth, it will teach you;
The fish of the sea, they will inform you.
9 Who among all these does not know
That the hand of the LORD has done this?
10 In His hand is every living soul
And the breath of all mankind.
11 Truly, the ear tests arguments
As the palate tastes foods.
12 Is wisdom in the aged
And understanding in the long-lived?
13 With Him are wisdom and courage;
His are counsel and understanding.
14 Whatever He tears down cannot be rebuilt;
Whomever He imprisons cannot be set free.
15 When He holds back the waters, they dry up;
When He lets them loose, they tear up the land.
16 With Him are strength and resourcefulness;
Erring and causing to err are from Him.
17 He makes counselors go about naked[b]
And causes judges to go mad.
18 He undoes the belts of kings,
And fastens loincloths on them.
19 He makes priests go about naked,[b]
And leads temple-servants[c] astray.
20 He deprives trusty men of speech,
And takes away the reason of elders.
21 He pours disgrace upon great men,
And loosens the belt of the mighty.

a-a Meaning of Heb. uncertain. *b A sign of madness.*
c Cf. Ugaritic ytnm, *a class of temple servants; others “the mighty.”*

Job’s citations becomes clear in his next address to the companions at vv. 7–8. **4:** The (pseudo) quotation of wisdom begins in the first line. Read somewhat differently from the received text, the line would mean: “One who laughs at calamity”—one who trusts in God, like the person Eliphaz described in 5.19ff., will receive an answer to one’s prayers.

5: The first line is notoriously challenging. Read somewhat differently, the sense is: “He shows contempt for disaster, at times of catastrophe is complacent.” *It is ready,* rather, “he (the one who trusts in God) is steady when the *foot slips.*” **6:** Rather, “The tents (of the pious) are untroubled by robbers; they *are secure* from those *who provoke God.*” *Those whom,* rather, “that which”—the disaster. **7–8:** Job interrupts his recitation of mock wisdom and parodies a traditional text, Deut. 32.7, which says that the elders are meant to convey proper teaching. Job replaces the sources of his companions’ wisdom with creatures in nature. *The beasts,* rather, “behemoth,” a semi-mythological version of the hippopotamus, celebrated by God in 41.15–24. *The earth,* many understand the reference as the animals of the earth. *Sky, earth* or land, and *sea* are the three domains of the world. **9:** Rather, “Who does not know all these (things)?” (see vv. 2–3 n.). The rest of the v. is an exact quotation from Isa. 42.20, which accounts for the unique use of the proper name of Israel’s God, YHVH, in the discourse of Job and his companions (see the intro.). **11:** *Tastes,* the term also connotes reason (e.g., v. 20), making the analogy even sharper. Elihu will adduce the same line (34.3). **12:** *Is wisdom:* This is a mock traditional assertion: “Wisdom is in the aged” (cf. Eliphaz in 15.9–10). **13:** Because the wisdom sayings are in somewhat random sequence, there is no proximate antecedent for *With him;* but the reference to God is clear. **14:** A parodic inversion of Eliphaz in 5.18. **15:** A parodic inversion of Eliphaz in 5.10. **16–21, 23–25:** God is credited with confounding political and religious leaders. This is a parody of Eliphaz in 5.11–14. **18:** *And fastens loincloths:* Since “ʾezor” denotes a “belt” rather than a *cloth,* the verb should be read slightly differently: “And removes the belt from their loins.” Warriors would gird their loins for combat; cf. 38.3. Perhaps the poet is punning—writing “fastens” and reading “removes.” The verb already puns on the terms for “belt.” **20:** *Trusty men,* or slightly

22 He draws mysteries out of the darkness,
And brings obscurities to light.
23 He exalts nations, then destroys them;
He expands nations, then leads them away.
24 He deranges the leaders of the people,
And makes them wander in a trackless waste.
25 They grope without light in the darkness;
He makes them wander as if drunk.

13 My eye has seen all this;
My ear has heard and understood it.
2 What you know, I know also;
I am not less than you.
3 Indeed, I would speak to the Almighty;
I insist on arguing with God.
4 But you invent lies;
All of you are quacks.
5 If you would only keep quiet
It would be considered wisdom on your part.
6 Hear now my arguments,
Listen to my pleading.
7 Will you speak unjustly on God's behalf?
Will you speak deceitfully for Him?
8 Will you be partial toward Him?
Will you plead God's cause?
9 Will it go well when He examines you?
Will you fool Him as one fools men?
10 He will surely reprove you
If in [a-]your heart[-a] you are partial toward Him.
11 His threat will terrify you,
And His fear will seize you.
12 Your briefs are empty[b] platitudes;
Your responses are unsubstantial.[c]

13 Keep quiet; I will have my say,
Come what may upon me.
14 How long! I will take my flesh in my teeth;
I will take my life in my hands.
15 [d-]He may well slay me; I may have no hope;[-d]
Yet I will argue my case before Him.
16 In this too is my salvation:
That no impious man can come into His presence.

17 Listen closely to my words;
Give ear to my discourse.

revocalizing and deriving the term from "na'am," "to speak"—"orators." **21:** Cf. Ps. 107.40. **22:** An apparent parody of Zophar (11.7–9); cf. 28.3, 11. **24:** Cf. Ps. 107.40. **25:** Cf. Deut. 28.29 and Isa. 19.14.

13.1–2: Job has made his point and summarizes: through experience and knowledge of wisdom, he knows what his companions know. His controversy with them is based on a difference in experience, not conventional knowledge. On "seeing" and "hearing," see 42.5. **3:** Job accepts Eliphaz's challenge (5.8) and asserts that he will speak to God. **4:** *Invent lies,* rather, "smear lies." "Smear" has the dual sense of slander and applying ointment, like the *quack* doctors. **7–10:** The friends do not constitute a tribunal, but they should nevertheless remain impartial during the juridical proceedings. Favoritism and deceit are forbidden in rendering justice (Exod. 23.3–7). God Himself would take offense—does He need a biased court in order to win? **13–15:** Job attempts to overcome his fear of divine intimidation (see 9.34–35). He reiterates (see 6.8–9) his readiness to die in order to make his case. **14:** *How long:* These two words are probably an accidental scribal repetition of the preceding two words. **15:** *I may have no hope:* The MT writes "not" but reads "for Him." The sense is therefore either "I will (no longer) wait" or "I will wait for Him." *Argue my case,* rather, read "derakhav," "His ways" (see 21.31) and interpret: "I will charge Him of His ways to His face." **16:** The idea is rather: "He (God) will be my salvation," for He will reject only a blasphemer—and I am not that.

a-a Lit. "secret." *b Lit. "ashen."* *c Lit. "clayey."*
d-d So with kethib; *others with* qere *"Though He slay me, yet will I trust in Him."*

18 See now, I have prepared a case;
I know that I will win it.
19 For who is it that would challenge me?
I should then keep silent and expire.
20 But two things do not do to me,
So that I need not hide from You:
21 Remove Your hand from me,
And let not Your terror frighten me.
22 Then summon me and I will respond,
Or I will speak and You reply to me.
23 How many are my iniquities and sins?
Advise me of my transgression and sin.
24 Why do You hide Your face,
And treat me like an enemy?
25 Will You harass a driven leaf,
Will You pursue dried-up straw,
26 That You decree for me bitter things
And make me [a]answer for[a] the iniquities of my youth,
27 That You put my feet in the stocks
And watch all my ways,
[b]Hemming in my footsteps?[b]
28 Man wastes away like a rotten thing,
Like a garment eaten by moths.

14 Man born of woman is short-lived and sated with trouble.
2 He blossoms like a flower and withers;
He vanishes like a shadow and does not endure.
3 Do You fix Your gaze on such a one?
Will You go to law with me?
4 [b]Who can produce a clean thing out of an unclean one? No one![b]
5 His days are determined;
You know the number of his months;
You have set him limits that he cannot pass.
6 Turn away from him, that he may be at ease
Until, like a hireling, he finishes out his day.

7 There is hope for a tree;
If it is cut down it will renew itself;
Its shoots will not cease.
8 If its roots are old in the earth,
And its stump dies in the ground,

a-a Lit. "inherit." *b-b Meaning of Heb. uncertain.*

19: Job's question provides a transition to his direct address to God. **20–24:** On the one hand, Job fears he will need to *hide* from God's intimidation; on the other, he fears God will *hide* [His] *face* and withhold from him the cause of his torment. In Jewish tradition, the notion of God's concealing or withdrawing His divine Presence is expressed by the phrase "hester panim," "hiding (God's) face." **24:** *Treat me like an enemy,* Heb "'oyeb." Job makes a serious pun on his name—"'iyyob." Recall 7.12 and cf. 19.11: Job thinks the Deity must reckon him an enemy in order to pummel him so. **26:** *Bitter things,* more poignantly, "poison"; cf. Deut. 32.32; Job 20.14. Job imagines there is a writ of indictment issued against him. **27:** *Put my feet in the stocks:* If Job's feet were in stocks, he could not walk. Rather, he likens the negative attention he receives from God to spreading "lime" (vocalizing "sid," lime," for "sad," "stocks") on the bottom of his feet and tracking him. The image rests on the widespread biblical metaphor that one's behavior is one's path in life. Here Job utterly contradicts his claim of divine indifference in 3.23. **28:** The images used to figure human decay either provide a transition to the next part of the discourse, or are misplaced and should follow 14.1–2.

14.1: *Man born of woman,* a derogatory epithet, a mere human, whose life is short and difficult (cf. 15.14; 25.4). **2:** For the same combination of images, see Ps. 102.12; cf. Isa. 40.6–8; Ps. 144.4. **3:** Although Job is summoning God to court, he blames God for "bringing [him] to court." From Job's perspective the Deity started by punishing him for undisclosed charges. **4:** Job echoes the sentiment of the spirit in 4.17–21 and protests: humans should not be persecuted for being impure—that fact cannot be changed. In rabbinic literature the v. is taken as praise of God: Who has the power to convert the impure (like Abraham's idolatrous father) into the pure (like Abraham)? Only the One, namely, God (*Pesik. Rav Kah.* 4). **5:** Cf. Ps. 90.9–10. **6:** *Turn away:* Job reiterates his plea from 7.16, 19. *Like a hireling,* an image from 7.2. **7–9:** The image of the tree challenges Bildad's metaphor of the righteous as a flourishing tree in 8.16–18. From Job's perspective the analogy cannot work because a human cannot rejuvenate

9 At the scent of water it will bud
And produce branches like a sapling.
10 But mortals languish and die;
Man expires; where is he?
11 The waters of the sea fail,
And the river dries up and is parched.
12 So man lies down never to rise;
He will awake only when the heavens are no more,
Only then be aroused from his sleep.
13 O that You would hide me in Sheol,
Conceal me until Your anger passes,
Set me a fixed time to attend to me.
14 If a man dies, can he live again?
All the time of my service I wait
Until my replacement comes.
15 You would call and I would answer You;
You would set Your heart on Your handiwork.
16 Then You would not count my steps,
Or keep watch over my sin.
17 My transgression would be sealed up in a pouch;
You would coat over my iniquity.

18 Mountains collapse and crumble;
Rocks are dislodged from their place.
19 Water wears away stone;
Torrents wash away earth;
So you destroy man's hope,
20 You overpower him forever and he perishes;
You alter his visage and dispatch him.
21 His sons attain honor and he does not know it;
They are humbled and he is not aware of it.
22 He feels only the pain of his flesh,
And his spirit mourns in him.

15 Eliphaz the Temanite said in reply:
2 Does a wise man answer with windy opinions,
And fill his belly with the east wind?

like a tree. The rare word for *shoots* links the passages. **11:** *Fail,* rather, "run out." **12:** Job denies resurrection, as he does also in v. 14, although there he imagines being in Sheol as a temporary hiding place from God's anger. For the analogy of *sleep* as death, cf. 3.13. With a belief in resurrection, one can *awake* from the *sleep* of death; see Isa. 26.19; Dan. 12.2. **13:** Job wishes God would allow him to lie among the dead, where he would not feel God's oppression; cf. 3.13–24. *To attend to me,* or "*Set me a fixed time* and then [after my period of my suffering has passed] pay me mind again." **14:** *Time of my service,* Job revisits 7.1, but this time he is referring to a fixed period when he is hidden away in Sheol, waiting for God's anger to pass. **15:** When Job's place in Sheol is filled by someone else, he will be returned to the realm of the living by a God who will care about His *handiwork;* contrast Job's dismay in 10.8–13. **16:** Job is hoping the Deity will change His ways; contrast 13.27 and 10.6, respectively. **17:** *Sealed up in a pouch:* In the ancient Near East evidence was bound up and stored for use at trials. If God would put away hypothetical evidence against Job, Job would emerge innocent and free from punishment. **18–22:** Job abandons his fantasy of a compassionate God and returns to images of a repressive one. **18:** *Rocks are dislodged,* cf. Job's characterization of the Deity in 9.5. **19:** *Torrents,* the translation assumes a metathesized root ("s-ḥ-p"), known from Akkadian and Arabic. **21:** The dead do not know what happens to their children. **22:** An enigmatic v. It might describe the decay of the dying body—first the *flesh* suffers pain and then the *spirit* "dries up" (not *mourns*). But perhaps *his flesh* denotes his family (e.g., Gen. 37.27) and *his spirit* the members of his household (e.g., Gen. 12.5), in which case it would describe the *mourning* over the dead person: "Only his family are pained over him, and his household mourns him."

15.1–35: Eliphaz begins the second round of dialogues. There are two parts. The first (vv. 2–16) is a diatribe against Job for claiming to have heard secrets from the divine circle (see 4.12–21 n.). The second part (vv. 17–35) is a lengthy defense of the doctrine of just retribution, concentrating on the ill fate of the wicked. In both parts Eliphaz elaborates points he had made in his first discourse, where he had mocked Job's claim to have received a divine word (5.1, 8), and described the miserable end that the wicked inevitably suffer (4.8–11). Eliphaz does not repeat his initial appeal to Job to maintain his renowned piety. Apparently he has surmised from Job's accusations of God that Job has turned sinful. On the other hand, emphasis on the fate of the wicked may be intended as a warning to Job to avoid a similar fate. Eliphaz sets the tone

3 Should he argue with useless talk,
With words that are of no worth?
4 You subvert piety
And restrain prayer to God.
5 Your sinfulness dictates your speech,
So you choose crafty language.
6 Your own mouth condemns you—not I;
Your lips testify against you.

7 Were you the first man born?
Were you created before the hills?
8 Have you listened in on the council of God?
Have you sole possession of wisdom?
9 What do you know that we do not know,
Or understand that we do not?
10 Among us are gray-haired old men,
Older by far than your father.
11 Are God's consolations not enough for you,
And His gentle words to you?
12 How your heart has carried you away,
How your eyes [a]-have failed-[a] you,
13 That you could vent your anger on God,
And let such words out of your mouth!
14 What is man that he can be cleared of guilt,
One born of woman, that he be in the right?
15 He puts no trust in His holy ones;
The heavens are not guiltless in His sight;
16 What then of one loathsome and foul,
Man, who drinks wrongdoing like water!

17 I will hold forth; listen to me;
What I have seen, I will declare—
18 That which wise men have transmitted from their fathers,
And have not withheld,

a-a Meaning of Heb. uncertain.

and the topic for the second cycle of speeches, and for some of the third. **2–3:** Eliphaz rudely dismisses Job's efforts to demonstrate his wisdom in the preceding discourse. **4–6:** Eliphaz regards Job's claims to have heard secrets from the divine realm (4.12–21) as blasphemy. V. 4 should be understood in the light of v. 8 below: "You go so far as to abrogate piety / as you (mis)appropriate conversation in the presence of God." The NJPS translation follows the interpretation in the Talmud, but it overturns the ordinary meanings of the words. **7–8:** From Eliphaz's wisdom perspective, Job could only have had a direct experience of God in two ways: either by being present at the creation, when divine wisdom was exposed (see Prov. 8.22–31; note that Eliphaz in v. 7b here is quoting Prov. 8.25); or by participating in the divine *council.* Prophets are privileged to listen in on the divine *council* (e.g., Jer. 23.22), but Eliphaz does not see Job as a prophet. **8:** *Have you sole possession,* rather, as in v. 4: "Have you appropriated to yourself." **9:** A direct rebuff of Job's assertions in 12.3 and 13.1–2. **10:** Those who put their stock in traditional wisdom venerate the aged, who have accumulated more wisdom; cf. 32.6–7; Sir. 25.4–6. See v. 17 below. **11:** God has given Job no consolation, so this v. is better rendered, "Are the consolations of these (viz., Job's companions; so Gersonides) too little for you?" that you need to claim that "a word in stealth is with you" (instead of *And His gentle words to you*). **12:** *How your eyes have failed* ("yirzemun"): Many moderns, including S. D. Luzzatto, follow the Gk and a Masoretic mss and read "yerumun": "How your eyes have risen," i.e., how haughty you have turned. **13:** In the first line Eliphaz complains that Job has, literally, "returned wind[y speech] to God," meaning that he has spoken unseemly things to the Deity; cf. Job 35.4 ("I shall give you a reply"). In the second line Eliphaz reuses a line that Bildad had employed in 8.10 to introduce quoted discourse. **14–16:** Thus, what follows is a parody of the message from the spirit that Job had reported in 4.17–19. The lack of an antecedent in this passage for the possessive pronouns in v. 15 *(His holy ones ... His sight)* suggests that these vv. are indeed a quotation. **14:** *One born of woman,* a parodic echo of Job in 14.1; cf. 25.4. **15:** *Holy ones,* see 5.1. *The heavens,* a metonym for God's messengers and other beings who reside in the sky (the angels); cf. Isa. 24.21; Job 25.5. *Guiltless,* a double entendre in Heb: clear and *guiltless.* **16:** Cf. Ps. 14.1, 3. In mocking Job's report of the spirit, Eliphaz turns the fact of humanity's humble origins from clay (4.19) into *foul* character. In 34.7 Elihu will parody the image of *drink*ing *wrongdoing like water* in reference to Job. **17:** Eliphaz counters Job's visual and aural experiences (see

19 To whom alone the land was given,
No stranger passing among them:
20 The wicked man writhes in torment all his days;
Few years are reserved for the ruthless.
21 Frightening sounds fill his ears;
When he is at ease a robber falls upon him.
22 He is never sure he will come back from the
    dark;
A sword stares him in the face.
23 He wanders about for bread—where is it?
He knows that the day of darkness has been
    readied for him.
24 Troubles terrify him, anxiety overpowers him,
Like a king [a]-expecting a siege.-[a]
25 For he has raised his arm against God
And played the hero against the Almighty.
26 He runs at Him defiantly[b]
[a]-With his thickly bossed shield.
27 His face is covered with fat
And his loins with blubber.-[a]
28 He dwells in cities doomed to ruin,
In houses that shall not be lived in,
That are destined to become heaps of rubble.
29 He will not be rich;
His wealth will not endure;
[a]-His produce shall not bend to the earth.-[a]
30 He will never get away from the darkness;
Flames will sear his shoots;
[a]-He will pass away by the breath of His mouth.
31 He will not be trusted;
He will be misled by falsehood,
And falsehood will be his recompense.-[a]
32 He will wither before his time,
His boughs never having flourished.
33 He will drop his unripe grapes like a vine;
He will shed his blossoms like an olive tree.
34 For the company of the impious is desolate;
Fire consumes the tents of the briber;
35 For they have conceived mischief, given
    birth to evil,
And their womb has produced deceit.

16

Job said in reply:

2 I have often heard such things;
You are all mischievous comforters.

a-a Meaning of Heb. uncertain. *b Lit. "with neck."*

13.1) with the traditional wisdom he has *seen*—to this Job should *listen*. **19:** Eliphaz counters Job's contention that "the land has been given to the hand of the wicked" (9.24) and defends God's justice. *No stranger:* The tradition has not been corrupted by foreign influence; cf. Joel 4.17. **20–24:** The misfortunes that are said to bedevil the wicked resemble those that Eliphaz had assured Job he would escape—if he maintains his piety—in 5.19–22. **20:** Formerly (4.10–11) Eliphaz had suggested that the wicked may thrive for a time. **21:** Compare Job's pseudo-wisdom in 12.6: the righteous will be spared the torments of the wicked. **24:** *Like a king expecting,* more likely, "(disaster attacks him) like a king armed for the fray." **25:** *For he,* the wicked, who receives his just deserts. *Played the hero,* said of God in Isa. 42.13. The wicked's arrogance knows no bounds. **26:** "With neck" (see translators' note *b)* is an ellipsis for "with strong neck" (Ps. 75.6), a gesture of haughtiness. **27:** Putting on fat is symbolic of arrogance; see Deut. 32.15. **28:** Eliphaz resumes his delineation of the disastrous fate of the wicked, recalling Bildad's image of the wicked's collapsing home in 8.14–15. **29:** *His produce,* an Akkadian word suggests that "wealth" is a better rendition, yielding tighter parallelism; the last line should be rendered "His wealth will not spread over the land." **30:** In contrast to Bildad's metaphor of the righteous as a plant flourishing in the sunlight, whose *shoots* can even survive transplantation (8.16–18), Eliphaz depicts the wicked as plants stunted in the dark, whose *shoots* are "dried out" and who perish *by the breath* of the Deity (cf. 4.9). **32:** The subject of the feminine verb *wither* is the last word of v. 31, "temurato," which should be attached to the first line of this v. and revocalized as a term for a "palm tree" ("timorah," e.g., 1 Kings 6.29); cf. LXX. The wicked's "palm" *will wither before his time.* **34–35:** Eliphaz concludes with his thesis of just retribution: the wicked who *produced deceit* will have their homes

3 Have windy words no limit?
What afflicts you that you speak on?
4 I would also talk like you
If you were in my place;
I would barrage you with words,
I would wag my head over you.
5 I would encourage you with words,[a]
My moving lips would bring relief.
6 If I speak, my pain will not be relieved,
And if I do not—what have I lost?
7 Now He has truly worn me out;
You have destroyed my whole community.
8 You have shriveled me;
My gauntness serves as a witness,
And testifies against me.
9 In His anger He tears and persecutes me;
He gnashes His teeth at me;
My foe stabs me with his eyes.
10 They open wide their mouths at me;
Reviling me, they strike my cheeks;
They inflame themselves against me.
11 God hands me over to an evil man,
Thrusts me into the clutches of the wicked.
12 I had been untroubled, and He broke me in pieces;
He took me by the scruff and shattered me;
He set me up as His target;
13 His bowmen surrounded me;
He pierced my kidneys; He showed no mercy;
He spilled my bile onto the ground.

a *Lit. "my mouth."*

burned. In these and the preceding vv. Eliphaz employs terms used by Job in his opening discourse (ch 3).

16.1–17.16: Eliphaz turns more strident, Job turns more sympathetic. If Job were confronted with the same conundrum, a pious man apparently punished by God, he would speak as they do (16.4–5). Yet Job knows he has nothing to lose by speaking truth to his companions and to God. The former show him no support; the latter brutally assails him as though he were a military target. Job's response is to bewail his victimization (16.15–16) and make a plea to God, who knows the truth (16.19). Speaking more in monologue than conversation, Job laments his loss of dignity (17.2, 6), leading to dejection and culminating in his anticipation of death. **16.2–3:** V. 3 is a pseudo-quotation of the friends (cf. Job in 6.24–26) by Job, introduced by *such things,* lit. "these [things]" (see 12.2–3 n.). Note that *you* in v. 3 is in the singular, as though spoken to Job. **4:** *Wag my head,* a gesture made at a wretched sight, an expression of sympathy, but perhaps also intended to ward off demonic agency; cf. Jer. 18.16; Lam. 2.15. **5:** *Moving lips,* a gesture of consolation; see 2.11; 42.11. Job was known to have fortified the fallen; see 4.3–4. **6:** *What have I lost,* more precisely, "(My pain) will not leave me" (cf. Ibn Ezra). **7–17:** Job gives voice to his protest against a persecuting God. **7:** In mid-verse Job switches from speaking of God in the third person to addressing Him in the second person; this is a common switch in psalms and other biblical and general literature (enallage). *Community,* Job's household and social circles, which became alienated from him; see chs 19 and 29; cf. Ps. 88.9. The term *community* (Heb "ʿedah") puns on "witness" (Heb "ʿed") in the next v. **8:** The v. appears to be in some disorder. A more literal rendering is: "*You have shriveled me* has become *a witness; my gauntness* has risen against me; *testify*ing in my face." Job would seem to be complaining that his affliction has stigmatized him, making him appear to be rejected by God; cf. 9.30–31. **9:** Job returns to speak of God in the third person. *In His anger He tears,* rather, "His anger rages" (for the idiom, see Amos 1.11). *Persecutes:* The verb ("satam") is related to the root of "Satan," and in later Jewish literature, another name for Satan is "Mastema." *Gnashes His teeth,* a gesture attributed to the wicked in Ps. (e.g., 37.12; 112.10); the wicked are figured as predators (e.g., Ps. 17.12), and so is the Deity here and elsewhere (e.g., Lam. 3.10). *My foe,* God; cf. 10.16–17. *Stabs me with his eyes,* perhaps giving an evil eye; cf. Ps. 35.19. **10:** The perpetrators are people who gesture in reaction to Job's stigma; cf. Lam. 2.16. *Strike my cheeks,* a widespread ancient Near Eastern gesture of shaming; cf. Lam. 3.30. *Inflame themselves,* more likely, "will amass against me"; cf. Gen. 48.19; Isa. 31.4. **11:** A typical petition in Ps. is that God protect the pious from the wicked (e.g., 17.8–9). **12:** The Deity's actions are like those of the lion in 10.16; cf. Gen. 49.8. The verbs are of matched alliterative reduplicated stems ("pirper," "pitspets"). *Target:* The divine image turns here into a military commander, calling out his archers (v. 13); cf. 6.20; Lam. 3.12. Job elaborates the image he drew in 14.20. **13:** *He pierced:* Although technically, Job is wounded by God's *bowmen,* he perceives that his tormentor is singular—the Deity, who has commanded his persecution. *Showed no mercy,* a refrain in Lam. (2.2, 7, 21; 3.43).

14 He breached me, breach after breach;
He rushed at me like a warrior.
15 I sewed sackcloth over my skin;
I [a]buried my glory[a] in the dust.
16 My face is red with weeping;
Darkness covers my eyes
17 [b]For no injustice on my part
And for the purity of my prayer![b]

18 Earth, do not cover my blood;
Let there be no resting place for my outcry!
19 Surely now my witness is in heaven;
He who can testify for me is on high.
20 O my advocates, my fellows,
Before God my eyes shed tears;
21 Let Him arbitrate between a man and God
As between a man and his fellow.
22 For a few more years will pass,
And I shall go the way of no return.
17 My spirit is crushed, my days run out;
The graveyard waits for me.

2 Surely mocking men keep me company,
And with their provocations I close my eyes.
3 Come now, stand surety for me!
Who will give his hand on my behalf?
4 You have hidden understanding from their minds;
Therefore You must not exalt [them].
5 He informs on his friends for a share [of their property],
And his children's eyes pine away.

6 He made me a byword among people;
I have become like Tophet[c] of old.
7 My eyes fail from vexation;
All shapes seem to me like shadows.
8 The upright are amazed at this;
The pure are aroused against the impious.

a-a Lit. "made my horn enter into."
b-b Or "Though I did no injustice, / And my prayer was pure."
c That consumed children; cf. Jer. 7.31.

14: For *breach*ing an enemy, cf. 2 Sam. 5.20. The verb echoes those of v. 12. *Like a warrior:* Characteristically, Job turns a favorable image of God (e.g., Isa. 42.13) into a negative one. **15:** *Sackcloth,* serves the dual purpose of indicating mourning and treating the wounds. *Buried my glory,* lit. "sunk my horn"—the opposite of God raising one's horn in triumph (e.g., Ps. 75.5–6). **16:** Darkened eyes signify gloom; cf. Lam. 5.17. **17:** *My prayer:* Job introduces his prayer, whose words are given in the immediately following vv. He appeals both to God and to his companions. **18:** If the earth were to *cover* [Job's] *blood,* the symbol of his affliction, his claim to innocence would be buried with it; cf. Gen. 4.10; Ezek. 24.7–8. *Resting place,* more likely, "hiding place"; cf. Job 28.1, 6, 12. This v. is used in many holocaust memorials. **19:** The *witness ... in heaven* is God; that is why Job insists on eliciting testimony from the Deity (13.22). **20:** *O my advocates,* there is a double entendre that can also be rendered "my taunters" (cf. Ps. 119.51). **21:** *Let Him arbitrate:* Job has made clear that God cannot be both judge and prosecutor, the one to decide between him and God (9.32–34). The phrase must mean something like: "So that a man can argue a case with God." **16.22–17.1:** Job returns to his refrain: I have one foot in the grave; cf. e.g., 7.16, 21; this anticipates the unit's conclusion at 17.11–16. **17.2:** A difficult v., as are many in this ch. It may mean: mockery is my lot, and my eyes tire (reading "til'enah ʿenay" for "talan ʿeni") of its increasing bitterness. Job is apparently addressing God (see v. 4). **3:** Striking hands is a gesture of providing surety for someone (e.g., Prov. 17.18). *Who will,* i.e., who else will? Job seeks divine support, as he had suggested in 16.19. **4:** The object of *exalt* is uncertain. Some vocalize in the passive: "You will not be exalted." **5:** A gnomic saying. Perhaps: a man invites his friends for a portion (to eat), while his children's eyes languish for lack of food. Similarly, Job's companions dispense wisdom to Job without taking any for themselves. **6:** Ironically, Job, having presented a proverbial saying, cites himself as a *byword*—he has become an object of derision. *Like Tophet,* more likely, "like spit in the face," following an Aram. root; for the same juxtaposition of ideas see 30.9–10. **7:** Having described his social reversal, Job relates again to his physical deterioration. *All shapes,* better, "my limbs wear away," reading "kalim" for "kullam" (rendered here as *all*). **8–10:** Job's diminution ought to shock good people, as it had at first stunned his friends (2.12–13),

9 The righteous man holds to his way;
He whose hands are clean grows stronger.
10 But all of you, come back now;
I shall not find a wise man among you.
11 My days are done, my tendons severed,
The strings of my heart.
12 They say that night is day,
That light is here—in the face of darkness.
13 If I must look forward to Sheol as my home,
And make my bed in the dark place,
14 Say to the Pit, "You are my father,"
To the maggots, "Mother," "Sister"—
15 Where, then, is my hope?
Who can see hope for me?
16 Will it descend to Sheol?
Shall we go down together to the dust?

18 Then Bildad the Shuhite said in reply:

2 How long? Put an end to talk!
Consider, and then we shall speak.
3 Why are we thought of as brutes,
Regarded by you as stupid?
4 You who tear yourself to pieces in anger—
Will [a]earth's order be disrupted[a] for your sake?
Will rocks be dislodged from their place?
5 Indeed, the light of the wicked fails;
The flame of his fire does not shine.
6 The light in his tent darkens;
His lamp fails him.
7 His iniquitous strides are hobbled;
His schemes overthrow him.
8 He is led by his feet into the net;
He walks onto the toils.
9 The trap seizes his heel;
The noose tightens on him.
10 The rope for him lies hidden on the ground;
His snare, on the path.
11 Terrors assault him on all sides
And send his feet flying.

a-a Lit. "the earth be abandoned."

who by their lack of understanding have proved unwise. **11:** Rather, "My days have passed, my plans have been driven asunder, (as have) the desires (cf. "'areshet" in Ps. 21.3) of my heart." **12:** Apparently referring to Job's companions, who see a dark situation *(night)*—Job's misery—and portray it as nothing terrible *(day),* for "light is nearer (i.e., preferable) than darkness" to them. Cf. Isa. 5.20. For "near" in the sense of favored, cf. the phrase "the people close to Him" in Ps. 148.14 and "(wisdom) is near to those who seek it" in Sir. 51.26. **13–16:** *If I must look forward ... Where, then is my hope?* The passage is structured around the same verbal stem ("q-w-y"), which lies at the root of *look forward* (but see next n.) and *hope,* creating a brilliant irony. **13:** *Look forward,* better (with Yellin): "If I measure (i.e., build) my home in Sheol ... ," which better parallels *And make my bed ...* (cf. "natah qaw," "measure with a line" in 38.5).

18.1–21: Bildad's response. After berating Job for insulting his companions' wisdom (vv. 2–4), Bildad resumes the argument initiated by Eliphaz (15.17–35), claiming in great detail that there is just retribution for the wicked (vv. 5–21), implying that the righteous receive their due as well. **2:** The plural *(we)* shows that Bildad is addressing his colleagues, who, he suggests, need to regroup in arguing with Job. **3:** *Regarded by you,* the Heb has the plural, but LXX and the translators here read the singular. **4:** Bildad transforms Job's idiom, charging God with wild rage (16.9), into a new expression, accusing Job of tearing himself apart in his anger; cf. Eliphaz's warning in 5.2. *Rocks be dislodged,* a response to Job in 14.18. **5–6:** Bildad cites and elaborates traditional wisdom (Prov. 13.9)—except that he neglects the favorable fate of the righteous, whose light will shine. The burning light is that of the family hearth. **7–10:** In 17.11 Job complained that his plans would never be fulfilled. Bildad responds that the wicked's schemes, analogized to footsteps, will be thwarted, as their feet will be ensnared. **7:** According to Prov. 4.12, "shortened strides" can be avoided by adopting wisdom. *Overthrow,* more likely, "cause to stumble" (reading with metathesis, "k-sh-l" for "sh-l-kh," as in Prov. 4.12). **9:** *Noose,* probably a kind of snare. **10:** *The rope,* a type of trap. The sequence of six different terms for snare manifests the poet's love of vocabulary that is characteristic of this book. **11–12:** The enumerated disasters recall the seven cited by Eliphaz in 5.19–22. **11:** *Send ...*

12 His progeny hunger;
Disaster awaits his wife.[a]
13 The tendons under his skin are consumed;
Death's first-born consumes his tendons.
14 He is torn from the safety of his tent;
Terror marches him to the king.[b]
15 It lodges in his desolate tent;
Sulfur is strewn upon his home.
16 His roots below dry up,
And above, his branches wither.
17 All mention of him vanishes from the earth;
He has no name abroad.
18 He is thrust from light to darkness,
Driven from the world.
19 He has no seed or breed among his people,
No survivor where he once lived.
20 Generations to come will be appalled at his fate,
As the previous ones are seized with horror.
21 "These were the haunts of the wicked;
Here was the place of him who knew not God."

19

Job said in reply:

2 How long will you grieve my spirit,
And crush me with words?
3 [c]Time and again[-c] you humiliate me,
And are not ashamed to abuse me.
4 If indeed I have erred,
My error remains with me.
5 Though you are overbearing toward me,
Reproaching me with my disgrace,
6 Yet know that God has wronged me;
He has thrown up siege works around me.
7 I cry, "Violence!" but am not answered;
I shout, but can get no justice.
8 He has barred my way; I cannot pass;
He has laid darkness upon my path.
9 He has stripped me of my glory,
Removed the crown from my head.

a Lit. "rib" (cf. Gen. 2.22); or "stumbling." *b Viz., of the netherworld.*
c-c Lit. "Ten times."

flying, or reading "va-hiplitsuhu" for "ve-hepitzuhu" (cf. 21.6 and Isa. 21.4) "scared off." **12:** Another possible interpretation: "He starves on account of his sin; disaster is ready at his side." **13:** *Death's first-born,* probably an allusion to the Canaanite god of death, Mot, who is imaged ravenously devouring the dead (cf. Hab. 2.5). Job alludes to Canaanite mythology in 5.7; 7.12; 26.13; 38.8–11 as well. **14:** *From ... his tent,* contrast the fate of the righteous (5.24; 12.6 and n.). *To the king,* Mot is not known as "king," and the reference remains enigmatic. **15:** Bildad's use of *home* (or "estate") recalls Eliphaz's remarks in 5.3–4 and, on the positive side, 5.24. **16:** Bildad evokes the images in 8.11–3 and 15.32–34. **17:** *He has no name abroad,* more likely, "he loses his reputation in the streets," precisely what Job bemoans of himself in chs 29–30. **19:** Contrast the fate of the pious, as Eliphaz describes it in 5.25. **20:** A response to 17.8, where Job maintained that good people would be appalled at a situation like his—an innocent sufferer. **21:** *Haunts,* rather, "dwellings."

19.1–29: Job's answer and his appeal. Job does not yet engage in the debate over whether the wicked get what they deserve—he will do that in his next discourse (ch 21). Here he appeals to his friends to cease persecuting him together with the Deity (vv. 2–5, 21–22, 28–29), trying to get them to understand that God has been wrongfully tormenting him (vv. 6–12), focusing in particular on how the stigma of divine disfavor has alienated family, friends, and even his once-faithful servants from him (vv. 13–20). Job desperately seeks vindication, first, by inscribing his claims on a monument (vv. 23–24), where they will be preserved for all to see, and second, by confronting God in person (vv. 25–27). **2:** As the rogue spirit had said (4.19–20), humans are *crush*ed in the space of a short lifetime. Job's companions do it *with words.* The Talmud (*b. B. M.* 58b) criticizes the unsympathetic manner of Job's companions. **3:** "Ten times" (see translators' note *c-c*) is a biblical convention for "several"; e.g., Num. 14.22. *Humiliate:* Zophar (11.3) had complained that no one had yet "humiliated," or confuted, Job. **6:** *God has wronged:* The Heb is more forceful, "has perverted" my justice; cf. Eccl. 7.13—exactly what the friends had denied in the first round (esp. 8.3). *Siege works:* Job elaborates the image of God as military commander that he had introduced before (16.12–14); he extends the image in v. 12. **7:** Job draws on Jer. 20.8. **8:** Job draws on

10 He tears down every part of me; I perish;
He uproots my hope like a tree.
11 He kindles His anger against me;
He regards me as one of His foes.
12 His troops advance together;
They build their road toward me
And encamp around my tent.
13 He alienated my kin from me;
My acquaintances disown me.
14 My relatives are gone;
My friends have forgotten me.
15 My dependents and maidservants regard me as a stranger;
I am an outsider to them.
16 I summon my servant but he does not respond;
I must myself entreat him.
17 My odor is repulsive to my wife;
I am loathsome to my children.
18 Even youngsters disdain me;
When I rise, they speak against me.
19 All my bosom friends detest me;
Those I love have turned against me.
20 My bones stick to my skin and flesh;
I escape with the skin of my teeth.

21 Pity me, pity me! You are my friends;
For the hand of God has struck me!
22 Why do you pursue me like God,
[a]-Maligning me insatiably?-[a]
23 O that my words were written down;
Would they were inscribed in a record,
24 Incised on a rock forever
With iron stylus and lead!
25 But I know that my Vindicator lives;
In the end He will testify on earth—
26 This, after my skin will have been peeled off.
But I would behold God while still in my flesh,
27 I myself, not another, would behold Him;
Would see with my own eyes:
My heart[b] pines within me.
28 You say, "How do we persecute him?
The root of the matter is in him."[c]

a-a Lit. "You are not satisfied with my flesh." *b Lit. "kidneys."*
c With many mss. and versions; printed editions, "me."

Hos. 2.8. **10:** A tree cannot rejuvenate (see 14.7) if it is *uproot*ed. Job harks back to his hopelessness (17.15–16). **11:** Job reiterates his contention of 13.24, but uses a different word for "enemy" for the sake of wordplay ("tsar" sounds like "zar," used three times in three different senses in vv. 13 ["disown"], 15 ["stranger"], and 17 ["repulsive"]). **13:** *Disown,* rather, "withdraw from me," in keeping with *alienated,* which is more precisely, "removed far away from me." The motif of being alienated is a widespread individual complaint; e.g., Pss. 31.12; 88.9, 19. **14:** *Are gone,* more precisely, "stay away." *Forgotten,* or "reject." **16:** Job's servant, like God, refuses to respond. *I must . . . ,* better, "even when I entreat him." **17:** Job's *children* have died (1.18–19), suggesting that the poem and narrative framework have different sources (see intro.). The phrase, lit. "sons of my womb," refers in Job (see 3.10) to those who came from the same womb, his siblings. **18:** *Youngsters,* "urchins"; the term is homonymous with "wicked man" in 16.11. Cf. 30.1. **20:** Being so dejected, Job cannot eat and becomes so thin that his bones show through his skin (see Ps. 102.6). *I escape:* The root is more likely the Semitic term for "cement"—Job's jaws are cemented together, preventing normal speech. The same symptoms and many others figure in the complaints of the Babylonian sufferer ("Let Me Praise the Lord of Wisdom"). This is a literary conceit, since Job continues his eloquent discourse. **21:** *Hand of God,* an affliction, understood as divine in origin; e.g., 1 Sam. 6.9; Ruth 1.13. **22:** *Pursue,* cf. 13.25. To eat a person's flesh is a Semitic expression for defamation; e.g., Ps. 27.2; Dan. 3.8. **23:** *In a record,* there is likely a double entendre: "in bronze" (from Babylonian). **24:** *On a rock,* possibly an allusion to the huge and highly visible Behistun inscription of Darius of Persia (late 6th c. BCE), inscribed on a cliff overlooking a road. Cf. Jer. 17.1; Ps. 102.19. **25:** Classical Christianity interprets this v. to refer to salvation after death, but Job insists on a divine hearing in his lifetime; cf. 16.19–22. *Testify,* lit. "arise"; see e.g., Deut. 19.15. *Vindicator,* Heb "go'el," "redeemer," the person, usually a relative, who stood up for his kinsman's rights; the word is also used of God in His relationship with Israel.

29 Be in fear of the sword,
For [your] fury is iniquity worthy of the sword;
Know there is a judgment!

20

Zophar the Naamathite said in reply:
2 In truth, my thoughts urge me to answer
(It is because of my feelings
3 When I hear reproof that insults me);
A spirit out of my understanding makes me reply:
4 Do you not know this, that from time
immemorial,
Since man was set on earth,
5 The joy of the wicked has been brief,
The happiness of the impious, fleeting?
6 Though he grows as high as the sky,
His head reaching the clouds,
7 He perishes forever, like his dung;
Those who saw him will say, "Where is he?"
8 He flies away like a dream and cannot be found;
He is banished like a night vision.
9 Eyes that glimpsed him do so no more;
They cannot see him in his place any longer.
10 His sons ingratiate themselves with the poor;
His own hands must give back his wealth.
11 His bones, still full of vigor,
Lie down in the dust with him.
12 Though evil is sweet to his taste,
And he conceals it under his tongue;
13 Though he saves it, does not let it go,
Holds it inside his mouth,
14 His food in his bowels turns
Into asps' venom within him.
15 The riches he swallows he vomits;
God empties it out of his stomach.
16 He sucks the poison of asps;
The tongue of the viper kills him.
17 Let him not enjoy the streams,
The rivers of honey, the brooks of cream.
18 He will give back the goods unswallowed;
The value of the riches, undigested.

29: Rather than cautioning Job that if he does not maintain his erstwhile piety, disaster will befall him, the testy companions should themselves worry about disasters such as the *sword* and "demons" (reading "shedin," with Luzzatto and others, for *judgment,* "shadin")—two of the calamities against which Eliphaz had warned (5.19–23 n.).

20.1–29: Zophar picks up the defense of the principle of just retribution. He argues, like Eliphaz and Bildad before him, that the wicked get their just deserts. After a brief introduction (vv. 2–4), he develops the theme in three parts, richly depicted in images: the happiness of the wicked does not last (vv. 5–9); the wicked will not be able to hold on to their ill-gotten gain (vv. 10–15); and God will inflict one or another of several calamitous fates on him (vv. 16–28). The entire discourse is presented as traditional wisdom (v. 4). **2–3:** Zophar's address to Job echoes Job's opening in 19.2–3. **3:** *Insults,* the same term as "humiliate" in 19.3 (see n.). *Spirit,* perhaps an allusion to the "spirit" that spoke to Job in 4.12–21; see 4.12–21 n. **5:** Cf. Ps. 37.2. **6:** *He grows,* better, "His haughtiness *grows.*" **7:** The wicked will be brought down from the heights to the depths; cf. e.g., Isa. 13.11; Ps. 147.6. **8:** *Dream,* cf. Isa. 29.8. *Night vision,* possibly a counterclaim against Job's contention to have experienced one (4.13). **9:** *They ... his place,* i.e., the people of his place, will *see him* no more. Zophar uses the language of Job in 7.8, 10; and cf. 8.18. **10:** *Ingratiate:* The ancient translations (and cf. Rashi and many others) parse the verb from the root "r-ts-ts," "to smash, crush," in which case the sense would be: "the poor (who had been exploited by the wicked) will crush the (wicked's) children," until the wicked pays them back. In the light of vv. 19–20, this fate would be measure-for-measure. **12–14:** Zophar begins a conceit that continues in the following vv. as well: the ill-gotten gain of the wicked is food—the wicked will not be able to retain it but will have to return it. **15:** This v. makes clear that it is *God* (and not chance) who maintains the moral equilibrium. *Empties,* lit. "dispossesses"; the v. mixes metaphorical and literal language; see 7.6 n. **16–17:** As Ibn Ezra points out, the contrast between snake venom and flowing *honey* and *cream* evokes images from Deut. 32.13 and 33. **18:** *Undigested,* or "he will not enjoy" the wealth he must return.

19 Because he crushed and tortured the poor,
He will not build up the house he took by force.
20 He will not see his children tranquil;
He will not preserve one of his dear ones.[a]
21 With no survivor to enjoy it,
His fortune will not prosper.
22 When he has all he wants, trouble will come;
Misfortunes of all kinds will batter him.
23 Let that fill his belly;
Let Him loose His burning anger at him,
And rain down His weapons upon him.
24 Fleeing from iron arrows,
He is shot through from a bow of bronze.
25 Brandished and run through his body,
The blade, through his gall,
Strikes terror into him.
26 Utter darkness waits for his treasured ones;
A fire fanned by no man will consume him;
Who survives in his tent will be crushed.
27 Heaven will expose his iniquity;
Earth will rise up against him.
28 His household will be cast forth by a flood,
Spilled out on the day of His wrath.
29 This is the wicked man's portion from God,
The lot God has ordained for him.

21 Job said in reply:

2 Listen well to what I say,
And let that be your consolation.
3 Bear with me while I speak,
And after I have spoken, you may mock.
4 Is my complaint directed toward a man?
Why should I not lose my patience?
5 Look at me and be appalled,
And clap your hand to your mouth.
6 When I think of it I am terrified;
My body is seized with shuddering.

7 Why do the wicked live on,
Prosper and grow wealthy?
8 Their children are with them always,
And they see their children's children.

a *For this meaning of* beṭen *and* ḥamud, *cf. Hos. 9.16.*

19–20: See v. 10 n. **19:** *Tortured:* This translation of "ʿazav" is not tenable. Samuel ben Nissim Masnut (13th c. Syria) compares a rabbinic term for "roof" ("ʿazivah")—"*because he crushed* the roof of *the poor.*" Alternatively, possibly related to "wares" ("ʿizzavon," several times in Ezek. ch 27)—"*because he crushed* the wares of *the poor.*" **20:** More likely, "because his belly knows no rest, he will not save (himself) with the wealth he holds dear"; cf. Ps. 39.12. **22:** *Misfortunes of all kinds,* rather, "he will be beset by the hand of everyone who suffers"—measure-for-measure (cf. vv. 10, 19–20 above). **23:** But if the wicked does manage to satisfy his desires, God will take violent action against him. **24:** *Iron arrows,* rather, "a weapon of iron," most likely a sword (see v. 25). *He is shot through,* rather, if he escapes from the thrust of a sword, the sword "will be replaced," namely followed by *a bow of bronze,* the arrows of which can reach a person *fleeing.* **25:** God "thrusts" (rather than *brandishes*) the "lightning" *blade* of a sword; cf. Deut. 32.41. **26:** *Treasured ones,* probably his family (see Ps. 83.4) but possibly his possessions; cf. Ps. 17.14. *Who survives,* possibly here and in v. 21 above the reference is to possessions that survive. **28:** *Will be cast forth,* more precisely, *a flood* will "wash away" *his household* (or house). "Wash away" ("yigel") puns on "will expose" ("yegalu") in v. 27. *Spilled out,* more likely, "an inundation."

21.1–34: Job again begs his companions to listen (cf. 13.5–6) and to appreciate the grief that impels him to speak so bitterly (cf. 7.11). Now he responds to the subject of the fate of the wicked, raised by each of his companions in round two, and mounts a counter-argument, based not on conventional wisdom but on empirical observation—just ask the man in the street (see v. 29): the wicked thrive because God allows it (e.g., vv. 9, 17, 19, 21). This theme was earlier adumbrated by Jeremiah (12.2–3) and Habakkuk (ch 1). **4:** Cf. 13.3. Job feels his friends should not be taking God's side (13.7–8), and he is frustrated that he receives no response from God (David Altschuller, 18th c.). **5:** "Placing" (not *clapping*) the *hand to your mouth* signifies a readiness to listen (so Rashbam; and see 40.4). **6:** Job is distressed both mentally and physically. **8–9:** Ironically, this picks up on the earlier promise of Eliphaz that Job would have many descendants and a secure homestead should he remain pious (5.24–26). **10–11:** The wicked enjoy those things that Job has lost (1.13–19). **13:** *In peace,* so Rashi. The translators read "roga‘" ("rest," "repose") for "rega‘" "in a moment." **14:** The wording is the opposite of the righteous attitude; see Isa. 58.2. **16:** Job seems to be saying that the prosperity of the wicked is *not their own doing* but God's—because He tolerates them (v. 17). *Beyond me,* more likely, a pious scribal correction for "remote from Him"—God pays no mind to the schemes of the wicked. **17:** A direct denial of the proverbial claim made by Bildad (18.5–6). *Apportion [their] lot,* or, "disseminate ruin" (to the wicked). **18:** Probably also governed by "How seldom" (v. 17). The tradition teaches that the wicked will be blown away like *chaff* (see Ps. 1.4), but they rarely are. **19:** Probably not a quotation (there are no indicators of such) but an injustice cited by Job: God suspends the "misfortune" due the wicked and metes it out later to his presumably innocent children. The switch from the plural to a singular wicked person is not unusual in Job. **20:** *Wrath,* the primary meaning is "venom"; Job is countering Zophar in 20.14, 16. **21:** Sequel to the thought of v. 19. **22:** The sense may be: because God *judges* from high in the clouds (see 22.12–14), He does not teach *knowledge* to the wicked. **23–26:** An embellishment of Job's point in 9.22 (see n.). **27:** *Devise,* reading "tahmosu" with "he" (a root known from Aram.) rather than "ḥet." **28–33:** *The great man,* ordinarily a term for a benefactor, here it may denote the wealthy wicked who exploits the poor (see 20.19; so Ibn Ezra). The implication is that the friends claim that the wicked's tent collapses (see, e.g., 8.13–15; 15.28; 18.14–15; 20.26); but if you would ask *wayfarers* (v. 29), they will attest to a different set of facts (vv. 30–33): The wicked person enjoys a good life and an honorable burial.

9 Their homes are secure, without fear;
They do not feel the rod of God.
10 Their bull breeds and does not fail;
Their cow calves and never miscarries;
11 They let their infants run loose like sheep,
And their children skip about.
12 They sing to the music of timbrel and lute,
And revel to the tune of the pipe;
13 They spend their days in happiness,
And go down to Sheol in peace.
14 They say to God, "Leave us alone,
We do not want to learn Your ways;
15 What is Shaddai that we should serve Him?
What will we gain by praying to Him?"
16 Their happiness is not their own doing.
(The thoughts of the wicked are beyond me!)
17 How seldom does the lamp of the wicked fail,
Does the calamity they deserve befall them,
Does He apportion [their] lot in anger!
18 Let them become like straw in the wind,
Like chaff carried off by a storm.
19 [You say,] "God is reserving his punishment for his sons";
Let it be paid back to him that he may feel it,
20 Let his eyes see his ruin,
And let him drink the wrath of Shaddai!
21 For what does he care about the fate of his family,
When his number of months runs out?
22 Can God be instructed in knowledge,
He who judges from such heights?
23 One man dies in robust health,
All tranquil and untroubled;
24 His pails are full of milk;
The marrow of his bones is juicy.
25 Another dies embittered,
Never having tasted happiness.
26 They both lie in the dust
And are covered with worms.

27 Oh, I know your thoughts,
And the tactics you will devise against me.
28 You will say, "Where is the house of the great man—
And where the tent in which the wicked dwelled?"
29 You must have consulted the wayfarers;
You cannot deny their evidence.
30 For the evil man is spared on the day of calamity,
On the day when wrath is led forth.

31 Who will upbraid him to his face?
Who will requite him for what he has done?
32 He is brought to the grave,
While a watch is kept at his tomb.
33 The clods of the wadi are sweet to him,
Everyone follows behind him,
Innumerable are those who precede him.
34 Why then do you offer me empty consolation?
Of your replies only the perfidy remains.

22 Eliphaz the Temanite said in reply:

2 Can a man be of use to God,
A wise man benefit Him?
3 Does Shaddai gain if you are righteous?
Does He profit if your conduct is blameless?
4 Is it because of your piety that He arraigns you,
And enters into judgment with you?
5 You know that your wickedness is great,
And that your iniquities have no limit.
6 You exact pledges from your fellows without reason,
And leave them naked, stripped of their clothes;
7 You do not give the thirsty water to drink;
You deny bread to the hungry.
8 The land belongs to the strong;
The privileged occupy it.
9 You have sent away widows empty-handed;
The strength of the fatherless is broken.
10 Therefore snares are all around you,
And sudden terrors frighten you,
11 Or darkness, so you cannot see;
A flood of waters covers you.

12 God is in the heavenly heights;
See the highest stars, how lofty!
13 You say, "What can God know?
Can He govern through the dense cloud?
14 The clouds screen Him so He cannot see
As He moves about the circuit of heaven."
15 Have you observed the immemorial path
That evil men have trodden;

33: *Are sweet,* or "cling." **34:** *Of your replies,* rather, "and your responses remain useless" (read "ʿamal" ["useless"] for "maʿal" *[perfidy];* see 16.2).

22.1–30: Eliphaz opens the third cycle of dialogue in three parts. In the first (vv. 2–11) he mocks Job's desire to litigate with God. In the second (vv. 12–20) he counters Job's argument that God is too remote from earth to notice what goes on among the wicked. In the third (vv. 21–30) he urges Job to return to God in piety, assuring him that, as a just Deity, He will bless him again. Eliphaz here elaborates the appeals that he and Zophar made in the first cycle (esp. 11.13–19). **2–11:** Eliphaz assumes (after the first round) that God is afflicting Job for a reason, and explains that He has no reason to engage in a courtroom debate with Job. In v. 4 Eliphaz adopts Job's position that God has *arraigned* Job, and in vv. 5–11 he offers a hyperbolic parody of the bill of indictment that Job imagines God has issued against him (so n. H. Tur-Sinai). The extreme charges against Job are not accusations made by Eliphaz, as most commentators assume, but are those that Job imputes to God, and Eliphaz is mocking them tongue in cheek. *The land belongs to the strong,* v. 8, could not be the words of the pious Eliphaz; it is a parody of Job's caustic remark in 9.24. Vv. 5–11 should therefore be surrounded by quotation marks. (Quotation marks did not exist in antiquity, and one of the most difficult issues in Job is understanding when the protagonists are quoting ancient sayings, or each other, and in the latter case, if these are real quotations or pseudo- or mock quotations.) Job will deny these mock charges and other potential challenges to his integrity in chs 29 and 31. Eliphaz thinks of himself as pious, but later Jewish tradition (e.g., *Shulhan Arukh,* Hoshen Ha-Mishpat, 228:4) forbids blaming a person's suffering for his own sins. **5:** In contrast to his first, tentative speech, here Eliphaz directly impugns Job's justice; see 2–11 n. **8:** Cf. the Talmud (*b. Sanh.* 58b): "Land is given to none other than the powerful." **9:** This v. evokes a classic passage from the 13th c. Canaanite (Ugaritic) Epic of Kirta, in which an ailing king is accused of malfeasance by his elder son. **11:** *Flood of waters,* or "a thundercloud." **13–14:** Eliphaz is parodying Job in 3.23 (see n.) and 21.22. **15–20:** Eliphaz revisits the arguments of all the companions in the second cycle that the wicked do receive their due. **15:** A revocalization of *immemorial* ("ʿolam") yields "evil men" ("ʿavilim," cf. 16.11),

16 How they were shriveled up before their time
And their foundation poured out like a river?
17 They said to God, “Leave us alone;
What can Shaddai do about it?”
18 But it was He who filled their houses with
good things.
(The thoughts of the wicked are beyond me!)
19 The righteous, seeing it,[a] rejoiced;
The innocent laughed with scorn.
20 Surely their substance was destroyed,
And their remnant consumed by fire.

21 Be close to Him and wholehearted;
Good things will come to you thereby.
22 Accept instruction from His mouth;
Lay up His words in your heart.
23 If you return to Shaddai you will be restored,
If you banish iniquity from your tent;
24 If you regard treasure as dirt,
Ophir-gold as stones of the wadi,
25 And Shaddai be your treasure
And precious silver for you,
26 When you seek the favor of Shaddai,
And lift up your face to God,
27 You will pray to Him, and He will listen to you,
And you will pay your vows.
28 You will decree and it will be fulfilled,
And light will shine upon your affairs.
29 When others sink low, you will say it is pride;
For He saves the humble.
30 He will deliver the guilty;
He will be delivered through the cleanness of your
hands.

23

Job said in reply:

2 Today again my complaint is bitter;
[b-]My strength is spent[-b] on account of my groaning.
3 Would that I knew how to reach Him,
How to get to His dwelling-place.
4 I would set out my case before Him
And fill my mouth with arguments.
5 I would learn what answers He had for me
And know how He would reply to me.
6 Would He contend with me overbearingly?
Surely He would not accuse me!

yielding *Have you observed the path* “of the evil.” **16:** *Shriveled,* cf. Job’s complaint in 16.8. **17:** Echoing Job in 21.14–15. **18:** Echoing Job in 21.16 (see n.). **19:** Cf. Ps. 107.42. *With scorn,* the Heb adds “at them.” **23:** An echo of Zophar (11.14). **27:** Ancient petitionary prayer was typically accompanied by vowing—people did not make a request of God without promising a gift. See 1 Sam. 1.10–12, Jonah 2.10; Ps. 116.14, 18. **28:** *Light will shine,* contrast v. 11 above. **29:** The v. draws on wisdom as in Prov. 29.23. In view of the second clause, the verb in the first clause should probably be singular and the v. interpreted: when He (God) brings you low, you should say, “it is pride.” **30:** The term *guilty* is lit. “not innocent”; but the particle “not” (“ʾiy”) is postbiblical and so could not be original here; furthermore the sense is difficult, for God punishes rather than *delivers the guilty!* Probably, a letter has fallen out; read: “an innocent man (“ʾish”; supplying a shin)” (with Ibn Janah, 11th c.). *He will be delivered,* more likely, “you *will be delivered.*”

23.1–24.25: Job responds at length to two contentions of Eliphaz: that there is no point in litigating with God (22.2–11) and that He watches and punishes the wicked (22.12–20). In ch 23 Job reiterates his desire to seek justice from the Deity, in spite of His being remote and intimidating; and in ch 24 Job describes how God lets the wicked get away with their crimes, provoking him to curse them (vv. 18–24). **23.2:** *Today again,* even after listening to your appeal. Cf. 10.1. **3–7:** If Job could reach God in His own realm, he believes He would need to deal with him justly. Cf. 13.18–14.3.

a Referring to v. 16. b-b Lit. “My hand is heavy.”

7 There the upright would be cleared by Him,
And I would escape forever from my judge.

8 But if I go East—He is not there;
West—I still do not perceive Him;
9 North—since He is concealed, I do not behold Him;
South—He is hidden, and I cannot see Him.
10 But He knows the way I take;
Would He assay me, I should emerge pure as gold.
11 I have followed in His tracks,
Kept His way without swerving,
12 I have not deviated from what His lips commanded;
I have treasured His words more than my daily bread.
13 He is one; who can dissuade Him?
Whatever He desires, He does.
14 For He will bring my term to an end,
But He has many more such at His disposal.
15 Therefore I am terrified at His presence;
When I consider, I dread Him.
16 God has made me fainthearted;
Shaddai has terrified me.
17 Yet I am not cut off by the darkness;
He has concealed the thick gloom from me.

24

Why are times for judgment not reserved by Shaddai?
Even those close to Him cannot foresee His actions.[a]
2 People remove boundary-stones;
They carry off flocks and pasture them;
3 They lead away the donkeys of the fatherless,
And seize the widow's bull as a pledge;
4 They chase the needy off the roads;
All the poor of the land are forced into hiding.
5 Like the wild asses of the wilderness,
They go about their tasks, seeking food;
The wilderness provides each with food for his lads;
6 They harvest fodder in the field,
And glean the late grapes in the vineyards of the wicked.
7 They pass the night naked for lack of clothing,
They have no covering against the cold;
8 They are drenched by the mountain rains,
And huddle against the rock for lack of shelter.
9[b] They snatch the fatherless infant from the breast,
And seize the child of the poor as a pledge.

a *Lit. "days."* *b* *This verse belongs to the description of the wicked in vv. 2–4a.*

7: See 9.15 n. **8–9:** Contrast Ps. 139.7–10; while that psalmist asserts he cannot avoid God, Job laments he cannot find Him. **10:** *But He knows,* or, "if He would know." **12:** *Have not deviated,* rather, "have not neglected." *More than ...,* more likely, revocalize and read with the LXX and Latin translations: "in my bosom"; cf. 10.13. **13:** *He is one* (Heb "ve'eḥad"). A scribal error for "If He has chosen" ("vaḥar"; cf. Ps. 132.13). **14:** *My term,* rather, "my allotment" of afflictions. **17:** More likely, "*I am not cut off* from *the darkness; thick gloom* covers (all) that is before *me*"—cf. 22.11.

24.1–16: The wrongs people do to each other are lamented in many works of ancient Near Eastern wisdom, such as "The Tale of the Eloquent Peasant," and "The Admonitions of Ipu-Wer," from Egypt, and "The Babylonian Theodicy." **1:** *For judgment,* added by the translation by inference. Job may allude to Deut. 32.34–35, in which case the "days" that cannot be *foreseen* are those of doom for the wicked. The "Day of the LORD" is a frequent prophetic image of retribution. **2:** Cf. Deut. 19.14; Prov. 22.28; 23.10. The subject *(People)* is not explicit, although from context the wicked are intended. Perhaps the antecedent is in v. 1, reading "evil ones" ("we-ra'im"; cf. e.g., Prov. 4.14) for the graphically similar "those close to Him." **3:** See Deut. 24.6. **4–11:** The poor are driven to misery and desperate acts. **5:** *Provides,* lacking in the Heb; the line is difficult. **6:** *Fodder* (Heb "blylw"): The poor seek food, not fodder for animals. When the word is divided, the line reads: *they harvest* "in a field not his" ("bly lw," so Ibn Ezra and see 18.15).

10–11: The poor overcome hunger and thirst by taking on menial jobs. **11:** *Between* [their] *rows:* There is no antecedent; divide the first three words into two, and read perhaps: "as the olives drop" ("binshor zeitim"). **14–17:** Criminals operate under cover of darkness. For them, night is day; cf. 38.15. **14–15:** Violating the sixth, seventh, and eighth statements of the Decalogue; cf. Hos. 4.2. **15:** See Prov. 7.9. **16:** Cf. Exod. 22.1. **20:** *The womb,* apparently, his own mother. *May he be sweet,* or "may the *worm* stick to him," referring to death; cf. 17.14. *Wrongdoers,* more precisely, "corruption." **21:** *Leave his widow,* or "(he will consort with) a widow and produce no good" (i.e., offspring). **23–24:** If this is still part of the curse: may God let the wicked feel secure until He suddenly brings them down.

10 They go about naked for lack of clothing,
And, hungry, carry sheaves;
11 Between rows [of olive trees] they make oil,
And, thirsty, they tread the winepresses.
12 Men groan in the city;
The souls of the dying cry out;
Yet God does not regard it as a reproach.

13 They are rebels against the light;
They are strangers to its ways,
And do not stay in its path.
14 The murderer arises [a]in the evening[a]
To kill the poor and needy,
And at night he acts the thief.
15 The eyes of the adulterer watch for twilight,
Thinking, "No one will glimpse me then."
He masks his face.
16 In the dark they break into houses;
By day they shut themselves in;
They do not know the light.
17 For all of them morning is darkness;
It is then that they discern the terror of darkness.
18[b] May they be flotsam on the face of the water;
May their portion in the land be cursed;
May none turn aside by way of their vineyards.
19 May drought and heat snatch away their snow waters,
And Sheol, those who have sinned.
20 May the womb forget him;
May he be sweet to the worms;
May he be no longer remembered;
May wrongdoers be broken like a tree.
21 May he consort with a barren woman who bears no child,
Leave his widow deprived of good.
22 Though he has the strength to seize bulls,
May he live with no assurance of survival.
23 Yet [God] gives him the security on which he relies,
And keeps watch over his affairs.
24 Exalted for a while, let them be gone;
Be brought low, and shrivel like mallows,
And wither like the heads of grain.

25 Surely no one can confute me,
Or prove that I am wrong.

a-a *Cf. Mishnaic Heb.* ʿor, *Aramaic* ʿorta, *"evening"; others "with the light."*
b *From here to the end of the chapter the translation is largely conjectural.*

25 Bildad the Shuhite said in reply:

2 Dominion and dread are His;
He imposes peace in His heights.
3 Can His troops be numbered?
On whom does His light not shine?
4 How can man be in the right before God?
How can one born of woman be cleared of guilt?
5 Even the moon is not bright,
And the stars are not pure in His sight.
6 How much less man, a worm,
The son-of-man, a maggot.

26 Then Job said in reply:

2 You would help without having the strength;
You would deliver with arms that have no power.
3 Without having the wisdom, you offer advice
And freely give your counsel.
4 To whom have you addressed words?
Whose breath issued from you?

5 The shades tremble
Beneath the waters and their denizens.
6 Sheol is naked before Him;
Abaddon has no cover.
7 He it is who stretched out Zaphon[a] over chaos,
Who suspended earth over emptiness.
8 He wrapped up the waters in His clouds;
Yet no cloud burst under their weight.
9 [b-]He shuts off the view of His throne,
Spreading His cloud over it.[-b]
10 He drew a boundary on the surface of the waters,
At the extreme where light and darkness meet.

a Used for heaven; cf. Isa. 14.13; Ps. 48.3. *b-b Meaning of Heb. uncertain.*

25.1–26.14: Speech from Bildad. Ch 25—only six vv. long—is attributed to Bildad, but it is very short. Most modern commentators realize that in chs 25–28 there is some textual disorder; parts of one ch belong with parts of another and some material may have been lost. In addition to the overly short final speech of Bildad in ch 25, ch 26, attributed to Job (but more probably by Bildad), is also short; 26.2–4 are addressed to an individual, but Job always addresses his companions in the plural; 25.4–6 are a parody of the words of the rogue spirit (4.17–19; cf. 15.14–16), which means a mockery of Job (see at 4.12–21 and at 15.13); 26.5–14 describe the Deity's prowess in creating and dominating the world; in the present text Job's discourse is peculiarly divided into two sections (ch 26 and ch 27). To account for these facts, the third speech of Bildad may be provisionally reconstructed as 26.2–4, introducing a (parodic) quotation: 25.4–6; 25.2–3, the beginning of the doxology; 26.5–14, the continuation of the doxology. The annotations will follow the arrangement of the Heb text, but the interpretations follow the reconstructed sequence (where chs 25–26 are both by Bildad). Job's discourse is now incomplete, and found in 27.2–7 (see 27.1–23 n.). **25.2–3:** Bildad may be responding to Job's claim that God's remoteness from the world in the heavens is negative, preventing him from maintaining a just order (3.23; 21.22; cf. 22.13–14). Bildad, like Eliphaz (22.12), regards God's loftiness as the best vantage from which to govern all creation. **3:** *His troops,* the stars; cf. Isa. 40.26. *His light,* Bildad counters Job's claim that God ignores the "rebels against the light" (24.13). **4–6:** Bildad's mockery of the spirit's message is even more extreme than Eliphaz's (22.5–11). The spirit had imaged human beings as those who live in clay houses (4.19); Bildad turns the metaphor into the literal: if they live in dirt, they are worms (v. 6)!

26.2–4: Bildad's opening address to Job (see 25.1–26.14 n.). V. 4 introduces a quotation (cf. at 8.10 and 15.13)—the parody of the spirit's discourse in 25.4–6. **4:** *Whose breath:* Bildad challenges Job's claim to be quoting a divine spirit in 4.17–21. **5–14:** The continuation of 25.2–3 (see 25.1–26.14 n.). Having established God's preeminent position in creation, Bildad specifies some features of that creation, drawing on the Canaanite and Israelite myths of how God as storm-god vanquished the sea (cf. 7.12 n.), created the world, and established His dominion; cf. e.g., Ps. 74.13–17. **5:** *Shades,* of the dead; contrast the tranquil state of the dead imagined by Job in 3.13–19. **6:** God sees through the earth all the way down to the netherworld. **9:** *His throne,* rather, slightly revocalized, "the full moon" (e.g., Ps. 81.4). The storm god's cloud is thick enough to block the light of a full moon, just as it is strong enough to hold all the rainwater (v. 8). The conventional Jewish reading is that *throne* (ordinarily spelled differently in the Heb) refers to the heavens (see e.g., Ps. 103.19). **10:** Cf. Prov. 8.27.

11 The pillars of heaven tremble,
Astounded at His blast.
12 By His power He stilled the sea;
By His skill He struck down Rahab.
13 By His wind the heavens were calmed;
His hand pierced the [a]Elusive Serpent.[a]
14 These are but glimpses of His rule,
The mere whisper that we perceive of Him;
Who can absorb the thunder of His mighty deeds?

27 Job again took up his theme and said:

2 By God who has deprived me of justice!
By Shaddai who has embittered my life!
3 As long as there is life in me,
And God's breath is in my nostrils,
4 My lips will speak no wrong,
Nor my tongue utter deceit.
5 Far be it from me to say you are right;
Until I die I will maintain my integrity.
6 I persist in my righteousness and will not yield;
[b]I shall be free of reproach[b] as long as I live.

7 May my enemy be as the wicked;
My assailant, as the wrongdoer.
8 For what hope has the impious man when he is cut down,
When God takes away his life?
9 Will God hear his cry
When trouble comes upon him,
10 When he seeks the favor of Shaddai,
Calls upon God at all times?
11 I will teach you what is in God's power,
And what is with Shaddai I will not conceal.
12 All of you have seen it,
So why talk nonsense?
13 This is the evil man's portion from God,
The lot that the ruthless receive from Shaddai:
14 Should he have many sons—they are marked for the sword;
His descendants will never have their fill of bread;
15 Those who survive him will be buried in a plague,
And their widows will not weep;
16 Should he pile up silver like dust,
Lay up clothing like dirt—

a-a Cf. Isa. 27.1. *b-b Meaning of Heb. uncertain.*

11: Cf. 9.6. **12:** *Stilled,* the verb ("raga'") ironically has the opposite meaning as well (Isa. 51.15). *Rahab,* see 9.13 translators' note. **13:** *The heavens were calmed,* the Heb cannot bear this sense. Many scholars divide the word *heavens* ("shamayim") and read: "He put Sea ("sam yam") in his net" (cf. Ps. 56.9 and probably Jer. 43.10), comparing the actions of the Babylonian god Marduk in *Enuma Elish.* **14:** *Absorb,* more precisely, "fathom."

27.1–23: Job's speech continues. This ch, attributed entirely to Job in the present translation, contains two thematically different sections, comprising the truncated discourse of Job (vv. 2–7) and the response of Zophar (vv. 8–23), who is otherwise not represented in the third cycle. Job forcefully reiterates his commitment to speak only truth, and Zophar, returning to the subject of his last discourse (ch 20) and of the speeches of Bildad (ch 18) and Eliphaz (22.15–20), counters Job's claims that the wicked prosper (ch 21) and escape punishment (ch 24). **1:** The odd introductory line is copied from 29.1. **2:** Cf. Ruth 1.20. **4:** Cf. 13.7. **5:** *Maintain my integrity,* cf. 2.3, 9. **6:** *Be free of reproach,* rather, "my heart (as an organ of speech; see 8.10 n.) has never blasphemed." **7:** Cf. e.g., 2 Sam. 18.32; Ps. 6.11.

27. 8: Response of Zophar. *When he is cut down,* cf. Job's death wish in 6.9. **11–12:** It is curious that the speaker addresses a plural audience. **13:** Cf. Zophar's conclusion in 20.29. **15:** *Widows,* cf. Ps. 78.64. **16:** For the phraseology cf. Zech. 9.3, and for the theme cf. Eccl. 6.1–2. Clothing was expensive in the ancient world and people had few garments.

17 He may lay it up, but the righteous will wear it,
And the innocent will share the silver.
18 The house he built is like a bird's nest,
Like the booth a watchman makes.
19 He lies down, a rich man, with [his wealth] intact;
When he opens his eyes it is gone.
20 Terror overtakes him like a flood;
A storm wind makes off with him by night.
21 The east wind carries him far away, and he is gone;
It sweeps him from his place.
22 Then it hurls itself at him without mercy;
He tries to escape from its force.
23 It claps its hands at him,
And whistles at him from its place.

28 There is a mine for silver,
And a place where gold is refined.
2 Iron is taken out of the earth,
And copper smelted from rock.
3 He sets bounds for darkness;
To every limit man probes,
To rocks in deepest darkness.
4 [a-]They open up a shaft far from where men live,
[In places] forgotten by wayfarers,
Destitute of men, far removed.[-a]
5 Earth, out of which food grows,
Is changed below as if into fire.
6 Its rocks are a source of sapphires;
It contains gold dust too.
7 No bird of prey knows the path to it;
The falcon's eye has not gazed upon it.
8 The proud beasts have not reached it;
The lion has not crossed it.
9 Man sets his hand against the flinty rock
And overturns mountains by the roots.
10 He carves out channels through rock;
His eyes behold every precious thing.
11 He dams up the sources of the streams
So that hidden things may be brought to light.

a-a Meaning of Heb. uncertain.

18: *Bird's nest,* an interpretation based on Arabic; alternatively, a cocoon or a spider's web (reading "'aqqabish" for "'ash"). In either case, the idea is that the structure is impermanent, like the *booth;* cf. 8.14–15. **20:** Cf. 20.28. **22:** Cf. 20.24. **23:** The east wind, personified, mocks him by its gestures (cf. Lam. 2.15) when he tries to flee its destructive force.

28.1–28: Conclusion of Elihu's speeches. The MT understands the dissertation on wisdom to be Job's; but its topic and style are discontinuous with ch 27. Most modern scholars regard the poem as self-contained and assign it to neither Job nor his friends. This is unlikely. It begins with "ki" ("for, because"), which typically connects to something preceding, and there is no antecedent for *He* in v. 3, which also suggests that something precedes. The motif of esoteric wisdom, which lies at the heart of the poem, conventionally describes it as beyond human reach—in the sky and under the earth; e.g., 11.7–8; Jer. 31.36; cf. Deut. 30.11–13. Here there is no reference to the sky; however, the end of Elihu's discourse in 37.21 refers to the sky; in addition, chs 28 and 37 share much vocabulary. Taking all this into consideration, and comparing 37.24 with 28.28, which both place a premium on awe/*fear* of God as the ultimate wisdom, it becomes clear that ch 28 is the misplaced conclusion of the Elihu speeches. (For other misplaced sections in Job, see 25.1–26.14 n.) The ch is structured by two questions about where wisdom might be found (vv. 12, 20). The riddle-like question is given a surprising answer in vv. 25–27. Having established that only God knows what is below the stratum where precious ore can be found (vv. 1–11), an excursus is presented on the idea that wisdom cannot be purchased with gold or precious stones (vv. 15–19). Most modern commentators think that the subject of vv. 3–11 is a miner, but there is not a single term relating to mining or digging in the entire passage. Traditional Jewish commentary correctly understands that the subject is God. **1:** *Mine,* the Heb has only "place of origin." **3:** *He,* the antecedents are the names of the Deity in 37.22–23 (see 28.1–28 n.). Cf. 12.22; Isa. 42.16—both said of God—and see 38.19–20. *Man probes,* the word for *man* is lacking; *probes* has God as its subject, as in Jer. 17.10; Pss. 44.22; 139.1, 23. **4:** *They* is lacking in Heb, rather, He (God) "bursts open a stream" (not *shaft*); cf. v. 10 below. **9:** *Overturns,* a divine activity; see 9.5. The word *man* is lacking. **10:** *He carves,* cf. Hab. 3.9; Pss. 74.15; 78.15; 114.8—all said of God. **11:** *Dams up,* more likely, "exposes" (reading

12 But where can wisdom be found;
Where is the source of understanding?
13 No man can set a value on it;
It cannot be found in the land of the living.
14 The deep says, "It is not in me";
The sea says, "I do not have it."
15 It cannot be bartered for gold;
Silver cannot be paid out as its price.
16 The finest gold of Ophir cannot be weighed against it,
Nor precious onyx, nor sapphire.
17 Gold or glass cannot match its value,
Nor vessels of fine gold be exchanged for it.
18 Coral and crystal cannot be mentioned with it;
A pouch of wisdom is better than rubies.
19 Topaz from Nubia cannot match its value;
Pure gold cannot be weighed against it.

20 But whence does wisdom come?
Where is the source of understanding?
21 It is hidden from the eyes of all living,
Concealed from the fowl of heaven.
22 Abaddon and Death say,
"We have only a report of it."
23 God understands the way to it;
He knows its source;
24 For He sees to the ends of the earth,
Observes all that is beneath the heavens.
25 When He fixed the weight of the winds,
Set the measure of the waters;
26 When He made a rule for the rain
And a course for the thunderstorms,
27 Then He saw it and gauged it;
He measured it and probed it.
28 He said to man,
"See! Fear of the Lord is wisdom;
To shun evil is understanding."

29

Job again took up his theme and said:

2 O that I were as in months gone by,
In the days when God watched over me,
3 When His lamp shone over my head,
When I walked in the dark by its light,
4 When I was in my prime,
When God's company graced my tent,

"ḥasap"); cf. 12.22. **13:** *Can set a value:* The context concerns finding wisdom, not assessing it; read with LXX and others: "knows the way to it" ("darkah") instead of *set a value on it* ("ʿerkah"); cf. v. 23. **14:** *Deep ... sea,* the subterranean ocean (e.g., Gen. 7.11; 49.25). The *Deep* is where the Mesopotamian god of wisdom Ea, and El, the wise head of the Canaanite pantheon, reside. **15–19:** A list of expensive and exotic metals and minerals. Wisdom cannot be obtained at any price. An elaboration of the motif in Prov. 3.14–15; 8.10–11. **16:** *Ophir,* cf. Isa. 13.12; Ps. 45.10. **18:** Cf. Prov. 8.11. **21:** Cf. vv. 7–8 above. **22:** *Abaddon* is a biblical term for the netherworld (e.g., 26.6). *Death* is the name of the Canaanite god of death and his dominion (e.g., 30.23). **25–27:** The secrets of divine wisdom are not found in a place but were revealed at a primordial time—when God created the world; cf. Prov. 8.22–31. **28:** By this definition of *wisdom,* Job is, or was, a true sage (1.1, 8; 2.3).

29.1–31.40: Job's lengthy final discourse (see 31.40) comprises five main parts. In the first (ch 29), a reverie, Job waxes nostalgic over his former life, when he was blessed with status and respect. In the the second (30.1–19) he laments the loss of his position and the public honor and acknowledgement that went with it. Moving from circumstances to cause, Job lays his miserable situation in protest before God (30.20–31). In the fourth and longest segment (31.1–34, 38–40) he takes an oath of innocence, swearing that he did not commit any number of offenses. Reminiscent of the assertions people make in the Egyptian Book of the Dead as they are judged upon entry to the afterlife, the oaths have a juridical function. By denying any possible charges of misconduct that God might hold against him, Job compels God to testify and support any and all charges He might be making; cf. e.g., Exod. 22.9–10. Job's purpose all along was to extract from God the accusations he assumes are being made against him (see 13.23). Job concludes (31.35–37) by reiterating his wish for a fair hearing. **29.2–6:** Job acknowledges that his good life was a blessing

5 When Shaddai was still with me,
When my lads surrounded me,
6 When my feet were bathed in cream,
And rocks poured out streams of oil for me.
7 When I passed through the city gates
To take my seat in the square,
8 Young men saw me and hid,
Elders rose and stood;
9 Nobles held back their words;
They clapped their hands to their mouths.
10 The voices of princes were hushed;
Their tongues stuck to their palates.
11 The ear that heard me acclaimed me;
The eye that saw, commended me.
12 For I saved the poor man who cried out,
The orphan who had none to help him.
13 I received the blessing of the lost;
I gladdened the heart of the widow.
14 I clothed myself in righteousness and it robed me;
Justice was my cloak and turban.
15 I was eyes to the blind
And feet to the lame.
16 I was a father to the needy,
And I looked into the case of the stranger.
17 I broke the jaws of the wrongdoer,
And I wrested prey from his teeth.
18 I thought I would end my days with my family,[a]
And [b-]be as long-lived as the phoenix,[-b]
19 My roots reaching water,
And dew lying on my branches;
20 My vigor refreshed,
My bow ever new in my hand.
21 Men would listen to me expectantly,
And wait for my counsel.
22 After I spoke they had nothing to say;
My words were as drops [of dew] upon them.
23 They waited for me as for rain,
For the late rain, their mouths open wide.
24 When I smiled at them, they would not believe it;
They never expected[c] a sign of my favor.
25 I decided their course and presided over them;
I lived like a king among his troops,
Like one who consoles mourners.

from God. **5:** *Lads,* servants (cf. 1.15–16). **6:** *Rocks,* rather, "the Rock," a metaphor for God (e.g., Deut. 32.4, 18, 31) and an allusion to the provision of water to the Israelites in the wilderness, depicted as "honey" and "oil" in Deut. 32.13b. **7–11:** The public recognition accorded to Job. People rose and fell silent in his presence. **9:** *Clapped,* cf. v. 22 below and see 21.5 n. **10:** *Their tongues stuck to their palates,* they uttered no sound; cf. Ps. 137.6; Lam. 4.4. **12–17:** Job protected the most vulnerable members of society, a significant theme of Israelite and ancient Near Eastern wisdom literature. **12:** Cf. Ps. 72.12. **14:** Cf. Isa. 61.10. **15:** *I was eyes:* The unique phrase may allude to another righteous gentile, Jethro (Num. 10.31). **16:** *Looked into the case:* Job has described himself as the local magistrate (vv. 7–17), who would insure justice for the powerless. By stigmatizing Job, God has not only done Job an injustice—He has prevented Job from executing justice. **17:** For the imagery of the wicked as predators, see 4.10–11 and elsewhere. **18:** *As the phoenix,* so Rashi and other commentators, drawing on a postbiblical term; but more likely, "(I thought) I would multiply days like the sand(s at the seashore)"; cf. e.g., Gen. 22.17. **21–23:** Job had hoped his friends would listen in silence and hang on his every word; see 13.5–6; 21.2–3. **22:** *Drops [of dew],* cf. Deut. 32.2. **24:** *They would not believe,* rather: "They would not deviate (lit. turn to the right [—or left])"; see 39.24; Isa. 30.21. *Never expected,* rather, "And at the shining of my face, they would uphold (lit. not allow to fall) [my word]"; see e.g., 1 Sam. 3.19. **25:** *Like one who consoles mourners,* more likely means something like: "wherever I lead them they camp."

a Lit. "nest." *b-b Others "multiply days like sand."*
c Taking yappilun *as from* pll; *cf. Gen. 48.11.*

30 But now those younger than I deride me,
[Men] whose fathers I would have disdained to
put among my sheep dogs.
2 Of what use to me is the strength of their hands?
All their vigor[a] is gone.
3 Wasted from want and starvation,
They flee to a parched land,
To the gloom of desolate wasteland.
4 They pluck saltwort and wormwood;
The roots of broom are their food.
5 Driven out [b-]from society,[-b]
They are cried at like a thief.
6 They live in the gullies of wadis,
In holes in the ground, and in rocks,
7 Braying among the bushes,
Huddling among the nettles,
8 Scoundrels, nobodies,
Stricken from the earth.

9 Now I am the butt of their gibes;
I have become a byword to them.
10 They abhor me; they keep their distance from me;
They do not withhold spittle from my face.
11 Because God[c] has disarmed[d] and humbled me,
They have thrown off restraint in my presence.
12 Mere striplings assail me at my right hand:
They put me to flight;
They build their roads for my ruin.
13 They tear up my path;
They promote my fall,
Although it does them no good.
14 They come as through a wide breach;
They roll in [b-]like raging billows.[-b]
15 Terror tumbles upon me;
It sweeps away my honor like the wind;
My dignity[e] vanishes like a cloud.
16 So now my life runs out;
Days of misery have taken hold of me.
17 By night my bones feel gnawed;
My sinews never rest.
18 [b-]With great effort I change clothing;
The neck of my tunic fits my waist.[-b]
19 He regarded me as clay,
I have become like dust and ashes.

30.1–8: Adding insult to injury, Job is berated by the lowest members of society. **1:** *Younger,* cf. 19.18. *Deride,* ironically, the same verb as "smiled" in 29.24. **2:** *All their vigor,* or, "on their account the harvest has perished"; see 5.26 n. **4:** *Are their food,* rather, "for their warmth" (see Isa. 47.14); the *broom* (or "juniper") bush is used for kindling (see Ps. 120.4). **8:** *Nobodies,* more precisely, "sons of nobodies." **9:** Cf. 17.6; Lam. 3.14. **11:** *Because God,* the first line is difficult, but the first verb *(disarmed)* is written ("ketiv") plural—"they ...." *Humbled,* more likely, a misread Arabic term for "bridle"—"they have loosened my bridle." **12:** Cf. 19.12. **14:** *As through ...*, or, "like a flood-burst." **15:** *My honor,* "my nobility"; cf. Isa. 32.5. **17:** The subject of *gnawed,* here an active verb in the singular, is "misery" in v. 16. **18:** *I change clothing,* in view of the parallel line that follows, "it seizes ("yitpos" for "tithapes") my robe violently." *Fits my waist,* rather, "constricts me." **19:** *He regarded,* more likely, "it has cast me down"; cf. Nah. 3.14. *Dust and ashes,* a figure for the wretched human condition; cf. Gen. 18.27; and see Job 42.6 n.

a *Meaning of Heb. uncertain.* b-b *Meaning of Heb. uncertain.*
c *Lit. "He."* d *Lit. "loosened my [bow] string."*
e *Heb.* yeshu'athi *taken as related to* shoa', *"noble."*

20 I cry out to You, but You do not answer me;
I wait, but You do [not] consider me.
21 You have become cruel to me;
With Your powerful hand You harass me.
22 You lift me up and mount me on the wind;
You make my courage melt.
23 I know You will bring me to death,
The house assigned for all the living.
24 [a]Surely He would not strike at a ruin
If, in calamity, one cried out to Him.[a]
25 Did I not weep for the unfortunate?
Did I not grieve for the needy?
26 I looked forward to good fortune, but evil came;
I hoped for light, but darkness came.
27 My bowels are in turmoil without respite;
Days of misery confront me.
28 I walk about in sunless gloom;
I rise in the assembly and cry out.
29 I have become a brother to jackals,
A companion to ostriches.
30 My skin, blackened, is peeling off me;
My bones are charred by the heat.
31 So my lyre is given over to mourning,
My pipe, to accompany weepers.

31 I have covenanted with my eyes
Not to gaze on a maiden.
2 What fate is decreed by God above?
What lot, by Shaddai in the heights?
3 Calamity is surely for the iniquitous;
Misfortune, for the worker of mischief.
4 Surely He observes my ways,
Takes account of my every step.

5 Have I walked with worthless men,
Or my feet hurried to deceit?
6 Let Him weigh me on the scale of righteousness;
Let God ascertain my integrity.
7 If my feet have strayed from their course,
My heart followed after my eyes,
And a stain sullied my hands,
8 May I sow, but another reap,
May the growth of my field be uprooted!
9 If my heart was ravished by the wife of my neighbor,
And I lay in wait at his door,
10 May my wife grind for another,

a-a Meaning of Heb. uncertain.

21: *Harass,* the same as "persecutes" in 16.9. **22:** The second line should probably read: "A surge (deriving "tushiya" from "sha'ah") overwhelms me." The word puns on *you lift me up* ("tisa'eni") of the preceding line. **23:** *Death,* the realm of the dead; cf. 28.22. *House assigned for all the living* becomes a Jewish term for a cemetery. **24:** *At a ruin,* more likely, read "at a poor person ("be'ani" instead of "be'i"); the term puns on "misery" ("'oni") in vv. 16 and 27. **25:** Because Job had shown compassion for the unfortunate, he expects providential care from God. **29:** Job lives in desolation with jackals and ostriches which inhabit the wasteland (e.g., Jer. 49.33); cf. Mic. 1.8. **30:** Cf. Lam. 4.8. **31:** Or *lyre* and *pipe* are metonyms for song—Job's cheerful song has turned to weeping; cf. the reverse in Ps. 30.12.

31.1–4: Job begins to review his righteous acts, which should have led to reward had God been observing his conduct—just as the sinful should suffer *misfortune* in Job's wishful thinking. Earlier, Job had seen divine surveillance as harassment (cf. 13.27). **4:** *Observes,* lit. "sees"—the proper response to Job who had "covenanted with [his] eyes" (v. 1). **5:** Job begins a series of oaths, swearing that he has not committed this and that transgression. *Worthless men,* rather, "falsity." **6:** *Scale of righteousness:* God should act according to the ethics He demands from people. **8:** Cf. the curses in Deut. 28.30, 33, 38–41. The penalty is measure-for-measure: if I take what belongs to another, may I be deprived of what belongs to me. **9:** Two of the most severe prohibitions in the Decalogue—adultery and murder. *Lay in wait* may imply a fatal ambush (Deut. 19.11). Another possible scenario: waiting for the husband to leave the house in order to sleep with the wife; cf. Prov. 7.6–22, where the faithless woman invites another man into her home when her husband is away. **10:** Traditional commentators follow the Talmud (*b. Sot.* 10a) and interpret *grind* and *kneel* to refer to sexual intercourse—which makes sense in context. **12:** *Consuming,* read perhaps "burn" ("tisrof" for "tesharesh," a difference of one letter). **13:** *Did I ever,* here and below, more precisely, "(I swear) I have not ..." **14:** *Arises,* like a witness in court; see at 19.25. **15:** *Make him,* referring to the servant in the singular. **16–17:** Job denies the charges imagined hyperbolically by Eliphaz in 22.7, 9. **18:** *He grew up,* the orphan (v. 17). Cf. Sir. 4.10. **19–20:** Job rebuts Eliphaz in 22.6. **21:** Job had never taken advantage of his judicial position, as does God, in Job's charges (see v. 23 and cf. 9.16–20; 13.20–21). **24–25:** Job distinguishes himself from the wicked who pursue only gain (e.g., 20.10, 15, 18–19). **26–27:** Though not an Israelite, Job is a monotheist who renounces worship of the *moon* and stars (see the use of the verb "shine" in Isa. 13.10 and cf. Isa. 14.12). Cf. Deut. 4.19. The *kiss* is a gesture of worship. **29:** *Thrill,* reading "hitroʿaʿti," "to jubilate" (Pss. 60.10; 65.14) for "hitʿorarti." Prov. (17.5; 24.17) denounces rejoicing at another's downfall.

May others kneel over her!
11 For that would have been debauchery,
A criminal offense,
12 A fire burning down to Abaddon,
Consuming the roots of all my increase.
13 Did I ever brush aside the case of my servants, man or maid,
When they made a complaint against me?
14 What then should I do when God arises;
When He calls me to account, what should I answer Him?
15 Did not He who made me in my mother's belly make him?
Did not One form us both in the womb?
16 Did I deny the poor their needs,
Or let a[a] widow pine away,
17 By eating my food alone,
The fatherless not eating of it also?
18 Why, from my youth he grew up with me as though I were his father;
Since I left my mother's womb I was her[b] guide.
19 I never saw an unclad wretch,
A needy man without clothing,
20 Whose loins did not bless me
As he warmed himself with the shearings of my sheep.
21 If I raised my hand against the fatherless,
Looking to my supporters in the gate,
22 May my arm drop off my shoulder;
My forearm break off [c]at the elbow.[-c]
23 For I am in dread of God-sent calamity;
I cannot bear His threat.
24 Did I put my reliance on gold,
Or regard fine gold as my bulwark?
25 Did I rejoice in my great wealth,
In having attained plenty?
26 If ever I saw the light shining,
The moon on its course in full glory,
27 And I secretly succumbed,
And my hand touched my mouth in a kiss,
28 That, too, would have been a criminal offense,
For I would have denied God above.
29 Did I rejoice over my enemy's misfortune?
Did I thrill because evil befell him?
30 I never let my mouth[d] sin
By wishing his death in a curse.

a Lit. "the eyes of a." *b Viz., the widow's.*
c-c Lit. "from its shaft," i.e., the humerus. *d Lit. "palate."*

31 (Indeed, the men of my clan said,
"We would consume his flesh insatiably!")
32 No sojourner spent the night in the open;
I opened my doors to the road.
33 Did I hide my transgressions like Adam,
Bury my wrongdoing in my bosom,
34 That I should [now] fear the great multitude,
And am shattered by the contempt of families,
So that I keep silent and do not step outdoors?

35 O that I had someone to give me a hearing;
O that Shaddai would reply to my writ,
Or my accuser draw up a true bill!
36 I would carry it on my shoulder;
Tie it around me for a wreath.
37 I would give him an account of my steps,
Offer it as to a commander.

38 If my land cries out against me,
Its furrows weep together;
39 If I have eaten its produce without payment,
And made its [rightful] owners despair,
40 May nettles grow there instead of wheat;
Instead of barley, stinkweed!

The words of Job are at an end.

32 These three men ceased replying to Job, for he considered himself right. 2 Then Elihu son of Barachel the
Buzite, of the family of Ram, was angry—angry at Job because
he thought himself right against God. 3 He was angry as well
at his three friends, because they found no reply, but merely

31: *Consume his flesh,* see 19.22 n. **32:** *To the road,* rather, with slight revocalization, "to the wayfarer" (cf. Jer. 14.8). **33:** *Like Adam,* or "like any man." **34:** *That I ... fear,* more likely, "because I fear"; a person is often intimidated from baring one's sins for fear of public shame. **35:** The second line more likely means: "Here is my mark. Let Shaddai answer me!" Job has all along been seeking the formal charges he imagines are leveled against him. **37:** *Offer it ... ,* rather, "I would approach Him (in court)" with all the boldness I can muster. **38–40:** For good measure, Job offers a final denial of misdeed.

32.1–37.24: The appearance of a fourth companion, Elihu the Buzite, is unexpected (see the intro.). He is specially introduced in prose (32.1–5); his name is Heb, not taken from the lists of Edomites in Gen. ch 36 like the first three companions (see 2.11 n.); and he is identified with his father's name, which is also not pseudo-Edomite. The speeches, which uniquely lecture Job in direct address, receive no response. These are among the signs that the Elihu discourses were secondarily added to an earlier form of the book. At the same time, its author adopts a language and style only subtly different from the rest of the book. Elihu figures prominently in the postbiblical *T. Job,* and his theology was favored by the classical Rabbis and medieval Jewish philosophers. Elihu's discourses perform two functions: they improve the arguments of the three companions, Eliphaz, Bildad, and Zophar, and better refute Job's claims; and they add a dimension of providential care and justice to the God speeches. In context, however, the effects may be ironic. Elihu's bombast makes him an unattractive speaker; and in the current form of the book, it looks like God is correcting Elihu rather than the other way around. Elihu's discourse responds to all of Job's contentions in several parts: a self-acknowledged (see 32.18–19) long-winded justification of his address to Job (32.6–33.12); an argument for divine providence over individuals (33.13–33); a theoretical argument for divine justice and retribution (34.1–37); a claim that, although God is transcendent, He will nonetheless respond to Job when He is ready (35.1–16); an empirical argument for divine justice and retribution (36.1–17); a reproach of Job for questioning the magnificent and awesome Deity (36.18–37.13); a challenge to Job's understanding, by appeal to the awe and mystery of God's acts of creation in the sky above (37.14–24) and in the earth below (ch 28). **32.1:** *Himself right,* a subjective judgment; cf. Prov. 16.1. **2:** *Elihu,* the name means "He is God"; Rashi, Ibn Ezra and others take him for an Israelite, but since he never uses the Israelite divine name YHVH, this conclusion is improbable. *Barachel,* elsewhere unattested, the name means "God has blessed"—once true of Job, but not since his trials began. *Buzite,* apparently affiliated with the family of Nahor, Abraham's Aramean brother (Gen. 22.21); Buz is said to be a brother of Uz, the name of Job's homeland (1.1). Buz is also a place listed with Tema, in northern Arabia, in Jer. 25.23. Buzi is the father of the prophet Ezekiel, who shows an acquaintance with the story of Job (see Ezek. 14.14, 20). *Ram:* Rabbeinu Tam (12th c. France) identifies the name with Aram, in

condemned Job. 4 Elihu waited out Job's speech, for they were
all older than he. 5 But when Elihu saw that the three men had
nothing to reply, he was angry.

6 Then Elihu son of Barachel the Buzite said in reply:

I have but few years, while you are old;
Therefore I was too awestruck and fearful
To hold forth among you.
7 I thought, "Let age speak;
Let advanced years declare wise things."
8 But truly it is the spirit in men,
The breath of Shaddai, that gives them understanding.
9 It is not the aged who are wise,
The elders, who understand how to judge.
10 Therefore I say, "Listen to me;
I too would hold forth."
11 Here I have waited out your speeches,
I have given ear to your insights,
While you probed the issues;
12 But as I attended to you,
I saw that none of you could argue with Job,
Or offer replies to his statements.
13 I fear you will say, "We have found the wise course;
God will defeat him, not man."
14 He did not set out his case against me,
Nor shall I use your reasons to reply to him.
15 They have been broken and can no longer reply;
Words fail them.
16 I have waited till they stopped speaking,
Till they ended and no longer replied.
17 Now I also would have my say;
I too would like to hold forth,
18 For I am full of words;
The wind in my belly presses me.
19 My belly is like wine not yet opened,
Like jugs of new wine ready to burst.
20 Let me speak, then, and get relief;
Let me open my lips and reply.
21 I would not show regard for any man,
Or temper my speech for anyone's sake;
22 For I do not know how to temper my speech—
My Maker would soon carry me off!

33 But now, Job, listen to my words,
Give ear to all that I say.
2 Now I open my lips;
My tongue forms words in my mouth.

keeping with the Aramean flavored framework of the book; otherwise Ram is known as an ancestor of David (e.g., Ruth 4.19). *Angry,* thrice repeated in this brief introduction (vv. 2, 3, 5). **3:** *Merely condemned Job,* a pious scribal correction for "allowed God to be condemned" (Rashi and Ibn Ezra). **6–22:** Elihu first addresses the friends, who have failed in their arguments with Job as they did in their defense of God, before speaking specifically to Job in ch 33. **8–9:** Elihu rejects the traditional claim (see 15.9–10) that wisdom is of the wise, insisting that God imparts wisdom directly. This will accord with his view that God reveals himself directly to people (33.14–17). **11:** *Insights,* excuses; reading "te'onot" (cf. Judg. 14.4; so Rashi) instead of "tevunot." *The issues,* lit. "the words." The entire discourse revolves around whose words will be effective. **14:** *He did not* ("we-lo'") *set:* Samuel ben Nissim Masnuth (13th c. Syria) more sensibly reads: "Had he ("we-lu") *set out his case ...*" *Nor shall I use* is better rendered "I would not have used ..." **15:** Elihu speaks of the companions in the third person as he slowly transitions to addressing Job (33.1). **18:** *I am full of words,* strongly alliterative—"maleiti millim." *Wind in my belly,* ironically pejorative—see 15.2. **21:** *For any man:* Elihu fails to avoid the charge of favoring God that Job had leveled at his companions in 13.8. *Temper my speech,* more precisely, "address by title," speak deferentially. **22:** Rather, "Were I ("lu" instead of "lo'") wont to defer, then my Maker would *carry me off.*" *Carry me off* puns on "show regard" in v. 21.

3 My words bespeak the uprightness of my
heart;
My lips utter insight honestly.
4 The spirit of God formed me;
The breath of Shaddai sustains me.
5 If you can, answer me;
Argue against me, take your stand.
6 You and I are the same before God;
I too was nipped from clay.
7 You are not overwhelmed by fear of me;
My pressure does not weigh heavily on you.

8 Indeed, you have stated in my hearing,
I heard the words spoken,
9 "I am guiltless, free from transgression;
I am innocent, without iniquity.
10 But He finds reasons to oppose me,
Considers me His enemy.
11 He puts my feet in stocks,
Watches all my ways."

12 In this you are not right;
I will answer you: God is greater than any man.
13 Why do you complain against Him
That He does not reply to any of man's
charges?
14 For God speaks [a]time and again[a]—
Though man does not perceive it—
15 In a dream, a night vision,
When deep sleep falls on men,
While they slumber on their beds.
16 Then He opens men's understanding,
And by disciplining them leaves His signature
17 To turn man away from an action,
To suppress pride in man.
18 He spares him from the Pit,
His person, from perishing by the sword.
19 He is reproved by pains on his bed,
And the trembling in his bones is constant.
20 He detests food;
Fine food [is repulsive] to him.
21 His flesh wastes away till it cannot be seen,
And his bones are rubbed away till they are
invisible.
22 He comes close to the Pit,
His life [verges] on death.

a-a Lit. "once ... twice."

33.3: Elihu counters Job's commitment to honesty (27.2–4) with his own. **6:** *Nipped from clay,* a widespread ancient Semitic expression, reflecting the creation of the human from clay (cf. Gen. 2.7), like a ceramic vessel. **7:** Elihu averts the reticence Job expressed in confronting God; see 13.20–21; cf. 9.34–35; 23.15–16. **9:** Elihu typically quotes Job in the somewhat distorted ways he has been cited by the friends—in this instance Zophar (11.4). Job had never claimed to be thoroughly innocent; see 7.20–21. **10:** *Considers ...*, see 13.24; 19.11. **11:** See 13.27 n. **13:** Cf. 9.16. Elihu takes issue with Job's most extreme position, on which Job has expressed ambivalence; see e.g., 13.22; 16.19, 21; 19.25–27; 23.3–7. **14–19:** Job had reported a disquieting *night vision* (see 4.12–21 n.) and suffered nightmares (7.13); Elihu explains that nocturnal revelations are divine warnings—to protect one from punishable acts. **15:** Elihu quotes 4.13, which he understands to be part of Job's discourse. **16:** *Leaves His signature,* more likely, "He frightens them ("yehittem" for "yaḥatom," assuming one letter has been mistranscribed) with His means of discipline; cf. 5.17–18; and see v. 19 below. **17:** *Suppress,* Heb "cover." Read perhaps, "yissah" instead of "yekhaseh," "extract (pride from a man)"; cf. Prov. 15.25. **18:** *Perishing by the sword,* rather, "passing into ruin"; cf. v. 28 below. **19:** *Bones,* more properly, "limbs." **20–22:** A morbid description of the fate of the admonished. **21:** *Rubbed away,* better "were laid bare"—not lit. but made visible by protruding through the emaciated skin. *Till ... invisible,* or "not thriving" (from "raveh").

23 If he has a representative,
One advocate against a thousand
To declare the man's uprightness,
24 Then He has mercy on him and decrees,
"Redeem him from descending to the Pit,
For I have obtained his ransom;
25 Let his flesh be healthier[a] than in his youth;
Let him return to his younger days."
26 He prays to God and is accepted by Him;
He enters His presence with shouts of joy,
For He requites a man for his righteousness.
27 He[b] declares[a] to men,
"I have sinned; I have perverted what was right;
But I was not paid back for it."
28 He redeemed [c]him from passing into the Pit;
He[-c] will enjoy the light.
29 Truly, God does all these things
Two or three times to a man,
30 To bring him back from the Pit,
That he may bask in the light of life.

31 Pay heed, Job, and hear me;
Be still, and I will speak;
32 If you have what to say, answer me;
Speak, for I am eager to vindicate you.
33 But if not, you listen to me;
Be still, and I will teach you wisdom.

34 Elihu said in reply:

2 Listen, O wise men, to my words;
You who have knowledge, give ear to me.
3 For the ear tests arguments
As the palate tastes food.
4 Let us decide for ourselves what is just;
Let us know among ourselves what is good.
5 For Job has said, "I am right;
God has deprived me of justice.
6 I declare the judgment against me false;
My arrow-wound is deadly, though I am free from transgression."
7 What man is like Job,
Who drinks mockery like water;
8 Who makes common cause with evildoers,
And goes with wicked men?

a Meaning of Heb. uncertain. *b I.e., the contrite man.*
c-c Or with kethib, *"me ... I."*

23: *Representative,* a guardian "angel." *Against ...*, rather, "even one out of a thousand"—one is enough to stand up in the divine council and—in a role opposite to that of the Satan (see 1.6 n.)—defend the person being disciplined, preventing the monitory affliction from going too far. Medieval Jewish philosophers tend to rationalize the angel as a person's good deeds (e.g., Saadia) or a timely force of nature (e.g., Maimonides). **27:** *He,* the admonished person (not "the contrite man" as in the translators' note *b*). God disciplines those whom He cares about; see 5.17–18 n. *Declares,* more precisely, "sings" or "declaims"; the unusual verb ("yashor") puns on *what was right* ("yashar"). *I have sinned,* see Job's admission in 7.20. *I was not paid back,* rather, "it was not worth it to me" (cf. e.g., Esth. 3.8). **31:** *Be still,* echoing Job in 13.13. **33:** Elihu takes on the self-imposed role of Eliphaz in 15.17.

34.1–37: On divine providence. **3:** Paraphrasing Job in 12.11. **5:** Quoting Job in 27.2. **6:** Alluding to Job in 6.4. **8:** Elihu's claim seems baseless, but he may be trying to save Job's reputation: he is not bad, but he has come under bad influences; cf. e.g., Ps. 1.1; Prov. 1.10–19.

9 For he says, "Man gains nothing
When he is in God's favor."

10 Therefore, men of understanding, listen to me;
Wickedness be far from God,
Wrongdoing, from Shaddai!
11 For He pays a man according to his actions,
And provides for him according to his conduct;
12 For God surely does not act wickedly;
Shaddai does not pervert justice.
13 Who placed the earth in His charge?
Who ordered the entire world?
14 If He but intends it,
He can call back His spirit and breath;
15 All flesh would at once expire,
And mankind return to dust.

16 If you would understand, listen to this;
Give ear to what I say.
17 Would one who hates justice govern?
Would you condemn the Just Mighty One?
18 Would you call a king a scoundrel,
Great men, wicked?
19 He is not partial to princes;
The noble are not preferred to the wretched;
For all of them are the work of His hands.
20 Some die suddenly in the middle of the night;
People are in turmoil and pass on;
Even great men are removed—not by human hands.
21 For His eyes are upon a man's ways;
He observes his every step.
22 Neither darkness nor gloom offers
A hiding-place for evildoers.
23 He has no set time for man
To appear before God in judgment.
24 He shatters mighty men without number
And sets others in their place.
25 Truly, He knows their deeds;
Night is over, and they are crushed.
26 He strikes them down with the wicked
Where people can see,
27 Because they have been disloyal to Him
And have not understood any of His ways;
28 Thus He lets the cry of the poor come before Him;
He listens to the cry of the needy.
29 When He is silent, who will condemn?
If He hides His face, who will see Him,
Be it nation or man?

9: A paraphrase of Job by Eliphaz in 22.2. **12:** Echoing Bildad in 8.3; cf. Job in 19.6. **14–15:** Human life is animated by the breath of God (Gen. 2.7), and if He takes it back, they *expire.* Cf. Ps. 104.29. **16:** Elihu now addresses Job specifically. **19–20:** In line with Job's mock wisdom in 12.17–21. **20:** *People are in turmoil:* Dividing the two words differently yields a better reading: "the noble die" ("yigwe'u sho'im"). *Not by human hands,* cf. Lam. 4.6. **21:** Elihu sees the positive side of divine tracking; cf. Job in 31.4. For the negative side see Job in 14.16 and elsewhere. **22:** A rebuttal of Job in 24.14–17. **23–27:** God stamps out the wicked without trial; a rebuttal of Job in ch 21. **28:** Consideration of the *poor* is a widespread ancient Near Eastern sign of a just monarch (e.g., Ps. 72.4). **29:** *Who will condemn* seems out of context; rather, "If He makes calm, who will agitate?" (Ibn Ezra, Naḥmanides; see 3.17 n.).

30 The impious man rule no more,
Nor do those who ensnare the people.
31 Has he said to God,
"I will bear [my punishment] and offend no more.
32 What I cannot see You teach me.
If I have done iniquity, I shall not do so again"?
33 Should He requite as you see fit?
But you have despised [Him]!
You must decide, not I;
Speak what you know.
34 Men of understanding say to me,
Wise men who hear me,
35 "Job does not speak with knowledge;
His words lack understanding."
36 Would that Job were tried to the limit
For answers which befit sinful men.
37 He adds to his sin;
He increases his transgression among us;
He multiplies his statements against God.

35 Elihu said in reply:

2 Do you think it just
To say, "I am right against God"?
3 If you ask how it benefits you,
"What have I gained from not sinning?"
4 I shall give you a reply,
You, along with your friends.
5 Behold the heavens and see;
Look at the skies high above you.
6 If you sin, what do you do to Him?
If your transgressions are many,
How do you affect Him?
7 If you are righteous,
What do you give Him;
What does He receive from your hand?
8 Your wickedness affects men like yourself;
Your righteousness, mortals.

9 Because of contention the oppressed cry out;
They shout because of the power of the great.
10 But none says, "Where is my God, my Maker,
Who gives strength in the night;
11 Who gives us more knowledge than the beasts of the earth,
Makes us wiser than the birds of the sky?"
12 Then they cry out, but He does not respond
Because of the arrogance of evil men.

30: *The impious ...*, better "So that the impious ..." **31:** The following is an appeal to Job, based on different word boundaries in the Heb: "You must say to God ..." (read "'el 'eloah 'emor"; so Tur-Sinai [a modern commentator]). **33:** *Should He ...* : The idea is that God will not give retribution to Job in a manner he "rejects" (not *you have despised*). *Speak what you know,* rather, "Why do you speak of what you do not know?" See v. 35 and 35.16.

35.1–16: Elihu responds mainly to Job's complaint in 7.16–21. **2:** Rather, "Did you plan on getting a trial, thinking: 'My vindication is from God'?" See 16.19; 19.25. **3:** Job has expressed such thoughts, not as his own, but as those of the wicked (see 21.14–15). **6–9:** Job does not understand what harm he can do to God by sinning (7.20). Elihu replies that God is looking out for people who suffer from the wrongdoing of others. **9:** *Because of contention,* or "From so much oppression (see Eccl. 4.1) people cry out." **10–12:** The oppressed should appeal to God, but they fail to do so, out of ignorance or pride (v. 12). **10:** *Strength,* rather, "song"; see Ps. 42.9. **11:** A cut at Job's facetious suggestion in 12.7–8.

13 Surely it is false that God does not listen,
That Shaddai does not take note of it.
14 Though you say, "You do not take note of it,"
The case is before Him;
So wait for Him.
15 [a]But since now it does not seem so,
He vents his anger;
He does not realize that it may be long drawn out.[-a]
16 Hence Job mouths empty words,
And piles up words without knowledge.

36

Then Elihu spoke once more.
2 Wait a little and let me hold forth;
There is still more to say for God.
3 I will make my opinions widely known;
I will justify my Maker.
4 In truth, my words are not false;
A man of sound opinions is before you.

5 See, God is mighty; He is not contemptuous;
He is mighty in strength and mind.
6 He does not let the wicked live;
He grants justice to the lowly.
7 He does not withdraw His eyes from the righteous;
With kings on thrones
He seats them forever, and they are exalted.
8 If they are bound in shackles
And caught in trammels of affliction,
9 He declares to them what they have done,
And that their transgressions are excessive;
10 He opens their understanding by discipline,
And orders them back from mischief.
11 If they will serve obediently,
They shall spend their days in happiness,
Their years in delight.
12 But if they are not obedient,
They shall perish by the sword,
Die for lack of understanding.
13 But the impious in heart become enraged;
They do not cry for help when He afflicts them.
14 They die in their youth;
[Expire] among the depraved.
15 He rescues the lowly from their affliction,
And opens their understanding through distress.

a-a Meaning of Heb. uncertain.

14: A response to Job, who had said he could not wait for a hearing (13.15). **15–16:** Rather, although Job asserts that God's "anger does not visit" punishment on the wicked, and that He "cares little about transgression (read "be-pesha'" for "bapash")," his argument is ignorant.

36.1–17: More on providence. 2: As Rashi points out, this v. "is entirely in Aram." Although Elihu's comments are for the most part in Heb, this v. serves as a reminder that Elihu is an Easterner, not an Israelite (see the intro.). **4:** Elihu pits his truth against Job's (see 27.2–4). **5:** *He is not contemptuous:* The verb should probably be connected with the following line: "He does not despise the pure of heart" (reading "bar leb" in the second line). **8–9:** People should understand their affliction as a punishment for their transgressions. **10–11:** God will reward repentance. **12:** *Perish by the sword,* see 33.18 n. *Die . . . ,* echoing 4.21. **14:** *The depraved,* technically, "(young) male prostitutes" (e.g., Deut. 23.18; 1 Kings 14.24). **15:** *Distress,* puns ironically on *rescues;* cf. v. 10.

16: *Distress,* rather, "an adversary"; the v. alludes to Ps. 23.5. **17:** Job has complained at length of the apparent successes of the wicked (chs 21; 24). **18:** *Let* [not] *anger* ("ḥemah"): Read rather "beware" ("hemeh"; cf. Arabic)—of being tempted by profit to sin; cf. v. 21. This section is particularly difficult. It is hard to believe that Elihu would suspect Job of an inclination to rob the helpless; the address is more likely made to the wicked or any listener. *His affluence: His* is not in the Heb—no one should be tempted by *affluence.* **20:** *When peoples vanish,* more likely, "to take advantage of (lit. to go up against) people right where they are (i.e., right under their noses)"; the wicked rob people while they sleep (see 24.14–17). **21:** *Because of that . . . ,* perhaps: "for you have chosen wrong-doing ("ʿavlah"; see Prov. 22.8 for the pairing of "wrong-doing" and *mischief* ["ʾaven"]) over *affliction*"—you would prefer to do wrong than worry over punishment. **22:** *Beyond reach,* rather, "is exalted." **23:** Job has accused God of unjust "ways"; see 13.15 n. **27:** Beginning here, Elihu anticipates the God speeches (esp. ch 38), enumerating some marvels of nature; however, he intermixes assertions about divine care for humanity, which is absent in the divine speeches from the tempest. **28:** *On all* ("rav") *mankind,* more likely, "they pour rain ("raviv") on humanity"; cf. Deut. 32.2. **31:** *Controls,* rather, "provides justice (providence)." **33:** *Tells of him,* or, "announces itself." *Against iniquity,* difficult; read probably (with several moderns) "storm" (Aram. "ʿalʿolah"): the storm (announces) the burning rage (of God).

37.1–5: Elihu is enthralled by God's thunder, which in the ancient Near East was identified as the voice of the storm god (e.g., Ps. 18.14). Dwelling on the divine voice, as expressed in nature, anticipates the divine speeches from the "tempest" (chs 38–41). **3:** *Lets it loose,* rather, "flashes lightning" ("yishreh" instead of "yishrehu"; said of the god Baal in Ugaritic epic). **4:** Cf. *roar*ing like a

16 Indeed, He draws you away from the brink of distress
To a broad place where there is no constraint;
Your table is laid out with rich food.
17 You are obsessed with the case of the wicked man,
But the justice of the case will be upheld.
18 Let anger at his affluence not mislead you;
Let much bribery not turn you aside.
19 [a]Will your limitless wealth avail you,[-a]
All your powerful efforts?
20 Do not long for the night
When peoples vanish where they are.
21 Beware! Do not turn to mischief;
Because of that you have been tried by affliction.
22 See, God is beyond reach in His power;
Who governs like Him?
23 Who ever reproached Him for His conduct?
Who ever said, "You have done wrong"?
24 Remember, then, to magnify His work,
Of which men have sung,
25 Which all men have beheld,
Men have seen, from a distance.
26 See, God is greater than we can know;
The number of His years cannot be counted.
27 He forms the droplets of water,
Which cluster into rain, from His mist.
28 The skies rain;
They pour down on all mankind.
29 Can one, indeed, contemplate the expanse of clouds,
The thunderings from His pavilion?
30 See, He spreads His lightning over it;
It fills the bed of the sea.
31 By these things He controls peoples;
He gives food in abundance.
32 Lightning fills His hands;
He orders it to hit the mark.
33 Its noise tells of Him.
[a]The kindling of anger against iniquity.[-a]

37 Because of this, too, my heart quakes,
And leaps from its place.
2 Just listen to the noise of His rumbling,
To the sound that comes out of His mouth.
3 He lets it loose beneath the entire heavens—
His lightning, to the ends of the earth.
4 After it, He lets out a roar;
He thunders in His majestic voice.

a-a Meaning of Heb. uncertain.

No one can find a trace of it by the time His voice
is heard.
5 God thunders marvelously with His voice;
He works wonders that we cannot understand.
6 He commands the snow, "Fall to the ground!"
And the downpour of rain, His mighty downpour
of rain,
7 Is as a sign on every man's hand,
That all men may know His doings.
8 Then the beast enters its lair,
And remains in its den.
9 The storm wind comes from its chamber,
And the cold from the constellations.
10 By the breath of God ice is formed,
And the expanse of water becomes solid.
11 He also loads the clouds with moisture
And scatters His lightning-clouds.
12 [a]He keeps turning events by His stratagems,[a]
That they might accomplish all that He commands
them
Throughout the inhabited earth,
13 Causing each of them to happen to His land,
Whether as a scourge or as a blessing.

14 Give ear to this, Job;
Stop to consider the marvels of God.
15 Do you know what charge God lays upon them
When His lightning-clouds shine?
16 Do you know the marvels worked upon the expanse
of clouds
By Him whose understanding is perfect,
17 [a]Why your clothes become hot[a]
When the land is becalmed by the south wind?
18 Can you help him stretch out the heavens,
Firm as a mirror of cast metal?
19 Inform us, then, what we may say to Him;
We cannot argue because [we are in] darkness.
20 Is anything conveyed to Him when I speak?
Can a man say anything when he is confused?
21 Now, then, one cannot see the sun,
Though it be bright in the heavens,
Until the wind comes and clears them [of clouds].
22 By the north wind the golden rays emerge;
The splendor about God is awesome.
23 Shaddai—we cannot attain to Him;
He is great in power and justice

a-a Meaning of Heb. uncertain.

lion as a metaphor for divine thunder in Jer. 25.30; Amos 1.2. Elihu's positive image of God as a mighty lion contrasts with Job's characterization of God as a predator in 10.16. *No one can find a trace ...*, more likely, "He does not hold back lightning ("we-lo' yeʿaqqeb beraqim") / when his voice (thunder) is sounded." **5:** A transition to other celestial wonders. **6:** *And the downpour ...*, perhaps: "The *downpour of rain* is the rods ("mattot," not "mitrot"; cf. Ezek. 19.11) of His might." **7:** *Is as ...*, rather, "He seals people in ... " (cf. "seals up" in 9.7). The torrential rain keeps both humans and animals (v. 8) indoors. **9:** God stores the wind in *chambers* until He wants to release it; cf. 9.9; cf. Ps. 135.7 and Job 38.22 (snow and hail). *Constellations,* more likely, cold "scattering" winds from the north; cf. v. 10 (cf. e.g., Exod. 15.8). **12:** *He ... events,* rather, "it (the cloud) moves to and fro." **13:** Extreme weather may be a reward or punishment for the land (see e.g., Deut. 11.14–17). **14–24:** Elihu's rhetorical questions on the same theme anticipate the God speeches (esp. ch 38). It is important to remember that the Elihu material was written later than the divine speeches, to anticipate them. **18:** *Can you stretch out,* more likely, "can you hammer out (the heavens like Him)?"; cf. Isa. 44.24. **19:** *Because ... darkness,* Elihu anticipates the divine challenge in 38.2. Here he intermixes "being in the dark" both physically and mentally. **20:** *When he is confused,* for "balaʿ" in this sense see, e.g., Isa. 28.7. **21:** *Though it be bright,* rather, "it is obscure" (cf. "baheret," "discoloration" in Lev. 13.2). **22:** *By the north wind,* more likely, "from the north," a possible reference to the Northern Lights.

And abundant in righteousness; He does not torment.
24 Therefore, men are in awe of Him
Whom none of the wise can perceive.

38 Then the LORD replied to Job out of the tempest and said:

2 Who is this who darkens counsel,
Speaking without knowledge?
3 Gird your loins like a man;
I will ask and you will inform Me.

4 Where were you when I laid the earth's foundations?
Speak if you have understanding.
5 Do you know who fixed its dimensions
Or who measured it with a line?
6 Onto what were its bases sunk?
Who set its cornerstone
7 When the morning stars sang together
And all the divine beings shouted for joy?

24: Elihu's discourse may continue in ch 28 (see 28.1–28 n.), where the concluding v. resembles this.

38.1–42.6: The LORD's speeches to Job and Job's responses. God responds to Job in two parts (38.1–40.2; 40.6–41.26), and Job replies to each (40.3–5; 42.1–6). The discourses are structured as rhetorical questions posed by God, designed to show that Job cannot equal His cosmic power and knowledge. The first discourse deals with the panorama of the natural world and esp. the animals; the second, after an introduction, with two curious specimens, the Behemoth and Leviathan. The divine discourses are complex and rather enigmatic, so that interpretations differ and are sometimes multi-layered. What is clear is that Job receives no clear answer to his burning question—why is he afflicted? Some understand that by pointing out the wonders of the created world, much of it is beyond human knowledge and some of it lacking sense, God demonstrates to Job that His ways are different from human ways (cf. Isa. 55.8–9). Some suggest that there is an implicit analogy: just as people do not comprehend the mysteries of nature, and yet perceive that there is order in it, so do they fail to comprehend divine justice, although there is an order in it, known only to God. By indicating how God understands and appreciates the animals, God is taken by many to display providential care for all creatures, including humans (see Jonah 4.11). The dressing down of Job is interpreted as a message to humanity: contrary to the impression that Gen. 1.26–30 and other passages may give, humans are not the center of the world—animals and nature are equally important. And as for Job's complaint—he should be contented with the fact that God has answered him.

However, it is also possible to regard the divine response as an avoidance of the issue. Not only does Job receive no response; God does not reveal to him the test of his devotion that is the real source of Job's suffering. Moreover, by ignoring the matter of just retribution and exhibiting His marvelous world, God only confirms Job's fear all along—that the Deity is about power, and not justice.

On the most fundamental level, God responds to Job in order not to forfeit the lawsuit Job has mounted against Him (see 29.1–31.4 nn.). However, by showing Job that he has no direct knowledge of His ways, God dismisses the case pro forma—Job is not a competent witness and cannot therefore bring charges against the Deity. It is often assumed that Job is somehow satisfied or convinced by God's presentation; but this depends on the understanding of Job's responses below. **38.1:** *Out of the tempest:* YHVH often appears in a storm god image (e.g., Exod. ch 19; Pss. 18; 29). Ancient Near Eastern storm gods were warriors, and this may account in part for the Deity's belligerency in accosting Job. Given that "wind," a main characteristic of a storm, is often used in the dialogues between Job and his companions as a disparaging term for poor argument (e.g., 8.2; 15.2; 16.3, though using a different word than here), what are we to make of God's speaking out of the wind? **3:** A challenge to an opponent in combat or perhaps belt-wrestling. **4–6:** The image of God as builder of the world, found in many places (e.g., Prov. 8.22–29), is most striking here. **4:** *Where were you,* etc. The questions put to Job are intended to demonstrate his lack of knowledge. They evoke Egyptian and Mesopotamian texts in which a senior scribe or teacher mocks a junior colleague's ignorance. The Deity's rhetoric seems overly-aggressive, perhaps mean-spirited. Of course, Job was not present at the creation, when God made use of His esoteric wisdom (see Prov. 8.22–31; cf. Job 15.7–11). **7:** For the *stars* as divine beings or angels see 25.3 n. The v. echoes Deut. 32.43a as preserved in a Qumran fragment: "Sing of his people, all you heavens; pay homage to him, all you divine beings." This biblical understanding is based on the ancient idea of stars and planets as manifestations of deities.

8 Who closed the sea behind doors
When it gushed forth out of the womb,
9 When I clothed it in clouds,
Swaddled it in dense clouds,
10 When I made breakers My limit for it,
And set up its bar and doors,
11 And said, "You may come so far and no farther;
Here your surging waves will stop"?

12 Have you ever commanded the day to break,
Assigned the dawn its place,
13 So that it seizes the corners of the earth
And shakes the wicked out of it?
14 It changes like clay under the seal
Till [its hues] are fixed like those of a garment.
15 Their light is withheld from the wicked,
And the upraised arm is broken.

16 Have you penetrated to the sources of the sea,
Or walked in the recesses of the deep?
17 Have the gates of death been disclosed to you?
Have you seen the gates of deep darkness?
18 Have you surveyed the expanses of the earth?
If you know of these—tell Me.

19 Which path leads to where light dwells,
And where is the place of darkness,
20 That you may take it to its domain
And know the way to its home?
21 Surely you know, for you were born then,
And the number of your years is many!

22 Have you penetrated the vaults of snow,
Seen the vaults of hail,
23 Which I have put aside for a time of adversity,
For a day of war and battle?
24 By what path is the west wind[a] dispersed,
The east wind scattered over the earth?
25 Who cut a channel for the torrents
And a path for the thunderstorms,
26 To rain down on uninhabited land,
On the wilderness where no man is,
27 To saturate the desolate wasteland,
And make the crop of grass sprout forth?
28 Does the rain have a father?
Who begot the dewdrops?

a *As Aramaic* 'urya.

8–11: A mythological scene in which the Deity held the god Sea (Yam; see 7.12 n.) in his celestial womb and controlled its release so as not to flood the earth. The birth imagery ironically evokes Job (3.10), who wanted to be kept inside the womb so as never to be born. The image of holding back the sea with a door-bolt may be influenced by *Enuma Elish* IV 139. In both the Bible and other ancient Near Eastern texts, these myths explain why the sea does not inundate the earth. **12–15:** The day is personified as a person rising in the morning and shaking off the blanket of earth to remove the bedbugs—the wicked, who operate by night (24.14–17). The earth becomes distinct like the design in a clay seal, and the wicked are exposed like a garment on a person. **15:** *Their light,* the day-time of the wicked is night. **16–38:** God's survey moves upward, from the subterranean to the horizon to the sky. **17:** The realm of Death (perhaps the Canaanite deity Mot; see 18.13 n.) is the netherworld (28.22). For *gates of death,* see Pss. 9.14; 107.18; cf. Isa. 38.10. **18:** *Earth,* in this context, as elsewhere, referring to the netherworld (cf. e.g., Exod. 15.12; Ps. 22.30). **19–20:** Light and darkness are personified. **21:** Sarcasm. **23:** Note the overtones of warfare. *Adversity,* or "the enemy." **25:** The Talmud (*b. B. M.* 16a) enhances the marvel: God creates a separate "path" for each thunderclap. **26–27:** Contrast Eliphaz in 5.10, where God has the rain fall where humans can use it. The Torah (Deut. 11.13–15) represents rainfall as the emblem of divine reward for fulfilling God's commands. Here God appears to undermine the concept of just retribution, while at the same time implicitly rejecting the idea of providential care for people. **28–29:** Cf. the personification of Sea (vv. 8–11 above). V. 28 presents the male side of procreation, v. 29 the female. The riddle-like questions call for a negative answer (cf. "ha-yesh" [*does,* lit. "is there"] in 5.1; 6.30; 25.3): God is responsible for all (cf. Jer. 14.22).

29 From whose belly came forth the ice?
Who gave birth to the frost of heaven?
30 Water congeals like stone,
And the surface of the deep compacts.

31 Can you tie cords to Pleiades
Or undo the reins of Orion?
32 Can you lead out Mazzaroth[a] in its season,
Conduct the Bear with her sons?
33 Do you know the laws of heaven
Or impose its authority on earth?

34 Can you send up an order to the clouds
For an abundance of water to cover you?
35 Can you dispatch the lightning on a mission
And have it answer you, "I am ready"?
36 Who put wisdom in the hidden parts?
Who gave understanding to the mind?[b]
37 Who is wise enough to give an account of the heavens?
Who can tilt the bottles of the sky,
38 Whereupon the earth melts into a mass,
And its clods stick together.

39 Can you hunt prey for the lion,
And satisfy the appetite of the king of beasts?
40 They crouch in their dens,
Lie in ambush in their lairs.
41 Who provides food for the raven
When his young cry out to God
And wander about without food?

39

Do you know the season when the mountain goats give birth?
Can you mark the time when the hinds calve?
2 Can you count the months they must complete?
Do you know the season they give birth,
3 When they couch to bring forth their offspring,
To deliver their young?
4 Their young are healthy; they grow up in the open;
They leave and return no more.

5 Who sets the wild ass free?
Who loosens the bonds of the onager,
6 Whose home I have made the wilderness,
The salt land his dwelling-place?

a *Evidently a constellation.* b *Or "rooster"; meaning of Heb. uncertain.*

31–32: Cf. 9.9. The identification of the constellations is uncertain, although there is wide agreement concerning *Pleiades* and *Orion.* The *cords* and *reins* suggest they are imagined as large animals (*Pleiades* is located within Taurus, the bull). Alternately, they may reflect the notion that the constellations are moved across the sky with bands as in *Enuma Elish* V 1–10. *Bear … sons,* probably Aldebaran (eye of the Bull) and the Hyades (cf. *b. Ber.* 58b). **34:** Cf. 22.11. **35:** *I am ready,* that is, "yes"—there is not a single word equivalent to "yes" in biblical Heb. **36:** *The mind:* The second half of the v. is used in the morning liturgy in a blessing that commends God for giving the rooster discernment to distinguish between day and night, based on the classical rabbinic interpretation of "sekhvi," here rendered *mind,* as "rooster." This understanding does not fit the present context, dealing with the sky. **38.39–39.30:** God exhibits a variety of animals, most of them wild and predatory, alternating between mammals (earth) and birds (sky). **38.39–40:** Eliphaz had likened the wicked to lions (4.10–11). Job had depicted the Deity as a predatory lion (10.16; 16.12). Here God provides food for the lion (cf. Ps. 104.21). **41:** Ravens feed on carrion; see 1 Kings 17.6. God hears the cry of the young ravens (cf. Ps. 147.9), but not Job's cry for justice (19.7).

39.1–4: Job may not know much about the calving and maturation of the ibex (mountain goat), but the poet does. **4:** *Return no more,* to their mothers. From the human perspective, this describes parental abandonment, a theme elaborated on more extremely in vv. 14–16.

7 He scoffs at the tumult of the city,
Does not hear the shouts of the driver.
8 He roams the hills for his pasture;
He searches for any green thing.

9 Would the wild ox agree to serve you?
Would he spend the night at your crib?
10 Can you hold the wild ox by ropes to the furrow?
Would he plow up the valleys behind you?
11 Would you rely on his great strength
And leave your toil to him?
12 Would you trust him to bring in the seed
And gather it in from your threshing floor?

13 The wing of the ostrich beats joyously;
Are her pinions and plumage like the stork's?
14 She leaves her eggs on the ground,
Letting them warm in the dirt,
15 Forgetting they may be crushed underfoot,
Or trampled by a wild beast.
16 Her young are cruelly abandoned as if they were not hers;
Her labor is in vain for lack of concern.
17 For God deprived her of wisdom,
Gave her no share of understanding,
18 Else she would soar on high,
Scoffing at the horse and its rider.

19 Do you give the horse his strength?
Do you clothe his neck with a mane?
20 Do you make him quiver like locusts,
His majestic snorting [spreading] terror?
21 He[a] paws with force, he runs with vigor,
Charging into battle.
22 He scoffs at fear; he cannot be frightened;
He does not recoil from the sword.
23 A quiverful of arrows whizzes by him,
And the flashing spear and the javelin.
24 Trembling with excitement, he swallows[b] the land;
He does not turn aside at the blast of the trumpet.
25 As the trumpet sounds, he says, "Aha!"
From afar he smells the battle,
The roaring and shouting of the officers.

26 Is it by your wisdom that the hawk grows pinions,
Spreads his wings to the south?

a Lit. "They ..." *b Or "digs up."*

7: *Shouts of the driver:* The wild ass is more fortunate than the human prisoner, who will escape "the taskmaster's voice" only after death (3.18). **9–12:** The horned *wild ox* is dangerous; cf. Ps. 22.22, where it is paired with the lion. **13–16:** Cf. Lam. 4.3. **17:** God unapologetically credits Himself, in the third person, for "causing" the callous mother ostrich "to forget wisdom." Ostriches were thought to be bad parents; Lam. 4.3. **18:** Because the ostrich cannot fly, it can fall victim to a stomping *horse* just as its young can be "trampled by a wild beast" (v. 15). Alternatively, the v. may mean that the ostrich "flaps" its wings and scoffs at the horse, which it can actually out-run. Reference to the *horse* provides a transition to the following description of the war horse. **19–25:** Contrast Ps. 147.10, according to which God does not prize the might of horses. **20:** *Quiver,* more likely, "leap"; cf. Joel 2.4–5. *Snorting ... terror,* cf. Jer. 8.16. **21:** *Battle,* lit. "weapon"; cf. the mention of specific weapons below (vv. 22–23). **24:** *Swallows the land,* better, "devours the ground," an image known in Arabic poetry. **25:** The blast of the "ram's horn" *(trumpet)* heralds battle (Amos 3.6). **26:** *Is it by your wisdom:* God reminds Job that the divine intelligence that informed creation is inaccessible to him.

27 Does the eagle soar at your command,
Building his nest high,
28 Dwelling in the rock,
Lodging upon the fastness of a jutting rock?
29 From there he spies out his food;
From afar his eyes see it.
30 His young gulp blood;
Where the slain are, there is he.

40 The LORD said in reply to Job.

2 [a]Shall one who should be disciplined complain against Shaddai?[a]
He who arraigns God must respond.

3 Job said in reply to the LORD:

4 See, I am of small worth; what can I answer You?
I clap my hand to my mouth.
5 I have spoken once, and will not reply;
Twice, and will do so no more.

6 Then the LORD replied to Job out of the tempest and said:

7 Gird your loins like a man;
I will ask, and you will inform Me.
8 Would you impugn My justice?
Would you condemn Me that you may be right?
9 Have you an arm like God's?
Can you thunder with a voice like His?
10 Deck yourself now with grandeur and eminence;
Clothe yourself in glory and majesty.
11 Scatter wide your raging anger;
See every proud man and bring him low.
12 See every proud man and humble him,
And bring them down where they stand.
13 Bury them all in the earth;
Hide their faces in obscurity.
14 Then even I would praise you
For the triumph your right hand won you.

a-a Meaning of Heb. uncertain.

27: Cf. Obad. 1.4. **30:** The final image of God's world is gruesome.

40.1–2: God concludes His first discourse. 2: *One who should be disciplined,* or "one who is afflicted." *Must respond:* The second line of the couplet continues the question: "Must one who accuses God be answered (reading "ye'anneh" for "ya'anenah")?" Just because Job suffers does not mean he is owed a response from God, who has not replied to Job's charges.

40.3–5: Job's response. Commentators typically interpret Job's gesture of "placing his hand on his mouth" to indicate acquiescence; however, the gesture signifies Job's waiting for further speech by the other party (see 21.5 n. and 29.9 n.). This gesture indicates that Job believes he has not yet received a proper reply, which is why God continues. *Of small worth:* The Heb has "I am light-weight"—he is no match for the powerful Deity, who put His challenge in physical terms (38.3).

40.6–41.26: The LORD's second discourse is a response to Job's dissatisfaction with the first. Here, after a brief introduction (40.7–14) God takes special pride in two terrifying creatures. Behemoth (40.15–24) would seem to be a semi-mythological version of the hippopotamus and Leviathan (40.25–41.26) a semi-mythological version of the crocodile, both animals foreign to the Land of Israel and native to Egypt. Comparing the creatures' composition to inanimate materials, like metal, wood, and stone (e.g., 40.17–18; 41.16, 19), has parallels in Mesopotamian descriptions of divine figures. Both Behemoth and Leviathan have been anticipated in the dialogues (3.8; 12.8). **40.7:** See 38.3 n. and vv. 3–5 n. above. **8:** God is being disingenuous—He knows Job's claim is just. But He immediately turns the contest back into one of power (v. 9 and passim). **10:** God thinks in terms of *majesty;* Job prides himself on having clothed himself with justice (29.14). **12:** *Them,* "the wicked." God challenges Job to perform His traditional responsibility (see e.g., ch 20; 34.24–27). This is the only section of the divine speeches that directly discusses divine justice.

15 Take now behemoth, whom I made as I did you;
He eats grass, like the cattle.
16 His strength is in his loins,
His might in the muscles of his belly.
17 [a]He makes his tail stand up[a] like a cedar;
The sinews of his thighs are knit together.
18 His bones are like tubes of bronze,
His limbs like iron rods.
19 He is the first of God's works;
Only his Maker can draw the sword against him.
20 The mountains yield him produce,
Where all the beasts of the field play.
21 He lies down beneath the lotuses,
In the cover of the swamp reeds.
22 The lotuses embower him with shade;
The willows of the brook surround him.
23 He can restrain the river from its rushing;
He is confident the stream[b] will gush at his command.
24 Can he be taken by his eyes?
Can his nose be pierced by hooks?
25 Can you draw out Leviathan by a fishhook?
Can you press down his tongue by a rope?
26 Can you put a ring through his nose,
Or pierce his jaw with a barb?
27 Will he plead with you at length?
Will he speak soft words to you?
28 Will he make an agreement with you
To be taken as your lifelong slave?
29 Will you play with him like a bird,
And tie him down for your girls?
30 [a]Shall traders traffic in him?[a]
Will he be divided up among merchants?
31 Can you fill his skin with darts
Or his head with fish-spears?
32 Lay a hand on him,
And you will never think of battle again.

41 See, any hope [of capturing] him must be disappointed;
One is prostrated by the very sight of him.
2 There is no one so fierce as to rouse him;
Who then can stand up to Me?

a-a Meaning of Heb. uncertain. *b Lit. "Jordan."*

15–24: The *behemoth* is described mainly in terms of strength that cannot be surmounted by humans. In rabbinic literature it is described as huge, capable of drinking six months of the Jordan River's flow (cf. v. 23, where *at his command* is interpreted as "into his mouth") at once (*Num. Rab.* 21:17). **19:** *First of God's works:* In traditional wisdom thinking it is wisdom that is "the first of His works" (Prov. 8.22). Here we find a different theological conception! **20:** The *mountains* are personified as vassals "bearing" tribute to their monarch (cf. Ps. 72.3). The unusual form of *produce* is identical with the Babylonian word for "wild animals," suggesting a secondary meaning: "The animals of the mountains raise (their voices) to Him." **24:** A transition to the description of the Leviathan. *Hooks,* reading "kemoshim," "barbs" (e.g., Isa. 34.13) for "bemokshim," which elsewhere mean "stumbling blocks" or "traps."

40.25–41.26: The description of the *Leviathan* is more detailed, dwelling on how it is impregnable, untamable, and frightening—even to "divine beings" (41.17). It is a terrifying horror, but God implies it is His amusement (40.29; cf. Ps. 104.26). The Talmud relates that in the messianic era the Leviathan will be slain and served as food at a banquet for the righteous, and its skin will be made into "sukkot" (festival booths) for the righteous (*b. B. Bat.* 74b–75a). In this conception, evil, symbolized by the monstrous creature, will be vanquished only in an idealized future. **40.25:** *Press down,* more likely, "bind" (cf. Samaritan Aram.). **26:** *Ring,* rather, "a reed" (e.g., Isa. 9.13). **27:** The Leviathan is not apt to succumb to Job gently. **28:** Eliphaz had ironically promised Job that if he would adhere to his piety, he would enjoy a "pact" (or covenant) with the wild animals (5.23). **29:** *For your girls,* as a pet. **30:** *Traffic,* understood as "dine" in the Talmud, giving rise to the idea of the messianic feast (see 40.25–41.26 n.). *Merchants,* lit. "Canaanites" (cf. Prov. 31.24). **31:** The Leviathan's *skin* is too tough to be penetrated. **32:** The Leviathan is intimidating, as the Deity has been for Job (e.g., 13.21).

41.1–3: The shift between references to the Leviathan *(him)* and the Deity *(Me)* is puzzling, and many moderns emend the text to

3 Whoever confronts Me I will requite,
For everything under the heavens is Mine.
4 [a-]I will not be silent concerning him
Or the praise of his martial exploits.[-a]
5 Who can uncover his outer garment?
Who can penetrate the folds of his jowls?
6 Who can pry open the doors of his face?
His bared teeth strike terror.
7 His protective scales are his pride,
Locked with a binding seal.
8 One scale touches the other;
Not even a breath can enter between them.
9 Each clings to each;
They are interlocked so they cannot be parted.
10 His sneezings flash lightning,
And his eyes are like the glimmerings of dawn.
11 Firebrands stream from his mouth;
Fiery sparks escape.
12 Out of his nostrils comes smoke
As from a steaming, boiling cauldron.
13 His breath ignites coals;
Flames blaze from his mouth.
14 Strength resides in his neck;
Power leaps before him.
15 The layers of his flesh stick together;
He is as though cast hard; he does not totter.
16 His heart is cast hard as a stone,
Hard as the nether millstone.
17 Divine beings are in dread as he rears up;
As he crashes down, they cringe.
18 No sword that overtakes him can prevail,
Nor spear, nor missile, nor lance.
19 He regards iron as straw,
Bronze, as rotted wood.
20 No arrow can put him to flight;
Slingstones turn into stubble for him.
21 Clubs[b] are regarded as stubble;
He scoffs at the quivering javelin.
22 His underpart is jagged shards;
It spreads a threshing-sledge on the mud.
23 He makes the depths seethe like a cauldron;
He makes the sea [boil] like an ointment-pot.
24 His wake is a luminous path;
He makes the deep seem white-haired.
25 There is no one on land who can dominate him,
Made as he is without fear.

a-a Meaning of Heb. uncertain. *b Meaning of Heb. uncertain.*

make all references to the Leviathan. Thus v. 3a would read: "Who has confronted him and come out whole?" (cf. 9.4a). **4:** The translation of the second line is a paraphrase; read perhaps: "(nor will I keep silent concerning) his might ("gevurato" instead of "gevurot") and the grace of his combat"—God is proud of His creature's fighting power. **5:** *His outer garment,* his hide. *Folds of his jowls,* read with LXX: "his double coat of armor" ("siryono" instead of "risno"; cf. Jer. 46.4; 51.3). **7:** *His pride,* read with LXX and Latin: "his back" ("gevo" instead of "gaʾava"). **8:** *Breath,* more likely, "(no) space" (instead of "ruaḥ," read "revaḥ"; Gen. 32.17). **10:** *Glimmerings of dawn,* an echo of 3.9. **11–13:** In this respect the Leviathan is a clone of the Deity (see Ps. 18.9), reinforcing the idea that God is powerful and to be feared. **14:** *Power,* reading "dobʾah" (Deut. 33.25 and cf. in Ugaritic) for "deʾava." **17:** *As he rears up,* rather, "of his majesty" (rendered "threat" in relation to God in 13.11); the Leviathan's dread demeanor is a double of the Deity's aspect. **22:** *Jagged shards,* or "flashes of the sun" (Rashi). **23:** The thrashing of the Leviathan causes the water to roil, as though it were *seeth*ing. **24:** The wake of the "sea" (rather than *deep*) turns *white* with foam. **25:** *Who can dominate him,* more usually understood, "(no one) like him." *Made . . . :* The Leviathan fears nothing; to the contrary, he horrifies and terrifies—as though Job had not suffered enough.

26 He sees all that is haughty;
He is king over all proud beasts.

42 Job said in reply to the LORD:

2 I know that You can do everything,
That nothing you propose is impossible for You.
3 Who is this who obscures counsel without knowledge?
Indeed, I spoke without understanding
Of things beyond me, which I did not know.
4 Hear now, and I will speak;
I will ask, and You will inform me.
5 I had heard You with my ears,
But now I see You with my eyes;
6 Therefore, I recant and relent,
Being but dust and ashes.

7 After the LORD had spoken these words to Job, the LORD
said to Eliphaz the Temanite, "I am incensed at you and your
two friends, for you have not spoken the truth about Me as did
My servant Job. 8 Now take seven bulls and seven rams and go
to My servant Job and sacrifice a burnt offering for yourselves.
And let Job, My servant, pray for you; for to him I will show
favor and not treat you vilely, since you have not spoken the
truth about Me as did My servant Job." 9 Eliphaz the Temanite
and Bildad the Shuhite and Zophar the Naamathite went and
did as the LORD had told them, and the LORD showed favor to
Job. 10 The LORD restored Job's fortunes when he prayed on behalf of his friends, and the LORD gave Job twice what he had
before.
11 All his brothers and sisters and all his former friends came
to him and had a meal with him in his house. They consoled
and comforted him for all the misfortune that the LORD had
brought upon him. Each gave him one *kesitah*[a] and each one
gold ring. 12 Thus the LORD blessed the latter years of Job's life
more than the former. He had fourteen thousand sheep, six
thousand camels, one thousand yoke of oxen, and one thousand she-asses. 13 He also had seven sons and three daughters.

a A unit of unknown value.

26: *Proud beasts,* cf. 28.8.

42.1–6: Job's second response to God is conventionally understood as a capitulation. Attention to the parody in vv. 2–4 and to the language in v. 6 yields the interpretation Elie Wiesel has famously sought but did not find: Job's disappointment and continuing defiance. **2:** *Nothing you propose is impossible,* a nearly verbatim allusion to God's condemnation of the builders of Babel in Gen. 11.6. **3:** *Who obscures,* a nearly verbatim parody of God in 38.2, except that *obscures* has a double entendre: "who causes to know" (cf. Arabic). *Indeed, I spoke ...,* in view of the parody, ironic. **4:** *Hear now ...,* a parody of Elihu in 33.1. *I will ask,* a parody of God in 38.3; 40.7. **5:** Job has already claimed to have seen and heard all (13.1)—the divine address has only confirmed his perspective. **6:** The Heb can sustain neither this nor most other translations. The verb rendered *recant* requires a direct object, which is lacking. *Dust and ashes* is a figurative expression referring to the abject human condition (see Gen. 18.27; Job 30.19); but the preposition "'al" cannot mean "being." This key v. should thus be rendered: "Therefore I am disgusted (see 7.16), and I take pity (cf. e.g., 2 Sam. 13.39) on wretched humanity." This understanding of the Heb is reflected in a liturgical poem recited on the evening of Yom Kippur: "Take pity on (pathetic) humanity!"

42.7–9: As we return to the prose framework, God's reply is not only unexpected but radical: Job had spoken "truthfully" (see the intro., "Subject and Theme"), and the companions, rehearsing traditional theology, have not. The companions can be forgiven only after atoning through sacrifices (cf. Num. 23.1) and having Job pray on their behalf. Job's intercessory role evokes those of Abraham (Gen. 20.7), Moses (e.g., Num. 12.13), Samuel (e.g., 1 Sam. 15.11), and Jeremiah (e.g., Jer. 7.16). Rabbis such as Rava, who maintained that Job's assertions were heresy, learn from God's approbation that a person is not responsible for what he may say in pain (*b. B. Bat.* 16b). **10–17:** Job's restoration does not explicitly include his healing. **10:** *Restored ... fortunes,* the expression elsewhere refers only to the restoration of a people (e.g., Jer. 30.3; 33.11; 48.47; 49.6, 39). Some see the restoration as evidence of God's justice; others understand it as starting over at the end of the test. **11:** *Consoled and comforted,* like the companions in 2.11. *The LORD,* and not the Satan, who is absent from the narrative conclusion (see 1.13 n.; 2.3 n.). *Kesitah,* a payment, originally a "lamb," evoking the patriarchal era (Gen. 33.19). **12:** Job's wealth (livestock) is restored in double measure (see 1.3). **13:** Job is

[14] The first he named Jemimah, the second Keziah, and the third Keren-happuch. [15] Nowhere in the land were women as beautiful as Job's daughters to be found. Their father gave them estates together with their brothers. [16] Afterward, Job lived one hundred and forty years to see four generations of sons and grandsons. [17] So Job died old and contented.

blessed with another ten children, to compensate for the ones he lost (the number of children is not doubled). Naḥmanides (13th c.) cannot believe that God would have allowed for the death of Job's original children, so he explains that the ten restored children are the original ones, secreted away by the Satan along with the cattle and servants, to execute the test. **14:** *Jemimah,* "Dove." *Keziah,* "Cassia." *Keren-happuch,* "Horn of kohl (mascara)." The naming of the daughters, and not the sons, recalls the episode of Zelophehad's daughters in Num. 27.1–11, which established that daughters may inherit from their father when there are no sons. **15:** The beauty of Job's daughters recalls Esth. chs 1–2. *Gave them estates:* In characteristically radical fashion, the book of Job has the daughters inheriting from their father along *with their brothers; with* is lit. "in the midst of," a usage that indicates an equal share (e.g., Num. 27.7). Cf. Gen. 31.14, which implies that a wealthy father may assign part of his estate to his daughters. **16:** A long life and many progeny is a biblical ideal esp. in wisdom literature (e.g., Ps. 1.3). *One hundred and forty years* is twice the natural human lifespan (Ps. 90.10). We do not know how long Job lived prior to this. **17:** A patriarchal death; cf. Gen. 35.29; 25.8. In a long addition drawing on Gen. ch s36 (see the intro., "Setting and Language"), the LXX adds that Job is Jobab (known from Gen. 36.32–33), Uz ("Ausis") is situated on the border of Idumea and Arabia, and his companions were kings.

חמש מגלות

The Five Megillot (Scrolls)

IN PRINTED EDITIONS OF THE TANAKH, the three initial books of Kethuvim—Psalms, Proverbs, and Job (sometimes ordered Psalms, Job, Proverbs)—are followed by five shorter books called *ḥamesh megillot,* "the five scrolls." These books were likely copied together on one scroll (much like the prophetic collection of the Twelve) because they fit the size of an average scroll (parchment was expensive and large sections of one would not be left empty) and also perhaps because they all were read liturgically. The order in which the five books appear varies in different texts. These five books were not always perceived as a single unit nor were they grouped together. In the Septuagint (LXX), Ruth, which opens "In the days that the judges ruled," appears after Judges, and Lamentations is placed after Jeremiah since an ancient tradition ascribes the authorship of Lamentations to Jeremiah. The Babylonian Talmud as well does not know the term *ḥamesh megillot* nor the order in which they are arranged today; it suggests (*b. B. Bat.* 14b) that the order of the beginning of the Kethuvim is: Ruth, Psalms, Job, Proverbs, Ecclesiastes, Song of Songs, Lamentations. A small number of medieval Hebrew manuscripts follow this tradition, as well as other orders that do not place these five books together.

The order in the NJPS Tanakh translation is a common one, found in numerous medieval manuscripts. The arrangement follows the order in which the books are read liturgically in the annual cycle, beginning with the spring new year (see Exod. 12.2): Song of Songs is read on Passover (April), Ruth on Shavuʿot (May–June), Lamentations on the Ninth of Av (July–August), Ecclesiastes on Sukkot (September–October), and Esther on Purim (March). Another common arrangement, found in the best early manuscripts (Aleppo Codex, the first complete Masoretic manuscript [10th c.], and Leningrad Codex B19A, the earliest extant complete manuscript [11th c.]; see essay "Masoretic Bible," pp. 2159–65), places the *megillot* in chronological order according to theories of traditional authorship: Ruth (Samuel), Song of Songs (Solomon in his youth), Ecclesiastes (Solomon in his old age), Lamentations (Jeremiah), and Esther (Mordecai, after the Babylonian exile). Many other arrangements are known. The grouping together of the five books reflects their common liturgical use, and perhaps a desire to have another pentad, to parallel the five books in the Torah and the five books within the book of Psalms.

[ADELE BERLIN AND MARC ZVI BRETTLER]

שיר השירים

The Song of Songs

THE SONG OF SONGS is the Tanakh's only extensive discourse on human, erotic love. The book consists of a series of poems in which the speech of two lovers is interspersed with occasional comments by other voices. Throughout the poems, the lovers describe themselves and each other, and their feelings of love, desire, and longing. While the book has no narrative plot, the relationship between the lovers is marked by cycles of absence and presence, with poems that celebrate the presence of a lover alternating with poems of longing and poems of invitation. While both lovers speak, the woman is the more active and articulate character. Her experiences, feelings, and perceptions are the central focus.

The Song is characterized by a wide range of literary techniques including wordplay, pun and soundplay, repetition, simile, metaphor, and double entendre. These literary features are powerful tools for communicating the experience of the lovers and the nature of their relationship. The frequent shifts in the poem—from praise to adjuration, from playfulness to violence, and from third-person to second-person address—draw the audience in to the dynamic energy and immediacy of the lovers' relationship.

The dense web of echoes and repetitions in the poem gives the audience a non-linear, cyclical experience that echoes the cycles of seeking and finding and desire and fulfillment that characterize the relationship. While the Song of Songs is not a linear narrative, these repetitions and echoes encourage it to be read as an unfolding story about two characters whom the audience comes to know better as the poem progresses. The frequent use of double entendre creates the impression of veiled, but undeniable sexuality that mimics the references to the lovers hiding and seeking and their coy flirtation.

The lush imagery of the poem, which draws on the beauty of the natural world, the royal court and other luxurious settings, mirrors the exuberance and sensual lushness of the lovers' relationship. The imagery is indeed sensual in that it appeals to all the senses: hearing, seeing, tasting, smelling, and touching. The poem's varied imagery and motifs reflects the variety and scope of the lovers' feelings for one another. Because the imagery and tone of the poem is so varied, it has generated many different interpretations of the lovers' relationship. While most readers see the relationship as an idyllic and romantic one, other readers have understood it to be more complex—marked not only by intimacy and desire but also by objectification and the constraints of conventional Israelite gender relationships.

The compositional history and origin of the Song of Songs remain matters of debate. Most commentators agree that the book is a collection of poetic units which are linked by theme, language, and style. There are disagreements, however, over the extent of each unit and the degree of coherence of the collection. Some scholars assert that the canonical text is the product of a redactor who edited together preexistent poems and poetic fragments. However, an increasing number of scholars argue that the poem is the work of a single author who drew on earlier sources, traditions, and poetic conventions.

The date of composition of the Song is also unclear. With the exception of the few references to King Solomon, there is no mention of known historical figures or events. Nor do the references to human behavior correlate to the attitudes or situations of a particular historical period. In addition, the book contains both archaic language and relatively late words, which makes it difficult to establish a date on linguistic grounds. Contemporary scholarly consensus hypothesizes that the poem probably has its roots in early folk and literary traditions but was composed or redacted in the 4th or 3rd c. BCE.

The original genre and function of the text have also been the subject of much research and debate. Over the past century, three major theories have been adduced. The first is that the Song is the script of a drama which told the story of a love affair. This theory was quite popular in the 19th c., but has since been abandoned. The second theory holds that the Song evolved from a Mesopotamian liturgical context which described the sacred marriage of a god and goddess. This theory is based on perceived similarities between the Song and ancient Mesopotamian sacred marriage texts. Like the dramatic theory, this theory has become less popular in recent years, but it remains possible that some of the images of the poem originate in liturgical or mythological traditions. The third, most satisfactory theory maintains that the text is a collection of poems about human love, some of which may have originally been used in wedding celebrations. While it is difficult to determine the poem's original setting, the poem was certainly composed to be performed orally. Consequently the sounds of the words, and other elements of the poem that would have been perceptible to listening audiences would have been particularly important in communicating the meanings of the poem.

The Song's positive focus on human, erotic love and its silence regarding the central theological and historical themes of the rest of the biblical text make it unique within the biblical canon. Some scholars have argued that already by the time of its inclusion in the canon, the Song was understood not only as human love poetry but also, and perhaps primarily, as a description of the love relationship between God and Israel. This theory rests partly on the use of the human love relationship as a metaphor for the God-Israel relationship in the prophetic literature (e.g., Isa. 54.4–8; Jer. 2.1–2; Ezek. chs 16, 23; Hos. chs 1–3). While it is possible that the allegorical understanding of the poem was already current at the time of the book's canonization, it is also possible that the poems were introduced into the canon because, as secular love songs, they occupied an important place in the culture of ancient Israel in Second Temple times. Once the book became part of the canon, the tendency to interpret it allegorically increased (see below). Within contemporary scholarship, the poem's distinctive focus on human love relations, the centrality of the woman character, and its intense sensuality have become predominant concerns. Scholars have explored the poem both within the context of ancient Israelite attitudes regarding gender and sexuality and as an expression of timeless human experiences of love and desire. For feminist scholars and scholars of gender and queer theory, the poem provides a powerful alternative to the patriarchal view of women's sexuality that is far more common in the Bible.

Song of Songs in Jewish Tradition

THE HISTORY OF INTERPRETATION of the Song in Jewish tradition is well documented. From as early as the 2nd c. CE it was understood in both human and divine terms. In rabbinic tradition, the Song narrates the words which God and Israel spoke to each other at the Red Sea, at Sinai, or in the Tent of Meeting. The descriptions of the male lover are understood as allegorical descriptions of God while the descriptions of the female lover are understood as divine praise of Israel. The statements of desire and love are read as expressions of love and intimacy between God and Israel. The Targum to the Song employs a similar strategy of expounding the Song as a historical allegory; it interprets the Song as a description of Israel's ongoing history of redemption by God. The allegorical interpretation plays a particularly important role in early Jewish mysticism. In medieval mystical texts, the theme of love remains constant but the identification of the protagonists changes. The lovers are sometimes identified as God and Israel, and sometimes interpreted as God and the individual soul or, alternatively, as the male and female aspects of the divine. The Song of Songs also plays a role in the Jewish liturgical tradition. It is recited at Passover and, in some communities, is recited or sung as part of the *kabbalat shabbat* (welcoming the Sabbath) service on Friday night.

While there has been a constant tradition of theological interpretation of the Song within Judaism, there has also been a tradition of secular, humanistic interpretation. The Talmud (*b. Sanh.* 101a) testifies to the singing of the Song in the secular settings of feasts and drinking halls, though it polemicizes against this use. In addition, words and images from the Song of Songs have figured prominently in Jewish marriage art, music, and liturgy since at least the Middle Ages. Only one anonymous medieval commentary that does not partake in allegorical interpretation has survived from the Middle Ages. The Song was also a popular biblical text for the early Zionist movement. Its lush descriptions of the natural world and the flora and fauna of the land of Israel gave voice to the early Zionist love for the land.

[ELSIE STERN]

1 The Song of Songs, by[a] Solomon.

2 [b]Oh, give me of the kisses of your mouth,[b]
For your love is more delightful than wine.
3 Your ointments yield a sweet fragrance,
Your name is like finest[c] oil—
Therefore do maidens love you.
4 Draw me after you, let us run!
[d]The king has brought me to his chambers.[d]
Let us delight and rejoice in your love,
Savoring it more than wine—
[e]Like new wine[e] they love you!

a *Or "concerning."* *b-b* *Heb. "Let him give me of the kisses of his mouth!"*
c *Meaning of Heb. uncertain.*
d-d *Emendation yields "Bring me, O king, to your chambers."*
e-e *Understanding* mesharim *as related to* tirosh; *cf. Aramaic* merath.

1.1: Title. Internal evidence suggests that this v. was added after the book was completed. *Song of Songs* is a superlative (like "king of kings"), meaning "the greatest or preeminent song." *By Solomon,* or "about Solomon." According to biblical tradition, Solomon authored the books of Prov. (Prov. 1.1), Eccl. (Eccl. 1.1), and Song. This tradition conforms with Solomon's attributes as a wise man, an expert in flora and fauna (1 Kings 5.9–14), and a lover of many women (1 Kings 11.1). Modern scholars do not accept the ascription of authorship to Solomon since the book refers to Solomon in the third person (3.7, 9, 11; 8.11) and uses late biblical language. In both the Tg. and the midrash, the name "Shlomo" (Solomon) is interpreted as a reference to God. The Song is interpreted metaphorically as a description of the love between God and Israel.

1.2–4: The woman expresses her desire for her lover. 2: *Oh, give me of the kisses of your mouth:* The direct address of the opening line as well as the shifting subjects and breathless quality of these vv. introduce a sense of immediacy that is one of the Song's distinctive literary features. *Wine:* The repeated references to wine (2.4, 7; 4.10; 5.1; 7.10; 8.2) may suggest an original context in wedding feasts or other celebrations where wine was drunk. Wine also functions poetically as a symbol of intoxicating sensuous pleasure. **3:** *Finest oil,* or, "oil poured out," the Heb is obscure; the lover's excellent reputation is widespread. **4:** *The king:* References to a king and to King Solomon and his queens (1.12; 3.9, 11; 6.8–9; 7.6) support interpretations of the Song as a royal wedding song or cultic song. In rabbinic interpretations, the king is understood as God, and the royal chambers as the Temple. In most modern readings, the references to the king are understood as complimentary references to the male lover The royal references throughout the poem also communicate the richness and luxuriousness of the lovers' experience.

1.5–6: The woman describes herself. 5: *Dark, but comely,* or "dark and comely." In 5.10, fair skin is a sign of masculine beauty. Here, the woman's darkness may be either an asset or a liability, and is the likely result of her work outdoors, described in the following vv. *Kedar,* northern Assyrian nomadic tribe. Kedar means "dark." The woman's dark complexion is compared to the black tents of Kedar, parallel to the "pavilions" (Heb "curtains") of Solomon. The word "Shelomoh," "Solomon," is perhaps better read as Shalmah, the name of an ancient Arabian tribe. *Daughters of Jerusalem:* The group appears repeatedly (3.5, 10–11; 5.8–9; 6.1; 8.4), and some have compared them to a Greek chorus. Like readers/hearers of the poem, these characters are invited to witness and eavesdrop on the woman's desire for her lover. **6:** *Vineyard:* In the Song, the vineyard often represents both a physical place and the woman's sexuality (1.14; 2.15; 7.13; 8.12).

1.7–17: Dialogue between the lovers. 7: *Tell me, ...* Though playful, this dialogue introduces the recurrent theme of the woman's search for her absent lover. **9:** *I have likened ... :* Throughout the Song, the lovers use comparison to praise one another's beauty and charm. *Mare in Pharaoh's chariots,* either an image of adorned majesty (the horses were decorated with ornaments) or a reference to an ancient battle strategy in which a mare was let loose among cavalry to distract the stallions. **12–14:** The physical closeness of the lovers—their scent—is described. *Nard ... myrrh ... henna,* precious spices used in perfumes. Nard and myrrh were exotic imports while henna was indigenous to biblical Israel. **14:** *En-gedi,* a lush, garden-like oasis in the Judean wilderness, near the Dead Sea. Given that wine grapes did not grow there, this too is a likely allusion to the woman's own sexuality. **17:** The lovers' "home" is among fragrant and protecting trees. *Cedars* and *cypresses* are tall trees with scented wood.

5 I am dark, but comely,
O daughters of Jerusalem—
Like the tents of Kedar,
Like the pavilions of Solomon.
6 Don't stare at me because I am swarthy,
Because the sun has gazed upon me.
My mother's sons quarreled with me,
They made me guard the vineyards;
My own vineyard I did not guard.

7 Tell me, you whom I love so well;
Where do you pasture your sheep?
Where do you rest them at noon?
Let me not be [a]as one who strays[a]
Beside the flocks of your fellows.
8 If you do not know, O fairest of women,
Go follow the tracks of the sheep,
And graze your kids[b]
By the tents of the shepherds.

9 I have likened you, my darling,
To a mare in Pharaoh's chariots:
10 Your cheeks are comely with plaited wreaths,
Your neck with strings of jewels.
11 We will add wreaths of gold
To your spangles of silver.

12 While the king was on his couch,
My nard gave forth its fragrance.
13 My beloved to me is a bag of myrrh
Lodged between my breasts.
14 My beloved to me is a spray of henna blooms
From the vineyards of En-gedi.

15 Ah, you are fair, my darling,
Ah, you are fair,
With your dove-like eyes!
16 And you, my beloved, are handsome,
Beautiful indeed!
Our couch is in a bower;
17 Cedars are the beams of our house,
Cypresses the rafters.

2 I am a rose[c] of Sharon,
A lily of the valleys.

a-a Meaning of Heb. uncertain. *b As a pretext for coming.* *c Lit. "crocus."*

2 Like a lily among thorns,
So is my darling among the maidens.

3 Like an apple tree among trees of the forest,
So is my beloved among the youths.
I delight to sit in his shade,
And his fruit is sweet to my mouth.
4 He brought me to the banquet room
[a]-And his banner of love was over me.-[a]
5 "Sustain me with raisin cakes,
Refresh me with apples,
For I am faint with love."
6 His left hand was under my head,
His right arm embraced me.
7 I adjure you, O maidens of Jerusalem,
By gazelles or by hinds of the field:
Do not wake or rouse
Love until it please!

8 Hark! My beloved!
There he comes,
Leaping over mountains,
Bounding over hills.
9 My beloved is like a gazelle
Or like a young stag.
There he stands behind our wall,
Gazing through the window,
Peering through the lattice.
10 My beloved spoke thus to me,
"Arise, my darling;
My fair one, come away!
11 For now the winter is past,
The rains are over and gone.
12 The blossoms have appeared in the land,
The time of pruning[b] has come;
The song of the turtledove
Is heard in our land.
13 The green figs form on the fig tree,
The vines in blossom give off fragrance.
Arise, my darling;
My fair one, come away!

14 "O my dove, in the cranny of the rocks,
Hidden by the cliff,
Let me see your face,
Let me hear your voice;

a-a *Meaning of Heb. uncertain.* *b* *Or "singing."*

2.1–3: The lovers praise one another for their uniqueness. **1:** *Sharon,* a fertile plain in northern Israel. **3:** *Apple tree:* The precise type of fruit is unknown; perhaps quince or apricot. Perhaps Heb "tapuaḥ" is a generic term for fragrant fruit; compare "pomme" in French. Just as the woman is "a lily among thorns" (v. 2), so is the man a tree with blossoms and fruit compared with the non-fruit-bearing trees of the forest.

2.4–7: The woman reminisces about her lover. **4:** *He brought me:* This is the first of several episodes that the woman recounts throughout the poem (3.1–4; 5.2–7; 8.5). These snippets of narrative are unique to the woman's voice in the Song. **7:** *I adjure you ... :* This recurring refrain (3.5; 5.8; 8.4), whose exact meaning is ambiguous, is addressed to the woman's female companions. *By gazelles ... :* In Heb, the names of these animals function as wordplays on the name of God (e.g., *gazelles,* "tzeva'ot," also means "hosts," as in "Lord of hosts"), which would be expected in such an adjuration; they also underscore the earthy quality of the oath and resonate with the use of these animals as symbols of love and beauty throughout the Song.

2.8–17: The woman's wish for the couple to run away together, to be alone in nature in the springtime. This passage is full of flora and fauna. **9:** *My beloved is like a gazelle:* Throughout the poem, the woman invokes the man's freedom and mobility which contrast with expectations regarding women's behavior that were common in the ancient Near East. The image of the man looking through the window contrasts with the image elsewhere in the Bible of women looking out of windows from private interior spaces into the more public arenas outside. **10–13:** *Arise, my darling .... Arise, my darling:* The repetition of the phrase sets these vv. apart as a separate unit. While many biblical texts are concerned with the land of Israel and its fertility, this is one of the few that celebrate the beauty of

For your voice is sweet
And your face is comely."
15 Catch us the foxes,
The little foxes
That ruin the vineyards—
For our vineyard is in blossom.

16 My beloved is mine
And I am his
Who browses among the lilies.
17 When the day [a-]blows gently[-a]
And the shadows flee,[b]
Set out, my beloved,
Swift as a gazelle
Or a young stag,
For the hills of spices![c]

3 Upon my couch at night[d]
I sought the one I love—
I sought, but found him not.
2 "I must rise and roam the town,
Through the streets and through the squares;
I must seek the one I love."
I sought but found him not.
3 [e-]I met the watchmen[-e]
Who patrol the town.
"Have you seen the one I love?"
4 Scarcely had I passed them
When I found the one I love.
I held him fast, I would not let him go
Till I brought him to my mother's house,
To the chamber of her who conceived me
5 I adjure you, O maidens of Jerusalem,
By gazelles or by hinds of the field:
Do not wake or rouse
Love until it please!
6 Who is she that comes up from the desert
Like columns of smoke,
In clouds of myrrh and frankincense,
Of all the powders of the merchant?
7 There is Solomon's couch,
Encircled by sixty warriors
Of the warriors of Israel,

a-a Emendation yields "declines"; cf. Jer. 6.4.
b Septuagint reads "lengthen"; cf. Jer. 6.4.
c Heb. bather *of uncertain meaning; 8.14 reads* besamim, *"spices."*
d I.e., in a dream.
e-e Lit. "The watchmen met me."

the land of Israel. **14:** *O my dove:* The dove, a symbol of purity, gentleness, and fidelity, is a frequent epithet for the woman in the Song (cf. 2.15; 5.2; 6.9). **15:** *Catch us ... :* The relationship of this fragment to the surrounding vv. is unclear. It may be either a fragment of a separate poem or proverb or the woman's response to the man's request in v. 14. **16:** *My beloved is mine:* This declaration of mutual love is frequently reused in wedding liturgies, music, and art. *Who browses among the lilies*: Like many others in the Song, this v. functions as a double entendre, echoing the themes of hiding and seeing. The sexual meaning of the images, where *the lilies* represent the erotic female body, is present but not fully visible. The double entendre functions like clothing that covers a body while revealing, or hinting at, its sexuality. **17:** This v. is mirrored in the conclusion of the Song.

3.1–6: The woman searches for her lover. The dreamlike quality of the episode (*upon my couch at night*), found here and at the beginning of ch 5, is one of the many poetic techniques employed in the Song. **1:** *I sought, but found him not:* A refrain (see v. 2 and 5.6) that highlights the desperate tone that contrasts with the playful, hide-and-go-seek mode of the previous ch. **4:** *My mother's house:* Motherhood is a central image in the Song (cf. 3.11; 6.9; 8.1, 5). Here, the mother represents security and support for the lovers. **5:** See 2.7.

3.6–11: Vision of royal wedding procession. The unit may be intended as a description of an actual royal wedding procession or as the woman's imaginative description of her lover. It consists of two parallel descriptions. The first (vv. 6–8) employs the language of war and has an undertone of violence; the second (vv. 9–11) employs the language of royalty and romance. Literarily, this unit mimics the experience of seeing an object become progressively clearer as it approaches from a distance. **6:** *Who is she,* or, what is this? The feminine form of the pronoun

8 All of them trained[a] in warfare,
Skilled in battle,
Each with sword on thigh
Because of terror by night.

9 King Solomon made him a palanquin
Of wood from Lebanon.
10 He made its posts of silver,
Its back[b] of gold,
Its seat of purple wool.
Within, it was decked with [c-]love
By the maidens of Jerusalem.[-c]
11 O maidens of Zion, go forth
And gaze upon King Solomon
Wearing the crown that his mother
Gave him on his wedding day,
On his day of bliss.

4 Ah, you are fair, my darling,
Ah, you are fair.
Your eyes are like doves
Behind your veil.
Your hair is like a flock of goats
Streaming down Mount Gilead.
2 Your teeth are like a flock of ewes[d]
Climbing up from the washing pool;
All of them bear twins,
And not one loses her young.
3 Your lips are like a crimson thread,
Your mouth is lovely.
Your brow behind your veil
[Gleams] like a pomegranate split open.
4 Your neck is like the Tower of David,
Built [e-]to hold weapons,[-e]
Hung with a thousand shields—
All the quivers of warriors.
5 Your breasts are like two fawns,
Twins of a gazelle,
Browsing among the lilies.
6[f] When the day blows gently
And the shadows flee,
I will betake me to the mount of myrrh,
To the hill of frankincense.

a Cf. Akkadian aḫāzu, *"to learn."* *b Meaning of Heb. uncertain.*
c-c Emendation yields "ebony, / O maidens of Jerusalem!"
d Cf. 6.6; exact nuance of qeṣuboth *uncertain, perhaps "shorn ones."*
e-e Apparently a poetic figure for jewelry; meaning of Heb. uncertain.
f See notes at 2.17.

(she) probably refers to Solomon's couch. **9–11:** *Solomon made . . . :* These vv. may be among the oldest parts of the Song. *Palanquin,* a covered chair that was set on poles and carried on the shoulders of four men. **10:** *Silver . . . gold . . . purple wool,* symbols of wealth and royalty. They were also used in the construction of the Tabernacle (Exod. ch 26). Consequently, the rabbinic commentators interpreted these vv. in reference to the Tabernacle. **11:** *Wearing the crown:* Grooms wore crowns in the Second Temple period, though after the destruction of the Second Temple, the practice was abolished as a sign of mourning. *On his wedding day:* Rabbinic interpreters understood this as a reference to the giving of Torah at Mt. Sinai. The idea that God and Israel were married at Sinai appears in *Song Rab.*, other midrashic texts, and liturgical texts from the rabbinic and medieval periods.

4.1–5.1: Dialogue about the woman's beauty and charms. The beginning of this unit corresponds to a genre called the "waṣf," known from Arabic poetry and ancient Egyptian love poetry. Each part of the body is compared to a different object with which it shares one trait. As a result, the comparisons are often surprising and whimsical. In this "waṣf," the objects of comparison are drawn primarily from the pastoral and natural spheres. The literary effects of the "waṣfs" have been interpreted in a variety of ways: they lead the reader/hearer to engage playfully with the poem by finding the resemblance at the heart of the comparison; they communicate the lovers' exuberant delight in one another; they alienate and objectify the lover by itemizing the parts of her body; they dissolve the boundaries between the lover and the natural world in a way that parallels other dissolving of boundaries in the poem (e.g., between the lovers themselves, past and present, dream and reality, the natural and human worlds). **4.1:** The woman's wavy hair flows down her back. *Mount Gilead,* rich pastureland in

7 Every part of you is fair, my darling,
There is no blemish in you
8 From Lebanon come with me;
From Lebanon, my bride, with me!
Trip down from Amana's peak,
From the peak of Senir[a] and Hermon,
From the dens of lions,
From the hills[b] of leopards.

9 You have captured my heart,
My own,[c] my bride,
You have captured my heart
With one [glance] of your eyes,
With one coil of your necklace.
10 How sweet is your love,
My own, my bride!
How much more delightful your love than wine,
Your ointments more fragrant
Than any spice!
11 Sweetness drops
From your lips, O bride;
Honey and milk
Are under your tongue;
And the scent of your robes
Is like the scent of Lebanon.

12 A garden locked
Is my own, my bride,
A fountain locked,
A sealed-up spring.
13 Your limbs are an orchard of pomegranates
And of all luscious fruits,
Of henna and of nard—
14 Nard and saffron,
Fragrant reed and cinnamon,
With all aromatic woods,
Myrrh and aloes—
All the choice perfumes.
15 [d-][You are] a garden spring,
A well of fresh water,[-d]
A rill of Lebanon.

16 Awake, O north wind,
Come, O south wind!

a Cf. Deut. 3.9. *b Emendation yields "lairs"; cf. Nah. 2.13.*
c Lit. "sister"; and so frequently below.
d-d Emendation yields "The spring in my garden / Is a well of fresh water."

the Transjordan region. **2:** *A flock of ewes ... her young,* an extended simile for the whiteness and evenness of the woman's teeth. The similarity in sound between the Heb words "shekulam" ("all of them") and "shakulah" ("loses her young") reinforces the notion of symmetry on the level of sound. **3:** *Pomegranate,* common symbol in the Song for color and taste. Here, either a reference to the color or shape of her brow or of the play of light and dark between her skin and her veil. **4:** *Tower of David:* This structure is not mentioned elsewhere in the Bible, and is not identical with the tower of the same name in modern Jerusalem. The image is that of a long neck adorned with necklaces. **6:** *When the day blows gently:* This echoes 2.17. The repetition of words, phrases and images in the Song contributes to its poetic unity and reinforces, on the level of word and sound, the portrayal of love as a never-ending cycle of seeking and finding, desire and fulfillment. *The mount of myrrh* and *the hill of frankincense* most likely refer to the woman's breasts. **8:** *Lebanon, Amana, Senir, Hermon,* mountains in the north of Israel. In the midrash, this v. is used as a prooftext for the idea that God goes into exile with Israel and will return to the land of Israel with the people (cf. Ezek. 11.16). **9:** *You have captured my heart:* Throughout the poem, the man uses language of power, military might and even slight danger to describe the woman's effect on him (cf. 1.9; 4.8; 6.4; 7.6) *My own,* lit. "my sister." Brother and sister are also used as terms of endearment in Egyptian love poetry. They symbolize closeness here, and are not to be taken literally as biological siblings. See 8.1. **10:** *How much more delightful ... :* The man's praise echoes the woman's in 1.2. **11:** *Sweetness drops:* The Heb words "nofet titofnah" form an onomatopoetic phrase which mimics the sound of dripping liquid. *Honey and milk,* symbols of agricultural plenty. "Land of milk and honey" is a frequent epithet for the land of Israel (e.g., Exod. 3.8). **12–16:** The garden represents the

Blow upon my garden,
That its perfume may spread.
Let my beloved come to his garden
And enjoy its luscious fruits!

5 I have come to my garden,
My own, my bride;
I have plucked my myrrh and spice,
Eaten my honey and honeycomb,
Drunk my wine and my milk.

Eat, lovers, and drink:
Drink deep of love!

2[a] I was asleep,
But my heart was wakeful.
Hark, my beloved knocks!
"Let me in, my own,
My darling, my faultless dove!
For my head is drenched with dew,
My locks with the damp of night."
3 I had taken off my robe—
Was I to don it again?
I had bathed my feet—
Was I to soil them again?
4 My beloved [b-]took his hand off the latch,[-b]
And my heart was stirred [c-]for him.[-c]
5 I rose to let in my beloved;
My hands dripped myrrh—
My fingers, flowing myrrh—
Upon the handles of the bolt.
6 I opened the door for my beloved,
But my beloved had turned and gone.
I was faint [d-]because of what he said.[-d]
I sought, but found him not;
I called, but he did not answer.
7 I met the watchmen[e]
Who patrol the town;
They struck me, they bruised me.
The guards of the walls
Stripped me of my mantle.
8 I adjure you, O maidens of Jerusalem!
If you meet my beloved, tell him this:
That I am faint with love.

a In vv. 2–8 the maiden relates a dream. *b-b Meaning of Heb. uncertain.*
c-c Many manuscripts and editions read "within me" ('alai).
d-d Change of vocalization yields "because of him." *e See note at 3.3.*

woman's sexuality; in v. 12, it is inaccessible; in v. 16 she invites her lover in. **5.1:** The man responds. The string of four first-person *(I)* verbs followed by direct objects with possessive suffixes communicates a sense of completion and possession. *Eat, lovers, and drink:* The unidentified speaker is perhaps the daughters of Jerusalem or an unnamed speaker, or the man himself, speaking to his companions.

5.2–7: Second nighttime episode. This unit echoes the dreamlike sequence in 3.1–4. Vv. play out in slow motion the woman's dream of hearing her lover approach, trying to rise from her bed to open the door for him, and when she finally does, he is gone. Here, however, unlike 3.1–4, the ending is dark and violent, suggesting unfulfilled desire. The unit's imagery is replete with sexual innuendo, where the house may represent the woman's body. **5–6:** *I rose .... I opened:* The repetition of the personal pronoun *I* ("'ani") lends emphasis to the woman's actions. **6–7:** *I sought ... him .... my mantle:* The repetition of the word "found" (*I ... found him not* and *I met the watchmen* [lit. "the watchmen found me"]) and the symmetrical structure of v. 7 lend coherence to this darkly ironic episode in which the watchmen, who are supposed to protect the city, perpetrate an act of unexplained, and seemingly unmotivated, violence. The ironic tone is compounded by the tension between the suggestions of sexual intercourse in vv. 5–6 and the explicit plot of the episode. **8:** *I adjure you,* variation of 2.7; 5.8; 8.4.

9: *How is your beloved,* either a request for identifying information or a question regarding the reasons for the woman's intense love.

5.10–16: The woman praises the man's beauty. This unit corresponds to the "waṣf" in 4.1–7 (see n.) and is the only extended description of the male body in the Song. The imagery is drawn from the realms of animals, plants, and precious metals and stones, and is more static than the "waṣfs" of the woman. It is also the only "waṣf" which is addressed to a third party rather than to the described lover.

6.1–3: Dialogue between the woman and the daughters of Jerusalem. 2: *My beloved has gone down to his garden,* description of a sexual encounter. The identification of the garden with the woman's body generates the double entendre here—see 2.16 n. **3:** *I am my beloved's,* see 5.5–6 n.

9 How is your beloved better than another,[a]
O fairest of women?
How is your beloved better than another[a]
That you adjure us so?

10 My beloved is clear-skinned and ruddy,
Preeminent among ten thousand.
11 His head is finest gold,
His locks are curled
And black as a raven.
12 His eyes are like doves
By watercourses,
Bathed in milk,
[b-]Set by a brimming pool.[-b]
13 His cheeks are like beds of spices,
[c-]Banks of[-c] perfume
His lips are like lilies;
They drip flowing myrrh.
14 His hands are rods of gold,
Studded with beryl;
His belly a tablet of ivory,
Adorned with sapphires.
15 His legs are like marble pillars
Set in sockets of fine gold.
He is majestic as Lebanon,
Stately as the cedars.
16 His mouth is delicious
And all of him is delightful.
Such is my beloved,
Such is my darling,
O maidens of Jerusalem!

6 "Whither has your beloved gone,
O fairest of women?
Whither has your beloved turned?
Let us seek him with you."
2 My beloved has gone down to his garden,
To the beds of spices,
To browse in the gardens
And to pick lilies.
3 I am my beloved's
And my beloved is mine;
He browses among the lilies.

a *Or "What sort of beloved is your beloved?"*
b-b *Meaning of Heb. uncertain.*
c-c *Septuagint vocalizes as participle, "producing."*

4 You are beautiful, my darling,
as Tirzah,
Comely as Jerusalem,
*a-*Awesome as bannered hosts.*-a*
5 Turn your eyes away from me,
For they overwhelm me!
Your hair is like a flock of goats
Streaming down from Gilead.
6 Your teeth are like a flock of ewes
Climbing up from the washing pool;
All of them bear twins,
And not one loses her young.
7 Your brow behind your veil
[Gleams] like a pomegranate split open.
8 There are sixty queens,
And eighty concubines,
And damsels without number.
9 Only one is my dove,
My perfect one,
The only one of her mother,
The delight of her who bore her.
Maidens see and acclaim her;
Queens and concubines, and praise her.

10 Who is she that shines through like the
dawn,
Beautiful as the moon,
Radiant as the sun
*a-*Awesome as bannered hosts?*-a*

11 I went down to the nut grove
To see the budding of the vale;
To see if the vines had blossomed,
If the pomegranates were in bloom.
12 *a-*Before I knew it,
My desire set me
Mid the chariots of Ammi-nadib.*-a*

7 Turn back, turn back,
O maid of Shulem!
Turn back, turn back,
That we may gaze upon you.
"Why will you gaze at the Shulammite
In[b] the Mahanaim dance?"

a-a Meaning of Heb. uncertain.
b With many manuscripts and editions; others read "like." Meaning of entire line uncertain.

6.4–9: The man describes his lover. Some of the imagery of this "waṣf" parallels the beginning of ch 4. **4:** *Tirzah,* capital of the Northern Kingdom of Israel in the late 10th and early 9th centuries BCE. It was replaced by Samaria and is here perhaps serving as a fabled royal city. *Jerusalem:* Biblical (e.g., Ps. 48.3; Lam. 2.16) and later Jewish texts ascribe legendary and mythic beauty to the city. *Awesome as bannered hosts,* or visions. This quasi-military reference which follows references to the highly fortified capitals of Israel and Judah underscores the double meaning of awesome—as both amazing and daunting. **5–7:** *Your hair .... split open,* cf. 4.1b–3. **8:** *There are sixty queens ... :* The man's praise echoes the woman's praise in 2.2–3; 5.10. **9:** *Mother,* see 3.4 n. **10:** *Beautiful ... sun:* The terms for sun ("the hot one") and moon ("the white one") here are highly poetic. The woman is like the breaking of the dawn, or perhaps like the morning star; even more, she is as radiant as the moon and the sun.

6.11–12: Episode fragment. Again a seeming escape to the world of nature, the site of lovemaking. The meaning of v. 12 eludes scholars.

7.1: Address to the woman. The speaker is ambiguous. Possibilities include the man, the women of Jerusalem or another unidentified group. *Maid of Shulem:* Shulem as a place name is unattested elsewhere in the Bible. It may be a variation of Shunem, a shortened form of Jerusalem, or a derivation from the root "shalem," "whole," which refers to Solomon or to the woman's wholeness and perfection. *In the Mahanaim dance:* Mahanaim, a place in the Northern Kingdom of Israel, can mean "two camps." This v. has been read alternatively as a serious rebuke or a coy invitation. The exhortation not to look, followed by an extended physical description in the following vv. highlights the pattern of hiding and revealing that permeates the poem.

2 How lovely are your feet in sandals,
O daughter of nobles!
Your rounded thighs are like jewels,
The work of a master's hand.
3 Your navel is like a round goblet—
Let mixed wine not be lacking!—
Your belly like a heap of wheat
Hedged about with lilies.
4 Your breasts are like two fawns,
Twins of a gazelle.
5 Your neck is like a tower of ivory,
Your eyes like pools in Heshbon
By the gate of Bath-rabbim,
Your nose like the Lebanon tower
That faces toward Damascus.
6 The head upon you is like [a-]crimson wool,[-a]
The locks of your head are like purple—
[b-]A king is held captive in the tresses.[-b]
7 How fair you are, how beautiful!
O Love, with all its rapture!
8 Your stately form is like the palm,
Your breasts are like clusters.
9 I say: Let me climb the palm,
Let me take hold of its branches;
Let your breasts be like clusters
of grapes,
Your breath like the fragrance of apples,
10 And your mouth like choicest wine.
"Let it flow to my beloved as new wine[c]
[b-]Gliding over the lips of sleepers."[-b]

11 I am my beloved's,
And his desire is for me.
12 Come, my beloved,
Let us go into the open;
Let us lodge [d-]among the henna shrubs.[-d]
13 Let us go early to the vineyards;
Let us see if the vine has flowered,
If its blossoms have opened,
If the pomegranates are in bloom.
There I will give my love to you.
14 The mandrakes yield their fragrance,
At our doors are all choice fruits;

a-a So Ibn Janah and Ibn Ezra, taking karmel *as a by-form of* karmil: *cf. 2 Chron. 2.6, 13; 3.14.*
b-b Meaning of Heb. uncertain. *c See note at 1.4 end.*
d-d Or "in the villages."

7.2–7: Description of the woman. While other "waṣfs" (see 4.1–5.1 n.) describe the body from top down, this "waṣf," which may describe the woman dancing, begins at the woman's feet and moves up and uses artisanal, natural and architectural imagery. **2:** *Daughter of nobles:* "Bat-nadiv" echoes the enigmatic phrase in 6.12. **3:** *Heap of wheat,* a reference either to the shape and color of her belly or to its fertility. **4:** See 4.5. **5:** *Tower of ivory,* cf. 4.4. *Heshbon,* city in ancient Moab. *Bath-rabbim:* The location is unattested elsewhere in the Bible. *Nose:* This comparison has troubled commentators. Some have suggested "face" instead of "nose" and read the simile as a symbol of stateliness; others understand this as a comic comparison. **6:** *Crimson wool,* or, "like the Carmel mountain range," another image of stateliness. **8–10:** The "waṣf" serves as a kind of sexual foreplay that the lover wishes to consummate.

7.11–14: The woman speaks to her lover. Again, nature is the setting for love. **11:** *I am my beloved's . . . ,* explicitly erotic variation on the mutual declaration of love (cf. 5.6; 6.3). **12:** *Come, my beloved:* This v. is the opening line of the song, "lekha dodi," which was incorporated by kabbalists in early modern times into the Sabbath eve liturgy. **13:** *Vineyards,* see 1.6 n. **14:** *Mandrakes,* understood as an aphrodisiac and fertility plant (cf. Gen. 30.14–15). *At our doors . . . for you,* cf. 1.6 in which the woman states that she has not kept her vineyard.

Both freshly picked and long-stored
Have I kept, my beloved, for you.

8 If only it could be as with a brother,
As if you had nursed at my mother's breast:
Then I could kiss you
When I met you in the street,
And no one would despise me.
2 I would lead you, I would bring you
To the house of my mother,
Of her who taught[a] me—
I would let you drink of the spiced wine,
Of my pomegranate juice.

3 His left hand was under my head,
His right hand caressed me.
4 I adjure you, O maidens of Jerusalem:
Do not wake or rouse
Love until it please!

5 Who is she that comes up from the desert,
Leaning upon her beloved?

Under the apple tree I roused you;
It was there your mother conceived you,
There she who bore you conceived you.

6 Let me be a seal upon your heart,
Like the seal upon your hand.[b]
For love is fierce as death,
Passion is mighty as Sheol;
Its darts are darts of fire,
A blazing flame.
7 Vast floods cannot quench love,
Nor rivers drown it.
If a man offered all his wealth for love,
He would be laughed to scorn.

8 "We have a little sister,
Whose breasts are not yet formed.
What shall we do for our sister
When she is spoken for?
9 If she be a wall,
We will build upon it a silver battlement;
If she be a door,
We will panel it in cedar."

a Emendation yields "bore"; cf. 6.9; 8.5. *b Lit. "arm."*

8.1–6: The woman speaks of her love and desire. 1: The woman longs for closeness with her lover and an openly affectionate relationship. **2:** *House of my mother,* see 3.4 n. **4:** *I adjure you,* see 2.7 n. **5:** *Who is she ... :* This fragment seems unconnected to the surrounding vv. It echoes 3.6a and 6.10. *Apple tree,* see 2.3 n.

8.6–7: Testimony to the power of love. These vv. are unique in the poem because they deal with love in the abstract. In addition, the cosmic, mythic language contrasts with the bucolic, pastoral, and artisanal images that dominate the rest of the poem. **6:** *Seal upon your heart,* sign of intimate connection and identity. Seals of semiprecious stones were worn around the neck and were used to prove identity, as we use a signature. See Gen. 38.18. *Sheol,* land of the dead. The connection between love and death is particularly evocative. **7:** *If a man:* This v. returns to the humanistic language which is more typical of the poem. The final phrase may also be read as a question: If a man ... would he be laughed to scorn?

8.8–10: Dialogue between the woman and unnamed characters. The speaker in v. 8 is not identified. Possibilities include the woman's brothers, either in the present or in a remembered conversation, or the women of Jerusalem. The *little sister* might be the woman herself or another character. **8–9:** Scholars disagree over the relationship between wall and door here. Some read the two terms as synonyms. In this case, the speakers vow to protect her inviolability. Others read them as opposites. If the woman is inaccessible like a wall, her brothers will reward her. If she is open like a door, they will board her up.

8.11–12: The woman compares herself to Solomon's vineyard. *I have my very own vineyard,* cf. 1.6. Solomon's vineyard had many keepers, but this vineyard (the beloved) is kept by and for one person only.

8.13–14: The woman's final invitation to her lover. The final vv. of the poem return to the imagery of the garden, spices, and gazelles. Is it the woman suggesting that she will flee with her lover, or is she telling him to flee from her? In line with this ambiguity, the hills of spices may refer to a place outside, or to the woman herself (see 4.6 n.). Just as the poem began in the middle of an encounter, so too does it end without strong closure. This structure contributes to the immediacy of the poem, giving the reader the impression of witnessing an ongoing relationship, not one confined to the past. It also underscores the cyclical nature of love.

10 I am a wall,
My breasts are like towers.
So I became in his eyes
As one who finds favor.

11 Solomon had a vineyard
In Baal-hamon.
He had to post guards in the vineyard:
A man would give for its fruit
A thousand pieces of silver.
12 I have my very own vineyard:
You may have the thousand, O Solomon,
And the guards of the fruit two hundred!

13 O you who linger in the garden,[a]
A lover is listening;
Let me hear your voice.
14 "Hurry, my beloved,
Swift as a gazelle or a young stag,
To the hills of spices!"

a *Heb. plural. Meaning of verse uncertain.*

רות

Ruth

THIS BEAUTIFUL SHORT STORY revolves around the relationship between Naomi, a woman from Bethlehem, in Judah, and her Moabite daughter-in-law, Ruth. Naomi, her husband, and their two sons have come to Moab to escape from famine in Bethlehem. The first chapter recounts, in short order, the death of Naomi's husband, the marriage of her sons to Moabite women, the sons' deaths ten years later, and Naomi's decision to return to Bethlehem. One daughter-in-law, Orpah, returns to her Moabite family. The other, Ruth, declares allegiance to Naomi and to the God of Israel and returns with Naomi. Despite Ruth's company, Naomi is embittered at her many losses. In the course of the book, however, these losses are all reversed. In the second chapter, Ruth gleans in the field of Naomi's kinsman, Boaz, and acquires enough grain to sustain Naomi and herself for some time. In the third chapter, Naomi devises a plan for Ruth's future security: Ruth will pay a nighttime visit to the threshing floor where Boaz has been winnowing the barley harvest, and will thereby elicit a promise of marriage. The plan is successful and culminates, in chapter four, in the marriage of Ruth and Boaz and the birth of their child, Obed. The book ends with a genealogy which traces the line of Obed back to Perez, the child of Judah and Tamar (Gen. ch 38), and forward to King David.

The simplicity of the story belies the literary craft of the book. Its central theme is the movement from emptiness to fulfillment. This theme is expressed on various planes, the agricultural, or national, and the personal, with the agricultural sequence anticipating the personal sequence all through the plot. The famine, affecting all of Judah, precedes Naomi's own bereavement, and the renewed harvest during which Ruth gleans in Boaz's fields anticipates the abundance and fulfillment that awaits Naomi through Obed's birth. Obed's birth, in turn, foreshadows David, the symbol par excellence of the nation. The fidelity and love between Naomi and Ruth is the most well-developed and positive portrayal of women's relationships in biblical literature. The centrality of women is also emphasized by the references in Ruth 4.11–12 to other prominent biblical women, namely, Leah and Rachel, the two wives of Jacob, and Tamar, whose son by Judah, who himself is Jacob's son, is an ancestor of Boaz, and therefore of Obed and David as well. Whether the book's author was male or female cannot be determined, but the prominence of women has allowed the book to be a resource for reflection on women's relationships and other aspects pertinent to the representation of gender in the Hebrew Bible.

The story portrays Ruth, Naomi, and Boaz as models of *ḥesed,* that is, of loyalty and commitment that go beyond the bounds of law or duty. *Ḥesed* is exemplified in the fidelity of Ruth to Naomi, the loving concern of Naomi for Ruth, and the kindness of Boaz to both women. Related to the motif of *ḥesed* is the role of God. God is mentioned numerous times by the three main characters, but the actions of the story are never explicitly said to have been caused by God. Rather, God remains in the shadows, implying that God rewards such acts of *ḥesed,* and that divine activity lies behind the reversal of the deprivations that have afflicted Naomi and the nation as a whole.

The author of the book is unknown and its date is difficult to establish. Many earlier scholars proposed a date between 950 and 700 BCE, that is, between the time of David and the Assyrian conquest of the Northern Kingdom of Israel. More recently, scholars opt for a date during the period of the Babylonian exile or in the early period of the return (586–500 BCE). In that case, the book may be read as a story of return, promising that those who return from exile will be blessed with family continuity in their land just as Naomi was blessed when she returned from Moab to Bethlehem. A story recounting the lineage of David would also have had special meaning in exilic or postexilic times, when the Davidic monarchy had come to an end, and the hope for its restoration blossomed. If the story was written in the early exilic period, its positive depiction of Ruth the Moabite may be polemicizing against the strong opposition in Ezra-Nehemiah to intermarriage (see esp. Ezra 9.2, 10; Neh. 13.23–30), claiming instead that foreigners may be integrated into the Jewish community.

In the Jewish Scriptures, Ruth is included among the Five "Megillot" (scrolls) in the third division, namely, the "Writings" (Kethuvim). (See those introductions, p. 1557 and 1263–64.) Because the book is read in the synagogue on Shavuʿot, the Feast of Weeks, it usually appears second among the megillot, after Song of Songs, which is read at Passover, though other sequences for these five books are found in manuscripts. The association with Shavuʿot is appropriate. The events told in Ruth span a period somewhat equivalent to that of Passover to Shavuʿot, that is, a seven-week period from the beginning of the barley harvest to the end of the wheat harvest. Furthermore, King David, the culmination of the genealogy in Ruth 4.18–22, was traditionally thought to have been born and to have died on Shavuʿot (*b. Ḥag.* [*Chagiga*] 12a). Finally, Shavuʿot has been identified since early postbiblical times as the time of the giving of the Torah to Moses on Mount Sinai (cf. Exod. chs 19–20). This element of the festival is related to the prevalent rabbinic theme of Ruth as the ideal convert to Judaism who takes the Torah upon herself just as the Israelites did at Mount Sinai.

In Christian Bibles, Ruth is placed between Judges and the books of Samuel, following the order of the Septuagint (LXX), which arranged these books chronologically, according to their setting; Ruth is set in the period of the judges (1.1) and ends with a genealogy of David (4.18–22).
It therefore provides a link between the chaotic period when Israel was ruled by judges and the stories that lead up to the establishment of the monarchy, which reaches its highest point in the reign of David.

[ADELE REINHARTZ]

1 In the days when the chieftains[a] ruled, there was a famine in the land; and a man of Bethlehem in Judah, with his
wife and two sons, went to reside in the country of Moab. 2 The
man's name was Elimelech, his wife's name was Naomi, and his two sons were named Mahlon and Chilion—Ephrathites of Bethlehem in Judah. They came to the country of Moab and remained there.
3 Elimelech, Naomi's husband, died; and she was left with her
two sons. 4 They married Moabite women, one named Orpah

a I.e., the leaders who arose in the period before the monarchy; others "judges."

1.1–22: From Moab to Bethlehem. 1.1–5: Naomi and her family in Moab. 1: The judges *(chieftains)* were tribal leaders of Israel in the period before the monarchy. Several biblical texts reflect tension between the Israelites and the Moabites, who lived east of the Dead Sea (see Num. 21.29–30; Deut. 23.4; Jer. 48.1–9). This tension, however, is not apparent in the book of Ruth (cf. 1 Sam. 22.3–4). *Bethlehem* means "house of bread"; this v. therefore puns by describing a *famine* in "the house of bread." **2:** *Ephrathites:* Ephrathah (see 4.11) is another name for Bethlehem. **3–5:** The names of Naomi and her family members may have symbolic significance. *Elimelech* literally means "my God is king"; *Mahlon* means "sickness"; *Chilion* may mean "consumptive"; *Orpah* is interpreted as "back of the neck"; *Ruth* may be

and the other Ruth, and they lived there about ten years. 5 Then
those two—Mahlon and Chilion—also died; so the woman was
left without her two sons and without her husband.
6 She started out with her daughters-in-law to return from
the country of Moab; for in the country of Moab she had heard
that the LORD had taken note of His people and given them
food. 7 Accompanied by her two daughters-in-law, she left the
place where she had been living; and they set out on the road
back to the land of Judah.
8 But Naomi said to her two daughters-in-law, "Turn back,
each of you to her mother's house. May the LORD deal kindly
with you, as you have dealt with the dead and with me! 9 May the
LORD grant that each of you find security in the house of a husband!" And she kissed them farewell. They broke into weeping
10 and said to her, "No, we will return with you to your people."
11 But Naomi replied, "Turn back, my daughters! Why should
you go with me? Have I any more sons in my body who might be
husbands for you? 12 Turn back, my daughters, for I am too old
to be married. Even if I thought there was hope for me, even if I
were married tonight and I also bore sons, 13 should you wait for
them to grow up? Should you on their account debar yourselves
from marriage? Oh no, my daughters! My lot is far more bitter
than yours, for the hand of the LORD has struck out against me."
14 They broke into weeping again, and Orpah kissed her
mother-in-law farewell. But Ruth clung to her. 15 So she said,
"See, your sister-in-law has returned to her people and her
gods. Go follow your sister-in-law." 16 But Ruth replied, "Do not
urge me to leave you, to turn back and not follow you. For wherever you go, I will go; wherever you lodge, I will lodge; your people shall be my people, and your God my God. 17 Where you
die, I will die, and there I will be buried. [a]Thus and more may
the LORD do to me[-a] if anything but death parts me from you."
18 When [Naomi] saw how determined she was to go with her,
she ceased to argue with her; 19 and the two went on until they
reached Bethlehem.

When they arrived in Bethlehem, the whole city buzzed with
excitement over them. The women said, "Can this be Naomi?"
20 "Do not call me Naomi,"[b] she replied. "Call me Mara,[c] for

a-a A formula of imprecation. *b I.e., "Pleasantness."* *c I.e., "Bitterness."*

"friend" or "companion"; *Naomi* is "pleasant"; and *Boaz* (2.1) is "in him is strength." These traits describe, to some degree, the role of the character within the story.

1.6–18: Naomi plans her return to Bethlehem. 6: Naomi attributes relief from the famine to God. This is one of several hints that a divine hand is guiding the events in the story. **8:** The term *mother's house* occurs elsewhere (Gen. 24.28; Song 3.4; 8.2). Childless widows are normally portrayed as returning to their fathers' homes (Gen. 38.11; Lev. 22.13). The unusual formulation is appropriate because Naomi is asking the young women to return to their mothers rather than remaining with their mother-in-law. **11:** According to Deut. 25.5–10, a childless widow is bound to marry her dead husband's brother. This is referred to as levirate law (from Latin "levir," "brother-in-law"). The first son of a levirate marriage will legally be the dead man's son for purposes of inheritance. Even were Naomi to give birth to more sons, they would not be obligated by levirate law to marry the widows, because they would not have had the same father as did her dead sons. **12:** *Ruth Rab.* points out that Naomi urges her daughters-in-law to turn back three times (vv. 8, 11, 12). This threefold admonition corresponds to later Jewish tradition and practice, according to which potential converts were to be strongly discouraged three times; those who persisted, however, were to be educated and accepted as sincere converts. **14:** *Ruth clung to her:* Ruth's attachment to Naomi is reminiscent of Gen. 2.24, which refers to the "clinging" of husband to wife. The connotation here is probably not sexual, but rather signifies Ruth's unswerving devotion to Naomi. **16–17:** This moving plea is among the best-known lines of the book. It expresses Ruth's devotion and loyalty to Naomi. *Ruth Rab.* and Rashi view Ruth's passionate declaration of allegiance as the point at which Naomi instructs Ruth in a formal process of conversion. The story, however, contains no reference to formal conversion, since that institution did not come into existence until rabbinic times. However, non-Jews did join the Jewish community in earlier times even in the absence of a formal procedure or ceremony: Ruth is an example. *Thus ... do to me:* Ruth's oath underscores the seriousness of her declaration. It has been interpreted to mean "only death will part us" or "not even death will part us."

1.19–23: Naomi and Ruth arrive in Bethlehem. 20–21: *Shaddai,* a divine epithet, perhaps used here as an archaism; in Job, where it is

Shaddai[a] has made my lot very bitter. 21 I went away full, and the LORD has brought me back empty. How can you call me Naomi, when the LORD has [b-]dealt harshly with[-b] me, when Shaddai has brought misfortune upon me!"

22 Thus Naomi returned from the country of Moab; she returned with her daughter-in-law Ruth the Moabite. They arrived in Bethlehem at the beginning of the barley harvest.

2 Now Naomi had a kinsman on her husband's side, a man of substance, of the family of Elimelech, whose name was Boaz.

2 Ruth the Moabite said to Naomi, "I would like to go to the fields and glean among the ears of grain, behind someone who may show me kindness." "Yes, daughter, go," she replied; 3 and off she went. She came and gleaned in a field, behind the reapers; and, as luck would have it, it was the piece of land belonging to Boaz, who was of Elimelech's family.

4 Presently Boaz arrived from Bethlehem. He greeted the reapers, "The LORD be with you!" And they responded, "The LORD bless you!" 5 Boaz said to the servant who was in charge of the reapers, "Whose girl is that?" 6 The servant in charge of the reapers replied, "She is a Moabite girl who came back with Naomi from the country of Moab. 7 She said, 'Please let me glean and gather among the sheaves behind the reapers.' She has been on her feet ever since she came this morning. [c-]She has rested but little in the hut."[-c]

8 Boaz said to Ruth, [d-]"Listen to me, daughter.[-d] Don't go to glean in another field. Don't go elsewhere, but stay here close to my girls. 9 Keep your eyes on the field they are reaping, and follow them. I have ordered the men not to molest you. And when you are thirsty, go to the jars and drink some of [the water] that the men have drawn."

10 She prostrated herself with her face to the ground, and said to him, "Why are you so kind as to single me out, when I am a foreigner?"

11 Boaz said in reply, "I have been told of all that you did for your mother-in-law after the death of your husband, how you left your father and mother and the land of your birth and came to a people you had not known before. 12 May the LORD reward your deeds. May you have a full recompense from the LORD, the God of Israel, under whose wings you have sought refuge!"

a Usually rendered "the Almighty." *b-b Others "testified against."*
c-c Meaning of Heb. uncertain. *d-d Lit. "Have you not heard, daughter?"*

frequent (5.17ff.), it is translated "the Almighty" (see translators' note *a*). **22:** *The beginning of the barley harvest* in the spring is associated in Lev. 23.10 with the Passover festival.

2.1–23: The field. 2.1–7: Ruth's plan. 1: *Boaz,* see 1.3–5 n. **2:** According to biblical law, the poor were permitted to walk behind the harvesters and gather the grain that they left behind (Lev. 19.9; 23.22; Deut. 24.19). Ruth's remark is puzzling in that she apparently plans to work *among the ears* themselves, that is, in the area that has not yet been harvested. This differs from what was permitted in extant biblical law, as do the institutions of the redeemer and the levirate marriage. Here as in other cases, Torah norms were either not known or not normative for the author, or were intentionally being reinterpreted. The fact that Naomi calls Ruth *daughter*—for the first time in this book—suggests that Ruth's love, devotion, and sense of responsibility is now reciprocated by Naomi. **3:** *Luck:* By coincidence—or perhaps divine providence—the field in which Ruth hopes to glean belongs to Naomi's husband's relative Boaz. Ruth is apparently unaware of the connection between Boaz and Naomi. **7:** *Among the sheaves:* Some interpreters suggest that Ruth's request (which goes against the biblical norm) was a ploy to meet the owner of the field, since special permission to glean among the sheaves is granted in 2.15. *She has rested ... hut:* The literal translation is "this is her sitting the house a little." Some commentators emend the text by omitting "the house," in conformity with the LXX. The overall sense is clear, however. The servant is commenting with some admiration on Ruth's stamina and perseverance.

2.8–16: Ruth meets Boaz in the field where she is gleaning.
8: Like Naomi, Boaz refers to Ruth as *daughter.* This form of address conveys his warm attitude toward her, and also stresses the generational difference between them, though their ages are never specified. **12:** This v. summarizes the message of the book: Whoever seeks shelter with the God of Israel will be rewarded. Rabbinic interpreters understand this phrase as a reference to Ruth's conversion. **14:** *Vinegar,*

13 She answered, "You are most kind, my lord, to comfort me
and to speak gently to your maidservant—though I am not so
much as one of your maidservants."
14 At mealtime, Boaz said to her, "Come over here and partake of the meal, and dip your morsel in the vinegar." So she
sat down beside the reapers. He handed her roasted grain, and
she ate her fill and had some left over.
15 When she got up again to glean, Boaz gave orders to his
workers, "You are not only to let her glean among the sheaves,
without interference, 16 but you must also pull some [stalks] out
of the heaps and leave them for her to glean, and not scold her."
17 She gleaned in the field until evening. Then she beat out
what she had gleaned—it was about an *ʾephah* of barley—18 and
carried it back with her to the town. When her mother-in-law
saw what she had gleaned, and when she also took out and gave
her what she had left over after eating her fill, 19 her mother-
in-law asked her, "Where did you glean today? Where did you
work? Blessed be he who took such generous notice of you!" So
she told her mother-in-law whom she had worked with, saying,
"The name of the man with whom I worked today is Boaz."
20 Naomi said to her daughter-in-law, "Blessed be he of the
LORD, who has not failed in His kindness to the living or to the
dead! For," Naomi explained to her daughter-in-law, "the man
is related to us; he is one of our redeeming kinsmen."[a] 21 Ruth
the Moabite said, "He even told me, 'Stay close by my workers
until all my harvest is finished.'" 22 And Naomi answered her
daughter-in-law Ruth, "It is best, daughter, that you go out with
his girls, and not be annoyed in some other field." 23 So she
stayed close to the maidservants of Boaz, and gleaned until the
barley harvest and the wheat harvest were finished. Then she
stayed at home with her mother-in-law.

3 Naomi, her mother-in-law, said to her, "Daughter, I must
seek a home for you, where you may be happy. 2 Now
there is our kinsman Boaz, whose girls you were close to. He
will be winnowing barley on the threshing floor tonight. 3 So
bathe, anoint yourself, dress up, and go down to the threshing
floor. But do not disclose yourself to the man until he has finished eating and drinking. 4 When he lies down, note the place
where he lies down, and go over and uncover his feet and lie

a Cf. Lev. 25.25 and note and Deut. 25.5–6. The fact that Boaz was a kinsman of Ruth's dead husband opened up the possibility of providing an heir for the latter.

actually a refreshing drink of sour wine and oil. Boaz's generosity, in providing drink and *roasted grain,* foreshadows the important role he will come to play in providing (sustenance and offspring) for Ruth and Naomi.

2.17–23: Ruth reports back to Naomi. 17: An *ʾephah* is approximately two-thirds of a bushel, a substantial amount for one day of gleaning. **20:** By identifying Boaz as *one of our redeeming kinsmen,* Naomi suggests his potential role in providing for Ruth and herself, since a "go'el" (redeeming kinsman: see translators' note *a*) had a special obligation to the family.

3.1–18: The threshing floor.
3.1–6: Naomi's plan. 2: The *threshing floor* is an elevated open space where the kernels of grain were separated from the chaff (winnowed). *Winnowing* was done in the evening when strong breezes would carry the light-weight chaff away while the kernels would drop to the ground. **3:** Rashi, following *b. Shab.* 113b, comments that Ruth reversed the order of preparation that Naomi had proposed. First she went down to the threshing floor and then beautified herself, lest passers-by believe her to be a harlot. According to Rashi, following *y. Pe'ah* 8.7, Ruth's preparations related directly to her conversion. In washing herself, Ruth purified herself from her earlier idolatry; in anointing herself, she took upon herself the commandments; in dressing, she put on Sabbath garments, that is, full observance of the Sabbath. This is a most remarkable transformation of a seduction scene. **4:** The most important aspect of Naomi's instructions to Ruth, to *uncover* Boaz's *feet* and *lie down,* is also the most ambiguous. Naomi may simply mean that Ruth should uncover a place at Boaz's feet and lie down. The word *feet,* however, may also be a euphemism for sexual organs (see Isa. 7.20). In this case, Naomi may have a bolder act in mind. Similarly, the verb *lie down,* which appears eight times in this ch, may be a euphemism for sexual intercourse. The frequent use of the verb "to know" also contributes to the sexual innuendo. Most commentators state that sexual intercourse did not actually take place, though several suggest that after awakening from a drunken stupor after a long day's work (3.7), Boaz was unsure whether or not he had intercourse

down. He will tell you what you are to do." 5 She replied, "I will
do everything you tell me."

6 She went down to the threshing floor and did just as her
mother-in-law had instructed her. 7 Boaz ate and drank, and
in a cheerful mood went to lie down beside the grainpile. Then
she went over stealthily and uncovered his feet and lay down.
8 In the middle of the night, the man gave a start and pulled
back—there was a woman lying at his feet!

9 "Who are you?" he asked. And she replied, "I am your
handmaid Ruth. [a]Spread your robe over your handmaid,[a] for
you are a redeeming kinsman."

10 He exclaimed, "Be blessed of the LORD, daughter! Your
latest deed of loyalty is greater than the first, in that you have
not turned to younger men, whether poor or rich.[b] 11 And now,
daughter, have no fear. I will do in your behalf whatever you
ask, for all the [c]elders of my town[c] know what a fine woman
you are. 12 But while it is true I am a redeeming kinsman, there
is another redeemer closer than I. 13 Stay for the night. Then in
the morning, if he will act as a redeemer, good! let him redeem.
But if he does not want to act as redeemer for you, I will do so
myself, as the LORD lives! Lie down until morning."

14 So she lay at his feet until dawn. She rose before one person could distinguish another, for he thought, "Let it not be
known that the woman came to the threshing floor." 15 And he
said, "Hold out the shawl you are wearing." She held it while he
measured out six measures of barley, and he put it on her back.

When she[d] got back to the town, 16 she came to her mother-
in-law, who asked, "How is it with you, daughter?" She told her
all that the man had done for her; 17 and she added, "He gave
me these six measures of barley, saying to me, 'Do not go back
to your mother-in-law empty-handed.'" 18 And Naomi said,
"Stay here, daughter, till you learn how the matter turns out.
For the man will not rest, but will settle the matter today."

a-a A formal act of espousal; cf. Ezek. 16.8.

b I.e., she sought out a kinsman of her dead husband; see note at 2.20 above. Her first act of loyalty had been to return with Naomi.

c-c Lit. "gate of my people."

d So in many Heb. mss; most mss. read "he."

with Ruth. The language conveys a sense of sexual tension that contributes to the sheer entertainment value for the reader.

3.7–13: Ruth meets Boaz at the threshing floor after he has winnowed. 9: Rather than wait for Boaz's instruction, as Naomi had proposed, Ruth takes the initiative. She asks him to *spread* his *robe* ("kanaf") over her, because he is a *redeeming kinsman.* In doing so, she echoes his own words in 2.12, in which he describes her as seeking shelter under God's wing (also "kanaf"). Ruth's words are also a marriage proposal (see translators' note *a-a*). In referring to Boaz as a *redeeming kinsman,* Ruth links the concepts of land redemption and levirate marriage that are not otherwise connected in the Bible (see 4.3–5). The situation is not precisely that of levirate marriage specified in Deut. 25.5–10, however, since Boaz in fact is not the brother of Ruth's dead husband, Mahlon. Had he been, no elaborate pretense would have been required. **10:** Boaz may be hinting that Ruth's proposal of marriage is an even more daring and comprehensive attempt to provide for Naomi's well-being than was her gleaning in the field. Ruth's decision to link her life with him is clearly flattering, particularly because she could have had her choice of young men.

3.14–18: Ruth reports back to Naomi. 15: Here, as at the end of ch 2, Ruth is provided with a large amount of grain to bring home to Naomi. The grain that Boaz gives her symbolizes the "seed" that he will later provide for the conception of their child. Noting that *six measures of barley* is far too much for a single person to carry, the Rabbis suggested symbolic interpretations. Rashi, following *Ruth Rab.* and various talmudic traditions, claimed that the text literally meant "six grains of barley," as a portent that their future son would be blessed with six blessings: the spirit of wisdom and discernment, counsel and might, the spirit of knowledge, and the fear of the LORD (see Isa. 11.2). *Ruth Rab.* suggests that the six grains of barley refer to six righteous descendants: David, Hezekiah (a righteous Judean king—see 2 Kings 18.1–5), Josiah (a righteous Judean king—see 2 Kings 23.24, 25), Hananiah, Mishael, and Azariah (see Dan. chs 1–3). **16:** Naomi's question means, "How do things stand with you, my daughter?" It echoes that of Boaz in v. 9 and thereby links the two older people, though they do not encounter one another directly. **17:** Here, as in 2.21, the words that Ruth reports to Naomi are not part of Boaz's original words to Ruth. Ruth may be fabricating or embroidering in order to emphasize that Boaz's care for Ruth extended to his concern for Naomi.

4 Meanwhile, Boaz had gone to the gate and sat down there. And now the redeemer whom Boaz had mentioned passed by. He called, "Come over and sit down here, So-and-so!" And he came over and sat down. 2 Then [Boaz] took ten elders of the town and said, "Be seated here"; and they sat down.

3 He said to the redeemer, "Naomi, now returned from the country of Moab, must sell the piece of land which belonged to our kinsman Elimelech. 4 I thought I should disclose the matter to you and say: Acquire it in the presence of those seated here and in the presence of the elders of my people. If you are willing to redeem it, redeem! But if you[a] will not redeem, tell me, that I may know. For there is no one to redeem but you, and I come after you." "I am willing to redeem it," he replied. 5 Boaz continued, "When you acquire the property from Naomi [b-]and from Ruth the Moabite, you must also acquire the wife of the deceased,[-b] so as to perpetuate the name of the deceased upon his estate." 6 The redeemer replied, "Then I cannot redeem it for myself, lest I impair my own estate.[c] You take over my right of redemption, for I am unable to exercise it."

7 Now this was formerly done in Israel in cases of redemption or exchange: to validate any transaction, one man would take off his sandal and hand it to the other. Such was the practice[d] in Israel. 8 So when the redeemer said to Boaz, "Acquire for yourself," he drew off his sandal. 9 And Boaz said to the elders and to the rest of the people, "You are witnesses today that I am acquiring from Naomi all that belonged to Elimelech and all that belonged to Chilion and Mahlon. 10 I am also acquiring Ruth the Moabite, the wife of Mahlon, as my wife, so as to perpetuate the name of the deceased upon his estate, that the name of the deceased may not disappear from among his kinsmen and from the gate of his home town. You are witnesses today."

11 All the people at the gate and the elders answered, "We are. May the LORD make the woman who is coming into your house like Rachel and Leah, both of whom built up the House of Israel! Prosper in Ephrathah[e] and perpetuate your name in Bethlehem! 12 And may your house be like the house of Perez whom Tamar bore to Judah—through the offspring which the LORD will give you by this young woman."

a So many Heb. mss., Septuagint, and Targum; most mss. read "he."

b-b Emendation yields "you must also acquire Ruth the Moabite, the wife of the deceased"; cf. v. 10.

c I.e., by expending capital for property which will go to the son legally regarded as Mahlon's; see Deut. 25.5–6.

d Understanding Heb. te'udah *in the sense of the Arabic* ʿādah *and Syriac* ʿyādā. *Cf. Ibn Ezra.*

e Ephrathah is another name applied to Bethlehem; cf. 1.2; Gen. 35.16, 19; 48.7; Mic. 5.1.

4.1–22: The gate. 4.1–12: Boaz "acquires" Ruth. 1: *The gate* was the commercial and judicial center of the town, where legal, business, and political transactions were conducted. Here Boaz encounters "Ploni ʾAlmoni," "Mr. So-and-So," the unnamed *redeemer* (3.12). Although Boaz must have known the name of the kinsman, the narrative does not report it. According to Rashi, following *Ruth Rab.*, and many contemporary commentators, the anonymity expresses the narrator's disapproval of the man's behavior. **2:** *Ten* as the number of a quorum (Heb "minyan") is derived by some from this v. (*b. Ketub.* 7b). **3–4:** It is difficult to reconstruct the precise legal background of these proceedings. Only now do we learn of Elimelech's land, which needs to be redeemed in order to provide for Naomi and Ruth. On redemption of land, see Lev. 25.24–34, 47–55; Jer. 32.7–15. **5:** Boaz implies that the acquisition of Ruth as wife is necessarily tied to the redemption of land (see 3.9 n.). According to Torah law, levirate marriage pertains only to the brother of the dead husband (Deut. 25.5–10) and not to other kinsmen. For this reason, neither Boaz nor the other kinsman is legally bound to marry Ruth. Nor does biblical law link levirate marriage with redemption of the land. Nevertheless, within this story, the link that is articulated by Ruth on the threshing floor is accepted as a fundamental premise by the other characters as well as by the narrator. **8:** The *sandal* represents the conveying of goods or rights from one party to another. In Heb it is not clear whether it was the redeemer who gave his sandal to Boaz or the other way around. *Ruth Rab.* opts for the latter, on the principle that it is the purchaser who gives the pledge. Modern interpreters generally prefer the former. In their view, the act symbolizes the fact that "Ploni ʾAlmoni" relinquishes the obligation and the privilege of redeeming the land and marrying Ruth.

[13] So Boaz married Ruth; she became his wife, and he cohabited with her. The LORD let her conceive, and she bore a
son. [14] And the women said to Naomi, "Blessed be the LORD,
who has not withheld a redeemer from you today! May his
name be perpetuated in Israel! [15] He will renew your life and
sustain your old age; for he is born of your daughter-in-law,
who loves you and is better to you than seven sons."

[16] Naomi took the child and held it to her bosom. She became its foster mother, [17] and the women neighbors gave him
a name, saying, "A son is born to Naomi!" They named him
Obed; he was the father of Jesse, father of David.

[18] This is the line of Perez: Perez begot Hezron, [19] Hezron begot Ram, Ram begot Ammi-nadab, [20] Amminadab begot Nahshon, Nahshon begot Salmon,[a] [21] Salmon begot Boaz, Boaz
begot Obed, [22] Obed begot Jesse, and Jesse begot David.

a Heb. "Salmah."

4.13–17: The birth of Obed. **15:** Though Ruth has disappeared from the story, she is acknowledged and given her due by the women who speak to Naomi after the birth of Boaz and Ruth's son. **16:** It is unlikely that Naomi has become, literally, the child's wet-nurse or adoptive parent; symbolically, however, this child represents Naomi's full recovery from the emotional and spiritual famine she suffered in the book's opening, and symbolizes the complete reversal of Naomi's ill-fortune, her restoration to fullness, and the continuation of her family.

4.18–22: Generations from Perez to David. Obed's genealogy is traced through Boaz, and not through Mahlon as it would be in the case of levirate marriage. The genealogy draws a direct line between *Perez* (son of Tamar) through *Obed* (son of Ruth) to *David.* In this way the theme of family continuity and divine favor through Ruth is extended to embrace national continuity and divine favor through David. The genealogy also helps to frame the book, which opens with Bethlehem, the home of David, and concludes with the genealogy of David.

איכה

Lamentations

THE HEBREW NAME FOR THE BOOK is "'Ekhah" ("How" or "Alas") after its initial word. The name Lamentations is a translation of Greek "Threnoi," the Septuagint's (LXX's) title for the book. The Talmud refers to the book as "Qinot," which means "Elegies" or "Laments." Ancient tradition (see *b. B. Bat.* 15a) ascribes the book's authorship to Jeremiah, a prophet who lived during the last days of the kingdom of Judah and prophesied its demise, and the two books share several significant phrases. The idea that Jeremiah composed laments is found already in 2 Chron. 35.25, which says that Jeremiah composed laments for the death of King Josiah. Modern scholars do not take the ancient ascriptions of authorship literally; they conclude that Lamentations, like most ancient Near Eastern compositions, was written anonymously, and its authors are unknown. The five chs probably originated as independent poems composed by different authors and were later drawn together to form the book.

The book is comprised of five poems about the destruction of the Temple and the city of Jerusalem that occurred in 586 BCE. This was an unprecedented event in Jewish history, both politically—for Judah lost its independence—and religiously—for the Temple, the main locus of sacrificial worship, was destroyed. Lamentations is an outpouring of mourning and grief over this catastrophe, but even more, it is a commemoration, a memorialization, of that event. It eternalizes the experience—the siege, the destruction, the exile—probing it from different perspectives and preserving it with astonishing vividness and immediacy. Lamentations helps to make the destruction a central event in the Jewish memory.

Ancient empires, especially Assyria and Babylonia, engaged in wars of conquest to expand their territory and to increase their resources, and so it was that Babylonia attacked and defeated Judah. The rules of ancient warfare did not distinguish between civilian and military targets. A common tactic was siege warfare. Since cities were walled for protection, they could not be easily defeated by a direct attack initially and were therefore besieged or blockaded until the population that had taken refuge inside was decimated by starvation and disease. At the same time, the attackers employed various technologies (ramps, battering rams, projectiles) to undermine the structure of the walls. Eventually, resistance from within diminished and the walls could be scaled or breached by the enemy. The people who survived the siege and the attack became captives of war, and many were deported to the conquering empire. This is the historical reality underlying the poetic expression of Lamentations.

Each of the five poems has its distinctive tone and theme, and offers a different perspective on the catastrophic defeat. In ch 1 we see Jerusalem, the lonely and shamed city, grieving for her lost inhabitants. Feminine imagery is especially prominent in this chapter, conveying the shameful and the shamed woman, abandoned by her lovers (her supposed allies), emptied of all she holds dear, mocked by passers-by, mourning and deprived of comfort. Ch 2 shifts to the siege of the city and all the horror of starvation and disease that accompanied it. Ch 3 speaks in the voice of a lone man who experiences the deportation into exile. Ch 4 returns to the city in its last days before destruction and gazes upon the degradation that has befallen the population. Ch 5, a prayer, may be read as the view of those who remained in Judah after the destruction, when it had become a Babylonian possession.

The book's first four chs are alphabetic acrostics, a literary device found elsewhere in the Bible (e.g., Pss. 111; 112; 145; Prov. 31.10–31), in which each v. or stanza begins with successive letters of the Hebrew alphabet, twenty-two in all. Ch 3 is a triple acrostic; all three vv. of each stanza begin with the same letter. Ch 5, although not an acrostic, also contains twenty-two vv. In Lamentations this formal device gives expression to the enormity or totality of the destruction (extending "from A to Z") and also provides a structure for the incomprehensible events and unstructured pain that engulfed Judah and its inhabitants. The alphabet helps to render order out of the chaos of destruction.

The language of the book, at times difficult, is highly poetic and extraordinarily moving. Even though at many points it is stereotypical, it is very effective in portraying the violence and suffering of the events described. The experiences of warfare, siege, famine, and death are individualized—brave men reduced to begging, mothers unable to nourish their children and resorting to cannibalism. The national catastrophe is thus made real, as society disintegrates and people die or are deported. All of this outpouring is addressed to God, so that He may feel the suffering of His people, rescue them, and restore them to their country and to their former relationship with Him. The entire book may be thought of as an appeal for God's mercy. Yet God remains silent.

If the book fails to move God, it fulfills another function, that of public mourning which simultaneously relives, commemorates, and attempts to understand a catastrophe of incomprehensible proportion. Lamentations does not create a new theology. It assumes the theology of Deuteronomy, where the sin of disloyalty to God, that is, idolatry, leads to divine punishment and exile (see Deut. ch 28; Lamentations, however, stresses the punishment and minimizes mention of the sin). God is responsible for the disaster; the Babylonians (never mentioned by name in the book) are merely divine agents (as Assyria was in an earlier time; see Isa. 10.5–11), although not altogether blameless. So, God, whose power is not diminished despite the Temple's destruction, must be the one to end the Babylonian dominance and bring about the return from exile. Repentance, the antidote to sin, is mentioned but is not central (this is not penitential prayer); rather, the idea in Lamentations is that the punishment, even though deserved, outweighs the sin (see similarly Isa. 40.2). The immediacy of the disproportionate punishment drowns out everything else.

The book was written after 586 BCE and before the end of the 6th c. BCE, when the Temple was rebuilt, but the exact time, place, and reason for its composition are unknown. Although the poems might sound like eye-witness accounts, they were likely composed some time after the events they describe and not necessarily by someone who experienced them, as most literature of destruction is (this is true of the literature about the destruction of the Second Temple and also of Holocaust literature). Perhaps the poems were used at the site of the ruined Temple to commemorate its loss (see Jer. 41.4–9 n.). The prophet Zechariah (7.5) speaks of fasting and lamenting in the fifth and seventh months (Zech. 8.19 adds the fourth and tenth months)—which commemorated the events leading to the destruction (mentioned by dates in 2 Kings ch 25). It is possible that some of the laments that accompanied these fasts included those in our book.

An ancient Near Eastern tradition of laments over the destruction of cities goes back to the Sumerian laments of the early second millennium BCE (e.g., "Lamentation over the Destruction of Ur," "Lamentation over the Destruction of Sumer and Ur," "Nippur Lament"). Despite the generic similarity, however, no direct line of influence can be drawn from the Sumerian laments to the book of Lamentations. Moreover, the Sumerian laments were recited on the occasion of the rebuilding of a temple, so their "story" has a happy ending. Not so in the book of Lamentations, where hopes for the rebuilding of the Jerusalem Temple remain unrealized, and God, who is so movingly implored to end His people's suffering and exile and to restore them to their former condition, never responds. Some scholars have suggested the existence of a native Israelite city lament tradition that arose from earlier destructions of cities, especially the Northern Kingdom, but the evidence for this is scant and indirect; no pre-586 BCE Israelite city laments have survived (although there are laments for individuals). The poems in the Bible that most resemble Lamentations are Pss. 74 and 79, also written in the aftermath of Jerusalem's destruction (see also Ps. 137).

In Masoretic manuscripts and in Jewish Bibles, Lamentations is located in the Writings, among the Five Scrolls (the ordering of the scrolls differs in various manuscripts), all of which are recited publicly on different occasions throughout the year. (In the LXX and in Christian Bibles, the book follows Jeremiah, who, according to ancient Jewish tradition, wrote it.) Lamentations is read liturgically on Tishʿah beʾav, the Ninth of Av (in July or August), the day of public mourning and fasting in commemoration of the destruction of the First Temple in 586 BCE and of the Second Temple in 70 CE, and around which the commemoration of other Jewish destructions and catastrophes has coalesced. As part of the rites of mourning on this day, the reader and congregation sit on the floor or on low benches when Lamentations is recited by candlelight or dim light, during the evening service (and in some places also during the morning service). Additional poems of lament, composed later, are customarily added afterwards.

[ADELE BERLIN]

1[a] א Alas!
Lonely sits the city
Once great with people!
She that was great among nations
Is become like a widow;
The princess among states
Is become a thrall.
2 ב Bitterly she weeps in the night,
Her cheek wet with tears.
There is none to comfort her
Of all her friends.

a Chaps. 1–4 are alphabetical acrostics, i.e., the verses begin with the successive letters of the Heb. alphabet. Chap. 3 is a triple acrostic. In chaps. 2–4 the letter pe *precedes the* ʿayin.

1.1–22: Jerusalem in mourning, with no one to comfort her. First the poet and then the city lament the destruction of Jerusalem. The ch falls into two parts, two speaking voices: vv. 1–11, the poet, and vv. 12–22, the city (in v. 17 the poet's voice is interjected). Shame, mourning, and suffering are the main themes. The phrase "none [or "no one"] to comfort her/me" occurs four times (vv. 2, 9, 17, 21; cf. vv. 7, 16) and emphasizes unceasing mourning.

1.1–11: The poet laments Jerusalem. Jerusalem is personified as a woman, widowed, abandoned, and shamed. **1:** *Alas!* or "woe" is a mournful cry often at the beginning of dirges (Isa. 1.21; Jer. 48.17; Lam. 2.1; 4.1). It suggests a contrast between a former glorious state and the current state of misery. The widow image evokes loneliness and bereavement, and also vulnerability. Jerusalem's "husband" is God. The poetry in this v., and in many others, has more assonance than the translation reflects. NJPS has rearranged the third and fourth lines, construing the structure of the v. as three sets of two parallel lines instead of a two-part v. with three lines each. Heb reads "Alas, Lonely sits the city, Once great with people, She has become like a widow; She that was great among nations, the princess among states, Is become a thrall." **2:** *Bitterly she weeps,* Heb "bakhoh tivkeh," "weeping she weeps": a common grammatical construction indicating intensity. The Talmud (*b. Sanh.* 104.2) explains that this doubling of the verbal root refers to the destruction of both Temples. *Friends,* political allies who should have come to her aid. Heb "ʾohaveha," lit "lovers," points to Judah's idolatry, her pursuit of "lovers" other than her "husband," God (see e.g., Ezek. chs 16 and 23). **3:** *Misery and harsh oppression* recall the enslavement in Egypt (Gen. 15.13; Exod. 1.11; Deut. 26.6), to which Judah's exile to Babylonia is likened. The v. makes more sense if translated "after misery ... " rather than "because of misery ... " *No rest,* no resting place, no place to dwell secure. **4:** The once-busy thoroughfares are empty of pilgrims to the Temple, for the Temple is destroyed and the people are gone. (The idea that Judah was totally depopulated is a rhetorical exaggeration; many people remained behind in Judah.) **5:** *Her many transgressions,* first of several admissions in this ch (vv. 8, 9, 14, 18, 20) that the sins of Israel brought on the destruction. **6:** *Fair Zion,* (lit. "Daughter of Zion"), the designation of the personified city that appears most frequently throughout Lam. and the Prophets (e.g., 2.1, 4, 8, 10, 13, 18; 4.22; Isa. 1.8; 52.2; Jer. 4.31; Mic. 4.8). It conveys the sense of "dear little Zion." **8:** *A mockery,* or, alternatively, she has been banished. *Seen her disgraced:* lit. "seen her nakedness," meaning her shame. **9:** *Her uncleanness:* The metaphor of ritual impurity (Lev. 15.16–24) is used to indicate Fair Zion's moral impurity. Zion has "exposed herself" immodestly and is sexually immoral. Sexual immorality is, in turn, a metaphor for idolatry, the sin which caused the exile according to many biblical texts. *See, O Lord, my misery* personified Zion's words (1.12), introduced into the poet's lament, integrate the two parts of ch 1.

All her allies have betrayed her;
They have become her foes.
3 ג Judah has gone into exile
Because of misery and harsh oppression;
When she settled among the nations,
She found no rest;
All her pursuers overtook her
[a]-In the narrow places.-[a]
4 ד Zion's roads are in mourning,
Empty of festival pilgrims;
All her gates are deserted.
Her priests sigh,
Her maidens are unhappy—
She is utterly disconsolate!
5 ה Her enemies are now the masters,
Her foes are at ease,
Because the LORD has afflicted her
For her many transgressions;
Her infants have gone into captivity
Before the enemy.
6 ו Gone from Fair Zion are all
That were her glory;
Her leaders were like stags
That found no pasture;
They could only walk feebly
Before the pursuer.

7 ז All the precious things she had
In the days of old
Jerusalem recalled
In her days of woe and sorrow,
When her people fell by enemy hands
With none to help her;
When enemies looked on and gloated
Over her downfall.
8 ח Jerusalem has greatly sinned,
Therefore she is become a mockery.
All who admired her despise her,
For they have seen her disgraced;
And she can only sigh
And shrink back.
9 ט Her uncleanness clings to her skirts.
She gave no thought to her future;
She has sunk appallingly,
With none to comfort her.—
See, O LORD, my misery;

a-a *Meaning of Heb. uncertain.*

How the enemy jeers!
10 י The foe has laid hands
On everything dear to her.
She has seen her Sanctuary
Invaded by nations
Which You have denied admission
Into Your community.
11 כ All her inhabitants sigh
As they search for bread;
They have bartered their treasures for food,
To keep themselves alive.—
See, O LORD, and behold,
[a]How abject[a] I have become!

12 ל [b]May it never befall you,[b]
All who pass along the road—
Look about and see:
Is there any agony like mine,
Which was dealt out to me
When the LORD afflicted me
On His day of wrath?
13 מ From above He sent a fire
Down into my bones.
He spread a net for my feet,
He hurled me backward;
He has left me forlorn,
In constant misery.
14[c] נ The yoke of my offenses is bound fast,
Lashed tight by His hand;
Imposed upon my neck,
It saps my strength;
The Lord has delivered me into the hands
Of those I cannot withstand.
15 ס The Lord in my midst has rejected
All my heroes;
He has proclaimed a set time against me
To crush my young men.
As in a press the Lord has trodden
Fair Maiden Judah.
16 ע For these things do I weep,
My eyes flow with tears:
Far from me is any comforter
Who might revive my spirit;
My children are forlorn,
For the foe has prevailed.

10: The looting of the Temple treasures by the victors (cf. 2 Chron. 36.10) is expressed in sexual terms. The Babylonians, who as foreigners had no rights of access to the Temple, raped it. **11:** A second interjection of personified Zion's words into the poet's lament, leading into Jerusalem's lament in the next section. *See, O LORD, and behold,* a cry to God for compassion.

1.12–22: Jerusalem's lament. The pain of Jerusalem and the harsh treatment she has suffered. 12: Jerusalem calls out for sympathy to passers-by as she called out to God in the previous v. *His day of wrath:* God's destruction is often depicted as transpiring in a single day, the Day of the LORD (e.g., Isa. 13.13; Joel 2.1; Amos 5.18; Obad. 1.15). **13:** The imagery of war—fire and nets to capture prisoners—conveys God's actions against Judah. **14:** The yoke of submission is constructed from Judah's sins; that is, it is the sins that led to this situation. **15:** Judah is crushed and her blood seeps out like wine in a winepress (in contrast to the promise in Deut. 32.14; see also translators' note *d* at Isa. 63.2). **16:** *Comforter:* The absence of a comforter (see vv. 2, 9, 16, 17, 21) is a major theme in the ch. With no one to comfort her, Jerusalem's mourning cannot be completed.

a-a Or (ironically) "What a glutton"; cf. Prov. 23.20–21.
b-b Meaning of Heb. uncertain. *c Meaning of parts of vv. 14 and 15 uncertain.*

17: The poet interrupts Jerusalem's speech, just as she did his (1.9c). *Jacob,* a common term for Judah in postexilic literature. *A thing unclean,* better, "an impure thing," literally, a menstruating woman, who is ritually impure and off limits for sexual relations. Judah's "lovers" (vv. 2, 19; NJPS "friends") do not want to have relations with her because she is in a state of impurity (see Ezek. 36.17 and Radak). **18:** An admission of sin, but the emphasis is on the suffering. **20:** *I know how wrong I was to disobey:* An alternate translation is "How very bitter I am." *Outside,* outside the city walls where the fighting took place. *Indoors,* inside the besieged city the inhabitants were ravaged by famine and disease (see Ezek. 7.15). **22:** The enemy is no more righteous than Judah, and deserves a punishment like hers. *Are many,* Heb "rabot," recalls Heb "rabati" ("great"; twice in 1.1). The city once "great with people" and "great among nations" is now great with respect to sighs. The trope of retribution against the enemy is common in psalms of lament. More than a vindictive call for revenge, it is a plea to restore the world order in which God protects Israel and banishes its enemies. Chs 3 and 4 end in a similar manner.

2.1–22: The Lord is Judah's enemy; in His anger He destroyed the physical structures of Jerusalem with violent force. The angry tone of ch 2 contrasts with the despair of ch 1, and the focus is on God, the perpetrator, rather than on the victim. Many verbs of strong military action portray God as a destroying enemy: e.g., "cast down," "razed," "cut down," "ravaged," "bent his bow," "slew."

2.1–9: God destroys Judah. 1: *Alas!* See 1.1 n., cf. 4.1. *Has shamed:* Heb "yaʿiv" occurs only here and may be interpreted to mean that God has made His holy Temple into an abomination (a term often associated with idolatry), or that He brought a cloud of darkness to the Temple. *The majesty of Israel,* epithet for the

17 פ Zion spreads out her hands,
She has no one to comfort her;
The LORD has summoned against Jacob
His enemies all about him;
Jerusalem has become among them
A thing unclean.

18 צ The LORD is in the right,
For I have disobeyed Him.
Hear, all you peoples,
And behold my agony:
My maidens and my youths
Have gone into captivity!
19 ק I cried out to my friends,
But they played me false.
My priests and my elders
Have perished in the city
As they searched for food
To keep themselves alive.
20 ר See, O LORD, the distress I am in!
My heart is in anguish,
[a-]I know how wrong I was[-a]
To disobey.
Outside the sword deals death;
Indoors, the plague.
21 ש When they heard how I was sighing,
There was none to comfort me;
All my foes heard of my plight and exulted.
For it is Your doing:
[b-]You have brought on the day that You
threatened.
Oh, let them become like me![-b]
22 ת Let all their wrongdoing come before You,
And deal with them
As You have dealt with me
For all my transgressions.
For my sighs are many,
And my heart is sick.

2 א Alas!
The Lord in His wrath
Has shamed[c] Fair Zion,
Has cast down from heaven to earth
The majesty of Israel.

a-a Lit. "My heart has turned over within me"; cf. Exod. 14.5; Hos. 11.8.
b-b Emendation yields "Oh, bring on them what befell me, / And let them become like me!" *c Meaning of Heb. uncertain.*

He did not remember His Footstool[a]
On His day of wrath.
2 ב The Lord has laid waste without pity
All the habitations of Jacob;
He has razed in His anger
Fair Judah's strongholds.
He has brought low in dishonor
The kingdom and its leaders.
3 ג In blazing anger He has cut down
All the might of Israel;
He has withdrawn His right hand
In the presence of the foe;
He has ravaged Jacob like flaming fire,
Consuming on all sides.
4 ד He bent His bow like an enemy,
Poised His right hand like a foe;
He slew all who delighted the eye.
He poured out His wrath like fire
In the Tent of Fair Zion.
5 ה The Lord has acted like a foe,
He has laid waste Israel,
Laid waste all her citadels,
Destroyed her strongholds.
He has increased within Fair Judah
Mourning and moaning.
6 ו He has stripped His Booth[a] like a garden,
He has destroyed His Tabernacle;[b]
The LORD has ended in Zion
Festival and sabbath;
In His raging anger He has spurned
King and priest.
7 ז The Lord has rejected His altar,
Disdained His Sanctuary.
He has handed over to the foe
The walls of its citadels;
They raised a shout in the House of the
LORD
As on a festival day.
8 ח The LORD resolved to destroy
The wall of Fair Zion;
[c-]He measured with a line,[-c] refrained not
From bringing destruction.
He has made wall and rampart to mourn,
Together they languish.

a *I.e., the Temple.*
b *Lit. "(Tent of) Meeting."*
c-c *I.e., He made His plans.*

Temple. *His Footstool,* a designation for the Temple. God is sometimes envisioned as a king sitting in heaven with His feet touching the Temple (see Isa. 60.13; Ezek. 43.7; Ps. 132.7; 1 Chron. 28.2). *Day of wrath,* with echoes in vv. 21 and 22, frames and characterizes ch 2. (See 1.12 and n.) **3:** *All the might of Israel,* lit. "Horn of Israel," signals power and pride (e.g., Jer. 48.25; Ps. 75.11). *His right hand,* this symbol of divine power (e.g., Exod. 15.6, 12) is intentionally withheld, allowing the Babylonians to conquer the city and despoil the Temple. **4:** *The Tent,* the homes in Judah or the Temple (Ps. 27.5). **6:** *His Booth* is the Temple (Ps. 27.5 ["pavilion," "tent"]; 76.3 ["den"]). *Like a garden:* The grammar is difficult. It may mean "as in a garden," that is, that God destroyed the Temple ("His booth") as easily as if it were a hut ("booth") in a garden (a temporary structure used during the harvest). *Festival and sabbath,* God has ended the Temple sacrifices on those days. This v. is a rare but significant indication of the importance of the Sabbath in the preexilic period. **7:** *They raised a shout ... as on a festival day:* The joyous sounds of Temple worship, now silenced, have been replaced by the enemies' exultant crowing. **8:** *Measured with a line:* Instead of using the plumbline to calculate how to erect a building, God is using it to calculate how to destroy it (see Amos 7.7–9). In vv. 8–10 the towers, walls, and gates disintegrate. The movement is from top to bottom, ending with the inhabitants sitting on the ground in mourning.

2.10–19: The survivors bewail their suffering. 10: Each action is a sign of mourning (see Ezek. 27.30; Job 2.12–13). Current Jewish mourning practices that reflect these ancient gestures include sitting on low chairs and wearing clothing that has been torn. **11:** The phrase "shever bat ʿami," *the ruin of my poor people,* occurs also in 3.48; 4.10 ("disaster") and Jer. 8.11 ("wounds"), 21 ("my people is shattered"); 14.17 ("my hapless people has suffered a grievous wound"). **12:** *Where is bread and wine?* Where are the stored up food supplies, the staples. *Bread:* Heb "dagan," "grain," can be stored for a long time, as can wine. But now all the basic supplies have been exhausted. *In their mothers' bosoms,* or "laps." The mothers are holding their children as they starve to death. **14:** Denunciation of false prophets. *Oracles of delusion and deception,* see Jer. 14.13–16; 23.25–27. The Heb here has no word for false prophets, using simply "prophets" ("seers"). **15:** Passers-by make gestures of shock or derision to register Jerusalem's changed state. A similar idealized depiction of Jerusalem, a large village in preexilic times, is found in Ps. 48.2–3.

9 ט Her gates have sunk into the ground,
He has smashed her bars to bits;
Her king and her leaders are [a]in exile,[a]
Instruction[b] is no more;
Her prophets, too, receive
No vision from the LORD.
10 י Silent sit on the ground
The elders of Fair Zion;
They have strewn dust on their heads
And girded themselves with sackcloth;
The maidens of Jerusalem have bowed
Their heads to the ground.
11 כ My eyes are spent with tears,
My heart is in tumult,
[c]My being melts away[c]
Over the ruin of [d]my poor people,[d]
As babes and sucklings languish
In the squares of the city.
12 ל They keep asking their mothers,
"Where is bread and wine?"
As they languish like battle-wounded
In the squares of the town,
As their life runs out
In their mothers' bosoms.
13 מ What can I [e]take as witness[e] or liken
To you, O Fair Jerusalem?
What can I match with you to console you,
O Fair Maiden Zion?
For your ruin is vast as the sea:
Who can heal you?
14 נ Your seers prophesied to you
Delusion and folly.
They did not expose your iniquity
So as to restore your fortunes,
But prophesied to you oracles
Of delusion and deception.
15 ס All who pass your way
Clap their hands at you;
They hiss and wag their head
At Fair Jerusalem:[f]
"Is this the city that was called

a-a *Lit. "among the nations."*
b *Heb.* torah, *here priestly instruction; cf. Jer. 18.18; Hag. 2.11; Mal. 2.6.*
c-c *Lit. "My liver spills on the ground."*
d-d *Lit. "the daughter of my people"; so elsewhere in poetry.*
e-e *Emendation yields "compare."*
f *These gestures were intended to ward off the calamity from the viewer; cf., e.g., Jer. 18.16 and note; Job 27.23.*

Perfect in Beauty,
Joy of All the Earth?"
16 פ All your enemies
Jeer at you;
They hiss and gnash their teeth,
And cry: "We've ruined her!
Ah, this is the day we hoped for;
[a]We have lived to see it!"[a]

17 ע The LORD has done what He purposed,
Has carried out the decree
That He ordained long ago;
He has torn down without pity.
He has let the foe rejoice over you,
Has exalted the might of your enemies.
18 צ [b]Their heart cried out[b] to the Lord.
O wall of Fair Zion,
Shed tears like a torrent
Day and night!
Give yourself no respite,
Your eyes no rest.
19 ק Arise, cry out in the night
At the beginning of the watches,
Pour out your heart like water
In the presence of the Lord!
Lift up your hands to Him
For the life of your infants,
Who faint for hunger
At every street corner.

20 ר See, O LORD, and behold,
To whom You have done this!
Alas, women eat their own fruit,
Their new-born[c] babes!
Alas, priest and prophet are slain
In the Sanctuary of the Lord!
21 ש Prostrate in the streets lie
Both young and old.
My maidens and youths
Are fallen by the sword;
You slew them on Your day of wrath,
You slaughtered without pity.
22 ת You summoned, as on a festival,
My neighbors from roundabout.
On the day of the wrath of the LORD,

a-a Lit. "We have attained, we have seen." *b-b Emendation yields "Cry aloud."*
c The root has this meaning in Arabic; others "dandled."

16: The enemies jeer and mock, as they take credit for Jerusalem's downfall. In this acrostic, and in the following two chs, the letter "pe" precedes the "'ayin," reflecting an alternative order of the alphabet, attested in inscriptions from Izbet Sartah and Kuntillet Ajrud. **17:** *Has carried out the decree,* that if Judah sinned, the Temple would be destroyed and the people exiled from their land (1 Kings 9.6–9). **18–19:** A call to Zion (according to the emendation adopted by NJPS). The "wall" is personified as a supplicant to God on behalf of the city. **19:** *Watches,* the night was divided into three watches (see Exod. 14.24; 1 Sam. 11.11; Song 3.1–3; 5.7). Nighttime is when suffering seems hardest to bear and when many prayers are offered, with the expectation that God will respond in the morning (cf. Ps. 30.6).

2.20–22: Jerusalem's address to God. 20: *Eat their ... babes:* Cannibalism was the extreme result of the famine during a siege (4.10; 2 Kings 6.28) and a punishment for violating the covenant (Deut. 28.53–57); this is a common trope in describing a siege. In this complete reversal of normal behavior, mothers, who cannot nourish their children, eat them when they have died. **21:** *Slaughtered,* as if preparing meat for a sacrifice. **22:** God invites the enemies *as on a festival* when they would participate in a sacrificial meal in the Temple. *Day of the wrath,* see 1.12 n., and 2.1 n.

None survived or escaped;
Those whom I bore[a] and reared
My foe has consumed.

3

א I am the man [b-]who has known affliction
Under[-b] the rod of His wrath;
2 Me He drove on and on
In unrelieved darkness;
3 On none but me He brings down His hand
Again and again, without cease.
4 ב He has worn away my flesh and skin;
He has shattered my bones.
5 All around me He has built
Misery[c] and hardship;
6 He has made me dwell in darkness,
Like those long dead.
7 ג He has walled me in and I cannot break out;
He has weighed me down with chains.
8 And when I cry and plead,
He shuts out my prayer;
9 He has walled in my ways with hewn blocks,
He has made my paths a maze.

10 ד He is a lurking bear to me,
A lion in hiding;
11 [d-]He has forced me off my way[-d] and mangled me,
He has left me numb.
12 He has bent His bow and made me
The target of His arrows:
13 ה He has shot into my vitals
The shafts of His quiver.
14 I have become a laughingstock to all people,
The butt of their gibes all day long.
15 He has filled me with bitterness,
Sated me with wormwood.

a *The root has this meaning in Arabic; others "dandled."*
b-b *Emendation yields "whom the Lord has shepherded with."*
c *Taking* rosh *as equivalent to* resh.
d-d *Meaning of Heb. uncertain.*

3.1–66: Lament and Hope. Lament is mixed with theological reflection, of the type found in the book of Job; hope alternates with despair. This is the longest and most complex poem of the book, arranged as a triple alphabetic acrostic: each letter has three short vv. assigned to it. The subdivisions according to content do not correspond to the alphabetic structure, with the result that the reader is pulled along from one thought to the next and interrupted by a new stanza in mid-thought. There is no logical or organized argument; emotional outpouring shifts back and forth to reasoned thought. The identity of the male speaker has long been debated. Some think he was a historical individual (Jeremiah, Jehoiachin, or Zedekiah have been suggested), but it seems preferable to take him as a literary persona, the counterpart of the female city speaking in 1.12–22, or the collective voice of the people (later in the ch, the "I" merges with the "we"). He is a Job-like figure, using some phraseology similar to Job's (esp. in vv. 25–39; see also v. 4), crying out to God from his suffering, trying to make sense of the terrible event, and to provoke God's response. But unlike Job, he never receives a response from God.

3.1–20: The lament of the male persona, who appears to be describing the deportation into exile. Vv. 1–13 are constructed on the image of God as a bad shepherd who leads His flock into dark and dangerous places (exile), in stark contrast to God as a good shepherd who leads His flock to good grazing land and water (as in Pss. 23; 78.52–53). **1:** *Rod of His wrath,* the shepherd's crook used for divine punishment (e.g., 2 Sam. 7.14; Isa. 10.5; Ps. 89.33). **2:** *Me He drove,* as with the shepherd's rod. *On and on in unrelieved darkness,* to a death-like state (Job 10.21–22; Lam. 3.6). Exile is often compared to darkness, prison, and death (see vv. 6–7), for in exile, as in death, a person has no access to God. **6:** *Long dead,* the eternally dead, who have no hope of life. **8:** *He shuts out my prayer,* see 3.44 n. **10:** *Bear ... lion,* God changes from being a bad shepherd into the dangerous wild animals from whom the shepherd is supposed to protect his flock (cf. David in 1 Sam. 17.34–37). **12–13:** Instead of shooting arrows at the wild animals, God shoots at the speaker. God is elsewhere a divine archer who shoots disaster from His bow; cf. Deut. 32.23–24; Ps. 38.2–3; Job 16.12–13. **15:** *Bitterness ... wormwood,* drinking bitter liquid is a common symbol of suffering, see 3.19; 4.21; Jer. 9.14; Job 9.18. **16:** *He has broken my teeth on gravel:* The Midrash (*Lam. Rab.* 3:16) explains

16 ו He has broken my teeth on gravel,
Has ground me into the dust.
17 My life was bereft of peace,
I forgot what happiness was.
18 I thought my strength and hope
Had perished before the LORD.
19 ז To recall my distress and my misery
Was wormwood and poison;
20 Whenever I thought of them,
I was bowed low.

21 But this do I call to mind,
Therefore I have hope:
22 ח The kindness of the LORD has not ended,
His mercies are not spent.
23 They are renewed every morning—
Ample is Your grace!
24 "The LORD is my portion," I say with full heart;
Therefore will I hope in Him.
25 ט The LORD is good to those who trust in Him,
To the one who seeks Him;
26 It is good to wait patiently
Till rescue comes from the LORD.
27 It is good for a man, when young,
To bear a yoke;
28 י Let him sit alone and be patient,
When He has laid it upon him.
29 Let him put his mouth to the dust—
There may yet be hope.
30 Let him offer his cheek to the smiter;
Let him be surfeited with mockery.
31 כ For the Lord does not
Reject forever,
32 But first afflicts, then pardons
In His abundant kindness.
33 For He does not willfully bring grief
Or affliction to man,
34 ל Crushing under His feet
All the prisoners of the earth.
35 To deny a man his rights
In the presence of the Most High,

this literally, saying that on their way into exile, Israelites kneaded dough on the ground, picking up grit along with the dough. The custom of dipping hard-boiled eggs or bread into ashes at the meal preceding the Fast of the Ninth of Av commemorating the Temples' destruction, derives from this midrash. **18:** *The LORD,* mentioned by name for the first time in the ch. **19:** *Wormwood and poison,* see 3.15.

3.21–24: Expression of faith and hope. 22–23: *Kindness,* Heb "ḥasdei," means acts of loyalty. God's loyalty to Israel, owed by virtue of His covenant, is unbroken, as is His mercy. *Kindness ... mercies,* with *grace* (or "faithfulness" in v. 23) constitute three of the Thirteen Attributes of God (Heb "shelosh ʿesreh middot," Exod. 34.6–7). The Thirteen Attributes are often cited in biblical texts; they are also recited on festivals and fast days, and in penitential prayers during the High Holy Day period. In many of these recitations, only the positive attributes, like God's mercy, are mentioned while punishment for sin is omitted. Similar praise of God's goodness appears in promises to David (Ps. 89). **23:** *They are renewed ... Ample is Your grace!* It is through God's grace that the poet wakes up every morning from sleep, a mini-death. This v. is the basis for the Jewish prayer recited upon waking from sleep: "I thank You, everliving King, who has mercifully restored my soul within me; ample is Your grace." In *Lam. Rab.* 3:16, the midrash interprets, "Because You renew us every morning, we know that ample is Your grace to redeem us." **24:** The word *hope* appears in vv. 21, 24, framing the thought.

3.25–39: Pious wisdom on human suffering. Suffering should be borne submissively yet not hopelessly. God does not punish capriciously; moreover He is merciful and will not reject the sufferer forever. **27:** *Bear a yoke,* submit to God's will. **28:** *Let him sit alone,* cf. 1.1. *It,* His chastisement. **29:** *Let him put his mouth to the dust,* accepting God's discipline submissively. **30:** *Let him offer his cheek ... be surfeited with mockery,* suffering abasement with resignation. **32:** *Pardons, kindness,* Heb terms are the same as "kindness" and "mercies" in v. 22. **33–39:** A restatement of standard biblical theology: All is according to the divine will; both good and bad come from God (cf. Isa. 45.7; Job 2.10). Suffering is the divine punishment for sin, to be accepted willingly. This passage

36 To wrong a man in his cause—
This the Lord does not choose.
37 מ Whose decree was ever fulfilled,
Unless the Lord willed it?
38 Is it not at the word of the Most High,
That weal and woe befall?
39 Of what shall a living man complain?
Each one of his own sins!

40 נ Let us search and examine our ways,
And turn back to the LORD;
41 Let us lift up our hearts with[a] our hands
To God in heaven:
42 We have transgressed and rebelled,
And You have not forgiven.
43 ס You have clothed Yourself in anger and pursued us,
You have slain without pity.
44 You have screened Yourself off with a cloud,
That no prayer may pass through.
45 You have made us filth and refuse
In the midst of the peoples.
46 פ All our enemies loudly
Rail against us.
47 Panic and pitfall are our lot,
Death and destruction.
48 My eyes shed streams of water
Over the ruin of my poor[b] people.

49 ע My eyes shall flow without cease,
Without respite,
50 [c-]Until the LORD looks down
And beholds from heaven.
51 My eyes have brought me grief[-c]
Over all the maidens of my city.
52 צ My foes have snared me like a bird,
Without any cause.
53 They have ended my life in a pit
And cast stones at me.
54 Waters flowed over my head;
I said: I am lost!

55 ק I have called on Your name, O LORD,
From the depths of the Pit.

is Job-like. **37:** A likely allusion to the creation story in Gen. ch 1. **39:** It is better to be alive than dead, even if one is suffering; and in any case, the suffering is due to the person's sins.

3.40–47: Communal lament. The confession of guilt has not resulted in God's forgiveness. God is addresssed by the speaker on behalf of the people, using the first-person plural. At the beginning the tone is conciliatory (vv. 40–41), but then becomes accusatory. **41:** *Lift up our hearts with our hands* stresses sincerity, not merely the outward gesture of prayer (cf. Joel 2.13). Lifting up the hands is a gesture of prayer. **42–44:** A devastating accusation against God that He has failed to forgive the repentant people. **42:** *We have transgressed and rebelled:* The Yom Kippur Confession of Sin ("viduy") today exhibits the same use of multiple terms for sin and is preceded by recitation of the Thirteen Attributes of God (see 3.22–23 n.). **44:** *Screened Yourself off with a cloud:* The cloud through which God revealed Himself at Sinai (Exod. 19.16), and which protects the people from fatal direct contact with the divine, is here re-envisioned as a barrier that God erected to prevent prayer from reaching Him.

3.48–66: Return to lament of the individual. 48: *The ruin of my poor people.* See 2.11 n. **52:** The letter "tzadi" occurs in the first three words, creating alliteration. **53:** *Pit,* the grave, the realm of the dead (cf. Isa. 14.15; Pss. 30.4; 88.5). **54:** *Waters flowed over my head,* a metaphor for desperation (see Jonah 2.6–7; 2 Sam. 22.5–6; Ps. 18.5–6).

a *Lit. "to"; emendation yields "rather than"; cf. Joel 2.13.*
b *Lit. "the daughter of my"; so frequently in poetry.*
c-c *Emendation yields: [50]"Until the LORD looks down from heaven / And beholds [51]my affliction. / The LORD has brought me grief."*

56 Hear my plea;
Do not shut Your ear
To my groan, to my cry!
57 You have ever drawn nigh when I called You;
You have said, "Do not fear!"
58 ר You championed my cause, O Lord,
You have redeemed my life.
59 You have seen, O LORD, the wrong done me;
Oh, vindicate my right!
60 You have seen all their malice,
All their designs against me;
61 שׁ You have heard, O LORD, their taunts,
All their designs against me,
62 The mouthings and pratings of my adversaries
Against me all day long.
63 See how, at their ease or at work,
I am the butt of their gibes.
64 ת Give them, O LORD, their deserts
According to their deeds.
65 Give them anguish[a] of heart;
Your curse be upon them!
66 Oh, pursue them in wrath and destroy them
From under the heavens of the LORD!

4 א Alas!
The gold is dulled,[a]
Debased the finest gold!
The sacred[b] gems are spilled
At every street corner.
2 ב The precious children of Zion;
Once valued as gold—
Alas, they are accounted as earthen pots,
Work of a potter's hands!
3 ג Even jackals offer the breast
And suckle their young;
But my poor people has turned cruel,
Like ostriches of the desert.
4 ד The tongue of the suckling cleaves
To its palate for thirst.
Little children beg for bread;
None gives them a morsel.

a Meaning of Heb. uncertain. *b Emendation yields "precious."*

56: Many verbs translated as imperatives in vv. 56–66 are in the past tense in the Heb, reflecting a hope, or the poet's confidence in God's response. **57–60:** Legal language. The poet casts himself as a plaintiff in court where God will judge him innocent and the enemy guilty (cf. vv. 34–36). We may understand these past-tense verbs as futures or imperatives: *drawn nigh .... champion my cause* and so forth. **63:** *At their ease or at work,* lit. "at their sitting and at their standing," at all times. **64–66:** Having described the enemy's wrongful treatment, the poet calls for retribution; see 1.22 n. **66:** *Pursue them in wrath* appears in the Passover Haggadah in "shefokh ḥamatkha," "Pour out Thy wrath," a section added in response to the Crusades petitioning God to wreak vengeance on the nations oppressing Israel. *From under the heavens of the LORD,* there is no place in God's world for wicked nations.

4.1–22: Description of the siege of Jerusalem and the suffering and degradation of its inhabitants, ending in threats against Edom and the hope for Israel's expiation. The physical and social effects of starvation are graphically described. Degradation is the main theme; those once well-off are now destitute, those once healthy are dying or dead. Much of the effect is achieved by the contrast in color; the rich palette of the colors of wealth and health (gold, purple, white, red, sapphire in vv. 1, 2, 5, 7, 8) is drained away to blackness. Heat is another dimension, the unrelenting heat of the summer siege, the dry and blackened skin (v. 8), the parched mouths (v. 4), God's burning anger setting fire to Zion (v. 11). There is no shade, no protection provided by God (contrast Ps. 121.5) or the king (v. 20). Like chs 1 and 2, this ch contains a single alphabetic acrostic and opens with the word *Alas!* (see 1.1 n.).

4.1–10: Contrasts between former grandeur and wretched present. **1:** *Alas!,* see 1.1 and n.; 2.1. **1–2:** *Gold* and *gems,* metaphors for people (v. 2) who, though precious are now treated as worthless, throw-away objects (potsherds). **3:** *Jackals,* considered despicable scavengers. *Ostriches,* thought to be cruel and neglectful parents (cf. Job 39.13–18). *My poor people has turned cruel,* not willingly but from desperation; they are no longer able to care for their children. **4:** *The tongue ... cleaves to its palate,* meaning they cannot utter a sound (Ezek. 3.26; Ps. 137.6; Job 29.10). The starving infants are too weak even to cry. **6:** *Sodom,* whose sudden destruction was legendary (Gen. 19.24–25), was overthrown in an instant, whereas Jerusalem was made to suffer long agony. **7–8:** The colors associated with vigor have disappeared; now people are dried up. **9:** A quick death in battle would be preferable to slow starvation. **10:** See 2.20 n.

4.11–16: God's fury against Jerusalem surprises even foreigners and is blamed on the Judean leadership. 11: *Fire,* symbol of divine wrath (e.g., 2.3; Deut. 32.22; Isa. 10.17; Jer. 17.27) and the actual fire that burned down the city. **12:** The Judean belief in the inviolability of Zion, that God would never permit His city to be destroyed (see Pss. 46.5; 48.3–8; it is also a theme in First Isaiah [see intro. to Isa.]), is here attributed even to foreigners, who are shocked when it proves wrong. **13–14:** *Prophets … priests,* religious leaders, who "shed blood," that is, acted immorally, causing the land to become impure or polluted, for which the punishment is exile. Shedding blood is sometimes a cypher for idolatry (Ezek. 22.1–5; Ps. 106.37–40). Those most associated with purity and vision are described as the most blind and defiled. The condemnation of the leaders here is even more severe than 2.14 where the prophets prophesied "delusion and deception." **15:** *Away! Unclean!* The formerly respected are now scorned and shunned as lepers (cf. Lev. 13.45–46). In the second part of the v., Judah, like its "leprous" leaders, is a pariah among the nations, having lost its proper place.

5 ה Those who feasted on dainties
Lie famished in the streets;
Those who were reared in purple
Have embraced refuse heaps.
6 ו The guilt[a] of my poor[b] people
Exceeded the iniquity[a] of Sodom,
Which was overthrown in a moment,
Without a hand striking it.
7 ז Her elect were purer than snow,
Whiter than milk;
Their limbs were ruddier than coral,
Their bodies[c] were like sapphire.
8 ח Now their faces are blacker than soot,
They are not recognized in the streets;
Their skin has shriveled on their bones,
It has become dry as wood.
9 ט Better off were the slain of the sword
Than those slain by famine,
[d]Who pined away, [as though] wounded,
For lack of[d] the fruits of the field.
10 י With their own hands, tenderhearted women
Have cooked their children;
Such became their fare,
In the disaster of my poor[b] people.

11 כ The LORD vented all His fury,
Poured out His blazing wrath;
He kindled a fire in Zion
Which consumed its foundations.
12 ל The kings of the earth did not believe,
Nor any of the inhabitants of the world,
That foe or adversary could enter
The gates of Jerusalem.
13 מ It was for the sins of her prophets,
The iniquities of her priests,
Who had shed in her midst
The blood of the just.
14 נ They wandered blindly through the streets,
Defiled with blood,
So that no one was able
To touch their garments.
15 ס "Away! Unclean!" people shouted at them,
"Away! Away! Touch not!"
So they wandered and wandered again;

a I.e., punishment. b See note at 3.48. c Meaning of Heb. uncertain.
d-d Meaning of Heb. uncertain.

For the nations had resolved:
"They shall stay here no longer."
16 פ [a]The LORD's countenance has turned away from them,
He will look on them no more.
They showed no regard for priests,
No favor to elders.
17 ע Even now our eyes pine away
In vain for deliverance.
As we waited, still we wait
For a nation that cannot help.
18 צ Our steps were checked,
We could not walk [b-]in our squares.[-b]
Our doom is near, our days are done—
Alas, our doom has come!
19 ק Our pursuers were swifter
Than the eagles in the sky;
They chased us in the mountains,
Lay in wait for us in the wilderness.
20 ר The breath of our life, the LORD's anointed,
Was captured in their traps—
He in whose shade we had thought
To live among the nations.
21 ש Rejoice and exult, Fair Edom,
Who dwell in the land of Uz!
To you, too, the cup shall pass,
You shall get drunk and expose your nakedness.
22 ת Your iniquity, Fair Zion, is expiated;
He will exile you no longer.
Your iniquity, Fair Edom, He will note;
He will uncover your sins.

5

Remember, O LORD, what has befallen us;
Behold, and see our disgrace!
2 Our heritage has passed to aliens,
Our homes to strangers.
3 We have become orphans, fatherless;
Our mothers are like widows.

a *Meaning of line uncertain.* *b-b* *Or "With long strides."*

16: *LORD's countenance,* the sign of divine favor (Lev. 6.26–27), is averted from Israel.

4.17–22: The voice of the community. As in 3.40–47, the speaker is "we," describing the final days of the siege and the fall of Jerusalem. **17:** *A nation,* Egypt (see Jer. 37.5–10; Isa. 30.7), the major power opposed to Babylonia, to which Judah had looked in vain for aid. **19:** Perhaps referring to events after the fall of Jerusalem, when Zedekiah and his soldiers fled the city and were pursued and captured by the Babylonian army (2 Kings 25.4–5). **20:** *The breath of our life, the LORD's anointed, ... in whose shade,* striking epithets for the divinely ordained kings (1 Sam. 24.7, 11; 2 Sam. 1.14, 16; Pss. 17.8; 91.1). The reference is likely to Zedekiah, the last king of Judah, whose defeat signaled the failure of the Davidic dynasty to protect the people. **21–22:** A curse on Edom, a neighbor of Judah who was a vassal to Babylonia. Edom is often singled out for negative comment (Ezek. ch 35; Obad. 1.10; Ps. 137.7) for its participation alongside the Babylonians. Edom is synonymous with Esau (Gen. 36.1) and therefore the traditional enemy or rival of Jacob/Israel (= Judah). **21:** *Rejoice and exult,* an ironic statement. *Fair Edom,* an epithet parallel to *Fair Zion* (v. 22); the two will exchange places in terms of misery. *Uz,* a region in southern Jordan or northwestern Arabia, often connected with Edom (Gen. 36.28; Jer. 25.20; Job 1.1; 1 Chron. 1.42). *The cup,* of God's wrath, a metaphorical wine goblet from which the wicked drink their punishment (the image is linked with drunkenness and nakedness, forms of public shaming; see 3.15; Jer. 25.15–29; 49.12; 51.7; Hab. 2.15–16). *Expose your nakedness,* and be shamed as Jerusalem was (1.8–10). **22:** *Your iniquity,* i.e., punishment for your iniquity. *Is expiated,* lit. "is complete," and therefore the exile will end (cf. Isa. 40.2).

5.1–22: A prayer for restoration. It may be read as the voice of the survivors in Judah, now occupied by Babylonia. The ch resembles communal laments and also penitential prayers of the Second Temple period. The lines are shorter and less complex. **1:** The plea to God to *remember* (that is, to pay mind to) is framed by *Why have You forgotten* (ignored) in v. 20. **2–3:** The breakdown of the institution of the family. **2:** *Heritage,* ancestral land was to be kept within the family. Here the reference may be to individual land holdings or to the country as a whole. *Aliens,* those outside the family. *Strangers,* foreigners. **3:** *Fatherless,* an orphan is a person without a father, a protector (see Exod. 22.21–23; Job 29.12). Widows and orphans are defenseless and required special protection (e.g., Isa. 1.23; Ps. 68.5–6).

4 We must pay to drink our own water,
Obtain our own kindling at a price.
5 We are hotly[a] pursued;
Exhausted, we are given no rest.
6 We hold out a hand to Egypt;
To Assyria, for our fill of bread.
7 Our fathers sinned and are no more;
And we must bear their guilt.
8 Slaves are ruling over us,
With none to rescue us from them.
9 We get our bread at the peril of our lives,
Because of the [b-]sword of the wilderness.[-b]
10 Our skin glows like an oven,
With the fever of famine.
11 They[c] have ravished women in Zion,
Maidens in the towns of Judah.
12 Princes have been hanged by them;[c]
No respect has been shown to elders.
13 Young men must carry millstones,
And youths stagger under loads of wood.
14 The old men are gone from the gate,
The young men from their music.
15 Gone is the joy of our hearts;
Our dancing is turned into mourning.
16 The crown has fallen from our head;
Woe to us that we have sinned!

17 Because of this our hearts are sick,
Because of these our eyes are dimmed:
18 Because of Mount Zion, which lies desolate;
Jackals prowl over it.

19 But You, O LORD, are enthroned forever,
Your throne endures through the ages.
20 Why have You forgotten us utterly,
Forsaken us for all time?

a Lit. "on our neck"; meaning of Heb. uncertain.
b-b Or "heat (cf. Deut. 28.22) of the wilderness"; meaning of Heb. uncertain.
c I.e., the slaves of v. 8.

4–5: Harsh economic conditions; rampant inflation. Water and wood are basic necessities and normally the cheapest commodities. **6:** *Egypt ... Assyria,* the two dominant powers of the ancient Near East, figurative for "east and west." They are often used in parallelism even when, as in this period, Assyria was long gone (Isa. 52.4; Zech. 10.10–11). **7:** *Our fathers sinned ... we must bear their guilt,* better "we must bear their punishment" (see Exod. 20.5; 34.7). Israel's sin goes back many generations, to the time of the wilderness when it first became a nation, and was especially prominent in the late monarchy, in the generation preceding the destruction. It includes the present generation; but only the present generation has suffered the punishment. **8:** *Slaves,* Judah is now governed by the lackeys of the Babylonian king (cf. 2 Kings 25.24). **9:** Food is scarce. *The sword of the wilderness,* a difficult phrase which may mean that scavenging in the countryside was dangerous because of marauders. Alternatively, it is a metaphor for the dehydration and starvation of the inhabitants of Judah, who suffer famine that resembles the famine of the siege (v. 10 and cf. 4.8). **11–14:** Social order has disintegrated; violence and indignity abound. Women are shamed sexually; leaders are shamed publicly; young and old are denied their proper calling and subjected to abusive labor. **12:** *Hanged,* refers either to the display of corpses or to torture and humiliation of the living. **13:** *Carry millstones:* Grinding, usually the work of women, slaves, and prisoners (Exod. 11.5; Judg. 16.21; Isa. 47.2; Job 31.10), is now forced upon the young men. The reference may be to a large milling operation in which a donkey would normally pull the heavy millstone, making this line parallel in meaning to the next one. *Youths stagger under loads of wood,* humans are made to do the work of animals, beasts of burden. **14:** *Old men* administered justice at the city gates (Deut. 22.15; 25.7; Ruth 4.1–2, 11), the location of business and legal transactions. **15:** *Joy of our hearts,* worship at the Temple (Ibn Ezra, based on Ezek. 24.25). **16:** *The crown,* the emblem of kingship, the Davidic dynasty or perhaps the crenellated walls of the city. *We have sinned,* an admission of guilt (cf. 3.42 and 5.7). **17:** *Because of this* refers back to vv. 2–16 as well as forward to v. 18. **18:** *Jackals,* or "foxes," proverbial inhabitants of ruined cities (see 4.3; Isa. 34.11–17; Ezek. 13.4; Zeph. 2.13–15; and in ancient Near Eastern curses). **19:** A strong theological expression of eternal divine sovereignty: God remains King even though His earthly throne, the Temple, has been destroyed. **20:** God is enthroned forever and forever forsakes Israel.

21 Take us back, O LORD, to Yourself,
And let us come back;
Renew our days as of old!
22 For truly, You have rejected us,
Bitterly raged against us.

Take us back, O LORD, to Yourself,
And let us come back;
Renew our days as of old!

21: A call to God to reinstate His former relationship with Israel. *Take us back,* see Jer. 31.18. The days as of old, i.e., days evoked in 1.1 when Jerusalem was "great with people," "great among nations," and "princess among states." Or, more generally, the time when Israel dwelled in her land under the protection of God. A fuller expression of God's returning the people from exile (after they have learned their lesson) is in Deut. 30.1–11. **22:** The hope for reinstatement is unrealized. Israel's rejection continues. In public readings of Lam., in order not to conclude on a dire note, it is the Jewish custom to repeat the last positive phrase (v. 21). Similar repetitions of the penultimate v. apply to the final chs of Isa., Mal., and Eccl.

קהלת

Ecclesiastes

AS LITERATURE, ECCLESIASTES BELONGS, along with Proverbs, Job, and—though the identifications are sometimes controversial—portions of other biblical books like Psalm 1, to the category of wisdom. That is, it is a set of observations on the nature of the world and the God who created and controls it, and on where humans fit and how they should behave in this divine creation. These observations are usually presented as the work of one or more sages, who arrive at the observations by exercising wisdom—a faculty based on their own experience and that of other sages before them, and sometimes also on divine revelation. But whether from experience or revelation, the wisdom is regularly understood to have God as its ultimate source. In the case of Ecclesiastes, such wisdom presents itself as experiential. The sage responsible for it is designated, in the Hebrew original, Koheleth, (see 1.1 n.), and so supplies the Hebrew title for the book as a whole. Koheleth remains the identification in subsequent Jewish tradition and will be used here; Christian tradition generally uses, for book and sage, Ecclesiastes, which is the Greek rendering of Koheleth (see 1.1 n.) devised by the translators of the book into Greek (the so-called Septuagint [LXX]) in the final three centuries BCE.

The twelve chs of the book cover a miscellany of topics. The cycles of the natural order; the amassing of wealth in property and other forms; the opposing forces that govern life; friendship, particularly as an antidote to life's wearying uncertainties; the virtues and difficulties of human authority; the nature of folly and the possibilities and limitations of wisdom; the enjoyment of one's toil; the terrors of old age—these are the sorts of issues on which Koheleth comments. His observations are bound together by certain fundamental themes. The first is expressed by the term "futility" *(hevel)* (see 1.2 n.). For Koheleth, this is foremost the inability of humans to make sense of the world around them—to see a coherent pattern, a plan to their lives and to nature, in the sense of a movement toward lasting goals, a line of development or progress. Koheleth, it appears, does not deny that there may be coherent patterns of activity for each human, animal, and other phenomenon, and he uses the word *maʿaseh* ("deed, work, action") for these patterns (ch 8), indicating also that they seem folded into the larger *maʿaseh* of God (see esp. 8.16–17). But the human ability to discern what these all are is frustrated, he argues, again and again, as evident by the fact that the traditional doctrine of reward and punishment for the good and the wicked does not appear to work. In this regard, Koheleth is arguing against the sort of position evident in the book of Deuteronomy or the bulk of Proverbs, for which the covenant tradition and experience provide certainty about what God demands of humans and so about His reward and punishment justice.

The one thing that is clear for Koheleth is death. It is the final point in each one's *maʿaseh,* the one immutable event in life that every human, animal, and other organism must succumb to, and that cuts across, therefore, all categories of morality, class and being. If there is any survival beyond death, either physically or in terms of memory and influence, humans cannot know this, and so cannot rely on it. What is left to humans, then, as Koheleth sees it—though he does raise an occasional doubt (e.g., 6.1–12 nn.)—is principally to enjoy their toil while they are alive. This "portion" *(ḥeleq)* (ch 2) is granted to them by God as part of their activity. Rewards and punishments, however, have no significant, no enduring role, for their effects are canceled out by the deaths of the persons concerned and the inability of such persons to direct the fruits of their labors to future generations.

The capacity to discern all of this—to understand what can be known and what cannot—is for Koheleth the task of wisdom. Wisdom, therefore, is most effective when it is used to clarify its own limits. In so doing, wisdom need not deny—nor does Koheleth deny—that God is in control, and has, as noted, a coherent pattern of activity that will bring every creature to account. Accordingly, it makes sense not to tempt the anger of God, say, by making rash prayer at the sanctuary or rash vows (4.17–5.5). This affirmation of God's authority and judgment is what rabbinic interpreters have emphasized as the central element in Koheleth's book, and while some modern critics have assigned the vv. that express it to later, orthodox editor(s) of the book, it comports well with the limits on human wisdom that all interpreters agree belong to the original author.

The topics and themes just outlined are not presented in a readily digestible, clear, linear form; that is, they are not developed in a systematic exposition from the beginning to the end of the book. Rather, a number of the topics, like futility and enjoyment of toil, are revisited, even several times. Yet there is no bland repetition at work here, since the recurrences often involve new perspectives that build on, nuance, and even contradict what has come before (e.g., ch 8; 9.1–12; ch 10 nn.). These recurrences and contradictions can at times be confusing, and they certainly make the reading of Koheleth difficult, even confusing. Countervailing these difficulties are occasional indications of structure in the book. Thus, a frame surrounds most of the book, as 1.2 is essentially repeated in 12.8. This frame, asserting that everything is futility reflects the book's main theme. In turn, within the frame are various smaller units defined by formal markers, balance in the placement of vv., or a certain connectedness in the flow of narrative. The catalogue of polarities in 3.1–8 is the most obvious example here, with the opposites arranged in syntactic parallel. Other examples are considered in the annotations below. These structures, however, do not clearly add up to a pattern that integrates the book as a whole, although scholars have tried to find one. What we appear to have, rather, is a loose coherence established by the recurrence of certain nouns for key concepts, like "futility" *(hevel)* and "portion" *(ḥelek)*, and of certain verbs, like "I set my mind" *(natatti et-libbi)* and "probe" *(tur)* (e.g., 2.1–3; 7.25). Put together, then, the recurrences of themes and terminology testify to the leisurely, self-conscious, ruminative process in which Koheleth is engaged, meandering through, around, and back to his favorite issues, considering them now from one angle, then from another, as he tries to come to grips with them.

If the Koheleth of the book is depicted throughout as a sage, he is also, in the first two chs, described as a king, who is recognized from the earliest ancient commentary (e.g., LXX; Tg.), as Solomon son of David. Although the name Solomon is nowhere used in the book and Koheleth does not occur elsewhere in the Bible, the genealogy and descriptions given of Koheleth in his book (1.1, 12, 16; 2.7, 9) make the identification with Solomon clear. While the Solomonic depiction is not maintained beyond ch 2, it does not contradict the depiction of Koheleth as sage, given the biblical tradition of Solomon as wise man (1 Kings ch 3; 5.9–14), and the larger ancient Near Eastern association of kingship and wisdom. On the other hand, the book does not abstain from queries about kingship, and at times is critical of that institution (ch 2; 4.13–14; 5.7–8; 7.19; 8.2–5; 9.14–15; 10.4–5, 16–20).

In any case, classical rabbinic tradition generally accepted that Koheleth was really Solomon, and that the book originated from the Solomonic period. Specific features of the book, however, point to a much later origin. Thus, the book's two Persian words, *pardes* ("grove"; 2.5) and *pitgam* ("sentence"; 8.11) indicate that in its present form it does not date from before the postexilic period (latter 6th c. BCE on) when the Achaemenid Persian empire emerged that ruled Judah and much else of the ancient Near East. This date comports with the variety of late grammatical features of Koheleth's Hebrew, e.g., the use of the feminine singular demonstrative pronoun, *zo,* and the negative particle, *ʾeyn,* used with infinitive constructs. At the other chronological end, Koheleth cannot be later than the first half of the 2nd century BCE, the date of a fragment of Koheleth found among the Dead Sea Scrolls and the implicit references to Koheleth in the Wisdom of Solomon and, perhaps, Sirach. Within the resulting chronological limits, approximately 580 to 200 BCE, scholars continue to debate whether Koheleth belongs in the Achaemenid Persian period (late 6th- end of 4th centuries BCE) or to the following early Hellenistic period, perhaps during the 3rd century BCE. Key to this debate is whether Koheleth was influenced by Greek philosophical ideas. In either instance, the several positive references to political hierarchy, wealth in land, and money *(kesef)* all mark the author of Koheleth as probably of the landed gentry.

In post-Talmudic Jewish tradition, that is, sometime between the 8th and 10th centuries CE, the book came to be classified as one of the five biblical megillot (scrolls), alongside of Ruth, Esther, Song of Songs, and Lamentations (see the intro. to The Five Megillot, p. 1557), each of them to be read on a religious occasion of the year. In Koheleth's case, it is the festival of Sukkot, originally celebrating the completion of the fall harvest and later also of the yearly cycle of reading the Torah. This celebration of work completed, expressed both as joy and as a mood of reflection on memory and time past, resonates with themes in Koheleth, and so may have helped to establish the connection between the book and the festival.

Despite the firm place Koheleth has in the biblical canon, rabbinic tradition shows some ambivalence toward the book. The evidence is rather laconic and concerns, in particular, the debates attributed to the 1st century BCE through the early 2nd century CE, which also included Ezekiel and the Song of Songs. Two features of Koheleth, and in varying fashion of these other books, appear to have provoked discussion: that they exhibit contradictions, in the case of Koheleth, self-contradictions; and that they offer unorthodox views that do not comport with the mainstream of Jewish thinking about God and Torah in the Bible. The result was, as various rabbinic Sages argued—others disagreeing—that Koheleth and these other books were not divinely inspired or canonical, or, in the ancient terminology, "did not make the hands unclean/impure" and thus deserved to "be removed from use and stored away" (e.g., *b. Shab.* 30b; *m. ʿEd.* 5.3; *b. Meg.* 7a). This rabbinic evidence, however, is all post facto, after Koheleth and the other books had already been included in the biblical canon. While it may possibly contain some memory of earlier debates about canonicity, even more it appears to reflect an ongoing challenge of how to correlate the ideas and formulations of Koheleth and the other books with the rest of the biblical canon. It is matched by the efforts of many later classical Jewish commentators on Koheleth to make this correlation, both by reinterpreting and so taming various troublesome sections of the book (e.g., annotations on 3.9–12; 6.1–12; ch 7), and by asserting that the statements in the epilogue, which appear orthodox, represent, indeed, the basic sense of the book. In the latter effort, the commentators may not be far wrong (12.9–14 n.).

[PETER MACHINIST]

1 The words of Koheleth[a] son of David, king in Jerusalem.
2 Utter futility!—said Koheleth—
Utter futility! All is futile!
3 What real value is there for a man
In all the gains[b] he makes beneath the sun?

4 One generation goes, another comes,
But the earth remains the same forever.
5 The sun rises, and the sun sets—
And glides[c] back to where it rises.
6 Southward blowing,
Turning northward,
Ever turning blows the wind;
On its rounds the wind returns.
7 All streams flow into the sea,
Yet the sea is never full;
To the place [from] which they flow
The streams flow back again.[d]
8 All such things are wearisome:
No man can ever state them;
The eye never has enough of seeing,
Nor the ear enough of hearing.
9 Only that shall happen
Which has happened,
Only that occur
Which has occurred;
There is nothing new
Beneath the sun!

a *Probably "the Assembler," i.e., of hearers or of sayings; cf. 12.9–11.*
b *So Rashbam. Heb.* ʿamal *usually has this sense in Ecclesiastes; cf. Ps. 105.44.*
c *So Targum; cf. Bereshith Rabbah on Gen. 1.17.*
d *According to popular belief, through tunnels; so Targum and Rashi.*

1.1: Introductory caption. As in some other biblical wisdom texts (e.g., Prov. 30.1), this introduction classifies the reflections and sayings that follow and identifies the sage who is responsible for them. Koheleth here, as the bulk of traditional Jewish and modern scholarly commentary agree, is not the personal name of, but a sobriquet for, this sage, who is described here as if he were Solomon. That Koheleth is a sobriquet comports with the fact that the word occurs elsewhere in the book with the definite article (12.8 and perhaps, with correction, 7.27). That it is also of feminine grammatical gender, even if applied to someone obviously male, poses no problem, since analogous formations in the Bible are known (e.g., Ezra 2.55, 57 || Neh. 7.57, 59); some Jewish and other commentaries, however, assume the feminine represents a feminine noun, like wisdom ("ḥokhmah"), which they argue stands for Solomon here. As to the meaning of Koheleth, opinion has ranged around "assemble," which is the basic sense of the root of the word ("k-h-l") and which the Gk translators fastened onto in their rendering, "Ecclesiastes," "the one of the assembly." But whether Koheleth means "the one who has assembled wisdom" (Rashi, etc.) or "assembled conflicting opinions and decided on the correct ones" *(Metzudat Zion)*, or "assembled the people around to speak or preach wisdom to them" (cf. 12.9, as well as the LXX, *Eccl. Rab.*, and much modern scholarship)—no one of these and other solutions has emerged as the decisive solution to the word, although they all fit its context in the book.

1.2: The theme. *Futility* here translates Heb "hevel," the most frequent technical term in Koheleth (38 occurrences). From its literal meaning, "air, breath," the word has acquired the sense of something fleeting, without substance (cf. its occurrence as the name "Abel," in Gen. ch 4), or even unreliable. In Koheleth, the literal meaning "air/breath" has not fully disappeared, since "hevel" is paired six times with the phrase "pursuit of wind" (e.g., 2.26). The acquired sense, however, is what dominates, adapted in the book to describe actions and work that do not last, or appear to lead to no lasting goal, or cannot be explained in any rational, i.e., human, way. Within Jewish commentary, one emphasis applies *futility* to actions performed by humans for themselves alone, which are not involved with Torah and labor for God.

1.3–11: Round and around. This section provides the first illustration of what Koheleth means by "futility." Vv. 4–8 give several examples of the ceaselessly circular, or oscillating, movement that for him governs all activity in the world: the passage of generations, the cycle of the sun, the flow of the water. There is, in short, no linear, goal-oriented activity, and the result is that the world never changes. The surrounding vv. 3 and 9–11 draw out the implications of these examples to affirm that nothing new occurs, and so there is nothing one can show for his toil, nothing to learn (to "remember," v. 11) and to build on. **9:** Put another way, as the sun cycles, so there is *nothing new beneath the sun.* Some Jewish

10 Sometimes there is a phenomenon of which they say,
"Look, this one is new!"—it occurred long since, in ages that
went by before us. 11 The earlier ones are not remembered; so
too those that will occur later [a]will no more be remembered
than[a] those that will occur at the very end.

12 I, Koheleth, was king in Jerusalem over Israel. 13 I set my
mind to study and to probe with wisdom all that happens under the sun.—An unhappy business, that, which God gave men
to be concerned with! 14 I observed all the happenings beneath
the sun, and I found that all is futile and pursuit[b] of wind:

15 A twisted thing that cannot be made straight,
A lack that cannot be made good.

16 I said to myself: "Here I have grown richer and wiser than
any that ruled before me over Jerusalem, and my mind has
zealously absorbed wisdom and learning." 17 And so I set my
mind to appraise wisdom and to appraise madness and folly.
And I learned—that this too was pursuit of wind:

18 For as wisdom grows, vexation grows;
To increase learning is to increase heartache.

2 I said to myself, "Come, I will treat you to merriment. Taste
mirth!" That too, I found, was futile.

2 Of revelry I said, "It's mad!"
Of merriment, "What good is that?"

3 I ventured to tempt my flesh with wine, and to grasp folly,
while letting my mind direct with wisdom, to the end that I
might learn which of the two was better for men to practice
in their few days of life under heaven. 4 I multiplied my possessions. I built myself houses and I planted vineyards. 5 I laid
out gardens and groves, in which I planted every kind of fruit
tree. 6 I constructed pools of water, enough to irrigate a forest
shooting up with trees. 7 I bought male and female slaves, and I
acquired stewards. I also acquired more cattle, both herds and
flocks, than all who were before me in Jerusalem. 8 I further

a-a Lit. "will not be remembered like…" For ʿim *meaning "like," cf. 2.16; 7.11; Job 9.26.*
b Lit. "tending," from root raʿah, *"to shepherd."*

commentators argue, following on v. 2, that the problem under discussion here is a wrong-headed focus on daily human or natural activities, rather than on the spiritual, which would not leave one with futile emptiness. Rashi, in particular, elaborates on this in a midrashic play on the phrase *nothing new beneath the sun*—a phrase that is unique to Koheleth in the Bible, although with antecedents and parallels both in the ancient Near East (e.g., Mari and Phoenicia) and in the Greek world. In Rashi's interpretation, the phrase comes out more positively than the conventional interpretation given above, as it contrasts futile daily activity done "in place of the Sun (= Light = Torah)," i.e., in contrast to the spiritual activity of Torah study and living.

1.12–18: Koheleth sets his task. *Koheleth* introduces himself in the first person, probably drawing upon a style used in royal inscriptions throughout the ancient Near East. His aim here, expressed particularly through his persona as Solomon, is to establish his preeminent ability to investigate wisdom, over against folly and madness, for which he uses a variety of technical terms that recur in the book (see intro.). Yet, anticipating the book's continuation, Koheleth admits that the investigation yields no happy, satisfying outcome, only pain and vexation from the futility of explaining and correcting the crooked. If this conclusion seems contrary to the wisdom successes of the Solomon in the biblical historical books, especially 1 Kings, various rabbinic commentators (e.g., Rashi, following earlier rabbinic traditions) suggested that Koheleth/Solomon is here looking back from the end of his life, after the excesses of his material and religious policies (cf. 1 Kings ch 11) had gone far to undermine his achievements. Alternatively, the Tg. saw this pessimism as growing out of the entire book being a prophecy of Solomon forecasting the collapse of his kingdom by division after his death.

2.1–26: Experiments with wisdom and their results. Having set his task to discover what, if anything, wisdom can yield, Koheleth now turns to find the answer. Vv. 1–2, serving as a bridge to the preceding vv., introduce, with a note of pessimism, that task. They do so by proposing, as a point of argument, that life appears to furnish no enjoyment. To test this proposition, vv. 3–11 and 12–16 describe two experiments Koheleth undertakes. **3–11:** In the first, he acquires material property and other wealth—the regular mark of royal power and success (cf. Solomon in 1 Kings chs 4–10). **5:** Among this wealth is the building of a *garden*, which, although unattested for Solomon, is familiar from other monarchs in the ancient Near East and beyond. **10:** His wealth gives him momentary pleasure as his "portion" ("ḥeleq") from his labor. (For this key term, see also 2.11; 3.22; 5.17, 18; 9.6, 9. NJPS freely translates here: *And that was all I got out of my wealth.*) **11–12:** But the wealth has no lasting value for him (v. 11), especially since it will fall to an unknown successor (v. 12a, though NJPS's positioning of this half-verse is debatable; in any case note the resumption of the theme in v. 21). **12–16:** The second experiment is determining if there is an advantage to *wisdom* over *folly.* **13–14:** Here, while *wisdom* does confer the advantage of "finding/observing" ("ra'ah")—perhaps of understanding the limits of one's situation (v. 13; see later)—it is negated by the fact that wise and fool alike have the same *fate* ("miqreh," another key word: lit. "happening"; see also 3.19–20; 9.2, 3, 11). *Fate* here means death, which wipes out the advantage of the wise over the fool, since both are equally forgotten (vv. 13–16).

2.17–23: The negative conclusions to the two experiments of vv. 1–16 are here elaborated.

amassed silver and gold and treasures of kings and provinces;
and I got myself male and female singers, as well as the lux-
uries of commoners—coffers[a] and coffers of them. 9 Thus, I
gained more wealth than anyone before me in Jerusalem. In
addition, my wisdom remained with me: 10 I withheld from my
eyes nothing they asked for, and denied myself no enjoyment;
rather, I got enjoyment out of[b] all my wealth. And that was all I
got out of my wealth.

11 Then my thoughts turned to all the fortune my hands had
built up, to the wealth I had acquired and won—and oh, it was
all futile and pursuit of wind; there was no real value under the
sun! 12 [c]For what will the man be like who will succeed [d-]the
one who is ruling[-d] over what was built up long ago?

My thoughts also turned to appraising wisdom and madness and folly. 13 I found that

Wisdom is superior to folly
As light is superior to darkness;
14 A wise man has his eyes in his head,
Whereas a fool walks in darkness.

But I also realized that the same fate awaits them both. 15 So I
reflected: "The fate of the fool is also destined for me; to what
advantage, then, have I been wise?" And I came to the conclusion that that too was futile, 16 because the wise man, just
like[e] the fool, is not remembered forever; for, as the succeeding
days roll by, both are forgotten. Alas, the wise man dies, just
like[e] the fool!

17 And so I loathed life. For I was distressed by all that goes
on under the sun, because everything is futile and pursuit of
wind.

18 So, too, I loathed all the wealth that I was gaining under the sun. For I shall leave it to the man who will succeed
me—19 and who knows whether he will be wise or foolish?—
and he will control all the wealth that I gained by toil and
wisdom under the sun. That too is futile. 20 And so I came to
view with despair all the gains I had made under the sun.
21 For sometimes a person whose fortune was made with wisdom, knowledge, and skill must hand it on to be the portion
of somebody who did not toil for it. That too is futile, and a
grave evil. 22 For what does a man get for all the toiling and
worrying he does under the sun? 23 All his days his thoughts
are grief and heartache, and even at night his mind has no
respite. That too is futile!

a The Heb. shiddah *occurs only here in the Bible; in the Mishnah it designates a kind of chest.*

b Septuagint and a few Heb. manuscripts have "(in exchange) for"; cf. 2.24; 3.13, 22; 5.17.

c The order of the two sentences in this verse is reversed in the translation for clarity.

d-d Change of vocalization yields "me, and who is to rule"; cf. vv. 18–19.

e See note on 1.11.

24 There is nothing worthwhile for a man but to eat and drink
and afford himself enjoyment with his means. And even that,
I noted, comes from God. 25 For who eats and who enjoys but
myself?[a] 26 To the man, namely, who pleases Him He has given
[b-]the wisdom and shrewdness to enjoy himself;[-b] and to him
who displeases, He has given the urge to gather and amass—
only for handing on to one who is pleasing to God. That too is
futile and pursuit of wind.

3 A season is set for everything, a time for every
experience under heaven:[c]
2 A time for [d-]being born[-d] and a time for dying,
A time for planting and a time for uprooting the
planted;
3 A time for [e-]slaying and a time for healing,[-e]
A time for tearing down and a time for building up;
4 A time for weeping and a time for laughing,
A time for wailing and a time for dancing;
5 A time for throwing stones and a time for gathering
stones,
A time for embracing and a time for shunning
embraces;
6 A time for seeking and a time for losing,
A time for keeping and a time for discarding;
7 A time for ripping and a time for sewing,
A time for silence and a time for speaking;
8 A time for loving and a time for hating;
A time for war and a time for peace.

9 What value, then, can the man of affairs get from what he
earns? 10 I have observed the business that God gave man to
be concerned with: 11 He brings everything to pass precisely at
its time; He also puts eternity in their mind,[f] but without man
ever guessing, from first to last, all the things that God brings

a *Some mss. and ancient versions read* mimmennu, *"by His doing."*
b-b *Lit. "wisdom and knowledge and enjoyment."*
c *I.e., all human experiences are preordained by God; see v. 11.*
d-d *Lit. "giving birth."*
e-e *Emendation yields "wrecking... repairing"; cf. 1 Kings 18.30.*
f *I.e., He preoccupies man with the attempt to discover the times of future events; cf. 8.17.*

2.24–26: Koheleth now offers a way to deal with the situation. He reorients the argument by proposing—and this is the interpretation of various classical Jewish commentators (e.g., *Eccl. Rab.;* Rashi)—that it is God's plan that one should at least enjoy the work while one does it, and by implication not worry about what will come afterward. This kind of enjoyment, Koheleth affirms, is an outgrowth of the wisdom and knowledge that together are God's gift to one He finds pleasing. The one who displeases God, on the other hand, suffers the fate lamented in the experiments above, namely, that God makes him focus simply on accumulating wealth, only then to see it handed over to one who pleases God.

3.1–8: The catalogue of polarities. Koheleth's interest in life's polarities, found often in the book (e.g., 4.13–14), is most strikingly expressed in this poem. It moves across various kinds of human activity, arranged in pairs that are either constructive-destructive or the reverse; the ordering of these pairs is often difficult to discern. Rabbinic commentary frequently, but not always, tried to go beyond the contextual meaning of the pairs, which refers to universal human activities, to something more specific, concerning biblical history or the proper behavior of Israel as mandated by God. **5:** For example, the contextual meaning of *throwing* or *gathering stones,* may refer to demolishing or constructing a building, sexual profligacy vs. restraint, or destroying the fertility of a field by throwing stones on it or promoting its fertility by gathering and removing them. For *Eccl. Rab.* followed by Rashi, however, the gathering of stones indicates the end of Jewish exile and the ingathering of Israel.

3.9–22: Reflections on the catalogue. 9: The first comment questions whether there is for one's labor any "advantage" or "profit" ("yitron"—another favorite word of Koheleth and exclusive to him in the Bible: see 1.3; 2.11, 13; 5.8, 15; 7.12; 10.10, 11; it is often used negatively as here). The questioning in this instance must arise out of the constructive and destructive actions catalogued in vv. 1–8: they suggest life is an endless circle of such actions, canceling or balancing each other out, and thus, once more, leading toward no goal, no "advantage." This cannot, however, be understood to deny God's control. Indeed vv. **10–15** affirm that God controls everything, echoing and extending 2.24–26. One part of this control, in v. **11**, is the fact that God puts *eternity* into human minds, i.e., gives humans a sense that there is a level of divine activity which determines events, beyond what they can see and understand, and so defines for them the limits of their reason.

to pass. 12 Thus I realized that the only worthwhile thing there
is for them is to enjoy themselves and do what is good[a] in their
lifetime; 13 also, that whenever a man does eat and drink and
get enjoyment out of all his wealth, it is a gift of God.
14 I realized, too, that whatever God has brought to pass will
recur evermore:

Nothing can be added to it
And nothing taken from it—

and God has brought to pass that men revere Him.

15b What is occurring occurred long since,
And what is to occur occurred long since:

and God seeks the pursued. 16 And, indeed, I have observed
under the sun:

Alongside justice there is wickedness,
Alongside righteousness there is wickedness.

17 I mused: "God will doom both righteous and wicked, for
[c-]there is[-c] a time for every experience and for every happening." 18b So I decided, as regards men, to dissociate them [from]
the divine beings and to face the fact that they are beasts.[d] 19 For
in respect of the fate of man and the fate of beast, they have one
and the same fate: as the one dies so dies the other, and both
have the same lifebreath; man has no superiority over beast,
since both amount to nothing. 20 Both go to the same place;
both came from dust and both return to dust. 21 Who knows if
a man's lifebreath does rise upward and if a beast's breath does
sink down into the earth?

22 I saw that there is nothing better for man than to enjoy his
possessions, since that is his portion. For who can enable him
to see what will happen afterward?

4 I further observed[e] all the oppression that goes on under
the sun: the tears of the oppressed, with none to comfort
them; and the power of their oppressors—with none to comfort them. 2 Then I accounted those who died long since more
fortunate than those who are still living; 3 and happier than
either are those who have not yet come into being and have
never witnessed the miseries that go on under the sun.

4 I have also noted that all labor and skillful enterprise come
from men's envy of each other—another futility and pursuit of
wind!

5 [True,]
The fool folds his hands together[f]
And has to eat his own flesh.

a I.e., what the author has already concluded (2.24) is good.
b Meaning of parts of verse uncertain.
c-c Shift of a diacritical point yields "He has set."
d Contrast Ps. 8.5–6. *e Cf. 3.16.* *f I.e., does not work; cf. Prov. 6.10; 24.33.*

12: By compensation, God allows humans, in another part of His control, to enjoy if not the "advantage" of their labor, then their labor while they are doing it. **16–22:** God's control is further explored. It is applied to two new pairs of opposites, not mentioned in the earlier catalogue of vv. 1–8. **16–17:** The first is *wickedness* vs. *justice,* both of which God allows (using the same language as for the opposites in the earlier catalogue), to occur each in its own time and season. **18–22:** The second pair is animals vs. humans. **19–21:** Here Koheleth questions the difference that evidently others in his community were asserting: that humans have an afterlife above (= in heaven) and *beasts* only one below (= in the netherworld). All Koheleth can see, however, is the same *fate* of the *dust* of death for both. (On the other hand, some rabbinic Sages, trying to harmonize Koheleth with their own beliefs, reinterpret these lines to make Koheleth finally affirm a human afterlife with God.) **22:** But, once again, the best thing for Koheleth is that humans focus on enjoying what they have—here the familiar term, their *portion*—now in their lifetimes.

4.1–16: Futility and human relationships. This ch explores several kinds of human interactions and their consequences. Comprised of five sections, vv. 1–3, 4–6, 7–8, 9–12, and 13–16, it is bound together through the repetition (though not in every section) of a clause of self-reference, "I have observed/noted" ("ra'ah": vv. 1, 4, 7, 15), and of comparisons in the form "better than" ("tov min": vv. 3, 6, 9, 13; cf. in a different form v. 8). Of these five sections, four describe negative interactions and only one positive. **1–3:** The first negative is the oppressor overwhelming the oppressed—a constant occurrence that makes death, or even not being born, better options (cf. 6.3 and Job ch 3, but, for the opposite view, Eccl. 9.4–6). **4–6:** The second negative is *envy* leading to futile labor. **7–8:** The third is the situation of a person *alone,*

6 [But no less truly,]
Better is a handful of gratification
Than two fistfuls of labor which is pursuit of wind.

7 And I have noted this further futility under the sun: 8 the
case of the man who is alone, with no companion, who has
neither son nor brother; yet he amasses wealth without limit,
and his eye is never sated with riches. For whom, now, [a-]is he
amassing it while denying himself[-a] enjoyment? That too is a
futility and an unhappy business.

9 [b]Two are better off than one, in that they have greater [c-]ben-
efit from[-c] their earnings. 10 For should they fall, one can raise
the other; but woe betide him who is alone and falls with no
companion to raise him! 11 Further, when two lie together they
are warm; but how can he who is alone get warm? 12 Also, if
one attacks, two can stand up to him. A threefold cord is not
readily broken!

13 Better a poor but wise youth than an old but foolish king
who no longer has the sense to heed warnings. 14 For the former can emerge from a dungeon to become king; while the
latter, even if born to kingship, can become a pauper.[d] 15 [How-
ever,] I reflected about [e-]all the living who walk under the sun
with[-e] that youthful successor who steps into his place. 16 Unnumbered are the multitudes of all those who preceded them;[f]
and later generations will not acclaim him either.[g] For that[h] too
is futile and pursuit of wind.

17 [i-]Be not overeager to go[-i] to the House of God: more acceptable is obedience than the offering of fools, for they know
nothing [but] to do wrong.

5 Keep your mouth from being rash, and let not your throat[j]
be quick to bring forth speech before God. For God is in
heaven and you are on earth; that is why your words should be
few. 2 Just as dreams come with much brooding, so does foolish utterance come with much speech. 3 When you make a vow
to God, do not delay to fulfill it. For He has no pleasure in fools;
what you vow, fulfill. 4 It is better not to vow at all than to vow
and not fulfill. 5 Don't let your mouth bring you into disfavor,

a-a Lit. "am I amassing … myself."

b 4.9–5.8 consists of a series of observations, each of which is introduced by some slight association with what precedes. The theme of 4.4–8 is not resumed until 5.9.

c-c Emendation yields "hope for"; cf. 2.20.

d Taking rash *as a verb; cf. Ps. 34.11.* *e-e I.e., "the contemporaries of."*

f And so never heard of the gifted youth.

g For despite his wisdom, he too will be forgotten; cf. 2.16.

h I.e., the advantage of wisdom over folly.

i-i Lit. "Guard your foot when it [or, you] would go."

j Heb. leb, *lit. "heart," sometimes designates the organ of speech; cf. Isa. 33.18; 59.13; Pss. 19.15; 49.4; Job. 8.10.*

and the *futility,* thus, of having no one to pass on the fruits of his labor. **13–16:** The fourth negative interaction depicts a poor, though wise, *youth* who succeeds where an old, foolish *king* fails, but whose achievement does not last because it was never known by the many generations before him and will be forgotten by those coming after (cf. 2.16). **9–12:** The one positive interaction comes between the third and fourth negatives; it celebrates the advantages and rewards of companionship over against the third negative of being alone, indeed against the polar divisiveness of all four negatives. The strength of companionship is compared (v. 12) to that of a three-ply cord, an image that appears to go back to the Sumerian Gilgamesh stories from early Mesopotamian literature of the late 3rd millennium BCE. Rabbinic commentary, however, took this cord to imply the advantages and greater strength of three persons functioning as companions, particularly in the matter of living and transmitting Torah, as against the two with which this section in vv. 9–12 otherwise deals.

4.17–5.6: Responding properly to God. 4.17 begins a new unit, since 4.16 ends with a statement of futility that is intended to close off the discussion that precedes it (cf. e.g., 2.26). The new unit comprises a set of warnings against various kinds of behavior that might at first seem acceptable, but when carried to extremes, without a balanced sense of context, become objectionable and even dangerous, as they could provoke God's anger. **4.17:** The first warning is against false sacrifice, which, as rabbinic commentary recognized, tries to cover up intentional, premeditated sinful acts (cf. such prophets as Amos 5.21–24). **5.1–2:** It is followed by a warning against uncontrolled speech, a common motif in biblical and other ancient Near Eastern wisdom, where it is often juxtaposed to the virtue of silence; Rashbam here understands it as excessively long prayer. **3–5:** Then comes making rash *vows* that cannot or are not intended to be

and don't plead before the messenger[a] that it was an error,
[b-]but fear God;[-b] else God may be angered by your talk and destroy your possessions. 6 [c]For much dreaming leads to futility
and to superfluous talk.

7 If you see in a province oppression of the poor and sup-
pression of right and justice, don't wonder at the fact; for one
high official is protected by a higher one, and both of them by
still higher ones. 8 Thus the greatest advantage in all the land is
his: he controls a field that is cultivated.[d]

9 A lover of money never has his fill of money, nor a lover of
wealth his fill of income. That too is futile. 10 As his substance
increases, so do those who consume it; what, then, does the
success of its owner amount to but feasting his eyes? 11 A
worker's[e] sleep is sweet, whether he has much or little to eat;
but the rich man's abundance doesn't let him sleep.
12 Here is a grave evil I have observed under the sun: riches
hoarded by their owner to his misfortune, 13 in that those riches are lost in some unlucky venture; and if he begets a son, he
has nothing in hand.
14 [f-]Another grave evil is this: He must depart just as he
came.[-f] As he came out of his mother's womb, so must he
depart at last, naked as he came. He can take nothing of his
wealth to carry with him. 15 So what is the good of his toiling
for the wind? 16 Besides, all his days [g-]he eats in darkness,[-g] with
much vexation and grief and anger.
17 Only this, I have found, is a real good: that one should eat
and drink and get pleasure with all the gains he makes under
the sun, during the numbered days of life that God has given
him; for that is his portion. 18 Also, whenever a man is given
riches and property by God, and is also permitted by Him to
enjoy them and to take his portion and get pleasure for his
gains—that is a gift of God. 19 For [such a man] will not brood
much over the days of his life,[h] because God keeps him busy
enjoying himself.

a Some ancient versions read "God."
b-b Moved up from v. 6 for clarity.
c Meaning of verse uncertain. Emendation yields "Much brooding results in dreams; and much talk in futilities"; cf. v. 2.
d I.e., the high official profits from the labor of others; but meaning of verse uncertain.
e Some ancient versions have "slave's." *f-f Moved up from v. 15 for clarity.*
g-g Septuagint reads "are [spent] in darkness and mourning."
h The thought of which is depressing; see v. 16.

paid (cf. Deut. 23.22–24; Prov. 20.25; Sir. 18.21). **2, 6:** Weaving through these warnings is yet another that concerns *dreams,* which may stand as a negative image for anything ephemeral and unstable (e.g., Job 20.8 and ancient Egyptian literature). More specifically, the reference may be to the widespread Near Eastern, including biblical, appeal to dreams as a form of divine communication, here warning against undue reliance on them because they could be vague and misleading (cf. dreams of false prophets in Deut. 13.2, 4, 6; Jer. 23.25, 27, 28, 32; 27.9; 29.8; Zech. 10.2).

5.7–8: The virtues of authority. 7: The hierarchy of authority may be modeled on the actual system of Koheleth's time, whether Achaemenid or, more likely, early Hellenistic (see intro.). The system serves justice, it appears, because the possible failures of the lower-ranking officials are watched over and corrected by the higher ranks (cf. in an earlier Egyptian wisdom text of the 2nd millennium BCE, "Tale of the Eloquent Peasant"). If the higher ranks here ultimately include God—though this is not specified—then the v. would connect with the preceding 4.17–5.6, where failures of human behavior are answerable to God. **8:** This v. has been a long-standing interpretive problem, though it seems to describe, as classical rabbinic tradition already saw, the value and "advantage/profit" that agriculture brings. More precisely, the emphasis may be not on the wealth of owning land, which is criticized in 2.1–11, but on the enjoyment and value of toiling on the land, as in vv. 11, 17–18 ahead (and also 2.24; 3.22; 8.15).

5.9–20: The problem of wealth and the solution. 9–16: The value of toil in 5.8 stands in deliberate contrast with the main focus here, which is on the futility of accumulating wealth. That theme had already been discussed in chs 2 and 4; here some of the earlier reasons for the futility are resumed, and added, in v. **9**, the particular problem of accumulating *money* (lit. "silver" ["kesef"]), which once acquired leaves one insatiable for more. **11, 17–20:** The contrasting and more positive situation, namely, the value of toil, is now reintroduced. Particularly in vv. 17–20 it is God who is said to preside over the whole matter (cf. 2.24–25; 3.12–13; 8.15; 9.7, 9; cf. 3.22; 11.8). And while He here grants humans wealth and goods, the focus

6 There is an evil I have observed under the sun, and a grave
one it is for man: [2] that God sometimes grants a man riches,
property, and wealth, so that he does not want for anything his
appetite may crave, but God does not permit him to enjoy it; instead, a stranger will enjoy it. That is futility and a grievous ill.
[3] Even if a man should beget a hundred children and live many
years—no matter how many the days of his years may come to,
if his gullet is not sated through his wealth, I say: The stillbirth,
though it was not even accorded a burial,[a] is more fortunate than
he. [4] Though it comes into futility and departs into darkness, and
its very name is covered with darkness, [5] though it has never
seen or experienced the sun, it is better off than he—[6] yes, even
if the other lived a thousand years twice over but never had his
fill of enjoyment! For are not both of them bound for the same
place? [7] [b]All of man's earning is for the sake of his mouth, [c]yet his
gullet is not sated. [8] What advantage then has the wise man over
the fool, what advantage has the pauper who knows how to get
on in life?[-c] [9] [d]Is the feasting of the eyes more important than the
pursuit of desire? That, too, is futility and pursuit of wind.
[10] Whatever happens, it was designated long ago and it was
known that it would happen; as for man, he cannot contend with
what is stronger than he. [11] Often, much talk means much futility. How does it benefit a man? [12] Who can possibly know what is
best for a man to do in life—the few days of his fleeting life? For[e]
who can tell him what the future holds for him under the sun?

7 [f]A good name is better than fragrant oil, and the day of
death than the day of birth.[g]

a *Stillbirths were cast into pits or hidden in the ground in no recognizable graves; cf. v. 4 end.* b *Cf. Prov. 16.26.*
c-c *Meaning of Heb. uncertain; emendation yields "And if the gullet is not sated, [8]what advantage has the wise man over the fool, he who knows how to get on in life over the pauper?"*
d *Meaning of first half of verse uncertain.*
e *Lit. "according to the shadow that"; cf. Qumran Aramaic* betel *and Syriac* meṭṭol; *and see 8.13.*
f *The author now offers a number of practical maxims, which, however, he concludes (vv. 23–24) are of limited value.*
g *Until a man dies, there is always danger that he may forfeit his good name.*

is not on these per se, but on God's grant of the power to enjoy them and the toil associated with them. Some rabbinic commentators (e.g., Rashi and Sforno) reconcile this text with later beliefs by asserting that God's gift of enjoyment is for those humans who earn it by meritorious deeds, and who would enjoy the blessing of their deeds not only on earth, but finally in the afterlife (cf. above on 3.9–22, where there is also a rabbinic effort to restore an afterlife orientation, against the plain sense of the biblical text).

6.1–12: Again, wealth, toil, and the meaning of life. 1–6: The first unit continues the focus on the futility of accumulating wealth (see earlier 2.18–19; 5.12–16 and the immediately preceding 5.17–20). But here Koheleth adds a sharper and more negative twist to these earlier occurrences by noting that if God can give humans wealth and possessions, as in 5.18, He can also deny humans, against 5.17–18, the power to enjoy them. He can even give that wealth to someone else; this recalls 2.18–19, and extends that text by noting that the recipient may be a stranger, someone outside the kin group of the possessor, who could thus alienate the wealth from the group. **3b–5:** The language reaches its climax in these sharply worded vv., which recall the image of the unborn in 4.3, but substitute for it what for the biblical author is the uglier and more horrible image of the stillborn. And yet even the stillborn is said to be more fortunate in his briefly earned rest than the living possessor of wealth who long accumulates but is not allowed to enjoy that wealth. The pessimism that all of this manifests is deepened in the second and third units of the ch. **7–9:** The second unit questions whether a human can ever find satisfaction in his toil, and so whether it makes any difference to be wise, foolish, or poor. **10–12:** The third unit, going farther, returns to an earlier theme of time's circularity and the lack of anything new (e.g., 1.9–10), and draws out of this circularity the conclusion, also found earlier (5.2, 6; 2.11–13), that human efforts are futile, in the light of God's strength in power and argument, to determine what sense life has or will lead to. The pessimism here was recognized by and sometimes alleviated in the rabbinic tradition (e.g., the Tg.) by claiming that these vv. intend to teach that human meaning can be satisfied not by material pursuits, but through spiritual goals, such as study of Torah, and by understanding that the final reward is to be sought in the afterlife (cf. 3.9–22 n.).

7.1–29: Proverbial sayings and the problem of wisdom. The pessimism of ch 6 is here examined further. **1–10:** The ch begins with a section of proverbs, the largest part of which, as in 4.3, 6, 9, 13, is arranged in a series of "better than" comparisons concerning wisdom and folly.

2 It is better to go to a house of mourning than to a house
of feasting; for that is the end of every man, and a living one
should take it to heart.
3 Vexation is better than revelry;[a] for though the face be sad,
the heart may be glad. 4 Wise men are drawn to a house of
mourning, and fools to a house of merrymaking.
5 It is better to listen to a wise man's reproof than to listen
to the praise of fools. 6 For the levity[b] of the fool is like the
crackling of nettles under a kettle. [c]But that too is illusory; 7 for
cheating[d] may rob the wise man of reason and destroy the prudence of the cautious.[e]
8 The end of a matter is better than the beginning of it.
Better a patient spirit than a haughty spirit.
9 Don't let your spirit be quickly vexed, for vexation abides in
the breasts of fools.
10 Don't say, "How has it happened that former times were
better than these?" For it is not wise of you to ask that question.
11 Wisdom is as good as a patrimony, and even better, for those
who behold the sun. 12 For to be in the shelter of wisdom is to be
also in the shelter of money,[f] and the advantage of intelligence is
that wisdom preserves the life of him who possesses it.
13 [g]Consider God's doing! Who can straighten what He has
twisted? 14 So in a time of good fortune enjoy the good fortune;
and in a time of misfortune, reflect: The one no less than the
other was God's doing; consequently, man may find no fault
with Him.[h]
15 In my own brief span of life, I have seen both these things:
sometimes a good man perishes in spite of his goodness, and
sometimes a wicked one endures in spite of his wickedness.
16 So don't overdo goodness and don't act the wise man to excess, or you may be dumfounded. 17 Don't overdo wickedness
and don't be a fool, or you may die before your time. 18 It is best
that you grasp the one without letting go of the other, for one
who fears God will do his duty[i] by both.
19 Wisdom is more of a stronghold to a wise man than [j-]ten
magnates[-j] that a city may contain.
20 [k]For there is not one good man on earth who does what is
best[l] and doesn't err.

a For empty revelry precludes real happiness; cf. 2.2.
b Emendation yields "praise" (shbḥ).
c This section, to end of verse 7, is apparently a continuation of the thought in vv. 11–12 and 19.
d Emendation yields "riches." *e Lit. "caution"; cf. postbiblical* mathun, *"cautious."*
f Emendation yields "For the possessor of wisdom becomes a possessor of money."
g Vv. 13–14 continue the thought of v. 10. *h So Rashi; cf. the same thought in Job 1.22; 2.10.*
i Cf. postbiblical yaṣa yede.
j-j Emendation yields "the riches of the magnates"; cf. Prov. 18.11.
k Apparently continuing the thought of v. 16. *l Refers back to 6.12.*

Wisdom here, in line with 4.2 (cf. 4.3; 6.3–5), is what recognizes that the only certain thing in life is its end, death; fools, on the contrary, focus on life and its illusory pleasures of laughter and feasting. If the valuation of wisdom over foolishness thus seems strong, doubts begin to enter toward the end of the first section, which notes the capacity of wise men to be corrupted (v. 7), and questions the conventional appeal to the superiority of wisdom inherited from the past (v. 10). **11–29:** These doubts lead to broader reflections on the nature of wisdom in the next two sections (vv. 11–14, 15–29). Here, while the power of wisdom and the punishment of the sinner are affirmed (vv. 11–12, 19, 26), questions about the human practice of wisdom resurface. Thus, in an echo of vv. 7, 10, righteous humans—who are equated with the wise (cf. v. 16)—are said not to be immune from sin (v. 20), and (excessive) reliance on the opinions of others is warned against (vv. 21–22).

A central claim of this ch is that reward and punishment do not always work as they should for righteous and wicked people (v. 15), leading Koheleth to recommend that a person avoid being too righteous and wise, and too wicked and foolish (vv. 16–18). This advice is unclear, although it recalls the Greek philosophical adage (e.g., Theognis, Aristotle), to do "nothing overmuch." Perhaps the point is more intellectual than practical: do not act as if you know completely and certainly what is right and wicked; human beings do not have that wisdom; only God does, who is the source of both good ("tov") and evil ("ra'")—perhaps here to be translated with NJPS, *good fortune* and *misfortune* (v. 14). At the most, then, human wisdom teaches the limits of what that wisdom can know (vv. 23–24, 27–28) and, therefore, the need for moderate, balanced behavior, which Koheleth connects with the fear of God (v. 18). But these limits and moderation, Koheleth concedes, are something humans generally will not recognize and accept,

21 Finally, don't pay attention to everything that is said, so
that you may not hear your slave reviling you; 22 for well you remember[a] the many times that you yourself have reviled others.
23 All this I tested with wisdom. I thought I could fathom
it,[b] but it eludes me. 24 [The secret of] what happens is elusive
and deep, deep down; who can discover it? 25 I put my mind
to studying, exploring, and seeking wisdom and the reason of
things, and to studying wickedness, stupidity, madness, and
folly. 26 Now, I find woman more bitter than death; she is all
traps, her hands are fetters and her heart is snares. He who
is pleasing to God escapes her, and he who is displeasing is
caught by her. 27 See, this is what I found, said Koheleth, item
by item in my search for the reason of things. 28 As for what I
sought further but did not find, I found only one human being
in a thousand, and the one I found among so many was never
a woman. 29 But, see, this I did find: God made men plain, but
they have engaged in too much reasoning.

8 [c-]Who is like the wise man,[-c] and who knows the meaning
of the adage:

"A man's wisdom lights up his face,
So that his deep discontent[d] is dissembled"?

2 I do! "Obey the king's orders—and [e-]don't rush[-e] into uttering an oath by God."[f] 3 [g-]Leave his presence; do not tarry[-g] in a
dangerous situation, for he can do anything he pleases; 4 inasmuch as a king's command is authoritative, and none can say
to him, "What are you doing?" 5 One who obeys orders will not
suffer from the dangerous situation.
A wise man, however, will bear in mind[h] that there is a time
of doom.[i] 6 For there is a time for every experience, including
the doom; for a man's calamity[j] overwhelms him. 7 Indeed, he
does not know what is to happen; even when it is on the point

a Lit. "your heart knows"; the same idiom occurs again in 8.5.
b Refers back to 6.12. *c-c Some ancient versions read "Who here is wise."*
d Lit. "face"; cf. 1 Sam. 1.18; Job 9.27. *e-e Moved up from v. 3 for English word order.*
f The answer to the inquiry about the implications of the proverb in v. 1 is given in the form of another proverb, of which only the first half is relevant and is enlarged upon.
g-g Or "Give ground before him; do not resist." *h The same idiom as in 7.22.*
i Lit. "time and doom"; cf. the synonymous "time of misfortune," lit. "time and misfortune," 9.11.
j Still another term for death; cf. "the time of calamity" for "the hour of death," 9.12.

tempted as they are to use their own "rational devices" (v. 29; NJPS: *too much reasoning*) to reach for certain truth. To underscore the point, the author introduces the image, known in other Near Eastern wisdom, both biblical (e.g., Prov. 2.16–19; 7.5–27) and nonbiblical (Egyptian and Mesopotamian), of the woman who waits to entrap the unwary and the sinner, that is, the one not favored by God (v. 26).

The difficult and troubling character of Koheleth's thoughts in this ch was, once more, recognized by the classical rabbinic interpreters, even as they sought to clarify and tame it. For example, the apparent pessimism of wisdom's focus on the end, not the beginning, of life (vv. 1–4) was understood positively by Joseph Albo, among others. He argued that death is to be celebrated because only then can a human being know and have realized his intellectual and spiritual potential. Similarly, for the pessimism of v. 14. Here it is said that a human being cannot make sense of his life and of what will come after him (lit. "will not find anything after him"), given that he has to endure, evidently in a way difficult to predict, both fortune and misfortune, which God has created. In Rashi's view, however, followed by NJPS, v. 14 refers to God's creating good and evil, and the reward and punishment that go respectively with each; humans, therefore, cannot and should not find any fault with Him (i.e., the "him" = God, not the human being) about unjust punishment.

8.1–17: Wisdom and its limits, again. This ch is framed by two statements about wisdom. **1:** The first appears, in the MT, to be positive, affirming the power of wisdom to make sense of things (translating v. 1a, against NJPS, as "who knows the meaning of a thing?") and so to produce contentment. This contradicts the final vv. of the ch (vv. 16–17), in which Koheleth argues, as he has in the preceding and earlier chs (3.11, 22; 6.12; 7.14, 23–24, 27–28), that his investigation of the nature of wisdom reveals wisdom's limits—its inability to find out the ultimate goal and meaning of the "activity" ("ma'aseh"; for this characteristic word of Koheleth, see also 3.11; 8.14, 17; 9.10; 11.5) of God and the world.

The contradiction between these two sets of vv. is not easy to resolve, if indeed it can be. One possibility is to note that v. 1 begins its affirmation of wisdom with a question, which might suggest uncertainty about the affirmation—an uncertainty that would then be confirmed by the final vv. (16–17). Alternatively, one might accept the contradiction—first,

of happening, who can tell him? 8 No man has authority over
the lifebreath—to hold back the lifebreath;[a] there is no authority over the day of death. There is no mustering out from that
war; wickedness[b] is powerless to save its owner.
9 All these things I observed; I noted all that went on under
the sun, while men still had authority over men to treat them
unjustly. 10 And then I saw scoundrels [c]coming from the Holy
Site and being brought to burial,[-c] while such as had acted
righteously were forgotten in the city.
And here is another frustration: 11 the fact that the sentence
imposed for evil deeds is not executed swiftly, which is why
men are emboldened to do evil—12 the fact that a sinner may
do evil a hundred times and his [punishment] still be delayed.
For although I am aware that "It will be well with those who revere God since they revere Him, 13 and it will not be well with
the scoundrel, and he will not live long, because[d] he does not
revere God"—14 here is a frustration that occurs in the world:
sometimes an upright man is requited according to the conduct
of the scoundrel; and sometimes the scoundrel is requited according to the conduct of the upright. I say all that is frustration.
15 I therefore praised enjoyment. For the only good a man can
have under the sun is to eat and drink and enjoy himself. That
much can accompany him, in exchange for his wealth, through
the days of life that God has granted him under the sun.

16 For I have set my mind to learn wisdom and to observe
the business that goes on in the world—even to the extent of
going without sleep day and night—17 and I have observed all
that God brings to pass. Indeed, man cannot guess the events
that occur under the sun. For man tries strenuously, but fails
to guess them; and even if a sage should think to discover them
he would not be able to guess them.

9 For all this I noted, and I ascertained[e] all this: that the actions of
even the righteous and the wise are determined by God. [f]Even
love! Even hate! Man knows none of these in advance—2 none![-f]

a From leaving the body when the time comes; see 12.7; cf. Pss. 104.29; 146.4.
b Emendation yields "riches."
c-c Meaning uncertain; emendation yields "approaching [to minister]. They would come and profane the Holy Site."
d See note on 6.12.
e Meaning of verb uncertain; construction as in Hos. 12.3; Ezra 3.12.
f-f Emendation yields "Even love, even hate, no man can know in advance. All [2]are insignificant."

affirmation and in the end, sharp restriction of the power of wisdom—and regard it as a reflection of Koheleth's slow, ruminative approach, as he tries to figure out what value wisdom may have. This would comport well with the vv. between the two wisdom statements. **2–9:** Thus, "power" or *command* (v. 4, "shilton") is first something positive and effective: the property of the king, who must be obeyed because with it he is irresistible and because his commands are even like oaths to God (vv. 2–4). **8:** But, as Koheleth then observes (see also Rashi, Rashbam, and others), no person, royal or otherwise, is "powerful" enough ("shalit," "shilton"), to hold on to his *lifebreath* ("ruaḥ") on the day of his death and to do battle, that is, with the angel of death. **9:** Indeed, finally, a person can use his "power/authority" ("shalat") to do harm to another. This progressive qualification of human "power," from royal authority commanding obedience to the evil ability to cause harm, leads to a second theme in which Koheleth also plays with different views. **9–15:** The theme is the treatment of the good and wicked. Here Koheleth goes beyond what he has said earlier (e.g., 7.15) to express directly the tension between his personal conviction, following traditional wisdom, that the good are rewarded and the wicked punished (vv. 12–13), and his observation that in reality this does not always work out (vv. 10, 14). The conclusion to this dilemma is Koheleth's favorite: it is all "hevel"—beyond human comprehension (vv. 10, 14; cf. 1.2, etc.); and the recommendation is likewise familiar (cf. e.g., 2.24–25): to enjoy the toil that one does while one is alive and doing it (v. 15). **16–17:** This conclusion and recommendation, then, are reinforced by the assertion that human wisdom cannot indeed make any sense of the divine "activity" ("ma'aseh") of the world.

9.1–12: Death is the final equalizer. Like ch 8, these vv. are also framed by two statements at the beginning and end (vv. 1–6, 10b–12). In this instance the theme is death as the final end or *fate* ("mikreh") for all humans, regardless of a person's moral or ritual behavior, power, or ability. While this theme and language are familiar (2.13–16; 3.19–21), they have here

For the same fate is in store for all: for the righteous, and for
the wicked; for the good and pure,[a] and for the impure; for
him who sacrifices, and for him who does not;[b] for him who
is pleasing,[c] and for him who is displeasing; and for him who
swears, and for him who shuns oaths.[d] 3 That is the sad thing
about all that goes on under the sun: that the same fate is in
store for all. (Not only that, but men's hearts are full of sadness,
and their minds of madness, while they live; and then—to the
dead!) 4 For he who is [e-]reckoned among[-e] the living has something to look forward to—even a live dog is better than a dead
lion—5 since the living know they will die. But the dead know
nothing; they have no more recompense,[f] for even the memory of them has died. 6 Their loves, their hates, their jealousies
have long since perished; and they have no more share till the
end of time in all that goes on under the sun.

7 Go, eat your bread in gladness, and drink your wine in
joy; for your action was long ago approved by God.[g] 8 Let your
clothes always be freshly washed, and your head never lack
ointment. 9 Enjoy happiness with a woman you love all the
fleeting days of life that have been granted to you under the
sun—all your fleeting days. For that alone is what you can get
out of life and out of the means you acquire under the sun.
10 Whatever it is in your power to do, do with all your might.
For there is no action, no reasoning, no learning, no wisdom in
Sheol, where you are going.

11 I have further observed under the sun that
The race is not won by the swift,
Nor the battle by the valiant;
Nor is bread won by the wise,
Nor wealth by the intelligent,
Nor favor by the learned.

For the time of mischance[h] comes to all.[i] 12 And a man cannot
even know his time. As fishes are enmeshed in a fatal net, and
as birds are trapped in a snare, so men are caught at the time of
calamity,[h] when it comes upon them without warning.

13 This thing too I observed under the sun about wisdom,
and it affected me profoundly. 14 There was a little city, with
few men in it; and to it came a great king, who invested it and
built mighty siege works against it. 15 Present in the city was a
poor wise man [j-]who might have saved[-j] it with his wisdom, but
nobody thought of that poor man. 16 So I observed: Wisdom is
better than valor; but

a I.e., those who observe the laws of ritual purity. *b Cf. 4.17.*
c I.e., to God; cf. 2.26; 7.26. *d Cf. 8.2.* *e-e Lit. "joined to all."*
f Emendation yields "hope." *g Cf. 2.24–25; 3.13; 5.18.* *h Euphemism for death.*
i I.e., the insignificant duration of life renders all successes illusory; cf. 4.15–16.
j-j Others "who saved."

some new emphases. **1:** The first is that *righteous* and *wise* people and their deeds are under God's control, but whether the deeds turn out to involve *love* or *hate,* humans cannot know beforehand. **4–6:** Moreover, contrary to 4.2–3; 7.11, being alive is better than being dead, because in the netherworld (Sheol), no labor, reward, emotions, or thought is possible (see also v. 10b). **7–10a:** These vv. then offer a practical response to this situation, which Koheleth has also sounded before (2.24–25; 8.15): enjoy life while you live it. Yet in this advice, again, are new motifs. **8:** One motif connects enjoyment with symbols of purity, a white garment and the head anointed with oil. Some rabbinic Sages (e.g., *b. Shab.* 153a; Ibn Paquda) understood this to mean that one's behavior in life should always be morally exemplary and spiritually elevated: ready at any time for death and God's judgment, and avoiding the excesses that would stain one's character as they would stain a white garment. **9:** Another new motif stresses that enjoyment should include having a wife to love—a sentiment that appears to vary from an earlier one that looked at women negatively (7.26, 28). A third new motif about enjoyment comes in the final statement of this unit, in v. **12**. Here you should delight in life while you can, because your end may well come suddenly and unexpectedly, like *fish* or *birds* caught in a trap.

9.13–18: Again the problematic of wisdom. The challenge posed by deciding how to live in the face of death brings Koheleth back to the theme of wisdom and its limits. First, in a parable (vv. 14–16), recalling 4.13 (cf. also 7.19), and then in a final declaration (vv. 17–18), the author asserts the potential value of wisdom over royal authority and military prowess, and yet the vulnerability of that wisdom, of its effectiveness, to human neglect and sin. Some rabbinic commentators (e.g., Rashi; Ibn Ezra) sought to mitigate the expression of vulnerability by proposing that the v. (15), *nobody thought of that poor*

A poor man's wisdom is scorned,
And his words are not heeded.
17 [a]Words spoken softly by wise men are heeded [b-]sooner
than those shouted by a lord in folly.[-b]
18 Wisdom is more valuable than [c-]weapons of war,[-c] but a
single error destroys much of value.

10 Dead flies turn the perfumer's ointment fetid and
putrid;[d] so a little folly outweighs massive wisdom.
2 A wise man's mind tends toward the right hand, a fool's toward the left.[e] 3 A fool's mind is also wanting when he travels,
and he lets everybody know he is a fool.
4 If the wrath of a lord flares up against you, don't give up your
post;[f] for [g-]when wrath abates, grave offenses are pardoned.[-g]
5 Here is an evil I have seen under the sun as great as an error
committed by a ruler: 6 Folly was placed on lofty heights, while
rich men sat in low estate. 7 I have seen slaves on horseback,
and nobles walking on the ground like slaves.
8 He who digs a pit will fall into it; he who breaches a stone
fence will be bitten by a snake. 9 He who quarries stones will [h-]be
hurt by them; he who splits wood will be harmed by[-h] it. 10 [i]If the
ax has become dull and he has not whetted the edge, he must
exert more strength. Thus the advantage of a skill [depends on
the exercise of] prudence. 11 If the snake bites because no spell
was uttered, no advantage is gained by the trained charmer.
12 A wise man's talk brings him favor, but a fool's lips are his
undoing. 13 His talk begins as silliness and ends as disastrous
madness. 14 Yet the fool talks and talks!
[j]A man cannot know what will happen; who can tell him
what the future holds?
15 [k]A fool's exertions tire him out, for he doesn't know how
to get to a town.

a Verses 9.17–10.19 constitute a group of loosely connected aphorisms.
b-b Lit. "than the scream of a lord in [the manner of] the fools."
c-c Emendation yields "everything precious." *d Meaning of Heb. uncertain.*
e I.e., a wise man's mind brings him good luck; a fool's brings him bad luck.
f Emendation yields "hope."
g-g Lit. "abatement (2 Chron. 36.16) remits grave offenses." For hinniaḥ, *"to remit," cf. Abodah Zarah 13a; cf.* hanaḥah, *"remission of taxes," Esth. 2.18.*
h-h Emendation yields "profit . . . shall make use of." *i Meaning of verse uncertain.*
j The thought of this sentence is resumed at v. 20.
k This verse continues the thought of v. 3.

man, does not refer to the time after he had saved the city, when people forgot his achievement, but to the time before, when his true wisdom was not yet known.

10.1–20: Maxims on wisdom and folly. The miscellany of maxims in this ch, a number of them expressed in oppositions between *wisdom* and *folly,* picks up several themes adumbrated earlier, but, again, with some new images. Thus, v. 1 links with the preceding 9.13–18 to describe how wisdom can be undone by just a little folly, but compares this now to the spoiling of fragrant oil by the presence in it of dead flies—which incidentally also recalls the theme of death's finality in 9.1–12. **4, 5–7, 16–17, 20:** In turn, the recognition of, respect for, even fear of social and political hierarchy, and the rulers at its top, which was evident in 5.7–8 and 8.2–5, reappears here. **5–7:** But this recognition is formulated in a new image for Koheleth, though one well known elsewhere in the Bible (e.g., Prov. 30.21–23) and in other ancient Near Eastern traditions, especially Egyptian and Mesopotamian, namely, the reversal of hierarchy as a sign of chaos and destruction and of the triumph of folly. The last point suggests that Koheleth in this ch has not given up on the rightness and power of wisdom. **8–11:** Accordingly, Koheleth offers a series of maxims appealing to the honored convention of wisdom born of experience to show that there are rules in the world which dictate that certain actions, here largely negative, will inevitably bring their negative consequences. **12–14:** This is extended to an observation about speech, specifically about the contrast between a wise man's presumably measured speech and the favor it brings him over against the fool's uncontrolled prattling and its disastrous results—all of this recalling earlier admonitions about the fool and the avoidance of excess (5.6; 6.11; 7.16–18). What follows, then, is a statement that no one can know what the future will bring (v. 14b). This, of course, is a characteristic sentiment of Koheleth, expressed several times before (e.g., 3.22; 6.12). But as expressed here, it might be taken to undermine the confidence Koheleth has been showing in the value of wisdom, unless one returns to the view that wisdom is above all the faculty of knowing clearly what one cannot know. An alternative explanation, embraced by various traditional Jewish commentators (e.g., Joseph ben David Ibn Yachya; Moshe Alshich), begins with the fact that this statement about ignorance of the future follows

16 Alas for you, O land whose king is a lackey and whose ministers dine in the morning! 17 Happy are you, O land whose king
is a master and whose ministers dine at the proper time—with
restraint, not with guzzling!

18 Through slothfulness the ceiling sags,
Through lazy hands the house caves in.

19 They[a] make a banquet for revelry; wine makes life merry,
and money answers every need.

20 Don't revile a king even among your intimates.[b]
Don't revile a rich man even in your bedchamber;
For a bird of the air may carry the utterance,
And a winged creature may report the word.

11 Send your bread forth upon the waters; for after many
days you will find it. 2 Distribute portions to seven or
even to eight, for you cannot know what misfortune may occur
on earth.

3 If the clouds are filled, they will pour down rain on the
earth; and [c]if a tree falls to the south or to the north, the tree
will stay where it falls.[-c] 4 If one watches the wind, he will never
sow; and if one observes the clouds, he will never reap. 5 Just
as you do not know how the lifebreath passes into[d] the limbs
within the womb of the pregnant woman, so you cannot foresee the actions of God, who causes all things to happen. 6 Sow
your seed in the morning, and don't hold back your hand in
the evening, since you don't know which is going to succeed,
the one or the other, or if both are equally good.

7 How sweet is the light, what a delight for the eyes to behold
the sun! 8 Even if a man lives many years, let him enjoy himself
in all of them, remembering how many the days of darkness
are going to be. The only future is nothingness!

a I.e., the ministers of v. 16. *b Others "thoughts"; meaning of Heb. uncertain.*
c-c Emendation yields, "if a thunderbolt (lit. arrow, cf., e.g., 2 Sam. 22.15) falls ... where the thunderbolt falls, only there will it strike."
d So many mss. and Targum; most mss. read "like."

directly on the rebuke of the fool's prattling, and is then itself followed by another rebuke of the fool's wearisome behavior (v. 15). So connected, our statement becomes an example of the fool's prattling—and, consequently, an implied criticism of Koheleth's earlier affirmation of the view it expresses. **16–18:** One additional statement about the rightness and power of wisdom concludes the present unit. Here the necessity of kingship is granted, but a sharp distinction is made between wise and foolish rulers (cf. 4.13–14): between those who govern with propriety and restraint and those who endanger the community by acting like a simple, untested "young man" ("na'ar" in v. 16; cf. the parallel of it with "simple-minded" in Prov. 1.4; NJPS translates, however, *lackey*) and carousing lazily at all hours.

11.1–10: Seize the day, for the future is dark and uncertain. Three sections take up this theme, vv. 1–6, 7–8, 9–10. **1–6:** The initial advice, about casting bread and giving a portion (vv. 1–2), was understood by rabbinic sages (e.g., *Eccl. Rab.*) as acting generously to others, because it may be repaid you, and even in a time of your own misfortune. The misfortune here, however, refers probably to the general uncertainty Koheleth has elsewhere expressed about the course of life, with the addition that one should not be cowed by this uncertainty into avoiding a charitable deed. **2:** The sequence *seven ... eight* is one form of a convention, in biblical and Canaanite literature (e.g., Amos chs 1–2), for expressing a significant quantity. **3:** The following observations appear to move away from uncertainty as they describe regular cause-and-effect actions in the natural world: of the *clouds, rain,* and *trees*. Yet uncertainty can be detected here indirectly as concerns the matter of timing—a matter that Koheleth has already discussed explicitly several times, especially in 3.1–11. The point seems to be that even if humans know that the clouds drop rain and the trees fall, they cannot predict when these actions will occur. **4–5:** Thus anyone who wastes (too much) time contemplating the timing of such events will not get on with the activity of planting and reaping, which is basic to the life of Koheleth's world (v. 4). What humans do not know about nature, then, is confirmed by what they do not know about their own birth, and all of this only underscores that they do not understand the essential *actions* ("ma'aseh") of God who is behind all of these and everything else. **6:** This last v. of the first section sums up the whole matter, as it returns to agriculture: faced with uncertainty about the future, it is better to sow and till than to do nothing, because at least there, is a chance of success. **7–8:** The second section looks at the "seize the day" theme by contrasting the pleasure of living, expressed as the sweet goodness of experiencing the *light* of *the sun* (cf. 6.6; 7.11), with the

9 O youth, enjoy yourself while you are young! Let your heart
lead you to enjoyment in the days of your youth. Follow the desires of your heart and the glances of your eyes—but know well
that God will call you to account for all such things—10 and
banish care from your mind, and pluck sorrow out of your
flesh! For youth and black hair are fleeting.

12 So appreciate your vigor[a] in the days of your youth, before those days of sorrow come and those years arrive of
which you will say, "I have no pleasure in them"; 2 before sun
and light and moon and stars grow dark, and the clouds come
back again after the rain:

3 When the guards of the house[b] become shaky,
And the men of valor[c] are bent,
And the maids that grind,[d] grown few, are idle,
And the ladies that peer through the windows[e] grow dim,
4 And the doors to the street[f] are shut—
With the noise of the hand mill growing fainter,
And the song of the bird [g]growing feebler,[g]
And all the strains of music dying down;[h]
5 When one is afraid of heights
And there is terror on the road.—
For the almond tree may blossom,
[i]The grasshopper be burdened,[i]
And the caper bush may bud again;[j]

a *Cf. postbiblical* bori; *others "Remember thy Creator."*
b *I.e., the arms.* c *I.e., the legs.* d *I.e., the teeth.* e *I.e., the eyes.*
f *I.e., the ears.* g-g *Exact meaning of Heb. uncertain.* h *Cf. 2 Sam. 19.36.*
i-i *Emendation yields "The squill (postbiblical Heb.* ḥaṣab*) resume its burden," i.e., its blossom-stalk and its leaves.*
j *These plants, after seeming dead for part of the year, revive, unlike man; cf. Job 14.7–10.*

coming days of darkness and the *nothingness* ("hevel") they bring—the days here referring to death and perhaps to the pains of old age that immediately precede it (cf. 6.3–4; 12.1–2). Given the darkness that is to come, Koheleth concludes, as he often has before, that what humans must do is to enjoy life while they have it. **9–10:** This enjoyment, as the third and final section asserts, is something best suited to the *young,* and so Koheleth advises them not to lose that opportunity, since youth is *fleeting* ("hevel" again, but in another of its senses than that in v. 8). The further observation (v. 9c), that the way a young person behaves will eventually be judged by God, has been regarded by some modern interpreters as an orthodox addition to the original text of Koheleth, since it presumably clashes with the uncertainty about knowing God that Koheleth otherwise expresses. But Koheleth's hope in the possibility of divine judgment was already stated in 3.17, where it seems natural to the context, and so it could be here. Rabbinic commentators, not surprisingly, were perfectly comfortable with it in this section.

12.1–8: The terrors of old age. The comment about youth and enjoyment that concludes the previous ch contrasts deliberately with this unit, which describes old age—the contrast made explicit in v. 1 between *the days of your youth* and *those days of sorrow.* That vv. 1–8 comprise the last unit attributed to Koheleth in the book is signaled by the final v., 8; this is a virtual repetition of 1.2, which, following the introductory rubric, opens the book. To be sure, 1.2 gives the phrase *Utter futility* twice, while here in 12.8, in the main MT, it is given only once; however, it does appear twice in several other Heb mss and the ancient Syriac version of 12.8. The virtual identity of 1.2 and 12.8 forms, thus, an inclusio, giving the book closure by symmetry, and this is confirmed by the editorial nature of the following vv. (see 12.9–14 n.). That Koheleth's book ends on the dark note of old age is no accident; rather, it reaffirms the transitory nature of life, with no certainty of continuity or afterlife, that has been stated throughout (e.g., 2.18–21; 5.12–16; 9.5–6). In the present instance we have a graphic picture of the decrepitude of old age in a variety of images. **2:** The first is that of darkness and light, last discussed in 11.7–8. Here it is elaborated and intensified: the *dark*ness (of old age) envelops the light (of vigorous life), whether that *light* comes during the day (the *sun*) or the night (the *moon* and the *stars*) (cf. e.g., Isa. 13.10; Ezek. 32.7–8). **3–4a:** This darkness, in turn, is connected with the weakening of basic human vocations—house managers, men of wealth or warriors, grinders of flour, sequestered women who have to look through windows—and of basic human activities—doors opening on the bustling business of the street-market, and grinding. **4b–5a:** All of these are finally linked up with nature—*birds, almond trees, grasshoppers*—and their decline or expressions of fear at the approaching darkness. What these images denote has been debated. Classical rabbinic thought (e.g., Tg.; *Eccl. Rab.;* and Rashi, and adopted in NJPS), has suggested an allegory,

But man sets out for his eternal abode,
With mourners all around in the street.—
6 Before the silver cord snaps
And the golden bowl crashes,
The jar is shattered at the spring,
And the jug[a] is smashed at the cistern.[b]
7 And the dust returns to the ground
As it was,
And the lifebreath returns to God
Who bestowed it.
8 Utter futility—said Koheleth—
All is futile!

9 A further word: Because Koheleth was a sage, he continued
to instruct the people. He listened to and tested the soundness[c]
of many maxims. 10 Koheleth sought to discover useful sayings
and recorded[d] genuinely truthful sayings. 11 The sayings of the
wise are like goads, like nails fixed [e-]in prodding sticks.[-e] [f-]They
were given by one Shepherd.[-f]

12 A further word: [g-]Against them,[-g] my son, be warned!
The making of many books is without limit
And much study[h] is a wearying of the flesh.
13 The sum of the matter, when all is said and done: Revere
God and observe His commandments! For this applies to all

a So in Punic; others "wheel." *b Poetic figure for the end of life.*
c A noun, like dibber *(Jer. 5.13), which occurs in such postbiblical phrases as* shanim kethiq(qe)nan, *"normal years" (lit. "years according to their propriety").*
d Wekhathub *is equivalent to* wekhathob, *an infinitive employed as in Esth. 9.16 and elsewhere.*
e-e Meaning of Heb. uncertain. Others "are those that are composed in collections."
f-f Meaning of Heb. uncertain. Emendation yields "They are accounted as a sharp ox goad" (post-biblical mardeaʿ*).*
g-g Emendation yields "Slow, there!" Cf. Arabic mah *and* mah mah; *so also* mah (meh) *in Prov. 31.2.*
h Meaning of Heb. uncertain.

wherein the words for managers, men of wealth, etc. denote the different parts of the human body, here deteriorating rapidly. Alternatively, the images could pertain to an estate of a wealthy landowner—echoing Koheleth's experiment in ch 2—now in serious decline. **5b–7:** Whatever the precise solution, the imagery clearly points to human death, given the references to funeral mourning, to the breaking of a device that uses a pitcher to raise water from a well (so Ibn Ezra; cf. Zech. 4.2–3), and to the return of each human body to dust, so echoing 3.19–20 and Gen. 3.19. **7:** Significantly, each human *lifebreath* ("ruaḥ"; cf. 11.5) will return to God who gave it, thus demonstrating a spirit-body distinction not expressed in 3.19–20 and Gen. 3.19.

12.9–14: Editorial reflections. Interpreters, whether traditional Jewish or modern critical, generally agree that these final vv. constitute an epilogue, after the conclusion of the book of Koheleth proper. Many traditional Jewish interpreters assume that it is still Koheleth/Solomon who is speaking here, but some (e.g., Rashbam) suppose that it is later editors, and the latter is the common opinion of modern critics. The formal indications of the separation of vv. 9–14 from the core of the book are twofold: the framework, noted above, that encloses 1.2–12.8; and the shift here to third-person discussion of Koheleth from the first-person remarks by him within 1.2–12.8. Since this third-person discussion echoes that in the introductory rubric of 1.1, the two together provide a second, larger framework around the one within 1.2–12.8 (note, however, the brief third-person references in 1.2 and 7.27). A third formal marker breaks vv. 9–14 into two parts, reflecting perhaps two separate editorial additions, 9–11 and 12–14, for each part begins with the phrase *A further word* (actually the Heb varies slightly in each: "ve-yoter she-" in v. 9; and "ve-yoter me-" in v. 12). **9–11:** The first part identifies Koheleth as a sage and describes his characteristic activity of teaching by means of wise sayings, emphasizing the careful construction of the sayings (v. 9c) and their provocative impact, like the goads and pricks of a shepherd (v. 11) to control the animals under his supervision. **11:** Interestingly, classical Jewish commentary (e.g., Tg.; *Eccl. Rab.;* and Rashi) identifies the *Shepherd* with Moses. **12–14:** The second part goes on not to criticize Koheleth's teaching, but to assert that with his sayings collected, it is not necessary, indeed not desirable, to add anything more (cf. Deut. 4.2; 13.1). Further, this second part strives to sum up Koheleth's teaching with the imperatives: fear (NJPS: *revere*) God and keep *His commandments* (v. 13b)—phrases frequent in other parts of the Bible (e.g., Deut. 6.2; Prov. 1.7; Job 28.28).

mankind: 14 that God will call every creature to account for [a]everything unknown,[a] be it good or bad.

The sum of the matter, when all is said and done: Revere God and observe His commandments! For this applies to all mankind.

a-a Emendation yields "all their conduct."

14: The reason given for this instruction is that God will bring every action, even if kept hidden up to this point, into judgment, whether for good or for ill. That rabbinic thought may have regarded this instruction to fear and keep as the center of Koheleth is suggested in the Masoretic note, reproduced in NJPS, that public readings of Koheleth must repeat v. 13 after v. 14, and so end the reading of the book with this v. (Similar Masoretic notes occur for the books of Isa., Mal., as the last in order of the twelve minor prophets, and Lam.) Some modern critics, on the other hand, have understood this instruction to fear and keep as the work of a later orthodox editor, who wished to tone down, if not to reshape, what he regarded as the radical challenge of Koheleth to the tradition of God's covenantal demands with their assurance of a strict reward and punishment justice. It is true that the instruction here to keep God's commandments does not appear elsewhere in Koheleth, but the other clause, to fear God, is found (3.14; 5.6; 7.18; 8.12–13), as is the statement about God's judgment (3.17; cf. 3.5; 11.9). It may be, then, that the traditional interpreters were correct after all, and that this concluding instruction, whether contributed by a later editor or by Koheleth himself, is in fact congruent with the views in the rest of the book. The point would be, in sum, that just because human rational inquiry leads nowhere, in terms of "demonstrating" a system of reward and punishment justice or of goal-oriented activity that leads to lasting achievements, it does not invalidate the power and sovereignty of God nor disprove the possibility that in some way He does call everyone and everything to account. (His existence is not an issue for the book.) Indeed, human rational inquiry affirms the divine power to allow humans the pleasures of enjoying their work while they are alive, if they would but take advantage of them. Therefore, when all is said and done, God and His power remain, and in the words of this final instruction, humans should recognize and acknowledge that.

אסתר

Esther

IN JEWISH TRADITION, THE BOOK OF ESTHER, called "megillat ʾester," "the scroll of Esther," is inextricably bound up with the holiday of Purim. The book provides the etiology (story of its origin) for Purim, authorizes its annual observance, and models how it is to be celebrated. Purim, the only biblical festival not mentioned in the Torah, needed a reason and an authorization. (Hanukkah, which commemorates the rededication of the Temple in 164 BCE, is based on events narrated in the extrabiblical books of 1 and 2 Maccabees.) Purim gets its reason in the pseudo-historical tale of how the Jews were saved from their archenemy and it gets its authorization in the letter of Mordecai (and Esther) which this book includes. The book of Esther is the centerpiece of the observance of Purim; it is read publicly on Purim eve and the following morning, accompanied by the noisy blotting out of Haman's name by children and adults, many of them dressed in funny costumes. Purim is a holiday replete with mock re-enactments of the Esther story, partying and excessive drinking, carnivals and masquerades, and a general sense of frivolity uncharacteristic of Jewish festivals. The Talmud (*b. Meg.* 7b) encourages one to get so drunk that he cannot distinguish between "Cursed be Haman" and "Blessed be Mordecai." Like Purim, the book is full of boisterous merrymaking—a comic farce for a carnivalesque holiday. The book sets the tone for the holiday, "days of feasting and merrymaking" (9.22). It also initiates the other customs of the holiday: sending (food) gifts to friends and neighbors and presents to the poor (9.22).

Esther is best read as a comedy. Rabbinic midrashim seem to have intuited this, and they add to the fun by their preposterous embellishments of the story and its characters, extending in the most unsubtle ways the farce or burlesque inherent in the book—with its bawdiness and slap-stick humor. The voyeurism of ch 1—drunken nobles hoping to ogle the queen—is made more explicit in the midrash (e.g., *Esth. Rab.*) on 1.11 that says that Vashti was bidden to appear "wearing a royal diadem" and nothing else, that is, naked. Ch 2, with its inside view of the harem, where the girls apply their cosmetics for a year in preparation for a night in the king's bed, is no less sexually suggestive. The lavishness of the Persian court and the ten drinking banquets in the story add to the aura of comic excess. The misunderstandings between Ahasuerus and Haman in chs 6 and 7, the climax of the plot, produce belly laughs. All of these attributes are characteristic of low comedy.

The story's plot is structured on improbabilities, exaggerations, misunderstandings, and reversals. Esther keeps her identity hidden although her relationship to Mordecai the Jew was known; an insignificant Jewish minority killed 75,000 of its enemies; Haman erected a seven-story stake for impaling his enemy. The characters are caricatures. Ahasuerus is a buffoon, never sure quite what to do, completely at the mercy of his ministers and servants, giving away his power without a thought. Haman is an erratic egomaniac, with wild mood swings, concerned only for his own honor and his enemy's disgrace. Even the heroes, Mordecai and Esther, seem one-dimensional and unrealistic. In fact, nothing about the events of the story is realistic, and therefore attempts to read history from it are misguided. The setting of the Persian court is authentic, as are a number of Persian words, but the events are fictional. There was no known Jewish queen of Persia. Moreover, the Persian empire was tolerant of its ethnic minorities and is an unlikely place for an edict to eradicate the Jewish population.

The story draws on conventional themes of ancient storytelling known from the Bible and from extrabiblical sources from the Persian period (especially in Greek sources): a rivalry between courtiers (this one focusing on honor and shame), a woman who uses her charm to save her people, an ancient ethnic feud, hidden identities, and the triumph of the forces of good over the forces of evil. The portrayal of the Persian court is equally conventional, if at times made into a burlesque. Like the many Greek stories about Persia (in Herodotus and other works from his time), Esther features royal luxury bordering on decadence, concern for protocol and legalities, wine parties, and the renowned communication system. Esther is, then, in tune with contemporary literary descriptions of Persia and its royal court. At the same time, it draws on biblical traditions, most obviously those about Saul and Agag, king of the Amalekites (1 Sam. ch 15), who are reincarnated, as it were, in Mordecai and Haman. The stories of Joseph and Daniel share with Esther the theme of Jewish courtiers in foreign courts. (The stories in Dan. chs 1–6 are roughly contemporary with Esther.) Finally, Esther echoes the book of Kings in its reference to royal annals, and some scholars have found additional similar phraseology in the two books.

Noticeably absent is any mention of God or of religious observance (prayer, Jewish dietary restrictions, traditional modesty, and endogamous marriage). The Rabbis were troubled by Esther's marriage to a non-Jew, and solved the problem by explaining that she remained completely passive in the king's bed or that she never actually consummated the marriage. They also provide her with kosher food, although the Bible is silent about her diet (unlike Daniel, who became a vegetarian so as to maintain Jewish dietary laws; see Dan. ch 1). Mordecai and the Jews mourn and fast, but do not pray—a most striking omission (Daniel also prays). In its omission of God and religion, the Hebrew text is highly unusual, so much so that in the Greek version of Esther there are prayers, the name of God occurs, and Esther desists from eating forbidden food or drinking forbidden wine. (There are other major differences in the Greek Esther as well, especially its tone.) It is not clear whether any of these religious items were part of the original story and then removed, or added to an original story that lacked them. The best explanation for their absence, especially the absence of God's name, is that, given that the story is so comic, at times bordering on lewd, such reticence about things religious is preferable, lest religion be debauched.

The book does have a serious side, and an important function as a Diaspora story, a story written about and for (and perhaps by) Jews of the Diaspora. As such, it promotes Jewish identity, solidarity within the Jewish community, and a strong connection with Jewish (biblical) tradition. It is more centered on the Diaspora than most Jewish works of its time; it does not refer to the land of Israel (other than the mention of the exile of Jeconiah in 2.6) or to the Temple. It addresses the inherent problems of a minority people, their vulnerability to political forces and government edicts, their lack of autonomy, and their dependence on royal favor and on the sagacity of their own leaders. More specifically, Haman's false claim about the Jews is a prototype of anti-Judaism, which must have been familiar enough to resonate with the book's original audience. In the end, though, the message is positive: good triumphs and evil is eradicated; the threat of Jewish annihilation is averted, and the Jewish community is assured of continuity and prosperity. No wonder that Haman became the symbol of later enemies of the Jews, and that other "Purims" were celebrated in medieval and early modern times in communities where great danger was averted. The psychological release provided in a carnivalesque holiday like Purim and in the book of Esther lends itself to similar celebrations of the communal triumph over danger. The book succeeds in putting a serious message in a comic form.

The book was probably written about 400–300 BCE, toward the end of the Persian period or the beginning of the Hellenistic period. It apparently adopted an earlier tale about Mordecai, Esther, and Haman (tales of wise courtiers and heroic queens were popular at that time) and shaped it into an etiology of Purim (mentioned only at the end of the book, after the main plot is completed, a holiday whose origin is lost in obscurity). The story appears in rather different form in the Greek version of Esther (LXX), where it has six major additions not found in the Masoretic version plus a number of other significant differences throughout the story. The Greek version is less comic and more melodramatic, and in its present form it reflects Hellenistic concerns (Jewish ritual observance, including circumcision) not found in the Hebrew version. An ancient body of midrashic interpretation attaches to Esther, found in the Talmud (*b. Meg.* 10b–17a), in Josephus's paraphrase (*Ant.,* Book 11, ch 6), in the two Targumim (Aramaic renderings) to Esther, and in several midrashic collections. There is no consensus on the date of the book's canonization, partly because there is no consensus on the date of the canonization of the Kethuvim. Strikingly, Esther is the only biblical book of which no remnant has been found at Qumran; apparently the Dead Sea community did not preserve this book (although they apparently had stories of the same genre), perhaps because they did not observe Purim, which according to their 364-day calendar would always fall on the Sabbath, creating a conflict of observance. (According to the Jewish calendar now in use, Purim (14 Adar) can never fall on the Sabbath.)

[ADELE BERLIN]

1 It happened in the days of Ahasuerus—that Ahasuerus
who reigned over a hundred and twenty-seven provinces
from India to Ethiopia. 2 In those days, when King Ahasuerus
occupied the royal throne in the fortress[a] Shushan, 3 in the
third year of his reign, he gave a banquet for all the officials and
courtiers—the administration of Persia and Media, the nobles
and the governors of the provinces in his service. 4 For no fewer
than a hundred and eighty days he displayed the vast riches of
his kingdom and the splendid glory of his majesty. 5 At the end
of this period, the king gave a banquet for seven days in the

a *I.e., the fortified city.*

1.1–22: Wine and Women. This ch is a prologue to the main story, setting the scene and the tone: luxury, bureaucracy, and bawdiness—all to excess. The Persian court is decadently lavish and mired in protocol. King Ahasuerus is all powerful and totally inept. The dismissal of Vashti paves the way for Esther's entrance.

1.1–8: Wine: Partytime in Persia. We enter the opulent Persian court, filled from ceiling to floor with expensive and exotic furnishings, exquisite drinking-vessels, and then the wine, the cause of all that is to follow. **1:** *Ahasuerus,* usually identified with the Persian king Xerxes I (reigned from 486–465 BCE), although the LXX and the Peshitta read Artaxerxes (reigned 465–424 BCE). But this Ahasuerus is a fictional character, a comic figurehead concerned with the trappings of power but exercising little of his own. *From India to Ethiopia:* The extent of his sovereignty shows how powerful he was. The Persian empire stretched from "Hi(n)dush"—the area in the Indus valley, in the modern province of Sind in southern Pakistan—to "Nubia," south of Egypt, and is described in these terms in Persian documents. *A hundred and twenty-seven provinces:* This is one of several large numbers that adds to the tone of exaggeration. Persian documents list 20–32 provinces. **2:** *The fortress Shushan:* Susa, one of the four Persian capitals (besides Ecbatana [Hamadan], Babylon, and Persepolis), was the main administrative capital and the king's winter residence. The *fortress* refers to the acropolis, the seat of the government, and *Shushan* or "the city of Shushan" refers to the lower city. **3–5:** The king displays his wealth. This scene parodies the Persian institution of the "King's Table," an occasion for the bringing of tribute from the provinces

court of the king's palace garden for all the people who lived in
the fortress Shushan, high and low alike. 6 [a][There were hangings of] white cotton and blue wool, caught up by cords of fine
linen and purple wool to silver rods and alabaster columns;
and there were couches of gold and silver on a pavement of
marble, alabaster, mother-of-pearl, and mosaics. 7 Royal wine
was served in abundance, as befits a king, in golden beakers,
beakers of varied design. 8 And the rule for the drinking was,
"No restrictions!" For the king had given orders to every palace steward to comply with each man's wishes. 9 In addition,
Queen Vashti gave a banquet for women, in the royal palace of
King Ahasuerus.

10 On the seventh day, when the king was merry with wine,
he ordered Mehuman, Bizzetha, Harbona, Bigtha, Abagtha,
Zethar, and Carcas, the seven eunuchs in attendance on King
Ahasuerus, 11 to bring Queen Vashti before the king wearing
a royal diadem, to display her beauty to the peoples and the
officials; for she was a beautiful woman. 12 But Queen Vashti
refused to come at the king's command conveyed by the eunuchs. The king was greatly incensed, and his fury burned
within him.

13 Then the king consulted the sages learned in procedure.[b]
(For it was the royal practice [to turn] to all who were versed
in law and precedent. 14 His closest advisers were Carshena,
Shethar, Admatha, Tarshish, Meres, Marsena, and Memucan,
the seven ministers of Persia and Media who had access to
the royal presence and occupied the first place in the kingdom.) 15 "What," [he asked,] "shall be done, according to law,
to Queen Vashti for failing to obey the command of King Ahasuerus conveyed by the eunuchs?"

16 Thereupon Memucan declared in the presence of the
king and the ministers: "Queen Vashti has committed an offense not only against Your Majesty but also against all the officials and against all the peoples in all the provinces of King
Ahasuerus. 17 For the queen's behavior will make all wives
despise their husbands, as they reflect that King Ahasuerus
himself ordered Queen Vashti to be brought before him, but
she would not come. 18 This very day the ladies of Persia and
Media, who have heard of the queen's behavior, will cite it to

a Meaning of part of this verse uncertain.
b Lit. "the times."

and the bestowing of gifts from the king to high officials. Persian palaces at Persepolis and Susa had large assembly halls (Persian "apadana," Heb "bitan") separate from the palace. **7:** Persian parties were famous for their wine-drinking. Herodotus (*Histories* 1.133) remarks that the Persians decided important issues when they were drunk and reconsidered them when they were sober, and vice versa. Ahasuerus will not have a chance to reconsider (cf. 2.1–2). The drinking-ware carries on the theme of opulence. Compare Dan. 5.2 where Belshazzar and his guests drank wine from the vessels that his father had looted from the Temple. **8:** *The rule for the drinking was, "No restrictions!":* The usual drinking practice was not followed. The best explanation is that the wine normally reserved "by royal law" for the exclusive use of the king was served to the guests. The phrase is then better translated "As for drinking according to the rule, no one enforced it." Many commentaries, however, take the phrase as a reference to the amount of wine: each man could drink as much or as little as he liked.

1.9–22: Women: The Vashti incident. 9: It was considered indecent for wives of the Persian nobility to attend male drinking parties; the only female attendees were dancing girls. For that reason the queen hosted a separate party for the women. **10:** The tongue-twisting names of the servants are Persian-sounding, but probably fake. The names in v. 14 mirror this list (*Mehuman/Memucan,* and so forth). **11:** Just as the king has displayed his wealth, so he wishes to display his queen. Just as the royal wine is not reserved exclusively for the king, so the king's wife is not kept for his eyes alone. *A royal diadem,* a mark of belonging to the royal household. **12:** Vashti tries to protect her own honor and her drunken husband's, but must disobey a royal command to do so. **13:** Ever concerned with the proper way of doing things, the king consults *sages learned in procedure,* the legal experts, or better, the experts in protocol. *Law,* Heb "dat," from the Persian "data," occurs nineteen times in the book, with meanings ranging from "law" to "custom" to "practice." In later Heb, it means "religion"; there is no biblical word for "religion." **16–22:** A domestic incident becomes a national crisis. The danger Memucan sees in Vashti's refusal is preposterous, as is his solution. His attempt to preserve the king's honor makes the king look even sillier and more

all Your Majesty's officials, and there will be no end of scorn
and provocation!
19 "If it please Your Majesty, let a royal edict be issued by you,
and let it be written into the laws of Persia and Media, so that
it cannot be abrogated, that Vashti shall never enter the presence of King Ahasuerus. And let Your Majesty bestow her royal
state upon another who is more worthy than she. 20 Then will
the judgment executed by Your Majesty resound throughout
your realm, vast though it is; and all wives will treat their husbands with respect, high and low alike."
21 The proposal was approved by the king and the ministers,
and the king did as Memucan proposed. 22 Dispatches were
sent to all the provinces of the king, to every province in its own
script and to every nation in its own language, that every man
should wield authority in his home and speak the language of
his own people.

2 Some time afterward, when the anger of King Ahasuerus
subsided, he thought of Vashti and what she had done and
what had been decreed against her. 2 The king's servants who
attended him said, "Let beautiful young virgins be sought out
for Your Majesty. 3 Let Your Majesty appoint officers in every
province of your realm to assemble all the beautiful young virgins at the fortress Shushan, in the harem under the supervision of Hege, the king's eunuch, guardian of the women. Let
them be provided with their cosmetics. 4 And let the maiden
who pleases Your Majesty be queen instead of Vashti." The proposal pleased the king, and he acted upon it.
5 In the fortress Shushan lived a Jew by the name of Mordecai, son of Jair son of Shimei son of Kish, a Benjaminite. 6 [Kish]
had been exiled from Jerusalem in the group that was carried
into exile along with King Jeconiah of Judah, which had been

vulnerable. **19:** Vashti refused to appear, and now she may never appear again. While the book is silent about what became of Vashti, many midrashim interpret her punishment as execution. *Cannot be abrogated,* Generally understood to mean that a law cannot be revoked, but the Heb means "may not be broken" or "to which there is no exception," (cf. 8.5, 8). Memucan may have said this out of concern that the king himself will want to make an exception and take Vashti back. That a domestic spat resulted in a royal edict is another comic exaggeration. Furthermore, it is hardly appropriate for an edict since it concerned only one person. **22:** *Dispatches were sent:* The Persians were noted for their excellent communications network. See also 3.12–13 and 8.9–14, where the dispatches become progressively more urgent. *To every province in its own script and to every nation* [or "people"] *in its own language,* to ensure that the edict could be understood by all in the multi-ethnic empire. The usual practice was to promulgate communications in Aram., the common language of the empire, and then to translate them locally. *That every man should wield authority in his home:* This is not the wording of the edict but the reason for its publication. Cf. 3.14; 8.13; and perhaps 9.21. Vashti's punishment is presumably meant to be a deterrent to other wives who might disobey their husbands. *Speak the language of his own people,* a difficult phrase, perhaps meaning that the dispatches were sent in vernacular languages so that they could be directly comprehended by all and that whatever language the husband spoke, his orders to his wife were authoritative.

2.1–18: Mordecai enters the story and Esther enters the harem. 2: The advisors suggest a replacement for Vashti lest Ahasuerus, now no longer angry and thinking of Vashti, decides to take her back. **4:** A beauty contest is hardly the way real queens of Persia were chosen. In fact, Persian queens had to come from the Persian nobility. **5–7:** Mordecai is a prominent upper-class Jew of the Babylonian exile, with an obliquely expressed link to King Saul. **5:** *A Jew by the name of Mordecai:* "Yehudi" (Jew) does not refer to a member of the tribe of Judah (Mordecai was from the tribe of Benjamin), but to a Jew from the kingdom of Judah (where all the Babylonian exiles were from); this is an early usage of "Jew" in the sense that we now know it. "Mordecai" was a common personal name in the Persian period (cf. Neh. 7.7); "Marduka" in its Babylonian form. (The older view that the name is a direct reference to the Babylonian god Marduk, and that Esther is a reference to the goddess Ishtar, is no longer accepted.) *Shimei:* According to rabbinic interpretation, this is Shimei son of Gera, the member of Saul's clan who supported him against David (2 Sam. 16.5–8); this book, in contrast to Samuel, reflects favorably on Saul and his household and on the tribe of Benjamin. **6:** *[Kish]:* Heb reads "who," leaving the antecedent vague. Was it Kish, the last person listed in v. 5, as traditional Jewish exegetes understood? More likely, the reference is to Mordecai, the subject of v. 5, who, like Daniel, is said to have been exiled from Jerusalem—a sign of authentic Jewish pedigree in the Diaspora—even though this would make Mordecai incredibly old (115 years). **7:** Esther is introduced indirectly, through the introduction of Mordecai; her patronymic is not given until v. 15. *Hadassah* means "myrtle." *Esther* is probably derived from the Persian name for "star." It was not uncommon for Diaspora Jews to have both a Heb and a vernacular name, as did Daniel and his friends (see Dan. 1.6–7), and Judah Maccabee. No Heb name is mentioned for Mordecai. **10:** It stretches credibility that Esther could keep her ethnic identity secret when Mordecai's was so public, but it is vital to the plot. **12:** *Oil of myrrh:* Myrrh is associated with love-making (Song 1.13; Prov. 7.17). The excess continues, along with the bureaucracy. **14:** *Second harem:* Perhaps there was a second harem, but more likely the women return to the same harem, this time to be looked after by *Shaashgaz.* **16:** *The tenth month, which is the month of Tebeth:* In Zech., Ezra, Neh., and Esth. a double system of naming months is used: the ordinal number (beginning with the spring) of the more ancient Israelite calendar and the month name, adopted from the Babylonian calendar via Aramaic (the latter is still in use). **17:** *Women ... virgins,* all the women who have already come and all the virgins yet to come. *A royal diadem,* perhaps the same diadem that Vashti was bidden to appear with in 1.11. **19:** This v. is difficult, and may be a scribal error.

driven into exile by King Nebuchadnezzar of Babylon.—7 He was foster father to Hadassah—that is, Esther—his uncle's daughter, for she had neither father nor mother. The maiden was shapely and beautiful; and when her father and mother died, Mordecai adopted her as his own daughter.

8 When the king's order and edict was proclaimed, and when many girls were assembled in the fortress Shushan under the supervision of Hegai,[a] Esther too was taken into the king's palace under the supervision of Hegai, guardian of the women. 9 The girl pleased him and won his favor, and he hastened to furnish her with her cosmetics and her rations, as well as with the seven maids who were her due from the king's palace; and he treated her and her maids with special kindness in the harem. 10 Esther did not reveal her people or her kindred, for Mordecai had told her not to reveal it. 11 Every single day Mordecai would walk about in front of the court of the harem, to learn how Esther was faring and what was happening to her.

12 When each girl's turn came to go to King Ahasuerus at the end of the twelve months' treatment prescribed for women (for that was the period spent on beautifying them: six months with oil of myrrh and six months with perfumes and women's cosmetics, 13 and it was after that that the girl would go to the king), whatever she asked for would be given her to take with her from the harem to the king's palace. 14 She would go in the evening and leave in the morning for a second harem in charge of Shaashgaz, the king's eunuch, guardian of the concubines. She would not go again to the king unless the king wanted her, when she would be summoned by name. 15 When the turn came for Esther daughter of Abihail—the uncle of Mordecai, who had adopted her as his own daughter—to go to the king, she did not ask for anything but what Hegai, the king's eunuch, guardian of the women, advised. Yet Esther won the admiration of all who saw her.

16 Esther was taken to King Ahasuerus, in his royal palace, in the tenth month, which is the month of Tebeth, in the seventh year of his reign. 17 The king loved Esther more than all the other women, and she won his grace and favor more than all the virgins. So he set a royal diadem on her head and made her queen instead of Vashti. 18 The king gave a great banquet for all his officials and courtiers, "the banquet of Esther." He proclaimed a remission of taxes[b] for the provinces and distributed gifts as befits a king.

19[c] When the virgins were assembled a second time, Mordecai sat in the palace gate. 20 But Esther still did not reveal her kindred or her people, as Mordecai had instructed her; for

a Identical with Hege in v. 3. *b Or "an amnesty."*
c Meaning of verse uncertain.

Esther obeyed Mordecai's bidding, as she had done when she was under his tutelage.

21 At that time, when Mordecai was sitting in the palace gate, Bigthan and Teresh, two of the king's eunuchs who guarded the threshold, became angry, and plotted to do away with King Ahasuerus. 22 Mordecai learned of it and told it to Queen Esther, and Esther reported it to the king in Mordecai's name. 23 The matter was investigated and found to be so, and the two were impaled on stakes. This was recorded in the book of annals at the instance of the king.

3 Some time afterward, King Ahasuerus promoted Haman son of Hammedatha the Agagite; he advanced him and seated him higher than any of his fellow officials. 2 All the king's courtiers in the palace gate knelt and bowed low to Haman, for such was the king's order concerning him; but Mordecai would not kneel or bow low. 3 Then the king's courtiers who were in the palace gate said to Mordecai, "Why do you disobey the king's order?" 4 When they spoke to him day after day and he would not listen to them, they told Haman, in order to see whether Mordecai's resolve would prevail; for he had explained to them that he was a Jew.[a] 5 When Haman saw that Mordecai would not kneel or bow low to him, Haman was filled with rage. 6 But he disdained to lay hands on Mordecai alone; having been told who Mordecai's people were, Haman plotted to do away with all the Jews, Mordecai's people, throughout the kingdom of Ahasuerus.

7 In the first month, that is, the month of Nisan, in the twelfth year of King Ahasuerus, *pur*—which means "the lot"—was cast before Haman concerning every day and every month, [until it

a I.e., that as a Jew he could not bow to a descendant of Agag, the Amalekite king; see 1 Sam. 15, and cf. Exod. 17.14–16; Deut. 25.17–19.

2.21–23: Mordecai uncovers a plot against the king. 21: *In the palace gate,* "the king's gate." More than a physical location, this is Mordecai's official position at court. Mordecai is a member of the king's "secret police," official spies who protected the king. **22:** Mordecai's job is to ferret out plots against the king. *In Mordecai's name:* Mordecai's loyalty to the king is demonstrated but he is not rewarded; the lack of reward will be remembered in 6.2. A rabbinic principle is derived from this verse: A person who quotes something in the name of the one who said it brings about the redemption of the world (*m. 'Avot* 6.6). **23:** *Impaled on stakes:* Heb "talah" may mean "to hang" or "to impale a dead body." Impalement was not the method of execution but a way of disgracing a person through the public display of his corpse. (Cf. Gen. 40.19; Deut. 21.22; Josh. 8.29; 10.26; 1 Sam. 31.10.) Herodotus (*Histories* 3.125; 7.238; cf. 9.79) also mentions the impalement of corpses as a sign of great disgrace. This first impalement in the story foreshadows Haman's plot to impale Mordecai.

3.1–15: Haman plots to kill the Jews. The main plot, the rivalry between the two courtiers, begins here. This personal rivalry quickly takes on national implications. **1:** *Promoted Haman:* Mordecai's good deed in saving the king's life goes unrewarded while Haman is promoted for no apparent reason. *The Agagite,* a descendent of Agag, the Amalekite king responsible for Saul's loss of the kingship (1 Sam. 15.8). The ancient enmity between Israel and Amalek informs the relationship between Haman and Mordecai. The Amalekite connection is reinforced in the synagogue lectionary cycle by the reading, on the Sabbath preceding Purim, the passage in Deut. 25.17–19 ("Remember what Amalek did to you .... you shall blot out the memory of Amalek") and the "haftarah" from 1 Sam. ch 15 (containing the story of Saul and Agag). On Purim itself the Torah reading is Exod. 17.8–16, the battle between Israel and Amalek. Both Targumim to Esther extend Haman's genealogy back to Esau, echoing Gen. 36.12, thereby extending the rivalry between Mordecai and Haman even further back to Esau and Jacob. **2:** *Would not kneel or bow low:* Mordecai's refusal is not based on religious principles, for biblical Jews or Israelites may bow to superiors (Gen. 23.7; 43.28; Exod. 18.7; 1 Kings 1.23), but on ethnic grounds so as not to give honor to an enemy of Israel. A rabbinic interpretation in *Tg. Rishon* recasts the refusal in terms of a religious prohibition, saying that Haman was wearing an image of an idol on his chest and that in bowing to him Mordecai would be bowing to an idol. Another rabbinic explanation (also found in the LXX and at home in the Hellenistic and Roman periods) is that it was improper to bow to anyone but God. **5:** *Filled with rage:* The mercurial mood-swings of Haman begin. Haman is a glutton for honor, as will become more evident in ch 6. **6:** *Mordecai's people:* Haman is motivated by both personal and ethnic reasons. **7:** *Pur,* an Akkadian word; the practice of casting lots by means of a small stone die is known from ancient Mesopotamia. Similar

fell on] the twelfth month, that is, the month of Adar. [8]Haman then said to King Ahasuerus, "There is a certain people, scattered and dispersed among the other peoples in all the provinces of your realm, whose laws are different from those of any other people and who do not obey the king's laws; and it is not in Your Majesty's interest to tolerate them. [9]If it please Your Majesty, let an edict be drawn for their destruction, and I will pay ten thousand talents of silver to the stewards for deposit in the royal treasury." [10]Thereupon the king removed his signet ring from his hand and gave it to Haman son of Hammedatha the Agagite, the foe of the Jews. [11]And the king said, "The money and the people are yours to do with as you see fit."

[12]On the thirteenth day of the first month, the king's scribes were summoned and a decree was issued, as Haman directed, to the king's satraps, to the governors of every province, and to the officials of every people, to every province in its own script and to every people in its own language. The orders were issued in the name of King Ahasuerus and sealed with the king's signet. [13]Accordingly, written instructions were dispatched by couriers to all the king's provinces to destroy, massacre, and exterminate all the Jews, young and old, children and women, on a single day, on the thirteenth day of the twelfth month—that is, the month of Adar—and to plunder their possessions. [14]The text of the document was to the effect that a law should be proclaimed in every single province; it was to be publicly displayed to all the peoples, so that they might be ready for that day.

[15]The couriers went out posthaste on the royal mission, and the decree was proclaimed in the fortress Shushan. The king and Haman sat down to feast, but the city of Shushan was dumbfounded.

4 When Mordecai learned all that had happened, Mordecai tore his clothes and put on sackcloth and ashes. He went through the city, crying out loudly and bitterly, [2]until he came in front of the palace gate; for one could not enter the palace gate wearing sackcloth.—[3]Also, in every province that the king's command and decree reached, there was great mourning among the Jews, with fasting, weeping, and wailing, and everybody lay in sackcloth and ashes.—[4]When Esther's maidens and eunuchs came and informed her, the queen was greatly agitated. She sent clothing for Mordecai to wear, so that he might take off his sackcloth; but he refused. [5]Thereupon Esther summoned Hathach, one of the eunuchs whom the king had appointed to serve her, and sent him to Mordecai to learn

techniques were used in Israel and Greece. The propitious month is Adar but no date is given until v. 13. **8:** Haman's accusation against the Jews contains the essence of what was later to grow into the classic anti-Jewish argument that the Jews are xenophobic and misanthropic. The earliest attested characterization of the Jews as misanthropic is attributed to Hecataeus of Abdera (or Pseudo-Hecataeus) (4th c. BCE), quoted in Diodorus Siculus. Haman is implying (falsely) that the Jews do not acknowledge the sovereignty of the king, and are therefore guilty of treason. The irony is that Mordecai demonstrated his loyalty to the king at the end of ch 2. *It is not in Your Majesty's interest:* Heb "shoveh" may also mean "profit," that is, there is no profit for the king in letting the Jews live. **9:** Haman offers an inducement in the form of revenue for the royal treasury, perhaps to offset any loss of taxes that might have been paid by the Jews, or perhaps simply as a bribe. *Ten thousand talents of silver,* estimated to be 302 metric tons or 333 tons of silver—an enormous amount, close to the total sum of the annual tribute of the entire Persian empire—another exaggerated number. **10:** *Signet ring,* the authority to sign and seal a royal edict. **12:** *Its own script ... its own language,* see 1.22. **13:** *To plunder their possessions,* cf. 8.11 and 9.10 n. **15:** *The couriers went out posthaste,* cf. 8.14. *Sat down to feast,* more partying, as if nothing out of the ordinary had happened; in contrast with the reaction of the city and of the Jews in 4.1. *The city of Shushan was dumbfounded:* The decree is shocking to normal people. The counterpart is 8.15, where "the city of Shushan rang with joyous cries."

4.1–17: Mordecai and Esther plan to save their people. Mourning replaces partying, at least among the Jews. Although not mentioned, God's Presence is most strongly felt in this ch. **1:** Typical signs of grief (Jonah 3.6; Neh. 9.1), which also serve here as a public protest. **4:** The harem, before a place of indulgence, is now a place of constriction for Esther. She cannot leave it and Mordecai cannot enter it. *So that he might take off his sackcloth,* in order to enter the palace precinct, as in 2.11.

the why and wherefore of it all. 6 Hathach went out to Mordecai in the city square in front of the palace gate; 7 and Mordecai told him all that had happened to him, and all about the
money that Haman had offered to pay into the royal treasury
for the destruction of the Jews. 8 He also gave him the written
text of the law that had been proclaimed in Shushan for their
destruction. [He bade him] show it to Esther and inform her,
and charge her to go to the king and to appeal to him and to
plead with him for her people. 9 When Hathach came and delivered Mordecai's message to Esther, 10 Esther told Hathach
to take back to Mordecai the following reply: 11 "All the king's
courtiers and the people of the king's provinces know that if
any person, man or woman, enters the king's presence in the
inner court without having been summoned, there is but one
law for him—that he be put to death. Only if the king extends
the golden scepter to him may he live. Now I have not been
summoned to visit the king for the last thirty days."
12 When Mordecai was told what Esther had said, 13 Mordecai had this message delivered to Esther: "Do not imagine
that you, of all the Jews, will escape with your life by being in
the king's palace. 14 On the contrary, if you keep silent in this
crisis, relief and deliverance will come to the Jews from another quarter, while you and your father's house will perish.
And who knows, perhaps you have attained to royal position
for just such a crisis." 15 Then Esther sent back this answer to
Mordecai: 16 "Go, assemble all the Jews who live in Shushan,
and fast in my behalf; do not eat or drink for three days, night
or day. I and my maidens will observe the same fast. Then I
shall go to the king, though it is contrary to the law; and if I am
to perish, I shall perish!" 17 So Mordecai went about [the city]
and did just as Esther had commanded him.

5 On the third day, Esther put on royal apparel and stood in
the inner court of the king's palace, facing the king's palace, while the king was sitting on his royal throne in the throne
room facing the entrance of the palace. 2 As soon as the king
saw Queen Esther standing in the court, she won his favor. The
king extended to Esther the golden scepter which he had in his
hand, and Esther approached and touched the tip of the scepter. 3 "What troubles you, Queen Esther?" the king asked her.
"And what is your request? Even to half the kingdom, it shall be
granted you." 4 "If it please Your Majesty," Esther replied, "let
Your Majesty and Haman come today to the feast that I have
prepared for him." 5 The king commanded, "Tell Haman to
hurry and do Esther's bidding." So the king and Haman came
to the feast that Esther had prepared.
6 At the wine feast, the king asked Esther, "What is your wish?
It shall be granted you. And what is your request? Even to half

11: Esther takes the initiative, hinting at the strategy she will use to carry out Mordecai's instructions. *Man or woman,* even a woman of whom the king may be enamored. Esther has no special privilege in this regard. *Enters the king's presence in the inner court:* Mordecai said nothing about going to the *inner court;* this is Esther's idea. There were other ways to communicate with the king, as we know from 2.2. (No such Persian regulation is known.) Esther is not refusing to plead for the Jews. Rather, she is outlining a daring plan to do so. **14:** *From another quarter:* "Mi-makom ʾaḥer" is interpreted in Jewish tradition as a reference to God, who is called "Ha-makom," i.e., "Omnipresent," in rabbinic writings. *You and your father's house will perish:* Mordecai is all that is left of Esther's father's house. The point is to personalize the danger to Esther (cf. Amos 7.17). **16–17:** Esther now gives the orders and Mordecai carries them out; a reversal from 2.10, 20. **16:** *Do not eat or drink for three days,* an unrealistically long fast. The post-Talmudic Fast of Esther lasts from sunrise until sundown on ʾAdar 13, immediately preceding Purim, not the date given here. *If I am to perish, I shall perish:* Mordecai says she will perish if she doesn't go to the king (v. 14); here Esther is resigned to the possibility of perishing if she does go to the king.

5.1–8: Esther's audience with the king. Esther carries out the first part of her strategy. The happy mood returns and the partying resumes. **1:** *Royal apparel,* her official garb as queen, for a formal audience with the king. *Inner court,* where it was forbidden to come unsummoned (4.11). **3:** *Even to half the kingdom,* an idiom for a large gift, cf. "half your wealth" (1 Kings 13.8). **4:** Esther's language is overly formal but she deflects the king's magnanimous offer and instead invites him to a banquet.

the kingdom, it shall be fulfilled." 7 "My wish," replied Esther,
"my request— 8 if Your Majesty will do me the favor, if it please
Your Majesty to grant my wish and accede to my request—let
Your Majesty and Haman come to the feast which I will prepare for them; and tomorrow I will do Your Majesty's bidding."
9 That day Haman went out happy and lighthearted. But
when Haman saw Mordecai in the palace gate, and Mordecai
did not rise or even stir on his account, Haman was filled with
rage at him. 10 Nevertheless, Haman controlled himself and
went home. He sent for his friends and his wife Zeresh, 11 and
Haman told them about his great wealth and his many sons,
and all about how the king had promoted him and advanced
him above the officials and the king's courtiers. 12 "What is
more," said Haman, "Queen Esther gave a feast, and besides
the king she did not have anyone but me. And tomorrow too
I am invited by her along with the king. 13 Yet all this means
nothing to me every time I see that Jew Mordecai sitting in the
palace gate." 14 Then his wife Zeresh and all his friends said to
him, "Let a stake be put up, fifty cubits high, and in the morning ask the king to have Mordecai impaled on it. Then you can
go gaily with the king to the feast." The proposal pleased Haman, and he had the stake put up.

6 That night, sleep deserted the king, and he ordered the
book of records, the annals, to be brought; and it was read
to the king. 2 There it was found written that Mordecai had denounced Bigthana and Teresh, two of the king's eunuchs who
guarded the threshold, who had plotted to do away with King
Ahasuerus. 3 "What honor or advancement has been conferred
on Mordecai for this?" the king inquired. "Nothing at all has
been done for him," replied the king's servants who were in attendance on him. 4 "Who is in the court?" the king asked. For
Haman had just entered the outer court of the royal palace, to
speak to the king about having Mordecai impaled on the stake
he had prepared for him. 5 "It is Haman standing in the court,"
the king's servants answered him. "Let him enter," said the
king. 6 Haman entered, and the king asked him, "What should
be done for a man whom the king desires to honor?" Haman
said to himself, "Whom would the king desire to honor more
than me?" 7 So Haman said to the king, "For the man whom
the king desires to honor, 8 let royal garb which the king has
worn be brought, and a horse on which the king has ridden

7–8: On the verge of stating her request, Esther interrupts herself with another invitation—the result is comic. **8:** *I will prepare for them,* cf. v. 4: "I have prepared for him." Now the party is as much for Haman as for the king—a clever rhetorical move to make Haman think he is the center of attention. And so he will be. The pronouns change to fit the audience. In v. 4, only the king was present; now both the king and Haman are present. Cf. the words of Potiphar's wife in Gen. 39.14, 17. **9–14:** Haman's mood swings. Seeing Mordecai spoils all the fun. **9:** *Did not rise or even stir:* Worse than not bowing (3.2), here Mordecai makes no motion at all to acknowledge Haman. **11:** *His great wealth and his many sons,* signs of success (cf. Job 1.1–3). Haman will lose both (8.1; 9.6–10). **12:** The invitation to dine privately with the king and queen is the most recent and highest in a string of honors. **13:** *That Jew Mordecai:* The person and his people continue to irritate Haman. *Sitting in the palace gate:* Mordecai's very presence is enough to upset Haman. Moreover, Mordecai is *sitting;* he did not rise or stir (v. 9). **14:** *Fifty cubits high,* about twenty-three meters (seventy-five feet), seven stories tall, higher than any Persian building; another exaggerated number. *Impaled on it,* the ultimate form of disgrace; see 2.23.

6.1–11: Haman designs a ceremony to honor himself, but must honor Mordecai instead. 1: *That night,* the same night that Haman erected a stake for Mordecai. *The book of records,* cf. 2.23. **2:** *Mordecai had denounced:* The plot had been reported in Mordecai's name (2.22). **4:** *Haman had just entered the outer court,* to obtain approval to dishonor (impale) Mordecai. No royal summons was needed to enter the *outer* court. **6:** The comic misunderstanding begins: Mordecai is on the king's mind and on Haman's, but for opposite reasons. The king speaks first, as is proper, and Haman never gets a chance to state why he came. **8:** The ceremony that Haman designs goes beyond the conventional ways of bestowing honor. It is calculated to make Haman appear to be the king. *Royal garb which the king has worn:* According to Plutarch, *Artaxerxes* 5, this is tantamount to asking for the kingship. *A horse on which the king has ridden and on whose head a royal diadem has been set,* the king's own horse, marked as such by a special diadem on its head. Another sign that Haman wants to replace

and on whose head a royal diadem has been set; 9 and let the attire and the horse be put in the charge of one of the king's noble courtiers. And let the man whom the king desires to honor be attired and paraded on the horse through the city square, while they proclaim before him: This is what is done for the man whom the king desires to honor!" 10 "Quick, then!" said the king to Haman. "Get the garb and the horse, as you have said, and do this to Mordecai the Jew, who sits in the king's gate. Omit nothing of all you have proposed." 11 So Haman took the garb and the horse and arrayed Mordecai and paraded him through the city square; and he proclaimed before him: This is what is done for the man whom the king desires to honor!

12 Then Mordecai returned to the king's gate, while Haman hurried home, his head covered in mourning. 13 There Haman told his wife Zeresh and all his friends everything that had befallen him. His advisers and his wife Zeresh said to him, "If Mordecai, before whom you have begun to fall, is of Jewish stock, you will not overcome him; you will fall before him to your ruin."

14 While they were still speaking with him, the king's eunuchs arrived and hurriedly brought Haman to the banquet which Esther had prepared.

7 So the king and Haman came to feast with Queen Esther. 2 On the second day, the king again asked Esther at the wine feast, "What is your wish, Queen Esther? It shall be granted you. And what is your request? Even to half the kingdom, it shall be fulfilled." 3 Queen Esther replied: "If Your Majesty will do me the favor, and if it pleases Your Majesty, let my life be granted me as my wish, and my people as my request. 4 For we have been sold, my people and I, to be destroyed, massacred, and exterminated. Had we only been sold as bondmen and

the king. Cf. 1 Kings 1.32–49. The nexus between the throne and the horse (a portable throne, as it were), is found in *m. Sanh.* 2.5, which forbids one to ride on the king's horse, to sit on his throne, or to use his scepter. Another obvious sign of a grab for the throne is taking the king's wife (see 1 Kings 2.22), and that is what Ahasuerus accuses Haman of in 7.8. **9:** *One of the king's noble courtiers:* The king will choose the noblest, Haman himself. Be *paraded,* Heb means "be mounted." The honoree should be mounted on a *horse* in *the city square,* visible to all. If this is where Mordecai was stationed in 4.6, then Haman would be publicly honored right in front of Mordecai. **10:** *Mordecai the Jew, who sits in the king's gate:* Ahasuerus's description of Mordecai includes exactly those characteristics that antagonize Haman (5.9, 13). **11:** The last time Mordecai was in the city square (4.6) he was dressed in mourning garb. What a reversal! Some midrashim embellish the scene, adding to Haman's subservience and dishonor, by imagining the preparations to include Haman's washing of Mordecai, since he was still covered in the ashes of mourning (and even having to wash the bath house), dressing him, and lowering himself so that Mordecai could step upon his neck in order to mount the horse. **12–14:** Haman is crestfallen. *His head covered in mourning,* ashamed and dejected (2 Sam. 15.30; Jer. 14.3). The reversal between Haman and Mordecai is complete; Mordecai has gone from mourning to splendor and Haman has gone from splendor to mourning. His wife and friends understand that he is doomed, but the final step in Haman's fall remains for the next ch.

7.1–10: The villain is unmasked and dispatched. As in the preceding ch, a comic misunderstanding is the centerpiece. The rivalry between Mordecai and Haman will come to a permanent end, and the evil Haman will be dispatched. But it remains in the following ch for the plot against the Jews to be successfully countered. **3:** Esther's words are heavy with formal language. She builds her case on her personal relationship to the king (cf. 8.5). *My life ... my people:* Esther equates her life (self) with her people, but does not name them as the Jews. **4:** *We have been sold,* perhaps a hint of Haman's attempted bribe, which Esther learned about from Mordecai in 4.7; or, perhaps the sense is "handed over, betrayed" as in Judg. 2.14; 3.8. *To be destroyed, massacred, and exterminated:* The same three terms are in Haman's edict (3.13). *Had we only been sold as bondmen and bondwomen:* The hypothetical threat of slavery is ironic, part of the rhetorical build-up. But Esther may be subtly recasting Haman's offer of money as a treasonous act against the king. An entire people could become enslaved only if another political entity conquered them. The implication is that Haman wanted to take ownership of some of the king's subjects—an act of treason. How ironic, for in 3.8 Haman had framed the Jews as traitors.

bondwomen, I would have kept silent; for [a]the adversary[a] is
not worthy of the king's trouble."
5 Thereupon King Ahasuerus demanded of Queen Esther,
"Who is he and where is he who dared to do this?" 6 "The adversary and enemy," replied Esther, "is this evil Haman!" And Haman cringed in terror before the king and the queen. 7 The king,
in his fury, left the wine feast for the palace garden, while Haman
remained to plead with Queen Esther for his life; for he saw that
the king had resolved to destroy him. 8 When the king returned
from the palace garden to the banquet room, Haman was lying prostrate on the couch on which Esther reclined. "Does he
mean," cried the king, "to ravish the queen in my own palace?"
No sooner did these words leave the king's lips than Haman's
face [b]was covered.[b] 9 Then Harbonah, one of the eunuchs in
attendance on the king, said, "What is more, a stake is standing at Haman's house, fifty cubits high, which Haman made for
Mordecai—the man whose words saved the king." "Impale him
on it!" the king ordered. 10 So they impaled Haman on the stake
which he had put up for Mordecai, and the king's fury abated.

8 That very day King Ahasuerus gave the property of Haman, the enemy of the Jews, to Queen Esther. Mordecai
presented himself to the king, for Esther had revealed how he
was related to her. 2 The king slipped off his ring, which he had
taken back from Haman, and gave it to Mordecai; and Esther
put Mordecai in charge of Haman's property.
3 Esther spoke to the king again, falling at his feet and weeping, and beseeching him to avert the evil plotted by Haman
the Agagite against the Jews. 4 The king extended the golden
scepter to Esther, and Esther arose and stood before the king.
5 "If it please Your Majesty," she said, "and if I have won your
favor and the proposal seems right to Your Majesty, and if I am
pleasing to you—let dispatches be written countermanding
those which were written by Haman son of Hammedatha the
Agagite, embodying his plot to annihilate the Jews throughout
the king's provinces. 6 For how can I bear to see the disaster
which will befall my people! And how can I bear to see the destruction of my kindred!"
7 Then King Ahasuerus said to Queen Esther and Mordecai
the Jew, "I have given Haman's property to Esther, and he has

a-a Emendation yields "a trifle" (ḥiṣṣar), *lit. "little finger."*
b-b Meaning of Heb. uncertain. Emendation yields "blanched"; cf. Ps. 34.6.

Not worthy of the king's trouble: Heb "nezek" means "trouble, annoyance" (cf. Akkadian "niziqtu" and "nizqu"). There is, however, a tradition of interpreting "nezek" in its Mishnaic Heb sense of "damage." **5:** *Who is he and where is he:* The culprit is sitting right there. An alternative rendering, "which one is he" (cf. Jonah 1.8; Eccl. 2.3; 11.6; *m. 'Abot* 4.1), conveys Ahasuerus's sputtering in confusion. **6:** *The adversary and enemy,* not only an enemy of the Jews, but of the queen, and hence of the king. **7:** *The king, in his fury, left:* Physical movements form a chain reaction pantomime: Haman cringes, Ahasuerus rises, Haman stands, the king returns, and Haman falls. *Haman remained,* "'amad" means "to stand, to take up a position." Haman had been reclining on his couch, as one did at ancient banquets, and now he stands to approach Esther to plead for his life. **8:** *Lying prostrate:* lit. "to fall," the gesture of a supplicant, as in 8.3 (cf. 1 Sam. 25.24). In the mode of a comic farce, Ahasuerus misinterprets Haman's pose, casting the supplicant as a seducer. *To ravish the queen in my own palace:* The pretext to punish Haman, for Haman's real wrong, plotting to kill the Jews, had the king's full endorsement. An attempt to take a king's wife or concubine has the political connotation of attempting to take the kingship (see Ibn Ezra; 2 Sam. 3.7; 2 Sam. 16.21–22; 1 Kings 2.15–17, 22; Gen. 35.22; Plutarch, *Artaxerxes* 26.2). *Haman's face was covered,* perhaps signaling that Haman was condemned to death or even put to death, since his body is impaled on a stake in v. 10. Alternatively, emend to "ashamed, downcast," (cf. Ps. 34.6). **9.** Another touch of irony and reversal: the stake prepared by Haman for Mordecai will conveniently be used for Haman himself. Once again, a switch from the dishonor of Mordecai to the dishonor of Haman. **10:** *The king's fury abated:* As in 2.1, a replacement will be needed for the person dispatched when the king was angry.

8.1–17: Haman's edict is countermanded. Esther will again step forward to save her people. **1–2:** The reversal between Haman and Mordecai (and Esther) is complete. **3–14:** Haman is gone but his decree remains in force. Esther has it revoked. The scene replays parts of chs 3 and 5. **3:** *Beseeching,* cf. 4.8. Esther is now fulfilling Mordecai's instructions. **7:** The king has done his part; now Esther and Mordecai must

been impaled on the stake for scheming against the Jews. [8] And
you may further write with regard to the Jews as you see fit.
[Write it] in the king's name and seal it with the king's signet,
for an edict that has been written in the king's name and sealed
with the king's signet may not be revoked."

[9] So the king's scribes were summoned at that time, on the
twenty-third day of the third month, that is, the month of Sivan; and letters were written, at Mordecai's dictation, to the
Jews and to the satraps, the governors and the officials of the
one hundred and twenty-seven provinces from India to Ethiopia: to every province in its own script and to every people in
its own language, and to the Jews in their own script and language. [10] He had them written in the name of King Ahasuerus
and sealed with the king's signet. Letters were dispatched by
mounted couriers, riding steeds [a-]used in the king's service,
bred of the royal stud,[-a] [11] to this effect: The king has permitted
the Jews of every city to assemble and fight for their lives; if
any people or province attacks them, they may destroy, massacre, and exterminate its armed force together with women and
children, and plunder their possessions—[12] on a single day in
all the provinces of King Ahasuerus, namely, on the thirteenth
day of the twelfth month, that is, the month of Adar. [13] The text
of the document was to be issued as a law in every single province: it was to be publicly displayed to all the peoples, so that
the Jews should be ready for that day to avenge themselves on
their enemies. [14] The couriers, mounted on royal steeds, went
out in urgent haste at the king's command; and the decree was
proclaimed in the fortress Shushan.

[15] Mordecai left the king's presence in royal robes of blue
and white, with a magnificent crown of gold and a mantle of
fine linen and purple wool. And the city of Shushan rang with
joyous cries. [16] The Jews enjoyed light and gladness, happiness
and honor. [17] And in every province and in every city, when
the king's command and decree arrived, there was gladness
and joy among the Jews, a feast and a holiday. And many of the
people of the land professed to be Jews, for the fear of the Jews
had fallen upon them.

9 And so, on the thirteenth day of the twelfth month—that
is, the month of Adar—when the king's command and decree were to be executed, the very day on which the enemies

a-a Meaning of Heb. uncertain.

do the rest. **8:** A new law is written to offset the old law, which *may not be revoked* (unlike at 1.19, see n.). A legal system in which this principle obtains is unwieldy, to say the least; another example of the lighthearted mocking of Persian culture. **9:** *To the Jews in their own script and language:* The message affects the Jews in particular. **10:** *Steeds used in the king's service, bred of the royal stud:* Horses specially bred for speed were used in the Persian postal system. **11:** *To assemble and fight for their lives:* Permission is given for defensive measures. *Destroy, massacre, and exterminate its armed force together with women and children,* wording similar to the original edict in 3.13. *Together with women and children:* Although distasteful to the modern reader, this was normal in the ancient world. *Plunder their possessions,* as in Haman's edict (3.13), but see 9.10, 15, 16. **13:** *Avenge themselves* signifies justified retaliation. **14:** *Urgent haste,* even more urgently than in 3.15. **15–17:** Mordecai emerges triumphant and the Jews rejoice. **15:** *Royal robes of blue and white:* Mordecai's upgraded attire reminds us that Joseph and Daniel, two other successful Jewish courtiers, were also invested in royal clothing and accessories (Gen. 41.42; Dan. 5.7, 29). The colorful textiles recall the tapestries in 1.6. *The city of Shushan rang with joyous cries,* a reversal of 3.15. **16:** This v. is recited in the "havdalah" service, marking the conclusion of the Sabbath, when it is supplemented with the words "and may this befall us as well!" **17:** *Holiday,* "Yom tov," "good day" or sometimes simply "day"; also in 9.19, 22, 28, 31, 32. Esther is the only place in the Bible where "yom tov" is used in its later sense of a set festival. *People of the land,* non-Jews. *Professed to be Jews,* or, identified with the Jews. Though there was not yet a process of formal conversion, non-Jews during the Persian period could attach themselves to the Jewish community or adopt particular Jewish customs. *Fear of the Jews:* Non-Jews perceived the Jews to be strong and so they wished to join them; another unlikely scenario.

9.1–19: The Jews triumph over their enemies. The events of the story are connected with the establishment of the festival of Purim; the reason for the holiday and instructions for its celebration are provided. The gleeful violence that permeates this ch is part of the carnivalesque character of the book, and should not be taken

of the Jews had expected to get them in their power, the opposite happened, and the Jews got their enemies in their power.
2 Throughout the provinces of King Ahasuerus, the Jews mustered in their cities to attack those who sought their hurt; and
no one could withstand them, for the fear of them had fallen
upon all the peoples. 3 Indeed, all the officials of the provinces—the satraps, the governors, and the king's stewards—
showed deference to the Jews, because the fear of Mordecai
had fallen upon them. 4 For Mordecai was now powerful in the
royal palace, and his fame was spreading through all the provinces; the man Mordecai was growing ever more powerful. 5 So
the Jews struck at their enemies with the sword, slaying and
destroying; they wreaked their will upon their enemies.

6 In the fortress Shushan the Jews killed a total of five hundred men. 7 They also killed[a]

Parshandatha,
Dalphon,
Aspatha,
8 Poratha,
Adalia,
Aridatha,
9 Parmashta,
Arisai,
Aridai,
and Vaizatha,

10 the ten sons of Haman son of Hammedatha, the foe of the
Jews. But they did not lay hands on the spoil. 11 When the number of those slain in the fortress Shushan was reported on that
same day to the king, 12 the king said to Queen Esther, "In the
fortress Shushan alone the Jews have killed a total of five hundred men, as well as the ten sons of Haman. What then must
they have done in the provinces of the realm! What is your wish
now? It shall be granted you. And what else is your request? It
shall be fulfilled." 13 "If it please Your Majesty," Esther replied,
"let the Jews in Shushan be permitted to act tomorrow also as
they did today; and let Haman's ten sons be impaled on the
stake." 14 The king ordered that this should be done, and the
decree was proclaimed in Shushan. Haman's ten sons were
impaled: 15 and the Jews in Shushan mustered again on the
fourteenth day of Adar and slew three hundred men in Shushan. But they did not lay hands on the spoil.

16 The rest of the Jews, those in the king's provinces, likewise
mustered and fought for their lives. They disposed of their enemies, killing seventy-five thousand of their foes; but they did
not lay hands on the spoil. 17 That was on the thirteenth day of
the month of Adar; and they rested on the fourteenth day and

a. Moved up from v. 10 for greater clarity.

seriously; this is a fictional orgy, not a real massacre. To be sure, this section has struck many readers as offensive and anti-Gentile, and out of proportion to the threat against the Jews that had been neutralized. But the "overkill" should be understood in the context of the farcical nature of the book, with its extreme exaggerations, reversals, and implausibilities. This mock battle serves as a safety-valve for the release of feelings of endangerment—that is one of the purposes of the carnivalesque. **2:** *To attack those who sought their hurt,* in self-defense, not revenge, according to the edict in 8.11. *The fear of them,* the fear that the Jews were stronger (8.17). **3:** The enemy masses were deterred by fear of the Jewish masses and the officials were deterred by fear of an official. **7–10:** The list of foreign-sounding names is amusing, like the names in 1.10, 14; and the tradition of reading them all out in one breath when the megillah is read publicly on Purim (*b. Meg.* 16b) adds to the amusement. The killing of Haman's sons is one more way that Haman's glory is diminished. It also brings his line to an end; no future threat to the Jews will come from him. Amalek is at last wiped out. **10:** *They did not lay hands on the spoil:* Taking spoil, a normal practice in warfare, was permitted in Haman's decree and in Mordecai's counterdecree. The notice that the Jews did not take spoil (also vv. 15, 16) reinforces the connection with 1 Sam. ch 15, where Saul took the Amalekite spoil, contrary to God's command. The Jews of Persia, led by Mordecai, apparently a descendent of Saul, replay, as it were, the battle against Amalek and "correct" Saul's error, enabling the descendants of Saul to triumph at last over the descendants of Agag. **16:** *Seventy-five thousand* is another exaggerated number. These battles are the mock battles of carnivalesque literature. **18–19:** These vv. reflect where the festival was observed on Adar 14 and where on Adar 15. According to rabbinic tradition, Jews, in all cities that had been walled since the time of Joshua, are to celebrate Purim

made it a day of feasting and merrymaking. ([18] But the Jews in Shushan mustered on both the thirteenth and fourteenth days, and so rested on the fifteenth, and made it a day of feasting and merrymaking.) [19] That is why village Jews, who live in unwalled towns, observe the fourteenth day of the month of Adar and make it a day of merrymaking and feasting, and as a holiday and an occasion for sending gifts to one another.

[20] Mordecai recorded these events. And he sent dispatches to all the Jews throughout the provinces of King Ahasuerus, near and far, [21] charging them to observe the fourteenth and fifteenth days of Adar, every year—[22] the same days on which the Jews enjoyed relief from their foes and the same month which had been transformed for them from one of grief and mourning to one of festive joy. They were to observe them as days of feasting and merrymaking, and as an occasion for sending gifts to one another and presents to the poor. [23] The Jews accordingly assumed as an obligation that which they had begun to practice and which Mordecai prescribed for them.

[24] For Haman son of Hammedatha the Agagite, the foe of all the Jews, had plotted to destroy the Jews, and had cast *pur*—that is, the lot—with intent to crush and exterminate them. [25] But when [Esther] came before the king, he commanded: [a-]"With the promulgation of this decree,[-a] let the evil plot, which he devised against the Jews, recoil on his own head!" So they impaled him and his sons on the stake. [26] For that reason these days were named Purim, after *pur.*

In view, then, of all the instructions in the said letter and of what they had experienced in that matter and what had befallen them, [27] the Jews undertook and irrevocably obligated themselves and their descendants, and all who might join them, to observe these two days in the manner prescribed and at the proper time each year. [28] Consequently, these days are recalled and observed in every generation: by every family, every province, and every city. And these days of Purim shall never cease among the Jews, and the memory of them shall never perish among their descendants.

[29] [b]Then Queen Esther daughter of Abihail wrote a second letter of Purim for the purpose of confirming with full authority the aforementioned one of Mordecai the Jew. [30] Dispatches were sent to all the Jews in the hundred and twenty-seven provinces of the realm of Ahasuerus with an ordinance of "equity and honesty:"[c] [31] These days of Purim shall be observed at

a-a Meaning of Heb. uncertain.

b Force of vv. 29–31 uncertain in part. Verse 29 reads literally, "Then Queen Esther, daughter of Abihail, and Mordecai the Jew, wrote with full authority to confirm this second letter of Purim."

c I.e., of new holidays, the instituting of which is linked to love of equity and honesty in Zech. 8.19.

on Adar 15—Shushan Purim—and Jews elsewhere were to celebrate on Adar 14. Thus, following rabbinic tradition, Purim is celebrated on Adar 15 in Jerusalem. **20–28:** The festival is established in perpetuity. **20:** *Mordecai recorded these events:* Rashi takes the book of Esther to be Mordecai's record of events (according to tradition, Mordecai wrote the book of Esther); modern interpreters take vv. 24–25 as Mordecai's record. **21:** *To observe the fourteenth and fifteenth days of Adar,* whichever day was appropriate to the location of the celebrant. **22:** *Feasting and merrymaking ... sending gifts ... presents to the poor:* These elements, along with the recitation of the scroll of Esther, constitute the halakhic requirements for the celebration of the festival. **24–26:** A summary of the story, emphasizing the etiology of the festival's name, *pur* and Purim, and the defeat of Haman, with credit to the king. **26:** *Purim:* Our earliest reference outside of Esther calls it "The Day of Mordecai" (2 Macc. 15.36). **28:** The festival is to be celebrated by Jews in all places for all time. **29–32:** The second Purim letter, further confirming the festival. The writer is either Esther, or Esther along with Mordecai. There is some tension in the book regarding whether to highlight Mordecai or Esther. The book is called "the scroll of Esther" and she certainly plays a pivotal role, but Mordecai is introduced before Esther (ch 2) and figures prominently at the end, where Esther is absent entirely (ch 10). **31:** Just as the Jews took upon themselves new fast days not mentioned in the Torah (Zech. 8.19) so will they now take upon themselves the celebration of a new festival, likewise not in the Torah. This first post-Torah festival recorded in the Bible is hereby authorized.

10.1–3: The accomplishments of King Ahasuerus and his Jewish courtier, Mordecai. 1: *Tribute:* Levying tribute signifies having sovereignty over the area. *The mainland and the islands,* a merismus for the entire inhabited world (cf. Isa. 42.4, 10). Now Ahasuerus's control extends beyond the 127 provinces of 1.1. **2:** Ahasuerus here is a true sovereign, no longer a pompous bumbler controlled by his advisors. *Are recorded in the Annals of the Kings of Media and Persia,* presumably the same annals mentioned in 6.1. This imitates the summary statements in the book of Kings (e.g., 1 Kings 14.19, 29; 15.31), lending a historical tone to the story and official authority to the recounting of it. **3:** In a story where honor is paramount, *Mordecai* has achieved the highest honor possible. He is a model of Jewish success in the Diaspora. The ending shows that the Jewish community is secure.

their proper time, as Mordecai the Jew—and now Queen Esther—has obligated them to do, and just as they have assumed for themselves and their descendants the obligation of the fasts with their lamentations.[a]
32 And Esther's ordinance validating these observances of Purim was recorded in a scroll.

10 King Ahasuerus imposed tribute on the mainland and the islands. 2 All his mighty and powerful acts, and a full account of the greatness to which the king advanced Mordecai, are recorded in the Annals of the Kings of Media and Persia.
3 For Mordecai the Jew ranked next to King Ahasuerus and was highly regarded by the Jews and popular with the multitude of his brethren; he sought the good of his people and interceded for the welfare of all his kindred.

a The Jews had long been observing fast days in commemoration of national calamities; see Zech. 7.5; 8.19.

דניאל

Daniel

THE BOOK OF DANIEL, probably written in its final version in 164 BCE, is thought to be the latest composition of the Hebrew Bible. Its narrative, however, is set much earlier, during the reigns of the powerful kings of Babylonia, Media, and Persia in the 6th century BCE. The figure of Daniel may have been influenced by Danel, a legendary ancient hero known from the *Aqhat Epic* found at Ugarit and mentioned in Ezek. 14.14; 28.3. Here, however, Daniel and his three friends provide a less elevated, more "Everyman" model of Jewish faithfulness to God. A member of the exile community in Babylonia, Daniel soon rises to become an important Jewish courtier. The anonymous author thus uses the period of exile as a setting to address the challenging issues of Jews living under foreign kings.

Problems in the Text and Structure of Daniel

DANIEL IS COMPRISED of two equal halves of different genres and different origins. Chs 1–6 consist of six "court legends" that utilize third-person narration to recount the adventures of wise Jewish heroes in the highest court in the land (cf. the Joseph story in Gen. chs 37–50; Esther). The legends reflect an entertaining, humorous, even satirical side. Chs 7–12 are made up of four apocalyptic visions, told in the first person, that are revelations of the events that lead to the cataclysmic end and transformation of history. The two halves of the book appear to arise at different times in Israel's history. Chs 1–6, probably originally oral, circulated most likely in the 4th to 2nd centuries BCE, when they were collected into a cycle of Daniel legends. Chs 7–12 are most likely written compositions, datable to the last year of the Maccabean revolt (164 BCE). In editing chs 1–12 together, the author of the visions made the whole into an apocalyptic book. (Apocalypses often mix different genres.) Several themes hold the two halves of the book of Daniel together: God's sovereignty over history and foreign monarchs, the special wisdom and insight of the one devoted to God, and the ideal of heroic obedience, even to the point of death. Dan. chs 7–12 is the only apocalypse in the Hebrew Bible; Ezekiel and Zechariah both have apocalyptic elements but are still within the genre of prophetic books. Jewish apocalypses were written earlier than Daniel (parts of *1 Enoch; Jub.*), and after Daniel (other parts of *1 Enoch, 4 Ezra* [2 Esd. chs 3–14], and in the New Testament, Revelation), but these were not incorporated into the Hebrew Bible.

Another peculiar characteristic of Daniel is its use of two languages (also present in Ezra and Neh.): 1.1–2.4a and 8.1–12.13 are in Heb, while 2.4b–7.28 are in Aram. (This does not correspond to the division by genre noted above.) Scholars have proposed two explanations for this: Either two languages were used in the original work, a combination that was retained in the multilingual world of the land of Israel in the 2nd century BCE; or the whole work was originally composed in one language, and one part was later translated into the other language. In this latter theory, Aram., the common international language of the ancient Near East at that time, is usually suggested as the original language of the whole. Neither explanation has met with complete scholarly agreement, but the most likely reconstruction is that chs 2–6 and separately, ch 7, were written in Aram., and chs 8–12, at a date slightly later than ch 7, in Heb. Ch 1 may have been written in Heb, or translated from Aram. into Heb as a more appropriate language for the introduction.

Historical and Political Context of Daniel

THE BOOK OF DANIEL, like many texts of the Jewish Bible, reflects a strong interest in the surrounding empires. Familiarity with the political history of the entire region is assumed in both the court legends of chs 1–6 and the apocalyptic visions of chs 7–12. The narrative of Daniel begins during the Neo-Babylonian empire. It was Nebuchadnezzar (also called Nebuchadrezzar), king of the Babylonians, who conquered Jerusalem and destroyed the first Temple in 586 BCE, and exiled many Judeans to Babylonia (2 Kings chs 24–25; Jer.). Contemporary with the Babylonian empire was the empire of the Medes, east of Babylonia. Cyrus of Persia arose in the mid-6th century BCE and conquered first the Medes and then the Babylonians in 539. In Judea the Medes and Persians were sometimes perceived as a joint kingdom, and at other times as following one after the other.

The Persian kings—the first four were Cyrus, Cambyses, Darius, and Xerxes—ruled the Jews more benevolently than did the Babylonians. Cyrus, encouraged the Judeans to return from their exile in 538, and allowed them to rebuild their Temple, which was constructed in 520–515 BCE. This state of affairs—very limited autonomy under Persian rule—continued until the rise of Alexander the Great (356–323), the Macedonian-Greek king who defeated the Persians to found a new empire. Alexander conquered the land of Israel in 332. He died young, however, and his vast empire split into several Greek-ruled kingdoms, the most important of which for the book of Daniel were the Seleucid, centered in Syria and Babylonia, and the Ptolemaic in Egypt. Judea lay at the intersection between the two empires, and the influences of these empires over Jerusalem ebbed and flowed; Jews were often split in their allegiances to one or the other. After gaining control of Judea at the beginning of the 2nd century BCE, the Seleucid kings suffered reversals, and their king Antiochus IV Epiphanes turned his attention to the control of the Jerusalem Temple and the gold that was stored there.

Because of the detailed nature of apocalyptic timetables, the dating of at least the last chs of Daniel can be established precisely. Scholars consider the predictions in this book, as in other apocalypses, to be prophecies after the fact, purportedly written down centuries earlier and kept secret in order to give credence to other predictions about the end of history. The recounting of history, then, though symbolic, can be matched quite easily with the history of the ancient Near East in the Greek period. The predictions are detailed and accurate until near the end of the Maccabean revolt in 164. At that point they veer dramatically from what we know of the actions of the Seleucid king (see annotations to ch 11), and scholars assume that the author lived and wrote at the precise time when the predictions are no longer accurate.

The scribal visionaries who produced Daniel were strongly opposed to Antiochus IV Epiphanes (whose name meant "god manifest"), yet they were probably not closely aligned with the Maccabees. The group is probably to be identified with those who are "knowledgeable" in 11.33, 12.3. (The same word in its verbal form, "to give understanding," is used at 9.22.) Their instruction includes the knowledge of future events that is contained in the visions, and their role is one of guardian to the "many."

Daniel in Jewish Tradition

THE BOOK OF DANIEL has been evaluated differently in Jewish and Christian tradition. Daniel was evidently considered a prophet at Qumran and elsewhere in early Judaism (*Ant.* 10.266–68), but because prefigurations of Jesus and Christian resurrection were seen in Daniel by the early church, the rabbinic tradition hesitated to embrace the visions of Daniel. The Rabbis denied that Daniel was predicting events after the Maccabean revolt, and especially not the end of time, and assigned him a role as seer, not prophet (*b. Meg.* 3a; *b. Sanh.* 94a). Jewish tradition was also sometimes critical of what appeared to be a positive relationship between Daniel and Nebuchadnezzar. The different status of Daniel in Judaism and Christianity is thus reflected in the position of the book in the two canons. In the Christian Old Testament Daniel is placed with the major prophets, Isaiah, Jeremiah, and Ezekiel, while in the Jewish Scriptures it is placed with the Kethuvim, or Writings. (Additional factors, including the late date of the book, may have also played a role in the book's placement in Kethuvim rather than in Prophets.) Although the book of Daniel has not held central importance in Jewish tradition, it has had an influence on Jewish liturgy—probably because of its late date, when proto-liturgy was being formed—and it is significant in revealing a great deal about the social and theological world of Jews at the end of the biblical era.

[LAWRENCE M. WILLS]

1 In the third year of the reign of King Jehoiakim of Judah, King Nebuchadnezzar of Babylon came to Jerusalem and laid siege to it. [2]The Lord delivered King Jehoiakim of Judah into his power, together with some of the vessels of the House of God, and he brought them to the land of Shinar to the house of his god; he deposited the vessels in the treasury of his god. [3]Then the king ordered Ashpenaz, his chief officer, to bring some Israelites of royal descent and of the nobility—[4]youths without blemish, handsome, proficient in all wisdom, knowledgeable and intelligent, and capable of serving in the royal palace—and teach them the writings and the language of the Chaldeans. [5]The king allotted daily rations to them from the king's food and from the wine he drank. They were to be educated for three years, [a-]at the end of which they[-a] were to enter the king's service.

a-a Or "and some of them."

1.1–6.29: Collection of court legends. Chs 1–6 probably circulated as independent stories before being collected and edited together (see the intro.). Chs 2, 4, and 5 demonstrate that Daniel is superior to the king's other courtiers, while chs 3 and 6 dramatically depict the persecution and vindication of the Jewish protagonists at the hands of the other courtiers. Ch 1 serves as an introduction to this collection. The positive resolution of the narrative in chs 1–6 and the sometimes humorous tone indicate that the tension did not result from the national crisis of the Maccabean revolt, but rather from the more general conflict of loyalties that existed for Jews living in the Diaspora in the centuries preceding that.

1.1–21: Daniel and his three companions are introduced and tested. This ch introduces the main Jewish characters—Daniel and his three friends—as well as Nebuchadnezzar and also the Temple vessels, which will figure in ch 5. In addition, though God's great power is emphasized, it is power that is exercised at a distance and through intermediaries, a theme that will be developed in terms of God's role in the court of the great foreign kings in chs 1–6 and in world history in chs 7–12. **1–2:** The fall of Judah and the beginnings of exile are introduced quickly. To establish the pedigree of the hero, the book of Daniel does not dwell here on Nebuchadnezzar as the archvillain of ancient Jewish history, or on the exile as tragedy. *The Lord* still controls human events, even the successes of foreign kings over Judah. The dating of events is not accurate: The third year of *King Jehoiakim* was 606 BCE, but *Nebuchadnezzar* captured Jerusalem in 597 BCE. *Vessels,* Ezra 1.7–8. *Shinar,* Babylonia. **3:** The "history" of the exile quickly turns to the fortunes of the four Jewish protagonists at the court of Nebuchadnezzar. They are heroic and aristocratic in bearing. Compare the treatment of the fallen king Jehoiachin in 2 Kings 25.27–30; Jer. 52.31–34. **4:** *Chaldeans:* A name for a region and language of Babylonia, it was also associated with the wisdom and learning of Eastern courtiers. In some passages in Daniel it refers to the ethnic group, in others it means courtiers. *The language of the Chaldeans* was Akkadian. **5:** The training of courtiers in languages, court protocol, and international relations was common in the ancient world.

6 Among them were the Judahites Daniel, Hananiah,
Mishael, and Azariah. 7 The chief officer gave them new
names; he named Daniel Belteshazzar, Hananiah Shadrach,
Mishael Meshach, and Azariah Abed-nego. 8 Daniel resolved
not to defile himself with the king's food or the wine he drank,
so he sought permission of the chief officer not to defile himself, 9 and God disposed the chief officer to be kind and compassionate toward Daniel. 10 The chief officer said to Daniel, "I
fear that my lord the king, who allotted food and drink to you,
will notice that you look out of sorts, unlike the other youths of
your age—and you will put my life[a] in jeopardy with the king."
11 Daniel replied to the guard whom the chief officer had put
in charge of Daniel, Hananiah, Mishael and Azariah, 12 "Please
test your servants for ten days, giving us legumes to eat and
water to drink. 13 Then compare our appearance with that of
the youths who eat of the king's food, and do with your servants as you see fit." 14 He agreed to this plan of theirs, and tested
them for ten days. 15 When the ten days were over, they looked
better and healthier than all the youths who were eating of the
king's food. 16 So the guard kept on removing their food, and
the wine they were supposed to drink, and gave them legumes.
17 God made all four of these young men intelligent and proficient in all writings and wisdom, and Daniel had understanding of visions and dreams of all kinds. 18 When the time the king
had set for their presentation had come, the chief officer presented them to Nebuchadnezzar. 19 The king spoke with them,
and of them all none was equal to Daniel, Hananiah, Mishael
and Azariah; so these entered the king's service. 20 Whenever
the king put a question to them requiring wisdom and understanding, he found them to be ten times better than all the magicians and exorcists throughout his realm. 21 Daniel was there
until the first year of King Cyrus.

2 In the second year of the reign of Nebuchadnezzar, Nebuchadnezzar had a dream; his spirit was agitated, [b]yet he
was overcome by[b] sleep. 2 The king ordered the magicians, exorcists, sorcerers, and Chaldeans to be summoned in order to
tell the king what he had dreamed. They came and stood before
the king, 3 and the king said to them, "I have had a dream and
I am full of anxiety to know what I have dreamed." 4 The Chaldeans spoke to the king in Aramaic, "O king, live forever! Relate
the dream to your servants, and we will tell its meaning." 5 The
king said in reply to the Chaldeans, "I hereby decree: If you will
not make the dream and its meaning known to me, you shall be
torn limb from limb and your houses confiscated.[c] 6 But if you

a Lit. "head." *b-b Meaning of Heb. uncertain; others "and he could not."*
c Meaning uncertain; or "turned into ruins."

7–8: *Belteshazzar,* see 4.5 n. Prominent Jews sometimes took Babylonian names, and at Gen. 41.45 Joseph is given an Egyptian name. The names *Shadrach, Meshach,* and *Abed-nego* have not been satisfactorily explained. Daniel and his friends refuse *the king's food,* presumably because it violated the food laws in Lev. ch 11 and Deut. ch 14. This v. also offers the only biblical indication of the later rabbinic law that Jews should not drink pagan wine. **8:** A stronger emphasis on dietary laws as a way of living a pious life away from the Temple developed in the Diaspora, as reflected here and in many works in the Apocrypha (Tobit 1.10–11; Judith 10.5; 12.1–2; 1 Macc. 1.62–63; 2 Macc. 5.27).

2.1–49: Daniel is able to interpret the king's dream. 1: *Second year* is inconsistent with 1.1–4. **2:** Lists of court officers—and other items as well—occur often in chs 1–6. The humorous tone of the pretentiousness of the list is meant to contrast with the understated power of Daniel's abilities. Unlike 1.4, *Chaldeans* here means courtiers, since the king would have been a Chaldean as well. **4:** With the words *O king,* the text switches from Heb to Aram. The interpretation of royal dreams was common in the ancient Near East (cf. ch 4; Gen. ch 41), but a twist is introduced when the king demands that the courtiers tell him the content of his dream as well as its interpretation. The king's threat indicates the high stakes and potential danger to the life of the courtier (cf. 2.12). Although there are many records of dream interpretation from the ancient Near East, there is no record of a courtier recounting the content of someone else's dream. The courtiers raise an objection on these grounds, setting the stage for Daniel, with the help of God (v. 30), to do what no ordinary human being could do. As in the other chs, Daniel serves as a vehicle for expressing God's great power.

tell the dream and its meaning, you shall receive from me gifts, presents, and great honor; therefore, tell me the dream and its meaning." [7] Once again they answered, "Let the king relate the dream to his servants, and we will tell its meaning." [8] The king said in reply, "It is clear to me that you are playing for time, since you see that I have decreed [9] that if you do not make the dream known to me, there is but one verdict for you. You have conspired to tell me something false and fraudulent until circumstances change; so relate the dream to me, and I will then know that you can tell its meaning." [10] The Chaldeans said in reply to the king, "There is no one on earth who can [a-]satisfy the king's demand,[-a] for great king or ruler—none has ever asked such a thing of any magician, exorcist, or Chaldean. [11] The thing asked by the king is difficult; there is no one who can tell it to the king except the gods whose abode is not among mortals."[b] [12] Whereupon the king flew into a violent rage, and gave an order to do away with all the wise men of Babylon.

[13] The decree condemning the wise men to death was issued. Daniel and his companions were about to be put to death [14] when Daniel remonstrated with Arioch, the captain of the royal guard who had set out to put the wise men of Babylon to death. [15] He spoke up and said to Arioch, the royal officer, "Why is the decree of the king so urgent?" Thereupon Arioch informed Daniel of the matter. [16] So Daniel went to ask the king for time, that he might tell the meaning to the king. [17] Then Daniel went to his house and informed his companions, Hananiah, Mishael, and Azariah, of the matter,[18] that they might implore the God of Heaven for help regarding this mystery, so that Daniel and his colleagues would not be put to death together with the other wise men of Babylon.

[19] The mystery was revealed to Daniel in a night vision; then Daniel blessed the God of Heaven. [20] Daniel spoke up and said:

"Let the name of God be blessed forever and ever,
For wisdom and power are His.
21 He changes times and seasons,
Removes kings and installs kings;
He gives the wise their wisdom
And knowledge to those who know.
22 He reveals deep and hidden things,
Knows what is in the darkness,
And light dwells with Him.
23 I acknowledge and praise You,
O God of my fathers,
You who have given me wisdom and power,
For now You have let me know what we asked of You;
You have let us know what concerns the king."

a-a Lit. "tell the king's matter." *b Lit. "flesh."*

13–23: It is possible that these vv. were added to tie the initial six chs together; the mention of the three friends connects this episode with chs 1 and 3, and the prayer is similar to those in chs 3, 4, and 6; see also Neh. 9.5; 1 Sam. ch 2; Prov. ch 8. Cf. 5.11–12 n. **18:** *Mystery,* "raz," a Persian word, generally used in Jewish apocalypticism to mean the special, restricted knowledge of the heavens and what is to happen in the future. Daniel's wisdom and knowledge provides another connection between chs 1–6 and chs 7–12. He is capable of receiving extraordinary revelations from God. **20:** The central words of the later Jewish kaddish prayer are based on the beginning of this v., whose theme, that ultimate wisdom only lies with God, is common in wisdom literature, esp. Job.

31–45: Portentous dreams of the fate of kingdoms were common in the ancient world; cf. Herodotus, *Histories* 1.108; 7.19. Here, however, the author uses an older prediction of four world kingdoms—understood as Babylonia, Media, Persia, and Greece—and emphasizes their decreasing value. They are followed by a mixed kingdom of *iron* and *clay,* which signifies the divided Greek kingdom and the Ptolemaic and Seleucid kings who ruled in the eastern Mediterranean (see the intro.). Although Daniel predicts the demise of the Babylonian kingdom and its ultimate replacement by the *kingdom* of the *God of Heaven,* Nebuchadnezzar nevertheless reveres Daniel for his insight.

24 Thereupon Daniel went to Arioch, whom the king had appointed to do away with the wise men of Babylon; he came and said to him as follows, "Do not do away with the wise men of Babylon; bring me to the king and I will tell the king the meaning!"
25 So Arioch rushed Daniel into the king's presence and said to him, "I have found among the exiles of Judah a man who can make the meaning known to the king!"
26 The king said in reply to Daniel (who was called Belteshazzar), "Can you really make known to me the dream that I saw and its meaning?"
27 Daniel answered the king and said, "The mystery about which the king has inquired—wise men, exorcists, magicians, and diviners cannot tell to the king.
28 But there is a God in heaven who reveals mysteries, and He has made known to King Nebuchadnezzar what is to be at the end of days. This is your dream and the vision that entered your mind in bed:
29 O king, the thoughts that came to your mind in your bed are about future events; He who reveals mysteries has let you know what is to happen.
30 Not because my wisdom is greater than that of other creatures has this mystery been revealed to me, but in order that the meaning should be made known to the king, and that you may know the thoughts of your mind.

31 "O king, as you looked on, there appeared a great statue. This statue, which was huge and its brightness surpassing, stood before you, and its appearance was awesome.
32 The head of that statue was of fine gold; its breast and arms were of silver; its belly and thighs, of bronze;
33 its legs were of iron, and its feet part iron and part clay.
34 As you looked on, a stone was hewn out, not by hands, and struck the statue on its feet of iron and clay and crushed them.
35 All at once, the iron, clay, bronze, silver, and gold were crushed, and became like chaff of the threshing floors of summer; a wind carried them off until no trace of them was left. But the stone that struck the statue became a great mountain and filled the whole earth.

36 "Such was the dream, and we will now tell the king its meaning.
37 You, O king—king of kings, to whom the God of Heaven has given kingdom, power, might, and glory;
38 into whose hands He has given men, wild beasts, and the fowl of heaven, wherever they may dwell; and to whom He has given dominion over them all—you are the head of gold.
39 But another kingdom will arise after you, inferior to yours; then yet a third kingdom, of bronze, which will rule over the whole earth.
40 But the fourth kingdom will be as strong as iron; just as iron crushes and shatters everything—and like iron that smashes—so will it crush and smash all these.
41 You saw the feet and the toes, part potter's clay and part iron; that means it will be a divided kingdom; it will have only some of the stability of iron, inasmuch as you saw iron mixed with common clay.
42 And the toes were part iron and part clay; that [means] the

kingdom will be in part strong and in part brittle. 43 You saw iron mixed with common clay; that means: [a]they shall intermingle with the offspring of men,[a] but shall not hold together, just as iron does not mix with clay. 44 And in the time of those kings, the God of Heaven will establish a kingdom that shall never be destroyed, a kingdom that shall not be transferred to another people. It will crush and wipe out all these kingdoms, but shall itself last forever—45 just as you saw how a stone was hewn from the mountain, not by hands, and crushed the iron, bronze, clay, silver, and gold. The great God has made known to the king what will happen in the future. The dream is sure and its interpretation reliable."

46 Then King Nebuchadnezzar prostrated himself and paid homage to Daniel and ordered that a meal offering and pleasing offerings be made to him. 47 The king said in reply to Daniel, "Truly your God must be the God of gods and Lord of kings and the revealer of mysteries to have enabled you to reveal this mystery." 48 The king then elevated Daniel and gave him very many gifts, and made him governor of the whole province of Babylon and chief prefect of all the wise men of Babylon. 49 At Daniel's request, the king appointed Shadrach, Meshach, and Abednego to administer the province of Babylon; while Daniel himself was at the king's court.

3 King Nebuchadnezzar made a statue of gold sixty cubits high and six cubits broad. He set it up in the plain of Dura in the province of Babylon. 2 King Nebuchadnezzar then sent word to gather the satraps, prefects, governors, counselors, treasurers, judges, officers, and all the provincial officials to attend the dedication of the statue that King Nebuchadnezzar had set up. 3 So the satraps, prefects, governors, counselors, treasurers, judges, officers, and all the provincial officials assembled for the dedication of the statue that King Nebuchadnezzar had set up, and stood before the statue that Nebuchadnezzar had set up. 4 The herald proclaimed in a loud voice, "You are commanded, O peoples and nations of every language, 5 when you hear the sound of the horn, pipe, zither, lyre, psaltery, bagpipe, and all other types of instruments, to fall down and worship the statue of gold that King Nebuchadnezzar has set up. 6 Whoever will not fall down and worship shall at once be thrown into a burning fiery furnace." 7 And so, as soon as all the peoples heard the sound of the horn, pipe, zither, lyre, psaltery, and all other types of instruments, all peoples and nations of every language fell down and worshiped the statue of gold that King Nebuchadnezzar had set up.

a-a Meaning uncertain.

46: *Prostrated ... paid homage* implies that the king worshipped Daniel, but Jewish interpreters assumed that Daniel declined this reverence (*Gen. Rab.* 96.5). The Rabbis were often quite critical of Daniel, however, for enjoying such a positive relationship with the tyrant who destroyed the First Temple (see 4.16–24 n.). The original narratives in chs 1–6 were probably oriented toward entertainment at the expense of the pagan kings.

3.1–33: Daniel's three companions are tested in the fiery furnace. Daniel himself is not mentioned in ch 3. The story about the three young men may have circulated as an independent oral legend, later incorporated into the tradition of Daniel narratives because of thematic similarities. The religious intolerance depicted in the ch is very atypical of the ancient Near Eastern world. Although the king's demand that Jews worship a statue has parallels to the events of the Maccabean revolt, the parallels are not close, and this section of Daniel is likely pre-Maccabean. It is unclear whether this story is based on a real event or is created to illustrate the power of God. **1:** *Statue of gold:* Herodotus 1.183 mentions a giant figure made of gold in the temple of Bel in Babylon. **2:** In this ch, lists, which are characteristic of Daniel, are used particularly often, perhaps for satirical effect. Even the names of the protagonists in their Babylonian form, "Shadrach, Meshach, and Abed-nego," are repeated often. The comic effect of the lists is even more marked if the narrative is read aloud, as it was probably originally recounted. The pomp and organization of officials, including the title *satrap,* seem to be more indicative of Persian administration, when the story may have been composed, rather than the Neo-Babylonian empire when the story is set. Ch 6 indicates that the editor of the collection is familiar with Persian administration. **5:** Some of the musical instruments mentioned are loanwords from Gk, the only certain Gk loanwords in Daniel.

8 Seizing the occasion, certain Chaldeans came forward to
slander the Jews. 9 They spoke up and said to King Nebuchadnezzar, "O king, live forever! 10 You, O king, gave an order that
everyone who hears the horn, pipe, zither, lyre, psaltery, bagpipe, and all types of instruments must fall down and worship
the golden statue, 11 and whoever does not fall down and worship shall be thrown into a burning fiery furnace. 12 There are
certain Jews whom you appointed to administer the province
of Babylon, Shadrach, Meshach, and Abed-nego; those men
pay no heed to you, O king; they do not serve your god or worship the statue of gold that you have set up."

13 Then Nebuchadnezzar, in raging fury, ordered Shadrach,
Meshach, and Abed-nego to be brought; so those men were
brought before the king. 14 Nebuchadnezzar spoke to them and
said, "Is it true, Shadrach, Meshach, and Abed-nego, that you
do not serve my god or worship the statue of gold that I have
set up? 15 Now if you are ready to fall down and worship the
statue that I have made when you hear the sound of the horn,
pipe, zither, lyre, psaltery, and bagpipe, and all other types of
instruments, [well and good]; but if you will not worship, you
shall at once be thrown into a burning fiery furnace, and what
god is there that can save you from my power?" 16 Shadrach,
Meshach, and Abed-nego said in reply to the king, "O Nebuchadnezzar, we have no need to answer you in this matter,
17 for if so it must be, our God whom we serve is able to save us
from the burning fiery furnace, and He will save us from your
power, O king. 18 But even if He does not, be it known to you,
O king, that we will not serve your god or worship the statue of
gold that you have set up."

19 Nebuchadnezzar was so filled with rage at Shadrach, Meshach, and Abed-nego that his visage was distorted, and he
gave an order to heat up the furnace to seven times its usual
heat. 20 He commanded some of the strongest men of his army
to bind Shadrach, Meshach, and Abed-nego, and to throw them
into the burning fiery furnace. 21 So these men, in their shirts,
trousers, hats, and other garments, were bound and thrown
into the burning fiery furnace. 22 Because the king's order was
urgent, and the furnace was heated to excess, a tongue of flame
killed the men who carried up Shadrach, Meshach, and Abed-
nego. 23 But those three men, Shadrach, Meshach, and Abed-
nego, dropped, bound, into the burning fiery furnace.

24 Then King Nebuchadnezzar was astonished and, rising in
haste, addressed his companions, saying, "Did we not throw
three men, bound, into the fire?" They spoke in reply, "Surely,
O king." 25 He answered, "But I see four men walking about unbound and unharmed in the fire and the fourth looks like a
divine being." 26 Nebuchadnezzar then approached the hatch
of the burning fiery furnace and called, "Shadrach, Meshach,

8: The threat from other courtiers, who are presumably jealous, is emphasized here and at 6.1–5; cf. also Esth. ch 3. **11:** Being thrown into the fiery furnace appears in postbiblical literature in reference to Abraham, based on this passage and the notice that he came from Ur of the Chaldeans; the Heb word "ur" also means fire (see e.g., *Gen. Rab.* 38.13). **15:** *What god is there:* Without realizing it, the king invokes the God who does have the power to save the three Jews, unlike the many gods whom the king worships. **19:** The bluster of the king is emphasized, perhaps also for comic effect. **25:** *The fourth looks like a divine being,* an angel. Angels become particularly important in this period; cf. 7.13–14 n.; 8.15–16 n.

Abed-nego, servants of the Most High God, come out!" So Shadrach, Meshach, and Abed-nego came out of the fire. 27 The satraps, the prefects, the governors, and the royal companions gathered around to look at those men, on whose bodies the fire had had no effect, the hair of whose heads had not been singed, whose shirts looked no different, to whom not even the odor of fire clung. 28 Nebuchadnezzar spoke up and said, "Blessed be the God of Shadrach, Meshach, and Abed-nego, who sent His angel to save His servants who, trusting in Him, flouted the king's decree at the risk of their lives rather than serve or worship any god but their own God. 29 I hereby give an order that [anyone of] any people or nation of whatever language who blasphemes the God of Shadrach, Meshach, and Abed-nego shall be torn limb from limb, and his house confiscated, for there is no other God who is able to save in this way."

30 Thereupon the king promoted Shadrach, Meshach, and Abed-nego in the province of Babylon.

31 "King Nebuchadnezzar to all people and nations of every language that inhabit the whole earth: May your well-being abound! 32 The signs and wonders that the Most High God has worked for me I am pleased to relate. 33 How great are His signs; how mighty His wonders! His kingdom is an everlasting kingdom, and His dominion endures throughout the generations."

4 I, Nebuchadnezzar, was living serenely in my house, flourishing in my palace. 2 I had a dream that frightened me, and my thoughts in bed and the vision of my mind alarmed me. 3 I gave an order to bring all the wise men of Babylon before me to let me know the meaning of the dream. 4 The magicians, exorcists, Chaldeans, and diviners came, and I related the dream to them, but they could not make its meaning known to me. 5 Finally, Daniel, called Belteshazzar after the name of my god, in whom the spirit of the holy gods was, came to me, and I related the dream to him, [saying], 6 "Belteshazzar, chief magician, in whom I know the spirit of the holy gods to be, and whom no mystery baffles, tell me the meaning of my dream vision that I have seen. 7 In the visions of my mind in bed

I saw a tree of great height in the midst of the earth;
8 The tree grew and became mighty;
Its top reached heaven,
And it was visible to the ends of the earth.
9 Its foliage was beautiful
And its fruit abundant;
There was food for all in it.
Beneath it the beasts of the field found shade,
And the birds of the sky dwelt on its branches;
All creatures fed on it.

31–33: The first doxology (praise of God) of the pagan kings; cf. 4.31–34; 6.27–28. The theme of all the doxologies is that God's kingship is superior to any earthly kingship. The implausibility of the Babylonian king Nebuchadnezzar blessing the God of Israel and making a decree of protection argues for a humorous interpretation of this ch. These vv. are sometimes taken as the introduction to ch 4 rather than concluding ch 3.

4.1–34: Daniel predicts Nebuchadnezzar's madness. 1: *I, Nebuchadnezzar:* The narrative begins in the first person, recounted by Nebuchadnezzar himself, which is typical of Neo-Babylonian royal inscriptions and of royal letters. Nebuchadnezzar was never absent from office for any extended period, but the king's temporary absence here likely suggests that the model for this story is not Nebuchadnezzar but Nabonidus, the last Babylonian king (556–539 BCE), who spent ten years at Teima, in the Arabian peninsula, allowing his son Belshazzar to reign as viceroy in his stead (see ch 5). The "Prayer of Nabonidus" (4Q242) from Qumran presents Nabonidus's first-person account of being cured by an unnamed Jewish seer after an affliction of seven years. The author's confusion between Nebuchadnezzar and Nabonidus suggests that he lived long after Babylonia had fallen. **5:** *Belteshazzar ... the name of my god,* see 1.7–8 n. Although the author understandably assumes that the name is related to the Babylonian god Bel, it actually means "protect his life" or perhaps "protects the prince's life," and is not based on the god Bel. **6:** *Mystery,* see 2.18 n. **7:** The "world-tree" is often used in the ancient Near East as a symbol of a great empire; cf. Ezek. 17.1–10; 31.3–14; Herodotus 1.108; 7.19.

10: *Watcher,* an angelic figure, common in Jewish apocalyptic literature (*Jub.* 4.15), who executes God's justice. In some texts watchers are fallen angels (*1 Enoch* chs 10–16).
16–24: The story slips into third-person narration with Daniel's role, but returns to first-person narration at v. 31. Daniel urges the king to reform his practices (v. 24), but in light of Nebuchadnezzar's conquest of Judah and the destruction of the Temple, his repentance could not have been seriously maintained. Daniel's concern for Nebuchadnezzar did not always meet with approval in rabbinic tradition (*b. B. Bat.* 4a); some rabbis, however, assumed that "my lord" (v. 16) must refer to God and the "enemy" must be Nebuchadnezzar himself. The point of these episodes, though told whimsically, seems to be that even Nebuchadnezzar could be forced to recognize the sovereignty of the one true God (cf. the book of Jonah).

10 In the vision of my mind in bed, I looked and saw a holy Watch-
er coming down from heaven. 11 He called loudly and said:
'Hew down the tree, lop off its branches,
Strip off its foliage, scatter its fruit.
Let the beasts of the field flee from beneath it
And the birds from its branches,
12 But leave the stump with its roots in the ground.
In fetters of iron and bronze
In the grass of the field,
Let him be drenched with the dew of heaven,
And share earth's verdure with the beasts.
13 Let his mind be altered from that of a man,
And let him be given the mind of a beast,
And let seven seasons pass over him.
14 This sentence is decreed by the Watchers;
This verdict is commanded by the Holy Ones
So that all creatures may know
That the Most High is sovereign over the realm of man,
And He gives it to whom He wishes
And He may set over it even the lowest of men.'
15 "I, King Nebuchadnezzar, had this dream; now you, Belteshazzar, tell me its meaning, since all the wise men of my
kingdom are not able to make its meaning known to me, but
you are able, for the spirit of the holy gods is in you."
16 Then Daniel, called Belteshazzar, was perplexed for a
while, and alarmed by his thoughts. The king addressed him,
"Let the dream and its meaning not alarm you." Belteshazzar
replied, "My lord, would that the dream were for your enemy
and its meaning for your foe! 17 The tree that you saw grow and
become mighty, whose top reached heaven, which was visible
throughout the earth, 18 whose foliage was beautiful, whose
fruit was so abundant that there was food for all in it, beneath
which the beasts of the field dwelt, and in whose branches the
birds of the sky lodged— 19 it is you, O king, you who have grown
and become mighty, whose greatness has grown to reach heav-
en, and whose dominion is to the end of the earth. 20 The holy
Watcher whom the king saw descend from heaven and say,
Hew down the tree and destroy it,
But leave the stump with its roots in the ground.
In fetters of iron and bronze
In the grass of the field,
Let him be drenched with the dew of heaven,
And share the lot of the beasts of the field
Until seven seasons pass over him—
21 this is its meaning, O king; it is the decree of the Most High
which has overtaken my lord the king. 22 You will be driven
away from men and have your habitation with the beasts of
the field. You will be fed grass like cattle, and be drenched with

the dew of heaven; seven seasons will pass over you until you
come to know that the Most High is sovereign over the realm of
man, and He gives it to whom He wishes. 23 And the meaning
of the command to leave the stump of the tree with its roots is
that the kingdom will remain yours from the time you come to
know that Heaven is sovereign. 24 Therefore, O king, may my
advice be acceptable to you: Redeem your sins by beneficence
and your iniquities by generosity to the poor; then your serenity may be extended."
25 All this befell King Nebuchadnezzar. 26 Twelve months
later, as he was walking on the roof of the royal palace at Babylon, 27 the king exclaimed, "There is great Babylon, which
I have built by my vast power to be a royal residence for the
glory of my majesty!" 28 The words were still on the king's lips,
when a voice fell from heaven, "It has been decreed for you,
O King Nebuchadnezzar: The kingdom has passed out of your
hands. 29 You are being driven away from men, and your habitation is to be with the beasts of the field. You are to be fed
grass like cattle, and seven seasons will pass over you until you
come to know that the Most High is sovereign over the realm
of man and He gives it to whom He wishes." 30 There and then
the sentence was carried out upon Nebuchadnezzar. He was
driven away from men, he ate grass like cattle, and his body
was drenched with the dew of heaven until his hair grew like
eagle's [feathers] and his nails like [the talons of] birds.
31 "When the time had passed, I, Nebuchadnezzar, lifted my
eyes to heaven, and my reason was restored to me. I blessed
the Most High, and praised and glorified the Ever-Living One,

Whose dominion is an everlasting dominion
And whose kingdom endures throughout the
generations.
32 All the inhabitants of the earth are of no account.
He does as He wishes with the host of heaven,
And with the inhabitants of the earth.
There is none to stay His hand
Or say to Him, 'What have You done?'

33 There and then my reason was restored to me, and my majesty
and splendor were restored to me for the glory of my kingdom.
My companions and nobles sought me out, and I was reestablished over my kingdom, and added greatness was given me.
34 So now I, Nebuchadnezzar, praise, exalt, and glorify the King
of Heaven, all of whose works are just and whose ways are right,
and who is able to humble those who behave arrogantly."

5 King Belshazzar gave a great banquet for his thousand nobles, and in the presence of the thousand he drank wine.
2 Under the influence of the wine, Belshazzar ordered the gold
and silver vessels that his father Nebuchadnezzar had taken out

28: *Voice,* cf. Dan. ch 5. **31–34:** Cf. 3.32–33; 6.27–28.

5.1–29: Daniel interprets the writing on the wall. 1–2: *Belshazzar* was the son of Nabonidus. He was never king, and only reigned as viceroy during his father's absence. *Great banquet:* Babylonian and Persian royal feasts were notorious for their excess; cf. Esth. ch 1. It is the sacrilege of drinking from the Temple vessels, however, especially by the *concubines,* that is most emphasized. According to rabbinic tradition (*b. Meg.* 11b–12a), Belshazzar was celebrating because he thought that the prediction of the demise of the Babylonian kingdom after seventy years (Jer. 25.11; cf. Dan. ch 9) had been proven wrong. He had miscalculated, however, by one year. *Vessels,* see 1.2.

of the temple at Jerusalem to be brought so that the king and his
nobles, his consorts, and his concubines could drink from them.
3 The golden vessels that had been taken out of the sanctuary
of the House of God in Jerusalem were then brought, and the
king, his nobles, his consorts, and his concubines drank from
them. 4 They drank wine and praised the gods of gold and silver,
bronze, iron, wood, and stone. 5 Just then, the fingers of a human hand appeared and wrote on the plaster of the wall of the
king's palace opposite the lampstand, so that the king could see
the hand as it wrote. 6 The king's face darkened, and his thoughts
alarmed him; the joints of his loins were loosened and his knees
knocked together. 7 The king called loudly for the exorcists, Chaldeans, and diviners to be brought. The king addressed the wise
men of Babylon, "Whoever can read this writing and tell me its
meaning shall be clothed in purple and wear a golden chain on
his neck, and shall rule as [a]one of three[a] in the kingdom."
8 Then all the king's wise men came, but they could not read
the writing or make known its meaning to the king. 9 King Belshazzar grew exceedingly alarmed and his face darkened, and
his nobles were dismayed. 10 Because of the state of the king
and his nobles, the queen came to the banquet hall. The queen
spoke up and said, "O king, live forever! Let your thoughts not
alarm you or your face darken. 11 There is a man in your kingdom who has the spirit of the holy gods in him; in your father's
time, illumination, understanding, and wisdom like that of
the gods were to be found in him, and your father, King Nebuchadnezzar, appointed him chief of the magicians, exorcists,
Chaldeans, and diviners. 12 Seeing that there is to be found
in Daniel (whom the king called Belteshazzar) extraordinary
spirit, knowledge, and understanding to interpret dreams, to
explain riddles and solve problems, let Daniel now be called to
tell the meaning [of the writing]."
13 Daniel was then brought before the king. The king addressed Daniel, "You are Daniel, one of the exiles of Judah
whom my father, the king, brought from Judah. 14 I have heard
about you that you have the spirit of the gods in you, and that
illumination, knowledge, and extraordinary wisdom are to be
found in you. 15 Now the wise men and exorcists have been
brought before me to read this writing and to make known its
meaning to me. But they could not tell what it meant. 16 I have
heard about you, that you can give interpretations and solve
problems. Now if you can read the writing and make known its
meaning to me, you shall be clothed in purple and wear a gold-
en chain on your neck and rule as one of three in the kingdom."
17 Then Daniel said in reply to the king, "You may keep your
gifts for yourself, and give your presents to others. But I will

4: *Gods of gold and silver:* A common feature of Judaism at this time was the "parody of idols," usually focusing on their material origin and their inability to respond to prayer; cf. 5.23; Isa. 44.9–20; Ps. 115.4–8; in the Apocrypha, Wisdom of Solomon 13.1–15.17; Bel and the Dragon; and at Qumran, 4QPrNab ar. **5:** *The fingers of a human hand:* Compare the finger of God that brings the plagues in Exod. 8.19, or writes the ten commandments in Exod. 31.18. **10:** *Queen,* probably the queen-mother, the wife of Nebuchadnezzar. **11–12:** Daniel's wisdom is spelled out by the queen-mother. Evidently she alone remembers his service to Nebuchadnezzar and his extraordinary abilities. This is one of the few places in chs 1–6 that connects the individual stories, and it is likely a redactional addition to make the book more coherent. See 2.13–23 n.

a-a *Cf. Dan. 6.3; or "third in rank."*

read the writing for the king, and make its meaning known to him. [18] O king, the Most High God bestowed kingship, grandeur, glory, and majesty upon your father Nebuchadnezzar. [19] And because of the grandeur that He bestowed upon him, all the peoples and nations of every language trembled in fear of him. He put to death whom he wished, and whom he wished he let live; he raised high whom he wished and whom he wished he brought low. [20] But when he grew haughty and willfully presumptuous, he was deposed from his royal throne and his glory was removed from him. [21] He was driven away from men, and his mind made like that of a beast, and his habitation was with wild asses. He was fed grass like cattle, and his body was drenched with the dew of heaven until he came to know that the Most High God is sovereign over the realm of man, and sets over it whom He wishes. [22] But you, Belshazzar his son, did not humble yourself although you knew all this. [23] You exalted yourself against the Lord of Heaven, and had the vessels of His temple brought to you. You and your nobles, your consorts, and your concubines drank wine from them and praised the gods of silver and gold, bronze and iron, wood and stone, which do not see, hear, or understand; but the God who controls your lifebreath and every move you make—Him you did not glorify! [24] He therefore made the hand appear, and caused the writing to be inscribed. [25] This is the writing that is inscribed: MENE MENE TEKEL UPHARSIN. [26] And this is its meaning: MENE—God has numbered[a] [the days of] your kingdom and brought it to an end; [27] TEKEL—[b]you have been weighed[b] in the balance and found wanting; [28] PERES—your kingdom [c]has been divided[c] and given to the Medes and the Persians." [29] Then, at Belshazzar's command, they clothed Daniel in purple, placed a golden chain on his neck, and proclaimed that he should rule as one of three in the kingdom.

[30] That very night, Belshazzar, the Chaldean king, was killed,

6 [1] and Darius the Mede received the kingdom, being about sixty-two years old. [2] It pleased Darius to appoint over the kingdom one hundred and twenty satraps to be in charge of the whole kingdom; [3] over them were three ministers, one of them Daniel, to whom these satraps reported, in order that the king not be troubled. [4] This man Daniel surpassed the other ministers and satraps by virtue of his extraordinary spirit, and the king considered setting him over the whole kingdom. [5] The ministers and satraps looked for some fault in Daniel's conduct in matters of state, but they could find neither fault nor corruption, inasmuch as he was trustworthy, and no negligence or corruption was to be found in him. [6] Those men then said, "We are not going to find any fault with this Daniel, unless we

a Aramaic mena. *b-b Aramaic* tekilta. *c-c Aramaic* perisat.

23: Because of the sacrilege of the Temple vessels, the sins of Belshazzar are more pointedly *against the Lord of Heaven* than was the case with Nebuchadnezzar. **25–28:** The words are interpreted on two levels. They are weights: *MENE* in Aram. is a mina (a little more than half a kg, about 20 oz); *TEKEL* is a shekel (11 g or less than half an oz); and *UPHARSIN* (a dual form of "peres") is two half-minas. They also sound like verbs: *MENE* sounds like the verb "to number," *TEKEL* "to weigh," and *UPHARSIN* "to divide." The last is also similar to the word "Persians." It is possible that the words originally referred only to the decreasing "weight" or importance of particular Babylonian monarchs, and the dynasty was thereby condemned. A more explicit level of prophetic condemnation was then added in terms of the verbal meanings.

5.30–6.29: Daniel in the lions' den. **5.30–6.1:** These vv. were likely added to provide a smooth transition between the separate stories in chs 5 and 6. **1:** *Darius the Mede* is unhistorical. Darius was a famous Persian king (522–486 BCE) responsible for organizing his empire into provinces headed by "satraps" or governors. According to Herodotus, *Histories* 3.89, Darius established twenty satrapies; contrast the exaggerated tradition of Esth. 1.1. The four-empires schema requires that Media be represented in chs 2 and 7, and it is possible that a story originally involving Darius of Persia has been altered to fit this schema. The events of 5.30 are likewise ahistorical. **3:** In the stories of court conflict, an initial balance among the courtiers is disturbed when one of them is promoted above the others; cf. 2.49 (in reference to ch 3); Esth. 3.1.

find something against him in connection with the laws of his
God." 7 Then these ministers and satraps came thronging in to
the king and said to him, "O King Darius, live forever! 8 All the
ministers of the kingdom, the prefects, satraps, companions,
and governors are in agreement that a royal ban should be issued under sanction of an oath that whoever shall address a
petition to any god or man, besides you, O king, during the
next thirty days shall be thrown into a lions' den. 9 So issue the
ban, O king, and put it in writing so that it be unalterable as
a law of the Medes and Persians that may not be abrogated."
10 Thereupon King Darius put the ban in writing.

11 When Daniel learned that it had been put in writing, he
went to his house, in whose upper chamber he had had windows made facing Jerusalem, and three times a day he knelt
down, prayed, and made confession to his God, as he had always done. 12 Then those men came thronging in and found
Daniel petitioning his God in supplication. 13 They then approached the king and reminded him of the royal ban: "Did
you not put in writing a ban that whoever addresses a petition
to any god or man besides you, O king, during the next thirty
days, shall be thrown into a lions' den?" The king said in reply, "The order stands firm, as a law of the Medes and Persians
that may not be abrogated." 14 Thereupon they said to the king,
"Daniel, one of the exiles of Judah, pays no heed to you, O king,
or to the ban that you put in writing; three times a day he offers
his petitions [to his God]." 15 Upon hearing that, the king was
very disturbed, and he set his heart upon saving Daniel, and
until the sun set made every effort to rescue him. 16 Then those
men came thronging in to the king and said to the king, "Know,
O king, that it is a law of the Medes and Persians that any ban
that the king issues under sanction of oath is unalterable." 17 By
the king's order, Daniel was then brought and thrown into
the lions' den. The king spoke to Daniel and said, "Your God,
whom you serve so regularly, will deliver you." 18 A rock was
brought and placed over the mouth of the den; the king sealed
it with his signet and with the signet of his nobles, so that nothing might be altered concerning Daniel.

19 The king then went to his palace and spent the night fasting; no diversions were brought to him, and his sleep fled
from him. 20 Then, at the first light of dawn, the king arose and
rushed to the lions' den. 21 As he approached the den, he cried
to Daniel in a mournful voice; the king said to Daniel, "Daniel, servant of the living God, was the God whom you served
so regularly able to deliver you from the lions?" 22 Daniel then
talked with the king, "O king, live forever! 23 My God sent His
angel, who shut the mouths of the lions so that they did not
injure me, inasmuch as I was found innocent by Him, nor have
I, O king, done you any injury." 24 The king was very glad, and

8: The interdict is historically implausible. No king of this period who claimed divine status forbade the worship of other gods. Darius the Persian was supportive of local religions, including that of the Jews. The exclusive worship of one god was a Jewish view, and this exclusive notion is projected onto an Eastern divine monarch. The narrative thus reflects Jewish tensions about remaining monotheistic in a mixed Diaspora culture. **9:** Some ancient authors believed that the law of the Persian king, once enacted, could not be altered (Esth. 1.19; 8.8; Diodorus Siculus 17.30). This is likely only a popular tradition, however, and is emphasized for dramatic effect (cf. 6.14–17). **11:** Praying *three times a day* became a common Jewish practice by the mishnaic period, though it has earlier precedents (Ps. 55.18; Jdt. 9.1). Likewise, the Mishnah legislates praying toward Jerusalem (*m. Ber.* 4.5).

ordered Daniel to be brought up out of the den. Daniel was
brought up out of the den, and no injury was found on him, for
he had trusted in his God. 25 Then, by order of the king, those
men who had slandered Daniel were brought and, together
with their children and wives, were thrown into the lions' den.
They had hardly reached the bottom of the den when the lions
overpowered them and crushed all their bones.
26 Then King Darius wrote to all peoples and nations of every
language that inhabit the earth, "May your well-being abound!
27 I have hereby given an order that throughout my royal domain men must tremble in fear before the God of Daniel, for
He is the living God who endures forever; His kingdom is indestructible, and His dominion is to the end of time; 28 He delivers and saves, and performs signs and wonders in heaven and
on earth, for He delivered Daniel from the power of the lions."
29 Thus Daniel prospered during the reign of Darius and during
the reign of Cyrus the Persian.

7 In the first year of King Belshazzar of Babylon, Daniel saw a
dream and a vision of his mind in bed; afterward he wrote
down the dream. Beginning the account, 2 Daniel related the
following:
"In my vision at night, I saw the four winds of heaven stirring up the great sea. 3 Four mighty beasts different from each
other emerged from the sea. 4 The first was like a lion but had
eagles' wings. As I looked on, its wings were plucked off, and
it was lifted off the ground and set on its feet like a man and
given the mind of a man. 5 Then I saw a second, different beast,
which was like a bear but raised on one side, and with three
fangs in its mouth among its teeth; it was told, 'Arise, eat much
meat!' 6 After that, as I looked on, there was another one, like a
leopard, and it had on its back four wings like those of a bird;
the beast had four heads, and dominion was given to it. 7 After that, as I looked on in the night vision, there was a fourth
beast—fearsome, dreadful, and very powerful, with great iron
teeth—that devoured and crushed, and stamped the remains
with its feet. It was different from all the other beasts which
had gone before it; and it had ten horns. 8 While I was gazing
upon these horns, a new little horn sprouted up among them;

25: The importance of family identity in the ancient Near East could result in family members receiving the punishment of the male heads; cf. Num. 16.25–33; 2 Sam. 21.1–9; Esth. 9.13–14; but in contrast to this, Jer. 31.28–29; Ezek. ch 18. **26–28:** A concluding doxology similar to 3.28, 32–33; 4.31–34. The story is told for dramatic effect. It is unlikely that Darius would invoke Daniel's God, although this has been the theme of chs 1–6, as it was in "Prayer of Nabonidus" (4QPrNab ar) and Bel and the Dragon from the Apocrypha. Keeping lions in an underground den is unknown; this and the sealing of the stone with the king's ring heighten the drama. **29:** *Cyrus the Persian* was the first Persian king (559–530 BCE). He was followed by Cambyses, Darius, and Xerxes; see 9.1.

7.1–12.13: Daniel's apocalyptic visions. This is the second half of the book; see the intro. on the difference in genre, date, and political situation of chs 7–12, and the difference in language between ch 7 and chs 8–12.

7.1–28: Vision of the four beasts. Ch 7, in Aram., may have been composed before chs 8–12. Like ch 2, it involves a dream interpretation and a four-kingdom schema, and like chs 2–6 it is in Aram. The depiction of the end of time in apocalyptic visions is often similar to biblical depictions of the beginning of time, that is, creation. The sea and monsters here are paralleled in many stories of creation (Gen. ch 1; Job 26.12–13; Pss. 33.6–7; 74.12–14; Isa. 27.1). **1:** *First year of King Belshazzar,* 553 BCE. The author of ch 7, like the author of ch 5, incorrectly thinks of Belshazzar as king. **2–3:** *Four winds ... four mighty beasts:* The tumult of all four winds blowing at once and the violence of the sea portend threatening events. The recurrence of the number four evokes the four kingdoms of ch 2, and ch 7 will develop a four-kingdom schema further. **4–8:** The animals are like the mythological figures of ancient Near Eastern art, but are also ferocious predators known to Israelite imagery, e.g., Hos. 13.7–8. (On the empires symbolized here, see the intro.) The winged *lion* represents the Babylonian kingdom, the ravenous *bear* the Medes, the winged *leopard* the Persians, and the last *beast* the Greek empire of Alexander the Great, with the *ten horns* representing the Seleucid successors of Alexander in the Near East. The last beast is the most fearsome and chaotic, and the last horn represents the Seleucid Antiochus IV Epiphanes, who killed some of his rivals. The human transformation of the first beast may be an allusion to ch 4. The general cast of this scene is also like Ezek. ch 1, with

three of the older horns were uprooted to make room for it.
There were eyes in this horn like those of a man, and a mouth
that spoke arrogantly. 9 As I looked on,

Thrones were set in place,
And the Ancient of Days took His seat.
His garment was like white snow,
And the hair of His head was like lamb's[a] wool.
His throne was tongues of flame;
Its wheels were blazing fire.
10 A river of fire streamed forth before Him;
Thousands upon thousands served Him;
Myriads upon myriads attended Him;
The court sat and the books were opened.

11 I looked on. Then, because of the arrogant words that the
horn spoke, the beast was killed as I looked on; its body was
destroyed and it was consigned to the flames. 12 The dominion
of the other beasts was taken away, but an extension of life was
given to them for a time and season. 13 As I looked on, in the
night vision,

One like a human being
Came with the clouds of heaven;
He reached the Ancient of Days
And was presented to Him.
14 Dominion, glory, and kingship were given to him;
All peoples and nations of every language must serve
him.
His dominion is an everlasting dominion that shall not
pass away,
And his kingship, one that shall not be destroyed.

15 As for me, Daniel, my spirit was disturbed within me and the
vision of my mind alarmed me. 16 I approached one of the attendants and asked him the true meaning of all this. He gave
me this interpretation of the matter: 17 "These great beasts, four
in number [mean] four kingdoms[b] will arise out of the earth;
18 then holy ones of the Most High will receive the kingdom,

a *Or "clean."* *b* *Lit. "kings."*

its composite creatures and symbolic weight. **9–14:** The chaos and destructive power of the beasts is followed by an even more awesome judgment scene. The model for the judgment scene is the ancient Near Eastern council of gods in heaven, often utilized in the Bible to depict God's council (Ps. 82.1; Job ch 1). The *throne* formed from *tongues of flame* echoes Isa. ch 6; Ezek. 1.25–28. **9:** *Ancient of Days:* God is described in corporeal terms in the way that El is pictured in Canaanite myth, with the warrior-god Baal coming before him after slaying the sea monster. It is significant, however, that combat is not mentioned here in Daniel, only judgment. As in Gen. ch 1, God has absolute sovereignty over the world, and does not need to establish authority through conflict. Cf. the role of angels in 10.20–21. **10:** As befits a great and absolute king, the divine retinue is large, comprised of *thousands upon thousands* and *myriads upon myriads.* **11:** The arrogance of the last horn is now seen as provocation for the most severe punishment. In ch 5 it was the arrogance and sacrilege of the latecomer Belshazzar, not the destructive history of Nebuchadnezzar, that provoked the strongest condemnation. **13–14:** *Human being,* lit. "son of man," which in the Bible is idiomatic for human being (Dan. 8.17; Ezek. 2.1; Job 25.6). Here, however, the celestial being is *like* a human being, i.e., has a human countenance. For the author it most likely represents a heavenly figure who will exercise judgment, perhaps Michael (see 10.13 n.). Christian tradition, especially in the Gospels, saw this as a prediction of Jesus as a heavenly "son of man." This messianic use of this title is a Jewish idea as well (*1 Enoch* 46.1; 48.10; *4 Ezra* [2 Esd.] ch 13; *b. Sanh.* 98a). Some Rabbis rejected the future messianic interpretation by arguing either that the predictions had all been fulfilled in the past (*b. Sanh.* 97b), or that Daniel's predictions did not include the end of time (*Gen. Rab.* 98.2). Later in Jewish tradition the messianic interpretation faded and the *one like a human being* was seen as representing Israel (Ibn Ezra, Rashi). **14:** *Dominion ... peoples and nations:* The tone and the words used here and in 7.27 tie this ch to the doxologies of chs 1–6 (see 3.31–33 n.). **16:** In chs 2 and 4 Daniel's extraordinary spiritual insights, bestowed by God, allowed him to interpret the dreams successfully, but the apocalyptic genre typically included a divine interpreter; cf. 8.15–16; 9.21–23; chs 10–12; Zech. chs 1–6. *Interpretation:* The word used here ("peshar") is the Aram. form of the word "pesher" used later at Qumran for a type of interpretation of prophetic literature, where the biblical book was seen as fulfilled in the time of the interpreter. (It is translated as "meaning" at 4.13; 5.15, 26.) **18:** *Holy ones of the Most High:* Some scholars see here a reference to the pious Jews of Daniel's circle, called "knowledgeable" in ch 12, but

and will possess the kingdom forever—forever and ever.'
19 Then I wanted to ascertain the true meaning of the fourth beast, which was different from them all, very fearsome, with teeth of iron, claws of bronze, that devoured and crushed, and stamped the remains; 20 and of the ten horns on its head; and of the new one that sprouted, to make room for which three fell—the horn that had eyes, and a mouth that spoke arrogantly, and which was more conspicuous than its fellows. 21 (I looked on as that horn made war with the holy ones and overcame them, 22 until the Ancient of Days came and judgment was rendered in favor of the holy ones of the Most High, for the time had come, and the holy ones took possession of the kingdom.) 23 This is what he said: 'The fourth beast [means]—there will be a fourth kingdom upon the earth which will be different from all the kingdoms; it will devour the whole earth, tread it down, and crush it. 24 And the ten horns [mean]—from that kingdom, ten kings will arise, and after them another will arise. He will be different from the former ones, and will bring low three kings. 25 He will speak words against the Most High, and will harass the holy ones of the Most High. He will think of changing times and laws, and they will be delivered into his power for a [a]time, times, and half a time.[a] 26 Then the court will sit and his dominion will be taken away, to be destroyed and abolished for all time. 27 The kingship and dominion and grandeur belonging to all the kingdoms under Heaven will be given to the people of the holy ones of the Most High. Their kingdom shall be an everlasting kingdom, and all dominions shall serve and obey them.' " 28 Here the account ends.

I, Daniel, was very alarmed by my thoughts, and my face darkened; and I could not put the matter out of my mind.

8 In the third year of the reign of King Belshazzar, a vision appeared to me, to me, Daniel, after the one that had appeared to me earlier. 2 I saw in the vision—at the time I saw it I was in the fortress of Shushan, in the province of Elam—I saw in the vision that I was beside the Ulai River. 3 I looked and saw a ram standing between me and the river; he had two horns; the horns were high, with one higher than the other, and the higher sprouting last. 4 I saw the ram butting westward, northward, and southward. No beast could withstand him, and there was none to deliver from his power. He did as he pleased and grew great. 5 As I looked on, a he-goat came from the west, passing over the entire earth without touching the ground. The goat had a conspicuous horn on its forehead. 6 He came up to the two-horned ram that I had seen standing between me and the river and charged at him with furious force. 7 I saw him

a-a I.e., a year, two years, and a half a year.

others argue, noting v. 27 and using the analogy of texts from Qumran, that *the holy ones* are the angelic host.

8.1–27: Vision of the ram and the he-goat. With the beginning of ch 8, the language changes from Aram. back to Heb, and continues in Heb to the end. The symbolic visions of chs 8–12 are less poetic, more detailed, and more focused on recent events from the author's perspective. **1:** *Third year ... Belshazzar,* see 7.1. **2:** *Shushan,* Susa, the winter capital of the Persian empire. *Ulai River:* Daniel twice has visions by a river (cf. 10.4), modeled after Ezekiel (Ezek. 1.1). Rivers create a natural boundary, and in the ancient world boundaries and crossroads were considered ideal locations for communication with the divine. **3–14:** *Ram ... he-goat:* The traditional four-kingdom schema is abandoned here in favor of one that is less compelling but better symbolizes the recent past from the author's perspective. The two-horned ram represents the Medes and Persians, and the he-goat represents Alexander the Great, who died *at the peak of his power* (v. 8). The *four conspicuous horns* (v. 8) represent the four kingdoms that succeeded Alexander, one of which was the Seleucid, over which Antiochus IV Epiphanes came to rule. This vision thus overlaps to a large extent with ch 7.

9: *Beautiful land,* Judea. **11:** *Regular offering ... abandoned:* Antiochus IV suppressed the practice of Judaism and turned the Temple into a non-Jewish worship site (1 Macc. 1.54–61; 2 Macc. 4.11–6.11). **14:** *Twenty-three hundred evenings and mornings,* i.e., 1,150 days, about the same as the three-and-a-half years of 7.25; 9.27; 12.7. **15–16:** *One who looked like a man:* An expression different from 7.13–14 is used here, which is a play on the name of *Gabriel.* Angels appear in the Bible, but only in Daniel and postbiblical texts do they have names; see also 12.1. **17–19:** Here and elsewhere (e.g., 8.26–27) a number of literary devices are used, typical of apocalypses, that increase the sense of awe, secrecy, and mystery, even though the events predicted seem very clear. The command to "keep the vision a secret" (v. 26) emphasizes that it was supposedly received by Daniel centuries earlier, but was not known until now at the *time of the end* when it finds its realization. This secret vision, though quite bizarre to us, would have been transparent to the author's audience in the 2nd c. BCE.

reach the ram and rage at him; he struck the ram and broke
its two horns, and the ram was powerless to withstand him.
He threw him to the ground and trampled him, and there was
none to deliver the ram from his power. 8 Then the he-goat
grew very great, but at the peak of his power his big horn was
broken. In its place, four conspicuous horns sprouted toward
the four winds of heaven. 9 From one of them emerged a small
horn, which extended itself greatly toward the south, toward
the east, and toward the beautiful land. 10 It grew as high as the
host of heaven and it hurled some stars of the [heavenly] host
to the ground and trampled them. 11 It vaunted itself against
the very chief of the host; on its account the regular offering
was suspended, and His holy place was abandoned. 12 [a-]An
army was arrayed iniquitously against the regular offering;[-a] it
hurled truth to the ground and prospered in what it did.
13 Then I heard a holy being speaking, and another holy being said to whoever it was who was speaking, "How long will
[what was seen in] the vision last—[a-]the regular offering be
forsaken because of transgression; the sanctuary be surrendered and the [heavenly] host be trampled?"[-a] 14 He answered
me,[b] "For twenty-three hundred evenings and mornings; then
the sanctuary shall be cleansed." 15 While I, Daniel, was seeing the vision, and trying to understand it, there appeared before me one who looked like a man. 16 I heard a human voice
from the middle of Ulai calling out, "Gabriel, make that man
understand the vision." 17 He came near to where I was standing, and as he came I was terrified, and fell prostrate. He said
to me, "Understand, O man, that the vision refers to the time of
the end." 18 When he spoke with me, I was overcome by a deep
sleep as I lay prostrate on the ground. Then he touched me and
made me stand up, 19 and said, "I am going to inform you of
what will happen when wrath is at an end, for [it refers] to the
time appointed for the end.
20 "The two-horned ram that you saw [signifies] the kings of
Media and Persia; 21 and the buck, the he-goat—the king of
Greece; and the large horn on his forehead, that is the first king.
22 One was broken and four came in its stead—that [means]:
four kingdoms will arise out of a nation, but without its power.
23 When their kingdoms are at an end, when the measure of
transgression[c] has been filled, then a king will arise, impudent
and versed in intrigue. 24 He will have great strength, but not
through his own strength. He will be extraordinarily destructive; he will prosper in what he does, and destroy the mighty
and the people of holy ones. 25 By his cunning, he will use deceit successfully. He will make great plans, will destroy many,

a-a *Meaning of Heb. uncertain.* b *Several ancient versions "him."*
c *Lit. "transgressors."*

taking them unawares, and will rise up against the chief of chiefs, but will be broken, not by [human] hands. [26] What was said in the vision about evenings and mornings is true. Now you keep the vision a secret, for it pertains to far-off days." [27] So I, Daniel, was stricken,[a] and languished many days. Then I arose and attended to the king's business, but I was dismayed by the vision and no one could explain it.

9 In the first year of Darius son of Ahasuerus, of Median descent, who was made king over the kingdom of the Chaldeans—[2] in the first year of his reign, I, Daniel, consulted the books concerning the number of years that, according to the word of the LORD that had come to Jeremiah the prophet, were to be the term of Jerusalem's desolation—seventy years. [3] I turned my face to the Lord God, devoting myself to prayer and supplication, in fasting, in sackcloth and ashes. [4] I prayed to the LORD my God, making confession thus: "O Lord, great and awesome God, who stays faithful to His covenant with those who love Him and keep His commandments! [5] We have sinned; we have gone astray; we have acted wickedly; we have been rebellious and have deviated from Your commandments and Your rules, [6] and have not obeyed Your servants the prophets who spoke in Your name to our kings, our officers, our fathers, and all the people of the land. [7] With You, O Lord, is the right, and the shame is on us to this very day, on the men of Judah and the inhabitants of Jerusalem, all Israel, near and far, in all the lands where You have banished them, for the trespass they committed against You. [8] The shame, O LORD, is on us, on our kings, our officers, and our fathers, because we have sinned against You. [9] To the Lord our God belong mercy and forgiveness, for we rebelled against Him, [10] and did not obey the LORD our God by following His teachings that He set before us through His servants the prophets. [11] All Israel has violated Your teaching and gone astray, disobeying You; so the curse and the oath written in the Teaching of Moses, the servant of God, have been poured down upon us, for we have sinned against Him. [12] He carried out the threat that He made against us, and against our rulers who ruled us, to bring upon us great misfortune; under the whole heaven there has never been done the like of what was done to Jerusalem. [13] All that calamity, just as is written in the Teaching of Moses, came upon us, yet we did not supplicate the LORD our God, did not repent of our iniquity or become wise through Your truth. [14] Hence the LORD was intent upon bringing calamity upon us, for the LORD our God is in the right in all that He has done, but we have not obeyed Him.

a *Meaning of Heb. uncertain.*

9.1–27: Daniel reinterprets Jeremiah's prophecy of seventy years. **1:** *Darius ... Ahasuerus:* On Darius, see 6.1 n. Ahasuerus is Xerxes, like Darius a Persian and not a Mede, and was the son, not father, of Darius. *Of Median descent,* possibly an effort to harmonize the fact that Ahasuerus and Darius were Persian with the statement in 6.1 that Darius was a Mede. **2:** The author grapples with the prophetic prediction in Jer. 25.11–12 that Babylon would fall after *seventy years.* This is one of the few explicit references in a biblical book to another biblical book; it does not necessarily reflect the canonization of the Prophets as a corpus, but suggests that like the Torah, certain prophetic texts were studied intensively at this time. **3:** *Fasting, sackcloth,* and *ashes* were aspects of ritual mourning in the Bible, but were also signs of penitence as well as preparation for fervent prayer and for visions (*4 Ezra* [2 Esd.] 5.13; 9.24). The rise of penitential theology in postbiblical Judaism suggests that, although Daniel's prayer is a response to particular historical events, it also reflects in Judaism a new personal, penitential religious life that is taken up in various ways by the Qumran sectarians, Pharisees, and Christians. This can also be found in some strands of rabbinic tradition (*b. Ta'an.* 11b–12a), but there is also found in the Talmud a tendency to rein in excessive penitential asceticism (*b. Ta'an.* 11a; *b. B. Bat.* 60b). **5:** Later Jewish confessions, culminating in the lengthy, formulaic confessions in the Yom Kippur liturgy, share this structure of listing words for various prohibited activities in the first-person plural.

15 “Now, O Lord our God—You who brought Your people
out of the land of Egypt with a mighty hand, winning fame for
Yourself to this very day—we have sinned, we have acted wickedly. 16 O Lord, as befits Your abundant benevolence, let Your
wrathful fury turn back from Your city Jerusalem, Your holy
mountain; for because of our sins and the iniquities of our
fathers, Jerusalem and Your people have become a mockery
among all who are around us.
17 “O our God, hear now the prayer of Your servant and his
plea, and show Your favor to Your desolate sanctuary, for the
Lord’s sake. 18 Incline Your ear, O my God, and hear; open Your
eyes and see our desolation and the city to which Your name is
attached. Not because of any merit of ours do we lay our plea
before You but because of Your abundant mercies. 19 O Lord,
hear! O Lord, forgive! O Lord, listen, and act without delay for
Your own sake, O my God; for Your name is attached to Your
city and Your people!”
20 While I was speaking, praying, and confessing my sin and
the sin of my people Israel, and laying my supplication before
the LORD my God on behalf of the holy mountain of my God—
21 while I was uttering my prayer, the man Gabriel, whom I
had previously seen in the vision, was sent forth in flight and
reached me about the time of the evening offering. 22 He made
me understand by speaking to me and saying, “Daniel, I have
just come forth to give you understanding. 23 A word went forth
as you began your plea, and I have come to tell it, for you are
precious; so mark the word and understand the vision.
24 “Seventy weeks[a] have been decreed for your people and
your holy city until the measure of transgression is filled and
that of sin complete, until iniquity is expiated, and eternal
righteousness ushered in; and prophetic vision ratified,[b] and
the Holy of Holies anointed. 25 You must know and understand: From the issuance of the word to restore and rebuild
Jerusalem until the [time of the] anointed leader is seven
weeks; and for sixty-two weeks it will be rebuilt, square and
moat, but in a time of distress. 26 And after those sixty-two
weeks, the anointed one will disappear and vanish.[c] The
army of a leader who is to come will destroy the city and the
sanctuary, but its end will come through a flood. Desolation
is decreed until the end of war. 27 During one week he will
make a firm covenant with many. For half a week he will put
a stop to the sacrifice and the meal offering. At the [d-]corner
[of the altar][-d] will be an appalling abomination until the decreed destruction will be poured down upon the appalling
thing.”

a Viz., of years. *b Lit. “sealed.”*
c Meaning of Heb. uncertain. *d-d Meaning of Heb. uncertain.*

15–19: The penitential prayer and confession of Israel’s sins expresses Deuteronomistic theology, i.e., a view expressed often in the books from Deut. through 2 Kings: Israel has sinned, and if it repents, God will act graciously once more (see e.g., Deut. ch 30; 2 Kings ch 17). **24:** *Seventy weeks* [of years], that is, 490 years, the true prediction of Jeremiah according to this interpretation (see v. 2 and n.). This interpretation is based on reading a single word in Jer. 25.11–12 in two different ways, as “shavʿuim” (weeks) and “shivʿim” (seventy). This is facilitated by the writing system at that time, which indicated consonants only, and not vowels. Such close textual study and revocalization of texts for interpretive purposes would characterize later rabbinic interpretation. *Holy of Holies anointed,* finally accomplished by Judas Maccabee in 164 BCE (1 Macc. 4.26–59), shortly after the final editing of Daniel. **25–26:** *Anointed leader .... anointed one:* The word *anointed* in vv. 25 and 26 is the Heb “mashiaḥ” (Messiah); thus these vv. have given rise to much Christian speculation. In the context of the other historical references, however, the *anointed leader* probably refers to either Zerubbabel or the high priest Joshua (Ezra 3.2; Hag. ch 1; Zech. 6.9–15), while the *anointed one* is most likely the high priest Onias III, killed in 171 BCE (2 Macc. 4.30–34). In the Bible, “mashiaḥ” never refers to the future ideal Davidic king; this use is postbiblical. The prince is Antiochus IV Epiphanes. **27:** *Half a week,* the three-and-a-half years of the Maccabean revolt that had transpired to that time. See 7.25 translators’ note; cf. 8.14 and n. *Appalling abomination,* probably new altar stones placed upon the altar in the Temple, upon which non-Jewish sacrifices were offered to foreign deities (1 Macc. 1.54; 2 Macc. 6.5).

10 In the third year of King Cyrus of Persia, an oracle was
revealed to Daniel, who was called Belteshazzar. That
oracle was true, [a]but it was a great task to understand the
prophecy; understanding came to him through the vision.[a]
[2] At that time, I, Daniel, kept three full weeks of mourning. [3] I
ate no tasty food, nor did any meat or wine enter my mouth. I
did not anoint myself until the three weeks were over. [4] It was
on the twenty-fourth day of the first month, when I was on the
bank of the great river—the Tigris—[5] that I looked and saw a
man dressed in linen, his loins girt in [b]fine gold.[b] [6] His body
was like beryl, his face had the appearance of lightning, his
eyes were like flaming torches, his arms and legs had the color
of burnished bronze, and the sound of his speech was like the
noise of a multitude.
[7] I, Daniel, alone saw the vision; the men who were with me
did not see the vision, yet they were seized with a great terror
and fled into hiding. [8] So I was left alone to see this great vision.
I was drained of strength, my vigor was destroyed, and I could
not summon up strength. [9] I heard him speaking; and when I
heard him speaking, overcome by a deep sleep, I lay prostrate
on the ground. [10] Then a hand touched me, and shook me onto
my hands and knees. [11] He said to me, "O Daniel, precious
man, mark what I say to you and stand up, for I have been sent
to you." After he said this to me, I stood up, trembling. [12] He
then said to me, "Have no fear, Daniel, for from the first day
that you set your mind to get understanding, practicing abstinence before your God, your prayer was heard, and I have
come because of your prayer. [13] However, the prince of the
Persian kingdom opposed me for twenty-one days; now Michael, a prince of the first rank, has come to my aid, after I was
detained there with the kings of Persia. [14] So I have come to
make you understand what is to befall your people in the days
to come, for there is yet a vision for those days."
[15] While he was saying these things to me, I looked down and
kept silent. [16] Then one who looked like a man touched my lips,
and I opened my mouth and spoke, saying to him who stood
before me, "My lord, because of the vision, I have been seized
with pangs and cannot summon strength. [17] How can this servant of my lord speak with my lord, seeing that my strength has
failed and no spirit is left in me?" [18] He who looked like a man
touched me again, and strengthened me. [19] He said, "Have
no fear, precious man, all will be well with you; be strong, be
strong!" As he spoke with me, I was strengthened, and said,
"Speak on, my lord, for you have strengthened me!" [20] Then
he said, "Do you know why I have come to you? Now I must
go back to fight the prince of Persia. When I go off, the prince

10.1–12.13: Vision of the last days. Chs 10–12 constitute one extended vision that is much more detailed and focused on events contemporary with the author.

10.1–21: Daniel is strengthened by a heavenly being. 1: *Third year ... Cyrus,* 536 BCE. **2–3:** Daniel's preparation is common for fervent prayer or visions (see 9.3 n.); here, however, it is particularly lengthy and detailed. **4:** *Bank ... river,* see 8.2 n. **5–6:** The appearance of the man is described like other divine beings (Ezek. 1.4–14; 9.2–3). **7:** Daniel's ability to clearly see this angelic figure, while others only sense his presence, serves to legitimate him and the visions he recounts. **12:** Being told not to fear continues an earlier prophetic motif (e.g., Jer. 1.8). **13:** *Prince of the Persian kingdom,* the guardian angel of Persia. *Michael* was a warrior angel, found in later Jewish and Christian literature (*1 Enoch* 9.1; 1QM 9.15–16; Revelation 12.7). See also 8.15–16 n. **20:** *Prince of Greece,* the guardian angel of the Seleucid empire. The guardian angels of Israel battle those of Persia and Greece in turn. The battle of the heavenly forces is also found at Qumran.

a-a Meaning of Heb. uncertain. *b-b Or "gold of Uphaz."*

of Greece will come in. [21] [a]No one is helping me against them
except your prince, Michael. However, I will tell you what is
recorded in the book of truth.[-a]
11 "In the first year of Darius the Mede, I took my stand to
strengthen and fortify him. [2] And now I will tell you the
truth: Persia will have three more kings, and the fourth will be
wealthier than them all; by the power he obtains through his
wealth, he will stir everyone up against the kingdom of Greece.
[3] Then a warrior king will appear who will have an extensive
dominion and do as he pleases. [4] But after his appearance, his
kingdom will be broken up and scattered to the four winds of
heaven, but not for any of his posterity, nor with dominion like
that which he had; for his kingdom will be uprooted and belong to others beside these.
[5] "The king of the south will grow powerful; however, one of
his officers will overpower him and rule, having an extensive
dominion. [6] After some years, an alliance will be made, and the
daughter of the king of the south will come to the king of the
north to effect the agreement, but she will not maintain her
strength, nor will his strength endure. She will be surrendered
together with those who escorted her and the one who begot
her and helped her during those times. [7] A shoot from her stock
will appear in his place, will come against the army and enter
the fortress of the king of the north; he will fight and overpower
them. [8] He will also take their gods with their molten images
and their precious vessels of silver and gold back to Egypt as
booty. For some years he will leave the king of the north alone,
[9] who will [later] invade the realm of the king of the south, but
will go back to his land.
[10] "His sons will wage war, collecting a multitude of great armies; he will advance and sweep through as a flood, and will
again wage war as far as his stronghold. [11] Then the king of the
south, in a rage, will go out to do battle with him, with the king
of the north. He will muster a great multitude, but the multitude will be delivered into his [foe's] power. [12] But when the
multitude is carried off, he will grow arrogant; he will cause
myriads to perish, but will not prevail. [13] Then the king of the
north will again muster a multitude even greater than the first.
After a time, a matter of years, he will advance with a great
army and much baggage. [14] In those times, many will resist the
king of the south, and the lawless sons of your people will assert themselves to confirm the vision, but they will fail. [15] The
king of the north will advance and throw up siege ramps and
capture a fortress city, and the forces of the south will not hold
out; even the elite of his army will be powerless to resist. [16] His
opponent will do as he pleases, for none will hold out against

a-a Order of clauses inverted for clarity.

11.1–45: The heavenly being reveals future events. A detailed description follows representing events in the conflicted relations between the Seleucid empire of Syria and Babylonia and the Ptolemaic empire of Egypt. The symbolic aspect of the vision is less compelling than ch 7 or even ch 8; it also sometimes bogs down in historical correspondences. Apocalyptic writings, as well as some of those from the Dead Sea Scrolls, typically refer to historical figures indirectly, in code, rather than by name. Daniel follows this practice. As the visions progress, and relate to the time of the author rather than to earlier times, they become more detailed. Thus, the detail allows a precise dating of the final composition and editing of Daniel. **1:** *First year of Darius the Mede,* see 9.1 n. **2–4:** It is unclear what Persian kings are intended; the *fourth* may be the last Persian king, Darius III (336–331 BCE). The *warrior king* is Alexander the Great, whose kingdom was broken up after his death, and ruled by various successor kingdoms. **5:** *The king of the south,* Ptolemy I Soter (323–285 BCE), who established the Ptolemaic kingdom in Egypt; one of his officers is Seleucus I, who founded the Seleucid kingdom in Babylonia, which expanded into adjacent areas, including Syria. **6:** An *alliance* based on marriage was effected between the Ptolemies and the Seleucids. The *daughter* of Ptolemy II and others were murdered. **7–8:** Her brother, Ptolemy III (246–221 BCE), a *shoot from her stock,* retaliated. **9:** Seleucus II, the *king of the north* (v. 7), invaded Egypt, *the realm of the king of the south,* but returned north. **10–13:** The *sons* of Seleucus II grew in strength and attacked Egypt. One of them, Antiochus III the Great (223–187 BCE), finally defeated Ptolemy V. There were Jews sympathetic to both sides (2 Macc. chs 3–4). **14:** The *lawless sons of your people* probably refers to the Seleucid sympathizers. **15–16:** The Battle of Paneas in 200 BCE gave Antiochus III control of

him; he will install himself in the beautiful land with destruction within his reach. 17 He will set his mind upon invading the strongholds throughout his [foe's] kingdom, but in order to destroy it he will effect an agreement with him and give him a daughter in marriage; he will not succeed at it and it will not come about. 18 He will turn to the coastlands and capture many; but a consul will put an end to his insults, nay pay him back for his insults. 19 He will head back to the strongholds of his own land, but will stumble, and fall, and vanish. 20 His place will be taken by one who will dispatch an officer to exact tribute for royal glory, but he will be broken in a few days, not by wrath or by war. 21 His place will be taken by a contemptible man, on whom royal majesty was not conferred; he will come in unawares and seize the kingdom through trickery. 22 The forces of the flood will be overwhelmed by him and will be broken, and so too the covenant leader. 23 And, from the time an alliance is made with him, he will practice deceit; and he will rise to power with a small band. 24 He will invade the richest of provinces unawares, and will do what his father and forefathers never did, lavishing on them[a] spoil, booty, and wealth; he will have designs upon strongholds, but only for a time.

25 "He will muster his strength and courage against the king of the south with a great army. The king of the south will wage war with a very great and powerful army but will not stand fast, for they will devise plans against him. 26 Those who eat of his food will ruin him. His army will be overwhelmed, and many will fall slain. 27 The minds of both kings will be bent on evil; while sitting at the table together, they will lie to each other, but to no avail, for there is yet an appointed term. 28 He will return to his land with great wealth, his mind set against the holy covenant. Having done his pleasure, he will return to his land. 29 At the appointed time, he will again invade the south, but the second time will not be like the first. 30 Ships from Kittim will come against him. He will be checked, and will turn back, raging against the holy covenant. Having done his pleasure, he will then attend to those who forsake the holy covenant. 31 Forces will be levied by him; they will desecrate the temple, the fortress; they will abolish the regular offering and set up the appalling abomination. 32 He will flatter with smooth words those who act wickedly toward the covenant, but the people devoted to their God will stand firm. 33 The knowledgeable among the people will make the many understand; and for a while they shall fall by sword and flame, suffer captivity and spoliation. 34 In defeat, they will receive a little help, and many will join them insincerely. 35 Some of the knowledgeable

a I.e., his followers.

the *beautiful land,* Judea. **17:** Another *marriage* is arranged to normalize relations, but it did not achieve its end. **18–19:** Antiochus III turns his attentions elsewhere but is unsuccessful and ultimately dies. **20:** Seleucus IV Philopator, who succeeded Antiochus III, sent Heliodorus to rob the Jerusalem Temple treasury. According to 2 Macc. ch 3, this attempt was unsuccessful because Heliodorus was chastised by a divine apparition, i.e., *not by wrath or by war.* **21–22:** Antiochus IV Epiphanes (175–164 BCE) succeeds Seleucus IV. Under his rule the *covenant leader,* the high priest Onias III, was murdered (see 9.26). **24:** Antiochus IV (Epiphanes) was notoriously lavish with sacrifices. **25–27:** Antiochus IV again defeats Egypt. **28:** In the midst of his constant campaigns, Antiochus IV had designs once again on the gold in the Jerusalem Temple (1 Macc. ch 1). **29–31:** When Antiochus IV invades Egypt once more, he is opposed by ships from *Kittim,* or Rome, now a Mediterranean power. Jewish sympathizers, along with Antiochus's appointed high priest, will forsake the covenant and introduce new sacrifices, including the *appalling abomination.* **32–35:** Some faithful Jews resist, and those who are *knowledgeable* will instruct the *many* (cf. 12.3). On the identity of the knowledgeable, see the intro. Many will, for the first time in Jewish history, suffer martyrdom (1 Macc. 1.63), namely death due to their religious beliefs. The *little help* they receive perhaps indicates the lack of an effective alliance between the militant Maccabees and Daniel's circle (cf. 1 Macc. 2.29–38).

will fall, that they may be refined and purged and whitened
until the time of the end, for an interval still remains until the
appointed time.
36 “The king will do as he pleases; he will exalt and magnify
himself above every god, and he will speak awful things against
the God of gods. He will prosper until wrath is spent, and what
has been decreed is accomplished. 37 He will not have regard
for the god of his ancestors or for the one dear to women;
he will not have regard for any god, but will magnify himself
above all. 38 He will honor the god of fortresses on his stand; he
will honor with gold and silver, with precious stones and costly
things, a god that his ancestors never knew. 39 He will deal with
fortified strongholds with the help of an alien god. He will heap
honor on those who acknowledge him, and will make them
master over many; he will distribute land for a price. 40 At the
time of the end, the king of the south will lock horns with him,
but the king of the north will attack him with chariots and riders and many ships. He will invade lands, sweeping through
them like a flood; 41 he will invade the beautiful land, too, and
many will fall, but these will escape his clutches: Edom, Moab,
and the chief part of the Ammonites. 42 He will lay his hands
on lands; not even the land of Egypt will escape. 43 He will gain
control over treasures of gold and silver and over all the precious things of Egypt, and the Libyans and Cushites will follow
at his heel. 44 But reports from east and north will alarm him,
and he will march forth in a great fury to destroy and annihilate many. 45 He will pitch his royal pavilion between the sea
and the beautiful holy mountain, and he will meet his doom
with no one to help him.

12 “At that time, the great prince, Michael, who stands
beside the sons of your people, will appear. It will be
a time of trouble, the like of which has never been since the
nation came into being. At that time, your people will be rescued, all who are found inscribed in the book. 2 Many of those
that sleep in the dust of the earth will awake, some to eternal
life, others to reproaches, to everlasting abhorrence. 3 And the
knowledgeable will be radiant like the bright expanse of sky,
and those who lead the many to righteousness will be like the
stars forever and ever.

36–39: The author depicts the arrogance of Antiochus IV as conflict in the divine council (cf. Isa. 14.12–21; Ezek. 28.1–10). The offense of Antiochus IV is not only against the God of gods, but also against his own ancestral god and the *one dear to women,* the Mesopotamian god Tammuz (Ezek. 8.14). Scholars have thought that Antiochus elevated the cult of Zeus Olympios above all other gods, but ancient authors depicted him as active in the worship of many deities and divine heroes. To the author of Daniel, however, the installation of Zeus Olympios in the sanctuary was *alien* both to Jews and to the Seleucid dynasty, which had previously favored Apollo as a patron deity. **40–45:** From this point, the predictions do not correspond to events as known from other sources, and scholars agree that the author must have been writing at the time of the events described in the preceding vv. (see the intro.). What is described is a cataclysmic battle of the major powers that would mark the end of the present age (cf. Ezek. chs 38–39), but the campaigns predicted here did not occur. This indicates that the date of Daniel is in the middle of the persecutions of Antiochus IV, before his defeat and the purification of the Jerusalem Temple, commemorated with Hanukkah.

12.1–13: Vision of the end. 1: A judgment scene similar to ch 7. *Michael,* see 8.15–16 n.; 10.13 n. *Book:* The book of life, prominent in the Jewish liturgy of the high holidays, is borrowed from Mesopotamia and is found in the Bible (e.g., Exod. 32.32–33; Isa. 4.3). Here it is more eschatological, i.e., oriented toward the end of time, and may have inscribed only a small subset of the people Israel, as it does in other Jewish apocalyptic texts. **2–3:** *Many ... will awake,* i.e., not all; presumably *some* who deserve *eternal life, others* who deserve *everlasting abhorrence.* The doctrine of resurrection and judgment probably came about during the persecutions of Antiochus IV as a means to discern justice at a time when pious people, the *knowledgeable,* were being martyred. Unlike Ezekiel's vision of dry bones (Ezek. ch 37), the resurrection here is not a metaphor for the rebirth of Israel, but individual resurrection for judgment. Whether bodily resurrection or some form of spiritual resurrection is intended is not stated. This is the only certain biblical reference to this doctrine, a doctrine that became central in Christian theology and remained a strong current in Judaism as well. It was a tenet of belief for the Pharisees, and Maimonides, centuries later, included it among his thirteen principles of Jewish faith.

[4] "But you, Daniel, keep the words secret, and seal the book
until the time of the end. Many will range far and wide and
knowledge will increase."
[5] Then I, Daniel, looked and saw two others standing, one on
one bank of the river, the other on the other bank of the river.
[6] One said to the man clothed in linen, who was above the water of the river, "How long until the end of these awful things?"
[7] Then I heard the man dressed in linen, who was above the
water of the river, swear by the Ever-Living One as he lifted his
right hand and his left hand to heaven: "For a [a]time, times, and
half a time;[a] and when the breaking of the power of the holy
people comes to an end, then shall all these things be fulfilled."
[8] I heard and did not understand, so I said, "My lord, what
will be the outcome of these things?" [9] He said, "Go, Daniel,
for these words are secret and sealed to the time of the end.
[10] Many will be purified and purged and refined; the wicked
will act wickedly and none of the wicked will understand;
but the knowledgeable will understand. ([11] From the time the
regular offering is abolished, and an appalling abomination
is set up—it will be a thousand two hundred and ninety days.
[12] Happy the one who waits and reaches one thousand three
hundred and thirty-five days.) [13] But you, go on to the end; you
shall rest, and arise to your destiny at the end of the days."

a-a See note at 7.25.

4: See 8.17–19 n. **11–12:** Other time predictions are added, pushing the expected end slightly later than those that have come before. It is possible that the failure of the end to come prompted successive adjustments.

עזרא

Ezra

EZRA-NEHEMIAH, WHICH BEGINS where Chronicles ends, is written as a continuation of Chronicles. It contains historical traditions, records significant liturgical developments in the newly reconstituted Second Temple community, and preserves important genealogical lists of returnees, priests, Levites, and other leadership and Temple personnel. In presenting this material concerning the early postexilic period, Ezra-Nehemiah emphasizes repeatedly their continuity with the Israelite preexilic past. Ezra explicitly appropriates Mosaic authority as he is represented as regiving the Torah in a kind of repetition of the Sinai event. Indeed, Ezra and Nehemiah insist that their legal innovations are already part of Mosaic Torah, i.e., that they are accurate applications of Mosaic Torah and have authoritative Mosaic status. Furthermore, the narrative of Ezra-Nehemiah repeatedly invokes and identifies with the "conquest" of the land of Israel during the time of Joshua as a way of authorizing the returnees' appropriation of Judah and their insistence on rebuilding the Temple and the wall of Jerusalem. The narrative of Ezra-Nehemiah thus represents the self-understanding of the reconstituted Second Temple community as fulfilling the Abrahamic covenant of promised land, a land which, in their textual memory, had been violently torn from them by the Babylonian king Nebuchadnezzar. Ezra-Nehemiah also repeatedly invokes the prophetic traditions of promise for return after the exile. They see themselves as part of the divine fulfillment of earlier prophecies for return and hope uttered by Isaiah, Jeremiah, and others. This identification was meant, in part, to encourage the returnees to identify with and revere their past textual history and overcome the profound disappointment that must have overwhelmed the exiles in Babylonia.

During the reign of Cyrus II (559–530 BCE), the king issued a proclamation encouraging nations to establish their own temples in their indigenous lands. At this time Sheshbazzar was the appointed governor (or leader) of Judah, now a province in the Persian empire, known as Yehud. As a result of Cyrus's decree of 538, known in different forms in Ezra 1.1–4 (see 2 Chron. 36.22–23) and Ezra 6.1–5, some Judahite exiles returned to Israel. Returnees began to reconstruct the Jerusalem Temple and resettle in Judah and surrounding environs. During the reign of Cambyses (530–522), Zerubbabel was governor of Judah and the rebuilding of the Jerusalem Temple continued. During the reign of Darius I (522–486) Haggai and Zechariah prophesied in Jerusalem, and the Jerusalem Temple was rebuilt and dedicated in 516. The rebuilding of the Jerusalem wall and surrounding areas continued under Xerxes I (486–465) and Artaxerxes I Longimanus (465–424). Ezra arrived in Jerusalem in 458. Nehemiah, governor of Judah, was sent to Jerusalem to rebuild the city in 445 and served under both Artaxerxes I and Darius II (423–405), who, following the general Persian policy of religious tolerance, continued to support Judah during his reign.

Date and Composition of Ezra-Nehemiah

MOST SCHOLARS DATE THE PRESENT VERSION of Ezra-Nehemiah to the 4th C. BCE. Ezra-Nehemiah describes events that occurred, for the most part, in the 5th C. BCE, but there are a number of references to later events and important figures. For instance, the Persian king Darius II (423–405) is mentioned in Neh. 12.22; this is the latest king mentioned and would support the claim that the traditions were compiled and completed by the early 4th c., and not later. Other significant details that would be expected in a late-4th-c. or later composition are totally lacking.

Some scholars have suggested that Ezra-Nehemiah is produced by the same author(s) and editor(s) responsible for producing Chronicles, and thus Chronicles-Ezra-Nehemiah should be understood to form a single literary work. This proposal stems from the following arguments: The three share major themes; the conclusion of 2 Chronicles (36.22–23) overlaps with the introduction of Ezra (1.1–3); and 1 Esdras (in the Septuagint [LXX]) combines parts of all three works. This thesis was first articulated in 1832 by the German-Jewish scholar Leopold Zunz and has since received wide support from other scholars. More recently scholars have challenged this theory on the basis of significantly different theological assumptions and differences in use of language in Ezra-Nehemiah and Chronicles; this newer position, which does not assign the same authorship to these works, is now widely accepted.

There is significant ancient debate surrounding the question of the unity of Ezra-Nehemiah. In rabbinic tradition Ezra-Nehemiah was recognized as a single work authored by Ezra (*b. B. Bat.* 15a). Ezra-Nehemiah is considered a single unified work in early Heb biblical manuscripts, in the Greek version of the Bible (LXX), and in later Jewish traditions.

The first formal division of Ezra-Nehemiah into two separate works appears in the 3rd c. CE, among Christians, in the work of the early church father, Origen. This division is also reflected in Jerome's extremely influential Latin translation, the Vulgate (Vg), which was completed in the 4th c. CE. The division of the book into Ezra and Nehemiah among Jews appears in the first printed editions of the Heb text in the 15th c. CE. However, in spite of this borrowed division, Masoretic tradition reflects that the end of the book is at the conclusion of Nehemiah. Titles for Ezra-Nehemiah differ in the various translations. Ezra is titled 2 Esdras in the LXX and 1 Esdras in the Vulgate. Nehemiah is titled 3 Esdras in the LXX and 2 Esdras in the Vulgate.

The LXX and Vulgate also preserve books related to the Ezra-Nehemiah narrative. The apocryphal work called 1 Esdras in the LXX (3 Esd. in the Vg; 1 Esd. in modern Bibles) preserves a translation of 2 Chron. chs 35–36; Ezra chs 1–10; Neh. 8.1–13; and a major addition that is lacking in the Heb version in 1 Esd. 3.1–5.6. Another related book is called "the Apocalypse of Ezra" or *4 Ezra* in the Vulgate and 2 Esdras in modern Bibles. These related versions preserve interpretations and alternate versions of the Ezra-Nehemiah narrative and are very important for acquiring a more complete understanding of this period and the development of Judaism.

Although Ezra-Nehemiah is presented as a single unified work in the Masoretic tradition, recent scholarship has debated its unity, suggesting that Ezra and Nehemiah are separate works, each drawn from various sources. As stated previously, the significant linguistic differences between Ezra and Nehemiah suggest that they were not written by the same author. The inclusion of overlapping but inconsistent genealogical lists also suggests that these two works were originally two independent texts. Finally, the entire book of Ezra focuses on the restoration of the Temple, establishing a community in Jerusalem, and the implementation of the Mosaic law. Nehemiah, on the other hand, focuses on resettlement of the returnees, rebuilding the Jerusalem wall, and insuring the economic stability of the people and of the Temple staff (the priests and Levites). These thematic differences further suggest that Ezra and Nehemiah were originally composed as two independent works.

Underlying Ezra-Nehemiah are earlier sources that were incorporated and then reworked into a largely coherent narrative. In fact, Ezra-Nehemiah, like other works of this period, is fond of quoting official documents. The authenticity of these documents, however, and their historical accuracy are debated by modern scholars. Below is a list of the likely sources that have been woven together to form the current book:

- Cyrus's decree: Ezra 1.2–4 (Heb); Ezra 6.3–5 (Aram.); Ezra 5.13–15 (paraphrase of the decree)
- List of returnees: Ezra 2.1–67, thought to be taken from Neh. 7.6–68, which is a combination of lists of different returns in the early Persian period
- Rehum's letter to Artaxerxes and Artaxerxes' reply: Ezra 4.7–22
- Tattenai's letter to Darius and Darius's reply: Ezra 5.6–17; 6.6–12
- Artaxerxes justifies the return and rebuilding: Ezra 7.12–26
- List of families who journeyed to Jerusalem: Ezra 8.1–14
- List of families who intermarried: Ezra 10.18–43
- Ezra's confession: Ezra 9.6–15
- Nehemiah's memoir: Neh. 1.1–7; 9.1–2; 12.27–43; 13.3, 31
- Authentic part of the Ezra narrative: Neh. 7.72b–9.5
- Confession: Neh. 9.6–37
- Temple archives material: Neh. 9.38–10.39
- Wall dedication: Neh. 12.27–33
- Purification of the Jerusalem community: Neh. 12.44–13.3

Ezra and Nehemiah are unique among biblical books in that they also include a genre identified as memoirs. These include both first-person and third-person narratives concerning Ezra and Nehemiah. The first-person narratives are typically considered to be authentic autobiographical accounts of Ezra and Nehemiah. The third-person parts of the memoirs are attributed to the editors of the final version of Ezra-Nehemiah. The Ezra memoir is thought to consist of parts of Ezra and Nehemiah and should be ordered in the following manner: Ezra chs 7–8; Neh. ch 8; Ezra chs 9–10; Neh. ch 9. Nehemiah's memoir is thought to consist of Neh. 1.1–7.72a (although some scholars have excluded 3.1–32 and 5.14–19 from the Nehemiah memoir); 11.1–2; 12.31–43; 13.4–31.

Guide to Reading Ezra-Nehemiah

THE NARRATIVE OF EZRA-NEHEMIAH begins with a lengthy account of the returnees' arrival in Jerusalem and the rebuilding of the Jerusalem Temple (Ezra chs 1–6). The memoirs of Ezra and Nehemiah follow. Ezra's memoir consists of Ezra chs 7–10 and Neh. chs 8–10. Chs 7 and 8 of Ezra contain reports of the initial difficulties Ezra confronted when he first began to build and the repeated appeal he made to Cyrus's initial decree. In addition, an elaborate account is presented of the legal crises that the returnees faced in light of the widespread practice of intermarriage. Finally, in ch 10 of Ezra, Ezra resolves the legal crisis and completes the rebuilding of the Temple. The conclusion of the Ezra memoir is preserved in the text of Nehemiah (7.27–10.40). Here Ezra conducts a public reading of the law, holds a celebration of the festival of Booths, a delayed Yom Kippur, and finally presents a covenant that is signed by the leaders of the community with the entire community present.

The Nehemiah memoir (Neh. 1.1–7.72) begins by focusing on a different project of restoration, namely the challenge of rebuilding the wall around Jerusalem. Nehemiah was determined to rebuild the wall, despite extensive harassment from the local peoples. The final section of the book (11.1–13.31) recounts a number of political and religious measures taken by Nehemiah in order to ensure the economic and religious preservation of the returnees and of the Temple personnel.

Importance for Judaism

THE IMPORTANCE OF EZRA for the creation and formation of what came to be known as rabbinic Judaism cannot be overestimated. According to the Bible, Ezra was the one who brought the Torah to the returning exiles, read and interpreted it publicly, and oversaw the people's solemn recommitment to its teachings (Neh. chs 8–10). Thus Ezra is like a second Moses. The Rabbis imply this by stating: "Ezra was sufficiently worthy that the Torah could have been given through him if Moses had not preceded him" (*t. Sanh.* 4.4). A number of ordinances called the ten *takanot* (regulations) are attributed to Ezra, although they are nowhere mentioned in the text of Ezra-Nehemiah. In addition, he is celebrated for other important accomplishments: He is said to be involved in the writing of the book of Psalms (*Song Rab.* 4.19), and he had the Torah restored to its "original Mosaic" Assyrian characters, thereby leaving the old Heb characters for the Samaritans (e.g., *b. Sanh.* 21b). These legal innovations, along with other notable accomplishments, reflect the way Ezra is received and embraced by rabbinic Judaism. Ezra is both an authoritative scribe and priest, as well as a kind of proto-Rabbi who also has the authority of a prophet. His legal innovations are not seen as such, but are depicted as proper interpretations of eternally binding Mosaic law (see Ezra 7.10; Neh. 8.1). This principle is at the heart of rabbinic interpretation, and his authenticity is never called into question within rabbinic Judaism.

Summary of Contents

I. Return from Babylonian exile and Temple restoration (Chs 1–6)
- A. Cyrus allows Jewish exiles to return and restore Temple (Ch 1)
  1. Jeremiah's prophecy and Cyrus's decree (1.1–4)
  2. Exiles prepare for return (1.5–6)
  3. Cyrus returns Temple vessels to returnees (1.7–11)
- B. List of exiles who returned to Jerusalem and Judah (Ch 2)
- C. Jeshua and Zerubbabel restore Temple rituals and celebrate (Ch 3)
  1. Temple sacrifice restored at festival of Tabernacles (3.1–7)
  2. Priests and Levites appointed supervisors (3.8–9)
  3. Temple foundations laid with a joyous celebration (3.10–13)
- D. Conflict concerning Temple restoration (Ch 4)
  1. Locals offer to help and are rejected (4.1–3)
  2. Locals try to undermine the Temple restoration *(Aramaic narrative: 4.8–6.18)* (4.4–7)
  3. Letter from locals to Artaxerxes to stop the restoration (4.8–16)
  4. Letter from Artaxerxes to locals (4.17–22)
  5. Temple restoration interrupted (4.23–24)
- E. Temple restoration resumed and completed (Chs 5–6)
  1. Temple restoration resumed with prophetic support (5.1–2)
  2. Tattenai's inquiry and God's protection (5.3–5)
  3. Letter from Tattenai to Darius (5.6–17)
  4. Darius finds Cyrus's decree in Ecbatana (6.1–2)
  5. Letter from Darius to Tattenai ordering Temple restoration (6.3–12)
  6. Temple restoration completed (6.13–15)
  7. Dedication of the Temple (6.16–18)
  8. Celebration of Passover in the first month *(Hebrew)* (6.19–22)

II. Ezra's mission to Jerusalem (Chs 7–10)
- A. Ezra joins the returnees *(Hebrew)* (7.1–10)
- B. Artaxerxes' letter commissioning Ezra's mission *(7.12–26 are Aramaic)* (7.11–26)
- C. Ezra's memoir *(the rest of the book is Hebrew)* (7.27–9.15)
  1. Ezra's prayer (7.27–28)

2. List of returnees who accompanied Ezra (8.1–14)
3. Ezra's preparations for the journey to Jerusalem (8.15–30)
4. Ezra's arrival in Jerusalem (8.31–36)
5. Crisis concerning intermarriage with foreigners (9.1–2)
6. Ezra's public confession and prayer (9.3–15)

D. Covenant to renounce all intermarriages (10.1–14)

E. List of returnees who had intermarried (10.15–44)

[HINDY NAJMAN]

1 In the first year of King Cyrus of Persia, when the word of the
LORD spoken by Jeremiah was fulfilled,[a] the LORD roused the
spirit of King Cyrus of Persia to issue a proclamation throughout
his realm by word of mouth and in writing as follows:
2 "Thus said King Cyrus of Persia: The LORD God of Heaven
has given me all the kingdoms of the earth and has charged
me with building Him a house in Jerusalem, which is in Judah.
3 Anyone of you of all His people—may his God be with him,
and let him go up to Jerusalem that is in Judah and build the
House of the LORD God of Israel, the God that is in Jerusalem;
4 and all who stay behind, wherever he may be living, let the
people of his place assist him with silver, gold, goods, and livestock, besides the freewill offering to the House of God that is in
Jerusalem."
5 So the chiefs of the clans of Judah and Benjamin, and the
priests and Levites, all whose spirit had been roused by God,
got ready to go up to build the House of the LORD that is in Jerusalem. 6 All their neighbors supported them with silver vessels,
with gold, with goods, with livestock, and with precious objects, besides what had been given as a freewill offering. 7 King
Cyrus of Persia released the vessels of the LORD's house which

a *Cf. Jer.* 29.10.

1.1–4: Jeremiah's prophecy is fulfilled through the decree of King Cyrus of Persia. This introductory section, until the words *let him go up* (v. 3), also appears as 2 Chron. 36.22–23. **1:** *In the first year of King Cyrus of Persia:* Although Cyrus became king of Persia in 559 BCE, the v. refers to Cyrus's first year as the ruler of Babylonia, 539–538. Cyrus granted the nations under his control the right to worship their own gods and build their temples. This decree typifies the tolerant religious policy of the Persians. *When the word of the LORD spoken by Jeremiah was fulfilled:* Throughout the book of Jeremiah the people of Judah are instructed to accept as a divine decree Babylonian rule and exile from their land. In some of the Jeremianic prophecies Nebuchadnezzar is even identified as the servant of God. However, Jeremiah also prophesies that there will eventually be a return to Judah in which the people of Judah will rebuild the Temple (e.g., Jer. 29.4–10; 31.27–34; 32.36–44). In the Second Temple period Cyrus's decree was interpreted as the fulfillment of Jeremiah's prophecy; it is possible that this was seen as a specific fulfillment of Jer. ch 25, a widely cited ch in other books, that suggested that Babylonia would dominate the world for seventy years. *The LORD roused the spirit of King Cyrus of Persia:* The intimate relationship between the LORD and Cyrus is emphasized in Isa. 44.28, where the LORD says, "He is my shepherd; He shall fulfill all My purposes!" Josephus suggests that Cyrus knew this passage from Isa. (*Ant.* 11.1.2). Cyrus is also referred to as the anointed one of the LORD in Isa. 45.1. In rabbinic traditions Cyrus is praised as a sage for his decree of 538 which permitted the rebuilding of the Jerusalem Temple. Cyrus is also held up as a model in Gk writings of the Persian period. **3–4:** The narrative of Ezra understands Cyrus's decree to rebuild the Temple to require all of the Jewish exiles to support the rebuilding of the Temple, but not necessarily to return to Judah. It appears from Ezra-Nehemiah that many exiles were reluctant to give up the lives they had established for themselves in Babylonia and to return to Judah where their sustenance and future seemed less certain. *The God that is in Jerusalem:* This follows the typical ancient Near Eastern pattern in which gods are viewed as national deities, localized at their capitals. In rabbinic traditions Cyrus's wisdom is said to be limited because he appears to confine to Jerusalem the power of the God of Israel and thereby to deny God's dominion over the world (*Esth. Rab.* proem 6 and 1.5).

1.5–11: The exiles return to Judah with the original Temple vessels. 5–6: Whoever shares Cyrus's divine inspiration returns. Those who choose to remain in exile, although they support the rebuilding project financially, are implicitly

Nebuchadnezzar had taken away from Jerusalem and had put
in the house of his god. 8 These King Cyrus of Persia released
through the office of Mithredath the treasurer, who gave an
inventory of them to Sheshbazzar the prince of Judah. 9 This is
the inventory: 30 gold basins, 1,000 silver basins, 29 knives, 10 30
gold bowls, 410 silver [a]double bowls,[a] 1,000 other vessels; 11 in
all, 5,400 gold and silver vessels. Sheshbazzar brought all these
back when the exiles came back from Babylon to Jerusalem.

2 [b]These are the people of the province who came up from
among the captive exiles whom King Nebuchadnezzar of
Babylon had carried into exile to Babylon, who returned to
Jerusalem and Judah, each to his own city, 2 who came with
Zerubbabel, Jeshua, Nehemiah, Seraiah, Reelaiah, Mordecai,
Bilshan, Mispar, Bigvai, Rehum, Baanah:

The list of the men of the people of Israel: 3 the sons of Parosh—2,172; 4 the sons of Shephatiah—372; 5 the sons of Arah—
775; 6 the sons of Pahath-moab: the sons of Jeshua and Joab—2,812;
7 the sons of Elam—1,254; 8 the sons of Zattu—945; 9 the sons of
Zaccai—760; 10 the sons of Bani—642; 11 the sons of Bebai—623;
12 the sons of Azgad—1,222; 13 the sons of Adonikam—666; 14 the
sons of Bigvai—2,056; 15 the sons of Adin—454; 16 the sons of
Ater: Hezekiah—98; 17 the sons of Bezai—323; 18 the sons of Jo-
rah—112; 19 the sons of Hashum—223; 20 the sons of Gibbar—95;
21 the sons of Bethlehem—123; 22 the sons of Netophah—56; 23 the
sons of Anathoth—128; 24 the sons of Azmaveth—42; 25 the sons
of Kiriath-arim: Chephirah and Beeroth—743; 26 the sons of
Ramah and Geba—621; 27 the men of Michmas—122; 28 the men
of Beth-el and Ai—223; 29 the men of Nebo—52; 30 the sons of
Magbish—156; 31 the sons of the other Elam—1,254; 32 the sons of
Harim—320; 33 the sons of Lod, Hadid, and Ono—725; 34 the sons
of Jericho—345; 35 the sons of Senaah—3,630.

36 The priests: the sons of Jedaiah: the house of Jeshua—973;
37 the sons of Immer—1,052; 38 the sons of Pashhur—1,247;
39 the sons of Harim—1,017.

40 The Levites: the sons of Jeshua and Kadmiel: the sons of
Hodaviah—74.

a-a Meaning of Heb. uncertain.

b This chapter appears as Neh. 7.6–73 with variations in the names and numbers.

reproached. **7–11:** Cyrus's return of the Temple vessels is also reported in Ezra 5.14; 6.5. A corroborating account of Nebuchadnezzar's removal of the Temple vessels appears in 2 Chron. 36.10, 18. The removal is also reported in 2 Kings 24.13, but there it also notes that Nebuchadnezzar "stripped off" the gold from all of the Temple vessels. This is not mentioned in Ezra, which has as a major theme the continuity between the Second Temple and the preexilic past.

2.1–70: List of exiles who return to Jerusalem and Judah (= Neh. 7.6–72). Neh. 7.5 titles this list "the genealogical register of those who were the first to come up." Although both lists purport to record the same group of returnees, they exhibit significant differences. Scholars suggest that both lists were in fact compiled later than the first wave of return, on the basis of either censuses or tax registers. The present place of the lists thus exaggerates the extent of response to Cyrus's decree. The Rabbis ask why Ezra did not return to Jerusalem immediately following Cyrus's decree in 538 BCE, and suggest that Ezra delayed his return because he was deeply immersed in the study of Torah under the tutelage of Jeremiah's scribe, Baruch son of Neriah. Thus, according to the Rabbis, Ezra was correct to delay his return in order to better prepare himself in the area of Torah study, which takes precedence even over the rebuilding of the Temple (*b. Meg.* 16b; *Song Rab.* 5.5). This tradition reflects a general tendency in classical rabbinic thought to privilege Torah study over Temple service and worship, and to find virtue in situations that may raise questions. **2:** The genealogical record is prefaced by a list of prominent returnees. It is unclear whether these leaders returned together. *Zerubbabel,* governor of the province of Judah during the reign of Darius I. Intimately involved in the rebuilding of the Temple, Zerubbabel is mentioned in the narratives of Haggai and Zechariah as the person who will finish the work of rebuilding the Temple. Yet he vanishes from the scene and is never heard of again. There is some speculation that he was removed by the Persians because he was perceived to be too powerful, especially since he was a descendant of the Davidic king Jehoiachin. In some rabbinic traditions, Zerubbabel becomes an Elijah-like figure who will explain the unanswered questions of Torah study in the time to come. Other rabbinic traditions identify him as one of the men of the great assembly, a group of sages imagined by the later Rabbis to have functioned as a judicial body in this period and

41 The singers: the sons of Asaph—128.
42 The gatekeepers: the sons of Shallum, the sons of Ater, the sons of Talmon, the sons of Akkub, the sons of Hatita, the sons of Shobai, all told—139.
43 The temple servants: the sons of Ziha, the sons of Hasupha, the sons of Tabbaoth, 44 the sons of Keros, the sons of Siaha, the sons of Padon, 45 the sons of Lebanah, the sons of Hagabah, the sons of Akkub, 46 the sons of Hagab, the sons of Salmai, the sons of Hanan, 47 the sons of Giddel, the sons of Gahar, the sons of Reaiah, 48 the sons of Rezin, the sons of Nekoda, the sons of Gazzam, 49 the sons of Uzza, the sons of Paseah, the sons of Besai, 50 the sons of Asnah, the sons of Meunim, the sons of Nephusim, 51 the sons of Bakbuk, the sons of Hakupha, the sons of Harhur, 52 the sons of Bazluth, the sons of Mehida, the sons of Harsha, 53 the sons of Barkos, the sons of Sisera, the sons of Temah, 54 the sons of Neziah, the sons of Hatipha.
55 The sons of Solomon's servants: the sons of Sotai, the sons of Hassophereth, the sons of Peruda, 56 the sons of Jaalah, the sons of Darkon, the sons of Giddel, 57 the sons of Shephatiah, the sons of Hattil, the sons of Pochereth-hazzebaim, the sons of Ami.
58 The total of temple servants and the sons of Solomon's servants—392.
59 The following were those who came up from Tel-melah, Tel-harsha, Cherub, Addan, and Immer—they were unable to tell whether their father's house and descent were Israelite:
60 the sons of Delaiah, the sons of Tobiah, the sons of Nekoda—652.
61 Of the sons of the priests, the sons of Habaiah, the sons of Hakkoz, the sons of Barzillai who had married a daughter of Barzillai and had taken his[a] name—
62 these searched for their genealogical records, but they could not be found, so they were disqualified for the priesthood.
63 The Tirshatha[b] ordered them not to eat of the most holy things until a priest with Urim and Thummim should appear.
64 The sum of the entire community was 42,360,
65 not counting their male and female servants, those being 7,337; they also had 200 male and female singers.
66 Their horses—736; their mules—245;
67 their camels—435; their asses—6,720.
68 Some of the chiefs of the clans, on arriving at the House of the LORD in Jerusalem, gave a freewill offering to erect the House of God on its site.
69 In accord with their means, they donated to the treasury of the work: gold—6,100 drachmas, silver—5,000 minas, and priestly robes—100.
70 The priests, the Levites and some of the people, and the singers, gatekeepers, and the temple servants took up residence in their towns and all Israel in their towns.

a *Lit. "their."* *b* *A Persian title.*

who served as an important link in the transmission of the Torah from biblical to rabbinic times. Zerubbabel is also said to have succeeded Daniel in the service of Darius I and is said, like Daniel, to be an interpreter of secrets, signs, and dreams. In another tradition he is said to be identical with Nehemiah (*b. Sanh.* 38a). *Jeshua,* the head of a prominent priestly family who returns from exile with Zerubbabel. He is credited with reinstituting the ritual functions of the priesthood and with rebuilding the altar. According to 1 Chron. 5.41, Jeshua is the descendant of Jozadak, the last high priest, who was exiled by Nebuchadnezzar to Babylonia. Thus, Jeshua's genealogical connection to the preexilic priesthood authorizes him to re-establish the rituals of the priestly practices. In Haggai and Zechariah, but not in Ezra-Nehemiah, he is called "high priest." *Mordecai,* named after the Babylonian god, Marduk. Some rabbinic sources suggest that this is the same Mordecai mentioned in the book of Esther and that he returned to Judah with the exiles mentioned in ch 2, though this is unlikely. *Bigvai,* the governor of the province of Judah 410–407 BCE, also listed as the leader of a prominent family in Neh. 7.19, and is connected to the covenant in Neh. 10.17. **41:** *Asaph:* The Asaphites are a group of musicians from the tribe of Levi. Pss. 50 and 73–83 are attributed to Asaph, and the Asaphites are also mentioned in 1 Chron. 6.24; 16.5–7, 37; 25.2, 9; 2 Chron. 5.12. **62:** The search for accurate and convincing genealogical connection is a theme throughout Ezra-Nehemiah, reflecting the growing concern for preserving hierarchy and lineage that persisted throughout the exilic and postexilic periods. On the disqualification of questionable priests from the eating of "terumah" (sacred gifts belonging to the priests), see *b. Ketub.* 24b; *b. Kid.* 69b. **63:** *Tirshatha,* an Old Persian term meaning "revered," often taken to mean governor in rabbinic traditions. 1 Esd. 5.40 and later rabbinic tradition understand *Tirshatha* to be

3 When the seventh month arrived—the Israelites being settled in their towns—the entire people assembled as one
man in Jerusalem. 2 Then Jeshua son of Jozadak and his brother priests, and Zerubbabel son of Shealtiel and his brothers set
to and built the altar of the God of Israel to offer burnt offerings
upon it as is written in the Teaching of Moses, the man of God.
3 They set up the altar on its site because they were in fear of
the peoples of the land, and they offered burnt offerings on it
to the LORD, burnt offerings each morning and evening. 4 Then
they celebrated the festival of Tabernacles as is written, with
its daily burnt offerings in the proper quantities, on each day
as is prescribed for it, 5 followed by the regular burnt offering
and the offerings for the new moons and for all the sacred fixed
times of the LORD, and whatever freewill offerings were made
to the LORD. 6 From the first day of the seventh month they began to make burnt offerings to the LORD, though the foundation of the Temple of the LORD had not been laid. 7 They paid
the hewers and craftsmen with money, and the Sidonians and
Tyrians with food, drink, and oil to bring cedarwood from Lebanon by sea to Joppa, in accord with the authorization granted
them by King Cyrus of Persia.

8 In the second year after their arrival at the House of God, at
Jerusalem, in the second month, Zerubbabel son of Shealtiel
and Jeshua son of Jozadak, and the rest of their brother priests
and Levites, and all who had come from the captivity to Jerusalem, as their first step appointed Levites from the age of twenty

referring to Nehemiah in his role as governor (see Rashi's commentary to *b. Ketub.* 24b in a discussion of Ezra 2.62). *Urim and Thummim:* These were used to divine the opinion of God and were consulted on a variety of matters. See, e.g., Exod. 28.30; Lev. 8.8; Num. 27.21; Deut. 33.8; and 1 Sam. 28.6. Rabbinic tradition does not understand Ezra 2.63 to suggest actual postexilic use of the Urim and Thummim. It is unclear why this system of lot setting was not re-established in this period, though the Rabbis suggest that the Urim and Thummim are akin to prophecy and are thus considered to have become unusable once prophecy ceased, after the latter prophets (Haggai, Zechariah, and Malachi), or perhaps even after the former prophets (*b. Sot.* 48a). Although Ezra lived after the time of prophecy, he is nevertheless said by the Rabbis to have been worthy of receiving divine inspiration "ruaḥ hakodesh," the holy spirit (*t. Sot.* 13.3). Nonetheless, in rabbinic interpretation, even Ezra could not resolve genealogical questions about all those who claimed to be priests.

3.1–7: Resuming Temple ritual and sacrifice on Sukkot (festival of Booths). The returnees are preparing to celebrate the festival of Booths in Tishri, the seventh month. According to 2 Chron. 7.8, the dedication of Solomon's Temple took place during the festival of Tabernacles. Ezra deliberately invokes preexilic Temple practice in order to authorize the Second Temple as an authentic restoration of the First Temple. **1:** The building begins under the governorship of Sheshbazzar (1.8–14; 5.14–16). After an interruption, the building resumes under the governorship of Zerubbabel and the priestly instruction of Jeshua. Some scholars identify Zerubbabel with Sheshbazzar because both are credited with building the Second Temple. However, it seems most likely that Sheshbazzar initiated the rebuilding and that Zerubbabel completed it. **2:** The combination of *Jeshua,* the priest, and *Zerubbabel,* a governor of Davidic descent, establishes an authoritative link to preexilic times; though in preexilic texts such close cooperation between the Davidic king and the Aaronide (high) priest is rarely recorded. There is no king because Judah remained under Persian sovereignty. *Teaching:* The returnees understand themselves to live in accordance with the very same law and Temple ritual that governed the preexilic community in Judah. The exact nature of this Teaching or Torah is unclear from the texts in Ezra-Nehemiah, though it seems likely to be very similar to the current form of the Torah. **3:** *They set up the altar:* In later midrashic traditions, the Rabbis point out that the altar was prioritized, not only in Ezra, but also when the Israelites first entered the land in Josh. 8.31 (*Midr. Ha-gadol,* Yitro [Exod.] 20.21). Ezra-Nehemiah repeatedly alludes to Joshua's conquest in order to authorize the returnees' claim to the land. *Because they were in fear of the peoples:* The returnees are intimidated by the hostile behavior of the local peoples, and are offering sacrifices to God in order to appeal for divine protection. This conflict between the returnees and the local people, many of whom were likely Judahites who were not exiled to Babylonia, is a major theme of the book. 1 Esd. 5.50, in contrast, mentions that some of the local peoples joined Ezra in the rededication. **4:** See Num. 29.12–32 for a detailed description of the prescribed sacrifices. **7:** Note the echoes of Solomon's practices: 1 Kings 5.15–32; 2 Chron. 2.2–4.22.

3.8–9: Reappointing priests and Levites to conduct the service in the house of God. 8: *Age of twenty:* This age limit also appears in the divisions of the Levites in 1 Chron.

and upward to supervise the work of the House of the LORD.
9 Jeshua, his sons and brothers, Kadmiel and his sons, [a]the
sons of Judah,[a] together were appointed in charge of those
who did the work in the House of God; also the sons of Henadad, their sons and brother Levites.
10 When the builders had laid the foundation of the Temple
of the LORD, priests in their vestments with trumpets, and Levites sons of Asaph with cymbals were stationed to give praise
to the LORD, as King David of Israel had ordained. 11 They sang
songs extolling and praising the LORD, [b]"For He is good, His
steadfast love for Israel is eternal."[b] All the people raised a
great shout extolling the LORD because the foundation of the
House of the LORD had been laid. 12 Many of the priests and
Levites and the chiefs of the clans, the old men who had seen
the first house, wept loudly at the sight of the founding of this
house. Many others shouted joyously at the top of their voices. 13 The people could not distinguish the shouts of joy from
the people's weeping, for the people raised a great shout, the
sound of which could be heard from afar.

4 When the adversaries of Judah and Benjamin heard that
the returned exiles were building a temple to the LORD
God of Israel, 2 they approached Zerubbabel and the chiefs of
the clans and said to them, "Let us build with you, since we
too worship your God, having offered sacrifices to Him since
the time of King Esarhaddon of Assyria, who brought us here."
3 Zerubbabel, Jeshua, and the rest of the chiefs of the clans of
Israel answered them, "It is not for you and us to build a House
to our God, but we alone will build it to the LORD God of Israel,
in accord with the charge that the king, King Cyrus of Persia,
laid upon us." 4 Thereupon the people of the land undermined
the resolve of the people of Judah, and made them afraid to
build. 5 They bribed ministers in order to thwart their plans all
the years of King Cyrus of Persia and until the reign of King
Darius of Persia.

a-a I.e., Hodaviah of 2.40. *b-b Cf. Pss. 106.1; 136.*

23.24, 27. **3.10–13: Laying the foundations for the Temple and the dedication. 10:** *As King David of Israel had ordained:* David's authority with respect to Temple sacrifice and practice is also invoked, e.g., in Neh. 12.45; 1 Chron. 6.31; 15.1–24; 16.4–42; 25.1; 2 Chron. 29.25, 30; 35.4. **11:** *They sang songs extolling and praising the LORD, "For He is good, His steadfast love ... is eternal":* This phrase, found in several psalms (106.1; 107.1; 118.1, 29; 136.1) became particularly prominent in Second Temple liturgy (see 1 Chron. 16.34; 2 Chron. 5.13; 7.3). **12–13:** Although continuity with preexilic practices is emphasized, the loss of the First Temple and its glory is still mourned. Cf. the returnees' response to the dedication of the walls in Neh. 12.43. Josephus emphasizes the irrevocable loss of the First Temple by interpreting the v. to mean that the sound of the elders and priests wailing was louder than the sound of joy and trumpets (*Ant.* 11.4.2). Similarly, the Rabbis interpret these vv. to suggest that the majority of the returnees could recall the First Temple and its glory.

4.1–5: Building is interrupted during the reign of Cyrus. 1: *Adversaries of Judah and Benjamin:* The adversaries are presumably the same peoples of the land who are harassing and intimidating the returnees. See 3.3. **2:** *King Esarhaddon of Assyria* (681–669 BCE): This seems to reflect the resettlement of people from elsewhere in the Assyrian empire by Esarhaddon, after the exile of the Northern Kingdom of Israel to the Assyrian empire in 722 BCE, when Shalmaneser V was king. In subsequent Assyrian campaigns, foreign nations were resettled in northern Israel by Esarhaddon and later by Osnappar (see 4.10 n.). Cf. 2 Kings 17.6, 24–44. **3:** *In accord with the charge that the king, King Cyrus of Persia:* The returnees use the decree of Cyrus in their struggle to preserve control over the rebuilding of the Temple and the wall, over the ritual practices, and over the genealogical purity of the reconstituted community in Judah. Josephus explains that only the returnees, namely the Jews, were permitted to participate in the rebuilding of the Temple, while the local peoples were told that they were permitted to worship at the Temple once it was completed (*Ant.* 11.4.3). Rabbinic interpretations justify the exclusion of the local peoples by claiming either that they were not descendants of Israel but Cutheans (*Pirqe R. El.* 38), or that they were idol worshippers (*b. 'Arak.* 5b) and therefore prohibited from involvement in the rebuilding and rededication of the Temple.

4.6–24: Opposition to building during the reigns of Xerxes and Artaxerxes. The narrative shifts forward in time, giving a more extensive account of the complaints raised by local peoples against the recent returnees. The letter recorded here is dated to the period after Darius I (522–486 BCE), prior to Ezra's mission. The section in 4.8–6.18 incorporating several official Aram. documents is in Aram., the lingua franca of this period. **6:** *In the reign of Ahasuerus:* This is apparently Xerxes (486–465), who ruled over Persia after Darius I. Rabbinic interpretations identify Artaxerxes with the Persian king in the book of Esther. **10:** The name *Osnappar* does not occur in the Assyrian chronicles, and is most likely a corruption of the name of the Assyrian king, Assurbanipal (669–627), who immediately succeeded Esarhaddon (681–669). *Beyond the River:* This large Persian province was west of the Euphrates River and extended as far as Egypt (including Judah). **11:** *King Artaxerxes:* This is Artaxerxes I Longimanus (Long Hand), who ruled 465–424. **14:** *We eat the salt of the palace,* an expression signifying the common interests of loyal allies. Apparently an oath was taken and solemnized through participation in a common meal. **15:** *Search the records of your fathers:* The book relies heavily on official documents. Artaxerxes (465–424) is asked to consult the Babylonian and Assyrian chronicles for records of the rebellions and eventual exiles of both the Northern Kingdom of Israel and the Southern Kingdom of Judah. He is asked, in particular, for records of the Judean rebellions against Babylonia and Nebuchadnezzar's eventual destruction of Jerusalem. **16:** This is the crux of their argument: The province of Yehud will rebel, trying to assert its independence, and others will follow suit. **17–22:** In rabbinic traditions both Darius I and Artaxerxes are identified with Cyrus (see 6.14 n.). Cyrus is therefore regarded as retracting the permission to rebuild the Temple which he had previously granted, hence losing his wisdom and becoming a fool (*Eccl. Rab.* 10.1).

6 And in the reign of Ahasuerus, at the start of his reign, they
drew up an accusation against the inhabitants of Judah and Jerusalem.

7 And in the time of Artaxerxes, Bishlam, Mithredath, Tabeel,
and the rest of their colleagues wrote to King Artaxerxes of Persia, a letter written in Aramaic and translated.[a]

Aramaic:[b] 8 Rehum the commissioner and Shimshai the
scribe wrote a letter concerning Jerusalem to King Artaxerxes
as follows: ([c]9 Then Rehum the commissioner and Shimshai
the scribe, and the rest of their colleagues, the judges, officials, officers, and overseers, the men of Erech, and of Babylon, and of Susa—that is the Elamites—10 and other peoples
whom the great and glorious Osnappar deported and settled
in the city of Samaria and the rest of the province Beyond the
River [wrote]—and now 11 this is the text of the letter which
they sent to him:)—"To King Artaxerxes [from] your servants, men of the province Beyond the River. And now 12 be
it known to the king that the Jews who came up from you to
us have reached Jerusalem and are rebuilding that rebellious
and wicked city; they are completing the walls and repairing
the foundation. 13 Now be it known to the king that if this city
is rebuilt and the walls completed, they will not pay tribute,
poll-tax, or land-tax, and in the end it will harm the kingdom.
14 Now since we eat the salt of the palace, and it is not right
that we should see the king dishonored, we have written to
advise the king [of this] 15 so that you may search the records
of your fathers and find in the records and know that this city
is a rebellious city, harmful to kings and states. Sedition has
been rife in it from early times; on that account this city was
destroyed. 16 We advise the king that if this city is rebuilt and
its walls are completed, you will no longer have any portion in
the province Beyond the River."

17 The king sent back the following message: "To Rehum the
commissioner and Shimshai the scribe, and the rest of their
colleagues, who dwell in Samaria and in the rest of the province of Beyond the River, greetings. 18 Now the letter that you
wrote me has been read to me in translation.[d] 19 At my order a
search has been made, and it has been found that this city has
from earliest times risen against kings, and that rebellion and
sedition have been rife in it. 20 Powerful kings have ruled over
Jerusalem and exercised authority over the whole province of
Beyond the River, and tribute, poll-tax, and land-tax were paid
to them. 21 Now issue an order to stop these men; this city is

a *Cf. below v. 18 and note d.*
b *A note indicating that what follows is in the Aramaic language.*
c *Vv. 9–11 amplify v. 8.* d *I.e., from Aramaic to Persian.*

not to be rebuilt until I so order. 22 Take care not to be lax in this matter or there will be much damage and harm to the kingdom."

23 When the text of the letter of King Artaxerxes was read before Rehum and Shimshai the scribe and their colleagues, they hurried to Jerusalem, to the Jews, and stopped them by main force. 24 At that time, work on the House of God in Jerusalem stopped and remained in abeyance until the second year of the reign of King Darius of Persia.

5 Then the prophets, Haggai the prophet and Zechariah son of Iddo, prophesied to the Jews in Judah and Jerusalem, [a]inspired by the God of Israel.[a] 2 Thereupon Zerubbabel son of Shealtiel and Jeshua son of Jozadak began rebuilding the House of God in Jerusalem, with the full support of the prophets of God. 3 At once Tattenai, governor of the province of Beyond the River, Shethar-bozenai, and their colleagues descended upon them and said this to them, "Who issued orders to you to rebuild this house and complete its furnishing?" 4 Then we[b] said to them, "What are the names of the men who are engaged in the building?" 5 But God watched over the elders of the Jews and they were not stopped while a report went to Darius and a letter was sent back in reply to it.

6 This is the text of the letter that Tattenai, governor of the province of Beyond the River, and Shethar-bozenai and his colleagues, the officials of Beyond the River, sent to King Darius. 7 They sent a message to him and this is what was written in it: "To King Darius, greetings, and so forth. 8 Be it known to the king, that we went to the province of Judah, to the house of the great God. It is being rebuilt of hewn stone, and wood is being laid in the walls. The work is being done with dispatch and is going well. 9 Thereupon we directed this question to these elders, 'Who issued orders to you to rebuild this house and to complete its furnishings?' 10 We also asked their names so that we could write down the names of their leaders for your information. 11 This is what they answered us: 'We are the servants of the God of heaven and earth; we are rebuilding the house that was originally built many years ago; a great king of Israel built it and completed it. 12 But because our fathers angered the God of Heaven, He handed them over to Nebuchadnezzar the Chaldean, king of Babylon, who demolished this house and exiled the people to Babylon. 13 But in the first year of King Cyrus of Babylon, King Cyrus issued an order to rebuild this House of God. 14 Also the silver and gold vessels of the House of God that Nebuchadnezzar had taken away from the temple

a-a *Lit. "with the name of the God of Israel upon them."*

b *The officials of v. 3; cf. v. 10. Greek and Syriac read "they."*

23: *Stopped them by main force:* Neh. 1.3 suggests that the objectors not only prevented further rebuilding, but also destroyed what had already been built. **24:** *The second year of the reign of King Darius of Persia:* Here Ezra-Nehemiah resumes the narrative of 4.5, returning to the resumption of building in the time of Darius.

5.1–2: Under Darius's reign the rebuilding of the Temple resumes and is completed. 2: *With the full support of the prophets of God:* The rebuilding of the Temple by Zerubbabel and Jeshua is connected to the divine prophecy received by Haggai and Zechariah (v. 1), which is preserved in the books by those names.

5.3–17: Tattenai writes to Darius and questions the authenticity of the returnees' claim. 3: *Tattenai:* During the reign of Darius, Tattenai is the *governor of the province of Beyond the River.* As is clear from 6.13, Tattenai adheres to the ruling of Darius and does not interfere with the rebuilding of the Jerusalem Temple. *Shethar-bozenai:* This name always appears just after Tattenai. Some scholars suggest that this is an official title of Tattenai; others suggest that it was the name of Tattenai's official scribe. **6:** *King Darius:* Darius I ruled the Persian empire 522–486 BCE. He is highly regarded for extending Cyrus's generous policy toward non-Persian peoples. **11:** *God of heaven and earth,* a very universalistic expression, appropriate when identifying God to non-Judahites. The narrative of Ezra recalls the building of the first, preexilic Temple in order to authorize and justify the building of the Second Temple. The *great king* is Solomon.

14: *Sheshbazzar* is the first governor of Judah under Cyrus. His appointment began at the time of Cyrus's decree in 538; see 3.1 n. 1 Esd. 6.18 inserts Zerubbabel in this v. as having received gifts along with Sheshbazzar.

6.1–5: Locating Cyrus's decree in the citadel of Ecbatana. 2: *Citadel of Ecbatana,* an important center for the Persian empire. Perhaps the phrase refers to the general area of Ecbatana (modern Hamadan) rather than a location within Ecbatana. The citadel of Ecbatana was a summer palace in the eastern part of the Persian empire. Although mentioned nowhere else in the Bible, Ecbatana is mentioned in three apocryphal traditions: 2 Macc. 9.3; Jdt. 1.1, 2, 14; and many times in Tobit. **4:** *The expenses shall be paid by the palace:* In contrast, according to the Heb version in Ezra ch 1, the Temple is paid for by the Judahite exiles, not by the Persian government. This is one of several discrepancies, sometimes irreconcilable, in Ezra-Nehemiah. These may reflect conflicting accounts or records.

6.6–12: Response of Darius. Darius's reply to Tattenai seems not to reflect an actual historical event, but rather to be an elaboration of Cyrus's decree of 538 BCE.

in Jerusalem and brought to the temple in Babylon—King
Cyrus released them from the temple in Babylon to be given to
the one called Sheshbazzar whom he had appointed governor.
15 He said to him, "Take these vessels, go, deposit them in the
temple in Jerusalem, and let the House of God be rebuilt on its
original site." 16 That same Sheshbazzar then came and laid the
foundations for the House of God in Jerusalem; and ever since
then it has been under construction, but is not yet finished.'
17 And now, if it please the king, let the royal archives there in
Babylon be searched to see whether indeed an order had been
issued by King Cyrus to rebuild this House of God in Jerusalem. May the king convey to us his pleasure in this matter."

6 Thereupon, at the order of King Darius, they searched
the archives where the treasures were stored in Babylon.
2 But it was in the citadel of Ecbatana, in the province of Media, that a scroll was found in which the following was written:
"Memorandum: 3 In the first year of King Cyrus, King Cyrus
issued an order concerning the House of God in Jerusalem:
'Let the house be rebuilt, a place for offering sacrifices, with
a base built up high. Let it be sixty cubits high and sixty cubits
wide, 4 with a course of unused timber for each three courses
of hewn stone. The expenses shall be paid by the palace. 5 And
the gold and silver vessels of the House of God which Nebuchadnezzar had taken away from the temple in Jerusalem and
transported to Babylon shall be returned, and let each go back
to the temple in Jerusalem where it belongs; you shall deposit
it in the House of God.'

6 "Now[a] you, Tattenai, governor of the province of Beyond
the River, Shethar-bozenai and colleagues, the officials of the
province of Beyond the River, stay away from that place. 7 Allow the work of this House of God to go on; let the governor of
the Jews and the elders of the Jews rebuild this House of God
on its site. 8 And I hereby issue an order concerning what you
must do to help these elders of the Jews rebuild this House of
God: the expenses are to be paid to these men with dispatch
out of the resources of the king, derived from the taxes of the
province of Beyond the River, so that the work not be stopped.
9 They are to be given daily, without fail, whatever they need
of young bulls, rams, or lambs as burnt offerings for the God
of Heaven, and wheat, salt, wine, and oil, at the order of the
priests in Jerusalem, 10 so that they may offer pleasing sacrifices to the God of Heaven and pray for the life of the king and
his sons. 11 I also issue an order that whoever alters this decree
shall have a beam removed from his house, and he shall be

a This introduces the text of the reply of Darius that doubtless contained the preceding narrative (vv. 1–5) as a preliminary.

impaled on it and his house confiscated.[a] [12]And may the God
who established His name there cause the downfall of any king
or nation that undertakes to alter or damage that House of God
in Jerusalem. I, Darius, have issued the decree; let it be carried
out with dispatch."

[13]Then Tattenai, governor of the province of Beyond the
River, Shethar-bozenai, and their colleagues carried out with
dispatch what King Darius had written. [14]So the elders of the
Jews progressed in the building, urged on by the prophesying
of Haggai the prophet and Zechariah son of Iddo, and they
brought the building to completion under the aegis of the
God of Israel and by the order of Cyrus and Darius and King
Artaxerxes of Persia. [15]The house was finished on the third of
the month of Adar in the sixth year of the reign of King Darius.
[16]The Israelites, the priests, and the Levites, and all the other
exiles celebrated the dedication of the House of God with joy.
[17]And they sacrificed for the dedication of this House of God
one hundred bulls, two hundred rams, four hundred lambs,
and twelve goats as a purification offering for all of Israel, according to the number of the tribes of Israel. [18]They appointed
the priests in their courses and the Levites in their divisions for
the service of God in Jerusalem, according to the prescription
in the Book of Moses.

[19][b]The returned exiles celebrated the Passover on the fourteenth day of the first month, [20]for the priests and Levites had
purified themselves to a man; they were all pure. They slaughtered the passover offering for all the returned exiles, and for
their brother priests and for themselves. [21]The children of Israel who had returned from the exile, together with all who
joined them in separating themselves from the uncleanliness
of the nations of the lands to worship the LORD God of Israel,
ate of it. [22]They joyfully celebrated the Feast of Unleavened
Bread for seven days, for the LORD had given them cause for
joy by inclining the heart of the Assyrian king toward them so
as to give them support in the work of the House of God, the
God of Israel.

a *Meaning uncertain; or "turned into ruins."* b *Hebrew resumes here.*

6.13–18: Completion of the Temple and its dedication. 14: *By the order of Cyrus and Darius and King Artaxerxes of Persia:* Rabbinic interpretations suggest that these three names refer to the very same king of Persia. This leads to a significant misrepresentation of Persian chronology in rabbinic traditions (*Seder 'Olam Rab.* 30; *b. Rosh Hash.* 3b). **15:** *The house was finished on the third of the month of Adar:* 1 Esd. 7.5 and *Ant.* 11.4.7 mention the twenty-third of Adar as the day of completion. **18:** *They appointed the priests in their courses and the Levites in their divisions for the service of God in Jerusalem, according to the prescription in the Book of Moses:* The courses of priests and divisions of Levites are not mentioned in any preexilic or exilic tradition, suggesting that this is an attempt to legitimate a later institution by false connection to the Torah. In 2 Chron. 35.4–5 the organization of the priests is also said to be preexilic, but is attributed to David and Solomon, not to Moses.

6.19–22: Celebration of the festival of Passover. The text returns to Heb from 6.19 through 7.11. In Josh. 5.10 the Israelites were able to offer the Passover sacrifice following their circumcision. Here too, purification is followed by the Passover sacrifice. Priestly texts in particular, which became notably authoritative in this period, suggest the importance of eating the Passover offering in a state of ritual purity (Num. 9.6–13; see also "Concepts of Purity," pp. 1998–2005). **21:** On the Passover celebration, cf. Exod. 12.16–51; Lev. 23.4–8; Num. 28.16–25; Deut. 16.1–8. As in some of these texts, the practice here reflects a one-day Passover celebration, followed by a seven-day "Matzot" (unleavened bread) festival (see esp. Lev. 23.5–8). **22:** *They joyfully celebrated the Feast of Unleavened Bread:* Cf. this to 2 Chron. 30.21, describing Hezekiah's Passover, and 2 Chron. 35.17, describing Josiah's Passover—the continuity between First and Second Temple practice is again emphasized. *The LORD had given them cause for joy by inclining the heart of the Assyrian king toward them:* Just as Cyrus is said in Ezra 1.1 to be inspired by the LORD, so is Darius's decree said to be under divine influence. Josephus refers to the "Persian king," not to the *Assyrian king,* in his retelling of the Ezra narrative (*Ant.* 11.4.8). Perhaps the reference to Assyria here alludes to the continuity between the Assyrian empire which destroyed the Northern Kingdom (722 BCE), the Babylonian empire which destroyed the Southern Kingdom (586 BCE), and the Persian empire which now fulfills the divine promise of restoration.

7 After these events, during the reign of King Artaxerxes of
Persia, Ezra son of Seraiah son of Azariah son of Hilkiah
2 son of Shallum son of Zadok son of Ahitub 3 son of Amariah
son of Azariah son of Meraioth 4 son of Zerahiah son of Uzzi
son of Bukki 5 son of Abishua son of Phinehas son of Eleazar
son of Aaron the chief priest—6 that Ezra came up from Babylon, a scribe expert in the Teaching of Moses which the LORD
God of Israel had given, whose request the king had granted in
its entirety, thanks to the benevolence of the LORD toward him.
(7 Some of the Israelites, the priests and Levites, the singers,
the gatekeepers, and the temple servants set out for Jerusalem
in the seventh year of King Artaxerxes, 8 arriving in Jerusalem
in the fifth month in the seventh year of the king.) 9 On the first
day of the first month the journey up from Babylon was started,
and on the first day of the fifth month he arrived in Jerusalem,
thanks to the benevolent care of his God for him. 10 For Ezra
had dedicated himself to study the Teaching of the LORD so as
to observe it, and to teach laws and rules to Israel.

11 The following is the text of the letter which King Artaxerxes
gave Ezra the priest-scribe, a scholar in matters concerning the
commandments of the LORD and His laws to Israel:

12 [a]"Artaxerxes king of kings, to Ezra the priest, scholar in the
law of the God of heaven, [b-]and so forth.[-b] And now, 13 I hereby
issue an order that anyone in my kingdom who is of the people
of Israel and its priests and Levites who feels impelled to go to
Jerusalem may go with you. 14 For you are commissioned by
the king and his seven advisers to regulate Judah and Jerusalem according to the law of your God, which is in your care,
15 and to bring the freewill offering of silver and gold, which

a Aramaic resumes here through v. 26. *b-b Meaning uncertain.*

7.1–10: Ezra joins the Jerusalem returnees. The introduction to Ezra's mission illustrates what was considered necessary to preserve and perpetuate the newly reconstituted Jerusalem community. The information that is included is intended to demonstrate that Ezra possessed the required authority and sufficient preparation for the job. First, Ezra is included in the Aaronide line of priests and is therefore a priest with the highest pedigree, authorized to conduct Temple sacrifice and ritual, perhaps even a high priest himself. (It is odd, however, that Ezra is never included in any of the high priestly lineages.) Second, Ezra is a scribe who is an "expert in the Teaching of Moses" (v. 6). He therefore provides an authoritative link to the returnees' preexilic past. Third, Ezra is said to have "dedicated himself to study the Teaching of the LORD" (v. 10). Thus, Ezra is prepared for the task of interpreting, explaining, and applying the ancient law to a new context in which Israel is ruled, not by a Davidic monarch, but by a Persian king. Finally, Ezra is said to be in the favor of the LORD (v. 6) and of God (v. 9). Ezra continues to be celebrated in later Jewish traditions, and is often compared to Ezekiel and Moses. See, for example, *t. Sanh.* 4.4: "Ezra was sufficiently worthy that the Torah could have been given through him if Moses had not preceded him." **1–5:** Ezra's lineage establishes authentic priestly credentials. The Rabbis write that if Aaron had been living during the time of Ezra, he would have been considered inferior to Ezra (*Eccl. Rab.* 1.4). **6:** Ezra will assume the position of instructor of the people in the *Teaching of Moses;* thus it is very important to establish his reliability as a scribe and knowledge of the text itself (see v. 10) early in Ezra's memoir (Ezra chs 7–10). *Came up:* Rabbinic interpretation makes an analogy between Moses and Ezra and states that just as Moses went up to Sinai to receive the Torah, so too Ezra went up to Jerusalem to receive the Torah (*b. Sanh.* 21b). *A scribe expert in the Teaching of Moses:* Some rabbinic traditions attribute the special markings over selected words in the Bible to the hand of Ezra, who, as the expert scribe, was privy to secret interpretive traditions concerning Mosaic Torah (*Num. Rab.* 3.13). **7–8:** The *seventh year* of Artaxerxes I Longimanus is 458 BCE. **9:** Ezra is perhaps alluding to the exodus from Egypt, which also occurred in the first month of the year. If so, as in Deutero-Isaiah (e.g., Isa. 52.12), the return of the Babylonian exiles is implicitly connected to the Israelites' original journey to the promised land after their enslavement and years of wandering in the desert. In addition, the celebration of the first and subsequent Passovers also occurred in the first month (Exod. 12.2; Num. 33.3). **10:** The language in this passage is highly influenced by Deut.; cf. e.g., Deut. 4.14. Ezra is here envisioned as a lawgiver like Moses, who will provide the people with the law along with its "correct" interpretation. According to the Rabbis, Ezra restored the Torah to the Assyrian script (the Heb letters in their current form, not their older, paleo-Heb form) in which it was originally given to Moses (*b. Sanh.* 21b).

7.11–26: Artaxerxes' letter commissioning Ezra's mission. **12–26:** The narrative at this point is written in Aram. and purports to preserve the correspondence between the Persian kings and their officials in Judah.

the king and his advisers made to the God of Israel, whose
dwelling is in Jerusalem, [16] and whatever silver and gold that
you find throughout the province of Babylon, together with
the freewill offerings that the people and the priests will give
for the House of their God, which is in Jerusalem. [17] You shall,
therefore, with dispatch acquire with this money bulls, rams,
and lambs, with their meal offerings and libations, and offer them on the altar of the House of your God in Jerusalem.
[18] And whatever you wish to do with the leftover silver and
gold, you and your kinsmen may do, in accord with the will
of your God. [19] The vessels for the service of the House of your
God that are given to you, deliver to God in Jerusalem, [20] and
any other needs of the House of your God that it falls to you to
supply, do so from the royal treasury. [21] I, King Artaxerxes, for
my part, hereby issue an order to all the treasurers in the province of Beyond the River that whatever request Ezra the priest,
scholar in the law of the God of Heaven, makes of you is to be
fulfilled with dispatch [22] up to the sum of one hundred talents
of silver, one hundred *kor* of wheat, one hundred *bath* of wine,
one hundred *bath* of oil, and salt without limit. [23] Whatever is
by order of the God of Heaven must be carried out diligently
for the House of the God of Heaven, else wrath will come upon
the king and his sons. [24] We further advise you that it is not permissible to impose tribute, poll tax, or land tax on any priest,
Levite, singer, gatekeeper, temple servant, or other servant of
this House of God. [25] And you, Ezra, by the divine wisdom you
possess, appoint magistrates and judges to judge all the people
in the province of Beyond the River who know the laws of your
God, and to teach those who do not know them. [26] Let anyone
who does not obey the law of your God and the law of the king
be punished with dispatch, whether by death, corporal punishment, confiscation of possessions, or imprisonment."
[27] [a]Blessed is the LORD God of our fathers, who put it into the
mind of the king to glorify the House of the LORD in Jerusalem,
[28] and who inclined the king and his counselors and the king's
military officers to be favorably disposed toward me. For my
part, thanks to the care of the LORD for me, I summoned up
courage and assembled leading men in Israel to go with me.

8 These are the chiefs of the clans and the register of the genealogy of those who came up with me from Babylon in the
reign of King Artaxerxes: [2] Of the sons of Phinehas, Gershom;
of the sons of Ithamar, Daniel; of the sons of David, Hattush.
[3] Of the sons of Shecaniah: of the sons of Parosh, Zechariah; through him the genealogy of 150 males was registered.
[4] Eliehoenai son of Zerahiah, of the sons of Pahath-moab, and

a Hebrew resumes here.

26: *The law of the king,* imperial law of Persia, which all Persian subjects must obey. The Persian legal system permitted the observance of both local law (here called *the law of your God*) and imperial law.

7.27–28: Ezra's prayer. 28: Ezra regards the gathering of some of Israel's leaders to return to Israel as partial fulfillment of the prophecies of Isaiah and Jeremiah.

8.1–14: Returnees who accompanied Ezra on his mission to Jerusalem. Josephus maintains that the ten tribes (apart from Judah and Benjamin) are still living beyond the Euphrates and did not return with Ezra (*Ant.* 11.5.2). While by this time, these tribes had assimilated due to the Assyrian policy of forced population exchanges, the tradition of their continued existence is found in, for instance, Tobit. **2:** Emphasis is placed on genealogical connections to the priesthood and to the Davidic line. These links are necessary if the preexilic and exilic Israelite prophecies of return are to be fulfilled. (See, e.g., Ezek. 37.24–28.) Moreover, authentic genealogies provide the returnees with the authority to oversee Temple ritual and to legislate to the people.

with him 200 males. 5 Of the sons of Shecaniah son of Jahaziel; and with him 300 males. 6 And of the sons of Adin, Ebed
son of Jonathan; and with him 50 males. 7 And of the sons of
Elam, Jeshaiah son of Athaliah; and with him 70 males. 8 And
of the sons of Shephatiah, Zebadiah son of Michael; and with
him 80 males. 9 Of the sons of Joab, Obadiah son of Jehiel; and
with him 218 males. 10 And of the sons of Shelomith, the son of
Josiphiah; and with him 160 males. 11 And of the sons of Bebai, Zechariah son of Bebai; and with him 28 males. 12 And of
the sons of Azgad, Johanan son of Hakkatan; and with him 110
males. 13 And of the sons of Adonikam, who were the last; and
these are their names: Eliphelet, Jeiel, and Shemaiah; and with
them 60 males. 14 And of the sons of Bigvai, Uthai and Zaccur;
and with them 70 males.

15 These I assembled by the river that enters Ahava, and we
encamped there for three days. I reviewed the people and the
priests, but I did not find any Levites there. 16 I sent for Eliezer,
Ariel, Shemaiah, Elnathan, Jarib, Elnathan, Nathan, Zechariah, and Meshullam, the leading men, and also for Joiarib and
Elnathan, the instructors, 17 and I gave them an order for Iddo,
the leader at the place [called] Casiphia. I gave them a message to convey to Iddo [and] his brother, temple-servants at the
place [called] Casiphia, that they should bring us attendants
for the House of our God. 18 Thanks to the benevolent care of
our God for us, they brought us a capable man of the family of
Mahli son of Levi son of Israel, and Sherebiah and his sons and
brothers, 18 in all, 19 and Hashabiah, and with him Jeshaiah
of the family of Merari, his brothers and their sons, 20 in all;
20 and of the temple servants whom David and the officers had
appointed for the service of the Levites—220 temple servants,
all of them listed by name.

21 I proclaimed a fast there by the Ahava River to afflict ourselves before our God to beseech Him for a smooth journey
for us and for our children and for all our possessions; 22 for
I was ashamed to ask the king for soldiers and horsemen to
protect us against any enemy on the way, since we had told the
king, "The benevolent care of our God is for all who seek Him,
while His fierce anger is against all who forsake Him." 23 So we
fasted and besought our God for this, and He responded to
our plea. 24 Then I selected twelve of the chiefs of the priests,
namely Sherebiah and Hashabiah with ten of their brothers,
25 and I weighed out to them the silver, the gold, and the vessels, the contribution to the House of our God which the king,

8.15–20: Ezra's examination and instruction of those who accompanied him. Ezra must check the genealogical links of those who accompany him, because of the importance of authentic lineage. These examinations also prepare the reader for the long discussion concerning the intermarriage crisis in chs 9 and 10. The crisis in finding Levites may be because they had a subsidiary role to the priests in the Temple service, and preferred to remain in Babylonia, without these Temple responsibilities. **15:** *These I assembled:* The narrative resumes here from 7.28. To emphasize this resumption, Ezra uses the very same verb, "to assemble," used at the conclusion of the prayer in 7.28. *Ahava:* The precise location of this river (or, perhaps, town) is not known. It may have been one of Babylonia's waterways, and it appears to be located on the route of Ezra's return to Judah. 1 Esd. 8.41, 61 mention the river "Thares" instead of the river *Ahava*. **17:** *Casiphia:* This place-name occurs only here. Since Ezra calls it *the place,* an expression used for places of Jewish worship in, e.g., Gen. 28.17; Deut. 12.5; 1 Kings 8.29, it may have been a religious center for Babylonians. Some scholars suggest that *Casiphia* may be related to "kesef," the Heb word for silver, and that the place may have been associated with silver production. **18–19:** *Mahli son of Levi:* Mahli was one of Merari's children (Num. 3.20). *Sherebiah, Hashabiah* and *Jeshaiah* are all from the line of Merari, one of the three sons of Levi (Num. 3.14, 20), to whom was assigned the responsibility for carrying the Tabernacle and related objects (Num. 4.29–33). **20:** *David and the officers had appointed for the service of the Levites:* Ezra's mission will reinstitute preexilic Davidic and priestly authority.

8.21–23: Ezra proclaims a fast. Though he is designated by the king, Ezra, a religious functionary, is fearful; contrast Nehemiah, appointed as governor, in Neh. 2.7–9. **21:** *I proclaimed a fast:* In the Second Temple period, fasting becomes a particularly important rite, and is generally accompanied by prayer and confession (see Zech. 7.1–7; 8.18–19; Esth. 4.15–16; Dan. 9.3–4; Neh. 9.1). *A smooth journey:* The phrase "derekh yesharah" appears in a number of exilic texts prophesying the return to Judah (see, e.g., Isa. 40.3; Jer. 31.9).

his counselors and officers, and all Israel who were present
had made. [26] I entrusted to their safekeeping the weight of six
hundred and fifty talents of silver, one hundred silver vessels
of one talent each, one hundred talents of gold; [27] also, twenty
gold bowls worth one thousand *daric*s and two vessels of good,
shining bronze, as precious as gold. [28] I said to them, "You are
consecrated to the LORD, and the vessels are consecrated, and
the silver and gold are a freewill offering to the LORD God of
your fathers. [29] Guard them diligently until such time as you
weigh them out in the presence of the officers of the priests
and the Levites and the officers of the clans of Israel in Jerusalem in the chambers of the House of the LORD."
[30] So the priests and the Levites received the cargo of silver
and gold and vessels by weight, to bring them to Jerusalem
to the House of our God. [31] We set out for Jerusalem from the
Ahava River on the twelfth of the first month. We enjoyed the
care of our God, who saved us from enemy ambush on the
journey.
[32] We arrived in Jerusalem and stayed there three days. [33] On
the fourth day the silver, gold, and vessels were weighed out in
the House of our God into the keeping of Meremoth son of Uriah the priest, with whom was Eleazar son of Phinehas. Jozabad
son of Jeshua, and Noadiah son of Binnui, the Levites, were
with them. [34] Everything accorded as to number and weight,
the entire cargo being recorded at that time.
[35] The returning exiles who arrived from captivity made
burnt offerings to the God of Israel: twelve bulls for all Israel,
ninety-six rams, seventy-seven lambs and twelve he-goats as
a purification offering, all this a burnt offering to the LORD.
[36] They handed the royal orders to the king's satraps and the
governors of the province of Beyond the River who gave support to the people and the House of God.

9 When this was over, the officers approached me, saying,
"The people of Israel and the priests and Levites have not
separated themselves from the peoples of the land whose

8.24–30: Ezra appoints the priests and entrusts them with the Temple vessels. 28: *"You are consecrated to the LORD, and the vessels are consecrated":* Here the Heb word "kadosh" signifies separation, distinction, and chosenness. The assertion that *you are consecrated to the LORD* recalls assertions of the consecrated status of the people throughout the Priestly narratives in the Torah. At the same time, the assertion that *the vessels are consecrated* serves as a warning that with consecrated status comes the responsibility to care for the Temple vessels and to ensure that they are not removed from their sacred place.

8.31–36: Ezra and returnees travel to Jerusalem. 32: The arrival occurred on the first day of the fifth month, Av, according to 7.8–9. Since, according to 2 Kings 25.8, it was in the fifth month that the First Temple was destroyed (see also Zech. 7.3), the occurrence of the return in Av may be therapeutic. This is also a solemn time for the returnees as they recall the lost glories of their past (cf. 3.12). In later Jewish traditions, the Ninth of Av is the day when the Jewish community mourns the destruction of both the First and Second Temples. *And stayed there three days:* In *Gen. Rab.* 56.1, the Rabbis connect Ezra's third day to the third day of Abraham's final trial at the binding of Isaac, on which Abraham received divine revelation. Cf. Exod. 19.16. *Three days,* used frequently in the Bible, may simply signify a short time. **35:** The Rabbis are puzzled by the fact that the returnees, who were considered to have sinned willfully, were permitted to offer sacrifices. This is said to be a legal exception to the rule that would ordinarily allow only those who had sinned inadvertently to offer a sacrifice of atonement (*b. Hor.; b. Tem.* 15b).

9.1–2: Intermarriage crisis. According to rabbinic tradition (e.g., *Num. Rab.* 19.3; *Eccl. Rab.* 7.23, §4) and many modern scholars, the prohibition of intermarriage is rooted in Deut. 7.3: "Do not give your daughters to their sons or take their daughters for your sons." However, Ezra insists on two points that are not explicit in any earlier text. First, intermarriage with any non-Israelite people is prohibited, not only intermarriage with the Canaanite nations referred to in Deut. (see also Deut. 20.16–18). Second, if one has intermarried, one must divorce one's foreign wife and expel any children resulting from the prohibited marriage. When Ezra says that the prohibition—including the aforementioned two points—is from the Teaching ("torah") and the commandment of our God (10.3), he seems to presuppose that Mosaic authority should be ascribed not only to the law explicitly stated in Deut. 7.3, but also to its interpretation or elaboration. This is similar to 1 Kings 11.1–2, an exilic text which suggests that Solomon's marriage to various foreign wives is a violation

abhorrent practices are like those of the Canaanites, the Hittites, the Perizzites, the Jebusites, the Ammonites, the Moabites, the Egyptians, and the Amorites. 2 They have taken their
daughters as wives for themselves and for their sons, so that
the holy seed has become intermingled with the peoples of the
land; and it is the officers and prefects who have taken the lead
in this trespass."

3 When I heard this, I rent my garment and robe, I tore hair
out of my head and beard, and I sat desolate. 4 Around me
gathered all who were concerned over the words of the God
of Israel because of the returning exiles' trespass, while I sat
desolate until the evening offering. 5 At the time of the evening
offering I ended my self-affliction; still in my torn garment and
robe, I got down on my knees and spread out my hands to the
LORD my God, 6 and said, "O my God, I am too ashamed and
mortified to lift my face to You, O my God, for our iniquities
[a-]are overwhelming[-a] and our guilt has grown high as heaven.
7 From the time of our fathers to this very day we have been
deep in guilt. Because of our iniquities, we, our kings, and our
priests have been handed over to foreign kings, to the sword,
to captivity, to pillage, and to humiliation, as is now the case.
8 "But now, for a short while, there has been a reprieve from
the LORD our God, who has granted us a surviving remnant
and given us a stake in His holy place; our God has restored
the luster to our eyes and furnished us with a little sustenance
in our bondage. 9 For bondsmen we are, though even in our
bondage God has not forsaken us, but has disposed the king of
Persia favorably toward us, to furnish us with sustenance and
to raise again the House of our God, repairing its ruins and giving us a hold[b] in Judah and Jerusalem.
10 "Now, what can we say in the face of this, O our God, for
we have forsaken Your commandments, 11 which You gave us
through Your servants the prophets when You said, 'The land
that you are about to possess is a land unclean through the uncleanness of the peoples of the land, through their abhorrent
practices with which they, in their impurity, have filled it from
one end to the other. 12 Now then, do not give your daughters
in marriage to their sons or let their daughters marry your
sons; do nothing for their well-being or advantage, then you
will be strong and enjoy the bounty of the land and bequeath
it to your children forever.' 13 After all that has happened to us
because of our evil deeds and our deep guilt—though You, our
God, have been forbearing, [punishing us] less than our iniquity [deserves] in that You have granted us such a remnant as
this—14 shall we once again violate Your commandments by
intermarrying with these peoples who follow such abhorrent

a-a *Lit. "are numerous above the head."* b *Lit. "fence."*

of Torah law. In *b. Meg.* 15a, Ezra is identified with the prophet Malachi because of the reference to a prohibition against intermarriage in Mal. 2.11. **1:** 1 Esd. 8.69 mentions the Edomites but does not mention *the Ammonites* or *the Amorites.* **2:** *It is the officers and prefects who have taken the lead in this trespass:* For a list of the transgressors, see the conclusion of Ezra (10.18–44). Even the priest, Jeshua, is included in the list of offenders (10.18). Though other biblical texts prohibit intermarriage to varying extents, nowhere else is it described in such highly charged theological language: *the holy seed has become intermingled with the peoples of the land.* This may be a reference to Isa. 6.13, which suggests that the exile will purify "a holy seed," making them unsuitable for mixture with anyone else, likely including those of Judean descent who did not experience the purifying power of the exile.

9.3–15: Ezra's public repentance and prayer. 3: Ezra's behavior is similar to that of earlier Jewish leaders who tried to avert a national disaster. For example, Josiah tears his clothing upon hearing the reading of the discovered Torah scroll (2 Kings 22.11); Mordecai and Esther fast and engage in mourning practices (Esth. 4.1–3, 16); and Jehoshaphat proclaims a fast and prays for deliverance from Israel's enemies (2 Chron. 20.1–13). Josephus states that Ezra and the returnees were concerned that God would punish them as He did in the past and therefore they fast and repent (*Ant.* 11.5.3). **5:** Ezra takes the typical position of the praying individual in the Bible (see, e.g., 1 Kings 8.22, 38). **6–7:** Cf. Daniel's prayer (Dan. 9.4–19), where the exiles' responsibility for the destruction of Jerusalem and the Temple is fully accepted. In Ezra's view, if the crisis of intermarriage is not averted, the returnees will risk losing Jerusalem, Judah, and the right to practice Temple ritual. These confessions of communal guilt typify postexilic liturgy. **12:** The concern for intermarriage in terms of both

practices? Will You not rage against us till we are destroyed without remnant or survivor? 15 O LORD, God of Israel, You are benevolent,[a] for we have survived as a remnant, as is now the case. We stand before You in all our guilt, for we cannot face You on this account."

10 While Ezra was praying and making confession, weeping and prostrating himself before the House of God, a very great crowd of Israelites gathered about him, men, women, and children; the people were weeping bitterly. 2 Then Shecaniah son of Jehiel of the family of Elam spoke up and said to Ezra, "We have trespassed against our God by bringing into our homes foreign women from the peoples of the land; [b]but there is still hope for Israel despite this.[-b] 3 Now then, let us make a covenant with our God to expel all these women and those who have been born to them, in accordance with the bidding of the Lord and of all who are concerned over the commandment of our God, and let the Teaching be obeyed. 4 Take action, for the responsibility is yours and we are with you. Act with resolve!"

5 So Ezra at once put the officers of the priests and the Levites and all Israel under oath to act accordingly, and they took the oath. 6 Then Ezra rose from his place in front of the House of God and went into the chamber of Jehohanan son of Eliashib; there, he ate no bread and drank no water, for he was in mourning over the trespass of those who had returned from exile. 7 Then a proclamation was issued in Judah and Jerusalem that all who had returned from the exile should assemble in Jerusalem, 8 and that anyone who did not come in three days would, by decision of the officers and elders, have his property confiscated and himself excluded from the congregation of the returning exiles.

9 All the men of Judah and Benjamin assembled in Jerusalem in three days; it was the ninth month, the twentieth of the month. All the people sat in the square of the House of God, trembling on account of the event and because of the rains. 10 Then Ezra the priest got up and said to them, "You have trespassed by bringing home foreign women, thus aggravating the guilt of Israel. 11 So now, make confession to the LORD, God of your fathers, and do His will, and separate yourselves from the peoples of the land and from the foreign women."

12 The entire congregation responded in a loud voice, "We must surely do just as you say. 13 However, many people are involved, and it is the rainy season; it is not possible to remain out in the open, nor is this the work of a day or two, because we have transgressed extensively in this matter. 14 Let our officers remain on behalf of the entire congregation, and all our

genders is unusual in the Bible; most texts emphasize the danger of foreign wives rather than husbands.

10.1–4: Community repents and empowers Ezra to act on their behalf. See 9.1–2 n. **2:** *Shecaniah* speaks in the first-person plural. For this reason, he is listed in rabbinic traditions as one of several exemplary leaders who take responsibility for the sins of the community and are thereby able to take the lead in resolving a problem (*b. Sanh.* 11a). **3:** The decision to expel all foreign wives and the children who were born to them is understood in rabbinic traditions to be the basis for the laws concerning matrilineal descent as a defining marker of Jewish identity (*Gen. Rab.* 7.2); biblical narratives suggest the priority of patrilineal descent in matters of genealogy and inheritance.

10.6–11: Ezra takes legal action to resolve the intermarriage crisis. Ezra requires the leadership of the returning community to take an oath to act in accordance with the law. Perhaps this is necessary in light of the charges that are made against the community leaders in 9.2. **6:** The sin is seen as so extreme that, like Moses after the construction of the golden calf, Ezra fasts completely (see Exod. 34.28; Deut. 9.18). **8:** The Rabbis take this v. as a legal precedent for their power to expropriate when it is beneficial for the community (*b. Git.* 36b).

10.12–14: Community accepts Ezra's legal action. This section of the narrative is deeply influenced by numerous Torah narratives involving the Israelites' willingness to accept the authority of Moses and to agree to obey particular laws.

a Or "*in the right.*" *b-b* Or "*Is there ... ?*"

townspeople who have brought home foreign women shall appear before them at scheduled times, together with the elders and judges of each town, in order to avert the burning anger of our God from us on this account." [15] Only Jonathan son of Asahel and Jahzeiah son of Tikvah remained for this purpose, assisted by Meshullam and Shabbethai, the Levites. [16] The returning exiles did so. Ezra the priest and the men who were the chiefs of the ancestral clans—all listed by name—sequestered themselves on the first day of the tenth month to study the matter. [17] By the first day of the first month they were done with all the men who had brought home foreign women. [18] Among the priestly families who were found to have brought foreign women were Jeshua son of Jozadak and his brothers Maaseiah, Eliezer, Jarib, and Gedaliah. [19] They gave their word[a] to expel their wives and, acknowledging their guilt, offered a ram from the flock to expiate it. [20] Of the sons of Immer: Hanani and Zebadiah; [21] of the sons of Harim: Maaseiah, Elijah, Shemaiah, Jehiel, and Uzziah; [22] of the sons of Pashhur: Elioenai, Maaseiah, Ishmael, Nethanel, Jozabad, and Elasah; [23] of the Levites: Jozabad, Shimei, Kelaiah who is Kelita, Pethahiah, Judah, and Eliezer. [24] Of the singers: Eliashib. Of the gatekeepers: Shallum, Telem, and Uri. [25] Of the Israelites: of the sons of Parosh: Ramiah, Izziah, Malchijah, Mijamin, Eleazar, Malchijah, and Benaiah; [26] of the sons of Elam: Mattaniah, Zechariah, Jehiel, Abdi, Jeremoth, and Elijah; [27] of the sons of Zattu: Elioenai, Eliashib, Mattaniah, Jeremoth, Zabad, and Aziza; [28] of the sons of Bebai: Jehohanan, Hananiah, Zabbai, and Athlai; [29] of the sons of Bani: Meshullam, Malluch, Adaiah, Jashub, Sheal, and Ramoth; [30] of the sons of Pahath-moab: Adna, Chelal, Benaiah, Maaseiah, Mattaniah, Bezalel, Binnui, and Manasseh; [31] of the sons of Harim: Eliezer, Isshijah, Malchijah, Shemaiah, and Shimeon; [32] also Benjamin, Malluch, and Shemariah; [33] of the sons of Hashum: Mattenai, Mattattah, Zabad, Eliphelet, Jeremai, Manasseh, and Shimei; [34] of the sons of Bani: Maadai, Amram, and Uel; [35] also Benaiah, Bedeiah, Cheluhu, [36] Vaniah, Meremoth, Eliashib, [37] Mattaniah, Mattenai, Jaasai, [38] Bani, Binnui, Shimei, [39] Shelemiah, Nathan, Adaiah, [40] Machnadebai, Shashai, Sharai, [41] Azarel, Shelemiah, Shemariah, [42] Shallum, Amariah, and Joseph; [43] of the sons of Nebo: Jeiel, Mattithiah, Zabad, Zebina, Jaddai, Joel, and Benaiah.

[44] All these had married foreign women, among whom were some women [b-]who had borne children.[-b]

a *Lit. "hand."* *b-b* *Meaning of Heb. uncertain.*

10.15–44: Determining which returnees intermarried. Though this list would seem to be an odd conclusion to a biblical book, it is quite suitable for the middle of the larger book Ezra-Nehemiah, especially since the theme of intermarriage will return in Nehemiah. **15:** *Jonathan son of Asahel,* who is mentioned first, is said by the Rabbis to have carried out the work with a special zeal (*Exod. Rab.* 50.5). **16:** *To study the matter:* This apparently refers to the study of existing legal traditions and to the interpretation emerging from that study. The v. recalls Ezra's priestly lineage (7.1–5), perhaps to authorize Ezra as an interpreter. He has already been authorized by being described as a scribe (chs 6 and 7), as one who is well-versed in biblical interpretation (7.10), and as a priest whose known lineage qualifies him to participate in Temple rituals. See 7.1–10 n. **18:** *Jeshua*'s intermarriage implicates even the priestly leadership in the intermarriage crisis. In 1 Esd. 9.19 only the descendants of Jeshua are said to have foreign wives, not Jeshua himself. **44:** *Who had borne children,* cf. 1 Esd. 9.36.

נחמיה

Nehemiah

FOR INTRODUCTION TO NEHEMIAH, see introduction to Ezra.

Summary of Contents

- I. Nehemiah rebuilds the walls of Jerusalem (1.1–7.72a)
  - A. Nehemiah hears Jerusalem's wall is destroyed (1.1–3)
  - B. Nehemiah's prayer (1.4–11a)
  - C. Artaxerxes authorizes Nehemiah to return and rebuild the wall (1.11b–2.10)
  - D. Nehemiah inspects the Jerusalem wall at night (2.11–16)
  - E. Nehemiah encourages the rebuilding of the wall (2.17–18)
  - F. Nehemiah's rebuilding is opposed by Sanballat, Tobiah, and Geshem (2.19–20)
  - G. List of returnees who worked on rebuilding the wall (3.1–32)
  - H. Sanballat tries to interfere with the rebuilding, but is not successful (3.33–38)
  - I. The people work on the walls and guard the wall (4.1–17)
  - J. Nehemiah resolves socioeconomic crises (5.1–13)
  - K. Nehemiah refrains from taking the governor's allowance (5.14–19)
  - L. Nehemiah avoids murderous plots to interfere with the completion of the Jerusalem wall (6.1–14)
  - M. Nehemiah completes the wall amidst ongoing harassment from Tobiah (6.15–19)
  - N. Nehemiah appoints guards for the gates of Jerusalem (7.1–3)
  - O. Nehemiah makes plans for the repopulation of Judah (7.4–5)
  - P. Genealogical register of those who returned from Babylonia (7.6–72a)
- II. Liturgical practices in the reconstituted community (7.72b–10.40)
  - A. Ezra reads from the Mosaic Torah and the people celebrate (7.72b–8.12)
  - B. Celebration of the festival of Sukkot (Booths) (8.13–18)
  - C. Public confession of sins (9.1–5)
  - D. Confessional prayer (9.6–37)
  - E. Nehemiah's covenant (10.1–40)
- III. Legislative acts of Nehemiah (11.1–13.31)
  - A. List of settlers in Jerusalem (11.1–24)
  - B. List of distribution of village settlers in Judah (11.25–36)
  - C. List of priests, Levites, and gatekeepers of the Temple (12.1–26)
  - D. The dedication of the wall (12.27–43)
  - E. Ensuring support of Temple clergy through tithing (12.44–47)

F. Prohibition against intermarriage (13.1–3)
G. Threat to Temple purity is resolved by Nehemiah (13.4–9)
H. Nehemiah re-establishes Temple tithes (13.10–14)
I. Nehemiah emphasizes the observance of Sabbath laws (13.15–22)
J. Prohibition against intermarriage (13.23–27)
K. Purification of the returnees and concluding prayer (13.28–31)

[HINDY NAJMAN]

1 The narrative of Nehemiah son of Hacaliah:
In the month of Kislev of the twentieth year,[a] when I was in
the fortress of Shushan, 2 Hanani, one of my brothers, together
with some men of Judah, arrived, and I asked them about the
Jews, the remnant who had survived the captivity, and about
Jerusalem. 3 They replied, "The survivors who have survived
the captivity there in the province are in dire trouble and disgrace; Jerusalem's wall is full of breaches, and its gates have
been destroyed by fire."

4 When I heard that, I sat and wept, and was in mourning
for days, fasting and praying to the God of Heaven. 5 I said,
"O LORD, God of Heaven, great and awesome God, who stays
faithful to His covenant with those who love Him and keep
His commandments! 6 Let Your ear be attentive and Your eyes
open to receive the prayer of Your servant that I am praying to
You now, day and night, on behalf of the Israelites, Your servants, confessing the sins that we Israelites have committed
against You, sins that I and my father's house have committed.
7 We have offended You by not keeping the commandments,
the laws, and the rules that You gave to Your servant Moses.
8 Be mindful of the promise You gave to Your servant Moses: 'If
you are unfaithful, I will scatter you among the peoples; 9 but if
you turn back to Me, faithfully keep My commandments, even
if your dispersed are at the ends of the earth,[b] I will gather them
from there and bring them to the place where I have chosen to
establish My name.' 10 For they are Your servants and Your people whom You redeemed by Your great power and Your mighty
hand. 11 O Lord! Let Your ear be attentive to the prayer of Your
servant, and to the prayer of Your servants who desire to hold

a *I.e., of King Artaxerxes; cf. 2.1.* *b* *Lit. "sky."*

1.1–3: News of Jerusalem in crisis. Although both the Masoretic tradition and the LXX present Ezra-Nehemiah as a single work, the transition from the conclusion of Ezra to the opening section of Nehemiah is awkward. **1:** *Nehemiah* means "the LORD is compassionate." Most date this event to 445 BCE (the twentieth year of Artaxerxes I), shortly after some kind of attack on the returnees reflected in the narrative of v. 3. **3:** *Jerusalem's wall is full of breaches, and its gates have been destroyed by fire:* The language recalls the destruction and burning of Jerusalem under the direction of Nebuzaradan, the chief of the guards under Nebuchadnezzar some 140 years earlier. Nehemiah expresses an urgent need to prevent what threatens to be a second destruction of the Jerusalem Temple. Cf. 2 Kings 25.8–12.

1.4–11a: Prayer of Nehemiah. **4:** Nehemiah's behavior accords with mourning and supplication practices that are characteristic of exilic and Second Temple narratives. Cf. Ezra 9.3–15, where Ezra participates in mourning rituals, fasts, confesses his sins, and then offers an elaborate prayer to the LORD. Similarly, in Dan. 9.3ff., Daniel prays while fasting and wearing sackcloth and ashes, then confesses and offers an elaborate prayer to the LORD. **5:** Petitionary prayers typically start with an invocation, often just "LORD" or "God." The unusually long invocation of this v. is meant to remind God of both His power and His obligation to redress the situation. **6:** Nehemiah employs the formula used by priests in the confession on Yom Kippur when he says: *Confessing the sins that we Israelites have committed against You, sins that I and my father's house have committed.* See Lev. ch 16 and *m. Yoma* 6.2. **7–11:** By recalling the history of Israel, Nehemiah reminds God of the promises made to Israel and also of God's own compassion at times when the Israelites strayed from their course. Much of this passage is a paraphrase of sections of Deut., though conceptions from Priestly literature, such as Israel being *unfaithful* (v. 8) are mixed in, suggesting that the author

Your name in awe. Grant Your servant success today, and dispose that man to be compassionate toward him!"

I was the king's cupbearer at the time.

2 In the month of Nisan, in the twentieth year of King Artaxerxes, wine was set before him; I took the wine and gave it to the king—I had never been out of sorts in his presence. [2] The king said to me, "How is it that you look bad, though you are not ill? It must be bad thoughts." I was very frightened, [3] but I answered the king, "May the king live forever! How should I not look bad when the city of the graveyard of my ancestors lies in ruins, and its gates have been consumed by fire?" [4] The king said to me, "What is your request?" With a prayer to the God of Heaven, [5] I answered the king, "If it please the king, and if your servant has found favor with you, send me to Judah, to the city of my ancestors' graves, to rebuild it." [6] With the consort seated at his side, the king said to me, "How long will you be gone and when will you return?" So it was agreeable to the king to send me, and I gave him a date. [7] Then I said to the king, "If it please the king, let me have letters to the governors of the province of Beyond the River, directing them to grant me passage until I reach Judah; [8] likewise, a letter to Asaph, the keeper of the King's Park, directing him to give me timber for roofing the gatehouses of the temple fortress and the city walls and for the house I shall occupy." The king gave me these, thanks to my God's benevolent care for me. [9] When I came to the governors of the province of Beyond the River I gave them the king's letters. The king also sent army officers and cavalry with me.

[10] When Sanballat the Horonite and Tobiah the Ammonite servant heard, it displeased them greatly that someone had come, intent on improving the condition of the Israelites.

[11] I arrived in Jerusalem. After I was there three days [12] I got up at night, I and a few men with me, and telling no one what my God had put into my mind to do for Jerusalem, and taking no other beast than the one on which I was riding, [13] I went out by the Valley Gate, at night, toward the Jackals' Spring and the Dung Gate; and I surveyed the walls of Jerusalem that were breached, and its gates, consumed by fire. [14] I proceeded to the Fountain Gate and to the King's Pool, where there was no room for the beast under me to continue. [15] So I went up the wadi by night, surveying the wall, and, entering again by the Valley Gate, I returned. [16] The prefects knew nothing of where I had gone or what I had done, since I had not yet divulged it to the Jews—the priests, the nobles, the prefects, or the rest of the officials.

[17] Then I said to them, "You see the bad state we are in—Jerusalem lying in ruins and its gates destroyed by fire. Come, let us rebuild the wall of Jerusalem and suffer no more disgrace."

was working from a complete Torah similar to our own.

1.11b–2.9: Nehemiah's request to return to Jerusalem is granted. **1.11b:** As the *cupbearer,* Nehemiah occupies a significant and trusted position in the palace of Artaxerxes. **2.3:** Nehemiah either demonstrates quick thinking or he has planned this response in advance. Josephus seems to prefer the first option, reporting this event as occurring on the same day on which Nehemiah is informed of Jerusalem's present situation (*Ant.* 11.5.6). **2.8:** This v. is adduced as proof that it is permissible to accept a gift for the Temple from an idol worshipper only if the gift is from the government (*b. 'Arak.* 6a).

2.10: Report of opposition to Nehemiah's arrival in Judah. *Sanballat the Horonite* is mentioned in documents from Elephantine in Egypt as the governor of Samaria. This v. is anticipatory; a major theme of Nehemiah is the opposition of these people to his restoration of Jerusalem.

2.11–16: Nehemiah secretly assesses the damage to Jerusalem. The secret nighttime evaluation of the walls begins and ends at the *Valley Gate.*

2.17–18: Nehemiah charges his attendants to assist him in rebuilding Jerusalem. 17: *Suffer no more disgrace:* The term "disgrace" is used elsewhere to characterize the destruction of the Temple and the exile. See Isa. 4.1–3; 22.18; 25.6–8; Jer. 23.39–40; 24.8–10; 25.8–11; Ezek. 16.52–58; 22.1–5; Lam. 5.1; Dan. 9.16.

18 I told them of my God's benevolent care for me, also of the things that the king had said to me, and they said, "Let us start building!" They were encouraged by [His] benevolence.

19 When Sanballat the Horonite and Tobiah the Ammonite servant and Geshem the Arab heard, they mocked us and held us in contempt and said, "What is this that you are doing? Are you rebelling against the king?" 20 I said to them in reply, "The God of Heaven will grant us success, and we, His servants, will start building. But you have no share or claim or stake[a] in Jerusalem!"

3 Then Eliashib the high priest and his fellow priests set to and rebuilt the Sheep Gate; they consecrated it and set up its doors, consecrating it as far as the Hundred's Tower, as far as the Tower of Hananel. 2 Next to him, the men of Jericho built. Next to them,[b] Zaccur son of Imri. 3 The sons of Hassenaah rebuilt the Fish Gate; they roofed it and set up its doors, locks, and bars. 4 Next to them, Meremoth son of Uriah son of Hakkoz repaired; and next to him,[c] Meshullam son of Berechiah son of Meshezabel. Next to him,[c] Zadok son of Baana repaired. 5 Next to him,[c] the Tekoites repaired, though their nobles would not [d-]take upon their shoulders[-d] the work of their lord. 6 Joiada son of Paseah and Meshullam son of Besodeiah repaired the Jeshanah Gate; they roofed it and set up its doors, locks, and bars. 7 Next to them, Melatiah the Gibeonite and Jadon the Meronothite repaired, [with] the men of Gibeon and Mizpah, [e-]under the jurisdiction[-e] of the governor of the province of Beyond the River. 8 Next to them,[b] Uzziel son of Harhaiah, [of the] smiths, repaired. Next to him, Hananiah, of[f] the perfumers. They restored Jerusalem as far as the Broad Wall. 9 Next to them, Rephaiah son of Hur, chief of half the district of Jerusalem, repaired. 10 Next to him,[c] Jedaiah son of Harumaph repaired in front of his house. Next to him, Hattush son of Hashabneiah repaired. 11 Malchijah son of Harim and Hasshub son of Pahath-moab repaired a second stretch, including the Tower of Ovens. 12 Next to them,[b] Shallum son of Hallohesh,[g] chief of half the district of Jerusalem, repaired—he and his daughters. 13 Hanun and the inhabitants of Zanoah repaired the Valley Gate; they rebuilt it and set up its doors, locks, and bars. And [they also repaired] a thousand cubits of wall to the Dung Gate. 14 Malchijah son of Rechab, chief of the district of Beth-haccerem, repaired the Dung Gate; he rebuilt it and set up its doors, locks, and bars. 15 Shallun son of Colhozeh, chief of the district of Mizpah, repaired the Fountain

a *Lit. "record."* *b* *Lit. "him."* *c* *Lit. "them."* *d-d* *Lit. "bring their neck into."*
e-e *Lit. "of the throne"; meaning of Heb. uncertain.*
f *Lit. "son of," i.e., member of the guild of.* *g* *I.e., the charmer.*

2.19–20: Confrontation between Nehemiah and local leaders: Sanballat, Tobiah, and Geshem. 19: *Geshem* or "Gashmu" (6.6, see translators' note *b*) may be a king of Kedar, since a recovered bowl from the Persian period is inscribed: "Cain son of Gashmu king of Kedar." The Kedarites are referred to in Gen. 25.13; Isa. 21.16–17; 42.11; 60.7; Jer. 2.10; 49.28–30; Ezek. 27.21; Ps. 120.5; Song 1.5; 1 Chron. 1.29. They likely originated in the Arabian peninsula. By the middle of the 5th c. BCE, they may have been a significant presence in the land of Israel. **20:** The success of the small community due to divine support becomes an increasingly prominent theme in postexilic literature, especially in Chronicles.

3.1–38: Nehemiah and returnees repair the wall. 1: The high priest *Eliashib* was the grandson of the priest Jeshua. He is mentioned elsewhere in Neh. (12.10, 22; 13.4). **1–5:** The northern section with eight work assignments. **6–13:** The western section with ten work assignments. **14–15:** The southern section with two work assignments.

Gate; he rebuilt it and covered it, and set up its doors, locks,
and bars, as well as the wall of the irrigation[a] pool of the King's
Garden as far as the steps going down from the City of David.
16 After him, Nehemiah son of Azbuk, chief of half the district
of Beth-zur, repaired, from in front of the graves of David as far
as the artificial pool, and as far as the House of the Warriors.
17 After him, the Levites repaired: Rehum son of Bani. Next to
him, Hashabiah, chief of half the district of Keilah, repaired for
his district. 18 After him, their brothers repaired: Bavvai son of
Henadad, chief of half the district of Keilah. 19 Next to him, Ezer
son of Jeshua, the chief of Mizpah, repaired a second stretch,
from in front of the ascent to the armory [at] the angle [of the
wall]. 20 After him, Baruch son of Zaccai zealously repaired a
second stretch, from the angle to the entrance to the house of
Eliashib, the high priest. 21 After him, Meremoth son of Uriah
son of Hakkoz repaired a second stretch, from the entrance to
Eliashib's house to the end of Eliashib's house. 22 After him,
the priests, inhabitants of the plain, repaired. 23 After them,[b]
Benjamin and Hasshub repaired in front of their houses. After
them,[b] Azariah son of Maaseiah son of Ananiah repaired beside his house. 24 After him, Binnui son of Henadad repaired a
second stretch, from the house of Azariah to the angle, to the
corner. 25 Palal son of Uzai—from in front of the angle and the
tower that juts out of the house of the king, the upper [tower]
of the prison compound. After him, Pedaiah son of Parosh.
(26 The temple servants were living on the Ophel, as far as a
point in front of the Water Gate in the east, and the jutting tower.) 27 After him, the Tekoites repaired a second stretch, from in
front of the great jutting tower to the wall of the Ophel. 28 Above
the Horse Gate, the priests repaired, each in front of his house.
29 After them,[b] Zadok son of Immer repaired in front of his
house. After him, Shemaiah son of Shechaniah, keeper of the
East Gate, repaired. 30 After him, Hananiah son of Shelemiah
and Hanun, the sixth son of Zalaph, repaired a second stretch.
After them,[b] Meshullam son of Berechiah repaired in front of
his chamber. 31 After him, Malchijah of the smiths repaired as
far as the house of the temple servants and the merchants,
[from] in front of the Muster Gate to the corner loft. 32 And
between the corner loft to the Sheep Gate the smiths and the
merchants repaired.

33 When Sanballat heard that we were rebuilding the wall,
it angered him, and he was extremely vexed. He mocked the
Jews, 34 saying in the presence of his brothers and the Samar-
ian force, "What are the miserable Jews doing? Will they restore, offer sacrifice, and finish one day? Can they revive those

16–32: The eastern section with twenty-one work assignments. **33–35:** Sanballat and Tobiah discourage the building. Cf. Ezra 4.4.

a Following Kimhi; cf. Mishnaic Heb. bet hashelaḥin, *irrigated field.*
b Lit. "him."

36–37: Nehemiah offers a lament over the destruction. **38:** Completion of the wall.

4.1–6: Repeated opposition by local people. 3: Nehemiah's response is both religious and pragmatic. **4:** The people appear very disheartened in their lament.

4.7–17: Nehemiah empowers the returnees. Nehemiah calls upon God as a divine warrior; thus Nehemiah's subjects seem to be participating in a religious war for the future of the returnees and their families. **8:** Just a little over a century prior to Nehemiah, Jeremiah was exhorting the people to build homes in Babylonia and plant gardens there (Jer. 29.5, 28). Now, Nehemiah tells the people to fight for their recovered land and for their right to live in their land.

stones out of the dust heaps, burned as they are?" 35 Tobiah
the Ammonite, alongside him, said, "That stone wall they are
building—if a fox climbed it he would breach it!"

36 Hear, our God, how we have become a mockery, and return their taunts upon their heads! Let them be taken as spoil
to a land of captivity! 37 Do not cover up their iniquity or let
their sin be blotted out before You, for they hurled provocations at the builders.

38 We rebuilt the wall till it was continuous all around to half
its height; for the people's heart was in the work.

4 When Sanballat and Tobiah, and the Arabs, the Ammonites, and the Ashdodites heard that healing had come to
the walls of Jerusalem, that the breached parts had begun to
be filled, it angered them very much, 2 and they all conspired
together to come and fight against Jerusalem and to throw it
into confusion. 3 Because of them we prayed to our God, and
set up a watch over them[a] day and night.

4 Judah was saying,

> "The strength of the basket-carrier has failed,
> And there is so much rubble;
> We are not able ourselves
> To rebuild the wall."

5 And our foes were saying, "Before they know or see it,
we shall be in among them and kill them, and put a stop to
the work." 6 When the Jews living near them[b] would arrive,
they would tell us [c-]time and again[-c] [d-]"... from all the places
where ... you shall come back to us ... "[-d] 7 I stationed, on the
lower levels of the place, behind the walls, on the bare rock—I
stationed the people by families with their swords, their lances, and their bows. 8 Then I decided to exhort the nobles, the
prefects, and the rest of the people, "Do not be afraid of them!
Think of the great and awesome Lord, and fight for your brothers, your sons and daughters, your wives and homes!"

9 When our enemies learned that it had become known to
us, since God had thus frustrated their plan, we could all return to the wall, each to his work. 10 From that day on, half my
servants did work and half held lances and shields, bows and
armor. And the officers stood behind the whole house of Judah 11 who were rebuilding the wall. The basket-carriers were
burdened, doing work with one hand while the other held a
weapon. 12 As for the builders, each had his sword girded at
his side as he was building. The trumpeter stood beside me.

a I.e., the workers on the walls. *b I.e., the foes.* *c-c Lit. "ten times."*
d-d Heb. seems to be abbreviated; a possible restoration of the sentence, with the missing elements enclosed in brackets, is: [of their evil plan; and we would say to them,] "From all the places where [you get such information] you shall come back to us [and convey it]."

13 I said to the nobles, the prefects, and the rest of the people,
"There is much work and it is spread out; we are scattered over
the wall, far from one another. 14 When you hear a trumpet call,
gather yourselves to me at that place; our God will fight for us!"
15 And so we worked on, while half were holding lances, from
the break of day until the stars appeared.

16 I further said to the people at that time, "Let every man
with his servant lodge in Jerusalem, that we may use the night
to stand guard and the day to work." 17 Nor did I, my brothers, my servants, or the guards following me ever take off our
clothes, *a-*[or] each his weapon, even at the water.*-a*

5

There was a great outcry by the common folk and their
wives against their brother Jews. 2 Some said, "Our sons
and daughters are numerous; we must get grain to eat in order that we may live!" 3 Others said, "We must pawn our fields,
our vineyards, and our homes to get grain to stave off hunger."
4 Yet others said, "We have borrowed money against our fields
and vineyards to pay the king's tax. 5 Now *b-*we are as good as*-b*
our brothers, and our children as good as theirs; yet here we
are subjecting our sons and daughters to slavery—some of our
daughters are already subjected—and we are powerless, while
our fields and vineyards belong to others."

6 It angered me very much to hear their outcry and these
complaints. 7 After pondering the matter carefully, I censured the nobles and the prefects, saying, "Are you pressing
claims on loans made to your brothers?" Then I raised a large
crowd against them 8 and said to them, "We have done our
best to buy back our Jewish brothers who were sold to the
nations; will you now sell your brothers so that they must be
sold [back] to us?" They kept silent, for they found nothing
to answer. 9 So I continued, "What you are doing is not right.
You ought to act in a God-fearing way so as not to give our
enemies, the nations, room to reproach us. 10 I, my brothers,
and my servants also have claims of money and grain against
them; let us now abandon those claims! 11 Give back at
once their fields, their vineyards, their olive trees, and their
homes, and [abandon] the claims for the hundred pieces
of silver, the grain, the wine, and the oil that you have been
pressing against them!" 12 They replied, "We shall give them
back, and not demand anything of them; we shall do just as
you say." Summoning the priests, I put them under oath to
keep this promise. 13 I also shook out the bosom of my garment and said, "So may God shake free of his household and
property any man who fails to keep this promise; may he be

a-a Meaning of Heb. uncertain. *b-b Lit. "our flesh is as good as the flesh of."*

15: *From the break of day until the stars appeared:* This v. offers one definition of daytime; the Rabbis use it to argue that one can fulfill the commandment of reciting the evening Shema (Deut. 6.4) only once the stars appear (*b. Ber.* 2b). In addition, this v. is used to define the beginning of night for purposes of purification (*b. Meg.* 20b).

5.1–5: Economic crisis among the returnees. The claim is that the creditors are seizing property that the returnees pledged when they needed to take loans. This is forbidden in the case of the poor (see Exod. 22.24–26). In earlier periods, such concerns fell under the purview of the prophets such as Amos, but prophecy as an institution was weakened in the postexilic period, so Nehemiah takes control of the situation. **1:** *Outcry* refers to a legal challenge as in Gen. 18.20–21; Job 34.28. **5:** *Daughters to slavery—some of our daughters are already subjected:* According to Exod. 21.7–11, an enslaved female loses the possibility of liberation if she is taken as a wife by her master, excluding maltreatment by her new master.

5.6–13: Nehemiah resolves the economic crisis. Nehemiah uses this occasion to declare a jubilee. See Lev. 25.1–55; Deut. 15.1–18. Due to his great power, Nehemiah is heeded (contrast Jer. 34.8–22), the community is stabilized, and work on the walls is resumed. Both civic and religious leaders seem to have been involved in these crimes, according to 6.7, 12.

5.14–19: Nehemiah does not make use of the governor's food allowance. Nehemiah leads by example even to the point of refusing what is legally his allotment. **14:** *Twelve years in all:* Nehemiah served two terms as governor, according to 13.6. The first one lasts twelve years, while the second is not specified. **19:** *Remember to my credit:* Similar prayers are found in 13.14, 23, 31. In the Bible, they typify Nehemiah, though similar requests are common in a variety of ancient Near Eastern prayers.

6.1–13: Opposition tries to distract and harm Nehemiah. 5–9: In a second attempt to stop the rebuilding, an unsealed—i.e., publicly accessible—letter accuses Nehemiah and his supporters of rebelling against Artaxerxes. Nehemiah is clear and direct in his rejection of these false claims: *They are figments of your imagination* (v. 8). **6–7:** The accusation is that Judah wants to become independent of Persia, with its own king, anointed by a prophet, as was the case before 586 BCE. There is no evidence to suggest that this ever was the intention of the returnees.

thus shaken out and stripped." All the assembled answered,
"Amen," and praised the LORD.
The people kept this promise.
14 Furthermore, from the day I was commissioned to be governor in the land of Judah—from the twentieth year of King
Artaxerxes until his thirty-second year, twelve years in all—
neither I nor my brothers ever ate of the governor's food allowance. 15 The former governors who preceded me laid heavy
burdens on the people, and took from them for bread and
wine more than[a] forty shekels of silver. Their servants also tyr-
annized over the people. But I, out of the fear of God, did not
do so. 16 I also supported the work on this wall; we did not buy
any land, and all my servants were gathered there at the work.
17 Although there were at my table, between Jews and prefects,
one hundred and fifty men in all, beside those who came to us
from surrounding nations; 18 and although what was prepared
for each day came to one ox, six select sheep, and fowl, all prepared for me, and at ten-day intervals all sorts of wine in abundance—yet I did not resort to the governor's food allowance,
for the [king's] service lay heavily on the people.
19 O my God, remember to my credit all that I have done for
this people!

6 When word reached Sanballat, Tobiah, Geshem the Arab,
and the rest of our enemies that I had rebuilt the wall and
not a breach remained in it—though at that time I had not yet
set up doors in the gateways—2 Sanballat and Geshem sent a
message to me, saying, "Come, let us get together in Kephirim
in the Ono valley"; they planned to do me harm. 3 I sent them
messengers, saying, "I am engaged in a great work and cannot come down, for the work will stop if I leave it in order to
come down to you." 4 They sent me the same message four
times, and I gave them the same answer. 5 Sanballat sent me
the same message a fifth time by his servant, who had an open
letter with him. 6 Its text was: "Word has reached the nations,
and Geshem[b] too says that you and the Jews are planning to
rebel—for which reason you are building the wall—and that
you are to be their king. [c]Such is the word.[-c] 7 You have also set
up prophets in Jerusalem to proclaim about you, 'There is a
king in Judah!' Word of these things will surely reach the king;
so come, let us confer together."
8 I sent back a message to him, saying, "None of these things
you mention has occurred; they are figments of your imagination"—9 for they all wished to intimidate us, thinking,

a *Lit. "after"; meaning of Heb. uncertain.* b *Heb.* Gashmu.
c-c *Meaning of Heb. uncertain.*

"They will desist from the work, and it will not get done." Now strengthen my hands!

10 Then I visited Shemaiah son of Delaiah son of Mehetabel when he was housebound, and he said,

"Let us meet in the House of God, inside the
sanctuary,
And let us shut the doors of the sanctuary, for they are
coming to kill you,
By night they are coming to kill you."

11 I replied, "Will a man like me take flight? Besides, who such as I can go into the sanctuary and live? I will not go in." 12 Then I realized that it was not God who sent him, but that he uttered that prophecy about me—Tobiah and Sanballat having hired him—13 because he was a hireling, that I might be intimidated and act thus and commit a sin, and so provide them a scandal with which to reproach me.

14 "O my God, remember against Tobiah and Sanballat these deeds of theirs,[a] and against Noadiah the prophetess, and against the other prophets that they wished to intimidate me!"

15 The wall was finished on the twenty-fifth of Elul, after fifty-two days. 16 When all our enemies heard it, all the nations round about us were intimidated, and fell very low in their own estimation; they realized that this work had been accomplished by the help of our God.

17 Also in those days, the nobles of Judah kept up a brisk correspondence with Tobiah, and Tobiah with them. 18 Many in Judah were his confederates, for he was a son-in-law of Shecaniah son of Arah, and his son Jehohanan had married the daughter of Meshullam son of Berechiah. 19 They would also speak well of him to me, and would divulge my affairs to him. Tobiah sent letters to intimidate me.

7 When the wall was rebuilt and I had set up the doors, tasks were assigned to the gatekeepers, the singers, and the Levites. 2 I put Hanani my brother and Hananiah, the captain of the fortress, in charge of Jerusalem, for he was a more trustworthy and God-fearing man than most. 3 I said to them, "The gates of Jerusalem are not to be opened until the heat of the day,[b] and [c]before you leave your posts[c] let the doors be closed and barred. And assign the inhabitants of Jerusalem to watches, each man to his watch, and each in front of his own house."

4 The city was broad and large, the people in it were few, and houses were not yet built. 5 My God put it into my mind to assemble the nobles, the prefects, and the people, in order to register them by families. I found the genealogical register

a *Lit. "his."* *b* *Lit. "sun."* *c-c* *Lit. "while they are still standing."*

10–13: In the final attempt to distract Nehemiah, a false prophet is hired to lure him into a situation that would brand him as a transgressor of Temple law. Nehemiah uncovers the plot and escapes in time.

6.14: Nehemiah prays to God for protection. While Nehemiah has Persian authority to control the political situation in Jerusalem, he must rely completely on God to handle external conflict. *Noadiah* is one of a few named female prophets; others are Miriam (Exod. 15.20), Deborah (Judg. 4.4), and Huldah (2 Kings 22.14).

6.15–16: The rebuilding of the wall is complete. *Fifty-two days:* This incredibly short time indicates the blessing and protection of God over the work. Cf. Ezra 6.14–15.

6.17–19: Tobiah tries to intimidate Nehemiah. While most of the surrounding peoples are said to desist from opposition because they recognize that the work on the wall was the work of God, *Tobiah* is still trying to harass and intimidate Nehemiah. Tobiah is to be contrasted with the two men Nehemiah places in charge of Jerusalem because they are "God fearing" (7.2). Some scholars suggest that Tobiah's attempted intimidation may in fact have occurred prior to the completion of the wall.

7.1–3: Nehemiah appoints gatekeepers, singers, and Levites to protect the gates and the doors. 1: *Tasks were assigned:* The service of these Temple personnel as protectors may have a precedent in the protection of Jehoash recorded in 2 Kings ch 11. The Levites are also charged with this duty in Neh. 13.22. **2:** *Hanani my brother:* This is the same individual who brought word about the condition of Jerusalem in 1.2. *And Hananiah:* Some scholars suggest that, since the verb is singular, only one person known by two similar names (*Hanani* and *Hananiah*) is intended, not two people.

7.4–72a: The genealogical register. 4–5: Nehemiah assembles the people and discovers a *genealogical register.*

6–72a: See Ezra 2.1–70 n. According to the Rabbis, the genealogical list in Ezra reflects the initial return from Babylonia, and the list in Neh. reflects a return that is linked to the dedication of the Temple. According to *b. Meg.* 16b, Nehemiah's return occurs twenty-four years after the initial return of Ezra.

of those who were the first to come up, and there I found written:

6[a]These are the people of the province who came up from among the captive exiles that Nebuchadnezzar, king of Babylon, had deported, and who returned to Jerusalem and to Judah, each to his own city, 7 who came with Zerubbabel, Jeshua, Nehemiah, Azariah, Raamiah, Nahamani, Mordecai, Bilshan, Mispereth, Bigvai, Nehum, Baanah.

The number of the men of the people of Israel: 8 the sons
of Parosh—2,172; 9 the sons of Shephatiah—372; 10 the sons
of Arah—652; 11 the sons of Pahath-moab: the sons of Jeshua
and Joab—2,818; 12 the sons of Elam—1,254; 13 the sons of Zattu—845; 14 the sons of Zaccai—760; 15 the sons of Binnui—648;
16 the sons of Bebai—628; 17 the sons of Azgad—2,322; 18 the
sons of Adonikam—667; 19 the sons of Bigvai—2,067; 20 the
sons of Adin—655; 21 the sons of Ater: Hezekiah—98; 22 the
sons of Hashum—328; 23 the sons of Bezai—324; 24 the sons of
Hariph—112; 25 the sons of Gibeon—95; 26 the men of Bethlehem and Netophah—188; 27 the men of Anathoth—128; 28 the
men of Beth-azmaveth—42; 29 the men of Kiriath-jearim,
Chephirah, and Beeroth—743; 30 the men of Ramah and
Geba—621; 31 the men of Michmas—122; 32 the men of Bethel
and Ai—123; 33 the men of the other Nebo—52; 34 the sons of
the other Elam—1,254; 35 the sons of Harim—320; 36 the sons
of Jericho—345; 37 the sons of Lod, Hadid, and Ono—721; 38 the
sons of Senaah—3,930.

39 The priests: the sons of Jedaiah: the house of Jeshua—973;
40 the sons of Immer—1,052; 41 the sons of Pashhur—1,247;
42 the sons of Harim—1,017.

43 The Levites: the sons of Jeshua: Kadmiel, the sons of Hodeiah—74.

44 The singers: the sons of Asaph—148.

45 The gatekeepers: the sons of Shallum, the sons of Ater, the sons of Talmon, the sons of Akkub, the sons of Hatita, the sons of Shobai—138.

46 The temple servants: the sons of Ziha, the sons of Hasupha,
the sons of Tabbaoth, 47 the sons of Keros, the sons of Siah, the
sons of Padon, 48 the sons of Lebanah, the sons of Hagabah, the
sons of Shalmai, 49 the sons of Hanan, the sons of Giddel, the
sons of Gahar, 50 the sons of Reaiah, the sons of Rezin, the sons
of Nekoda, 51 the sons of Gazzam, the sons of Uzza, the sons
of Paseah, 52 the sons of Besai, the sons of Meunim, the sons

a Vv. 6–43 appear as Ezra 2 with variations in the names and numbers.

of Nephishesim, 53 the sons of Bakbuk, the sons of Hakupha,
the sons of Harhur, 54 the sons of Bazlith, the sons of Mehida,
the sons of Harsha, 55 the sons of Barkos, the sons of Sisera, the
sons of Temah, 56 the sons of Neziah, the sons of Hatipha.
57 The sons of Solomon's servants: the sons of Sotai, the sons
of Sophereth, the sons of Perida, 58 the sons of Jala, the sons of
Darkon, the sons of Giddel, 59 the sons of Shephatiah, the sons
of Hattil, the sons of Pochereth-hazzebaim, the sons of Amon.
60 The total of temple servants and the sons of Solomon's
servants—392.
61 The following were those who came up from Tel-melah,
Tel-harsha, Cherub, Addon, and Immer—they were unable to
tell whether their father's house and descent were Israelite:
62 the sons of Delaiah, the sons of Tobiah, the sons of Nekoda—642.
63 Of the priests: the sons of Habaiah, the sons of Hakkoz, the
sons of Barzillai who had married a daughter of Barzillai the
Gileadite and had taken his[a] name—64 these searched for their
genealogical records, but they could not be found, so they
were disqualified for the priesthood. 65 The Tirshatha[b] ordered
them not to eat of the most holy things until a priest with Urim
and Thummim should appear.
66 The sum of the entire community was 42,360, 67 not counting their male and female servants, these being 7,337; they also
had 245 male and female singers. 68 [c-][Their horses—736, their
mules—245,][-c] camels—435, asses—6,720.
69 Some of the heads of the clans made donations for the
work. The Tirshatha donated to the treasury: gold—1,000
drachmas, basins—50, priestly robes—530.
70 Some of the heads of the clans donated to the work treasury: gold—20,000 drachmas, and silver—2,200 minas.
71 The rest of the people donated: gold—20,000 drachmas,
silver—2,000, and priestly robes—67.
72 The priests, the Levites, the gatekeepers, the singers, some
of the people, the temple servants, and all Israel took up residence in their towns.

8 When the seventh month arrived—the Israelites being
[settled] in their towns—1 the entire people assembled as
one man in the square before the Water Gate, and they asked
Ezra the scribe to bring the scroll of the Teaching of Moses with
which the LORD had charged Israel. 2 On the first day of the
seventh month, Ezra the priest brought the Teaching before
the congregation, men and women and all who could listen
with understanding. 3 He read from it, facing the square before

a *Lit. "their."* *b* *A Persian title.*
c-c *These words are missing in some mss. and editions; but cf. Ezra 2.66.*

7.72b–8.8: Ezra reads from the Mosaic Torah ("torat moshe"). Cf. the narrative of the discovered Torah scroll during the reign of Josiah, king of Judah, in 2 Kings chs 22–23 (esp. 23.1–3). This narrative's use of exactly the same time description as Ezra 3.1 may indicate that the passage about the dedication of the altar and the passage about the reading of the Torah of Moses are to be read together. **8.1:** *Water Gate,* on the east side of Jerusalem and directly opposite the Temple. **2:** *On the first day of the seventh month,* later known as Rosh Ha-Shanah, the New Year festival (see also Lev. 23.23–25; Num. 29.1–6). The community here includes women, as in Deut. 1.12; contrast Exod. 19.14–15.

the Water Gate, from the first light until midday, to the men
and the women and those who could understand; the ears of
all the people were given to the scroll of the Teaching.
4 Ezra the scribe stood upon a wooden tower made for the
purpose, and beside him stood Mattithiah, Shema, Anaiah,
Uriah, Hilkiah, and Maaseiah at his right, and at his left Pedaiah, Mishael, Malchijah, Hashum, Hashbaddanah, Zechariah,
Meshullam. 5 Ezra opened the scroll in the sight of all the people, for he was above all the people; as he opened it, all the people stood up. 6 Ezra blessed the LORD, the great God, and all the
people answered, "Amen, Amen," with hands upraised. Then
they bowed their heads and prostrated themselves before the
LORD with their faces to the ground. 7 Jeshua, Bani, Sherebiah,
Jamin, Akkub, Shabbethai, Hodiah, Maaseiah, Kelita, Azariah,
Jozabad, Hanan, Pelaiah, and the Levites explained the Teaching to the people, while the people stood in their places. 8 They
read from the scroll of the Teaching of God, translating it and
giving the sense; so they understood the reading.
9 Nehemiah the Tirshatha, Ezra the priest and scribe, and
the Levites who were explaining to the people said to all the
people, "This day is holy to the LORD your God: you must not
mourn or weep," for all the people were weeping as they listened to the words of the Teaching. 10 He further said to them,
"Go, eat choice foods and drink sweet drinks and send portions to whoever has nothing prepared, for the day is holy to
our Lord. Do not be sad, for your rejoicing in the LORD is the
source of your strength." 11 The Levites were quieting the people, saying, "Hush, for the day is holy; do not be sad." 12 Then all
the people went to eat and drink and send portions and make
great merriment, for they understood the things they were
told.
13 On the second day, the heads of the clans of all the people and the priests and Levites gathered to Ezra the scribe to
study the words of the Teaching. 14 They found written in the
Teaching that the LORD had commanded Moses that the Israelites must dwell in booths during the festival of the seventh
month, 15 and that they must announce and proclaim throughout all their towns and Jerusalem as follows, "Go out to the

4: Elevated upon a wooden platform, Ezra reenacts the Sinai event and the people, like their ancestors, publicly accept the law. Whereas at Sinai Moses records what God reveals, Ezra now reads what Moses has written. Cf. the earlier, preexilic, public reading of the Torah of Moses in Josh. 8.30–35. Rabbinic traditions state that the wooden platform upon which Ezra stood was the Temple Mount (e.g., *t. Sot.*, 7.13; *b. Yoma* 69b; *b. Sot.* 40b–41a). The Rabbis state that the six people called to read publicly from the Torah scroll on the Day of Atonement represent the six people who stand at Ezra's left and the six people who stand at Ezra's right during the public reading of the Torah. (The Rabbis take Meshullam as another name for *Zechariah,* so there are six, not seven people [see *b. Meg.* 23a].) **5:** *All the people stood up:* The Rabbis use this v. to illustrate correct conduct during the public reading of a Torah scroll. The people's standing is understood to reflect complete silence. A contemporary reflection of this v. is seen in synagogue worship: When the Torah scroll is raised, the congregation rises. **6:** *Ezra blessed the LORD, the great God:* The Rabbis explain that the phrase *the great God* refers to Ezra's use of the Tetragrammaton, the four-letter name of God (YHVH) (*b. Yoma* 69b). By the rabbinic period pronouncing this name had become taboo, and it begins to fall out of use in postexilic texts. **8:** The exact meaning of each of these words is uncertain, though together they reflect the idea that the Torah text cannot simply be read and understood in a straightforward way, an idea that is particularly prominent within rabbinic culture. *Translating it:* Rabbinic interpretation understands the Heb "meforash" to refer to the Tg., the Aram. translation of the v., which was recited in public along with the v. Unable to understand the Heb text, the returnees required both Aram. translation and interpretation (*b. Meg.* 3a; *b. Ned.* 37b; *Gen. Rab.* 36.8).

8.9–12: The people celebrate the first of Tishri, a holy and joyful festival. Cf. the response following the laying of the foundations of the Temple in Ezra 3.10–13. Nehemiah's attitude is that this reenacted revelation must be characterized by joy, not mourning, as in 2 Kings 22.11, or fear, as in the Sinai revelation (Exod. ch 19).

8.13–18: Ezra and the people celebrate the festival of Sukkot (the feast of Booths). Compare Solomon's celebration of Sukkot in 2 Chron. 7.8–10. **14:** See Exod. 23.16; 34.22; Lev. 23.33–43; Num. 29.1–38. **15:** These four species *(olive trees, pine trees, myrtles, palms and [other] leafy trees)* differ from the four species (palm, myrtle, willow, etrog) understood from later tradition based on Lev. 23.40 (see 2 Macc. 10.7; *Ant.* 3.10.4; *m. Sukk.* 4.1–7; *Lev. Rab.* 30.15; and *b. Sukk.* 12a and 38a, where the Rabbis attempt to resolve

mountains and bring leafy branches of olive trees, pine[a] trees, myrtles, palms and [other] leafy[a] trees to make booths, as it is written." 16 So the people went out and brought them, and made themselves booths on their roofs, in their courtyards, in the courtyards of the House of God, in the square of the Water Gate and in the square of the Ephraim Gate. 17 The whole community that returned from the captivity made booths and dwelt in the booths—the Israelites had not done so from the days of Joshua[b] son of Nun to that day—and there was very great rejoicing. 18 He read from the scroll of the Teaching of God each day, from the first to the last day. They celebrated the festival seven days, and there was a solemn gathering on the eighth, as prescribed.

9 On the twenty-fourth day of this month, the Israelites assembled, fasting, in sackcloth, and with earth upon them. 2 Those of the stock of Israel separated themselves from all foreigners, and stood and confessed their sins and the iniquities of their fathers. 3 Standing in their places, they read from the scroll of the Teaching of the LORD their God for one-fourth of the day, and for another fourth they confessed and prostrated themselves before the LORD their God. 4 On the raised platform of the Levites stood Jeshua and Bani, Kadmiel, Shebaniah, Bunni, Sherebiah, Bani, and Chenani, and cried in a loud voice to the LORD their God. 5 The Levites Jeshua, Kadmiel, Bani, Hashabniah, Sherebiah, Hodiah, and Pethahiah said, "Rise, bless the LORD your God who is from eternity to eternity: 'May Your glorious name be blessed, exalted though it is above every blessing and praise!'

6 "You alone are the LORD. You made the heavens, the highest[c] heavens, and all their host, the earth and everything upon it, the seas and everything in them. You keep them all alive, and the host of heaven prostrate themselves before You. 7 You are the LORD God, who chose Abram, who brought him out of Ur of the Chaldeans and changed his name to Abraham. 8 Finding

a *Meaning of Heb. uncertain.* b *Heb.* Jeshua.
c *Lit. "the heavens of the."*

this inconsistency). Most remarkable, rabbinic tradition suggests that these four species should be taken in hand, while here, perhaps based on the contiguity of Lev. 23.40, 42, they are used for constructing the *booths*. **18:** Cf. Lev. 23.33–36; Num. 29.35 regarding the festival of Sukkot, particularly the *solemn gathering* on the eighth day; this is lacking in Deut. 16.15; 1 Kings 8.66.

9.1–5: People fast and confess their sins. 1: This passage suggests that a festival similar to Yom Kippur is observed on the 24th day of Tishri, after the celebration of Sukkot, not on the 10th of Tishri as reflected in other biblical texts (Lev. 16.29; 23.27–28; 25.9; Num. 29.7) and later rabbinic traditions. **2:** *Separated themselves from all foreigners:* This may refer to a crisis similar to the one recorded in Ezra chs 9–10; Neh. 10.31; 12.23–31. **3:** This passage is cited in rabbinic literature as an example of how one should divide one's day between study and prayer. One should divide the period from midday until the evening into two parts. In the first part, one should study the weekly portion of the Torah and the haftarah. In the second part, one should confess one's sins to God (*b. Meg.* 30b; *b. Ta'an.* 12b). **4:** *And cried in a loud voice to the LORD their God:* The Rabbis understand the people's cry as a confession for idolatrous practices that are said to have caused the destruction of the sanctuary, the burning of the Temple, the murder of the righteous, and the Babylonian exile (*b. Sanh.* 64a; *b. Yoma* 69b). **5:** Introduction to the confession. Cf. Dan. 2.20–23. The Rabbis comment that Neh. 9.5 reflects the fact that in the Temple liturgy the people did not respond to blessings with "Amen," but rather gave praise to God following each blessing (*b. Ber.* 63a; *b. Sot.* 40b; and the more extensive discussion of Temple liturgy in *b. Ta'an.* 16b).

9.6–37: Communal confession. Cf. Nehemiah's prayer to Joshua's recounting of Israelite history in Josh. ch 24. Like all historical retellings, it is remarkably selective in what it narrates. For example, for the ancestral period, only Abraham is mentioned. This prayer is incorporated into the daily morning prayer in Jewish liturgy. **6:** The prayer begins with a declaration of God as Creator. This relies mainly on the Priestly account of creation in Gen. 1.1–2.4. *The highest heavens, and all their host* is found elsewhere, though these are not Priestly terms (see, e.g., Deut. 10.14; 1 Kings 8.27; 2 Chron. 6.18). The author of this prayer is thus combining concepts from originally separate sources that have become integrated in the Torah. R. Oshaia uses this v. as a proof that the "Shekhinah" (divine Presence) is in every place (*b. B. Bat.* 25a). **7–8:** The prayer alludes to the following events: Abraham was brought out of Ur (Gen. ch 12), God changed Abram's name to Abraham (Gen. ch 17); Abraham's heart was found to be faithful (Gen. ch 22); God made a covenant with Abram to give him and his descendants the land of the surrounding peoples (Gen. ch 15). As in later retellings of biblical events, the order of events may be rearranged. **9–12:** The prayer continues with the retelling of the miraculous exodus from Egypt. The relatively extensive space given to the exodus reflects its general importance in biblical tradition and its special significance for those who have undergone an "exodus" of their own. **9:** Here, the prayer alludes to God's speech to Moses at the burning bush in Exod. 3.7 and later in the exodus narrative, Exod. 14.10. **10:** The language in Nehemiah seems closest to Exod. 9.16. **11:** In Nehemiah's recounting of the splitting of the sea, Moses' role is limited, as in Ps. 78.13. In the exodus narrative Moses plays a much more active role (Exod. 14.16, 21, 27). **12:** The language here is almost a verbatim quotation from Exod. 13.21. **13–14:** Giving of the Torah at Sinai. This is lacking in the shorter historical retellings in Deut. 26.5–9; Josh. 24.2–13. **13a:** Here Nehemiah preserves, side by side, two different accounts of the Sinai theophany. *You came down on Mount Sinai* reflects the tradition in Exod. 19.11, 20 where God is said to have come down on Mount Sinai. *And spoke to them from heaven* reflects the tradition in Exod. 20.19 that God communicated to Israel from the heavens and not from an earthly location. **13b:** See Mal. 2.6; Ps. 119.137, 142. **16–21:** The prayer emphasizes God's compassion despite Israel's continued transgression. **18:** Nehemiah's retelling of the golden calf episode omits the role played by Aaron. Cf. Exod. 32.1–4, 21–24. **22–25:** Conquest of Israel and settlement. **22:** See Num. 21.21–35; Deut. chs 2–3.

his heart true to You, You made a covenant with him to give the
land of the Canaanite, the Hittite, the Amorite, the Perizzite,
the Jebusite, and the Girgashite—to give it to his descendants. And You kept Your word, for You are righteous. 9 You took
note of our fathers' affliction in Egypt, and heard their cry at
the Sea of Reeds. 10 You performed signs and wonders against
Pharaoh, all his servants, and all the people of his land, for You
knew that they acted presumptuously toward them. You made
a name for Yourself that endures to this day. 11 You split the sea
before them; they passed through the sea on dry land, but You
threw their pursuers into the depths, like a stone into the raging waters.

12 "You led them by day with a pillar of cloud, and by night
with a pillar of fire, to give them light in the way they were to
go. 13 You came down on Mount Sinai and spoke to them from
heaven; You gave them right rules and true teachings, good
laws and commandments. 14 You made known to them Your
holy sabbath, and You ordained for them laws, commandments and Teaching, through Moses Your servant. 15 You gave
them bread from heaven when they were hungry, and produced water from a rock when they were thirsty. You told them
to go and possess the land that You swore to give them. 16 But
they—our fathers—acted presumptuously; they stiffened their
necks and did not obey Your commandments. 17 Refusing to
obey, unmindful of Your wonders that You did for them, they
stiffened their necks, and in their defiance resolved to return
to their slavery. But You, being a forgiving God, gracious and
compassionate, long-suffering and abounding in faithfulness,
did not abandon them. 18 Even though they made themselves a
molten calf and said, 'This is your God who brought you out of
Egypt,' thus committing great impieties, 19 You, in Your abundant compassion, did not abandon them in the wilderness.
The pillar of cloud did not depart from them to lead them on
the way by day, nor the pillar of fire by night to give them light
in the way they were to go. 20 You endowed them with Your
good spirit to instruct them. You did not withhold Your manna from their mouth; You gave them water when they were
thirsty. 21 Forty years You sustained them in the wilderness so
that they lacked nothing; their clothes did not wear out, and
their feet did not swell.

22 "You gave them kingdoms and peoples, and [a]allotted
them territory.[a] They took possession of the land of Sihon,
the land of the king of Heshbon, and the land of Og, king of
Bashan. 23 You made their children as numerous as the stars of
heaven, and brought them to the land which You told their fathers to go and possess. 24 The sons came and took possession

a-a Meaning of Heb. uncertain.

of the land: You subdued the Canaanite inhabitants of the
land before them; You delivered them into their power, both
their kings and the peoples of the land, to do with them as they
pleased. [25] They captured fortified cities and rich lands; they
took possession of houses filled with every good thing, of hewn
cisterns, vineyards, olive trees, and fruit trees in abundance.
They ate, they were filled, they grew fat; they luxuriated in Your
great bounty. [26] Then, defying You, they rebelled; they cast
Your Teaching behind their back. They killed Your prophets
who admonished them to turn them back to You; they committed great impieties.
[27] "You delivered them into the power of their adversaries
who oppressed them. In their time of trouble they cried to You;
You in heaven heard them, and in Your abundant compassion
gave them saviors who saved them from the power of their
adversaries. [28] But when they had relief, they again did what
was evil in Your sight, so You abandoned them to the power of
their enemies, who subjugated them. Again they cried to You,
and You in heaven heard and rescued them in Your compassion, time after time. [29] You admonished them in order to turn
them back to Your Teaching, but they acted presumptuously
and disobeyed Your commandments, and sinned against Your
rules, by following which a man shall live. They turned a defiant shoulder, stiffened their neck, and would not obey. [30] You
bore with them for many years, admonished them by Your
spirit through Your prophets, but they would not give ear, so
You delivered them into the power of the peoples of the lands.
[31] Still, in Your great compassion You did not make an end of
them or abandon them, for You are a gracious and compassionate God.
[32] "And now, our God, great, mighty, and awesome God, who
stays faithful to His covenant, do not treat lightly all the suffering that has overtaken us—our kings, our officers, our priests,
our prophets, our fathers, and all Your people—from the time
of the Assyrian kings to this day. [33] Surely You are in the right
with respect to all that has come upon us, for You have acted faithfully, and we have been wicked. [34] Our kings, officers,
priests, and fathers did not follow Your Teaching, and did not
listen to Your commandments or to the warnings that You gave
them. [35] When they had their own kings and enjoyed the good
that You lavished upon them, and the broad and rich land that
You put at their disposal, they would not serve You, and did
not turn from their wicked deeds. [36] Today we are slaves, and
the land that You gave our fathers to enjoy its fruit and bounty—here we are slaves on it! [37] On account of our sins it yields
its abundant crops to kings whom You have set over us. They
rule over our bodies and our beasts as they please, and we are
in great distress.

26–31: Repeated transgression of Israel in the land, following a pattern already established in the desert (v. 18). Nehemiah recounts the period of the judges and the kings. The main theme is God's continued forgiveness and forbearance, which Nehemiah is invoking as paradigmatic for his own situation. (Ps. 106 has a similar function and structure.) **32–37:** Returnees confess their sins. **32:** The words *and now* mark a transition. Nehemiah turns his attention from the past to the present. This is common in many other biblical prayers, e.g., Num. 14.17; Dan. 9.15; Ezra 9.10. **34–35:** List of people who are guilty and responsible for the exile. Cf. Jer. 24.1–10; 44.17; Zech. 1.5–6; 7.8–14; Dan. 9.6, 8; and 2 Chron. 36.14–16.

10 "In view of all this, we make this pledge and put it in
writing; and on the sealed copy [are subscribed] our officials, our Levites, and our priests.
2 "On the sealed copy[a] [are subscribed]: Nehemiah the Tirshatha son of Hacaliah and Zedekiah, 3 Seraiah, Azariah, Jeremiah, 4 Pashhur, Amariah, Malchijah, 5 Hattush, Shebaniah,
Malluch, 6 Harim, Meremoth, Obadiah, 7 Daniel, Ginnethon,
Baruch, 8 Meshullam, Abijah, Mijamin, 9 Maaziah, Bilgai, Shemaiah; these are the priests.
10 "And the Levites: Jeshua son of Azaniah, Binnui of the
sons of Henadad, and Kadmiel. 11 And their brothers: Shebaniah, Hodiah, Kelita, Pelaiah, Hanan, 12 Mica, Rehob, Hashabiah,
13 Zaccur, Sherebiah, Shebaniah, 14 Hodiah, Bani, and Beninu.
15 "The heads of the people: Parosh, Pahath-moab, Elam,
Zattu, Bani, 16 Bunni, Azgad, Bebai, 17 Adonijah, Bigvai, Adin,
18 Ater, Hezekiah, Azzur, 19 Hodiah, Hashum, Bezai, 20 Hariph,
Anathoth, Nebai, 21 Magpiash, Meshullam, Hezir, 22 Meshezabel, Zadok, Jaddua, 23 Pelatiah, Hanan, Anaiah, 24 Hoshea,
Hananiah, Hasshub, 25 Hallohesh, Pilha, Shobek, 26 Rehum,
Hashabnah, Maaseiah, 27 and Ahiah, Hanan, Anan, 28 Malluch,
Harim, Baanah.
29 "And the rest of the people, the priests, the Levites, the
gatekeepers, the singers, the temple servants, and all who
separated themselves from the peoples of the lands to [follow]
the Teaching of God, their wives, sons and daughters, all who
know enough to understand, 30 join with their noble brothers,
and take an oath with sanctions to follow the Teaching of God,
given through Moses the servant of God, and to observe carefully all the commandments of the LORD our Lord, His rules
and laws.
31 "Namely: We will not give our daughters in marriage to the
peoples of the land, or take their daughters for our sons.
32 "The peoples of the land who bring their wares and all
sorts of foodstuff for sale on the sabbath day—we will not buy
from them on the sabbath or a holy day.
"We will forgo [the produce of] the seventh year, and every
outstanding debt.
33 "We have laid upon ourselves obligations: To charge ourselves one-third of a shekel yearly for the service of the House
of our God— 34 for the rows of bread, for the regular meal offering and for the regular burnt offering, [for those of the] sabbaths, new moons, festivals, for consecrations, for purification
offerings to atone for Israel, and for all the work in the House
of our God.
35 "We have cast lots [among] the priests, the Levites, and the
people, to bring the wood offering to the House of our God by

a *Heb. plural.*

10.1–40: The covenant of Nehemiah and the returnees. 1–28: There is considerable overlap between this list and the priests listed in 1 Chron. ch 24. **29:** *The rest of the people* do not sign the covenant, but take part in the oath to keep the law. **30:** Josiah's covenant, like Nehemiah's, is preceded by a public reading of the text of the covenant, the Torah (2 Chron. 34.30–32). Hezekiah's covenant, like Nehemiah's, follows a communal confession (2 Chron. 29.5–10). **31:** Intermarriage, mentioned first, is a major theme in Ezra-Nehemiah. **32:** The *sabbath,* mentioned second, became especially significant in the exilic period. This v. represents one of many attempts to develop and establish a coherent definition of the type of work that is prohibited on the Sabbath. (See also Isa. 56.1–8; 58.13–14; Jer. 17.21–24; and Ezek. 20.12, 16, 20, 24.) *We will forgo [the produce of] the seventh year,* see Exod. 21.2–6; 23.10–11; Lev. 25.1–7; Deut. 15.1–18. **33–34:** This is related to Torah law, which requires every Israelite to pay half a shekel (Exod. 30.1–16; 38.25–26). See also 2 Kings 12.2–16; 2 Chron. 24.4–14, where payment is required for repair of the Temple. **35:** Torah laws concerning support of the Temple do not mention this tax. However, there is a requirement that the priests keep the fire burning continuously for the sacrifices in the sanctuary (Lev. 6.2–23). It may have been understood at the time of Nehemiah that this requirement could not be fulfilled unless a supply of wood was guaranteed. (See 13.31; *m. Ta'an.* 4.5; *b. Ta'an.* 28a.)

clans annually at set times in order to provide fuel for the altar
of the LORD our God, as is written in the Teaching.
[36] "And [we undertake] to bring to the House of the LORD
annually the first fruits of our soil, and of every fruit of every
tree; [37] also, the first-born of our sons and our beasts, as is written in the Teaching; and to bring the firstlings of our cattle and
flocks to the House of our God for the priests who minister in
the House of our God.
[38] "We will bring to the storerooms of the House of our God
the first part of our dough, and our gifts [of grain], and of the
fruit of every tree, wine and oil for the priests, and the tithes of
our land for the Levites—the Levites who collect the tithe in all
our towns [a-]subject to royal service.[-a] [39] An Aaronite priest must
be with the Levites when they collect the tithe, and the Levites
must bring up a tithe of the tithe to the House of our God, to
the storerooms of the treasury. [40] For it is to the storerooms that
the Israelites and the Levites must bring the gifts of grain, wine,
and oil. The equipment of the sanctuary and of the ministering
priests and the gatekeepers and the singers is also there.
"We will not neglect the House of our God."

11 The officers of the people settled in Jerusalem; the rest
of the people cast lots for one out of ten to come and
settle in the holy city of Jerusalem, and the other nine-tenths
to stay in the towns. [2] The people gave their blessing to all the
men who willingly settled in Jerusalem.
[3] These are the heads of the province who lived in Jerusalem—in the countryside[b] of Judah, the people lived in their
towns, each on his own property, Israelites, priests, Levites,
temple servants, and the sons of Solomon's servants, [4] while in
Jerusalem some of the Judahites and some of the Benjaminites
lived:
Of the Judahites: Athaiah son of Uzziah son of Zechariah son
of Amariah son of Shephatiah son of Mahalalel, of the clan of
Periz, [5] and Maaseiah son of Baruch son of Col-hozeh son of
Hazaiah son of Adaiah son of Joiarib son of Zechariah son of
the Shilohite. [6] All the clan of Periz who were living in Jerusalem—468 valorous men.
[7] These are the Benjaminites: Sallu son of Meshullam son
of Joed son of Pedaiah son of Kolaiah son of Maaseiah son of
Ithiel son of Jesaiah. [8] After him, Gabbai and Sallai—928.
[9] Joel son of Zichri was the official in charge of them, and
Judah son of Hassenuah was the second-in-command of the
city.
[10] Of the priests: Jedaiah son of Joiarib, Jachin, [11] Seraiah
son of Hilkiah son of Meshullam son of Zadok son of Meraioth

a-a For this sense of ʿabodah, *"service," cf.* 5.18. *b Lit. "towns."*

37: As in the case of the prohibition against intermarriage, the laws of tithing and priestly support are given in more detail than in the Torah. The claim that these laws are *as is written in the Teaching* ("torah") should be understood to mean that the authoritative interpretation of Torah has the same authority as Torah itself. These stipulations of their covenant are violated by the people, and Nehemiah must reinforce them in 5.1–5; 13.1–3, 10–12, 15–17, 19–22, 23–28.

11.1–24: The list of those who settled in Jerusalem. 2: *Who willingly settled:* Despite its status as "the holy city," for economic reasons settlement in Jerusalem was not attractive, as recognized by the Rabbis (*b. Ketub.* 110b).

11.25–36: The distribution of village settlements in Judah. Eleven of the listed settlements are said to be in territory known to be under Edomite-Arab control after the destruction of the First Temple, and scholars have questioned the historical reliability of this source. Some scholars have suggested that the settlement list reflects the conquest list in Josh. chs 14–15.

12.1–26: Lists of priests, Levites, and gatekeepers of the Temple. This list supplements 11.10–24. It postdates Nehemiah and is dated to the 4th c. BCE. **1–7:** This list of priests overlaps significantly with the list of priests who signed the covenant document in ch 10.

son of Ahitub, chief officer of the House of God, 12 and their
brothers, who did the work of the House—822; and Adaiah
son of Jeroham son of Pelaliah son of Amzi son of Zechariah
son of Pashhur son of Malchijah, 13 and his brothers, heads of
clans—242; and Amashsai son of Azarel son of Ahzai son of
Meshillemoth son of Immer, 14 and their brothers, valorous
warriors—128. Zabdiel son of Haggedolim was the official in
charge of them.
15 Of the Levites: Shemaiah son of Hasshub son of Azrikam
son of Hashabiah son of Bunni, 16 and Shabbethai and Jozabad
of the heads of the Levites were in charge of the external work
of the House of God. 17 Mattaniah son of Micha son of Zabdi
son of Asaph was the head; at prayer, he would lead off with
praise; and Bakbukiah, one of his brothers, was his second-
in-command; and Abda son of Shammua son of Galal son of
Jeduthun. 18 All the Levites in the holy city—284.
19 And the gatekeepers: Akkub, Talmon, and their brothers,
who stood watch at the gates—172.
20 And the rest of the Israelites, the priests, and the Levites in
all the towns of Judah [lived] each on his estate.
21 The temple servants lived on the Ophel; Ziha and Gishpa
were in charge of the temple servants.
22 The overseer of the Levites in Jerusalem was Uzzi son of
Bani son of Hashabiah son of Mattaniah son of Micha, of the
Asaphite singers, over the work of the House of God. 23 There
was a royal order concerning them, a stipulation concerning
the daily duties of the singers.
24 Petahiah son of Meshezabel, of the sons of Zerah son of
Judah, advised the king concerning all the affairs of the people.
25 As concerns the villages with their fields: Some of the Judahites lived in Kiriath-arba and its outlying hamlets, in Dibon and its outlying hamlets, and in Jekabzeel and its villages;
26 in Jeshua, in Moladah, and in Beth-pelet; 27 in Hazar-shual,
in Beer-sheba and its outlying hamlets; 28 and in Ziklag and in
Meconah and its outlying hamlets; 29 in En-rimmon, in Zorah
and in Jarmuth; 30 Zanoah, Adullam, and their villages; Lachish and its fields; Azekah and its outlying hamlets. They settled from Beer-sheba to the Valley of Hinnom.
31 The Benjaminites: from Geba, Michmash, Aija, and Bethel
and its outlying hamlets; 32 Anathoth, Nob, Ananiah, 33 Hazor, Ramah, Gittaim, 34 Hadid, Zeboim, Neballat, 35 Lod, Ono,
Ge-harashim. 36 Some of the Judahite divisions of Levites were
[shifted] to Benjamin.

12 These are the priests and the Levites who came up with
Zerubbabel son of Shealtiel and Jeshua:
Seraiah, Jeremiah, Ezra, 2 Amariah, Malluch, Hattush,
3 Shecaniah, Rehum, Meramoth, 4 Iddo, Ginnethoi, Abijah,

[5] Mijamin, Maadiah, Bilgah, [6] Shemaiah, Joiarib, Jedaiah, [7] Sallu, Amok, Hilkiah, Jedaiah. These were the heads of the priests and their brothers in the time of Jeshua.

[8] The Levites: Jeshua, Binnui, Kadmiel, Sherebiah, Judah, and Mattaniah, in charge of thanksgiving songs,[a] he and his brothers; [9] and Bakbukiah and Unni [and] their brothers served opposite them by shifts.

[10] Jeshua begot Joiakim; Joiakim begot Eliashib; Eliashib begot Joiada; [11] Joiada begot Jonathan; Jonathan begot Jaddua.

[12] In the time of Joiakim, the heads of the priestly clans were: Meriaiah—of the Seraiah clan; Hananiah—of the Jeremiah clan; [13] Meshullam—of the Ezra clan; Jehohanan—of the Amariah clan; [14] Jonathan—of the Melicu clan; Joseph—of the Shebaniah clan; [15] Adna—of the Harim clan; Helkai—of the Meraioth clan; [16] Zechariah—of the Iddo clan; Meshullam—of the Ginnethon clan; [17] Zichri—of the Abijah clan... of the Miniamin clan; Piltai—of the Moadiah clan; [18] Shammua—of the Bilgah clan; Jehonathan—of the Shemaiah clan; [19] Mattenai—of the Joiarib clan; Uzzi—of the Jedaiah clan; [20] Kallai—of the Sallai clan; Eber—of the Amok clan; [21] Hashabiah—of the Hilkiah clan; Nethanel—of the Jedaiah clan.

[22] The Levites and the priests were listed by heads of clans in the days of Eliashib, Joiada, Johanan, and Jaddua, down to the reign of Darius the Persian. [23] But the Levite heads of clans are listed in the book of the chronicles to the time of Johanan son of Eliashib.

[24] The heads of the Levites: Hashabiah, Sherebiah, Jeshua son of Kadmiel, and their brothers served opposite them, singing praise and thanksgiving hymns by the ordinance of David the man of God—served opposite them in shifts; [25] Mattaniah, Bakbukiah, Obadiah, Meshullam, Talmon, and Akkub, guarding as gatekeepers by shifts at the vestibules of the gates.

[26] These were in the time of Joiakim son of Jeshua son of Jozadak, and in the time of Nehemiah the governor, and of Ezra the priest, the scribe.

[27] At the dedication of the wall of Jerusalem, the Levites, wherever they lived, were sought out and brought to Jerusalem to celebrate a joyful dedication with thanksgiving and with song, accompanied by cymbals, harps, and lyres. [28] The companies of singers assembled from the [Jordan] plain, the environs of Jerusalem, and from the Netophathite villages; [29] from Beth-hagilgal, from the countryside of Geba and Azmaveth, for the singers built themselves villages in the environs of Jerusalem.

[30] The priests and Levites purified themselves; then they purified the people, and the gates, and the wall.

a Meaning of Heb. uncertain.

23: *The book of the chronicles* is not the book of Chronicles included in the Tanakh, but rather a collection of genealogical lists that was presumably preserved among the Temple documents. **24:** *David the man of God:* Cf. Ezra 3.10, where David, who is traditionally viewed as the author of Psalms, is considered the author of the Temple liturgy. The title *the man of God* may reflect a tradition that David was a prophet, since he composed parts of the Bible. In rabbinic traditions David is listed as one of ten figures (e.g., Moses, Elkana, Elisha, Micha), each of whom is said to be a "man of God," "ʾish ʾElohim" (*Sifre Devarim,* piska 342 on Deut. 33.1; *ʾAvot R. Nat.,* version B, ch 37).

12.27–43: The dedication of the wall. Scholars note that this section resumes the Nehemiah memoir from 7.5. After a long interruption from the Ezra memoir, which is inserted into the book of Nehemiah, the dedication of the Jerusalem wall provides closure. **27:** Cf. Ezra 3.10–13; 2 Chron. 23.18; 29.26–30; 30.23. For additional mention of these musical instruments, see the postexilic 1 Chron. 13.8; 15.16; 25.1, 6; 2 Chron. 5.12; 29.25.

31 I had the officers of Judah go up onto the wall, and I appointed two large thanksgiving [choirs] and processions. [One
marched] south on the wall, to the Dung Gate; 32 behind them
were Hoshaiah and half the officers of Judah, 33 and Azariah,
Ezra, Meshullam, 34 Judah, Benjamin, Shemaiah, and Jeremiah, 35 and some of the young priests, with trumpets; Zechariah son of Jonathan son of Shemaiah son of Mattaniah son
of Micaiah son of Zaccur son of Asaph, 36 and his brothers
Shemaiah, and Azarel, Milalai, Gilalai, Maai, Nethanel, Judah,
and Hanani, with the musical instruments of David, the man
of God; and Ezra the scribe went ahead of them. 37 From there
to the Fountain Gate, where they ascended the steps of the City
of David directly before them, by the ascent on the wall, above
the house of David, [and onward] to the Water Gate on the east.
38 The other thanksgiving [choir] marched on the wall in
the opposite direction, with me and half the people behind it,
above the Tower of Ovens to the Broad Wall; 39 and above the
Gate of Ephraim, the Jeshanah Gate, the Fish Gate, the Tower of Hananel, the Tower of the Hundred, to the Sheep Gate;
and they halted at the Gate of the Prison Compound. 40 Both
thanksgiving choirs halted at the House of God, and I and
half the prefects with me, 41 and the priests Eliakim, Maaseiah, Miniamin, Micaiah, Elioenai, Zechariah, Hananiah, with
trumpets, 42 and Maaseiah and Shemaiah, Eleazar, Uzzi, Jehohanan, Malchijah, Elam, and Ezer. The the singers sounded
forth, with Jezrahiah in charge.
43 On that day, they offered great sacrifices and rejoiced, for
God made them rejoice greatly; the women and children also rejoiced, and the rejoicing in Jerusalem could be heard from afar.
44 At that time men were appointed over the chambers that
served as treasuries for the gifts, the first fruits, and the tithes,
into which the portions prescribed by the Teaching for the
priests and Levites were gathered from the fields of the towns;
for the people of Judah were grateful to the priests and Levites
who were in attendance, 45 who kept the charge of their God and
the charge of purity, as well as to the singers and gatekeepers
[serving] in accord with the ordinance of David and Solomon
his son— 46 for the chiefs of the singers and songs of praise and
thanksgiving to God already existed in the time of David and
Asaph. 47 And in the time of Zerubbabel, and in the time of Nehemiah, all Israel contributed the daily portions of the singers and
the gatekeepers, and made sacred contributions for the Levites,
and the Levites made sacred contributions for the Aaronites.

13 At that time they read to the people from the Book of
Moses, and it was found written that no Ammonite or
Moabite might ever enter the congregation of God, 2 since they
did not meet Israel with bread and water, and hired Balaam

43: *And the rejoicing in Jerusalem could be heard from afar:* As at the beginning of the rebuilding, the sound of joy can be heard from afar. See Ezra 3.13.

12.44–47: Ensuring support of Temple clergy through tithing. 45: The Temple staff are authorized to dedicate, sacrifice, and continue the Temple service. Nehemiah emphasizes direct continuity with David and Solomon. **47:** *Zerubbabel* and *Nehemiah* are treated as contemporaries, which is historically inaccurate.

13.1–3: Prohibition against intermarriage with an Ammonite or Moabite. Cf. Ezra chs 9–10. **2:** Cf. Deut. 23.3–5. *Balaam,* see Num. chs 22–24.

against them to curse them; but our God turned the curse into a blessing. [3] When they heard the Teaching, they separated all the alien admixture from Israel.

[4] Earlier, the priest Eliashib, a relative of Tobiah, who had been appointed over the rooms in the House of our God, [5] had assigned to him[a] a large room where they used to store the meal offering, the frankincense, the equipment, the tithes of grain, wine, and oil, the dues of the Levites, singers and gatekeepers, and the gifts for the priests. [6] During all this time, I was not in Jerusalem, for in the thirty-second year of King Artaxerxes of Babylon, I went to the king, and only after a while did I ask leave of the king [to return]. [7] When I arrived in Jerusalem, I learned of the outrage perpetrated by Eliashib on behalf of Tobiah in assigning him a room in the courts of the House of God. [8] I was greatly displeased, and had all the household gear of Tobiah thrown out of the room; [9] I gave orders to purify the rooms, and had the equipment of the House of God and the meal offering and the frankincense put back.

[10] I then discovered that the portions of the Levites had not been contributed, and that the Levites and the singers who performed the [temple] service had made off, each to his fields. [11] I censured the prefects, saying, "How is it that the House of God has been neglected?" Then I recalled [the Levites] and installed them again in their posts; [12] and all Judah brought the tithes of grain, wine, and oil into the treasuries. [13] I put the treasuries in the charge of the priest Shelemiah, the scribe Zadok, and Pedaiah of the Levites; and assisting them was Hanan son of Zaccur son of Mattaniah—for they were regarded as trustworthy persons, and it was their duty to distribute the portions to their brothers.

[14] O my God, remember me favorably for this, and do not blot out the devotion I showed toward the House of my God and its attendants.

[15] At that time I saw men in Judah treading winepresses on the sabbath, and others bringing heaps of grain and loading them onto asses, also wine, grapes, figs, and all sorts of goods, and bringing them into Jerusalem on the sabbath. I admonished them there and then for selling provisions. [16] Tyrians who lived there brought fish and all sorts of wares and sold them on the sabbath to the Judahites in Jerusalem. [17] I censured the nobles of Judah, saying to them, "What evil thing is this that you are doing, profaning the sabbath day! [18] This is just what your ancestors did, and for it God brought all this misfortune on this city; and now you give cause for further wrath against Israel by profaning the sabbath!"

a I.e., Tobiah.

3: As in Ezra chs 9–10, not just Moabites and Ammonites are separated, but all foreigners.

13.4–9: Tobiah the Ammonite compromises the purity of the Temple and Nehemiah resolves the crisis. 6: Nehemiah returned to Artaxerxes for an unknown time, during which problems arose. Cf. 2.6.

13.10–14: Re-establishing the tithes.

13.15–22: Observance of the Sabbath day. The closest parallel to this prohibition of business on the Sabbath day is Jer. 17.21–24 (cf. Amos 8.5). For other exilic and postexilic discussion of Sabbath observance, see Isa. 56.1–8; Ezek. ch 20. As is clear from the covenant in ch 10 and the discussion here, Sabbath observance is seen as inextricably linked to the fulfillment of the covenant between God and Israel. Violation of the Sabbath would result in the loss of Jerusalem and Judah again, as it did earlier, according to Jer. 17.1–24. **15:** The Rabbis explain that this v. reflects an early stage in the application of Sabbath law, when lax observance demanded a strict response, and the use of all but three utensils on the Sabbath day was forbidden. Later on, as reflected in *m. Shab.* 17.4, the Rabbis were more lenient (*b. Shab.* 123b and Rashi ad loc.).

[19] When shadows filled the gateways of Jerusalem at the approach of the sabbath, I gave orders that the doors be closed, and ordered them not to be opened until after the sabbath. I stationed some of my servants at the gates, so that no goods should enter on the sabbath. [20] Once or twice the merchants and the vendors of all sorts of wares spent the night outside Jerusalem, [21] but I warned them, saying, "What do you mean by spending the night alongside the wall? If you do so again, I will lay hands upon you!" From then on they did not come on the sabbath. [22] I gave orders to the Levites to purify themselves and come and guard the gates, to preserve the sanctity of the sabbath.

This too, O my God, remember to my credit, and spare me in accord with your abundant faithfulness.

[23] Also at that time, I saw that Jews had married Ashdodite, Ammonite, and Moabite women; [24] a good number of their children spoke the language of Ashdod and the language of those various peoples, and did not know how to speak Judean. [25] I censured them, cursed them, flogged them, tore out their hair, and adjured them by God, saying, "You shall not give your daughters in marriage to their sons, or take any of their daughters for your sons or yourselves. [26] It was just in such things that King Solomon of Israel sinned! Among the many nations there was not a king like him, and so well loved was he by his God that God made him king of all Israel, yet foreign wives caused even him to sin. [27] How, then, can we acquiesce in your doing this great wrong, breaking faith with our God by marrying foreign women?" [28] One of the sons of Joiada son of the high priest Eliashib was a son-in-law of Sanballat the Horonite; I drove him away from me.

[29] Remember to their discredit, O my God, how they polluted the priesthood, the covenant of the priests and Levites. [30] I purged them of every foreign element, and arranged for the priests and the Levites to work each at his task by shifts, [31] and for the wood offering [to be brought] at fixed times and for the first fruits.

O my God, remember it to my credit!

13.23–27: Prohibition against intermarriage. 23: Though the book draws to a conclusion by restating one of its main themes, the dangers of intermarriage, the conception here is quite different from Ezra 9.2. **26:** See 1 Kings 11.1–13.

13.28–31: Purification of the returnees and concluding prayer. The final vv. in Neh. re-emphasize the careful exclusion of any person who compromised the purification of the returnees and the rebuilding of the Temple. **28:** The perceived vulnerability of the newly constituted Jewish community in Jerusalem; even someone with authentic lineage must be banished because of a relation through marriage to *Sanballat the Horonite*. **29:** Here there is an emphasis on the inextricable link between the defilement of the priesthood and the vulnerability of the renewed covenant with the recent returnees. The re-established community still perceives itself to be vulnerable to destruction and defilement. **30–31:** The final vv. are a repeated expression of the hope that the purification and the sacrifices will continue to be received as genuine and authentic by God and, furthermore, that God will consider the re-established community to be genuine and authentic. Thus, the concluding vv. seem intended to link the reforms inextricably to the figure of Nehemiah. While the ending is certainly abrupt and arguably anticlimactic, it nevertheless seems to fit with the overall themes and focus of Ezra-Neh.

דברי הימים א

1 Chronicles

THE TITLE "THE BOOK OF CHRONICLES", a rendering of the Hebrew *divrei hayyamim* (e.g., 1 Kings 14.19, "Annals"), is a misnomer. The book is neither a dry chronicle nor an analytic work, but a complex theological-historical composition beginning with Adam and concluding with the Cyrus declarations (538 BCE). Chronicles should not be identified with the Annals of the Kings of Israel or the Annals of the Kings of Judah that are frequently mentioned in Kings, since Chronicles was written after Kings. Furthermore, even though in English Bibles, following the tradition of the Septuagint (the ancient Greek Bible translation, abbreviated LXX), Chronicles is divided into two books like Samuel and Kings, in the Hebrew tradition it is a single book. It is thus proper to speak of the book of Chronicles rather than the books of Chronicles.

Rabbinic tradition assigns authorship of Chronicles to Ezra the scribe and his circle. Modern scholarship remains divided over the book's relationship to Ezra; though most of the 19th- and 20th-c. scholars accepted the rabbinic position, based on several considerations, including linguistic similarities between Ezra-Nehemiah and Chronicles, similarity in outlook and theology, and the fact that the conclusion of Chronicles is identical to the introduction of Ezra. These scholars used the term "the Chronicler" to refer to the single author of Chronicles-Ezra-Nehemiah. Most scholars now reject this position, arguing that the two works, though somewhat similar because they were written in approximately the same period, differ substantively in their outlook and theology. Three key examples of this difference in outlook are: (1) the uncompromising stance of Ezra-Nehemiah regarding all forms of exogamy (marrying outside of the clan), as opposed to Chronicles' relatively liberal attitude on exogamy; (2) Chronicles' inclusive definition of the true Israel, which contrasts sharply with Ezra-Nehemiah, in whose view only those Jews returning from the Babylonian captivity are the true Israel; and (3) the heightened place of the Davidic covenant in Chronicles, in contrast to the emphasis on the exodus-Sinai traditions in Ezra-Nehemiah. In addition, there are significant linguistic and stylistic differences between the two corpora. Most scholars now use the term "the Chronicler" to refer to the author of Chronicles only and believe that he was likely a member of Levitical circles. Some suggest that the Chronicler was aware, and made use, of Ezra-Nehemiah in formulating his own positions.

The book's date of composition has also been much debated, with estimates ranging from approximately 500 (the early Persian empire) through the late 2nd c. BCE (in the Hellenistic age). All in all, the late middle or, possibly, early 4th c.—i.e., mid-late Persian period (375–325)—appears the most likely. As for the literary growth of Chronicles—that is, the number of authors responsible for the book's final form—most scholars maintain that the main body of the book is the product of one author or circle. Nonetheless, some passages are commonly viewed as later additions to the book's basic stratum; therefore Chronicles probably reached its final form after the 4th c. BCE.

Awareness of the provenance of Chronicles has significant implications for understanding its purpose and methods. Three basic approaches have been advanced regarding the process(es) and stages involved in its composition. The most commonly held position views the main body of Chronicles (after the initial genealogies in chs 1–9) as a retelling of the books of Samuel and Kings. The material selected or omitted, however, along with the new formulations and literary "spins" given to older material, indicate that the author imbues this material with new perspectives and meanings, in order to address the needs of his audience. To be sure, many of the differences between the formulations of Samuel-Kings and Chronicles are not the result of tendentious rewriting; rather, they are believed to reflect the use of a *Vorlage* (i.e., the text used by the translator) of Samuel-Kings that differed from the present Masoretic Text of Samuel-Kings and, at least in some cases, was identical to that reflected in the LXX and attested in copies of Samuel-Kings found among the Dead Sea Scrolls at Qumran. The existence of these textual differences in the author's *Vorlage* does not, accordingly, affect the fundamental nature of the relationship between Chronicles and Samuel-Kings. A second understanding of the compositional process(es) maintains that Chronicles' text antedates the Samuel-Kings corpus (at least in their present form) and that it is the latter corpus that has introduced changes. Finally, a third school of thought holds that both corpora stem from a common literary ancestor or ur-composition (original, underlying text); the differences between Chronicles and Samuel-Kings are simply the result of independent (literary/scribal) growth. On this last approach the question of chronological primacy of one set of traditions over the other is of little consequence. It must be emphasized that these diverse views regarding the relationship obtaining between Chronicles and Samuel-Kings concern the origins of material shared by Chronicles and Samuel-Kings (the "synoptic passages"). It is entirely possible that other discrepancies between the two corpora—i.e., the presence of passages in Samuel-Kings not attested in Chronicles, or vice versa—are, by all accounts, the result of *independent* ongoing compositional and redactional activity peculiar to each work. Thus, for example, the absence of the David-Bathsheba episode (2 Sam. 11.2–12.25) from the Chronicler's work may stem from the fact that this narrative was added to the book of Samuel later, following the composition (and final redaction) of Chronicles, rather than, as frequently maintained, resulting from a tendentious deletion on the part of the Chronicler.

One of the key factors mustered by scholars in their attempts to establish the chronological—and, hence, literary—relationship between Chronicles and Samuel-Kings involves the chronological stratification of biblical Hebrew employed in each of the two corpora. Most scholars have favored the view that Chronicles is composed in a stratum of Hebrew known as "LBH" (late biblical Hebrew, from postexilic times), whereas the bulk of Samuel-Kings employs "CBH" (classical biblical Hebrew, from preexilic times). Naturally, this position lends support to the claim that Samuel-Kings, the older corpus, was reworked by the Chronicler. Other scholars, however, have challenged the methodology and assumptions employed by some scholars in dating the stages of biblical Hebrew and, accordingly, reject the claim of the chronological priority of Samuel-Kings. Not surprisingly, these scholars prefer to explain the divergent linguistic data attested in the two corpora along other—i.e., non-diachronic—lines (e.g., standard-vs.-colloquial Hebrew usage). In principle, this approach could allow for *both* Chronicles and Samuel-Kings—or, at the least, significant parts thereof—to be assigned to either the early biblical (i.e., preexilic) or late (exilic/postexilic) periods. In light of the clear indicators of late provenance attested in several passages in Chronicles, however, most proponents of this latter position prefer to view both corpora as relatively late (i.e., postexilic) compositions. While some of the linguistic differences between the two corpora may, indeed, be explained along non-diachronic lines, the overall weight of evidence—including the absence of discernibly late linguistic features from Samuel-Kings—favors the proposed preexilic provenance of these books.

An altogether different approach to the relationship between Chronicles and Samuel-Kings—and the implications of the numerous differences between them—takes its cue from the study of orality in the ancient world. Studies of this feature have revealed that in semi-literate societies such as ancient Israel, in which oral transmission of traditions is the primary force in shaping societal norms and identity, the exact wording of a given "text" is of relatively little significance; what is essential is the core content or message of the (overall) tradition being conveyed. In other words, in such societies, textual/lexical variation is taken for granted and ought not be seen as necessarily bearing substantive import. This observation bears significant implications regarding the content of Chronicles and its formulations vis-à-vis those of Samuel-Kings: if many variants between the two corpora are viewed as simply "free-variants," many so-called differences between them, including those of a substantive nature, may in fact be inconsequential. Similarly, though to a lesser extent, the issue of orality may bear on the diachronic relationship obtained between both corpora. For, if it is the oral aspect of the material (or, tradition) that is primary, linguistic differences between the two corpora may well reflect colloquial usage and, hence, lessen the importance or relevance of diachronic explanations of the differences between them. The importance of orality studies notwithstanding, the following caveat is apposite. Determining and applying criteria that allow for objective controls on the scope of such "free" (oral) variants is an elusive endeavor; while it is clear that minor, inconsequential variations are to be expected—as indeed is the case among manuscripts of the very same composition—distinguishing between those textual variants that reflect a substantive alteration on the part of an ancient author/scribe and those that do not involves no small measure of subjectivity. Accordingly, despite the contribution of research in orality to the study of Chronicles and its relationship to its sources, the vast number of substantive, and fundamental, differences between Chronicles and Samuel-Kings, and the worldviews reflected therein, cannot be gainsaid.

The numerous and substantive differences between Chronicles and earlier sources have led to widely divergent views concerning the quintessential nature and purpose of Chronicles. Many earlier scholars labeled Chronicles a biased falsification of Israel's past. More recent students have viewed Chronicles as a kind of edifying fiction or "exegetical" companion to Samuel-Kings. Others, noting that the presence of much nonsynoptic and wholly rewritten passages does not allow for application of the term "exegesis," have argued that the work is an independent, genuine piece of historical writing—presented, like all "history," through the (idiosyncratic) prism of its author. Of particular note is whether the Chronicler should be viewed as a "genuine" historian or, rather, a theologian, a question prompted by the ubiquitous role of theologically motivated formulations in Chronicles. The historian-theologian dichotomy, however, is inappropriate, as are the other attempts to provide facile and only partially correct depictions of the author and his work. Chronicles is, in its own right, a comprehensive, systematic (re)writing of Israel's history, formulated on the basis of, and expressive of, a distinctive worldview (i.e., theology). Indeed, Chronicles constitutes a prime source for understanding how biblical authors utilized, interpreted, supplemented and reformulated earlier source materials; this has far-reaching implications for our understanding of biblical "historiography," law, inner-biblical exegesis, and, more generally, the reformulation of existing authoritative/sacred texts, a phenomenon amply documented throughout the Second Temple period.

The very nature of Chronicles' composition raises fundamental questions about the author's intentions and his expectations of his audience. On one hand, the book's relatively late date of composition means that its author was probably familiar with the (completed, redacted) Torah in a form similar, though not fully identical, to that preserved in our own day, and in some form of almost all of the prophetic, narrative, and poetic works (e.g., some form of Ps.) which comprise the present canon of the Hebrew Bible. Accordingly, the author's understanding of a given subject or passage is likely to reflect not only the developed belief systems of his own period, but the other relevant passages from the earlier biblical corpus, as they were understood in his time. Indeed, the author's interest in harmonizing various biblical passages informs much of the author's reformulation of earlier texts. At the same time, the very novelty of the book's (re)formulations begs the following question: on the assumption that Chronicles is, as discussed above, a rewriting of Samuel-Kings and other sources, did the author expect his audience to be familiar with the earlier texts and/or traditions upon which he drew, or not? In other words, did he intend his work to supplement the earlier compositions or, rather, to supersede the earlier histories? To be sure, this question has been raised about other biblical books (e.g., Deut.'s reformulation of earlier sources), but it is especially important in connection with Chronicles, given the vast amount of overlap between Chronicles and Samuel-Kings. (This issue will be noted in the annotations to several passages.) Several passages (e.g., 1 Chron. 2.7, 10; 2 Chron. 10.15) presuppose the audience's familiarity with earlier narrative traditions. Yet, the radical reformulation of much of the book's source material is difficult to explain on this basis. On balance, it appears that the Chronicler presupposes the audience's familiarity with earlier traditions; it is likely, however, that these traditions were (assumed to be) known by his audience only in a general, elastic form, allowing for alterations—and/or alternate explanations—where necessary.

The difficulty in resolving this matter is further complicated by the ambivalent nature of Chronicles' treatment of earlier legal and religious traditions, namely, the seemingly inconsistent or ad hoc fashion in which the book treats and reacts to earlier sources of biblical law. On the one hand, several passages implicitly reflect acceptance of the authoritative, perhaps even semi-canonical, status of earlier legal and cultic norms, in particular those attested in pentateuchal sources (see, e.g., nn. to 1 Chron. 15.2–11, 13–15; 2 Chron. 35.12–13). On the other hand, Chronicles' willingness to ignore, modify, or override pentateuchal norms at several junctures (see, e.g., 1 Chron. 23.24–27; 2 Chron. 22.11–12; 30.10–20) would seem to call into question the authoritative (or, perhaps, semi-canonical) status of these earlier compositions. Though some scholars have attempted to resolve this and other difficulties by depicting the book as belonging to the genre of "utopian" literature—such that the author's purpose is to set forth his view of the world as it should be—this explanation is ill-defined and, ultimately, unsatisfying. An alternative is that the Chronicler viewed the legal norms of the Bible as guidelines rather than fixed, binding regulations. What is clear is that the Chronicler was selective in his approach, accepting many earlier legal and religious positions while rejecting or modifying others. Less clear is whether the Chronicler's positions were actually implemented during his —or any other—time in Israelite/Jewish history. In this sense, the many positions unique to Chronicles may, indeed, reflect a utopian view of a properly constituted Israelite/Jewish society; this is true of other Israelite and ancient Near Eastern historical works as well.

The existence of many discrepancies between Chronicles and other biblical compositions, most notably Samuel-Kings, was noted already by Jews living shortly after the book's composition. Ancient readers of the Bible, as well as virtually all premodern exegetes, assumed as a matter of course that there could be no substantive contradictions between Chronicles and its earlier biblical sources. The earliest testimony to the awareness of the differences between Chronicles and Samuel-Kings is reflected in the very name given to Chronicles by the translators of the LXX. The Jewish translators of Chronicles, living in the mid-2nd c. BCE, called

Chronicles by the Greek term "Paraleipomenon," in the LXX translation, i.e., a "(supplement to) things omitted." This title implies an exegetical stance, according to which the additional material of Chronicles is not the literary creation of the author of Chronicles, but includes genuine "historical" traditions which, for one reason or another, were not included in Samuel. This harmonistic approach was also adopted by Eupolemus, an historian of the 2nd c. BCE, and is especially manifest in Josephus's approach as is well documented already in his *Ant.*, which superimposes the narratives of Samuel-Kings and Chronicles. While this approach is incorrect, it does reflect that at points Chronicles presupposes the reader's familiarity with earlier sources, or at least traditions now found from those sources (see e.g., 1 Chron. ch 10, which assumes knowledge of Saul's kingship). Rabbinic tradition, which clearly indicates awareness of the numerous differences between Chronicles and its sources, tends to view the earlier biblical compositions as historically true, while viewing Chronicles as a kind of midrash to these works. (See essay on "Midrash," pp. 1879–91). At the same time, it is important to note that the Rabbis of antiquity produced no systematic commentary to Chronicles, so there is little way to determine how they resolved the many discrepancies—or, for that matter, what they viewed as a true "discrepancy"—between Chronicles and its sources. This state of affairs improved only marginally in the post-Talmudic and medieval periods, when Chronicles, in the final canonical sections of Writings, was largely neglected in favor of Samuel and Kings, in the Prophets section, which served a more significant role in Jewish liturgy. (The Prophets are used for haftarah readings, while the Writings are not.) Indeed, one prominent medieval exegete openly acknowledged that he had hardly studied the book. Against this backdrop, it is noteworthy that at least one early renaissance exegete, Isaac Abravanel (d. 1508), acknowledged the tendentious nature of Chronicles, comparing it to the politically motivated treatises of monarchies in his own time. In general, the available evidence suggests that, at least with respect to historical traditions, Jews of antiquity accepted the version of the accounts as preserved in the earlier Deuteronomistic sources of Samuel and Kings over that of Chronicles. The relative unimportance of Chronicles among ancient Jews correlates with the fact that only one copy of Chronicles was uncovered among the literary finds of the Second Temple community at Qumran (the Dead Sea Scrolls). In light of this state of affairs, it is noteworthy that one leading 18th-c. Talmudist, R. Aryeh Loeb ben Asher (Gūnzberg) (Metz, France; d. 1785) was willing to acknowledge that the incompatibility of the genealogical data attested in 1 Chronicles with that preserved in Ezra was, indeed, irreconcilable, the result of the biblical editors incorporating conflicting sets of traditions and data in the two works.

Chronicles advances several major themes and religious perspectives. In some cases Chronicles has merely reworked and highlighted positions addressed, in different form, in other biblical books; in other instances, Chronicles charts a wholly new course. A brief overview of some of the salient issues follows. Other issues will be addressed in the annotations.

The central topic in Chronicles is the Temple service, the institution that lies at the center of Jewish/Israelite life, and around which Chronicles weaves its view of Israel's history. This position reflects the religio-political reality of Second Temple life, in which the cult, rather than the (defunct) Davidic monarchy, occupied center stage. For much of this period the Temple remained a modest structure and support for its personnel was not always forthcoming; accordingly, Chronicles' formulations reflect a call for rejuvenating the national cult.

One of the principles long viewed as a hallmark of Chronicles is its strict notion of divine providence and retribution. On this view, virtuous deeds lead to a reward (wealth, children, etc.), while bad deeds bring punishment and suffering. Similarly, so it is held, Chronicles rejects the notion of vicarious punishment and/or reward (see Exod. 20.5, 6 nn.); individuals are neither punished nor rewarded for the actions of another individual. This theology has generally been understood as largely, but not exclusively, retrospective in nature, accounting for national (and personal) misfortunes of the past, but also offering Jews of the Second Temple period theological guidance in their day-to-day lives. Indeed, some have argued that this position is Chronicles' raison d'être. However, Chronicles is inconsistent in applying this principle; this has led some scholars to suggest that Chronicles does not differ fundamentally from other biblical books in its understanding of vicarious punishment and retribution. Rather, the book's uniqueness lies in its view of divine compassion or grace as the operative principle. It is this quality, so it is argued, which allows for repentance and forgiveness of transgressions, thereby conveying the message of eternal hope. Stated differently, the divine punishment is a last resort measure, imposed only if the offender has obstinately refused to mend his ways. Chronicles' approach is thus seen as primarily forward-looking and hope-inspiring, rather than retrospective and expressive of a systematic theological stance. Although a definitive assessment of Chronicles' position remains elusive, this latter approach appears closer to the mark.

A potentially related issue concerns Chronicles' realpolitik and the place of messianic or eschatological expectations in the work. Scholarly views differ widely, largely as a result of differing uses of the term "eschatology." To be sure, Chronicles—perhaps because of its nature as a rewriting of First Temple material, perhaps out of fear of upsetting the contemporary hegemony—contains no explicit statement on either matter. This has led to the view that the author of Chronicles was a "pragmatist" who saw contemporary Jewish society, with its functioning cult, as the fulfillment of Israel's role; Persian hegemony, which allowed for such cultic activity, is accepted with no monarchic or royalist expectations (no hope for the reinstitution of the Davidic monarchy). This view, however, is less than convincing. The Chronicler's apparent acceptance of the status quo and the foreign monarch's role as supporter of the cultic establishment may simply mean that, even under less than optimal conditions, Israel has not been abandoned by its deity. In addition, Chronicles' vastly expanded depiction of David's and Solomon's accomplishments in various spheres and the glorified depiction of the Davidic dynasty—and denigration of all other monarchs, including David's predecessor, Saul—along with the book's emphasis on "all Israel" suggests that anticipation of a Davidic, "messianic" figure is a central feature of Chronicles. Indeed, some see this messianic/eschatological yearning as the driving force behind Chronicles' forward-looking notion of grace: proper conduct, trust in the omnipotent deity, and divine compassion, can bring about Israel's restoration with a Davidic king at its head.

Chronicles' view regarding the northern monarchy is quite clear: in contrast to the book of Kings, which justifies the existence of the northern monarchy (see esp. 1 Kings ch 11), its very existence is illegitimate, since the Davidic kings alone constitute the earthly expression of the LORD's kingdom. For this reason, Chronicles discusses the fortunes of the northern monarchy only to the extent that they impact Judah. This was easy to accomplish in his time-period, several centuries after the exile of the north. Positions differ, however, regarding the importance of the populace of the northern tribes. Many scholars now acknowledge that the book's frequent use of the expression "all Israel," and its references to pan-Israelite participation in various passages (both synoptic and otherwise) indicate that Chronicles' author, in contrast to Ezra-Nehemiah, viewed the unification of (northern) Israel and Judah, as well as the ingathering of all exiled Israelites/Judahites, as an issue of paramount importance. Indeed, even allowing for the existence of some inaccuracies and fictitious material, the structure of the genealogical lists of Benjamin, Ephraim, Manasseh—and, possibly, (southern) Asher—suggests that these lists were formulated on the basis of ongoing, roughly contemporaneous tribal traditions, indicating that significant portions (i.e., descendants) of these tribes had survived intact and constituted part of the Chronicler's audience. This does not, however, entail the position that the (descendants of the) northern tribes, especially those to the north of Ephraim, lived on their ancestral lands, an issue for which Chronicles offers no explicit evidence (see 1 Chron. ch 9). This approach contrasts with the view of earlier scholars, who understood the "all-Israel" passages to mean that the true claim to the title "Israel" rests exclusively with Judah and those northern tribes aligned with her or living within her borders, yielding a position close to that of Ezra-Nehemiah.

Chronicles, like other biblical compositions, attaches great importance to the role of prophecy in Israelite (and Judean) life. At the same time, it also attests several unique positions regarding prophets and prophecy. It contains a relatively large number of instances in which lay persons spontaneously serve as conduits for ad hoc prophecy. While these individuals are accorded the titles reserved for "professional" prophets, they play no less important a role in providing divine guidance to the nation. Failure to pay heed to any of these prophetic warnings and guidance resulted in catastrophe. In addition to the novelty of ad hoc prophecy, Chronicles assigns new roles to professional prophets, most notably that of recording the official biographies ("chronicles") of kings. Chronicles' unique depictions of prophecy and the prophetic role(s) convey the conviction that although circumstances in postexilic society may be quite different from those before the Babylonian exile, the lines of communication with the deity remain intact.

Another significant contribution of Chronicles is the important role played by women. Although virtually all of the book's major characters—i.e., monarchs and prophets—are men, the book preserves some notable exceptions of women who play significant roles in Israel's life. These women are depicted as heads of families (or clans) and their land holdings, and are even credited with accomplishments generally associated only with successful monarchs (e.g., building of cities). This motif may reflect the socio-economic reality and exigencies of postexilic and Second Temple society, wherein all members of society were called upon to contribute to all venues of life, including those that, in earlier times, would have been deemed the exclusive domain of men.

A notable feature of Chronicles is its reticence concerning several pivotal events in the nation's history, e.g., the exodus from Egypt, the theophany at Sinai, and the "conquest" of Canaan. Many scholars see in these omissions Chronicles' expression of the eternal connection between the people of Israel and its land as an unbroken chain, having no real starting point, nor involving a hiatus after the First Temple period. At the time of Chronicles' composition, Jews constituted only one part of a heterogeneous population in their ancestral land, while a significant proportion, perhaps even a majority, of Jews lived in foreign lands. Chronicles makes a clear statement regarding the true owners of the land as well as the need for all Jews to return to their homeland.

Several aspects of Chronicles' worldview are reminiscent of views encountered in rabbinic literature. Two examples are: the importance of intention (e.g., joy, sincerity) as opposed to concrete deeds alone in the service of the LORD, and the view that people are legally culpable for wrongdoing only if duly warned prior to committing the offense. In light of this, some scholars have described Chronicles as a bridge between the "classical period" of the Bible and later rabbinic society. While there is some truth in this depiction, the points of similarity between Chronicles and rabbinic thought may have other explanations. Chronicles' frequent insistence on warning the king and/or people of Israel as a sine qua non for religious culpability may simply be part of the book's view of grace, with its repeated attempts to steer Israel in the right path. Similarly, the importance of joy, appearing mostly in connection with divine worship, may be the author's way of highlighting the centrality of the cult, rather than constituting a general theological principle regarding the importance of intentions. Hence, while Chronicles certainly reflects positions differing from those of other biblical works, the scope of views common to Chronicles and earlier biblical works places the book squarely within the biblical matrix, rendering the depiction of Chronicles as a "bridge" somewhat exaggerated.

The following is a schematic description of Chronicles' structure.

1 Chronicles chs 1–9: The genealogical tables
1 Chronicles ch 10: The reign of Saul
1 Chronicles chs 11–29: The reign of David
2 Chronicles chs 1–9: Solomon's reign
2 Chronicles 10.1–36.16: Post-Solomonic kings
2 Chronicles 36.17–23: Destruction of Temple, exile, and Cyrus's proclamation

[DAVID ROTHSTEIN]

1 Adam, Seth, Enosh; 2 Kenan, Mahalalel, Jared; 3 Enoch, Methuselah, Lamech; 4 Noah, Shem, Ham, and Japheth.
5 [a]The sons of Japheth: Gomer, Magog, Madai, Javan, Tubal,
Meshech, and Tiras. 6 The sons of Gomer: Ashkenaz, Diphath,
and Togarmah. 7 The sons of Javan: Elishah, Tarshish, Kittim,
and Rodanim.
8 The sons of Ham: Cush, Mizraim, Put, and Canaan. 9 The
sons of Cush: Seba, Havilah, Sabta, Raama, and Sabteca. The
sons of Raama: Sheba and Dedan. 10 Cush begot Nimrod; he
was the first mighty one on earth.
11 Mizraim begot the Ludim, the Anamim, the Lehabim, the
Naphtuhim, 12 the Pathrusim, the Casluhim (whence the Philistines came forth), and the Caphtorim.
13 Canaan begot Sidon his first-born, and Heth, 14 and the Jebusites, the Amorites, the Girgashites, 15 the Hivites, the Arkites,
the Sinites, 16 the Arvadites, the Zemarites, and the Hamathites.
17 The sons of Shem: Elam, Asshur, Arpachshad, Lud, Aram,
Uz, Hul, Gether, and Meshech. 18 Arpachshad begot Shelah;
and Shelah begot Eber. 19 Two sons were born to Eber: the
name of the one was Peleg (for in his days the earth was divided), and the name of his brother Joktan. 20 Joktan begot Almodad, Sheleph, Hazarmaveth, Jerah, 21 Hadoram, Uzal, Diklah,
22 Ebal, Abimael, Sheba, 23 Ophir, Havilah, and Jobab; all these
were the sons of Joktan.
24 Shem, Arpachshad, Shelah; 25 Eber, Peleg, Reu; 26 Serug,
Nahor, Terah; 27 Abram, that is, Abraham.
28 [b]The sons of Abraham: Isaac and Ishmael. 29 This is their
line: The first-born of Ishmael, Nebaioth; and Kedar, Abdeel,
Mibsam, 30 Mishma, Dumah, Massa, Hadad, Tema, 31 Jetur, Naphish, and Kedmah. These are the sons of Ishmael. 32 The sons
of Keturah, Abraham's concubine: she bore Zimran, Jokshan,

1.1–9.44: The genealogies. Genealogies are important in many ancient societies, especially those structured on familial relationships. They should not always be understood literally and are used in the Bible, as elsewhere, to express the relationships between various clans and peoples as well as to highlight the place of prominent individuals or to give them a pedigree. They play an especially important role in Priestly thinking, and are reflected in postbiblical literature as well, for example in Matt. 1.1–17. Given the interests of the Chronicler, it is not surprising that the genealogies of David and the descendants of Levi, the Levites and priests, play a particularly prominent role in this section. Some of these chs have their source in other biblical material, while other parts do not, reflecting likely access to sources beyond what is now found in the canonical Bible.

1.1–2.2: Adam to Israel. Although this material follows Gen. (5.3–32; 11.10–27; 36.1–43), its selection and arrangement (e.g., placing secondary lines of descent before the primary) emphasize the line culminating in Israel. There is no elaboration concerning Abraham, a point which, together with other hints in Chronicles, suggests that Chronicles views Jacob/Israel (consistently referred to as Israel in Chronicles) as the central patriarch; see 16.13. This may be part

a *With vv. 5–23, cf. Gen. 10.1–30.* b *With vv. 28–33, cf. Gen. 25.1–16.*

Medan, Midian, Ishbak, and Shuah. The sons of Jokshan: Sheba and Dedan. 33 The sons of Midian: Ephah, Epher, Enoch,
Abida, and Eldaah. All these were the descendants of Keturah.
34 Abraham begot Isaac. The sons of Isaac: Esau and Israel.
35 The sons of Esau: Eliphaz, Reuel, Jeush, Jalam, and Korah.
36 The sons of Eliphaz: Teman, Omar, Zephi, Gatam, Kenaz,
Timna, and Amalek. 37 The sons of Reuel: Nahath, Zerah,
Shammah, and Mizzah.
38 The sons of Seir: Lotan, Shobal, Zibeon, Anah, Dishon, Ezer,
and Dishan. 39 The sons of Lotan: Hori and Homam; and Lotan's
sister was Timna. 40 The sons of Shobal: Alian, Manahath, Ebal,
Shephi, and Onam. The sons of Zibeon: Aiah and Anah. 41 The
sons of Anah: Dishon. The sons of Dishon: Hamran, Eshban,
Ithran, and Cheran. 42 The sons of Ezer: Bilhan, Zaavan, and
Jaakan. The sons of Dishan: Uz and Aran.
43[a] These are the kings who reigned in the land of Edom before any king reigned over the Israelites: Bela son of Beor, and
the name of his city was Dinhabah. 44 When Bela died, Jobab
son of Zerah from Bozrah succeeded him as king. 45 When
Jobab died, Husham of the land of the Temanites succeeded
him as king. 46 When Husham died, Hadad son of Bedad, who
defeated the Midianites in the country of Moab, succeeded
him as king, and the name of his city was Avith. 47 When Hadad died, Samlah of Masrekah succeeded him as king. 48 When
Samlah died, Saul of Rehoboth-on-the-River succeeded him
as king. 49 When Saul died, Baal-hanan son of Achbor succeeded him as king. 50 When Baal-hanan died, Hadad succeeded
him as king; and the name of his city was Pai, and his wife's
name Mehetabel daughter of Matred daughter of Me-zahab.
51 And Hadad died.
The clans of Edom were the clans of Timna, Alvah, Jetheth,
52 Oholibamah, Elah, Pinon, 53 Kenaz, Teman, Mibzar, 54 Magdiel, and Iram; these are the clans of Edom.

2 These are the sons of Israel: Reuben, Simeon, Levi, Judah,
Issachar, Zebulun, 2 Dan, Joseph, Benjamin, Naphtali,
Gad, and Asher. 3 The sons of Judah: Er, Onan, and Shelah;

a With vv. 43–50, cf. Gen. 36.31–43.

of the book's "inclusivist," pan-Israel tendency. **1.43–54:** The list of Edomite rulers from Gen. 36.31–43 is seemingly superfluous. Chronicles' point may be that physical descent alone is not determinative of one's worthiness; alternately, the list appears for the sake of completeness. **2.1–2:** With the exception of Dan (the son of Bilhah), the children of Israel are listed according to their mothers, beginning with the children of Leah, then Rachel, then the concubines Bilhah and Zilpah.

2.3–9.1: The tribes of Israel and Judah. Although thought by some to be a later addition to the book, this listing of Israel's forebears is an integral part of Chronicles and its literary plan. It establishes the book's audience: pedigreed Jews of the Second Temple period as the only genuine heirs to the ancestral covenant, which has its most tangible expression in possession of the land of Canaan and the functioning of the Temple cult. The historicity of this list is far from certain. The issue is particularly acute in connection with several key figures, such as the priest Zadok, in ch 5, for whom Chronicles appears to have supplied an entirely new pedigree. The appearance in these chs of many otherwise unknown names was noted by the early Rabbis, who, consistent with their tendency attested elsewhere, employed midrash-type interpretations of these names in order to link them with better-known individuals known from other biblical passages. In some cases the Rabbis' motive appears to have been to explain (away) the seemingly non-Israelite origin of many of these individuals; in other cases, the Rabbis are attempting to harmonize divergent traditions. The structure of this list has been variously explained. Two likely explanations follow. The list reflects geographical location; it begins with the southern tribe of Judah, the leading non-sacral tribe, and then proceeds in counter-clockwise fashion, moving to the east (Transjordan) before returning westward to address the northern and, then, central tribes. At the center of this list is the tribe of Levi, reflective of the tribe's central role in Chronicles. The fact that this geographical depiction is not fully accurate suggests that the author was primarily, though not exclusively, interested in Judah, Levi, and Benjamin, the tribes that remained loyal to the Davidic monarchy and the Jerusalem Temple. This accounts for the framework: Judah (at the beginning of the list), Benjamin (at the end), and Levi (in the middle). The order of the remaining tribes was deemed not particularly important. The tribes of Dan and Zebulun are missing from the list, possibly as the result of scribal error. Some maintain that Chronicles intentionally

these three, Bath-shua the Canaanite woman bore to him. But
Er, Judah's first-born, was displeasing to the LORD, and He took
his life. 4 His daughter-in-law Tamar also bore him Perez and
Zerah. Judah's sons were five in all.
5 The sons of Perez: Hezron and Hamul. 6 The sons of Zerah:
Zimri, Ethan, Heman, Calcol, and Dara, five in all. 7 The sons of
Carmi: Achar, the troubler of Israel, who committed a trespass
against the proscribed thing; 8 and Ethan's son was Azariah.
9 The sons of Hezron that were born to him: Jerahmeel,
Ram, and Chelubai. 10 Ram begot Amminadab, and Amminadab begot Nahshon, prince of the sons of Judah. 11 Nahshon was the father of Salma, Salma of Boaz, 12 Boaz of Obed,
Obed of Jesse. 13 Jesse begot Eliab his first-born, Abinadab the
second, Shimea the third, 14 Nethanel the fourth, Raddai the
fifth, 15 Ozem the sixth, David the seventh; 16 their sisters were
Zeruiah and Abigail. The sons of Zeruiah: Abishai, Joab, and
Asahel, three. 17 Abigail bore Amasa, and the father of Amasa
was Jether the Ishmaelite.

omitted Dan because of its association with apostasy (see Judg. chs 17–19; 1 Kings 12.29–30); this allows Chronicles to portray a religiously idealized Israel.

2.3–4.23: Judah. Judah was especially important since the majority of the Jews living in this period traced themselves to Judah, and because the Davidic king was descended from Judah. In addition to material preserved elsewhere, this list contains traditions without parallel; e.g., the claim that Caleb and Jerahmeel were brothers, and sons of Hezron. The author's acknowledgment of six marriages with foreigners is ample testimony to his willingness to integrate non-Israelite/Judahite individuals and, perhaps, communities into the body of Israel. It is likely that the genealogy here reflects an attempt to include peoples who had not been part of preexilic Judah but whose incorporation during the Persian period would have been helpful in solidifying relations with the Persian government. **2.3–4:** A condensation of the narrative of Gen. ch 38. **5:** Reflecting Gen. 46.12. **7:** Chronicles' laconic formulation presupposes the reader's familiarity with the episode in Josh. 7.1–26, either in its present canonical form or in some other, possibly oral, form—this is one of many instances that indicate that while creating a fundamentally new narrative framework, Chronicles draws upon the audience's (presumed) familiarity with earlier traditions. The passage in Josh. expresses the importance of observing divine regulations, especially those pertaining to the realm of the sacred, and makes the point that possession of the promised land, one of Chronicles' central themes, is contingent upon compliance with biblical law. In particular, the reference to Achar's act of trespass ("maʿal") is consistent with Chronicles' frequent use of this term. Here the term denotes personal use of/benefit from property devoted to the deity; elsewhere the author uses it to denote sin, in general. The name "Achar" (literally, "bring calamity") appears in this form in LXX to Josh. ch 7; the MT there reads "Achan." Hos. 2.17 may reflect LXX's form. **10–17:** David's ancestors. Chronicles' emphasis on David's genealogy reflects the monarch's central role within the book's theology. **10–15:** Cf. Ruth 4.18–22. **12–15:** David is the youngest of seven sons according to Chronicles, but 1 Sam. lists him as the youngest of either four or eight sons (see, e.g., 1 Sam. 16.7–11; 17.12–14, 17). Although some scholars maintain that Chronicles reflects a mistaken understanding of 1 Sam. 16.10, this placement as the seventh is more likely meant to glorify David since the number "seven" signifies completion in the Bible. The literary (i.e., artificial) nature of this datum is buttressed by the typological number of seven generations from Ram to Jesse and by the use of a similar technique in connection with Solomon (see 3.5 n.). The depiction of 1 Sam. ch 16 in the Dura Europos synagogue (one of the oldest synagogues in the world, uncovered in Syria in 1932) reflects Chronicles' position. The Peshitta harmonizes this v. with 1 Sam. 16.10. **16–17:** Joab is listed as the son of David's sister, as are Abishai and Asahel. Neither Zeruiah nor Abigail is ever identified as David's sister in the earlier biblical sources. The depiction of women as heads of their respective families is noteworthy; the husbands have been either omitted (v. 16) or demoted in importance (v. 17). While all of the social ramifications of this position remain unclear, it points, at the least, to the woman's status as legal owner of family property and family provider. Similar implications regarding (some) women's socio-economic status may be implied by the appearance of women's names in Heb and Aram. seals uncovered in (the Land of) Israel and at the site of the Jewish colony at Elephantine (Egypt). It is likely that this datum reflects the social reality of the author's period rather than that of preexilic Israel/Judah. Indeed, many extrabiblical sources attest to the fact that women of the Persian period (in Babylonia, Elephantine, and elsewhere) were actively involved in various fields of commerce. Additional examples of women as heads of households appear in vv. 34–35, 48–49. The importance of women's contribution to family life in Persian period Judean society is also reflected in Prov. 31.10–31, likely a composition of the Persian period, which describes the ways in which a wife's

18 Caleb son of Hezron had children by his wife Azubah, and
by Jerioth; these were her sons: Jesher, Shobab, and Ardon.
19 When Azubah died, Caleb married Ephrath, who bore him
Hur. 20 Hur begot Uri, and Uri begot Bezalel.
21 Afterward Hezron had relations with the daughter of
Machir father of Gilead—he had married her when he was sixty
years old—and she bore him Segub; 22 and Segub begot Jair; he
had twenty-three cities in the land of Gilead. 23 But Geshur and
Aram took from them Havvoth-jair, Kenath and its dependencies, sixty towns. All these were the sons of Machir, the father of
Gilead. 24 After the death of Hezron, in Caleb-ephrathah, Abijah, wife of Hezron, bore Ashhur, the father of Tekoa.
25 The sons of Jerahmeel the first-born of Hezron: Ram his
first-born, Bunah, Oren, Ozem, and Ahijah. 26 Jerahmeel had
another wife, whose name was Atarah; she was the mother of
Onam. 27 The sons of Ram the first-born of Jerahmeel: Maaz,
Jamin, and Eker. 28 The sons of Onam: Shammai and Jada.
The sons of Shammai: Nadab and Abishur. 29 The name of
Abishur's wife was Abihail, and she bore him Ahban and Mo-
lid. 30 The sons of Nadab: Seled and Appaim; Seled died childless. 31 The sons of Appaim: Ishi. The sons of Ishi: Sheshan. The
sons of Sheshan: Ahlai. 32 The sons of Jada, Shammai's brother:
Jether and Jonathan; Jether died childless. 33 The sons of Jonathan: Peleth and Zaza. These were the descendants of Jerahmeel. 34 Sheshan had no sons, only daughters; Sheshan had an
Egyptian slave, whose name was Jarha. 35 So Sheshan gave his
daughter in marriage to Jarha his slave; and she bore him Attai. 36 Attai begot Nathan, and Nathan begot Zabad. 37 Zabad
begot Ephlal, and Ephlal begot Obed. 38 Obed begot Jehu, and
Jehu begot Azariah. 39 Azariah begot Helez, and Helez begot
Eleasah. 40 Eleasah begot Sisamai, and Sisamai begot Shallum.
41 Shallum begot Jekamiah, and Jekamiah begot Elishama.
42 The sons of Caleb brother of Jerahmeel: Meshah his first-
born, who was the father of Ziph. The sons of Mareshah father
of Hebron. 43 The sons of Hebron: Korah, Tappuah, Rekem, and
Shema. 44 Shema begot Raham the father of Jorkeam, and Rekem begot Shammai. 45 The son of Shammai: Maon, and Maon
begot Bethzur. 46 Ephah, Caleb's concubine, bore Haran, Moza,
and Gazez; Haran begot Gazez. 47 The sons of Jahdai: Regem,

resourcefulness, wisdom, and industry—inside the home and out—are responsible for her family's well-being. Indeed, the opening v. of this composition ("What a rare find is a capable wife! / Her worth is far beyond that of rubies") expresses the view that the true value—monetary and otherwise —of a capable wife far exceeds any amount paid as part of her marriage dowry. Prov. 31.14–16 depict the capable wife as overseeing female workers (of the family estate) and actively involved in commerce and land acquisition. The concluding section, v. 30, also states that a God-fearing woman, rather than a woman of beauty, is truly praiseworthy, a sentiment that the Chronicler would endorse. The listing of Joab prepares the reader for ch 11, which credits Joab with the capture of Jerusalem. The description of Amasa as the son of an Ishmaelite is significant (see 2 Sam. 19.13, which indicates that Amasa was related to David). The MT of 2 Sam. 17.25 refers to Yether as an "Israelite," a difficult reading, which is emended by some scholars. Some medieval exegetes adopted a harmonistic approach: Yithra was an Israelite who lived in Ishmaelite territory. Chronicles' text probably indicates that its author was not bothered by Amasa's Ishmaelite descent nor by Abigail's marriage to an Ishmaelite, a position that differs markedly from Ezra-Neh. (see intro.). Some scholars argue that Ezra's hard-line position may have applied only to members of his generation, and that the presence of non-Israelite ancestors in Israel's (distant) past was not problematic. Rabbinic tradents were clearly aware of the difficulties posed by passages such as these. They often resolved such passages by claiming that the foreign spouse had undergone religious conversion, an institution that is not attested in the biblical period. **18–20:** Bezalel was the most prominent member of Caleb's family, owing to his role as head craftsman of the Tabernacle; this explains the juxtaposition of vv. 18, 19 with v. 20. **34–35:** Although Chronicles nowhere spells out its views on exogamy, the present passage attests to the book's relatively open stance on the issue, in contrast to Deut. 23.8–9; Ezra 9.1–2. No less important is the fact that the descendants of this marriage are assigned the lineage of their mother, i.e., Judahite, implying that the woman here functions in the socio-legal capacity of a man. **42–49:** Many of the children mentioned here (e.g., *Hebron*) are known as geographical locations in Judah; the genealogical language here connects the founding of these cities to descendants of *Caleb* (cf. Josh. 14.12–14; Judg. 1.10), emphasizing the role of this important Judean in the foundation of important cities throughout Judah. In Torah tradition,

Jotham, Geshan, Pelet, Ephah, and Shaaph. [48] Maacah, Caleb's
concubine, bore Sheber and Tirhanah. [49] She also bore Shaaph
father of Madmannah, Sheva father of Machbenah and father
of Gibea; the daughter of Caleb was Achsah. [50] These were the
descendants of Caleb.

The sons of Hur the first-born of Ephrathah: Shobal father of
Kiriath-jearim, [51] Salma father of Bethlehem, Hareph father of
Beth-gader. [52] Shobal father of Kiriath-jearim had sons: Haro-
eh, half of the Menuhoth. [53] And the families of Kiriath-jearim:
the Ithrites, the Puthites, the Shumathites, and the Mishraites;
from these came the Zorathites and the Eshtaolites. [54] The sons
of Salma: Bethlehem, the Netophathites, Atroth-beth-joab,
and half of the Manahathites, the Zorites. [55] The families of the
scribes that dwelt at Jabez: the Tirathites, the Shimeathites, the
Sucathites; these are the Kenites who came from Hammath,
father of the house of Rechab.

3 These are the sons of David who were born to him in Hebron: the first-born Amnon, by Ahinoam the Jezreelite; the
second Daniel, by Abigail the Carmelite; [2] the third Absalom,
son of Maacah daughter of King Talmai of Geshur; the fourth
Adonijah, son of Haggith; [3] the fifth Shephatiah, by Abital;
the sixth Ithream, by his wife Eglah; [4] six were born to him in
Hebron. He reigned there seven years and six months, and in
Jerusalem he reigned thirty-three years. [5] These were born to
him in Jerusalem: Shimea, Shobab, Nathan, and Solomon,
four by Bath-shua daughter of Ammiel; [6] then Ibhar, Elishama,
Eliphelet, [7] Nogah, Nepheg, Japhia, [8] Elishama, Eliada, and
Eliphelet—nine. [9] All were David's sons, besides the sons of the
concubines; and Tamar was their sister.

[10] The son of Solomon: Rehoboam; his son Abijah, his son
Asa, his son Jehoshaphat, [11] his son Joram, his son Ahaziah,
his son Joash, [12] his son Amaziah, his son Azariah, his son
Jotham, [13] his son Ahaz, his son Hezekiah, his son Manasseh,

Caleb attains prominence as a loyal spy (see Num. chs 13–14), but since Chronicles deemphasizes the exodus and "conquest," his significance is given a different reason here. *Ephah* and *Maacah* are the only women in Chronicles identified by name as concubines; by contrast, the mothers of the children in vv. 42–45 bear no name. This suggests that the concubines' secondary spousal status does not prevent them from attaining distinction, as evidence by the fact that Maacah's sons are credited with establishing three towns (v. 49; see Josh. 15.31, 57); this is consonant with the emphasis that Chronicles places on individual merit and achievements. **49:** More than simply completing the list of Caleb's offspring, the reference to *Achsah* is another example of Chronicles' recognition, albeit implicit, of the importance of industrious women; see Josh. 15.17–19; Judg. 1.12–15, which describe (with some variation in LXX) Achsah's initiative and claim that Caleb is the son of Jephunneh (Num. 13.6; Josh. 15.13). **55:** The v. may describe the migration of three Kenite families from lands belonging to one *Hammath*—who founded Beth-rechab—to Kiriath-Sepher and their eventual settling at *Jabez*. This explanation takes the Masoretic "Sopherim" as denoting inhabitants of Kiriath-Sepher (rather than denoting a guild/family of scribes). Though Beth-rechab may refer to Beth-marcaboth (Josh. 19.5; 1 Chron. 4.31), the identity of this and other sites mentioned here remains uncertain. The *Kenites,* who appear elsewhere as pre-Israelite inhabitants of the land (Gen. 15.19), were viewed at some point as descendants of Caleb's; they are depicted elsewhere as maintaining peaceful relations with Israelite tribes (Judg. 4.17–21; 5.24–27). The v. remains opaque.

3.1–24: David's descendants. See 2.10–17 n. **1:** 2 Sam. 3.3 states that Abigail's son was named Kileab. Rabbinic and medieval commentators (*Tg. Chron.,* Radak; cf. *b. Ber.* 4a) maintained that the child bore both names; his given name was Daniel, meaning "God has judged me (innocent of any guilt in the death of Abigail's husband, Nabal)"; the name Kileab, meaning "like the father" (or "entirely the father"), was given later, when it became clear that the son bore a striking resemblance to David, thereby removing any suspicion of Nabal's paternity. (Note that this tradition views Chronicles as maintaining the original name.) The actual facts remain uncertain. Chronicles nowhere records the circumstances surrounding David's marriage to Abigail (1 Sam. ch 25), possibly because they present a less than flattering picture of David or because the author may not have been interested in purely personal aspects of David's life. **2:** The author does not hesitate to mention David's marriage to a foreign woman, *Maacah.* Such marriages often served political purposes in antiquity. **4:** The reference to *Jerusalem* at this juncture anticipates its importance for the Chronicler, who mentions the city by this name 153 times. For a discussion of David's regency, see 1 Chron. 27.1–34 n. **5:** Solomon appears as the

14 his son Amon, and his son Josiah. 15 The sons of Josiah: Johanan the first-born, the second Jehoiakim, the third Zedekiah, the fourth Shallum. 16 The descendants of Jehoiakim: his
son Jeconiah, his son Zedekiah; 17 and the sons of Jeconiah,
the captive: Shealtiel his son, 18 Malchiram, Pedaiah, Shenaz-
zar, Jekamiah, Hoshama, and Nedabiah; 19 the sons of Pedaiah:
Zerubbabel and Shimei; the sons of Zerubbabel: Meshullam
and Hananiah, and Shelomith was their sister; 20 Hashubah,
Ohel, Berechiah, Hasadiah, and Jushab-hesed—five. 21 And
the sons of Hananiah: Pelatiah and Jeshaiah; the sons of [Je-
shaiah]: Rephaiah; the sons of [Rephaiah]: Arnan; the sons of
[Arnan]: Obadiah; the sons of [Obadiah]: Shecaniah. 22 And
the sons of Shecaniah: Shemaiah; and the sons of Shemaiah:
Hattush, and Igal, and Bariah, and Neariah, and Shaphat—six.
23 And the sons of Neariah: Elioenai, and Hizkiah, and Azrikam—three. 24 And the sons of Elioenai: Hodaviah, and Eliashib, and Pelaiah, and Akkub, and Johanan, and Delaiah, and
Anani—seven.

4 The sons of Judah: Perez, Hezron, Carmi, Hur, and Shobal. 2 Reaiah son of Shobal begot Jahath, and Jahath begot
Ahumai and Lahad. These were the families of the Zorathites.
3 These were [the sons of] the father of Etam: Jezreel, Ishma,
and Idbash; and the name of their sister was Hazlelponi, 4 and
Penuel was the father of Gedor, and Ezer the father of Hu-
shah. These were the sons of Hur, the first-born of Ephrathah,
the father of Bethlehem. 5 Ashhur the father of Tekoa had two
wives, Helah and Naarah; 6 Naarah bore him Ahuzam, Hepher,
Temeni, and Ahashtari. These were the sons of Naarah. 7 The
sons of Helah: Zereth, Zohar, and Ethnan. 8 Koz was the father
of Anub, Zobebah, and the families of Aharhel son of Harum.
9 Jabez was more esteemed than his brothers; and his mother
named him Jabez, "Because," she said, "I bore him in pain."[a]
10 Jabez invoked the God of Israel, saying, "Oh, bless me, enlarge my territory, stand by me, and make me not suffer pain
from misfortune!" And God granted what he asked. 11 Chelub
the brother of Shuhah begot Mehir, who was the father of Eshton. 12 Eshton begot Bethrapha, Paseah, and Tehinnah father of
Ir-nahash. These were the men of Recah. 13 The sons of Kenaz:
Othniel and Seraiah; and the sons of Othniel: 14 Hathath and
Meonothai. He begot Ophrah. Seraiah begot Joab father of

a Heb. ʿoṣeb, *connected with "Jabez."*

fourth son born to David in Jerusalem, and the fourth son of Bath-shua (= Bathsheba). The form of this name is identical to that borne by Judah's wife, mentioned above (2.3; cf. Gen. 38.2, 12). LXX, in both Samuel-Kings and Chronicles, refers to her as "Bersabee." According to 2 Sam. 12.24, Solomon is the second of as many sons born to Bathsheba. Chronicles' version glorifies Solomon, by claiming that despite having three older brothers, he alone was chosen to be king. The "three-four" number scheme, where the fourth is climactic (as in Judah, the fourth son of Jacob), is common in the Bible. The Syriac translation (Peshitta) omits "four by Bathshua," thereby harmonizing the v. with 2 Sam. 5.14. **17–24:** Exilic and postexilic line, until Chronicles' time. This passage contains many otherwise unknown traditions, and there are substantive differences among the ancient versions. The presence of six generations following Zerubbabel (ca. 520 BCE), entails a final date for Chronicles' composition of no earlier than ca. 400 BCE or, perhaps, the early 4th c. BCE. LXX here adds yet another five generations, requiring a final date no earlier than the mid-3rd c., and possibly as late ca. 200 BCE. Scholars who posit a late 6th-c. date for Chronicles' composition attribute this extended genealogy (whether that of LXX or the MT) to a later author/redactor. The updating of the genealogy of David well into the postexilic period likely reflects, on any of the preceding approaches, the hope that one of his descendants would again assume the throne.

4.1–20: Sons of Perez. This list adds to that of Gen. 46.12 and Num. 26.20–22; see also Ruth 4.18–22. The line which eventually produced David; this genealogy continues the end of ch 2, which has been disrupted by the insertion of the genealogy of David. **9:** Despite the mention of the (Judahite/Kenite?) town Jabez above (2.55), this v. and the following one bear no genealogical connection to Judah. The two vv., probably the creation of the Chronicler, serve the theological purposes of the author; see the following v. Once again, it is the mother who names the child, here on the basis of her experiences. **10:** This opaque v., as translated here, expresses the view that by means of sincere prayer Jabez managed to overcome the limitations seemingly inherent in the name given to him by his mother. The author thus reinforces

Ge-harashim,[a] so-called because they were craftsmen. 15 The
sons of Caleb son of Jephunneh: Iru, Elah, and Naam; and the
sons of Elah: Kenaz. 16 The sons of Jehallelel: Ziph, Ziphah,
Tiria, and Asarel. 17 The sons of Ezrah: Jether, Mered, Epher,
and Jalon. She[b] conceived and bore Miriam, Shammai, and
Ishbah father of Eshtemoa. 18 And his Judahite wife bore Jered
father of Gedor, Heber father of Soco, and Jekuthiel father
of Zanoah. These were the sons of Bithiah daughter of Pharaoh, whom Mered married. 19 The sons of the wife of Hodiah
sister of Naham were the fathers of Keilah the Garmite and
Eshtemoa the Maacathite. 20 The sons of Shimon: Amnon, Rin-
nah, Ben-hanan, and Tilon. The sons of Ishi: Zoheth and Ben-
zoheth. 21 The sons of Shelah son of Judah: Er father of Lecah,
Laadah father of Mareshah, and the families of the linen fac-
tory at Beth-ashbea; 22 and Jokim, and the men of Cozeba and
Joash, and Saraph, who married into Moab and Jashubi Lehem
(the records are ancient). 23 These were the potters who dwelt
at Netaim and Gederah; they dwelt there in the king's service.

24 The sons of Simeon: Nemuel, Jamin, Jarib, Zerah, Shaul;
25 his son Shallum, his son Mibsam, his son Mishma. 26 The
sons of Mishma: his son Hammuel, his son Zaccur, his son
Shimei. 27 Shimei had sixteen sons and six daughters; but his
brothers had not many children; in all, their families were not
as prolific as the Judahites. 28 They dwelt in Beersheba, Moladah, Hazar-shual, 29 Bilhah, Ezem, Tolad, 30 Bethuel, Hormah, Ziklag, 31 Beth-marcaboth, Hazar-susim, Beth-biri, and
Shaaraim. These were their towns until David became king,
32 together with their villages, Etam, Ain, Rimmon, Tochen,
and Ashan—five towns, 33 along with all their villages that were
around these towns as far as Baal; such were their settlements.

Registered in their genealogy were: 34 Meshobab, Jamlech,
Joshah son of Amaziah, 35 Joel, Jehu son of Joshibiah son of Se-
raiah son of Asiel. 36 Elioenai, Jaakobah, Jeshohaiah, Asaiah,
Adiel, Jesimiel, Benaiah, 37 Ziza son of Shiphi son of Allon son

a *Lit. "the valley of the craftsmen."* *b* *Apparently Bithiah; cf. v. 18.*

the following recurring claims. First, sincere prayer is always effectual, difficult circumstances notwithstanding; second, such dependence on the deity yields positive results, including the acquisition of more land, itself an important motif in Chronicles. Contrary to some explanations, this passage does not reflect a pacifistic approach, preferring prayer over battle; indeed, the author does not state how, precisely, the divine response was manifest (i.e., commerce, battle). Vows are a popular sign of biblical religiosity (see Judg. 11.30–31; 1 Sam. 1.11). Such short notices, which interrupt the genealogies, are found throughout the introduction of Chronicles (e.g., 4.39–41; 5.19–22; 7.22–23) and are most likely the creation of the Chronicler. **21–23:** The presentation of *Shelah*'s descendants suggests that Shelah and his descendants remained in Canaan and were not subjected to Egyptian bondage, a datum which contradicts Gen. 46.12; Num. 26.20; see 7.20–29 n. In Gen. ch 38 Er is Judah's eldest son. Er dies and his brother, Onan, refuses to perform the levir's duty, and he, too, dies. Er's widow (Tamar), having been denied levirate marriage to Shelah, initiates a rendezvous with her father-in-law, Judah. Having then given birth to twins—neither of whom is named after the deceased Er (see Deut. 25.6; Ruth 4.10) or becomes his heir—Tamar does not remarry. No mention is made of the lot of Judah's youngest son. The present v. may reflect an attempt to bring the narrative into line with Deut. 25.6 by claiming that Shelah named his eldest son after his deceased brother, Er—this, despite the fact that Shelah's son was, presumably, not borne by Tamar but by another woman. If correct, this passage presupposes familiarity with the narrative of Gen. ch 38. This passage would be signaling the importance of fidelity to one's family and the preservation of family lineage (and, possibly, property). **22:** The Heb text behind *married into Moab* is opaque and variously translated. The present translation follows the Aram. Tg. LXX renders "settled in Moab"; others, "ruled in Moab" or "worked for Moab." **24–43:** *Simeon:* This tribe was traditionally associated with Judah (so, e.g., Judg. 1.3), which explains its position in the list. The relatively brief treatment of Simeon reflects its virtual disappearance over the course of time; indeed, biblical traditions in general regarding this tribe are limited. **28:** It is unclear whether the vv. here formed part of Persian Yehud; they may simply have been inhabited by families claiming Simeonite ancestry. **33–38:** The inconsistent manner in which the identity of the princes is formulated makes it likely that the list is not the Chronicler's creation. The list may correspond to the thirteen cities listed in Josh. 19.2–6. **33:** Chronicles, though following much of the data regarding Simeon in Josh. ch 19, omits Josh. 19.8–9, which refers to the "inheritance of the tribe of Simeon"; this may reflect Simeon's eventual absorption into Judah. The latter part of this v. is viewed by some as

of Jedaiah son of Shimri son of Shemaiah—38 these mentioned by name were chiefs in their families, and their clans increased greatly. 39 They went to the approaches to Gedor, to the eastern side of the valley, in search of pasture for their flocks. 40 They found rich, good pasture, and the land was ample, quiet, and peaceful. The former inhabitants were of Ham; 41 those recorded by name came in the days of King Hezekiah of Judah, and attacked their encampments and the Meuṇim who were found there, and wiped them out forever, and settled in their place, because there was pasture there for their flocks. 42 And some of them, five hundred of the Simeonites, went to Mount Seir, with Pelatiah, Neariah, Rephaiah, and Uzziel, sons of Ishi, at their head, 43 and they destroyed the last surviving Amalekites, and they live there to this day.

5 The sons of Reuben the first-born of Israel. (He was the first-born; but when he defiled his father's bed, his birthright was given to the sons of Joseph son of Israel, so he is not reckoned as first-born in the genealogy; 2 though Judah became more powerful than his brothers and a leader came from him, yet the birthright belonged to Joseph.) 3 The sons of Reuben, the first-born of Israel: Enoch, Pallu, Hezron, and Carmi. 4 The sons of Joel: his son Shemaiah, his son Gog, his son Shimei, 5 his son Micah, his son Reaiah, his son Baal, 6 his son Beerah—whom King Tillegath-pilneser of Assyria exiled—was chieftain of the Reubenites. 7 And his kinsmen, by their families, according to their lines in the genealogy: the head, Jeiel, and Zechariah, 8 and Bela son of Azaz son of Shema son of Joel; he dwelt in Aroer as far as Nebo and Baal-meon. 9 He also dwelt to the east as far as the fringe of the wilderness this side of the Euphrates, because their cattle had increased in the land of Gilead. 10 And in the days of Saul they made war on the Hagrites, who fell by their hand; and they occupied their tents throughout all the region east of Gilead.

11 The sons of Gad dwelt facing them in the land of Bashan as far as Salcah: 12 Joel the chief, Shapham the second, Janai, and Shaphat in Bashan. 13 And by clans: Michael, Meshullam, Sheba, Jorai, Jacan, Zia, and Eber—seven. 14 These were the sons of Abihail son of Huri son of Jaroah son of Gilead son of Michael son of Jeshishai son of Jahdo son of Buz; 15 Ahi son of Abdiel son of Guni was chief of their clan, 16 and they dwelt in Gilead, in Bashan, and in its dependencies, and in all the pasturelands

properly belonging to the following v., which lacks an introduction. For discussion of family registries see 1 Chron. 5.17 n. **39–41:** The wording of these vv. is reminiscent of Gen. ch 26 and Judg. ch 18, which also involve struggles for land. The cities listed in vv. 39–41 are located in the western Negev, beyond the boundaries of Persian Yehud. The historicity of vv. 39–41 is uncertain. **41:** Several questions arise in connection with this v. First, *the days of King Hezekiah* may refer either to the time at which the names were recorded or when the attack occurred. The latter possibility is supported by 2 Kings 18.8 (without parallel in Chronicles), where Hezekiah is engaged in battle north of Gerar. However, this passage may simply form part of the book's motif, wherein righteous kings (here, Hezekiah) are rewarded, though the fact that the Simeonites, rather than Hezekiah, are credited with the victory argues against this. The identity of the *Meunim* is debated; they may have been a north-Arabian tribe, a south-Arabian group, or Idumeans. **43:** Chronicles employs the phrase *to this day* on only one other occasion, see 5.26. It is unclear whether the phrase here implies that the Simeonites inhabited the area in the author's day or, rather, whether this reflects a "utopian" formulation, expressive of hopes for the future. Amalek was a grandson of Esau (Gen. 36.10–12 || 1 Chron. 1.35–36). The "remnants" of Amalek may refer to descendants of survivors of the battles waged by Saul (1 Sam. 14.48; 15.2–3) and David (2 Sam. 8.12).

5.1–22: Reuben, Gad, Transjordan. The author explains (vv. 1–10) why it is that Reuben, Jacob's firstborn according to Gen., did not occupy a leading role; see Gen. 35.22; 49.3–4. The formulation of vv. 1–2 highlights Judah's central role, while recognizing the significant role of the Joseph tribes (Ephraim and Manasseh). This picture neatly summarizes Chronicles' depiction of the true (i.e., pan-) Israel. Chronicles' emphasis on Judah is the reason that the genealogies do not begin with Reuben. **3–10:** The boundaries of the territory inhabited by Reuben are not clearly defined, but they suggest an area well to the east of the territory generally depicted in biblical sources as having been under Israelite control and settlement. This is consonant with Chronicles' expansive view of the boundaries of Israel's patrimony; see 13.5 n.

of Sharon, to their limits. [17] All of them were registered by genealogies in the days of King Jotham of Judah, and in the days of King Jeroboam of Israel.

[18] The Reubenites, the Gadites, and the half-tribe of Manasseh had warriors who carried shield and sword, drew the bow, and were experienced at war—44,760, ready for service. [19] They made war on the Hagrites—Jetur, Naphish, and Nodab. [20] They prevailed against them; the Hagrites and all who were with them were delivered into their hands, for they cried to God in the battle, and He responded to their entreaty because they trusted in Him. [21] They carried off their livestock: 50,000 of their camels, 250,000 sheep, 2,000 asses, and 100,000 people. [22] For many fell slain, because it was God's battle. And they dwelt in their place until the exile.

[23] The members of the half-tribe of Manasseh dwelt in the land; they were very numerous from Bashan to Baal-hermon, Senir, and Mount Hermon. [24] These were the chiefs of their clans: Epher, Ishi, Eliel, Azriel, Jeremiah, Hodaviah, and Jahdiel, men of substance, famous men, chiefs of their clans. [25] But they trespassed against the God of their fathers by going astray after the gods of the peoples of the land, whom God had destroyed before them. [26] So the God of Israel roused the spirit of King Pul of Assyria—the spirit of King Tillegath-pilneser of Assyria—and he carried them away, namely, the Reubenites, the Gadites, and the half-tribe of Manasseh, and brought them to Halah, Habor, Hara, and the river Gozan, to this day.

[27][a] The sons of Levi: Gershom, Kohath, and Merari. [28] The sons of Kohath: Amram, Izhar, Hebron, and Uzziel. [29] The children of Amram: Aaron, Moses, and Miriam. The sons of Aaron: Nadab, Abihu, Eleazar, and Ithamar. [30] Eleazar begot Phinehas, Phinehas begot Abishua, [31] Abishua begot Bukki, Bukki begot Uzzi, [32] Uzzi begot Zerahiah, Zerahiah begot Meraioth, [33] Meraioth begot Amariah, Amariah begot Ahitub, [34] Ahitub begot Zadok, Zadok begot Ahimaaz, [35] Ahimaaz begot Azariah, Azariah begot Johanan, [36] and Johanan begot Azariah (it was he who served as priest in the House that Solomon built in Jerusalem). [37] Azariah begot Amariah, Amariah begot Ahitub, [38] Ahitub begot Zadok, Zadok begot Shallum, [39] Shallum begot Hilkiah, Hilkiah begot Azariah, [40] Azariah begot Seraiah, Seraiah begot Jehozadak; [41] and Jehozadak went into exile when the LORD exiled Judah and Jerusalem by the hand of Nebuchadnezzar.

a In some editions, chap. 6 begins here.

17: The importance of registering by genealogical records (Heb "hityahes") is attested only in Chronicles and Ezra-Neh. For the latter, this expresses an exclusivist worldview; Chronicles, however, employs genealogical record keeping as part of its programmatic broadening of the definition of "Israel." Rabbinic sources (*m. Kidd.* 4.1–6) also reflect the need to establish one's genealogy, albeit primarily in marriages involving the priestly line, for whom priestly law prescribes greater restrictions (Lev. 21.7, 13; Ezek. 44.22). These legal concerns are not reflected in Chronicles' genealogy (cf. Ezra 2.62). Pentateuchal precedent for family and tribal registry is found at Num. 1.1–18, though (presumably) as part of a military arrangement.

5.23–26: Half-tribe of Manasseh. Significantly, Chronicles limits mention of the northern exile to the Transjordan, never alluding to that suffered by the Cisjordanian tribes of northern Israel. The implication is that the Assyrian exile of the northern tribes was limited in scope, in contrast to 2 Kings 17.18–23, and the Assyrian sources. This passage is an example of the intimate bond between Israel and its land in Chronicles; see 2 Chron. 30.5 n. For the expression *they trespassed* (v. 25), see 9.1. *Pul* is a late Babylonian variant of the name Tiglath Pil(n)eser III, the great Assyrian expansionist king who reigned 745–727 BCE. The author has employed this form of the name on the basis of 2 Kings 15.19, 29. V. 26 parallels 2 Chron. 36.22–23 (|| Ezra 1.1–4), reflective of the author's belief that all such matters are the direct result of the divine will (cf. 2 Chron. 21.16). By contrast, 2 Kings 16.7 states that Tiglath-pileser came at Ahaz's request. The reference to *Halah, Habor,* and *Gozan* constitutes an anachronistic conflation of the Assyrian attack of 732 BCE (2 Kings 15.29) and that of 721 BCE (2 Kings 17.6; 18.11).

5.27–41: The high priestly line. Zadok's Aaronide pedigree does not appear in Samuel; many scholars thus assume that he was of foreign, possibly Jebusite, origin. The motive behind Chronicles' position is that Torah (Priestly) law requires that all priests be descendants of Moses' brother, Aaron (see esp. Num. ch 18). Since, according to Chronicles, David is the archpatron of all matters pertaining to Israel's sacrificial cult, Zadok had to be provided with an acceptable pedigree.

6 The sons of Levi: Gershom, Kohath, and Merari. 2 And these are the names of the sons of Gershom: Libni and Shimei. 3 The sons of Kohath: Amram, Izhar, Hebron, and Uzziel. 4 The sons of Merari: Mahli and Mushi. These were the families of the Levites according to their clans. 5 Of Gershom: his son Libni, his son Jahath, his son Zimmah, 6 his son Joah, his son Iddo, his son Zerah, his son Jeatherai. 7 The sons of Kohath: his son Amminadab, his son Korah, his son Assir, 8 his son Elkanah, his son Ebiasaph, his son Assir, 9 his son Tahath, his son Uriel, his son Uzziah, and his son Shaul. 10 The sons of Elkanah: Amasai and Ahimoth, 11 his son Elkanah, his son Zophai, his son Nahath, 12 his son Eliab, his son Jeroham, his son Elkanah. 13 The sons of Samuel: his first-born [a]Vashni, and[a] Abijah. 14 The sons of Merari: Mahli, his son Libni, his son Shimei, his son Uzzah, 15 his son Shimea, his son Haggiah, and his son Asaiah.

16 These were appointed by David to be in charge of song in the House of the LORD, from the time the Ark came to rest. 17 They served at the Tabernacle of the Tent of Meeting with song until Solomon built the House of the LORD in Jerusalem; and they carried out their duties as prescribed for them. 18 Those were the appointed men; and their sons were: the Kohathites: Heman the singer, son of Joel son of Samuel 19 son of Elkanah son of Jeroham son of Eliel son of Toah 20 son of Zuph son of Elkanah son of Mahath son of Amasai 21 son of Elkanah son of Joel son of Azariah son of Zephaniah 22 son of Tahath son of Assir son of Ebiasaph son of Korah 23 son of Izhar son of Kohath son of Levi son of Israel; 24 and his kinsman Asaph, who stood on his right, namely, Asaph son of Berechiah son of Shimea 25 son of Michael son of Baaseiah son of Malchijah 26 son of Ethni son of Zerah son of Adaiah 27 son of Ethan son of Zimmah son of Shimei 28 son of Jahath son of Gershom son of Levi. 29 On the left were their kinsmen: the sons of Merari: Ethan son of Kishi son of Abdi son of Malluch 30 son of Hashabiah son of Amaziah son of Hilkiah 31 son of Amzi son of Bani son of Shemer 32 son of Mahli son of Mushi son of Merari son of Levi; 33 and their kinsmen the Levites were appointed for all the service of the Tabernacle of the House of God.

a-a Some ancient versions read "Joel, and the second"; cf. 1 Sam. 8.2.

6.1–66: Levi. The descendants of *Gershom, Kohath,* and *Merari* are each divided into "Levites" (vv. 1–15) and musicians/singers (vv. 16–31). Kohath contains a third group, the high priests, descended from Amram. The placement of this last group in the middle position (fourth among seven) reflects its central role. **8–13:** The appearance of *Elkanah* and the prophet Samuel in the list of Levites is unparalleled in other sources. 1 Sam. ch 1 indicates that Samuel was of either Ephraimite or, less plausibly, Judahite origin. Chronicles' revised position is informed by the fact that 1 Sam. chs 2–3 present Samuel as having ministered in the Shiloh Tabernacle, an activity typically identified with (later) Levitic service. Inasmuch as Torah law (e.g., Num. ch 18) proscribes cultic service by anyone not of Levitic descent, the author felt compelled to attach an explicit Levitic pedigree to Samuel. Some argue that 1 Sam. views Samuel's family as a Levitical family hailing from Ephraim or Judah. **16–17:** Outside of Chronicles, there is no indication that Levites were responsible for cultic music in the First Temple, and many scholars maintain that this institution is a Second Temple innovation. On this view, Chronicles' claim is part of its broadly attested tendency to attribute the cultic practices of its day to hoary antiquity; antiquity implies authenticity and greater sanctity, and allows the Jews of Chronicles' time to see their (modest) Temple as part of an illustrious tradition requiring their continued support. Scholars who hold this view also suggest that this section is to be connected to the narrative sections later in Chronicles (much of chs 15–29) that tendentiously suggest that David established the basic institutions and framework for the Temple though only Solomon his son built the actual structure. Other scholars, however, accept as authentic Chronicles' tradition regarding a First Temple Levitical musical guild. This position is supported by the depiction of David's personal connection with music (1 Sam. chs 16–18; 2 Sam. 6.5; 23.1) and the evidence of other ancient Near Eastern cultures that suggests that music was an important part of the cult, often under royal patronage, from an early period. Chronicles' list suggests data differing from those reflected in the superscriptions to Psalms, suggesting different (possibly preexilic) traditions. Cf. Ezra ch 2; Neh. ch 7. **33:** The formulation *Tabernacle of the House* of *God* (Elohim) is sui generis, a conflation of two appellations that generally appear individually. The conflate usage may reflect the Chronicler's insistence that the Jerusalem Temple is the legitimate heir to the desert Tabernacle; see 2 Chron. 3.11–13 n. and 5.5. The

34 But Aaron and his sons made offerings upon the altar of burnt offering and upon the altar of incense, performing all the tasks of the most holy place, to make atonement for Israel, according to all that Moses the servant of God had commanded. 35 These are the sons of Aaron: his son Eleazar, his son Phinehas, his son Abishua, 36 his son Bukki, his son Uzzi, his son Zerahiah, 37 his son Meraioth, his son Amariah, his son Ahitub, 38 his son Zadok, his son Ahimaaz. 39[a] These are their dwelling-places according to their settlements within their borders: to the sons of Aaron of the families of Kohathites, for theirs was the [first] lot; 40 they gave them Hebron in the land of Judah and its surrounding pasturelands, 41 but the fields of the city and its villages they gave to Caleb son of Jephunneh. 42 To the sons of Aaron they gave the cities[b] of refuge: Hebron and Libnah with its pasturelands, Jattir and Eshtemoa with its pasturelands, 43 Hilen with its pasturelands, Debir with its pasturelands, 44 Ashan with its pasturelands, and Beth-shemesh with its pasturelands. 45 From the tribe of Benjamin, Geba with its pasturelands, Alemeth with its pasturelands, and Anathoth with its pasturelands. All their cities throughout their families were thirteen.

46 To the remaining Kohathites were given by lot out of the family of the tribe, out of the half-tribe, the half of Manasseh, ten cities. 47 To the Gershomites according to their families were allotted thirteen cities out of the tribes of Issachar, Asher, Naphtali, and Manasseh in Bashan. 48 To the Merarites according to their families were allotted twelve cities out of the tribes of Reuben, Gad, and Zebulun. 49 So the people of Israel gave the Levites the cities with their pasturelands. 50 They gave them by lot out of the tribe of the Judahites these cities that are mentioned by name, and out of the tribe of the Simeonites, and out of the tribe of the Benjaminites.

51 And some of the families of the sons of Kohath had cities of their territory out of the tribe of Ephraim. 52 They gave them the cities of refuge: Shechem with its pasturelands in the hill country of Ephraim, Gezer with its pasturelands, 53 Jokmeam with its pasturelands, Beth-horon with its pasturelands, 54 Aijalon with its pasturelands, Gath-rimmon with its pasturelands; 55 and out of the half-tribe of Manasseh: Aner with its pasturelands, and Bileam with its pasturelands, for the rest of the families of the Kohathites.

56 To the Gershomites; out of the half-tribe of Manasseh: Golan in Bashan with its pasturelands and Ashtaroth with its pasturelands; 57 and out of the tribe of Issachar: Kedesh with its pasturelands, Dobrath with its pasturelands, 58 Ramoth with its pasturelands, and Anem with its pasturelands; 59 out of the

expression "House of God" appears thirty-one times in Chronicles. In priestly sources "tabernacle" (Heb "mishkan") simply denotes the structure; a second appellation, "Tent of Meeting," conveys the sense of proximity to the deity, i.e., the place where humans may approach and meet the deity. Chronicles, for whom participation by all members of society in the Temple service is important, probably did not have this distinction in mind and employs both terms indiscriminately. **34:** The author's high regard for Levites notwithstanding, this v. defines the unique responsibilities of the priestly class, set forth at Num. 18.1–5. *Performing all the tasks of the most holy place* refers generally to the inner sanctum of the Temple; here it may refer to either that part that housed the lampstand, table of the bread of presence, and the golden incense altar ("hekhal") or the innermost part ("debir"), wherein the Ark was housed and to which only the high priest had access (Lev. 16.1–2). **54–66:** The list of dwelling places parallels Josh. 21.5–39, though there are several differences with respect to sequence. The chronological relationship between the passages is uncertain.

a With vv. 24–51, cf. Josh. 21.3–42. *b Josh. 21.13, "city."*

tribe of Asher: Mashal with its pasturelands, Abdon with its pasturelands, 60 Hukok with its pasturelands, and Rehob with its pasturelands; 61 and out of the tribe of Naphtali: Kedesh in Galilee with its pasturelands; Hammon with its pasturelands, and Kiriathaim with its pasturelands. 62 To the rest of the Merarites, out of the tribe of Zebulun: Rimmono with its pasturelands, Tabor with its pasturelands; 63 and beyond the Jordan at Jericho, on the east side of the Jordan, out of the tribe of Reuben: Bezer in the wilderness with its pasturelands, Jahaz with its pasturelands, 64 Kedemoth with its pasturelands, and Mephaath with its pasture lands; 65 and out of the tribe of Gad: Ramoth in Gilead with its pasturelands, Mahanaim with its pasturelands, 66 Heshbon with its pasturelands, and Jazer with its pasturelands.

7 The sons of Issachar: Tola, Puah, Jashub, and Shimron—four. 2 The sons of Tola: Uzzi, Rephaiah, Jeriel, Jahmai, Ibsam, Shemuel, chiefs of their clans, men of substance according to their lines; their number in the days of David was 22,600. 3 The sons of Uzzi: Izrahiah. And the sons of Izrahiah: Michael, Obadiah, Joel, and Isshiah—five. All of them were chiefs. 4 And together with them, by their lines, according to their clans, were units of the fighting force, 36,000, for they had many wives and sons. 5 Their kinsmen belonging to all the families of Issachar were in all 87,000 men of substance; they were all registered by genealogy.

6 [The sons of] Benjamin: Bela, Becher, and Jediael—three. 7 The sons of Bela: Ezbon, Uzzi, Uzziel, Jerimoth, and Iri—five, chiefs of clans, men of substance, registered by genealogy—22,034. 8 The sons of Becher: Zemirah, Joash, Eliezer, Elioenai, Omri, Jeremoth, Abijah, Anathoth, and Alemeth. All these were the sons of Becher; 9 and they were registered by genealogy according to their lines, as chiefs of their clans, men of substance—20,200. 10 The sons of Jediael: Bilhan. And the sons of Bilhan: Jeush, Benjamin, Ehud, Chenaanah, Zethan, Tarshish, and Ahishahar. 11 All these were the sons of Jediael, chiefs of the clans, men of substance—17,200, who made up the fighting force. 12 And Shuppim and Huppim were the sons of Ir; Hushim the sons of Aher.

13 The sons of Naphtali: Jahziel, Guni, Jezer, and Shallum, the descendants of Bilhah.

14 The sons of Manasseh: Asriel, whom his Aramean concubine bore; she bore Machir the father of Gilead. 15 And Machir took wives for Huppim and for Shuppim. The name of his sister was Maacah. And the name of the second was Zelophehad; and Zelophehad had daughters. 16 And Maacah the wife of Machir bore a son, and she named him Peresh; and the name of his brother was Sheresh; and his sons were Ulam and

7.1–12: Issachar and Benjamin. The Benjamin list occasions surprise: (1) It opens with the word "Benjamin" instead of "the sons of Benjamin" (NJPS adds "The sons of"); (2) the detailed list of Benjamin also appears in ch 8; and (3) there is little shared material with Torah sources (Gen. 46.21; Num. 26.38–42). These data suggest that this passage draws on a source that is no longer extant outside of the Torah.

7.13: Naphtali. This passage's brevity may indicate that material has been lost.

7.14–19: Manasseh. This passage claims that *Manasseh* and his son, *Machir,* were born in trans-Jordanian territory (with no indication that either ever left Egypt), consistent with the Chronicler's ideological de-emphasis of the exodus, whereas Torah tradition (Gen. 41.51–52; Num. 27.1–4; 32.39–42; Deut. 3.14–15) records their birth in Egypt. Similarly, the claim that *Asriel* was Manasseh's son contradicts Num. 26.31, which mentions Asriel as Manasseh's great-grandson. Some medieval commentators argued that the Asriel mentioned here is, in fact, consistent with Num., and that Chronicles mentions him first because only he was born to a full wife, whereas Machir was born to Joseph's concubine. The difficulties are plain; note, e.g., that the brothers of Asriel (according to Num.) are not mentioned here. Recent attempts at textual reconstruction of the passage remain speculative. The absence of criticism regarding marriage with foreigners as discussed above, is again noteworthy. The reference to an *Aramean concubine* as standing at the head of a major clan of Manasseh is no less significant. The role of women in this passage is underscored by the appearance of *Maacah* in v. 16, who names her son, and especially the role played by *Hammolecheth,* whose husband is not mentioned at all.

Rekem. [17] The sons of Ulam: Bedan. These were the sons of
Gilead son of Machir son of Manasseh. [18] And his sister Hammolecheth bore Ishhod, Abiezer, and Mahlah. [19] The sons of
Shemida were Ahian, Shechem, Likhi, and Aniam.
[20] The sons of Ephraim: Shuthelah, his son Bered, his son
Tahath, his son Eleadah, his son Tahath, [21] his son Zabad, his
son Shuthelah, also Ezer and Elead. The men of Gath, born
in the land, killed them because they had gone down to take
their cattle. [22] And Ephraim their father mourned many days,
and his brothers came to comfort him. [23] He cohabited with
his wife, who conceived and bore a son; and she named him
Beriah, because it occurred when there was misfortune[a] in his
house. [24] His daughter was Sheerah, who built both Lower and
Upper Beth-horon, and Uzzen-sheerah. [25] His son Rephah, his
son Resheph, his son Telah, his son Tahan, [26] his son Ladan,
his son Ammihud, his son Elishama, [27] his son Non, his son
Joshua. [28] Their possessions and settlements were Bethel and
its dependencies, and on the east Naaran, and on the west
Gezer and its dependencies, Shechem and its dependencies,
and Aiah and its dependencies; [29] also along the borders of the
Manassites, Beth-shean and its dependencies, Taanach and
its dependencies, Megiddo and its dependencies, Dor and its
dependencies. In these dwelt the sons of Joseph son of Israel.
[30] The sons of Asher: Imnah, Ishvah, Ishvi, Beriah, and their
sister Serah. [31] The sons of Beriah: Heber and Malchiel, who
was the father of Birzaith. [32] Heber begot Japhlet, Shomer,
Hotham, and their sister, Shua. [33] The sons of Japhlet: Pasach,
Bimhal, and Ashvath. These were the sons of Japhlet. [34] The
sons of Shemer: Ahi, Rohgah, Hubbah, and Aram. [35] The sons
of Helem his brother: Zophah, Imna, Shelesh, and Amal. [36] The
sons of Zophah: Suah, Harnepher, Shual, Beri, Imrah, [37] Bezer,
Hod, Shamma, Shilshah, Ithran, and Beera. [38] The sons of
Jether: Jephunneh, Pispa, and Ara. [39] The sons of Ulla: Arah,
Hanniel, and Rizia. [40] All of these men of Asher, chiefs of the
clans, select men, men of substance, heads of the chieftains.
And they were registered by genealogy according to fighting
force; the number of the men was 26,000 men.

a *Heb.* beraʿah.

7.20–29: Ephraim. This passage maintains that Ephraim and his family remained in Canaan, contradicting Gen. chs 41–50, which states that Ephraim and his brother, Manasseh, were born, and died, in Egypt. The Aram. Tg. along with several rabbinic sources (*Mek. de R. Ishmael, beshallaḥ* (introduction); *b. Sanh.* 92b) resolved this contradiction by claiming that some members of Ephraim left Egypt and infiltrated Canaan before the divinely "appointed time" of redemption had arrived; their failure was a sign (esp. for later generations) that one ought not to "play God" and try to expedite (messianic) redemption. Other traditional sources (*b. Sanh.* 92b; *Tg. Ps.-J.* and *Frg. Tg.* to Exod. 13.17) claim that the fiasco was the result of faulty computation of the period of enslavement imposed by Gen. 15.13, while some sources conflate the two explanations (*Song Rab.* to 2.7). Some medieval exegetes (e.g., Radak) argued that the words "born in the land" refer to the people of Ephraim and that the event described herein took place in either the desert or Transjordan. Some modern scholars simply emend the text, viewing the word "Ephraim" as a gloss, or maintain that the name refers to a later descendant. Others, declining to emend, say that this passage is part of Chronicles' portrayal of the eternal bond between Israel and its land. **24:** The reference to a woman who built several cities is remarkable within Chronicles and in the Hebrew Bible, generally. Indeed, only one other instance of city-building attributed to a commoner is mentioned in the entire genealogical section (1 Chron. 8.12). Elsewhere in Chronicles, the motif of city-building appears exclusively as a marker of upright kings (see 2 Chron. 8.2–7 and 8.1–6 n.). Some view Chronicles' relatively positive depiction of women (i.e., as city-builders and heads of households) as reflecting the needs of a pioneer-like society, as presumably existed in Persian Yehud, wherein all members are called upon to contribute in any way possible. At the same time, it is noteworthy that Chronicles' atypical empowerment of women is restricted to the family setting and is not extended to the public domain (political, cultic, prophetic). Finally, virtually all the instances of non-Judahite empowerment of women appear in connection with Ephraim and Manasseh. Given that Ephraim and Manasseh play the most significant role in Chronicles and are a cipher for the northern tribes, the focus on women's roles in these tribes is paradigmatic.

7.30–40: Asher. While similar to the data at Gen. 46.17; Num. 26.44–46, the numbers reflect a dramatic decrease compared to Num. 1.40–41; 26.47; and 1 Chron. 12.37. Chronicles omits the descendants of three of Asher's sons and his daughter,

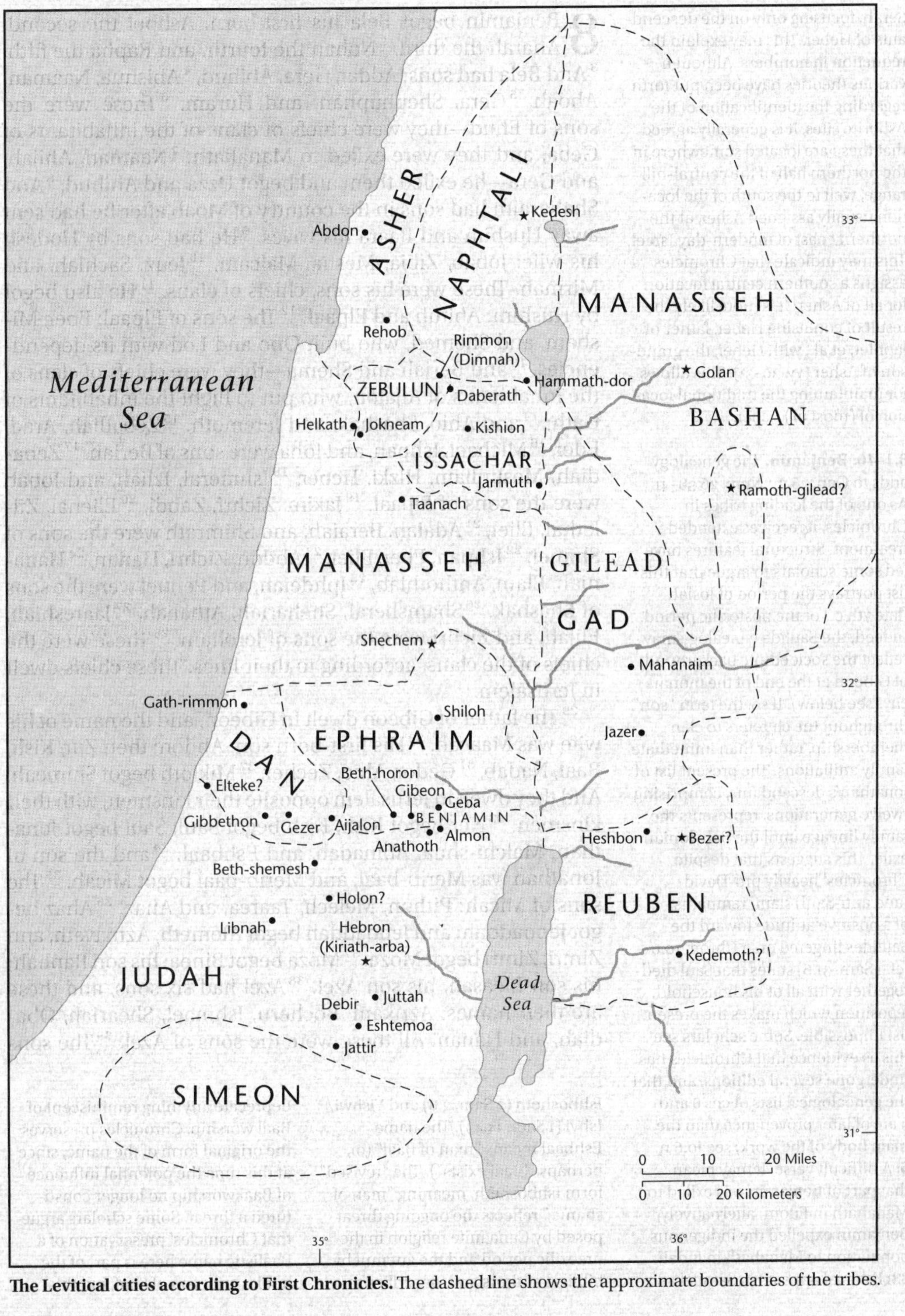

The Levitical cities according to First Chronicles. The dashed line shows the approximate boundaries of the tribes.

8 Benjamin begot Bela his first-born, Ashbel the second,
Aharah the third, 2 Nohah the fourth, and Rapha the fifth.
3 And Bela had sons: Addar, Gera, Abihud, 4 Abishua, Naaman,
Ahoah, 5 Gera, Shephuphan, and Huram. 6 These were the
sons of Ehud—they were chiefs of clans of the inhabitants of
Geba, and they were exiled to Manahath: 7 Naaman, Ahijah,
and Gera—he exiled them and begot Uzza and Ahihud. 8 And
Shaharaim had sons in the country of Moab after he had sent
away Hushim and Baara his wives. 9 He had sons by Hodesh
his wife: Jobab, Zibia, Mesha, Malcam, 10 Jeuz, Sachiah, and
Mirmah. These were his sons, chiefs of clans. 11 He also begot
by Hushim: Abitub and Elpaal. 12 The sons of Elpaal: Eber, Mi-
sham, and Shemed, who built Ono and Lod with its dependencies, 13 and Beriah and Shema—they were chiefs of clans of
the inhabitants of Aijalon, who put to flight the inhabitants of
Gath; 14 and Ahio, Shashak, and Jeremoth. 15 Zebadiah, Arad,
Eder, 16 Michael, Ishpah, and Joha were sons of Beriah. 17 Zebadiah, Meshullam, Hizki, Heber, 18 Ishmerai, Izliah, and Jobab
were the sons of Elpaal. 19 Jakim, Zichri, Zabdi, 20 Elienai, Zillethai, Eliel, 21 Adaiah, Beraiah, and Shimrath were the sons of
Shimei. 22 Ishpan, Eber, Eliel, 23 Abdon, Zichri, Hanan, 24 Hananiah, Elam, Anthothiah, 25 Iphdeiah, and Penuel were the sons
of Shashak. 26 Shamsherai, Shehariah, Athaliah, 27 Jaareshiah,
Elijah, and Zichri were the sons of Jeroham. 28 These were the
chiefs of the clans, according to their lines. These chiefs dwelt
in Jerusalem.
29 The father of Gibeon dwelt in Gibeon, and the name of his
wife was Maacah. 30 His first-born son: Abdon; then Zur, Kish,
Baal, Nadab, 31 Gedor, Ahio, Zecher. 32 Mikloth begot Shimeah.
And they dwelt in Jerusalem opposite their kinsmen, with their
kinsmen. 33 Ner begot Kish, Kish begot Saul, Saul begot Jonathan, Malchi-shua, Abinadab, and Eshbaal; 34 and the son of
Jonathan was Merib-baal; and Merib-baal begot Micah. 35 The
sons of Micah: Pithon, Melech, Taarea, and Ahaz. 36 Ahaz begot Jehoaddah; and Jehoaddah begot Alemeth, Azmaveth, and
Zimri; Zimri begot Moza. 37 Moza begot Binea; his son Raphah;
his son Eleasah, his son Azel. 38 Azel had six sons, and these
are their names: Azrikam, Bocheru, Ishmael, Sheariah, Obadiah, and Hanan. All these were the sons of Azel. 39 The sons

Serah, focusing only on the descendants of Heber. This may explain the reduction in numbers. Although various theories have been put forth regarding the identification of the Asherite sites, it is generally agreed that these are located somewhere in the northern half of the central-hill range, well to the south of the location usually assigned Asher, at the northern coast of modern-day Israel. This may indicate that Chronicles assigns a southern central location for all of Asher; it is more likely the result of confusing Heber, father of Japhlet, et al., with Heber, the grandson of Asher (vv. 30–31). This allows for maintaining the traditional location of (most of) Asher.

8.1–40: Benjamin. The genealogy adds to Gen. 46.21; Num. 26.38–41. As one of the leading tribes in Chronicles, it receives extended treatment. Structural features have led some scholars to argue that this list portrays the period of Josiah (late 7th c.) or the postexilic period. Indeed, the Saulide genealogy may reflect the socioethnic background of Gibeon at the end of the monarchy (see below). If so, the term "son" throughout the ch refers to clan membership, rather than immediate family affiliations. The present list of Jonathan's descendants, comprising twelve generations, represents the family lineage until the Babylonian exile. This suggests that despite Chronicles' heavily pro-David (and anti-Saul) slant, remnants of a positive attitude toward the Saulides lingered on. 1 Chron. 10.6 (cf. 1 Sam. 31.6) states that Saul died together with all of his household, a position which makes the present list impossible. Some scholars see this as evidence that Chronicles has undergone several editions, and that the genealogical lists of chs 8 and 9 are of later provenance than the main body of the work; see 10.6 n. **6:** A difficult verse. It may mean that part of Benjamin was exiled to Manahath in Edom; alternatively, Benjamin expelled the indigenous population to Manahath in Judah. **33:** Eshbaal appears in Samuel as Ishbosheth (2 Sam. 2.8) and Yishwi/Ishvi (1 Sam. 14.49). The name Eshbaal means "man of Baal" (or, perhaps, "Baal exists"). The "revised" form Ishbosheth, meaning "man of shame," reflects the ongoing threat posed by Canaanite religion in the preexilic period and the attempt by biblical authors and/or scribes to deprecate anything reminiscent of Baal worship. Chronicles preserves the original form of the name, since at this time the potential influence of Baal worship no longer constituted a threat. Some scholars argue that Chronicles' preservation of a Baalistic name here is part of the book's criticism of Saul, but this

of Eshek his brother: Ulam his first-born, Jeush the second, and Eliphelet the third. [40] The descendants of Ulam—men of substance, who drew the bow, had many children and grandchildren—one hundred and fifty; all these were Benjaminites.

9 All Israel was registered by genealogies; and these are in the book of the kings of Israel. And Judah was taken into exile in Babylon because of their trespass. [2][a] The first to settle in their towns, on their property, were Israelites, priests, Levites, and temple servants, [3] while some of the Judahites and some of the Benjaminites and some of the Ephraimites and Manassehites settled in Jerusalem; [4] Uthai son of Ammihud son of Omri son of Imri son of Bani, from the sons of Perez son of Judah; [5] and of the Shilonites: Asaiah the first-born and his sons. [6] Of the sons of Zerah: Jeuel and their kinsmen—690. [7] Of the Benjaminites: Sallu son of Meshullam son of Hodaviah son of Hassenuah, [8] Ibneiah son of Jeroham, Elah son of Uzzi son of Michri, and Meshullam son of Shephatiah son of Reuel son of Ibneiah; [9] and their kinsmen, according to their lines—956. All these were chiefs of their ancestral clans.

[10] Of the priests: Jedaiah, Jehoiarib, Jachin, [11] and Azariah son of Hilkiah son of Meshullam son of Zadok son of Meraioth son of Ahitub, chief officer of the House of God; [12] and Adaiah son of Jeroham son of Pashhur son of Malchijah, and Maasai son of Adiel son of Jahzerah son of Meshullam son of

a With vv. 2–17, cf. Neh. 11.3–19.

is unlikely, since the same phenomenon is attested in connection with David's sons and, possibly, Solomon's officials (see 14.7 || 2 Sam. 5.16; 2 Chron. 10.18 || 1 Kings 4.6; 12.18). Several biblical passages highlight the military prowess of the Benjaminites; see Judg. 20.16; 2 Sam. 1.22. This v. accords prestige to the forces of Ulam by identifying them as descendants of Saul, Israel's first king. Thus, while portraying Saul in harsh terms (1 Chron. ch 10), the author recognizes that his descendants are not tainted by Saul's conduct.

9.1–44: Identity of the community. **1:** Note the key word "trespass" (Heb "maʿal"). In Priestly texts from the Torah, the term denotes encroachment upon (personal use of) sacred items; in Second Temple sources its semantic field expands to cover more general offenses. It appears frequently as part of Chronicles' theology, e.g., 10.13 (Saul's death); 2 Chron. 36.14 (Judah's exile). For the role of genealogies, see 1 Chron. 5.17 n. and Num. 1.18. **2–17:** Though parallel to Neh. 11.3–19, there are many differences; some may be the result of variant traditions, while others reflect Chronicles' ideological revisions. **2:** The opening words may refer to Second Temple society, requiring the translation "The first to settle again…." On this reading, the v. emphasizes that First Temple Israel, with all of its tribes, is still alive and has its direct continuation in Second Temple society centered in Jerusalem, i.e., the Babylonian exile effected little change in the nation's structure. This is part of Chronicles' inclusivist approach to Israel's identity, as opposed to Ezra-Neh., which privileges the returnees from the exile. Alternatively, the v. has been translated "The former settlers," referring to the (early) pre-exilic settlement in Jerusalem. On this approach, the concluding words of v. 1 *(And Judah was taken into exile …)* are a gloss added to restore the reality of exile which the original Chronicles had tried to avoid. Related to this issue is the question of the fate of the northern Cisjordanian tribes following the destruction of the First Temple; Chronicles never states what their fate was following the Babylonian conquest. This, in turn, begs the question as to whether the Ephraimites and Manassites—who are generally emblematic for all of the northern tribes—mentioned here relocated from the north or, rather, had somehow formed part of the returning exiles. **3:** See Neh. 11.4, which makes no reference to Ephraim and Manasseh. Chronicles' version (if understood as referring to Second Temple society) underscores the inclusivist tendency of Chronicles vis-à-vis Ezra-Neh. Unlike Neh. ch 11, Chronicles implies no criticism of those not living in Jerusalem. This is reflective of Chronicles' position of the timeless bond between Israelites-Judahites and their national patrimony and, on the view that northerners had never been removed from their ancestral lands (see above), it is to be expected. **11:** The Heb term employed, "negid [bet ha-elohim]" *(chief officer of the House of God)* is unusual; it generally denotes a military and/or political leader and, rarely, crown prince. Its precise meaning here is unclear, as is the intended bearer of this name. It may denote Jedaiah, though no high priest bearing this name appears in the Persian period. The syntax of this v. makes the bearer of the title "chief officer of the House of God" uncertain; the relatively rare title appears at 2 Chron. 31.13; 35.8 (see also Jer. 20.1), and may refer to the high priest. A notable feature of Chronicles is its use of divine names and epithets. Two issues stand out. First, many passages in Chronicles employ the generic "Elohim/elohim" rather than the name "YHVH" appearing in parallel texts.

Meshillemith son of Immer, 13 together with their kinsmen,
chiefs of their clans—1,760, men of substance for the work of
the service of the House of God.
14 Of the Levites: Shemaiah son of Hasshub son of Azrikam
son of Hashabiah, of the sons of Merari; 15 and Bakbakkar,
Heresh, Galal, and Mattaniah son of Mica son of Zichri son
of Asaph; 16 and Obadiah son of Shemaiah son of Galal son of
Jeduthun, and Berechiah son of Asa son of Elkanah, who dwelt
in the villages of the Netophathites.
17 The gatekeepers were: Shallum, Akkub, Talmon, Ahiman;
and their kinsman Shallum was the chief 18 hitherto in the
King's Gate on the east. They were the keepers belonging to the
Levite camp. 19 Shallum son of Kore son of Ebiasaph son of Korah, and his kinsmen of his clan, the Korahites, were in charge
of the work of the service, guards of the threshold of the Tent;
their fathers had been guards of the entrance to the camp of
the LORD. 20 And Phinehas son of Eleazar was the chief officer
over them in time past; the LORD was with him. 21 Zechariah
the son of Meshelemiah was gatekeeper at the entrance of the
Tent of Meeting. 22 All these, who were selected as gatekeepers at the thresholds, were 212. They were selected by genealogies in their villages. David and Samuel the seer established
them in their office of trust. 23 They and their descendants were
in charge of the gates of the House of the LORD, that is, the
House of the Tent, as guards. 24 The gatekeepers were on the
four sides, east, west, north, and south; 25 and their kinsmen in
their villages were obliged to join them every seven days, according to a fixed schedule. 26 The four chief gatekeepers, who
were Levites, were entrusted to be over the chambers and the
treasuries of the House of God. 27 They spent the night near the
House of God; for they had to do guard duty, and they were in
charge of opening it every morning.
28 Some of them had charge of the service vessels, for they
were counted when they were brought back and taken out.
29 Some of them were in charge of the vessels and all the holy

(A complicating factor is the use of different divine names/epithets in the MT and LXX in the parallel passages of Chronicles and the Samuel-Kings corpus.) This has led some scholars to posit a tendency to minimize the use of YHVH, a phenomenon explicitly attested in the Dead Sea Scrolls and reflective of the sense of distance between humans and the deity. While YHVH appears over four hundred fifty times in Chronicles, there are thirty-two occasions in which Chronicles replaces the reading "YHVH", appearing in the Masoretic version of the earlier biblical passage, with the term "elohim." Various explanations for this state of affairs have been proffered. It may reflect a tendency, attested elsewhere in postexilic and Second Temple sources, to minimize use and articulation of the divine proper name; it may reflect a perceived distancing between the (transcendent) deity and humans, a tendency reflected in many postexilic sources (see 1 Chron. 21.1 n.). Alternatively, this may reflect a "universalization" of the deity, now perceived as the deity of all humankind. Undermining these explanations is the fact that many purported alterations on the part of Chronicles disappear once it is recognized that the LXX versions of these earlier passages read "YHVH," rather than "elohim," a phenomenon further complicated by textual variants among the many mss of LXX themselves. The most likely explanation of the data in Chronicles is that the data reflect stylistic variants of the Chronicler; while some of these variants bear substantive implications and, thus, may be intentional, they are not generally indicative of a systematic shift in the author's perception of the deity. A second issue concerning the use of the divine name(s) centers around the pronunciation of the name Y(a)HV(e)H by the Chronicler and his audience. Postbiblical sources—most notably the Dead Sea Scrolls, rabbinic texts, and, possibly, LXX—indicate that the articulation of the name YHVH was minimized, if not avoided altogether. There are indications that this phenomenon was already underway in Chronicles, as exemplified by the frequent replacement of "Adonai Y(a)HV(e)H" (in Samuel) by the form "Adonai Elohim" in Chronicles. While there may be other factors responsible for this development, this explanation is a plausible one. Finally, it is not clear whether the various meanings originally conveyed by the different forms of the divine name—e.g., "YHVH Seba'ot" (YHVH/Creator of [heavenly] hosts; see, e.g., 1 Chron. 11.9)—were understood by the Chronicler or whether they had become "frozen" and emptied of their original semantic content. **17–33:** These vv., which have no extant source, outline various functions of the gatekeepers, who may have attained added significance in the Second Temple period. Ezra (2.42, 70; 7.7) and Neh. (7.1, 45) mention this role, but only Chronicles places its origins in the preexilic era. Gatekeepers, in Chronicles and the ancient Near East generally, bore a

vessels, and of the flour, wine, oil, incense, and spices. 30 Some
of the priests blended the compound of spices. 31 Mattithiah,
one of the Levites, the first-born of Shallum the Korahite, was
entrusted with making the flat cakes. 32 Also some of their Kohathite kinsmen had charge of the rows of bread, to prepare
them for each sabbath.
33 Now these are the singers, the chiefs of Levitical clans who
remained in the chambers free of other service, for they were
on duty day and night. 34 These were chiefs of Levitical clans,
according to their lines; these chiefs lived in Jerusalem.
35 The father of Gibeon, Jeiel, lived in Gibeon, and the name
of his wife was Maacah. 36 His first-born son, Abdon; then Zur,
Kish, Baal, Ner, Nadab, 37 Gedor, Ahio, Zechariah, and Mikloth; 38 Mikloth begot Shimeam; and they lived in Jerusalem
opposite their kinsmen, with their kinsmen. 39 Ner begot Kish,
Kish begot Saul, Saul begot Jonathan, Malchi-shua, Abinadab,
and Eshbaal; 40 and the son of Jonathan was Merib-baal; and
Merib-baal begot Micah. 41 The sons of Micah: Pithon, Melech, Taharea; 42 Ahaz begot Jarah, and Jarah begot Alemeth,
Azmaveth, and Zimri; Zimri begot Moza. 43 Moza begot Binea;
his son was Rephaiah, his son Eleasah, his son Azel. 44 Azel had
six sons and these were their names: Azrikam, Bocheru, Ishmael, Sheariah, Obadiah, and Hanan. These were the sons of
Azel.

10 [a]The Philistines attacked Israel, and the men of Israel
fled before the Philistines and [many] fell on Mount Gilboa. 2 The Philistines pursued Saul and his sons, and the Philistines struck down Jonathan, Abinadab, and Malchi-shua,
sons of Saul. 3 The battle raged around Saul, and the archers hit
him, and he [b]was wounded[b] by the archers. 4 Saul said to his
arms-bearer, "Draw your sword and run me through, so that
these uncircumcised may not come and make sport of me."
But his arms-bearer, out of great awe, refused; whereupon Saul
grasped the sword and fell upon it. 5 When the arms-bearer saw

a With vv. 1–12, cf. 1 Sam. 31.1–13. *b-b Meaning of Heb. uncertain.*

broad range of cultic, security, and financial responsibilities. Martial depictions of levitic guards are in evidence elsewhere; see 1 Chron. 25.9–31; 2 Chron. 23.3–5. Gatekeepers are also involved with the Temple finances, Temple offerings (including baking; 2 Chron. 31.14–16), and even appear as counselors to the kings (1 Chron. 26.14). Priestly sources, while not employing the term "gatekeeper," assign the role of guarding (the Tabernacle) to Levites as well as priests (Num. 18.3–5). Rabbinic sources (*m. Mid.* 1:1), which apply the codes of royal guardsmen to the gatekeepers, similarly attest this bifurcation, stating that priests guarded at three inner Temple posts, while Levites were assigned to twenty-one (or, on another view, twenty-four) stations on the outer perimeter of the Temple. V. 33 appears to imply that the Temple singers worked day and night, whereas gatekeepers were granted time for rest. Medieval tradents differed with regard to the role of the gatekeepers; some maintained that their role was only at night, while others argued that they served during the day, as well. The claim regarding the singers is opaque and resists a definitive explanation; there is no indication in the Bible that sacrificial activity took place at night and the Rabbis similarly maintained that no cultic activity was performed at night other than the burning (on the altar) entrails of animals slaughtered earlier in the day. If taken at face value this v. would indicate the important role that music had taken on in the Temple worship, perhaps surpassing, to some extent, that of sacrifice (cf. Ps. 134.1, where the identity of those who "stand nightly" is not stated). Alternatively, the v. may have actions other than performance, e.g., attending to instruments, rehearsals, etc., in mind (cf. Ezek. 40.44) or, less plausibly, "day and night" may mean "long hours." **34–44:** A repetition (with variations) of part of the Benjaminite genealogy of 8.28–38; it here serves to introduce King Saul, a Benjaminite.

10.1–14: Saul's death and transfer of the monarchy to David. 1 Sam. devotes approximately twenty chs to the reign of Saul; Chronicles deems one ch, focusing on Saul's death, sufficient. This is a clear statement of Chronicles' primary interests, that is to say, David and the Davidic dynasty, and of the author's negative assessment of Saul. In addition to the paucity of material, Chronicles' overall depiction of Saul is decidedly different from that in Samuel. The latter contains a block of material sympathetic to Saul, which emphasizes his courage and leadership and the esteem in which he was held. Overall, Samuel portrays Saul as a multi-dimensional, tragic figure. Chronicles knows none of this; Saul is a one-dimensional figure, whose demeaning death is just desert for a host of offenses he committed. Chronicles' version of Saul's death and the readiness

that Saul was dead, he too fell on his sword and died. 6 Thus
Saul and his three sons and his entire house died together.
7 And when all the men of Israel who were in the valley saw
that they[a] had fled and that Saul and his sons were dead, they
abandoned their towns and fled; the Philistines then came and
occupied them.

8 The next day the Philistines came to strip the slain, and they
found Saul and his sons lying on Mount Gilboa. 9 They stripped
him, and carried off his head and his armor, and sent them
throughout the land of the Philistines to spread the news to
their idols and among the people. 10 They placed his armor in
the temple of their god, and they impaled his head in the temple of Dagan. 11 When all Jabesh-gilead heard everything that
the Philistines had done to Saul, 12 all their stalwart men set out,
removed the bodies of Saul and his sons, and brought them to
Jabesh. They buried the bones under the oak tree in Jabesh,
and they fasted for seven days. 13 Saul died for the trespass that
he had committed against the LORD in not having fulfilled the
command of the LORD; moreover, he had consulted a ghost to
seek advice, 14 and did not seek advice of the LORD; so He had
him slain and the kingdom transferred to David son of Jesse.

a I.e., Israel.

of some of the population to bury his mutilated corpse presents a far less flattering picture than that in Samuel. **6:** See 8.1–40 n. The present v. clashes with 15.29, which indicates that (at the least) Saul's daughter Michal remained alive. This v. has been explained as a compositional oversight on the author's part. Others argue that this inconsistency is the price that Chronicles had to pay in order to promote two distinct positions: The Chronicler wanted to show that David fulfilled his promise to Saul and his household concerning the continued wellbeing of Saul's descendants (1 Sam. 20.15; 24.22–23), but at the same time Chronicles was concerned that David not appear as a usurper—thus the notice that David ascended an heirless throne following Saul's death (vv. 1–3). Chronicles' version of the episode may be the original, arguing that it forms a coherent narrative with other sections of 1 Sam. Even if this is so, this version is entirely in keeping with key motifs in Chronicles. **7:** The words *they had fled* are ambiguous; the present translation understands them to refer to the Israelite forces, while others take them to mean that Saul and his sons first fled, before giving up all hope. This offers a sharp contrast to David's valor; see 14.8–17 n. Saul's demoralizing defeat, resulting in whole tracts of Israel's land being overrun by the enemy, must be seen against the backdrop of Chronicles' "land-theology" which, as noted, portrays a picture of continuous Israelite settlement in its land and, moreover, maintains that the entire territory of Canaan had already been settled by the patriarchs (see 13.5 n.). This may also explain the fact that in 1 Sam. ch 31 the Philistine presence in the land is more extensive than that suggested by Chronicles' reticence. Since expanding Israel's hegemony and/or building Israel's land is a topos expressive of monarchic express (see 1 Chron. 18.1–17; 2 Chron. 8.3–7; 11.5–12), the reverse state of affairs, viz., loss of land to the Philistines, indicates the author's negative assessment of Saul. **8–12:** 1 Sam. 31.11 states that the king's armor was placed in the temple of Ashtaroth, rather than the temple of "their god(s)". It is possible that the two readings are mere variants; it is also possible that the use of the term "god(s)" (Heb "'elohim") is intended to create a contrast with the use of this term at 1 Chron. 14.12, offering a contrast between the victorious David who burns the (vanquished) "god(s)" captured from the vanquished Philistines vs. Saul's armor that is captured by the Philistines and offered to the (victorious) Philistine god(s) in recognition for their assistance. For the connection between Saul and the people of Jabesh, see 1 Sam. ch 11. 1 Sam. ch 31 claims that Saul's corpse, with his head attached, was taken from the battlefield and impaled on the wall of Beth-shan. Retrieving the corpse entailed a dangerous operation: The people of Jabesh, operating by night, would have had to penetrate enemy territory under the very noses of the Philistine guards, suggesting that Saul was truly venerated by the people of Jabesh. By contrast, Chronicles states that Saul's head was taken to the temple of Dagon while the rest of his corpse was left at the battle site. According to this scenario, the people of Jabesh were willing to attend to Saul's corpse left on Mount Gilboa, but they were not prepared to endanger their own lives by approaching the (Philistine) temple of Dagon. Additionally, Saul was never buried fully and properly, a sign of disgrace. This reflects Saul's diminished image in Chronicles. **13–14:** Chronicles routinely explains death as punishment for sins, and so here, unlike in 1 Sam., attributes Saul's death to his sins. To do so, it must rewrite some of the material that is known from Samuel (e.g., 1 Sam. 28.8–23). Chronicles highlights Saul's failure to seek advice (Heb "darash") of the LORD before going to battle, in contrast to 1 Sam. ch 28, where Saul was prevented from receiving divine guidance. This also creates a clear contrast with David's conduct (see 14.10, 14). The concluding words emphasize that the transfer of power to David was both immediate and decreed in heaven, a point

11 [a]All Israel gathered to David at Hebron and said, "We are
your own flesh and blood. 2 Long before now, even when
Saul was king, you were the leader of Israel; and the LORD your
God said to you: You shall shepherd My people Israel; you shall
be ruler of My people Israel." 3 All the elders of Israel came to
the king at Hebron, and David made a pact with them in Hebron before the LORD. And they anointed David king over Israel, according to the word of the LORD through Samuel.
4 David and all Israel set out for Jerusalem, that is Jebus,
where the Jebusite inhabitants of the land lived. 5 David was

a *With vv. 1–9, cf. 2 Sam. 5.1–10, and with vv. 11–41, cf. 2 Sam. 23.8–39.*

restated several times in the ensuing chs. For *trespass,* see 9.1 n. The motif of a monarch rising to power by both divine decree and overwhelming popular support (as described in the ensuing two chs) is a literary topos of the ancient Near East.

11.1–29.30: David's rule. The portrait of David is greatly enhanced. Many unflattering episodes found in Samuel are deleted, while positive aspects of David's career are embellished. (See the intro. for a discussion of theories regarding the literary relationship between Chronicles and Samuel-Kings.) There is, however, no attempt to whitewash all of David's misdeeds. The most striking change in Chronicles' portrayal concerns David's role in the religious cult: Whereas Samuel describes the political and personal experiences of David the warrior, Chronicles' David is, first and foremost, the patron of the cult. This portrayal, together with David's association with (parts of) the book of Psalms, casts him as a spiritual figure, leading to the rabbinic depiction of David as a Torah scholar, as well as the composer of most of the Psalms and the compiler of psalms composed by earlier and contemporary figures (e.g., Asaph, sons of Korah; see *b. B. Bat.* 15a). This spiritualization of David is also attested in the Dead Sea Scrolls of Qumran, where David is credited with composition of the book of Psalms and more than 4,000 psalms. By, contrast, the LXX explicitly attributes some Psalms to later figures (e.g., 145 [LXX, attributes to Haggai and Zecharaiah] = 146 [Heb, no attribute]), as did several medieval exegetes.

11.1–3: David's ascension to the throne. The parallel version at 2 Sam. chs 1–5 differs substantially. The formulation here conveys the unmistakable impression that the transition between Saul's demise and David's rule was the result of divine decree and unanimous popular support, and therefore both immediate and smooth; there was neither void nor period of political instability. This differs dramatically from 2 Sam. chs 1–4, which describe the power struggle following Saul's death. Additionally, Chronicles never mentions David's having been a local chieftain; he is instead portrayed as going from private citizen to monarch over a united Israel-Judah. This, too, contradicts Samuel, which presents David as a local, Judahite leader, whose leadership over a united confederation of tribes comes about gradually, following years of friction between him and the regnant Saul. Chronicles thus avoids portraying David as a possible usurper since for the Chronicler, the "true" or "ideal" Israel consists of a unity of all the tribes headed by one legitimate monarch. In 2 Sam. (5.1–2) this declaration of support for, and recognition of, David as Israel's true leader, even during Saul's reign, is probably nothing more than a pro forma statement, meant to allow the northern tribes to save face while (outwardly) acknowledging David's superiority. By contrast, Chronicles' reticence regarding the war between the supporters of David and those of Saul indicates that the author viewed this declaration as genuine; see 1 Chron. 12.1–23 n. **1:** Whereas 2 Sam. 5.1 speaks of all the tribes coming to Hebron, Chronicles says that all Israel came, reflecting the outpouring of unanimous support for David. This point is reiterated at 12.24–41. The participation by the entire nation in important events is a recurring motif in Chronicles. **4–9:** The conquest of Jerusalem. The appearance of this passage at this juncture is prompted by literary, rather than chronological, considerations—its placement conveys the impression that David's first official act consisted of capturing Jerusalem. It is true that, according to Chronicles, Jerusalem attains its special status only later (see 1 Chron. chs 21–22). Still, the centrality of Jerusalem was so deeply rooted by the time of Chronicles that his readers would probably have seen this story as suggestive of David's (prophetically) inspired leadership. According to biblical tradition, Jerusalem had been a Jebusite city, so that no Israelite tribe had a stronger claim to it than any other—a sort of Washington, D.C. In 2 Sam., David's decision to establish Jerusalem as his new capital was designed to consolidate his hold over a newly united entity (Israel and Judah), which emerged only after a lengthy period of political instability. In Chronicles, however, David's ascension to the throne receives unanimous support; there is no need to seek a capital that will give stability to his regime. Accordingly, the conquest of Jerusalem takes on a different meaning in Chronicles: David intuitively sensed Jerusalem's (future) importance. Chronicles again claims that all Israel participated in this venture, whereas 2 Sam. ch 5 states that David was accompanied by "his men"; David's venture in 2 Sam. is a private one, whereas Chronicles views it as a religious priority, involving the entire nation. **5:** Chronicles deletes 2 Sam. 5.6b, 8, either because that passage was deemed incomprehensible or because it was seen as attributing to

told by the inhabitants of Jebus, "You will never get in here!"
But David captured the stronghold of Zion; it is now the City
of David. 6 David said, "Whoever attacks the Jebusites first will
be the chief officer"; Joab son of Zeruiah attacked first, and became the chief.

7 David occupied the stronghold; therefore it was renamed
the City of David. 8 David also fortified the surrounding area,
from the Millo roundabout, and Joab rebuilt the rest of the city.
9 David kept growing stronger, for the LORD of Hosts was with
him.

10 And these were David's chief warriors who strongly supported him in his kingdom, together with all Israel, to make
him king, according to the word of the LORD concerning Israel.
11 This is the list of David's warriors: Jashobeam son of Hachmoni, the chief officer; he wielded his spear against three hundred and slew them all on one occasion. 12 Next to him was
Eleazar son of Dodo, the Ahohite; he was one of the three warriors. 13 He was with David at Pas Dammim when the Philistines gathered there for battle. There was a plot of ground full
of barley there; the troops had fled from the Philistines, 14 but
they took their stand in the middle of the plot and defended it,
and they routed the Philistines. Thus the LORD wrought a great
victory.

15 Three of the thirty chiefs went down to the rock to David, at
the cave of Adullam, while a force of Philistines was encamped
in the Valley of Rephaim. 16 David was then in the stronghold,
and a Philistine garrison was then at Bethlehem. 17 David felt a
craving and said, "If only I could get a drink of water from the
cistern which is by the gate of Bethlehem!" 18 So the three got
through the Philistine camp, and drew water from the cistern
which is by the gate of Bethlehem, and they carried it back to
David. But David would not drink it, and he poured it out as a
libation to the LORD. 19 For he said, "God forbid that I should
do this! Can I drink the blood of these men who risked their
lives?"—for they had brought it at the risk of their lives, and he
would not drink it. Such were the exploits of the three warriors.
20 Abshai, the brother of Joab, was head of another three. He
once wielded his spear against three hundred and slew them.
He won a name among the three; 21 among the three he was
more highly regarded than the other two, and so he became

David a degrading prejudice toward the blind and lame. **6–8:** The role of Joab in capturing and providing for Jerusalem does not appear in 2 Sam. The mention of Joab here foreshadows the following chs, which list David's warriors and their achievements, requiring that Chronicles establish Joab's credentials. While it is unclear whether this datum is based on historical records or is the Chronicler's invention, the net result is a more positive image of Joab than that in the Deuteronomistic History (see 20.1; 21.3–6; cf. 1 Kings 2.5–6). The glorification of David's closest officers adds to David's glorification. In addition, Chronicles' version enhances the importance of Jerusalem: He who captures Jerusalem attains glory and leadership. Chronicles further claims that the name "City of David" was given to Jerusalem by the people of Israel, another sign of public support for David. 2 Sam., however, suggests that David, who alone (without Joab) was responsible for the capture of Jerusalem, introduced the new name. This fits the personal nature of David's venture, according to Samuel, and also makes for a less modest David.

11.10–46: Warriors who joined David. This material is largely similar to that of 2 Sam. ch 23, often viewed as part of an appendix to Samuel; this is one of several places where the Chronicler has rearranged his source material. Its placement at the end of Samuel allows for the reasonable inference that these warriors joined David over the course of his forty-year rule, while the Chronicler's sequence implies that these elite fighters joined the king at the very outset of his rule, supporting the notion that David enjoyed unanimous support. The historicity of the sixteen warriors in vv. 41b–47 added by Chronicles to the list in 2 Sam. is uncertain. **13–14:** In contrast to 2 Sam. 23.10, the MT of Chronicles indicates that the Philistines were routed by Eleazar and David; cf. Saul's conduct in 10.7 and see n. LXX and other ancient versions of Chronicles read the singular form, indicating that it was Eleazar alone who defeated the enemy. Both readings accomplish the same goal, namely, exaltation of David. The Masoretic reading does so by stressing that David's valor was a crucial factor in the victory; the other versions do so by highlighting the truly extraordinary abilities of the warriors who saw fit to join David. **16–19:** Realizing that his actions needlessly endangered his men, and that drinking the water would be tantamount to drinking blood—an act proscribed by Lev. 17.11–12; Deut. 12.23–25—he offers it as a libation (offering) to God.

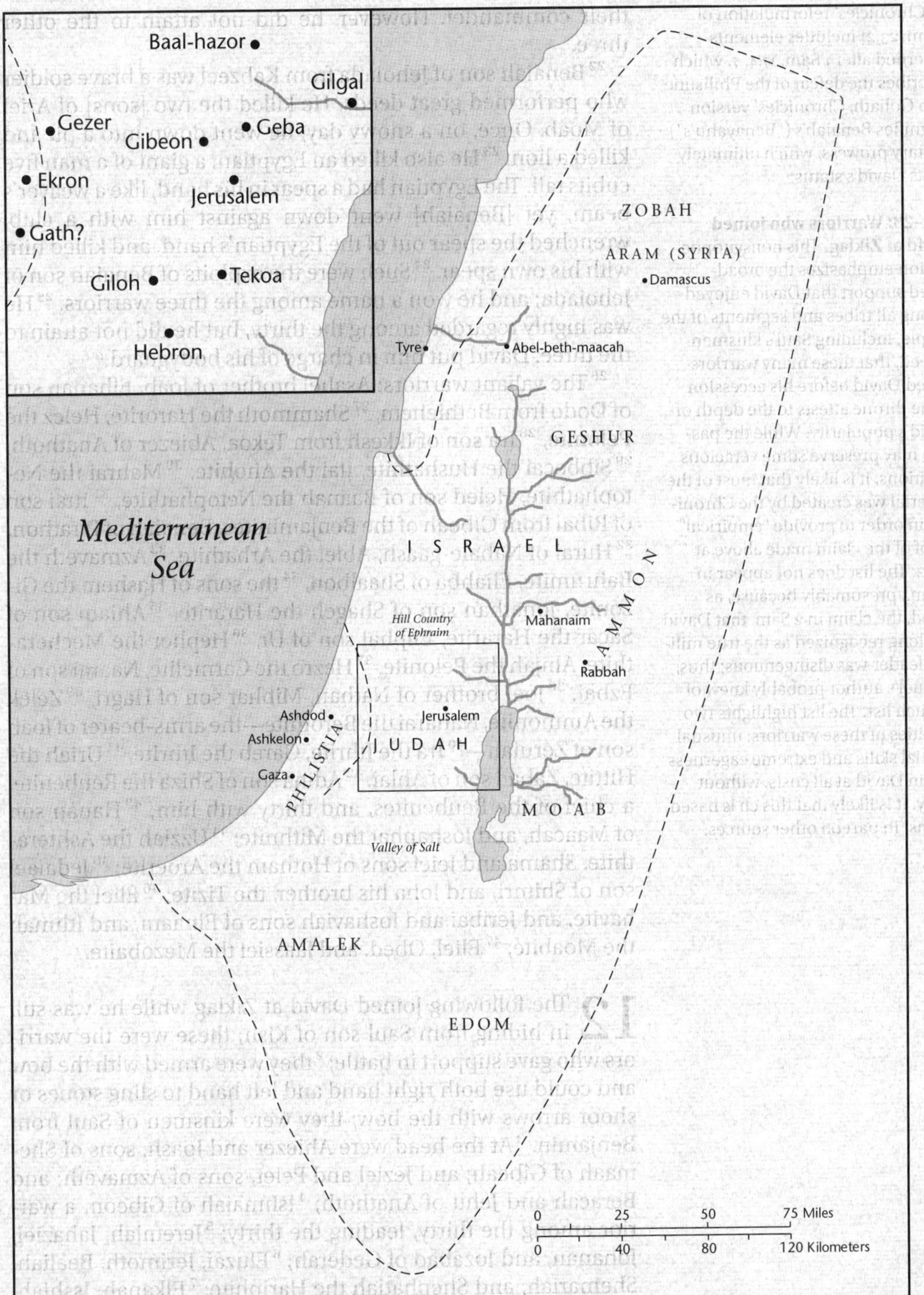

The kingdom of David according to First Chronicles. The dashed line shows the approximate boundary of the kingdom at its greatest extent.

23: Chronicles' reformulation of 2 Sam. 23.21 includes elements patterned after 1 Sam. 17.4, 7, which describes the defeat of the Philistine hero Goliath. Chronicles' version magnifies Benaiah's ("Benayahu's") military prowess, which ultimately exalts David's status.

12.1–23: Warriors who joined David at Ziklag. This nonsynoptic section emphasizes the broad-based support that David enjoyed among all tribes and segments of the people, including Saul's kinsmen. Indeed, that these many warriors joined David before his accession to the throne attests to the depth of David's popularity. While the passage may preserve some veracious traditions, it is likely that most of the material was created by the Chronicler in order to provide "empirical" proof of the claim made above at 11.1–2. The list does not appear in 2 Sam., presumably because, as noted, the claim in 2 Sam. that David was long recognized as the true military leader was disingenuous; thus, Samuel's author probably knew of no such list. The list highlights two qualities of these warriors: unusual martial skills and extreme eagerness to join David at all costs, without delay. It is likely that this ch is based at least in part on other sources.

their commander. However, he did not attain to the other
three.
22 Benaiah son of Jehoiada from Kabzeel was a brave soldier
who performed great deeds. He killed the two [sons] of Ariel
of Moab. Once, on a snowy day, he went down into a pit and
killed a lion. 23 He also killed an Egyptian, a giant of a man five
cubits tall. The Egyptian had a spear in his hand, like a weaver's
beam, yet [Benaiah] went down against him with a club,
wrenched the spear out of the Egyptian's hand, and killed him
with his own spear. 24 Such were the exploits of Benaiah son of
Jehoiada; and he won a name among the three warriors. 25 He
was highly regarded among the thirty, but he did not attain to
the three. David put him in charge of his bodyguard.[a]
26 The valiant warriors: Asahel brother of Joab, Elhanan son
of Dodo from Bethlehem, 27 Shammoth the Harorite, Helez the
Pelonite, 28 Ira son of Ikkesh from Tekoa, Abiezer of Anathoth,
29 Sibbecai the Hushathite, Ilai the Ahohite, 30 Mahrai the Netophathite, Heled son of Baanah the Netophathite, 31 Ittai son
of Ribai from Gibeah of the Benjaminites, Benaiah of Pirathon,
32 Hurai of Nahale-gaash, Abiel the Arbathite, 33 Azmaveth the
Bahrumite, Eliahba of Shaalbon, 34 the sons of Hashem the Gi-
zonite, Jonathan son of Shageh the Hararite, 35 Ahiam son of
Sacar the Hararite, Eliphal son of Ur, 36 Hepher the Mechera-
thite, Ahijah the Pelonite, 37 Hezro the Carmelite, Naarai son of
Ezbai, 38 Joel brother of Nathan, Mibhar son of Hagri, 39 Zelek
the Ammonite, Naharai the Berothite—the arms-bearer of Joab
son of Zeruiah—40 Ira the Ithrite, Gareb the Ithrite, 41 Uriah the
Hittite, Zabad son of Ahlai. 42 Adina son of Shiza the Reubenite,
a chief of the Reubenites, and thirty with him; 43 Hanan son
of Maacah, and Joshaphat the Mithnite; 44 Uzziah the Ashtera-
thite, Shama and Jeiel sons of Hotham the Aroerite; 45 Jedaiael
son of Shimri, and Joha his brother, the Tizite; 46 Eliel the Ma-
havite, and Jeribai and Joshaviah sons of Elnaam, and Ithmah
the Moabite; 47 Eliel, Obed, and Jaassiel the Mezobaite.

12 The following joined David at Ziklag while he was still
in hiding from Saul son of Kish; these were the warriors who gave support in battle; 2 they were armed with the bow
and could use both right hand and left hand to sling stones or
shoot arrows with the bow; they were kinsmen of Saul from
Benjamin. 3 At the head were Ahiezer and Joash, sons of She-
maah of Gibeah; and Jeziel and Pelet, sons of Azmaveth; and
Beracah and Jehu of Anathoth; 4 Ishmaiah of Gibeon, a warrior among the thirty, leading the thirty; 5 Jeremiah, Jahaziel,
Johanan, and Jozabad of Gederah; 6 Eluzai, Jerimoth, Bealiah,
Shemariah, and Shephatiah the Hariphite; 7 Elkanah, Isshiah,

a Meaning of Heb. uncertain.

Azarel, Joezer, and Jashobeam the Korahites; 8 Joelah and Zebadiah, sons of Jeroham of Gedor.[a] 9 Of the Gadites, there withdrew to follow David to the wilderness stronghold valiant men,
fighters fit for battle, armed with shield and spear; they had
the appearance of lions, and were as swift as gazelles upon the
mountains: 10 Ezer the chief, Obadiah the second, Eliab the
third, 11 Mashmannah the fourth, Jeremiah the fifth, 12 Attai
the sixth, Eliel the seventh, 13 Johanan the eighth, Elzabad the
ninth, 14 Jeremiah the tenth, Machbannai the eleventh. 15 Those
were the Gadites, heads of the army. The least was equal to a
hundred, the greatest to a thousand. 16 These were the ones
who crossed the Jordan in the first month, when it was at its
crest, and they put to flight all the lowlanders to the east and
west. 17 Some of the Benjaminites and Judahites came to the
stronghold to David, 18 and David went out to meet them, saying to them, "If you come on a peaceful errand, to support me,
then I will make common cause with you, but if to betray me
to my foes, for no injustice on my part, then let the God of our
fathers take notice and give judgment." 19 Then the spirit seized
Amasai, chief of the captains:

"We are yours, David,
On your side, son of Jesse;
At peace, at peace with you,
And at peace with him who supports you,
For your God supports you."

So David accepted them, and placed them at the head of his
band.

20 Some Manassites went over to David's side when he came
with the Philistines to make war against Saul, but they were of
no help to them, because the lords of the Philistines in council
dismissed him, saying, "He will go over to the side of his lord,
Saul, and it will cost us our heads"; 21 when he went to Ziklag,
these Manassites went over to his side—Adnah, Jozabad, Jediael, Michael, Jozabad, Elihu, and Zillethai, chiefs of the clans
of Manasseh.

22 It was they who gave support to David against the band,[b]
for all were valiant men; and they were officers of the force.

23 Day in day out, people came to David to give him support,
until there was an army as vast as the army of God.

24 These are the numbers of the [men of the] armed bands
who joined David at Hebron to transfer Saul's kingdom to him,
in accordance with the word of the LORD:

25 Judahites, equipped with shield and spear—6,800 armed
men; 26 Simeonites, valiant men, fighting troops—7,100; 27 of
the Levites—4,600; 28 Jehoiada, chief officer of the Aaronides;

a *Or, "the troop," reading Heb.* gedud *with several mss.*
b *I.e., the band of Amalekite raiders; cf. 1 Sam. 30.8, 15.*

17–18: It is not immediately apparent why this group is singled out or, put differently, why David suspected them more than the others, though it is likely that, given the historical differences between Judah and Benjamin, the mere presence of warriors from both tribes in the same military unit aroused David's suspicion. Some note that this group parallels the one that remained loyal to the Davidic dynasty at the time of its schism; see 1 Kings 12.16; 2 Chron. 10.16. Because of this and other similarities and contrastive elements shared with those passages (see also, 2 Sam. 20.1), it is likely that this passage is Chronicles' way of reinforcing the divine election of David and his successors. Perhaps this section highlights the fact that even Benjaminites, of Saul's tribe, followed David (see v. 2). **19:** This reflects Chronicles' innovative view on prophets and prophecy. Whereas many biblical books view prophecy as the exclusive prerogative of "professional" prophets whose activity centers on the monarchy, Chronicles maintains that any individual, even a non-Israelite, may, under the proper circumstances, serve as a conduit for conveying the divine will; hence, *Amasai,* a military man, experiences ad hoc prophecy. The possession formulae *(the spirit seized)* introduce the speeches of "non-prophets" only, indicating that Chronicles differentiates between this group and "professional" prophets.

12.24–41: Fighting forces at Hebron. Chronicles again stresses that the selection of David was by divine decree, both explicitly in v. 24, "in accordance with the word of the LORD," and through the structure and contents of the narrative. **25–39:** The total number of the fighting men who arrived at Hebron, 340,822, does not take into account other (male) Israelites who supported David from afar. While Chronicles is not the only biblical book to employ hyperbolic numbers in its narratives, it does so on an unusually broad scale—in numerous scenes involving military might, public support for the king, financial and material support for the

with him, 3,700; 29 Zadok, a young valiant man, with his clan—
22 officers; 30 of the Benjaminites, kinsmen of Saul, 3,000 in
their great numbers, hitherto protecting the interests of the
house of Saul; 31 of the Ephraimites, 20,800 valiant men, famous in their clans; 32 of the half-tribe of Manasseh, 18,000,
who were designated by name to come and make David king;
33 of the Issacharites, men who knew how to interpret the signs
of the times, to determine how Israel should act; their chiefs
were 200, and all their kinsmen followed them; 34 of Zebulun,
those ready for service, able to man a battle line with all kinds
of weapons, 50,000, giving support wholeheartedly; 35 of Naphtali, 1,000 chieftains with their shields and lances—37,000;
36 of the Danites, able to man the battle line—28,600; 37 of
Asher, those ready for service to man the battle line—40,000;
38 from beyond the Jordan, of the Reubenites, the Gadites, and
the half-tribe of Manasseh, together with all kinds of military
weapons—120,000.

39 All these, fighting men, manning the battle line with whole
heart, came to Hebron to make David king over all Israel. Likewise, all the rest of Israel was of one mind to make David king.

40 They were there with David three days, eating and drinking, for their kinsmen had provided for them.

41 And also, their relatives as far away as Issachar, Zebulun,
and Naphtali brought food by ass, camel, mule, and ox—provisions of flour, cakes of figs, raisin cakes, wine, oil, cattle, and
sheep in abundance, for there was joy in Israel.

13 Then David consulted with the officers of the thousands
and the hundreds, with every chief officer. 2 David said
to the entire assembly of Israel, "If you approve, and if the LORD
our God concurs,[a] let us send far and wide to our remaining
kinsmen throughout the territories of Israel, including the
priests and Levites in the towns where they have pasturelands,
that they should gather together to us 3 in order to transfer the
Ark of our God to us, for throughout the days of Saul we paid
no regard to it." 4 The entire assembly agreed to do so, for the
proposal pleased all the people. 5 David then assembled all Israel from Shihor of Egypt to Lebo-hamath, in order to bring the

a Meaning of Heb. uncertain.

Temple, and the numbers of animals sacrificed on festive occasions. This incredibly large number, and others in Chronicles, has led some scholars to argue that Heb "ʾelef," in these passages does not mean "thousand," but denotes, rather, a clan-based militia unit consisting of perhaps fifteen to twenty members, a usage attested in, e.g., Judg. 6.15 ("clan"). Closer examination of the relevant passages, however, reveals that Chronicles did, in fact, have the meaning "thousands" in mind. The passage emphasizes the enormous number of Israelites who not only supported David but traveled from afar in order to demonstrate support for him. It is striking that the largest contingents hail from the most distant regions, indicating complete and far-reaching support for David.

13.1–14: Transferring the Ark: The failed attempt. 1 Chron. ch 13 reflects 2 Sam. ch 6, while 1 Chron. ch 14 reflects 2 Sam. ch 5, another example of the Chronicler's rearrangement of his source material (see 11.10–46 n.). The reason for this rearrangement is explored below (see 14.1–17 n.). **1–4:** In 2 Sam. ch 6, David's transfer of the Ark to his new capital is intended to consolidate his position as leader of the newly unified nation; accordingly, he is accompanied by thirty thousand "picked men." Historically, this is a reasonable motive, inasmuch as the establishment of a functioning cult was, in the ancient Near East, a measure of a monarch's success and stability. By contrast, Chronicles presents David's act as expressing genuine concern for the cult (see Ps. 132), requiring the support and participation of the entire nation. Moreover, Chronicles' David seeks the nation's consent. This portrays Israel's only legitimate monarchy in a "democratized" fashion; David consults with his subjects or, more precisely, his kinsmen (v. 2). This utopian depiction may be an expression of Chronicles' messianic yearnings (See the intro.). In addition, the author again makes the claim that important historical events were approved, and attended, by the population at large—a clarion call to his contemporaries for similar support. **2:** Heb "p-r-tz," lit. "to break forth," (here rendered "far and wide") recurs in various forms in this and the following ch. Its use in the present v. is particularly unusual, serving to alert the reader that David has "broken forth/out," i.e., acted impetuously. As emerges in ch 15, David's intentions were sincere, but his rash decision, which ignored critical cultic norms, resulted in disaster. See ch 15 nn. **4–6:** Chronicles' version reflects its portrayal of Solomon and David as parallel or continuous figures; David is in no

Ark of God from Kiriath-jearim. 6[a]David and all Israel went up
to Baalah, Kiriath-jearim of Judah, to bring up from there the
Ark of God, the LORD, Enthroned on the Cherubim, to which
the Name was attached. 7 They transported the Ark of God on
a new cart from the house of Abinadab; Uzza and Ahio guided
the cart, 8 and David and all Israel danced before God with all
their might—with songs, lyres, harps, timbrels, cymbals, and
trumpets. 9 But when they came to the threshing floor of Chi-
don, Uzza put out his hand to hold the Ark of God because the
oxen had stumbled.[b] 10 The LORD was incensed at Uzza, and
struck him down, because he laid a hand on the Ark; and so
he died there before God. 11 David was distressed because the
LORD [c]had burst out[c] against Uzza; and that place was named
Perez-uzzah, as it is still called.

12 David was afraid of God that day; he said, "How can I bring
the Ark of God here?" 13 So David did not remove the Ark to his
place in the City of David; instead, he diverted it to the house
of Obed-edom the Gittite. 14 The Ark of God remained in the
house of Obed-edom, in its own abode, three months, and the
LORD blessed the house of Obed-edom and all he had.

a With vv. 6–14, cf. 2 Sam. 6.2–11. *b Meaning of Heb. uncertain.*
c-c *Heb.* paraṣ … pereṣ.

way inferior to Solomon. This was important since only Solomon constructed the Temple itself, and thus he might be seen as more significant than David. Thus, since 1 Kings ch 8 (compare 2 Chron. 5.2) states that the elders and tribal heads participated in the relocation of the Ark into the Temple, the author provided a similar scene for David. David's intention is to make sure that all Israel, including those who could not attend his coronation, would take part in the transferal of the Ark. Since those assembled for the coronation had not yet returned home, their consent entails their remaining in Hebron for an (indefinite) period, until the remaining Israelites join them; their consent thus reflects their awareness of the Ark's importance and willingness to do whatever necessary to further the cause of the cult. It is generally assumed that the Ark did not exist in the Chronicler's time (see 2 Chron. 35.3 n.). Perhaps the Ark is a cipher for worship generally, or the author wished to convey his expectation that the Ark would one day again be part of the religious practice. **5:** This v. conveys two important views. First, as understood by most scholars, Chronicles maintains a position attested only rarely in the Bible (see Josh. 13.3), that Israel's southern border extends to the easternmost branch of the Nile *(Shihor),* i.e., Pelusium, located on the western coast of the Sinai Peninsula. Second, in contrast to the early history, which portrays a gradual expansion of Israelite control culminating in the conquests of David, Chronicles claims that all of Canaan had already been populated by Israelites at an early stage in the nation's history. This is another expression of Chronicles' position regarding Israel's continuous presence in its land. Most scholars identify *Lebo-hamath* with Lebweh in modern Syria. These borders are ideal; it is doubtful that Israel ever controlled such an extensive area. Some argue that this v. does not express a (unique) view of Israel's boundaries but, rather, alludes to the presence of Israelites/Jews in foreign lands, all of whom are expected to participate in religious events and support the religious establishment no less than Israelites/Jews living in Israel and Judah. In other words, the author is, in this view, addressing (the religious obligations of) contemporary Jews residing in the diaspora. While the motif of support by Jews everywhere for religious observance is ubiquitous in Chronicles, this latter explanation is less than convincing, primarily because Lebo-Hamath appears in the Bible exclusively as a marker of Israel's north(east)ern boundary. **6:** *Cherubim:* Traditional Jewish sources, using an Aram. wordplay, view the cherubs as angel-like figures, having the face of a child (*b. Sukk.* 5b); several medieval exegetes, however, reject this position (e.g., Rashbam; Hezekiah ben Manoah [Hizkuni]). The cherubs were actually griffin-like or sphinx-like, composite creatures, similar to those attested in other cultures of the ancient Near East. Their role was twofold: to protect sacred or important precincts by warding off evil forces, and to serve as a throne for gods and/or kings (see Exod. 25.17–22; 26.31–35; Ezek. 1.4–28a; 10.8–22; see nn. to these vv.). This latter role explains why it is that the LORD is referred to as *Enthroned on the Cherubim,* as well as the Ark's unique status: It symbolizes the presence of the LORD. **9–14:** Obed-edom is a Gittite, probably hailing from the city of Gath, in Philistine territory. Nothing in 2 Sam. ch 6 suggests that he was a Levite. Nonetheless, the ample attestation of Levitical guards and musicians bearing this name in 1 Chron. (e.g., ch 16) implies that Chronicles views him as a Levite. Some scholars defend this pedigree, arguing that Chronicles understood Gath to refer to Gath-rimmon, a Levitical city (Josh. 19.45; 21.24). It is more likely, however, that Chronicles could not portray David as abandoning the Ark in a house of a foreigner that just happened to be close to the site of Uzza's death. Thus, the Chronicler reworked the genealogies to suggest that David placed the Ark in the hands of a person formally charged with this cultic task.

14 [a]King Hiram of Tyre sent envoys to David with cedar
logs, stonemasons, and carpenters to build a palace for
him. 2 Thus David knew that the LORD had established him as
king over Israel, and that his kingship was highly exalted for
the sake of His people Israel.
3 David took more wives in Jerusalem, and David begot more
sons and daughters. 4 These are the names of the children born
to him in Jerusalem:[b] Shammua, Shobab, Nathan, and Solomon; 5 Ibhar, Elishua, and Elpelet; 6 Nogah, Nepheg, and Japhia; 7 Elishama, Beeliada, and Eliphelet.
8 When the Philistines heard that David had been anointed
king over all Israel, all the Philistines went up in search of David; but David heard of it, and he went out to them. 9 The Philistines came and raided the Valley of Rephaim. 10 David inquired
of God, "Shall I go up against the Philistines? Will You deliver
them into my hands?" And the LORD answered him, "Go up,
and I will deliver them into your hands." 11 Thereupon David
ascended Baal-perazim, and David defeated them there. David said, "God [c]burst out[c] against my enemies by my hands
as waters burst out." That is why that place was named Baal-
perazim. 12 They abandoned their gods there, and David ordered these to be burned.
13 Once again the Philistines raided the valley. 14 David inquired of God once more, and God answered, "Do not go up

a With vv. 1–16, cf. 2 Sam. 5.11–25.
b With the list in vv. 4–7, cf. also 1 Chron. 3.5–8. *c-c Heb.* paraṣ.

14.1–17: David's palace, family, and battles. The material found in this ch appears in 2 Sam. in a different arrangement. 2 Sam. ch 5 places this material between David's coronation and his capture of Jerusalem, allowing the inference that David occupied himself with personal matters (e.g., construction of his palace) before attending to the Ark. Chronicles, by placing this material between the two attempts at transferring the Ark, conveys the impression that the delay in attending to the Ark was because David was occupied with other matters (rather than lack of motivation). Chronicles deletes 2 Sam. 6.12, which indicates that David renewed his efforts only after being informed that Obed-edom had prospered as a result of the Ark's presence because this portrayal reflects poorly upon David and his veneration of the cult—two important emphases of the book. Chronicles offers no clear explanation regarding the timing behind David's decision to again attend to the Ark; this implies that David returned to this task at the first opportunity following the activities described in ch 14 or, more precisely, once he had come to understand the reasons for the failure of the first attempt. The claim that chronologically ch 14 precedes the events of ch 13 (as in 2 Sam. ch 5–6), and that the present arrangement of chs 13–15 is motivated by the desire for literary (and theological) effect (see 1 Chron. 13.1–14 nn.; 14.8–17 n. below) is unlikely. One of the important motifs in Chronicles' depiction of David is his alacrity in attending to all matters pertaining to the cult, rendering all personal matters of secondary importance. The significance of this depiction may be fully grasped by viewing it against the matrix of ancient Near Eastern sources, which assign especial importance to the accomplishments of kings during their first year of reign *(rēš šarrūti).* Clearly, this all-important motif is vitiated by the claim that (as in 2 Sam.) David occupied himself with personal matters before attending to the Ark.

1–2: The placement of this passage in Chronicles may indicate that, despite David's culpability in the failure of the first attempt to relocate the Ark and Uzza's death, he was still the object of divine favor, since his intentions concerning the cult were sincere. **3–7:** Having many wives and children is a sign of success and divine favor in Chronicles; hence the passage's juxtaposition to the preceding vv.

14.8–17: David defeats the Philistines. These vv. convey a fundamental difference between David and Saul: Unlike Saul, David inquires of God in time of need (war), thereby assuring victory. They also anticipate the reason (given in ch 15) for the disastrous results of David's first attempt to move the Ark. The Heb root "p-r-tz" in v. 11 connects this ch with chs 13 (vv. 2, 11) and 15 (v. 13), indicating that when Israel follows the divine lead, all goes well; when they act rashly ("p-r-tz") and without due concern for the law, punishment follows. **12:** Cf. 2 Sam. 5.21. The latter states that David and his men "carried off" the enemies' idols. Chronicles' formulation is designed to reconcile David's conduct with Deut. 7.25, which demands that such paraphernalia be burnt. Deut. in its final form was not authoritative for the author of Samuel, but was for the Chronicler; given his interest in depicting David as righteous, the v. needed to be adjusted so David would follow "Mosaic" law. It is unclear whether the Chronicler simply changed his text or, as some aver, he interpreted the Heb term in 2 Sam., "vayisa'em" "he carried them off," to mean "burnt them"; evidence from the Dead Sea Scrolls may also suggest that this particular change predated the Chronicler.

after them, but circle around them and confront them at the
baca[a] trees. 15 And when you hear the sound of marching in
the tops of the *baca* trees, then go out to battle, for God will be
going in front of you to attack the Philistine forces." 16 David did
as God had commanded him; and they routed the Philistines
from Gibeon all the way to Gezer. 17 David became famous
throughout the lands, and the LORD put the fear of him in all
the nations.

15 He had houses made for himself in the City of David, and
he prepared a place for the Ark of God, and pitched a tent
for it. 2 Then David gave orders that none but the Levites were
to carry the Ark of God, for the LORD had chosen them to carry
the Ark of the LORD and to minister to Him forever. 3 David assembled all Israel in Jerusalem to bring up the Ark of the LORD
to its place, which he had prepared for it. 4 Then David gathered together the Aaronides and the Levites: 5 the sons of Kohath:
Uriel the officer and his kinsmen—120; 6 the sons of Merari:
Asaiah the officer and his kinsmen—220; 7 the sons of Gershom: Joel the officer and his kinsmen—130; 8 the sons of Elizaphan: Shemaiah the officer and his kinsmen—200; 9 the sons
of Hebron: Eliel the officer and his kinsmen— 80; 10 the sons of
Uzziel: Amminadab the officer and his kinsmen—112.

11 David sent for Zadok and Abiathar the priests, and for the
Levites: Uriel, Asaiah, Joel, Shemaiah, Eliel, and Amminadab.
12 He said to them, "You are the heads of the clans of the Levites;
sanctify yourselves, you and your kinsmen, and bring up the
Ark of the LORD God of Israel to [the place] I have prepared
for it. 13 [b-]Because you were not there the first time,[-b] the LORD
our God burst out against us, for we did not show due regard
for Him."

14 The priests and Levites sanctified themselves in order to
bring up the Ark of the LORD God of Israel. 15 The Levites carried the Ark of God by means of poles on their shoulders, as Moses had commanded in accordance with the word of the LORD.
16 David ordered the officers of the Levites to install their kinsmen, the singers, with musical instruments, harps, lyres, and
cymbals, joyfully making their voices heard. 17 So the Levites
installed Heman son of Joel and, of his kinsmen, Asaph son of
Berechiah; and, of the sons of Merari their kinsmen, Ethan son

a Meaning of Heb. uncertain. *b-b Meaning of Heb. uncertain.*

15.1–29: The Ark successfully moved to Jerusalem. The primary purpose of this ch is to explain, in theological terms, the reason(s) behind David's ultimate success in transporting the Ark. Two issues inform the Chronicler's reformulation of 2 Sam.: the author's need to account for the failure of the first attempt at relocating the Ark, a point not addressed in 2 Sam., and the author's unwillingness to accept material concerning cultic norms which Samuel's version contains because these conflict with Torah texts and Second Temple practices. **1:** In contrast to 2 Sam. 6.12, Chronicles omits the point that David's renewed effort at transferring the Ark was motivated by his hearing of the blessings that accrued to Obed-edom while the Ark was in his possession. This omission lets Chronicles avoid the impression that David was concerned primarily with advancement of his own political career and, indeed, had entertained the possibility of leaving the Ark at Obed-edom's house indefinitely. Chronicles' formulation indicates that the delay was necessary simply to allow David to determine why the first attempt had failed. This is reinforced by the placement of this v., which claims that David had prepared a tent-structure in anticipation of the eventual arrival of the Ark before uncovering the reason for the failure of the first attempt. **2–11:** The second attempt at bringing the Ark to Jerusalem is successful because David observes the cultic norms of the Torah; see Deut. 10.10 and Num. 7.9, which suggest that Levites and priests must lead all cultic events and ceremonies. The Levitical tribe consists of three clans: Kohath, Merari, and Gershom. Four of the chiefs are descendants of Kohath, consistent with Kohath's preeminent role in connection with transport of the Tabernacle and Ark (Num. 4.1–15). Two chiefs belong to the clans of Merari and Gershom, respectively. *Uriel* is either the fifth or eight generation scion of Kohath. *Joel* does not appear among the earlier listings of Gershom's descendants; cf. 1 Chron. 23.7–8; 26.21–22. The reading *Amminadab* in v. 10 has been questioned, leading to various proposed restorations. *Abiathar* appears in Chronicles only here; elsewhere the high priests of David's time are Ahimelech, son of Abiathar, and Zadok. **12:** The holiness of the Ark requires that those handling it sanctify themselves; cf. Josh. 3.5–6. **13–15:** David complies with Torah legislation; see Num. 6.9. **16, 19:** The *cymbals,* like the trumpets, were not used for musical accompaniment; rather, they

of Kushaiah. [18]Together with them were their kinsmen of second rank, Zechariah, Ben, Jaaziel, Shemiramoth, Jehiel, Unni, Eliab, Benaiah, Maaseiah, Mattithiah, Eliphalehu, Mikneiah, Obed-edom and Jeiel the gatekeepers. [19]Also the singers Heman, Asaph, and Ethan to sound the bronze cymbals, [20]and Zechariah, Aziel, Shemiramoth, Jehiel, Unni, Eliab, Maaseiah, and Benaiah with harps [a]on *alamoth;*[-a] [21]also Mattithiah, Eliphalehu, Mikneiah, Obed-edom, Jeiel, and Azaziah, with lyres to lead [a]on the *sheminith;*[-a] [22]also Chenaniah, officer of the Levites in song;[b] he was in charge of the song[b] because he was a master. [23]Berechiah and Elkanah were gatekeepers for the Ark. [24]Shebaniah, Joshaphat, Nethanel, Amasai, Zechariah, Benaiah, and Eliezer the priests sounded the trumpets before the Ark of God, and Obed-edom and Jehiah were gatekeepers for the Ark. [25][c]Then David and the elders of Israel and the officers of the thousands who were going to bring up the Ark of the Covenant of the LORD from the house of Obed-edom were joyful. [26]Since God helped the Levites who were carrying the Ark of the Covenant of the LORD, they sacrificed seven bulls and seven rams. [27]Now David and all the Levites who were carrying the Ark, and the singers and Chenaniah, officer of song of the singers, [a]were wrapped[-a] in robes of fine linen, and David wore a linen ephod. [28]All Israel brought up the Ark of the Covenant of the LORD with shouts and with blasts of the horn, with trumpets and cymbals, playing on harps and lyres. [29]As the Ark of the Covenant of the LORD arrived at the City of David, Michal daughter of Saul looked out of the window and saw King David leaping and dancing, and she despised him for it.

16 [d]They brought in the Ark of God and set it up inside the tent that David had pitched for it, and they sacrificed burnt offerings and offerings of well-being before God. [2]When David finished sacrificing the burnt offerings and the offerings of well-being, he blessed the people in the name of the LORD. [3]And he distributed to every person in Israel—man and woman alike—to each a loaf of bread, [a]a cake made in a pan, and a raisin cake.[-a] [4]He appointed Levites to minister before

a-a Meaning of Heb. uncertain. *b Meaning of Heb. uncertain.*
c Vv. 25–29 are found also in 2 Sam. 6.12–16. *d With vv. 1–3, cf. 2 Sam. 6.17–19.*

announced the beginning of a song; see 23.5 n. **20:** The Heb *alamoth,* a term attested in the Psalms and in Phoenician inscriptions, has been variously explained. It may denote young women vocalists, indicating the active participation of women in the Temple service or, perhaps, to (young) women musicians. If correct, this datum adds to the Chronicler's depiction of women's contributions to postexilic society; see the intro. and 25.6–8 n. Rabbinic sources, which do not acknowledge women functionaries in the Temple, maintained that the tonal quality of young Levite boys' voices—which resembles that of young women—made it possible for them to take part in the Temple choir, despite their being under the minimal age of twenty (23.27–28); the Aram. Tg. renders the Heb "(with) sweetness and pleasantness," reflecting a similar understanding. Medieval tradents understood the term to mean "forcefully, with insight," reflecting the root's other meanings in Heb and Arabic (anonymous disciple of Saadia Gaon). **22:** *Chenaniah* is not identified with any of the three Levitical clans. The nature of his duty is uncertain, possibly being that of carrying the Ark, singing, or supervising contributions. **23:** David assigns gatekeepers to the Ark, as well as to the Tabernacle in Gibeon and the yet to be built Temple. **25:** The recurring use of "joy" in Chronicles emphasizes the importance of the occasion. 2 Sam. 6.12 also mentions this element, but assigns it only to David. Chronicles apparently sought to apply 2 Chron. 8.1, which states that the elders and heads of tribes participated in the dedication of Solomon's Temple, to David's celebration; see 13.4–6 n. **26–27:** In contrast to the wording of 2 Sam. 6.13, Chronicles' listing of sacrificial animals reflects the influence of Priestly formulations in the Torah. In addition, Chronicles' formulation suggests that it is the people, rather than David, per se, who provide the sacrificial animals (see 1 Chron. 16.1–6 n. and 29.21 n.). This is consonant with the Chronicles' emphasis on the communal nature of the procession. **28–29:** Since Chronicles has deleted references to David's excessive ecstasy and the subsequent confrontation between Michal and David (see 2 Sam. 6.20–23), the reference to Michal's response might seem out of place. In fact, it is Chronicles' way of saying that Michal resented David's immense joy in attending to the Ark, which indicates that Saul's disregard for the cult was shared by other members of his family, continuing the theme of Saul's illegitimacy.

16.1–6: The Ark is placed in the tent. 4–6: Following the Priestly tradition incorporated in the Torah (contrast Deut.'s Levitical priests;

the Ark of the LORD, to invoke, to praise, and to extol the LORD
God of Israel: 5 Asaph the chief, Zechariah second in rank,
Jeiel, Shemiramoth, Jehiel, Mattithiah, Eliab, Benaiah, Obed-
edom, and Jeiel, with harps and lyres, and Asaph sounding the
cymbals, 6 and Benaiah and Jahaziel the priests, with trumpets,
regularly before the Ark of the Covenant of God. 7 Then, on that
day, David first commissioned Asaph and his kinsmen to give
praise to the LORD:

8[a] "Praise the LORD;
call on His name;
proclaim His deeds among the peoples.

a With vv. 8–22, cf. Ps. 105.1–15.

see Deut. 17.9), Chronicles, here and elsewhere, insists on a strict separation between the roles of Levites and priests. The Levites are assigned the duties of singing, guarding the sacred precincts, and generally assisting the priests. The role of blowing the cultic trumpets is reserved for priests, in accordance with Num. 10.8. The trumpets have several functions: to proclaim the presence of the LORD/Ark (here and 15.24, 28), to call for the people to prostrate themselves (2 Chron. 29.27–28), and to give the signal for prayer (2 Chron. 13.14). For a different function, see Num. 10.9–10. The role of Levites in connection to Temple song is very prominent in Chronicles, but is not clearly attested in earlier sources; it is thus unclear whether this is a new role developed during the Second Temple period. As in 15.26, Chronicles differs from 2 Sam. (6.13, 17) in crediting the people, rather than David, with provision of the sacrifices. **4:** The verbs *invoke, praise,* and *extol* all recur in the medley that follows. The Heb form of "invoke" may refer simply to expressing the name of YHVH, but the Heb root also allows the meaning "remind/cause remembrance." This allows for two plausible interpretations: Israel is to be reminded (of YHVH's providential care) and/or YHVH is to be reminded (of Israel and His past deeds on their behalf). The idea of YHVH's remembering of Israel appears, inter alia, at Num. 10.9–10. **5:** Nine Levites are called upon to perform with harps and lyres; the arrangement of names, taken together with 15.20–21, suggests that six were to play the harps, while three were assigned to the lyres. It is possible that this reflects some sort of archetypal arrangement of the Temple music, but this is uncertain. Rabbinic sources (*m. ʿArak.* 2:3; *t. ʿArak.* 2:1; *b. ʿArak.* 10a–10b) set minimal requirements for the number of musicians assigned to each instrument—including the number of trumpets. Only one cymbal is required, reflecting the formulation of v. 5, wherein only Asaph plays the cymbal. Rabbinic sources also attest the use of flutes on selected occasions (*m. Sukk.* 4:1; 5:1; *m. ʿArak.* 2.3), something not attested in Chronicles.

16.7–36: A medley of parts of Pss. 96; 105; and 106. The presence of poetic passages within a narrative framework is well attested in the Bible. The literary history of the present medley and its relationship to the surrounding narrative has been the subject of diverse opinions. In addition, the exact relation between Chronicles and these psalms has been debated. It is most likely that the Chronicler had the book of Psalms more or less in the form we have it, and here copied out sections of psalms that were relevant to this occasion and were popular among Jews of his time, while omitting or altering parts of these same psalms. The key messages of the Chronicler's new literary creation concern Israel's unique position among the nations and the deity's universal hegemony. This piece forms an inclusio with David's prayer in ch 29. In addition to several substantive changes introduced by the author (discussed below), there are several minor textual deviations from the text of Psalms, frequently reflecting a later stage of Biblical Heb and poetic style (e.g., v. 12 || Ps. 105.5; v. 32 || Ps. 96.12; v. 33 || Ps. 96.12).

16.7: The institution of cultic music. The Rabbis, noting the absence of pentateuchal precedent for the institution of cultic music and praise, found legal justification for the practice in Deut. 18.5 (*b. ʿArak.* 11a). Rabbinic sources debate which aspect, the instrumental or choral, constituted the essential component of cultic music (*b. Sukk.* 50b–51a). Rabbinic texts express various views regarding the composition of the Levitical orchestra. They also preserve diverse views, variously interpreted and reformulated by medieval tradents, regarding the occasions on which the instrumental and choral accompaniment were to be performed. The plethora of rabbinic sources relating to these issues notwithstanding, many rabbinic tradents did not view the musical repertoire as a *sine qua non* of sacrificial and cultic activity (see *m. ʿArak.* 2.3–4; *t. ʿArak.* 2.1–4; *b. ʿArak.* 10a–11a). *Asaph* is one of the leading Levitical figures and appears (as does Korah) in many superscriptions in the book of Psalms. Some consider him to be a founder of a guild of Temple singers, while others doubt that he was a historical figure; see 6.16–17 n. The other leaders of song are Heman and Jeduthun. The medley highlights the importance of the deity's fulfillment of His promise regarding Israel's sovereignty over its land; in particular, it stresses the role of the Temple and its attendant activities as the center of life in the promised land and as the ultimate goal and expression of that sovereignty. **8–22:** These vv. (= Ps. 105.1–15) describe the LORD's covenant with Abraham. Significantly,

9 Sing praises unto Him;
speak of all His wondrous acts.
10 Exult in His holy name;
let all who seek the LORD rejoice.
11 Turn to the LORD, to His might;[a]
seek His presence constantly.
12 Remember the wonders He has done;
His portents and the judgments He has pronounced,
13 O offspring of Israel, His servant,
O descendants of Jacob, His chosen ones.
14 He is the LORD our God;
His judgments are throughout the earth.
15 Be ever mindful of His covenant,
the promise He gave for a thousand generations,
16 that He made with Abraham,
swore to Isaac,
17 and confirmed in a decree for Jacob,
for Israel, as an eternal covenant,
18 saying, 'To you I will give the land of Canaan
as your allotted heritage.'
19 You were then few in number,
a handful, merely sojourning there,
20 wandering from nation to nation,
from one kingdom to another.
21 He allowed no one to oppress them;
He reproved kings on their account,
22 'Do not touch My anointed ones;
do not harm My prophets.'

23[b] "Sing to the LORD, all the earth.
proclaim His victory day after day.
24 Tell of His glory among the nations,
His wondrous deeds among all peoples.
25 For the LORD is great and much acclaimed,
He is held in awe by all divine beings.
26 All the gods of the peoples are mere idols,
but the LORD made the heavens.
27 Glory and majesty are before Him;
strength and joy are in His place.

28 "Ascribe to the LORD, O families of the peoples,
ascribe to the LORD glory and strength.

a I.e., the Ark; cf. Pss. 78.61; 132.8. *b With vv. 23–33, cf. Ps. 96.1–13.*

Chronicles deletes the subsequent vv. of the psalm, in which Joseph and then the Israelites are in Egypt. This excision is part of Chronicles' reticence concerning periods during which Israel was absent from its land. **13:** Ps. 105.6 reads, "Abraham...." This reading is part of Chronicles' emphasis on Jacob/Israel, rather than on Abraham. This phenomenon is part of the book's highlighting its view that all of the tribes belong to the nation of Israel—so long as they remain faithful to Jerusalem, its Temple, and the Davidic monarchy. At the same time, it underscores the fact that the people of Israel alone, among Abraham's descendants, are the legitimate heirs of the Abrahamic promises. This is reinforced by vv. 16–17 (|| Ps. 105.9–10), the only passage in Chronicles to mention the patriarchal covenant, which states that the promise was made to Abraham, Isaac and Jacob—to the exclusion of all others. **15:** In order to conform Ps. 96.8 to the present context, prior to the Jerusalem Temple's existence, Chronicles calls on all people to come "before Him" rather than coming "(in)to His (Temple) courts. **19:** The formulation has the Levites addressing the people in second person (cf. Ps. 105.12, which reads, "they [i.e., Israel's forebears] were then few in number"). This reading, like several others in this medley, speaks to the recent past and the author's time, when exiled Judahites found themselves in foreign lands and benefitted from providential protection; it thereby creates a bond and sense of continuity between the present generation and Israel's earliest forebears who experienced similar situations. **22:** Though the context of this v. indicates that *anointed ones* refers to the patriarchs, the Chronicler's elsewhere usage may indicate that the present v. was intended to anticipate the future, when Israel's monarch and, perhaps, all Israelites would be considered "anointed ones"; see 2 Chron. 6.41–42. **23:** Taken from Ps. 96.1–13a, these vv. (23–35) invite the nations to recognize the LORD's glory and His actions on behalf of Israel. The "universalistic" approach is seen by some as a late biblical (i.e., Second Temple) phenomenon, reflecting the contact between Jews and other peoples; it is unlikely that such an appeal would have been made during David's days.

29 Ascribe to the LORD the glory of His name,
bring tribute and enter before Him,
bow down to the LORD majestic in holiness.
30 Tremble in His presence, all the earth!
The world stands firm; it cannot be shaken.
31 Let the heavens rejoice and the earth exult;
let them declare among the nations, "The LORD is King!"
32 Let the sea and all within it thunder,
the fields and everything in them exult;
33 then shall all the trees of the forest shout for joy
at the presence of the LORD,
for He is coming to rule the earth.
34 Praise the LORD for He is good;
His steadfast love is eternal.
35 [a]Declare:
Deliver us, O God, our deliverer,
and gather us and save us from the nations,
to acclaim Your holy name,
to glory in Your praise.
36 Blessed is the LORD, God of Israel, from eternity to eternity."
And all the people said, "Amen" and "Praise the LORD."-[a]
37 He left Asaph and his kinsmen there before the Ark of the
Covenant of the LORD to minister before the Ark regularly as
each day required, 38 as well as Obed-edom with their kinsmen—68; also Obed-edom son of Jedithun and Hosah as gatekeepers; 39 also Zadok the priest and his fellow priests before
the Tabernacle of the LORD at the shrine which was in Gibeon;
40 to sacrifice burnt offerings to the LORD on the altar of the
burnt offering regularly, morning and evening, in accordance
with what was prescribed in the Teaching of the LORD with
which He charged Israel. 41 With them were Heman and Jeduthun and the other selected men designated by name to give
praise to the LORD, "For His steadfast love is eternal." 42 Heman
and Jeduthun had with them trumpets and cymbals to sound,

a-a Cf. Ps. 106.47–48.

29: The vexing Heb formulation, "hadrat qodesh," here translated *the LORD majestic in holiness.* Rabbinic sources, on the basis of metathesis and interchange of "he" and "het" (yielding, "hdrt" to "ḥrdt"), proffer the meaning "reverence/trembling (in the presence of) the Holy [One]," a position adopted, on other grounds, by some moderns. The phrase has also been rendered "holy sanctuary" and "in/before the holy theophany." This approach yields the position that the Temple houses a tangible presence or manifestation of deity and, in the case of 2 Chron. 20.21, that a tangible manifestation of the deity leads the people in warfare (cf. 2 Chron. 20.21 n.). There is no consensus regarding this expression. There are several differences between Ps. 96.6 and this v. Whereas Ps. 96 reads "[strength and] glory," Chronicles reads "[strength and] joy," referring to the pilgrims' state of mind. (For the importance of joy, in particular in the context of the Temple and its worship, see 1 Chron. 29.11–19). The term "place" (Heb "makom") is applied rather than in place of Ps. 96's "temple." Chronicles reads "place" (Heb "makom")—a term pregnant with cultic meanings in Heb and other Semitic languages—thereby avoiding anachronism. **34:** A common postexilic liturgical refrain; see v. 41; 2 Chron. 5.13; 7.3, 6; 20.21. Praise or "give thanks" (Heb "hodu") forms an inclusio with the opening, v. 8. **35–36:** Conclusion of prayer (= Ps. 106.47–48). Chronicles has added the word *Declare* to the text of Ps. 106.47; it thereby calls on the public gathered at the time of the Levitic recital—and, indeed, the people of Israel, generally—to participate in petitioning the deity. V. 35 is anachronistic: In Chronicles' time most Jews lived in foreign lands, but in David's time all of Israel resided within the borders of its promised land, as understood by Chronicles; see 13.5. (Ps. 106 is generally viewed as an exilic or postexilic composition.) Perhaps the author was willing to allow for this inconsistency in order to tell his contemporaries that the rightful place of every Israelite/Jew is in the land of Israel. The author adds the words "and save us" to the text of Ps. 106.47. In addition to being of immediate relevance to his audience, this alteration mitigates somewhat the anachronism noted above, since salvation—as opposed to ingathering—from the nations of the world would have been appropriate even in David's time. The entire medley is traditionally recited as part of the "pesukei dezimrah" ("verses of song"), the opening section of the daily morning prayers. **37–38:** Members of Merari, whose Tabernacle duties are set forth at Num. 4.20-33, attend to both the Ark and the Tabernacle, an expression of the complementary nature of the two sacred sites; see the following n. **39:** The reference to *Gibeon* is part of a tradition unique to Chronicles, though it may be based on 1 Kings chs 3–5. In the earlier books, the Tabernacle or the Ark is the focus of cultic concern, but not both. Moreover, nothing is heard of the Tabernacle after its destruction in

and instruments for the songs of God; and the sons of Jeduthun were to be at the gate. 43 Then all the people went every one to his home, and David returned to greet his household.

17 [a]When David settled in his palace, David said to the prophet Nathan, "Here I am dwelling in a house of cedar, while the Ark of the Covenant of the LORD is under tent-cloths." 2 Nathan said to David, "Do whatever you have in mind, for God is with you."

3 But that same night the word of God came to Nathan: 4 "Go and say to My servant David: Thus said the LORD: You are not the one to build a house for Me to dwell in. 5 From the day that I brought out Israel to this day, I have not dwelt in a house, but have [gone] from tent to tent and from one Tabernacle [to another]. 6 As I moved about wherever Israel went, did I ever reproach any of the judges of Israel whom I appointed to care for My people Israel: Why have you not built Me a house of cedar?

7 "Further, say thus to My servant David: Thus said the LORD of Hosts: I took you from the pasture, from following the flock, to be ruler of My people Israel, 8 and I have been with you wherever you went, and have cut down all your enemies before you. Moreover, I will give you renown like that of the greatest men on earth. 9 I will establish a home for My people Israel and will plant them firm, so that they shall dwell secure and shall tremble no more. Evil men shall not wear them down anymore as in the past, 10 ever since I appointed judges over My people Israel. I will subdue all your enemies.

And I declare to you: The LORD will build a house[b] for you. 11 When your days are done and you follow your fathers, I will raise up your offspring after you, one of your own sons, and I will establish his kingship. 12 He shall build a house for Me, and I will establish his throne forever. 13 I will be a father to him, and he shall be a son to Me, but I will never withdraw My favor

a With this chapter, cf. 2 Sam. 7.

b I.e., a dynasty; play on "house" (i.e., Temple) in v. 4.

Shiloh. Chronicles maintains that both the Ark and Tabernacle were concurrently important, with the Ark located in one place and the Tabernacle in another. No explanation is given as to how this situation came about. The idea that this tradition is Chronicles' way of claiming that Lev. 17.8–9 was observed in every generation is difficult (see vv. 1–2). See also 2 Chron. 1.3–6.

17.1–15: Rejection of David's request to build an edifice for the Ark and the "dynastic oracle." This is a revision of 2 Sam. 7.1–17, often seen as the culminating center of Samuel. Many differences exist among the MT of Samuel, the corresponding LXX, and Chronicles. Some explain Chronicles as reflecting an underlying Heb text different from Masoretic 2 Sam.; others claim that Chronicles used a proto-Samuel source, and that 2 Sam. is secondary. At least some of the differences should be attributed to Chronicles' creative reworking of its sources; Chronicles' version of 2 Sam. ch 7 is consistent with its emphases in other parts of Chronicles. (LXX to 2 Sam., while different from Chronicles, agrees with the latter on many substantive points, further suggesting that both result from tendentious reworking.) **1:** 2 Sam. 7.1 concludes "the LORD had granted him [David] safety from all the enemies around him." Chronicles' deletion is informed by two considerations: David's alacrity, leading to the request to build a Temple immediately and, second, the fact that David will have more battles to wage, a fact which contradicts 2 Sam. ch 7. See v. 10 n.; 22.9. **4–14:** The cultic norms of the ancient Near East dictated that the deity determine the time (and place) of construction of his/her temple. Unlike the version of 2 Sam. 7.5–16, Chronicles takes the eventual building of a temple to be a given. Similarly, it employs a less strident tone than 2 Sam. ch 7; moreover, it is not clear whether the present passage is intended as a censure of David. While these vv. may convey the same meaning as that expressed in 2 Sam. ch 7, they may also be read as implying that since David's request was made with pure intentions, he will be rewarded with the promise of a royal dynasty. See 1 Chron. 22.8–9 and v. 9 n. for Chronicles' explanation of the denial of David's request. **4:** *You are not the one to build a house for Me:* Chronicles' reformulation indicates that the construction of a Temple (by someone) is not in doubt (as in 2 Sam. ch 7; see below, v. 15) but that David will not be the builder. **10:** 2 Sam. 7.11 reads: "I will give you safety from all your enemies"; Chronicles' reading again avoids the idea of David's safety. **13:** Most scholars understand the dynastic promise in 2 Sam. 7.14–16 to be absolute; should David's successors sin they will be chastised, but the dynasty will remain intact. (This is a clear reference to the sins committed by Solomon and, perhaps, later Judahite kings; Chronicles omits any mention of such potential sins, so as to avoid even the hint of Solomon's sinning.) Chronicles, by

from him as I withdrew it from your predecessor. [14] I will install
him in My house and in My kingship forever, and his throne
shall be established forever."
[15] Nathan spoke to David in accordance with all these words
and all this prophecy. [16] Then King David came and sat before
the LORD, and he said, "What am I, O LORD God, and what
is my family, that You have brought me thus far? [17] Yet even
this, O God, has seemed too little to You; for You have spoken of Your servant's house for the future. [a-]You regard me as
a man of distinction,[-a] O LORD God. [18] What more can David

a-a Meaning of Heb. uncertain.

contrast, elsewhere explicitly adopts the position found in some places in Kings (1 Kings 2.1–4 n.) that the dynastic promise is contingent upon fidelity to the commandments (e.g., 28.9; 2 Chron. 7.17–20). The present passage, by its omission of part of 2 Sam. 7.14–15, allows for the possibility that the promise is granted conditionally. The unconditional dynastic promise has been seen by most scholars as chronologically prior; later biblical thought, reflecting the reality of the end of the Davidic dynasty, claims that the divine promise was contingent upon proper religious conduct. Recent scholars, however, argue that the conditional and unconditional views of the dynastic promise are coeval. They argue, less convincingly, that the present passage, with its deletion of part of 2 Sam. 7.14–15, adopts the unconditional view, while other Chronicles passages endorse the opposing position. The Chronicler's emphasis on religious fealty renders this approach unlikely. A more plausible explanation takes the passages expressing the condition view as the author's way of clarifying the intent of the present passage. One Qumran composition (4Q252 vi, 1–4) resolved the dilemma created by the cessation of the Davidic monarchy by (implicitly) claiming that David was promised not that there would be no break in the continuation of his dynasty but, rather, that, henceforth, his descendants alone would be the legitimate heirs to the throne—to the exclusion of, e.g., the Hasmonean dynasty. See also Pss. 89; 132.

14: *Kingship* (Heb "malkhut") may refer generally to Solomon's role as representative of the LORD's kingdom or, more likely, to Solomon's palace; see 2 Chron. 1.18; 2.11. Chronicles views the establishment of a dynasty as directed primarily toward Solomon, since he gives complete expression to divine rule in both religious and political spheres. (Cf. 2 Sam. 7.16: "your house ... your kingship ... your throne.") Chronicles claims that David's dynasty is not his own; rather, he and his descendants sit on the LORD's throne, i.e., they are His representatives on earth (see 1 Chron. 28.5; 29.11; 2 Chron. 13.8). 2 Sam. ch 7, however, views the dynasty as being David's possession or grant, given to him and his descendants. Stated differently, Chronicles views the Davidic monarchy as a vehicle for the theocratic kingdom, and therefore, anyone who challenges (or does not await the renewal of) the Davidic dynasty rejects the LORD; see, e.g., 2 Chron. 13.8, 12. **15:** A close reading of 2 Sam. ch 7 suggests David's request is rejected because it stems largely from personal motives (2 Sam. 7.5: "Are you the one to build a house for Me to dwell in?"; cf. v. 4, above). All successful dynasties in the ancient Near East were expected to establish and maintain a functioning religious establishment. Accordingly, David is rebuffed and told that he has it backwards: It is the LORD who will grant him a stable dynasty. David cannot use God to further his own political ambitions and the Temple will be built only when the LORD deems fit. This explanation, as noted, will not suffice for Chronicles, for which tending to the cult was paramount. Moreover, Chronicles' David has little reason to be concerned over lack of stability, since (in contrast to Samuel's David) he has never been the object of opposition and, indeed, was accepted by the entire nation. The reason that David cannot build the Temple is supplied by the Chronicler only at 22.8–9: The Temple could not be built by one whose hands were sullied with the blood of human beings (see 22.5–10 n.). Reading the present ch in the light of ch 22 allows for the following understanding of ch 17. Israel's leaders prior to David were not commanded or expected to build a Temple for the simple reason that Israel was in an ongoing state of war with its neighbors; hence, all its leaders were rendered unfit by dint of having been involved in bloodshed. On this reading of the present ch, David is not rebuked for being presumptuous; rather, he is told that, despite his sincere intentions, he is in no more of a position to build the Temple than were his predecessors. Hence, the stinging tenor of 2 Sam. 7.5 has been replaced in Chronicles by the matter-of-fact declaration that David will not be the one to build the Temple but, rather, his son. As for the dynastic promise, Chronicles probably intended this as a reward for David's well-intended offer. See further, ch 22. The phrasing "I will install" ("we-ha-amadtihu") conveys the nuance that Solomon's office will be comparable to that of priests and Levites installed in their positions. Solomon's function, unlike that of other Temple officiants is to oversee all matters pertaining to the Temple and its construction.

17.16–27: David's response. The unambiguous reference to the sojourn in Egypt (vv. 21–22) is relatively rare in Chronicles; see intro. Chronicles, like other biblical texts, is not fully consistent in its editing or its incorporation of earlier traditions. Cf. Solomon's reticence concerning this issue and his emphasis on the

Davidic covenant (2 Chron. ch 6), suggesting that the latter has surpassed the former in significance.

18.1–17: David's victories. This ch presents David's military victories and the extension of his empire, particularly to the north/northeast. **1:** 2 Sam. 8.1 states "David attacked the Philistines and subdued them; and David took Metheg-Ammah from the Philistines." Chronicles' shorter version may indicate that its author found Samuel incomprehensible. **2:** The Chronicler shortens the parallel v. at 2 Sam. 8.2, perhaps because David's orders that two-thirds of the Moabites be killed appear to be both ruthless and arbitrary. **3:** Setting up a monument was a means of fixing the boundaries of a ruler's sovereignty. The second half of this v. (in Heb) is syntactically ambiguous; it is unclear if David or Hadadezer was going to set up his monument. If Hadadezer is the subject of the second half of the v., it then describes David's response to Hadadezer's attempt to free himself from David's subjugation. **4:** Hamstringing horses rendered them unusable for military (or other) purposes. This v. fits nicely with Chronicles' view of military success as determined by religious merit, not military prowess; see also Deut. 17.16, 20. **8–9:** Chronicles' claim that the copper taken by David was used by Solomon in fashioning Temple appurtenances does not appear in 2 Sam. ch 8. This passage again suggests continuity between David and Solomon as Temple builders, and furthers David's image as the arch patron of the Temple, and as one whose personal wealth was of secondary importance. This v. forms part of a recurring motif, an increase in Temple revenue —particularly in warfare—bespeaks a successful king and loss of Temple holdings—either in warfare or as a result of tribute paid to foreign rulers—attests to a monarch's failed status. **10:** *Hadoram*'s name appears at 2 Sam. 8.9 as Joram. Hadoram means "Had(d)u (i.e:, Baal) is exalted." Such a name would be natural among Arameans.

add regarding the honoring of Your servant? You know Your
servant. 19 O LORD, [a-]for Your servant's sake, and of Your own
accord,[-a] You have wrought this great thing, and made known
all these great things. 20 O LORD, there is none like You, and
there is no other God but You, as we have always heard. 21 And
who is like Your people Israel, a unique nation on earth, whom
God went and redeemed as His people, winning renown for
Yourself for great and marvelous deeds, driving out nations
before Your people whom You redeemed from Egypt. 22 You
have established Your people Israel as Your very own people
forever; and You, O LORD, have become their God.

23 "And now, O LORD, let Your promise concerning Your
servant and his house be fulfilled forever; and do as You have
promised. 24 Let it be fulfilled that Your name be glorified forever, in that men will say, 'The LORD of Hosts, God of Israel,
is Israel's God'; and may the house of Your servant David be
established before You. 25 Because You, my God, have revealed
to Your servant that You will build a house for him, Your servant has ventured to pray to You. 26 And now, O LORD, You are
God and You have made this gracious promise to Your servant.
27 Now, it has pleased You to bless Your servant's house, that it
abide before You forever; for You, O LORD, have blessed and
are blessed forever."

18 [b]Sometime afterward, David attacked the Philistines
and subdued them; and David took Gath and its dependencies from the Philistines. 2 He also defeated the Moabites; the Moabites became tributary vassals of David.

3 David defeated Hadadezer, king of Zobah-hamath, who
was on his way to set up his monument at the Euphrates River. 4 David captured 1,000 chariots and 7,000 horsemen and
20,000 foot soldiers of his force; and David hamstrung all the
chariot horses except for 100, which he retained. 5 And when
the Arameans of Damascus came to the aid of King Hadadezer
of Zobah-hamath, David struck down 22,000 of the Arameans.
6 David stationed [garrisons] in Aram of Damascus, and the
Arameans became tributary vassals of David. The LORD gave
David victory wherever he went. 7 David took the gold shields[c]
carried by Hadadezer's retinue and brought them to Jerusalem; 8 and from Tibbath and Cun, towns of Hadadezer, David
took a vast amount of copper, from which Solomon made the
bronze tank, the columns, and the bronze vessels.

9 When King Tou of Hamath heard that David had defeated
the entire army of King Hadadezer of Zobah, 10 he sent his son
Hadoram to King David to greet him and to congratulate him

a-a Meaning of Heb. uncertain. *b With this chapter, cf. 2 Sam. 8.*
c Or "quivers."

on his military victory over Hadadezer—for Hadadezer had
been at war with Tou; [he brought with him] all manner of
gold, silver, and copper objects. 11 King David dedicated these
to the LORD, along with the other silver and gold that he had
taken from all the nations: from Edom, Moab, and Ammon;
from the Philistines and the Amalekites.

12 Abshai son of Zeruiah struck down Edom in the Valley of
Salt, 18,000 in all. 13 He stationed garrisons in Edom, and all
the Edomites became vassals of David. The LORD gave David
victory wherever he went.

14 David reigned over all Israel, and David executed true
justice among all his people. 15 Joab son of Zeruiah was commander of the army; Jehoshaphat son of Ahilud was recorder;
16 Zadok son of Ahitub and Abimelech son of Abiathar were
priests; Shavsha was scribe; 17 Benaiah son of Jehoiada was
commander of the Cherethites and the Pelethites; and David's
sons were first ministers of the king.

19 [a]Sometime afterward, Nahash the king of the Ammonites died, and his son succeeded him as king. 2 David
said, "I will keep faith with Hanun son of Nahash, since his
father kept faith with me." David sent messengers with condolences to him over his father. But when David's courtiers came
to the land of Ammon to Hanun, with condolences, 3 the Ammonite officials said to Hanun, "Do you think David is really
honoring your father just because he sent you men with condolences? Why, it is to explore, to subvert, and to spy out the
land that his courtiers have come to you." 4 So Hanun seized
David's courtiers, shaved them, and cut away half of their garments up to the buttocks, and sent them off. 5 When David was
told about the men, he dispatched others to meet them, for the
men were greatly embarrassed. And the king gave orders, "Stay
in Jericho until your beards grow back; then you can return."

6 The Ammonites realized that they had incurred the wrath
of David; so Hanun and the Ammonites sent 1,000 silver talents to hire chariots and horsemen from Aram-naharaim,

a With this chapter, cf. 2 Sam. 10.

By contrast, the typically Israelite Joram, meaning "the LORD is exalted," is surprising, suggesting that Samuel reflects a censored form of the name, whereas Chronicles retains the original form; see 8.33 n. **14:** True justice (Heb "mishpat u-tzedakah") refers, in the Bible and the ancient Near East, to the establishment of social order ("law and order"), the sine qua non of any society. This, together with the establishment and maintenance of a functioning sacrificial cult, was the sign of a successful monarch who was fulfilling his divinely given mandate. **17:** The *Cherethites* and the *Pelethites* were mercenary troops whose origin probably lay in the Aegean Sea; see 2 Sam. 15.18; 20.7, 23. 1 Sam. 30.14 suggests that they joined David's forces during his stay at Ziklag. The origin of the Pelethites is unknown. *Sons ... first ministers:* 2 Sam. 8.18 states that "David's sons were priests" (Heb "kohanim"). Since Torah (Priestly) sources mandate that only descendants of Aaron, Moses' brother, could be priests, traditional commentators have labored to explain the term "kohanim" in 2 Sam. as referring to some office other than priesthood, e.g., (leading) court officials or military advisers; others emend the text of 2 Sam. The simplest explanation is that the Chronicler could not accept the idea that the sons of David, a Judean, functioned as priests, so he revised the tradition. This explanation also accounts for another difference between Chronicles and Samuel. 2 Sam. 20.26 refers to "Ira, the Yairite ... "; no such notice appears in Chronicles. The gentilic "Yairite" probably refers to a clan within the Transjordanian tribe of Manasseh, or, possibly, to the town of Kiriath-jearim (see 13.6). Some traditional sources (Tg. to 2 Sam.; tosafists to *b. ʿEruv.* 63a) understood Ira to be a court official or military adviser, a position adopted by some moderns. Another view found in traditional sources (e.g., tosafists *ad b. ʿEruv.* 63, s.v. "kol") maintains that Ira's father, but not his mother, was a descendant of Aaron. Chronicles' omission of this datum indicates that its author probably understood 2 Sam. as maintaining that Ira was a priest.

19.1–19: More victories for David. This passage is a light reworking of 2 Sam. ch 10. **1–2:** *Nahash* respected the terms of his treaty (performed "ḥesed," "faith") with David and, for that reason, David saw fit to send his condolences. Rabbinic tradents, who understood the Heb term "ḥesed" to mean "acts of kindness," were perplexed by the absence of any unusual expressions of friendship on the part of Nahash. Accordingly, they claimed that David's family members had been killed while in the custody of the king of Moab, save for one brother; the brother found refuge with Nahash, who refused Moab's request to

Aram-maacah, and Zobah. [7] They hired 32,000 chariots, the
king of Maacah, and his army, who came and encamped before Medeba. The Ammonites were mobilized from their cities
and came to do battle.
[8] On learning this, David sent out Joab and the whole army,
[including] the professional fighters. [9] The Ammonites marched
out and took up their battle position at the entrance of the city,
while the kings who came [took their stand] separately in the
open. [10] Joab saw that there was a battle line against him both
front and rear. So he made a selection from all the picked men
of Israel and arrayed them against the Arameans, [11] and the rest
of the troops he put under the command of his brother Abishai
and arrayed them against the Ammonites. [12] Joab said, "If the
Arameans prove too strong for me, you come to my aid; and
if the Ammonites prove too strong for you, I will come to your
aid. [13] Let us be strong and resolute for the sake of our people
and the towns of our God; and the LORD will do what He deems
right."
[14] Joab and the troops with him marched into battle against
the Arameans, who fled before him. [15] And when the Ammonites saw that the Arameans had fled, they too fled before his
brother Abishai, and withdrew into the city. So Joab went to
Jerusalem.
[16] When the Arameans saw that they had been routed by
Israel, they sent messengers to bring out the Arameans from
across the Euphrates; Shophach, Hadadezer's army commander, led them. [17] David was informed of it; he assembled
all Israel, crossed the Jordan, and came and took up positions
against them. David drew up his forces against Aram; and they
fought with him. [18] But the Arameans were put to flight by Israel. David killed 7,000 Aramean charioteers and 40,000 foot-
men; he also killed Shophach, the army commander. [19] And
when all the vassals of Hadadezer saw that they had been routed by Israel, they submitted to David and became his vassals.
And the Arameans would not help the Ammonites anymore.

20 [a] At the turn of the year, the season when kings go out
[to battle], Joab led out the army force and devastated
the land of Ammon, and then besieged Rabbah, while David remained in Jerusalem; Joab reduced Rabbah and left it
in ruins. [2] David took the crown from the head of their king;

a With vv. 1–3, cf. 2 Sam. 11.1; 12.30–31.

extradite him (*Num. Rab.* 14:3; *Tanh.-Yelammedenu, Va-Yera'*). **13:** The formulation of this v., like its parallel in 2 Sam., expresses the generals' trust in God, the key factor, according to Chronicles, in assuring victory over the enemy. This is a good example of an idea that appears in the sources of Chronicles but gains new importance in Chronicles. **18–19:** The Chronicler expands the number found in 2 Sam. 10.18 tenfold to glorify David and to emphasize the power of divine assistance.

20.1–8: Defeating Ammon and the Philistines.

20.1–3: Capture of Rabbah. 2 Sam. 12.26–30 states that Joab sent a message reminding David that if he remained in Jerusalem, he would be denied the glory accompanying the impending capture of Rabbah. David then joins his troops and takes part in the conquest. 2 Sam.'s version portrays David as a monarch guilty of adultery with Bathsheba and of the abuse of power (leading to the death of Uriah), who also takes the credit for a military victory whose groundwork has been laid by someone else. Chronicles presents a more flattering picture; it makes no mention of Joab's message or David's motive in joining his troops, and states simply that Joab captured and then destroyed Rabbah. See 11.6–8 n. Chronicles' omission, however, makes David's sudden appearance at Rabbah awkward. Some LXX mss harmonize this passage with 2 Sam. Following v. 1, 2 Sam. 11.1 presents the story of David and Bathsheba. Chronicles deletes the entire episode, because of its damaging portrayal of David. The disturbing implications of 2 Sam. chs 11–12 were not lost upon rabbinic tradents and medieval exegetes who offered various attempts at mitigating the severity of David's deeds (see *b. Shab.* 56a-b; Isaac Abravanel to 2 Sam.). Some scholars maintain that, as in other instances of deletion, Chronicles is not attempting to deny the tradition of 2 Sam., which would have been known to his readers; rather, the author has simply selected the material that best suited his interests and goals. **2:** In place of Heb "malkam," "(the crown of) their king," several versions read "Milkom," i.e., the (crown of) the national god of Ammon. (Cf. Zeph. 1.5 n. The early Heb text was written without vowels, so the consonantal text may be read either way.) Rabbinic sources (*b. A. Z.*

he found that it weighed a talent of gold, and in it were precious stones. It was placed on David's head. He also carried
off a vast amount of booty from the city. 3 He led out the people who lived there and [a]-he hacked them-[a] with saws and iron
threshing boards and axes;[b] David did thus to all the towns of
Ammon. Then David and all the troops returned to Jerusalem.
4 After this, fighting broke out with the Philistines at Gezer; that
was when Sibbecai the Hushathite killed Sippai, a descendant
of the Rephaim, and they were humbled.
5 Again there was fighting with the Philistines, and Elhanan
son of Jair killed Lahmi, the brother of Goliath the Gittite; his
spear had a shaft like a weaver's beam. 6 Once again there was
fighting at Gath. There was a giant of a man who had twenty-
four fingers [and toes], six [on each hand] and six [on each
foot]; he too was descended from the Raphah. 7 When he
taunted Israel, Jonathan son of David's brother Shimea killed
him. 8 These were descended from the Raphah in Gath, and
they fell by the hands of David and his men.

21 [c]Satan arose against Israel and incited David to number
Israel. 2 David said to Joab and to the commanders of
the army, "Go and count Israel from Beer-sheba to Dan and

a-a Meaning of Heb. uncertain. 2 Sam. 12.31 has "set them to work."
b Heb. megeroth; *cf. 2 Sam. 12.31* magzeroth, *"axes."*
c With vv. 1–26, cf. 2 Sam. 24.

44a) reflect the same understanding. Similar uncertainty attends 2 Sam. ch 12. *A talent of gold:* The immense weight, approximately 34 kg (75 lbs), has been variously explained. **3:** The words *he hacked them* have been variously interpreted, e.g., "he ruled over them, placing upon them hewing of stones."

20.4–8: Battles with the Philistines. Cf. 2 Sam. 21.18–19. The term *Rephaim,* in various Semitic languages and biblical Heb, has several meanings; here the reference is to "giants" or "megaliths." The Bible frequently ascribes Transjordanian provenance to these beings. Vv. 6–8 discuss one whose origin lay in the city of Gath, along the coastal plain. **6:** 2 Sam. 21.19 states: "Elhanan son of Jaare-oregim the Bethlehemite killed Goliath the Gittite, whose spear had a shaft like a weaver's bar." This seems to contradict 1 Sam. ch 17, which states that David killed Goliath. Although it is likely that Samuel preserves two variant traditions, a rabbinic tradition (Tg. to 2 Sam. ch 21; *Ruth Rab.* 2.2) claimed that David and Elhanan were one and the same. A similar position is adopted by some modern commentators, who argue that David was a throne name, while Elhanan was the king's given name. One medieval exegete (Isaiah of Trani) argued that Goliath of 2 Sam. ch 21 was not the same warrior referred to in 1 Sam. ch 17. Chronicles' formulation probably reflects the author's attempt to reconcile the two different traditions preserved in Samuel; thus, David killed Goliath, while Goliath's brother was slain by Elhanan. Alternatively, Chronicles may result from textual corruption, or a different underlying text, of 2 Sam. 21.17.

21.1–26: David's census and consequences. The differences between Chronicles' version and 2 Sam. ch 24 are numerous and substantive, leading to divergent views regarding the textual history of both passages. Chronicles shares many features with 4QSam[a] (one of the Dead Sea Scroll Samuel mss from Qumran), yet still differs from it in fundamental respects. The following remarks relate to the MT alone. In 2 Sam. this episode appears in a closing addendum or appendix to the book. It concludes with the notice that the plague has come to a close, with no hint of a logical nexus between this incident and the immediately following opening chs of 1 Kings. Indeed, the first chs in Kings deal with David's last days and the rocky transition to Solomon's rule. Finally, 2 Sam. does not indicate when in David's career this episode took place. In Chronicles this story, which takes place while David is relatively young (see 23.1), serves as a prelude to the choice of the Temple site. In the last century, several scholars saw the divinely guided selection of the Temple site as part of the book's polemic—and that of Second Temple Judaism, generally—against the Samaritans, who maintained that Mt. Gerizim (in Shechem), rather than Jerusalem, constituted the "chosen place." This position is unlikely, since tensions between Samaritans and Jews reached their height during the Hasmonean period and the establishment of the cultic site on Mt. Gerizim can be dated no earlier than the early 2nd c. BCE, well after the likely date of Chronicles' composition. More likely, Chronicles' point is that all aspects of the Israelite/Jewish Temple and cult are determined by the divine will, not human caprice, a theme repeated elsewhere. **1:** 2 Sam. 24.1 states that "the anger of the LORD again flared up against Israel" and, consequently, incited David to sin so as to bring (further) guilt upon the people. There is no hint as to the cause of this state of affairs, however. Chronicles resolves some of the difficulty by eliminating reference to the LORD's anger. Furthermore, Chronicles mitigates the difficulties created by 2 Sam. by claiming that David was incited by an intermediary, Satan. Many scholars understand the Heb

bring me information as to their number." [3] Joab answered,
"May the LORD increase His people a hundredfold; my lord
king, are they not all subjects of my lord? Why should my lord
require this? Why should it be a cause of guilt for Israel?"
[4] However, the king's command to Joab remained firm, so
Joab set out and traversed all Israel; he then came to Jerusalem. [5] Joab reported to David the number of the people that
had been recorded. All Israel comprised 1,100,000 ready to
draw the sword, while in Judah there were 470,000 men ready
to draw the sword. [6] He did not record among them Levi and
Benjamin, because the king's command had become repugnant to Joab. [7] God was displeased about this matter and He
struck Israel.
[8] David said to God, "I have sinned grievously in having done
this thing; please remit the guilt of Your servant, for I have acted foolishly." [9] The LORD ordered Gad, David's seer: [10] "Go and
tell David: Thus said the LORD: I offer you three things; choose
one of them and I will bring it upon you." [11] Gad came to David and told him, "Thus said the LORD: Select for yourself [12] a
three-year famine; or that you be swept away three months before your adversaries with the sword of your enemies overtaking you; or three days of the sword of the LORD, pestilence in
the land, the angel of the LORD wreaking destruction throughout the territory of Israel. Now consider what reply I shall take
back to Him who sent me." [13] David said to Gad, "I am in great
distress. Let me fall into the hands of the LORD, for His compassion is very great; and let me not fall into the hands of men."
[14] The LORD sent a pestilence upon Israel, and 70,000 men
fell in Israel. [15] God sent an angel to Jerusalem to destroy it,
but as he was about to wreak destruction, the LORD saw and
renounced further punishment and said to the destroying angel, "Enough! Stay your hand!" The angel of the LORD was then
standing by the threshing floor of Ornan the Jebusite. [16] David
looked up and saw the angel of the LORD standing between
heaven and earth, with a drawn sword in his hand directed
against Jerusalem. David and the elders, covered in sackcloth,
threw themselves on their faces. [17] David said to God, "Was it
not I alone who ordered the numbering of the people? I alone
am guilty, and have caused severe harm; but these sheep, what

"satan" to refer to the infamous heavenly being, arguing that the v.'s formulation reflects a growing tendency in postexilic Judaism to distance the deity from direct contact with human affairs, especially those involving suffering, but it is more likely that it here refers to a human adversary, its meaning elsewhere in the Bible. (Only in postbiblical literature does the word come to mean the Satan.) The ascription of David's incitement to a divine being accomplishes little, since he is submissive to the divine will; ultimately, then, the LORD stands behind David's offense. For these reasons, the term has been interpreted as referring here to a human (possibly, military) adversary, who sought to cause David harm by inciting him to execute the census. **3–5:** Israel, like other ancient societies, viewed census taking, unless given explicit divine sanction, as taboo (e.g., Exod. 30.11–16). While the reasons for this taboo are not clearly explained in biblical texts, it is likely that Chronicles opposed this practice, frequently associated with military preparations, because it implies that martial strength, rather than religious merit and divine providence, is primarily responsible for victory in battle. **6:** 2 Sam. makes no reference to the exclusion of Levi and Benjamin. The common denominator between the two tribes is their intimate connection to Israel's cultic worship. The Levites were central to the cult, and, according to Jewish tradition, the southern edge of Benjamin included part of Jerusalem. Moreover, Gibeon, the site of the Tabernacle (see 16.39), was also in Benjamin. Thus, Chronicles distances these tribes from any involvement in David's misdeed. Some see Chronicles' position as related to its view of theodicy: Jerusalem was spared because the Levites and Benjamin had no part in the census. The Jewish historian Josephus (late 1st c. CE) claims that the exclusion of these two tribes was the result not of Joab's refusal, but of David's regret (over his decision) during the course of the census (*Ant.* 7.320). **8–17:** David's request that he and his household alone be punished is surprising, if one attributes to Chronicles a strict view of retribution and personal accountability. What sin have the family members committed, not to mention the seventy thousand citizens who perished? It is possible that the taboo associated with census taking is sui generis. Alternatively, this passage may indicate that Chronicles, in principle, accepts the prevalent biblical notion of vicarious punishment; see intro. The description of the angel in v. 16 is more detailed than that of Samuel, and may reflect more developed notions of angelology in Second Temple times.

have they done? O LORD my God, let Your hand fall upon me
and my father's house, and let not Your people be plagued!"
[18] The angel of the LORD told Gad to inform David that David
should go and set up an altar to the LORD on the threshing
floor of Ornan the Jebusite. [19] David went up, following Gad's
instructions, which he had delivered in the name of the LORD.
[20] Ornan too saw the angel; his four sons who were with him
hid themselves while Ornan kept on threshing wheat. [21] David came to Ornan; when Ornan looked up, he saw David and
came off the threshing floor and bowed low to David, with his
face to the ground. [22] David said to Ornan, "Sell me the site of
the threshing floor, that I may build on it an altar to the LORD.
Sell it to me at the full price, that the plague against the people will be checked." [23] Ornan said to David, "Take it and let
my lord the king do whatever he sees fit. See, I donate oxen for
burnt offerings, and the threshing boards for wood, as well as
wheat for a meal offering—I donate all of it." [24] But King David replied to Ornan, "No, I will buy them at the full price. I
cannot make a present to the LORD of what belongs to you, or
sacrifice a burnt offering that has cost me nothing." [25] So David paid Ornan for the site 600 shekels' worth of gold. [26] And
David built there an altar to the LORD and sacrificed burnt offerings and offerings of well-being. He invoked the LORD, who
answered him with fire from heaven on the altar of burnt offerings. [27] The LORD ordered the angel to return his sword to
its sheath. [28] At that time, when David saw that the LORD answered him at the threshing floor of Ornan the Jebusite, then
he sacrificed there—[29] for the Tabernacle of the LORD, which
Moses had made in the wilderness, and the altar of burnt offerings, were at that time in the shrine at Gibeon, [30] and David
was unable to go to it to worship God because he was terrified
22 by the sword of the angel of the LORD. [1] David said,
"Here will be the House of the LORD and here the altar
of burnt offerings for Israel."

[2] David gave orders to assemble the aliens living in the land
of Israel, and assigned them to be hewers, to quarry and dress
stones for building the House of God. [3] Much iron for nails for

18–27: 2 Sam. ch 24 states that David paid fifty shekels of silver. Chronicles' version may reflect a different economic system; alternatively, Chronicles is making the point that no amount is too great concerning the cult. **28–30:** This is part of Chronicles' view that the locus for sacrifice was the altar (made in Moses' day) located in the Tabernacle. See 16.37–39 nn.

22.1: Selection of the Temple site. The heavenly fire pinpoints the precise location chosen by the LORD for construction of the Temple and also serves as a sign of divine favor; see Lev. 9.24; 1 Kings 18.38; 2 Chron. 7.1–3 n., in connection with Solomon's dedication of the Temple. Chronicles again views David and Solomon as two parallel, continuous personalities. David's reasoning here is simple: Since the altar and Tabernacle built in Moses' day were located in Gibeon, the divine instruction concerning the locus for David's offering (along with the heavenly fire) proves that Gibeon is merely a temporary phase; the permanent "chosen" site is in Jerusalem. This v.'s formulation informs the rabbinic tradition that demands the utmost precision in the location of the altar (see *b. Zevaḥ.* 62a and 2 Chron. 3.1–2 n.).

22.2–29.25: David's preparations for the Temple, its service, and transfer of power to Solomon. This entire section has no parallel in other biblical sources. The Chronicler composed it to bolster David's image by suggesting that he did everything allowable for building the Temple short of constructing the structure itself. The Chronicler thus presents the construction of the Temple as a two-part venture, begun by David and completed by Solomon, again suggesting strong continuity between David and Solomon. **22.2–19:** Chronicles repeatedly makes the point that, although David was denied the honor of building the Temple, he did everything in his power to lay its groundwork (see below, vv. 11–16). Accordingly, David prepares the labor force and raw materials ; because of the magnitude and majesty of the Temple, they are described as being without limit (v. 16). The recurring reference to abundance is a leitmotif in the present passage and continues throughout the book's treatment of the Temple and the cult. The point: there is never enough when dealing with the all-important cult. Since the Second Temple, until its reconstruction by King Herod in the 1st c. BCE, was a modest structure, this theme is Chronicles' clarion to his contemporaries to "recreate" the Temple's grandeur. **2:** The term "gerim," aliens, here refers to the indigenous peoples of Canaan who had been subdued, but retained a distinct identity. Chronicles does not address their legal status; their use as forced laborers may reflect Deut. 20.10–18 and, especially, Josh. 9.27. The claim that the arduous work was carried out by

the doors of the gates and for clasps did David lay aside, and so
much copper it could not be weighed, 4 and cedar logs without
number—for the Sidonians and the Tyrians brought many
cedar logs to David.
5 For David thought, "My son Solomon is an untried youth,
and the House to be built for the LORD is to be made exceedingly great to win fame and glory throughout all the lands; let
me then lay aside material for him." So David laid aside much
material before he died. 6 Then he summoned his son Solomon and charged him with building the House for the LORD
God of Israel.
7 David said to Solomon, "My son, I wanted to build a House
for the name of the LORD my God. 8 But the word of the LORD
came to me, saying, 'You have shed much blood and fought
great battles; you shall not build a House for My name for you
have shed much blood on the earth in My sight. 9 But you will
have a son who will be a man at rest, for I will give him rest
from all his enemies on all sides; Solomon[a] will be his name
and I shall confer peace[b] and quiet on Israel in his time. 10 He
will build a House for My name; he shall be a son to Me and I
to him a father, and I will establish his throne of kingship over
Israel forever.' 11 Now, my son, may the LORD be with you, and
may you succeed in building the House of the LORD your God

a Heb. Shelomoh. *b Heb.* shalom.

the labor of aliens may indicate that the ideal king spares his own people from such labor; see 2 Chron. 2.16–17; 8.8–9. **4:** For a similar statement concerning Tyrians and Sidonians, see 2 Chron. 2.1–15. The present v. implies that these northern neighbors donated their services and materials, a sign of their admiration for David or the importance that they attached to the Temple project; cf. 14.1. **5–10:** This explanation of David's disqualification from building the Temple, put in the form of a divine oracle (v. 8), is unique to Chronicles; Temple and bloodshed do not go hand in hand. True, David's wars were justified and, moreover, a sign of David's righteousness and success; still, tainted hands cannot build the Temple. This explanation differs fundamentally from 1 Kings 5.17, which claims that David was engaged in warfare throughout his life, leaving no time for Temple building. The explanation of 1 Kings may be understood as a ramification of the denial of David's request to build a temple in 2 Sam. ch 7. By contrast Chronicles claims that David's wars came to a close well before his demise (see 22.18 and 23.1). David thus becomes the paradigmatic Temple patron who, knowing full well that he would not witness the Temple's construction, selflessly devoted all his energy to the realization of that goal. Moreover, Chronicles' justification implies that no factor, other than divine decree, could have prevented David from realizing his most prized dream of constructing the Temple. This religious teaching could not, of course, be conveyed by the version of the events in 1 Kings ch 5. The legal basis behind Chronicles' disqualification has been variously explained (e.g., bloodshed in warfare, David's removal of internal dissidents); it is most likely, however, that Chronicles' justification is sui generis, lacking any scriptural basis. **5:** Solomon's age at this juncture is unknown, but it is likely that he was not a *youth*. As emerges at 2 Chron. 13.7–8, where similar phrasing is applied in connection with the mature Rehoboam, *untried youth* denotes, simply, lack of experience. The point here is that whatever Solomon's age, the preparations for Temple-building, as envisaged by the Chronicler, are so daunting that waiting for a new king to begin the process will result in unavoidable delay; hence, David's all-out efforts. **9:** This v. puns on Solomon's name: "Shelomoh" expresses the idea that in his day peace ("shalom") and quiet will prevail (see translators' notes *a, b*). Chronicles employs this literary technique elsewhere. By calling Solomon a man at rest, Chronicles shifts the rest required for the Temple's construction from David's reign (as in 2 Sam.) to Solomon. Chronicles' description, here and elsewhere, ignores 1 Kings chs 1–2, which states that Solomon's accession involved subterfuge and elimination of competitors and other "undesirables." Chronicles' reformulation expresses the view that the two earthly expressions of divine sovereignty—the Temple cult and the Davidic dynasty—were divinely determined, leaving no room for dissent. **10:** The terms *father* and *son* here denote covenantal relationships between the two parties. The term *son* may also signify legal adoption, in which the son represents the interests of the family (Ps. 2.5–7). **11–16:** This literary unit is framed by the words *the LORD be with you*. The use of such devices is common in Chronicles. David encourages Solomon, reminding him that success in executing construction of the Temple hinges on God's granting him wisdom and on his observance of God's Torah. Whereas Kings' Solomon is renowned for his judicial wisdom and general knowledge, Chronicles focuses on Solomon's wisdom as manifest, primarily, in connection with organization of all aspects of the Temple's construction; see, e.g., 2 Chron. 2.11. This emphasis, part of the book's pro-Temple bias, is part of a well-attested ancient Near Eastern and biblical motif (e.g., Prov. 3.19–20; 24.3–4), wherein construction (of homes, palaces, the cosmos) is the

as He promised you would. 12 Only let God give you sense and
understanding and put you in charge of Israel and the observance of the Teaching of the LORD your God. 13 Then you shall
succeed, if you observantly carry out the laws and the rules
that the LORD charged Moses to lay upon Israel. Be strong and
of good courage; do not be afraid or dismayed. 14 See, [a]by denying myself,[a] I have laid aside for the House of the LORD one
hundred thousand talents of gold and one million talents of
silver, and so much copper and iron it cannot be weighed; I
have also laid aside wood and stone, and you shall add to
them. 15 An abundance of workmen is at your disposal—hewers, workers in stone and wood, and every kind of craftsman in
every kind of material—16 gold, silver, copper, and iron without
limit. Go and do it, and may the LORD be with you."
17 David charged all the officers of Israel to support his son
Solomon, 18 "See, the LORD your God is with you, and He will
give you rest on every side, for He delivered the inhabitants of
the land into my hand so that the land lies conquered before
the LORD and before His people. 19 Now, set your minds and
hearts on worshiping the LORD your God, and go build the
Sanctuary of the LORD your God so that you may bring the Ark
of the Covenant of the LORD and the holy vessels of God to the
house that is built for the name of the LORD."

23 When David reached a ripe old age, he made his son
Solomon king over Israel. 2 Then David assembled
all the officers of Israel and the priests and the Levites. 3 The
Levites, from the age of thirty and upward, were counted; the

a-a With Targum; or "in my poverty."

ultimate sign of wisdom, whether human or divine; see, further, 2 Chron. 1.14–17 n. This section anticipates many of the qualities of Solomon that are depicted in 1 Kings and 2 Chron. **12:** The phrase *observance of the Teaching ["torah"] of the LORD your God* is reflective of Chronicles' era, in which proper conduct was defined exclusively in accordance with the laws of the (authoritative form of the) Torah; cf. the less legal formulation at 1 Kings 8.25. These vv., especially 12–13, employ a Moses-Joshua typology in their depiction of the relationship of David and Solomon (see Deut. 3.28; 31.7–8; Josh. 1.5–9), expressing the view that David, like Moses, laid the groundwork for Israel's future life, though he himself did not live to see its realization. In addition, the smooth transition from Moses to Joshua, decreed by God and warmly endorsed by the people (Josh. 1.16–18), parallels Chronicles' depiction of the transfer of power from David to Solomon. Finally, the days of Moses and Joshua constitute Israel's classic "golden age," much as the reigns of David and Solomon form the golden age of Judah's monarchy. For Moses-David typology, see 2 Chron. chs 13–14. **14–16:** David again claims that he has prepared building materials, as well as workers and craftsmen. This formulation is reminiscent of Exod. 31.1–6; 35.10ff. Chronicles, here and elsewhere, draws an analogy between the Mosaic Tabernacle and the First Temple, in order to accentuate the continuity, authenticity, and antiquity of Israel's sacrificial cult. The call to Solomon to add to the already massive quantities of materials anticipates 2 Chron. 2.7–8. **17–19:** David employs the same terms, used in the previous vv., when addressing the nation's officers; compare Moses' charge in Deut. 30.6–8. **18:** This v. contains paraphrases of Exod. 23.31; Num. 32.22, 29; Deut. 12.10. The allusions convey the view that the divinely promised "rest" and security have now been achieved and, thus, the time has come to build the Temple. (Note esp., that Deut. 12.10–11 relates to Temple and pilgrimage themes.) As discussed above, in Chronicles this means that there is no taint of bloodshed on the new generation. **19:** *Worshiping* (Heb "lidrosh"), specifically, attending to the Temple cult. As in Deut. (e.g., 12.11), God's name rather than God resides in the Temple.

23.1–27.34: David's administration. On the basis of repetitions and contradictions, many scholars argue that parts of this section are secondary, disagreeing only on the particulars. Others, however, maintain that these chs are an integral part of the original, and explain the repetitions and contradictions as either intentional literary flourishes or the result of Chronicles' incorporation of variant traditions. **23.1:** This v. implies that David had undertaken his preparations for the Temple while still young, following his years of warfare (cf. 1 Kings 5.17–18). This makes the crucial point that David devoted many years on behalf of the Temple, knowing all the while that he would not merit seeing its construction; see 1 Chron. 22.5–10 n. **2–3:** David takes a census of the Levites. The Levites, who were not included in David's earlier census, are now counted. Context suggests that this census was probably carried out in order to assess the organization of the Temple, not for David's own sake; hence, there is no criticism of David. This separate census parallels the practice of Moses' day; see Num. 3.14–39. The introduction to the ch suggests a smooth transition

head-count of their males was 38,000: 4 of these there were 24,000 in charge of the work of the House of the LORD, 6,000 officers and magistrates, 5 4,000 gatekeepers, and 4,000 for praising the LORD "with instruments I devised for singing praises." 6 David formed them into divisions:

The sons of Levi: Gershon, Kohath, and Merari. 7 The Gershonites: Ladan and Shimei. 8 The sons of Ladan: Jehiel the chief, Zetham, and Joel—3. 9 The sons of Shimei: Shelomith, Haziel, and Haran—3. These were the chiefs of the clans of the Ladanites. 10 And the sons of Shimei: Jahath, Zina, Jeush, and Beriah; these were the sons of Shimei—4. 11 Jahath was the chief and Zizah the second, but Jeush and Beriah did not have many children, so they were enrolled together as a single clan. 12 The sons of Kohath: Amram, Izhar, Hebron, and Uzziel—4. 13 The sons of Amram: Aaron and Moses. Aaron was set apart, he and his sons, forever, to be consecrated as most holy, to make burnt offerings to the LORD and serve Him and pronounce blessings in His name forever. 14 As for Moses, the man of God, his sons were named after the tribe of Levi. 15 The sons of Moses: Gershom and Eliezer. 16 The sons of Gershom: Shebuel the chief. 17 And the sons of Eliezer were: Rehabiah the chief. Eliezer had no other sons, but the sons of Rehabiah were very numerous. 18 The sons of Izhar: Shelomith the chief. 19 The sons of Hebron: Jeriah the chief, Amariah the second, Jahaziel the third, and Jekameam the fourth. 20 The sons of Uzziel: Micah the chief and Isshiah the second. 21 The sons of Merari: Mahli and Mushi. The sons of Mahli: Eleazar and Kish. 22 Eleazar died having no sons but only daughters; the sons of Kish, their kinsmen, married them. 23 The sons of Mushi: Mahli, Eder, and Jeremoth—3.

24 These are the sons of Levi by clans, with their clan chiefs as they were enrolled, with a list of their names by heads, who did the work of the service of the House of the LORD from the age of

between David and Solomon, in sharp contrast to the end of 2 Sam. and the beginning of 1 Kings. V. 3 makes no mention of the upper age limit prescribed in priestly sources, viz., fifty years (Num. 4.2–3; 8.24–25). Some rabbinic sources maintained that the limits imposed in pentateuchal sources were intended only for the duration of the wilderness trek. In addition, rabbinic and medieval tradents averred that the roles assigned to Levites in Chronicles—inner-Temple service and cultic song—are not subject to the limitation of Num. 8.25, but are determined by the Levite's ability to perform the assigned task (*b. Ḥul.* 24a). Rabbinic sources differ, however, as to whether there is an upper age limit to priestly service (see *t. Ḥul.* 1:16, *b. Ḥul.* 24a). **5:** Chronicles credits David with another feature of Temple worship: fashioning the instruments; see 2 Chron. 7.6; 29.26–27. 2 Chron. 29.25 claims that the use of these instruments was, ultimately, divinely ordained. **13:** The end of this v. is reminiscent of Deut. 10.8 which, however, applies to the entire tribe of Levi (the "Levitical priests"); following Priestly norms found in the Torah, it is applied to priests only. The first part of Deut. 10.8 has informed the Levites' role at 1 Chron. 15.2. *Amram*'s marriage to a Levite woman (see Exod. 2.1) results in a "fully" levitic lineage for Moses, Aaron, and Miriam, all of whom attain greatness. A Qumran text (4Q452) claims that Kohath instructed his son, Amram, to take care of (and heed) the writings of Levi, the family patriarch. The term *most holy* is generally applied to objects, e.g., tithes, various offerings, the inner and outer (priestly) altars, and the innermost part ("debir") of the Temple/Tabernacle. This v. is unique in its application of the term to humans, leading some to understand the v. to mean that Aaron was set apart to offer the most holy offerings. This is unlikely, both for syntactic reasons and because it allows for the inference that non-priests may offer "standard" holy offerings. Israel is frequently called "holy" (e.g., Deut. 14.2, 21 ["consecrated" in these vv.]; Jer. 2.3; Ezra 9.2); it is therefore reasonable to apply the term "most holy" to Aaron and his sons. **24–32:** This passage involves a shift from v. 2, leading some scholars to posit different authorship for the vv.; this argument, however, is not compelling. David introduces an innovation by allowing (or, perhaps, requiring) Levites to assume their duties at the age of twenty, rather than the age of thirty or twenty-five, as set forth in the Torah (Num. 4.3, 23, 30, 39, 47; 8.24). The rationale is that the age of thirty was necessary in the wilderness period, when carrying the Ark required stronger or more responsible and experienced cultic personnel; a permanent cult made such age restrictions unnecessary. This is apparently an example of Chronicles attributing contemporary cultic norms to hoary antiquity, here, specifically to David. Historically, the change in policy may reflect the need for more personnel for a functioning cultic establishment or, as indicated by biblical sources, that the number of Levites in postexilic and Second Temple Judah was quite small (see

twenty and upward. 25 For David said, "The LORD God of Israel
has given rest to His people and made His dwelling in Jerusalem forever. 26 Therefore the Levites need not carry the Tabernacle and all its various service vessels." 27 Among the last acts
of David was the counting of the Levites from the age of twenty
and upward. 28 For their appointment was alongside the Aaronites for the service of the House of the LORD, to look after the
courts and the chambers, and the purity of all the holy things,
and the performance of the service of the House of God, 29 and
the rows of bread, and the fine flour for the meal offering, and
the unleavened wafers, and the cakes made on the griddle and
soaked, and every measure of capacity and length; 30 and to
be present every morning to praise and extol the LORD, and at
evening too, 31 and whenever offerings were made to the LORD,
according to the quantities prescribed for them, on sabbaths,
new moons and holidays, regularly, before the LORD; 32 and so
to keep watch over the Tent of Meeting, over the holy things,
and over the Aaronites their kinsmen, for the service of the
House of the LORD.

Ezra 8.15–20); accordingly, it was necessary to enlist all those of adult age. David is presented as a legislator, again signaling a role parallel to that of Moses. **24-27:** Several pentateuchal sources (Num. 4.3, 23, 30, 39, 47) indicate that Levitical conscription begins at the age of thirty; Num. 8.24, however, fixes twenty-five as the age. (Cf. LXX, which reads "twenty-five" in all pentateuchal passages.) It is unclear whether the present vv. reflect the exigencies of the period (i.e., shortage of man-power or the like), or whether this was simply a measure to increase the scope of Levitical involvement in the cult. In either event, Chronicles' willingness to depart from pentateuchal norms is noteworthy; its apparent need to justify the novel practice is no less significant (see intro.). **26:** *Need not:* The Aram. Tg. understands this v. to mean that Levites were no longer allowed to move the cultic vessels. **28–32:** Chronicles both expands the roles of the Levites and upgrades their status vis-à-vis priests to an extent not attested in pentateuchal sources. With regard to the former, Chronicles assigns to Levites not only orchestral and minstrel roles but, moreover, responsibility for care and maintenance of the holy vessels (or, perhaps, holy foodstuffs) as well as guard duty (a role also attested at Num. 3.8–10; 4.18–20; and 18.1–7, and, for different reasons, at Ezek. 44.14). The elevated status of Levites is evident in their depiction as ministering *alongside* (v. 28) their priestly *kinsmen*/"brothers" (v. 32), implying relative equality; by contrast, the depiction of Num. 3.5–9; 18.2–6 defines their roles as one of serving the priests. In short, the status of Levites in Chronicles is somewhere between that prescribed in Priestly pentateuchal sources and that reflected in Deut., which, for the most part, classifies priests and Levites as one group. Finally, it is instructive that, in contrast to its extended discussion of Levites and their responsibilities, Chronicles devotes little attention to the office of high priest or, for that matter, priestly families, despite the exclusive nature of their role in the performance of sacrifices. This bespeaks the author's pro-Levitic stance and bolsters the likelihood that the author was a member of one of the Levitic clans. **28:** The duties assigned to the Levites include tasks wholly unattested in earlier sources, as well as tasks mentioned in these sources but not assigned to any specific group (see, e.g., Lev. 24.5–9). Num.(3.5–9; 18.2–6) does state that the Levites shall guard the Tabernacle and serve the priests, but the precise nature of their service is not explained; the Chronicler fills in this gap, most likely attributing practices of his period to that of David. The net result is that the Levites perform most of the Temple duties and make the daily Temple service possible. The priests are limited to sacrificing, blowing the trumpets (Num. 10.1–10), and "blessing" in the LORD's name (see Num. 6.22–27). **30–31:** The cultic songs accompany the morning and afternoon or evening services together with the burnt offering, i.e., they have no independent role. They are also performed on the Sabbath, new moon, and pilgrimage festivals; 2 Chron. 2.4; 8.13; 31.3. In Psalms, we only have a single psalm attributed to one of these occasions, to the Sabbath (Ps. 92), though LXX Psalms assigns additional psalms to various festivals (e.g., Ps. 29) and liturgical texts found among the Dead Sea Scrolls reflect a more extensive Sabbath and festival liturgy, including prayers for festivals unique to the Qumran writings. **32:** *Service* (Heb "ʿavodah") as a generic term for Levitical responsibilities is unattested in Torah texts, where it refers to physical labor (portage). Development of this word continues in postbiblical Heb, where "ʿavodah," sometimes called "ʿavodah shebalev," "ʿavodah," of the heart, refers to "prayer."

24 The divisions of the Aaronites were:
The sons of Aaron: Nadab and Abihu, Eleazar and Ithamar. [2] Nadab and Abihu died in the lifetime of their father, and they had no children, so Eleazar and Ithamar served as priests.

[3] David, Zadok of the sons of Eleazar, and Ahimelech of the sons of Ithamar divided them into offices by their tasks. [4] The sons of Eleazar turned out to be more numerous by male heads than the sons of Ithamar, so they divided the sons of Eleazar into sixteen chiefs of clans and the sons of Ithamar into eight clans. [5] They divided them by lot, both on an equal footing, since they were all sanctuary officers and officers of God—the sons of Eleazar and the sons of Ithamar. [6] Shemaiah son of Nathanel, the scribe, who was of the Levites, registered them under the eye of the king, the officers, and Zadok the priest, and Ahimelech son of Abiathar, and the chiefs of clans of the priests and Levites—[a]one clan more taken for Eleazar for each one taken of Ithamar.[a]

[7] The first lot fell on Jehoiarib; the second on Jedaiah; [8] the third on Harim; the fourth on Seorim; [9] the fifth on Malchijah; the sixth on Mijamin; [10] the seventh on Hakkoz; the eighth on Abijah; [11] the ninth on Jeshua; the tenth on Shecaniah; [12] the eleventh on Eliashib; the twelfth on Jakim; [13] the thirteenth on Huppah; the fourteenth on Jeshebeab; [14] the fifteenth on Bilgah; the sixteenth on Immer; [15] the seventeenth on Hezir; the eighteenth on Happizzez; [16] the nineteenth on Pethahiah; the twentieth on Jehezkel; [17] the twenty-first on Jachin; the twenty-second on Gamul; [18] the twenty-third on Delaiah; the twenty-fourth on Maaziah.

[19] According to this allocation of offices by tasks, they were to enter the House of the LORD as was laid down for them by Aaron their father, as the LORD God of Israel had commanded him.

[20] The remaining Levites: the sons of Amram: Shubael; the sons of Shubael: Jehdeiah; [21] Rehabiah. The sons of Rehabiah: Isshiah, the chief. [22] Izharites: Shelomoth. The sons of Shelomoth: Jahath [23] and Benai, Jeriah; the second, Amariah; the third, Jahaziel; the fourth, Jekameam. [24] The sons of Uzziel: Micah. The sons of Micah: Shamir. [25] The brother of Micah: Isshiah. The sons of Isshiah: Zechariah. [26] The sons of Merari: Mahli and Mushi. The sons of Jaazaiah, his son—[27] the sons of Merari by Jaazaiah his son: Shoham, Zakkur, and Ibri. [28] Mahli: Eleazar; he had no sons. [29] Kish: the sons of Kish: Jerahmeel. [30] The sons of Mushi: Mahli, Eder, and Jerimoth. These were the sons of the Levites by their clans.

[31] These too cast lots corresponding to their kinsmen, the sons of Aaron, under the eye of King David and Zadok and

a-a Meaning of Heb. uncertain.

24.1–19: Sons of Aaron. Chronicles claims that the existence of twenty-four priestly divisions, a familiar part of Second Temple life, was David's innovation. These divisions are a practice reflected in the Mishmarot Texts from Qumran (4Q320–30), rabbinic sources (*b. Taʿan.* 27a), as well as post-rabbinic liturgical compositions ("piyyutim") and tablets that were placed on ancient synagogue walls. (Cf. 1QM, the War Scroll from Qumran, which recognizes twenty-six such divisions, reflecting the solar calendar adopted by the Qumran community; cf, also, Josephus, Ant. 7.365–368.) This passage is viewed by many as secondary. **2:** Cf. Lev. 10.2; 16.1; Num. 3.4; 26.61. Chronicles omits mention of the cultic offense committed by *Nadab and Abihu* and in place of the priestly claim that they "died before (in the presence of) YHVH," Chronicles states that they *died in the lifetime of their father,* shifting the focus to Aaron's remaining descendants. Since the Chronicler elsewhere highlights the dire consequences of cultic violations or imprecision (see 15.2, 13), it is unclear whether the reticence regarding the two sons demise is intended to avoid mention of cultic malfeasance in Aaron's family. **5:** *Officer of God,* an uncommon title, reflects the importance and uniqueness of the priestly caste. The title "Officer of God" has also been translated as a superlative, meaning, "highest officials," but this is unlikely. **6:** Chronicles' interest in scribal activity and record keeping is again attested (see 5.17 n.). This *Shemaiah* appears only here. **7:** Order established by lot. The Maccabees trace their lineage to *Jehoiarib,* which has led some to argue that the list is of 2nd-c. provenance; this is unconvincing.

24.20–31: More sons of Levi. This list is frequently thought to reflect an updated version of 23.6–23.

Ahimelech and the chiefs of the clans of the priests and Levites, on the principle of "chief and youngest brother alike."

25 David and the officers of the army set apart for service the sons of Asaph, of Heman, and of Jeduthun, who prophesied to the accompaniment of lyres, harps, and cymbals. The list of men who performed this work, according to their service, was:

2 Sons of Asaph: Zaccur, Joseph, Nethaniah, and Asarelah—sons of Asaph under the charge of Asaph, who prophesied by order of the king. 3 Jeduthun—the sons of Jeduthun: Gedaliah, Zeri, Jeshaiah, Hashabiah, Mattithiah—6, under the charge of their father Jeduthun, who, accompanied on the harp, prophesied, praising and extolling the LORD. 4 Heman—the sons of Heman: Bukkiah, Mattaniah, Uzziel, Shebuel, Jerimoth, Hananiah, Hanani, Eliathah, Giddalti, Romamti-ezer, Joshbekashah, Mallothi, Hothir, and Mahazioth; 5 all these were sons of Heman, the seer of the king, [who uttered] prophecies of God for His greater glory. God gave Heman fourteen sons and three daughters; 6 all these were under the charge of their father for the singing in the House of the LORD, to the accompaniment of cymbals, harps, and lyres, for the service of the House of God by order of the king. Asaph, Jeduthun, and Heman—7 their total number with their kinsmen, trained singers of the LORD—all the masters, 288.

8 They cast lots for shifts on the principle of "small and great alike, like master like apprentice."

9 The first lot fell to Asaph—to Joseph; the second, to Gedaliah, he and his brothers and his sons—12; 10 the third, to Zaccur: his sons and his brothers—12; 11 the fourth, to Izri: his sons and his brothers—12; 12 the fifth, to Nethaniah: his sons and his brothers—12; 13 the sixth, to Bukkiah: his sons and his brothers—12;

25.1–31: The musicians/singers. The placement of this group following the Levites reflects their related roles in the cult. **1–3:** Another facet of Chronicles' views on prophecy. It is possible that the Levitical prophecy of these vv. is a kind of cultic and musically inspired prophecy, but more likely Chronicles viewed the musical performance itself as a form of prophecy, i.e., written or performed under prophetic inspiration. Chronicles claims that the musical aspects of the Levites' activity are, like other features of Israel's cultic service, the product of divine inspiration. (Even so, precisely what is intended by this position, viz., the "lyrics" or musical arrangement, etc., is uncertain.) For earlier examples of music as part of prophetic ecstasy, see 1 Sam. 10.5. The reference to prophecy in connection with cultic music (i.e., psalms) served as a basis for the claim of Saadia Gaon (9th c. CE) that the Psalms were not (contra the claims of Karaite scholars) a book of spontaneous prayers emanating from the human heart but were, rather, prophetically "dictated" vv. to be used only as directed. **1:** *Asaph, Heman,* and *Jeduthun* (elsewhere: Ethan) appear in the superscriptions (introits) to several compositions in the book of Psalms (e.g., 39, 50, 88). These figures, about whom little (historically reliable) information is known, are viewed here as the founders of the cultic guilds bearing their names; these guilds may indeed extend into First Temple times. **4:** The latter part of this difficult v., preserving names otherwise unattested in the Bible, has been emended and reconstructed by many scholars, resulting in a song of praise, rather than the present list of sons. One such reconstruction, entailing different vocalization of the names, is: "Be compassionate to me, O YHVH; be compassionate to me. You are my God; I magnify/have magnified and exalt/exalted my helper (or: warrior). Living in adversity, I have spoken (your praise?); Be generous with (your) revelations." **5:** The description of Heman as *the seer of the king* (LXX: royal musicians) is an expression of the inspired nature of the cultic music and the activity of the leaders of the Levitical singers/musicians (see v. 1 n.). Contrary to some opinions, Chronicles does not portray all Levites as prophets. For many children are a sign of divine favor, see 14.3–7. **6–8:** Some scholars understand v. 6 to mean that Heman's daughters were part of the Temple orchestra (cf. Ezra 2.65; Neh. 7.67); the v. probably refers only to the sons listed in v. 4, however. **9–31:** Chronicles again credits David with establishing cultic norms. Division of the Levites into twenty-four watches appears only in Second Temple sources. The Levites are assigned by Num. 18.4–6 to guard the Tabernacle against encroachment by outsiders, an act which unleashes the divine wrath. Chronicles assigns the Levite clans specific locations, but does not indicate whether their primary role is to prevent encroachment or simply as a kind of "honor guard," a notion which appears in later Jewish sources (*Sifre Zuta,* Korah, Num. 18.4; Maimonides, *Book of Commandments,* 22). The Rabbis (*Sifre Num.* 116, *b. ʿArak.* 11b) understood the division of labor to be absolute, such that a Levite may not perform the task(s) assigned to another Levitical clan.

26.1–19: Gatekeepers. The list of gatekeepers follows the cultic singers.

[14] the seventh, to Jesarelah: his sons and his brothers—12; [15] the
eighth, to Jeshaiah: his sons and his brothers—12; [16] the ninth,
to Mattaniah: his sons and his brothers—12; [17] the tenth, to
Shimei: his sons and his brothers—12; [18] the eleventh to Azarel: his sons and his brothers—12; [19] the twelfth, to Hashabiah:
his sons and his brothers—12; [20] the thirteenth, to Shubael: his
sons and his brothers—12; [21] the fourteenth, to Mattithiah: his
sons and his brothers—12; [22] the fifteenth, to Jeremoth: his sons
and his brothers—12; [23] the sixteenth, to Hananiah: his sons and
his brothers—12; [24] the seventeenth, to Joshbekashah: his sons
and his brothers—12; [25] the eighteenth, to Hanani: his sons and
his brothers—12; [26] the nineteenth, to Mallothi: his sons and
his brothers—12; [27] the twentieth, to Eliathah: his sons and his
brothers—12; [28] the twenty-first, to Hothir: his sons and his
brothers—12; [29] the twenty-second, to Giddalti: his sons and his
brothers—12; [30] the twenty-third, to Mahazioth: his sons and
his brothers—12; [31] the twenty-fourth, to Romamti-ezer: his sons
and his brothers—12.

26 The divisions of the gatekeepers: Korahites:
Meshelemiah son of Kore, of the sons of Asaph. [2] Sons
of Meshelemiah: Zechariah the firstborn, Jediael the second,
Zebadiah the third, Jathniel the fourth, [3] Elam the fifth, Jehohanan the sixth, Eliehoenai the seventh. [4] Sons of Obed-edom:
Shemaiah the first-born, Jehozabad the second, Joah the third,
Sacar the fourth, Nethanel the fifth, [5] Ammiel the sixth, Issachar
the seventh, Peullethai the eighth—for God had blessed him.
[6] To his son Shemaiah were born sons who exercised authority
in their clans because they were men of substance. [7] The sons
of Shemaiah: Othni, Rephael, Obed, Elzabad—his brothers,
men of ability, were Elihu and Semachiah. [8] All these, sons of
Obed-edom; they and their sons and brothers, strong and able
men for the service—62 of Obed-edom. [9] Meshelemiah had
sons and brothers, able men—18. [10] Hosah of the Merarites
had sons: Shimri the chief (he was not the first-born, but his
father designated him chief), [11] Hilkiah the second, Tebaliah
the third, Zechariah the fourth. All the sons and brothers of
Hosah—13.

[12] These are the divisions of the gatekeepers, by their chief
men, [who worked in] shifts corresponding to their kinsmen,
ministering in the House of the LORD. [13] They cast lots, small
and great alike, by clans, for each gate.

[14] The lot for the east [gate] fell to Shelemiah. Then they cast
lots [for] Zechariah his son, a prudent counselor, and his lot
came out to be the north [gate]. [15] For Obed-edom, the south
[gate], and for his sons, the vestibule. [16] For Shuppim and for
Hosah, the west [gate], with the Shallecheth gate on the ascending highway. Watch corresponded to watch: [17] At the

east—six Levites; at the north—four daily; at the south—four daily; at the vestibule—two by two; [18] at the colonnade on the west—four at the causeway and two at the colonnade. [19] These were the divisions of the gatekeepers of the sons of Korah and the sons of Merari.

[20] And the Levites: Ahijah over the treasuries of the House of God and the treasuries of the dedicated things. [21] The sons of Ladan: the sons of the Gershonites belonging to Ladan; the chiefs of the clans of Ladan, the Gershonite—Jehieli. [22] The sons of Jehieli: Zetham and Joel; his brother was over the treasuries of the House of the LORD.

[23] Of the Amramites, the Izharites, the Hebronites, the Uzzielites: [24] Shebuel son of Gershom son of Moses was the chief officer over the treasuries. [25] And his brothers: Eliezer, his son Rehabiah, his son Jeshaiah, his son Joram, his son Zichri, his son Shelomith—[26] that Shelomith and his brothers were over all the treasuries of dedicated things that were dedicated by King David and the chiefs of the clans, and the officers of thousands and hundreds and the other army officers; [27] they dedicated some of the booty of the wars to maintain the House of the LORD. [28] All that Samuel the seer had dedicated, and Saul son of Kish, and Abner son of Ner, and Joab son of Zeruiah—or [what] any other man had dedicated, was under the charge of Shelomith and his brothers.

[29] The Izharites: Chenaniah and his sons were over Israel as clerks and magistrates for affairs outside [the sanctuary]. [30] The Hebronites: Hashabiah and his brothers, capable men, 1,700, supervising Israel on the west side of the Jordan in all matters of the LORD and the service of the king. [31] The Hebronites: Jeriah, the chief of the Hebronites—they were investigated in the fortieth year of David's reign by clans of all their lines, and men of substance were found among them in Jazer-gilead. [32] His brothers, able men, 2,700, chiefs of clans—David put them in charge of the Reubenites, the Gadites, and the half-tribe of Manasseh in all matters of God and matters of the king.

27 The number of Israelites—chiefs of clans, officers of thousands and hundreds and their clerks, who served the king in all matters of the divisions, who worked in monthly

26.20–32: Officers and judges. The listing of officials most removed from cultic responsibilities appears toward the end of the block extending from ch 23 through ch 27, following priests and Levites. It offers a bridge to the following ch that outlines noncultic functionaries. **28:** This passage offers a more positive view of Saul than that encountered earlier, suggesting that the author here may have drawn on popular tradition. More likely, the author means to say that if a person like Saul was aware of the importance of the cult, it follows that any self-respecting Jew must do no less. *Abner* was the commander of Saul's army; *Joab* was the commander of David's. **29–32:** These vv. are noteworthy because they refer to various secular duties of the Levites, a phenomenon which elsewhere appears only in the late biblical period (Neh. 11.16; 2 Chron. 19.8–11). This section's historicity is debated.

27.1–34: Non-cultic arrangements. This ch deals with general organizational features of David's reign; it is likely of secondary origin, added by a later hand, a fact suggested by the overlap between it and ch 11, as well as parts of chs 23–26. Though it has been argued that the Chronicler would not have fabricated so detailed a list as that found in vv. 1–15, this argument is not convincing. Whether stemming from a genuine source or created by the author, the list serves as a supplement to the data of ch 11; i.e., whereas the latter source cites warriors who joined David at the outset of his reign, the present ch describes the royal guard contingent of David's final days. The concern with such issues reinforces the likelihood that the author anticipated the renewal, at some future point, of the Davidic glory. David's reign is depicted as one of order, with the nation centered on the Jerusalem cult. Chronicles' depiction of Israel's governance during the monarchic period involves a melding of earlier biblical traditions. Most striking is the appearance of "officers of thousands and hundreds (v. 1)" titles attested in pentateuchal priestly sources (e.g., Num. chs 1–4), in passages which, in contrast to Chronicles, reflect no awareness of a monarch(y). Chronicles' formulation involves a huge number of civil servants serving on a rotating basis. The delegation of responsibility is not intended to minimize the role and authority of the kings; rather it suggests a society wherein various responsibilities are shared by the nation. The Israelite social structure depicted never existed; it is unclear whether the Chronicler actually anticipated the eventual implementation of this form of governance and national service. **1–15:** The monthly shifts. Chronicles'

shifts during all the months of the year—each division, 24,000. 2 Over the first division for the first month—Jashobeam son of Zabdiel; his division had 24,000. 3 Of the sons of Perez, he, the chief of all the officers of the army, [served] for the first month. 4 Over the division of the second month—Dodai the Ahohite; Mikloth was chief officer of his division; his division had 24,000. 5 The third army officer for the third month—Benaiah son of Jehoiada, the chief priest; his division had 24,000. 6 That was Benaiah, one of the warriors of the thirty and over the thirty; and [over] his division was Ammizabad his son. 7 The fourth, for the fourth month, Asahel brother of Joab, and his son Zebadiah after him; his division had 24,000. 8 The fifth, for the fifth month, the officer Shamhut the Izrahite; his division had 24,000. 9 The sixth, for the sixth month, Ira son of Ikkesh the Tekoite; his division had 24,000. 10 The seventh, for the seventh month, Helez the Pelonite, of the Ephraimites; his division had 24,000. 11 The eighth, for the eighth month, Sibbecai the Hushathite, of Zerah; his division had 24,000. 12 The ninth, for the ninth month, Abiezer the Anathothite, of Benjamin; his division had 24,000. 13 The tenth, for the tenth month, Mahrai the Netophathite, of Zerah; his division had 24,000. 14 The eleventh, for the eleventh month, Benaiah the Pirathonite, of the Ephraimites; his division had 24,000. 15 The twelfth, for the twelfth month, Heldai the Netophathite, of Othniel; his division had 24,000.

16 Over the tribes of Israel: Reuben: the chief officer, Eliezer son of Zichri. Simeon: Shephatiah son of Maaca. 17 Levi: Hashabiah son of Kemuel. Aaron: Zadok. 18 Judah: Elihu, of the brothers of David. Issachar: Omri son of Michael. 19 Zebulun: Ishmaiah son of Obadiah. Naphtali: Jerimoth son of Azriel. 20 Ephraimites: Hoshea son of Azaziah. The half-tribe of Manasseh: Joel son of Pedaiah. 21 Half Manasseh in Gilead: Iddo son of Zechariah. Benjamin: Jaasiel son of Abner. 22 Dan: Azarel son of Jeroham. These were the officers of the tribes of Israel.

23 David did not take a census of those under twenty years of age, for the LORD had promised to make Israel as numerous as the stars of heaven. 24 Joab son of Zeruiah did begin to count them, but he did not finish; wrath struck Israel on account of this, and the census was not entered into the account of the chronicles of King David.

25 Over the royal treasuries: Azmaveth son of Adiel. Over the treasuries in the country—in the towns, the hamlets, and the citadels: Jonathan son of Uzziah. 26 Over the field laborers in agricultural work: Ezri son of Chelub. 27 Over the vineyards: Shimei the Ramathite. And over the produce in the vineyards for wine cellars: Zabdi the Shiphmite. 28 Over the olive trees and the sycamores in the Shephelah: Baal-hanan the Gederite.

notion of monthly shifts is probably inspired by 1 Kings 4.7, which details the monthly arrangements for Solomon's household. Note the typological number twenty-four (thousand) in this passage. **16–24:** A listing of tribal chiefs. The tribes of Asher and Gad are missing, perhaps in order to keep the number of tribes at twelve. The passage, esp. the appearance of twelve figures, alludes to the census of Num. ch 1, wherein tribal heads were responsible for their respective tribes. **23–24:** The census of ch 21 is here presented in terms more favorable to David, less favorable to Joab This passage, almost certainly a later addition, is opaque. Does the census refer to vv. 1–15, that of ch 21, or possibly, both? The most likely explanation is that the formulation here seeks to exonerate David's actions in ch 21 by offering a new version of it, while attempting to place some of the blame for that fiasco on Joab. Alternatively, its purpose may be to explain that a second census, that of the current ch (vv. 1–15, was successfully completed, owing to the fact that it was conducted in accordance with priestly law (see Exod. 30.12–16), which calls for census taking only of males twenty years of age and upward. Several traditional exegetes (e.g., Naḥmanides, Malbim [Rabbi Meir Leibush ben Yehiel Michal]), averred that the v. merely clarifies the nature of David's offense in ch 21, viz., David's error lay in counting all males, including those under the age of twenty, when in fact, priestly law (reformulated here) allows census only of males twenty years of age and above; accordingly, no blame is laid at the feet of Joab. **25–31:** Stewards of David's holdings. Like most kings in the ancient Near East, David acquired large tracts of property. The description of these holdings is part of Chronicles' glorification of David. The large number of non-cultic servants and non-Temple related land holdings indicate that, the importance of the Temple notwithstanding, the monarchy attended to and developed successfully the economy and other mundane aspects of society. Chronicles' depiction of the

Over the oil-stores: Joash. 29 Over the cattle pasturing in Sharon: Shirtai the Sharonite. And over the cattle in the valleys: Shaphat son of Adlai. 30 Over the camels: Obil the Ishmaelite. And over the she-asses: Jehdeiah the Meronothite. 31 Over the flocks: Jaziz the Hagrite. All these were stewards of the property of King David. 32 Jonathan, David's uncle, was a counselor, a master, and a scribe: Jehiel son of Hachmoni was with the king's sons. 33 Ahitophel was a counselor to the king. Hushai the Archite was the king's friend. 34 After Ahitophel were Jehoiada son of Benaiah and Abiathar. The commander of the king's army was Joab.

28 David assembled all the officers of Israel—the tribal officers, the divisional officers who served the king, the captains of thousands and the captains of hundreds, and the stewards of all the property and cattle of the king and his sons, with the eunuchs and the warriors, all the men of substance—to Jerusalem. 2 King David rose to his feet and said, "Hear me, my brothers, my people! I wanted to build a resting-place for the Ark of the Covenant of the LORD, for the footstool of our God, and I laid aside material for building. 3 But God said to me, 'You will not build a house for My name, for you are a man of battles and have shed blood.' 4 The LORD God of Israel chose me of all my father's house to be king over Israel forever. For He chose Judah to be ruler, and of the family of Judah, my father's house; and of my father's sons, He preferred to make me king over all Israel; 5 and of all my sons—for many are the sons the LORD gave me—He chose my son Solomon to sit on the throne of the kingdom of the LORD over Israel. 6 He said to me, 'It will be your son Solomon who will build My House and My courts, for I have chosen him to be a son to Me, and I will be a father to him. 7 I will establish his kingdom forever, if he keeps firmly to the observance of My commandments and rules as he does now.' 8 And now, in the sight of all Israel, the congregation of the LORD, and in the hearing of our God, [I say:] Observe and apply yourselves to all the commandments of the LORD your God in order that you may possess this good land and bequeath it to your children after you forever.

9 "And you, my son Solomon, know the God of your father, and serve Him with single mind and fervent heart, for the LORD searches all minds and discerns the design of every thought; if you seek Him He will be available to you, but if you forsake Him He will abandon you forever. 10 See then, the LORD chose you to build a house as the sanctuary; be strong and do it."

11 David gave his son Solomon the plan of the porch and its houses, its storerooms and its upper chambers and inner chambers; and of the place of the Ark-cover; 12 and the plan of all that he had by the spirit: of the courts of the House of the

monarchic role in these aspects of society, without parallel in biblical sources, buttresses the claim of some scholars that the Chronicler viewed the monarchy as having importance beyond the limited role of Temple patron; indeed, this suggests that the Chronicler anticipated a renewed, vibrant monarchy for Israel. **32–34:** Important figures in the king's entourage; some but not all of these are known from the lists and narratives in Samuel.

28.1–21: David encourages Solomon and the people. 2: The footstool refers to the Ark. The expression reflects the belief that the LORD was seated upon a throne created by the (wings of the) cherubs—situated above the Ark—so that His feet rested on the Ark itself (cf. Lam. 2.1). **3–7:** This passage is a reprise of earlier passages. V. 3 refers back to 1 Chron. 22.8. For the selection of David in v. 4, see 1 Sam. 16.10–12; for the selection of Judah, see 1 Chron. 5.2 and Gen. 49.8–10. For v. 5, see 1 Chron. 3.1–9 and 14.3–7. Davidic kings "sit on the LORD's throne"; see 17.14. **7:** Continuity of the monarchy is here contingent upon observance of the divine commandments; see 17.13 n. **8–9:** The importance of serving the LORD wholeheartedly; see 29.9–19. The Heb root, "d-r-sh," so prominent and semantically rich throughout Chronicles (see 1 Chron. 10.13–14 ["to seek advice"]; 13.3 ["paid ... regard"]; 16.11 ["see His presence"]), takes on a different meaning in this v., where it refers to "seeking out" performance—i.e., conform to/observing—the laws of the pentateuch. In making pentateuchal law, rather than the Deity or the Temple, the object of such inquiry, the author expresses his view of the pentateuch as an inspired text, observance of whose laws enables Israel to fulfill their divine mission; cf. Ezra 7.10. The sense of "searching (for)/expounding (the true meaning[s] of) the biblical text/teachings," is ubiquitous in the Dead Sea Scrolls and rabbinic texts. See 2 Chron. 13.22–23 n. and 24.27. **12:** *Spirit* here refers to prophetic inspiration, as

LORD and all its surrounding chambers, and of the treasuries of the House of God and of the treasuries of the holy things; 13 the divisions of priests and Levites for all the work of the service of the House of the LORD and all the vessels of the service of the House of the LORD; 14 and gold, the weight of gold for vessels of every sort of use; silver for all the vessels of silver by weight, for all the vessels of every kind of service; 15 the weight of the gold lampstands and their gold lamps, and the weight of the silver lampstands, each lampstand and its silver lamps, according to the use of every lampstand; 16 and the weight of gold for the tables of the rows of bread, for each table, and of silver for the silver tables; 17 and of the pure gold for the forks and the basins and the jars; and the weight of the gold bowls, every bowl; and the weight of the silver bowls, each and every bowl; 18 the weight of refined gold for the incense altar and the gold for the figure of the chariot—the cherubs—those with outspread wings screening the Ark of the Covenant of the LORD. 19 "All this that the LORD made me understand by His hand on me, I give you in writing—the plan of all the works."

20 David said to his son Solomon, "Be strong and of good courage and do it; do not be afraid or dismayed, for the LORD God my God is with you; He will not fail you or forsake you till all the work on the House of the LORD is done. 21 Here are the divisions of the priests and Levites for all kinds of service of the House of God, and with you in all the work are willing men, skilled in all sorts of tasks; also the officers and all the people are at your command."

29 King David said to the entire assemblage, "God has chosen my son Solomon alone, an untried lad, although the work to be done is vast—for the temple[a] is not for a man but for the LORD God. 2 I have spared no effort to lay up for the House of my God gold for golden objects, silver for silver, copper for copper, iron for iron, wood for wooden, onyx-stone and inlay-stone, stone of antimony and variegated colors—every

a *Lit. "fortress."*

clarified in v. 19. **18:** Chronicles refers to the Ark/cherubim combination as constituting a chariot, reflecting a mobile aspect of the deity. The precise import of this depiction in the present context is unclear; it may reflect the fact that the deity is capable of departing the Temple (in response to sins that defile the Temple; cf. Ezek. chs 1 and 10) or, alternatively, bespeak a martial aspect of the deity. **19:** Chronicles' David is not explicitly labeled a prophet or seer, but is the recipient of prophetic revelation or inspiration. This v. is consistent with Chronicles' glorification of David, as well as the recurring theme of the divine source of all things pertaining to the Temple. Ancient Near Eastern norms emphasize the need for precisely situating the Temple structure and its components, so as to comport with the deity's instructions; failure to properly execute the construction—and reconstruction—of temples inevitably leads to disaster. David's prophetic status is explicitly acknowledged in the writings of the Dead Sea Scrolls (11QPs[a]) and some traditional Jewish sources (*Tg. Chron.;* Isaac Abravanel). Even so, other sources (*y. Meg.* 1.1 [70a], Rashi ad *b. Sukk.* 51b) claim that the Temple plans were given to David via the prophets Samuel, Gad, or Nathan; see above, 9.22, and 2 Chron. 29.25. Radak averred that David experienced not prophecy but, rather, a lesser degree of divine inspiration (Heb "ruaḥ ha-kodesh," lit. "the holy spirit"; compare *y. Meg.*). **20:** These words are reminiscent of Moses' words of exhortation to Joshua, which also employ the phrases "be strong and resolute ("ḥazaq ve'ematz")," "fear not and be not dismayed," "YHVH is/will be with you," and "(YHVH) will not fail you or forsake you" (Deut. 31.7–8, 23; Josh. 1.7, 9). David and Solomon are viewed like Moses and Joshua (see 22.12 n.).

29.1–9: The call to support Solomon in building the Temple. Chronicles describes the grandeur of the Temple, requiring participation of the entire population; for similar description, see 2 Chron. 2.3–8. The willing participation of the people mirrors the construction of the Tabernacle in Exod. 35.4–29. **1:** The Heb term here translated "temple/fortress" is "birah," itself a Hebraized form of Akkadian "birtu," meaning "fortress." In its present context the term, which appears in connection with Jerusalem and/or the Temple only here and at Neh. 2.8; 7.2, has been understood by some (ancients and moderns) as denoting a Temple chamber; others (ancients and moderns) understand the term as synonymous with the Temple (see *b. Yoma* 2a; *b. Zevaḥ.* 104b). If the latter, the term's usage here may reflect the combined military and religious role of temple complexes in the ancient world. The author may also be hinting at his belief that the true source of Israel's security and strength is to be found in the Temple

kind of precious stone and much marble. 3 Besides, out of my
solicitude for the House of my God, I gave over my private
hoard of gold and silver to the House of my God—in addition
to all that I laid aside for the holy House: 4 3,000 gold talents of
Ophir gold, and 7,000 talents of refined silver for covering the
walls of the houses 5 (gold for golden objects, silver for silver
for all the work)—into the hands of craftsmen. Now who is going to make a freewill offering and devote himself today to the
LORD?"

6 The officers of the clans and the officers of the tribes of Israel and the captains of thousands and hundreds and the supervisors of the king's work made freewill offerings, 7 giving for the
work of the House of God: 5,000 talents of gold, 10,000 darics,
10,000 talents of silver, 18,000 talents of copper, 100,000 talents
of iron. 8 Whoever had stones in his possession gave them to
the treasury of the House of the LORD in the charge of Jehiel the
Gershonite. 9 The people rejoiced over the freewill offerings
they made, for with a whole heart they made freewill offerings
to the LORD; King David also rejoiced very much.

10 David blessed the LORD in front of all the assemblage; David said, "Blessed are You, LORD, God of Israel our father, from
eternity to eternity. 11 Yours, LORD, are greatness, might, splendor, triumph, and majesty—yes, all that is in heaven and on
earth; to You, LORD, belong kingship and preeminence above
all. 12 Riches and honor are Yours to dispense; You have dominion over all; with You are strength and might, and it is in
Your power to make anyone great and strong. 13 Now, God, we
praise You and extol Your glorious name. 14 Who am I and who
are my people, that we should have the means to make such
a freewill offering; but all is from You, and it is Your gift that
we have given to You. 15 For we are sojourners with You, mere
transients like our fathers; our days on earth are like a shadow,
with nothing in prospect. 16 O LORD our God, all this great mass
that we have laid aside to build You a House for Your holy name
is from You, and it is all Yours. 17 I know, God, that You search
the heart and desire uprightness; I, with upright heart, freely
offered all these things; now Your people, who are present

and (proper) performance of its attendant rituals. **3:** Heb "segullah" [NJPS *private hoard*] is cognate with several semitic attestations of this word. The term is most frequently employed in the Bible to express the exclusive relationship between Israel and YHVH (e.g., Exod. 19.5; Deut. 7.6; 14.2; 26.18), reflective of its use in the ancient Near East to denote the special status accorded the highest ranking vassal. The term in these passages is sometimes rendered "(most precious) treasure/treasured people"; here, too, it denotes the most precious of possessions.

29.11–19: David's thanksgiving prayer. This prayer is structurally and thematically similar to the Psalms anthology in ch 16; together they form an inclusio of David's cultic activity. Both passages contain the following themes: transition from landless patriarchs to landed society, the LORD's kingship, and a closing petition. Another significant element now appears: Deeds are truly virtuous only if accompanied by proper intentions. Humans cannot gloat in the act of contributing to the LORD's Temple, since all human success and wealth come from Him. But people can take pride that their donations are given with joy and not as a result of coercion; see intro. This prayer, however, seems to be an original composition of the Chronicler, and it does not have any parallels in Psalms. Its late provenance is indicated, inter alia, by its lexical features and its explicit profession of a universal, rather than national, deity. Like 16.8–36, vv. 10–13 are traditionally recited as part of the "pesukei de-zimrah" of the morning prayers. David's claim of willful contributions on his part and that of the populace is part of Chronicles' oft-encountered emphasis on unlimited assistance to the Temple; it also forms part of an ancient Near Eastern norm demanding that all cult-related contributions (as opposed to wealth taken in battle with enemies) be given without duress; cf. Exod. 25.2; 35.22, 29. Thus, while the primary responsibility in Chronicles, as in the ancient Near East generally, devolves upon the monarch, Chronicles makes the point that the populace is also expected to play its role in support of the cult. **15:** This v. contains allusions to Lev. 25.23 (which declares Israel's patrimony as properly belonging to the deity); Pss. 39.13; 144.4; and Job 8.9, all of which emphasize the ephemeral nature of human existence. The v. not only highlights the fleeting nature of human existence but also underscores the message of the preceding v., namely, that all wealth, and even life itself, is granted by the Deity alone; it is entirely in keeping with Chronicles' emphasis on human frailty and the Deity's control of all aspects of life. Highlighting the brevity of life also underscores the importance of prompt commitment to truly cardinal matters, i.e., the Temple, as personified by David's life.

here—I saw them joyously making freewill offerings. [18] O LORD
God of Abraham, Isaac, and Israel, our fathers, remember this
to the eternal credit of the thoughts of Your people's hearts,
and make their hearts constant toward You. [19] As to my son
Solomon, give him a whole heart to observe Your commandments, Your admonitions, and Your laws, and to fulfill them
all, and to build this temple[a] for which I have made provision."
[20] David said to the whole assemblage, "Now bless the LORD
your God." All the assemblage blessed the LORD God of their
fathers, and bowed their heads low to the LORD and the king.
[21] They offered sacrifices to the LORD and made burnt offerings to the LORD on the morrow of that day: 1,000 bulls, 1,000
rams, 1,000 lambs, with their libations; [they made] sacrifices
in great number for all Israel, [22] and they ate and drank in the
presence of the LORD on that day with great joy. They again
proclaimed Solomon son of David king, and they anointed
him as ruler before the LORD, and Zadok as high priest. [23] Solomon successfully took over the throne of the LORD as king instead of his father David, and all went well with him. All Israel
accepted him; [24] all the officials and the warriors, and the sons
of King David as well, gave their hand in support of King Solomon. [25] The LORD made Solomon exceedingly great in the eyes
of all Israel, and endowed him with a regal majesty that no king
of Israel before him ever had.

a Lit. "fortress."

29.21: Once again, it appears to be the people—possibly, but not necessarily, together with David— who offer the sacrifices; see 15.26–27 n. It is likely that the sacrifices celebrate the occasion of public contributions to the Temple building fund and the accompanying prayers, constituting another expression of the people's support for Temple-related matters; it is possible, if less likely, that they were offered in response to the formal appointment of Solomon as crown prince, which is not mentioned until v. 22. The statement that the people fell prostrate to both the deity and the king is highly irregular; the "king" may refer either to Solomon, whose coronation is mentioned in v. 22, or David. **22:** The reference to a "second time" (NJPS *again*) is not attested in LXX and Peshitta, and is probably secondary. Some have posited 1 Kings 1.38–49 as constituting the first coronation. The point of the second one is, accordingly, to declare the public support for Solomon, the private coronation by Nathan and Zadok in 1 Kings being insufficient. It is more likely that the implied first coronation is that mentioned at 1 Chron. 23.1. On this view, too, the present ch seeks to highlight the unquestioned support of Solomon and, thereby, jettison the uncertainty regarding David's successor described in 1 Kings ch 1. Solomon's anointing at this juncture is taken by some to mean that he served as co-regent with David. This is unlikely, given the book's predilection for one leader exclusively occupying the divinely appointed position. It is likely that this action, performed during David's lifetime, establishes Solomon as crown prince, and is intended to preclude the possibility of a power vacuum and struggle following David's demise. This is reinforced by 2 Chron. 19.11, which indicates that the term "nagid," denotes an official subservient to another. Rabbinic tradents, noting that anointing of monarchs in the Bible appears only rarely, and conflating the present passage with the episode in 1 Kings ch 1, maintained that its performance is limited to instances where the new monarch's legitimacy is in question (*b. Ker.* 5b). Zadok's anointment is also vexing. Though Aaron and his sons were anointed as part of the priestly ordination, Zadok functioned in the capacity of high priest. This may be an oblique reference to Zadok's less than stable position, reflected at 1 Kings 1.8, 26. Alternatively, this may be the author's way of expressing some sort of dual leadership, a position attested in various forms in Zech. chs 3–4, as well as in the Dead Sea Scrolls. This stance, however, is not reflected elsewhere in Chronicles, rendering it problematic. **24:** Chronicles is oblivious to 1 Kings chs 1–3, which describe the struggles concerning David's succession. **25:** This formulation may indicate that Chronicles viewed Solomon as no less important a figure than David; others reject this, noting that David is Chronicles' king, par excellence. Alternatively, this formulation may anticipate Chronicles' use of a Solomonic typology in its depiction of Hezekiah's magnificent wealth; see 2 Kings 20.13. The formulation *regal majesty* (Heb "hod malkhut"), which appears only in postexilic sources, is most likely a calque of the Akkadian "melam šarrūti," and expresses both legitimation of the king (by the deity) and royal power. Thus, the v. states that Solomon's popularity and legitimacy were brought about by God (cf. 10.13–14) and that his imperial dominion reached proportions not attained by any predecessor (cf. 1 Kings 1.37, 47; 5.1–4; Ezra 5.11, where the phrase "great king" is likely a calque of another Akkadian formulation, "šarru rabû"). To be sure, the claim that Solomon attained power "that no king before him ever had" is surprising; since Chronicles considers Saul to have been a failed king, this leaves only David. This may be

26 Thus David son of Jesse reigned over all Israel; 27 the length
of his reign over Israel was forty years: he reigned seven years
in Hebron and thirty-three years in Jerusalem. 28 He died at a
ripe old age, having enjoyed long life, riches and honor, and
his son Solomon reigned in his stead. 29 The acts of King David,
early and late, are recorded in the history of Samuel the seer,
the history of Nathan the prophet, and the history of Gad the
seer, 30 together with all the mighty deeds of his kingship and
the events that befell him and Israel and all the kingdoms of
the earth.

the author's elliptical way of stating Solomon's superiority while avoiding denigration of David, whose stature in Chronicles has been established. **26–27:** Whereas 1 Kings 2.11 states that David ruled over Judah in Hebron, and over a united Israel in Jerusalem, Chronicles avoids this dichotomy. Chronicles' position carries a price: If David ruled from Hebron over all Israel for seven years, then his move to Jerusalem has no clear motive. Chronicles' presentation of the capture of Jerusalem as a national-religious issue raises the unanswered problem of why the move was postponed seven years; see 11.1–3, 4–9 nn. More fundamentally, Chronicles' claim begs the question: when, precisely, did David actually rule as king in Hebron? No such period is described above and the sequence of events in 1 Chron. chs 10–29 offers no hint of an extended period during which David ruled over all Israel from Hebron. On the other hand, the seven years cannot refer to a period overlapping Saul's regency (as claimed by 1 Sam. and 2 Sam.), since that would imply rivalry and bifurcation in Israel's leadership, a position in tension with Chronicles' belief that there can be only one divinely-appointed monarch (see 1 Chron. 11.1–3 n.; 2 Chron. 13.5, 8, and intro.); indeed, Chronicles never depicts David as ruling during Saul's lifetime. Perhaps the author lifted this datum from 2 Sam. 5.4–5 without adjusting it to its new context. It is more likely, though, that the author employs the forty-year period because of its typological importance (e.g., the leadership of Moses and Solomon), and has chosen to pass over the difficulty in silence. **28–30:** A recurring feature of Chronicles is the claim that the official royal chronicles were composed by prophets. This is another example of the changed role and nature of prophets in Chronicles; they are, among other things, historians who record, study, interpret, and assess past events. In addition, Chronicles' claim implies that everything contained in these official accounts—and, by implication, the book of Chronicles itself—is fully accurate and credible. Many modern scholars, however, doubt that these works, typically mentioned at the end of the kings' reign, ever existed. **30:** The phrase *all the kingdoms of the earth* (lit., "of the lands") refers to neighboring nations (see 2 Chron. 12.8; 17.10; 20.29), and reflects the international status and power achieved by David (cf. 1 Chron. 14.17; 17.8). This phrase recurs at the book's close (2 Chron. 36.23), though with the singular form "kingdoms of the earth/land." The different forms of the Heb word for "land/lands" may be a mere variant; in this case, the passages indicate that the divinely granted reign has passed (for the present, at least) to Cyrus and the Persians. However, the two forms may bear different nuances, viz., regional lands (David) vs. earth (Cyrus).

דברי הימים ב

2 Chronicles

AN INTRODUCTION TO THE BOOK of Chronicles precedes 1 Chronicles.

[DAVID ROTHSTEIN]

1 Solomon son of David took firm hold of his kingdom, for
the LORD his God was with him and made him exceedingly
great. 2 Solomon summoned all Israel—the officers of thousands and of hundreds, and the judges, and all the chiefs of all
Israel, the heads of the clans. 3 [a]Then Solomon, and all the assemblage with him, went to the shrine at Gibeon, for the Tent of
Meeting, which Moses the servant of the LORD had made in the
wilderness, was there. (4 But the Ark of God David had brought
up from Kiriath-jearim to the place which David had prepared
for it; for he had pitched a tent for it in Jerusalem.) 5 The bronze
altar, which Bezalel son of Uri son of Hur had made, was also
there before the Tabernacle of the LORD, and Solomon and
the assemblage resorted to it. 6 There Solomon ascended the
bronze altar before the LORD, which was at the Tent of Meeting,
and on it sacrificed a thousand burnt offerings.

7 That night, God appeared to Solomon and said to him,
"Ask, what shall I grant you?" 8 Solomon said to God, "You
dealt most graciously with my father David, and now You have
made me king in his stead. 9 Now, O LORD God, let Your promise to my father David be fulfilled; for You have made me king
over a people as numerous as the dust of the earth. 10 Grant me

a With vv. 3–13, cf. 1 Kings 3.4–15; with vv. 14–17, cf. 1 Kings 10.26–29.

1.1–9.31: Solomon's reign. Chronicles presents a much more favorable depiction of Solomon than the book of Kings, omitting passages which reflect poorly upon him. In general, Chronicles portrays Solomon as a near mirror-image of David. Solomon's reign is marked by the realization of David's cultic preparations and economic growth. Thus, the continuity between David and Solomon in Chronicles is greater than in Samuel-Kings. The precise nature of the relationship between the Solomon narrative in Chronicles and its parallel text (1 Kings ch 1–11) is a more complex issue than that obtaining in connection with the David narrative. This is due to the many differences, in both content and structure, between the Masoretic and LXX versions of 1 Kings ch 1–11, a prime example of which is the generally more positive portrait of Solomon in LXX Kings. There are differing assessments as to which version of 1 Kings is of earlier provenance, but the evidence favors the view that LXX attests a later reworking of an earlier text. While this issue bears on the interpretation of the relationship between Chronicles and 1 Kings (including the question of the chronological primacy of the Solomon narrative in 1 Kings vs. that of Chronicles; see intro.), the annotations below relate, in most cases, to the Masoretic reading of 1 Kings.

1.1–13: Solomon travels to Gibeon. In the "incubation" story of 1 Kings 3.4–14 Solomon makes a private pilgrimage to Gibeon in the hope of receiving divine communication. Chronicles views this pilgrimage as a sign of Solomon's devotion to the Temple service cult and, thereby, having national-religious significance. In line with the tendency to create greater continuity between David and Solomon, Solomon's actions parallel those of David; see 1 Chron. 11.4–8 and esp. 13.1–5. **1:** David's prayers on behalf of Solomon have materialized (1 Chron. 28.20). *The LORD his God was with him*, language used of David (e.g., 2 Sam. 5.10), creating continuity between David and Solomon. **3:** 1 Kings (3.2–3) acknowledges that Israel offered local sacrifices before the construction of Solomon's Temple; Chronicles

then the wisdom and the knowledge [a]to lead this people,[a] for who can govern Your great people?" 11 God said to Solomon, "Because you want this, and have not asked for wealth, property, and glory, nor have you asked for the life of your enemy, or long life for yourself, but you have asked for the wisdom and the knowledge to be able to govern My people over whom I have made you king, 12 wisdom and knowledge are granted to you, and I grant you also wealth, property, and glory, the like of which no king before you has had, nor shall any after you have." 13 From the shrine at Gibeon, from the Tent of Meeting, Solomon went to Jerusalem and reigned over Israel.

14 Solomon assembled chariots and horsemen; he had 1,400 chariots and 12,000 horses that he stationed in the chariot towns and with the king in Jerusalem. 15 The king made silver and gold as plentiful in Jerusalem as stones, and cedars as plentiful as the sycamores in the Shephelah. 16 Solomon's horses were imported from Egypt and from Que; the king's traders would buy them from Que at the market price. 17 A chariot imported from Egypt cost 600 shekels of silver, and a horse 150. These in turn were exported by them[b] to all the kings of the Hittites and the kings of the Arameans.

18 Then Solomon resolved to build a House for the name of the LORD and a royal palace for himself.

a-a Lit. "that I may go out before this people and come in."
b That is, Solomon's dealers.

consistently avoids mention of any such possibility. The Tabernacle and altar were, for Chronicles, the mobile "chosen place" for cultic activity, in accordance with Lev. 17.8; Deut. 12.4–28. For this reason Chronicles claims that Gibeon was the site of the Mosaic Tabernacle (and sacred appurtenances), whereas 1 Kings 3.4 states only that the "great altar"—i.e., one of many—was there (see 1 Chron. 16.39). For Chronicles, but not for Kings, Lev. as well as Deut. was authoritative; this explains the revision here. Rabbinic tradition (*m. Zevaḥ.* 14.4–7; *t. Zevaḥ.* 13.19) reconciles the divergent biblical traditions (Lev. ch 17; Deut. ch 12; 1 Kings; Chron.) by arguing that prior to the construction of the Temple, local cultic slaughter was permitted so long as there was no central tabernacle housing both the "great altar" and the Ark (as in Chronicles' description of Gibeon); when such existed, as in the rabbinic understanding of the Shiloh Tabernacle (see Josh. 18.1; 1 Sam. 3.3), sacrifice was permitted only at the central site. This accounts for David's sacrifices, in Jerusalem, at 1 Chron. 16.2. As previously noted, Chronicles omits reference to the dynastic struggle during David's old age. Chronicles also defers mention of Solomon's marriage to Pharaoh's daughter (1 Kings 3.1) until 8.11. By doing so, Chronicles seeks to convey the impression that Solomon's first act as monarch pertained to religious, Temple-related matters. Additionally, the Chronicler depicts Solomon's marriage to Pharaoh's daughter is a "political" one, intended to consolidate his position; only after this stability is assured does Solomon, according to 1 Kings, go to Gibeon. Chronicles, however, maintains that Solomon's rule was divinely ordained and had never been in doubt; hence, the diplomatic motive behind this marriage was irrelevant. **11:** The reference to Solomon's detractors is surprising, inasmuch as there is no hint of opposition to Solomon's accession in 1 Chron. chs 28–29. This may indicate that the Chronicler acknowledged that there was some opposition to Solomon; alternatively, the formulation may allude to opponents that may conceivably arise at some future date. **13:** Chronicles omits Solomon's sacrifice before the Ark upon his return to Jerusalem; cf. 1 Kings 3.15. This probably reflects Chronicles' slant concerning centralization of worship even before the construction of the Temple; see, however, 1 Chron. 16.2.

1.14–17: Economic growth. Almost identical wording appears at the close of Solomon's life in 2 Chron. 9.27–28 (= 1 Kings 10.23–28); it is not unusual for Chronicles to rearrange source material for literary or ideological reasons. This use of inclusio (2 Chron. 1.14–17 || 2 Chron. 9.27–28) may be nothing more than a literary device; it is more likely, however, that Chronicles here portrays God's promise as being realized without delay, such that the entire period of Solomon's reign was marked by economic prosperity. There is no hint here of the hardships endured during the course of this economic boom; see 10.1. The passage also implies that the generous contributions made by the people towards the end of David's life (1 Chron. 29.6–9) had not brought about financial hardship; on the contrary, there ensued a period of unprecedented national prosperity. Chronicles omits 1 Kings 3.16–28, Solomon's first successful adjudication, because Chronicles maintains that Solomon's wisdom was manifest, first and foremost, in executing the Temple project; see 2 Chron. 2.11. **15:** 1 Kings 10.27 mentions only plentitude of silver; Chronicles adds the words "and gold," emphasizing the economic boom in Solomon's day.

1.18–2.17: Preparation of work force and Solomon's negotiations with Huram. There are many

2 [a]Solomon mustered 70,000 basket carriers and 80,000
quarriers in the hills, with 3,600 men supervising them.
2 Solomon sent this message to King Huram of Tyre, "In view
of what you did for my father David in sending him cedars
to build a palace for his residence—3 see, I intend to build a
House for the name of the LORD my God; I will dedicate it to
Him for making incense offering of sweet spices in His honor,
for the regular rows of bread, and for the morning and evening
burnt offerings on sabbaths, new moons, and festivals, as is
Israel's eternal duty. 4 The House that I intend to build will be
great, inasmuch as our God is greater than all gods. 5 Who indeed is capable of building a House for Him! Even the heavens
to their uttermost reaches cannot contain Him, and who am I

a Cf. 1 Kings 5.

differences between this ch and 1 Kings ch 5. The fundamental difference between the two versions may be summarized as follows: the story in 1 Kings is about political alliances and the fulfillment of YHVH's promise to bless Solomon with wisdom in political matters (1 Kings 3.11–13), whereas Chronicles' version is about Solomon's zeal and alacrity in advancing the cause of the Temple construction and shows no concern for political alliances. Kings calls the king Hiram, while in Chronicles he is Huram. Both forms are shortened forms of the name "Ahiram (Ahuram)." The change may be the result of scribal confusion between the graphically similar letters "yod" (y/î) and "vav" or "waw" (v or w/û). Alternatively, it may reflect a change in the name's morphology. Ahiram means "the/my (divine) brother is exalted"; Ahuram may be parsed as an archaic form, with a nominative case ending following the word "brother," yielding the meaning "the brother [is exalted]." The presence of a nominative case vowel in similar formations in other Semitic languages (Eblaite and, of greater relevance, Punic) bolsters the likelihood that the Chronicler's vocalization is historically authentic. In Kings Hiram establishes diplomatic contact with Solomon, to continue the beneficial (and lucrative; see below) relations which he had enjoyed with David; he therefore does this only after Solomon's rule has been fully stabilized. By contrast, Chronicles claims that Solomon initiates the diplomacy shortly after his visit to Gibeon and his conscription of Temple workers; his alacrity demonstrates his commitment to executing the construction of the Temple. Second, the negotiations in 1 Kings are based on a quid pro quo; Solomon pays for needed services, while the terms of payment are dictated by Hiram. In Chronicles Solomon unilaterally dictates the terms, while Huram is presented as a "believing," monotheistic Gentile, whose motive for assisting Solomon is largely, or even exclusively, religious. Third, the cost in Kings involves yearly provisions for Hiram's household; Chronicles speaks of a one-time payment. Fourth, in 1 Kings Solomon's description of the planned Temple is terse and businesslike; Chronicles' Solomon describes the magnitude of the Temple project in superlative terms and spells out the specific cultic activities (integrating Priestly perspectives) to take place in the Temple. Fifth, by having Huram refer to Solomon as "my lord" (v. 14), Chronicles portrays Solomon as the dominant monarch; see 8.1–6 n. Finally, according to 1 Kings 5.26, the wisdom that God bestowed upon Solomon is demonstrated by Solomon's execution of a treaty with Hiram. Chronicles makes no reference to this treaty nor to its constituting the realization of Solomon's wisdom. As noted above, Chronicles maintains that Solomon's wisdom was manifest primarily in connection with the Temple building, and only secondarily in other spheres. Chronicles' omission of the treaty reflects two factors. Since Chronicles presents Solomon as the most powerful and wealthy monarch in the region, there is no reason for Solomon to limit himself by a political treaty. Second, Chronicles' omission reflects the book's ideological stance, according to which a truly believing individual must trust in God's ability to provide for all needs, making treaties with foreigners (and wicked Israelites) superfluous and even improper. Although some scholars have interpreted the version in 1 Kings ch 5 as reflective of Solomon's cunning in dealing with Hiram, to whom he had consented to pay an exorbitant amount of foodstuffs in exchange for assistance with the Temple's construction (1 Kings 5.20–25), it is unlikely that the Chronicler would have understood 1 Kings' formulation in this manner. **2.3:** The addition of details of the sacrifices in vv. 3–4, not found in 1 Kings, reflects Chronicles' incorporation of the Priestly perspective found in Lev. and elsewhere. **5:** Chronicles expresses the divine transcendence; the Temple does not actually "house" the LORD (contrast 1 Kings 8.13). This formulation may be informed by Deut.'s "name theology," according to which only the LORD's name is localized at the Temple (see, e.g., Deut. 12.5, 11). Read together with v. 2, this v. emphasizes that the temple that Solomon has in mind will make the palace that Huram built for David pale by comparison, since the latter was meant for (human) residence; the Temple, while not capable of housing the Deity, must be a on a scale fitting that of the universe. This v. has no parallel in the negotiations of 1 Kings ch 5.

that I should build Him a House—except as a place for making
burnt offerings to Him? [6] Now send me a craftsman to work in
gold, silver, bronze, and iron, and in purple, crimson, and blue
yarn, and who knows how to engrave, alongside the craftsmen I have here in Judah and in Jerusalem, whom my father
David provided. [7] Send me cedars, cypress, and algum wood
from the Lebanon, for I know that your servants are skilled at
cutting the trees of Lebanon. My servants will work with yours
[8] to provide me with a great stock of timber; for the House that
I intend to build will be singularly great. [9] I have allocated for
your servants, the wood-cutters who fell the trees, 20,000 *kor*
of crushed wheat and 20,000 *kor* of barley, 20,000 *bath* of wine
and 20,000 *bath* of oil."

[10] Huram, king of Tyre, sent Solomon this written message in
reply, "Because the LORD loved His people, He made you king
over them."

[11] Huram continued, "Blessed is the LORD, God of Israel, who
made the heavens and the earth, who gave King David a wise
son, endowed with intelligence and understanding, to build a
House for the LORD and a royal palace for himself. [12] Now I am
sending you a skillful and intelligent man, my master[a] Huram,
[13] the son of a Danite woman, his father a Tyrian. He is skilled
at working in gold, silver, bronze, iron, precious stones, and
wood; in purple, blue, and crimson yarn and in fine linen; and
at engraving and designing whatever will be required of him,
alongside your craftsmen and the craftsmen of my lord, your
father David. [14] As to the wheat, barley, oil, and wine which my
lord mentioned, let him send them to his servants. [15] We undertake to cut down as many trees of Lebanon as you need,
and deliver them to you as rafts by sea to Jaffa; you will transport them to Jerusalem."

a Lit. "my father."

6: The formulation reflects the list of materials found in construction of the Tabernacle; see Exod. 25.4–7; 35.5–9. While 1 Kings 7.13–14 mentions the Phoenician craftsman in charge, this v. has no parallel in 1 Kings ch 5. **8:** At 1 Kings 5.20 Solomon openly acknowledges the superior skills of Hiram's workers and, thereby, the fact that Hiram holds the high ground in negotiations over the Temple project. In Chronicles Solomon acknowledges the need for assistance from Huram's (Hiram's) workers but lessens the nature of his dependence on them, thereby revealing a shrewder and more dominant Solomon. **9:** Chronicles' version presents Solomon as making a one-time payment (as opposed to the yearly payment made by Solomon [1 Kings 5.25]), consisting only of food for Huram's workers. The implication is that all other expenses and building materials were assumed by Huram. For similar altruism on Huram's part, but apparently for other reasons, see 2 Chron. 8.1–2. The motif of abundance ("great stock," [v. 8]) again expresses the grandeur of the Temple (see 1 Chron. ch 29), as well as Huram's willingness to absorb the great expense involved. **10–13:** Huram's reply: The implication of Huram's readiness to assist Solomon is that if a foreigner—albeit righteous—recognizes the importance of the Israelite Temple, how much more so should be the response of all Israelites/Jews. The depiction of foreign rulers here and elsewhere as acknowledging Israel's deity—and in some instances (2 Chron. 36.23), their own role as His earthly agent—is seen by some as evidence of thoroughgoing monotheism; similarly, some scholars view the important role played by Huram (and Cyrus) as expressing the view that the Davidic dynasty is not a sine qua non for Israel's well-being and the fulfillment of its role in this world. The latter point, however, is not compelling; the author may simply be stating that Israel is always, at all times and in all circumstances, under divine protection, as expressed at 1 Chron. 16.19–22, 35. For discussion of the Davidic monarchy, see intro. **11:** A patent formulation of the view that the wisdom granted Solomon was realized primarily in the building of the Temple, not in domestic and international leadership. The wording recalls 1 Chron. 22.12, indicating that David's hopes for Solomon have materialized. **12–14:** The materials listed are reminiscent of the Tabernacle account in Exod. 25.3–7; 35.5–9; see the "continuity theme" in 1 Chron. ch 21. This motif also explains the name and tribal background of the chief Temple craftsman. Whereas 1 Kings 7.14 assigns his mother to the northern tribe of Naphtali, Chronicles claims that his mother was from the northern tribe of Dan, while his father was a Tyrian; the (half-) Danite lineage of Huramabi thus parallels the Tabernacle account in Exod., wherein one of the head artisans, Oholiab, was a Danite (Exod. 31.6). The Tyrian origin of the craftsman's father, which clearly did not bother the Chronicler, troubled Jewish exegetes. Josephus *(Ant.)* and some medieval commentators argued that his father was Jewish, by taking "Tyre" to refer to the mainland Tyre, apportioned to Asher (Josh. 19.29), rather than the

16 Solomon took a census of all the aliens who were in the
land of Israel, besides the census taken by his father David,
and they were found to be 153,600. 17 He made 70,000 of them
basket carriers, and 80,000 of them quarriers, with 3,600 supervisors to see that the people worked.

3 Then Solomon began to build the House of the LORD in
Jerusalem on Mount Moriah, where [the LORD] had appeared to his father David, at the place which David had designated, at the threshing floor of Ornan the Jebusite. 2 [a]He began
to build on the second day of the second month of the fourth

a With vv. 2–17, cf. 1 Kings 6; 7.1–22.

Phoenician city. Others suggested that his father was originally from the fort-city of Ser, which formed part of Naphtali, but subsequently moved to Tyre. The Chronicler's statement here reflects his relatively moderate position on intermarriage and lineage; see intro. **16–17:** Solomon again prepares the work force. Significantly, he uses only *aliens* for the work force; Kings is ambivalent on this matter (cf. 1 Kings 5.27; 9.21). In addition, Chronicles has omitted the covenant between Solomon and Hiram (1 Kings 5.26).

3.1–2: The Temple site. The "Land of Moriah" appears elsewhere only at Gen. 22.1 in connection with the ʿAkedah, Abraham's binding of Isaac. Chronicles claims that David's altar was erected on the very spot where Abraham prepared to sacrifice Isaac. Other allusions to Gen. ch 22 include the words "who was seen/appeared to David," (Heb "r-'-h"), reminiscent of Gen. 22.4, 8, 13 and, esp. v. 14. Chronicles thus emphasizes the "chosen" nature of the Temple site, which reaches back to Israel's earliest forebear, suggesting that the site's uniqueness is almost ontological. This may also be another expression of the fulfillment of the divine promise to Abraham; see 1 Chron. 16.8–18. A rabbinic tradition (*Pirqe R. El.* 31; see also *y. Naz.* 7.2 [56a]; *Gen. Rab.* 34; *b. Zevaḥ.* 62a) further maintains that the locus of the Temple altar was the place from which Adam was created, and where Cain and Abel made their respective offerings (Gen. 4.3–4), suggesting that the locus of humankind's creation is also the locus of atonement (i.e., "rejuvenation"). The Samaritan community preserves a parallel tradition, wherein the binding of Isaac took place on Mt. Gerizim, the religious center of the Samaritans. **1:** While Chronicles emphasizes that the importance of Jerusalem and the Temple Mount has its roots in hoary antiquity, it stops short of explicitly assigning an ontologically unique status to the Temple locus, an idea amply attested in the ancient Near East and in the Bible (see, e.g., Jer. 17.12; Pss. 24.9–10; 48.2–3). **2:** The delay in building the Temple at 1 Kings 6.1 is reasonable, since Solomon had been forced to first secure his throne. Chronicles, however, omits the entire episode (see 1.3 n.); indeed, Chronicles implies that Solomon's negotiations with Huram took place immediately upon his return from Gibeon, i.e, within days of Solomon's accession to the throne. Furthermore, David had already laid most of the groundwork. Nevertheless, Chronicles

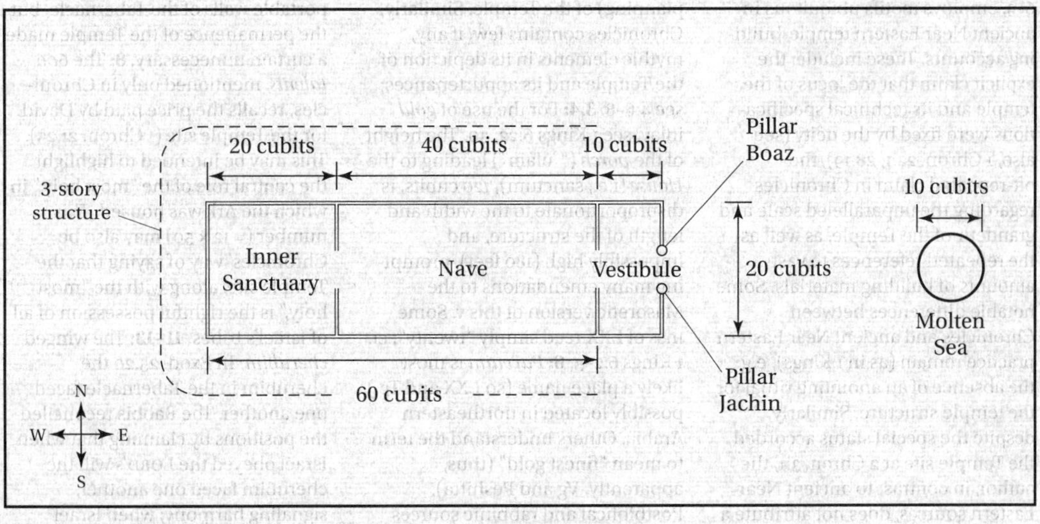

The Temple of Solomon according to Second Chronicles

year of his reign. 3 These were the dimensions Solomon established for building the House of God: its length in cubits,
by the former measure, was 60, and its breadth was 20. 4 The
length of the porch in front [was equal] to the breadth of the
House—20 cubits, and its height was 120. Inside he overlaid
it with pure gold. 5 The House itself he paneled with cypress
wood. He overlaid it with fine gold and embossed on it palms
and chains. 6 He studded the House with precious stones for
decoration; the gold was from Parvaim. 7 He overlaid the House
with gold—the beams, the thresholds, its walls and doors; he
carved cherubim on the walls. 8 He made the Holy of Holies: its
length was [equal to] the breadth of the house—20 cubits, and
its breadth was 20 cubits. He overlaid it with 600 talents of fine
gold. 9 The weight of the nails was 50 shekels of gold; the upper
chambers he overlaid with gold. 10 He made two sculptured
cherubim in the Holy of Holies, and they were overlaid with
gold. 11 The outspread wings of the cherubim were 20 cubits
across: one wing 5 cubits long touching one wall of the House,
and the other wing 5 cubits long touching the wing of the other
cherub; 12 one wing of the other [cherub] 5 cubits long extending to the other wall of the House, and its other wing 5 cubits
long touching the wing of the first cherub. 13 The wingspread
of these cherubim was thus 20 cubits across, and they were

portrays Solomon as waiting until the fourth year perhaps because the period of three years in Chronicles is typological, signifying a (relatively) short period (see 11.7; 17.7) and the magnitude of the Temple project, emphasized repeatedly in Chronicles, required several years of preparation. Chronicles omits 1 Kings' reference to 480 years from the exodus (6.1); this omission is another instance of Chronicles' reticence concerning Israel's sojourn in, and deliverance from, Egypt (see intro.).

3.3–5.1: Solomon's Temple. Chronicles' description of the Temple and appurtenances differs considerably from that in 1 Kings chs 6–7, in two respects. First, Chronicles' account is much shorter. Second, Chronicles' version brings Kings' description into closer harmony with the Mosaic Tabernacle described in the Priestly source of the Torah, another example of the "continuity theme." (The Priestly account was not known or authoritative to the author of Kings.) Beginning with v. 8, and with the exception of 4.11–16, the syntactic subject of these vv. is Solomon, thus emphasizing Solomon's role as executor of David's preparations. Chronicles, to a greater extent than the parallel passage in 1 Kings chs 6–9, employs motifs ubiquitous in ancient Near Eastern temple-building accounts. These include: the explicit claim that the locus of the temple and its technical specifications were fixed by the deity (see also, 1 Chron. 22.1; 28.19), the oft-repeated claim in Chronicles regarding the unparalleled scale and grandeur of the Temple, as well as the repeated references to vast amounts of building materials. Some notable differences between Chronicles and ancient Near Eastern practice remain (as in 1 Kings), e.g., the absence of an anointing ritual for the temple structure. Similarly, despite the special status accorded the Temple site at 2 Chron. 3.1, the author, in contrast to ancient Near Eastern sources, does not attribute a unique status to the Temple site or the materials used in the Temple's construction. Other instances of the author's departure from ancient Near Eastern norms include the absence of an important (or, in fact, any) role to Solomon in the actual construction (as opposed to planning) of the Temple. Similarly, Chronicles contains few, if any, mythic elements in its depiction of the Temple and its appurtenances; see 4.6–8. **3.4:** For the use of *gold* inlay, see 1 Kings 6.22, 30. The height of the *porch* ("'ulam") leading to the *House* (i.e., sanctum), *120* cubits, is disproportionate to the width and length of the structure, and impossibly high (180 feet), prompting many emendations to the Masoretic version of this v. Some mss of LXX read simply "twenty"; cf. 1 Kings 6.2–3. **6:** *Parvaim* is most likely a place name (so LXX and Tg.), possibly located in northeastern Arabia. Others understand the term to mean "finest gold" (thus, apparently, Vg and Peshitta). Postbiblical and rabbinic sources understood the term as denoting either a mythical location or quality. **7:** 1 Kings 6.22 makes no mention of *cherubim* being engraved on the walls of the Temple. Chronicles' position, informed by Exod. 26.1, 31, appears to be an artificial construct. In Exod. the curtain encloses the portable walls of the Tabernacle, but the permanence of the Temple made a curtain unnecessary. **8:** The *600 talents,* mentioned only in Chronicles, recalls the price paid by David for the Temple site (1 Chron. 21.25). This may be intended to highlight the central role of the "most holy," in which the Ark was housed. This number (= 12 × 50) may also be Chronicles' way of saying that the Temple site, along with the "most holy," is the rightful possession of all of Israel's tribes. **11–13:** The winged *cherubim:* In Exod. 25.20 the cherubim in the Tabernacle faced one another. The Rabbis reconciled the positions by claiming that when Israel obeyed the LORD's will the cherubim faced one another, signaling harmony; when Israel veered from the path, the cherubim

standing up facing the House. [14] He made the curtain of blue,
purple, and crimson yarn and fine linen, and he worked cherubim into it. [15] At the front of the House he made two columns
35 cubits high; the capitals[a] on top of them were 5 cubits high.
[16] He made chainwork in the inner Sanctuary and set it on the
top of the columns; he made a hundred pomegranates and set
them into the chainwork. [17] He erected the columns in front of
the Great Hall, one to its right and one to its left; the one to the
right was called Jachin, and the one to the left, Boaz.

4 [b]He made an altar of bronze 20 cubits long, 20 cubits wide,
and 10 cubits high.
[2] He made the sea[c] of cast metal 10 cubits across from brim to
brim, perfectly round; it was 5 cubits high, and its circumference
was 30 cubits. [3] Beneath were figures of oxen set all around it, of
10 cubits, encircling the sea; the oxen were in two rows, cast in
one piece with it. [4] It stood upon twelve oxen: three faced north,
three faced west, three faced south, and three faced east, with
the sea resting upon them; their haunches were all turned inward. [5] It was a handbreadth thick, and its brim was made like
that of a cup, like the petals of a lily. It held 3,000 *bath*.
[6] He made ten bronze lavers for washing; he set five on the
right and five on the left; they would rinse off in them the parts
of the burnt offering; but the sea served the priests for washing.
[7] He made ten lampstands of gold as prescribed, and placed
them in the Great Hall, five on the right and five on the left. [8] He
made ten tables and placed them in the Great Hall, five on the
right and five on the left. He made one hundred gold basins.

a Meaning of Heb. uncertain. *b Cf. 1 Kings 7.23–50.* *c I.e., a large basin.*

faced outwards, toward the Temple courts (*b. B. Bat.* 99a). **14:** There is no mention of a curtain, cherub-adorned or otherwise, separating the Holy from the Most Holy in either 1 Kings (6.21) or the (future) temple of Ezekiel. Indeed, 1 Kings 6.31–32 mentions doors at this juncture. The Heb word for veil, "parokhet," appears twenty-four times in the Priestly source[s], and nowhere else in the Bible. Moreover, the very existence of such a curtain contradicts 4.22, and 1 Kings 7.50; 6.31–32, where permanent doors separate the courts. Chronicles' account is, again, informed by the description of the Priestly Tabernacle (Exod. 26.31–37; 36.35). Despite the seemingly artificial nature of Chronicles' position, several Second Temple sources (e.g., Josephus) mention the "parokhet" or veil as a feature of the Second Temple, suggesting that this feature was, indeed, part of the Temple structure at the time of the Chronicler, whose formulation here reflects an attempt at legitimation. Chronicles claims that this structural feature had existed in Solomon's Temple, as well. Rabbinic tradition preserves two positions. On one view, Solomon's Temple had one curtain separating the Holy and Most Holy, while the Second Temple had two such curtains; a second view maintained that both temples had one curtain (*m. Yoma* 5:1, *b. Yoma* 51b). **15–17:** 1 Kings 7.15–22 states that Hiram (Huram) had the pillars built; Chronicles implies that Solomon was responsible for them. The position of these pillars—on either side of the entrance to the sanctum, a point not specified in the Kings account—corresponds to archeological evidence of the sanctuaries at Hazor and Arad. **4.1:** The *altar of bronze* is missing in 1 Kings. The reference here may be a scribal error; more likely Chronicles has added it under the influence of Exod. 27.1; 38.1. The dimensions probably describe the altar base, from which steps led to the altar itself. **2–5:** *The sea:* The differences between this v. and 1 Kings 7.23–26 have generated many explanations. The difference in size may reflect a cylindrical shape (Chronicles) vs. a hemisphere (Kings). Chronicles' reference to *oxen* may result from Chronicles' difficulty in understanding the Kings passage. Some postbiblical sources (Josephus, *Ant.*) maintained that production of the oxen violated the anti-iconic position of Deut. 4.16–18; see 9.18–19. **6–8:** The purpose of the *lavers,* not found in 1 Kings, reflects the influence of Exod. 30.17–21; here too the Priestly description of the Tabernacle is used to fill in the description in Kings. Though the purpose of the tank ("sea") at 1 Kings 7.23–24 is not specified, the presence of vegetation as part of the sea suggests a mythic role symbolizing the cosmic source of water and fertility. Chronicles' sea has no vegetation and serves a purely cultic-legal function, supplying clean, pure water, reflecting the influence of Exod. 30.17–21; here, too, the Priestly description of the Tabernacle is used to fill in the depiction in Kings. (Ezek. [esp. 47.1–12], prescribes no tank for the (future) Temple, but describes a wondrous life-giving source of water that emanates from the Temple.) Rabbinic sources reflect a hybrid tradition, stating that a stream whose source lay in the Temple replenished the water in the tank (*y. Yoma* 3.10 [41a]). **7:** Cf. Exod. 25.31–39; 37.17–24. Rabbinic sources say that there were ten candelabra in addition to that fashioned in Moses' day; the present v. was explained to mean that five were placed to the

[9] He built the court of the priests and the great court, and doors
for the great court; he overlaid the doors with bronze. [10] He set
the sea on the right side, at the southeast corner.
[11] Huram made the pails, the shovels, and the basins. With
that Huram completed the work he had undertaken for King
Solomon in the House of God: [12] the two columns, the globes,
and the two capitals on top of the columns; and the two pieces
of network to cover the two globes of the capitals on top of the
columns; [13] the four hundred pomegranates for the two pieces
of network, two rows of pomegranates for each network, to cover
the two globes of the capitals on top of the columns; [14] he made
the stands and the lavers upon the stands; [15] one sea with the
twelve oxen beneath it; [16] the pails, the shovels, and the bowls.[a]
And all the vessels made for King Solomon for the House of the
LORD by Huram his master were of burnished bronze. [17] The king
had them cast in molds dug out of the earth, in the plain of the
Jordan between Succoth and Zeredah. [18] Solomon made a very
large number of vessels; the weight of the bronze used could not
be reckoned. [19] And Solomon made all the furnishings that were
in the House of God: the altar of gold; the tables for the bread of
display; [20] the lampstands and their lamps, to burn as prescribed
in front of the inner Sanctuary, of solid gold; [21] and the petals,
lamps, and tongs, of purest gold; [22] the snuffers, basins, ladles,
and fire pans, of solid gold; and the entrance to the House: the
doors of the innermost part of the House, the Holy of Holies, and
the doors of the Great Hall of the House, of gold.

5 [b]When all the work that King Solomon undertook for the
House of the LORD was completed, Solomon brought the
things that his father David had consecrated—the silver, the
gold, and the utensils—and deposited them in the treasury of
the House of God.
[2] Then Solomon convoked the elders of Israel—all the heads
of the tribes and the ancestral chiefs of the Israelites—in Jerusalem, to bring up the Ark of the Covenant of the LORD from
the City of David, that is, Zion.
[3] All the men of Israel assembled before the king at the Feast,[c]
in the seventh month. [4] When all the elders of Israel had come,
the Levites carried the Ark. [5] They brought up the Ark and the
Tent of Meeting and all the holy vessels that were in the Tent—
the Levite priests brought them up. [6] Meanwhile, King Solomon
and the whole community of Israel, who had gathered to him

a *Or "forks."* *b* *Cf. 1 Kings 7.51–8.11.* *c* *I.e., of Tabernacles.*

right of Moses' candelabrum and five to its left. Some rabbinic tradents say that all ten candelabra were used (i.e., lighted) daily, like that of Moses (see 13.11), while others say that only Moses' candelabrum was lighted (*t. Menaḥ.* 11.10; *y. Shek.* 6.3 [50b]). Some commentators argue that the elevenfold increase in the number of candelabra corresponds, roughly, to the ratio of the area of the Temple court to that of Moses' Tabernacle (12:1 ratio). **9:** In contrast to 1 Kings (6.36; 7.12), Chronicles claims that the inner court was for priests and the outer for lay Israelites. This position, informed by Ezek. chs 40–48, is reflected in postbiblical and rabbinic sources. The "Temple Scroll" from Qumran (11QTemple) speaks of three courts, the outermost being designated for women and minors under the age of twenty. **10–22:** This passage is very similar to 1 Kings 7.39–50. The many apparent contradictions between it and other aspects of Chronicles' description have led many scholars to view this passage as a late addition to the book; particularly noteworthy is the claim (vv. 11 and 16) that Huram made these vessels, contradicting the claim elsewhere that Solomon was responsible for their production. This point is not convincing; Chronicles is following the lead of 1 Kings 7.13ff. The claim that Huram produced some vessels does not belie the position that Solomon had built (i.e., been in charge of building) the Temple. **11:** The wording is reminiscent of the completion of the Tabernacle at Exod. 39.32, again emphasizing the continuity theme. Similarly, the following vv. here parallel Exod. 39.33–41, which list the Tabernacle vessels. **5.1:** For David's role, see, e.g., 1 Chron. 18.8, 10–11; 22.3–4, 14, 16; 29.2–9.

5.2–7.11: Dedication of the Temple. The culmination of all that has transpired since 1 Chron. ch 11. Patterned after 1 Kings 8.1–66, this section consists of three parts: (1) transfer of the Ark into the Temple, (2) Solomon's dedicatory prayer, (3) descent of divine fire and concluding ceremonies. Chronicles adds, at several points, descriptions of the Levitical choral rite, indicative of the enhanced role of Levitical service in Chronicles.

5.2–6.11: Transfer of the Ark. This section may also be titled "The Consecration of the Temple," since the placement of the Ark in

before the Ark, were sacrificing sheep and oxen in such abundance that they could not be numbered or counted.
[7] The priests brought the Ark of the LORD's Covenant to its
place in the inner Sanctuary of the House, in the Holy of Holies, beneath the wings of the cherubim; [8] for the cherubim
had their wings spread out over the place of the Ark so that
the cherubim covered the Ark and its poles from above. [9] The
poles projected beyond the Ark and the ends of the poles were
visible from the front of the inner Sanctuary, but they could
not be seen from the outside; and there they remain to this
day. [10] There was nothing inside the Ark but the two tablets
that Moses placed [there] at Horeb, when the LORD made [a
Covenant] with the Israelites after their departure from Egypt.
[11] When the priests came out of the Sanctuary—all the priests
present had sanctified themselves, without keeping to the set
divisions—[12] all the Levite singers, Asaph, Heman, Jeduthun,
their sons and their brothers, dressed in fine linen, holding
cymbals, harps, and lyres, were standing to the east of the altar, and with them were 120 priests who blew trumpets. [13] The
trumpeters and the singers joined in unison to praise and extol
the LORD; and as the sound of the trumpets, cymbals, and other musical instruments, and the praise of the LORD, "For He is
good, for His steadfast love is eternal," grew louder, the House,
the House of the LORD, was filled with a cloud. [14] The priests
could not stay and perform the service because of the cloud,
for the glory of the LORD filled the House of God.

6 [a] Then Solomon declared:
"The LORD has chosen
To abide in a thick cloud;
2 I have built for You
A stately House,
And a place where You
May dwell forever."

[3] Then, as the whole congregation of Israel stood, the king
turned and blessed the whole congregation of Israel. [4] He said,
"Blessed is the LORD God of Israel, [b]who made a promise to
my father David and fulfilled it.[-b] For He said, [5] 'From the time I
brought My people out of the land of Egypt, I never chose a city
from among all the tribes of Israel to build a House where My
name might abide; nor did I choose anyone to be the leader of
my people Israel. [6] But then I chose Jerusalem for My name to
abide there, and I chose David to rule My people Israel.'
[7] "Now my father David had wanted to build a House for
the name of the LORD God of Israel. [8] But the LORD said to

a Cf. 1 Kings 8.12–53.
b-b Lit. "who spoke with His own mouth a promise to my father David and has fulfilled with His own hands."

the Temple constitutes the latter's consecration. **5.11–14:** Based upon 1 Kings 8.10–11. Vv. 11b–13a are the Chronicler's addition. V. 11b adds to 1 Kings the claim that on this occasion all of the priestly divisions participated equally; see 1 Chron. 24.1–19. **12–13:** Whereas Kings assigns no role to the Levites, Chronicles states that immediately upon transferal of the Ark, the Levites perform, whereupon the LORD's glory appears, veiled in a cloud and hidden from the people's sight. The coincidence of the sacred song with the divine cloud may indicate divine approval of the choral song; alternatively, the choral service, specifically mentioning the divine name and His virtuous acts, evokes the divine Presence. This latter approach sees the daily recital of the choral service as serving to announce, and procure, the LORD's protective presence in the Temple. See 7.1–3. On the phrase *For He is good, for His steadfast love is eternal,* see 1 Chron. 16.34 n.

my father David, 'As for your wanting to build a House for My
name, you do well to want that. 9 However, you shall not build
the House; your son, the issue of your loins, he shall build the
House for My name.' 10 Now the LORD has fulfilled the promise
that He made. I have succeeded[a] my father David and have ascended the throne of Israel, as the LORD promised. I have built
the House for the name of the LORD God of Israel, 11 and there
I have set the Ark containing the Covenant that the LORD made
with the Israelites."

12 Then, standing before the altar of the LORD in front of the
whole congregation of Israel, he spread forth his hands. 13 Solomon had made a bronze platform[b] and placed it in the midst
of the Great Court; it was 5 cubits long and 5 cubits wide and 3
cubits high. He stood on it; then, kneeling in front of the whole
congregation of Israel, he spread forth his hands to heaven
14 and said, "O LORD God of Israel, there is no god like You in
the heavens and on the earth, You who steadfastly maintain
the Covenant with Your servants who walk before You with all
their heart; 15 You who have kept the promises You made to
Your servant, my father David; You made a promise and have
fulfilled it—as is now the case. 16 And now, O LORD God of Israel, keep that promise that You made to Your servant, my father
David, 'You shall never lack a descendant in My sight sitting
on the throne of Israel if only your children will look to their
way and walk in the [path] of My teachings as you have walked
before Me.' 17 Now, therefore, O God of Israel, let the promise
that You made to Your servant, my father David, be confirmed.

18 "Does God really dwell with man on earth? Even the heavens to their uttermost reaches cannot contain You; how much
less this House that I have built! 19 Yet turn, O LORD my God,
to the prayer and supplication of Your servant, and hear the
cry and the prayer that Your servant offers to You. 20 May Your
eyes be open day and night toward this House, toward the
place where You have resolved to make Your name abide; may
You heed the prayers that Your servant offers toward this place.
21 And when You hear the supplications that Your servant and
Your people Israel offer toward this place, give heed in Your
heavenly abode—give heed and pardon.

22 "If a man commits an offense against his fellow, and an
oath is exacted from him, causing him to utter an imprecation against himself, and he comes with his imprecation before Your altar in this House, 23 may You hear in heaven and
take action to judge Your servants, requiting him who is in the
wrong by bringing down the punishment of his conduct on his
head, vindicating him who is in the right by rewarding him according to his righteousness.

a Lit. "risen in place of." *b Meaning of Heb. uncertain.*

6.10: The phrase *throne of Israel* appears only here in Chronicles (cf. 1 Kings 2.4). Together with the more frequent depiction of David and Solomon as occupying the deity's throne, this passage emphasizes that the king's role is that of serving the people, rather than serving his own self-interest; cf. 2 Chron. 2.10; 9.8.

6.12–42: Solomon's dedicatory prayer. This section, together with 7.1–11, may also be titled the "Consecration of the Altar." Though fundamentally similar to 1 Kings 8.22–53, several differences stand out. Chronicles omits 1 Kings 8.50–51, wherein Solomon asks YHVH to grant the exiled people of Israel favor in the eyes of their "captors" and reminds Him of His role in the exodus from Egypt (see 2 Chron. ch 36 nn.). Vv. 36–39 thus jettison the notion of an "acceptable" form of exile; rather, the proper divine response is the ingathering of all exiles (see 2 Chron. 36.22–23 n.). In addition, 2 Chron. 6.12–42 contains fewer references to the exodus (it is omitted from 1 Kings 8.21, 51) and places greater emphasis on the role of the Davidic covenant. **12–17:** Chronicles' citation of these vv. bolsters the stance of those scholars who claim that the author looked forward to a renewal (at some future date) of the Davidic monarchy. 1 Kings 8.22 makes no mention of the bronze altar; Chronicles' text remedies this. Solomon is positioned in front of the bronze altar (2 Chron. 4.1). **13–14:** V. 13 is absent in Kings. The platform's size is identical to that of the Tabernacle altar (Exod. 27.1–2; 38.10). The motive behind this addition is unclear; it is possible that the Chronicler is projecting a practice of his day into the Solomonic Temple. Similar uncertainty obtains regarding the location of this platform; it may have been in the inner (priestly court), though it is more likely to have been in the outer (lay) court. **16:** 1 Kings 8.25 reads "to walk before me." Chronicles expresses the "Torah-centered" perspective, wherein proper service of God is defined, exclusively, by observance

24 “Should Your people Israel be defeated by an enemy because they have sinned against You, and then once again acknowledge Your name and offer prayer and supplication to You in this House, 25 may You hear in heaven and pardon the sin of Your people Israel, and restore them to the land that You gave to them and to their fathers.

26 “Should the heavens be shut up and there be no rain because they have sinned against You, and then they pray toward this place and acknowledge Your name and repent of their sins, because You humbled them, 27 may You hear in heaven and pardon the sin of Your servants, Your people Israel, when You have shown them the proper way in which they are to walk, and send down rain upon the land that You gave to Your people as their heritage. 28 So, too, if there is a famine in the land, if there is pestilence, blight, mildew, locusts, or caterpillars, or if an enemy oppresses them in any of the settlements of their land.

“In any plague and in any disease, 29 any prayer or supplication offered by any person among all Your people Israel—each of whom knows his affliction and his pain—when he spreads forth his hands toward this House, 30 may You hear in Your heavenly abode, and pardon. Deal with each man according to his ways as You know his heart to be—for You alone know the hearts of all men—31 so that they may revere You all the days that they live on the land that You gave to our fathers.

32 “Or if a foreigner who is not of Your people Israel comes from a distant land for the sake of Your great name, Your mighty hand, and Your outstretched arm, if he comes to pray toward this House, 33 may You hear in Your heavenly abode and grant whatever the foreigner appeals to You for. Thus all the peoples of the earth will know Your name and revere You, as does Your people Israel; and they will recognize that Your name is attached to this House that I have built.

34 “When Your people take the field against their enemies in a campaign on which You send them, and they pray to You in the direction of the city which You have chosen and the House which I have built to Your name, 35 may You hear in heaven their prayer and supplication and uphold their cause.

36 “When they sin against You—for there is no person who does not sin—and You are angry with them and deliver them to the enemy, and their captors carry them off to an enemy land, near or far; 37 and they take it to heart in the land to which they have been carried off, and repent and make supplication to You in the land of their captivity, saying, ‘We have sinned, we have acted perversely, we have acted wickedly,’ 38 and they turn back to You with all their heart and soul, in the land of their captivity where they were carried off, and pray in the direction of their land which You gave to their fathers and the

of the commandments. The Heb word “torah,” in this and other contexts, has been rendered by some commentators *teachings* (as here) and by others as “the Torah (i.e., Pentateuch)”; in Chronicles, the latter is more likely. **23–33:** The foreigner. This passage encourages the participation of non-Israelites in recognizing YHVH (though not explicitly requiring the denial of other deities) and the Jerusalem Temple. The passage does not spell out the nature of foreign presence within the Temple precincts; the formulation “toward this house” suggests that foreigners may enter only the outer court(s) of the Temple. 1 Chron. 16.11, 29 (“enter before Him”) however, may permit foreigners to enter the inner court as well. Neither this passage nor others in Chronicles acknowledges the active participation of foreigners in sacrificial activity, as does Isa. 56.6–8. Chronicles expresses a more welcoming position than Ezek. 44.9.

city which You have chosen, and toward the House which I
have built for Your name—39 may You hear their prayer and
supplication in Your heavenly abode, uphold their cause, and
pardon Your people who have sinned against You. 40 Now My
God, may Your eyes be open and Your ears attentive to prayer
from this place, and now,

41 Advance, O LORD God, to your resting-place,
You and Your mighty Ark.
Your priests, O LORD God, are clothed in triumph;
Your loyal ones will rejoice in [Your] goodness.
42 O LORD God,
do not reject Your anointed one;
remember the loyalty of Your servant David."

7 [a]When Solomon finished praying, fire descended from
heaven and consumed the burnt offering and the sacrifices, and the glory of the LORD filled the House. 2 The priests
could not enter the House of the LORD, for the glory of the
LORD filled the House of the LORD. 3 All the Israelites witnessed
the descent of the fire and the glory of the LORD on the House;
they knelt with their faces to the ground and prostrated themselves, praising the LORD, "For He is good, for His steadfast
love is eternal."

a Cf. 1 Kings 8.54–9.9.

41–42: These vv. appear (with some variation) in Ps. 132.8–10; since they are contextually appropriate, Chronicles places them here, in Solomon's mouth. The concluding words *(the loyalty of Your servant David)* in Heb are ambiguous, referring either to David's acts of steadfast love toward the LORD or the LORD's steadfast love toward David (see Isa. 55.3); here they emphasize the fulfillment of David's role in establishing the cult. In either case, the passage is noteworthy because of its implicit recognition of the notion of transferring the merits (or special relation with the deity) from one individual to another; see the discussion of divine retribution in the intro. The singular *Your anointed one,* attested in most mss, refers to Solomon; Codex Leningrad (the oldest complete mss of the Bible in Heb) reads the plural "anointed ones," probably referring to Solomon and David, both of whom worked tirelessly on behalf of the Temple. These vv. differ from the concluding part of Solomon's prayer in 2 Kings (8.54–61). There, Solomon petitions the LORD to accept Israel's future prayers in the Temple; here, Solomon's words form part of the present consecration of the altar. Citation of Psalms in Chronicles, but not in Kings may suggest that some form had become known by the time of the Chronicler; since Ps. 132 addresses many topics central to Chronicles (e.g., the dynastic promise, David's devotion to the cult), it is especially suitable for quotation. The phrase *mighty Ark* (v. 41) reflects the Ark's function as divine throne-footstool (see 1 Chron. 13.6) and the view that the divine warrior, seated upon the Ark/cherubs, would lead His people in (victorious) battle (e.g., Num. 10.35; 1 Sam. 4.3–8; see also Ps. 78.61). Chronicles has left its mark on traditional Jewish prayer, in that it is customary in many congregations to recite the Psalms version of these vv. when returning the Torah scroll to the synagogue "Ark," its "resting place." The conclusion to the prayer omits the reference to the exodus from Egypt as the basis for invoking divine favor (1 Kings 8.50–51); the Davidic covenant of Ps. 132 appears in its place. In contrast to Ps. 132.9, which lit. reads "don righteousness" ("sedeq"), Chronicles asks that the priests be "clothed" in salvation; this term may refer to protection from harm potentially resulting from lack of precision in the performance of Temple responsibilities (see 1 Chron. 13.10). Similarly, Chronicles' Solomon requests that the people of Israel rejoice in "goodness," which may reflect belief in the Temple's role (as the Deity's residence) in assuring the people's welfare and prosperity. This echoes Ps. 132.15; but, whereas that v. addresses the welfare of the chosen city (Jerusalem), the present passage concerns all upstanding Israelites and is consonant with the book's depiction of national prosperity throughout Solomon's tenure.

7.1–11: Descent of divine fire and concluding ceremonies. 1–3: The divine Presence fills the Temple, in response to Solomon's prayer; these vv. are absent in 1 Kings. Vv. 1 and 3 echo the dedication of the Mosaic Tabernacle at Lev. 9.24; in both passages a divine fire consumes the sacrifice in the presence of the people, who then prostrate themselves and sing the LORD's praise. (See also the reference to the divine Presence three times in these three vv. and in Lev. 9.23.) The Chronicler thus again establishes a continuum between the Tabernacle and Temple, including, by implication, the Second Temple of his own day; see 1 Chron. 21.26, which forms the connecting link between Lev. ch 9 and the present v. The recurring refrain, "for He is good ... eternal" (see 1 Chron. 16.34 n.) expresses the belief in the beneficence and protection of Him whose glory resides in the Temple. The present passage complements the appearance of the divine glory ("kavod") at 5.11–14. The former marks the dedication of the Temple, accomplished by placement of the Ark within it, the latter the dedication of the altar.

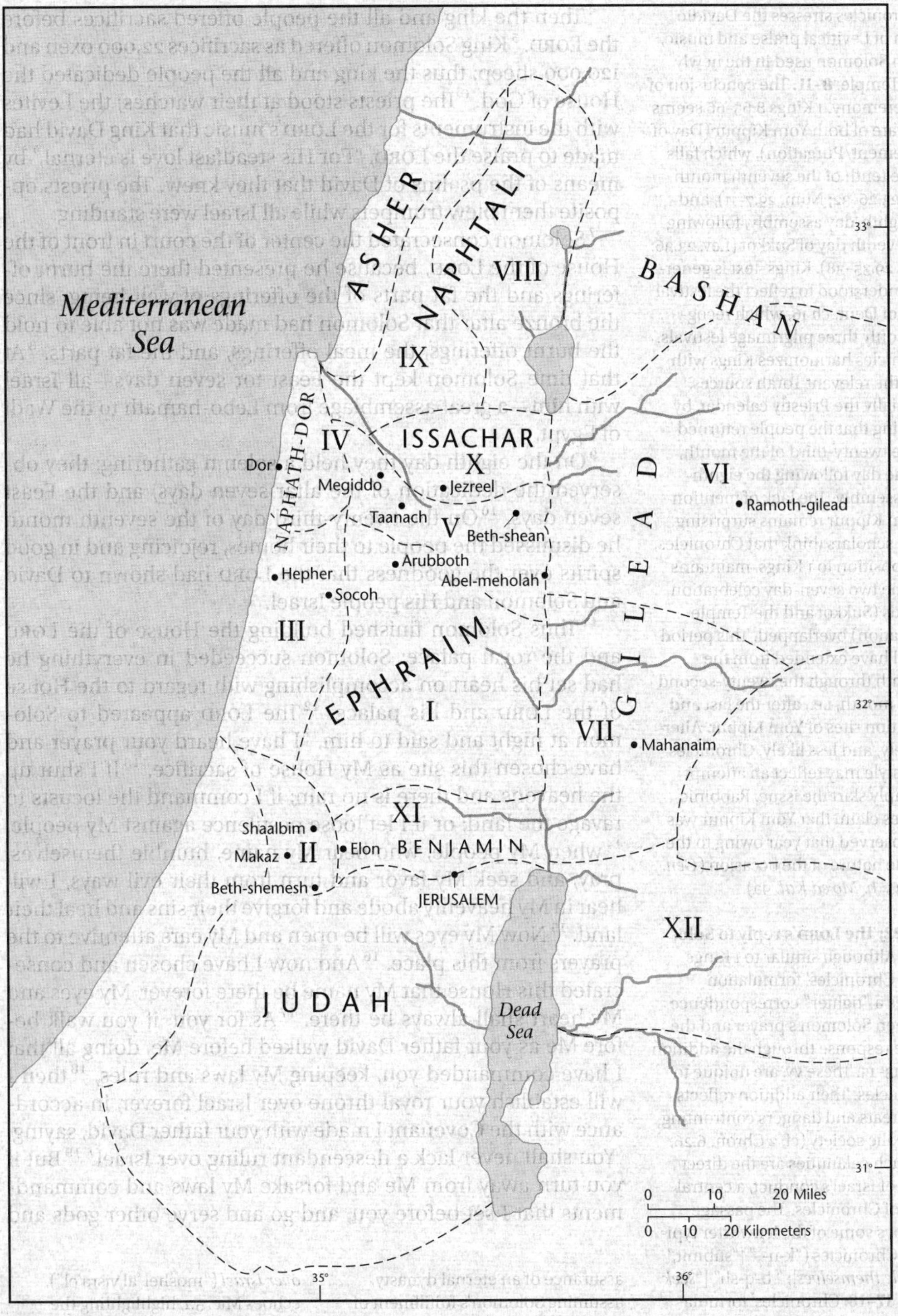

The kingdom of Solomon according to Second Chronicles

4 Then the king and all the people offered sacrifices before the LORD. 5 King Solomon offered as sacrifices 22,000 oxen and 120,000 sheep; thus the king and all the people dedicated the House of God. 6 The priests stood at their watches; the Levites with the instruments for the LORD's music that King David had made to praise the LORD, "For His steadfast love is eternal," by means of the psalms of David that they knew. The priests opposite them blew trumpets while all Israel were standing.

7 Solomon consecrated the center of the court in front of the House of the LORD, because he presented there the burnt offerings and the fat parts of the offerings of well-being, since the bronze altar that Solomon had made was not able to hold the burnt offerings, the meal offerings, and the fat parts. 8 At that time Solomon kept the Feast for seven days—all Israel with him—a great assemblage from Lebo-hamath to the Wadi of Egypt.

9 On the eighth day they held a solemn gathering; they observed the dedication of the altar seven days, and the Feast seven days. 10 On the twenty-third day of the seventh month he dismissed the people to their homes, rejoicing and in good spirits over the goodness that the LORD had shown to David and Solomon and His people Israel.

11 Thus Solomon finished building the House of the LORD and the royal palace; Solomon succeeded in everything he had set his heart on accomplishing with regard to the House of the LORD and his palace. 12 The LORD appeared to Solomon at night and said to him, "I have heard your prayer and have chosen this site as My House of sacrifice. 13 If I shut up the heavens and there is no rain; if I command the locusts to ravage the land; or if I let loose pestilence against My people, 14 when My people, who bear My name, humble themselves, pray, and seek My favor and turn from their evil ways, I will hear in My heavenly abode and forgive their sins and heal their land. 15 Now My eyes will be open and My ears attentive to the prayers from this place. 16 And now I have chosen and consecrated this House that My name be there forever. My eyes and My heart shall always be there. 17 As for you, if you walk before Me as your father David walked before Me, doing all that I have commanded you, keeping My laws and rules, 18 then I will establish your royal throne over Israel forever, in accordance with the Covenant I made with your father David, saying, 'You shall never lack a descendant ruling over Israel.' 19 But if you turn away from Me and forsake My laws and commandments that I set before you, and go and serve other gods and

6: Chronicles stresses the Davidic origin of Levitical praise and music, which Solomon used in the newly built Temple. **8–11:** The conclusion of the ceremony. 1 Kings 8.65–66 seems unaware of both Yom Kippur (Day of Atonement/Purgation), which falls on the tenth of the seventh month (Lev. 23.26–32; Num. 29.7–11), and the eighth-day assembly, following the seventh day of Sukkot (Lev. 23.36; Num. 29.35–38). Kings' text is generally understood to reflect the festival cycle of Deut. ch 16, which recognizes only three pilgrimage festivals. Chronicles harmonizes Kings with all of the relevant Torah sources, especially the Priestly calendar, by claiming that the people returned on the twenty-third of the month, i.e., the day following the eighth-day assembly. The lack of mention of Yom Kippur remains surprising. Some scholars think that Chronicles, in opposition to 1 Kings, maintains that the two seven-day celebration periods (Sukkot and the Temple dedication) overlapped. This period would have extended from the fifteenth through the twenty-second of the month, i.e., after the fast and purgation rites of Yom Kippur. Alternatively, and less likely, Chronicles' terse style may reflect an attempt to simply skirt the issue. Rabbinic sources claim that Yom Kippur was not observed that year owing to the unique nature of the occasion (*Gen. Rab.* 35; *b. Mo'ed Kat.* 9a).

7.12–22: The LORD's reply to Solomon. Although similar to 1 Kings 9.2–9, Chronicles' formulation creates a "tighter" correspondence between Solomon's prayer and the divine response through the addition of vv. 13–15. These vv. are unique to Chronicles. Their addition reflects the threats and dangers confronting postexilic society (cf. 2 Chron. 6.26, 28); such calamities are the direct result of Israel's conduct, a central tenet of Chronicles. The passage employs some of the leitwörter typical of Chronicles ("k-n-ʿ" ["submit," *humble themselves*]; " b-q-sh" ["*seek* out"]) **17–18:** Chronicles' formulation (cf. 1 Kings 9.5) highlights the assurance of an eternal dynasty, assuming Solomon's fulfillment of the necessary conditions. V. 18, *ruling over Israel* ("moshel ʿal yisraʾel"), echoes Mic. 5.1, highlighting the dynastic promise.

worship them, 20 then I will uproot them[a] from My land that
I gave them, and this House that I consecrated to My name I
shall cast out of my sight, and make it a proverb and a byword
among all peoples. 21 And as for this House, once so exalted,
everyone passing by it shall be appalled and say, 'Why did the
Lord do thus to this land and to this House?' 22 And the reply will be, 'It is because they forsook the Lord God of their
fathers who freed them from the land of Egypt, and adopted
other gods and worshiped them and served them; therefore
He brought all this calamity upon them.'"

8 [b]At the end of twenty years, during which Solomon constructed the House of the Lord and his palace—2 Solomon
also rebuilt the cities that Huram had given to him,[c] and settled Israelites in them—3 Solomon marched against Hamath-
zobah and overpowered it. 4 He built Tadmor in the desert and
all the garrison towns that he built in Hamath. 5 He built Upper Beth-horon and Lower Beth-horon as fortified cities with
walls, gates, and bars, 6 as well as Baalath and all of Solomon's
garrison towns, chariot towns, and cavalry towns—everything
that Solomon desired to build in Jerusalem and in the Lebanon, and throughout the territory that he ruled. 7 All the people that were left of the Hittites, Amorites, Perizzites, Hivites,
and Jebusites, none of whom were of Israelite stock—8 those of
their descendants who were left after them in the land, whom
the Israelites had not annihilated—these Solomon subjected
to forced labor, as is still the case. 9 But the Israelites, none of
whom Solomon enslaved for his works, served as soldiers and
as his chief officers, and as commanders of his chariotry and
cavalry. 10 These were King Solomon's prefects—250 foremen

a I.e., Israel; cf. 1 Kings 9.7. *b Cf. 1 Kings 9.10–28.* *c Lit. "Solomon."*

8.1–16: Other projects. 1–6: Solomon expands Israel's territory. 1 Kings 9.10–13 states that Solomon relinquished twenty cities to Hiram (Huram) in payment for material. Hiram there addresses Solomon as "my brother," a technical term used in the ancient Near East between sovereigns of equal stature, and then reproves him for having made payment with land of poor quality. Some medieval and modern commentators adopt a harmonistic approach to the parallel passages, arguing that Kings and Chronicles complement each other. Attempts at harmonizing the accounts of Chronicles and 1 Kings 9.10–13 date back to Josephus, who maintained that upon seeing the poor quality of the land given to him by Solomon, Hiram decided to return it Solomon. The harmonistic approach has been buttressed by the fact that Israel's northern frontier shifted during the early monarchy between Israelite and Phoenician rule. Even allowing for the plausibility of such a scenario, the question remains: why did neither biblical source relate the "facts" in their entirety? The ineluctable conclusion is that Chronicles' text is tendentious. Chronicles could not accept the fact that Solomon, the wealthiest of kings, would be forced to relinquish land in payment. This is especially problematic for Chronicles, given its maximalistic approach to Israel's borders and its view that the entirety of Israel's territory had been settled before David's time (see 1 Chron. 13.5; cf. the critique of Saul at 1 Chron. 10.7). In addition, the absence of any apparent motive for Huram's (unilateral) gesture suggests that Chronicles' position is tendentious. Furthermore, Huram's reproof of Solomon as depicted in Kings is unacceptable to Chronicles (see 1.18–2.17 n.). The stature of Chronicles' Huram, portrayed as a vassal, is consistently lessened vis-à-vis that detailed in 1 Kings, where he is the dominant figure. Vv. 3–6, which have as their theme "Solomon as successful builder of Israel," then form a seamless continuation of v. 2. Indeed, this passage mentions only Solomon's achievements; setbacks mentioned in 1 Kings, e.g., Pharaoh's incursion into Israel and capture of the city of Gezer (1 Kings 9.16), are omitted by Chronicles. **1–2:** Huram's unexplained act of altruism may be Chronicles' way of depicting Huram not just as an admirer of Solomon and the Israelite cult but as a vassal who willingly conveys tribute to the sovereign; in this singular instance, the tribute takes the form of land rather than movable or fungible items. For other forms of tribute presented to Solomon, see 2 Chron. 9.23–24. Chronicles, unlike 1 Kings 6.38–7.1, nowhere specifies that the Temple was built in seven years and Solomon's palace in thirteen. Josephus (*Ant.*, 8.5.1. [8:130–32]) explained the difference between the two projects as reflecting Solomon's alacrity in dealing with the Temple, not as indicative of Solomon's greater concern for the opulence of his palace. Chronicles' reticence, however, suggests that the author may have sensed that the data in 1 Kings undermine his idealized portrayal of Solomon. **3–10:** *Lebanon,* the mountains of eastern Lebanon. **10:** *250:* 1 Kings 9.23 reads "550." Medieval commentators (Rashi, Radak) averred that the present v. refers only to Israelites, whereas 1 Kings ch 9 includes the foreign officials. Some

over the people. 11 Solomon brought up Pharaoh's daughter
from the City of David to the palace that he had built for her,
for he said, "No wife of mine shall dwell in a palace of King
David of Israel, for [the area] is sacred since the Ark of the LORD
has entered it."
12 At that time, Solomon offered burnt offerings on the altar
that he had built in front of the porch. 13 What was due for each
day he sacrificed according to the commandment of Moses
for the sabbaths, the new moons, and the thrice-yearly festivals—the Feast of Unleavened Bread, the Feast of Weeks, and
the Feast of Booths. 14 Following the prescription of his father
David, he set up the divisions of the priests for their duties, and
the Levites for their watches, to praise and to serve alongside
the priests, according to each day's requirement, and the gatekeepers in their watches, gate by gate, for such was the commandment of David, the man of God. 15 They did not depart
from the commandment of the king relating to the priests and
the Levites in all these matters and also relating to the treasuries. 16 And all of Solomon's work was well executed from the
day the House of the LORD was founded until the House of the
LORD was completed to perfection.
17 At that time Solomon went to Ezion-geber and to Eloth on
the seacoast of the land of Edom. 18 Huram sent him, under the
charge of servants, a fleet with a crew of expert seamen; they
went with Solomon's men to Ophir, and obtained gold there
in the amount of 450 talents, which they brought to King Solomon.

9 [a] The queen of Sheba heard of Solomon's fame, and came
to Jerusalem to test Solomon with hard questions, accompanied by a very large retinue, including camels bearing
spices, a great quantity of gold, and precious stones. When
she came to Solomon, she spoke to him of all that she had on

a *Cf. 1 Kings 10; 11.41–43.*

have observed that the differential of "300" corresponds to a similar difference between 2.17 (3,600 supervisors) and 1 Kings 5.30 (3,300 supervisors); thus the total number is the same in each book. This explanation is problematic; Chronicles plainly states that Gentile supervisors are involved at 2.17, Israelites here. The present v. may simply be the result of scribal error. **11:** 1 Kings 9.10–13, Chronicles' source, functions as part of the "Solomon as builder" theme; he fortifies cities throughout his domain, including Jerusalem, and suggests that his wife's move was the result of personal motives. Chronicles gives the incident a religious motive; he moves his wife into another domicile, because her presence in the sacred precincts is improper. The juxtaposition of this v. to the following (reworked) passage, along with the shared Heb term "heʿelah" *(brought up,* "offered"*),* suggests a shared theme: Solomon as guardian and patron of the Temple and its environs. Chronicles' depiction of Solomon is at polar odds with that of Kings. The latter has Solomon tolerating and even supporting the foreign worship of his many wives (1 Kings 11.1). Chronicles not only omits this entire issue—Solomon's numerous wives as well as their religious offenses—but stresses that Solomon exhibited religious zeal precisely by "cracking down" on his wife. It is likely that the term here translated *City of David* denotes the earlier location of the palatial complex or its wings (cf. LXX, which renders "city" throughout the v.). It is uncertain whether Solomon's concern was the impurity caused by menstruation (see Lev. 15.19–24) or by sexual intercourse (Lev. 15.16–18). That Solomon takes this step only after the Temple's construction raises the question as to whether Chronicles' explanation reflects a "genuine" legal position or is merely an ad hoc comment, intended to highlight Solomon's extreme zeal in protecting the sanctity of the Temple complex. For discussion of Solomon's marriage to a foreigner, see intro. **12–16:** Chronicles elaborates on 1 Kings 9.25, bringing it into harmony with Num. chs 28–29 and Deut. ch 16. In general the Chronicler "updates" his sources by bringing them in conformity with Priestly and Deuteronomic Torah material; the Chronicler assumes that righteous kings such as Solomon knew the entire Torah and certainly followed its laws. **14:** *Man of God,* a title also applied to Moses (Deut. 33.1; Ps. 90.1) as well as to several other biblical figures. Its purpose here is to highlight the parallel between David and Moses as founders of Israel's cult and its norms.

8.17–9.31: Solomon's grandeur. 8.17–18: Solomon is again depicted as the dominant monarch. That Huram's ships were transported either by land or by a canal connecting the Red Sea and the Nile is historically improbable. Chronicles' formulation here, while differing only slightly from 1 Kings 9.26–28, may indicate that Huram (again) unilaterally and altruistically aided Solomon; note that there is no suggestion here that Huram's men brought gold to Huram. **9.1–12:** Queen of Sheba visits. This

her mind. 2 Solomon had answers for all her questions; there was nothing that Solomon did not know, nothing to which he could not give her an answer.

3 When the queen of Sheba saw how wise Solomon was and the palace he had built, 4 the fare of his table, the seating of his courtiers, the service and attire of his attendants, his butlers and their attire, and the procession with which he went up to the House of the LORD, it took her breath away. 5 She said to the king, "What I heard in my own land about you and your wisdom was true. 6 I did not believe what they said until I came and saw with my own eyes that not even the half of your great wisdom had been described to me; you surpass the report that I heard. 7 How fortunate are your men and how fortunate are these courtiers of yours who are always in attendance on you and can hear your wisdom! 8 Blessed is the LORD your God, who favored you and set you on His throne as a king before the LORD. It is because of your God's love for Israel and in order to establish them forever that He made you king over them to execute righteous justice."

9 She presented the king with 120 talents of gold, and a vast quantity of spices and precious stones. There were no such spices as those which the queen of Sheba gave to King Solomon—10 also, the servants of Huram and Solomon who brought gold from Ophir brought algum-wood and precious stones. 11 The king made of the algum-wood ramps for the House of the LORD and for the royal palace, and lyres and harps for the musicians, whose like had never before been seen in the land of Judah—12 King Solomon, in turn, gave the queen of Sheba everything she expressed a desire for, exceeding a return for what she had brought to the king. Then she and her courtiers left and returned to her own land.

13 The gold that Solomon received every year weighed 666 gold talents, 14 besides what traders and merchants brought, and the gold and silver that all the kings of Arabia and governors of the regions brought to Solomon. 15 King Solomon made 200 shields of beaten gold—600 shekels of beaten gold for each shield, 16 and 300 bucklers of beaten gold—300 [shekels] of gold for each buckler. The king placed them in the Lebanon Forest House. 17 The king also made a large throne of ivory, overlaid with pure gold. 18 Six steps led up to the throne; and the throne had a golden footstool attached to it, and arms on either side of the seat. Two lions stood beside the arms, 19 and twelve lions stood on the six steps, six on either side. None such was ever made for any other kingdom. 20 All of King Solomon's drinking vessels were of gold, and all the utensils of the Lebanon Forest House were of pure gold; silver counted for nothing in Solomon's days. 21 The king's fleet traveled to Tarshish with Huram's servants. Once every three years, the Tarshish fleet came in, bearing gold and silver, ivory, apes, and peacocks.

passage is largely identical to 1 Kings 10.11–13; it furthers Chronicles' depiction of Solomon's success and majesty. **8:** This v. forms an inclusio with the blessing uttered by Huram at 2.11. (Kings mentions this only once; see 1 Kings 10.9.) Huram, a northern neighbor of Israel, and the queen of Sheba, from a country to the south, together symbolize universal recognition of Solomon's importance and, specifically, that the Davidic monarch is a concrete sign of the LORD's love for Israel. This is another expression of Chronicles' messianic aspirations. Chronicles again claims that the Davidic monarchs are the earthly representatives of divine rule; see 1 Chron. 17.14 and cf. 1 Kings 10.9. **12:** *Gave [her] ... everything she expressed a desire for:* The exchange of gifts is a mark of cordial relations between sovereigns; Chronicles probably did not view it as signifying a formal treaty; see 2.16–17. **13–28:** Miscellaneous notices. Following 1 Kings 10.14–28, with minor differences. **18–19:** The use of *twelve lions* probably reflects the unity of Israel's tribes. Rabbinic sources deal extensively with the design and significance of Solomon's throne; some (*Tg. Esth. II*, 1.1) attribute its production to Huram. Although the reticence of rabbinic sources implies no criticism of Solomon's use of iconography, Josephus (*Ant.* 8.195–96) states that Solomon's production of the lion images was sinful, as was the production of the molten sea (1 Kings 7.23–26); see 4.2–5. **21–23:** Solomon's commercial ventures. Chronicles views the opulent throne positively. Elsewhere the Bible identifies *Tarshish* as a source of silver, iron, and lead—not gold, ivory, apes, etc. 1 Kings 10.22 refers to "Tarshish vessels," with no reference to the vessels' destination. Some scholars locate Tarshish in Africa, along the Red Sea, and historical sources indicate that Tarshish lay in the Mediterranean basin, not along the Red Sea, as emerges from Chronicles. Chronicles' text may reflect an ancient misunderstanding of a technical term, a phenomenon attested in LXX to 1 Kings 10.22, as well.

22 King Solomon surpassed all the kings of the earth in wealth
and wisdom. 23 All the kings of the earth came to pay homage
to Solomon and to listen to the wisdom with which God had
endowed him. 24 Each brought his tribute—silver and gold objects, robes, weapons, and spices, horses and mules—in the
amount due each year. 25 Solomon had 4,000 stalls for horses
and chariots, and 12,000 horsemen, which he stationed in the
chariot towns and with the king in Jerusalem. 26 He ruled over
all the kings from the Euphrates to the land of the Philistines
and to the border of Egypt. 27 The king made silver as plentiful
in Jerusalem as stones, and cedars as plentiful as sycamores
in the Shephelah. 28 Horses were brought for Solomon from
Egypt and all the lands. 29 The other events of Solomon's reign,
early and late, are recorded in the chronicle of the prophet
Nathan and in the prophecies of Ahijah the Shilonite and in
the visions of Jedo the seer concerning Jeroboam son of Nebat. 30 Solomon reigned forty years over all Israel in Jerusalem.
31 Solomon slept with his fathers and was buried in the city of
his father David; his son Rehoboam succeeded him as king.

10 [a]Rehoboam went to Shechem, for all Israel had come
to Shechem to acclaim him king. 2 Jeroboam son of Nebat learned of it while he was in Egypt where he had fled from

a Cf. 1 Kings 12.1–19.

Tarshish fleet or Tarshish ships originally denoted a type of maritime vessel, not the ship's destination or route; see 20.36–37. **25–28:** Solomon's extreme wealth would seem to be in violation of Deut. 17.17 and may have led the translators of LXX to 1 Kings to bring Solomon's depiction more in line with Deut. ch 17. Indeed, rabbinic sources are critical of the excessive number of horses, in violation of the same v. (see *b. Sanh.* 21b). Some medieval Jewish scholars maintained that Deut.'s limitation on royal wealth refers only to wealth gained by levying of taxes (commentaries of R. Meir Abulafia, Nissim Gerondi ad *b. Sanh.* 21b). Alternatively, some explained that the monarch was prohibited only from amassing wealth for purely personal glory, whereas wealth used to bring honor to the kingdom was permitted (Maimonides, *Laws of Kings and their Wars,* Menahem ha-Meiri, *b. Sanh.* 21b). **26:** Solomon's empire. Consistent with its depiction above (1 Chron. 13.5; 2 Chron. 7.8; 8.3–8) of expanded borders, Chronicles portrays Solomon as having ruled over a (relatively) large region. **29–31:** No mention is made of Solomon's offenses or of Jeroboam (who would later be the first king of the Northern Kingdom) noted in 1 Kings ch 11. Following a model established with David, Solomon's official biography was composed by prophets; see 1 Chron. 29.28–30. Solomon's reign of forty years parallels that of David, a further example of the way these monarchs mirror each other for the Chronicler. Many scholars maintain, with Josephus's *Ant.*, that Iddo (Jedo), the seer, is to be identified with the anonymous prophet of 1 Kings 13.1–10; see 12.15; 13.22. The mention of the prophet *Ahijah the Shilonite* is especially surprising, since according to 1 Kings 11.29–30; 12.15, omitted by Chronicles, he tells Solomon of the dissolution of the united monarchy.

10.1–36.23: From Rehoboam to the exile. This section builds on the parallels in Kings, but offers much new information and many differing assessments of monarchs. The literary motifs (or topoi) in this section are: building reports, military stock and capabilities, sickness and death, military victories and defeats. With regard to each of these, arguments have been made in support of both their (purported) fictional character as well as their (purported) factual nature, based on authentic sources that Chronicles, but not the author of Kings, had. Perhaps the most salient topos of this section is that of war accounts. Fifteen such reports appear, all without parallel in Kings. The novel features of Chronicles' formulation are viewed by some as the creation of its author, who sought to portray the first four post-Solomonic kings positively, so as to establish the legitimacy of Judah over its northern neighbor, the Samaritans. It is further argued that the battles reported here reflect Second Temple reality, when Judah was surrounded by neighbors who posed a territorial and religious threat. The message of these reports is understood to be that salvation lies in cultic fidelity. Other scholars counter, more persuasively, by noting that Chronicles' treatment of the first four post-Solomonic kings is not uniformly positive in nature. With regard to the battle accounts, these scholars acknowledge that they are all characterized by chronistic style and moralizing, but argue that the numerous details (of geography, proper nouns, etc.) point to a genuine historical basis. In addition, it is argued that most of the battles involve Israelite military activity, such that Israel's victories cannot be attributed, exclusively, to religious fidelity. The bulk of this section, 10.1–28.27, describes a divided "house." Judah, and parts of the other tribes who identify with Judah, remain faithful to the Davidic monarchy and the Jerusalem Temple. The bulk of the northern tribes follow the illegitimate kings

King Solomon, and Jeroboam returned from Egypt. 3 They sent for him; and Jeroboam and all Israel came and spoke to Rehoboam as follows: 4 "Your father made our yoke heavy. Now lighten the harsh labor and the heavy yoke that your father laid on us, and we will serve you." 5 He answered them, "Come back to me in three days." So the people went away.

6 King Rehoboam took counsel with the elders who had served during the lifetime of his father Solomon. He said, "What answer do you counsel to give these people?" 7 They answered him, "If you will be good to these people and appease them and speak to them with kind words, they will be your servants always." 8 But he ignored the counsel that the elders gave him, and took counsel with the young men who had grown up with him and were serving him. 9 "What," he asked, "do you counsel that we reply to these people who said to me, 'Lighten the yoke that your father laid on us'?" 10 And the young men who had grown up with him answered, "Speak thus to the people who said to you, 'Your father made our yoke heavy, now you make it lighter for us.' Say to them, 'My little finger is thicker than my father's loins. 11 My father imposed a heavy yoke on you, and I will add to your yoke; my father flogged you with whips, but I [will do so] with scorpions.'"

12 Jeroboam and all the people came to Rehoboam on the third day, since the king had told them, "Come back on the third day." 13 The king answered them harshly; thus King Rehoboam ignored the elders' counsel. 14 He spoke to them in accordance with the counsel of the young men, and said, [a-]"I will make[-a] your yoke heavy, and I will add to it; my father flogged you with whips, but I [will do so] with scorpions." 15 The king did not listen to the people, for God had brought it about in order that the LORD might fulfill the promise that He had made through Ahijah the Shilonite to Jeroboam son of Nebat. 16 When all Israel [saw] that the king had not listened to them, the people answered the king:

"We have no portion in David,
No share in Jesse's son!
To your tents, O Israel!
Now look to your own house, O David."

So all Israel returned to their homes.[b] 17 But Rehoboam continued to reign over the Israelites who lived in the towns of Judah.

a-a Some mss. and printed editions read "my father made"; cf. 1 Kings 12.14.
b Lit. "tents."

of (northern) Israel. As noted in the intro., Chronicles focuses exclusively on Judah (and its supporters), mentioning the northern empire only where it affects Judah's fortunes. Though some scholars see the "anti-northern" critique as applying to the populace of the north, namely the Samaritans who were contemporaries of the Chronicler, the evidence of Chronicles favors the view that the Chronicler inveighs only against the northern monarchs and their supporters.

10.1–11.4: Rehoboam's coronation and division of the monarchy. Shechem was an ancient religious center of the northern tribes. The choice of this northern site, rather than Jerusalem, for Rehoboam's coronation indicates that there was opposition among the northern tribes to Rehoboam's accession, most likely because they feared that he would continue Solomon's policies of conscription for forced labor. Thus, although Chronicles' description of Solomon's reign creates the impression of prosperity and almost utopian social harmony, this passage, along with the ensuing episode, indicates that the actual situation was quite different. **10.1:** Alternatively, given the author's claim (13.7–8) that the blame for the dissolution of the united monarchy lay entirely with the northern leaders—despite the lack of any factual basis for their claims (see 1.14–17)—the present v. may simply indicate that Rehoboam was aware of the growing (and unjustified) agitation among the northern leaders for independence from Judah. **2–3:** These vv. are problematic in Chronicles, since the relevant background material in Kings has been omitted. 1 Kings 11.29–40 relates the story of Jeroboam as told by Ahijah the prophet: Owing to Solomon's role in his wives' cultic offenses, the northern tribes will be taken away from Solomon and Jeroboam will rule over these tribes. Thereafter, Jeroboam flees to Egypt and returns to the land of Israel following Solomon's demise. Chronicles deletes all of this material since it indicates that the period of Solomon's rule was not quite so idyllic, nor was his personal conduct exemplary and Chronicles views the very existence of a non-Davidic dynasty as both treasonous and rebellion against God. Chronicles' omission of this material creates several problems. First, the reader of Chronicles has no prior acquaintance with Jeroboam,

18 King Rehoboam sent out Hadoram, who was in charge of the
forced labor, but the Israelites pelted him to death with stones.
Thereupon, King Rehoboam hurriedly mounted his chariot
and fled to Jerusalem. 19 Israel has been in revolt against the
house of David to this day.

11 [a]When Rehoboam arrived in Jerusalem, he mustered the
house of Judah and Benjamin, 180,000 picked fighting
men, to make war with Israel in order to restore the kingdom to
Rehoboam. 2 But the word of the LORD came to Shemaiah, the
man of God: 3 "Say to Rehoboam son of Solomon king of Judah,
and to all Israel in Judah and Benjamin: 4 Thus said the LORD:
You shall not set out to make war on your kinsmen. Let every
man return to his home, for this thing has been brought about
by Me." They heeded the words of the LORD and refrained from
marching against Jeroboam. 5 Rehoboam dwelt in Jerusalem
and built fortified towns in Judah. 6 He built up Bethlehem, and
Etam, and Tekoa, 7 and Beth-zur, and Soco, and Adullam, 8 and
Gath, and Mareshah, and Ziph, 9 and Adoraim, and Lachish,
and Azekah, 10 and Zorah, and Aijalon, and Hebron, which are
in Judah and in Benjamin, as fortified towns. 11 He strengthened the fortified towns and put commanders in them, along
with stores of food, oil, and wine, 12 and shields and spears in
every town. He strengthened them exceedingly; thus Judah
and Benjamin were his.

13 The priests and the Levites, from all their territories
throughout Israel, presented themselves to him. 14 The Levites
had left their pasturelands and their holdings and had set out
for Judah and Jerusalem, for Jeroboam and his sons had prevented them from serving the LORD, 15 having appointed his
own priests for the shrines, goat-demons, and calves which he
had made. 16 From all the tribes of Israel, those intent on seeking the LORD God of Israel followed them to Jerusalem, to sacrifice to the LORD God of their fathers. 17 They strengthened the
kingdom of Judah, and supported Rehoboam son of Solomon

a With 11.1–4, cf. 1 Kings 12.21–24.

unless he has previously read 1 Kings. Many scholars therefore argue that Chronicles, here and elsewhere, presumes the reader's familiarity with the earlier sources. Indeed, v. 15, contains a clear allusion to 1 Kings 11.29–39. It is, indeed, likely that the Chronicler assumes that his readers are familiar with some form of the tradition as preserved in 1 Kings, but seeks to substantively recast the information found there. **18:** The name *Hadoram* appears in 1 Kings (12.18) as Adoram. This is another instance in which Chronicles has preserved the original form of a name; see 1 Chron. 18.10 n. **19:** It is unclear whether Chronicles views Rehoboam as culpable for the division of the monarchy or, rather, as a victim of inexperience and bad counseling. Given Chronicles' view of retribution, and the fact that Chronicles makes no mention of Solomon's offenses and the punishment pronounced in 1 Kings, it would seem that the secession of the northern tribes would be attributed to Rehoboam's wrongful conduct. But v. 15 indicates that the entire episode was divinely guided so as to allow for fulfillment of Ahijah's royal oracle. Moreover, as explained below, Chronicles seems to exonerate Rehoboam by claiming that his miscalculations were the result of youthful inexperience in handling a northern "rebellion." Although a definitive answer eludes us, it is likely that Chronicles does not view the divine decree regarding secession and Rehoboam's own actions as mutually exclusive. **11.1:** Chronicles omits Jeroboam's election by the north (1 Kings 12.20), a point that typifies Chronicles' reticence on matters concerning the northern monarchy. **2–4:** Whereas v. 3 states that *Shemaiah*'s prophecy was to be addressed to *all Israel in Judah and Benjamin,* 1 Kings 12.23 reads "the House of Judah"; Chronicles here integrates Benjamin into the Southern Kingdom. **4:** By referring to the people of the north as *kinsmen*/brethren, the author expresses his inclusive, "pan-Israel" worldview; the leaders of the North are, indeed, scoundrels, but the populace at large remains part of the true Israel, i.e., those who acknowledge the unique status of Jerusalem and the Davidic monarchy.

11.5–12: Rehoboam's building projects. Building projects are a sign of a king's success and divine favor. This favorable evaluation of Rehoboam suggests that he is not the cause of the secession but, rather, its victim. In addition, the juxtaposition of Rehoboam's acceptance of the prophetic directive to refrain from warfare and his successful building ventures also expresses another Chronicles theme, viz., the importance of heeding the prophetic word. This section has no parallel in Kings.

11.13–17: Rehoboam's support for the Levites. This section has no parallel in Kings, but reflects the Chronicler's attitude toward the

for three years, for they followed the ways of David and Solomon for three years.

18 Rehoboam married Mahalath daughter of Jerimoth son of David, and Abihail daughter of Eliab son of Jesse. 19 She bore him sons: Jeush, Shemariah, and Zaham. 20 He then took Maacah daughter of Absalom; she bore him Abijah, Attai, Ziza, and Shelomith. 21 Rehoboam loved Maacah daughter of Absalom more than his other wives and concubines—for he took eighteen wives and sixty concubines; he begot twenty-eight sons and sixty daughters. 22 Rehoboam designated Abijah son of Maacah as chief and leader among his brothers, for he intended him to be his successor. 23 He prudently distributed all his sons throughout the regions of Judah and Benjamin and throughout the fortified towns; he provided them with abundant food, and he sought many wives for them.

12 When the kingship of Rehoboam was firmly established, and he grew strong, he abandoned the Teaching of the LORD, he and all Israel with him.

2 In the fifth year of King Rehoboam, King Shishak of Egypt marched against Jerusalem—for they had trespassed against the LORD—3 with 1,200 chariots, 60,000 horsemen and innumerable troops who came with him from Egypt: Lybians, Sukkites, and Kushites. 4 He took the fortified towns of Judah and advanced on Jerusalem. 5 The prophet Shemaiah came to Rehoboam and the officers of Judah, who had assembled in Jerusalem because of Shishak, and said to them, "Thus said the LORD: You have abandoned Me, so I am abandoning you to Shishak." 6 Then the officers of Israel and the king humbled themselves and declared, "The LORD is in the right." 7 When the LORD saw that they had submitted, the word of the LORD came to Shemaiah, saying, "Since they have humbled themselves, I will not destroy them but will grant them some measure of deliverance, and My wrath will not be poured out on Jerusalem through Shishak. 8 They will be subject to him, and they will know the

importance of the Levites. Whereas 1 Kings 12.31–32 suggests that priests and Levites were appointed indiscriminately, Chronicles claims that Jeroboam excluded all "genuine" cultic personnel—leaving him with none (see 2 Chron. 13.9–12). The disenfranchised priests and Levites understood that their only option was to abandon the plots that had been given them by the lay Israelites (1 Chron. 6.49) and relocate to the south, which they gladly did. The reference to goat-demons in v. 15 alludes to Lev. 17.7; the author thus claims that the sacrificial service in the northern tribes was both illicit and tantamount to worship of other deities.

11.18–23: Rehoboam's family. This section has no parallel in Kings. Rehoboam's many wives are further evidence of Chronicles' positive evaluation of Rehoboam. While Kings focuses on Jeroboam, devoting only eleven vv. to Rehoboam (1 Kings 14.21–31), Chronicles devotes 11.5–12.16 to Rehoboam, a clear statement of its concern with Judahite kings at the expense of the northern monarchy. Many of the names appearing here are otherwise unattested (e.g., v. 19); others stand in tension with other passages, probably indicating that Chronicles has used an independent source. **20:** *Maacah,* see 13.2 and 1 Kings 15.2, 10.

12.1–12: Shishak's invasion. Chronicles expands upon the parallel passage found at 1 Kings 14.25–28. Chronicles' explanation, seen by many as part of its view on providence and retribution, is that Rehoboam's conduct was virtuous during the initial three years of his reign. During the fourth year he began to sin and, was consequently punished. The impressive fortifications undertaken by Rehoboam, reflective of the boom enjoyed during the years of his fidelity to God, were ultimately of no avail, since Israel's "true" defense system is none other than the Deity. This point is underscored by the huge size of Pharaoh's force: their sudden and inexplicable retreat conveys the miraculous (i.e., divinely guided) nature of the episode (vv. 6–7). The entire passage shows Chronicles' one-dimensional depiction of the nature of warfare. **1–8:** Chronicles specifies that the king, his officers, and the people were all guilty; hence, all were punished—the nation cannot be punished for the acts of the king alone. As soon as the king repents, he is forgiven. **1:** Significantly, Chronicles does not charge Rehoboam with idolatry or any particular offense. The vague formulation probably denotes a generally "disinterested" or "slovenly" approach to observance of precepts; cf. 36.12–14 n.; 15–17 n. **6–12:** This contrasts with 2 Kings 14.23–24, which charges the kings and the people with idolatrous practices. Chronicles thereby makes the claim that sustained refusal to repent from wrongful conduct, even that of a less heinous nature than idolatry, will result in catastrophe; see 2 Chron. 36.12–14 n. Chronicles employs the Heb root "k-n-'" ("be humbled, submit"), in the sense of submission to the divine will, far more than any

difference between serving Me and serving the kingdoms of
the earth." King Shishak of Egypt marched against Jerusalem.
9 [a]He took away the treasures of the House of the LORD and the
treasures of the royal palace; he took away everything; he took
away the golden shields that Solomon had made. 10 King Rehoboam had bronze shields made in their place, and entrusted
them to the officers of the guard[b] who guarded the entrance to
the royal palace. 11 Whenever the king entered the House of the
LORD, the guards would carry them and then bring them back
to the armory of the guards. 12 After he had humbled himself,
the anger of the LORD was averted and He did not destroy him
entirely; in Judah, too, good things were found.

a With vv. 9–16, cf. 1 Kings 14.26–31. *b Lit. "runners."*

other biblical book, indicating its importance; in this passage alone it occurs four times. This root, while rare in the Pentateuch, appears at Lev. 26.41 in connection with Israel's acknowledgement of their sinful conduct; Lev. ch 26 also serves as the backdrop for Chronicles' formulation of Judah's exile (2 Chron. 36.20–21). **9–12:** The claim that *good things* (v. 12) were also found among the people may mean either that the people, too, repented, or that they had to their credit good deeds that offset their sins. Typically, Chronicles claims that contrition effects God's

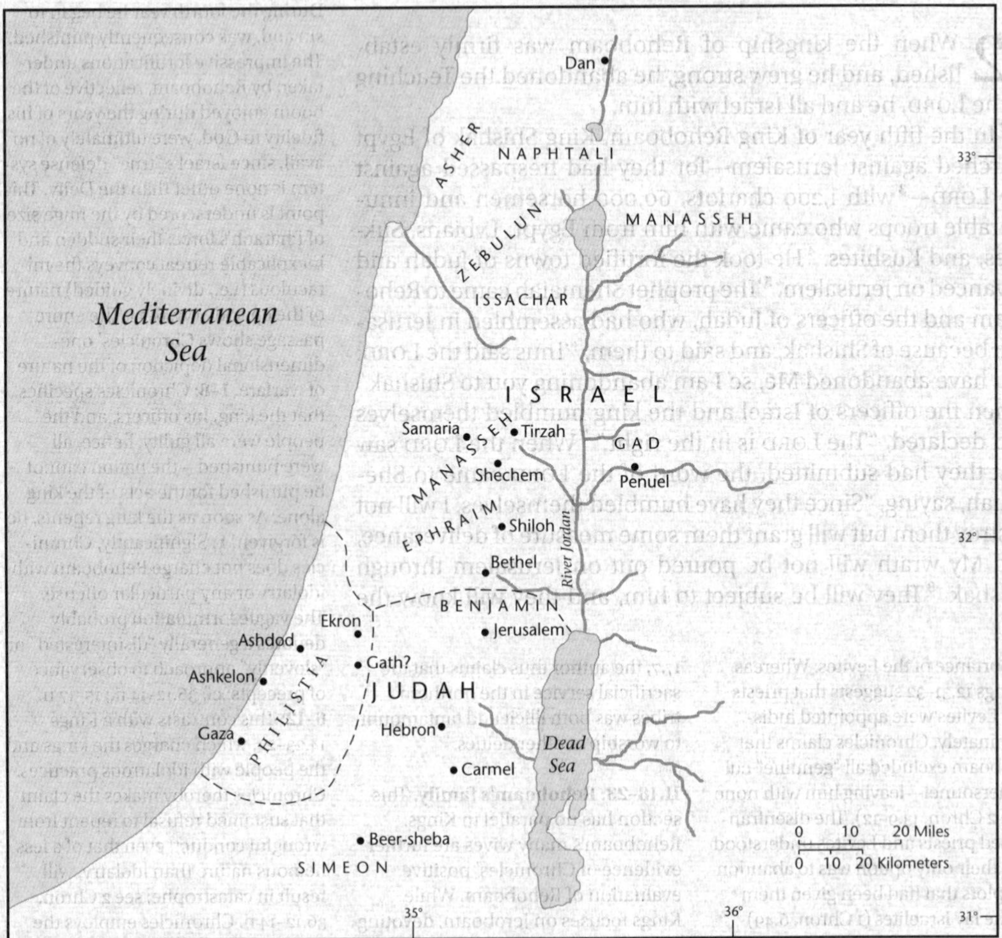

The divided monarchy according to Second Chronicles. The dashed line shows the approximate boundaries between Israel, Judah and Philistia.

13 King Rehoboam grew strong in Jerusalem and exercised
kingship. Rehoboam was forty-one years old when he became
king, and he reigned seventeen years in Jerusalem—the city
the LORD had chosen out of all the tribes of Israel to establish
His name there. His mother's name was Naamah the Ammonitess. 14 He did what was wrong, for he had not set his heart to
seek the LORD. 15 The deeds of Rehoboam, early and late, are
recorded in the chronicles of the prophet Shemaiah and Iddo
the seer, in the manner of genealogy. There was continuous
war between Rehoboam and Jeroboam. 16 Rehoboam slept
with his fathers and was buried in the City of David. His son
Abijah succeeded him as king.

13

In the eighteenth year of King Jeroboam, Abijah became
king over Judah. 2 He reigned three years in Jerusalem;
his mother's name was Micaiah daughter of Uriel of Gibeah.
There was war between Abijah and Jeroboam. 3 Abijah joined
battle with a force of warriors, 400,000 picked men. Jeroboam
arrayed for battle against him 800,000 picked men, warriors.
4 Abijah stood on top of Mount Zemaraim in the hill country of
Ephraim and said, "Listen to me, Jeroboam and all Israel. 5 Surely you know that the LORD God of Israel gave David kingship
over Israel forever—to him and his sons—by a covenant of salt.
6 Jeroboam son of Nebat had been in the service of Solomon
son of David, but he rose up and rebelled against his master.

immediate forgiveness, a sign of divine compassion or grace (see intro.). The invading force suddenly departs, with no apparent loss of life. Chronicles offers no details, military or otherwise. This is an example of Chronicles' use of "one-dimensional" causality, the idea that events have only one cause. For the topos of Temple holdings lost/gained as a result of warfare and how that reflects on the king, see 1 Chron. 18.8–9 n.

12.13–15: End of Rehoboam's reign. By mentioning Rehoboam's mother, v. 13 acknowledges (at least some of) Solomon's foreign wives. For prophetic court biographers, see 1 Chron. 29.28–30. Chronicles' overall evaluation of Rehoboam is not one-dimensional. The assessment here is essentially negative. Yet, the following ch offers an apologia on his behalf; see 13.7; 11.3–17. In contrast, 1 Kings 15.3 offers no hint that Rehoboam or the people repented from their idolatrous ways. **14:** Typical of Chronicles' understanding of religious fidelity, it does not specify idolatry or any other specific offense. The formulation allows for a wide range of religious improprieties, including a general sort of religious malaise, wherein the deity is not sought out as the source of blessing.

13.1–23: Abijah's reign. Chronicles' account of *Abijah* shares virtually nothing with the much briefer account (eight vv.) in 1 Kings ch 15 (where his name is Abijam). Chronicles' form of the name—which bears the meaning "YaH(VH) is the/my (divine) father"—may reflect the author's positive assessment of this figure, whom 1 Kings portrays in less than flattering terms. Abijam, by contrast, means "Yam (the sea divinity) is my/the (divine) father"; however, it may also bear the same meaning as Abijah, with the "am" ending being the result of phonological factors. Alternatively, the two forms may be the result of scribal error, owing to graphic similarity between the letters "heh" and "mem." Furthermore, Chronicles contains not the slightest criticism of Abijah, whereas 1 Kings 15.3–4 states that Abijam was evil and that his rule was preserved merely for the sake of the Davidic dynasty. Chronicles' reworking may have been informed by its theology of retribution; since Kings does not indicate that Abijam was punished for his misdeeds, Chronicles concluded that Abijah could not have been so bad. Alternatively, the tradition concerning Abijah's victory over the north, which many view as authentic, may have led Chronicles to conclude that Abijah was an upright king. (The details of that victory, however, reflect the Chronicler's terminology and ideology, and were likely his creation.) Still, Chronicles does not depict Abijah in the same laudatory terms typical of other righteous kings; the assessments of Kings and Chronicles are therefore not radically different. This position is buttressed by the reference to reforms executed by his son (e.g., 14.2–4), suggesting some shortcomings on Abijah's part. **1–3:** The incredibly large military forces recorded here are typical of Chronicles; see 1 Chron. 12.25–39 n. Note that some mss read 14,000 in place of *400,000.* Perhaps the *800,000* of the northern forces is the same as the number of "warriors" mentioned at 2 Sam. 24.9, highlighting that Jeroboam mustered every available fighter and outnumbered the enemy but was, nonetheless, defeated. **4:** The location of *Mount Zemaraim* is uncertain, but a Benjaminite town of that name appears at Josh. 18.21–24. LXX reads "Mount Samaria." The use of oration as a rhetorical device in the nonsynoptic passages is a ubiquitous feature of Chronicles. Like Herodotus and other Hellenistic historians, the author uses these speeches to express his position on a variety of subjects. **5–12:** This passage is a parade example of Chronicles'

7 Riffraff and scoundrels gathered around him and pressed hard
upon Rehoboam son of Solomon. Rehoboam was inexperienced and fainthearted and could not stand up to them. 8 Now
you are bent on opposing the kingdom of the LORD, which is in
the charge of the sons of David, because you are a great multitude and possess the golden calves that Jeroboam made for you
as gods. 9 Did you not banish the priests of the LORD, the sons of
Aaron and the Levites, and, like the peoples of the land, appoint
your own priests? Anyone who offered himself for ordination
with a young bull of the herd and seven rams became a priest
of no-gods! 10 As for us, the LORD is our God, and we have not
forsaken Him. The priests who minister to the LORD are the sons
of Aaron, and the Levites are at their tasks. 11 They offer burnt offerings in smoke each morning and each evening, and the aromatic incense, the rows of bread on the pure table; they kindle
the golden lampstand with its lamps burning each evening, for
we keep the charge of the LORD our God, while you have forsaken it. 12 See, God is with us as our chief, and His priests have
the trumpets for sounding blasts against you. O children of Israel, do not fight the LORD God of your fathers, because you will
not succeed." 13 Jeroboam, however, had directed the ambush to
go around and come from the rear, thus [a]the main body was[a]
in front of Judah, while the ambush was behind them. 14 When
Judah turned around and saw that the fighting was before and
behind them, they cried out to the LORD, and the priests blew
the trumpets. 15 The men of Judah raised a shout; and when the
men of Judah raised a shout, God routed Jeroboam and all Israel
before Abijah and Judah. 16 The Israelites fled before Judah, and
God delivered them into their hands. 17 Abijah and his army inflicted a severe defeat on them; 500,000 men of Israel fell slain.
18 The Israelites were crushed at that time, while the people of
Judah triumphed because they relied on the LORD God of their
fathers. 19 Abijah pursued Jeroboam and captured some of his
cities—Bethel with its dependencies, Jeshanah with its dependencies, and Ephrain with its dependencies. 20 Jeroboam could
not muster strength again during the days of Abijah. The LORD
struck him down and he died. 21 But Abijah grew powerful; he
married fourteen wives and begat twenty-two sons and sixteen
daughters.

22 The other events of Abijah's reign, his conduct and his
acts, are recorded in the story of the prophet Iddo. 23 Abijah

a-a Lit. "they were."

critique of the northern dynasty. The appeal to the populace of the north reflects the book's "inclusivist" slant; see intro. This paradigmatic oration, with its emphasis on the Jerusalem cult and Davidic monarchy, explains the basis for the divided kingdom and Judah's supremacy, as narrated through ch 28. **5–8:** The Chronicler expresses his view that any monarchy other than the Davidic one is illegitimate. Moreover, since the Davidides are God's proxies, opposition to, and armed struggle against, their rule is tantamount to rebellion against God (see 1 Chron. 17.14 n.). V. 7 indicates that the inexperienced Rehoboam fell victim to a more powerful group of scoundrels. Josephus (*Ant.* 8.277), along with some modern students of Chronicles, understood the *riffraff and scoundrels* to be Rehoboam's inexperienced advisors; Chronicles' critique of the northern leaders makes this unlikely. **7–8:** Repetition (in Heb) of "become strong" at the end of v. 7 and the beginning of v. 8 *(stand up to ... opposing)* is Chronicles' way of saying, "you are attempting to impose your monarchy upon God's representatives, just as you did at the inception of Rehoboam's rule"; see 12.13–15 n. **9–12:** The only true and proper religious practice is that observed in the Jerusalem Temple, in accordance with the Torah, especially the Priestly laws; treason against the Davidic monarchy and religious apostasy thus go hand in hand. **12:** The role of trumpet blasts in assuring military victory appears at Num. 10.9. **13–14:** Chronicles is consistent that the *trumpets* are to be blown, in warfare and on religious occasions, by *priests* only; see 1 Chron. 16.4–6 n. The much larger Israelite force succumbs to Abijah's forces. Here, as in so many other instances, Chronicles jettisons any concrete physical description of the battle; what is recorded is not human military tactics, but the divine will, which responds to human petition and trust in the divine. **19–21:** The expansion, as well as the development, of territory is a sign of success and divine favor; see 8.1–3; 11.5–12. **22–23:** *Story* (Heb "midrash," used only here and in 24.27). The term in postbiblical literature becomes a common term for exegesis (see 1 Chron. 28.8–9 n.) and exposition; here it means simply "narrative." Still, the choice of this term reflects Chronicles' view that such stories are the product of prophetic exposition and interpretation; see 1 Chron. 29.29.

slept with his fathers and was buried in the City of David; his
son Asa succeeded him as king. The land was untroubled for
ten years.

14 Asa did what was good and pleasing to the LORD his
God. 2 He abolished the alien altars and shrines; he
smashed the pillars and cut down the sacred posts. 3 He ordered Judah to turn to the LORD God of their fathers and to
observe the Teaching and the Commandment. 4 He abolished
the shrines and the incense stands throughout the cities of Judah, and the kingdom was untroubled under him. 5 He built
fortified towns in Judah, since the land was untroubled and he
was not engaged in warfare during those years, for the LORD
had granted him respite. 6 He said to Judah, "Let us build up
these cities and surround them with walls and towers, gates
and bars, while the land is at our disposal because we turned
to the LORD our God—we turned [to Him] and He gave us respite on all sides." They were successful in their building.
7 Asa had an army of 300,000 men from Judah bearing shields
and spears, and 280,000 from Benjamin bearing bucklers and
drawing the bow; all these were valiant men. 8 Zerah the Cushite marched out against them with an army of a thousand
thousand and 300 chariots. When he reached Mareshah 9 Asa
confronted him, and the battle lines were drawn in the valley
of Zephat by Mareshah. 10 Asa called to the LORD his God, and
said, "O LORD, it is all the same to You to help the numerous
and the powerless. Help us, O LORD our God, for we rely on
You, and in Your name we have come against this great multitude. You are the LORD our God. Let no mortal hinder You."
11 So the LORD routed the Cushites before Asa and Judah, and
the Cushites fled. 12 Asa and the army with him pursued them
as far as Gerar. Many of the Cushites fell wounded beyond
recovery, for they broke before the LORD and His camp. Very
much spoil was taken. 13 All the cities in the vicinity of Gerar
were ravaged, for a terror of the LORD seized them. All the cities were plundered, and they yielded much booty. 14 They also
ravaged the encampment of herdsmen, capturing much sheep
and camels. Then they returned to Jerusalem.

14.1–16.14: Asa's reign. Chronicles expands upon 2 Kings' version (15.9–24), dividing it into two periods: the period of fidelity (14.1–15.19) and the period of faithlessness (16.1–14). The reigns of Asa and Ahijah are bound by the shared motif of reliance upon the LORD. **14.1–8:** Reform and prosperity. This is an expansion of 1 Kings 15.11–12. Chronicles' presentation is, at this stage, unambiguously positive, as emphasized by the repeated reference to *his God* (vv. 1, 10). **2–4:** This passage is best viewed as an elaboration of an independent source used by Chronicles, but influenced by 2 Kings 18.4. Cf. 1 Kings 15.14 regarding shrines. The presence of paraphernalia of foreign cultic worship is assumed but never explained. The Heb "ḥamanim" has been the subject of various interpretations. These include: *incense stands,* incense altars, pillars for sun worship, and (wayside) chapel. **5–6:** For building cities as a sign of monarchic success and divine favor, see 11.5–12 n. **7–14:** Asa battles Zerah the Cushite. There is no extrabiblical evidence for this account, whose historicity is debated. Most of the scholars who see the account as factual agree that the expedition was led by a commander of Nubian extraction, supported by Nubian forces; others, less convincingly, maintain that the original confrontation involved Bedouin tribes south of Judah. The numbers of the enemy force are again fantastic, though. The Syriac translation (Peshitta) reads "thirty thousand chariots." On either reading, the point is the same: Asa's extremely large force, outnumbered nearly two-to-one and lacking a large chariot force, manages to defeat the enemy force by virtue of exclusive trust in, and supplication to, God. Chronicles does not explain the circumstances surrounding the incursion of the Cushites.

15 The spirit of God came upon Azariah son of Oded. [2] He came to Asa and said to him, "Listen to me, Asa and all Judah and Benjamin; the LORD is with you as long as you are with Him. If you turn to Him, He will respond to you, but if you forsake Him, He will forsake you. [3] Israel has gone many days without the true God, without a priest to give instruction and without Teaching. [4] But in distress it returned to the LORD God of Israel, and sought Him, and He responded to them. [5] At those times, [a]no wayfarer[a] was safe, for there was much tumult among all the inhabitants of the lands. [6] Nation was crushed by nation and city by city, for God threw them into panic with every kind of trouble. [7] As for you, be strong, do not be disheartened, for there is reward for your labor."

[8] When Asa heard these words, the prophecy of Oded the prophet, he took courage and removed the abominations from the entire land of Judah and Benjamin and from the cities that he had captured in the hill country of Ephraim. He restored the altar of the LORD in front of the porch of the LORD. [9] He assembled all the people of Judah and Benjamin and those people of Ephraim, Manasseh, and Simeon who sojourned among them, for many in Israel had thrown in their lot with him when they saw that the LORD his God was with him. [10] They were assembled in Jerusalem in the third month of the fifteenth year of the reign of Asa. [11] They brought sacrifices to the LORD on that day; they brought 700 oxen and 7,000 sheep of the spoil. [12] They entered into a covenant to worship the LORD God of their fathers with all their heart and with all their soul. [13] Whoever would not worship the LORD God of Israel would be put to death, whether small or great, whether man or woman. [14] So they took an oath to the LORD in a loud voice and with shouts, with trumpeting and blasts of the horn. [15] All Judah rejoiced over the oath, for they swore with all their heart and sought Him with all their will. He responded to them and gave them respite on every side.

a-a Lit. "one who goes out and one who comes in."

15.1–7: Azariah's address. This Azariah is otherwise unattested. Since the situation described in vv. 3–7 does not correspond to events of Asa's reign, some commentators view these vv. as a prophetic pronouncement regarding the future, a view reflected in LXX. The Aram. Tg. interprets them as alluding to the conduct of Jeroboam and his supporters. Alternatively, they may allude to the reigns of Rehoboam and Abijah or, less plausibly, the period of the judges (e.g., Judg. 2.11–13). Others maintain that the passage may, indeed, have Asa's reign in mind; the rhetorical style reflects Chronicles' thematic concerns, and need not refer to specific events of Asa's reign. Vv. 2–7 draw on several biblical passages; see Hos. 3.4 (v. 3); Amos 3.17 (v. 5b); Deut. 4.29–30 (vv. 2–4); and Zech. 8.9–11 (vv. 4–7). **1:** For similar use of the "possession formula," see 1 Chron. 12.19 n.; 2 Chron. 20.14; 24.20. This formula appears only in Chronicles' nonsynoptic passages and only in connection with "nonprofessional prophets." Chronicles distinguishes between professional prophets, who address the monarchy exclusively, and other "temporary prophets/messengers," whose messages are directed at the people at large (including the king). **3:** Some medievals (Radak, and an anonymous disciple of Saadia) interpreted Heb "ʾelohim," here rendered "God," to mean "magistrates"; hence, the phrase *without the true God* is to be rendered "without magistrates who judge honestly." **8–19:** Religious reform. This passage, a doublet of 14.2–4, was probably taken from an independent source, which has not been fully harmonized with the surrounding passages. Note, specifically, that the reference to Asa's capture of territory in Ephraim (v. 8) has no antecedent, since Asa's reign is depicted as peaceful. The covenant described in this passage is reminiscent of the theophany and lawgiving related in Exod. chs 19–20; both take place in the third month. The present passage probably informs the book of *Jubilees* and other writings of the Qumran community, the earliest sources that view the festival of Shavuʿot, celebrated in the third month, as the annual occasion for renewal of the covenant and acceptance of new members. As in *Jub.* and the Qumran compositions, commitment to the covenant is enforced by means of oaths, a word whose Heb form (root "sh-b-ʿ") is homologous with the festival name. The members of the Qumran community maintained that all outsiders were doomed to perdition. The severity of the punishment in this passage is consonant with other passages of Persian provenance that address failure to observe the law; see Ezra 7.26; 10.7–8. The presence of Simeon, the southernmost tribe, together with northern tribes remains anomalous; see 34.6–7. **8:** *Oded the prophet:* The words are syntactically problematic and have been variously rendered. In addition, attribution of the prophetic message to Oded contradicts v. 1. The ancient versions (LXX; Vg; Peshitta) harmonize with v. 1. The words may be a gloss.

16 [a]He[b] also deposed Maacah mother of King Asa from the
rank of queen mother, because she had made an abominable
thing for [the goddess] Asherah. Asa cut down her abominable thing, reduced it to dust, and burned it in the Wadi Kidron.
17 The shrines, indeed, were not abolished in Israel; however,
Asa was wholehearted [with the LORD] all his life. 18 He brought
into the House of God the things that he and his father had
consecrated—silver, gold, and utensils. 19 There was no war
until the thirty-fifth year of the reign of Asa.

16 [c]In the thirty-sixth year of the reign of Asa, King Baasha
of Israel marched against Judah and built up Ramah to
block [d-]all movement[-d] of King Asa of Judah. 2 Asa took all the
silver and gold from the treasuries of the House of the LORD
and the royal palace, and sent them to King Ben-hadad of
Aram, who resided in Damascus, with this message: 3 "There
is a pact between me and you, as there was between my father
and your father. I herewith send you silver and gold; go and
break your pact with King Baasha of Israel so that he may withdraw from me." 4 Ben-hadad acceded to King Asa's request;
he sent his army commanders against the towns of Israel and
ravaged Ijon, Dan, Abel-maim, and all the garrison towns of
Naphtali. 5 When Baasha heard about it, he stopped building
up Ramah and put an end to the work on it. 6 Then King Asa
mustered all Judah, and they carried away the stones and timber with which Baasha had built up Ramah; with these King
Asa built up Geba and Mizpah.
7 At that time, Hanani the seer came to King Asa of Judah and
said to him, "Because you relied on the king of Aram and did
not rely on the LORD your God, therefore the army of the king
of Aram has slipped out of your hands. 8 The Cushites and Lybians were a mighty army with chariots and horsemen in very
great numbers, yet because you relied on the LORD He delivered them into your hands. 9 For the eyes of the LORD range
over the entire earth, to give support to those who are wholeheartedly with Him. You have acted foolishly in this matter,

a With vv. 16–19, cf. 1 Kings 15.13–16. *b I.e., Asa.* *c Cf. 1 Kings 15.17–24.*
d-d Lit. "one who goes out and one who comes in."

16–19: Cultic reforms. *Queen mother* (Heb "gevirah"): Some maintain that the "gevirah" held an official position within the monarchy, and wielded significant political power, perhaps second only to the king. Others have gone further, arguing that the "gevirah" regulated aspects of the official Temple cult, as suggested by the fact that *Maacah* had been responsible for the production of "the abominable thing," likely a (proscribed) cultic mask. Others believe that the "gevirah" enjoyed no formal status, and that the influence wielded by various queen mothers was a function of their personalities. Despite the importance of women in Chronicles (esp. prominent in its genealogical section), the book offers little information regarding the "gevirah."

16.1–10: Asa's fateful alliance. A reversal of Asa's previous exclusive reliance on the LORD, and the resulting rebuke by the prophet Hanani. **2:** 1 Kings 15.18 states that Asa had relinquished "all" of the silver and gold that "remained" in the Temple treasury (and palace); Chronicles omits "all" and the phrase "that remained," meaning that the Temple's stock of valuables was depleted, but not decimated. While Asa's alliance led to substantial loss of Temple holdings, Rehoboam's more egregious conduct, consisting of abandonment of (or laxity in) religious observance generally, led to greater financial devastation; see 2 Chron. 12.1–12. For the topos of Temple holdings lost/gained as a result of warfare and how that reflects on the king, see 1 Chron. 18.8–9 n. **7–10:** *Hanani,* the father of Jehu the prophet; see 1 Kings 16.1, 7; 2 Chron. 19.2; 20.34. Chronicles thus has Jehu's father prophesying during the reign of Jehoshapat's father. This prophetic rebuke is reminiscent of others in Chronicles (e.g., 2 Chron. 12.5; 19.1–2) and other biblical sources (1 Kings 20.35–43; 2 Kings 13.14–19; Isa. 10.20), wherein proper conduct assures military success. V. 7 is especially reminiscent of Isa. 31.1, which employs the Heb roots "sh-ʿ-n" (rely)—which appears thrice in the present vv.—"b-t-h" (trust in), as well as "sh-ʿ-y/h" (look to), and "d-r-š" (seek out), a lexical favorite of Chronicles. One LXX tradition goes beyond the MT, implying that had Asa acted properly he would have defeated the Israelite forces. **7:** Some mss of LXX read "Israel" in place of *Aram,* probably a secondary reading. According to the MT, had Asa remained faithful he would have conquered Baasha as well as his confederates, the Arameans. **9:** The root "s-k-l" (act foolishly) also appears at 1 Chron. 21.8, where David's census-taking, reflecting a lack of trust in the Deity, brought about disaster.

and henceforth you will be beset by wars." 10 Asa was vexed at
the seer and put him into the stocks,[a] for he was furious with
him because of that. Asa inflicted cruelties on some of the people at that time.
11 The acts of Asa, early and late, are recorded in the annals
of the kings of Judah and Israel. 12 In the thirty-ninth year of
his reign, Asa suffered from an acute foot ailment; but ill as he
was, he still did not turn to the LORD but to physicians. 13 Asa
slept with his fathers. He died in the forty-first year of his reign
14 and was buried in the grave that he had made for himself in
the City of David. He was laid in his resting-place, which was
filled with spices of all kinds, expertly blended; a very great fire
was made in his honor.

17 His son Jehoshaphat succeeded him as king, and took
firm hold of Israel. 2 He stationed troops in all the fortified towns of Judah, and stationed garrisons throughout
the land of Judah and the cities of Ephraim which his father
Asa had captured. 3 The LORD was with Jehoshaphat because
he followed the earlier ways of his father David, and did not
worship the Baalim, 4 but worshiped the God of his father and
followed His commandments—unlike the behavior of Israel.
5 So the LORD established the kingdom in his hands, and all
Judah gave presents to Jehoshaphat. He had wealth and glory
in abundance. 6 His mind was elevated in the ways of the LORD.
Moreover, he abolished the shrines and the sacred posts from
Judah.
7 In the third year of his reign he sent his officers Ben-hail,
Obadiah, Zechariah, Nethanel, and Micaiah throughout the
cities of Judah to offer instruction. 8 With them were the Levites, Shemaiah, Nethaniah, Zebadiah, Asahel, Shemiramoth,
Jehonathan, Adonijah, Tobijah and Tob-adonijah the Levites;
with them were Elishama and Jehoram the priests. 9 They offered instruction throughout Judah, having with them the
Book of the Teaching of the LORD. They made the rounds of

a *Meaning of Heb. uncertain.*

16.11–14: Conclusion of Asa's reign. 12: Asa's affliction may be punishment for his alliance with Benhadad, though the text does not quite say as much. The episode involves another instance of paranomasia (wordplay or punning), here based on the name Asa ("'asa'"), since the Aram. root "'-s-y/'-s-'" means "heal." The use of Aram. is hardly surprising in a book of the Second Temple period, given how widespread this language was throughout the Near East. The exact intent of the criticism leveled against Asa is not clear. The passage probably faults him for seeking "natural" cures while not beseeching God, though it may imply that he should have relied exclusively on the Deity; either way, it certainly suggests that Asa failed to recognize God's power to cure illness. **14:** The burial description is fuller than that of 1 Kings 15.24, yielding a fundamentally positive assessment of Asa's reign.

17.1–20.37: Jehoshaphat's reign. Chronicles' portrayal of Jehoshaphat differs dramatically from that in 1 Kings. The latter (quite correctly from a historical perspective) views Jehoshaphat's northern counterpart, Ahab, as the more important of the two kings; accordingly, Kings contains only occasional notices concerning Jehoshaphat. Chronicles, however, devotes a total of four chs to Jehoshaphat, with only passing reference to his northern counterparts. Several features reflect a Solomon typology, where features of Jehoshaphat are modeled after those of his illustrious forebear, since in Chronicles all good and successful monarchs embody the qualities manifest by David and Solomon. Despite Chronicles' critique of Jehoshaphat's alliance with the wicked, which apparently reflects the book's understanding of the parallel passages in Kings, Chronicles' overall assessment of the king is positive, leading some scholars to argue that Chronicles has drawn on extrabiblical material. This position is unwarranted; the portrait of Jehoshaphat is illustrative of the Chronicler's view that personal piety is not sufficient; avoidance of illicit alliances is sine qua non of upright conduct. Moreover, Chonicles' portrait expresses a holistic view of divine justice, such that improper conduct, while requiring divine chastisement, is viewed in the broader context of one's actions. **17.3–4:** This ch has no parallel and forms part of the book's expanded role for Levites. Chronicles presupposes the reader's familiarity with 1 Kings ch 17ff., which relate the prevalence of Baal worship in northern Israel. **5:** The wording of this v. is reminiscent of Solomon. **7–9:** *Levites* stand out among those sent to educate the people; Deut. 33.10 may inform the v. Debate surrounding the account's historicity notwithstanding, it almost certainly reflects Second Temple, rather than First Temple, reality. The itinerant instructors are

all the cities of Judah and instructed the people. [10]A terror of
the LORD seized all the kingdoms of the lands around Judah,
and they did not go to war with Jehoshaphat. [11]From Philistia a
load of silver was brought to Jehoshaphat as tribute. The Arabs,
too, brought him flocks: 7,700 rams and 7,700 he-goats. [12]Je-
hoshaphat grew greater and greater, and he built up fortresses
and garrison towns in Judah. [13]He carried out extensive works
in the towns of Judah, and had soldiers, valiant men, in Jerusalem. [14]They were enrolled according to their clans. Judah:
chiefs of thousands, Adnah the chief, who had 300,000 valiant men; [15]next to him was Jehohanan the captain, who had
280,000; [16]next to him was Amasiah son of Zichri, who made
a freewill offering to the LORD. He had 200,000 valiant men.
[17]Benjamin: Eliada, a valiant man, who had 200,000 men
armed with bow and buckler; [18]next to him was Jehozabad,
who had 180,000 armed men. [19]These served the king, besides
those whom the king assigned to the fortified towns throughout Judah.

18 [a]So Jehoshaphat had wealth and honor in abundance,
and he allied himself by marriage to Ahab. [2]After some
years had passed, he came to visit Ahab at Samaria. Ahab
slaughtered sheep and oxen in abundance for him and for the
people with him, and persuaded him to march against Ramoth-
gilead. [3]King Ahab of Israel said to King Jehoshaphat of Judah,
"Will you accompany me to Ramoth-gilead?" He answered
him, "I will do what you do; my troops shall be your troops and
shall accompany you in battle." [4]Jehoshaphat then said to the
king of Israel, "But first inquire for the word of the LORD."
[5]So the king of Israel gathered the prophets, four hundred
men, and asked them, "Shall I march upon Ramoth-gilead for
battle, or shall I not?" "March," they said, "and God will deliver it into the king's hands." [6]Then Jehoshaphat asked, "Is
there not another prophet of the LORD here through whom we
can inquire?" [7]And the king of Israel answered Jehoshaphat,
"There is one more man through whom we can inquire of the
LORD; but I hate him, because he never prophesies anything
good for me but always misfortune. He is Micaiah son of Imlah." Jehoshaphat replied, "Let the king not say such a thing."
[8]So the king of Israel summoned an officer and said, "Bring
Micaiah son of Imlah at once."
[9]The king of Israel and King Jehoshaphat of Judah, wearing their robes, were seated on their thrones situated in the

a Cf. 1 Kings 22.

sent only to the cities of Judah, not Ephraim; this may be the author's way of expressing Judah's religious superiority. *Book of the Teaching ["torah"] of the LORD:* This term, used in 34.14 and Neh. 9.3, likely refers to the Torah. **10–19:** The offering of royal tribute by foreign kings, a clear statement of geopolitical dominance, is reminiscent of Solomon and David. **12:** The Heb words rendered *greater and greater* are virtually identical with those depicting Solomon; see 1.1.

18.1–34: Jehoshaphat joins forces with Ahab. The details are identical to 1 Kings ch 22, with a few notable exceptions. The primary difference concerns the episode's purpose in the context of Kings and Chronicles. Kings focuses on the question of true vs. false prophecy, while Chronicles' focus is on the impropriety of forging an alliance (military or political) with foreign or wicked entities (see 19.1–3). Thus the opening vv., unattested in Kings, explain that Jehoshaphat's error had its roots in the marriage between his son and Ahab's daughter. **1–2:** An implicit rebuke: Jehoshaphat has wealth and honor in abundance—what enticement could there be for creating a family bond with a wicked northern king? The harsh indictment is reaffirmed by v. 2, Ahab *persuaded* ("hesit," lit. "enticed/incited") Jehoshaphat. Heb "incite" has, throughout the Bible, a decidedly negative connotation, generally involving sedition to idolatry. Moreover, this same verb appears at a crucial point later in the story, indicating that Jehoshaphat has become the victim of sedition. The enticement was apparently the abundance of animals slaughtered in honor of Jehoshaphat. *Ramoth-gilead* (lit. "heights of Gilead") is located on the eastern bank of the Jordan, south of the present-day Golan Heights. **3:** In contrast to 1 Kings ch 22, Jehoshaphat here makes no mention of his horses joining the horses of Ahab, perhaps because Chronicles saw it as implying that victory is determined largely by military might, an unacceptable position in Chronicles' worldview, even for a king who has been "enticed." **4:** On inquiring of the LORD before warfare as a sign of righteousness, see 1 Chron. 10.14; 14.10.

27–28: *Come home safe* (lit. "return in peace"): "In peace," Heb "be-shalom," is a leading idea in this story. This v. anticipates v. 34, which states that the (basically) upright Jehoshaphat returned "in peace," whereas the wicked Ahab was killed, as prophesied by Micaiah. **27:** The words *Listen, all you peoples* appear at Mic. 1.2, possibly indicating that Chronicles identified Micaiah, the prophet of the present episode, with the prophet Micah, one of the twelve "minor prophets"; this identification is historically problematic.

threshing floor at the entrance of the gate of Samaria; and all
the prophets were prophesying before them. 10 Zedekiah son of
Chenaanah had provided himself with iron horns; and he said,
"Thus said the LORD: With these you shall gore the Arameans
till you make an end of them." 11 All the other prophets were
prophesying similarly, "March against Ramoth-gilead and be
victorious! The LORD will deliver it into Your Majesty's hands."

12 The messenger who had gone to summon Micaiah said to
him, "Look, the words of the prophets are unanimously favorable to the king. Let your word be like that of the rest of them;
speak a favorable word." 13 "By the life of the LORD," Micaiah
answered, "I will speak only what my God tells me." 14 When
he came before the king, the king said to him, "Micah,[a] shall
we march against Ramoth-gilead for battle or shall we not?"
He answered him, "March and be victorious! They will be delivered into your hands." 15 The king said to him, "How many
times must I adjure you to tell me nothing but the truth in the
name of the LORD?" 16 Then he said, "I saw all Israel scattered
over the hills like sheep without a shepherd; and the LORD
said, 'These have no master; let everyone return to his home
in safety.' " 17 The king of Israel said to Jehoshaphat, "Did I not
tell you that he would not prophesy good fortune for me, but
only misfortune?"

18 Then [Micaiah] said, "Indeed, hear now the word of the
LORD! I saw the LORD seated upon His throne, with all the host
of heaven standing in attendance to the right and to the left of
Him. 19 The LORD asked, 'Who will entice King Ahab of Israel
so that he will march and fall at Ramoth-gilead?' Then one said
this and another said that, 20 until a certain spirit came forward
and stood before the LORD and said, 'I will entice him.' 'How?'
said the LORD to him. 21 And he replied, 'I will go forth and become a lying spirit in the mouth of all his prophets.' Then He
said, 'You will entice with success. Go forth and do it.' 22 Thus
the LORD has put a lying spirit in the mouth of all these prophets of yours; for the LORD has decreed misfortune for you."

23 Thereupon Zedekiah son of Chenaanah came up and
struck Micaiah on the cheek, and exclaimed, "However did the
spirit of the LORD pass from me to speak with you!" 24 Micaiah
replied, "You will see on the day when you try to hide in the
innermost room." 25 Then the king of Israel said, "Take Micaiah
and turn him over to Amon, the governor of the city, and to
Prince Joash, 26 and say, 'The king's orders are: Put this fellow
in prison, and let his fare be scant bread and scant water until
I come home safe.' " 27 To which Micaiah retorted, "If you ever
come home safe, the LORD has not spoken through me." He
said further, [b-]"Listen, all you peoples!"[-b]

a A shortened form of Micaiah. *b-b Cf. Mic. 1.2.*

28 The king of Israel and King Jehoshaphat of Judah marched
against Ramoth-gilead. 29 The king of Israel said to Jehoshaphat, [a-]“I will disguise myself and go[-a] into the battle, but you,
wear your robes.” So the king of Israel disguised himself, and
they went into the battle. 30 The king of Aram had given these
instructions to his chariot officers: “Do not attack anyone,
small or great, except the king of Israel.” 31 When the chariot officers saw Jehoshaphat, whom they took for the king of Israel,
they wheeled around to attack him, and Jehoshaphat cried out
and the LORD helped him, and God diverted them from him.
32 And when the chariot officers realized that he was not the
king of Israel, they gave up the pursuit. 33 Then a man drew his
bow at random and hit the king of Israel between the [b-]plates
of the[-b] armor and he said to his charioteer, “Turn around and
get me behind the lines; I am wounded.” 34 The battle [b-]raged
all day long,[-b] and the king remained propped up in the chariot
facing Aram until dusk; he died as the sun was setting.

19 King Jehoshaphat of Judah returned safely to his palace,
to Jerusalem. 2 Jehu son of Hanani the seer went out to
meet King Jehoshaphat and said to him, “Should one give aid
to the wicked and befriend those who hate the LORD? For this,
wrath is upon you from the LORD. 3 However, there is some
good in you, for you have purged the land of the sacred posts
and have dedicated yourself to worship God.”
4 Jehoshaphat remained in Jerusalem a while and then went
out among the people from Beer-sheba to the hill country

a-a Infinitives used for finite verb; cf. note at 1 Kings 22.30.
b-b Meaning of Heb. uncertain.

31: 1 Kings reads “he cried out,” which denotes either a shout of desperation or an attempt to muster the troops. Chronicles’ text, which adds *and the LORD helped him,* explains this call as a shout of prayer, emphasizing that prayer and repentance are efficacious, even in seemingly hopeless situations. Jehoshaphat is thus implicitly contrasted with Saul who, in similar circumstances, chose to take his life, rather than engage in prayer. *God diverted them* (Heb “wayesitem,” “he enticed them”): LXX’s reading suggests the graphically similar “wayesirem,” i.e., “he moved them away,” but this is likely a secondary reading. The very strangeness of “wayesitem” however, is part of Chronicles’ literary strategy. Chronicles applies a kind of talion (measure-for-measure) principle: He who was previously “enticed” to commit an egregious act by trusting in the might of alliances with the wicked (v. 2) is saved by the LORD, who “entices” the attacking force to suddenly desist, merely by virtue of his recognition that salvation comes only from trust in divine omnipotence. This is a further instance of Chronicles’ view that outcomes have only a single cause; there is no explanation of the military means by which Jehoshaphat’s deliverance came about. The Chronicler’s programmatic dismissal of northern monarchs and Ahab in particular, leads him to omit Ahab’s post-mortem treatment, including his burial, recorded in 1 Kings 22.35b–40.

19.1–20.30: This entire section has no parallel in Kings. 19.1–3: Prophetic rebuke. **2:** *Befriend* (Heb “teʾehav,” root “ʾ-h-v,” “to like, love”), like its semantic cognate in other Semitic languages, connotes treaty or covenant fidelity; the same idea is present in *give aid.* This usage figures prominently in Deut.; see Deut. 6.5 and 11.13 (both part of the “Shema” prayer traditionally recited twice daily); 10.12; 11.1 and 30.20. By employing this pregnant lexeme these passages command Israel to remain loyal to the divine Overlord, rather than any human sovereign. These vv. are not present in the Deuteronomistic version in Kings, since that source focuses on the person of Ahab and, more fundamentally, because the Deuteronomist sees no religious dilemma in joining forces with a northern king (or other wicked individual) so long as one does not adopt his sinful ways. Chronicles, however, takes the position that the mere act of displaying tolerance toward the wicked is wrong, since it countenances the LORD’s enemies (see Ps. 139.21). Moreover, such tolerance and cooperation signals a lack of exclusive trust in God and His ability to provide for one’s every need. Chronicles’ view of separation from the wicked informed postbiblical literature (see, e.g., 1QS 5:1–20; *ʾAvot R. Nat.,* A, 16). Chronicles explains the absence of punishment for this breach of faith—for which no remorse is expressed—by the fact that Jehoshaphat has many good deeds to his credit that offset the present offense. For this reason, Chronicles prefaces this story with an account of Jehoshaphat’s worthy acts in ch 17. Since the question of differentiating true from false prophecy is not at issue in Chronicles, it is quite natural that Jehoshaphat is not blamed for having gone to battle, per se.

19.4–11: Establishment of judiciary. Jehoshaphat responds to the prophetic rebuke by promoting justice throughout the land. The historicity of this passage, unattested in Kings, has been debated at

of Ephraim; he brought them back to the LORD God of their
fathers. 5 He appointed judges in the land in all the fortified
towns of Judah, in each and every town. 6 He charged the
judges: "Consider what you are doing, for you judge not on
behalf of man, but on behalf of the LORD, and He is with you
when you pass judgment. 7 Now let the dread of the LORD be
upon you; act with care, for there is no injustice or favoritism
or bribe-taking with the LORD our God." 8 Jehoshaphat also appointed in Jerusalem some Levites and priests and heads of
the clans of Israelites for rendering judgment in matters of the
LORD, and for disputes. Then they returned to Jerusalem. 9 He
charged them, "This is how you shall act: in fear of the LORD,
with fidelity, and with whole heart. 10 When a dispute comes
before you from your brothers living in their towns, whether
about homicide, or about ritual, or laws or rules, you must instruct them so that they do not incur guilt before the LORD and
wrath be upon you and your brothers. Act so and you will not
incur guilt. 11 See, Amariah the chief priest is over you in all
cases concerning the LORD, and Zebadiah son of Ishmael is the
commander of the house of Judah in all cases concerning the
king; the Levitical officials are at your disposal; act with resolve
and the LORD be with the good."

20 After that, Moabites, Ammonites, together with some
Ammonim,[a] came against Jehoshaphat to wage war.
2 The report was brought to Jehoshaphat: "A great multitude is
coming against you from beyond the sea, from Aram, and is
now in Hazazon-tamar"—that is, En-gedi. 3 Jehoshaphat was
afraid; he decided to resort to the LORD and proclaimed a fast
for all Judah. 4 Judah assembled to beseech the LORD. They also
came from all the towns of Judah to seek the LORD.

a Probably for m'nym *"Meunites" (1 Chron. 4.41); cf. Kimhi.*

length. The formulation and content of this ch are highly reminiscent of Deut. 1.13–17; 16.18; 17.8–12. The use of paranomasia—the name Jehoshaphat means "the LORD has judged" (Heb "shafat")—bolsters the likelihood of this passage's literary, rather than historical, value. They thus view the passage as a type of midrash on Jehoshaphat's name: The king whose name includes the root "to judge" established the judicial system in Judah. Others, pointing to various differences between Chronicles and Deut. (e.g., the cities in which courts were established, the absence of vocabulary characteristic of Chronicles), have argued that Chronicles' story is factual, and draws on pre-Chronicles, non-Deuteronomic material. **4:** In contrast to ch 17, here Jehoshaphat's reform was applied not only to Judah but up through the hill country of Ephraim, as well. (This action is described as "returning" the people to the LORD.) This is another example of Chronicles' inclusivist position. This position may also reflect Deut. 16.18, which refers to cities located in (all of) Israel's tribes. **6:** For similar phrasing and notions, see Deut. 1.17. **7:** See Deut. 10.17. **10:** See Exod. 18.16; Deut. 17.8.

20.1–21.1: Jehoshaphat defeats an eastern confederation. The historicity of this ch is, again, much debated. Some scholars argue that the entire account is a historical "midrash" on either 2 Kings ch 3 or Exod. ch 14 and Isa. 7.9b. Others accept a historical kernel to the account, seeing it as a magnified version of a local conflict (in the postexilic period) or drawing on a credible local tradition. Still others see the reference to *Meunites* in v. 1 (see translators' note *a*) as indicating that the attacking force involved Nabateans from Meun/Maʿanthe, near Petra, in the 4th or 3rd c. BCE. Finally, some accept Chronicles' claim that the battle occurred in Jehoshaphat's time. Note that Chronicles does not offer any theological explanation for the outbreak of war during the reign of a (basically) righteous king. Chronicles thereby acknowledges that some wars come about not as punishments but, rather, as a means of testing the religious commitment of the king and his people, or for some other (unexplained) reason. This may be further proof that Chronicles does not maintain a rigorous theology of retribution. **20.1–2:** The redundant *some Ammonim* has prompted several exegetes to read "Meunim." On the basis of the biblical site Maʿon and Arabic Maʿan, it appears that the Meunites lived either in the southern Negev, i.e., west of the Arabah, or slightly to the Arabah's east, near Petra. LXX reads here "Minaeans." **2:** The MT entails a geographical difficulty: Peoples coming *from beyond the sea* (whomever this might refer to) and Arameans, whose territory lay to the northeast of Israel, would not be expected to gather at En-gedi, located at roughly the middle of the length of the Dead Sea. The old Latin translation renders "Edomites" in place of Arameans, a reading adopted by many moderns, especially since the two words are graphically similar in Heb. **3–5:** These vv. again refer only to the cities of Judah, either because the impending battle was due to take place in Judah's territory or, once

5 Jehoshaphat stood in the congregation of Judah and Jerusalem in the House of the LORD at the front of the new court.
6 He said, "LORD God of our fathers, truly You are the God in
heaven and You rule over the kingdoms of the nations; power
and strength are Yours; none can oppose You. 7 O our God, you
dispossessed the inhabitants of this land before Your people
Israel, and You gave it to the descendants of Your friend Abraham forever. 8 They settled in it and in it built for You a House
for Your name. They said, 9 'Should misfortune befall us—the
punishing sword, pestilence, or famine, we shall stand before
this House and before You—for Your name is in this House—
and we shall cry out to You in our distress, and You will listen and deliver us.' 10 Now the people of Ammon, Moab, and
the hill country of Seir, into whose [land] You did not let Israel come when they came from Egypt, but they turned aside
from them and did not wipe them out, 11 these now repay us
by coming to expel us from Your possession which You gave us
as ours. 12 O our God, surely You will punish them, for we are
powerless before this great multitude that has come against us,
and do not know what to do, but our eyes are on You." 13 All
Judah stood before the LORD with their little ones, their womenfolk, and their children.

14 Then in the midst of the congregation the spirit of the
LORD came upon Jahaziel son of Zechariah son of Benaiah son
of Jeiel son of Mattaniah the Levite, of the sons of Asaph, 15 and
he said, "Give heed, all Judah and the inhabitants of Jerusalem
and King Jehoshaphat; thus said the LORD to you, 'Do not fear
or be dismayed by this great multitude, for the battle is God's,
not yours. 16 March down against them tomorrow as they come
up by the Ascent of Ziz; you will find them at the end of the
wadi in the direction of the wilderness of Jeruel. 17 It is not for
you to fight this battle; stand by, wait, and witness your deliverance by the LORD, O Judah and Jerusalem; do not fear or be
dismayed; go forth to meet them tomorrow and the LORD will
be with you.'" 18 Jehoshaphat bowed low with his face to the
ground, and all Judah and the inhabitants of Jerusalem threw
themselves down before the LORD to worship the LORD. 19 Levites of the sons of Kohath and of the sons of Korah got up to
extol the LORD God of Israel at the top of their voices.

20 Early the next morning they arose and went forth to the
wilderness of Tekoa. As they went forth, Jehoshaphat stood
and said, "Listen to me, O Judah and inhabitants of Jerusalem:
Trust firmly in the LORD your God and you will stand firm;

again, as a sign of Chronicles' preferential treatment of Judah, whose residents understand the importance of seeking out the LORD. Fasting in the Bible appears in many contexts; for examples of such conduct before engaging in battle, see 1 Sam. 7.6; 14.24; Joel 2.15; Jdt. 4.1–15. **5:** *The new court,* a third (outer) court or, alternatively, a newly formed division within Chronicles' second (i.e., lay) court. **6–12:** Jehoshaphat's prayer contains a reprise of Israel's early history. V. 9 portrays this public gathering as a fulfillment of Solomon's prayer at 2 Chron. 6.24–25, again linking Jehoshaphat and Solomon. **10:** This v. adopts the tradition regarding *Seir* preserved in Deut. 21.2–8; cf. Num. 20.14–21. **12:** *Punish them* (lit. "judge them," Heb "tishpot-bam") is another example of paranomasia. The LORD is asked to judge (Israel's enemies), precisely as the literal meaning of "Jehoshaphat" indicates. **13–14:** The leading role of the Levites is once again in evidence, as the critical oracle is delivered by one of the Temple minstrels. This v. should not be taken to indicate that "Levitic prophecy" always, or even generally, involved an oracular saying; instead it reflects the type of ad hoc prophetic activity favored by Chronicles. **15–17:** The wording of these vv. draws on earlier works, most notably Exod. 14.13–14. Like Moses in the latter instance, Jahaziel tells Judah that the war is the LORD's battle. This passage is perhaps the clearest example of Chronicles' one-dimensional approach to human endeavors. The view of some scholars that Chronicles' formulation is advocating a pacifistic policy is unlikely given the depiction of warfare elsewhere in the book; more likely, the Chronicler simply sought to explain that no situation, however bleak, is without hope; ultimately, the outcome in all battles (as in other spheres of life) is determined exclusively by divine intervention. **20:** Jehoshaphat, the fundamentally good king, addresses his people, reminding them that trust in the LORD and his prophets brings success. Trust in God, along with proper cultic activity (including prayer) centered on the Temple, ensures victory. Indeed, in contrast to previous military encounters, this passage makes no mention of the number of the Judahite forces, for Israel's strength is not responsible for victory. True to form, the righteous monarch engages his people in the decision making, rather than

trust firmly in His prophets and you will succeed." 21 After taking counsel with the people, he stationed singers to the LORD
extolling the One majestic in holiness as they went forth ahead
of the vanguard, saying, "Praise the LORD, for His steadfast love
is eternal." 22 As they began their joyous shouts and hymns, the
LORD set ambushes for the men of Amon, Moab, and the hill
country of Seir, who were marching against Judah, and they
were routed. 23 The Ammonites and Moabites turned against
the men of the hill country of Seir to exterminate and annihilate them. When they had made an end of the men of Seir, each
helped to destroy his fellow.

24 When Judah reached the lookout in the wilderness and
looked for the multitude, they saw them lying on the ground
as corpses; not one had survived. 25 Jehoshaphat and his army
came to take the booty, and found an abundance of goods,
corpses, and precious objects, which they pillaged, more than
they could carry off. For three days they were taking booty,
there was so much of it. 26 On the fourth day they assembled in
the Valley of Blessing—for there they blessed the LORD; that is
why that place is called the Valley of Blessing to this day. 27 All
the men of Judah and Jerusalem with Jehoshaphat at their
head returned joyfully to Jerusalem, for the LORD had given
them cause for rejoicing over their enemies. 28 They came to
Jerusalem to the House of the LORD, to the accompaniment of
harps, lyres, and trumpets. 29 The terror of God seized all the
kingdoms of the lands when they heard that the LORD had
fought the enemies of Israel. 30 The kingdom of Jehoshaphat
was untroubled, and his God granted him respite on all sides.

31[a] Jehoshaphat reigned over Judah. He was thirty-five years
old when he became king, and he reigned in Jerusalem for
twenty-five years. His mother's name was Azubah daughter of
Shilhi. 32 He followed the course of his father Asa and did not
deviate from it, doing what was pleasing to the LORD. 33 However, the shrines did not cease; the people still did not direct
their heart toward the God of their fathers. 34 As for the other
events of Jehoshaphat's reign, early and late, they are recorded
in the annals of Jehu son of Hanani, which were included in
the book of the kings of Israel.

35 Afterward, King Jehoshaphat of Judah entered into a partnership with King Ahaziah of Israel, thereby acting wickedly.
36 He joined with him in constructing ships to go to Tarshish;
the ships were constructed in Ezion-geber. 37 Eliezer son of
Dodavahu of Mareshah prophesied against Jehoshaphat, "As
you have made a partnership with Ahaziah, the LORD will
break up your work." The ships were wrecked and were unable
to go to Tarshish.

a With vv. 31–37, cf. 1 Kings 22.41–49.

dictating to them. The people's ready assent shows they are worthy of the LORD's intervention. *Trust firmly ... and you will stand firm* ("ha'minu ... vete'menu") reflects the similar paronomasia in Isa. 7.9. **21:** *The One majestic in holiness:* The Heb is unclear, and others render "in holy attire," "His holy splendor," or "the holy place of His appearing"; see 16.29. The "democratization" theme appears at 1 Chron. 13.1–4 (see n.); 2 Chron. 1.2; 30.2; 32.3. Note the refrain *"Praise ... for His steadfast love is eternal."* **22–24:** In contrast to other passages, where the priestly trumpet blasts lead the army into victory (e.g., Josh. 6.8–10, 16), here the Levitical choral rite dominates. The victory begins as soon as the Levites break forth in chant; Judah engages in no military activity. No explanation is offered for how the internecine fighting broke out in the enemy camp (cf. Judg. 11.19–22). Since the Jewish community of Chronicles' time was in no position to wage war, the message of the Levitic role here seems to be that it is their cultic chant, whether performed in battle or in the Temple, which invokes divine favor and protects Israel. **25–30:** All of the enemy force has been decimated, another feature appearing in Exod. (14.28; see above, vv. 15–17 n.). The only task left for Judah's "army" is scavenging and collection of the spoils. **35–37:** The story of Jehoshaphat's joint maritime venture differs markedly from 1 Kings 22.49–50, either because Chronicles' text reflects a different source or due to its own tendentious reworking. Kings states that Jehoshaphat prepared ships for sailing but these were destroyed in Ezion-geber (near present-day Eilat) and did not sail. Jehoshaphat then refused Ahaziah's offer of assistance. No reason is offered there for Jehoshaphat's refusal. Chronicles' version results in a second offense on the part of Jehoshaphat, one that appears to be identical to his wrongdoing in ch 18. It is possible that this latter episode teaches that any form of cooperation with the wicked is forbidden, i.e., even where

21 [a]Jehoshaphat slept with his fathers and was buried with
his fathers in the City of David; his son Jehoram succeeded him as king. 2 He had brothers, sons of Jehoshaphat:
Azariah, Jehiel, Zechariah, Azariahu, Michael, and Shephatiah; all these were sons of King Jehoshaphat of Israel. 3 Their father gave them many gifts of silver, gold, and [other] presents,
as well as fortified towns in Judah, but he gave the kingdom to
Jehoram because he was the first-born.
4 Jehoram proceeded to take firm hold of his father's kingdom and put to the sword all his brothers, as well as some of
the officers of Israel. 5 Jehoram was thirty-two years old when
he became king, and he reigned in Jerusalem eight years. 6 He
followed the practices of the kings of Israel doing what the
House of Ahab had done, for he married a daughter of Ahab;
he did what was displeasing to the LORD. 7 However, the LORD
refrained from destroying the House of David for the sake of
the covenant he had made with David, and in accordance with
his promise to maintain a lamp for him and his descendants
for all time. 8 During his reign, the Edomites rebelled against
Judah's rule and set up a king of their own. 9 Jehoram advanced
[against them] with his officers and all his chariotry. He arose
by night and attacked the Edomites, who surrounded him
and the chariot commanders. 10 Edom has been in rebellion
against Judah, to this day; Libnah also rebelled against him at
that time, because he had forsaken the LORD God of his fathers.
11 Moreover, he built shrines in the hill country of Judah; he led
astray the inhabitants of Jerusalem and made Judah wayward.
12 A letter from Elijah the prophet came to him which read,
"Thus says the LORD God of your father David: Since you have
not followed the practices of your father Jehoshaphat and the
practices of King Asa of Judah, 13 but have followed the practices of the kings of Israel, leading astray Judah and the inhabitants of Jerusalem as the House of Ahab led them astray, and
have also killed your brothers of your father's house, who were
better than you, 14 therefore, the LORD will inflict a great blow
upon your people, your sons, and your wives and all your possessions. 15 As for you, you will be severely stricken with a disorder of the bowels year after year until your bowels drop out."
16 The LORD stirred up the spirit of the Philistines and the
Arabs who were neighbors of the Cushites against Jehoram.
17 They marched against Judah, breached its defenses, and carried off all the property that was found in the king's palace, as

a Cf. 2 Kings 8.17–24.

the upright individual participates purely for his own benefit and with no regard for the welfare of the wicked. Chronicles claims that the ships were intended to sail for Tarshish, whereas 1 Kings states that the ships' destination was Ophir, located in Africa, at the mouth of the Red Sea; see 9.21. As elsewhere in Chronicles, a prophet not known from other sources appears to offer a short speech to the king.

21.2–20: Jehoram's reign. An expanded version of 2 Kings 8.16–24; some of Chronicles' added material probably draws on additional written sources. **2–4:** *Jehoram* establishes his rule. These vv. are unique to Chronicles. Jehoram is the eldest of seven sons, signaling the blessing bestowed upon Jehoshaphat. Like many other leaders—most commonly, of the northern tribes—Jehoram seeks uncontested control by the execution of all potential claimants; cf. Judg. ch 9; 1 Kings 15.29; 16.11–12; 2 Kings 10.11 || 2 Chron. 22.8. The placement of these vv. highlights the theme of the threat of extinction to the Davidic line which unites chs 21–22 (see 21.17; 22.8–9; 22.10–11). **5–11:** The passage, aside from v. 11, is taken from 2 Kings 8.17–22. **6:** Athaliah was probably a daughter of Omri, King of Israel, and hence sister of Ahab. **7:** Chronicles' reformulation of 2 Kings 8.19 highlights the divine promise to the Davidic dynasty. **8–11:** Chronicles suggests that Jehoram's troubles are the result of his religious infidelity. **10–19:** These vv. have no parallel in Kings. **12–15:** Letter from Elijah. The prevalent view maintains that this letter is Chronicles' creation. The choice of Elijah was probably informed by his role as zealous champion of the worship of YHVH against the influence of Baalism in northern Israel during the rule of Ahab and Ahaziah. Given Jehoram's marriage to Ahab's daughter, Elijah was the natural choice. Because of uncertainty surrounding the chronology of the period (see 2 Kings 1.17; ch 2; 3.11), it is unclear whether Chronicles thought that Elijah was still alive or had perished after composing the prophetic letter.

21.16–20: End of Jehoram's reign. **17:** LXX reads "daughters" in place of *wives*. The form "Jehoahaz" in place of the standard "Ahaziah" (see

well as his sons and his wives. The only son who remained was
Jehoahaz, his youngest. 18 After this, the LORD afflicted him with
an incurable disease of the bowels. 19 Some years later, when a
period of two years had elapsed, his bowels dropped out because of his disease, and he died a gruesome death. His people
did not make a fire for him like the fire for his fathers. 20 He was
thirty-two years old when he became king, and he reigned in
Jerusalem eight years. He departed unpraised,[a] and was buried
in the City of David, but not in the tombs of the kings.

22 [b]The inhabitants of Jerusalem made Ahaziah, his youngest son, king in his stead, because all the older ones had
been killed by the troops that penetrated the camp with the
Arabs. Ahaziah son of Jehoram reigned as king of Judah. 2 Ahaziah was forty-two years old when he became king, and he
reigned in Jerusalem one year; his mother's name was Athaliah
daughter of Omri. 3 He too followed the practices of the house
of Ahab, for his mother counseled him to do evil. 4 He did what
was displeasing to the LORD, like the house of Ahab, for they
became his counselors after his father's death, to his ruination.
5 Moreover, he followed their counsel and marched with Jehoram son of King Ahab of Israel to battle against King Hazael of
Aram at Ramoth-gilead, where the Arameans wounded Joram.
6 He returned to Jezreel to recover from the wounds inflicted
on him at Ramah when he fought against King Hazael of Aram.
King Azariah son of Jehoram of Judah went down to Jezreel to
visit Jehoram son of Ahab while he was ill. 7 God caused the
downfall of Ahaziah because he visited Joram. During his visit
he went out with Jehoram to Jehu son of Nimshi, whom the
LORD had anointed to cut off the house of Ahab. 8 In the course
of bringing the house of Ahab to judgment, Jehu came upon
the officers of Judah and the nephews of Ahaziah, ministers of
Ahaziah, and killed them. 9 He sent in search of Ahaziah, who
was caught hiding in Samaria, was brought to Jehu, and put
to death. He was given a burial, because it was said, "He is the
son of Jehoshaphat who worshiped the LORD wholeheartedly."
So the house of Ahaziah could not muster the strength to rule.
10 When Athaliah, Ahaziah's mother, learned that her son
was dead, she promptly did away with all who were of the royal

a Following Septuagint; cf. Arabic ḥamada, *"praise."*

b With vv. 1–6, cf. 2 Kings 8.25–29; with vv. 8–9, cf. 2 Kings 9.27–28; with vv. 10–12, cf. 2 Kings 11.1–3.

22.1) supports the likelihood that this v. is taken from an independent source. Both names mean "YHVH has grasped/strengthened." "Jehoahaz" places the theophoric element ("Jeho") first, followed by the verb "grasp/strengthen"; Ahaziah places the theophoric element ("yah"/"iah") after the verb. **18–20:** The king's disease is not recorded in Kings; it is unclear whether Chronicles draws on a genuine source or has created this account in fulfillment of v. 15. Chronicles' version highlights the ignominious nature of Jehoram's demise; cf. 2 Kings 8.23–24.

22.1–9: Ahaziah's reign. This account, not preserved elsewhere, is reminiscent of 14.9–15 and may derive from the same source. Two features continue from Jehoram's reign to Ahaziah's: the influence of Athaliah and the threat to the Davidic line. The passage contains several allusions to the disastrous reign of Saul (1 Chron. ch 10); compare, esp., vv. 7 and 9 with 1 Chron. 10.6, 13–14. **1–3:** The age, *forty-two,* is impossible, since it would make Ahaziah older than his father. Many LXX mss read "twenty"; Peshitta reads "twenty-two," as does 2 Kings 8.26. **4–5:** Added by Chronicles; contacts with the north bring disaster. **7–9:** A condensed and extensively reworked version of 2 Kings 9.1–28; 10.12–14, provided with an introductory sentence explaining that the events befalling the dynasty are the result of backsliding. Chronicles differs from 2 Kings in the following respects: The princes of Judah die before Ahaziah (cf. 2 Kings 10.12–14); the circumstances of his death are different (cf. 2 Kings 9.27); the circumstances surrounding his burial are different (cf. 2 Kings 9.28). Chronicles' text may be based on an independent source, but the presence of several Chronistic motifs suggests that it is the creation of its author. Specifically, the emphasis on God's complete control of history (v. 7, *God caused the downfall of Ahaziah*) is consistent with Chronicles' theology, as is the emphasis on the impropriety of association with northern monarchs.

22.10–24.27: Joash's reign. With the possible exception of parts of ch 24, this section is based on 2 Kings chs 11–12. Joash's reign consists of three periods: (1) the Davidic dynasty at its lowest point; (2) a period of revitalization, echoing the upswing

stock of the house of Judah. 11 But Jehoshabeath, daughter of
the king, spirited away Ahaziah's son Joash from among the
princes who were being slain, and put him and his nurse in a
bedroom. Jehoshabeath, daughter of King Jehoram, wife of the
priest Jehoiada—she was the sister of Ahaziah—kept him hidden from Athaliah so that he was not put to death. 12 He stayed
with them for six years, hidden in the House of God, while Athaliah reigned over the land.

23 [a]In the seventh year, Jehoiada took courage and brought
the chiefs of the hundreds, Azariah son of Jeroham, Ishmael son of Jehohanan, Azariah son of Obed, Maaseiah son of
Adaiah, and Elishaphat son of Zichri, into a compact with him.
2 They went through Judah and assembled the Levites from all
the towns of Judah, and the chiefs of the clans of Israel. They
came to Jerusalem 3 and the entire assembly made a covenant
with the king in the House of God. He[b] said to them, "The son of
the king shall be king according to the promise the LORD made
concerning the sons of David. 4 This is what you must do: One
third of you, priests and Levites, who are on duty for the week,
shall be gatekeepers at the thresholds; 5 another third shall be
stationed in the royal palace, and the other third at the Foundation Gate. All the people shall be in the courts of the House
of the LORD. 6 Let no one enter the House of the LORD except
the priests and the ministering Levites. They may enter because
they are sanctified, but all the people shall obey the proscription of the LORD. 7 The Levites shall surround the king on every
side, every man with his weapons at the ready; and whoever enters the House shall be killed. Stay close to the king in his comings and goings." 8 The Levites and all Judah did just as Jehoiada
the priest ordered: each took his men—those who were on duty
that week and those who were off duty that week, for Jehoiada
the priest had not dismissed the divisions. 9 Jehoiada the priest
gave the chiefs of the hundreds King David's spears and shields
and quivers that were kept in the House of God. 10 He stationed
the entire force, each man with his weapons at the ready, from
the south end of the House to the north end of the House, at
the altar and the House, to guard the king on every side. 11 Then
they brought out the king's son, and placed upon him the crown
and the insignia. They proclaimed him king, and Jehoiada and
his sons anointed him and shouted, "Long live the king!"
12 When Athaliah heard the shouting of the people and the
guards and the acclamation of the king, she came out to the
people, to the House of the LORD. 13 She looked about and saw
the king standing by his pillar at the entrance, the chiefs with
their trumpets beside the king, and all the people of the land

a Cf. 2 Kings 11.4–20. *b I.e., Jehoiada.*

upon Joash's ascension; (3) religious backsliding, including rejection of the prophetic word, leading to military defeat and the king's death.

22.10–23.21: Joash takes power. 22.10–12: Following Kings, the standard opening and closing formulae are lacking, indicating that Athaliah's reign is not formally recognized. **12:** It is unclear where, precisely, in the Temple complex Joash was hidden, though the fact that he was successfully hidden for six years suggests that he was placed in the Temple's inner chambers, possibly those normally accessible only to priests. If so, this may constitute a break with the Priestly sources of the Pentateuch, which proscribe non-priestly presence in the sanctuary (i.e., Tent of Meeting; see also, 2 Chron. 29.16). Alternatively, it may constitute an early precedent for the rabbinic view (*b. Yoma* 82a, *b. Sanh.* 74a) that saving of human lives ("piqquaḥ nefesh") supercedes virtually all other religious precepts. **23.1–21:** Joash's coronation and removal of Athaliah. Cf. 2 Kings 11.4–20. Two key alterations appear: (1) Joash's rule is welcomed and supported by the populace (it is a personal affair in Kings); this is reminiscent of Chronicles' depiction of David and Solomon. (2) Chronicles adjusts the cultic details to its view of proper cultic procedure, as it pertains to priests and Levites. The importance of the Levites is again in evidence, as the author places the king's welfare primarily in their hands, with the priests playing a secondary role. **1–16:** Blessings. The period focuses on restoration of the Temple. Chronicles claims that Jehoiada, the high priest, married Jehoshabeath (22.11), the daughter of Ahaziah, who was not of priestly lineage. This datum appears to be in tension with Lev. 21.14, which requires that high priests marry only priestly virgins/nubile women. It is possible, however, that the Heb term for "his own kin" used there was understood to mean simply "his people" (see Samaritan Pentateuch to Lev. 21.14). **1:** Most of these names

rejoicing and blowing trumpets, and the singers with musical
instruments leading the hymns. Athaliah rent her garments
and cried out, "Treason, treason!" 14 Then the priest Jehoiada
ordered out the army officers, the chiefs of hundreds, and said
to them, "Take her out between the ranks, and if anyone follows her, put him to the sword." For the priest thought, "Let her
not be put to death in the House of the LORD." 15 They cleared a
passage for her and she came to the entrance of the Horse Gate
to the royal palace; there she was put to death.
16 Then Jehoiada solemnized a covenant between himself
and the people and the king that they should be the people
of the LORD. 17 All the people then went to the temple of Baal;
they tore it down and smashed its altars and images to bits,
and they slew Mattan, the priest of Baal, in front of the altars.
18 Jehoiada put the officers of the House of the LORD in the
charge of Levite priests whom David had assigned over the
House of the LORD to offer up burnt offerings, as is prescribed
in the Teaching of Moses, accompanied by joyful song as ordained by David. 19 He stationed the gatekeepers at the gates of
the House of the LORD to prevent the entry of anyone unclean
for any reason. 20 He took the chiefs of hundreds, the nobles,
and the rulers of the people and all the people of the land, and
they escorted the king down from the House of the LORD into
the royal palace by the upper gate, and seated the king on the
royal throne. 21 All the people of the land rejoiced, and the city
was quiet. As for Athaliah, she had been put to the sword.

24 [a]Jehoash was seven years old when he became king,
and he reigned in Jerusalem forty years. His mother's
name was Zibiah of Beer-sheba. 2 All the days of the priest Jehoiada, Jehoash did what was pleasing to the LORD. 3 Jehoiada
took two wives for him, by whom he had sons and daughters.
4 Afterward, Joash decided to renovate the House of the
LORD. 5 He assembled the priests and the Levites and charged
them as follows: "Go out to the towns of Judah and collect
money from all Israel for the annual repair of the House of your
God. Do it quickly." But the Levites did not act quickly. 6 The
king summoned Jehoiada the chief and said to him, "Why have
you not seen to it that the Levites brought the tax imposed by
Moses, the servant of the LORD, and the congregation of Israel from Judah and Jerusalem to the Tent of the Pact?" 7 For
the children of the wicked Athaliah had violated the House of
God and had even used the sacred things of the House of the
LORD for the Baals. 8 The king ordered that a chest be made and
placed on the outside of the gate of the House of the LORD. 9 A
proclamation was issued in Judah and Jerusalem to bring the

a *Cf.* 2 Kings 12.1–22.

are borne elsewhere in Chronicles by priests and Levites. Admittedly, the name *Ishmael* does not appear elsewhere bearing priestly or Levitic lineage, his father's name, *Jehohanan,* does so appear (1 Chron. 26.3). Similarly, Elishaphat is not attested as a priestly/Levitic name, but his father, *Zichri,* is a Levite living in Jerusalem. Despite the common nature of these names, their presence in the Temple here suggests that they are also of priestly/Levitic lineage. The officers in 2 Kings 11.4 appear to fill a military role.

24.1–2: Joash's reign begins. Chronicles' depiction is more favorable than that of 2 Kings ch 12; it omits the notice about sacrifice at the local shrines or high places ("bamot"; 2 Kings 12.4).

24.4–14: Temple restoration. The passage differs substantially from 2 Kings 12.4–16 and conveys several of Chronicles' recurring themes. The claim that there was a surplus of money for other purposes (cf. 2 Kings 12.13–14) due to generosity of the people is to be expected; see 1 Chron. 29.11–19. Contra 2 Kings 12.8, wherein Jehoiada and other priests are reproved for failure to attend to Temple repairs, Chronicles has the Levites execute collection of Temple donations, an example of the book's pro-Levite stance. **6:** The term *Tent of the Pact* alludes to the Mosaic Tabernacle (Num. 9.15; 17.22–23; 18.2). Although this term appears nowhere else in Chronicles, it forms part of the Chronicler's continuity motif, wherein the Temple is the direct successor to the Tabernacle; see 2 Chron. 1.3–6; 5.5; 6.33.

tax imposed on Israel in the wilderness by Moses, the servant
of God. 10 All the officers and all the people gladly brought it
and threw it into the chest till it was full. 11 Whenever the chest
was brought to the royal officers by the Levites, and they saw
that it contained much money, the royal scribe and the agent
of the chief priest came and emptied out the chest and carried
it back to its place. They did this day by day, and much money
was collected. 12 The king and Jehoiada delivered the money to
those who oversaw the tasks connected with the work of the
House of the LORD. They hired masons and carpenters to renovate the House of the LORD, as well as craftsmen in iron and
bronze to repair the House of the LORD. 13 The overseers did
their work; under them the work went well and they restored
the House of God to its original form and repaired it. 14 When
they had finished, they brought the money that was left over to
the king and Jehoiada; it was made into utensils for the House
of the LORD, service vessels: buckets and ladles, golden and
silver vessels. Burnt offerings were offered up regularly in the
House of the LORD all the days of Jehoiada. 15 Jehoiada reached
a ripe old age and died; he was one hundred and thirty years
old at his death. 16 They buried him in the City of David together with the kings, because he had done good in Israel, and on
behalf of God and His House.

17 But after the death of Jehoiada, the officers of Judah came,
bowing low to the king; and the king listened to them. 18 They
forsook the House of the LORD God of their fathers to serve
the sacred posts and idols; and there was wrath upon Judah
and Jerusalem because of this guilt of theirs. 19 The LORD sent
prophets among them to bring them back to Him; they admonished them but they would not pay heed. 20 Then the spirit
of God enveloped Zechariah son of Jehoiada the priest; he
stood above the people and said to them, "Thus God said: Why
do you transgress the commandments of the LORD when you
cannot succeed? Since you have forsaken the LORD, He has
forsaken you." 21 They conspired against him and pelted him
with stones in the court of the House of the LORD, by order of
the king. 22 King Joash disregarded the loyalty that his father Jehoiada had shown to him, and killed his son. As he was dying,
he said, "May the LORD see and requite it."

10: The importance of divine service, esp. that connected with the Temple, being performed with joy is a recurring motif. In addition, this passage highlights the collective nature of this endeavor. For discussion of both points, see 1 Chron. 29.11–19 n. **14:** The reference to *vessels* made from money left over contradicts 2 Kings 12.14, which precludes using the donations for these items; the vessels—in particular, the (ubiquitous) trumpets and snuffers (2 Chron. 4.22)—would have been of importance to the Chronicler and his audience. Several of these utensils are mentioned in Priestly sources, constituting another example of the nexus between the Temple and the desert Tabernacle. In addition, no mention is made here of money for guilt offerings and sin offerings being given towards support of the priests, reflecting a relative "downgrading" of priests vis-à-vis Levites.

24.15–16: The death of Jehoiada. The burial notice indicates Chronicles' positive evaluation of Jehoiada, Joash's mentor. Jehoiada enjoys one of the longest life spans of any postdiluvian figure. In addition, this is the only time that the author addresses the burial arrangements of a non-monarchic figure, according him the status of quasi-monarch. While this may point to the growing stature of the high priest in postexilic society (see 1 Chron. 23.28–32), the sui generis nature of this report warrants caution; the royal-like homage extended to Jehoiada may be due to his role in protecting the integrity of the monarchic line.

24.17–27: Judgment. 2 Kings 12.17–21 states that Joash submitted to the Arameans and was assassinated, but offers no theological explanation. Chronicles provides it by claiming that Joash's death resulted from his refusal to heed the teachings of Jehohiada, who had just died. This passage exemplifies Chronicles' view of the divine capacity for forgiveness, and of the importance of prophetic forewarning before punishment. Much of the core material, especially that concerning Zechariah and the Aramean invasion, may be taken from sources other than Kings. **17–22:** Unknown from other sources. Zechariah here is a foil to Joash and highlights the difference between the several periods in Joash's reign. The sermonic style is typical of Chronicles. **21–22:** Jehoiada is killed in the very place where he crowned Joash; see also 23.14, where Jehoiada refuses to allow Athaliah's killing in the sacred precincts. This passage contains one of only two attestations of the Deity as the subject of the root "seek"; for similar depiction of God as one who "seeks [payment/

23 At the turn of the year, the army of Aram marched against him; they invaded Judah and Jerusalem, and wiped out all the officers of the people from among the people, and sent all the booty they took to the king of Damascus. 24 The invading army of Aram had come with but a few men, but the LORD delivered a very large army into their hands, because they had forsaken the LORD God of their fathers. They inflicted punishments on Joash. 25 When they withdrew, having left him with many wounds, his courtiers plotted against him because of the murder[a] of the sons of Jehoiada the priest, and they killed him in bed. He died and was buried in the City of David; he was not buried in the tombs of the kings. 26 These were the men who conspired against him: Zabad son of Shimeath the Ammonitess, and Jehozabad son of Shimrith the Moabitess. 27 As to his sons, and the many pronouncements against him, and his rebuilding of the House of God, they are recorded in the story in the book of the kings. His son Amaziah succeeded him as king.

25 [b]Amaziah was twenty-five years old when he became king, and he reigned twenty-nine years in Jerusalem; his mother's name was Jehoaddan of Jerusalem. 2 He did what was pleasing to the LORD, but not with a whole heart. 3 Once he had the kingdom firmly under control, he executed the courtiers who had assassinated his father the king. 4 But he did not put their children to death for [he acted] in accordance with what is written in the Teaching, in the Book of Moses, where the LORD commanded, [c-]"Parents shall not die for children, nor shall children die for parents, but every person shall die only for his own crime."[-c]

a Lit. "blood." *b Cf. 2 Kings 14.* *c-c Cf. Deut. 24.16.*

revenge for spilt] blood," see Ps. 9.13. **23–24:** Aramean invasion. Other than the mention of war spoil, this passage differs markedly from 2 Kings 12.7–18. There, the Aramean king, Hazael, is bought off and does not attack. Here, it appears that the Aramean force attacks while Hazael remains at home. Finally, the two versions of the battle differ substantively. Chronicles' text is probably a tendentious reformulation of earlier material, emphasizing that (only) those who sinned were now being punished. **25:** Chronicles explains the king's assassination as retribution for his treatment of Zechariah, highlighting the explanation through several key words ("ʿ-z-b [abandon]," "q-sh-r [conspire]") shared by this v. and vv. 21–22; cf. 2 Kings 2.20. The problematic phrasing of 2 Kings 12.20 is replaced here by *in bed*, perhaps indicating that Chronicles no longer understood the reference in Kings. The "bed" may also be an allusion to the bedroom mentioned above (22.11), indicating a total lack of appreciation on Joash's part. Chronicles' statement regarding Joash's burial is likely tendentious, suggesting a more negative evaluation of Joash; cf. 2 Kings 12.22, where Joash is buried with his fathers in the city of David. **26:** Cf. the names at 2 Kings 12.22. The claim that two of the conspirators were foreigners may bear a talionic or measure-for-measure message: When Israel turns to foreign gods their (divinely ordained) punishment comes at the hands of foreigners. **27:** On *story*, "midrash," see 13.22–23 n. The term "midrash" in this v. has been interpreted as denoting an expanded form of the 1–2 Kings account (see 1 Chron. 28.8–9 n.) and has served as a basis for various theories regarding the Chronicler's use of extrabiblical sources. In fact, it probably means something like "story, record, protocols."

25.1–28: Amaziah's reign. Amaziah's reign, like that of Joash and others, is divided into periods of fidelity and infidelity. As in other cases, divine forbearance and grace require that a prophet be sent to warn Amaziah, but to no avail. **1–4:** Chronicles' less than fully positive evaluation reflects the book's criticism of Amaziah's dependence on mercenaries. V. 4 is a reformulation of 2 Kings 14.5–6, itself based on Deut. 24.16. Whereas Deut. and Kings employ the Heb form meaning "be executed" ("yumtu"), Chronicles employs the form meaning "die" ("yamutu"). This may be merely a textual or linguistic variant, although some see it as proof of Chronicles' (purported) strict theory of retribution, namely, that an innocent individual cannot be punished, either by society or the deity, for the offense of another. **5–13:** Campaign against Edom. Chronicles expands greatly upon 2 Kings 14.7. The expansion contains motifs characteristic of Chronicles' worldview, in particular: unity and harmony among all of the people/tribes of Israel, the belief that success in all matters—here, military and financial—are determined exclusively by the Deity, and the rewards reaped for heeding the prophetic message. The number "ten thousand" (vv. 11–12) though small by comparison with numbers appearing in other Chronicles passages, is employed elsewhere in typological fashion, where it denotes a large force; see (in addition to 2 Kings ch 14), Judg. 1.4; 3.29; 4.6; 6.3–4.

5 Amaziah assembled the men of Judah, and he put all the men of Judah and Benjamin under officers of thousands and officers of hundreds, by clans. He mustered them from the age of twenty upward, and found them to be 300,000 picked men fit for service, able to bear spear and shield. 6 He hired 100,000 warriors from Israel for 100 talents of silver. 7 Then a man of God came to him and said, "O king! Do not let the army of Israel go with you, for the LORD is not with Israel—all these Ephraimites. 8 But go by yourself and do it; take courage for battle, [else] God will make you fall before the enemy. For in God there is power to help one or make one fall!" 9 Amaziah said to the man of God, "And what am I to do about the 100 talents I gave for the Israelite force?" The man of God replied, "The LORD has the means to give you much more than that." 10 So Amaziah detached the force that came to him from Ephraim, [ordering them] to go back to their place. They were greatly enraged against Judah and returned to their place in a rage.

11 Amaziah took courage and, leading his army, he marched to the Valley of Salt. He slew 10,000 men of Seir; 12 another 10,000 the men of Judah captured alive and brought to the top of Sela. They threw them down from the top of Sela and every one of them was burst open. 13 The men of the force that Amaziah had sent back so they would not go with him into battle made forays against the towns of Judah from Samaria to Beth-horon. They slew 3,000 of them, and took much booty.

14 After Amaziah returned from defeating the Edomites, he had the gods of the men of Seir brought, and installed them as his gods; he prostrated himself before them, and to them he made sacrifice. 15 The LORD was enraged at Amaziah, and sent a prophet to him who said to him, "Why are you worshiping the gods of a people who could not save their people from you?" 16 As he spoke to him, [Amaziah] said to him, "Have we appointed you a counselor to the king? Stop, else you will be killed!" The prophet stopped, saying, "I see God has counseled that you be destroyed, since you act this way and disregard my counsel."

17 Then King Amaziah of Judah took counsel and sent this message to Joash son of Jehoahaz son of Jehu, king of Israel, "Come, let us confront each other!" 18 King Joash of Israel sent back this message to King Amaziah of Judah, "The thistle in Lebanon sent this message to the cedar in Lebanon, 'Give your daughter to my son in marriage.' But a wild beast in Lebanon passed by and trampled the thistle. 19 You boast that you have defeated the Edomites and you are ambitious to get more glory. Now stay at home, lest, provoking disaster you fall, dragging Judah down with you." 20 But Amaziah paid no heed—it was God's doing, in order to deliver them up because they worshiped the gods of Edom. 21 King Joash of Israel marched up,

5: *Judah and Benjamin* is probably an attempt at identifying the composition of "Judah" mentioned earlier. The size of Amaziah's force, though certainly exaggerated, is considerably smaller than that mentioned in earlier accounts (1 Chron. 21.5–6; 2 Chron. 17.14–18). True to Chronicles' view, it is not the size of one's army that counts; victory and defeat in this episode are determined by one's loyalty to God. **6:** The tradition regarding mercenaries may be historically authentic. **7:** The reference to *Ephraimites* probably indicates that the mercenaries were hired from territory bordering on Judah. **12–13:** *Sela* is often identified as Petra, in southern Jordan, but this remains uncertain (cf. Ps. 137.8–9 n.). **14–16:** Worship by a victorious Judean king of the gods of a defeated enemy is unparalleled elsewhere in the Bible and quite surprising. This is likely Chronicles' creation, intended to explain Amaziah's defeat at the hands of Joash; see v. 20. **17–24:** These are largely identical to 2 Kings 24.8–14, with the addition of the phrase *it was God's doing, in order to deliver them up because they worshiped the gods of Edom* (v. 20), which makes explicit the Chronicler's theology. This v. also anticipates 26.5, below; Chronicles stresses the difference between father and son, and, accordingly, the vastly different outcomes (cf. 26.6–8). **17:** The wording here is anomalous, stating that Amaziah *took counsel,* but without noting the presence of a second party. Given that this passage plays on the Heb root "y-ʿ-ts" (advice/counsel) in the preceding v., it is likely that the v. means he took counsel with himself, refusing to consult and heed the prophetic word. There is irony in the fact that the treasure that had once been entrusted to Obed-edom ("servant/worshipper of Edom") has been lost because of the king's worship of foreign gods.

and he and King Amaziah of Judah confronted each other at
Beth-shemesh in Judah. 22 The men of Judah were routed by
Israel, and they all fled to their homes. 23 King Joash of Israel
captured Amaziah son of Joash son of Jehoahaz, king of Judah,
in Beth-shemesh. He brought him to Jerusalem and made a
breach of 400 cubits in the wall of Jerusalem, from the Ephraim
Gate to the Corner Gate. 24 Then, with all the gold and silver
and all the utensils that were to be found in the House of God
in the custody of Obed-edom, and with the treasuries of the
royal palace, and with the hostages, he returned to Samaria.
25 King Amaziah son of Joash of Judah lived fifteen years
after the death of King Joash son of Jehoahaz of Israel. 26 The
other events of Amaziah's reign, early and late, are recorded in
the book of the kings of Judah and Israel. 27 From the time that
Amaziah turned from following the LORD, a conspiracy was
formed against him in Jerusalem, and he fled to Lachish; but
they sent men after him to Lachish and they put him to death
there. 28 They brought his body back on horses and buried him
with his fathers in the city of Judah.

26 Then all the people of Judah took Uzziah, who was sixteen years old, and proclaimed him king to succeed his
father Amaziah. 2 It was he who rebuilt Eloth and restored it to
Judah after King [Amaziah] slept with his fathers.
3 Uzziah was sixteen years old when he became king, and
he reigned fifty-two years in Jerusalem; his mother's name
was Jecoliah of Jerusalem. 4 He did what was pleasing to the
LORD just as his father Amaziah had done. 5 He applied himself to the worship of God during the time of Zechariah, instructor in the visions[a] of God; during the time he worshiped
the LORD, God made him prosper. 6 He went forth to fight the
Philistines, and breached the wall of Gath and the wall of Jab-
neh and the wall of Ashdod; he built towns in [the region of]
Ashdod and among the Philistines. 7 God helped him against
the Philistines, against the Arabs who lived in Gur-baal, and
the Meunites. 8 The Ammonites paid tribute to Uzziah, and his
fame spread to the approaches of Egypt, for he grew exceedingly strong. 9 Uzziah built towers in Jerusalem on the Corner
Gate and the Valley Gate and on the Angle, and fortified them.
10 He built towers in the wilderness and hewed out many cisterns, for he had much cattle, and farmers in the foothills and
on the plain, and vine dressers in the mountains and on the
fertile lands, for he loved the soil.
11 Uzziah had an army of warriors, a battle-ready force who
were mustered by Jeiel the scribe and Maasseiah the adjutant
under Hananiah, one of the king's officers. 12 The clan chiefs,

26.1–23: Uzziah's reign. The treatment of Uzziah's reign is divided into two parts: the king's lengthy reign and his affliction with skin disease. This division is an attempt to deal with the source material: 2 Kings 14.21–15.4 depict Uzziah in a positive fashion, while 15.5–7 describe his affliction. Perhaps using some additional sources, Chronicles fills in both periods, and explains why the king is punished. **1–4:** 2 Kings generally employs the name Azariah. This difference is explained either as a regnal, rather than personal, name; or, since the Heb roots "ʿ-z-z" (the root of *Uzziah*) and "ʿ-z-r" (the root of Azariah) both mean "strong," as an interchangeable alternate form of the name. **5:** *Zechariah,* not otherwise attested, may have appeared in an earlier source available to Chronicles. Some exegetes argued that he is synonymous with Azariah, the priest, of 26.17. **6–8:** The literary features connecting these vv. with 25.20 have led some to doubt their historicity here.

a Some Heb. mss. read byrʾt; *compare ancient versions, "fear."*

valiants, totaled 2,600; [13] under them was the trained army of 307,500, who made war with might and power to aid the king against the enemy. [14] Uzziah provided them—the whole army—with shields and spears, and helmets and mail, and bows and slingstones. [15] He made clever devices in Jerusalem, set on the towers and the corners, for shooting arrows and large stones. His fame spread far, for he was helped wonderfully, and he became strong.

[16] When he was strong, he grew so arrogant he acted corruptly: he trespassed against his God by entering the Temple of the LORD to offer incense on the incense altar. [17] The priest Azariah, with eighty other brave priests of the LORD, followed him in [18] and, confronting King Uzziah, said to him, "It is not for you, Uzziah, to offer incense to the LORD, but for the Aaronite priests, who have been consecrated, to offer incense. Get out of the Sanctuary, for you have trespassed; there will be no glory in it for you from the LORD God." [19] Uzziah, holding the censer and ready to burn incense, got angry; but as he got angry with the priests, leprosy broke out on his forehead in front of the priests in the House of the LORD beside the incense altar. [20] When the chief priest Azariah and all the other priests looked at him, his forehead was leprous, so they rushed him out of there; he too made haste to get out, for the LORD had struck him with a plague. [21] King Uzziah was a leper until the day of his death. He lived in [a-]isolated quarters[-a] as a leper, for he was cut off from the House of the LORD—while Jotham his son was in charge of the king's house and governed the people of the land.

[22] The other events of Uzziah's reign, early and late, were recorded by the prophet Isaiah son of Amoz. [23] Uzziah slept with his fathers in the burial field of the kings, because, they said, he was a leper; his son Jotham succeeded him as king.

27 Jotham was twenty-five years old when he became king, and he reigned sixteen years in Jerusalem; his mother's name was Jerushah daughter of Zadok. [2] He did what was pleasing to the LORD just as his father Uzziah had done, but he did not enter the Temple of the LORD; however, the people still acted corruptly. [3] It was he who built the Upper Gate of the House of the LORD; he also built extensively on the wall of Ophel. [4] He built towns in the hill country of Judah, and in the woods he built fortresses and towers. [5] Moreover, he fought with the king of the Ammonites and overcame them; the

a-a Meaning of Heb. uncertain.

18–19: The consequences of cultic infractions are severe. The punishment is equally severe, since this skin affliction (traditionally translated as leprosy, but actually reflecting a range of skin lesions) renders the afflicted person so contaminated that he or she must dwell outside of the city (see Lev. 13.44–46). Another instance of retributive justice may be seen here: He who treads upon forbidden soil—the inner sanctum—is ultimately removed beyond the physical bounds of society (owing to skin disease). The theme of "trespass" (Heb "maʿal") recurs throughout the remainder of Chronicles; see, inter alia, 2 Chron. 26.16; 28.19; 29.6; 30.7; 36.14; as well as 1 Chron. 9.1; 10.13. There are similarities between this passage and the Korah rebellion of Num. ch 16. Though regents in the ancient Near East frequently assumed priestly roles (cf. 1 Kings 12.33; 13.1), Chronicles precludes any such practice; see 2 Chron. 13.10–11. **23:** Instead of 2 Kings 15.7, "in the City of David," Chronicles here reads *in the burial field of the kings.* A burial inscription was found in Jerusalem describing the transport of Uzziah's bones. No similar inscriptions have been found for other kings, suggesting that the tradition found here that Uzziah was not buried with his ancestors is accurate.

27.1–9: Jotham's reign. Jotham's reign is depicted in decidedly positive terms. His religious obedience brings prosperity; even the notice at 2 Kings 15.37 concerning the military campaign by Aram and the northern king Pekah are omitted here, being diverted to the reign of Ahaz. This contrasts markedly with the reign of his son, Ahaz, whom Chronicles portrays as wicked in the extreme (see ch 28). This pattern may reflect the influence of Ezek. ch 18, which explains that parents are not held accountable for their sons'/children's misconduct and grandsons/grandchildren are not responsible for the misdeeds of their fathers; each is judged in his/her own right (see intro.). **3–4:** Chronicles adds details to the terse description in 2 Kings 15.32–38. **5–9:** The historicity of this campaign, not recorded elsewhere, is debated. Some scholars emend "Ammonites" to "Meunites" (see 20.1 n.), believing that Jotham continued his father's policy (see 26.7).

Ammonites gave him that year 100 talents of silver and 10,000
kor of wheat and another 10,000 of barley; that is what the Ammonites paid him, and [likewise] in the second and third years.
6 Jotham was strong because he maintained a faithful course
before the LORD his God.

7 The other events of Jotham's reign, and all his battles and
his conduct, are recorded in the book of the kings of Israel and
Judah. 8 He was twenty-five years old when he became king,
and he reigned sixteen years in Jerusalem. 9 Jotham slept with
his fathers, and was buried in the City of David; his son Ahaz
succeeded him as king.

28 Ahaz was twenty years old when he became king, and
he reigned sixteen years in Jerusalem. He did not do
what was pleasing to the LORD as his father David had done,
2 but followed the ways of the kings of Israel; he even made
molten images for the Baals. 3 He made offerings in the Valley of Ben-hinnom and burned his sons in fire, in the abhorrent fashion of the nations which the LORD had dispossessed
before the Israelites. 4 He sacrificed and made offerings at the
shrines, on the hills, and under every leafy tree. 5 The LORD his
God delivered him over to the king of Aram, who defeated him
and took many of his men captive, and brought them to Damascus. He was also delivered over to the king of Israel, who
inflicted a great defeat on him. 6 Pekah son of Remaliah killed
120,000 in Judah—all brave men—in one day, because they
had forsaken the LORD God of their fathers. 7 Zichri, the champion of Ephraim, killed Maaseiah the king's son, and Azrikam
chief of the palace, and Elkanah, the second to the king. 8 The
Israelites captured 200,000 of their kinsmen, women, boys,
and girls; they also took a large amount of booty from them
and brought the booty to Samaria.

9 A prophet of the LORD by the name of Oded was there,
who went out to meet the army on its return to Samaria. He
said to them, "Because of the fury of the LORD God of your fathers against Judah, He delivered them over to you, and you
killed them in a rage that reached heaven. 10 Do you now intend to subjugate the men and women of Judah and Jerusalem to be your slaves? As it is, you have nothing but offenses

28.1–27: Ahaz's reign. The low point of the preexilic Judahite monarchy. Besides the sharp contrast with his father, Ahaz's wickedness creates a foil for his son, Hezekiah, the most righteous of the post-Solomonic Davidides. In many ways, this reign marks a complete reversal of 2 Chron. ch 13 and the lessons of Chronicles' Abijah. Thus, the present ch portrays the northern tribes in a most positive light, including a sincere self-reckoning of their sinful ways (cf. 2 Chron. 13.4–12). Chronicles maintains that the Northern Kingdom fell to Assyria during this reign. This paves the way for a single sovereign (Hezekiah) to reunify Judah and the northern tribes, another key theme of 2 Chron. ch 13. The antithetical nature of Judah's fate in the two chs is expressed via the polar approaches to the cult. Ch 13 contrasts Judah's cultic fealty with the cultic fraud perpetrated by the northern leaders; the present ch emphasizes Judah's cultic offenses and the ensuing consequences. Like the episode of Manasseh (see 33.1–20), with which this ch shares several motifs, the reign of Ahaz serves as a precursor to exile. The combination of northern and southern incursions, together with a preponderance (nine times) of references to captives and captivity (Heb "sh-b-y") convey the dire nature of the circumstances. The following ch, with its depiction of the cultic reforms of Hezekiah, reverses the state of captivity and expresses the view that contrition and fealty to the cult can rectify even the most egregious wrongdoings (and ensuing punishments) and lead to reunification of the people. **1–4:** Ahaz's idolatrous ways are more pronounced than in 2 Kings 16.12–18, justifying the exile for much of the population. **5–7:** Chronicles' description of the Syro-Ephraimite war differs from other biblical versions (2 Kings 15.37; 16.5; Isa. ch 7; Hos. 5.8–6.6). Chronicles probably draws on earlier sources, but formulates them in accordance with its overall depiction of Ahaz; cf. 2 Kings 16.5. **5:** A complete reversal of 13.15–17. **6:** While the numbers and time frame may reflect literary embellishment, the defeat of Judah is quite plausible; see 2 Kings 16.5, where the confederation puts Jerusalem to siege. **8–15:** The names in v. 12, along with the (unexpected) mention of Jericho, further the likelihood that Chronicles has drawn on an earlier source. The description of the prophetic activity of Oded (v. 9) and its aftermath, however, comports with the theology of Chronicles and was likely composed for illustrative purposes, filling in gaps in the story line. **9:** The appearance of the prophet *Oded* among the northerners and their willingness to heed his message reflect the author's

against the LORD your God. 11 Now then, listen to me, and send back the captives you have taken from your kinsmen, for the wrath of the LORD is upon you!" 12 Some of the chief men of the Ephraimites—Azariah son of Jehohanan, Berechiah son of Meshillemoth, Jehizkiah son of Shallum, and Amasa son of Hadlai—confronted those returning from the campaign 13 and said to them, "Do not bring these captives here, for it would mean our offending the LORD, adding to our sins and our offenses; for our offense is grave enough, and there is already wrath upon Israel." 14 So the soldiers released the captives and the booty in the presence of the officers and all the congregation. 15 Then the men named above proceeded to take the captives in hand, and with the booty they clothed all the naked among them—they clothed them and shod them and gave them to eat and drink and anointed them and provided donkeys for all who were failing and brought them to Jericho, the city of palms, back to their kinsmen. Then they returned to Samaria.

16 At that time, King Ahaz sent to the king of Assyria for help. 17 Again the Edomites came and inflicted a defeat on Judah and took captives. 18 And the Philistines made forays against the cities of the Shephelah and the Negeb of Judah; they seized Beth-shemesh and Aijalon and Gederoth, and Soco with its villages, and Timnah with its villages, and Gimzo with its villages; and they settled there. 19 Thus the LORD brought Judah low on account of King Ahaz of Israel,[a] for he threw off restraint in Judah and trespassed against the LORD. 20 Tillegath-pilneser, king of Assyria, marched against him and gave him trouble, instead of supporting him. 21 For Ahaz plundered the House of the LORD and the house of the king and the officers, and made a gift to the king of Assyria—to no avail.

22 In his time of trouble, this King Ahaz trespassed even more against the LORD, 23 sacrificing to the gods of Damascus which had defeated him, for he thought, "The gods of the kings of Aram help them; I shall sacrifice to them and they will help me"; but they were his ruin and that of all Israel. 24 Ahaz collected the utensils of the House of God, and cut the utensils of the House of God to pieces. He shut the doors of the House of the LORD and made himself altars in every corner of Jerusalem. 25 In every town in Judah he set up shrines to make offerings to other gods, vexing the LORD God of his fathers.

26 The other events of his reign and all his conduct, early and late, are recorded in the book of the kings of Judah and Israel. 27 Ahaz slept with his fathers and was buried in the city, in Jerusalem; his body was not brought to the tombs of the kings of Israel. His son Hezekiah succeeded him as king.

a Some mss. and ancient versions read "Judah."

view that the ordinary citizens of the North were true members of the people of Israel; their compassion towards their southern brethren expresses the author's view of the importance of national unity. **16–17:** An Edomite attack is consistent with historical evidence of Edomite expansion at this time. **19:** The title, "King of Israel" here may reflect the adoption by Ahaz of the practices of the Kings of the North ("Israel"). **22–25:** Ahaz, whose egregious conduct is similar to that of the notorious Manasseh, serves as an example of the consequences of refusal to change one's sinful ways. 2 Kings 16.10–16 states that Ahaz sought to build a replica (in the JerusalemTemple) of the altar that he had seen in Damascus. The wording of v. 23, especially the claim that the Aramean gods became a stumbling block (Heb "le-hakhšilo") for Ahaz and the nation, may be informed by Isa. 8.14–15, which employs similar phrasing. **24–25:** Chronicles repeats *every* to emphasize the extent of Ahaz's cultic sins, which go beyond those attested in 2 Kings ch 16. The formulation in v. 24 anticipates 29.6–7.

29 Hezekiah became king at the age of twenty-five, and he
reigned twenty-nine years in Jerusalem; his mother's
name was Abijah daughter of Zechariah. 2 He did what was
pleasing to the LORD, just as his father David had done.
3 He, in the first month of the first year of his reign, opened
the doors of the House of the LORD and repaired them. 4 He
summoned the priests and the Levites and assembled them
in the east square. 5 He said to them, "Listen to me, Levites!
Sanctify yourselves and sanctify the House of the LORD God
of your fathers, and take the abhorrent things out of the holy
place. 6 For our fathers trespassed and did what displeased the
LORD our God; they forsook Him and turned their faces away
from the dwelling-place of the LORD, turning their backs on it.
7 They also shut the doors of the porch and put out the lights;

29.1–32.33: Hezekiah's reign. The form Jehezekiah, Heb "Yeḥizkiyahu," (lit. "the LORD is strong") is the standard form in Chronicles—which, in fact, preserves almost all of the attestations of this form—whereas Kings prefers the shorter form Hezekiah (Heb "Ḥizkiyahu" [lit. "the LORD is my strength"]). Cuneiform evidence, which preserves the vocalization "ḫa-za-qi-ya-u" and similar formulations, indicates that the form preserved in Kings is older. The form in Chronicles fits patterns of names in later Heb, and is secondary. Hezekiah is, after David and Solomon, the outstanding Judean monarch in Chronicles, equivalent in stature to Josiah in Kings. It is likely that Chronicles viewed Jerusalem's survival of the Assyrian onslaught during Hezekiah's reign—together with (the embellished depiction of) his devotion to the Temple—as indicative of the king's piety; by contrast, Josiah's inability to halt the backsliding that had already begun, together with Chronicles' charge regarding his failure to heed the prophetic word (see 2 Chron. 35.22), relegated him to a lower status. Furthermore, whereas Josiah fails to heed the prophetically inspired message conveyed by Necho (35.21–22), Hezekiah exhibits no such weakness and works in tandem with the prophet Isaiah (32.20). Finally, the expanded role of Hezekiah in Temple-related matters in Chronicles reinforces Hezekiah's stature. In addition to the bulk of material devoted to his reign, several features and lexical links suggest that Chronicles sought to portray him as a second Solomon or, possibly, a combination of David and Solomon. Most fundamentally, Hezekiah symbolizes the reunification of all Israel around the Jerusalem Temple, as in the days of David and Solomon. Other typological features will be noted below. The high esteem in which Hezekiah was held is reflected in a rabbinic statement that, despite some failings, he had been worthy to be Israel's messiah (*b. Sanh.* 94a). The key difference between Kings' treatment of Hezekiah and that of Chronicles is that while the former concentrates on Hezekiah's military and geopolitical engagements, especially with Assyria, the latter minimizes these in favor of Hezekiah's religious achievements. (This is reminiscent of Chronicles' treatment of David.) Chronicles' treatment may be divided into two units. Chs 29–31 address Hezekiah's religious reforms, a topic that Kings treats in one v. The remaining ch, 32, is a condensed, and radically rewritten, description of the fortunes of the faithful king.

29.1–26: Purging and rededication of the Temple. Aside from the first two vv., there is no extant source for this account. It is unclear if Chronicles has drawn on an independent source, but it is likely the creation of the author; certainly the passage's formulation reflects the author's style and interests. The beginning of this ch, claiming that Hezekiah attended to the cultus immediately upon ascending the throne, together with its conclusion, are part of the Solomonic typology applied to Hezekiah. **1–18:** Reflective of Chronicles' pro-Levitical stance, it is they who are called upon to oversee purification of the Temple and its appurtenances. **1:** Chronicles' chronology, wherein Ahaz died at thirty-six years of age and Hezekiah ascended the throne at the age of twenty-five, yields the result that Ahaz begat Hezekiah at the age of eleven. Some scholars resolve this by positing that Ahaz and Hezekiah were siblings. **3–11:** Charge to the Levites. V. 3 contains two novel points with respect to Kings. Chronicles claims that the king opened the doors to the Temple. No such datum appears in 2 Kings; the closest source is found at 2 Kings 18.16, though the reference there is quite different. (See also 2 Kings 16.18, in connection with Ahaz.) Second, Chronicles makes the highly improbable and tendentious claim that this action was undertaken during Hezekiah's *first year*—according to some interpretations of this v., the first day—of rule (see v. 17). Chronicles' date means that Hezekiah attended to the cult on the very day on which he ascended the throne and, moreover, that the priests gathered and sanctified themselves on this same day. Chronicles portrays Hezekiah as wasting no time in attending to cultic matters—a clear echo of David and Solomon. The first month of the Heb year (roughly April) marks not only the renewal of the festal cycle but, according to Exod. ch 40, also the time when Moses' Tabernacle was erected; thus, typologically, Hezekiah is depicted as a new Moses. **3:** As in the case of David (and Solomon; see 1 Chron. 14.1–17 n.; 2 Chron. 1.3), Hezekiah begins his cultic activity shortly after assuming power, viz., in the first year of his reign. **4–6:** The only sin cited in v. 6 is rejection of the cultus (not idolatry), succinctly expressing they did not offer incense and did not make burnt offerings in the holy place to the God of Israel. 8 The wrath of the LORD was upon Judah and Jerusalem; He made them an object of horror, amazement, and hissing[a] as you see with your own eyes. 9 Our fathers died by the sword, and our sons and daughters and wives are in captivity on account of this. 10 Now I wish to make a covenant with the LORD God of Israel, so that His rage may be withdrawn from us. 11 Now, my sons, do not be slack, for the LORD chose you to attend upon Him, to serve Him, to be His ministers and to make offerings to Him."

12 So the Levites set to—Mahath son of Amasai and Joel son of Azariah of the sons of Kohath; and of the sons of Merari, Kish son of Abdi and Azariah son of Jehallelel; and of the Gershonites, Joah son of Zimmah and Eden son of Joah; 13 and of the sons of Elizaphan, Shimri and Jeiel; and of the sons of Asaph, Zechariah and Mattaniah;14 and of the sons of Heman, Jehiel and Shimei; and of the sons of Jeduthun, Shemaiah and Uzziel—15 and, gathering their brothers, they sanctified themselves and came, by a command of the king concerning the LORD's ordinances, to purify the House of the LORD. 16 The priests went into the House of the LORD to purify it, and brought all the unclean things they found in the Temple of the LORD out into the court of the House of the LORD; [there] the Levites received them, to take them outside to Wadi Kidron. 17 They began the sanctification on the first day of the first month; on the eighth day of the month they reached the porch of the LORD. They sanctified the House of the LORD for eight days, and on the sixteenth day of the first month they finished. 18 Then they went into the palace of King Hezekiah and said, "We have purified the whole House of the LORD and the altar of burnt offering and all its utensils, and the table of the bread of display and all its utensils; 19 and all the utensils that King Ahaz had befouled during his reign, when he trespassed, we have made ready and sanctified. They are standing in front of the altar of the LORD."

a See note at Jer. 18.16.

the central role of the cultus in Chronicles. **11:** The words *to attend upon Him, to serve Him, to be His ministers* are taken from the Levitical role as formulated in Deut. 18.5. The reference to *make offerings to Him* in the present v. reflects the wording of Deut. 33.10, which assigns the performance of the incense offering to Levites. (Deut. makes no distinction between priests and Levites.) In following the lead of Deut. 33.10, Chronicles departs from the Priestly position, where incense offerings are performed by priests (see Num. 17.5). At the same time, Chronicles' formulation, employing the verb indicating an "offering," has no explicit object, leaving open the precise nature of the sacrificial activity. **12–14:** The fourteen Levites fall into two groups. The first eight consist of *Kohath, Merari,* Gershon, and *Elizaphan;* a similar ordering appears at 1 Chron. 15.5–6. The second group consists of *Asaph, Heman,* and *Jeduthun;* this grouping appears in 1 Chron. chs 15–16 and 25.1. The message here is that all Levitic clans responded with equal alacrity. **15:** The king's directives receive divine imprimatur (see also, vv. 20–21); he thus functions as a mouthpiece, if not quite prophet, of the Deity. The significance of this is underscored by the innovative nature of the cultic practices involved; see the following vv. **16:** Informed by Priestly Torah law (Num. 3.10; 4.19; 18.3–7), Chronicles emphasizes that the innermost Temple precincts were accessible only to (pure) priests; Levites served in the other precincts, see 2 Chron. 5.7. **17:** Completion of the Temple purification *on the eighth day* (of the first month) is unmistakably reminiscent of Exod. 40.17, which, together with Lev. 8.33–9.24, indicates that the Tabernacle dedication ceremonies lasted eight days. **18–29:** Chronicles' description of the purification and rededication reflects the terminology of the Priestly source. Two divergences, however, bear comment. First, Chronicles has the burnt offering presented before the "ḥat'at" (purificatory/expiatory/propitiatory) offering (cf. Lev. 5.8). While a similar sequence appears at Ezra 8.35, that passage may reflect the sequence in prescriptive sacrifice texts of the Bible, where the burnt offerings precede all others, and may not be indicative of actual sacrificial practice in Ezra; by contrast, the present ch presents a descriptive narrative. Additionally, whereas Priestly sources prescribe the "ḥat'at" only for unwitting or unintentional offenses (Lev. ch 4; Num. 15.22–29), here the "ḥat'at" is offered in response for willful wrongdoings, a practice also reflected at Ezra 8.35. All this indicates that Chronicles and, apparently, Ezra reflect postexilic norms that diverge from Priestly law. Rather than viewing these norms as examples of Chronicles' independent approach to cultic/legal matters, some rabbinic tradents explained them as ad hoc (prophetically sanctioned) practices ("hora'at sha'ah"; see *y. Hor.* 1:8 [46b]). **21:** This evokes the Tabernacle dedication ceremony of Num. 7.9ff. A similar arrangement of cultic offerings appears at Ezra 8.35, which also echoes Num. ch 7 (see *b. Menaḥ.* 45a); see v. 31, below. **22:** The absence of a subject in this v., in contrast to the following v., suggests that non-priests, probably Levites, were called upon to slaughter. Although most exegetes and scholars maintain that Lev. 1.2–4 permits cultic slaughter by laypersons (cf. Philo, *Spec. Laws*; idem

20 King Hezekiah rose early, gathered the officers of the city,
and went up to the House of the LORD. 21 They brought seven
bulls and seven rams and seven lambs and seven he-goats as
a purification offering for the kingdom and for the Sanctuary
and for Judah. He ordered the Aaronite priests to offer them
on the altar of the LORD. 22 The cattle were slaughtered, and the
priests received the blood and dashed it against the altar; the
rams were slaughtered and the blood was dashed against the
altar; the lambs were slaughtered and the blood was dashed
against the altar. 23 The he-goats for the purification offering
were presented to the king and the congregation, who laid
their hands upon them. 24 The priests slaughtered them and

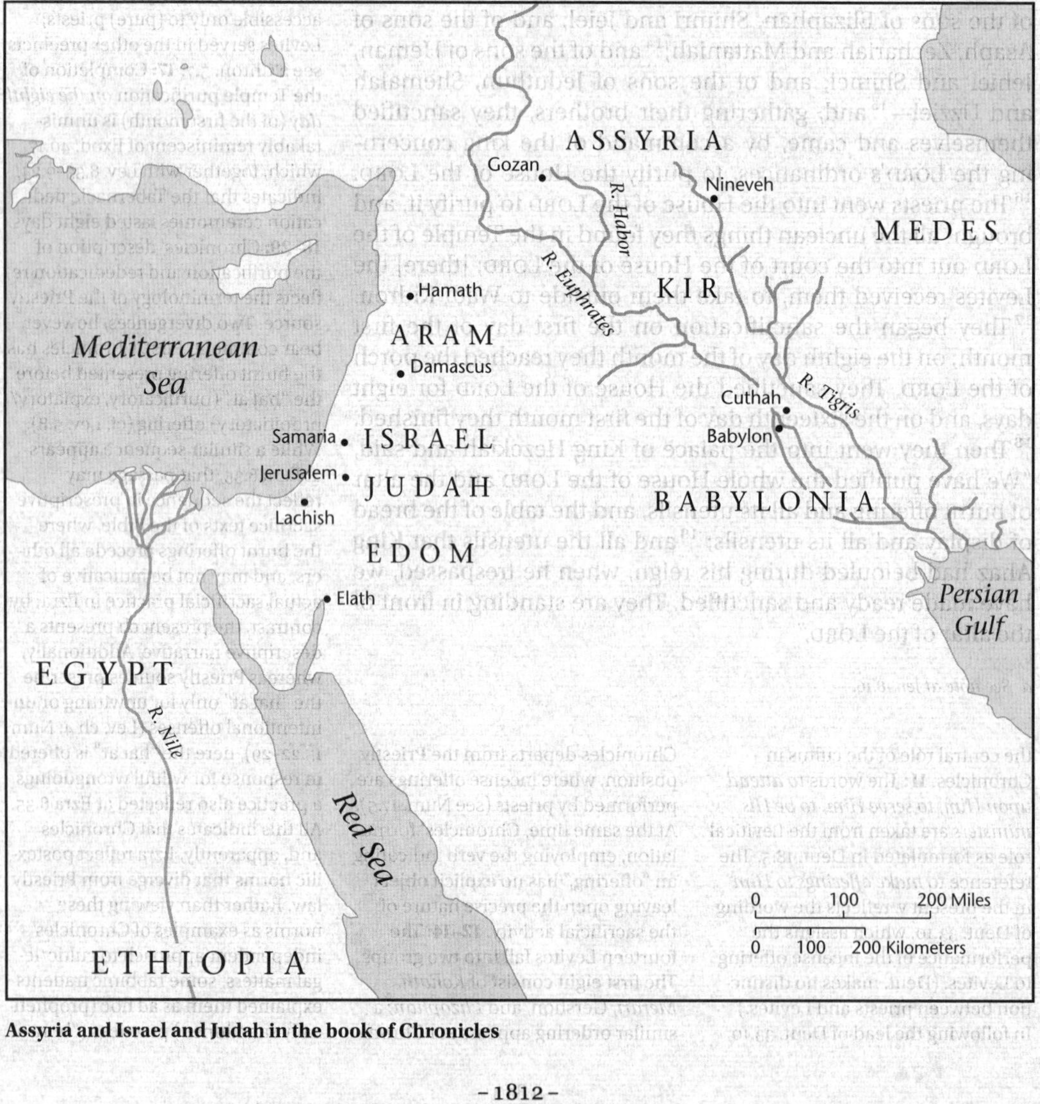

Assyria and Israel and Judah in the book of Chronicles

performed the purification rite with the blood against the altar,
to expiate for all Israel, for the king had designated the burnt
offering and the purification offering to be for all Israel. 25 He
stationed the Levites in the House of the LORD with cymbals
and harps and lyres, as David and Gad the king's seer and Nathan the prophet had ordained, for the ordinance was by the
LORD through His prophets.
26 When the Levites were in place with the instruments of
David, and the priests with their trumpets, 27 Hezekiah gave the
order to offer the burnt offering on the altar. When the burnt
offering began, the song of the LORD and the trumpets began
also, together with the instruments of King David of Israel. 28 All
the congregation prostrated themselves, the song was sung and
the trumpets were blown—all this until the end of the burnt offering. 29 When the offering was finished, the king and all who
were there with him knelt and prostrated themselves. 30 King
Hezekiah and the officers ordered the Levites to praise the
LORD in the words of David and Asaph the seer; so they praised
rapturously, and they bowed and prostrated themselves.
31 Then Hezekiah said, "Now you have consecrated yourselves to the LORD; come, bring sacrifices of well-being and
thanksgiving to the House of the LORD." The congregation
brought sacrifices of well-being and thanksgiving, and all who
felt so moved brought burnt offerings. 32 The number of burnt
offerings that the congregation brought was 70 cattle, 100 rams,
200 lambs—all these for burnt offerings to the LORD. 33 The
sacred offerings were 600 large cattle and 3,000 small cattle.
34 The priests were too few to be able to flay all the burnt offerings, so their kinsmen, the Levites, reinforced them till the end
of the work, and till the [rest of the] priests sanctified themselves. (The Levites were more conscientious about sanctifying
themselves than the priests.) 35 For beside the large number of
burnt offerings, there were the fat parts of the sacrifices of well-
being and the libations for the burnt offerings; so the service of
the House of the LORD was properly accomplished. 36 Hezekiah and all the people rejoiced over what God had enabled the
people to accomplish, because it had happened so suddenly.

30 Hezekiah sent word to all Israel and Judah; he also wrote
letters to Ephraim and Manasseh to come to the House
of the LORD in Jerusalem to keep the Passover for the LORD
God of Israel. 2 The king and his officers and the congregation

Sacr., 5; idem, *QE*, 10; and *Lev. Rab.* 22.7), the fact that Levites are again involved (if they are, indeed the subject of the v.) is another example of the ubiquitous role of Levites (see 1 Chron. 23.28–32 nn.; 2 Chron. 35.3). **24:** Possibly an allusion to the ordination rites of Exod. 29.12, 36–37. *All Israel* may refer to those exiled as well as those remaining in the land, or may indicate that the king made the offerings on behalf of a wider group than that envisaged by the priests and Levites above. The reference to the cultic vessels here, following their desecration by Ahaz (28.24), may allude to the pristine conditions of Solomon's reign. In contrast to burnt offerings, priestly law (Lev. 9.15; 16.15) requires that the "ḥat'at" *(purification offering)* be slaughtered by priests. **25–30:** Hezekiah's reestablishment of the choral rite casts him as a second David, who was, according to Chronicles, the composer of psalms and the fashioner of musical instruments employed in the Temple. **25:** The formulation suggests that the people recognized that the success of the Temple purification was brought about by divine will, rather than by (primarily) their own work; see 1 Chron. 15.26. **29–30:** The combination of bowing and prostration appears elsewhere in Chronicles only at 2 Chron. 7.3, where the heavenly fire signals divine approval and inauguration of the Temple. While this fact may imply the occurrence of a divine manifestation here, the author's silence suggests that this did not happen; the similar formulation simply reflects the importance of the purification and rededication. **31:** The reference to "consecration" and *all who felt so moved* (lit. "those of a generous heart") echoes the Tabernacle project; see Exod. 36.3–7. **34:** The author treats the Levites preferentially. **36:** As with David (1 Chron. 29.9) and elsewhere (2 Chron. 7.10; 30.21–26), cultic activity is accompanied by joy. The alacrity with which the successful sanctification had taken place was a sign of the people's zeal and the divine assent to Hezekiah's actions.

30.1–27: Celebration of the Passover festival. The historicity of this ch, along with its literary development, is much debated. Some scholars maintain that Chronicles has drawn upon earlier sources, based on the anomalous date and duration of the festival, along with various other details, which would hardly

in Jerusalem had agreed to keep the Passover in the second
month, [3] for at the time, they were unable to keep it,[a] for not
enough priests had sanctified themselves, nor had the people
assembled in Jerusalem. [4] The king and the whole congregation
thought it proper [5] to issue a decree and proclaim throughout
all Israel from Beer-sheba to Dan that they come and keep the
Passover for the LORD God of Israel in Jerusalem—not often did
they act in accord with what was written. [6] The couriers went out
with the letters from the king and his officers through all Israel
and Judah, by order of the king, proclaiming, "O you Israelites!
Return to the LORD God of your fathers, Abraham, Isaac, and Israel, and He will return to the remnant of you who escaped from
the hand of the kings of Assyria. [7] Do not be like your fathers and
brothers who trespassed against the LORD God of their fathers
and He turned them into a horror, as you see. [8] Now do not be
stiffnecked like your fathers; submit yourselves to the LORD and
come to His sanctuary, which He consecrated forever, and serve
the LORD your God so that His anger may turn back from you.
[9] If you return to the LORD, your brothers and children will be
regarded with compassion by their captors, and will return to
this land; for the LORD your God is gracious and merciful; He
will not turn His face from you if you return to Him."

[10] As the couriers passed from town to town in the land of
Ephraim and Manasseh till they reached Zebulun, they were
laughed at and mocked. [11] Some of the people of Asher and
Manasseh and Zebulun, however, were contrite, and came
to Jerusalem. [12] The hand of God was on Judah, too, making
them of a single mind to carry out the command of the king
and officers concerning the ordinance of the LORD. [13] A great

a I.e., on its proper date; cf. Num. 9.1–14.

have been concocted by Chronicles, for whom proper cultic procedure was paramount. Some argue that Chronicles reflects a pre-Priestly tradition of the Unleavened Bread festival, as preserved in Exod. 34.18. In fact, the ch is best understood as Chronicles' creation, which combines the Unleavened Bread festival with the Passover feast; this reflects Deuteronomic (hence, Josianic) influence. Accordingly, Chronicles' version cannot be historical; it is intended to highlight the cult as observed in the postexilic era, and Hezekiah's status (cf. Chronicles' treatment of Josiah, below). Chronicles' pan-Israel orientation is evident at several points in the episode. While scholars disagree on the historicity of Hezekiah's attempt to unite north and south at this juncture, as well, there is good reason to accept this depiction. First, the Assyrians, following their conquest of the northern tribes, were occupied for a short period with other matters, thus creating a window for Hezekiah's expansion. Second, Hezekiah's son is named Manasseh; this name, together with the name Ephraim, forms a recurring pair that together connotes the confederation of northern tribes in Chronicles. In selecting this name for his son Hezekiah was signaling, at least according to the Chronicler, the importance that he attached to the northern tribes. This pan-Israel attitude is evident in all of Hezekiah's preparations. Rabbinic tradents interpreted the name on the basis of the root whose meaning is "forget," reflecting the fact that Manasseh was destined to "forget" the biblical precepts and, similarly, cause Israel to forget the deity (*b. Sanh.* 102b). **1–3:** In addition to expressing Chronicles' pan-Israel view, this passage also conveys the importance of the Temple service. The inclusion of all segments of the population in the decision-making process is typical of upright "democratic" kings; see 1 Chron. 13.1. **1:** *Sent word:* The use of letters for royal proclamations reflects the practice of the Persian period, and is thus anachronistic here. **5:** *From Beer-sheba to Dan,* i.e., the full expanse of Israelite settlement in the ancestral land; this is consonant with Chronicles' view of the ongoing Israelite presence in the land. **6:** The use of "runners" or *couriers* reflects the reality of the Persian empire (see above, v. 1), whose vast territory was connected by a system of horsemen and stations located along the routes (see Esth. 3.15; 8.14). Measure-for-measure reward is expressed: If the people *return to the LORD ... He will return to the remnant.* V. 9 continues this motif with a slight twist: The captives will be returned to the land. **8–9:** These vv. employ the root "š-w-b (return)" twice, as well as the similar sounding word for captors (root "š-b-y"). Several locutions are reminiscent of other biblical passages expressive of divine compassion (e.g., Exod. 34.6–7; Joel 2.13; Jonah 4.2; Pss. 112.4; 145.8); in particular, these vv. bear resemblance to Solomon's prayer at 2 Chron. 6.38–39 || 1 Kings 8.48–50. In harking back to Solomon's prayer concerning exiled Israelites, the passage makes clear that true repentance, including proper cultic observance, are the sure means of returning all Israel/Jews to their homeland. The phrase *gracious and merciful* ("rahum we-hannun"), is a feature of Late Biblical Hebrew; the locution in Standard Biblical Hebrew is "merciful and gracious." **13:** The celebration of the festival in the *second month,* contrary to the first month legislated in Torah sources (e.g., Exod.

crowd assembled at Jerusalem to keep the Feast of Unleavened Bread in the second month, a very great congregation. [14] They set to and removed the altars that were in Jerusalem, and they removed all the incense stands and threw them into Wadi Kidron. [15] They slaughtered the paschal sacrifice on the fourteenth of the second month. The priests and Levites were ashamed, and they sanctified themselves and brought burnt offerings to the House of the LORD. [16] They took their stations, as was their rule according to the Teaching of Moses, man of God. The priests dashed the blood [which they received] from the Levites. [17] Since many in the congregation had not sanctified themselves, the Levites were in charge of slaughtering the paschal sacrifice for everyone who was not clean, so as to consecrate them to the LORD. [18] For most of the people—many from Ephraim and Manasseh, Issachar and Zebulun—had not purified themselves, yet they ate the paschal sacrifice in violation of what was written. Hezekiah prayed for them, saying, "The good LORD will provide atonement for [19] everyone who set his mind on worshiping God, the LORD God of his fathers, even if he is not purified for the sanctuary." [20] The LORD heard Hezekiah and healed the people.

[21] The Israelites who were in Jerusalem kept the Feast of Unleavened Bread seven days, with great rejoicing, the Levites and the priests praising the LORD daily with powerful instruments for the LORD. [22] Hezekiah persuaded all the Levites who performed skillfully for the LORD to spend the seven days of the festival making offerings of well-being, and confessing to the LORD God of their fathers. [23] All the congregation resolved to keep seven more days, so they kept seven more days of rejoicing. [24] King Hezekiah of Judah contributed to the congregation 1,000 bulls and 7,000 sheep. And the officers contributed to the congregation 1,000 bulls and 10,000 sheep. And the priests sanctified themselves in large numbers. [25] All the congregation of Judah and the priests and the Levites and all the congregation that came from Israel, and the resident aliens who came from the land of Israel and who lived in Judah, rejoiced. [26] There was great rejoicing in Jerusalem, for since the time of King Solomon son of David of Israel nothing like it had happened in Jerusalem. [27] The Levite priests rose and blessed

12.2–3; Deut. 16.1–8) may reflect a northern calendar, which lagged behind the Judahite calendar by one month. Alternatively, Chronicles is applying to the community the legislation concerning an individual in Num. 9.6–12, which addresses the "Second Passover," i.e., the paschal sacrifice offered by those unable to participate in the regular paschal offering due to ritual impurity or other legitimate reasons; see *t. Pisha* 8.4, where this point is debated. Some rabbinic sources (*m. Pes.* 4.9; *t. Pisha* 8.5) explain Hezekiah's controversial move as based on intercalation, in which an additional (i.e., thirteenth) month is added to the concluding year; thus he did not really change the month of the festival. Some Israelites accepted Hezekiah's intercalation, while others did not, and so refrained from participating. **18–20:** This is a remarkable deviation from Priestly norms, which are punctilious concerning matters of ritual purity. Sincere prayer from a righteous king (v. 20) trumps typical concerns. **21:** Some exegetes take the words *kept the Feast … seven days* as an ellipsis for "consumed the festal offerings." **23:** Note the popular nature of this decision. **24-26:** The most likely explanation is that the incident was, at least from the author's perspective, entirely without precedent. Hezekiah's action is, thus, another example of the Chronicler's willingness to legislate (or, acknowledge) cultic/legal practices inconsistent with pentateuchal norms; cf. 2 Chron. 35.13, where the author emphasizes the king's compliance with earlier (conflicting) cultic norms. No less surprising is Chronicles' depiction of a wrongful ritual act whose severity is somehow mitigated by Hezekiah's petition for divine forgiveness. Perhaps the willingness of the author to attribute to Hezekiah conduct that deviates from (presumable earlier) cultic norms suggests that this episode draws on historical records and is not the de novo creation of the author. However, even granting the basic facticity of this narrative, the fact that the author was prepared to incorporate it and acknowledge its cultic "aberrations" bespeaks his tolerance of divergence from standard cultic practice under extenuating circumstances, such as securing the unification of the nation in religious commitment and observance (see intro.). The word "joy/rejoice," a favorite topos of Chronicles, appears four times in vv. 21–26, reflective of its importance in service of the deity and, in particular, Temple worship. **25:** The reference to *resident aliens* recalls Num. 9.14; some medieval exegetes (Gersonides [Ralbag]) averred that *aliens* refers to northerners who had relocated in Judah. Moreover, the text may indicate that all those

the people, and their voice was heard, and their prayer went up to His holy abode, to heaven.

31 When all this was finished, all Israel who were present went out into the towns of Judah and smashed the pillars, cut down the sacred posts, demolished the shrines and altars throughout Judah and Benjamin, and throughout Ephraim and Manasseh, to the very last one. Then all the Israelites returned to their towns, each to his possession.

2 Hezekiah reconstituted the divisions of the priests and Levites, each man of the priests and Levites according to his office, for the burnt offerings, the offerings of well-being, to minister, and to sing hymns and praises in the gates of the courts of the LORD; 3 also the king's portion, from his property, for the burnt offerings—the morning and evening burnt offering, and the burnt offerings for sabbaths, and new moons, and festivals, as prescribed in the Teaching of the LORD.

4 He ordered the people, the inhabitants of Jerusalem, to deliver the portions of the priests and the Levites, so that they might devote themselves to the Teaching of the LORD. 5 When the word spread, the Israelites brought large quantities of grain, wine, oil, honey, and all kinds of agricultural produce, and tithes of all, in large amounts. 6 The men of Israel and Judah living in the towns of Judah—they too brought tithes of cattle and sheep and tithes of sacred things consecrated to the LORD their God, piling them in heaps. 7 In the third month the heaps began to accumulate, and were finished in the seventh month. 8 When Hezekiah and the officers came and saw the heaps, they blessed the LORD and his people Israel. 9 Hezekiah asked the priests and Levites about the heaps. 10 The chief

living in the land were, de facto, part of an extended pan-Israelite entity. This has led to the reasonable suggestion that the sojourners were, in fact, proselytes (even if no formal conversion process existed). It is also possible, however, that the author is implementing the Deuteronomic directive to incorporate sojourners in festal and cultic celebrations (Deut. 14.29; 16.11, 14; 26.11–12). If so, Chronicles has gone beyond Deut. (16.1–8), which does not mention participation of sojourners in the paschal ritual, and, presumably, the position of Exod. 12.47–49. The referent of *land of Israel,* though opaque, is all of Israel's patrimony outside Judah. The reference to Solomon's period is a clear example of Chronicles' Solomon typology (see 29.1–32.33 n.). The Chronicler again emphasizes the role of joy in religious, especially Temple, service; see 1 Chron. 29.11–19. The passage employs an allusion to Deut. 26.15, a passage that beseeches the Deity to bless Israel and its land with abundance.

31.1–21: Cultic arrangements. The cultic reform is executed by the entire population, both Judah and the northern regions. The overwhelming response of the people indicates the nation's worthy and upright nature. This state of affairs offers a theological explanation for the miraculous deliverance from the Assyrians in the following ch. This is summarized in the ch's final v., which emphasizes that "he prospered" because of his concern for the Temple and for the "torah" *(teaching).* **2:** Hezekiah reestablishes the Temple service as it was prior to Ahaz. The v. specifies the various activities, those of the priests (sacrificing) and those of the Levites. The wording, *to minister ... to sing ... in the gates,* has troubled translators and commentators, since it seems to suggest that all of these Levitical activities, including singing, took place "in" the Temple gateways. In fact, the phrase simply means within the gates/precincts of the Temple. "Camp" appears in this sense at 1 Chron. 9.19; it may reflect an allusion to the Israelite desert encampment or, more likely, part of the book's use of martial imagery in connection with the Temple and its attendants. The Rabbis *(t. Kelim; b. B. K.* 1:13; *Sifre Num., Naso'* 1) employed the terms "divine camp" ("mahaneh šekhinah") in connection with the priestly and inner lay court; similarly, "levitical camp" in connection with the Temple Mount, generally, reflecting the encampment of Levites and priests around the Tabernacle (Num. 1.50). **4–19:** Consumption of priestly perquisites: This passage appears to contradict Lev. 22.11–13 and Num. 18.11–20, which grant priestly women and children access to priestly (agricultural) perquisites. Attempts at harmonization notwithstanding (e.g., Radak [v. 16]), it is likely that Chronicles here departs from pentateuchal norms. The reason is unclear, though it may reflect the diminished availability of priestly perquisites during the Chronicler's time. **6:** The opaque phrase *tithes of sacred things* ("qodashim") most likely refers to tithes separated from consecrated offerings. Since Torah law nowhere requires tithing such offerings, the latter explanation reflects either a novel legal position on the part of Chronicles or the fact that the people gave generously, going beyond the requirements of cultic norms (note the emphasis on abundance in v. 5), a motif amply attested in Chronicles. **10:** This v. spells out what is implicit in other passages, especially the David and Solomon

priest Azariah, of the house of Zadok, replied to him, saying,
"Ever since the gifts began to be brought to the House of the
LORD, people have been eating to satiety and leaving over in
great amounts, for the LORD has blessed His people; this huge
amount is left over!" [11] Hezekiah then gave orders to prepare
store-chambers in the House of the LORD; and they were prepared. [12] They brought in the gifts and the tithes and the sacred
things faithfully. Their supervisor was Conaniah the Levite,
and Shimei his brother was second in rank. [13] Jehiel and Azaziah and Nahath and Asahel and Jerimoth and Jozabad and
Eliel and Ismachiah and Mahath and Benaiah were commis-
sioners under Conaniah and Shimei his brother by appointment of King Hezekiah; Azariah was supervisor of the House
of God. [14] Kore son of Imnah the Levite, the keeper of the East
Gate, was in charge of the freewill offerings to God, of the allocation of gifts to the LORD, and the most sacred things. [15] Under him were Eden, Miniamin, Jeshua, Shemaiah, Amariah,
and Shecaniah, in offices of trust in the priestly towns, making allocation to their brothers by divisions, to great and small
alike; [16] besides allocating their daily rations to those males
registered by families from three years old and up, all who
entered the House of the LORD according to their service and
their shift by division; [17] and in charge of the registry of priests
by clans, and of the Levites, from twenty years old and up, by
shifts, in their divisions; [18] and the registry of the dependents
of their whole company—wives, sons, and daughters—for, relying upon them, they sanctified themselves in holiness. [19] And
for the Aaronite priests, in each and every one of their towns
with adjoining fields, the above-named men were to allocate
portions to every male of the priests and to every registered
Levite. [20] Hezekiah did this throughout Judah. He acted in a
way that was good, upright, and faithful before the LORD his
God. [21] Every work he undertook in the service of the House of
God or in the Teaching and the Commandment, to worship his
God, he did with all his heart; and he prospered.

32 [a]After these faithful deeds, King Sennacherib of Assyria invaded Judah and encamped against its fortified towns with the aim of taking them over. [2] When Hezekiah
saw that Sennacherib had come, intent on making war against

a Cf. 2 Kings 18–20; Isa. 36–39.

narratives: financial support for the Temple and its maintenance bring about blessing and wealth; see Hag. 1.3–11 and Mal. 3.10–11. **11–13:** Storage of contributions. This is the only passage in Chronicles that assigns Zadokite lineage to an individual; cf. 1 Kings 4.2, which refers to an earlier Azariah. The identity of the twelve figures listed here is unknown; their role here again highlights the ubiquitous presence of Levites. It is further possible that the use of otherwise unknown individuals is intended to amplify the broad participation of all of the Levites. The number "twelve" occurs at 1 Chron. 16.5–6, in connection with the musicians attending the Ark; the recurring of this typological number may be symbolizing the participation (and representation) of all of the tribes. V. 12 employs the term "faithfully" ("'emunah"), a term/motif that looms large in the following vv., esp. in connection with Hezekiah (see below, v. 20), as well as at other junctures (1 Chron. 9.22, 26, 31; 2 Chron. 19.9). Hezekiah and Azariah work in tandem; cf. the following n. **20:** Whereas *good, upright,* and the phrase "good and right" are amply employed elsewhere in connection with praiseworthy conduct (e.g., Deut. 6.18; 12.25; 13.19), the addition of faithful is surprising. It highlights Hezekiah's truly upright nature and anticipates the use of the term ("faithful") at 32.1. LXX here omits "faithful."

32.1–33: Assyrian invasion and Hezekiah's faithfulness. A highly revised version of 2 Kings chs 18–19 and its parallel in Isa. chs 36–39. The negative features of Hezekiah's conduct, e.g., pride and removal of Temple vessels, surrender to the Assyrians, are omitted. Similarly, Hezekiah's military preparations, severely criticized by Isaiah, are here presented as being accompanied by the king's hortatory speech stressing trust in the LORD; this results in a positive assessment of Hezekiah's preparations. In v. 1, Chronicles omits the reference in 2 Kings 18.4 to the bronze serpent fashioned by Moses—which later became a source of cultic offense—presumably out of respect for Moses and Mosaic law. **1–6:** 2 Kings 18.13 and Isa. 36.1 state that Sennacherib's invasion took place in the fourteenth year and that the Assyrians managed to capture (many of) the cities of Judah, but not Jerusalem (see v. 10 n. below). Chronicles omits the date; in its place it employs a connective link, *after these faithful deeds,* whose function is to explain theologically the reason for the Assyrians' defeat.

Jerusalem, [3] he consulted with his officers and warriors about stopping the flow of the springs outside the city, and they supported him. [4] A large force was assembled to stop up all the springs and the wadi that flowed through the land, for otherwise, they thought, the king of Assyria would come and find water in abundance. [5] He acted with vigor, rebuilding the whole breached wall, raising towers on it, and building another wall outside it. He fortified the Millo of the City of David, and made a great quantity of arms and shields. [6] He appointed battle officers over the people; then, gathering them to him in the square of the city gate, he rallied them, saying, [7] "Be strong and of good courage; do not be frightened or dismayed by the king of Assyria or by the horde that is with him, for we have more with us than he has with him. [8] With him is an arm of flesh, but with us is the LORD our God, to help us and to fight our battles." The people were encouraged by the speech of King Hezekiah of Judah.

[9] Afterward, King Sennacherib of Assyria sent his officers to Jerusalem—he and all his staff being at Lachish—with this message to King Hezekiah of Judah and to all the people of Judah who were in Jerusalem: [10] "Thus said King Sennacherib of Assyria: On what do you trust to enable you to endure a siege in Jerusalem? [11] Hezekiah is seducing you to a death of hunger and thirst, saying, 'The LORD our God will save us from the king of Assyria.' [12] But is not Hezekiah the one who removed His shrines and His altars and commanded the people of Judah and Jerusalem saying, 'Before this one altar you shall prostrate yourselves, and upon it make your burnt offerings'? [13] Surely you know what I and my fathers have done to the peoples of the lands? Were the gods of the nations of the lands able to save their lands from me? [14] Which of all the gods of any of those nations whom my fathers destroyed was able to save his people from me, that your God should be able to save you from me? [15] Now then, do not let Hezekiah delude you; do not let him seduce you in this way; do not believe him. For no god of any nation or kingdom has been able to save his people from me or from my fathers—much less your God, to save you from me!" [16] His officers said still more things against the LORD God and against His servant Hezekiah. [17] He also wrote letters

The invasion by a foreign army at this juncture would appear to undermine Chronicles' strict view of retribution. This passage's purpose may be to teach the proper response to "trials": Trust and piety are more potent than military might. Cf. 14.9–15. **3:** The democratization principle at work. Rabbinic sources differ over the propriety of the decision to stop the springs: *m. Pes.* 4.9 expresses criticism, while *ʾAvot R. Nat.* A, 2, informed by v. 30, below, lauds the move (see also, *Pirqe R. El.* 9). Most scholars see vv. 3–8 in a positive light, as part of the "building" motif characteristic of successful monarchs; others, less plausibly, see the decision to build before turning to the deity for assistance as a sign of arrogance and excessive confidence. **7–8:** The words *be strong and of good courage* are highly reminiscent of David and Solomon; see 1 Chron. 22.13. These vv. are a potent expression of one of Chronicles' main themes, a theme that would have resonated deeply with his audience in the postexilic period, when Israel lacked military power. **10:** As noted above, some understand Chronicles' text to mean that the Assyrian forces did not reach Jerusalem, a position which comports with 2 Kings 19.32–33 (= Isa. 37.33–34). This v., however, does suggest that Jerusalem was under siege. Chronicles' depiction thus magnifies the miracle of Jerusalem's remaining unharmed. Extrabiblical data supports the historicity of a limited Jerusalem siege. **13:** Sennacherib's *fathers* refers to his predecessors. The formulation here conflates 2 Kings 18.35 (|| Isa. 36.20), which states that no god had managed to save his/her land from the Assyrian advance, and 2 Kings 19.11–12 (|| Isa. 37.11–12), which lists some of the decimated nations. Vv. 13–15 here conflate these passages. The upshot is that all of the Assyrian bravado amounts to naught; as indicated by Chronicles' formulation at v. 15, the claim that YHVH, like other gods, is un*able* ("y-kh-l") to save His people is unfounded. **19:** An added summary v., accusing Sennacherib and his officials of blasphemy, thus justifying their defeat. **20:** Chronicles conflates the prayers of the kings and the prophet in 2 Kings 19.2–4 (|| Isa. 37.2–4) and 19.14–19 (|| Isa. 37.14–20), while omitting the specific content of Hezekiah's prayer and Isaiah's message at 2 Kings 19.15–33. Chronicles also omits 2 Kings 19.34, which implies that Hezekiah's own merit would not have sufficed to save Jerusalem and its environs. The terse formulation here does not convey the sense of despair evident in 2 Kings, reflecting Chronicles' belief that trust in the Deity, accompanied by sincere prayer, is always effectual. Chronicles' formulation implies a sort of partnership with Isaiah,

reviling the LORD God of Israel, saying of Him, "Just as the gods
of the other nations of the earth did not save their people from
me, so the God of Hezekiah will not save his people from me."
18 They called loudly in the language of Judah to the people of
Jerusalem who were on the wall, to frighten them into panic,
so as to capture the city. 19 They spoke of the God of Jerusalem as though He were like the gods of the other peoples of the
earth, made by human hands. 20 Then King Hezekiah and the
prophet Isaiah son of Amoz prayed about this, and cried out
to heaven.
21 The LORD sent an angel who annihilated every mighty
warrior, commander, and officer in the army of the king of Assyria, and he returned in disgrace to his land. He entered the
house of his god, and there some of his own offspring struck
him down by the sword. 22 Thus the LORD delivered Hezekiah
and the inhabitants of Jerusalem from King Sennacherib of Assyria, and from everyone; He provided for them on all sides.
23 Many brought tribute to the LORD to Jerusalem, and gifts to
King Hezekiah of Judah; thereafter he was exalted in the eyes
of all the nations.

suggesting that upright monarchs work in tandem with prophetic guidance. **21–23:** The LORD *provided for them* (the people) and *exalted* Hezekiah *in the eyes of all the nations,* acts that are reminiscent of Jehoshaphat and especially Solomon (1 Chron. 22.9) and David (1 Chron. 14.17). The stark contrast between Hezekiah's fate and that of Sennacherib could hardly be clearer: One is *exalted in the eyes* of the entire world, the other is murdered by *his own offspring.*

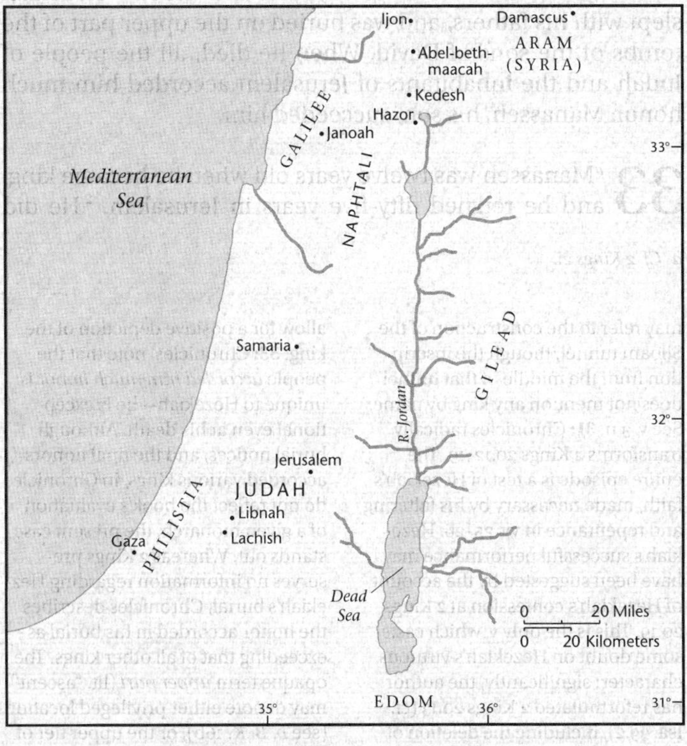

Places associated with Sennacherib's invasion of Judah

24 At that time, Hezekiah fell deathly sick. He prayed to the
LORD, who responded to him and gave him a sign. 25 Hezekiah
made no return for what had been bestowed upon him, for he
grew arrogant; so wrath was decreed for him and for Judah and
Jerusalem. 26 Then Hezekiah humbled himself where he had
been arrogant, he and the inhabitants of Jerusalem, and no
wrath of the LORD came on them during the reign of Hezekiah.
27 Hezekiah enjoyed riches and glory in abundance; he filled
treasuries with silver and gold, precious stones, spices, shields,
and all lovely objects; 28 and store-cities with the produce of
grain, wine, and oil, and stalls for all kinds of beasts, and flocks
for sheepfolds. 29 And he acquired towns, and flocks of small
and large cattle in great number, for God endowed him with
very many possessions. 30 It was Hezekiah who stopped up the
spring of water of Upper Gihon, leading it downward west of
the City of David; Hezekiah prospered in all that he did. 31 So
too in the matter of the ambassadors of the princes of Babylon,
who were sent to him to inquire about the sign that was in the
land, when God forsook him in order to test him, to learn all
that was in his mind.

32 The other events of Hezekiah's reign, and his faithful acts,
are recorded in the visions of the prophet Isaiah son of Amoz
and in the book of the kings of Judah and Israel. 33 Hezekiah
slept with his fathers, and was buried on the upper part of the
tombs of the sons of David. When he died, all the people of
Judah and the inhabitants of Jerusalem accorded him much
honor. Manasseh, his son, succeeded him.

33 [a]Manasseh was twelve years old when he became king,
and he reigned fifty-five years in Jerusalem. 2 He did

a Cf. 2 Kings 21.

24–26: This passage contains but a fleeting allusion to 2 Kings 20.1–11, which states that Hezekiah, stricken by illness, beseeched the LORD; he requested and was shown a portent signaling his recovery, and his life is extended by fifteen years. Chronicles' omission of the substance of this passage may indicate that Chronicles viewed Hezekiah's request for an explicit sign as indicating less than full trust in the prophetic word (2 Kings 20.8). Also, Hezekiah's petition contains self-descriptions that do not reflect the submissive stance that Chronicles requires. A rabbinic tradition states that Hezekiah's illness was the punishment incurred for refusal to beget children, a decision motivated by his foreknowledge of the fact that his son, Manasseh, would be evil (*b. Ber.* 10a). This explanation, which may be read into Isa. 38.18–19, is not borne out by Chronicles' claim that his illness was the result of hubris. The Rabbis resolve this issue by claiming that Hezekiah's hubris lay in his refusal to defer to Isaiah. Josephus acknowledged that Hezekiah's illness occurred before the birth of Manasseh and that the king prayed that he be given a son, but does not claim that this was the reason for his punishment (*Ant.* 10.25–28). **25–26:** This may reflect an understanding of the previously narrated siege of Jerusalem as punishment for Hezekiah's arrogance, but as a result of proper penitence, the siege was not successful. It is more likely that the king's hubris was manifest following the failed siege; some midrashic sources embellish this point by criticizing Hezekiah's failure to offer thanksgiving following the failed onslaught (*Shir haShir. Rab.* 4:19). **27–29:** Solomon typology: great wealth and honor. Chronicles' text presupposes the reader's familiarity with 1 Kings ch 1 through 2 Kings ch 19. While describing Hezekiah's wealth and glory in terms reminiscent of David, Solomon, and Jehoshaphat, Chronicles is unusual insofar as it twice employs the term *in abundance, very* (Heb "me'od"). **30:** This action guaranteed a constant water supply for Jerusalem. This may refer to the construction of the Siloam tunnel, though the inscription from the middle of that tunnel does not mention any king by name. See v. 3 n. **31:** Chronicles radically transforms 2 Kings 20.12–19. The entire episode is a test of Hezekiah's faith, made necessary by his faltering and repentance in vv. 25–26. Hezekiah's successful performance may have been suggested by the account of Hezekiah's confession at 2 Kings 20.19. This is the only v. which casts some doubt on Hezekiah's virtuous character; significantly, the author has reformulated 2 Kings 20.13 (cf. Isa. 39.2), including the deletion of all its incriminating aspects, so as to allow for a positive depiction of the king. **33:** Chronicles' note that the people *accorded him much honor* is unique to Hezekiah—he is exceptional even at his death. Although burial notices, and the final honors accorded various kings, in Chronicles do not reflect the book's evaluation of a given monarch, the present case stands out. Whereas 2 Kings preserves no information regarding Hezekiah's burial, Chronicles describes the honor accorded in his burial as exceeding that of all other kings. The opaque term *upper part* (lit. "ascent") may denote either privileged location (see *b. B. K.* 16b), or the upper tier of a multi-level tomb.

what was displeasing to the LORD, following the abhorrent
practices of the nations that the LORD had dispossessed before
the Israelites. 3 He rebuilt the shrines that his father Hezekiah
had demolished; he erected altars for the Baals and made sacred posts. He bowed down to all the host of heaven and worshiped them, 4 and he built altars [to them] in the House of the
LORD, of which the LORD had said, "My name will be in Jerusalem forever." 5 He built altars for all the host of heaven in the two
courts of the House of the LORD. 6 He consigned his sons to the
fire in the Valley of Ben-hinnom, and he practiced soothsaying, divination, and sorcery, and consulted ghosts and familiar
spirits; he did much that was displeasing to the LORD in order
to vex Him. 7 He placed a sculptured image that he made in the
House of God, of which God had said to David and to his son
Solomon, "In this House and in Jerusalem, which I chose out
of all the tribes of Israel, I will establish My name forever. 8 And
I will never again remove the feet of Israel from the land that I
assigned to their fathers, if only they observe faithfully all that I
have commanded them—all the teaching and the laws and the
rules given by Moses." 9 Manasseh led Judah and the inhabitants of Jerusalem astray into evil greater than that done by the
nations that the LORD had destroyed before the Israelites.

10 The LORD spoke to Manasseh and his people, but they
would not pay heed, 11 so the LORD brought against them the

33.1–20: Manasseh's reign. Chronicles' presentation of Manasseh is the subject of widely divergent views. Some have sought a historical basis behind this version—or parts thereof—arguing, for example, that Manasseh may have appeared before the Assyrian king as part of a tribute brought to the sovereign. This explanation misses the mark; the lack of any historical and/or geopolitical detail bespeaks the Chronicler's lack of interest in purely "historical" matters. Thus, vv. 11–19, the story of Manasseh's captivity and repentance, are the creation of Chronicles, intended to resolve the theological difficulties engendered by the Kings' version. The portrayal of this monarch in 2 Kings ch 21 is unambiguously negative. He exceeded all previous Judahite kings (and the kings who lived in the land before Israel came there, as well) in his wickedness. Indeed, rabbinic sources embellish the biblical accounts of Manasseh's wickedness; see *b. Yebam.* 49, which states that Manasseh had Isaiah executed, and *b. Zevaḥ.* 61b, which accuses the king of extinguishing the heavenly fire that had descended upon the altar in Solomon's dedication. His fostering of idolatry is cited as the reason for the ultimate destruction of Jerusalem (2 Kings 21.12–16; 24.3). Despite all this, he manages to reign for fifty-five years, longer than any other monarch. Chronicles knows none of this. Chronicles' radical revision is generally explained as reflecting the author's theological stance; his view on retribution left no room for the notion that the most wicked of kings managed to rule longer than any other monarch—and, apparently, enjoyed a peaceful life, to boot!—or that Manasseh's egregious sins could be visited upon a later generation. Hence, Chronicles simply had to delete these troublesome issues, while creating a much more positive image of the king. According to others, however, Chronicles' portrayal is to be explained on the basis of divine compassion, which allows even the most wicked of individuals to repent and start anew (see intro.). Later Jewish tradition (e.g., *b. Sanh.* 102b–103a) understood the two accounts as complementary. See vv. 10–13 n. **1–6:** Unlike 2 Kings 21.16, Chronicles refers only to cultic offenses, and makes no reference to Manasseh's execution of innocents. (Rabbinic sources [*y. Sanh.* 10.2; *b. Yebam.* 49b] state that, in addition to the offenses cited herein and at 2 Kings ch 21, Manasseh had the prophet Isaiah killed.) Other scholars, less plausibly, have understood 2 Kings 21.16 as referring to social injustice, rather than (mass) murder. Chronicles' reticence may reflect its highlighting of cultic issues; it may also reflect discomfort with the notion that a Davidic monarch guilty of abusing his role as society's caretaker—whether by murdering or simply exploiting them—could be forgiven so easily and continue his role as a leading proponent of religious fidelity. **6:** Chronicles enlarges Kings' sin by changing "his son" to *his sons;* either is a violation of Deut. 18.10–13. **7:** Manasseh places the forms in the very Temple wherein the LORD has "placed" His name. **9:** Chronicles states that Manasseh and the people at large were guilty of foreign worship. Accordingly, both the king and the people are the object of the Assyrian assault. **10–13:** Some scholars view the story of Manasseh's exile as wholly artificial, while others accept the story's general historicity, suggesting that it transpired between 677 and 648 BCE. The "true" reason for his presence in the Assyrian court is also debated, with some arguing that, in fact, Manasseh actually came to proclaim his fidelity to the throne. Whether true or not, the style of these vv., which ignore any attention to geopolitical and military details (e.g., who governed Judah in Manasseh's absence), is typical of Chronicles' one-dimensional perspective, which emphasizes only religious/theological factors. Finally, Chronicles implies that the people of Judah were not punished, despite

officers of the army of the king of Assyria, who took Manasseh
captive in manacles, bound him in fetters, and led him off to
Babylon. 12 In his distress, he entreated the LORD his God and
humbled himself greatly before the God of his fathers. 13 He
prayed to Him, and He granted his prayer, heard his plea, and
returned him to Jerusalem to his kingdom. Then Manasseh
knew that the LORD alone was God. 14 Afterward he built the
outer wall of the City of David west of Gihon in the wadi on the
way to the Fish Gate, and it encircled Ophel; he raised it very
high. He also placed army officers in all the fortified towns of
Judah. 15 He removed the foreign gods and the image from the
House of the LORD, as well as all the altars that he had built
on the Mount of the House of the LORD and in Jerusalem, and
dumped them outside the city. 16 He rebuilt the altar of the
LORD and offered on it sacrifices of well-being and thanksgiving, and commanded the people of Judah to worship the LORD
God of Israel. 17 To be sure, the people continued sacrificing at
the shrines, but only to the LORD their God.
18 The other events of Manasseh's reign, and his prayer to
his God, and the words of the seers who spoke to him in the
name of the LORD God of Israel are found in the chronicles
of the kings of Israel. 19 His prayer and how it was granted to
him, the whole account of his sin and trespass, and the places
in which he built shrines and installed sacred posts and images before he humbled himself are recorded in the words of
Hozai.[a] 20 Manasseh slept with his fathers and was buried on
his palace grounds; his son Amon succeeded him as king.
21 Amon was twenty-two years old when he became king,
and he reigned two years in Jerusalem. 22 He did what was
displeasing to the LORD, as his father Manasseh had done.
Amon sacrificed to all the idols that his father Manasseh
had made and worshiped them. 23 He did not humble himself before the LORD, as his father Manasseh had humbled
himself; instead, Amon incurred much guilt. 24 His courtiers
conspired against him and killed him in his palace. 25 But
the people of the land struck down all who had conspired
against King Amon; and the people of the land made his son
Josiah king in his stead.

a Or "seers."

their role in the foreign worship. It is possible that their eventual return to proper religious worship atoned for their misdeeds; cf. 2 Chron. 12.12. Chronicles' terse formulation of Manasseh's prayer and contrition, along with his seemingly immediate pardon, was problematic for Jews in antiquity. LXX traditions (and the *Didaskalia Apostolorum* ii.22; *Apostolic Constitutions* 2.xxii) preserve an apocryphal "prayer of Manasseh"; the Dead Sea Scrolls preserve a different prayer attributed to him (4Q380–381). A rabbinic tradition states that Moses had prayed that Manasseh's prayer be accepted (*Sifre Deut.* 348). Similarly, rabbinic (and early Christian) sources attempt to explain the means by which Manasseh (miraculously) managed to return to Jerusalem. **11–13:** The detail that Manasseh was led off *to Babylon* by the Assyrian king is impossible; the Assyrian king would have led him to an Assyrian rather than a Babylonian city. Some scholars therefore view the text symbolically, with Manasseh prefiguring the later exile of the Judeans to Babylonia. The story thus emphasizes the efficacy of repentance, for even the wicked Manasseh is returned to Judah after he is contrite. **14–17:** Signs of divine favor and monarchical success; see 2 Chron. 8.3–8; 11.5–12. The image/idol (Heb "semel") is that referred to above, v. 7. Whereas 2 Kings 21.7 states that Manasseh had placed an image of Asherah, Chronicles replaces "Asherah" with the rare term "semel," a term possibly of Phoenician origin. Chronicles here may be influenced by the "statue ("semel") of outrage" (NJPS, *image that provokes fury*) in Ezek. 8.3, which forms part of a passage detailing defilement of the Temple, as well as Deut. 4.16. **18:** Chronicles emphasizes that Manasseh had been forewarned by the LORD's messengers; hence, his failure to heed them justified his punishment. The claim that explicit warning is a sine qua non for punishment is seen by many scholars as a forerunner of the rabbinic view that courts may punish offenders only if the latter had been warned of the sinful nature of their actions prior to commission of their offense. More likely, Chronicles' position may be viewed as part of its notion of divine grace (see intro.). **19–20:** Chronicles' omission of Manasseh's culpability in Judah's exile demands an alternate explanation or justification for this national catastrophe. Chronicles addresses this point in ch 36.

33.21–25: Amon's reign. Humbling oneself (or not; see 1 Kings 21.29) is the theme that emphasizes the fundamental difference between Amon and Manasseh: Amon is killed in his palace, whereas Manasseh enjoyed

34 [a]Josiah was eight years old when he became king, and
he reigned thirty-one years in Jerusalem. 2 He did what
was pleasing to the LORD, following the ways of his father David
without deviating to the right or to the left. 3 In the eighth year
of his reign, while he was still young, he began to seek the God
of his father David, and in the twelfth year he began to purge
Judah and Jerusalem of the shrines, the sacred posts, the idols,
and the molten images. 4 At his bidding, they demolished the
altars of the Baals, and he had the incense stands above them
cut down; he smashed the sacred posts, the idols, and the images, ground them into dust, and strewed it onto the graves of
those who had sacrificed to them. 5 He burned the bones of
priests on their altars and purged Judah and Jerusalem. 6 In the
towns of Manasseh and Ephraim and Simeon, as far as Naphtali, [lying] in ruins on every side, 7 he demolished the altars
and the sacred posts and smashed the idols and ground them
into dust; and he hewed down all the incense stands throughout the land of Israel. Then he returned to Jerusalem.
8 In the eighteenth year of his reign, after purging the land
and the House, he commissioned Shaphan son of Azaliah,
Maaseiah the governor of the city, and Joah son of Joahaz
the recorder to repair the House of the LORD his God. 9 They
came to the high priest Hilkiah and delivered to him the silver
brought to the House of God, which the Levites, the guards of
the threshold, had collected from Manasseh and Ephraim and
from all the remnant of Israel and from all Judah and Benjamin
and [b]the inhabitants of Jerusalem.[-b] 10 They delivered it into
the custody of the overseers who were in charge at the House

a Cf. 2 *Kings* 22; 23.1–20.
b-b With kethib *and ancient versions;* qere, *"they returned to Jerusalem."*

an honorable burial in the same place. These vv. imply a retributive punishment.

34.1–35.27: Josiah's reign. Although Chronicles incorporates much material here from Kings, its depiction of Josiah differs in significant ways, both in detail and in overall assessment. Kings claims that Josiah ascended the throne at age eight; discovery of the "scroll" took place ten years later and was followed by Josiah's cultic and religious reforms, which were undertaken in response to the warnings of divine wrath and punishment that Josiah found in the discovered scroll. Chronicles, however, offers a different chronology, portraying Josiah as having sought the LORD at the age of sixteen, *while he was still young* (v. 3), and undertaking cultic purification at the age of twenty, prior to the discovery of the (missing) scroll. This version creates a more flattering image of this righteous king, employing motifs familiar from the David, Solomon, and Hezekiah episodes. Some scholars, in support of Chronicles' version, argue that the prophets Zephaniah and Jeremiah exerted influence on Josiah before 621 BCE, the year in which the scroll was found. Others have attempted to correlate each step of Josiah's reform in Chronicles with a corresponding wane in Assyrian influence. No consensus exists as to which version is more reliable, and whether or not Chronicles has rearranged these events for theological reasons. Chronicles' enhanced image of much of Josiah's reign highlights the ultimately less than positive assessment of Josiah, as indicated by Chronicles' description of his death. Overall, Chronicles' Josiah is a less significant monarch than Kings' Josiah. Whereas Josiah is the leading monarch in Kings, in Chronicles it is Hezekiah. **34.3:** *The eighth year of his reign,* i.e., when Josiah was sixteen years of age. Some premodern commentators (Josephus, *Ant.;* Radak) maintain that Josiah began his reform at the age of eight, the age at which he ascended the throne. It is generally agreed that the scroll discovered by Hilkiah in 2 Kings is some form of the book of Deut. More likely, Chronicles understands the referent to be the entire Torah; this would explain Chronicles' omission of 2 Kings' claim (22.8) that Shaphan read the scroll (see also 35.6). **6–7:** Chronicles' version entails a serious difficulty: Since Josiah had already purged the Temple and people of illicit practices; this passage makes clear what remained for him to correct following discovery of the scroll. Josiah now extended his reform even to more distant points within the northern tribes, following his illustrious ancestor Hezekiah. **8–13:** Cf. 2 Kings 22.3–7; there the Temple repairs simply set the stage for discovery of the scroll. Chronicles maintains that the repairs were part of Josiah's religious reform, already underway, during which the scroll was discovered. **8:** The date, *the eighteenth year,* marks one stage in the activities begun in v. 3. Chronicles' formulation suggests that discovery of the scroll was a reward for Josiah's cultic zeal, which the king displayed from an early age. Chronicles makes limited mention of Josiah's cleansing of the Temple, since Chronicles claims that such action had already taken place under Manasseh (33.15–16); cf. 2 Kings 23.4–6. **9:** The reference to *Manasseh, Ephraim,* et al., is another example of Chronicles' inclusivist slant; see v. 21.

of the LORD, and the overseers who worked in the House of the LORD spent it on examining and repairing the House. 11 They paid it out to the artisans and the masons to buy quarried stone and wood for the couplings and for making roof-beams for the buildings that the kings of Judah had allowed to fall into ruin. 12 The men did the work honestly; over them were appointed the Levites Jahath and Obadiah, of the sons of Merari, and Zechariah and Meshullam, of the sons of Kohath, to supervise; while other Levites, all the master musicians, 13 were over the porters, supervising all who worked at each and every task; some of the Levites were scribes and officials and gatekeepers.

14 As they took out the silver that had been brought to the House of the LORD, the priest Hilkiah found a scroll of the LORD's Teaching given by Moses. 15 Hilkiah spoke up and said to the scribe Shaphan, "I have found a scroll of the Teaching in the House of the LORD"; and Hilkiah gave the scroll to Shaphan. 16 Shaphan brought the scroll to the king and also reported to the king, "All that was entrusted to your servants is being done; 17 they have melted down the silver that was found in the House of the LORD and delivered it to those who were in charge, to the overseers." 18 The scribe Shaphan also told the king, "The priest Hilkiah has given me a scroll"; and Shaphan read from it to the king. 19 When the king heard the words of the Teaching, he tore his clothes. 20 The king gave orders to Hilkiah, and Ahikam son of Shaphan, and Abdon son of Micah, and the scribe Shaphan, and Asaiah the king's minister, saying, 21 "Go, inquire of the LORD on my behalf and on behalf of those who remain in Israel and Judah concerning the words of the scroll that has been found, for great indeed must be the wrath of the LORD that has been poured down upon us because our fathers did not obey the word of the LORD and do all that is written in this scroll."

22 Hilkiah and those whom the king [had ordered] went to the prophetess Huldah, wife of Shallum son of Tokhath son of Hasrah, keeper of the wardrobe, who was living in Jerusalem in the Mishneh,[a] and spoke to her accordingly. 23 She responded to them: "Thus said the LORD God of Israel: Say to the man who sent you to Me, 24 'Thus said the LORD: I am going to bring disaster upon this place and its inhabitants—all the curses that are written in the scroll that was read to the king of Judah—25 because they forsook Me and made offerings to other gods in order to vex Me with all the works of their hands; My wrath shall be poured out against this place and not be quenched.' 26 But say this to the king of Judah who sent you to inquire of the LORD: 'Thus said the LORD God of Israel: As for the words which you have heard, 27 since your heart was

a A quarter in Jerusalem; cf. Zeph. 1.10.

12: Chronicles expands the role of the Levites; cf. 2 Kings 22.7. **21:** *Those who remain in Israel and Judah* replaces "all Judah" of 2 Kings 22.13, and *the word of the LORD* replaces "the words of this scroll" in 2 Kings 22.13. The first change reflects the inclusivist tendency of Chronicles. The "word of the LORD" refers in other biblical books to prophecy, but Chronicles employs it also in connection with Torah legislation (see 1 Chron. 10.13; 15.15; 2 Chron. 35.6). This probably indicates that for Chronicles, and the postexilic period generally, Torah replaced prophecy; stated differently, the prophet was already understood as the transmitter or interpreter of Mosaic law, as in the Rabbis. **24:** Some explain Chronicles' reference to *curses* as an allusion to Deut. 29.20, thus indicating that Chronicles understood the discovered scroll to be Deut. **27:** 2 Kings 22.19b reads: "... I decreed against this place and its inhabitants—that it will become a desolation and a curse." The word "place" may refer to either Jerusalem or the Temple. In either case, Chronicles could not tolerate the "place" being cursed and so omitted the words "I decreed ... curse" in the Heb. **30:** Chronicles reads *Levites* in place of 2 Kings' "prophets" (23.2) to reflect the social makeup of Second Temple society and/or Chronicles' view of Levites as involved in prophetic activity; see 1 Chron. 25.1–5.

35.1–19: The Passover celebration. With the exception of the last two vv., none of this material is found in Kings. When compared to 2 Kings 23.21–23, Chronicles' version involves two important developments: the prominence of Levites in cultic affairs and the transformation of the Paschal offering, which Exod. ch 12 depicts as a family offering, into a Temple sacrifice like all others. Chronicles' much extended treatment, which involves elements from various Torah sources (see below), reflects Chronicles' view that the scroll found by Hilkiah was the entire Torah (more or less), whereas Kings maintains that only "a scroll of the

softened and you humbled yourself before God when you
heard His words concerning this place and its inhabitants, and
you humbled yourself before Me and tore your clothes and
wept before Me, I for My part have listened, declares the LORD.
28 Assuredly, I will gather you to your fathers, and you will be
laid in your grave in peace; your eyes shall see nothing of the
disaster that I will bring upon this place and its inhabitants.' "
They reported this back to the king.

29 Then the king sent word and assembled all the elders of
Judah and Jerusalem. 30 The king went up to the House of the
LORD with all the men of Judah and the inhabitants of Jerusalem and the priests and the Levites—all the people, young and
old—and he read to them the entire text of the covenant scroll
that was found in the House of the LORD. 31 The king stood in
his place and solemnized the covenant before the LORD: to
follow the LORD and observe His commandments, His injunctions, and His laws with all his heart and soul, to fulfill all the
terms of the covenant written in this scroll. 32 He obligated all
the men of Jerusalem and Benjamin who were present; and the
inhabitants of Jerusalem acted in accord with the Covenant of
God, God of their fathers. 33 Josiah removed all the abominations from the whole territory of the Israelites and obliged all
who were in Israel to worship the LORD their God. Throughout
his reign they did not deviate from following the LORD God of
their fathers.

35 [a]Josiah kept the Passover for the LORD in Jerusalem; the
passover sacrifice was slaughtered on the fourteenth
day of the first month. 2 He reinstated the priests in their shifts
and rallied them to the service of the House of the LORD. 3 He
said to the Levites, consecrated to the LORD, who taught all

a Cf. 2 *Kings* 23.21–30.

Teaching," which most scholars identify as an early form of Deut. alone, had been discovered. **1:** Chronicles omits the words "as it is written in this book of the covenant" found in Kings, avoiding the inference that the religious reforms were based exclusively on the discovery of the scroll and, hence, that before that discovery such reforms had not taken place. **2–15:** An instance of innerbiblical legal interpretation, in which earlier legal texts are, in this case, harmonized. (The translations of the various texts somewhat obscure this harmonization.) Exod. 12.3–5 specifies that the Paschal offering may be brought only from sheep or goats and must be roasted, not cooked in water ("b-sh-l") or consumed raw. By contrast, Deut. 16.2 states that cattle, as well as sheep and goats, are acceptable. Furthermore, Deut. 16.7 specifies that the offering must be boiled ("b-sh-l"—the NJPS translation there, "cook," is imprecise). Chronicles reconciles the two sources. The result is that the Paschal offering must be either *lambs* or *goats,* following Exod. ch 12; Deut.'s reference to "cattle" is interpreted as denoting a distinct offering—which Chronicles calls simply *sacred offerings* (v. 13)—and is intended as an adjunct to the Paschal offering. Chronicles further claims that Deut.'s use of the term "boil" means "boiled [as in Deut.] in fire [as in Exod.]." This incorporates the language of both Exod. and Deut., while the accompanying sacred offerings may, like most sacrifices, be boiled or poached, following Deut. (The beginning of v. 13, translated literally, is "They boiled the passover sacrifice in fire.") Chronicles' formulation reflects a bold step: Chronicles has changed the simple, straightforward meaning of Deut. and, moreover, the interpretation creates a previously nonexistent accompanying sacrifice. Chronicles' innovations were adopted, in varying form, in later Second Temple compositions (e.g., the book of *Jub.*) as well as rabbinic circles (see the variant traditions in *Sifre Deut.* 129; *Mek. R. Ishmael, Pisha,* 4; *y. Pes.* 6.1 [33a]; *b. Pes.* 66b; *Tg. Onk.* and, esp., *Tg. Ps.-J.* to Deut. 16.2; cf. LXX Deut. 16.7, which mandates that the paschal offering be both cooked and broiled). Harmonistic exegesis is especially well attested at Qumran (e.g., 11QT^{a}, 11QMelch) and other postbiblical sources (e.g., *Jub.*), and is a hallmark of rabbinic legal exegesis. (For more on this type of innerbiblical interpretation, see "Innerbiblical Interpretation," pp. 1835–41.) **3:** Since the Ark will presumably have been in the Temple since the latter's dedication by Solomon (2 Chron. 5.7–9), this opaque v. was interpreted by the Rabbis (*m. Shek.* 6.1; *t. Sot.* 13.1; *b. Yoma* 52b, 53b; *b. Hor.* 12a; see also, *m. Yoma* 5.2 and *b. Yoma* 21b) and other premodern sources (e.g., Karaite exegete, Japheth ben Eli) to mean that the Ark was hidden (or, perhaps, buried) in the Temple complex, so as to prevent its capture during the eventual Babylonian onslaught. These traditions notwithstanding, the v. remains opaque. The role of Levites as teachers and guardians of the law is in evidence in Deut. 33.10 (where the referent may include priests); Mal. 2.4–7; Neh. 8.7, 9; and 2 Chron. 17.8–9; and may have expanded primarily during the late preexilic and exilic period. It is also well attested in later Second Temple sources, including *Jub.* and several of the Qumran Dead Sea Scrolls (Aram. Levi; 4Q540; 4Q541), though there is evidence that some biblical works of this period (Dan.) may have challenged the exclusivity of this role. The phenomenon of teachers suggests not only the growth and formalization of a fixed body of literature as well as an increasingly educated society—at least in the author's view—alongside the centralized power base of the Temple. The importance of some form of recitation/study of texts by the people at large is already in evidence in Deut. At a later stage of Jewish history, study of "Torah" and its teachers would replace and supersede Temple worship and its officiants in importance. **10:** The implication of this v. is that all of the animals had been sacrificed by the end of the fourteenth of the month; given the large number slaughtered this process must have begun several hours earlier; cf. the times prescribed at Exod. 12.6 and Deut. 16.6. Rabbinic tradents, too, allowed for slaughtering of the paschal sacrifice to begin during the afternoon hours and, when required, as early as one-half hour after noon (*m. Pes.* 5.1). **12–13:** *As prescribed in the scroll of Moses* and *as prescribed* signify Chronicles' claim of authentic legal interpretation. **16–19:** Summary of events. **18:** The phrase *no Passover like that one* cannot refer, as in 2 Kings, to the centralization of sacrificial worship, since such had taken place during Hezekiah's reign. Rather, it probably refers to the prominence of the Levites or to the performance of the offerings in this precise fashion. **19:** LXX adds here (the translation of) 2 Kings 23.4–27, which states that despite Josiah's piety the decree regarding Jerusalem's eventual destruction (as a consequence of Manasseh's sins) remained in effect. LXX's text may convey an attempt at mitigating Chronicles' rather harsh indictment of Josiah; in any event, the attempt at harmonization flounders in the face of Chronicles' fundamentally different approach to the causes of the destruction.

Israel, "Put the Holy Ark in the House that Solomon son of
David, king of Israel, built; as you no longer carry it on your
shoulders, see now to the service of the LORD your God and
His people Israel, 4 and dispose yourselves by clans according
to your divisions, as prescribed in the writing of King David of
Israel and in the document of his son Solomon, 5 and attend
in the Sanctuary, by clan divisions, on your kinsmen, the people—by clan divisions of the Levites. 6 Having sanctified yourselves, slaughter the passover sacrifice and prepare it for your
kinsmen, according to the word of God given by Moses." 7 Josiah donated to the people small cattle—lambs and goats, all for
passover sacrifices for all present—to the sum of 30,000, and
large cattle, 3,000—these from the property of the king. 8 His
officers gave a freewill offering to the people, to the priests, and
to the Levites. Hilkiah and Zechariah and Jehiel, the chiefs of
the House of God, donated to the priests for passover sacrifices
2,600 [small cattle] and 300 large cattle. 9 Conaniah, Shemaiah,
and Nethanel, his brothers, and Hashabiah and Jeiel and Jozabad, officers of the Levites, donated 5,000 [small cattle] and
500 large cattle to the Levites for passover sacrifices.

10 The service was arranged well: the priests stood at their
posts and the Levites in their divisions, by the king's command.
11 They slaughtered the passover sacrifice and the priests [re-
ceived its blood] from them and dashed it, while the Levites
flayed the animals. 12 They removed the parts to be burnt, distrib-
uting them to divisions of the people by clans, and making the
sacrifices to the LORD, as prescribed in the scroll of Moses; they
did the same for the cattle. 13 They roasted the passover sacrifice
in fire, as prescribed, while the sacred offerings they cooked in
pots, cauldrons, and pans, and conveyed them with dispatch to
all the people. 14 Afterward they provided for themselves and the
priests, for the Aaronite priests were busy offering the burnt offerings and the fatty parts until nightfall, so the Levites provided
both for themselves and for the Aaronite priests. 15 The Asaphite
singers were at their stations, by command of David and Asaph
and Heman and Jeduthun, the seer of the king; and the gatekeepers were at each and every gate. They did not have to leave
their tasks, because their Levite brothers provided for them.
16 The entire service of the LORD was arranged well that day, to
keep the Passover and to make the burnt offerings on the altar
of the LORD, according to the command of King Josiah. 17 All the
Israelites present kept the Passover at that time, and the Feast of
Unleavened Bread for seven days. 18 Since the time of the prophet Samuel, no Passover like that one had ever been kept in Israel;
none of the kings of Israel had kept a Passover like the one kept
by Josiah and the priests and the Levites and all Judah and Israel
there present and the inhabitants of Jerusalem. 19 That Passover
was kept in the eighteenth year of the reign of Josiah.

20 After all this furbishing of the Temple by Josiah, King Necho of Egypt came up to fight at Carchemish on the Euphrates,
and Josiah went out against him. 21 [Necho] sent messengers
to him, saying, "What have I to do with you, king of Judah? I do
not march against you this day but against the kingdom that
wars with me, and it is God's will that I hurry. Refrain, then,
from interfering with God who is with me, that He not destroy you." 22 But Josiah would not let him alone; instead, [a]he
donned [his armor][a] to fight him, heedless of Necho's words
from the mouth of God; and he came to fight in the plain of
Megiddo. 23 Archers shot King Josiah, and the king said to his
servants, "Get me away from here, for I am badly wounded."
24 His servants carried him out of his chariot and put him in
the wagon of his second-in-command, and conveyed him to
Jerusalem. There he died, and was buried in the grave of his
fathers, and all Judah and Jerusalem went into mourning over
Josiah. 25 Jeremiah composed laments for Josiah which all the
singers, male and female, recited in their laments for Josiah, as
is done to this day; they became customary in Israel and were
incorporated into the laments. 26 The other events of Josiah's
reign and his faithful deeds, in accord with the Teaching of the
LORD, 27 and his acts, early and late, are recorded in the book of
the kings of Israel and Judah.

a-a With Targum.

35.20–27: Josiah's death. 2 Kings 23.28–31 offers a laconic account, whose historical background and veracity are uncertain. Chronicles' longer text probably reflects an elaboration upon Kings or perhaps a slightly longer text of Kings that has not been preserved. Chronicles' formulation suggests that the incursion of the Egyptian forces took place shortly after the Passover celebration. The formulation of v. 20 is reminiscent of 32.1, appearing in connection with the Assyrian assault on Hezekiah's kingdom. By emphasizing the achievements of both monarchs in the cultic realm, and the polar differences in their respective fates, the author emphasizes that despite his many meritorious deeds, Josiah died because of his failure to heed the LORD's word conveyed by Necho. The episode is reminiscent of Ahab's death in ch 18: He died because of his failure to heed prophetic warning. Chronicles thus portrays Josiah, a symbol of piety in Kings, in a more negative fashion. He must do so to explain Josiah's surprising death. **20–21:** While the details of this incident are not certain, it is likely that Necho was on his way to assist his Assyrian allies who had been driven to Carchemish by the Babylonians (cf. formulation of 2 Kings 23.29). The use of Necho as a conduit for the LORD's word constitutes the clearest statement of Chronicles' view on "spontaneous" prophecy: Even a foreign king may be chosen to convey the divine message, putting him (temporarily) on the same footing as an Israelite prophet. The anomalous nature of this episode is reflected in postbiblical works. 1 Esd. 1.26 replaces "Necho's words" with "the words of Jeremiah" (a position reflected in Radak's commentary), while the Aram. Tg. (35.23) offers the generic formulation, "Josiah died because he did not seek instruction from the LORD." **22–24:** *He donned [his armor]:* Heb "hitḥapes" is the term employed at 18.29 with Ahab, where it means "disguise," so its use here may be intended to connect Josiah to Ahab's folly. 2 Kings 23.29 states that Josiah was slain at *Megiddo;* this is not repeated in Chronicles, perhaps in an attempt to minimize (but not resolve) the discrepancy between 2 Kings 23.29 and the prophecy of Huldah, which promised that the king would be gathered unto his grave in peace (2 Kings 22.20 || 2 Chron. 34.28). Some see the claim that Josiah died in Jerusalem (consonantal "yršlm") as punning on, and giving credence to, Huldah's assurance that the king would be buried in peace (consonantal "bšlm"). It is possible that, aside from any punning, the mere fact of the king's death at home, presumably surrounded by family, allows his death to be seen as "peaceful rest." If so, the motif "resting/returning in peace" is another datum shared with the Ahab narrative who, as warned by the prophet Micaiah (2 Chron. 18.27), dies in battle and does not return in peace, whereas Jehoshaphat does (2 Chron. 19.1). Taken together, both narratives express the Chronicler's views concerning failure to heed the prophetic word. Josiah is the only king concerning whom it is stated that the nation mourned. The present v. may reflect the people's appreciation for Josiah's concern for the nation's lot, as manifest in his mourning upon hearing the dire news regarding Jerusalem (34.19, 27). In addition, the people's mourning makes clear their admiration of/support for Josiah; he, thereby, joins David, Solomon, Jehoshaphat, and Hezekiah, all of whom were the beneficiaries of wide support. **25–27:** The *laments* were understood by rabbinic tradents (*t. Ta'an.* 2:10) and, possibly, Josephus *(Ant.),* as referring to part of the book of Lam. (in their view, composed by Jeremiah): more likely, the reference is to an unknown collection of laments. For *Teaching* ("torah") *of the LORD,* see 34.1–3. **26:** Chronicles attributes "(acts of) loyalty" (NJPS, *faithful deeds*) to Josiah and Hezekiah (2 Chron. 32.32, "faithful acts") alone. Josiah's loyalty,

36 [a]The people of the land took Jehoahaz son of Josiah
and made him king instead of his father in Jerusalem.
[2] Jehoahaz was twenty-three years old when he became king
and he reigned three months in Jerusalem. [3] The king of Egypt
deposed him in Jerusalem and laid a fine on the land of 100
silver talents and one gold talent. [4] The king of Egypt made his
brother Eliakim king over Judah and Jerusalem, and changed
his name to Jehoiakim; Necho took his brother Joahaz and
brought him to Egypt.
[5] Jehoiakim was twenty-five years old when he became king,
and he reigned eleven years in Jerusalem; he did what was displeasing to the LORD his God. [6] King Nebuchadnezzar of Babylon marched against him; he bound him in fetters to convey
him to Babylon. [7] Nebuchadnezzar also brought some vessels
of the House of the LORD to Babylon, and set them in his palace in Babylon. [8] The other events of Jehoiakim's reign, and the
abominable things he did, and what was found against him,
are recorded in the book of the kings of Israel and Judah. His
son Jehoiachin succeeded him as king.
[9] Jehoiachin was eight years old when he became king, and
he reigned three months and ten days in Jerusalem; he did
what was displeasing to the LORD. [10] At the turn of the year,
King Nebuchadnezzar sent to have him brought to Babylon
with the precious vessels of the House of the LORD, and he
made his kinsman Zedekiah king over Judah and Jerusalem.

a With vv. 1–13, cf. 2 Kings 23.28–37; 24.1–20.

in accordance with the Torah/teaching of YHVH, harks back to 34.14–20. The upshot is that sincere devotion to God notwithstanding, failure to heed the prophetic word leads to disaster.

36.1–21: Judgment and exile. Chronicles' narration of the stages of Judah's exile differs in several significant respects from the Deuteronomistic version in Kings. Chronicles abbreviates the parent text (2 Kings chs 23–24), omitting the death notices of each king, while highlighting the ever-worsening state of the cult. While Chronicles does acknowledge the role of previous generations in connection with the Temple's destruction, its emphasis and perspective differ from that of 2 Kings. Manasseh is not held responsible by Chronicles (see above, 33.10–13); rather, the people as a whole—particularly those alive in the final years before the destruction—are culpable. In addition, whereas 2 Kings' (23.25–25.25) description of spiritual decline during the three/four generations prior to the destruction reflects a well-attested biblical motif of trans-generational punishment (see, e.g., Exod. 20.5; 34.7; Num. 14.18), Chronicles neither invokes nor alludes to this motif. Rather, it acknowledges Judah's gradual decline while at the same time placing the ultimate responsibility upon the generation of the destruction who, despite repeated divine calls to change course, continued, and even exceeded, the sinful ways of previous generations. Thus, Chronicles suggests that the destruction, although foreseen and foresworn, was not tied to any predetermined chronological scheme. Moreover, Chronicles' emphasis on the (failed) efforts of God's messengers to warn the people demonstrates the Deity's reluctance to carry out the punishment. By contrast, the repeated statement in 2 Kings that even the improved conduct of Judah's kings and society (esp. during the reign of Josiah) could not assuage God's anger reflects the pessimistic tone and forgone nature of Jerusalem's destruction in 2 Kings. Finally, the scope and severity of the punishment predicted in 2 Kings is more extreme, and detailed, than that spelled out in 2 Chron. ch 36. **1–4:** A condensed version of 2 Kings 23.30–34; Chronicles omits the negative appraisal of *Jehoahaz.* Chronicles also omits discussion of the fate of the kings and Temple spoils following their removal from the land; this may be another expression of the centrality of Israel's attachment to its land in Chronicles. **5–8:** The description of *Jehoiakim* being bound and led to Babylon in v. 6 contradicts 2 Kings 24.1. Some explain the Heb, which employs an infinitive verbal form, to mean that the king need not have actually been taken to Babylon, merely that he was bound and threatened with such a punishment. Others aver, more plausibly, that the author maintains that he was taken to Babylon as a vassal to participate in the victory celebrations, a position spelled out explicitly in LXX and 1 Esd. and suggested by the similarity of the punishment to that meted out against Manasseh (2 Chron. 33.11) The removal of Temple *vessels* (v. 7), not mentioned in Kings, was carried out in order to serve as royal tribute. **7:** The Heb "hekhal" (of Sumerian origin, where it means "large house") can denote either a temple or palace. Chronicles' reticence suggests that the latter is more likely, particularly in light of the importance it places on the eventual return of the Temple vessels as part of its continuity theme. **9–10:** Chronicles' text is terse, focusing on the exile of *Jehoiachin* and the spoiling of the Temple; cf. 2 Kings 24.8–17.

11 Zedekiah was twenty-one years old when he became king,
and he reigned eleven years in Jerusalem. 12 He did what was
displeasing to the LORD his God; he did not humble himself
before the prophet Jeremiah, who spoke for the LORD. 13 He
also rebelled against Nebuchadnezzar, who made him take an
oath[a] by God; he stiffened his neck and hardened his heart so
as not to turn to the LORD God of Israel. 14 All the officers of
the priests and the people committed many trespasses, following all the abominable practices of the nations. They polluted the House of the LORD, which He had consecrated in

a Viz., a vassal oath.

11–23: Zedekiah and Chronicles' justification of the destruction of Judah and the exile. As noted above, 2 Kings claims that the main cause of the destruction and exile of Judah was the foreign worship sponsored by Judah's kings, Manasseh in particular. Chronicles, however, minimizes the role of Manasseh's sins, claiming that the exile was (primarily) the result of the sins of Zedekiah's generation. **12–14:** Specific significant sins (not heeding prophets, false oaths) are attributed to Zedekiah, as well as the people as a whole—the king's sins alone cannot explain the national disaster. The oath alluded to is that referred to at Ezek. 17.11–21. Chronicles' treatment of Zedekiah omits the king's failed attempt at escape from the hands of the Babylonian forces and his subsequent torture (2 Kings 25.1–7 || Jer. 52.3b–11), as well as the limited sovereignty granted him (2 Kings 24.17). Some view Chronicles' omission of 2 Kings 24.14 as indicating that the author attached no particular significance to the restoration of the Davidic monarchy. This is unlikely; the fact that the sovereignty granted Zedekiah was so limited together with the fact that by the author's time it had become clear that this sovereignty had not led to reestablishment of the Davidic monarchy would justify the decision to omit the 2 Kings passage. The importance of "return," and submission to God is again in evidence in this passage. Thus, while v. 13 specifies one offense, it is noteworthy that v. 12 emphasizes that a key element of the king's sinful conduct, and cause of the exile, was his refusal to submit (k-n-ʿ) to the prophetic instructions proclaimed by Jeremiah, a fact not mentioned at 2 Kings 24.19 || Jer. 52.2, but entirely consistent with Chroniclers' outlook. As in 2 Chron. 12.1–8, the implication is that while repentance and divine compassion make possible remission of even the most heinous offenses (viz., idolatry) continued refusal to mend one's sinful conduct—even that of a less egregious nature—will lead to disaster. In v. 14, Chronicles places blame on the *priests* as well as laity, but notably omits reference to the Levites. Like Jer. (16.18) and Ezek. (5.11 and 8.6, 13,

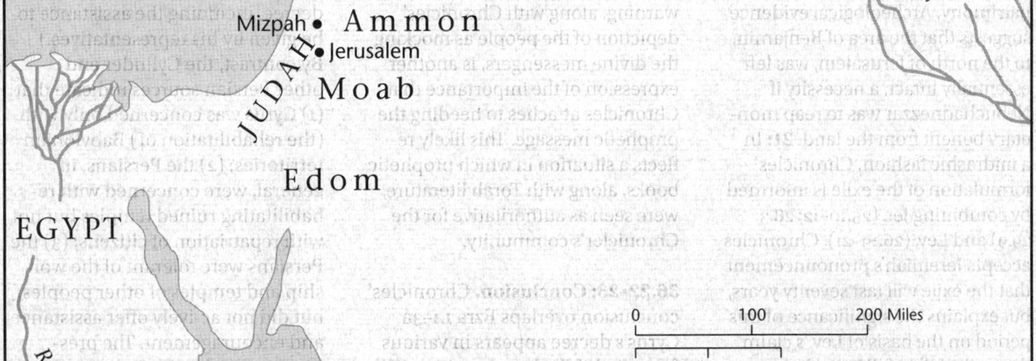

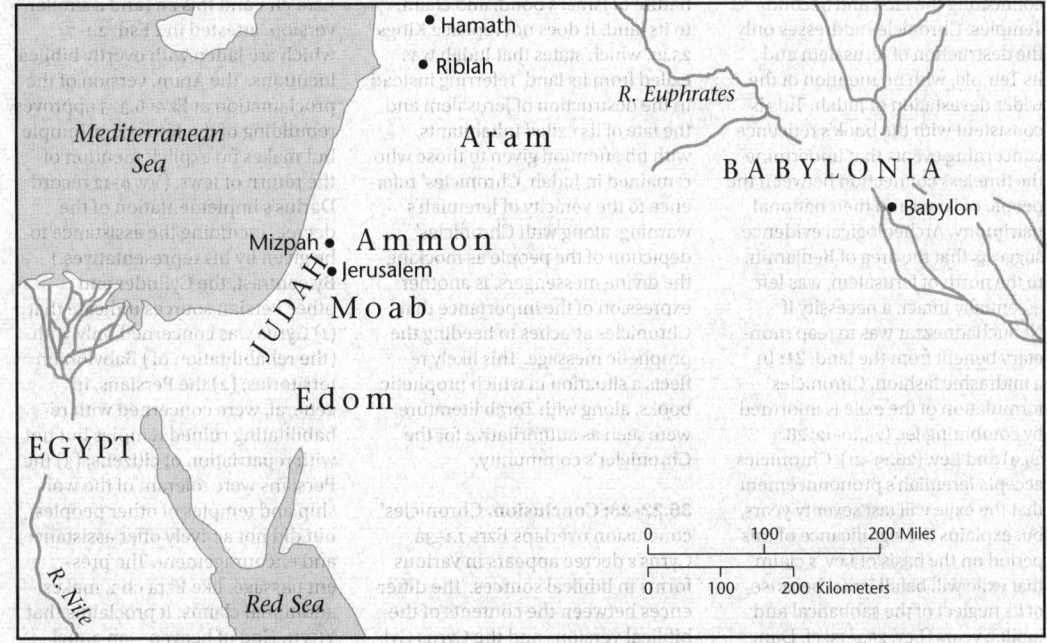

Babylonia and Judah ca. 600 BCE

Jerusalem. 15 The LORD God of their fathers had sent word to
them through His messengers daily without fail, for He had
pity on His people and His dwelling-place. 16 But they mocked
the messengers of God and disdained His words and taunted
His prophets until the wrath of the LORD against His people
grew beyond remedy. 17 He therefore brought the king of the
Chaldeans upon them, who killed their youths by the sword in
their sanctuary; He did not spare youth, maiden, elder, or graybeard, but delivered all into his hands. 18 All the vessels of the
House of God, large and small, and the treasures of the House
of the LORD and the treasures of the king and his officers were
all brought to Babylon. 19 They burned the House of God and
tore down the wall of Jerusalem, burned down all its mansions,
and consigned all its precious objects to destruction. 20 Those
who survived the sword he exiled to Babylon, and they became
his and his sons' servants till the rise of the Persian kingdom,
21 in fulfillment of the word of the LORD spoken by Jeremiah,
until the land paid back its sabbaths; as long as it lay desolate
it kept sabbath, till seventy years were completed.

22 And in the first year of King Cyrus of Persia, when the
word of the LORD spoken by Jeremiah was fulfilled, the LORD

15), Chronicles accuses the people of defiling the Temple; no details are provided here. The use of the ubiquitous Heb term "m-ʿ-l" forms an inclusio with the first full narrative of the book, viz., Saul's downfall. **15–17:** Another instance of warning preceding divine punishment. Chronicles' formulation emphasizes the extent of the people's sin: Despite the numerous opportunities for repentance, the people persist in their sinful ways. The absolute decadence is highlighted by three verbs in v. 16 to express the people's disdain for the prophetic word. V. 17 contains allusions to Lam. 1.12, 15; 2.21; 5.11–13, all of which describe the devastation and suffering of Jerusalem and its inhabitants. Like Lam. 2.1–9, this v. makes clear that it is YHVH who hands His own people over to the Babylonians. The lack of compassion contrasts with the Deity's patience and compassion mentioned in v. 15; and is reminiscent of 2 Chron. 12.8. **18–20:** See 2 Kings 24.13. Chronicles maintains that all of the vessels were taken to Babylonia (during the first deportation); their return to Jerusalem is part of the continuity theme connecting the First and Second Temples. Chronicles addresses only the destruction of Jerusalem and its Temple, with no mention of the wider devastation of Judah. This is consistent with the book's reticence concerning events that undermine the timeless connection between the people of Israel and their national patrimony. Archeological evidence suggests that the area of Benjamin, to the north of Jerusalem, was left essentially intact, a necessity if Nebuchadnezzar was to reap monetary benefit from the land. **21:** In a midrashic fashion, Chronicles' formulation of the exile is informed by combining Jer. (25.10–12; 28.3; 29.9) and Lev. (26.19–21). Chronicles accepts Jeremiah's pronouncement that the exile will last seventy years, but explains the significance of this period on the basis of Lev.'s claim that exile will befall Israel because of its neglect of the sabbatical and jubilee years (Lev. 25.1–13; cf. Dan. 9.2, 22–27). Whereas *seventy years* signifies in Jer. a lengthy stay in captivity, Chronicles views this period as a brief hiatus in Israel's history, which did not significantly alter the nature of Israel's bond, and claim, to its land. It does not repeat 2 Kings 25.21, which states that Judah was exiled from its land, referring instead to the destruction of Jerusalem and the fate of its exiled inhabitants, with no attention given to those who remained in Judah. Chronicles' reference to the veracity of Jeremiah's warning, along with Chronicles' depiction of the people as mocking the divine messengers, is another expression of the importance that Chronicles attaches to heeding the prophetic message. This likely reflects a situation in which prophetic books, along with Torah literature, were seen as authoritative for the Chronicler's community.

36.22–23: Conclusion. Chronicles' conclusion overlaps Ezra 1.1–3a. Cyrus's decree appears in various forms in biblical sources. The differences between the contents of the biblical versions and the Cyrus Cylinder, as well as the very nature of the biblical accounts, has led most scholars to doubt the historicity of the biblical versions of the decree. This is especially true regarding Ezra ch 1 and this ch (and a similar version, attested in 1 Esd. 2.1–7), which are laden with overtly biblical locutions. The Aram. version of the proclamation at Ezra 6.3–5 approves rebuilding of the Jerusalem Temple but makes no explicit mention of the return of Jews. (Vv. 6–12 record Darius's implementation of the decree, including the assistance to be given by his representatives.) By contrast, the Cylinder and other Persian sources indicate that: (1) Cyrus was concerned only with (the rehabilitation of) Babylonian territories; (2) the Persians, in general, were concerned with rehabilitating ruined temples but not with repatriation of citizens; (3) the Persians were tolerant of the worship and temples of other peoples, but did not actively offer assistance and encouragement. The present passage, like Ezra ch 1, makes additional claims. It proclaims that YHVH, God of heaven—an appellation found primarily in Persian

roused the spirit of King Cyrus of Persia to issue a proclamation throughout his realm by word of mouth and in writing, as follows: 23 "Thus said King Cyrus of Persia: The LORD God of Heaven has given me all the kingdoms of the earth, and has charged me with building Him a House in Jerusalem, which is in Judah. Any one of you of all His people, the LORD his God be with him and let him go up."

unity of Chronicles and Ezra-Neh. and their relative dates of composition (see intro.). Some scholars who accept the unity of the two works argue that these common vv. join the two works together. Others, rejecting the works' unity, argue that these vv. were added to the original conclusion of Chronicles to avoid ending on a pessimistic note.

period documents and sources—has given to Cyrus sovereignty over the world and he (Cyrus) orders both the rebuilding of the Temple and the right of all (exiled) Jews to return to Jerusalem. In contrast to Ezra 1.4, Chronicles omits mention of Cyrus's call for Jews who do not wish to return to support those seeking to do so, since this statement provides a pretext for Jews remaining in exile, a position that runs counter to the book's emphasis on the eternal bond between the people of Israel/Judah and their national patrimony (see 1 Chron. 16.7–36). This is consonant with the book's omission of 1 Kings 8.50–51, noted at 2 Chron. 6.41–42. The actual duration of the Babylonian exile, beginning with the second stage of deportations, was forty-eight years. The author may have felt that he had no choice but to employ the number seventy, because of the precedent of Jeremiah, alternatively, he may have had in mind the time at which (in his view) the postexilic prophets Zechariah and Haggai prophesied concerning the rehabilitated Temple, rather than the beginning of the return from exile. For implications of the view of the role of foreign leaders vis-à-vis that of the Davidic monarchy, see 2 Chron. 2.10–13 n. The numerous explanations proffered depend, to some extent, on the question of the However, given the importance of this theme elsewhere in Chronicles, the passage is most likely part of the original composition. Unlike Ezra 1.3, which says "May his God be with him," Chronicles adds *the LORD.* The attribution of monotheism to foreign nations and their leaders is attested above (1 Chron. 16.23; 2 Chron. 1.18–2.15). Finally, the grammatical form of the concluding Heb word, *and let him go up,* is taken by some to indicate that the process of redemption is ongoing. Cyrus's edict is depicted as the fulfillment of prophecy; with it, Israel's sins have been requited and the brief period of Israel's rupture from its land has ended.

Introduction to the Essays

THE FORTY ESSAYS IN THIS SECTION set the annotations to the biblical books in a broader context, enhancing our goal of representing Jewish academic scholarship on the Bible. They offer a wealth of supplementary material, not easily accessible elsewhere, and they represent the best of current scholarship. There is some overlap from essay to essay, but we view this as a positive feature. As in the case of the annotations, we have given our authors free rein to shape their material, and their essays manifest, as do the annotations, the variety of approaches that is typical of Jewish biblical interpretation.

The first set of essays, "Jewish Interpretation of the Bible," surveys, in chronological order, Jewish biblical interpretation in various periods, from earliest times to the present. These essays explain and model what is quintessentially Jewish about Jewish interpretation. They convey a flavor of each age, its distinctive modes of interpretation. Taken as a whole, they form a study in the continuities and discontinuities that mark the history of Jewish biblical interpretation.

The second set of essays, "Biblical Ideas and Institutions," surveys various concepts that stand behind the biblical text. This section begins with a broad overview of "The Religion of the Bible," and then presents significant ideas and institutions to which the biblical authors often refer, including purity, the festivals, David, and war and peace. The emphasis here is not specifically Jewish, but some of the topics explored, such as purity, the festivals, or the calendar, are areas where Jewish biblical scholars have shown particular interest and have made important contributions.

The third set of essays, "The Bible in Jewish Life," gives some intimation of the importance of the Bible for Judaism and the Jewish community, an importance that cannot be overstated. The Bible is *the* key text of Jewish life. The essays in this section are largely arranged chronologically, from antiquity to the present. They describe the place of the Bible in different communities and intellectual contexts, from the Jewish community that composed and preserved the Dead Sea Scrolls through the modern State of Israel and America, and in the scholarly writings of contemporary Jewish women. No description of the Bible in Jewish life would be complete without a discussion of the role of the Bible in the synagogue and in the liturgy, the part the Bible has played in forging and justifying Jewish customs, or the making of Jewish translations of the Bible from antiquity to modern times.

The fourth set of essays, "Backgrounds for Reading the Bible," provides contemporary scholarly background material for understanding the Bible. Like much of the second section of essays, the emphasis here is not specifically Jewish. The topics addressed reflect the editors' sensibilities of what an informed reader might want to know about how contemporary scholars study the Bible. Included here are essays on the historical, geographic, archeological, linguistic, and literary contexts from which the Bible emerged; essays on the development of the biblical text; and modern ways of reading various types of biblical literature.

The fifth and last set of essays, "The Hebrew Bible in Other Scriptures" recognizes that the authors of both the New Testament and the Qur'an knew and were influenced by the Hebrew Bible, in different ways and to different extents. The two essays juxtapose the uses of Hebrew Scriptures in emerging Christianity and early Islam.

In the final section of this volume, following "Tables and Charts," the "Translations of Primary Sources" and the "Glossary" are of particular importance. The Translations offer an introductory English bibliography of many primary sources mentioned in the annotations and the essays, including ancient Near Eastern, early postbiblical, classical rabbinic, medieval, philosophical, and mystical works. The Glossary explains both Hebrew and Jewish terms, as well as technical terms used in modern biblical scholarship. The material in all five sections following the annotated biblical books—the essays, tables and charts, and other supplementary materials—is intended to inform the reader, concisely but still preserving high academic quality, about the Bible and its world, from both Jewish and academic perspectives.

[ADELE BERLIN AND MARC ZVI BRETTLER]

Inner-biblical Interpretation

The interpretation of the Bible begins in the Bible itself. Biblical authors frequently commented on other biblical texts; they revised them, they argued with them, and they alluded to them. In so doing, they conveyed an understanding of the texts they utilized—in short, they interpreted earlier biblical writings. This tendency became especially prominent at the end of the preexilic period and during the exilic and postexilic periods, in other words after an early protocanonical set of texts became sacred. These reader-writers understood older texts in original ways, applied their principles to new situations, or borrowed from their prestige. In this respect the biblical authors resemble later Jewish (and Christian) writers, who constantly look back to biblical models as they create new texts, ideas, and practices. Thus the religion that *generated* the Bible foreshadows the religions *generated by* the Bible: Israelite thinkers, like those of various forms of Judaism and Christianity, constructed their works by recasting language and themes found in earlier ones. Biblical authors bequeathed their successors not only a text, but ways of relating to that text, reacting to that text, recreating that text, and allowing that text to remain alive.

It will be helpful to discuss both the forms that inner-biblical revision takes and the effects of those revisions at the level of ideas—both *how* and *why* biblical authors borrow from their predecessors. In examining both these issues, this essay will also compare the ways biblical authors used biblical texts with the ways postbiblical authors did so.

To begin, then, with the rhetoric of reuse and re-reading: Biblical authors utilized the work of their predecessors in several ways. Some biblical passages use a formula when they quote an older text, thus making the borrowing explicit. (This practice resembles the modern.) 2 Kings 14.5–6 tells us of King Joash, "Once he had the kingdom firmly in his grasp, he put to death the courtiers who had assassinated his father the king. But he did not put to death the children of the assassins, in accordance with what is written *[kakatuv]* in the Book of the Teaching of Moses *[torat moshe]*, where the LORD commanded, 'Parents shall not be put to death for children, nor children be put to death for parents; a person shall be put to death only for his own crime.' " The formula "in accordance with what is written" (or, more simply, "as it is written") introduces a nearly word-for-word quotation from Deut. 24.16. In other instances this formula introduces quotations or refers to ideas found elsewhere in the Torah (1 Kings 2.3; Ezra 3.2; 2 Chron. 23.18). This formula (*kakatuv* or *kemo shekatuv*) is also used to introduce quotations from Scripture in rabbinic literature, the Dead Sea Scrolls, and (in Gk translation) the New Testament.

In a much larger number of cases, however, biblical texts borrow phrasing or imagery without citing the source explicitly; rather, the shared items help the knowledgeable reader identify the source. The prophet responsible for the latter part of the book of Isa. (see the intro. to Isa.) comforted Judeans after the destruction of Jerusalem with these words:

> The LORD comforts *Zion,* comforts all her ruins. He makes *Zion's* wasteland an Eden; her desert, a garden of the LORD ... Listen to Me, My *people,* and My nation, give ear! *For teaching goes forth from Me,* and I will give *My judgment* as a light of the peoples ... My arms will *judge peoples.* Islands will look eagerly to Me, and in My arms they will have hope. *Lift up* your eyes towards heaven and look at

> the earth below! For the heaven can melt away like smoke, and the earth can wear out like a garment ... But My salvation will endure forever (Isa. 51.3–6, author's translation).

In issuing this prediction, the exilic author borrows from a passage found in the work of two prophets who lived more than a century and a half earlier, (First) Isaiah and Micah:

> In the future, the mountain of the LORD's House will be established as the greatest of mountains and *lifted up* above the hills. All nations will flow towards it, and many *peoples* will come and say, "Let us go up to the LORD's mountain, to the House of Jacob's God," ... *For teaching goes forth from Zion,* and the LORD's word from Jerusalem. And God will *judge* the nations, ... and they will beat their swords into plowshares and their weapons into pruning forks; nation will not lift up sword against nation, and they will learn war no more (Isa. 2.2–4, author's translation; Mic. 4.1–4 is almost identical).

The author of Isa. ch 51 borrowed the items printed in italics above. In addition, *ḥorvoteha* ("her ruins") in Isa. ch 51 is an intentional pun, hinting at *ḥarvotam* ("their swords") in Isa. ch 2 and Mic. ch 4, a word that has a different meaning but sounds nearly identical. The passages share several images as well. The idea of peoples gathering appears in both passages, and both predict that the LORD will teach nations and judge them at His mountain. In both passages agricultural images (plowshares and pruning hooks in Isa. ch 2 and Mic. ch 4, gardens in Isa. ch 53) take the place of figures of destruction. The new text reworks the old one. It repeats the earlier prediction, but it shifts attention from the nations who come in pursuit of instruction and peace to the benefits that Jerusalem will gain from her newly exalted position. The later author does not use a citation formula to tell the reader that the new text depends on the older one, but the many items they share indicate their relationship. We may characterize this relationship as a literary allusion. A great many biblical texts utilized their predecessors in this way, and some postbiblical writers continued the tradition of allusion. Based on similarity of vocabulary and phraseology, it is clear that many of the Dead Sea Scrolls borrow and rework texts from the Bible; the same is true of the New Testament. On the other hand, the central works of rabbinic literature (the Talmuds and the midrashim) allude to the Bible much less frequently. They tend instead to cite the Bible explicitly by using citation formulas like "as it is written" or "as it was said." Other rabbinic works, however, often borrow vocabulary and images from the Bible in a style that recalls the Bible itself; these rabbinic works include prayers found in the Siddur (prayerbook), moralistic books, and some mystical texts. Allusions to the Bible continue throughout the development of Hebrew literature; they are very frequent in medieval Hebrew poetry and in the work of modern Israeli writers such as Bialik, Agnon, Amichai, and others.

Some biblical works borrow whole sections from older texts. For example, the book of Chron. repeats, more or less verbatim, large parts of Sam. and Kings. The legal collection in Deut. chs 12–26 includes laws similar to those in Exod. chs 21–23. According to most modern source-critical biblical scholars, the books of Gen. through Num. incorporate several older texts that are no longer available to us in their original form. In all these cases, the new works make small but highly significant changes in the borrowed material. Thus the theological and historical outlook of Chron. differs from that of Sam.-Kings, even as Chron. reports the same events using many of the same words (see the intro. to Chron.). Some modern scholars maintain that a group of priests copied an older form of the festival law now found in Lev. ch 23, but they added vv. 9–22 and vv. 39–44 when they did so (see nn. there). By making the additions, these priests radically altered the religious outlook of the original document. They acknowledged the validity of popular ritual observances deliberately shunned by the more elite priests responsible for the older version of the ch. Revising a text by copying it with significant variations or additions remained a common form of Jewish writing in the period immediately following the completion of the Bible. Works such as *Jub.* and some of the Dead Sea Scrolls retold the stories of the Torah or repeated and modified laws found there. These works were not preserved by later Jewish groups, however, and they did not continue to be studied, read, or chanted in Jewish communities. The Rabbis did not incorporate large sections of the Bible into new works that they wrote; instead, they typically compiled collections of interpretive comments on the Bible (known as midrashim), included interpretive comments in legal works (such as the Talmud), and, beginning with the Middle Ages, wrote verse-by-verse commentaries on the Bible.

Finally, some later comments on biblical passages occur within those passages themselves, at least in the text of the Bible that has been in use for the past two millennia. Like modern readers, ancient readers penned explanations or reactions to the text they were reading in margins or between the lines. Some of these marginal comments were subsequently inserted into the text itself by scribes who copied the scroll containing the marginal comment. (It is also possible that some of these comments were inserted to begin with by scribes who made them as they were copying a scroll.) For example, 1 Kings 15.5 originally limited itself to a comment praising King David, and one important ms of the ancient Gk translation of Kings preserves that original text. A later scribe found the fulsome praise of David inconsistent with the story in 2 Sam. ch 11. That story is exceedingly critical of David for committing adultery with the wife of Uriah the Hittite (one of his own soldiers) and for having Uriah murdered to ensure that the adultery was not discovered. Therefore, the scribe added a qualification in 1 Kings 15.5: "except in the matter of Uriah the Hittite." These words became part of the Masoretic Text (MT), which thus contains both the original author's evaluation of David and a later reader's reaction to that evaluation. Similarly, Exod. 22.24 originally read, "If you lend money to My "*'am,*" do not act toward them as a creditor; exact no interest from them." Now, the Heb word "*'am*" usually means "people," but it can also mean "the poor" or "common folk, peasantry" (see Isa. 3.15; Ps. 72.2; Neh. 5.1). To make clear that in this case the second of these meanings was to be understood, a later scribe added the words "to the poor among you" immediately after "*'am.*" Since the meaning of "*'am*" as "people" was more common, the scribe worried that without clarification the v. would be misread.

The goals of other biblical authors and scribes who borrowed material from older biblical texts were varied. As we can see from the scribal insertion in Exod. ch 22 just discussed, they sometimes wanted to explain a passage that seemed ambiguous, problematic, or somehow relevant to their own situation. In other words, they wrote an interpretation. A famous example occurs in Dan. 9.2: "I, Daniel, consulted the books concerning the number of years that, according to the word of the LORD that had come to Jeremiah the prophet, were to be the term of Jerusalem's desolation—seventy years." In this v. the author of Daniel cited a passage from the book of Jer. explicitly. Jeremiah wrote that passage shortly after the Babylonians deported many of Jerusalem's leaders in 597 BCE: "Thus said the LORD: When Babylon's seventy years are over, I will take note of you, and I will fulfill to you My promise of favor—to bring you back to this place" (Jer. 29.10). The author of Dan. wrote at a time when the Second Temple was being desecrated and Jerusalem's status as a holy city was in peril (in the middle of the 2nd C. BCE). Therefore, that author felt that the redemption and favor promised in Jer.

29.10 had still not materialized, even though seventy years had long passed. How, then, to understand Jeremiah's prophecy as a true prophecy? Daniel reports that the angel Gabriel answered this question: "Seventy weeks have been decreed for your people and your holy city until ... eternal righteousness [is] ushered in; and prophetic vision ratified" (Dan. 9.24). According to Gabriel's interpretation, Jeremiah's words were really a sort of code. When Jeremiah said "seventy *[shiv'im]* years" he meant "seventy weeks" or "seventy sevens" *(shavu'im shiv'im)* of years; the consonants *shv'ym* had to be read twice, with slightly different vocalization each time. As a result what seems like one word is really two. The redemption would occur not seventy years after Jeremiah issued the prophecy, but four hundred and ninety years afterwards. This interpretation of Jer. ch 29 confirms the prophecy as a true one, and makes it applicable to a current situation. The interpretation is certainly a novel one, and not what Jeremiah himself meant; it makes it seem that Jeremiah was speaking for the benefit of the audience at the time of Daniel, not for Jeremiah's own audience. Nevertheless, Daniel's reading of Jeremiah follows a recognizable logic. The word of God is not like the word of a human; divine speech is infinitely more meaningful. When a human utters the consonants of the word *shiv'im,* it means only one thing ("seventy"), but when God does so they have (at least) another layer of meaning, and thus they can be read twice in two different ways *(shavu'im shiv'im),* to mean seventy sevens. Precisely the same theory of divine language as supercharged with meaning underlies biblical interpretations found in postbiblical Jewish literature, such as the midrashim (see "Midrash," pp. 1879–91). Indeed, this passage in Dan. is an early case of classical Jewish scriptural interpretation. Midrash, then, is not just a postbiblical invention used by the Rabbis to revise the Bible as they saw fit. It is a biblical means of relating to the Bible, which the Rabbis inherited from the biblical authors themselves.

One more case in which a biblical author explicitly interprets older biblical texts: Both Exod. and Deut. provide regulations concerning the Passover sacrifice, but these regulations differ in several respects. According to Deut. 16.7, the Passover sacrifice should be boiled. The law concerning the Passover sacrifice in Exod. 12.9 takes issue with Deut. on this point, warning its audience, "Don't eat it raw or boiled in water; rather, [eat it] roasted in fire" (author's translation; the NJPS translation obscures this point by translating the verb "cook" in Deut.). That such a disagreement *(maḥloket)* occurs in this ancient Jewish literature is not surprising: Two groups in the biblical period agreed that the Passover sacrifice was important but disagreed on its precise details. Such disagreements over the precise requirements of a ritual are a regular feature of Jewish law in all ages. Classical rabbinic authorities, for example, agree that one should not eat dairy products for some time after eating meat but disagree concerning the exact length of the waiting period (some say it should be three hours; others, six); contemporary Jewish groups agree that communal prayers are important but disagree concerning whether women should be allowed to lead them. The authors of the book of Chron., however, cannot tolerate disagreement between two texts in the Torah; unlike most modern scholars, they view the Torah not as an anthology of differing opinions (comparable to the Talmud), or as a compendium of different sources, but as a single work, written by Moses (comparable to a law code such as Maimonides' *Mishneh Torah*). Consequently, they deny that a legal disagreement or *maḥloket* can occur in the Torah. When narrating the Passover observances during the reign of the righteous King Josiah, Chron. tells us that "they slaughtered the Passover sacrifice ... according to what is written in the Book of Moses ... and they boiled the Passover sacrifice in fire, in accordance with the law" (2 Chron. 35.11–13, author's translation). Precisely what Chron. means by the phrase "boiled in fire" is not clear. What is evident, however, is that Chron. insists the sacrifice was performed in accordance with the Torah *as a whole:* somehow the priests simultaneously *boiled* it (as per Deut.) and roasted it *in fire* (as per Exod.). The interpretive principle that the book of Chron. advocates here is shared by classical rabbinic commentators: The Torah is a single document, and therefore what seem to be contradictions within it must be explained away through harmonization. (Rabbinic interpreters on these passages in Exod. and Deut. devised several ways of showing that they do not really disagree with each other; see, e.g., the Talmud's explanation in *b. Pes.* 70b.)

In the cases just examined, the goal of the later passage is to illuminate the earlier one. In many other instances of inner-biblical borrowing, however, the new text presents an innovative variation of the older text's ideas or even argues against it. Instead of saying, "Here is how you ought to understand the older text," the new composition tells the reader, "There are some ideas in the older text that need to be revised or extended or discarded. Here's my proposal for a replacement." Exod. 34.6–7 informs us that God sometimes punishes children for their parent's sin—indeed, even grandchildren and great-grandchildren can be punished:

> *The LORD! the LORD!* a God *compassionate and gracious, slow to anger, abounding in kindness* and faithfulness, *extending* kindness to the thousandth generation, forgiving iniquity, transgression, and sin; yet He does not remit all punishment, but visits the iniquity of parents upon children and children's children, upon the third and fourth generations.

According to this formulation (which appears in condensed form in Exod. 32.1–6, 34; Num. 14.1–20; 2 Kings 20.12–19; Ps. 99.8), God punishes children for the sins of their parents, apparently as a sign of mercy to the parents: When sinners repent, their punishment is deferred to their offspring. Other biblical writers, however, rejected this notion. Ps. 103.8–10, for example, notes: "*The LORD* is *compassionate and gracious, slow to anger, abounding in kindness.* He will not *extend* his anger forever, nor will He fight for all time" (author's translation).

The psalmist quotes the text from Exod. ch 34, which was already an authoritative and holy text, but revises the morally troubling part: Where the older text informed us that God punishes a sin for generations, the psalm maintains that God does not contend forever. A similar quotation-with-revision occurs in Deut. 7.9–10, Jonah 4.2, and Joel 2.12. These texts do not attempt to tell us how to read Exod. ch 34; that is, they do not argue that Exod. ch 34 somehow means something other than what it seems to say. Rather, they repeat it while also disagreeing with part of it. The same phenomenon occurs in rabbinic liturgy. During the introduction to the Torah service on festivals and throughout the Yom Kippur service, the first part of the statement from Exod. ch 34 is quoted, but the section at the end describing the intergenerational punishment is omitted. In purposefully misquoting the scriptural passage, then, the Rabbis who created the festival liturgy follow a scriptural precedent.

Sometimes it is difficult to be sure whether a later biblical author means to interpret an earlier text or to revise it. Exod. 23.9 reads, "Do not oppress *the foreigner.* You experienced the life of the foreigner, *for you were foreigners in the land of Egypt*" (author's translation). Deut. 10.19 echoes but amplifies the v. from Exod.: "Love *the foreigner, for you were foreigners in the land of Egypt.*" Does Deut. intend to explain that "not oppressing" really means "loving," and that Exod. 23.9 at a deeper level commands us to love the foreigner? Or does Deut. rather mean to say that not only is what Exod. commanded right, but we should go further and actively love the foreigner? It is difficult to be sure, but given the many other cases in which Deut. clearly disagrees with Exod. (e.g., the law of the Passover sacrifice discussed above, or the law of the slave in Deut. 15.12–18, which revises Exod. 21.2–7), the latter explanation seems more likely.

Biblical writers often use older texts to bolster their own writing or to help make some claim in a particularly clear or lively fashion. According to Jer. 2.3:

> Israel is the LORD's *holy item,* the *first-fruits* He produced. All who *consume* Israel will *incur guilt;* disaster will befall them (author's translation).

In making this assertion, Jeremiah relies on the ritual law found in Lev. 22.14–16:

> If a man *consumes* a *holy item* by mistake he must give a *holy item* to the priest plus one-fifth of its value. The priests must not let the *holy items* donated to the LORD by the Israelites be defiled, nor may they allow the Israelites to *incur punishment* by *consuming holy items* (author's translation).

Jeremiah suggests an analogy in order to make his own point more vivid: According to ritual law, certain agricultural products (esp. *first-fruits,* according to Num. 18.11–13) are holy items. They belong to the Temple and cannot be consumed (i.e., eaten) as regular food; those who do so incur guilt. So too the nation Israel is sacred to the LORD; the nation is, metaphorically, a holy item. Therefore, any who would consume (i.e., attack or destroy) that nation will incur guilt and suffer disaster. This sort of literary allusion differs from the examples of inner-biblical interpretation and revision we saw above. Jeremiah neither explains the passage from Lev. nor repeats it while modifying its message. He does not claim that the older passage is really a geopolitical warning to Israel's enemies rather than a law concerning the sacrificial rites. Nor does he suggest that the text ought to be such a warning and needs to be rewritten. In fact, Jeremiah's statement does not affect the meaning of the older text at all. Rather, Jeremiah evokes the law from Lev. in order to make his own message readily understood by analogy. In so doing, he also aligns himself with an authoritative text and thus bolsters his own status as prophet.

The following case of inner-biblical allusion, on the other hand, at once enriches the text that makes the allusion and illuminates the source. When two Israelite spies venture into Jericho at the outset of the book of Josh., the Canaanite harlot Rahab allows them to hide in her house, thus disobeying an edict of her own Canaanite king. She explains her reasons to the Israelite spies:

> I know that the LORD has given you the land. Indeed, *fear* of you has *overtaken* us, and *all the inhabitants of* the land *are trembling* because of you (Josh. 2.9, author's translation).

Rahab's words closely resemble a line from the song Moses and the Israelites sang at the Reed Sea after they escaped from Egypt:

> *All the inhabitants of* Canaan *will tremble; fear* and terror will *overtake* them (Exod. 15.15–16, author's translation).

The allusion in Josh. (which was written after the poem in Exod. ch 15) works on several levels. It establishes a link between the events described in the first chs of Josh. and the exodus from Egypt, a link that other passages in Josh. strengthen. (E.g., the crossing of the River Jordan in Josh. chs 3–4 reenacts the crossing of the Sea of Reeds in Exod. chs 14–15.) This brief allusion helps the author make a central point: The grand act of salvation that the LORD performed for Israelite slaves in the past was not the last such act; in each and every generation Jews should see themselves as participating in that miracle, because similar miracles may well save them, too. By repeating vocabulary from Exod. ch 15, the author of Josh. forges a parallel between two moments in time and hence expresses a philosophy of history: History repeats itself, and the activities of earlier generations are a sign for what will happen to their offspring. At the same time, this allusion also tells us something about the song in Exod. It is possible to read that poem as prophetic, and to view the line describing the Canaanites' fear as a prediction made by Moses well before the Canaanites actually heard of the Israelites' good fortune. By paraphrasing that line in the past tense, the author of Josh. confirms the accuracy of the older prediction and thus reinforces Moses' prestige. Allusions to biblical texts occur with enormous frequency in later Jewish literature. One cannot move through a page of the Dead Sea Scrolls' *Community Rule,* a paragraph from the rabbinic liturgy, a poem by Yehudah Halevi or Nathan Zach or Dan Pagis, or a novel by A. B. Yehoshua or Amos Oz without finding vocabulary and images that evoke particular passages from the Bible. Indeed, the constant reworking of biblical material is a hallmark of Jewish literature, a hallmark that is already prominent in the Bible itself.

It is often stated that postbiblical Judaism is a religion of the Book, and that interpretation and debate are quintessentially rabbinic activities. In light of the phenomenon of inner-biblical exegesis and allusion, it becomes evident that these characteristics of Jewish creativity did not begin with the Rabbis. Biblical authors themselves regarded older biblical texts as authoritative, sacred, and worthy of study. Close examination of some biblical documents, especially those composed toward the end of the biblical period but including some from the preexilic era, shows something extraordinary: Priests and prophets, psalmists and scribes composed Scripture by recycling Scripture, by turning it and turning it to find new truths in it. For many biblical writers, new words from God emerged from intense examination and reordering of old ones. The interpretation of a sacred text could yield revelation, as much as revelation yielded a sacred text. If this is so, then the gulf that separates the Bible or *Torah shebikhtav* ("Written Torah") from rabbinic tradition or *Torah shebeʿal peh* ("Oral Torah") is smaller than one might think. The Rabbis stand alongside their biblical forebears when they interpret the Bible, even when they interpret the Bible in surprising or radical ways. It is perhaps for this reason that they portrayed biblical figures as the first biblical commentators. "Moses wrote many things in an obscure way [in the Torah], and then came King David [in the book of Psalms] who explained them," we read in a midrash on Exod. (*Exod. Rab.* 15:22). By reading and revising, explaining and debating, the authors of the Bible as well as those who follow them demonstrate that many different texts, biblical and otherwise, contain the living words of God.

[BENJAMIN D. SOMMER]

Early Nonrabbinic Interpretation

A variety of extrabiblical texts preserve ancient interpretations of biblical law and narrative. Many motifs from these interpretations are found in later rabbinic (as well as Christian and Islamic) sources. But the interpretive texts were, for the most part, not preserved within rabbinic corpora and libraries, and they often represent legal and theological views that diverge sharply from those found within rabbinic Judaism. Scholars use these texts—recovered from Christian libraries and from the Dead Sea Scrolls at Qumran—both to reconstruct the diverse character of the Second Temple community before the emergence of rabbinic Judaism and Christianity, and to illuminate later interpretations. (For an explanation of the Dead Sea Scrolls and the ways in which they are named and referenced, see "The Bible in the Dead Sea Scrolls," pp. 1850–59.)

These interpretive texts vary greatly in the way they present their relationship to the biblical texts they interpret. At one extreme are interpretive texts that efface themselves, presenting themselves as nothing more than editions, retellings, or translations of biblical passages. Translations and interpretations that claim divine authority are less self-effacing, but claim to present nothing but the one true meaning of biblical passages. At the opposite extreme are the interpretive writings of individuals such as Josephus and Philo of Alexandria, who self-consciously occupy particular points of view, which they know to be at some distance—perspectivally, historically, linguistically—from the biblical passages they interpret.

Biblical Retellings

Examples of self-effacing texts, which present themselves as editions or retellings of biblical texts, include *Jubilees (Jub.),* the *Genesis Apocryphon* (1QapGen ar), *Reworked Pentateuch* (4Q158, 4Q354, 4Q365, 4Q366, 4Q367), and the *Temple Scroll* (11QT). These texts are often characterized as "pseudepigrapha"—as writings falsely attributed to earlier authoritative figures, such as Moses, Ezekiel, or Ezra. However, this term is misleading and anachronistic. It is misleading because it presupposes that, in contrast to these extrabiblical texts, the biblical texts are authentically attributed to certain authors—a presupposition that biblical scholars no longer maintain. In addition, the term is anachronistic, because it assumes a conception of authorial attribution—as marking a historical and proprietary fact—which was operative in some Gk-speaking circles in late antiquity, long after the last scriptural works had been written and, indeed, canonized. There is no evidence, however, that this conception was operative for Second Temple writers and readers.

Self-effacing texts rewrite traditions familiar from the Bible, sometimes in strikingly unfamiliar ways, in order to resolve interpretive questions and to serve particular theological and legal agendas, of which there were many in the diverse atmosphere of Second Temple Judaism. Since their authors do not identify themselves, they seem more like inner-biblical than rabbinic interpretations (which generally ascribe interpretations to a named Rabbi). In fact, it is anachronistic to apply the distinction between inner-biblical and extrabiblical interpretations to Second Temple reworkings because, when these works were composed, there was no rigidly defined and universally accepted biblical canon. These works aspired not to replace, but rather to accompany traditions already regarded as authoritative, and thus to provide those traditions with their proper interpretive contexts. Just as the Deuteronomic law collection came to be accepted within the Torah alongside the earlier Covenant Collection in Exod. chs 20–23, so it is possible to see the aforementioned extrabiblical works as accompanying the Torah texts at Qumran, where they have been found.

It was in this spirit that *Jub.*, a work written in the land of Israel during the first third of the 2nd c. BCE, rewrote Gen. and the first part of Exod. These sections of the Torah appear to be concerned exclusively with narratives about the patriarchs and matriarchs and about Israel's sojourn in Egypt. The absence of legal significance was problematic for *Jub.*, as it would be, centuries later, to Rashi, the great medieval commentator (see "Medieval Jewish Interpretation," pp. 1891–1915). Rashi's solution was the suggestion, derived from classical rabbinic sources, that the initial, nonlegal sections of the Torah serve to establish the Jewish people's right to the land of Israel. In contrast, the solution of *Jub.* was to rewrite the narratives as stories with legal implications. These implications were explained in accordance with a particular (nonrabbinic) view of law, especially regarding the calendar, which *Jub.* insists should be solar. For example, *Jub.* was bothered—like many other ancient, medieval, and modern interpretations—by a narrative in Gen. ch 38 in which Judah, son of Jacob, has sexual relations with his daughter-in-law, Tamar. To make matters even worse, according to Ruth ch 4, the line of David springs from this illicit union! *Jub.* offers an exegetically ingenious solution. In its version of the story, neither of Judah's sons, Er and Onan, consummated his marriage with Tamar (*Jub.* 41.2–5):

> He hated (her) and did not lie with her because his mother was a Canaanite woman and he wanted to marry someone from his mother's tribe. But his father Judah did not allow him. That Er, Judah's firstborn, was evil, and the Lord killed him. Then Judah said to his brother Onan: "Go in to your brother's wife, perform the levirate duty for her, and produce descendants for your brother." Onan knew that the descendants would not be his but his brother's, so he entered the house of his brother's wife and poured out the semen on the ground. In the Lord's estimation it was an evil act, and He killed him.

Consequently, although Judah transgressed, he did not, strictly speaking, commit the serious sin of adulterous union with his daughter-in-law. He therefore did not deserve the death penalty, and was able to achieve atonement through his remorse and through his expression of commitment to the law (*Jub.* 41.27–28):

> We told Judah that his two sons had not lain with her. For this reason his descendants were established for another generation and would not be uprooted. For in his integrity he had gone and demanded punishment because Judah had wanted to burn her on the basis of the law which Abraham had commanded his children.

Interpretations of this kind were not presented by *Jub.* merely as plausible solutions to exegetical problems, which would have allowed them to compete with other possible solutions. Instead, *Jub.* purports to be a text dictated to Moses, at God's command, by the angel of the Presence at Sinai. In some ways, this is similar to the notion of an authoritative Oral Torah that would become so central to rabbinic theology (see "Classical Rabbinic Interpretation," pp. 1859–78). Here is the prologue to the book of *Jub.*:

> These are the words regarding the divisions of the times of the law and of the testimony, of the events of the years, of the weeks of their jubilees throughout all the years of eternity as He related (them) to Moses on Mt. Sinai when he went up to receive the stone tablets—the law and the commandments—on the Lord's orders as He had told him that he should come up to the summit of the mountain.

Toward the end of the first ch Moses receives his command to record what is dictated to him (*Jub.* 1.26):

> Now you write all these words which I will tell you on this mountain: what is first and what is last and what is to come during all the divisions of time which are in the law and which are in the testimony and in the weeks of their jubilees until eternity—until the time when I descend and live with them throughout all the ages of eternity.

Many of the laws expounded in *Jub.* were also said to be inscribed on heavenly tablets (following Mesopotamian models), and to have been transmitted by angels to a select line of humans, beginning with Enoch. Clearly, the stakes were very high in Second Temple contests of biblical interpretation. How else may we explain the need for so many modes of self-authorization?

In addition to solving exegetical problems, another function of ancient reworkings was to spell out in detail what older traditions had expressed with great concision. For example, in Gen. 12.11, Abram briefly acknowledges his wife's beauty: "[*Hineh na*] I know what a beautiful woman you are." The first two words are left untranslated by NJPS, but may be translated as "now." This immediately raises the question: What event had brought about Abram's recognition *now*? To answer this question the *Genesis Apocryphon,* a Dead Sea text written in Aram., expands the biblical passage as follows (column 20.1–12):

> 1 ... [...] How ... and pretty is the shape of her face, and how [l]ovely and how smooth the hair of her head! How lovely are her eyes; how pleasant her nose and all the blossom of her face ... How graceful is her breast and how lovely all her whiteness! How beautiful are her arms! And her hands, how perfect! How alluring is the whole appearance of her hand[s]! How pretty are the palms of her hands and how long and supple all the fingers of her hands! Her feet, how lovely! How perfect her thighs! No virgin or wife who enters the bridal chamber is more beautiful than her. Above all women her beauty stands out; her loveliness is far above them all. And with all this beauty there is in her great wisdom. And everything she does with her hands is perfect. When the king heard the words of Hirqanos and the words of his companions, which the three of them spoke in unison, he desired her greatly and sent immediately for her to be fetched. He saw her and was amazed at all her beauty, and took her for himself as a wife. He wanted to kill me, but Sarai said to the king: He is my brother, so that I could profit at her expense. I, Abram, was spared on her account and I was not killed. But I wept bitterly that night, I, Abram, and my nephew Lot with me, because Sarai had been taken away from me by force.

The language of praise used here is from the Song of Songs. Use of traditions from other biblical books, which presupposes that all the biblical books bear one on the other, is characteristic of ancient reworkings, as well as of later rabbinic interpretations. But the above passage does more than expand Abram's remark. It justifies Abram's lying to Pharaoh, while also providing the careful reader of Gen. with a more complete picture of Abram's own inner spiritual struggles. The continuation of the passage challenges God to "do justice for me against him and show your mighty arm against him." Such boldness is not out of character for Abram, as his challenges to God in Gen. chs 15 and 18 show. But it is not to be found in Gen. ch 12. Motifs are thus moved from one section to another where they might appropriately belong. Clearly, one motive for the reworking is to emphasize central features of Abram's personality. Thus ancient reworkings seek to explain not only the legal, but also what we might call the literary aspects of the text, giving insights into character and plot.

Translations

Ancient translations of the Torah into Gk, Aram., and Latin are governed by the original texts in ways that reworkings are not. Nevertheless, these translations were often interpretive; they solved interpretive problems, took sides in theological and legal controversies, and expanded narrative and legal material, while purporting merely to convey the meaning of the texts they translate. That this phenomenon was originally connected to the linguistic and cultural difficulties facing those who returned from Babylonia to reconstruct the Temple is suggested by Neh. 8.1–8:

> All the people gathered together ... They asked Ezra the scribe to bring the book of the Torah of Moses ... Ezra the priest brought the Torah before the assembly, men, women, and all who could hear with understanding ... He read aloud from ... dawn until midday facing the men, women, and the interpreters, and ... all the people were attentive to the

> book of Torah ... Ezra the scribe opened the book before the eyes of the entire people ... When he opened it all of the people stood. Ezra blessed the LORD, the great God and the entire people answered: "Amen, Amen" while raising their hands, bowing down, and prostrating themselves before the LORD with their faces upon the ground ... Those interpreting the Torah ... read aloud from the book of the Torah of God, explaining, applying insight, and making the reading comprehensible (author's translation).

Evidently, the audience could not understand the text without some help, and translators (later called *meturgemanim*) continued to provide such help in rabbinic times. The Rabbis dated the earliest Targumim (plural of "Targum," Aram. "translation") to the time of Ezra (*b. Meg.* 3a and *b. Ned.* 37b) and, in even the earliest rabbinic sources, refer to the public reading of Targum alongside the recitation of the weekly Torah portion. Thus, for example, the halakhot associated with reading and translating are discussed in the Mishnah (*Meg.* 4:4): "The reader of Torah is not to read less than three vv. He is to read to the *meturgeman* not more than one v. at a time, or in a reading from the Prophets [i.e., haftarah] not more than three." It was the responsibility of the *meturgeman* (translator) not only to translate the text, but to render it comprehensible. The Aram. Targumim (e.g., *Tg. Onk.; Tg. Neof.; Frg. Tg.; Tg. Ps.-J.*) often supplement and gloss biblical narratives, and they take special pains to avoid any suggestion of inappropriate anthropomorphism. For example, in Exod. ch 33, Moses asks God to see His Presence (33.18). Here is the NJPS translation of God's response (Exod. 33.19–23):

> And He answered, "I will make all My goodness pass before you, and I will proclaim before you the name LORD, and the grace that I grant and the compassion that I show. But," He said, "you cannot see My face, for man may not see Me and live." And the LORD said, "See, there is a place near Me. Station yourself on the rock and, as My Presence passes by, I will put you in a cleft of the rock and shield you with My hand *[kapi]* until I have passed by. Then I will take My hand away and you will see My back; but My face must not be seen."

Here *kapi* is translated "My hand." For the Targumim, however, such a translation would have been problematic, because it suggested that God is embodied and anthropomorphic. Accordingly, the Targumim wanted to emphasize that *kapi* is used metaphorically to mean "my instrument." They differ, however, in their views about the instrument used. Thus *Tg. Onk.* writes, "I will shield you with My *Memra*," understanding *Memra* (Aram. for "word" or "utterance") to be a mediating power through which God communicates with human beings. In other Targum traditions *(Tg. Neof.; Tg. Ps.-J.; Frg. Tg.) kapi* is translated as "the group of angels who stand and minister before Me."

Commentary

Some ancient interpretations are more forthright about what they are doing than these reworkings and translations, such as the *pesharim* found at Qumran, e.g., *Pesher Habakkuk* [1QpHab]; *Pesher Psalms* [4Q171]; *Pesher Nahum* [4Q169]; *Pesher Hosea* [4Q166 and 4Q167]; *Pesher Isaiah* [4Q161–165]. These compositions clearly distinguish between the biblical texts and their interpretations. In this respect, they differ from *Genesis Apocryphon, Jub., 1 Enoch, 4 Ezra,* and many other Second Temple interpretive texts, and they anticipate later rabbinic midrash. To describe themselves, they use the word *(p-sh-r),* which has a biblical precedent in Dan., where this verb is used (Dan. 2.5ff.) to refer to the authorized interpretation of dreams. Consider, for example, this passage from *Pesher Habakkuk* (1QpHab VII, 1–8):

> And God told Habakkuk to write what was going to happen to the last generation, but he did not let him know the consummation of the era. *Blank* And as for what he says: "So that /may run/ the one who reads it." (Hab. 2.2) Its interpretation concerns the Teacher of Righteousness, to whom God has made known all the mysteries of the words of His servants, the prophets. (Hab. 2.3) For the vision has an appointed time, it will have an end and not fail. *Blank* Its interpretation: the final age will be extended and go beyond all that the prophets say, because the mysteries of God are wonderful.

Note that the authority of divine revelation is claimed, not only for the prophetic text, but also for its interpretation, which has been given to the Teacher of Righteousness, a figure of great importance to the Qumran community. In Second Temple biblical interpretation, even when interpretation and text were distinguished, interpretations were not presented as personal opinions, or as plausible solutions to exegetical problems. Instead they were presented as having an authority based on divine revelation, thus as originating in the very same source as the text itself. Thus it might be most appropriate to refer to Second Temple writings not as extrabiblical, but rather as authoritative literature. To be sure, many of the interpretive texts which are contemporaneous with some of the exilic texts in the Bible, although not ultimately included in the Jewish canon, were considered to be inspired and to have assumed scriptural stature in various late Second Temple Jewish communities. However, this cannot be stated as a general characterization of all of the materials from Qumran or from Gk-speaking Jewish communities of the late Second Temple period.

Inspired Interpretive Texts by Named Individuals

Philo of Alexandria (ca. 20 BCE–50 CE) left behind a rich legacy of writings including theological essays, allegorical interpretations, explications of biblical laws, and questions and answers on Gen. and Exod. Composed in Gk within the Hellenized community of Alexandria, which never recovered from its decimation in the 2nd c. CE, his works, which interpret the Septuagint (LXX, Gk) rather than Heb texts, were apparently lost to later Jewish exegetes and philosophers. Indeed, he was appropriated so completely by some Christians that he was retrospectively regarded as a Christian. Only centuries later, during the Reformation, was it recalled that Philo Christianus had in fact been Philo Judaeus. This recognition generated renewed interest by Jewish scholars and repudiation by some Christian theologians. To this day, some scholars interpret Philo as a proto-Christian, while others view him as a proto-rabbinic Jew.

Philo's challenge was different from the challenge confronting the authors of *Jub.* or the *Genesis Apocryphon.* They had to authorize, to an exclusively Jewish audience, what they took to be authentic Judaism, in the face of rival practices and interpretations. Philo, in contrast, had to authorize Judaism itself to both Jews and non-Jews, within the relatively new context of the Hellenistic competition of cultures, a competition that was at the same time political, especially in light of the even newer Roman empire's quest to authorize itself through the appropriation of the Greek philosophical and literary heritage.

The place of Judaism within this new Roman world was far from clear. On the one hand, the significance of the Greek heritage was now as universal as the empire itself sought to be. Near Eastern cultures, which enjoyed the mystique of antiquity and exoticism, could legitimize themselves by identifying their gods with Greek gods and their teachings with Greek teachings. On the other hand, religious syncretism did not cohere easily with Jewish monotheism, and the Mosaic law, which seemed primarily to address Jews alone, was in danger of appearing parochial, thus rendering it potentially threatening to Rome and potentially insignificant to Hellenized Jews.

Thus, in Philo's world, the authority of Mosaic law itself was a live issue. One of his primary objectives was to show through interpretation that biblical texts have universal significance. Philo claimed (*Mos.* 2:12):

> That Moses himself was the best of all lawgivers in all countries, better in fact than any that have ever arisen among either the Greeks or the barbarians, and that his laws are most excellent and truly come from God....

To be sure, Mosaic law is particular in the sense that it is binding in all its details only for the particular people of Israel. This law does, however, have universal significance in virtue of its special relation to natural law (*Mos.* 2:14):

> But Moses is alone in this, that his laws, firm unshaken, immovable, stamped, as it were, with the seals of nature herself, remain secure from the day when they were first enacted to now, and we may hope that they will remain for all future ages as though immortal, so long as the sun and moon and the whole heaven and universe exist.

Philo used a variety of methods to demonstrate this point. For example, he read the creation story in Gen. as a treatise on philosophical cosmology, akin to Plato's *Timaeus,* and he interpreted many laws and rituals as having an allegorical level of meaning, at which they signify philosophical doctrines of importance to Gentiles as well as Jews. Philo's immediate influence seems to have been greatest upon Christian interpreters, such as Origen and Clement of Alexandria. But his methods and ideas, transmitted through various intermediaries, resurfaced among medieval Jewish philosophers, for whose biblical interpretation his works serve as a paradigm, although it is likely they did not directly know his writings.

As in *Jub.,* Philo perceived the need to explain why the Torah begins not with the revelation of the law at Sinai, but with the stories of creation and the ancestors (*Abr.* 5):

> First he [Moses] wished to show that the enacted ordinances are not inconsistent with nature; and secondly that those who wish to live in accordance with the laws as they stand have no difficult task, seeing that the first generations before any at all of the particular statutes was set in writing followed the unwritten law with perfect ease, so that one might properly say that the enacted laws are nothing else than memorials of the life of the ancients, preserving to a later generation their actual words and deeds.

The point of the narratives was not to convey laws written on heavenly tablets, as it was for *Jub.* Instead, their point was to convey the unwritten law of nature, which was embodied in the exemplary lives of the ancestors. Indeed, the enacted laws peculiar to Israel had to be understood solely as memorials of the lives of these sages. This universalistic interpretation was intended to emphasize, not to undermine, the need for Jews to preserve their particular traditions and observances. But it implied that Jews could only observe the law properly if they understood it not only legally, but also philosophically.

In this spirit, Philo found in biblical narratives a meaning that was both cosmological and psychological. For example, he read the conflict between Cain and Abel as a conflict between the archetype of evil and the archetype of holiness, hence as an allegorical representation of moral conflict within a single human soul. Every detail related about the brothers—their names, their chosen professions, their conceptions of God and their actions—conveyed a moral lesson about the impression of vice or virtue. Thus Cain's name, which Philo derives from the Heb verb meaning "to possess," shows that the root of all evil is the belief that humans are possessors of what properly belongs to God. In contrast, Abel's "name means 'one who refers (all things) to God' " (*Sacr.* 2). Similarly, Cain chose to till the soil, a profession that involved him with earthly and inanimate objects, not with preparation for a future life. In contrast (*QG* 1:59): "Abel's choice of work as a shepherd is understood as preparatory to rulership and kingship." It is hardly surprising, then, that God preferred Abel's sacrifice. Cain's reaction—the jealous fratricide—only exacerbated his problem by removing the possibility of coming under Abel's virtuous influence (*Det.* 68):

> It would have been to the advantage of Cain, the lover of self, to have guarded Abel; for had he carefully preserved him, he would have been able to lay claim only to a mixed "half and half" life indeed, but would not have drained the cup of sheer unmitigated wickedness.

Thus vice is self-destructive. To be sure, Abel died while Cain survived (*Post.* 39):

> But in my judgment and in that of my friends, preferable to life with impious men would be death with pious men; for awaiting those who die in this way there will be undying life, but awaiting those who live in that way there will be eternal death.

But hope never perishes. When God asks Cain, "Where is your brother?" this shows, according to Philo, that repentance is always possible and that we are consequently responsible for our actions (*QG* 1:68):

> Why does he who knows all ask the fratricide, "Where is Abel, your brother?" He wishes that man himself of his own will shall confess, in order that he may not pretend that all things seem to come about through necessity. For he who killed through necessity would confess that he acted unwillingly; for that which is not in our power is not to be blamed. But he who sins of his own free will denies it, for sinners are obliged to repent. Accordingly he (Moses) inserts in all parts of his legislation that the Deity is not the cause of evil.

Philo's philosophical approach to biblical narratives differed significantly from the approach of *Jub.* and kindred works. But Philo also repeatedly connected these narratives to laws mentioned later in the Torah. For example, he connected the story of Cain and Abel to the law that requires that first fruits be brought as an offering. The point was not to show, as *Jub.* intended, that the narratives were implicitly legal texts, but that Mosaic law provided solutions for the moral problems confronting all humans. The law is designed to implant healthy theological convictions, to efface evil impressions and to reinforce good ones. Thus, for example, the tiller of soil is commanded to bring the first fruits as an offering to God, and to profess God's dominion over a land to which the farmer is ultimately foreign. Philo's analysis of Cain brings out the wisdom of this law, which is shown to manifest a deep understanding of the human soul.

Thus Philo's interpretations are not wholly unlike the reworkings of biblical traditions found in *Jub.* and similar works. But Philo does not present his interpretations as versions of the texts they interpret. Indeed, he could not "rewrite the Bible," since he accepted the story told by the *Let. Aris.* to authorize the LXX (see "Jewish Translations of the Bible," pp. 2091–2106). According to the *Let. Aris.,* Ptolemy Philadelphus had commissioned a Gk translation of the Bible, which was then produced by seventy Jewish elders who worked in isolation on the island of Pharos, but miraculously produced a single text. Thus, in his relationship to the biblical texts, Philo was more like interpreters after canonization than like his Second Temple contemporaries in the land of Israel.

Philo occasionally presented his interpretations as results of his own insight, but he did this only on occasion, and more frequently appealed to other sources of authority. He invoked "the traditions of the fathers" and claimed divine inspiration. He even insisted, when he interpreted the creation story in Gen. as a philosophical cosmology, that "it is Moses who lays this down, not I" (*Opif.* 24–25). On the one hand, Philo's self-conscious use of the first-person pronoun exhibits his sense of his own independent activity as an interpreter. On the other hand, he continues to efface himself.

Another important source for pre-rabbinic Jewish interpretations is the voluminous writings of Flavius Josephus, or Joseph bar Matthias (37–100 CE). From the age of 30, Josephus spent his life in Rome during the reigns of Vespasian, Titus, and Domitian. He devoted his life to retelling the history of the Jewish people from the creation of the world (i.e., retelling the history of the Jews beginning with the beginning of Gen.) until the destruction of the Second Temple and the Roman conquest, focusing on the Jewish war with Rome, in which he had participated. At a time when the Jews were under severe attack and criticism, he sought to explain and glorify those who lived in accordance with the law of Moses.

Josephus himself was a member of the priestly aristocracy and was well educated in the traditions of Jewish interpretation. Scholars have noted his extensive supplementation and interpretation of biblical passages. Yet he claimed only to present Scripture itself (*Ant.* 1.17):

> The precise details of our Scripture records will, then, be set forth, each in its place, as my narrative proceeds, that being the procedure that I have promised to follow throughout this work, neither adding nor omitting anything.

This self-effacing claim is, perhaps, best understood in light of Josephus's understanding of what it means to "read" Scripture, i.e., interpret the authoritative texts in the context of the wealth of authoritative interpretation. It is clear that, by the time of Josephus, there was already an extant body of interpretive material that shaped the way Jews read and transmitted the books of Tanakh. When Josephus promised neither to add nor to omit, he did not mean that he would convey only the letter of these books, without also conveying the expansions and interpretations which he considered authoritative.

For example, while in Gen. ch 18 we are told only of Sodom's wickedness, Josephus provides his readers with an extensive gloss on the nature of that wickedness (*Ant.* 1.194–95):

> Now, about this time the Sodomites, overweeningly proud of their numbers and the extent of their wealth, showed themselves insolent to men and impious to the Divinity, insomuch that they no more remembered the benefits that they had received from Him, hated foreigners and avoided any contact with others. Indignant at this conduct, God accordingly resolved to chastise them for their arrogance, and not only to uproot their city, but to blast their land so completely that it should yield neither plant nor fruit whatsoever from that time forward.

Other Second Temple texts—e.g., Wisd. 19.14 and Sir. 16.8—reflect the tradition that arrogance was the principal sin of the Sodomites. In addition, Josephus often explains and justifies actions that may have seemed morally questionable. So, for example, Josephus explained or even justified Joseph's concealment of his own identity (*Ant.* 2.99):

> It was in order to discover news of his father and what had become of him after his own departure that he so acted; he moreover desired to learn the fate of his brother Benjamin, for he feared that by such a ruse as they had practiced on himself, they might have rid the family of him also.

This expansion resembles other Second Temple attempts to explain the characters and motivations of biblical personalities. But, living in Rome immediately after the Roman conquest, Josephus had an additional reason to cast Jewish tradition in a light that was morally favorable.

Like Philo, Josephus sometimes claimed divine authority for his writings. Thus he claimed to be a divine messenger who had to present the inspired word of God (*J.W.* 3.392–408; *Ant.* 10.78–79). Indeed, as an eyewitness to the destruction of the Second Temple, he implicitly and repeatedly identified himself with the prophet Jeremiah, who both prophesied and witnessed the destruction of the First Temple. Like Josephus, Jeremiah was also a priest—hence one of those entrusted with the faithful preservation of the records of the history of the Jewish people, which, as Josephus adds, "will continue to be preserved with scrupulous accuracy" (*Ag. Ap.* 1.29). Clearly, Josephus understood himself to be exercising this priestly and prophetic office, carrying on the work of Scripture transmission through his own inspired interpretations.

Conclusion

While nonrabbinic interpretive texts of the Second Temple period varied significantly in form, they shared two basic assumptions: a commitment to render the Scriptures relevant to the communities they addressed, and a belief in the inspired status of their own interpretations.

[HINDY NAJMAN]

The Bible in the Dead Sea Scrolls

Until the discovery in the Judean Desert, near the Dead Sea, of more than 200 scrolls containing various parts of the Bible, historical and textual analysis of the biblical text relied on ancient translations and medieval mss. The Judean Desert discoveries brought to light Heb mss older by 1,000 years than the ones previously known, and document a period of pluriformity in the biblical text. Although no original copy of any biblical text has survived, these mss not only greatly enhance our knowledge of textual features in general but also have a significant impact on central issues in biblical scholarship.

Before proceeding to a discussion of their effect on biblical scholarship, a brief aside to explain the conventional scholarly signs or sigla commonly used for Qumran and Judean Desert scrolls is in order. The elements included comprise the number of the cave (for Qumran, 1–11); identification of the site (Q = Qumran, Mas = Masada, Ḥev = Naḥal Ḥever); an abbreviated name of the biblical book (e.g., Gen = Genesis); number of the copy (in superscript; the first copy is ^{a}, the second is ^{b}, etc.). Other details sometimes indicated include the material on which the scroll is written (pap = papyrus), the language (gr = Greek; ar = Aram.), the script (paleo = Paleo-Heb [the ancient Heb script]), or the literary genre (p = *pesher*). For example, 11QPs is a scroll from Qumran Cave 11 and contains material from the book of Psalms. A provisional list of documents from the Judean Desert, containing text numbers, sigla, and names is found in the *Encyclopedia of the Dead Sea Scrolls* (Oxford, 2000). For a categorized list of the biblical texts and an index list of all passages preserved in biblical mss from the Judaean Desert, see *The Texts from the Judaean Desert: Indices* (DJD 39; Oxford 2002).

Finds

The story of the discovery of the Dead Sea Scrolls in the mid-20th c. needs no retelling.

What is significant are the large numbers of biblical and especially Torah books preserved in the Judean Desert. The bulk of these mainly fragmentarily-preserved biblical scrolls come from caves located near Qumran, a site occupied from ca. 150 BCE to 68 CE. Smaller numbers of scrolls were found elsewhere in the Judean Desert: at Masada, Naḥal Ḥever, and Wadi Murabbaʿat. Of a total of 900 separate scrolls found at Qumran, 200 are biblical. At Masada, seven of the fifteen literary texts found, that is, nearly half, are biblical. Within the biblical corpus itself, proportionally more copies of Torah books were found: at Qumran they comprised 43.5 percent of the biblical corpus, and at other sites in the Judean Desert a full 64 percent of the biblical scrolls. Paleographical analysis shows that the script of the Qumran scrolls dates from 250 BCE (the earliest scroll is 4QExod[f]) to the mid-1st c. CE, with most of the mss dating from the 1st c. BCE to the 1st c. CE. In addition, two types of Heb scripts were found at Qumran: Thirteen texts were written in paleo-Heb ("archaic" Heb, used mainly in the First Temple period and on Second Temple coins), but the overwhelming majority of the texts were written in square script (also called Assyrian or Jewish, borrowed during the Babylonian exile, and used from the Second Temple period on). The non-Qumran Judean Desert scrolls were written exclusively in square script and date to the 1st and 2nd centuries CE.

The table on p. 1852 summarizes the data for the numbers of biblical scrolls found in the Judean Desert. A brief glance at the table not only reveals the prominence of Torah books in general, but also the greater popularity of specific biblical books, as evidenced, for example, by the relatively large number of copies of Deut., Ps., and Isa. These latter works are also the ones most often cited in sectarian compositions at Qumran as well as in the New Testament and later rabbinic literature.

A small number of the scrolls found at Qumran contained more than a single book; thus two scrolls from Cave 4 contained Gen. and Exod., one combined Exod. and Lev., and another Lev. and Num. This perhaps suggests the writing of the books of the Torah on one scroll, but there is too little evidence to prove it. On the other hand, essential to any consideration of the Judean Desert finds is the rarity of a fully preserved text of any biblical work; fragmentary preservation is the rule. Most of the 200 biblical scrolls from the eleven Qumran caves contain no more than one-tenth of a biblical book; the complete Isaiah scroll (1QIsa[a]) is the exception.

The table also indicates that, excluding Esth. (but see discussion below), all the books of what was to become the Hebrew canon are represented in the Judean Desert corpus. Direct evidence for Neh. is also missing; however, as Ezra-Neh. was perceived as a single book in antiquity, scholars posit its presence at Qumran indirectly, from the Ezra scroll from Qumran Cave 4.

Text Type Classification

Although higher concentrations of biblical texts were found in Qumran Caves 4 and 11, almost without exception the finds in the caves are not homogeneous; thus no one cave contained the "biblical library shelf" at Qumran. Nor does it necessarily follow that a text found at Qumran was written or copied there; it is now widely held that many of the texts found at Qumran were imported from elsewhere. Thus, these finds have important implications for our general understanding of the biblical text and the canon in the late Second Temple period.

Even prior to the discovery of the Dead Sea Scrolls, scholars were aware of the existence of more than one biblical text type. Scholarly division of biblical texts according to three main types—the Masoretic Text (MT) as reflected in medieval mss; the Septuagint (LXX), the ancient Gk translation of the Bible; and the Samaritan Pentateuch (SP), that is, the version preserved by the Samaritan community—received confirmation from Qumran finds. Ancient Heb exemplars of

BIBLICAL BOOKS FROM JUDEAN DESERT FINDS

Biblical Book (some scrolls contain two books)	Qumran	Scripts at Qumran		Other Judean Desert Sites
		"Square"	Paleo-Hebrew	
Genesis	19	16	3	4
Exodus	15	13	2	1
Leviticus	12	8	4	2
Numbers	5	4	1	4
Deuteronomy	30	28	2	3
Joshua	2	2		1
Judges	3	3		1
1–2 Samuel	4	4		
1–2 Kings	3	3		
Isaiah	21	21		1
Jeremiah	6	6		
Ezekiel	6	6		1
Minor Prophets	8	8		1
Psalms	36	36		3
Proverbs	2	2		
Job	4	3	1	
Song of Songs	4	4		
Ruth	4	4		
Lamentations	4	4		
Ecclesiastes	2	2		
Esther	0			0
Daniel	8	8		
Ezra-Nehemiah	1	1		
Chronicles	1	1		
Total	200	187	13	22

each of these three later text types were found at Qumran. As they predate the above-mentioned exemplars, in speaking of these text types at Qumran, they are more aptly labeled proto-Masoretic, proto-Septuagintal, and pre-Samaritan (or harmonistic; see below). The Qumran biblical texts shed light on the formation and the relationship between these types. They do not, however, represent the full variety of texts discovered at Qumran. A quarter of all of the biblical texts discovered there cannot be assigned to a type and are best referred to as independent or nonaligned texts, raising questions about the earlier scholarly tripartite division. Some Qumran texts display distinctive orthography (spelling), morphology (grammatical word formation), and scribal practices, and it has been suggested that they represent particular scribal habits or even a scribal school of the Qumran community itself.

Proto-Masoretic Scrolls

The largest group of biblical scrolls at Qumran, about 40 percent, resembles the consonantal text in medieval Masoretic mss, as documented in some of the earliest medieval codices; for example, in Codex Leningrad (dated 1009) and the 10th-c. Aleppo Codex. (Both of these codices are authoritative copies of the Bible with vocalization and cantillation traditions; all Qumran texts lack these signs, which developed in the late first millennium CE.) Some scholars prefer the label "proto-rabbinic" for this category. The high proportion of texts belonging to this type at Qumran, as opposed to the lesser representation of other text types there, evidently reflects their dominant, though not exclusive, status. The proportionate predominance of this text type perhaps reflects a crucial stage in the process that resulted in its emergence as the authoritative text (see below). Among the Qumran texts the ones that bear the most remarkable affinity to medieval ones are 4QGen[b] and 1QIsa[b]. Other closely related texts are 4QJer[a] and 4QJer[c].

Proto-Septuagintal Texts

A significant legacy of the discovery of the Dead Sea Scrolls is related to their attestation to the reliability of ancient translations. It is no longer possible to argue that differences from the MT preserved in the ancient translations all reflect intentional changes introduced by the translator rather than a different underlying text *(Vorlage);* it is clear that multiple text types circulated at the same time. One small group of texts found at Qumran, four in number, includes scrolls closely resembling the presumed Heb parent *(Vorlage)* of the LXX translation. Of the texts found at Qumran, 4QJer[b] and 4QJer[d] are closest to LXX, resembling both its shorter text and its v. arrangement. Other texts exhibiting close affinities to LXX are 4QDeut[q] and 4QSam[a]. Readings from the ancient translations hitherto regarded as questionable have now been shown to preserve authentic Heb ones.

Harmonistic Editing

A few texts are often called pre-Samaritan, since they share certain features of the Samaritan text, but lack the distinctive ideology of the Samaritans (references to Mt. Gerizim, e.g.). This small group of five texts from Qumran—4QpaleoExod[m], 4QpaleoExod-Lev[f], 4QNum[b], 4QDeut[n], and 4Q364 (4QRP[b]; see below)—is better characterized by a different feature: the presence of harmonizing alterations, that is, changes or additions that create concord between two separate but parallel Torah texts. The two texts undergoing harmonization can be contextually close, such as the addition to Exod. 7.8 based on 7.15–18, or remote, such as the two versions of the Decalogue (Exod. ch 20 and Deut. ch 5). Alterations can be of different kinds: additions of a "source" for a quotation, mostly insertions from Deut. to the parallel sections in the earlier books of the Torah, or provision of a missing command or its fulfillment. Harmonistic editing is also found in some nonbiblical texts from Qumran, including quotations in *Reworked Pentateuch* (4QRP), excerpts cited for liturgical purposes, phylacteries, and mezuzot.

As compared to some of the later Qumran biblical scrolls, the Samaritan Pentateuch (SP) itself reflects a limited degree of harmonization, a fact that has bearing on the question of its dating. SP includes, in addition to harmonizing alterations, particularistic changes introduced by the Samaritans—related mainly to the sanctity of Mt. Gerizim—before the destruction of the Samaritan temple on Mt. Gerizim in 111 BCE. On this basis, it appears that the specifically sectarian changes and additions now found in the SP were introduced during the 2nd c. BCE to pre-Hasmonean Jewish harmonizing texts of the Torah. Although biblical texts continued to undergo harmonistic editing at Qumran, the Samaritans did not continue to update their texts with the more extensive changes attested in Qumran texts from the final two centuries of the Second Temple period.

Nonaligned Texts

The remaining texts, about 25 percent of the biblical corpus, may combine readings belonging to one or more traditional categories alongside independent variants; they are not easily assigned to a particular text type and are therefore classified as independent or nonaligned. To this group also belong the so-called vulgar (in the sense of popular) texts, exemplified by 1QIsa[a], which exhibit a freer approach to the text. The scribal changes introduced into vocabulary and grammar reflect, on the whole, an attempt either to simplify the difficult biblical text, or to remove grammatical and contextual difficulties.

In addition, also related to this group are some texts of doubtful biblical nature, among them the so-called *Reworked Pentateuch*. This group is composed of six Heb mss, in which a running biblical text is reworked by scribal intervention, characterized by omissions of, additions to, and rearrangements of biblical passages, and, in some cases, the introduction of nonbiblical passages as well. We must also bear in mind that no external features or headings distinguish between biblical and nonbiblical texts at Qumran. Scholars debate these texts' classification: Some assign them to the biblical corpus, others define them as *Reworked Pentateuch,* whereas still others view them as nonbiblical. These texts stand on the boundary between text and interpretation.

Translations

Also of notable importance as witnesses to the development of the biblical text during the late Second Temple period are the Gk and Aram. translations of the Bible. Among the Qumran scrolls Gk translations were found: two scrolls of Lev. and one scroll each of Exod., Num., and Deut. These texts are reliable witnesses to an early stage of the transmission of LXX, preceding the one in which revisions bringing LXX into line with MT are attested. In addition, a Gk copy of the Minor Prophets was found in Naḥal Ḥever (8Ḥev XII gr); it belongs however to the latter type, being the earliest extant revision bringing LXX into line with MT (mid-1st c. BCE). Aram. Targumim, of lesser importance than LXX as witnesses to an early stage of the Heb biblical text, were also found at Qumran. The oldest extant Targum texts (to Lev., 4QtgLev; and Job, 4QtgJob and 11QtgJob) are extremely literal in contrast to the exegetical expansions characteristic of later Targumim.

Quotation and Use of Scriptures

Other biblically related texts found at Qumran, which will not be discussed at length here, are excerpted and abbreviated texts probably used for liturgical purposes, such as phylacteries (tefillin) and mezuzot. (There is a significant amount of variation in the texts found in these, and many do not agree with the later rabbinic prescriptions concerning their content.) Texts such as 4QExod[d] which contains Exod. 13.15–16 and 15.1, and 4QDeut[n] where Deut. ch 8 precedes Deut. chs 5–6, also belong to this category. Also found in Qumran texts, both sectarian and nonsectarian, are free quotations of and allusions to biblical texts. Another genre found at Qumran, *pesher,* also incorporates biblical quotations. The works in question take selected biblical texts and apply them to the contemporary sectarian setting. From the formal viewpoint they resemble later medieval commentaries; the basic structure includes citation of a biblical text (the lemma), an introductory formula containing the word *pesher* (actualized interpretation), and the interpretation, which is an application of the text to a contemporary reality typically unrelated to its original context. Thus the lemmata of the *pesharim* also serve as witnesses to the biblical text of the mainly prophetic books they interpret. In some cases, more than one text to the same v. seems to be interpreted. In other cases, the biblical lemma may have been changed to fit the *pesher* interpretation. In addition to these obvious uses of biblical texts, there are, scattered throughout the sectarian writings of the Qumran community, many allusions to and citations of biblical vv, or parts of vv. The Qumran community was "Bible-centric"; its literature was saturated with biblical phrases.

Literary Development and Textual Transmission

Higher Criticism

Of the contributions made by the discovery of the Qumran scrolls, one of the most telling belongs to the realm of higher criticism (see "Modern Study of the Bible," pp. 2166–77). The scrolls brought to light unambiguous witnesses to textual differences belonging to earlier stages of the literary growth of various biblical books; before their discovery, these differences were only attested indirectly, especially in the ancient translations or versions. The discovery of the Qumran scrolls has had a particularly significant impact on our understanding of the text of Judg., Sam., Jer., Esth., and Dan. The examples below demonstrate how Qumran texts bear witness to what is believed to represent an earlier editorial stage of a biblical work. Qumran texts also support hitherto unattested variants or different readings found in LXX. Additionally, some texts found at Qumran are believed to represent possible sources for biblical books.

Additions Not Found in MT

As witnessed by MT (and Vg, Syriac, and the Tg.), Nahash, king of Ammon, agreed to make a treaty with the people of Jabesh-gilead on condition that he gouge out their right eyes (1 Sam. 11.1–2). In the context of these textual witnesses this seems an unusually brutal act. An additional passage preserved in 4QSam[a], which unfolds the story of how Nahash oppressed the tribes of Gad and Reuben, inflicting terror by gouging out their right eyes, and how 7,000 men escaped mutilation by fleeing to Jabesh-gilead, provides a more natural link between the election of Saul as king in Mizpah (1 Sam. 10.27a) and his Ammonite campaign (10.27b). Moreover, the reading found in 4QSam[a], "it was about a month's time" *(k-m-ḥ-d-sh),* provides a more logical connection between the additional passage and the one following, than MT's "he pretended not to mind" (*k-m-ḥ-r-sh,* 11.1). (In Heb script, *d* and *r* are almost identical and easily confused.)

Although some scholars explain the additional passage in 4QSam[a] as a secondary midrashic addition, it is more likely that 4QSam[a] has preserved the original reading and that MT's reading is based on scribal error, that is, an accidental omission during an early stage of the book's literary development or transmission. In general, the text of Sam. as reflected by MT is problematic, and LXX and the fragments discovered at Qumran reflect a better-preserved text.

Witness to an Earlier Editorial Stage

Judg. 6.7–10 is missing from a text found at Qumran, 4QJudg[a]. Evidently not the result of scribal error, this omission can be seen as reflecting an earlier stage in the editing of the book of Judg. The section found in MT, in which a prophet tells the Israelites that God will save them even though they have sinned in the past, has clear parallels to vv. 11–24, in which the angel of the LORD appears to Gideon; it is also very similar to other texts found in Deut. and related literature. It appears, then, that Judg. 6.7–10 was a later addition by the so-called Deuteronomistic Historian, the editor of Deut., Josh., Judg., 1–2 Sam., and 1–2 Kings, who focused on the centralization of the cult in Jerusalem.

Attestation to LXX

The organizational complexity of Jer. and the relationship between MT and other ancient versions, especially LXX, enhances the importance of the Qumran finds. Two of the six fragmentary mss of Jer. found there (4QJer[b] and 4QJer[d]) are close in nature to the so-called original LXX version of Jer. (to be distinguished from later revisions correcting the translation to reflect MT and from Syriac, Vg, and the Targumim). LXX to Jer. differs from MT in two ways: first, in ch and v. order; second, in the length of the text, where the LXX is one-eighth shorter than MT, missing words, phrases, or even entire sections. Evidently, the LXX was translated from a Heb text close in nature to these two mss, which reflects a first, short edition of the book of Jer. that differs from the longer, differently ordered text documented in MT and other related versions. The Qumran texts support the view that LXX reflects an authentic Second Temple period variant tradition of the biblical text.

Possible Sources for Biblical Books

As opposed to the above examples, the following ones do not reflect stages in the editing of a biblical work; rather they relate to possible sources for biblical books.

Esther. As mentioned earlier, all the books of the Hebrew canon were represented among the Qumran scrolls, with the exception of Esth. The different explanations for its absence range from the vagaries of chance, to suggestions that the Qumran community did not observe the holiday of Purim and/or the book had not yet achieved "canonical" status. The exact nature of a text from Cave 4 labeled Proto-Esther (4Q550–550e) is also a matter of debate. Some identify it as an Aram. prototype or source underlying the various Heb, Gk, Latin, and even Armenian versions of Esth., while others find only a general resemblance between the book of Esth. and this composition, and still others argue that this text has very little in common with the Heb story of Esther, and is simply a hitherto unknown Aram. text. Even if this Qumran text has no direct relationship to Esth., it is another example of a story with a Persian court setting.

Daniel. Cave 4 at Qumran contained some Heb and Aram. texts exhibiting varying degrees of connection to Dan. The most clear-cut link is that between Dan. and the *Prayer of Nabonidus* (4QPrNab ar). Long before the latter text's publication, the resemblance between the story of Nabonidus's illness while in exile at Teima and the legend of Nebuchadnezzar's madness in Dan. ch 4 was noted. The author of Dan. ch 4 adapted this material to his worldview, most significantly by changing the name of the king to that of the better-known one—Nebuchadnezzar—and by identifying the anonymous Jew who assisted the king with Daniel.

Another fragmentary text found at Qumran, labeled Historical Text A (4Q248), resembles Dan. ch 11. This text mentions, in an extremely condensed manner, a number of events pertaining to Antiochus IV Epiphanes, also referred to in Dan. These chronologically arranged events start with Antiochus IV's first invasion of Egypt (170–169 BCE) and end with his second inroad into Egypt in 168. Following the last event mentioned in the Qumran text, which is the second invasion of Egypt, words parallel to Dan. 12.7 appear: "and when the shattering of the power of the ho[ly] people [... comes to an end, then shall all] these things [be fulfilled]." The absence of references to Antiochus's religious persecutions, as compared with ample references of this nature in Dan. (7.25; 11.30–33; 12.1), makes it clear that 4Q248's composition preceded 167 BCE. If so, this work was composed before the completion of the final edition of Dan., commonly dated to ca. 165 BCE, and may have been part of an apocalyptic work that served as a source for this book.

Finally, another possible source for Dan. is found in the throne-theophany of the *Book of Giants* (4Q530, col. ii). Comparison of this text to Dan. 7.9–10 shows that the book of Dan. preserved a more expanded form of the vision.

Text Criticism

Another important aspect of the contribution of biblical Dead Sea Scrolls to biblical studies belongs to text criticism (sometimes called "lower criticism"). As opposed to the literary-historical bent of higher criticism, this field relates to the technical aspect of establishing the best readings of the wording of the text. The examples demonstrate how the scrolls enhance our understanding of the development of variants created in the course of textual transmission. On occasion the Qumran texts preserve superior readings; in other instances, they represent vulgarization of the text.

Haplography

1QIsaª, which is the oldest ms of Isa. that has been preserved, dated ca. 125 BCE, is of a vulgar or popular text type (see above). Its fifteen surviving fragments contain about forty, mostly minor, variants from MT, some of which shed light on the development of variants in the biblical text.

1QIsaª usually has the secondary variant, that is, scribal changes and "corrections" made to proto-MT not based on ancient witnesses. Two instances of haplography (an erroneous omission of one or two identical or similar adjacent letters or words) include the omission by the original copyist of 1QIsaª of part of Isa. 40.7–8 because of the double repetition of "grass withers, flowers fade," or Isa. 26.3–4, where 1QIsaª has reduced the double occurrence of "trust" to a single one. In both these cases MT has the superior reading.

Nevertheless, 1QIsaª also provides an example where MT's reading reflects haplography. MT (Peshitta and Vg) reads Isa. 40.12 as: "Who measured *the waters (mayim)* with the hollow of his hand, and gauged the sky with a span?" This question seems out of place in the context of a rhetorical list with negative answers. 1QIsaª has a slightly different but superior reading: "Who measured *the waters of the sea (mei yam)* with the hollow of his hand...." A similar reading is also attested in a paraphrase found in an apotropaic prayer, 4Q511, which reads: "Can *the waters of the sea (mei rabah)* be gauged in the hollow of a man's hand?"

Another original reading preserved in the Dead Sea Scrolls comes from 4QSamª. MT to 1 Sam. 1.24 has the double reading *ve ha-naʿar naʿar:* "And though the boy was still very young" whereas 4QSamª has an expanded reading: "... and *the boy (ve ha-naʿar)* [with] them. And they went before the LORD, and his father slaughtered the sacrifi[ce as] it happened [every year to the LORD. And she brought *the boy (ha-naʿar)*]...." MT reflects a case of parablepsis (or homoioarcton), that is, the identical beginning ("the boy") caused the erroneous omission of a section.

Matres Lectionis

In its most ancient form the Heb alphabet contained only consonants. It is well known that *matres lectionis,* literally "mothers of reading," that is consonants used to indicate vowel length and quality, were secondarily introduced into the text, sometimes relatively late in its development. Variants in the use of *matres lectionis* usually do not affect the biblical text, but in some cases they provide evidence for a different scribal understanding. Such is the case in 1 Sam. 1.24, where MT reads three bulls *(parim sheloshah),* while 4QSamª reads: three-year-old bull *(be par meshulash).* Both MT and 4QSamª presumably derive from the same common consonantal source: *b-p-r-m-sh-l-sh,* with a difference of opinion about where to divide the words. The Qumran scroll's variant seems more reasonable contextually, as the following v. refers only to an offering of one bull. When *matres lectionis* were later introduced, 4QSamª (and LXX and the Peshitta) were in a better position to indicate the proper reading, while MT (Tg. and Vg), lacking *matres lectionis,* have a corrupt reading.

Original Reading Preserved in a Qumran Text

Testimonia (4QTest) is one of the few almost completely preserved texts found at Qumran. Written on one sheet of skin (parchment), this text is a collection of quotations directly linked to each other without quotation formulas or interpretations.

A superior reading is documented in the quotation of Deut. 33.9 in *Testimonia.* Where MT has the singular "him" following a reference to mother and father, a reconstructed reading of 4QTest restores the original parallel structure: "Who said of his father, 'I consider you not' and to his mother 'I ignore you.' His brother he disregarded, ignored his own children."

Canon at Qumran

The discoveries at Qumran, while shedding light on the pluriformity of biblical texts in the Second Temple period, do not provide the means to definitively establish which books the sect held sacred. Nor do the finds of large numbers of copies of particular biblical alongside other apocryphal (*Jub., Enoch,* etc.) or sectarian works necessarily indicate their sanctification in the eyes of the Qumran sect. Moreover, as not all of the texts found at Qumran were copied there and it is impossible to establish who wrote or copied them, we cannot determine their canonical status.

Nonetheless, the biblical scrolls found at Qumran do bear on the question of the growth of the Hebrew canon, which was, according to many scholars, fixed only at a later period. The presence at Qumran of all of the books found in the Hebrew canon (with the exception of Esth.) may support the inference that these books already had canonical status. What was not yet agreed upon was the *exact* boundaries of the canon as well as the final textual form of the individual works. Thus it is that we find proto-Septuagintal and harmonistic texts alongside the prevailing proto-Masoretic type. In the course of less than a century after the scrolls were hidden, however, the proto-MT type emerged as the accepted one.

On the other hand, using the multiformity of the biblical texts found at Qumran as evidence, some scholars argue that the canon was not yet fixed and even postulate a broader canon. Some claim that the examples of *Reworked Pentateuch* reflect a free approach to the Bible. Others base their argument against a fixed canon at this date on the existence of various editions of Ps. at Qumran, including some with additional psalms (some of which are attested in the LXX and other versions), submitting that this indicates the fluidity of the collection at that time. However, many of these psalm texts may have been liturgical rather than biblical texts, and reflect a different order for this reason, just as we find a different ordering of psalms in the present-day *siddur.* We must also bear in mind that multiple copies of a text can testify to alternative uses: liturgical, for study, for copying, and so on. Therefore, notwithstanding the variety of text types preserved in the Qumran library, it seems that at that period the canon itself, that is, the identity and number of biblical books it encompassed, was already well on the way to becoming fixed.

The Emergence of MT as the Authoritative Text

There is no scholarly consensus regarding the history of the biblical text. Some argue for a gradual development between the 5th and 1st centuries BCE in three geographical areas: the land of Israel, Egypt, and some third locality, in all probability Babylonia. Others suggest that the Rabbis, the Samaritans, and the Christians each preserved a particular collection of biblical texts, derived from a larger variety of text forms, which were lost with the disappearance of the groups that had presumably saved them.

The presence of diverse texts and text types at Qumran led other scholars to argue for a paradigm reflecting textual variety, based on three main text types but including texts with a free approach to the biblical one. Clearly, based on the Qumran evidence, plurality of texts was the rule from the 3rd to the 1st c. BCE. The additional finds from the Judean Desert document a shift in this state of affairs, however. At Masada, the much more limited number of biblical finds represents only the so-called proto-Masoretic (or proto-rabbinic) type, as is the case for the later finds from the Bar Kokhba Revolt refuge caves. This supports the view that this text type achieved authoritative status during the period between the Great Revolt and the Bar Kokhba Revolt (between 70 and 135 CE), pushing the other variants out. Thus, by the end of the Bar Kokhba Revolt, the textual pluriformity attested in the pre-destruction period gave way to the exclusive choice of the already prominent proto-MT type as binding. Thus, the destruction of the Temple and its aftermath served as a strong impetus for creating a more unified text. Given the lack of evidence for the biblical libraries in the possession of the different groups in Second Temple Judaism—with the Qumran library serving as perhaps only a sampling of biblical texts circulating among various groups—it is impossible to establish a definite link between particular groups and specific text types. The sole known exception is the Samaritan community, which chose harmonistic texts for its Holy Writings at a date preceding the acceptance of MT as the authoritative text version. It is possible that, in the absence of a tradition similar to rabbinic oral law, the Samaritans preferred a text relatively free of internal contradictions as the basis for their Holy Writings.

In sum, the discovery of biblical texts in the Judean Desert has been of inestimable value for biblical scholarship. By significantly enlarging the number of ancient witnesses to the biblical text, the finds shed light on manifold aspects of the development of the biblical canon and text as represented by MT and the other variants and facilitate better understanding of when MT emerged as the authoritative witness to the biblical text.

[ESTHER ESHEL]

Classical Rabbinic Interpretation

By the 1st c. CE, Jewish interpretation was beginning a long process of standardization and development. The Rabbis who carried out this program clearly believed that sacred texts contain timeless wisdom; but when preserved in writing, this timeless wisdom becomes in time obscure or difficult to understand, and must therefore be explained. This necessity is the origin of commentary, which can run along a continuum between "pure" types: from the effort to explain the text as it is in itself—what might be called the "original intent" or "plain sense" of the writing—to the effort to interpret the text in contemporary terms in the commentator's day—the "application" or "practical intent" of the writing. In this sense, rabbinic interpretation functions much as other interpretation does.

The Classical Rabbinic Period

Covering nearly a millennium (1st c.–11th c.), the rabbinic period is a lengthy and complex era, during which exegetical approaches and traditions developed that link up with inner-biblical and early postbiblical interpretation at one end and with medieval interpretation at the other. Rabbinic tradition developed primarily in two centers: the land of Israel and Babylonia, with the latter gradually becoming more important and influential. In many ways the rabbinic approach to interpretation—comparison of texts, inference according to established procedures, and intense argument over approaches and outcomes—established the "ground rules" for most of subsequent Jewish exegesis until the modern era.

The Historical Background

The Roman empire ruthlessly put down two Jewish efforts at rebellion, in 70 and 135 CE. These events were not the sole cause of the increasing emphasis on study in Judaism, but the first put an end to Temple worship and

SOME TANNAITIC RABBIS

First generation

Gamaliel (sometimes called "the Elder"; late 1st century BCE)

Shimeon ben Gamaliel (1st century CE)

Yoḥanan ben Zakkai (1st century CE)

Second generation

Elder

Gamaliel II (of Yavneh; son of R. Shimeon; born ca. 50 CE)

Eliezer ben Hyrcanus (pupil of R. Yoḥanan ben Zakkai; 1st–2nd century)

Yehoshua ben Ḥananiah (pupil of R. Yoḥanan ben Zakkai; 1st–2nd century)

Younger

Akiva ben Yosef (ca. 40–135)

Ishma'el (or Yishma'el) ben Elisha (early 2nd century)

Third generation

Students of Akiva

Meir (2nd century)

Shimeon bar Yoḥai (2nd century)

Yose ben Ḥalafta (2nd century)

Yehudah bar Ilai (2nd century)

Shimeon ben Gamaliel II (2nd century)

Fourth generation

Judah ha-Nasi ("Rabbi"; ca. 135–220)

Eleazar bar Shimeon (2nd century; son of Shimeon bar Yoḥai)

Fifth generation

Gamaliel III (2nd century)

the second crushed any hope of its restoration. Thereafter, Jewish religious practice was marked to an even greater extent by study of the Bible, and comment on it, as a major religious activity. There had been study before, of course; rabbinic tradition had been handed on. The concerns and universe of discourse of MMT, the halakhic letter from Qumran, indicate that such debates date back to the 2nd c. BCE, even in detail and language. Hillel and Shammai and their schools (1st c. BCE to 1st c. CE) argued points of law during the late Second Temple period, up to the time of the Temple's destruction in 70 CE. That date is a convenient marker for the start of the classical rabbinic era, which is conventionally divided into four periods, with overlapping beginnings and endings for each. Periods are subdivided into generations, with a "generation" generally indicating the passing of a school of teaching from master to student.

Rabbinic Periods

The early period, beginning from the followers of Hillel, is that of the *tanna'im.* A *tanna'* is one who "repeats" (traditions), i.e., a transmitter or tradent of oral teaching. This period began around 70 CE and extended into the early 3rd c. Prominent in the tannaitic period are Rabbis Gamaliel, Akiva, and Judah ha-Nasi (the last being the rabbi credited with the redaction of the Mishnah; see below). There are five generations of *tanna'im,* beginning with the schools of Hillel and Shammai and extending to the era of Gamaliel III.

The second period is that of the *'amora'im.* An *'amora'* is a "speaker" or interpreter. This period, beginning in the 3rd c., lasted until about the 6th c. The amoraic period was the talmudic era (see below). The Babylonian *'amora'im* are divided into seven "generations" and the land of Israel *'amora'im* into five.

SOME AMORAIC RABBIS

Land of Israel	Babylonia
First generation	
Elder	
Ḥiyya (2nd–3rd century)	
Bar Kappara (3rd century)	
Levi bar Sisi (3rd century)	
Ḥaninah bar Ḥama (2nd–3rd century)	
Younger	
Yannai (known as Rabbah, "the Great," or Sabba, "the Elder"; 3rd century)	Rav (Abba Arikha, "the Tall"; d. ca. 248)
Yehoshua ben Levi (of Lydda; 3rd century)	Mar Shemuel (d. ca. 254)
Second generation	
Yoḥanan (ca. 240–279)	Yehudah ben Yeḥezkel (d. 291)
Simeon ben Lakhish (d. ca. 275)	
Third generation	
Yosi bar Ḥanina	Rabba bar Naḥmani (d. ca. 321)
Abbahu (ca. 300)	Yosef (d. 333)
Eleazar ben Pedat (3rd century)	
Ammi bar Natan (ca. 279)	
Assi (3rd century)	
Ze'era (3rd century)	
Fourth generation	
Ḥaggai	Abbayei (ca. 278–338)
Yirmiyahu ben Abba (4th century)	Rava (Abba ben Yosef bar Ḥama; 4th century)
Yonah (4th century)	
Yosa	
Aḥa	
Fifth generation	
Mana	Papa (d. 376)
Yose bar Abin	
Ḥizkiya	
Sixth generation	
	Ashi (ca. 335–427)
Seventh generation	
	Yemar
	Mar bar R. Ashi

The third, little-known period is that of the *savora'im.* A *savora'* is an "expositor." These rabbis were members of academies in Babylonia in the 6th c.

The fourth period, which at its end crosses over into medieval interpretation, is that of the *ge'onim.* A *ga'on* is the leader of one of the academies in Babylonia; *ga'on* means "pride" and is a short form of the title *ro'sh yeshivat ga'on Ya'akov* "head of the academy [that is] the pride of Jacob." The geonic period extends from the mid-6th c. to the 11th c., and saw the first efforts at systematic legal commentary of the Talmud. The greatest among these Rabbis was Saadia ben Joseph Gaon (10th c.), who began rabbinic study of philosophy and literature, as well as study of the Bible (rather than only study of the Talmud).

The Texts of the Rabbinic Periods

The major works of the rabbinic period are of two types: those arranged topically, of which the main ones are the Mishnah and the Talmud; and those arranged around the biblical text, midrash, including the ten collections in the so-called *Midrash Rabbah.* We will describe these works, noting their types and approximate dates of composition or compilation.

Works arranged topically. The Mishnah is a compilation of the written records of oral discussions of various laws. "Mishnah" means "oral instruction" (from Heb *shanah,* "repeat," equivalent to Aram. *teni'*, from which *tanna'* is derived). It is divided into six "orders," each of which has numerous subsections, called "tractates." The orders are: *Zeraʿim,* "Seeds" (rules about agriculture); *Moʿed,* "Appointed Times" (rules about Sabbaths and festivals); *Nashim,* "Women" (primarily marriage laws); *Nezikin,* "Damages" (rules about money and legal disputes); *Kodoshim,* "Holy Things" (Temple procedures); and *Teharot,* "Purities" (ritual impurities and purification). The Mishnah is believed to have been compiled in its final form by Rabbi Judah ha-Nasi ("the Prince," or more correctly, "the Patriarch," the title of the head of the Jewish community in the land of Israel; he is known as "Rabbi") around 200 CE, though it contains material from generations before Rabbi's time.

Other material from the same period, more or less, is contained in the Tosefta ("addition"), a collection of further rabbinic comments on most of the topics covered in the Mishnah. The structure of the Tosefta (t.) parallels that of the Mishnah, though it is composed of extra-Mishnaic material.

The Talmud, the major work of Jewish rabbinical interpretation, exists in two forms: "Talmud Yerushalmi," the Jerusalem Talmud (sometimes more accurately called the Talmud of the land of Israel or the Palestinian Talmud) and "Talmud Bavli," the Babylonian Talmud. In references these are abbreviated *y.* and *b.* respectively. The Talmud consists of pericopes of the Mishnah, accompanied by a commentary called the Gemara ("learning"). The Talmuds were compiled during the 3rd through the 6th centuries CE, first in Israel (until 370), and later in Babylonia (6th c.).

Works organized around the biblical text. The *Midrash Rabbah* ("Great Midrash") is a collection of rabbinic comments on the biblical text, which in its final form (Venice, 1545) contains ten midrashim: the five books of the Torah, Gen. through Deut., and the Five Scrolls, Song, Ruth, Lam., Eccl., Esth. Individual sections are referred to by their biblical title, for instance, *Genesis Rabbah* (or *Bereshit Rabbah*), *Lamentations Rabbah,* and so on. Despite their final publication in one volume, however, these works arose at widely different times, with *Gen. Rab.* generally regarded as the earliest (ca. 5th c. CE), followed by *Lev. Rab.* (slightly later). The latest are *Exod., Num.,* and *Deut.* To complicate matters further, some of these works are composite arrangements of works from different periods.

Halakhah and Aggadah. Cutting across the categories of separate works are the two main descriptive types of rabbinic comment: halakhah, or legal comment, and aggadah, or non-legal comment. Halakhah (from *halakh,* "go, walk") refers to the "way" of Torah; halakhah itself is concerned with explicating, applying, and in general making sense of the legal materials in the Bible. Aggadah is a much more amorphous category: it includes theology, lore, legend, sayings, prayer and praise—in fact, it seems to be a catch-all for whatever is not halakhah.

Principles of Rabbinic Interpretation

Rabbinic interpretation is characterized by several methods, the principles and illustrations of which we will examine below. The Rabbis themselves proposed various descriptive lists of types of interpretation, of which the shortest and best-known is attributed to Hillel (1st c. BCE). Hillel found seven types of interpretation:

- *Qal vaḥomer:* the deduction from a minor case to a major case.
- *Gezerah shavah:* drawing an analogy between texts based on a word in common
- *Binyan ʾav mikatuv ʾeḥad:* applying a principle derived from one verse
- *Binyan ʾav mishenei ketuvim:* applying a principle derived from two verses
- *Kelal uferat uferat ukelal:* modification of a general principle derived from a particular principle; modification of a particular principle derived from a general principle
- *Kayotzeʾ bo bemakom ʾaḥer:* principles derived from similar passages
- *Davar halamed meʿinyano:* deduction from context

Rabbinic method also included such ancient types as *notarikon,* where each consonant of a Heb word was taken as an abbreviation for a different word. The Rabbis, for example, parsed the first word of the Decalogue, *ʾanokhi,* "I," as an acronym of the (Aram.) words *ʾanaʾ ketavit yehavit*—"I [God] wrote it [and] gave it." This method was employed by Babylonian and Assyrian scribes long before the rabbinic era.

The earliest texts containing rabbinic interpretation were edited after 200 CE, and the origins of the system that gave birth to these texts must be inferred from texts of earlier groups (see "Early Nonrabbinic Interpretation," pp. 1841–50).

For two reasons we will concentrate on halakhah rather than aggadah. First, the Talmuds were much more explicitly consistent in their presentation of such texts, their methods are easier to understand, and consequently their development is also easier to trace. Second, these texts and methods are relatively unexplored in modern academic discourse. Nevertheless, more purely homiletical methods will also be described at the end of this essay.

Broadly speaking, rabbinic exegesis may be explained in three ways: historically, phenomenologically, and functionally. The historical approach looks at the *development* of interpretation. The functional approach seeks to understand the *purposes* of interpretation. Finally, the phenomenological approach studies *methods* of interpretation. This study combines all these perspectives.

Omnisignificance

James Kugel has proposed the term "omnisignificance" to describe the essential stance of rabbinic interpretation. These interpreters assume that there is no detail of the text, however insignificant it may seem, that does not carry meaning. Further, this meaning is not merely a matter of emphasis or rhetorical variation; the text intends to teach, and it intends this with every part of itself. The interpreter must find the correct analytical tool to make the teaching clear.

This is a restatement of the rabbinic interpretation of Deut. 32.47: "'For it is not an empty thing for you, it is your very life,' and if [it appears] devoid [of moral or halakhic meaning]—it is you [who have not worked out its moral or legal significance]" (*y. Ketub.* 8:11 [32c]). In rabbinic terms omnisignificance has a sharply limited and highly focused range: It is restricted to moral, theological, or legal interpretations. A rabbinic comment attributed to the mid-3rd c. scholar in the land of Israel, R. Simeon ben Lakhish, will illustrate this: "There are verses which are worthy of being burnt, but they are [after all, when properly understood,] essential components of Torah" (*b. Ḥul.* 60b). "Omnisignificance" is not only a fundamental assumption of the rabbinic view of Scripture, it also guides interpretation into well-defined channels and establishes a hierarchy of exegetical alternatives.

It also presents a challenge. Having claimed such profundity for *all* of Scripture, the rabbinic program should deliver on its promise. But the Bible contains a great deal of material which, by rabbinic standards, is not legal, ritual, moral, ethical, or theological: stories of Israelite ancestors, genealogies, poetry (not all of it religious), census lists, geographical and dynastic information of dubious interest to a legal scholar. Thus the *Mekhilta* (*Mek.*, a halakhic midrash on Exod.) runs only from Exod. 12.1 to 35.3, and skips long passages about the construction of the Tabernacle in Exod. chs 25–40, except for brief sections relating to 31.12–17 and 35.1–3. There is no halakhic midrash on Gen. at all. A truly omnisignificant program would fit in all the nonlegal and non-edificatory passages. It would also cover what is missing. For instance, the Torah lacks explicit mention of matters that the Rabbis—and most Jews—would consider essential, such as the obligation to pray regularly. True, Abraham, Isaac, and Jacob pray, Moses prays, Joshua prays, but regular prayer is not mandated, nor is its structure laid down. The Rabbis settled on Deut. 11.13, "serving Him with all your heart," as referring to prayer, which is "the service of the heart" (*b. Taʿan.* 2a), but this reference is very vague.

Thus the promise was never totally fulfilled. Omnisignificance is a rabbinic view of Scripture rather than a complete exegetical program, and an ideal which was never actually realized. Not every scriptural text has been interpreted as a strictly "religious" one. The available collections of classic rabbinic texts do not constitute an omnisignificant corpus; not only do they fail to deal with many vv., and even whole biblical chs, but features which are considered significant—legally or morally—in one context are ignored in others. The rabbinic program or programs do not even attempt to provide a complete commentary, in whatever mode, to any biblical book, ch, or passage, though in some heavily halakhic chs in Lev. something resembling a complete commentary could be composed (an attempt to do so was the Vilna Gaon, in *ʾAderet ʾEliyahu*). Indeed, the statement quoted above, "if [it appears] devoid [of moral or halakhic meaning]—it is you [who have not worked out its moral or legal significance]," which is reported in the name of the fifth-generation authority, R. Mana, is an admission of this failure and a rebuke to his colleagues or disciples.

There is another aspect to this problem. The doctrine of omnisignificance assumes a uniform narrative or expositional density in Scripture; the biblical text is presumed to be uniformly informative on some level. The preserved rabbinic exegetical materials available to us do not bear out this assumption, however. For example, the phrases *ʾish ʾish,* "every man," (Lev. 15.2; 17.3, 8, 10, 13; 18.6; 20.2, 9; 22.4, 18; 24.15; Num. 1.4; 4.19, 49; 5.12; 9.10) and *ʾish,* "a man," (Lev. 19.20) are sometimes interpreted as including women (*b. Zevaḥ.* 108b), but at other times not, since the v. itself includes them within its purview when it employs the phrase, *ʾish ʾo ʾishah,* "a man or a woman" (Lev. 13.29, 38). Why does Scripture employ these variations? The impression one receives is that rabbinic exegesis reflects a concerted effort to harmonize such expressions and level their applications. Women are included in the expression "every man," as they are in the expression "a man," and of course explicitly in the expression "a man or a woman." The Rabbis never raise these questions in a systematic way.

The omnisignificant imperative proceeds directly from the view of the Torah and the entire Bible as divine revelation; it serves to justify interpretive approaches to biblical texts. Nevertheless, in practice this principle was not universally applied to all biblical texts nor was the meaning restricted to narrow halakhic or moral categories. Indeed, plain-sense interpretations are not excluded, so long as they have legal, ritual, or edificatory value. At times, then, the interpretation borders on what we would consider the plain sense of the text, so long as it has omnisignificant ramifications.

Goals and Methods of Rabbinic Interpretation

Rabbinic interpretation was concerned to increase the understanding of the text and its acceptability. The Rabbis also aimed to define legal requirements more exactly. The resulting explanations were primarily concerned with interpreting biblical passages in terms that were more understandable or palatable to their contemporaries, and to provide exact definitions and interpretations for biblical vv. that had legal or ritual significance.

An example of the first is found in the rabbinic dispute over whether the case of a "rebellious son" of Deut. 21.18–21 ever occurred, or whether it was presented as part of the Deuteronomic legislation merely as an object lesson.

> R. Judah said: If [the "stubborn and rebellious" son's] mother is not like his father in voice, appearance and stature, he does not become a stubborn and rebellious son [and thus subject to the death penalty]. Why so? Scripture said: "he will not obey our voice" (Deut. 21.20), and since they must be identical in voice, they must also be [identical] in appearance and stature.… There never has been a "stubborn and rebellious" son, and never will be. Why then was the law written? That you may expound it and receive a reward.… [This may agree with R. Simeon, who said:] Because one [= the son] eats a *tartemar* (about 180 grams) of meat and drinks half a *log* (about a cup) of Italian wine, shall his father and mother have him stoned? But it never happened and never will happen. Why then was the law written? That you may expound it and receive a reward (*b. Sanh.* 71a).

R. Judah interprets the biblical description of the parents' complaint that their son does "not obey *our* voice" as mandating that their *voices* be identical, and the Talmud takes this as an impossible condition. How often will a father and mother have the same "voice, appearance and stature"?

Precise interpretation of a grammatical element is commonly used for legal or ritual texts which are intended to be carried out. Indeed, in other cases, the requirement that two elements of the act be identical is not absolute: for instance, the Mishnah prescribes that the sin offerings brought on the Day of Atonement be alike, but that requirement may be waived (*m. Yoma* 6:1). It is clear, however, that the imperatives of the two cases are different. Sacrifices must be offered, but executing a rebellious son for being a glutton and a drunkard seemed excessive to R. Simeon. This insistence on the exactitude of biblical expressions is typical of rabbinic interpretation of biblical texts, even when there is no apparent cultural disparity between the biblical and rabbinic worlds. It is bound up with the rabbinic view of Scripture's exceedingly precise mode of expression. While it was in all likelihood Scripture's divine origin that allowed such a mode of interpretation to gain sway, once established, this mode was adopted for rabbinic texts as well, and we find 4th- and 5th-c. Rabbis applying similar modes of interpretation to the Mishnah and other rabbinic texts, and later authorities doing the same to the Talmuds and later texts.

Duplications and Redundancies

Of particular concern to the Rabbis were two challenges to the omnisignificant view: duplications and contradictions. How could an omnisignificant text tolerate either of these departures from the precision posited of it? If every letter were weighed, how could Scripture seemingly contradict itself, repeat itself, or deal with matters that seemed not terribly significant to the Rabbis? We will examine their methods for dealing with duplications, which probably concerned them as much as contradictions, if only because, from their point of view, there were so many of them.

Generally speaking, redundancies and duplications are interpreted as they may be applied to actual cases, so as to draw distinctions between apparently similar, identical, or contradictory passages. While the Babylonian Talmud states this principle only for legal texts (as in *b. Bek.* 6b), it clearly also applies, though with different methods, to nonlegal passages. This method of dealing with redundancies expanded to include all sorts of interpretation, and became typical of the traditional approach to most of the problems outlined above. As the medieval tosafists (commentators on the Talmud during the 12th–14th centuries) noted, only when these methods fail should one fall back on the plain sense (see *Tosafot Sot.* 3a, s.v. *lo*).

Examples of the Rabbis dealing with duplicate passages are numerous in the interpretive material from the 2nd c. onward. One example is found in the various Torah passages regarding the law of a "Hebrew slave." The *Mek.* on Exod. chs 21–22 includes a section on the laws pertaining to a "Hebrew slave" in Exod. 21.4–7, which must be coordinated with another passage relating to slavery in Lev. 25.39–46, and, ultimately, to Deut. 15.12–18. It does so by distinguishing between the application of each of these passages.

> You say that Scripture here deals with one sold into servitude by the court for stealing, telling us that such a one must serve not only the one who bought him but also the latter's son after him. Perhaps however it deals only with one who sells himself? When it says: "And if thy brother be waxen poor with thee and sell himself unto thee" (Lev. 25.39), behold the one selling himself is here spoken of. Why then should Scripture say here: "If thou buy a Hebrew slave?" It must therefore deal with one sold into slavery by the court for stealing, telling that such a one must serve not only the one who bought him but also the latter's son after him. (*Mek.,* ed. Lauterbach, vol. III, p. 3)

Since the Exod. passage does not specify the cause of the sale into slavery while the Lev. passage does, the Rabbis might have simply harmonized the two. The essential difficulty, that Exod. 21.2 specifies a six-year term of servitude, while Lev. 25.40 mandates a variable term, depending on when in the jubilee cycle the sale took place, could perhaps have been reconciled in some way; for example, the six-year term could have been required, while serving until the jubilee would have applied to a case in which the slave wanted to continue with his master, as, indeed, the *Mek.* itself does suggest in the case of an Israelite sold by the court. No new category would have had to be created. But by creating a new distinction, the Rabbis accounted not only for the overlap between the two passages but the very existence of two separate passages ostensibly dealing with but one topic: the Hebrew slave.

Finally, there is the third passage, Deut. 15.12–18, which specifies a term of six years, with the slave going out in the seventh loaded down with gifts. *Sifre Deut.* 119 deals explicitly with the relationship of this passage to the two categories of Hebrew slave already established, and to the Hebrew maidservant of Exod. 21.7–12.

> When you set him free, do not let him go empty-handed. Furnish him out of the flock, threshing floor, and vat.... Perhaps we only furnish the one who goes out in six years (Exod. 21.2); whence [do we know that this applies also] to the one who departs in the jubilee (Lev. 25.40) or with the death of the master (referring to Exod. 21.2–6) and the Hebrew maidservant with her displaying signs of puberty (Exod. 21.7–12)? Scripture says: "You shall set free" (Deut. 15.12), "when you shall set free" (Deut. 15.13), "when you shall set him free" (ibid.)—[thus applying to all three cases].

This passage thus harmonizes and distinguishes among the various Torah texts referring to Hebrew servitude. These texts display differing emphases and phraseology, and thus offer opportunities for both means of exegesis.

What then do the Rabbis do when the repetition or repetitions are identical? Such a problem is posed by the threefold appearance of the prohibition of seething a kid in its mother's milk in Exod. 23.19; 34.26; and Deut. 14.21.

> Why is this law stated in three places? To correspond to the three covenants which the Holy One, blessed be He, made with Israel: One at Horeb (Exod. 24.7–8), one in the plains of Moab (Deut. 29.11), and one on Mount Gerizim and Mount Ebal (Deut. 28.69) ...
>
> R. Jonathan says: Why is this law stated in three places? Once to apply to domestic animals, once to apply to wild animals, and once to apply to fowl.
>
> Abba Ḥanin states in the name of R. Eliezer: Why is this law stated in three places? Once to apply to large cattle, once to apply to goats, and once to apply to sheep.
>
> R. Simeon ben Eleazar says: Why is this law stated in three places? Once to apply to large cattle, once to apply to small cattle, and once to apply to wild animals.
>
> R. Simeon ben Yoḥai says: Why is this law stated in three places? One is a prohibition against eating it, one is a prohibition against deriving any benefit from it, and one is a prohibition against the mere cooking of it.

Here the threefold mention is interpreted by means of standard matrices involving three classes, either of animals or of prohibited actions (eating, drinking, or deriving benefit). In the nature of things, as we might expect, not all of these matrices are equally compelling. In rabbinic literature, the animal world is regularly divided into domestic animals, wild animals, and fowl, and domestic animals in turn are subdivided into large and small cattle, so that R. Simeon ben Eleazar's division into large and small cattle, and wild animals, while somewhat unusual, is certainly in line with convention (though Abba Ḥanin's statement dividing animals into large and small cattle, and then subdividing small cattle into goats and sheep, does seem simply to be an effort to use the three repetitions). Thus, rabbinic exegesis combines the attempt to relate scriptural texts with rabbinic categories (which are often based on Scripture in any case; e.g., Gen. 2.20 for domestic animals, wild animals, and fowl) with the modification of those categories to fit a particular distribution of vv. This can often result in an elaborate series of arguments designed to demonstrate that each v., though seemingly redundant, is intended to counter a particular hypothetical argument.

Though it is not explicitly stated, these examples illustrate the use of a principle attributed to R. Ishmael, an authority of the first half of the 2nd c. and colleague of R. Akiva: "Every passage that is said and repeated is repeated only for the sake of the new information [contained] in it." This principle underwent an interesting and characteristic metamorphosis in the course of time. Originally it seems to have been intended as a "cap" on expositions: In the case of the duplicate passages, only the *differences,* or more precisely the pluses in the duplicate passage, are expounded, not the repetitions themselves, which by definition contain no new information. Thus, in the case of the duplicate lists of animals forbidden to be eaten in Lev. 11.1–28 and Deut. 14.3–21, the Babylonian Talmud first cites a view which explains the repetitive mention of the camel (in Deut. 14.7 as opposed to Lev. 11.4) as an animal which is forbidden to be eaten as coming to include as forbidden the offspring of a camel which resembles a clean animal. Later in the discussion, the following teaching is quoted:

> Why is [the list of clean and unclean animals] repeated? Because of the *shesuʿah* [according to rabbinic interpretation, an animal with two backs and two spinal columns, which is mentioned only in the Deuteronomic passage]. Why with regard to birds? Because of the *raʾah* [a bird mentioned only in Deut. 14.13].—Then,

> perhaps, [the repetition of] "camel," "camel" [in both books] comes for the same purpose [that is, the camel "comes along for the ride" in order to provide a context for the two additions, and not for any other purpose]?—Nevertheless, whenever we can derive [a lesson from the biblical text], we do so (*b. Bek.* 6b).

The ideal here is to derive a lesson *from every repetition.* Every part of it is subject to interpretation, if only we can interpret it. If we cannot, a lacuna exists, which may be filled later or in messianic times, in accord with R. Yoḥanan's fervent wish as expressed in *b. Menaḥ.* 45a: "This passage will be interpreted by Elijah in the future [in the messianic era]." Maimonides (1135–1204 CE), on the other hand, rejected such amplifications; he seems to have been of the opinion that post-Talmudic authorities could not multiply "counts" on their own, but only when they had already been made by a Talmudic source.

This is not to say that the Rabbis did not have other methods of dealing with such problems. But for all their ingenuity, a not insignificant amount of Scripture escaped their treatment, at least as we may judge from the surviving compilations of late antiquity. We may understand the well-known rabbinic story of *b. Menaḥ.* 29b in this light.

> R. Judah said in the name of Rav: When Moses ascended on high he found the Holy One, blessed be He, engaged in affixing coronets [small strokes on the tops of certain letters in a Torah scroll] to the letters. Said Moses: "Lord of the Universe, who prevents You [from giving the Torah without these coronets]?" He answered: "There will arise a man at the end of many generations, Akiva ben Joseph by name, who will expound heaps and heaps of laws upon each stroke." "Lord of the Universe, let me see him." He said: "Turn around." Moses went and sat down behind eight rows [of R. Akiva's disciples and listened to his expositions of the Torah]. He was not able to follow the arguments and was depressed, but when they came to a certain subject and the disciples said to the master, "How do you know it?" and [R. Akiva] replied: "It is a law given to Moses at Sinai," he was comforted. He then returned to the Holy One, blessed be He, and said, "Lord of the Universe, You have such a man and you give the Torah through me?" He replied: "Be silent, for such is My decree." Moses then said, "Lord of the Universe, You have shown me his Torah [teaching], show me his reward." "Turn around," said He. Moses turned around and saw them weighing out [R. Akiva's] flesh in the market stalls [after his martyrdom in the Hadrianic persecutions]. "Lord of the Universe! Such Torah, and such a reward!" He replied: "Be silent, for such is My decree."

We have no legal expositions based on the coronets of the letters of the Torah in the name of R. Judah or Rav, or, indeed, any earlier or later authorities. Unless we posit a tremendous ("heaps and heaps") amount of lost interpretation, we must assume that this story refers to those parts of the Torah which still lacked a definitive rabbinic exposition.

Argument by Analogy and the *Ribbuy* ("Extension")

The argument by analogy is characteristic of rabbinic interpretation as a whole. For example, the common biblical Heb phrase *ʾish ʾish,* "a man, a man," i.e., "every man," "each man," by extension "every person," is often interpreted as including classes of people other than males. This is because the phrase is considered redundant, since *ʾish* alone may mean the same. From that phrase the Rabbis derive, in various contexts, the applicability of the relevant rule to women, children, proselytes, their wives, non-Jews, or, in some cases, people of indeterminate sex or hermaphrodites. The fact that all of these are derived by analogy does not mean that there is a uniformity of choice, though. The form the analogy takes depends on the context. Thus, the prohibition of incest (Lev. 20.2) includes non-Jews:

> "And say *(to'mar)* to the Children of Israel," "and speak *(tedaber)* to the Children of Israel," "say *('emor)* to the Children of Israel," "speak *(daber)* to the Children of Israel," "instruct *(tzav)* the Children of Israel," "and you shall instruct *(tetzaveh)* the Children of Israel"—R. Yose says: "The Torah speaks in the human language in many expressions, and all must be expounded *(lehidaresh)*: 'Israel'—this refers to Israel (i.e., male Jews); 'sojourner' *(ger)*—this refers to the proselyte *(ger)*; "*the* proselyte"—this includes the wives of proselytes; 'in Israel'—this includes women and slaves. If so, why does [Scripture] say *''ish 'ish'*? To include non-Jews" (*Sifra Kod.* 10:1–2, ed. Weiss 91b).

Nevertheless, *'ish* is always taken to exclude minors, even when some other means is employed to bring them within the applicability of the rule in question. Thus, in regard to the skin diseases commonly rendered as "leprosy" in Lev. 13.44, we find the following:

> *'ish,* "a man"—From where [do we know this] to include a woman or a minor? Scripture states: *"tzaru'a,"* "one suffering from a skin disease," whether a man or a woman or a minor. If so, why is *'ish* stated? For a matter [stated] below: a man unbinds his hair and undoes his clothes but a woman does not unbind her hair or undo her clothes (*Sifra Tzri'a* 12:1, ed. Weiss, 67d).

Minors are included by means of an interpretation of the word *tzaru'a,* despite the exclusion signalled by *'ish.* Note also that the definite article, which in Heb is registered by a one-letter prefix, may also be used as a hook on which to hang an analogical interpretation. The word *ha-ger,* "the sojourner," or rather the *"ha-"* prefix, is taken to include the wives of proselytes, while the word *be-Yisrael,* "in Israel" is taken to include women and slaves. Ordinarily, the category of "women" is included by the repetition of the word *'ish,* as in the expression *'ish 'ish* noted above. Here there is only one *'ish,* and, instead, women are included in this way.

Rava and the Omnisignificant Revolution

Over time these inconsistencies in the application of methods became a matter of concern to later scholars, especially the great fourth-generation Babylonian *'amora'* of the second quarter of the 4th c., Rava, and some of his predecessors in the land of Israel as well, particularly the third-generation *tanna'* R. Ilai. Both were concerned with inconsistent uses of analogy, but Rava was concerned with the inconsistent use of the omnisignificant principle itself. Rava's concern manifested itself in a systematic research program into the limits of the application of omnisignificance, motivated, it would seem, both by his own powers of systematization, his apparently strong interest in the subject of halakhic interpretation, and by challenges to rabbinic interpretation and authority in his own time and place. Unlike most other rabbinic authorities, he seems to have had wide communal responsibilities in the city of Mahoza, which was located on the west bank of the River Tigris directly across from the Persian capital of Ctesiphon. The political head of Babylonian Jewry, the Head of the Exile, who also had standing as a Persian nobleman, was headquartered there, and adjacent to Mahoza was the *catholicos,* the head of the Nestorian Church, in Seleucia, then known as Veh-Ardaxshir. The cosmopolitan population that Rava ministered to was skeptical of rabbinic authority and exegesis, and this undoubtedly helped lead him to searching examinations of its aims and methods.

Rava was concerned with why the Rabbis interpreted some words and phrases in certain texts but not in others. Beyond that, he was concerned with why Scripture itself expends greater effort in expositing certain matters while leaving others relatively unexamined. In all these ways, and others, Rava explores the limits of omnisignificant interpretation as it existed in his day. In ten passages in the Babylonian Talmud (nine attributed to Rava [*b. Kid.* 9a; *B. K.* 77b; *Mak.* 8a; *Tem.* 6b; *Yoma* 63b; *ʿArak.* 30b; *Ned.* 80b; the tenth, *Tem.* 28b, is anonymous and may be redactional]), and in four similar cases in the Talmud of the land of Israel (all attributed to R. Ilai [*y. Yoma* 3.6 (40c); *Meg.* 1:12 (72a) = *Hor.* 3.3 (47c–d); *Yebam.* 6.4 (7c)]), the inconsistency of the application of rabbinic exegetical principles to specific texts is examined. For example, in *b. Kid.* 9a we have the following:

> Our Rabbis taught: [A woman is acquired in marriage] by a document: How so? If A writes for B on a paper or a shard, even if not intrinsically worth a *perutah:* "Your daughter be consecrated to me," "your daughter be betrothed to me," [or] "your daughter be my wife," she is betrothed.
>
> R. Zera ben Memmel objected: But this document is unlike a deed of purchase: there the seller writes: "My field is sold to you," while here the husband [i.e., the "acquirer"] writes: "Your daughter be consecrated to me."
>
> Rava replied: There [the form is determined] by scriptural context, and here [likewise it is determined] by scriptural context. There it is written, "and *he sell* some of his possessions" (Lev. 25.25), thus Scripture made it dependent on the seller; while here it is written "when a man [takes a woman]" (Deut. 24.1), thus making it dependent on the husband."

Thus, legal rules based on scriptural texts are expected to be consistent, and their inconsistencies must be accounted for.

This insistence on consistency extends to a demand for a minimally uniform density of scriptural interpretation even within one passage. For example, in Deut. 22.1, 3, Scripture states: "If you see your fellow's ox or sheep gone astray, do not ignore it; you must take it back to your fellow.... You shall do the same with his ass; you shall do the same with his garment; and so too shall you do with anything that your fellow loses and you find: you must not remain indifferent."

> Said Rava: Why does the All Merciful mention "an ox, a donkey, a sheep and a garment" [in Deut. 22.1, 3]?
>
> For had the All Merciful mentioned "garment" [alone], I would have thought [that] that applies only if the object [can be identified] by witnesses or the object itself has a mark [of distinction by which it may be identified], but not in the case of a donkey [for which these means of identification do not apply]. [That is,] if its saddle [can be identified] by witnesses or its saddle has a mark [of distinction by which it may be identified], I might think that it need not be returned to him. Therefore the All Merciful mentioned "a donkey" to show that even the donkey [too is returned] by virtue of the mark of the saddle.
>
> Why did the All Merciful mention "ox" and "sheep"? "Ox"—that even the shearing of its tail, and "sheep"—that even its shearings [must be returned]. Then the All Merciful should have mentioned [only] "ox" for the shearings of its tail, and the shearings of a sheep would follow *a fortiori!*
>
> But, says Rava, "donkey" mentioned in connection with a pit [in Exod. 21.33: "And if a man should open a pit ... and an ox or a donkey should fall therein.... "] on R. Judah's view [which rejects the rabbinic use of the term to exclude vessels

damaged in such a case] and "sheep" in connection with a lost article [in Deut. 22.1, 3] on all views, are difficult [in that they do not seem to serve any exegetical purpose] (*b. B. M.* 27a).

Clearly, Rava's concern with the interface of rabbinic interpretation and the formulation of biblical laws borders onto questions involving the construction of the biblical text itself.

According to geonic tradition, Rava was the head of the combined Babylonian academy, so that most of the authorities of the fifth generation were his disciples and continued to carry on this program. The Babylonian Talmud contains long passages working out the details of Rava's concerns, passages that have almost no parallels in the Talmud of the land of Israel.

Other Developments in Rabbinic Interpretation

Taking Contradictory Verses into Account

Various passages in both Talmuds show methodological concerns that parallel those of Rava. For instance, there is the phenomenon of a sort of "round-robin" of queries designed to elucidate how an interpreter deals with the vv. or phrases which seem to counter his own interpretation, or for which his own interpretation does not account. The Talmud of the land of Israel presents a dialogue between the schools of Shammai and Hillel. The school of Shammai maintains that not only is labor *on* the Sabbath prohibited, but one may not even initiate a process that proceeds automatically, on its own, *during* the Sabbath. The school of Hillel, however, permits this. The Talmud inquires into the scriptural support for the two positions.

Mishnah: The school of Shammai say: Ink, dyes and alkaline plants may not be steeped [in water in order to further the dyeing process] unless they can be dissolved while it is still daylight [before the Sabbath begins], but the school of Hillel permit it.

Talmud: And what is the reason of the school of Shammai [to prohibit]? "Six days shall you labor and do all your work" (Exod. 20.9)—complete *all* your work while it is still daylight [before the Sabbath, that is, during the six days of the week, and not on the Sabbath].

And what is the reason of the school of Hillel? "Six days shall you labor ... and [the seventh] day" (Exod. 20.9–10)—[that is, you may complete your work on the seventh day—the Sabbath—so long as it is done as the automatic continuation of a process that began before the Sabbath] (*y. Shab.* 1:5 [3d–4a]).

How do the school of Hillel interpret the [verse used by the school of Shammai to justify] their reason? "Six days shall you labor and do all your work" [but not on the Sabbath]—this refers to working actually done by hand [and not automatically].

And how do the school of Shammai interpret the [verse used by the school of Hillel to justify] their reason? "Six days shall you labor ... and on [the seventh] day"—this refers to [the following permitted process]: One may open a water-canal to a garden on the eve of the Sabbath [that is, before the Sabbath begins,] and [the garden] is watered [automatically] on the Sabbath.

Thus, each position must not only be justified on the basis of its own independent interpretation of the relevant biblical vv., but *it must account for the vv. or phrases employed by its opponents.* This form of debate eventually made its way into nonlegal contexts, more often in the Babylonian Talmud. Ultimately, the legal point was seen to hinge on a methodological disagreement as to the proper interpretation of the biblical v. This formal disagreement served to underline the essential biblical basis of these disputes.

Assessing Analogies

Since much of rabbinic interpretation is based on some form of analogy, there are cases in which the Rabbis were faced with competing analogies, and had to decide which to choose. When these choices were made early on, and appear later without explicit justifications, redactors must somehow account for them. Thus, for example, one midrashic text on Deut. 15.12 and Exod. 21.2 ("six years must he serve") proposes that a Hebrew slave may serve not only his master but his master's son, but not his master's heir.

> Who whispered to you to include the son [in the "he shall serve" of the v., as one whom the slave must serve] and to exclude the heir? I include the son who takes his father's place in regard to affiancing a Hebrew maidservant [as laid down in Exod. 21.9–10] and a field of inheritance [as per Lev. 25.25–28], and I exclude the heir who does not take the father's place [that is, the place of the master, who in this case is *not* the son of the father but merely his heir] and for a field of inheritance (*Sifre Re'eh* 118, ed. Finkelstein, pp. 177–178).

Thus, the rule regarding whom a Hebrew slave must serve may be likened to one in which only the son has a part, or to one in which (as in the case of Num. 27.6–11, which sets out the order of inheritance, though the son has priority) other heirs have a place. In this case, since the son has an exclusive right in the cases enumerated, he is assumed to have exclusive rights here too, and not merely priority as in the case of inheritance.

The Beginning of the End

Ironically, by the time Rava began his efforts at systematization, some of the options available were already being eliminated. A Babylonian version of an anecdote about the great second-generation *'amora'* of the land of Israel, R. Yoḥanan, the most frequently cited authority in either Talmud, whose disciples made up the greater part of the third generation of *'amora'im,* is depicted as declaring that the exposition of the letter *vav* was no longer possible.

> R. Yoḥanan was [once] sitting and expounding: *"Notar* [a portion of a sacrifice left over beyond the prescribed time for eating it and which must be burnt on the third day, see Lev. 7.17] must be burnt in its [proper] time during the day; when not in its proper time, it may be burnt during the day or at night."
>
> R. Eleazar [ben Pedat] raised an objection to R. Yoḥanan: "'I only [know] that a child which must be circumcized on the eighth day must be circumcized during the day; how do I [know this of] a child circumcized on the ninth, tenth, eleventh or twelfth? It is stated: *"And on* the day" [Lev. 12.3].' And even one who does not expound a *vav* will expound a *vav-heh* ("and" and "the")."
>
> [R. Yoḥanan] remained silent. After [R. Eleazar] left, R. Yoḥanan said to Resh Laqish: "Did you see [Eleazar] ben Pedat sitting and expounding like Moses in the name of the Almighty!"
>
> Said Resh Laqish to him: "Is it then his [teaching]? It is really a baraita."
>
> "Where is it taught?"
>
> "In *Torat Kohanim* [= *Sifra,* the halakhic midrash on Leviticus]."
>
> [R. Yoḥanan] went out, memorized it in three days and mastered it in three months (*b. Yebam.* 72b).

The parallel in the Talmud of the land of Israel is couched in different terms (*y. Shab.* 2:1 [4c]), but the essential point is that neither Talmud records *any such exposition* of a *vav* by any authority *after R. Yoḥanan's time.* (See *b. Yebam.* 68a, b for Rav and *b. B. M.* 8b, both first-generation Babylonian *'amora'im* and senior to R. Yoḥanan.) R. Yoḥanan's decision thus seems to have marked a turning point in amoraic midrashic exposition.

This does not mean that *ʾamoraʾim* abandoned the field of *ribbuy*—expounding extensions based on Heb particles or single letters. Though we do not find the letter *vav* expounded for this purpose, R. Yoḥanan himself does expound other Heb prepositions and conjunctives: *ʾo,* "or" (*b. Shab.* 63b), *ʾim,* "if" (*b. B. K.* 43b), *gam,* "also" (*b. ʾArak.* 7a). But over time the *ʾamoraʾim* did less and less of this type of exposition. On the other hand, we find authorities of the fourth generation, both in Israel and Babylonia, treating duplications in the Mishnah not too differently from the way they treated biblical vv. One example, which is expounded in both Talmuds, will illustrate the point.

> Mishnah *Shabbat* 11:4: If one throws [an object over a distance of] four cubits in the sea, he is not liable [for transgressing the Sabbath law]. *If there is a water pool and a public road traverses it, and one throws [an object] four cubits therein, he is liable.* And what depth constitutes a pool? Less than ten handbreadths. *If there is a water pool and a public road traverses it, and one throws [an object] four cubits therein, he is liable.*
>
> Gemara: One of the rabbis said to Rava: As for "traversing" [mentioned] twice, that is well, [as] it informs us this: (1) traversing with difficulty is designated "traversing" [for purposes of the Sabbath laws]; (2) use with difficulty is not designated use. But why state "pool" twice?—One refers to summer and one to winter, and both are necessary. For if only one were stated, I would say: That is only in summer, when people walk therein to cool themselves, but in winter [this is] not [the case]. And if we were told [this] of winter, [I would say that] they do not object [to wading through the pool], but not in summer.

The Talmud of the land of Israel on this Mishnah also adverts to this problem, and expounds the duplicate text in a similar way, and also in the name of a fourth-generation authority, R. Pinḥas (*y. Shab.* 11:4 [13a]).

> Why was it taught twice? R. Ḥanina in the name of R. Pinḥas: [This text refers to a case in which there were] two pools, one through which people walked and one through which people did not walk, except when they were forced to, so that you do not say that since people do not walk through [it] except when they are forced to, it is not [considered] public ground but private ground; accordingly, you must say that it is public ground.

Thus, in the course of time, less and less recourse was made to the midrashic exposition of biblical vv., and more and more emphasis was given to extracting what information was available—even quasi-midrashically—from early rabbinic sources themselves. By the geonic period, under challenge from the Karaites, the system of halakhic midrash had closed down. Rava's work is to be dated closer to the beginning of this process than to its end, and he does make use of particular rabbinic exegetical principles. But, as we have seen, and as he admits, he cannot fill in every gap.

Nonlegal Interpretation

There is nothing like this systematic concern for nonlegal or "aggadic" interpretation in rabbinic literature, though here too the principle of omnisignificance holds sway. On the whole, the rabbinic collections of aggadic material were directed at the common people, and reflect their interests and concerns. Judging from this huge literature, theosophic and mystical concerns were then, as later, esoteric and limited to small numbers of adepts. Thus, the problems of interpreting the Bible as an omnisignificant text as described above were shaped by yet another concern: making the Bible relevant not only to rabbinic disciples but also to the nonscholarly audience who heard the Torah in synagogue rather than studying it in the *bet midrash.*

The Rabbis acknowledged the relative disproportion in the biblical text between rabbinic concerns and other material, as in this comment from R. Aḥa, perhaps the fourth-generation *ʾamoraʾ* in Israel of that name:

> The conversation of the servants of the Patriarchs is more pleasing before the Holy One, blessed be He, than the Torah [-learning] of the[ir] descendants, for the passage [dealing with the journey] of Eliezer, [the servant of Abraham, in seeking a wife for Isaac takes up] two or three columns [of text in a Torah scroll], is said and repeated [i.e., the passage describes the journey and then quotes Eliezer describing the journey], while the [rule that] the blood of a [dead] creeping thing causes impurity as does its flesh, [which is] among the essential parts of the Torah *(migupei Torah)* [but is derived] from an inclusion [of one letter] (*Gen. Rab.* 60:32, ed. Theodor-Albeck, p. 650).

Later on another comment by the same sage is quoted, even more poignantly:

> The foot-washing of the servants of the Patriarchs is more pleasing before the Holy One, blessed be He, than the Torah[-learning] of the[ir] descendants, for even the washing of [his] feet [in Gen. 24.32] must be recorded, [while the rule that] the blood of a [dead] creeping thing causes impurity as does its flesh, [which is] among the essential parts of the Torah *(migupei Torah)* [but is derived] from an inclusion [of one letter] (p. 651).

R. Aḥa's comment clearly calls attention to the disparity in Torah's treatment of halakhic matters versus the detail in the patriarchal narratives—and by extension, the non-halakhic parts of the Torah. But his intent is less clear. To his successors, the Torah could hardly be conceived as intending to *devalue* the halakhot derived by one letter, or the halakhic process in general. The case of the patriarchs, or the subjects of biblical narratives in general, must have an importance in God's scheme of things that warrants such attention to their doings.

This led, in later times, to the idea that the lives of the patriarchs prefigured the history of their descendants. The kernel of this idea may be seen in the Gen. narrative of the Covenant Between the Pieces, where God informs Abram of the future Egyptian bondage, the exodus and the entrance into the land of Israel (Gen. ch 15). Thus, R. Aḥa (4th c.), in describing the creation of Adam, concludes that God gives Adam his discharge after Adam's sin and says:

> This is a sign for you: just as you have come in judgment before Me and been discharged, so too your descendants will come in judgment before Me and I will give them their discharge. When? On Rosh Hashanah, [the Day of Judgment] (*Lev. Rab.* 29:1, ed. Margoliot, p. 669).

Without specifying this principle of patriarchal anticipation of the history of the people of Israel, R. Joshua of Sikhnin (4th c., a younger contemporary of R. Aḥa) comments on Abraham's battle with the Mesopotamian kings in Gen. ch 14:

> The Holy One, blessed be He, gave a sign to Abraham that whatever would befall him would befall his descendants. How? He chose Abraham from among his entire father's house ... and he chose his descendants from the Seventy Nations *(Midr. Tanḥ.)*.

On the whole, typical rabbinic midrash was intended to attract people and inculcate moral, ethical and religious values, particularly in preaching. In the process, a good deal of folkloric material was incorporated. At times, however, the folklore is brought in for its own sake, in order to appeal to the preacher's listeners. Thus, for example, in *Lev. Rab.* 19:6 (ed. Margaliot, p. 438), we find the following discussion regarding the name of Nebuchadnezzar's wife.

> What was the name of the wife of Nebuchadnezzar? R. Ḥananiah said: Semiram was her name; R. Abin said: Semiramis was her name; and the Rabbis said: Semiraʿam was her name, because she was born in *raʿam* during an earthquake [or, in thunder].

While the names come from Hellenistic sources, and at least one partly Hebrew folk-etymology was provided for one name, no moral lesson is drawn. The motive for the explanation of the names would seem to be the need to satisfy the curiosity of the listeners. In contrast, Noah's (scripturally anonymous) wife is identified with another biblical woman, and the name is expounded homiletically.

> "And the sister of Tubal Cain was Naamah" (Gen. 4.22). Said R. Abba ben Kahana: Naamah was the wife of Noah [the assonance of Noah and Naamah should not be overlooked], and why was she called Naamah? Because her deeds were pleasant *(neʿimim)*. The rabbis said: [She] was another Naamah, who would play her tambourine sweetly for idol worship (*Gen. Rab.* 23:22, p. 224).

The purpose of this identification is more complex. It serves to connect two vv. which are otherwise disconnected; it also serves to explain why Naamah is mentioned at all, since she plays no role in the events depicted by Scripture. And, finally, the identification allows the Rabbis to comment obliquely on the nature of the sinfulness of the generation before the flood. According to R. Abba ben Kahana, Noah, the righteous man, married a righteous woman, whose deeds were pleasant. According to the Rabbis, this Naamah was typical of her sinful generation, and her deeds helped bring on the flood. Needless to say, these identifications would also have satisfied the curiosity of the people who came to hear the scriptural portion expounded. Indeed, the Bible itself provides a precedent for such exegetical elaboration. The prophet Jehu ben Hanani is mentioned in 1 Kings 16.1–12, and his father, Hanani, appears only in his patronym. But in 2 Chron. 16.7, we find the father playing a more active role: "At that time Hanani the seer came to King Asa of Judah and said to him, 'Because you relied on the king of Aram and did not rely on the LORD your God, therefore the army of the king of Aram has slipped out of your hands.' " This then illustrates the rule expounded by R. Yoḥanan, that every prophet's father who is mentioned along with his son was also a prophet (*b. Meg.* 15a, *Lev. Rab.* 6:6, pp. 142–143). Such an assumption made sense in a society where sons most often followed their fathers' occupation. It also illustrates the idea that a person or family is to be judged as a whole: If a family is known for its piety, it (or, for that matter, a nation) is judged by its reputation. The result is the far-ranging rabbinic principle that "one attributes meritorious behavior to the meritorious *(megalgelin zekhut ʿal yedei zakai)*, and sinful acts to the sinful" (*Sifre Num.* 114, p. 123) and its closely associated principle that if a person or nation performs a certain (minimally) meritorious or sinful deed, it is accounted as though she or they had performed a much greater one *(maʿaleh ʿalav/ ʿalehen keʾilu)* (*Sifre Deut.* 253, p. 279).

In particular, when Scripture attributes a sinful act to an otherwise righteous character, or one whose reputation was considered, for one reason or another, sacrosanct, the Rabbis did not hesitate to reinterpret the relevant v. or vv. A case in point is David's adulterous relationship with Bathsheba and his plotting the death of her husband, Uriah the Hittite (a story omitted in Chron. because it does not comport with David as an ideal king). A long disquisition on David is included as one of a long series of defenses of biblical characters to whom sin is imputed (*b. Shab.* 55b–56b).

> R. Samuel ben Naḥmani said in R. Jonathan's name: Whoever says that

David sinned is merely in error, for it is said, "And David behaved wisely in all his ways: and the LORD was with him" (1 Sam. 18.14). Is it possible that sin came to his hand, yet the divine Presence was with him? Then how do I interpret [the v.] "Wherefore have you despised the word of the LORD, to do that which is evil in His sight?" (2 Sam. 12.9)—he wished to do [evil] but did not.

Rav observed: Rabbi, who is descended from David, seeks to defend him! [Not so, for] the "evil" [mentioned] here is unlike any other evil [mentioned] elsewhere in the Torah. For of every other evil [mentioned] in the Torah it is written, "and he did," whereas here it is written, "to do"—this means that he desired to do, but did not (*b. Shab.* 56a).

The various vv. that accuse David of adultery and murder are thereby reinterpreted; Uriah was guilty of disobeying the king's order to go home, and was therefore worthy of death as a rebel (see 2 Sam. ch 12). David was criticized for arranging his death in battle rather than having him arraigned before the Sanhedrin; again, his relationship with Bathsheba was not adulterous because all of David's soldiers gave their wives divorces before setting out to battle. Thus, Bathsheba was a divorced woman when David had his affair with her, and her husband was guilty of traitorous insubordination.

Unlike much of rabbinic midrash, which adds further layers of interpretation onto the plain meaning of the v., the Rabbis' treatment of such incidents and vv. runs counter to that plain meaning. For the Rabbis and for the communities they represented, the stakes were simply too high to allow the plain sense to stand.

Similarly, at least for some Rabbis, the theological stakes were too high to maintain the plain sense of those vv. which express an anthropomorphic view of God.

"And rested on the seventh day" (Exod. 20.11). But is He subject to such a thing as weariness? Has it not been said: "The creator of the ends of the earth is not faint or weary" (Isa. 40.28)? And it says, "He gives power to the faint" (Isa. 40.29). And it also says, "By the word of the LORD were the heavens made" (Ps. 33.6). How then can Scripture say, "And rested on the seventh day"? Rather, so to speak, God allowed it to be written about Him that He created His world in six days and rested on the seventh. Is it not an *a fortiori* argument? If He, for Whom there is no weariness, allowed it to be written about Him that He created His world in six days and rested on the seventh, how much more should man, of whom it is written, "But man is born to toil" (Job 5.7), rest on the seventh day (*Mek. Yitro,* 7, end, ed. Lauterbach, vol. 2, pp. 255–256).

In this interpretation the Rabbis accomplish two objectives. First, any suggestion that weariness may be attributed to God is rejected, but, equally important, the v. in question is turned into one which stresses the importance of the Sabbath for humans.

Nevertheless, some Rabbis seem to have reveled in these anthropomorphic depictions of the Deity, and even added to them (*b. Ber.* 6a):

R. Abin son of R. Adda in the name of R. Isaac says: How do we know that the Holy One, blessed be He, puts on phylacteries (tefillin)? For it is said, "The Lord has sworn by His right hand, and by the arm of His strength" (Isa. 62.8). "By His right hand"—this [refers] to the Torah, for it is said, "At His right hand was a fiery law to them" (Deut. 33.2). "And by the arm of His strength"—this [refers] to the phylacteries, as it is said, "The Lord will give strength to His people" (Ps. 29.11). And how do we know that the phylacteries are a strength to Israel? For it is written, "And all the peoples of the earth shall see that the name of the Lord is called upon you, and they shall be afraid of you" (Deut. 28.11 [10]), and it has been

> taught: R. Eliezer the Great says: This refers to the phylactery of the head.

This is not meant as a metaphysical statement, however, for the Talmud goes on to inquire as to what vv. are written on the parchments of God's phylacteries. According to R. Ḥiyya ben Abin, "And who is like Your people Israel, a unique nation on earth" (1 Chron. 17.21). The phylacteries become a visible symbol of the relationship of God and Israel, and God's love for His people.

God's love for Israel is one of the constant themes of aggadic interpretation. In a sense, we have seen it at work in the interpretation of the ancestral narratives as foreshadowings of the future history of the Jewish people. It also serves as a powerful exegetical tool for other nonlegal or nontheological passages. Any passage that has some relation to Israelite history, sociology, demography (as the various census lists), etc., may be viewed as a manifestation of God's love for His people. Such a love is expressed as a concern for anything that relates to the beloved.

> "These were the marches of the Israelites" (Num. 33.1). A parable; to what may this be compared? To a king whose son was ill; he took him to one place to cure him, and on the way back, the father began to recount all the marches [they had undertaken], saying to him: Here we slept, here we were cold, here your head hurt. So too did the Holy One, blessed be He, say to Moses: Recount for them all the places they had angered Me. For that reason it is written: "These were the marches of the Israelites" (*Tanḥ. Masʿei* 3).

Thus is a rather bare-bones list of camping places in the wilderness converted into an expression of God's love for Israel. This interpretive tool serves several functions: It explains the omnisignificant worth of many biblical passages by allegorizing them as reflecting in some way the relationship of God the Father to the Israelites; and in doing so, it responded to an urgent need for the reassurance of God's love for Israel and Israel's chosenness at a time when Christianity challenged both notions.

Conclusion

Scripture, according to the Rabbis, is the abiding evidence of God's presence and continued love for His people, but the rabbinic relationship to Scripture is not one of passive acceptance. Scripture provides the basic material and some of the ground rules for rabbinic interpretation, but the elements of Scripture—passages, vv., words, even individual letters—are integrated in a way that is both scriptural *and* rabbinic. One consequence of this mutuality is the assumption that a reasoned argument has the force of a scriptural decree [*b. Pes.* 21b; *b. Ketub.* 22a; *b. B. K.* 46b; *b. Ḥul.* 114b; *b. Nid.* 25a]. The sovereignty of reason and of rabbinic authority is thereby affirmed.

> It has been taught: On that day R. Eliezer brought forth every imaginable argument, but they did not accept them. [Finally, in frustration,] he said: If the law follows my opinion, let this carob-tree prove it! Thereupon the carob-tree was torn a hundred cubits out of its place—others affirm, four hundred cubits. No proof can be brought from a carob-tree, they retorted. Again he said to them: If the law agrees with my opinion, let the stream of water prove it! Thereupon the stream of water flowed backwards. No proof can be brought from a stream of water, they rejoined. Again he urged: If the law agrees with my opinion, let the walls of the schoolhouse prove it! Thereupon the walls inclined to fall. But R. Joshua rebuked them, saying: When scholars are engaged in a legal dispute, what have you to interfere? Hence [the walls] did not fall, out of deference to R. Joshua, nor did they resume standing, in deference to R. Eliezer, and they still stand inclined. Finally he said to them:

If the law follows my opinion, let it be proved from Heaven! Thereupon a heavenly echo cried out: Why do you dispute with R. Eliezer, seeing that in all matters the law agrees with his opinion? But R. Joshua arose and exclaimed: "It is not in Heaven!" (Deut. 30.12).

What did he mean by that? Said R. Jeremiah: Since the Torah has already been given at Mount Sinai, we pay no attention to a heavenly echo, because You have long since written in the Torah at Mount Sinai: "After the majority must one incline" (Exod. 23.2).

R. Nathan met Elijah [the Prophet] and asked him, What did the Holy One, blessed be He, do at that time [in response to this statement]? He laughed [with joy], he replied, saying: My sons have defeated Me, My sons have defeated Me! (*b. B. M.* 59b.)

Appendix: The Orders and Tractates of the Mishnah

Zera'im ("Seeds"):
- *Berakhot*
- *Pe'ah*
- *Demai*
- *Kil'ayim*
- *Shevi'it*
- *Terumot*
- *Ma'aserot*
- *Ma'aser Sheni*
- *Ḥallah*
- *'Orlah*
- *Bikkurim*

Mo'ed ("Season" or "Festival"):
- *Shabbat*
- *'Eruvin*
- *Pesaḥim*
- *Shekalim*
- *Yoma*
- *Sukkah*
- *Betzah*
- *Rosh Ha-Shanah*
- *Ta'anit*
- *Megillah*
- *Mo'ed Katan*
- *Ḥagigah*

Nashim ("Women"):
- *Yebamot*
- *Ketubbot*
- *Nedarim*
- *Nazir*
- *Sotah*
- *Gittin*
- *Kiddushin*

Nezikin ("Damages"):
- *Bava Kamma*
- *Bava Metzi'a*
- *Bava Batra*
- *Sanhedrin*
- *Makkot*
- *Shevu'ot*
- *'Eduyyot*
- *'Avodah Zarah*
- *'Avot*
- *Horayot*

Kodoshim ("Sacred Things"):
- *Zevaḥim*
- *Menaḥot*
- *Ḥullin*
- *Bekhorot*
- *'Arakhin*
- *Temurah*
- *Keritot*
- *Me'ilah*
- *Tamid*
- *Middot*
- *Kinnim*

Teharot ("Purifications"):
- *Kelim*
- *'Ohalot*
- *Nega'im*
- *Parah*
- *Teharot*
- *Mikva'ot*
- *Niddah*
- *Makhshirin*
- *Zavim*
- *Tevul Yom*
- *Yadayim*
- *'Uktzin*

[YAAKOV ELMAN]

Midrash and Jewish Exegesis

It is often remarked that what is Jewish about the Bible is not the Bible itself, not even the Heb text of the Bible, but the Jewish *interpretation* of the Bible. And of all the types of Jewish biblical interpretation, none have been identified so closely with the Jewish Bible as midrash. Indeed, the two have been so closely identified that for some, midrash has become a virtual trope for Judaism, a figure for all that is distinctive and different about the Jews, their religion, and culture.

Midrash is the specific name for the activity of biblical interpretation as practiced by the Rabbis of the land of Israel in the first five centuries of the common era. The Heb word derives from the root, *d-r-sh,* which literally means "to inquire" or "to search after." In the earlier books of the Bible, the root is used to refer to the act of seeking out God's will (e.g., Gen. 25.22; Exod. 18.15), particularly through consulting a figure like Moses or a prophet or another type of oracular authority. By the end of the biblical period, the locus for that search appears to have settled on the text of the Torah where, it was now believed, God's will for the present moment was to be found. Thus the scribe Ezra, we are told in the book by his name, "had dedicated himself to study the Teaching *(torah)* of the LORD so as to observe it" (Ezra 7.10). The Heb word for "study" used in the v., *lidrosh,* has the same root as midrash. By late antiquity, midrash had come to designate Bible study in general. The Rabbis called their academy a *bet midrash,* literally "a house of study," and from such usage, midrash came to be the term the Rabbis themselves employed to designate the way they studied Scripture and interpreted its meaning.

In its primary sense, then, midrash refers to an *activity,* a mode of study. Somewhat confusingly, the same word is also applied to the products of that activity, namely, individual interpretations—a specific midrash of a v. or word, for example. These midrashic interpretations originally circulated and were transmitted orally, both in rabbinic schools and through synagogue sermons. Around the 3rd or 4th c. CE, the oral traditions of the Rabbis began to be collected in literary anthologies, and these collections also came to be known as midrashim, as in *Midrash Rabbah,* the folio-sized collection of homiletical midrashim on the Torah which was first published in Constantinople in 1512. For the past hundred years, however, some scholars have appropriated the word "midrash" as a collective term to describe ancient biblical interpretation in general. For example, the French scholar Renee Bloch used the term "midrash" to describe any ancient "meditation on the sacred texts," an activity that could be found equally in the Aram. translations of the Bible, in many of the books of the Apocrypha and Pseudepigrapha, and in the New Testament, as well as in later rabbinic texts. And still more recently, the term has passed into popular circulation as a name for all "creative" interpretations of the Bible that seek to move beyond the historical, "original" sense of the biblical text. In this usage, the word "midrash" stands for everything from novelistic retellings of biblical episodes to postmodernist essayistic explorations of Gen. and Exod., New Age homilies, and contemporary poems that re-imagine the biblical text.

Language, of course, follows usage, not the strictures of scholars. Even if the latter (including myself) would prefer to restrict the use of the word "midrash" to the ancient biblical interpretations of the Rabbis—who, if they did not invent the term, nonetheless were the first ones to use it extensively—scholars do not control the fates of words. On the other hand, while contemporary efforts at "neo-midrash" are not direct descendants of the classical midrashic tradition of the Rabbis, it is also not entirely inappropriate to call these latter-day compositions living examples of the midrashic "spirit," motivated by some of the same desires that inspired the Rabbis to interpret the Bible. Yet precisely how to define that "spirit" is not an easy task. Perhaps the closest thing to a definition might be the classical midrashic statement attributed to the early sage Akiva (d. ca. 135 CE), a comment on Deut. 32.47, "[This law] is no empty thing for you *(lo' davar reik mekem).*" Exploiting the fact that the preposition *mekem* literally means "from," not "for," you, Akiva explained: "If it seems empty, it is *from* you—on account of your own failure—for you do not know how to study *(lidrosh)* its meaning properly" (*Gen. Rab.* 1:14). The imperative facing every Bible interpreter is, to paraphrase E. M. Forster, to *connect,* to find the text's significance for the present moment, to make it speak to us now. Nothing in the Bible is without such significance. If the interpreter can't find it, the fault is his or her own, not the Bible's. Akiva's elaboration might be called the credo of Jewish biblical interpretation.

In fact, the precise relation of midrash to other types of Jewish biblical interpretation and to Jewish tradition at large involves a truly complex set of questions, and these become even more complicated if the relationship of midrash is considered in connection with the competing traditions of Christian and Islamic interpretation. Ultimately, these questions boil down to some of the most fundamental issues that involve the study of biblical interpretation in general, and Jewish interpretation in particular. What does it mean to call a type of interpretation like midrash "Jewish"? Is there a distinctively or uniquely "Jewish" way of reading the Bible? Is a Jewish reading of the Bible distinguished merely by its content and by the theological beliefs it brings to its reading, or is there something intrinsically different about the very procedures of interpretation that Jews employ as opposed to those of, say, Christian readers of the Bible?

Within the context of this *Jewish Study Bible,* it would seem especially opportune to consider these questions even if there are no definitive answers to them. We may begin with a historical sketch of midrash's development. The origins of midrash lie in biblical tradition itself where many biblical passages self-consciously look back upon earlier passages and, in one way or another, reinterpret their meaning. The book of Chron., for example, consciously recasts the history of the earlier books of Sam. and Kings, adding some episodes and omitting others, and generally spinning the earlier narrative in the course of retelling it in a politically tendentious direction amenable to its author. Elsewhere, many "later" vv. in the Bible recycle allusions and imagery from "earlier" biblical texts in order to apply them to new contexts and situations. The laws of marital divorce become the imagery to describe God's punishment of the people of Israel (cf. e.g., Deut. 24.1–4 and Jer. 3.1); the exodus from Egypt (Exod. chs 1–15), the paradigm for all future redemptions (see, e.g., Isa. 43.16–20; 51.9–11; Ezek. ch 20).

In a very few cases it is possible even to see how certain textual "problems" are solved within the Bible itself. For example, in the year 605 BCE, some twenty years before the destruction of the First Temple and the exile of the Judeans to Babylonia, the prophet Jeremiah prophesied that Judea "shall be a desolate ruin, and those nations shall serve the king of Babylon seventy years" (Jer. 25.11). In a second prophecy, somewhat later, he went on to prophesy that "when Babylon's seventy years are over, I will fulfill to you My promise of favor—to bring you back to this place" (29.10). And some seventy years later, in 538 BCE, when the Judean exiles did indeed return to Judea from Babylonia, they must doubtless have believed that Jeremiah's prophecy had been fulfilled. Some 370 years later, however, around the year 165 BCE, in despair over the Hellenistic persecution of their religious practices, Jews had greater difficulty believing in the fulfillment of Jeremiah's promise of redemption even if they were physically living in the land of Israel. The author of the book of Dan., in order to bolster faith in the apocalypse he believed was imminent, reinterpreted Jeremiah's earlier prophecy so that seventy years became seventy "weeks" of years—490 years, in other words—a date that brought the ancient prophecy close enough to his own time so as to convince his audience of its truth. Or to give a second example of a different type of "interpretation," here is a case where two earlier vv. seemed to a later biblical author to contradict each other: Exod. 12.8 stipulates emphatically that the Passover sacrifice must be roasted *(tzli ʾesh).* Speaking about the same sacrifice, however, Deut. 16.7 says, "You shall cook *(uvishalta)* it"—a verb implying that the meat should be boiled (as in a stew). 2 Chron. 35.13, obviously troubled by the discrepancy between the two Torah vv., "solved" the textual problem (if not the culinary one) by maintaining both locutions: The Jews "cooked the paschal sacrifice in fire" *(vayvashlu hapesaḥ baʾesh)*—"they boiled the paschal sacrifice in fire" (which probably means that they braised it).

The scholar Michael Fishbane, who has exhaustively studied these and similar cases in the Bible, has described them as part of a larger phenomenon which he calls inner-biblical exegesis (see "Inner-biblical Interpretation," pp. 1835–41). Although most of these examples are not, strictly speaking, exegeses (insofar as they do not explain or clarify anything about the earlier v.), they nonetheless exhibit certain tendencies—inner dynamics, as it were—that are, at the least, exegetical reflexes. These include the tendencies (as we have seen) to harmonize conflicting or discordant vv.; to reemploy and reapply biblical paradigms and imagery to new cases; to reinvest "old" historical references with "new" historical contexts; and to integrate nonhistorical portions of the Bible within the larger context of biblical history (e.g., by giving individual psalms historical superscriptions that "identify" the precise biblical episode during which David composed the psalm; e.g., Pss. 18 and 34).

Once the Bible was closed, Fishbane argues, these inner-biblical tendencies emerged as full-fledged, consciously applied interpretive techniques (demonstrating, if nothing else, the deep continuity of early postbiblical interpretation with the preceding tradition). Our earliest genuine commentaries on the Bible are the *pesharim,* or apocalyptic commentaries, found among the Dead Sea Scrolls at Qumran, and the allegorical treatises on the Bible written by Philo of Alexandria. The vast amount of early postbiblical interpretation is found, however, not in formal commentaries but in nonexegetical works that span the entire range of ancient postbiblical Jewish literature. These include the Aram. Targumim (or translations); the various works of the Apocrypha and Pseudepigrapha which claim to "fill in" missing episodes or accounts from the Bible; and the various types of compositions sometimes called "the Re-Written Bible," works like the *Genesis Apocryphon,* the book of *Jub.*, and Pseudo-Philo's *L.A.B.* These last works claim merely to "retell" the biblical narrative. They do so, however, by adding in, without comment, numerous details and events nowhere to be found in the Bible itself that are really implied interpretations, that is, solutions to "problems" ancient readers may have had with the biblical text.

Such is the context within which rabbinic midrash emerged in Roman Palestine as one type of Jewish exegesis among many others in the first centuries of the common era. We know very little about the inner history of midrash or about its practice, presumably in schools, academies, and synagogues. The one thing we do know is that, with a few scattered exceptions, the Rabbis did not explicitly theorize about their mode of interpretation or formally legislate its procedures. As a result, nearly everything we can say about midrash must be adduced from the texts themselves.

Generally speaking, the underlying interpretive assumptions that the Rabbis brought to midrash were not different from those of their nonrabbinic contemporaries, Jewish or Gentile. As scholars have shown repeatedly over the last century, the Rabbis shared hermeneutical techniques and procedures with their Greco-Roman neighbors as well as with the larger and more ancient Near Eastern culture into which ancient Judaism was born. Midrash dealing with halakhah, or legal matters, uses many of the same hermeneutical principles used by Greek and Roman jurists, and the Rabbis seem to have borrowed at least the names for some of those principles from their pagan contemporaries. In the realm of aggadah—narrative and lore—midrash applied to the Bible techniques known to be used in ancient literary and dream interpretation. Such, for example, seems to be the origin of *gematria,* perhaps the most "notorious" type of hermeneutical technique in midrash wherein the numerical sum of a word's letters is used to decode its meaning. A good example of this type of technique is an interpretation attributed to R. Levi for the word *ʾekhah* ("alas"), the first word in the book of Lam., a book that the Rabbis read not only as a lament but also as a prophecy of the destruction of the Temple. The numerical sum of the word's four letters (*alef* = 1; *yod* = 10; *kaf* = 20; *heh* = 5) is 36, and this number, according to R. Levi, points to the 36 transgressions punishable by excommunication that the Jews committed, thereby bringing upon themselves the destruction of the Temple. The unusual word *ʾekhah,* with its archaic elongated form (rather than the shorter, more common *ʾekh*) was understood, in other words, to be the hermeneutical key to the meaning of the entire scroll of Lamentations—the reason the Jews were forced to lament their fate. Along the same lines, in a related but different form of interpretation—*notarikon* (lit. "stenographic interpretation"), or interpretation by acrostics—ben Azzai used the same word's four letters as a key to showing that the Jews were not punished until they had denied the One *(alef)* God; transgressed all Ten *(yod)* Commandments; spurned circumcision (which was given after twenty *[kaf]* generations), and—on top of everything else!—rejected all the commandments in the Five *(heh)* Books of Moses. Both types of hermeneutical principles are attested in ancient handbooks for dream-interpreters.

Beyond these particular techniques, however, nearly all ancient readers of the Bible also shared four basic beliefs about the nature of Scripture, as James Kugel has cogently argued. First, they believed that the Bible was essentially a cryptic document—that its true meaning was not to be found on the surface but had to be discovered within the text, and that this discovery required special skills and wisdom. (In this, ancient readers of the Bible would have found themselves in agreement with ancient philosophers for whom it was no less axiomatic that all truth is obscure, never obvious or manifest to all; otherwise, anybody could be a philosopher or, for that matter, a scriptural exegete!) Second, the Bible was believed to be a perfect document, without contradiction, inconsistency, or superfluity. What might seem to be a contradiction or to be superfluous, even a word or phrase, was really an occasion—for some, a tip-off—for interpretation. Third, the Bible is always relevant—that is to say, its true meaning is always one that has import for the present moment. Nothing in the Bible—neither genealogies nor prophecies—is in Scripture for purely historical reasons, preserved for its antiquarian interest alone. Fourth, the Bible was believed to be of divine origin. As Kugel notes, however, this last feature was probably the least simple, since the Bible's divinity was not seen necessarily to preclude Moses' authorship. Furthermore, attributing divinity to the Bible means little if one does not define the nature of that divinity more closely. The God whom the Rabbis believed authored the Bible was hardly the same author as the God of an early Christian reader of the Bible like Origen.

Still, while the Rabbis shared these assumptions about the Bible with other ancient readers, Jews and Christians alike, they also brought some distinctive convictions of their own to their study. First and foremost, the

Rabbis believed that the Bible—or what they called the Written Torah—was only one of two revelations God had given to the children of Israel at Mt. Sinai. Alongside the Written Torah, they believed, God had also revealed to the Israelites an Oral Torah which, as its name indicates, was delivered and transmitted orally. Precisely how to define the Oral Torah is one of the great debates among Jewish scholars. For our present purposes we may say that it comprises everything that the Rabbis believed was "Judaism" that is not *explicitly* written in the Torah; admittedly, this is a vast and heterogeneous body of material that encompasses everything from the many laws not spelled out in the Bible to the Rabbis' own beliefs and theology as well as all their folk wisdom and lore. Midrash itself is part of the Oral Torah, but the most important fact for understanding the role of the Oral Torah *in* midrash is that, for the Rabbis, these two Torahs—the Written and the Oral—were understood to be complementary. The "relevance" of the Written Torah for the Rabbis lay, we may say, in its application as Oral Torah; the two were not only in absolute agreement but deeply intertwined and mutually embedded. As a result, a great part of the Rabbis' midrashic efforts are devoted either to finding the roots of the Oral Torah in the Written Torah, or to elucidating the hidden truths of the Written Torah so as to make it yield the insights of what they already knew to be Oral Torah.

Nowhere is this more evident than in midrash halakhah, or legal exegesis. One passage will suffice to illustrate the point—a series of interpretations connected with the laws of kashrut, the dietary laws, and specifically the regulations pertaining to the separation of meat and milk products. Few laws are more closely associated with classical Judaism. Yet the source of these laws is a single injunction in the entire Bible, "You shall not boil a kid in its mother's milk" (Exod. 23.19) which, as we know today, was originally a cultic regulation, not a dietary rule. Curiously, that injunction also happens to be repeated verbatim twice more in the Bible (Exod. 34.26; Deut. 14.21), raising the additional problem of the vv.' superfluity: Why say the same thing three times? Not surprisingly, the Rabbis exploited the multiple appearances of the injunction in order to expand the range of the single law. In the *Mek.* (*Kaspa* 5, Lauterbach III, 187–190), the earliest collection of midrashim on the book of Exod., nine interpretations are offered to explain why the v. is repeated, and seven more simply to explain the full significance of the Exod. v. alone. Here is a small sampling of the interpretations:

> R. Jonathan says: Why is this law stated in three places? Once to apply to domestic animals, once to apply to the beast of chase, and once to apply to fowl.
>
> Abba Ḥanin said in the name of R. Eliezer: Why is this law stated in three places? Once to apply to large cattle, once to apply to goats, and once to apply to sheep....
>
> R. Simon ben Yoḥai says: Why is this law stated in three places? One is a prohibition against eating it, one is a prohibition against deriving any benefit from it, and one is a prohibition against the mere cooking of it ...
>
> R. Yosi the Galilean: Scripture says, "You shall not eat anything that dies a natural death" (Deut. 14.21), and in the same passage, it is said, "You shall not boil a kid in its mother's milk." [From this it follows that] the flesh of any animal which is forbidden to be eaten if the animal dies a natural death [and is not ritually slaughtered according to the laws of kashrut] is also forbidden to be cooked with milk. Now one might think that fowl, since it becomes forbidden to eat if it dies a natural death, should also be forbidden to be cooked with milk. Scripture, however, stipulates, "in its mother's milk." This excludes fowl because it has no mother's milk. And the unclean animal [an animal like pig that Scripture forbids one to eat in any case] is also excluded

from the prohibition [of cooking it with milk] because it is forbidden to be eaten whether it is ritually slaughtered properly or whether it dies a natural death.

The first two opinions in the passage use "the extra vv."—the multiple occurrences of the v.—to extend its application from a goat, the actual subject of the v., to other species of animals. R. Jonathan and Abba Ḥanin both adopt the same interpretive strategy, but they divide the animal kingdom in different cuts, as it were. The third opinion, of Rabbi Simon ben Yoḥai, uses the extra vv. to extend the prohibition from cooking milk and meat together (which is itself already an interpretation, since the biblical v. prohibits only cooking a kid in its mother's milk) to eating it and even deriving benefit from it (by, e.g., selling meat and milk cooked together); this interpretation takes the biblical v. even closer to the complete dietary regulation in its full rabbinic form.

Now clearly, these opinions are being used to justify and to legitimate existing practices, which must have developed out of their own logic. The interpretations were not invented to derive the practices anew or for the first time. There is simply no way that any interpreter could have looked at the three identical vv. and extrapolated from them the different prohibitions that, say, R. Simon bar Yoḥai proposes. With the fourth and final interpretation of R. Yosi the Galilean, however, the interpretations take a very different turn. The very form and style of Yosi's interpretation is of a very different nature than the first three—not only more expansive but also more academic in tone. The interpretation is based on the fact that Deut. 14.21 contains not only the prohibition against boiling a kid in its mother's milk but also the additional prohibition against eating an animal that has died a natural death and not been ritually slaughtered. From the fact that the two prohibitions are stated in the same v., R. Yosi initially hypothesizes that all animals that fall under one prohibition should fall under the other one as well. This would seem to be a completely unexceptionable assumption, but R. Yosi himself immediately argues against it—and here the real gist of his interpretation emerges. For the v. prohibiting boiling a kid in milk explicitly states that the milk must be "its mother's," thereby excluding fowl from the prohibition since, as R. Yosi explains, they do not give milk. Similarly, he continues, an unclean animal—that is, an animal like pig that cannot be eaten under any circumstances—also does not fall under the prohibition, which is to say, it *could* be boiled in its mother's milk as long as one didn't eat it!

The structure of argument in this interpretation is very different from that in the first three. Essentially, R. Yosi builds upon the contiguity of the two prohibitions in the same v. to draw a general principle, and then uses that generalization to highlight a specific detail in the same v. ("its mother's milk") to prove an exception to the generalization. This technique (in Heb known as *kelal uferat,* a general rule followed by a particular) is one of the legal principles that the Rabbis share in common with ancient jurists in general. Yet even more striking about Yosi's interpretation, which *excludes* fowl from the prohibition, is the fact that it conflicts with that of R. Jonathan, who *did* include fowl under the prohibition. Exactly what is at stake in this disagreement is intriguing but unclear—whether their dispute really extends to practice (for some contemporary Jewish readers, it would be wonderful news to learn that a great sage like R. Yosi ate chicken with dairy products!), or whether it is a purely theoretical, academic argument. The more relevant observation to make is that the editor of the midrashic collection himself makes no note of the disagreement. He records the two interpretations along with the others as though there were absolutely no significant difference between them, no disagreement, no inconsistency.

This feature is common to the editing of many midrashic collections, but nowhere is it more the case than in midrash aggadah, that is, interpretations dealing with legend and lore, the vast terrain of nonlegal and homiletical material which effectively includes everything in rabbinic tradition from narrative to theology. In theory, midrash aggadah does not differ substantively or methodologically from midrash halakhah, and most midrashic collections mix halakhah and aggadah indiscriminately. As rabbinic literature developed, however, midrash became increasingly identified with aggadah, and it is for its aggadic interpretations that midrash has become most famous (or infamous, depending on your perspective) for its creative, playful, and multiple interpretations.

As a typical example of such multiple interpretations, consider the following passage. Gen. 25.19–36.42 is largely devoted to the story of Jacob and Esau and their rivalry from the time of their conception to their mature middle age. This rivalry began *in utero.* Rebekah, like all the matriarchs, cannot initially conceive, but once she does become pregnant with the two boys, Scripture tells us, *vayitrotzetzu habanim bekirbah,* "the children struggled in her womb" (Gen. 25.22). On this phrase, *Gen. Rab.,* the classical midrash on Gen., offers the following four interpretations:

> R. Yoḥanan and R. Shimon ben Lakhish [both offered opinions]. R. Yoḥanan said: This one ran *(ratz)* to kill the other, and the other ran *(ratz)* to kill the first one. [Namely, R. Yoḥanan associates the word *vayitrotzetzu* with the word for "run" *(ratz).*]
>
> R. Shimon ben Lakhish said: This one permitted [what was forbidden] by command *(hitir tzivuyav)* to the other, and the other one permitted [what was forbidden] by command to the first [meaning, in other words, that from the beginning each one's laws and practices seem to have been diametrically opposed, in conflict with each other. The interpretation puns *vayitrozetzu* and *hitir tzivuyav;* say the two words quickly, and they'll begin to sound alike.]
>
> R. Berechyah said in the name of R. Levi: Lest you think that it was only after they left the womb that the one attacked the other, [this v. teaches us] that even while they were in the womb [Esau] raised his fist *(zeirteih)* against [Jacob]. This is what is written, "The wicked are defiant *(zoru)* from the womb" (Ps. 58.4) [playing on the word *zoru* and the Aram. word for fist. This interpretation seems to emphasize the word *bekirbah,* "in her womb" as the basis for its interpretation.]
>
> *"Vayitrotzetzu habanim bekirbah"* ("the children struggled in her womb") means that they tried to run out of her womb. When Rebekah passed by a pagan temple, Esau would kick her to let him leave; this is what is written, "The wicked are defiant *(zoru)* from the womb" (Ps. 58.4) [playing on the word *zoru* and the second half of the term *ʿavodah zarah,* literally "strange worship," i.e., idolatry]. And when Rebekah passed by a synagogue and a study-hall *(bet midrash),* Jacob would kick her to let him out, this is what is written, "Before I created you in the womb, I knew you *(yedatikha)*" (Jer. 1.5) [probably reading the last phrase as *yidatikha,* "I caused you to know"] (*Gen. Rab.,* ed. J. Theodor and H. Albeck, 63:6, pp. 682–83).

Each of these four interpretations offers a slightly different though equally typical midrashic way of reading the word *vayitrotzetzu:* Some break it up into smaller words like *ratz* ("run"), or pun it with a similarly sounding phrase like *hitir tzivuyav* ("permitted the commands"), or connect the Gen. base-verse with another v. in Scripture (e.g., Ps. 58.4) which, through more punning interpretations, is enlisted to gloss the meaning of the base-verse. In the very last interpretation of Jer. 1.5, the anonymous Rabbi exploits the fact that the Heb text of the Bible in a Torah scroll records only consonantal letters, and no vowels—a fact that, somewhat ironically, now allows the midrashic reader to change the vowels of certain biblical words and thus their meaning, as here from the active form, *yedatikha* ("I knew") to the causative *yidatikha* ("I caused you to know").

What leads the Rabbis to base so many of their interpretations on phonetic puns, on associations between the sound of a word like *vayitrotzetzu* and other similarly sounding words and phrases? In part, this strongly aural dimension of midrash may derive from the Bible's own use of oral puns and soundplay—a habit facilitated by the very nature of spoken Heb—but it also probably reflects the way the Bible was learned by the Rabbis. Most likely, Jews in the land of Israel during the rabbinic period did not study the Bible by reading it directly in scrolls, which were doubtless scarce and, because of their size, rather unwieldy; rather, they learned Scripture from hearing it read aloud during the synagogue service or in classes in the academy. From such repeated auditory experiences, one assumes the Rabbis memorized the scriptural text and carried it around in their heads as a *heard* text. As we now know, a text learned this way is "known" differently than one learned from having read it on a page (or scroll). For one thing, the page itself does not figure as a primary unit in one's memory of the text. Another thing is that one "hears" the text rather than "sees" it (even in the mind's eye), and as a consequence, one is more likely to associate like-sounding words or phrases or vv. (the latter probably having been the main units of memorization) rather than those connected by visual elements (either physical proximity in the written text or on a page, or matters of orthography). And while it may seem paradoxical, it is in fact perfectly explicable why the Rabbis tend to atomize vv. or words into their constituent sounds, *and* simultaneously to associate otherwise unrelated vv. or phrases on the basis of shared phonetic elements; in both cases, they are responding to the phonetic/aural element of the text. This is not to say that the Rabbis did not know the Bible as a written text; it was, in fact, the only text normatively written down in rabbinic culture. It was, however, also the only text in rabbinic culture to be regularly read aloud from the written scroll. Indeed, the Bible's most common name in rabbinic Heb is *miqra'*, "that which is read aloud."

Midrash, then, is very much an exegesis of the *heard* text. This does not, of course, explain everything in midrash. For while they are willing to take the boldest liberties in interpreting Scripture, the Rabbis are also the closest "readers" of Scripture imaginable, with an almost preternatural sensitivity to the least "bump" in the scriptural text—an unnecessary repetition or superfluity, any kind of syntactical or lexical peculiarity, a mere hint at something unseemly in the way of behavior, or the smallest possibility of an inconsistency between vv. or even between a v. and what the Rabbis believed must be the case.

Since we have been considering Jacob and Esau, let us look at an interpretation of another v. from their narrative, from the story in Gen. ch 27 of Jacob's deception of Isaac, where he fools his aged blind father into giving him the blessing intended for Esau, the first-born son. Jacob's wiliness (of which this episode was not the first case) may or may not have been in itself a cause for embarrassment to the Rabbis, but Gen. 27.19 posed a very concrete problem for them. In response to Isaac's question, "Which of my sons are you?" Jacob tells his father an outright lie, "I am Esau, your first-born." How does the midrash deal with this problem?

The answer is quite simple: By re-reading the v. so that it no longer says, "I am Esau, your first-born" but "I am [that is, Jacob]; Esau is your first-born" (*Tanḥ.,* ed. S. Buber, Genesis, p. 131). Now this interpretation may seem overly clever, especially as an attempt to whitewash Jacob's reputation, but in fact the interpretation exploits a genuine "problem" in the v. For why does Jacob need to tell his father that Esau is his first-born son? As an answer to Isaac's question, the detail is irrelevant; and as a piece of familial information, it is obviously something Isaac knows. Further, the Heb word that Jacob uses in the v. to identify himself, *ʾanokhi,* "I," is itself noteworthy as a somewhat archaic locution that every Rabbi would have instantly recognized as the opening word of the Decalogue—indeed, as the word with which God introduces Himself: "I am/*ʾanokhi* the LORD your God" (Exod. 20.2). (In fact, another, somewhat more expansive version of this midrash states that Jacob said, "I am he who will receive the Decalogue, but Esau is your first-born" [*Gen. Rab.* 65:18, p. 730].) Faced with all these textual "facts," along with the ethical problem raised by Jacob's outright lie, the midrashic reading might appear almost inevitable.

Almost, but not quite. Did the Rabbis believe that this was the "real" meaning of the v., or what Jacob actually meant to say? This question takes us to the very heart of midrash and its hermeneutics. Some scholars have suggested that midrashim like this are midrashic "jokes," the humor lying in the self-conscious dissonance between what the Rabbis know the Bible is saying, and what they wish it to say. This is undoubtedly true: What midrash continually demonstrates is the possibility that Scripture may mean something other than what it says. But there is also a way in which the playfulness of midrash may be interpreted as the Rabbis' sense of the playfulness of Scripture itself. After all, could God have ever really allowed Jacob to mislead Isaac and let the blessing be given to the wrong son? Could Isaac, *our* ancestor, have been so easily misled? Must he not have known to whom he was giving the blessing? Were not Isaac and Jacob merely *pretending* to deceive and to be deceived? Isn't this pretence at deception the subtext of the story in which Isaac and Jacob act out their roles of deceiver and deceived so that providential history, the history of Israel and of the Jews, can take place despite history?

The Rabbis, after all, fully knew who Jacob and Esau *really* were—not just biblical figures, not merely their ancestors. They were also the progenitors of Israel and Rome—the latter was almost as ancient an identification as the former—and, in a certain sense, they *were* Judaism and Rome. "The voice is the voice of Jacob, yet the hands are the hands of Esau," Isaac announces as the disguised Jacob approaches (Gen. 27.22). On which the midrash comments: "Jacob attains domination through his voice [i.e., the power of language], and Esau through [the power of] his hands." R. Yehuda bar Ilai is said to have added that R. Judah the Prince interpreted the latter v. in even more contemporary terms: "The voice of Jacob cries out for what the hands of Esau have done to him" (*Gen. Rab.* 65:21, pp. 733–34, 740). The Rabbis knew that the story of Jacob and Esau and their rivalry was not simply biblical history. It was also their own history, the contemporary reality in which they had to struggle daily merely to survive.

With this understanding of the hermeneutical background behind midrash, let us return to the question with which we began this essay: What is Jewish about midrash? It would be tempting to say that interpretations like the preceding one, identifying Jacob with Judaism and Esau with Rome, point to the inherently Jewish nature of midrash. This is certainly true of the content of the interpretation, but it is worth recalling that ancient and medieval Christian students of the Bible used the same hermeneutical principle to identify Jacob with the church and Esau with Judaism. The same is true by and large of the ancient Jewish and Christian interpretations of the Song of Songs; both traditions interpret the poem as a love song between God and His chosen nation—the major difference being that in one case the beloved nation is Israel, in the other Christianity (or the church). Is the difference between Jewish and Christian interpretation then merely one of theological preferences?

Some scholars have posited the differences between the two interpretive traditions as being that between midrash and allegory. In fact, over the past twenty years, as they have awakened to the existence of midrash, literary theorists in particular have sought to see in rabbinic hermeneutics an alternative mode of interpretation to allegory. Where the latter is said to posit the existence of a reference or meaning "behind" the text as a kind of static metaphysical presence, midrash has been celebrated for seeing meaning "in front" of the text, in the intertextual play between vv., in the deferral of a single absolute meaning in favor of a multiplicity of provisional and possible meanings, and not least of all, for its far more open complicity between the interpreter and the act of interpretation as a subjective exercise whose interest lies less in the outcome of interpretation than in the process itself. Some scholars have even identified midrash with a kind of uniquely Jewish "ontology," or at least a mode of thinking whose difference from the so-called Greco-Christian logocentric tradition, usually identified with allegory, has been seen as closer to that of poststructuralism.

The difficulty with this comparison is not only that its view of midrash is overly romanticized but that it fails to take into account the fact that midrash is itself a form of allegory—not philosophical allegory, to be sure, but nonetheless a form of interpretation that seeks to show how the text means something other than what it says. In this, midrash is not different from other types of ancient interpretation. There is, in fact, much in early Christian interpretation from the New Testament itself through Augustine and the Antiochene fathers that is midrash-like. The main hermeneutical difference between the two is that Christian exegesis is far more systematic. Because of its greater intimacy with classical philosophical culture, Christian interpretation is heavily theorized and more programmatic (and to that extent, more obviously tendentious than rabbinic interpretation). It is also driven, as it were, by a different set of anxieties. The main anxiety for Christian interpreters is the knowledge that the New Testament is indeed a belated document, a late-comer, as it were, and hence the main challenge faced by Christian exegetes is to prove that the New Testament is in fact the key to understanding the Old Testament, and that the latter cannot properly be understood without the full knowledge afforded by the New Testament. In contrast, the anxiety driving the Rabbis is the worry that the Bible itself foresees their rejection and obsolescence; hence the constant challenge they face is to find through midrash a way for God to address them anew, to prove through the study of Scripture that they remain His chosen people, and that their interpretation, as embodied in the Oral Torah, is in fact the true and legitimate interpretation of the Bible's meaning.

The other feature that truly distinguishes rabbinic midrash is its singular literary form, the modes of discourse in which its hermeneutics are articulated. These literary forms show the close connection between rabbinic interpretation of the Bible and synagogue homilies. The most characteristic of all these forms is the proem or *petiḥta,* a form that may have served (as Joseph Heinemann has suggested) as a kind of mini-sermon that introduced the initial v. of the weekly Shabbat Torah reading. Instead of beginning with that v., however, the proem opens with another v. taken from a completely different part of Tanakh; this v. is typically called the "remote" v. because it is, for all practical purposes, unrelated to the weekly Torah reading and its opening v. It is this v. that the proem actually "interprets," building in the process a kind of exegetical bridge that eventually culminates in its true subject, the opening v. of the weekly reading.

As a brief example of the form, consider the following *petiḥta* for the weekly Torah reading that begins with Lev. 24.2, "Command the Israelite people to bring you clear oil of beaten olives for lighting, so as to maintain lights regularly."

> Bar Kapparah (d. 230 CE) recited a *petiḥta:* "It is You who light my lamp; the LORD, my God, lights up my darkness" (Ps. 18.29).

> The Holy One, blessed be He, said to man: Your lamp is in my hand, as it is said, "The lifebreath of man is the lamp of the LORD" (Prov. 20.27). And my lamp is in yours: [this is the meaning of the phrase] "so as to maintain lights regularly" (Lev. 24.2). To which the Holy One, blessed be He, added: If you light my lamp, I will light yours. That is the meaning of "Command the Israelite people ... " (Lev. 24.2).

Perhaps the most remarkable thing about this particular *petiḥta* is the speech the author of the proem puts into God's mouth—a speech that is actually an interpretation of Ps. 18.29; God Himself confirms, as it were, the meaning of the v. in the psalm, but it is also through God's "interpretation" that the preacher or author of this sermon speaks to his audience. While the interpretation itself, as well as that of Prov. 20.27, are independent exegeses, the proem joins them in order to make its own point about Lev. 24.2. Contrary to how it looks in Scripture, this v. is not simply a commandment from God to the Israelites to light a special candelabrum in the sanctuary. Rather, it is testimony to the reciprocity of the deeds of God and man: If Israel lights God's lamp in the sanctuary, then He will light man's lamp, namely, his soul. Or to put the same point in more general terms, human life is God's response to human observance of the commandments!

The *petiḥta* epitomizes the characteristic type of midrashic literary form that exists precisely in the gray area between pure commentary, on the one side, and an original, creative composition. Indeed, it is precisely in this gray area between the two separate realms of commentary and literature that midrash takes seed and grows, never crossing over entirely into either realm, flourishing in the space precisely in-between. The *petiḥta* is also only one among several literary forms of this kind that come into existence in midrash as the discourse of its exegesis. These relatively short literary units—which include the parable, the extrabiblical legend, pronouncement and fulfillment stories (in which interpreted biblical vv. serve as punchlines or prophetic realizations of unusual narratives), and various types of lists and testimony forms—are the real literary units of rabbinic midrash.

Unlike their contemporaries, the Rabbis did not write treatises on the Bible and its meaning (as did Philo, e.g.), nor did they initially compose tracts in which they sought to "rewrite" the Bible (although such works do come into existence in the early post-rabbinic period). It is not even clear that they wrote commentaries as did the members of the apocalyptic community at Qumran. We know very little about the composition or process of editing of the various midrashic collections, but from their contents and overall skeletal style, it would seem that they were compiled to serve as source-books for "professionals"—that is, rabbinic preachers and teachers who used them to prepare sermons and lessons. There is little indication that they were originally meant to serve as commentaries to be studied alongside the Bible nor were they, as were a number of early Christian exegetical texts, transcripts of actual sermons or lessons in Scripture. As anthologies of interpretations, with multiple interpretations recorded side-by-side with no comments and few attempts to navigate between them, these midrashic collections embody the delight of midrash in always yet *another* additional interpretation. Yet unlike their postmodern descendants, in which polysemy signifies an indeterminacy that reflects the fundamental instability of meaning, multiple interpretation as found in midrash is actually a sign of its stability, the guarantee of a belief in Scripture as an inexhaustible fount of meaningfulness.

That the Rabbis preferred this type of anthological composition to systematic treatises or formal commentaries is in itself a revealing fact about the way they saw biblical interpretation. For them, Bible study was an ad hoc activity directed essentially to an audience

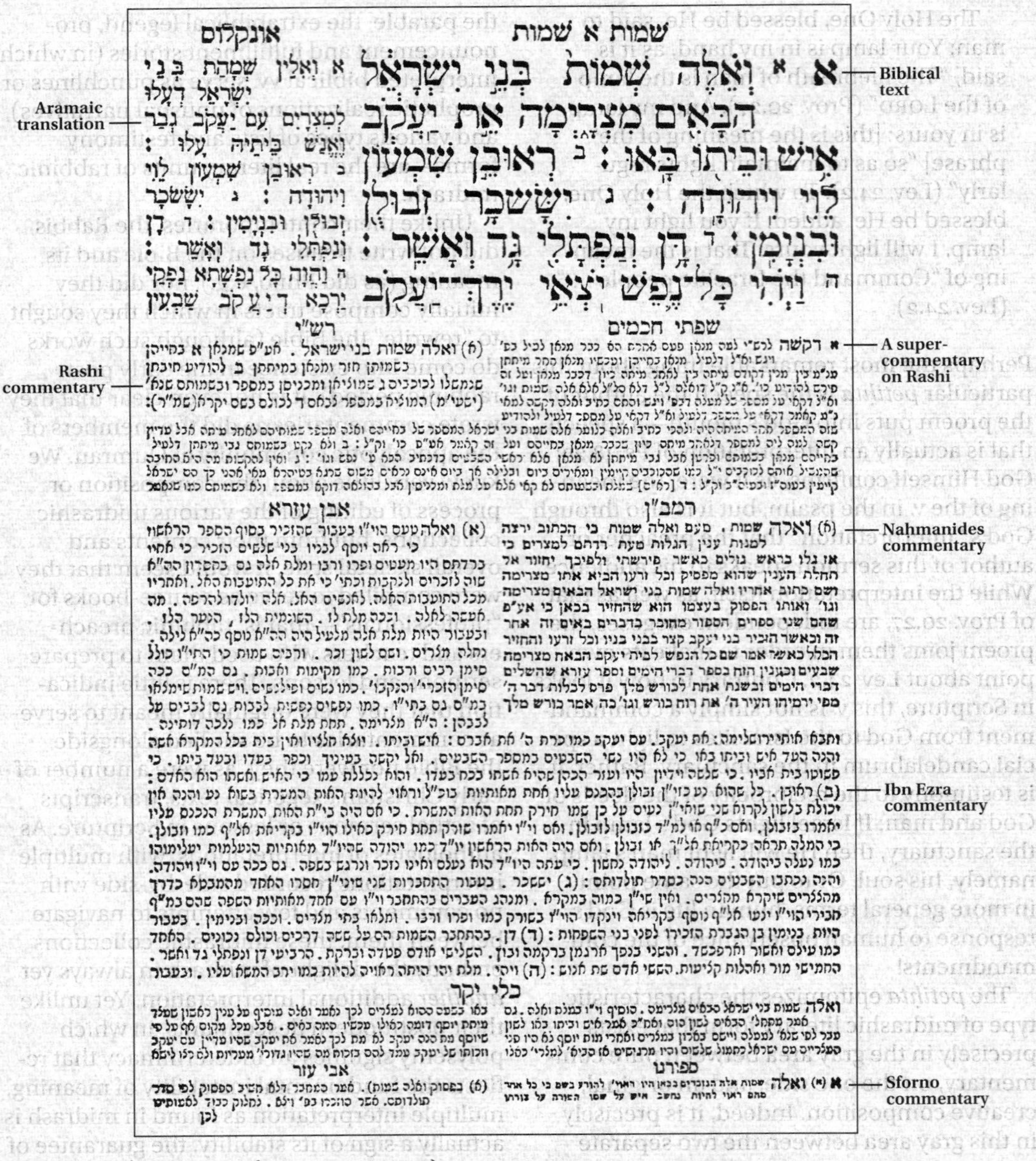

A *Miqra'ot Gedolot* (RABBINIC BIBLE), VILNIUS 1907, FROM THE BEGINNING OF EXODUS 1
The page includes the biblical text, the standard Aramaic translation *(Targum Onkelos)*, Rashi, a super-commentary on Rashi, Naḥmanides, Ibn Ezra, Sforno, and two other commentaries.

hungry for a response to its immediate needs and to the desire to have Scripture speak in the present moment. This feature of midrash is also one that seems to have troubled some later rabbinic authorities and even led them to dismiss midrash as at best a poetic form of speech that need not be taken too seriously. Partly because of such ambivalence, midrash's fortunes following the rabbinic period decidedly waned. The high point of classical midrashic creativity was reached in the first five centuries in the common era, but while encyclopedias of midrash continued to be composed throughout the Middle Ages, original midrashic composition declined until, ultimately, the new forms of *peshat*-oriented exegesis—so-called contextual or plain-sense interpretation—emerged in the late 10th c. in the Islamic world and the 11th c. in Europe. What has survived in the popular Jewish tradition of Bible study from the classical midrashic traditions are primarily those interpretations that were selected by Rashi (R. Shlomo Yitzhaki, 1040–1105) for inclusion in his commentary to the Bible. Finally, in the 12th and 13th centuries, the literary forms of classical midrash were appropriated and revived by the fledgling kabbalistic movement in such works as the *Sefer Bahir* and the *Zohar,* where they were infused with a new mystical content and thereby transformed into a medium for esoteric teachings. At this point, however, another literary tradition had begun.

For much of the past two centuries, since the beginnings of the Jewish Enlightenment and of modern critical study of the Bible among Jewish scholars, most interest in premodern Jewish biblical interpretation has centered upon the *peshat* interpreters of the Middle Ages, with their more contextual, grammatically informed, and rationalistic exegesis of the biblical text. And yet, as has become increasingly clear in the last half-century, *peshat* exegesis has been more of an exception, almost a blip, in the long history of Jewish biblical exegesis. If there has been a dominant mode of Jewish reading of the Bible, it has been more in the "spirit" of midrash—if not classical midrash itself—with its imperative to connect to the biblical text, its irrepressible playfulness, and its delight in multiple, polyvalent traditions of interpretation. And nowhere is this more visible than in the very page layout of what becomes the true Jewish study Bible—that is, the Rabbinic Bible, the *Miqraʾot Gedolot*—as it was first published in 1516 (2nd edition 1524–25) by the Christian printer Daniel Bomberg and then successively built upon and expanded by subsequent publishing houses. On the previous page, as one can see, the biblical text is surrounded by commentaries and para-exegetical works—the Aram. Targum next to the biblical text, with the commentaries of Rashi, Ibn Ezra, Naḥmanides, Sforno, and others below. Although most of these commentaries are *peshat* commentaries, each one explicitly or implicitly insisting upon the univocal truth of its particular interpretation, here they all lie next to each other on the same page, as though there were no significant difference or disagreement between them, awaiting the reader who will study them all, gleaning each for its own contribution and added significance. In its celebration of the possibilities of multiple interpretation, this very page layout is "midrashic"—and powerful testimony in itself to the supreme power midrash continues to wield in the Jewish study of the Bible.

[DAVID STERN]

Medieval Jewish Interpretation

The Way of the *Peshat*

The Bible has been the focus of a rich exegetical tradition, which began to evolve even before the canonization process was completed. The techniques of inner-biblical exegesis, *pesher*-type interpretation as practiced at Qumran, and rabbinic midrash are all examples of the application of the Bible to the changing spiritual needs of a faith-community. (See "Inner-biblical Interpretation," pp. 1835–41; "The Bible in the Dead Sea Scrolls," pp. 1850–59; and "Midrash," pp. 1879–91.) Rabbinic midrash treated the entire Bible as an organic whole, whose parts were infinitely significant and ripe for interpretation. This led to atomizing the text, reading words and vv. out of context, and making connections between vv. from various biblical books. Halakhic midrash attempted to anchor current practice in the biblical text, while aggadic midrash shed light on the character of biblical personalities and derived moral, educational, and theological lessons from biblical narrative through a variety of creative techniques, which often had little regard for the literary coherence or earlier meanings of the text. The midrashic method adequately satisfied the community's needs well into the early Middle Ages, when significant forces came to bear which called for new approaches to the biblical text and gave birth to the commentary genre. In contrast to midrashic collections, which are anthologies of comments by various sages, arranged either as a commentary on a biblical book or as a collection of sermons, the commentary bears the distinct stamp of a single author. From the 8th c. onward, in Iraq, Judeo-Arabic paraphrases of biblical texts begin to appear, replacing Aram. works of a similar nature. These are the precursors of the commentary genre. By the middle of the 9th c., a steady stream of commentaries begins to flow through the veins of the Jewish body politic, nourishing and invigorating it, and providing instruction and inspiration for each succeeding generation.

Karaites and *Geonim* (9th–11th Centuries)

Jewish scholars were doubtless aware of the importance of the Bible for Christians and its use as a source of inspiration and prooftexts. Indeed, Christians were already producing commentaries on biblical books in the 3rd c. However, only with the rise of Islam and the challenge posed by its claim of religious superiority did new approaches to the study of the biblical text seem imperative for Jewish scholars. The engagement of Muslim scholars in Qur'anic exegesis directly influenced the approach of their Jewish counterparts to the Hebrew Scriptures. The exposure to Islamic philosophy, especially rationalist Mutazilite Kalam, was also a powerful factor and left a distinct stamp of rationalism on the works of the period. Under the influence of Arabic philology and linguistics the serious study of the Heb language was undertaken, dictionaries were written, and rules, often derived from the Arabic grammarian's study of Qur'anic grammar, began to be defined for Heb grammar. One of the distinctive features of the commentary genre is the recognition that language follows specific rules and that these must be taken into account when explaining the text. Thus, although the message of the Bible is still seen as divine, the medium is human, and follows the conventions of human speech and communication.

It was at this time in Iraq, newly conquered by the Arabs from the Persians, that the Karaite movement began to take shape. By questioning the validity of the oral law and its supremacy over the written, and its sometimes idiosyncratic interpretations and occasional contradictions of the biblical text, this movement challenged the authority of the rabbinic leadership of the period. The Karaites advocated a return to Scripture and ridiculed the rabbinic readings of the text, which indeed were often difficult to justify on rational grounds. The movement's founding father, or better, precursor, was Anan ben David (mid-8th c.), who according to recent scholarship, was not really the first Karaite, but rather the founder of a rival legal school which promoted a different interpretation of the halakhah, while using the same techniques of midrash halakhah as the Rabbis. Anan promoted an extreme ascetical form of religion, which he buttressed with midrashic exegetical methods, and many of his views were rejected by later Karaites. Anan, at least according to later tradition, seems to have coined the slogan "search diligently the Scriptures and do not rely on my opinion," thus inspiring an efflorescence of biblical scholarship in both the Karaite and Rabbanite (the term used for Rabbinic in Karaite contexts) camps that would reach its zenith in the 10th and 11th centuries.

The Karaites, who coalesced into a movement in the 10th c., were the first Jewish group to produce full-fledged scriptural commentaries. The earliest exegete seems to have been the Karaite Benjamin al-Nahawandi (first half of the 9th c.), who wrote commentaries on the Torah and several other biblical books, of which only fragments remain. The earliest extant complete Jewish commentary is Daniel al-Qumisi's commentary on the Minor Prophets, the only part of his oeuvre to have survived intact. Al-Qumisi flourished in the last quarter of the 9th c., during which time he emigrated to Jerusalem where he helped found the Karaite community of Mourners of Zion. His commentary, written in Heb, bears a distinct authorial stamp, and presents a running verse-by-verse exposition of the biblical text, incorporating occasional Arabic and Persian glosses. Al-Qumisi demonstrates a distinct awareness of the literary nature of the biblical text, pointing out connections between vv. and sections, and offering philological analysis where necessary. On occasion he will apply certain prophetic statements to his own era, specifically engaging in polemics against the Rabbanites. But such interpretations are always offered as a second level of meaning after the v. has been subjected to philological and literary analysis. Take for example, Hos. 2.8–9: "Assuredly, I will hedge up her roads with thorns and raise walls against her, and she shall not find her paths. Pursue her lovers as she will, she will not overtake them; and seek them as she may, she shall never find them. Then she will say, 'I will go and return to my first husband, for then I fared better than now.'" After explaining the difficult words in the text and placing the vv. in the general context of Hosea's prophecy, al-Qumisi then applies these vv. to the Karaite-Rabbanite controversy, explaining that many will seek enlightenment through the teachings of the Rabbanites but will be disappointed ("seek them as she may, she shall never find them," 2.8) and as a result, there will be some who wish to "return to the first husband" (2.9), i.e., to the proper worship of God as prescribed in the Bible (the Karaite way), while there are those who "pursue their lovers" (ibid.), i.e., engage in improper acts, as did the early nations, in which men would marry their nieces and sisters-in-law and perform other forbidden unions, use candlelight on the Sabbath, etc., as did the Rabbanites. But the shepherds who mislead their flocks (i.e., the Rabbanites) will be dismissed and Israel will not find them, as it is written "I will dismiss them from tending the flock" (Ezek. 34.10). While this type of exegesis is somewhat reminiscent of the *pesharim* of the Dead Sea sectarians, there is a wide gap between the latter, which use the biblical text as a key for predicting the future, particularly the fate of their community, and those Karaites like al-Qumisi, who occasionally offer a midrashic type of gloss applying the text to their present situation. In general, in contrast with the Sages, who spoke of the multivalency of Scripture, al-Qumisi insisted that every word in the Bible had but one true interpretation. Unfortunately, this interpretation was not always immediately obvious. Therefore, multiple meanings could vie with each other, until the true meaning would be clarified at the End of Days when the Teacher of Righteousness *(moreh tzedek)*, a messianic figure who is also prominent in Qumran *pesher* texts, would clarify ambiguities and decide on the one true interpretation.

The most prominent Rabbanite exegete of this period is Saadia Gaon (882–942), a polymath, who did pioneering scholarly work in many areas, including grammar and exegesis. Saadia was born in Egypt and later moved to Iraq, where he was eventually chosen to be *gaon,* or head of the Sura academy, the leading Talmudic academy of his time. Saadia translated most of the Bible into Arabic and wrote commentaries on many books including the Torah, Isa., Prov., Job, and some of the Five Scrolls. He prefaced his commentaries with detailed introductions discussing grammatical, exegetical, and philosophical issues and polemicizing extensively against the Karaites. Saadia set down several principles of interpretation, which guided him in his work of translation and exegesis. These are most explicit in the introduction to his Torah commentary, where he affirmed the necessity of understanding the biblical text according to the plain meaning of the words, with the following exceptions: (1) if experience and sense perception contradict the plain meaning (e.g., that Eve was the mother of all living things [Gen. 2.20]); (2) if reason contradicts the plain sense (e.g., Deut. 4.24, that "the LORD your God is a consuming fire," which must be interpreted metaphorically); (3) when vv. contradict each other (e.g., Mal. 3.10, "thus put Me to the test," which must be interpreted so as not to contradict Deut. 6.16, "do not test the LORD, your God," which takes precedence); (4) when a v. contradicts established tradition (e.g., in the prohibition against seething a kid in its mother's milk [Exod. 23.19; 34.26; Deut. 14.21]). In the last case, an oral tradition (the complete separation of meat and milk products) was transmitted by the people, who saw how the prophets behaved in this matter. One of Saadia's key exegetical principles was maintaining a balance between the freedom of the interpreter and the authoritative tradition. This issue must have been heatedly discussed in Islamic circles as well, but for Saadia it was probably primarily motivated by the need to defend the oral tradition from the attacks of the Karaites. For Saadia unlimited freedom of interpretation, which the Karaites advocated, was unthinkable, since it would lead to religious anarchy. Exegetical freedom had to be limited by the dictates of tradition, which sometimes led to interpretations far from the plain sense.

Another important rabbinic exegete of this period was Samuel ben Ḥofni (d. 1013), *gaon* of Sura, who wrote an extensive commentary on the Torah in Judeo-Arabic, only part of which survives. This commentary follows in Saadia's footsteps but has its own unique features as well. It takes a rationalistic approach to the text and features extensive excursuses on various topics, which go far beyond the explication of the text and for which he was criticized by later exegetes. For example, his comment on Gen. 41.49 ("So Joseph collected produce in very large quantity, like the sands of the sea") includes a lengthy discourse on hoarding, and he appends to his commentary on the death of Jacob a long discussion of the laws of death and burial (Gen. 47.29).

One of the most prominent Karaite scholars of the period was Yaʿqub al-Qirqisani, a native of Iraq and a younger contemporary of Saadia, who wrote two major works in Arabic, a legal code called *Kitab al-anwar wa'l maraqib (Book of Lights and Watchtowers),* and a commentary on the Torah titled *Kitab al-Riyad wa'l ḥadaʾiq (Book of Gardens and Parks).* These two works constituted a unified exegetical project encompassing the legal and narrative portions of the Torah. In the latter work he sets down thirty-seven principles of exegesis and explains his exegetical aims and methods. Examples include the Mosaic authorship of the entire Torah and the necessity to interpret Scripture literally unless this would lead to a contradiction. Another important principle is that "Scripture addresses human beings in a manner accessible to them and about matters familiar to them from their own experience," which is reminiscent of the rabbinic principle "Scripture speaks in human language" (e.g., *b. Ber.* 31b). His works demonstrate a wide knowledge of contemporary philosophical and intellectual trends, as was typical for his time and environment.

In the 10th c. Jerusalem became the spiritual center of Karaism. The greatest Karaite exegete was Japheth ben Eli, who flourished in the second half of the 10th c. and was part of this Jerusalem school of Karaite scholars. He is the only exegete to have translated and commented on the entire Bible. He seems to have undertaken this task in order to provide the Karaite community with an adequate treatment of Scripture, which could hold its own against traditional rabbinic exegesis, especially the sophisticated treatment of his formidable Rabbanite opponent Saadia Gaon. While not as sophisticated and well developed in his understanding of Arabic linguistics and Mutazilite (rationalist Islamic) philosophy as his 11th-c. successors, such as Yusuf al-Basir, Jeshuah ben Judah, and Abu'l-Faraj Harun, his originality and literary-contextual approach set the tone for succeeding generations of exegetes and were profoundly influential. Japheth's Karaite successors used his commentaries as the foundation for their remarks, expanding and elaborating upon them, and his comments also found their way into the rabbinic *peshat* tradition, mainly through the mediation of Abraham Ibn Ezra.

Japheth's commentaries are divided into two sections. Each biblical book begins with a programmatic introduction, followed by a section-by-section translation and commentary. The translation and commentary are intimately related: The translation represents the distillation of the exegete's understanding of the meaning of the text, while the commentary discusses in depth the various options for its interpretation. Like Daniel al-Qumisi, Japheth also interpreted the text according to two methods, one the linguistic-contextual, the other, the *pesher*-like or prognostic, in which allusions are sought in the text to the exegete's own time, and to the struggle of the Karaite movement against its opponents. For Japheth and other Karaite members of the Mourners of Zion, such as Salmon ben Jeroḥam (mid-10th c.), this second method, which had a strong messianic tone to it, replaced the rabbinic method of midrash, which they had rejected. However, this method was used selectively, only on works or vv. deemed appropriate for such treatment (e.g., the poetic passages in the Torah and Early Prophets; Ps.; Dan.; Song).

In the late 10th c. the Karaite Abu Yaʿaqov Yusuf Ibn Nuḥ published a grammatical commentary on the Bible, the *Dikduk* (Grammar), which bears witness to an early Karaite tradition of Heb grammatical thought which originated in Persia and Iraq in the 8th to 9th centuries and was at first shared by Rabbanites and Karaites alike. The intention of this work was to use the tools of grammar and linguistics to elucidate the biblical text; it is thus distinguished from the grammars of Saadia and the Karaite Abu'l-Faraj Harun, which were more theoretical grammars arranged systematically. Ibn Nuḥ also wrote a long commentary on the Torah, only part of which survives.

The most important Karaite exegete of the 11th c. is Jeshuah ben Judah, author of several exegetical works, including long and short commentaries on the Torah, and *Genesis Rabbah,* a theological commentary on the opening chs of Gen. (not to be confused with the rabbinic midrash of the same name). His commentaries, scholastic in nature, are imbued with the teachings of Mutazilite Kalam and include lengthy halakhic discussions. They also include extensive quotations from rabbinic literature, some of them cited approvingly.

By the 11th c. a Karaite community had taken hold in Byzantium, and soon Karaites from this community were traveling to Jerusalem to study at the feet of the great sages of the Jerusalem school. Led by Tobias ben Moses, these Byzantine sectarians translated into Heb and epitomized large portions of the Karaite exegetical and halakhic tradition of the time and brought them back to Byzantium. Thus were the Arabic works of Japheth, Jeshuah, and the great theologian Yusuf al-Basir salvaged and transmitted to new generations of students, albeit in rather inferior translations that did not do justice to the eloquence of their authors.

The *geonim* and their Karaite contemporaries are the pioneers of Jewish biblical exegesis, the first to produce systematic biblical commentaries. They influenced succeeding schools of interpretation, especially those in the Arabic sphere: e.g., exegetes such as Judah Ibn Balʿam and Abraham Ibn Ezra (Muslim Spain), Abraham Maimonides (Egypt) and the Yemenite midrashic commentaries such as *Midrash ha-gadol.*

The Spanish School (10th–11th Centuries)

In the late geonic period (10th–11th centuries), the intellectual and spiritual center of medieval Jewry moved to Muslim Spain, where the grammatical and exegetical work begun by Saadia Gaon and the Karaites was continued and reached new levels of sophistication. The first significant work to be produced in Spain was the *Maḥberet (Notebook)* of Menaḥem ben Jacob Ibn Saruq, (mid-10th c.) the secretary of Ḥisdai Ibn Shaprut (ca. 915–ca. 970), a prominent minister in the court of the Caliph ʿAbd al-Raḥman. The *Maḥberet* is a Heb dictionary of biblical roots, the first of its kind to be produced in Heb. Though not a commentary, this work elucidated many difficult biblical vv., and represented the purest form of philological exegesis. The *Maḥberet* proved to be controversial and elicited a spirited response from Menaḥem's contemporary Dunash ben Labrat. The students of these grammarians carried on the discussion in a series of exchanges. They focused on the basic meaning of biblical roots and vv., many of which had theological and doctrinal implications. For instance, Dunash accused Menaḥem of preferring Karaite interpretations to those of the Rabbanites. Indeed, Menaḥem is singleminded in his devotion to the biblical language and text, insisting that they needed to be understood on their own terms, without recourse to other sources. Thus, he avoids comparative philology as much as possible, even shunning Aram. and Mishnaic Heb for the most part. Dunash is much more of a traditionalist, relying on the Masorah, comparative philology (Arabic, Aram.), and traditional rabbinic interpretation. The works of these early grammarians would soon be surpassed by their successors, but the fact that they were written in Heb made them accessible to and extremely influential among the northern French exegetical school of Rashi and his disciples.

One of the weaknesses of the grammatical theories of Menaḥem and Dunash was their adherence to the biliteral theory of "weak" Heb verbs (instead of the triliteral root theory that was later accepted). Indeed, in the case of some weak verbs, Menaḥem assigned them only one root letter. This understanding of the verbal root and other linguistic matters was improved considerably by the important grammatical work of Judah Ḥayyuj (ca. 945–ca. 1000) and Jonah Ibn Janaḥ (11th c.), who raised the scientific study of Heb grammar to new heights. Ḥayyuj wrote three grammatical treatises, including *Sefer ha-Shorashim (Book of Roots),* and a grammatical commentary on the Prophets entitled *Kitab al-Nutaf (Book of Plucked Feathers).* These works contain a great deal of exegetical material, which greatly influenced subsequent exegetes. Ḥayyuj is credited with introducing the concept of the triliteral Heb root, which he applied to the weak verbs and which revolutionized the study of Heb grammar.

Ibn Janaḥ refined Ḥayyuj's theories in several grammatical treatises, including *Kitab al-Luma (Sefer ha-Riqmah, Book of Variegated Flowerbeds)* and *Kitab al-Usul (Sefer ha-Shorashim, Book of Roots).* Much of the former deals with exegetical tools, including various kinds of substitutions, perhaps the most daring and controversial of his methods. For example at Eccl. 1.8, he explains *kol ha-devarim yegeʿim* (lit. "all things are weary") as *kol ha-devarim meyageʿim* ("all things make one weary, are wearisome," substituting a verb for an adjective). At Exod. 21.8, "he shall not have the right to sell her to a foreign people *(ʿam nokhri),* he substitutes *ʾish* (man) for *ʿam.* Similarly, when Abimelech pleads with God, "will You slay a nation *(goy)* though it be innocent?" (Gen. 20.4), Ibn Janaḥ insists that one must substitute *ʾish* (man) for *goy* (nation). Many believe that Ibn Janaḥ is here anticipating the conjectural emendation, a significant tool of modern biblical scholarship, but it is more likely that these interpretations are based on established exegetical principles, many borrowed from Qurʾanic exegesis. Most of these substitutions were accepted by his contemporaries, but some were criticized for exceeding the limits of the acceptable. For instance, Ibn Janaḥ proposes that in 1 Kings 2.28, "for Joab sided with Adonijah, and did not side with Absalom," Absalom should be replaced with Solomon, which makes more sense in the context. However, most of Ibn Janaḥ's critics accept the Masoretic Text and interpret the text as referring to Joab's lack of support for Absalom in the past. Ibn Janaḥ was also a pioneer in comparative philology and solved many an exegetical difficulty through recourse to Rabbinic Heb, Aram. or Arabic. Some of his solutions have been proposed by modern Bible scholars who were unaware that Ibn Janaḥ had anticipated them. An example of his technique is his explanation of Num. 16.1: *vayikaḥ koraḥ,* "and Korah took." Exegetes throughout the ages, beginning with the Targumim and midrashim, have puzzled over what it was that Korah took and made various proposals for filling the gap. Ibn Janaḥ, on the basis of comparison with the Arabic equivalent of the word *lakaḥ* (the root of *vayikaḥ*), suggests that the word here means "to begin" and does not require a direct object. It is rather connected to the verb in the following v. *vayakumu,* "they rose up," and means Korah and his men began to rise up against Moses.

In another important contribution, Ibn Janaḥ applied rhetorical principles to biblical usage, especially with regard to poetic repetition or parallelism. Thus, for example, one finds synonyms in Isa. 41.4, "Who has made and done?" and in Isa. 43.7, "I have created, fashioned and made him." Are these synonyms to be explained as having different meanings? The midrashic tradition and many medieval exegetes saw a distinct meaning in each word, assuming that since in the Bible no words are superfluous, each word had its own meaning. Ibn Janaḥ argued that the use of such synonyms and repetitions is rhetorical, to add elegance and beauty to the language; they do not add further meaning. If one should ask, then, why bother repeating the same idea in different words, Ibn Janaḥ would respond that in the art of rhetoric, elaboration is more elegant and artistic. This view was adopted by many Spanish and Provençal exegetes, especially Abraham Ibn Ezra and Radak, and was criticized by others who favored the midrashic method. In recent times, this question has again become a topic of dispute among interpreters of the Bible.

The two most important exegetes in Muslim Spain were Moses ben Samuel Gikatilla of Saragossa and Judah ben Samuel Ibn Balʿam of Toledo and later Seville, who were both active in the second half of the 11th c. Gikatilla translated the Arabic grammar books of Ḥayyuj into Heb and wrote a commentary on the Bible; most of it is lost. From the extant fragments of his commentary one can see that he was heavily influenced by Ibn Janaḥ in matters grammatical, but did not confine his exegesis to grammar and philology; he also commented on matters of content and general meaning. Notable is his severe rationalism, especially in dealing with miracles. He was also the first exegete to assign the second part of the book of Isaiah (chs 40–66) to a second prophet (called by modern scholars Second Isaiah or Deutero-Isaiah).

Judah Ibn Balʿam's works have fared better than Gikatilla's and most have survived, although, until recently, few had been published. His commentaries are very selective, focusing on vv. about which he disagrees with his predecessors. In his introduction to the Prophets, he spells out his exegetical method, explaining that he will treat difficult words in three ways: by translating them into Arabic, by comparing them with cognate words in the Bible, and, wherever possible, by relating them to equivalents in Rabbinic Heb, Aram., or Arabic. Although some have considered him an epigone (a follower of lesser abilities) of Ibn Janaḥ, he was clearly an independent thinker, who struggled with the text, rejected opposing views, and offered many innovative interpretations. In some cases, if he was not satisfied with previous solutions to a problem and could not provide a better solution of his own, he preferred to leave the problem unsolved. Only in matters of halakhah did he bow to tradition, as did most of the *peshat* (contextual) exegetes of the Middle Ages. Like his mentor Ibn Janaḥ, he was concerned with identifying geographical names, objects, flora, and fauna.

Abraham Ibn Ezra (1089–1164)

The commentaries of Abraham ben Meir Ibn Ezra mark the culmination of the Spanish-Arabic period of exegesis. Ibn Ezra lived in Spain most of his life, but in 1140 he abandoned his homeland, probably for personal reasons, and set out on a journey that would take him to Rome and through much of France, arriving finally in England, where he died in 1164. As he traveled, he produced, often by commission, commentaries on various biblical books; in some cases, such as Exod., Minor Prophets, Ps., Esth., and Dan., he produced two commentaries, one considerably longer and more detailed than the other. Ibn Ezra, in the Spanish tradition, based his methodology on the twin pillars of grammar and reason. He argued that only an exegete thoroughly grounded in Heb grammar and lexicography could properly understand the meaning of the biblical text. For him the text had but one meaning, which could be obtained only through the application of the rules of grammar. Furthermore, an acceptable interpretation had to be logically consistent and stand up to the test of reason.

In the introduction to his Torah commentary, he discusses four earlier approaches to biblical exegesis which he found wanting: (1) the geonic, which tended to stray from the matter at hand and lapsed into lengthy discussions of matters not germane to the text; (2) the Karaite, which rejected the oral tradition of the Sages, allowing every exegete to interpret according to his own understanding, even in matters of halakhah, thus undermining rabbinic authority; (3) the Christian, which tended to allegorize the text, including matters of halakhah, thus robbing it of its basic meaning and calling into question the necessity for religious observance; and (4) the midrashic, the way of the Sages, whose interpretations defied logic and reason and ignored context. This lack of exegetical control was totally unacceptable.

Ibn Ezra then articulates his own methodology: he will explain the grammar of each word only once, at its first occurrence, and then explain its meaning in context. He also declares that he will ignore the comments of the Masoretes, which he claims have no exegetical value, though they provided much material for homilists.

Ibn Ezra's exegesis represents a distillation of the finest achievements of the Spanish philological school of exegesis, avoiding its more radical elements such as Ibn Janaḥ's methods of lexical and consonantal substitution. He adopted Moses Ibn Ezra's stance (see below) that Scripture uses human language and therefore must conform to the rules of syntax and rhetoric; this led him to reject midrashim which tampered with the syntax, or interpretations based on plene or defective spellings since these had no effect on the meaning of the text. Furthermore, the Bible speaks of God and the elements of nature in human terms, so that human beings can understand what it is saying. Expressions such as the "mouth of the earth" (Num. 16.32) or "the heart of the sea" (Exod. 15.8) are figures of speech and should not be understood literally.

Ibn Ezra fully accepted the Spanish exegetical tradition that did not assign significance to changes in spelling or wording if the meaning was not affected. As a result, he paid little attention to textual nuance, unusual spellings, and stylistic variations, which are popular now among modern students of the Bible. He ignored the differences in parallel passages, e.g., the two versions of the Decalogue, or Pharaoh's two dreams, and, saw no significance in the unusual form *ʾoholoh* (Gen. 9.21), instead of *ʾoholo,* which Rashi as well as the midrash interpreted to refer to the fall of Samaria (called *ʾOholah*), brought down by drunkenness and depravity.

In his firm belief that Scripture could not contradict the demands of reason, he was a faithful follower of Saadia Gaon, invoking the method of *tikun* (correction or adaptation, based on the *tawil* of Qurʾanic exegesis) in order to make a v. conform to reason by means of allegory or metaphor. But in order to avoid undermining the validity of the commandments, the historicity of the patriarchal narratives, or the truthfulness of the prophetic messages, he insisted, as did Saadia, that the method of *tikun* had to be applied only when absolutely necessary.

Ibn Ezra also followed Saadia in his steadfast defense of the oral tradition (kabbalah) of the Sages, particularly in matters of halakhah. In practical terms this meant that Ibn Ezra could not accept a *peshat* interpretation that contradicted halakhah, in contrast to other *peshat* exegetes, such as Rashbam, of the northern French school, or Radak. Thus, for example, Exod. 13.9 and other passages which provide the scriptural basis for tefillin (phylacteries) are accepted as referring to the halakhic requirement to actually bind copies of these passages on the arm and place them on the head in leather boxes (phylacteries, or tefillin). Ibn Ezra argues that since the literal interpretation does not contradict reason and that the commandment it entails can be carried out, it must be accepted, unlike the v. "and you should circumcise the foreskin of your heart" (Deut. 10.16), which cannot be interpreted literally. The Karaites and Rashbam, on the other hand, interpret both these vv. metaphorically as merely urging constant vigilance in remembering the commandments. But while the oral tradition of the Sages, the vast body of halakhah gathered in the Mishnah and Talmud, was sacrosanct, the same authority was not ascribed to the *midreshei halakhah,* the halakhic midrashim of the Sages meant to provide scriptural justification for the actual laws themselves. He felt no compulsion to defend these in the same way he defended the halakhic decisions of the Talmud (see, e.g., his short commentary to Exod. 21.8). Similarly, despite his respect for the halakhic decisions of the rabbinic Sages, Ibn Ezra feels no compulsion to accept their assignations of authorship to the various biblical books (e.g., he questions whether Jeremiah wrote Lam.), or the midrashic identification of biblical characters (e.g., contra Rashi, he rejects the midrashic view that the prophet Joel was the son of the prophet Samuel).

Ibn Ezra had a very conservative view of the biblical text and rejected all attempts at emendation. On the other hand, he did have a penchant for higher criticism, pointing to later additions in the text (e.g., Gen. 12.6; 22.14; Deut. 3.11), and especially the last twelve vv. of Deut. ("the secret of the twelve"), which he claims were written prophetically by Joshua. Similarly, following Moses Gikatilla, he advocates the postexilic dating of the second part of Isaiah and of some of the psalms (e.g., Ps. 69).

Ibn Ezra was a serious philosopher, a Neoplatonist, heavily influenced by astrology. Although he never wrote any systematic theological or philosophical treatises, his thought may be gleaned from his biblical commentaries. Indeed, many of Ibn Ezra's allusions to secrets *(sodot)* refer to his views on central issues of Jewish theology, such as God's relation to the land of Israel, the people of Israel, and the role of the sacrificial cult, especially the scapegoat (Lev. 16.8) in determining the fate of the Jewish people. His referring to these views as secrets, and alluding to them obliquely, may be an indication that they might be threatening to the religious well-being of the Jewish masses and could only be tolerated and properly understood by the intellectual elite.

Ibn Ezra was one of the main conduits of Spanish-Jewish culture to the rest of Western Europe, and as such his legacy is of inestimable value. Despite the impression given by his "modern" critical allusions and his tendency to be overly critical of his predecessors and contemporaries, he was not a radical exegete. His importance lies in his position at the end of a productive period in Jewish intellectual history and his ability to summarize in Heb the exegetical achievements of this period clearly, succinctly, and judiciously. Nevertheless, his commentaries presented challenges to the reader because of their concise, difficult nature, and scattered cryptic comments, which stimulated the production of a whole corpus of super-commentaries that elucidate and elaborate upon them.

Interest in Ibn Ezra has continued down through the ages, making him one of the most influential cultural icons in Jewish history. In the Late Middle Ages, he was appropriated by nearly every intellectual school. Though he was a Neoplatonist, Maimonidean Aristotelians found common ground in him. Though he polemicized fiercely against the Karaites, these sectarians also claimed him as one of their own, perhaps because he often cited works by Karaite scholars. Baruch Spinoza cited him as the first biblical critic, making much of his so-called higher-critical comments and using his name to justify his own much more radical views. He was also much admired by the Christian Hebraists in the early modern period, who translated many of his works and quoted him approvingly. In the modern period, Jewish reformers and biblical critics saw him as a precursor of their views, as someone who was dedicated to the pursuit of truth but could not express his views openly, and as someone, who, like Maimonides, was open to the outside world, willing to accept the truth from whatever source it came.

Aesthetics and Philosophy

At the same time that grammarians were refining their tools to better explain the biblical text, another school of thought was approaching the Bible from a different direction. Scholars trained in philosophy were using their newfound knowledge to reexamine the biblical text and then reinterpret it in the light of their philosophical insights. While none utilized the commentary genre, their works are full of comments on the biblical text, which they attempt to harmonize with their philosophical teachings. (See "The Bible in the Jewish Philosophical Tradition," pp. 1916–43.) Although he did not write biblical commentaries as such, Moses ben Jacob Ibn Ezra (ca. 1055–1138), a relative and friend of Abraham Ibn Ezra, made an important contribution to biblical hermeneutics by developing a literary exegetical theory based on Arabic theories of aesthetics. His Arabic treatise, *Book of Discussion and Conversation,* provides guidelines for writing Heb poetry in the Arabic style. To illustrate his points Ibn Ezra brings examples from the Bible and thereby indirectly provides an analysis of biblical stylistics in comparison with the ideal of Arabic poetry. Applying his theory to prophecy, he portrayed biblical prophets as poets, who supplied the literary form for the divine message. The implications for exegesis are obvious, since this means that biblical prophecies can be analyzed like any other poetry. Furthermore, if the ideas expressed are paramount, then the stylistic embellishments of these ideas do not have interpretive significance and can be ignored. This leads to the principle, characteristic of the Spanish school of *peshat* exegesis, that the Bible may repeat the same idea in different words for stylistic, aesthetic purposes, and that such repetition is not exegetically significant. Thus, for example, in "Abraham breathed his last and died" (Gen. 25.8), "breathed his last" *(vayigva')* renders "and died" *(vayamot)* superfluous. As part of his theory, Ibn Ezra enumerates literary ornaments of poetry, known in Arabic as *badi,* which he proceeds to identify in the Bible. Some, such as metaphor, simile, and allegory, were commonly recognized; for others, he could not find good examples. Nevertheless, in the attempt, he revealed many characteristics of biblical style, which had hitherto not been recognized. Ibn Ezra's aesthetic exegesis, written in Arabic, towards the end of the Golden Age of Spanish-Jewish culture (10th–12th centuries, when Muslims controlled most of Spain), remained untranslated until recently, and thus had little impact on subsequent generations, living in Christian Europe with limited exposure to Arabic language and culture.

Baḥya Ibn Pakuda (ca. 1100) in his *Duties of the Heart,* elaborates a theory of biblical exegesis in which he identifies several levels of understanding, from the basic linguistic to the lexical to the contextual and finally to the esoteric, which is only attainable by those who have intellect and understanding. Baḥya was greatly influenced by the Sufi mystics of his time. Moses Maimonides (Rambam; 1138–1204) devoted much of his major philosophical work, the *Guide of the Perplexed,* to the interpretation of particular biblical texts. His primary purpose is to demonstrate that the inner meaning of the biblical text is compatible with Aristotelian philosophy. The whole first section is devoted to the elucidation of equivocal terms in the Bible, and sections of the Bible are interpreted or explained at various points in the work. Another major concern of his was the elucidation of parables, which he viewed as having two levels of meaning, revealed and hidden. Maimonides spends a great deal of effort in elucidating the biblical prophecies as well as the book of Job. For the former, a major concern was harmonizing the biblical text with reason and logic; the latter he read as a parable on divine providence and the problem of evil. He often used midrashic interpretations as an aid for his exegesis, interpreting them philosophically as well. Maimonides' exegetical approach was very influential on succeeding generations of scholars. He was the prime representative and major spokesman for the Aristotelian school in Jewish philosophy, and subsequent Jewish philosophical exegesis shows strong signs of his influence.

Provençal School (12th–13th Centuries)

The lore of the Spanish *peshat* tradition was brought to Provence by the Kimḥi family. The father Joseph (ca. 1105–1170) moved his family, which already included his elder son Moses, from Spain to Narbonne in Provence around 1150, in the wake of the Almohade persecutions. His second son David (ca. 1160–1235) was born in Narbonne. David lost his father at the tender age of ten years and was raised by his brother. The Kimḥis were an impressive family, all steeped in the Sephardic tradition of philosophical rationalism and scientific study of the Heb language. All wrote biblical commentaries and grammatical works. Joseph is probably best known for his anti-Christian polemic *Sefer ha-Berit (The Book of the Covenant),* which contains much material of an exegetical nature, Moses for his grammatical work, *Mahlakh shevilei ha-daʿat (The Course of the Paths of Knowledge),* which was translated into Latin in 1508 and became a favorite of 16th-c. Christian Hebraists. Both Joseph and Moses left commentaries on Prov. and Job; the latter's Prov. commentary was attributed until recent times to Abraham Ibn Ezra. But the family's most distinguished exegete was David (better known by the acronym Radak), who surpassed his father and brother in celebrity. He produced commentaries on the Torah, Prophets, Ps., Prov., Job, and Chron. These commentaries along with his grammatical works, *Sefer ha-Shorashim (Book of Roots)* and *Sefer Mikhlol* (*Comprehensive Hebrew Grammar*), became standard works in the field and epitomized the best of the Spanish *peshat* tradition. Growing up in Provence, with its history of midrashic exegesis, Radak was exposed to the positive aspects of this tradition; and in his commentaries he does justice to both *peshat* and midrash, quoting *derashot* (homiletical interpretations of the Sages) and also incorporating midrashic methods and sensibilities into his *peshat* exegesis. For instance, while Radak opposes the midrashic tendency to glorify the patriarchs and matriarchs, preferring to view them as having human strengths and weaknesses, he does derive moral encouragement and religious inspiration from their actions. For example, at Gen. 21.15, concerning Hagar and Ishmael, he teaches the lesson of patience and fortitude in the face of adversity, for if God can perform a miracle for Abraham's maidservant, anyone may benefit from such divine attention.

In similar fashion, Radak does not shy away from applying biblical prophecies and psalms to the situation of the Jews in their present exile and to the long awaited messianic salvation. Thus, in commenting on Isa. 52.1, "Awake, awake, O Zion! / Clothe yourself in splendor; / put on your robes of majesty, / Jerusalem, holy city! / For the uncircumcised and the unclean / shall never enter you again," he explains "the uncircumcised and the unclean" as referring to the two nations of Edom (Christianity) and Ishmael (Islam) who have fought incessantly over Jerusalem, but who will eventually have to surrender it when the Messiah comes. In this contemporizing tendency he reacts against the extreme historicization of those exegetes such as Moses Gikatilla, who, perhaps for apologetic reasons, explained all the biblical prophecies as referring to past events.

A philosophically trained Maimonidean, Radak introduces philosophical ideas into his commentaries and vigorously defended the Maimonidean position both in writing and orally, participating in his later years in the first Maimonidean controversy. Radak also had a keen historical sense, which he applied judiciously to various biblical issues. For example, he explains the existence of variant readings for the same words, called *ketiv* (written) and *qere* (to be read) as the result of the confusion generated by the first exile (6th c. BCE), when books were lost and traditions forgotten. In cases when the men of the Great Synagogue (a group believed by the Sages to have begun functioning in the early postexilic period) could not determine which of two variants was the correct one, they recorded both. In general, on matters concerning the transmission of the biblical text, he is relatively progressive.

The works of Radak, alongside those of Ibn Ezra, exerted tremendous influence in subsequent generations. His grammar books became the standard in the field, and were copied and printed numerous times. His grammatical works and his commentaries were very popular among Christian Hebraists of the 16th–19th centuries, and are consulted and cited by modern Bible scholars to this day.

Northern France (11th–12th Centuries)

During the heyday of the Spanish school (the second half of the 11th c.), there developed in northern France another school of *peshat* exegesis, with similar goals and slightly different results. Anonymous glossators called *poterim,* who taught the Bible through the vernacular and are the school's precursors, were active during the early part of the century. In the middle of the century Menaḥem ben Ḥelbo (1015–1085) was writing complete commentaries on the Prophets and Writings, characterized by, among other things, a concern for the plain meaning, the interpolation of foreign words *(leʿazim),* and an attempt to show connections between various passages. Unfortunately very little of his work has survived. The true inspiration for this efflorescence in biblical scholarship was the 11th-c. scholar, R. Shlomo Yitzhaki (Rashi [an acronym for Rabbi Shlomo son of Isaac], 1040–1105). Rashi wrote commentaries on almost the entire biblical corpus as well as on the Talmud. They draw heavily on the rabbinic tradition and also display a newly discovered sensitivity to context, which influences his choice of midrashic material. The genius of Rashi's commentaries lies in their clarity, concision, felicity of expression, and skillful selection and editing of sources. On numerous occasions, Rashi modifies midrashic sources to accommodate his exegetical goals. In one of his few methodological statements (at Gen. 3.8), he states, "there are many aggadic interpretations, and our Sages have already arranged them in their proper place in *Genesis Rabbah* and other midrashic collections. I, however, am only concerned with the contextual meaning of Scripture (*peshuto shel miqra'*, from the same root as *peshat*) and with such *'aggadot* that properly explain the word and meaning of Scripture." Rashi is thus saying that he will be very selective in his choice of rabbinic material and will not include rabbinic comments which read the text out of context. One puzzling aspect of Rashi's commentaries is the double comment, in which he explains a v. according to context and then follows this with a citation from a midrashic source. It has been the generally accepted opinion that Rashi adds these rabbinic comments only if he is not completely satisfied with his *peshat* explanation. Thus, a weak midrash is used to strengthen a weak *peshat*. Recently, however, it has been suggested that each part of these double interpretations is actually complementary, representing a dualistic approach to the biblical text. The two interpretations when combined, produce a fuller, more satisfying picture, enabling the reader more fully to grasp the meaning of Scripture in all its complexity. Rashi was very sensitive to the nuances of biblical language, and though he lacked the training of his Spanish colleagues who read and wrote in Arabic, he knew the work of Menaḥem ben Saruq and Dunash ben Labrat, whom he quotes in his commentaries. In addition his commentaries are replete with hundreds of *le'azim*, or word definitions in Old French. Although he does not reveal a great deal about himself in his commentaries, he does refer occasionally to realia or to social conditions in his own time. Rashi was a brilliant Heb stylist; this feature, as well as his ability to create a commentary with a didactic and moral thrust that had popular appeal, have helped assign his commentary pride of place in the Ashkenazi canon of classic Jewish texts which are still studied widely today. His commentary on the Torah became immensely popular, achieving near-canonical status, as an acceptable substitute for the required weekly reading of the Targum in preparation for the Torah reading on Sabbath mornings. Rashi's commentary also spawned an impressive number of super-commentaries, beginning with the commentary of Ramban (see below). Among the most famous are those of Judah Khalatz (Spain-Morocco, 15th c.), Abraham Bukarat (Spain, Tunis, late 15th–early 16th c.), Elijah Mizraḥi (Constantinople, ca. 1450–1526), Judah Loew ben Bezalel (Maharal) of Prague (ca. 1525–1609), and Shabbetai Bass (Prague, 1641–1718). Indeed the production of translations and super-commentaries continues to this very day. Rashi's blend of contextual exegesis and ethical homiletics was a winning combination. His reputation as a Talmudist further strengthened his authority and assured that his Bible commentary would never be neglected.

Rashi's sense of *peshuto shel miqra'*, the plain or contextual sense of scripture, developed over the course of his lifetime. He reworked some of his commentaries and was constantly looking for new insights into the text. His grandson, Samuel ben Meir, relates that he admitted to him that if he had more time he would write new commentaries "based on the insights into the contextual meanings of Scripture which are being thought up every day" (commentary to Gen. 37.2). This indicates that there was a great deal of activity in biblical study at the time in the school of Rashi and the trend was away from the exclusive use of rabbinic material. For Rashi, *peshat* and *derash* coexisted in a state of tension, and *derashot* that did not violate the integrity of the text and taught an important lesson were still favored.

With Rashi's students and younger contemporaries in the *peshat* school, the balance shifted away from the rabbinic in favor of the biblical. This can be seen already in the work of Joseph Kara (1050–1125), who applied the principles of contextual exegesis to the biblical text with greater rigor and consistency. The name Kara indicates that he dealt with the Bible *(miqra')* in his professional life, either as a teacher or an exegete, or both. Kara produced commentaries for most of the books of the Bible, of which the commentaries on the Former and Latter Prophets, Ps., Job, and the Five Scrolls have survived. Recently significant portions of his Commentary on the Torah have been discovered. Kara was also an important exegete of religious poetry *(piyyut),* his commentaries attaining great renown. In Kara, we find considerable progress away from the reliance on midrashic sources for exegesis, a fact which sets him apart from Rashi. In a lengthy programmatic statement in his commentary on 1 Sam. 1.17, Kara makes a strong case for the independent integrity of the text and its ability to stand alone without midrashic embellishment: "One should know that when the prophecies were written they were written complete, with nothing missing and with adequate interpretation, so that subsequent generations would not be led astray by them. It is not necessary to bring a proof from anywhere else, including the midrash, because the Torah was given and recorded in perfect form, lacking nothing. The purpose of the midrash of our Sages is to exalt and glorify the Torah." He compares someone who inclines towards the midrash to a drowning person desperately grabbing for something to hold on to. Had he heeded God's word and made the effort to grasp the contextual meaning, he would have been rewarded by deeper insight. For Kara, then, the contextual meaning of the text has religious significance, in that it brings one closer to the true word of God. Kara was an independent thinker, not afraid to criticize his predecessors or to find fault with the interpretations of the Rabbis. He was concerned with methodology and his commentaries abound with statements proposing various hermeneutical rules. He was particularly sensitive to literary issues and pointed out instances of parallelism, metaphor and other aspects of biblical style. Kara was also noted for his rationalism, which manifests itself in his quest for reasons for the commandments, and rational explanations for characters' actions and for seemingly miraculous events.

The school of *peshat* exegesis reached the zenith of its achievements with the commentaries of Samuel ben Meir (Rashbam) (ca. 1080–ca. 1160), the grandson of Rashi. His greatest achievement was his Torah commentary, in which he diligently persevered in elucidating the contextual meaning of Scripture *(peshat)* without regard for the interpretations of the Sages. He took his grandfather Rashi to task for his deviations from the *peshat;* indeed, his commentary may be seen as a reaction and critical response to that of Rashi. In most cases, he provides a *peshat* explanation only if he feels that Rashi's comment does not do the job. In an interesting methodological statement, Rashbam makes it clear that his goal in his commentary is only to understand the text as it was written. This includes texts of a legal nature which supposedly govern Jewish practice.

Rashbam sees the halakhot (legal pronouncements) as primary, but recognizes that their connection with the text is often not that easy to justify. Nevertheless this does not detract from their primary importance: "All those with wisdom should know and understand that I have not come to explain halakhot, even though they are primary.... Since from the superfluity of Scripture one derives halakhot and aggadot; some of these are found in the comments of R. Solomon, my mother's father. But I have come to explain Scripture contextually" (Exod. 21.1). In other words, Rashbam recognizes two legitimate modes of exegesis. The rabbinic mode is legitimate in its own right and does not need justification; in this context, it is noteworthy that Rashbam (in contrast, e.g., to Abraham Ibn Ezra) was an important halakhic scholar. But the *peshat* mode is also valid in and of itself and operates within its own methodological confines. The two are complementary. Rashbam was the most consistent exegete in insisting on a strict separation between the two. In some cases, he even interpreted the text in opposition to the halakhah. For example, at Exod. 21.6 he explains that after having his ear pierced, the servant is bound to his master for life, even though the halakhah determines that he goes free in the jubilee year, following Lev. 25.40. At Exod. 21.34, in the case of an animal that falls into an open pit, Rashbam's interpretation is that the carcass should go, according to *peshat,* to the owner of the pit, while pointing out that the halakhah determines that it goes to the owner of the animal. Regarding the famous prohibition against seething a kid in its mother's milk (Exod. 23.19 and elsewhere), Rashbam offers a historical, cultural explanation: "Goats generally give birth to two kids at the same time. It was customary to slaughter one of them. Since goats produce much milk ... it was the custom to boil the kid in its mother's milk. The text deals with the most likely case [which can be applied to other animals]. It is disgraceful, voracious and gluttonous to consume a mother's milk together with her offspring.... The intention of the text is to teach civilized behavior." At the end of his lengthy comment, he adds, however, that "this is the case for all meat and milk, as our Sages have explained in the Talmud Tractate *Ḥullin.*"

Rashbam showed interest in linguistic and literary matters and had the most sophisticated approach to grammar of all the members of his school. He even wrote a book, called *Sefer Dayekut (Book of Precision),* which deals with grammatical questions in the Bible. But like other members of his school, his efforts were hampered by a lack of familiarity with the major Arabic works of grammar produced by the Spanish school. Only the works of Menaḥem and Dunash were available to him. Rashbam was the first medieval exegete to point out the literary technique of foreshadowing, providing information in anticipation of the later need for it. For example, Gen. 9.18, "Ham was the father of Canaan," is seemingly out of place in its context. However, it prepares the reader for the cursing of Canaan later on. Similarly, Num. 13.20 "Now it happened to be the season of the first ripe grapes," prepares the reader for the return of the spies with a cluster of grapes (Num. 13.23, 27). Rashbam points out many other instances of this feature of biblical stylistics.

The last major representative of the *peshat* school is Eliezer of Beaugency (mid-12th c.), who may have been a student of Rashbam. He wrote commentaries on most of the books of the Bible, but only a few, on the Latter Prophets, have survived; therefore our knowledge of his methodology is scant. Eliezer is extreme in his avoidance of midrash; one finds few references to it in his writings. His style is paraphrastic, creating a seamless weave of text with his own words intermingled with the text of Scripture. He stressed the importance of context for explaining difficult words and passages (*davar lamed meʿinyano,* [the meaning of] a word is learned from its context). Like Joseph Kara, he proposed many rules for understanding the biblical text, and many of his comments deal with literary issues. He shows a sensitivity to nuance and devotes much more attention than his colleagues to matters of redaction and the ordering of the biblical books.

Joseph Bekhor Shor (1130–1200) was the last member of this school and his work already shows signs of a decline. He can be seen as a transitional figure situated between the most important members of the *peshat* school (Kara, Rashbam, Eliezer) and the tosafists (see below). His Torah commentary has characteristics of both schools. Although mainly devoted to *peshat* exegesis, his commentary includes more midrashic material than those of his predecessors. He also makes use of *gematria* (the numerical value of letters), which was in vogue among the Pietists in Germany. Among his most significant contributions were his psychological insights into the motivations of the characters in the Bible. He is also concerned with literary structure and connections between passages. His interpretations are often innovative, and even fanciful.

By the turn of the 13th c., just as the mini-renaissance of the 12th c. died out and rationalism lost its luster, so too did the *peshat* school fade away. It may very well have been that the radical nature of the enterprise contributed to its lack of appeal to future generations of scholars and laity. The study of Scripture, as opposed to Talmud, was never primary in the curriculum in Ashkenaz, and an exegetical enterprise which could be seen as undermining the authority of rabbinic interpretation and halakhic rulings based on Scripture was simply not sustainable. The influence of this school, with the exception of Rashi, whose commentary managed to strike the right balance between *peshat* and *derash,* was minimal. The small number of surviving mss of the commentaries of Rashbam and Eliezer bears this out. Joseph Kara fared slightly better, although much of his oeuvre was also lost. It seems that these types of commentaries had little appeal to the masses, and even among the intellectuals, changing currents in thinking and an anti-rationalist movement contributed to the neglect of the works of this school for the rest of the Middle Ages.

The Northern French School's Encounter with Christianity

Biblical exegesis among the northern French was influenced by the Jewish encounter with Christianity in several ways. The interest in the biblical text shown by this school of northern French exegetes has invited comparisons with similar trends in Christian scholarly circles at the time, notably the School of St. Victor in Paris, where the canon, Andrew of St. Victor, pursued the *hebraica veritas* with the same assiduousness as Rashbam and his colleagues pursued the *peshat.* Though names are not mentioned, Andrew, who was not well-versed in Heb, consulted Jews regularly and cites Jewish exegesis frequently in his commentaries. Some of the sources he cites can be traced to members of the northern French school. It is not unreasonable to assume that the winds of influence blew in the other direction as well. Indeed it has been argued convincingly that the focus of the exegetes of this school, especially Rashi, on the construction of a narrative that the Jewish people could identify with and be proud of was a primary concern, and was stimulated by the competing narrative presented by the Christian side in what was an ongoing debate and struggle for legitimacy. So, while there is definitely evidence of shared concerns and techniques, made possible by the atmosphere of tolerance and open rationalistic inquiry fostered by the 12th c. renaissance, there is also evidence of competition, rivalry, and struggle for supremacy, which can be seen clearly in the polemical aspects of these exegetes' commentaries.

Indeed, it is likely that the exigencies of polemic and disputation stimulated study of the biblical text unencumbered by traditional non-literal interpretation. The New Testament interprets many vv. in the Hebrew Bible christologically, as referring to the life or significance of Jesus of Nazareth. This method was continued in the writings of the Church Fathers and in the medieval Christian commentaries, and such comments loom large in the polemical works written by Jews and Christians in the later medieval period. One area which received special attention was the interpretation of the legal parts of the Torah. Christians argued that many of these laws, such as the dietary laws, were no longer applicable as they had been abrogated by the advent of Jesus as Messiah. Jews contended that all the laws remained valid, even if they lacked a rational explanation, since their fulfillment was an act of faith in God. Another issue was the status and interpretation of the words of the prophets, many of which the Christians applied to Jesus. Jewish exegetes tried to put these prophecies in their historical context, applying them to events in the past, either in the time of the prophet or immediately thereafter. Another important strategy of the Jewish polemicists was to argue from context, showing the indefensibility of the Christian interpretation if the context was considered. This approach, of course, militated against midrashic interpretation as well and contributed to the decline in its use during the Middle Ages. Many of the exegetes of the northern French school were involved in polemics with Christians and these are alluded to in their commentaries either directly or obliquely. The impact of the Crusades is especially felt in Rashi's commentary on Ps., written after 1096, in which he applies numerous vv. to the struggle of the Jewish people in exile with Christianity (symbolized by Esau or Edom), in many cases reading these vv. against the thrust of traditional commentary, in order to avoid any possible misuse of them by Christians. On the other hand his commentary on Song, in which on numerous occasions he uses the term *dugma'* in the sense of figure, shows the influence of contemporary Christian exegesis, where typology was an important exegetical tool. Joseph Kara's comments on the meaning and dates of prophecies of comfort, the meaning of the exile, and the continuing value of the observance of the commandments are apologetically motivated. He was also sensitive to comments that Christians might use for their own polemical purposes. Thus, he criticizes Rashi for explaining *ma'aseh merkavah,* the chariot vision in Ezek. ch 1, as wheels being held together by crossed bars, for fear that this explanation might be used by Christian polemicists to argue that God's chariot was supported by a cross (1 Kings 7.33). Another tendency evident in Kara, but especially in Rashbam and Joseph Bekhor Shor, is to explain the actions of the patriarchs in as positive a manner as possible. Thus according to Rashbam, Abraham had given enough water to Hagar to last her and Ishmael until they reached the next inn. But because she lost her way in the desert, the water ran out (commentary to Gen. 21.14). Jacob dealt honestly with his brother and bought the birthright from him outright at its fair market value. He served him a meal of bread and lentil soup afterwards in order to confirm the transaction (commentary to Gen. 25.31–33). An especially sensitive topic was the despoiling of the Egyptians (Exod. 3.22). Rashbam explains that the Israelite women asked the Egyptians to give them the vessels as outright gifts, and adds that this is the literal meaning and an answer to the sectarians *(teshuvat ha-minim).* This last comment is a clear indication of the direct relationship between the contextual meaning and anti-Christian polemic. This type of interpretation was the best response to Christian allegorization, which tended to read a reference to Jesus and his life into every v. possible. Nevertheless, not all of these Jewish interpreters were equally engaged in anti-Christian polemic, and the development of *peshat* interpretation should not be seen entirely as a reaction to Christianity.

Ashkenaz in the Late Middle Ages

Biblical commentary in Ashkenaz in the later Middle Ages was produced by the tosafists, a school of students of the Talmud, which flourished between the 12th (from the time of Rashbam and his brother Jacob Tam) and 14th centuries, and German Pietists (Ḥasidei Ashkenaz), a pietistic school, which flourished from the mid-12th to the mid-13th centuries. The tosafist commentaries, mostly produced in the latter part of the tosafist period, were almost all anonymous and have only recently begun to be studied. Many were largely compilations. Very little attention was paid to linguistic matters. Rabbinic midrash was again favored, as were numerological techniques such as *gematria* (explaining a word or group of words according to the numerical value of the letters) and *notarikon* (interpreting every letter in a particular word as the first letter of a whole word, or interpreting a word by breaking it up into its components). The commentaries produced in this period were influenced by the methods of Talmud study of the tosafists, but did not neglect the *peshat* entirely. The best known is that of Hezekiah ben Manoaḥ (Ḥizekuni; mid-13th c.), which incorporates a good deal of commentary by Joseph Bekhor Shor and other members of the *peshat* school. The commentaries of the German Pietists are of two types. Some, such as the commentary of Judah ben Samuel (ca. 1150–1217) as recorded by his son Zaltman, are rather undisciplined *peshat* commentaries intended for a wide audience; others, especially those of Eleazar ben Judah of Worms (ca. 1165–ca. 1230), are full of *gematriot, notarikonim,* and other esoteric methods of exegesis, and were intended for the small circle of initiates schooled in the particular brand of mysticism practiced by this group.

Naḥmanides (1194–1271)

Naḥmanides (Moses ben Naḥman; Ramban) marks a new stage in the history of exegesis, since he was the first scholar who wrote his commentaries under the influence of both the Sephardic Andalusian (the region of southern Spain) and Ashkenazic traditions. Naḥmanides was a product of Christian Spain, but he unquestionably felt himself to be in the line of the Andalusian exegetical tradition and indeed advanced the cause of *peshat* exegesis with many insightful comments. At the same time he had absorbed the work of Rashi and the northern French school and held it in high regard. He also did not hesitate to utilize the vast resources of rabbinic literature—Talmudim, halakhic and aggadic midrashim, as well as geonic and mystical works. In his introduction he speaks of his attitudes to both Abraham Ibn Ezra and Rashi, the dean of northern French exegetes. He shows respect for both of his predecessors, but also is not afraid to criticize what he found wanting. Though certainly trained in grammar and philology, he found the Spanish approach as exemplified by Ibn Ezra to be excessively philological and therefore limiting. He was sympathetic to Rashi and his judicious selection of midrashic material, but here too, he did not hesitate to criticize a choice of midrash that he felt was too distant from the *peshat.* Thus he sought to strike a balance between the two approaches and to adopt a more holistic approach to the text. His commentaries are substantially longer than those of Rashi or Ibn Ezra, as he expanded the exegetical enterprise to encompass issues of theology, mysticism, ethics, history, or character analysis, thus weaving a particularly colorful and variegated tapestry which operated on several levels. His commentary is famous for its psychological insights and deep understanding of human nature. Although most Jewish exegetes avoided typology and pre-figuration, because of their extensive use by Christian exegetes and theologians, Naḥmanides uses them extensively in his Torah commentary, connecting the deeds and travels of the patriarchs with subsequent events in Jewish history. To a larger extent than most exegetes, he was concerned with problems of structure, order, and thematic unity, explaining the reasons for the sequence of the books in the Torah and also for sequences of sections, vv., or even items in lists. For instance he invests a great deal of effort in explaining the order of the vv. and sections in the parashah of *Mishpatim* (Exod. chs 21–23), a section of laws in no apparent logical order. Scholars have identified at least fourteen categories of hierarchies in his Torah commentary, including birth order, order of importance, order of preference, and increasing or decreasing order of severity (for sins). In this tendency he follows the rabbinic mindset for which nothing in the Torah is arbitrary or haphazard, but rather, as the word of God, has significance on multiple levels. Naḥmanides was also a kabbalist, steeped in mystical traditions of the Provençal school of kabbalah. He included in his commentary, which was intended for a popular audience, numerous allusions to hidden meanings of the vv. of the Torah and interpretations of obscure, difficult midrashim, thereby stimulating kabbalistic activity and lending an aura of legitimacy to the esoteric understanding of the Torah as propounded by kabbalistic theosophy.

Kabbalistic Exegesis and *Pardes*

Naḥmanides was active in Gerona, Spain, in the second half of the 13th c., in the generation preceding Moses de Leon and his circle who composed or compiled the zoharic corpus of mystical texts. (See "The Bible in the Jewish Mystical Tradition," pp. 1943–63.) While one can distinguish levels of interpretation in Naḥmanides' commentary, it is in the last quarter of the 13th c., particularly in the *Zohar* and other writings often attributed by modern scholars to Moses de Leon that one first encounters the acronym *pardes* to refer to the four levels of interpretation of the biblical text, *peshat, remez, derash,* and *sod,* or historical, philosophical, homiletic, and mystical. This usage is primarily restricted to kabbalistic writings and did not achieve the almost universal application that the four senses achieved in medieval Christian exegesis. The first three methods of interpreting the text—the *peshat,* philosophical, and homiletical—already existed and were widely applied by exegetes of various persuasions up until that time. By introducing a fourth level and presenting it as the culmination of the exegetical process, the most profound understanding of the biblical text attainable, the kabbalists were validating the work of their predecessors while at the same time claiming pride of place for their own innovative approach to the text. The commentary of Naḥmanides' student Baḥya ben Asher (late 13th c.) was more formally organized along the lines of the commentaries of the medieval Christian exegetes, with several levels of interpretation, although there are few vv. which are interpreted on all four levels. But with the exception of Baḥya, there are few examples of exegetes who analyze a book using all four methods consistently as did the Christians. Rather than being a methodology, *pardes* is a convenient way of describing the four approaches that medieval exegetes took in commenting on a biblical book. Some exegetes would use only one approach, some would combine two or three, but seldom would all four be consistently applied.

Eastern Post-Maimonidean School (13th Century)

Exegesis in the Middle East after Maimonides bears the unmistakable imprint of the thought of this greatly revered Sage. Of great significance are the commentaries of Abraham, Maimonides' son (1186–1237), who was a great scholar, theologian and mystic in his own right. Abraham had hoped to fulfill his father's dream of producing a commentary on the Torah, but succeeded in completing only the first two books. His commentaries are eclectic, devoted in the main to *peshat* exegesis, in the tradition of scholars and grammarians of Andalusia, but also incorporating philosophical insights, and taking a critical stance vis-à-vis midrashic homilies. Abraham was greatly influenced by the pietistic Sufi (Muslim mystical) movement, which spread through Egypt in his day, and his commentaries are suffused with pietism. Indeed, he goes so far as to portray the patriarchs and the prophets as engaging in Sufi-style meditation and the pursuit of spiritual perfection. Abraham's commentaries, written in Judeo-Arabic, did not fare well, and survived in a single ms, published only in the mid-20th c.

The last significant *peshat* exegete in the Middle East was Ṭanḥum ben Joseph Yerushalmi (ca. 1220–1291, originally from the land of Israel; died in Egypt). Tanḥum was an anthologist, who compiled the best of the contextual exegesis of his predecessors, including Ibn Ezra, Radak, and Japheth ben Eli and other Karaites, often expressing his preferences. In his *Kitab al-Bayan (Book of Explanation),* he commented on the entire Bible, but only sections on the Former Prophets, Latter Prophets (except Isa.), Five Scrolls, Dan., and parts of Ps. have survived. This work is preceded by an introduction which deals with many principles of scriptural exegesis, such as grammatical issues, textual difficulties, internal contradictions, and problems in chronology. In his commentaries he identifies many rhetorical devices, following in the tradition of Moses Ibn Ezra and other Spanish exegetes. Like Maimonides' son, Abraham, he too was profoundly influenced both by Maimonidean rationalism and by Sufi mysticism. Although primarily concerned with *peshat* exegesis, he often gives both exoteric and esoteric interpretations to specific passages. In the case of the book of Jonah, he deviates from his normal practice and interprets the entire book as an allegory of the soul.

The 14th and 15th Centuries

In the 14th and 15th centuries, commentaries tended to veer away from the *peshat* to follow homiletical, philosophical, or mystical lines. Nevertheless, *peshat* commentary was never completely abandoned. Jacob ben Asher (1270?–1340), who immigrated to Toledo, Spain, with his family in the early 14th c. and was the author of a famous law code, *Sefer ha-Turim (The Book of Columns),* wrote a lengthy *peshat* commentary in which he anthologized many of his famous predecessors, but also included many original comments. He prefaced each section with *gematriot* and explanations of the Masoretic tradition, in order to whet his reader's appetite. Ironically, it is these comments that proved to be most popular, and were frequently reprinted, while his long commentary languished in ms until 1806 and has never gained a wide readership. This is an indication of the low level of interest in *peshat* commentary in the later Middle Ages.

Exegetes of a philosophical bent tended to interpret Scripture through the prism of the philosophical school to which they adhered. (See "The Bible in the Jewish Philosophical Tradition," pp. 1916–43.) Two important examples are Levi ben Gershom (Ralbag; 1288–1344) and Joseph Ibn Kaspi (1279–1340), both Aristotelian rationalists, who followed the teachings of Maimonides. Ralbag was probably the most significant and original Jewish thinker of the later medieval period. He was also a prolific exegete, writing lengthy commentaries on the Torah, Early Prophets, Five Scrolls and Job. While his exegesis is certainly informed by his philosophical worldview, there is much in it that can be characterized as *peshat.* To give but one example of his rationalistic exegesis, he offers a daring interpretation of Joshua's miraculous victory at Gibeon (Josh. 10.12): the miracle that occurred was not that the sun actually stood still for Joshua and the Israelites, but that the Israelites enjoyed such a swift victory that it made it seem as if the sun stood still. In general, except for his commentary on Song, Ralbag did not engage in philosophical allegory. He typically divided his commentaries into three sections: (1) an explanation of the difficult words in a passage; (2) an expanded paraphrase of the text; and finally, at the end of the section, (3) a list of lessons, both moral and philosophical, which could be derived from it. Ralbag was the first exegete to provide such lessons in his commentaries, and in this he may have been influenced by Christian exegesis.

Ibn Kaspi, who hailed from Argentière in Provence (hence his name, meaning "silver"), wrote commentaries on almost the entire Bible. While primarily devoted to an understanding of *peshat,* these display his philosophical learning and his knowledge of Christian sources as well. He stresses numerous times in his commentaries the importance of a thorough knowledge of Heb grammar and a mastery of the science of logic in order to properly understand the Bible. For example, his entire commentary on the book of Esth. is a critique of a comment by Ibn Ezra, which he refutes through logical analysis.

In this period, the Karaite community in Byzantium continued to develop biblical studies as it struggled to maintain its identity in the face of the overwhelming influence of the great medieval Rabbanite thinkers such as Maimonides and Ibn Ezra. The two great Karaite exegetes of the period were Aaron ben Joseph, the "elder" (ca. 1250–1320), and Aaron ben Elijah, of Nicomedia, "the younger" (ca. 1317–1369). Aaron ben Joseph produced commentaries on the Torah *(Sefer ha-Mivḥar; The Book of the Most Select),* on the Former Prophets, Isa., and Ps. *(Mivḥar yesharim; The Most Select of the Righteous),* and on Job (lost), while Aaron ben Elijah produced, inter alia, a commentary on the Torah *(Keter Torah; The Crown of the Torah).* Both authors cite Rabbanite sources extensively, including Rashi, Ibn Ezra, Maimonides, Radak, and Ramban. Ibn Ezra was especially popular, as he was among Rabbanite authors of the period. The commentaries of these exegetes follow in the Spanish tradition, relying on grammar and reason, rejecting aggadah, and, in halakhic matters, highlighting the differences between Rabbanites and Karaites.

In rabbinic circles, the sermons on the Torah (*ʿAkeidat Yitzḥak; The Binding of Isaac*) and the commentaries on the Five Scrolls of Isaac Arama (ca. 1420–1494) are exemplary models of homiletic exegesis, blending exegetical innovation and homiletic genius with psychological and philosophical insight. Arama was one of the first exegetes to use the method of problematization consistently, whereby the exegete raises a number of issues at the beginning of a passage, and then proceeds to solve the problems in the course of his discussion. This method was also followed by Don Isaac Abravanel (1437–1508), Arama's student, undoubtedly the greatest exegete of the 15th c. Abravanel produced voluminous commentaries on the Torah, Prophets, and Dan., which are thoughtful, thought-provoking, and challenging. Abravanel was very much concerned with *peshat* exegesis, which he declared to be his primary focus. He also grapples seriously with the rabbinic midrashic tradition, displaying a nuanced approach to midrashic interpretations, carefully selecting those that he found acceptable and rejecting others. More traditional in his theology than the rationalists of the later Middle Ages, he advocated a faith-based religious position which he considered to be more in line with the rabbinic tradition. For instance, he rejects Ralbag's rationalization of Joshua's miracle (10.12; see above) and declares that this was a divinely decreed deviation from the natural order. A true child of the Renaissance, he was open to the cultural innovations being articulated in his times and introduced much contemporary thought into his exegesis. He was particularly well-versed in Christian theological and exegetical literature, often quoting approvingly from Christian sources. Especially important are his ideas on the monarchy, expressed in his commentaries on Sam. and Kings. Drawing on his experience as a courtier and his deep familiarity with medieval history and political theory, he made a strong case against the monarchy, which he considered to be an inferior form of government.

Midrashic Exegesis

In the Middle Ages, the midrashic tradition was attacked on several fronts, especially by Karaites and Christians. As a result of these attacks, and because of the increased preference for *peshat,* many exegetes avoided rabbinic midrash as much as possible, while others incorporated it into their commentaries only sparingly, or else interpreted it philosophically or kabbalistically. Nevertheless, a strand of midrashic exegesis was maintained throughout the Middle Ages, quite possibly as a reaction to the elimination of such commentary from the medieval commentary tradition and out of a desire to hold up the standard of the rabbinic tradition and assure that it not be forgotten among Jews. Another reason could be the utility of midrashic material as a source for sermons, the demand for which seemed to increase as the Middle Ages waned. After the classical period of midrashic creativity during the late Talmudic and geonic periods, the Middle Ages witnessed the production of many midrashic compilations. The largest and most comprehensive was the 13th c. *Yalkut Shimʿoni* (attributed to Simeon the Preacher of Frankfurt), an attempt at producing a comprehensive verse-by-verse midrashic anthology for the entire Bible. Others in this vein were *Midrash ha-Gadol*

(The Great Midrash) by David Ha-Adani (Yemen, 14th c.), *Yalkut (ha)-Makhiri* on the Latter Prophets and Writings by Makhir ben Abba Mari (Spain? 14th c.?), and *Yalkut Re'uveni* (17th c.), a kabbalistic-midrashic compilation by Reuben Ha-Kohen. There were also commentaries produced in the midrashic style, which included a great deal of *peshat* interpretation as well as midrashic material. Examples are the *Lekaḥ Tov (Good Instruction)* by Tobiah ben Eliezer (11th c., Byzantium) and *Sekhel Tov (Sound Understanding)* by Menaḥem ben Solomon (12th c., Italy?). Some anthologists had very ambitious goals for their work; for example, Jacob Sikili (Sicily, Damascus), stated in his anthology *Talmud Torah* (1366) that he included in it all halakhic and aggadic statements from all available sources, thus obviating the need to consult any other work.

Midrashic-style commentary was especially popular in Yemen, which witnessed the production of, among others, *Me'or ha-'afelah (The Luminary of the Darkness)* by Netanel ben Isaiah (1328–29), *Midrash ha-ḥefetz (The Midrash of Desire)* by Zekhariah ha-Rofe (1430), and *Midrash ha-be'ur (The Midrash of Explanation)* by Saadia ben David (1441). These editors were not mere compilers, but often edited their texts and added comments of their own, including many of a philosophical nature. Also unique to the Yemenite midrashim are numerous citations from Muslim lore and literature, as well as folkloristic material. Anthological commentaries such as these remained popular through the late Middle Ages and into the early modern period.

The 16th Century

The upheaval of the expulsion from Spain (1492) and its aftermath scattered much of Spanish Jewry across Turkey, Greece, Italy, and North Africa. Biblical exegesis was produced in great abundance in all of these countries as well as in centers in central and eastern Europe. In Italy, the most famous exegete of the 15th c. was Obadiah Sforno (ca. 1475–1550). He produced commentaries on the Torah and Ps., which are dedicated above all to elucidating the *peshat*. Sforno, a rabbi, was also a trained physician and a cultured individual, a fine product of the world of Renaissance humanism, whose values infuse his exegesis. His Torah commentary became one of the mainstays of the biblical commentary tradition.

In the Ottoman Empire, important centers of study arose in Salonika and Constantinople. Rabbi Isaac ben Joseph Karo, a Spanish Jew, survived the Spanish and Portuguese exiles, ending up in Constantinople. In 1518 he published his commentary on the Torah, *Toledot Yitzḥak (The Story of Isaac)*, which proved to be one of the most popular and influential commentaries of the 16th c. The commentary is eclectic, incorporating comments in all four of the traditional modes of interpretation, and reveals the author's cultural sophistication. Its immense popularity is indicated by the fact that it went through four editions in fourteen years and is often quoted by later exegetes.

In Salonika, the yeshiva of Joseph Taitatzak flourished between 1525 and 1540, training many rabbis and scholars who produced vast quantities of biblical commentary, which far surpassed those produced in the Middle Ages in quantity if not in quality. For the book of Esth. and other scrolls, for example, more commentaries were written in the 16th c. than in all the centuries preceding. This surge in commentary production can be explained by the needs of the various communities for relevant biblical commentary; most arose out of sermons preached in public on the Sabbaths and holidays which were later committed to writing. Many of the commentaries produced are characterized by their prolixity, tendentiousness, inconsistencies, and homiletical nature. Yet there is still much of value that can be gleaned from them, and they deserve more attention than they have received in the past. Of particular interest is Eliezer Ashkenazi (1513–1586), a student of

Joseph Taitatzak's who was one of the leading scholars of his generation. Ashkenazi was a Talmudist and rationalist who knew many languages and was scientifically trained. He advocated the unfettered search for truth in Scripture. His greatest work is *Maʿasei ʾAdonai (Acts of God),* a four-part commentary on the narrative portions of the Torah. In this work, he urges the student to search diligently for the truth without regard for the opinions of the Sages or previous exegetes, especially the latter, since they may have become corrupted over time. He develops a theory concerning the nature and purpose of the biblical stories, according to which the events narrated in the Torah actually occurred, but the stories which relate these events are parables. The plain sense of the text can be found in the parables and not in the events themselves. In his commentary, Ashkenazi grapples with important theological issues, such as divine providence and the influence of astrology over Jewish destiny.

Other contemporary exegetes worthy of mention are Moses Alshekh (d. 1593) and Solomon ben Moses ha-Levi Alkabetz (ca. 1505–1584), both members of the Safed school of mystics. The exegetes of this period took a particular interest in the Kethuvim, especially Ps., Job, and the Five Scrolls. Alshekh, a Talmudist and kabbalist, had studied at Joseph Taitatzak's yeshiva in Salonika and later moved to Safed. Like many of his contemporaries, he preached on the Sabbaths and holidays on the weekly Torah readings and other biblical books and later edited his sermons for publication. He produced commentaries on almost the entire Bible. Solomon Alkabetz, another student of Taitatzak, and one of the more important members of the kabbalistic circle of Safed, produced compendious commentaries on the Minor Prophets, Ps., Job, Song, Ruth, and Esth., incorporating the comments of many of his contemporaries and predecessors. His commentaries are characterized by their extreme reverence for the words of the Sages, which he considered to be authentic traditions reflecting the true meaning of the text, and not mere homiletical interpretations, which could be accepted or rejected at will.

Meanwhile, in Aleppo, Syria, Samuel ben Abraham Laniado (d. 1605) was composing an impressive body of commentary, covering most of the Bible (Torah, Prophets, Ps., Lam.). Laniado's commentaries are especially noteworthy for their sensitivity to literary nuance and structural patterns in the text, thus making them quite "modern" in their orientation.

In eastern Europe at this time, Talmudic studies were dominant and biblical studies were in a state of decline. The output of biblical commentary, while significant, was dwarfed by the production in other fields. Even so, much of the commentary literature of this period was written in homiletic style, with constant recourse to rabbinic sources, and often to philosophical and mystical sources as well. Particularly popular as sources were the commentaries of Isaac Arama and Isaac Karo. *Peshat* commentaries were relatively uncommon. Among the better known commentaries was the *Gur Aryeh* by Judah Loew ben Bezalel of Prague (Maharal; 1525–1609), a super-commentary on Rashi, which combines concern with the *peshat* with reference to rabbinic sources as deep *peshat,* the true meaning of the text, which goes deeper than the literal. He also does not neglect mystical traditions. In general, however, Maharal and other exegetes of the period did not innovate methodologically and did not advance Bible study beyond the stage it was at by the end of the Middle Ages.

The 17th and 18th Centuries

In the 17th c., several noteworthy commentaries were produced. In Poland, Ephraim Solomon ben Aaron of Luntshits (1550–1619), a gifted *darshan,* or sermonizer, produced several collections of sermons and a commentary on the Torah in the homiletic style, called *Keli Yakar* (1st ed. Lublin, 1602), which enjoyed immense popularity and was included in many editions of the Rabbinic Bible.

More than a century later, Ḥayyim ben Moses Ibn ʿAttar (1696–1743), a rabbi and kabbalist of Moroccan origin, who led a group of rabbis and students to settle in the land of Israel in 1740, wrote a commentary titled *ʾOr ha-Ḥayim,* first published in Venice in 1742. This commentary was often published alongside that of Ephraim of Luntshits in East European editions of the Rabbinic Bible (*Miqraʾot Gedolot,* see below) and was especially popular among the Ḥasidim.

In Jaworow, Galicia, David Altschuler began to produce a commentary on the Prophets and Writings in order to promote the study of the Bible. His work was continued by his son, Jehiel Hillel, who in 1780–82 published the entire commentary. It was divided into two sections, *Metsudat Tsiyon (Fortress of Zion)* and *Metsudat David (Fortress of David).* The former explains the meanings of individual words, the latter the meaning of the text. The commentary, based for the most part on the medieval *peshat* exegetes such as Radak and Ibn Ezra, was very popular and has been frequently republished. (It appears in most editions of *Miqraʾot Gedolot,* see below.)

This period also saw the production of vernacular commentaries on the Bible in various parts of the Jewish world. At the end of the 16th or beginning of the 17th c., Jacob ben Isaac Ashkenazi, of Janow (d. 1623), produced a Yiddish translation with commentary on significant liturgical portions of the Tanakh, namely the Torah, Haftarot (Prophetic Readings) and Megillot (Five Scrolls). The book, *Tzene-rene* (i.e., *Tzeʾenah u-reʾenah,* or *Go Forth and Gaze* [based on Song 3.11, which is addressed to the daughters of Zion]), proved to be the most popular work in the history of Yiddish literature. Over 210 editions of this work have appeared to date. The oldest extant edition, which is not the first, appeared in Basel in 1622. At least three others had preceded it. The book was written in a popular style, intended for Yiddish-speaking Jewish men and women who lacked the education necessary for understanding the Bible in the original. In this work, the author does not provide a word-for-word translation of the text, but rather weaves together the biblical text, midrashim, medieval commentaries, elements of halakhah, and ethical admonition into a pleasing, harmonious whole. The author drew on a wide variety of rabbinic and medieval sources, not only commentaries, but also ethical *(Sefer Ḥasidim, Sefer ha-Mevakesh),* philosophical (Saadia, Ibn Gabirol, Maimonides), and mystical works (*Zohar,* Cordovero's *Palm Tree of Deborah*). The author's major medieval source seems to have been the commentary of Baḥya ben Asher. He also drew heavily on Isaac Karo's *Toledot Yitzḥak.* The work became especially popular with women, who would read it religiously every Sabbath. Its success can be attributed to the author's skill in selecting his material and finding those sources which would appeal to his unschooled readers. He was especially successful in selecting sources that would appeal to his female readers, injecting comments of a midrashic and moralistic nature, relating to marital relations and childrearing. *Tzene-rene* went through numerous editions, first in Western, then in Eastern Europe, and some editions bore the ideological stamp of the maskilic rationalists or their Hasidic opponents. Editions, translations, and adaptations of this ever-popular work are still being produced. A similar work on the Prophets and Writings, called *Sefer ha-Magid (The Book of the Storyteller)* mistakenly attributed to Ashkenazi, also attained considerable popularity, but nothing approaching that of *Tzene-rene.*

In the 18th c., a parallel phenomenon to *Tzene-rene* was the publication in Constantinople of *Meʿam Loʿez (From a Foreign People),* a Ladino (Judeo-Spanish) commentary on the Bible, which is considered to be the outstanding work of Judeo-Spanish literature. Conceived by Jacob Culi as a response to the havoc wrought by the Sabbatean heresy of the previous century (Shabbetai Tzevi was followed by many as Messiah, but converted to Islam in 1666, precipitating a great crisis), it was aimed at the masses who had strayed from observant Judaism and could no longer read the texts in Heb. Culi produced the volume for Gen., which wove together in a pleasing and appealing manner a variety of sources dealing with the text, including much ancillary material such as anecdotes, ethical admonitions, folklore, and historical narratives. After Culi's death, his work was continued by others. The rest of the Torah was completed and published by 1772, and other volumes, published in a similar style, were produced over the following centuries. In recent years a Heb translation has been produced. It is difficult to overstate the importance of *Meʿam Loʿez* in Sephardic culture. It spread all over the Sephardic world and for many families it was the only literature that they read. Unlike *Tzene-rene,* it was never considered only suitable for women, and so was equally popular among men, women, and children.

By the mid-18th c., the winds of change were blowing through the Jewish communities of Europe, and the stage was being set for the Haskalah and the revolution in study that would follow in its wake. (See "Jewish Biblical Scholarship from the 17th to the 19th Centuries," pp. 1963–71, and "The Bible in the Jewish Philosophical Tradition," pp. 1916–43.)

Miqra'ot Gedolot

The production of Bibles with the biblical text surrounded by a number of commentaries and translations began in the late Middle Ages, as scribes copied for themselves or patrons commissioned such works for their own use. With the introduction and spread of the printing press, commentaries were first produced individually, or accompanying the biblical text. The first Rabbinic Bible was published by Daniel Bomberg in 1516 in Venice and included the commentaries of Rashi, Ibn Ezra, and Ramban. Other editions soon followed (Venice, 1524–25, 1544). The second Rabbinic Bible (1524–1525), edited by Jacob ben Ḥayyim ben Isaac Ibn Adonijah (ca. 1470–ca. 1538), an apprentice of Bomberg's who converted to Christianity late in life, is especially important, because of the editor's attention to the accuracy of the text, seeking out mss to help in this task, and his attempt to produce an edition faithful to the Masoretic tradition. (See "Masoretic Bible," pp. 2159–65.) He also succeeded in printing more commentaries than had his predecessors. His edition set the standard for generations to come and served as the basis for many subsequent editions. Another important edition was *Kehilat Mosheh* (*The Congregation of Moses;* Amsterdam, 1724–1727), edited by Moses Frankfurter, which had sixteen commentaries never before included, such as those of Ralbag. In the 19th c. in Eastern Europe, the production of such editions of the Bible became extremely popular and publishers in Warsaw, Vilna, and Cracow vied for customers' attention, competing for the distinction of having the greatest number of commentaries in their editions. It was early in the 19th c. that the title *Miqra'ot Gedolot (Great Scriptures)* for such editions was first introduced. Besides the classical triumvirate of Rashi, Ibn Ezra, and Naḥmanides, the *Keli yakar (Precious Vessel)* by Ephraim of Luntshitz and *Or ha-Ḥayim (Light of Life)* by Ḥayyim Ibn ʿAttar seem to have been immensely popular and gained a wide readership. For Prophets and Writings, the *Metzudot* of the Altschulers were constant companions of Rashi. Depending on the book, they were usually joined by Ibn Ezra, Radak, Ralbag, and Sforno. There can be no doubt that these editions had a tremendous influence on which commentaries were read and which were neglected. Inclusion in an edition of *Miqra'ot Gedolot* would ensure a wide audience. The juxtaposition of commentaries from different locations and periods also influenced how the Bible was studied (see p. 1890). Such editions facilitate a dialogue across generations and cultures mediated by the reader, who thus becomes another link in the ongoing tradition of biblical study and interpretation.

[BARRY D. WALFISH]

The Bible in the Jewish Philosophical Tradition

Understanding what the Bible says and means has been the central concern of the Jewish philosophical tradition. Jewish philosophers have assumed that the biblical text, as God's revealed word, is true. In principle, then, what is true in the Bible must cohere with what is known to be true from other sources of knowledge. Given the limitations of human knowledge, however, no one philosophical reading of the Bible can be definitive; all readings are necessarily partial, incomplete, and amenable to correction. Committed to the pursuit of truth, Jewish philosophers "translated" the Bible into other languages, composed commentaries on the Bible, expounded the particularly difficult or significant sections of the Bible, and theorized about the relationship between knowledge discovered by human reason and knowledge revealed by God. All of these activities were regarded as expressions of the religious obligation to love God.

Although the Bible played an important role in all phases of Jewish philosophy, the philosophical tools for reflections about the Bible have changed over time, reflecting the transformation of Jewish culture as influenced by its general surroundings. In ancient Alexandria, medieval Spain, Provence, and Italy, modern Germany, and contemporary America, Jewish philosophers have engaged diverse philosophical schools, including Platonism, Stoicism, Kalam, Aristotelianism, Enlightenment, Kantianism, Existentialism, Phenomenology, and Post-Structuralism. By thinking about Judaism in light of these philosophical traditions, Jewish philosophers not only fathomed the depth of the Bible anew but also acted as cultural mediators between Judaism and surrounding cultures.

The Greco-Roman World

The Bible itself laid the foundation for the pursuit of wisdom in Judaism, even though the Bible is not a philosophical text. Fusing ancient Israelite wisdom with covenantal theology, the book of Deut. stated that the laws given to Israel are wisdom that the people of other nations can appreciate and the *torah* or teaching (understood in postbiblical Judaism as the Torah) is wisdom proper to Israel (4.5–8). The identification of Torah and wisdom meant that the scholar of Torah is also the carrier of the sapiential tradition and that to stand in a proper relationship with God, the wise person must fathom the truth of the Torah. As attested in the Wisdom of Ben Sirach, by the 2nd c. BCE, the fusion of Torah and wisdom was fully in place: The Torah was understood to contain not only divine commands that regulate social relations and Israel's relationship with God, but also information about God's created world. Since Torah is revealed wisdom, the pursuit of wisdom about the world, which is the task of philosophy, would have to be linked to the interpretation of the divinely revealed text.

Jewish philosophy began in earnest during the Hellenistic period, when Diaspora Jews encountered Greek philosophy. As Gk-speaking Egyptian Jews lost their facility in Heb, they translated the Bible into Gk—the Septuagint (LXX)—and began to study it in light of Greek philosophy. The first Jewish philosopher known by name, Aristobulus (ca. 180–145 BCE), wanted readers to understand the Torah philosophically in order to demonstrate the rationality of the Jewish religion. (A few extant fragments of his work are in *The Old Testament Pseudepigrapha* [ed. James Charlesworth, Garden City: Doubleday, 1985], pp. 831–42.) Writing in Gk to Jews and Gentiles, Aristobulus presented Judaism as a type of philosophical school. He did not wish to assimilate the Jewish religion into Greek philosophy, but rather to argue that Judaism is superior to other philosophical schools because "Plato and the philosophers borrowed from Moses." Though Aristobulus equated the God of the Jews and the God of the Gentile philosophers, his teachings were thoroughly Jewish because he also identified the rational wisdom of the philosophers with "Torah." Precisely because the Torah teaches philosophical truths, it must *not* be taken literally. Through allegorical reading of the LXX, Aristobulus and other educated Jews could explain to themselves and to non-Jews the meaning of Jewish practices, beliefs, and sacred texts that kept the Jews a people apart in the Greco-Roman world. Allegory would typify much of the early Jewish Hellenistic philosophical tradition.

Another typical example of Judeo-Hellenistic philosophical writing was the author of the Wisdom of Solomon, who was conversant in Middle Platonism (a philosophical school that flourished from 80 BCE to 220 CE and was steeped in Stoicism), as well as in Israelite Wisdom tradition. The Wisdom of Solomon was an attempt to place the Jewish religion within a broad philosophical text, intelligible to educated contemporaries who are at home in Hellenistic philosophy. The author identifies himself with King Solomon and, on the basis of 1 Kings ch 3, presents King Solomon as achieving a union with Wisdom through searching and praying (Wisd. 7.7–9; 9.1–8). For the duration of Jewish philosophy, the belief that King Solomon was the prototype of the sage and patron of arts and sciences would legitimize the study on philosophy and science and would make Eccl. and Song, two works attributed to him, central texts for philosophical commentaries.

The most important and prolific Jewish philosopher of the Hellenistic period was Philo of Alexandria (15 BCE–50 CE). At home in the culture of the Greek polis and thoroughly proficient in the philosophy of the major Greek schools of Plato, Aristotle, the Stoics, and the Pythagoreans, Philo's allegiance to Scripture was never in question. He rejected a radical allegorical reading of the Bible and argued that those who advocated it merely wished to assimilate into Hellenistic Roman society and abandon Judaism. For Philo, true philosophical life is to be found in the divine law of Moses, which leads its adherents to the attainment of the ultimate end of human life—the seeing of God. Philo's exposition of Scripture's truths was meant to prove the uniqueness and epistemological superiority of the Jewish tradition over other intellectual and religious traditions.

The prophecy of Moses plays an important role in establishing the perfection of the Hebrew Scriptures. For Philo, Moses was the most perfect of men with reference to his priestly piety (*Mos.* 2:66) and his constant and unbroken nobility of life and other virtues (*Mos.* 1:24, 29; 2:58). With no sin and imperfection, Moses was "king, lawgiver, high priest, prophet," and "in each function he won the highest place" (*Mos.* 2:292). Philo provides a highly idealized account of Moses' life, illustrating his outstanding moral and religious qualities. Moses' prophecy itself proved his intellectual perfection since he comprehended the incorporeal, intelligible world of Ideas. Using the language of allegory to do it, Moses wrote down what he had seen of the incorporeal world of real essences. The intellectual study of "mental things and real existences" is the allegorical study of Scripture. In accordance with the Platonic schema of the *Republic,* Philo portrays Moses as the philosopher-king who "attained the very summit of philosophy," and he is credited with discoveries wrongly attributed to others (*Mos.* 2:2). While Moses was not God, he was not merely human either. Philo applies to Moses the same title—*theos*—that he applies also to the Logos. Indeed, Moses receives a "divine communication," meaning that "all that follows in the wake of God is within the good man's apprehension while he himself is beyond it." As the embodiment of Logos, Moses is called "the law-giving Word," by which humanity could be rescued from the bondage of matter. Thus Moses is the supreme high priest, who bestows "a blessing which nothing in the world can surpass" (*Mos.* 2:67). Moses rescued mankind from the bondage of matter.

Philo adapted to Scriptures the same method that the Stoics used to interpret Homer and Greek mythology. The Hebrew Scriptures for him are the inspired word of God. Moses' utterances were "absolutely and entirely signs of the divine excellence, conduct and particularly the nation of his worshippers, for whom he opens up the road which leads to happiness" (*Mos.* 2:189). The Bible was composed in a state comparable to that of the philosopher when he is inspired to recall intelligible ideas beyond the world of sense and matter. That means that for Philo, the Torah is inspired, but Moses and not God was its author, a daring notion indeed as far as later rabbinic Judaism is concerned. The same inspiration also filled the LXX translators who preserved the true meaning of the mysteries conveyed by Moses.

At Sinai Moses' purified soul was engraved or inscribed by God. By virtue of this divine impression of knowledge, Moses was a "living law" even before he composed the written laws. In his own person Moses functioned as a kind of seal designed to impress the law in the shape of his life on those who would become his followers (*Mos.* 1:158–59). Moses expressed his extraordinary knowledge through the act of writing (rather than speaking) when he composed the Torah, which contains laws of proper conduct and facts about the structure of the cosmos. The language at his disposal, however, was post-lapsarian; it was no longer the original Adamic language, which had been mimetic. Whereas Adamic language presented reality by giving names to things on the basis of direct apprehension of the essences of things, Moses could only use an imperfect language. Moreover, since Moses addressed all Israelites, who by definition were imperfect and ill prepared, he had to use audio-visual aids to convey his conceptual message. The result was the anthropomorphic language of the Bible, which requires allegorical interpretation.

The upshot of Philo's analysis is that only the Mosaic law enables those who follow it to live by the Stoic mandate of life in accordance with nature. The zenith of the well-lived life is an individual, ecstatic, unmediated experience of coming to know the transcendent and immaterial God. This is a contemplative, mystical experience in which the "eye of the mind" or the soul comes "to see God." As the goal of human life, this mystical experience governs the direction of the happy life, organizing all human activities to attain it. Since for Philo the revealed law of Moses is the ideal law, which God implanted in nature at creation, the universal goal of "seeing God" is achievable only for those who live by the law of Moses, since it alone guides humanity in accordance with nature. Hence the experience of "seeing God" constitutes the community of "Israel" which for Philo is a nonethnic intellectual-religious category ("those who see God") rather than an ethnic or national category. This view would enable Christian readers to adapt Philo for their own needs, making him into a Church Father, and explains why the works of Philo were preserved in the church rather than in the synagogue.

Philo illustrates the extent to which a Jewish intellectual in 1st-c. Alexandria could creatively reconcile the Greek philosophical tradition with Scripture-based religion. Yet Philo did not chart the future development of Judaism. Instead, the Rabbis of the land of Israel and Babylonia articulated what became normative Judaism. Although the Rabbis reflected on the same themes of concern to Philo, they did not adopt his allegorical method of interpretation. Similarly, while the rabbinic academy shared many features with Greco-Roman philosophical schools, including the total commitment to the love of wisdom (which the Rabbis equated with Torah), and the life-long cultivation of moral and intellectual virtues, rabbinic speculations about God, the universe, the problem of evil, and the purpose of human life proceeded hermeneutically and homiletically rather than systematically and demonstratively. In addition, rabbinic views developed from the Heb text, rather than from the LXX. These views, found in a wide variety of early and late rabbinic texts, are extremely diffuse and diverse and are extremely difficult to categorize and to compare to the oeuvre of a single individual like Philo.

Medieval Jewish Philosophy

The Greco-Roman period in Jewish history ended with the redaction of the Talmud, the Jerusalem Talmud (ca. 400 CE) and the Babylonian Talmud (after 500 CE). Soon afterwards, with the rise and expansion of Islam, the life of Jews in the Middle East radically changed. The new religion recognized the Bible as revealed Scripture and granted Jews the status of protected subjects *(dhimmi)*. As a monotheistic religion, Islam did not pose a theoretical challenge to Jews. But when Greek and Hellenistic philosophy and science were translated into Arabic during the 8th and 9th centuries, Islamic civilization gave rise to a new systematic philosophy *(falsafah)* and speculative theology *(kalam)*. The latter two did pose an intellectual challenge to which Jewish thinkers, who were conversant in Arabic language and culture, had to respond. In the new rationalist climate, which sets up reason as a judge of religion, Judaism had to be proven to be a rational religion.

Most problematic were the anthropomorphic depictions of God in the Bible and in rabbinic texts. In the ecstatic and visionary strand of rabbinic thought, known as the *heikhalot* and *merkavah* literature (see "The Bible in the Jewish Mystical Tradition," pp. 1943–63), God was not only imaged as a king seated on the Throne of Glory as in the Bible, but the limbs of God's body were given precise (albeit fantastic) measurements. In the new intellectual climate of the 9th c., the corporeal depiction of God in rabbinic Judaism became an intellectual embarrassment and a target of severe criticism from rationalist skeptics such as Hiwi al-Balkhi (whose "Two Hundred Questions Concerning Scripture" are known only through Saadia's response to them). The most scathing critique of rabbinic Judaism came from the Karaites, who denied the validity of the oral tradition and regarded only written law as sacred. But how is Scripture to be interpreted without the rabbinic tradition? Following the Kalam theologians of the Muʿtazilite school, the Karaite thinkers posited human reason and the sciences of grammar and philology as the way to fathom the meaning of divinely revealed Scripture. The Karaites' exposition of the biblical text would give rise to their articulation of the dogmas of Judaism and to the formal distinction between ceremonial and rational commandment. The Karaites were thus the first Jewish philosophers in the Middle Ages. Their critique of rabbinic Judaism put them outside normative Judaism, but their influence on the way normative Judaism formulated its philosophical beliefs was profound.

It was the great foe of Karaism, Saadia Gaon (882–942), who articulated the philosophic defense of rabbinic Judaism. Like the Karaite philosophers, Saadia Gaon's theology was shaped by the Muʿtazilite Kalam, but he applied its claim that human reason is compatible with a divinely revealed religion not only to Scripture but to the entire rabbinic tradition. There is nothing in rabbinic Judaism that is contradictory to reason, provided the written law and the oral law are properly interpreted. To prove the first claim, Saadia translated almost the entire Bible into Arabic. This literal translation *(Tafsir)* was accompanied by an extended paraphrastic commentary on the biblical text *(Sharḥ)* intended for the more learned reader. To prove the latter claim, Saadia composed thematic monographs on rabbinic law. In his main theological treatise, *Kitab al Amanat wa'l itiqadat (Book of Doctrines and Beliefs)*, Saadia delineated the circumstances that legitimized a nonliteralist understanding of the biblical text.

Saadia's *Book of Doctrines and Beliefs* had a clear polemical intent: to reject all forms of Jewish skepticism and disbelief rife in his time and to place rabbinic Judaism on a firm rationalist foundation. Saadia's method of reasoning was not significantly different from that of the Karaites, but his conclusions were. Like the Karaites, he regarded the rationalist inquiry into the meaning of the received tradition by the tools that God implanted in humans (namely, human reason) to be a religious obligation. Saadia believed that his method of exposition could help turn religious belief, affirmed on the basis of tradition, into firmly held convictions that are corroborated by rational proofs. For Saadia, the revealed tradition is a source of valid knowledge that complements what can be known through the other three sources: sense perception, self-evident truths, and logical inference. A revelation from God is necessary because human beings are not intellectually equal; some are more gifted than others. Furthermore, the pursuit of truth by natural human reason is very arduous, time-consuming, and prone to errors. Divine revelation is necessary to compensate for human limitations, making truth available to all, including women and children.

A superb close reader of the Bible, Saadia found scriptural support for almost every detail of rational argument. Saadia's rationalist exposition of Scripture demanded that whenever Scripture appears to be in conflict with what is known to be true from the other three sources of knowledge, it is necessary to submit the text to careful examination and interpret the scriptural text in question allegorically. This is especially necessary in regard to the corporeal depiction of God in the Bible. Since reason independently demonstrates that God is the creator of the universe and that, therefore, God is not corporeal, it follows that the literal meaning of the biblical text cannot be true. Saadia proposes how to decode the corporeal language of the Bible. For example, when the term *head* is applied to God it must mean "excellence and elevation"; *eye* means "supervision"; *ear* "denotes acceptance"; *mouth* and *lip* mean "teaching and command"; *heart* "signifies wisdom"; *bowels* "denote amiability"; *foot* denotes "coercion." Since these words are used in the Bible also in nonanthropomorphic senses, it is most appropriate that the nonanthropomorphic sense will be used in scriptural utterances about God. Thus the rationalist conception of God recommended the allegorical interpretation. After Saadia, the allegorical interpretation of the text was applied not only to divine attributes but also to human agents in biblical narratives.

The intellectualization of rabbinic Judaism reached its zenith in Muslim Spain during the 11th and 12th centuries. The unique cultural symbiosis between Judaism and Islam flourished under the Ummayad Caliphate in Cordoba and its successor petty kingdoms, where outstanding Jews rose to power in the administration of the Muslim state, creating a Jewish culture suffused with the sensibilities and ideals of *adab,* namely, the broad scientific and rhetorical learning that made one courteous and urbane. The *adib* (the man schooled in *adab*) was a highly refined person who was expected to know a little about many topics in order to add brilliance to the court. The key for success in the court was possession of rhetorical skills, poetic eloquence, and calligraphic excellence, all of which were cultivated through the study and production of prose and poetry. The *adib* culled his knowledge from prose books that encompassed tales, fables, anecdotes, practical advice, and popularization of scientific information, all gleaned from the philosophical-scientific heritage of the Hellenistic world, interspersed with some material from India.

Jewish culture in Muslim Spain changed profoundly as Jewish courtiers absorbed the *adab* program, but without compromising their Jewish identity or their conviction about the spiritual superiority of Judaism. Indeed, the Bible anchored the Jewish response to the attraction of the dazzling Islamic civilization in Andalusia. Fully aware of Islamic claims about the Qur'an's divinity and perfection, including the superiority of Qur'anic Arabic to all other languages, Jewish scholars asserted the uniqueness of the Tanakh and its pure language and applied the sciences of grammar and philology to prove the perfection of the Bible. This perfection was not merely linguistic or rhetorical; it was scientific and philosophic as well. The linguistic analysis of the Bible by grammarians such as Judah ben David Ḥayyuj (ca. 950–ca. 1000), Isaac ben Levi Ibn Mar Shaul, Samuel Ibn Naghrella (933–1056), Judah ben Samuel Ibn Balʿam (d. ca. 1090), Moses ben Samuel Ibn Gikatilla (or Chiquitilla) (d. ca. 1080), Jonah Ibn Janaḥ (ca. 985–c. 1040) and Shmuel Alkanzi (1050–1130), enabled a deeper philosophical understanding of the Bible to emerge. It was through the literal meaning of the text (later called *peshat*) that the deeper philosophical meaning could be accessed.

The most outstanding exponent of the link between the linguistic analysis of Heb and the philosophical exposition of the Bible was Abraham Ibn Ezra (1089–1167). A poet, liturgist, grammarian, translator, mathematician, astronomer, astrologer and philosopher, Abraham Ibn Ezra's interpretation of Judaism was naturalist and rationalist. Regarding the Jews as unique mediators between cultures, Ibn Ezra was committed to imparting knowledge of Greek and Arabic cultures to his Jewish audience and even wrote scientific works in Latin to make the work of Jews known to Christians. He began to comment on the biblical canon rather late in life after migrating from Muslim Spain to Italy with the intention of teaching the correct reading of the Bible to Jews who were not yet familiar with the Jewish rationalist tradition and Judeo-Hispanic biblical exegesis. Though Ibn Ezra composed commentaries to the entire Bible, the extant texts include commentaries (some preserved in two versions) on the Torah, Isa., the Twelve Minor Prophets, Ps., Job, the Five Scrolls, and Dan. The style of the commentary is terse and cryptic, full of allusions to philosophical and scientific (esp. astrological) theories, purportedly contained in the Bible, but which should not be expounded in full in the context of the biblical commentary.

Ibn Ezra claimed that the Bible itself attests to the fact that ancient Israelites were versed in the sciences, so that the study of the sciences is an inherently Jewish activity. Therefore, only a scholar who is deeply proficient in the sciences, especially astronomy and astrology, can properly understand the meaning of the biblical text. For Ibn Ezra the exposition of the text by means of astrological references does not mean imposing science on the Bible, but rather showing how the biblical text itself actually enlarges the scope of the scientific discourse known to him from extrabiblical, Muslim and Hermetic sources. At times the biblical text is used by Ibn Ezra to address questions that are raised by other sciences or resolve tensions between various scientific theories, for example, between the assumption of astrology that ascribes to celestial bodies the physical properties such as hot and cold, and the Aristotelian views according to which the celestial bodies are made of a refined substance that does not carry physical properties. The Bible can also remove a contradiction between the assumptions of astrology and the physical view that Ibn Ezra accepted as correct. For example, Ps. 148 teaches not only about the cosmological differentiation between the lower and supernal worlds, but also about the physical composition of objects in the supralunar world and the fixed cyclical motion.

For Ibn Ezra, the science of astrology captures the fixity of natural laws, even though he maintained that the predictive power of astrology is not perfect. Although Ibn Ezra did not consider astrology to be practically useful, he made many allusions to astrological theories when he explained animal sacrifices, the festivals, the scapegoat ritual, and the uniqueness of the Holy Land, among other aspects of Israelite religion. The prevalence of astrology in the exposition of the biblical text, however, should not obscure the main claim of Ibn Ezra about the relationship between astrology and the Torah. Precisely because Israel is in possession of the revealed Torah, Israel alone can be free from the influences of astral forces, provided Israel studies the Torah and observes its commandments. As

Ibn Ezra teaches in the commentary on Exod. 3.21, the very commitment to Torah study and the life that flows from it ensures that Israel is not subject to astrological influence.

Ibn Ezra's naturalism went hand in hand with his esoteric style of biblical commentaries and, in turn, with his intellectual elitism. He made a clear distinction between the masses, who lack the capacity to engage in philosophy and science, and the few who possess the "heart," which is the seat of reason in Ibn Ezra's psychology. Only the very few who are scientifically educated can attain the ultimate end of human life and enjoy the bliss of immortality reserved to the individual soul. For the educated reader, laconic allusions are sufficient to direct him to the deep philosophic and scientific matters taught by the Torah. These are the "secrets" *(sodot)* of the Torah that remain obscure to the masses. In the 14th c., as we shall see below, several Jewish philosophers composed supercommentaries on Ibn Ezra's commentaries, spelling out (not always correctly) the precise meaning of these secrets.

Until the second half of the 14th c. it was Moses Maimonides, Rambam (Rabbi Moses son of Maimon 1138–1204), rather than Abraham Ibn Ezra who dominated the Jewish philosophical approach to the Bible. Although Maimonides perpetuated many ideas of Ibn Ezra, Maimonides also vigorously rejected the science of astrology, highlighted the limitation of human knowledge in metaphysics, and recognized naturalist causality only as far as the sublunar world is concerned. At the heart of Maimonides' approach to the Bible stood his theory of prophecy, which is remarkably similar to that of Philo, even though the immediate source of inspiration for Maimonides was not Philo but the Muslim philosopher Abu Nasr Alfarabi (d. 950). Adopting Plato's political theory to the case of Islam, Alfarabi portrayed the founder of the true religion as a philosopher-prophet-legislator-imam whose perfect law contains the translation of philosophic truths into figurative speech.

Following Alfarabi, Maimonides understood prophecy as a cognitive activity by an intellectually perfect person. All prophets must be philosophers, though not all philosophers are endowed with the imaginative faculty that can translate philosophic knowledge into figurative speech characteristic of prophecy. Maimonides, however, took pains to differentiate between the prophecy of Moses and the prophecy of all other prophets: Moses received his prophecy in broad daylight, and he prophesied whenever he wished, without fear or trembling, and without any input from his senses or the imagination. Moses' prophecy was qualitatively different because he transcended human corporeality and "attained the angelic." Suppressing his senses, appetites, and desires to the utmost minimum, Moses transcended human embodiment, and his body no longer functioned as a "veil" between him and God. Mosaic prophecy was, therefore, purely intellectual, the result of the conjunction between Moses' perfected intellect and the Active Intellect. In knowing what the Active Intellect knows, Moses apprehended the pattern of the law of nature. Therefore, the Torah of Moses "enters into what is natural" (*Guide* II:40), that is to say, it fits the structure of reality. The perfection of the Torah is thus completed in the perfection of the agent that received the Torah—the prophet Moses.

Moses was not only cognitively perfect; his imaginative faculty was also the most perfect. While Moses' prophecy was itself strictly conceptual or cognitive, the transmission of its content to the Israelites required the use of the imagination, since this faculty is the difference between philosopher and prophet. Because of Moses' perfect imagination, the Torah of Moses is the most perfect poetic text, one in which there is a perfect fit between the cognitive, esoteric core of the philosophic truths and figurative language of Torah narratives, a fit that justifies *allegoresis.* In Aristotelian language this is to say that the narratives, poetic imagery, and laws of the Torah function as Matter for the cognitive truths that are their

Form. In its figurative language, the Torah teaches the sciences of physics and metaphysics. The task of the philosophic reader of the Bible is to remove the figurative veils of the Torah in order to fathom its philosophic content.

For the philosophically inclined reader, Maimonides composed *The Guide for the Perplexed,* whose first part contains a philosophical dictionary of the most problematic terms in the Bible. For example, Scripture uses the terms *image* and *likeness* to refer to God. These terms, Maimonides explains, are equivocal terms: When applied to natural things they refer to shapes of natural bodies, but when applied to God they mean something altogether different, because God is noncorporeal. Maimonides proceeds to explain the meaning of other terms such as *figure, shape, place, throne, to descend, to ascend, sitting, standing, rising, to stand, to approach, to rise,* and others, all in order to teach the reader how to read the Bible correctly in a manner that does not violate the radical otherness of God.

Maimonides held that there is an unbridgeable ontological gap between God, the Necessary Existent, and all other things. It is therefore impossible for humans to know the essence of God. Human beings can only know who God is not, although from the observation of the natural world and the science of physics, human beings can know a lot about the actions of God. The radical negative theology of Maimonides entails that all terms applied to God in the Torah are either equivocations or absolute equivocation, which would suggest that the term "prophecy" as applied to Moses and any other prophet is also absolutely equivocal. Maimonides, however, does not go that far, because he could not make Moses into a deity; Moses can only be a unique human being. Because Maimonides insisted that Moses remain a human being and the Torah rationally intelligible, he had to explain in what sense the Torah of Moses is from God. This is the purpose of talking about "divine ruse" (Heb *ʿormah,* Arabic *talattuf*) in the *Guide* III:30 and 32.

The "divine ruse" was to give Israel the Torah through the intermediacy of Moses who communicated with Israel at a level that Israel could accept. Since God is an absolute unity, in God will and wisdom are the same: What God wills and what God knows are the same, and both are manifested in the way God governs the world. And since God governs through natural causes, divine management of human affairs takes into consideration the particular conditions of humanity. Given the prevalence of idolatrous practices and beliefs, the "divine ruse" was evident both in forcing Israel to live in the desert in order to improve its character, and in using Moses as the intermediary to address Israel at a level at which it could comprehend God's word. Concomitantly, in order to make sure that we will not conclude erroneously that the Torah of Moses is merely contingent, the eighth principle of Maimonides' "Thirteen Principles of Jewish Faith" specifies dogmatically that the Torah cannot change.

The cognitive perfection of Moses yielded a perfect text, but the divinity of the Torah can also be determined by an examination of its function. The Torah is divine because it can be shown that the Torah brings about the perfection of the body *(tikkun ha-guf)* and perfection of the soul *(tikkun ha-nefesh)*. The Torah is a prescription for human well-being, because the inner meaning of the Torah corresponds to the structure of reality. By living according to the regimen articulated in the Torah, human beings can attain well-being of body and soul, when the former is understood as a means to the attainment of the latter. By observing the commandments of the Written Torah as interpreted by the Oral Torah, one ensures physical health, the acquisition of the requisite virtues, culminating in the perfection of the intellect. It is the perfection of the intellect through cognition of intelligibles that constitutes the immortal life that the Jewish tradition denotes as "world-to-come." Whether this cognitive state constitutes personal immortality and whether this is the correct interpretation of rabbinic Judaism would become a major theme in the debate about Maimonides's legacy during the 13th c.

Maimonides did not compose a linear commentary on the Bible, but only articulated general hermeneutical principles. The application of Maimonides' hermeneutical principles to the Bible was carried out by his followers, beginning with Samuel Ibn Tibbon (d. 1232), who translated the *Guide* from Arabic into Heb, composed a glossary of philosophical terms in the *Guide,* explained the esoteric meaning of Eccl., and composed a systematic exposition of the biblical creation narrative in light of Aristotle's physics. To master the latter and make it accessible to Jewish seekers of wisdom, Ibn Tibbon also translated Aristotle's *Meteora* into Heb in 1210. Samuel Ibn Tibbon inaugurated the tradition of philosophical biblical commentaries that read the Bible as an encoded Aristotelian, philosophical text.

Jewish philosophers in 13th c. Spain vacillated between two conflicting goals: On the one hand, the philosophers wished to teach philosophy to the many in order to raise the intellectual level of Jews and enable them to perfect their soul so as to attain immortality. On the other hand, the philosophers believed that ordinary Jews lacked the intellectual preconditions to engage in philosophy; they may misunderstand philosophic teachings and harbor erroneous views. The followers of Maimonides attempted to bridge the gap between the philosophers and the public by composing summaries of philosophical texts, popularizing philosophy in prose studded with rhymed poetry, and by writing philosophical commentaries on the Bible in which they made clear what Maimonides only hinted at in the *Guide.* With the treatment of the Bible as a philosophic-scientific text, opposition to rationalist philosophy was unavoidable. Throughout the 13th c., Jewish communities in Spain, Provence, France, Italy, the land of Israel, Egypt, and Iraq were engaged in a bitter controversy about the status of philosophy within Jewish traditional society.

R. David Kimḥi (Radak; 1160–1235), a biblical exegete, grammarian, and translator, whose family migrated from Muslim Spain to Provence, played a major role in what we now call the Maimonidean Controversy of the 1230s. He is an example of a militant rationalist commentator on the Bible for whom the Torah was intentionally written by Moses with a "double meaning, one obscuring the other ... the exoteric for the masses and the esoteric for the Sages" (Frank Talmage, *David Kimhi: The Man and the Commentaries* [Cambridge, MA: Harvard University Press, 1975], p. 120). Although Radak retains the *peshat* level of the biblical text and contributed greatly to its understanding, his commentaries also provided an elaborate allegorical reading. For example, "the Garden of Eden represents the Active Intellect and the Tree of Life the human Intellect, while the Tree of Knowledge of Good and Evil symbolized the material intellect" (Talmage, p. 121). Radak goes on to interpret biblical personae allegorically. Cain, for example, was a farmer and devoid of intellectual accomplishments, whereas Abel was occupied with the vanities of life, even though he was endowed with material intellect. In Radak's reading, it was the third son, Seth, who ate from the Tree of Life and was created in the image of Adam. It was he who shared with Adam the human intellect. Seth was the good seed and the true founder of mankind. In this allegorical fashion Radak explicates the two main bodies of esoteric teachings in the Torah, the Account of Creation *(maʿaseh bereshit),* based on the creation narrative of Gen., and the Account of the Chariot *(maʿaseh merkavah),* based on the first ch of Ezek. Based on Maimonides's reading of the latter, Radak was even more elaborate and specific than was Maimonides in reading this ch as expression of Aristotelian cosmology whose principles are explained in "ch headings" in the *Guide.*

The rationalist philosophers insisted that to worship God correctly Jews must know philosophy. Therefore, the controversy during the 13th c. concerned the cultural boundaries of Judaism and the degree to which the Bible contains truths articulated in other sources. Yet, if the Torah is indeed divine Wisdom, as the philosophers argued, then one could argue that there is no need to consult philosophy and science at all since Scripture already contains all the knowledge necessary for its correct interpretation. Kabbalists (see "The Bible in the Jewish Mystical Tradition," pp. 1943–63) such as Jacob Ibn Sheshet (13th c.) advanced that claim and rejected the Maimonidean interpretation of the creation narrative. Yet the kabbalists too developed their ideas and exegetical strategies through familiarity with Jewish philosophy, and like the philosophers the kabbalists endorsed the distinction between the exoteric *(nigleh)* and esoteric *(nistar)* levels of the biblical text. Likewise, the kabbalists accepted Maimonides' claim that the Torah is the prescription for human well-being, or happiness, culminating in personal immortality. For this and other reasons, the impression often given of an absolute difference between the medieval philosophical and kabbalistic tradition is incorrect.

The primary difference between the rationalist philosophers and the kabbalists concerned the nature of the Heb language. Whereas to the Maimonidean philosophers Heb was a conventional, human language, the kabbalists maintained that Heb is literally the language of God whose elements—the Heb letters—are the "building blocks," so to speak, of the created universe. The revelation of the Torah and the creation of the universe are two sides of the same coin. For the kabbalists, then, *ma'aseh bereshit* and *ma'aseh merkavah* refer not to the physical universe of the sublunar and supralunar worlds, respectively, but to processes within the Godhead. In other words, Scripture, according to the kabbalists, is a symbolic manifestation of God's essence, the very thing that Maimonides claimed lies beyond the ken of human knowledge. Although both rationalist philosophers and kabbalists asserted that the Hebrew Scriptures contain salvific truths about God, for the philosophers these truths concern the created world and its relationship with God, whereas for the kabbalists these truths are of God's very essence.

The final phase of the Maimonidean Controversy took place in 1303–1305 and ended on July 31, 1306, when R. Solomon Ibn Adret imposed a ban on the study of philosophy for men under twenty-five years of age. The ban signaled the complex status of philosophy within traditional Jewish society, but it by no means ended the philosophical interpretation of the Bible. In the first half of the 14th c., especially in Provence, additional philosophical commentaries on the Bible were composed in which rationalist philosophers, such as Joseph Ibn Kaspi (1279–ca. 1331) and Nissim ben Moses of Marseilles (active 1320s), expounded the philosophic import of the biblical text and attempted to solve various exegetical problems that arise by reading the Bible in light of Aristotelian philosophy. The most extensive and philosophically sophisticated of these commentaries are those composed by Rabbi Levi ben Gershom, known as Ralbag or Gersonides (1288–1344).

Gersonides was a first-rate scientist, specializing in astronomy, who mastered the Aristotelian corpus by writing supercommentaries on commentaries of Averroes (1126–1198). Intimately versed with the legacy of Maimonides, Gersonides took issue with his Jewish predecessor on many points, radicalizing the intellectualist tenor of Jewish rationalist naturalism. Most importantly, Gersonides rejected Maimonides' esoteric method of teaching philosophy. Philosophy need not and must not be kept secret from the masses but must be taught openly, systematically, and without allusions and hints. Accepting Aristotelian philosophy wholeheartedly, Gersonides was determined to teach the Jewish public at large the correct meaning of the doctrines of creation, prophecy, providence, miracles, and the chosenness of Israel in his systematic philosophical work *Milḥamot ha-Shem (The Wars of the Lord)* as well as in his biblical commentaries. Like Ibn Ezra, Gersonides launched his philosophical exegesis only after composing scientific-philosophic works; proficiency in philosophy was a necessary condition to the proper understanding of the revealed text.

In agreement with Maimonides, Gersonides held that "the Torah is the written record of Moses' prophetic revelation, and, therefore, its value for guiding the Israelites to perfection is determined by the nature and quality of Moses' prophetic capabilities" (Robert Eisen, *Gersonides on Providence, Covenant, and the Chosen People: A Study in Medieval Jewish Philosophy and Biblical Commentary* [Albany: State University of New York, 1995], p. 73). But unlike Maimonides, Gersonides considered the prophet's ability to predict the future as the major difference between philosophers and prophets. The predictive capacity of the prophets follows from their perfect knowledge of causal relations in the natural world governed by astral forces. Contrary to Maimonides, who vehemently rejected the science of astrology, Gersonides, like Ibn Ezra, was an expert astrologer who attempted to shed light on the remote past on the basis of his astrological and astronomical knowledge. This knowledge is especially relevant to the interpretation of the commandments, whose allegorical meaning Gersonides spells out. Contrary to Maimonides, for whom the masses at the time of Moses were incapable of philosophical sophistication, Gersonides held that Moses taught the entire nation of uneducated Israelites the full range of philosophical doctrines, natural science, and metaphysics after their exodus from Egypt.

The pedagogic function of the Torah and the need to teach philosophy openly do not mean that Gersonides renounced the elitism characteristic of the Jewish philosophical tradition. He too believed that different audiences understand the Torah on different levels in accord with their level of intellectual perfection. Because of their lack of philosophical training the masses cannot appreciate the deep philosophical meaning of the Torah. Yet Gersonides was much more optimistic than Maimonides and Ibn Ezra about the ability of the philosopher to bring the masses to a higher level of knowledge. His philosophical commentaries accomplished that task for the general Jewish reader, but they did not simply rehash his philosophical-scientific views. Sometimes the exposition of the biblical text provided Gersonides an opportunity to offer new insights and revisions of what he said in his earlier philosophical text *The Wars of the Lord*.

Gersonides's commentaries on the Torah were written to be accessible, and followed a rigid structure: He first explained the meaning of the words, then provided a statement of the import of the section under consideration, and concluded the discussion with a summary of the "lessons" *(toʿaliot)* to be derived from the Torah portion. In his *Commentary on the Song of Songs* Gersonides departed from that style. Writing for a generally educated reader who has just embarked on the study of philosophy, Gersonides presented the Song as a philosophical allegory about the path toward ultimate felicity. From Abraham Ibn Ezra, through Joseph Ibn Aqnin (ca. 1150–1220), Moses Ibn Tibbon (active 1240–1270), and Immanuel of Rome (ca. 1261–ca. 1328), Jewish philosophers read the Song as a philosophical allegory about the human path of spiritual improvement. But unlike his predecessors, who interpreted the Song as an intellectual process culminating in the conjunction between the human rational soul and the Active Intellect, Gersonides interpreted the text to refer to internal processes, namely, the relationship between the human rational soul and the imagination. Reviewing the fundamentals of philosophy for his reader, Gersonides instructs the reader of the Song to understand the obstacles to the attainment of felicity and the ways to overcome them. Though relatively few could reach the lofty goal of spiritual perfection by which humans attain personal immortality, the goal is in principle attainable by the students of science and philosophy.

Gersonides's commitment to the dissemination of scientific knowledge was shared by Jewish philosophers in Spain and Provence during the second half of the 14th c. By then, however, what were considered sound scientific theories included not only the teachings of Aristotle, but also Neoplatonic and Hermetic theories about the natural world. This syncretistic mixture was used as a new interpretative grid for the Bible, deriving its inspiration from Abraham Ibn Ezra. In Spain during the second half of the 14th c., Samuel Ibn Motot, Joseph Tov Elem, Ezra Gatingo, Shlomo Franco, and Shem Tov Ibn Shaprut composed super-commentaries on Ibn Ezra's biblical commentaries, openly using astrology and astral magic to decode the hints of Ibn Ezra so as to explain ancient Israelite practices such as the tabernacle, the sacrifices, and the priestly vestments.

The main claims of their astral theology include the following: The Torah was given at Sinai on the basis of astrological calculation. Biblical events reflect the influences of the stars, and biblical personalities and rabbinic sages were expert astrologers. Prophecy is predicated on knowledge of astrology. Miracles are understood to be the results of the prophet's intellectual perfection. Moses was able to overcome Egyptian magicians because he was a superior astrologer. His intellectualist perfection included the knowledge of astrology, culminating in the conjunction of his intellect with the Active Intellect. He was a practicing magician who correctly understood the link between earthly and celestial powers. The knowledge of astrology enables the intellectually perfect to extricate themselves from astral causality. Moreover, the uniqueness of the people of Israel is explained in its ability to transcend the impact of astral influences through Israel's mastery of the astrological sciences. Most importantly, the commandments themselves function as tools in the manipulation of astral forces. The commandments either manifest the influence of a given celestial body, or were given as techniques to draw spiritual energy from the celestial spheres into the corporeal world. In this regard, the commandments are effective tools in the attempt to prosper in this world. The performance of the commandments mitigates the destructive forces of the corporeal world that are regulated by the celestial bodies. Observance of the commandments thus has an instrumental value, for the more consistently one performs them the more one can extricate oneself from the impact of astral forces.

In short, by the turn of the 15th c. the scientists-philosophers proposed a strictly naturalistic interpretation of Torah on the basis of astral determinism. As Judah Halevi in the 12th c. rejected such a naturalist approach to the Bible, so in the early 15th c. did Hasdai Crescas (d. ca. 1412), who set out to extricate Judaism from the clutches of philosophy. Crescas himself was a well-trained philosopher, but he was convinced that the intellectualization of Judaism by the rationalists was responsible for the mass conversion of Jews to Christianity during and after the anti-Jewish riots and massacres of 1391. To rejuvenate Iberian Jewish life, Crescas subjected Aristotle's physics to minute critique, manifesting familiarity with contemporary scholastic critique of Aristotle's conception of motion. If Aristotle's philosophy can be proven to be either nondemonstrative or patently mistaken, Aristotle's philosophy could not constitute the true meaning of the Torah. Crescas, however, advanced his critique of Aristotle by using Aristotelian logic so that the novelty and full implications of it were either not fully understood by Jewish philosophers, or dismissed outright as evidence of his philosophical limitations.

Crescas was not alone in his displeasure with the naturalist exposition of the Bible, in which the Torah was viewed as a means to an end. Similar claims were voiced by other Jewish thinkers in Spain and Portugal in an attempt to rethink the relationship between Torah and philosophy. Continuing to uphold the Aristotelian worldview, Jewish philosophers in the 15th c. increasingly acknowledged that the Torah is not identical with philosophy, but is rather superior to it. Whereas philosophy is grounded merely in knowledge of created things, Torah is revealed knowledge that can be explained by reason but not exhausted by it. Thus Simon ben Tzemach Duran (1361–1444), who was well-versed in Aristotelian philosophy, maintained that it only serves to shed light on the meaning of Torah and that philosophy alone could not possibly lead to the attainment of ultimate felicity. A similar position was espoused by Joseph Ibn Shem Tov (ca. 1400–ca. 1460), who composed commentaries to Aristotle and who interpreted the ultimate end of human life in terms of Averroes's theory of cognition.

The philosophers' own admission that knowledge of philosophy alone fails to secure personal immortality and that it must be complemented by revealed knowledge gave 15th c. Jewish philosophy its conservative posture as much as this viewpoint served an important polemical purpose against Christianity. As Spanish Jewry was fighting for its physical and spiritual survival, Jewish intellectuals were increasingly engaged in philosophical polemics against Christianity either through systematic exposition of Jewish dogmas, or through philosophical examination of Christian readings of the biblical text. The gist of this defense was that Judaism is superior to Christianity because Judaism is a rational religion. The God of Judaism does not do what is logically impossible; only what is naturally impossible. Whether rational arguments sustained Jewish believers is hard to determine; what is clear is that by the 15th c. in Spain allegiance to Judaism became harder and harder.

In the 15th c., the philosophical defense of Judaism became more difficult because the opponents were often Jewish apostates with illustrious rabbinic backgrounds. Thus the Jewish delegation to the forced disputation in Tortosa (1413–1414) performed rather poorly against the apostates Jeronimo de Santa Fe and Pablo de Santa Maria who presented the Christian understanding of the messianic meaning of biblical and rabbinic texts. The rivalry between the two religions in Spain ended with the mass expulsion of Jews from Spain and the possessions of the Spanish Crown (1492), whose main goal was to end any contacts between professing Jews and *conversos* (Jewish converts to Christianity), to make Spain a unified, Catholic kingdom.

The Early-modern Period

The traumatic expulsion from Spain, and soon thereafter from Portugal, did not extinguish Jewish culture. In the Sephardi diaspora in North Africa, Italy, and the Ottoman Empire, Jewish culture continued to flourish and even experience a Renaissance of sorts. The interpretation of the Tanakh stood at the center of the cultural renewal, although there were two distinctive approaches to the Bible. On the one hand, there was the growing familiarity with Renaissance humanism and a willingness to adopt its historical sensibility to the interpretation of the Bible. The science of history was added to the list of sciences relevant to tease out the true meaning of Scriptures. On the other hand, the historical approach of kabbalah influenced Jewish philosophers who were seeking to fathom the infinite, eternal meanings of the canonical text, which could be penetrated but not exhausted by human reason.

The most innovative interpreter of the Bible in the generation of the expulsion from Spain was Isaac Abravanel (1437–1508), the illustrious diplomat, financier, and royal adviser to the kings of Portugal, Spain, and Naples. Familiar with Renaissance humanism (which had penetrated Iberia in the 1440s and flourished under the patronage of Queen Isabella during the 1480s), Abravanel introduced historical sensibility to the exposition of the Bible, while defending the inviolability of the rabbinic tradition. Abravanel's biblical commentaries are replete with quotations from Greek, Roman, Christian, and Muslim sources along with references to medieval Jewish biblical interpreters such as Rashi, Ibn Ezra, Radak, Gersonides, Naḥmanides, and Ibn Kaspi, and philosophers such as Maimonides and Crescas. Paying due respect to his predecessors, Abravanel also criticizes Maimonides for harmonizing the Torah with Aristotelian philosophy, chides Ibn Ezra for speaking in riddles, and rebukes Gersonides for deducing moral lessons from the Bible. The Torah must not be read reductively or allegorically.

Under the influence of contemporary humanists, Abravanel was the first to ponder the historical process that brought about and shaped the making of the biblical texts qua texts. He began his commentaries with extensive introductions in which he discussed the character of the book, the author, the date of composition, the content, and the structure of the book under consideration. Abravanel also noted textual problems such as inconsistencies and discrepancies in a given biblical text or between biblical books. Abravanel's novel literary criticism of the Bible broke new ground in regard to questions about the structure and divisions of the biblical canon as a whole and the interrelationship of its parts. Thus Abravanel attempted to account for divergences between the books of Sam. and Chron., suggested that the author of Chron. was Ezra, paid attention to the human dimension of biblical narratives, assessed the stylistic differences between various prophetic books against the psychological makeup of the prophets as reflecting their particular historical circumstance, discussed biblical geography, investigated chronological quandaries, and examined the actual political circumstances at a given time in order to shed light on the narrative. Abravanel's astute historical observations yielded many insights that anticipated the biblical criticism of Spinoza in the mid-17th c. But unlike Spinoza, Abravanel remained deeply committed to the tradition and was aware of the potential danger that critical thinking could pose to Judaism. To address this danger Abravanel developed the construct of the "Torah of Moses" as a "central theological prop" (Eric Lawee, *Isaac Abrabanel's Stance toward Tradition: Defense, Dissent, and Dialogue* [Albany: SUNY Press, 2001, p. 185]), often endorsing views that were even more conservative than those of his medieval predecessors.

Similarly, Abravanel's exposure to humanism did not come at the expense of his familiarity with scholastic philosophy. He quotes directly from Thomas Aquinas (ca. 1225–1274), Albertus Magnus (1206–1280), and Nicholas de Lyra (ca. 1270–1340), and from the Christian scholastics Abravanel derived the distinction between human government and divine government which parallels the scholastic distinction between temporal and spiritual authorities. The scholastic philosophers developed their political theory on the basis of Aristotle's *Politics,* though most Jewish thinkers did not use it. Abravanel, by contrast, made massive use of the third book of the *Politics* in his commentary on 1 Sam. ch 8, although he did not quote the text directly. With Aristotle's analysis of political regimes and his own experience in European courts, Abravanel could read the biblical text as a political document, but without concluding that the Bible as a whole is a human document.

The inquiry into the literary and historical dimensions of Scriptures continued throughout the 16th c., especially in Italy. The Heb grammarian Elija Levita (d. 1549) was the first Jew to show that the vocalization of the biblical text and the system of accents were the work of the Masoretes of Tiberias, after the Talmud had been completed in the 6th c. The Masoretes concretized the tradition of how the Bible should be read, how it should be transmitted in writing, and, concomitantly, how the Bible should be understood. Since prior to the Masoretes the biblical text was handed down without vocalization, punctuation, or other signs, the lateness of the Masoretic Text indicates that the biblical text itself has a history. Levita's grammatical studies added yet another rationale for studying the Bible as any other ancient, human, literary text.

The best example of the historical awareness of Italian Jewish intellectuals was Azariah di Rossi (1512–1575). Familiar with classical and Renaissance historiography, Azariah composed his *Me'or 'Einayim (Light of the Eyes)* "to advance the legitimacy of objective historical inquiry into the Jewish past by establishing the total adequacy of religious tradition for purposes of moral edification, independent of any outside sources" (Lester A. Segal, *Historical Consciousness and Religious Tradition in Azariah de Rossi's Me'or Einayim* [Philadelphia: Jewish Publication Society, 1989], p. 30). Committed to the pursuit of truth, which Azariah regarded as "the seal of the truthful God, the quality of the beautiful soul, and it is well that all pursue it" (Segal, p. 32), Azariah moved to examine some of the problematic aspects of biblical chronology, such as "the uncertain duration of the First Temple period" (Segal, p. 31). Azariah did not intend to challenge the validity of the rabbinic tradition but rather to provide new evidence to prove the uniqueness of the people of Israel and their spiritual superiority in all aspects of human culture. Along with other Jewish apologists who argued for the doctrine of the divine election of Israel by showing that the Jews were the creators of music, di Rossi claimed that Moses was the author of the book of Job and the composer of the first known dialogue. While Azariah (like Abravanel before him) validated the authority of rabbinic tradition, his examination of the rabbinic past with references to non-Jewish texts and his observation about the historical origins of Jewish philosophy in the Greco-Roman world gave rise to a heated public controversy. Other contemporaries of di Rossi, such as Abraham ben David Portaleone (1542–1612), also affirmed the authority of the rabbinic tradition and the ideals of Torah study while at the same time providing rich historical and scientific information about aspects of the biblical text.

Awareness of the history of the biblical text itself was common among Jewish thinkers exposed to Renaissance humanism, especially in Italy. In the Ottoman Empire, however, most Sephardic intellectuals shared the kabbalistic notion that the revealed Torah is the manifestation of a supernal, primordial Torah that has infinite meanings. The task of the Jewish philosopher was to fathom the endless meaning of the Torah, knowing full well that it cannot be exhausted. In the Ottoman Empire, even more than in 15th c. Spain, the Bible became the focus of philosophical midrash. Applying the analytic procedures of talmudic scholars to the biblical text, the philosopher-preachers attempted to penetrate the meaning of Scripture with scientific precision. The homilies of Isaac Karo (1458–1535) illustrate this tendency.

Assuming that his audience was fully familiar with the biblical text, Karo did not provide a running commentary but aimed at explicating Scripture in its complexity. In accord with the medieval assumption that Scripture is a scientific text, Karo held that the role of the commentator is to elucidate the practical and theoretical wisdom in the Bible because such understanding enables the soul of the learner to cling to God and to enjoy the bliss of immortality. Other contemporaries and successors of Karo, such as Joseph Taitatzak (ca. 1477–1545), Moses Almosnino (ca. 1515–1580), Isaac Aderbi (16th c.), Isaac Arroyo (16th c.), and Moshe Alshekh (d. after 1593) also considered the scrutiny of the Bible a religious activity par excellence leading to the attainment of immortal life. The philosophical exegesis of sacred texts reflects the theological postures that the exiles brought with them from Iberia, namely, that revealed religion perfects natural human reason and that the divinely revealed Torah contains all human wisdom because it is identical with the infinite wisdom of God.

The exegetical unveiling of the infinite meanings of Scripture required linguistic sophistication and rhetorical versatility. The Sephardic philosophers in the Ottoman

Empire selectively adopted the Renaissance cult of rhetorica. Though the exiles did not boast a recovery of the ancient sources, living either in the land of Israel itself or merely getting closer to it did inspire the Jewish exegete to present the Bible as a perfect text, aesthetically, morally, and intellectually, measuring or surpassing the achievements of the classics. Thus Moses Almosnino (ca. 1515–1580), for example, presented King Solomon as the embodiment of Renaissance *homo universalis* and the wisest of all ancient sages, and the religious poetry of King David was favorably compared to Greek and Roman poetry. By the same token, the moral teachings of King David and King Solomon recorded in Ps., Prov., and Eccl., and interpreted by the rabbinic sages, were claimed to have surpassed the moral wisdom of Aristotle, Cicero, and Seneca, along with other ancient moral philosophers.

During the 16th c., then, the historical-literary investigation of the Bible coexisted with the philosophical-homiletical approach. If the first approach regarded the Bible as a text like all others, the second approach accentuated the exceptionality of the Bible and its divine perfection. In the mid-17th c., especially in the Dutch Republic, the tension between the two approaches could not be glossed over, but resulted in open doubts about the divinity, authority, and exceptionality of the Bible. The most consistent and radical critic of the Bible and of the Jewish philosophical exposition of the Bible was Baruch (Benedict) Spinoza (1632–1676). A child of ex-*conversos* who received traditional Jewish education, Spinoza was familiar with the biblical commentaries of Abraham Ibn Ezra and Maimonides's *Guide*. Spinoza praised Ibn Ezra's linguistic insights, but vehemently rejected the philosophical hermeneutics of Maimonides. It is doubtful that Spinoza was informed of the biblical commentaries of Isaac Abravanel or that he was familiar with Azariah di Rossi's work. Yet Spinoza's challenge appears less radical if it is viewed in light of his Jewish predecessors.

Spinoza argued that the Bible could not be proven to be a divinely revealed text, and even if the Bible was revealed by God, its meaning is accessible only through human interpretation. Spinoza applied the historical-philological method to demonstrate inconsistencies—logical and temporal—in the Bible. The Bible, according to Spinoza, is a human document that must be studied like any other ancient text, a product of the imagination of its human authors. With a thorough knowledge of the Heb language and an understanding of the historical past, the Bible can be seen precisely for what it is: a book that teaches morality and politics rather than philosophy and science.

Rejecting Maimonides' claim that the Bible contains philosophical truths expressed in figurative language, Spinoza argued that the Bible has nothing to do with philosophy and science because it is a product of prophetic imagination. The prophets were neither scientists nor philosophers; they were people with limited knowledge of nature who were endowed with vivid imaginations, very much like poets. Unlike natural knowledge, prophecy cannot be taught and cannot be imitated; it is a special gift. Prophecy must not be regarded as the "highest degree of men" or the "ultimate term of perfection," as Maimonides held, for which reason prophecy requires an external "sign" to verify its authenticity. With his critique of prophecy Spinoza not only denied the epistemic superiority of the biblical text, which has been presupposed by all Jewish philosophers since Philo, he also rejected the Maimonidean attempt to interpret the Bible esoterically. Because there is no hidden truth behind the surface of the Bible, Spinoza charged Maimonides and his followers with an attempt to make Scripture present the same teachings as pagan philosophers.

For Spinoza truth is not a property of Scripture, as Jewish philosophers since Philo had maintained, but a characteristic of the method of interpreting Scripture. Differentiating between the meaning of Scripture and its truth, Spinoza asserted that the meaning must be found solely from the usage of language, for which mastery of Heb grammar is absolutely necessary. The Bible does not accommodate itself to human limitations; rather, radicalizing earlier ideas found in rabbinic literature, the Bible speaks the only language it can speak, namely, a human language. To the extent that the Bible does have a universal message, it has nothing to do with philosophy or science but with morality, namely, the commandment to love one's neighbor. This message, Spinoza believed, is the reason why the Bible is still politically relevant, even though the political order established by Moses in the Bible no longer exists. The Bible teaches against religious intolerance and persecution, and in this regard the Bible is the basis of universal ethics; yet the Bible is not an exceptional, or privileged text. To treat the Bible as such is itself the result of "prejudice," a harmful habit of thought that hinders clear thinking. In short, the Bible has no cognitive significance or authority. It rather reflects the ordinary conception of God as imagined by common people of the time, among whom were the prophets.

Spinoza regarded the editorial work of the Bible, which he ascribed to Ezra, as far from perfect, because the text of the Bible was put together at a considerably later time from the events recorded. Through close reading of the text, Spinoza attempted to show that biblical religion developed over time. Spinoza portrayed Moses strictly as a legislator and political leader who single-handedly ruled a mass of ex-slaves who were incapable of self-governance. The law that Moses gave Israel left no free choice for individuals, and Moses could induce the Israelites to observe the law only by promising material benefits. Spinoza then rehashed some of the Christian arguments about the nature of Mosaic law, which highlighted its earthly nature of biblical rewards and the absence of spiritual rewards. Biblical religion then deals only with temporal matters and has nothing to do with ultimate felicity, even though biblical religion provided a universal, ethical basis to a society.

Spinoza's devastating critique of the Bible undermined the foundation of rabbinic Judaism. Though Spinoza articulated his biblical criticism after he was excommunicated on July 27, 1657, his challenge was correctly assessed by the leaders of the Jewish community who expelled him. Refusing conversion to Christianity, Spinoza socialized with the Collegiants, an offshoot of a radical Calvinist group whose liberal theological and political views had been condemned by official Calvinism early in the century and who were hospitable to people alienated from their own religious communities. Spinoza also rejected a post at the University of Heidelberg in order to maintain his intellectual freedom, preferring to correspond with contemporary scientists such as Henry Oldenburg, the secretary of the Royal Society in London. Spinoza's critique of the Bible became known in England and inspired the English Deists of the late 17th and early 18th centuries. Some Deists attacked the Bible for its lack of a doctrine of immortality, whereas for others the dubious moral character of the prophets and other biblical heroes was a sign of the inferior quality of the Bible.

Spinoza's challenge to traditional Judaism would continue to reverberate throughout the modern period as biblical criticism became prevalent, especially among Protestant scholars. That challenge of biblical criticism, on the one hand, and the determination of Jews to integrate into European society, on the other hand, necessitated a reinterpretation of Judaism. The traditional belief in the revealed status of Scripture would have to be rethought with new philosophical tools during the modern period. Modern Jewish philosophy would be articulated on the basis of Judaism's conversation with the Enlightenment, Kantianism, Hegelianism and Romanticism, affecting the approaches to the Bible. In modern times, as in the Middle Ages, the Bible continued to serve as the bridge between the particularistic beliefs of Judaism and non-Jewish cultures.

Modern Jewish Philosophy

Moses Mendelssohn (1729–1786) captures the transition from premodern to modern philosophy. Although he was a staunch advocate of Jewish emancipation and a proponent of the Jewish Enlightenment (Haskalah), Mendelssohn remained deeply committed to traditional Jewish life. At the same time, he also socialized with the leading intellectuals in Germany, who regarded him as spokesman of the German Enlightenment. Mendelssohn's views were shaped by German philosophers such as Gottfried Wilhelm Leibniz (1646–1716), Christian Wolff (1679–1754), and Gothold Ephraim Lessing (1729–1781) no less than by Maimonides and Spinoza.

Endorsing the Enlightenment concept of natural religion, Mendelssohn maintained that reason alone can prove that God exists, that God governs the universe through providence, and that the human soul is immortal. These three universal propositions are accessible to the human mind without a special revelation from God. In contrast to Jewish medieval philosophers, Mendelssohn held that revelation does not disclose any ideas that cannot be discovered by human reason. In terms of truth, there is only one source (viz. reason) rather than two (viz. reason and revelation). If natural religion requires no additional revelation, what then is Judaism? Mendelssohn answers that Judaism is not a revealed religion but a "revealed legislation." At Sinai God did not reveal any truths or doctrines, but only laws. Prior to the Sinaitic event, the ancient Israelites already reached a level of intellectual development resulting in the knowledge of three pillars of natural religion. What distinguishes Jews from non-Jews is not religion, which is common to all humans endowed with reason, but a specific legislation obligatory to Jews only. The revealed legislation charts the particular path that Israel alone must follow in order to attain the felicity to which all human beings aspire. And since the laws were revealed by God rather than discovered by humans, they could neither be changed nor abrogated. In Mendelssohn's mind, loyalty to the laws of Judaism was fully compatible with the rationalist universalism of the Enlightenment.

The Bible stood at the center of Mendelssohn's attempts to modernize the Jews and prepare them for integration into European society. He translated parts of the Bible into German but printed the translation in Heb characters in order to make it accessible to Yiddish-speaking Jews whom he wished to wean away from the language that symbolized Jewish cultural backwardness. In additional to the translation of the Bible, Mendelssohn composed and edited commentaries in Heb in order to offer Jews an alternative to Protestant biblical commentaries. Like his medieval predecessors, Mendelssohn began his exegetical endeavor by composing a commentary on Eccl. (1768–1769), but in contrast to them Mendelssohn saw Eccl. in a philosophical light that attributed its skepticism to imagined conversation partners. On the basis of medieval commentaries, especially by Rashi, Radak, and Abraham Ibn Ezra, Mendelssohn focused on the literal meaning of the biblical text and on the accent marks of the Masoretic Text (MT) in order to clarify Eccl.'s philosophical stance. Eccl., Mendelssohn argued, taught no theoretical knowledge but only practical knowledge conducive to moral improvement and in accord with contemporary science. Nonetheless, Mendelssohn still defended the traditional Jewish view that King Solomon was the author of Eccl. and perpetuated the notion that the ancient king was the source of all known sciences. Hence, there is no surprise that even Harvey's theory of blood circulation (1628) is alluded to, according to Mendelssohn, in Eccl. 12.6: "Before the silver cord snaps and the golden bowl crashes, the jar is shattered at the spring and the jug is smashed at the cistern" (David Sorkin, *Moses Mendelssohn and the Religion of Enlightenment* [Berkeley and Los Angeles: University of California Press, 1996], p. 43). While few Jews paid attention to Mendelssohn's commentary on Eccl., German biblical scholars translated it into German and published it in 1771.

During the 1770s Mendelssohn worked on the German translation of the Ps., which he regarded as a seminal biblical text for moral and spiritual edification. Familiar with the aesthetic theories of the 18th c., Mendelssohn considered the Ps. the highest exemplar of the sublime and believed that the Ps. illustrate how theology and aesthetics are intertwined. He translated the Ps. into German in order to show the glory of Hebrew lyric poetry alongside classical and Nordic poetry and also in order to replace existing German translations of the Ps., especially Luther's, even though Mendelssohn held that translation in great esteem and retained some of its most elegant parts. The translation of the Ps. was published in 1785 and was well received by Jews throughout Europe.

The crown of Mendelssohn's biblical studies and educational activities was the translation of the Torah into German with an accompanying Heb commentary (known as *Bi'ur,* 1780–1783). With the help of the grammarian Solomon Dubno (1738–1813), Mendelssohn focused on the literal meaning of the text *(peshat),* often relying on the commentary of Abraham Ibn Ezra, in an attempt to respond to the challenges of contemporary biblical criticism. While Mendelssohn considered the literal meaning to be primary, he still defended the legitimacy of rabbinic homiletical exegesis *(derash).* Mendelssohn's translation and commentaries on the Torah was a true group effort. Dubno departed from the project before completing the assigned commentary on Gen., but other Jewish Enlightenment figures joined it. Naftali Herz Wessely (1725–1805) wrote the commentary on Lev., and Hertz Homberg (1749–1841) and Aaron Jaroslav commented on Num. and Deut. When the five volumes were reissued as one volume, under the title *Sefer Netivot ha-Shalom (The Book of the Paths of Peace),* Mendelssohn composed a new introduction, titled *'Or Netivah (Light for the Path),* spelling out the principles of the entire enterprise.

According to Mendelssohn the Bible is not about revealed truth but about "trust and faith that result in Israel's obedience through the Commandments, which are the preeminent form of practical knowledge" (Sorkin, p. 55). Since Mendelssohn understood the Bible as a record of the unique covenantal relationship between God and Israel, his views were closer to Judah Halevi's than to Maimonides's. With Halevi, Mendelssohn held that Sinai was a historical, collective event in which Moses directly heard God's speech and wrote it down. Contrary to Maimonides, Mendelssohn regarded the Heb language not as a conventional human language but as a divine language. Even the accents of the MT, said Mendelssohn, have a divine source. Moses could transmit divine communication to Joshua so accurately because of the unique features of the Heb language: It is the only language whose written form retains the oral nature of all languages. The task of the translator and commentator is to capture the sense of the text, and Mendelssohn took as his model the ancient Aram. translator of the Bible, Onkelos, regarded as authoritative by the rabbinic tradition. The emphasis on the unique orality of the biblical text was Mendelssohn's best proof against the Documentary Hypothesis, which was based on the lateness of the MT. In Mendelssohn's view the oral tradition preserved the way God had spoken, which Moses duly recorded. Mendelssohn was not oblivious to the historical study of the Bible, but he believed that it could only help establish the traditional Jewish faith.

Mendelssohn's idiosyncratic blend of Jewish traditionalism and Enlightenment rationalism was difficult to perpetuate to the next generation. Traditional Jews, suspicious of the Emancipation and its perils, were critical of his biblical translation and commentaries; and the more radical disciples who desired full integration into German culture found his observance of Jewish law a hindrance to their goal. Even Mendelssohn's own children failed to reconcile the two worlds of their father;

all but one of his six children converted to Christianity. Ironically, Christian contemporaries of Mendelssohn understood his claim that Judaism is a revealed legislation to mean that Judaism is a legalistic, obsolete fossil of an ancient era, a ceremonial law that has no vitality. This view was accepted by Immanuel Kant and through him became commonplace among German intellectuals of the 19th c.

For Jews in Germany and Central Europe, the 19th c. consisted of the relentless struggle to gain civil rights and social acceptance, the rise of *Wissenschaft des Judentums* (the scientific study of Judaism), and the drive to reform Judaism from within. Whereas the emancipation of the Jews was possible because of the French Revolution, the defeats of Napoleon rolled the process back as anti-Jewish fulminations swept through Germany. The violence against Jews in Bavaria during the Hep! Hep! riots of 1819 accentuated Jewish insecurity and manifested the unwillingness of German society to see Jews as equals. In response, a group of Jewish scholars convened in Berlin in November 1819 to found the Society *(Verein)* for the Culture and Scientific Study of the Jews. Its agenda was to examine the entire records of the Jewish past—biblical and rabbinic—from a scientific perspective and aided with new tools of contemporary science, especially history and philology. The members of the society had different interests and agendas: Some wished to show how Judaism contributed to Western civilization, in order to secure a position in German academia, while others were mostly interested in ameliorating the situation of the Jews and improving Jewish education. Still others were primarily concerned with determining what is subject to change in Judaism, and hence obsolete, as opposed to the eternal essence of Judaism that is not subject to change. Although their research into the Jewish past was of highest academic quality, it did not lead to university posts. In frustration, the Jewish scholars created their own institutions of higher learning, that is, rabbinical seminaries in which Jewish students studied the entire gamut of Jewish literary heritage scientifically and objectively.

The critical stance of *Wissenschaft des Judentums* scholarship was mainly directed toward postbiblical Judaism, but the Bible could not remain immune to it. In 1810 a student of Mendelssohn, Yehuda Leib ben Zeʾev, published his *Mavoʾ ʾel Mikraʾey Kodesh (Introduction to Holy Scriptures),* which was modeled after J. C. Eichhorn's study by the same title, in which he established the composite nature of the book of Isa., among other critical observations. Leopold Zunz (1794–1886) in his *The Religious Teachings of the Jews, Historically Developed* (*Die gottesdienstlichen Vortrage der Juden, historisch entwickelt* [1832]) advanced daring new theses regarding the books of Chron. and the Psalter. Isaac Samuel Reggio (1784–1855) and Shlomo Yehudah Rapoport (1790–1867) also advanced critical theses regarding Isa. and Ps. What was commonplace among Protestant biblical critics of the 19th c. was beginning to make inroads in Jewish scholarship. A new Jewish philosophy was needed to integrate contemporary historical research into a new schema. It was provided by Naḥman Krochmal (1785–1840).

Krochmal was the first modern Jewish philosopher to make not only the Jewish religion but also the Jewish people a subject for philosophic investigation, thereby providing a philosophic explanation of Jewish history. His philosophic model was Georg Wilhelm Friedrich Hegel (1770–1831), though he was also deeply influenced by Giambattista Vico (1668–1744), Johan Gottfried Herder (1744–1803), and the German Idealists, Friedrich von Schlegel (1772–1829) and Friedrich Wilhelm Joseph von Schelling (1775–1854). No less central to Krochmal's reinterpretation of Judaism were the views of Maimonides, Ibn Ezra, Spinoza, and Mendelssohn, as well as the teachings of kabbalah. Krochmal's *Moreh Nevukhei Ha-Zeman (The Guide for the Perplexed of This Time)* was written in 1840 and published posthumously in 1851, edited by Leopold Zunz. The title, a play on

Maimonides's great work, was no accident: Krochmal wished to accomplish for the Jews of his generation what Maimonides did for his contemporaries: a comprehensive reconciliation of Judaism with the reigning philosophy. Since the Aristotelianism of Maimonides was now obsolete, and Maimonides's emphasis on God's radical otherness was religiously unsatisfying, a reconceptualization of Judaism in terms of the reigning Idealist philosophy was now in order. The Neoplatonic ontology of Ibn Ezra's philosophy and the teachings of kabbalah served Krochmal to prove that Judaism is a metaphysical system that is not only compatible with German Idealism, but that Judaism is the most refined expression of the Absolute Spirit.

Writing in Heb to the proponents of Jewish Enlightenment in Galicia, Bohemia, Moravia, and Italy, who were disoriented by modernity but who had not lost their Jewish commitment, Krochmal introduced the post-Kantian understanding of the relationship between religion and philosophy. For Krochmal "religion and philosophy are essentially identical, in that both represent processes of speculation, which are equal in their apprehension of truth" (Jay M. Harris, *Nachman Krochmal: Guiding the Perplexed of the Modern Ages* [New York: New York University Press, 1991], p. 26). But whereas philosophy conceives of Spirit in the form of concepts, religion does so through representations *(Vorstellungen)*. The representation is a form of consciousness higher than that of sensation and observation but lower than that of concept. The representations of religion (i.e., the metaphors and symbols) "are not expressions of poetic genius and creativity; rather, they are rooted in the universal mind—the essence of human spirituality—and therefore virtually all metaphors are equivalent in many different languages" (Harris, p. 27). Krochmal's view of prophetic activity would thus place him between Maimonides and Spinoza. While agreeing with Maimonides that there is a relationship between theology and truth, Krochmal also was in agreement with Spinoza that prophets and theologians cannot be considered philosophers.

For Krochmal, who defined religion as the belief in spiritual powers, biblical religion is the highest form of religion; it contains the same faith in the Absolute Spirit which is present in the ultimate truth of philosophy. Krochmal's biblical studies and his philosophy of history were to document this claim. Krochmal was fully aware that much of biblical criticism was at odds with prevailing Jewish traditional ideas, but he believed that proper understanding of the Bible and post-biblical history could show both the continuity of Jewish faith and its evolution over time. With detailed knowledge of rabbinic Jewish exegesis and modern biblical criticism, Krochmal was intent to prove that the Rabbis in fact shared the assumptions of the modern critics. Thus in regard to the book of Isa., Krochmal argues that the Rabbis themselves were aware of the composite nature of the book and its rather late date of composition. To his satisfaction, he manages to prove that critical conclusions about Isa. are compatible with traditional sensibilities.

Similarly, Krochmal uses the rabbinic debate about the doubtful sanctity of Eccl. (*m. Yad.* 3:5) to prove that "wisdom, and especially Solomon's wisdom, is acknowledged to be a gift from God, and therefore the Rabbis could not have denigrated Qohelet [Eccl.] for being simply a product of Solomon's mind, for this would, in fact, confer upon it sufficient status to be worthy of canonization" (Harris, p. 176). The very fact that the Rabbis debated it proved to him that they entertained the possibility that the book was not authored by Solomon but by a later author. The Rabbis, Krochmal maintains, were equally aware of the late date of composition of some of the psalms, even as late as 2nd c. BCE, notwithstanding the fact that the tradition ascribed them to King David. Traditional Jews, then, should not ignore contemporary biblical scholarship but rather incorporate it into their own understanding of the tradition since it is in many ways consonant with earlier traditions. Krochmal believed that contemporary modern biblical scholarship proves his philosophy of history: Jewish creativity and vitality is eternal and ever-evolving. Unlike any other nation that exhibits the finite cycle of growth, maturation, and disintegration, the Jewish people is eternal. Due to its special relationship with God, the Absolute Spirit, the Jewish people repeatedly renews its national life, manifesting the eternal Absolute Spirit.

Whereas Krochmal articulated a Jewish philosophy that addressed the perplexity of East European Enlightened Jews who wished to remain loyal to Judaism, in Germany the dominant secular philosopher who shaped Jewish thinking was not Hegel and other Idealist philosophers, but Immanuel Kant (1724–1804). His claim that human beings are in principle unable to have certain knowledge about God, the soul, and the origin of the universe was intended not to abolish faith, but to make room for it. For Kant, faith was rational, an apprehension of the greatest good and striving toward it. Although Kant denied the possibility of metaphysics and limited the scope of theoretical, demonstrative knowledge to the phenomenal world of sense perception, he did not deny the existence of God. Indeed, reason must postulate the existence of God, but the "only content we can ascribe to our idea of God is moral." God is not the giver of the moral law but the "necessary condition for the possibility of the summum bonum," i.e., for the "distribution of happiness in exact proportion to morality" (*Critique of Practical Reason,* trans. Beck [1956], p. 129). The existence of God is postulated in order to fulfill a fundamental requirement of the moral law, namely, that the virtuous man is worthy of happiness. True religion, in contrast to clericalism, is, therefore, an ethical religion in which the kingdom of God is nothing else than the ethical commonwealth: "If God is to be found at all, it is not behind nature but behind moral law" (Kenneth Seeskin, *Jewish Philosophy in a Secular Age* [Albany: State University of New York Press, 1990], p. 58). So long as we think about God as a moral agent, we cannot be accused of anthropomorphism, since morality has no empirical content. God cannot do otherwise than act as is morally required. Yet Kant also showed that historical religion did not develop in ignorance of the moral law. He wants to claim that actual religions have in one way or another approached the ideal of the pure founded on a universal conception of humanity and a commitment to its moral improvement. Unless actual religion approached this ideal it would be impossible for Kant to argue that it is engraved on each of our hearts. Not surprisingly, Kant's depiction of Judaism was anything but complimentary. Following Spinoza and Mendelssohn, Kant viewed Judaism as a mere national-political entity, contending that it fails to satisfy the essential criteria of religion in that it fails to inculcate the appropriate inner morals, demanding only external obedience to statutes and law. Judaism, Kant said in accord with traditional Christian perception, is concerned only with things of this world and lacks any formulation of the concept of immortality.

Kant's philosophic formulation of religion accorded with the orientation of modern liberal Judaism. Seeking to distill the essence of Judaism that remained constant throughout the process of change over time, Reform theologians defined the essence of Judaism as ethical monotheism. Kant's understanding of the moral law as rational self-legislation was believed to be totally congruent with the biblical emphasis on "duty" and "right." The Jewish followers of Kant reinterpreted Judaism in such a way that it would conform to Kant's formulation of religion, while at the same time rejecting Kant's critique of Judaism.

Hermann Cohen (1842–1918), the towering Jewish philosopher of the late 19th c., was able to show how a Neo-Kantian reading of Judaism leads to universalizing the revealed message of the Bible. Benefiting from the final success of the Emancipation in Germany, Cohen held a regular academic post at the University of Marburg, reformulating the principles of Kantian philosophy. While rethinking Kant during the 1870s, Cohen also witnessed the rise of modern anti-Semitism as a backlash to the Emancipation. In his *A Public Declaration Concerning the Jewish Question* (*Ein Bekenntnis zur Judenfrage* [1880]), Cohen called for the total integration of German Jewry into German society, but while calling for Jews to take their religion seriously. Cohen got involved in a public defense of Judaism against anti-Semitic charges that according to the Talmud the laws of the Torah apply only to Jews and not to relations between Jews and Christians. He rejected this reading and published his view that Israel's chosenness by God from the outset had universal scope: Since God is the one who loves the stranger, Israel is chosen as a mission to mankind.

Cohen did not write a commentary on the Bible, but his main exposition of Jewish philosophy—*Religion of Reason out of the Sources of Judaism*—takes most of its data from the Bible. Rejecting Kant's portrayal of Judaism, Cohen argued that when properly understood "the ancient sources and their received interpretation are much closer to a morally pure faith than Kant thought" (Seeskin, *Jewish Philosophy,* p. 160). Cohen does not say that Judaism is the religion of reason, but rather that the ideas of a purely rational faith can be found in Jewish sources, first among them the Bible. At the University of Marburg, Cohen's colleagues included Julius Wellhausen, the most important biblical scholar of the time. Cohen's reformulation of biblical religion could be viewed as an attempt to reject some of the claims of Wellhausen and his followers. Cohen's religion is strictly ethical religion or religion of ethics. Morality is an infinite task of self-sanctification, precisely as Lev. 11.44 ("For I the LORD am your God: you shall sanctify yourselves and be holy, for I am holy") teaches. For Cohen, however, the laws of ancient Israel are of universal scope. Precisely because there is only one God, there can be only one law applicable to all people who share a common dignity (Lev. 19.34; 24.22). The social legislation of the Bible is not restricted to Jews only but applies to the "stranger," namely to all humans. Cohen interpreted the command to love the stranger along the lines of Kantian philosophy: It is not a commandment forced on us by a supernatural being but a duty that we in our better moments would impose on ourselves. The Bible itself, especially the book of Deut., spells out the need to bridge the gap between what is and what ought to be.

Following a Protestant model, in the teachings of prophets Cohen found the most refined expression of the relationship between humanity and God. The prophets made pity and sympathy for others the cornerstone of their moral teachings. Through empathy with the suffering of my neighbor I am able to encounter the person as a Thou rather than merely as an instance of humanity. The main challenge to humanity is not impending death but the experience of poverty, about which the prophets were deeply concerned (Cohen, *Religion of Reason,* tr. Kaplan [New York, 1972], pp. 135–136). Ethics, then, needs the idea of a perfect being to guarantee that our effort to perfect the world has some hope of succeeding. God does not only sustain the world but shows compassion for those who suffer and forgives those whose quest for self-sanctification falls short. The forgiveness of sin brings God into relation with each person, who remains a sinner in constant need of God. Thus, religion goes beyond ethics; religion does not negate our duties as moral agents but provides us with a richer conception of the task of fulfilling them.

Hermann Cohen influenced an entire class of German Jewish philosophers, including Ernest Cassirer (1874–1945), Julius Guttmann (1880–1950), Leo Baeck (1873–1956), Joseph B. Soloveitchik (1903–1993), and Steven Schwarzchild (1924–1989), as well as the work of the biblical scholar Yehezkel

Kaufmann (1889–1963). After resigning from his post in Marburg, Cohen joined the *Academie für die Wissenschaft des Judentums* in Berlin, calling on Jewish scholars not to divorce scientific study from inner piety. His aim was to encourage Jewish scholars to establish an intimate bond between their scholarly and spiritual interests. Cohen's disciple Franz Rosenzweig would later perpetuate the fiction that in later life Cohen renounced his commitment to religion of reason; in truth Cohen remained consistent throughout his life, advocating the idealization of Judaism through a correct reading of the Bible.

After Cohen's death in 1918, Jewish philosophy in Germany would be dominated by two main figures—Martin Buber (1878–1965) and Franz Rosenzweig (1886–1929)—who also collaborated on a new translation of the Bible into German. The goal of that translation was precisely the opposite of Mendelssohn's enterprise a century and a half earlier: Whereas Mendelssohn wanted the Jews of his day to master the German language in order to integrate into German society, the Buber-Rosenzweig translation of the Bible intended to Hebraicize the Bible for German Jewish readers who had been thoroughly integrated into German culture and who had been emotionally and practically distanced from Judaism. The translation begun in 1925 was completed in 1961 by Buber alone after many intermissions, and long after Rosenzweig's untimely death in 1929. Tragically, when that new translation of the Bible into German was completed, German Jewry, for whom it was intended, was no longer in existence.

Despite their collaboration and deep respect for each other, Buber and Rosenzweig did not share the same understanding of the Bible. For Buber the language of the Bible was inseparable from the living Heb language and the foundational stratum of Jewish culture. Along with other Jewish biblical scholars such as Simon Bernfeld (1860–1940), Abraham Kahana (1874–1946), Benno Jacob (1862–1945), Moses David Cassuto (1883–1951), Yehezkel Kaufmann (1889–1963), Moses Hirsch Segal (1877–1968), and Naphtali Herz Tur-Sinai (1886–1973), Buber rejected the dominant readings of the Bible by Protestant theologians. Instead of theologizing the Bible, these scholars attempted to listen to the Bible's own unique voice, emphasize the rhythm of living utterance reflected in it, trace the associative elements that lead the attentive listener to the original meaning of the living utterance, and explore the concrete meaning and original dynamics of basic words. Unlike some of his Jewish cohorts, Buber had no difficulty maintaining a critical distance from the biblical text or sorting out the seeming contradictions and inconsistencies of the Bible without feeling apologetic about it. At the same time, Buber developed distinctive linguistic tools that enabled him to wrest the lived experience from the biblical text.

With Rosenzweig, Buber introduced the search for key-words *(Leitwörter)* repeated in a given text with stubborn consistency, conveying its meaning. The key words force the listener not only to concentrate in a particular manner but also to participate in the experience evoked by the biblical text. Buber's translation attempted to retain the identity of each Heb root without blurring its manifold associations; if the semantic field of German words was too narrow in scope, Buber created new compound words in which the added word or root explained the particular development of a basic root. Through this message, Buber attempted to penetrate the primordial life of the spoken word as it reflected the unique otherness of the speaker. In this regard, Buber's translation/interpretation of the Bible stood in diametrical opposition to medieval philosophical commentaries that highlighted the abstract, philosophical content of the Bible.

Buber's attempt to recapture the concrete, living, unique human utterance of the biblical text differed from the approach of his collaborator, Franz Rosenzweig. For him, the goal of the translation was to break through the linguistic particularity of the text to the supralinguistic language without word. He did not compose a commentary on the Bible but his philosophical magnum opus, *Der Stern der Erlosung (The Star of Redemption),* presented his biblical theology as an alternative to Western philosophy. For Rosenzweig, not only is revelation an encounter with the Other, revelatory speech is dialogical. Rosenzweig states: "The ways of God are different from the ways of man, but the word of God and the word of man are the same. What man hears in his heart as his own human speech is the very word which comes out of God's mouth" (*The Star of Redemption,* trans. William W. Hallo [Boston: Beacon Press, 1972], p. 151). Accordingly Rosenzweig reinterpreted the prophetic speech: "The prophet does not mediate between God and man. He does not receive revelation in order to pass it on; rather, the voice of God sounds forth directly from within him, God speaks as 'I' directly from within him" (*Star,* p. 178). In the Bible Rosenzweig found the "I" addressed by God. Biblical literature is unique because it authenticates the renewal of the divine word.

Buber, by contrast, did not believe that through the Bible one can still hear the voice of the living God, because he considered the Bible itself to be a human response to the encounter with God. Though we cannot hear the voice of God, we can hear the voice of those who were in the presence of God. In doing so, the listener/reader stands again in the presence of God. The encounter with God, according to Buber, is a contentless experience that cannot be rendered propositionally. Developing Cohen's emphasis on correlation, Buber highlighted the relational nature of reality. All existence has two relational modalities: an I-It or an I-Thou. In Kantian terms, the former modality treats the other as a means to an end, whereas the latter treats the other as an end for its own sake. The I-Thou is the ideal relationship that, alas, cannot be maintained over time, since it necessarily disintegrates into I-It, objectifying the other. The only Thou that cannot be objectified is God, the Eternal Thou. Revelation, for Buber, is not a single event in the remote past, but an ongoing encounter with the presence of God. Similarly, the revelation at Sinai did not signify the disclosure of a legal code but a living experience of God's immediate presence. The spokenness *(Geschprochenheit)* of the Bible captures that direct encounter between God and the people of the time. The intent of the new German translation was to come as close as possible to the raw spokenness of the Bible. For Buber the engagement in biblical studies in Nazi Germany was an act of spiritual resistance. He finally departed from Germany in 1938 and settled in Israel (then called Palestine) where he continued the translation enterprise and went on to compose various essays on the Bible, the most important of which was *Moses,* written in 1944 and published in 1946. These midrashic essays illustrated Buber's own dialogical relationship with the biblical text, attempting to retrieve the past experience in order to stand once again in the presence of God.

In 1937, just a year before he departed from Germany, Buber appointed Abraham Joshua Heschel (1907–1972) to succeed him as supervisor of adult education in Germany and director of the *Jüdisches Lehrhaus* at Frankfurt am Main, the main institutional context for the revitalization of Jewish life in Germany since the 1920s. The Nazis, however, deported Heschel (who was a Polish Jew) back to Poland in 1938, and after several months of teaching in Warsaw he was able to immigrate to England and from there to the United States in 1940. What Buber attempted to accomplish for the Jews of Germany, Heschel attempted to accomplish, with partial success, for American Jews. It was a dialogical reinterpretation of Judaism that addressed the predicament of modernity, its gnawing doubts and rootlessness. The tragedy of the modern person is the loss of the ability to ask the right questions to which the Bible is the answer. Heschel powerfully stated the challenge facing humanity in the second half of the 20th c.: "Our problem ... is how to share the certainty of Israel that the Bible contains that which God wants us to know and to hearken to; how to attain a collective sense for the presence of God in the biblical words. In this problem lies the dilemma of our fate, and in the answer lies the dawn or the doom" (*God in Search of Man: A Philosophy of Judaism* [New York: Farrar Straus and Giroux, 1955], p. 246). In the return to the Bible lies the solution to the modern predicament of Jews and non-Jews alike.

In continuity with Buber, Heschel denied that the Bible is a philosophical text or that the God of the Bible is a philosophical abstraction or a psychological projection. Rather, God is a living reality who takes passionate interest in the life of His creatures, or as Heschel's celebrated title put it, God is in search of man. Indeed, "the Bible is not primarily man's vision of God, but God's vision of man" (*Man Is Not Alone: A Philosophy of Religion* [New York: Farrar Straus and Giroux, 1951], p. 129). Heschel then placed God at the center of the divine-human drama told in the Bible, a long story of God's active pursuit of a rebellious Israel. The biblical text itself came into being as a response to God's revealing power. In Heschel's understanding of the Bible, the question of authorship, which exercised so much of modern biblical scholarship, is a moot point. The Bible is a product of divine and human authorships.

Heschel viewed attachment to the Bible to be essential to continued Jewish existence. The destiny of the Jewish people is to be a "community in whom the Bible lives on." Israel must remain dedicated to the Bible in order for the Bible to remain "a sublime challenge and source of illumination for the world." Since the Bible is "the frontier of the spirit" that "shows the way of God with man and the way of man with God," had the Bible not been preserved, an invaluable pathway to God would be lost. The current spiritual poverty throughout the world is due largely to a "growing alienation from the Bible" (*God in Search of Man*, pp. 252, 238). Heschel viewed the Bible as the deepest alternative to the spiritual malaise of the 20th century, the only hope for the revival of divine wisdom, justice and compassion. Heschel was committed to reengagement with the Bible in order to preserve the Jewish faith for the future.

In his doctoral dissertation at the University of Berlin, *Die Prophetie* (1933), which was later published in an expanded form in *The Prophets* (1962), Heschel articulated the doctrine of divine pathos according to which "God does not reveal himself in an abstract absoluteness, but in a personal and intimate relation to the world.... God is also moved and affected by what happens in the world, and reacts accordingly" (Heschel, *The Prophets* [New York: Harper and Row, 1962], pp. 223–224). "It is precisely because God is filled with pathos for human beings that they may respond with sympathy to God.... The prophetic faith is thus a sympathetic response to divine pathos" (John C. Merkle, "Heschel's Theology of Divine Pathos," in John C. Merkle (ed.), *Abraham Joshua Heschel: Exploring His Life and Thought* [London and New York, 1985], p. 81).

Heschel's uncanny ability to present the biblical faith as the answer to the modern predicament was partially responsible for the spiritual revival of Judaism in America during the 1960s and 1970s. Yet it is hard to gauge whether Heschel's enormous fame as a cultural icon actually led American Jews in search of Jewish renewal back to the study of the Bible. Jewish Studies programs began to sprout in the 1970s at the same time that Religious Studies departments were established in secular universities. Courses in the Bible were then offered as part of the academic study of religion, and the Bible was now studied either as an ancient Near Eastern document, or as sophisticated "literature" that illustrated many of the linguistic subtleties of contemporary literary theories, or as a source of information about the sociocultural setting of the framers of the biblical canon. For Jewish Studies professors in American universities, the philosophic import of the Bible has become neglected, presumably because taking the biblical text as Scripture, namely, as an existentially meaningful text, is perceived as belonging in the denominational seminaries but not in the secular university.

Three contemporary Jewish philosophical theologians—Norbert M. Samuelson (b. 1936), David R. Blumenthal (b. 1938) and Judith Plaskow (b. 1947)—challenge this convention, illustrating the continued relevance of the Bible for contemporary Jewish thought and the indebtedness to Buber and Heschel. Samuelson illustrates how the Bible is engaged in the context of the dialogue between science and religion. Though his academic training was in analytic philosophy and medieval Jewish philosophy, Samuelson regards the task of Jewish philosophy to be predominantly constructive rather than historical or analytical. Since what is true in the Bible must be in accord with what is known to be true in contemporary science, if the literal meaning of the biblical text is in conflict with contemporary science, it could not be the correct reading of the text. Samuelson's reading of the creation narrative shows how the biblical story of creation accords with contemporary physics. (See Norbert M. Samuelson, *The First Seven Days: A Philosophical Commentary on the Creation of Genesis* [Atlanta: Scholars Press, 1992]; *Judaism and the Doctrine of Creation* [Cambridge: Cambridge University Press, 1994].) Samuelson's theory of revelation is very much in accord with Buber's, but his approach to the biblical text is similar to medieval biblical exegesis, in that it pays close attention to contemporary science.

Like Samuelson, David Blumenthal was trained as a historian of medieval Jewish philosophy, but has devoted his efforts to writing constructive Jewish philosophy. If for Samuelson contemporary science is the main challenge to the meaning of the Bible, for Blumenthal the point of departure is the trauma of the Holocaust. Applying post-Structuralist strategies to the Ps., Blumenthal attempts to construct a post-Holocaust Jewish theology by therapeutically confronting the personal God of Israel as an abusive deity (David R. Blumenthal, *Facing the Abusing God: A Theology of Protest* [Louisville: Westminster/John Knox Press, 1993], esp. pp. 57–192). Selecting Pss. 128, 44, 109, and 27 for close reading, Blumenthal offers not only his own new translation of the psalms but also four simultaneous commentaries. The first commentary is a philological commentary based on existing biblical scholarship. The second commentary is written under the influence of Heschel, Blumenthal's teacher, in an attempt to capture the spiritual tradition of Hasidism. The third commentary focuses "on the emotional attitudes which the psalmist tradition wishes us to cultivate," and the fourth commentary attempts "to respond to Jacque Derrida, Michel Foucault, Sigmund Freud, Alice Miller, Carol Gilligan, Jessica Benjamin, Elie Wiesel and others in the calling-reading-proclaiming of the psalms" (pp. 58–60). By writing four simultaneous glosses on the biblical text, Blumenthal intentionally mimics the medieval Jewish exegetical tradition, clearly implying that he sees his work in continuity with medieval predecessors no less than an attempt to respond to psychoanalysis, deconstruction, feminism, and the Holocaust. It remains to be seen whether this reading will catch the imagination of American Jews.

At present the one contemporary Jewish theologian who has succeeded in influencing how some American Jews approach the Bible is Judith Plaskow, perhaps the best-known Jewish feminist (see "Jewish Women's Scholarly Writings," pp. 2086–91). She has argued that Judaism is in need of healing not because of the Holocaust but because of the systematic and pernicious exclusion of women from the activity of scriptural interpretation. (See Judith Plaskow, *Standing Again at Sinai* [San Francisco: Harper and Row, 1990].) Women were present at Sinai but it was the male-centered rabbinic tradition that ignored, silenced, and marginalized women. A new reading of the Bible is necessary if Jewish women are to be restored to their rightful place within the tradition and become creative readers of their own sacred texts. Plaskow inaugurated an insightful feminist engagement with the Bible and rekindled a feminist midrashic discourse, but since most of those who engage in this enterprise are not philosophically trained, feminist biblical interpretations to date lack philosophical rigor.

Conclusion

In sum, our survey of the Bible in the Jewish philosophical tradition makes it clear that the Bible stood at the center of the Jewish philosophical enterprise. Through translations, interpretations, and commentaries, Jewish philosophers were able not only to negotiate the differences between Judaism and other cultures, but also to rethink Judaism anew by using new philosophic tools and theoretical paradigms. As each generation of Jewish philosophers asked, "What does the Bible say and what does it mean?" they were able to respond flexibly to changing historical circumstances and ponder the meaning of Judaism. Premodern and modern Jewish philosophers approached the Bible quite differently. Whereas the former presupposed that the Bible contains abstract, universal truths that are either identical to philosophy or can be explicated by philosophy, most (though not all) modern Jewish philosophers regarded the Bible as the record of divine-human direct, unmediated encounter. Accordingly, whereas the premodern Jewish philosophers composed philosophical commentaries on the Bible, modern Jewish philosophers have regarded the Bible as the source from which springs their Jewish theology. For all Jewish philosophers the pursuit of wisdom to which Israel is called by God can be accomplished through the encounter with the Bible itself.

[HAVA TIROSH-SAMUELSON]

The Bible in the Jewish Mystical Tradition

[Please note that the Scripture quotations in the following article are the author's.
—the Editors.]

The Hebrew Bible, Sacred Scripture, is the core text of Jewish religious culture, the foundational document of its creative life in every respect. All of its contents—from the opening account of the creation to concluding traditions about national exile and return, with emphasis on the lives of its religious leaders and the legal traditions recorded in the Torah, plus its collections of prayer and wisdom teachings—all these comprise the authoritative canon of Judaism. This written record was complemented from biblical antiquity to the present day by an oral tradition, for its understanding and interpretation in a wide variety of ways and contexts. Commentary is thus a core practice of Jewish religious culture; and the Hebrew Bible is its principal subject and prooftext. Much of this commentary, beginning with legal and theological midrash in rabbinic antiquity (see "Midrash," pp. 1879–91), was grounded in the ongoing study and preaching of Scripture. Originally oral in both form and function, it was eventually written down, and supplemented by further study and other written traditions—for the past two thousand years.

The Jewish mystical tradition is also founded upon Scripture. This is its primary subject and prooftext. The many rabbinic comments on Scripture are also woven into the mystical imagination, for Scripture was always read in Judaism through rabbinic lenses. Built upon these foundations, the Jewish mystical tradition is thus fundamentally a tradition of commentary. This anchors the mystical spirit and imagination in the sources of revelation and tradition. It keeps its soaring spirit and imagination normative.

Sacred Scripture

Mystical experiences and reports of these experiences occur in the Hebrew Bible, and two of them became foundational texts for study and mystical visions. The most important is Ezekiel's vision of God upon a cosmic throne (Ezek. ch 1; mid-6th c. BCE). Set upon a heavenly firmament, beneath which were four fiery figures at the four corners (each one with wings and a different visage), the Divine Figure enthroned above had the "appearance of the likeness of a man" (v. 26). It too had a fiery appearance—appearing "like a rainbow," with a luminous aura roundabout. Since the four divine creatures moved upon "wheels," the entire complex resembled a chariot; and so the entire vision (in Ezek. ch 1) came to be called in rabbinic literature "The Account of the Chariot" (*Maʿaseh Merkavah*)—and all its textual details were scrutinized and meditated upon for millennia. This process of contemplation and interpretation may have begun by the prophet or his disciples, as the fiery figures (called *ḥayyot*) seen in the first experience are identified with the "cherubs" envisioned in a later one (Ezek. 10.20). In a much less detailed heavenly vision, a century earlier, the prophet Isaiah called these creatures "seraphs"—a term that personified the "searing flames" of their appearance (Isa. 6.2). (The Heb root *s-r-f* means "to burn.") This designation also became one of the core "scriptural" terms studied and envisioned over the ages, as did the angels' three-fold chant of Divine praise: "Holy, Holy, Holy! The LORD of Hosts! The entire earth is filled with His Glory *[kavod]*" (Isa. 6.3). Like Isaiah, Ezekiel also envisioned what seemed to him as the "likeness of the Glory *[kavod]* of the LORD" (Ezek. 1.28). *Kavod,* this epithet for the Divine Glory, became a standard trope for the Throne Figure as an embodied presence.

Ezekiel's commentary on his own experience was a prelude of things to come, as the Torah (and Scripture as a whole) came to be regarded as an inscription of special import. "Open my eyes", O LORD, said a later psalmist-sage, "that I may perceive wonders through [or from] Your Torah [or Teachings]" (Ps. 119.18). And so when Daniel once studied the old prophetic "books," in an attempt to figure out the chronology of Jeremiah's oracle of a seventy-year time of destruction (Jer. 25.11–12) his prayer for Divine deliverance was answered by a mystical vision in which the angel Gabriel instructed him in the meaning of that prophecy (Dan. ch 9). We thus find, by the close of the biblical period (2nd c. BCE), an explicit expression of what would later become a major component of Jewish mysticism: the experience of visions (or inner illuminations) through the study of authoritative sources. It is therefore not surprising that Daniel's account alludes to Isa. 6.6–7 when it wants to indicate the way this angel approached and came into direct contact with the human visionary (Dan. 9.21). Already in Scripture there is both mystical experience and mystical commentary.

Ancient Rabbinic Traditions

The earliest stratum of rabbinic sources contains a ruling designed to restrict the public exposition of certain texts. Two of these were works with mystical content. The first noted in *m. Ḥag.* (2.1) refers to the secrets of Gen. ch 1: "It is forbidden to expound (*ʾein dorshin*) ... the Account of the Creation in a pair" (that is by two students together; though "it may be expounded by an individual," explains the *Tosefta* [2.1], a parallel legal source of the 3rd c. CE); and the second is the Account of the Chariot, which may not even be expounded "by an individual" ("unless he is wise and can understand [it] on his own," according to the *Tosefta*). Thus two entire chs of the Bible were deemed to encode mystical secrets, which could be further explicated for intellectual knowledge or spiritual experience.

Presumably both rabbinic passages were designed to restrict such study to single persons without the aid of a teacher (and the two rulings and versions suggest as much). And presumably not all those who expounded these passages achieved mystical visions. Thus, in one comment we are told: "Many expounded the *Merkavah* and never saw it in their life" (*t. Ḥag.* 3.28); though another tradition states: "There are those who expound properly but do not practice (*meqqayem*; or enact the exposition), (and) those who practice properly but do not expound properly" (*t. Ḥag.* 2.1).

Tradition preserves a striking instance of the conjunction of vision and exposition while studying Gen. ch 1. Once, we are told, R. Yehoshua came upon Ben Zoma, who did not respond to his greeting while he was in a mystical trance. When R. Yeshoshua then asked him, "Whence and whither, Ben Zoma"? (i.e., 'where were you at?!'); he said: "I was gazing at the Account of Creation, and there is not even a handbreadth between the upper and lower waters, as it is said: 'The Spirit of God was hovering *(meraḥefet)* over the face of the waters' (Gen. 1.2). And it (also) says: 'As an eagle stirs up its nest [and hovers *(yeraḥef)* over its young]' (Deut. 32.11). Just as an eagle flies over its nest, touching and not touching, so there is not even a handbreadth between the upper and lower waters." This act of scriptural exposition, whereby a passage in Gen. was interpreted esoterically via another in Deut., included an ecstatic vision—but with dire consequences. R. Yehoshua told his disciples that "Ben Zoma is already outside" (i.e., 'gone' from this world, mentally unstable); and he died shortly thereafter (*y. Ḥag.* 2.1).

Other traditions of Ben Zoma's mystical madness are included in reports of other visionaries and their fate. The account in the Babylonian Talmud (*Ḥag.* 14b) is the most mystical of the versions. It refers to "Four (persons) who entered the 'Garden' (presumably an exalted state)," adding biblical vv. Two of these vv. reflect certain kinds of applications of Scripture to mystical events. The first of these passages is from Ps. 101.7, "No one who practices deceit shall stay within My House." The editor of the Talmud (or the tradition he represented) clearly understood this v. to refer to the heavenly Temple (where one might envision God on His Throne). The second passage is from Prov. 25.16, "Have you found honey? Eat only what you need, lest surfeiting on it you vomit it up." This v. was applied to Ben Zoma, with the sense that he grossly overdid what was right or needful in his ecstatic experience. By choosing this passage, the editors are likely referring to a related word of caution concerning proper mystic practice. For once in the academy of Pumbeditha, after the elders taught R. Joseph the Account of Creation, they asked him to teach them the Account of the Chariot. But he demurred, saying: "'Honey and milk are under your tongue' (Song 4.11)—the things that are sweeter than honey and milk (should remain) under your tongue," namely they should remain esoteric and not be taught in public (*b. Ḥag.* 13a).

We now return to the list of prohibited passages. In a valuable tradition preserved by the Church Father Origen (ca. 185–253 CE), reporting "the custom of the Jews," he lists not only the Accounts of Creation and the Chariot as texts of special status, but refers to the account of the Cherubs in the final part of Ezek. (chs 40–48 depict the future Temple) and to the Song. The reason for restricting the concluding chs from Ezek. was undoubtedly related to the imagery of the Divine Figure and Heavenly Chariot involved (cf. Ezek. 43.1–7); but the reason for restricting study of the Song is not immediately clear. Most likely, a similar esoteric issue was involved. Indeed, later Jewish mystics referred to the figure of the male beloved portrayed in Song 5.10–16 as the *Shiur Qomah*, lit. the "Measure of the [Divine] Stature," and envisioned (and even speculated on) its enormous size and specified its features by citing this passage from the Song (citations of this text also recurs in the *heikhalot* literature, from the 3rd–8th c. CE). Hence this scriptural depiction was believed to be related to the Divine Form upon the Heavenly Chariot. In fact, this complex of features is preserved in an old midrash (reported in the Middle Ages, in various circles in Gerona). In it we are told that the various colors used in the Song passage to depict the Beloved (white, red, black, gold, and pale-green [beryl]) comprised the color spectrum seen on the "rainbow" which irradiated the Divine Form (upon its Chariot) in Ezek. 1.28. Undoubtedly, this text preserves an exposition of the biblical vv. in Song ch 5 in conjunction with the throne vision of Ezekiel. No wonder that such a text was only preserved in esoteric channels from antiquity until the 13th c.

An additional aspect of mystical speculations on the Creation focuses on the significance of the Divine Name, Y *(yod)* H *(heh)* V *(vav)* H *(heh)*, especially the first two letters of that name. A passage that is part of an old homily condensed and reported in the Jerusalem Talmud (at *Ḥag.* 2.1, our vaunted source for such matters) notes:

> Rabbi Abbahu [said] in the name of R. Yoḥanan: With two letters were two worlds created—this world and the world to come: one with the letter *heh* and one with the letter *yod*. And what is the proof (text) for this? 'For *be-YaH* [with the letters *y*(*od*) and *h*(*eh*) the Lord *tzur ʿolamim* (Isa. 26.4; read as if *tziyyer ʿolamim*, 'formed worlds'; though literally, 'the Lord is an everlasting Rock'). But [from this v.] we do not know with which letter God created which world. However, since it is also written: 'These are the generations of heaven and earth *be-hibarʾam*ʾ (Gen. 2.4), [we may infer that] He created them (the heavens and the earth of this world) with the letter *heh* (and thus He created the world to come with the letter *yod*; reading *be-hibarʾam*, 'when He created them' as if *be-heh barʾam*, 'He created them with a *heh*'!) ..." [Author's translation]

This interpretation is more than idle speculation. Triggering such exegesis was the belief that God created the world through letters of the Divine Name—thus, the letters of this Name had creative powers. Such speculation extended in mystical circles to the Tetragrammaton, YHVH, which regarded its four letters as the fundamental components of all Being, not only the creation. On the way to that major belief, we turn to a text that had enormous importance for the Jewish mystical tradition. It was called *Sefer Yetzirah (The Book of Creation)*, which may have had various early formulations until it was finally edited in the early medieval period (about the 9th c.), and had an enormous importance for the Jewish mystical tradition, expounding on the mystical importance of Heb letters. It teaches that the entire universe was formed from the twenty-two letters of the Heb alphabet (its shapes and sounds). According to the grammatical speculations of this work, these letters were "engraved" and "hewed" out of the primordial ether by the Spirit of God (this refers to Gen. 1.2, where the word "wind" may also mean "spirit"), and grouped them in many combinations according to various linguistic criteria (*Sefer Yetzirah*, ch 6ff.). Furthermore, it claimed that sets of letters are juxtaposed to others in patterns of primal pairs, for which the v. in Eccl. (7.10), "So God has created every object, opposite the other" is the paradigm text. This notion is also given profound theological significance: "Good opposite evil—good from good and evil from evil. God brings evil to light and evil brings good to light. Good is stored up for the good and evil is kept for the evil" (ibid., ch 60).

Even more significant in that work are ten primary "numbers" or "elements" (called *sefirot*—a term later used to designate the ten 'gradations' emanated from God). These are without any dimension and the fundamental basis of All (they are called "ten *sefirot belimah*," the latter word marking the fact that they are "without any what"—an allusion to Job 26.7, "God hung the earth on *beli-mah*, "nothingness"). This primal number (ten) is also connected to the four elements (earth, air, fire, and water), and to the primary seals of the emergent creation (which were fixed by different combinations of the three principal letters of the Divine Name YHV). Clearly, diverse speculations coalesce in this text. A citation from Isa. 57.15 is used to mark one major belief about the relationship between the primary letters and various Divine Names: "These are the twenty-two letters [upon which] Yah, Yahveh, God, the Lord of Hosts, the Living God, the God of Israel, God Almighty 'high and lofty, dwelling forever, and Holy is his Name' (Isa. 57.15) [founded] the universe" (*Sefer Yetzirah*, ch 56). Each of these elements is found in later mystical works. Particularly important is the combination of the ten primal numbers and twenty-two letters into a sum of thirty-two. This total would be canonized as the "thirty-two paths of primal wisdom" in later writings. The Heb letters for thirty-two, *lamed* and *bet* compose the word *leb*, "heart," thus marking (by a mystical acronym) the "heart" of esoteric truth.

In sum, the early sources contain four fundamental features that will all recur in the panoply of speculations and experiences of the medieval and early modern periods: (1) The combination of Scripture and commentary—interpretation of biblical vv. is primary, both to anchor speculations and to justify intuitions; (2) The conjunction of scriptural interpretation and mystical experience—experiences being derived from or explained by biblical v.; (3) The importance of Divine Names, especially the fundamental significance of the Names of God in the creation, topics explained via biblical interpretation or speculation; (4) The primacy and significance of the Heb alphabet viewed as the fundamental components of the creation of the world (and by extension all speech and texts, components of this Divine Speech).

The Medieval Traditions

Primary Precursors (12th Century CE)

One of the important early centers of philosophical kabbalah was in Provence (southeastern France), and it centered around R. Abraham ben David of Posquières and his son R. Isaac the Blind. R. Isaac composed the central document of early kabbalah—a commentary on the *Sefer Yetzirah*, and with it broke the code of oral transmission and allowed its arcane dicta to be disclosed. His commentary drew on the entire fund of rabbinic tradition from Scripture on, and revealed its theosophical significance. Thus in commenting on the fact that the ten *sefirot* ("emanations"; lit. "counting, numbers") are derived from the "one" spirit of God, R. Isaac states: " 'One' (ch 10) is the beginning of the essences. 'One': the breath of the living God, for from the breath is all ... for the voice is by breath ... By the voice is the hewing, for the drawing forth of the voice is interior. With 'breath He engraved' (ch 12): engraving is by voice and hewing is by breath by way of voice." He says further on, " 'Engraved in voice' (ch 17): in the drawing out of the tone of the voice the letters are emanated and engraved, as it is written, 'the voice of God engraves flames of fire' (Ps. 29.7), for the voice divides one letter into many letters through its drawing out." All these matters pertain to primordial Divine processes, concerning which some passages in Scripture preserve traces. In subsequent centuries these features of voice and breath, and the carving out of letters through their articulation, will be techniques of mystical practice, as explained through an example below.

As noted above, portions of Gen. ch 1 were believed to refer to mystic events. The nephew of R. Isaac, R. Asher ben David, was a principal recipient of his master's esoteric wisdom. His compositions (dealing with the Supernal Emanations), reflect an early example of a mystical exposition of Gen. ch 1. It focuses on its letters and words, and purports to show that the sentences of this text encode the primordial emanation of Divinity from its infinite concealment, and that these gradations (here called *sefirot* explicitly) are symbolized by epithets related to their major modalities in the Divine Hierarchy. He begins his teaching (quoting and interpreting Gen. 1.1):

> "In the beginning (*be-reishit*)." The letter *bet* [the consonant of the preposition *be-*] is [symbolically identified with] the exalted Crown (*Keter*), and therefore this letter is larger than all the other *bets* [for it is written in majuscule at the beginning of the Bible]. The word "beginning (*reishit*)" refers to Wisdom (*Ḥokhmah*). And thus, in truth, the two [highest and most primordial] *sefirot* [the Crown of all Being and the taproot of all Wisdom] are conjoined in one word. From what [text in Scripture] do we know that "Wisdom" is "beginning"? From the passage, "The *beginning* of *wisdom* is the fear of the LORD" (Psalms 111.10). [Hence, the mystical secret is:] With both the Crown and Wisdom He "created *ʾet* [the Heb particle that precedes a definite direct object] the heavens and *ʾet* the earth." These [dual references to the heavens and the earth] refer to [the *sefirot* called] Beauty (*Tiferet*) and Diadem (*ʿAtarah*) [the middle and lowest gradations, respectively]. He also created the [two particles called] *ʾet*; [and though they have no linguistic meaning in ordinary speech, symbolize mystically] the supernal powers called Lovingkindness (*Ḥesed*) and Fear (*Paḥad*). All the creation [and thus all the supernal gradations] are summarized up in this [opening biblical v.]."

This is clearly a teaching of secret wisdom for those already in the know—this wisdom being the symbolic meaning of Scripture, which is nothing less than an account of the supernal mysteries. The contemplative intuitions that originally produced this teaching are not mentioned, and we only have some indications of their scriptural justification. The entire matter is beyond ordinary sense, and some of the topics elicit amazement—particularly the remark that the two occurrences of the identical particle *ʾet* (mere markers of a definite direct object) symbolize two different Divine acts in the process of emanation. We thus have a precious early witness to a bifurcation of scriptural meaning. At the level of its plain sense, Scripture purports to speak of worldly events in worldly terms, and using ordinary forms of syntax, but on the symbolic plane these formulations are traces of spiritual events in the supernal realm. The only correspondence to ordinary understanding is that the sequence of the words conforms to a primordial sequence as well. The mystery of scriptural language (in all its features) will be one of the true kabbalistic mysteries and lead to mystical expositions of all its words. It will also state explicitly what is here only implied: that Scripture and the supernal realities are (mystically) one and the same.

Among the works of mystical theology composed during this period, is *Sefer Ha-ʿIyyun*, or *Book of Contemplation,* which deals with the "topic of the innermost" reality *(penimiyut)*—within which is "the essence of the entire existence of the Glory." This work notes that there is a limit to such exoteric contemplation, and one cannot speculate on anything before the Account of the Creation. This is stated explicitly, with biblical texts adduced to support this crucial concern:

> Before the Holy One, Blessed be He, created any power from among the [primordial] powers, His power was indiscernible—until something appeared from Nothing, in the actualization of Primordial Wisdom, called ... Hiddenness (*taʿalumah*). It came into being from Utter Inscrutability (*ʾain ḥeqer*) through the power of the unified conjunction; as it is written, "And Wisdom, from Nothingness (*me-ʾayin*) it shall come into Being" (Job 28.12)—from on high (*me-ʿal*), above all that is hidden (*ʿal kol neʿelam*) "it shall come into Being." It is concealed in the mysteries of Wisdom; as it is written, "And He told you the Hidden [Mysteries] (*taʿalumot*) of Wisdom' (Job 11.6). "From Nothingness it shall come into

Being"—[meaning:] from [through] contraction (*me-mi'ut*) it [Wisdom] shall come into Being"!

The terms and texts of this passage are based on the interpretation of two vv. in the book of Job. Most notably, Job 28.12 is reconstructed to justify and authorize the mystical teaching that Wisdom emanates from the primal Nothingness. The original biblical phrase is actually a statement stressing that lack of human knowledge of the origin of Wisdom, "Where *(me-'ayin)* can wisdom be found?" whereas its midrashic reconstruction turns it into a teaching about esoteric gnosis (Wisdom derives from the Nothingness before all Being)! Moreover, the primal Wisdom is said to emerge from a depth within the primal Hiddenness—an assertion based on an explication of the preposition *min/me-* ("from"), taken in the first instance to indicate that Wisdom comes from the totality of Nothingness, and in the second to mark that its emergence from Hiddenness to Being brings a diminution or contraction of the Primal Totality into Something (even primordial Wisdom is something less than it was in its infinite original boundlessness). All this was conveyed by God to the mystics in some gnostic revelation, in some contemplative state of super consciousness. Job 11.6 records this Divine communication, and also provides the term for this primordial Hiddenness. Such a revelation would undoubtedly have preceded the mystic's ability to perceive in Job 28.12 a clue of this ultimate and secret truth.

Another important work from the same mystical circle is the *Fountain of Wisdom*, and it deals with the most esoteric secrets of the overflowing Divine emanation. Once again (as already noted in R. David's caution) there is a limit to speculation. In this case it is directed to the most exalted of spiritual masters, the prophet Moses, in response to his request for supernal knowledge. We are told that when Moses had fixed the knowledge of God in his heart, so that it would be "unchanged" and "true and clear," he turned to God and asked:

"Show me Your ways" (Exod. 33.13). Whereupon the Holy One, Blessed be He, responded and said: "You cannot see My face" (v. 20). That means: concerning the darkness of which you have requested knowledge [the primordial "fountain" of darkness, derived from a primeval ether], and which is prior to all [entities, and is] from Me [alone] and My own [created] source—you are unable to achieve any comprehensible clarity. Therefore God said, "You shall see my back, but My face shall not be seen" (v. 23). This means (based on the Aramaic Targum translation), that "that" which preceded the existence of the universe [and is from Me] you cannot comprehend, that you might say that I [God] am like other entities, of which one can say "this thing comes from this place." Therefore you cannot apprehend knowledge of this darkness which was set over against My existence. But from that point on, you may know all things: that is, everything from and below this darkness—even My emanated essence, and the power of My Name and Glory (paragraphs 36–37).

The mystic master has interpreted the dialogue between Moses and God in Exod. 33.12–23 as Moses' request for esoteric instruction (in the course of his spiritual apprenticeship and development), and God's delimitation of the kinds of theosophical knowledge that might be attained. The interpretation of v. 23 deftly understood "my back" and "my face" in terms of the "before" and "after" of such permissible wisdom, based on a mystical reinterpretation of the Aram. translation's own reinterpretation of the stark anthropomorphism of the biblical phrase. But despite such hidden knowledge, the mystic instruction does inform us that the primeval ether had "darkened" in the process of emanation, producing a spectrum of hues (presumably perceived in the mind's eye, in a state of meditation), which was nevertheless incomprehensible to all rational "inquiry" (called *ḥaqirah*). Thus, the most esoteric "ways" of the Divine emanation are beyond all mental apprehension—and the student learns all this from an exegesis of Moses' own example in Scripture.

Major Sources (13th Century CE*)*

The appearance in Provence of the *Sefer Bahir* (Book of Radiance), the ambience of R. Isaac the Blind's oral and elite mystical teachings, was a major event. Suddenly a document circulated that gave full expression to many topics of present and future concern to the Jewish mystical tradition. It "records" sages responding to questions by their students, and a common setting of many teachings is: "Rabbi X sat and exposited *(darash)*." These questions were related to the secret meanings of scriptural phrases (or even letters), often with discussion interposed in order to clarify certain points. Significantly, here sages are explicitly and publically expositing Scripture with respect to the supernal Divine emanations, in the context of circles of mystical adepts. Mystical discourses in fellowship settings would then be a major feature of various classical works in Spain and elsewhere. This work's correlation of vv. of Scripture with the ten emanations and their dynamics resulted in giving new scriptural epithets to these processes (distinct from their main designations—like Crown, or Wisdom, or Diadem, as noted earlier). Additionally, certain ritual texts specified in Scripture were also correlated with the supernal emanations, such that ritual performance was in fact an earthly (human) actualization of esoteric (Divine) realities. These issues of capital importance are spelled out in the following examples.

A major symbol of the sefirotic structure was an image of a Tree—actually inverted, with its roots in the Infinite Hiddenness of Divinity and its branches and fruit extending outward, symbolizing the (six) dimensions of Being and its creative offshoots. Images of water and planting were also correlated with this tree; and the implanting, as it were, of the flowing creativity of Divinity from its heights to the lower realms of the hierarchy, was sometimes portrayed as a garden planted by streams. In some schemes, this would symbolize the emanation of Divine Wisdom, from its origins in luminous clarity, to its lower manifestations (the inner wisdom of all things). One passage in the *Bahir* cites Song 4.15 to symbolize this esoteric truth. It explains the phrase "A fountain of gardens, a well of living waters, flowing from the Lebanon" as referring to the channels of Divine spiritual creativity that flow from a primordial and supernal fountain or well of absolute purity called "Lebanon" *(levanon)*, because of the luminal "whiteness" *(lavan)* in that sphere, unsullied by shadow or subject or specificity. Another term for this flowing "stream" of supernal powers is *naḥal;* and in the same passage the phrase *ʿarvei naḥal*, "willows of [growing by] a stream", which were among the four species specified for the celebration of the harvest Festival of Tabernacles (Lev. 23.40), becomes a symbolic epithet for the "two wheels of the Chariot," which emit beneficence to Israel (through the streams of the emanations)—God's own *naḥalah* ("inheritance"). Thus, the supernal Throne of Divinity is now designated a fount of this heavenly "gift" (par. 121). In the meditative and exegetical imagination of the mystic, scriptural vv. coalesce and co-symbolize the most esoteric matters. The Account of the Chariot is never far from the speculations of these Jewish mystics.

Lev. 23.40 reads: "On the first day [of the festival] you shall take the product [fruit] of a *hadar*-tree, branches of palm trees, boughs of leafy trees, and willows of the stream—and you shall rejoice before the LORD your God seven days." Several features of this command are uncertain, and have been discussed since antiquity, with the Rabbis determining (for ritual purposes) that the *hadar* fruit was an etrog, a citron; that the boughs of leafy trees were myrtle branches; and that the entire complex of four species (being one palm frond, one citron, two willow branches, and three myrtle sprigs, totaling seven, to match the days of the festival week) were to be taken and held together as a ritual bouquet, in thanksgiving to God for the harvest. But the mystical meaning far exceeded this common sense and public purpose. According to the teacher in the Book of *Bahir*, six of the species (the palm frond and the five willow and myrtle twigs and leaves) symbolized the six middle dimensions of the sefirotic hierarchy (levels four to nine; located beneath the supreme triad of Crown, Wisdom, and Understanding). The palm frond was thus like a cosmic tree, the twigs were like its branches, symbolizing the extensions of Divinity throughout Being. Altogether, this group was deemed masculine, over against the seventh species, the citron, which symbolized the lowest (tenth) level of the hierarchy, and was deemed feminine (and elsewhere called the Queen or the lower *Shekhinah*). This final level is impregnated with all the creative energies of the higher spheres, and functions as a Cosmic Mother for the materialization of these qualities in our world.

The teacher adds that the female entity was necessary for the vitality of existence (both Divine and worldly) to be sustained; "for it is impossible for the upper and lower worlds to endure without a female"! Holding the species together during the ritual, the celebrant not only dramatizes (and actualizes) Divine Unity, but performs a conjunction of opposites. Hence, Scripture symbolically encodes aspects of the most supernal Divine reality, and when the words of Scripture are actualized through ritual performance their energy is materialized concretely by the worshipper who enacts theological truths—such as Divine unity and the male-female fabric of Being (par. 117). This account is not some isolated oddity; for the mystics it was a fundamental truth. Not far from Provence, in Guadalajara (Spain), another teacher, named R. Moses de Leon, composed a ritual handbook around this time and called it *Sefer Ha-Rimmon* (The Book of the Pomegranate). In it he explained the kabbalistic significance of the Divine commandments. When he came to the ritual of the four species, to be taken in hand on Sukkot, he similarly divided them in to a grouping of six and one; he called the former masculine and the latter feminine, and even specified that the worshipper must hold the frond and the sprigs in the right hand (this being the male side), and the citron in the left (it being the female)—and bring them together in the ritual act.

De Leon underscored the esoteric quality of this ritual, saying:

> There are things that we do [on earth] which hint at a Great Thing [i.e., the Divine Hierarchy] ... For you will find that there is nothing in the lower world that doesn't have its Great Power in the supernal realms ... And the mystery of the [gathering together of the] four species [written in Scripture and enacted by persons] ... is that all shall be One (folios 65a–67a).

The underlying unity of Divine Being is thus deeply encoded in the language of Scripture, and can be enacted in and through its ritual commandments. Hence a person may proclaim God's Unity in words (esp. the Shema prayer from Deut. 6.4, "Hear, O Israel, the LORD our God, the LORD is One"), and exemplify it through the commandments as well. The words of Scripture thus crystallize in human language transcendent spiritual truths of Divinity. Mystics imbued with the hidden code, and the proper methods of interpretation, can penetrate the skein of words and their symbolic secrets. The very act of interpretation is thus a spiritual and mystical act—the precursor to knowing the hints in heaven of what is done on earth.

Other Major Sources of the 13th Century

We are now in a position to say more of the mystical texture of the scriptural text. Two major Spanish kabbalists who were both heir to major oral traditions, and offer different but still reluctant peeks through the formulations of Scripture into the supernal Beyond are Naḥmanides and R. Joseph Gikatilla. R. Moses ben Naḥman, also known as Naḥmanides (or by the acronym Ramban), was intent on keeping the secrets of Scripture oral and reserved for the spiritual elite. He therefore says in the Introduction to his commentary on the Torah that the kabbalistic teachings are not in any way encoded in Scripture, and no one can ever deduce anything in the supernal realms from a particular scriptural word or phrase. There is thus no secret exegetical tradition that he could (or would) disclose, and the most that he tells us is that one or another word or passage is a "sufficient hint to the wise." This is not a hint for any exegetical use or intuitive technique, but suggests that profound mysteries are linked (or related) to such passages, such that the person who had received oral instruction from a master, might be reminded of some traditions or be able to ponder further. Ordinary people would have no clue from such clues. Indeed, Naḥmanides stated explicitly that he wrote his commentary for the populace at large, so that they might find comfort in his expositions and spiritual rest on the holy Sabbath, while in exile. Hence his hints are mere allusions, and without allusive content.

But if Naḥmanides only hints at esoteric particulars, he nevertheless states explicitly in the Introduction some of the most astounding things about the esoteric 'nature' of Scripture:

> We also have in our possession a True Tradition (Kabbalah) that the entire Torah is [composed of] the Names of the Holy One, Blessed be He; [that is,] the words [of the Torah] may be divided up [reconstituted] into Names of a [totally] different [linguistic] order—as if you were to think, by way of parabolic example, that the verse [beginning] *Bereishit [bara' Elohim*; "In the beginning, God created"] were divided into other words, like *Be-rosh yitbarakh Elohim* ["May God be blessed above all" or "most of all"]. And the entire Torah is like this, not including the combinations or numerical equivalents of the Names [i.e., hyperlinks producing new Names, or algorithmic combinations correlated the Names with other topics]! ... Hence if a Torah Scroll is missing [even] one letter [even like the letter *vav*, only used as an orthographic aid for pronunciation] ... we would be required to render such a text invalid ... And thus it appears that [the primordial] Torah written with [letters of] black fire upon white fire [as per an esoteric teaching first found in the Jerusalem Talmud], was [composed] in the manner just mentioned; [namely,] the writing was continuous without breaks between the word; and it was thus possible to read it both according to the [Divine] Names [encoded therein] and in our [conventional] way, dealing with the Torah and the commandments. It was given to Moses our master in the latter manner, along with the oral tradition of how to read it according to its [esoteric] Names ...

Naḥmanides thus believed that the Torah is a texture of Divine Names at the esoteric and non-semantic level of Scripture, and that its original and primordial inscription is a series of fiery configurations from God. In esoteric truth, the core of Scripture is not a human communication, but a primordial Divine enunciation of holy hieroglyphs: God only enunciated God's Names, as a profound expression of (modalities of) His Being. But this articulation of Divinity (a mystery conveyed to Moses, the first master of such secrets) was formulated simultaneously (through an exoteric division of these Names), as an instruction for human beings. Hence Naḥmanides adds that he has composed his commentary for those who read it during the liturgical year and wish to find instruction in it—mostly through its plain sense, but also by means of some other "pleasant" matters for those who can appreciate them, including those "who know esoteric wisdom" [called *ḥen*, lit. "grace," but here an acronym for *ḥokhmah nisteret*]. But he warns his readership not to engage in logical deductions or rational presumptions about the hints "which I write as secrets of the Torah *(sitrei Torah)*" because no one will be able to ascertain their meanings in this way (of ratiocination), "but only from the mouth of a kabbalist to a discerning ear." Any speculation rooted in the human mind will lead one astray and prove of "great harm." The inner sense of God's true Word is a truth about God, and so earthly knowledge follows the wrong track. This is an explicit word to the unwise!

R. Joseph Gikatilla offers another mystical tradition on Scripture as a texture of Divine Names in his 'Bible Code' called *Sha'arei Orah* (Gates of Light). According to Gikatilla, Scripture contains a hierarchy of Names corresponding to the hierarchy of the *sefirot*, along with numerous different epithets of these Names also keyed to the Divine gradations emanated from the Hidden Depths of the Godhead. At the core of all these Names is the Holy Tetragrammaton, Y-H-V-H, which is deemed the innermost truth of Divine Being (the other Names are derivative modalities or expressions, according to different Divine attributes of action). This ultra-core Name is "like the image *(ke-dimyon)* of the trunk of a tree," upon which the other Names and nominal epithets "depend," and from which "all the holy Names are rooted and extend in every direction like *(be-dimyon)* branches and shoots ... and every one of which produces fruits according to its kind." Now these multiple Names and epithets (the epithets being nominal terms like "Rock" or "Well," but also particles like "thus" or "this") mean more than they say, for they are (in esoteric truth) mere traces of the most transcendent and spiritual realities—beyond human cognition and only verbal springboards for meditation, for the person initiated into the esoteric code.

Gikallita compares the reality of the biblical Divine Names to the way nouns and names function in human discourse; namely, they are only hints and reminders of certain realities. To make his point he uses the example of the name 'Reuben,' whose orthographic form and vocal enunciation are hardly the same as the actual person Reuben, though the name may evoke, recall, or refer to him in one way or another. In an analogous manner, the epithets and Names of Scripture may aide the mystic in meditative prayer or in contemplative intentions of various sorts. Scripture can serve that purpose because there is an ontological link (a link of "being") between the expressible form and the ultimate Divine reality. And thus Scripture is a most holy text, whose deepest sense transcends ordinary narrative and ordinary discourse, just as the meanings of the laws are similarly keyed to supernal dimensions. Pronouncing Scripture is ever and always a pronunciation of the Names of God. Knowing this, the adept loves God all the more and binds his human consciousness to them in a chain of Names that link the human mind to God. Scripture is thus a holy litany of Divine Names, expressed in human forms by God through Moses. Correspondingly, the enunciation of this Scripture by humans is a sacred chant that weaves the soul of the speaker into the ultimate texture of God.

The Major Exemplar of 13th Century Kabbalah: The Book of Zohar

The most wondrous work of mystical teachings in the Jewish spiritual canon is *Sefer Ha-Zohar* (The Book of Splendor). Deriving from ancient sources and traditions, and transformed by diverse medieval sensibilities and techniques, this work suddenly appeared in Castile (north-central Spain) in the mid-13th c., as a book of mystical study and discourse by Rabbi Shimon bar Yoḥai, one of the great sages of rabbinic antiquity, and his disciples. This (pseudepigraphic) ancient aura deepened the mysterious enchantment of the work, filled with wonders and marvels of the imagination, as the sages roamed the Land of Israel and spoke words of Torah. The work claims to reflect their mystical study of Scripture, often in modes that reflect ancient rabbinic homilies, but with the aim of penetrating the "hierognosis" or holy wisdom of the text, as one visual event or another in the world evoked scriptural passages and associations, all leading to meditations on the supernal realities to which such matters appeared to correspond. The Book of *Zohar* is thus the product of circles of sages, disciples and seekers, and reflects diverse orientations to similar subjects—not solely because the work is a repository of diverse groups of esoteric devotees, but because of the infinite fullness of Scripture, which human hermeneutics could hardly exhaust. Often the only confirmation of the truth or viability of a given teaching (even on the same topic) was that it fit the flow of biblical language and led to mystical insights and ecstatic transports. When this happened, the interpreter would be kissed on the forehead by his companion who proclaimed: "O what joy. If I only came into this world to hear this [teaching], it would be sufficient"!

This joy reflects the idea that "there is no word of Torah, or even small letter of Torah, lacking a hint of supernal wisdom *(ḥokhmeta 'ila'ah),* and from which devolve myriads *(tilei tilin)* of mysteries of supernal wisdom" (*Zohar* III. 79b). This statement is significant both for what it says explicitly (that Scripture is saturated with supernal mysteries), and for what it only implies. Those in the know would perceive in this comment about the myriads of mysteries an allusion to a comment in the midrash to the Song. In it, the "curled" black locks of the beloved's hair (called *taltalim* in Song 5.11) are deemed the very words and interpretations of Torah—itself associated with God. That is, there is a trace in this old midrash of a mystic belief that the primordial Torah was somehow expressed upon a spiritual configuration of Divinity (a belief articulated quite explicitly in other sources); this notion is given a most supreme esoteric confirmation in the *Zohar*. For it was a mystic truth since antiquity that the figure of the beloved in Song ch 5 was the Majestic Form of God (called *Shiur Qomah*)—a spiritual configuration which later mystics deemed the holy hierarchy of the Divine Gradations (the *sefirot*). Thus the myriads of esoteric truths referred to in the preceding passage are aspects of the Godhead manifest in the supernal realms. No wonder (or what a great wonder!) that another source tells the student "to meditate" on Scripture and the images perceived thereby (to the inner eye of thought), in order "to know" the mystery of God and "fix the wisdom of His Name in his heart" (*Zohar* I. 217a).

Given the vast variety of materials in the Book of *Zohar*, this essay will focus on several cases that exemplify the spiritual passage of the interpreter of Scripture into the Divine Depths. As already observed, the act of exegesis is a sacred rite, not separable from mystical experiences attained in and through this process. Study of Scripture is thus a spiritual pedagogy for the achievement of a higher consciousness—but remarkably one not separable from the ritual and ethical behaviors linked to it.

Many teachings in the *Zohar* imitate (or revive) older rabbinic homiletic styles, composed for congregants on Sabbaths and Festivals. Perhaps in some instances this mode of scriptural inquiry may have originated in the prayer groups of mystical adepts; otherwise they are entirely literary constructs. Either way, their purpose is to address issues of concern to individuals with mystical proclivities and interests. The teachings in *Zohar* I. 103a-b are a splendid case in point, and take their departure from a citation of Gen. 18.1, "And he [Abraham] was sitting at the entrance of the tent" (words that follow the announcement that "Then the LORD appeared *[Va-yera']* to him at the tents of Mamre," which begins a Sabbath Torah recitation). As is common in ancient homilies, the Torah passage is immediately juxtaposed to another biblical passage, far removed from the first, whose theological pertinence to the primary passage is initially tenuous, but worked out in the homily. In this instance, Rabbi Judah "opened" his instruction by citing Prov. 31.23, "Her husband is known in the gates." At first glance one might think that "her husband" alludes here to Sarah and Abraham (since Sarah heard the message of the angels to Abraham "from the opening of the tent"; Gen. 18.10), and that the "gates" allude to the entrance of the tent. But this apparent correlation is only at the level of plain sense. Mystics require more, and so the first glance is not sufficient for an esoteric eye.

The teaching begins obscurely, with only a hint of who the "husband" is. Rabbi Judah starts by saying that the Holy One, Blessed be He, has ascended into the supernal heights, utterly hidden and concealed, and beyond any and all human comprehension. Even the angels are dumbfounded, and can only proclaim, "Blessed is the Glory of YHVH *from His Place*" (Ezek. 3.10)—because God and God's place is unknowable even to them. So how then, the teacher asks, can Scripture say, "her husband is known in the gates"? And with one fell swoop we are thrown into a mystical reading of Scripture, which identifies the husband with the Holy One ("Her husband is the Holy One"!) and the female (by implication) with the Shekhinah. But this still leaves the initial quest for knowledge unsatisfied, along with the ancillary question of who has this knowledge—seemingly so impossible. Obviously, this is an issue that perplexed all mystics. If there is no true human comprehension of God, to what extent is there positive theological knowledge? Rabbi Judah now offers an answer based on the passage in Prov. interpreted with a mystical twist. To say that God can be known in the "gates" *(she'arim)* means that God can be "grasped" to the extent that one "opens the gates of the imagination *(she'urei de-libba)*" and connects with "the spirit of wisdom." The greater the development the individual's spiritual capacity and purification of consciousness, the greater will be the imaginative truth fixed in one's mind. But to say that anyone really and truly knows God "as He truly is"—that is utterly impossible, "for no one has ever been able to attain such knowledge of Him."

The teacher walks a narrow ridge across a cognitive abyss. Negative theology denies that one can say anything positive about God, let alone have any positive knowledge of Him. This is the ultimate mystical assertion of Rabbi Judah. But he also indicates the limited (imperfect and inconclusive) role of the imagination, which suggests that certain images might produce positive assertions—for the individual attached to the spirit of wisdom. But how can anyone be sure of that, and not be swept away by images deriving from one's imperfect spiritual state, or even choose incorrect images or use them incorrectly? This is a great problem, and addressed head-on by the Sage. The person who asks, "Who are these gates?" learns from the psalmist that they are "the openings of eternity" through which "the King of Glory may come" (Ps. 24.7) and be present (in some measure) to human consciousness. The *Zohar* also observes that the word "openings" (in the Ps. passage) is in the plural, suggesting that the first opening of the imagination is but the first of a series of spiritual openings that would purify consciousness of its pretentions of positive knowledge.

But this realization doesn't quell the problem. The seeker still wonders how to "attain the clarity of the first opening," so that the others might be discovered. And with that complication the teacher retreats in temporary despair. For since Israel is now in exile, this initial opening is "unknown," and it will remain so until they come forth from exile. Thus the physical dislocation of the people is an outer expression of a deeper inner rupture of religious consciousness, an exile from true wisdom. If the hope of higher awareness lies in the future; the present is darkened by alienation from God and any awareness of the openings that might enlarge the mind. Paradoxically, the teacher says all this through the interpretation of Scripture. Thus the initate may wonder whether the spiritual imagination might be guided through the images of Scripture itself—these being true traces of primordial truths.

The bulk of the Book of *Zohar* is predicated on this possibility. Repeatedly, the verbal images of Scripture are deemed the gateways to a higher consciousness and its ritual and moral challenges, and some images challenge one not to let older images become reified or routinized, but constantly to recover or renew their spiritual potential. An example of the first issue revolves around the word "day," and focuses on a ritual prescription in Scripture; an example of the second takes the word "well" into account, and involves a historical narrative. In both cases, of course, more is involved than temporal units or cisterns—because the words of Scripture are not like any other words we use, even if they sound like normal human words, and refer to quite ordinary things.

Earlier, this essay looked at the Festival of Sukkot, a holiday that was a religious event that had been historicized in the Bible (see "Biblical Festivals and Fast Days," pp. 2025–34) and given spiritual significance by the Sages. For the *Zohar* (III. 103b–104a), however, all its ritual features are but worldly manifestations of spiritual realities, encoded in the biblical text. To understand the mystical perception one must attend to the language of the commandment. "On the fifteenth day of this seventh month there shall be a Festival of Booths [Sukkot] to the LORD, seven days ... You shall dwell in booths seven days" (Lev. 23.33, 42). On the face of it, the ritual rule is clear: the people are enjoined to celebrate a festival "to the LORD" (*la*-YHVH), for "seven days"; and also to reside in booths for the duration of the festival. But the formulation is concise, and symbolic to a mystical mind of supernal events. The seven days of the week cannot be separated from the seven days of creation, which the mystics of the *Zohar* understood to symbolize the seven lower *sefirot* (from *Ḥesed*, Kindness or Generosity, the virtue of Abraham, down to *Malkhut*, the Dominion or Kingdom of this supernal Heaven). Hence the phrase "to YHVH, seven days" could refer to the "seven days *of* YHVH," such that each of the days of the festival week was a different manifestation of Divinity. From this perception it was a small step to understand the final clause as an injunction for these seven gradations to dwell in the earthly booths for the ritual week, reading it: "Seven days: dwell in the booths"!

Rabbi Eleazar, the purported teacher of this text, makes all these grammatical points, and notes their profound theological import. For him, the booth symbolizes the Divine Hierarchy, and the days manifest the Divine aspects of the gradations. The days are spoken to directly, and thus personified; this allows the master to indicate that the various Biblical personages whose virtues were linked to the virtues of the gradations, would be symbolically present in successive days—beginning with Abraham, who was famously hospitable (according to tradition), and repeatedly opened his tent and set a table for guests. Thus the festival week, a time of earthly bounty, celebrates the gifts of God, manifest in a supernal generosity. And just as God cares for the needy on earth, so must all worshippers care for the poor in their midst and invite them to dwell in the booth and eat at its table. Hence another ethical dimension is added: celebrating the Divine bounty each of the days requires acts of sustenance for the needy who must be invited. Feeding the poor thus returns the bounty of God to God each day via the needy who are present at the table. Not to do so, says the Sage, is to pervert the offering to God and make the entire celebration worthless. The Divine "days" will dwell on earth when these earthly days are filled with human generosity. Ritual and ethics are thus intertwined; sustaining the poor recycles the bounty of God to people in need and this makes the festival of God a festival for God. The mystic does works on earth for the sake of Heaven, serving Heaven through ritual generosity. All this is derived from Scripture, which anchors ethics through images of Divinity. This is imagination in the service of God. The booth and its days become openings to a higher consciousness.

The *Zohar* similarly finds deep, ethical and esoteric meanings in the wells described in the Bible. The well is understood as a symbol of the source of the highest Divine Wisdom that flows ceaselessly from the ultra-cosmic springs of Divinity, and thus one who wishes "to know the mystery of Wisdom *(raza de-ḥokhmeta)*" must labor (spiritually) and dig a well that opens his consciousness to the Mystery of Faith (namely entire Divine Hierarchy). We learn this lesson from the patriarchs who all dug wells to create spiritual channels into the Divine realm, and be strengthened thereby in their religious life. Isaac is a strong example of this activity, for he re-dug the wells that his father Abraham had hewn (Gen. 26.18), and thus renewed and deepened his ancestor's spiritual wisdom. We are also told that those persons who are able to "envision" such wells will penetrate to a supreme level of Divine understanding. And this is hinted at in Scripture by the fact that one of the wells that Isaac dug was called Reḥovot (from the Heb root, *r-ḥ-v*, "to expand"), for by his spiritual labors his mind was "expanded." But the deeds that were effective in the time of the patriarchs, who lived before Sinai, change for subsequent generations. It is now by means of the Divine commandments that persons may strengthen and enhance their spiritual capacities—or conversely diminish them through a slackening of religious duties (*Zohar* I. 140a-b). The Torah is now the well of living waters, flowing from supernal wisdom, and by enacting it persons may ascend to spiritual heights and be fortified in their faith. The commandments are the new portals of spiritual growth.

Human prayer is also an opening of the supernal well, when performed out of the depth of one's heart. This is taught through another act of mystical interpretation, which begins with a seeming contradiction, and resolves into a spiritual instruction. The contradiction or puzzlement is focused on David, traditionally the author of Ps. David had already said "With my whole heart I have sought You" (in Ps. 119.10), so why did he also say "Out of the depths I have called (to) You, O LORD" (in Ps. 130.1–2)? The resolution lies in the fact that the second psalm "stands without [explicit] name of author," so that people "of all generations can take this psalm for their own"—and be instructed that one must pray to God from the "depths of his soul" so that heart and mind will be intently focused on God and the prayer. The new emphasis is for the inner spiritual self. But there is yet another dimension that pertains to the spiritual realities of Divinity, and it is this: proper intention in prayer should be directed to the Source of All Sources, so that one "may draw up blessings from [the spheres called] 'the depths of the well,' the source of all life—this being 'the stream that comes forth from Eden' (Gen. 2.10)," the realm of the *sefirot* that endows the world with beneficence. True prayer is thus "a drawing of this water from Above to Below" [that is, from the Divine "Depths" in the ultimate supernal realm, to the lower spheres; hence the Psalm v. was read as if it said, "Out of the Supernal Depths I have called You forth"]—such that the human word conjoins with God's desire to bless the world, and draws God's "bounties" into the supernal well, from which they may flow to the world (*Zohar* II. 63b) Thus the "depth" of the soul calls to the "Depth" of Divinity for spiritual beneficence, and the "well" of the imagination calls to the Heavenly "Well"; as a result, Scripture and the heart are renewed. The efficacy of prayer and the soul are thus founded upon Scripture and revealed through it. The two are intertwined.

The 16th Century (Safed): Mystical Ethics, Meditation and Prayer

The Jewish mystical tradition continues through the reformulation of its own sources, in a series of spiritual renaissances. The Book of *Zohar* is one such use and renewal of tradition; the works produced by several interrelated coteries of mystics in Safed, in the Upper Galilee of the Land of Israel in the 16th c., is another case in point. One influential expression of this renewal is based on the massive commentaries and reinterpretations of the *Zohar* produced by R. Moses Cordovero (in written form) and R. Isaac Luria Ashkenazi (known as "the Ari"; his teaching were transmitted orally for centuries). Another creative expression of renewal was through the formulation and systematization of Jewish ethics. The treatise called *Tomer Devorah (The Palm Tree of Deborah)*, by Cordovero, is a classic of this genre, and exemplifies the intense behavioral spirituality of the mystics in Safed, grounded in the mystical belief, hinted at in Gen. 1.27, that the human being is a microcosm of the macrocosmic Divine Being (the supernal Divine hierarchy in human form, called the *Shiur Qomah*). The human task was to imitate the patterns and flow of Divine vitality in and through their body and its actions, and thus irradiate the world with such primal Divine qualities as Mercy, Humility, and Lovingkindness *(Ḥesed)*. Within a century this work was incorporated into another classic of Jewish mysticism, the *Shnei Luḥot Ha-Berit (The Two Tables of the Covenant;* popularly called by its acronym, the *Shelah*), by R. Isaiah Horovitz. The *Tomer Devorah* was widespread and influential on its own, but in its new venue it reached many other spiritual adepts over the centuries. Like other Jewish mystical texts, the book is founded upon Scripture and on its interpretation.

One of the core passages of Scripture that expresses the Divine attribute of mercy is Exod. 34.6–7, where God tells Moses that He is a God "Compassionate and gracious, slow to anger, abounding in kindness and faithfulness, [who] ... forgives *(nose')* iniquity ... and sin, ... " Many kabbalists, Cordovero among them, believed that the qualities of Mercy are rooted in the Supernal Crown of Divinity—in a realm above the Hierarchy, where such love and care "is" in its purest and most spiritual form. One of the later biblical reformulations of these attributes was by the prophet Micah, who said, "Who is a God like You, who forgives *(nose')* iniquity ... and does not keep His anger forever, because He delights in mercy ..." (Mic. 7.18–20). This formulation is the principle text of *Tomer Devorah*. Each one of its phrases is discussed in terms of purely Divine attributes, and then supplemented with how a person might imitate God and develop these traits through mindfulness and practice. Not only do these human actions benefit the performer of the action and the receivers of this beneficence, they also (and this is a particularly kabbalistic emphasis) benefit Divinity—insofar as lack or need in the world indicates something that needs repair in the totality of Being, and which only a human can heal or help. All human actions thus have ultimate Divine effects and reverberations, though Cordovero's work was especially valued for the way it trained personal dispositions and traits within a theological framework. The following two examples highlight this point.

One of the Divine attributes mentioned by Micah is that God "forgives" iniquity. Literally, the Heb word *nose'* means "to carry" or "to bear" or endure something. This concrete meaning is given a profound theological meaning in our text. Since God is Merciful in the highest and most perfected degree, God emanates mercy continuously into the world; even if humans sin or pervert the good, God "bears and endures" their sin and keeps nourishing the sinner with love and mercy, until a person might repent. This is truly a mystical attribute of infinite Divine love. And it "is the greatest quality of tolerance that God nourishes and sustains the ... sinner until the latter repents. From which a person should learn the degree of patience [necessary] in bearing his neighbor's yoke [burden] and the evils done by his neighbor even when those evils still exist. So that even when his neighbor offends he bears with him until the wrong is righted, or until it disappears on its own accord, and so forth." Such then is one feature of the imitation of God. Another relates to the quality of not remaining angry, even as God "does not retain His anger forever." Cordovero observes: "This is a quality which a person should make his own in dealings with his neighbor. For even if it is permitted to chastise one's neighbor or children, who [would] suffer as a result, one should not persist in such a rebuke precisely because of this [harm]."

A scriptural lesson on this point is derived from Exod. 23.5: "When you see the ass of your enemy crouching under its burden, you shall surely help it/him." This strong ethical injunction is now taken much further. The Rabbis had interpreted this text (in *b. Pes.* 113b) to mean that this enmity refers to a person who sees his neighbor sin but, since he is the sole witness and cannot testify in court, may "hate the sinner for the offense" (in Cordovero's words). Neverthless, *ʿazov taʿazov ʿimmo* means "you shall abandon [or leave aside] the anger in your heart" (and not just "help" with the burden). This literal reading of the scriptural phrase has profound spiritual significance and imposes a great ethical demand upon the religious person. "It is a religious duty," Cordovero concludes, "to encourage [the neighbor] lovingly, and perhaps this way of dealing with him will succeed. This is precisely the [Divine] quality of which we have spoken, 'He does not retain His anger forever.'" The human heart must therefore divest itself of anger and imitate the attribute of endless Divine mercy. This is not simply biblical or rabbinic ethics. It is a mystical ethic based on Scripture and developed through interpretation.

Alongside such instances of mystical exegesis and normative ethics in a kabbalistic key, others in Safed were intent to develop practices based on the word and letter mysticism of the *Sefer Yetzirah*. One such master was R. Judah Albotini, whose manual *Sulam Ha-ʿAliyah* (The Ladder of Ascension) is a detailed description of techniques for ecstatic prayer based on the twenty-two letters of the alphabet in multiple arrangements and combinations. These letters, as the core elements of the created universe (and the linguistic core of Scripture), provided the adept with methods of spiritual ascension into the highest spheres where contact with God might be attained and prayers fulfilled. In an expository section, Albotini refers to the passage in the *Sefer Yetzirah* that discussed the issues of engraving and hewing letters, and goes on to indicate just what this means for a prophet-kabbalist seeking to cultivate the Divine Spirit through the letters of creation. In his words, this involved a "hewing" of these letters "in interior prophetic visions, after one's mind has transcended the human domain and enters the Divine domain" (ch 7). In some cases this is done through types of visualization and impressing the letters in one's mind or "soul" in the process of meditation.

Albotini also refers to breathing and vocalization techniques that required highly intense articulations of the vowels and letters of the Heb alphabet along with related body and head movements (ch 10). Some verbal patterns follow alphabetic sequences (like "a-b-c-d") and their multiple combinations; others follow certain words and their innumerous variations. One such word (developed in ch 1) is the first word of the Bible, *Be-Reishit* ("In the beginning"), it being initially rendered by the letter pattern *b-r-ʾ-sh-y-t* (its scriptural form; but then with such variations as *b-r-sh-y-t-ʾ*, *b-r-y-t-ʾ-sh*, etc.). The initial orthographic pattern starts with the letter *bet* throughout; successive ones begin with other letters of the word. Albotini warns the reader that this technique is powerful, involves out-of-the-body experiences, and should only be performed after much training and self-purification. Thus the letters of Scripture are elements to conjure with. Broken up into their orthographic components to produce holy sounds and Divine Names, the letters of Scripture, being primary expressions of Divine Breath, are sounds that may be vocalized with most awesome results.

Naḥmanides had already hinted of such matters, and chose the opening words of Gen. as his "figurative" case. He undoubtedly knew more than he said.

Magical prayer was only one dimension of the use of Scripture and its words. The intense spiritual fellowships in Safed also gave vent to their longing for God through poignant prayers. One such prayer (still recited by Jews on the Sabbath, at the onset and conclusion) was *Yedid Nefesh* ("Beloved of My Soul"), written by R. Eliezer Azikri. Its yearning and pathos are felt in every line, which are studded with phrases from Scripture. Particularly evident are passages taken from the Song to express spiritual longing. The prayer opens with a call to God, the dearly beloved of the speaker's soul, to "draw forth" His servant to heavenly favor, that he might "run" like a deer towards God, whose love is "sweeter than the dripping honeycomb"—for, he cries, "my soul is sick for Your love"; "please, O God, heal her" and show her the great radiance of Your splendor. Readers will readily recognize the traces of the Song in two of the phrases—namely, the request that God "draw" the "love-sick soul" to Him, so that it might "run" and bask in the Divine light (see Song 1.4; 2.5); and also the deft use of Moses' request of God to "heal" Miriam (Num. 12.13), now applied to the speaker's soul. In addition, the poem refers to the "honeyed sweetness" of spiritual bliss, derived from a hymn to Torah (Ps. 19.11). Azikri undoubtedly also mentions the sweetness of superior "taste" to allude, in fitting emphasis, to the psalmist's words, "Taste and see that the LORD is good"! (Ps. 34.9). Through such citations and a verbal texture drawn from Scripture, the speaker articulates an overwhelming desire to come into God's presence, and to savor its spiritual bounty. All this is a mystic desire, poignant and powerful, from a soul in love.

17th through 20th Centuries: Hasidism

Spiritual adepts were called "pious ones" *(ḥasidim)* at various points over the centuries. For example, some individuals whose spiritual practices included long periods of meditation prior to prayers were called *ḥasidim re'shonim* ("the first pious ones") in rabbinic antiquity. Another circle of mystics that bore this name were the saintly pious individuals of the Rhineland in the 13th c., often referred to as *Ḥasidei Ashkenaz*, or the German Pietists. The circles that produced a revival of intense piety and fellowship in the 18th c. drew from all their predecessors and all their literary precedents—including kabbalistic sources and techniques, and also traditions of ethics and spirituality cultivated in medieval and later groups. The spiritual founder of the revival of Hasidism is acclaimed to be R. Eliezer Baʿal Shem Tov (popularly known as the Besht, an acronym of his epithet 'Master of the Good Name'—an indication that he was also adept in letter and Name mysticism). This spiritual revival movement was characterized by the spiritual individualization of the teachings of earlier kabbalah, and an intense focus on the cultivation of inwardness and proper mindfulness on God at all times—not just while performing the commandments and during prayer, but in all worldly actions, even those not regulated by normative religious practice. Features of their reinterpretation of tradition, through reinterpretations of Scripture, will be especially evident through the following examples from successive centuries, which pick up materials discussed earlier.

The first example is from a teaching cited in the name of the Besht (18th c.) by R. Menaḥem Naḥum of Chernobyl (in his work *Me'irat ʿEinayim*), who was a student of the Great Maggid of Mezritch (Dov Baer), himself a direct disciple of the Besht. Hence, oral traditions were preserved and transmitted by disciple circles, and disseminated in the oral teachings of other masters. This particular teaching is based upon, but also transforms, the Zoharic teaching about the wells dug by the patriarch Isaac. The particular emphasis is on the digging of the wells that had been stopped up by the Philistines, in order to find the "living water" under the earth that had been thrown in to block them up (Gen. 26.15). According to the Besht, as reported by the later disciple, the "earth" *(ʿafar)* symbolizes all the places in the lower world where one might have access to the higher Divine worlds, but these have been covered over by material shards of all sorts (the Philistines symbolize these negative shards, called *qelipot*), and thus require spiritual repair and intense "focus" *(histaqlut)* in order for the underlying spiritual waters to be perceived. Abraham dug such wells in the course of his life, and through his actions revealed ways to ascend to God through ordinary life activities (a revelation of Torah before the Torah of Sinai); and Isaac followed suit, continuing his father's spiritual example for his time and place. Their example and the Torah of Moses thus open portals towards Divinity in the everyday. The lesson of the Besht is that spiritual life is to be found in the ordinary course of life, but requires spiritual focus in order to find its hidden potential.

A 19th c. teacher, R. Aaron of Zhitomir, whose Torah teachings are collected in a work called *Toledot Aharon*, adds to this teaching and reinforces it. He too was concerned to maintain the chain of spiritual instruction inherited from the first teachers. He was a disciple of the acclaimed R. Levi Yizḥak of Berdichev, and was careful "not to recite anything that he had not heard from his master [R. Levi], who had heard it from the Maggid, who had heard or seen it [directly] from the Besht." Concerning the subject of digging wells and finding spiritual resources in this world, R. Aaron tells us that Isaac proceeded with "mental thoughtfulness" *(sikhliyut)*, conditioned by the love and fear of God. But this was an ongoing struggle against external and internal factors; hence the biblical text refers to strife and contention in this process (thus one well [Gen. 26.20] was explicitly named *ʿEiseq* ["wrangling"], to mark this "difficulty"). At the point when such spiritual difficulties abated, Isaac uncovered the well called Reḥovot. In R. Aaron's teaching, this well is not so much symbolic of an expansion of Isaac's mind (as in the earlier interpretation in the *Zohar*), but of a profound "attachment" *(devequt)* of his mind to the Divine realities, through an intense concentration on "every letter in [the course of] his prayer." This Divine connection gave Isaac (and his spiritual heirs) the wherewithal to remain spiritually focused at all times. Significantly, the way the point is established is by a recombination of the letters of Reḥovot *(r-ḥ-b-t)* to yield the word *ḥavurot* ("connections"; formed of the letters *ḥ-b-r-t*). This recombination of the letters of Scripture is for the sake of spiritual mindfulness—not for ecstasy. R. Aaron concludes with a remark that ordinary speech requires a special effort, since it is not grounded in the holy words of Torah and prayer. In these circumstances, he says, the spiritually adept should make all the spoken words a "garment" for proper "thought," thereby investing it with proper intentions.

R. Aaron offers another spiritual reading of Isaac's ordinary activities that turns another episode in Scripture into a profound instruction. It harks back to a passage discussed earlier from the *Zohar*, but now with a twist that accords with the new concerns of Hasidism. To give a flavor of the style, the overall teaching, containing the theological and spiritual message, will be presented; then it can be seen how the master establishes this teaching through a deft reinterpretation of the words of Scripture. His homily is based on the v. "And Isaac sowed in that land and reaped a hundredfold the same year" (Gen. 26.12):

> The concern here is that it is impossible for any person to come to any [spiritual] level, be it the attainment of supernal Reverence or Love [exalted *sefirot*], or the Holy Spirit, or the supernal Lights, unless he divest himself of all his materiality, earthiness and physicality. For how can he attain holiness if he is still embodied and attached to the shards

of physicality—since these two qualities [holiness and physicality] contradict each other? It is only by divesting oneself of materiality and physicality, and coming gradually closer to holiness. This process is similar to seed sown in the earth. One cannot reap any growth until the seed sinks into the ground, rain falls, and the seed sprouts into many shoots. In like manner, it is only when persons annul their physicality that they can attain a higher level.

This strong condemnation of the physical body allows the spiritual capacities to flourish. The analogy used is induced by the v. in Scripture that triggers the teaching, but for this master more is involved. As he proceeds to teach these comments more precisely, he reveals the exegetical basis of his remarks, and thus brings the reader into his spiritual world. It is a teaching of Scripture through its most radical reinterpretation. He specifies that persons can begin to break their physicality and its consequences (sin) through the "fear" of God who judges individuals for every transgression. This "fear" is symbolized by Isaac, who is the supernal prototype of Fear or Reverence for God. Accessing this consciousness inaugurates the process of trying to suppress earthy qualities, symbolized in the text by the sowing of seed into the earth (until it breaks or bursts and yields a new produce). That is why Scripture says that Isaac sowed seed "in the ground" *(ba-ʾaretz);* for one has first to break one's "earthiness" *(ʾartziyut)* and its traits; only then is change possible. And that is why Scripture also says that after the sowing Isaac reaped produce that "year" *(ba-shanah);* since it is by virtue of self-negations that an individual is able to "change" *(meshaneh)* into a new person. This leads to a higher spirituality—from fear to reverence and humility; and that is why the text also refers to a reaping of a hundredfold *(meʾah).* The word *meʾah* is spelled *mem-ʾalef-he.* It can thus be read as saying that a person who truly relates to the "Primary Principle of the Universe" *(ʾalufo shel ʿolam)*—that is, God, the word for whom *(ʾElohim)* begins with *ʾalef*—and who does so with true humility, in the sense meant by Moses who said, "What (*mah*—spelled *mem-he*) are we?" (Exod. 15.7), has thereby broken the natural self and entered on a godly path. This is a gradual process, hence Scripture spoke of this hundredfold with the expression *meʾah sheʿarim,* to indicate that the path of humility takes one through the "measures *(sheʿurim)*" of one's ability; for it is only through the "preparations of one's heart," according to one's capacity, that one will work on this self-suppression of physical needs and urges, and develop a reverence for God that leads to their spiritual transformation.

This teaching is entirely predicated on Scripture and its interpretation, even though the spiritual insight and type of counsel may have derived from other sources. Teaching spiritual growth and self-transformation through Scripture give the master's words a venerable authority—and reveals Scripture anew as a work of spiritual instruction (and in this case, not merely a piece of narrative with odd details). In the words of another 19th c. master, R. Abraham Joshua Heschel of Apt (great ancestor of the 20th c. Jewish theologian and scholar of the same name), "The Torah is eternal *(nitzit),*" hence all of its words and teachings must teach and "apply to all generations." This principle inspired all these masters to look deeply into Scripture for its hidden truths. Commenting on Ps. 19.10, which states that the Torah is "sweeter than honey, than the drippings of the honeycomb," a great spiritual master of the 20th c., R. Abraham Isaac Kook, the first chief rabbi of mandatory Palestine, said that its spiritual boon is not solely the transcendent joy one may derive in and through a life of Torah, filled with its observance and its contemplation. Its sweetness, so surpassing, is the realization that the Infinite and Unknowable God has given traces of His sweet goodness in the small letters of the Torah, so that one may seek God through Scripture and find in its words appropriate direction for living one's life.

Conclusion

Scripture and tradition undergo ever new permutations of sense and purpose in the Jewish mystical tradition. In the multivalent Jewish mystical traditions Scripture is revealed as multifaceted—a voice of spiritual instruction from Divinity, and thus more than words and more than human language. The language of Scripture depicts God through all sorts of verbal hieroglyphs, from single words and their epithets, or chains of words as traces of supernal processes. God's speech is godly even in its human transformations, and God's Torah is an expression of God in human language and its images. Reading and studying this sacred Scripture is thus a sacred act; it is a holy ritual even in its mere recitation, let alone in its meditative perusal. To know the right way to read and interpret Scripture is a key to its sacred secrets. But let the student beware and know one only enters the gates of Scripture through the measures of one's mind and imagination. For this reason mystics stress that one has to fit the measure of one's mind to the measures of Scripture, not fit Scripture to the individual's natural state of mind. One has to grow into the text, and it will enlarge the mind through its largesse. To think otherwise is self-idolatry. For spiritual seekers must become worthy of Scripture, and this is a gradual process, which Scripture itself can guide. This is the lesson of the ages.

[MICHAEL FISHBANE]

Jewish Biblical Scholarship from the 17th to the 19th Centuries

The period between 1650 and 1900 forms a particularly rich and variegated chapter in the history of Jewish biblical interpretation, particularly within the European Ashkenazic communities. Over the course of these two and a half centuries, hundreds of Bible commentaries and supercommentaries came to be written and published, and although the vast majority have fallen into obscurity, a few have exerted considerable influence and continue to be studied to this day. The substantial scholarly output of this period was broadly due to three historically related factors: the growth and relative stability of communities in both western and eastern Europe, a flourishing religious and scholarly life, and an active Jewish printing industry.

The biblical scholarship of this period is particularly important because of the way in which it reflected and even shaped the far-reaching historical, religious, and cultural shifts taking place within European Jewry. Through most of the 17th and 18th centuries, the interpretation of the Bible was largely derivative of medieval exegesis, particularly the didactic and homiletical modes of late medieval scholarship. As the 18th c. progressed, the textual and linguistic interests of medieval Spanish exegesis began to be revived, and by 1800, biblical interpretation was given new impetus by the Jewish Enlightenment, and to a lesser degree, by the reinvigorated scholarly circles that emerged in Lithuania in opposition to the spread of Hasidism. In the 19th c., as the cultural and religious insularity of traditional Jewish life gave way to the external pressures of emancipation, and as internal divisions weakened the authority of rabbinic Judaism, the interpretation of Scripture became a central factor in the struggle to determine the meaning and relevance of inherited Jewish traditions.

The vast majority of Jewish Bible commentaries that appeared in the 17th and 18th centuries were methodologically unoriginal and substantively unremarkable. The Sephardic communities of North Africa, the Middle East, and western Europe (e.g., Amsterdam and Hamburg) retained the traditions of Heb language and Bible study pioneered by medieval Spanish scholars, but did not offer new linguistic or exegetical advances. Among the Ashkenazic communities of western and eastern Europe, the reality was more complex. On the one hand, biblical commentaries were a time-honored scholarly endeavor, many of them centered around the careful parsing of midrashic texts and Rashi's commentary which had attained near-canonical status. On the other hand, there was a pronounced ambivalence, if not indifference, toward Bible study, especially of the philological or grammatical kind. The study of Talmud and its commentaries and the medieval codes of law were given pride of place, and the study of the Bible was relegated to a respectful, honored, but secondary position. These realities are reflected in the fact that some of the best and most enduring writings of this era emerged from non-Ashkenazic Mediterranean communities: *Meʿam Loʿez*, the mid-18th c. popular Ladino compilation of rabbinic writings (Constantinople, 1730–1772); Ḥayyim ben Moses Attar's *Or ha-Ḥayyim* (Venice, 1742) which became very popular among Ashkenazic Jewry; and David Samuel Pardo's, *Maskil le-David* (Venice, 1761), a supercommentary to Rashi.

Modern scholars have often credited a group of 17th-c. thinkers, among them Benedict Spinoza (1634–77), for anticipating the emergence of biblical criticism by eschewing traditional modes of interpretation and by raising questions concerning the reliability, authenticity, and even authorship of the Bible. In his *Theologico-Political Treatise* (1670) Spinoza set out to employ "the true method of Scriptural interpretation," which would entail examining the Bible afresh "in a careful, impartial, and unfettered spirit, making no assumptions concerning it" (Benedict Spinoza, *Theologico-Political Treatise*, transl. R.H.M. Elwes, New York: Dover Publications, 1951; preface and pp. 98–119). Spinoza's intention was to undermine the presumption of a seamless, consistent text that could be ascribed to the hand of Moses and to convince his readers that the Hebrew Bible was so confused and beset with problems that a clear understanding of its meaning was often beyond reach. A careful reading of the *Theologico-Political Treatise*, however, belies the scholarly value of his biblical insights by revealing the arbitrary nature of his methods and the capricious quality of many of his conclusions. Spinoza's discussion was far less interested in the interpretative difficulties and challenges of the Hebrew Bible than in undermining the authority of Scripture for a variety of philosophical and political reasons. Moreover, Spinoza's handling of the Hebrew Bible had no impact on 17th- and 18th-c. Jewish interpretation of the Hebrew Bible. It is often assumed that European scholars who launched the serious critical study of the Bible drew upon Spinoza's writing, although a careful examination of their scholarship might suggest far more limited influence.

The Ashkenazic ambivalence towards the Bible began to change slowly in the 18th c., as some rabbinic authorities and scholars decried the neglect of Bible study and the absence of the requisite grammatical and textual skills. A few grammarians, most notably Solomon Hanau (1687–1746), tried to revive interest in the study of Heb grammar, and the *peshat*-oriented commentary of Rashbam was printed for the first time in 1705. There was also renewed interest in the writings of David Kimḥi (Radak) and Abraham Ibn Ezra later in the century.

The most important development in the 18th c. was the appearance of the Haskalah (Jewish Enlightenment) in late 18th-c. Prussia and its impact on the culture of European Jewry. As part of their effort to promote the integration of Jews into European society, these Jewish Enlightenment figures, or maskilim as they came to be known, were highly attuned to the literary-aesthetic sophistication of contemporary German culture while also sensitive to the poor state of Jewish biblical scholarship and its disregard of earlier Jewish textual traditions.

Both tendencies were evident in the new edition of the Torah published by Moses Mendelssohn (1729–1786), a highly regarded German philosopher and man of letters who was also the most prominent individual associated with the Berlin Haskalah. Appearing in Berlin between 1780 and 1783 as *Sefer Netivot ha-Shalom*, Mendelssohn's Pentateuch was a collaborative affair that included two of the finest scholars associated with the Haskalah, Naftali Herz Wessely (1725–1805) and Solomon Dubno (1738–1813). *Sefer Netivot ha-Shalom* included a new German translation, an extensive Heb commentary, and a series of highly technical Masoretic notes that attempted to fix the precise morphology and pointing of the text. The German translation, printed in Heb script and rendered into a good contemporary *hochdeutsch* ("high," or "literary," German), served the same function as earlier Bible translations, namely, to make the text accessible to a growing number of Jews who felt less comfortable with Heb than with their native tongue. More importantly, the translation also set out to capture the prosaic and poetic qualities of the Heb original in order to offer Jews a text that was as aesthetically sophisticated as any German Bible in circulation, but without Christologically-informed readings and interpretations, and without the textual emendations being introduced by contemporary German scholars. In this regard, Mendelssohn offered his co-religionists a Bible translation that conformed to both Jewish textual traditions and rabbinic interpretations.

The Heb commentary to this Bible embraced the same twofold orientation. On the one hand, the commentary (simply titled *Bi'ur* or "explanation" in Heb) culled the medieval exegesis of Rashi, Rashbam, Ibn Ezra, and Naḥmanides (see "Medieval Jewish Interpretation," pp. 1891–1915) for the best of their *peshat*-oriented interpretations, while also contributing its own linguistic and literary insights. In the face of broad European disregard for the scholarly value of rabbinic literature, on the other hand, Mendelssohn, Dubno and Wessely tried to demonstrate the exegetical acuity of midrashic interpretations by pointing to the sound philological, syntactical, and narrative insights exhibited by the Sages of late antiquity. This commentary thus incorporated rabbinic literature, both *midrash halakhah* (legal interpretation) and *midrash aggadah*, (interpretation of narratives) and sought to explain its relationship to *peshuto shel mikra*—the "plain" sense of the text. Mendelssohn and his fellow contributors adopted differing strategies with regard to the articulation of this relationship: Mendelssohn viewed *peshat* (the plain sense) and *derash* (rabbinic-homiletical interpretation) as eliciting two hermeneutically distinct yet equally veracious layers of the text, while Wessely was more inclined to conflate the two by suggesting that the rabbinic reading represented nothing but the true depths of *peshat*. In either case, their commentaries displayed serious regard for the linguistic qualities of Scripture, using it to elicit fresh approaches to the biblical text as well as a better appreciation for the substantive exegetical legacy of rabbinic Judaism. The Mendelssohn commentary was reprinted in dozens of 19th-c. editions, making it by far the most popular Jewish Bible and second only to the traditional texts published with Targum and Rashi.

In Eastern Europe, meanwhile, many Jewish communities had been swept up by the social and religious revivalism of Hasidism, and with it came a number of scholarly and popular commentaries to the Bible. The opposition to this movement, centered in the leadership of Elijah b. Solomon Zalman (the Vilna Gaon; 1720–97) and his Lithuanian-based disciples, was no less intensely committed to the study of kabbalistic traditions, and they too incorporated these scholarly pursuits into their study of Scripture. R. Elijah and his followers, however, also cultivated an interest in the Bible that roughly paralleled, and may even have been informed by, maskilic developments in Western Europe. In his *ʾAderet ʾEliyahu*, first published posthumously in an 1804 edition of the Pentateuch, R. Elijah called attention to the importance of *peshat*-oriented readings of Scripture, while at the same time probing the nature of rabbinic exegesis. His expression of concern for the biblical text and its traditional rabbinic interpretation, however, was aimed at underscoring the far-reaching, even radical, nature of rabbinic *derashot* (homiletical expositions). As such, this commentary did not in itself set out to advance fresh approaches to the biblical text, nor, in the end, did it substantively explicate the exegetical discernment of the Sages. With this emphasis on the distinction of *peshat* and *derash*, R. Elijah sought to highlight the interpretative creativity and profundity of rabbinic Judaism, an endeavor that would shape the intellectual and spiritual character of Lithuanian scholarship well into the 20th c.

In the 19th c., the most significant developments in Jewish biblical scholarship took place among the Jews of German-speaking Europe. As these Jews began their century-long struggle for civic equality and social integration, their approach to the Hebrew Bible came to reflect the cultural and religious vicissitudes of the age. One can discern three different though somewhat overlapping trends, all of them cognizant of the relationship of Bible study to the broader challenges of modernity, and all of them staking out a set of assumptions regarding Scripture and its religious and cultural meaning to contemporary Jews.

One trend found primary expression in the continued promotion of the maskilic revival of Heb and Bible study, which in some cases was spurred on by a growing awareness of increasing sophisticated and critical scholarship emanating from European universities. Within a decade after the publication of Mendelssohn's Pentateuch, a group of younger maskilim had extended the project to cover all the books of the Prophets and Writings, and some of these were even replaced in the 1830s by new commentaries. In 1810, Judah Leib ben Zeʾev (1764–1811) contributed a set of introductory essays to the Prophets and Writings which focused mainly on the historical and literary features of those books. Ben Zeʾev's introductions made use of contemporary German scholarship, including an acknowledgement—and ambivalent rejection—of critical notions regarding the authorship of some prophetic books. The interest in Heb and Bible study was also taken up by those who straddled the maskilic and rabbinic circles: Solomon Pappenheim (1740–1814), a rabbinic court judge in Breslau, wrote a multi-volume study of Heb synonyms, while Wolf Heidenheim (1757–1832), an important publisher and editor of liturgical texts, penned a series of commentaries on the Masorah and a supercommentary to Rashi.

Maskilically-inspired biblical scholarship also began to flourish beyond the German-speaking lands of Central Europe. In Italy, Isaac Samuel Reggio (1784–1855) translated the Torah into Italian and added a Heb commentary that drew extensively from the *Biʾur*. Samuel David Luzzatto (1800–1865), an original and independent-minded scholar, also penned a Heb commentary to the Pentateuch, as well as two Heb grammars, a study of *Tg. Onk.*, and numerous essays on Heb philology. His lectures on the Pentateuch, including introductions to issues regarding the biblical text and modes of interpretation, were collected and published posthumously. In France, Samuel Cahen (1796–1862) penned a French translation and produced a remarkably ambitious and wide-ranging commentary to the Tanakh, one which drew upon the classics of Jewish scholarship (which now included the Mendelssohn Bible) as well as nonrabbinic and non-Jewish translations and writings. An important center of biblical scholarship also emerged in Galicia, where maskilically-oriented scholars began to publish essays and biblical studies in new maskilic journals such as *Bikkurei ha-Ittim* and *Kerem Ḥemed.* Naḥman Krochmal (1785–1840) addressed himself to questions regarding Isa., Eccl., and Ps., embracing the late dating of sections of this literature and arguing that such critical awareness was already evident in rabbinic literature. His one-time student and friend Solomon Judah Rapoport (1790–1867) also included in his writings similar critical ideas regarding the books of Isa. and Ps. There also emerged a group of Lithuanian maskilim who produced a number of commentaries, supercommentaries, and journal articles that took up various linguistic and exegetical issues pertaining to the study of the Bible.

Taken together, these writings endeavored to expand the intellectual, religious, and cultural horizons of European Jews. This body of literature was largely traditionalist in its commitments and sensibilities, and although aware in varying degress of the critical approaches emanating from European universities, they chose not to engage them in any sustained manner. Critical notions regarding the text, its editing and its historical context were raised only with regard to the non-pentateuchal books, and generally where medieval scholars had either opened the door to such notions or when there existed sufficient ambiguity to allow for new ideas. While most of these writings did not have enduring value, they did make the engagement with Scripture a more central part of European Jewish culture.

The second salient trend that characterized the 19th-c. study of Scripture emanated from a group of Jews invested in academic methods and intellectual discourse of contemporary German scholarship. Emerging in the 1810s, this group began to promote the *Wissenschaft des Judentums*, the critical-academic ("scientific") study of Jewish history and literature, with particular emphasis on texts, languages, and philosophical issues not generally studied in traditional settings. Up until the second half of the century, these proponents of *Wissenschaft* formed a broader circle with the maskilic writers cited above and shared their cautiousness, focusing on the Prophets and Writings and venturing fairly circumscribed forays into text-critical and authorial issues. One exception was the early work of Isaac Jost (1793–1860), in which he lauded the importance of critical approaches to the Pentateuch and subscribed to the fragmentary theories of its composition. A decade later Jost retreated from this position and assumed a more agnostic view regarding traditional and critical approaches; but he also insisted on the distinction between historical and theological issues, such that the spirit embedded in the teachings of the Pentateuch trumped questions of historical provenance of the text.

The proponents of *Wissenschaft des Judentums* shed some of their biblical conservatism in the second half of the century, when scholars such as Leopold Zunz (1794–1886), Abraham Geiger (1810–1874), and Heinrich Graetz (1817–1891) began to apply their considerable talents to the text-critical study of the Hebrew Bible. Two scholars, Julius Popper (1822–1884) and Marcus Kalisch (1828–1885), offered important insights into the composition of the Pentateuch that engaged and the central theories then being formulated by the leading critical scholars. Younger scholars such as Kaufmann Kohler (1843–1926) and Sigmund Maybaum (1844–1919), rabbinic leaders in the Reform movement, also embraced the premises and conclusions of contemporary documentary analysis as a natural extension of the advancement of science and scholarship. Despite their embrace of the critical study of the Bible, however, these Jews never really joined their European peers in common scholarly cause. Biblical scholarship remained institutionally and theologically based in faculties with deep Christian commitments into which Jews were not admitted, and even their scholarly publications tended to appear in separate journals.

One partial exception to this and perhaps the most noteworthy contribution of *Wissenschaft des Judentums* was Geiger's *Urschrift und Übersetzungen der Bibel* (1857). Geiger set out to demonstrate the originally fluid nature of the biblical text and the presence of competing versions, a phenomenon that he substantiated by pointing to the varying translations of Scripture that emerged in late antiquity. Underlying his approach was the notion that the Bible was not a "sealed book of antiquity, whose meaning the student had to unlock in order to acquaint himself with the ideas of a day long past." Rather, "every age, every movement and every personality in history has brought its own ideas to bear upon the Bible." (Abraham Geiger, *Urschrift und Übersetzungen der Bibel*, Breslau, 1857, p. 72) This was not merely a programmatic outline of an important subfield of biblical scholarship; Geiger's statement that the Bible was all things to all people was predicated upon his insistence that an objective interpretation of Scripture could not be achieved, and as such, was not a particularly valuable endeavor to pursue. Deeply committed as he was to the religious reformation of Judaism, Geiger sought to emphasize the early historical flexibility of Jewish traditions as an instructive guidepost to contemporary Judaism.

Broadly seen, Geiger and other proponents of *Wissenschaft* engaged the Bible in a rather limited way, one that remained an internally directed endeavor framed in terms of Jewish traditions and sensibilities. These Jews were less interested in the development of new critical perspectives relating to the origins of the Bible or to the serious study of biblical history or philology than in the textual and interpretative *reception* of the biblical text. The cultural and religious needs of the moment manifested themselves in a primary focus upon the manifold ways in which the Bible had been read, pointing clearly to the possibility of other, more contemporaneous readings rather than on the original meaning of the text. Jewish critical scholarship would eventually free itself of these constraints, but at this juncture, the social and cultural bases upon which to develop such interests were as yet undeveloped.

The third trend that characterized the 19th-c. study of the Bible arose out of the most traditionalist element of European Jewry, that which came to be identified by its orthodoxy. Traditionalist leaders were largely unwilling to address text-critical questions, but they were acutely sensitive to other 19th-c. developments that they perceived to be far more pressing: the growing abandonment of traditional Jewish practices and learning, and the Reform eschewal of rabbinic authority in general and ancient rabbinic readings of Scripture in particular. In their struggle against the burgeoning Reform movement, a number of traditional defenders of rabbinic Judaism sought to buttress their orthodoxy by turning to the Bible and trying to demonstrate the fundamental accord between Scripture and its rabbinic elucidations. The resulting commentaries contributed an important and lasting corpus of traditional scholarship to the history of biblical interpretation.

The first of these commentaries was *Ha-Ketav veha-Kabbalah (The Written Text and [Rabbinic] Tradition)*, published in 1839 by Jacob Zvi Meklenburg (1785–1865) of Königsberg. This exegete exhibited an impressive scholarly range that included not only rabbinic and medieval texts, but also a rudimentary knowledge of classical languages and a familiarity with maskilic and *Wissenschaft* writings. Meklenburg was most concerned about the perceived inauthenticity of oral traditions, particularly the idea that rabbinic readings were foisted unnaturally upon Scripture. In response, he suggested that a refined grasp of the biblical language and idiom would demonstrate that "the Written Torah and the Oral Torah are twins, stuck one to the other such that they could not be sundered" (*Ha-Ketav veha-Kabbalah* , Leipzig 1839, introduction, p. xiii). Meklenburg did not intend to collapse the distinction between *peshat* and *derash*. His aim, rather, was to defuse any apparent tension between them and to legitimate midrashic and Talmudic readings by grounding them in the biblical text with subtlety and sophistication. In the body of the commentary itself, his explication of the rabbinic interpretations of Scripture was undertaken only on a selective basis, and his limited attempts at laying out a systematic approach to the problem relied substantially on Mendelssohn's writings. Instead, Meklenburg's work was devoted first and foremost to an explication of *peshuto shel mikra'* (the plain sense of the biblical text), drawing extensively and in an undifferentiated manner on Mendelssohn's *Sefer Netivot ha-Shalom*, the Vilna Gaon's *'Aderet 'Eliyahu*, and the scholarly contributions of Pappenheim, Heidenheim, Luzzatto and others. This commentary served as an excellent anthology of late 18th and early 19th-c. *peshat* exegesis, a collection that reflected the reinvigoration of Jewish Bible study.

Responding to similar religious challenges and drawing upon some of the same scholarly traditions, R. Meir Leibush ben Yehiel Michel (1809–1879) also set out with the aim of joining the Written and Oral Torahs, but he approached the undertaking in a far more systematic and substantive fashion. Commonly known by his acronym Malbim, he served as a communal rabbi in the Posen region (Eastern Prussia) at a time when proponents of Reform began to articulate their positions with greater forcefulness. He authored commentaries to Isa., Song, and Esth., and in 1866 he produced a commentary to the Prophets and Writings. In 1860 he published an edition of the *Sifra*, the early rabbinic midrash to Lev., which interpolated the relevant biblical vv. at the head of each midrashic segment, and to which he wrote a commentary titled *Ha-Torah veha-Mitzvah*. It is significant, in terms of understanding Malbim's methods and aims, that it was this rabbinic commentary that appeared with the full text of the *Sifra* as his commentary to Lev. Over the next two decades he applied this approach to the other books of the Torah, producing a commentary to the *Mek.* (Exod.) and *Sifre* (Num. and Deut.); for sections of the Bible without midrash halakhah, Malbim posed a series of questions to which he supplied lengthy answers, somewhat reminiscent of the style employed by Abravanel and other late medieval scholars. Judging by its numerous reprintings, this work proved to be one of the most popular Bible commentaries of late 19th-c. European Jewry.

In his extensive two-part introduction to the original *Sifra* commentary, Malbim was unequivocal about his overarching objective: to develop tools that would demonstrate the veracity of rabbinic traditions. The Sages, he asserted, had a profound knowledge of Heb that included a firm grasp of grammatical principles, sensitivity to the subtlest of differences among apparently synonymous nouns and verbs, and an appreciation of biblical style and idiom, all of which he detailed in a separate section of the introduction. Malbim explicitly rejected the well-attested medieval notion that rabbinic teachings were merely traditions that used scriptural vv. as props or as a kind of subscript. Moreover, unlike Mendelssohn and Meklenburg, and more akin to the approach taken by Wessely, his demonstration of the linguistic profundity of rabbinic literature tended to blur the distinction between *peshat* and *derash*. After all, if the Sages were superb linguists and readers of texts, then all their interpretations could be identified with *peshuto shel mikra*. The words of the Oral Torah, he wrote, "are compelled by and ingrained in the scriptural *peshat* and in the depths of the language. *Derush* [sic] alone is the simple *peshat* that is based upon the true and clear rules of language" (Malbim, *Sifra de-Bei Rav ... im Peirush Ha-Torah veha-Mitzvah*, Bucharest, 1860, p. 2a).

The reawakened interest in Heb and Bible study and the need to reinforce the integrity of traditional Judaism found different expression in the approach of Samson Raphael Hirsch (1808–1888), a a prominent and outspoken leader of German Orthodoxy.

In the late 1860s, Hirsch began to publish a translation and lengthy German commentary to the Pentateuch (*Der Pentateuch, übersetzt und erläutert,* Frankfurt am Main, 1867–78). No less committed to the defense of normative rabbinic Judaism than Meklenburg and Malbim, Hirsch took the position that the corpus of rabbinic teachings could not—and for polemical purposes, should not—be derived from the biblical text. Although the Bible served as a kind of a mnemonic primer that elicited the particulars of the Oral Torah, this was possible only in the presence of a revealed tradition that Moses and the Israelites had already absorbed (see Hirsch's commentary to Exod. 21.2). Instead, highly sensitive to the prevailing European-Protestant depreciation of Judaism, Hirsch used his commentary to demonstrate the thoroughly integrated spiritual and ethical worldview of the Torah. Leavening his homiletical approach with some questionable philology, Hirsch produced what could be described as a theosophical commentary which made heavy use of biblical symbolism and which mined biblical narratives and strictures for their sublime moral teachings. In tenor and substance, as in language and style, Hirsch's commentary remained a distinct contribution to 19th-c. biblical interpretation.

More than a generation later, R. David Zvi Hoffmann (1843–1921), rector of the Orthodox rabbinic seminary of Berlin (Hildesheimer Seminary) and an important leader of German Jewry in his own right, produced German commentaries to the books of Lev. and Deut. (*Das Buch Leviticus, übersetzt und erklärt,* Berlin, 1905–06; *Das Buch Deuteronomium, übersetzt und erklärt,* Berlin, 1913–22). Hoffmann's biblical scholarship combined the overlapping traditionalist elements of Haskalah and *Wissenschaft* scholarship with the orthodox apologia of scholars like Meklenburg. Academically trained and well-versed in contemporary European biblical scholarship, Hoffmann was as concerned with defending the integrity of the Bible as displaying its ultimate concordance with rabbinic oral traditions. Beginning in 1879, Hoffmann was the first Jewish scholar to attempt a serious challenge to aspects of Wellhausen's writings, directly addressing himself to its central assertions regarding the postexilic dating of the Priestly Code and drawing attention to what he claimed were internal inconsistencies and false assumptions. With regard to his exegesis, Hoffmann, like Malbim, devoted a considerable amount of scholarly attention to the study of midrash halakhah, but the methodological conclusions he drew were different. Hoffmann allowed that in many instances rabbinic traditions either preceded or appeared concurrently with their scripturally based articulation in midrashic literature, and as such, could not be independently derived from the biblical text. Nevertheless, the task of the modern exegete was to connect the Bible with tradition, even if retrospectively. Hoffmann's biblical writings, however, were not focused solely on this issue, and their scholarly range was broader than any other 19th-c. commentary, incorporating linguistic and scientific insights alongside philosophy and comparative anthropology.

The revival of Bible study took root and flourished in Eastern Europe as well, and although the commentaries that emerged from there shared the traditionalist concern for the integrity of rabbinic interpretations, they tended to approach the problem in a more selective and discerning fashion. The head of the prestigious Volozhin Yeshivah, R. Naftali Zvi Yehudah Berlin (1817–93; known by his acronym as Netziv), penned a commentary to the Pentateuch titled *Ha-ʿAmek Davar* which first appeared in an 1879–80 Vilna edition of the Bible. Like Malbim and Hoffmann, Berlin had elsewhere devoted significant scholarly energy to the study of early rabbinic midrash, but his Bible commentary engaged both Scripture and rabbinic literature in ways that tried to develop an appreciation for their independent literary qualities. Berlin spoke incisively about the limitless interpretative possibilities that inhered in the biblical text, and at the same time allowed that earlier rabbinic modes of interpretation had been independently and creatively derived. At the turn of the century, Barukh Ha-Levi Epstein (1860–1942) also set out to show the fundamental accord between the Bible and the Oral Law in an edition of the Torah named *Torah Temimah* (Vilna, 1904). Epstein went about this task by anthologizing rabbinic uses of Scripture and appending a series of notes which proved to contain original and insightful comments regarding the rabbinic interpretation of Scripture. In many ways, the real scholarly achievement of this work may have been the anthology itself, in which Epstein culled a large corpus of rabbinic literature and edited and condensed his findings with masterful scholarship. Perhaps the most original of the late 19th-c. traditionalist commentaries, however, was the posthumously published *Meshekh Ḥokhmah* (1927) of R. Meir Simhah Ha-Kohen of Dvinsk (1843–1926). Like Berlin, this exegete was an outstanding rabbinic scholar who appreciated not only the quality of rabbinic scriptural interpretation, but also its ongoing creativity. As such, he asserted the right of rabbinic scholars of all generations to venture beyond attested readings in order to derive new halakhah from scriptural *peshat*.

Conclusion

While the beginning of our survey clearly marked a new chapter in the history of Jewish biblical interpretation, the point we have reached here at the end of this overview does not represent its closing or conclusion. Rather, with the end of the 19th and beginning of the 20th centuries, we leave behind only the first stages of the Jewish encounter with modernity and its concomitant reengagement with the Hebrew Bible. By the end of our period, to be sure, the traditionalist attempt to demonstrate the textually-grounded nature—and hence presumed correctness—of rabbinic exegesis had effectively run its creative course. The 19th-c. scholarship of the maskilim and the *Wissenschaft des Judentums*, which was ground-breaking and innovative for its time, nevertheless remained in many ways stunted and undeveloped. With some noteable exceptions, the scholars we surveyed here did not seriously engage European biblical scholarship and some of its most challenging and critical developments. As such, while Jewish biblical interpretation of the 18th and 19th centuries forms a distinct and historically important corpus, it must also be seen as a period that cultivated new cultural and intellectual commitments that would express themselves fully only in the next century.

[EDWARD BREUER]

Modern Jewish Interpretation

Academic biblical interpretation by Jewish scholars from the beginning of the 20th c. shows some continuity with what preceded, but by the end of the century, becomes quite distinct from it. While building on the insights of the enlightenment and Spinoza, the Haskalah (Jewish Enlightenment Movement) and Mendelssohn, and Geiger and Zunz and other *Wissenschaft* scholars, modern Jewish interpretation is not best appreciated in terms of intellectual movements or seminal figures. Instead, the last century is better understood as the gradual acculturation of Jewish scholarship into mainstream academic biblical scholarship; for this reason, this essay will focus less on individual scholars and more on general trends. By the beginning of the 21st c., it is difficult to see a distinction between most Jewish biblical interpretation and general biblical interpretation; for that reason, this essays highlights, by and large, developments in the 20th rather than the 21st c.

This process of gradual acculturation of Jewish Bible scholars into general biblical scholarship began slowly, and most Jewish scholars in the early 20th c. were antagonistic toward the methods developed within mainline (Protestant) biblical scholarship, as illustrated in the previous essay ("Jewish Biblical Scholarship from the 17th to the 19th Centuries") by the career of R. David Zvi Hoffmann (1843–1921). Many of the students at the Hildesheimer Seminary in Berlin at which he taught and later served as rector were also enrolled at the University of Berlin, where they came into contact with Pentateuchal (Source) criticism. Hoffmann, however, rejected and encouraged his students to reject the academic, university perspectives and conclusions, noting "the entire Torah is true, holy and given by God—every single word was written by divine command." He also defended the rabbinic tradition as correct and authoritative.

Hoffmann's polemical stance was adopted by Solomon Schechter, who stated in his famous lecture "Higher Criticism—Higher Anti-Semitism":

> Wellhausen's Prolegomena and History are *teeming with aperçes* full of venom against Judaism, and you cannot wonder that he was rewarded by one of the highest orders which the Prussian Government had to bestow.... But this Higher anti-Semitism has now reached its climax when every discovery of recent years is called to bear witness against us and to accuse us of spiritual larceny.... The Bible is our sole *raison d'être,* and it is just this which the Higher anti-Semitism is seeking to destroy, denying all our claims for the past, and leaving us without hope for the future.

This perspective was later popularized in the 1929–1936 publication by J. H. Hertz (1872–1946), the Chief Rabbi of the British Empire, of *The Pentateuch and Haftorahs,* which served as the standard Torah of the Jewish community for home and synagogue for over half a century. Hertz was deeply critical of Wellhausen and condemned many of the ideas that were current in mainstream biblical scholarship of his day, including the claims that the Pentateuch was written late, was influenced by other ancient Near Eastern cultures, and is historically inaccurate; he called such notions "a perversion of history and a desecration of religion." He selectively cited several conservative non-Jewish scholars when they supported his position. Many traditionalists criticized him for this, believing that non-Jewish scholarship should not be integrated at all into the study of the Jewish Bible.

Text-criticism of the Bible—comparing the different early versions of the Bible produced in different languages in an attempt to recreate a more original text and to understand how various readings are related (see "Textual Criticism," pp. 2149–52)—did not present the same sort of problems to some Jewish scholars as other branches of historical-critical study. Medieval precedents existed for the textual criticism of the Bible, and it could be engaged in without the deeply theological, Protestant suppositions concerning source-criticism. Felix Perles (1874–1933) and Hirsch Perez Chajes (1876–1927), who toward the end of his life served as chief rabbi of Vienna and wrote on the Bible, the New Testament, and rabbinic literature, engaged extensively in text criticism. At the same time, they criticized their Christian counterparts for offering emendations that indicated a lack of feel for biblical Heb diction and style. Perles was among the first Jewish biblical scholars to be widely read and acknowledged in mainstream Protestant biblical scholarship.

The German scholar and liberal rabbi Benno Jacob (1862–1945), author of significant commentaries on Gen. and Exod., was one of the few Jewish scholars of the early 20th c. who explicitly adopted the stance that the Torah did not originate with Moses. Yet, he did not accept the dominant system of Wellhausen, suggesting instead a unified spiritual origin of the Torah. He also developed some novel models for the literary study of the Bible; these would have a significant influence on the Buber-Rosenzweig translation, and on the scholarship of Umberto (Moshe David) Cassuto, though not on the broader world of biblical scholarship.

Institutional constraints, and later historical events, are to a large extent responsible for the lack of serious Jewish engagement with critical biblical studies in Europe. Jews were welcome to study Semitics, and in some cases Bible, at European universities, but could not teach Bible, which was typically undertaken in the context of Catholic or Protestant theological faculties. Jewish Semitists such as Jakob Barth [1851–1914] were nevertheless very involved in several disputes concerning the Bible, especially in taking the Bible's side in the *Babel und Bibel* controversy, which began with Friedrich Delitzsch's suggestion that the Bible was derivative of, and inferior to, Babylonian civilization.

The German Jewish community was on a trajectory to produce serious mainstream biblical scholarship, but this was prevented by the rise of Nazism and its tragic aftermath, including the rise of the Iron Curtain. The highly innovative Bible translation of Martin Buber (1878–1965) and Franz Rosenzweig (1886–1929), which attempted to recreate as much of the feel and rhythm of the Heb for German speakers, was begun in 1926 and completed only in 1962, at which point there was scarcely an audience to read it. Instead, the traditions of European biblical scholarship developed in Israel and in America, with European émigrés playing a crucial role, especially through the middle of the 20th c.

The Hebrew University in Jerusalem, which opened in 1925, should have become the natural place for the critical study of the Hebrew Bible for Jews. Perles was a strong advocate for this; in his 1927 address at the dedication of the Institute for Jewish Studies at Hebrew University, "Why Do We Need Biblical Studies," he observed to his "great regret ... that the number of Jewish scholars who work in this field [modern biblical studies] is still very small. I see in this a great embarrassment and a great loss to Israel." In its initial years, Hebrew University was deeply conflicted about how the Bible should be taught. A compromise suggested hiring two professors, one teaching a critical, one a more traditional perspective. In 1932 the university established a department called *Miqra'*, the less-used Jewish rabbinic name for the Tanakh, signaling that the Bible would not be taught in a totally traditional fashion. It took several decades, however, for critical approaches to become entrenched. The main instructors in the early period of the department were the Lithuanian-born British scholar Moshe Zvi Segal, who did not believe in the source-critical approach to the Torah (although he divided the book of Samuel into many sources), and later the Italian Moshe David (Umberto) Cassuto, best known for his work on the recently found Ugaritic material as it related to the Bible and for his polemics against the documentary hypothesis.

Beginning in 1949, biblical studies was taught by the Ukrainian-born, Swiss-trained scholar Yehezkel Kaufmann (1889–1963), who emigrated to Palestine in 1928, and the Dutch holocaust survivor Isac Leo (Aryeh) Seeligmann (1907–1982); these were the first fully critical biblical scholars to teach at the university, though neither was formally trained primarily in biblical studies. Kaufmann, who wrote in Heb, had a significant influence on Jewish biblical scholarship, and to some extent on general biblical scholarship once his *Toldot Ha-'emunah Ha-Yisre'elit* [The History of Israelite Religion (8 vols., 1937–1956)] was abridged and translated by Moshe Greenberg in 1960 (published as *The Religion of Israel: From Its Beginnings to the Babylonian Exile*). Kaufmann accepted source-criticism, but attempted to reclaim the Bible for the Jewish community, in part by insisting on the early date of the Priestly source, which most Protestant scholars saw as late and legalistic. Kaufmann also claimed that biblical religion was originally monotheistic, and he insisted on the basic historicity of the biblical text, a position upheld until the late 20th c. by most Israeli biblical scholars and archeologists.

Seeligmann was quite different. He played an important role in mainstream biblical scholarship, publishing in European languages as well as Heb. Although an observant Orthodox Jew (and rabbi), his perspective was critical and non-apologetic. He trained two generations of scholars who taught at the Israeli universities, and he opened up Israeli biblical scholarship and scholars to mainstream European biblical scholarship, with which he was deeply connected. He and his students, however, avoided the study of biblical theology, which was so prevalent in the broader field. Members of the *Miqra'* Department were supplemented, among others, by the Semitics scholar and text-critic Moshe Goshen-Gottstein (1925–1991), one of the main forces behind the Hebrew University Bible Project, aimed at producing a comprehensive critical edition of the Bible based on the Aleppo Codex, and incorporating all known variants from Heb mss and rabbinic texts (see "Masoretic Bible," pp. 2159–65). It also highlights many Masoretic items, another significant focus of Israeli biblical studies. At its zenith in the 1970s and 80s, the Hebrew University had one of the largest and strongest faculties of biblical studies ever assembled, distributed among five departments (Bible, Archeology, Semitic Languages, Hebrew Language, and Assyriology). Its size has since diminished, along with the rest of the humanities faculty. The Bible does continue to have a special role in the Israeli academy in departments of archeology, which were initially very interested in connecting the land of Israel and its material remains to the biblical story, as seen in the works of Benjamin Mazar (1906–1995), Yohanan Aharoni (1919–1976), and Yigael Yadin (1917–1984). Although some Israeli archeologists continue to pursue this approach, others take the position that the Bible and the archeological record need to be considered separately, and that the two often diverge.

The Israeli academic Bible establishment has spearheaded several major Hebrew projects, including the extensive *Entsiḳlopedyah Miḳra'it (Encyclopaedia Biblica;* published in 9 vols., 1950–1988), the partially completed *Miqra' Leyisra'el* (The Bible for Israel), a series of critical commentaries geared toward a secular Israeli audience, and *Mikra'ot Gedolot 'HaKeter,'* a new critical edition of the rabbinic Bible (see p. 1890 of "Midrash") whose first volume was published in 1992. The last is a project of Bar-Ilan University, which fosters religious Jewish education; its Bible department shies away from source-critical approaches, emphasizing literary approaches, which tend to view the text as a unity, and the history of Jewish biblical interpretation. Jewish scholars in Israel and abroad, in comparison with other biblical scholars, have had a disproportionate interest in the publication and analysis of the Dead Sea Scrolls (see "The Bible in the Dead Sea Scrolls," pp. 1850–59), considered the greatest archeological find of the 20th c.; given their place of discovery in the Judean desert in 1946–47, and the purchase of several scrolls just as Israel was declaring statehood in 1947, this is not surprising. Although much initial study of the scrolls by Christian scholars focused on their contribution to the understanding of the background to early Christianity, Jewish scholars in Israel and the U.S. have explored the scrolls in relation to the Jewish communities of the period, especially to their religious movements and to incipient halakhah.

The university was not the only home for Jewish biblical studies in Israel. The study of Bible is compulsory in Israeli (Jewish) schools, and there is still, among many, an interest in the Bible as Israel's national book (see "The Bible in Israeli Life," pp. 2071–81). This was especially facilitated by Israel's first prime minister David Ben-Gurion, who organized a regular Bible study-group. Study of the Bible, at least as it is represented in rabbinic literature and medieval Jewish commentary, is strong among the large ultra-Orthodox religious community, although there, engagement with postbiblical rabbinic literature predominates. Some tentative approaches have recently been developed in Israel that attempt to bridge critical biblical perspectives and more traditional religious ones, but much work remains in this area.

Biblical study in the U.S. developed in parallel to its study in Europe and Israel. But Americans had a need that Israelis did not—the translation of the Bible into English. The latter half of the 19th c. saw the appearance of a handful of English translations (see "Jewish Translations of the Bible," pp. 2091–2106). A plan to publish a new American Jewish Bible was first devised in the 1890s, and *The Holy Scriptures According to the Masoretic Text* was finally published by the Jewish Publication Society in 1917. (See "The Jewish Bible in America," pp. 2081–85.) A revision of the 1885 English Revised Version of the OT, this translation attempted to "remove all un-Jewish and anti-Jewish phrases, expressions, renderings, [and] usages." By the 1950s, as new Protestant and Catholic Bibles were being prepared, the Jewish Publication Society undertook a fresh translation of the Hebrew Bible, which appeared between 1962 and 1985 under the self-consciously Hebraic title *Tanakh*. The Jewish biblical scholars who served on the translation committees were H. L. Ginsberg, Moshe Greenberg, Jonas C. Greenfield, Harry M. Orlinsky, Nahum M. Sarna, and Ephraim A. Speiser. This version serves as the basic reference Bible in Jewish religious, educational, and scholarly circles.

The Bible was taught, to varying degrees, in the Jewish seminaries in the U.S. that trained rabbis. In Orthodox seminaries, the emphasis was and remains much more on the history of traditional Jewish biblical interpretation and on what the Bible might mean for today's readers, than on the use of historical-critical methods to discern what the Bible meant in its original contexts. Under the influence of Solomon Schechter, the same was true for much of the 20th c. at The Jewish Theological Seminary, which ordained Conservative rabbis. Later in the century, however, The Jewish Theological Seminary adopted historical-critical scholarship, and many of its professors played a leading role in general academic biblical scholarship. By the early 20th c. the Reform position was influenced by the movement's highly influential 1885 Pittsburgh Platform, which stated: "We hold that the modern discoveries of scientific researches in the domain of nature and history are not antagonistic to the doctrines of Judaism, the *Bible* reflecting the primitive ideas of its own age, and a time clothing its conception of Divine Providence and Justice dealing with man in miraculous narratives." In contrast to the other rabbinical seminaries, Reform Judaism was open to Wellhausen and other historical-critical European scholars. For example, Julian Morgenstern (1881–1976), an ordained Reform rabbi who received his Ph.D. at Heidelberg, was a professor of Bible at Hebrew Union College and served as its president; at the same time, he was well-accepted among academic biblical scholars and even served as the president of the Society of Biblical Literature, the guild's professional association.

As in Europe in the early 20th c., Jews in North America were not welcome to teach in colleges and universities, which often did not veer far from their denominational origins, and discriminated against Jewish students and professors. Until the middle of the 20th c., there were few exceptions, especially the University of Pennsylvania, and for a brief period, Columbia University. The institutional realities concerning Jewish and biblical studies in the U.S. provided the impetus for the founding of Philadelphia's Dropsie College in 1907 "for the study of Hebrew and Cognate Learning." Granting over two hundred Ph.D.s before closing as a degree-granting institution in 1986, it was for much of the 20th c. an important center for academic Jewish studies, including biblical and Semitic studies.

Jewish participation in mainstream biblical studies began for earnest only after WWII. Brandeis University, founded in 1948 by the Jewish community as a non-sectarian university, began training students in biblical and Semitic studies. At the same time, the University of Pennsylvania, which, unlike most of the other Ivy League universities, never housed a divinity school, trained a disproportionate number of Jewish biblical scholars who held major positions when these became available to Jews. The Jewish Galician-born E. A. Speiser (1902–1965), a noted Assyriologist and biblical scholar, was a significant figure at Penn at mid-century; he published the first volume that appeared in the Anchor Bible Series (Genesis, 1964).

As part of the foment and openness of the 1960s in the U.S., the Ph.D. programs related to Biblical Studies at Yale and Harvard University, which previously had few Jewish students, took in a significant number of Jews, and the American academy appointed more Jewish professors of Bible. This was in part connected to the relocation of biblical studies at American universities from a subfield of Christianity to the history of religion and to ancient Near Eastern studies. The philo-Semitic attitude of several professors at these institutions facilitated this development. At the same time, American universities were developing Jewish Studies programs that invariably included biblical studies. Jews were, then, encouraged to complete Ph.D.s in biblical studies, knowing that they could find employment in programs of Ancient Near Eastern Studies, Religious Studies, and Jewish Studies. These Ph.D.s, holding varying and differing Jewish commitments and perspectives, found congenial homes at many leading colleges, universities, and (Jewish and non-Jewish) seminaries, where they have trained much of the current generation of biblical scholars, both Jews and non-Jews. Their contributions to many areas of biblical scholarship utilize standard academic methods of biblical studies. They have found different ways of reconciling these principles with Jewish belief and practice.

Not all American Jewry accepts the perspective of academically trained biblical scholars. Much of Orthodox American Jewry has embraced the highly traditional and staunchly anti-critical ArtScroll series, which draws exclusively on premodern Jewish exegesis and the modern rabbinic approaches and shows no interest in the ancient Near East or in literary features of the text. This American series contrasts with the Israeli Bible commentary *Daʿat Miqraʾ (Knowledge of the Bible)* published by the Rav Kook Institute, which draws on literary insight and realia, though not on historical-critical scholarship. Indeed, even some volumes of the JPS Torah commentary, published by the Jewish Publication Society (1989–1996) and written by U. S. academics are less critical than many other commentary series. For example, even when they discuss textual sources, they usually eschew the standard sigla JEPD. Unlike standard critical commentary series, the JPS Torah commentary gives much more emphasis to integrating postbiblical Jewish texts into a critical biblical commentary. JPS has now expanded the series to include other biblical books, under the rubric of the JPS Bible Commentary.

The current volume, *The Jewish Study Bible*, first published in 2004, reflects the extent to which Jewish biblical scholarship has come of age. Its publication highlights the existence of a sufficient number of academically trained English-speaking biblical scholars to write from a critical perspective, with Jewish sensitivity, on the entire Hebrew Bible. Such a coterie of scholars did not exist several decades ago, and reflects a "sea-change" concerning the openness of general biblical scholarship to Jewish scholars and scholarship. It is equally noteworthy that non-Jewish scholars routinely ask their students to use this Bible as well as other works by Jewish scholars. But Jewish scholars do not, as they once did, only publish in Jewish venues for Jewish readers; in the last half-century, Jewish scholars have contributed significantly to many major commentary series, and have published in the major journals in the field.

The Introduction to this volume highlights some distinctive features of Jewish biblical interpretation (see p. x); the current essay offers an opportunity to explain and expand upon those brief observations. Most Jewish biblical scholars are quite conservative in their use of the Masoretic Text and tend to focus on the final form of the text; this may be motivated by the acceptance of the MT as the authoritative text in Jewish life and the lack of importance of the LXX within the Jewish community. Jewish scholars have until recently been less interested than their Protestant counterparts in biblical theology, since it was seen as a Protestant sub-discipline of the field; this is now changing. Conversely, several Jewish scholars have shown greater interest than their Protestant colleagues in particular biblical books (esp. Lev., Num., and Chron.) that had been neglected by Protestant scholars because they had been characterized until recently as legalistic, late, and irrelevant. Jewish scholars have also devoted particular attention to the rich world of medieval Jewish commentary, and how it may be used to elucidate linguistic, stylistic, literary, and canonical issues. Several Jewish scholars, some biblical scholars, such as the Israeli biblical scholar Meir Weiss (1908–1998), and the American literary scholar Robert Alter (1935–), have played an especially significant role in the development of certain types of literary study of the Bible. Similarly, female Jewish scholars (see "Jewish Women's Scholarly Writings," pp. 2086–91) such as Tikva Frymer Kensy (1943–2006) have played a crucial role in the new field of feminist studies of the Bible. Finally, some Israeli Jewish biblical scholarship continues, to some extent, to be typified by a strong interest in the connection between the Bible and the land of Israel, including a focus on archeology and realia, though now serious discussion of the Bible as Israel's national book, a position fostered by Ben-Gurion but that lessened in the recent past, are increasingly being heard.

While in the past one could speak of the distinctive features of Jewish biblical scholarship, that is becoming harder to do, for as Jewish scholars have been well-integrated into the field of biblical scholarship, the lines between Jewish and non-Jewish critical biblical scholarship have begun to blur significantly. Jews now partake of and contribute to mainstream critical biblical scholarship as it develops in different directions. In fact, the area of medieval Jewish biblical interpretation, once an almost exclusively Jewish concern, is now of interest to a wide variety of biblical scholars. For the first time in history, it is becoming more difficult to establish a clear set of distinguishing characteristics of Jewish biblical scholarship.

[MARC ZVI BRETTLER]

BIBLICAL IDEAS AND INSTITUTIONS

The Religion of the Bible

We must first understand that biblical religion is not, strictly speaking, "biblical" because, unlike Judaism and Christianity, it is not a religion based on the Bible—i.e., the canonized record of past divine revelation—but on that revelation itself. Also, it is not a "religion," in the sense of the beliefs and practices of an actual community. Rather, biblical religion was a minority, dissident phenomenon, always at odds, as the Bible itself states, with the actual religions of the small kingdoms of Israel and Judah. The religion of the latter might better be termed Israelite-Judean religion. For more than a century the difference between biblical and Israelite-Judean religion has been an axiom of modern biblical studies (see discussion below).

Moreover, biblical religion is not a unity but rather a congeries of differing and often competing opinions and traditions. Historical scholarship has isolated at least three major forms of biblical religion in the Bible:

(1) Deuteronomic-covenantal religion, based on the legal form of a treaty between Israel and its deity, emphasizing Israelite loyalty and the performance of divine commandments, viewed as stipulations of the treaty.

(2) Priestly religion, centering on the cult and emphasizing purity and punctilious observance of rituals.

(3) Wisdom religion, focusing on understanding the cosmos and the laws of human nature, and dealing with such general problems of human existence as suffering and theodicy.

Despite considerable mutual influence and interpenetration, these three major types of biblical religion are best examined individually.

We shall first summarize the little that is known, or surmised, about Israelite-Judean religion, and then take up each of these major streams of biblical religion in turn.

Israelite-Judean Religion

The actual religion of the states of Israel and Judah from ca. 900 to 600 BCE can be partially reconstructed from archeological and inscriptional evidence and from some evidence in the biblical text, which must be interpreted with caution, because the Bible stands in a polemical relationship to the contemporary religions of Israelites and Judeans, consistently distorting the real meaning of such features as the "high places" (*bamot,* translated "open shrines" in NJPS [e.g., 1 Kings 3.2]). Northern, Israelite religion was especially misrepresented by the propaganda of the predominantly southern, Judean authors and editors of most of the Tanakh. For these reasons the following sketch is conjectural, but represents the generality of current scholarly opinion.

There is no question that the national deity of both Israel and Judah was YHVH (LORD in NJPS), but the relationship to this deity might be better called monolatrous, the worship of one god without denying the existence of others, rather than strictly monotheistic. YHVH is the name regularly, but not exclusively, appearing as the theophoric or divine element in Israelite-Judean names. YHVH's attributes, as expressed in the oldest examples of Israelite poetry, such as the Song of Deborah (Judg. ch 5) and the Blessings of Jacob (Gen. ch 49) and Moses (Deut. ch 33) seem to be a mixture of features attested in Canaanite and Ugaritic religions for the ancient creator god El, the "old god" (*ʾilu du ʿalami* = Heb *ʾel ʿolam,* "Everlasting God" [Gen. 22.33]) and the young vigorous fertility-storm god, Baal. YHVH is usually portrayed as seated on His heavenly throne, surrounded by the angelic host waiting in attendance, like Canaanite El; or, like Baal, either mounted in the divine chariot, or riding on the "wings of the wind/cherubim." Derived from the latter deity is the pervasive theophanic imagery, namely depictions of the deity appearing with storm clouds, thunder, lightning, earthquake, etc., so familiar to Bible readers. Holy war themes, in which YHVH leads His hosts in battle, are also similar to those elsewhere in the ancient Near East. YHVH is often portrayed as setting out for battle, armed with the divine spear, bow and arrows, against Israel's foes (Ps. 18.7–16; Deut. 32.22–25, 41–42; Hab. 3.3–13; etc.).

Perhaps mingled with, and partially absorbed by, YHVH was a type of god reflecting an older type of religion centering on a familial deity, often referred to simply as the "god of X" (X being the name of an ancestor of the family or clan) or, more generally, as the "god of the fathers." Evidence for this kind of religion comes mainly from the patriarchal narratives of Gen. ("God of Abraham, Isaac and Jacob") and is otherwise attested in the Near East from Mesopotamia in the second millennium BCE to, much later, the region of the Nabatean Arabs (centered in Jordan) in Roman times.

In sum, the major attributes of YHVH that continued in biblical religion were already found in Israelite-Judean religion: king, creator, father, warrior, provider of fertilizing rain. Since many of the oldest texts (e.g., Judg. 5.4) refer to YHVH as "coming from the south" (Seir, Paran, Sinai/Horeb), He originally may have been a god of one of the regions south of Judah. But even in old texts He has already absorbed the attributes of several kinds of ancient Near Eastern deities, to become a kind of over-arching deity. The name YHVH may be attested in pre-Israelite documents from the Amorite region of upper Mesopotamia. In the Bible the name is explained as referring to His ability to protect Israel (*ʾehyeh asher ʾehyeh,* "I shall be what I shall be" [Exod. 3.14]) interpreted in context as "I shall be with you." The original sense of the name may refer to God as creator (taking "YHVH" as causative *hiphil,* "He brings into being") or it may have some other, lost connotation.

One of the most discussed issues in recent years is whether YHVH had a female consort, the ancient Canaanite mother/fertility goddess Asherah, identified with the tree of life. Two Heb inscriptions contain benedictions in the name of "YHVH and his Asherah." Scholars are divided in opinion whether Asherah here referred to the goddess herself, or whether the term has been reduced to an abstract hypostatization of YHVH's power to provide fertility. More evidence is needed, but in any case it is certain that biblical religion, in possible contrast to Israelite-Judean religion, viewed Asherah simply as a Canaanite deity and her symbol, reduced to a wooden pole, as idolatrous.

YHVH was worshipped at "high places" scattered around the country, which varied from simple hilltop shrines with stone or earthen altars, cultic pillars *(matzevot),* and wooden poles *(ʾasherim),* to larger structures such as the main high places in the Northern Kingdom, Dan and Bethel, where YHVH was worshipped as a calf. In biblical religion the high places are viewed propagandistically as totally idolatrous from the time of Solomon on, since all "legitimate" worship was to be confined to the Jerusalem Temple. Ironically, the latter itself was a typical Canaanite shrine, built by the Phoenicians, with three divisions, the last of which was the "Holy of Holies," with altar, cultic pillars, elaborate decoration of palmettes, lotus, bulls, and cherubim. According to the main traditions of the Bible, the Holy of Holies contained no divine image, as in typical ancient shrines, but only the Ark of the Covenant containing the stone tablets given by YHVH to Moses. The Ark seems to have had its origin in the kind of box-like palladium still used by some Bedouin tribes. Mounted on a camel, it leads their migrations, as the Israelite Ark is said to have led Israel in the desert (Num. 10.33). The Ark also led the army into battle according to texts describing the early period. Its capture by the Philistines caused a major religious crisis

(1 Sam. chs 4–6). According to the Bible, the Ark was brought to newly conquered Jerusalem by David and was placed by Solomon in the Temple, where it was viewed by many as the throne of YHVH. It is not mentioned thereafter, and its later fate is unknown.

Israelite-Judean religion seems to have had aniconic tendencies; it avoided depicting YHVH through any image or icon. Later biblical religion condemns images of deities vehemently, and has suppressed all evidence of their legitimate use, except for the cryptic reference to human-like statues called teraphim, attested in a few places, like Gen. 31.34 and 1 Sam. 19.13, which seem to have been family deities, or talismans. It is possible that the strange story in Judg. chs 17–19 of the image stolen by the Danites, which became the center of a cult served by a priesthood descended from Moses, preserves the memory of an image of YHVH worshipped in some circles. Archeological evidence has as yet turned up no divine images in an excavated shrine, though of course such valuable objects probably would have been removed or looted in antiquity. Israelite-Judean sites do contain large numbers of different types of female figurines, some of which probably represent the fertility goddess Asherah. Such images are usually viewed by scholars as amulets, and as belonging to "popular," not "official," religion (see below).

Worship of YHVH consisted of sacrifices, the oldest of which seem to have been the "whole offering" *(ʿolah),* the "communal offering" *(shelem)* and, probably, the "purification (or sin) offering" *(ḥataʾt).* Pilgrimages were made to local shrines on sacred occasions. Old biblical texts show that the three major festivals, two in the spring, one in the fall (later called Passover-Matzot, Shavuʿot, and Sukkot), along with the new moon and Sabbath were occasions for such visits, though it is unclear if in Israelite-Judean religion the Sabbath was already associated with the seven-day week. A yearly pilgimage is also attested at which a communal offering was made and consumed by the family (1 Sam. ch 1). The elaborate cultic establishment described in the Torah, especially in Lev., is held by most scholars to be a development of later biblical religion projected back into the past, but it undoubtedly contains elements reflecting the actual cults of Israel and Judah, such as the scapegoat ritual on the Day of Atonement, itself probably originally a shrine-cleansing rite.

Curiously, the Bible contains no reference to a New Year festival (the references in Lev. 23.24 and Num. 29.1, later taken to refer to the New Year festival, do not mention that name); yet it is scarcely likely that Israel was the only Near Eastern people without such an event, so crucial to ancient thinking and the actual lives of people. It is likely that biblical religion has expunged all reference to the New Year festival, except for an enigmatic reference to a "Day of Acclaim" *(yom teruʿah).* Some scholars have hypothesized a New Year festival based on the evidence of some biblical psalms, especially the so-called "enthronement psalms" (Pss. 93; 96–98), and comparative evidence, primarily the Babylonian *akitu* festival. The event might have proclaimed YHVH's victory over cosmic chaos (see below), and His kingship as creator. Certainly, the themes of creation and kingship survive in the later Jewish Rosh Ha-Shanah; but that Israel also had such a festival remains conjectural. If the New Year rituals were as close to those of the ancient Near East as suggested by some scholars, biblical religion may have edited the festival out as too redolent of idolatrous practices. Some scholars have also suggested a festival celebrating covenant renewal, held every seven years, based on Deut. 31.10–11; but the existence of such a cultic event is even more conjectural than that of a New Year festival.

Prophets played a prominent role in both Israel and Judah. Prophecy of various kinds is attested in practically all ancient cultures. In the ancient Near East prophets are found in Egypt and Mesopotamia, where their function was secondary to the dominant oracular means employed. But in western Asia ecstatic prophecy seems to have had a more central significance. The closest parallels to biblical prophecy are found in the Mari texts (in modern Syria on the Euphrates) of the middle second millennium BCE, reflecting an Amorite (West Semitic) culture related to Israel in many respects. There, as in the Bible, prophets, both men and women, are sent to kings to deliver messages, and sometimes rebukes, from deities. Prophets are well attested from areas around Israel, from Phoenicia to Transjordan, where texts have been found mentioning a seer Balaam, evidently the prophet described in Num. chs 22–24.

But in Israel and Judah prophets seem to have been even more important than in neighboring cultures. Mechanical forms of divination played a less significant role; there is reference to what were probably a sort of sacred dice, the Urim and Thummim, which could give a simple yes-or-no answer to questions. Later, they are said to be stones set in the breastplate of the high priest. There are also references to consulting the spirits of the dead, such as Saul's visit to the woman of En-dor, who raised the ghost of Samuel (described as a "god" *['elohim]*) (1 Sam. ch 28). But from an early period, the standard means of "inquiring of God" was through a prophet *(navi')*, also called "seer" *(ro'eh)*, "visionary" *(ḥozeh)*, and "man of God" *('ish ha-'elohim)*.

Prophets were characterized by a nonnormal psychological state: ecstasy. When the "spirit of God" entered them they fell (sometimes literally) into a trance and received messages from God. They might appear to be asleep, or babble uncontrollably. Prophecy might be stimulated by music (1 Sam. 10.5; 2 Kings 3.15) and was always related to music through the art of poetry, because much biblical prophecy was composed in rhythmical parallelistic discourse, that is, poetry. The early prophets traveled in bands with a leader in their midst, who might be called their "father"; they themselves were "sons of the prophets." They delivered oracles on everything from lost asses (1 Sam. ch 9) to campaigns in war to the appointing of kings. It is likely that groups of cultic prophets were found at shrines, and royal prophets at the courts of kings. In all of this the role of prophets was probably similar to that in surrounding cultures.

However, some prophets took on a more exalted, and isolated, function in Israel and Judah. Prophecy, represented by the seer Samuel, seems to have been centrally involved in the founding of the monarchy, in the transition from charismatic to royal leadership in the 10th c. BCE. The Bible attests to prophetic figures who claim to be empowered to appoint kings, and who presume to remain censors of monarchy and state. They deliver unbidden oracles, often unwelcome to rulers, on state policies, both religious and military. They criticize the people for lack of social concern and for oppressing the poor. Such independent prophets, great figures like Samuel and Nathan in the 10th c., Elijah and Elisha in the 9th, Amos, Hosea, Isaiah in the 8th, Jeremiah, Ezekiel and others in the 7th and 6th centuries, far surpass the prophets in the surrounding cultures and are of great importance in the biblical tradition.

The prophets' dominant literary form was the "messenger speech," a discourse purporting to be the direct words of the deity—in structure these were often similar to the message a messenger might deliver on behalf of a king. Many genres were used: laments, parables, hymns, etc., but the central type of speech was the "lawsuit" *(riv)*, which used legal forms to excoriate Israel. The basic outline was a statement of the crime, of an individual, like a king or priest, or of the people as a whole, followed by the sentence passed by the divine court in heaven (of which prophets seem to have been viewed as human members, transported there in their visions). One often finds also a call to "heaven and earth" to serve as witnesses. Lawsuit oracles were delivered not only against Israel and Judah, but also against surrounding peoples (sometimes called "oracles against the nations"). Although the implied audience is the other nations, the actual audience was Israel-Judah, who was to learn a lesson from these speeches. Most prophets also gave "salvation oracles," predictions of weal and assurances of divine protection, a function that may originally have belonged to cult prophets at shrines. It has also been suggested that many psalms reflect an oracle of salvation delivered by priests, or cult prophets, at the shrine. We shall see below that it was the independent, fearless brand of prophecy that provided the stimulus for the growth of biblical religion out of Israelite-Judean religion, but that prophecy itself eventually became effectively outlawed by later biblical religion.

Did Israelite-Judean religion practice child sacrifice, as surrounding Canaanite religions did? To be sure, the Bible condemns "passing children through the fire to Molech" (probably a form of Baal), but Israelites were acquainted with the practice, and recognized its numinous terror when performed by others (2 Kings ch 3). The prophets condemn those who sacrifice their children at the tophet outside Jerusalem, a place of such horror that it gave its name, Gehenna *(ge' ben hinom)*, to the later concept of hell. Biblical religion recognized that the first-born "belong" to YHVH and must be "redeemed." The story of Abraham's binding of Isaac implies that child sacrifice has been superseded, but it also recognizes the significance of the rite as the supreme test of loyalty to YHVH. The story of the unhappy fate of Jephthah's daughter (Judg. ch 11) suggests that the practice of child sacrifice in connection with a strong oath was not unknown in Israel. Certain prophetic texts as well suggest that it was practiced (see, e.g., Mic. 6.7).

Very little is known about the official cult of the Northern Kingdom, beyond the establishment of two royal shrines in Dan and Bethel by Jeroboam I in the 9th c., where worship centered on the images of two calves set up by him, mentioned above. Jeroboam is also said to have established a festival in the eighth month to replace the festival in the seventh month (the New Year festival?) in Judah (1 Kings 12.33).

More is known about the state cult of Judah, which centered in the shrine on Mt. Zion in Jerusalem. Judean religion seems to have reflected a royal theology, or ideology, based on a covenant *(berit)*, an unconditional divine promise to David that his dynasty would rule forever, "as long as the sun and moon exist" (Ps. 89.37–38). The king was viewed as the "son" of God (2 Sam. 7.14; Pss. 2.7; 89.27), though whether this implied actual royal divinity is questionable. There is little doubt that this royal religion was imported into Judah from primarily Egyptian and Phoenician sources. The terms used to describe the king in the biblical texts that most directly reflect Judean royal tradition, the "royal psalms" (Pss. 2; 20; 21; 45; 72; 89) are used elsewhere only of God. Also prominent in this royal cult were notions of unconditional divine protection of Zion and Jerusalem, amounting to what has been termed a doctrine of the "inviolability of Zion." (This notion is also expressed in Isa. chs 1–39.) It was believed that no enemy could capture the city in which was located God's sacred house, the Temple built and maintained by the king, which was viewed as the royal chapel. The "Zion Psalms" (Pss. 46; 47; 48) are possibly early expressions of this doctrine, which also figures prominently in later prophetic messianic visions (see below). The aim of this political, religious, and cultic complex was undoubtedly to strengthen the claim of the monarchy to legitimacy. It seems to have succeeded, because Judean dynastic kingship remained stable for over three centuries (the brief usurpation by Athaliah is the only exception, and she was a northerner, the daughter of Phoenician Jezebel). Northern Israel, by contrast, probably lacking such a royal ideology, saw the rise and fall of many ruling houses. The main ideas of royal religion became transmuted in biblical religion into messianic eschatology (see below).

What can reasonably be conjectured about the belief system of ancient Israel and Judah? If one relies only on the biblical evidence, very little can be extrapolated that is not dependent on the dating of the texts—a highly debated enterprise—so that any interpretation must remain to some extent circular. For example, was covenant already a feature of early Israelite religion, or did it rise to prominence only later, in biblical religion? The answer to this question depends on how one dates the biblical covenantal traditions, a topic with little scholarly consensus. The only religious complex of ideas that is more or less unanimously accepted for ancient Israel is the "monomyth" of the primeval battle between YHVH and the dragon-like Sea (Yam, also called Rahab, Serpent, Leviathan, River[s], etc.). This myth is found throughout biblical literature and is usually connected with creation (cf. Isa. 51.9–10; Pss. 74.13–15; 89.10–11; Job 26.12–13, etc.; ch 1 in Gen. reflects biblical religion and has been largely demythologized, with the exception of a reference to sea monsters in 1.21). But what did the myth mean to ancient Israel? Was it reflected, even reenacted in the cult? Had it been reduced to merely a literary motif? We have no answer for such questions.

The extrabiblical archeological and epigraphic evidence points to little overt difference between Israelite-Judean religion and the religions of surrounding peoples. The religious picture that emerges from the great Moabite inscription of the mid-9th c. BCE does not differ from what is described in, and may reasonably be extrapolated from, the older texts of the Bible; except that it is Chemosh, national deity of Moab, who wages holy war on YHVH and puts Israel itself to the ban of extermination *(ḥerem)*. Iconography points in the same direction. Israel and Judah made unrestrained use of the typical Levantine Egypto-Phoenician and Mesopotamian repertoire of motifs: winged sun discs, scarabs, moon god symbols, sacred trees of life, paradise imagery, cherubim (a composite beast with the body of a lion, the wings of eagles, and a human head), winged cobras (seraphim?), etc. Many of these symbols were used on seals, the most personal representation of individual identity, and it is therefore difficult to dismiss them as mere "art." But it is a mystery what such things meant to the Israelites. The full significance of the amulets, especially female figurines, abundant at Israelite sites also escapes us.

Amulets and "pagan" visual symbols are commonly ascribed to "popular" rather than to "official" religion, which supposedly shunned them. Worship at the high places and consultation with the spirits of the dead *(ʾovot veyidʿonim)* are similarly ascribed to "folk religion." But the opposition of "popular or folk vs. official" is inherently polemical and is dependent on individual interpretation; this dichotomy may not reflect the reality of Israelite-Judean religion. For example, it is well known that the Bible presents only a gloomy picture of the afterlife in Sheol, as a shadowy, listless realm cut off from contact with God. But it is becoming ever clearer that the high places and especially the cultic pillars *(matzevot)* associated with them, point to a belief in some kind of active contact with long-dead ancestors, perhaps even a cult of dead heroes. The communal *marzeaḥ* drinking bouts, condemned by the prophets as "pagan," may also have been thought to enable one to commune with ancestors. Is one to label such things as reflecting only "popular religion"? Or is it more likely that developed biblical religion has edited these practices out and declared them to be "idolatrous?" Similarly, biblical religion reduced the heavenly assembly of divine beings, called "sons of God" (Ps. 29.1), "holy ones" (Ps. 89.6–7) and even "gods" (Ps. 82.1) in older biblical texts, to colorless and nameless "messengers" (angels). But there is every reason to suspect that in Israelite-Judean religion the angels were the same type of potent, named heavenly forces so prominent in postbiblical religion, especially apocalyptic, and also in rabbinic midrash.

The general picture of Israelite-Judean religion that emerges is of a cult along the same pattern of other cults in the ancient Near East. If the surface conceals some "elusive essence" of an already totally monotheistic, covenantal, Torah-oriented faith, scholarship has not yet discerned it with certainty (see below). It is likely not in Israelite-Judean, but rather in biblical religion—what might be termed the Biblical Revolution—that the essential developments lie.

Biblical Religion

Revolution or Reform?

The complexes of traditions in edited texts that form the evidence for biblical religion date, for the most part, from the 7th to 5th centuries BCE: the Torah, the historical works, the beginnings of the compilation of the prophetic books, and the chief wisdom books. Embedded in these works are materials that reflect older stages of biblical religion—its prehistory, as it were—and many traditions of Israelite-Judean religion that have, in the main, been altered to reflect later viewpoints.

A key question is whether biblical tradition is merely a later, more developed stage of Israelite-Judean religion, continuing the same basic religious ideas and tendencies, a viewpoint that posits essential continuity; or whether, conversely, biblical religion marks a basic shift in religion, a reinterpretation of older traditions so radical as to be revolutionary. Continuity or revolution?

The Bible claims continuity from Moses on, with no meaningful development. This single authentic tradition was constantly violated by apostasy, but was also restored in a series of "reforms" by figures such as Josiah and Ezra. Modern critical scholarship overturned the traditional viewpoint by emphasizing the principle of change and development. The classic late 19th c. synthesis of Julius Wellhausen posited discontinuity between older Israelite and later biblical traditions. The former was a "nature" religion, not essentially different from the cults of surrounding ancient peoples; the latter was a new kind of faith, rooted in prophetic inspiration. Later, according to Wellhausen, it became a fossilized text-centered religion dominated by Priestly ritual and petty legalism. Such value judgments, reflecting Social Darwinist prejudices, seemed to invalidate Wellhausen's synthesis to many 20th c. scholars. William F. Albright and his students tried to show that archeology could demonstrate substantial continuity between Israelite and biblical religions. For example, the covenant traditions were held to go back to recently discovered second millenium models. Some of the patriarchal traditions were demonstrated to have had early roots. Monotheism was related to trends in the late Bronze Age Near East, and so on. A similar attempt at demonstrating essential continuity was made by the Israeli scholar Yehezkel Kaufmann, who attacked Wellhausen's synthesis and tried to show that Israel's religion reflected the same basic ideas from beginning to end. By the end of the 20th c. a revisionist reaction against the claims of continuity set in, with claims of discontinuity much stronger than those made by Wellhausen. Some claimed that biblical religion was mainly a product of the Persian and even Hellenistic eras, and that the existence of Israelite-Judean religion, and even of "Israel" itself was chimerical. Some revisionist scholars were justly accused of having political goals.

Which approach is the most justified, on the basis of the biblical and extrabiblical evidence, including archeology? This is not a matter in which one can simply allow the "facts" to speak for themselves, because interpretation plays a key role at every stage of the discussion. But it is possible to list a few major differences between what scholarship generally considers to be typical of earlier vs. later religion:

(1) *Monotheism.* Older, especially poetic, texts portray the deity as seated among the assembly of divine beings, who are sometimes, as noted above, called *bene ʾel(im),* ("sons of gods"), *kedoshim* ("holy ones"), among other terms. Statements of divine incomparability echo those commonly found also in extrabiblical hymns; for example "Who is like you among the gods?" (Exod.

15.11). Now, monotheism is really a complex philosophical idea that is very hard to express in biblical language, but later texts, especially Deut., do seem to be struggling to make overt statements about God's oneness and uniqueness, most famously in Deut. 4.35: "It has been clearly demonstrated to you that the LORD alone is God; there is none beside Him," and (depending on one's interpretation) in the Shema: "Hear, Israel, the LORD, our God, the LORD is one" (Deut. 6.4). In the Bible, key ideas are generally expressed peripherally, especially by concrete, often ritual actions. A probable sign of real monotheism is the active polemic against idolatry one finds in Deuteronomic texts and in late prophets, like Jeremiah and, especially, Second Isaiah. It (mis)represents other ancient religions as mere fetishism, the foolish worship of images of "wood and stone."

(2) *Centralization of worship.* A potent ritual expression of absolute monotheism is the attempt to reflect God's oneness by insisting on one legitimate shrine, the Jerusalem Temple. This is a cultic development of the Deuteronomic movement, perhaps first attempted by Hezekiah in the late 8th c. (1 Kings ch 18), and later effected by Josiah in his famous "reform" in 621 BCE (2 Kings chs 22–23). Earlier religion tolerated a multiplicity of altars, a fact obscured by the Deuteronomic editing of most of the historical books. But actions speak louder than words. The fact that Josiah, the paragon of militant piety, did not kill the priests of the "high places" (except for Bethel, the main rival of Jerusalem), but rather allowed them to share the Priestly income of the Jerusalem shrine (2 Kings 23.9) is a tacit admission that local shrines had been considered quite legitimate before. In the context of ancient religion, centralization of worship, which is also reflected in the contemporary Priestly writings (despite some signs of earlier decentralization), was an extremely radical step that deserves to be viewed as revolutionary in the extreme.

(3) *Myth vs. history.* It is often said that biblical religion broke with the kind of mythical thinking characteristic of the religions of the ancient Near East in favor of history. God was praised for His great acts of national redemption, such as the exodus from Egypt and the conquest of Canaan ("salvation history"). It is true that biblical religion has ousted most of the mythology of the ancient world, with the exception of a few stock themes, like creation, the garden of Eden and YHVH's cosmic battle in primeval times with the Sea. Especially the sexual aspects of mythology, involved with the birth and procreation of the gods, have been eliminated (except for a few relics like Gen. 6.1–4). Indeed, it can fairly be stated that the processes of demythologization and desexualization of religion are related to each other and go hand-in-hand in biblical religion.

But it is less certain that biblical religion broke with the concept of myth itself. If one defines myth as narrative that expresses a culture's deepest attitudes and emotions about the origin and nature of the world in which it lives, it is correct to say that biblical religion created new but potent myths of its own. And it is certainly incorrect to hold that biblical religion is historical in any modern, scientific sense. Rather, the unique creation of biblical religion is a blend of history and myth that might best be termed typology, the cyclical recurrence of a few historical patterns, such as national apostasy and repentance, which serve as the basis of a vital historiography. Events are made to reflect, anticipate, and explain each other typologically. For example, the patriarchal narratives foreshadow later Israelite settlement in many ways (a fact the Rabbis recognized and expressed in the principle that "the deeds of the fathers prefigure what will occur to their descendants" *(ma'ase 'avot siman levanim).* Disparate events are united by extended and intertwining typologies of creation and redemption. So, the return from exile in Babylonia is viewed as a second exodus from Egypt; the exodus itself is described in such a way as to evoke creation typology, as is the Sinai theophany, and so on. History is valued not for the unique, but for the recurrence of these repeated patterns. It is in this sense that biblical religion may be termed a historical faith.

Was Israelite-Judean religion already historical in this sense? The answer depends on the dating of the texts. Numerous typical ancient Near Eastern mythological themes are, however, prevalent in creation accounts outside Gen. ch 1. Moreover, texts that reflect the royal theology of Judah, which are mostly very old, are also replete with language and themes drawn from ancient mythology. Indeed, that tradition does not even shrink from calling the king the "son of God" (albeit adoptive). Such facts lead one to suspect that the characteristic use of historically rooted typology is likely a feature of biblical, not earlier, religion.

(4) *Individualism.* Older religion viewed the individual as a member of society: family, clan, tribe, and nation. Corporate, transgenerational responsibity for sin was the rule, as in the Decalogue ("punishing children for the crime of their fathers to the third, even the fourth generation" [Exod. 20.5]). This notion is often evident even in Deut., where the Heb text often refers to the plural rather than the singular Israelite, suggesting that he or she will be punished or rewarded with the larger group (see e.g., Deut. 11.13–21). Evidence of an overt challenge to this doctrine first appears in the prophets of the late 7th and 6th centuries BCE, Jeremiah and, especially, Ezekiel (Ezek. ch 18). In late texts individual responsibility for sin has become the standard doctrine, as in the book of Chron. The belief in individual responsibility for sin went along with an elevated position for women and a new formulation of the nation Israel as a community of committed believers *('edah, kahal).*

The change was also reflected in new models of piety. Older psalms remain more or less on the level of similar compositions from the ancient Near East. But a new inwardness, focused on individual relationship to God, appears prominently in later psalms, like Pss. 139 and 119. A new concept of the religious individual, totally devoted to God, is especially a feature of developed Deuteronomic religion, and is linked to the new emphasis on the oneness of God. It will be remembered that the Shema continues: "You shall love the LORD, your God, with all your heart, and all your life" (Deut. 6.5). Another sign of the new individualism is a much heightened concern with the problem of individual suffering and the concomitant theological issue of theodicy. It finds expression mainly in later texts such as the "confessions" of Jer. (e.g., Jer. 11.18–12.6) and, above all, the book of Job.

(5) *Text religion and canon.* The older forms of Israelite religion probably were mainly oral, especially prophecy (at least before the 7th c.). But Deuteronomic religion introduced a new text-centeredness by insisting on the unchangeability of the written form of the *torah* ("instruction") given to Moses on Horeb (Sinai). More than any other Torah book, Deut. emphasizes the *sefer* or written document. Nothing may be added or taken away (Deut. 4.2; 13.1). This is the beginning of the notion of immutable canon, an approach to sacred texts quite at variance with the liberal attitude toward textual transmission of most ancient cultures. Indeed, despite this injunction, even biblical traditions remained astonishingly fluid for several centuries after Deut. But eventually the process of codification, standardization, and canonization set in, beginning with the Torah (probably in the 5th c.) and extending gradually to the Prophets and the Writings, a development that was completed by the 1st c. CE (or several centuries earlier, according to several scholars). Along with the increasing textualization and literariness of biblical religion went an intertextual aspect of internal commentary and inner-biblical interpretation.

(6) *Forms of piety.* A new kind of piety also arose, fostered especially by Deut., focused on prayer and study. Ritual was not ignored, but it became secondary to teaching and meditation. Attitudes and themes native to the older wisdom tradition were adapted to this new piety, which emphasized study of the written record of divine revelation. It should be

noted that biblical religion makes no claim for Mosaic authorship of the Torah as a whole, but only of Deut. (Deut. 31.9). In addition, the older liturgical tradition was revised to make it compatible with strict monotheism, resulting in the type of prayer found in most of the book of Ps. (see discussion below).

These developments fit the general historical and cultural context of the centuries between about 800 and 400 BCE. It was a time of extreme change and uncertainty in the Near East, marked by the rise of a radically new form of political organization, the empire, first of the Assyrians, later of the Neo-Babylonians and the Persians. These world empires made imperial religious as well as political claims, and the policies of mixing of populations through exile and resettlement weakened the old polities of the region. The chief gods of the imperial states were raised to supremacy over other deities. Henotheism, if not true monotheism, and syncretism were tendencies of the age. But uncertainty led to its opposite: cultural, including religious, conservatism, a focus on ancient traditions, and an attempt to present the new as authentically old. The typical literary production of the time is the pseudonymous *fraus pia,* a document that claims to have been written by a sage in hoary antiquity, but which actually fulfills some current need. The "finding" of the book of Deut. in the Temple in 621 BCE, corresponds nicely to this contemporary model. In sum, biblical religion fits the period in question in a general way, and sometimes very specifically.

To return to the original question: Do all of these new developments of the 7th to 5th centuries BCE mark a radically new departure, or only a later stage in the development of Israelite religion? The explosion of new features in the period in question is undeniable, from the scholarly point of view. But at what point does a difference in degree become a difference in kind? At what point is one justified of speaking of something as revolutionary, as radically new, especially if the tradition in question keeps insisting it is really very old, and merely being stripped of later accretions, "reformed"? Probably the claims of continuity vs. discontinuity cannot be judged only on the basis of logic. Rather, one must choose the answer one judges to be best supported by the evidence one accepts, and, it must be admitted, one's private religious convictions. To me, it seems clear that biblical religion possesses such a cohesiveness, even in its disparity of traditions; so clearly reflects the needs of its times; and, above all, so evidently represents a heightening and sharpening of traditional ideas, that it deserves to be viewed as revolutionary. The following discussion reflects this judgment.

The Development of Biblical Religion: From Prophecy to Text

Whether biblical religion marks a radical break with older Israelite-Judean religion, or only a new, heightened phase, its formative stimulus seems to have been in the Northern Kingdom of Israel in the 9th c. BCE. The attempt of Jezebel to import the worship of Tyrian Baal, along with its rites and coterie of prophets, into Israel stirred the violent opposition of the prophets of the native deity YHVH. The leaders of the "YHVH-only" party, as Morton Smith called it, Elijah and his disciple Elisha, inspired a military coup against the northern monarchs, the Omrides. Elijah was filled with exclusive "zeal" *(kin'ah)* for God, an intolerance of other deities that remained one of the hallmarks of biblical religion. The struggle with Baalism in the North continued into the 8th c., as evidenced by the activity of Hosea, who seems to have introduced a number of other key ideas, such as the use of pungent sexual terminology to describe apostasy ("whoring after foreign gods"). Biblical religion was thus Northern in origin, which explains why, as a religious reference (as opposed to political and cultural), the name of the community that accepted biblical religion was to remain "Israel" long after the late 8th-c. demise of the historical kingdom of Israel.

After the fall of the Northern Kingdom in the 8th c., this prophetically rooted, exclusive faith migrated south to Judah, perhaps already at the end of the 8th c., when it may have inspired the reforming efforts of King Hezekiah. By the late 7th c. biblical religion had become consolidated into the Deuteronomic "movement," probably a loose confederation of priests, prophets and their disciples, and royal officials. King Josiah was induced, by the "finding" of a "Book of the Instruction" (*sefer* hatorah—probably a form of Deut.) in the Temple, and by political motives (the weakening of Assyria) to undertake the great revolutionary "reform" of 621 BCE. The traditional high places were proscribed, worship was centralized in Jerusalem; images, stelae *(matzevot),* wooden poles *('asherim),* and the other paraphernalia of "idolatry" were destroyed (2 Kings chs 22–23); and the worship of the "Queen of Heaven" (Astarte) was forbidden (Jer. 44.18).

The reform, or revolution, lapsed after Josiah's ignominious death in battle, which could hardly have been interpreted by most contemporaries other than as divine judgment on his impiety in uprooting so many traditional forms of worship (see Jer. 44.15–19). But the ruling classes of Judah were soon exiled to Babylonia. The exile community of the 6th c. BCE, centered near Nippur in southern Babylonia, was a crucible of religious activity: prophetic (Second Isa.; Ezek.) and historical (the work of the Deuteronomistic Historian, editor of the first edition of the Former Prophets, the historical books from Josh. to Kings). The basic theological ideas of the Deuteronomic and Priestly tradition began to take their classic written forms, as did the first editions of some of the prophetic writings.

The most active period in the establishment of biblical religion thus took place in the exile, and it was this religion that was transplanted back into the tiny Judean community of returned exiles in the late 6th and mid-5th centuries BCE. The first attempts at return were feeble and indecisive. The final reforms of Ezra and Nehemiah (after 450 BCE) imposed the standards of developed biblical religion on the community, with the Torah, probably in more or less its present form, as the constitution. The development of biblical religion was therefore gradual, stretching from at least the late 9th or 8th to the 5th centuries. In its final form it marks an attempt to restore preexilic Judah, reinterpreted as a religious community of Israel, by restructuring old institutions and formulating new theological ideas projected back into a Mosaic age that was now viewed as uniquely authoritative. Contemporary prophecy was demoted and all but abolished in favor of the written documents that contained past revelation, so that biblical religion became a completely textual religion, requiring a body of approved interpreters, the scribes. Interpretation of the old revelation displaced the new revelations of contemporary prophets. The final form of biblical religion was supported by the Persian state, which may have stimulated the formation of the Torah, a compromise document of the two major ongoing traditions of biblical religion, the Deuteronomic-covenantal and the Priestly-cultic, both of which will now be briefly described.

Deuteronomic-covenantal Religion

The dominant stream of biblical religion is the Deuteronomic, or covenantal tradition. It conceives of the relationship between God and Israel as a legal form, a *berit* or *'edut,* a covenant, i.e., a contract, or treaty, made between God and the escapees from Egypt at Horeb (in other traditions, Sinai) with the mediation of the prophet Moses. The people had a direct mass revelation of the divine Presence for the announcement of the Decalogue; the rest of the laws, the terms of the covenant, were transmitted privately to Moses on the mountain and read to the people later. The people agreed to the treaty freely, binding themselves and their descendants by an oath and covenant ceremony. By this treaty YHVH became Israel's God, with an obligation to give them the land of Canaan and otherwise protect them and provide for their needs; and Israel became God's people, with a permanent obligation to fulfill the divine commandments, the laws of the covenant. Horrendous curses are threatened for Israel's breach of the contract (see esp. Deut. 28.15–68). The Horeb/Sinai covenant is therefore conditional, unlike the covenant with David, which is strictly promissory. The most explicit and complete form of the covenant is in the book of Deut., whose core is a work of the 7th c. BCE. Fragmentary and perhaps older covenantal traditions are found in Exod. chs 19–24 and 32–34.

It is now known that the conditional covenant between God and Israel generally follows the form of the treaty between a suzerain and his vassals, attested from the second millennium on. The covenant patterns of Deut. have been shown to follow most closely later, Assyrian, treaty forms of the first millennium. Whether other covenant traditions can be shown to go back to earlier forms, attested among the Hittites of the late Bronze Age, is a matter of scholarly dispute. It is possible that covenant *(berit)* was first applied in the Judean royal tradition to the divine promise of protection to the House of David, as the unconditional, promissory type of covenant (itself based on ancient royal grants by kings to favored vassals). It was later said to have been prefigured by a similar "covenant," a promise to the national patriarch Abraham (Gen. chs 15, 17). Finally, the covenant idea, in its conditional form, was extended to the whole nation as a unique mass divine revelation. It is also possible that some traditions of the conditional type of national covenant precede the monarchy, and that the two types of covenant, conditional and unconditional, competed with each other already in Israelite-Judean religion. But the virtual absence of references to the Horeb/Sinai event in definitely old, especially poetic, texts, suggests the greater likelihood of the sequence described above.

Whatever its age and provenance, the covenant idea, as expressed in the Deuteronomic tradition, now dominates the Bible, not only the Torah, but also the work of the historical books, which have undergone a Deuteronomic edition, and some of the prophets, especially Hos. and above all, Jer. (though curiously, the covenant with Israel is hardly mentioned at all outside the Torah). The leading religious ideas of this tradition, in their classic Deuteronomic form, may be summarized as follows:

Deuteronomic religion is strictly monolatrous and probably monotheistic; i.e., not only insisting on the worship of one God, but positing the effective existence only of this deity. Other gods are mere breaths, nothings *(hevel);* all idols are but material objects. Monotheism was an abstract idea difficult to express in ancient language, but it is palpable in Deuteronomic theology, if only by inference. As noted above, the abstract notion of monotheism is manifested in the strong Deuteronomic insistence that God be worshipped at only one shrine.

Deuteronomic religion places central stress on the name of God, and for this reason has been called by scholars a "name theology." The name (rather than the deity!) is said to "rest" *(shakan)* on the place God has chosen, i.e., the sole legitimate shrine (Jerusalem). It is a religion that implies divine transcendence. Direct divine contact with the world is strongly denied, except for the Horeb/Sinai revelation (and Deut. ch 4 seems to deny that God appeared on earth even then). Rather, God remains in heaven, from which He hears human prayer (1 Kings 8.30–49). This type of religion placed great stress on the word, both as name and prayer; and concomitantly on the sense of hearing, as manifested not only in God's hearing of prayer, but also in human hearing of the words of the covenant and transmitting them to the young through teaching. The divine instruction *(torah)* must be the sole topic of human religious thought and meditation; it is Israel's true "wisdom" (Deut. 4.6). Deut. places great emphasis on mind and inner thought. It contains a certain rationalizing, even rationalistic tendency, often offering reasons and explanations for the commandments of the covenant (Deut. 5.15; 15.18; etc.).

The focus on the oneness of God, shrine, and thought, extends also to emotion. Israel is enjoined not only to fear and obey, but also to love God, with total, singular inner devotion. The commandment to love, a seeming paradox, has its roots in the legal language of the ancient Near East, as an expression of volition, insuring that the terms of an agreement are entered into freely; for example, a vassal king may be commanded to "love" his overlord. But in Deut., loving God has become more than a legal metaphor. It is a total commitment, expressive of the emotion of *kin'ah,* which not only means "zeal," but also "jealousy." Stemming from this deep emotional bond between deity and individual (for Deuteronomic religion has a pronounced focus on the individual in the group) is a certain tendency toward intolerance and even totalitarianism, which has manifested itself often in later, biblically-based religions. But it is also true that covenant religion is the locus of an implicit doctrine of free will, because Israel is always confronted with the choice to obey or not obey, even if the promised reward for the former is life and the threatened punishment for the latter is death (see esp. Deut. 30.15–20).

Covenant faith is also a militant religion. It draws upon and reinterprets the holy war traditions of the ancient Near East and of Israelite-Judean religion, but focuses them not on any actual national foe but on what must be regarded, in Deut.'s day, as a quite fictitious enemy, the Canaanites, demanding their complete destruction (see esp. Deut. 20.16–18). Since the latter no longer existed as a group in the period in question, it is difficult to escape the impression that by "Canaanites" is meant an inner foe, Canaanizers, as it were, most likely adherents of older Israelite-Judean religion.

Covenant religion is a text religion, limiting itself to the written record of the contract between God and Israel. Creation themes are practically absent; reference to nature as "heaven and earth" is limited to invoking them as witnesses to the covenant, a literary survival of the list of gods in ancient treaties. Although it has prophetic roots, and reveres Moses as a unique super-prophet, Deuteronomic religion all but abolishes future prophetic revelation, lest new divine communications compete with the single authoritative written revelation at Horeb/Sinai (see below).

Deuteronomic religion has little interest in the cult, apart from insisting that it be limited to one spot. Otherwise, its major interest in ritual is in linking observance with the exodus, as it does with the Sabbath (Deut. 5.15), or in highlighting the Passover, by its nature already linked with the exodus. Passover seems to have played a key role in Deuteronomic-covenantal religion, since the "reforms" of Hezekiah and Josiah are described as being accompanied by special Passover ceremonies.

Priestly-cultic Religion

The Priestly tradition, the core of which is the mass of cultic legislation including the end of Exod., all of Lev., and parts of Num., represents a type of religion that, like Deuteronomic faith, is also monotheistic and centered on one place of worship. It, too, presents itself as the result of revelation in a covenant, which it also terms *berit,* although unlike Deuteronomic texts, it does not avoid adding the word "eternal" *(berit ʿolam).* It views the sacrificial cult as an unconditional and permanent establishment, like the Davidic covenant, and unlike the Sinai/Horeb covenant, which was dependent on Israel's obedience and was therefore conditional. Like the Deuteronomic tradition, the Priestly tradition uses the term "rest" *(shakan)* to describe God's link to the shrine *(mishkan),* but what "rests" on it is not the divine name, but the "glory" *(kavod).* For this reason it is often said that the Priestly texts reflect a "glory" theology, in opposition to Deuteronomic "name" theology, expressive of an implied idea of divine immanence rather than transcendence. *Kavod* is the term already used in Israelite-Judean religion to describe the manifestation in theophany of the divine Presence as storm cloud, lightning, earthquake, and, above all, as refulgent radiance. These ideas are rooted in the ancient Near East; a similar light surrounded the gods (a late relic of this belief is the halo around saints' heads in Christian art, prefigured by the light that streamed from Moses' face [Exod. 34.30]). But in Priestly thinking the ancient concepts and images have become more systematic. The divine glory, which was the main manifestation of the Sinai experience (Exod. 24.16–18) in the Priestly worldview, is said to have entered the completed Mosaic Tabernacle, model of future shrines, at its dedication (Exod. 40.34–35) and to return each year on the Day of Atonement to the Holy of Holies in the Temple, where it appeared over the cherub lid of the Ark (Lev. 16.2) (an alternative interpretation is that it was always immanent in the shrine but became visible only on that day). To be sure, it was seen only by the high priest on that day, but Priestly religion is nevertheless in general a religion of seeing, not hearing, like Deuteronomic religion. It is also a religion of touching, and smelling of the propitiating odor *(reaḥ niḥoaḥ)* of sacrifice and of the sweet savour of incense and spices. In other words, it is a religion of the physical, in which language, even prayer, plays little role, being quite absent from Torah texts reflecting this tradition. The contrast with Deuteronomic religion on this point could not be greater.

The Priestly tradition includes not only cultic texts dealing with sacrifice and ritual, but also the Priestly narrative source, responsible for the creation account of Gen. 1.1–2.4 and other key stories in Gen. and later in the Torah. If the narrative materials are viewed in conjunction with the cultic ones, it is possible to extrapolate an implicit Priestly theology that blends ritual and theology. The central ritual substance is the blood of sacrifice, and the central religious idea is atonement. The only explicit statement of the connection between the two is Lev. 17.11, where it is said that the blood of sacrifice effects atonement for the lives of Israelites. The underlying theology is not explained, since, unlike Deut., the Priestly authors eschew explanation and rationalization; but in the preceding ch, Lev. ch 16, it is said that the high priest is to attain atonement for Israel by entering the Holy of Holies and sprinkling sacrificial blood before the divine Presence. The link between atonement and blood is therefore quite firm. According to another Priestly text, Gen. ch 9, avoiding consumption of blood is part of a complex of themes, in which the eating of the meat of animals is presented in the context of a divine concession to inherent human sinfulness. But the preceding ch (Gen. ch 8) contains an eternal divine promise never to allow human sin to lead to another catastrophic flood. It may perhaps be extrapolated that blood is a reminder to God both of human sin and of His promise to forgive. Perhaps it is safer to say that the link between sacrificial blood and forgiveness for sins is a mystery, because the Priestly tradition cultivates mystery and a sense of the immanently numinous. The Priestly complex of blood and atonement was to have a great effect on Christian theology. After the destruction of the Temple, the Rabbis stated that prayer, rather than blood, attains forgiveness for Israel; this reflects a melding of Deuteronomic and Priestly worldviews.

Priestly religion has reinterpreted the old cult of Israelite-Judean religion to focus less on the ancient whole, communal, and thank offerings *(ʿolah, shelem, todah),* than on the expiatory sacrifices, the "purification offering" *(ḥatʾat)* (sometimes translated "sin offering") and "trespass offering" ("guilt offering") *(ʾasham).* Old festivals were reinterpreted, the ancient probable New Year, as noted above, all but disappearing in the process.

The Priestly tradition also continues the ancient insistence that worshippers be morally as well as ritually pure. It has been suggested that some psalms, especially Pss. 15 and 24, reflect ancient "entrance liturgies," declarations of moral purity pilgrims were obliged to make before they could enter the sacred precincts of the shrine. The moral aspect finds expression in the Priestly tradition of later biblical religion primarily in the "Holiness Collection" (Lev. chs 17–26), especially in Lev. ch 19 (the command to "love thy neighbor as thyself" comes from Lev. 19.18). In these chs, worshippers are enjoined to be "holy as the LORD, your God is holy." To the developed Priestly tradition holiness means not just the numinous "other," or moral perfection, but physical and spiritual separation from the impure: clean from unclean, sinner from wicked, Israel from the nations. Gen. ch 1 represents creation itself as a series of separations and distinctions by means of which primeval chaos became ordered. Similarly, the Temple consists of a complex of precincts of increasing holiness. This reclusive, segregating notion of the holy is derived from ancient Near Eastern, ultimately mythically rooted models, like much of Priestly thinking. But in its final form this definition of holiness as separation and exclusion fits especially well with the milieu of postexilic Judah in the 5th c. BCE, in which, as the books of Ezra and Neh. show, separation from other groups was the key issue. Gone is the broad view of holiness as the divine Presence that fills the whole earth (Isa. 6.3). Also reflecting postexilic circumstances is the ritual prominence in the Priestly codes of the Sabbath as a weekly day of rest memorializing creation, and the rite of circumcision as a sign of the Abrahamic covenant, distinguishing Jews from their neighbors.

Other Traditions of Biblical Religion

The Liturgical Tradition

As noted above, the Deuteronomic tradition exalts prayer (though mainly in the deuteronomistic historical books of Former Prophets), while the Priestly tradition seems to all but ignore it (the high priest's confession on the Day of Atonement is a notable exception). Prose prayer plays a prominent role in the historical works edited by the Deuteronomic school, as well as in the later book of Chron. Poetic prayer is mainly found in the book of Ps., the history and development of which is very complex and poorly understood. Chron. states that liturgical pieces, such as hymns and petitions, were composed by Levitical guilds in Second Temple times (1 Chron. chs 15–16). This may also have been true in earlier periods as well, but the only liturgical situation that can definitely be reconstructed for Israelite-Judean religion is the one associated with the large genre of the "petitions of the individual." A worshipper in distress vowed to make a sacrifice of thanksgiving *(todah)* if rescued by God, and to declare God's praise to those assembled for the communal sacrificial meal. There is evidence that in some cases the prayer and praise would be written down, sometimes on a stele. This form of prayer is also attested elsewhere in the ancient Near East, but is most highly developed in the book of Ps. Doubtless the cult of Israelite-Judean religion included hymns to the deity, of which old psalms like Pss. 29 and 68 may be examples. Prayers were also offered at the Jerusalem Temple on behalf of the king, of which the small number of "royal psalms" are probable survivors (Pss. 2; 20; 21; 45; 72; 89).

The canonical book of Ps. reflects biblical religion and was collected in the postexilic period of the 5th and 4th centuries. Many psalms are assigned pseudepigraphically to David, others to Levitical figures such as Asaph, Ethan, and Korah. Many are unascribed. The work is divided into five "books," likely on the model of the Torah. The old traditions of Israelite-Judean prayer have been reinterpreted and reworked to supply models of approved monotheistic piety. Prayers are addressed only to YHVH; there is no mention of the mediating angelic figures that seem to have played a role in "popular" religion (Ps. 91.11; Job 33.23). Numerous genres are represented: petitions of the individual (the largest group), communal petitions and complaints, historical hymns, nature hymns, "enthronement psalms" (describing God as king), "royal psalms" (praise and petition for the Davidic king), "Zion psalms" (hymns about Jerusalem and the Temple mountain), "songs of ascent" (for pilgrimages), wisdom and Torah psalms. There is a scholarly debate about the extent to which the canonical psalms represent actual liturgical pieces written for and used in the cult. Opinions range from the view that practically all of the psalms, except for wisdom and Torah, were used in the cult, to the view that almost all psalms have been freed from their cultic roots and have become "spiritualized" literary expressions of a dominantly individual, Temple-focused piety. There is little doubt the "royal psalms" are intended by the editors to be taken eschatologically, as referring to the future messianic (not, as they originally did, the current Davidic) king. It is likely that the other genres had many functions; as is often the case with liturgical texts, actual usage and inner meaning are not always apparent from the bare text, because the same words can be applied to many, and ever-changing, circumstances. This fact, though inconvenient for scholarship, no doubt partially accounts for the great popularity of the book of Ps. to this day.

Prophetic Tradition in Biblical Religion

The role of prophets in Israelite-Judean religion was sketched above, as well as the prophetic background to the development of biblical religion, specifically, the Deuteronomic-covenantal tradition. Strangely enough, however, biblical religion has a divided attitude toward the phenomenon of prophecy. On the one hand, prophecy was exalted in the figure of Moses, and revelation, by origin a purely prophetic phenomenon and limited to individuals, was made a constitutive national experience at Horeb/Sinai, albeit limited to that one occurence. On the other hand, prophecy as a living phenomenon was discouraged. Future prophets had to prove they were "true" and not "false" by producing prophecies that came true before their messages would be heeded (Deut. 18.21), a tautologous condition that effectively abolished prophecy as a living institution after the 5th c. BCE, at least in "official" religion. No future revelation could compete with Moses or amend what he had said.

The books of the Latter Prophets (Isa., Jer., Ezek., the Twelve), which purport to be a record of the great literary prophets of the past, were composed and edited in such a way that the viewpoint of developed biblical religion was dominant. The ecstatic aspect of the prophetic experience was downplayed, and visions were usually reported in some detail only for the inaugural of the prophet. Otherwise, the visual aspect, while definitely present, is secondary to the auditory. This produces the impression that the prophets were motivated by some vague kind of "inspiration" akin to that experienced by artists or writers, and that they were mainly preachers of morality, rather than the strange, antisocial, conflicted, and—if we can judge from the "Confessions" of Jeremiah—doubt-tortured individuals they often were. Jeremiah rails against his prophetic mission, but feels an irresistible inner compulsion ("a burning fire imprisoned within my bones, which I struggle to contain but cannot") to deliver God's words (Jer. 20.9). Biblical religion has flattened the prophets (a process continued by later tradition) but could not obliterate all evidence of their powerful personalities.

The Latter Prophets were also edited with much interpolation of later tradition, so that it is often difficult to tell in a book like Isa. which speeches go back to the prophet himself (chs 24–27, 40–66 are definitely non-Isaianic). Many of the later additions are eschatological and messianic. Eschatology, "the doctrine of the end," is the prophetic tradition that expresses hopes for the coming of an era of perfect peace, often brought about by a messianic ruler. The ancient Near

Eastern background seems to have been in a type of oracle that predicted the coming of such a ruler after a time of troubles and disorder. The royal tradition of Judah (and perhaps even of Northern Israel) may already have contained such visions of a future king, but the attestations of messianism are in the literary prophets, especially Isaiah of Jerusalem, who seems to have been the first to introduce eschatology in a major way. The oracles in Isa. from chs 7–11 predict the birth of several royal or royal-like children. The paradigmatic oracle is Isa. ch 11, which describes the reign of the future king in terms of a return to paradise. Peace will reign over the whole earth; even predatory animals will lose their urge to harm. Edenic themes dominate the developing messianic tradition in the later prophets, so that messianic oracles have been said to express an underlying belief in the cyclical, or at least circular nature of history, reflected in the dictum that "the end of time will be like the beginning of time" (Hermann Gunkel, the great German biblical scholar active in the late 19th and early 20th centuries). The messianic age will witness the submission of the nations to Israel, its king and its God, the cessation of war, the exaltation of the Temple on Mt. Zion, and so on. The eschatological tradition became the focus of the hopes of an exiled and subjected people. This accounts for its popularity after the exile, and the fact that the prophetic books were edited with many eschatological additions. Contemporary prophecy after the 5th c. may have been viewed as dangerous, but the prophets of the past, now made into canonical texts, could be studied for their glowing predictions, actual or interpolated, of the reversal of Israel's lowly state among the nations. Some scholars have tried to find a social milieu for the development of messianism, and posited an opposition in the postexilic period between conservative and privileged Priestly circles, who eschewed messianic enthusiasm, and oppressed circles of "visionaries," who cultivated it as a form of protest. In fact, messianism is entirely absent from the Torah, the central document of postexilic official religion; but it is uncertain that one is justified in positing a societal opposition of the type just described to explain the cultivation of messianic themes. Even the rich can long for the coming of the messiah.

By the 3rd to 2nd centuries BCE eschatology had developed into apocalyptic (a Gk term meaning "to uncover"), a form of literature combining many strands of tradition. The only representative of apocalyptic in the Bible is Dan. chs 7–12, but it was the subject of vast literature from the 3rd c. BCE to the 3rd c. CE, eventually becoming a Christian genre. The Dead Sea community is held by most scholars to have been the Essenes, an apocalyptic sect; and Christianity grew from apocalyptic roots as well. Apocalyptic differs from earlier prophetic eschatology in being deterministic, hermetic, and systematic; it typically also uses an intermediary angelic figure as a conduit for its revelations. The pattern of history was fixed by God at creation; free will is therefore an illusion. A great crisis, in the form of the persecution of the righteous, viewed as a small group of the faithful who are "in the know" and who can interpret the meaning of the strange and wild imagery that fills apocalyptic texts, will trigger divine intervention and the final cosmic battle between good and evil, waged on an earthly and angelic plane. The holy war traditions of the ancient world find their apotheosis in Armageddon. Apocalyptic literature has a definite concept of an afterlife, linked to reward and punishment, unlike biblical religion: The dead will be resurrected on the Day of Judgment, some for eternal punishment, others for eternal bliss in paradise. The apocalyptic concept of resurrection and judgment was accepted by the Rabbis and by Christians as a dogma.

The Wisdom Tradition

The wisdom tradition is found in many places in the Bible, but it especially dominates the Writings, not only "proper" wisdom books like Prov., Job, and Eccl., but also some psalms (1, 19, 37, 119, etc.) and other texts. Wisdom *(ḥokhmah)* is the term used to describe the intellectual and educational tradition of the ancient Near East, the province of scribal schools, teachers and students, but also elders, wise fathers and mothers. Wisdom was a determinedly international and humanistic tradition. The wise of all nations communicated with each other; genres, themes, and even language crossed boundaries freely. Parts of the book of Proverbs are virtually translations of an Egyptian work of wisdom; and biblical wisdom texts are replete with themes and language drawn from foreign wise men. The themes of traditional wisdom were the training of the young, expressed in maxims for correct living that would produce prosperity and esteem, so called "practical wisdom." But there also was so-called "speculative wisdom," which dealt with philosophical and religious issues, above all the problem of suffering and theodicy, the justifying of the ways of God: Why do the righteous often suffer and the wicked prosper? There are Babylonian and Egyptian "Jobs" as well as the biblical figure; and even the latter, in consonance with the international focus of wisdom, is portrayed not as an Israelite but as an Aramean from Uz. Wisdom was also a tradition interested in creation, in the workings of nature. Natural imagery abounds in wisdom texts, like proverbs and fables; and Solomon is said to have delivered parables about plants, animals, fish, and trees (1 Kings 5.13).

Many scholars hold that there was a kind of incipient natural philosophy in the ancient world shared also by Israel. The world was created by wisdom, and reflects an underlying unity of natural and moral orders, called *ma'at,* "truth," in Egypt, *mesharum,* "right," in Mesopotamia, and by various terms in Israel, among them *'emet,* "stability, truth," and *tzedek,* "righteousness, order." In Israel, it was believed that the world was created by God with the help of wisdom (Prov. ch 8; Job ch 28), so that His plan is manifested in the order of the cosmos.

Up to the 7th c. the wisdom tradition seems to have shown little interest in the particular religious traditions of Israel-Judah (though the prophets make increasing use of wisdom themes, esp. Jer., Second Isa., and Ezek.); this explains the absence of references to cultic worship and to covenant in wisdom books. The development of full biblical religion, in the form of the Deuteronomic-covenantal complex, created a crisis of the wise. Deut. rejects wisdom that does not concern itself with revelation and covenantal law. In the exile and afterwards, some of the wise began to accommodate their views to biblical religion, in varying degrees. Some refused all but superficial adherence to the new order. Although it is a very late book, Eccl. remains almost wholly on the level of traditional old wisdom, except for the last vv. (probably added by an editor). The book shows no concern for covenant religion and in its gentle cynicism is close to the ancient Near Eastern wisdom tradition (esp. in regard to its *carpe diem* philosophy) and also to contemporary Epicurean philosophy.

But much of wisdom compromised with biblical religion by combining themes of traditional wisdom with the new faith. A strange deterministic theology of retribution developed that dominates much of Prov., some Ps. (esp. 37) and, most strikingly, the speeches of Job's "friends": The righteous are always rewarded, the wicked always punished. Combined with this belief in strict reward and punishment was a doctrine of absolute cause and effect, derived from the nature interest of old wisdom, but now distorted into this new deterministic theology. Since only the wicked suffer, Job's friends say, Job must have committed some crime since he is clearly suffering. This doctrine is really a hybrid wisdom-covenantal faith, though it avoids explicit mention of covenant and presents itself as a form of natural law.

The greatest rebel against this deterministic and pitiless pseudo-piety was the author of Job, who rejects the arguments of the friends. Job is a radical rebel, who refuses to admit he is being punished for sin. With astounding hubris he demands that God appear to justify His ways. Job forces the deity to intervene to save His reputation. In a set of great speeches (Job chs 38–41), some of the most magnificent poetry of the Bible, God challenges Job to explain the works of creation. The problem with the divine "answer" is that God does not seem to address Job's challenge that He must explain why He is making Job suffer. Interpretations of the meaning of the book are numerous. Some maintain that God is simply overwhelming Job by confronting him with his human ignorance of the ways of God. Who are you to challenge the deity? A more modern reading holds that God is confirming the lack of congruence between natural and moral realms, a total rejection of traditional wisdom philosophy. A more positive interpretation is that God, even as He reminds Job of his human weakness, rouses him to awe and wonder at the greatness of nature, so that human suffering, even Job's, sinks into relative insignificance, at least temporarily. Probably the meaning of the book, like the meaning of *Hamlet* or any great work of literature, will always remain a riddle. Eventually wisdom's focus on nature gave way entirely to a focus on covenant, with results we see in the "Torah psalms," of which Ps. 119 is the longest, if not the most stirring, example.

Conclusions and Synthesis

Can one summarize biblical religion in a way that will organize its disparate traditions? The Bible is the most unsystematic of sacred texts, representing 1,000 years of textual development from different areas and social and religious groups. The several traditions of biblical religion we have listed, and the added complication of their superimposition on an earlier, and in many ways quite different, stage and type of religion, are so complex and confusing that one despairs of finding meaning in the whole, rather than in the parts. The historical discipline of source criticism has isolated the traditions and strands, without explaining their presence combined in the same work, often next to each other, in a way that seems intended to bewilder the reader. The traditional Jewish strategy in dealing with the multifariousness of the Bible is midrash, with its joyously insouciant ability to connect both the similar and the contradictory with a leap of imagination. However, historical scholarship, more limited in its agility than midrash, seems to be faced with two stark choices: to renounce interpretation of the whole and consider only the parts; or, conversely, to overlook the diversity and deal only with the whole on the canonical level. Indeed, canonical criticism, which views the Bible in the light of the communities that regard it as their Scripture, is one of the most important hermeneutical developments of recent years.

Yet there is a middle way: to recognize in the multiplicity of viewpoints not the result of incompetent editing, but the intent to express new religious insights in a culture that had as yet developed no theological, philosophical language adequate to describe them—a culture that, in addition, was conscientious about preserving old texts and traditions. In place of a harmonized, systematized theology, the Bible presents conflicting traditions, often next to each other: two creation narratives in Gen. chs 1–3; two forms of covenant tradition in the Torah, Deuteronomic and Priestly; two forms of prophetic speech, excoriating *riv* and comforting eschatology, and so on. Since biblical religion is textual, the believer is also necessarily a reader and an interpreter. Therefore a literary approach, a reading of God, as it were, may be preferable to a systematic theological approach that seeks to reconcile contradictions. Sympathy, not sophistry or scholasticism is required. The Bible must be read with the same freedom one has in all literary, especially poetic, interpretation, with concern for language and nuance, with awareness of the device of the juxtaposition of opposites, with delight in the kind of ambiguities that give texts deeper meaning. The later Rabbis recognized this freedom in midrash, and even in matters of halakhic disagreement sometimes allowed that both opinions were the "words of the Living God," a God made living precisely by the play of debate.

Indeed, biblical religion seems to go out of its way to cultivate and display disunity, to express religious ideas in terms of paired themes in tension, even opposition. For example, it can speak of God in one v. in a way that emphasizes the austere transcendence of the Deity; in the next v. it can use the most earthy and explicit anthropomorphism. The Bible is the least ecclesiastical, scholastic, and dogmatic of texts. As a transitional form of religion, biblical traditions had the luxury not to systematize, which is precisely what made the Bible the fertile ground from which its daughter religions could grow.

Yet there is an underlying unity in the varying traditions: the development of the characteristically biblical notion of faith in God. Faith is a much more complex idea than it is commonly held to be, so accustomed are we to speaking of "simple" faith. In fact it is a very complicated concept, the result of a long process of development. Its roots are probably in the ancient institution of holy war. Warriors were commanded to have confidence in God's protection, not to fear or let their hearts become weak (Deut. 20.3). This idea of trust or confidence in God's protection in battle did not become the truly biblical concept of faith until it was taken over by prophecy, from which it passed into the Deuteronomic-covenantal tradition and from thence into the other major traditions of biblical religion. Diagnostic of the idea of faith in its biblical form is that it has not only a primary object, God, but also a secondary one, the prophet. Moreover, the trust it demands is total and unconditional. This is the sort of faith Isaiah demanded of King Ahaz (Isa. 7.9): "If you do not have faith you will not be established!" (The Heb is a play on words, and says literally, "If you do not display firmness you will not be made firm.") The faith demanded here is not only that God will rescue Judah in a time of grave peril, but that Ahaz must also believe Isaiah is a true, not a false prophet. The sign of Immanuel (Isa. 7.14–17) that Isaiah gives Ahaz is unique, a test rather than a confirmation of confidence. Biblical faith involves absolute trust in the prophet as well as in God. This was later transmuted into faith in the authenticity of the textual record of past revelation. This mediated type of faith is the essential uniting core of all forms and all major traditions of biblical religion, and the unique contribution of biblical religion to world religion.

Faith, in the sense just described, pervades the whole Bible. Gen. has been edited to represent a struggle for faith on the part of the patriarchs, especially Abraham, who proves his faith only with the binding of Isaac. The narratives of the rest of the Torah record the people's struggle to maintain absolute trust in God, a test they repeatedly fail, despite the prevalence of overwhelming miracles. The prophets wrestle with faith constantly, especially with faith in the fact that they themselves are true and not deluded false prophets. Job, whatever the exact meaning of the book, certainly implies faith in divine Providence, despite all evidence to the contrary. The Ps., especially the petitions of the individual, represent the struggle for firm, if not unquestioning, conviction despite suffering, doubts, and inner weakness. This biblical faith has as its locus a new kind of religious individual, the believing self, united in its devotion to the Deity. The tension between the faith-filled self, its own doubts, and the new type of community of believers posited by biblical religion as the true "Israel," is what gives the Bible its paradoxical unity in disparity, and its great religious power.

[STEPHEN A. GELLER]

Concepts of Purity in the Bible

As in many religious traditions past and present, ancient Israelites categorized persons, places, and other things as "holy" *(kodesh)* or "common" *(ḥol)* and as "pure" *(tahor)* or "impure" *(tame')* (Lev. 10.10). These sets of categories are not identical: What is pure is not necessarily holy, nor is the common necessarily impure. Moreover, ancient Israel had multiple conceptions of purity, each of which developed over time, possibly under the influence of distinct religious ideologies. One notion of impurity, moral impurity, concerned the dangers of defilement associated with grave sins such as idolatry, incest, and murder. Another notion of impurity, ritual impurity, concerned contact with various natural substances relating to birth, death, and genital discharges. Contact with ritual impurity had serious consequences in one's religious life, rendering one temporarily unfit to encounter holy space and objects. To understand and appreciate these distinctions is a challenge for modern readers who are accustomed to looking down on hierarchy in general and to scoffing at seemingly irrational avoidances, especially when they pertain to death and sex.

In the early days of modern biblical scholarship, conceptions of defilement were treated with outright scorn. James Frazer (1854–1941) and William Robertson Smith (1846–1894), two founders of modern anthropology, could barely conceal their disgust for the avoidance behaviors of the Jewish Bible. Smith, Frazer, and others approached purity rules as if they were a random collection of primitive taboos. Their origin lay in savage fears of blood and demons; their preservation by Israel was simply a matter of perpetuating ancient custom. Making matters worse, Sigmund Freud (1856–1939) in *Totem and Taboo* famously compared religious avoidances with the obsessive behavior of psychotics. Whether they were seen as the products of primitive fears or primeval obsessions, ritualized avoidances were dismissed by many as irrational, pointless, and just plain foolish.

The situation changed dramatically only in the 1960s. Under the influence of structural anthropology in general and the works of Mary Douglas (1921–2007) in particular, biblical scholars began approaching purity rules in new ways. Scholars came to recognize that avoidance behaviors could no longer be dismissed as something inherently or distinctly primitive. Many societies draw boundaries around certain behaviors (esp. when it comes to death and sex), and these boundaries are certainly not always rational. Second, scholars also began to recognize that the avoidances of any religious tradition or culture had to be treated *systemically* or *structurally*. While earlier scholars would collect and analyze taboos in an encyclopedic fashion—comparing, for instance, various cultures' attitudes toward blood or hair—scholars would now focus on how the avoidance rules of any single culture work together to form a coherent conception of things permitted and prohibited, of things sacred and defiled.

A third important development was the willingness of scholars to recognize that a system of avoidance behaviors may be symbolic in nature. Where earlier scholars had assumed that the laws must be connected to primitive notions of health or hygiene, scholars now recognize that there might be more to these rules than a simple desire to avoid dirt or disease. In line with this perspective, scholars are increasingly translating the Heb terms *tame'* and *tahor* as "impure" and "pure," instead of as "unclean" and "clean."

Yet some interpretive challenges remain. One error introduced under the influence of some anthropologists is the assumption that the ancient Israelite purity system was put in place in order for priests to subordinate

Israelites and for Israelite men to subordinate their wives and daughters. Yet it is increasingly recognized that the ancient Israelite purity system affects men and women, priests and Israelites. While Israelite society was hierarchical and patriarchal, the ritual purity system did little to enforce these social demarcations; in any case, this certainly was not the system's primary purpose. Another common error is the identification of ritual impurity with sinfulness. The distinction between ritual and moral purity—also increasingly recognized by scholars—allows us to see better the complex relationship between impurity and sin.

Ritual Impurity

The bulk of the biblical purity laws concerns the situations and substances that render one ritually impure, and therefore temporarily unfit to encounter the sacred. Ritual impurity results from direct or indirect contact with any one of a number of natural sources or processes including childbirth (Lev. 12.1–8), certain skin diseases (13.1–46; 14.1–32), funguses in clothes (13.47–59) and houses (14.33–53), genital discharges (15.1–33), the carcasses of certain impure animals (11.1–47), and human corpses (Num. 19.1–22). Paradoxically, ritual impurity also comes about as a byproduct of some sacrificial procedures (Lev. 16.28; Num. 19.7–8). The durations of these impurities differ, as do the requisite cleansing processes. In general, however, there are three distinct characteristics of ritual impurity: (1) The sources of ritual impurity are natural and more or less unavoidable. (2) It is not sinful to contract these impurities. (3) These impurities can convey an impermanent contagion to people (priests and Israelites) and to many items within close proximity.

That the sources of ritual impurity are natural is really quite clear. Birth, death, sex, disease, and discharge are part of life. Ritual impurity is also generally unavoidable. While certain defiling substances are relatively avoidable (e.g., touching carcasses), others are inescapable (discharge, disease, and death). Some ritual impurities are not just inevitable, but obligatory. All Israelites (priests included) are obligated to reproduce (Gen. 1.28; 9.7). All Israelites (except the high priest) are required to bury their deceased close relatives (Lev. 21.10–15; cf. 21.1–4). Priests are also obligated to perform cultic procedures that result in their defilement (Lev. 16.28; Num. 19.8).

It is not a sin to contract these ritual impurities. This idea proceeds logically from the observations drawn above. While priests must limit their contact with corpse impurity (Lev. 21.1–4), they are not prohibited from contracting other impurities (22.3–7). To be sure, priests and non-priests alike are sternly warned against eating sacred food or entering sacred precincts when in a state of ritual impurity (Lev. 7.19–21; 22.3–7), lest they defile holy food or space. Yet the primary concern incumbent upon the priests is not to avoid ritual impurity at all times, but to safeguard the separation between ritual impurity and purity (Lev. 10.10; cf. Ezek. 44.23). By extension, Israelites are obliged to remain aware of their ritual status, lest they accidentally come into contact with the sacred while in a state of ritual impurity (Lev. 15.31). Because ritual impurity is contagious, the danger here is that defilement if left unchecked will accumulate and defile the Tabernacle or Temple, rendering it impure and unfit for divine habitation. It is for this reason that the refusal to purify oneself would constitute a transgression (Num. 19.20). But this does not make being ritually impure sinful in and of itself. As long as Israelites remain aware of their status and avoid contact with the Temple and holy objects while impure—and do what is necessary to ameliorate the situation—there is little chance of danger or transgression.

A few biblical narratives nevertheless view at least one form of ritual defilement as a punishment for moral shortcomings. Miriam was afflicted with a "leprous" or "scale" ailment when she spoke against Moses' Cushite wife (Num. 12.10); the Judean King Uzziah was similarly afflicted when he sinfully asserted priestly prerogatives (2 Chron. 26.16–21). But viewing one particular skin disease as a possible punishment for sin is not tantamount to viewing ritual impurity as sinful in and of itself. If it were, the sinner would be defiling even without the manifestation of a defiling affliction. Thus the following claim still stands: It is not sinful to be ritually impure, and ritual impurity does not result directly from sin.

The third characteristic of ritual impurity is that it conveys to persons (priests and Israelites, men and women) an impermanent contagion. This is obviously true of the ritual impurity that Israelites contract from direct or indirect contact with a ritually impure carcass or another ritually impure Israelite. In such a case, the period of defilement can be as brief as less than one day, until the setting of the sun (Lev. 11.24; 15.7; Num. 19.22). The same holds for persons who engage in permitted sexual relations (Lev. 15.16–18). A man who has sexual contact with a menstruant or a person who comes into contact with a corpse will be ritually impure for a week (Lev. 15.24; Num. 19.11). Other defiling conditions can result in even longer periods of defilement; for example, the ritual impurity following childbirth lasts, in its less severe form, either thirty-three or sixty-six days (Lev. 12.1–8). Finally, irregular genital flows (for both men and women), scale disease, and house funguses last an unspecified amount of time. But even these forms of impurity are conceived of as impermanent—that is why the biblical tradition records purificatory procedures for all of them. There is no form of ritual impurity that does not have purificatory procedures; they may include waiting until sundown, bathing, washing clothes, and performing sacrificial rites. Even when long-lasting, the status of ritual defilement is an impermanent one.

Clearly, ritual impurity cannot be understood simply as a concern with health or hygiene. There is no direct correspondence between what is unhealthy or unclean and what is impure. Some sources of impurity (such as a pig's carcass) may strike some as dirty in some way. But some things that even ancient Israelites considered to be dirty were not necessarily ritually defiling: Excrement, human and animal, is not impure according to the Priestly system described in the Torah, despite the fact that it was recognized to be dirty and contrary to holiness (Deut. 23.13–15; but cf. Ezek. 4.12–15).

The idea that ancient Israelites viewed what is unhealthy as impure finds only scant support in Lev. chs 13–14, which discuss the ritual impurity that results from various obscure skin diseases and other funguses. Other biblical texts suggest that ancient Israelites knew about all sorts of diseases. If the concern with purity were the concern with health, we would expect all known diseases to be defiling. Yet only one kind of illness is defiling, and it defiles even when it affects a house or clothing, without affecting people. The concern in Lev. chs 13–14 is not with the spreading of the disease so much as with the spreading of impurity. All who come into contact with what is deemed "leprous" are impure, and are so for a day, whether or not they show signs of the disease.

It is also commonly believed that the dietary prohibitions extend from rules concerning health. (This view can be traced back, in part, to the medieval Jewish philosopher and physician Moses Maimonides.) This is nowhere explicit in biblical texts. Furthermore, while this is arguably true of certain defiling foods (e.g., pork), there is no known health risk associated with the majority of defiling land animals and birds. On the other hand, there are many known health risks associated with the consumption of various plants, but not even poisonous plants are viewed as defiling. There is, in the end, no direct association between health and purity, or between disease and defilement.

It can also be clearly seen now that ritual impurity is not a system put into place in order for priests to subordinate Israelites or for men to subordinate women. The subordination of classes—where it exists—needs to be supported by permanent or at least long-lasting social stigmas that are selective in such a way as to support the intended social agenda. Ritual impurity, however, is impermanent and applies to all Israelites—men and women, priests and laypersons. The system is therefore not well suited to reinforce any specific social hierarchies.

Traditional Judaism—in both the medieval and modern periods—has been primarily interested in the ritual impurity associated with menstruation. For a variety of reasons, this remains the only aspect of the biblical ritual impurity system that was maintained for very long after the destruction of the Second Temple in 70 CE. But the Bible knows of no such selective focus. In Lev., genital flows from both men and women are sources of ritual defilement. "Leprous" impurities affect men and women equally, and the corpses of men and women equally constitute the most severe form of ritual defilement.

Even in the case of defilements pertaining to women, it is difficult to understand the rules as intending to subordinate them or exclude them. One must bear in mind that women would only experience menstrual impurity after puberty, before menopause, and when not pregnant or lactating. For most ancient Israelite women, periodic ritual defilement was probably not a monthly affair. Moreover, the procedures of ritual purification require women to come into the sanctuary and to actively participate in sacrificial procedures (Lev. 12.6–8). If the rules were meant to exclude women, one should wonder why rituals of purification serve to bring women into the sanctuary.

If ritual impurity is not directly related to sin, health, or hygiene, or the desire to subordinate laypersons or women, what then is its basis?

The common denominators of the varied sources of ritual defilement are death and sex. Concerns with death-avoidance explain the defilements associated with corpses, carcasses, and the loss of reproductive genital fluids. Death-avoidance can also explain the concern with the skin disease, which is explicitly described as decomposition of the flesh (Num. 12.12). Yet death-avoidance on its own does not explain why sex and birth defile. The only substances that flow from the body and defile are sexual/genital in nature. (Even blood flowing from the veins of a dying person is not ritually defiling.) The dual concerns with death and sex provide the basis for understanding all of the ritual purity rules.

The ritual purity system of ancient Israel serves to force a separation between the experience of encountering God's sanctity and matters pertaining to death and sex. Because God is eternal, God does not die. Because God has no consort, God does not have sex. Therefore, by separating from sex and death—by following the ritual purity regulations—ancient Israelites separated themselves from what made them least God-like. Only a heightened God-like state—the state of ritual purity—made one temporarily eligible to approach the sanctuary, God's holy residence among the Israelites (Exod. 24.8). Following the ritual purity laws is yet another way of behaving in accordance with the theological underpinning of the Holiness Collection: *imitatio Dei* (Lev. 11.44–45; 19.2; 20.7, 26).

Ritual impurity is for these reasons diametrically opposed to holiness. And as noted, ritual purity—the established absence of any ritual defilement—is the prerequisite for encountering God's holy presence, as manifest in the Tabernacle or the Temple. But this formula is not reversible: The lack of holiness does not necessarily constitute ritual impurity. There are in fact four possible states. At either end of the spectrum are the diametrically opposed statuses of ritual impurity and holiness. In between the extremes are two intermediary—and in many cases, overlapping—positions. Working in from one end, in the absence of impurity one can be considered to be pure *(tahor)*. Working in from the other end, in the absence of holiness one can be considered to be "common" *(ḥol)* (Lev. 10.10). It has been emphasized that the prohibitions related to ritual impurity primarily involve the dangers associated with bringing what is impure into contact with what is holy. It remains permitted for pure and impure persons and things to commingle in non-holy, "common" space. For instance, when Israelites consumed food that was permitted but not sacrificial (and thus not holy), ritually pure and impure persons were permitted to consume such food together (Deut. 12.15).

It is difficult to know how widely these regulations were followed in ancient Israel. They are reflected in detail only in Priestly literature, and in related texts such as Ezek. Priestly material is particularly concerned with these issues, since priests were responsible for the ritual purity of the Temple. References to ritual impurity can nonetheless be identified in a variety of other texts (e.g., Deut. 23.11–12; 2 Sam. 11.4; Isa. 52.11). Ritual purity should not therefore be understood as an issue of concern only to priests.

Moral Impurity

As noted above, the Bible is concerned with another form of purity and impurity, often referred to as "moral." (Some scholars draw this distinction in different terms, speaking of "permitted" [ritual] and "prohibited" [moral] impurities.) Moral impurity results from committing certain acts so heinous that they are considered defiling. Such behaviors include certain sexual sins (e.g., Lev. 18.24–30), idolatry (e.g., 19.31; 20.1–3), and bloodshed (e.g., Num. 35.33–34). These "abominations" bring about an impurity that *morally*—but not *ritually*—defiles the sinner (Lev. 18.24), the land of Israel (Lev. 18.25; Ezek. 36.17), and the sanctuary of God (Lev. 20.3; Ezek. 5.11). This defilement, in turn, leads to the expulsion of the people from the land of Israel (Lev. 18.28; Ezek. 36.19). The bulk of the references to these ideas can be found in Priestly traditions (esp. the Holiness Collection) and in the most Priestly of prophetic books, Ezek. Additional articulations of the notion or echoes of it can be found in various strands of biblical tradition, including Gen. 34.5; Deut. 24.1–4; 1 Kings 14.24; Jer. 2.7, 23; 3.1; Hos. 5.6; 6.10; and Ps. 106.34–40.

There are seven important differences between moral and ritual impurity.

(1) While ritual impurity is generally not sinful, moral impurity is a direct consequence of grave sin.

(2) A characteristic feature of moral impurity is its deleterious effect on the land of Israel. Ritual impurity, in contrast, may threaten the sanctity of the Temple, but poses no threat to the land.

(3) While ritual impurity often results in a contagious defilement, there is no personal contact-contagion associated with moral impurity. Moral impurity does defile the sinners themselves (Lev. 18.24; 19.31; cf. Gen. 34.5; Deut. 24.1–4). But one need not bathe subsequent to direct or indirect contact with an idolater, a murderer, or an individual who committed a sexual sin.

(4) While ritual impurity results in an impermanent defilement, moral impurity leads to a long-lasting, if not permanent, degradation of the sinner and, eventually, of the land of Israel.

(5) While ritual impurity can be ameliorated by rites of purification, that is not the case for moral impurity. Moral purity is achieved by punishment, atonement, or, best of all, by refraining from committing morally impure acts in the first place.

(6) Since moral impurity does not produce ritual defilement, sinners—in contrast to those who are ritually impure—are not excluded from the sanctuary. In the case of the suspected adulteress (Num. 5.11–31), the woman is brought into the sanctuary itself in order to determine her moral status. It also appears that Israelite murderers sought sanctuary *in the sanctuary* (Exod. 21.14; cf. 1 Kings 1.50–53; 2.28–30). Moral impurity does indeed defile the sacred precincts (e.g., Lev. 20.3), but the effect of moral impurity does

BIBLICAL IMPURITIES

Type	Source	Effect	Resolution
Ritual	Bodily flows, corpses, etc.	Temporary, contagious defilement of persons and objects	Bathing, waiting
Moral	Sins: idolatry, sexual transgression, bloodshed	Long-lasting defilement of sinners, land, and sanctuary	Atonement or punishment, and ultimately, exile

not penetrate the holy realm by the entrance of sinners into it. Moral impurity is a potent force unleashed by sinful behavior that affects the sanctuary even from afar, in its own way.

(7) In addition to these phenomenological differences between ritual and moral defilements, there are also terminological distinctions drawn in the texts themselves. Although the term "impure" *(tame')* is used in both contexts, the terms "abomination" *(to'evah)* and "pollute" *(ḥanaf)* are used with regard to the sources of moral impurity, but not with regard to the sources of ritual impurity. For all of these reasons, it is imperative to distinguish between moral and ritual impurity.

Ritual and Moral Impurities

For reasons that are not entirely clear, the passages that articulate the idea of moral impurity are often understood as metaphors. Metaphor is a complex phenomenon; even its definition is still debated by linguists and philosophers. According to some, metaphor is so pervasive that it could accurately be argued that all rituals involve metaphor on one level or another. But when scholars refer to moral impurity in particular as metaphorical, the implication is that the passage is not to be taken literally: The defilement in question is not real. There is, however, no reason why the defilement of the land by blood shed upon it (Num. 35.33–34) ought to be a metaphor, while the defilement of a person who merely enters a tent in which a corpse lies is real (Num. 19.14). Though the sources and modes of transfer of moral and ritual impurity differ, we are dealing, nonetheless, with two analogous *perceptions of contagion,* each of which brings about effects of religious, legal, and social consequence. There are indeed differences between ritual and moral defilements. But the difference between ritual and moral defilement is not accurately understood by describing one (ritual impurity) as literal and the other (moral impurity) as metaphorical.

The ritual impurity rules constitute a set of avoidances that symbolically express the notion of *imitatio Dei.* The moral impurity rules constitute a set of danger beliefs, and the symbolism involved here works differently. When ancient Israelites believed that the land and sanctuary were defiled by idolatry, sexual sin, and murder, they believed that God finds these behaviors so abhorrent that He would not and could not abide on a land that is saturated with residue left by their performance. It is precisely this ramification of moral defilement that is depicted quite dramatically in Ezek. chs 8–11. Upon Israel's performance of grave sins, God's "glory" departs from the sanctuary and Israel's exile then ensues. The doctrine of moral defilement underscores the fact that grave sins affect not only their perpetrators and victims, but also Israelite society as a whole. If God cannot abide in His earthly sanctuary because it has been defiled, then all Israel will suffer exile together.

Purity Disputes in Ancient Judaism

Disputes among Jews with regard to the nature and force of the purity laws are in evidence throughout the Second Temple period. Purity debates among Pharisees and Sadducees are preserved in the Mishnah (*m. Yad.* 4:6–7), and heightened concerns with purity are also characteristic of the sectarian literature discovered at Qumran. In the Dead Sea Scrolls we find stricter rules concerning ritual impurity in the *Temple Scroll* (11QSTemple), and stricter rules concerning moral impurity in, especially, the *Community Rule* (1QS). And some important Dead Sea texts (e.g., again, the 1QS) display a blending of the notions of ritual and moral impurity, such that sinners were considered ritually impure and moral purity achieved, in part, by water rites. Early Christianity was characterized, among other things, by a heightened interest in certain aspects of moral purity over and against a reduced focus on ritual purity (e.g., Mark 7.1–23). The later Rabbis, operating in the middle of this spectrum, exerted much more effort in discussing the rules of ritual purity (to which much of the Mishnah is devoted), while exhibiting less interest in moral defilement (but see *Sifra* on Lev. 18.24–30). Unlike the Christians of their day, the Rabbis maintained interests in both ritual and moral purity; and unlike the earlier sectarians, the Rabbis struggled to maintain distinctions between the two notions.

One purity dispute in particular is already reflected in the early Second Temple period, and the documents pertaining to the dispute can be found within the Bible. During the Persian period, both Ezra and Nehemiah confronted situations in which a number of the Jews had married local non-Jewish women. Both Ezra and Nehemiah urged the dissolution of these marriages (Ezra 9.1–10.44; Neh. 13.23–31). It is rather clear that purity in some form was at issue. Terms of defilement are used with reference to the problem (Ezra 6.21; 9.1, 11–14), and the proposed solution—divorce—is referred to as a purification (Neh. 13.30). This has led many scholars to the view that these books considered the foreign wives to be ritually impure, presumably as the result of their status as Gentiles. The passages in question, however, echo not the Priestly traditions relating to ritual impurity, but the Holiness Collection traditions relating to moral impurity: What is being said here by Ezra, Nehemiah, and their supporters is that the foreign women are in an inherent state of moral defilement and that inevitably the defilement will be passed to their progeny as well.

The view of Ezra and Nehemiah met with considerable opposition. The book of Ruth, according to some interpretations, effectively counters the prejudiced perspective of Ezra-Neh., as do various Second Temple prophetic passages (Isa. 56.3–8). When one looks back at the Priestly traditions on these matters, it also becomes clear that Ezra's position is by no means clearly articulated there. One can find in the Torah limited prohibitions of intermarriage (e.g., Deut. 7.1–5) and even passages ascribing moral impurity to foreigners (e.g., Lev. 18.24). Yet one cannot find a clear, Priestly prohibition of intermarriage, justified by appeal to the notion of moral defilement (cf. Ezra 9.11–12). This may reflect the fact that the prohibition only emerged in the Second Temple period. Alternatively, this may reflect the continuing influence of Ezra's Priestly opponents, who certainly had a more welcoming attitude toward foreigners. Looking back on the Torah from the vantage point of Ezra ch 9, one can imagine a group of priests maintaining strong systems of ritual and moral purity while at the same time establishing a society with relatively open social boundaries.

The biblical traditions, from Lev. to Ezra, leave a legacy that is not only challenging to contemporary scholars, but was likely equally challenging to ancient Jews themselves—giving rise to the purity disputes of the Second Temple period. When evaluating purity disputes among various ancient Jewish groups (early Christians included), it is imperative to understand well the complex and symbolic character of the purity systems, and it is equally important to appreciate the distinct natures of the ritual and moral purity systems. The purity rules are often disparaged as blunt instruments of social control, put in place by the priestly few to enforce their hegemony over laypersons and women. Alternatively, some still see purity rules as vestiges from primitive times. The challenge is to recognize purity rules (of the ritual and moral sort) as meaningful and yet nuanced ways of highlighting issues of social and theological significance.

[JONATHAN KLAWANS]

Daily Life in Biblical Times

This essay provides an overview of the day to day living of ordinary people in ancient Israel, focusing on both rural and urban lifestyles, general household and life cycles, the arts and literacy.

Rural Life

Throughout the pre-monarchal and monarchal periods (ca. 1200–586 BCE), most Israelites lived in small towns, villages, and farmsteads. Their livelihood depended mostly on tilling the land and herding. Most families were self-sufficient, sometimes producing small amounts of surplus to exchange for items of necessity. The social structure was patrilineal and patrilocal; that is, the father was the head of the household, inheritance was through male descendants, and upon marriage the newlywed couple resided in the groom's father's house.

The Village: Physical Layout

Villages, as well as towns, were built on uncultivable land, on an elevated spot that provided a certain amount of security. They were located close to a water source, not far from the fields, and in close proximity to a road leading to the close by town and its markets. When a water source was unavailable or insufficient, cisterns were constructed to catch and store run-off rainwater. Villages were ring-shaped, agglomerated or farmsteads. In ring-shaped villages several houses were built around the perimeter, with a low-lying wall marking the limits of the settlement and serving as a fence to keep the animals in. Sometimes the houses were built next to each other with the outer wall forming a perimeter wall. Agglomerated villages were formed by constructing house complexes indiscriminately, leaving open spaces and "streets" of varying width in between. Farmsteads contained a single building or a group of buildings with a surrounding perimeter wall. In all of these structures, the gate to the settlement, and the open area surrounding the gate, were public space used for transacting public business, including commercial and judicial proceedings.

The common house during the Israelite (preexilic) period, whether in the village or the city, was the "Four-Room House" or the "Pillared House." These terms stem from certain architectural elements typical to this structure. The "Four-Room House" is a misnomer; it contains three long rooms with a broad room in the back. Entrance to the house was gained generally through the middle long room. These are also called "Pillared Houses" based on the two rows of three to four monolithic pillars that ran between the two side rooms and the central room. When monoliths were not available, the pillars were made of stacked large stones, or "drums." The size of the pillars, the thickness of the outer walls, stairs, and the remains found inside indicate that these houses had an upper floor, and thus more than four rooms. Whether the central room was open or roofed and what the configuration of the house was (esp. the second floor) is debated. Space and other factors sometimes dictated that some houses had fewer than four rooms.

The side rooms of the house were divided by thin, low curtain-walls, forming smaller rooms that created spaces devoted to various activities such as storage, textile production, etc. Some rooms were cobbled and were used for stabling animals—a few sheep or goats, a donkey, or even a cow. Food preparation took place on the ground floor, and archeologists have recovered remains of grinding, cooking and baking installations and associated ceramic vessels and tools. The second floor was the family's living quarters. In the summer, the family might sleep on the flat roof.

Most houses accommodated an extended family, which included three generations (grandparents, nuclear family with children, unmarried members of the family) joined by hired hands and/or slaves.

Sociopolitical Structure of the Village

Villages were occupied by nuclear families known as *bet ʾab*, "the house of the father," that belonged to a larger kinship group, *mishpaḥa*, "the clan." The latter belonged to a larger unit, *shevet/matteh*, "tribe."

The head of the household (the father) had authority over the household and was responsible for law and order as well as all economic decisions, sometimes together with the mother. The heads of the households within the village or town constituted the council of the elders, who were charged in making judicial decisions and other matters that could not be handled within the family. The parents were responsible for the education and training of their children; the young children who stayed at home were mostly educated by the mother who carried out mostly house-related duties. Education was comprised of practical matters, and did not typically include training in reading and writing.

The Economy

The economy was agrarian and most households were largely self-sufficient, though bartering for commodities they could not produce. During the period of the settlement (ca. 1200–1000 BCE) the Israelites practiced subsistence agriculture; during the monarchical period new opportunities, such as trade, were introduced. The unification of the land under a central government enabled the more efficient exchange of goods and commodities, and the improvement of means of production, such as the introduction of the beam press for oil pressing, facilitated the creation of surplus for trade. The extensive implementation of land-use methods such as terraces in the hill country and runoff agriculture in semi-arid regions like the Negev helped extend agriculture into previously uncultivated areas.

Agriculture

Agriculture was the mainstay of the Israelite economy. The farmer's primary occupation was cultivating and processing field crops, followed by fruit trees, vegetables and herbs. Cereals, chiefly wheat and barley, were the most prevalent field crops, supplemented by legumes, including peas, chickpeas, grasspeas, broad beans, and fenugreek. Other crops included millet, flax, sesame, and spices including dill, cumin, black cumin, coriander, and marjoram. Produce such as cucumbers, water- and muskmelons, leeks, onions, garlic, and gourds were cultivated mainly in plots close to the house.

A major agricultural undertaking was the cultivation of fruit trees and the processing of their byproducts. The most important fruit trees common to the region were grape vines and olive trees, which produced wine and oil, respectively. Other fruit trees included fig, pomegranate, date, sycamore, carob, black mulberries, and a variety of nuts including almonds, pistachios, and walnuts.

Agriculture is a seasonal occupation determined by the types of plants cultivated and the times during the year in which they were planted, cared for, ripened and harvested. The Bible provides us with the names of agricultural seasons but does not mention their order or length. The Gezer Calendar (see below, Literacy), a seven-line document in early Phoenician/Heb script, outlines the various agricultural chores, their order and approximate length. The beginning and end of the agricultural seasons were celebrated with feasts (pilgrimage holidays): Passover *(pesaḥ),* Weeks *(shavu'ot),* and Tabernacles or Ingathering (*sukkot* or *'asip*).

Herding

The second most important economical endeavor was herding, of both the seminomadic and sedentary types. In the former, shepherds led their animals on seasonal grazing expeditions along a prescribed circuit within a given territory while maintaining a home base; in the latter, they were part of a village community that was involved in herding to a limited extent mostly for its own consumption. Even when sedentary herding was practiced, the need to feed and water the animals forced the shepherds out of the settlement in search of grazing land and water sources.

The two most frequently herded animals were sheep and goats. Other animals, such as cattle or donkeys, were kept in small numbers as draft and transport animals. Sheep and goats were valued for their byproducts: milk for several dairy products, meat, bones for tools and other objects, wool and hair for textile production, and skins for use as liquid containers and footwear.

Other occupations

The Israelites developed various skills or crafts that for some turned into full-time occupations. Among these crafts were pottery making, textile production, dyeing, tanning, carpentry, masonry, and metallurgy.

Transport

Moving materials and people from one place to another was done mostly by donkeys and mules, though at times camels and horses were also employed. The use of pack animals was necessary because of the hilly terrain and the lack of wide roads. Wagons and carts were used only in a limited way where appropriate roads were available. Cattle were utilized mostly in agricultural work such as plowing and threshing; however, textual and artistic evidence show that they were needed also to pull vehicles.

Seafaring

The Israelites were not, by and large, seafaring people although a few biblical references (e.g., Judg. 5.17) suggest that some Israelites were engaged in this endeavor. For much of the First Temple period, the Philistines controlled access to the Mediterranean coast, and the Phoenicians dominated maritime activities in the Mediterranean during the biblical period (see Ezek. chs 27–28). 1 Kings records that King Solomon cooperated with the Phoenicians in some expeditions to secure raw materials and other exotic items.

Urban life

The rise of the monarchy influenced the development of urban life in ancient Israel. Centralized government required an administration that could control collection of taxes, public works, and the defense of the country.

The City – Physical Layout

Several features differentiated cities from villages. Cities were planned and had fortifications that included walls, sloping ramparts *(glacis),* gate complexes, moats, etc. They had public structures such as storage facilities, administrative and religious centers, water systems, and more. While the ordinary people lived in the typical pillared house (see above), the nobility lived in mansions and palaces.

Population

Cities had larger populations than villages and towns. While the population in the village was of homogeneous background, the city had an ethnic mixture since the city served as a commercial hub that attracted people from various regions. The local population was hierarchical and included bureaucrats, religious functionaries, military commanders and the like, all of whom made up the nobility that were served by the common people who carried out the daily chores.

While it is hard to estimate the size of the population of a particular site or region, fluctuations can be observed and connected with trends; for example, the increase of population in the hill country during the Iron Age I (1200–1000 BCE) is related to the appearance of the Israelites, while a decrease in the number of villages in the hill country at the end of this period is attributed to the rise of the monarchy and migration to the cities. Likewise, the increase of population in Jerusalem at the end of the 8th c. BCE is attributed to a migration of refugees from the north after the fall of the Northern Kingdom of Israel.

The Economy

The move from rural to urban life also caused a change in the economic system of the newly formed communities. While in the pre-monarchical and in the monarchical periods villages were self-sufficient, urban settlements were made of non-productive populations (e.g., administration, military) that needed outside support. This was achieved by the creation of tax collecting and distribution systems that were supervised by the monarchy; this in turn established the hierarchical order of towns and cities. An example of the tax collecting system is documented by the Samaria Ostraca, which records contributions made by individuals and estates to the crown, in this case the Northern Kingdom. The *LMLK* (ancient Heb seals) stamped jar handles illustrate a commodities distribution system by the central government in the Southern Kingdom of Judah. These systems provided for the non-productive segments of Israelite society that lived mostly in the urban centers.

Household and Life Cycles

The *bet ʿab* (see above) was the basic social unit dominating Israelite society. Loyalty was first to the family, which was the engine driving all aspects of life including the economy, social and legal matters, and rites of passage.

Diet

Recent interest in nutrition led to the awareness of the so-called Mediterranean diet. This brought the publication of popular as well as scholarly works related to the topic of the ancient Israelite cuisine. The Israelite diet contained baked goods, dairy products, vegetables, herbs, fruits and their byproducts, and small amounts of meat and fish. Bread, made of wheat or barley, was the basic and constant element of every meal, though other baked goods were eaten as well. Other field crops, such as legumes (peas, beans, etc.), used mainly in stews or gruels, were also a common part of the meal. Food was spiced with salt that had to be imported and with domesticated and wild herbs. Vegetables—including cucumbers, onions, garlic, greens—and melons, were available only in season. Dairy products, such as fresh milk, butter, and yogurt were available while fresh and dry cheese was available year round.

Fruit—including figs, pomegranates, grapes, apricots, dates, apples, carob—were available in season; some were processed either as wine or as dried fruit (raisins) and could be eaten throughout the year. Olives were used only for their oil since treating olives for consumption was unknown till later times.

Sources of meat included domestic (beef, veal, mutton, lamb) and wild animals. The latter included fowl, deer, and fish. While pork was available, archeological evidence indicates that the Israelites, like some other surrounding ethnic groups in this period, did not eat pork. Meat of domestic animals was eaten only on special occasions such as festivals, and the most common preparation was by boiling it, though roasting was also practiced. Preserving meat is not mentioned in the Hebrew Bible, but is known to have been practiced in the ancient world, especially in Egypt, and involved salting, drying, and smoking. However, it seems that the preferable way of meat consumption for the Israelites was to have it during family gatherings when the whole animal could be consumed.

Storage

Surplus of byproducts (grain, wine, oil, dried fruit) had to be stored for future use. Individuals stored their goods in jars in storerooms at the house, and in stone-lined storage pits. The central government stored the commodities produced on royal estates or collected as taxes in jars in storehouses, mostly tripartite pillared buildings, and in silos. These commodities were used to maintain the royal house and pay functionaries such as priests, the bureaucracy, and the military.

Food Preparation

Preparing food was a daily chore. In the home, women were the cooks and they started the day by grinding grain for flour and baking bread. Grinding was done by placing the grain between two stones and moving the upper one back and forth to produce flour; this could take several hours a day. The Israelites ate three meals daily, one in the morning, one at midday, and the main meal in the evening at the conclusion of the workday when the whole family had returned to the house. Food was prepared on the ground floor, where installations for grinding, baking, and cooking were located. The shape and size of the cooking pots depended on the type of food prepared. Besides bread, the most common foods were stews, gruels, and soups. All were served in large bowls (kraters) and then distributed to individual small bowls.

Hygiene and Sanitation

Sanitary conditions in antiquity were primitive to non-existent. Refuse was dumped into the street or thrown over the city wall. Very few latrines were recovered archeologically suggesting that relieving was done in the open (see Deut. 23.13–14). These habits affected the quality of the water drawn from cisterns that provided water for drinking, cooking, and washing because they were filled with runoff rainwater from the streets. Lack of running water determined the number of times people could bathe or wash their clothes. Water quality and other unsanitary conditions affected health and quality of life; often wine, rather than water (which might be polluted), was used for drinking.

Health and Sickness

Biblical vocabulary and archeological evidence suggest very strongly that the Israelites suffered from a variety of diseases. Furthermore, many suffered from handicaps (Lev. 21.17–18) while mental illness was also recognized. Incidents of plagues and other devastating epidemics are mentioned in the Bible.

The Israelites identified two sources of sickness: (1) ideological, namely, God's response to disobedience; and (2) close contact with a sick person which led to contagion. To remedy the first, prayer, covenant observance, and sacrifice were prescribed. The second was dealt with by quarantine and sacrifice, both supervised by the priests, who also acted as physicians.

Life Cycles

Several life-cycle events were marked and celebrated; these included birth and circumcision (for boys), coming of age (menstruation for women), marriage, motherhood, death and burial. All of these milestones were observed in the family. Other happenings that did not call for celebration but were marked included levirate marriage, divorce, and widowhood. Old age was recognized as the age of wisdom and entitled those who reached it to become members of "the

Council of the Elders," which had certain social and judicial responsibilities.

Arts

Performing arts and visual arts were part of Israelite culture. The performing arts included playing music, singing, and dancing, in religious and secular contexts. Formal or official performances, carried out by professionals, took place in the central Temple, other religious centers, and in the royal court. Spontaneous performances took place at work, during the execution of mundane chores, and at family gatherings.

The visual arts included works in ivory, clay, metal, stone, mixed media, and graffiti. Ivory carving was done mostly by Phoenician artists inspired by motifs taken from the local and surrounding cultures. These objects were considered luxury items. Clay was used not only to make pottery vessels, but also in the production of cult stands, incense burners, and figurines, the most common of which were the "horse and rider" type and the so-called female pillar figurines. These figurines were most likely used in house shrines. A small number of figurines were made of metal. Stone carving was used to produce scarabaeid stamp seals, cosmetic palettes, and stone weights. Jewelry—rings, earrings, bracelets, and necklaces—were made out of a variety of materials including gold, silver, precious and semi-precious stones. The large pithoi (water jars) found at Kuntillet ʿAjrud, in the south, suggest that some Israelites had artistic talent.

Literacy

Writings in ancient Israel can be divided into private and official, with some overlap between the two. Some scholars suggest that only about one percent of the population of Israel and Judah during the Iron Age was literate. The archeological evidence indicates that literacy was higher in Israel and Judah in the 8th–6th centuries BCE, but it is impossible to assess to what degree. Furthermore, it is hard to tell when literacy began to play a role in ancient Israel. The archeological evidence for literacy includes seals and seal impressions, ostraca, graffiti, monumental inscriptions, and more. This is complemented by some references in the Bible to reading and writing (e.g., Isa. 8.1; 29.11; Jer. 36.2).

Writing was done on a variety of materials including stone, metal, clay, potsherds, wood, papyrus, and leather (sheep, goat, and calf hides). Sometimes, stone walls were coated with plaster and inscribed with ink as attested in the 8th c. sites of Deir ʿAlla (in the Jordan Valley) and Kuntillet ʿAjrud (in the Sinai).

Attempts to learn writing are known from some early inscriptions. Two abecedaries—alphabet written in sequence—are known from ʿIzbet Sartah, an 11th c. BCE small village between the Shephelah and the Coastal Plain, and from Tel Zayit, a 10th c. BCE town in the Shephelah. Both were inscribed in the Phoenician (or early Heb) script. Another early inscription dated to the early 10th c. BCE and considered a writing exercise is the "Gezer Calendar" that according to some scholars was also written in the Phoenician script, forerunner of the Heb script. These examples, together with the abecedary from Kuntillet ʿAjrud, an 8th c. BCE fort/shrine/caravansary on the border between the Sinai and the Negev, illustrate that throughout Israelite history attempts were made by individuals (coached by others) to learn writing.

Some scholars suggest that during the monarchy schools developed for scribes, but if indeed there were such institutions, they were meant for members of the elite class and the bureaucracy. This is well illustrated in Lachish Letter 3 (586 BCE), where the officer Hoshayahu maintains that he had read every letter sent to him (Pritchard 1969:321–22; Hallo and Younger 1996:3:79). However, an 8th c. BCE Jerusalemite tomb belonging to "... yahu, the royal steward" telling tomb-robbers that inside "... there is [he]re no silver or gold ..." may suggest that literacy was not extremely limited.

Amulets, requests for blessings, graffiti, and other inscriptions of a personal nature are examples of private writing. This includes two silver amulets found in the early 6th c. BCE burial caves at Ketef Hinnom. They are inscribed with a text closely resembling Num. 6.24–26: "May YHVH bless you and watch over you! May YHVH make his face shine upon you and grant you peace!" (McCarter 1996:121–22). Other requests for blessings were found inscribed in ink on large pithoi and door-jambs at Kuntillet ʿAjrud and scratched on the walls of a burial cave at el-Qom, in the Hebron Mountains. One inscription from the former site reads: "Message of [...] so[n of] ʿAmaryaw: Speak to my lord.... ʻI bless you by YHVH of Teman and by his Asherah! May he bless you and watch over you and be with my lord...!ʼ" One inscription from el-Qom reads: "Blessed be your stonecutter! May he lay old people to rest in this!" Another inscription there is reminiscent of the one from Kuntillet ʿAjrus: "Belonging to ʿUriyahu, the governor. This is his inscription. Blessed be ʿUriyahu by YHVH: He has been saved from his enemies by his Asherah. (Written) by ʿOniyahu." These suggest that a reasonable number of people not belonging to the elite could read and write.

The "Letter of Complaint" from Mesad Hashavyahu at Yavneh-Yam was probably dictated by an illiterate reaper to a scribe sitting at the entrance to the governor's residence. The worker complains that his garment was confiscated under the pretense that he had not fulfilled his daily quota of work. The complaint echoes the biblical law of Exod. 22.25–26 (see also Deut. 24.12–13). This is probably as close as we can get to hearing the voice of an average Israelite. A document called by modern scholars "The Widow's Plea," the authenticity of which is questioned by some, is very similar and belongs to the same genre.

Other inscriptions reflecting daily use include those found on stone weights and inscriptions made by individuals on pottery before and after firing designating ownership or content.

Official writings include correspondence, record keeping, monumental inscriptions, seals and seal impressions. Examples of official correspondence are the Lachish Letters (McCarter 1996:116–19) and the Arad Ostraca (McCarter 1996:119–20). The Samaria Ostraca (Pritchard 1969:281; McCarter 1996:103–105) illustrate accounting practices that took place at tax collection and commodities distribution centers. Seals and seal impressions illustrate the lively activity related to official business that took place in many aspects of daily life. The *LMLK* ("to/of the king") seal impressions are the best example for monarchical involvement in the economy and politics of the time.

While several monumental inscriptions dedicated by non-Israelite kings are known from biblical times (e.g., Moabite Stone, Tel Dan Inscription, Tel Miqne-Ekron Inscription), only one can be attributed to the Israelites, the Siloam Inscription. This well-executed inscription was discovered in the Siloam (or Hezekiah) Tunnel and commemorates the completion of the project. The location of the inscription, at the end of the tunnel, suggests that it was not meant for public view, and thus should not be considered a typical royal inscription; indeed, it lacks the king's name.

[ODED BOROWSKI]

The Temple

Temples in the Bible and Ancient Near East

Throughout the ancient Near East the major religious institution and locus of encounter between humans and the deity was the temple. Temples were not primarily places of public prayer as are today's synagogues, churches, and mosques, but divine residences; it is therefore preferable to refer to temples of foreign deities by their native nomenclature, "the house of (the divine) X" and to Israel's temples as "the house of God" and "the house of YHVH" (see e.g., 1 Kings 6.37; Ps. 52.10). Some tangible representation of divine presence stood within the temple: a cult statue, a standard, or a symbol. The god present could be worshipped and paid homage by presenting gifts (including animal and vegetable sacrifices), uttering prayers, or simple prostration. Cultic activities performed in Israelite temples were performed "before the LORD," *lifnei* YHVH (e.g., Lev. 1.3); and there was some sort of sign of Divine presence, such as a cult statue in Micah's private temple in Dan, the golden calves in Bethel, Dan and Samaria, the pillars at Arad or Bethel, or the Ark and *Kavod*, "Divine Majesty/Glory," in Shiloh and subsequently in Jerusalem.

Although ordinary citizens were not excluded from the temples, their presence was not obligatory; the cult could go on without them. The regular cult, or the "the caring and feeding of the god," as the Assyriologist A. Leo Oppenheim termed it, was observed by a permanent, professional clergy, according to the Bible, the presiding priests, sons of Eli, Abiathar, Zadok, Levi, Moses, or Aaron. However, temple visits by the public on fixed festivals and sporadic public or private occasions are well attested in biblical literature. So, for example, Elkanah and his family frequent Shiloh, Absalom pays a vow in Hebron, and the people of Israel and Judah make annual pilgrimages individually or en masse to Jerusalem or Bethel.

The Bible indicates that ancient Israel knew several temples at various sites including Shiloh, Nob, Gilgal, Bethel, Shechem, Hebron, Mizpah, and, of course, Jerusalem. Even the Tabernacle, described in Exod., that stood at the center of the Israelite camp during their wilderness wanderings was depicted as a temple. Although it was assembled and disassembled as the Israelites traveled from one desert encampment to the next, it was no different conceptually or functionally from any other House of God. The God of Israel was imagined as present within, and worshipped publicly by a family of priests. A building was uncovered in Arad that was apparently a temple, although it is not mentioned in the Bible, and outside the Land of Israel, in Elephantine in Egypt, documents attest to a temple to YHV the God of Israel.

The First Temple

The most prominent, ancient Israelite House of God was the Temple that, according to the Bible, stood in Jerusalem on Mt. Zion from the time it was built in the 10th c. BCE by King Solomon until destroyed by King Nebuchadrezzar (Nebuchadnezzar) II of Babylon in 586 BCE.

Nothing remains of this Temple, so it may be viewed only from descriptions in the Hebrew Bible, especially in 1 Kings chs 6–7 and in scattered allusions in the book of Kings, the books of prophets of the First Temple period, and perhaps some Ps. The description of the Temple in the book of Chron. is late and imposes on the First Temple certain features of the Tabernacle and perhaps the postexilic, Second Temple. Even so, some relevant information can be gleaned from it as well as from the descriptions of the Tabernacle in

Exod. chs 25–40, and the Temple of the future in Ezekiel's vision (chs 40–48).

Some scholars have claimed that the Jerusalem Temple, if it existed at all, was not built by Solomon and certainly did not resemble the magnificent edifice described in Kings and Chron. Whatever the historical reality may be, the biblical text enables the reader to conjure up a coherent portrait of the Temple as envisaged by the biblical authors; and with the help of ancient Near Eastern artifacts and textual parallels it is possible to reconstruct its form and develop an understanding of its design, significance, and symbolism. It is this biblical image, rather than the real First Temple, which will be the focus of this section; the structure of the real First Temple cannot be recovered beyond what the biblical texts suggest. Furthermore, it is likely that the First Temple was renovated during the hundreds of years it stood (see esp. 2 Kings chs 12 and 22), but any structural changes can no longer be ascertained.

Solomon's Temple, the First Temple, was primarily a luxurious house in which the people worshipped God who dwelled within as a king resided in his palace. The people would frequent the courtyards; the priests would serve God in the court and in the outer sanctum, providing His daily needs; and He would sit in his throne room with supernatural creatures guarding the entrance. The building materials and furnishings of the Temple focused the visitor or onlooker on the divine resident in its midst, sitting on the cherub throne. Inside the House, in the most important place, were the stored tablets of the covenant attesting to the special relationship between the Divine resident and the people of Israel who built the house. The precinct in which the Temple stood was a garden, resembling the garden of Eden, marked by tranquility in nature, and watered by rivers going out of it to irrigate the entire world around it. All this was on a cosmic mountain, linking heaven with earth.

The Bible speaks of "going up" or ascending to Mt. Zion or the Mountain of the LORD. The toponym Zion *(tziyyōn)*, whose meaning remains elusive, originally designated the site of the fortress captured by David where he took up residence and then called it "the City of David," indicating that it was the hill overlooking the royal compound in Jerusalem. In the course of time the term was applied to all of Jerusalem. The Mountain of the LORD is not particularly high, and Ps. 125.2 even states that Jerusalem is surrounded by mountains; but the modest topographic reality need not detract from the emotional experience of the ascent. The prophets Isaiah, Micah, Ezekiel, Second Isaiah, and Deutero-Zechariah, predict that in the end of days, as a result of apocalyptic catastrophes and upheavals, "the Mount of the LORD's House / Shall stand firm above the mountains" (Isa. 2.2). This picture of the future with its ideal Temple reflects the aspirations and desires of the prophets' present; and pilgrims going up to the House of the LORD assumedly felt themselves symbolically uplifted or spiritually ascending a much loftier mountain.

A number of gates provide access to the Temple. We cannot know their description or their number at various times in the First Temple period; but assuming the gates Ezekiel envisions for the future Temple reflect those he saw in the Jerusalem Temple on the eve of its destruction, we see that at some time during its long history the Temple was outfitted with gates resembling those found in excavations at Megiddo and Gezer, dating from the time of Solomon or later.

According to Priestly texts, any ritually pure person could enter the Temple (see the converse in Num. 3.10). Additionally, certain Psalms and prophecies express ethical requirements, which have parallels in temples of other ancient Near Eastern religions. According to Ps. 15:

LORD, who may sojourn in Your tent,
  who may dwell on Your holy mountain?
He who lives without blame,
  who does what is right,
  and in his heart acknowledges the truth;

whose tongue is not given to evil;
who has never done harm to his fellow,
or borne reproach for [his acts toward]
his neighbor;
for whom a contemptible man is
abhorrent,
but who honors those who fear
the LORD;
who stands by his oath even to his hurt;
who has never lent money at interest,
or accepted a bribe against the
innocent.
The man who acts thus shall never be
shaken.

This passage is comparable to an inscription at the entrance to the temple in Edfu in Egypt in which Sheshet, goddess of writing, says to Horus:

I have come before you to write down
before you the ones who do right
and the ones who do wrong:
The one who enters when impure,
and who speaks lies in your house;
The one who distinguishes between
good and bad, the pure one;
The perfect one who walks in
righteousness ... who greatly loves
your servants;
He who receives bribes and covets
the property of your temple;
He who is careful ... the man who doesn't
take from his fellow's portion;
I decree good for he who does good
in your city; I hate the evildoer ...
[He who does righteous] in your house
will last forever; and the sinner will
be eternally destroyed.

How these ethical mandates were enforced is unknown.

Upon entering the Temple compound the worshipper would stand in a large outer court. In the courtyard, people recite prayers and hymns, and prepare or consume sacrifices. This court is paved with large hewn stones, and surrounded by service chambers called *leshakhot* (sg. *lishkah*), used by priests, prophets, and courtiers for eating sacrificial meat, storage, and other functions. Similar structures with like purposes were present at Shiloh, Ramah, and perhaps Dan. Narratives in Jer. and Ezekiel's vision show that by the end of the First Temple's existence there were numerous *leshakhot* that were loci of royal and clerical activity, not of a strictly cultic nature.

Continuing on, one enters the inner court, permitted only to priests (according to Lev.). In this court stands a large, bronze altar for sacrifices and libations. The priests tend the fire on the altar, arrange cuts of sacrificial animals, gather the animal blood, and pour it at the base of the altar using special bronze implements. Under King Ahaz this altar was replaced by one in an Aramaean style; while the older, Solomonic altar was pushed to the side, serving now for special rituals, perhaps divination by extispicy, performed for the king. The old altar was simple, having only a single upper surface and a set of horns, quarter-round protubrances, resembling the bronze altar described for the Tabernacle or the stone altar found in Tel-Sheva (Beersheba). The new altar, which Ezekiel saw as the basis for the altar in the future Temple, is stepped having three stages. It also has horns, and resembles in form and the names of its parts the Mesopotamian stepped temple towers called *ziqqurat*s. Ezekiel's altar had steps leading up to it on the east side, contradicting the law of the altar in Exod. 20.23 and differing from the Tabernacle altar. Whether the original altar in the Temple had such steps is unknown.

The Temple itself stands in the middle of the court. In front of the building, to the right and left of the entrance, stand enormous bronze implements filled with water. Left of the entrance as one faces the building is a huge basin, or Sea *(Yam),* which rests on twelve bronze cattle, four facing each direction of the compass. Along with them are ten immense wheeled stands, or *mekhonot*, made of bronze. Each stand is decorated with lions, cattle, and cherubs, and atop each one rests a bronze basin *(kiyyor).* According to the book of Chron., the *Yam* served for Priestly ablutions, while the smaller basins on the *mekhonot* held water for washing the flesh and entrails of the sacrificial animals.

The number, size, location and decoration of these vessels indicate that they also have a symbolic role, whose meaning is revealed by Ezekiel's concluding vision of the Temple of the future. This future Temple contains no such vessels. Instead, at exactly the place where the Sea stood in Solomon's Temple, Ezekiel (ch 47) sees welling up from under the Temple threshold a steady stream flowing out and down into the *Yam Haʿaravah*, the Dead Sea. But the Dead Sea, after receiving the waters of the stream flowing from the Temple, is no longer dead, that is inimical to life, for this stream is a source of life for animals and plants grazing and growing on its banks, and the stream "heals" the Dead Sea itself into which it flows.

This river of the future, also described by Joel, recalls the river flowing from the garden of Eden (God's private garden) where it watered the garden, and then branched into four streams. If so, the river flowing from Ezekiel's Temple and the bronze water implements in Solomon's Temple symbolized the river flowing forth from the garden of Eden to water the world. Other ancient Near Eastern temples as well had in them streams or waterworks of various sorts. An inscription of Ilu-shuma, king of Ashshur (early second millennium BCE), tells that from the Ishtar temple in the city Ashshur, situated on Mt. Ebih, two streams flowed forth to different gates, just as we find in Deutero-Zech. The waterworks of the Jerusalem Temple thus helped mark it as the natural habitat of the Divine resident.

Ugaritic mythology also helps us understand the water symbolism of the First Temple. El's abode on Mt. Zaphon, a name borrowed to designate Jerusalem and Mt. Zion (see esp. Ps. 48.3), was located at "the underground wellspring of the rivers, the course of the two seas." Solomon's waterworks consisting of a Sea and two rows of water wagons are comparable, in which case the Temple resembles El's abode, and reflects the well-known adoption of Ugaritic El imagery applied to YHVH. Finally, a large water basin found at Ashshur was decorated with *apkallu* (primordial sages) and divine figures holding jugs from which streams of water flows. The *apkallu* figures, resembling men with fish bottoms, mark the basin as belonging to Ea, the Mesopotamian god of wisdom, crafts, and the subterranean waters, who is identified eventually with Canaanite El.

An additional aspect of the water vessels ties them to both the ideal world of the future and the primordial divine garden. The *mekhonot* are decorated with lions, bulls, and cherubs. Cherubs are winged creatures, mythological denizens of the divine realm in general and divine gardens in particular. Furthermore, the combination of lions and bulls recalls Isaiah's prophecy (Isa. 11.6–7):

The wolf shall dwell with the lamb,
The leopard lie down with the kid;
The calf, the beast of prey, and the
  fatling together
With a little boy to herd them.
The cow and the bear shall graze,
Their young shall lie down together;
And the lion, like the ox, shall eat straw.

The prophecy then says "In all of My sacred mount / Nothing evil or vile shall be done" (v. 9). If so, harmony and serene coexistence between carnivorous and herbivorous animals is connected with the Holy Mountain where the Temple will stand. Again, the decorations of the Temple implements in the present reflect the ideal divine dwelling of the future, while the Temple of the future provides the key for understanding the symbolism of the Temple of the present.

Beyond the rows of *mekhonot*, is the entrance to God's House. This building, a long-room structure consisting of a forecourt, a large anteroom, and a smaller inner room resembles in overall internal layout various ancient Near Eastern temples, but in particular two early first millennium temples at Tel-Tayanat in Turkey, one discovered in the 1930s and the other discovered in the early 21st c., and a late second millennium temple at Ain-Dara discovered in the 1980s.

The materials of the building contrast with those of the courtyards. It is not made of hewn stone with which the courtyards are paved, but of rough, unhewn, whole stones. The builders may have applied to the Temple building itself the ancient law prohibiting an altar of hewn stone (Exod. 20.22; see parallel [which Solomon could not know] at Deut. 27.6). According to Jewish tradition the altar that brings peace should not be desecrated by iron used to make swords symbolizing war; this is yet another expression of the paradise-like tranquility of the divine dwelling.

The stone structure is encased on its right, rear, and left sides by a three story cedar-wood structure reaching half the height of the building. A unique parallel to this wooden surrounding structure is found in the Ain-Dara temple, which is surrounded on two sides and from behind by a chambered, stone corridor. The upright boards of this structure are called *tselaʿot* (lit. "ribs"), while the ones lying horizontally, connecting the *tselaʿot* with the stone walls, are called *yetsiʿim* (lit. "mattresses"). The *tselaʿot* and *yetsiʿim* made up together a type of cedar-wood box enveloping the building, recalling the forest of Lebanon, considered by ancient Near Eastern peoples a pure or holy divine residence. Here too the Temple resembles the natural habitat of resident God.

The horizontal *yetsiʿim* divide the structure into three stories, the middle story opening to the left of the entrance to the Temple itself. Worshippers ascended and descended through trap doors or spiral staircases called *belulim*. This structure stores Temple treasures, including all valuable objects dedicated to God as royal presents or items taken as booty in war. Some of the valuables in these stores pre-dated Solomon, for Solomon is said to have put in the stores sacred objects belonging to David, and temple treasuries are mentioned as early as the time of Joshua and the conquest of Jericho. These treasures were used from time to time to pay tribute.

A small forecourt *(Ulam)* was in front of the main entrance of the Temple, extending the width of the building. Twenty cubits wide and ten deep, it was enclosed by a low wall whose height equals that of the wall around the Temple courtyard itself. These walls are decorated with an enigmatic feature called *ḥalonei shekufim ʾatumim*, "blocked, transparent windows," probably, false windows, of the type found in the Ain Dara Temple and a temple of the Storm God at Aleppo. (In this period windows were simply openings in the wall; the technology for producing glass windows had not yet developed.) In the *Ulam* stand two immense hollow pillars cast from bronze and topped with floral motifs. These free-standing pillars, with no architectural function, have decorative and symbolic significance. Perhaps they flank the entryway as silent witnesses to the great event of God's entry into the new Temple when it was dedicated. As such, they bear constant witness to God's presence in the Temple, resembling the giant footprints leading from the entry to the inner sancta in the Ain-Dara temple. The physical shape of the pillars is also suggestive. Each pillar was topped with a lotus-shaped capitol, decorated with pomegranates, and intertwined, tangled branches, making them stylized trees. Thus, they may represent the two trees growing in the middle of the garden of Eden, the tree of knowledge of good and bad and the tree of life. This symbolic interpretation accords well with the other motifs connecting the Temple with the divine garden.

The pillars were given the enigmatic names *Yakhin* and *Boʿaz*. The pillars may be functionally related to cult objects mentioned in an inscription from Kar-Tukulti-Ninurta that describes two wooden pillars dedicated to the god Ashur, each one engraved with an inscription. The names may also be words of a blessing or a prayer for the king who built the Temple and made the pillars, perhaps "may YHVH establish *(yakhin)* the throne of his David and his kingdom to his descendants forever" and "by might *(be'oz)* of YHVH may the king rejoice." The first of these suggested names resembles the name of a gate of Nineveh given it by Sennacherib, "Enlil makes stable *(mukīn)* my regnal period."

Passing between the two pillars, the worshipper reaches the Temple's entrance, framed by four interlocking doorframes, one inside the other. The frames are of "oil wood," a type of olive wood or pine. The stepped doorframes resemble those found in a model shrine unearthed at Khirbet Qeiyafah, from the early 10th c. (the time of David), which displays an entrance surrounded by four interlocking door frames. These resemble an architectural feature representing temples *pars pro toto* in divine symbols used in Mesopotamian iconography, such as on the relief atop the stele of Hammurabi where Shamash sits upon a temple entrance consisting of four interlocking frames. Some Mesopotamian reliefs depict gods framed within such entryways, so this particular type of frame may be symbolic of divine presence in the Temple.

In the doorframe hang two doors, each made of two planks of cypress or juniper wood. The doors are engraved with cherubs, palmettes and open calyxes, and the decorations are covered with gold applied in a way designated enigmatically as *meyushar*, "straightened." These doors are opened and closed every morning and evening with golden implements, a type of key, called *potot,* which should be corrected on the basis of Chron. to *poteḥot,* "openers." Door-opening rituals are known from other biblical and ancient Near Eastern temples, such as 1 Sam. 3.15, where Samuel opened the doors of the Shiloh sanctuary in the morning.

The Temple itself is comprised of one long room measuring twenty by forty cubits (approximately thirty by sixty ft) known as the *heykhal,* a term derived from Sumerian "é.gal," "big house," via the Akkadian *ekallu.* The Sumerian and Akkadian terms usually designate a royal palace, but in Ugaritic and biblical Heb the word is often applied to earthly temples or to a deity's heavenly dwelling place.

Like the doors, the floor of this room is of cypress (or perhaps juniper) wood. But the walls and ceiling are of cedar wood, lending fragrance to the room. The two sidewalls as well as the entrance wall are engraved with gourds and calyxes. But the wall at the back of the *heykhal,* leading to the inner chamber, is decorated more ornately; it is covered with calyxes, palmettes and cherubs. The cherubs engraved on the doors to the *heykhal* represent guards and recall the cherubs holding the ever-turning sword guarding the entry to the garden of Eden and the way to the tree of life. The cherubs on the back wall of the *heykhal* represent, in contrast, the honor guard standing outside the throne room in which the Divine King sits enthroned in all His radiant Glory.

The main daily ritual was performed in the *heykhal*. It was furnished with appropriate cultic furnishings, and the ritual performed aimed at arousing the worshippers' emotions and providing the daily needs of the divine resident.

Along the side walls stood ten golden lampstands *(menorot),* five to the right and five to the left. On the *menorot* rested golden oil lamps which burned from dusk to dawn, as God's lamp did at Shiloh. Each lampstand probably held only a single lamp, although some scholars think that the lampstands were more elaborate with seven branches as in the Tabernacle. The priest tended these lamps with golden implements.

In the middle of the *heykhal* was a table set with loaves of bread and pouring and drinking vessels, all for the divine repast. A bread table was likely found in the pre-Jerusalem temple at Nob. If the offering table resembled that in the Tabernacle, then it finds parallels in tables depicted on various monuments such as the sarcophagus of Ahiram, king of Byblos, the Assyrian reliefs of Ashurbanipal, and the table of showbread from the Second Temple depicted on the Arch of Titus. The meals served periodically on this table were accompanied by music played upon gold covered instruments called *mezammerot*. The Israelite temples with an internal table alongside an altar for burnt offerings in the courtyard may reflect a blending of different cultic traditions.

An altar for incense, made of cedar wood overlaid with gold stood in front of the door leading into the inner chamber. The attending priests place incense upon it using golden spoons, called *kappot* (lit. "palms"); to burn the incense, coals were brought from the courtyard altar upon golden pans *(maḥtot)*.

The *Devir* or "Holy of Holies" was entered by passing through a short corridor surrounded by five interlocking frames. The doors to the Holy of Holies were made of "oil wood" and decorated with cherubs, palmettes, and calyxes and covered with gold applied by a process called *radad*. The *Devir* itself was cubic, twenty cubits to each dimension, and made entirely of cedar wood. Its walls were covered with gold and decorated with calyxes, palmettes, and cherubs, representing God's heavenly retinue, recalling the Divine throne-room scenes described in the prophecy of Michaiah son of Imlah (1 Kings ch 22), Isaiah's throne vision (Isa. ch 6), and the opening chs of the book of Job. Above the *Devir* was an attic or loft. This secret room may have been the bedroom used by Ahaziah's sister Jehosheba to hide her nephew Jehoash from wicked Queen Athalyah (2 Kings 11.2); one scholar has suggested that it was used for performing a sacred marriage rite, though there is scant evidence for the practice of this ritual.

In the middle of the *Devir* stood two enormous cherubs, each ten cubits high with ten-cubit wingspans. The outstretched wings fill the chamber from side to side. These cherubs are usually taken to represent God's throne, or the supports for it, and are the basis of the divine epithet, "He who sits upon the cherubs," *yoshev hakkeruvim*; according to Chron., this cherub throne is a model of the *Merkavah*, a term used in postbiblical Heb to designate the Divine chariot described in Ezek. chs 1 and 12. A more recent suggestion sees the cherubs as erect creatures who shield God with their outstretched wings; they resemble erect, winged beings known mainly from Egyptian-inspired iconography.

Under the wings of the cherubs stood the Ark (*'aron*, lit. a box). This Ark, brought to Jerusalem from Shiloh where it stood earlier, is God's footstool. Just like other footstools known from the ancient Near East into which copies of treaties were placed, this one stored the tablets of the Covenant recording the covenant between God and His people Israel. The tablets of the Covenant stored in the Holy of Holies have a parallel in the discovery of a copy of Esarhaddon's Vassal Treaty found in the holy of holies of the temple uncovered at Tel-Tayanat in the excavations of 2010.

The importance of this inner room was emphasized by its grand entrance doors, and also by the form of the Temple in its entirety. The worshipper who passed from the courtyard into the Holy of Holies viewed cultic implements and decorations which progressively increased in value and technological sophistication. Everything in the courtyard was made of bronze, but inside the building was of gold only, with the amount of gold increasing from the *heykhal* into the *Devir*. The wood in the *heykhal* was both cedar and cypress, while in the *Devir* it was cedar with the cherubs of oil wood. The outer door was surrounded by a four-tiered doorframe, while the frame of the inner door was five-tiered. The walls of the *heykhal* were decorated with gourds and calyxes, while the walls of the *Devir* bore calyxes, palmettes and cherubs. The gradual increase parallels an increase in sanctity and in strictness on who may enter. The outer court was visited by the people at large, while the inner court was the domain of the priests, and the inside of the Temple was open only to the high priest. All in all, Solomon's Temple is a luxurious divine residence in a mountaintop pleasure garden; its general design focuses on the inner room, and is meant to glorify and magnify the divine resident sitting on the cherub throne.

The Second Temple

The Bible offers much less information about the form and symbolism of the Second Temple, whose construction is related in Ezra chs 1–6 and is alluded to in Hag. and Zech. chs 1–9. It is described very briefly in Ezra 6.3–5 in a scroll said to have been found in the citadel of Ecbatana in the province of Media. According to this passage, Cyrus ordered that the "House of God in Jerusalem" be constructed on a high foundation platform, and be "sixty cubits high and sixty cubits wide." It should be "a course of unused timber for each three courses of hewn stone." The Judeans were to deposit there the vessels of gold and silver which Nebuchadnezzar had removed from the Temple in Jerusalem and brought to Babylonia.

According to this brief, laconic description, the Temple would have been cubic in shape. This is peculiar, but perhaps using the form of the First Temple, this refers to the cubic Holy of Holies. The building then consists of a core identical to the First Temple, namely twenty cubits in width, and sixty cubits long, divided into an ante-room called *heykhal* (Neh. 6.10) which was twenty cubits wide and forty long, and an inner sanctuary or Holy of Holies which was twenty cubits square. There were doors to the *heykhal* (Neh. 6.10). On either side of the core were side structures of the same dimensions, paralleling the *tsela'ot* and *yetsi'im* of the First Temple. This building would have been thirty cubits high, leaving thirty cubits for height of the foundation platform, for a total of sixty cubits. The three courses of stone and one of wood probably refer to the walls of the courtyards surrounding the Temple (cf. 1 Kings 6.12). Use of the plural forms *ḥatsrey* and *ḥatsrot* (Isa. 62.9; Neh. 8.16; 13.7) indicates that there were two courts, an inner and an outer, and in the wall to the inner court in which the altar stood was a double door (Mal. 1.10). The book of Joel, probably composed in the early Second Temple period, refers to priests crying "between the Ulam and the altar" (2.17) suggesting that a portico was placed before the entrance to the Temple.

The courts contained "chambers," *leneshkhot,* used for storing valuable Temple property (Ezra 8.29), cultic vessels (Neh. 10.40; 13.4–9), and sacrificial material and income from tithes, first-born, etc. (Neh. 10.38–39). As such, these chambers were kept in a state of cultic purity.

Likewise, little is said about the furnishings and decorations of the Second Temple. Cedar wood from Lebanon (Ezra 3.7) was used, probably in the walls and roof, in addition to the courses of wood in the courtyard walls. The Temple had an altar for burnt offerings, which was set up even before the Temple was founded (Ezra 3.2–6; cf. 7.17). The Temple vessels returned to Sheshbazzar were probably vessels from the Temple treasuries and not implements used in the cult proper (Ezra 1.7–11). The vessels brought by Ezra which are designated by Artaxerxes to be cultic vessels are of an uncertain nature (Ezra 7.19). The Ark was not reproduced in the Second Temple, having been carried away before the First Temple was destroyed in 586 BCE.

The Second Temple period prophet Malachi refers to the altar as "YHVH's Table" (NJPS: "the table of the LORD"; Mal. 1.7, 12), a term used otherwise for the table of showbread (Exod. 25.23). He may thereby be alluding as well to the table of showbread which in Ezek. 41.22 is called both *mizbeaḥ* and *shulḥan*. The gold menorah described by Zechariah (4.1–4, 10b–14) may have been the menorah in the Second Temple, in which case it is different in form from the Tabernacle Menorah and those in the First Temple.

Although the Second Temple may have had the same form and total dimensions as the First, it was much less elaborate. According to Ezra 3.12–13, the surviving elders who had seen the First Temple wept profusely when they saw the foundation of the Second

Temple. Later on Hag. 2.3 tells us that those elders living at the time of the Temple's reconstruction who were old enough (more than seventy years old) to remember the First Temple in its glory, thought the Second as nothing in comparison.

Several Psalms composed during the period of the Second Temple may offer additional information about its form and function. Finally, the book of Chron., composed in the late Persian period, may have added to its description of Solomon's Temple certain details that reflect the Second Temple.

Divine Presence in the Temple

In what form did God dwell in the Temple? This question is answered in varying manners in the Bible. As noted above, ancient Near Eastern peoples regarded temples as earthly residences for their gods. The gods were manifest in the temples in physical embodiments as cult statues or other sorts of symbols. Such a way of representing the God of Israel in an Israelite temple would be possible as long as it was believed that divinity could be imbued in a physical object; and, indeed, the book of Judg. mentions a cult statue in the private temple of Micah in the tribe of Dan, while other temples such as at Bethel and Arad housed stone pillars, or *matsevot*. The temple in Gideon's town of Ophrah (Judg. 8.27) seems to have represented God in the form of a golden divine garment known as an Ephod. Certain recent scholars suggest that representing God by an anthropomorphic statue was common in ancient Israel, and that even the Jerusalem Temple hosted such an icon at certain times.

According to 1 Kings 8.13, Solomon pronounces "I have surely built for You an exalted house; a place for your eternal dwelling" (author's translation). Since the Ark served as God's sedan-chair and throne, introducing the Ark into the Temple and placing it in the Holy of Holies, as reported in 1 Kings ch 8, brought with it the invisible God seated upon it. This has been designated "empty seat aniconism." Authors of the Priestly School, responsible for composition of one of the main literary strata in the Torah, did not suffice with an invisible, transcendent God, and in their opinion, God manifested Himself first in the Tabernacle and subsequently in Shiloh and then Jerusalem through His *Kavod*, often translated "glory," or "majesty," but better understood as "glorious substance." This Priestly term does not reflect the abstract idea of "honor" or "glory," but signifies something quite concrete and perceptible. The divine *Kavod* is the shining radiance which enveloped God and which radiated from Him, similar to the divine radiance called *melammu* in Akkadian. This radiance overwhelmed and could knock off his feet anyone who gazed upon it, and it in turn was shrouded by a cloud. Ezekiel, a priest who lived at the time of the destruction of the Temple and who was influenced by the Priestly School, describes the step-by-step exiting from the Temple of the *Kavod* before the destruction, and in his vision of reconstruction he sees it return. Zechariah shares Ezekiel's view.

But in striking contrast to the Priestly School and these two prophets, the Deuteronomic School places God in His heavenly dwelling-place, limiting His presence in the Temple to His name that is called upon. According to this school, God looks down from His heavenly residence. The Deuteronomists turned the earthly Temple in Jerusalem into a type of "switchboard" that would redirect heavenwards any prayer directed towards it, as noted, e.g., in 1 Kings 8.42–43: "... when he comes to pray toward this House, oh, hear in Your heavenly abode ...," God sees the supplicant in the Temple and hears his prayer, but is not present Himself.

A compromise position is found in Isa. 6.1, where the prophet Isaiah sees God sitting on a high and exalted throne, in the Temple, but according to the *Seraphim* His *Kavod* fills the entire earth. A similar compromise was accepted by the prophet of the restoration period, whom modern scholars call Trito-Isaiah, who quotes God as saying "The heaven is My throne / And the earth is My footstool: / Where could you build a house for Me, / What place could serve as My abode?" (Isa. 66.1). The same prophet says: "My House shall be called / A house of prayer for all the peoples" (Isa. 56.7), and in this he accepts the concept of Solomon's prayer and of the Deuteronomists. Trito-Isaiah construes the *Kavod*, as the light of God which will shine upon His people as well as the glorious building materials which the peoples will bring to the Temple (Isa. 60.13).

The prophet Haggai predicts that God's *Kavod* will enter the Temple as the heavens and earth quake, and in this he is very close to Ezekiel. But he empties the crucial concept of *Kavod* of theological meaning, for the *Kavod* that is to fill the Temple is not God's radiant *kavod* that stuns any onlooker, but vast wealth. Similarly, God says that He will be desirous of the Temple and will be "glorified" by it, using the word *'ekkaveda*, "I will be honored," namely, the new Temple will be for God's glory and honor. Both Third Isaiah and Haggai exploit the multi-valance of the word *kavod* in order to span the theological abyss separating two radically different concepts of divine Presence in the Temple.

The two concepts exist to this day. The *kavod* has changed, developed and metamorphosed into the rabbinic *Shekhinah* which is a restricted divine presence focused in a particular locus; according to some Rabbis the *shekhinah* during the Second Temple period was found in one of the lamps burning on the Temple lampstand, so that the radiance of the *Kavod* persists even though it is, so to speak "on a low flame." This concept of *Kavod* might even be expressed in *Shiviti* ("I am ever mindful of the LORD's presence," Ps. 16.8) decorations commonly found in synagogues of Sephardic Jews. The decorations are pictures of seven-branched lampstands upon which the Tetragrammaton is written, and by way of these signs God, in the form of His name and the cult object bearing or embodying His presence, is literally placed before the worshipper in the synagogue.

According to biblical texts, when the Second Temple was dedicated after the exile there is no hint that God's *kavod* entered the newly rebuilt Temple as expected, and the dedication festivities of this Temple, which should have climaxed with the entry of the divine resident into the rebuilt Temple, were limited to offering sacrifices. This is because, as it turned out, the Temple is devoid of its Divine resident. Indeed, the concept that God is not restricted to the Temple complements the concept that God is found everywhere and can be worshipped anywhere and everywhere. This concept permits, probably beginning in the 3rd c. BCE, the construction of synagogues, the Jewish institution that eventually replaced the lost Temple.

[VICTOR AVIGDOR HUROWITZ] Z"L

EDITED FOR PUBLICATION BY ADELE BERLIN AND MARC ZVI BRETTLER

Biblical Calendars

Dates are frequently used in the Bible for indicating the time of events and prescribing when festivals should be observed. Most dates in the Bible consist of a numbered day in the month, the number (sometimes name) of the month, and in narratives, the number of the year, as in 2 Kings 25.1. The year number is nearly always of the reign of the ruling king—Israelite or sometimes foreign (e.g., Persian: Ezra 1.1), i.e., the 'regnal year'—but in some cases, years are counted with reference to a major event such as the exodus (e.g., Num. 33.38; 1 Kings 6.1) or the exile (Ezra 1.2). Days of the week are never specified in such formulae, even though the concept of the seven-day week, ending with the Sabbath, is attested in several places in the Torah and elsewhere. Similarly, the seven-year sabbatical cycle and the fifty-year jubilee cycle of Lev. 25.1–24 are never explicitly used in the Bible for dating or chronological purposes. Weekdays, sabbatical cycles, and jubilees were only used regularly for such purposes in postbiblical literature (e.g., in the book of *Jub.*, and in Roman period documents and inscriptions).

A date only makes sense in relation to a known calendar; and yet, remarkably, the calendar (or calendars) that the Bible assumes for dating purposes is never described in full. The Bible does not indicate the length of its months, or how many months are in a year; it does not explain whether the calendar is based on the cycle of the sun and seasons, on the phases of the moon, on the observation of the stars, or on any other cycle or scheme. The Bible's remarkable reticence about its own calendar is significant, and can be taken in itself as evidence that the calendar was lunar, just as were all other calendars in the ancient Near East (with the only exception being Egypt). It is precisely because all ancient Near Eastern calendars were lunar that the Bible sees no need to explain this.

Like all ancient Near Eastern calendars, the calendar of ancient Israel and of the Bible is likely to have been based on observations of the moon, with months beginning at or around the first sighting of the new moon, and a normal month length of twenty-nine or thirty days. The recurrence of some festivals at particular agricultural seasons during the year—such as Passover at the time of *ʾaviv* (Exod. 23.15), i.e., an early stage in the maturation of the grains (Exod. 9.31), Sukkot at the time of the ingathering of the harvest (Lev. 23.39)—indicates that the calendar was kept in alignment with the seasonal or solar year. (See "Biblical Festivals and Fast Days," pp. 2025–34.) This would have been achieved by counting twelve months in the year, with the occasional intercalation of a thirteenth month, as was normal practice throughout the ancient Near East.

More tangible evidence of a lunar calendar in the Hebrew Bible is difficult to find. Intercalation, for example—a distinctive feature of ancient lunar calendars—is never mentioned in the Bible, and there is no evidence of which month in the year was intercalated. Gen. 1.14, "Let there be lights in the expanse of the sky to separate day from night; they shall serve as signs for the set times—the days and the years," suggests that both the sun and the moon are to be used for reckoning festivals, days, and years; Ps. 104.19 (a later text), is more ambiguous: "He made the moon to mark the seasons; / the sun knows when to set," marks the significance of only the moon in relation to the calendar. The dates of the flood, according to the Masoretic, Samaritan and most other texts of Gen. chs 7–8, run from the seventeenth of the second month to the twenty-seventh of the same month of the next year, thus lasting one year and ten days. As pointed out already in rabbinic sources (*Gen. Rab.* 33:7), these ten days may represent the difference between the solar and the lunar year, which would suggest that the biblical calendar year was lunar, while the flood lasted the equivalent of one solar year. However, the reverse may be argued by comparing Exod. 19.1 to Num. 10.11, which notes that the Israelites arrived at Sinai on the first of the third month, and left Sinai on the twentieth of the second month; this means that they resided at Sinai for one year *less* approximately ten days, which would suggest in turn that the biblical calendar year was solar, and the Israelites resided at Sinai for the equivalent of one lunar year. It has long been argued that the Heb word for month, *ḥodesh*, is itself an indication that the calendar was lunar, since the notion of "newness" implicit in the root *ḥ-d-sh* can only refer to the new moon; likewise, the other word for month, *yeraḥ*, is clearly derived from *yareaḥ*, "moon" (see e.g., Abraham Ibn Ezra, in his commentary on Lev. 25.9). This argument, however, is flawed, because the etymology of a word does not necessarily indicate how it was used in any later period, and it is common for the terminology of lunar calendars to be applied to non-lunar calendars (thus the etymology of the English word "month" is "moon," even though the calendar of English speakers today is solar).

In the 1950s, Annie Jaubert put forward the theory that the calendar assumed in the Hebrew Bible (or at least in its Priestly narratives) was not lunar, but based on a 364-day year. This calendar is explicitly attested in later, extrabiblical works (see below). Jaubert acknowledged that a lunar calendar must also have been used in ancient Israel, but suggested that the latter was a "civil" calendar, whereas the 364-day year served as the cultic, priestly calendar. (It is not unusual for societies to use simultaneously more than one calendar.) The latter, she argued, was abolished by Hellenistic rulers in the early 2nd c. BCE, and replaced by the lunar calendar. This theory enables dated events in biblical narratives to occur consistently only on "significant" weekdays—Sunday, Wednesday, and Friday, which correspond to the weekdays when, in the 364-day calendar, the biblical festivals occur—and significantly (almost) never on the Sabbath. However, the pattern of event dates in the Bible which is used as the basis of her argument can be explained entirely as a literary predilection, in the Bible, for round or other standard numbers, and her theory has also been refuted on other grounds. The 364-day calendar would be so unique in the context of the ancient world that the Bible is unlikely to have used it without explicitly describing it. Thus, although a lunar calendar is equally impossible to prove, it remains inherently more likely.

Another calendar can be inferred from the count of fifty days between Passover and Shavuʿot (Lev. 23.15–16), to which other festivals at further fifty-day intervals were later added in Qumran's *Temple Scroll* (11Q19 [The Temple Scroll[a]] xviii-xix, xxi; also in 4QMMT[a] frg. 2, col. v). This has been interpreted as the survival of an ancient pentecontad calendar of seven fifty-day periods, amounting to a 350-day year; Philo may imply that such a calendar was followed by the 1st-c. Jewish Egyptian sect of Therapeutai (Philo, *Contempl.* 8 [65]). This theory is possible, although this calendar would be marginal at best to the Hebrew Bible.

In a rare passage of the Bible that addresses calendrical issues, King Jeroboam is accused of establishing a festival "on the fifteenth day of the eighth month; in imitation of the festival in Judah ... On the fifteenth day of the eighth month—the month in which he had contrived of his own mind to establish a festival for the Israelites" (1 Kings 12.32–33). In this, he departed from the festival calendars of the Torah (e.g., Lev. ch 23; Num. chs 28–29; Deut. ch 16), where there is no festival in the eighth month. The "festival in Judah" is most likely a reference to Sukkot, on the fifteenth of the seventh month, whereas Jeroboam held it one month later, in the eighth month. However, the precise meaning of "month in which he had contrived of his own mind" remains unclear. Some have suggested that Jeroboam was reinstating a traditional northern calendar in which this harvest festival was celebrated in the eighth month, thus one month later than in the southern Judean calendar, claiming (problematically) that grain ripened later in the north. It is equally possible that after rebelling against the Davidic dynasty and establishing himself as king in the north, Jeroboam intercalated in the calendar one extra month, largely to demonstrate his political independence; the result would have been that his eighth month, according to his own reckoning, corresponded to the seventh month in the Judean calendar.

The months in the Hebrew Bible are normally numbered, not named. Numbered months make a first appearance in the story of the flood (Gen. 7.11: the second month), then in Exod., when God commands Moses to count the month of *ʾaviv* (in the spring: see above) as the first month (Exod. 12.2; 13.4). This numbering implies that the year begins in the spring. An autumn New Year, which became normative in later Judaism, is implicit perhaps in one, relatively late passage, Ezek. 40.1, which places the "tenth of the month"—an apparent allusion to the Day of Atonement—at the "beginning of the year." The Feast of Ingathering (later called the festival of Sukkot), in the seventh month, is referred to as the "end of the year" in Exod. 23.16 (see also 34.22), but this does not necessarily mean the end and beginning of a new calendar year; more likely, it indicates the end of the year's agricultural cycle or cycle of festivals, with the new year beginning in the following spring. Although numbered months are the norm in the Bible, some month names make rare appearances in the book of Kings: besides *ʾaviv* (which may be a seasonal identifier of the first month, rather than its name), that book refers to *Ziv*, identified as the second month (1 Kings 6.1, 37), *bul*, the eighth month (ibid., 38), and *ʾeitanim* (NJPS: Ethanim), the seventh month (ibid., 8.2); these names are probably of extra-Israelite origin.

In the postexilic period, in some later biblical books, Babylonian month names begin to appear on their own or alongside numbered months: Nisan (e.g., Neh. 2.1), Sivan (Esth. 8.9), ʾElul (Neh. 6.15), Kislev (Neh. 1.1), Tevet (NJPS: Tebeth; Esth. 2.16), Shevat (Zech. 1.7), ʾAdar (Ezra 6.15). These names are all Akkadian, the Semitic language of ancient Mesopotamia, and they entered Heb via Aram. In this system, Nisan is consistently equated with the first month, as in the Babylonian calendar. These month names—which were later to become normative in Judaism—suggest not merely a change of language, but also that the Jews had in fact adopted entirely the Babylonian calendar, a lunar calendar that served as the official calendar of the Persian Achaemenid empire (and later, of the Seleucid empire). That Jews were using the Babylonian calendar to determine the dates of biblical festivals is evident, at least, from the "Passover papyrus" from Elephantine (southern Egypt), which indicates that in 419 BCE, the festivals of Passover and Unleavened Bread were observed on the month days prescribed in the Torah, but in the Babylonian month of Nisan.

After the Hasmonean state broke off from its Seleucid overlords in the mid-2nd c. BCE, the Judean (or "Jewish") calendar soon acquired a separate identity of its own. Although retaining Babylonian month names (as evidenced in the books of Macc.), intercalations were probably no longer made at the same time as the Babylonians, which presumably led sometimes to one month discrepancies between the calendars.

In approximately the same period, in the late 3rd c. BCE – 1st c. CE, a dissident, nonlunar calendar appears in Jewish literary sources: the books of *1 Enoch*, *Jub.*, and the Dead Sea Scrolls. This calendar does not depend on the moon or other natural phenomena, but is completely fixed and schematic. It consists of a year of 364 days (with months of thirty or thirty-one days), or fifty-two weeks exactly, which means that the New Year and festivals recur every year on the same day of the week. It is slightly shorter than the solar or seasonal year (which counts approximately 365 and one-fourth days), which makes it gradually drift away from a correct alignment with the seasons. The extent to which this calendar was used in practice, for example at Qumran (where most of the Dead Sea Scrolls were discovered), and its relevance to Qumran sectarianism remain unclear. Although dissident, this is the earliest calendar to be explicitly described in any Jewish source. Its origins are much debated: some argue in favor of Babylonian origins (as indeed, the astronomical sections of *1 Enoch* are clearly derived from Mesopotamian astronomy), but Egyptian influence is more likely (the Egyptian calendar consisted similarly of a fixed, schematic year, although of 365 days; Judea was under Ptolemaic rule in the 3rd c. BCE). In Qumran calendar texts, the 364-day calendar is synchronized with a schematic lunar calendar (in a three-year cycle), priestly courses (a twenty-four-week cycle), and in one text (4Q319), the cycle of jubilees. Months are numbered and not named, which is not surprising given that this calendar bears no relation to the Babylonian calendar. The chronology of biblical narratives is interpreted in *Jub.* and in Qumran sources (e.g., 4Q252: the flood) on the basis of the 364-day calendar.

After the 1st c. CE, the lunar calendar prevailed entirely among the Jews, in contrast with other calendars in the Roman East that adapted almost universally to the solar, Julian calendar. Jewish communities reckoned this calendar independently of one another and in very different ways, in the Diaspora as well as in Palestine. But in late antiquity and through the Middle Ages, a standard, rabbinic lunar calendar—only finalized in the 10th c.—was gradually accepted as normative by all Jews. In early rabbinic and in Jewish medieval tradition, the chronology of biblical narratives and the biblical liturgical year were interpreted on the basis of this lunar calendar.

[SACHA STERN]

Biblical Festivals and Fast Days

[Please note that the Scripture quotations in the following article are the author's.
—the Editors.]

The festivals and fast days of the Hebrew Bible are realizations of "sacred time," and they were most often celebrated in "sacred space," at temples and other designated worship sites. These celebrations mark the separation of the sacred from the profane, and help define Israel as a people. The festivals and commemorative fast days of the Hebrew Bible are observed in Judaism until the present day, although their significance and manner of observance have changed over time. As this essay will note, already in the course of the biblical period the festivals underwent modifications.

Almost all that we know about the ancient celebration of these festivals and fast days comes from the Hebrew Bible; extrabiblical sources provide very little information. Reconstructing the biblical festivals is complicated by two factors: It is unclear which biblical laws and narratives reflect actual ancient Israelite practice, and in tracing the development of the festivals and fast days, it is often uncertain how the relevant biblical sources should be dated and chronologically arranged. The approach taken here is that the biblical reports on the festivals and fast days are largely realistic, although they may be somewhat idealized. Indeed, there is no reason to doubt that harvest festivals were celebrated in ancient Israel, sacrifices were offered, and pilgrimages undertaken. Concerning the second issue, this essay follows the position that the festival texts of Priestly authorship in Exod., Lev., and Num. were composed after Deut., associated with Josiah's reform of 622 BCE that made the Jerusalem Temple the only legitimate place of worship. (See the intro. to Torah, pp. 1–6; intro. to Deut., pp. 339–45.) This centralization of worship changed religious practice in ancient Israel in fundamental ways.

The Heb word for "festival" is *moʿed*, "set time" (Lev. 23.2, 4), reflecting the scheduling of festivals in accordance with accepted calendars (see "Biblical Calendars," pp. 2021–25), the Sabbath and the new moon, which did not need to be scheduled, are sacred days, nonetheless, and their provisions are sometimes set forth together with those of the festivals. Three annual festivals, Pesaḥ-*matzot*, and the two harvest festivals (later called Shavuʿot or Weeks and Sukkot or Booths) are designated *ḥag*, "pilgrimage festival," meaning that their proper celebration required attendance at a sacred site where sacrifice could be offered. These pilgrimage festivals *(ḥaggim)* are thus a subcategory of the general festivals *(moʿadim)*.

The following presentation begins with Torah passages; these are supplemented with other biblical sources, and, when available, non-biblical texts.

The Sabbath (Heb *shabbat*)

Heb *shabbat* derives from the verb *sh-b-t*, "to cease, desist," and its particular nominal form connotes regularity rather than a single act, that is: "a regular cessation." It designates the seventh day of the week, from Friday evening through Saturday evening, as a day of obligatory rest, and overrides all other religious events. Its occurrence is never interrupted, and in the Priestly view, it never has been since creation (Gen. 2.1–3). Sabbaths are unrelated to the phases of the moon; hence the suggestion that Heb *shabbat* is cognate with Akkadian *sapattu*, a similar sounding word for the fifteenth of the month, misses the point. Rather, the Sabbath is to be regarded as an original Israelite-Jewish contribution to world culture. It reflects ancient notions concerning the number seven, an important number in Semitic cultures, and seven-day units of repeated time. Unprecedented, however, is the rule that all members of society are entitled to respite from daily labors, which is the essential message of the Sabbath.

The earliest statement related to Shabbat is in Exod. 23.12, taken from an agrarian calendar of sacred celebrations:

> For six days you shall produce your products, but on the seventh day you must desist *[tishbot]*, in order that your ox and your mule may rest, and the son of your handmaiden and the resident alien may regain strength.

This is repeated with minor variations in Exod. 34.21:

> For six days shall you work [the land], but on the seventh day you must desist *[tishbot]*; even at the time of plowing and the time of reaping shall you desist.

Although both texts use the verb *sh-b-t*, neither uses the noun *Shabbat*, "the Sabbath."

In contrast, the Torah preserves two versions of the Decalogue, each expressing its own concept of the Sabbath (Exod. 20.8–11; Deut. 5.12–15). The version in Deut. is by and large earlier than Exod., and is quoted below:

> Observe *[shamor]* the Sabbath day *[yom hashabbat]* so as to sanctify it, as the LORD, your God, has commanded you. Six days shall you labor *[taʾabod]*, performing all of your tasks *[melaʾktekah]*, but the seventh day is a Sabbath of the LORD. You may not perform any tasks *[melaʾkah]*, neither you, nor your son or your daughter, your male or female slave, your ox or your mule, or any of your cattle, or the resident alien who is in your gates, so that your male and female slave may rest as you do. Remember that you were a slave in the land of Egypt, and the LORD, your God, freed you from there with a strong hand and an outstretched arm. It is for this reason that the LORD, your God, has commanded you to keep the Sabbath day.

Deut. broadens the agrarian-humanitarian frame of reference by introducing the element of *melaʾkah*, "tasks." Putting Exod. ch 23, and Deut. ch 5 together, we have three avoidance categories that define the Sabbath: not to produce (agricultural) product, not to labor, and not to perform tasks.

Although the Decalogue versions generally agree, and both speak of sanctifying the Sabbath, they differ from each other in several ways. Whereas Deut. has "to keep, observe," Exod. has *zakor*, "to mark" (usually translated "to remember"), the Sabbath day. More significant is Deut.'s view that the Sabbath symbolizes the liberation from Egyptian bondage. The Exod. version of the Decalogue, in accord with the Priestly tradition (see Gen. 2.1–3), has God resting on the Sabbath of creation, offering a fundamentally different reason for the day's observance: The Israelites are to emulate their Creator. No biblical Shabbat text defines *mela'kah*; this would only be done systematically in the Dead Sea Scrolls (see the *Damascus Document* [4Q266] 10.14–11.18) and in *m. Shab.* (esp. 7.2–4).

The Sabbath is especially important in the Priestly tradition in the Torah, as seen for example in Lev. 19.3: "Each one of you is to revere his mother and his father, and my Sabbaths shall you observe." According to that tradition, violation of the Sabbath is punishable by death (see e.g., Exod. 31.14–15).

The calendar of festivals begins in Lev. 23.3:

> For six days you shall perform tasks, but on the seventh day, it is a Sabbath of complete cessation *[shabbat shabbaton]*, a sanctuary convocation *[mikra' kodesh]*. You may not perform any tasks; it is a Sabbath day in all your settlements.

Lev. 23.3 thus adds the Sabbath's status as a sanctuary convocation, thereby treating it as a public occasion for worship. Num. 28.9–10, part of a still later Priestly text, outlines special sacrifices for the Sabbath.

Clues to the celebration of the Sabbath appear in other Torah passages. Exod. ch 16, in narrating the manna episode in the wilderness, forbids gathering that heavenly food on the Sabbath, and further stipulates that cooking and baking are forbidden on the Sabbath. Exod. 35.3 forbids lighting fire on the Sabbath, presumably for the purpose of cooking. Num. ch 15, shows that gathering wood was forbidden on the Sabbath; an Israelite who did so was executed.

Several texts outside the Torah teach us different aspects about the Sabbath, mostly from negative inference. Thus, Hos. (2.13), where the LORD threatens Israel: "I will bring a halt *(wehishbatti)* to all her rejoicing: her pilgrimages, her new moons and her Sabbaths, and all her festivals," implies that the Shabbat was a joyous occasion. Amos (8.4–5) suggests that acquiring provisions and unpacking grain were prohibited on the Sabbath, as on the new moon. Isaiah (1.12–14) speaks at the close of the 8th c. BCE. He connects Sabbaths and new moons to "convoking sacred gatherings," informing us that these occasions brought Israelites to the Temple in Jerusalem. The husband of a Shunammite woman asked his wife, who intended to visit the prophet Elisha: "Why are you going to him today? It is neither new moon nor Sabbath" (NJPS, 2 Kings 4.23), suggesting that this was a special day in which prophetic advice might be solicited. Finally, 2 Kings chs 11 and 16 describe special royal activities in the Jerusalem Temple on the Sabbath (cf. similar activities prescribed for the *nasi'*, "chieftain, prince" of a later period in Ezek. ch 46).

The Sabbath law of Lev. 23.3 ordains that the Sabbath be observed "in all your settlements," that is, not just at a sanctuary. Sabbath observance at a local sanctuary became especially difficult after 622 BCE, when Josiah, king of Judah, issued an edict restricting all sacrifice to the Jerusalem Temple (2 Kings chs 22–23). Soon thereafter, the Judean kingdom was conquered by the Babylonians (586 BCE), part of the population was exiled, and the Temple was destroyed; the Second Temple only resumed partial operations seventy years later. Thus after 586 new forms of Sabbath (and new moon) worship would have developed in the "settlements," removed from any temple or sanctuary.

The Hebrew Bible provides information about observance of the Sabbath in the exile and beyond. Jer. ch 17, generally regarded as postexilic, notes that the Sabbath was being violated in Jerusalem and the countryside, and includes carrying as one of the tasks forbidden on the Shabbat:

> Thus said the LORD: Take safe care of yourselves! Do not carry merchandise on the Sabbath, bringing it in through the gates of Jerusalem. And do not carry merchandise from your homes on the Sabbath day or engage in any tasks. You

> must sanctify the Sabbath day as I commanded your ancestors (Jer. 17.21–22).

Other exilic and postexilic statements reinforce the concept of the Sabbath as sacred time. The prophet Ezekiel (22.8, 26) condemns the Temple priests for desecrating the Sabbath, failing "to differentiate between the sacred and the profane." Ezek. chs 40–48, describe in great detail rites performed in the Temple on the Sabbath, with the participation of the *nasi'* (Ezekiel's title for the Davidic king). On a more positive note, [Trito]-Isaiah (56.1–2) praises those who honor the Sabbath, and later (58.13–14) asserts that God will bring joy to those who rejoice on the Sabbath. The book of Neh. opens a window onto the life of the community in postexilic Jerusalem and Yehud, as that leader endeavors to maintain Sabbath observance under Persian imperial rule (Neh. 10.32; 13.14–22). In order to prevent commerce on the Shabbat, Nehemiah (Neh. 13.19) ordered the gates of Jerusalem bolted as the shadows of evening darkened before the Sabbath.

An incidental reference to the Sabbath is in a Heb inscription from Yavneh Yam, dated ca. 625 BCE: *lpny shbt (= lipne shabbat),* "before the Sabbath," the same phrase used in Neh. 13.19. The Sabbath is also mentioned in two Aram. inscriptions from Jewish colonies in Egypt of the 5th c. BCE. These inscriptions make clear that the Sabbath was not merely a theoretical festival, but was observed in preexilic and postexilic times, in the land of Israel and in the diaspora.

The New Moon (Heb *ḥodesh*)

In biblical times, the birth of the new moon (*ḥodesh*, also "month") was reported by visual sighting, at which point counting would begin, when applicable, to days in the month when the annual festivals occurred. In ancient Israel, as in most ancient Near Eastern societies, luni-solar calendars were in use to reconcile seasonal festivals (linked to the earth's position in respect to the sun) with the months of the year (determined by the moon).

Moon gods, most notably Sin in Mesopotamia, were widely worshipped in the ancient Near East. Although moon worship was forbidden in biblical religion (see Deut. 17.2–5), the monthly phases of the moon were expressed in the religious calendar. A late statement on public celebration of the new moon appears in Num. 28.11–16. There is, however, no statement in the Torah that tasks are prohibited on the new moon, or that it is to be celebrated as a sanctuary convocation.

Non-Torah texts offer a different picture. The prophet Amos (8.5), in the mid-late 8th c. BCE, censures greedy and dishonest merchants who say: "If only the new moon would pass so that we could sell grain, and the Sabbath, so that we could market wheat," suggesting that commercial activities were prohibited on the new moon as well as on the Sabbath. 1 Sam. ch 20, where David makes repeated references to a feast on the new moon, also mentions a "sacred feast of the clan." In the postexilic period, [Trito]-Isaiah (66.23) says: "It shall happen, one new moon after another, and one Sabbath after another, that all flesh shall come to worship Me"; this reflects the importance of the new moon in the postexilic period. Its importance became much less significant by the rabbinic period.

The Annual Festivals (Heb *mo'ed*), and Pilgrimages (Heb *ḥag*)

The early agrarian calendar of festivals in Exod. 23.14–18 (cf. the later Exod. 34.18–23) reads:

> Three times a year shall you undertake a pilgrimage on My behalf. You shall observe the pilgrimage festival of unleavened bread *[ḥag hammatzot]*. For seven days you shall eat unleavened bread as I have commanded you, at the set time of the new moon of Abib *[lemo'ed ḥodesh ha'abib]*, for it was then that you went forth out of Egypt; and you may not appear before Me empty-handed. Also,

> the pilgrimage festival of reaping *[weḥag hakatzir]*, the first fruits of your agricultural product which you sowed in the field. Also, the pilgrimage festival of ingathering *[ḥag haʾasip]*, at the end of the year, when you gather in your products from the field.

The clause "as I have commanded you" refers to the obligation to eat unleavened bread (Exod. 12.21–27, 29–42; 13.1–16). These texts are rich in descriptive information about the two conjoined celebrations that may have once been separate: the pilgrimage festival of unleavened bread, and the Passover sacrifice. In earlier times, such festivals would have brought worshippers to local, or regional cult sites where celebratory sacrifices could be offered. The term *moʿed*, used here and in other Torah texts (Exod. 34.18; Deut. 16.6) indicates that these festivals were scheduled on a precise date (see the NJPS translators' note to Exod. 13.4); Heb *ḥodesh* here means "new moon," not "month." This suggests that at one time, the Passover-*matzot* celebrations occurred on the new moon, not on the full moon, at mid-month, as in the later Priestly festival calendar of Lev. ch 23. The other two pilgrimage festivals were likely also celebrated on the new moon as well.

The early calendar of Exod. ch 23, and the similarly early sections in Exod. chs 12–13 note the Passover sacrifice, but also stipulate: "And you may not appear before Me empty-handed," suggesting that other offerings were expected as well. The month name during which this festival was celebrated, Abib, literally means "budding grain" (Exod. 9.31; Lev. 2.14). This does not suggest, however, that the festival of unleavened bread celebrated the new grain crop; rather, from the outset it commemorated the exodus. The requirement of eating unleavened bread is explained as a consequence of leaving Egypt in haste, unleavened bread being a kind of "hard-tack" carried on long marches. The Passover sacrifice in the evening commemorated the night of the exodus, when the Israelites in Egypt were cautioned to remain indoors, hence the unique, domestic sacrifice, the *pesaḥ*, offered household by household in the evening, without recourse to priest or altar, and offered up whole. Hyssop was to be dipped in the blood of the sacrifice, and applied to the lintels and doorposts of Israelite homes. It was prophylactic, intended to ward off the "destroyer" *(mashit)*, sent by God to punish the Egyptians (see Exod. 12.23 n.). The God of Israel was pictured as "straddling" the houses of the Israelites in order to protect them. This is the correct meaning of the Heb verb *pasaḥ*, which means "to protect," rather than "to pass over" (see Isa. 31.5 n.).

Part of the commemorative process was the injunction to relate the exodus saga to the children, who will predictably inquire: "What is this ritual celebration?" (Exod. 12.26; 13.8, 14). The early narratives of Exod. 12.29–42, and all of Exod. ch 13, effectively answer the question, describing the midnight exodus after Pharaoh finally allowed the Israelites to leave Egypt with their herds and flocks. Much later this would develop into the standardized rituals of the Passover *seder*.

The festival calendar in Exod. ch 23, and its parallel in Exod. ch 34, also legislate two harvest festivals, both termed *ḥag*. *Qatzir*, "reaping," referring to the wheat or barley harvest, and *ʾasip* "ingathering," of fruits such as olives, at the end of the agricultural year. No precise dates are here given for these two celebrations.

The festival calendar in Deut. ch 16 reworks and expands the earlier calendar in Exod. ch 23, especially in light of the innovation of Deut. ch 12, restricting all sacrifice to one, central Temple. Vv. 1–8 restate the laws of Passover, which is now celebrated "at the place where the LORD chooses to install his name" (Deut. 16.6), not in individual households, as originally prescribed, nor at local cult sites. (See similarly 2 Kings 23.21–23.)

It would have been difficult to undertake a long pilgrimage that would keep worshippers away from home for a week or more during the grain harvest season. Thus, Deut. ch 16 would permit a person to celebrate the Passover sacrifice, now cooked at the central sanctuary in the evening, to return home the next morning. Nevertheless, the text legislates the prohibition of *ḥametz,* "leavened bread" for six additional days, and the celebration of an *ʿatzeret,* "solemn assembly" on the seventh day, back home, on which tasks were prohibited.

Deut. 16.9–12 presents the revised calendar for the pilgrimage of the grain harvest:

> Seven weeks shall you count off from when you first put the sickle to the standing grain; [then] shall you begin to count seven weeks. You shall celebrate a pilgrimage festival of weeks *[ḥag shabhuʿot]* to the LORD, your God, donating your generous offering according as the LORD, your God, will have blessed you. You shall rejoice in the presence of the LORD, your God; you and your son and your daughter, your male and your female servant, and the Levite in your gates, and the resident alien and the orphan and widow who are in your midst, at the cult site where the LORD, your God, chooses to install his name. Remembering that you were a slave in Egypt, you must obey these statutes.

This festival is commemorated later than its counterpart in Exod.; this is best explained as a practical response to the centralization of worship, allowing people to complete the wheat harvest before undertaking a distant Temple pilgrimage. This new name of the festival, *Shavuʿot,* "weeks," rather than "harvest" reflects its new nature.

Deut. 16.11–17 ordains the last of the three pilgrimage festivals, whose name has also been changed from "ingathering" to *Sukkot,* "booths," perhaps reflecting the practice of living in booths in the fields until the harvest was completed (see Isa. 1.8). The festival lasts seven days but no beginning date is provided, and once again, the Israelites are enjoined not to appear in God's presence empty-handed. The passage concludes with the repeated listing of the three annual pilgrimage festivals.

The presentation of "first fruits," (Heb *reʾsit*) at the Temple according to Deut. ch 26 is not directly associated with the pilgrimage festival of Weeks, and no precise date is set, but it would be appropriate at that time, or even earlier, at the presentation of the first sheaf. It may have been intended as an annual event. In addition, this passage contains a dramatic declaration of thanksgiving for the exodus and for the grant of the promised land. The rhetoric is reminiscent of the Deuteronomic version of the Decalogue regarding the Sabbath. A process of historicizing has begun, whereby a seasonal harvest festival has appropriated aspects commemorating past events (deemed to be historical). Deut. ch 26, in addition, dramatizes desacralization, a process by which the deity is offered a portion of the new crop before the people may partake of it. This is because the earth and all that is in it belong, in the first instance, to the LORD (Pss. 24.1; 98.7), and the offering of a portion to the deity allows human consumption of the rest. This passage in Deut. may well be the basis for the Priestly provisions for celebrations to occur between Passover and Shavuʿot, as set forth in Lev. 23.9–14, to which we now turn.

The Priestly festival calendar is in Lev. ch 23 of the Holiness Collection (Lev. chs 17–27). After opening with the Sabbath (see above), the actual festival calendar begins in v. 4, with the law of Pesaḥ (vv. 4–8):

> These are the set times of the LORD [*moʿade* YHVH], sanctuary convocations, which you shall convene at their set time: In the first month, on the fourteenth of the month, at twilight, is a Pesaḥ [Passover] sacrifice to the LORD. And on the fifteenth day of this month is the pilgrimage festival of unleavened bread to the LORD; for seven days you shall eat unleavened bread. And you shall offer up a fire-offering to the LORD for seven days; on the seventh day is a sanctuary convocation. You may not perform any work tasks.

An exact date is set for the Passover festival, and the same will be true for the other two festivals, and other sacred occasions. The months of the year are indicated by ordinal numbers ("the first month," and so forth), a practice found in Heb inscriptions. The Passover sacrifice is to be brought at twilight, not at sunset as in Deut., while the festival of Matzot itself commences on the next day, the fifteenth of the month. The first and seventh days are designated a sanctuary convocation, when tasks are forbidden.

Lev. ch 23, like Deut. ch 15, which it probably knows, accepts the deferral of the grain harvest festival for seven weeks, but it deals with it in a different way. Lev. 23.9–14 prescribe a ceremony in the Temple "on the morrow of the Sabbath day," namely, the day after the first Sabbath that follows the seven day festival of unleavened bread. (Various Jewish groups would later debate the meaning of the phrase "On the morrow of the Sabbath day"; see Lev. 23.11 n.) On that date, the priest "raises" the first sheaf *(ʿomer)* of the barley crop, whereas in Deut., he places it before the LORD. The objective is the same: to display the offering, rather than burning it on the altar. This ceremony affords the use of the barley harvest right after the Passover festival, as stated in Lev. 23.14, which explicitly prohibits consumption of the new crop "until that very day," that is, until the ceremony for the new harvest had taken place. After part of the new crop is offered as a gift to God, the Israelites may then use the remainder.

The Leviticus calendar continues by mandating counting seven "Sabbatical weeks" *(shabbatot),* namely, weeks ending on the Sabbath. The wheat harvest festival is then commemorated fifty days after the counting started, when "a grain offering from the new crop" *(minḥah ḥadashah)* is to be brought as "first fruits" *(bikkurim)*. In contrast to the other two festivals, this occasion is not called *ḥag* (pilgrimage festival) here in Lev. The section ends with a thematically related order to leave the edges of the field and gleanings for the poor and the resident alien at harvest time (probably copied from Lev. 19.9–10).

Lev. 23.23–25 continues with the new moon of the seventh month, celebrated as a sanctuary convocation when tasks are prohibited, and special sacrifices are offered. None of the earlier calendars mandate this festival, which is the precursor of the Jewish New Year, Rosh Ha-Shanah; that cannot be its function here since it takes place at the beginning of the seventh month. Instead, that occasion, on which the shofar was blown, heralded the upcoming pilgrimage on the annual harvest festival, at mid-month. The new moon of the seventh month is called "a Sabbath-like (day), commemorated by the shofar blast," or just "day of the (shofar) blast." Ps. 81.4: "Blast the shofar on the new moon, and on the full moon, for the day of our pilgrimage festival" may refer to this festival, if the "new moon" of that v. is that of the seventh month.

This special new moon is followed by "the Day of Atonement" *(yom hakkippurim)* to be observed annually on the tenth day of the seventh month (Lev. 23.26–32). The prescribed rites overlap with those, given in greater detail in Lev. ch 16. Israel is commanded to "afflict [them]selves" (or: "practice self-denial") on that day, which is taken to mean fasting. An unspecified fire-offering is to be brought, and tasks are prohibited on that day, designated a sanctuary convocation. V. 32 gives the day an added designation:

> It is a Sabbath of complete cessation *[shabbat shabbaton]* for you; you shall afflict yourselves *[weʿinnitem ʾet napshotekem],* on the ninth day in the evening, from one evening to the next evening shall you observe your Sabbath.

The concept of *kippurim,* usually translated "atonement," more precisely connotes "purgation" or "riddance," the wiping away of ritual impurities generated during the year that would detract from the holiness of the Sanctuary. This is in preparation for the Sukkot pilgrimage festival scheduled to begin five days later. Lev. ch 16 clarifies how this process was implemented (see Lev. 16.1–34 n.).

Lev. 23.33–44 relate to "the Sukkot pilgrimage festival" *(ḥag hassukkot),* and present two overlapping instructions. Vv. 33–37a are composed in the general style of Lev. ch 23:

> The LORD spoke to Moses as follows: Speak to the Israelites as follows: On the fifteenth day of the seventh month is the pilgrimage festival of Sukkot for seven days, to the LORD. On the first day is a sanctuary convocation; you shall not perform any work tasks. For seven days you shall bring an offering by fire to the LORD. On the eighth day is a sanctuary convocation and you shall bring an offering by fire to the LORD; it is a solemn assembly; you may not perform any work tasks. These are the set times of the LORD which you shall proclaim as sanctuary convocations.

In its final form, Lev. (23.40–43) adds another passage on the Sukkot festival, repeating the same provisions, in substance, but adding the following:

> On the first day you shall take for yourselves the fruit of the hadar tree, branches of palm trees, and boughs of leafy trees, and willows of the brook, and you shall rejoice before the LORD, your God, for seven days ... all citizens in Israel shall live in booths, in order that future generations may know that I made the Israelite people live in booths when I brought them out of the land of Egypt.

Only here does the Torah connect Sukkot, originally an agricultural festival, with a historical event.

The calendar in Num. chs 28–30 incorporates most of the provisions of the preceding sources, but restricts itself to the public sphere. There is no reference to the Passover sacrifice, for example, only to the festival sacrifice, termed *ḥag.* The major innovation in Num. is the *tamid,* "daily sacrifice," which overrides all other sacred occasions. This calendar further prescribes a detailed regimen for each occasion—Sabbath, new moon, Pesaḥ-*matzot,* the festival of weeks, the new moon of the seventh month, the Day of Atonement, and Sukkot. In fact, different sacrifices are prescribed for each of the eight days of the Sukkot festival. This calendar lacks any reference to the presentation of the first sheaf and to the counting of fifty days, or to the notion of Sabbatical weeks, or to a pilgrimage during the grain harvest.

Although the Torah contains the only detailed prescriptive texts about the festivals, various festivals are mentioned outside of the Torah. Some of these overlap with the Torah festivals, while others suggest that at various times and places in ancient Israel, additional or different festivals were celebrated. For example, Judg. 21.19 mentions an unspecified "pilgrimage festival *[ḥag]* of the LORD" in Shiloh, where there stood "a temple of the LORD" (*bet* YHVH). This may be related to the report in 1 Sam. 1.3, 7 that Elkanah, the father of the prophet Samuel, made an annual pilgrimage to Shiloh. Nothing connects such events with the annual festivals known from the Torah, yet these accounts suggest that annual pilgrimages to sacred sites were customary in early biblical times.

As in the case of the Sabbath and the new moon, most of what we know about the observance of pilgrimage festivals derives from the prophetic condemnation of practices associated with these festivals. Hosea (9.5), in the mid-8th c., chastises northern Israelites who defile the sacrifices: "What will you do for the day of the set festival and for the day of the pilgrimage festival of the LORD?"

At approximately the same period, also in Northern Israel, Amos (5.21) transmits the LORD's first-person condemnation of northern Israelite religious practice: "I detest, I abhor your pilgrimage offerings, and I will not inhale (the aroma) of your solemn assemblies." The prophet predicts that festivals will turn into times of mourning (Amos

8.10). Later, in Jerusalem, Isaiah criticizes the meaningless sequence of annual festivals (Isa. 29.1; cf. Mal. 2.3). In contrast, Isa. 30.29 foresees the LORD's punishment of the nations and the subsequent restoration of Judah, when there will again be rejoicing in the Jerusalem Temple:

> For you, there shall be singing,
> As on a night when a pilgrimage festival
> is sanctified.
> There shall be rejoicing as when they
> march
> With flute, with timbrels, and with lyres,
> To the Rock of Israel, on the Mount of
> the LORD.

Similarly, the prophet Nahum (2.1) heralds the joyous celebration of festivals:

> Behold on the hills the footsteps of
> a herald! He announces peace.
> Celebrate your pilgrimage festivals, Judah;
> fulfill your vows.
> For never again shall the evildoer invade
> you; He has been totally cut-off!

The postexilic prophet known as Second Zechariah (14.16) foresees a major pilgrimage of defeated nations on "the day of the LORD," when the survivors of the LORD's wrath will bow to His sovereignty. That pilgrimage will take place on Sukkot, the major pilgrimage festival in ancient Israel, for only then had the people completed the harvest and so could gather in large numbers at the Jerusalem Temple.

Several of the annual festivals are mentioned in the Former Prophets. Most significant is the record of Solomon's dedication of the Temple in Jerusalem, which was celebrated "on *the* pilgrimage festival" (1 Kings 8.2, 65), namely, on Sukkot in the seventh month, called "the month of the perennial streams," at the beginning of the rainy season in October. The importance of the pilgrimage festivals in Israel's life is illustrated by the fact that the secessionist king, Jeroboam I, changed the date of the Sukkot pilgrimage from the seventh to the eighth month, and routed it to Bethel rather than to Jerusalem—in an effort to consolidate his rule over northern Israel (1 Kings 12.32–33), and to establish its independence from the kingdom of Judah. Calendars help determine national identity, and this calendrical change reflected a strong break with Judean religious institutions and the Jerusalem Temple.

The late books of Ezra-Neh. and Chron. report on the dutiful observance of the annual festivals in Jerusalem in postexilic times (Ezra 3.4; 6.22; Neh. 8.14, 18; 2 Chron. 30.1). Ezek. 45.21; 46.11, probably to be dated as well to the postexilic period, contain references to festivals in the style of the Priestly Torah texts; given the late date of the text, and the fact that Ezekiel was a priest and his work was edited in priestly circles, this is expected.

A biblical festival that came into being after the Torah festivals, and is therefore not mentioned in the Torah, is Purim. The raison d'etre for its observance—to commemorate the rescue from annihilation of the Jews of Persia—is given in the book of Esth. Esth. 8.12 records that this festival should be celebrated "on the thirteenth of the twelfth month, that is the month of Adar." The name Purim refers to the "lots" cast so that Haman could determine the day on which to destroy the Jews (Esth. 3.7). The rites specified in the biblical observance of Purim differ from all earlier festivals: feasting and merry-making, exchanging gifts and giving presents to the poor (Esth. 9.20–23).

Hanukkah, commemorating the ritual cleansing of the Temple in 164 BCE is never mentioned in the Bible; the latest of the biblical books, Dan., seems to know of the persecutions that led up to Hanukkah, but not of the cleansing of the Temple (see Dan. 11.21–45 nn.), and the holiday that commemorated it.

Annual Fast Days

Fasting was a widely attested religious practice in the ancient Near East, as in ancient

Israel. The key term is Heb *tzom,* "fast, fast day" (Jer. 36.6) and related verbs. The underlying phenomenology is self-mortification, or self-denial, whereby the renunciation of normal gratifications, and the consequent deprivation suffered by the worshipper, are seen as ways of entreating the deity to be gracious and forgiving. Fasting can be part of mourning and the grieving process, or markers of individual and communal ad hoc fasts. Annual days of communal fasting were instituted to commemorate national disaster; some of these continue to be observed.

The annual Day of Atonement, already discussed as part of the religious calendar, incorporates a complex of phenomena, only one of which is fasting. In a ritual context, fasting represents an aspect of purification. While the Day of Atonement is never actually called a "fast," Isa. 58.3, which says, most likely in reference to that day, "Why, when we fasted, did You not see? When we starved our bodies, did You pay no heed?" suggests that already in the biblical period the Day of Atonement was characterized by fasting.

The primary source for annual communal fasts is the postexilic prophet Zechariah (8.19):

> Thus says the LORD of Hosts: The fast of the fourth (month), and the fast of the fifth, and the fast of the seventh, and the fast of the tenth shall become occasions of joy and gladness, and happy festivals for the House of Judah. But you must love truth and peace!

These fast days, all commemorating tragic events associated with the Babylonian destruction of Jerusalem and its Temple, may be identified by reference to 2 Kings ch 25, and the parallel account in Jer. ch 52, (see also Jer. chs 39 and 41). The fast days are listed in the order of the months of the year, beginning with Nisan in the spring, not in the chronological order of the historical events that they commemorate:

(1) The fast of the fourth month (Tamuz). This commemorates the breach of the walls of Jerusalem by the Babylonians in the fourth month, after a long siege, on the ninth of the month in 586 BCE. (See 2 Kings 25.3–4; Jer. 39.2–3; 52.6–7.).

(2) The fast of the fifth month (Av), commemorating the day the Babylonian commander burned the Temple of Jerusalem and smashed the city walls, on the tenth of the month in 586 (See 2 Kings 25.8–10; Jer. 52.12–14.)

(3) The fast of the seventh month (Tishri), commemorating the assassination in 586 of the Babylonian appointed governor, Gedaliah, by Judean zealots. (See 2 Kings 25.25; Jer. ch 41.)

(4) The fast of the tenth month (Tevet), when Nebuchadnezzar initiated the siege of Jerusalem on the tenth of the month in 588. (See 2 Kings 25.12; Jer. 52.4–5.)

Three of these disasters were brought upon Judah and Jerusalem directly by the Babylonians, but the third, later called the Fast of Gedaliah, was attributed to a group of Judeans, of the royal family, whose actions brought harsh reprisals by the Babylonians, adding to the national tragedy.

Religious practice changes over time, and these biblical fast days and festivals underwent changes in meaning and in ritual practice throughout the biblical period; and new festivals, such as Hanukkah, were added to the Jewish calendar. In addition, many of the festivals that were originally occasioned by the agricultural cycle were reinterpreted over time, and connected to historical events. For example, by the rabbinic period, Shavuʿot, in the Bible a grain harvest festival, became associated with the giving of the Torah on Mt. Sinai, an association never made explicit in the Bible. The process of reinterpretation of the significance of festivals and their observances that we see in the Bible continued afterwards, from postbiblical times until our own day.

[BARUCH A. LEVINE]

Historical and Ideal Davidic Kingship

The Bible's presentation of the royal House of David, which ruled Israel and Judah ca. 1000–586 BCE, constitutes an important source for the development of messianism in both Judaism and Christianity.

Historical Background

The earliest historical evidence for the royal House of David in Judah appears in the Tel Dan Inscription and the Mesha Inscription (the Moabite Stone), which both date to the second half of the 9th c. BCE and contain references to "the house of David." Thus, they do not provide definitive proof for the existence of a historical King David. Nevertheless, on the basis of the biblical record, most scholars generally date David's reign to the first half of the 10th c. BCE, ca. 1000–960 BCE. The Hebrew Bible, particularly the books of Sam. and Chron., are our main source for the reconstruction of the origins of the Davidic dynasty. Although both Sam. and Chron. present accounts of the early history of the House of David, both are the products of later writers with their own historiographical viewpoints that shape their presentations of David's rise to power; they cannot be used as straightforward historical accounts.

The power vacuum left in western Asia by the withdrawal of the Egyptian empire from the region in the late-13th and early-12th centuries BCE offers the background for the rise of the House of David. The Assyrian empire did not engage western Asia until the mid-9th c. BCE, so the region was relatively free from outside political control and therefore able to develop its own political structures in the late second millennium and the early first millennium. Historical evidence points to the influx of two major population groups into Canaan during this period. The first were semi-nomadic Semitic-speaking groups who entered Canaan from the Arabian Desert, east of the Jordan River. Ancient records identify these peoples with the Akkadian term, *ḫabiru/apiru*, which some identify with the Heb word, *ʿivri*, "Hebrew." The Akkadian term means "barbarian," i.e., people who stand outside the boundaries of normative civilization. The second group, identified in Egyptian sources as "the Sea Peoples," originated in the Greek islands and entered Canaan from the west by way of the Mediterranean Sea after they failed to conquer Egypt in 1196 BCE. Both groups melded with the local Canaanite populations. The *ḫabiru* settled in the hill country of Canaan to form the Israelite and Judean peoples, and the Sea Peoples settled along the Canaanite coastal plain to form the Philistines. Archeological evidence indicates conflict between the two peoples from ca. 1200 BCE through ca. 1000 BCE when Israel/Judah emerged as the dominant political power of the region.

The books of Judg. and Sam. present an account of the origins of kingship in Israel from a decidedly pro-Davidic viewpoint. The Heb term, "judge," *(shophet)* refers to political rather than judicial leaders. Although the framework of Judg. portrays a unified twelve-tribe Israel under the leadership of a succession of judges, a closer reading of the individual narratives indicates that each judge exercised authority over only a handful of tribes. Within these narratives, it is clear that the tribe of Ephraim attempts to play a leading role, threatening Gideon of Manasseh with war when he assembles a small band of three hundred men to fight the Midianites (Judg. chs 6–8) and actually waging war against Jephthah of Gilead when he battles the Ammonites (Judg. chs 11–12). In both cases, the tribe of Ephraim apparently saw itself as the leading tribe of a coalition and attempted to assert its authority over Manasseh and Gilead. Judg. ch 9 presents an account of the failed attempt by Abimelech ben Gideon to claim the kingship of Israel following the death of his father. At the conclusion of the book, Judg. chs 19–21 present an account of the rape of the Levite's concubine and its consequences in the Benjaminite city of Gibeah, Saul's later capital, in a blatant attempt to discredit the first known king of Israel. Thus, Judg. deals with kingship in a variety of ways, (re)writing traditions about earlier local leaders, and putting them in a pro-Davidic framework. (See intro. to Judg., pp. 495–97.)

1 Sam. portrays the selection of Saul ben Kish of the tribe of Benjamin as a reaction to the attempts by the Philistines to dominate Israel. Given the archeological evidence concerning conflict between the Israelites in the hill country and the Philistines in the coastal plain, such a scenario is reasonable. The underlying issue is not simply control of the land of Canaan, but economic power in western Asia as well; Israel sits astride the trade routes between Egypt to the southwest, Africa and the Arabian Peninsula to the south, Phoenicia and Asia Minor to the north and northwest, and Aram and Mesopotamia to the northeast. Whoever would control those routes, particularly in a period when the superpowers of the time, viz., Egypt and Mesopotamia, were not engaged in Canaan, would dominate the ancient Near Eastern economy.

Even apart from the pro-Davidic perspective of Sam., it is clear that Saul's kingship was a dismal failure. The Philistines were able to contain Israel in the hill country, and Saul eventually committed suicide according to 1 Sam. ch 31, defending Beth Shean in the eastern Jezreel Valley, the last strongpoint protecting the route from Israel to Aram and Mesopotamia.

The Rise of David

1 Sam. also makes it clear that Saul was unable to bring David under his influence. David appears as a tribal leader of Judah, who married Saul's daughter Michal to become son-in-law to the king. In the ancient world, such a marriage would have signaled a political alliance between the kingdom of Israel ruled by Saul and the tribe of Judah ruled by David. Such a scenario suggests that Saul already served as king of what would later be known as the ten tribes of northern Israel, and that an alliance with Judah would bring the southern hill country under Saul's control. Such a move by Saul would strengthen his hand against the Philistines.

It is impossible to determine what historical reality, if any, stands behind the Bible's depiction of the rift between Saul and David. 1 Sam. indicates that Saul was afflicted by an evil spirit (e.g., 1 Sam. 18.10) that looks very much like a form of manic-depressive syndrome—but interpreters must bear in mind that Sam. was written in the aftermath of Saul's death by pro-Davidic authors. The Bible suggests that the conflict between David and Saul presented the Philistines with an opportunity to turn David against Saul. When David went over to the Philistine side to escape Saul's pursuit, the Philistines granted David rule over a small town called Ziklag along the Philistine-Judean border and charged David with the task of harassing Judah while they launched a major assault against Saul. David used his position to protect the people of Judah and thereby to build support for himself, and his position left him conveniently far from the site of Saul's demise at Mt. Gilboa.

2 Sam. portrays the process by which David became king, first of Judah and then over all Israel. The death of Saul and three of his sons left David free to move from Ziklag to the ancient, important city of Hebron to assume kingship over the tribe of Judah. David was still a Philistine vassal at the time, and the Philistines would have seen David's move as serving their own interests. Israel was left under the rule of one of Saul's surviving sons, identified as Ish-bosheth, "man of shame," in Sam. and as Eshbaal, "man of Baal," and likely his real name in Chron. (8.33). As a Philistine vassal, David went to war against Ish-bosheth/Eshbaal for some seven years until he won a victory over the Israelite forces at Gibeon. David's victory at Gibeon apparently

tipped the balance of power against Israel. Shortly thereafter, Ish-bosheth's general, Abner, defected to David only to be assassinated by David's general, Joab, and two Gibeonite army officers assassinated Ish-bosheth/Eshbaal. With Ish-Bosheth/Eshbaal dead, the elders of Israel (namely the north) approached David to invite him to serve as king over Israel, and David readily accepted.

But David was faced with a political problem, viz., if he remained at Hebron, the northern Israelite tribes would not follow him for long; if he moved his capital to the north, he would lose the tribe of Judah. His solution, the conquest of Jebusite Jerusalem, on the border between Judah and the northern tribes, using only his own mercenary troops, gave David a capital that would enable him to unite the two major portions of his kingdom. 2 Sam. ch 6 maintains that David also made Jerusalem the religious capital of Israel by moving the Ark of the Covenant from Kiriath-jearim, where it had resided after having been seized by the Philistines, to Jerusalem. When the Philistines sent armies to ensure David's continued submission to their role, David decisively defeated them, something Saul had never been able to do. Finally, according to the Bible, with David's subjugation of the Philistines, Israel/Judah emerged as the regional power in western Asia. But David came to power as a member of the ruling house of Saul. 2 Sam. ch 6 relates (and justifies) David's refusal to have relations with Michal, which ensures that no children of Saulide blood would be born to her. 2 Sam. ch 20 relates David's handing over of the surviving descendants of Saul to the Gibeonites for execution eliminating further Saulide challengers to David. And 2 Sam. chs 9 and 19 relate David's care for Saul's grandson, Mephibosheth, identified as Merib-baal in Chron., as Mephibosheth ultimately relinquishes any claims to his grandfather's throne.

The House of David in History

The Bible suggests that upon David's death, Solomon (ca. 960–921 BCE), son of David's favorite wife Bathsheba, emerges as the next king of Israel. 1 Kings chs 1–11 portray Solomon's reign in a mixture of adulatory and critical terms. Solomon's rule saw the foundation of the Jerusalem Temple (the First Temple), the building of cities, and the establishment of trade relations that enriched Israel and extended its power. Archeology points to extensive building throughout the land beginning in the 10th c. BCE, although some archeologists place the strata previously associated with Solomon at a later period. The Bible suggests that Solomon's reign also saw the imposition of heavy taxation and even forced labor on the northern tribes that eventually led to their revolt against the House of David following Solomon's death.

Whereas David rose to kingship by marrying into the royal house of Saul, 1 Kings ch 1 asserts that Solomon attained kingship through the efforts of his mother, Bathsheba and the prophet Nathan. Bathsheba was the latest of David's wives and Solomon was one of his youngest sons. Insofar as the earlier wives and sons were from David's days in Hebron and Bathsheba was from Jerusalem, the rise of Solomon to kingship and Bathsheba to the important role of *Gebirah* or "Queen Mother" constituted a coup within the harem culture of the Davidic house that defined the future course of the dynasty. When Solomon succeeded his father, many of David's supporters from his Hebron days, such as his general Joab and his high priest Abiathar, were either killed or expelled from Jerusalem to be replaced by a new set of Jerusalemite figures, such as Benaiah the military commander and Zadok the new high priest (1 Kings 1.1–40).

Indeed, marriage is a key factor in political power in the ancient world. Treaties between nations are sealed by the marriage of members of the two royal houses. Thus David married Michal the daughter of Saul, Ahinoam who some identify as Saul's former wife, Abigail of Carmel who gave him control of Judah, Maacah of Geshur who became a key ally on Israel's northern border, and others.

1 Kings ch 11 charges Solomon with apostasy for marrying foreign women and allowing them to worship their foreign gods in Jerusalem, but Solomon's many marriages are actually testimony to his political standing in the world. Yet the account of his son Rehoboam's interview with the northern tribes in 1 Kings ch 12 to determine if they would accept him as king suggests Solomon's heavy hand and excessive taxation policy in ruling the northern tribes was the true cause of the northern revolt.

With the revolt of the northern tribes at the outset of Rehoboam's reign, the House of David was left to rule only the tribe of Judah and perhaps Benjamin as well. Indeed, for most of the next two hundred years, Judah was generally a vassal to its far larger and more powerful neighbor, Israel. But with the destruction of the Northern Kingdom of Israel by the Assyrian army in 722/721 BCE, the House of David had the opportunity to re-establish its rule over the former Northern Kingdom of Israel and thereby to regain Judah's status as a minor regional power. In order to pursue such a goal, King Hezekiah of Judah (715–687 BCE) allied with Prince Merodach Baladan of Babylonia to revolt against their Assyrian overlords. Hezekiah's alliance included all of the small city-states of western Asia, and the Egyptians promised him support. When the Assyrian King Sennacherib invaded western Asia in 701 BCE to put down the revolt, Hezekiah's alliance quickly collapsed, and he was left in Jerusalem to face Sennacherib alone. Although much of Isa. chs 36–39 and 2 Kings chs 18–20 claim that YHVH came to Hezekiah's aid to deliver Jerusalem, Sennacherib's records indicate that Hezekiah did submit to him, enabling the Assyrian army to march against Merodach Baladan in Babylonia.

King Manasseh son of Hezekiah (687–642 BCE) spent much of the 7th c. rebuilding Judah following the devastation left by the Assyrian army. But when the Assyrian empire was on the verge of collapse, King Josiah of Judah (640–609 BCE) once again saw an opportunity to reunite Israel and Judah under independent Davidic rule. The Egyptian Pharaoh, Necho II, saw things differently, and when Josiah marched the Judean army to Megiddo in 609 BCE in an effort to stop Necho from aiding his beleaguered Assyrian allies against the Babylonian army, Necho killed Josiah in battle and brought an end to the Davidic monarch's program of religious reform and national restoration.

When King Nebuchadnezzar of Babylonia defeated the Egyptians at Carchemesh in 605 BCE, Babylonia became Judah's new overlord. Although King Jehoiakim son of Josiah of Judah (609–598 BCE) submitted to Nebuchadnezzar, he owed his throne to Necho and ultimately revolted against Babylonia in 598 BCE with promises of Egyptian support. The revolt failed miserably, and Jehoiakim died of unknown causes, leaving his eighteen-year-old son Jehoiachin (597 BCE) to face the Babylonians alone. Nebuchadnezzar deported the young king to Babylonia, where he lived for the rest of his life, along with several thousand educated and skilled Judeans to serve the needs of the Babylonian empire. He appointed Jehoiachin's uncle, Zedekiah son of Josiah (597–587/586 BCE), as a puppet monarch, whose job it was to keep Judah quiet. Zedekiah failed in that task and when Judah revolted a second time in 588 BCE, Nebuchadnezzar attacked a second time, destroying Jerusalem and Solomon's Temple and deporting even more Judeans to Babylonian Exile (586 BCE). Although 2 Kings 25.27–30 reports that the Babylonian King Evil-merodach (562–560 BCE) released Jehoiachin from prison, he never returned to Jerusalem. Jehoiachin's grandson, Zerubbabel ben Shealtiel, later led a delegation of Judean exiles back to Jerusalem to rebuild the Temple in 522 BCE. Hag. 2.20–23 suggests that there were plans to reinstate Davidic kingship to coincide with the rebuilding of the Temple, but those plans were never realized and Zerubbabel disappeared from the records by the time the Second Temple was completed in about 515 BCE. No Davidic monarch ever regained the throne in Jerusalem after this time.

The Idealization of the House of David

The idealization of the House of David begins already in Judg., Sam., Kings, and Chron. Judg. portrays Othniel of Judah in ideal terms (Judg. 2.7–11), but each of the subsequent judges, each from a northern tribe, is flawed to one degree or another. Judg. concludes with the narrative concerning the rape and murder of the Levite's concubine in Judg. chs 19–21 in a clear polemic against Saul and underscores its anticipation of the rise of kingship by concluding that "there was no king in Israel; everyone did as he pleased" (Judg. 21.25). When 1 Sam. portrays David in relation to Saul, David is always idealized as favored by YHVH. 2 Sam. chs 1–8 note the many deaths that occur as David rises to power, e.g., Saul, Abner, Ish-bosheth, the sons of Saul, etc., but at each point exonerates David of any responsibility and grants him eternal kingship (2 Sam. ch 7). This contrasts with Saul, who is depicted as killing, and attempting to kill many innocent people, including his own son Jonathan, and David. David is condemned when he commits adultery with Bathsheba and sees to the murder of her husband, Uriah the Hittite, but he is immediately forgiven by YHVH when he repents (2 Sam. chs 10–12). 1 Chron. chs 11–29 idolize David even beyond Sam. and Kings. Chron. does not include an account of David's affair with Bathsheba, and it lionizes him as the designer of the Temple. Throughout Kings and Chron., David is frequently the benchmark for the evaluation of each member of the House of David who is judged according to the degree to which he did what was right in the eyes of YHVH like his father David or not (see e.g., 2 Kings 18.3). Other kings of the House of David are also idealized to a degree. 1 Kings chs 3–10 praise Solomon for his wisdom, wealth, building of the Temple, etc., although 1 Kings chs 1–2 and 11 give a far more critical portrayal of his reign. 2 Chron. chs 1–9, however, make no mention of Solomon's elimination of rivals or the apostasy of his wives; instead, it focuses on his wisdom, wealth, and building of the Temple. Eight Davidic monarchs are praised for their righteousness, i.e., Asa son of Abijam (1 Kings 15.11; 2 Chron. 14.1), Jehoshaphat son of Asa (1 Kings 22.43; 2 Chron. 17.3), Jehoash son of Ahaziah (2 Kings 12.3; 2 Chron. 24.2), Amaziah son of Joash (2 Kings 14.3; 2 Chron. 25.2); Azariah/Uzziah son of Amaziah (2 Kings 15.3; 2 Chron. 26.4); Jotham son of Uzziah (2 Kings 15.34; 2 Chron. 27.2); Hezekiah son of Ahaz (2 Kings 18.3; 2 Chron. 29.2), and Josiah son of Amon (2 Kings 22.2; 2 Chron. 34.2). Indeed, Josiah is described as the greatest of all the kings of the House of David, as a second Moses, insofar as 2 Kings 23.25 states, "There was no king like him before who turned back to YHVH with all his heart and soul and might according to all the Torah of Moses, and afterwards there was none like him" (author's translation). Chron. lauds many of the figures even more so by describing Jehoshaphat's judicial reforms (2 Chron. 19.4–11), enhancing Hezekiah's Temple reform and celebration of Passover (2 Chron. 29.1–30.27), Manasseh's repentance (2 Chron. 33.10–17), and Josiah's celebration of Passover (2 Chron. 35.1–19).

But the full idealization of the House of David appears in the books of the Latter Prophets. Isaiah looks forward to an ideal Davidic monarch who will be known as the Prince of Peace who will rule in justice (Isa. 9.1–6); who will preside over a kingdom in which the wolf will lie down with the lamb, all of Israel's enemies will be conquered, and the exiles from Assyria and Egypt will return home (Isa. 11.1–16); and whose reign will open the eyes, ears, and minds of the people to YHVH's restoration (Isa. 32.1–20). Isa. chs 36–39 present a far more idealized view of Hezekiah than its counterpart in 2 Kings chs 18–20 by eliminating any sense of Hezekiah's wrongdoing. (Chron. also presents a more idealized Hezekiah than its main source, Kings.) While Isa. chs 40–66 envision no restoration of a Davidic monarch, it maintains that YHVH's promise to the House of David applies generally to the people of Israel (Isa. 55.1–5).

Jeremiah is far more willing to judge Jerusalem and the House of David, but he holds out for an ideal Davidic monarch in Jer. 23.1–8 who will represent "the righteous branch" of David (v. 5). Like Second Isa., Jer. 33.14–26 recognizes that there will not be another Davidic monarch and argues that the righteous branch of David will be realized by the city of Jerusalem and the Levitical priesthood. Ezek. 37.15–28 envisions the reunification of northern Israel (the House of Joseph) and southern Judah under the rule of a Davidic king with the Temple at their center. Ezekiel's vision of the restored Temple in Ezek. chs 40–48 envisions the Davidic prince (not king) leading the people in the worship of YHVH—this represents a compromise position, where David is central, but as a diminished prince rather than king.

Many of the Twelve Prophets likewise idealize the House of David. Hos. 3.5 anticipates northern Israel's return to YHVH and David their king. Amos 9.11–15 views the restoration of the fallen booth of David as the key to Israel's restoration. Mic. chs 4–5 portray a monarch from Bethlehem as the key figure who will defeat Israel's oppressors and thereby bring about the idyllic vision of peace in Mic. 4.1–5. Hag. 2.20–23 envisions Zerubbabel ben Shealtiel, the grandson of Jehoiachin, as YHVH's signet who will rule following the overthrow of the throne of nations, i.e., the Persian monarch. And Zech. chs 9–14 look forward to the victory of Judah and the House of David as YHVH fights against the nations to ensure divine recognition throughout the entire world following the restoration of the Temple.

Finally, the book of Ps. also contributes to the idealization of David. David is already identified in the narrative literature as a musician who is able to comfort the distressed Saul in 1 Sam. 16.14–23 and as the royal patron of the Temple who established the Levitical choirs and musicians in 1 Chron. ch 25 (cf. 2 Chron. 23.18). He sings a lament for Saul and Jonathan in 2 Sam. 2.17–27; a song of thanksgiving for divine deliverance from his enemies in 2 Sam. ch 22 (cf. Ps. 18); and his last words are in 2 Sam. ch 23. 1st Chron. ch 16 indicates that Pss. 96, 105, and 106 were sung by the Levites when David brought the Ark to Jerusalem. Rabbinic tradition credits David with presenting the book of Ps. to Israel: "Moses gave the Five Books of the Torah, and corresponding to them, David gave the Five Books of Psalms to Israel (*Midr. Tehillim* 1:2). The book of Ps. itself credits David with the authorship of many psalms that were inspired by events in the monarch's life, i.e., Pss. 3; 7; 18; 34; 51; 52; 54; 56; 57; 59; 60; 63; 142, and others are simply ascribed to David, i.e., Pss. 4–6; 8–9; 11–17; 19–32; 35–41; 53; 55; 58; 61–62; 64–66; 68–70; 101; 103; 108–109; 122; 124; 131; 133; 138; and 139–145. Ps. 72.20 marks the conclusion of the second book of Ps. with the statement, "The Prayers of David ben Jesse are Concluded" (author's translation). Other psalms point to David's efforts to serve God, such as his tireless efforts to find a suitable place for the Ark of the Covenant (Ps. 132), God's defense of the (Davidic) King in Zion from enemies (Ps. 2); and God's grant to David of an eternal covenant (Pss. 89; 110).

Some biblical texts present an idealized David, and even suggest that an ideal Davidic leader, or perhaps even David himself, will return as an ideal king at some unspecified time in the future. Biblical texts also use the term *mashiaḥ*, "messiah," for the anointed king; the term refers to the anointing of the king with oil as part of the coronation ceremony (see e.g., 1 Sam. 16.13). Yet, within the Bible itself, the term "messiah" is only used for past kings, and never for the future ideal Davidic king, as the term came into use in postbiblical literature, where Judaism and Christianity employed idealized images of David as the basis for their respective theological world views. Christianity presents Jesus as a descendant of the House of David who is sent as God's Messiah to redeem humankind. Judaism views the Davidic Messiah as a figure who will come when the

Jerusalem Temple is re-established. Indeed, Hillel, one of the founding figures of the Rabbinic movement in Judaism, is identified as a descendant of the House of David. Messianic expectations would wax and wane throughout Jewish history, but remain at the core of Judaism, expressed in the daily liturgy and elsewhere.

[MARVIN A. SWEENEY]

War and Peace in the Bible

Permeated with depictions of military conflicts, the Bible has profoundly shaped the way many cultures—from West to East—think about war and peace. But why did the biblical authors devote so much space to this subject? With the aim of offering an informed response to this question, this essay begins by surveying the diverse war ideologies reflected throughout the corpus of biblical literature.

The Book of Genesis

The political ideal of the book of Gen. is a plurality of peoples living in peaceful coexistence. Thus Isaac avoids conflict over access to water sources (a typical *casus belli*) by opting to move on and build other wells (Gen. 26.15–22, see also ch 13). The book's most poignant expression of rapprochement is the scene in which Jacob makes reconciliation with Esau (chs 32–33); this scene may be compared to the later reconciliation between Joseph and his brothers (chs 44–45). In both accounts, the individuals represent (or anticipate) the actions of later, larger political collectivities. In addition to the gifts exchanged by Jacob and Joseph, two other popular peace strategies in the ancient Near East were intermarriage and alliances. While Gen. agrees with Deut. in rejecting intermarriage with the native Canaanites as an option for Israel (Gen. 24.2–4; 26.34–35; 38.1–30), it does not share its opposition to peace treaties (14.13; 21.22–34; 26.28; 31.44; contrast Deut. ch 7).

The authors of Gen. are ambivalent with respect to the military aggression of the kind displayed by Simeon and Levi against the city of Shechem (Gen. ch 34; see also 49.5–7). Yet they do not present the patriarchs as pacifists. Abr[ha]am goes to war in order to defend his southern Canaanite neighbors against external aggression (ch 14). Even so, he does not engage in this military campaign to establish territorial rights in Canaan or to increase his personal wealth (contrast the description of Jacob's behavior in 48.22).

The Narrative in Exodus-Joshua

The narrative beginning in the book of Exod. and extending to the book of Josh. presents a much different view of Israel. Instead of originating in the Land, the nation comes from Egypt and takes possession of Canaan through military conquest. The linking of Gen. to Exod.–Josh. alters their interpretation, so that their competing conceptions of Israel's history are not to be read in a sequence: the conquest of the Land is preceded by an epoch of the peaceful patriarchs. The war ideology in Exod.–Josh. could also not be more different than that of Gen. Whereas Abraham fought in solidarity with his neighbors, the Israelites now wage war in order to wipe out the Land's former inhabitants and their military success is due to divine rather than human heroic action.

Israel's most formative war is also her first war. The climax of the exodus itself is presented as a battle between the Pharaoh and his select armies against YHVH, the divine warrior (Exod. 15.3) who fights for Israel (Exod. 14.13–14). As Israel's first war hero in Exod.–Josh., YHVH is also Israel's first and rightful ruler who "will reign for ever and ever" (Exod. 15.18). Before divine kingship is replaced by that of a human war hero (see below on 1–2 Sam.), the Israelites fight against a series of rulers and the descriptions of these battles have a pronounced anti-monarchic tendency (Num. chs 21–24; 31.8; Deut. 2.26–3.11; 4.47; 7.24; 29.7–8; Josh. chs 2–13; see also Judg. chs 3–5; 11). In Exod.–Deut., a non-royal leader Moses and his successor Joshua fill the role otherwise assigned to kings.

Throughout Exod.–Josh., war is not the special responsibility of a stratified professional military force. Instead, all Israel is expected to fight (see esp. Num. chs 1–3). Military service is obligatory for all members of the nation and is in fact one of the primary means by which an Israelite man performs his membership. As such, this generation of Israel is designated the "generation of warriors" in Deut. 2.14–16. Likewise, Israelite society is conceived as a war camp, which is organized around the Tabernacle housing the Ark of the Covenant, which itself had a central military function (see 1 Sam. 4.4, where the Ark is called "the Ark of the Covenant of the LORD of Hosts Enthroned on the Cherubim"; "Hosts" refers to the heavenly figures who join God in battle).

The Ark leads Israel on its journey through the wilderness, which is conceived as a battle (Num. 10.35–36). Any military action without the Ark is doomed to failure (Num. 14.39–45; cf. Deut. 1.42). The Ark plays a central role in the momentous victory at Jericho (Josh. ch 6). Moses presents the Torah to the Levites who carry the Ark (Deut. 31.9, 25–26), suggesting that what might have originally served as a means of transporting a cultic figurine into battle (cf. "Ark of God/YHVH" in 1 Sam. chs 4–7 et passim) later came to symbolize the covenant as the guarantee of Israel's military success and political prosperity. This is similar to the late idea that Joshua would succeed in conquering the land as long as he remained steadfast in meditating upon the Torah (Josh. 1.8).

Another strand of the narrative in Exod.–Josh. emphasizes the holiness/purity of the war camp. In order that the divine Presence would continue to protect Israel from its position in the midst of the camp, Israel must maintain high standards of purity—both cultic and ethical, which are depicted as gradually developing along the journey. (See "Concepts of Purity," pp. 1998–2005.) Infractions of this behavior result in either a departure of the divine Presence or the people's total annihilation (Exod. chs 32–33; Num. ch 16). Going to war against the Midianites, Moses orders, in a gruesome scene, the execution of the non-virgin women and male children. Virgin women are spared perhaps because they are neutral, not yet having been "contaminated" by contact with the seed of Midianite men (see Judg. 21.11). Insofar as war involves contact with corpses, it defiles. Rituals of purification are therefore required for the troops to reenter the camp/Israelite society (Num. ch 31).

A prominent theme in the war accounts of Exod.–Josh. is faith in YHVH. At the Sea of Reeds, Moses orders Israel to be still and to allow YHVH to fight for them (Exod. 14.13–14). In the end, the people "trust" YHVH and Moses his servant (Exod. 14.31; cf. Isa. 7.9 and 2 Chron. 20.20). At the next stage of their journey, the spies return with conflicting reports and the people express their desire to return to Egypt, which provokes YHVH's consternation over their disbelief (Num. 14.31; cf. Deut. 1.32; 9.23).

Deuteronomy and Joshua

The book of Deut. depicts the time after the "generation of warriors" had finally passed away, when Moses addresses Israel in preparation for the impending wars of conquest. Reviewing past battles (Deut. chs 1–3; 7.18–19; 8.14–15; 29.1–7) and emphasizing that it is YHVH who fights the nation's wars (7.17–24; 9.1–7; 31.1–8, 23), Moses declares that Israel's God will not dislodge the inhabitants of the land all at once lest wild animals rise up in unoccupied regions (7.22, see Exod. 23.29–30). He also reflects upon the reason for YHVH's military assistance: In addition to the covenant with the patriarchs and YHVH's own honor, the wars are presented as divine judgment on the wicked indigenous inhabitants (e.g., 7.7–8; 9.4–7, 27–29).

Moses' discourses in Deut. frame a law collection that aims to regulate life once the land is conquered. Within this collection, rules pertaining to war and the military occupy a considerable amount of space (Deut. 20.1–20; 21.10–14; 23.10–14; 25.17–19) and reflect a range of perspectives. Such regulations are distinctive in the ancient Near East and represent the earliest known written war conventions. The laws in Deut. 23.10–14 are priestly in character: Because YHVH moves to and fro in the midst of the camp to protect and ensure victory, the camp (an idealistic image of Israelite society) must be kept holy. The rules of engagement in Deut. ch 20 anticipate principles of just war theory insofar as they require Israelite armies to demonstrate restraint. Similarly, 21.10–14 refers to marriage to and ethical treatment of captive women (contrast 7.3–5).

An important aspect of the Torah's war ideology is found in Deut. ch 28 (and Lev. ch 26), which delineates the blessings/curses for obedience/disobedience. Among the various blessings, Israel is promised military success and political strength. Failure to keep the commandments will be punished with defeat on the battlefield and exile, which are described at greater length. These curse-texts introduce the idea that it is Israel's God who afflicts the nation with war. In Gen. chs 6–9 the whole earth is wiped out by a flood, which often symbolizes war elsewhere (Isa. 8.7–8; Dan. 11.10, 40 as well as many ancient Near East texts); the divine "bow" that YHVH places in the clouds serves as a sign of the promise never again to cause this kind of devastation (Gen. 9.13–17)—that is why it faces heaven rather than earth. In the passages from Deut. and Lev., however, YHVH threatens to wage war against not the whole earth but rather solely against Israel. Josh. and Judg. split the double role played by war in Deut. ch 28, the former portraying compliance and military conquest, and the latter transgression and the loss of parts of the Land on a temporary basis.

With respect to the ban *(ḥērem),* Deut. and Josh. present a distinctive approach. Most often this practice functions as a form of severe punishment and retribution (e.g., Isa. 34.2), which resembles the practice of the ban elsewhere in the ancient Near East. Other texts view the ban as limited, and link it with special gratitude for divine assistance inasmuch as the victor forgoes any material gain (see e.g., Num. 21.1–3). In Deut. and Josh., Israel wipes out the prior inhabitants of the Land (the "seven nations") in order to avoid their cultural influence (Deut. 7.1–5; 20.15–18). Deut. confines the application of the forgoing lenient regulations solely to very distant cities (20.15–18). The transmitted shape of the book of Josh. presupposes these advanced compositional stages of Deut. insofar as it portrays how Joshua executes the ban on all the cities he conquers. The only group not wiped out is the Hivites/Gibeonites, who pretend to come from a distant country (Josh. ch 9). While Joshua is said not to have left a soul alive of all the cities he conquered (11.10–22), the second half of the book reflects a different tradition, affirming that many of the Land's prior inhabitants survived (see e.g., 16.10; 17.12–18).

The Book of Judges

In order to explain how the hegemony established by Joshua had been largely forfeited by the time of Samuel, the book of Judg. creates an intermediate era initiated by a generation "who did not know YHVH" (author's translation, Judg. 2.10; see "who did not know Joseph" [Exod. 1.8] in the redactional bridge between Gen. and Exod.–Josh.). The national unity that characterized Joshua's conquest dissolves as Israel abandons YHVH in a favor of a plurality of other deities (Judg. 2.12). This in turn leads to tribulations in the form of war: YHVH withdraws protection so that Israel is both assaulted by her enemies and no longer witnesses success on her military campaigns (2.15–16). The "rest" from wars enjoyed by the Land at the climax of the book of Josh. (Josh. 11.23) is replaced by perennial fighting with intermediate periods of "rest" (Judg. 3.11, 30; 5.31; 8.28). In the most desperate moments, "saviors" or "judges" (typically translated in NJPS as "chieftains") are divinely raised up to deliver Israel from its enemies. However, these engagements never lead to Israel's political centralization and consolidation. Indeed, victories often arouse intertribal jealousy and conflicts that evolve into protracted civil wars (e.g., 5.15–18; 8.1–3; 9.23–57; 12.1–6; chs 17–21). The generation that conquers the Land is depicted as successfully avoiding such conflict (Josh. 22.10–34).

The stories of the saviors/judges themselves consist in large part of older regional legends of military champions and warlords. As in the portrayals of Saul and David, these texts link military victory to the right to rule. Thus Jephthah becomes the "head" of Gileadite society for his success in battle (Judg. 11.4–10). The same ideology of monarchic rule is found in the stories of Gideon (8.22–23), Saul (1 Sam. 11.14–15), and David (2 Sam. 5.1–3). Other features of these texts include pre-battle oracles, valor, chivalric code of conduct, dueling, taunts, kinship, sharing the booty, capturing divine images and symbols, tricksterism, etc. According to these earlier texts, war is not the divine punishment for sin but rather a natural activity through which both rulers and groups consolidate their power.

In drawing upon these older legends to write a history from a pan-Israelite perspective, the authors of Judg. portray YHVH exploiting the military prowess and personal agendas of individual warriors (Othniel, Ehud, Barak, Gideon, Jephthah, and Samson) for the welfare of the people as a whole. This characteristic feature is accompanied by a shift of attention from the human heroes to divine involvement (this is esp. apparent in the core stories of Deborah and Gideon). The book often casts shadows on individual warriors, emphasizing their hubris and tragic deaths (Judg. 8.24–27; 9.53–55; 11.30–40; 16.4–31). Another prominent feature of the book's redaction is the way it negotiates belonging in Israel by appeal to wartime contributions of various regions, tribes, clans, and cities (see 5.13–23; 8.1–9; 12.1–6). Yet the book's most central message is that these post-conquest generations of Israel must fight wars because of their collective *sin*. In contrast to the depiction in the older legends, the editors responsible for the book's narrative framework present a *punitive conception of war* rather than identifying it as an unavoidable condition of the nation's existence.

Samuel and Kings

While Judg. presents war as the means through which Israel forfeits the unity she enjoyed in the age of Joshua, the book of Sam. portrays war as the path to Israel's political consolidation. In this work, war is not linked to Israel's prior transgressions, as it is in the narrative framework of Judg. War is part of the natural political order. This perennial view of war (as opposed to Judg.'s punitive view) provides the basis for the book's argument for a permanent, centralized monarchy.

Inasmuch as war is fought for self-defense, political autonomy and territorial conquest, Sam. presents a view of war similar to that in Exod.–Josh. Likewise, the book of Judg. may be compared to Kings, which begins with a period of peace and unity (the reign of Solomon) followed by downward spiral.

In recounting the emergence of the monarchy, the book of Sam. emphasizes the changes this institution would bring to Israelite society. In the period in which YHVH reigned as king, Israel lacked a sophisticated arsenal and depended upon divine assistance. In the final battle depicted before the establishment of the monarchy, YHVH throws the Philistines (who are a new national menace in Sam.) into confusion so that they could be routed by the Israelites (1 Sam. 7.10). The immediately following ch marks the introduction of a new order: In his address to the nation, Samuel describes the chariot-warfare and the weapons industry that will accompany the establishment of a centralized kingdom (8.11–12; see the references to chariots in anti-monarchic texts such as Exod. chs 14–15; Josh. ch 11; Judg. chs 4–5). When pleading for a monarchy, the people refer to the king's role in battle (Judg. 8.20), and beginning with Saul's first battle against the Ammonites (1 Sam. ch 11), it is this function that dominates the subsequent narrative.

Kings has many themes in common with Sam., even though Kings presents war more as a divine punitive measure. The greatest cause of anxiety for the authors of both of these works is Israel's civil wars. One of the overarching emphases of both books is adherence to the prophetic word, not least in wartime situations (1 Sam. chs 15; 28; 30.8; 2 Sam. 2.1; 5.19, 23; 1 Kings chs 20; 22; 2 Kings chs 3; 6–7; 9–10; 14.25; chs 18–20). Because Israel does not heed the prophets and turns to the sins of Jeroboam, it suffers defeat in war and is exiled from the Land (2 Kings ch 17). Imperial armies later devastate Judah. Yet because Hezekiah seeks Isaiah's assistance and repents (chs 18–19), Jerusalem and Judah are spared this fate for several generations.

The Latter Prophets

War looms large in the Latter Prophets. Although this corpus of literature mirrors a variety of perspectives on war, the disparate books in this corpus have much in common—not least a will to perceive divine judgment in Israel's catastrophic defeat and to pinpoint exactly what elicited that judgment. By identifying various abuses in a society that would be wiped out in war, they lay the groundwork for the restoration of a society after war.

In addition to drawing attention to various social injustices and cultic impurities, the prophets are presented as speaking out against what they deem to be quick fixes that avoid an honest confrontation with the problem. Thus Isaiah reminds Judah that she made many physical preparations for war (Isa. 22.8–11) but failed "to consider the One who planned [the war] and gave no thought to the One who designed it long before" (author's translation; Isa. 22.11).

Most of the prophets repudiate treaty politics. Supported by those who wished to maintain their positions of power, military alliances jeopardized the welfare of the people as a whole. The prophets refer to the ratification of these treaties as acts of harlotry. Enchanted by what others had to offer, the nation abandons her divine husband. It is consequently punished in war, and the descriptions of these scenes are graphic in their sexual metaphors (see e.g., Ezek. ch 23 and Hos. ch 2).

YHVH's warring against Israel and Judah at times contravenes the very restrictions YHVH places on Israel's military conduct in laws contained in the Torah. For example, many passages in the Latter Prophets refer to the devastation of Israel's and Judah's lands: "I will lay waste her vines and her fig trees, ... I will make them a forest, and the wild animals shall devour them" (author's translation; Hos. 2.14). Israel is, however, forbidden to treat her enemies this way (Deut. 20.19–20). The same applies to YHVH's indiscriminate slaughter of women and children (e.g., Nah. ch 3; cf. Deut. 20.10–14; 21.10–14).

The prophets often refer to the divine mercy that brings Israel back to the land after the exile brought about by enemies: "After I have plucked them up, I will again have compassion on them, and I will bring them again to their heritage and to their land, every one of them" (NRSV; Jer. 12.15). Other texts limit the survivors to a small remnant (e.g., Isa. 10.21–22). There is also the promise of cessation of war against YHVH's people: "I will not again destroy Ephraim; for I am God and no mortal ..." (NRSV; Hos. 11.9). This declaration is compared to the promise never again to destroy the earth after the flood (Isa. 54.9–10).

Finally, much of the prophetical writings include oracles against the surrounding nations that consist in large part of descriptions of the wars. These texts make the claim of divine sovereignty over the international sphere and an expectation of fair "rules of engagement" in the international sphere. Amos attributes divine punishment to the ruthless way contemporary states waged war (Amos chs 1–2). A more common cause of divine wrath is the hubris of their rulers (e.g., Isa. ch 16). These foreign peoples serve as instruments of judgment, yet they fail to recognize the source of their strength and so are punished (Isa. 10.5–15). The hope expressed in Isa. 2.4/Mic. 4.3, Zech. 9.10, and Hos. 2.18–23 is that the weapons of war used by these nations, and indeed war itself, will be abolished.

The Writings

War represents a central theme of the book of Ps. In many of the older songs and prayers, the king requests deliverance from his enemies, who threaten not only him but also his people (e.g., Ps. 3); at other moments, the psalmist laments defeat or gives thanks for victory (e.g., Pss. 18; 54). In appropriating and reworking these older songs/prayers, the book collectivizes the voice to include all members of Israel, emphasizing justice and piety as the conditions for deliverance. This process of expansion, juxtaposition, and adaptation transforms the identity of the enemy, who is now no longer merely a military aggressor but also an opponent to a particular group (e.g., the righteous, the poor, and the lowly). Many of the communal laments devote special attention to war, reflecting upon its causes and pleading for salvation. While most identify sin as the cause, some affirm innocence despite punishment (e.g., Ps. 44).

Reflecting upon the destruction wrought by war, the book of Lam. cries out in anger against Israel's God for wiping out Jacob and Zion without mercy. In verbalizing their rage and demanding explanations, the voices of the book discover solidarity as a community of mourners. They begin with the most basic form of language (the alphabet) and, by means of acrostics and poetry, undertake the daunting task of reordering the fundamental components of life that were torn apart as YHVH acted the part of Israel's enemy (Lam. 2.4–5). Although culpability is confessed (2.17), it does not obviate the need to draw attention to the suffering (e.g., 1.18–20) and to pose the accusative question whether the punishment fits the crime (2.20; 3.42–54; 4.1–20; 5.20–22).

Dan. espouses a unique historical perspective in the Hebrew Bible. According to the (proto-) apocalyptic outlook of this book's final form, political turmoil in world history should not warrant despair. The war waged against YHVH's people will eventually come to an end. All transpires according to the divine plan written in the "book of truth" (Dan. 10.21), and the community of the faithful is made privy to this plan thanks to the writings of a key figure, whose righteous deeds are rewarded with visions (chs 9 and 10). According to the visions, there is a struggle in heaven between "the chief princes," representing various peoples, and this struggle directly affects the political events on earth. All empires ultimately perish and in the end are replaced by an everlasting kingdom established by the God of Heaven and governed by the holy ones. In the meantime, it is improper to seek military liberation. One should engage instead in textual study, pious behavior, and confession for the sins that occasioned Israel's exile (see esp. chs 6, 9, and 10).

Similar to Dan., the books of Ezra-Neh. and Esth. depict survival strategies in an age of empires. In Ezra-Neh., the fate of the Judean people and their land is subject ultimately to the will of the God of Heaven rather than that of the foreign ruler. Nevertheless, Israel's God works through foreign rulers to secure the nation's welfare. In this new political order, it is imperative for Jews to use whatever political influence they have to prompt the foreign king to action on their behalf. Thus Esther persuades the king to permit Jews throughout the empire to defend themselves (Esth. 8.11). Nehemiah presents the inhabitants of Judah arming themselves against external aggression (Neh. ch 4). In none of these books is military force used to rebel against the empire.

The book of Chron., composed during the late Persian or Hellenistic period, shares Judg.'s punitive conception of war (see above). It also shares its cyclical understanding of history by presenting the behavior of each generation determining Israel's fate ("rest from war"). Its authors identify pious kings as aggressive military leaders and ambitious builders, whose construction projects often include fortifications and other military installations in Judah and Jerusalem (e.g., 2 Chron. 8.1–6). Threatened with invasions, Israel/Judah is spared punishment when the nation repents (e.g., 2 Chron. 12.1–12). YHVH actively fights for Israel/Judah, with cultic officials, musicians, and cultic objects playing leading roles (e.g., 2 Chron. 13.3–19; 20.1–30). The surrounding nations are unified in their animosity for Judah. They threaten the existence of the people as a whole rather than solely the political autonomy of the kingdom.

The Significance of War in the Bible

Some scholars claim that so much of the Bible focuses on war because ancient Israel was an especially bellicose society. Such was the conviction of a formative generation of scholars, who explained the relative absence of war in Gen. on the assumption that the book's stories are either completely divorced from historical reality (Julius Wellhausen) or pre-Israelite (Hermann Gunkel). A subsequent generation of scholars (under the influence of Gerhard von Rad after World War II) viewed the focus on war in terms of an apolitical theology of "Holy War," with the ideal of Israel's God fighting alone to the exclusion of a direct involvement of the people.

A more tenable approach to the question views the Bible as a project of constructing a (new) *national identity* for Israel. From this perspective we can appreciate why the biblical authors devote so much space to the subject of war. For a political community, war constitutes the ultimate threat. Floods, famine, and other natural catastrophes afflict regions defined according to natural geographical boundaries; they are oblivious to political borders. In contrast, war is directed against peoples and states. For this reason, nations commonly define and redefine themselves in relation to wars and battles, both real and imagined. War monuments and memorials serve as spaces in which political communities negotiate belonging and status by commemorating those who sacrificed on their behalf. Competing with hegemonic memories are counter-memories created by social, political, and ethnic actors, all of whom seek to call attention to their contributions or to the "real" causes of victory and defeat. By reminding others of the part they played in the collective war effort, they affirm their membership within the larger community and lay claim to political rights. The identity of the nation assumes definition in these conflicts over war memories.

The Bible may be understood as a type of war memorial. War pervades its pages because its authors are engaged in an effort to forge a corporate identity for Israel, one that can both transcend deep divisions within the population and withstand military conquest by imperial armies. The biblical authors, like the architects of national identities in more recent times, construct this identity in direct relation to memories of war (both real and imagined). The main subject of the Bible is the people of Israel and its Land. Therefore war, as a force that threatens to break an established bond between a people and a land, is a natural theme for biblical literature.

From the evidence in Kings and the Latter Prophets, this nation-building project seems to have attained new dimensions with the onslaught of the Assyrian empire, beginning in the 8th c. BCE. This unprecedented military challenge (Assyria was the first empire to encroach on Israel's territories) prompted in some circles a project of reconceptualizing Israel's identity. This effort continued in the following centuries, which witnessed the demise and transformation of Israel's political institutions. As part of this effort, the biblical authors imagine Israel as a people that existed long before the establishment of the centralized state(s) destroyed by enemy armies. According to this understanding, the unifying and sustaining factor in Israel's history was not its institutions of statehood but rather its deity and the covenant that the deity entered directly with the nation, a covenant that included a promise by YHVH to protect Israel from its enemies if Israel adheres to the covenant stipulations.

With respect to war, the Hebrew Bible is quite distinct from the Christian New Testament. Very few passages in the latter treat the subject of war, and most of those passages that do treat the subject do so in spiritual, non-political terms. (The warlike imagery in the book of Revelation, if taken literally, would be an exception, but if it is read metaphorically it refers to spiritual struggles, not actual battles.) This tendency is in keeping with the Church's emerging identity as a *transnational community of faith*. In contrast, the authors of the Hebrew Scriptures are concerned to fashion a corporate identity for the people of Israel—one that may be properly designated "national." War plays a central role in this venture.

[JACOB L. WRIGHT]

THE BIBLE IN JEWISH LIFE

The Bible in the Synagogue

During the period of the Second Temple (from the return to Zion [538 BCE] until the destruction of the Temple [70 CE]), and in particular after the conquest of the entire Near East by the armies of Alexander the Great (ca. 330 BCE), numerous upheavals occurred in the religious-spiritual world of the Jewish people. Two of the fundamental changes caused by these upheavals are important for our discussion, having left their mark on Judaism, in all places, in every era, and upon the various forms of Jewish expression, up to the present day: the growth and establishment of the synagogue, and the central role played by the Bible in the religious and spiritual existence of the Jewish people. Since then, a Jewish community without a synagogue at its center is unimaginable, nor could one conceive of a synagogue in which a central place was not reserved, both physically and in terms of its activities, for the three sections of the Tanakh: the Torah, the Prophets, and the Writings.

During the era of the First Temple (until its destruction in 586 BCE), and to some extent during the ensuing two or three centuries, the word of God was perceived to be revealed to humanity in numerous ways. First and foremost, it came through the prophet through whom God revealed His will or His plans. God also answered the people's questions, both by way of the priests, using the Urim and Thummim, as well as through dreams (see 1 Sam. 28.6: "But the LORD did not answer him, either by dreams or by Urim or by prophets"). Thus the prophet, the priest, and the interpreter of dreams served as intermediaries between God and human beings. In this respect, a major upheaval occurred when it was believed that prophecy had departed from Israel after the prophets Haggai, Zechariah, and Malachi (*b. B. Bat.* 14b), that the Urim and Thummim had disappeared (*y. Mak.* 5:2), and that dreams are not divine messages from heaven but a result of human self-reflection (*b. Ber.* 55b). All of these methods of discovering the divine will were then replaced by texts, the Holy Scriptures. The nation of Israel became what was later termed the "People of the Book." The intermediary between God and humanity was henceforth the Rabbi, the wise man who knew how to read Scriptures and to hear through them God's voice. Instead of one-time divine revelations through dreams or prophets or priests, the Jewish people were given a book which was understood to contain God's revelation for all time. The era of revelation to individuals at appointed times came to a close, and was replaced by a new era with continuous revelation for all, by way of the Holy Scriptures. From this point on, the religion and culture of Israel developed around the twenty-four books of the Tanakh: in Houses of Study and in schools, at particular events such as eulogies or festive religious celebrations, but first and foremost in the synagogues.

It would appear that, as the prestige of the Temple began to decline, the need to continue hearing the word of God was among the central factors leading to the ascent of the synagogue as an institution, or perhaps even to its creation. Parallel to the sacrificial service which was practiced in the Jerusalem Temple only, it became necessary to create an institution in which Jews, wherever they might be, could gather on special occasions, to listen together to the word of God and to discover what it implies (as is described in the Bible itself, in Neh. ch 8). In the course of time these gatherings became formalized in fixed, obligatory forms, but the exact process through which they took shape is for the most part unknown, due to the dearth of extant sources from the Second Temple period. However, aided by the Jewish philosopher Philo (*De Somnis* 2:127), by the historian Flavius Josephus (*Ag. Ap.* 2:175), and by early Christian literature (Acts 15.21), we can pinpoint some early stages of this process in the 1st c. CE, though the origin of the synagogue may be several centuries earlier. We may reasonably assume that slowly and gradually, the idea of the synagogue began to crystallize. That which eventually coalesced during the period of the rabbinic Sages (from the 1st c. CE until the Islamic conquest [ca. 640 CE]) attained its ultimate form in the geonic period (which ended just beyond 1000 CE). It was at that time that the first Jewish prayer books were compiled. Despite all the social and cultural metamorphoses that the Jewish people have undergone subsequently, the position of the Bible in the synagogue has remained basically unchanged. There are regular readings from the Torah, fixed readings from the Prophets, reading of the Five Scrolls on specific days, explication of Scriptures during or close to their public reading, including their translation into different languages, and extensive use of Scripture in the liturgy. Liturgical use includes the recitation of various psalms, reading of additional scriptural excerpts such as the Song of the Sea (Exod. ch 15) or the story of the binding of Isaac (Gen. ch 22) in the daily morning prayer, recitation of *piyyutim* (liturgical poetry) that draws on Scripture in various ways, as well as extensive use of biblical Heb and its expressions within the prayers (see "The Bible in the Liturgy," pp. 2057–67).

Reading from the Torah

According to a tradition recorded in the Talmud (*b. B. K.* 82a), a custom had already been established during the time of Moses—and later reaffirmed by Ezra the Scribe—to read from the Torah every Monday, Thursday, and Sabbath, so that the Jewish people would not remain without Torah for three consecutive days. This tradition, even if it cannot be substantiated, confers great antiquity and considerable importance on the custom of reading from the Torah. It seems likely that initially people gathered for the reading and study of selected sections of the Torah on festivals or other special days, but that during the Second Temple period the custom of a weekly reading from the Torah, in order, from beginning to end, was gradually established.

The reading of the Torah in most Jewish communities (at least until the 19th c., when some modern movements introduced changes) follows the custom consolidated by Babylonian Jewry during the period of the Sages and the *geonim*. There is some indication that this custom originated in the land of Israel, but even if this is so, it was the Babylonian Jewry that granted it pivotal status. According to this custom, the Torah is read in an annual cycle, divided into fifty-four fixed sections, called *parashiyot* (sg.: *parashah*). The full parashah is read in the synagogue on Sabbath morning, between the *Shaḥarit* and *Musaf* prayer services. On Sabbath afternoon (during the *Minḥah* service) and during *Shaḥarit* on Monday and Thursday mornings, the beginning vv. from the parashah that will be read in full on the following Sabbath are read. Designated sections of the Torah whose themes are appropriate are also read on special days such as festivals, Rosh Ḥodesh (the new moon), and public fast days, as well as other special occasions. For example, the passage describing the religious precept of blotting out the remembrance of Amalek (Deut. 25.17–19) is read on the Sabbath preceding Purim, due to the connection between Haman and the Amalekites (Esth. 3.1). Most of these special excerpts were already selected for this purpose during the rabbinic period (*b. Meg.* 31a–b, etc.).

The division of the Torah into fifty-four parashiyot (instead of the expected fifty-two) stems from the fact that in certain years there are fifty-four Sabbath days. This is possible only in a leap year, which contains thirteen lunar months, and even then provided that hardly any festivals occur on Sabbath. (When a festival does occur on Sabbath, the passage which is read from the Torah is one associated with that festival rather than the weekly parashah.) In a year that has fewer Sabbath days, as is the case in most years, two consecutive parashiyot are joined in accordance with predetermined rules (e.g., *Mattot* and *Masʿei* from the book of Num. [30.2–32.42 and 33.1–36.13], or *Nitsavim* and *Va-yelekh* from Deut. [29.9–30.20 and 31.1–30]), so that the entire reading will be concluded within one year and by a fixed date in the calendar. This date is the day after the Sukkot festival, which is called *Simḥat Torah* (Rejoicing of the Torah); on the following Sabbath, referred to as *Shabbat Bereshit* (the sabbath of the parashah of Bereshit, the first parashah), the Torah reading recommences with Gen. The division of the Torah into parashiyot and the assignment of each parashah to a given week are essentially identical in all Jewish communities throughout the world. They are predictable and follow a fixed routine.

The Torah is read in the synagogue from a parchment scroll and seven (or more) people are called up to the Torah for the reading, one after the other. The parchment scroll contains the unvocalized text of the Torah without the diacritical marks (for chanting), so that the reading requires skill and preparation. In antiquity, each person called to the Torah would read his own passage (*b. Kid.* 49a), but as time passed, it became customary for each person called up to the Torah (who had an *ʿaliyah*) to recite only the blessings before and after the reading, while another individual designated for this task, and who had prepared himself for it, would read the parashah. The regulations for reading from the Torah were fashioned by halakhah and custom into clear rules: the order of those called to the Torah, their number, the passages apportioned to each of them, the blessings recited by those called up, and the manner in which the congregation congratulates them, etc. The blessings recited by each honoree before and after the reading are noteworthy (*b. Ber.* 11b). Their main emphasis is on the choosing of the Jewish People, expressed among other things, in the giving of the Torah, the "Torah of truth" with its promise of "everlasting life."

It becomes apparent that in the land of Israel during the period of the Rabbis or Sages and that of the *geonim* (as well as in some communities outside the land of Israel that assumed its custom), a different mode of reading from the Torah was widespread, referred to inaccurately as the "triennial cycle" (cf. *b. Meg.* 29b). Here, too, the Torah was read in sequence, but it was divided into a greater number of readings, called *sedarim* (sg.: *seder*). The length of each seder and the overall number of sedarim in the Torah varied from one synagogue to another. That which was read in one synagogue on Sabbath was not necessarily identical to that read on the same Sabbath in another synagogue. Moreover, even the seder read in a particular synagogue on a certain Sabbath did not have to be identical in length with what would be read in later years in the same synagogue when the same Torah portion was reached.

Each synagogue and community on each Sabbath would determine for itself the length of the Torah reading, according to its custom or requirements: the desire to honor more people with the Torah reading, the presence of a groom in the synagogue, the time available, and so forth. The earliest halakhah (*m. Ber.* 4:4) requires that each reader recite at least three vv. from the Torah, but it does not specify the maximum number permitted. The Mishnah (ibid., 4:1) further requires that at least seven people should read from the Torah every Sabbath, but it allows additional participants. In other words, at least twenty-one vv. were read on each occasion, but apparently the reading would often be extended, in accordance with the desires of the readers and their number, or in order to conclude the reading at an appropriate point, rather than in the middle of a subject. If we assume that eight or nine people read from the Torah each Sabbath, and that each of them would read about four or five vv., we can conclude that at this pace each synagogue completed its Torah reading in approximately three years. The evidence we possess (mostly from discoveries over the past century, primarily from the Cairo Genizah) indicates numerous Torah reading cycles that extended over 141–175 Sabbaths. Thus, it is also clear that it would have been impossible to set any fixed date in the annual calendar at which the Torah reading would either conclude or recommence. The festival we now call *Simḥat Torah* was celebrated in the land of Israel at the very most on the Sabbath on which the Torah reading was concluded, approximately once in three years, and at a different time in each synagogue because in the land of Israel there was no fixed date to conclude the Torah reading in the annual calendar.

A person attending a synagogue in the land of Israel in ancient times, who had not been present there on the previous Sabbath, could not know beforehand which seder he was about to hear. Reading over a cycle of three years resulted in a particular story in the Torah being read at one time in winter and at another in the summer; or in a legal portion such as our parashah of *Mishpatim* (Exod. chs 21–24) being subdivided in different ways in different years. A preacher who came to the synagogue to give a sermon on a subject arising from the Torah reading and who had not previously enquired as to where the congregation stood in their Torah reading cycle would likely find himself more than surprised or even totally unprepared—a situation not entirely unknown (see *Lev. Rab.* 3:6). A person who wandered from one synagogue to the next would read about the birth of Moses on one Sabbath, mourn his death with another congregation on the following Sabbath, and then hear of Moses walking upon the face of the earth if he came the next Sabbath to a synagogue in the process of reading from Lev. or Num. Flexible reading systems like these may possibly fit the customs of smaller congregations permanently located in one place, but it would be most difficult to utilize them to construct a national religious system extending over distant locations. This, then, would seem to be the reason why the Babylonian custom eventually won out, replacing the customs of the land of Israel in a process which reached its final stages around the 12th c. From then on, all those attending synagogue would hear the entire Torah every year, and this undoubtedly was sufficient to forcefully instill the Torah into the cultural agenda.

The Haftarah

The last of those called up to the Torah on Sabbath and festivals remains on the podium after the reading has concluded, and then reads (usually from a printed vocalized text, not a scroll) an additional portion from Scripture, taken from the Prophets. This reading is termed "haftarah" (a word that means conclusion), as it brings the readings from Scripture on Sabbath and festivals to their end.

The haftarah section is often connected either linguistically or in content with the weekly parashah, e.g., the haftarah which begins with the v. "King David was now old and advanced in years" (1 Kings 1.1) is read on the Sabbath when the passage "Abraham was old and advanced in years" is read (Gen. ch 24); or the Prophet Isaiah's mention of the flood (ch 54) is read on the Sabbath when the story of the flood is read from the Torah. At other times, however, the haftarah has a particular connection with the occasion upon which it is read, such as the haftarah beginning with the words "Comfort, oh comfort my people" (Isa. ch 40), which is always recited on the Sabbath after Tishʿah beʾav (a day of national mourning), or the haftarah which begins "Return, O Israel, to the LORD your God" (Hos. 14.2ff.), which is read in the Sabbath preceding Yom Kippur.

It is most likely that the institution of the haftarah was created at the close of the Second Temple era, during the great dispute between the Jews and the Samaritans, the latter deeming the Torah to be holy, but not accepting the sanctity of the prophetic books. The decision to read something from the Prophets every Sabbath was apparently part of the polemic against the Samaritans, as though the Jews wished to state: The books of the Prophets are also holy, and are also the word of God, so it is appropriate to read them publicly and to recite a blessing upon their reading. The blessings recited before and after the haftarah ("... Who has chosen good prophets, and desires their words, which are spoken in truth ..."; "... Who has chosen the Torah and His prophet Moses and His people Israel and prophets of truth and righteousness") clearly emphasize this point. Evidence for the reading of the haftarah may already be found in the Apocrypha (2 Macc. 15.9) and in the New Testament (Luke 4.16–30). The subject is also discussed extensively in various contexts in the literature of the Sages (e.g., *m. Meg.* 4:1–3; 3:5–6).

It seems that initially the choice of passage to be read from the Prophets and its precise length was made by the the reader of the haftarah himself (called the *maftir*), or according to the custom of his congregation. As time passed, however, these readings also became formalized, attaining permanent status. Here, too, halakhah and custom brought about orderly, fixed lists of haftarot. But certain differences are notable even today among the various communities of the Jewish people—Ashkenazic, Sephardic, Yemenite, and Italian Jews—being the heritage of those flexible and dynamic times in antiquity. Needless to say, in ancient times in the land of Israel, where the extent of the Torah readings was irregular and flexible, there were numerous alternative customs for the haftarot. (A modern commentary on the haftarot is *Haftarot: The Traditional Hebrew Text with the New JPS Translation,* commentary by Michael Fishbane [Philadelphia: The Jewish Publication Society, 2002].)

Thus, with regard to the manner in which reading from the Torah and the haftarah were consolidated, the land of Israel and Babylonia reveal two opposite conceptions concerning uniformity and permanence, the quantity of Torah and prophetic readings to which the synagogue congregation was exposed on Sabbath and festivals, and the total annual extent.

The Five Scrolls

On five occasions during the year, one of the five scrolls is read in the synagogue: Song (during the week of Passover); the Scroll of Ruth (Shavuʿot); Lam. (Tishʿah beʾav); Eccl. (during the week of Sukkot); and the Scroll of Esth. (Purim). Evidence shows that during the geonic period some parts of the scrolls were also read on the Sabbaths prior to these occasions, in preparation for them.

The reading of the Scroll of Esth. on Purim appears to be the most ancient of all (see *m. Meg.* 1:1). This is self-evident, since the whole story of the origin of Purim is contained in this scroll. The second scroll to be introduced into the synagogue would appear to be Lam., which relates to the story of the destruction of the Temple. Evidence of its recitation on Tishʿah beʾav may already be found in the writings of the Sages (e.g., *Lam. Rab.,* petiḥta 17). The other three scrolls, which are read on the three pilgrimage festivals, apparently were not read liturgically in the synagogue until the end of the period of the Sages, or even until the geonic period (see the minor tractate *Soferim* 14:3). An adequate explanation has yet to be offered as to why a certain scroll is read on a given festival. The links between the scrolls and the festivals on which they are recited are vague and mainly of a homiletic nature. Apparently, once Esth. and Lam. came to be read in the synagogue, because of their close ties with the occasions on which they were read, a need was felt to grant the other three scrolls a similar status. Thus, for reasons we cannot fully discern, they slowly entered the world of the synagogue. The result was that those attending synagogue on the three festivals were exposed to all portions of Scriptures (Torah, Prophets, Writings), which marked the synagogue activities in an especially vigorous and emphatic manner.

The Bible in "The Literature of the Synagogue": Translation, Sermon, *Piyyut*

The regular reading of Torah, Prophets, and the Scrolls served as a permanent basis for relating to Scriptures within the framework of synagogue life. We can point to three types of literary activities which accompanied the Bible as it reached the synagogue congregation (as noted, besides the prayers): (1) translation of Scripture into the vernacular (in the ancient context, primarily into Aram.); (2) homilies and explication of the passages read; (3) extensive use of their themes and content for composition of *piyyutim* (liturgical poems).

The Translation

Once part of the synagogue congregation had a limited command of Heb, and especially once the Rabbis began to find multiple and varied halakhic and aggadic meanings in Scriptures, it became impossible to separate the reading of the holy texts (the Torah and probably the haftarot and scrolls as well) from their fixed companion: the translation into Aram. (in its various dialects) in the land of Israel and Babylonia, or into Gk in Hellenistic centers such as Alexandria. The Aram. translations (the Targumim), as described below, preserved the vitality of the ancient texts and prevented them from becoming merely a fossilized heritage of the past (regarding the translation of Scripture, see also "Jewish Translations of the Bible," pp. 2091–2106).

Based on the sources (e.g., *m. Meg.* 4:6), it appears that next to the readers of the Torah a man stood translating the reading into Aram.: the *meturgeman* (translator). The reader and the translator alternated, v. following v. (but in the haftarah several vv. could be translated together). They were required to respect each other by not beginning to speak before the other had concluded his words (*b. Sot.* 39b). This ensured that there was no overlap or confusion between the Torah text and its translation. The *meturgeman* may possibly have been a professional who earned his living from this work, but he could also have been a learned member of the congregation who knew how to fulfill the religious duty of translation.

In the same way that there was a difference between the land of Israel and Babylonia regarding the customs of Torah and haftarah readings, there was a difference concerning the translations into Aram. that were customary in both places. The Targum that was customary in Babylonia (*Tg. Onk.* on the Torah and the Tg. by Yonatan ben ʿUziʾel on the Prophets) tended to be a literal translation, adhering as closely as possible to the biblical text. In passages containing poetry (such as Gen. ch 49), in ambiguous vv., and in a few other cases, the Babylonian Targum permitted minor additions or even deviations from the Scriptural source, for exegetical or theological purposes, such as the removal of what seemed to be contradictions in the biblical text and anthropomorphic expressions relating to God or the need to preserve the honor of the fathers of the nation. But even more important is the fact that these two translations were the exclusive, authorized translations of Scripture, and on every Sabbath those attending the synagogue would be exposed to their single, fixed text. Although there was a clear risk of monotony and routine, this was the way in which the Babylonian Rabbis sought to present the biblical text to its listeners.

Such was not the practice of Jews in the land of Israel. The *meturgeman* wove into the words of the Torah a long series of exegetic, literary, haggadic, and halakhic traditions, remonstrations or words of encouragement for the congregation. He thus brought to their ears the biblical text, readapted and refashioned in many ways, in accordance with the intellectual competence of different congregations, current and local occurrences, and the *meturgeman's* own tendencies. It is also worthy to note that in the land of Israel—as opposed to Babylonia—no single biblical v. was translated in an identical, uniform manner in every place or at all times. The *meturgeman* was permitted to choose the manner of translation that seemed proper to him, to add his own comments to the traditions he had imbibed from his teachers, to omit or to expand on words, and thus to emphasize one or other aspect of the translated text. This picture of variation and flexibility is clearly reflected in the Aram. translations of the Torah and Prophets that have come down to us from the land of Israel. They are referred to by name, such as the *Targum Yerushalmi* or *Targum Yonatan ben ʿUziʾel on the Torah* (Tg. Ps.-J.; even though its composer is not the same person of similar name who composed the Tg. on the Prophets), and so on. If we recall that in the land of Israel a reading of about forty vv. was deemed adequate for any occasion, it would seem that ample time remained for the *meturgeman* to expand on the passage. Indeed, the amount of material inserted by the meturgeman is often greater than the text itself. The translator would sometimes even weave a long poem into his translation, if he thought that it would add majesty and beauty to his words and enhance their dramatic potential (e.g., within the narrative of the parting of the Red Sea [Exod. chs 14–15], or the Binding of Isaac [Gen. ch 22]). The aggadic traditions embedded in the various translations are frequently colorful and exciting, with a distinct educational and popular tone, and shed new light on the text that was just read. These traditions stress the importance of prayer or extol the patriarchs of the nation, describe in bold colors the days of redemption or emphasize the principle of reward and punishment, and so forth. Not only was the length of the passages read from the Torah and Prophets variable and flexible, but even the manner in which these passages were presented to the congregation by way of the Aram. translation was constantly changing. The audience in the land of Israel could not then be lulled by feelings of familiarity and routine.

The Sermon

Besides the Torah reading and its translation, there was often a public sermon, given on various occasions, festivals, and Sabbaths, usually during the *Shaḥarit* (morning) prayer or in the afternoon, sometimes prior to the Torah reading and sometimes afterwards. The preacher, either a local sage or a guest, an elder of the congregation or one of their teachers, dealt with various and sundry topics, educational, academic, and issues of contemporary concern, according to his understanding of the task at hand.

Naturally, the sermons differed from one Sabbath to the next and from festival to festival, adding another dimension to the use of the Bible in the synagogue. In nearly every case the preacher dealt with the subject of the Torah reading, together with the haftarah or the scroll for that day, contributing his part to what the congregation had learned from the reading and its Aram. translation.

There are thousands of literary units in the literature of the Sages, especially in midrashic literature (e.g., *Gen. Rab.* or *m. Tanḥ.*) that originally served as public sermons offered prior to scriptural readings. These literary units demonstrate the remarkably rhetorical character of the public sermon, relating various topics that would be of concern to its audience: the reason for suffering, the nature of religious life without the Temple, relations between Jews and Gentiles, the difficulty of observing the commandments, the hope for redemption, and others. Such sermons were studded with innumerable biblical vv., together with their explication, so that the realm of Scriptures was broadened to include excerpts from texts that were not read on that Sabbath or festival.

In the land of Israel—but seemingly hardly ever in Babylonia—the preachers would often expound on an issue arising from the biblical reading, through the use of a widespread literary pattern referred to as *petiḥta* (usually translated as "proem"). According to this pattern the preacher would first choose a v. from the Prophets or the Writings, a v. that appeared to have no connection whatsoever with the topic in the Torah, haftarah, or scroll read that day. He would then spiral from this v., from topic to topic, until he arrived at the opening v. of the reading and by that gave closure to his sermon. This pattern, which connected two unrelated vv., allowed the preacher to illuminate different issues while piquing the congregation's curiosity. The listeners knew from the outset what the preacher's concluding v. would be, and they must certainly have attempted to surmise how the preacher would eventually make the connection between the opening and the concluding vv. of his sermon. The choice to open the sermon with vv. from books that were usually not read in the synagogue (those Prophets that were not used as haftarot, the book of Prov., the book of Job, etc.) was another way to expose all portions of Scripture to the synagogue congregation, and to emphasize that the entire Bible is interconnected. On Sabbath and festivals they would then read from the Torah and the Prophets, and would hear a sermon based to a large extent on the Writings. Thus all portions of Scripture would be reviewed once again, and the audience would see the full extent of Scripture.

The Piyyut

Piyyut refers to the poetical religious compositions, nearly all in Heb, recited in liturgical contexts in the synagogue or outside it, such as at wedding ceremonies or at festive meals. These compositions maintain the various characteristics of poetry in general, such as rhythm, meter, refrains, and acrostics of various kinds.

During the era of the Sages and the geonic period, the *piyyut* blossomed primarily in the land of Israel, mainly for use in the synagogue. The *piyyutim* were not composed as adornments for the prayers or as supplements to them, but rather, first and foremost, as lyrical alternatives for the fixed and obligatory prayers. If the congregation or its leaders desired, the standard prayer would be recited by the cantor in prose (as it is recited to this day), but if they wished to vary the expression of their feelings through a *piyyut,* this option was also open to them. For this reason hundreds and even thousands of *piyyutim* were composed by many poets, only some of whom are known to us by name: Yose ben Yose (4th to 5th c.); Yannai (5th to 6th c.); Rabbi Elazar Ha-Kalir (6th to 7th c.); and others. Those attending synagogue could occasionally hear, for example, a one-time lyrical substitution for the *ʿAmidah* or for the blessings enveloping the reciting of the Shema. At times, the poet was accompanied by a small choir, contributing a further dimension to the experience the *piyyutim* brought with them.

Since the *piyyut* was essentially a lyrical substitute for prayer, its themes were primarily drawn from that realm, but it appears that the poets frequently dealt as well with the topics of the Torah reading, the haftarah, or, when appropriate, one of the five scrolls. Thus we can also view their words as a kind of poetic sermon on the themes associated with that day. For example, through his poetic substitute for the second blessing of the *ʿAmidah,* the blessing of "He who revives the dead," the poet could relate in his own way to the story of the Binding of Isaac, who according to a rabbinic tradition was slain by Abraham, but revived; or through his poetic version of the blessing before reciting the Shema, the blessing of "Who creates the heavenly lights," he could relate to the story of the creation of the world and the heavenly lights in his own way. Within the *piyyutim,* the poet was also permitted to introduce explicit quotations of vv. from the entire Bible, as many did. Since the number of poets and *piyyutim* was virtually unlimited, the person listening to them in the synagogue could on nearly every occasion sample another new composition, different from those he recognized, and in this way he would also come to know many varied scriptural passages.

As time went on, and in no small part due to the opposition of Babylonian Sages to the use of the *piyyut* in the synagogue, the status of the *piyyut* as a substitute for prayers was reduced to a mere embellishment, recited in various Jewish communities primarily on Rosh Ha-Shanah and Yom Kippur, and in a minority of congregations on festivals and other occasions as well. We see, therefore, another example of the triumph of the Babylonian view over that of the land of Israel in regard to the reading of Scripture in the synagogue and to matters associated with it (Tg., sermon, and *piyyut*).

Conclusion

It is difficult to know whether on any given Sabbath or festival, the Targum, sermon, and *piyyut* would all have been heard together in the synagogue. It would seem logical that when one was expanded, the others would have been curtailed. But needless to say, the existence of these three components in proximity to the scriptural texts that were read in the synagogue made Scripture into a magnet, which attracted various literary forms through which it was presented to the community.

No synagogue lacks a central and impressive place designated to house the Torah scroll(s), or a special spot assigned for the reading of the Torah, haftarah, and the five scrolls. There is no Sabbath or festival when the congregation does not hear portions of Scripture, as the focus of synagogue activity and its climax. In the light of what we have seen, there is no way whatsoever to comprehend the history of the synagogue and what was taking place within its walls without fully comprehending that the foundation of all synagogue activity is the Bible.

[AVIGDOR SHINAN]

The Bible in the Liturgy

Rabbinic liturgy gradually became the dominant form of Jewish worship after the Roman destruction of the Temple in 70 CE. This liturgy is related, to different extents, in form, content and language to biblical prayer. In the post-Temple world, the Rabbis adopted, transformed, and expanded this biblical model. This essay understands the liturgy's use of the Bible through four categories: (1) Reading Scripture: the public reading or recitation of substantial selections from the Bible in a liturgical context, probably arising from general study of Scripture; (2) *Intact Biblical Passages as Rabbinic Prayers*: passages from the Bible, whether or not they were originally prayers, are used as prayers in the context of the liturgy, probably a continuation of already established practices; (3) *Biblicizing Prayers*: the composition of new prayers whose language is richly allusive to biblical language but that revise the original freely as needed, probably characteristic of prayer from the Second Temple period; and (4) *Prayers Composed from Biblical Verse*: individual biblical vv. (or fragments) combined with other vv. and used in new compositions, a practice that arose later in prayer development and is not as central to rabbinic liturgies as the previous three types. Before elaborating on these four modes, however, it is helpful to review the basic features of the Second Temple and the early rabbinic liturgy.

Second Temple-Era Liturgy

The most fundamental discontinuity between the Second Temple era and the rabbinic period is the nature of worship itself. The Bible prescribes and describes formal public worship as consisting of a sacrificial system, conducted by priests, centered (eventually) exclusively in the Jerusalem Temple (see "Religion of the Bible," pp. 1978–97). Psalms sung by the Levites accompanied and/or paralleled this sacrificial worship, giving it an explicit verbal component. By means of this sacrificial worship, Jews fulfilled a significant element of their covenantal obligations to God. However, because most Jews were generally unable to be present for the daily, Sabbath, and festival covenantal offerings, they participated in this sacrificial worship only vicariously. Even those in the Diaspora contributed to this sacrificial system through regular payment of Temple taxes.

We know little about the liturgical life of Jews who could not be present in Jerusalem while the Second Temple still stood. We do know that at least some Jews resident in the Land of Israel were able to participate more actively through the institution of the *ma'amad*, described by the Rabbis in the Mishnah (*Ta'an.* 4:2–3). This institution divided the entire nation into twenty-four groups, each responsible for two weeks of annual service in the Temple. When their priests and Levites went to Jerusalem to serve, the Israelites, at least those living at a distance, would gather in their local synagogues and read from the first ch of Gen. This system, however, apparently excluded any diaspora Jews.

Beyond this, we learn from the Bible itself that Jews prayed and that norms for how to construct such prayers were emerging. The Bible includes numerous examples of verbal prayers that individuals offered on occasions ranging from joy and thanksgiving to utter distress. These biblical texts, both in poetry and prose, demonstrate that preferred vocabularies and patterns for expressing ideas had emerged as part of a Jewish ritual language. Prayer texts embedded in the later books of the Bible and in extrabiblical Jewish literature of the Second Temple period provide examples of appropriate prayer language. This language used for prayer in the late Second Temple period demonstrates deep knowledge of the Bible, often alluding to or reusing earlier biblical phraseology (e.g., Dan. ch 9; Tobit 3.1–6; 3 Macc. 6.2–15).

Such biblicizing language also appears in Hebrew prayers found among the Dead Sea Scrolls (see "The Bible in the Dead Sea Scrolls," pp. 1850–59). Many of these late Second Temple period texts belonged to an apocalyptic community that chose to absent itself from the Jerusalem Temple whose leadership it considered illegitimate. This community substituted a system of verbal worship, and among their surviving scrolls are various prayer texts, some complete with instructions. While this community did employ Ps.—indeed, more copies of Ps. were found among the Dead Sea Scrolls than of any other book—their liturgy included additional psalm-like compositions not found in the Masoretic psalter (e.g., *Hodayot* hymns, non-canonical psalms), as well as nonbiblical, probably new compositions in a Heb deeply influenced by the Bible (e.g., *Words of the Luminaries*; *Songs of the Sabbath Sacrifice*). Very similar linguistic modes, albeit in Gk, appear in the prayers embedded in the New Testament and other early Christian writings (e.g., the Magnificat in Luke 1.46–55). Biblicizing language thus formed an obvious precedent and model for the prayers that emerged among the Rabbis.

The Rabbis record that some extrabiblical verbal prayer was part of the Temple liturgy as well. However, these texts date from more than a century after the destruction of the Temple and must be used with caution to reconstruct actual Temple practices. *M. Tamid* (4:3, end-5:1) records that the priests would interrupt their daily morning sacrificial offering in order to convene in the Chamber of Hewn Stone for the recitation of the Shema (see below for discussion of Shema itself). All the elements that the Mishnah lists for this ritual appear in subsequent rabbinic liturgy, albeit not all in conjunction with the Shema. The Mishnah's description also omits key elements of the earliest known rabbinic formulations. *M. Sot.* 7:7–8 depicts the rituals surrounding the high priest's reading Torah every Yom Kippur and the king's reading of the Torah during Sukkot every seventh year (based on Deut. 31.9–13). In both cases, the rituals described in the Mishnah go beyond the biblical prescriptions: Lev. ch 16, which describes the Yom Kippur ritual, does not command Torah reading on Yom Kippur; Deut. ch 31 does not give the responsibility to read aloud "this Teaching" to the king. In addition, the Mishnah includes lists of blessings that follow each of these readings, lists that cohere in style but not in all their specifics with models found in later rabbinic practice.

That all these examples differ from later rabbinic liturgy and from the biblical commandments raises significant questions: are they authentic memories of Second Temple era realities, do they reflect rabbinic liturgical realities at the time the Mishnah was redacted, or are they rabbinic projections of an ideal state in a rebuilt Temple? Whatever the case may be, these examples point either to historical continuity between the official Second Temple worship systems and rabbinic liturgy or to a continuity that the Rabbis constructed to fit their ideology and the way they wanted to present their liturgical system.

Rabbinic Liturgy

After the destruction of the Jerusalem Temple in 70 CE, the official biblically commanded Jewish sacrificial worship ceased, creating a situation of extreme discontinuity. The Rabbis responded by calling for a purely verbal worship system. This was significantly radical and discontinuous with biblical models; it largely marginalized the priests and Levites, who had been the officiants for the sacrifices, and concomitantly called for universal participation in covenantal worship. However radical this new rabbinic mode of worship may have been, it nevertheless contained numerous elements of continuity, elements that undoubtedly aided in the eventual universal acceptance of the rabbinic system.

The most significant continuities relate directly to the Bible. First, by the time the Temple was destroyed, the synagogue had already become a widespread institution, both in the Land of Israel and in the greater Jewish Diaspora. However, the late Second Temple period synagogue served primarily, if not exclusively, as a place of study and education rather than of prayer; indeed the Gk term *synagogos*, like the Heb *beit k'nesset*, refers to a gathering place, with no specific reference to prayer. Biblical texts were read and studied there; this includes Torah and Prophets (as we learn from Luke 4.16–21 where Jesus reads from Isa.), and probably other books as well, like Esth. on Purim. The Rabbis integrated this regular reading of Scripture into their new liturgical structure, gradually regulating and regularizing it. For details, see "The Bible in the Synagogue," pp. 2049–57.

It is not clear how quickly all synagogues adopted rabbinic liturgy, though. The process of integration likely took several centuries. Some rabbis avoided local synagogues or formed their own. The need for 9th-c. Babylonian *geonim* to instruct two different Spanish Jewish communities in the fundamentals of rabbinic prayer suggests that at least in some places, the process took almost a millennium. However, synagogue communities eventually accepted rabbinic guidance and synagogues universally became the locus of communal liturgy performed according to rabbinic directives. The Karaites, a movement begun in the late first millennium, dissented, rejecting rabbinic teachings, including most of their prayer traditions, and seeking to live entirely by the Bible (see below).

The second way that the Rabbis injected continuity into their fundamentally discontinuous ritual world was in their choice of prayer language. The Rabbis lived in a world that was deeply multilingual, in which most Jews in the Land of Israel spoke Gk as well as the languages of the Bible, Heb and Aram. Jews in Babylonia spoke a form of Persian as well as an eastern Aram. dialect and Heb. Contemporary scholars suggest that this knowledge of biblical languages was not unique to the rabbinic class. Each of these languages was preferred for use in different social contexts. The Rabbis' deep preference for Heb as the language of prayer placed that prayer in direct continuity with the language of divine revelation (the Bible) and engagement with this revelation through study of the Bible. Heb thus marked the sanctity that they ascribed to their liturgical system. Although the Rabbis did allow those who did not know Heb to recite even the most important prayers of their liturgical system in another language (*m. Sot.* 7:1), this was clearly not ideal, and *t. Sot.* 7:7 debates whether this leniency applies to the recitation of Shema.

We now come to the four different ways in which the Bible appears in rabbinic liturgy, mentioned at the beginning of this essay.

1. Reading Scripture

As an integral part of their liturgical structure, the Rabbis adopted or continued the existing synagogue practice of regular reading of Scripture, not on a daily basis, but organized week by week with a primary reading on the morning of the Sabbath and shorter readings from the following week's portion, begun at the Sabbath afternoon service and repeated on Monday and Thursday mornings. As the essay "The Bible in the Synagogue" (pp. 2049–57), covers the content of this first category, this essay focuses instead on its liturgical context.

The Rabbis transformed this act of study into a liturgical act by introducing blessings that framed the reading, originally just before and after the entire reading, but later, at some point before the close of the Talmud, to before and after every single subsection (*'aliyah*) into which the reading was divided (*b. Meg.* 21b). The first blessing praises God "who chose us from all the peoples and gave us His Torah" and the second one "who gave us the teaching (Torah) of truth and implanted eternal life in our midst"; both conclude by blessing God as the "Giver of Torah." The iteration and reiteration of these blessings express the ideas that the ritual reading of Torah is not just simple study, but rather is a ritual reenactment of God's revelation at Sinai, now in the context of each and every synagogue. Participation in the recitation of these blessings and the scriptural reading constitutes an act of acceptance of this divine covenantal offering by the gathered community, expressed in its affirmation, "amen," to these blessings.

The performance of the reading reinforces this message. The Torah scroll must be letter-perfect; the reader must read with absolute precision as if the voice of Sinai itself; and the reader must stand to read, without even leaning on the table on which the scroll rests. In addition, the Torah must be in a form that communicates its antiquity, even though the technology for thinning leather that allowed the entire Torah to be written on a single, manageable scroll emerged only in the early centuries CE. The Torah (and scroll of Esth.) must be handwritten on animal skin; it may never be in the form of a codex (bound book), (or, in later periods) a text to which the vowels and musical notation have been added, or a printed text.

Emerging in the post-Talmudic period and expanding incrementally ever since has been a liturgy celebrating the presence of the Torah scroll in the midst of the human community and expressing this message with greater elaboration. Particularly noteworthy is the sense that the very presence of the Torah scroll provides a potent point of access to God and thus an efficacious time for prayers. The earliest prayer books (late first millennium CE) contain prayers for the leaders of the Jewish community and for the community itself. With time, customary prayers recited in the presence of the Torah expanded to include prayers for the non-Jewish governing powers, prayers for the people called to the Torah and those for whom they would like to pray, prayers for healing of the sick, naming of baby girls, blessings on the coming month, memorials for the deceased, and much more.

The liturgical settings of other scriptural readings suggest different meanings for them. Although all biblical books may be read from a scroll, only the book of Esth. must be read in its ancient scroll form (because Esth. 9.26 commands reading "this letter," taken to mean the letter in its original form). The blessings framing the haftarah (supplementary readings taken from the Prophets) are elaborate but more diffuse in their message. The blessing before the reading emphasizes that the words of the prophets did receive divine approbation. Its conclusion establishes a theological hierarchy; it praises God who chooses "the Torah, Moses His servant, Israel His people, and the prophets of truth and righteousness." Following the reading are a series of blessings that speak to the larger occasion of the day as well as to the specificity of a prophetic reading. The first addresses God as faithful to the content of divine revelation. The next two blessings are messianic, asking God to re-establish Jewish life in Zion and re-establish the anointed Davidic monarchy (the Messiah). The whole concludes with a blessing thanking God "for the Torah, for the worship, for the prophets" and then for the Sabbath or festival day. The main purpose of these blessings is the middle expression of messianic expectation, an expectation that, of course, finds its primary biblical expression in the prophetic writings. The prophetic readings thus include an element of anticipating future redemption and go beyond a reliving of the past. The content of any individual reading does not necessarily support this meaning, but many readings do, such as the haftarot for the seven weeks of consolation between the Ninth of Av and Rosh Ha-Shanah.

Most of the Five Megillot, or Scrolls (Song, Ruth, Lam., Eccl., Esth.), read on specific occasions in the annual cycle (see "The Five Megillot," p. 1557) receive no specific liturgical structure; when read from a printed book, not even a blessing is recited. Esth., however, as it is always read from a scroll, does receive an elaborate liturgical setting. Before the reading, the reader recites not only the blessing for reading the scroll and for the occasion (*sheheḥiyanu*, during the evening reading only), but also a blessing praising God "who performed miracles for our ancestors in those days at this time." These blessings thus add the ideas, not named in Esth. itself, that God was responsible for the ancient victory celebrated and that the salvation experienced then has relevance today. The blessing following the reading reinforces these teachings. Through the first person plural, it praises God "who participates in *our* struggles, who judges *our* court cases, who wreaks vengeance for *us*, who repays all *our* enemies, and who punishes *our* foes for *us*." For Jews personally suffering any persecution or injustice, this blessing states with utter clarity that, like in ancient times, God remains today the source of their hoped-for release from their current situation.

2. Intact Biblical Passages as Rabbinic Prayers

In contrast to the first category, wherein Scripture read from scriptural books became part of the worship service, the second category consists of direct integration of biblical selections into the liturgical text itself. These appear in two forms: texts that are already prayer texts in the Bible that rabbinic liturgy integrates without changes; and biblical texts that are not originally prayer texts whose function the Rabbis transform. Both cases demonstrate the fundamental centrality of the Bible in the liturgy in a straightforward manner.

The predominant source for the biblical prayers from the first category is Psalms. Likely even before the destruction of the Temple, Jews associated Pss. 113–118 with festive days. The Rabbis call this cluster the Egyptian Hallel ("praise") because of the content of Ps. 114 ("When Israel went forth from Egypt ..."). Rabbinic liturgy incorporates some form of the recitation of these psalms into the liturgy of almost all festive days at the conclusion of the morning service before the Torah reading as well as into the Passover Seder (the evening home liturgy celebrating the exodus).

The process by which rabbinic liturgy came to integrate other psalms is less clear, but the Talmud praises recitation of Ps. 145 thrice daily (*b. Ber.* 4b) and praises those who complete the *hallel* daily. This is not a reference to the Egyptian Hallel, but to something else included in a liturgical element called the "Verses of Song" (*pesukei d'zimra; b. Shab.* 118b). Texts of the latter centuries of the first millennium CE clarify that this refers to the central element of the preliminary prayers of the daily morning service, Pss. 145–150. Jews further expanded the "Verses of Song" with additional biblical passages: a prayer of David (1 Chron. 29.10–13), a levitical prayer from the time of Ezra and Nehemiah (Neh. 9.6–11), both followed by Moses' Song of the Sea (Exod. 14.30–15.21). Especially on Sabbaths and holidays, different regional rites recite numerous additional Psalms before this *hallel* as well. Psalms also begin the Friday evening service. Originally just Pss. 92 (the Ps. for the Sabbath day) –93, Pss. 95–99 and 29 were added in the early modern period under the influence of Lurianic kabbalah.

Just as the Rabbis expressed the meaning and function of scriptural readings by adding blessings before and after them, so too they communicated the meaning and function of *hallel*. Except at the Passover Seder, the Egyptian Hallel always begins with a blessing acknowledging the rabbinic understanding that its recitation is a commanded act (*mitzvah*). The Seder provides a lyric introduction to the Hallel instead that expresses this same meaning, albeit without the technical blessing formula. It asserts effusively that because God saved us from Egypt, we have an obligation in return to offer God our praise. The introductory blessing to the "Verses of Song" is similarly lyric, establishing that the praise expressed in the Ps. is due to God as the God of all history from creation to redemption. The Talmudic corpus preserves fragmentary texts for most of the concluding prayers for these recitations of psalms. These blessings are all ecstatic and effusive in their language, multiplying praises of God to express the human inability adequately to verbalize their magnitude. Israel joins with all of creation in this praise in order to construct a deafening, resounding chorus. In this, these liturgical settings transform these received biblical texts into the personal praise of those actually reciting them again.

Many other Pss. are or may be recited on particular occasions (see the list in the addendum to this article). These too become the personal prayers of those reciting them, sometimes with the particular purpose expressed through prefixed statements of personal or communal intention. Some communities today will recite Pss. 121 and 130 responsively at every service in times of communal crisis. However, none of these recitations are accompanied by blessings, so remain outside the formal liturgy.

Some other recitations of Pss. were added over time, less as expressions of prayer than as additional study texts that would create opportunities for the recitation of *kaddish*, the doxological praise of God that medieval Jews understood to aid the souls of the departed. Primary among these are Ps. 130 added just before the "Verses of Song," and the Psalm of the Day at the conclusion of each day's service. This last draws on the mishnaic memory that Levites had recited a particular Ps. each day of the week in the Jerusalem Temple (*m. Tamid* 7:4). The new month, some holidays, and the penitential season around Rosh HaShanah and Yom Kippur in the fall contribute their own Pss. as well.

The recitation of this Psalm of the Day is closer in function to the recitation of another group of biblical texts than it is to that of the Hallel Psalms, in that they retain the quality of study texts and are not fully transformed into liturgy. The preliminary rites in the morning, before the "Verses of Song," include a number of biblical passages whose recitation falls fully into this world of study. Most of the passages have a connection, explicit or implicit, to the sacrificial worship of the Temple, and they enter the rabbinic liturgical system from the understanding that, in the absence of the possibility of actual sacrifice, study of these passages is a covenantal act that is pleasing to God. The actual passages chosen differ from rite to rite. Common Ashkenazi practice includes passages arranged into a rough description of the actual Temple ritual, moving from the basin for preliminary hand washing (Exod. 30.17–21), to clearing the ashes (Lev. 6.1–6), then the daily sacrifice (Lev. 1.11; Num. 28.1–8), and finally the incense offering (Exod. 30.7–8, 34–36). Later practice also adds the binding of Isaac (Gen. ch 22), explicitly to remind God of the covenantal promises made then.

We turn now to the Shema, probably the best-known and most important example of biblical texts that enter rabbinic liturgy. In its biblical context, it is not a ritual text, but it certainly becomes one in rabbinic usage. The Shema consists of three biblical passages that have been juxtaposed: Deut. 6.4–9 (interrupted with a rabbinic interjection between the first and second vv. in response to hearing God's name), Deut. 11.13–21, and Num. 15.37–41. It is recited daily, morning and evening. The Rabbis specifically title this a "recitation," (from the root *q-r-ʾ*) pointing to the biblical origin *(miqraʾ)* of these passages. Like the passages about the sacrifices, but unlike the recitation of entire Psalms, these texts are all extracted from their larger narrative contexts in the Torah. Their content interlinks them one with the other, particularly their commandments of various practices, like donning *tefillin* (phylacteries), marking one's doorpost with a *mezuzah*, or wearing *tzitzit* (ritual fringes on a *tallit*), that serve to construct a constant consciousness of God's presence and His commandments.

The lifting of these passages out of their biblical context may have originated in the Second Temple period, as indicated in *m. Tamid*. However, there is no evidence for their liturgical recitation in the Dead Sea Scrolls or other Second Temple descriptions of Jewish piety. The so-called Nash papyrus, discovered in Egypt in 1898 and perhaps dating from the first half of the 2nd c. CE contains the text of the Ten Commandments and the beginning of the Shema. Although not necessarily meant for liturgical use, this verifies the rabbinic memory that the Shema's three passages were originally linked with a fourth, the Ten Commandments. To delegitimize those privileging the Ten Commandments over the rest of Torah, the Rabbis forbade their continued inclusion.

The Rabbis understand the recitation of the first two passages to constitute acceptance of God's sovereignty and commandments respectively, while they refer to the third passage as either commanding the *tzitzit* or reminding Jews of the exodus. The Shema sometimes stands on its own, as it needs to be recited at specific times of day that may not coincide with synagogue services. However, in its full liturgical context, the Rabbis embed it in a matrix of elaborate blessings, which develop the primary historical and theological claims, on the basis of which God expects Israel to accept their relationship with Him: God's creative work, both at the beginning of history and in ongoing ways; God's particular love for Israel as expressed by giving them the Torah; and God's redeeming Israel from Egyptian slavery. It is this setting that makes these passages into a liturgical performance.

3. Biblicizing Prayers

These blessings, along with those of the other central prayers of the rabbinic liturgical system (the *ʿAmidah* [standing prayer], also called *ha-tefillah* [the prayer], or *Shemonah ʿEsrei* [eighteen benedictions]; and the *birkat ha-mazon* [grace after meals]), are new compositions, not excerpts from the Bible. However, the language of these prayers retains a close connection to the Bible, especially at the symbolic level. The Heb of these prayers is grammatically and syntactically closer to rabbinic Heb than to biblical Heb, but, like the prayer language that had emerged in the Second Temple period, it is richly allusive to the language of the Bible, drawing on its vocabulary and imagery for almost every phrase. Because most of these allusions are to Psalms or other poetic texts, the result is a highly poetic prose.

Sometimes shorter (occasionally longer) biblical phrases appear verbatim. Frequently, though, they appear with their language tweaked so as to fit their new syntactic context. Many other changes derive from the rabbinic requirement that prayers be voiced in the first person plural (*b. Ber.* 29b–30a, 49b–50a). Not infrequently, the texts presume that the allusions will be understood; the original context of the language continues to inform the meaning of the prayer. On other occasions, the rabbinic linguistic decision seems to reflect a search for the best theological statement in their own context (see the discussion about proper adaptations to Isa. 45.7 in the opening line of the first morning blessing before Shema; *b. Ber.* 11b).

Different modes of biblicizing language may appear within any given prayer. The first blessing of the *ʿAmidah*, called *ʾAvot* (patriarchs, ancestors) is typical. A translation of the prayer reads:

> Blessed are You, Lord our God and God of our fathers, God of Abraham, God of Isaac, and God of Jacob, great, mighty, and awesome God, God Most High, who bestows acts of loving-kindness and creates all, who remembers the loving-kindness of the fathers and will bring a Redeemer to their children's children for the sake of His name, in love. King, Helper, Savior, Shield: Blessed are You, Lord, Shield of Abraham. (Sacks, Rabbi Sir Jonathan, transl. and comm., *The Koren Sacks Siddur*. Jerusalem: Koren Publishers Jerusalem Ltd., 2009.)

It begins, not with its expected blessing formula, "Blessed are You, Lord our God, King of the universe, who ..." but with the seemingly anomalous "Blessed are You, Lord our God and God of our fathers, God of Abraham, God of Isaac, and God of Jacob." The unusual words here are a direct citation of Exod. 3.15, where God instructs Moses to tell the Israelites that this is the divine name, adding, "This shall be My name forever, / This My appellation for all eternity." This name proves to have particular power. Elijah invokes it when defeating the priests of Baal (1 Kings 18.36). The ʾAvot prayer continues addressing God as "the great, the mighty and the awesome God," language found verbatim in Deut. 10.17, but cited with slight variations in later books of the Bible, suggesting that it had entered into the vocabulary of Hebrew prayer more generally. Next we find God addressed as "God Most High," language taken from Melchizedek's blessing of Abraham in Gen. 14.19. The rite used in the Land of Israel contained a longer citation at this point, concluding the prayer here with the rest of the v., "Creator of heaven and earth." Today's rites paraphrase this, after an interruption, as "creates all." "Who bestows acts of loving-kindness" alludes to Isa. 63.7 and its discussion of God's acts of lovingkindness. "Who remembers the lovingkindness of the fathers" alludes to language about God's remembering earlier generations in Jer. 2.2 or Lev. 26.45. "And will bring a Redeemer to their children's children for the sake of His name, in love" is a freer use of biblical language, vaguely allusive to themes found in Isa. 59.20 or Ps. 103.17–18. Similarly, "King, Helper, Savior, Shield" echo themes of Pss. 18.36 and 79.9. Finally, the concluding blessing here calls on God as "shield of Abraham," alluding to God's promise to Abram in Gen. 15.1, "Fear not, Abram, / I am a shield to you; / Your reward shall be very great."

As is evident from this description, prayers of this type integrate phrases cited directly from the Bible along with others that are, to varying degrees, allusive to it. These prayers can include entire vv. as well, especially as responses. For instance, two vv. from the Song of the Sea (Exod. 15.11, 18) conclude the blessing following Shema that celebrates God's past redemptive acts. Another set of vv., appearing in three different liturgical contexts, draw primarily from the angelic liturgies witnessed by Isaiah (6.3) and Ezekiel (3.12). These contexts either recall or participate in this angelic praise. In both cases, the liturgy gives these vv. a new verbal context, including the worshipping community in the event the Bible describes.

A third set of vv. operates differently. The priestly benediction of the community (Num. 6.24–26) was one of the Temple rituals that the Rabbis adapted to the post-Temple context. These blessings are still recited by *kohanim*, Jewish males of priestly descent. In this, they retain their original function; they might better belong in our second category of types of liturgical texts. However, the Rabbis integrated this blessing into their *ʿAmidah*, and when no priests are available, or, in the Diaspora, on all days except for festivals, the precentor simply recites these vv. as part of the larger context of the *ʿAmidah*, hardly differentiated from much of the rest of that complex of prayers.

This third category thus most characterizes both the language of the pre-rabbinic liturgies known from Second Temple sources as well as the prayers that received sustained attention in the Mishnah and Talmud, particularly, the blessings surrounding the Shema, the *ʿAmidah*, and the Grace after Meals.

4. Prayers Composed from Biblical Verses

The three types of uses of biblical material in Jewish liturgy so far discussed are substantially distinct from our fourth and last category of prayers: those composed entirely of direct citations from the Bible, of individual but intact vv. strung together from various biblical contexts to form an entirely new composition. Most likely these prayers are later liturgical creations than the prayers of the previous category. This last category appears only outside the core statutory prayers, suggesting that this literary mode reflects a post-Talmudic aesthetic. Such prayers are found, for instance, in the "Verses of Song," preceding its *hallel*, in the supplicatory prayers *(taḥanun)* that follow the *ʿAmidah* on weekdays, in the liturgies that accompany the taking out and returning the Torah from the Ark, in the additions at the conclusion of the Grace after Meals, in the introduction to *havdalah* (the ritual ending the Sabbath), and among the penitential prayers of the High Holy Day season. In addition, this is the style of liturgical composition that most characterizes the prayers of the Karaites, an anti-rabbanite movement that emerged towards the end of the first millennium. Presumably, the rabbanite Jews were already producing compositions in this style when Karaism emerged or they might have rejected it as characteristic of the group that was challenging their authority.

In our third category of prayers, *Biblicizing Prayers,* every word adds to the text's meaning in some way. In contrast, compositions in our fourth category express their meaning by combining vv. containing similar words. Only the echoes of words from one v. to another create the prayer's meaning. There are precedents for this literary mode even within biblical poetry, especially where the demands of an acrostic limits freer expression, as, for example, in Ps. 145. However, the actual rabbinic liturgical performance of this Ps., which adds biblical vv. to its beginning, brings it into our fourth category as well. Vv. from elsewhere in the Psalter beginning with the word *ʾashrei* ("happy is ...") introduce Ps. 145 and give it its more familiar name. The most common vv. are Ps. 84.5 and the last v. of the preceding Ps. (Ps. 144), but various rites add many more. Ps. 115.18 also concludes the composition. We do not know how early this complex should be dated, but it may represent a transitional stage between reciting intact Psalms and concatenating vv.

A hymn that is fully characteristic of our fourth category, known by its opening words, *Yehi Khavod* ("May God's glory ..."), consists of eighteen vv., only three of which form a cluster in the Bible. It consists of: Pss. 104.31; 113.2–4; 135.13; 103.19; 1 Chron. 16.31; Pss. 10.16; 33.10; Prov. 19.21; Pss. 33.11; 33.9; 132.13; 135.4; 94.14; 78.38; 20.10. In addition, after 1 Chron. 16.31, it includes one line, familiar from many prayers of this genre, that consists of three v. fragments (The LORD reigns, the LORD reigned, the LORD will reign forever and ever). Not a single phrase is nonbiblical.

Because they incorporate (with a few exceptions) complete vv., much of the content of any one v. is incidental or even occasionally contradictory to the overall intent of the composition. A good example of this is the prayer recited when removing the Torah from the Ark, Num. 10.35, "When the Ark was to set out, Moses would say: Advance O LORD! / May Your enemies be scattered, / and may Your foes flee before You!" This v. appears in both the Ashkenazi and Sephardi rites, but with opposite emphases. In the Ashkenazi rite, the partial v. following is Isa. 2.3, "For instruction shall come forth from Zion, / The word of the LORD from Jerusalem." The emphasis, thus, is on the motion of God's teaching, first from Sinai, then emanating from Zion, and now in the synagogue, where the Torah is about to emerge from the Ark. The second half of the Num.'s v. with its call for God's protection of Israel thus plays no role in the meaning of the composition. In contrast, the Sephardi rite embeds this v. (in its Sabbath and festival liturgy) following a v. calling on God's salvific powers and before another that similarly calls on God to "advance." The emphasis here is thus on Moses' request for protection from Israel's enemies in the second part of the v. and not on its description of the movement of the Ark. The contrast is even starker in the Italian rite's elaborate festival liturgy for this moment which includes at this point a series of nine vv. calling on God to "advance."

Concluding Observations

The Jewish liturgical world that emerged after the destruction of the Temple was profoundly biblical, albeit through the four different modes discussed above. All four of these modes continued to shape traditional Jewish liturgy, often enriched further by liturgical poetry (*piyyut*), itself intensely biblicizing. Challenges to this biblical character of Jewish liturgy did arise over time. While existing compositions in the fourth mode aggregated additional vv., there is little evidence that new prayers of this type continued to be created, probably because of the challenges to communicating in this fashion. Kabbalists added prose statements of intention to received prayers, but with biblical echoes only in prooftexts. Modern translated prayers often poorly communicate the biblicizing analogies and authors of new prayers do not always successfully write in this mode. Today's feminist concerns also challenge those elements of the received language of the prayers that reflect the biblical preference for masculine references to God and the elevation of male members of the community over the female. Prayer is a living tradition that cannot be entirely represented schematically, and that will continue to grow in new directions as worshippers find themselves in new contexts.

Addendum: Some Liturgical Uses of Psalms in Jewish Tradition

Ps. 1: unveiling of tombstone
Ps. 3: recitation of the Shema before going to sleep
Ps. 6: vv. 2–11 are in *Tahanun*
Ps. 8: daily evening service
Ps. 15: dedication of a new house; unveiling of a tombstone
Ps. 16: funeral; unveiling; in a house of mourning
Ps. 19: introductory prayers *(pesuqei de-zimra)* in the morning service for Sabbath and festivals
Ps. 20: daily morning service
Ps. 23: for the sick; funeral; unveiling
Ps. 24: psalm for Sunday; on festivals when the Torah is returned to the Ark
Ps. 27: from 1 Elul through Hoshana Rabbah
Ps. 29: Friday evening service; on Sabbath when the Torah is returned to the Ark
Ps. 30: introductory prayers for the daily, Sabbath, and festival morning service; dedication of a new house
Ps. 33: introductory prayers for the Sabbath and festival morning service

Ps. 34: introductory prayers for the Sabbath and festival morning service
Ps. 39: house of mourning
Ps. 47: before the blowing of the shofar (ram's horn) on Rosh Ha-Shanah
Ps. 48: psalm for Monday
Ps. 49: house of mourning; funeral
Ps. 63: consecration of a cemetery; funeral
Ps. 67: evening service at the conclusion of Sabbath
Ps. 81: psalm for Thursday
Ps. 82: psalm for Tuesday
Ps. 83: daily morning service when *Taḥanun* is recited
Ps. 90: introductory prayers for the Sabbath and festival morning service
Ps. 91: recitation of the Shema before going to sleep; before going on a journey; introductory prayers for the Sabbath and festival morning service
Ps. 92: Friday evening service; introductory prayers for the Sabbath and festival morning service
Ps. 93: psalm for Friday; Friday evening service; introductory prayers for the Sabbath and festival morning service
Ps. 94: psalm for Wednesday
Pss. 95–99: Friday evening service
Ps. 100: introductory prayers for the daily morning service
Ps. 102: consecration of a cemetery
Ps. 103: for the sick; consecration of a cemetery
Ps. 104: new moon; Sabbath afternoon service (fall and winter); consecration of a cemetery
Pss. 113–118: Hallel on new moon, festivals, and Hanukkah
Pss. 120–134: Sabbath afternoon service (fall and winter)
Ps. 126: introduction to grace after meals on Sabbath and festivals
Ps. 130: morning service of Ten Days of Repentance
Pss. 135–136: introductory prayers for the Sabbath and festival morning service
Ps. 137: introduction to grace after meals on weekdays
Ps. 139: for the sick
Ps. 144: evening service at the conclusion of Sabbath
Pss. 145–150: introductory prayers for the daily, Sabbath, and festival morning service

[RUTH LANGER]

Jewish Customs

Many contemporary Jewish observances and customs do not reflect ancient biblical practices and laws. Contemporary practices derive from a wide variety of sources over different times and places: Some have biblical precedent, some reflect classical rabbinic interpretation of the Bible, while others are more recent, and reflect Jewish adaptations of local customs.

Customs are known by their Heb name *minhag* (plural *minhagim*). The word *minhag* appears (twice) in the Hebrew Bible, in 2 Kings 9.20: "And the lookout reported, 'The messenger has reached them, but has not turned back. And it looks like the driving (*keminhag*) of Jehu son of Nimshi, who drives wildly.'" The word takes on its new meaning in rabbinic literature of the early centuries of the Common Era (and perhaps earlier) with the sense of "practice," such as in "this was the practice of R. Akiva that when he prayed with the congregation, he would shorten his prayers ..." (*b. Ber.* 35b). This reflects a personal, very individual, practice that did not necessarily obligate others. The custom of the Babylonians described there encompassed a broader section of the community, but did not obligate their Palestinian co-religionists. Rabbinic literature also tells of more localized customs, such as those of (probably an elite class of) Jerusalemites of the late Second Temple period. In fact, a whole ch (number 4) in the tractate *Pes.* deals with the obligations of a person coming from a locality with one set of customs, who goes to another with a different set.

Local, perhaps familial custom is reflected already in Gen., in reference to marriage practices, when Laban, in reference to his giving Leah rather than Rachel to Jacob as a wife says (Gen. 29.26): "It is not the practice in our place to marry off the younger before the older."

Strikingly, although this statement by a non-Israelite was before the revelation at Sinai, which for the Rabbis was the point of origin of law, in later rabbinic times it was regarded as a binding rule. Thus the early medieval tosafists (Franko-German commentators on the Talmud *b. Kid.* 52 b) rule that if a father received a bride-price for one of his unspecified daughters, we assume that it is for the older one, because "it is not the practice in our place to marry off the younger before the older." Not all medieval Sages, however, agreed with this ruling, though more recently, R. Moses Schrieber (also known as the Chatam Sofer), an important Orthodox leader and Rabbi of Pressburg in the early 19th c., stated, "It is very difficult for me to go against an explicit statement in the Bible. And I have been told that such a case came before my teacher, R. Nathan Adler, and he failed—erred [in his ruling of this matter]." This issue occupied many later authorities who discussed it from a variety of different standpoints. So we see, that even the *local practice* of Laban, prior (in the Bible's chronology) to the receipt of the Torah of Sinai, and from a non-Israelite whom the Bible depicts in an unsavory manner, nonetheless was a matter of considerable concern throughout Jewish legal history. This demonstrates the tremendous importance of *minhag* in Jewish tradition.

The prominent place of *minhag* is especially odd since it has no real source in the canons of Jewish law, i.e., the Bible, or the later codices, such as the Mishnah and Talmud, or the later great legal compilations of Maimonides, Rabbenu Jacob ben Asher (author of the *Turim*), and the *Shulhan Aruch* of R. Yosef Caro with the annotations of R. Moshe Isserles [the *Rema* or *Remo*]). Indeed, Jewish law knows a tripartite hierarchy, with biblical law at the top rung (these laws are called *mi-de-Oraita*, Aram. for "from the Torah"), postbiblical rabbinic rulings (*Mi-de-Rabbanan*—rules established by the Rabbis) in second place, and *minhag* in the lowest position. The laws which the Rabbis see as biblical are most authoritative, least flexible, and are applied with a clear tendency to stringency; the rabbinic laws are less stringent; and *minhag* is the least authoritative. Moreover, while the highest two categories are seen as obligating more or less all segments of the Jewish community, *minhag* was generally speaking localized, and consequently it differed greatly from one area to another, and was authoritative only in its specific locale. It is thus especially remarkable that *minhag* has played such a central role within Judaism.

During the early Middle Ages *minhag* was upgraded, and a number of great authorities in France, Provence, and Spain, state (in a variety of formulations with only slight differences) that the "*minhag* of our fathers is Torah," meaning that *minhag* has very weighty authority, perhaps even as weighty as that of the Bible. Although this created a new status for *minhag*, which gained even greater currency in later generations, this statement equating *minhag* with Torah was not meant to be taken literally, and *minhag* was not accorded all the regulatory prescriptions pertaining to biblical law. This in part reflects the rabbinic understanding that biblical law was divinely given; rabbinic law was enacted by the Rabbis in court rulings or even in individual decisions; but customs evolved, perhaps spontaneously, or sometimes through emulating the personal practices of great individuals, who took upon themselves, and themselves alone, specific practices, usually in the form of stringencies. These customs had a dynamic evolution of their own, evolving sometimes in one place and spreading to another, sometimes remaining in their own locality, and at times waning and/or disappearing completely. Very commonly their origins and rationale were forgotten, and new reasons were offered to explain, justify, and legitimate them.

A whole corpus of literature grew up first recording, and then explicating customs, beginning in early Medieval Ashkenaz (Germany) and Provence, and later spreading throughout the whole of the Jewish world. Frequently these *minhagim* (customs) morphed into laws—i.e., binding rulings, and local communities drew up their own lists of customs, often bolstering their authority by redefining them as "regulations" (*gezerot* or *takkanot*). However, the classic codices, such as the *Shulhan Aruch*, took care to distinguish between "absolute rulings" *(dinim),* and customs, prefixing the latter with phrases such as "there are who practice" *(yesh nohagim)* as "the people practiced" *(nahagu ha-am),* and such like.

As the following examples illustrate, often biblical vv. were attributed as the source for a *minhag,* with the explicit recognition, however, that the *minhag* does not represent, or carry the weight of, biblical law.

For example, an annotation of R. Mosheh Isserles (the main halachic authority for Ashkenazic Jewry) to the *Shulhan Aruch* (the main Jewish code of law) reads: "It is good to blow [the shofar, ram's horn, on Rosh Ha-Shanah] from the right side" (Orah Hayyim 585:2). The latter-day authority, the Hafetz Hayyim (Rabbi Yisrael Meir Kagan, 1838–1933), quotes in the name of R. Meir Simha of Dvinsk, that the true reason for this is because we pattern the blowing of the shofar on the trumpets blown at battle according to the book of Judg., which describes Gideon's battle, noting: "and the three columns blew their horns and broke their jars. Holding the torches in their left hands and the horns for blowing in their right hands ..." (Judg. 7.20). Similarly, the custom to blow the shofar one hundred times on Rosh Ha-Shanah, was stated by Gaonic authorities (ca. 10th c.) to be in accordance with the hundred cries that the mother of Sisera cried out in anguish (see Judg. 5.28). Although the biblical text nowhere explicitly states that she cried out one hundred times, this interpretation is likely based on the presence of one hundred letters in Judg. 5.20–30! This follows a common hermeneutical practice in rabbinic homiletic, and thus connects the *minhag* of blowing the shofar on Rosh Ha-Shanah to Sisera's mother in Judg., giving it biblical precedence.

The custom of leaving a stone upon a grave site when visiting a burial place of a family member is similarly given biblical precedence, and is connected to Gen. 35.20. There, when Rachel passed away on the road to Ephrath, "Over her grave Jacob set up a pillar *(matzevah);* it is the pillar at Rachel's grave to this day." The 11th c. *Midrash Lekah Tov* comments on this v.: "From this we learn that each of the children placed a stone upon those stones ... and Jacob's stone was on top of them all." Thus, the Bible is used to justify later *minhag.*

A biblical source is also adduced by some for the custom that when someone is called up to the synagogue reading of the Torah (has an *ʿaliyah*), that person ascends the *bimah* (podium) from one side, and descends from the other (*Shulhan Aruch*, Orah Hayyim 141:7). The v. cited for this practice is Ezek. 46.9, "But on the fixed occasions, when the common people come before the LORD, whoever enters by the north gate to bow low shall leave by the south gate; and whoever enters by the south gate shall leave by the north gate. They shall not go back through the gate by which they came in, but shall go out by the opposite one." No matter that this v. deals with the ideal future Jerusalem Temple, and has no explicit connection to the reading of the Torah. Other biblical vv. fill in *minhagim* related to other parts of the Torah service ritual. When concluding the reading of a pentateuchal book in the synagogue service, the congregation declaims: "Be strong, be strong, and let us strengthen ourselves" (ibid., 139:11). This, it is claimed, is based on the vv. in Josh. 1.8–9: "Let not this Book of the

Teaching cease from your lips ... I charge you: Be strong and resolute...." The vv. in Josh., however, are the divine charge to Joshua, and are not connected to the communal reading of the Torah! Biblical vv. that are not connected to the Torah at all are also cited to justify the *minhag* that when the Torah scroll is returned to the Ark, those whom it passes should accompany it part of the way (ibid., 149:11), as it is written, "Follow none but the LORD your God ..." (Deut. 13.5).

The use of biblical "precedent" in customs is found in a variety of areas outside of synagogue practice. For example, it is customary at the wedding ceremony for the bride to stand to the right of the bridegroom under the *huppah* (canopy). The reason given for this accepted practice is that it is based on the v. in Ps. 45.10, "the consort stands at your right hand." The final letters of these three relevant words *(nitzvah shegal liyminekha)* spell in reverse order *kallah*, bride. Here a common hermeneutical technique has been used to identify the source of this custom; the identification of the consort with the bride is also facilitated by the numerous rabbinic sources that liken a bride to royalty.

There was, and continues to be, a definite tendency to find a biblical source for common customs, many of which can be demonstrated to be quite late in origin, and may even have totally foreign—i.e., non-Jewish roots. The development of such *minhagim* reflects the dynamic nature of Jewish law and practice, while the attempts to find biblical roots for them reflects the continuing importance of the Bible throughout Jewish tradition.

Over the generations, the distinction between law and custom has largely become blurred. In the words of Belgian philosopher of law, Chaim Perelman, in his important book *Justice* (New York: Random House, 1967, pp. 9–12):

> A mode of behaviour that has been adopted without protest creates a precedent, and no one will object to actions that conform to precedents. The principle of inertia transforms every habitual way of thinking ..., and it is the basis for the rules that develop spontaneously in any given society. A customary form of behaviour, one which conforms to the expectations of the members of the group, needs no justification; it will be accepted spontaneously as just, because it is as it should be.... It is only when someone maintains that what ought to be is different than what is that proof has to be supplied.... Only in upsetting a presumption must proof be given. The principle of inertia thus plays an indispensable stabilizing rule in social life. This does not mean that what is must remain forever, but rather that there are no change without reason ...

So customs come and go, altering, evolving, disappearing with the changes in circumstances, population movements, crises and catastrophes, and new social order, etc. But custom, in whatever variegated forms it takes, constitutes a major element in Jewish law and life. Indeed if the *dinim*—regulations, are the outlines, custom is the color and the fleshing out of the character of Jewish ritual; it is the chiaroscuro of Jewish life.

[DANIEL SPERBER]

The Bible in Israeli Life*

The Bible, once at the center of the cultural scene in Israel, has become marginalized; its magic has faded. A new Israeli generation no longer believes that, to be considered educated, one must be well-versed in the canonical national literature; to a greater or lesser degree, it rejects Bible study as a required subject. Pride in the greatness of the Bible is giving way to alienation; instead of proficiency in Scripture one finds unashamed ignorance of its content. Before we can measure the depth of the change and trace its causes, we must examine the situation as it was until recently, when the Bible proudly held sway over the Israeli scene.

Early Days: The Holy Scripture of Secular Zionism

The Zionist endeavor defined itself from the start in biblical language, as the "return to Zion" (Ps. 126.1), and by placing Bible study at the center of the school curriculum made it an integral component of national rebirth, rebuilding the ancestral land, and revival of its language. The return to the land, cultivation of the land, national independence, military valor, speaking the tongue of Amos and Isaiah, received quasi-religious inspiration from the Bible; it embodied that generation's tasks and visions as if the present were recapturing the past. Leaders, authors, and teachers all believed that the Bible legitimized Zionism: It testified to Jewish ownership of the land and foretold the return, the rebuilding, and the ingathering. Conversely, Zionism enhanced Scripture: It was realizing prophecy and thereby confirming the Bible's eternal truth. The Bible was an inspiring commentary on the present, and the present was a concrete interpretation of the Bible. The immediacy and reality of the biblical saga—from the immigration of individuals in obedience to the command, "Go forth from your native land" (Gen. 12.1) and the mass exodus from the house of bondage, through the frailty of the "desert generation" and the virility of the conquerors of Canaan, culminating in the defensive wars waged by the Judges and the establishment of the monarchy—invested the present with an aura of ancient splendor. Biblical history gave the Zionist endeavor roots in time; geography, with its memory-laden sites, confirmed its ties to place; and archeology provided the newcomers with material proof of their "nativity" in this old-new land.

Literature, particularly poetry, played a major role in this two-way association of Zionism with the Bible. The power of poetry can be seen in two poems about Saul's heroic death by Natan Alterman and Amir Gilboa, both published in the first decade of the State of Israel. Alterman's ballad, "The Day of Battle and Its Eve are Ended" (*'Ir ha-Yonah,* Tel Aviv, 1957, pp. 184–185) begins with a brief reference to the biblical story of the overthrow of Israel's army on Mt. Gilboa: defeat, flight, and King Saul's suicide. The poet then goes on to describe in detail how the wounded herald rides a whole night from the battlefield to the queen mother's home and, upon arriving, falls to the ground, speechless. His blood, staining her feet, and the news of the king's death implied by his silence, have brought the battlefield to her doorstep. Her heroism is no less impressive than Saul's in this struggle for the national spirit. "Rise, my son," she commands the herald, and upon hearing his tearful description of the king's falling on his sword, she responds, expressing the heroism of mothers:

> Then spake she to the youth: Blood
> Will cover mother's feet,

*A longer version of this article appeared in Hebrew in *Yeri'ot* 1, 1999; an English translation by Mr. David Louvish was published in *Modern Judaism,* 19.3, 1999, pp. 217–239. This adaptation is published with the kind permission of *Modern Judaism.*

But the nation will rise seven times
If it be defeated on its own land.
Judgment has been visited upon the king,
But a successor will arise in due time,
For it was upon his own land that
He leaned the sword upon which he died.
Thus she spake and her voice trembled.
And so it was. And David heard.

She neither weeps nor holds her tongue, but her voice trembles. David, and with him the readers, heard in her words the essence of Zionism: A defeat in exile is final, but a defeat in the homeland is temporary. The blood-soaked soil of the land strengthens the resolve of its sons and their mothers: Vanquished in exile by death and its terror, here they will prevail over both.

Alterman speaks through the mouth of a fictitious biblical character, whereas Amir Gilboa in his poem "Saul" (*Keḥullim va-Adummim,* Tel Aviv, 1963, p. 216) bridges the time gap by having a contemporary speak to Saul. While the courage of Saul's mother is superhuman (in a sense even inhuman), Gilboa's narrator expresses amazement at Saul's awe-inspiring death by describing his own weaknesses and doubts:

Saul! Saul!
I do not know whether it was shame
or fear of a bodiless head—
But upon passing by the wall of
Beth-Shean
I turned my head away.

Then, when your arms-bearer refused
you the sword you commanded,
I stood dumb, speechless,
and my blood flowed from my heart.
I really cannot say what I would have
done in his place
had I been your arms-bearer.

And you are the king.

And it is your honor as king when you
command.
I really cannot say what I would have
done in his place.

Saul, Saul, come!
In Beth-Shean the Children of Israel
now live.

Saul's head is impaled upon the (Roman) wall of Beth-Shean at this day (1952), and the speaker, averting his gaze, admits that he does not know whether he did so out of shame at what the Philistines did to his king or out of fear of the terrible sight. Uncertainty as to the real reason for his behavior is also expressed in a further, even more heartrending, quandary: He is present at Gilboa when Saul's arms-bearer disobeys the king's command to bring him his sword so that he can commit suicide. The speaker does not know whether he himself would have been brave enough to disobey his monarch, or whether he would have obeyed, recognizing that the king's honor required him to obey even unto death. The solemnity of the biblical scene is expressed through the narrator's insignificance and doubts: It does not occur to him to identify with the king, and while he is identifying with the arms-bearer, he is still no more than a silent observer, his heart bleeding at the gravity of the dilemma. Only toward the end of the poem does a new certainty seize him, enabling him to address the live Saul and inform him of the great Zionist message of comfort; the story of Israel's defeat on Mt. Gilboa and the abuse of Saul's body has a happy ending: Beth-Shean is being rebuilt and settled by new immigrants!

Alterman delivers the message in loud, resonant tones; Gilboa whispers: By virtue of national continuity, geographic identity, and Scripture's eternal truth, we are living in the Bible and the Bible lives in us. Thus the Bible had become the Holy Scriptures of Zionism, but there was a profound difference between those who considered it a heroic *epos,* to be released from the heavy shackles of prophetic ethics, and those for whom it was a source of ethical lore and Jewish spiritual life. The latter considered the ethical values underlying the laws of the Torah, as well as the courageous social censure and vision of national redemption pronounced by the prophets, as a firm basis for a new version of Judaism: neither halakhic, traditional, nor exilic; but authentic by virtue of being neo-biblical.

In addition to these groups of writers, however, there were radical discreditors of Judaism, for whom clinging to the national heritage and accepting authority, excess spirituality, moral scruples, the claim to national uniqueness, were obstructions on the path to a natural, free life. They rejected the Bible entirely, or expressed their adoption of alternative values by such means as giving poetic expression to the false prophets or explicitly rejecting David.

Method of Interpretation: *Derash* Claiming to Be *Peshat*

Accompanying the return to the Bible was an enthusiastic devotion to *peshat* (contextual and philological interpretation). *Peshat* alone would reveal the text's authentic meaning, extricating it from talmudic midrash (homiletics) and medieval commentaries, and from the confining authority of the Rabbis. Part of the magic of *peshat* was that it extended the secular hegemony (already effective in society, politics, and culture) to the realm of Bible commentary, freeing it from religious tradition. David Ben-Gurion does not say this explicitly in his article, "The Bible Shines with Its Own Light" (*Iyyunim ba-Tanakh,* Tel Aviv, 1969, pp. 41–45) but conveys it indirectly by three examples of the superiority of *peshat:* "an eye for an eye" cannot possibly refer to payment of damages, as taught by the Rabbis; the biblical David was no scholar, poring night after night over the oral law, but an intrepid warrior-king, capable of committing grave sins; and "the truth obliges us" to recognize that "The Song of Songs is (in its plain meaning, as a love song) one thing, while the midrash of the Song of Songs is another." But then Ben-Gurion declares, "The books of the Bible declare the glory of Israel. As to the glory of God—that is declared by the heavens, and the 'heavens' belong not to our nation only, not even to humankind, but to infinity.... The Bible is our own creation.... The Holy One, blessed be He, does not need an identity card." With that he abandons a contextual, philological reading of innumerable passages that speak in God's name or magnify and glorify Him; through radical midrash, he ignores the active, clearly manifest deity, and replaces Him by the spirit of the nation or the soul of the universe.

Indeed, although Zionism promoted understanding of the Bible (through biblical realia and analogy between the two periods), it also obstructed understanding (since the modern Return responded to a national, not divine, imperative). The secular generation, eager to find its reflection in the text and guide itself by its light, could ardently embrace such vv. as "doing work with one hand while the other held a weapon" (Neh. 4.11), but was puzzled and repelled by "you shall be holy, for I, the LORD your God, am holy" (Lev. 19.2). To bridge the gap, they had to resort to quasi-midrashic interpretation, which sanctified biblical values while rejecting the plain meaning of divine revelation. "Thus says the LORD" and "I the LORD am your God, who brought you out of the land of Egypt" (Exod. 20.1), were metaphorical, archaic expressions that actually represented a psychological reality: an ethical imperative emerging from the depths of the soul, or the national spirit inspiring the liberators. But since midrash was considered invalid, contrary to *peshat,* and identified with the disparaged *pilpul* (hair-splitting, legalistic reasoning), such naïve explanations had to obscure their remoteness from *peshat.*

By using one of the most characteristic tools of midrash, metaphor, the authors of the Declaration of Independence of Israel could substitute for the transcendent "God of Israel" the national "Rock of Israel" (this too purged of its plain religious meaning, as in 2 Sam. 23.3: "The God of Israel has spoken, the Rock of Israel has said..."). Similarly, midrashic license divorced the words "the guardian of Israel neither slumbers nor sleeps" from their context in Ps. 121 (where the name of God occurs five times), interpreting "guardian of Israel" not as the omnipotent heavenly guardian but as the brave human guards on earth. One popular Hanukkah song used the quite radical technique of *al tikre* (substitution of one word for another) to transform "Who can tell the mighty acts of the LORD" (Ps. 106.2) into "Who can tell the mighty acts of Israel." A song for the fifteenth day of Shevat (the New Year for trees) took the first phrase of the v. "When you enter the land and plant any tree for food, you shall regard its fruit as forbidden...." (Lev. 19.23) and made of it a separate commandment by cutting the v. in half, the syntax in Heb allowing the remaining words to be understood as: "When you enter the land, you shall plant every tree...." The song then added a rhyme in biblical Heb: "... /And the tree shall give its fruit and the land its yield." Even the injunction to donate money to the Jewish National Fund was traced to the Torah by a kind of modern halakhic midrash, so convincing that everyone was sure that the words "redemption shall be granted to the land" (Lev. 25.24) are an imperative to purchase Gentile land by peaceful means; the context of the phrase, however, calls for restoring a family's ancestral holdings, sold to strangers because of poverty, to the family's ownership. Similarly, the emblem of the Reali School in Haifa urged its students, "Walk modestly," dropping the words, "with your God" (Mic. 6.8); and the words "Let My people go" were likewise taken from the ritual context "that they may worship Me in the wilderness" (Exod. 7.16), thereby severing them from context, detaching them from their history, and obscuring the identity of the divine speaker. Anyone could thus claim that the rousing challenge to a tyrannical government had sprung from the nation's spirit, uttered by its heroic fighters.

One might think that this Zionist midrash had no place in academia, which is committed to philological and historical study of the biblical text. Nevertheless, despite the detachment of the academy from the social world and its resistance to any ideological manipulation of the Bible, scholars also have reinforced the Zionist-worldly conception of the Bible. Engagement in critical study of the Bible in itself is an expression of the Zionist ambition to normalize all aspects of our life and resume our place in the family of nations. Owing to these efforts, the Bible is studied in Israel, too, in light of scientific criteria developed in the last few centuries, mainly by Protestant scholars, thus breaking free of the Jewish study tradition (which subordinates the written law to the oral). Bible research in Israel has become an active partner in international Bible study, as noted with pride by the editors of the Heb-language *Encyclopedia Biblica* (preface, Vol. I, 1950): "The nation that created the Bible is gradually taking its rightful place in the study of its eternal book" (p. 9). The critical study of Scripture, with no prior assumption of sanctity or overt superiority, makes its own contribution to the national midrash, undermines the perfection of Scripture, and considerably dims its brilliance; but it also provides a scientific-rationalistic justification for the secular view of the Bible as a human, national creation. Moreover, the academic definition of Bible studies agreed with the spirit of the times, treating the oral law as irrelevant to understanding the Bible. In the early 1950s, when I was pursuing my studies in the Hebrew University's Bible Department, one could not study midrashic exegesis there, as it ran counter to *peshat.* Nor was any course devoted even to those of the medieval commentaries that were based on *peshat,* as they were not sufficiently critical (the situation has since changed quite radically). The spirit of the times also molded the scientific principles guiding the *Encyclopedia Biblica;* it, too, reinforced the secular-material view. The encyclopedia was indeed committed to "the original meaning of the texts, in accordance with the intentions of the authors, as they were understood at the time of writing and by the audiences for whom they were originally written" (preface, p. 11). But the editors' understanding of *peshat* was so one-sided that the ancient authors would probably have been amazed at the extraordinary emphasis on realia, archeology, and the world of the ancient Near East, and the utter neglect of theological, ideological, and literary aspects (as evident, e.g., in the almost complete disregard for the writings of the Israeli scholars Yehezkel Kaufmann and Martin Buber). As the times changed, this distortion, too, was somewhat mitigated in the last volumes; but the encyclopedia still lacks entries on memory, labor, property, peace, and remnant, on the one hand, and speech, humor, satire, and narrative, on the other. In sum: Bible scholars, high in their ivory towers, who had no part in the creation of the national midrash, were influenced by it unawares and indirectly helped to buttress it.

The secularizing national midrash also gave schoolchildren a social motive to study the Bible: it prepared them for "life," because minimal knowledge of the Bible was necessary for participation in the collective discourse. The Bible was not only one of the founts of Israel's literary and artistic creation, its inventory of associations (as it still is to some extent), but also the key to the values and ideas current in society. Incoming immigration is referred to in Heb, contrary to geography, as *ʿaliyah,* "coming up," while outgoing emigration is *yeridah,* "going down," to take one example; and native-born Israelis, looking down upon the so-called primitive culture of the new immigrants, could invoke the term "desert generation" to justify their attitudes (and their budgetary priorities). A person who did not study the Bible was a stranger in Israeli society.

Religious Zionism, too, was an integral part of this collective discourse. Children in religious schools also "granted redemption to the land" with their mothers' pennies; they marched on the fifteenth of Shevat, holding saplings and singing "When you enter the land"; and at Hanukkah parties they sang "Who can tell the mighty acts of Israel," entertaining no doubts that the words had religious validity. Clearly, despite religious Zionism's efforts to contend with the predominantly secular bent of Zionism, it, too, was charmed by the national midrash. Perhaps this was because of the remarkable ability of that midrash, on the one hand, to provide biblical confirmation for the truth of Zionism, and, on the other, to guarantee on behalf of Zionism that the Bible would continue to occupy a central position in Jewish society. Thus, a fierce controversy raged as to the religious sanctity of the Bible, but at the same time no one denied that it belonged to the entire nation—a shared, unifying, and inspiring possession.

The Crisis of Secular Zionism Undermines the Validity of the National Midrash

One does not have to be a "post-Zionist" to realize that Zionism, as an ideology and a mass movement, is in deep trouble, and this has implications for the place of the Bible in contemporary Israeli society.

The establishment of the State of Israel brought about major changes in the country: Voluntarism gave way to state-run action, donations to taxation; governmental relief labor made tree-planting on the fifteenth of Shevat an anachronism, and the Land Administration took over "redemption of the land" from the Jewish National Fund. Manual labor has become the province of foreign workers. Finally, the Yom Kippur War (1973) revealed for all to see that the institutionalized Israel Defense Forces could no longer be compared to the Israelite army of the time of the judges and the early monarchy.

Along with social, economic, and political change has come a mental revolution: Romantic dreams and utopian aspirations have given way to concrete, short-term realism; a self-assured ideology, ignoring anything that clashed with its all-embracing concepts and not averse to shallow conformism, has become unfashionable. There is a strong bias for skepticism and open-mindedness, avoiding bombastic phraseology (embellished with biblical quotations) and preferring understatement—a descent from declamation to stammering; a systematic demythologization of Zionism is underway in the name of one's right—and obligation—to know the complex truth underlying appearance and pretension. The cult of heroism, with its implied contempt for human weakness and disregard for the enemy's suffering, has been discredited. The collective vision, which demanded bravery and self-sacrifice, has been supplanted by personal goals, in which individuals make their own choices and decide what demands to make on themselves. Spontaneity and permissiveness are preferred to normativity and moderation; education has shifted from nurturing values to developing aptitudes, advocating extracurricular studies rather than youth-movement activities. The humanities and natural sciences are neglected in favor of social and applied sciences, law, and business administration. The ambition of the second-generation *sabra* [native Israeli] is no longer to put down roots in this country but to spread his or her wings and explore the world.

Some consider this crisis to be the beginning of the end of Zionism, for better or for worse. I, however, see the process not as disintegration but as maturation, which is a precondition for any new growth. At any rate, Zionism is gradually losing its power as a secular religion, and the Bible is no longer the Scripture of that religion. The allure of romantic Zionism has dimmed, the sensation of miracle in Israel's revival has faded, and feelings of national pride have weakened; the abyss between the real present and the mythological past has deepened. As a result, the national midrash has lost its potency, no longer able to bridge the chasm between life and the Book. We increasingly lack a link with the Bible; it is no longer a source of inspiration and guidance. It has lost its magic.

A brief hermeneutic excursion will explain. The interpretive power of *peshat* derives not from religious common ground but only from philological credibility. In contrast, the interpretive validity of a midrashic system, the confidence that the content attributed to the text is indeed concealed between its lines, is limited a priori to believers. For the members of that audience to embrace the proposed midrashic commentary as an authentic, binding interpretation, they must agree on:

(1) The overall truth of the values, ideas, and ideals that they are supposed to believe: Zionism as renaissance and redemption; Eretz Israel as the promised land; the duty of self-sacrifice to pioneering and security goals; and so on.

(2) The supreme position of the Book in the community, its ability to reinforce the beliefs, precepts, and hopes to which it is committed: the Bible as the peak of creativity in the era of our national splendor and an embodiment of eternal truths.

(3) The capacity of quasi-homiletical exegesis—despite its relative methodological freedom—to reveal an inner truth behind the linguistic exterior.

The first two assumptions taken together—the truth of the values the audience embraces and their acceptance of the eternal truth of the Book—clearly justify an interpretive technique flexible enough to adapt those eternal truths to the needs of the times: The secularizing national midrash is indeed revealing and faithfully representing the message of Scripture to our generation, which is once again implementing, "for the first time in two thousand years," the injunction to return to Zion and to rebuild the land. But once the force of Zionist values has faded, their brilliance dimmed, with the concomitant weakening of the need to connect with the Bible as the values' source of inspiration, the methodological weakness of the national midrash is clear: It is artificial, empty, meaningless. Interpretive flexibility, tolerated because it was necessary to bridge the gap between the Bible and its readers, is now seen as illusion, repugnant manipulation. Once the national midrash has lost its allure, it has also lost its creative power.

These days, appeals to the Bible for inspiration or motivation are rare indeed, and they are generally low-key; perhaps the only instance in recent years was the use of the anti-pharaonic call "Let my people go" as a unifying slogan in the struggle for liberation of the Soviet Jews. Another echo of biblical language is the Heb name of the Israeli association for the protection of human rights in the Occupied Areas, *Be-Tzelem,* "in the image" ("in the image of God," Gen. 1.27), implying that the association's work is a true expression of the biblical ethic. The secular nature of this midrash is brought out by divorcing the word from its context—whose "image"?—but the link with the Bible is highlighted by printing the word with the traditional vowel points and cantillation accents. A similar technique is employed on the title page of Arieh (Lova) Eliav's anthology, *On Peace in Jewish Tradition* (Heb.: Tel Aviv, 1975), where the word *shalom* is printed in the same way. In this book, however, even the sympathetic reader senses that the author is seeking in the Bible not inspiration but "proofs" for his values. Similarly—though the differences are greater than the comparison—Member of Kenesset (Israel's Parliament) Yael Dayan's attempt to anchor her campaign for gay rights in David's lament for Jonathan was seen not as authentic, merely provocative. On the other hand, Meir Shalev's humorous midrash, *The Bible Now* (Heb.: Jerusalem and Tel Aviv, 1985), was received enthusiastically and widely circulated because, in contrast to the traditionally adulatory attitude, he has brought the Bible down to our own level. His readers willingly swallow even his entirely imaginary additions (such as the idea that Abigail poisoned her husband Nabal in order to marry David) because the humorous midrash provides us with a kind of biblical confirmation for a realistic, forgiving view of ourselves.

In contrast to Ben-Gurion's ideals, not only has the Bible lost its hold on young people but Israeli youth has rallied to the Diaspora's characteristic issue: the Holocaust. This may be an attempt to atone for early condescending *sabra*-Zionist attitudes to the Diaspora and the hasty judgment of the millions of victims as "lambs led to slaughter"; it may also represent a desire to exchange the imperative of Return implicit in the biblical promise, grounds for fervent, ideological Zionism, for the imperative of preventing a further Holocaust, grounds for pragmatic Zionism. Perhaps it also expresses a craving for a national ideal protected by a universal, unchallenged taboo, uniting the entire nation in the face of a calamity whose uniqueness and exclusiveness are vehemently defended.

None of these revolutionary developments have affected the *ḥaredi* [ultra-Orthodox] community. One component of that community's opposition to Zionism is a firm refusal to detach the Bible from the oral law and make it shine "with its own light" in the center of national existence. The Talmudic worldview considers the written law first in sanctity but not in authority. That privilege is reserved for the oral law, which, as the authoritative interpretation of the Bible, also determines which of its contents are effective today. The hierarchy is also reflected in the curriculum of the *ḥaredi* schools: The Bible is studied by children, both boys and girls, but when the boys are ready to study Talmud they no longer study the Bible (except for the weekly Torah portion). The Talmud itself, it is true, lists the Bible as a subject for study in its own right, binding for adults: "Man should always divide his time into three: a third [spent] studying Bible, a third Mishnah, a third the Talmud" (*b. Kid.* 30a). In the Middle Ages, however, it was ruled that that injuction is fulfilled—in all three parts—by studying the Babylonian Talmud, since it includes all three.

With the Talmud occupying center stage, contextual, philological interpretation of the text, *peshat,* is not a challenge (except for the two centuries between Rashi and Ḥizkuni, the Golden Age of the French school of *peshat,* which flourished in the explicitly Talmudic culture of northern France); besides, over the last few generations, the creativity of homiletic interpretation in general has declined. As a result, contemporary *ḥaredi* society has raised the exclusivity of Talmud study to an unprecedented level, and accordingly has not been affected by the changing attitudes to the Bible in the Zionist camp. One cost of this stability has been a loss of creativity: There are among this group no new commentaries on the Bible; they prefer instead to publish anthologies of classical commentaries. Examples are the eclectic commentaries published in English in the United States by the *ḥaredi* Art-Scroll Publishing House, and the popular book by Yehudah Nashoni, *Hagut be-Parshiyot ha-Torah,* i.e., *Meditation on the Portions of the Torah,* subtitled "Original Exegesis according to *Pardes,* as directed by Early and Late Authorities, with the Addition of Innovations and Insights" (2nd ed., Benei Berak, 1979).

The national-religious public, too, believes in the unity of the oral and written law, while insisting that this principle in no way bars its participation in the Zionist return to the Bible. On its face this should be easy: it requires a clear differentiation between *peshat* and midrash, as taught by the great exponents of *peshat,* mainly in medieval Spain and northern France. Since both modes of exegesis are legitimate, each can be considered for its specific purpose: midrash explains the written law in accordance with the oral, while *peshat* extracts the primary meaning of the biblical text. In fact, however, the paths blazed by the medieval commentators cannot simply be resumed, for in modern biblical studies the *peshat* method is immeasurably more critical than in the medieval period: It challenges not only the unity of the written and oral law but even the sanctity of the Bible itself—at least, in the traditional definition.

Orthodox Bible scholars, therefore, who teach at Bar-Ilan University and other academic institutions, must contribute to the development of *peshat* while meeting the double criterion of scientific method and religious faith. In answering this challenge they are motivated, among other things, by the belief that the quest for truth is a religious duty—a *mitzvah*—and that intellectual integrity is an ethical-religious virtue. In this endeavor they indeed require no little courage to face opposition from both right and left.

The great majority of religiously observant Bible teachers, however, prefer not to confront the tension between *peshat* and *derash,* or the critical bent of modern *peshat,* instead adopting various pragmatic solutions. Quite typical, for example, is the inclusion of Bible lessons in almost all the yeshivah high schools, in the category of "secular" rather than "sacred" studies. Moreover, most Bible teachers in these schools—and in the parallel girls' *ulpenot*—are not university graduates with degrees in Bible studies, but yeshivah graduates whose studies have centered on the Talmud. Not only are they unqualified, having professionally studied neither the Bible itself nor the related tools; but, lacking the aptitude to explain the *peshat* consistently and systematically (particularly as they sometimes view it contemptuously as overly "simple" and superficial), they tend to offer their own fanciful interpretations in the spirit of *derash.* Even when teaching the Torah with the standard commentators, they generally fail to distinguish between *peshat* and *derash,* preferring to present their students with a harmonistic hodgepodge of "pretty" explanations, unsystematic and uncontrolled.

Observant Jews are exposed in the synagogue to signficant sections of the Bible: the weekly Torah portions, the haftarot, and the Five Scrolls; and a good many psalms in the prayers. They regard study of the Torah (including the Written Torah) as a major religious duty *(mitzvah).* Consequently, their sons and daughters rival each other in the worldwide Bible Quiz for Youth, with no secular competitors on the scene. Nevertheless, whether they are slowly edging to the right and adopting *ḥaredi* ways, or maintaining their involvement in society as a whole, they cannot evade their part in the process of the deterioration of the Bible's status.

Now that the Bible has been divested of the colorful cloak created by the national midrash, it emerges in its primary light, as a religious document. As long as the national midrash ruled, the secular public thought it understood the Bible better than did the religious public, which was still shackled by the bonds of rabbinic midrash. Now, however, with the religious nature of the Bible rediscovered, secular Israelis have seemingly renounced such pretensions, and are perhaps even willing to relinquish possession, and restore the Bible to the believers in its sanctity. The latter, for their part, are quick to cite the relative short-livedness of the secular interpretation as historical proof of its illegitimacy; intoxicated by this newfound power, they are inclined to arrogate to themselves the exclusive right to interpret and explain the Bible. Moreover, as religiosity is generally perceived today from the outside and from a distance, in its fundamentalist-nationalist guise, secular Israelis are increasingly distancing themselves from the Bible. This has been reinforced by yet another development: As the secular-national midrash has lost its cogency, it has been supplanted by a new national midrash, which places the values of a maximalist—at times brutal—religious Zionism on what seems like the plain meaning of the biblical text. Thus, exclusive Jewish ownership of the land is justified by Rashi's comment on the first v. of the Torah; commitment to the territorial integrity of Greater Israel is derived from Abraham's "Covenant of Pieces" with God in Gen. ch 15; triumphalist isolationism is substantiated by Balaam's blessing, "A people that dwells apart, not reckoning itself among the *goyim*" (Num. 23.9); and the taking of excessive political and military risks is based on "Israel, trust in the LORD! He is their help and shield" (Ps. 115.9); not to mention the Kahanist glorification of Simeon's and Levi's killing in Shechem (Gen. ch 34) and the topical espousal of the book of Josh. and the war against Amalek. If this is indeed the true message of the Bible, little wonder that many secular Israelis, who believed with all their heart that justice and humanity, if applied only to our own people, are no better than injustice and inhumanity, draw back and reject the Bible. It has lost its universality; once a unifier, it has become divisive.

Existential *Peshat* as a Possible Response to Current Needs

The time is not ripe for a new collective midrash. We have only just emerged from an era of collective certainties, and a time of searching may follow the current transitional period of alienation. *Peshat* is essentially an open-ended quest. While *derash* is generally founded on a priori acceptance of certain truths, *peshat* depends on the credibility of method. The seeker of *peshat* is not supposed to know in advance what may be found in the text; the only prerequisites are philological exactitude, common sense, intellectual honesty, an open mind, and an awareness of the distinctiveness of the ancient text. If its religious nature, which can no longer be denied, is not to erect a barrier between an avowed nonbeliever and the Book, he or she must be on guard against secular arrogance toward religious faith, and perhaps also overcome the fear of being bewitched by its charms, and listen with an open mind and heart to the direct voice of the text. Intelligence, imagination, and empathy will help to understand the meaning of the words "says the LORD" when uttered by a prophet, as well as their implications for the messenger's attitude to his Master and to his mission. On the other hand, one can understand a biblical passage properly without having to accept it as factual truth or normatively binding. One must refrain from negating the text a priori, enter into a dialogue with the text, and thereby enhance one's ability to listen to it on its merits.

The national midrash built an educational analogy between past and present, but the seeker of *peshat*, in the quest for the primary meaning of the text, does not ignore the differences between past and present. A heightened awareness of passing time teaches one that even religious values and institutions are dependent on historical context. This historical sense can protect us from the fundamentalism that uncritically embraces biblical norms (such as political violence) in utterly changed circumstances. The seeker of *peshat* must also scrutinize the Bible against the background of its environment, gaining a broad perspective that indicates the limits of our national uniqueness, the relationship between adoption (say, of Canaanite language and poetics) and rejection (for instance, of Babylonian ethical and legal norms). Identification with biblical heroes, too, is no longer romantic but critical, in the spirit of the fervent inner criticism discernible in the Bible itself. This sober realism of *peshat* is accompanied by the quest for truth, and this may enhance the attraction of *peshat* for those who have lost trust and interest in the high-flown idealism of the national midrash.

Peshat is inconceivable without methodological awareness: It is relative, derived from scant information (because of the extreme brevity of biblical historiography and the scarcity of contemporary extrabiblical documentation), and constrained by the scholar's scientific school and personality. This methodological awareness must go hand in hand with hermeneutic awareness that a text may tolerate more than one interpretation. The time of arrogant *peshat,* professing to be the supreme, exclusive, scientific truth, is over; the time has come for *peshat* which, though conscious of its advantages—rigorous discipline, rationality, consistency, independence, immediacy—is also acutely aware of the attendant disadvantages—clinging to the past, exclusive attention to the rational, and aversion to ambivalence. This *peshat,* far from disdaining midrash, recognizes its contribution. It is therefore vital that departments of biblical studies at universities and high schools introduce the thorough, systematic study of rabbinic midrash. Students at all levels should be capable of evaluating the nature of creative, nonphilological exegesis and thereby of understanding the sterling value of midrash down through the generations, from those remote times when religious creativity shifted from revelation to interpretation, to the recent times when a modern national movement found it necessary to connect with its ancient source of inspiration. The attraction of Bible studies will be enhanced if students realize that they demand not only proficiency and understanding of the text, but also methodological sophistication. One cannot simply say anything that comes to mind; but differences of opinion and variant exegetical methods are legitimate, each generation having its own interpreters.

Existential *peshat* is based on critical *peshat,* but the two are not identical. While many scholars must keep the text at a distance, behind a barrier, an interpreter seeking to make the Bible relevant to his or her personal existence is thereby regarding him- or herself as one of those to whom it is addressed. The Bible's role as the foundation text of the Jewish people is not dissimilar to the role of parents: One can develop relationships of all kinds toward them, but one cannot relate to them as strangers. Just so, a member of the Jewish people may respect the Bible, love it, obey it; but may equally well disobey it, rebel against it, or feel estranged from it. Whatever the case, that person cannot view the Bible as "just another book." This is aptly demonstrated by a 1990s show, *"Va-yo'mer va-yelekh"* ("And he said, and he went"), staged by the *Ittim* ensemble under the direction of Rina Yerushalmi, who writes in the program notes that, after staging two Shakespeare plays, "we felt that the time had come to reach out to our own text, and the Bible is our primeval text." As a prodigal son returning to his parents, this powerful show comes back to the Bible, with admiration, love, anger, bitter mockery, and pain.

Existential *peshat* will never be able to place the Bible at the center of public life. Instead of struggling in vain to recreate a bygone situation, it is more realistic to promote understanding of the Bible as it is, with its beliefs, inner tensions, and chronological and geographical contexts; and, at the same time, to bring out the relevance of the Torah, the Prophets, and the Writings for our own time. No exegetical technique, however, can create unassisted the motivation for its use. Lacking thirst, there is no sure need for the well or the pump. Good teachers are capable of provoking thirst, but their numbers are steadily decreasing for lack of a supportive public atmosphere. Nevertheless, if we can believe the many signs that herald the beginning of a new era, marked by reaction to the prevalent cynicism and nihilism, by growing awareness of the benefit inherent in a definition of personal and collective identity, in a commitment to norms and values, and in the awe confronting spiritual greatness—if we can trust these signs, there are good prospects that all these will be sought first and foremost in that wonderful book which rests, well-nigh forgotten, on the bottom shelf of the "Jewish bookcase."

[URIEL SIMON]

The Jewish Bible in America

Wherever Jews migrate, the Bible follows them, for Jewish communal life is impossible without it. So late in 1655, perhaps a year after the first Jewish communal settlement in New Amsterdam (today New York), a Sephardic merchant named Abraham de Lucena (d. ca. 1670) arrived in town bearing a Torah scroll, borrowed from the Jewish community of Amsterdam. The presence of this Torah scroll served as a defining symbol of Jewish communal life and culture, creating a sense of sacred space.

Wherever Jews later created communities in North America, they either brought Torah scrolls with them from home, which is what the Jews who emigrated to Savannah did in 1733, or they quickly borrowed Torah scrolls from elsewhere, as the Jews of Newport did in 1760. Some individual Jews brought privately-owned Torah scrolls with them to the New World. Jewish religious life in smaller 18th-c. colonial Jewish settlements like Lancaster and Reading, Pennsylvania revolved around these privately-owned Torahs. Whenever a *minyan* (prayer quorum) could be gathered, usually in the owner's private home, the presence of the Torah scroll defined the worship service as authentic, for the scroll contains the sacred teachings of Jewish religious life.

While the ritualized public reading of the Torah from a properly written scroll naturally focused attention on the Torah, the first five books of the Bible, which Jews continue to privilege and know best, some early American Jews also possessed printed Heb copies of all twenty-four books of the Jewish Bible, imported from Europe. Others relied upon less expensive Christian editions of the Bible in English, even though these contained the "Old Testament" and New Testament bound together in one volume, following the Christian canon, with headings that highlighted how the "Old Testament" prefigured the New.

Millions of Christian Americans likewise possessed that Bible, which they read, pondered, preached from, and debated. In the early decades of the 19th c., historian Mark Noll shows, belief in the Protestant notion of the "Bible alone" *[sola Scriptura]* "constituted an anchor of religious authority in a churning sea of demographic, social and political turmoil."

Even if they owned the same Bibles, however, American Jews never viewed them the same way as their neighbors did. They accorded sanctity only to the books that formed part of the Jewish Bible, resisted Christological interpretations, and recalled that their own tradition ordered the books of Scripture in a different way than did Christians.

Jewish biblical interpretation, by its very existence, complicated American Christian ideas of following the "Bible alone." If, after all, there were Jewish and Christian Bibles and Jewish and Christian interpretations of those Bibles, how could all of them be true? The *sola Scriptura* concept, moreover, ran counter to Jewish teachings concerning the

"Oral Torah." Judaism in that period stressed that there is a wealth of tradition preserved by the ancient Rabbis of the Talmud and other rabbinic sources that had been handed down at Sinai, though not found in the written biblical text itself.

For their part, Christians viewed Jews as "keepers of the Old Testament" who obstinately misunderstood the Jewish Bible's central message. William McGuffey's *Eclectic Third Reader* (1836–37), a widely used elementary school textbook, for example, taught a generation of American schoolchildren that the "Old Testament" was Jews' "own sacred volume, which contained the most extraordinary predictions concerning the infidelity of their nation, and the rise, progress, and extensive prevalence of Christianity." To Jews, of course, such Christological readings of the Jewish Bible were anathema.

Simultaneously, then, the Bible served both as a bridge and as a boundary marker between Jews and Christians in America. It linked the two great faiths around commonly-cherished biblical teachings. And it demarcated differences over what the term "Bible" connotes, and how the Bible's sacred words should be understood.

The vast majority of American Jews, until comparatively recent times, privileged the Jewish Bible over the Talmud, which few could read. This distinguished them from traditional European Jews, whose educational priorities were precisely the reverse. In 19th-c. America, it was the Bible and not the Talmud that bound Jews together and linked them to their neighbors. Leading Jews, like the editor, politician and dramatist Mordecai Noah (1785–1851), believed that God's word, as found in the Jewish Bible, was "our safest guide." He once advised the American Jewish religious leader Isaac Leeser (1806–1868) to "shut the Talmud and open the Bible."

Indeed, it was a Jew, Jonathan (Jonas) Horwitz (d. 1852), who, in 1812, "proposed the publication of an edition of the Hebrew Bible," the first of its kind in the United States. Many Christian clergy subscribed to the project, and it was brought to fruition two years later by the Scottish printer, Thomas Dobson. In 1826, another Jew, printer Solomon Jackson (d. ca. 1847), proposed the publication of a Heb-English linear Bible. Six leading Jews and three Christian clergy recommended the project, one of the latter highlighting the fact that the "author and editor belong to the *literal* family of Abraham."

While that Bible never appeared, Isaac Leeser in Philadelphia published a handsome edition of the Hebrew Bible in 1848. Six years later, in 1854, he produced the world's first full-scale Jewish translation of the Bible into English. That translation freed Jews from their reliance on Christian translations of the Bible and taught Christians who consulted it much about the Jewish view of Scripture. By contrast, the Talmud remained neglected on the part of 19th-c. American Jews. The first printed American edition of the Talmud and its commentaries only appeared in 1919.

Rightly or not, many in America looked upon Jews as experts on everything connected to the Jewish Bible, since leading rabbis could read its text in the original Heb and cite a chain of traditional Jewish interpretations concerning what that text meant. When controversies arose over such topics as temperance, capital punishment, and slavery, the Jewish view of Scripture was regularly solicited.

In the case of slavery, Rabbi Morris Raphall (1798–1868) of New York, in a celebrated address delivered on the National Fast Day (January 4, 1861) at the request of the American Society for Promoting National Unity, concluded that even if Southern slave holders had acted wrongly, slave holding as such was "no sin" for slave property was "expressly placed under the protection of the Ten Commandments." (Slaves are mentioned explicitly in Exod. 20.10, 14.) His address reinforced familiar Protestant arguments, but nevertheless received wide circulation, coming as it did from a learned rabbi. One enthusiastic Protestant minister was so persuaded by Raphall's reading, based on the Heb original, that he declared the rabbi's lecture to be "as true almost as the word of God itself." Unsurprisingly, opponents of slavery, significant Jewish leaders among them, condemned Raphall's reading of the biblical text and insisted on a more historically contextualized reading or one that focused on the spirit rather than on the letter of Divine law. Rabbi David Einhorn (1808–1879), for example, argued vehemently that it was "rebellion against God to enslave human beings created in His image." What is significant is that both sides in this debate appealed to the Jewish Bible, as interpreted by rabbis who could read it in Heb, and were familiar with its traditional commentaries.

Americans continued to look to Jews as experts on the Hebrew Bible long after the Civil War. Popular 19th-c. Bible magazines, such as *The Old Testament Student,* welcomed Jewish participation and brought Jewish teachings concerning the Bible to non-Jewish readers. Chautauqua and other lecture forums regularly featured Jewish speakers on biblical subjects. Thanks to the Jewish philanthropist Jacob Schiff (1847–1920), Harvard University created its Semitic Museum and funded the first American archeological excavation in Palestine, which Schiff saw as the fountainhead of Semitic civilization. Elsewhere, in many parts of the country, Christians consulted with knowledgeable Jews concerning what the Heb of the Jewish Bible originally meant and how Jews understood difficult biblical passages.

These developments went hand in hand with the first flickers of Jewish Bible scholarship on American shores. The initial group of American Jewish Bible scholars was trained in Europe, immigrated with the great wave of Central European Jews that swelled America's Jewish population from less than 15,000 in 1840 to about 250,000 just forty years later, and most were active rabbis. Some, like Isidor Kalisch (1816–1886) and Isaac M. Wise (1819–1900), sought to strengthen the hands of the faithful against missionaries and higher biblical critics. Others, like Benjamin Szold (1829–1902), whose commentary on Job was the first commentary on a book of the Bible by an American Jew, wrote primarily for his peers abroad; he has been described as a "conservative critic." Meanwhile, Michael Heilprin (1823–1888), the only member of this early group who was not a rabbi, enthusiastically promoted biblical criticism and did much to familiarize Americans of all faiths with the fruits of German scholarship. Perhaps the most creative of all the early Jewish Bible scholars in America was the eccentric Arnold Bogumil Ehrlich (1848–1919). Ehrlich, though like Heilprin not a rabbi, taught Heb and rabbinic thought for many years in New York City. His scholarly writings in German and Heb, replete with suggested emendations of the biblical text, continue to be widely consulted.

The lonely efforts of these scholarly pioneers contrast with the poor knowledge of the Bible that characterized the mass of American Jews at that time. Like so many of their Protestant and Catholic peers, they revered the Bible more than they actually knew it. They formally studied the Bible for only a few years as youngsters in supplementary schools that met mostly on Sundays.

The textbooks Jews employed to teach the Bible were similar to Christian volumes. Instead of word-for-word translations from the original Heb, common in traditional Jewish pedagogy, American Jewish textbooks mostly relied upon catechisms with posed questions and memorized answers, as well as moralistic Bible stories (including folk legends such as the extrabiblical story of Abraham smashing his father's idols), and, for older children, abridged translations known as "junior Bibles." For all that these resembled Christian textbooks in form, the Jewish texts emphasized Jewish interpretations in place of Christian ones, and sought to ensure that Jewish children identified the Bible as a Jewish book and the source of Jewish law. For example, the popular Protestant *Child's Scripture Question Book* (1853) depicted the prophet Malachi as foretelling the coming of John the Baptist, "to prepare the way before Christ." Its closely related Jewish counterpart,

Elementary Introduction to the Scriptures for the Use of Hebrew Children (1854) depicted Malachi instead as one who came to "reform the people," and who foretold the coming of "Elijah the prophet."

The mass migration of over two million east European Jews to America's shores in the late 19th and early 20th centuries brought to America a community of Jews who knew and respected the Jewish Bible; many of them could read it in the original. Their numbers elevated the American Jewish community into one of the world's largest, with a new responsibility to advance Jewish learning at all levels. Publication in New York of the *Jewish Encyclopedia* (1901–1906), a grand synthesis of Jewish scholarship, reflected this responsibility and heralded American Jewry's cultural arrival. The encyclopedia devoted substantial attention to biblical subjects, making available to lay English readers both traditional Jewish approaches to the Bible and the fruits of modern critical scholarship.

The Jewish Publication Society, established in 1888, likewise committed itself to advancing knowledge of the Bible among Jews. In 1917, it published a new Jewish translation of the Bible, under the chief editorship of the Russian-born Max Margolis (1866–1932), one of America's foremost biblical scholars (see "Jewish Translations of the Bible," pp. 2091–2106). Significantly, a majority of the members of the translation committee for the new Bible, including Margolis, had received at least an important part of their formal Jewish education in the United States, a signal of how quickly serious study of the Jewish Bible in the country was developing. "It was a Bible translation to which American Jews could point with pride as the creation of the Jewish consciousness on a par with similar products of the Catholic and Protestant churches ...," historian Abraham Neuman explained, "To the Jews it presented a Bible which combined the spirit of Jewish tradition with the results of biblical scholarship, ancient, mediaeval and modern. To non-Jews it opened the gateway of Jewish tradition in the interpretation of the Word of God."

Interest in the Bible likewise spread at the popular level. The *American Jewish Year Book,* in 1923, provided a list of some sixty volumes on Bible and Biblical Literature, which it described as "standard books in English" on the subject, numbers of them written by American Jews. The Jewish Chautauqua Society produced educational materials on the Bible for teachers. Educator Joseph Magil (1871–1945) created a series of linear Bibles to facilitate word-by-word translations from biblical Heb into Yiddish or English. For Yiddish-speaking Jews, the poet Yehoash Solomon Bloomgarden (d. 1927) also produced a lyrical Yiddish translation of the Bible ("the greatest single achievement of American Yiddish poetry" according to David Roskies) that began to appear serially in the New York daily *Der Tog* from 1922.

Popular interest in the Bible soon spilled over into American Jewish literature and popular culture. The poet Delmore Schwartz (1913–1966), for example, wrote a series of dramatic monologues expounding on the biblical stories of Abraham, Sarah, and Jacob. The prolific novelist Sholem Asch (1880–1957) produced novels on Moses and Isaiah. Between 1939 and 1949 he published a trilogy on New Testament characters—*The Nazarene, The Apostle,* and *Mary*—which involved him in controversy within the Jewish community. Charles Reznikoff (1894–1976) penned *By the Waters of Manhattan,* as if reimagining Ps. 137 ("By the rivers of Babylon ...") for a new diaspora land. Later, under the influence of the Holocaust, novelists like Bernard Malamud (1914–1986) drew upon themes from the book of Job.

Film-makers likewise turned to biblical themes. The world's first Yiddish talkie film, produced in the United States by Joseph Green (1900–1996), was titled *Joseph in the Land of Egypt* (1932). Other Yiddish-language films featured titles like *The Sacrifice of Isaac* and *The Destruction of Jerusalem,* recycled from biblical epics originally produced for the silent screen. These stories from the Jewish Bible proved popular with Jewish audiences; they reinforced Judaism's central narratives and helped to legitimate film as an acceptable form of mass entertainment.

The religious revival that followed World War II led to a series of film epics from the Jewish Bible for broader English-speaking audiences, notably such titles as *Samson and Delilah* (1949), *The Ten Commandments* (1956) and *Esther and the King* (1960). All three, according to film scholar Patricia Erens, employed biblical themes to "provide a commentary on the recent suffering of the Jewish people, their miraculous survival and their hope for reconstitution in the new State of Israel." To date, more than fifty films based on themes from the Jewish Bible have been produced in the United States. Their subjects, selected both for their dramatic power and for their familiarity to viewers, include widely-known stories from Gen. and Exod., the tale of Samson and Delilah from the book of Judg., episodes from the lives of King David and King Solomon, and the thrilling story of Esther.

The post-war revival also witnessed new interest on the part of Jews in the study of the Jewish Bible, paralleling renewed Christian interest in the "Book of Books." Rabbis in the 1950s spoke of the need "to reclaim the Bible for the Jews." Sales of the 1917 Jewish Bible translation boomed. A new Heb-English version of that Bible was produced. Synagogue Bible classes and home study programs proliferated. Bible-themed art books, and illustrated Jewish editions of individual books of the Bible, such as Jonah and Ruth, sold thousands of copies.

Against this background, the Jewish Publication Society decided to undertake a new Jewish translation of the Bible, on different principles than the 1917 translation. Protestants had produced the highly successful Revised Standard Version and Catholics had likewise begun to translate the Bible anew. The Jewish translation promised to take full advantage of modern scholarship, to render the Bible into modern (as opposed to King James) English, and to print the Bible according to the highest standards of contemporary typographical design (see also "Jewish Translations of the Bible," pp. 2091–2106).

The scholars and rabbis who worked on the new translation were, for the most part, American-born and trained. Several taught at major universities, reflecting both the growing acceptance of Jewish studies as a legitimate academic discipline and the increased willingness on the part of universities to permit biblical studies to be taught by Jews. The goal of these rabbis and scholars was to produce a *Jewish* Bible translation, based on the accepted Heb MT and sensitive to Jewish interpretive tradition, that would be respected by Jews and non-Jews alike.

The completed Torah translation, when published in 1963, was warmly welcomed by Catholic and Protestant, as well as Jewish scholars. Its appearance was judged an important event, and was covered in major newspapers and magazines. The Torah translation also achieved wide sales—a quarter of a million copies were printed within a decade.

Twenty more years would pass before the Jewish Publication Society celebrated the translation of the whole Bible in 1982. Three years later, all three parts of the Bible translation, with revisions, were brought together in one volume entitled *Tanakh*—from the Heb acronym for *Torah* (Pentateuch), *Nevi'im* (Prophets), and *Kethuvim* (Writings). That title, carefully chosen, underscored the Jewishness of the new translation. A "Judeo-Christian" title like "The Holy Scriptures," the title of the 1917 translation, was consciously rejected.

Tanakh thus encapsulated an important message not only about the Bible translation but about the whole story of the Jewish Bible in America. It underscored the fact that Jews, even as they shared the Hebrew Bible in common with their Christian neighbors, understood much of it differently, and even called it by a different name.

[JONATHAN D. SARNA]

Jewish Women's Scholarly Writings on the Bible

Recent biblical scholarship has been witness to the growing visibility of women scholars, and the profound impact of feminist criticism. Jewish women have participated actively in these trends, and there now exists a corpus of Jewish women's biblical scholarship, some of which also partakes of and contributes to the area of feminist criticism. What follows is a brief survey that outlines its range of subject matter and methodologies, examines its presuppositions, and assesses its place in the field of biblical studies in general and feminist biblical criticism more specifically. The works cited are only a small sample of an ever-growing library, but they illustrate the diversity of current approaches and interests that are addressed in Jewish women's writing on the Bible.

Subject Matter

The studies undertaken by Jewish women address a range of topics similar to that found in women's biblical scholarship more generally. First and foremost, Jewish women's writing on the Bible had focused on the representation of women both within and outside of their family contexts. *Countertraditions in the Bible: A Feminist Approach,* by Ilana Pardes (Cambridge, MA: Harvard University Press, 1992), for example, analyzes stories about women as well as the female imagery in Song, while *Taboo or not Taboo: Sexuality and Family in the Hebrew Bible,* by Ilona N. Rashkow (Minneapolis: Fortress, 2000) explores incest and other aspects of sexuality within the family unit. Athalya Brenner's study, *The Intercourse of Knowledge: On Gendering Desire and "Sexuality" in the Hebrew Bible* (Leiden: Brill, 1997), examines both the semantics and the narratives of gender and sexuality, including the broad range of what she refers to as "deviations from socio-sexual boundaries." Yet not all books by women scholars pay special attention to issues of gender and the representation of women. For example, *From Father to Son: Kinship, Conflict, and Continuity in Genesis,* by Devora Steinmetz (Louisville, KY: Westminster John Knox Press, 1991), focuses primarily on male relationships and pays little attention to the presence and absence of women in the Gen. narratives.

By contrast, other works incorporate a strong emphasis on gender issues into their treatments of topics that extend beyond women, family, and female imagery. Susan Niditch's study, *War in the Hebrew Bible: A Study in the Ethics of Violence* (New York: Oxford University Press, 1993), is not explicitly a feminist reading of the Bible; indeed, it is much more concerned with addressing the anti-Jewish interpretations in which biblical Israel, and, by extension, Judaism, are viewed as war-mongering and parochial. Nevertheless, Niditch examines such female figures as Jael (Judg. chs 4–5) and Esther, and addresses issues such as the fate of women in time of war. Adele Reinhartz's *Why Ask My Name? Anonymity and Identity in Biblical Narrative* (New York: Oxford University Press, 1992) focuses on the unnamed characters in the Bible, both male and female, but it too pays special attention to issues related to gender, particularly because so many of the Bible's anonymous figures are women.

Whereas the above studies focus primarily on biblical texts as such, others place them within the broader context of the ancient Near Eastern world. Tikva Frymer-Kensky's *In the Wake of the Goddesses: Women, Culture, and the Biblical Transformation of Pagan Myth* (New York: Fawcett, Columbine 1992) examines the biblical transformation of ancient Near Eastern goddess mythology and its impact on sexuality, gender, and wisdom as expressed in the Bible. Other writers look at biblical women as a starting point for a broader discussion of the role of women in Judaism or in Jewish literature. Nehama Aschkenasy's book, *Eve's Journey: Feminine Images in Hebraic Literary Tradition* (Philadelphia: University of Pennsylvania Press, 1986), for example, traces the ongoing influence of female archetypes back to the "otherness" of women in ancient Hebrew literature. Helena Zlotnick's *Dinah's Daughters: Gender and Judaism from the Hebrew Bible to Late Antiquity* (Philadelphia: University of Pennsylvania Press, 2002) looks at the ways in which Judaism contrasts Jewish and Gentile women in the context of national identity. Leila Leah Bronner's *From Eve to Esther: Rabbinic Reconstructions of Biblical Women* (Louisville, KY: Westminster John Knox, 1994) examines the treatment of key biblical women in rabbinic literature. These studies are based on the assumption that the biblical portrayal of women has profoundly informed the ways in which women are described in later Jewish literature, and in the laws and customs that have determined women's roles in postbiblical Jewish law and everyday life.

Finally, there is a growing body of literature that takes biblical narratives about women as a basis for more personal responses, in the form of meditations and creative retellings. For example, Alicia Suskin Ostriker's book, *The Nakedness of the Fathers* (New Brunswick: Rutgers University Press, 1994), combines poetry, biblical interpretation, and autobiography in a uniquely refreshing and illuminating way. In doing so, she also exhorts Jewish women to do their own interpretations of biblical texts, thereby engaging in their own acts of discovery and creativity. Such works mark the intersection of scholarship and creative literature. They do not so much elucidate the possible meanings of the Bible in its original context as they explore its possibilities for contemporary Jewish women. Yet in the very process of doing so, they often draw attention to the ways in which, and the degree to which, these narratives themselves reflect a particular time and place.

Methodologies

In contrast to the field of biblical studies more generally, Jewish women's biblical scholarship does not focus very much on source analysis and other historical-critical issues, nor is there much concern about "what really happened," an issue that is of great interest in feminist New Testament scholarship (e.g., concerning the role of female disciples of Jesus, and the role of women as deacons in early Christian worship). One exception is the work of Savina Teubal (*Sarah the Priestess: The First Matriarch of Genesis* [Athens, OH: Swallow Press, 1984]; *Hagar the Egyptian: The Lost Tradition of the Matriarchs* [San Francisco: HarperSanFrancisco, 1990]), which attempts to treat Hagar and Sarah as historical figures and account for their biblical representations on the basis of the history, politics, and demographics of Israelite society. Most scholars, however, refrain from such specific historical reconstructions, due to the paucity of evidence (but see the discussion below on social-scientific methodologies).

If the Bible does not provide a clear window into Israelite history, it does provide ample basis for other types of approaches. Most prevalent among women writers on the Bible have been literary-critical methodologies, either on their own or in combination with other methods. From Adele Berlin's *Poetics and Interpretation of Biblical Narrative* (Sheffield: The Almond Press, 1983) to Yairah Amit's introduction, *Reading Biblical Narratives: Literary Criticism and the Hebrew Bible* (Minneapolis: Fortress, 2001), a central concern has been to explore the workings of biblical narrative by employing the categories and methods applied to the genres of narrative and poetry. Such works consider the fundamental building blocks of narrative, including plot, character, and setting, as well as more subtle dimensions such as narrative point of view and linguistic elements such as morphological and syntactical parallelism (e.g., Adele Berlin, *The Dynamics of Biblical Parallelism* [Bloomington: Indiana University Press, 1985]).

In most cases, literary approaches are seasoned with a strong dose of historical consciousness. Exemplary in this regard is the work of Susan Ackerman (*Warrior, Dancer, Seductress, Queen: Women in Judges and Biblical Israel* [New York: Doubleday, 1998]). While Ackerman does not assume a historical reality for the stories or characters of the book of Judg., she does take seriously the historical reality of the authors and their audiences. In analyzing Judges' stories about women, she discerns six character types and compares their stories to others from the ancient Near East in order to discern the ways in which they were imagined and developed over the thousand-year period of Israelite history.

Other scholars explicitly combine literary approaches with social-scientific methodologies. Athalya Brenner (*The Israelite Woman: Social Role and Literary Type in Biblical Narrative* [Sheffield: JSOT Press, 1985]) draws on biblical narratives in order to examine the social roles available in ancient Israelite society outside of the family and household contexts. Carol Meyers (*Discovering Eve: Ancient Israelite Women in Context* [New York: Oxford, 1988]) uses a socio-historical method that draws upon archeology, feminist criticism, anthropology, and social-scientific theory more generally to discern the social world of ancient Israel, in particular women's lives within the household in relation to the larger community.

Another fruitful combination has involved literary studies and psychoanalysis. For example, Ilona N. Rashkow draws on psychoanalysis in *The Phallacy of Genesis: A Feminist-Psychoanalytic Approach* (Louisville, KY: Westminster John Knox Press, 1993) and, more recently, *Taboo or not Taboo: Sexuality and Family in the Hebrew Bible.* In a category all its own is the work of Aviva Gottlieb Zornberg (*Genesis of Desire: Reflections on Genesis* [Philadelphia: Jewish Publication Society, 1995]; *Particulars of Rapture: Reflections on Exodus* [New York: Doubleday, 2001]), which draws both from traditional Jewish sources and from a broad range of philosophical, literary, and psychoanalytical works in her struggles with the meaning of the biblical text.

On the whole, these varied approaches and areas of investigation coexist amicably within the field of biblical studies. This state of affairs may reflect not only the desire of women to be supportive of women's study of the Bible generally, but also a postmodern ethos that validates the notion that a given text may be subject to a plurality of interpretations. Nevertheless, there is one contentious issue that also makes its way, at least occasionally, into the literature, and that is the extent to which Jewish women's writings on the Bible may confirm rather than resist or subvert the biases of mainstream biblical criticism, whether of "secular" scholars or traditional Jewish interpretation. In particular, the literary critical enterprise is sharply criticized by Esther Fuchs in her book *Sexual Politics in the Biblical Narrative: Reading the Hebrew Bible as a Woman* (Sheffield: Sheffield Academic Press, 2000). Fuchs argues that literary-critical works are often fundamentally androcentric; by admiring "the virtuosity of the biblical narrator" they "ignore the patriarchal ideology that inspires so much of what they glorify" (Fuchs, p. 7). She is similarly dismissive of postmodern approaches that, in her view, implicitly or explicitly condone patriarchal readings (p. 9). Fuchs advocates a resistant reading that "questions the ways in which the biblical narrative universalizes and legislates its hierarchical endorsement of the power relations between male and female characters" (p. 9). Despite these views, her own approach is literary, in that it focuses on the Bible as a literary text or texts, at the same time as it is also ideological, in that it exposes the ideological tendencies within these literary texts.

The questions raised in these works, the approaches they take, and the audiences that they address, all place them firmly within the spectrum of biblical studies more generally, including feminist biblical criticism. The participation of Jewish women in the larger enterprise is illustrated by the multi-volume anthologies titled *A Feminist Companion to the Bible* (edited by Athalya Brenner, first series, 11 volumes [Sheffield: Sheffield Academic Press, 1993–1997], second series, 7 volumes [Sheffield: Sheffield Academic Press, 1998–2000]), in which chs by North American and European authors—Christian, Jewish, and neither—sit side by side and often engage in dialogue with one another. These collections provide readers from many different social locations and levels of knowledge with access to the range of feminist scholarship, including the European and Jewish voices that are often not well known to North American and non-Jewish readers.

In keeping with this broad range of approaches, Jewish women's writings on the Bible draw upon a wide variety of sources, from the classics of biblical scholarship, to works in other fields that develop the methodologies that women apply to the Bible, to a range of religious and other literature from which parallels can be drawn and to which connections can be made. While some women situate their work firmly within the spectrum of critical biblical scholarship, others draw liberally from traditional Jewish sources. This is apparent not only in the apologetic works, in which traditional Jewish exegesis is often seen as the key to the meaning of the text, but in a number of other creative works, including the work of Elyse Goldstein (*ReVisions: Seeing Torah through a Feminist Lens* [Woodstock, VT: Jewish Lights, 1988]), Norma Rosen (*Biblical Women Unbound* [Philadelphia: Jewish Publication Society, 1986]), Alicia Ostriker (*The Nakedness of the Fathers*), and Ellen Frankel (*The Five Books of Miriam: A Woman's Commentary on the Torah* [San Francisco: HarperSanFrancisco, 1996]).

All four of these books evoke the genre of midrash, that is, classic Jewish biblical interpretation, as a resource for their own creative approaches. Goldstein and Frankel both intend their books as contributions to the Jewish commentary genre that has its roots in rabbinic midrash and is exemplified in medieval Jewish interpretation. Frankel's book reflects this genre not only in its content but also in its formal structure, in which biblical passages are quoted, and then the imagined responses of a range of collective ("our daughters," "our mothers," "our bubbes [grandmothers]," "the rabbis") and individual (such as Lilith, Sarah, Hagar, Dinah, and Miriam) commentators are recorded, in a way that imparts a sense of lively dialogue. Books that fall more squarely into the genre of critical biblical scholarship, however, draw much less frequently upon classic Jewish sources such as midrash or medieval exegesis. Some refer occasionally to specific midrashim (Reinhartz, Steinmetz, Pamela Tamarkin Reis, *Reading the Lines: A Fresh Look at the Hebrew Bible* [Peabody, MA: Hendrickson, 2002]), or discuss midrash as a genre (Berlin, Meyers, Steinmetz), but their primary frame of reference is critical biblical scholarship.

Basic Assumptions

Despite these diverse interests and approaches, Jewish women's writings on the Bible share a number of presuppositions. Most important is the need to include women and gender issues in the overall study of the Bible. Implicit in this assumption is the view that biblical scholarship, while not ignoring women entirely, has generally overlooked the presence and importance of women. Thus to some extent women's biblical scholarship aims to correct a bias in mainstream scholarship. Second, while few of these works concern themselves directly with textual or literary reconstruction, many of them, with the exception of those taking a very traditional stance, do presume the results of standard source criticism, that is, they agree that the Bible in its present form took shape over a number of centuries and drew upon several written sources. They also agree that it is important to situate biblical writings within their context in the ancient Near Eastern world, and to consider social and historical circumstances to the extent that these can be ascertained.

Most controversial, perhaps, is the degree to which Jewish women writers accept or reject the fundamental assumptions of feminist biblical scholarship more generally: that the society reflected in the Bible was patriarchal in that it privileges men, and that the Bible itself is an androcentric text, written from the perspective of male interests, concerns, and activities. On one end of the spectrum we find apologetic works, often written by Orthodox women (e.g., Tamar Frankiel, *The Voice of Sarah: Feminine Spirituality and Traditional Judaism* [San Francisco: HarperSanFrancisco, 1990]) with the intention of affirming the traditional separation of gender roles according to which women are relegated to the private, domestic sphere and hence excluded from public roles, particularly within the synagogue service. Such works reflect the influence of feminism insofar as they focus on the role of women in a way that is not usually apparent in traditional Jewish men's writings on the Bible, but they reject the feminist emphasis on liberation due to its implied critique of traditional Judaism. Such works will argue that traditional women's roles stem from the Torah and hence are divinely mandated; furthermore, they do not oppress women or imply their secondary status, but, on the contrary, affirm their elevated spiritual status.

Many other works, whether written by secular women (e.g., Pardes) or by women who affiliate themselves with the established Jewish denominations (Goldstein, Reinhartz), either implicitly or explicitly accept the feminist argument regarding the Bible's androcentrism and patriarchy. Rashkow (*Taboo or not Taboo*), for example, views biblical patriarchy and androcentrism as mechanisms by which heterosexual males defined themselves as the norm (p. 10). Niditch ("Portrayals of Women in the Hebrew Bible," in Judith R. Baskin, ed., *Jewish Women in Historical Perspective* [Detroit: Wayne State University Press, 1991], p. 28) and Pardes both acknowledge the Bible as patriarchal and androcentric, but argue for the presence of "nuances" (Niditch) or "countertraditions" (Pardes) that subtly subvert or undermine the predominant patriarchal ideology.

Context in Biblical Scholarship

Jewish women writers on the Bible differ fundamentally from non-Jewish women to the extent that they relate in some way to classical Jewish sources as being part of their own heritage; that they in some way or another incorporate Jewish sensibilities or experiences, however these may be defined, into their scholarship and writing; and that they envisage Jews, or more specifically Jewish women, as an important part of their audiences. In other ways, however, the concerns and perspectives of Jewish women parallel those of non-Jewish women, particularly women who explicitly identify themselves as Christian, who examine issues that arise in Christian contexts and address their studies primarily to Christian women. In both cases there are interpreters who read the Scriptures with a "hermeneutics of suspicion" (Elisabeth Schüssler Fiorenza) in order to identify patriarchal and androcentric tendencies, those who creatively fill the gaps of the text to create new texts, those who find "countertraditions" in the Bible that can be used as a basis for subverting or correcting the text's patriarchal biases, and those who believe that the Bible is beyond redemption. These similarities exist because of mutual influence, but also because Jewish and Christian women are engaged in parallel struggles against the ways that the biblical text has been used to restrict women's activities and possibilities.

The value of Jewish women's writings on the Bible as scholarship can be measured by their contributions to the understanding of the Bible, its narrative, theology, ideology, and all other aspects. In the context of feminist scholarship, however, their value can be measured in terms of their liberative potential. The latter can be seen most clearly in those works that draw on the creative imagination of the author. These works may fall at or outside the margins of the scholarly world, but as personal reflections that attempt to address contemporary women through ancient texts, they have the potential to reach a general audience that may also be open to a new way of reading the Bible. Nevertheless, the proliferation of Jewish women's writing on the Bible, in its very diversity, is a force for liberation and transformation. It exemplifies women's access to education and to the institutions of higher education and publication, and allows women's views to stand alongside those of male scholars in shaping the field of biblical studies. Whether they do or do not view the Bible as a positive force in women's lives, women writers on the Bible themselves model the possibilities for Jewish women to become engaged and make strong contribution in the form of works that will be read and have influence both within the academy and in the broader community.

[ADELE REINHARTZ]

Jewish Translations of the Bible

Jews first translated the Bible approximately 2,300 years ago, and Jews continue—as individuals and as members of committees—to translate the Bible to the present day. The first translation was the Septuagint (LXX) or Old Gk version of the Bible, produced in Alexandria for use by Gk-speaking Jews. Translations such as the Jewish Publication Society's new Tanakh, therefore, on which this study Bible is based, have a considerable lineage.

In spite of a rich and varied heritage, Jewish translations have not received the attention accorded to Christian versions. This has only partly to do with the relative sizes of the Jewish and Christian communities. It has much more to do with the role of translation in the history of Christianity. Translation was present from the beginning: Although Jesus (presumably) primarily spoke Aram., his words were preserved and disseminated in Gk. Translation, therefore, as a function of mission, was present in Christianity from the beginning.

In Judaism, by contrast, respect for the original Heb wording has been maintained through the intervening centuries. Even when substantial numbers of Jews have not understood Heb—as occurred during the Hellenistic period, when many adopted Gk as their primary language—those who translated the Heb text produced a version that was markedly influenced by Heb phrasing, idiom, and syntax. This points to a distinctive feature of Judaism: the desire to preserve some familiarity with the Heb text and language in at least some part of the community. Thus, for instance, chanting of the Bible in Heb remains a part of liturgical practice in almost all contemporary synagogues—whether or not most worshippers can understand the text in its original tongue.

Thus for Jews a translated Bible is an accompaniment to, not replacement for, the original Heb. This helps explain the prominence of Jewish versions that display the Heb and English (or other foreign language text) on facing pages. Even when the Heb text is not physically present in its entirety, it is typically brought to the reader's attention through numerous notations and references.

On the other hand, another tradition attempted to make the Bible available in more idiomatic versions to the increasing number of Jews who had little or no acquaintance with Heb and no desire to learn it. These two impulses have continued in the history of Jewish translation to the present.

From these remarks it can be deduced that for many in the Jewish community Bible translations have had an ambivalent status:

The Bible has needed to be translated so it would be understood; at the same time, this translation typically pointed to the importance of the original Heb. These translations have followed the Jewish tradition in terms not only of contents and order, but with familiar divisions into weekly Torah portions, inclusion of haftarot (the readings from the Prophets that accompany the weekly Torah readings), and other features associated with synagogue usage. Moreover, such a version reflects the richness of the exegetical traditions, both halakhic and midrashic; christological interpretations have no place in such editions.

Early Versions

The earliest Jewish Bible translation, the Torah translated into Gk, dates to approximately 275 BCE in Alexandria, the Egyptian capital city. As recorded in the *Let. Aris.,* which was composed at least a century after the events it purports to narrate, the second ruler of Hellenistic Egypt, Ptolemy II Philadelphus, was persuaded by his librarian to initiate and support a Gk translation of the Jewish laws or *torah.* This text was to occupy a place of honor at the great library Ptolemy was assembling at Alexandria. Ptolemy arranged for seventy-two elders—each renowned for his scholarship and unblemished morality—to be brought in from Jerusalem to ensure that the translation would meet the highest standards of both Hellenistic and Jewish scholarship. Ptolemy welcomed them with lavish entertainment, after which they set about their task. They finished their work in seventy-two days, dividing themselves into subcommittees and consulting with each other. This story has parallels, with variants and embellishments, in rabbinic literature, as well as in Josephus, Philo, and other ancient Jewish sources.

The last part of the *Let. Aris.* narrates a formal ceremony during which the Jews of Alexandria accepted this Gk translation of the Torah as Sacred Writ. Details of this ceremony call to mind, intentionally so, the account of Moses' giving of the law in the biblical book of Exod. To underscore the seriousness of this action, a curse was uttered against anyone daring to alter the wording of this Gk version.

It is unlikely that this lofty view of translation accords with what its translators actually had in mind. If we examine the LXX version of the Torah, we find a fairly literal reflection of its Heb *Vorlage* (underlying text). It is not difficult to see in this approach the desire to produce something on the model of a Heb-Gk interlinear version, which would presuppose at least rudimentary knowledge of both languages on the part of its originally intended audience.

Such a Gk text, especially when it circulated independently among people who had little or no knowledge of Heb, could well become a substitute for the original, as the *Let. Aris.* envisions. That is not necessarily the case, however. In fact, numerous revisers of this earliest version of the Gk, of whom Aquila (2nd c. CE), Theodotion (2nd c. CE), and Symmachus (2nd–3rd c. CE) are the best known, regularly displayed their acceptance of the subservience of the Gk to the Heb when they "corrected" older Gk texts to accord with the Heb wording in use within their community. In this way they reflected the view, described above, of the foreign-language text as at most the next-best thing to the Heb. At the same time, the care with which they fashioned their Gk version demonstrates the seriousness with which they carried out their craft.

We cannot know for certain what led the author of the *Let. Aris.* to promote the LXX as a document with sanctity and authority equal to the original. The fact that Jewish revisers, presumably active before and during the period when the *Letter* was composed, continued their work in spite of the threats of anathema might lead to the conclusion that the *Letter*'s author was an idiosyncratic or at least ineffective proponent of his point of view. But that is certainly not so. The 1st-c. CE Jewish philosopher Philo, himself a native of Alexandria, equated the LXX translators with the biblical prophets, thus according their words—and especially the differences between the Gk and the Heb texts—the status of inspired revelation. Philo knew no Heb; for such an individual, the Bible in translated form assumed preeminent importance.

While Philo was undoubtedly not the sole Jew to feel this way, his point of view is more characteristic of early Christians. It was in their communities that the relatively sober account of Aristeas acquired its miraculous characteristics: Each scholar worked alone to produce, under divine intervention, exactly the same text as his colleagues. And until Jerome (ca. 345–420 CE), hardly any church leader studied Heb or sought to learn the language so as to read the Old Testament in its original formulation. The Gk text served that purpose, as it continues to do for Orthodox Christians to this very day.

Was this earliest Gk version the result of internal Jewish concerns about the need for authoritative interpretation as the Heb grew increasingly foreign to the community? Or was the impetus, as asserted in the *Let. Aris.*, external, the result of intellectual curiosity on the part of the Ptolemaic leadership? As is so often the case, the response need not be either/or. Rather, it is perfectly understandable that a convergence of compatible motives led to this development.

The *Let. Aris.* deals only with the translation of the Torah. In the absence of external evidence, even sources as problematic as the *Let. Aris.*, it is difficult to speak with certainty about the order, provenance, and *tendenz* (ideological slant or general orientation) of other books or blocks of material for the LXX. We can note, nonetheless, that some later translators consciously modeled their renderings on the generally literal approach taken by the translators of the Torah, while other translators apparently felt free to modernize, harmonize, and otherwise modify the underlying Heb text, presumably to accord with their perception of audience needs. Among revisers such as Theodotion and Aquila, there is a noticeable tendency toward more literal representation of the Heb, not only in quantitative terms, but also qualitatively, whereby even the fairly limited freedom of lexical and stylistic variation in the Torah yielded to standardization. No matter what we may think of the literary value of the resultant Gk, such texts were popular, as witnessed by the continued use and development of the extremely literal version of Aquila by Gk-speaking Jews throughout the Byzantine period.

The sources cited above witness to differing views about the value of the Gk version, but none condemns translation per se. Such condemnations are found in rabbinic sources, along with positive statements, often directed specifically at the Gk text, about biblical versions in languages other than Heb. Such divergent opinions likely reflect deep divisions among rabbinic authorities, linked to factors such as chronology (pre- or post- 70 CE), geography (in the land of Israel or the Diaspora), and ideology. Although Christians disputed—sometimes heatedly, as in the case of Jerome and Augustine—about which text to translate, the question of whether to translate never arose.

According to rabbinic tradition, there is evidence of scriptural translation in Scripture itself. As depicted in Neh. ch 8, Ezra, standing before the people at Jerusalem's Water Gate, read from the Book of the Law (essentially the Torah) in Heb, with others providing an explanation. (The exact meaning of the Heb terminology used in Neh. 8.8 is debated; see nn. there.) In this scenario, the explanation or interpretation was in Aram.; interpreters were utilizing Aram. to supplement and explain, but not replace, the Heb original, and in an oral rather than scribal context.

At some point in the pre-Christian era, scribes put Aram. renderings of the Bible into written form. Among the Dead Sea Scrolls are two small Aram. Lev. fragments, alongside a far longer Aram. text of Job. Although it has become conventional to speak of this material as targumic—the noun form is Targum (Tg.) (pl. Targumim or Targums)—it is more precise to limit this term to materials that date from the rabbinic period of the first centuries CE. There are several important Targumim for the Torah, the Former Prophets, the Latter Prophets, and the Writings. The most influential Targumim were composed in Palestine, with later developments in Babylonia.

It is often asserted that the texts of the Targumim, which initially functioned liturgically as supplements to the Heb, were essentially paraphrases. This is not so. A considerable portion of almost all of the Targumim represents a formal or rather literal rendering of a Heb that generally coincides with the traditional or MT. When targumists did depart from their Heb, however, it is the case that they exercised considerably more freedom than most LXX translators in introducing extensive blocks of "nonbiblical" material in both narrative and legal sections. Among the techniques they adopted were circumlocutions for the name of God. They also incorporated a broad range of updatings to conform to their perceptions of both communal needs and the Oral Tradition. But this additional material is hardly ever a free translation of the Heb or paraphrase.

As part of Christian Scripture, the books of the Old Testament were also circulated in Syriac, or Eastern Aram., and Latin. Jews may well have been responsible for some of the early (3rd c. CE and before) Syriac versions that played a part in the later development of the standard Syriac Bible or Peshitta. On the other hand, there is no sure evidence that Jews produced Latin versions of the Bible, in spite of their presence in North Africa, where Christians prepared their earliest biblical texts in Latin. As noted above, Jerome made a point of learning Heb and of consulting Jewish teachers to produce the Latin text ultimately adopted by the Catholic Church as the Vulgate (Vg). For this, he was roundly attacked on philological, theological, and religious grounds; in terms of the latter, he was almost universally condemned for consorting with Jews who would infect him with their perverse interpretations (or rather misinterpretations) of sacred Scripture. It is nonetheless true that almost all subsequent translators (e.g., Martin Luther) and translation committees (such as those responsible for the King James Version [KJV]) made use, often extensive use, of Jewish sources.

The Medieval and Renaissance Periods

The preeminence of the Arabic language accompanied the rapid rise of Islam in the mid-7th c. CE. Jews living in the East and in North Africa quickly adopted it, as they had earlier Latin, Gk, and Aram. Sporadic efforts at rendering the biblical text into Arabic were made in the first few centuries, but only a few remnants of this tradition survive. For the achievement of a full-blown, well-conceived project of Bible translation, we must wait until the early 10th c. It was then that Saadia ben Joseph, a *gaon* (head of a Babylonian rabbinic academy, took it upon himself to prepare an Arabic translation of the Bible. Originally written in Heb characters (as was most Judeo-Arabic), Saadia Gaon's version was destined to be the standard biblical text for Arabic-speaking Jews—a status it still retains for certain Yemenite communities. Saadia's goal, which he magnificently achieved, was to produce a clear, unadorned Arabic rendering of what he understood the Heb original to mean. Where this practice came into conflict with the presentation of distinctive features of Heb grammar or syntax, he readily jettisoned the latter. In the process, Saadia championed the rabbinic understanding of Scripture that was opposed by another group of Jews active at this period, the Karaites.

As Jews settled throughout Europe, they did not at first translate the Bible. Their adherence to the Bible in Heb ran parallel to, albeit at some distance from, the aversion of the Catholic Church to vernacular versions (the official Bible of the Roman Catholic Church is the Latin Vg). In fact, Jewish translations of the Bible were rarely among the earliest literary achievements of European Jewry.

In the case of the Spanish Jews, for example, the most influential version, the Ferrara

Bible, postdates the expulsion of 1492 by half a century, taking its name from the northern Italian city to which many prominent Jews had fled. Although this text ultimately formed the basis for other Spanish-language Bibles in wide use among Catholics, its Jewish origins are securely fixed by a number of distinctive features: use of Heb characters in its first printings, close adherence to Heb grammar, transcription of proper names, and its division according to traditional synagogal practice. It is also worthy of note that a rabbi, Moses Arragel, was responsible for the Spanish-language text of the Alba Bible and some of the illustrations that filled this lavishly produced volume. Arragel, who completed his work in 1430, was commissioned by a high-ranking Spanish leader who was Catholic.

Among German-speaking Jews translation of the Hebrew Bible goes back to the 1200s. These early exemplars, shaped primarily for the home and school, were often excruciatingly literal representations of a single book or block of biblical material. The implicitly "female" orientation of such versions—after all, women had charge of the home and elementary education, but no public role in the synagogue—became explicit in the *Teutsch Ḥumash* of Jacob ben Isaac of Yarnow, from the mid-1600s. Better known as the *Tzena Ure'ena* or "Women's Bible," this rendering incorporated an enormous amount of extrabiblical, largely aggadic, material. This development seems to support the prevailing view of the time that women could comprehend the Bible only when it was augmented with stories and concrete examples; men, on the other hand, could be trusted with the Heb original. All of these versions were in Judeo-German or Yiddish.

A century before Jacob ben Isaac, and unnoted by him, Martin Luther had produced his landmark German version of the Bible, laboring on the Old Testament from 1522 to 1534. As part of his efforts to reform Christianity, he shaped a German text characterized by forceful language and direct diction. A literary masterpiece against which all subsequent German Bibles would be measured, Luther's version, like Jerome's some 1,100 years earlier, reflected the Jewish interpretive tradition—in Luther's case, Rashi, as refracted through Christian sources, influenced him more than he would probably have been comfortable admitting.

Early Modern Translations

Two and a half centuries later, it was to Luther, or at least to the language of Luther, that the Jewish intellectual Moses Mendelssohn (1729–1786; see "Jewish Biblical Scholarship from the 17th to the 19th Centuries," pp. 1963–71) turned. He was not happy with the Yiddish "jargon" used in previous Jewish Bible translations and, more generally, in Jewish society. He looked to language, in this case the higher form of German that prevailed in cultured circles, as a means to bring his fellow Jews into closer contact with German society, its ideas and ideals. To achieve this end, he adopted the language, but not the theological outlook or presuppositions, of Luther. Only Jews, Mendelssohn argued, could produce a proper version for Jews. Moreover, in common with Saadia Gaon and the Ferrara Bible, Mendelssohn's text at first circulated in Heb characters. From his perspective, it was a singular mark of success that the Mendelssohn translation was soon thereafter printed in German script, facilitating for Jews even greater familiarity with that language and for Christians a firsthand acquaintance with an elevated Jewish view of Scripture.

Mendelssohn's efforts, like those of many translators before and after him, resulted in a translation that in effect brought the biblical text to the contemporary reader. For Mendelssohn, this movement from antiquity to the modern world served to acquaint both Jews and non-Jews with traditional Jewish interpretation in a style that was already familiar to Christians and, it was hoped, in which cultured Jews would also immerse themselves. For his opponents, on the other hand, Mendelssohn's renderings of the Bible were more likely than not to lead Jewish youth astray as they ventured into the decidedly "foreign" realm of German literature in general.

Successive editions of Mendelssohn's translation bear witness to a growing market that he both reflected and stimulated. The rise of Reform and neo-Orthodox communities among German-speaking Jews was a further impetus to the preparation and publication of biblical versions in German and Judeo-German or Yiddish. While Orthodox constituencies favored renderings that adhered to traditional Jewish sources, especially the translation and commentary by Samson Raphael Hirsch, others were receptive to editions that incorporated the fruits of the new, critical schools then taking hold among Protestants, as found in editions by Leopold Zunz and Ludwig Philippson. Increased sales also resulted from the packaging of some editions as family Bibles.

Other Translations

The 20th c. witnessed another major Jewish translation into German that took a decidedly different approach to the entire enterprise of Bible translation. This version grew out of a collaboration between the philosophers Martin Buber (1878–1965) and Franz Rosenzweig (1886–1929) (see "The Bible in the Jewish Philosophical Tradition," pp. 1916–43). The resultant text, begun before World War I but completed only after World War II and the Holocaust, did not read like anything else in German literature—and this was precisely the point. The Bible was a product of an ancient society, chronologically and geographically far removed from 20th-c. Europe. In order to experience it in an authentic way, the reader needed to be transported, as it were, back into antiquity. For those without the knowledge of Heb, precisely the audience for a Bible translation, the best way to do this was to experience a modern language text that sounded, looked, and functioned as much as possible like the ancient original. Reading Buber-Rosenzweig was not intended to be an easy task, but the rewards—in terms of discovering many literary and theological features otherwise obliterated through translation—were well worth the struggle, at least for some.

By the time Buber-Rosenzweig appeared in its entirety, most of European Jewry, including the Jews of Germany, had been destroyed. A similar, though not identical circumstance occurred in connection with Yiddish translation, in that one of its most notable achievements did not appear until well after the high point of Yiddish cultural and linguistic dominance. In this case it was one individual, Solomon Bloomgarden—better known by his pen name Yehoash—who was responsible for the text. Beginning in 1910, he published his version in serialized form, revising and perfecting it until he died in 1927. It was the eve of World War II, however, before his work appeared as a whole. By that time, Yiddish had lost or was soon to lose its prominence as a living language.

As noted above, Jews had been preparing Yiddish translations long before Yehoash's time. But Christians, or more precisely Jews who had converted to Christianity, were also active in this field during the 19th c. Supported by the British and Foreign Bible Society, among others, such individuals produced Yiddish-language Old Testaments compatible with Christian theology that missionary societies distributed widely throughout Eastern Europe and among immigrant Jewish communities in the West. Together with Yiddish versions of the New Testament, these Yiddish Bibles were intended to provide the "Good News" in an attractive and accessible format. Bible Society records indicate that such theological motivations were accompanied by the desire to raise the quality of Yiddish from jargon to a standardized, recognized language.

English Translations

The history of Jewish translation of the Bible into English shares many of the features of

Jewish versions in other modern languages. At the same time, distinctive elements mark its development, culminating in the proliferation of texts during the past several decades.

In some ways, the KJV of 1611 functions for English speakers as Luther's version has for those who speak German. Although not the earliest English rendering, KJV is by far the most influential. The members of its translation committee resemble Luther's individual effort in two other respects: They were deeply indebted to Jewish scholarship, in their case the work of David Kimḥi (Radak); but they themselves had no recorded contact with Jews who, having been expelled from England several centuries earlier, were not officially welcomed back until the mid-1600s.

The cadence, vocabulary, and overall structure of the KJV strongly resemble the Heb original. Any number of memorable turns of phrases ("tender mercies," Ps. 25.6 and elsewhere) or lingering verbal pictures ("the face of the waters," Gen. 1.2, and "the LORD make his face shine upon thee," Num. 6.26) we associate with KJV are in fact quite literal renderings of the Heb lost in freer translations into English or other modern languages. Whether through recognition of this indebtedness, a desire to fit in, a lack of interest in making a new English translation, or a combination of such factors, KJV apparently served the needs of England's growing Jewish community for the first c. of its post-expulsion existence.

The first Jewish versions of the Bible in English appear in the 1780s and are limited to the Torah. They are not in fact new translations: A page of Heb text faces the corresponding version of KJV, with a scattering of notes (in English and Heb) from traditional Jewish sources such as Rashi. Such editions may represent a reaction to Heb-English texts published in the preceding decades under Protestant auspices. In any event, the materials in these versions, consciously shaped as they are for English-speaking Jews, represent an important step—and not an isolated one.

Earlier in this essay, both internal and external causes or stimuli were identified for the Gk translation of the Torah (the LXX). A similar complex of concerns was operative in England at the turn of the 19th c. It is clear that by that time most Jews, those who immigrated from Spanish-speaking lands as well as those from German and Yiddish backgrounds, were becoming increasingly familiar and comfortable with English. Synagogues established by both German and Spanish communities made use of prayerbooks with some English, and it was not uncommon to hear at least a few sermons in English. Under such circumstances the appearance of "Jewish Bibles" that combined English with Heb (and some traditional Jewish exegetical annotation) is not surprising.

External forces were active that would slowly propel the Jewish community in the same direction. Missionary societies had existed for some time, but by the early 1800s their number, and especially their focus on the conversion of Jews, increased considerably. Most notable in this respect was the London Society for Promoting Christianity among Jews, generally referred to simply as the London Jews Society. Their proselytizing was in turn greatly abetted by the British and Foreign Bible Society, founded in 1804. Although not a missionary society per se, this organization (and others founded throughout the world, including the American Bible Society), had as one of its principal goals the mass production of inexpensive Bibles that were useful in acquainting non-Christians with the New Testament gospel and the Old Testament as Christian texts. (Yiddish Bibles of this sort were noted above.) In what might appropriately be termed a measure of self-defense, the Jewish community would come to see the value of producing its own English-language versions.

An additional feature marks the introduction of English Bibles into London's Jewish community and from there throughout the Empire and to North America: the few known pre-1800 editions came not from the Jewish establishment, but from individuals on the periphery of the organized community or even at odds with its leadership. Perhaps

Jewish leaders of this period thought it imprudent to challenge, if only implicitly, the unique status of KJV. On the other hand, they may have been resisting the incursion of English into precincts where Heb and German (Yiddish) or Spanish had previously reigned unchallenged.

In any case, by the mid-1800s, individuals well connected by profession, relation, or both were preparing English versions, typically of the Torah or specific books rather than the entire Bible, for Jews. In an unmistakable sign that these versions had "arrived," the Chief Rabbi of the British Empire sanctioned two of them. Perhaps the better parallel is the term "authorized," as in the Authorized Version, another name for KJV. We must, nonetheless, be careful to distinguish the procedures, and especially the goals, envisioned in these two cases. When the Church of England "authorizes" a translation of Scripture, it signifies its suitability for liturgical use in a church. When the Chief Rabbi "sanctioned" Jewish versions, he pointedly did not refer to the synagogue, but to their use in schools and homes. It was not conceivable that the Chief Rabbi would have bestowed similar recognition for liturgical usage, where the Heb text retained its central role. Still, it is worthy of note that he at least tacitly recognized the increasing role of the home and school in transmitting and inculcating Jewish values as enshrined in the Bible.

By the end of the 19th c., the Jews of England had their choice of more than a dozen English-language versions specifically marketed to them. The translations themselves are admittedly not distinguished nor do they differ markedly from KJV. Efforts were made to excise christological language and to (re-) introduce traditional Jewish interpretations. Nevertheless, at the very time Protestants themselves were beginning to experiment with rather radical (for Victorian society) departures from KJV, Jews departed but rarely from its linguistic heritage and overall format. This may have stemmed from the desire "to be more English than the English," or (as noted above for the 18th c.) from the recognition of KJV's "Jewish" roots. It was left to the Jews of the United States, and then not until the middle of the 20th c., to devise new approaches to Bible translation.

Even with communal recognition, Jewish translators in England had, as had Jews in German-speaking lands, worked as individuals—unlike the committees that produced KJV and its successors (or the LXX, for that matter). This pattern prevailed throughout most of the 19th c. in the United States as well. One man, Isaac Leeser, is responsible for the most influential English-language translation on either side of the Atlantic. Like Saadia, Leeser was a communal leader of prodigious accomplishment and not a little controversy. Despite his notoriety in some circles, Leeser's Torah translation of the 1840s, followed a decade later by his rendering of the entire Bible, attracted considerable interest and resulted in a series of new editions and republications over seven decades. Unlike Saadia's flowing Arabic, Leeser's English was rather wooden and at many points essentially devoid of literary distinction. It is perhaps the existence of Leeser's work rather than its merits that marks it as a noteworthy achievement.

By the end of the 19th c., the American Jewish community had become sufficiently sophisticated to support a growing number of cultural organizations in addition to synagogues and other communal structures. Among the most important organizations is the Jewish Publication Society (JPS) of America. Founded in Philadelphia in 1888, JPS attracted the financial support of some of America's wealthiest Jews and the involvement of some of the country's leading Jewish intellectuals and writers. In 1917, JPS organized and published the first committee-produced English-language version of the Bible for Jews. The idea for such a version, which was to function as a replacement for Leeser, originated with the Central Committee of American Rabbis, made up of Reform clergy. Their plan, put into action in the 1890s, was to enlist individual rabbis and scholars to work on a given book or block of biblical material. An editorial committee was to ensure some measure of consistency and quality. But these procedures were difficult to implement, and by the early 20th c. little progress had been achieved.

At that point JPS took charge, having secured the cooperation and support of most of those involved in the earlier project. Rather than farming out sections of the text to individuals, they established a committee that would be responsible for the translation. This committee was composed of six men, two each from the three major Jewish institutions of higher learning: Hebrew Union College (HUC) in Cincinnati, affiliated with the Reform movement; the Jewish Theological Seminary (JTS) in New York City, part of the Conservative movement; and Dropsie College in Philadelphia, which was not a rabbinical seminary but a nondenominational graduate school that provided instruction in fields, such as biblical studies, that were not readily accessible to Jews elsewhere. No representative from an Orthodox institution was part of the committee. In terms of their ideological or theological stances, these men ranged from quite liberal to fairly traditional. None of the six, however, was a biblical scholar of any distinction.

In addition to these six translators, JPS selected as editor-in-chief the biblical scholar Max L. Margolis, who was among the best qualified, in terms of temperament as well as training, for the task at hand. He had taught at HUC in Cincinnati as well as at the University of California at Berkeley before being selected in 1908 as one of the original faculty members at Dropsie. He was thoroughly grounded in traditional Jewish learning, as might be expected, but was also well trained in the classics and in the critical approaches to biblical study then in vogue (in terms of the latter, he was generally skeptical, although appreciative). In one respect, the choice of Margolis was unusual: He had been born in Eastern Europe, educated there and in Berlin, and came to the United States only in the late 1880s. As it happened, the selection of an immigrant rather than a native speaker of English helped shape both the process that produced this version and the translation itself.

As an immigrant, Margolis was acutely aware of distinctions in English diction and the negative effects of improper language or slang as a newly arrived populace sought to improve its status in America. To Margolis, the language of King James, albeit lexically antiquated and stylistically out-of-date, was nonetheless the best possible model for his fellow immigrants. In his desire to inculcate the best of English, along with a Jewish understanding of the Bible, Margolis consciously emulated Moses Mendelssohn, whom he greatly admired.

Margolis's efforts were entirely consistent with the approach prescribed by JPS. Although most readers of its 1917 English translation did not know it, this version adhered quite closely to the (British) Revised Version of 1885, which constituted the first major revision of the 1611 KJV. Verse-by-verse comparisons between the Jewish Version of 1917 and the Revised Version reveal agreement, typically word-for-word agreement, in most passages. Where it was necessary to incorporate materials not found in KJV or its revision, Margolis deliberately chose KJV-sounding language, so as to achieve a text that seamlessly combined the "new" with the "old."

Margolis, of course, excised overtly christological renderings and introduced some traditional Jewish exegesis. But a well-educated, early 20th-c. Protestant would in no way have been put off by the JPS translation, and the same might well have been true for any Jewish reader of the Revised Version. This harmonious picture, which carried over to formatting and even binding, was surely consistent with the goals of the JPS leadership. Margolis, like Mendelssohn over a century earlier, could also derive considerable satisfaction from the recognition that one could learn to be a better Jew and a good citizen through one and the same process.

It was biblical scholar Harry M. Orlinsky who aptly remarked that the shelf life of translations for English-speaking Jews has averaged half a century. That was the case with Leeser and also, so it turns out, for the JPS version of 1917. That JPS itself initiated the project which resulted in a replacement for its earlier translation is due primarily to the energetic advocacy and leadership of Orlinsky. A longtime faculty member at New York City's Jewish Institute of Religion, later merged with Hebrew Union College, Orlinsky was singularly well placed to head the new translation project. He had been selected in the 1940s as the first Jewish member of the Revised Standard Version (RSV) translation committee; in fact, he was the first Jew to serve on any committee to prepare a mainstream (that is, Christian) Bible translation. His experience in this regard led to his subsequent selection as the only Jewish editor for the New Revised Standard Version (NRSV). By the late 1950s, when he began to lobby for a new Jewish translation, Orlinsky was well known and respected among a wide range of rabbis and Jewish scholars.

Moreover, Orlinsky had a clear vision of what a Jewish translation should look and sound like, a vision that marked a definite departure from the King James-type language characteristic of earlier Jewish versions. For Orlinsky, the effectiveness of any Bible translation was linked to its easy intelligibility by contemporary readers, who can be readily put off by antiquated or obscure words and stilted or foreign-looking syntax. The question translators should always have before them is this: What did the original authors intend to say to their audience and how can we convey that meaning to our audience? In short, this approach to translation seeks to bring the text to the reader. Although an admirer of Mendelssohn and Margolis, Orlinsky's model from within Judaism itself was Saadia Gaon. More broadly, Orlinsky was allying himself with a number of (mostly Protestant) scholars associated with the American Bible Society, who promoted and practiced a dynamic or functional equivalence approach to translation in two popular versions of the post–World War II era: Today's English Version *(The Good News Bible)* and the Contemporary English Version.

Orlinsky of course approached his task from what he understood to be a thoroughly Jewish stance. In his opinion, sensitivity to distinctively Jewish interpretations and exegetes produced a text that was not only more suitable for the Jewish community, but that often presented a more accurate rendering than those offered by other translations. When published in a volume that dispensed with hard-to-read type and the two-column-per-page format traditionally associated with Bibles, the New Jewish Publication Society translation (NJPS) was positioned to take its place among the other accessible, readable, and attractive English Bibles of the mid- to late 20th c.

Orlinsky served as editor-in-chief of the committee that prepared the NJPS translation of the Torah, which initially appeared in the mid-1960s; he was also part of the group that worked on the Prophets. Other scholars from North America and Israel composed the committee for the Writings. Their efforts were first published as separate volumes, 1962 (first edition of Torah, revised 1967), 1978 (Nevi'im), and 1982 (Kethuvim). It was 1985 before the entire Tanakh appeared, incorporating in revised form the efforts of all three translation committees. Until 1999, volumes of the Tanakh contained only the English version; in that year, a Heb-English language edition first came out, thereby facilitating comparison between text and translation.

It is instructive to compare the two JPS versions, 1917 and 1985, in order to gauge both the distance that separates them and the features they hold in common:

Genesis 1.1–2

1917: **In the beginning God created** the heaven and the earth.... And **the spirit of God hovered** over the face of the waters

1985: **When God began to create** heaven and earth.... And **a wind from God sweeping** over the water

The 1917 version retains the wording of KJV; it parts company with the Protestant text by replacing the upper case "s" of Spirit, a reference to the Trinity, with a lower case "s." In addition to rendering Heb *ruaḥ* with "wind" rather than with a form of "spirit," Orlinsky (in the 1985 version), in keeping with one line of Jewish exegesis, renders the notoriously difficult wording of Gen.' (and the Bible's) beginning as "When God began to create." In so doing, he excludes the theological doctrine of *creatio ex nihilo,* to the extent that this belief is dependent on the traditional English text. Moreover, it reflects the opening of the Babylonian creation story, *Enuma Elish,* which also begins with a "when" clause. It is also characteristic of Orlinsky's approach that the literal "face of the waters" yields to the simpler, more modern-sounding "the water."

Genesis 11.5 (Tower of Babel)

1917: And the LORD came down to see the city and the tower, which the **children of men builded.**

1985: The LORD came down to look at the city and tower that **man had built.**

It is characteristic of almost all post-World War II versions to update archaic verb forms, such as "had built" for "builded" in this passage. More noteworthy is the use of the generic "man" (but not "human" or "humankind" as in gender-neutral texts like the roughly contemporary NRSV) for the literal, but perhaps misleading, "children of men." In like manner, "Israelites" consistently replaces "children of Israel" in the 1985 version.

Exodus 21.15

1917: **And he that smiteth his** father, or **his** mother, shall be surely put to death.

1985: **He who strikes his** father or **his** mother shall be put to death.

"He who strikes" sounds far more natural to today's readers than "he that smiteth." The retention of the third sg. masculine pronoun, a precise reflection of the Heb wording, is avoided in certain other modern translations, most notably the NRSV. As mentioned above, Orlinsky played a role in the development of the NRSV as well as the JPS version of 1985. Although his sympathies in such passages lay with the gender-neutral approach taken by the NRSV, in these instances the NJPS Torah tended to resist any innovation. An important innovation, from Orlinsky's perspective, is found at the beginning of this v. (as in Gen. 11.5 and many other places), where the conjunction *vav*—typically translated as "and" in traditional English versions (esp. KJV)—is omitted. Elsewhere, its presence is signaled through the use of subordination where the paratactic structure of Heb favored coordination.

Deuteronomy 24.16

1917: The **fathers** shall not be put to death for the children, neither shall the children be put to death for the **fathers; every man** shall be put to death for **his** own sin.

1985: **Parents** should not be put to death for children, nor children be put to death for **parents: a person** shall be put to death only for **his** own crime.

In this case, NJPS shows considerable, although not consistent, sensitivity to gendered language. The version understands that "fathers," although a literal translation of the Heb, does not reflect the more inclusive meaning of the term here, hence "parents." In like manner, "every man" is more accurately rendered by "a person." The NRSV, although not the NJPS, manages to eliminate all vestiges of male-oriented language by the use of "their own" after "persons." Although more consistent in terms of gender language, such an approach involves more restructuring of the Heb than the NJPS Torah editors apparently found desirable.

Judges 12.9

1917: And he had thirty sons, and thirty daughters he sent **abroad,** and thirty daughters he brought in from **abroad** for his sons.

1985: He had thirty sons, and he married off thirty daughters **outside the clan** and brought in thirty girls from **outside the clan** for his sons.

In his own distinctively insightful way, Orlinsky used to point out how misleading the traditional rendering "abroad" is here. It is not that the judge Ibzan sought foreign spouses for his sons and daughters, but that he went "outside the clan" for prospective sons- and daughters-in-law. A small point perhaps, but instructive for showing what were, for Orlinsky, some of the benefits of the approach he championed.

Isaiah 7.14

1917: **Behold, the young woman shall conceive, and bear** a son.

1985: **Look, the young woman is with child and about to give birth to** a son.

With the rendering "a virgin," the KJV translation of this passage has been central to a christological interpretation of the Old Testament. In keeping with a long-standing Jewish understanding and with the philologically more correct meaning, both JPS and NJPS have "the young woman." For the rest, JPS 1917 retains the traditional KJV rendering, which places conception and child-bearing in the (distant) future. Although such a rendering of Heb present participles is possible, NJPS is surely on more solid ground, syntactically and contextually, when it portrays the women as pregnant and soon to give birth. It is noteworthy that the RSV Old Testament of 1952 was the first mainstream Christian translation to place "the young woman" in the text itself, relegating "a virgin" to the margins. Orlinsky's presence as an RSV editor did not go unnoticed by that translation's conservative critics.

Jeremiah 31.29–30 (similar expression found in Ezekiel 18.14)

1917: In those days they shall say no more: The **fathers** have eaten sour grapes, and the children's teeth are set on edge. But every one shall die for **his** own iniquity; **every man** that eateth the sour grapes, **his** teeth shall be set on edge.

1985: In those days they shall no longer say: The **parents** have eaten sour grapes, and the children's teeth are set on edge. But **all** shall die for **their** own sins; the teeth of **everyone** who eats sour grapes shall be set on edge.

It is instructive to compare the NJPS text here with a passage from the Torah, such as Deut. 24.16 above. In the earlier example, NJPS retained the sg. (with "person"; cf. "man" in traditional English versions), leading to the retention of the masculine sg. pronoun "his." In the Prophets, NJPS, in a move that could be characterized as quite bold if nonetheless consistent with NRSV, eliminates all exclusively male references. Such a practice, while less literal than the 1917 JPS version, does more accurately reflect the meaning of the Heb original, as understood by the committee responsible for the Prophets.

Ezekiel 2.1 (and frequently elsewhere in the book of Ezekiel)

1917: **Son of man**

1985: **O mortal**

Ben 'adam is the characteristic way in which God addresses the prophet Ezekiel throughout his book. The literal translation of this Heb phrase is "son of man," which the 1917 JPS version shares with many traditional and even modern English-language versions. The NJPS editors responsible for the Prophets determined that the main point of this appellation was not Ezekiel's maleness, but his humanness or mortality, vis-à-vis the divinity and immortality of the LORD. Hence, they decided to dispense with tradition, a decision found in several other contemporary versions as well.

Proverbs 31.10
1917: **A woman of valour** who can find? For her price is far above rubies.
1985: What a rare find is **a capable wife!** Her worth is far beyond that of rubies.

The expression "a woman of valour" is one of the few memorable phrases coined by the JPS 1917 translators. To this day, it is used to describe women of noteworthy achievement within the Jewish community. It is a rather literal rendering of the Heb, *ʾeshet ḥayil.* The NJPS editors for the Writings discarded this expression in favor of "a capable wife," which is to be sure a possible rendering of the Heb. Nonetheless, in this case it is difficult to see this newer wording as either a closer reflection of the Heb or a sensitive application of the ancient text to the modern world.

Other English Versions

The post-World War II period has witnessed the proliferation, some might call it explosion, of new, often competing English-language versions, especially among Protestants. The number of such versions is in effect multiplied by the seemingly endless variety of editions, often aimed at niche markets (recent widows, virgin teenagers, recovering alcoholics, e.g.) in which these translations appear. In comparison, the corresponding market for Jewish versions is quite limited, even when interested non-Jewish scholars, ministers, and laity are taken into account. Nonetheless, the NJPS is far from alone in finding supporters (as well as detractors!) in the contemporary English-speaking Jewish community, or better, communities.

Among the most widely advertised and beautifully produced versions is the ArtScroll's Tanach (Tanach, an alternate spelling of Tanakh, is an acronym reflecting the traditional tripartite Jewish division of the Bible: Torah, Nevi'im [Prophets], Kethuvim [Writings]), a product of Mesorah Publications of Brooklyn, New York. It is aimed primarily at more traditional or Orthodox segments of the Jewish community, but its appeal has gone beyond that market, in common with many of Mesorah's other publications in the ArtScroll series. For the Torah, its translators relied on the interpretations of the medieval exegete Rashi; elsewhere, they are more eclectic—but they never range beyond traditional sources. This leads to a number of distinctive English renderings, among which are:

Genesis 2.2: **By the seventh day** God completed His work which He had done, and He **abstained on the seventh day.**

For the first prepositional phrase, the Heb reads "on the seventh day," which is contextually difficult, given the fact that creation is elsewhere portrayed as a six-day event.

Exodus 12.15: For a seven-day period shall you eat matzos, but **on the previous day** you shall nullify the leaven from your homes.

The highlighted prepositional phrase is, literally in the Heb, "on the first day," which creates confusion when compared to other biblical passages in which the leaven was to be "nullified" before the Passover began.

Exodus 20.7: You shall not take the Name of **HA-SHEM,** your God, in vain, for **HA-SHEM** will not absolve anyone who takes His Name in vain.

Here, as frequently elsewhere, the tetragrammaton ("YHVH")—which in most English-language versions is represented by the title, the LORD—is replaced by an expression that literally means "the Name," reflecting the ineffability of God's proper name. *Ha-Shem* as a surrogate for YHVH is frequently used in Orthodox contexts.

Exodus 22.24: **When** you lend money to My people ... do not lay interest upon him.

The Heb word rendered here as "when" is the common Heb conjunction, *ʾim,* which in the vast majority of instances is translated literally as "if." The use of "when" here, paralleled in two other places in the Torah, is in accordance with the tradition that in Judaism charity is not a matter of "if," but "when."

Leviticus 23.11: He shall wave the Omer before HA-SHEM to gain favor for you; on the morrow **of the rest day** the Kohen shall wave it.

This v. describes a ceremony, still maintained among traditional Jews, in which the days from Passover to Shavuʿot (the Festival of Weeks or Pentecost) are enumerated by an offering called the Omer. The Heb text specifies that the counting of the Omer starts with the day after "the Shabbat." But rabbinic Judaism understands "Shabbat" here not in its usual sense, but as "the day of rest," that is, the first day of Passover. As in several examples above, the ArtScroll Tanach follows rabbinic interpretation rather than a more literal rendering of the biblical text itself, especially when the more literal rendering might create confusion on halakhic matter.

Another version intended primarily for Orthodox and other traditional Jews is *The Living Torah,* by Rabbi Aryeh Kaplan, and the *Living Nach,* three successive volumes covering the Prophets and the Writings, translated by Kaplan's followers after his death. Kaplan was a prolific writer on Jewish topics and often emphasized mystical elements in Jewish thought and practice. The volumes influenced by Kaplan reflect traditional Jewish sources—for legal interpretation especially the philosopher Maimonides—and also display a demonstrable interest in matters of spiritual import. Among characteristic Kaplan renderings are:

Exodus 20.8–10: Remember the Sabbath to keep it holy. You can work during the six weekdays and do all your tasks. But **Saturday** is the Sabbath to God your Lord.

Lest there be any doubt about when the "seventh day" falls, Kaplan explicitly introduces the modern-sounding expression "Saturday" into the ancient text.

Leviticus 17.14: Tell the Israelites not to eat any blood, since the **life-force** of all flesh is in its blood. Whoever eats it shall be cut off **[spiritually].**

The translation of this passage, along with Kaplan's rendering of Deut. 12.23 below and elsewhere, explicitly introduces a spiritual element into the biblical text that is, at best, implicit in the literal wording of the Heb text.

Leviticus 18.7: Do not **commit a sexual offense against** your father or mother. If a woman is your mother, you must not **commit incest with her.**

There is no specific Heb word for "incest" as opposed to the more general term translated here as "sexual offense." As in other examples, Kaplan's practice leads to modification of the literal text in the direction of specificity or explicitness.

Leviticus 19.14: Do not place a stumbling block before the **[morally]** blind.

Leviticus 19.29: Do not defile your daughter with **premarital sex.**

As elsewhere, Kaplan renders a fairly general term with a specific one; in this instance, "premarital sex." In a sense, he may be responding to those who, with some justification, make statements like, "there is no specific prohibition against premarital sex in the Old Testament." While that may otherwise be quite true, the explicit prohibition does appear in *The Living Torah*!

Deuteronomy 12.23: Be extremely careful not to eat the blood, since the blood is associated with the **spiritual nature** [other translations: "life"], and when you eat flesh, you shall not ingest the **spiritual nature** along with it.

Working on his own, the Jewish scholar Everett Fox has produced an English-language version of the Torah that draws its distinctive inspiration from the German translation of Buber-Rosenzweig. Like them, Fox endeavors to draw the contemporary reader into the world of antiquity through a modern-language version that incorporates many aspects of the ancient Heb text absent in most other English renderings. The flavor, as it were, of his *Schocken Bible: The Five Books of Moses,* can be appreciated through the following examples:

Genesis 1.1–2: **At the beginning of God's creating** of the heavens and the earth, when the earth was wild and waste, darkness rushed over the face of Ocean, **rushing-spirit of God hovering** over the face of the waters—

Genesis 1.8: God called the dome: **Heaven!**

There was **setting,** there was **dawning:** second day.

Genesis 17.5: No longer shall your name be called **Avram,** rather shall your name be **Avraham,** for I will make you ***Av Hamon Goyyim*/Father of a throng of Nations!**

Fox chooses to present the biblical names in their Heb form, thereby allowing English readers to hear more clearly what the ancient listener would have heard and to enjoy something of the wordplay hitherto accessible only to readers of Heb.

Genesis 25.30–31: *Esav* said to **Yaakov: Pray give me a gulp of the red-stuff, that red-stuff,** for I am so weary! Therefore they called his name: **Edom/Red-One. Yaakov** said: Sell me your **firstborn-right here-and-now.**

Although other versions note wordplays, here and elsewhere, in their notes, Fox presents wordplays associated with names in the text itself. It is also characteristic of Fox to use dashes to indicate that what takes more than one "word" to say in English required only one word in Heb.

Genesis 27.36: He [Esav] said: Is that why his name was called **Yaakov/Heel-Sneak?** For he has now **sneaked against me** twice.

Genesis 30.24: She [Rahel] became pregnant and bore a son. She said: God has **removed/*asaf*** my reproach! So she called his name: **Yosef,** saying: May **YHVH add/*yosef*** another son to me!

Genesis 42.7: When **Yosef** saw his brothers, he **recognized** them, but he **pretended-no-recognition** of them and spoke harshly with them.

Genesis 43.10: The man [Yosef] **warned, yes, warned us,** saying: You shall not see my face unless your brother is with you.

Where the Heb uses the same root (here, "warn") twice in proximity, most English translations either ignore it or paraphrase, as "surely" or "really warned us." Here and elsewhere, Fox represents this verbal repetition as literally as possible.

Genesis 45.12–13: Here, **your eyes see, as well as my brother Binyimin's eyes,** that it is **my mouth** that speaks to you. So tell my father of all **the weight I carry** in Egypt, and of all that you have seen, and **make haste,** bring my father down here!

Exodus 5.17: But he [Pharaoh] said: **Lax you are, lax.**

Exodus 12.42–43, 48: It is a night of **keeping-watch for YHWH.... YHWH** said to **Moshe** and **Aharon:** This is the law of the **Passover-meal.** Any **foreign son** is not to eat of it.... But any **foreskinned-man** is not to eat of it.

Exodus 13.1: **Hallow to me** every first-born, **breacher of every womb** among the **Children of Israel,** of man or of beast, it is mine.

These are among the most important English-language Jewish versions available today. They are by no means the only ones. Among other notable translations that have appeared in recent years are Richard Elliott Friedman, *Commentary on the Torah with a New English Translation* (2001), and Robert Alter, *The Five Books of Moses: A Translation with Commentary* (2004), and *The Book of Psalms* (2007). Especially among Orthodox Jews, individual rabbis or groups of rabbis are preparing their own translations, reflecting both distinctive elements in their teaching and the need for instruction in English even within the most traditional communities. In many ways, the production of such versions parallels developments within the far larger Protestant communities, where distinctive theologies stimulate an ever increasing number of translations.

In today's world there are many factors that promote the production and publication of Bible translations. Theological, literary, social, even fiscal forces have come to play their role in this phenomenon, which is as old as the LXX and as new as the latest version. For Jews, the questions that arise are ancient and perennial, modern and immediate: What is it that makes a Bible translation Jewish? Should a Jewish translation ever supplant, rather than supplement, the Heb original? Who, if anyone, should determine which mode of translation, or presentation, or annotation is best? Do differing versions serve to divide Jews, and, if so, should there be one unifying version? In the past, diverse responses have met such queries, giving rise to present circumstances. For the future, even greater diversity is likely. Nonetheless, it is possible to be optimistic that Jewish Bible translators will remain true to their task of finding and perfecting distinctive ways to link their communities with the sacred text of the Torah, the Prophets, and the Writings.

[LEONARD J. GREENSPOON]

The History of Israel in the Biblical Period

Methodological Considerations

Reconstructing the history of Israel is a complicated process. Evidence from the Hebrew Bible, from archeology, and from extrabiblical sources must first be interpreted independently of each other, and only then brought together and reinterpreted, in order to create a more complete and better-grounded historical picture.

The history of Israel as described in the Hebrew Bible, like most ancient historical writings, was not intended to be an accurate record of past events. Its purpose was, rather, didactic, illustrating the role of the God of Israel in history and, by so doing, shaping the identity of the people of Israel. The biblical historians were more interested in what the past, as they (re)constructed it, meant for the present, rather than in what actually had happened long ago. That does not mean that biblical history was a complete fabrication, but it does mean that the Bible, which incorporates sources from many different periods and authors, must be used very judiciously to reconstruct the history of ancient Israel. The modern historian must separate different editorial levels and revisions and evaluate them in terms of their origin and historical reliability. Only then is it possible to determine how a biblical text might be used for historical reconstruction.

The archeological research (see "Archeology," pp. 2124–36) is based on the interpretation of the finds discovered in excavations and surveys conducted in Israel and in neighboring countries, and is a very important independent extrabiblical source for the history of Israel. This data often offers background to the biblical texts; it depicts processes of settlement and destruction, prosperity and decline in the material culture, cultural connections and demographical relationships. It is also the main source for understanding the society and culture of the kingdoms of Israel (the Northern Kingdom) and Judah. Scientific information and methods—from the physical, biological, and social sciences—are used to analyze material remains, thereby clarifying important aspects of the society, economy and culture; they also assist the accurate dating of the finds. The archeological data provides information independent of the Bible; it may be in agreement with the biblical description or contradict it, or it may be silent on a given point. Often it raises new questions and areas of inquiry. Extrabiblical written sources from Israel and Judah, and written sources from neighboring kingdoms (mainly Phoenicia, Philistia, Ammon, Moab and Edom), as well as from the great empires of the ancient Near East (mainly Assyria, Babylonia, and Egypt), contribute valuable information on the specific periods and events that they describe. Many of these extrabiblical sources were written close to the time of the events they describe, which, to some extent, may make them seem more reliable than the biblical writings, composed at a greater distance from the events, and transmitted over a long period of time, although extrabiblical sources are no less subjective and agenda-driven than the Bible. This multi-pronged research, combining the conclusions of critical biblical scholarship, of the study of the archeological material, and of the research on the extrabiblical written sources, makes it possible to create, with some confidence, many facets of ancient Israelite history. Nevertheless, our picture of Israel's past is often incomplete and uncertain.

Periodization

Historians divide the past into eras or periods, often based on major political and/or social changes. For most historians of the biblical period, the Babylonian exile of Judah in the 6th c. is a central event. We are certain from a variety of ancient sources that it happened, we know when it began (the first wave was in 597, the second in 587 or 586, when the Temple was also destroyed), and we know when it ended (in 538, with the Cyrus proclamation, immediately after the Persian conquest of Babylonia). Thus, there is broad agreement that the biblical period can be divided into the preexilic (pre-586), the exilic (586–538), and the postexilic period.

Alternatively, the history of ancient Israel could be periodized based on the major empires that controlled Israel. In this scheme, the Assyrian period (through the late 7th c.) is replaced by the Babylonian (through 539), the Persian (through 333), and finally the Greek or Hellenistic.

Until recently, it was common to divide preexilic history into the premonarchic and the monarchic periods, and to divide the latter into the united monarchy in the 10th c., of (Saul,) David, and Solomon, followed by the period of the divided monarchy. As this essay will show, however, the premonarchic period long ago became a literary description of the mythological roots, the early beginnings of the nation and the way to describe the right of Israel on its land. The archeological evidence also does not support the existence of a united monarchy under David and Solomon as described in the Bible, so the rubric of "united monarchy" is best abandoned, although it remains useful for discussing how the Bible views the Israelite past.

Beginnings

As early as the end of the fourth millennium BCE, important centers of political, economic, and cultural power grew in Mesopotamia and Egypt. These dominated the Near East until the conquests of Alexander the Great in the final third of the first millennium BCE.

The land "between the rivers" ("Mesopotamia" in Gk) is located in the eastern part of the Fertile Crescent, between the Tigris and the Euphrates. The civilizations of Sumer, Akkad, Babylonia, and Assyria flourished here. The Euphrates delineates the western boundary of Mesopotamia, but the cultural impact of Mesopotamia was felt much farther westward—throughout Anatolia (Turkey), Syria, and even into the northern part of the Land of Israel. Nevertheless, only in the mid-8th c. BCE did Assyria succeed in conquering the entire region of Syria and the Land of Israel. Assyria established its control over the entire region up to the boundary of Egypt, and for a short period, ruled Egypt as well.

Egyptian civilization developed in the southwestern side of the Fertile Crescent. For long periods, the Egyptian economic and cultural influence was felt in the Land of Israel, Phoenicia (modern day Lebanon) and the southern part of Syria. While Egypt was developing as a political and military power, it also controlled parts of this expanse, and for a short period in the second half of the second millennium BCE, even ruled over most of this region. When Assyria declined in the late 7th c., Egypt inherited control of Syria, the Phoenician coast, and the Land of Israel. In the last quarter of the 7th c. BCE, Egypt established an empire that, at its peak, reached the banks of the Euphrates.

The vast region that included Syria, Phoenicia, and the Land of Israel lay between the two major centers of wealth and culture that bounded the Fertile Crescent. This region was immensely important; its resources (e.g., the timber of Lebanon) could be exploited, it served as a link for maritime and overland commerce, and the area served as a buffer zone, or as a starting point for attacks against the opposing empire.

The empires viewed this region as a single geographic unit, lumping together the various ethnic groups and city-states that were there. The Euphrates was its northeastern border, the area between the upper Euphrates and the Taurus and Amanus Mountains was the northern border, and Naḥal Besor (Wadi Shelaleh, south of Gaza) served as the southern boundary. The Mediterranean seaboard defined this area on the west, and the Arabian Desert, bordering the inhabited regions in Bashan, Gilead, Moab, Amon and Edom, was its eastern frontier. Nonetheless, before the Assyrian conquest in the 8th c. BCE, the small independent kingdoms in Syria and the Land of Israel did not belong to the same geopolitical unit. Apart from one fleeting episode in the 14th c. BCE, these areas were not included under one ruler and were never part of one administrative framework. This explains why in documents from the second millennium and the beginning of the first millennium BCE, there is no geopolitical designation for this region.

It was only after the Assyrian conquest (8th c. BCE) that the entire region between the Euphrates and the border of Egypt was united into one political and territorial unit, known by its Akkadian name, *eber nāri* ("Beyond the River"). At that point, the Assyrians put an end to the independence of the ethnic and political entities that had existed, and annexed most of them to Assyria, turning them into Assyrian provinces. The Assyrians brought about far-ranging changes in the cultural, economic, and demographic characteristics of the region, determining the region's fate for generations to come. Even after the fall of Assyria in the late 7th c., this situation continued to exist under the rule of Egypt, Babylonia, and even Persia, when all of the area west of the Euphrates was included in the fifth satrapy that was still called *eber nāri*.

A more limited area that included southern Syria and the Land of Israel is referred to in various documents from the second millennium BCE as Canaan. (See "Geography," pp. 2119–24.) This area corresponds to the land of Canaan as described in Num. 34.1–12 and, with minor changes, in Ezek. 47.13–20. In Egyptian sources from the early part of the second millennium BCE it is called Retenu, and in later periods in Egyptian history, it is also called Djahi and Ḫurru.

The Early History of Israel

The history of early Israel—until the 9th c.—as described in the Hebrew Bible diverges sharply from the history that can be reconstructed from the archeological finds and the ancient extrabiblical sources. Contemporary scholars tend to give greater weight to the archeological and epigraphic (written inscriptions and documents) evidence, as this essay will do.

The picture that can be reconstructed from archeology indicates the emergence of the kingdoms of Israel and Judah in the 9th c. BCE and the existence of the Northern Kingdom until the late 8th c. BCE and the existence of the Southern Kingdom until the early 6th c. BCE. In addition, in the few ancient inscriptions that have been preserved, only one kingdom—the Northern Kingdom—is given the name "Israel," and only its people are called "Israelites" (unlike the Bible, which uses "Israel" to encompass both kingdoms before the "divided monarchy"). Although the kingdom of Judah is mentioned in some ancient inscriptions, they never suggest that it was part of a unit comprised of Israel and Judah. There are no extrabiblical indications of a united monarchy called "Israel."

During most of the historical periods, the main urban centers in the Land of Israel were located along the coast, in the lowland and in the central valleys, especially in the northern parts of the land. The main trade routes passed through these areas, and the important commercial junctions and harbors were located there, enabling the development of urban society and small cities. The fertile soil and the plentiful water sources in these areas supported a stable agricultural society. On the other hand, the highland was usually sparsely inhabited, with few urban centers; it was predominantly rural, with many seminomadic groups at its periphery.

Such was the situation during the Late Bronze Period (1550–1200 BCE), when the entire land was under the rule of the Egyptian empire. Throughout this period, the Egyptian imperial centers were located along the coastal plain, while the key Canaanite cities were in the Lowland (e.g., Lachish, Gath, Gezer) and in the northern valleys (e.g., Megiddo, Hazor). The highlands were dominated by two cities: Jerusalem controlled a limited, poor territory in the southern hill country (Judean hills), and Shechem ruled over a more fertile and populated area in the north (later to be known as the Samaria hills). Throughout this period, the small sedentary population in the hill country was concentrated in the cities and their immediate territory, while many areas were "no-man's-land," partly occupied by nomads called "Shasu," and bands of outlaws called "'Apiru."

A shift occurred in the twilight of the Egyptian control, during the late 13th c. BCE, when the Egyptian kings of the nineteenth dynasty sent military campaigns against disobedient cities and the rising nomadic elements in the southern steppes and in the Highland. Seti I and his son, Ramses II, fought against the Shasu in the Negev Highland and the Gaza area, while Ramses' son, Merneptah (1213–1203 BCE) destroyed the rebellious cities of Gezer, Yenoam and Ashkelon, and fought against a group of people, explicitly called "Israel," probably one of the nomadic tribes on the fringe of Canaan. Merneptah's Stele claims that "Israel is laid waste, his seed is not." This is typical exaggerated Egyptian rhetoric, but it shows that by the end of the 13th c. BCE the Egyptians knew of the existence of a geopolitical entity called "Israel" in the land of Canaan.

The early rulers of the twentieth dynasty continued earlier policy, strengthening Egyptian control over the land. Their campaigns brought southern Canaan under direct Egyptian control, while all the major urban centers were destroyed by the Egyptian army, by revolting Canaanite cities, or by the outlaw bands. Only a handful of these urban centers were restored during the 12th c. BCE. As a result, much of its former population became refugees, joining the strengthening semi-nomadic/outlaw elements.

During the Iron Age I (1200–1000/950 BCE), the growth of these semi-nomadic and outlaw elements, and the decline of the urban culture, led to a process of settlement that took place mostly in the central highland, around the city of Shechem. (According to this picture, the origin of Israel is to be sought within the land of Israel, not from tribes who escaped from Egypt, as the Bible portrays Israel's origins.) Some 200 tiny settlements appeared in this region during this period, moving from semi-nomadic to a sedentary culture, from sheep herding to a horticultural and agricultural economy. During the same time, another settlement process took place in the southern coastal plain and the western Lowland, mostly around the city of Ekron (midway between the former cities of Gezer and Gath). Both populations were comprised of a variety of elements, with an Aegean-oriented population (Philistines) in the coastal plain and fringe-region nomads in the central hill country. The majority population of both areas, however, was comprised of local Canaanites. While the highland settlements show continuity with previous Canaanite material culture, the settlements in the southern coastal plain exhibit significant foreign traits, such as Aegean-styled pottery, cultic artifacts, and architecture. These are exemplified well in Ekron, where a fifty acre city was built, with satellite settlements in the coastal plain and the Lowland; it was the largest entity in the southern Levant until its destruction in the early 10th c. BCE.

The biblical description of the early periods of the history of Israel, its origins from the extended family of Jacob, the exodus from Egypt, the conquest and settlement of Canaan, and the early (united) monarchy, are problematic from a historical perspective. There is little or no explicit extrabiblical evidence of the names or events mentioned in Gen. through Sam.

The first possible synchronism between the biblical description and extrabiblical sources comes from the early period of the kingdom of Judah under the rule of Solomon's son Rehoboam. The Egyptian pharaoh Shishak (Sheshonq I) undertook a campaign in Western Asia, probably in 925 BCE, as explicitly indicated in Egyptian sources and as also confirmed by destruction layers at key cities in Israel. The pylon of Pharaoh Sheshonq I at the temple of Amun at Karnak (in Upper Egypt) mentions many identifiable sites in the territory that later became the kingdom of Israel, but mentions neither Judah nor Israel by name. Memories of this event are preserved in 1 Kings 14.25–28 (cf. 2 Chron. 12.2–9).

The History of the Kingdoms of Israel and Judah

During the Iron Age IIA (in the second half of the 10th and in the early 9th c. BCE), the settlements of the northern Highland and the city of Shechem became a single entity that expanded its control over vast areas in the Lowland and the northern valleys. During the early 9th c. BCE, the traditional center at Shechem was replaced by a new palatial complex that was erected in Samaria, several kilometers northwest of the traditional highland center. This complex included a podium built over casemate enclosure, reshaping the natural hill into a constructed box, with an elaborated palace built on it with ashlar masonry architecture, including decorated stone capitals. Similar architecture has been excavated in the former Canaanite centers of the neighboring regions—Megiddo and Jezreel in the Jezreel valley, Hazor to the north of the Sea of Galilee, En-Gev to the east, and Gezer in the northern Lowland; it is also found in Transjordan, in two strategically located sites monitoring the main routes passing across the plateau—Khirbet Atarus and Khirbet Mudeyine eth-Themed. This common architecture suggests that in this period, the kingdom of Israel under the rule of the Omrides (the descendants of King Omri) became one of the strongest kingdoms in the Levant; it is no coincidence that for the first time, it is mentioned in Moabite, Assyrian and Aramean inscriptions.

The earliest inscription to mention the kingdom of Israel is the 9th c. stele of Mesha the king of Moab, which refers to the Israelite King Omri by name. Shalmaneser III (reigned 859–824) reported in his Kurkh Inscription that "Ahab the Israelite" (Omri's son, according to the Bible) contributed a contingent of 2,000 chariots and 10,000 troops to the coalition that fought Assyria at the battle of Qarqar in northern Syria (853 BCE). The same Assyrian king mentioned "Jehu the son of Omri" in one of his inscriptions, as well as in the Black Obelisk, which also shows the portrait of Jehu kneeling before the Assyrian king. (Jehu was not in fact a descendent of Omri, but began a new dynasty; the ancient sources, however, recognize Omri as the central dynast in the Northern Kingdom.) The Aramaean stele found at Tel Dan in northern Israel records the killing of the king of Israel, probably Joram, and the king of the House of David, probably Ahaziah. The name, "the house of Omri," for the kingdom of Israel appears also in Adad-Nirari III's (811–783) inscription from Kalah, and in the inscription of Tiglath-pileser III (745–727) summarizing the annexation of the territory of Aram Damascus. The memory of this name over a century after Omri's death reflects that king's great power and reputation.

During the 9th c. BCE, at the same time when the Omrides established the kingdom of Israel, archeological remains suggest that a small entity arose in the south, with its center at Jerusalem; about a dozen of settlements surrounded the city. While the political vacuum around the hills of Samaria enabled Israel to expand, the kings of Jerusalem faced the Lowland, the realm of the powerful Philistine city of Gath, to their west. Gath controlled its own satellite settlements and had a rich material culture that included import ware, epigraphic finds and monumental architecture. Thus, the territorial extent of Jerusalem remained small, as in the Late Bronze period.

A major shift is reflected in the late 9th c. BCE wave of destructions, probably caused by the Arameans, which included all of the major Israelite sites outside of the Highland, from Hazor in the north to Gezer in the south and Khirbet Atarus in the east. A parallel wave of destruction is evident in the Lowland, affecting Gath and its satellite settlements. A bit later, fortified enclosures appear in the south above the villages of Lachish and Beth-shemesh. Another royal center was built at Tel Beersheba, controlling the trade route passing through the Beersheba-Arad Valley. The monumental architecture in these sites and their public character show that they do not reflect an organic, gradual internal development, but resulted from external efforts—in this case, from the rulers of Jerusalem. The control over the agricultural territories of the Lowland and over the trade routes of the Beersheba-Arad Valley reflects the administrative and economic development in Jerusalem itself, which at this point was undoubtedly the capital of the newly established kingdom: the kingdom of Judah. Thus the archeological record suggests that the united kingdom did not exist, and that Judah developed significantly later than the Northern Kingdom of Israel.

The kingdom of Israel survived the Aramaean expansion during the second half of the 9th c., and several decades afterwards, in the early 8th c. BCE, it restored the centers outside of the Highland. Gezer, Megiddo, and Hazor were rebuilt, and new centers, including Dan in the north, were constructed. The rulers at Samaria even reached as far south as the fringe of the Sinai desert, as the fortress at Kuntillet Ajrud testifies. (An inscription from that fortress refers to YHVH of Shomron, "YHVH of Samaria," indicating its connection to the Northern Kingdom, despite its southern location.) Samaria thus created an alternative trade route from Arabia to the coastal plain, parallel to the Judahite system in the Beersheba-Arad valley. The kingdom of Israel flourished, with rich material culture and an elaborate royal court, as testified by dozens of ivory objects and epigraphic finds that name officials in the service of the king.

To the south, the kingdom of Judah also enjoyed a period of prosperity, although on a smaller scale than Israel. The center at Lachish was rebuilt; in the northern Lowland, where the fortified center at Beth-shemesh was destroyed, it was replaced by a modest settlement, which housed facilities of olive oil industry. Similar installations were unearthed in the southern settlement of Tel Beit-Mirsim, which became the second center of this industry. To the south, the Beersheba-Arad valley was dotted with fortresses (like Arad) and small villages that enjoyed the growing trade with Arabia, which helped support the royal center at Tel Beersheba.

Changes on the larger international scene would increasingly affect the kingdoms of Israel and Judah. The kingdom of Assyria had consolidated its control over Babylonia in the south and adjacent regions to the north and east, and by the 9th c. BCE was poised to expand into the west. At this point the fairly complete Assyrian annals enable the construction of a relatively exact chronology, and provide numerous synchronisms with biblical texts. Beginning with Ahab, king of Israel in the mid-9th c., some of the rulers of both Israel and Judah are mentioned in Assyrian sources, an indication of the growing, and ominous, Assyrian interest in the region. The Assyrians were establishing an empire, a process which reached its zenith with the Assyrian king Esarhaddon's subjugation of Egypt in 671 BCE. They overwhelmed the smaller kingdoms to its west, usually incorporating their territories into the empire as provinces and deporting large groups of the elite population to other regions, destroying their national identity and thereby suppressing their desire to rebel. By the late 8th c. BCE this subjugation was virtually complete. The Aramean kingdoms had been taken, including Aram Damascus in 732, and during the same time, the kingdom of Israel was partially captured by Tiglath-pileser III (cf. 2 Kings

15.29). The capture of "the land of the House of Omri" is mentioned by the Assyrian king in some of his inscriptions. According to the biblical description, supported by Assyrian inscriptions and by archeological finds, Samaria was conquered in 722–720 BCE, its ruling class and large parts of its population were exiled, and the kingdom of Israel became an Assyrian province—the province of Samaria. Assyrian inscriptions ascribe this destruction to Sargon II, although some later Babylonian inscriptions, and the Bible, ascribe it to his predecessor, Shalmaneser V. Akkadian documents found at Gezer, Tel Hadid, Megiddo and other sites testify to the presence of deportees from Mesopotamia and the Iranian plateau. Judah's territory was diminished, and in part because of the remote location of Jerusalem, was allowed to exist in vassal status.

The History of the Kingdom of Judah (720–586 BCE)

At the end of the 8th c. BCE the kingdom of Judah was part of the Assyrian world, which took advantage of the local economy and its products—the olive oil of the Lowland and the trade routes of the Beersheba-Arad Valley. Traces of this prosperity are visible with the expansion of Jerusalem and its fortification, and the rich material culture that was unearthed in its regional centers, such as Lachish and Tel Beersheba. Furthermore, the royal economy of Judah was reorganized with the development of the administrative system that was based on royal estates that produced olive oil; this was stored in special jars, some of them stamped with a seal with the word *LMLK,* "belonging to the king," that designated them as part of the court's property. Most of these jars were unearthed at Lachish and at other important Judahite centers of the Lowland. Moreover, many epigraphic seals, private and official, were found all over Judah, alongside standardized weights; these further indicate the involvement of the central government in the kingdom's economy.

This situation did not last long, and a vast wave of destruction brought an end to all of the centers in the Lowland and the Beersheba-Arad valley. Toward the end of the 8th c. BCE the Judean king Hezekiah rebelled against Assyria and attempted to reassert Judean independence. He was ruthlessly quashed by the Assyrian king Sennacherib in a military campaign (701 BCE) that is well documented in both biblical and Assyrian sources, as well as in the archeological record. Though the Davidic dynasty survived, most of the cities and towns of Judah were razed and Jerusalem avoided destruction only by paying a heavy tribute. Thus, just like Israel in the middle of the 9th c., Judah of the late 8th c. BCE was reduced to the southern Highland alone, cut out of the major economic advantages of the lower regions.

Archeological excavations in the Lowland have shown that during the late 8th to early 7th c. BCE, another shift of power in the region occurred, altering the geopolitical array once again, this time from Judah in the Highland back to a Lowland city—Ekron. Following 200 years of being a small town in the fringe of Judah, Ekron expanded once again to comprise its earlier fifty acre extent, now containing more than 100 installations of olive oil industry. Similar installations were unearthed in its satellite town of Tel Batash. Other significant Judahite centers were left in ruins, both in the Lowland and in the Beersheba-Arad valley, while the region of Jerusalem flourished with many settlements in its vicinity and in the Benjamin Plateau, along with the foundation of an administrative center at Ramat Raḥel, dominating the royal estates in its vicinity.

This change occurred only in the late 7th c. BCE, after the withdrawal and fall of the Assyrian empire. By the late 7th c. the Assyrian empire was overextended, and was unable to prevent its former vassals from reasserting their independence; it was eventually overthrown at the end of the 7th c. by a resurgent Babylonia to its south. The Babylonians captured the Assyrian capital of

Nineveh in 612, and in effect took possession of the former Assyrian empire. In the initial years, Egypt and Judah attempted to reassert their independence from Babylonia. This was the time of the reign of the Judean king Josiah (640–609), whom the book of Kings compares to David, and whose accomplishments are magnified like those of his illustrious predecessor. Judah was likely able to re-establish control over some of the territory in the Lowland; Josiah's religious reforms of 622/21 (see 2 Kings chs 22–23) should be understood in this context. This is the historical background to the period when Judah re-established its Lowland center at Lachish, although Beth-shemesh was not rebuilt, probably due to the strength of Ekron, which still controlled major parts of the region. To the south, the center of the Beersheba-Arad Valley was established at Tel Iraʾ, alongside fortresses such as Arad, while the traditional Judahite center of Tel Beersheba was left in ruins. A further expansion occurred in the eastern fringe, where a royal estate was built at En-Gedi, on the shores of the Dead Sea, to exploit its natural resources.

The administrative system of the kingdom continued, as we know from the stamped storage jars, now stamped with a seal in the shape of a rosette (without the word *LMLK [lemelek]*). The control over the olive groves of the Lowland, alongside the trade routes of the Beersheba-Arad Valley helped foster a mature Judahite economy and culture. This maturity is seen in the use of written documents, unearthed at Jerusalem, Lachish, Tel Iraʾ and the Beersheba-Arad fortresses, as well as the finding of epigraphic bullae, used to seal written papyri and/or packs of commodities, and the presence of Mesopotamian, Egyptian and South-Arabian finds, brought in through trade, in Jerusalem.

This intermediate period of limited recovery was short-lived. After Josiah's death in Megiddo (609 BCE) by the hands of Pharaoh Necho, Judah was again reduced to the status of a vassal, first to Egypt, and then, by the end of the 7th c. BCE to Babylonia. Caught between two greater powers, the Judean kings Jehoiakim and Zedekiah successively allied themselves with Egypt, which proved to be the weaker partner. Under Nebuchadrezzar (also called Nebuchadnezzar) II, the Babylonians laid siege to Jerusalem in 597 and 586, in the second instance destroying the city, burning down the Temple, and bringing the Davidic dynasty to an end.

Archeological evidence reflects this destruction of Judah and Jerusalem. All of the major centers were destroyed, including the capital and the periphery centers of Lachish and Tel Iraʾ. The region of Benjamin, with its sites of Mizpah (Tel en-Nasbeh), Gibeon (el-Jib), Nebi-Samwil, and Tel el-Ful, was left intact, to serve the remnant of Judah in the 6th c. BCE.

This destruction by the Babylonians ushered in the end of an era. Despite the extravagant propaganda of the royal establishment, the Davidic dynasty was not permanent and its capital city was not impregnable. Jerusalem was destroyed, its Temple burned, and its population decimated by death and exile. Although a significant number of Judeans remained in Judah, autonomous control of the country became only a memory. Despite partial restoration later in the 6th c., exile in Babylonia transformed the religion of Judah into what would later be called Judaism. From this point on, a significant proportion of Jews would live outside of the land of Israel, without king, Temple, or priesthood. The Torah and other writings that would eventually comprise the Bible gained new importance in this period, filling the vacuum left by the destruction of the core institutions. The preservation and compilation of older texts, and the creation of new ones during and after the exilic period, preserved and developed the national identity of the Jews.

The Persian Period (539–333 BCE)

The Babylonian exile and the period of Persian domination that followed was a time of great transformation for Judean institutions, religious practices, and culture; it was also a time in which the fundamental continuity with preexilic traditions was reaffirmed and secured. When Nebuchadnezzar put down the rebellion of Judah in 586 BCE, he exiled to Babylonia a portion of the population, especially the ruling class and the skilled artisans. Most of the population, however, remained in Judah, where a subsistence economy was soon re-established. Although the system of regular sacrifices at the Temple was disrupted, the ruined Temple remained a focus for religious observances. The book of Lam. may preserve liturgical poems used on days commemorating the destruction of Jerusalem and its Temple. Little is known about the circumstances of those who went into exile, although it appears that the exiles were settled in a number of local communities in Babylonia, where they fared well, and were able to oversee their own internal and cultural affairs under the leadership of Jewish elders and prophets (see Ezek.; Isa. chs 40–55). Other exiles, it would seem, viewed the exile not as a sign of God's displeasure, but of divine weakness, and likely assimilated into the mainstream Babylonian culture (see Jer. ch 44).

The conquest of Babylonia by the Persian king Cyrus the Great in 539 BCE brought with it significant changes throughout the ancient Near Eastern world. In keeping with his policy of respecting the various deities worshipped throughout the empire, a decree by Cyrus in 538 (see Ezra 1.1–4; 6.1–5) authorized the rebuilding of the Temple in Jerusalem and the return of the Temple vessels captured by Nebuchadnezzar. In addition, Cyrus allowed the exiles who wished to return to Judah to do so. Within the exilic community in Babylonia the anonymous prophet known as "Second Isaiah" (Isa. chs 40–55) strongly supported Cyrus and urged the exiles to return to Judah. Although historical sources are few and ambiguous, it is likely that only a small minority of the exiles and their descendants returned to Judah, most choosing to remain in Babylonia. This latter group became the nucleus of a large and highly significant Jewish Diaspora community (Jews of "the dispersion," living voluntarily outside the land of Israel), which strongly influenced the development of Judaism and Jewish culture during the following centuries. A smaller Diaspora community also developed in Egypt, formed originally of Judeans (including the prophet Jeremiah) who fled there during the last days of Judah.

Notwithstanding the decree of Cyrus, the Temple in Jerusalem was not rebuilt until 520–515 BCE. The reasons for the delay may include the tentative Persian control over the western territories until after the Persians conquered Egypt in 525. In addition, the economy of Yehud (the name by which the Persian province of Judah was known) was weak, and various biblical texts attest to significant friction between the population that had remained in the land and the small but powerful group who returned to Jerusalem from exile with the authorization and financial backing of the Persian king. Conflicts with the neighboring territories also complicated the situation.

During the early part of Persian rule, the governors of Judah were prominent Jews from the Diaspora community, one of whom, Zerubbabel, was a member of the Davidic royal family. Davidic kingship, however, was not reinstituted because Yehud was not an independent country, but a province of the Persian empire. The province of Yehud itself was very small, consisting of Jerusalem and the territory surrounding it within a radius of about 24–32 km (15–20 mi).

Once the Temple was rebuilt, it became the nucleus of the restored community, and consequently a focus of conflict (Isa. chs 56–66; Mal.). The high priestly family, which had also returned from the Diaspora, became very powerful, and at least on one occasion clashed with the governor appointed by the Persian king. Those Jews whose ancestors had been in exile and those whose ancestors had remained in the land were at odds. Those who returned from the Diaspora styled themselves the "children of the exile" and referred rather contemptuously to the rest as "people of the land," as though their very status as Jews was in question.

In fact, the definition of the community was one of the most contentious issues of the period, reflected both in the controversy over mixed marriages between Jewish men and ethnically foreign women (Ezra ch 10; Neh. ch 13) and also in conflicts within the Jewish community over who had the right to claim the traditional identity as descendants of "Abraham" and "Israel" (see Isa. chs 55–66, esp. 63.16). Although cast in religious terms, these conflicts were also in part socioeconomic (see Neh. ch 5). All of these disputes and efforts toward redefinition of the community took place under Persian imperial control. Thus it is no accident that the two most prominent figures involved in various reforms of mid-5th c. Yehud, Ezra and Nehemiah, were Diaspora Jews of high standing, carrying out tasks that had been specifically authorized by the Persian kings.

Because this was a period of self-conscious reconstruction, it was also a time of immense literary activity, as traditional materials were collected, revised, and edited, and new works composed. Although much of the Torah may have existed earlier in various forms, it was probably reworked during the Persian period into something close to its final form. Although a work called by modern scholars the Deuteronomistic History (Deut. through 2 Kings), outlining the history of Israel from right before its entrance into Canaan until the end of the kingdom of Judah, had been composed during the latter years of the monarchy and updated during the exile, a new version of that history, forming most of the book of Chron., was prepared during the very end of the Persian period or even a bit later (ca. 350–300 BCE). It clearly reflects the concerns of the postexilic community, focusing almost exclusively on the history of Judah and placing particular emphasis on the institution of the Temple.

In addition to the prophetic books composed at this time (Isa. chs 56–66, Hag., Zech., Mal., and perhaps Joel), older prophetic writings were edited and reinterpreted. Psalmody is assumed to have been an important element of worship in the First Temple, but appears to have taken on an even more significant role in the Second Temple. Although the expansion and revision of the book of Ps. may have continued into later periods, an important shaping of the Psalter, perhaps including its division into five "books," was part of Persian period literary activity. Wisdom writing, too, flourished during this time. The book of Job, parts of the book of Prov., and perhaps Eccl. were likely composed then.

The Hellenistic Period (333–63 BCE)

The westward expansion of the Persian empire into the area of Asia Minor, where many cities had been founded and populated by Greeks, brought Persia into conflict with Greece. Twice the Persians invaded the Greek mainland, but were defeated on both occasions. Eventually, Philip of Macedon developed a plan to free the Greek cities of Asia Minor from Persian domination. Although he died before he could undertake the campaign, it was taken up by his son Alexander the Great in 334 BCE. Alexander, however, did not stop with the accomplishment of that initial goal. In 332 he continued down the Phoenician coast, subduing any city that resisted, conquered Egypt, then turning to the Persian heartland, defeating Darius III, the last Persian emperor, in 331. Alexander continued his conquest into the eastern reaches of the Persian empire before returning in 324 to Babylon, which he apparently intended to establish as the capital of the empire he now controlled. He died in 323, before he could successfully organize his enormous territory. His generals then fought for control of portions of the empire. By 301 an agreement gave Egypt to Ptolemy and Mesopotamia and the Levant to Seleucus. Ptolemy, however, occupied most of the Levant. After a series of five wars extending over more than 100 years, the Ptolemaic kings finally lost the Levant to the Seleucids in 198 BCE.

Jerusalem had surrendered to Alexander in 332 and was relatively undisturbed by the events of his conquest. Samaria, initially surrendered, but rebelled in 332 and was severely punished: its inhabitants were killed or sold into slavery, and the city was refounded as a Macedonian military colony. Documents belonging to a group of Samaritans who fled and were later tracked down and killed by Alexander's troops were excavated from the Wadi Daliyeh in the Jordan Valley. In contrast to the relatively settled conditions immediately following Alexander's conquest, the territorial dispute between the Ptolemies and the Seleucids had serious consequences for Jerusalem and Judea. The wars sometimes affected Judean territory, at the border between the two, but more seriously, the nation's leaders had to make difficult choices concerning which power to support. The conflict between pro-Ptolemaic and pro-Seleucid factions within the Judean community thus became a significant factor in internal politics during the 3rd c. BCE.

The Ptolemies considered their territories important sources of revenue. They employed "tax farmers," often local persons who bought the right to collect taxes for a specified area; their profit consisted of the difference between the amount they raised and the amount they had pledged to the government. Some of these positions were quite lucrative. The Ptolemies also engaged prominent landowners to keep the peace as the heads of locally organized military villages. The 1st c. CE Jewish historian Josephus preserves a long account of the Tobiad family, which served the Ptolemaic government in both capacities; his lively narrative reflects both the power and wealth such positions could afford as well as the dangers and conflict they often entailed.

The most significant cultural effect of Ptolemaic rule was the establishment of a large Jewish Diaspora community in Egypt, centered in the new city of Alexandria, founded by Alexander the Great. Jews had often migrated to Egypt during times of economic or political trouble (see Jer. chs 42–44). In the 5th c. a Jewish military colony in the service of the Persian army was established at Elephantine (Heb *Yev*, near modern Aswan). They worshipped at their own temple, though they did not offer animal sacrifices there, and remained in correspondence with Jerusalem concerning various religious matters. The various Aramaic documents found there (letters, contracts, marriage documents, records of legal disputes, etc.) provide an important glimpse into the daily life of this Jewish community in Egypt.

The Hellenistic Egyptian Diaspora was much larger and more influential than the previous small communities of Jews living in Egypt. Its origins are not clear, but during the initial Ptolemaic conquest of the eastern Mediterranean territory, Ptolemy I apparently captured Jerusalem and took many prisoners back to Egypt, where they settled. Later many other Jews migrated there, presumably for economic reasons. The community continued to grow, both in size and in prosperity. By the Roman period the Jewish population numbered in the hundreds of thousands, including many wealthy and prominent families.

By the middle of the 3rd c. BCE the Jewish community in Egypt had translated the books of the Torah into Gk, and over the next century or so, the other books of the Bible were also translated (resulting in the text we now call the Septuagint [LXX]). (See "Jewish Translations of the Bible," pp. 2091–2106.) A legendary account of this project is contained in the *Let. Aris.*, which claims that Ptolemy II Philadelphus (285–246 BCE) initiated this project so that he could have a copy of the Torah for the library of Alexandria. More likely, the translation was undertaken for the religious needs of a Jewish community that no longer understood Heb. The Jewish Diaspora in Egypt, as well as other Jewish communities, also produced a rich and varied literature in Gk and Gk language and customs influenced much of the Jewish community in profound ways.

Less is known about the Jews of the eastern Diaspora who remained under Seleucid control than about the Jews of Egypt and the land of Israel, but it appears that these Jews, like peoples of other ethnic groups, had access to economic and political advancement within the Seleucid empire. This success is reflected in some of the tales in the apocryphal book of Tobit and in Dan. chs 1–6. While they acknowledge that faithful Jews may be vulnerable because of their religion, on the whole these are optimistic stories with a positive view of the Gentile kings.

The eastern Diaspora was also the conduit for important religious developments that arose from the contact between Judaism and the religions of Babylonia and Persia. This influence is most clearly seen in the development of apocalyptic literature. Although it is more difficult to trace the path of influence in its earliest stages, the dualistic religious beliefs of Persian Zoroastrianism almost certainly contributed to the development of Jewish apocalyptic and to some of the ideas of the later sectarians at Qumran.

The eventual triumph of the Seleucid kingdom over the Ptolemies in the fifth Syrian war (198 BCE) had a profound impact, especially on the Jews of Judea. The Seleucid ruler Antiochus III treated the Judeans generously in appreciation for the support he received from the pro-Seleucid faction, granting an allowance for the Temple and various tax concessions, as well as confirming the Judeans' right to live "according to the laws of their country." Although relations began well, the more decentralized way the Seleucid empire governed its territories set the stage for a terrible conflict. The Seleuicid empire derived some unity, however, from a network of Greek cities established throughout the empire. These were not necessarily ethnically Greek but were cities that would receive a charter to organize as a *polis,* the Greek form of city government. Cultural prestige and economic advantages often led the leadership of Near Eastern cities to request such a charter.

The events leading up to the conflict between Judea and the Seleucid king Antiochus IV Epiphanes (175–164 BCE) are complex and not fully understood. In part they involved a struggle for succession to the high priesthood and the attempts of various contenders to secure the support of the king by paying him large sums of money. The first of the contenders, Jason, also paid to have Jerusalem established as a Greek *polis,* Antioch at Jerusalem. Neither of these acts in itself seems to have aroused much opposition in Jerusalem. The conflict was not a cultural conflict between Judaism and Hellenism, for Jews had already incorporated significant elements of Hellenistic culture, which they considered quite compatible with Judaism.

The crisis was sparked by the attempt by another contender, Menelaus, to buy the office of high priest. When he promised the king more than he could pay, he attempted to raise the money by taking golden vessels from the Temple. At this, a riot broke out in Jerusalem. Subsequent fighting between the forces of Jason and Menelaus convinced Antiochus that Judea was in revolt, and in 169 or 168 he retook the city and plundered the Temple. After further disturbances, Antiochus sent Syrian troops, which remained garrisoned in Jerusalem. Whether the status of Jerusalem at this point was a *polis* or a military colony is uncertain, but in 167 the Temple was reorganized to accommodate the religious needs of the Syrian-Greek troops. It was rededicated to Zeus Olympius, the Gk name for the Syrian god Baal Shamem, and an altar was established there to sacrifice to Zeus. Though Menelaus continued to preside as high priest, most Jews considered these actions to have profaned the Temple. In addition, the traditional practices of Judaism such as circumcision and observing the Sabbath were suppressed by Antiochus, perhaps with the cooperation of Menelaus. Since religious persecution in and of itself was virtually unknown in antiquity, it is likely that these changes were instituted to further economic and political goals. These decrees ignited the resistance known as the Maccabean revolt. Knowledge of this period is reflected in Dan. chs 7–12, most likely the latest composition in the Tanakh.

The Hasmoneans, Mattathias and his sons Judas Maccabeus, Jonathan, Simon, John (Heb *Yoḥanan*), and Eleazar led the revolt. Although Judas managed to retake control of the Temple in 164 (its rededication being the occasion for the institution of the festival of Hanukkah), it was not until 142 that the last of the Seleucid army was expelled and actual independence was secured by Simon. From then until the Roman conquest of Judea in 63 BCE, the small kingdom was ruled by the Hasmonean family, who ruled as both kings and high priests. The Romans would destroy the Second Temple in 70 CE, in response to a series of Jewish revolts.

[ODED LIPSCHITS]

Geography of Biblical Land of Israel

> I have come down to rescue them from the Egyptians and to bring them out of that land to a good and spacious land, a land flowing with milk and honey, the region of the Canaanites, the Hittites, the Amorites, the Perizzites, the Hivites, and the Jebusites (Exod. 3.8).

This divine decree reflects two fundamental aspects of the Land of Israel: its physical properties and its occupation by various peoples. This land, the homeland of the Bible, is shaped by a unique combination of topography, mountains, sea, and desert. The civilizations that developed in this land were affected by these local physical features, as well by its location at the crossroads of the great civilizations of the time, Egypt to the south, Hatti to the north and Assyria and Babylonia to the east.

The term *the Land of Israel* occurs infrequently in the Hebrew Bible, referring either generally to the territory inhabited by the Israelites or specifically to the territory of the Northern Kingdom of Israel. Much more common is the term *the Land of Canaan*. Referring to the former inhabitants of the promised land, from whom it was about to be conquered, this term occurs over fifty times in the first six books of the Bible. Its extent is described in different ways in several biblical texts, including Num. ch 34, which delineates an area from the Mediterranean Sea in the west to the Jordan River in the east, the Beer-sheba Valley in the south and the northern slopes of Mt. Lebanon in the north. This area—which excludes Transjordan, the area to the east of the Jordan River—overlaps approximately with the Asian territory that was ruled by Egypt during the second half of the second millennium BCE; the biblical term "Canaan" probably echoes one of the names of this province. Several biblical passages mention *the land of the Amorites*, typically referring to the Transjordan, though in some cases the Amorites are mentioned together with the Canaanites and other nations as the primary residents of the promised land (e.g., Exod. 3.17). These many, varying lists of the nations of Canaan, reflect the mixed ethnic population of the land during biblical times, and may echo the results of the turbulent demographic history of the Levant during the second millennium BCE. Several accounts of the promised land take the Euphrates and the Nile as its extremes (e.g., Gen. 15.18). Israel never controlled this vast territory; such accounts reflect a utopian vision that overlaps with the territory of the western provinces of the eastern empires of late biblical period (known as "Beyond the River"; e.g., Ezra 8.36), which stretches between Mesopotamia, Asia Minor, and Egypt.

Sources

Both ancient and modern sources aid in the reconstruction of the geography of the land. Ancient written documents are the bridge that enables the modern student to get closer to the ancient reality. Only a small number of extrabiblical sources from the biblical period are helpful (e.g., Egyptian topographical lists and the Amarna Letters), while several early postbiblical works, especially Jewish Hellenistic (e.g., the book of Macc.), rabbinic literature, and early Christian (e.g., the *Onomasticon* of Eusebius), provide useful geographical information that preserve local traditions concerning biblical places and events. The Bible is undoubtedly the most important source for geographical information concerning ancient Israel. All genres—e.g., narrative, prophecy and law—contain valuable geographical information either as a natural part of the content or as geographical notes or glosses.

Certain biblical genres contain specific and detailed geographical information. One such genre is topographical lists, which occasionally appear within a narrative, and provide a synchronic picture of a particular region at a certain historical moment. The original setting of such lists can be determined by comparison with other historical and archeological information. Border accounts and itineraries presenting place names in linear patterns provide especially invaluable topographical data. Border accounts preserve a synchronous picture of the land, its ethnic composition and administrative subdivision. The historian's task is to recover the most original form of such lists, and the accurate setting of the situation described. Itineraries systematically present information concerning journeys, and thus are of great help in reconstructing the toponymy of the land. Nevertheless, most biblical itineraries describe the journey of the Israelites in the wilderness of Sinai, and the sites mentioned seldom occur in other sources, limiting their usefulness to the general picture of these distant areas. Further geographical knowledge can be deduced from genealogies, many of which reflect geography. Using the common metaphor of family relationships, the authors of genealogies depicted the internal social, cultural, and political relationships between groups that were settled in a certain region at a particular time. (E.g., Ammon and Moab, both fathered by Lot, and cousins of Isaac [Gen. ch 19], represent adjacent, culturally related nations.) A careful examination of parallel genealogical accounts reveals the dynamic aspect of such relationships.

The archeological information recovered from excavations and regional surveys is the most significant modern source for understanding ancient settlement distribution and organization, as well as changes over time. Another important modern source is the Arabic toponymy of Palestine, that is, the names given to settlements after the Islamic conquest of the land in the 7th c. CE, after the decrease of the native Jewish population. These "modern" names preserve many biblical place names, despite changes in politics, religion, ethnics, and—above all—language during the last millennium and a half.

Physical features

Four parallel longitudinal features shape the landscape of the land. From west to east they are: the Mediterranean coastline and coastal plain, the central mountain range, the Great Rift Valley, and the Transjordan range. The features of each of these, as well as their interrelations, provide the background for most of the land's geographical characteristics, from natural features such as soils and precipitation, to man-made ones such as settlement patterns and road networks.

The coastline and the adjacent coastal plain are a strip of land, which varies in width from a few dozen meters (a few dozen yards; e.g., near Mt. Carmel) to several dozen kilometers (thirty-some miles; e.g., near Gaza), between the sea to the west and the hill country to the east (for this and the following discussion unless otherwise noted, see Map no. 1). The eastern part of this strip is mainly alluvial soil deposited by the streams flowing from the hill country, whereas in the southernmost part, the land of the Philistines, the soil is mostly loess, brought by the winds from the deserts of Negev and Sinai. Most parts of the coastal plain receive a fair amount of winter rain (on the average more than 400–600 mm [16–24 inches] a year), and several perennial streams are found from Jaffa (biblical Joppa) northward. From Mt. Carmel southward this strip accommodated an important international road (the "Way of the Sea"), and settlements tended to be located close to this route, to take advantage of land for agricultural purposes and to participate in international trade. Of less economic importance was the coastline, which consists mainly of various formations of sand brought from central Africa by the Nile and the Mediterranean, making it unsuitable for both agriculture and seafaring. On the other hand, from Mt. Carmel northwards, there is less sand and the coastline is occasionally rocky, a feature that makes it suitable for mooring, which prompted the development of several significant port cities, mostly further north along the Lebanese coastline (Phoenicia, see Map no. 7).

From the Israelite point of view, the most significant part of the land was no doubt the central mountain range that stretches, with only a few breaks, from the Negev (Negeb) Mountains in the south to the Lebanon Ridge. With only several peaks of more than 1000 m (3,288 ft) above sea level, the height of most peaks is seldom more than 600–800 m (1,969–2,625 ft), though the northernmost Lebanon Ridge averages 1500 m (4,921 ft). The central range receives an average of 600–800 mm (24–32 inches) of winter precipitation, and many springs of greater or lesser flow are scattered throughout the area. The economy of this part of the land depended on the deforested plots of fertile alluvial soils that accumulate either naturally in the mountainous valleys and plateaus, or artificially on the mountains' slopes.

The populated area tends to concentrate in a strip along the watershed, narrowed by the rugged mountain slopes to the west and the "rain shadow" deserts to the east. A "rain shadow" desert is an area that receives low precipitation because it is separated from the sea by a mountain range whose height causes a great part of the humidity brought by the winds to condense and fuse and then to fall down there as a rain, leaving a lesser amount of humidity for the farther lower areas on its other side. These areas, such as the Judean Desert, were usually used for seasonal grazing, whereas occasional relatively wet years or periods of security allowed the border of the sown area to move eastward. The Beersheba Valley separates the Negev Mountains and the Hebron Mountains, creating the southern border of the inhabited land during almost all historical periods. The southern part of the central hill country, that is, the territory of the kingdom of Judah, consists of numerous plateaus along the watershed.

Broadening Judah's sown area is the Shephelah (lit. "Lowland") along the western foothills. Its soft inclines and spacious valleys afforded easy living, agriculture, and transportation.

The territory of the kingdom of Israel, that is, the northern part of the central hill country, and Galilee, is different; it consists of several latitudinal valleys, such as the valleys of Shiloh, Shechem, and Dothan (see Map no. 5). Most important of these are the valleys of Jezreel and Beth-shean (see Map no. 3) that divide the hill country of Samaria and Galilee; these are the only real breaks in the mountainous chain. The area enjoys fair precipitation and has many springs of plentiful flow, and vast areas of rich alluvial soil, which were always of a great economic importance, in both aspects of agriculture and transportation.

The third longitudinal feature, the Great Rift Valley is a depression that stretches from the Red Sea through the Gulf of Eilat (biblical Elath) to the Orontes Valley in modern Syria and Turkey (see Map no. 6). Several hundred meters lower than the mountain range on both sides, this depression is from six to fourteen kilometers (3.7 to 8.7 mi) wide and in the land of Israel half of its length is below sea level. The abundant winter rains that drain into the Lebanon Valley find their way to the Mediterranean Sea through the Litani River, whereas the poor rains of the southernmost part of this strip drain southward towards the Gulf of Eilat, mostly being absorbed into the earth on their way. The middle and main section of this area stretches from north of the Hulah Valley to the saddle in the middle of the Arabah and is a closed basin. Water, mostly from the east, collects in the Hulah Lake, and then flows southward twenty kilometers (12.4 mi) in the Jordan River to the Sea of Galilee, and continues through the Jordan another hundred kilometers (62 mi) to lose its sweetness in the Dead Sea. Only limited sections of the Great Rift Valley (e.g., the Valley of Succoth) were used for either agriculture or transportation, thus this strip is of less importance for the geographical history of the land.

The Transjordan Range towers to the east of the Great Rift Valley. Mostly over 1,000 m (3,281 ft) high and occasionally over 1,500 m (4,921 ft) (east of the middle Arabah) and 2,000 m (1.24 mi; Mt. Hermon), the peaks of this range are often no more than twenty kilometers (12.43 mi) from the valley. Creating a dramatic elevation change, this range forces the humidity coming from the Mediterranean to reascend to a level where it condenses and fuses and falls as rain. This makes the Transjordan highlands relatively fertile, allowing for prosperous grazing as well as grain agriculture. For this reason the desirable *terra rosa* of the Moabite Tableland to the east of the Dead Sea became disputed territory between Israel and Moab. For similar reasons, the volcanic soil of the Bashan that stretches from the Golan Heights east- and southeastward was often fought over by Israel and Aram. The great Syro-Arabian Desert borders to the east the Transjordanian Range. Finally, a second international road that crossed the land (the so-called "King's Highway," see Map no. 2) enjoyed the relatively moderate elevation changes of this range, giving it an additional geopolitical and economic importance.

Civilization

The end of the pre-Israelite period coincided with a massive migration of peoples that changed the geopolitical map of the Fertile Crescent. Marked by the migration of the Sea Peoples from the Aegean, this colossal event concluded with the appearance of some of the famous biblical peoples, such as the Philistines who settled in southwestern Canaan, and the Arameans whose expansion reached its northeastern part. The appearance of the Israelite tribes, as well as of their neighbors to the east—the peoples of the Transjordan states: Ammon, Moab and Edom—should be seen as part of this great human migration. Adding to the already complex ethnic mix of the land, these peoples changed the Canaanite-Egyptian political order of the Late Bronze Age. The Canaanites maintained their political dominance mainly along the Lebanon coastline, where they were known from the post-Canaanite era as the Sidonians, now called Phoenicians.

This population was settled throughout the land in permanent settlements and nomadic encampments. The biblical Heb term for a settlement is *ʿir*, usually rendered in English as "city, town"; it could refer to a permanent settlement of any size, large or small. Other terms designate an open settlement as opposed to a settled area surrounded by protective walls, but the term *ʿir* occasionally refers to both types. Accordingly, there is no biblical term for "village." Most of the population lived in permanent settlements, great cities such as the capitals Jerusalem and apparently also Samaria, administrative centers such as Lachish and Megiddo, country towns such as Libnah and Mizpah, and their "daughters," i.e., surrounding unwalled settlements (ancient "suburbs"). (See Map no. 5

for these locations.) Most of the inhabitants of these settlements were farmers, who made their living from grain and fruit agriculture and pasturage. During the biblical period, a gradually decreasing part of the population dwelt in seasonal settlements on the skirts of the sown land, raising herds and flocks.

The social horizon of the inhabitants of the land was not limited to their own settlements. Biblical evidence for roads, as well as accounts of journeys, indicate the existence of a developed road system. Unfortunately, there are several difficulties in reconstructing this system; on the philological side, the term *derekh* functions as both noun ("way, road, journey") and preposition ("via"), and can be read as either the starting point of a designated road, or a description of the route of a one-time journey. On the archeological side, very limited physical evidence remains of the road system of biblical times. This system can, however, be traced by other means. Occasionally, archeological finds reflect a line of contemporary settlements that suggests that a road connected these settlements. This picture may be supported by the physical layout of the land, as well as the remains of later historical roads.

The overall picture suggests a road network of local, regional, national, as well as international importance. Of the latter, two roads appear to have been the main trade routes between Egypt and Arabia to the south and Anatolia and Mesopotamia to the north: the so-called "The King's Highway" (after Num. 20.17) along the Transjordan range, and the so-called "Way of the Sea" (after Isa. 8.23, or its medieval designation after Isa.'s Latin translation:, *via maris*) along the coastal plain and across the central hill country south of Mt. Carmel. These two longitudinal international roads were paralleled by a national road that mainly followed the watershed of the central range, and by a few shorter regional roads. Connected to one another by several shorter latitudinal roads, they created the skeleton of the countrywide network. Crossing the central hill country and the eastern valley, the latitudinal roads tend to follow either the leveled lower part of a valley or the leveled upper part of a mountain range, keeping the elevation change and the lengthening bends to the necessary minimum.

The central location of the land of Israel between Egypt, Asia Minor, and Mesopotamia made it both part of different civilizations and a land-bridge connecting them. The resulting compound cultural environment is illustrated by the history of the languages and writing systems that were used in this area. During the pre-Israelite period, the land was governed by the Egyptians, who used Egyptian Hieratic (a cursive writing system for scribal use) for their internal needs and the Akkadian language in cuneiform script (the language of international relations) for correspondence with their Canaanite subjects. After centuries of Egyptian rule, the area experienced a half millennium of reduced foreign involvement, with only rare and sporadic raids by either the Egyptians or the Assyrians. During this period—i.e., the first part of the Israelite period—the local emerging cultures made use of an alphabet script, a local Canaanite development derived from an Egyptian writing system. This period came to an end with the Assyrian conquest of the western part of the Fertile Crescent in the 8th c., which involved a reintroduction of Akkadian and cuneiform script. At this juncture the Aram. language and script were also introduced; they continued to be used by subsequent Egyptian, Babylonian and Persian empires, through the beginning of the Hellenistic period.

Like many other Semites, ancient Israel oriented their geographical world facing the rising sun. All three sets of cardinal directions reflected in the biblical Heb are directed eastward. Most common is the set that follows the movement of the sun: *mizraḥ*—"the place of sunrise," or *moza'*—"the place of (its) exit," for east; *ma'arav*—"the place of sunset," or *mavo'*—"the place of (its) entrance," for west; the root of the term for north, *zaphon*, means "hidden," possibly hinting at the part of the sky which the sun never visits; the term for south, *darom*, not impossibly derived from *dur* "circle" referring to the route the sun takes from east to west through the southern sky. The most primitive (and probably oldest) set of geographical designations follows the human body, in which *panim* (face) or *qedem* (front) designate the east. Thus, facing the rising sun, the back or behind *('aḥor)* is west, *yamin* (right) is south, and *smol* (left) is north. (Thus the phrase *liphne* [derived from *panim*, "face"]—lit. "before the face of, in front of" should be rendered "to the east of" much more frequently than reflected in translations.) The first two components of this set are used to describe the timeline as well; thus "face" and "front" designate the past time, whereas "behind" refers to the (unseen) future. Finally, a parallel set of terms for cardinal directions uses the map of the land: *Negev* is south; *yam* (sea) is west; and *zaphon* is north, possibly after Mt. Zaphon, by the northern part of the eastern Mediterranean coast. (No term for east is certain for this set, although it may be *qedem* after "the sons of Qedem" ["Kedemites," Judg. 8.10].) Thus Gen. 28.14 states:

> Your descendants shall be as the dust of the earth; you shall spread out to the *west* [lit. "toward the sea"] and to the *east* [lit. "toward the front," or "toward the land of the sons of Qedem"], to the *north* [lit. "toward the hiding place" or "toward Mt. Zaphon"] and to the *south* [lit. "toward the Negev"]. All the families of the earth shall bless themselves by you and your descendants.

Though probably of different historical and geographical origins, the components of these three sets are sporadically used in the Bible, with no apparent pattern or distribution. They all share the notion that there are four basic compass points, an idea first attested in Mesopotamia that continues to this very day.

[AMITAI BARUCHI-UNNA]

Archeology and the Hebrew Bible

Hand-in-hand with the development of the modern study of the Hebrew Bible, from the mid-19th c. CE onwards, archeology has been recognized as a crucial tool for the study of the Bible and its cultural and material backgrounds. While earlier research placed a strong emphasis on using the archeological finds to illustrate the historical veracity of events described in the Bible—at times based on rather tenuous connections—in more recent times, a more judicious use of archeological remains has become the dominant approach of most scholars of "Biblical Archeology."

In the following discussion, archeological dating corresponds to the following standard terminology. Archeologists use a system of dating that relies on the technological level of the society. The time from 3600 BCE to 586 BCE is divided as follows:

Bronze Age: 3600 BCE–1200 BCE
- Early Bronze Age: 3600–2000
- Middle Bronze Age: 2000–1550
- Late Bronze Age: 1550–1200

Iron Age: 1200–586 BCE
- Iron Age I: 1200–1000
- Iron Age II: 1000–586

After 586 BCE, time periods are based on historical and political factors, as follows:

- Babylonian Period: 586–539
- Persian Period: 539–332
- Hellenistic Period: Begins in 332

Nowadays, the study of Biblical Archeology, which some scholars prefer to call the Archeology of Syro-Palestine, involves the excavation and study of material remains of the periods, cultures, and regions in which the biblical texts were formed and relate to. This ranges from the appearance of early villages and city states in the Levant (from the late Prehistoric periods, ca. 10,000 BCE) and until the advent of Hellenism (ca. 4th c. BCE), and from the Southern Levant (the Land of Israel and its surroundings), Egypt, Mesopotamia, Syria, Anatolia (modern Turkey), and to a certain extent, even the Aegean region, Persia, and Sudan. While the archeological evidence can, at times, provide direct evidence for events, processes, and on occasion even people mentioned in the biblical text, first and foremost the archeological evidence should be used to provide a broad-based cultural background for the understanding of the biblical texts, enabling correlations between suggested periods of the formation and development of the biblical text and the material culture which are reflected in the texts, and if possible, assisting in determining the dating and cultural background of particular texts.

The field of Biblical Archeology covers an enormous range of topics. The following essay presents major biblical places and events that are (or in some cases, are not) reflected in the archeological record, major archeological sites in the Land of Israel, various topics on which archeology sheds light (including daily life in ancient Israel, social structure, and the Heb language), and some of the major issues and debates in current research.

Places and Events

In the earliest days of Biblical Archeology, excavators searched for material evidence that corroborates the biblical text. Although there is archeological and historical evidence (from extrabiblical documents) supporting various events of the monarchical period (esp. the later period) recorded in the Bible, there is little, if any evidence corroborating the biblical depiction of early Israelite or Judean history. Thus, although attempts have been made to identify an early, pre-Iron Age (ca. pre-1200 BCE) *Sitz im Leben* (i.e., historical context or "life-situation") for the patriarchal narratives, the many anachronisms in these narratives (e.g., mention of the domesticated camel and of the Philistines) preclude a pre-Iron Age date, and the overall setting of these stories fits an Iron Age background at the earliest.

Similarly, attempts to identify archeological evidence for the Israelite sojourn in Egypt and the exodus have been unsuccessful. Mainstream archeological research has not succeeded in identifying concrete, specific remains that verify any of the details of these biblical narratives, though these narratives may recall, in a broad sense, cultural memories of connections between Egypt and the Southern Levant during the late Bronze and early Iron Ages.

For close to a century, scholars have debated if the archeological record in Israel reflects the conquest and settlement stories in Josh. and Judg., and have deliberated more generally concerning the processes relating to the appearance of the early Israelites in the early Iron Age (ca. 1200–1000 BCE). While at first many scholars proposed archeological evidence for a large-scale destruction of Canaanite sites at the end of the Late Bronze Age (ca. 1200 BCE), save for a small number of sites (which may have been destroyed at different times and by different groups—e.g., Hazor, Lachish, Yarmuth [NJPS: Jarmuth]), there is no evidence for wide-scale destruction at the end of the Late Bronze Age; this contradicts the main story in Josh.

Others have suggested that a slow process of infiltration from outside of Canaan occurred at this time, but once again, this may be seen only in a small number of sites, and the very strong connections of the early Israelite culture to the preceding Canaanite culture speak against this model. Therefore, many scholars have suggested, most plausibly, that significant components of the early Israelite tribes in fact originated within Canaan. Perhaps the genesis of Israel should be seen in relation to social dislocation from urban Canaanite culture, or, as many presently agree, within the ongoing oscillation between nomadic, rural, and urban subsistence patterns of the autochthonous population of highland Canaan.

While it is clear that the early Israelites shared many features with Canaanite culture, differences existed as well. The very different characters of their subsistence, level of technological sophistication, socioeconomic development and other factors, make it possible to speak of Israelites as distinct from Canaanites by the end of the second millennium. Various early sites from the Israelite period (1000–600 BCE) have been identified, such as Giloh, Izbet Sartah (a site between Aphek and Shiloh), Khirbet Raddana (close to Ai), Shiloh, Mt. Ebal and perhaps several "sandal sites," so-called based on their shape, resembling a giant footprint or sandal. These early Israelite sites are characterized by simple architecture without fortifications, evidence of animal pens and silos, and a very basic material culture lacking wealth and prestige items.

Several early Israelite cultic sites have been identified as well, such as at Shiloh, Mt. Ebal and the "Bull Site" near Dothan in northern Samaria. These sites and their material assemblage represent a change from the Late Bronze Age Canaanite culture, but, once again it is unknown if they represent new populations, for example, Israel.

From the same period, a much clearer picture of Philistine culture is emerging from the southern coastal plain ("Philistia"). The appearance and character of the Philistine culture mirrors the biblical description of a largely foreign group that often conflicted with the Israelites and Judeans. While formerly it was assumed that the Philistines represented a relatively uniform group of more or less single origin, one of a so-called "Sea Peoples" who each captured and settled along different parts of the eastern Mediterranean littoral, current archeological evidence indicates that they were comprised of groups of various origins, non-Levantine and Levantine, who combined together to form a unique, "entangled" (that is, composite) culture. Contemporary scholarship does point to one Sea Peoples group that settled in the Amuq region in Southern Turkey, perhaps called the *Palistin*—possibly a "northern Philistine" entity. The Philistines in Philistia underwent a process of cultural change throughout the early Iron Age (continuing into later phases of the Iron Age as well), retaining some aspects of their unique culture, while shedding others.

The Early Monarchy

Archeological evidence for the early stages of the monarchy is minimal at best. The attempts to identify the formation of a polity in the region north of Jerusalem in the late Iron I/early IIA (ca. 11th/10th c. BCE), perhaps mirroring the biblical tradition of the kingdom of Saul, are tenuous. The question of the existence of archeological evidence for the "united monarchy" of David and Solomon is extensively debated in contemporary scholarship. Most scholars in the mid-to-late 20th c. CE believed that concrete evidence of the "united monarchy" could be identified (such as the so-called "Solomonic gates" at Hazor, Gezer and Megiddo); at present, this is a highly contested topic, dependent on complex stratigraphic-chronological issues. Some scholars continue to believe that the united monarchy was a large and prosperous kingdom, mirroring to a large extent the image portrayed in the biblical text; others suggest that there was a kingdom of David and Solomon but of a minor scale; still others question the very existence of this early kingdom and see it instead as a literary creation of the later Judean kingdom, or even post-Iron Age times, after the 6th c. BCE. This debate is connected to whether, in the eyes of various scholars, there was an initial "united monarchy" followed by a divided northern and southern kingdom, or whether the Northern Kingdom was the first substantial polity, and only later, with its weakening and destruction in the 8th c. BCE, did the southern Judean kingdom create a narrative claiming primacy. In any case, the lack of substantive epigraphic materials from this early stage of the Iron Age II (after 1000 BCE), and other extensive archeological evidence, indicate that even if an early united monarchy existed, its level of political and bureaucratic complexity was not as developed as the biblical text suggests. The mention of the "House of David" in the Tel Dan inscription, which dates to the mid/late 9th c. BCE, does not prove the existence of an extensive Davidic kingdom in the early 10th c. BCE, but does indicate a Judean polity during the 9th c. that even then associated its origin with David. In addition, the archeological record indicates that Judah was becoming more powerful by the late 9th c. Some scholars see the Tel Dan inscription as evidence for a historical David, and find a royal palace in the City of David in Jerusalem, and find Khirbet Qeiyafa (an ancient city overlooking the Elah Valley) in the Shephelah, to have been at one time an important Davidic city, but their evidence is inconclusive.

The Sheshonq/Shishaq campaign of ca. 925 BCE, in which this Egyptian Pharaoh of the 22nd Dynasty (Sheshonq I) campaigned to the Levant, may offer the first interface between the archeological remains, and biblical (see 1 Kings 14.25–26) and nonbiblical records. Some scholars have identified specific destruction layers from this period at sites in the Levant, even identifying finds relating to the campaign (such as the fragment of the Sheshonq stela at Megiddo, and most recently, a Sheshonq scarab at Faynan), or attempting to explain changes in settlement patterns as reflecting this event. Some scholars believe that the supposedly clear cut archeological evidence reflects an Egyptian attempt to curtail the geopolitical status of the "united monarchy" and its successor. Other scholars, however, have dated the various destruction levels that supposedly relate to this campaign differently; the very dating of specific archeological strata to the late 10th c. BCE is highly contested (see below).

Remains from the 9th c. BCE northern Israelite kingdom provide ample archeological evidence of a substantial rise in the level of sociopolitical complexity. Signs of developed urbanism—including fortifications, palaces, water systems, stables, socioeconomic hierarchy—along with evidence of international trade and the beginning of more extensive literacy, indicate that substantial change occurred during this period. This evidence accords well with Assyrian documents and inscriptions on the role that the kingdom of Israel, and the Omride Dynasty in particular, played in Levantine region politics, and is mirrored as well in the regional role of this kingdom in the biblical text. At this time, the kingdom of Israel was embroiled in a geopolitical struggle with the Arameans, in particular under the reign of Hazael of Damascus. Various destruction layers at sites in the north and south of the Levant have been related to these events (e.g., Reḥov [ca. 5 km south of Beth-shean], Jezreel, Gath, Beit Zayit [a modern village in Israel 7 km west of Jerusalem] and others).

During the 8th c. BCE, and in particular during its second half, both the kingdoms of Israel and Judah became much more visible, from an archeological and historical perspective. By then, both kingdoms had reached a higher level of sociopolitical complexity, as shown by the unambiguous archeological evidence in many urban and rural contexts. In addition, their expanding role in regional geopolitics is reflected in various Neo-Assyrian texts.

Several noteworthy events and processes are reflected in the archeological record. During the early 8th c. both Israel and Judah show evidence of expanded cities with various manifestations of socioeconomic complexity, such as foreign trade. Examples can be seen for the Northern Kingdom at sites such as Samaria, Megiddo, Hazor and Dor, and for the Southern Kingdom in Jerusalem, Beth-shemesh, Lachish and Tel Sheva (biblical Beer-sheba). The earthquake mentioned in Amos 1.1, dating to ca. 760 BCE, left a clear archeological imprint at several sites such as Hazor, Gezer and Tel es-Safi/Gath (35 km/22 mi northwest of Hebron; possibly the Philistine city of Gath). The archeological record clearly reflects the encroachment of the Neo-Assyrian empire into this region. Destructions relating to the 733 BCE campaign of Tiglath-pileser III are seen at various sites (e.g., Dan, Hazor, Tel Kinrot [biblical town of Chinnereth on the northwestern shore of the Sea of Chinnereth]), and the final destruction of the Northern Kingdom in 722/20 is evidenced at Samaria. The fall of Samaria had a direct influence on the southern kingdom of Judah as well, due to the influx of refugees from the Northern Kingdom.

In the south, the Assyrian campaigns are evident in Philistia (such as the destruction of Ashdod relating to Sargon II's campaign of 713 BCE), especially the campaign of Sennacherib in 701. Archeological evidence of this campaign is seen at several sites, most impressively at Lachish, Level III, where there is conclusive evidence of the Assyrian siege and conquest of the city. This dovetails nicely with the Assyrian reliefs in the palace of Sennacherib, and the biblical and Assyrian textual evidence.

Although the Assyrian and biblical texts inform us of the Assyrian siege of Jerusalem, very little, if any, archeological evidence corroborates this. Prior though to this campaign, Jerusalem was expanded, and the "Western Hill" was settled. In addition, the hinterland of Jerusalem and also in the Judean Hills and the Judean Shephelah saw a substantial expansion of the urban and rural settlement, and material evidence indicates that various sites and regions (such as the western Shephelah and eastern Philistia, including sites such as Tel es-Safi/Gath), were taken over by the Judeans. These processes are related both to the expansionist policies of King Hezekiah of Judah (late 8th to early 7th c.), and, perhaps, to the overflow of refugees from the Northern Kingdom to the south after the conquest of Samaria in 722/720.

Important evidence of the Judean preparations for the siege in 701 is seen in the evidence of fortification and supplies sent out before the campaign. The latter are reflected in the jars stamped with *LMLK*, "of/belonging to the king," which begin to appear in this period. As a result of the defeat in 701, the Judean settlements in the Shephelah and perhaps in other regions as well, were severely curtailed, and many of the sites that were occupied before the campaign were abandoned subsequently.

In the late 8th c., and throughout much of the 7th c., the Assyrian control in the Southern Levant in general, especially in the regions of Phoenicia, Israel, Judah, and Philistia, is strongly felt. Assyrian textual evidence celebrates their strong presence and influence in the region, and archeological sites attest directly to Assyrian presence, in the form of palaces and forts of the Assyrian administration, such as at Samaria, Ashdod, Jemmeh (a site 12 km / 7 mi due south of Gaza), and Tel Sera (Ziklag?). Similarly, economic developments in Phoenicia and Philistia, most clearly seen at Philistine Ekron, confirm the strong Assyrian economic and political influence in the region.

In the 7th c. (in particular in the second half) the Judean kingdom flourished, even if its expansion to the west was stopped by the Assyrians. Both in the heartland of Judah, in and around Jerusalem, but also in the northern Negev and the Judean desert, extensive settlement activities can be seen. Large-scale building in Jerusalem, along with that at many rural sites, indicates this prosperity, mirroring the Assyrian evidence that the Judean kingdom was a loyal Assyrian vassal at the time. This evidence that Judah flourished during the 7th c. BCE concurs with the commonly held view that this period, in particular the second half of this century, was a time of cultural "renaissance"—a time to which many scholars would date various biblical texts (in particular, those related to the "Deuteronomist").

Only towards the end of the 7th c. BCE, when the Assyrian control of the Levant waned, and the Babylonians and Egyptians vied for control of this region, is this growth and flourishing curtailed. This is blatantly indicated in the Bible both by the death of King Josiah of Judah at Megiddo in 609 BCE, and the following period of political instability and rapid changes in the Judean kingdom. The 7th c. BCE, in contrast to earlier periods, reflects more extensive evidence of writing and literacy in the Judean kingdom, including the Arad Letters, the Lachish Letters, and many inscribed bulla (seal-ring impressions)—including several which mention names found in the Bible. The Heb language used in these extrabiblical inscriptions is virtually identical to the "Classical Biblical Hebrew," the dialect of Heb found in large sections of the Torah, and most of the Former Prophets, and some of the classical prophets such as Amos and the first part of Isa. These inscriptions thus contain, according to most scholars, important circumstantial evidence for the dating of these biblical texts.

The Assyrian, Babylonian and biblical sources inform us that during the late 7th and early 6th c. BCE, the Judean kingdom was caught in a maelstrom of geopolitical interests, particularly those of the Babylonians and the Egyptians. While there is little archeological evidence of the dramatic political events depicted in the Bible, as various Judean kings decided whether they wanted to ally with Egypt or Babylonia, clear-cut evidence of the final destruction of the kingdom at the hands of the Babylonians ca. 586 BCE is seen at many sites, such as at Jerusalem and Lachish, and at other small sites throughout the kingdom. The fate of the Philistine cities was similarly sealed, and there is ample archeological evidence of the 604 BCE campaign of Nebuchadnezzar of Babylonia which destroyed the remaining Philistine cities (Ashkelon, Ashdod, Ekron and Gaza), and exiled the surviving population to Babylonia.

Following the Babylonian destructions, clear evidence points to a change in the character of the settlement patterns in Judah, Philistia and the surrounding regions. While scholars hotly debate whether or not the entire land of Judah was deserted and only repopulated decades later during the period of Persian rule (late 6th c. BCE), it is evident that major changes did occur which set the stage for the development of early Second Temple Judaism in the Persian province of Yehud, and in parallel, the development of other regional cultures, such as the Phoenicians along the coast and the Samaritans in the highlands north of Jerusalem.

Major Archeological Sites in the Land of Israel

Jerusalem

Early Jerusalem was concentrated on the southeastern ridge (the "City of David") with finds commencing from the late fourth millennium. The evidence for Iron Age Jerusalem is quite complex. The city of David contains some early Iron Age material, followed by, according to some scholars, evidence of 10th c. development. The City of David shows a continuous sequence of Iron Age settlement and construction, ending with impressive evidence of the fiery Babylonian destruction of 586. From the 8th c. through the end of the Iron Age, Jerusalem expanded to the west and north, with striking finds, including fortifications and houses and tombs, as well as the so-called "Broad Wall" in the Jewish Quarter of modern day Jerusalem, and various tombs—including those at Ketef Hinnom to the west of the city in which two silver scrolls containing a version of Num. 6.24–25 (the "priestly blessing") were found. The royal quarters and Temple area for the most part are located under the later remains of the present day Temple Mount, so they cannot be excavated. While it is very likely that the First Temple—possibly built already by Solomon as claimed in the Bible—was originally located in the same place as the Dome of the Rock, later building activities have obliterated all evidence for this structure.

Megiddo

This is one of the most important sites for biblical archeology; extensive excavations have uncovered remains of a more or less continuous settlement from late prehistoric through Classical periods. The Iron Age remains reflect various stages of the pre-monarchic and monarchic periods, particularly in relationship to the Northern Kingdom of Israel. The dating and historical relationships of various levels and features at the site have been debated for many years; scholars disagree on whether its fortifications and gates are to be dated to the time of Solomon, Ahab or Jeroboam II. The fortifications, palaces, houses, stables and water systems offer evidence of the rich culture of this kingdom.

Dan

The Iron Age I may show evidence of an early Israelite settlement, possibly connected with southern parts of the country, perhaps reflecting in some manner the biblical story of the southern origins of the Danites (see esp. Judg. chs 17–18). During Iron Age II, Dan became an important urban site, which was settled until late in the Iron Age. During the Iron IIA and IIB the site was fortified, and included an important cultic center (once again apparently referred to in the biblical texts as well—see e.g., 1 Kings 12.29), and was the focus of ongoing conflicts between Israel and the Arameans. This is reflected in the royal Aramean inscription (the so-called "Beth David" inscription), mostly likely set up at the site by Hazael of Aram-Damascus after conquering the site.

Hazor

Settled initially in the early Iron Age by people of apparent Israelite affiliation, during the Iron Age II it becomes a central city of the Northern Kingdom of Israel, with substantial evidence of fortifications, public and private architecture, a water system and other features. The site most likely served as a regional government center throughout the time of the monarchy. The site was destroyed by Tiglath-pileser III.

Reḥov

Excavations here provide one of the most complete archeological pictures of the Iron Age IIA in northern Israel, even though this site, in the Beth Shean Valley, is not mentioned in the Bible. This Late Bronze Age city continued without interruption through Iron Age I. The Iron Age IIA (10th–9th c. BCE) remains testify to a thriving urban environment. Various aspects of the material culture of this site indicate differences from other northern, Israelite material culture, suggesting a slightly different origin of its inhabitants (Canaanite? Aramean?). One of several small inscriptions from the 10th and 9th centuries BCE mentions the name Nimshi, the father/grandfather of biblical Jehu (1 Kings 19.16; 2 Kings 9.2). A large-scale honey and beeswax facility, unique in the ancient Near East, suggests that the honey was used in religious contexts there; this may explain the biblical prohibition of the use of honey in sacrificial offerings (e.g., Lev. 2.11).

Samaria

This site was founded in the Iron IIA, and soon became the capital of the Northern Kingdom. Although much of the Iron Age city was covered or destroyed by later levels, impressive evidence of the royal palace compound on the site's acropolis remains. The finds from this compound include a collection of ivory inlays, evidence of the riches of the Israelite monarchy (see e.g., Amos 3.15), with important cultural connections with Phoenicia, and the collection of ostraca (writing on broken pieces of pottery) recording taxation sent to the royal coffers, from various places and clans around the capital. These contain a wide variety of names, providing an excellent window to the language and onomastics of the Israelite kingdom in Iron II. Most agree that these ostraca date to the first half of the 8th c.

Shiloh

Identified in the Bible as the location of the Tabernacle after the Israelites enter Canaan, archeological evidence points to a substantial Iron I settlement, and hints of sacrificial activity have been found on the site. The Iron I settlement was destroyed in the late 11th c. BCE.

Jezreel

Poorly preserved remains of a royal palace of the Northern Kingdom were found on the site, apparently the same palace mentioned in biblical narratives on the Omride Dynasty and its aftermath.

Dor

This site was a large Canaanite city. According to some, it turned into a Sea Peoples (Sikil) site in the Iron Age I, while others have suggested that the Canaanite culture continued at the site, with some influences from new peoples and cultures in the early Iron Age. During Iron Age II, the site came under the rule of the Israelite kingdom, as identified by its fortifications.

Gezer

A central site on the southwestern edges of the Israelite (northern) kingdom, with remains representing the various stages of the Iron Age. As with Hazor and Megiddo, the dating of the Iron IIA levels, and in particular, the fortifications, are debated.

Jericho

Despite numerous excavations conducted on the site in the last century and a half, there are very few Iron Age finds at Jericho, contrary to the central role it has in the biblical narrative of the conquest of Canaan by Joshua. This raises serious questions about the account of the conquest in Josh.

Mt. Ebal

An ongoing and very thorough surface survey of the Northern Central Highlands (the "Manasseh Survey") has uncovered numerous sites, including many dating to the early Iron Age. Several of these were excavated, several "sandal sites," so called because they look like sandals or footprints. Only a small minority of scholars see any connection between the archeological evidence at Mt. Ebal and Deut. ch 27 and Josh. ch 8.

Ai

The site of et-Tell to the east of modern-day Ramallah is identified by most historical geographers as the location of biblical Ai. As with Jericho, despite the fact that this site plays a major role in the conquest narrative in the book of Josh., no Late Bronze, Canaanite remains were found on the site, and a small early Iron Age Israelite village was found there, indicating that the traditions of the destruction of this site do not reflect an actual event relating to the early Israelites. Suggestions to resolve this discrepancy by placing biblical Ai at another location (e.g., Khirbet Maqqatir) have not been accepted by most scholars.

Beth Shemesh

An important site located in the northwestern Shephelah (Judean foothills); according to the excavators it continued to be a Canaanite city into the Iron Age I. Iron IIA (10th–9th c. BCE) shows evidence of public building, perhaps pointing to Judean control of the site.

The site continues to have Judean cultural character until the end of the 8th c. BCE, when it was destroyed, and subsequently abandoned in the Assyrian campaign of 701 BCE.

Khirbet Qeiyafa

Located southeast of Beth Shemesh in the Elah Valley, this site was fortified during the late Iron I/early Iron IIA (late 11th/early 10th c. BCE), and soon afterwards destroyed. The excavator identifies this as a Judean site, with typical fortifications, pottery, diet, cult, and even inscriptions, and sees it as proof of the existence of a Judean state in the 10th c. BCE. Others have questioned the cultural/ethnic affiliation of the site, and its dating.

Hebron

Limited excavations at Tel Rumeida, biblical Hebron, have revealed evidence of both Iron I and Iron II levels, with typical Judean finds. While it is clear that this site was an important Judean site during the Iron Age II, little else is known.

Lachish

One of the most important tels in the Southern Levant, it was settled from the Early Bronze Age to the Persian period. The large Late Bronze Age Canaanite city was destroyed at the end of the 13th c. or the beginning of the 12th c. BCE, but was not subsequently settled during the Iron I. The site was reoccupied in the Iron Age IIA (10th and/or 9th c. BCE), and became a central site in the Judean kingdom, second only to Jerusalem. Impressive remains of fortifications, a series of forts/palaces, public and private buildings, a water system and other remains, illustrate the importance of the site. The destruction levels in Level III (701; Sennacherib) and Level II (586; Nebuchadnezzar), the impressive remains of the Assyrian siege of 701, fit well with several biblical accounts of this event; and the "Lachish Letters"—a collection of administrative ostraca found in the city gate of Level II, dating to the eve of the Babylonian destruction, offer an important picture of the Heb language at the end of the First Temple period, and reflect the impending destruction of Jerusalem.

Tel Sheva

A site to the west of modern-day Beer-sheba with a series of levels dating from the late Iron Age I until the end of the 8th c. BCE. Following a late Iron I/early Iron Age IIA village, a small fortified city was built, including various elements typical of Israelite/Judean urbanism, including a gate, a "casemate" (double) wall, a water system, public and private buildings, and perhaps even the remains of a temple. The site most likely served as an administrative and trade center for the kingdom of Judah and was apparently destroyed in Sennacherib's campaign of 701 BCE.

Kuntillet Ajrud

This was a caravanserai (roadside inn) in the eastern Sinai desert, on the route between the north Sinai coast and the Gulf of Aqaba. Despite its location south of Judah, the cultural affiliation of the site seems to be mostly Israelite (Northern Kingdom) and it most likely dates to the late 9th /early 8th c. BCE. Excavations here uncovered, in addition to the caravanserai building itself, important inscriptions written on pottery and plaster, including reference to the YHVH of Teiman and YHVH of Samaria, and to Asherah (a goddess, consort of YHVH, or a sacred pole).

Arad

A site occupied from the late Iron I until the end of the Iron Age; during Iron II it served as a fort of the kingdom of Judah. Important finds include a temple, which apparently went out of use in the late 8th c. BCE, perhaps as part of the religious reform during the time of Hezekiah. In addition, an important collection of letters written on ostraca was found there, relating the administration of the fortress in the late Iron Age.

Negev

Throughout the northern Negev, settlements and forts from various stages of the Iron Age II have been found. Some of these sites date to the Iron Age IIA, and some scholars see them as evidence of the activities of the united monarchy in this region, while others believe they reflect activities of either earlier or later periods. Later stages of the Iron Age reveal forts and sites related to the activities of the Judean kingdom in this region, but also of the encroachment of the Edomites during the end of the Iron Age. An Edomite shrine was found at Qitmit, and an Edomite cultic area found at the fort at Hazeva.

Gath

A multi-period site occupied during the Bronze Age and onwards, it was one of the important Late Bronze Age Canaanite cities. During the Iron Age, from the 12th c. until the late 9th c. BCE, it was one of the five central cities of the Philistines (the "Pentapolis"), and during the 10th and 9th centuries may have been the largest city in Philistia and in the Southern Levant in general. Gath most likely was the capital of one or more important regional polities in the Iron Age IIA, and most likely dominated, or at least overshadowed, the Judean kingdom up until the destruction of Gath ca. 830 BCE. Evidence of the siege and massive destruction of Gath, most likely by Hazael of Aram Damascus (an event mentioned in 2 Kings 12.17–18), marks the end of this important Philistine city, and the shifting of its role to nearby Philistine Ekron. During the late 8th c. BCE, as part of the Judean expansion to the west, the Judeans occupied the city, until the Assyrian campaign of 701 BCE.

Ashkelon

It was one of the largest and most continuously settled sites in the Land of Israel. During the Iron Age it was one of the five important Philistine cities, with impressive remains from all stages of the Philistine culture, from the early Iron I until the city's final destruction, by Nebuchadnezzar the Babylonian, in 604 BCE. Abundant remains of the thriving 7th c. BCE city have been excavated, reflecting robust commerce, international trade (with various parts of the Mediterranean), daily life, various inscriptions, and religious practices. Following its destruction at the end of the Iron Age, the city continued to be important in the Persian and Hellenistic period, but with a strong Phoenician cultural leaning.

Ashdod

An important Late Bronze Age city which may have been partially destroyed with the arrival of the Philistines; it, subsequently became one of the five cities of the Philistine Pentapolis. Archeological remains represent all phases of the Philistine culture, from the earliest stages with so-called "Mycenaean IIIC" pottery and other finds, through the Babylonian conquest of Philistia in 604 BCE. Evidence, including mass tombs, reflects the destruction of the city by Sargon II of Assyria in 713 BCE. Following the late Iron Age destruction, the city was only resettled in the late 6th c. BCE in the Persian period, with Phoenician-oriented cultural remains.

Ekron

This site was settled in the Middle and Late Bronze Age. In the latter it is a small settlement, but during the Iron Age it became one of the five cities of the Philistine Pentapolis. Rich evidence of all stages of the Philistine culture has been found, including fortifications, temples in several stages, public and private buildings, industrial activities, and more. Of particular significance is the Iron IIC temple (7th c. BCE), built with strong

Assyrian architectural influence, in which a royal inscription, mentioning five of Ekron's kings, including Padi and Achish known from the Bible and Assyrian inscriptions, and the name of the Goddess of Ekron—Patgaya—of apparent Aegean origin. The site contains the largest olive oil production center in the ancient Near East, reflecting the economic and political prosperity and stability in the early 7th c. BCE (the "Pax Assyriaca").

Edom and Faynan

The Edomite cultural remains are closely connected to the cultures west of the Jordan. Copper mining activities were carried out during the Iron I and Iron IIA at Faynan.

Topics

Daily Life

Excavations at urban and rural sites have revealed a wide array of the facets of daily life in Israel and Judah. While, by and large, much of it is quite similar to that of other Iron Age eastern Mediterranean cultures, some aspects were unique.

A prime example of this is the so-called "Four Room House" (or Pillared house), found in numerous Israelite and Judean sites. Various explanations of the function of this type of house have been suggested, and its prevalence indicates that it did have specific significance within the Israelite/Judean ethos. Yet, claims that these houses are a definitive marker of Israelite/Judean ethnicity, *sine qua non*, cannot be accepted, as there are Israelite/Judean sites without them, and these houses also appear in non-Israelite/Judean regions.

Most Israelites and Judeans, both in rural and urban settings, led a relatively simple life, at subsistence level, with very little evidence of wealth. Evidence of typical Mediterranean agricultural practices is common, as are household activities such as baking, cooking, weaving, and rudimentary household production. While it has often been stressed that an abstinence from pork was typical of Iron Age Israel and Judah, recent studies have shown that this, by and large, does not hold true for Israel, but does seem to be the case in Iron II Judah. Ceramics, stone implements, and metal objects, in small quantities and of simple design have been discovered in various excavations, and very few imported items are found.

Evidence of mortuary customs is particularly well-represented for Iron II Judah. The most common burial was in a cave, with a shape carved out that may imitate the Four Room House, with rather simple burial offerings. A small number of more sumptuous burial caves, most probably of the elites, have been unearthed in Jerusalem and in Samaria as well.

Social Structure

As the case with most other societies in the ancient Near East, the majority of the Israelite and Judean population were relatively poor and belonged to a low social strata. There is some minimal evidence, particularly in the large cities, and perhaps in some rural forts and farms, of more elevated and well-off portions of society, with more access to prestige items, sophisticated technology, imported goods, and other resources. In Iron II Jerusalem, in particular, elaborate burial complexes reflect elite status. Some hints concerning the tax structures may be gleaned from the lists appearing in the Samaria ostraca, and hints of inequality can also be seen in the Mesad Ḥashavyahu ostracon, in which a poor laborer complains of unjust treatment at the hand of an employer or master. Indications of state and temple-related bureaucracy include seals and stamps of various officials, official "supplies" given out by the kingdom's administration (such as the *LMLK* and "Rosette" jars in Iron II Judah), possible depictions of royalty (at Kuntillet Ajrud and Ramat Rachel), and apparent evidence of vessels designated for religious offerings. These indicate the existence of state and local level administrative structures alongside various levels of a religious hierarchy. Ancient Israel and Judah was strongly androcentric, with sharp gender distinctions, like most ancient Near Eastern societies. While examples of women who attained high levels are known from the textual, epigraphic, and even archeological evidence, this is by far the exception rather than the norm. As in most ancient societies, the public space and functions were dominated by males, while in the private, domestic realm women had a central, and even de facto dominant role.

Religion and Religious Reforms

While there is no unambiguous archeological evidence for the centralization of worship reflected in Deut. (see esp. ch 12), there is much data on religious practices both in Israel and Judah, including remains of religious sites from the early Iron Age Israelite sites, such as at Shiloh, the "Bull Site" (in northeastern Samaria), Hazor, and Mt. Ebal (see above). Several important temples have been found in the Iron II kingdom of Judah; the most noteworthy is at Arad, and temples have been unearthed at Mosa (near Jerusalem) and possibly at Khirbet Qeiyafa and Tel Sheva. Smaller Iron II worship structures and cultic sites are known from quite a few sites in Israel and Judah, such as at Megiddo, Ta'anakh (an area south of the Jezreel Valley), Lachish, Kuntillet Ajrud, and perhaps even Jerusalem. Knowledge of religions from the surrounding cultures sheds important light on Israelite/Judean religious practices. For example, while Philistine practice is different in many ways, their horned altars are very reminiscent of Israelite religious practices. Various aspects of Israelite/Judean religious iconography, as seen on figurines, cultic stands, and other objects, demonstrate strong connections with Canaanite practices. Important insights concerning Israelite religious architecture, in particular those shedding light on the depiction in 1 Kings of the Temple in Jerusalem, may be gleaned from comparisons to architectural features of other Levantine temples, from earlier periods (such as at Hazor, Megiddo and Shechem) and from various Iron Age sites (e.g., the Iron II temple at Ayn Dara in northern Syria). Overall, the archeological evidence indicates that during the Iron Age, Israelite and Judean religion was not of the aniconic and monotheistic character that the biblical texts, including the Decalogue, might suggest.

Inscriptions, Literacy, Language, and Dating of Biblical Hebrew

While the number of inscriptions from the region of the Southern Levant pales in comparison with those from Egypt and Mesopotamia, nevertheless, over the last century and a half, a significant corpus of inscriptions dating to the Iron Age has been discovered. This includes finds from across the Iron Age Levant, and although it does not include libraries or archives, it represents a broad range of genres.

It is clear that while there was some literacy in Iron Age Israel and Judah, it was limited, particularly prior to the later Iron Age. Only from the 9th c. BCE, and in particular the 8th c. BCE, is there some evidence of the spread of literacy in Israel and Judah.

The development of many of the local languages in the Iron Age Levant is well-illustrated through inscriptions. The development of Heb from a Canaanite-based language is well-documented, as is the gradual influence of Aram., Gk and Persian, in the late Iron Age and the Persian and Hellenistic periods. This is important, inter alia, when considering questions relating to the dating of various portions of the biblical texts based on linguistic criteria, suggesting that most Heb texts likely precede the Persian period.

As expected few inscriptions relate to specific events, processes and even figures mentioned in the biblical texts. Rather, the inscriptions provide general cultural and material background for the Bible.

Current Issues and Debates

The field of Biblical Archeology in general, and the study of Iron Age Judah and Israel in particular, is very dynamic and changes quickly. Much of what was accepted just a few decades ago is being revised, and new methods and theories are constantly being applied—so much so that Biblical Archeology of the early 21st c. CE is quite different from that of the mid-to-late 20th c. The conclusion of this essay discusses some of these newer debates and issues.

Biblical interface: One of the ongoing and pressing issues in Biblical Archeology is the interface between archeological and biblical research. Time and again, practitioners in one or the other of these two fields justifiably attempt to utilize the research of the other field. While this is laudable, much too often the biblical scholar is not up-to-date with archeological research, and the archeologist is not up-to-date with the biblical research. Some archeologists continue to read biblical texts in a simplistic and straightforward manner—and look for the archeological evidence for this reading—without realizing that biblical scholarship has demonstrated the complexity and date of composition of a given text. It is crucial that biblical scholars and archeologists work more closely with each other.

Chronology: The dating of various archeological sites, strata and features is a cardinal component of all archeological research, and is particularly important in connecting specific finds to biblical events, persons, or periods. For example, until recently it was widely accepted that the similar gates at Gezer, Hazor and Megiddo are related to Solomon and the united kingdom of the 10th c. BCE. In the last several decades, an intense debate has developed between the "High," "Modified High" and "Low" chronologies of the Iron Age (the two central figures in this debate are A. Mazar and I. Finkelstein), and the dating of the various levels between the early 12th c. and the beginning of the 8th c. BCE has been the subject of intense disputes. (With the beginning of the substantial Assyrian involvement in the Levant in the 8th c. BCE, the lack of chronological clarity is resolved.) Perhaps additional scientific tools will resolve this fundamental debate.

Historicity: The earliest practitioners of Biblical Archeology used archeological remains to prove the historicity of the Bible, especially of specific events, stories and processes depicted in the biblical text. As is clear from the evidence presented above in this essay, the archeological evidence does not support the historicity of a straightforward reading of much of the Bible. Only toward the end of the Iron Age is there significant correspondence between biblical texts and archeological evidence.

Israel/Judah: While the existence of two separate polities, the kingdoms of Judah and Israel are well-documented in the Bible, until recently most scholars have stressed the similarities between Israel and Judah, and lump them together as reflecting "Israelite culture." This obscures clear differences in language, material culture, diet, cult, and other elements between the two. In the coming years archeology may help clarify the differences and similarities between Israel and Judah, and how they influenced each other in various periods.

[AREN M. MAEIR]

On the Bible and the Ancient Near East

Reconnecting with the Ancient World

Ancient Near Eastern inscriptions, monuments, and artifacts (with the exception of the Egyptian pyramids), and the knowledge of the ancient cultures that they revealed, were largely unknown to Western culture throughout the Middle Ages and the Early Modern period. At the close of the 19th c. as the Ottoman empire was breathing its last, European powers posted many missions to the Middle East that included archeologists. At first, essentially they were looters who took back monuments, many with hieroglyphics and cuneiform writings. When these scripts were deciphered in the mid-19th c., the inscriptions told an eager public about the world in which Israel was formed.

Mesopotamia

From Nineveh (present day Mosul) in Assyria, a cavalcade of rulers mentioned in the Bible—among them Sargon II, Sennacherib, and Ashurbanipal—took flesh to validate elements of the biblical accounts of the Assyrian devastation of Israel and Judah. Yet nothing was as sensational as the presentation George Smith made to the British Society of Biblical Archaeology on December 3, 1872. Reading from a Nineveh tablet, Smith revealed how a Mesopotamian hero (Utnapishtim, then read as Hasisadra for Atraḫasis) survived a flood the gods had sent to destroy humanity. The news stunned: Could the account of God's command to Noah have been cribbed from Babylonian antecedents?

There were other jolts: abandoned as a baby, Sargon of Agade was shown (in 1870) to have survived in a reed basket, eventually to earn divine favor. The god Marduk (in some versions Assur) conquered Tiamat (possibly cognate to Gen. *tehom,* "the deep") and rearranged its corpse in terms reminiscent of the creation in Gen. ch 1 (1876). From Susa (1905) came Hammurabi of Babylon's imposing law code stela that questioned the distinctiveness of biblical divine legislation. With all these antecedents to biblical lore, the hot topic around the First World War was which to credit, the Bible or Babylon, for stimulating our culture? Some of the debate (pressed by the German Friedrich Delitzsch, and labeled *Babel und Bibel* in contemporaneous journalism) degenerated into anti-Semitic diatribes; but it did stimulate scholarship (e.g., Form Criticism, best associated with Hermann Gunkel) that interpreted biblical traditions though comparison with Near Eastern, especially Mesopotamian, lore. The aim was to illuminate the contexts for the production, application, adaptation, and diffusion of themes and motifs that excited the mind in antiquity. In this enterprise, the focus came to be less on when, where and by whom Hebraic traditions were created (the focus of the earlier Documentary Hypothesis), but on how, why, and under which circumstances ideas commonly shared in antiquity came to have their particular inflection among the Hebrews. In effect, the Bible had come to be one more source from the ancient Near East, and a latecomer at that.

An industry soon came to the fore in the late 19th and early 20th c. in which specialized compilations "paralleled" the Bible, book by book, through excerpts from mostly cuneiform documents. In this way, a treasure trove of ancient material came to the attention of a wider public, with mythological *(Enuma Elish, Atraḫasis),* epic *(Gilgamesh),* cultic (hymns and rituals), wisdom, juridical, annalistic, and divinatory contents. These publications are precursors to more recent reference sets such as J. B. Pritchard's *Ancient Near Eastern Texts Relating to the Old Testament* (3rd ed., 1969) and W. W. Hallo and K. L. Younger, *The Context of Scriptures* (3 vols., 1997–2003). Here, however, translated texts tend to be complete rather than extracts and are arranged by genre rather than following the sequence of biblical books. In these reference works, too, selections come from a broad horizon, including lands and subjects only remotely associated with the Bible. Among the translated sources are those from ancient Egypt, which outside of Mesopotamia was the other locus of scholarly attention.

Egypt

Given its accessible monumental remains (pyramids, temples, tombs, and mummies), Egypt has enticed the wider public without being linked to the Bible. Still, at least since Josephus (1st c. CE), there has always been interest in finding Egyptian sources to confirm biblical episodes: Had Joseph not governed Egypt, second only to Pharaoh? Did Israel not live in bondage there for centuries? Had God not deployed "signs and wonders" when confounding Pharaoh? Did Solomon not marry an Egyptian princess? Since the decipherment of hieroglyphics in the early 19th c., the brunt of biblical focus on Egypt has been on the Late Bronze Age, specifically from the Hyksos through the 21st Dynasty (ca. 1630 to 1100). Israel is thought to enter (eisodus) and leave (exodus) Egypt during that interval. In the absence of credible Egyptian testimony, establishing a date and condition for the exodus (however conceived) has required the juggling of a broad array of circumstantial evidence, from many sources, and not always fully compatible. Not surprisingly, proposals have a limited shelf-life or they appeal to narrow circles. Totally unexpected was the recovery (since the 1890s) of Aramaic archives affirming a 5th c. Jewish (mercenary) presence in Elephantine (near Aswan), with contracts for marriage (earliest in attestation), syncretistic worship (blessings by YHVH and other gods), and references to the Passover.

By contrast to evasive historical confirmations, Egypt's literature has contributed notable conjunctions with biblical equivalents. Its sun-splashed hymn to the god Aten (Amarna period, 14th c.) has reminded many of the great Ps. 104 (see Ps. 104 n.); but with this linkage came much speculation on an Amarna period birthplace for monotheism as well as sensationalizing rewrites of the early years of Moses. Egypt's courtly love lyrics (13th c.) have illumined the study of the Song of Songs, in particular accenting courtly setting and erotic desire. Egypt's rich display of wisdom treatises (esp. that of Amenemope) has nicely enhanced understanding of Prov. and the *carpe diem* ("seize the day") urgings of the Harper's Songs that are often cited along those of Eccl. Many episodes in Egypt's arsenal of delightful tales are brought into comparison with those in the Bible, none as frequently as the attempted seduction of an innocent youth by a married woman ("The Two Brothers"), the life that Sinuhe created for himself in Middle Bronze Canaan, or the neat magician's trick of dividing waters to reveal dry land (see the "Westcar Papyrus"). In addition, the 14th c. Amarna Letters have offered helpful background for understanding the early history of Israel, including the origin of the name "Hebrew," connected by many to the Hapirus/Habirus that were frequently mentioned in those documents.

Anatolia

The recovery of cuneiform tablets from *Boğazköy* in the heartland of Anatolia (Turkey) had occurred early in the 20th c. Because many were in Akkadian and could be read, they confirmed the site to be Hattushash, the capital of the Hittites. The Hittites turned out to be Indo-Europeans; but a disposition to connect them with the *ḥitti* ("Hittites") of Scripture proved tenacious despite evidence of vast differences. In fact, the Hittites of the Hebrew Bible were mostly northern Syrians with populations that included Indo-European Luwians, who also wielded a just recently deciphered hieroglyphic script. The Hebrew writers got to know them best after Arameans dominated the region; that is why practically all Hittites in the Bible have patently Semitic names and are not related to the much earlier Hittites of Hattushash.

The bulk of recovered Hittite documents came from elite circles, and although they contained ritual, legal, as well as literary texts, the material that has delivered the most satisfying correspondence with biblical thought is historiographic. Embedded in Hittite annals and in penitential prayers are a powerful sense of obligation (covenants and oaths), a visceral urge for expiation, and an obsessive need for absolution; these themes are exploited extensively by many biblicists despite the significant chronological gap present between the Hittite and biblical texts.

Northern Mesopotamia and Syria

After the collapse of the Ottoman empire, western Asia was administered by the French and British, an arrangement that for all practical purposes came to an end just after the Second World War. In the interval, a number of sites began to disgorge tablets. Through such outlets as the *Illustrated London News* (before it petered out in the 1970s), an eager public learned of major finds as they were being made and in the process supported investment in more expeditions. These are noted below by the sequence of their first discovery:

Nuzi

Nuzi is located at Yorghan Tepe, east of the Tigris River; excavated from 1925 to 1931. Its family archives were from the 14th c. and they gave detailed information on the social lives of a Ḫurrian community. They were widely exploited, at first to give a late Bronze Age setting for the patriarchal narratives (see works of Ephraim Speiser; Cyrus Gordon). Some spectacular Nuzi parallels that clarified the wife-sister connection between Abraham and Sarah (Gen. chs 12; 20; cf. ch 26) proved to have false foundations. Comparisons that explained the Laban-Jacob marriage arrangements and their sheep-herding provisions have fared better; but they cannot be used to date episodes in Gen. because such practices had long duration in the ancient Near East.

Ugarit

This is Ras Shamra, on the Syrian coast; excavated since 1929. Its Late Bronze Age archives came from the palaces of merchant-princes and the houses of learned priests. Although they include documents in many languages, those preserved in alphabetic cuneiform quickly captured the imagination of biblicists. Until their discovery, knowledge of Canaanite (and Phoenician) culture had been drawn largely from the Bible, where it had been caricatured as fickle (many gods), seductive (cheap thrills), brutal (human sacrifice), and depraved (orgies). The first charge is arguably true; the others hardly likely.

The Ugaritic literature proved to be especially fresh and stimulating. Among the texts were the saga of a king, Keret or Kirta, who risked losing it all by making an unnecessary vow; the tale of Danel, who begged for a son only to see him killed by a petulant goddess; and a grand myth, featuring a dysfunctional pantheon, about Baal's struggles to deserve leadership of the gods. Characters from these texts continue to inspire scholarship; none more so than Asherah, wife of El, and Anat, consort of Baal. Especially since the discovery of inscribed jars in Kuntillet el-Ajrud (Sinai Peninsula, since the mid-1970s), Asherah is commonly discussed as an erstwhile partner of the Hebrew God. Yet, it is not often kept in mind that Ugarit was much more cosmopolitan than Israel or Judah ever were. As such, its pantheon was by no means limited to those evoked in the Bible and its mythmaking had broader applications than that shaped in Israel.

The language of the alphabetic texts proved especially useful. It shared with Heb a vocabulary (esp. as it concerned the cult, including the names of deities like El, Baal, and Yam), some grammatical constructions, and its poetry was comparable to biblical psalms. After a period of undisciplined exegesis based on Ugaritic, a modest number of biblical passages have indeed found clarity through application of Ugaritic principles. Still under debate is the value of dating the production of biblical verse on the basis of Ugaritic poetics.

Mari

This site is Tel Ḫariri, on the right bank of the Euphrates, 50 kms north of the Iraqi frontier; excavated since 1933. Its palace archives were largely from the 18th c. and they gave insight into the lives of Amorite rulers in the age of Hammurabi of Babylon, with Aleppo and Qatna proving to be major Middle Bronze powers. The site preserved records of diplomatic relations with Mediterranean cities such as Ugarit, Byblos, and Hazor, and documentation of trade with Cyprus and Crete (but not yet with Egypt). No direct links can be made as yet between Mari's Amorites and the ancestors of Israel, although a Yaminite tribal branch that roamed the environs of Mari may have eventually settled Benjamin territory near Jericho. (The names "DUMU Yamina" and "Benjamin" are identical in meaning.) An 18th c. cuneiform fragment of local origin from the coastal region (Siyanu, near Latakia) shows scribal procedures that are similar to Mari's. Startling and most unlikely is a suggestion that Amutpiel of Qatna is Amraphel of Gen. ch 14.

Many practices and institutions recovered from the Mari tablets show remarkable affinity to those in the Bible, albeit without direct influence. In particular, the biblical gift for storytelling, with its lively phrasing, vivid pacing, fine structure, and wordplays, is nicely matched in Amorite letter writing. Details on tribal configuration, covenant ceremonials, battle strategies, third-party marriage arrangements (as was Isaac's), and *matzebot* (stone monuments) installations, have all shed light on biblical passages. In the Mari age, treaty obligations were limited to the lifetimes of the signatories—unlike what would later develop in the Amarna period, when covenants were deemed to be eternal and permanent. This perception too has had application in studying Hebrew historiography.

More widely discussed are the origins and development of prophecy. During the reign of King Zimri-Lim, a concerted effort to consult the gods left us a rich dossier of visions, dreams, and prophecies. None is more biblically evocative among the latter than an admonition attributed to the god Addu (Hadad) of Aleppo in which a just rule is the price for divine support:

> I had given all the land to (your father) Yaḫdun-Lim and by means of my weapons he had no opponent. But when he abandoned me, I gave (his enemy) Samsi-Addu the land I had handed to him.... I brought you back to your father's throne and I handed you the weapons with which I battled against Sea [*têmtum* = Yam]. I rubbed you with oil from my numinous glow so that no one could stand up to you. Now listen to my only wish: Whenever anyone appeals to you for judgment, saying, "I am aggrieved," be there to decide his case and to give him satisfaction. This is what I desire of you.

Alalaḫ

Known as Tel Achana, in the Turkish Amuq Valley; excavated intermittently since 1937, its royal archives—some from the 17th c. and others from the 14th c.—include a picaresque (auto) biography of King Idrimi. A refugee from Aleppo, Idrimi grasped fate by the horns and shaped for himself a throne in Alalaḫ. The story, inscribed on a homely likeness, is full of folkloristic touches, inviting comparisons with the rise to power of such figures as Abimelech (son of Gideon), Jephthah, and especially David. While many individual texts—dealing with marriage, loans, wills, and treaties—are readily presented in the reference collections mentioned above, their contribution to elucidating biblical passages is decidedly uneven.

Biblicizing

More recent are the discoveries at Emar (Tel Meskene-Balis, by the Upper Euphrates; rescue operation 1972–1976; resumed since 1996) and at Ebla (Tel Mardikh, not far from Aleppo; excavated since 1964, but with stunning results after 1975). These two discoveries exemplify an older phenomenon that has spiked in our days, as information is delivered online with little lead-time for proper scholarly evaluation, namely a tendency to *biblicize* Near Eastern records.

To *biblicize* is to attach Bible-derived explanations to details in Near Eastern documents and artifacts on first exposure to them. The result then becomes evidence by which to clarify biblical contexts and passages. The logic is circular; the goal is to draw reciprocal benefits for biblical and Near Eastern lore by highlighting proximal parallels—and over time such commissions correct themselves. Occasionally, however, the process gives permanence to misconceptions. For example, just after the First World War, Leonard Woolley excavated Tel el-Muqayyar in southern Iraq, a site that covered Sumerian Ur. There he found evidence of a flood so major that he imagined it impacting biblical historiography and his suggestion resurfaces periodically in the literature.

Of more consequence was his recovery of an early dynastic tomb (27th c.) with the remains of a beautiful statue of a "ram in the thicket." For Woolley, the pose evoked a detail in the aftermath of Abraham's near sacrifice of Isaac (Gen. 22.13); thenceforth, "Ur of the Chaldees" (Gen. ch 11) became the name of the site. Woolley had actually found a bejeweled goat that was likely paired and balanced to hold a bowl. But the explanation took hold and it is practically impossible today to locate a biblical map of the patriarchal period without finding in it Abraham trekking from Southern Mesopotamia, a region that has hardly any mention in Hebrew recall of its origins. Similarly, when *Enuma Elish* (often termed "the Babylonian Creation Epic") was being deciphered, how Marduk shaped the cosmos was first read with Gen. ch 1 as a guide. The pattern and sequence of Marduk's creative effort are often used to secure a Mesopotamian background to Gen. ch 1, even if no individual act in the accounts matches securely and no step in the transmission charts reasonably.

The evaluation of Emar's records is still ongoing. The site has delivered a large variety of texts from a building of an official titled, "diviner of the gods of Emar." Along with some literary documents several elaborate rituals were recovered, among them a libretto for the installation of the High Priestess of Baal. Gathering the attention of biblical scholars is the unique sequence of activities for the *zukru*-festival. Apparently recurring every seven years, the ritual involved the citizens of Emar on the first full moon of the year, and extended over a full week. There were processions beyond the city gate, with stops at blocks of standing stones, apparently in a renewal of pledge to the god Dagan. For some scholars, this type of ritual comes from beyond Canaan and so might remind of renewal ceremonies among the Hebrews who likewise moved from inland Syria into Canaan. Yet, as achieved, the balance between the two institutions relies on outlines crafted much too accommodatingly. More significant for understanding the background of the Bible are juridical documents, with women playing major roles in guiding family life, even with male kin around.

Logic might have discouraged linking the extensive Ebla archives with anything biblical, for most of them date from the 25th c. on, when Israel was yet to be conceived. Indeed, Ebla depicts a society where the elite owned huge herds of sheep, with scant evidence of the nomadic life that was the remembered trait of Israel's ancestry. Ebla was a wealthy city in a region teeming with urban settlements and with influence far and wide. While the scribes relied on Sumerian formulae to maintain their records, we now know that the written language of the archives is reminiscent of Akkadian (so East Semitic), but with many West Semitic words.

William F. Albright, the architect of a major American school of biblical scholarship, had relied on Near Eastern archives to buttress Israel's version of its patriarchal history; but after his death in 1971, studies challenged his approach and conclusions. His supporters, therefore, turned to the Ebla archives to reaffirm his vision. Read with the then imperfectly understood Ebla syllabary, documents were thought to reveal the names of cities that played a role in Hebrew historiography, among them Sodom, Gomorrah, Jerusalem, Hazor, Lachish, and Gaza. Ebla personal names also seemed to have a biblical calque to them, among them Eber, Abram, Esau, Saul, David, and Israel. Because some names ended in *-ya,* plausibly a shortened form of Yahveh, some argued that the Hebrew god was already worshipped in Canaan. Even family tombs, of the type known at Machpelah, were shown to be typical of Eblaite culture, hence proto-Hebraic. There could be little reason, these scholars claimed, to doubt the Bible's accurate memory of Israel's earliest past.

The debate about Ebla's role in sustaining biblical historiography was conducted by eminent scholars on both sides of the Atlantic. It stretched into the mid-1980s before sharper understanding of Ebla's records took out much of its steam. Better knowledge of the script soon taught that there was no equivalence to any personal name found in the Bible and no uncontested mention of any place familiar to us from the land of Israel. Ebla was abruptly dropped from several tours of the Holy Land, alas for the wrong reasons. When in the early 1990s similar archives were recovered from Tel Beydar in northeast Syria, hardly any biblical scholar paid them mind.

The "and" of the Matter

Yet the risk of *biblicizing* must not be overstated. Despite the occasional endurance of skewed or hyped evidence, the process nonetheless brings many discoveries to the attention of a public that focuses best with the Bible as lens. The better message here is how to think of the conjunction "and" in "The Bible *and* the Ancient Near East." The two entities are frequently linked in this way, yet there is only coarse equivalence or match to the components. The "ancient Near East" is a geographical area, generally stretching from Egypt through Iran, with records long before the invention of writing. The label has meaning only in reference to an aggregate of societies unequal in power, intellectual worth, and lasting contribution. Some of these powers achieved regional control or intellectual primacy that lasted over centuries and occasionally influenced ancient Israel. In the process, they have bequeathed humanity a treasury of enriching concepts and ideas as well as models for evaluating the social experiment that became Israel. These achievements and models are for us to reconstruct by evaluating thousands of records that the modern spade recovers. However, none of the component cultures has left us anything remotely comparable to the "Bible," that is a shared scripture that has codified a people's religious, social or religious mores and has sustained a vision of a narrated past covering many centuries.

In contrast, for many the "Bible" is a distinct entity, with iconic status and special sanctity. But the Bible also emerges as a highly processed compendium of distinct efforts, each of disputed origins. When we search it to learn how Israel conducted its life—how people married, raised children, worked, and died—we develop insights by capturing tidbits from across diverse types of literatures (narratives, love songs, prayers, and the like), not all of them as attached to actual ancient practice as we would wish. So, we welcome what the ancient Near East, with its accumulation of more precisely targeted testimony, has to tell us about the lives of Israel's neighbors, and try to reach applicable conclusions through judicious comparison—after all, Israel partook of that world. After a century of such proximation, the inventory of biblical practices that remain as yet exclusively Israel's is now slim but significant: beyond the adoption of monotheism by a substantial segment of the population, they include circumcising males a week after birth, observing a seventh-day Sabbath, excluding women from the priesthood and from juridical transactions, legalizing cultic instruction, codifying purity and diet taboos, and regulating aspects of intimacy, dressing, and grooming.

So far, Israel's soil has been uncommonly stingy in yielding independent and datable records that might confirm the Bible's march of events. It is really jolting for us to acknowledge that so far no record from Israel or its neighbors has had direct or specific recall of any of Israel's storied ancestors and leaders, the first such validation surfacing when Ahab ruled Israel (9th c.). We should reason, of course, that the dearth of evidence is never a cogent argument against historicity; still, we might also keep in mind that what Israel wanted most to communicate through its literature is embedded in momentous exchanges between God and Hebrew ancestors, dialogues that are largely impervious to historical appraisal. One day we might recover from some tel a document that mentions "Abram son of Terah"; but what possible source could there be to substantiate the divine revelations that sent him off to the promised land or had him ready to sacrifice his beloved son?

Finally, the arguments detailed in Israel's accounting of its past aim less to chart an exact accounting of events than to promote a set of principles articulated in some biblical texts, including the ideas that there can only be one God, with no heavenly lineage or a recognizable form; that this God displays divine will through interaction with a chosen people; that this people must meet an elevated code of behavior worthy of that God; and that history progresses by commitment to a divine covenant rather than by adherence to international treaties. For this reason, short of uncovering a nice cache of extrabiblical records from Judah or Israel that might give living testimony of their social culture and historical experience, matching ancient Near Eastern records with biblical accounts will continue to be a challenge. Nonetheless, as students of Israel and of the ancient Near East, we cannot deny the accuracy of two momentous contentions advanced in our Bible: That ancient Israel has been exceptional in its capacity to discover the logic of monotheism and that it remained stubborn in its resolve to broadcast it as a historical truth.

Beyond this Essay

A handy and (almost) painless guide into the world of Israel's neighbors is through Jack M. Sasson (et al., eds) *Civilizations of the Ancient Near East* (2 volumes; Hendrickson Publishers, 2001). Kenton L. Sparks's *Ancient Texts for the Study of the Hebrew Bible: A Guide to the Background Literature* (Hendricksons Publishers, 2005) is a truly remarkable synthesis, for it surveys literary treasures from the Levant in an elegant and judicious way. Many of the works mentioned in it can be found in Pritchard's *Ancient Near Eastern Texts* and in Hallo's and Younger's *The Context of Scriptures*, cited above. Those interested in how ancient documents have affected our knowledge of Israelite history can now turn to a masterly, if generally conservative, overview: *The Sacred Bridge: Carta's Atlas of the Biblical World* (Carta, 2005) by Anson F. Rainey and R. Steven Notley.

[JACK M. SASSON]

Languages of the Bible

Hebrew and the Semitic Languages

The bulk of the Bible was originally composed in Heb, the language of the biblical Israelites, and the language that was spoken in the land of Israel until the end of the tannaitic period (the time of the Mishnah, ca. 200 CE). During the amoraic period (the time of the later Talmudic Rabbis, ca. 200–500 CE) it ceased to be a living language, although for Jews it remained the language of liturgy and literature until its revival as a spoken tongue at the end of the 19th c. Heb is a member of the Semitic family of languages, which on the basis of geography has been divided into three groups: Northeastern Semitic (Akkadian and its dialects of Assyrian and Babylonian, and Eblaite), Southern Semitic (Old South Arabian and its modern descendants, Geʿez and the modern Ethiopic dialects, and Classical Arabic and its pre-classical and modern dialects), and Northwest Semitic (Ammonite, Aram., Deir ʿAlla, Edomite, Heb, Moabite, Phoenician and Punic, and Ugaritic). Some scholars today prefer a different classification in which they distinguish between West and East Semitic, the latter of which is furthered subdivided into Ethiopian, Modern South Arabian, and Central Semitic; Central Semitic in turn is composed of Northwest Semitic, Arabic, and Old South Arabian.

Within the Northwest Semitic family of languages, Heb is part of the "Canaanite" branch of languages. Other members of the Canaanite branch include Ammonite and Edomite, both of which are attested in a few poorly preserved inscriptions; Moabite, the language of the Mesha Stele erected by King Mesha, which boasts of Moab's victory over Israel (see 2 Kings 3.4–27 for the biblical account); and Phoenician and Punic (the form of Phoenician in the western Mediterranean), which are attested in inscriptions and in Gk and Latin transcriptions. These languages share several linguistic features that distinguish them from the other branches of Northwest Semitic: Aram., Ugaritic, and Deir ʿAlla (attested in a text from biblical Succoth that mentions Balaam the Seer).

Alphabet

The earliest Heb inscriptions are written in a consonantal script that was probably borrowed from the Phoenicians at the beginning of the first millennium BCE. This script, like its Phoenician ancestor, was at first purely consonantal and did not mark vowels. The use of a script that does not indicate vowels can create ambiguity for the reader since a sequence of consonants can often be read in different ways with different meanings, for example, *km* can represent *kam* "he arose," *kama* "she arose," *kamu* "they arose," *kum/kumi/kumu/kuma* "arise!," *kom/kum* "arising." Inscriptions from different centuries show that certain letters known as *ʾamot keriʾah, matres lectionis,* or vowel letters (*alef, heh, vav,* and *yod*) were gradually employed to represent vowels, at first at the end of words, and then in the middle, too. In the consonantal text of the Bible one can find both final and medial *matres lectionis.*

The Heb script that developed from the Phoenician is known as the Paleo-Heb script. Sometime in the centuries before the Common Era it was replaced by a descendant of the Aram. square script, which also originally developed from the Phoenician. It is known as the Jewish square script or *ketav ʾashuri* (Assyrian script), the latter name pointing to its origins in the Aram.-speaking East. By the time of the Dead Sea Scrolls (mid-3rd c. BCE to 1st c. CE), almost all mss were written in the square script, though a few were still written in the Paleo-Heb script, and in some documents the Tetragrammaton (YHVH) alone was written in Paleo-Heb. The Jewish square script is used today in printing modern Heb, and the Paleo-Heb script continues to be used by the Samaritan community.

There is evidence of graphic confusion of consonants in the Bible. Some of the confusion can be attributed to the similarity in form of letters in the Paleo-Heb script, and some is due to the similarity of letters in the square script. For example, it appears that *resh* and *dalet,* which are similar in the square script, have been confused in two parallel passages: *ʾadikem* "(Like dirt of the streets) I crushed them" (2 Sam. 22.43) vs. *ʾarikem* "(Like dirt of the streets) I cast them out" (Ps. 18.43).

Pronunciation of Biblical Hebrew

Evidence for the pronunciation of Heb during the biblical period comes from three main sources:

Transliterations of Hebrew into Akkadian, Gk, Latin, and Arabic. Some Heb proper nouns are transliterated into cuneiform in Akkadian tablets, for example, Ḫa-za-qi-a-u Ya-u-da-ai "Hezekiah the Judean" in Sennacherib's annals from the very beginning of the 7th c. BCE. The Septuagint (LXX, 3rd c. BCE) is a rich source for transliteration of proper nouns, though, as is the case with all transliterations, there are many unknown variables including the lack of a one-to-one correspondence between the Heb alphabet and the Gk alphabet and the possibility that the Heb tradition underlying the transliteration into Gk differs chronologically and possibly dialectically from the Heb of the Tiberian tradition that is found in Bibles currently used. See, for example, the difference in pronunciation between the Gk transliteration *Rebekka* and Tiberian Heb *Rivka.* The Hexapla of the church father Origen, a six-column work from the 2nd to 3rd centuries CE, is also of importance since column two (the "Secunda") contains the Biblical text (not only proper nouns) transliterated into Gk. Unfortunately, only fragments from the Ps. have survived. Transliteration of Heb into the Roman alphabet is attested in the 5th c. in the Latin works of Jerome. Biblical Heb transcribed into Arabic can be found in medieval Karaite works.

Vocalized Manuscripts. The oldest extant mss of the Bible are the Dead Sea Scrolls from Qumran, which are purely consonantal and have no vowel signs. The oldest mss with vowel signs (and cantillation signs that serve as musical notes and also mark word stress and punctuation) are attested only about a thousand years later toward the end of the first millennium. Four different vocalization systems were in use during the Middle Ages. The most prestigious system and the one that is still used today is that of the Tiberian Masoretes (see "Masoretic Bible," pp. 2159–65), who devised vowel and cantillation signs in order to preserve an ancient tradition of reading that had been passed down orally for centuries. There were also Masoretes in Babylonia who developed a separate graphic system of pointing, which reflects a slightly different pronunciation. The discovery of the Cairo Genizah at the end of the 19th c. revealed another system, known today as the "Palestinian," which appears to be the ancestor of the Sephardic pronunciation of Heb (both the *kamatz* and the *pataḥ* are pronounced as *a,* and both the *tzere* and *segol* are realized as *e*). A fourth system known as "the expanded Tiberian" or "Tiberian-Palestinian" makes use of Tiberian vowel signs to represent a "Palestinian" pronunciation.

Oral Traditions of the Recitation of the Bible. The oral traditions of the recitation of the Bible that have survived into the present also deserve mention, in particular that of the Yemenite Jews, whose reading tradition preserves many old features, for example, the hard/soft (stop/fricative) pronunciation of all six consonants *bgdkpt* (in contrast to Modern Heb where one finds an alternation of *b/v, k/kh,* and *p/f,* but not *g/gh, d/dh,* and *t/th*). Additional phenomena in the Yemenite reading tradition conform to what is described in the medieval treatises of the Tiberian Masoretes and thus demonstrate the antiquity of the tradition.

Dialects

It is widely assumed that there were different dialects of Heb during the biblical period. The biblical narrator at Judg. 12.6 notes a difference between the Gileadites and Ephraimites in pronouncing the sibilant (sh/s) in *shibbolet/sibbolet.* Scholars have suggested that stories that take place in the north (e.g., the Elijah and Elisha narratives in Kings) sometimes display dialectal forms that differ from the biblical norm, which is thought to reflect southern Heb, i.e., the Heb of the Judean kingdom. See, for example, the spelling of the second feminine singular independent pronoun "you" *ʾty (= ʾatti)* in northern stories as opposed to normal biblical *ʾat* (see, e.g., 2 Kings 4.16). The Samaria ostraca from the 8th c. BCE provide clear extrabiblical evidence of a northern Heb dialect. "Year" is written as *sht (= shat)* as against *shanah* in Judah, and "wine" spelled *yn* reflects *yen* as against southern *yyn (yayin).* On the basis of the contraction of *ay* to *e* in *yn,* scholars have suggested that the prophet Amos, who prophesied in the north, makes a linguistic pun (8.1–2) that is understandable only if one realizes that northern Heb contracted *ay* to *e:* He rhymes *kayitz* "summer fruit" and *ketz* "end" (probably pronounced the same).

Chronology and Periodization of Biblical Hebrew

All spoken languages develop over time and thus it is only natural that Heb too underwent changes during the lengthy biblical period, which stretches from sometime in the second millenium BCE almost down to the destruction of the Second Temple in 70 CE. In addition to differences in style and language between some biblical books, and between the literary sources (J, E, P, and D) that make up the Torah, scholars are able to discern four linguistic periods:

Early Biblical Hebrew. It is not known when Heb was first spoken and when it developed into a language that was distinct from other Canaanite languages. The earliest stories in Gen., for example, the account of creation and the flood, are not datable linguistically, since they are written in the same language as other stories from the First Temple period. The earliest datable Heb is an agricultural calendar found at Gezer, which is assigned to the latter part of the 10th c. BCE. There are two sources from the 15th to 13th centuries BCE that hint at what proto-Heb may have looked like—the language of the Ugaritic tablets from Ras Shamra in Syria and the Canaanitisms in the El-Amarna tablets found in Egypt. The former tablets include mythological stories of Canaanite gods that are echoed in motifs and language in the Bible. The latter include letters written by Canaanite-speaking scribes in the area of modern-day Lebanon, Syria, and Israel to the Pharoah in Egypt; the language of the tablets is Akkadian, yet the scribes inadvertently inserted features of their own Canaanite tongue and sometimes deliberately glossed Akkadian words with their Canaanite equivalents. Neither Ugaritic nor El-Amarna Canaanite, however, is a linear ancestor of Heb.

The oldest Heb in the Bible is found in several poems that are replete with archaic-looking features of morphology (e.g., the remains of case endings such as the final *o*-vowel in *ḥayto ʾeretz* "wild beasts" [Gen. 49.11]), syntax (the frequent absence of the definite article and the relative pronoun), and vocabulary. Among the most striking archaic poems are the Blessing of Jacob (Gen. ch 49), the Song of the Sea (Exod. ch 15), the Balaam parables (Num. chs 23–24), the Song of Moses (Deut. ch 32), the Blessing of Moses (Deut. ch 33), the Song of Deborah (Judg. ch 5), as well as some Psalms (e.g., Ps. 29). Many terms in these poems occur only once in the entire Bible *(hapax legomena)* and thus it is often difficult to pinpoint their precise meaning.

Classical Biblical Hebrew. This language, which includes most of the books of the Bible from Gen. through Kings as well as portions of the Latter Prophets and the Writings, is the Heb of the First Temple period. In general, when one talks of biblical Heb, one refers to the language of this period. Perhaps the most salient feature of the language is the use of verbal forms with the *vav conversive (vav ha-hipukh),* for example, *va-yakom va-yelekh* "and he arose and went" (Gen. 24.10), *ya'aleh ... ve-hishkah* "would go up ... and water" (Gen. 2.6). Other noteworthy features include lengthened and shortened modal forms, for example, *'eshmera* "I want to keep, allow me to keep" as opposed to regular *'eshmor* "I shall keep," *yehi* "let there be" as opposed to regular *yihyeh* "there will be."

Transitional Period between Classical and Late. The destruction of the First Temple and the Babylonian exile are a watershed in the history of biblical Heb. Postexilic Heb differs markedly from preexilic Heb. The language of the books of Jer. and Ezek. demonstrates features of Heb from both the First and Second Temple periods, and thus reflects a period of linguistic transition, for example, Ezekiel's use of both classical Heb *shesh* and late biblical Heb *butz* for the cloth "byssus." One of several grammatical peculiarities of this period that is particularly noticeable in the language of Jer. and Ezek. is the frequent spelling in the consonantal text of the second-person feminine perfect ending in *-ty,* for example, *lmdty (= limmadti)* "you taught" (Jer. 2.33) as opposed to regular *-t: lmdt (= limmadt).*

Late Biblical Hebrew. The Heb of the Second Temple period, the language of Esth., Ezra, Neh., Dan., and Chron., clearly reveals a late composition. The contrast in language is apparent when comparing passages in Chron. to parallel passages in Sam. and Kings. The verbal system of Late Biblical Hebrew is marked by the gradual disappearance of the classical verbal forms with *vav conversive* and the lengthened and shortened verbal forms. The language is also characterized by the adoption of loanwords from Aram. (e.g., *zman* "time" as opposed to classical Heb *mo'ed; madda'* "knowledge" as against classical *da'at*) as well as some from Persian (e.g., *pardes* "park," *pitgam* "decree"). The Heb of the period also evidences features that reflect Tannaitic Heb, the early stratum of Mishnaic Heb, for example, *nulledu* "they were born" (1 Chron. 20.8) reflecting the stem *nuf'al,* a combination of *nif'al* and *pu'al* as against classical biblical *noledu (nif'al).*

Extrabiblical Hebrew Sources

Our knowledge of the Heb of the biblical period is limited almost entirely to what is attested in the Bible. There is a relatively small corpus of Heb inscriptions from different sites in the land of Israel (e.g., Gezer, Samaria, Jerusalem, Arad, and Lachish) whose grammar corresponds to that of biblical Heb. These inscriptions have also slightly enriched our knowledge of the vocabulary of the biblical period. The Siloam Inscription (8th to 7th centuries BCE) describing the digging of a water tunnel (also mentioned in 2 Kings 20.20 and 2 Chron. 32.30) contributes a previously unattested word *zdh,* whose pronunciation is unknown since there is no internal *mater lectionis* to inform us what the medial vowel was (the final *heh* probably represents *a*). The word seems to mean "crack, fissure" since it occurs in a context in which something in a rock allowed masons wielding picks on either side of the rock to hear each other. A Lachish ostracon (6th c. BCE) also reveals a new form *tsbh (= tesibbah?)* "course" (from the root *s-b-b,* "to turn") in the phrase *tsbt hbkr (= tesibbat ha-boker)* "during the course of the morning."

In addition to inscriptions, archeological digs have turned up seals and bullae (seal impressions on clay) that contain names known from the Bible, for example, *lbrkyhw bn nryhw hspr* "belonging to Berekhyahu son of Neriyahu the scribe" (the amanuensis of Jeremiah known as *Baruch ben Neriyahu* in Jer. 36.32; it was not found in situ, however, and so its authenticity has been questioned). A few seals bear the title *'asher 'al ha-bayit,* "who is over the house," an official in charge of the royal palace mentioned several times in the Bible, for example, 1 Kings 4.6; 16.9; 18.3. Many of the seals and bullae reveal names from the ancient Heb onomasticon (inventory of names) that are not attested in the Bible.

The Qumran caves next to the Dead Sea have yielded hundreds of Heb documents. Multiple copies of biblical texts have been discovered (all books are attested except for the book of Esth.) as well as sectarian writings of the Qumran community. (See "The Bible in the Dead Sea Scrolls," pp. 1850–59.) The linguistic contribution of the Dead Sea Scrolls is considerable. Frequently one witnesses the linguistic modernization of biblical texts: Older, archaic forms found in the MT are replaced by more modern ones, for example, the archaic case ending on the first word of the Masoretic *ḥayto ba-saday* "beasts in the field" (Isa. 56.9) has been deleted in the Great Isaiah Scroll from Qumran (1QIsa[a]), and the archaic form of the second word *(saday)* has been changed to the classical *sadeh.* Some features in the language of the Dead Sea Scrolls are representative of Late Biblical Hebrew, for example, the expression *beshel she-* "so that," and even Tannaitic Heb phenomena crop up, for example, the idiom *nasa' ve-natan* "carried and took" (= "traded"). From the slightly later period of the Second Jewish Revolt one finds that the Heb of the Bar Kokhba letters from nearby Naḥal Ḥever and Wadi Murabbaʿat no longer reflect biblical Heb, but rather a Tannaitic-like Heb, for example, the use of final *nun* and the negative particle *lo'* in *wl' d'gyn l'ḥykhn (ve-lo' do'agin le-'aḥekhon)* "you do not care for your brethren" as against what in biblical Heb would have final *mem* and the negative particle *'en (ve-'en do'agim le-'aḥekhem).*

Aramaic in the Bible

There are a few passages in the Bible that were written in Aram. and not Heb. Aram. is attested in the Bible in two words in Gen. 31.48, *yegar sahaduta* (glossed into Heb as *gal ʿed,* "the heap of witness"), one v. in Jer. 10.11, four chs in Ezra (4.8–6.18 and 7.12–26) and six chs in Dan. (2.4–7.28). The use of Aram. in each of these sources is not surprising. In Gen. ch 31 Aram. is put into the mouth of Laban, who is an Aramean. The biblical narrative explicitly links the patriarchal families with the Arameans. By the time of Jeremiah, Aram. had already become a language of trade and diplomacy in the Neo-Assyrian and Neo-Babylonian empires. During the time when Ezra and Dan. were composed, Aram. had become the undisputed lingua franca of the ancient Near East. Biblical Aram. belongs to the period of Aram. known as "Official" or "Imperial" Aram. (ca. 700–200 BCE), the latter term emphasizing that Aram. was used throughout the Achaemenid Persian empire for communication and administration. Documents written in the Aram. of this period have been found in Egypt (Elephantine, Hermopolis), Mesopotamia, and even farther afield (Spain, Afghanistan, India). Although belonging to Official Aram., the one Aram. sentence in Jer. reveals a sign of older Aram. in the form *'arka'* "land" alongside the Official Aram. form *'arʿa.* The Aram. of Ezra shows signs of being older linguistically than the Aram. of Dan. (the pronouns with final *-m* in Ezra are older than the corresponding pronouns with final *-n* in Dan.).

The use of Aram. in the land of Israel spread with the return of the exiles from Babylonia, where Aram. was in the process of replacing Akkadian. Even when using Heb, scribes of this period typically employed the Aram. script rather than the paleo-Heb script, as noted above. During the Second Temple period it was spoken and written together with Heb, as evidenced by the Dead Sea Scrolls and the Bar Kokhba letters, both of which were written in Heb and in Aram. Aram. completely supplanted Heb as the spoken language by the end of the tannaitic period.

[STEVEN E. FASSBERG]

Textual Criticism

Textual criticism explores the origin and nature of all the forms of a composition, in our case the biblical books. It attempts to reconstruct the original or earliest form of a text, and describes how texts were written, changed, and transmitted over time. It also evaluates the different readings found in different versions of the text.

Textual criticism of the Hebrew Bible is like textual criticism of any work that is attested in multiple versions, with an additional complication: some of the earliest surviving biblical texts are not preserved in the original Heb or Aram., but in Gk or other languages. The earliest complete translations of the Hebrew Bible, known as the ancient versions, are the Gk Septuagint (LXX), the Aram. Targumim (Targums), the Syriac Peshitta, and the Latin Vulgate (Vg). It is not always easy to retrovert (or reconstruct) the Gk and other ancient translations into Heb or Aram. In addition, often the Gk and other versions require a textual analysis of their own before they can be compared to the Heb text(s). Thus, textual criticism is partly art and partly science, especially in the case of the Hebrew Bible.

Despite these uncertainties, textual criticism is essential for biblical interpretation; it is one of the first tasks an exegete must perform, since exegesis of a text depends on accurately determining its wording. Textual criticism is also important for other disciplines of biblical scholarship, including historical, geographical, and linguistic analysis of Scripture, where it is also important to determine on which text the analysis should be based.

Textual Witnesses

The biblical text has been transmitted in many ancient and medieval mss in different languages. We possess fragments of leather and papyrus scrolls that are approximately two thousand years old, written in Heb, Gk, and Aram., as well as mss in Heb and other languages from the Middle Ages. These mss shed light on the biblical text; they testify to the form of the text in a given ms, hence they are called "textual witnesses." All textual witnesses differ from one another to a greater or lesser extent. Since no ms contains what could be called *the* biblical text (the original text), biblical scholars study all of these witnesses, noting the agreements and differences among them. The comparison and analysis of these textual differences holds a central place within textual criticism.

Most texts—ancient and modern—that are transmitted from one generation to the next become corrupted (acquire errors) to some extent. For modern compositions, the process of textual transmission from the writing of the autographs (the original copies) until their final printing is relatively short, so the possibilities of mistakes are limited. In ancient times, however, copies were handwritten over a long time-span, greatly increasing the opportunity for errors to creep in. The Hebrew Bible had an especially long transmission period, and many copies were made of it. The complexities of writing on papyrus and leather (parchment), and the length of the transmission process, cause no two surviving copies to be exactly alike.

Biblical research postulates that many details in the text preserved in its various representatives (mss, early modern printed editions, modern scholarly editons) of what is commonly called the Masoretic Text (MT: see "Masoretic Bible," pp. 2159–65), do not preserve the original text of the biblical books. Even though the concept of an "original text" necessarily remains vague, differences between the MT and the other textual witnesses imply that the MT is not the (most) original text, and we should not automatically postulate that MT is better or more original than any other textual witness.

The textual witnesses of the biblical books often contain parallel versions of the same passage. Some of these reflect different formulations in the MT itself of the same psalm (Ps. 18 || 2 Sam. ch 22; Ps.14 || Ps. 53), a genealogical list (Ezra ch 2 || Neh. 7.6–72), segments of books (Jer. ch 52 || 2 Kings 24.18–25.30; Isa. 36.1–38.8 || 2 Kings 18.13–20.11), and even large segments of a complete book, viz., Chron., large sections of which parallel the books of Sam. and Kings. These parallel versions of the "same" passage are not identical, so even within the MT there is inconsistency regarding the exact wording of the passage.

The coming to light, beginning in 1947, of the Dead Sea Scrolls (see "The Bible in the Dead Sea Scrolls," pp. 1850–59), containing biblical texts written in Heb and Aram. dating from approximately 250 BCE until 135 CE, greatly increased our knowledge about the text of the Hebrew Bible. Prior to that discovery, no ancient Heb texts of the Hebrew Bible were known, except for the Nash papyrus of the Decalogue; the mss of the MT from the Middle Ages presented the earliest surviving Heb-Aram. copies of biblical books. Now, with the publication of the Dead Sea Scrolls, we have a broad understanding of the textual variety of the Hebrew Bible that existed for the last two centuries before the Common Era and the first two centuries of the Common Era. Valuable ancient variants are not only found in biblical texts such as the Dead Sea Scrolls, but also in *tefillin, mezuzot,* quotations in non-canonical works such as nonbiblical Qumran texts, and so-called rewritten Bible compositions found at Qumran and elsewhere. Multiple forms of wording and spelling were frequent and apparently acceptable, even in the Torah, held to be of the highest sacredness by all ancient Jewish communities.

The books of Hebrew Scripture were gradually accepted as authoritative by diverse ancient Jewish communities, who assembled them into collections of sacred writings, with the books arranged in different orders; some of these collections ultimately became the canons of the MT, the LXX, and the Samaritan Pentateuch. Sometimes the version preserved by one community represents an earlier tradition than that preserved by another. For example, an analysis of the MT and LXX versions of Jer. leads us to believe that the shorter LXX text represents an early stage in the *literary* development of that book, which preceded the edition of the MT that became authoritative (canonical) in Jewish tradition. Glimpses into that earlier edition of Jer. are also attested in some Dead Sea Scroll fragments of that book.

Finally, there is no connection between the sacred status of the Bible books and the nature of the scribal transmission—we learn from the Dead Sea Scrolls that sacred books existed in a single community in multiple, different versions.

The Practice of Textual Criticism

The first step of textual criticsm is collecting and comparing the variations in the textual witnesses. This process highlights the growth of the books through complex stages of editorial revision and textual transmission, even though these witnesses are but a fraction of the number that may once have existed. The process and the problem of the loss of witnesses is not confined to biblical research, since other literatures, especially Akkadian compositions, and Homer's *Iliad* and *Odyssey* developed in a similar fashion. But the textual criticism of the Hebrew Bible encounters added complexities because of the large number of witnesses, over an unusually long period of time, in many different languages.

Textual critics may choose a reading found in a Heb ms or ancient translation, or may offer a conjectural emendation of the biblical text when neither the Heb mss nor the ancient versions preserve satisfactory evidence. The first area may be called textual criticism proper, while the second is supplementary to it.

After collecting Heb readings and reconstructing them from the ancient versions, such readings are evaluated against the MT (usually Leningrad codex B19[A]), the earliest complete extant MT ms), which is regarded as the *textus receptus* (received text) of the Hebrew Bible, although, as noted, the MT does not necessarily contain the most ancient or the most accurate text. Differences from the MT, called variants, viz., pluses, minuses, differences in letters, words, and the sequence of words, as well as differences in vocalization, word division, and sense divisions, are observed.

As a rule, the collation of Heb variants from biblical mss is relatively simple. Somewhat more complicated is the collecting of variant readings from biblical quotations in nonbiblical sources. The reconstruction of variant readings from the ancient translations is equally complex.

After collecting variants from Heb and translated texts, they are compared with their counterparts in the MT. A particular reading is considered preferable when all other readings may be shown to have derived from that preferred reading. Due to the vicissitudes of the textual transmission, in any given verse, the MT may contain an original reading in one detail, while the original reading for another detail may be contained in the LXX.

There are no objective criteria or rules for the comparison and evaluation of readings. Certain criteria adopted by some, including preference for the MT, broad attestation, age of textual witnesses are of little help. Other principles may be more helpful. Among these, the rule of the *lectio difficilior* ("the more difficult reading is to be preferred") provides occasional help, although it is impractical since it fails to take simple scribal errors into consideration and scholars have different views on the nature of the difficulties of many readings. Other "rules" pertain to "the shorter reading is to be preferred" and assimilation to parallel passages (harmonization). Such rules should be used sparingly and with full recognition of their subjective nature.

NJPS and Textual Criticism

Each Bible translation has to decide which text is the basis of its translation, either the MT, a combination of texts (among which the MT typically dominates), or a different version, such as the LXX. While most translations use a combination of texts, several translations adhere closely to the MT, either for theological reasons or because the MT is the text that their community reveres and uses in liturgical contexts. Such adherence to the MT can be at times problematic because, as noted above, the MT does not always represent the best or most original text of the Hebrew Bible. (See "Jewish Translations of the Bible," pp. 2091–2106.)

NJPS (*"A New Translation of the Holy Scriptures According to the Traditional Hebrew Text"*), used throughout *The Jewish Study Bible*, is an excellent translation, claiming to represent the MT, but this ideal cannot always be achieved. When encountering textual problems, *NJPS* used several techniques when not providing a straightforward translation of the MT, not always consistently.

NJPS often playfully manipulates the English translation of textually difficult words to create an acceptable meaning. Thus in Ezek. 10.2 the MT includes an awkward repetition of *wayo'mer*, which is not felt in *NJPS*, which reads "spoke ... and said," translating the same word slightly differently in each occurrence. The LXX omits the second word. The last words in Josh. 10.39 in the MT are a clear afterthought, lacking in the LXX, and presented here in italics: "just as they had done to Hebron, they did to Debir and its king, *and as they had done to Libnah and its king.*" *NJPS* produces a smooth: "just as they had done to Hebron, and as they had done to Libnah and its king, so they did to Debir and its king"—it accomplishes this by adding a connecting word "and" not found in the mss and reversing the elements in the v. (For similar additional examples in *NJPS*, see Josh. 1.15; 5.2, 6; 10.4.)

In some especially difficult cases, *NJPS* includes Heb variants in the translation against its principle of always representing the MT; this is accompanied by a translators' note. Thus the MT at Ps. 64.7, *tamnu*, usually rendered "they have accomplished," is mentioned only in the note in *NJPS*, while the translation is based on a variant with a *tet*, namely *tamnu* ("they have concealed"). For this reading the translators' note in *NJPS* quotes "some mss. (cf. *Minḥat Shai*) and Rashi ..." Gen. 4.8, *wayo'mer qayin 'el hewel aḥiv* ("Cain said to his brother Abel") is not problematic by itself. But Cain's words are not cited, so this becomes a textually difficult passage. The missing words, probably originally included in the text but lost in transmission, are preserved in the ancient versions, as mentioned in a note in *NJPS*. The ellipsis in *NJPS* "Cain said to his brother Abel ... and" reflects an unusual technique attempting to overcome this problem. The resulting text is artificial, apparently close to the MT, but in fact far removed from it. The contextually difficult phrase in 1 Sam. 2.11 "Then Elkanah went home" was corrected in *NJPS* to "Then Elkanah [and Hannah] went home." The addition of Hannah, which would involve a plural verbal form in Heb, creates a new context. The likely mistake in 1 Sam. 13.1 "Saul was one year old when he began to reign" was corrected to "Saul was ... years old" (note added: "The number is lacking in the Heb. text"). Thus, on occasion *NJPS* uses ellipses and brackets to effectively emend the MT.

Sometimes *NJPS* emends the MT in the translation itself. In 1 Sam. 1.28 *wayishtaḥu* ("and he bowed low") is translated in *NJPS* as a plural form ("and they bowed low" = *wayishtaḥavu*) against all evidence. The *NJPS* note "A reading in the Talmud (Berakot 61a) implies that Elkanah was there" reflects an exegetical notion, and not an ancient ms. Likewise, the Vg (not mentioned in the *NJPS*) has a plural form, but this rendering, too, may be based on exegesis.

However, most emendations (phrased as "emendation yields ...") are mentioned in the translators' notes of *NJPS*, while the MT is left intact in the translation. Thus, in Isa. *NJPS* remarks almost one hundred times "Meaning of Heb. uncertain" or "Meaning of verse uncertain" and in all those cases it adds "emendation yields." Most of these so-called "emendations" are not really emendations (a technical term used for corrections by scholars), but involve cases supported by ms evidence—they are corrections of the MT based on preferred non-MT readings that are mentioned in the translators' notes. For example, in translating the middle of Jer. 27.1 as "Jehoiakim," but noting "emendation yields Zedekiah ...," the translators do not render the MT, but prefer the alternative reading found in some medieval Heb mss and the Peshitta.

In sum, even though *NJPS* bases its translation on the MT, it also alerts the reader to problematic words or contexts in the MT. In such cases the reading is described in the notes as "meaning of Heb. uncertain," or "meaning of verse uncertain." These and other corrections of the MT (named "emendations" in *NJPS*) for which notes are provided are explained on pp. xvii–xviii of the "Preface to the 1985 JPS Edition": "where the committee [of translators] had to admit that it did not understand a word or passage"; "where an alternative rendering was possible"; "where important textual variants are to be found"; "where the text remains obscure"; "where the Heb text permits, alternative renderings have been offered." Thus, *NJPS* walks a delicate line, affirming the importance of the MT for the Jewish community, for whom it is *the* text of the Bible, while acknowledging that the MT is not a perfect text. Other modern translations, however, are less attached to the MT, and often derive their translations from a combination of the MT, the LXX, the Dead Sea Scrolls, other ancient versions, and conjectural emendation.

[EMANUEL TOV]

The Canonization of the Bible

Canonization, the process through which the Bible became the Bible, is only imperfectly understood. We do not know when the concept of "the Bible" developed, exactly how various books came to be part of the Bible to the exclusion of others, how these books were put into a particular order and divided into sections, and how their precise wording was established. Since there are no contemporaneous descriptions of this process, it needs to be reconstructed from indirect evidence, namely, from the variety of biblical texts from different periods and places, and from later traditions in rabbinic, early Christian, and other sources that discuss the formation of the Bible. Thus, the reconstruction suggested below is tentative.

Definitions

"Canon" is a Gk word meaning "reed," and came to refer to any straight stick used for measuring. This basic meaning was extended to refer to any rule or standard by which things could be compared or judged—what is in, and what is out. The Alexandrian grammarians, classical Greek writers who were also literary critics, used "canon" for the list of standard or classic authors who were worthy of attention and imitation. These lists were not closed, and these scholars disputed adding or removing works from them. Furthermore, inclusion in the list merely recognized a work's quality; it did not confer upon it any new status. Thus, a canon of writings came to denote those texts that were of central importance to a given group. The term is applied somewhat imprecisely for the Bible, since the earliest evidence we have for understanding the development of the Tanakh does *not* come from book lists that delimit precisely what works are included. This is different from the situation concerning the early Christian Bible, where early book lists are found; other ideas known from the canonization of the Christian Bible have until recently been inappropriately assumed to be true for the Hebrew Bible as well.

When used in reference to the Bible, canon conveys something beyond its meaning in Greek culture: a closed list of approved writings. Not only is a given set of texts included, but all other texts—no matter how worthy or useful—are excluded. Canon in this sense is closed and unchangeable, and eventually, all canonical books were thought of as inspired. This is expressed in a rabbinic comment on Eccl. 12.12. The biblical text reads:

> "Of anything beyond these [Heb *mehemah*], my child, beware. Of making many books there is no end" (NRSV).

The rabbinic comment explains:

> Those who bring more than twenty-four books [the standard rabbinic number of books in the Tanakh; see below] into their house introduce confusion [Heb *mehumah*] into their house (*Eccl. Rab.* 12:12).

This suggests not only that the works in the canon are important, but that they, along with their authoritative interpretation, are sufficient in and of themselves. Once the biblical canon was fixed, there could be no additions to it or subtractions from it. It is likely, however, that before this idea of fixed, unchangeable canon developed, there was a looser idea, a canon concept, or an incipient canon.

The Tanakh

It is extremely difficult to trace how this conception of canon first developed, and how it is connected to associated but not identical notions, such as the eventual stabilization of the biblical text. Until the mid-20th c., many scholars thought that the canon of the Tanakh was established at Yavneh (Jamnia), a city near the Mediterranean coast, west of Jerusalem, that was a center of Jewish learning after the destruction of the Second Temple (70 CE). According to this theory, a group of Rabbis met there in about 90 CE and debated and voted on whether or not certain books were canonical; at the end of this meeting, the official contents of the Bible were supposedly established. This overly neat reconstruction was based on a misunderstanding of rabbinic texts and is now rejected. The rabbinic texts that tell of these debates do not concern granting canonical status to particular books, but reflect certain ambivalences toward particular biblical books, such as Song, which were already in the canon, and whose canonical presence needed to be justified. Unfortunately, evidence is not available to offer a clear picture of how the canon of the Bible was formed, since much of the material from early Jewish sources (including the Dead Sea Scrolls, rabbinic texts, and the 1st c. CE historian Josephus) and Christian sources, is ambiguous or biased.

This much is clear: the canon of the Bible did not develop at a single moment in time but rather in stages over many years. There is general agreement that the Torah was the first section of the Bible to be recognized as central by the Jewish community, as a document worthy of intensive study and interpretation. Exactly when this happened is uncertain. Many scholars associate this development with Ezra, and see the "law of your God" (Ezra 7.14), with which Ezra was entrusted in the 5th c. BCE, as the Torah. This assertion likely goes beyond the evidence of the text. Though the Jewish community had recognized the Torah as central to its identity by the Persian period (6th to 4th centuries), a conclusion suggested by citations of Torah material as authoritative in biblical books from this period (e.g., Chron.; Ezra-Neh.), it is unclear exactly how this happened, or whether this development was fostered by internal or external factors, and should be associated primarily with a single individual such as Ezra, or should be seen as part of a larger, gradual, more complicated process that likely began during the Babylonian exile.

According to rabbinic tradition, the Torah is the first part of a tripartite (three-part) canon, followed by Nevi'im (Prophets) and Kethuvim (Writings), forming a work that much later was known by the acronym Tanak(h), *T*orah, *N*evi'im, *K*ethuvim. Nevi'im (see intro., pp. 429–38) is composed of Josh., Judg., Sam. (seen as one book), Kings (seen as one book)—historical works known as "the former prophets"—and "the latter prophets," consisting of Isa., Jer., Ezek., and the twelve minor prophets (Hos. through Mal., seen as one book). The order of these eight books has been relatively stable (although the order of the three major prophets is different in the Talmud in *b. B. Bat.* 14b, and the LXX [Septuagint] has a slightly different order of the first half of the minor prophets). Kethuvim (see intro., pp. 1263–64) is composed of the following eleven books, which, by contrast, appear in a wide variety of orders in various book lists and biblical mss: Ps.; Prov.; Job; the "five scrolls," Song, Ruth, Lam., Eccl., and Esth.; Dan.; Ezra-Neh. (seen as one book); and Chron. (seen as one book). (The order of the "five scrolls" has been esp. variable.) This extreme variability suggests that Kethuvim was the latest section to be canonized. The number of canonical books according to traditional Jewish sources is thus twenty-four (five in the Torah, eight in Nevi'im, eleven in Kethuvim).

We do not know when the acronym "Tanakh" originated. Rabbinic texts recognize a tripartite canon, where Torah, Nevi'im and Kethuvim, are used for each part of the canon. Their Aram. equivalent *'oraita, nevi'ei ukhtivei* (*b. Kid.* 49a) could be used as a general term for the Bible as a whole, though in classical rabbinic literature this cumbersome locution is not generally employed. (Rabbinic literature prefers the terms *miqra'* [that which

CANONS OF THE BIBLE

Jewish Canon	Protestant Canon	Roman Catholic/Orthodox Canon
Torah (LAW)	PENTATEUCH	PENTATEUCH
Genesis	Genesis	Genesis
Exodus	Exodus	Exodus
Leviticus	Leviticus	Leviticus
Numbers	Numbers	Numbers
Deuteronomy	Deuteronomy	Deuteronomy
Nevi'im (PROPHETS)	HISTORIES	HISTORIES
FORMER PROPHETS	Joshua	Joshua
Joshua	Judges	Judges
Judges	Ruth	Ruth
Samuel (1 and 2)	1 and 2 Samuel	1 and 2 Samuel
Kings (1 and 2)	1 and 2 Kings	1 and 2 Kings
LATTER PROPHETS	1 and 2 Chronicles	1 and 2 Chronicles
Isaiah	Ezra	Ezra
Jeremiah	Nehemiah	Nehemiah
Ezekiel	Esther	Tobit
The Twelve	POETICAL/WISDOM BOOKS	Judith
Hosea	Job	Esther
Joel	Psalms	1 and 2 Maccabees
Amos	Proverbs	POETICAL/WISDOM BOOKS
Obadiah	Ecclesiastes	Job
Jonah	Song of Solomon	Psalms
Micah	PROPHETS	Proverbs
Nahum	Isaiah	Ecclesiastes
Habakkuk	Jeremiah	Song of Solomon
Zephaniah	Lamentations	Wisdom of Solomon
Haggai	Ezekiel	Sirach
Zechariah	Daniel	PROPHETS
Malachi	Hosea	Isaiah
Kethuvim (WRITINGS)	Joel	Jeremiah
Psalms	Amos	Lamentations
Proverbs	Obadiah	Baruch
Job	Jonah	Ezekiel
(Five Scrolls)	Micah	Daniel
Song of Songs	Nahum	Hosea
Ruth	Habakkuk	Joel
Lamentations	Zephaniah	Amos
Ecclesiastes	Haggai	Obadiah
Esther	Zechariah	Jonah
Daniel	Malachi	Micah
Ezra-Nehemiah	THE APOCRYPHA	Nahum
Chronicles (1 and 2)	1 and 2 Esdras	Habakkuk
There is no Apocrypha in the Hebrew Bible	Tobit	Zephaniah
	Judith	Haggai
	Esther (with additions)	Zechariah
	Wisdom of Solomon	Malachi
	Ecclesiasticus (Sirach)	Orthodox canons generally include
	Baruch	1 and 2 Esdras
	Letter of Jeremiah (Baruch ch 6)	Prayer of Manasseh
	Prayer of Azariah and Song of Three	Psalm 151
	Daniel and Susanna	3 Maccabees
	Daniel, Bel, & Snake	4 Maccabees (as an Appendix)
	Prayer of Manasseh	
	1 and 2 Maccabees	

is read] and *kitvei ha-kodesh* [the writings of holiness or holy writings], among others.) The acronym Tanakh is first found in Masoretic literature in the form of ʾn"k (from the Aram. *ʾoraita, neviʾei ukhtivei*—Masoretic notes are typically in Aram.). Tanakh, a Heb reflection of this Masoretic term, is also found in Masoretic literature. It would thus seem that the term originated in the late first millennium, with the flourishing of the "Masoretic movement," (see "Masoretic Bible," pp. 2159–65). In contrast to earlier Jewish terms for the Bible which did not explicitly distinguish between different parts of the canon, the term Tanakh may be understood as creating clearer dividing lines between the canonical sections, in some cases even (explicitly) suggesting priority of Torah over Nevi'im and Nevi'im over Kethuvim.

The origin of the tripartite canon has been a topic of debate, with several scholars suggesting that a two-part canon, the Torah and other works, was the original form, and that only later was it divided into three parts; references to "the law and the prophets," seemingly as synonymous with the Bible, in Matt. 7.12 and other New Testament books may support this. Evidence for a tripartite canon may appear in such sources as the prologue to the Wisdom of Jesus ben Sirach (2nd c. BCE), which says that "many great teachings have been given to us through the Law and the Prophets and the others [or, other books] that followed them" and Luke 24.44, which refers to "the law of Moses, the prophets, and the psalms [possibly a name for the third canonical division, named after its first book]." The tripartite canon, whenever it developed, is not fully logical or consistent in assigning books to particular canonical divisions. This likely reflects the gradual nature of the canonization process, with Nevi'im canonized before Kethuvim. This would explain why the Kethuvim contains the book of *the prophet* Daniel (dating from the 2nd c. BCE), which logically belongs with Isa., Jer., Ezek., and The Twelve. It would also clarify why Kethuvim contains several late historical books, such as Ezra-Neh. and Chron., which would seem more appropriately to belong with similar works such as Josh. and Kings. The tripartite canon most likely suggests, therefore, that Torah was canonized in the Persian period, followed by the canonization of Nevi'im in the late Persian or early Greek period, while the Kethuvim texts were canonized last, probably by the time of the destruction of the Second Temple (70 CE). It is difficult to determine exactly when the books of the Kethuvim were canonized beyond observing that this must have been after the completion of its latest book, most likely Dan. in 164 BCE.

The tripartite division is not the only one known in antiquity, nor is the number of twenty-four books the only number mentioned in ancient Jewish sources. The Samaritan community only had the Torah as its canon. Josephus is often cited as evidence for the Jewish canon in the 1st c. CE, but there may have been several competing notions of canon in this period, and he should not be taken as normative for all of Judaism in his time. He is, however, apparently the earliest source to suggest a closed canon, consisting of twenty-two biblical books; he also draws a striking contrast between the Jewish "justly accredited" books and Greek literature, noting that Jews would "cheerfully ... die" for their books (*Ag. Ap.* 1.38–43). Since he does not list his twenty-two books, it is not clear if he simply had a smaller canon than the rabbinic list of twenty-four books, or if, instead, his canon had the texts in a different order, combined in different ways, perhaps putting Ruth after Judg. and Lam. after Jer., and treating these smaller books as appendices to the ones they follow, rather than as independent works. Such an arrangement would yield twenty-two books, a number that conveniently corresponds to the number of letters in the Heb alphabet; some early Christian sources also cite this as the number of books in the Bible.

The placement of Ruth and Lam. mentioned above is found in the LXX, the Gk translation of the Bible begun in Alexandria,

Egypt, in the 3rd c. BCE for the Jewish community there (see "Jewish Translations of the Bible," pp. 2091–2106). According to this originally Jewish tradition, mentioned by some early church fathers from the 2nd c. CE and later, and reflected in the arrangement of the earliest extant comprehensive LXX mss (4th c. CE), the Hebrew Bible is divided into four parts: Torah, Histories, Poetical and Wisdom books, and Prophets. This division and order continue to be used in the Christian Old Testament (see chart on p. 2157). Older scholarship spoke of this four-part book arrangement as the Alexandrian canon, in contrast to the tripartite Palestinian canon, but scholars now acknowledge that such a clear geographical dichotomy never existed.

Scholars also now recognize that even when canonization took place, the wording of the Bible did not absolutely freeze. Evidence suggests that by the 2nd c. CE the biblical text had largely stabilized—this is reflected in the (few) mss we have from this period from near the Dead Sea, as well as the development of early rabbinic midrash, much of which presupposes a stable text. The destruction of the Second Temple and the Hadrianic persecution of the early 2nd c. CE may have also caused a type of conservatism which was responsible for establishing "the" biblical text. These were gradual and to some extent incomplete processes, and it is difficult to understand exactly how they were accomplished before the advent of the printing press. It is important to remember that different Jewish groups from the early first millennium CE may have had different ideas of what comprised scripture; for instance, it is unlikely that the Qumran community, most of whose texts date from a century or so immediately before and immediately after the Common Era, viewed Esth. as part of their Bible, since no ms of that biblical book has been found among the thousands of fragments discovered. In contrast, over a dozen mss of *Jub.*, a work similar to Gen. and Exod., have survived, and it is referred to as authoritative in that community's work (CD 16:1–3); given this work's affinities with the practices of the Dead Sea community, it was probably a very significant text for them. Yet, using the term canon in reference to this community is problematic since their many writings never contain a term that seems to mean the Bible, nor is it clear that they had a notion of a closed set of texts that was special. In rabbinic literature, the Wisdom of Jesus ben Sirach (Sir. or Ecclesiasticus), a book in the Apocrypha but not in the Hebrew Bible, is occasionally cited with the same formula used for introducing biblical texts and was thus, in some sense, canonical for some Rabbis. Therefore, although we can probably speak of "the" canon having formed by the 1st c. CE, there was a certain amount of fluidity or variability around the fringes.

This fluidity also applies to the extensive divergence in the wording of the biblical text as shown in mss from Qumran, in translations of the Bible in the LXX and elsewhere, and to a lesser extent in early rabbinic citations (see "Textual Criticism," pp. 2149–52). Some of these differences are small and insignificant, such as a variant spelling, but some are of major significance, and affect the meaning of the text. There are cases where the text is found in two or more different recensions—identifiably different versions, not merely two different copies of the same original with minor variants—which may vary the order of materials or may exhibit fundamentally different text-types (e.g., short types vs. expansive types, as with the text of Jer.; see the intro. to Jer.). One Ps. scroll from Qumran (11QPs) contains many different wordings for psalms preserved in our Bible, a different order for some psalms, and some additional compositions not found in our Psalter. This evidence suggests that, at least in the early stages of the canonization process, it was quite acceptable for a book to circulate in different versions and that different communities may have canonized different versions of the same book. Comparative evidence indicates that a community could hold a book to be sacred without a definitive notion of the precise wording of the book.

The most basic question is why certain books were canonized while others were not. Books that were excluded from the Jewish canon had in some cases been translated in the LXX and were therefore canonized in the Christian community as Apocrypha; others were lost, or survived as pseudepigrapha (writings falsely attributed to major biblical figures), and/or were preserved only in fragmentary form in the Dead Sea Scrolls. Some of these excluded books explicitly date from after the Persian period (later than 332 BCE), and thus were seen as too recent to be eligible for inclusion in the canon. (The book of Dan., and perhaps Eccl., is from this late date, but they profess to have been written earlier, and thus could be included in the Bible.)

In various ways, the canonical status of a book or group of books arises from the community's view of their centrality, authority, sacredness, and inspiration—all terms that are difficult to define and disentangle. The Song, for instance, was originally an erotic love poem; by the early rabbinic period, it had come to be interpreted allegorically as a love poem between God and Israel. The book's superscription suggests that it was seen as the inspired composition of Solomon himself. The superscription and the allegorical reading are two pieces of evidence suggestive of the process whereby Song was transformed from a love poem into a biblical book. We do not know when either of these ways of reading the Song began, but the result was the transformation of secular love poetry into a holy book, understood as written under divine inspiration and recounting the relationship between God and Israel.

Despite major uncertainties in our understanding of the process of canonization, several points seem fairly certain. First, the process of canonization was gradual and it began long before the Rabbis. It is likely that its final stages were reached by (if not before) the 1st c. CE, perhaps as a reaction to the destruction of the Second Temple in 70 CE and its aftermath. (Some believe that the idea of canon developed a bit later in reaction to the emergent Christian community, which viewed a different, broader set of texts as central.) This crisis in 70 intensified a development that had begun over half a millennium earlier, with the destruction of the First Temple (586 BCE). Through this development Israel gradually became the People of the Book (a term first found in the Qur'an in reference to Jews and Christians). Second, it is unlikely that canonization represents a purely top-down process, through which a small group of leaders (Rabbis) determined the canon; instead, the designation of certain works as canonical was more the official recognition of the works that a large or important segment of the community had already held to be central, holy, or authoritative. Finally, the act of canonization was remarkably inclusive, creating a body of works richly textured by a wide variety of genres, ideologies, and theologies. This is, fundamentally, a typical ancient Near Eastern process: Instead of creating a small, highly consistent text, as we perhaps would now do, those responsible for the process made efforts to include many of the viewpoints in ancient Israel, incorporating differing and even contradictory traditions into this single, and singular, book that came to be called the Bible.

[MARC ZVI BRETTLER]

The Development of the Masoretic Bible

The transmission of the Bible may be divided into four broad periods: (1) the era of Qumran (3rd c. BCE–1st c. CE); (2) the era of the Sages until the Masoretic codices (2nd c.–8th/9th c.); (3) the era of the Masoretic codices (9th/10th c.–15th c.); (4) the era of the printed editions (15th/16th c.–21st c.). We will survey these periods below, briefly summarizing the first two eras, and concentrating on the latter two.

The Era of Qumran

Our knowledge of the early history of the transmission of the Bible was greatly expanded with the discoveries in the mid-20th c. in the Judean Desert (Qumran and other sites) of Bible mss ranging from the 3rd c. BCE to the 1st c. CE (and beyond); there are no extant mss before this era, though some mss predate the actual Qumran community. (See "The Bible in the Dead Sea Scrolls," pp. 1850–59.) All the books of the Bible (except Esth.) were found, typically in fragmentary mss, with the books of Gen., Exod., Deut., Isa., and Ps. most frequently represented. These discoveries caused a reexamination and reevaluation of other early witnesses of the biblical text, such as the text of the Septuagint (LXX; the Gk translation of the Bible) and the Samaritan Pentateuch (SP). Heb variants which had been surmised on the basis of the Gk in LXX were now shown to have actually existed. Many scholars tried to categorize the Qumran material in its relationship to these known versions, as well as to the current standard Bible text, MT (Masoretic Text). Some noted that the Qumran material does not always fit into the categories of the previously known witnesses. The Qumran era reflects a multiplicity of texts (i.e., of variants), with witnesses for all three of the previously known text-types (MT [at that time: the proto-Masoretic text-type, which seems to have been the dominant text-type then, and which later attained exclusivity among the Heb texts], LXX, SP), as well as other previously unknown variants. It is this era that preserves substantial variants in the reading of a word, a phrase, a verse, or larger units.

Notwithstanding the multiplicity of texts, it seems that within the Jerusalem Temple circles there was a clear preference for the one textual tradition that we call the proto-Masoretic text-type (because of its close affinities to the later Masoretic Bibles). Thus, the consonantal text of fragments of biblical mss found at Masada (brought there by the fighters) conforms closely to MT. Some rabbinic evidence may substantiate this conclusion (see *y. Ta'an.* 4:2 [fol. 68a] and *b. Ketub.* 106a).

The current text of the Bible (MT) preserves evidence of variant texts from an early period. This can be seen especially in the transmission of parallel texts in the Bible, which preserve early variants of the same text (e.g., in the list of names of David's warriors [2 Sam. 23.8ff.; 1 Chron. 11.11ff.], or in various parallel psalms [e.g., Pss. 14 || 53]). Another phenomenon that preserves early variants is "double readings," where two variants appear consecutively in the text (e.g., 1 Sam. 28.3, lit. "they buried him in Ramah and in his city"); this phenomenon also occurs in LXX and the Aram. Targumim.

The Era of the Sages till the Masoretic Codices

It is especially difficult to reconstruct this period because we lack direct witnesses to the Heb text; i.e., we do not have Hebrew Bible mss from most of this period. (We have some evidence from the Bar-Kokhba period, found in Wadi Murabba'at and Naḥal Ḥever, and perhaps some from its end.) Instead, the vast literature of the Sages serves as a significant secondary witness to the Bible text in this period, both in its constant citations of biblical texts and its various statements about the text. For example, *b. ʿEruv.* 13a/*Sot.* 20a admonishes to be careful while copying biblical texts, for even one letter added or omitted can destroy the world. We also have many statements of R. Naḥman ben Yitzḥak, noting explicitly "x *ketiv,*" that a word in the Bible is to be spelled in a specific way (usually defective spelling; this spelling, e.g., without a *yod* or a *vav,* serves as the basis for his midrashic re-vocalization of the word); for example, *b. Shab.* 28b; 55b.

Once we enter the era of the Sages, the quality and quantity of variants of the Bible, as known from the prior period, disappear almost entirely. This is due to the fact that the Sages rejected both the LXX and the Samaritan text (accepted by the Christians and the Samaritans, respectively), and accepted the proto-Masoretic text-type as their Bible text. So, in effect, we are now left with only one text-type for the Bible. Although within this text-type there still remains a range of variants, they are minor; they are almost never of the substantial type known from the earlier era.

During this period the Sages continued to develop the concept of the sanctity of the biblical text which included the details of its spelling (including whether it was plene or defective, that is, written, e.g., with a *vav,* or without it). This can be seen in the numerous *derashot,* or expositions, both halakhic (legal) and aggadic (nonlegal), that hinge on the details of the spelling, and which assume only one correct way of spelling. (E.g., see *Gen. Rab.* 12:6 [Theodor-Albeck edition, Jerusalem 1965, pp. 101–102, 104], on the exact spelling of *toldot* in the Bible and *b. Menaḥ.* 34b/*Zevaḥ.* 37a/*Sanh.* 4b on the plene/defective spellings of *(u)le-totafot* in Exod. 13.16; Deut. 6.8; 11.18.)

According to the conception of the Sages there was one accurate text—in all its details. Nevertheless, a range of (minor) variants in the texts that circulated continued to exist, though these now all belonged to one text-type. Occasionally, these variants are reflected in the literature of the Sages itself (see, e.g., the list of R. Akiva Eiger in his *Gilyon Ha-Shas* to *b. Shab.* 55b; V. Aptowitzer, *Das Schriftwort in der Rabbinischen Literatur;* and the apparatus in the Hebrew University Bible).

The Era of the Masoretic Codices

The third period differs from the earlier ones in a number of ways. First, the form of transmission changed. Previously, all Heb texts were written in scroll format; now, in addition to the continued use of scrolls for ritual reading (e.g., the Torah scroll), the codex—a ms in book form—was introduced. The earliest extant dated Heb biblical codex is from 916 CE; however, the Heb codex format had apparently been in use since the 8th c. CE (when it was mentioned by R. Yehudai Gaon).

Second, *nekudot* (vowel points) and *teʿamim* (cantillation marks) were introduced into the text. These signs—reflecting the pronunciation and accentuation that had previously been transmitted orally—were the work of the Masoretes. Scholars in the 19th and 20th centuries have shown, especially based on mss in the Cairo Genizah, that in addition to the well-known system of vocalization and accentuation currently in use, which was developed in Tiberias, there were two other systems that were developed, but which were later abandoned. All three systems differ in the choice of signs. One was developed in Babylonia, and the other in the land of Israel, though perhaps not in Tiberias. Both of these latter systems (which place their signs on top of the letters) reflect a slightly different pronunciation than that of Tiberias. For example, the other systems have only five, and not seven, vowels; i.e., only one sound for *pataḥ-qamatz; tzere-segol;* akin to current "Sephardi" pronunciation. In addition to these three major systems, other subsystems, variants of the major systems, developed.

The introduction of the different systems of signs in different geographical areas at about the same time (apparently the 7th–8th centuries CE) seems to reflect the need felt by various experts to preserve in written form the oral tradition of pronunciation and accentuation of the biblical text before it would be lost. It is possible that the upheavals associated with the Arab conquests in this period served as a major impetus for this development.

The third difference between the third period and the previous ones was the introduction of the Masorah, an extensive system of notes intended to preserve the written text of the Bible. This Masorah was recorded in both biblical codices and in independent works. The scholars who composed these notes, and who are also responsible for the introduction of the vocalization and cantillation marks, are called Masoretes. Here, too, as in the case of the systems of vocalization, different Masorahs developed in different locations; in addition to the Tiberian Masorah, there was an independent development of Masorah in Babylonia. These Masorahs have as their goal the preservation of a sanctified text, accurate in all its details, including plene-defective spelling (as noted above, this view developed in the second era, with roots in the Temple circles in the first era). In short, the goal of the Masorah apparatus is to preserve the one correct or authoritative biblical text.

Two stages were usually involved in producing a Masoretic codex: First a scribe would write the biblical text, and then the Masorete would add the vocalization, accentuation, and the Masorah. The Masorah on the page was of two types. The first type was the Masorah Parva or small Masorah—short notes in between the columns (usually three) of the page, which referred to specific words in the text (those words were marked by a little circle above them). The note would often just note *"l"* (Aram. *leita* = there is no other; it is unique), opposite a given word. At other times, it would note the number of times a word occurs in a particular form, for example, *"b"*; *"d"* (it occurs twice; it occurs four times). As a rule, the Masorah would take note of the exceptions in any given case, preventing a copyist from normalizing an odd form to a more common one. The second type was the Masorah Magna—longer notes on the top and/or bottom of the page, repeating select phenomena marked in the Masorah Parva, and adding the references to the vv. involved. This was done by quoting a few words of the given vv., since v. and ch numbers were not yet used. Due to space limitations, there were many more Masorah Parva notes on the page than there were Masorah Magna notes.

Two main types of masoretic lists were compiled: (a) elaborative Masorah *(masorah mefaretet)*—this is the type noted above, for example, elaborating how many times a word occurs in a given form, for example, six times with defective spelling; (b) collative (or cumulative) Masorah *(masorah metzarefet)*—which collates the various unusual forms or words that appear (but not plene-defective spelling), and arranges them according to the alphabet or the order of biblical books. For example, a well-known list organizes all cases of words in the Bible that occur once without, and once with, a *vav* at their beginning (e.g., *ʾokhlah* [1 Sam. 1.9], *ve-ʾokhlah* [Gen. 27.19]). As the lists of the collative Masorah are sometimes very long, they cannot be copied in full on a given page in a Bible codex, but are usually copied there only in part (in those codices that bring these types of lists). In addition, the lists of the collative Masorah were edited early-on as a separate work, sometimes called *ʾOkhlah ve-ʾOkhlah,* based upon the first example of the first list.

The sources available to the Masorete were sometimes different from those of the original scribe who wrote the consonantal text. If the Masorete found a contradiction between his source (Bible ms or Masorah note) and the Bible codex he was working on, he would correct the codex (sometimes adding a corresponding Masorah Parva note). At first, both the Masorah Parva and the Masorah Magna played a role in the correction of the codices, and were copied diligently. With time, however, the Masorah Magna took on a formalistic function, with the scribe filling up a set number of lines, for example, two lines on top and three lines on the bottom, with Masorah Magna, thereby giving the codex the "masoretic codex format"—but without using it for correcting the biblical text. (In fact, in some mss the copyist would on occasion simply cut off the list to fit the space available). Occasionally, the Masorah Magna was written in micography, using the letters of the Masorah Magna decoratively to form different shapes, both geometrical (Sepharad) and even zoomorphic (animals and other shapes; Ashkenaz). At this later stage of transmission, then, the Masorah Parva was still often used for text-critical purposes, but the more complex Masorah Magna had, in effect, lost its original purpose, and had become decorative.

The medieval Masoretic codices may be divided into various groups based on geographical areas: (1) accurate Tiberian mss (10th–11th centuries); (2) Sephardi mss (13th–15th centuries); (3) Ashkenazi mss (12th–15th centuries); (4) Italian mss (12–15th centuries); (5) Yemenite mss (15th–16th centuries). Most of these mss are now held in state and university libraries around the world.

The accurate Tiberian mss (mss from the land of Israel and Egypt, with Tiberian Masorah) form a group whose text accurately reflects the Bible as reflected in the Tiberian Masorah. The most accurate ms among this group is the Aleppo Codex (= A) (ca. 930), whose Masorete was Aharon ben Asher, the last and most famous of the renowned ben Asher family of Masoretes. The other mss in this group are close to this text.

The Sephardi mss can be subdivided into three subgroups: those whose text is very close to A; those close to A (these were called "accurate Sephardi mss" in the Middle Ages); those further away from A.

The Ashkenazi mss can generally be divided into two groups: those whose text is far from A; those whose text is very far from A. (At least in the Torah, however, there are some that are close to A.)

The Italian mss show somewhat similar characteristics to those in the Ashkenazi mss.

The Yemenite mss are very accurate in the Torah text, as they reflect A, because they conformed to the rulings of Maimonides, who followed A.

The Bible text in any medieval ms depended on the sources available to the scribe and to the Masorete; i.e., on the Bible mss and on the Masorah. Throughout the Middle Ages, there were often minor differences between the various sources available. There is clear evidence of places where mss are corrected (usually differences in plene-defective spelling) based upon another Bible ms or upon a Masoretic note; we can still see in the mss cases where a letter is erased and an adjacent letter is extended to fill in, or a letter is erased by crossing it out, or a letter is added above the line. This is seen most often in Ashkenazi mss, where the original text represents an alternate subtradition in spelling, whereas the Masorah represents the "accurate" tradition. The extant evidence points to the second half of the 13th c. as the beginning of the awareness among certain Ashkenazim that the Sephardi mss are accurate and differ from their own. These adaptations continued until the era of the printed Bible, and all reflect minor variants, very rarely affecting meaning.

The Torah was always regarded with special care and attention. In addition to the Masoretic codices, Torah scrolls continued to be written for ritual use. Special halakhic regulations legislated issues, such as where different types of paragraph spaces should be inserted *(parshiyot petuḥot u-setumot)* and song layout (Exod. ch 15; Deut. ch 32). Indeed, Maimonides legislated in his Code (*Hilkhot Sefer Torah* 10:1) that deviations in spelling, in section division, and in song layout render a scroll unfit for ritual use.

Given the many variants that Maimonides was confronted with, he had to decide what, in fact, was the accurate Torah text; i.e., what should be the standard text that others must copy. Maimonides chose the Aleppo Codex. He wrote a Torah scroll based upon it, and he included in his Code (*Hilkhot Sefer Torah* 8:4) a list of the sections and the layout of the songs based upon it. As we now know, he chose wisely; for the Aleppo Codex is, in fact, the most accurate among the accurate mss in that it reflects the Tiberian Masorah most accurately. The Yemenites followed Maimonides, first basing their work upon his Code, and then apparently making a model based upon his Torah scroll. Therefore, their Torah scrolls by and large reflect the Aleppo Codex in the text, sections and songs (excluding some minor variants).

Others, however, followed different options. R. Jacob Tam (France; 12th c.), a significant French halakhist, wrote a work that determined the sections and song layout based on French sources (he also attended there to unique letters and special *tagim* [tittles]). Ramah, R. Meir ha-Levi ben Todros Abulafia (d. 1244), a major Spanish halakhist, though he mostly followed Maimonides in the layout of sections and songs, decided on a different tactic for the text. He chose to follow the well-known halakhic rule of following the majority, and thus followed a selective majority of Sephardi mss (using only ancient "accurate" ones, rather than a single ms). In addition, he made use of the Masorah. In the 13th c., we have evidence of Ashkenazi scholars coming to Spain (1250; 1273) to make an accurate copy based on Ramah's work, in order to serve as a model in Ashkenaz. R. Menaḥem ha-Meiri, a significant Provencal halakhist, also used the method of majority when determining the text in his *Kiryat Sefer* (1306), but allowed a wider selection of sources. (In addition, he attended to unique letters and special *tagim.*) He also allowed himself to deviate from Maimonides in various section divisions, basing himself on French/Ashkenazi sources as well as logic. Later, R. Yom Tov Lipman Muelhausen (15th c.; Ashkenaz) reverted to exclusively following Maimonides concerning the sections and the layout of the songs.

Thus, we see that there were different tactics used by different decisors in determining the proper text, sections, and song layout. Some followed a single ms, while others decided on the basis of several mss. Regional variation was significant. The net result was that there was no absolute unity during the Middle Ages concerning the details of the Torah scrolls, even though the halakhah required unity.

The Era of the Printed Editions

The fourth era differs from the previous three by the change in medium—from handwritten mss to print. This eventually gave rise to a major change in the transmission of the text, as totally identical volumes could be printed in multiple copies and distributed to diverse geographical areas. At the outset of printing, different Bible editions reflected the different types of sources available to the editors. Thus, for example, the first dated edition of the complete Bible in Heb, Soncino 1488, reflected Ashkenazi sources (e.g., with many variants in the text, mostly plene-defective variants, but also other types of variants).

Printing proceeded apace, each editor relying on the sources at hand, until the first edition of the Rabbinic Bible *(Miqra'ot Gedolot),* Venice 1517 (referred to as RB1517), edited by the convert Felix Pratensis for the Christian publisher Daniel Bomberg. This edition not only included the complete Bible (there had previously appeared four or five other complete editions and over fifty partial editions, e.g., just Torah), but also the Aram. Targum to each book (excluding Ezra, Dan., Chron.), and one or two commentaries to each book. The editor also often listed in the margin variants in the biblical text or vocalization that he found in the mss. He also listed in the margin cases of *qere* (where a word is to be read differently than it is written), but omitted the term *qere;* this made it impossible to distinguish between cases of *qere* and cases of other variants. The introduction and the closing remarks to the work highlight that the editor and publisher were very proud of this edition and felt that it reflected the accurate Bible text. In reality, the editor created a new hybrid biblical text, of the Sefardi tradition mixed with certain Ashkenazi phenomena.

Eight years after this first edition of the Rabbinic Bible, Bomberg issued a second edition of the Rabbinic Bible, this time edited anew by Jacob ben Ḥayyim Ibn ʾAdoniyahu, a Jew (who later converted to Christianity) learned in Talmud, halakhah, and kabbalah. This Venice 1525 edition (referred to as RB1525) differed from the first in a number of areas. First, it presented two or three commentaries on each book. Second, it presented for the first time the apparatus of the Masorah on every page: Masorah Parva and Masorah Magna; it presented the masorah finalis—over 5,000 masoretic lists at the end of the edition, arranged alphabetically, and cross-referenced to the lists in the edition; it also included at the end of the edition the variants between various Masoretic schools, namely between ben Asher and ben Naphtali, and the textual variants between the West and the East (Eretz Israel and Babylonia; beginning with the Prophets). Third, this edition was more accurate in its marking of the *qere-ketiv,* adding *q'[ere]* to the variant, thus clearly identifying it as such; and was more accurate in marking other phenomena, such as majuscular (large) and minuscular (small) letters, etc. Fourth, this edition differed from the first in details of the text, vocalization, and accentuation.

This edition is based upon Sephardi mss; unlike the first Rabbinic Bible, it does not reflect a hybrid edition. RB1525 was the initiative of Jacob ben Ḥayyim Ibn ʾAdoniyahu who convinced Bomberg that the first edition, RB1517, could not serve as a model edition, unlike other editions of basic works undertaken by Bomberg, for example, the Babylonian Talmud; Maimonides' *Mishneh Torah*. Jacob ben Ḥayyim felt that the first edition contained inaccuracies in the text, vocalization, and accentuation. Furthermore, it was not accurate enough concerning Masoretic issues. These matters were important to him especially because of his kabbalistic background. Though at first glance these were minor variants (e.g., plene-defective spelling), which did not affect the meaning of the text, in kabbalistic terms these were often of major importance. The kabbalists envisaged the Torah text as the name(s) of God, and any variant would thus cause damage to the name. Therefore, they venerated the work of the Masoretes in preserving the accurate text. So, too, the various unique phenomena of the biblical text, for example, majuscular and minuscular letters, all had kabbalistic import; it was therefore, important to reproduce these, too, accurately in the Bible edition.

Using these kabbalistic arguments, Jacob ben Ḥayyim was able to convince Bomberg of the importance of undertaking a new Bible edition with the Masorah. Bomberg, as a Christian Hebraist (he had learned Heb from Felix Pratensis), was aware of the newer phenomenon of Christian kabbalah (using the kabbalah for Christian purposes), and in fact wished to promote it. A few vestiges of the kabbalistic factor can be found in RB1525 itself. Thus, we find that Jacob ben Ḥayyim in his introduction to the edition explained the *qere-ketiv* in a kabbalistic vein; we find him bringing a few references to kabbalistic issues in the Masorah Parva; and we even find one note in the Masorah Magna (Exod. 10.5) where Jacob ben Ḥayyim uses the kabbalah as a criterion to decide between two conflicting masoretic notes.

RB1525 together with its Masoretic apparatus became the standard for the accurate Bible text for the next four centuries. This edition was reproduced again in Venice in 1548; 1568; 1618, and Basel 1618; and later in Amsterdam 1724; and still later in Warsaw 1860–1866.

The medium of print allowed this text to become the standard text *(textus receptus),* for now there was the ability to distribute one text in many copies among many geographical areas. Furthermore, now it was possible to refer to this work as a standard, even when suggesting that it must be modified. For example, Menahem di Lonzano's *ʾOr Torah* (in: *Shetei Yadot;* Venice 1618) was devoted to corrections in the Torah, and Yedidya Norzi's *Minḥat Shai* (Mantua 1626; first published Mantua 1742–1744; and later republished e.g., in RB1860–1866; introduction—Pisa 1819) was devoted to corrections in the whole Bible. Both of these critics, following the lead of Ramah (Abulafia), and somewhat similar to Jacob ben Ḥayyim, used Sephardi mss and Masoretic notes as their criteria of accuracy. Using these criteria they corrected various cases of textual variants, mostly plene-defective spelling, and certain cases of vocalization and accentuation. This corrected text, Jacob ben Ḥayyim-(Ramah)-Lonzano-Norzi, then became the *textus receptus.*

With time, this text also became the standard in Torah scrolls both for Sephardim and Ashkenazim. Only the Yemenites continued to follow the tradition of Maimonides (i.e., the Aleppo Codex). As it turned out, these two crystallizations (the joint text; the Yemenite text) are very close in the Torah, with only a few variants between them.

A new era in the printed Bible began with the Stuttgart 1937 edition of the *Biblia Hebraica.* Here P. Kahle abandoned the RB1525 text (which had still served C. D. Ginsburg in his London 1926 edition), and in its place used the text of ms Leningrad B19[A] (1008 CE), which belongs to the accurate Tiberian mss. This ms is quite close to the Aleppo Codex, and in some cases is corrected to agree with it. (Kahle had wanted to reproduce the Aleppo Codex, *the* ms of Aharon ben Asher, then still in Aleppo, Syria, but was unable to do so.) Kahle also printed there for the first time the Masorah Parva (but not the Masorah Magna) of ms L.

The Aleppo Codex arrived in Israel in 1958 and became the spur for renewed activity in this field. It was chosen as the base text for the Hebrew University Bible Project's Bible edition, a critical edition of the Bible incorporating variants from the ancient translations, Dead Sea Scrolls, and rabbinic literature. So far, only a small part of this important edition, which also reproduces the Masorah Parva and the Masorah Magna in A, has appeared. In addition, various complete Bibles have appeared that are based on A (edited by M. Breuer); so, too, M. Cohen's CD-ROM of the Bible (with vocalization and accentuation searchable; with both Masorahs of A, as well as a selection of medieval Jewish commentators), and his *Miqra'ot Gedolot Ha-Keter* (which will encompass the complete Bible [15 vols. to date], and which also reproduces the Masorah Parva and the Masorah Magna of A). All of these editions involve some reconstruction and conjecture, since the Aleppo Codex is now missing almost all of the Torah (except for the last eight chs), as well as the end of the ms, and several leaves in between. This material is filled in by using Yemenite Torah mss, which are believed to represent the Aleppo Codex closely, and the extant Masoretic notes from the Aleppo Codex. After 500 years of printing the Bible, we can thus turn back from the *textus receptus* based on Sefardi mss to the accurate Tiberian mss, and indeed to the most accurate of these mss, the Aleppo Codex.

Using the many ms sources available today, it is now possible to trace the vicissitudes of the Bible from the era of Qumran to today. The earliest period shows significant textual variation, but by the second period, once one text-type was accepted, the many variants in the Bible mss that continued to circulate were mostly of a minor nature. By the third period, the sanctity of the Bible text, as well as the apparatus of the Masorah, kept the biblical variants in a minor mode. This was even more the case in the fourth period, under the influence of printing, but most especially in the modern period, where ancient reliable mss can be reproduced with great accuracy and disseminated widely.

[JORDAN S. PENKOWER]

The Modern Study of the Bible

Background

Modern study of the Bible focuses on analysis of the biblical text as well as the historical, social, cultural, linguistic, and religious contexts in which the Bible was written and in which it is read. This is often called critical analysis, referring to the ideal of the objective, analytical study of the Bible guided by current scientific methodology rather than by the interpreter's theological or ideological presuppositions. (Thus, critical scholarship does not refer to an interest in criticizing the Bible and its beliefs.) In practice, however, full objectivity is difficult to attain, and the interpreter's presuppositions frequently influence critical readings of the Bible even when the interpreter self-consciously attempts to avoid such influence.

The modern critical study of the Bible began during the 17th and 18th centuries with the onset of the European Enlightenment in which human reason supplanted religious dogma as the primary means to interpret the world at large. The result was an intellectual revolution that saw the development of empirical method as the basis for modern philosophical, scientific, literary, linguistic, and historical study.

New empirical and historically-based exegetical methods posited that the Bible was the product of human authors and therefore must be studied like any other literature in relation to the sociohistorical contexts in which it was written. Enlightenment biblical exegesis (interpretation) therefore provided the means to argue for a historical development of the ideas in the Bible. In practice, Enlightenment rationalism enabled the newly emerging Protestant Christianity to employ scientific methods in the study of the Bible and of theology to argue for an evolution in the history of religion. Such evolutionary religious models would then point to Protestant Christianity as the highest form of human religious thought.

Although Jews were largely marginalized in the overwhelmingly Protestant Christian emergence of modern critical biblical scholarship, some did play major roles, ranging from Baruch, later Benedict Spinoza (1632–1677), who was expelled from the Jewish community of Amsterdam, and Moses Mendelssohn (1729–1786), who defended Judaism as a true religion of reason and urged Jews to take part in Gentile culture while affirming their distinctive religious identity and practices. Jewish scholars frequently had to defend Judaism as they worked in a hostile environment that viewed Judaism as a backwards example of human religious expression that should be left behind. Indeed, one of the early examples of the modern scientific study of the Bible and of rabbinic literature by a Jewish scholar was Leopold Zunz's 1809 volume, *Die gottesdienstlichen Vorträge der Jüden (The Liturgical Sermons of the Jews),* written to demonstrate that the expository sermon had been a feature of Judaism from the time of the Bible through the present. The study forced the Prussian government to withdraw its opposition to the licensing of rabbis as legitimate clergy like their Christian counterparts.

As Zunz's study demonstrates, modern religious practice and the modern study of the Bible are heavily indebted to earlier Jewish scholarship and practice. For example, the Babylonian Talmud preserves an opinion that Moses could not have written the account of his death in Deut. ch 34, that Hezekiah and his colleagues edited the book of Isa., and that the Men of the Great Assembly (a group of scholars who emerged, according to the Rabbis, in the Persian period—their existence is doubted by many modern scholars) edited the books of Ezek. and the book of the Twelve Prophets (*b. B. Bat.* 14b–15a). Medieval Jewish exegetes, such as Saadia Gaon (892–942), Rashi (1040–1105), Abraham Ibn Ezra (1089–1167), Moses Maimonides (1135–1204), David Kimḥi (1160–1235), and others, laid the foundations for rational analysis of the Bible and Jewish thought as well as the grammatical underpinnings for the philological study of the Bible in response to challenges from the Karaites, Christians, and Muslims. Indeed, Ibn Ezra pointed to a number of passages in the Torah, such as Gen. 12.6; 13.7; Deut. 1.1; and 34.5–12, that could not have been written by Moses, and he observed difficulties in the view that Isaiah ben Amoz could have written Isa. chs 40–66. (See "Medieval Jewish Interpretation," pp. 1891–1915.) Similar premodern views questioning the Mosaic authorship of the entire Torah were also voiced by Judah ha-Hasid (1140–1217).

Source Criticism

With the burgeoning interest in the historical context of the Bible, early critical study focused especially on the identification of the earlier written sources that were combined to form the Torah. Christian scholars espoused the historical study of the Torah in an effort to show that the Pentateuch was indeed the product of evolutionary human thinking that would then lead ultimately to the emergence of Christianity from its Israelite roots. Pre-Enlightenment thinkers argued that Moses could not have been the author of the Pentateuch. Jean Astruc (1684–1766) employed methods developed in the study of the classics to argue that the various names used for the deity in the Pentateuch pointed to a number of earlier documentary sources that preceded the final form of Gen. and that could be found within it; he believed that Moses combined these documents. Wilhelm Martin Leberecht de Wette (1780–1849) and Karl Heinrich Graf (1815–1869), applied Astruc's methods and insights to the entire Pentateuch and the book of Josh. to posit an early form of the documentary hypothesis that identified the Priestly writings of Exod., Lev., and Num. as later works than Deut.; they also abandoned the notion of the Mosaic compilation of the Torah.

These were the predecessors to Julius Wellhausen (1844–1918), a German Old Testament scholar, who is generally credited with developing the classical form of the documentary hypothesis for the composition of the Pentateuch as part of his larger effort to write a history of Israelite religion. Wellhausen's *Die Composition des Hexateuchs und der historischen Bücher des Alten Testaments* ("The Composition of the Hexateuch and the Historical Books of the Old Testament," 1876–77; 3rd edition, 1899) and *Prolegomena zur Geschichtes Israels* ("Prolegomena to the History of Israel," 1878/1882; English edition, 1886; this work was first published in 1878 as *Geschichte Israels, The History of Israel*). Based upon his observations of the different forms of the name of the deity, literary styles, religious ideas, and geographical locations, Wellhausen illustrated the development of the four classic sources of the Pentateuch: J, E, D, and P, in that order. He posited that the Torah is the result of long historical development, in parallel to the prophetic corpus, and thus the Torah should not been seen as influencing the prophets, but was, in places, influenced by them.

The earliest source was the J source, named for its use of the personal name, JHVH (the German rendition of YHVH), as the primary designation for the deity. Wellhausen argued that J, the earliest of the sources, was written in the 9th c. BCE. (Gerhard von Rad later pushed the date of J back to the early years of the Davidic monarchy, 10th c. BCE.) Wellhausen maintained that J represented a very primitive religious worldview in which animals could talk (the snake in the garden of Eden in Gen. ch 3 and Balaam's ass in Num. chs 22–24). The J source reflected a folkloristic literary style in which human beings could interrelate face-to-face with a very anthropomorphically-defined YHVH (Gen. chs 2–4). J was frequently morally neutral, as exemplified by Abraham's decision to call Sarah his sister and her subsequent entry into Pharaoh's harem (Gen. 12.10–20). It emphasized Judean locations, such as Hebron, where the ancestors were buried (Gen. ch 23) and which served as David's capital during his seven years of Judean rule (2 Sam. chs 1–5).

The second source was the E source, named for its use of the generic designation, Elohim, "God," for the deity until the burning bush episode in Exod. ch 3. Wellhausen dated the E source to the 8th c. BCE, the apex of the history of the Northern Kingdom of Israel, which was destroyed by the Assyrian empire in 722–721 BCE. In contrast to the anthropomorphic portrayal of the deity by the J source, E presented a more reserved portrayal of the deity, who communicated with human beings by means of intermediaries, such as dreams, angels (Gen. ch 22) and burning bushes (Exod. ch 3). E was less folkloristic and far more moralistic than J, as indicated by its efforts to explain that Sarah really was the half-sister of Abraham (Gen. ch 20). Since it tended to emphasize northern Israelite locations, such as Bethel (Gen. ch 28) and Penuel (Gen. ch 32), and figures associated with the north, such as Joseph (Gen. chs 37–50), it was thought to have been of northern origin. The E source was brought south to Judah following the destruction of northern Israel and combined with the J source.

Wellhausen's third source was D, which was constituted largely by the bulk of the book of Deut. Deuteronomy has a distinctive exhortational style designed to appeal to its audience. It employs expressions, such as "Hear, O Israel" (Deut. 6.4 and elsewhere), "And you shall observe the commandments and statutes and laws that I command you this day to do them" (author's translation; Deut. 7.11), to motivate its audience to action to observe the word of YHVH. Indeed, YHVH's word served as a more developed mediatory role for communication between YHVH and human beings than those in the E source. Wellhausen, following de Wette, identified Deut. with the book of the Torah discovered ca. 622 in the Jerusalem Temple during the religious reforms of King Josiah of Judah (reigned 640–609 BCE; 2 Kings chs 22–23). Insofar as Deut.'s laws appear to have served as the basis for Josiah's reforms, Wellhausen dated D to the mid-7th c. BCE and argued that it was written by northern reform circles before it was brought south to be discovered in the Jerusalem Temple.

Wellhausen's fourth and final source was P, named for its Priestly character and interests. P displayed a keen interest in ritual and legal matters pertaining to the priesthood, such as observance of the Shabbat (Gen. 2.1–3); circumcision (Gen. ch 17); and sacrificial offerings (Lev. chs 1–16). Its literary style was formalized and stereotypical, employing phrases such as, "and there was evening and there was morning, a first day" (Gen. 1.5) and "this is the instruction (Heb *torah*) concerning the whole burnt offering" (author's translation; Lev. 6.2). The interrelationship between YHVH and human beings was even more formally defined by the mediating role of the priesthood than the angels of E or the word of YHVH in D. Like E, P did not use the personal name of YHVH until the time of Moses (Exod. ch 6). Wellhausen dated the P source to the reforms of Ezra and Nehemiah during the postexilic Persian period of the 6th–4th centuries BCE when—in his view—Judah emerged as a theocracy governed by the priesthood under Persian rule.

Although conceived as a work of objective literary-historical criticism, Wellhausen's reconstruction of his sources reflects his own Protestant religious views. He gives priority to the J source as the most authentic representation of the face-to-face relationship between YHVH and human beings, much like the relationship between YHVH and the prophets, upon which Protestant Christianity modeled its own understanding of its relationship with the deity. In Wellhausen's view, the P source represented a decline in Israelite religion into mindless legalism and ritual, which reflected Protestant Christianity's conflict with the Roman Catholic Church and its low view of rabbinic Judaism.

Wellhausen's grand reconstruction is problematic in several other ways as well. He was unable to reconstruct a full narrative sequence for each source, and he frequently could not distinguish between J and E. Finally, the relative absence of priestly concerns in J, E, and D was a remarkable omission for sources allegedly written in a society in which the Temple and priesthood played a central role throughout its history. These problems have prompted major rethinking of Wellhausen's results; some interpreters reject source analysis altogether and focus on literary plot and characterization in the study of the Pentateuch, and others have suggested that J is much later than Wellhausen suggested.

Wellhausen was not the only source critic of his time, although he is the best known. Another prominent figure is Bernard Duhm (1847–1928), another German biblical scholar who identified the three major portions of the book of Isa., viz., Proto- or First Isaiah in Isa. chs 1–39 from the late 8th c. BCE; Deutero- or Second Isaiah in Isa. chs 40–55 from the 6th c. BCE; and Trito- or Third Isaiah from the postexilic period in Isa. chs 56–66. Duhm built upon earlier observations going all the way back to Ibn Ezra concerning an exilic component to the book beginning in Isa. ch 40. This position had been argued before by critical scholars, such as Wilhelm Gesenius (1786–1842), based upon stylistic difference and references to the 6th c. Persian monarch, Cyrus, in Isa. 44.28 and 45.1. Nevertheless, Duhm achieved a breakthrough by recognizing that chs 56–66 were even later than chs 40–55. He likewise analyzed the book of Jer. and posited four different sources, beginning with the prophet's own words, continuing with a narrative revision of the prophet's words, a biographical source based especially on the theological viewpoint of the book of Deut., and a small segment concerned with restoration. Although some of Duhm's views have been challenged, for example, Trito-Isaiah appears to be the work of multiple prophets, his work on Isa. and Jer. continues to form important foundations for contemporary research on both prophetic books.

Redaction Criticism

Redaction criticism is a literary-critical method for studying the editorial (redactional) shaping, combination, and expansion of earlier literary sources. It emerged from Source Criticism as a means to explain how the various sources underlying the various biblical books were brought together to produce the present form of the biblical books.

Because of the influence of German philosophical and theological idealism, source critics tended to privilege the earliest levels of composition, such as the J source or the authentic oracles of the prophets, as the most creative and theologically important works of the Bible. Later tradents and editors were generally considered as mere literary mechanics who understood little of the creative works of the earliest biblical authors and frequently distorted those works as they supplemented them with editorial comments that frequently served their own later interests. Because later tradents and redactors were understood to be legalistically minded Jews from the postexilic period, early redaction criticism functioned as a means to charge that Jewish editors had corrupted the true meaning of the original biblical compositions and to call for modern critical scholars to strip away these theologically irrelevant additions to reconstruct the authentic text and message of the Bible.

But as redaction-critical work proceeded through the early 20th c., interpreters increasingly recognized the theological insights and literary creativity of the editors or redactors who produced the final forms of the biblical texts. The works of Gerhard von Rad (1901–1971) and Martin Noth (1902–1968) were especially important in this regard. Building upon insights of Hermann Gunkel (1862–1932), von Rad's 1938 study of the J source argued that the J writer of the Pentateuch had collected and assembled a large number of oral traditions from various sanctuaries throughout Israel to construct the initial J stratum of the Pentateuch. The J stratum of the Pentateuch therefore constituted the first national history of Israel from the early Davidic monarchy and played an important role in forging the identities of the tribes of Israel into a coherent Israelite nation. Martin Noth's 1943 study of the Deuteronomistic History argued that the Former Prophets, i.e., Josh., Judg., Sam., and Kings, likewise demonstrated the work of writers, heavily influenced by Deut., who collected and assembled earlier traditions to form a unified historical work that explained the Babylonian exile as the result of Israel's failure to observe divine instruction as presented in Deut. In both cases, the J writer of the Pentateuch and the Deuteronomistic authors of the Former Prophets were both redactors and writers, i.e., both were creative authors and theologians in their own rights who deserved the attention of biblical scholars.

Redaction-critical work flourished in the latter half of the 20th c. as scholars began to recognize the theological and literary importance of the redactors who produced the final forms of the biblical books. Frank Moore Cross (1921–2012) wrote important studies of the P stratum of the Pentateuch and the Deuteronomistic History. In the case of the P, Cross demonstrated that the Priestly writer was both a redactor and an author who gave shape to the earlier JE narratives of the Pentateuch and worked them into an overarching Priestly narrative that would produce the final form of the Torah that would stand as the basis for Jewish identity through the present day. Cross's work on the Deuteronomistic History similarly demonstrated that it was not simply a narrative of Israel's demise in the Babylonian exile, but an earlier edition of the work had been written in the late-7th c. BCE to support the program of religious reform and national restoration of King Josiah of Judah (reigned 640–609 BCE). Redaction-critical work was especially influential in the study of the prophetic literature as interpreters sought to explain how the oracles of the prophets were edited into the great prophetic books of the Bible. Isa. was a particularly important focus as scholars attempted to trace the process by which the works of First, Second, and Third Isaiah were brought together to produce the present form of the book of Isa., and newer models developed, suggesting that the voices of Second and Third Isaiah are not confined to chs 40–66, but were active in chs 1–39 as well. Jer. remains the subject of ongoing discussion as interpreters have attempted to explain the book's Deuteronomistic outlook and its relation to the Former Prophets. Recent discussion has focused especially on the formation of the book of the Twelve Prophets as scholars have attempted to explain how twelve discrete prophetic works were brought together into a single scroll, and the means by which the completed book views the past and future of the city of Jerusalem.

Tradition and Form Criticism

Although source criticism proved to be a dominant form of biblical exegesis through the first half of the 20th c., the study of ancient Near Eastern literatures demonstrated the tremendous influence of neighboring cultures on the composition of biblical literature. Wellhausen and others had constructed models for the composition of biblical literature during the monarchic period and beyond, but were less interested in the prehistory of biblical literature. The emergence of the interrelated fields of tradition and form criticism provided the means to answer such questions. Tradition criticism attempts to identify and study earlier traditions on which the present biblical literature is based. Early expressions of form criticism attempt to study the oral speech forms that would have been employed to convey those early traditions.

The key figure in the development of tradition criticism and form criticism is Hermann Gunkel (1832–1932), who was deeply influenced by the developing German "history of religions school." Given the influence of ancient Near Eastern literature and the growing field of folklore studies, Gunkel reasoned that biblical literature must have gone through a long period of (oral) development before it reached its current written forms. In an effort to recover the oral traditions or text forms on which the written forms of biblical literature were based, Gunkel posited that ancient Israel would have developed its own speech forms to give expression to such oral traditions. Because in his view ancient Israel originated as a primitive, preliterate, semi-nomadic culture that evolved into a landed agriculturally-based monarchy, Gunkel maintained that early speech forms would have played a role in producing the narrative cycles, prophetic oracles, and hymnic compositions that now appear in biblical literature. Such oral forms would be short and self-contained textual units or genres (German, *Gattungen*) that were easily memorized and passed on the oral culture of early Israel.

Gunkel's 1901 commentary on Gen. provided a systematic form- and tradition-critical analysis of the book, within a source critical framework. He argued that oral genres had informed the composition of the major sources of the book of Gen. and that those genres could be recovered by attention to their characteristic self-contained motific concerns and structures and the social setting (German, *Sitz im Leben*, lit. "life setting") in which they arose. Typical genres in Gen. included sagas concerning the founding figures in the history of Israel, such as Abraham and Moses; legends concerning the exemplary traits and actions of the ancients, such as Noah's righteousness (Gen. ch 6) or Abraham's fidelity to God (Gen. ch 22); or etiological narratives, such as Jacob's foundation of the sanctuary at Bethel (Gen. ch 28). Such narratives played a role in defining early Israelite cultural and national identity, much like *Grimm's Fairy Tales* that were then serving the same role in German society, and they would have been transmitted in social settings such as the family hearth or the local sanctuaries, such as Shiloh, Bethel, Gilgal, and others. Likewise, Gunkel's posthumously published 1933 study of the Psalms, *Einleitung in die Psalmen* ("Introduction to the Psalms") identified the basic genres used in Israelite worship, such as the hymn of praise, the individual and communal laments, the thanksgiving psalms, the wisdom psalms, and royal psalms, all of which would have functioned in the Jerusalem Temple and other earlier worship sites.

Later form critics drew insights from redaction criticism and other methods to further develop form criticism into a tool for literary study of the Bible as well as for the reconstruction of oral speech forms. Klaus Koch (b. 1926) presented a general introduction of the method to both German- and English-reading audiences that emphasized the study of structure, genre, setting, and intention as the basic elements of form critical study. German scholar Wolfgang Richter recognized the importance of the literary character of the text and its linguistic formation. Rolf Knierim (b. 1928) laid new foundations for understanding the classic form critical categories of structure, genre, setting, and intent. The present writer employs a revamped understanding of form criticism in conversation with text linguistics, narrative analysis, and intertextuality to study both the synchronic (final literary form) and the diachronic (the compositional history) forms of entire biblical books and indeed of the Bible itself.

Form criticism has emerged as a foundational exegetical method in contemporary biblical interpretation. It analyzes the formal features of a text, including its unique syntactical and semantic form or literary structure and its typical linguistic genres that shape the text and facilitate its expression. Form criticism is used both to analyze the present literary form of the text and to ascertain its compositional history in relation to its postulated written and oral stages. It works in tandem with other critical methodologies, such as rhetorical criticism, redaction criticism, tradition-historical criticism, textual criticism, canonical criticism, newer literary criticisms, the social sciences, and linguistics in the interpretation of biblical texts.

Textual Criticism

Although Judaism reads the Heb Masoretic Text (MT) as its authoritative form of the Bible, a variety of ancient textual versions appear in Heb, Gk, Aram., Syriac, Latin, Ethiopic, and other languages. (Biblical scholars typically call the ancient translations "versions.") Textual criticism is the study of the text of the Bible, sometimes to correct the text in cases of textual corruption and sometimes to understand the hermeneutical and interpretative viewpoints of the ancient versions in which the Bible appears. (See "Textual Criticism," pp. 2149–52 and "Masoretic Bible," pp. 2159–65.)

The basic form of the text of the Bible in Judaism is the Heb MT. The Bible was transmitted in handwritten mss throughout antiquity until the advent of printing in the 16th c. CE, and most Jewish scribes took great care to ensure the accurate transmission of biblical mss. Such efforts were necessary not only to ensure an accurate text but to defend Judaism against charges by Christians, Muslims, and others that the Jewish Bible had been corrupted and that rabbinic Judaism was therefore in error. The Masoretes, best known by the works of 10th c. CE figures as Moses ben Asher and his son Aaron ben Asher, produced authoritative mss of the Bible that employed a combination of the Heb consonantal text, vowel pointing to give the correct vocalization to the text, a system of accents that defined the syntax and cantillation of the text, and extensive marginal notes on readings; they also composed treatises on grammar. Because Jews buried or stored away mss in the Cairo Genizah when they were no longer usable, our oldest Masoretic mss are the Cairo Codex of the Prophets (895 CE), the Aleppo Codex of the Hebrew Bible (10th c. CE)—perhaps the first time the entire Hebrew Bible was written in a single volume, and the Leningrad/St. Petersburg Codex of the entire Hebrew Bible (1008 CE). Maimonides declared the Aleppo Codex to be most authoritative, at least in terms of how the biblical texts should be divided into paragraphs and lines. Unfortunately, the Aleppo Codex is no longer complete, so modern critical text editions rely on the Leningrad/St. Petersburg Codex as the oldest complete Hebrew Bible ms, although new text editions have begun to employ the Aleppo Codex when its text is extant. The differences between Aleppo and Leningrad are relatively minor.

A major question in modern text-critical research is the interrelationship between the Gk Septuagint (LXX) and the MT. The LXX was originally translated from Heb into Gk beginning in the 3rd pre-Christian c. by Jews living in Egypt (and perhaps elsewhere in the Hellenistic diaspora). The LXX was adopted by early Christianity as an authoritative form of the text of the Old Testament for Gk-speaking Christians. The 4th c. CE Codex Vaticanus is the oldest complete text of the LXX, and the 4th c. Codex Sinaiticus is also an important witness, although portions of its text were inadvertently destroyed by the monks at St. Catherine's Monastery on the traditional site of Mt. Sinai. Ironically, then, the earliest extant copies of the entire Hebrew Bible are in Gk, more than half a millennium earlier than Aleppo or Leningrad (although the Dead Sea Scrolls, from the 3rd c. BCE through the early 2nd c. CE, preserve a significant part of the Hebrew Bible). The LXX often presents a smoother more readable text than the Heb, and in some cases, such as Jer., Dan., and Esth., it presents a text that is markedly different from that of the Masoretic version. Although a small number of Jewish early modern text critics, such as Zecharias Frankel (1801–1875), whose philosophy was foundational for the later founding of Conservative Judaism, held to the priority of the MT, most modern text critics maintain that the Old Greek text of the LXX may represent an earlier Jewish text of the Bible. Consequently, many critical text editions and translations of the Bible will correct the MT on the basis of the LXX and other versions. In many cases, however, text critics are too quick to emend the MT as the Gk frequently represents an attempt to interpret and render a difficult Heb expression.

A major advance in modern text criticism took place beginning in 1947 with the discovery of the Dead Sea Scrolls near the ancient site of Qumran at the northwest shores of the Dead Sea. (See "The Bible in the Dead Sea Scrolls," pp. 1850–59.) Following the accidental discovery of seven mss in Qumran Cave 1 by Arab shepherds in the 1940s, some eleven ms caves and other ms sites from Wadi Muraba'at, Naḥal Ḥever, and Masada eventually came to light with the remains of some eight hundred ancient Heb, Aram., and Gk mss. Although there was considerable delay in the publication of the scrolls, the appointment of Emanuel Tov (1941–) as chief editor ensured the timely completion of the publication process. Every book of the Bible except the book of Esth. was represented among the finds as well as many works of the Apocrypha, the pseudepigrapha, and works that were previously unknown. The proto-Masoretic text (namely the consonantal MT, without the vowel points and cantillation marks that developed later) is well represented, such as the Isa. scrolls of Cave 1 and the Twelve Prophets Murabba'at Scroll. Many Heb mss display variations, some in keeping with the Samaritan Pentateuch (SP; the Torah text used by the Samaritan community, which broke off from Judaism in the pre-rabbinic period) or the Heb text that would have served as a basis for LXX readings, and some that represent free variation and interpretation by the scribes who wrote them. A particularly noteworthy find is the B and G ms of Jer. from Qumran Cave 4 that represents the shorter Heb text underlying the LXX form of Jer. Likewise, the Cave 4 Sam. mss represent considerable affinities with the Gk versions. On the other hand, the Gk Twelve Prophets Scroll from Naḥal Ḥever represents a Gk translation of an underlying proto-Masoretic Text.

Research on the other textual versions, such as the Aram. Targums, the Syriac Peshitta, the Latin Vulgate (Vg), and the Ethiopian Bible, is a major concern in modern biblical study. Although most text critics focus on the reconstruction of the Heb text of the Bible, many are beginning to recognize that the versions constitute literary works of Scripture in their own right that represent translation and interpretation of the underlying Heb text.

Rhetorical Criticism and Literary Approaches

The exegetical methods discussed above, including source criticism, redaction criticism, tradition and form criticism, and textual criticism, are largely diachronic methods of biblical exegesis. Diachronic methods are concerned especially with the historical dimensions of the biblical text, such as the identity and perspective of the author, the sociohistorical setting in which the text is written, and the history of the text's composition. Oftentimes, such methods left the interpreter with a fragmented text. But during the second half of the 20th c., many interpreters began to turn to synchronic issues of biblical interpretation, which look at the final form of the text, and were especially concerned with the literary form and function of the text apart from its historical dimensions. Synchronic methods therefore take up the text's communicative functions, its interrelationships with other texts, whether contemporaneous or not, and the role of the reader in constructing meaning in the text. Most recent literary studies, especially postmodern studies, drawing on the literary schools and movements from the humanities, dissolve the sharp distinction between synchronic and diachronic; they are, like historical critics, interested in the time and place of the authors and the authors' issues and ideologies.

The emergence of rhetorical criticism in the latter 20th c. was an important move in this direction. James Muilenberg (1896–1974) was an American scholar who began to employ synchronic literary methods in his 1956 commentary on Isa. chs 40–66 to interpret the literary features, rhetorical dimensions, and coherence of the final form of the Isaian text. He treated Isa. as a work of poetry that employed poetic devices such as chiastic structure, rhyme and alliteration, motific development, etc. His 1969 presidential address to the Society of Biblical Literature, "Form Criticism and Beyond," proposed rhetorical criticism as an outgrowth of form critical method. Whereas form critical method had focused on the reconstruction of smaller oral text units based on genre, rhetorical criticism would study how these units worked together to create a wholistic, communicative text. Later rhetorical critics, such as Phyllis Trible (1932–), would turn to the classical Greek and Roman rhetoricians to develop models for understanding the means by which biblical texts were designed to interact and communicate with their intended audiences.

Although Moshe Greenberg's (1928–2010) wholistic method for reading biblical texts was not an example of rhetorical criticism per se, his commentary on Ezek. and other works have much in common with rhetorical criticism due to his focus on interpreting the final form of the text with a combination of ancient Near Eastern literature, rabbinic interpretation, and modern critical scholarship combined.

As the study of the Bible moved out of the theological seminaries and into secular universities during the latter half of the 20th c., particularly in America, interpreters increasingly began to explore the role of the Bible as literature. Jewish scholars were especially well represented, particularly because of their dissatisfaction with the atomization of the Bible in the hands of German source, redaction, and form critics. Robert Alter (1935–), a specialist in comparative literature, wrote *The Art of Biblical Narrative* (1981) and *The Art of Biblical Poetry* (1985). Although both studies focus on the synchronic dimensions of biblical text, his interest in type scenes, conventional forms used by biblical authors, constitutes an important link with the interest in genre in form critical studies. Meir Sternberg's *The Poetics of Biblical Narrative* (1987) emphasizes plot development, characterization, and the role of gapping in biblical narrative. Whereas source critics viewed breaks in narrative flow as evidence of literary seams among the various earlier sources that comprise a narrative, Sternberg viewed them as a sign of literary coherence in which readers were expected—whether consciously or unconsciously—to fill in missing information, motivations, and viewpoint based on their perspectives and familiarity with plot, setting, and character.

A major development in newer literary study was the shift from author-based reading strategies to reader-based strategies. The reconstruction of a historically-based author whose viewpoints and intentions had come to expression in a text proved to be a very elusive goal, and was abandoned by some. Early literary study of the Bible was heavily influenced by New Criticism, which posited that a literary work was an artifact, an autonomous work of art, independent of the intentions and viewpoints of its authors and the socio-historical context in which it was written. Early structuralist interpretation drew upon the linguistic work of Ferdinand de Saussure (1857–1913), who posited that meaning in language was determined not by historical usage, but by the system of relationships within a language (i.e., a tree is a woody plant that is not a bush or a shrub) that make communication possible. The anthropologist, Claude Lévi-Strauss (1908–2009), posited that such binary structures of life/death, male/female, hunting/farming, etc., represented universal structures of thinking in all human societies that would come to expression in literature.

But whereas these early models were author-oriented, later models began to stress the role of the reader or audience in interpretation. Stanley Fish's (1938–) 1980, *Is There a Text in this Class? The Authority of Interpretive Communities*, signaled the advent of Reader Response Criticism, where scholars began to ask how the perspectives, agendas, and biases of the reader influenced the interpretation of a text and attempts to reconstruct its author and historical setting. Such a shift allowed for the introduction of the subjectivity of the reader—or better interpretive communities—in the overall interpretation of biblical literature.

Deconstructionist models of reading, especially influenced by the work of Jacque Derrida (1930–2004), question the metaphysical assumptions of western philosophy, particularly its interests in positing a central deity, reason, or even the human being as the central principle around which all reality is organized. Deconstruction posits that language is incomplete, self-contradictory, and inconsistent. Therefore the point of reading is not to reconstruct and restate meaning as intended by an author, but to engage the text itself in conversation to tease out a variety of meanings, much like rabbinic midrash.

Intertextual studies, especially those influenced by the work of Mikhail Bakhtin (1895–1975), focus on the dialogical character of the reading process. He argues that meaning in the reading of texts emerges through the "primacy of context over text" (heteroglossia), the hybrid nature of language (polyglossia), and the relation between texts or utterances (intertextuality). The process of communication entails appropriating language from other writers or speakers and filling it with content based on new agendas and understandings. Likewise, the process of reading entails that readers bring their own understandings of text and language to the reading process to interpret the text at hand.

The work of Emmanuel Levinas (1906–1995) likewise builds an intertextual model of communication and reading insofar as he posits that readers encounter "the Other" during the reading process. Encounter with the Other according to Levinas denies the drive toward unity and demands recognition that the Self is not alone in the world. Recognition of the Other therefore entails the moral obligation to recognize the Other and to establish relation with the Other that will advance the world toward ideal existence. When applied to the reading process, the reader enters into a dialog with the text and interpretation flows from that encounter.

Social Scientific Criticism

Social scientific criticism, which applies insights and methodologies from the fields of sociology, anthropology, and ethnography, has also emerged as a major sub-field in the study of the Bible in the late-20th and early-21st centuries. To a certain extent, the form critical preoccupation with *Sitz im Leben* or "social setting" anticipated this concern. Late-19th and early 20th c. scholars, such as Julius Wellhausen and William Robertson Smith (1846–1894), studied Islamic and Bedouin social organization as means to understand ancient Israel. Indeed, Wellhausen left the field of theology following his work in the Hebrew Bible to pursue sociohistorical study of early Islam. Perhaps the best-known early social historian of ancient Israel was Max Weber (1864–1920), who in his *Ancient Judaism* (1917–1920), studied sociohistorical and institutional change in ancient Israel (and in ancient China and early Protestant Christianity as well). Weber's understanding of charismatic figures in ancient Israelite society, for example, Saul, David, prophetic figures, etc., still continues to play a role in the field.

The mid-20th c. saw little interest in social scientific criticism by biblical scholars, but the 1960s and 1970s saw the re-emergence of the field as biblical studies were increasingly taught in secular universities where biblical scholars interacted with colleagues in the social sciences. George Mendenhall (b. 1916) and Norman Gottwald (b. 1926) pursued socioeconomic research to argue that ancient Israel emerged as the result of a peasant revolt against Canaanite urban culture with its hierarchical systems of overlords to form a new egalitarian culture in the highlands of Israel. Gottwald in particular was influenced by Marxist social theory and the model is largely rejected in biblical scholarship, but the work of these two scholars opened the way for others to pursue social scientific studies in conjunction with archeology. Gösta Ahström's *The History of Ancient Palestine* (1993) is an example of a major history that is informed by social scientific research. Major insights of such work include the recognition that ancient Israel developed from tribal societies, to chiefdoms, and ultimately to monarchies. The kingdom of Saul and the early kingdom of David appear to be chiefdoms; indeed, Saul appears to have ruled over the northern tribes of Israel whereas David ruled over Judah and eventually united the two chiefdoms following the death of Saul's son Eshbaal (Ish-bosheth according to 2 Sam.) to form the basis for the early monarchy.

Social scientific criticism has been useful in clarifying the social roles of prophets in ancient Israel and Judah. Although many early theologians presupposed an ideal model of Martin Luther standing alone against the Roman Catholic Church as the basis for their views of prophets, ancient Near Eastern comparative evidence points to prophets as a professional class who were largely organized around temples and their associated monarchies. Even a figure like Jeremiah, who is portrayed in conflict with the late Judean kings and the Jerusalem Temple, was supported by the family of Shaphan, who had played an important role in the pro-Babylonian monarchy of King Josiah. Social scientific research has also done much to clarify the social role of women in ancient Israelite and Judean societies, including the concern with the social and economic rights of women in the Deuteronomic law code, family structure, i.e., the *beit ab*, "house of the father," in Persian-period Judah (Yehud), and the purity laws of the Torah and their impact on the priesthood, gender roles, and social relations.

Contexts for Reading the Bible

For much of its history modern critical scholarship on the Bible has focused on an allegedly objective scholarly interpretation of the Bible in relation to the intentions of its authors and their historical context. But the increasing impact of contemporary literary criticism with its interest in the synchronic dimensions of a text and the role of its readers who construct its interpretation has called such methods into question. Indeed, many believe that the earlier historical-critical study of the Bible actually served the interests of Protestant European and American Christianity that aimed to arrive at a "true" understanding of the Bible apart from its interpretation in the Roman Catholic Church or in Judaism. By the late-20th and early 21st centuries, interpreters have turned to a variety of means to interpret the Bible in the various contexts—ethnic, cultural, canonical, religious, and others—in which it is read.

The late-20th c. saw the emergence of a variety of liberation theologies that would play a major role in shifting the reading of the Bible away from its ancient contexts and into direct conversation with contemporary ethnic and cultural communities. One of the earliest of the liberationist movements was Latin American Liberation Theology. This movement began in Central and South America as Roman Catholic clergy serving local Christians communities sought means to relate the message of the Bible to needs of their very poor and oppressed working class communities who often lived under dictatorial rule. The Exod. narratives and the prophetic literature proved to be especially relevant to such contexts insofar as both call for the overthrow of oppressors and the unjust in society in order to allow the righteous in Israel to thrive in freedom under the protection of the divine. Liberation theology also struck deep roots in the African-American Christian religious community and the women's liberation movement in both Judaism and Christianity as a means to look to the Bible for models of empowerment and change.

The recognition that ancient Israel was not a white European society but a western Asian culture with extensive influence from the

African culture of Egypt has prompted many interpreters to rethink their views concerning the ethnic makeup of Israel and the means by which the Bible might be employed to address contemporary communities. The feminist movement has likewise called for greater attention to the construction of gender roles in ancient Israel and the modern world as well as new models for feminist exegesis and hermeneutics. As Christianity grows in Asia, Asian and Asian-American scholars are examining the interrelationships between Confucian and Buddhist hermeneutics in biblical interpretation. Post-colonial hermeneutics are also growing, although such perspectives often view both ancient and modern Israel as an imperial power when in fact ancient Israel and Judah were overrun by the ancient empires of Egypt, Aram, Assyria, Babylon, and Persia.

Theological and religious contexts are also playing important roles in the contemporary reading of the Bible. As more and more Roman Catholic and Jewish scholars have entered the field of modern biblical scholarship, they have paid increasing attention to their respective theological and religious contexts in biblical interpretation. Modern biblical scholarship began as a branch of Protestant theology, and the contexts of both Christian theology and Jewish thought provide rich resources for reading the Bible in relation to both traditions. One important movement in this regard is canonical criticism. As noted above, many interpreters became dissatisfied with the so-called "atomistic" tendencies of modern source criticism and called for wholistic models for reading the Bible, reasoning that Christian (and Jewish) communities read biblical books in their final forms, not as early or later J sources, original oracles of Isaiah, or other critical reconstructions. Early canonical criticism emerged in the work of Brevard Childs (b. 1923), who called for reading the books of the Bible as Christian Scripture while recognizing the Bible's historical roots. Such a strategy meant reading biblical books in their final forms and in relation to the New Testament, although other canonical critics, such as James A. Sanders (b. 1927), pointed out that Christianity has a number of canonical forms, such as the LXX, the Latin Vg, the Syriac Peshitta, the Ethiopian Bible, and others in addition to the Jewish MT. Moshe Greenberg, mentioned above, with his "wholistic" approach, may be seen as a representative of a Jewish canonical perspective.

[MARVIN A. SWEENEY]

Gender in the Bible

Gender and Sex

Gender study encourages the constant negotiation between the categories of "sex" and "gender": "sex" and "male/female" are biological terms whereas "gender" and "masculine/feminine" refer to social constructs or behaviors. Stated differently, "sex" is biological and physiological, while "gender" is enacted. Most societies have particular roles or conduct expected of people belonging to particular groups (and some societies have more than two genders, though the Bible depicts gender as dichotomous—either male or female). As we will see, these norms are not uniform in a text as complex as the Bible; they changed over time and place, and varying norms could exist even at the same time and place. Gender studies in relation to the Bible asks how males were expected to enact their masculinity and how females were expected to enact their femininity. This differs from the feminist study of the Bible, which specifically explores women.

I begin with an example about males. In 1 Kings ch 2, David, on his deathbed, tells his son Solomon "be strong and show yourself a man" (1 Kings 2.2). What did he mean? Furthermore, was there only one way of "show[ing] yourself [to be] a man" in ancient Israel, or could maleness or femaleness be enacted in a variety of ways? The remainder of 1 Kings 2 defines David's and Solomon's masculinity: being strong, and avenging and killing the king's foes. This is the predominant biblical model of masculinity, and involves dominance and violence; many scholars call this model the hegemonic male. In fact, throughout the ancient Near East, to ascribe feminine characteristics to a warrior or king is an insult, suggesting that he is weak. The expectation of male dominance, and non-parity of genders is expressed, for example, in the story in 2 Sam. 11.21, which refers to the incident when a woman killed the judge Abimelech by throwing a millstone at his head from the city wall: "Who struck down Abimelech son of Jerubbesheth? Was it not a woman who dropped an upper millstone on him from the wall at Thebez, from which he died?" (See Judg. ch 9.) The story of the death of Abimelech at the hands of a woman has here become paradigmatic for a shameful, unmanly death.

There are, however, other images of the ideal man. Ps. 1 notes the ideal male as studying the Torah "day and night." This different masculine ideal, which likely developed late in the biblical period when Israel lacked political power, became especially significant in the later rabbinic period. It also existed earlier, overlapping with the model of the hegemonic man and other models that existed at different times and places in ancient Israel for how masculinity and femininity should be enacted. This diversity of models should not be surprising, since the Bible is a complex work with multiple perspectives on many issues.

Israel was a polygynous society, in which a man could have many sexual partners (wives, concubines, and even prostitutes), and not a polyandrous society, in which a woman could have many partners. A woman may have only one sexual partner. Therefore, the definition of adultery is the occurrence of sexual relations between a man (regardless of his marital status) and a woman who was married or betrothed to another man (who "owned" her sexuality). Sex between a married man and an unmarried woman was not considered adultery. Before marriage, a girl's father owned her sexuality and was therefore paid for his daughter's virginity by the man who married her, or illicitly had sex with her (see Deut. 22.28–29). Nothing comparable existed for males; they owned their own sexuality and that of their wives. In fact, among the curses that Deuteronomy declares for Israel's sins, which upend the natural order of society, is "If you pay the bride-price for a wife, another man shall enjoy her" (Deut. 28.30). While prostitution existed and was not illegal (and some prostitutes were portrayed positively, as in 1 Kings 3.16–28), no man would want his daughter to become a prostitute; Deut. 23.18–19 strongly discourages female and male prostitution. In the case of a priest, who was subject to special laws of purity, Lev. 21.9 warns: "When the daughter of a priest defiles herself through harlotry, it is her father whom she defiles; she shall be put to the fire." The gender disparity caused by polygyny but not polyandry, and the various institutions established to reinforce this norm are often subsumed under the term "patriarchy." This word's exact meaning is debated, and some find it inappropriate for ancient Israel. Nevertheless, as the following examples illustrate, in terms of gender relations, Israel was, in many respects, a male-favoring or male-privileging society, and not egalitarian with respect to gender.

Gender Roles in the Public Sphere

Women were excluded, or played secondary roles, in many of the leadership positions in ancient Israel. Much of the Bible is characterized by the monarchy, and monarchs were men—although royal women sometimes had great power (esp. the queen mother and, of course, Queen Esther, who was queen of Persia, not of Israel), the Bible never depicts a woman in Israel as a legitimate monarch. Although in 2 Kings ch 11 Athaliah serves as a queen, or regent-queen, since the legitimate king was a minor and had been placed in protective hiding from her, the manner in which she is portrayed is aimed at delegitimizing her. Kingship—an institution sanctioned by God in the Bible, is the domain of men. The various lists and names of royal officials preserved in the Bible are all male. This evidence shows that in the natural order of things, positions of political power and leadership were held by males, at least in the monarchic period.

The book of Judg. offers a different model. Chs 4–5 feature Deborah as one of the major judges, and Jael as a laudatory protagonist, responsible for the death of Sisera, the Canaanite army leader. It may indicate that some ancient Israelites believed that women could lead, and do so strongly and effectively, although these women are exceptions to the general rule of male leadership. Other scholars, however, point out that this story is placed in the prehistory of Israel, in a topsy-turvy anarchic period, and thus does not reflect an ideal in which women had power, but suggests just the opposite: women only have power when the world is turned upside down.

Women also could not be priests, the most significant role in the religious hierarchy. According to the Priestly system and Deut., Levites, priests, and the high priest were all male, patrilineal descendants of Levi or Aaron. Yet, they could take upon themselves certain religious duties and roles. Num. 6.1–21, which outlines the laws of the nazirite, who according to some scholars is an individual who assumes some priestly responsibilities, notes (v. 2): "If anyone, man or woman, explicitly utters a nazirite's vow, to set himself apart for the Lord." It is striking, nevertheless, that the continuation of the nazirite law never mentions women, and the Bible notes several male nazirites, but none who are female. Samson's mother, who takes on some of the requirements of a nazirite because she is carrying a child who will become a nazirite (Judg. 13.4, 7), is a partial exception. Two biblical passages contain intriguing references to "the women who performed tasks at the entrance of the Tent of Meeting" (Exod. 38.8; 1 Sam. 2.22), but the Bible is totally silent about what these tasks were. Women, just like men, could and did worship at sanctuaries and temples, praying (see esp. 1 Sam. chs 1–2), and sacrificing there. However, some texts mandated that at specific festivals, this was only a male responsibility (Exod. 23.17; 34.23; Deut. 16.16: contrast Deut. 31.12). Comparative evidence suggests that women may have been more involved in family religious practices (previously called "popular religion"), but these are not well-attested in the Bible, which is more concerned with "official religion," that is, religion in the public sphere. Also absent are prayers in Psalms that specifically relate to women's concerns, such as the safe birth of a healthy child, while male concerns, such as victory in war, predominate.

The Bible knows of women prophets; this term is used of Miriam (Exod. 15.20), in the early biblical period, of Huldah, in the later monarchical period (2 Kings 22.14), and Noadiah, late in the biblical period (Neh. 6.14). Joel 3.1 prophesies that in the future "I will pour out My spirit on all flesh; Your sons and daughters shall prophesy." The named women prophets have comparable roles and authority as their male counterparts, but they are few and less well known. Many more male prophets are recorded in the Bible than female prophets, and no woman has a book dedicated to her prophetic revelations; the Latter Prophets are all male.

This brief survey of women as kings, judges, priests, and prophets suggests a picture where women rarely held significant public power.

Gender Roles in the Private Sphere

Within the family, a woman was subordinate to her husband. Amos 4.1 condemns women who say to their husbands "bring, so we may drink!" (author's translation); women should serve men (see Gen. 18.6), but not be served by them. It is equally evident in the strong statement to Eve who is told after eating of the tree (Gen. 3.16) "And he shall rule over you." The Heb for "rule," uses the root *m-sh-l*, a root suggesting mastering, dominating, and exercising authority over someone; Gen. 3.16 thus suggests a divinely ordained gender hierarchy. The long parables in Ezek. chs 16 and 23 suggest that in some circles husbands had the right to humiliate—in an extreme, extra-judicial fashion—wives who have had sex outside of marriage. Men are supposed to command women, not the other way around; cases such as (Judg. 13.11) "Manoah [Samson's father] promptly followed his wife" are anomalous, and reflect poorly on the man involved, who cannot uphold masculine values. (See also Judg. 4.9.)

Main female roles revolved around giving birth to children and caring for them; when a sick child complains of a severe headache, his father sends him to his mother (2 Kings 4.19). Children offered women, according to the Bible, a basic sense of fulfillment and social status; Gen. 30.1 observes: "When Rachel saw that she had borne Jacob no children, she became envious of her sister [Leah]; and Rachel said to Jacob, 'Give me children, or I shall die.'" Ps. 128.3 notes a predominant biblical ideal of a woman: "Your wife shall be like a fruitful vine within your house." In the tragic story at the end of Judg. ch 11, Jephthah's daughter, before being sacrificed, asks her father "let me be for two months, and I will go with my companions and lament upon the hills and there bewail my maidenhood [dying as a childless virgin]" (v. 37).

Within the family, women were generally responsible for preparing food, cooking and preparing clothing. This is illustrated most clearly in Gen. ch 27, where Rebekah prepares foodstuffs and clothing so that Jacob might trick Isaac. Men were engaged in hunting (ibid., v. 7) and in the more physical agricultural work in the field (see esp. the book of Ruth, where the women glean between the men who are harvesting the crops), including sheep-shearing (2 Sam. 13.23–27). It is difficult to ascertain if women in ancient Israel were expected to avoid public places. Some texts suggest that they had an active public role (e.g., Prov. 31.10–31), while others may suggest that public spaces could be dangerous for women (Song 5.7).

In legal matters, women were treated the same as men when they committed crimes or were the victims of crimes. Exod. 21.29, for example, deals with an ox that "kills a man or a woman," and the penalty is the same in either case. Similarly, in Lev. 20.9 "If anyone insults his father or his mother, he shall be put to death; he has insulted his father and his mother—his bloodguilt is upon him."

Equality under the law, however, took second place to the family hierarchy, wherein women were subordinate to their father or husband. Thus a father could annul his (unmarried) daughter's vow and a husband could annul his wife's vow (Num. ch 30). Num. 30.10 notes, however, that "The vow of a widow or of a divorced woman, however, whatever she has imposed on herself, shall be binding upon her," since widows and divorcees are not under the authority of a husband or father. But, although widows were independent legally, they were often impoverished, lacking the support that a male would provide (see esp. Ruth). They are therefore included, along with orphans and the poor, in the laws that mandate care for the underprivileged (e.g., Exod. 22.21; Deut. 24.19–21), and most starkly by Isa. 4.1, which notes that after a period of destruction "seven women shall take hold of one man, saying, 'We will eat our own food / And wear our own clothes; / Only let us be called by your name—/ Take away our disgrace!'"

The Bible shows several different views on whether or not women were part of the covenantal community. Exod. 19.15, immediately before the revelation on Sinai, has Moses telling the people "Be ready for the third day: do not go near a woman." In that passage, the "people" to whom the chapter is addressed are men only. The Decalogue that follows is addressed explicitly to males when it prohibits coveting "your neighbor's wife" (20.14). In fact, these women are viewed as the man's property: "You shall not covet your neighbor's house: you shall not covet your neighbor's wife, or his male or female slave, or his ox or his ass, or anything that is your neighbor's." In contrast, Deut. 31.12 includes women in its covenant ceremony: "Gather the people—men, women, children, and the strangers in your communities—that they may hear and so learn to revere the LORD your God and to observe faithfully every word of this Teaching." (Cf. Neh. 8.2–3; 10.29.)

Women as Authors

We know little about gender and the authorship of literature in ancient Israel, including the involvement of women in producing or writing parts of the Bible. The Bible associates some works with female authorship, such as the songs of Deborah (Judg. ch 5) and Miriam (Exod. 15.20–21); it is not surprising that women composed songs to welcome home the male warriors on whom they depend. Literacy rates were very low in ancient Israel (probably below 5 percent), and it is likely, based on ancient Near Eastern and other analogies, that many fewer women than men could read and write. (We have, e.g., the names of many more male than female scribes from Mesopotamia.) It has been suggested that perhaps a small number of biblical books were written by women (Ruth and sections of Song are leading candidates), but it is exceedingly difficult to determine this. Some biblical writings contain a female voice or take a woman's perspective, but this has little bearing on authorship. Even when a woman plays a central role or is a main protagonist, as in Esth., the book should not be seen as having been written by a woman.

The observations above are a sketch, and no more. Exceptions exist to almost every generalization adduced. Conceptions of gender are fluid over time and place, and differ between classes—then, as now. For example, Prov. 31.10–31 depicts an independent, wealthy, property-owning, entrepreneurial woman, most likely representing the rights of some upper-class women in the Persian period. In contrast, the initial chs of Prov. depict certain women very negatively; they are temptresses who "lurk at every corner" (Prov. 7.12), whose "house is a highway to Sheol [the underworld] / Leading down to Death's inner chambers" (v. 27). These contrasting depictions remind us that understandings of gender changed over time, and even at a single time, differed widely within the ancient population, as they do now. Furthermore, it is difficult to know how representative the Bible is of ancient Israel's life and practices.

Are particular texts descriptive or prescriptive? Are the descriptions commonplace or exceptional? Broadly illustrative or paradigmatic? These issues are often difficult to resolve. In addition, modern biblical translations often obscure many gender-related issues; they may mistake gender-neutral terms for gender-specific ones (e.g., translating *'adam* as "man" in Gen. 1.27, rather than "person"—see below), and sometimes, for reasons of modern gender-inclusivity, are gender-inclusive when the text is gender-specific (see e.g., the NRSV rendering of Ps. 128.1, "Happy is everyone," which is clearly incorrect given v. 4 "Thus shall the man *[gaver]* be blessed"). Thus, all issues concerning gender and the Bible must be studied with great care, looking at the original Heb terms, some of which are ambiguous. For example, the common word *'ish* may mean man or person, depending on context.

Gender in the Divine Sphere

Since many of the biblical descriptions of God are metaphorical, it is natural to wonder to what extent gender in the divine sphere mirrors the human. Does the biblical God have a biological sex? Is God imagined as a man or a woman, as both or as neither?

And even if the Bible does not depict God as sexed, is God gendered as male or female?

In exploring all issues concerning gender and the Bible, but especially concerning God's gender and sex, it is important not to fall into anachronism. A fundamental feature of all religions is that they change over time. Thus, it is imperative not to accept as factual for the biblical period the belief expressed by the important medieval philosopher and legal sage Maimonides (1135[?]–1204) that God

> is incorporeal, that His unity is physical neither potentially nor actually. None of the attributes of matter can be predicated of Him ... If He were a body, He would be like other bodies. Whenever Scripture describes Him in corporeal terms ... it speaks metaphorically. Thus our sages said: "The Torah speaks in human language" (*Berakhot* 31b). This ... is taught in the Biblical verse: "You have seen no image" (Deut. 4:14 [sic—should be v. 15]). This verse means to say, one cannot conceive of Him as one would a Baal image, since, as we have shown, He has no body at all, actually or potentially. (Translation from Isadore Twersky, *A Maimonides Reader* [NY: Behrman, 1972], 418.)

In fact, a large number of texts do depict various body parts of God such as arms, hands, legs, and fingers. Texts such as Deut. 4.15 say that at Horeb (Deut.'s name for Mt. Sinai), the Israelites saw no image or shape of God, but never say in the categorical terms represented by Maimonides that God has no image. Vv. such as Isa. 40.18, "To whom, then, can you liken God, / What form compare to Him?" (cf. 40.25; 46.5) represent a small minority opinion in the Bible, and are part of a polemic saying that God should not be represented in a physical, "plastic" shape, as was common in the ancient Near Eastern world; they do not mean that their author believed in an incorporeal God.

Thus, did the corporeal God that ancient Israelites believed in have a sex or a gender? Although some scholars suggest that some biblical texts contain echoes or remnants of a sexually active male deity, and thus this idea may have existed in ancient Israel, it is not found explicitly in any biblical text. In fact, in Ezek. 1.26, where God is depicted as being in "the semblance of a human form," the following verse makes clear that the divine genitalia, if they exist at all, are hidden: "and from what appeared as his loins down, I saw what looked like fire." It is likely that this depiction is an attempt to say that God is sexless.

But is God genderless in the Bible? Biblical Hebrew, like French, Spanish, German, Arabic and many other languages, but unlike English, has only two grammatical genders. There is no neuter; all nouns are either masculine or feminine, and when replaced by pronouns, masculine or feminine pronouns must be used. Nouns govern verbs that are conjugated in the masculine or feminine. This is a ubiquitous feature of Heb (and all Semitic languages). The grammatical gender of God is *always* masculine and *never* feminine—in other words, no biblical sentence ever uses the pronoun "she" of God or has God as the subject of a feminine verb. Fewer than ten biblical texts use unambiguous feminine imagery of God (see e.g., Isa. 42.14, where God is compared to "a woman in labor"), but in none of these is God construed as grammatically feminine. Although scholars debate the relevance of this grammatical fact, many modern linguistic studies suggest that such grammatical features are significant, and that the repeated use of masculine pronouns and verbs with God, was part of, and would have fostered, a belief in a masculine deity.

Other factors would have furthered this belief. A variety of biblical texts use the marriage metaphor to express the (covenantal) relationship between God and Israel—these are, for example, especially prominent in the first three chs of Hos. In *all* of these texts God is the husband and Israel is the wife—*never* is God the wife. Given that the husband-wife relationship in ancient Israel was one where the husband (Heb *ba'al*, lit. "owner") had power over his wife, it is not surprising that God is always husband, and never wife. Thus, the use of the metaphor "God is Israel's husband" would have also fostered the idea of God as male.

The same notion is strengthened by the many masculine images used of God in the Bible. Exod. 15.3, for example, depicts God as a man ['ish] of war, and many passages throughout the Bible depict God as a strong, victorious male warrior. In contrast, a very small number of texts, all in Deutero-Isaiah (Isa. chs 40–66), use feminine imagery of God, as in Isa. 49.15–16: "Can a woman forget her baby, / Or disown the child of her womb? / Though she might forget, / I never could forget you. / See, I have engraved you / On the palms of My hands, / Your walls are ever before Me." Scholars have suggested that this imagery, which genders God as female, developed in response to the Babylonian exile, which fostered the need among some for a more feminine, nurturing deity.

Gen. 1.27 is often cited in discussions concerning the gender of God. In the NJPS translation, it reads: "And God created man in His image, in the image of God He created him; male and female He created them." This translation is problematic; the word rendered "man" is Heb *'adam,* which is typically a gender-neutral term that should be translated as "person" (or "humanity"). Thus, this text is talking about the creation of the first human, or of humanity as a whole, but not the first male.

Although not printed as such in the NJPS, the repetitions and other features suggest that Gen 1.27 is poetry (see "Biblical Poetry," pp. 2184–91), and thus best translated:

> And God created person in His image,
> in the image of God He created it/him;
> male and female He created them.

Given that a predominant form of biblical poetry is where each verse-part more or less says the same thing (the older term for this is synonymous parallelism), perhaps this v. should be analyzed as: And God created person in His image = in the image of God He created it/him = male and female He created them. In that case, the v. suggests that God is both male and female, and therefore perhaps beyond sex and gender. However, this type of three-part poetic line (the tricolon) is somewhat uncommon in biblical poetry, which strongly favors two-part lines (bicola), and thus the line might also be analyzed as "And God created person in His image = in the image of God He created it/him; male and female He created them," where "male and female ..." is an additional statement introducing the following v. that deals with procreation. In that case, "male and female He created them" has no bearing on the gender of God according to the Bible's first creation story.

We do not have much evidence beyond the Bible to make broad statements about ancient Israel's beliefs concerning God's sex and gender. Yet, some findings suggest that some ancient Israelites believed that the world was governed by two main deities, a male and female couple, Yahveh and Asherah. (See "Religion of the Bible," pp. 1978–97.) There are some hints of this in the Bible, and some scholars believe that this idea was central to royal belief in some periods. Eighth c. inscriptions from Kuntillet Ajrud and Khirbet el-Qom refer to "Yahveh of Samaria and his Asherah," and many scholars believe that these refer to male and female deities. (The issue is complex, esp. since Asherah is both the name of a deity, and of a sacred tree or pole dedicated to her, and the grammar of the inscriptions is somewhat unexpected.) In contrast, we do know that the biblical authors fostered belief in a single high-God, YHVH, who was sexless and did not have a female consort, and, in almost all of their gender depictions of the deity, imagined God as male. This is captured properly in the NJPS translation, which uses male pronouns such as "He" and "Him" for God.

Despite these various uncertainties, what can be said is that the Bible, like many religious and social texts, is very concerned about gender. This comes out quite clearly in Deut. 22.5: "A woman must not put on man's apparel, nor shall a man wear woman's clothing; for whoever does these things is abhorrent to the LORD your God." Here the Bible makes explicit the notion of gender demarcation that is encoded throughout the Bible. Gender is central to one's identity and should be immediately evident. Males should act and look like males, and females should act and look like females, and both genders should worship a masculine God.

[MARC ZVI BRETTLER]

Reading Biblical Poetry

Most literary works, both narrative and non-narrative, from the ancient Near East are in poetry. In contrast, the Bible uses narrative prose, not epic poetry, to tell its traditional stories. Prose narrative dominates in the Torah, the Former Prophets, and several books in Kethuvim (The Writings). To be sure, there are a few narrative poems, for example, Judg. ch 5 and Ps. 136, but they exist along with, not in place of, the prose narratives that inform them. Poetry in the Bible is regularly used for non-narrative genres: prayers, laments, victory songs, love poems, wisdom instruction, and prophetic speeches. About one-third of the Bible is poetry, including the books of Ps., Prov., Job, Song, Lam., Eccl. Modern scholars also consider most of the speeches of the latter prophets (Isaiah, Jeremiah, Ezekiel, the Twelve) to be poetry. In addition to these large blocks of text, poems are interspersed in the prose narrative; examples are the Testament of Jacob (Gen. ch 49), the Song of the Sea (Exod. ch 15), the Sayings of Balaam (Num. 23.7–10, 18–24; 24.3–9, 15–24), the Song of Moses (Deut. ch 32), the Testament of Moses (Deut. ch 33), the Song of Deborah (Judg. ch 5), the Prayer of Hannah (1 Sam. ch 2), the Elegy over Saul and Jonathan (2 Sam. ch 1), and David's Song in 2 Sam. ch 22 (= Ps. 18).

Most individual poems are relatively short, about thirty vv. or less on average. (The longest single poem is Ps. 119, with 176 vv.) Long books like Ps., Job, and others are actually composed of series of, or collections of, poems.

Poetry, or more properly, verse, is a form of elevated discourse whose formal properties differ from prose (which is also somewhat elevated discourse, not a record of everyday speech). Some argue that these differences are a matter of degree rather than of kind, but at a certain point quantitative difference becomes qualitative difference. The attributes of poetry will be discussed below.

The identification of biblical poetry and the definition of what constitutes poetry in the Bible has been a vexed issue since early postbiblical times. Each generation of scholars has applied its own criteria, usually drawn from its own vernacular poetry, be it the classical meters of Greek and Latin poetry, the medieval Arabic systems of rhyme and meter, or the accentual meter of English poetry—but none of these fit biblical poetry. The Bible itself has little to say about its poetry, other than offering some terms that may indicate types of poems.

The most general term is *shir* or *shira*, "song." *Shir* may stand alone, as in Judg. 5.12; Ps. 65.1, or may be qualified, as in *shir hammaʿalot*, "song of ascents" (Pss. 120–134); *shir yedidot*, "A love song" (Ps. 45.1); "A song for the dedication of the House" (Ps. 30.1); *shir tziyyon* "song of Zion" (Ps. 137.3); *shir tehillah* "song of praise" (Neh. 12.46). The "feminine" form, *shira*, is found in Exod. 15.1; Deut. 31.30; Num. 21.17; Isa. 5.1, and elsewhere, and appears to be synonymous with *shir*. Another frequent term is *mizmor*, "psalm, a song sung to the accompaniment of a stringed instrument" commonly found in the superscriptions to psalms, sometimes in combination with *shir* (e.g., Pss. 67.1; 68.1). A third term, *qina*, "lament, dirge" is known from 2 Sam. 1.17; Amos 8.10, etc. These terms are suggestive of ancient notions of poetic genres, but they do not mark every passage that a modern reader would consider poetry.

Another suggestive feature of the Masoretic Text (MT) is the traditional scribal convention of stichography, whereby certain passages are written in verse-like lines (e.g., Exod. ch 15; Deut. ch 32; Judg. ch 5; 2 Sam. ch 22). This scribal convention, discussed in rabbinic literature, sets off certain sections from the blocks of surrounding text. There are two forms, called by the rabbis "small brick over large brick, large brick over small brick" and "small brick over small brick, large brick over large brick." Small brick over large brick looks like:

Small brick over small brick looks like:

The stichographic writing, too, is not a sufficient criterion by which to identify poetry by today's standards because it was used for only a fraction of passages that we would consider poetry (e.g., most mss do not use this stichography for Ps.); moreover, it is occasionally used for non-poetic lists (Josh. 12.9–24; 1 Sam. 6.17; Esth. 9.7–9).

A third potential indicator of poetry, in the MT, is the system of accents (tropes, or cantillation marks) used in the Tiberian Masorah, whereby the books of Ps., Prov., and most of Job are given a different system of accents from the other twenty-one books of the Bible. [These three books are referred to as *sifrei ʾemet*, *ʾemet* being an acronym from the initials of *ʾiyyov* (Job), *mishlei* (Prov.), and *tehillim* (Ps.).] Again, while we consider these three books to be poetic, there are additional poetic books and passages for which these accents are not used. It seems that this system of accents indicates only the cantillation and says nothing about poetry per se.

While the Bible does not define or describe its poetry, most scholars would accept the following description: *Biblical poetry is a type of elevated discourse, composed of terse lines, and employing a high degree of parallelism and imagery.* Other tropes and figures may also be present, most commonly word and sound repetition and patterning. Meter was apparently not required (see below).

Terseness is a feature of many of the world's poetries; lines of poetry tend to be shorter and more concise than prose clauses, whether or not a system of meter is present. Lines of biblical poetry are generally no longer than three or four words. Terseness is often achieved by the omission of the definite article, the accusative marker *ʾet*, and the relative pronoun *ʾasher*. Accompanying the terseness of the lines is the paratactic style by which lines are joined together. The connectives between lines may be missing altogether or may consist of the multivalent conjunction *vav*, "and, but, or." Thus the relationship between lines is often not explicit, opening up both difficulties and opportunities for interpretation. Terseness and parataxis make poetry seem more intense; they give the impression that each word is heavily laden with meaning.

Biblical poetry is characterized most of all by its binary form of expression known as parallelism. Parallelism is the pairing of a line (or part of a line) with one or more lines that are in some way linguistically equivalent. The equivalence is often grammatical—that is, both parts of the parallelism may have the same syntactic structure, as in

The LORD is my light and my help;
    whom should I fear?
The LORD is the stronghold of my life,
    whom should I dread? (Ps. 27.1).

Often, though, the grammatical structure is not identical, at least on the surface, as in

> Before I created you in the womb, ...
> Before you were born, ... (Jer. 1.5).

In this example, "you" (the prophet) is the grammatical object in the first line and the subject in the second. In Prov. 6.20, a positive clause is paired with a negative clause.

> My son, keep your father's
> commandment;
> Do not forsake your mother's teaching.

Grammar has many facets and any one of them can be brought into play in parallelism.

Another form of equivalence is semantic equivalence; the meaning of the lines is somehow related: perhaps synonymous, perhaps reflecting the converse or reverse, or perhaps extending the meaning in any one of a number of ways. Equivalence does not imply identity. The second line of a parallelism rarely repeats exactly the same words or exactly the same thought as the first; it is more likely to echo, expand, or intensify the idea in the first line in any one of a number of ways. For example,

> Women in Zion they raped;
> Maidens in the towns of Judah
> (Lam. 5.11, author's translation).

The parallelism intensifies from "women" (women in general) to "maidens" (women of marriageable age), making the second line a more poignant image of rape. It expands from "Zion" to "towns of Judah," making the atrocity more widespread—not only in the capital but throughout the country.

Grammatical and semantic equivalence account for most parallelisms (both are present in Lam. 5.11), but because there are so many equivalent permutations for any given line, the number of potential parallelisms is enormous, if not infinite. By shaping the parallel line, that is, by narrowing the potential choice to a single statement, the poet clarifies the first line and moves the poem forward. Compare, for example, two couplets that differ in only one word:

> But you, O Lord, are enthroned forever;
> Your *fame* endures throughout the ages
> (Ps. 102.13).

> But you, O Lord are enthroned forever,
> Your *throne* endures through the ages
> (Lam. 5.19).

Both vv. open with the image of God enthroned as a king. The slight difference in their second lines changes the thrust of the thought in their first lines. Ps. 102 is concerned with God's permanence, which it contrasts with the fleeting life of humans; it therefore focuses on God's fame, literally, the mention of His name, symbolizing His being. Lam. has a different concern: the existence of God when He has no Temple, no earthly locus for divine worship, no earthly throne to symbolize His kingship. The author of Lam. claims that God's throne is independent of the Temple and continues to exist despite the loss of the Temple. In parallelisms like these, the first line presents a picture and the second line shines a spotlight on a certain part of it.

Parallelism helps to bind together the paratactic lines. It works as a counterweight to the parataxis, forging a relationship between the lines that is otherwise unexpressed. The basic structuring unit of the poem is not a single line, but a set of parallel lines (a two-line set is sometimes called a couplet or a bicolon and a three-line set is a tricolon), as these examples demonstrate.

Another by-product of parallelism is the balance that it creates. Scholars have long sought metrical regularity in biblical poetry, but no metrical system—be it syllable counting, stress counting, thought-rhythm, or constraints on the number of syntactic units in a line—has met with unanimous acceptance. More likely, the ancient Hebrew poets embraced a system in which many lines of a poem are more or less the same length and partake of the rhythm of their parallelism, but without the requirement of precise measurement.

Beyond the level of sets of parallel lines one may find larger structural units, sometimes called strophes or stanzas. These are not units of a required number of lines, but merely a subdivision of a poem, not indicated formally, that modern readers make on the basis of the poem's contents or its structural or lexical repetitions (e.g., a refrain). Some translations indicate these subdivisions by leaving space between sections, but they are not indicated in the Heb text. Even when there are no discrete stanzas, couplets are woven into longer segments or entire poems so as to provide movement and development. A dramatic example is the "scene" at the end of the Song of Deborah (considered to be one of the oldest poems in the Bible), with a dialogue in which Sisera's mother answers her own question (Judg. 5.28–30).

> Through the window peered Sisera's
>   mother,
> Behind the lattice she whined:
> "Why is his chariot so long in coming?
> Why so late the clatter of his wheels?"
> The wisest of her ladies give answer;
> She, too, replies to herself:
> "They must be dividing the spoil they
>   have found:
> A damsel or two for each man,
> Spoil of dyed cloths for Sisera,
> Spoil of embroidered cloths,
> A couple of embroidered cloths
> Round every neck as spoil."

In these vv. some words repeat while others are echoed by words related in meaning. Redundancy is raised to an art-form. The terse lines—snapshots, as it were—grow into a larger moving picture as we imagine, through the eyes of Sisera's mother, that Sisera is bedecking himself with damsels and beautiful cloths obtained as the spoils of war (even as we know all the while that he lies dead in Jael's tent).

The unity of a poem is sometimes, but far from always, promoted by a formal device like an acrostic, an inclusio, or a refrain. Occasionally, an alphabetic acrostic forms the unifying structure of a poem, marking it as ordered and complete, from A to Z. Acrostics may have served also as a pedagogic or mnemonic device. Alphabetic acrostics (sometimes incomplete) are present in Pss. 9–10, 25, 34, 37, 111, 112, 119, 145; Prov. 31.10–31; Lam. chs 1, 2, 3, 4. A more common unifying device is "inclusio" (also called inclusion, frame or ring-composition) in which the poem begins and ends with a similar line, as in Ps. 104.1 and 35: "Bless the LORD, O my soul." Compare also Ps. 8.2, 10: "O LORD, our Lord, how majestic is Your name throughout the earth." Inclusio provides a strong sense of closure to a poem. Less common is refrain, the repetition of a chorus-like line, which, in the case of psalms, may have been sung antiphonally (e.g., Ps. 136); sometimes refrains are not repeated exactly.

We can see terseness and parallelism in operation, as well as larger structuring devices, in a segment of Ps. 136. The segment also illustrates how poetry differs from prose, since it is a poetic rendering of a prose narrative in the Torah.

> Who made the heavens with wisdom,
>   His steadfast love is eternal;
> Who spread the earth over the water,
>   His steadfast love is eternal;
> Who made the great lights,
>   His steadfast love is eternal;
> the sun to dominate the day,
>   His steadfast love is eternal;
> the moon and the stars to dominate
>   the night,
>   His steadfast love is eternal.
>   (Ps. 136.5–9)

Immediately evident is the refrain, which unambiguously separates each line of poetry, and also gives cohesion to the whole, as well as rhythm. Even in English translation (and more so in Heb) each line seems terse, and about the same length, so that reading the lines one after another creates a rhythm, although not a precise meter. Compare the Gen. account of the creation of the celestial bodies that the psalm encapsulates in vv. 7–9: "God made the two great lights, the greater light to dominate the day and the lesser light to dominate the night, and the stars" (Gen. 1.16). The prose account also has parallelism, but it is not as obvious or as pervasive as in the psalm. The psalm has broken up the prose verse into poetic lines, by the use of, and clearly marked by, the refrain.

In addition to terseness and parallelism, biblical poems may employ the repetition and patterning of words and sound clusters, sometimes producing word- or soundplay. An ABB'A' or chiastic word pattern occurs in Song 2.14:

A Let me see your *face*,
B Let me hear your *voice*;
B' For your *voice* is sweet
A' And your *face* is comely.

A classic example of soundplay is found in Isa. 5.7:

vayeqav lemishpat vehinneh mispaḥ
litzdaqah vehinneh tzeʿaqah,
"And He hoped for justice, / But behold injustice; / For equity, / But behold, iniquity!"

(Cf. also Isa. 61.3; Zeph. 2.4.) Repeated words may be key words, words that recur often and point to the message of the poem; for example, in Ps. 121 the word "guard/guardian" occurs six times within the eight verses of the psalm, and indeed the psalm is about God as Israel's guardian. In Ps. 122 the topic is Jerusalem, and the name of the city occurs three times. In addition, combinations of the letters that make up the name "Jerusalem" occur frequently throughout the poem; many words in the poem echo Jerusalem's name.

These are samplings of the myriad repetitions of words and sounds that enhance the poeticalness of biblical poetry, and often its rhetorical force as well. Poetry is an auditory medium. Sound—be it the repetition of sounds or the rhythm of lines—and the nexus of sound and meaning contribute to the heightening of the discourse and to the effect on the listener. Poetry is related to music, and some poetic genres, like the psalms, were publicly performed with musical accompaniment. (cf. Exod. 15.20–21; Ps. 137.2). Musical instruments are called *kelei shir*, "instruments of song/poetry" (Neh. 12.36). David, the psalmist par excellence (according to tradition), is a musician (1 Sam. 16.23). At the same time, poetry (*shir*) is associated with "speaking, reciting" (Judg. 5.12; Ps. 137.3). The combination of music and words, sound and meaning, is epitomized in poetry.

No discussion of poetry can omit imagery, or metaphor, often thought to be the essence of poetry. Metaphors are not merely decorative; they, like parallelism, are pervasive in poetry. Poetry envisions the world metaphorically, it offers an alternative way of seeing reality. As medieval Jewish scholars put it, "The best part of poetry is its falseness (that is, its figurativeness)." (They got this idea from Arabic sources, who got it from Aristotle *[Poetics]*.) Poetry, in this view, is not only elevated language, it is elevated vision.

A small example is in Ps. 136.6. We looked at this psalm earlier, noting how it poeticizes the creation story in Gen. ch 1. But the poetry of Ps. 136 is not merely a matter of breaking up prose sentences into terse, parallelistic poetic lines; it is a matter of re-envisioning the account of creation. Ps. 136.6 says that God "spread (Heb *roqaʿ*) the earth over the water." Gen. does not say this; in fact, according to Gen. 1.9, the water was gathered to one place so the dry land could appear—the land was actually under the water, visible when the water was removed. Moreover, the word that the psalm uses for "spread" is the same word that Gen. uses for "firmament." The psalmist has a different conception, or a different interpretation, of how the world was created. He sees the earth being spread, like a firmament, upon the water. The earth is a firm expanse set permanently in place over the waters (the forces of chaos, which cannot now escape); the earth is made analogous to the firmament of Gen. that separates the upper and lower waters. The psalm's conception of the creation of the earth is more mythological than that of Gen., more like, for instance, Ps. 24.2: "For He founded it [the world] upon the ocean, / set it on the nether-streams." Poetry can retain more mythological concepts than prose, not because it is earlier or more primitive (Ps. 136 is probably exilic, after 586 BCE), but because it is free to call upon more imaginative views of the universe than are found in the "logical" or "theological" discourse of prose.

Metaphor, rather like parallelism, juxtaposes similarities and differences in such a way that a relationship between them is created. In metaphor, two things are brought together that do not generally occur together; they collide, or explode, leaving in their wake a new way of seeing. Metaphors come in many shapes and sizes. Some take but a line, others inform an entire poem. Some are deeply embedded in the culture of Israel, like the parent-child relationship or the husband-wife relationship used to portray the relationship between God and Israel; others may be the new creation of the poet; and still others may be "dead metaphors," commonplace idioms that have lost their impact. Much of the difficulty in understanding poetry arises from the difficulty in recognizing what is metaphoric (and what is not) and in perceiving the meaning of the metaphor.

Ps. 133.1: "How good and pleasant it is / that brothers dwell together," contains a metaphor that is often overlooked. The verb "dwell together," *shevet yaḥad*, is a legal term that means to live in joint tenancy; that is, to hold land in joint ownership without dividing it up among separate owners (cf. Gen. 13.6; 36.7; Deut. 25.5). The psalm is not about harmonious family life, in my reading, but about brothers holding land together. This is a metaphor for the (re)unification of Israel and Judah, as observed in *Metzudat David*, an 18th c. commentary written by David Altschuler (and printed in most editions of *Miqra'ot Gedolot*), which explains:

> How very good and how very pleasant is the thing when the whole house of Israel will dwell on its land; they are called "brothers" for the great affection that is among them.... And they will be together in one kingship and will not be divided into two kingdoms any more.

Metaphors, again like parallelisms, can have many permutations. A common metaphor for human beings is a tree, with its leaves and fruit. The water that nourishes the tree/person is God's *torah* or trust in God. Prov. 11.28 and 30 capture the idea in pithy statements: "The righteous shall flourish like foliage" and "The fruit of the righteous is a tree of life." More embellishment is found in the following examples.

> The righteous bloom like a date-palm;
> they thrive like a cedar in Lebanon;
> planted in the house of the LORD,
> they flourish in the courts of our God.
> In old age they still produce fruit;
> they are full of sap and freshness
> (Ps. 92.13–15).

The image is of grandeur and vigor. Both the date-palm and the cedars of Lebanon are tall and stately and long-lived. So will be the righteous in the protection of the Temple: long-lived and vigorous in old age.

More famous is the tree imagery in Ps. 1.3, applied to the man who delights in God's teaching *(torah)*.

> He will be like a tree planted beside
> water channels,
> which produces its fruit in its season,
> and whose foliage does not wither;
> And all that he does will succeed.
> (author's translation).

Just as the tree is nourished by water channels that provide a constant supply of water, so the man is continually nourished by God's teaching *(torah),* a constant source of life. Just as the tree flourishes and accomplishes its purpose in life, so will the man succeed in his purpose. The rootedness and productiveness of the righteous man is contrasted with the transience and worthlessness of the wicked, who are like the chaff, the husks that are blown away in the winnowing process. A further implication of the metaphor: the tree's fruit and foliage also belong to the image of the man. The man, like the tree, will have fruit (= children) in its season (year after year) and unwithering foliage (= a long life). Children and long life are the ideal blessing in ancient Israel (cf. Job 42.16–17), and that blessing is achieved, says the psalm, through devotion to God's teaching.

Often compared to Ps. 1 is Jer. 17.5–8, which contrasts the man who trusts in humans with the man who trusts in God. The former will be like a tamarisk, a desert shrub with small, narrow leaves.

He shall be like a tamarisk in the desert,
which does not sense when good (= rain)
comes.
It dwells in the parched wilderness,
in salt-lands, without inhabitants.
As for the man who trusts in God,
He will be like a tree planted beside water,
sending forth its roots by a stream.
It does not sense when heat comes,
Its leaves remain fresh,
And in a drought year it does not worry;
It does not cease to produce fruit.
(Jer. 17.6–8, author's translation)

The man who trusts in humans lives in a permanent desert, without nourishment; even when a bit of water reaches him, he cannot make use of it. On the other hand, the man who trusts in God is constantly nourished, and because he has sunk his roots deep into water sources, he can easily survive a drought with no loss of productivity.

These tree metaphors show how the same basic image may be altered or embellished to fit different contexts. Now let us see how the same concept may be conveyed through different images. Wisdom is an abstract concept that is expressed metaphorically in different ways in Prov. and in Job. Prov. 1.20–33 personifies Wisdom as a woman calling aloud in the public square, scolding those who reject her and warning them that she will be gleeful when they fail in life (cf. also Prov. chs 8–9). Lady Wisdom is certainly advertising her availability and urging everyone to pay heed to her. This is firmly in keeping with the main purpose of the book of Prov., to provide Wisdom to everyone so that all may prosper.

Job, on the other hand, has a very different notion of Wisdom. Wisdom is desirable but elusive, unattainable. Job 28.1–2 implicitly compares Wisdom to precious metals and gems hidden deep in the earth. This suggests that Wisdom is more precious than metals and gems (a comparison that Prov. often makes) but at the same time it says that Wisdom is difficult to find (Prov. would disagree). Like the other poems in Job, this ch employs difficult language and develops its images in detail. Its first section (vv. 3–11) have been interpreted as either a picture of human metal mining or as the acts of the deity in the course of creation. Especially evocative are vv. 5–6:

Earth, out of which food grows,
Is changed below as if into fire.
Its rocks are a source of sapphires;
It contains gold dust too.

The world below the surface is a very different place from the world above. Above is the soil that provides bread, below is a hot colorful fantasy-world of potential riches. But, though humans can find the riches under the ground, can they find Wisdom?

But where can wisdom be found;
Where is the source of understanding?
(Job 28.12)

The link between the first section (v. 1) and the second section (v. 12) is forged by the repetition of two words (the Heb root for the first is *m-tz-ʾ*).

There is a mine *(motzaʾ)* for silver,
And a place *(maqom)* where gold is refined. (Job 28.1)

But where can wisdom be found *(timatzeʾ)*;
Where is the source [place] *(maqom)* of understanding? (Job 28.12)

Vv. 13–19 echo the first section by saying that no one can put a price on wisdom, its value is beyond all the precious materials in the world. Moreover, its location is not anywhere in the natural world, nor even in the mythological world of the "deep" and the "sea" (the primordial waters).

Where, then, does wisdom come from, asks the third section of the poem (Job 28.20–28).

It hidden from the eyes of all living,
Concealed from the fowl of the sky.
Abbadon and Death say,
"With our ears we have heard a rumor of it" (vv. 21–22, author's translation)

A number of parallels are invoked: earth, sky, and the netherworld; the living and the dead; eyes and ears and seeing and hearing—to the effect that no creature, earthly or not, alive or dead, anywhere in the cosmos, has perceived Wisdom.

Only God knows where it is and how to reach it, for He is all-seeing and in the course of creating the world, He saw and gauged Wisdom. The poet here borrows the well-known idea that Wisdom was present at creation—compare Prov. 8.22–31. But the picture of creation in vv. 25–26 is not at all like Gen. ch 1, or like Ps. 136, or even like Prov. ch 8.

When He fixed the weight of the winds,
Set the measure of the waters;
When He made a rule for the rain
And a course for the thunderstorms
(Job 28.25–26).

This description focuses on God's power over meteorological or mythological forces. The creation is not centered on the earth, or below the earth where the mines are (where men can penetrate to), or even in the watery deep or in the realm of Death (below the ground); but far above the earth, in the home of the wind and the rain—the heavens. Wisdom was and remains in the domain of God, not in the domain of human beings. How, then, can humans achieve wisdom? Only through the fear of the Lord (v. 28). "Fear of the Lord" is the essence of wisdom according to all the biblical wisdom books, but Job ch 28 dramatizes that principle according to its conception of Wisdom.

It is not easy to sum up what biblical poetry is. More than just a set of formal features or structures, poetry is sound and vision compressed for intensity and expressed with potency. Biblical poetry struggles to probe and stretch the important cultural concepts and issues of ancient Israel in exquisitely distilled Heb. In that sense, it is the purest, most rarefied, expression of biblical thought.

[ADELE BERLIN]

Reading Biblical Narrative

Much of the Bible is narrative. Gen. through Kings, as well as the books of Jonah, Ruth, Esth., Dan. chs 1–6, Ezra, Neh., and Chron., consist primarily of narrative, though they incorporate other genres such as law, poetry, and lists. Other narrative pieces can be found in biographical elements in the book of Jer. and in the frame story (the outer tale within which the dialogues take place) of Job. Biblical narrative texts share some of the same conventions as Western or English literature, but also use some non-Western conventions that they share with ancient Near Eastern literature.

Stories in the Bible are generally short, consisting of a few vv. (see e.g., some of the Elisha miracle-tales [2 Kings 2.19–21; 4.38–41, 42–44]) and up to some forty vv. (e.g., the story of the prophecy of Micaiah son of Imlah about the death of Ahab [1 Kings 22.1–38]). Longer works, though found, are atypical: the Joseph narrative (Gen. chs 37; 39–48; 50), the succession narrative (2 Sam. chs 11–20; 1 Kings chs 1–2), Ruth (eighty-five vv.), and the book of Esth. (ten chs). Many of the smaller stories have been woven together into what may be called biographies—multiple episodes that center on events in the lives of individuals, like Noah, Abraham, Jacob, David, and so on.

It is often not advisable to break down these larger biographies into their constituent units. For example, it is wrong to remove from its context the short story about Elisha's curse of the boys who insult him by calling out "Go away, baldhead!" (2 Kings 2.23–24). The story opens with the words "From there he went up"—from Jericho, whose waters he healed, thus curing the town of its bereavement over the death of its children. This is connected to the prophet's anger in the baldhead story: the children of Jericho who show him dishonor are indebted to him, since he saved them from death, and therefore they now deserve—in the opinion of the redactor of Elisha's biography—death. This brief story does not mention the prophet's name, knowing that readers are familiar with him from the previous stories; this, too, highlights the dependence of 2 Kings 2.23–24 on its broader context.

Another important story in the Elisha cycle concerns his interactions with the Shunammite woman (2 Kings 4.8–37), a story I will use as a paradigm for the nature of biblical narrative, and how such narrative should be interpreted. The prophet Elisha, wishing to reward this barren woman for the generous hospitality she has shown him, announces how she will give birth to a son by her aged husband. The pronouncement is fulfilled, but the boy dies. The woman insists that the prophet perform another miracle and return her son to life.

The story's opening assumes familiarity with Elisha and presents the story as one more link in the chain of tales about him: "One day Elisha visited Shunem. A wealthy woman lived there, and she urged him to have a meal; and whenever he passed by, he would stop there for a meal" (v. 8). The v. presents readers with the story's second protagonist, the woman, a wealthy woman of influence (the Heb *gadol*, "big, great," may also mean "rich"; see e.g., Lev. 19.15; 2 Sam. 19.33)—from Shunem. The v.'s second half reveals how the prophet stops regularly for meals at her house. No details are told of the woman's marital status, but her strong, decisive nature is alluded to with the words "she urged him *[vataḥazek-bo]* to have [lit. 'eat'] a meal."

This v. also opens the first scene, and includes the formula that the narrator uses to divide his story into three sections, *vayehi hayom*, "One day" (vv. 8, 11, 18). In this, the first section, the woman suggests to her husband that they build a small "upper chamber" and furnish it for Elisha (vv. 9–10). The husband's response is not mentioned, but at the start of the next section it is evident that the deed has been completed. That section, which is longer than the first, describes how Elisha rewards the woman by giving her news of her imminent motherhood, tidings that are soon fulfilled (vv. 11–17). The third section, the longest of the three (vv. 18–37), presents a complication and its resolution: the boy dies but, thanks to his mother's keen determination, Elisha returns him to life.

The story has two protagonists, Elisha and the Shunammite woman. Alongside them are two secondary figures: the Shunammite's husband and Gehazi, the prophet's servant. The chief role of secondary characters is to illuminate the primary figures: through her husband we see the woman's determination and strength of character. This is already highlighted at the story's beginning, which does not mention the husband's response to his wife's suggestion to build the chamber for the prophet. When the boy collapses in the field, the husband-father hurries to transfer responsibility to his wife, telling his servant, "Carry him to his mother" (v. 19). When the boy dies, the mother hides the tragedy from her husband. She will need his minimal assistance—the transportation he can provide, an ass and a servant who will bring her to the man of God—though when he questions her trip, noting, "It is neither new moon nor sabbath" (v. 23; these were most likely the typical occasions to visit a prophet), she does not answer and leaves with only one word, *shalom* (rendered in NJPS "It's all right"). This is not necessarily a sign of disrespect towards the husband; the woman is determined to meet the man of God, whom she expects will save her son. The husband will not be mentioned again.

If the weakness of the husband highlights the strength of his wife, Gehazi, Elisha's servant, helps to reveal his master's weakness: Elisha uses his servant to enforce his notion of what it means to be "a man of God," and the appropriate distance between himself and others. In the story's second section, when he desires to repay the Shunammite for her hospitality, Elisha turns to her by way of Gehazi: "He said to his servant Gehazi, 'Call that Shunammite woman.' He called her, and she stood before him. He said to him, 'Tell her, "You have gone to all this trouble for us. What can we do for you? Can we speak in your behalf to the king or to the army commander?"'" (vv. 12–13). Her polite refusal of his generosity, "I live among my own people" (ibid.), reveals the confused prophet's embarrassing ignorance: "What then can be done for her?" (v. 14). It is Gehazi, the sensible servant, who knows the neighborhood gossip and understands what the prophet does not; he suggests the solution: "The fact is ... she has no son, and her husband is old" (ibid.).

Gehazi is again instrumental in revealing Elisha's lack of understanding when the bereaved mother appears before him on Mt. Carmel. The insensitive Gehazi approaches in order to push her away, since that is his job—to separate and moderate between the man of God and the common people. This act enables the prophet to voice his own failure: "Let her alone, for she is in bitter distress; *and the* L*ORD has hidden it from me and has not told me*" (v. 27). Elisha fails for a third time when he tries to revive the boy by sending Gehazi with his staff (v. 30), but the attempt fails and, in any case, the Shunammite does not let Elisha escape, insisting that he accompany her to her home.

Alongside these two pairs, a few other figures appear momentarily on the stage: the son who says but two words, *roshi roshi*, "my head, my head" (v. 19), and the servants, one of whom brings messages between the woman and her husband when the latter is in the field, and the other who brings the bereaved mother to the prophet on Mt. Carmel. Neither speaks a word.

Only Elisha and Gehazi are given names. The woman, though she is a primary character (and even the most dominant, as we will soon see) is called by her hometown: "the Shunammite." The missing name reflects a social norm: even if our story places a woman at the center and shines a kindly light on her, the narrative reflects the socially superior position of men by leaving this woman unnamed. (Another example of this is the wife of Manoah [Judg. ch 13], who stands at the center of a story that relates how an angel of God announces the impending birth of a son [Samson] to her—and not her husband; she is also smarter and more daring than her husband. When Manoah expresses his fears at the end of the story, "We shall surely die, for we have seen a divine being" [v. 22], she answers astutely, "Had the LORD meant to take our lives, He would not have accepted a burnt offering and meal offering from us, nor let us see all these things; and He would not have made such an announcement to us" [v. 23]. Still, Manoah, the husband is named, while the woman is not.)

The designations used to refer to characters are significant, and these change with the circumstances related in the narrative. In Elisha's first appearance in our story, the narrator calls him by name: "One day Elisha visited Shunem" (2 Kings 4.8). The woman, who suggests to her husband that they build an annex for the prophet in their home, refers to him as "a holy man of God" (v. 9), an epithet that justifies the initiative and expense, and that is fully realized by the miracles that Elisha will perform. The woman again calls him "man of God" when she turns to him later (v. 16), and again, in her words to her husband when she relates her wish to go to the prophet on Mt. Carmel (v. 22); the narrator also uses the epithet in the vv. that deal with the subsequent meeting between the bereaved mother and the prophet (vv. 25, 27).

The woman, we recall, is referred to as a "wealthy [great] woman," but the prophet, when he speaks of her to Gehazi, says, "Call *that Shunammite woman*" (v. 12). This designation is repeated twice more, when he sees her approaching on Mt. Carmel, "There is *that Shunammite woman*" (v. 25), and again, in his final words to Gehazi, after he has revived the boy, "Call *the Shunammite woman*" (v. 36). The prophet's designation conveys the lack of feeling he has for her, and perhaps even a bit of condescension. (See similarly the way in which the proud Gehazi refers to Naaman, commander of the Aramean army, in the next ch: "... My master has let *that Aramean* Naaman off without accepting what he brought!" [2 Kings 5.20].)

The Shunammite's husband, who shirks his responsibilities when his son becomes ill, tells his attendant: "Carry him to his mother" (2 Kings 4.19). The narrator calls her "the boy's mother" when she stands firm against Elisha, determined that he and only he must restore the life of her son (v. 30). The woman calls herself a "maidservant" when the prophet promises that she will become a mother, "Please, my lord, man of God, do not delude your maidservant" (v. 16).

The son is called *hayeled*, "the child" (vv. 18, 20, 34) or *hana'ar*, "the boy" (vv. 30, 32, 35). By the end of the story, however, he is referred to in relation to his mother: "Elisha says to her, "Pick up your son" (v. 36), and the narrator relates: "then she picked up her son and left" (v. 37). The change illustrates the crucial role played by the mother's determination in saving the boy's life and in fulfilling the prophet's words that "you will be embracing a son" (v. 16).

Another figure who plays a central role in most of the Bible's stories is God, though His involvement in our story is relatively modest. The woman and the narrator call Elisha "man of God" in order to remind us that the prophet's power derives from God. The prophet himself does not mention God when he declares the miracle, "At this season next year, you will be embracing a son" (2 Kings 4.16), reflecting a carelessness that will blow up in his face with the boy's death. Elisha remembers God only after his miracle fails, when the woman comes to the Carmel and clings to his legs. To Gehazi, who tries to push the woman away, he says: "... *the LORD* has hidden it from me and has not told me" (v. 27). The Shunammite also mentions God when she vows not to leave until Elisha makes things right: "As the LORD lives and as you live, I will not leave you!" (v. 30). When the prophet revives the boy, his actions suggest that he is performing magic; the three Heb words reflected in "and prayed to the LORD" (v. 33) do little to correct this impression.

Apart from the distinctive sobriquets that contribute to the story's characterizations, characters are also depicted by their descriptions of each other. Gehazi describes the husband as "old" (v. 14), and Elisha characterizes the woman's state of mind by saying that she is "in bitter distress" (v. 27).

The biblical narrator rarely reveals a character's thoughts or emotions, nor does he tend to explicitly express his opinions of characters and their behavior; we must instead infer these from characters' actions and words. The Shunammite's resolute doggedness is never stated, but expressed through her interaction with other characters: her proposal-announcement to her husband concerning their building the extra chamber (2 Kings 4.10), and her insistence that the prophet accompany her, "As the LORD lives and as you live, I will not leave you!" (v. 30). The Shunammite is entirely focused on her objective; to both her husband's inquiry about her journey to the Carmel (v. 23), and the prophet's question posed by Gehazi, "How are you? How is your husband? How is the child?" (v. 26), she answers with one word: *shalom*. Her resolve is apparent also in the directions she gives the servant: "Urge [the beast] on; see that I don't slow down unless I tell you" (v. 24). The similar instructions of Elisha to Gehazi, "Tie up your skirts, take my staff in your hand, and go. If you meet anyone, do not greet him; and if anyone greets you, do not answer him. And place my staff on the face of the boy" (v. 29), highlight an essential difference: the Shunammite's resolve is to save her son, while the prophet's resolve is to dodge responsibility. Moreover, Elisha errs in thinking that his staff has the power to produce miracles. But reality will again loom before him when Gehazi reports that "the boy has not awakened" (v. 31).

In contrast to Elisha's negligence, we see the woman's forthright pragmatism when he first proclaims the miracle (without referring to God) and she replies, "do not delude your maidservant" (v. 16). Perhaps we hear here, too, a fear of disappointment, after having given up the hope of motherhood. Afterwards, with the boy's death, her doubt turns into rebuke, "Did I ask my lord for a son? Didn't I say: 'Don't mislead me'?" (v. 28).

The woman's resolve is reflected also in her acts. The verb *ḥ-z-q* is twice used to describe her actions: first, at the story's beginning, "she *urged* him to have a meal" (2 Kings 4.8), and then after the most awful of things, her son's death, occurs, "she *clasped* his feet" (v. 27), the first sign that she will not leave him until he comes and performs his work. The prophet's feet reappear at the end of the story, when she prostrates herself before them (v. 37), an expression of gratitude for the son's return to life.

We have already seen the elements of Elisha's character that are reflected in his availing himself of Gehazi's help, whether this expresses his own failings or whether it involves using his attendant to help keep a safe distance from the woman. But when Elisha proclaims the miracle, he dispenses with all aloofness and announces to her, directly: "At this season next year, you will be embracing a son" (v. 16). Also after the boy's successful resurrection he turns directly to her with an abrupt command to "pick up your son" (v. 36). While the character of the Shunammite is delineated both by her words and her actions, it is almost impossible to point to any actions by Elisha apart from his (successful) attempt to revive the boy (vv. 32–35), an act which, as already noted, leaves God aside.

The biblical narrator avoids descriptions, whether of scenery or people. And indeed, our story contains no descriptions whatsoever of characters' physical appearance, since these have no function in the story. (On the rare occasions when the Bible provides such information, it is usually to offer a detail that is crucial to the story's development.) We note, too, that few characters occupy the stage—two or three, at the most—the Shunammite and her husband (vv. 9–10), the prophet, Gehazi and the woman (vv. 12–16), the son, his father, and the servant (vv. 18–20), the boy and his mother (vv. 20–21), and so on. In other stories we find collective characters, choruses with numerous participants, but these constitute one speaking voice.

Biblical narrative may take place in multiple settings. In our story, the first two sections transpire in the Shunammite's home, but the third section (2 Kings 4.18–33) takes place in different locations: the field in which the son and his father are situated (vv. 18–19); their home, where the boy dies (vv. 20–24); Mt. Carmel, where the prophet resides (vv. 25–30); the road from the Carmel to the woman's home (v. 31); and again, the woman's home, where the story ends, with the resuscitation of the boy and his return to his mother's arms (vv. 32–37). The story closes with the emptying of the stage: the woman takes her son and exits (v. 37).

Biblical narratives often leave gaps, which the reader is expected to fill. Thus, for example, the Shunammite tells her husband her plans to build the extra room in order to host the man of God (vv. 9–10), but his response and the building of this room are not recorded. From the next v. the reader learns that the prophet indeed stays in the additional room, from which we conclude that the husband consented to his wife's initiative. The narrator avoids giving the husband's response in order to minimize his stature, or the credit due him: it is the great woman who decides.

The story contains many chronological ellipses: it omits any mention of the year that passes between the prophet's prophecy and the boy's birth (v. 17), and likewise the time between the boy's birth and the day of his death is passed by in silence. Immediately following the v. that reports the boy's birth, the third section, the heart of the story, opens schematically, "The child grew up. One day, he went out ..." (v. 18). This abrupt jump brings us quickly from the birth to the moment when the youngster can participate in the plot. (See similarly Gen. 25.26–27, "... Isaac was sixty years old when they were born. And the boys grew up, Esau became a skillful hunter, a man of the outdoors; but Jacob was a mild man who stayed in camp" and Exod. 2.11, "Some time after that, when Moses had grown up, he went out to his kinsfolk and witnessed their labors.")

The hours the boy spends on his mother's lap, as he moves between life and death, are described very tersely: "and the child sat on her lap until noon; and he died" (2 Kings 4.20). As long as the boy lives, the mother waits and hopes for improvement; when he dies, she becomes intensely active. In order to express her fierce resolve, the narrator avoids describing the woman's journey to the man of God on Mt. Carmel; her rush is only reflected in her own words to her husband, "so *I can hurry* to the man of God and back" (v. 22), in the impatience reflected in the enigmatic answer she gives her husband, *shalom* (v. 23), and in her words to the rider, "see that I don't slow down unless I tell you" (v. 24). The journey itself is conveyed with the utmost brevity: "She went on until she came to the man of God on Mount Carmel" (v. 25).

The biblical narrator treats the passing of time according to his needs, shortening or expanding his narrative. Dialogue faithfully represents the time that passes within a story, but events are hurriedly recounted. The narrator even avoids unnecessary repetitions that might interrupt the story's rapid pace; this is quite different from epic poetry, where repetitions, even when verbatim repetitions, are commonplace. The foundations of epic poetry were oral, when the creator stood before his audience. That storyteller had many choices: to raise his voice or to whisper, to pronounce words quickly or to take his time, to accompany his words with facial expressions or with gestures. Moreover, audiences love repetitions, which allow them to chime in and recite the repeating lines together. In the Bible, a written medium, the storytelling effects of the performer are lost, and effort is expended to avoid unnecessary repetitions. Epic poetry narrates repeated commands and reports of the commands' execution: X tells Y to convey his commands to Z; Y conveys X's commands, and Z carries them out. This occurs less often in biblical narrative, and when it does, it is for a specific purpose. In our story, Elisha tells Gehazi, "Tell her [the Shunammite], 'You have gone to all this trouble for us. What can we do for you? Can we speak in your behalf to the king or to the army commander?'" (2 Kings 4.13). Instead of repeating the message when Gehazi relates it to the Shunammite, the biblical narrator jumps directly to her answer: "She replied, 'I live among my own people'" (ibid.), and the reader easily fills in the gap.

Events progress in a similar fashion when the Shunammite travels to Mt. Carmel. The prophet dispatches Gehazi to meet her: "Go, hurry toward her and ask her, 'How are you? How is your husband? How is the child?'" (v. 26), and the questions are followed immediately by her answer: "We are well" (ibid.).

Occasionally, for dramatic effect, the narrator lingers over the command's execution: Elisha rushes to dispatch his assistant to revive the boy (in a desire to evade a troublesome task?): "Tie up your skirts, take my staff in your hand, and go. If you meet anyone, do not greet him; and if anyone greets you, do not answer him. And place my staff on the face of the boy" (v. 29). The narrator repeats part of the command when he reports Gehazi's actions, in order to spotlight his failure: "Gehazi had gone on before them and had placed the staff on the boy's face; but there was no sound or response ..." (v. 31).

The narrator's manipulation of the timeline is noticeable also in his ability to recount synchronous events: the mother does not put much faith in the mission the prophet gives to Gehazi, and she compels the prophet to accompany her to her home: "But the boy's mother said, 'As the LORD lives and as you live, I will not leave you!' So he arose and followed her" (v. 30). The two journeys now occur simultaneously, that of Gehazi and that of the prophet and the woman; as the prophet is still seen walking after the woman, Gehazi arrives at the destination, attempts to revive the boy and fails, and on his return trip, the two routes coincide: "He turned back [along the way] to meet him and told him, 'The boy has not awakened'" (v. 31).

The narrator can also disrupt the timeline by moving back to the past or jumping ahead to the future. Into the mouth of the bereaving Shunammite the narrator places the words, "Did I ask my lord for a son? Didn't I say: 'Don't mislead me?'" (2 Kings 4.28). The second half of the v. returns us to the woman's words following the prophet's initial pronouncement of the miracle, "do not delude your maidservant" (v. 16). This time, she replaces the root *k-z-b* ("mislead") with its synonym, *sh-l-h,* because the latter creates a wordplay with the verb *sh-ʾ-l* in the first part of the v., "Did *I ask (sh-ʾ-l)* my lord for a son?" She no longer doubts the prophet's ability to fulfill his promise but she criticizes both the prophet and his God. It was better for her to be barren than to give birth to a son and lose him. She now interprets her initial intent differently, as though she had foreseen the coming disaster. Indeed, her initial words appear now as a prophecy or, using rabbinic terminology, as an "unwitting prophecy," when "they foresee and know not what they foresee; they mutter and know not what they mutter" (*b. Sot.* 12b). A jump from the present to the future is found in Elisha's promise/prophecy, "At this season next year, you will be embracing a son" (v. 16), words that cause us to wonder whether the promise will be fulfilled, especially in light of the doubt thrown onto it in the Shunammite's response.

The narrative contains some flexible elements, such as in the multiple sobriquets that designate the characters, each matching the particular circumstances in which it is used, or in the substitution of a synonym in place of another word, such as that of *sh-l-h* for *k-z-b.* On the other hand, the story also repeats words and expressions, creating similar or parallel situations. We saw this in the repetition of the word *shalom* (vv. 23, 26), which points to the woman's unyielding determination to achieve her objective, and in the repetition of the root *ḥ-z-q,* "to urge," "to clasp." A further example is the repetition of the root *n-s-ʾ* ("carry, pick up") which marks the story's complication and resolution: when the boy becomes ill, "[the father commands] his servant, '*Carry* him to his mother.' He *carried* him ..." (vv. 19–20). The same verb is used later, when the prophet commands the mother, "'*Pick up [s'i]* your son.' ... then she *picked up [vatisa']* her son and left" (vv. 36–37). We have already noted an example of a parallel situation—when the Shunammite first grabs hold of the prophet's legs (v. 27), expressing both her deep despair as well as her determination, and then when she falls to his feet, in an expression of gratitude (v. 37). A final parallel situation is the Shunammite's command to her servant in v. 24 and Elisha's command to Gehazi in v. 29, which spotlights the contrast between the two protagonists.

Many of the features that we have mentioned testify to the biblical narrative's dramatic quality and to its similarities to theater. The narrative is, as it were, performed in front of us, which is why there is no place for descriptions of characters or landscapes, or for representing the inner worlds or thoughts of the characters. Actions and words convey all the reader needs to know about the plot and the relations between characters. To be sure, the narrator occasionally gives some "director's notes." This is the function of the exposition and also of the directions for creating sets: the woman's plan for building the added room and furnishing it prepares the stage for the dramatic scene in which the boy later lies on the prophet's bed in that upper chamber (vv. 32–36).

Familiarity with the features of the biblical narrative, as expressed in our story, helps us trace its underlying message, since the biblical narrator, like a playwright, generally does not explicitly state his intentions or his evaluation—positive or negative—of his characters; this is accomplished through characters' actions, words, and relationships with one another. The superior status of men in the Bible and its general male-orientation are well-known: at the center of the Bible we find the patriarchs, Joseph, Moses, Joshua, the judges, the kings, and the prophets, who occupy center stage. If a main role is occasionally given to a woman, it is to teach a lesson, or even to humiliate the male. Our story presents two protagonists, one opposite the other. Elisha, the man of God, certain of himself and of his power, takes care to keep a formal distance between himself and the Shunammite. He speaks to her through his messenger and, in a patronizing way, seeks to repay her by using his connections with the authorities (v. 13). Elisha also avoids invoking the name of God when he pronounces the miracle, a clear sign of his confidence and even pride. The great, strong woman of Shunem teaches Elisha an important lesson in humility. She has no need of his interference in the corridors of government on her behalf; the embarrassed prophet, following her polite refusal, needs the guidance of his servant (v. 14). The prophet keeps stumbling; he, who has been referred to repeatedly as the "man of God," will not involve God in pronouncing the miracle, and God will not inform him of the boy's death. Elisha again voices his embarrassment to Gehazi, "the LORD has hidden it from me and has not told me" (v. 27). The prophet's third failure comes when he, who did not hesitate to promise the woman a son, does not hurry to confront the boy's death. On the contrary, he prefers to dodge his responsibility and pass off the task to his attendant. Once again, the woman prevails over the prophet, compelling him to follow her and bring her son back to life. With the conclusion of the story, the social hierarchy is returned to the normal state: the prophet commands Gehazi to call the woman and, when she stands before him, he commands her to take her son (v. 36). She expresses her gratitude by falling at his feet and then picks up her son and leaves, at which point the curtain falls. But the reader is not deluded: the prophet's authority has been fractured, and his position has been diminished in the shadow of the woman's stronger character.

As noted earlier, the Bible's "biographies" are formed from a chain of stories. The continuation to 2 Kings ch 4 is found later in the Elisha cycle, in 2 Kings 8.1–6, a brief narrative about the power of a story. A number of the characters from our story appear also there: Elisha, the woman—who is no longer called by her hometown but by the miracle that Elisha performed for her—"the woman whose son he revived" (2 Kings 8.1), the son, and "Gehazi, the servant of the man of God" (v. 4). Elisha sends the woman abroad for seven years, due to a famine that he prophesied, and on her return, she "went to the king to complain about her house and farm" (v. 3) over which she seems to have lost ownership. The woman arrives to make her complaint at the exact hour that Gehazi stands before the king, at the king's request, relating "all the wonderful things that Elisha has done" (v. 4), including Elisha's having revived the Shunammite's son. Due to the fortuitous timing of the Shunammite's arrival, the king commands a eunuch to restore her property and even increase it, "and all the revenue from her farm from the time she left the country until now" (v. 6). This story was meant to demonstrate the truth of all the Elisha stories, and also to show how a story, in itself, can effect positive change (the root *s-p-r*, "to tell," appears in vv. 4, 5, 6). The story's tone is also ironic: when Elisha initially offered to interfere on the woman's behalf before the king (4.13), she answered "I live among my own people" (ibid.), but now she is in need of the king's protection and it is the prophet's name that induces the king to help. The prophet's first apparent failure now appears otherwise.

Connections between stories are not limited to a single story-cycle. The Elisha/Shunammite story is connected to other stories in the Bible, and these connections are meaningful. The story of the Shunammite converses with Gen. ch 18, the story about the news of Isaac's impending birth, where the news is primarily directed at Sarah (despite the fact that the three visitors initially appear to Abraham). The guests ask of Sarah's whereabouts (Gen. 18.9), and the language of the divine pronouncement revolves around her, "I will return to you next year, and your wife Sarah shall have a son" (Gen. 18.10; see also v. 14). Sarah laughs (v. 12), and the reader understands the implicit etymology of the boy's name, Isaac, *yitzḥak*, "he will laugh."

These two stories share certain elements. In Elisha's promise, "At this season next year, you will be embracing a son" (2 Kings 4.16), we hear an echo of God's words to Abraham (quoted above). In both stories we hear about the fulfillment of the promise (Gen. 21.2; 2 Kings 4.17); the husbands of both women are old: Sarah saying concerning Abraham "with my husband so old" (Gen. 18.12), while Gehazi says that "her husband is old" (2 Kings 4.14). Also the doubt expressed by the women is shared in both stories, in Sarah's laughter and words (Gen. 18.12) and in the Shunammite woman's words (2 Kings 4.16), discussed above.

The difference between the two stories is also very clear: it is God Himself who pronounces the news in Gen. ch 18, while in our story it is the prophet who does not bother to even mention God's name that speaks the promise. This comparison diminishes Elisha's reputation.

The story of Samuel's birth in 1 Sam. ch 1 has also influenced our story. Like Elisha, who is ignorant of the woman's needs, the priest Eli also fails, thinking that the praying Hannah is drunk (1 Sam. 1.13–14). In the Shunammite's rhetorical question, "Did I ask *[ha-sh'alti]* my lord for a son?" (2 Kings 4.28), we hear an echo of Samuel's name derivations in his birth story, "and may the God of Israel grant you what you have asked *[e'et shelatekh 'asher sha'alt]* of Him" (1 Sam. 1.17; see also vv. 27, 28). The woman who prayed for a son receives a son who lives, while the woman who did not pray for a son—and who even doubted the promise for a son, will, in the end, need to explicitly petition the prophet to intervene so that the boy will live. This suggests that a woman must actively desire a child for that child to live.

Our story also contains an echo of the story about the death of the son of Jeroboam (1 Kings 14.1–18). Our story seems to be a mirror reflection of this story, in which, after the son falls ill, Jeroboam instructs his wife to go to the prophet for help (v. 2). In our story, it is the woman who initiates action while the husband is passive, and she goes to the prophet only after the boy has died (2 Kings

4.22ff.). In the 1 Kings story, despite the woman's arrival in disguise, and despite his own blindness, the prophet Ahijah identifies the woman as the wife of Jeroboam because God had told him of her impending arrival (1 Kings 14.5); Elisha, on the other hand, testifies that God has hidden the boy's death from him (2 Kings 4.27). Ahijah tells Jeroboam's wife that her son will die (1 Kings 14.12), which soon occurs (v. 17), while Elisha will bring the Shunammite's son back to life (2 Kings 4.33–35) and informs her that the son is alive (v. 36). The son of Jeroboam dies because of his father's sins; the son of the Shunammite lives because of the respect his mother shows God and the man of God.

The story of Elisha's revival of the Shunammite's son left its mark on the Elijah cycle. Even though Elijah is depicted as Elisha's teacher, parts of the Elijah cycle developed after the Elisha cycle, and are dependent on it. In order to temper Elijah's zealous nature, and to show another, more merciful side of him, the episode of the death and revival of the son of the woman from Zarephath (1 Kings 17.17–24) was embedded into the story of the drought declared by Elijah. The episode is intrusive there, breaking the natural continuity of the drought story. In that story's first scene, Elijah "stayed by the Wadi Cherith," where he is miraculously fed until the riverbed dries up (vv. 5–7). At that point, God sends him to Zarephath, in Sidon, where God designates a widow to feed him, "and she and he and her household had food for a long time" (v. 15). The immediate continuation of this story is in 18.1, "Much later, in the third year, the word of the LORD came to Elijah, 'Go, appear before Ahab; then I will send rain upon the earth.'" After a year in Wadi Cherith and a year in Zarephath, two years that emphasize the famine's severity, God—and not the prophet—has mercy on His people and sends rain.

The episode of the woman of Zarephath's son's death, and his revival by Elijah, has nothing to do with the famine. On the contrary, it interrupts and disrupts that story. The story of the boy's death and revival was created under the influence of the Elisha—Shunammite woman story, as seen in the following points:

(1) Only in this scene of the famine story, and in one late story in the Elijah cycle, is Elijah referred to as the "man of God" (1 Kings 17.18, 24), a sobriquet commonplace in the Elisha cycle and in our story, in particular.

(2) God designates a woman to feed Elijah but not to house him in her home. And yet, in vv. 17–24, he is seen as a guest in her house (v. 20), like Elisha in the Shunammite's house.

(3) The "upper chamber" appears totally unexpectedly in Elijah's story. Elijah takes the child from his mother and "carried him to the upper chamber where he was staying" (v. 19). In the story of Elisha, the upper chamber is an integral part of the story.

(4) Elisha—and not Elijah—is known as the prophet who revives the dead. His ability to bring people back to life is so established that even after death his grave maintains that power (2 Kings 13.20–21).

(5) The drought story, particularly in the encounter scene between the woman from Zarephath and Elijah, contains a change that eased the insertion of the interpolated episode. In the Masoretic Text (MT) of 1 Kings ch 17, the woman tells Elijah, "I am just gathering a couple of sticks, so that I can go home and prepare it for me *and my son*; we shall eat it and then we shall die" (v. 12). In v. 13, the prophet answers her, "... but first make me a small cake from what you have there, and bring it out to me; then make some for yourself *and your son*." The Septuagint (LXX), on the other hand, speaks of *sons*, in the plural, in both vv. The LXX preserves the original text, and the transition from the plural to singular was meant to reshape the woman into a mother of a single child that will die and be revived, like the Shunammite woman.

This similarity between the two revival stories explains, in turn, why the Shunammite story appears in the Elisha cycle immediately following the story of the increase of the widow's oil by the prophet (2 Kings 4.1–7).

That story was inspired by Elijah's multiplication of flour and oil. Because of the juxtaposition of the story of Elijah's multiplication of flour and oil with the episode about the death of the woman of Zarephath's son in the current form of the famine stories (1 Kings chs 17–18), the stories of the multiplication of the oil and the death and revival of the Shunammite's son were also juxtaposed to one another. Moreover, this juxtaposition serves another purpose: at the end of the story of Elisha's multiplication of oil, Elisha promises the debt-ridden widow that "you and your children *will live* on [the remaining oil after your debts are paid]" (2 Kings 4.7, author's translation). The story of the Shunammite, of course, revolves around Elisha's giving life to the woman's son. We see here how the juxtaposition of stories is not coincidental: there is a message behind the order of stories and episodes. The juxtaposition of these two episodes shows how Elisha helps both the poor and the rich, giving life to all. This juxtaposition also illustrates how various contexts can influence one another in a variety of ways over time; this may be termed "the boomerang effect."

Our story concerning Elisha and the Shunammite is juxtaposed meaningfully with 2 Kings 4.38–41, a story that again deals with life and death. The disciples of the prophets eat poisoned food, and "they began to cry out: 'O man of God, there is death in the pot!'" (v. 40). Elisha throws flour into the pot, "and there was no longer anything harmful in the pot" (v. 41). The juxtaposition of these three stories solidifies the image of Elisha as the ultimate life-giver.

The story of Elisha and the Shunammite woman contains a sharp criticism of the prophet since, despite the happy ending, readers remember that the role of the woman in saving her son was greater than the prophet's. The criticism of the prophet should not surprise us: biblical narrative, especially that written in the First Temple period, typically presents flawed figures. Perfect characters are liable to give rise to personality cults and the worship of the characters, thereby diminishing God's stature. Furthermore, humans, imperfect figures, can learn best from other imperfect figures. The biblical narrative aims to educate its readers, and education is made possible through stories about imperfect people. The Bible's heroes err and sin like all human beings, "for there is no man who does not sin" (1 Kings 8.46), and they pay for their mistakes and sins.

[YAIR ZAKOVITCH]

Reading Biblical Law

Law and legal practice are represented in many books of the Bible. The Torah, which contains all of the Bible's formal legal collections, is the most important locus of biblical law, but laws are mentioned in prophetic speeches, narratives throughout the Bible, wisdom literature and other genres as well.

In the ancient Near East laws were promulgated by the king; the Torah, in contrast, uniquely within the ancient Near Eastern world, views law as divine revelation. There could be no more compelling authority for them and no more compelling motivation to obey them. More specifically, the Torah's laws are formulated as stipulations of the covenant *(berit)* between God and Israel. The covenant assures divine protection and blessing if Israel obeys God's laws or commandments. This is reflected, for example, in what God tells Israel just before the revelation at Sinai: "Now then, if you will obey Me faithfully and keep my covenant, you shall be My treasured possession among all the peoples" (Exod. 19.5). According to Exod. 24.3, after narrating the commandments, the content of the covenant, "Moses went and repeated to the people all the commands of the LORD and all the rules; and all the people answered with one voice, saying, 'All the things that the LORD has commanded we will do!'" The surrounding vv. detail the ceremony solemnizing this covenant.

Terminology

Various Heb terms introduce and describe biblical laws. These include *torah* ("instruction"), *ḥoq* ("law") or *mishpat* ("rule"), as in the introduction to the collection of laws in Exod. chs 21–23: "These are the rules *[mishpatim]* that you [Moses] shall set before them" (Exod. 21.1). Alongside these markers, the Torah often uses the Heb word *mitzva* ("commandment" or "instruction"), which characterizes the laws' place within the Torah as God's commandments to the Israelite community. The Decalogue, or the Ten Commandments, is called simply *devarim*, "words" (Exod. 20.1; Deut. 4.12; 8.19). While rabbinic interpreters find significance in these different terms, at the basic level they are largely synonymous.

On the basis of form, modern scholars have suggested classifying biblical laws into two major categories: apodictic and casuistic. Apodictic laws, like those in the Decalogue, are commands, formulated in the imperative ("Honor your father and your mother") or prohibitive ("You shall not murder"). Casuistic laws present cases or situations (if a certain thing has happened) and the law pertaining to them (then this is what you should do): "If a man is guilty of a capital offense and is put to death, and you impale him on a stake, you must not let his corpse remain on the stake overnight, but must bury him the same day" (Deut. 21.22–23a). Each casuistic law begins with a protasis ("If such-and-such occurs") that narrates a set of circumstances. The latter part of the law, called the apodosis ("then such-and-such must happen"), prescribes the legal action to be taken. In contrast, apodictic laws, like those in the Decalogue, do not describe the case; rather they require or prohibit the performance of certain actions in a "do this/do not do that" style.

It is uncertain why laws appear in both of these forms, and if each form represents a distinct social setting *(Sitz im Leben)*. As discussed below ("Biblical Law in the Context of Mesopotamian Law"), casuistic law is the more common form of law in the ancient Near East, though some Mesopotamian legal collections, such as the Laws of Eshnunna (20th c. BCE), contain both types of laws.

Many laws are presented with no reason associated with them, while others contain reasons, or more specifically motivations, for observing the specific law. Examples of the latter include Deut. 21.22–23: "If a man is guilty of a capital offense and is put to death, and you impale him on a stake, you must not let his corpse remain on the stake overnight, but must bury him the same day. For an impaled body is an affront to God; you shall not defile the land that the LORD your God is giving you to possess," and Deut. 22.8: "When you build a new house, you shall make a parapet for your roof, so that you do not bring bloodguilt on your house if anyone should fall from it." The conclusions of both these laws ("For an impaled body is an affront to God ..."; "so that you do not bring bloodguilt on your house ...") explain the laws' requirements. Such "motive clauses" are found throughout the Torah, but especially typify Deut., which has a hortatory character; they contribute to the book's overall structure as Moses' valedictory address to Israel.

Law in the Torah

The most famous biblical set of laws, the Decalogue, or Ten Commandments, is narrated twice in the Torah, in Exod. ch 20 and Deut. ch 5. The two versions of the Decalogue contain both minor and major variations; attempts to reconstruct an original Decalogue, the source of both Exod. and Deut., have not proved convincing.

A set of laws is presented in Exod. 20.19 [Heb 22]–23.33. Since the following 24.7 refers to *sefer ha-berit*, "the record of the covenant" or "the book/scroll of the covenant," these laws are referred to as the "Covenant Collection." The laws in Deut. chs 12–26 often modify these laws from Exod., and are called the "Deuteronomic Law Collection." Lev. also contains many laws. Those at the beginning of the book focus on sacrifices, while chs 17–26 contain a broader collection, often called the "Holiness Collection" because of the refrain insisting that all Israel must be holy, as seen, for example, in 19.2: "You shall be holy, for I, the LORD your God, am holy." As this refrain shows, in contrast to the earlier part of Lev., which emphasizes the holiness of the priests only, this collection insists that all Israel, priests and non-priests, must be holy.

Examining each of these collections on its own reveals complexity that confounds smooth readings one might expect from a unified composition. For example, the Covenant Collection repeats the same law concerning proper treatment of the alien in Exod. 22.20 and 23.9. Although this is not clear in translation, the laws in Deut. often switch between addressing the single Israelite and addressing the community, in the plural. (See e.g., Deut. 14.3–4: "You [sg.] shall not eat anything abhorrent. These are the animals that you [pl.] may eat: the ox, the sheep, and the goat ....") These variations suggest that there is not only development between the various law collections, but within them, as well.

In some cases, laws on similar topics appear in each of these collections—for example, each deals with slavery (Exod. 21.2–11; Lev. 25.39–46; Deut. 15.12–18) and each contains a festival calendar (Exod. 23.14–17; Lev. ch 23; Deut. 16.1–17). Each collection legislates different, sometimes contradictory, norms, which suggests that each collection represents practices or ideals of different circumstances. Each collection also contains laws that are not found in the others. Most significantly, there are many areas of law that are not explicitly covered in any of these three major collections, including basic marriage law or laws concerning shepherds' responsibilities and payments. Thus, it is best to call these large groups of laws "collections" rather than "codes," since the latter term suggests a well-organized, complete set of laws that was used in the law courts; none of these characteristics clearly applies to the material in these collections.

The law collections are all situated in narrative frameworks that contextualize them. For example, the Covenant Collection is embedded within the description of the revelation at Sinai. The ritual laws at the beginning of Lev. are presented as God's revelation from the Tent of Meeting, after the completion of the Tabernacle at Sinai. The laws of Deut. are preceded by a long narrative introduction, set in the fortieth year after the exodus, immediately preceding the entrance into the land. The prominence of these collections within the Torah suggests that law is the Torah's main storyline, its very reason for telling its stories.

We do not have a deep understanding of how biblical law was practiced and enforced. At an even more basic level, some scholars have suggested, quite plausibly, that some of the legislation in the Bible was never meant to be observed, but reflects an ideal—what the law should really be, even though it would be impractical (see e.g., the jubilee year legislation in Lev. ch 25). This suggestion finds some support in other ancient Near Eastern law collections. Unfortunately, specific laws in the Bible (or the ancient Near East) are not marked as "real" or "ideal," and thus it is difficult to know which laws were meant to be broadly observed, and which represented societal ideals.

Outside the main law collections, individual laws appear within shorter narratives in the Torah. Even Gen. contains laws, though these are very few in number. For example, a group of instructions, including a prohibition against murder, accompanies God's blessings to Noah and his descendants as they leave the ark (Gen. 9.1–17). Abraham's story includes God's instruction to the patriarch to undergo circumcision, and mandates the practice of circumcision on the eighth day for all future males (Gen. 17.9–14). The exodus from Egypt brings in its wake several commandments, including the consecration of the first-born and the observance of a commemorative festival (Exod. ch 13). Similarly, the laws of inheritance occur in response to the inquiries of Zelophehad's daughters (Num. 27.1–11; cf. Num. ch 36).

As noted above, the legal collections are often inconsistent with each other, and the Torah's slave laws present some of the more famous examples of these inconsistencies. The laws in Exod. 21.2–11 govern the procedures for freeing Hebrew slaves, and distinguish between the processes that apply to male slaves and to female slaves. The laws in Deut. 15.12–18 collapse this gender distinction, and apply the rules governing male slaves in Exod. 21.2–6 (freedom after six years of service, with the option of entering permanent indenture) to both males and females. The laws in Lev. 25.39–46 mention only male Israelite hirelings (not slaves, as these are explicitly prohibited in Lev. 25.39), who are freed not in the sixth year of service, but in the jubilee year. These laws do not offer Israelite servants the option of permanent servitude along the lines of Exod. 21.6 and Deut. 15.17. Instead, according to Lev. 25.44–46, permanent servitude is reserved for non-Israelite male or female slaves (to whom the Heb text applies the usual words for slave).

Modern scholars have understood the repetitions and contradictions in the legal collections, as they have in Torah narratives, as evidence that the Torah was composed from multiple sources. This historical approach seeks to clarify why the Torah contains multiple sets of laws (and multiple narratives surrounding their origins) on any number of subjects (such as slaves) with little consistency between them. The contradictions are the result (and part of the proof) of the process that brought the variant sources, including their laws, together into the Torah. Thus, law constitutes an important building block of the modern documentary hypothesis; many of the central debates in the field of modern pentateuchal criticism focus on how multiple, contradictory laws came to be and how they were merged into the Torah. Debates continue about the chronological order of these laws and the degree to which any set of laws depends on, and may actually revise (and perhaps even subvert), another set.

Rabbinic interpreters, who faced the task of deriving practical law *(halakhah)* and who, moreover, assumed the Torah's basic unity, used midrash to explain the repetitions and to resolve apparent contradictions (see essays on "Classical Rabbinic Interpretation" pp. 1859–78, and "Midrash," pp. 1879–91). Thus, in the case of slavery, rabbinic *halakhah* eliminates these problems by, for instance, applying the jubilee-year release of Lev. ch 25 even to Jewish slaves who undergo the procedure for "permanent" indenture; the Rabbis accomplish this by interpreting the word "forever" (Exod. 21.6; Deut. 15.17) as until the jubilee year. This type of interpretation did not originate with the Rabbis, but is already found in late biblical literature, as Judaism first tried to make sense out of the composite Torah (see essay on "Inner-biblical Interpretation," pp. 1835–41).

Law in the Prophets and Writings

While the Torah contains the bulk of the Hebrew Bible's legislative texts, these law collections are not comprehensive. Material that explains, supplements, complements, and contradicts Torah law is found in the second two canonical divisions, Prophets and Writings. Continuing the example of slavery noted above, the prophet Jeremiah specifically refers to the seventh-year release law when he castigates the Judeans under Zedekiah for skirting the requirements of this law by reenslaving previously released slaves (Jer. 34.8–22; see esp. v. 14). Similarly, the circumstances of a "kinsman ... in straits" who would sell himself to a fellow Israelite (Lev. 25.39) are clarified by the story of a widow who turns to the prophet Elisha because "a creditor is coming to seize [her] two children as slaves" (2 Kings 4.1).

Passages in the Prophets and Writings also illuminate certain aspects of trial procedure in ancient Israel. Some laws in the Torah mention trials in passing (e.g., Deut. 17.2–13; 25.1–3), and several narratives describe the resolution of disputes informally, as in Laban's dispute against Jacob (Gen. 31.26–44), or before an authority, as in the "Judgment of Solomon" (1 Kings 3.16–28). Modern scholarship has shown that the trial is a central motif of both prophecy and prayer. Jeremiah, for instance, presents a message in terms of God's "accusation" (*riv*) against Israel (Jer. 2.9), and psalmists regularly say in essence "Judge me, O LORD" (e.g., Pss. 7.9; 35.24; 43.1), in apparent imitation of how plaintiffs might address human judges. In a similar vein, the main plot of the book of Job turns on Job's litigation against God, and the book is full of legal language that reflects ancient Israelite practices.

Prophetic passages in Isa. 1.13 and Amos 8.5 suggest that the new moon was celebrated as a festival by some in ancient Israel; this is an important case where non-Torah material reflects norms that are absent in the Torah. Prov. 6.31 notes concerning a thief "Yet if caught he must pay sevenfold; / He must give up all he owns," and a similar norm of sevenfold recompense is reflected in the LXX's translation of 2 Sam. 12.6. In contrast, the law on the comparable topic in Exod. 21.37 notes: "When a man steals an ox or a sheep, and slaughters it or sells it, he shall pay five oxen for the ox, and four sheep for the sheep." One way to resolve contradictions like these is to posit that the Torah reflects ideal legislation, while these other sources show us law as it was practiced in ancient Israel. Another solution attributes differences like these to historical change between the times in which the different legal practices were in effect.

Biblical Law in the Context of Mesopotamian Law

The recovery of legal texts from the ancient Near East has improved our understanding of the meaning and function of biblical law. These texts include collections of laws, most famously the "Laws of Hammurabi" (18th c. BCE), as well as several other collections and many, many more records of legal practice from throughout the Fertile Crescent and beyond. Most of the texts are in Sumerian or Akkadian, the languages of Mesopotamia written in cuneiform script on clay tablets, and date from ca. 3000 BCE through the 1st c. CE. Some are in Hittite, an Indo-European language spoken in Asia Minor, and date from the second millenium BCE. Legal documents in other languages, including Aram. and even Heb, are more rarely attested. All of these materials shed light on many aspects of law in ancient Israel and in the Hebrew Bible, including the interpretation of legal terms and procedures and legislation on specific topics. Many of the same legal cases are addressed throughout the ancient Near East, although the specifics of the actual law may differ from one place to another.

Biblical law's place within broader Near Eastern legal culture can be clearly seen in a comparison of the goring ox laws in Exod. 21.28–32, 35–36 with goring ox laws attested in two other Akkadian law collections from the early second millennium BCE, the Laws of Eshnunna and the more famous Laws of Hammurabi:

Exod. 21.28–32, 35–36

28. When an ox gores a man or a woman to death, the ox shall be stoned and its flesh shall not be eaten, but the owner of the ox is not to be punished.

29. If, however, that ox has been in the habit of goring, and its owner, though warned, has failed to guard it, and it kills a man or a woman— the ox shall be stoned and its owner, too, shall be put to death.

30. If ransom is laid upon him, he must pay whatever is laid upon him to redeem his life.
31. So, too, if it gores a minor, male or female, [the owner] shall be dealt with according to the same rule.
32. But if the ox gores a slave, male or female, he shall pay thirty shekels of silver to the master, and the ox shall be stoned.

...

35. When a man's ox injures his neighbor's ox and it dies, they shall sell the live ox and divide its price; they shall also divide the dead animal.
36. If, however, it is known that the ox was in the habit of goring, and its owner has failed to guard it, he must restore ox for ox, but shall keep the dead animal.

Laws of Eshnunna, §§53–54
[Author's translation]
53. If an ox gores another ox and kills (it), both ox owners shall divide the price of the living ox and the flesh of the dead ox.
54. If an ox is a gorer and the community informed its owner, but he did not set his ox straight, and the ox gored a man and killed (him), the owner of the ox shall weigh (and pay) 2/3 mina of silver.

Laws of Hammurabi, §§250–252
250. If an ox, while walking in the street, gored a man and caused (his) death, no claims will be allowed in that case.
251. If a man's ox is a gorer, and the community informed him that it is a gorer, yet he did not have its horns screened nor controlled his ox, and that ox gored a man and caused (his) death, he must pay 1/2 mina of silver.
252. If (it gored) a man's slave, he must pay 1/3 mina of silver.

The striking similarities between the Akkadian and the biblical laws, in substance and formulation, suggest that they must be related. In terms of substance, all address similar cases in the same order, and make the same legal distinction between an ox that has no previous history of goring and one that is a habitual gorer (Exod. 21.28–29, 35–36). All three share casuistic formulation, which is the hallmark of law, and more generally, of all writing considered "scientific" from the ancient Near East. In the case of the ox goring another ox (Exod. 21.35 and Laws of Eshnunna, section 53), the resemblance is extremely close—the Heb verb translated as "injures" *(yigof)* is atypical in context, and is probably borrowed from Akkadian *(nakāpu)*—suggesting some contact, direct or indirect, between the biblical law and some version of the law in Akkadian.

These similarities, and other examples like them, indicate that the biblical law collections drew on the legal traditions from the ancient Near East. At the same time, the Bible gives a uniquely Israelite expression to these traditions. The Akkadian laws emphasize economic compensation and establish, for example, monetary penalties even in the case when a habitually goring ox kills a human (i.e., a case of negligent homicide). In the Bible, this same case initially carries the death penalty; monetary compensation for homicide is allowed, but does not seem to be ideal, because human life is viewed as invaluable. Beyond these specifics, biblical law stands out, fundamentally, as an expression of a covenant between God and humans. In contrast, Hammurabi is depicted as a human lawgiver; he presents his laws to the gods as a sign that he is a proper king, but the gods, albeit present throughout the long royal inscription, have no claim to being the lawgivers.

In law, as in some other aspects of biblical literature, God assumes the role played by human kings in neighboring cultures. This basic point emerges from reading the Bible together with Hammurabi's laws, which shows that God replaces the king as the lawgiver. In the realm of biblical law, the extent of the analogy between the human kings of the ancient Near East and God in the Bible becomes apparent in light of ancient Near Eastern treaties. These treaties were imposed by powerful overlords, or suzerains, on their vassals. They stipulate the vassals' obligations to the overlords in a manner that closely resembles the presentation of laws in the Torah. Thus, they often include a historical introduction as a motivation for the vassal's loyalty, just as God recalls the exodus at the beginning of the Decalogue, or as Deut. introduces its laws with eleven chs of narrative material. Similarly, the suzerainty treaties conclude with blessings and curses, much like those in Deut. ch 28, which contain remarkable overlaps with the curses in Assyrian treaties (see Deut. 28.27–35 n.).

The Bible understands the relationship between God and Israel in terms of the relationship between the suzerain and the vassal that these treaties describe. The covenant is essentially a theologized legal-political concept. Comparison with extrabiblical legal texts not only shows the likely sources of some biblical laws, but more importantly exposes the origins of the covenant in the human realm, and thus affords a deeper appreciation of the place of law within biblical religion.

[SHALOM E. HOLTZ]

Use of the Hebrew Bible in the New Testament

In the early 2nd c. CE, Marcion, a bishop from Sinope, a city on the Black Sea, proposed that the Scriptures of the Jews were not sacred and that the God those texts proclaimed was not the same as the one Jesus revealed. Marcion may have developed the first Christian canon: a collection consisting of the Gospel of Luke, stripped of references to Israel's Scripture, and select letters of Paul. Despite Marcion's early popularity, the followers of Jesus soon rejected his views, proclaimed him a heretic, and adopted the scriptures of Israel—what they came to call the "Old Testament" (hence throughout this article OT)—as part of the church's canon.

What became the New Testament (hence NT) is infused with OT references. One generous count claims it contains approximately 350 quotations and close to 2,500 allusions, with Ps. and Isa. the most frequently adduced. Of the Tanakh's twenty-four books, only Judg., Song, Eccl., Ezra-Neh., and Chron. lack explicit quotations.

Although no definitive quotations or allusions appear in three short NT books (Philemon, 2 and 3 John), their authors also knew the OT. Paul composed Philemon, and the two Johannine Epistles are part of a literary family that also includes the Gospel of John, 1 John, and the book of Revelation (or Apocalypse of John): the Gospel and the first Epistle offer both allusions and direct quotations; Revelation presents no direct quotations but over 600 allusions. When the NT speaks of authoritative texts, including those read in community gatherings (see Rom. 15.4; 1 Corinthians 10.11; 2 Timothy 3.14–17; 2 Peter 1.20–21), it refers to the OT. Later NT books such as Acts of the Apostles (17.2; 18.24–28) and 1 Timothy (1.6–10) indicate that correct interpretation of the OT was of concern in both debates with Jews outside the church and within Christian contexts: Jesus' followers found their Lord and Savior present in and predicted by these texts; non-messianic Jews did not.

Jesus and his earliest followers, all Jews from Galilee and Judea, would have been familiar with the Heb texts through synagogue readings, family and village storytellers and teachers, or instructions from itinerant teachers. It is also highly likely that they knew various ways that the texts had been and were being interpreted, including through the nascent Targumim, Aram. translations that often contained elaborations (see essay "Jewish Translations of the Bible," pp. 2091–2106). However, the NT is written in Gk: whether the NT authors are citing the LXX (see previously mentioned essay), using an alternative Gk version, translating the Heb or Aram. themselves, paraphrasing, or citing from memory, must be determined on a case-by-case basis. Complicating the search for the antecedent text cited by or alluded to in the NT is that at the time of the NT's composition (ca. 40s–50s CE for Paul's Epistles through the early 2nd c. for texts such as 2 Peter), no standardized Hebrew or Greek canon existed, as we now appreciate from the diverse biblical texts found among the Dead Sea Scrolls (see "The Bible in the Dead Sea Scrolls," pp. 1850–59). Finally, appreciating how Jesus, the Gospel writers, Paul, and the other NT authors understood Israel's Scripture is complicated by the fact that we do not know which citations and allusions Jesus himself made and which were attributed to him by his followers who composed the Gospels.

The uses to which the NT authors put OT materials vary, just as do the uses found among the Qumran scrolls, rabbinic and Targumic texts, and by 1st-c. CE Jewish authors such as Josephus and Philo. Some NT passages present OT statements as prophecies that Jesus and the church fulfill, when the original context is clearly not prophetic; this happens among the Dead Sea Scrolls as well. Others rephrase prophetic statements in terms of past events. References are sometimes combined; words are strategically omitted or, perhaps changed, although, as noted above, we are often uncertain in what form(s) the text circulated at the time of Jesus and his followers. Although, like many biblical citations in rabbinic texts, some NT quotations and allusions appear to lack concern for their original literary context; most of this material takes on an enhanced meaning when understood in light of that context.

A few NT texts, notably the Epistle to the Hebrews, read the OT through *typology*, a literary form that sees in the earlier passage a blueprint for or foreshadowing of something that will come to fulfillment or perfection. The form appears in classical Greek as well as earlier biblical literature. For example, Gen. 12.10–20, the sojourn of Abram and Sarai in Egypt, can be seen as a type of Israel's descent to Egypt during the time of Joseph and their exodus under Moses. The NT sometimes utilizes *allegory*, in which symbolic meanings are assigned to OT characters or plot lines; this too is continuous with the earlier biblical material, as in Isa. 5.1–10.

Legal Discussions

NT citations of Torah vary from endorsement to modification to (rarely) rejection. (Here, and elsewhere in this essay, NT quotations are from the New Revised Standard Version [NRSV].) According to Matt. 5.17, Jesus insists, "Do not think that I have come to abolish the law or the prophets; I have come not to abolish but to fulfill." ("The law," following a Jewish usage, refers to the Torah.) Conversely, Mark 7.19 states that Jesus "declared all foods clean" (a line other Gospels lack; in some modern printings, the v. appears in parentheses to indicate that it expresses a conclusion the author drew and not something Jesus himself said). Jesus defines the "greatest commandment" as a combination of Deut. 6.4–5 ("Hear, O Israel: the Lord our God, the Lord is one; you shall love the Lord your God with all your heart, and with all your soul, and with all your mind, and with all your strength" ["mind," a translation of the difficult Heb word, *me'od*, may come from Gk versions]) and Lev. 19.18 ("You shall love your neighbor as yourself" [see Mark 12.29–31; also Matt. 22.37–39; in Luke 10.25–28, a "lawyer" combines the passages]).

The Gospels indicate that Jesus held Torah to be authoritative but rejected certain interpretations, such as the Pharisaic practice of hand-washing before meals, which is not explicitly mentioned in the Torah (Mark 7.1–23 || Matt. 15.1–20). At times, Jesus intensifies the commandments. To the injunction against murder (Exod. 20.13), Jesus adds anger (Matt. 5.21–22). To the injunction against adultery (Exod. 20.14), he includes the forbidding of lust (Matt. 5.27–30). Showing a more strict interpretation of Torah as well is Jesus' comment on divorce. Whereas Deut. (24.3) permits divorce, Jesus forbids it by appealing to Adam and Eve and concludes, "Therefore what God has joined together, let no one separate" (see Matt. 19.6 || Mark 10.9); a similar stringency may be reflected in some Dead Sea Scrolls.

Paul cites the OT with different emphases, in part because he is speaking primarily to Gentiles. To make his case that Gentiles in the churches should not follow Torah's distinctive practices, such as circumcision, Paul insists that the Torah was given "because of transgressions," "ordained through angels by a mediator," and designed to serve as a place-keeper "until the offspring would come to whom the promise [to Abraham] had been made" (Gal. 3.19). The "offspring" to whom Paul refers is Jesus: he draws this conclusion by interpreting the promise to Abraham (Gen. 13.14–16; 17.7–8; 22.17, and elsewhere) of "offspring" (Gk *sperma*; Heb *zerah*)—a collective noun in both Gk and Heb, and thus grammatically singular—as a singular, referring to one individual (Gal. 3.16). Thus Abraham's promises go not to the people of Israel, but to the singular Jesus, and through him to his followers. Perhaps tempering this view, Paul writes to the congregation at Rome that for Israel, "the gifts and the calling of God are irrevocable" (Rom. 11.29) and to the "Israelites" belong "the adoption, the glory, the covenants, the giving of the law, the worship, and the promises; to them belong the patriarchs, and from them, according to the flesh, comes the Messiah" (Rom. 9.4–5).

Legal and narrative traditions in the Torah as well as the Prophetic writings also provide Paul an explanation for Jesus' role as savior. In Gal. 3.13, he writes, "Christ redeemed us from the curse of the law by becoming a curse for us—for it is written, 'Cursed is everyone who hangs on a tree'"; the allusion is to Deut. 21.23, instructions on the interment of a hanged criminal. Here Paul takes the original v. out of context; this type of reading was common in early Jewish biblical interpretation. Similarly, Paul states in Gal. 3.8, "The Scripture, foreseeing that God would justify the Gentiles by faith, declared the gospel beforehand to Abraham, saying, 'All the Gentiles shall be blessed in you'"; the allusion is to Gen. 12.3; 18.18 (see also on Abraham's righteousness, Paul's citation of Gen. 15.6 in Rom. 4.3). Complementing this comment about Abraham is Rom. 1.17, "the righteousness of God is revealed through faith for faith; as it is written, 'The one who is righteous will live by faith'"; the citation is to Hab. 2.4b.

Prophecies and Verses Understood as Prophecy

A number of NT texts claim that Jesus fulfilled prophecy. Matthew (2.6) quotes Mic. 5.2 to indicate that the one to rule Israel will be from Bethlehem and concludes that this ruler is the Messiah. Later Targumic readings (e.g., *Tg. Ps.-J.* on Gen. 35.21) also take Micah's comment as having messianic implications. Elsewhere, the NT takes as prophecies statements that do not have predictive value in their original contexts. Matt. 2.15b describes the flight to Egypt and then the return to Israel by Joseph, Mary, and Jesus in terms of Hos. 11.1b, "This was to fulfill what had been spoken by the Lord through the prophet, 'Out of Egypt I have called my son.'" Hosea describes Israel's exodus from Egypt, a past event; for Matthew, the v. is prophetic and Jesus fulfills it. In Matt. 13.14–15, Jesus quotes Isa. 6.9–10, the prophet's lament about his lack of reception, to explain why those who are not Jesus' disciples do not understand his parables.

The famous prediction of the "virginal conception" in Matt. 1.23 is complicated by the translation of the original Heb into Gk. The Heb of Isa. 7.14 refers to a pregnant young woman (Heb *'almah*) whose child will be a sign to King Ahaz of Judah that his political concerns will shortly abate. The LXX describes this woman as a *parthenos*, a term that can mean "virgin" as well as "young woman" (see Gen. 34.3 LXX, in reference to Dinah, who has just had sexual relations with Shechem). For Matthew, *parthenos* means not simply young woman, but a sexually inexperienced one.

Descriptions of Jesus' crucifixion in Matt. and Mark (likely, Matthew used Mark as a source, so we have two versions of the same story rather than independent accounts) draw upon Ps. 22. (Ps. was generally understood in ancient Judaism as a prophetic book.) The lament psalm opens with the cry, "My God, my God, / why have You forsaken me?" (NRSV Ps. 22.1a; JPS [22.2a] has, "why have You abandoned me"), a v. that Matthew (27.46) and Mark (15.34) place on the lips of the dying Jesus. The opening word (*Eli* in Matt.; *Eloi* in Mark) is then understood by the people standing at the cross to be an invocation of the prophet Elijah (whose name begins with *Eli*), who was to herald the messianic age (see Mal. 3.23–24). The two Gospels then follow the same Ps. in describing the subsequent events, from the mocking of Jesus to the casting of lots for his clothes (Ps. 22.7, 18; cf. Matt. 27.41, 35; Mark 15.29, 24).

Other NT passages also draw on the OT to interpret Jesus' crucifixion. According to John's Gospel, soldiers broke the legs of the men crucified on either side of Jesus (the practice was designed to hasten death) but, determining Jesus was already dead, did not break his legs. John 19.36 explains, "These things occurred so that the scripture might be fulfilled, 'None of his bones shall be broken.'" The citation is to Exod. 12.46 (also Num. 9.12), a reference to the Passover offering. For John, Jesus *is* the Paschal lamb. Hebrews 9.11–28 also understands Jesus' death in sacrificial terms by alluding to different antecedent Scripture, including Exod. ch 24, Lev. ch 16 and Num. ch 19.

Scriptural Interpretation

In 2 Corinthians ch 3, Paul uses multiple references to the OT to make his point. First, he compares his Gentile readers to "a letter of Christ, prepared by us, written not with ink but with the Spirit of the living God, not on tablets of stone but on tablets of human hearts" (3.3). Then he develops the comparison of the Old and New Covenants (Testaments). His congregants are "ministers of a new covenant, not of letter but of spirit; for the letter kills, but the Spirit gives life" (3.6). Third, explaining that the law condemns but cannot save, he alludes to the veil Moses wore (Exod. 34.35): "Now if the ministry of death, chiseled in letters on stone tablets, came in glory so that the people of Israel could not gaze at Moses' face because of the glory of his face, a glory now set aside, how much more will the ministry of the Spirit come in glory?" (2 Corinthians 3.7–8). Paul then argues that Moses "put a veil over his face to keep the people of Israel from gazing at the end of the glory that was being set aside" (3.13). Finally, he dismisses the scriptural interpretations made by "the people of Israel" who do not follow Jesus: "their minds were hardened. Indeed, to this very day, when they hear the reading of the old covenant, that same veil is still there, since only in Christ is it set aside. Indeed, to this very day whenever Moses is read, a veil lies over their minds ... " (3.14–16). For Paul, Jesus' followers, both Jews and Gentiles, and those Jews who did not join the messianic movement take authority from the same text, but only the former understand what they are reading. John 5.39–47 offers a similar claim.

Allusion, Typology, and Allegory

Allusion, sometimes overt and sometimes subtle, enriches a later text by evoking images of an earlier one. For example, the famous "Parable of the Prodigal Son" begins, "There was a man who had two sons" (Luke 15.11). The description evokes Cain and Abel, Ishmael and Isaac, Esau and Jacob. References to a good "shepherd" (see Matt. 18.12; John 10.11; Hebrews 13.20; 1 Peter 2.25, etc.) have numerous connections to Moses, David, and God. When Jesus' opponents accuse him of being a "glutton and a drunkard" (Matt. 11.19 || Luke 7.34), listeners hear an allusion to Deut. 21.20, the law in which the "stubborn and rebellious" son should be put to death. When Persian astrologers or "magi" speak of the "star at its rising" appearing at the birth of the "king of the Jews" (Matt. 2.2), readers may hear a reference to Num. 24.17, "a star rises from Jacob," a v. that also had messianic significance in later Judaism.

Allusions enhance understandings of Jesus by associating him with numerous passages in the OT, and they do so as well for other NT figures. The first three Gospels present John the Baptist as "the voice of one crying out in the wilderness: 'Prepare the way of the Lord, make his paths straight'" (Mark 1.3 || Matt. 3.3 || Luke 3.4). This announcement cites a form of Isa. 40.3, the prophet's proclamation to the people in exile in Babylonia that they will soon return to their homeland. For Isaiah a voice instructs listeners to build a way or path (i.e., a "highway") in the wilderness; for Mark, John the Baptist is the wilderness voice, and the "way" (Gk, *hodos*; see Acts 9.2) is that of Jesus. Similarly, Matthew's genealogy (1.16;

contrast Luke 3.23) describes Joseph as the son of Jacob: this second Joseph, like his predecessor in Gen., also dreams dreams and rescues his family by taking them to Egypt.

As noted above, typology is a means of reading a text as a foreshadowing or first draft. For example, the Gospels take the "sign of Jonah" as a "type" or model of what Jesus will do. Matt. 12.39–40 interprets the sign in terms of resurrection ("as Jonah was three days and three nights in the belly of the sea monster, so for three days and three nights the Son of Man will be in the heart of the earth"); Matt. 12.41 (cf. 16.4) || Luke 11.29–32 go on to suggest the sign alludes to both the Gentile mission and anticipates that at the final judgment the people of Nineveh will fare better than Jesus' Jewish contemporaries.

Replete with typological imagery, the Epistle to the Hebrews, an anonymous text whose dating and provenance remain disputed, depicts the wilderness Tabernacle *(mishkan)* as the "type" or first draft of the heavenly altar at which Jesus serves as both high priest and offering. For Hebrews, Jesus is a priest "after the order of Melchizedek" (see Gen. 14.18–20; Ps. 110.4). Hebrews 8.6–13 draws upon the language of the "new covenant" in Jer. 31.31 (Gk *diatheke*; Heb *brit*) to announce that the first covenant had become obsolete. "And what is obsolete and growing old will soon disappear" (Hebrews 8.13).

Sometimes seen as typology and sometimes classified as a running commentary, much like rabbinic midrash, John 6.25–59 retells the story of the Israelites in the wilderness. Jesus says, "I am the bread of life" (6.35), comparable to but infinitely better than the "manna" that the Israelites ate. In another running commentary, Matt. chs 2–7 present Jesus as both a new Moses who survives when other children are slaughtered, enters and leaves Egypt, crosses water (the Baptism), enters the wilderness to face temptation, and ascends a mountain to proclaim instruction (the Sermon on the Mount). The long speech attributed to the martyr Stephen in Acts 7.2–53 can be similarly understood as a *midrash* on the history of Israel.

Allegory, a genre like typology present in Israel's Scriptures, classical sources, as well as the writings of Philo of Alexandria, establishes an equivalence between elements in two texts. For example, in Isa.'s "Song of the Vineyard," the vineyard is Israel, the owner is God, and the vineyard's failure to yield cultivated grapes stands for Israel's failure to repent and act with righteousness. Several Gospel parables draw on this image of Israel as the vineyard and Jesus/God as the landowner (e.g., Matt. 21.33–41 || Mark 12.1–9 || Luke 20.9–16).

Paul's allegory of Sarah and Hagar (Gal. 4.22–31) serves to encourage his Gentile audience to eschew teachers who maintain that Gentile followers of Jesus must practice the markers of Jewish identity (e.g., circumcision). According to Paul, "Hagar, from Mount Sinai, bearing children for slavery ... corresponds to the present Jerusalem, for she is in slavery with her children" (vv. 24–25), whereas Sarah (not explicitly named) "corresponds to the Jerusalem above; she is free, and she is our mother" (v. 26). Other allegorical readings include the citation of Deut. 25.4 in 1 Corinthians 9.9 and the presentation of Rome as the "whore of Babylon" in Revelation chs 17–18.

Understandings of Jesus in Terms of Israel's Scriptures

The Gospel of John opens with the famous line, "In the beginning *(en arche)* was the Word, and the Word was with God, and the Word was God ... " (John 1.1). The first words repeat the LXX version of Gen. 1.1: "In the beginning ...." John's Gospel thus locates Jesus, the Word who "became flesh" (John 1.14), as present at creation and as both distinct from and sharing the role of the biblical deity. (Cf. early Jewish traditions that focus on the preexistence of the Torah at creation.) John's prologue (1.1–14) also evokes images of Wisdom (Heb *hochmah*; Gk *sophia*), found in

Prov. 8.22–31 (and see, from the Deuterocanonical writings, Wisdom of Solomon ch 9). Matthew's Gospel opens by anchoring Jesus into the Scriptures of Israel via a genealogy of Jesus, "the son of David, the son of Abraham" (1.1). Matthew's first words, *biblos geneseos*, literally, "book of the genesis," repeat those of Gen. 2.4 LXX. According to Luke 3.38, Jesus' genealogy locates him as the "son of Adam, son of God." For Paul, Jesus is the "last Adam" who rectifies the sin of the first man (1 Corinthians 15.45; see also 15.22; Rom. 5.12). Extending the references to Adam, 1 Timothy—a text many scholars believe to have been written in Paul's name but not by the Apostle himself—states, "Adam was not deceived, but the woman was deceived and became a transgressor" (1 Timothy 2.14). Revelation 2.7 promises "permission to eat from the tree of life" as an eschatological reward to those who heed the Spirit.

In Luke 4.17–19, Jesus appears to read from as well as to offer a paraphrase of Isa. 61.1–2: "The Spirit of the Lord is upon me, / because he has anointed me to bring good news to the poor ...." Jesus' miracles, such as multiplying loaves and fishes (Matt. 14.13–21 || Mark 6.30–44 || Luke 9.10–17 || John 6.5–15), recollect the miraculous provisions of food offered to Israel in the wilderness (Exod. ch 16; Num. ch 11; Deut. ch 8) as well as by Elijah (1 Kings 17.8–16; see the recapitulation of this scene in Luke 4.25–26) and Elisha (2 Kings 4.1–7). Jesus' healings likewise recollect those performed by Elijah and Elisha (1 Kings 17.17–24; 2 Kings 5.1–19; see the recapitulation in Luke 4.27). Moses and Elijah, depicted as appearing at Jesus' Transfiguration (Matt. 17.3; Mark 9.4; Luke 9.30) may be understood symbolizing, respectively, Torah and the Prophetic corpus.

The book of Dan., a late OT text that quickly became very popular, provides background for Jesus' primary self-designation, "son of man" (Heb *ben adam*; Aram. *bar-enosh*; Gk *huios tou anthropou*). The Heb expression originally meant "human being" (e.g., Num. 23.19; Ezek. 2.1 and over ninety other times; Ps. 8.5). Dan. 7.13–14 describes "one like the Son of man" who comes "with the clouds of heaven" to the "Ancient of days"; to this Son of Man was given "dominion, and glory, and a kingdom, that all people, nations, and languages, should serve him ...." For Daniel, "Son of Man" (Aram. *bar-enosh*) refers to an eschatological figure, perhaps the angel Michael, perhaps a corporate symbol for the "saints of the most high." *1 Enoch* chs 37–71, to which some Jews of the Second Temple period may have accorded the status of Scripture, identifies the "Son of Man" as Enoch. In some Talmudic literature (*b. Sanh.* 98a; cf. *y. Taʿan.* 2.1), the term has eschatological and messianic connotations.

Complementing the "Son of man" references is the understanding of Jesus as the "suffering servant" mentioned in Isa., especially ch 53. For Isaiah, the servant is sometimes explicitly identified as Israel (see Isa. 44.1; 45.4; 49.3), suffering in exile yet to be redeemed and returned to the homeland by the gracious God. In explaining Jesus' healings and exorcisms, Matt. 8.17 paraphrases Isa. 53.4 by stating, "This was to fulfill what had been spoken through the prophet Isaiah, 'He took our infirmities and bore our diseases.'" In Acts 8.32–33, Philip explains to an Ethiopian officer who is reading from the Scroll of Isa. that the prophet's mention of "a sheep that before its shearers is silent" (Isa. 53.7) refers to Jesus (see for the same motif, Matt. 26.63; 27.12, 14). According to 1 Peter, an epistle ascribed to Peter although many scholars suggest it is pseudonymous, Jesus "committed no sin, / and no deceit was found in his mouth" (1 Peter 2.22); the comment recollects Isa. 53.9b, "and there was no deceit in his mouth."

Other passages combine various citations into new readings that summarize Christological claims (that is, attributions of messiahship to Jesus). For example, 1 Peter 2.4–8 combines Isa. 28.16; Ps. 118.22; and Isa. 8.14 describing Jesus as the "stone that the builders rejected," as the "cornerstone," and as a stumbling block. Similar imagery appears in Matt. 21.42 || Mark 12.10 || Luke 20.17; Acts 4.11; Rom. 9.33; and Ephesians 2.20.

Afterword

Literary texts require interpretation; each community, and each reader, sees new things in ancient writings. For the Christian Church, traditionally, Jesus is present throughout the pages of the OT; for the Jewish community, he is absent from the Hebrew Bible. This is not a matter of who reads correctly, as if biblical interpretation is a zero-sum game (here I take issue with 2 Corinthians ch 3). Many Christians, following the NT, will see Jesus in the Scriptures of Israel, just as many Jews will read those same Scriptures in light of midrashic commentaries. Whereas today Church and Synagogue see the shared materials through different lenses, in different canonical orders (see "Canonization," pp. 2153–58), in different languages, and with different emphases, these differences should not be the basis of polemic concerning who is reading the text correctly. Rather, they point to the richness of the text, of the traditions that hold them to be sacred, and of the human imagination.

[AMY-JILL LEVINE]

The Hebrew Bible and Biblical Exegesis in the Qur'an and Muslim Tradition

Muslim scripture and exegesis contain numerous allusions to biblical persons and events as well as to custom and law. These include references to the creation of the world, the early development of humankind, Noah and the flood, the patriarchal period, especially the life of Abraham, and the story of Moses and the Israelites. There are also allusions to the conquest of Canaan, mention of various biblical kings and prophets, most notably David and Solomon, and implicit references to the destruction of the Temples in Jerusalem (both the First and the Second). The Qur'an's (or "Koran's") rendering of biblical history is, however, often at variance with Hebrew Scripture and subsequent Jewish tradition. The differences between the versions became a point of contention between the two faith communities beginning with the Prophet Muhammad and the Jewish tribes of Arabia.

Although the Qur'an's links to the Hebrew Bible have long been recognized in the Western world—it also gave rise to a lively discussion among Muslims during the formative centuries of Islam—it was only with the publication of Abraham Geiger's *Was hat Mohammed aus den Judenthume aufgenommen* (Bonn, 1833; tr. by F. Young as *Judaism in Islam* [Madras, 1898]) that serious scholarly attention was devoted to the Qur'an's use of the Hebrew Bible and its postbiblical permutations. Since Geiger, one of the founders of the 19th c. movement called the "Science of Judaism" *(Wissenschaft des Judentums)*, scholars well versed in Arabic and Jewish sources have sought to trace how Jewish biblical texts and traditions might have made their way into Muslim scripture and, beyond that, into the vast literature that informs the Qur'an. In addition, modern scholars have raised questions about how this material served the Prophet Muhammad's mission and helped form contemporaneous and subsequent Muslim attitudes towards the Jews and Judaism. Among the subjects they discuss are references to biblical geography in Muslim scripture, the reshaping of biblical narratives in the Qur'an, the use of Heb and Aram. vocabulary, traces of Jewish legal practice and custom, and Muslim attitudes towards biblical tales of the people, and the value of studying Jewish sources.

The Land of the Bible and the Qur'an

Muslim scripture contains few references to specific geographical locations. Even the

Hijaz, the region of Arabia that gave rise to Islam, receives scant attention. Mecca, the Prophet Muhammad's birthplace, is mentioned once; Medina, where the Muslim community *(ummah)* took shape, only a few times. Beyond the Arabian peninsula, the Qurʾan refers only to Egypt *(Misr)* in tales linked to ancient Israel. There is no explicit mention of the Syro-Palestinian landscape or of ancient Mesopotamia, places central to the narratives of the Hebrew Bible. This is not surprising. The Qurʾan tends to be overly sparing in historical and geographical detail.

Muslim scripture, however, does contain a number of indirect references to biblical geography. For example the Qurʾan speaks of *al-ard al-Muqaddasah*, literally the "land made holy," or "the holy land," a reference connected to the Hebrew Bible, more specifically to the conquest of Canaan. For example, in Surah 5.21–26, Moses commands his followers to enter the holy land and not to turn back out of fear. By doing so they would then forfeit the land that God decreed was to be theirs (v. *[ayah]* 21). But the Israelites point to people of great strength who inhabit the land and block their path (v. 22). Then follows an account of two God-fearing men who commanded [the Israelites to] assault the [fierce enemy] at the gate [of the city] upon entering [the land]. Were the Israelites to put their faith in God [they will be conquerors] (v. 23). The following three vv. (24–26) speak of Moses' rebellious followers, and how their actions will force them to wander (in the wilderness) for forty years.

Surah 5.21 calls attention to Gen. 15.18–20 where God promises Abraham that his progeny will rule the land of Canaan, a promise later repeated to the patriarch's descendants. The following v. moves to the eve of the conquest and in speaking of "people of great strength" draws attention to the biblical Anakites, powerful giant-like warriors that awaited the Israelites on the other side of the Jordan, hence causing God's people to fear entering Canaan (Num. chs 13–14; Deut. 9.1–3). The next v. (v. 23) echoes the tale of two spies (Caleb and Joshua) who, unlike their compatriots, called for invading the land of the Canaanites. It is not clear what Muhammad's contemporaries made of these allusions to the Hebrew Bible. There could be little question, however, that later Muslim Qurʾan scholars were familiar with the biblical tale and some midrashic elements to which the biblical story gave rise. They mention inter alia that the Canaanite giants are the descendants of one ʿAnaq thus linking the Qurʾan's "powerful people" to the biblical Anakites, and the two unnamed spies of v. 23 are correctly identified as Joshua and Caleb, as in Hebrew Scripture.

The identity and territorial scope of the holy land are not denoted in the Qurʾan, and later Muslim scholars express divergent views on this matter. Some claim the "holy land" to be all of *al-Sham*, the great Arab province that encompassed a geographical expanse which covered all of the Syro-Palestinian landscape as well as parts of modern Iraq and Saudi Arabia. Others maintain that it signifies the *jund* or sub-district of Filastin (the Arab/Muslim equivalent of what had been Graeco-Roman Palaestina Prima), that is an area restricted to Jerusalem and its environs. Still others claim that it refers specifically to Jericho, which according to Josh. ch 2, was the Israelite's point of entry into Canaan. Still others suggest that it refers to the Filastin-Damascus axis and various areas east of the Jordan River from which the Israelites launched campaigns and where the Bible informs us various Israelite tribes came to settle (Josh. 13.8–13). There are even claims for Mount Sinai *(Tur)*, an interpretation favored by many who regard the holy land of the Qurʾan as the place where the Ten Commandments were revealed.

Nowhere, however, does Muslim scripture make explicit reference to Syria-Palestine or to any of its towns and cities. Jerusalem is never mentioned explicitly, though it is clear that Muhammad and his contemporaries knew of Jerusalem and its history in biblical and postbiblical times. Qurʾan 38.21–25 is linked, however loosely, with a well-known tale of David holding court, which is rendered in the Qurʾan as *mihrab*, and understood by Muslim scholars as referring to David's sanctuary in Jerusalem. Other vv. (17.2–8) almost certainly draw attention to the ancient Temples of Solomon and Herod; Qurʾan (2.114) speaks of blameworthy individuals who prohibit mention of the word of God in His places of worship and destroy them. Some exegetes understand this v. as referring to the polythiests and Mecca, but most think that these opaque references are to the Temples in Jerusalem and identify the unnamed blameworthy individuals as Nebuchadnezzar (who destroyed the First Temple), Antiochus (who despoiled the Second Temple in the 2nd c. BCE), and the Roman Titus (who looted and destroyed the Temple of Herod).

Among the vv. that allegedly refer to Jerusalem, the most noteworthy and certainly most discussed by Muslim scholars is the highly enigmatic first v. of Surah 17: "God took *(asra)* his servant ... one night from the sacred place of worship *(al-masjid al-haram)* to the furthest place of worship *(al-masjid al-aqsa)* whose surroundings [God] blessed *(barakna hawlahu)* so as to show him his manifest signs ...." By the 2nd Islamic c., most Muslim exegetes maintained that this v. refers to a nocturnal journey *(israʾ)* of the Prophet Muhammad, a journey which began at the mosque in Mecca, and took the Prophet to Jerusalem (the furthest place of worship), more specifically to the ancient platform where the Jewish Temples had stood. At that spot Muhammad began his ascent to Heaven and meeting with God, the *miʾraj*. Along the various stations of his route to Heaven, his presence was acknowledged by the prophets of old and the heavenly court, thus legitimizing Muhammad as a true prophet of God. The only question for most Muslim scholars was whether the Prophet's Jerusalem journey and ascent to Heaven was an actual journey or one that he encountered in a prophetic dream.

Modern Western scholars are skeptical of linking the Qurʾanic passage to any geographical or historical reality. In their view "the furthest place of worship" refers to an imagined place, the final destination of a mystical journey. Nocturnal visions were the stock and trade of those receiving God's revelation since most ancient times. Western scholars reading this v. in the Qurʾan draw attention to the account of the biblical prophet Ezekiel who relates how he experienced a vision in which he was miraculously transported from Babylon to Jerusalem's Temple complex where Ezekiel encountered the glory of the LORD (Ezek. ch 8). Most Western scholars suggest that the extended Muslim commentary linking the *israʾ* and *miʾraj* to Jerusalem was dictated by political events that took place well after the death of the Prophet, namely the need for the Syria-based Banu Umayyah, the first Islamic dynasty (661–750 CE) to endow Jerusalem with sacred credentials similar to those of Mecca and Medina, the holy cities of Arabia. In sum, the Prophet and his community surely knew something of Jerusalem but the extent of their knowledge is unknown. Outside of veiled references to having originally prayed in the direction of the city, as did Jews, there is no evidence that the earliest Muslim community regarded the holy city with fervor equal to that of the Jews and Christians. In any case, Muhammad later reoriented the direction of prayer towards Mecca (Qurʾan 2.142–50).

Biblical History and the Jews in the Qurʾan

Although the Qurʾan contains numerous references to persons and events linked to the Hebrew Bible, these are not presented in a systematic fashion; instead they are spliced into segments of texts. This comes as no surprise as, generally speaking, Muslim scripture contains no extensive historical framework, nor does it contain material that can be traced directly to typical biblical forms of historical writing. Written in rhymed prose, the Qurʾan's style is more similar to prophetic literature with its explosive linguistic cadences and ambiguous historical referents as opposed to the narrative structures of Gen. through Kings. The discrete divisions and clusters of vv. in Muslim scripture appear disjointed, with little if any evidence of a sustained, unified composition. Of the 114 *surahs* or segments ("chapters"), only the twelfth, the story of the biblical Joseph, here seen through the lens of a rabbinic permutation, has a beginning, middle, and end, all framed within a single tale. Instead, the few traces of the biblical past are presented in bits and pieces, given meaning by a unifying moral framework that calls for the belief in and obedience to the one true God of Heaven and His prophets.

References to the world of the Israelites *(Banu Isra'il)* appear in both the early Qurʾanic material, reflecting Muhammad's mission in Mecca, and the later material from the Prophet's sojourn in Medina, where he came into sustained contact with the local Jewish tribes. At first Muhammad saw the Jews, fellow monotheists, as his natural allies and made overtures in order to have them recognize the legitimacy of his prophetic calling and message. But as the Jews refused to accept the legitimacy of his mission, and as it was politically expedient to turn against them, Muhammad changed course. Like the Jews, Muslims originally prayed in the direction of Jerusalem, but the orientation of prayer was later directed to Mecca (Qurʾan 2.142–50). They also celebrated the fast of the Day of Atonement *(ashura)* on the tenth day of a prescribed month, a practice later superseded by an obligatory month-long fast from sunrise to sunset. Similarly, the Muslims embraced ritual slaughter and prohibited the eating of carrion and pork (Qurʾan 2.173) but the Qurʾan also mocks the further restrictive nature of Jewish dietary law. The Medina segments of scripture derive moral lessons from the events and persons of the Hebrew Bible, often citing the biblical past to indict the Jews of Medina for their current behavior. In the Qurʾan's brief against the Jews of Arabia, the rebellious Israelites confronting Moses are made the analogs of the Jewish tribes rejecting Muhammad. Given the criticism of the wayward Israelites and their leaders in the Hebrew Bible, the Qurʾan and subsequent Islamic tradition had a vast repertoire of stories with which to indict contemporaneous Jews.

This negative reading of the history of ancient Israel is reflected in the Qur'an's use of the term *Yahud*, which refers to Jews collectively (the sg. is *Yahudi* [Heb *Yehudi*]). This term is always applied with pejorative connotations, so a generic label to signify a faith community became a term that called to attention the wicked behavior of an entire people. The Jews are called blasphemers and the most hostile of men to the true believers (Qur'an 5.64, 82). The Jews, along with Christians, are not to be taken as friends (Qurʾan 5.51). Neither they (nor the Christians) will ever be satisfied unless the Muslims follow their religion *(millah)* instead of Islam as preached by Muhammad (Qurʾan 2.120). This description of the *Yahud* is a well-worn theme in Qurʾan commentary and in a wide variety of Muslim literary output inspired by scripture and its commentary. A second term, used more neutrally, with which the Qurʾan specifies Jews is *Banu Isra'il,* "The Israelites." As in the Hebrew Bible, the Qurʾanic reference is to the extended households formed by the progeny of the biblical patriarch Jacob, who was also known as Israel (Gen. 32.25–33). The Jews of Muhammad's time are thus linked once again in Muslim scripture to the Jews of biblical times.

There are occasions when the Israelites are mentioned favorably, as when they follow the dictates of their prophets and thus earn the favor of their God. Therefore much can be learned from the righteous among them, particularly from the prophets sent to lead them. Following the precedent set by the Israelites who obeyed their prophets and thus served their God, were those Jews in Muhammad's time, who, unlike their recalcitrant kinsmen, answered the Prophet's call (e.g., Qurʾan 4.46, 162). But there are, the Qurʾan reminds us (e.g., 20.85), many occasions when the biblical Israelites turned against these prophets, most notably Moses, the great law-giver who, time and again, was confronted by rebellion. The rebelliousness of the generation in the wilderness and subsequent Jewish sinners establishes a pattern of negative behavior embraced by the Arabian descendants of the "hard hearted" Israelites of old. The Qur'an reminds us that God does not give His followers license to choose which of His prophets to follow, nor can they pick their way through the revealed book given them by the prophets He sent them (Qur'an 2.85). Referring to Muhammad's Jewish adversaries and their blameworthy acts, Muslim scripture not only recalls the transgressions of their biblical ancestors—defiant acts for which they were duly punished—it notes that these acts are described in the Jews' own Scripture and hence are proof of their continuing inclination to defy God's wishes.

The Qur'an mentions the rebellion of Korah (Qur'an 28.76–82), the corrupting of God's law that led to the destruction of Solomon's Temple (Qur'an 17.4), and similar transgressions including the accusation of persecuting and killing their own prophets (Qur'an 2.61, 87, 91; 4.155; 5.70). These prophets were all righteous individuals, none more so than Moses, who is closely identified with Muhammad. As in rabbinic sources describing the life of Moses, a later Muslim legend reports the Muslim Prophet was born and died on the same day and the same month many decades apart. Like Moses, he was also born fully circumcised, a highly unusual occurrence considered by the Rabbis a sign of prophetic calling. The births of both prophets were also marked by miraculous happenings. For Muslims, these and other linkages with Moses are clearly taken as a sign that Muhammad was the last in a chain of messengers sent by God, proving thereby the legitimacy of Muhammad's mission and authority.

The Qur'an (3.81) indicates that God sent his prophets (to the Israelites) only after they had entered into a covenant concerning the Prophet with Him. That is, each successive prophet swore to reveal to their people Muhammad's future coming so as to pave the way for his acceptance among Muhammad's Jewish (and Christian) contemporaries. How is it then that the Jews do not accept the last of God's prophets, when his coming is foretold in their own sacred Scripture? There are two explanations, both found in the Qur'an, for why the Jews of Muhammad's time rejected the prophet sent by God to them. In denying veracity of the Prophet's version of biblical events, the Jews either lost the original revelation sent to them and thus were revering a defective biblical text *(tabdil)*, or they deliberately falsified their revealed book *(tahrif)* in order to deny the truth of the Prophet's claim contained within this more original scripture (Qur'an 2.75; 4.46; 5.13; also 3.71 and similar vv.), an act of malice consciously initiated. In sum, the Qur'an's version of the biblical past is the God-given version; the Hebrew Bible is either a falsehood occasioned by a historic accident, or a deliberate forgery perpetrated to deny what the Jews know in their hearts to be true.

This accusation coincides with the Arabization of Islam, in which elements from the life of Abraham, the second most prominent biblical figure in Muslim scripture—Moses being the first—were cast in a new and different light. Having been put in an adversarial position with the Jews, and having expanded his diplomatic and military efforts to more distant regions in the Arabian peninsula, it would appear that Muhammad began to stress the Arabian character of his faith. The Bible suggests that Abraham's monotheistic faith was forged before he arrived in Canaan, the land promised by God to his descendants. Aware of Jewish claims attached to Abraham's patrimony, the Qur'an declares explicitly that the biblical patriarch was a *hanif,* meaning a proto-Muslim who, although a monotheist, was neither Jew nor Christian (Qur'an 3.67). It stresses Abraham's role in developing the *Ka'bah,* the central shrine of Mecca, a role he shared with his son Ishmael who in Islamic tradition is considered a true prophet (Qur'an

2.127–29; 19.54). Monotheism was thus said to have originated in Mecca and not in Canaan. The linkage of Abraham and Ishmael to the Meccan shrine was an indication to later Muslims that the shrine at the place of Muhammad's birth took precedence over Jerusalem and the Temple later built by Solomon. In turn, Muslim tradition declared Ishmael to be the ancestor of the northern Arabs, with particular reference to the Prophet's tribe and clan and therefore Muhammad himself. Reversing the account of the Bible, Ishmael emerges as Abraham's favored son. In some post-Qurʾanic Muslim traditions, the story told is of the binding of Ishmael and not of Isaac.

The Transfer and Absorption of the Hebrew Bible and Postbiblical Tradition

Geiger was followed by other Western scholars who grappled with the Islamization of themes that originated in the Hebrew Bible and had been retold in postbiblical literature. The vaguest similarities in Jewish and Muslim tradition were often considered proof of direct borrowing; differences were ascribed to purposeful distortion. These charges, whether stated or implied, rest on two assumptions: that the transmission of biblical material was consciously initiated and carefully programmed, and that the borrowed biblical and Jewish texts and traditions themselves were always discernible to Muhammad and his followers and to subsequent generations of Muslims. Neither assumption reflects the complex process of cultures sharing the same sacred space and interacting with one another. In all likelihood, the earliest Muslims became acquainted with biblical lore through direct contact with the Jews of Arabia and perhaps through stories that had widely circulated among the Arab tribesmen as monotheistic ideas proliferated throughout the peninsula. Unfortunately, we know little, if indeed anything about the beliefs and practices of the Jews of west Arabia. After the Arab conquest of the Levant and Iraq, Muslims were drawn into direct contact with the other Jewish communities, who exhibited the beliefs, practices, and understandings of the Hebrew Bible known to us from a wide variety of rabbinic sources. Biblical lore from these rabbinic sources eventually percolated into Muslim tradition. Stories derived from the Hebrew Bible and postbiblical Jewish writings were labeled by the Muslims *Israʾiliyat*, "Israelitica."

Well aware that Jewish Scripture and lore deeply penetrated their own tradition, Muslim authorities discussed the potential impact of borrowing the cultural realia of the Jews. Relying on various vv. in the Qurʾan, some Muslims argued that the Hebrew Bible itself was not to be cited as it had been inaccurately transmitted and/or deliberately falsified. However other Muslims regarded the Torah *(tawrat)* revered by contemporaneous Jews as an authentic document of God's revealed word, albeit a Heb text that had been superseded by the Arabic Qurʾan. From this second perspective, there was no overriding reason to exclude references to the Hebrew Bible in Muslim writings, especially since they saw non-distorted readings of the biblical text as foretelling Muhammad's future coming.

The transmission of nonscriptural Jewish materials, that is, the midrashic lore of postbiblical times, was also discussed among Muslim scholars and it came to be looked upon with great favor. The Prophet himself was alleged to have given permission to transmit traditions about the Israelites provided that they would not be misinterpreted and lead the Muslim faithful astray. For properly understood, the nonscriptural Jewish sources foretold the future coming of Muhammad's mission, as did the Hebrew Bible when interpreted correctly. The Muslim authorities favoring the study of Jewish nonbiblical texts also claimed that these later sources predicted future events of Islamic history. Such accounts when transmitted were, therefore, likely to lead to the edification of the Muslims, so narrating all sorts of traditions about the Israelites was licit, and even desirable. Whether or not they actually read biblical lore, Muslim authors drew attention to it in their writings. Similarly, biblical and postbiblical Jewish themes appear in Muslim sources, although Muslims may not have been aware of the themes' Jewish origins. In these last instances, perhaps the Jewish material was transmitted by Jewish converts seeking to initiate an inner dialogue with their former co-religionists in order to demonstrate similarities between Judaism and their new faith.

By the 3rd c. of Islam (8th to 9th c. CE), the Muslim religious authorities looked with disfavor upon *Isra'iliyat*, but the stories about the Israelites, particularly of the biblical prophets, captured the imagination of Muslim readers and gave rise eventually to a genre of popular literature known as "Tales of the Prophets." In time, some of the Islamized literature about biblical events and persons found their way back to Jews and Jewish sources in the form of commonly shared folklore.

[JACOB LASSNER]

Weights and Measures

Modern equivalents for biblical weights and measures are presented in the following tables.

WEIGHTS

HEBREW	NJPS	EQUIVALENCE	U.S. AVOIRDUPOIS	METRIC UNITS
kikar	talent	60 minas	75.558 pounds	34.3 kilograms
maneh	mina	50 shekels	20.148 ounces	571.2 grams
shekel	shekel	2 bekas	176.29 grains	11.42 grams
pim (or *payim*)	pim	.667 shekel	117.52 grains	7.61 grams
beka'	half-shekel	10 gerahs	88.14 grains	5.71 grams
gerah	gerah		8.81 grains	.57 gram

The practice of weighing unmarked ingots of metal used in commercial transactions prior to the invention of money explains that the names of the units of weight were used later as indications of value, and as names for monetary standards.

LENGTH MEASURES

HEBREW	NJPS	EQUIVALENCE	U.S. MEASURES	METRIC UNITS
'amah	cubit	2 spans	17.49 inches	.443 meter
zeret	span	3 handbreadths	8.745 inches	.221 meter
tofaḥ, tefaḥ	handbreadth, hand's breadth	4 fingers	2.915 inches	.074 meter
'etzba'	finger		0.728 inch	.019 meter

The cubit described in Ezekiel 40.5; 43.13 is equal to seven (not six) handbreadths, namely 20.405 inches.

CAPACITY: LIQUID MEASURES

HEBREW	NJPS	EQUIVALENCE	U.S. MEASURES	METRIC UNITS
kor	kor	10 baths	60.738 gallons	230 liters
bat	bath	6 hins	6.073 gallons	23 liters
hin	hin	3 kabs	1.012 gallons	3.829 liters
kav	kab	4 logs	1.4349 quarts	1.276 liters
log	log		0.674 pint	.32 liter

CAPACITY: DRY MEASURES

HEBREW	NJPS	EQUIVALENCE	U.S. MEASURES	METRIC UNITS
ḥomer	homer	2 lethechs	6.524 bushels	229.7 liters
kor	kor	2 lethechs	6.524 bushels	229.7 liters
letekh	lethech	5 ephahs	3.262 bushels	114.8 liters
'efah	ephah, measure	3 seahs	20.878 quarts	22.9 liters
se'ah	seah	3.33 omers	6.959 quarts	7.7 liters
'omer	omer	1.8 kabs	2.087 quarts	2.3 liters
'isaron	tenth of a measure	.1 ephah	2.087 quarts	2.3 liters
kav	kab		1.159 quarts	1.3 liters

Timeline*

DATE	PERIOD	EGYPT
Ca. 3300–2000 BCE	EARLY BRONZE AGE	
3300–3100	Early Bronze I	Earliest forms of writing
3100–2700	Early Bronze II	Political unification; Early Dynastic period
2700–2300	Early Bronze III	Old Kingdom; Dynasties 3–5
2300–2000	Early Bronze IV	First Intermediate Period
Ca. 2000–1550 BCE	MIDDLE BRONZE AGE	
2000–1650	Middle Bronze I–II	Middle Kingdom; Dynasties 11–12
1650–1550	Middle Bronze III	Second Intermediate/ Hyksos Period
Ca. 1550–1200 BCE	LATE BRONZE AGE	New Kingdom; Dynasties 18–19: Thutmose III (1479–1425), Akenhaten (1352–1336), Seti I (1294–1279), Rameses II (1279–1213), Merneptah (1213–1203); Sea Peoples (groups including Philistines) invasions begin
Ca. 1200–586 BCE	IRON AGE	
Ca. 1200–1025	Iron I	Rameses III (1184–1153)**
Ca. 1025–586	Iron II	
Ca. 1025–928	Iron IIA	
Ca. 928–722	Iron IIB	Shishak I invades Palestine (925)

* Many dates before 1000 BCE are highly uncertain.
** For a more complete list of rulers, see "Chronological Table of Rulers," pp. 2226–29.

LAND OF ISRAEL		MESOPOTAMIA, ASIA MINOR
		Earliest forms of writing; Full urbanization; Sumerian culture develops
In Egyptian sphere		High point of Sumerian culture
Flourishing city-states		Sargon of Akkad; Naram-Sin of Akkad; Gudea of Lagash
Decline/abandonment of city-states		Third Dynasty of Ur
Revival of urbanism; Invention of alphabet		Amorite kingdoms: Shamshi-Adad of Assyria (ca. 1813–1781); Hammurabi of Babylon (ca. 1792–1750); Rise of Hittites
In Egyptian sphere; Rise of Mitanni in north; Ugarit flourishes; Presence of Israel in land of Israel		Hittites challenge Egypt for control of Western Asia
Collapse of city-states		Hittite empire collapses; Trojan War
Israel emerges in Canaan; Philistines settle on SW coast; Small city-states develop in Phoenicia, Aram, Transjordan		Resurgence of Assyria: Tiglath-pileser I (1114–1076)
United monarchy in Israel: Saul (1025–1005); David (1005–965); Solomon (968–928)		
Divided monarchy:		
JUDAH:	ISRAEL:	
Rehoboam (928–911)	Jeroboam I (928–907)	Rise of Neo-Assyrian empire
	Omri (882–871); Capital at Samaria	Shalmaneser III (858–824); Battle of Qarqar (853)
	Ahab (873–852)	
Jehoshaphat (867–846)	Prophet Elijah (mid-9th century)	
	Prophet Elisha (mid- to late 9th century)	
Athaliah (842–836)	Jehu (842–814)	
Jehoash (836–798)	Jehoash (800–788)	Adad-nirari III (811–783)
	Jeroboam II (788–747)	
	Prophet Amos (mid-8th century)	
	Prophet Hosea (mid-8th century)	Tiglath-pileser III (745–727); Assyrian conquest of the Levant
Ahaz (743/735–727/715)	Hoshea (732–722)	Shalmaneser V (727–722) Samaria captured (722)

TIMELINE *(continued)*

DATE	PERIOD	EGYPT
Ca. 722–586 BCE	Iron IIC	Egypt conquered by Assyria (671) Psammetichus I (664–610) Neco II (610–595)
Ca. 586–539 BCE	NEO-BABYLONIAN	
		GREECE AND ROME
539–333 BCE	PERSIAN	Greeks repel Persian invasions Peloponnesian War (431–404)
333–63 BCE	HELLENISTIC	Alexander the Great (336–323); Defeats Persians at Issus (332); Occupies the Levant and Egypt Rome gains control over Greece (ca. 188–146) Sack of Carthage and Corinth (146)
63 BCE–330 CE	ROMAN	Julius Caesar named dictator (49); assassinated (44) Octavian (Augustus) defeats Antony at Actium (31); (Emperor 27 BCE–14 CE) Tiberius (14–37 CE) Gaius (Caligula) (37–41) Claudius (41–54) Nero (54–68) Vespasian (69–79) Titus (79–81) Domitian (81–96) Nerva (96–98) Trajan (98–117) Hadrian (117–138)

LAND OF ISRAEL	MESOPOTAMIA, ASIA MINOR
JUDAH: Prophet Isaiah (late 8th to early 7th centuries) Prophet Micah (late 8th century) Hezekiah (727/715–698/687) Manasseh (698/687–642) Josiah (639–609) Prophet Zephaniah (late 7th century) Prophet Jeremiah (late 7th–early 6th centuries) Jehoahaz (609) Jehoiakim (608–598) Jehoiachin (597) Prophet Ezekiel (early 6th century) Zedekiah (597–586); Capture of Jerusalem (586)	Sargon II (722–705) Sennacherib (705–681); Attack on Judah and seige of Jerusalem (701) Esarhaddon (681–669) Ashurbanipal (669–627) Rise of Babylonia Assyrian capital of Nineveh captured (612) Nebuchadrezzar II (604–562) of Babylonia
	Nabonidus (556–539)
EASTERN MEDITERRANEAN Some exiles return from Babylonia (538) Second Temple built (520–515) Prophet Haggai (520); Prophet Zechariah (520–518) Nehemiah governor of Judah (ca. 445–430) Mission of Ezra the scribe (mid-5th [or early 4th] century)	Cyrus II (the Great) (559–530); Capture of Babylon (539) Cambyses (530–522); Capture of Egypt (525) Darius I (522–486) Xerxes I (486–465) Artaxerxes I (465–424) Artaxerxes II (405–359)
Seleucus I (312/311–281) controls Syria and Mesopotamia Ptolemy I (323–282) controls Egypt, Palestine, Phoenicia Antiochus III (223–187) gains control of southern Syria, Phoenicia, and Judea from Ptolemy IV (202–198) Ben Sira (Sirach) (early 2nd century) Antiochus IV Epiphanes (175–164) Revolt of the Maccabees (167–164) HASMONEAN RULE OF JUDEA (165–37): John Hyrcanus (135–104); Alexander Janneus (103–76); Salome Alexandra (76–67)	
Pompey conquers the Levant (66–62); Enters Jerusalem (63) Herod the Great king of Judea (37–4 BCE); Rebuilds Second Temple First Jewish Revolt in Judea against Rome (66–73 CE); Jerusalem is captured; Second Temple destroyed (70) Jewish revolts in Egypt, Libya, Cyprus (115–118) Second Jewish Revolt in Judea against Rome (132–135)	

Chronological Table of Rulers

DATE	EGYPT	ASSYRIA	BABYLONIA
1300 BCE	DYNASTY 19 (1295–1186): Seti I (1294–1279) Rameses II (1279–1213) Merneptah (1213–1203)		
1200	DYNASTY 20 (1186–1069)	Tiglath-pileser I (1114–1076)	
	DYNASTY 21 (1069–945)		
1000	DYNASTIES 22–24 (945–715): Shoshenq I (**Shishak**) (945–924)	Shalmaneser III (858–824) Shamshi-Adad V (824–811)	
	DYNASTY 25 (780–656):		
800		Adad-nirari III (811–783) Shalmaneser IV (783–773) Ashur-dan III (773–755) Ashur-nirari V (755–745) **Tiglath-pileser** III **(Pul)** (745–727) **Shalmaneser** V (727–722) Sargon II (722–705) **Sennacherib** (705–681)	Marduk-apal-iddina II **(Merodach-baladan)** (721–710, 703)
700	Taharqa **(Tirhakah)** (690–664) DYNASTY 26 (664–525): Psammetichus I (664–610) Neco II (610–595) Psammetichus II (595–589) Apries **(Hophra)** (589–570) Amasis II (570–526) Psammetichus III (526–525)	**Esarhaddon** (681–669) Ashurbanipal (669–627) Ashur-etil-ilani } Sin-shum-lishir } (627–612) Sin-shar-ishkun } Ashur-uballit II (612–609)	Nabo-polassar (625–605) **Nebuchadrezzar** II **(Nebuchadnezzar)** (605–562) Amel-Marduk **(Evil-merodach)** (562–560) Neriglissar (560–556) Labashi-Marduk (556) **Nabonidus** (556–539) **Belshazzar** (co-regent 553–543)
400			
325 BCE			

Note: Names in boldface occur in the Tanakh. Overlapping dates indicate co-regencies. Date ranges are reigns, not life spans. Many dates are uncertain or approximations.

DATE	PERSIA	ISRAEL	
1300 BCE			
1200			
		UNITED MONARCHY:	
1000		**Saul** (1025–1005); **David** (1005–965); **Solomon (Yedidiah)** (968–928)	
		DIVIDED MONARCHY:	
		JUDAH:	ISRAEL:
		Rehoboam (928–911)	**Jeroboam** I (928–907)
		Abijam (Abijah) (911–908)	**Nadab** (907–906)
		Asa (908–867)	**Baasha** (906–883)
		Jehoshaphat (870–846)	**Elah** (883–882); **Zimri** (882)
			Omri (882–871)
		Jehoram (Joram) (851–843)	**Ahab** (873–852)
			Ahaziah (852–851)
		Ahaziah (Jehoahaz) (843–842)	**Jehoram (Joram)** (851–842)
		Athaliah (842–836)	**Jehu** (842–814)
800		**Jehoash** (Joash) (836–798)	**Jehoahaz** (817–800)
		Amaziah (798–769)	**Jehoash (Joash)** (800–784)
		Azariah (Uzziah) (785–733)	**Jeroboam** II (788–747)
			Zechariah (747); **Shallum** (747)
			Menahem (747–737)
			Pekahiah (737–735)
		Jotham (759–743)	**Pekah** (735–732)
		Ahaz (743/735–727/715)*	**Hoshea** (732–722)
		Hezekiah (727/715–698/687)*	
700			
		Manasseh (698/687–642)*	
		Amon (641–640)	
		Josiah (640–609)	
		Jehoahaz (Shallum) (609)	
		Jehoiakim (Eliakim) (608–598)	
		Jehoiachin (Jeconiah, etc.**)** (597)	
		Zedekiah (Mattaniah) (597–586)	
	Cyrus II (559–530)		
	Cambyses (530–522)		
	Darius I (522–486)		
	Xerxes I **(Ahasuerus)** (486–465)		
	Artaxerxes I (465–424)		
	Darius II (423–405)		
400	Artaxerxes II (405–359)		
	Artaxerxes III (359–338)		
	Artaxerxes IV (338–336)		
325 BCE	Darius III (336–330)		

*Data are inconsistent for the dates of the reigns of Ahaz, Hezekiah, and Manasseh.

CHRONOLOGICAL TABLE OF RULERS *(continued)*

DATE	EGYPT	SYRIA
	HELLENISTIC PERIOD	Alexander (the Great) (336–323)
300 BCE	Ptolemy I Soter (305–282)	Seleucus I Nicator (305–281)
	Ptolemy II Philadelphus (285–246)	Antiochus I Soter (281–261)
		Antiochus II Theos (261–246)
	Ptolemy III Euergetes (246–221)	Seleucus II Callinicus (246–225)
	Ptolemy IV Philopator (221–204)	Seleucus III Soter Ceraunos (225–223)
	Ptolemy V Epiphanes (204–180);	Antiochus III (the Great) (223–187)
	Cleopatra I (180–176)	Seleucus IV Philopator (187–175)
		Antiochus IV Epiphanes (175–164)
	Ptolemy VI Philometor (180–145);	Antiochus V Eupator (164–162)
	Cleopatra II (175–116)	Demetrius I Soter (162–150)
	Ptolemy VII Neos Philopator (145)	Alexander Epiphanes (Balas) (150–145)
	Ptolemy VIII Euergetes II Physcon (170–116)	Demetrius II Nicator (145–141 and 129–125)
		Antiochus VI Epiphanes (145–142)
		Trypho (142–138)
		Antiochus VII Sidetes (138–129)
		Cleopatra Thea (126–121)
		Antiochus VIII Grypus (125–121 and 121–96)
	Cleopatra III (116–101)	Seleucus V (125)
	Ptolemy IX Soter II (116–107 and 88–80)	Antiochus IX Cyzicenus (115–95)
100 BCE	Ptolemy X Alexander I (107–88)	Seleucus VI (95)
		Antiochus X Eusebes (95–83)
		Antiochus XI Philadelphus (95)
	Cleopatra Berenice (101–88)	Demetrius III Eukairos (95–88)
		Philip I Epiphanes Philadelphus (95–84)
	Ptolemy XI Alexander II (80)	Antiochus XII Dionysus Epiphanes (87–84)
		Philip II (67–66)
	Ptolemy XII Auletes (80–59 and 55–51)	Antiochus XIII Asiaticus (69–68 and 65–64)
50 BCE	Cleopatra VII (51–30)	
	Ptolemy XIII (51–47)	
	Ptolemy XIV (47–44)	
25 CE		
50 CE		
100 CE		

DATE	ROMAN EMPIRE	LAND OF ISRAEL
300 BCE		
		HASMONEAN RULERS
		[Mattathias d. 166]
		Judas Maccabeus, son of Mattathias (165–160)
		Jonathan, son of Mattathias (160–142)
		Simon, son of Mattathias (142–135)
		John Hyrcanus I, son of Simon (135–104)
		Judah Aristobulus I, son of John Hyrcanus (104–103)
		Alexander Janneus, son of John Hyrcanus (103–76)
100 BCE		Salome Alexandra, wife of Alexander Jannaeus (76–67)
		Aristobulus II, son of Alexander Jannaeus and Salome Alexandra (67–63)
		Hyrcanus II, son of Alexander Jannaeus and Salome Alexandra (63–40)
50 BCE		
		Mattathias Antigonus, son of Aristobulus II (40–37)
		HERODIAN DYNASTY
		Herod the Great, king of the Jews (37–4)
	ROMAN EMPERORS	Herod Archelaus, son of Herod the Great, ethnarch of Judea, Samaria, Idumea (4 BCE–6 CE)
25 CE	Octavian (Augustus) (27 BCE–14 CE)	Herod Antipas, son of Herod the Great, tetrarch of Galilee and Perea (4 BCE–39 CE)
		Herod Philip, son of Herod the Great, tetrarch of Batanea, Trachonitis, Auranitis (4 BCE–34 CE)
	Tiberius (14–37)	
		Herod Agrippa I, grandson of Herod the Great, king of Batanea, Trachonitis, Aurantis (37–44) and of Judea,* Galilee, and Perea (41–44)
50 CE	Gaius Caligula (37–41)	
	Claudius (41–54)	
	Nero (54–68)	
	Galba (68–69); Otho (69); Vitellius (69)	Herod Agrippa II, son of Herod Agrippa I, king of Chalcis (50–53), king of Batanea, Trachonitis, Auranitis, Galilee, Perea (53–ca. 93)
	Vespasian (69–79)	
	Titus (79–81)	
	Domitian (81–96)	
	Nerva (96–98)	
100 CE	Trajan (98–117)	
	Hadrian (117–138)	

* In 41 Judea was made part of the kingdom of Herod Agrippa I, grandson of Herod the Great (see Herodian Dynasty, above). At his death in 44 it became a province again.

Calendar

The year was composed of twelve lunar months (beginning on the day of the new moon), with an intercalary month added periodically (see perhaps 1 Kings 12.33). In some traditions, and perhaps originally, the year began in the fall, at the autumnal equinox (see Exod. 23.16; 34.22). In others, following Babylonian practice, the new year was celebrated in the spring. The fall new year became standard in postbiblical Judaism.

Months in the Bible are usually identified by ordinal numbers, beginning with the spring new year. Some months (in boldface in the following list) are also designated with names derived either from a Canaanite calendar or, in postexilic texts, from a Babylonian one; the names of months not found in the Bible are known from other ancient sources.

	CANAANITE NAME	BABYLONIAN/ARAMAIC NAME	MODERN EQUIVALENT
First	**'Aviv**	**Nisan**	March–April
Second	**Ziv**	'Iyar	April–May
Third		**Sivan**	May–June
Fourth		Tamuz	June–July
Fifth		'Av	July–August
Sixth		**'Elul**	August–September
Seventh	**'Etanim**	Tishri	September–October
Eighth	**Bul**	Marḥeshvan	October–November
Ninth		Kislev	November–December
Tenth		**Tevet**	December–January
Eleventh		**Shevat**	January–February
Twelfth		**'Adar**	February–March

The Jewish calendar is based on the lunar month, which is a bit longer than 29½ days, so Jewish lunar months are 29 or 30 days long. Twelve lunar months usually amount to 354 days, 11 days short of a solar year. In order for the festivals to stay in the correct season in relation to the solar year, an extra month is added every few years. Following ancient Babylonian models, the calendar runs on a 19-year cycle: years 3, 6, 8,11, 14, 17, and 19 of the cycle are intercalated or "leap" years, containing an extra month of Adar, sometimes called *Adar Sheni* (second Adar). Adar was chosen for intercalation because it is the last month of the Babylonian year and of the biblical year beginning in Nisan (an alternate calendar, the one now in use, begins the year in Tishri with Rosh Ha-Shanah). The next 19-year intercalation cycle will begin in 5768 (2007–2008 CE).

Observances fall within the calendar as follows:

Rosh Ha-Shanah (the New Year)	1–2 Tishri
Yom Kippur (the Day of Atonement)	10 Tishri
Sukkot (Booths) begins	15 Tishri
Hanukkah begins	25 Kislev
Purim	14 Adar (15 Adar in Jerusalem and other ancient walled cities)
Passover begins	15 Nisan
Shavu'ot (Weeks) begins	6 Sivan
Tish'ah be' av	9 Av

Table of Biblical Readings

		TORAH	NEVI'IM
WEEKLY SABBATH READINGS			
Genesis			
בראשית	*Bere'shit*	1.1–6.8	Isaiah 42.5–43.10 (42.5–21)*
נח	*Noaḥ*	6.9–11.32	Isaiah 54.1–55.5 (54.1–10)
לך לך	*Lekh Lekha*	12.1–17.27	Isaiah 40.27–41.16
וירא	*Va-yera'*	18.1–22.24	2 Kings 4.1–37 (4.1–23)
חיי שרה	*Ḥayyei Sarah*	23.1–25.18	1 Kings 1.1–31
תולדות	*Toledot*	25.19–28.9	Malachi 1.1–2.7
ויצא	*Va-yetse'*	28.10–32.3	Hosea 12.13–14.10 (11.7–12.12)
וישלח	*Va-yishlaḥ*	32.4–36.43	Hosea 11.7–12.12 (Obadiah 1.1–21)
וישב	*Va-yeshev*	37.1–40.23	Amos 2.6–3.8
מקץ	*Mikkets*	41.1–44.17	1 Kings 3.15–4.1
ויגש	*Va-yiggash*	44.18–47.27	Ezekiel 37.15–28
ויחי	*Va-yeḥi*	47.28–50.26	1 Kings 2.1–12
Exodus			
שמות	*Shemot*	1.1–6.1	Isaiah 27.6–28.13; 29.22, 23 (Jeremiah 1.1–2.3)
וארא	*Va-'era'*	6.2–9.35	Ezekiel 28.25–29.21
בא	*Bo'*	10.1–13.16	Jeremiah 46.13–28
בשלח	*Be-shallaḥ*	13.17–17.16	Judges 4.4–5.31 (5.1–31)
יתרו	*Yitro*	18.1–20.26	Isaiah 6.1–7.6; 9.5, 6 (6.1–13)
משפטים	*Mishpatim*	21.1–24.18	Jeremiah 34.8–22; 33.25, 26
תרומה	*Terumah*	25.1–27.19	1 Kings 5.26–6.13
תצוה	*Tetsavveh*	27.20–30.10	Ezekiel 43.10–27
כי תשא	*Ki Tissa'*	30.11–34.35	1 Kings 18.1–39 (18.20–39)
ויקהל	*Va-yakhel*	35.1–38.20	1 Kings 7.40–50 (7.13–26)
פקודי	*Pekudei*	38.21–40.38	1 Kings 7.51–8.21 (7.40–50)
Leviticus			
ויקרא	*Va-yikra'*	1.1–5.26	Isaiah 43.21–44.23
צו	*Tsav*	6.1–8.36	Jeremiah 7.21–8.3; 9.22, 23
שמיני	*Shemini*	9.1–11.47	2 Samuel 6.1–7.17 (6.1–19)
תזריע	*Tazria'*	12.1–13.59	2 Kings 4.42–5.19
מצרע	*Metsora'*	14.1–15.33	2 Kings 7.3–20
אחרי מות	*'Aḥarei Mot*	16.1–18.30	Ezekiel 22.1–19 (22.1–16)
קדשים	*Kedoshim*	19.1–20.27	Amos 9.7–15 (Ezekiel 20.2–20)
אמר	*'Emor*	21.1–24.23	Ezekiel 44.15–31
בהר	*Be-har*	25.1–26.2	Jeremiah 32.6–27
בחקתי	*Be-ḥukotai*	26.3–27.34	Jeremiah 16.19–17.14

Local practice may differ from the selections listed. * Parentheses indicate Sephardi ritual.

		TORAH		NEVI'IM
Numbers				
במדבר	*Be-midbar*	1.1–4.20		Hosea 2.1–22
נשא	*Naso'*	4.21–7.89		Judges 13.2–25
בהעלתך	*Be-ha'alotekha*	8.1–12.16		Zechariah 2.14–4.7
שלח לך	*Shelaḥ-Lekha*	13.1–15.41		Joshua 2.1–24
קרח	*Koraḥ*	16.1–18.32		1 Samuel 11.14–12.22
חקת	*Ḥukat*	19.1–22.1		Judges 11.1–33
בלק	*Balak*	22.2–25.9		Micah 5.6–6.8
פינחס	*Pinḥas*	25.10–30.1		1 Kings 18.46–19.21
מטות	*Matot*	30.2–32.42		Jeremiah 1.1–2.3
מסעי	*Mase'ei*	33.1–36.13		Jeremiah 2.4–28; 3.4 (2.4–28; 4.1, 2)
Deuteronomy				
דברים	*Devarim*	1.1–3.22		Isaiah 1.1–27
ואתחנן	*Va-'etḥanan*	3.23–7.11		Isaiah 40.1–26
עקב	*'Ekev*	7.12–11.25		Isaiah 49.14–51.3
ראה	*Re'eh*	11.26–16.17		Isaiah 54.11–55.5
שפטים	*Shofetim*	16.18–21.9		Isaiah 51.12–52.12
כי תצא	*Ki Tetze'*	21.10–25.19		Isaiah 54.1–10
כי תבוש	*Ki Tavo'*	26.1–29.8		Isaiah 60.1–22
נצבים	*Nitzavim*	29.9–30.20		Isaiah 61.10–63.9
וילך	*Va-yelekh*	31.1–30		—
האזינו	*Ha'azinu*	32.1–52		2 Samuel 22.1–51
וזאת הברכה	*Ve-zo't Ha-berakhah*	33.1–34.12		Joshua 1.1–18 (1.1–9)

READINGS FOR SPECIAL SABBATHS

Sabbath coinciding with Rosh Ḥodesh	Weekly portion and Numbers 28.9–15	Isaiah 66.1–24
Sabbath immediately preceding Rosh Ḥodesh	Weekly portion	1 Samuel 20.18–42
Shekalim	Weekly portion and Exodus 30.11–16	2 Kings 12.1–17 (11.17–12.17)
Zakhor	Weekly portion and Deuteronomy 25.17–19	1 Samuel 15.2–34 (15.1–34)
Parah	Weekly portion and Numbers 19.1–22	Ezekiel 36.16–38 (36.16–36)
Ha-Ḥodesh	Weekly portion and Exodus 12.1–20	Ezekiel 45.16–46.18 (45.18–46.15)
Ha-Gadol	Weekly portion	Malachi 3.4–24
First Sabbath Hanukkah	Weekly portion plus the verses relating the prince *(nasi')* of the day corresponding to the day of Hanukkah	Zechariah 2.14–4.7
Second Sabbath Hanukkah	Weekly portion and Hanukkah portions as above	1 Kings 7.40–50

	TORAH	NEVI'IM
READINGS FOR THE DAYS OF AWE		
Rosh Ha-Shanah		
First Day	Genesis 21.1–34; Numbers 29.1–6	1 Samuel 1.1–2.10
Second Day	Genesis 22.1–24; Numbers 29.1–6	Jeremiah 31.2–20
Sabbath Shuvah	Weekly portion	Hosea 14.2–10; Micah 7.18–20; Joel 2.15–27 (Hosea 14.2–10; Micah 7.18–20)
Yom Kippur		
Morning	Leviticus 16.1–34; Numbers 29.7–11	Isaiah 57.14–58.14
Afternoon	Leviticus 18.1–30	Jonah 1.1–4.11; Micah 7.18–20
READINGS FOR THE FESTIVALS		
Sukkot (Tabernacles)		
First Day	Leviticus 22.26–23.44; Numbers 29.12–16	Zechariah 14.1–21
Second Day	Leviticus 22.26–23.44; Numbers 29.12–16	1 Kings 8.2–21
Sabbath during the Middle Days	Exodus 33.12–34.26; Daily portion from Numbers 29	Ezekiel 38.18–39.16
Eighth Day	Deuteronomy 14.22–16.17 (15.19–16.17); Numbers 29.35–30.1	1 Kings 8.54–66
Simḥat Torah	Deuteronomy 33.1–34.12; Genesis 1.1–2.3; Numbers 29.35–30.1	Joshua 1.1–18 (1.1–9)
Pesaḥ (Passover)		
First Day	Exodus 12.21–51; Numbers 28.16–25	Joshua 5.2–6.1; 6.27
Second Day	Leviticus 22.26–23.44; Numbers 28.16–25	2 Kings 23.1–9, 21–25
Sabbath during the Middle Days	Exodus 33.12–34.26; Numbers 28.19–25	Ezekiel 37.1–14
Seventh Day	Exodus 13.17–15.26; Numbers 28.19–25	2 Samuel 22.1–51
Eighth Day	Deuteronomy 15.19–16.17; Numbers 28.19–25	Isaiah 10.32–12.6
Shavu'ot (Pentecost)		
First Day	Exodus 19.1–20.23; Numbers 28.26–31	Ezekiel 1.1–28; 3.12
Second Day	Deuteronomy 15.19–16.17;* Numbers 28.26–31	Habakkuk 3.1–19 (2.20–3.19)
READINGS ON WEEKDAY OCCASIONS		
Purim	Exodus 17.8–16	—
Ninth of Av		
Morning	Deuteronomy 4.25–40	Jeremiah 8.13–9.23
Afternoon	Exodus 32.11–14; 34.1–10	Isaiah 55.6–56.8
Public Fast Days		
Morning	Exodus 32.11–14; 34.1–10	—
Afternoon	Exodus 32.11–14; 34.1–10	Isaiah 55.6–56.8
READINGS OF THE FIVE MEGILLOT		
The Song of Songs		Sabbath during Pesaḥ (Passover)
Ruth		Shavu'ot (Pentecost)
Lamentations		Ninth of Av
Ecclesiastes		Sabbath during Sukkot (Tabernacles)
Esther		Purim

* On the Sabbath, 14.22–16.17.

Chapter/ Verse Differences

Chapter/verse differences between standard English numbering and Hebrew text numbering used in NJPS. Books are listed in Hebrew canonical order.

ENGLISH	HEBREW
Gen. 31.55	Gen. 32.1
Gen. 32.1–32	Gen. 32.2–33
Exod. 8.1–4	Exod. 7.26–29
Exod. 8.5–32	Exod. 8.1–28
Exod. 22.1	Exod. 21.37
Exod. 22.2–31	Exod. 22.1–30
Lev. 6.1–7	Lev. 5.20–26
Lev. 6.8–30	Lev. 6.1–23
Num. 16.36–50	Num. 17.1–15
Num. 17.1–13	Num. 17.16–28
Num. 26.1a	Num. 25.19
Num. 29.40	Num. 30.1
Num. 30.1–6	Num. 30.2–17
Deut. 12.32	Deut. 13.1
Deut. 13.1–18	Deut. 13.2–19
Deut. 22.30	Deut. 23.1
Deut. 23.1–25	Deut. 23.2–26
Deut. 29.1	Deut. 28.69
Deut. 29.2–29	Deut. 29.1–28
1 Sam. 20.42b	1 Sam. 21.1
1 Sam. 21.1–15	1 Sam. 21.2–16
1 Sam. 23.29	1 Sam. 24.1
1 Sam. 24.1–22	1 Sam. 24.2–23
2 Sam. 18.33	2 Sam. 19.1
2 Sam. 19.1–43	2 Sam. 19.2–44
1 Kings 4.21–34	1 Kings 5.1–14
1 Kings 5.1–18	1 Kings 5.15–32
1 Kings 18.33b	1 Kings 18.34a
1 Kings 20.2b	1 Kings 20.3a
1 Kings 22.22a	1 Kings 22.21b
1 Kings 22.43b	1 Kings 22.44
1 Kings 22.44–53	1 Kings 22.45–54
2 Kings 11.21	2 Kings 12.1
2 Kings 12.1–21	2 Kings 12.2–22
Isa. 9.1	Isa. 8.23
Isa. 9.2–21	Isa. 9.1–20
Isa. 63.19	Isa. 63.19a
Isa. 64.1	Isa. 63.19b
Isa. 64.2–12	Isa. 64.1–11
Jer. 9.1	Jer. 8.23
Jer. 9.2–26	Jer. 9.1–25
Ezek. 20.45–49	Ezek. 21.1–5
Ezek. 21.1–32	Ezek. 21.6–37
Hos. 1.10–11	Hos. 2.1–2
Hos. 2.1–23	Hos. 2.3–25

ENGLISH	HEBREW
Hos. 11.12	Hos. 12.1
Hos. 12.1–14	Hos. 12.2–15
Hos. 13.6	Hos. 14.1
Hos. 14.1–9	Hos. 14.2–10
Joel 2.28–32	Joel 3.1–5
Joel 3.1–21	Joel 4.1–21
Jon. 1.17	Jon. 2.1
Jon. 2.1–10	Jon. 2.2–11
Mic. 5.1	Mic. 4.14
Mic. 5.2–15	Mic. 5.1–14
Nah. 1.15	Nah. 2.1
Nah. 2.1–13	Nah. 2.2–14
Zech. 1.18–21	Zech. 2.1–4
Zech. 2.1–13	Zech. 2.5–17
Mal. 4.1–6	Mal. 3.19–24
Ps. 3. title	Ps. 3.1
Ps. 3.1–8	Ps. 3.2–9
Ps. 4. title	Ps. 4.1
Ps. 4.1–8	Ps. 4.2–9
Ps. 5. title	Ps. 5.1
Ps. 5.1–12	Ps. 5.2–13
Ps. 6. title	Ps. 6.1
Ps. 6.1–10	Ps. 6.2–11
Ps. 7. title	Ps. 7.1
Ps. 7.1–17	Ps. 7.2–18
Ps. 8. title	Ps. 8.1
Ps. 8.1–9	Ps. 8.2–10
Ps. 9. title	Ps. 9.1
Ps. 9.1–20	Ps. 9.2–21
Ps. 11. title	Ps. 11.1a
Ps. 12. title	Ps. 12.1
Ps. 12.1–8	Ps. 12.2–9
Ps. 13. title	Ps. 13.1
Ps. 13.1–5	Ps. 13.2–6a
Ps. 13.6	Ps. 13.6b
Ps. 14. title	Ps. 14.1a
Ps. 15. title	Ps. 15.1a
Ps. 16. title	Ps. 16.1a
Ps. 17. title	Ps. 17.1a
Ps. 18. title	Ps. 18.1–2a
Ps. 18.1–50	Ps. 18.2–51
Ps. 19. title	Ps. 19.1
Ps. 19.1–14	Ps. 19.2–15
Ps. 20. title	Ps. 20.1
Ps. 20.1–9	Ps. 20.2–10

ENGLISH	HEBREW
Ps. 21. title	Ps. 21.1
Ps. 21.1–13	Ps. 21.2–14
Ps. 22. title	Ps. 22.1
Ps. 22.1–31	Ps. 22.2–32
Ps. 23. title	Ps. 23.1a
Ps. 24. title	Ps. 24.1a
Ps. 25. title	Ps. 25.1a
Ps. 26. title	Ps. 26.1a
Ps. 27. title	Ps. 27.1a
Ps. 28. title	Ps. 28.1a
Ps. 29. title	Ps. 29.1a
Ps. 30. title	Ps. 30.1
Ps. 30.1–12	Ps. 30.2–13
Ps. 31. title	Ps. 31.1
Ps. 31.1–24	Ps. 31.2–25
Ps. 32. title	Ps. 32.1a
Ps. 34. title	Ps. 34.1
Ps. 34.1–22	Ps. 34.2–23
Ps. 35. title	Ps. 35.1 (1st word)
Ps. 36. title	Ps. 36.1
Ps. 36.1–12	Ps. 36.2–13
Ps. 37. title	Ps. 37.1 (1st word)
Ps. 38. title	Ps. 38.1
Ps. 38.1–22	Ps. 38.2–23
Ps. 39. title	Ps. 39.1
Ps. 39.1–13	Ps. 39.2–14
Ps. 40. title	Ps. 40.1
Ps. 40.1–17	Ps. 40.2–18
Ps. 41. title	Ps. 41.1
Ps. 41.1–13	Ps. 41.2–14
Ps. 42. title	Ps. 42.1
Ps. 42.1–11	Ps. 42.2–12
Ps. 44. title	Ps. 44.1
Ps. 44.1–26	Ps. 44.2–27
Ps. 45. title	Ps. 45.1
Ps. 45.1–17	Ps. 45.2–18
Ps. 46. title	Ps. 46.1
Ps. 46.1–11	Ps. 46.2–12
Ps. 47. title	Ps. 47.1
Ps. 47.1–9	Ps. 47.2–10
Ps. 48. title	Ps. 48.1
Ps. 48.1–14	Ps. 48.2–15
Ps. 49. title	Ps. 49.1
Ps. 49.1–20	Ps. 49.2–21
Ps. 50. title	Ps. 50.1a

ENGLISH	HEBREW	ENGLISH	HEBREW	ENGLISH	HEBREW
Ps. 51. title	Ps. 51.1–2a	Ps. 79.1	Ps. 79.1b	Ps. 127. title	Ps. 127.1a
Ps. 51.1–19	Ps. 51.2b–21	Ps. 80. title	Ps. 80.1	Ps. 127.1	Ps. 127.1b
Ps. 52. title	Ps. 52.1–2a	Ps. 80.1–19	Ps. 80.2–20	Ps. 128. title	Ps. 128.1a
Ps. 52.1–9	Ps. 52.2b–11	Ps. 81. title	Ps. 81.1	Ps. 128.1	Ps. 128.1b
Ps. 53. title	Ps. 53.1	Ps. 81.1–16	Ps. 81.2–17	Ps. 129. title	Ps. 129.1a
Ps. 53.1–6	Ps. 53.2–7	Ps. 82. title	Ps. 82.1a	Ps. 129.1	Ps. 129.1b
Ps. 54. title	Ps. 54.1–2	Ps. 82.1	Ps. 82.1b	Ps. 130. title	Ps. 130.1a
Ps. 54.1–7	Ps. 54.3–9	Ps. 83. title	Ps. 83.1	Ps. 130.1	Ps. 130.1b
Ps. 55. title	Ps. 55.1	Ps. 83.1–18	Ps. 83.2–19	Ps. 131. title	Ps. 131.1a
Ps. 55.1–23	Ps. 55.2–24	Ps. 84. title	Ps. 84.1	Ps. 131.1	Ps. 131.1b
Ps. 56. title	Ps. 56.1	Ps. 84.1–12	Ps. 84.2–13	Ps. 132. title	Ps. 132.1a
Ps. 56.1–13	Ps. 56.2–14	Ps. 85. title	Ps. 85.1	Ps. 132.1	Ps. 132.1b
Ps. 57. title	Ps. 57.1	Ps. 85.1–13	Ps. 85.2–14	Ps. 133. title	Ps. 133.1a
Ps. 57.1–11	Ps. 57.2–12	Ps. 86. title	Ps. 86.1a	Ps. 133.1	Ps. 133.1b
Ps. 58. title	Ps. 58.1	Ps. 86.1	Ps. 86.1b	Ps. 134. title	Ps. 134.1a
Ps. 58.1–11	Ps. 58.2–12	Ps. 87. title	Ps. 87.1a	Ps. 134.1	Ps. 134.1b
Ps. 59. title	Ps. 59.1	Ps. 87.1	Ps. 87.1b	Ps. 138. title	Ps. 138.1a
Ps. 59.1–17	Ps. 59.2–18	Ps. 88. title	Ps. 88.1	Ps. 138.1	Ps. 138.1b
Ps. 60. title	Ps. 60.1–2	Ps. 88.1–18	Ps. 88.2–19	Ps. 139. title	Ps. 139.1a
Ps. 60.1–12	Ps. 60.3–14	Ps. 89. title	Ps. 89.1	Ps. 139.1	Ps. 139.1b
Ps. 61. title	Ps. 61.1	Ps. 89.1–52	Ps. 89.2–53	Ps. 140. title	Ps. 140.1
Ps. 61.1–8	Ps. 61.2–9	Ps. 90. title	Ps. 90.1a	Ps. 140.1–13	Ps. 140.2–14
Ps. 62. title	Ps. 62.1	Ps. 90.1	Ps. 90.1b	Ps. 141. title	Ps. 141.1a
Ps. 62.1–12	Ps. 62.2–13	Ps. 92. title	Ps. 92.1	Ps. 141.1	Ps. 141.1b
Ps. 63. title	Ps. 63.1	Ps. 92.1–15	Ps. 92.2–16	Ps. 142. title	Ps. 142.1
Ps. 63.1–11	Ps. 63.2–12	Ps. 98. title	Ps. 98.1 (1st word)	Ps. 142.1–7	Ps. 142.2–8
Ps. 64. title	Ps. 64.1	Ps. 100. title	Ps. 100.1a	Ps. 143. title	Ps. 143.1a
Ps. 64.1–10	Ps. 64.2–11	Ps. 100.1	Ps. 100.1b	Ps. 143.1	Ps. 143.1b
Ps. 65. title	Ps. 65.1	Ps. 101. title	Ps. 101.1a	Ps. 144. title	Ps. 144.1 (1st word)
Ps. 65.1–13	Ps. 65.2–14	Ps. 101.1	Ps. 101.1b	Ps. 145. title	Ps. 145.1a
Ps. 66. title	Ps. 66.1a	Ps. 102. title	Ps. 102.1	Ps. 145.1	Ps. 145.1b
Ps. 66.1	Ps. 66.1b	Ps. 102.1–28	Ps. 102.2–29	Song 6.13	Song 7.1
Ps. 67. title	Ps. 67.1	Ps. 103. title	Ps. 103.1 (1st word)	Song 7.1–13	Song 7.2–14
Ps. 67.1–7	Ps. 67.2–8	Ps. 108. title	Ps. 108.1	Eccl. 5.1	Eccl. 4.17
Ps. 68. title	Ps. 68.1	Ps. 108.1–13	Ps. 108.2–14	Eccl. 5.2–20	Eccl. 5.1–19
Ps. 68.1–35	Ps. 68.2–36	Ps. 109. title	Ps. 109.1a	Dan. 4.1–3	Dan. 3.31–33
Ps. 69. title	Ps. 69.1	Ps. 109.1	Ps. 109.1b	Dan. 4.4–37	Dan. 4.1–34
Ps. 69.1–36	Ps. 69.2–37	Ps. 110. title	Ps. 110.1a	Dan. 5.31	Dan. 6.1
Ps. 70. title	Ps. 70.1	Ps. 110.1	Ps. 110.1b	Dan. 6.1–28	Dan. 6.2–29
Ps. 70.1–5	Ps. 70.2–6	Ps. 120. title	Ps. 120.1a	Neh. 4.1–6	Neh. 3.53–58
Ps. 72. title	Ps. 72.1 (1st word)	Ps. 120.1	Ps. 120.1b	Neh. 4.7–23	Neh. 4.1–17
Ps. 73. title	Ps. 73.1a	Ps. 121. title	Ps. 121.1a	Neh. 9.38	Neh. 10.1
Ps. 73.1	Ps. 73.1b	Ps. 121.1	Ps. 121.1b	Neh. 10.1–39	Neh. 10.2–40
Ps. 74. title	Ps. 74.1a	Ps. 122. title	Ps. 122.1a	1 Chron. 6.1–15	1 Chron. 5.27–41
Ps. 74.1	Ps. 74.1b	Ps. 122.1	Ps. 122.1b	1 Chron. 6.16–81	1 Chron. 6.1–66
Ps. 75. title	Ps. 75.1	Ps. 123. title	Ps. 123.1a	1 Chron. 12.4	1 Chron. 12.4–5
Ps. 75.1–10	Ps. 75.2–11	Ps. 123.1	Ps. 123.1b	1 Chron. 12.5–40	1 Chron. 12.6–41
Ps. 76. title	Ps. 76.1	Ps. 124. title	Ps. 124.1a	2 Chron. 2.1	2 Chron. 1.18
Ps. 77. title	Ps. 77.1	Ps. 124.1	Ps. 124.1b	2 Chron. 2.2–18	2 Chron. 2.1–17
Ps. 77.1–20	Ps. 77.2–21	Ps. 125. title	Ps. 125.1a	2 Chron. 14.1	2 Chron. 13.23
Ps. 78. title	Ps. 78.1a	Ps. 125.1	Ps. 125.1b	2 Chron. 14.2–15	2 Chron. 14.1–14
Ps. 78.1	Ps. 78.1b	Ps. 126. title	Ps. 126.1a		
Ps. 79. title	Ps. 79.1a	Ps. 126.1	Ps. 126.1b		

Translations of Primary Sources

ANCIENT NEAR EASTERN DOCUMENTS

Coogan, Michael D. *A Reader of Ancient Near Eastern Texts: Sources for the Study of the Old Testament.* Oxford: Oxford University Press, 2012.

Coogan, Michael D., and Mark S. Smith. *Stories from Ancient Canaan.* 2d ed. Louisville, KY: Westminster John Knox Press, 2012.

Parker, Simon B. and Theodore Lewis, *Writings from the Ancient World.* A series produced by the Society of Biblical Literature (Atlanta, GA), with each volume devoted to a particular genre and language.

ANCIENT TRANSLATIONS OF THE BIBLE

Greek

Pietersma, Albert, and Benjamin G. Wright, eds. *A New English Translation of the Septuagint.* Oxford: Oxford University Press, 2007.

Aramaic

McNamara, Martin J.; Kevin Cathcart; Michael Maher. *The Aramaic Bible: The Targums.* Collegeville, Mn.: Liturgical Press, 1987– .

The Samaritan Pentateuch

Tsedaka, Benyamim, and Sharon Sullivan, eds. *The Israelite Samaritan Version of the Torah.* Translated by Tsedaka Benyamim. Grand Rapids, MI: William B. Eerdmans, 2013.

APOCRYPHA AND PSEUDEPIGRAPHA

Bauckham, Richard, James Davila, and Alex Panayotov, eds. *Old Testament Pseudepigrapha: More Noncanonical Scriptures.* Grand Rapids, MI: William B. Eerdmans, 2013– .

Charlesworth, James H., ed. *The Old Testament Pseudepigrapha.* 2 vols. New York: Doubleday, 1983–1985.

Schiffman, Lawrence H., James L. Kugel, and Louis H. Feldman, eds. *Outside the Bible: Ancient Jewish Writings Related to Scripture.* 3 vols. Philadelphia: Jewish Publication Society, 2013.

DEAD SEA SCROLLS

Abegg, Martin, Jr.; Peter Flint; and Eugene Ulrich, eds. *The Dead Sea Scrolls Bible: The Oldest Known Bible.* San Francisco: HarperSanFrancisco, 1999.

Charlesworth, James H., ed. *The Dead Sea Scrolls.* Louisville, KY: Westminster John Knox Press, 1994–.

Discoveries in the Judean Desert (various editors). Oxford and New York: Oxford University Press, 1977–2011.

García Martínez, Florentino, ed. *The Dead Sea Scrolls Study Edition.* 2 vols. Leiden: E. J. Brill, 1998.

Vermes, Geza. *The Complete Dead Sea Scrolls in English.* Rev. ed. London, England: Penguin Books, 2012.

Wise, Michael O., Martin Abegg Jr., and Edward Cook, eds. *The Dead Sea Scrolls: A New Translation.* Rev. ed. New York: HarperCollins, 2005.

JOSEPHUS

Mason, Steve, ed. *Flavius Josephus: Translation and Commentary.* Leiden: Brill, 1999– .

Thackeray, H. St. J. and Ralph Marcus, trans. *Josephus.* Loeb Classical Library. 9 vols. Cambridge, Ma.: Harvard University Press, 1976–1981.

Whiston, William, trans. *The Works of Josephus Complete and Unabridged.* 1736. New updated edition, Peabody, Ma.: Hendrickson Publishers, 1987.

Williamson, G. A., trans. *Josephus: The Jewish War.* New York: Penguin Books, 1984.

PHILO OF ALEXANDRIA

Colson, F. H. and Whitaker, G. H., trans. *Philo.* Loeb Classical Library. 10 vols. Cambridge, Ma.: Harvard University Press, 1961–1991.

Williamson, Ronald. *Jews in the Hellenistic World: Philo.* Cambridge, Eng.: Cambridge University Press, 1989.

Yonge, C. D., trans. *The Works of Philo.* 1854. New updated edition. Peabody, Ma.: Hendrickson Publishers, 1993.

RABBINIC TEXTS

Mishnah

Blackman, Philip. *Mishnayoth.* 7 vols. New York: Judaica Press, 1964.

Danby, Herbert. *The Mishnah: Translated from the Hebrew with Introduction and Brief Explanatory Notes.* Oxford: The Clarendon Press, 1933.

Kehati, Pinchas. *Mishnayot Kehati.* 21 vols. Nanuet, NY: Feldheim, 2005.

Neusner, Jacob. *The Mishnah: A New Translation.* New Haven: Yale University Press, 1988.

Tosefta

Neusner, Jacob. *The Tosefta: Translated from Hebrew with a New Introduction.* Peabody, MA: Hendrickson, 2014.

Talmud

Epstein, I. *The Babylonian Talmud.* 30 vols. London: Soncino Press, 1935–48.

Steinsaltz, Adin Even-Israel. *Koren Talmud.* Jerusalem: Koren Publishers, 2012– .

Zlotowitz, Meir. *Schottenstein Edition: Talmud Bavli.* 73 vols. Brooklyn, NY: Mesorah Publications, Ltd, 2004.

Midrash

Berman, Samuel A., trans. *Midrash Tanhuma-Yelammedenu.* New York: Ktav Publishing, 1996.

Bialik, Hayyim N. and Y. H. Ravinsky. *The Book of Legends: Sefer Ha-Aggadah.* New York: Schocken Books, 1992.

Braude, William G., trans. *Pesikta Rabbati.* New Haven: Yale University Press, 1968.

Braude, William G., and Israel J. Kapstein, trans. *Pesikta De-Rab Kahana.* 2d ed. Philadelphia, PA: Jewish Publication Society, 2002.

Freedman, H. and M. Simon, eds. *Midrash Rabbah.* 10 vols. London: Soncino Press, 1961.

Ginzberg, Louis. *The Legends of the Jews.* 8 vols. Philadelphia: Jewish Publication Society, 1968.

Hammer, Reuven. *Sifrei Deuteronomy: A Tannaitic Commentary on the Book of Deuteronomy.* New Haven: Yale University Press, 1986.

Kasher, Menahem. *Encyclopedia of Biblical Interpretation, A Millennial Anthology.* 9 vols. New York: American Biblical Encyclopedia Society, 1953–1979.

Lauterbach, J. Z. *Mekhilta of Rabbi Ishmael.* Philadelphia: Jewish Publication Society of America, 1976.

Nelson, W. David, trans. *Mekhilta de-Rabbi Shimon Bar Yoḥai.* Philadelphia, PA: The Jewish Publication Society, 2006.

Townsend, John T., trans. *Midrash Tanhuma.* 3 vols. New York: Ktav Publishing, 2003.

Medieval Jewish Commentaries

Baker, Joshua and Ernest Nicholson, trans. *The Commentary of Rabbi David Kimhi on Psalms 120–150.* Cambridge: Cambridge University Press, 1973.

Carasik, Michael. *The Commentators' Bible: The JPS Miqra'ot Gedolot.* Philadelphia: Jewish Publication Society, 2005– .

Chavel, Charles B., trans. *Ramban (Nachmanides): Commentary on the Torah.* 5 vols. New York: Shilo Publishing House, 1971–1976.

Gruber, Mayer, *Rashi's Commentary on the Psalms.* Atlanta: Scholars Press, 1998.

Japhet, Sara and Robert B. Salters, *The Commentary of R. Samuel ben Meir, Rashbam, on Qoheleth.* Jerusalem: Magnes, 1985.

Lockshin, Martin I, trans. *Rashbam's Commentary on Deuteronomy: An Annotated Translation.* Providence, RI: Brown Judaic Studies, 2004.

———. *Rabbi Samuel ben Meier's Commentary on Exodus: An Annotated Translation.* Brown Judaic Series, no. 310. Atlanta: Scholars Press, 1997.

———. *Rabbi Samuel ben Meier's Commentary on Leviticus and Numbers; An Annotated Translation.* Brown Judaic Series, no. 330. Providence, R. I.: Brown Judaic Studies, 2001.

Silbermann, A. M. and M. Rosenbaum, trans. *Pentateuch with Targum Onkelos, Haphtaroth and Rashi's Commentary.* 5 vols. New York: Hebrew Publishing Co., 1969.

Strickman, H. Norman and Arthur M. Silver, trans. *Ibn Ezra's Commentary on the Pentateuch.* 5 vols. New York: Menorah Publishing Co., 1988– .

Tomaschoff, Avner. *Abarbanel on the Torah: Selected Themes from the Five Books of Moses.* Jerusalem: The Jewish Agency for Israel, 2007.

Medieval Jewish Philosophy

Feldman, Seymour, trans. *Levi ben Gershom: The Wars of the Lord.* 3 vols. Philadelphia: Jewish Publication Society, 1999.

Frank, Daniel H., trans. *The Book of Doctrines and Beliefs.* Indianapolis: Hackett Publishing Co., 2002.

Lewy, Hans. *Three Jewish Philosophers: Philo, Saadya Gaon, Jehuda Halevi.* New York: Macmillan Publishing Co., 1972.

Pines, Shlomo, trans. *The Guide of the Perplexed.* Chicago: University of Chicago Press, 1963.

Mystical Texts

Cohen, Martin Samuel. *The Shiʿur Qomah: Texts and Recensions.* Tübingen: Mohr, 1985.

Green, Arthur, Ebn Leader, Ariel Evan Mayse, and Or N. Rose, eds. *Speaking Torah: Spiritual Teachings from Around the Maggid's Table.* 2 vols. Woodstock, VT: Jewish Lights Publishing, 2013.

Jacobs, Louis. *Jewish Mystical Testimonies.* New York: Schocken Books, 1996.

Kaplan, Aryeh. *The Bahir: An Ancient Kabbalistic Text Attributed to Rabbi Nehuniah ben HaKana, First Century, C. E.* New York: S. Weiser, 1979.

Matt, Daniel C., trans. *The Zohar: Pritzker Edition.* Stanford, CA: Stanford University Press, 2004– .

OTHER SCRIPTURES

Levine, Amy-Jill, and Marc Zvi Brettler, eds., *The Jewish Annotated New Testament.* New York and Oxford: Oxford University Press, 2011.

Abdel Haleem, M.A.S., trans., *The Qur'an.* Oxford and New York: Oxford University Press, 2004.

Glossary

Abarbanel an alternative pronunciation of **Abravanel.**

Abraham Ibn Ezra see **Ibn Ezra, Abraham.**

Abravanel, Isaac (1437–1508) a medieval philosopher and biblical commentator. He fled from Portugal to Spain to escape a sentence of death in a supposed plot against the king; in 1492, with the expulsion of Jews from Spain, he was forced to flee again and lived in Venice. His works include commentaries on the Torah and the Prophets, as well as philosophical works that followed, and were partly intended to correct, Maimonides. His biblical commentaries were, unlike most medieval commentary, not verse-by-verse or word-by-word, but were concerned with larger passages united by a single theme; he opens each unit with a set of questions that he answers in great detail. In philosophy he insisted on the primary importance of religion and wrote against efforts to explain biblical events in naturalistic terms; he also opposed efforts to formulate a set of dogmatic principles for Judaism.

Abravanel, Judah (1460–1521) physician, poet, and philosopher, and son of Isaac Abravanel. His *Dialogue on Love* (published posthumously) argued that love was the structural principle of the universe, and that the soul therefore sought and could reach God through love.

Abulafia, Abraham ben Shemuel (13th c.) a leading kabbalist and mystic of Spain. Abulafia taught a method of mystical insight that involved contemplating the letters of the Heb alphabet, seen as the elements of the names of God. His method was therefore called "The Path of the Names" *(Shemot),* in contrast to other kabbalistic methods called "The Path of the Numbers" *(Sefirot).*

acrostic a literary device in which the first letter of each line of poetry occurs according to a predetermined pattern. In the Bible acrostics only occur as alphabetical acrostics, in which the individual lines of a poem (or occasionally small groups of lines) begin with the twenty-two letters of the Heb alphabet in order. (This would be equivalent to the first line of an English poem beginning with A, the second with B, etc.) The acrostic form, besides giving the aesthetic pleasure of a pattern, may have been intended to make memorization easier. It may also have been intended as a way of expressing completeness: In Lam., for instance, the acrostic format of the individual chs might have been used to express both the completeness of the outpouring of grief and its finality. The following poems in the Bible are acrostics: Pss. 9–10, 25, 34, 37, 111, 112, 119, 145; Prov. 31.10–31; Lam. chs 1, 2, 3, 4; Nah. 1.2–8 (or 9) (incomplete).

Active Intellect in mystical thought, the repository of the intelligible forms that govern the sublunar world.

Adar the twelfth month (February–March) in the Jewish year. In order to bring the lunar calendar into alignment with the solar year, a leap year, in which there are two months of Adar, occurs seven times during each nineteen-year cycle of years (see p. 2230). This added month is called either *'adar sheni,* "second adar," or *ve'adar,* "and adar."

Adonai (Heb "my Lord") a divine title and the word generally substituted for the **Tetragrammaton,** YHVH, when the Bible is read aloud.

aggadah (or "haggadah," possibly from Heb *huggad,* "things said" or "what is told") the nonlegal portions of the Talmud and Midrash (see **halakhah**). Aggadah is concerned with explicating the meaning of Scripture in the moral sense, and with elaborating on the stories in the Bible. As such it is more akin to preaching than to legal analysis, and many aggadic collections are homiletical in character. The legal sections, halakhah, are concerned with understanding the obligations placed on the believer by the biblical text; aggadah, by contrast, contains ethical teaching as well as illustrative narrative, prayers, legends, and folklore.

Aḥad Ha'Am (Heb "one of the people" or "the people are one") pen-name of **Asher Ginzberg** (1856–1927), Zionist writer.

Ahikar the hero of an ancient Near East court story who is deprived of his position through a false accusation.

'Akedah (Heb "binding") the story of the binding of Isaac (Gen. ch 22).

Akiva (Aqiba) ben Yosef, Rabbi (ca. 50–135 CE), rabbi at Lydda, martyred in the Hadrianic persecutions. He played an instrumental role in the task of beginning to assemble and organize the oral law, which was continued by his pupil R. **Meir** and concluded by R. Judah *ha-Nasi'* (**Judah the Prince**), resulting in the **Mishnah** (see).

Akkadian the language of the Assyrian and Babylonian empires. Akkadian is a Semitic language related to Heb, and is written in cuneiform, wedge-shaped writing, typically on clay tablets.

'Aleinu prayer beginning *'aleinu leshabe-aḥ la'adon ha-kol,* "it is our duty to praise the Lord of all," recited at the conclusion of regular services.

ʿaliyah (Heb "ascent") pilgrimage or emigration to the land of Israel; being given the honor of "ascending" to read the Torah in synagogue worship.

allegory an extended comparison in which an author, while speaking directly of one reality, intends to mean, and is understood by the reader to be speaking indirectly about, something entirely different. Allegory uses action, setting, and character to point to a symbolic level. Some texts, e.g., the "Song of the Vineyard" in Isa. ch 5, expressly mark themselves as allegorical. "Allegorical interpretation," such as that used by Philo to draw out the meaning of the Bible, is an effort to make an allegory out of a writing that was not originally intended to be one, but that is, in the view of the interpreter, presenting a hidden meaning that the allegorical interpretation will reveal.

Amarna Letters Akkadian cuneiform tablets from the period of 1350 BCE or slightly earlier, containing diplomatic correspondence from the reigns of Pharaohs Amenophis III and Akhenaton and providing scholarly insight into the language of and the situation in Canaan in the period preceding the rise of the Israelite tribal confederation.

ʿAmidah (Heb "standing") the main prayer in Jewish worship. Also called the ***Shemonah ʿEsrei*** (eighteen [blessings]), although on regular weekdays (not Shabbat or festivals), it now consists of nineteen blessings: three at opening, followed by thirteen petitions and three at closing. For Shabbat and festivals, the three initial and final blessings frame a special blessing that focuses on the special day.

ʾamoraʾ (Aram. "speaker"; pl. *ʾamoraʾim*) a rabbinic teacher of the talmudic period. The name is used in both Babylonia and the land of Israel.

Amorites according to the Bible, one of the native nations of Canaan. Amorites are attested in other ancient Near Eastern documents from the third millennium and onwards as residents of western Asia who migrated to Mesopotamia and other areas. They spoke a language related to Heb.

amphictyony a social organization in ancient Greece where tribes are united around a central sanctuary and service this sanctuary on a rotating basis. Some scholars believe that a similar system existed in Israel in premonarchic times.

anaphora the repetition of a word or phrase at the beginning of successive lines or sentences. "As the eyes of slaves follow their master's hand, / as the eyes of a slave-girl follow the hand of her mistress, / so our eyes are toward the LORD our God, awaiting His favor" (Ps. 123.2).

anastrophe the repetition at the beginning of one line of the word or phrase concluding the previous line. "The voice of the LORD convulses the wilderness; / the LORD convulses the wilderness of Kadesh" (Ps. 29.7).

Anat a Canaanite goddess often depicted as a warrior.

anthropomorphic (Gk "human form") language that presents God in human or human-like terms. "Your right hand, O LORD, glorious in power, / Your right hand, O LORD, shatters the foe!" (Exod. 15.6).

antithesis the contrast of ideas through closely contrasted words. "A gentle response allays wrath; / A harsh word provokes anger" (Prov. 15.1). See **parallelism**, and essay "Biblical Poetry" (pp. 2184–91).

antithetic parallelism two parallel lines related to one another by opposition, e.g., Prov. 10.4, "Negligent hands cause poverty, / But diligent hands enrich."

apocalypse (Gk *apokalypsis* "revelation") a narrative literary genre in which an angel or other heavenly being communicates to a human being the divine plan for history and the arrangement of the supernatural order. Many apocalypses are a series of visions of heaven and earth that are then explained. Apocalypses are a feature of late biblical religion.

apocalyptic a worldview that assumes the disclosure of heavenly secrets, most typically to or for a community that perceives itself as suffering or victimized. Communities that espouse this worldview often interpret biblical passages (esp. in the Prophets) as pertaining to their own time.

Apocrypha (Gk "hidden things") a group of about twenty mostly Jewish writings (e.g., Ben Sirach; 1 Maccabees), many of which were included in the **Septuagint,** but that were ultimately not included in the Bible. They are, however, part of the canon of the Orthodox Christian churches, and most (though not all) of them are included in the canon of the Roman Catholic church.

apodictic law a law or regulation that is stated as a command ("You shall not murder").

apodosis (Gk "refer [lit. 'give'] back") the consequence in a conditional sentence: "When you build a new house, you shall make a parapet for your roof" contains a protasis ("When you build a new house") and an apodosis ("you shall make a parapet for your roof").

apophatic (from Gk for "deny") the theology that works by denying likenesses between God and anything that can be conceived, since God transcends all human thought and experience; the nature of God is thus inferred only negatively, by what God is not.

Apostolic Constitutions a Christian text of church order and worship from the 4th c. CE, in part a rewording of the **Didascalia Apostolorum;** it quotes the apocryphal Prayer of Manasseh (mentioned in 2 Chron. 33.13, 18)

apostrophe an address to an absent person or personified object. There is an apostrophe to Assyria in Isa. 10.5.

Aquila (lived 2nd c. CE) a Jewish reviser of the Greek Bible; Aquila tried to make the text, which had become the Bible of the early Christian church, less favorable to some christological exegesis. The translation follows the Heb very closely. According to tradition, he was a convert and a student of Akiva.

Aramaic a Semitic language used widely in Mesopotamia and the land of Israel during the Persian period, though it developed earlier. In the mid-first millennium, it eventually replaced Akkadian as the lingua franca of the ancient Near Eastern world. It became the ordinary language of Jews and is the language of much rabbinic literature. The Aram. translation of the Bible is the **Targum.**

Arameans a Semitic people living in the area of modern Syria from the second millennium onwards. Some biblical texts suggest particular kinship between Israel and the Arameans (see esp. Deut. 26.5). Damascus was their main city.

Ark (for the Torah) a box or cabinet, typically of wood, in which the Torah scrolls are stored at the front of the synagogue. It is often finely decorated, reflecting the centrality of the Torah scrolls to Judaism.

Ark of the Covenant the chest (Heb *ʾaron*) in the Tabernacle or Temple that contained the Pact (Heb *ʿedut*) (Exod. 40.20), or the tablets (Deut. 10.2), or that served as the throne of the LORD (1 Sam. 4.4).

Asherah (pl. Asherim) Canaanite goddess, wife or consort of El; her sacred symbol, a pole or tree, was the object of prophetic condemnation.

Ashi, Rabbana (ca. 335–427) Babylonian *ʾamoraʾ* of the Sura academy; one of the primary editors of the Babylonian Talmud.

Ashkenazi the name Ashkenaz appears in Gen. 10.3, as a descendant of Gomer, son of Japheth, son of Noah. In geonic tradition (ca. 9th c. CE) Ashkenaz became identified with Germany, and Jews living in the Rhineland, and their descendants in France and Bohemia, were called Ashkenazi(m). See **Sephardim.**

Ashtoreth the Canaanite goddess of love and fertility; worship of Ashtoreth is condemned in Judg. chs 2 and 10.

Assyria a Mesopotamian world power, in addition to Babylonia. Its capital cities included Ashur and Nineveh. The Assyrian empire conquered the Northern Kingdom of Israel in 722 and exiled its people. The Assyrians were well-known for their massive building projects and for their cruelty in war.

Astarte see **Ashtoreth.**

ʾatbash a form of cipher in which a word is transformed into a code by letter substitution, in which the last letter of the alphabet is substituted for the first, the next-to-last for the second, and so on: *alef* becomes *tav, bet* becomes *shin, gimel* becomes *resh,* etc. (In English, A would become Z, B would become Y, etc.) Using this method, Jeremiah transforms Babylon into Sheshach (Jer. 25.26; 51.41): ***b-b-l*** or ***bet-bet-lamed*** becomes ***sh-sh-k*** or ***shin-shin-kaf.***

atonement the expiation for sin, or reparation for an injury committed against another. Heb *kapparah* (with possible root meaning "to cover") refers to ritual cleansing of the Temple precincts.

Atrahasis hero of the Mesopotamian epic of Atrahasis, who survives the god Enlil's efforts to destroy humankind by, among other means, a flood (with some parallels to the story of Noah in Gen. chs 6–9). Sections of the epic are reworked in tablet 11 of the **Gilgamesh** Epic, which also recounts a flood story.

ʾAvot (Heb "fathers") the name of the first blessing in the ***ʾAmidah,*** from its reference to "the God of Abraham, the God of Isaac, and the God of Jacob"; also the name of a tractate in the **Mishnah;** see ***Pirkei ʾAvot.***

ʾAvot de Rabbi Nathan A rabbinic midrash on the mishnaic tractate of ***ʾAvot;*** see ***Pirkei ʾAvot.***

Baal the Canaanite storm god; also a word meaning "lord" or "master, owner."

Babylonia a Mesopotamian world power. It often competed against Assyria, which it conquered in 612 BCE. Its major city was Babylon, Akkadian for "gate of the gods." Its main god became Marduk, and its religion and literature were extremely influential, even on its arch-rival Assyria. Babylonia destroyed the First Temple in 586, and was conquered by Cyrus the Great in 539.

Babylonian Chronicles narratives of Babylonian history written on clay tablets.

Babylonian exile the forced relocation of some of the population of Judah, perhaps the ruling portion of it, after the conquest by Babylonia in 597–586 BCE. The exile ended with the permitted return to the land under Cyrus (beginning ca. 538 BCE).

Babylonian Talmud see **Talmud.**

Baer, Dov (1710–72) a Hasidic leader and follower of Isaac Luria; he became well known as a preacher *(maggid)* and is therefore known as "the **Maggid**."

ban (Heb *ḥerem*) the devotion of war booty (including people) in its entirety to the deity (see esp. Deut. 20.17), or the forfeiture of goods (e.g., idols) from which no benefit is permissible. See ***ḥerem.***

Baraita (Aram. "outside," i.e., external to the Mishnah) a section of rabbinic material with a ruling or interpretation like that in the Mishnah, that is from the tannaitic period but not contained in the Mishnah.

Barekhu (Heb "bless") the first word of the opening prayer for the main part of the morning and evening synagogue services, "Bless the Lord."

Bar Kappara 3rd c. CE scholar; he lived in the land of Israel.

Bar Kokhba, Shimeon (Aram. "son of a star") sobriquet of Shimeon Bar Kosiba (d. 135 CE), leader of the second Jewish revolt against Rome.

bar Yoḥai, R. Shimeon (also Simeon ben Yoḥai) a 2nd c. Rabbi, pupil of R. Akiva ben Yosef and teacher of R. Judah *ha-Nasi'* **(Judah the Prince)**. R. Shimeon began the classification of **halakhah.** He was the subject of legendary tales based on the period of his life in which he was in hiding from Roman persecution, reportedly living in a cave. The medieval kabbalists claimed that during this sojourn in the cave the doctrines of mysticism were revealed to him, and thus the ***Zohar*** is presented as teachings of, and tales about, R. Shimeon.

Bavli, Talmud the Babylonian Talmud; see **Talmud.**

BCE Before the Common Era, an alternative to BC.

Bedouin an Arab nomad; in general, a member of a nomadic desert tribe.

Bel Akkadian "master," (cognate to Baal) alternative name for **Marduk,** head of the Babylonian pantheon.

ben Asher, Aaron (9th–10th centuries) Masorete of Tiberias. Ben Asher was one of the primary scholars who established the Heb Masoretic Text.

ben Asher, Aryeh Loeb (Gunzberg) Lithuanian rabbi and legal commentator (c. 1695–1785).

ben Asher, Baḥya (d. 1320) biblical commentator of Spain. He used the ***Zohar***'s method of distinguishing four levels of meaning in Scripture: ***peshat*** (contextual sense), *remez* (allegorical sense), ***derash*** (homiletical sense), and ***sod*** (mystical sense). These were known by the acronym ***pardes.***

ben Gershon, R. Levi see **Ralbag.**

ben Ḥalafta, Yose (Yosi, Yossi) mid-2nd c. ***tanna'***. He was a pupil of R. Akiva and one of the Rabbis frequently quoted in the **Mishnah.**

ben Ḥofni, Samuel (also Shemuel ben Ḥofni) **gaon** of the Sura academy in Babylonia from ca. 997 CE until his death in 1013. He wrote commentaries in Judeo-Arabic on parts of the Torah (including a translation), and also philosophical and theological works.

ben Isaac, R. Shlomo see **Rashi.**

ben Maimon, R. Moshe see **Rambam.**

ben Meir, R. Shemuel see **Rashbam.**

ben Naḥman, R. Moshe see **Ramban.**

berit (Heb "treaty") a term that may be used of a treaty between two individuals, groups, or nations, or between God and Israel (see **covenant**).

bet midrash (Heb "house of study") a place with a traditional Jewish library where people study Jewish texts together and listen to classes on these texts. Along with the synagogue, to which it is often connected, this is the central Jewish institution.

bicolon unit of Heb poetry composed of two **cola,** or lines (sometimes called a *dístich*).

binding (of Isaac) see **'Akedah.**

birkhat ha-mazon (Heb "blessing for nourishment") the Jewish grace after meals.

Bonfils, Joseph 11th c. rabbi of Limoges, France; **tosafist,** biblical scholar, and author of liturgical poetry who introduced such poetry ***(piyyutim)*** into the synagogue service.

Booths, Festival of see **Sukkot.**

bulla a clay seal with the impression of a signet ring or other symbol of authority.

Cairo Genizah the storeroom (see **genizah**) of the synagogue of Fostat in Old Cairo (built 882 CE). In it were discovered many thousands of fragments of texts, including a portion of Ben Sirach (Ecclesiasticus) in Heb, and many early rabbinic documents, translations of the Bible, liturgical texts, poetry, letters, and other writings.

calendar see chart on p. 2230.

calque (French *calquer,* "to trace") a "loan translation" or word-for-word or element-for-element rendition of a word or phrase from one language into another.

Cambyses son of Cyrus and king of Persia 529–522 BCE. He conquered Egypt in 525.

Canaan a designation for the area roughly equivalent to the land of Israel in prebiblical Mesopotamian and Egyptian documents. In the Bible, it most often refers to the pre-Israelite land of Israel.

canon (Gk "reed" or "measuring stick") the group of writings considered to be holy or authoritative by a particular community. The canon of the Bible is the list of books in the Tanakh (see p. 2155).

cantillation the practice of chanting or intoning the biblical text in public reading, according to traditional systems of tone, pitch, and length; also, the written system of marks in the biblical text that serves as a guide to the systems of recitation.

casemate wall a double wall, usually the outside of a larger house or of a city wall, that is filled up with dirt or rubble.

casuistic law a law or regulation that is stated as the consequence of a particular situation or "case" ("If someone injures you, (then) he shall be liable").

CE Common Era; equivalent to the christological term AD.

charismatic (Gk "gifted, graced") characterized by the ability to influence or lead others; personally magnetic; talented.

Chemosh the chief god of **Moab.**

cherubim (pl. of *kerub*) composite, winged creatures; two carved cherubim guarded the Ark in the Temple, where they may have served as guardians of sacred places and attendants on YHVH.

chiasm, pl. **chiasmus** (from Gk *chi,* the letter that resembles an "X") inverting the second pair of terms in a parallel structure, so that the corresponding terms, if laid out in a square, would form an X. The resultant pattern is ABB'A', ABCB'A', ABCC'B'A', etc. For example: "Truthful speech (A) wins the favor of kings (B); / They love those (B') who speak honestly (A')" (Prov. 16.13). Chiasmus can also describe the structure of an entire passage, and it can involve several terms or parts of a passage, each of which has an analog that occurs in the reverse order of the original list of terms or sequence of parts.

Christian Hebraists Christian scholars, inspired by the examples of Origen and **Jerome,** who taught the importance of returning to the Heb text of the Christian Old Testament, and who therefore studied Heb with rabbinic scholars and influenced Christian Bible translation and commentary to rely on the Heb and not on the Latin Vulgate text. The beginnings of Christian Hebraism are generally traced to Andrew of St. Victor (d. 1175), a monk at the Abbey of St. Victor in Paris, where Hugh of St. Victor (d. 1141) had established a school specializing in biblical exposition. There was a significant renaissance of Christian Hebraism during the Renaissance.

Cisjordan "on this side of the Jordan," the west side the Jordan River.

citadel a stronghold or fortress, whether standing alone or serving as the inner fortification of a city.

Classical Biblical Hebrew the main dialect of biblical Heb, reflected in over half of the Bible. This dialect was used in Judah through the Babylonian exile of 586 BCE. Classical Hebrew was then replaced by Late Biblical Hebrew, comprised of Exilic and Postexilic Hebrew. Both of these latter forms were significantly influenced by Aram.

colon, pl. **cola** a single line of poetry (also known as a *stich*).

colophon (Gk "summit," by extension "finishing touch") an inscription at the end of a writing giving information about authorship.

Community Rule (or *Rule of the Community*) a scroll from the Dead Sea community, 1QS, that sets out the communal arrangements under which the community functioned, or at least those that they held up as an ideal: holding property in common; eating, blessing, and advising one another in unity; preparing for the eschaton; and training new members of the community in their responsibilities. Also called *The Manual of Discipline.*

concordance a word index to a given text, listing each occurrence of a given word along with a context line so that scholars may better see how a particular word is used.

concubine a woman who is the sexual partner of a man, and is legally recognized as such, but who does not have the full status of a wife.

Cordovero, Moses ben Jacob (Moshe ben Yaʿakov; 1522–1570) kabbalist, of Spain. Cordovero wrote commentaries on the Bible and on kabbalistic works; his interests were philosophical, but ultimately his views were mystical and esoteric.

corvée forced labor for the state

cosmology any account (mythical or otherwise) of the origin of the world.

covenant (Heb ***berit***) a treaty between God and Israel. Some covenants have specific conditions or treaty stipulations, while others are covenants of grant. The biblical notion of covenant between God and Israel, especially as it appears in Deut., may reflect a theologized reworking of treaties between Assyrian kings and their vassals.

cult, cultus the religious ritual and practice of a particular group; the rules governing worship, sacrifice, etc.

Cyrus king of Persia (559–530 BCE). He defeated Media in 550 and conquered most of the ancient Near East, including Babylonia, allowing the Jewish exiles in Babylonia to return to the land beginning ca. 538.

Cyrus Cylinder an Akkadian inscription describing the conquest of Babylon by Cyrus.

D the Deuteronomic source, which covers almost the entire book of Deut. (except for sections of the last few chs).

Daily Hallel see ***hallel.***

Davidic dynasty the direct descendants of King David, who reigned in Jerusalem from the 10th c. through the 6th c. An attempt to reinstitute this dynasty after the return from exile was not successful.

Day of Atonement (Heb ***Yom Kippur***) commemorated on the tenth day of the seventh month in the fall. It was a day of fasting and abstinence, as well as performance of certain key Temple rituals (see Lev. ch 16).

Day of the Lord a time mentioned in many prophetic books where God appears as a warrior, sometimes fighting against Israel, sometimes against Israel's enemies. The earliest text to mention this Day is Amos 5.18.

Dead Sea Scrolls a group of texts, mostly from the 2nd c. BCE through the 1st c. CE found in the area of the Dead Sea. Most are from eleven caves at Qumran. These scrolls, mostly preserved in fragmentary form, include biblical texts, ancient texts which were known in translation before the scrolls were discovered, and new texts. Often the nonbiblical texts are divided into sectarian documents, namely those unique to the group that lived in this area, and nonsectarian documents that were in the group's library, but were not unique to this group, often understood as the ancient Essenes (see essay, "The Bible in the Dead Sea Scrolls," pp. 1850–59).

defective spelling the form of a word in the Heb text that is missing one or more optional vowel letters. See **plene spelling.**

defilement a state of ritual impurity caused by contact with a corpse or other impure object. Priestly literature in the Torah is especially concerned with defilement and removing defilement (see essay, "Concepts of Purity," pp. 1998–2005).

de Leon, Moshe (ca. 1240–1305) kabbalist of Spain. He wrote kabbalistic books in Heb, but also wrote (in Aram.) large parts of the ***Zohar,*** a purported compendium of 2nd-c. rabbinic teachings that is the main work of kabbalistic commentary.

derash (Heb *d-r-sh,* "inquire") interpretation (see **midrash**).

derashah (pl. *derashot*) interpretation, particularly in a homiletic context; a sermon.

Deutero-Isaiah the general term for the portion of Isa. beginning with ch 40. Most scholars consider Deutero-Isaiah to consist of chs 40–55 (or 40–54). These chs are primarily concerned with the promise of return from exile and the events leading up to the decree of **Cyrus** (538 BCE) permitting the exiles to return to Judah and rebuild their city and Temple. See **Trito-Isaiah.**

Deuteronomistic having the qualities or the theology of the **Deuteronomistic History.**

Deuteronomistic Historian the presumed author or authors of the narrative history in the books of Deut., Josh., Judg., Sam., and Kings.

Deuteronomistic History the account in the books Deut., Josh., Judg., Sam., and Kings, that portrays the history of Israel as a partial failure to keep the covenant faithfully, and the consequences of that failure in the subsequent history of the people. These books show significant theological and linguistic similarities, suggesting that they have a common editor or editors.

Diaspora (Gk "dispersion") the places outside the land of Israel where Jews live.

diatribe an argument against a position or critical of a person holding it. Diatribe often includes an imagined dialogue between opposing viewpoints.

Didascalia Apostolorum (Latin "Teaching of the Apostles") a Christian text from the 3rd c. CE concerning church order and rules for worship services; it quotes various texts, including the apocryphal Prayer of Manasseh (mentioned in 2 Chron. 33.13, 18).

dittography (Gk "double writing") the inadvertent repetition of letters, words, or phrases in the process of copying a text.

divination the effort to learn about the future or the current situation, particularly such an effort undertaken by occult means, such as consulting mediums.

Documentary Hypothesis the theory that the Torah (Pentateuch) is a combination of sources or documents from different eras and different geographical or social groups: **J** or the Yahwist source, possibly reflecting the traditions of Judah during the monarchic period; **E** or the Elohist source, possibly from the Northern Kingdom; **D** or the Deuteronomistic source, possibly from a group involved in the reforms undertaken by Josiah and his successors; and **P** or the Priestly source, the groups that maintained Temple worship and the ritual and other practices, and who assembled these materials during or after the exile (see Torah intro, pp. 1–6).

E one of the four sources or traditions in the Torah, which characteristically refers to God as *'elohim.* More recently, as scholars have examined the texts more closely, they speak of a JE tradition, since E as a separate source is difficult to isolate entirely. It may represent the traditions and practices of the inhabitants of the northern areas of Israel.

Edom, pl. **Edomites** the territory and people to the southeast of Judah, first attested in late second millennium texts. Edom is identified in Gen. ch 36 with Esau, Jacob's brother. The enmity between these brothers and between Judah and Edom mirror each other.

Egyptian Hallel see ***hallel.***

El a Canaanite deity popular in the second millennium. In the texts from **Ugarit,** he is a significant deity, but is often depicted as old and is largely supplanted by Baal.

Elephantine Papyri Aram. documents, mostly from the 5th c. BCE, found on the island of Elephantine, near Syene (modern Aswan) in Egypt. The papyri show that among those who inhabited the colony on Elephantine were Jews who kept up religious observances, such as Passover, and had their own temple.

Eliezer, Rabbi two *tanna'im* are named Eliezer: Eliezer ben Hyrcanos (1st–2nd c.), teacher of R. Akiva ben Yosef; and Eliezer ben Yosei ha-Galili (2nd c.), a pupil of R. Akiva.

Elijah a biblical prophet and miracle worker living in the 9th c. in northern Israel. Much postbiblical folklore collected around Elijah, who is depicted as ascending to heaven rather than dying in 2 Kings ch 2. He was later thought of as the forerunner or announcer of the messiah.

Elohim the Heb word *'elohim* is usually translated "God," though its plural form is sometimes translated "gods" (e.g., Gen. 6.2, "sons of elohim," NJPS "divine beings"). It is originally a common noun (a god), though it is often used as a proper noun for The God of Israel, even though it is a plural form.

Elohist the putative author of the E source (see **E**).

Enki the Mesopotamian god of wisdom.

Enlightenment the philosophical movement that flourished in the 18th c. in continental Europe (primarily Germany and France) and England. It was characterized by an emphasis on the importance of human reason and reflection on actual experience, a tendency to favor materialist as opposed to religious views, optimism about human progress, and pragmatic approaches to politics and ethics. The movement within Judaism corresponding to the Enlightenment, and influenced by it, is called Haskalah.

Enlil a chief Mesopotamian god, ruler of earth and sky; he also decreed the fate of human beings and the other gods.

***Enoch,* books of** writings dating from the 3rd c. BCE to the 6th c. CE, attributed to Enoch (Gen. ch 5). They contain apocalyptic visions, describe visits to the heavenly places, and make use of the character of Enoch (who, according to the Gen. account, was believed to have been taken directly to heaven without dying) as a guide to and interpreter of the meaning of history. Portions of some of these works have been discovered among the Dead Sea Scrolls.

Enuma Elish a Babylonian creation epic, in which the god Marduk becomes king of the gods after creating the cosmos from the body of the goddess of the deep, Tiamat.

ephod the priestly garment similar to a tunic. It held the breastplate that contained the lots Urim and Thummim, used in casting lots to determine the divine will; this led to the use of the term ephod to mean the agency of divination.

eponym the use of a representative figure to stand for an entire group; the "Table of Nations" in Gen. ch 10 contains eponyms such as Canaan (v. 6).

eschatological, eschatology (Gk *eschata,* "last things") a concern with the end time, or the end of the world as we know it, whether that involves a new historical era radically discontinuous from this one, or an entirely new cosmos after the destruction of the current one.

Essenes a Jewish group that flourished from around the 1st c. BCE to the 1st c. CE. They kept the Jewish law with utmost rigor, living apart from other Jews in their own communities. Most scholars believe that the members of the Qumran community (where the Dead Sea Scrolls were discovered) were Essenes.

etiology (Gk *aition,* "cause") an explanation for a word, an event, or a natural phenomenon. An etiological story is one that posits a particular cause (not necessarily the right cause) for some event. For example, the story at the end of Gen. ch 32 explains why Israelites do not eat the thigh muscle.

euphemism the substitution of an inoffensive word for one that is too explicit. The word "legs" in Isa. 6.2; 7.20 is a euphemism for "genitals."

exegesis (Gk "lead into") the explanation or interpretation of the meaning of a written text, especially a biblical text.

exilarch (Heb *resh galuta'*) the title of the head of Babylonian Jewry.

exile the forced removal of a people from its land, and the community in which they lived in the foreign land. The Israelites of the Northern Kingdom were exiled by the Assyrians in the late 8th c., and the Judeans were exiled by the Babylonians in the early 6th c. Specifically, "the exile" is the period from 586 to approximately 539 BCE. During this time the ruling classes of Judah were forced to leave Judah and live in Babylonia. See **Babylonian exile.**

exodus the journey that Israel took from Egypt toward the land of Israel, according to the book of Exod.

fable an illustrative story in which animals or plants have speaking parts. Judg. 9.8–15 is a fable told against the proposal to establish a monarchy in Israel.

Fertile Crescent the agriculturally fertile areas of Egypt, Israel, and Mesopotamia, forming a rough arc from the Nile through the coastal regions of Israel to the Tigris-Euphrates basin.

Festival of Weeks see **Shavu'ot.**

First Temple the Temple in Jerusalem from Solomon's time (10th c.) until the destruction of Jerusalem by the Babylonians in 586 BCE. The First Temple period extends from the 10th to 6th centuries BCE.

form criticism a method of studying biblical texts that developed in Germany in the late 19th and early 20th centuries. This method isolates structures or forms of particular types or genres of biblical literature, and attempts to connect these forms to a particular social setting *(Sitz im Leben)* (see "Modern Study of the Bible," pp. 2166–77).

Former Prophets the subdivision of the Nevi'im section of the Bible that includes the books of Josh., Judg., Sam., and Kings (Heb title *nevi'im ri'shonim*). See also **Latter Prophets.**

Galilee the northernmost geographical area of Israel.

galut (Heb "exile") most often used of the **Babylonian exile** (see).

gaon, pl. ***geonim*** title of heads of rabbinic academies in Babylonia from the mid-6th to 11th centuries CE. The title is taken from the phrase, *ro'sh yeshivat ga'on Ya'akov,* "head of the academy [that is] the pride of Jacob."

Gaon, Saadia Saadia ben Joseph (882–942) was the ***gaon*** (head of the academy) of Sura in Babylonia and the greatest of the *geonim.* He translated the Torah and other books of the Bible into Arabic, along with a short commentary.

Gehenna Gk spelling of Heb *ge'hinnom,* "valley of Hinnom," the area outside Jerusalem where trash was burned. By metaphoric extension it came to mean a place of torment, and in postbiblical literature meant "hell."

Gemara (Aram. "completion") the commentary on the **Mishnah** that supplemented and extended the Mishnaic material, although not all of the Mishnah is treated in the Gemara. The **Mishnah** and the Gemara together form the **Talmud.**

gematria, pl. ***gematriot*** (*gimatriya,* likely from Gk *geometria*) a procedure for interpreting a word or phrase by its numerical value. Heb letters may represent numbers (*alef* = 1; *bet* = 2, etc.), and the letters of a word or phrase are added up and equated with other words having the same total. For example, according to Gen. 14.14, Abraham musters 318 retainers. Some rabbinic commentaries suggest that he merely mustered Eliezer, since the numerical value of Eliezer's name is 318 (*'-l-y-'-z-r* is 1+30+10+70+7+200).

genizah a storeroom in a synagogue used for keeping old books and objects, especially those that are too sacred to be thrown away. See **Cairo Genizah.**

geonic period the period characterized by the teachings of the academies in Babylonia that extended from roughly the mid-6th to the mid-11th c. CE. See ***gaon.***

ger (Heb) in biblical usage, a resident alien, a foreigner who sojourns in Israel. In rabbinic literature, the word means a convert; conversion did not exist in the biblical period.

Gersonides see **Ralbag.**

Gikatilla, Yosef ben Abraham (1248–ca.1325) kabbalist of Spain. He was a student of **Abraham Abulafia,** and later was associated with **Moshe de Leon,** author of much of the ***Zohar.*** Gikatilla was one of the main formulators of the kabbalistic view that the divine name, YHVH, implicitly contained all the letters of the Heb alphabet.

Gilgamesh the Babylonian and Assyrian epic whose hero, Gilgamesh, travels the world in search of immortality. Among the characters he encounters is Utnapishtim, whose tale of the flood has parallels with the biblical account of Noah (Gen. chs 6–9).

Ginsberg, Asher see **Aḥad Ha'Am.**

God, names for see **Adonai; Elohim; YHVH.**

God, titles for see **Tzevaot;** ***Melekh ha-'Olam;*** **ha-Shem** (see **Shem**).

Graf-Wellhausen Hypothesis the hypothesis developed in the 19th c. (primarily by the German biblical scholar J. Wellhausen) that the Torah is comprised of four more or less complete documents, J, E, D, and P, in that order. See **Documentary Hypothesis.**

Great Hallel see ***hallel.***

Greek Bible a general term for the variety of ancient translations of the Bible into Gk in antiquity, including the Septuagint and the translations of **Aquila, Symmachus,** and **Theodotion.**

Guide of the Perplexed (*Moreh Nevukhim*) the philosophical work by Maimonides (**Rambam**) that interpreted the Torah mainly in the light of Aristotelian philosophy with the aim of removing contradictions between the teaching of Torah and the understandings of philosophy.

Gunzberg see **ben Asher, Aryeh Loeb.**

H the Holiness Collection (imprecisely called the Holiness Code), the ritual and ethical laws found in Lev. chs 17–26. The author of these laws was affiliated with the Priestly school, but was probably writing after that school penned the bulk of its material that now appears in the Torah. The authors of the Holiness Collection likely wrote small sections dispersed throughout the first four books of the Torah. The collection is so named from the exhortation, "You shall be holy, for I, the LORD your God, am holy" (Lev. 19.2).

haftarah, pl. **haftarot** (Heb "conclusion") the reading from a prophetic book that follows the Torah reading in the Sabbath or festival service.

Ḥag festival, particularly one of the three Pilgrim Festivals (*shalosh regalim:* Passover [pesaḥ], Shavu'ot, Sukkot).

Ḥag Sameaḥ good wishes for a holiday: "joyous festival."

haggadah see **aggadah.**

Haggadah of Pesaḥ ("telling of Passover") the liturgical recitation used at the Passover **Seder;** also the book that contains the recitation and instructions of the Seder.

halakhah (Heb "way," from *halakh* "go"; pl. *halakhot*) the legal portions of the Talmud, or any legal ruling according to Jewish law.

Halevi, Judah (ca. 1075–ca. 1141; also Yehudah ha-Levi) Hebrew poet, of Spain, and author of the Arabic philosophical work, *The Kuzari,* a defense of Judaism.

hallel (Heb "to praise" [infinitive]) the name for various Psalms used in synagogue liturgies: the "Egyptian Hallel" refers to Pss. 113–118, recited on festivals and (in part) on new moons; the "Great Hallel" refers to Ps. 136; the "daily Hallel" refers to Pss. 146–150.

Hammurabi Babylonian monarch (reigned 1792–1750 BCE), responsible for the formulation of a legal collection (the Code [or Laws] of Hammurabi) that is one of the earliest collections of case law on various subjects.

Ḥanukkah (Heb "dedication") festival commemorating the rededication of the Temple in 164 BCE. See **Hasmonean Revolt.**

haplography (Gk "single writing") the inadvertent omission of a doubled letter, word, or phrase in the process of copying a text.

HaReuveni, Nogah Israeli botanist (d. 2007).

ha-Shem see **Shem.**

Hasidic, pl. **Hasidim** (Heb *Ḥasid,* "pious one") a renewal movement that began in the mid-18th c. in eastern Europe under the influence of the Ba'al Shem Tov ("master of the good Name"), R. Yisrael ben Eliezer (ca. 1700–1760).

Haskalah see **Enlightenment.**

Hasmonean Revolt the uprising led by the family of Mattathias Heshmon against the Seleucid ruler Antiochus IV Epiphanes beginning in 166 BCE, particularly by Mattathias's son Judah (or Judas) Maccabeus ("the hammer"), which succeeded in liberating Jerusalem and the surrounding territory from Seleucid rule in 164. When the Temple, which had been desecrated by Antiochus, was retaken by the Jews it was rededicated, an event commemorated in the festival of **Ḥanukkah** ("dedication").

Hebrew Bible a term used to refer to what Christians call the Old Testament. Though the two terms refer to basically the same body of writings, the order of books in the Hebrew Bible (that is, the Jewish Bible) differs from that found in the Old Testament.

heikhalot rabbati ("greater halls") mystical writings probably dating from the 3rd to 7th centuries CE. The "halls" (or "palaces, temples") are heavenly realms through which the narrative moves.

heikhalot zutarti ("lesser halls") mystical writings of the same type as the ***heikhalot rabbati.***

Hellenism a general term for the spread of Greek culture, politics, and language around the Mediterranean in the period after the conquests of Alexander the Great (d. 323 BCE).

hendiadys figure of speech that expresses a compound idea by two words linked by a conjunction. For example, "pain and childbearing" (Gen. 3.16) means "pangs in childbearing."

ḥerem (Heb "**ban**") the total dedication of conquest to God; later, the exile or suspension of someone from the community ("excommunication").

hermeneutic principles the rabbinic types of interpretation. A list attributed to Hillel (1st c. BCE) includes: *qal vaḥomer* (deduction from minor to major); *gezerah shavah* (analogy between texts based on a common word); *binyan ʾav mikatuv ʾeḥad* (applying a principle derived from one v.); *binyan ʾav mishenei ketuvim* (applying a principle derived from two vv.); *kelal uferat uferat ukelal* (modifying the general from the particular; modifying the particular from the general); *kayotzeʾ bo bemakom ʾaḥer* (principles developed from similar passages); *davar halamed meʿinyano* (deduction from context). See "Classical Rabbinic Interpretation" (pp. 1859–78.)

Hexapla the compendium of six Bible versions (in columns: (1) Heb, (2) Heb transliterated into Gk, (3) Gk **[Aquila]**, (4) Gk **[Symmachus]**, (5) **Septuagint,** (6) Gk **[Theodotion]**) compiled by the early Christian scholar Origen (d. 254). The original Hexapla, which ran to 7,000 pages, was lost, but quotations from it exist in various early writings and a Syriac translation of column five (known as the Syriac Hexapla or Syro-Hexapla), was prepared by a Christian bishop, Paul of Tella (who held office in 618–619), and it is an important witness to the transmission of the text of the Septuagint.

Hexateuch (Gk "six scrolls") a grouping of the first six books in the Bible—Gen. through Josh.—to complete the Torah narrative with the conquest of the land that is in Josh. See **Pentateuch; Tetrateuch.**

high places places of worship or sacrifice, often at the top of a hill or mountain. Under the influence of the centralization of worship in Jerusalem at the Temple, particularly in the Deuteronomic reform carried out under Josiah, the high places were vilified as idolatrous, though in earlier writings, and even in the narratives in Kings, there are clear indications that sacrifice and worship took place in numerous locations throughout the land of Israel.

higher criticism the effort to distinguish among the sources of biblical documents, and to trace them back to their origins, so far as that is possible; distinguished from textual criticism ("lower criticism"), which is concerned with establishing the most accurate text in its final form. See **Documentary Hypothesis.**

Hillel an important early rabbinic sage of the 1st c. BCE; according to tradition, he migrated from Babylonia to Israel. Tradition also suggests that he set up a "house" or scholarly school. The House of Hillel often differs with the House of Shammai in halakhic rulings, and is typically more lenient.

Ḥizkuni Rabbi Hezekiah ben Manoah (13th c. France), a biblical commentator; his commentary on the Pentateuch is known as "the Ḥazzekuni."

Holiness Collection see **H.**

homoioteleuton (Gk "similar [or same] ending") a scribal error in which a phrase is omitted when an immediately following phrase ends with the same word; the copyist's eye moved from the first occurrence of the word to the second, and left out the words in between.

hortatory characteristic of writing or speech that aims at changing the behavior of the hearers or inspiring them to a particular course of action.

ḥumash (from *ḥamishah ḥumshei Torah,* "five fifths of Torah") a synonym for the Torah, or the book used by a synagogue congregation to follow the Torah reading.

Hyksos the mostly Semitic rulers of Egypt during the period 1665–1560 BCE (approximately).

hyperbole exaggeration for effect. "Would the LORD be pleased with thousands of rams, / With myriads of streams of oil?" (Mic. 6.7).

hypostasis (Gk "that which stands under," i.e., the real nature or essence of anything; pl. *hypostases*) a Greek philosophical term, meaning both "essential being" or what defines a thing as a member of a class of things and "individual being" or what a thing is in itself. It was used by, among others, the neoplatonist mystics. It refers to the three constitutive orders of reality, the One, Mind, and Soul, each of which is an hypostasis. See "The Bible in the Jewish Mystical Tradition" (pp. 1943–63).

Ibn Aknin, Yosef ben Yehudah (ca. 1150–1220) philosopher and biblical commentator, of Spain and Morocco.

His commentary on the Song treated it as an allegory of the soul's effort to free itself from matter and unite with the intellect that emanates from God.

Ibn Balʿam, Yehudah (11th c.) biblical commentator and grammarian of Spain. His commentary on the Torah and the Prophets is a link between the work of **Saadia Gaon** and **Abraham Ibn Ezra.**

Ibn Daud, Abraham (ca. 1110–1180) philosopher and historian of Spain. His work was concerned to show the consonance of science and religion, and particularly of Aristotelianism and Judaism.

Ibn Ezra, Abraham (1089–1164) poet, biblical commentator, translator, philosopher, who lived in Spain, North Africa, Italy, France, and England. His biblical commentaries cover large portions of the text, and provided Hebrew readers with their first chance to read the comments of **Saadia Gaon,** which Ibn Ezra translated from Arabic.

Ibn Ezra, Moshe (1070–1138) philosopher and poet of Spain. He wrote on philosophical matters such as the nature of the divine, the intellect, and nature, but his best-known works are poems, particularly those sacred poems in the Sephardic prayer book.

Idumea Gk form of the name "Edom"; province in the land of Israel during Persian, Hellenistic, and Roman times, located south of Judah (Yehud), between the Dead Sea and the Mediterranean.

impurity a ritual state which forbade the impure individual to partake in Temple rituals (see **defilement,** and "Concepts of Purity," pp. 1998–2005).

Inanna Sumerian goddess of fertility and war; equivalent to the Babylonian **Ishtar.** She was similar to the Greek Persephone in being captive in the underworld, later released.

inclusio the use of the same word or phrase at the end of a passage as appeared at the beginning, thus rounding off or completing it. Inclusio may have been used to mark subsections of a work. It is also called inclusion, frame, and envelope structure.

incubation the practice of sleeping in a particular place, or in contact with particular things (animal skins, the ground) in order to induce dreams that might provide divine guidance.

Ingathering (*kibutz galuyot,* "ingathering of the exiles") the belief that the people will ultimately return to the land of Israel from their places of exile.

intercalation adding an extra time unit (day or month) to a calendar to compensate for the inexact fit between the solar year and the daily or lunar cycle. In the Jewish calendar, an extra month (a repetition of Adar) is intercalated in seven years of the nineteen-year cycle. See **Adar;** see also p. 2230.

interpolation an insertion of material into a previously existent text. In the absence of textual evidence—e.g., differing forms of a manuscript for a given text—interpolation must be inferred and is often the subject of scholarly disagreement.

interregnum an interruption or gap between the end of one reign or dynasty and the beginning of the next.

intertextuality the interrelationship between one part of a text (or collection of texts) and other parts. Intertextuality can take the form of recurrent images (the vineyard in Isa. 5.1–10 and 27.2–4), quotation and/or inner biblical interpretation (Jer. 25.11–12 is partly quoted in Dan. 9.2 before it is reinterpreted), or allusion (Isa. 54.8 alludes to the promise made to Noah in Gen. 9.11).

Ishtar the Mesopotamian goddess of fertility and war (the Gk spelling was Astarte); the Canaanite version of her name is Ashtar. See **Inanna.**

Isis the Egyptian mother-goddess, wife of Osiris, the god of vegetation and hence of regeneration.

J the posited document or narrative tradition that is one of the constituent parts of the Torah (Pentateuch), according to a scholarly hypothesis codified by J. Wellhausen and subsequently developed by numerous biblical researchers. J is usually understood to be the earliest source, and is Judean; it frequently depicts God, for whom it uses the **Tetragrammaton** (YHVH, misvocalized Jehovah, thus J), in very anthropomorphic terms. See intro. to the Torah (pp. 1–6).

Jerome (ca. 340–420 CE) Christian theologian and translator. Beginning in 382, he produced a Latin version of the Bible, the Old Testament of which was based not on a previous Latin version nor on the Gk text **(Septuagint)** but on the Heb. In order to do this Jerome studied Heb with rabbis of the time, an unusual step for a Christian. His version, which became known as the **Vulgate** ("common") because it was the translation into commonly used Latin in the western world, was completed in 405.

Jerusalem Talmud also called the Palestinian Talmud or the Talmud of the land of Israel, although none of these titles is fully accurate. This **Talmud,** mostly reflecting traditions of the Galilean ***'amora'im*** of the 3rd and 4th centuries CE, is a commentary on several tractates of the **Mishnah.** It was ultimately seen as less authoritative than the longer, more comprehensive, and more carefully edited Babylonian Talmud. See **Talmud.**

Josephus, Flavius Hellenistic Jewish historian (ca. 37–ca. 100 CE). Four of his writings have survived: *The Jewish War* (an account of the rebellion against Rome in 66–70 CE, with background information starting at about 200 BCE); *The Antiquities of the Jews* (a history from creation up to the start of *The Jewish War*); *Against Apion,* a defense of Judaism; and an autobiography. Josephus provides invaluable historical information about Judaism and its background from 200 BCE to 100 CE; his account of the rebellion, in which he was a participant, is partly that of an eyewitness. He also provides first-hand information about the Essenes and the Pharisees (he was at one time or another associated with both), as well as information about the Sadducees. Josephus is important in understanding Second Temple Judaism and the context in which rabbinic Judaism developed.

jubilee (Heb *yovel,* perhaps "ram" from the sounding of the ram's horn to mark the beginning of the observance) the year of release for slaves and return of ancestral lands to their original owners (or descendants of the owners), to occur every fifty years (after seven sabbaths of years) (Lev. ch 25). It is a cornerstone of Priestly ideology, but it is uncertain if it was ever practiced.

***Jubilees,* book of** a pseudepigraphic book, retelling much of Gen. and Exod., representing itself as a hidden revelation to Moses. It was most likely written in the 2nd c. BCE in the land of Israel. The book gets its name from its concern with cycles of time. *Jubilees* was apparently considered authoritative by the Qumran community. It is attributed to Moses and purports to be a revelation to him from the angel of the Presence.

Judaeus, Philo (ca. 20 BCE–50 CE) Hellenistic Jewish philosopher of Alexandria, Egypt. Philo worked out a system that tried to interpret biblical concepts and beliefs in terms of the philosophy of Plato and his follow ers. In this system, God cannot be known directly, but only through intermediate beings; the soul, the higher element in the human person, is always attempting to return to God, its origin, although if this task is not far enough along at the time of the individual's death, the soul may have to transmigrate into another body and try again. In trying to make this philosophy compatible with Judaism, Philo developed a highly allegorical exegesis of the Bible.

Judah the area of southern Israel. According to the biblical text, after the death of Solomon, the kingdom was divided into two, with Judah in the south and Israel in the north. The capital of Judah was Jerusalem.

Judah Halevi see **Halevi, Judah.**

Judah the Prince Rabbi. Judah ha-Nasi, the prince or patriarch (Heb *nasi'*) of the community in Israel in the late 2nd c. CE. He was very powerful, and had close relation with the Roman rulers. He played a central role in editing the Mishnah, and tradition sees him as the editor of that work.

Judahites the term for inhabitants of the tribal area of Judah in the period before the Persian, Greek, and Roman rule (during which time Judah is referred to as "Yehud," "Ioudaia," and "Judaea," and the inhabitants are Judeans).

Judea (Judaea) the Roman name for the area of Judah.

kabbalah "what is received," i.e., matter handed to one. In the 12th c. and later, however, kabbalah came to mean esoteric or in some sense mystical teaching. Kabbalah taught that God was inaccessible by direct experience, and could only be apprehended through emanations of the Godhead; Torah in kabbalistic teaching had a hidden meaning, and meditation on texts was a method of ascent to a mystical vision.

kaddish (Aram. "holiness, sanctification") prayer in praise of God that is recited at the conclusion of a principal section of the synagogue service; a special type of kaddish is also recited in memory of the deceased.

Kalam (Arabic "speech, reason") Islamic scholasticism, dating from the 8th c. CE, a theology that developed in response to the rediscovery of Aristotelian philosophy in the Islamic world. The earliest proponents of this school were called Mutazilite ("separatist") because they were seen as separate from orthodox Islamic teaching. The Kalam movement influenced both Karaite and rabbinic teaching, including among the latter the work of **Saadia Gaon.**

kapparah see **atonement.**

Karaites (lit. "Scripturists"; from Heb *Miqra'*) the theological movement in Judaism dating from Babylonia in the 8th c. CE. Karaites claimed to be restoring an original form of Judaism from the Second Temple period, and were opposed by the rabbis of their time, particularly **Saadia Gaon.** Karaite calendars, festivals, dietary restrictions, and other practices differed in various ways from rabbinic norms. The movement reached its height around the 11th c. though a small Karaite community is still in existence today in Israel.

Karo, Joseph (1488–1575) legal commentator and mystic, author of the Jewish code of law, **Shulḥan 'Arukh** (1563).

kashering the process of making a permissible food **kosher** or fit for consumption, especially soaking and salting meat to remove blood.

kashrut the system of dietary laws and restrictions; see **kosher.**

kataphatic (from Gk for "affirm") the theology that works by ascribing positive attributes to God, through which one understands the divine nature.

Kedushah (Heb "holiness") prayers of sanctification of God, especially the third blessing of the ***'Amidah,*** including the words "Holy, holy, holy" from Isa. 6.3.

kere see ***qere.***

ketiv ("what is written") the biblical text in its written form, in contrast, in certain cases, to the way it is to be read aloud. See ***qere.***

Kiddush short for *kiddush ha-yom,* "sanctification of the day," both the ceremony and the prayer that proclaims the holiness of the Sabbath (or festival), recited over wine before the Sabbath (or festival) meal.

Kimḥi a family of grammarians and exegetes in medieval France (originally from Spain); the three great scholars of this family were Yosef Kimḥi (ca. 1105–1170), who defended Jewish interpretation against Christian criticism in *Sefer ha-Berit,* and his two sons, Moshe and David. The latter, a prolific biblical commentator and grammarian, was known as **Radak.**

kitvei hakodesh (Heb "holy writings") a rabbinic term for the Bible; the Holy Scriptures.

kohen (Heb "priest") a member of the hereditary group within the Levites, traditionally supposed to be descended from Aaron or Zadok, who alone were allowed to serve as Temple priests.

kosher (Heb "fit" or "proper") a general term used in postbiblical texts for dietary laws; usually applied to food, but also to other ritual objects and practices. Most dietary laws apply to meat: It may not be consumed with blood in it, certain kinds of internal fat are not to be eaten, it may not be consumed along with dairy products, and some meats (e.g., pork), sea creatures (e.g., shellfish), and "creeping things" (e.g., snails) are not permitted.

Lachish ostraca letters or inscriptions written on shards (pieces of broken pottery) found at Lachish. Most are letters by Hoshaiah to Joash, both presumably military officers, during the Babylonian siege of Lachish in 586 BCE.

Latter Prophets the canonical division of Nevi'im that includes the books of Isa., Jer., Ezek., and the Twelve (Heb title *nevi'im aḥaronim*).

Laws of Eshnunna the legal collection of a Mesopotamian city-state, about 50 km (30 mi) from present-day Baghdad, that flourished in the early part of the 2nd millennium BCE. These laws include parallels to those found in the legal collections in the Torah.

LBH Late Biblical Hebrew, the dialect spoken during and after the Babylonian exile, when Aram. influenced Heb significantly.

leitmotif (German "leading theme") a term, borrowed from music criticism, for a repeated or recurrent idea, phrase, or image in a text.

leitwort (German "leading word") a repeated word that serves to unify a text or bring out a major idea.

Lekha Dodi the mystical 16th-c. hymn or song that is sung at the beginning of the Sabbath. The title means "Come, my friend," and the first line is: "Come, my friend, to meet the bride; let us welcome the presence of the Sabbath."

Letter of Aristeas an apocryphal work, the supposed eyewitness account of the translation of the Torah into Gk. It is the origin of the story that the translators numbered seventy-two (rounded off to seventy and therefore the reason that this Gk translation of the Bible is called the Septuagint [Gk "seventy"] and is abbreviated LXX).

Levant (Latin "rising") the eastern part of the Mediterranean with its islands and neighboring countries.

Leviathan the monster of the sea in Canaanite mythology, who is defeated by Baal. This has echoes in Ps. 74.14–17 and elsewhere.

levirate marriage (from Latin *levir,* "husband's brother") the provision that if a man died without an heir to carry on his name, his brother would marry the widow, and the first son she bore would be regarded as the dead brother's heir. This practice is dealt with in Deut. 25.5–10, but it is unclear whether it was actually carried out to any extent; by rabbinic times *ḥalitzah,* the ceremony that released the levir from this obligation, was preferred.

lex talionis (Latin "law [of retribution] in kind") punishment fitting the crime; see **talion.**

liminal (Latin *limina,* "threshhold") the term for rites or practices that governed life passages, such as entry into puberty or marriage.

lingua franca a common tongue or shared language that enables people with different native languages to converse, carry on commercial relationships, etc. In the Persian period Aram. replaced Akkadian as a lingua franca around the Near East; during the Hellenistic period Gk did the same for the lands surrounding the Mediterranean.

littoral a region lying along the shore of a large lake or sea.

liturgy the form or rite for communal, public worship.

LMLK a stamp or seal found on storage jars dating from the late 8th to early 7th c. BCE; it is an abbreviation of Heb *la-melekh,* "to the king" (referring perhaps to the government in general), "for the king," or "of the king."

lower criticism, textual criticism, as distinguished from source criticism ("higher criticism"). See "Textual Criticism" (pp. 2149–52).

Luria, Itzḥak (1534–1572) halakhic and kabbalistic teacher, active in Safed, Israel. Though he wrote little or nothing himself, his followers after his death produced a large amount of writing presenting his teaching, which basically stated the goal of all creation to be the gradual perfection of all realms, divine and human. This perfection was to be sought not just individually, but communally, and therefore fit with messianic expectations and other movements for renewal.

Lurianism the teachings of Itzḥak Luria or based on the writings of his followers.

Luzzato, Samuel David Italian Hebraist, scholar, exegete (1800–1865).

LXX the Roman numeral seventy, the standard abbreviation for the **Septuagint.**

Maʿariv (from *ʿerev,* "evening") the evening prayer service, held after nightfall. See ***Minḥah; Shaḥarit.***

Maʾat Egyptian goddess of reason and order; her name literally means "truth."

maftir (Heb "completer") the reader who completes the Torah portion by repeating the last three or so vv. of it, reciting the Torah blessing, and reading the **haftarah** (see).

"Maggid, the" see **Baer, Dov.**

Maimonides, Moses (also Moshe ben Maimon) see **Rambam.**

Malbim Rabbi Meir Leibush ben Yehiel Michal (1809–1879), biblical commentator in Russia.

malediction curse; opposite of benediction, "blessing."

manumission release from servitude.

Marduk chief god of Babylon; according to ***Enuma Elish,*** a Babylonian epic of creation, he formed the cosmos from the corpse of **Tiamat,** goddess of the deep.

maskil, pl. **maskilim** (lit. "knowledgeable") a title for an educated person; later, a kabbalist; still later, an adherent of Haskalah **(Enlightenment)**.

Masorah the system of markings (vowel signs, marginal notes, cantillation and accent marks, etc.) that were added to the consonantal Heb text by scribal scholars **(Masoretes)** in the early Middle Ages.

Masorete a scholar of the scribal schools that in the early Middle Ages established the basic Heb text for the Bible, fixed its accepted pronunciation, and ensured its accurate copying and transmission by a system of markings **(Masorah).**

Masoretic Text (MT) the Heb text as established by the Masoretes.

matrilineal tracing descent through female ancestors; see **patrilineal.**

matzah, pl. ***matzot*** unleavened bread, associated with Passover, but also used with certain sacrifices.

Megillot (Heb "scrolls") the five books of Kethuvim that are read during various festivals: Song in **Pesaḥ,** Ruth on **Shavuʿot,** Lam. on ***Tishʿah beʾav,*** Eccl. on **Sukkot,** and Esth. on **Purim.**

Meir, Rabbi 2nd c. pupil of Akiva who helped to reconstitute the Sanhedrin after the second (Bar Kokhba) revolt. R. Meir's teachings were partly aimed at organizing the oral law, and led to the compilation of the Mishnah under R. Judah ha-Nasi **(Judah the Prince)**.

Mekhilta two halakhic midrashic commentaries on sections of Exod., one attributed to R. Ishmael and the other to R. Shimeon bar Yoḥai.

Melekh ha-ʿOlam Heb "ruler of the universe," a title for God.

Mendelssohn, Moses (1729–1786) German scholar, defender of Judaism against Christian argument, and leader of the Haskalah or **Enlightenment** movement. He led the efforts of a team of scholars to translate the Bible into German (printed in Heb characters).

merism a figure of speech in which opposing terms, e.g., "good and bad," are combined to convey the idea of including both terms and everything in between. The "tree of knowledge of good and bad" (Gen. 2.17), therefore, may mean the tree of knowledge of everything.

merkavah a name for mystical writings, inspired by Ezek. ch 1, in which the visionary is conducted through the heavenly realms by a chariot *(merkavah).*

Merneptah Stele an Egyptian inscribed stone that includes the first mention of Israel outside the Bible. It celebrates the victories of Pharaoh Merneptah (ca. 1200 BCE) in the area of **Canaan.**

Merodach Heb version of **Marduk,** chief god of Babylon (Jer. 50.2).

Mesha Stele (also called the "Moabite Stone") a commemorative stone dating from about 830 BCE with engraved text celebrating the reign of King Mesha of Moab (2 Kings 3.4–5). Besides an account of the dealings of Mesha with the descendants of Omri, king of Israel, the text deals with the god of Moab, **Chemosh,** and the favor that Chemosh has shown to Mesha in contrast to his predecessors in allowing Mesha to reclaim territory from Israel. It also contains a reference to the ***ḥerem*** or **ban,** indicating that this idea was not unique to Israel.

Mesopotamia (Gk "between the rivers") the area between the Tigris and Euphrates rivers.

messiah (Heb *mashiaḥ,* "anointed [one]") a title for the king or other servant or agent of God (priest, prophet, or even non-Israelite Cyrus in Isa. 45.1). In the Tanakh, *mashiaḥ* never refers to the future ideal king.

metaphor a direct comparison between two unlike things: "The LORD is my shepherd" (Ps. 23.1). See **simile.**

metonymy a figure of speech in which a word is used in place of another word to which it is closely related. In Isa. 41.5 "the coastlands" is a metonymy for "the inhabitants of the coasts," i.e., foreigners.

meturgeman (Aram. "interpreter"; cf. **Targum**) the one who provided a running translation into the language of the congregation—Aram., in the origin of the practice—of the Torah reading (and other Scripture readings) in the synagogue service.

mezuzah, pl. **mezuzot** (Heb "doorpost") a parchment on which are written the paragraphs of the **Shema** (Deut. 6.4–9; 11.13–21), and on the back of which *sh-d-y* ("Shaddai," "Almighty") is written, often so as to be visible through a small opening in the case. *Sh-d-y* is interpreted as an acronym for *shomer delatot Yisra'el,* "guardian of the doors of Israel."

midrash, midrashic (Heb *derash,* "inquire") interpretation to draw out meanings from a text that are other than, or go beyond, the "plain sense" (see ***peshat***).

Milcom Heb form of the name of the god of Ammon. See **Molech.**

Minḥah (Heb "offering") the second of the daily prayer services. It occurs during the period between noon and sunset. See ***Shaḥarit; Maʿariv.***

miqra' ("that which is read [aloud]") the standard rabbinic way of referring to the biblical text.

Miqra'ot Gedolot the Rabbinic Bible, an edition of the Masoretic Text accompanied by the Aram. translation (Targum) and various commentaries such as Rashi, Ibn Ezra, Ramban, and Rashbam. See p. 1890.

Miqṣat Maʿaseh ha-Torah ("matters of the Torah") one of the Dead Sea Scrolls (4QMMT), in the form of a letter from the Qumran sect to its opponents, explaining, among other things, the differences in legal interpretation and application between the Qumran community and the Jerusalem establishment of the time.

Mishnah (Heb "oral instruction," from *shanah,* "repeat") the compilation of oral law and rabbinic commentary, edited ca. 200 CE, that is the basis of the **Talmud.** The Mishnah in its final form is generally attributed to R. Judah ha-Nasi (**Judah the Prince,** ca. 135–220), though it contains material that may go back centuries before R. Judah's time.

Mishneh Torah the first codification of Jewish law, by Maimonides (**Rambam**).

mitzvah, pl. ***mitzvot*** (Heb "commandment") a religious obligation; by extension, any good deed.

MMT see ***Miqṣat Maʿaseh ha-Torah.***

Moab/Moabites the territory and inhabitants southeast of the Dead Sea.

Moabite Stone see **Mesha Stele.**

Molech the title—"king"—of the Ammonite god. The worshippers of this god were accused of child sacrifice.

Mot the Canaanite god of death.

motif an image or character type that recurs throughout a literary work. The Servant motif occurs in Isa. at 42.1–4; 49.1–6; 50.4–11; 52.13–53.12.

Musaf ("addition") the extra service on a Sabbath or festival, after ***Shaḥarit*** (see).

Musar Movement a 19th-c. Lithuanian movement to promote piety and ethical behavior; its founder was R. Yisrael Salanter (1810–1883). Its practices continue in yeshivas influenced by followers of the movement.

Mutazilite Kalam see **Kalam.**

Naḥmanides Moshe ben Naḥman, known as **Ramban** (see).

narrative a connected account of an incident, or a longer account including many incidents. Narratives can be historical, fictional, legendary, mythical, or a combination of types.

necromancy the practice of divination by communication with the dead, who are presumed to have knowledge of the future.

Negev (Negeb) the high plateau south of the central hill country of Israel.

Neoplatonism the philosophical movement, originating with Plotinus (ca. 204–270), that saw the universe as a series of emanations flowing out from the One, the causeless, unknowable source of all that is. The emanations, Mind *(nous)* and Soul, are, along with the One, called **hypostases.** The individual's task is to return to the One by contemplation, involving a progressive detachment from the world of matter and sense and ultimately from all categories of thought until the One can be grasped in an indescribable void of thought.

Netziv Rabbi Naftali Zvi Yehuda Berlin (1816–1893), prominent Lithuanian educator and Talmudic scholar.

new moon see **Rosh Ḥodesh.**

Ninth of Av see ***Tishʿah beʾav.***

Noahide laws the basic commandments laid upon Noah, and therefore seen as binding upon all human beings, Jews and Gentiles alike: They prohibited blasphemy, idolatry, sexual immorality, murder, robbery, and eating blood; and they commanded justice.

notarikon, pl. ***notarikonim*** (from Gk *notarikon,* "shorthand") a method of interpretation that takes each letter of a word as the initial letter of another word, thereby creating a phrase that is treated as the full meaning intended by the word; also breaking a word into constituent parts and interpreting those parts in order to reveal a hidden meaning within the original word. For example, rabbinic interpretation treated the first word of the Decalogue, *ʾanokhi* (the longer word for "I"), as an acronym for the Aram. sentence *ʾanaʾ ketavit yehavit,* "I [God] wrote it [and] gave it."

obelisk a four-sided stone shaft, usually tapered and topped with a pyramid, characteristic of ancient Egypt.

ʿOlam the biblical Heb term for unending (time), extended in postbiblical Heb to mean all space, i.e., the world or universe.

oracle a unit of prophetic speech; usually translates *masaʾ* ("burden").

Oral Torah a synonym for the **Mishnah** and **Talmud.** According to traditional rabbinic belief, the oral law was given to Moses on Mount Sinai along with the written law, the Torah. The oral law was, however, as its name suggests, originally transmitted orally alongside the Torah, as the authoritative interpretation of the Torah. As a result of historical exigencies, it was committed to writing by the Rabbis, in stages, in the first millennium CE.

Ovadiah of Bertinoro (ca. 1450–1509) commentator on **Mishnah,** from Bertinoro (Italy). By treating the Mishnah itself, in isolation from its treatment in the **Talmud,** Ovadiah encouraged the study of Mishnah independently of the Talmud.

P the Priestly document in the Torah, comprised of both narratives and laws. It is concerned, among other things, with laws and regulations, ritual practices, the proper conduct of Temple worship, holiness and purity, and genealogies. P may also have had a hand in the shaping or redaction of the Torah. See intro. to the Torah (pp. 1–6).

Palestine a name derived from the Roman designation *Provincia Syria Palaestina,* "Syro-Palestinian Province," which replaced *Provincia Judaea* after the revolt of 135 CE; *Palaestina* was the Roman spelling of "Philistine," and the designation was probably intended as a derogation of Jewish claims to the territory.

Palestinian Talmud the **Jerusalem Talmud** or Talmud **Yerushalmi;** see **Talmud.**

parallelism a characteristic feature of biblical Hebrew poetry in which the second line of a unit in some way echoes the meaning or grammatical structure of the first line. This can take the form of a repetition of the meaning, or of a statement of opposites, or of a further statement that serves to extend or modify the first line in some way. See "Biblical Poetry" (pp. 2184–91).

parashah the portion of Torah designated to be read publicly for each week of the year. There are fifty-four parashiyot, to provide for the maximum possible number of Sabbaths in a year (that can only occur in an intercalated or leap year). In years with fewer Sabbaths, the readings are combined to produce fewer portions. The weekly portion is also sometimes improperly called the *Sidrah,* "arrangement."

pardes a Late Biblical Hebrew word borrowed from Persian, meaning "park, garden, orchard." It was later employed as an acronym for the four levels of meaning in Scripture according to the ***Zohar: peshat*** (contextual sense), ***remez*** (allegorical sense), ***derash*** (homiletical sense), and ***sod*** (mystical sense).

Paschal pertaining to the Passover (ultimately from the Gk *pascha,* derived from Heb *pesah*).

Passover see **Pesaḥ.**

Passover *Haggadah, Haggadah* of Pesaḥ the "telling" of the Passover story in the context of the household liturgy of Pesaḥ, which accompanies the ritual meal, the **Seder.**

patriarchs the founding fathers *(ʾavot)* of Israel: Abraham, Isaac, and Jacob.

patrilineal tracing one's descent through male ancestors; see **matrilineal.**

Pentapolis the five cities of the **Philistines** (see): Ashdod, Ashkelon, Ekron, Gath, and Gaza.

Pentateuch (Gk "five scrolls") the first five books of the Bible—Gen. through Deut.—regarded as a unit after its final editing during or after the exile. The traditional term in Judaism for this collection of books is Torah, "teaching." Although these five books are traditionally grouped together, they contain markedly different kinds of writing—prehistory, narrative, law, ritual instruction, etc.—and scholars have investigated the materials of which they are composed. Deut. is largely a separate work that was probably attached to the first four books at a later stage, leading some scholars to speak of a **Tetrateuch** consisting of Gen. through Num.; and it is also the case that the actual narrative climax of the story, the conquest of the land of Israel, is given in the book of Josh., leading other scholars to speak of a **Hexateuch** consisting of Gen. through Josh. See intro. to the Torah (pp. 1–6).

Persian period ca. 539–333 BCE, from the time of Cyrus the Great until the Greek conquest by Alexander.

Pesaḥ (probably "protection"; others "pass over") the name of the festival commemorating the exodus from Egypt. The first day involves the sacrifice of the lamb, which took place on the eve of the exodus (14 Nisan); the rest of the festival, *Ḥag ha-Matzot* or "festival of unleavened bread," was probably originally a festival marking the beginning of the spring barley harvest. Pesaḥ is the first of the ***shalosh regalim*** or "three pilgrim festivals."

peshat (Heb "simple") the "plain sense" or "contextual sense" of a text, often contrasted with ***derash,*** the homiletical meaning.

pesher, pl. ***pesharim*** (Heb "interpretation") a type of commentary on the Bible from the Qumran community in which the biblical text is understood to be actualized or fulfilled in the interpreter's time period. Some are comments on vv. in biblical order, while others group vv. by subject; typically, the comment contains the word *pesher.*

Peshitta (Syriac "simple") a translation of the Bible into Syriac (a dialect of Aram.) for the use of Syriac-speaking Jewish communities; it was largely taken over by Syriac-speaking Christians, who added a Syriac translation of the New Testament.

Pesikta de Rav Kahana and ***Pesikta Rabbati*** (Aram. *pesiktaʾ*, "section") two collections of midrash that deal with selected biblical passages, the first dating from the 5th–7th centuries, the second from the 9th–13th.

petiḥta ("opening") an introduction to a midrashic unit, often begun with a v. unconnected to the biblical text being interpreted. Sometimes termed "**proem.**"

Pharisees a movement among Jews in the 1st c. CE, according to Josephus and the writings in the New Testament. The Pharisees were concerned to extend Jewish practice into all areas of life, and followed the tradition of interpretation **(Oral Torah)** associated with the schools of **Hillel** and Shammai. They were thus proponents of a Jewish identity separate from the larger non-Jewish culture that surrounded Judea, but were also opponents of the more conservative Sadducees, who did not accept their traditions of oral law. See **Sadducees.**

Philistines a group from the **Sea Peoples,** who invaded and settled on the coastal region of Canaan. They had been repulsed from an invasion of Egypt (ca. 1190 BCE). The five major Philistine cities (the **Pentapolis**) were Ashdod, Ashkelon, Ekron, Gath, and Gaza.

Philo see **Judaeus, Philo**

Phoenicians the people who lived in the area north of Israel, in part of what is present-day Lebanon. Their chief cities were Tyre and Sidon. The Phoenicians were known throughout the eastern Mediterranean region as merchants, and for producing a reddish-purple dye, from which they apparently got their name (*phoinix* is the Gk word for the color of the dye).

phylacteries see **tefillin.**

pilpul dialectical argument; superseded in talmudic study in some locations by logical argument promoted by the followers of the **Vilna Gaon.**

Pirkei ʾAvot ("chapters of the Fathers") a tractate of the **Mishnah** (called *ʾAvot*) that begins by tracing the transmission of the oral law from Moses to the Rabbis; emphasizes the strong link between Torah study and ethical behavior; and contains non-legal, moralistic sayings of various Rabbis. *ʾAvot* is included in the traditional prayerbook and is made part of the liturgical recitation in many communities.

piyyut (formed from *payyetan,* the creator of a liturgical poem; from Gk *poietes,* "thing made," "poem") a liturgical poem accompanying the prayers in the synagogue service. *Piyyutim* began to be composed around the 5th c. in the land of Israel, and new ones continued to be created up until the 18th c.

plene spelling (from Latin "full") the form of a word in the Heb text that includes all of the vowel letters. See **defective spelling.**

primogeniture the social arrangement by which the eldest son inherits a father's title or the bulk of the father's property.

proem a short introduction or preface to a literary text. See ***petiḥta.***

proleptic anticipatory; literary device of foreshadowing or anticipating a later development in a narrative, or anticipating and answering an argument from an opponent.

prophet (Gk *prophetes,* "speak out" or "speak forth") the Septuagint translation of *navi'* ("one who is called"), the standard Heb term for prophet. Synonyms include "seer," "man of God," and "visionary." See the intro. to Nevi'im (pp. 429–38).

prophetic lawsuit see ***riv.***

pseudepigrapha (Gk "things falsely attributed") the name for a class of writings not included in the canon, many of which are ascribed to figures of antiquity like Enoch, Moses, and Solomon. Most of these works, which were not canonized by any community, were written by Jews in the Hellenistic period.

Purim the festival that commemorates the delivery of the Jews in Persia from destruction, as recounted in the book of Esth. It is celebrated on 14 or 15 Adar.

qal vaḥomer (Heb "light and heavy") a form of rabbinic argument that moves from a lesser case to a greater one; similar to the argument *a fortiori* (Latin "how much the more").

qere ("what is read") a biblical word as it should be pronounced, in contrast to what is written in the text. See ***ketiv.***

qinah Heb "lament."

qinah meter a metrical pattern consisting of a line with three stresses followed by a line with two stresses; it is primarily used in psalms of lament or complaint, and in the book of Lam., though it can also express joy (e.g., Ps. 65).

Qumran community the settlement near Wadi Qumran at the Dead Sea, most likely composed of Essenes. The Qumran group was a sectarian Jewish community that kept its own practices in opposition to the established community in Jerusalem and Judea; the library of this group was discovered in 1947 and is known as the Dead Sea Scrolls.

Rabbah (Heb "great") a general designation for collections (deriving from different periods) of midrashic comment on various books of the Bible, primarily Torah (*Gen. Rabbah,* etc.), but also the five Scrolls (*Song Rabbah,* etc.).

Rabbanite an adherent of the rabbinic teaching tradition, in contrast to the **Karaites,** who questioned or denied many halakhic interpretations of the Rabbis.

Radak acronym for Rabbi David **Kimḥi** (ca. 1160–1235), son of Yosef Kimḥi, biblical commentator, of France. He wrote commentaries on Gen., Ps., Prov., Chron., and the Prophets, as well as a Heb grammar and lexicon.

Ralbag acronym for Rabbi Levi ben Gershon, or Gersonides (1288–1344), medieval talmudic scholar of France. Ralbag wrote on philosophy, astronomy, and mathematics, in addition to his biblical exegesis and talmudic explications; his conception of God was philosophical, particularly Aristotelian. He wrote commentaries on most of the books of the Bible.

Rambam acronym for Rabbi Moshe ben Maimon (Moses Maimonides) (1135–1204), a philosopher and rabbi—also a practicing physician—was probably the greatest medieval Jewish philosopher. His writings include *Sefer ha-Mitzvot* ("Book of the Commandments"), ***Mishneh Torah,*** a code of Jewish law, and the philosophical work ***Guide of the Perplexed.*** Originally from Spain, he lived part of his life in Egypt.

Ramban acronym for Rabbi Moshe ben Naḥman (1194–1270), or Naḥmanides, rabbi and scholar of Spain. He defended Judaism against Christian arguments so effectively that he was persecuted and fled to Israel (city of Acre); his writings on the Torah and on early kabbalistic works were influential in the later kabbalistic movement.

Rashbam acronym for Rabbi Shemuel ben Meir (ca. 1080–1160), talmudic and biblical commentator of France. His biblical commentaries concentrated on explicating the literal sense of the text; he often disputed the commentary of his grandfather, Rashi.

Rashi acronym for Rabbi Shlomo ben Isaac (ca. 1040–1105), French talmudic and biblical scholar. He was the author both of a commentary on the whole Bible and of a commentary on the Talmud Bavli **(Babylonian Talmud),** both of which became extremely popular. His scriptural interpretation, largely taken from earlier sources, favored the contextual sense of the text rather than a set of atomistic interpetations to each phrase; his talmudic commentary was part of a greater effort to interpret Jewish law for an increasingly far-flung population.

Rav a 3rd c. Babylonian ***'amora'*** whose real name was 'Abba ben 'Aivu. "Rav" means "great" and is a tribute to the regard in which he was held by his students at the academy in Sura, which he founded. Rav and Mar Samuel are seen as the main teachers in the tradition that became the Babylonian **Talmud.** Rav's specialty was issues relating to religious law and interpretation.

Rava Rabbi Abba ben Joseph bar Ḥama (c. 280–352 CE), among the authorities most often referred to in the Talmud.

redaction criticism the study of how already existing textual units—narratives of incidents, laws, proverbs, or other isolatable pieces that can be disentangled by **source criticism**—were combined into larger texts by the activities of editors, called "redactors." Redaction criticism concentrates on the perspective of the editor, trying to deduce what editorial intentions can be understood from the way smaller units are arranged, expanded, and combined.

redactor an editor who works with already existing units to combine them into larger wholes.

riv (pronounced "reev") the literary form in the Prophets and elsewhere of a "covenant lawsuit."

Roman period the period from 63 BCE onwards, marking the beginning of Roman rule of Judea.

Rosh Ha-Shanah (Heb "head [i.e., beginning] of the year") the fall New Year in the Jewish calendar, 1 Tishri. (Rosh Ha-Shanah is now observed for two days.) The beginning of the religious calendar is 1 Nisan.

Rosh Ḥodesh (Heb "new moon") the beginning of the month, celebrated as a festival in biblical times (e.g., Isa. 1.13–14).

Sadducees a movement among Jews in the 1st C.CE, according to **Josephus** and the New Testament. They held to a strict application of Torah and to maintaining Temple worship according to its mandate; in order to continue the Temple practices without interference, the Sadducees were apparently willing to collaborate with the occupying Roman power to some extent, including accepting Roman interference in the choice of high priest. They were opposed to the Pharisees in not accepting the traditions of oral law as a guide to Torah practices, and they were also opposed to the political activists who wished to rebel against Roman rule, fearing that any rebellion would bring an end to the limited autonomy under which they could maintain Temple worship. See **Pharisees.**

Samaria ostraca broken pottery pieces on which are written notations of the amount of oil or wine received at various times, probably during the reigns of Jehoash and/or Jeroboam II.

Samaritan Pentateuch a text of the Torah in Heb used by the **Samaritans.** This text disagrees with the **Masoretic Text** at many points. Some of these disagreements reflect Samaritan beliefs (e.g., in the religious importance of Mt. Gerizim), but others are supported by the **Dead Sea Scrolls** and reflect an alternate textual tradition.

Samaritans the descendants of the population of Samaria (Northern Kingdom) after the invasion of that kingdom and the deportation of the inhabitants in 722 BCE. The Samaritans regard themselves as descended from the Jewish remnant after the deportation, but the returning exiles from the Southern Kingdom (after the Babylonian exile) did not regard them as Jews, seeing them rather as descendants of foreigners who had been settled there after the Jewish population had been removed. Therefore, beginning with Ezra and Nehemiah, the leadership forbade intermarriage between Samaritans and Jews. The Samaritans maintained worship (with a temple on Mt. Gerizim) and the Torah (but not the rest of the Bible), although their calendar is not the same as the Jewish calendar.

Samuel, Mar 2nd–3rd c. Babylonian ***ʾamora***, a contemporary of Rav and founder of the other great Babylonian academy at Nehardea. Samuel and Rav are the two sources of the teaching that became the Babylonian Talmud; Samuel specialized in issues related to civil law.

Sanhedrin (ultimately from Gk *synedria* from *syn-* and *hedra*, "with seat," i.e., "council") the religious court that held ruling authority over the Jewish people during the Roman period and into the Byzantine era; also, a tractate of the **Mishnah** dealing with issues of the law courts in general.

scroll a long strip of parchment (treated leather) or papyrus (reeds split, moistened, and pressed together), on which a text was written in columns. The scroll was read by unrolling one side while rolling up the other, to expose successive columns of text.

Sea Peoples remnants of the Mycenean or Aegean civilizations, which collapsed towards the end of the second millennium BCE. Some of these people sailed eastward on the Mediterranean and attacked those living along the **littoral;** they were repulsed from Egypt (ca. 1190) and settled along the coast of Canaan at about the same time the Israelites were entering the land from the other direction. The biblical **Philistines** are among the Sea Peoples.

Second Isaiah see **Deutero-Isaiah.**

Second Temple the Temple constructed ca. 515 BCE by the returning exiles, and continued and expanded over the course of time, until its destruction by the Romans in 70 CE.

Seder, pl. **Sedarim** (Heb "order") the ritual meal and recitation of Passover eve. Also, the major divisions of the **Mishnah.**

Seder 'Olam Rabbah (Heb "great order of the world") a chronology of biblical events from Creation to the time of Alexander the Great; the bulk of it dates from the early 2nd c. CE.

Sefirot ("ciphers" or numbers) the ten numbers that formed part of the basis of creation in mystical thought; primarily the emanations from the Godhead that correspond to these numbers.

Seleucid empire the political entity that ruled over Syria and (at times) Judea after the death of Alexander the Great. The Seleucid ruler Antiochus IV "Epiphanes" desecrated the Temple in 167 BCE, leading to the Maccabean revolt and the rededication of the Temple in 164 BCE, an event commemorated in the festival of **Ḥanukkah.**

Sephardim based on Sepharad, the early Jewish name for Spain (based on a misunderstanding of Obad. 1.20, which refers to Asia Minor, specifically Lydia); by extension the name of Jews living in Iberia or descended from those who did.

Septuagint the Gk translation of the Heb text of the Bible, begun with the Torah in Alexandria in the 3rd c. BCE. According to a legend repeated in the ***Letter of Aristeas,*** seventy-two scholars gathered to translate and finished their work in seventy-two days; this number, rounded to seventy and represented in Latin as LXX, became the standard symbol for the Septuagint.

Sforno, Ovadiah ben Yaakov (1475–1550) philosopher and Bible commentator of Italy. Sforno was concerned to explicate the plain meaning of the text, and was opposed to kabbalistic interpretation.

Shabbat (Heb "cessation") the Sabbath day; also, a Tractate in the **Mishnah** (order Mo'ed), in the **Tosefta** and in the **Talmud**s, dealing with the laws of Shabbat.

Shaḥarit (Heb "morning") the morning prayer service. See ***Minḥah; Ma'ariv.***

shalosh regalim "three pilgrimages," the three Pilgrim Festivals—**Pesaḥ, Shavu'ot, Sukkot,** when all Israelite males were expected to go up to the Jerusalem Temple.

Shammai an important early rabbinic sage of the 1st c. BCE who often differed from Hillel. The House of Shammai was generally strict in their halakhic rulings.

Shavu'ot the festival of "Weeks" (also "Pentecost," Gk for "fiftieth" [day]), the spring harvest, occurring according to Priestly texts fifty days (seven full weeks) after **Pesaḥ.** It is the second of the ***shalosh regalim.***

Shekhinah a postbiblical term for the "dwelling" or "presence" of God with Israel; by extension, the divine manifestation in the community's life, or the sense of divine immanence within the world. In kabbalistic thought, Shekhinah is the feminine aspect of God that must be reconciled with the masculine, higher aspects so that God's love can be manifested in the world.

Shem, ha-Shem "name" or "the Name," a locution for YHVH to avoid saying the actual name of God (see Deut. 28.58).

Shema the first word, used as a title, of the exhortation (Deut. 6.4), "Hear, O Israel, the LORD our God is one LORD" (or, "the LORD our God, the LORD is one"); also the name of perhaps the most important and best-known prayer in Judaism, comprised of Deut. 6.4–9; 11.13–21; Num. 15.37–41.

Shemini 'Atzeret "eighth [day] of assembly," following the seven days of Sukkot; in the Diaspora it is celebrated as two days, the second of which is ***Simḥat Torah.***

Shemoneh 'Esrei "the Eighteen," rabbinic name for the ***'Amidah,*** from the number of benedictions in the original prayer.

Sheol the underworld or abode of the dead. In the Bible, all deceased descended to Sheol; there is no concept of a separate heaven and hell.

Shephelah the foothills leading to the central hill country of the land of Israel.

Shi'ur Komah mystical work from the 10th c. CE or earlier, which tries to convey a sense of God's infinite greatness by a description of God's immense size.

Shiv'ah (Heb "seven") the seven days of mourning following the death of a near relative.

shofar the ram's horn for ceremonial use. In ancient Israel it was sounded to announce the anointing of a king or as a summons to war or to sound an alarm; today, in the synagogue, it is sounded on the High Holy Days.

Shulḥan 'Arukh (Heb "set table") the most widely-used code of Jewish law, written by **Joseph Karo.**

Siddur (Heb "order") the traditional Jewish prayerbook.

Sifra an early midrash halakha (legal exegesis) commentary on Lev.

Sifre the early midrash halakha (legal exegesis) for Num. and Deut.

signet ring a ring bearing a personal seal or impression, used to make an indentation in clay as a sign of authenticity of authorship.

Simḥat Torah "rejoicing of Torah," the second day of ***Shemini ʿAtzeret,*** marking the completion of the annual Torah reading cycle.

simile a comparison between two unlike things in which one is compared with the other on the basis of a posited similarity, usually using the terms "like" or "as": "My heart is like wax, melting within me" (Ps. 22.15).

sod (Heb "secret") in mystical interpretation, the hidden or inner meaning of a text; the hidden or inner life of God.

source criticism the effort to discover the written sources or documents behind a text and to explore how the sources were combined into larger units. See **Documentary Hypothesis.**

Spinoza, Baruch (Benedict) (1632–77) philosopher. Spinoza was born a Jew, but as his philosophy developed he became increasingly at odds with traditional Jewish teaching, and he was excommunicated at the age of 24. Besides his philosophical writings, Spinoza engaged in biblical criticism (see esp. his "Of the Interpretation of Scripture" in his *Theological-Political Tractate*), and in some respects anticipated critical findings that did not become established until well after his death, including the assertion that someone other than Moses wrote the Torah.

Sukkot (Heb "booths") the autumn harvest festival (*ḥag ha-ʾasif,* "festival of ingathering"), during which it is customary, following Lev. 23.42–43, to dwell in temporary booths. It is the third of the ***shalosh regalim.***

Sumer the civilization that arose in southern Mesopotamia during the late 4th millennium BCE. Organized around city-states, the Sumerian culture held sway for most of that time until it was finally superseded by Hammurabi in 1750 BCE. The Sumerians developed cuneiform writing, which involved using a wedge-shaped reed to press marks into wet clay. The clay was then baked and the resulting tablet could be stored. Many cuneiform tablets have been recovered from archeological sites in Mesopotamia, from Sumer and from later civilizations, such as Babylonia, that adopted the cuneiform method of writing.

Sura the southern Babylonian city that was the site of one of the two academies (the other was in Pumbedita) that were centers of rabbinic and geonic study. Sura was founded by **Rav** in the 3rd c. CE and continued in existence for more than 800 years.

suzerain the lord or ruler to whom loyalty is due in a covenant relationship. (Although the term is actually Old French for "sovereign," and originally applied to the feudal relationship of lord to peasant or subsidiary, it has been adapted for the ancient Near Eastern covenant system.)

Symmachus a 2nd–3rd c. translator of the Bible into Gk, whose translation was included in Origen's **Hexapla** (a compendium of six Bible versions). Most of the Hexapla, and therefore most of Symmachus's translation, has been lost, and nothing is known about Symmachus as a person.

syncretism the incorporation into one religion of practices and teachings derived from another, or the effort to combine two different religious traditions into a third, composite religion.

synecdoche figure of speech in which a part of a thing or concept is used to represent the whole—e.g., "hand" for "worker"—or the larger whole is used to represent the part—e.g., "the law" for "police."

synonymous parallelism an imprecise term used for the type of parallelism (see **parallelism**) where the second line or **colon** of a **bicolon** echoes the meaning of the first in different terms, e.g., Isa. 1.3, "An ox knows its owner, / An ass its master's crib: / Israel does not know, / My people takes no thought." See "Biblical Poetry" (pp. 2184–91).

synoptic (Gk "view together") the term for texts that, when compared directly, are seen to be verbally identical or to have similarities sufficient to suggest that one is derived from the other, or both are derived from a common source.

Tabernacle the temporary sanctuary for containing the Ark of the Covenant, and for worship and sacrifice in the wilderness according to Priestly tradition. Exod. chs 25–30 contain instructions for building it; the construction is narrated in Exod. chs 35–40.

tablet a slab, typically of clay, with a smoothed surface that can be inscribed with a text.

talion (Latin *talio,* "in kind" from *talis,* "like," "such like") a punishment that is of the same kind as the crime: exacting an equivalent penalty, such as an equal economic loss for theft, or death for murder, or "an eye for an eye." Talion is well-attested in Mesopotamian law, and in some biblical legal collections.

tallit four-cornered fringed shawl worn during prayer; also called *tallit gadol,* "large tallit," in contrast to *tallit katan,* "small tallit," worn throughout the day beneath the clothing by observant Jewish men (see Num. 15.38–39; Deut. 22.12).

Talmud (Heb "teaching") the title of the two great collections of rabbinic teaching, the Jerusalem Talmud or Talmud Yerushalmi and the Babylonian Talmud or Talmud Bavli. The Talmuds were compiled beginning after 200 CE, as an extensive commentary on the **Mishnah;** they consist of comments on, and extensions of, the Mishnah sections to work out the application of Jewish teaching to everyday life, but they also include much other material, and information and teaching on a wide range of topics. The form of the Talmuds is that passages of the Mishnah are commented on by rabbinic teachings (called **Gemara**). The Mishnah is not treated in its entirety. At the beginning of the Talmud's formation, the two centers of rabbinic study (the land of Israel and Babylonia) were in contact with each other and the commentary therefore reflected a common effort; later, especially with the completion of the Talmud in Israel (ca. 400 CE), the Babylonian effort continued to refine and extend the applications, and it was the Talmud developed in Babylonia (completion after 500 CE) that was distributed worldwide, under the auspices of the academies that continued to work in Babylonia until the beginning of the second millennium CE.

tanna' (Aram. "repeat" [traditions]) a rabbinic teacher during the period from the destruction of the Second Temple (70 CE) to the final form of the **Mishnah** (ca. 200 CE).

Targum, pl. **Targumim** Aram. translations of the Bible. There are two main texts on the Torah: *Targum Onkelos,* used by Babylonian Jews, and *Targum Yerushalmi* or the Jerusalem Targum (often mistakenly called Targum Jonathan), used in the land of Israel.

tefillin small black leather boxes containing biblical passages from Exod. 13.1–10; 13.11–16; Deut. 6.4–9; 11.13–21. Two are worn during weekday morning prayer: one on the head (above the space between the eyes, just below the hairline) and one on the (left) arm (see, e.g., Deut. 6.8).

tel a mound formed by repeated occupation and destruction on a particular site.

teshuvah (Heb "return") repentance.

Tetragrammaton (Gk "four letters") the divine name, **YHVH** (see).

Tetrateuch the first four books of the Bible, Gen. through Num., regarded by some scholars as an edited collection to which Deut. was then attached. See **Pentateuch.**

textual criticism the effort to establish, by scholarly assessment of manuscript copies and other sources, an accurate version of a text. See "Textual Criticism" (pp. 2149–52).

Textus Receptus (Latin "received text") the standard text in a tradition. For the Heb text the "received text" is understood to be the Masoretic Text, particularly that in the Rabbinic Bible ***(Miqra'ot Gedolot)*** in the 1525 edition published in Venice.

theodicy the theological effort to justify the goodness of God in the face of suffering.

Theodotion (ca. 2nd c. CE) a translator of the Bible into Gk and reviser of the **Septuagint.**

theophany (Gk "appearance of god") the temporary appearance or manifestation of a divine being in a form that can be apprehended by the human senses.

Third Isaiah see **Trito-Isaiah.**

Thirteen Attributes synagogue prayer (based on Exod. 34.6–7) listing the merciful qualities of God for forgiveness: (1) LORD (2) LORD; (3) great in compassion; (4) merciful; (5) gracious; (6) slow to anger; abounding in (7) mercy and (8) truth [or faithfulness]; (9) merciful to the thousandth [generation]; forgiving (10) iniquity, (11) transgression, and (12) sin; (13) pardoning.

threshing floor a location where the usable portion of grain is separated from its outer covering. Grain is threshed by being beaten to crack the husks and separate the grain from the stems. It is then winnowed by being tossed in a flat basket in a breeze, allowing the husks (chaff), which are lighter, to blow away. A good location for this process is a flat area on a hilltop; this was also an ideal spot for offering sacrifice (see 1 Chron. 21.18–27).

Tiamat goddess of the deep and mother of the Babylonian pantheon; she is sometimes portrayed as a dragon.

tikkunei soferim (Heb "emendations of the scribes") texts which according to rabbinic tradition were modified by scribes, typically to avoid an expression about God that would be offensive; some modern scholars use the term for additional scribal emendations that serve the same purpose.

Tish'ah be'av 9 Av, the day of mourning commemorating the destruction of the two Temples. 2 Kings 25.8–9 says that the First Temple was burned (by the Babylonians) on 7 Av, while Jer. 52.12 dates it on 10 Av; the **Talmud** places it on 9 Av. The Second Temple was destroyed (by the Romans) on 10 Av.

tosafist author of **tosafot** (see).

tosafot brief commentaries on the Talmud (12th–14th centuries) by rabbis in France and Germany, which are printed in the outer columns. The tosafot carry on the talmudic traditions of conversation and interaction with the text and with previous commentators, including resolving contradictions, extending applications, and revisiting matters previously discussed.

Tosefta (Aram. "addition") a compilation of oral law, of uncertain provenance and date, that follows the arrangement of the **Mishnah.**

tradents ("ones who hand on") those who transmit or repeat a tradition.

tradition criticism the investigation of the development of a text from its earliest stages (oral or original source documents) to the latest (canonical) stage.

Transjordan the area to the east of the Jordan River.

Trito-Isaiah the scholarly term for chs 56–66 (or 55–66) of Isa. These chs are primarily concerned with the life of the returned exiles in the province of Yehud (the Persian name for Judah) after 538 BCE. Some scholars doubt the separate existence of Trito-Isaiah; others maintain that it is not the product of one author, but a collection of diverse oracles by different members of a "school of Isaiah" collected during the Persian period.

Tzevaot, YHVH "LORD of Hosts," a title for God as leader of the heavenly armies (Ps. 89.6–9).

tzitzit the fringes attached to the four corners of a garment (Num. 15.38); also the entire garment that has such fringes, usually identical to the *tallit katan* (see **tallit**).

Ugarit city near the Mediterranean coast (Ras-Shamra in present-day Syria), source of an important store of Canaanite myths. Beginning in the 1920s archeological excavations in and around the area led to the discovery of a large number of cuneiform tablets in **Akkadian,** and others in a previously unknown language (subsequently named Ugaritic) which was related to Heb. The tablets also provided an archive of the political and economic activities of the rulers of Ugarit during the second half of the second millennium (1500–1200 BCE).

unleavened bread (Heb *matzah*, pl. *matzot*) bread made without yeast; also the festival, *Ḥag ha-Matzot,* that follows **Pesaḥ** (see).

Urim and Thummim a method of divination (the details of which are unclear) that the high priest used to discover God's response to yes-or-no questions.

vassal the underlord in a covenant relationship, who is granted power and control over people in a particular area in return for loyalty to the suzerain.

Vassal Treaty of Esarhaddon an Assyrian treaty document from the reign of the Assyrian king Esarhaddon (681–669 BCE), with parallels to parts of Deut.

Vilna Gaon see **Zalman, Elijah ben Solomon.**

Vorlage (German "preceding position," i.e., pattern) the underlying text of a translation.

Vulgate (Latin "common") the Bible translated by Jerome (completed 405 CE). The Old Testament of the Vulgate was translated directly from Heb, unlike that of the previous Latin version (the "Old Latin" or "Vetus Latina"), which was translated from the **Septuagint.**

wadi a seasonal watercourse, dry in the summer and full of water during the winter rainy period.

Weeks, Festival of see **Shavu'ot.**

Wisdom literature modern scholarship has identified the books of Prov., Eccl., and Job, and certain Psalms (e.g., Ps. 37) as examples of a type of literature with analogues in other ancient Near Eastern literatures. Wisdom is concerned with matters of insight and meditation on the meaning of life, moral exhortation, and the identification of recurrent patterns in nature and human life. Wisdom generally focuses on the individual rather than the nation, and therefore does not examine many of the events and teachings central to biblical literature, such as the exodus, Temple worship and sacrifice, the covenant, the monarchy, or prophecy.

Yehud designation of the province of Judah during Persian times.

Yerushalmi, Talmud the Jerusalem (sometimes called Palestinian) Talmud. See **Talmud.**

YHVH the name of God, which conventionally remains unpronounced and is represented in the text by the Heb letters *yod-he-vav-he* and the vowels for the title *Adonai,* "my Lord." In standard English translations, including NJPS, YHVH is represented by the word LORD written in capital and small capital letters. The original vocalization and meaning of this name is unknown, though it is connected to the verb *h-y-h,* "be" or "become," most likely in a causitive sense, "he who causes to be."

Yikum Purkan (Aram. "may deliverance arise") two synagogue prayers (in Ashkenazi communities) recited after the **haftarah** reading, one for the welfare of Torah students and scholars, the other for the welfare of the congregation.

Yom Kippur (Heb "day of atonement") the solemn fast observed each year on 10 Tishri, according to the command recorded in Lev. 23.26–32. The observance involves abstention of various kinds and focuses on personal and communal repentance ***(teshuvah)***. The prayer services begin with the evening service and continue through the next day, with a morning service, an additional service, an afternoon service, and a concluding service.

Zalman, Elijah ben Solomon (1720–1797) the **"Vilna Gaon,"** scholar of Vilna, Lithuania. He studied religious and secular subjects (such as mathematics and philosophy), arguing that knowledge in these areas was necessary for Torah study. For eight years he wandered throughout Europe, meeting with and teaching local rabbis and establishing his reputation for learning. He then returned to Vilna, where he spent the rest of his life expounding the Talmud. He strongly opposed the nascent Hasidic movement.

ziggurat a temple-tower in ancient Mesopotamia. Ziggurats are presumed to represent a mount, on the top of which the earthly and divine realms merged.

Z"L *zikhro l'bhrakhah,* "his memory for a blessing," or "of blessed memory."

Zohar ("Splendor") kabbalistic writing of the late 13th c., partly the work of **Moshe de Leon** (d. 1305).

Index

C

F

H

J

Q

T

THE NEW OXFORD

BIBLE MAPS

JEWISH STUDY BIBLE

Prepared by Oxford Cartographers
and based on the Oxford Bible Atlas

MAP 1

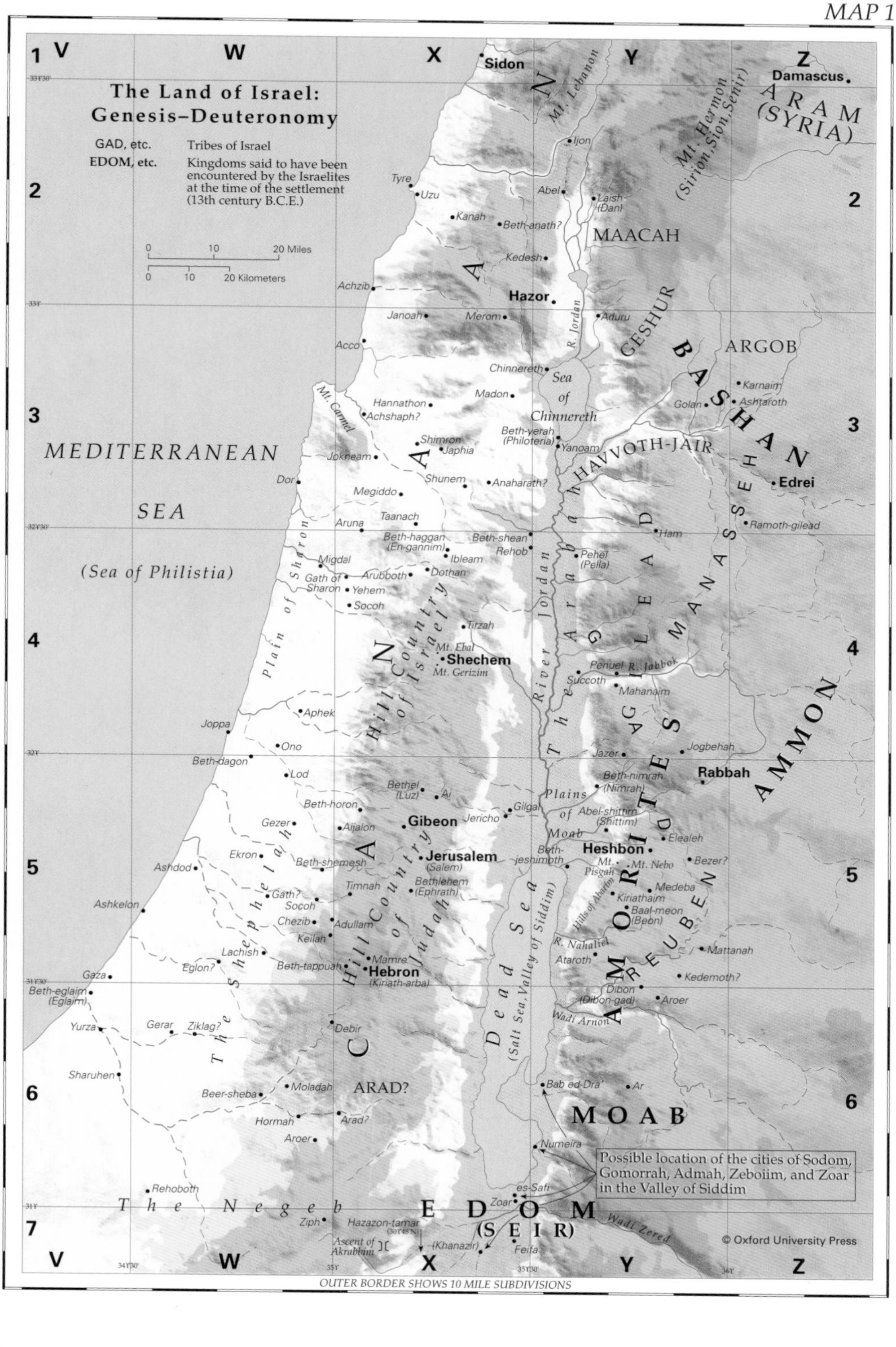

The Land of Israel: Genesis–Deuteronomy
GAD, etc. Tribes of Israel
EDOM, etc. Kingdoms said to have been encountered by the Israelites at the time of the settlement (13th century B.C.E.)
0 10 20 Miles
0 10 20 Kilometers
V W X Y Z
1 2 3 4 5 6 7
Sidon
Damascus
ARAM (SYRIA)
Mt. Lebanon
Mt. Hermon (Sirion, Sion, Senir)
Ijon
Tyre
Uzu
Abel
Laish (Dan)
Kanah
Beth-anath?
MAACAH
Kedesh
Achzib
Hazor
Janoah
Merom
R. Jordan
Aduru
GESHUR
Acco
ARGOB
BASHAN
Chinnereth
Sea of Chinnereth
Karnaim
Ashtaroth
Golan
Madon
Mt. Carmel
Hannathon
Achshaph?
MEDITERRANEAN SEA
(Sea of Philistia)
Shimron
Japhia
Beth-yerah (Philoteria)
Yanoam
HAVVOTH-JAIR
Jokneam
Dor
Megiddo
Shunem
Anaharath?
Edrei
Taanach
Aruna
Beth-haggan (En-gannim)
Ibleam
Beth-shean
Rehob
Ham
Ramoth-gilead
Pehel (Pella)
Migdal
Gath of Sharon
Arubboth
Dothan
Yehem
Socoh
Plain of Sharon
Hill Country of Israel
Tirzah
Mt. Ebal
Shechem
Mt. Gerizim
River Jordan
The Arabah
GILEAD
MANASSEH
Penuel
R. Jabbok
Succoth
Mahanaim
Aphek
Joppa
Ono
Beth-dagon
Lod
Jazer
Jogbehah
Rabbah
AMMON
GAD
AMORITES
Bethel (Luz)
Ai
Beth-nimrah (Nimrah)
Beth-horon
Gilgal
Plains of Moab
Abel-shittim (Shittim)
Gezer
Aijalon
Gibeon
Jericho
Elealeh
Ekron
Beth-shemesh
Jerusalem (Salem)
Beth-jeshimoth
Heshbon
Mt. Pisgah
Mt. Nebo
Bezer?
Ashdod
Timnah
Bethlehem (Ephrath)
Medeba
Gath?
Socoh
Kiriathaim
Hills of Abarim
Ashkelon
Chezib
Adullam
Baal-meon (Beon)
Keilah
Hill Country of Judah
Dead Sea (Salt Sea, Valley of Siddim)
R. Nahaliel
Lachish
Mattanah
Mamre
Eglon?
Beth-tappuah
Hebron (Kiriath-arba)
Ataroth
REUBEN
Kedemoth?
Gaza
Beth-eglaim (Eglaim)
Dibon (Dibon-gad)
Aroer
Wadi Arnon
The Shephelah
Yurza
Gerar
Ziklag?
Debir
CANAAN
Sharuhen
Bab ed-Dra'
Ar
Beer-sheba
Moladah
ARAD?
MOAB
Hormah
Arad?
Aroer
Numeira
Possible location of the cities of Sodom, Gomorrah, Admah, Zeboiim, and Zoar in the Valley of Siddim
Rehoboth
es-Safi
The Negeb
EDOM (SEIR)
Zoar
Wadi Zered
Ziph
Hazazon-tamar
Ascent of Akrabbim
(Khanazir)
Feifa
© Oxford University Press
OUTER BORDER SHOWS 10 MILE SUBDIVISIONS

MAP 2

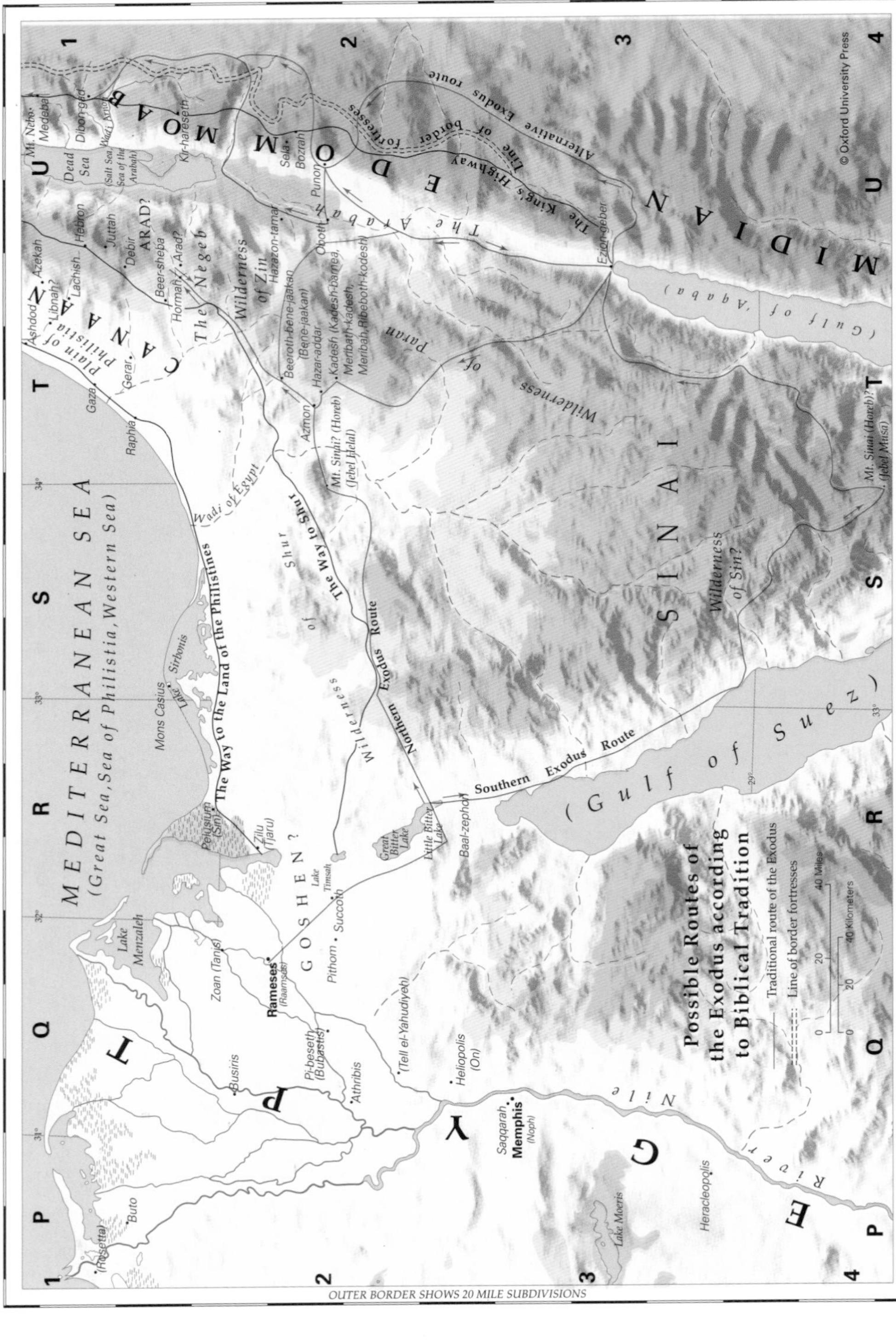

Possible Routes of the Exodus according to Biblical Tradition
Traditional route of the Exodus
Line of border fortresses
0 20 40 Miles
0 20 40 Kilometers
© Oxford University Press
MEDITERRANEAN SEA
(Great Sea, Sea of Philistia, Western Sea)
EGYPT
SINAI
MIDIAN
EDOM
MOAB
CANAAN
GOSHEN?
(Gulf of Suez)
(Gulf of 'Aqaba)
The Way to the Land of the Philistines
The Way to Shur
Wilderness of Shur
Northern Exodus Route
Southern Exodus Route
Alternative Exodus route
The King's Highway
Line of border fortresses
The Arabah
The Negeb
Wilderness of Zin
Wilderness of Paran
Wilderness of Sin?
Wadi of Egypt
Plain of Philistia
River Nile
Lake Menzaleh
Lake Sirbonis
Mons Casius
Pelusium (Sin)
Zilu (Tjaru)
Lake Timsah
Great Bitter Lake
Little Bitter Lake
Baal-zephon
Rameses (Raamses)
Zoan (Tanis)
Pithom
Succoth
Pi-beseth (Bubastis)
Busiris
Athribis
(Tell el-Yahudiyeh)
Heliopolis (On)
Saqqarah
Memphis (Noph)
Heracleopolis
Lake Moeris
Buto
(Rosetta)
Raphia
Gaza
Gerar
Ashdod
Libnah?
Azekah
Lachish
Hebron
Debir
Juttah
Beer-sheba
Hormah
Arad?
ARAD?
Dead Sea
(Salt Sea, Sea of the Arabah)
Mt. Nebo
Medeba
Dibon-gad
Wadi Arnon
Kir-hareseth
Sela
Bozrah
Punon
Oboth
Hazazon-tamar
Beeroth-bene-jaakan (Bene-jaakan)
Hazar-addar
Kadesh (Kadesh-barnea, Meribath-kadesh, Meribah, Ribeboth-kodesh)
Azmon
Mt. Sinai? (Horeb) (Jebel Helal)
Ezion-geber
Mt. Sinai (Horeb)? (Jebel Musa)
31°
32°
33°
34°
29°
P Q R S T U
1 2 3 4

OUTER BORDER SHOWS 20 MILE SUBDIVISIONS

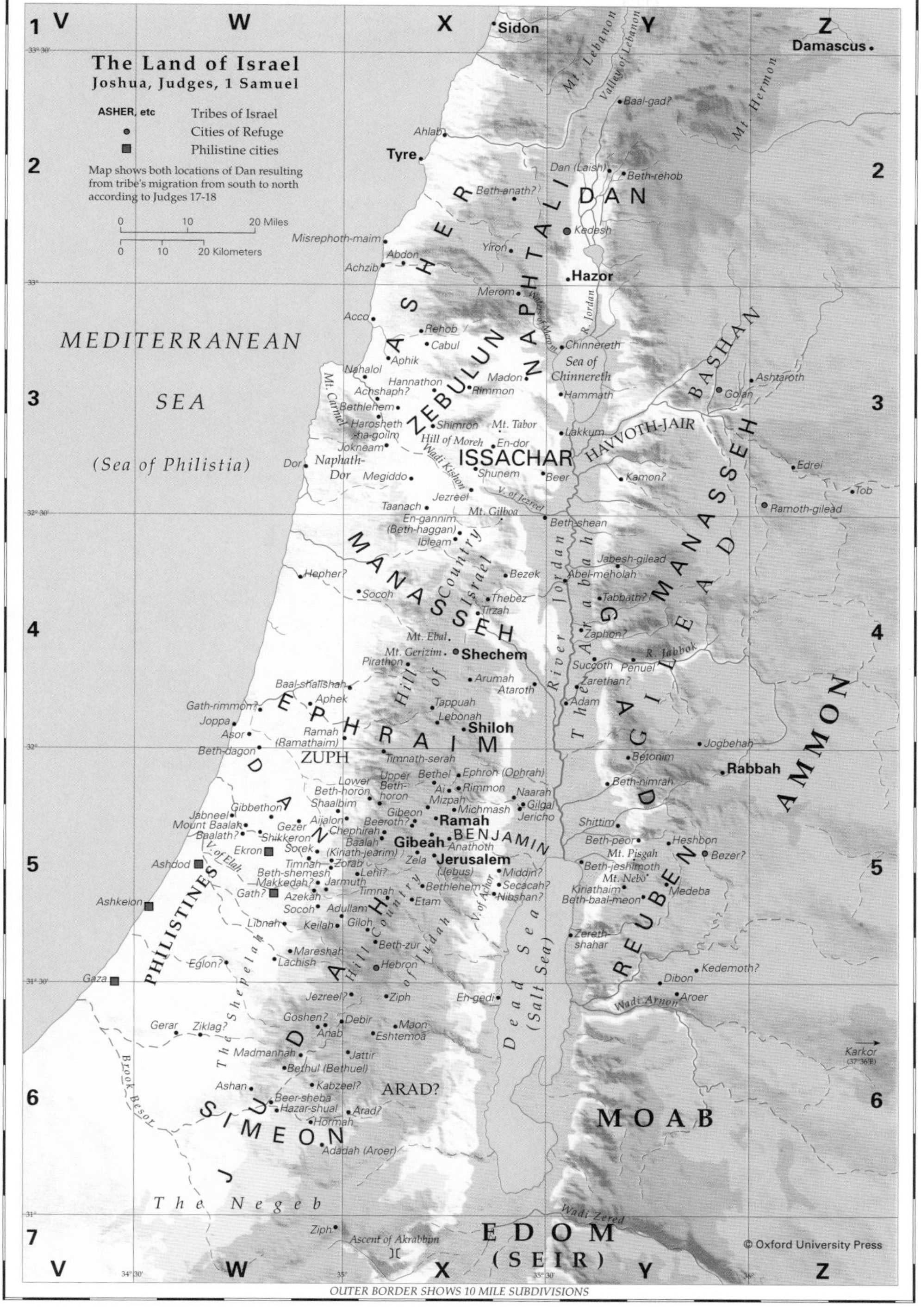

OUTER BORDER SHOWS 10 MILE SUBDIVISIONS

MAP 4

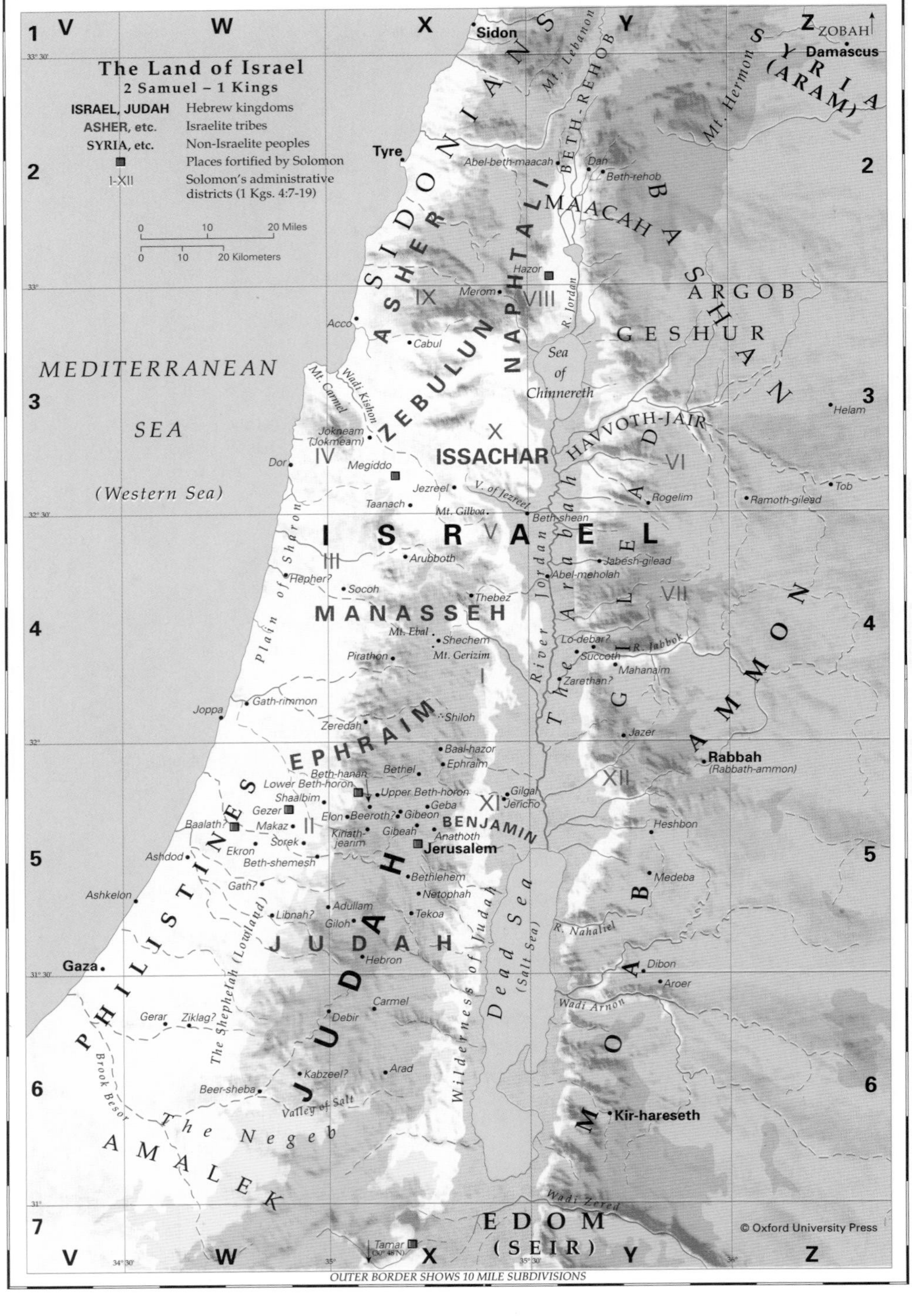

The Land of Israel
2 Samuel – 1 Kings
ISRAEL, JUDAH Hebrew kingdoms
ASHER, etc. Israelite tribes
SYRIA, etc. Non-Israelite peoples
Places fortified by Solomon
I-XII Solomon's administrative districts (1 Kgs. 4:7-19)
0 10 20 Miles
0 10 20 Kilometers
MEDITERRANEAN SEA
(Western Sea)
SIDONIANS
Sidon
Tyre
Mt. Lebanon
BETH-REHOB
Mt. Hermon
SYRIA (ARAM)
ZOBAH
Damascus
Abel-beth-maacah
Dan
Beth-rehob
MAACAH
BASHAN
ASHER
NAPHTALI
Hazor
Merom
VIII
IX
R. Jordan
ARGOB
GESHUR
Acco
Cabul
ZEBULUN
Sea of Chinnereth
Mt. Carmel
Wadi Kishon
Jokneam (Jokmeam)
X
ISSACHAR
HAVVOTH-JAIR
Helam
Dor
IV
Megiddo
VI
Jezreel
V. of Jezreel
Tob
Taanach
Mt. Gilboa
Rogelim
Ramoth-gilead
Beth-shean
ISRAEL
V
GILEAD
III
Arubboth
Jabesh-gilead
Hepher?
Abel-meholah
Socoh
Plain of Sharon
Thebez
VII
MANASSEH
The Arabah
Mt. Ebal
Shechem
Mt. Gerizim
Lo-debar?
R. Jabbok
Succoth
Mahanaim
Pirathon
I
River Jordan
Zarethan?
AMMON
Joppa
Gath-rimmon
Shiloh
Zeredah
Jazer
EPHRAIM
Baal-hazor
Ephraim
Rabbah
(Rabbath-ammon)
Bethel
Beth-hanan
Lower Beth-horon
Upper Beth-horon
Gilgal
Jericho
XI
XII
Shaalbim
Geba
Gezer
Elon
Beeroth?
Gibeon
BENJAMIN
Baalath?
Makaz
II
Heshbon
Kiriath-jearim
Gibeah
Anathoth
Sorek
Ekron
Jerusalem
Ashdod
Beth-shemesh
Bethlehem
Medeba
Gath?
Netophah
Ashkelon
Adullam
Libnah?
Giloh
Tekoa
PHILISTINES
JUDAH
Dead Sea (Salt Sea)
Wilderness of Judah
R. Nahaliel
Hebron
MOAB
Gaza
Dibon
Aroer
Carmel
Wadi Arnon
Gerar
Ziklag?
Debir
The Shephelah (Lowland)
Brook Besor
Kabzeel?
Arad
Beer-sheba
Valley of Salt
Kir-hareseth
The Negeb
AMALEK
Wadi Zered
EDOM (SEIR)
Tamar (30° 48'N)
© Oxford University Press
OUTER BORDER SHOWS 10 MILE SUBDIVISIONS

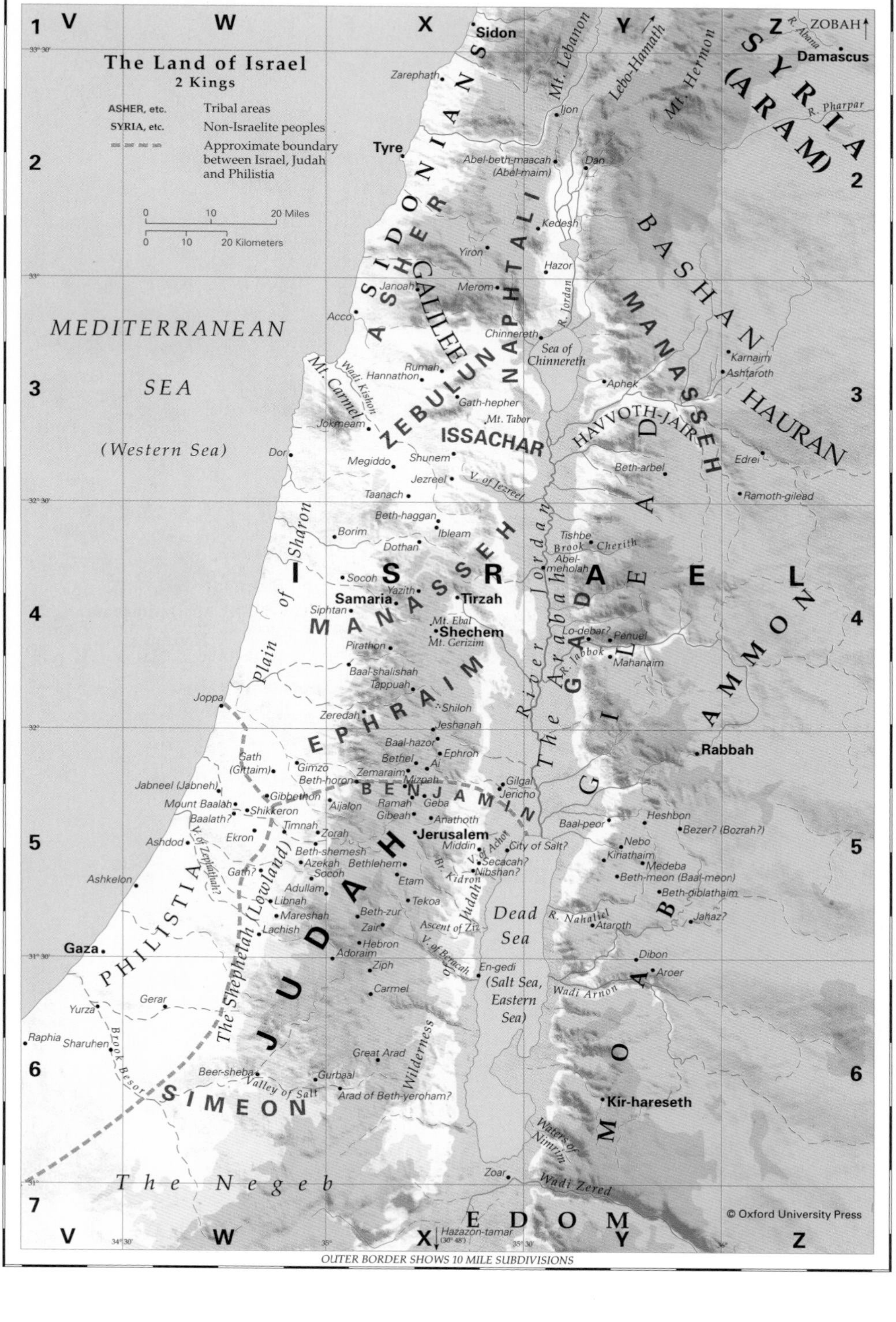

OUTER BORDER SHOWS 10 MILE SUBDIVISIONS

MAP 6

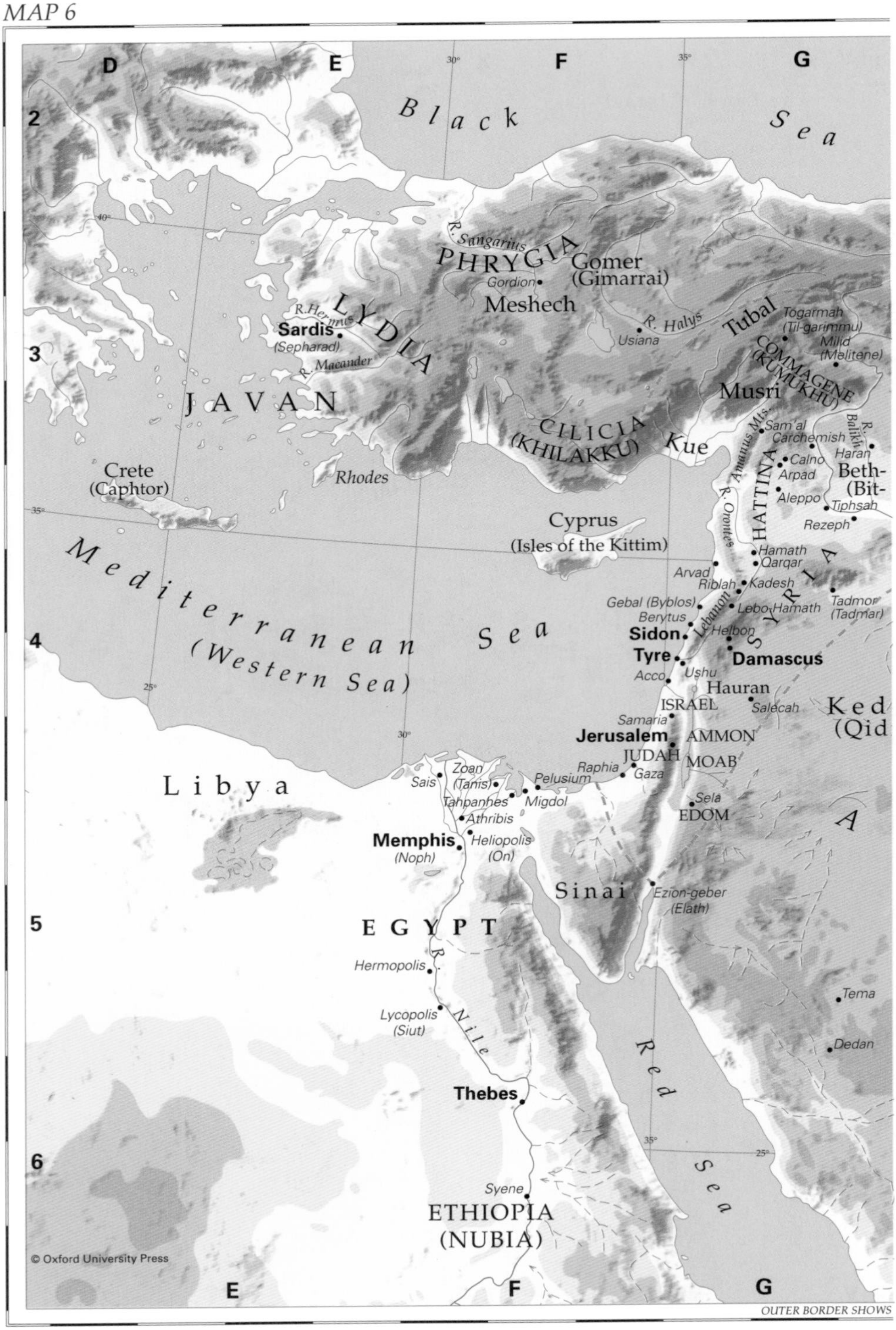
D
E
F
G
2
3
4
5
6
30°
35°
40°
25°
Black
Sea
R. Sangarius
PHRYGIA
Gomer
(Gimarrai)
Gordion
Meshech
LYDIA
R. Hermus
Sardis
(Sepharad)
R. Maeander
R. Halys
Usiana
Tubal
Togarmah
(Til-garimmu)
Milid
(Melitene)
COMMAGENE
(KUMUKHU)
Musri
JAVAN
CILICIA
(KHILAKKU)
Kue
Amanus Mts.
Sam'al
Carchemish
R. Balikh
Haran
Beth-
(Bit-
Calno
Arpad
HATTINA
Aleppo
Tiphsah
Rezeph
Crete
(Caphtor)
Rhodes
Cyprus
(Isles of the Kittim)
R. Orontes
Hamath
Qarqar
Arvad
Riblah
Kadesh
SYRIA
Tadmor
(Tadmar)
Gebal (Byblos)
Berytus
Lebo-Hamath
Lebanon
Mediterranean
Sea
(Western Sea)
Sidon
Helbon
Tyre
Damascus
Acco
Ushu
Hauran
ISRAEL
Salecah
Ked
(Qid
Samaria
Jerusalem
AMMON
JUDAH
MOAB
Raphia
Gaza
Libya
Zoan
(Tanis)
Sais
Pelusium
Tahpanhes
Migdol
Athribis
Sela
EDOM
Memphis
(Noph)
Heliopolis
(On)
A
Sinai
Ezion-geber
(Elath)
EGYPT
R. Nile
Hermopolis
Tema
Lycopolis
(Siut)
Dedan
Red
Sea
Thebes
Syene
ETHIOPIA
(NUBIA)
© Oxford University Press
OUTER BORDER SHOWS

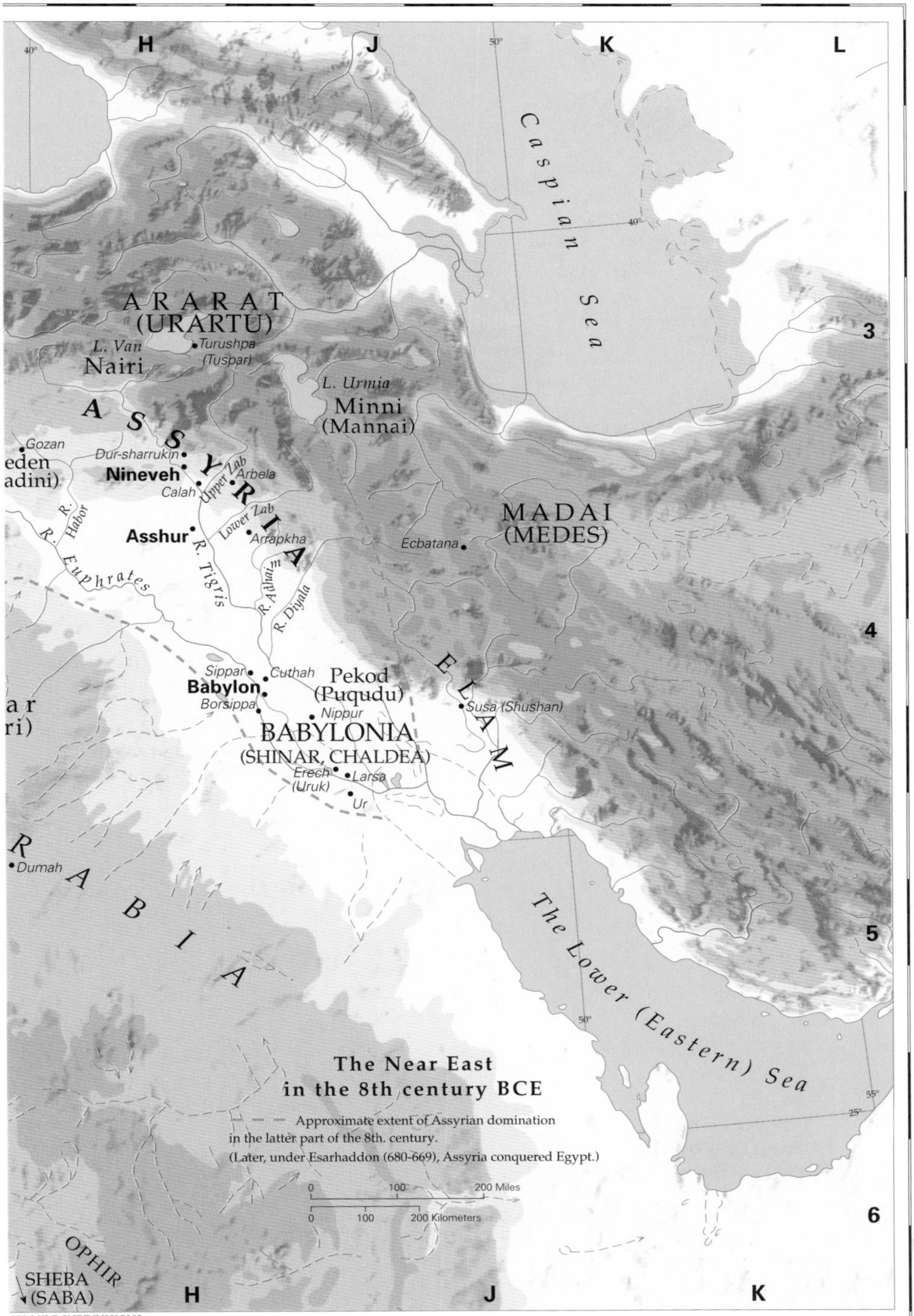

H
J
K
L
Caspian Sea
ARARAT (URARTU)
L. Van
Turushpa (Tuspar)
Nairi
L. Urmia
Minni (Mannai)
ASSYRIA
Gozan
eden adini)
Dur-sharrukin
Nineveh
Arbela
Calah
Upper Zab
Lower Zab
R. Habor
Asshur
Arrapkha
R. Euphrates
R. Tigris
R. Adhaim
R. Diyala
MADAI (MEDES)
Ecbatana
ELAM
Sippar
Cuthah
Babylon
Borsippa
Pekod (Puqudu)
Nippur
Susa (Shushan)
BABYLONIA (SHINAR, CHALDEA)
Erech (Uruk)
Larsa
Ur
ar ri)
Dumah
ARABIA
The Lower (Eastern) Sea
3
4
5
6
The Near East in the 8th century BCE
Approximate extent of Assyrian domination in the latter part of the 8th. century.
(Later, under Esarhaddon (680-669), Assyria conquered Egypt.)
0 100 200 Miles
0 100 200 Kilometers
OPHIR
SHEBA (SABA)
100 MILE SUBDIVISIONS

MAP 7

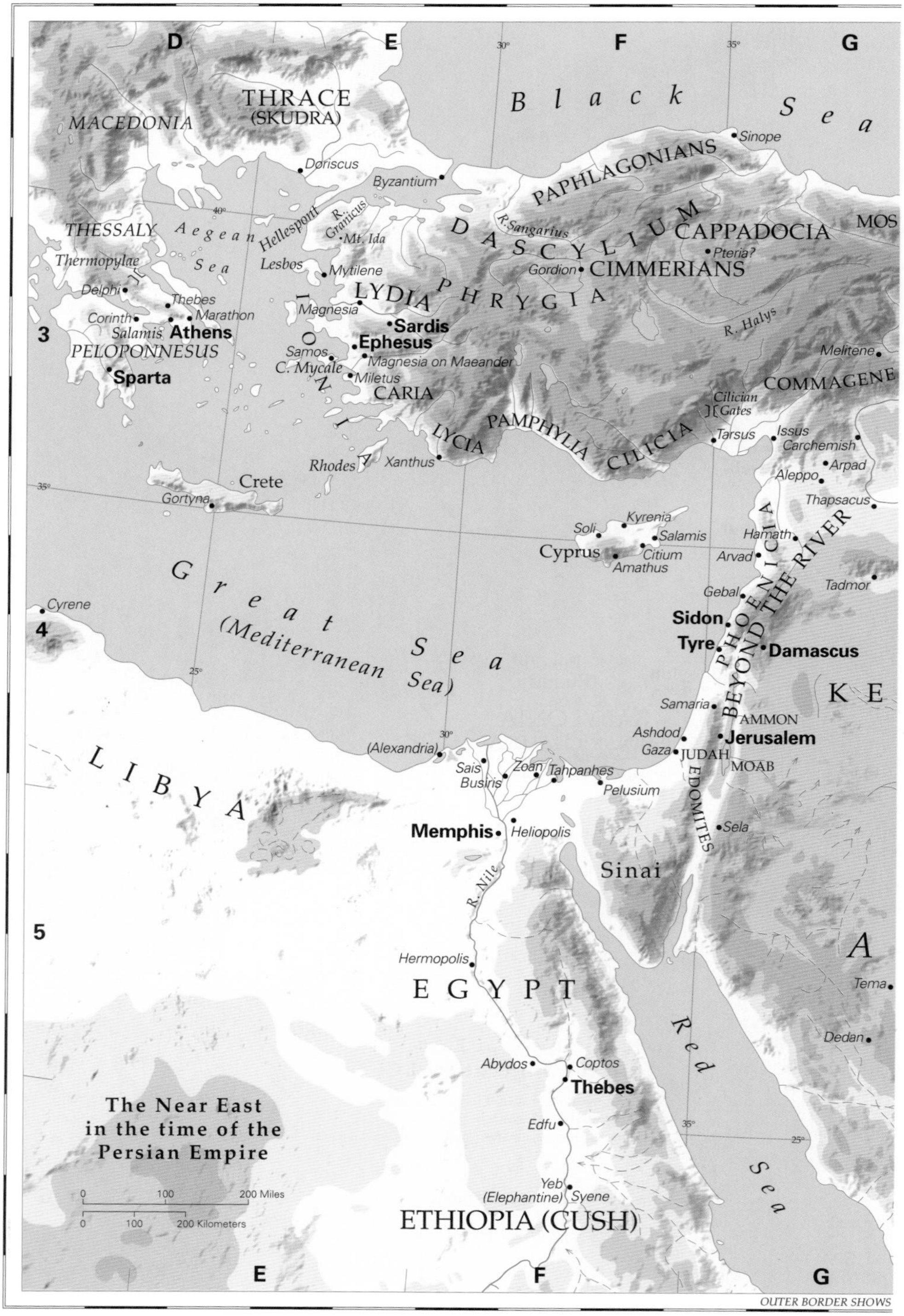

The Near East in the time of the Persian Empire
0 100 200 Miles
0 100 200 Kilometers
D
E
F
G
3
4
5
30°
35°
40°
25°
THRACE (SKUDRA)
MACEDONIA
Black Sea
Sinope
Doriscus
Byzantium
PAPHLAGONIANS
THESSALY
Aegean Sea
Hellespont
R. Granicus
Mt. Ida
R. Sangarius
DASCYLIUM
CAPPADOCIA
MOS
Thermopylae
Lesbos
Mytilene
Pteria?
Gordion
CIMMERIANS
Delphi
Thebes
LYDIA
PHRYGIA
Corinth
Marathon
Magnesia
Salamis
Athens
Sardis
R. Halys
PELOPONNESUS
Ephesus
Samos
Magnesia on Maeander
Melitene
Sparta
C. Mycale
Miletus
IONIA
CARIA
COMMAGENE
Cilician Gates
LYCIA
PAMPHYLIA
CILICIA
Tarsus
Issus
Carchemish
Rhodes
Xanthus
Arpad
Aleppo
Crete
Gortyna
Thapsacus
Kyrenia
Soli
Salamis
Hamath
Cyprus
Citium
Amathus
Arvad
Great Sea (Mediterranean Sea)
Tadmor
Gebal
Cyrene
PHOENICIA
BEYOND THE RIVER
Sidon
Tyre
Damascus
Samaria
KE
AMMON
Ashdod
Jerusalem
Gaza
JUDAH
MOAB
(Alexandria)
LIBYA
Sais
Busiris
Zoan
Tahpanhes
Pelusium
EDOMITES
Memphis
Heliopolis
Sela
Sinai
R. Nile
A
Hermopolis
Tema
EGYPT
Red Sea
Dedan
Abydos
Coptos
Thebes
Edfu
Yeb (Elephantine)
Syene
ETHIOPIA (CUSH)
OUTER BORDER SHOWS

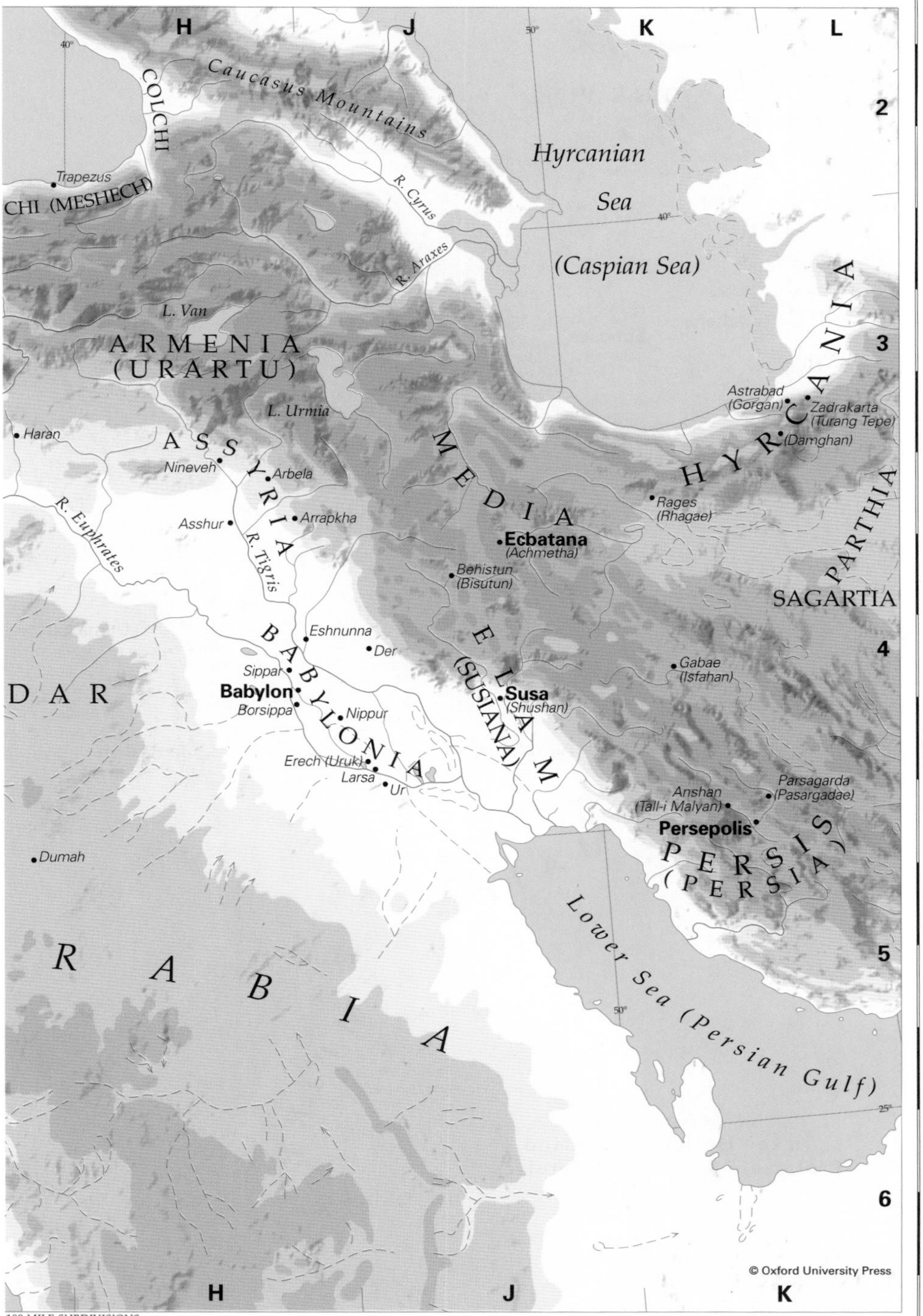

100 MILE SUBDIVISIONS

MAP 8

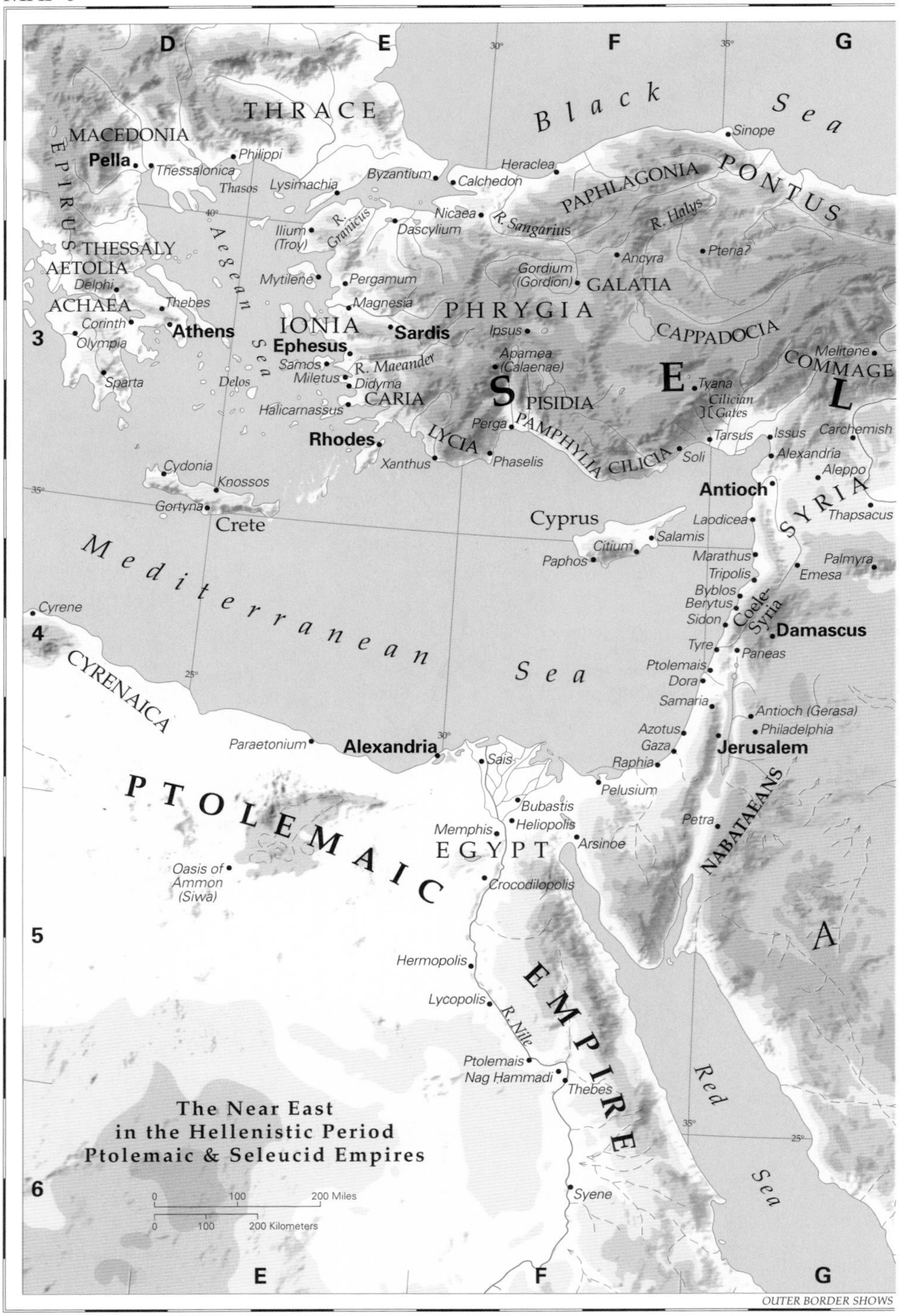

The Near East
in the Hellenistic Period
Ptolemaic & Seleucid Empires
D
E
F
G
3
4
5
6
30°
35°
40°
25°
Black Sea
THRACE
MACEDONIA
EPIRUS
Pella
Thessalonica
Philippi
Thasos
Lysimachia
Byzantium
Calchedon
Heraclea
Sinope
PAPHLAGONIA
PONTUS
R. Halys
Pteria?
Ancyra
Nicaea
R. Sangarius
Dascylium
R. Granicus
Ilium (Troy)
THESSALY
AETOLIA
Delphi
ACHAEA
Thebes
Corinth
Olympia
Athens
Sparta
Aegean Sea
Mytilene
Pergamum
Magnesia
IONIA
Sardis
Ephesus
Samos
Miletus
Didyma
R. Maeander
Delos
CARIA
Halicarnassus
Rhodes
Gordium (Gordion)
GALATIA
PHRYGIA
Ipsus
Apamea (Calaenae)
PISIDIA
CAPPADOCIA
Melitene
COMMAGENE
Tyana
Cilician Gates
Tarsus
Issus
Carchemish
Perga
PAMPHYLIA
LYCIA
Phaselis
Xanthus
CILICIA
Soli
Alexandria
Aleppo
Antioch
SYRIA
Thapsacus
SELEUCID
Cydonia
Knossos
Gortyna
Crete
Cyprus
Salamis
Citium
Paphos
Laodicea
Marathus
Tripolis
Byblos
Berytus
Sidon
Coele-Syria
Palmyra
Emesa
Damascus
Tyre
Paneas
Ptolemais
Dora
Samaria
Antioch (Gerasa)
Philadelphia
Azotus
Gaza
Jerusalem
Raphia
Mediterranean Sea
Cyrene
CYRENAICA
Paraetonium
Alexandria
Sais
Pelusium
Bubastis
Heliopolis
Memphis
Arsinoe
EGYPT
NABATAEANS
Petra
PTOLEMAIC EMPIRE
Oasis of Ammon (Siwa)
Crocodilopolis
Hermopolis
Lycopolis
R. Nile
Ptolemais
Nag Hammadi
Thebes
Red Sea
Syene
0 100 200 Miles
0 100 200 Kilometers
OUTER BORDER SHOWS

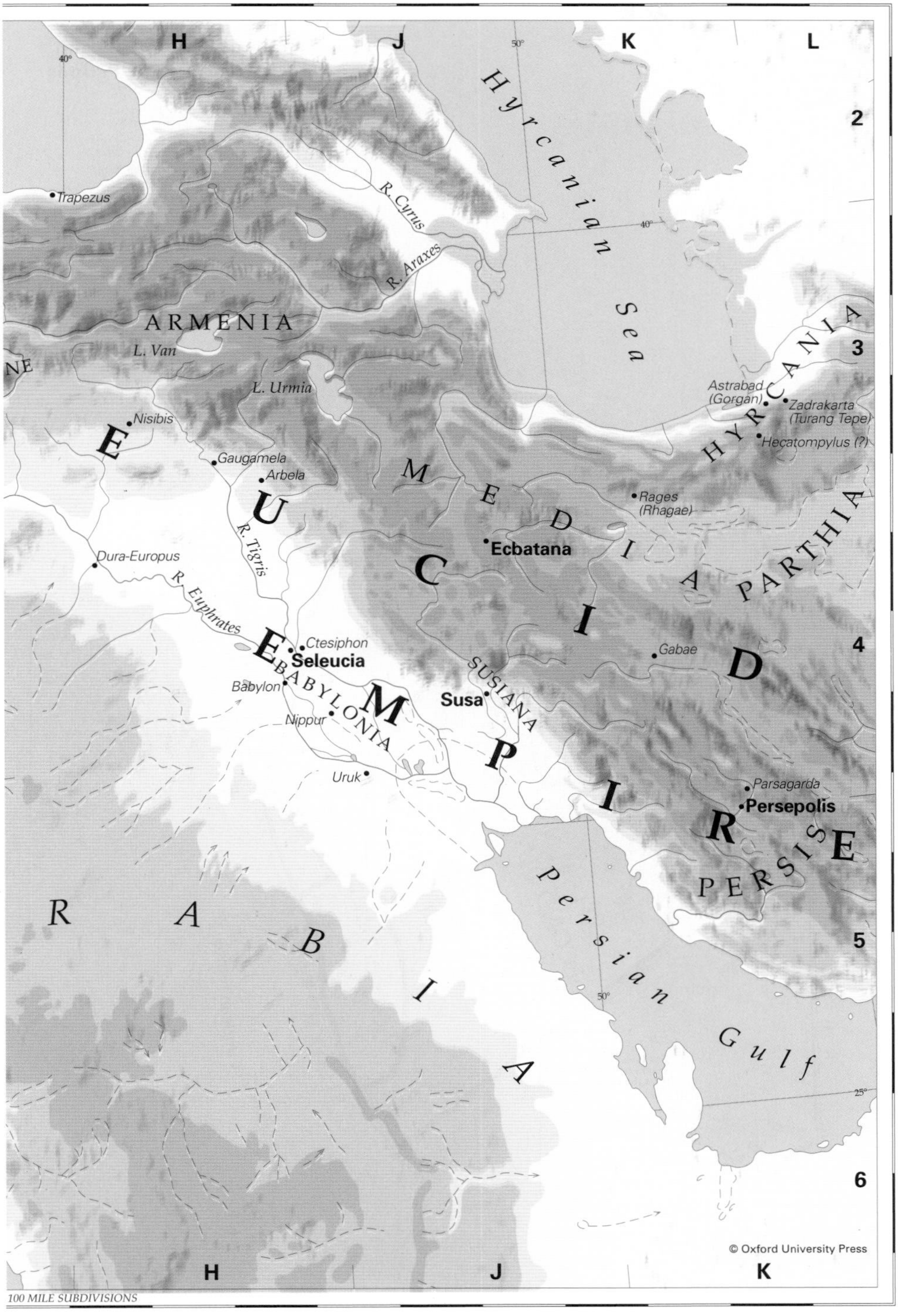
H
J
K
L
2
3
4
5
6
Hyrcanian Sea
Trapezus
R. Cyrus
R. Araxes
ARMENIA
L. Van
L. Urmia
NE
Astrabad (Gorgan)
Zadrakarta (Turang Tepe)
Hecatompylus (?)
HYRCANIA
Nisibis
Gaugamela
Arbela
MEDIA
Rages (Rhagae)
PARTHIA
Ecbatana
R. Tigris
Dura-Europus
R. Euphrates
SELEUCID EMPIRE
Ctesiphon
Seleucia
Gabae
SUSIANA
Babylon
BABYLONIA
Susa
Nippur
Uruk
Parsagarda
Persepolis
PERSIS
Persian Gulf
ARABIA
40°
50°
25°
© Oxford University Press
100 MILE SUBDIVISIONS

MAP 9

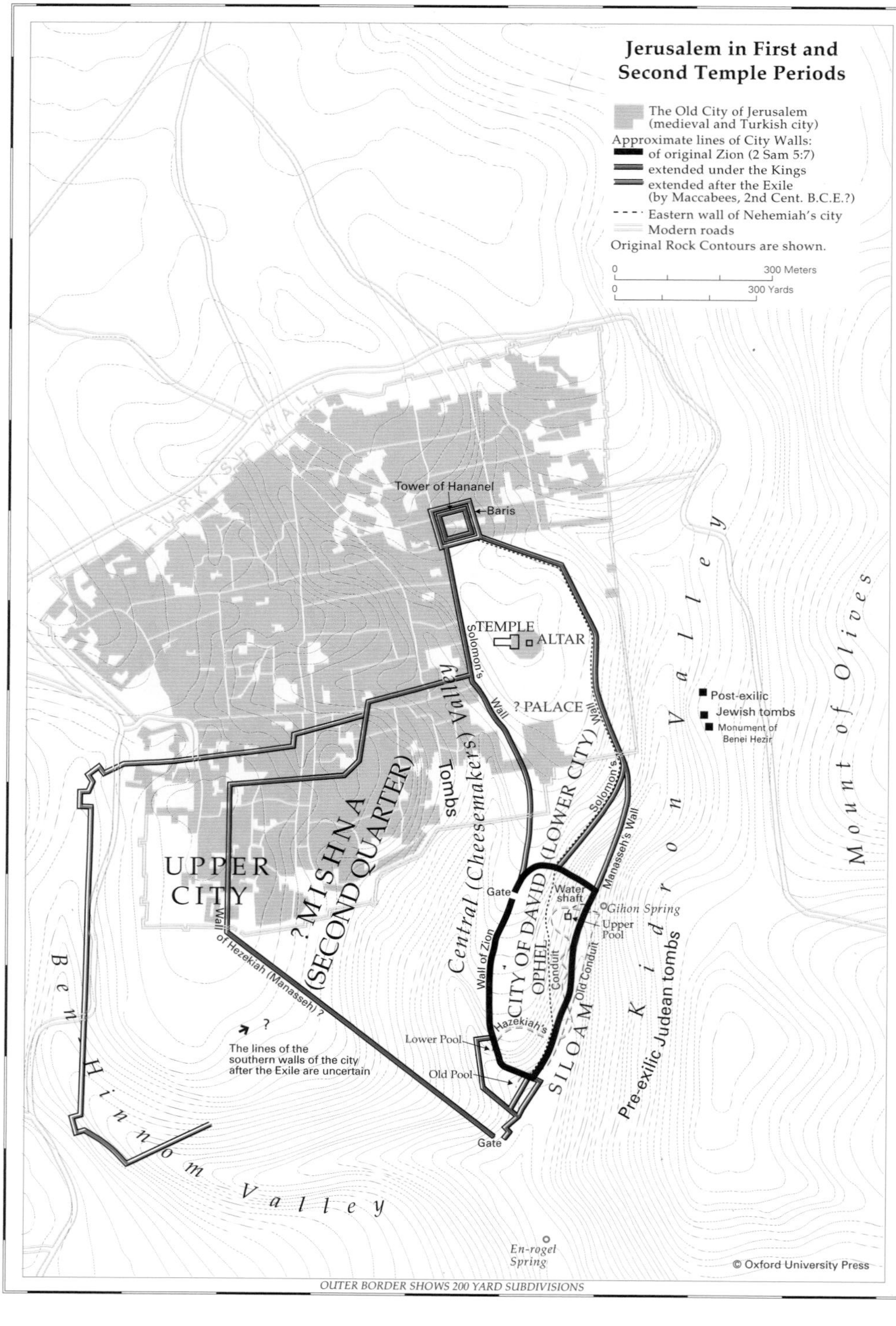

Jerusalem in First and Second Temple Periods
The Old City of Jerusalem (medieval and Turkish city)
Approximate lines of City Walls:
of original Zion (2 Sam 5:7)
extended under the Kings
extended after the Exile (by Maccabees, 2nd Cent. B.C.E.?)
Eastern wall of Nehemiah's city
Modern roads
Original Rock Contours are shown.
0 300 Meters
0 300 Yards
TURKISH WALL
Tower of Hananel
Baris
TEMPLE
ALTAR
Solomon's Wall
? PALACE
Wall
Solomon's
Manasseh's Wall
Kidron Valley
Mount of Olives
Post-exilic Jewish tombs
Monument of Benei Hezir
Central (Cheesemakers) Valley
Tombs
?MISHNA (SECOND QUARTER)
UPPER CITY
(LOWER CITY)
CITY OF DAVID
OPHEL
Gate
Water shaft
Gihon Spring
Upper Pool
Wall of Zion
Conduit
Old Conduit
Hazekiah's
SILOAM
Pre-exilic Judean tombs
Wall of Hezekiah (Manasseh) ?
?
The lines of the southern walls of the city after the Exile are uncertain
Lower Pool
Old Pool
Gate
Ben Hinnom Valley
En-rogel Spring
© Oxford University Press
OUTER BORDER SHOWS 200 YARD SUBDIVISIONS

INDEX TO MAPS